NELSON'S
CROSS REFERENCE
GUIDE TO THE BIBLE

NELSON'S
CROSS REFERENCE
GUIDE TO THE BIBLE

Edited by Jerome H. Smith

THOMAS NELSON
Since 1798

NASHVILLE DALLAS MEXICO CITY RIO DE JANEIRO BEIJING

Published in Nashville, TN, by Thomas Nelson.
Thomas Nelson is a trademark of Thomas Nelson, Inc.

Thomas Nelson, Inc. titles may be purchased in bulk for educational,
business, fundraising, or sales promotional use. For information,
please email SpecialMarkets@ThomasNelson.com

Published in association with the literary agency of Alive Communications, Inc.
7680 Goddard Street, Suite 200
Colorado Springs, CO 80920
www.alivecom.com

Book design and composition by Mark McGarry,
Texas Type & Book Works, Dallas, Texas

ISBN-10: 1418504599
ISBN-13: 9781418504595

Printed in China by CTPS
07 08 09 10 11—9 8 7 6 5 4 3 2 1

To My Wife, Susanne
And her Mother, Grace Opificius
Who have been of continuing assistance in producing this Work

To My Sons: Timothy and Daniel
Who have kept the computer and software working!

To my high school Sunday School class members
Colleen, Betty, Sandy, Donita, and Linda
Who personally tested my original unpublished work

And to the Members of the Cass Technical High School Bible Discussion Club
Pastor Emery Moss, Jr., Pastor Michael Martin
And ever so many more Bible Club members who challenged me to deeper study by their Bible questions

To the late Dr. Lehman Strauss, at Highland Park Baptist, for his Bible teaching ministry

To Miss Ellen Groh, who introduced me to the original Treasury of Scripture Knowledge
in her "How to Study the Bible" summer class

In memory of my Aunt Ethel, whose gift enabled me to get my first copy of the Treasury

And to all Bible readers, urging them to share the news that this Bible study tool
can help everyone to study the Bible to grow spiritually.

INTRODUCTION

If you have ever read a verse in the Bible and wanted to know what other verses said about that same subject, the *Nelson's Cross Reference Guide to the Bible* is the resource you need.

This guide works much like the cross references in the center column or side margins of a study Bible, but provides the help right where it is needed, at the verse being consulted. Whenever you read a verse in the Bible and think, "I would like to know more about this," turn to that verse in *Nelson's Cross Reference Guide*.

The *Nelson's Cross Reference Guide to the Bible* is arranged just like the Bible itself, with the same order of books, chapters, and verses. All you have to do is look any verse up as you would in any Bible.

To explore subjects further, turn in the *Cross Reference Guide* to the listed passage marked with the "+" symbol (which indicates "find more here") to do a full study of a particular Bible theme.

These very complete cross references make it possible to find all that the Bible says about any Bible subject. This is important, because failure to consult all the Bible evidence can lead to a mistaken conclusion-or at least an incomplete picture-of what the Bible really teaches.

This *Cross Reference Guide* is even more helpful than the most complete concordance, because it:

- Connects ideas, not just words, and leads the reader to verses related to the topic that may be expressed in different terms
- Connects quotations with their sources
- Connects prophetic predictions with their fulfillments

- Is the only study resource that connects verses and passages expressing cause/effect relationships for practical application Bible study (Psalm 9:10)
- Contains the most complete and accurate cross references to prophetic subjects found anywhere

Using *Nelson's Cross Reference Guide to the Bible* will help you mine far more from Biblical text than just reading alone. Jesus compared Scripture with Scripture (Luke 4:18), and Paul (Acts 17:3) used this technique to study and explain the Bible's mysteries to others, helping everyone fully understand the Word of God. Using this Bible study tool to search the Scriptures (John 5:39) can function as an essential step in promoting your spiritual growth (1 Peter 2:2; 2 Peter 3:18). To enrich your Bible study, you may easily use this resource every day (Joshua 1:8; Acts 17:11), every time you read the Bible.

The *Cross Reference Guide* is keyed to the Authorized or King James Version of the English Bible, chosen because this venerable version is still the only widely accepted standard Bible translation for reference work and study, to which all other translations are compared. However, the *Cross Reference Guide* will work equally well with all other Bible translations and versions.

Nelson's Cross Reference Guide to the Bible is the one Bible study tool that can help you understand the Bible in a comprehensive way, and it is an outstanding way to let the Bible explain itself.

CONVENTIONS

The conventions used in the *Cross Reference Guide* are few and simple:

- A "+" (plus) symbol marks where more verses on the theme are found: turn to the verse so marked in this *Cross Reference Guide* to find more references on that theme. The "+" means "Find more here."
- References in *Italic* type show where the Bible quotes itself, as when the New Testament quotes the Old Testament.
- References in ***Italic bold*** mark prophecies and their fulfillment.

Further conventions of less immediate concern to the general user include:

- Dates are given with the abbreviations A.M. (*anno mundi*, in the year of the world from Creation in 4004 B.C. following Usher), B.C. (year before Christ), A.D. (for dates after Christ), and An. Ex. Is. (Anno Exodus Israel, year since the Exodus from Egypt, see Joshua 13:1). In connection with dates "cir." (see Genesis 20:1) is an abbreviation for *circum* which means "about."
- LXX refers to the Greek Septuagint, the Greek translation used by Christ and the apostles, which sometimes reads differently than the Hebrew text of the Old Testament, most notably at Amos 4:13, noted in the cross references where it is cited at Revelation 1:8, and Deuteronomy 32:43, cited at Hebrews 1:6.
- References to Strong's Concordance word numbers (from its lexicon) are given in the form "**S#430h**" (see Genesis 1:1) for Old Testament Hebrew words, and "**S#622g**" (see Matthew 2:13) for New Testament Greek words.
- Sources cited include Young (author of *Young's Analytical Concordance*), a reference to his *Literal Translation of the Bible* and the accompanying *Concise Critical Comments*, the source of many Old Testament cross references at obscure places, many alternate renderings, and the meaning of Bible names; in the New Testament Alford's *The Greek Testament* has been drawn upon for a few cross references; CB, *Companion Bible*, cited at Isaiah 45:7 and Ezekiel 21:25.
- Alternate renderings provided by the King James translators are introduced by italicized words, most often an italicized *or*; words introducing alternate renderings from other sources are not italicized; the symbol "mg" for "margin" in a reference (like the reference Ps 69:34mg given at Genesis 1:28) refers to these alternate renderings traditionally given in the center or side margin of the Bible.
- Cross references are given in the normal Biblical order, except that references in the same Bible book are given first; references to certain key Bible words (like "soul," "spirit," and in the New Testament to "if") immediately follow the keyword, thus often out of the Biblical order, to connect the keyword reference (or references when separated by the semicolon) to that word. Keyword references show where the complete listing and analysis for the word is given. The subject cross references follow the keyword reference.
- The abbreviations for Bible book names are the standard ones (or should be!) and are given separately with the list of Bible books in canonical order.

CONVENTIONS

BIBLE BOOK ABBREVIATIONS

Ge	Genesis		Mt	Matthew
Ex	Exodus		Mk	Mark
Le	Leviticus		Lk	Luke
Nu	Numbers		Jn	John
Dt	Deuteronomy		Ac	Acts
Jsh	Joshua		Ro	Romans
Jg	Judges		1 C	1 Corinthians
Ru	Ruth		2 C	2 Corinthians
1 S	1 Samuel		Ga	Galatians
2 S	2 Samuel		Ep	Ephesians
1 K	1 Kings		Ph	Philippians
2 K	2 Kings		Col	Colossians
1 Ch	1 Chronicles		1 Th	1 Thessalonians
2 Ch	2 Chronicles		2 Th	2 Thessalonians
Ezr	Ezra		1 T	1 Timothy
Ne	Nehemiah		2 T	2 Timothy
Est	Esther		T	Titus
Jb	Job		Phm	Philemon
Ps	Psalms		He	Hebrews
Pr	Proverbs		Ja	James
Ec	Ecclesiastes		1 P	1 Peter
SS	Song of Solomon		2 P	2 Peter
Is	Isaiah		1 J	1 John
Je	Jeremiah		2 J	2 John
La	Lamentations		3 J	3 John
Ezk	Ezekiel		Ju	Jude
Da	Daniel		Re	Revelation
Ho	Hosea			
Jl	Joel			
Am	Amos			
Ob	Obadiah			
Jon	Jonah			
Mi	Micah			
Na	Nahum			
Hab	Habakkuk			
Zp	Zephaniah			
Hg	Haggai			
Zc	Zechariah			
Ml	Malachi			

BIBLE BOOK ABBREVIATIONS

Genesis	Ge		Matthew	Mt
Exodus	Ex		Mark	Mk
Leviticus	Le		Luke	Lk
Numbers	Nu		John	Jn
Deuteronomy	Dt		Acts	Ac
Joshua	Jsh		Romans	Ro
Judges	Jg		1 Corinthians	1C
Ruth	Ru		2 Corinthians	2C
1 Samuel	1S		Galatians	Ga
2 Samuel	2S		Ephesians	Ep
1 Kings	1K		Philippians	Ph
2 Kings	2K		Colossians	Col
1 Chronicles	1Ch		1 Thessalonians	1Th
2 Chronicles	2Ch		2 Thessalonians	2Th
Ezra	Ezr		1 Timothy	1T
Nehemiah	Ne		2 Timothy	2T
Esther	Est		Titus	T
Job	Jb		Philemon	Phm
Psalms	Ps		Hebrews	Hv
Proverbs	Pr		James	Ja
Ecclesiastes	Ec		1 Peter	1P
Song of Solomon	SS		2 Peter	2P
Isaiah	Is		1 John	1J
Jeremiah	Je		2 John	2J
Lamentations	La		3 John	3J
Ezekiel	Eze		Jude	Ju
Daniel	Da		Revelation	Re
Hosea	Ho			
Joel	Jl			
Amos	Am			
Obadiah	Ob			
Jonah	Jon			
Micah	Mi			
Nahum	Na			
Habakkuk	Hab			
Zephaniah	Zp			
Haggai	Hg			
Zechariah	Zc			
Malachi	Ml			

THE OLD TESTAMENT

GENESIS

GENESIS 1

1 beginning. Pr 8:22-24. 16:4. Mk 13:19. Jn 1:1-3. 15:27. Ac 1:1, 22. He 1:10. 1 J 1:1. Re 3:14.

God. Heb. *Elohim*. **S#430h**. Ge 2:2. +19:29. Ex +2:24. Ps +45:6. 89:11, 12. Ep 3:9. Col 1:16, 17, 18. He 1:2.

created. ver. 21, 27. Ge 2:3. Ne 9:6. Jb 38:4, 7. Is 42:5. 44:24. Je 27:5. Ml +2:10. Jn +1:3. Ac 17:24. Ro 1:19, 20. He 11:3.

heaven. Ge 2:4. 14:19, 22. Ex 20:11. 1 Ch 29:11. Jb 26:13. Ps 19:1. 89:11, 12. 102:25. 104:30. 121:2. Pr 8:22-30. Ec 12:1. Is 40:26. 65:17. Je 10:12. 32:17. 51:15. Zc 12:1. Ac 4:24. 14:15. 2 P 3:4, 5. Re 21:1, 6.

earth. Ex 19:5. Ps 90:2.

2 And. Ge +8:22.

was. or, became. Ge 2:7. 9:15. 19:26. Ex 32:1. Dt 27:9. 2 S 7:24. or, came to pass. Ge 4:3, 14. 22:1. 24:15. 27:1. Jsh 4:1. 5:1. 1 K 13:22. Is 14:24.

without form. Heb. *tohu*, **S#8414h**, Is +45:18. Ge +4:25. Jb 26:7. Is 24:1. 34:11. 45:18. Je 4:23. Jl 2:31. Na 2:10. Mt 27:45. Ep 5:11, 13. Col 1:13. Re 6:12. 8:12. 9:2. 16:10.

and void. Heb. *bohu*. Ge +4:25. **S#922h**. ver. 2. Is 34:11 (emptiness). Je 4:23.

and darkness. Jb +38:9.

deep. or, sea. Ps 42:7. 104:24. Is 51:10. 63:13. Jon +2:5. Hab 3:10. 2 C 11:25.

Spirit. Heb. *ruach*, Is +48:16. Ge 6:17. Jb 26:13. Ps 33:6. 104:30. Is 40:12-14. 42:1. Mt +12:32. Lk 24:49. Jn 3:6, 34. 7:39. Ac 1:5. 2:17, 18. 4:8. 10:38, 44. 1 Th 5:19. Ja 1:18.

moved. Heb. was brooding. **S#7363h**. Dt 32:11. Is 31:5. Jn 3:3-8. Ro 8:5, 9, 14. Ga 4:29. 2 C 5:17, 18.

face. ver. 29. 2:6. +11:8. Ex 32:12. 33:16. Dt 6:15. 1 K 13:34. Jb 37:12. Am 5:8. 9:6, 8. Lk 12:56.

waters. Ge 7:6. Ps 104:6.

3 God. Ps 33:6, 9. Mt 8:3. Jn 11:43, 44.

said. ver. 3, 6, 9, 11, 14, 20, 24, 26, 28, 29.

Let. Ge 13:8. Jb +42:2. Ec 8:4. Mt 13:30. Jn 14:1. Ph 2:5.

be. or, become. ver. 2.

light. Ps 97:11. 119:130. Is 45:7. Jn 1:5, 9. 3:19. 2 C 4:6. 1 J 1:5. 2:8.

was. or, became. ver. 14-19.

4 saw. ver. 10, 12, 18, 25, 31. Ec 2:13. 11:7. 1 P 2:9.

good. or, beautiful. ver. 10, 12, 18, 21, 25, 31. 2:18. Ps 145:9, 10. Ec 3:11.

divided. ver. 7. Is 5:20. 45:7. 2 C 6:14. Ph 1:10.

light. Ex 10:23.

darkness. Jb 26:10.

5 God. Ps 74:16.

called. ver. 5, 8, 10. Ge 5:2. Ps 92:2. Ec 3:11. Is 41:4. Re 1:8, 11, 17. 2:8. 21:6. 22:13.

Day, and. Ge 8:22. Ps 19:2. Is 45:7. Je 33:20. Jn 8:12. 2 Cor 4:6. 1 Th 5:5. He 1:2, 3.

And the. Heb. And the evening was, and the morning was. ver. 8, 13, 19, 23, +31. Ge 19:27. Le 23:32. Ps 104:20.

day. Ex 20:9, 10. Pr +4:18. 1 J 2:8.

6 Let there. ver. 14, 20. Ge 7:11, 12. Jb 9:8. 37:18. Ps 19:1. 33:6, 7, 9. 136:5. 148:4. Pr 8:27. Je 10:12. 51:15. Zp 3:5. Zc 12:1.

firmament. Heb. expansion. ver. 8. Jg 5:4. Jb 26:8. 37:18. Ps 104:5-9. 147:8. Pr 8:28, 29. Is 40:22. Da 7:13. 2 P 3:5-7.

7 made. ver. 16, 25, 31. Ge 2:2, 3. Ex 20:8-11. 31:17. firmament. or, expanse. ver. +6. Ge 7:11. Ps 19:1.

divided. Pr 8:28, 29.

were. or, are.

above. Ps 148:4.

and it. ver. 9, 11, 15, 24. Mt 8:27.

8 God called. ver. 5, 10. Ge 5:2. 32:28.

evening. ver. 5, 13, 19, 23, 31.

9 Let. Jb 26:7, 10. Ps 33:7. 136:5, 6. Ro 6:14. Col 3:1. Re 10:6.

one. Jb 38:8-11. Je 5:22. 2 P 3:5.

dry. Ge +7:11. Ps 104:8. Pr 3:19. 8:29. Is 51:13-16. The exodus through the Red Sea is compared to the third day of creation in the following passages: Ps 66:5, 6. 77:15. Is 8:5-10. 17:13.

10 Earth. Ge 2:5. Ps 24:2. Ec 1:4.

gathering. Ps 33:7. 95:5. 146:6.

Seas. Ge 9:2. Jb 38:8. Pr 8:29.

God saw. ver. 4. Dt 32:4. Ps 104:31.

11 **Let the**. Ge 2:5. Jb 28:5. Ps 147:8. Is 42:5. Mt 6:30. He 6:7.
grass. Heb. tender grass. Dt 32:2. Is 40:8. Da 4:15, 23. Mk 6:39.
seed. Ge +29.
fruit. ver. 29. Ge 2:9, 16. Ps 1:3. Je 17:8. Mt 3:10. Ro 6:22.
after. ver. 11, 12, 21, 24, 25. Ge 7:14. 8:22. Je 13:23. 33:20. Ga 6:7-9.
kind. Ge 6:20. Dt +14:13. Mt 7:16-20. Lk 6:43, 44. 1 C 15:36-38. Ja 3:12.

12 **earth**. Is 61:11. Mk 4:28.
herb. Is 55:10, 11. Mt 13:24-26. Lk 6:44. 2 C 9:10. Ga 6:7.
good. Ps 104:31. 1 T 4:4. Ja 1:17.

13 **evening**. Ps 65:8. 104:23. Ec 11:6. Zc 14:7. Lk 24:29. Jn 20:19. Ac 28:23.
morning. Ge 19:15. Ps 30:5. Mt 16:3. Mk 11:20. 16:2. Lk 21:38. Ac 5:21.
day. ver. 5, 14. Ge 2:4. 43:16. Ex 20:9. Le 23:32. Mt 27:64. Mk 9:31.

14 **Let there**. Dt 4:19. Ps 19:1-6. 74:16, 17. 136:7-9. Is 40:26. 45:7. Je 31:35. 33:20-26.
lights. or, light bearers. Or, rather, luminaries or light-bearers; being a different word from that rendered light, in ver. 3. Ex 25:6. Ps 74:16. 90:8. Pr 15:30.
firmament. ver. +6. Ps 19:1. 150:1. Da 12:3.
heaven. Dt 26:15. Ps 97:6. Mt 24:29. Ac 2:19.
the day. Heb. between the day and between the night.
and let. Ge 8:22. 9:13. Ps 81:3. Jl 2:10, 30, 31. 3:15. Am 8:9. Mt 2:2. Lk 21:25, 26. 23:45. Ac 2:19, 20. Re 6:12. 8:12. 9:2.
signs. 2 K 20:9. Ps 89:36, 37. Is 47:12-14. Je +10:2. Mt 16:1-3. 24:29-31. Lk 12:54-56.
seasons. Ge +17:21 18:14. 21:2. Ps 104:19. Je 31:36, 37. 33:25, 26. Jl 2:23. Ac 14:17.

15 **lights**. ver. 14-18. Dt 33:14. Jsh 10:12. Ps 8:3. Je 31:35. Hab 3:11. 1 C 15:51. Re 21:23.
firmament. ver. +14. Ps 19:1. 150:1. Da 12:3.
light. Is 45:7. 2 C 4:6.
earth. ver. 1. Ex 20:11. 2 K 19:15. Ne 9:6. Ps 90:2. Pr 8:22-26. Is 45:18. Je 27:5. 32:17. 33:25, 26. Jn 1:3. Re 10:6. 14:7.

16 **made**. or, appointed. Ps 104:19.
greater. Ge 15:12, 17. Jsh 10:12, 13. Is 38:8. Ml 4:2. Lk 4:40. Jn 9:5.
lesser. Mt 5:14. Ro 10:18. Ph 2:15.
to rule. Heb. for the rule, etc. Ps 19:4-6. 136:7-9. Is 13:10. 24:23. 40:26. Je 31:35. Jl 2:10, 31. 3:15. Am 8:9. Mt 24:29. 27:45. Ac 2:20. 1 C 15:41. Re 16:8, 9. 21:23.
he made the stars also. Or, with the stars also. Ge 11:4. 37:9. Jg 5:20. 2 K 23:5. Jb 9:9. 38:31, 32. Ps 147:2. Is 13:10. Je +10:2. Am 5:8.

17 **set them**. Ge 9:13. Ps 8:1, 3. Ac 13:47. 2 P 3:5-8.

18 **rule over**. Ps 19:6. Je 4:23-26.
darkness. Jb +38:9.

19 **fourth**. Ge 15:16. Ex 20:5. Le 19:24. Da 2:40. 3:25. 7:23. Zc 8:19. Re 4:7. 6:7, 8. 8:12. 16:8.

20 **Let the waters**. ver. 22. Ge 2:19. 8:17. Jb 12:7-10. Ps 104:24, 25.
bring. Ge 7:21. 8:17. 9:7. Ex 1:7.
moving. *or*, creeping. Ge 7:21. Le 5:2. Dt +14:19. 1 K 4:33.
creature. Ge +2:19.
life. Heb. a living soul. Heb. *nephesh*, soul, ver. 21, 24, 30. Ge +2:7, 19. 9:4, 5, 10, 12, 15, 16. Le 11:10, 46. 24:18. Nu 31:28. Jb 41:21. Ec +3:21. Ezk 47:9. Mt +10:28. 1 C +15:45. Here 'soul,' a part, is used for the whole animal or living creature. For other instances of this figure see ver. 21, 24, 30. Re 16:3.
fowl that may fly. Heb. let fowl fly. Ge 2:19.
open firmament. Heb. face of the firmament. ver. 7, 14.

21 **great**. Jb 7:12. Ps 104:24-26. Ezk 32:2. Jon 1:17. 2:10. Mt 12:40.
creature. Heb. *nephesh*, soul, ver. +20. Ge +2:7, 19.
brought. Ge 8:17. 9:7.
God saw. ver. 18, 25, 31.

22 **blessed**. ver. 28. Dt +28:3.
fruitful. ver. 28. Ge 8:17. 9:1, 7. 30:27, 30. 35:11. Jb 42:12. Ps 107:31, 38. 128:3. Pr 10:22.
fowl. Le 11:9, 13. 1 K 4:33. Ps 148:10.

23 **evening**. Ex 12:6. 18:13. 1 S 17:16. Ps 65:8. 104:23. Ec 11:6. Zc 14:7. Lk 24:29. Jn 20:19. Ac 28:23.
morning. ver. 5, 8, 13, 19, 31. Ge 19:15. Ex 16:21. Nu 9:21. 2 S 23:4. Ps 30:5. 59:16. Mt 16:3. 20:1. Mk 1:35. 11:20. 16:2. Lk 21:38. Ac 5:21.

24 **Let**. Ge 2:20. 6:20. 7:14. 8:19. Ps 50:9, 10.
creature. Heb. *nephesh*, soul, ver. +20. Ge +2:7, 19.
cattle. Cattle, denotes domestic animals living on vegetables; Beasts of the earth, wild animals; especially such as live on flesh; and Creeping things, reptiles; or all the different genera of serpents, worms, and such animals as have no feet.

25 **God made**. Ge 2:19, 20. Je 27:5.

26 **Let us**. Ge 3:22. 11:7. 18:1-3. 19:24. Ex 21:4, 6, 29. Dt +6:4. Jb 35:10. Ps 97:7. 100:3. Is 6:8. 40:25. 48:16. 64:8. Jn 5:17. 14:23. 17:5, 11, 21, 22. 1 J 5:7.
make. Is 54:5. 62:5. Je 3:1, 6. 4:30. Ezk 16:32. Ho 1:2. 2:19. 3:1.
man. In Hebrew, Adam; probably so called either from the red earth of which he was formed, or from the blush or flesh-tint of the human countenance: the name is intended to designate the species.

in our. Ge 5:1, 3. 9:6. Ex 20:4. Le 26:1. Ps 73:20. Is 45:20. 48:5. Je 10:14. Ac 17:26, 28, 29. Ro 1:20. 1 C 11:7. 15:49. 2 C 3:18. 4:4. Ep 4:24. Ph 2:7. Col 1:15. 3:10. He 1:3. Ja 3:9. 1 J 3:2. Re 3:14. 4:11.

image...likeness. Two words are used, but one thing is meant. One of the two words expresses the thing referred to, and the other intensifies and emphasizes it. The second word, if a noun, becomes in effect an adjective of the superlative degree, which is, by this means, made especially emphatic. The two words joined by "and" are always the same part of speech, such as two nouns or two verbs. This figure of speech is one of the most important figures in the Bible, and is very frequently used in both the Old and New Testaments. Here, "image and likeness" by Hendiadys is "in the likeness of our image," thus one thing, not two. For Hendiadys of verbs, see Is +66:11. For additional instances of the figure Hendiadys of nouns see Ge 2:9. 3:16. 4:4. 5:29. 13:13. 19:24. Dt 30:15. 1 S 28:3. 2 S 20:19. 1 K 20:33. 1 Ch 22:5. 2 Ch 2:9. 16:14. Jb 10:17, 21. Ps 74:16. 96:7. 116:1. 119:138. Is 57:8. Je 22:3, 15. 29:11. Da 8:10. Mi 2:11. Zp 1:16. Mt 3:11. 4:16. 24:30, 31. Lk 1:17. 21:15. Jn 1:17. 3:5. 4:23, 24. 11:25, 26. Ac 1:25. 3:14. 14:13. 23:6. Ro 1:5. 2:27. 8:6. 11:17. 1 C 2:4. 11:7. Ep 4:11. 5:5. 6:18. Col 2:8, 18. 1 Th 2:12. 1 T 3:15. 2 T 1:10. 4:1, 2. T 2:13. Ja 3:9. 2 P 1:16, 17. Re 5:10. 6:11. 13:5.

have dominion. ver. 28. Ge 9:2-4. Jb 5:23. Ps 2:8. 8:4-8. 47:3. +49:14. 104:20-24. 145:13. +149:4-9. Is 11:6, 9. Je 27:6. Da 2:38. Zc +14:9. Mt +5:5. Lk +1:32, 33. Ro 4:13. 8:19-23. 1 C +15:24-28. Ep 1:18-21. He +1:2. 2:6-9. 8:11. Ja 3:7. Re 11:15. +20:4.

27   created man. Ge 5:1. Ps 100:3. Ec 7:29. Is 64:8. Ac 17:26. Ja 3:9.

own image. Col 3:10.

in the image. ver. 26. Ps 139:14. Is 43:7. Ep 2:10. 4:24. Col 1:15.

male. 5:2. Ml 2:15. Mt 19:4. Mk 10:6. 1 C 11:8, 9. Ga 3:28.

28   blessed. ver. 22. Ge 2:3. 9:1. 17:16, 20. 22:17, 18. 24:60. 26:3, 4, 24. 49:25. Dt +28:3. 1 Ch 4:10. Jb 42:12. Ps 107:38. 128:4. 1 T 4:3.

them. Ge 2:18, 20-23.

fruitful. ver. 22. Ps +127:3. 128:3. 1 T 4:1, 3. He 13:4.

replenish. or, fill. ver. 22. Ge 9:1. Ex 32:29mg. 1 K 18:33. Is 2:6. 23:2. 45:18. Je 31:25. 51:11 (gather). Ezk 26:2. 27:25.

dominion. ver. +26. Ps 8:6. He 2:6-8.

moveth. Heb. creepeth. Ps 69:34mg.

29   I have. Ps 115:16. Ho 2:8. Ac 17:24, 25, 28. 1 T 6:17.

bearing. Heb. seeding. Here is an instance of

the Figure of speech Polyptoton, where words are repeated in different inflections or endings for emphasis. This figure is often preserved in the marginal renderings. For other instances of this figure see Ge 26:28. 28:20. 30:8. Ps 14:5. 53:5. 64:6. 106:14. Pr 30:24. Is 8:12. Je 22:16. 48:5mg. 51:2. Ezk 13:5mg. 38:12. Da 11:3. Ho 2:6mg. Jon 1:10. Mi 2:4. Na 1:15. Hab 3:2. Zc 1:2, 14, 15. 7:9. Mk 4:41. Lk 22:15. Jn 6:28. 7:24. Ac 23:12, 14. Ep 6:18. Col 2:19. 1 T 1:18. 2 T 4:7. Ja 5:17mg. Re 16:9. 17:6.

to you. Ge 2:16. 9:3. Ps 104:14, 15, 27, 28. 111:5. 136:25. 145:15, 16. 146:7. Is 33:16. Mt 6:11, 25, 26. Ac 14:17.

30   to every beast. Ge 9:3. Ps 104:14. 145:15, 16. 147:9.

life. Heb. a living soul. Heb. *nephesh*, ver. +20. Ge 2:+7, +19.

31   very good. Ge 6:6. Dt 32:4. Ps 19:1, 2. 104:24. 1 T 4:4.

the evening. Evening and morning are put for the full day; or, the whole of a day and night. ver. 5, 8, 13, 19, 23, 31. By this figure the beginning and end of anything is put for the whole of it. Compare Ps 92:2. Ec 3:11. 10:13. 11:6. Is 41:4. 44:6. 48:12. Re 1:8, 11, 17. 2:8. 21:6. 22:13.

and the. ver. 5, 8, 13, 23. Ge 2:2. Ex 20:11. 31:17.

GENESIS 2

1   Thus. ver. 4. Ge 1:1, 10. Ex 20:11. 31:17. Is 45:18. 55:9. 65:17. Ac 4:24. He 4:3. 2 P 3:5-8.

host. Dt +4:19. Is 24:21. 34:4. 40:26-28.

2   And on. Ge 1:31. Ex +20:8, 11. 23:12. 31:17. Dt 5:14. Jn 5:17. Lk 24:1. Col 2:16. He 4:4.

seventh day God. The LXX, Syriac, and the Samaritan Text read *the sixth day*, which is probably the true reading; as the Hebrew letter *vau*, which stands for *six*, might easily be changed into the Hebrew letter *zain*, which denotes *seven*.

rested. Is 40:28.

3   blessed. Ex +20:8-11. Pr 10:22. Is 56:2-7. +58:13, 14. Jn 20:19, 26. Ac 16:13. 20:7. 1 C 16:2. He 4:4-10.

the seventh day. Ge 1:28. 4:3mg. 29:27. Ex 16:26-30.

created and made. Heb. created to make.

4   the generations. Ge 1:4, 11-27. 5:1. 10:1. 11:10. 25:12, 19. 36:1, 9. Ex 6:16. Ps 90:1, 2.

in. Ge 1:3-31.

Lord. i.e. *owner, master*. **S#3068h**, Jehovah. Ex 15:3. 1 K 18:39. 2 Ch 20:6. Ps +9:10. 18:31. 86:10. Is 44:6. Re 1:4, 8. 11:17. 16:5. Jehovah-Elohim. First occurrence of this compound name. For other Jehovah compound names see Ge 15:2, 8. 22:8. Ex +15:26.

17:15. 20:2. 31:13. Jg 6:24. 1 S 1:3. Ps 7:17. 23:1. 95:6. 99:5. Je 23:6. Ezk 48:35. Zc 14:5.
earth. Jb 38:4. Is 45:18.

5 **plant**. Ge 1:12. Ps 104:14.
had not. Jb 5:10. 38:26-28. Ps 65:9-11. 135:7. Je 10:12, 13. 14:22. Mt 5:45. He 6:7.
to till. Ge 3:23. 4:2, 12.

6 **there went up a mist**. *or*, a mist which went up. ver. 5. Ge 7:4. Ps 135:7. 148:8. Je 10:12, 13.
face. Ge +1:2.

7 **Lord God**. ver. +4.
formed. ver. 19. 2 K 19:25. Ps 94:9. 95:5. 100:3. 139:14, 15. Is 45:18. 64:8. Note that man's body was formed, but soul and spirit were created, Ge 1:26, 27, proving man is a compound being.
man. ver. 8, 15. Note man is a compound being consisting of body and spirit, Jb +14:22. Ec +12:7. Mt +10:28. Lk 8:55. Ro 8:10. 1 C 5:3. *15:45*. 2 C 5:6, 8. 1 Th 5:23. He 4:12. 3 J 2.
of the. Heb. dust of the ground.
dust. Ge 3:19, 23. Jb 4:19. 33:6. Ps +103:14. Ec 3:20. +12:7. Is 64:8. Ro 9:20. 1 C 15:47. 2 C 4:7. 5:1. **S#6083h**, translated elsewhere "ashes," Nu 19:17. 2 K 23:4; "earth," Ge 26:15; "ground," Jb 14:8; "morter," Le 14:42, 45; "powder," 2 K 23:6, 15; "rubbish," Ne 4:2, 10.
and breathed. Jb 27:3. 33:4. Ezk 37:9. Jn 20:22. Ac 17:25.
nostrils. Ge 7:22. Ec +3:21. Is 2:22.
breath. Heb. *neshamah*, **S#5397h**. Ge 7:22. Dt 20:16. Jsh 10:40. 11:11, 14. 2 S 22:16. 1 K 15:29. 17:17. Jb 4:9. 26:4. 27:3. 32:8. 33:4. +34:14. 37:10. Ps 18:15. 150:6. Pr 20:27. Is 2:22. 30:33. 42:5. 57:16. Da 5:23. 10:17. Note that "spirit" or "soul" are not merely "breath." "Breath" constitutes function, "spirit" and "soul" often designate "being," or the immaterial part of man. "Breath" is distinct from "spirit" and "soul" as it cannot substitute for these terms in the following passages: Ge 34:3. 41:8. Le 20:27. Dt 2:30. 1 S 1:15. 28:7. 1 K 21:5. 22:21-24. Jb 34:14. Ps 16:10. 19:7. 34:18. 106:15. Pr 16:18, 19. 18:14. Ec 1:14. Is 29:24. 58:5. Mt +10:28. Lk 12:19. Jn 4:23. Ac 23:8, 9. Ep 4:23. 1 Th 5:23. He 4:12. 1 J 4:1. Re 6:9-11. 20:4. The human soul or spirit is distinguished from the divine Spirit from whom it proceeded, thus refuting pantheism, 1 C 2:11. Soul or spirit is distinguished from the body it inhabits, refuting materialism, Ge 35:18. 1 K 17:21. Jb +14:22. Ec +12:7. Zc +12:1. Ja 2:26.
life. Ge 6:17. 7:22. 17:15. Ac 17:25. 1 C 15:45. He 12:9.
became. Ge +1:2.
living. ver. 19. Ge 1:21, 24. Jb 27:3. 32:8. 33:4.

soul. Heb. **S#5315h**, *nephesh*. Ge +1:20. +12:5. 35:18. +41:8. Nu 16:22. 27:16. 1 K 17:21. 2 K 4:27. Jb +14:22. 34:14. Ps 63:1. Pr 20:27. Ec +12:7. Is 10:18. Da 7:15. Zc 12:1. Mt +10:28. Mk 12:26, 27. 1 C 15:45. 1 Th 5:23. He +12:9. Ja 2:26. 1 P +3:4. An examination of its lexical uses shows immediately that "nephesh" is used with a broader range of meaning than the more theological English term "soul." The 754 occurrences of the Hebrew word *nephesh* (most often rendered "soul") may be classified as to its different meanings or lexical uses as follows: (1) Ge +2:19, used of lower creatures; (2) Ge +9:15, used alike of lower creatures and man, rendered "creature," "life" (Le 17:11), "soul" (Nu 31:28); (3) Ge +12:5, used of man as an individual person; (4) Ge +12:13, used of mortal man, as though the soul could die or be destroyed; also rendered "life" (Ge +44:30), "ghost," etc. (Nu +23:10); (5) Ge +17:14, used of man as being "cut off" by God; (6) Ge +27:31, used of man, exercising certain powers, or performing certain acts, often rendered by emphatic pronouns; (7) Ge +34:3, used of man, exercising mental faculties, rendered "soul," "mind" (Ge +23:8), "heart" (Ex +23:9), "lust," etc. (Ex +15:9); also used of God, Le +26:11; (8) Le +19:28, used of man actually dead; (9) Nu +11:6, used of man as possessing animal appetites and desires; (10) Jsh +10:28, used of man being slain or killed by man. (11) Ps +30:3, used of man as going to a place described by the word "grave," etc. Compare the classification of the corresponding New Testament term *psyche* at Mt +2:20. For "spirit," Heb. *ruach*, see Ge +6:3.

8 **a garden**. Ge 13:10. SS 6:2. Is 51:3. Ezk 28:13. 31:8, 9. Jl 2:3. Jn 19:41.
eastward. Ge 3:24. 4:16. 2 K 19:12. Ezk 27:23. 31:16, 18.
Eden. LXX paradise. i.e. *delight*, **S#5731h**. ver. 8, 10, 15. Ge 3:23, 24. 4:16. 2 Ch 29:12. 31:15. Is 51:3. Ezk 28:13. 31:9, 16, 18. 36:35. Jl 2:3.
put the. ver. 15.
formed. Ro 9:20.

9 **every**. Ezk 31:8, 9, 16, 18.
tree of life. Ge 3:22. Pr 3:18. 11:30. Ezk 47:12. Jn 6:48, 51, 53. Re 2:7. 22:2, 14.
midst. Re 2:7.
tree of knowledge. ver. 17. Ge 3:3, 22. Dt 6:25. Pr 1:7. Is 44:25. 47:10. Ro 3:20. 1 C 8:1.
good and evil. Figure of speech Hendiadys, Ge +1:26. Thus here, tree of evil enjoyment.

10 **And a**. lit. And there was a.
river. Ps 36:8. 46:4. Ezk 47:1. Jl 3:18. Zc 14:8. Jn 7:38. Re 22:1.
thence it was parted. or, thence it will part, or gets parted, or parts itself.

11 **Pison**. i.e. *overflowing*, **S#6376h**, only here.
Havilah. Ge +10:7.

12　bdellium. Nu 11:7.
　　onyx. Ex 25:7. 28:9, 20. 35:9, 27. 39:6, 13. 1
　　Ch 29:2. Jb 28:16. Ezk 28:13.
13　Gihon. i.e. *the great breaking forth*, **S#1521h**. 1 K
　　1:33, 38, 45. 2 Ch 32:30. 33:14.
　　Ethiopia. Heb. Cush. **S#3568h**. Ge +10:6-8. 2
　　K 19:9. 1 Ch 1:8-10. Est 1:1. 8:9. Jb 28:19. Ps
　　7:t. 68:31. 87:4. Is 11:11. 18:1. 20:3-5. 37:9.
　　43:3. 45:14. Je 46:9. Ezk 29:10. 30:4, 5, 9.
　　38:5. Na 3:9. Zp 3:10. For **S#3569h**, see Nu
　　+12:1. Ac 8:27.
14　Hiddekel. i.e. *sharp voice or sound*, **S#2313h**. Da
　　10:4. The Tigris.
　　toward the east of. or, eastward to. Ge 4:16.
　　Assyria. i.e. *a step*, **S#804h**. Ge 10:11, 22.
　　25:18. Is 7:17, 18, 20. 8:4, 7. 10:12. 11:11, 16.
　　19:23-25. 20:1, 4, 6. 27:13. 36:1, 2, 4, 8, 13,
　　15, 16, 18. 37:4, 6, 8, 10, 11, 18, 21, 33, 37.
　　38:6. Je 2:18, 36. 50:17, 18. Ezk 23:7. Ho
　　7:11. 8:9. 9:3. 10:6. 11:11. Mi 5:6. 7:12. Na
　　3:18. Zp 2:13. Zc 10:10, 11.
　　Euphrates. i.e. *fruitfulness*, **S#6578h**. Ge 15:18.
　　Dt 1:7. 11:24. Jsh 1:4. 2 S 8:3. 2 K 23:29.
　　24:7. 1 Ch 5:9. 18:3. 2 Ch 35:20. Ps +72:8. Je
　　13:4-7. 46:2, 6, 10. 51:63. Re 9:14.
15　the man. or, Adam. Ge 5:2. Jb 31:33.
　　put. ver. 8. Ps 128:2. Ep 4:28. 2 Th 3:10. 1 T
　　5:8.
　　dress. Dt 28:39.
　　keep. Heb. keep diligently, watch, guard,
　　keep safe, protect, preserve. Same Heb. word
　　(**S#8104h**) used at Ge 3:24. Ex 22:7, 10. Dt 4:2.
　　5:12, 29. 7:8. Jsh 10:18. 2 Ch 34:31. Ps 19:11.
　　91:11. 119:4, 5, 57, 60, 106. Pr 6:24. 7:5. Ec
　　3:6. Ezk 17:14.
16　God. 1 S 15:22.
　　saying. Ge 1:3. 3:9. 6:13. 12:1. 13:14. 15:18.
　　Ex 3:4, 5.
　　thou mayest freely eat. Heb. eating thou
　　shalt eat. ver. 9. Ge 3:1, 2. 1 T 4:4. 6:17.
　　Repetition of the word "eat" in two different
　　grammatical forms is a form of strong empha-
　　sis known as the figure of speech Polyptoton.
　　When Eve omitted this figure in Ge 3:2, she
　　changed and thus "diminished" from the
　　word of God. For other instances of this figure
　　see ver. 17. Is 6:9. Da 11:13. Zc 8:21. Mt
　　13:13, 14. Mk 4:12. Lk 8:10. Ro 11:8. 12:15.
　　He 6:14.
17　of the tree. ver. 9. Ge 3:1-3, 11, 17, 19. Ac
　　5:30. 10:39. 1 P 2:24. Re 2:7. 22:2.
　　good and evil. Dt 6:4. Ro 3:20.
　　in the day. Ezk 33:12. Here, "in the day" is
　　put for an indefinite time and means simply
　　"when," or "after then," or "after that." For
　　other instances of this figure see ver. 4. Le
　　13:14. 14:57. Dt 21:16. 2 S 21:12. 1 K 2:37. 2
　　K 20:1. Ps 18:18. Is 11:16. Je 11:3, 4. 31:32.
　　34:13. Ezk 20:5, 6. 36:33. 38:18. The action is
　　put for the declaration concerning it. The

meaning is not that he would die that very
day, but that he would be sentenced to die "in
that day." For other instances of this figure
see Ge 27:37. 30:13. 34:12. Je 1:5, 10.
　　thou shalt surely die. Heb. dying thou shalt
die. Figure of speech Polyptoton, ver. +16.
Here again Eve in Ge 3:3 alters the Word of
God by saying "Lest ye die"! Thus she changes
a certainty into a contingency. Not only does
she thus diminish from and alter the Word of
God but she adds to it the words "neither
shall ye touch it," which the Lord God had
not spoken!
　　surely. Ge 3:3, 4, 19. 5:5. 20:7. Le 22:9. Nu
26:65. Dt 27:26. 30:15, 19, 20. Je 15:1, 2.
26:8. Ezk 3:18-20. 18:4, 13, 32. Ro 3:23. 5:12-
21. 6:16, 23. 7:10-13. 8:2. 1 C 15:22, 56. Ga
3:10. Ep 2:1-6. 4:18. Col 2:13. 1 T 5:6. He
+9:27. Ja 1:15. 1 J +5:16. Re 2:11. 20:6, 14.
21:8.
18　It. This is an example of the figure of speech
Heterosis of Gender; here, the masculine for
the neuter, as the Hebrew has no neuter gender. Translated literally from the Hebrew, this
would read "He is not good." The use of this
figure is highly significant in Jn 16:13, 14
where John violates Greek grammar to
emphasize the personality of the Holy Spirit.
For other instances of this figure, see Jn
16:13, 14. Ep 1:14.
　　good. Ge 3:12. 24:4. Ru 3:1. Pr 18:22. Ec 4:9-
12. Mt 19:5. 1 C 7:1, 2, 36. 1 T 4:1, 3. He 13:4.
　　I will. Ge 3:12. 1 C 11:7-12. 1 T +2:11-13. 1 P
3:7.
　　meet for him. Heb. as before him.
19　And out. Ge 1:20-25.
　　brought. ver. 22, 23. Ge 1:26, 28. 6:20. 9:2.
Ps 8:4-8.
　　Adam. or, the man. ver. 15mg. i.e. *red earth*,
S#120h. ver. 19, 20, 23. 3:8, 9, 20, 21. 4:1, 25.
5:1, 2. Dt 32:8. See **S#121h**: ver. 21. 3:17. 5:3,
4, 5. 1 Ch 1:1. Jb 31:33. Compare Jsh 3:16,
the name of a town.
　　to see. Ge 1:4, 10, 12, 18, 21, 25. +3:9. 6:5, 6.
7:1. 11:5. 16:13. +18:21. 1 S 16:7. Ps 1:6. 2 T
2:19.
　　creature. Mt +2:20. **S#5315h**. Heb. *nephesh*,
soul, used of lower creatures in Ge 1:20, 21,
24, 30. 9:4, 10, 12, 15, 16. Le 11:10, 46.
17:11, 14. 24:18. Nu 31:28. Dt 12:23. Jb
12:10. 41:21. Pr 12:10. Is 19:10. Je 2:24. Ezk
47:9. For the other uses of *nephesh*, see ver. +7.
20　gave names to. Heb. called.
　　but. ver. 18. 1 C 11:9.
21　deep. Ge 15:12. 1 S 26:12. Jb 4:13. 33:15. Pr
19:15. Da 8:18. Jn 12:24. 19:30. Ro 5:14.
22　rib. 1 C 11:8, 9.
　　made. Heb. builded. 1 K 18:32. Ps 127:1. 1 T
2:13.
　　brought. ver. 19. Pr 18:22. 19:14. He +13:4.

23 bone. Ge +29:14. He 2:14.
flesh. ver. 24. Mt 19:5, 6.
Woman. Heb. Isha. 1 C 11:8, 9.
taken. Pr 19:14. 1 C 11:8.
Man. Heb. Ish.
24 Therefore. Ge 10:9. 26:33. 32:32. Mt *19:5.*
Mk *10:7.* 1 C *6:16.* Ep *5:31.*
leave. Ge 24:58, 59. 31:14, 15. 39:6. Ps
45:10. Lk 14:26.
cleave. Le 22:12, 13. Dt +4:4. Pr 12:4.
31:10.
and they. The LXX, Vulgate, Syriac, Arabic,
and Samaritan read "they TWO;" as is also
read in several of the Parallel Passages. Ml
2:14-16. Mt 19:3-9. Mk 10:6-12. Ro 7:2. 1 C
6:16, 17. 7:2-4, 10, 11. Ep 5:28-31. 1 T 5:14. 1
P 3:1-7.
one. Ge 1:26, 27. Dt +6:4.
25 naked. Ge 3:7, 10, 11. 9:22. Is +20:2. He
4:13. Re 7:9-14.
ashamed. Ex 32:25. Ezr +9:6. Is +42:17.
47:3. Da 12:2. Jl +2:26. Mk 8:38. Ep 5:27. Ph
3:19. Col 1:22, 28. 2 P 3:11, 14. Ju 24.

GENESIS 3

1 Now. ver. 13-15. Is 27:1. Mt 10:16. 2 C 11:3,
14. Re 12:9. 20:2.
serpent. The Samaritan Copy, instead of
nachash, 'a serpent,' reads *cachash,* 'a liar, or
deceiver,' read Jn 8:44. Ezk 28:13, 14, 16, 17.
2 C 2:11. 11:3, 14.
subtil. This word means wise, sometimes in a
good sense, as in Ezk 28:12; rendered "prudent" frequently in Pr +22:3. For the evil
sense see Ezk 28:17. Jb 5:12. 15:5. 1 S 23:22.
Ps 83:3.
beast. or, living being or creature. Re 4:6-9.
5:6, 8, 14.
And. Ge 1:2. +8:22. Lk 14:21.
he said. Nu 22:28, 29. Ec 4:10. 1 P 3:7.
Yea, hath. Heb. Yea, because. Ps 35:10.
hath. Jb 1:7, 9-11. 2:2, 4, 5. Mt 4:3, 6, 9.
2 serpent. Ps 58:4.
may eat. Misquoted from Ge 2:16 by not
repeating the emphatic figure of speech
Polyptoton, and thus omitting the emphatic
"freely."
fruit. Ge 2:16, 17.
3 But. Ge 2:16, 17. Ja 2:19.
neither. Pr 30:6. Lk 19:21.
touch. Ge 20:6. Ex 19:12, 13. 1 Ch 16:22. Jb
1:11. 2:5. 19:21. 1 C 7:1. 2 C 6:17. Col 2:21.
lest. Eve's misquotation changed the
emphatic certainty expressed at Ge 2:17 into a
contingency by not retaining the figure of
speech Polyptoton preserved in the word
"surely."
4 serpent. Jn 8:44.
Ye. ver. 13. Dt 29:19. 2 K 1:4, 6, 16. 8:10. Ps

10:11. Ezk +13:22. 2 C 2:11. 11:3. 1 T 2:14.
not. Ge 2:17. Mt 2:8.
surely. Ge 2:16.
5 God. Ex 20:7. 1 K 22:6. Je 14:13, 14. 28:2, 3.
Ezk 13:2-6, 22. 2 C 11:3, 13-15.
your. ver. 7, 10. Mt 6:23. Ac 26:18. 1 C 2:9.
Ep 1:18.
ye. Is 14:14. Ezk 28:2, 12-17. Pr 2:6. Ph 2:6.
as gods. Ps 12:4. 82:6. Ezk 28:2, 9. Ac 12:22,
23. 2 C 4:4. 2 Th 2:4. Re 13:4, 14.
knowing. ver. 22. Ge 2:17.
6 saw. Jsh 7:21. Jg 16:1, 2. Ja 1:14, 15.
was good. Mt 4:3. 1 J 2:16.
pleasant. Heb. a desire. Ezk 24:16, 21, 25.
to the eyes. Ge 6:2. 39:7. Jsh 7:21. 2 S 11:2.
Jb 31:1. Ps +101:3. Mt 4:5, 8. 5:28. 1 J 2:16.
wise. Ne 8:13mg. 9:20. Pr 21:11. Da 9:22mg.
and did. 1 T 2:14.
and he did eat. ver. 12, 17. Ho 6:7mg. Ro
5:12-19.
7 And the. ver. 5. Dt 28:34. 2 K 6:20.
Lk 16:23.
opened. Ge 21:19. 1 Ch 21:16. Ps +119:18.
Lk 4:18. Jn 20:16. Ac 9:17, 18.
knew. ver. 10, 11. Ge 2:25. +4:1.
naked. Ge +2:25. Is +20:2.
and they. ver. 21. Jb 9:29-31. Ps 32:1. Pr
28:13. Is 28:20. 59:6.
sewed. Jb 16:15. Ec 3:7. Ezk 13:8.
fig. Mt 21:19. Ph 3:9.
aprons. or, things to gird about.
8 And they. ver. 10. Dt 4:33. 5:25, 26.
voice. Dt 18:16. 2 S 22:14. Jb 37:4. 38:1. Ps
29:3-9. 95:7. 106:25. Jl 2:11. Mt 3:17. 17:5.
Jn 10:27. 12:28. 2 P 1:17, 18.
walking. Ge 18:33. Le 26:12. Dt 23:14.
cool of the day. Heb. wind. Jb 34:21, 22. 38:1.
hid. Jb 31:33. Ps +11:4. 32:7. 94:9. 139:1-12.
Ho 10:8. Jon 1:3, 9, 10. Ro 2:15. Re 6:15-17.
9 the Lord. Ge 4:9. 11:5. 16:8. 18:20, 21. Jsh
7:17-19. Re 20:12, 13.
called. ver. 20. Ge 1:5. 2:19. 4:17, 25. Jn 10:3.
Where. Ge 18:9. 1 K 19:13. Mt 2:2.
10 voice. Lk 24:15, 32.
I was afraid. Ex 3:6. Dt 5:25. Jb 23:15. Ps
119:120. Is 33:14. 57:11. 1 J 3:20.
because. ver. +7.
11 hast thou. Ge 2:16, 17. 4:10. Ps 50:21. 90:8.
Ro 3:20. 5:12-21.
12 The woman. Ge 2:18, 20, 22. Ex 32:21-24. 1
S 15:15, 20-24. Jb 31:33. Pr 19:3. 28:13. Lk
10:29. Ro 10:3. Ja 1:13-15.
13 What. Ge 44:15. 2 S 3:24. 12:9-12. Jn
+18:35. Ga 6:7.
The serpent. ver. 1, 2, 4-6. 2 C 11:3, 14. 1 T
2:14.
14 thou art. ver. 1. Ge 9:6. Ex 21:28-32. Le
20:25. Dt 28:15-20.
upon. Ps 44:25.
dust. Ps 72:9. Is 29:4. 65:25. Mi 7:17.

15 enmity. Nu 21:6, 7. Ezk 25:15. Am 9:3. Mt 3:7. 12:34. 23:33. Lk 10:19. Ac 28:3-6. Ro 3:13. Ja +4:4. Re 12:7, 9.
thee. Ho +11:1. Mt +16:23.
thy seed. Ge 12:7. 17:7. 21:12. Mt 13:38. Jn 8:44. Ac 13:10. Ro 9:7. Ga 3:16. 1 J 3:8, 10.
her seed. Ge 12:1-3. +49:10. Nu 24:15-19. Dt 18:15-19. 2 S 7:16. Ps ch. 2. 16:9, +10, 11. ch. 22, 45, 72, 110. +132:11. Is 7:14. 9:6. 11:1-2, 10. 35:3-5, 10. Je 31:22, 31-34. Ezk 34:23, 24. 37:22-25. Da 9:24-27. Ho 6:1-3. Am 9:11-15. Mi 5:1-3. Hg 2:7. Zc 3:8. 6:12. 9:9-10. Ml 1:10-11. 3:1. 4:2. Mt 1:18, 23, 25. Lk 1:31-35, 76. Ro 16:20. Ga +4:4. 1 J 3:8. Re 12:5.
it shall. Ro 16:20. Col 2:15. He 2:14, 15. 1 J 3:8. Re 12:7, 8, 17. 20:1-3, 10.
bruise. Jb 9:17. Ps 139:11 (cover).
thou. Ge 49:17. Is 53:3, 4, 12. Da 9:26. Mt 4:1-10. Lk 10:17-20. 22:39-44, 53. Jn 12:31-33. 14:30, 31. 16:11. Ac 3:15. 1 C 15:55. 2 T 1:10. He 2:18. 5:7. Re 2:10. 12:9-13. 13:7. 15:1-6. 20:7, 8.

16 and. Ge +1:26.
conception. Ps 51:5.
in sorrow. Ge 5:29. 35:16-18. 1 S 4:19-21. Is 42:14. 53:11. Je +4:31. Mi 4:9, 10. Jn 16:21. 1 T 2:15.
thy desire. Ge 4:7. SS 7:10.
to. *or*, subject to.
rule. Nu 30:7, 8, 13. Est 1:20. 1 C 7:4. 11:3. 14:34. Ep 5:22-24. Col +3:18. 1 T 2:11, 12. T 2:5. 1 P 3:1-6.

17 Adam. Ho 6:7mg.
Because. Ge 16:2. 1 S 15:23, 24. Mt 22:12. 25:26, 27, 45. Ro 3:19.
hast eaten. ver. 6, 11. Ge 2:16, 17. Je 7:23, 24.
cursed. Ge 5:29. Ps 127:2. Is 24:5, 6. Ro 8:20-22.
in sorrow. Jb 5:6, 7. 14:1. Ps 90:7-9. 127:2. Ec 2:22, 23. 5:17. Jn 16:33.

18 Thorns. Nu 33:55. Jsh 23:13. Jg 8:7. Jb 5:5. Pr 22:5. Is 5:6. 55:13. Je 4:3. 12:13. Ho 2:6. Mt 13:7, 22. Jn 19:2. Ro 8:22. 2 C 12:7. He 6:8.
thistles. Jb 31:40. 2 K 14:9. Ho 10:8. Mt 7:16.
bring forth. Heb. cause to bud.
herb. Ps 104:14, 15. Ro 14:2.

19 In. Ep 4:28. 2 Th 3:10.
face. Ec 8:1. Is 3:15. 36:9. La 5:12. Ac 20:25, 38.
bread. Bread is put for all kinds of food. Ge 18:5. 39:6. 43:25, 31. Ex +18:12. Dt 8:3. Ps 41:9. 102:4. +107:18 (meat). 146:7. Ec 9:11. Is 33:16. +58:7. Je 52:33. Mt 4:4. 6:11. 15:2, 26. Lk 14:1, 15. Jn 13:18. Ac 2:42, 46.
till. Jb 1:21. Ps 90:3. 104:29.
return. He 9:27.
thou taken. Ge +2:7. 18:27.
for dust. Ge 2:7. 18:27. Ps 103:14. Ec 12:7.

unto dust. Jb 21:26. 34:15. Ps +103:14. 104:29. Ec 3:20. +12:7. Da 12:2. Ro 5:12-21. He +9:27.

20 Adam called. Ge 2:20, 23. 5:29. 16:11. Ex 2:10. 1 S 1:20. Mt 1:21, 23.
Eve. Heb. Chavah; that is, living. i.e. *life giver*, **S#2332h**. Ge 4:1. 2 C 11:3. 1 T 2:13.
of. Ac 17:26.
living. Ro 4:17.

21 make. ver. 7. Ps 32:1. Pr 28:13. Ro 3:22. 2 C 5:2, 3, 21.
coats. Is 61:10. 64:6. Mt 22:11. Lk 15:22. Ro 10:3. 13:14. Ph 3:9.
skins. Ge 27:16.

22 Behold. Ge 15:3, 12, 17. Ps 133:1.
become. Is 57:12. Zc 11:13 (goodly).
as one. ver. 5. Ge +1:26. 11:6, 7.
us. ver. 5. Ge +1:26. Dt 32:37. Jg 10:14. Ec 11:9. Is 2:10. 57:12, 13. Je 46:9, 11. Ezk 20:39. 28:3. Am 4:4, 5. Mk 7:9. Lk 11:41. 13:33. Jn 3:10. 1 C 6:4. 2 C 13:5.
good. Heb. *tov*, meaning general good. Ge 1:4. 6:2. Dt 1:25. 3:25. Est 1:11mg.
tree. Ge 2:9. Pr 3:18. Re 2:7. 22:2.
eat. Ps 22:26. Jn 6:48-58.
for ever. Heb. *olam*, Ex +12:24.

23 sent. Ge 21:14. 25:6. 28:5. 45:7.
to till. ver. 19. Ge 2:5. 4:2, 12. 9:20. Ec 5:9. Je 27:11.

24 drove. Ge 4:14, 16. Ezk 31:11.
east. Ge 2:8.
Cherubims. Ex 25:18, 20, 22. 36:8. 37:7-9. Nu 7:89. 1 S +4:4. 2 S 22:11. 1 K 6:23, 25-29, 32, 35. 8:6, 7. 1 Ch 13:6. 28:18. 2 Ch 3:7, 10, 11. 5:8. Ps 18:10. +104:4. Is 37:16. Ezk 9:3. 10:1, 2, 4, 19, 20. 11:22. 28:14, 16. 41:18. He 1:7, 14. 9:5.
a flaming. Nu 22:23. Jsh 5:13. 1 Ch 21:16, 17. He 1:7.
turned. Jb 37:12.
keep. Ge +2:15.
way. Jn 14:6. He 10:18-22.
tree. Ge 2:9.

GENESIS 4

1 knew. ver. +17, 25. Ge 3:7. +15:15. 19:5, 8. 24:16. 38:26. Nu 31:17. Jg 11:39. 19:25. 1 S 1:19. 1 K 1:4. Mt 1:25.
Cain. *That is*, gotten or acquired. i.e. *possession, acquisition*, **S#7014h**. ver. 1-3, 5, 6, 8, 9, 13, 15-17, 24, 25.
I have. ver. 25. Ge 3:15. 5:29. 1 J 3:12.
from the Lord. Ge 33:5. Ps +127:3.

2 Abel. Heb. Hebel. i.e. *vanity, transitory* **S#1893h**. ver. 4, 8, 9, 25.
And Abel. Ge 30:29-31. 37:13. Ex 3:1. Ps 78:70-72. Am 7:15. Lk 11:50, 51.
a keeper. Heb. a feeder. ver. 25. 46:32, 34. 47:3.

Cain. Jn 8:44. 1 J 3:10, 12, 15.
tiller. Ge 3:23. 9:20.
3　A.M. 129. B.C. 3875.
in the process of time. Heb. at the end of days. Either at the end of the year, or of the week, i.e. on the Sabbath. Ne +13:6mg.
the fruit. Ge 3:17. Le +23:10, 13.
4　**the firstlings**. Ex 13:2, 12. 34:19. Le 27:26. Nu 18:12, 17. Pr 3:9. He 9:22. 1 P 1:19, 20. Re 13:8.
flock. Heb. sheep, or, goats.
fat. Ex 29:13. Le 3:4, 16, 17.
had respect. Ge 15:17. Le 9:24. Nu 16:35. Jg 6:21. 1 S 15:22. 1 K 18:24, 38. 1 Ch 21:26. 2 Ch 7:1. Ps 20:3mg. He 11:4. 1 P 1:18, 19. Re 13:8.
5　**not respect**. Nu 16:15. 1 S 16:7. Pr 21:27. Ec 8:13. Ac 10:34. He 11:4. Ja 1:15.
wroth. Ge 31:2, 5. Jb 5:2. Is 3:9-11. Mt 20:15. Lk 15:28-30. 1 J 3:12. Ju 11.
countenance. Ge 31:2. Jb 29:24. Ps 4:6.
6　**Why**. 1 Ch 13:11-13. Jb 5:2. Is 1:18. Je 2:5, 31. Jon 4:1-4, 8-11. Mi 6:3-5. Mt 20:15. Lk 15:31, 32.
7　**If**. Ex 19:5, 6. Le 26:3, 14, 15, 18, 21, 23, 24, 27, 28, 40-42. Dt 4:26-29. 8:19, 20. 11:22, 26-28. 15:5. 19:9. 30:9, 10, 17, 18. Jsh 24:20. 1 S 7:3. 12:14, 15. 1 K 6:12. 8:31, 32, 46-50. 9:2-9. 1 Ch 28:6-9. 2 Ch +7:14. 15:1, 2. 30:9. Ne 1:8, 9. Is 1:19, 20. Je +7:5.
thou doest well. Ge 19:21. Jb 42:8. Pr 18:5. Ec 8:12, 13. Is 3:10, 11. Mi 7:18. Ml 1:8, 10, 13. Ac 10:35. Ro 2:7-11. 12:1. 14:18. Ep 1:6. 1 T 5:4. 1 P 2:5.
be accepted. *or*, have the excellency. Ge 49:3. Pr 21:27. He 11:4.
and if. Nu 32:23.
sin. ver. 8-13. Ro 7:8, 9. Ep 5:2. Ja 1:15. Sin is put for the offering for sin. For other instances of this figure see Ex 29:14. 30:10. Le 4:3. 6:25. 7:7. Nu 8:8. Ho 4:8. 2 C 5:21.
lieth. By the figure Personification the sin offering as a live animal is represented as a person waiting at the door. By this figure things are represented as persons and human actions are attributed to things. For other examples of this figure see Ge 18:20. 30:33. Ex 18:8. Dt 31:17, 21, 29. Jb 31:29. Ps 85:10. 116:3. 119:143. Ec 2:2. Is 59:12, 14. Je 14:7. 1 C 13:4, 5, 6, 7. Ja 1:15. Re 18:5.
unto thee. *or*, subject unto thee. Ge 3:16mg.
rule. Jb 11:14, 15. Ro 6:12, 16.
8　**talked**. 2 S 3:27. 13:26-28. 20:9, 10. Ne 6:2. Ps 36:3. 55:21. Pr 26:24-26. Mi 7:6. Lk 22:48.
Cain rose. 2 S 14:6. Ps 24:3-6. Mt 23:35. Jn 18:23. T 3:3. Ja 1:15. 1 J 3:12-15. Ju 11.
slew. He 12:24.
9　**Where is**. Ge 3:9-11. Nu +32:23. Ps 9:12.

I know. ver. +1. Ge 37:32. Jb 22:13, 14. Ps 10:13, 14. Pr +28:13. Jn 8:44. Ac 5:4-9.
10　**What**. Ge 3:13. 20:9. 31:26. Jsh 7:19. 1 S 13:11. Ps 50:21. Jn 18:35.
voice. Ge 18:20, 21. 19:13. Ex 3:7, 9. Nu 35:33. Dt 21:1-9. Is 26:21. Hab 2:11. Mt 27:25. Re 6:10.
blood. Heb. bloods. 2 K +9:26mg. The plural is used for the singular, to express great excellence or magnitude. For other examples of this usage see Ge 19:11. 2 K +9:26mg. Ps 42:5, 11. 51:17. 89:1. Is 58:11mg. Ezk 25:17mg. 28:10. Mt 26:65. Jn 1:13. Ac 1:7. Ro 12:1. 2 C 1:3. He 9:8, 12, 23. Ja 1:17. 1 P 5:3. 2 P 3:11. Re 5:10.
crieth. Ge +27:34. Ex +22:23. 2 K 9:26. Ps 9:12. 72:14. 116:15. Ac 5:3, 9. He 11:4. 12:24. Re 6:10. By the figure of speech Personification, intelligence, words, or actions are attributed to inanimate things. For other instances of this figure see ver. 11. Jsh 24:27. Jg 5:20. 2 K 3:19mg. Jb 31:38. 38:7. Ps 19:1. SS 1:6. Is 14:8. 55:12. Je 31:15. 51:48. Ro 8:19. 9:20. 10:6.
11　**cursed**. ver. 14. Ge 3:14. Dt 27:16-26. 28:15-20. 29:19-21. Ga 3:10.
opened. Jb 16:18. 31:38-40. Is 26:21. Re 12:16.
mouth. ver. +10.
hand. Dt 28:20.
12　**it**. Ge 3:17, 18. Le 26:20. Dt 28:15-24. Jl 1:10-20. Ro 8:20.
strength. Pr 5:10.
a fugitive. ver. 14. Le 26:17, 36. Dt 28:64-67. Ps 109:10. Je 20:3, 4. Ho 9:17.
13　**My punishment is greater than I can bear**. or, Mine iniquity is greater than that it may be forgiven. Ge +2:17. 19:15. 1 S 28:10. Jb 15:22. 21:19. Is 5:18. 55:7. Mt 12:31, 32. Jn 6:37. Ja +5:19, 20. 1 J +5:16. Re 16:9, 11, 21.
14　**driven**. Ge 3:24. Jb 15:20-24. Pr +14:32. 28:1. Is 8:22.
from thy. ver. 16. Jb 21:14, 15. Ps +51:11. Mt 25:41, 46. 2 Th 1:9.
face. Ge +1:2.
fugitive. ver. +12.
that. ver. 15. Ge 9:5, 6. Le 26:17, 36. Nu 17:12, 13. 35:19, 21, 27. 2 S 14:7. Jb 15:20-24. Pr. 28:1.
15　**And**. Ro 2:4.
Therefore. 1 K 16:7. Ps 59:11. Ho 1:4. Mt 26:52.
slayeth. Ge 9:6. Nu 35:21.
sevenfold. ver. 24. Le 26:18, 21, 24, 28. Ps 79:12. Pr. 6:31.
set a mark, etc. Or, rather, 'gave a sign or token to Cain, that those who found him should not kill him.'

mark (token). Ex 12:13. Ezk 9:4, 6. Re 14:9, 11.

16 **went**. ver. 14. Jb 1:12. 2:7. Ps 51:11. 68:2. Je 23:39. Jon 1:3, 10. Mt 18:20. 27:5. Lk 13:26, 27. Jn 13:30. 2 C 7:10. 1 Th 1:9.
Nod. i.e. *wandering*, **S#5113h**. So called from *nad*, a vagabond, which Cain is termed in ver. 12. Ge +2:8. Is 51:3.

17 **knew**. ver. +1. Ex +34:15.
Enoch. Heb. Chanoch. Ge 5:18, 22.
and he. Ge 11:4. Ps 127:1. Ec 2:4-11. Da 4:30. Lk 12:16-21. 17:28, 29.
city. He 11:9, 10.
the name. 2 S 18:18. Ps 49:11.

18 A.M. cir. 194. B.C. cir. 3810.
Irad. i.e. *fugitive*, **S#5897h**.
Mehujael. i.e. *grief*, **S#4232h**.
Methusael. i.e. *man of God*, **S#4967h**.
Lamech. Heb. Lemech. i.e. *powerful, over-thrower*, **S#3929h**. ver. 18, 19, 23, 24. 5:25, 26, 28, 30, 31. 1 Ch 1:3. Lk 3:36.

19 **two wives**. Ge 2:18, 24. 16:1-6. 25:1, 6. 26:34. 28:9. 29:25-30. 32:22. 36:2, 3. Le 18:18. Dt 17:17. 21:15-17. Jg 8:30, 31. Ru 4:11. 1 S 1:2, 4, 5. 25:42, 43. 27:3. 30:5. 2 S 2:2. 3:2-5, 7. 5:13. 12:8. 1 K 11:1-3. 1 Ch 4:5. 14:3. 2 Ch 11:18, 21. 13:21. 24:3. Ne 13:26. SS 6:8. Is 4:1. Da 5:2. Ml 2:15. Mt 19:4, 5, 8. 1 T 3:2, 12. 5:9. T 1:6.
Adah. i.e. *pleasure, ornament*, **S#5711h**. ver. 19, 20, 23. Ge 36:2, 4, 10, 12, 16.
Zillah. i.e. *a shade*, **S#6741h**. ver. 19, 22, 23.

20 **Jabal**. i.e. *flowing, leading, a river; nomad; a stream*, **S#2989h**.
the. ver. 21. 1 Ch 2:50-52. 4:4, 5. Jn 8:44. Ro 4:11, 12.
father. The inventor or teacher. 1 S 10:12.
dwell. ver. 2. Ge 9:21. 25:27. Je 35:7, 9, 10. He 11:9.
cattle. Ge 26:14. 47:17. Ex 34:19. Ec 2:7.

21 A.M. cir. 500. B.C. cir. 3504.
Jubal. i.e. *music*, **S#3106h**. ver. 21.
father. Ro 4:11, 12.
handle. Je 2:8. 46:9. Ezk 27:29. 38:4.
the harp. Ge 31:27. Am 6:5. Re +5:8.
organ (pipe). Jb 21:12. 30:31. Ps 150:4.

22 **Tubal-cain**. i.e. *possessor of the world*, **S#8423h**.
instructor. Heb. whetter, a sharpener. 1 S 13:20. Jb 16:9. Ps 7:12. 52:2.
artificer. 1 Ch 29:5. 2 Ch 34:11. Is 3:3.
brass and. Ge 27:40. Ex 25:3. Nu 31:22. 35:16. Dt 8:9. 27:5. 33:25. 2 S 12:31. 2 Ch 2:7. Jb 20:24. Is 2:4.
Naamah. i.e. *pleasant, pleasing*, **S#5279h**. Jsh 15:41. Ru 1:19, 20. 1 K 14:21, 31. 2 Ch 12:13.

23 **wives**. ver. +19.
Hear. Nu 23:18. Jg 9:7.
I have slain a man to my wounding. *or*, I would slay a man in my wound, etc. Ge 49:6.

to my hurt. *or*, in my hurt.
slain. Ex 20:13. 21:25. Le 19:18. Dt 32:35. Ps 94:1. He 10:30.

24 **if**. ver. 15.
avenged. Ex 21:21mg. Dt +19:6. Ps 18:47.
sevenfold. Le 26:21. 2 S 21:6. Ps 79:12. Pr. 6:31.
truly. Ps 94:4. Pr 27:1.
seventy. Mt 18:22.

25 A.M. 130. B.C. 3874.
Adam. Ge 5:3.
knew. ver. +1, 17.
and called. Ge 5:3, 4. 1 Ch 1:1. Lk 3:38.
Seth. Heb. Sheth; i.e. *appointed*, or *put*. i.e. *replacing*, **S#8352h**. ver. 25, 26. Ge 5:3, 4, 6, 7, 8. Nu 24:17. 1 Ch 1:1. There is an intended play on words here, involving the repetition of words similar in sound, but not necessarily in sense. Here, Seth (*Sheth*) and "appointed" (Heb. *shath*) are similar in sound. At Ge 1:2, the Hebrew words underlying our "form" and "void" (*tohu, bohu*) are similar in sound. For other instances of this figure see Ge 11:9. 18:27. Ps 56:8. 122:6. Ec 7:1, 6. Je 10:11. Da 5:26-28. Mt 24:7.
For God. ver. 1-3, 8, 10, 11. Ex 18:4.
seed. Here, "seed" is put for son or posterity, as also in Ge 15:13. For the same figure involving a different term, see Ge 3:19. Ge 21:13. 1 S 1:11mg. 2 S 7:12. 1 Ch 17:11.
whom. ver. 8.

26 A.M. 235. B.C. 3769.
Seth. Lk 3:38.
to him. Ge 5:6-8.
Enos. Heb. Enosh. i.e. *mortal man*, **S#583h**. ver. 26. Ge 5:6, 7, 9, 10, 11. 1 Ch 1:1.
to call upon the name of the Lord. *or*, call *themselves* by the name of the Lord. Ge 12:8. 1 K 18:24. Ps 79:6. 116:17. Is 43:22. Je 33:16. Jl 2:32. Zp 3:9. Jn 4:23, 24. Ac 2:21. 9:14. 11:26 22:16. Ro 10:13. 1 C 1:2. Ep 3:14, 15.
name. Is +30:27. Je +10:25. Mt 1:21, 23. 6:9. Lk 1:13. 2:21. 11:2. Jn 1:12. 2:23. 3:18. Ro 10:13.

GENESIS 5

1 **book**. Ex 17:14. Ne 7:5.
the generations. Ge +2:4. 6:9. 1 Ch 1:1. Mt 1:1. Lk 3:36-38.
in the likeness. Ge 1:26, 27. 3:5, 22. Ec 7:29. 1 C 11:7. 2 C 3:18. Ep 4:24. Col 3:10. He 1:3. 12:9.

2 **Male**. Ge 1:27. Ml 2:15. Mk *10*:6. 1 C 12:12. Ga 3:28.
blessed. Ge 1:28.
their. Ge 2:15, 23mg. Ac 17:26.

3 A.M. 130. B.C. 3874.
in his. Jb 14:4. 15:14-16. 25:4. Ps 14:2, 3.

51:5. Lk 1:35. Jn 3:6. Ro 5:12. Ep 2:3.
called. Ge 4:25.

4 And the. 1 Ch 1:1-3. Lk 3:36-38.
and he. ver. 7, 10, 13, 19, 22, 26, 30. Ge
1:28. 9:1, 7. 11:12. Ps 127:3. 144:12.
begat sons and daughters. Le 18:6, 10, 11.
20:17. Dt 27:22.

5 A.M. 930. B.C. 3074.
nine. ver. 8, 11, 14, 17, etc. with Dt 30:20. Ps
90:10.
and he died. ver. 8, 11, 14, etc. Ge 2:17.
3:19. 2 S 14:14. Jb 30:23. Ps 49:7-10. Ezk
18:4. Ro 5:12-14. 1 C 15:21, 22. He 9:27.

6 A.M. 235. B.C. 3769.
begat. Ge 4:26.

7 Seth. Ge 4:25.
Enos. 1 Ch 1:1.

8 A.M. 1042. B.C. 2962.

9 A.M. 325. B.C. 3679.
Cainan. Heb. Kenan. i.e. *possession, acquisition;
fixed*, **S#7018h**. ver. 10, 12, 13, 14. 1 Ch 1:2. Lk
3:37.

10 begat. ver. 4.

11 A.M. 1140. B.C. 2864.
died. ver. 5.

12 A.M. 395. B.C. 3609.
Mahalaleel. Gr. Maleleel. i.e. *praise of God*,
S#4111h. ver. 13, 15, 16, 17. 1 Ch 1:2. Ne 11:4.
Lk 3:37.

13 and begat. ver. 4.

14 A.M. 1235. B.C. 2769.
died. ver. 5.

15 A.M. 460. B.C. 3544.
Jared. i.e. *descent*, **S#3382h**. ver. 16, 18, 19, 20.
1 Ch 1:2. 4:18. Heb. Jered. 1 Ch 1:2.

16 and begat. See ver. 4.

17 A.M. 1290. B.C. 2714.
died. ver. 5.

18 A.M. 622. B.C. 3382.
Enoch. Ge 4:17. 1 Ch 1:3, Henoch. Lk 3:37.
Ju 14, 15.

19 and begat. ver. 4.

20 he died. ver. 5.

21 A.M. 687. B.C. 3317.
Enoch. i.e. *dedicated; teacher*, **S#2585h**. Ge 4:17,
18. 5:18, 19, 21, 22, 23, 24. 25:4. 46:9. Ex
6:14. Nu 26:5. 1 Ch 1:3, 33. 5:3.
Methuselah. i.e. *man of dart, or* he dies and it
is sent-namely, the flood. **S#4968h**. ver. 21, 22,
25, 26, 27. 1 Ch 1:3. Lk 3:37, Mathusala.

22 Walked. ver. 24. Ex 2:5. 14:29. Jsh 5:6. 1 S
8:3. 12:2.
with God. ver. 24. Ge 3:8. 6:9. +17:1. 24:40.
48:15. Dt 5:33. 13:4. 1 K 2:4. 3:3, 6, 14. 2 K
+20:3. 22:2. 23:3. Ne 5:9. Ps 16:8. 86:11.
89:30-32. 116:9. 128:1. Am 3:3. Mi 4:5. +6:8.
Ml 2:6. Lk 1:6. Ac 9:31. Ro 8:1. 2 C 5:7. Ga
5:16. Col +1:10. 1 Th 4:1. He 11:5, 6. 1 J 1:3,
6, 7. 2:6.
begat. Jn 17:15. 1 T 4:3. Ju 14.

23 A.M. 987. B.C. 3017.

24 walked. ver. +22.
he was not. Ge 37:30. 42:13, 32, 36. Jb 7:8.
Je 31:15. Mt 2:18.
for. 2 K 2:11. Lk 23:43. He 11:5, 6. Ju 14, 15.
took. 2 K 2:10. Ps 49:15. 73:24. Is 57:1. 1 C
15:51. 1 Th 4:17.

25 A.M. 874. B.C. 3130.
Lamech. Heb. Lemech. Ge 4:18mg.

26 begat sons and daughters. ver. 4.

27 A.M. 1656. B.C. 2348.
he died. ver. 5. Ec 11:8. Is 65:20.

28 A.M. 1056. B.C. 2948.

29 Noah. i.e. *rest* or *comfort*, **S#5146h**. ver. 30, 32.
Ge 6:8, 9, 10, 13, 22. 7:1, 5, 6, 7, 9, 11, 13,
15, 23. 8:1, 6, 11, 13, 15, 18, 20. 9:1, 8, 17,
18, 19, 20, 24, 28, 29. 10:1, 32. 1 Ch 1:4. Is
54:9. Ezk 14:14, 20. Lk +3:36, Noe.
comfort. Ge 27:42. 37:35. Ps 23:4. 71:21.
work. Ge 3:19. 6:3, 11, 12. Ex 23:24. Le 18:3.
Jb 33:17. Ec 4:3. Mi 6:16.
and. Ge +1:26.
because. Ge 3:17-19. 4:11, 12.
which. Ge 8:21. Ro 8:20-23.

30 begat sons. See ver. 4.

31 A.M. 1651. B.C. 2353.
he died. ver. 5.

32 A.M. 1556. B.C. 2448.
Noah. Ge 7:6.
Shem. i.e. *celebrated name*, **S#8035h**. Ge 6:10.
7:13. 9:18, 19, 23, 26, 27. 10:1, 21, 22, 31.
11:10, 11. 1 Ch 1:4, 17, 24. Lk 3:36.
Ham. i.e. *raging*, **S#2526h**. Ge 6:10. 7:13. 9:18,
22. 10:1, 6, 20. 1 Ch 1:4, 8. 4:40. Ps 78:51.
105:23, 27. 106:22.
Japheth. i.e. *enlargement*, **S#3315h**. Ge 6:10.
7:13. 9:18, 23, 27. 10:1, 2, 21. 1 Ch 1:4, 5.

GENESIS 6

1 A.M. 1556. B.C. 2448.
to multiply. Ge 1:28. Ac 6:1.
face. Ge +1:2.

2 the sons. Ge 4:26. Ex 4:22, 23. Dt 14:1. Ps
82:6, 7. Is 63:16. Jn 8:41, 42. Ro 9:7, 8. 2 C
6:18.
of God. ver. 4. Jb 1:6. 2:1. 38:7. Ps 29:1.
+36:6mg. 89:6. Da 3:25. Ho 1:10. 2 P 2:4. Ju
6. "Sons of God" denotes wondrous, mighty,
supernatural beings, frequently (but as here,
perhaps not always: see Mt 22:30) used of
angels in the O.T.
saw. Jb +31:1. 2 P 2:14.
that they. Ge 3:6. 39:6, 7. 2 S 11:2. 1 J 2:16.
were fair. 1 K 11:1, 3. Ne 13:25, 26.
they took. Ge 24:3. Jg +3:6. Mt 22:30. Lk
20:35, 36.

3 A.M. 810. B.C. 3194.
My. Nu 11:17. Ne 9:30. Is 1:5. 5:4. +63:10. Je
11:7, 11. Lk 19:42. Jn 16:8. Ac 7:51. Ga 5:16,

17. 1 Th 5:19. 2 Th 2:6, 7. 1 P 3:18-20. 2 P 3:9. Ju 14, 15.

spirit. Heb. *ruach*. Here *ruach* refers to the invisible psychological part of man given to him by God at man's formation at birth, and returning to God at his death. **S#7307h**. Nu 16:22. 27:16. Jb 27:3. 34:14. Ps 31:5. 104:30. Ec 3:21, 21. 8:8, 8. 11:5. 12:7. Is 42:5. Ezk 37:9 (wind). Zc 12:1. The word *ruach*, spirit, is used of (1) God, Is 40:13. (2) The Holy Spirit, Is +48:16. (3) The operations of the Holy Spirit in (a) creation, Ge 1:2; (b) giving life, Ezk 37:14; (c) executing judgment, Ex +15:8. (4) Invisible power from on high in giving spiritual gifts, Ge +41:38. (5) Psychological uses: 1) The invisible part of man, rendered "breath," ver. +17; "spirit," Ge +6:3. See Ge +41:8 on the interchangeable uses of "soul," Heb. *nephesh*, and "spirit," Heb. *ruach*. 2) The invisible characteristics of man, rendered "mind," Ge +26:35; "breath," Is 33:11; "courage," Jsh 2:11; "anger," Jg 8:3; "blast," Is 25:4; "spirit," Ge +41:8. (6) By Synecdoche, *spirit*, an integral part of man individually, is put for the whole person, Ps +106:33. (7) Invisible spirit beings, angels and cherubim, Ps +104:4. (8) Neutral spirit beings, Jb 4:15. Is 31:3. (9) Evil angels, Jg +9:23. (10) Wind, Ge 8:1. For the corresponding Greek word, *pneuma*, see Mt +8:16.

always. Heb. *olam*, **S#5769h**. 1 Ch 16:15. Jb 7:16. Ps 119:112. Je 20:17.

strive. Jb +36:9. Ps 81:11-15. Is 55:6. Ho 5:6. 9:12. Ro 1:24-28.

flesh. Jb 34:15. Ps 56:4. 78:37-39. Is 40:6-8. Je 17:5. Jn 3:6. Ro 8:1-13. 1 C 1:29. 15:39. Ga 5:16-24. 1 P 1:24.

yet. 1 P 3:20.

his days. Ge 47:9. Ps 39:5. Ja 4:14.

shall be. Ge 15:13-16. Is 38:5. Je 25:12. Da 9:2, 23-27. Jn 21:18, 19, 21, 22, 23. Ac 1:6. 1 Th 5:1-4.

4 giants. Dt +2:20.

after. ver. 3.

sons of God. ver. +2.

came in. Ge 38:18. Dt +22:13. Ru +4:13. Mt 1:18.

mighty. Ge 10:8, 9. Is 2:17. 1 C 1:26. 2 C 10:5.

of old. Heb. *olam*, **S#5769h**. Dt 32:7. 1 S 27:8. Ps 25:6. 119:52. Is 46:9. 57:11. 63:9, 11. Je 28:8. La 3:6. Ezk 26:20. Am 9:11. Mi 7:14. Ml 3:4.

men of. Ge 11:4. Nu 16:2.

5 God. Ge 13:13. 18:20, 21. Ps 14:1-4. 53:2. Ro 1:28-31. 3:9-19.

saw. Ge 7:1. 11:5. 29:31. Ex 3:4. Dt 32:19.

of man. Jg 20:48. Ac 8:12. 1 P 3:21.

every. Ep 4:17-19. 5:8. T 1:15.

imagination. *or*, the whole imagination,

with the purposes and desires of the heart. The Hebrew word signifies not only the imagination, but also the purposes and desires. Ge 8:21. Dt 29:19. 31:21. 1 K 8:46. 1 Ch +28:9. 29:18. Jb 15:14, 16. Ps 14:2, 3. Pr 6:18. 20:9. Ec 7:20, 29. 9:3. Is 26:3. Je 17:9. Ezk 8:9, 12. Mt 15:19, 20. Mk 7:21-23. Ro 1:28. 3:10, 18. 8:7. Ep 2:1-3. T 3:3.

thoughts. Is 66:4. Je 4:14. Ezk 14:3.

continually. Heb. every day. 1 S 18:29. 2 K 13:3. Jb 1:5mg.

6 repented. Ge 1:31. Nu 23:19. Jg 10:16. 1 S 15:11, 29, 35. 2 S 24:16. 1 Ch 21:15. Ps 110:4. Je +18:8. Ml +3:6. Ro +11:29. He 6:17, 18. Ja 1:17.

grieved. Nu 32:14. Dt 5:29. 25:16. 32:29. Ps 7:11-13. 10:3. 11:5. 78:40. 81:13. 95:8-10. 119:158. Pr 11:20. 15:9, 26. Is 48:18. +63:10. Je 12:8. Ezk 33:11. Ho 7:2. 9:15. 12:2. 13:7, 8. Mi 6:2. Na 1:6. Mk 3:5. Lk 19:41, 42. Ep 4:30. He 3:10, 17, 18. Re +6:16, 17.

heart. Ge 8:21. 1 S 13:14. Je 19:5 (mind). 32:41. Ac 13:22.

7 I will. Ps 24:1, 2. 37:20. Pr 10:27. 16:4. Is 48:18. Lk 19:41, 42.

destroy. Dt 28:63. 29:20. Ph 3:19. 2 Th 1:9.

face. Ge +1:2.

both man, and beast. Heb. from man unto beast. Je 4:22-27. 12:3, 4. Ho 4:3. Zp 1:3. Ro 3:20-22.

repenteth. Am 7:3, 6. He 3:11.

8 found. Ge 19:19. Ex 33:12-17. Ps 84:11. 145:20. Pr 12:2. Je 31:2. Lk 1:30. Ac 7:46. Ro 4:4. 11:6. 1 C 15:10. Ga 1:15. 2 T 1:18. T 2:11. 3:7. He 4:16. 2 P 2:5.

grace. Ex 22:27. 2 Ch 30:9. Ne 9:17, 31. Ps 103:8. Pr 3:34.

9 These. Ge 2:4. 5:1. 10:1.

just. Ge 7:1. Dt 32:4. Jb 12:4. Pr 4:18. Ec 7:20. Ezk 14:14, 20. Mi +6:8. Hab +2:4. Mt 1:19. 27:19. Mk 6:20. Lk 2:25. +16:10. 23:50. Ac 10:22. 22:14. Ro 1:17. He 11:7. 2 P 2:5, 7.

perfect. *or*, upright. Mt +5:48. Lk 1:6. Jn +17:6.

Noah walked. Ge +5:22. 1 P 2:5.

10 A.M. 1556. B.C. 2448.

Shem. Ge +5:32.

Ham. Ge 9:22-24.

Japheth. Ge 10:21.

11 earth. Ge 11:1. 18:25. Ps 66:1, 4. Ezk 14:13. Mt 5:13.

before. Ge 7:1. 10:9. 13:13. 2 Ch 34:27. Lk 1:6. Ro 2:13. 3:19.

violence. Ps 11:5. 140:11. Is 60:18. Je 22:3. Ezk 45:9. Ho 4:1, 2. Zp 3:4.

12 God looked upon. ver. 8. Ge 18:21. Jb 33:27. Ps 14:2, 3. Pr. 15:3.

corrupt. Ex 32:7. Dt 31:29. 32:5. Jg 2:19.

for. ver. 4, 5. Ge 7:1, 21. Jb 22:15-17. Ps 14:1-3. 1 P 3:19, 20. 2 P 2:5.

all. What is said of the whole, collectively, is sometimes said only of a part; and not all of the parts, precisely and singularly. Here, the "all" with the exception of Noah. Other examples where "all" in context admits of exceptions and is not universal include Ge 35:26 (except Benjamin: see ver. 16, 24). Mt 19:28 (except Judas Iscariot). 1 C 15:22 (except those who are "alive and remain" at Christ's coming: see ver. 51 and 1 Th 4:15, 17). He 11:13 (except Enoch: see ver. 5).
flesh. 2 Ch 32:8. Ps 56:4. 65:2. 145:21. Is 40:5, 6. 66:16, 23. Mt 19:5. Lk +3:6. Jn 6:51.
earth. 2 P 2:5. Re 11:18.

13 **The end**. Is 34:1-4. Je 51:13. Ezk 7:2-6. Am 8:2. Ro 3:19. 10:4. 1 P 4:7.
flesh. ver. +12, 17. Ps 136:25.
is come. Is 60:1. Mt 12:28. He 12:22.
filled. ver. 4, 11, 12. Ge 49:5. Ho 4:1, 2.
and, behold. ver. 17.
destroy. Ge 18:20, 21. 19:24, 25. Ex +22:23, 24. Nu +32:23. Dt 15:9. Jg 9:24. 2 S 3:39. 1 K +8:32. Jb +4:8. Ps 31:23. +37:9. 54:5. +58:11. 91:8. Pr 13:15. 22:22, 23. 24:17, 18. Is +66:24. Ezk +39:23. Ml +3:5. Mt 18:6, 10. Lk +18:7, 8. Ro +1:27. 12:19. Col 3:25. 2 P 2:4-7. Re +11:18.
with. or, from. Ge 7:23. Ps 37:9, 10.
the earth. Je 4:23-28. He 11:7. 2 P 3:6, 7, 10-12.

14 A.M. 1536. B.C. 2468.
Make. Mt 24:38. 1 P 3:20.
ark. Ex 2:3, 5. 1 Th 1:10. He 11:7.
wood. Ga 6:14.
rooms. Heb. nests.
shalt pitch. Ex 2:3. 30:10. Le 17:11 (atonement). Dt +32:43 (merciful).
within. Ex 25:2. 37:2.

15 **cubits**. Ge 7:20. Dt 3:11.

16 **window**. Ge 7:11. 8:6. 2 S 6:16. 2 K 9:30.
the door. Ge 7:16. Lk 13:25.
with. Ezk 41:16. 42:3. lower. **S#8482h**, *tahti*. Dt +32:22.

17 **behold**. ver. 13. Ge 9:9. Ex 14:17. 2 P 2:5.
I, even I. Le 26:28. Dt 32:39. Is 48:15. 51:12. Je 23:39. Ezk 5:8. 6:3. 34:11, 20. Ho 5:14.
bring. Ge 7:4, 17, 21-23. Jb 22:16. Ps 29:10. 93:3, 4. 107:34. Is 54:9. Am 9:6. Mt 24:39. Lk 17:27. He 11:7. 1 P 3:20.
is the. Ge +2:7. 7:15. Jb 27:3. Ps 31:5. Ec 3:19. 12:7. Mt 27:50.
breath. Heb. *ruach*. Here *ruach* has reference to the invisible and psychological part of man given to him by God at man's formation at birth, and returning to God at death. **S#7307h**. Ge 7:15, 22. Jb 9:18. 12:10. 17:1. Ps 104:29. 135:17. +146:4. Ec 3:19. Je 10:14. 51:17. La 4:20. Ezk 37:5, 6, 8, 9, 10. Hab 2:19. For the other uses of *ruach* see ver. +3.

shall die. ver. 7. Ps 104:29. 107:34. Ac 5:5. Ro 5:12-14, 21. 6:23. 8:20-22.

18 **establish**. Ge 9:9, 11. 17:4, 7, 21.
covenant. Ge 15:18. He 13:20.
come. Ge 7:1, 7, 13. Is 26:20. Ac +16:31. He 11:7. 1 P 3:20. 2 P 2:5, 9. Re 22:17.

19 **every**. Is 65:25. Ro 8:20, 21.
two. Ge 7:2, 3, 8, 9, 15, 16. 8:17. Ps 36:6. Am 3:3.

20 **fowls**. Ge 1:20-24. Ac 10:11, 12.
two. Ge 1:28. 2:19. 7:8-16. Jn 5:40. 6:37.

21 **all food**. Ge 1:29, 30. Jb 38:41. 40:20. Ps 36:6. 104:27, 28. 136:25. 145:16. 147:9. Mt 6:26.

22 **according to**. Ge 7:5, 9, 16. 17:23. Ex 40:16. Dt 12:32. Mt 7:24-27. Jn 2:5. 15:14. He 11:7, 8. 1 J 5:3, 4.

GENESIS 7

1 A.M. 1656. B.C. 2348.
Come. ver. 7, 13. Jb 5:19-24. Ps 91:1-10. Pr 14:26. 18:10. Is 26:20, 21. Ezk 9:4-6. Zp +2:3. Mt 11:28. 24:37-39. Ac 2:39. He 11:7. 1 P 3:20. 2 P 2:5.
house. "House" is put for household, descendants, or family. Ge 30:30. 43:16. Ex 1:21. Jsh 2:18, 19. 24:15. 2 S 7:11. 1 Ch 10:6. Ps 49:11. Is 36:3. Lk 19:9. Ac 10:2. 11:14. +16:15, 31. 18:8. 1 C 1:16. 1 T 3:4. 2 T 1:16. 3:6. 2 T 4:19. T 1:11. He 11:7.
thee. Ge +6:9. Ps 33:18, 19. Pr 10:6, 7, 9. 11:4-8. Is 3:10, 11. Ph 2:15, 16. 2 P 2:5-9.
seen righteous. Ge 6:9. Jn +17:6.

2 **every clean**. ver. 8. Ge 6:19-21. 8:20. Le ch. 11. Dt 14:1-21. Ac 10:11-15.
sevens. Heb. seven, seven.
not. Le 10:10. Ezk 44:23.

3 **face**. Ge +1:2.

4 **For**. ver. 10. Ge 2:5. 6:3. 8:10, 12. 29:27, 28. Jsh 6:3, 4. Am 4:7.
forty days. ver. 12, 17. Ex 34:28. Jon +3:4.
and every. ver. 21-23. Ge 6:7, 13, 17.
destroy. Heb. blot out. ver. 21, 23. Ge 6:7, 13, 17. Ex 32:32, 33. Jb 22:16. Ps 69:28. Re 3:5.
face. Ge +1:2.

5 **all that**. Ge 6:22. Ex 39:32, 42, 43. 40:16. Ps 119:6. Mt 3:15. Lk 8:21. Jn 2:5. 8:28, 29. 13:17. Ph 2:8. He 5:8.

6 **six hundred**. Ge 5:32. 8:13.

7 **Noah went in**. ver. 1, 13-15. Ge 6:18. Pr +22:3. Mt +24:37, 38. He 6:18.

8 **clean**. ver. 2, 3. Ge 6:19, 20.

9 **went in**. ver. 16. Ge 2:19. Is 11:6-9. 65:25. Je 8:7. Ac 10:11, 12. Ga 3:28.

10 **after seven days**. *or*, on the seventh day. ver. 4.
waters. ver. 4, 17-20. Ge 6:17. Jb 22:16. Lk 17:27.

11 second month. The first month was Tisri, which answers to the latter end of September and first half of October; the second was Marchesvan, which answers to part of October and part of November.
same day. Mt 24:27. Lk 17:26, 27. 1 Th 5:3.
all. Ge 1:7. 6:17. 8:2. Ps 33:7. Pr 8:28, 29. Je 5:22. 51:16. Ezk 26:19. Am 9:5, 6. Mt 24:38. 1 Th 5:3.
fountains. Ge +1:9. Ex 20:4. Le 11:36. Jb 38:16, 25. Ps 87:7. 104:10.
deep. Ge 1:2. 49:25. Dt 33:13. Ps 104:6.
windows. *or,* flood-gates. Ge 1:7. 8:2. 2 K 7:2, 19. Ps 78:23, 24. Ec 12:3. Is 24:18. 60:8. Ml 3:10.

12 forty. ver. 4, 17. Dt 10:10. Jon +3:4.

13 selfsame. Heb. In the body, or essence, or strength of the day. Dt +32:48.
entered. ver. 1, 7-9. Ge 6:18. He 11:7. 1 P 3:20. 2 P 2:5.
and Shem. Ge +5:32.

14 They. ver. 2, 3, 8, 9.
kind. Ge 1:21. Dt 14:13, 14.
sort. Heb. wing. Ge 6:20. Ps 148:10mg. Is +24:16mg.

15 went. Ge 6:20. Is 11:6.
two. ver. 9. Ge 6:19.
breath. Ge +2:7. 6:17. Jb 27:3. Ps +146:4.

16 as. ver. 2, 3.
and the. Dt 33:27. Ps 36:6. 46:1-3. 91:1-10. Pr 3:23. Jn 10:27-30. 1 P 1:5.
shut. Jg 9:51. 2 K 4:4, 5. Is 26:20. 55:6. Mt 25:10. Lk 13:25. Ro 8:1. Col 3:3. Re 3:20.

17 forty days. ver. +4, 12.
bare up. Ro 5:21.

18 waters prevailed. Ex 14:28. Jb 22:16. Ps 69:15. Jon 2:5.
ark. Ps 104:26.
face. Ge +1:2.

19 waters. Ps 69:1.
exceedingly. Ge 6:17. 17:2, 6, 20. Ex 1:7. Nu 14:7. 1 K 7:47.
all. Ge +41:56.
the high hills. Ps 46:2, 3. 104:6-9. Je 3:23. 2 P 3:6.

20 and the mountains. Ge 8:4. Ps 104:6. Je 3:23.

21 all flesh. ver. 4. Ge 6:6, 7, 13, 17. Nu 23:19. Is 24:6, 19. Je 4:22-27. 12:3, 4. Zp 1:3. Lk 17:27. Ro 8:20, 22. 2 P 2:5. 3:6.

22 breath of life. Heb. breath of the spirit of life. Ge +2:7. 6:17. Ps +146:4.

23 every living substance. ver. 21, 22. Jb 22:15-17. Pr 11:21. Is 24:1-8. Mt 24:37-39. 2 P 2:5.
face. Ge +1:2.
and Noah only. Ge +5:29. Ex 14:28-30. Ps 91:1, 9, 10. Pr 11:4. Ml 3:17, 18. Mt 25:46. Lk +3:36. 2 P 3:6.

24 an hundred and. ver. 11. Ge 8:3, 4. Jb 12:15.

GENESIS 8

1 God remembered. Ge 19:29. Ex 2:24. 1 S 1:19. Jb 14:13. Ps 94:14. 137:7. Am 8:7. Hab 3:2. Re 16:19. 18:5.
the cattle. Ge 6:20. Nu 22:32. Ps 36:6. 145:9. Jon 4:11. Mt 10:29. Ro 8:20-22.
a wind. Ex 14:21. Nu 11:31. Ps 104:7-9. Pr 25:23. Am 4:13.
waters. Jb 12:15. Ps 29:10. 33:7. Is 44:27. Na 1:4.

2 fountains. Ge +7:11. Pr 8:28. Jon 2:3.
windows. 2 K 7:2.
stopped. Jb 38:8.
rain. Ge 7:4, 12. Jb 37:11-13. 38:37. Mt 8:9, 26, 27.

3 continually. Heb. in going and returning.
hundred. Ge 7:11, 24.
abated. Jb 38:11. Ps 30:5. Is 30:18. Je 5:22.

4 the ark. Ge 7:17-19.
seventh month. That is, of the year, not of the deluge.
rested. Ro 6:9. Ep 2:6.
Ararat. i.e. *mountain of descent; the curse reversed,* **S#780h**. 2 K 19:37. Is 37:38. Je 51:27.

5 decreased continually. Heb. were in going and decreasing.
the tenth. Ge 7:11.

6 opened the window. ver. +13. Ge 6:16. 2 K 13:17. Da 6:10.

7 a raven. Ge 4:16. Le 11:15. 1 K 17:4, 6. Jb 38:41. Ps 147:9. Pr 30:17. SS 5:11. Is 34:11. Lk 12:24. Ep 4:20.
went forth to and fro. Heb. in going forth and returning.

8 a dove. ver. 10-12. SS 1:15. 2:11, 12, 14. Mt 10:16. Lk 3:22.
face. Ge +1:2.

9 found. Dt 28:65. Ps 55:6. Ezk 7:16. Mt 11:28. Jn 16:33. He 13:14.
and she. Ps 116:7. Is 60:8.
face. Ge +1:2.
pulled her. Heb. caused her to come.

10 stayed. Ps 40:1. Is 8:17. 26:8. Ro 8:25.
seven. ver. 12. Ge 7:4, 10.

11 dove. ver. +8.
evening. Ge 15:12. Zc 14:7.
an olive. Ne 8:15. SS 2:12. Zc 4:12-14. Ro 10:15. Ep 1:14.
abated. ver. +3.

12 And he. Ps +27:14. Is 30:18. Hab 2:3. Ja 5:7, 8.
seven. ver. 10. Ge 2:2, 3.
dove. ver. +8. Is 38:14. Je 48:28.
returned. 2 P 3:13. Re 21:4.

13 A.M. 1657. B.C. 2347.
six. Ge 7:6, 11.
first. Ex 40:2. 2 Ch 29:17. Ezr 7:9. 10:17. Ezk 45:18. Lk 1:5. 2:1, 2. 2 P 1:16. 1 J 1:1.
covering. Ex +26:14. 39:34. 40:19. Nu 3:25.

face. Ge +1:2.
dry. Ge 1:9.
14   **second month**. Ge 7:11.
dried. Ex 14:21. Is 19:5. Je 23:10. 50:38. Jl 1:20.
15   **And God spake**. Ge 6:8, 13-21. 21:17, 19. 22:12. 35:12, 13. Ex 19:19.
16   **Go forth**. Ge 7:1, 7, 13. Jsh 3:17. Ps 121:8. Da 3:25, 26. Ac 16:27, 28, 37-39.
17   **Bring**. Ge 7:14, 15.
flesh. Ge 7:15. Ac 17:26. 1 C 15:39.
fowl. Ge 1:20. 2:19. 6:20. 9:2. Dt 14:11. Ps 8:8. Da 2:38. Mt 6:26. Ja 3:7.
cattle. Ge 9:10. Ps 148:10.
creeping. Le 11:21. Dt 14:19. Ac 10:12. Ja 3:7.
breed. Ge 1:22, 28. 9:1, 7. Ps 107:38. 144:13, 14. Je 31:17, 28.
18   **went**. Ps 121:8.
sons. Ge 5:32. 6:10. +7:1.
19   **Every**. Ge 7:14.
kinds. Heb. families.
20   **builded**. Ge 4:4. +12:7. 35:1, 7. Ex 20:24, 25. 24:4-8. Le 17:11. Jg 6:24, 26. 13:19. Ro 12:1. He 13:10, 15, 16. 1 P 2:5, 9.
clean beast. Ge 7:2. Le ch. 11. 20:25. Dt 14:4.
fowl. Dt 14:11, 20.
burnt offerings. Le +23:12.
21   **Lord**. Ps 91:4. He 12:29.
smelled. Le 1:9, 13, 17. 26:31. SS 4:10, 11. Is 65:5. Ezk 20:41. Am 5:21, 22. 2 C 2:15. Ep 5:2. Ph 4:18.
sweet savour. Heb. savour of rest. Ge +1:29. 5:29mg. Ex 29:18, 25. Le 1:9, 13, 17. 2:9, 12. 3:5, 16. +4:31. 8:21. Nu 15:3, 7, 24. 28:2, 27. 29:2, 8, 13. Ezr 6:10. Ezk 16:19mg. 20:28, 41mg. Jn 4:24. Ep 5:2. He 13:15, 16.
said. Ge 24:45. 27:41. 1 S 27:1. Ho 7:2.
his heart. Ge +6:6. Je 3:15. 7:31.
curse. Ge 3:17. 4:12. 5:29. 6:7, 13, 17. Is 54:9. Col 3:13.
for. *or*, though.
imagination. Ge +6:5. 1 Ch +28:9. Ps 51:5. 58:3. Je 17:9. 18:12. Mt 15:19. Ro 1:21. 8:7, 8. Ep 2:1-3. Ja 1:14, 15. 1 J 5:19.
youth. 1 K 12:8. 2 Ch 13:7. Ps 51:5. Ec 12:1. Ep 2:3. 1 T 3:6. 4:12.
neither. Ge 9:11-15. Is +54:9, 10.
as I. 2 P 3:6, 7.
22   **While the earth remaineth**. Heb. as yet all the days of the earth. Ge +9:12. Ps +72:5, 7, 17. 78:69. 89:36, 37. 104:5. 119:90, 91. Ec +1:4. Mt 24:35.
seedtime. Ge 45:6. Ex 34:21. Ps 74:16, 17. SS 2:11, 12. Is +54:9. Je 5:24. Ja 5:7.
and. The repetition of the word "and" at the beginning of successive clauses asks us to unhurriedly stop and notice each point, weigh each matter, and consider each particular thus added and emphasized; there is never

any climax at the end. Contrast this with the opposite, successive clauses not joined by "and," Ge +10:1. Zc 6:12, 13. Mt 7:25. Lk 1:31, 32. 14:21. 15:20, 22, 23. Jn 10:27-28. Ac 1:8. Ro 9:4. 1 C 1:30. Ep 4:31. He 13:8. Ja 4:13. 2 P 1:5-7. Re 6:15. 12:11. 13:1. 18:12, 13.
day. Je 31:35, 36. 33:20-26.

GENESIS 9

1   **blessed**. ver. 7. Ge 1:22, 28. 2:3. 8:17. 24:60. Ps 112:1. 128:3, 4. Is 11:6-8. 51:2. Be. ver. 7, 19. Ge 1:28. 8:17. 10:32. Jn 12:24. 15:2.
2   **the fear**. Ge 1:28. 2:19. 35:5. Le 26:6, 22. Jb 5:22, 23. Ps 8:4-8. 104:20-23. Ezk 34:25. Ho 2:18. Ja 3:7.
3   **Every**. Le ch. 11. 22:8. Dt 12:15. 14:3-21. Jn 6:53. Ac 10:12-15. 1 T 4:3-5.
even. Ge 1:29, 30. Ps 104:14, 15. Ro 14:3, 14, 17, 20. 1 C 10:23, 25, 26, 31. Col 2:16, 21, 22. 1 T 4:3, 4.
green. Ge 1:30. Ex 10:15. Nu 22:4. Ps 37:2. Is 15:6.
4   **the life**. Ge +2:19.
blood. Ro 6:23. He 9:22.
not eat. Le +3:17.
5   **lives**. Heb. *nephesh*, Ge +44:30. "Soul" (the usual translation of *nephesh*) is used for "life," which is the effect of it. For other examples of this usage see Ge 37:21. Le 17:11. 1 K 2:23. Ps 38:12. Je 45:5. Mt +2:20. 16:25. 20:28. Mk 3:4. 10:45. Lk 9:56. 12:22, 23. 14:26. Jn 10:11. 12:25. Ph 2:30. 1 J 3:16. Re 12:11.
every beast. Ex 21:28, 29. Jb 12:7, 8.
require it. Lk +11:50. Ac 20:20, 26, 27.
and at. Ge 4:9, 10. Le 19:16. Nu 35:31-33. Dt 21:1-9. Ps 9:12. Mt 23:35. 1 J 3:15. Re 19:2.
hand. Ex 4:13. 1 K 8:53. Ps 7:3. 49:15mg. 107:2. Is 64:6. Mk 6:2. Lk 1:71. Ac 5:12. 7:25, 35.
brother. Ac 17:26.
I require the. ver. 6. Ex 21:12-17. Nu 35:30-34. Dt 19:18, 19. 25:1-3. 32:35. Pr 17:15. 20:26. 28:17. Ac 25:10, 11. Ro 13:4.
life. Heb. *nephesh*, Ge +2:7; +44:30.
6   **sheddeth**. Ex 21:25. Dt 32:43. Jn 19:11.
by man. Ex 21:12-14. 22:2, 3. Le 24:17. Dt 19:6. 2 S 4:8, 11. Mt 26:52. Ro 12:19. 13:4. Re 13:10. 19:11. 21:8.
in the image. Ge 1:26, 27. 5:1. Ps 51:4. 1 C 11:7. Ja 3:9.
7   **be ye fruitful**. ver. 1, 19. Ge 1:28. 8:17.
8   **God**. Heb. *Elohim*. Ge 1:1.
spake. Ge 3:8. +8:15.
Noah. Ge 5:28, 29, 32.
9   **establish my covenant**. ver. 11, +16, 17. Ge 6:18. +17:7, 8. 22:17. Is +54:9, 10. Je 31:35, 36. 33:20. Ro 1:3.
10   **with**. ver. 15, 16. Ge 8:1. Jb ch. 38, 41. Ps

36:5, 6. 145:9. Jon 4:11.
creature. Heb. *nephesh*, soul, Ge +2:19.

11 And I. Ge 8:21, 22. Is 54:9.
neither shall all. Ge 7:21-23. 8:21, 22. Is +54:9. 2 P +3:7, 11.

12 token. ver. 13, 17. Ge 17:11. Ex 3:12. +12:13. 13:16. Jsh 2:12. Ezk +9:4. Mt 26:26-28. 1 C 11:23-25. Ep 1:13.
creature. ver. 10. Ge +2:19.
perpetual. Heb. *olam*, s#5769h. Ex 29:9. 31:16. Le 3:17. 25:34. Je 23:40. 50:5. 51:39, 57. Zp 2:9.
generations. Ge +8:22. 13:15. 17:7, 19. Dt 5:29. 29:29. 2 S 7:24-26. Ps +72:5. 89:4, 29, 36, 37. 102:12, 28. 145:13. Ec +1:4. Is 9:6, 7. 34:17. 51:8. 59:21. Je 31:35-36. 32:38-40. Ezk 37:24-27. Da 2:44, 45. 7:13, 14, 18, 27. Mt 19:28. Lk 1:32, 33, 55. 13:28-30. Re 11:15. 21:3, 24. 22:4, 5.

13 bow. Ge 27:3. 48:22. Ezk 1:28. Re 4:3. 10:1.
cloud. Jg 5:4. Jb 22:14. 26:8. 37:16. 38:34, 37. Ps 104:3. Ec 11:4. Ezk 30:3. 34:12. Da 7:13. Jl 2:2. Zp 1:15. Mt 24:30. 26:64. Mk 13:26. 14:62. 1 Th 4:17. Re 1:7.
token. ver. +12.

14 bow. Ezk 1:28. Re 4:3. 10:1.
cloud. Ge 2:5, 6. 1 K 18:43-45. Jb 37:21-22. Ec 11:4. Mt 16:2, 3. Lk 12:54-57.

15 remember. Ge +8:1. Ex 28:12. Le +26:42.
creature. Heb. *nephesh*. Notice that *nephesh* is used alike of lower creatures and man; rendered *creature* here and ver. 16; *the life*, Le 17:11, 14; *soul*, Nu 31:28. ver. 10. Ge +2:7, 19. For the other uses of *nephesh* see Ge +2:7.
the waters. ver. 11. Ge 8:21. Is 54:8-10. 2 P 3:7.

16 bow. ver. 13, 14.
cloud. ver. +13.
remember. ver. +15.
everlasting. Heb. *olam*, Ge +17:7.
covenant. ver. 9-11. Ge 8:21, +22. 15:18. Ex 19:25. Dt 30:1. 2 S 7:10, 12, 13, 15, 16, 24-26. +23:5. Ps 105:8-10. Is 9:7. 24:5. +55:3. Je 31:31-34. 32:40. Ezk 37:26. He 6:18. 8:8. 13:20.
creature. Heb. *nephesh*, ver. +15. ver. 10. Ge +2:7. +2:19.

17 token. ver. +12, 13.
covenant. ver. +16.

18 sons. Ge 5:32. 7:7. Lk 3:36.
Shem. Ge +5:32.
Ham. Ge 7:13. 10:1, 6.
Japheth. Ge 7:13. 10:1, 2.
Canaan. Heb. Chenaan. Ge 10:6, 15.

19 These. Ge 5:32. 10:1. 1 Ch 1:4.
and of them. Ge 8:17. 10:2-32. 1 Ch 1:4-28. 1 P 3:20.
whole. Ge 11:4, 8. Ml 2:10. Ac 17:26.

20 began. Mt 26:47. Mk 10:41. 11:15. Lk 3:23.
an husbandman. Ge 2:15. 3:18, 19, 23. 4:2.

5:29. 2 K 25:12. Pr 12:11. Ec 5:9. Is 28:24-26. Zc 13:5. Mt 21:33-41. Jn 15:1. 2 T 2:6. Ja 5:7.
planted. Dt 20:6. 28:30. Pr 24:30. SS 1:6. 1 C 9:7.

21 wine. ver. +24.
drunken. Ge 6:9. 19:32-36. Pr 20:1. 23:31, 32. 31:4. Lk 21:34. Ro 13:13. 1 C 10:12. Ga +5:21. 1 T 4:4, 5. T 2:2.
uncovered. Ge 3:7. Hab 2:15, 16. Lk 10:30. Re 3:17, 18.

22 Ham. ver. +18, 25. Ge +5:32. 10:6, 15-19. 1 Ch 1:8, 13-16.
nakedness. Le 18:7. Ezk 22:10. Hab 2:15.
told. 2 S 1:19, 20. Ps 35:20, 21. 40:15. Pr 12:13. 17:9. 25:9. 30:17. Ob 12, 13. Mt 18:15. 1 C 13:6. Ga 6:1. Ep 5:3, 4.

23 garment. Ge 37:34. Ex 22:27.
and went. Ex +20:12. Ga 6:1. 1 P 4:8.
nakedness. Le 18:7. Is 58:7.

24 awoke. Pr 23:35. Jl 1:5. 1 C 15:34.
wine. 1 S 1:14. 25:37. Pr 20:1. 23:29-35. Hab 2:15.
younger. Ge 27:15, 42. 42:13, 32. 44:2. 1 S 17:14.

25 Cursed. ver. 22. Ge 3:14. 4:11. 27:12. 49:7. Ex +20:5. Dt 27:16. Pr 26:2. Mt 25:41. Jn 8:34.
Canaan. Dt. 7:1. 20:17. Le 18:3. Jsh 17:13. Ro 1:27.
servant of. Ge 10:15-20. 15:16. 25:23. 27:29. 37:10. 49:8. Jsh 9:23, 27. Jg 1:28-30. 1 K 9:20, 21. 2 Ch 8:7, 8. Pr 30:17. Jn 8:34.

26 Blessed. Ge 14:20. 24:27. Ex 18:10. Ps 144:15. Lk 1:68. Ro +9:5. 11:33. He 11:16.
the Lord. Ge 11:10-26. 12:1-3. Lk 3:23-36.
Shem. He 11:16.
his servant. *or*, servant to them. ver. +18, 27. Ge 27:37, 40. Jg 1:28. 2 Ch 8:8.

27 enlarge. *or*, persuade. Ge 10:2-5. Dt 32:8. 1 Ch 1:5. Is 54:2. 60:3-9. 66:19. Ml 1:11. Ep 2:19.
Japheth. Japheth is put for his posterity. For other examples of this usage see Ge 12:3. Nu 24:17. 1 K 18:17, 18. Ps 14:7. Ezk 34:23. Ml 1:2, 3. Ro 9:13.
dwell. Is 11:10. Ml 1:11. Ro 11:12. 15:12. Ep 2:13, 14, 19. 3:6. He 11:9, 10.

28 lived. Ge 17:18. 19:20. 25:7.
flood. Ge 7:6.

29 A.M. 2006. B.C. 1998.
nine. Ge 5:5, 20, 27, 32. 11:11-25. Ps 90:10.
died. Ge +2:17.

GENESIS 10

1 are the. Ge 2:4. 5:1. 6:9. Mt 1:1.
generations. Ge 17:20.
Shem. Ge +5:32. When a passage uses "no ands" this asks us to hurry past the details listed and focus upon the climax to which

they lead. Contrast the use of "many ands" at Ge 7:13 and +8:22. For other examples of "no ands" see Ge 19:17. Ex 15:9, 10. Is 33:7-12. Ezk 33:15, 16. Mk 7:21-23. Lk 14:13, 14. 17:27. Ro 1:29-31. 1 C 3:12, 13. 13:4-7. 13:13. Ga 5:19-21. 5:22, 23. Ep 4:32. 1 T 4:13-16. 2 T 3:1-5. 3:10, 11. 3:16, 17. 4:2, 3. Ja 1:19, 20.

Ham. ver. 6-20. Ge 9:24.

Japheth. ver. 2-5, 21. 1 Ch 1:5.

and unto. Ge 9:1, 7, 19.

flood. Ge 6:17. 8:13. 9:11, 15. 11:10. Jb 22:16. Ps 29:10. Is 54:9. Mt 24:38. Lk 17:27.

2   **sons**. ver. 21. 1 Ch 1:5-7. Is 66:19. Ezk 27:7, 12-14, 19. 38:2, 6, 15. 39:1. Re 20:8.

Gomer. i.e. *complete, perfect*, **S#1586h**. ver. 3. 1 Ch 1:5, 6. Ezk 38:6. Ho 1:3.

Magog. i.e. *expansion, extension; region of Gog*, **S#4031h**. 1 Ch 1:5. Ezk 38:2. 39:6. Re 20:8.

Madai. i.e. *extended of the Lord*, **S#4074h**. 2 K 17:6, Medes. 18:11. 1 Ch 1:5. Ezr +6:2, Medes. Est +1:3, Media. Da 11:2.

Javan. i.e. *supple; clay; mired; effervescing*, **S#3120h**. ver. 4. 1 Ch 1:5, 7. Is 66:19. Ezk 27:13, 19. Da 8:21. 10:20mg. 11:2mg. Jl 3:6. Zc 9:13.

Tubal. i.e. *flowing forth; carried or led*, **S#8422h**. Ge 4:22. 1 Ch 1:5. Is 66:19. Ezk 27:13. 32:26. 38:2, 3. 39:1.

Meshech. i.e. *drawing out*, **S#4902h**. 1 Ch 1:5, 17. Ps 120:5. Ezk 27:13. 32:26. 38:2, 3. 39:1.

Tiras. i.e. *desire, longing; destroyer*, 1 Ch 1:5. Not mentioned elsewhere in Scripture. Tiras has been identified with Tarshish by some. ver. +4.

3   **Gomer**. ver. +2.

Ashkenaz. i.e. *strong, fortified*, **S#813h**. 1 Ch 1:6. Je 51:27.

Riphath. i.e. *healing; bruising; a crusher, a terror*, **S#7384h**. 1 Ch 1:6.

Togarmah. i.e. *breaking or gnawing of bones*, **S#8425h**. 1 Ch 1:6. Ezk 27:14. 38:6.

4   A.M. 1666. B.C. 2338.

Elishah. i.e. *God of my salvation*, **S#473h**. 1 Ch 1:7. Ezk 27:7.

Tarshish. i.e. *breaking, subjection*, **S#8659h**. 1 K 10:22. 22:48. 1 Ch 1:7. 7:10, Tharshish. 2 Ch 9:21. 20:36, 37. Est 1:14. Ps 48:7. 72:10. Is 2:16. 23:1, 6, 10, 14. 60:9. 66:19. Je 10:9. Ezk 27:12, 25. 38:13. Jon 1:3. 4:2.

Kittim. i.e. *subduers, hidden; breaking, small*, **S#3794h**. Nu 24:24. 1 Ch 1:7. Is 23:1, 12. Je 2:10. Ezk 27:6. Da 11:30, Chittim.

Dodanim. or, Rodanim. i.e. *leaders*, **S#1721h**. 1 Ch 1:7.

5   A.M. 1757. B.C. 2247.

isles. ver. 25. Is +11:11. Je 25:22. 47:4mg. Ezk 26:15, 18.

Gentiles. i.e. *foreigners*, **S#1471h**. Jg 4:2, 13, 16. Is 11:10. 42:1, 6. 60:3, 5, 11, 16. Je 14:22.

divided. Dt +32:8.

in their lands. ver. 20, 31. Re 5:9. 7:9. 10:11. 11:9. 13:7. 14:6. 17:15.

after his. ver. 20. Ge 11:1-9.

6   A.M. 1676. B.C. 2228.

And the. Ge 9:22. 1 Ch 1:8-16. 4:40. Ps 78:51. 105:23, 27. 106:22. Ham. ver. 1.

Cush. i.e. *black; terror; blackness, burning; Ethiopian*, **S#3568h**. ver. 7, 8. Ge +2:13mg. 2 Ch 12:3. 14:9, 12, 13. 16:8. Je 13:23.

Mizraim. i.e. *double distress*, **S#4714h**. ver. 13. Ge 50:11. 1 Ch 1:8, 11. Is 7:18. 19:6. 37:25.

Phut. i.e. *extension; afflicted; a bow*, **S#6316h**. 1 Ch 1:8. Je 46:9mg. Ezk 27:10. 30:5mg. 38:5mg. Na +3:9, Put.

Canaan. i.e. *humiliated; subjection; merchant, servant*, **S#3667h**. ver. 15. Ge 9:18, 22, 25, 26, 27. 1 Ch 1:8, 13.

7   **Cush**. ver. 6.

Seba. i.e. *eminent; drink thou*, **S#5434h**. 1 Ch 1:9. Ps 72:10. Is 43:3.

Havilah. i.e. *circular; trembling; childbirth; anguish*, **S#2341h**. ver. 29. Ge 2:11. 25:18. 1 S 15:7. 1 Ch 1:9, 23.

Sabtah. i.e. *terror; breaking through*, **S#5454h**. 1 Ch 1:9.

Raamah. i.e. *thunder; quivering in the wind; trembling; roaring*, **S#7484h**. 1 Ch 1:9. Ezk 27:22.

Sabtecha. i.e. *beating, striking; terror*, **S#5455h**. 1 Ch 1:9.

Sheba. 1 K +10:1.

Dedan. i.e. *leading forward; low*, **S#1719h**. Ge 25:3. 1 Ch 1:9, 32. Is 21:13, Dedanim, **S#1720h**. Je 25:23. 49:8. Ezk 25:13. 27:15, 20. 38:13.

8   **Cush**. ver. 6.

Nimrod. i.e. *rebel*, **S#5248h**. ver. 9. 1 Ch 1:10. Mi 5:6.

mighty. Ge 6:4. Dt 10:17. Jsh 1:14. 6:2. 8:3. 10:2. Jg 5:13.

earth. Jb 24:13. 34:37.

9   **a mighty**. Ge 6:4. 25:27. 27:40. Je 16:16. Ezk 13:18. Mi 7:2.

before. Ge 7:1. Nu 16:2. Jsh 7:12, 13. 1 S 26:12. 1 Ch 14:8. 2 Ch 14:10. Jb 23:4.

Even as. 2 Ch 28:22.

mighty. ver. +8. 2 Ch 14:9. 16:8. Ps 52:1-3. 120:4. Is 5:22. 18:2. Je 9:23.

before the Lord. Ge 6:11. 13:13. 2 Ch 28:22. Ps 52:7. 66:7. Mi 7:2.

10   A.M. 1745. B.C. 2259.

And the. Je 50:21. Mi 5:6.

Babel. Gr. Babylon. i.e. *confusion, mixture*, **S#894h**. Ge 11:9. 2 K 20:14. Ps 137:1, 8. Is 13:19. 14:4, 22. 21:9. 39:1. 43:14. Je 50:1. 51:8. Da 4:30. Mi 4:10. Ac 7:43. 1 P 5:13. Re 14:8. 16:19. 17:5. 18:2, 10, 21.

Erech. i.e. *length*, **S#751h**.

Accad. i.e. *strengthen; fortress; band, fortification, castle; a vessel, pitcher*, **S#390h**.

Calneh. i.e. *fortified dwellings; the wail is complete*, **S#3641h**. Is 10:9. Am 6:2.

Shinar. i.e. *casting out, scattering*, **S#8152h**. Ge 11:2. 14:1, 9. Jsh 7:21mg. Is 11:11. Da 1:2. Zc 5:11.

11 A.M. 1700. B.C. 2304.

went forth Asshur. *or*, he went out *into* Assyria. Mi 5:6.

Asshur. ver. +22. Ge 2:14. 25:18. 2 K 15:19, 29.

Nineveh. i.e. *agreeable; offspring abiding*, **S#5210h**. ver. 12. 2 K 19:36. Is 37:37. Jon 1:2. 3:2-7. 4:11. Na 1:1, 14. 2:8. 3:7. Zp 2:13. Mt 12:41. Lk 11:32.

the city of. or, the streets of the city.

Rehoboth. i.e. *broad or wide places*, **S#7344h**. Ge 26:22. 36:37. 1 Ch 1:48. Am +5:16.

12 **Resen**. i.e. *bridle, curb*, **S#7449h**.

Nineveh. ver. +11.

Calah. i.e. *full or old age, completion*, **S#3625h**. ver. 11. 2 K 15:19, 29. 1 Ch 5:26.

13 **Mizraim**. ver. 6.

Ludim. i.e. *travailings, generation*, **S#3866h**. ver. +22. 1 Ch 1:11.

Anamim. i.e. *answer of the waters; affliction of the waters; fountains of waters*, **S#6047h**. 1 Ch 1:11.

Lehabim. i.e. *flames; scorching heat*, **S#3853h**. 1 Ch 1:11. 2 Ch 12:3. 16:8. Da 11:43. Na 3:9.

Naphtuhim. i.e. *openings*, **S#5320h**. 1 Ch 1:11.

14 **Pathrusim**. i.e. *southern region, Egypt*, **S#6625h**. 1 Ch 1:12. Is +11:11, Pathros.

Casluhim. i.e. *protected boundary; pardoned*, **S#3695h**. 1 Ch 1:12.

Philistim. i.e. *wallowing*, **S#6625h**. 1 Ch 1:12. Is 14:31. Je +47:4.

Caphtorim. i.e. *crowns, lintels*, **S#3732h**. Dt 2:23. 1 Ch 1:12, Caphthorim. Je +47:4, Caphtor. Am 9:7.

15 **Canaan**. ver. 6. 1 Ch 1:13.

Sidon. Heb. Tzidon. Ge +49:13, Zidon.

firstborn. Ge 41:51, 52 with Je 31:9. Ex 4:22. Dt 21:15-17. Ps 89:20, 27. Col 1:15, 18.

Heth. i.e. *terror; dread, fear, striking*, **S#2845h**. Ge 23:3, 5, 7, 10, 16, 18, 20. 25:10. 27:46. 49:32. 1 Ch 1:13.

16 **Jebusite**. i.e. *treading down*, **S#2983h**. Ge 15:21. Ex 3:8, 17. 13:5. 23:23. 33:2. 34:11. Nu 13:29. Dt 7:1. 20:17. Jsh 3:10. 9:1. 11:3. 12:8. 15:8, 63. +18:16, 28, Jebusi. 24:11. Jg 1:21. 3:5. +19:10, Jebus, 11. 2 S 5:6, 8. 24:16, 18. 1 K 9:20. 1 Ch 1:14. 11:4, 6. 21:15, 18, 28. 2 Ch 3:1. 8:7. Ezr 9:1. Ne 9:8. Ezk 16:3, 45. Zc 9:7.

Amorite. i.e. *mountaineers*, **S#567h**. Ge 14:7, 13. 15:16, 21. 48:22. Ex 3:8, 17. 13:5. 23:23. 33:2. 34:11. Nu 13:29. 21:13, 21, 25, 26, 29, 31, 32, 34. 22:2. 32:33, 39. Dt 1:4, 7, 19, 20, 27, 44. 2:24. 3:2, 8, 9. 4:46, 47. 7:1. 20:17. 31:4. Jsh 2:10. 3:10. 5:1. 7:7. 9:1, 10. 10:5, 6, 12. 11:3. 12:2, 8. 13:4, 10, 21. 24:8, 11, 12,

15, 18. Jg 1:34-36. 3:5. 6:10. 10:8, 11. 11:19, 21-23. 1 S 7:14. 2 S 21:2. 1 K 4:19. 9:20. 21:26. 2 K 21:11. 1 Ch 1:14. 2 Ch 8:7. Ezr 9:1. Ne 9:8. Ps 135:11. 136:19. Ezk 16:3, 45. Am 2:9, 10.

Girgasite. i.e. *dweller in loamy soil*, **S#1622h**. Ge 15:21. Dt 7:1. Jsh 3:10. 24:11. 1 Ch 1:14. Ne 9:8.

17 **Hivite**. i.e. *villager, serpent*, **S#2340h**. Ge 34:2. 36:2. Ex 3:8, 17. 13:5. 23:23, 28. 33:2. 34:11. Dt 7:1. 20:17. Jsh 3:10. 9:1, 7. 11:3, 19. 12:8. 24:11. Jg 3:3, 5. 2 S 24:7. 1 K 9:20. 1 Ch 1:15. 2 Ch 8:7.

Arkite. i.e. *fugitive; my gnawing*, **S#6208h**. 1 Ch 1:15.

Sinite. i.e. *dwellers in a marshy land*, **S#5513h**. 1 Ch 1:15.

18 **Arvadite**. 1 Ch 1:16. Ezk 27:8, 11.

Zemarite. Jsh 18:22. 1 Ch 1:16.

Hamathite. Nu +13:21. 1 Ch 1:16.

Canaanites. ver. 15, 19. Ge 12:6. 13:7. 15:21. +24:3, 37. 34:30. 38:2. 46:10. 50:11. Ex 3:8, 17. 6:15. 13:5, 11. 23:23, 28. 33:2, 11. 33:2. 34:11. Nu 13:29. 14:25, 43, 45. 21:3. 33:40. Dt 1:7. 7:1. 11:30. 20:17. Jsh 3:10. 5:1. 7:9. 9:1. 11:3. 12:8. 13:4. 16:10. 17:12, 13, 16, 18. 24:11. Jg 1:1, 3-5, 9, 10, 17, 27-30, 32, 33. 3:3, 5. 2 S 24:7. 1 K 9:16. 1 Ch 2:3. Ezr 9:1. Ne 9:8, 24. Ob 20. Zc 14:21. Mt 10:4. Mk 3:18.

19 **And the border**. Ge 13:12-17. 15:18-21. Nu 34:2-15. Dt 32:8. Jsh 12:7, 8. 14-21.

Sidon. i.e. *hunting, fishery; plenty of fish*, **S#6721h**. Ge +49:13, Zidon.

as thou comest. Ge +25:18. Ge 13:10.

Gerar. Ge 20:1, 2. 26:1, 6, 17, 20, 26. 2 Ch 14:13, 14.

Gaza. Heb. Azzah. i.e. *strong, fortified*, **S#5804h**. Dt 2:23. Jsh 10:41. 11:22. 15:47. Jg 1:18. 6:4. 16:1, 21. 1 S 6:17. 1 K 4:24. 2 K 18:8. 1 Ch 7:28. Je 25:20. 47:1mg, 5. Am 1:6, 7. Zp 2:4. Zc 9:5. Ac 8:26.

Sodom. i.e. *flaming, burning; mystery; dew, abundance; fettered*, **S#5467h**. Ge 13:10-13. 14:2, 8, 10-12, 17, 21, 22. 18:16, 20, 22, 26. 19:1, 4, 24, 28. Dt 29:23. 32:32. Is 1:9, 10. 3:9. 13:19. Je 23:14. 49:18. 50:40. La 4:6. Ezk 16:46, 48, 49, 53, 55, 56. Am 4:11. Zp 2:9. Mt 10:15. Mk 6:11. Lk 10:12. Ro 9:29. 2 P 2:6. Ju 7. Re 11:8.

Gomorrah. i.e. *people of fear; bondage; a ruined heap*, **S#6017h**. Ge 13:10. 14:2, 8, 10, 11. 18:20. 19:24, 28. Dt 29:23. 32:32. Is 1:9, 10. 13:19. Je 23:14. 49:18. 50:40. Am 4:11. Zp 2:9.

Admah. i.e. *earthy; red*, **S#126h**. Ge 14:2, 8. Dt 29:23. Ho 11:8.

Zeboim. i.e. *gazelles, gathering of troops; dyers, hyenas*, **S#6636h**. Ge 14:2, 8. Dt 29:23. Also **S#6650h**: 1 S 13:18, Ne 11:34. Also **S#6636h**: Ho 11:8.

20　sons of Ham. ver. 6. Ge 11:1-9.
21　Shem. ver. +1. Ge 9:26. Lk 3:36. Ro 9:4, 5.
　　the father. Ge 11:10-26.
　　Eber. ver. +24, 25.
　　the brother. ver. 2.
　　elder. ver. +1. Ge 5:32.
22　children. Ge 9:26. 1 Ch 1:17-27.
　　Elam. i.e. *eternal*, **S#5867h**. Ge 14:1, 9. 2 K
　　15:19. 1 Ch 1:17. 8:24. 26:3. Ezr 2:7, 31. 4:9.
　　8:7. 10:2, 26. Ne 7:12, 34. 10:14. 12:42. Jb
　　1:17. Is 11:11. 21:2. 22:6. Je 25:25. 49:34-39.
　　Ezk 32:24. Da 8:2. Ac 2:9.
　　Asshur. i.e. *a step, going*, **S#804h**. ver. 11. Nu
　　24:22, 24. 1 Ch 1:17. Ezr 4:2. Ps 83:8. Ezk
　　27:23. 31:3. 32:22. Ho 14:3.
　　Arphaxad. Heb. Arpachshad. i.e. *boundary of*
　　the Chaldeans; one that heals, **S#775h**. ver. 24. Ge
　　11:10-13. 1 Ch 1:17, 18, 24.
　　Lud. i.e. *bending, tortuous*, **S#3865h**. 1 Ch 1:17.
　　Is 66:19. Je 46:9mg. Ezk 27:10. 30:5mg.
　　Aram. Nu 23:7.
23　Uz. i.e. *counsel; impressible; fruitful in trees, fer-*
　　tile land, **S#5780h**. Ge 22:21, Huz. 36:28. 1 Ch
　　1:17, 42. Jb 1:1. Je 25:20. La 4:21.
　　Hul. i.e. *circle; to have pain*, **S#2343h**. 1 Ch 1:17.
　　Gether. i.e. *fear, turning aside; spying a neigh-*
　　bor; a proud spy; seeing a wine press, **S#1666h**. 1
　　Ch 1:17.
　　Mash. i.e. *drawn out, departed*, **S#4851h**. ver. 2.
　　1 Ch 1:17.
24　Salah. Heb. Shelah. i.e. *sent, shooting forth; a*
　　missile, **S#7974h**. Ge 11:12-15. 1 Ch 1:18, 24. Lk
　　3:35.
　　Eber. i.e. *the region beyond; a shoot*, **S#5677h**.
　　ver. 21, 25. Ge 11:14-17. 14:13. Nu 24:24. Jsh
　　24:2, 3, 14, 15. 1 Ch 1:18, 19, 25. 5:13. 8:12,
　　22. Ne 12:20. Lk 3:35.
25　A.M. 1757. **B.C.** 2247.
　　Eber. ver. 21, +24.
　　the name. Ge 11:16-19. Lk 3:35, 36.
　　Peleg. i.e. Division. **S#6389h**. i.e. *earthquake*.
　　Ge 11:16-19. 1 Ch 1:19, 25. Lk 3:35.
　　earth divided. ver. 32. Dt 32:8. Ac 17:26.
　　Joktan. i.e. *he will be small; small dispute*,
　　S#3355h. ver. 26, 29. 1 Ch 1:19, 20, 23.
26　Joktan. ver. +25. 1 Ch 1:20-23.
　　Almodad. i.e. *immeasurable*, **S#486h**. 1 Ch
　　1:20.
　　Sheleph. i.e. *extract, drawn out, selected*,
　　S#8026h. 1 Ch 1:20.
　　Hazarmaveth. i.e. *court of death*, **S#2700h**. 1 Ch
　　1:20.
　　Jerah. i.e. *moon, lunar*, **S#3392h**. 1 Ch 1:20.
27　And. 1 Ch 1:20-23.
　　Hadoram. i.e. *Hadar is high; exalted, power*,
　　S#1913h. 1 Ch 1:21. 18:10. 2 Ch 10:18.
　　Uzal. i.e. *going to and fro; wandering; shall be*
　　flooded, **S#187h**. 1 Ch 1:21. Ezk 27:19mg.
　　Diklah. i.e. *a palm tree*, **S#1853h**. 1 Ch 1:21.
28　A.M. cir. 1797. **B.C.** cir. 2207.

　　Obal. i.e. *bare; heaping confusion; bare district;*
　　stripped; bare of leaves, **S#5745h**.
　　Abimeal. i.e. *a father sent from God*, **S#39h**. 1
　　Ch 1:22.
　　Sheba. 1 K +10:1.
29　Ophir. i.e. *fruitful; abundance; reducing to ashes*,
　　S#211h. 1 K +9:28. 1 Ch 1:23.
　　Havilah. ver. +7. Ge 2:11. 25:18. 1 S 15:7.
　　Jobab. i.e. *a desert; crying out*, **S#3103h**. Ge
　　36:33, 34. Jsh 11:1. 1 Ch 1:23, 44, 45. 8:9, 18.
30　Mesha. i.e. *retreat; bringing deliverance*,
　　S#4852h.
　　Sephar. i.e. *numbering; census*, **S#5611h**.
　　mount. Ge 12:8. 14:10. 19:17, 30. 22:2.
　　31:21. Ex 3:1.
　　of the east. Ge +29:1.
31　after their families. ver. +5, 20. Ac 17:26.
32　are the. ver. 1, 20, 31. Ge 5:29-31.
　　nations. ver. 25. Ge 9:1, 7, 19. Ac 17:26.
　　divided. ver. +25. Ge 11:8. Dt 32:8. Da 4:37.
　　5:28. Lk 1:51.

GENESIS 11

1　A.M. 1757. **B.C.** 2247.
　　earth. Ge +6:11.
　　was of. or, was. Jb 12:20. Ps 81:5. Pr 17:7. Is
　　19:18. Zp 3:9. Ac 2:4-6. Re 7:9, 10.
　　language. Heb. lip. Pr 12:19, 22. Is 19:18mg.
　　33:19. Zp 3:9mg.
　　speech. Heb. words.
2　from the east. *or*, eastward. Ge 12:8. 13:11.
　　2 S 6:2. 1 Ch 13:6.
　　Shinar. ver. +9. Ge +10:10.
3　they said one to another. Heb. a man said
　　to his neighbor.
　　Go to. The Hebrew word signifies *come*, or
　　make preparation, as for a journey or the exe-
　　cution of a purpose. ver. 4, 7. Ps 64:5. Pr 1:11.
　　Ec 2:1. Is 5:5. 41:6, 7. Ja 4:13. 5:1.
　　us. ver. 7. He 3:13. 10:24.
　　burn thoroughly. Heb. burn to a burning.
　　brick. Ex 1:14. 5:7-18. 2 S 12:31. Is 9:10.
　　65:3. Na 3:14. 1 P 2:5.
　　stone. Ge 28:11. Is 9:10.
　　slime. Ge 14:10. Ex 2:3. Re 21:19.
4　Go to. ver. 3, 7. Ge 38:16. Ex 1:10.
　　and let. 2 S 8:13. Ps 49:11-13. Pr 10:7. Da
　　4:30. Jn 5:44.
　　city. Ge 4:17. 13:12. Pr 25:28. Re 18:10, 13,
　　16. 21:18, 21.
　　whose. Ge 28:12. Ps 107:26.
　　top. Dt 1:28. 9:1. Da 4:11, 22. Am 9:2.
　　name. Ge 6:4. Ex 9:16. Dt 22:14. Ru 4:10. 2 S
　　7:9, 23. 8:13. Jb 18:17. Pr 10:7. Is 42:8. Da
　　4:30. Mk 6:14. Jn 5:44. Ro 9:17. Re 3:1.
　　lest. ver. 8, 9. Dt 4:27. Ps 44:11. 92:9. Lk
　　1:51.
　　face. Ge +1:2.
5　came down. Ge 18:21. Ex 3:8. 19:11, 18, 20.

34:5. Nu 11:25. 12:5. Je 23:23, 24. Jn +3:13. He 4:13.

see. Ps 14:2.

children. Dt 9:2. 1 K 8:39. Mk 3:28. Ep 3:5.

6 **Behold**. Ge 3:22. Jg 10:14. 1 K 18:27. Ec 11:9.

the people. ver. 1. Ge 9:19. Ac 17:26.

one. Dt +6:4.

imagined. Ge 6:5. 8:21. Jb 5:12. Ps 2:1-4. Lk 1:51. 1 C 1:19.

7 **Go to**. ver. 4.

let us. ver. 5. Ge +1:26. 3:22. Pr 8:30. Is 6:8. Jn 1:1.

confound. Ex 4:11. Jb 5:12, 13. 12:20. Ps 2:4. 33:10. 55:9. Ac 2:4-11.

language. Is 28:11. Ac 2:4-6. 1 C 14:21, 22.

may. Ge 10:5, 20, 32. 42:23. Dt 28:49. Ps 55:9. Je 5:15. 1 C 14:2-11, 23.

8 **scattered**. ver. 4, 9. Ge 49:7. Dt 32:8. Ps 92:9. Is 8:9. Lk 1:51. Ac 8:1.

upon. Ge 10:25, 32.

face. Ge +1:2. 16:8. Jg 11:3mg. Is 14:21. Ac 17:26. Re 12:14.

left off. ver. 4. Pr 10:24.

city. ver. +4. Jb 12:14. Ps 127:1.

9 **name**. Ge 19:22.

Babel. *That is*, Confusion. Ge 10:5, +10, 20, 31. Is ch. 13, 14. Je ch. 50, 51. 1 C 14:23. 1 P 5:13. Re 18:2.

scatter. ver. +4. Ps 68:30. Lk 1:51.

the face. Ge 10:25, 32. Ac 17:26.

10 A.M. 1658. B.C. 2346.

generations. ver. 27. Ge 2:4. 5:1. 10:1, 21, 22. 1 Ch 1:17-27. Lk 3:34-36.

Shem. Ge +5:32.

Arphaxad. Ge +10:22.

11 A.M. 2158. B.C. 1846.

Shem. ver. 10. Ge 5:4, etc.

begat sons. Ge 1:28. 5:4. Ps 127:3, 4. 144:12.

12 A.M. 1693. B.C. 2311.

Arphaxad. Ge 10:22. 1 Ch 1:17, 18.

begat. Ge +10:24.

13 A.M. 2096. B.C. 1908.

14 A.M. 1723. B.C. 2281.

Eber. Ge +10:24.

15 A.M. 2126. B.C. 1878.

16 A.M. 1757. B.C. 2247.

Eber. Ge +10:24.

Peleg. Ge +10:25. Lk 3:35, Phalec.

17 A.M. 2187. B.C. 1817.

18 A.M. 1787. B.C. 2217.

Reu. i.e. *associate, friend*, S#7466h. ver. 19, 20, 21. 1 Ch 1:25. Lk 3:35, Ragau.

19 A.M. 1996. B.C. 2008.

two. Ge 5:27. 11:11. Dt 31:2. Ps 90:10.

20 A.M. 1819. B.C. 2185.

Serug. i.e. *a branch, shoot, intertwined*, S#8286h. ver. 21, 22, 23. 1 Ch 1:26. Lk 3:35, Saruch.

21 A.M. 2026. B.C. 1978.

22 A.M. 1849. B.C. 2155.

Nahor. i.e. *snorer; snorting; burning or drying up; white, splendid*, S#5152h. ver. 23, 24, 25, 26, 27, 29. Ge 22:20, 23. 24:10, 15, 24, 47. 29:5. 31:53. Jsh 24:2, Nachor. 1 Ch 1:26. Lk 3:34.

23 A.M. 2049. B.C. 1955.

24 A.M. 1878. B.C. 2126.

Terah. ver. +26. Lk 3:34, Thara.

25 A.M. 1997. B.C. 2007.

26 A.M. 1948. B.C. 2056.

Terah. i.e. *delay; breathing*, S#8646h. ver. 24, 25, 27, 28, 31, 32. Jsh 24:2. 1 Ch 1:26.

Abram. i.e. *exalted father; ambition*, S#87h. Ge 12:4, 5. 17:1, 3, 5. 18:19. 22:20-24. 29:4, 5. Ex 3:6. Jsh 24:2. 1 Ch 1:26, 27. Ne 9:7. Mt 22:31, 32. Mk 12:26, 27. Lk 20:37, 38. Jn 8:39, 52, 53, 56, +58. Ro 4:11. Ga 3:16. He 11:17. Ja 2:23.

Nahor. ver. +22.

Haran. i.e. *mountainous; parched*, S#2039h. ver. 27-29, 31, 32. Ge 12:4, 5. 27:43. 28:10. 29:4, 5. 2 K 19:12. 1 Ch 23:9. Is 37:12. Ezk 27:23. Ac 7:2-4, Charran.

27 A.M. 2008. B.C. 1996. Abram, though mentioned first, was born last. Ge 10:21. 17:15-21. 25:23. 27:15. +48:18, 20. Ex 7:7. Jg 6:15. 1 S 16:10-12. 1 K 1:6. 2:22. Col +1:15.

generations. ver. +10.

Lot. i.e. *a covering; myrrh*, S#3876h. ver. 31. Ge 12:4, 5. 13:1, 5, 7, 8, 10, 11, 12, 14. 14:12, 16. 19:1, 5, 6, 9, 10, 12, 14, 15, 18, 23, 29, 30, 36. Dt 2:9, 19. Ps 83:8. 2 P 2:7.

28 **Haran died before**. Thus, Lot was an orphan. Nu 3:4. 27:1-5. Dt +10:18. 21:16. 2 S 9:3. 2 K 11:1-12. Est 2:7. La 5:3.

Ur. ver. 31. Ge 15:7. Ne 9:7. Ac 7:2-4.

Ur. i.e. *fire, light, flame*, S#218h. ver. 31. Ge 15:7. 1 Ch 11:35. Ne 9:7.

Chaldees. Ge 15:7. 2 K 24:2. 25:4. 2 Ch 36:17. Ne 9:7. Jb 1:17. Je 39:5. Ac 7:4.

29 **Nahor**. ver. +22.

Sarai. Ge 17:15. 20:12. 1 P 3:6.

Milcah. i.e. *queen; counsel*, S#4435h. Ge 22:20, 23. 24:15, 24, 47. Nu 26:33. 27:1. 36:11. Jsh 17:3.

Iscah. i.e. *observant; she looks abroad*, S#3252h. Iscah is called the *daughter-in-law* of Terah, (ver. 31,) as being Abram's wife; yet Abram afterwards said, "she is the daughter of my father, but not the daughter of my mother." (Ge 20:12.) Probably Haran was the eldest son of Terah, and Abram his youngest by another wife: and thus Sarai was the daughter, or *grand-daughter* of Terah, Abram's father, but not of his mother.

30 **barren**. Ge 15:2, 3. 16:1, 2. 18:11, 12. 21:1, 2. 25:21. 29:31. 30:1, 2. Dt 28:18. Jg 13:2. 1 S 1:2, 5. 2 S 6:23. 2 K 4:14. Ps +113:9. +127:3. Is +54:1. Lk 1:7, 36. Ro 4:19. He 11:11.

31 A.M. 2078. B.C. 1926.

took. ver. 26, 27. Ge 12:1.

Lot. ver. 27.

Haran. ver. +26.

daughter-in-law. Ge 38:11. Le 18:15. 20:12. Ru 1:6, 22. 2:20. 4:15. Mi 7:6. Mt 10:35.

they went. ver. 28. Ge 12:1. Jsh 24:2, 3. He 11:8.

Ur. ver. 28. Ge 15:7. Jsh 24:2. Ne 9:7. Ac 7:2-4.

the land. Ge 10:19. 24:10.

Canaan. Ge 10:6, 18, 19. +48:3. Nu 34:2. Ac 13:19.

Haran. ver. +26. B.C. cir. 1923. A.M. cir. 2081.

and dwelt. Nu 32:1-5. Mt 8:21. He 4:1.

32　A.M. 2083. B.C. 1921.

Terah. ver. +26.

died. Ru 1:3. Ac 7:4.

Haran. ver. +31.

GENESIS 12

1　**had**. Ge 11:31, 32. 15:7. Ne 9:7. Is 41:9. 51:2. Ezk 33:24.

Get. Jsh 24:2, 3. Ps 45:10, 11. Lk 14:26-33. Ac 7:2-6. 2 C 5:16. 6:17. He 11:8. Re 18:4.

show. 1 C 2:9, 10. Ep 2:6. 1 J 3:2. Re 21:9.

2　**And I**. Ge 13:16. 15:5. 17:5, 6. 22:17, 18. 24:35. 26:4. 27:29. 28:3, 14. 32:12. 35:11. 46:3. 47:27. Ex 1:7. 32:10. Nu 14:12. 24:9, 10. Dt 26:5. 2 S 7:9. 1 K 3:8, 9. Mi 7:20. Ro 4:11. Ga 3:7.

bless thee. Ex 6:4-8. Dt 9:5. Is 19:24, 25. Hg 2:19. Ep 1:3.

great. Is 51:2. Ezk 33:24.

name. Ge 11:4. 17:5. 32:28. 1 Ch 17:8, 21. Ps 52:9. Mt 1:21. Ac 4:12. Ph 2:10.

thou shalt. Ge 14:14-16. 18:18. 19:29. 28:4. 1 K 1:47. Je 4:2. Zp 3:20. Zc 8:13. Jn 7:38. Ga 3:14. He 6:14.

3　**will bless**. Ge 27:29. Ps +122:6. Nu 24:9. Mt 25:40, 45.

them. Ge +18:18.

thee. Ge +9:27.

curse him. Ex 23:22mg. Nu 23:8. Dt +30:7. Je 30:16. Am 9:15.

in thee. Ge 18:18. +22:18. 26:3, 4. 28:14. 30:27, 30. 39:5. Ps 72:11, 17. Zc 8:23. Mt 1:1. Lk 1:55, 73. Ac 3:25, 26. Ro 4:11, 13. 1 C 1:30. Ga 3:8, 14, 16, 28. Ep 1:3. Col 3:11. He 6:12, 17. Re 7:9.

4　**departed**. Ex 12:38. Ne 13:3. Is 51:2. Mt 10:37.

and Lot. Ge 11:27.

departed out. He 11:8.

5　**Lot**. Ge 13:1.

son. Ac 12:25. Col 4:10.

substance. Ge 13:6. Ec 5:19.

the souls. ver. +13. Ge 14:14, 21mg. 46:5-26. Ezk 27:13. Re 18:13. Heb. *nephesh*, S#5315h, used of man as an individual person here and at Ge +2:7. 46:15, 18, 22, 25, 26, 27. Ex 1:5. 12:4. Le 22:11. Pr 10:3. 11:25, 30. 19:15. Ezk 18:4. *Nephesh* used in this same sense is rendered "person" at Ge 14:21. 36:6. Nu 31:40, 46. Dt 10:22. Je 43:6. 52:29, 30. Ezk 16:5. 27:13. It is otherwise rendered "persons," Nu 31:35; "any," Dt 24:7; "man," 2 K 12:4; "men," 1 Ch 5:21; and left untranslated at Nu 31:35, where it is literally "and the soul of man...were 32,000 souls." For the other uses of *nephesh* see Ge +2:7. "Soul," a part of man, is used of the whole person here and at Ge 14:21mg. 17:14. 46:15, 26, 27. Ex 12:19. 16:16mg. Le 5:2, 4. Ezk 18:4, 20. Lk 6:9. Ac 2:41, 43. 7:14. Ro 13:1. 1 P 3:20. Re 6:9. 20:4.

in Haran. Ge 11:31.

and into. Ge 10:19. Ac 7:4. He 11:8, 9.

land of Canaan. Ge +11:31. 26:3.

6　**passed**. He 11:9.

place. Ge 18:24. 19:12. 29:22.

Sichem. i.e. *shoulder; early in the morning*, S#7927h. Ge 33:18. 34:2. 35:4. Jsh 20:7. 24:32. Jg 9:1. 1 K 12:1, Shechem. Jn 4:5, Sychar. Ac 7:16, Sychem.

plain. The word rendered *plain* should be rendered *oak*, or according to Celsius, the *turpentine tree*. Ge 13:18. 14:13. 18:1. Jg 4:11. 9:6, 37. 1 S 10:3.

Moreh. i.e. *teacher; famous; dart flinger*, S#4176h. Dt 11:30. Jg 7:1.

And. Ge 13:7. Ps +23:5.

Canaanite. Ge +10:18.

7　**appeared**. Ge 17:1. 18:1. +32:30. +35:9. 46:29. Jn 1:18. 8:56, 58.

Unto thy. Ge +13:15. Ac 7:5. Ro 9:7, 8. Ga 3:16.

land. Ge 15:7. Dt 34:4.

builded. ver. 8. Ge 8:20. 13:4, 18. 22:9. 26:25. 33:20. He 11:13.

8　**removed**. 1 P 2:11.

Bethel. i.e. *house of God*, S#1008h. Ge 13:3. 28:19. 31:13. 35:1, 3, 6, 8, 15, 16. Jsh 7:2. 8:17. 12:9. 16:2. 18:13. Jg 1:22, 23. 4:5. 20:31mg. 1 S 10:3. 1 K 12:29. 13:1, 4, 10, 11, 32. 2 K 2:2, 3, 23. 10:29. 17:28. 23:4, 15, 17, 19. 1 Ch 7:28. Ne 11:31. Ho 10:15. 12:4. Am 3:14. 4:4. 5:5. 7:13.

tent. He 11:9.

Hai. i.e. *heap of ruins*, S#5857h. Ge 13:3. Jsh 7:2. 8:3, Ai. Ne 11:31, Aija. Is 10:28, Aiath.

altar. Ge 8:20. Dt 27:2, 12. Jsh 8:9, 30. 1 P 2:5.

called. Ge 4:26. 13:4. 21:33. 26:25. Ex 34:5. 1 Ch 4:10. Ps 99:6. 116:4. Pr 18:10. Jl 2:32. Ac 2:21. Ro 10:12-14. 1 C 1:2.

9　**going**. Ge 26:13. Ph 3:13.

on still. Heb. in going and journeying. Ge 13:3. 24:62. Ps 105:13. He 11:13, 14.

south. Ge 13:1, 3. 20:1. 24:62. Nu 13:17, 22, 29. Dt 1:7. Jsh 11:16. 15:3, 21. Jg 1:9, 15. 1 S

27:10. Ps 126:4. Is 21:1. 30:6. Je 13:19. 17:26. 32:44. 33:13. Ezk 20:46, 47. 21:4.

10 A.M. 2084. B.C. 1920.
was a. Ro 5:3.
famine. Ge 47:13. 1 K +8:37. ch. 17, 18. 2 K ch. 7. Ne 5:3. Ps 34:19. Is 51:19. Je 14:1, 15. 15:2. 24:10. 27:8. Ezk 12:16. Am 8:11. Jn 16:33. Ac 14:22.
went. Ge 26:2, 3. 43:1. 46:3, 4. 1 S 27:1. 2 K 8:1, 2. Ps 105:13. Is 30:2. 31:1.

11 **he said**. Ge 20:2. 26:7. 1 S 16:2. Lk 22:55-61. Ac 21:26. 23:6. Ga 2:12, 13. 6:12.
a fair. ver. 14. Ge +29:17. Pr 11:22. SS 1:14. 4:1, 7. 6:4, 10. Am 8:13.

12 **Egyptians**. i.e. *tribulation*, **S#4714h**. ver. 14. Ge 41:55, 56. 43:32. 46:34. 47:15. 47:20. 50:3, 11. Ex 1:13. 3:8, 9, 21, 22. 1 S 4:8. 2 K 7:6. Is 19:2, 4, 21, 23. Ezk 29:12, 13. Ac 7:22. He 11:29.
will kill. Ge 20:11. 26:7. 1 S 27:1. Pr 29:25. Mt 10:28. 1 J 1:8-10.

13 **Say**. Jn 8:44. Ro 3:6-8. 6:23. Col 3:6.
thou art. Ge +11:29. 20:2, 5, 12, 13. 26:7. Is 57:11. Mt 26:69-75. Ga 2:12, 13.
that it. Ge 20:11. Pr 29:25. Ec 7:20. Je 17:7.
and. Ps +146:3-5. Je 17:5-8.
soul. Heb. *nephesh*. Used here and in the following passages of mortal man, as though the soul could die or be destroyed (Mt +10:28. Ac 2:37. 2 T 1:10): Ge 17:14. Le 17:11. Jsh 2:13. 11:11. Jg 16:16, 30. 1 S 25:29. 1 K 17:21, 22. Jb 11:20. 18:4mg. 33:22. 36:14mg. Ps 22:29. 49:8, 15. Is +10:18. +55:3. Je 4:10. 40:14mg. Ezk 13:19. 14:14, 20. 18:4. Mt +2:20. +12:18. For the other uses of *nephesh* see Ge +2:7.
live. Je 38:17, 20.

14 **beheld**. Ge +3:6. 6:2. 39:7. Jb +31:1. Mt 5:28. He 13:4.

15 **princes**. Est 2:2-16. Pr 29:12. Ho 7:4, 5.
Pharaoh. i.e. *sun king*, **S#6547h**. Pharaoh was a common name of the Egyptian kings, and signified *a ruler*, or *king*, or *father of his country*. Ge 40:2. 41:1. Ex 2:5, 15. 1 K 3:1. 2 K 18:21. Je 25:19. 46:17. Ezk 32:2.
taken. Ge 20:2. Est 2:9. Ps 68:18. 105:4. Pr 6:29. Ep 4:8. He 13:4.

16 **And he**. Ge 13:2. 20:14.
well. Ge 13:10. 14:23.
he had. Ge 24:35. 26:14. 32:5, 13-15. Jb 1:3. 42:12. Ps 14:13, 14.
maid-servants. Ge 16:1. 20:14.

17 **plagued**. Ge 20:18. 1 Ch 16:21. 21:22. Jb 34:19. Ps 105:13-15. He 13:4.
plagues. 1 S 5:11.
wife. Ge +11:29. 17:15. 23:9. 1 Ch 16:21.

18 **What**. Ge 3:13. 4:10. 20:9, 10. 26:9-11. 31:26. 44:15. Ex 32:21. Jsh 7:19. 1 S 14:43. Pr 21:1.
why. Le 19:17. Is 43:27. Ep 5:11.
wife. Ro 7:3.

19 **Why**. Le 19:17. Ro 3:8. Ep 4:25. Col 3:9.
sister. Ge 20:2, 12. 26:9.

20 **sent**. Ge 26:16. Ex 11:8. Ps 105:14, 15. Pr 21:1. Lk 21:24.

GENESIS 13

1 A.M. 2086. B.C. 1918.
up. Ge 12:10.
the south. The south of Canaan; as in leaving Egypt, it is said he 'came from the south,' (ver. 3,) and the southern part of the promised land lay northeast of Egypt. Ge +12:9. 21:33. Jsh 10:40. 18:5. 2 S 24:7.
Egypt. i.e. *binds or oppresses*, **S#4714h**. ver. 10. Ge 12:10. 15:18. 21:21. 26:2. 37:25, 28, 36.

2 **rich**. Ge 24:35. 26:12, 13. Dt 8:18. 1 S 2:7. Jb 1:3, 10. 22:21-25. Ps 112:1-3. Pr 3:9, 10. 10:22. Mt 6:33. Lk 18:23. 1 T +4:8.

3 **from**. Ge 12:6, 8, 9.
south. Ge +12:9.
beginning. Ge 35:1. Re 2:4, 5.
Bethel and Hai. i.e. The place which was afterwards called *Bethel* by Jacob, and so called when Moses wrote; for its first name was *Luz*. Ge +28:19.

4 **Unto**. ver. 18. Ge 12:7, 8. 35:1-3. Ps 26:8. 42:1, 2. 84:1, 2, 10.
called. Ge 4:26. 21:33. Ps 65:1, 2. 107:1, 8, 15. 116:2, 17. 145:18. Is 12:4. 58:9. Je 29:12. Zep 3:9. Ro 10:13. 1 C 1:2. Ep 6:18, 19.

5 **Lot**. Ge 11:27, 31. 12:5.
tents. Ge 4:20. 25:27. Je 49:29.

6 **bear**. Ge 36:6, 7. Ec 5:10, 11. Lk 12:17, 18. 1 T 6:9.
substance. ver. 2. Ge 12:5, 16.

7 **a strife**. Ge 21:25. 26:20. Ex 2:17. 1 C 3:3. Ga 5:20. T 3:3. Ja 3:16. 4:1.
Canaanite. Ge +10:18. Ne 5:9. Ph 2:14, 15. Col 4:5. 1 Th 4:12. 1 P 2:12.
Perizzite. i.e. *villagers*, **S#6522h**. Ge 15:20. 34:30. Ex 3:8, 17. 23:23. 33:2. 34:11. Dt 7:1. 20:17. Jsh 3:10. 9:1. 11:3. 12:8. 17:15-18. 24:11. Jg 1:4, 5. 3:5. 1 K 9:20. 2 Ch 8:7. Ezr 9:1. Ne 9:8.
dwelled. i.e. They were *there* when Abram and Lot came to pitch their tents in the land.

8 **said**. Pr 13:10. 15:18. 20:3.
Let. 1 C 6:6, 7. He 12:14.
brethren. Heb. men, brethren. Ge 11:27-31. 45:24. Ex 2:13. 1 K +15:10. 2 Ch 2:17mg. Ps 133:1. Is +40:13mg. Ac 7:26. Ro 12:10. Ep 4:2, 3. 1 Th 4:9. He 13:1. 1 P 1:22. 2:17. 3:8. 4:8. 2 P 1:7. 1 J 2:9-11. 3:14-19. 4:7, 20, 21.

9 **Is not**. Ge 20:15. 34:10. 47:6. Ec 6:6. Mt 7:22. Mk 12:24. Jn 4:35.
if. Ep 4:1-3. Ph 2:1-4. 4:5.
thou wilt take. Ps 120:7. Ro 12:18. 1 C 6:7. He 12:14. Ja 3:13-18. 1 P 3:8-12.
left. Ge 24:49. Nu 20:17. 22:26.

10 lifted. Ge 3:6. 18:16. 2 T 4:10. 1 J 2:15.
and beheld. Ge +3:6. 6:2. Nu 32:1. 1 J 2:15, 16.
the plain. Ge 19:17, 24, 25. Dt 34:3. 1 K 7:46. Ps 107:33, 34. 1 J 2:15.
the garden. Ge 2:8-10. 19:28. Is 51:3. Ezk 28:13. 31:8. Jl 2:3.
land of. Ge 47:6.
Zoar. i.e. *little*, **S#6820h**. Ge 14:2, 8. 19:22, 23, 30. Dt 34:3. Is 15:5. Je 48:34. Instead of Zoar, which was situated at the extremity of the plain of Jordan, the Syriac reads *Zoan*, which was situated in the south of Egypt, and in a well-watered country. Nu +13:22.

11 A.M. 2087. B.C. 1917.
chose. Ge 15:1. 19:17. Jg 10:14. Pr 1:29. Is 65:12. 66:3.
they separated. ver. 9, 14. Ps 16:3. 119:63. Pr 27:10. He 10:25. 1 P 2:17.

12 Lot dwelled. Ge 19:29. Jn 17:15, 16. Ep +5:11, 12.
cities of. Ge +11:4. 14:2. 19:24, 25, 29.
pitched. Ge 14:12. 19:1. Ps 26:5. Is +66:4. 1 C 15:33. 2 P 2:7, 8.

13 the men. Ge 15:16. 18:20. 19:4, 5. 1 S 15:18. Is 1:9. 3:9. Ezk 16:46-50. Mt 9:10, 13. 11:23, 24. Jn 9:24, 31. Ro 1:27. 2 P 2:6-8, 10. Ju 7.
wicked. Ex 23:2 (evil). 2 Ch 7:14. Jb 2:10 (evil). 21:30. Ps 5:4 (evil). Pr 11:21. 15:26.
and. Figure of speech Hendiadys, "very wicked sinners," Ge +1:26.
sinners. Ge 39:9. Nu +32:23. Ps 1:1.
before. Ge 6:11. 10:9. 38:7. 2 K 21:6. Is 3:8. Je 23:24. He 4:13.

14 was. ver. 11.
Lift. ver. 10. Is 49:18. 60:4.
look. Ge 15:15. 18:2. 22:13. Dt 34:1-4.
northward. Ge 28:14. Dt 3:27.

15 For all. Je 30:3. Ezk 28:25. Ro 11:29.
land. Dt 11:12. Je 23:7, 8. Da 7:14. Mt 8:11.
to thee. ver. 17. Ge 12:7. 15:3, 7, 8, 18. 17:7, 8. 18:18. 24:7. 26:3, 4. 28:4, 13. 35:12. 48:4. 50:24. Ex 3:6. 6:8. 32:13. 33:1. Nu 32:11. 34:2, 12. Dt 1:8, 35. 4:31. 6:10, 18, 23. 7:13. 8:1. 9:5. 26:2-4. 30:20. 34:4. Jsh 1:6. 21:43. 2 Ch 20:7. Ne 9:7, 8, 15, 23. Ps 37:22, 29. 105:9-12, 42, 44. 112:1, 2. Is 63:18. Je 32:22. Mt +5:5. 8:11. 22:23-32. Lk 13:28. Ac 1:6. +7:5. Ro 4:13. +15:8. He +11:13, 39.
thy seed. Ga *3:16*.
for ever. Heb. *olam*, Ex +12:24. Ge +8:22. +9:12, +16. 17:8. Is +11:11. Je 31:36. 33:26. Ezk 36:24. Am +9:14, 15. Lk 1:32, 33, 55. Ro +11:1.

16 I will. Ge +12:2. +22:17. Ro 4:16-18. Re 7:9.
as the dust. Ge 16:10. 28:14. Nu 23:10. 2 Ch 1:9.

17 walk. Nu 13:17-24. Jsh 18:4. Ezk 43:7. Ep 1:18. 3:18. Col +1:10. 1 Th 4:1.
give. ver. +15.

18 plain. Heb. plains. Ge +12:6. Dt 11:30. Jsh 24:26. Jg 9:37. 1 S 10:3.
Mamre. i.e. *bitter; causing fatness*, **S#4471h**. Ge 14:13, 24. 18:1. 23:17, 19. 25:9. 35:27. 49:30. 50:13.
Hebron. Ge 23:2. 35:27. 37:14. Ex +6:18. Nu +13:22.
altar. ver. 4. Ge +8:20. Jsh 8:30. Jg 21:4. 1 S 7:17. 14:35. 2 S 24:25. 1 K 18:32. Ps 16:8. 1 T 2:8.

GENESIS 14

1 A.M. 2091. B.C. 1913.
came to pass. Ru 1:1. 2 S 21:1. Is 7:1. Je 1:3.
Amraphel. i.e. *speaker of hidden things; terrific giant*, **S#569h**. ver. 9.
Shinar. Ge +10:10. Is 39:6.
Arioch. i.e. *lion-like*, **S#746h**. ver. 9. Da 2:14, 15, 15, 24, 25.
Ellasar. i.e. *God is chastener*, **S#495h**. ver. 9. Is 37:12.
Chedorlaomer. i.e. *handful of sheaves*, **S#3540h**. ver. 4, 5, 9, 17.
Elam. Ge +10:22.
Tidal. i.e. *fear, reverence; breaking the yoke*, **S#8413h**. ver. 9.

2 Bera. i.e. *son of evil; excelling in science*, **S#1298h**.
Sodom. Ge +10:19. 13:10. 19:24. Is 1:9, 10.
Birsha. i.e. *son of wickedness*, **S#1306h**.
Shinab. i.e. *tooth of father; change of father*, **S#8134h**.
Admah. Dt 29:23. Ho 11:8.
Shemeber. i.e. *name of wing; flying wing; illustrious*, **S#8038h**.
Zeboiim. Dt 29:23. 1 S 13:18. Ne 11:34.
Bela. i.e. *consumption; swallowing up; destroying*, **S#1106h**. ver. 8. Also Ge 36:32, 33. 46:21. Nu 26:38, 40. 1 Ch 1:43, 44. 5:8. 7:6, 7. 8:1, 3.
Zoar. Ge +13:10.

3 joined. ver. 13. Jg 20:11.
vale. **S#6010h**. ver. 8, 10. 37:14. Rendered *valley*, ver. 17. Nu 14:25. Jsh 7:24, 26. SS 2:1.
Siddim. i.e. *furrows; open fields*, **S#7708h**. ver. 8, 10.
salt sea. Ge 19:24, 25. Nu 34:3, 12. Dt 3:17. Jsh 3:16. 12:3. 15:2, 5. 18:19. Ps 107:34mg.

4 Twelve. Ge 17:20. 35:22. 1 K 4:7. 10:20. Mt 26:53. Lk 2:42. 6:13. Re 21:21. 22:2.
they served. Ge 9:25, 26.
thirteenth. Ge 16:12 with 17:25. 1 K 7:1 with 11:6. Est 3:12, 13. Is 7:8.
they rebelled. Ezk 17:15.

5 Rephaims. i.e. *the dead; giants*, **S#7497h**. Dt +2:20.
Ashteroth. Dt 1:4. Jsh 9:10. 12:4. 13:12, 31.
Karnaim. i.e. *two horned Astartes*, **S#6255h**.
Zuzims. i.e. *commotions, arousings*, **S#2104h**. Dt

2:20-23. 1 Ch 4:40. Ps 78:51. 105:23, 27. 106:22.

Emims. i.e. *terrors, horrors*, **S#368h**. Dt 2:10, 11.
Shaveh Kiriathaim. *or*, the plains of Kiriathaim. i.e. *plain of the double city*, **S#7741h**. Nu 32:37. Jsh 13:19. Je 48:1, 23.

6 Horites. i.e. *cave dwellers*, **S#2752h**. Ge 36:8, 20-30. Dt 2:12, 22. 1 Ch 1:38-42.
Seir. A region south of the Dead Sea, **S#8165h**. Ge 32:3. 33:14, 16. 36:8, 9, 20, 21, 30. Nu 24:18. Dt 1:2, 44. 2:1, 4, 5, 8, 12, 22, 29. 33:2. Jsh 11:17. 12:7. 15:10. 24:4. Jg 5:4. 1 Ch 4:42. 2 Ch 20:10, 22, 23. 25:11, 14. Is 21:11. Ezk 25:8. 35:2, 3, 7, 15.
El-paran. *or*, the plain of Paran. i.e. *the power of their adorning*, **S#364h**. Ge 16:7. 21:21. Nu 10:12. 12:16. 13:3, 26. Dt 1:1. 33:2. 1 S 25:1. 1 K 11:18. Hab 3:3.

7 Enmishpat. i.e. *fount of judgment*, **S#5880h**.
Kadesh. i.e. *Sodomite; devoted to Venus; set apart; sacred*, **S#6946h**. Ge 16:14. 20:1. Nu 13:26. 20:1, 14, 16, 22. 27:14. 33:36, 37. Dt 1:19, 46. 32:51. Jg 11:16, 17. Ps 29:8. Ezk 47:19. 48:28.
country. Heb. field. A part of a thing is put for the whole of the thing. Here, "all the country" is Heb. "the whole field." See 1 S 27:7. Other examples of a part put for the whole include "gate" put for city, Ge 22:17. Ex 20:10. Dt 12:12. 14:27. 16:5. Ps 87:2. Je 15:7. "Gate" put for inhabitants or for the people who assemble at the city's gates, Ru 3:11. 4:10. Pr 31:23. "Stones" put for restored buildings, Ps 102:14. "Wall" put for whole city encompassed by it, Am 1:7, 10, 14. "Corner" put for "tower" which was usually placed at the corner, Zp 1:16. 3:6. "Gate" is put for place of business, 1 K 22:10. 2 K 7:1. Ezk 11:1; place of judgment or court, Dt +16:18. 17:8. 21:19. 22:15. 25:7. 2 S 15:2. Jb 31:21. Is 29:21. Am 5:15. Zc 8:16; place of audience with the king, 2 S 19:8. Est 2:19, 21. 3:2. Jb 29:7. La 5:14; place of legal transactions, Ge 23:10, 18; place of public assembly, 2 Ch 32:6. Ne 8:1, 3. Pr 1:21; place for public discourse, Je 17:19, 20. 26:10. 36:10. Am 5:10; place of honor, Ps 69:12. 127:5; symbol of power, Mt 16:18; symbol of entrance to life, death, or destruction, Jb 38:17. Ps 9:13. 107:18. Is 38:10. Mt 7:13, 14.
Amalekites. Ge 36:12, 16. Nu +14:45. 24:20.
Amorites. ver. 13. Ge +10:16.
Hazezontamar. i.e. *cutting off of the palm tree*, **S#2688h**. 2 Ch 20:2. Called by the Chaldee, *Engaddi*, a town on the western shore of the Dead Sea. Jsh 15:62. 2 Ch 20:2.

8 Zeboiim. i.e. *gazelles*, **S#6636h**. Ge +10:19.
same. ver. 2. Ge +13:10. 19:20, 22.
joined. ver. +3.
vale. ver. +3, 10.

9 four kings with. ver. 1.
10 slime. **S#2564h**. Ge +11:3. Ex 2:3.
pits. Heb. *beer*, Ge +16:14.
fell. Jsh 8:24. Ps 83:10. Is 24:18. Je 48:44.
the mountain. Ge 19:17, 30.
11 all the goods. ver. 16, 21. Ge 12:5. Dt 28:31, 35, 51.
12 took. 2 Ch 18:31. 1 T 5:22.
Lot. Ge 11:27. 12:5.
who dwelt. Ge 13:12, 13. 19:1. Nu 16:26. Jb 9:23. Je 2:17-19. 1 T +6:9-11. Ja 4:4. 2 P 2:6-9. 1 J 2:15-17. Re 3:19. 18:4.
13 one. 1 S 4:12. Jb 1:15.
the Hebrew. i.e. *descendant of Eber*, **S#5680h**. Ge 39:14, 17. 40:15. 41:12. 43:32. Ex 1:15, 16, 19. 2:6, 7, 11, 13. 3:18. 5:3. 7:16. 9:1, 13. 10:3. 21:2. Dt 15:12. 1 S 4:6, 9. 13:3, 7, 19. 14:11, 21. 29:3. Je 34:9, 14. Jon 1:9. Ac 6:1. 2 C 11:22. Ph 3:5. So called from "Eber," Ge 10:21, +24. 11:14.
dwelt. Ge 13:18.
Mamre. ver. 24. Ge +13:18.
Amorite. ver. 7. Ge +10:16.
Eschol. Nu 13:23. 32:9. Dt 1:24.
Aner. i.e. *cast out, an exile; sprout; a lamp swept away*, **S#6063h**. ver. 24. Jsh 21:25, Tanach. Jg 1:27, Taanach. 1 Ch 6:70.
and these. ver. 24. Ge 21:27, 32.
14 his brother. Ge 11:27-31. 13:8. Pr 17:17. 24:11, 12. Ga 6:1, 2. 1 P 3:9. 1 J 3:18.
armed. *or*, led forth. Ps 45:3-5. 68:12. Is 41:2, 3.
trained. *or*, instructed. Ge 12:5. 15:2. 18:19. 24:12-29. Pr 20:18. +22:6. 24:6. Lk 14:31.
born. Ge 12:5, 16. 15:3. 17:12, 27. +18:19. 23:6. Ec 2:7.
Dan. Nu +1:12. Dt 34:1. Jsh 19:40-47. Jg 18:29. +20:1. 1 K 12:29, 30. 15:20. 2 K 10:29. 2 Ch 16:4. Je 4:15. 8:16. Ezk 48:1, 2, 32. Am 8:14.
15 And he. Ps 112:5.
divided. Ge 32:7. Jg 7:16. 9:34, 43. 1 S 11:11.
smote. Is 41:2, 3.
Hobah. i.e. *hiding place, lurking place*, **S#2327h**.
Damascus. i.e. *silent is the sackcloth weaver; city of Ham*, **S#1834h**. Ge 15:2. 2 S 8:5, 6. 1 K 11:24. 15:18. 19:15. 20:34. 2 K 5:12. 8:7, 9. 14:28. 16:9-12. 1 Ch 18:5. 2 Ch 16:2. 24:23. 28:5, 23. SS 7:4. Is 7:8. 8:4. 17:1, 3. Je 49:23, 24, 27. Ezk 27:18. Am 1:3, 5. 3:12. 5:27. Zc 9:1. Ac 9:2.
16 And. Ge +8:22.
brought back. ver. 11, 12. Ge 12:2. 19:16. 1 S 30:8, 18, 19. Is 41:2, 3. Ga 6:1.
people. Ex 15:13.
17 to. Jg 11:34. 1 S 18:6. Pr 14:20. 19:4.
after. He 7:1.
Shaveh. i.e. *equalize*, **S#7740h**. Compare ver. 5.
king's. 2 S 18:18.

18 Melchizedek. i.e. *king of righteousness*, **S#4442h**. Ps 110:4. He 5:6. 6:20.
king. Ps 76:2. He *7:1, 2*.
Salem. i.e. *peace; complete, perfect*, **S#8004h**. Ge 33:18. Ps 76:2.
bread. Jg 19:19. Ps 104:15. Mt 26:26-29. Ga 6:10.
the priest. Ps 110:4. He 5:6, 10. 6:20. 7:1, 3, 10-22.
the most high. Ru 3:10. 2 S 2:5. Ps +7:17. Mi 6:6.

19 he blessed. Ge 27:4, 25-29. 47:7, 10. 48:9-16. 49:28. Nu 6:23-27. Mk 10:16. Ga 3:14. He 7:6, 7.
Blessed be. Ru 3:10. 2 S 2:5. Ep 1:3, 6.
most high. Nu 24:16. Ps +7:17. Mi 6:6.
possessor. ver. 22. Ps 24:1. 50:10. 115:15, 16. Mt 11:25. Lk 10:21. Re 10:6.

20 blessed. Ge 9:26. 24:27. 1 Ch 29:10-12. Ps 68:19. 72:17-19. 144:1. Ep 1:3. 1 P 1:3, 4.
which. Jsh 10:42. Ps 44:3.
tithes. Ge 28:22. Le 27:17, 18, 30-33. Nu 18:21, 24. 28:26. Dt 12:17. 14:23, 28, 29. 26:12-14. 2 Ch 31:5, 6, 12. Ne 10:37. 13:10, 12, 13. Am 4:4. Ml 3:8, 10. Mt 5:19. 23:23. Mk 7:11, 13. Lk 11:42. 18:12. Ac +20:35. Ro 12:8. 1 C 9:14. 16:2. 2 C 9:6-12. Ga 6:6, 7. 1 T 5:17, 18. He 7:4-9. 13:15, 16.

21 persons. Heb. *nephesh*, souls, Ge +12:5. 46:15. Je 39:18.

22 lift. Ge +21:23. Ex 6:8mg. Nu 14:30mg. Dt 32:40. Ps 106:26. Is 3:7mg. Ezk 20:5, 6, 15, 23, 28, 42. 36:7. 47:14. Da 12:7. Re 10:5, 6.
unto. Ge 21:23-31. Jg 11:35.
the most high God. Heb. *El Elyon*. ver 20. Ge 17:1. Ps 83:18. Is +57:15. Da 4:34. Hg 2:8.
possessor. ver. 19. Ge 21:23. Ps 24:1.

23 That I. Ge 21:23. 26:29. 42:15. Ps 95:11. He 4:5.
will not. Ge 23:13. 2 K 5:16, 20. 1 Ch 21:24. Da 5:17. Ac 20:33. 1 C 9:18, 19. 2 C 11:7, 9-11. 12:14. 3 J 7.
lest. 2 C 11:12. He 13:5.

24 Save. Pr 3:27. Mt 7:12. Ro 13:7, 8.
Aner. ver. 13.
let. 1 C 9:14, 15. 1 T 5:18.

GENESIS 15

1 A.M. 2093. B.C. 1911.
word. 1 S 15:10. Is 55:10, 11. Ezk 1:3.
in a vision. Ge 46:2. Nu 12:6. 24:4, 16. Ezk 1:1. 13:7. Da 10:1-16. Ac 10:10-17, 22. He 1:1.
Fear not. ver. 14-16. Ge 21:17. 26:24. 46:3. Ex 14:13. Ps +118:6. Is 35:4. Je 30:10. 46:27, 28. Da 10:12. Zp 3:13, 16. Zc 8:15. Mt 8:26. 28:5. Lk 1:13, 30. 2:10. 12:4, 5, 32. Jn 12:15. Ac 18:9. Re 1:17.
thy shield. Dt 33:29. 2 S 22:3, 31. Ps 5:12.

+84:11. 91:4. 119:114. Pr 30:5. Jn 8:56. Ep 6:16.
reward. Ps 58:11. La 3:24. Mt +5:12. He 11:9, 13, 16, 39. +13:5, 6. Re 21:3, 4.

2 what. Ge 12:1-3.
go. 2 Ch 21:20. Ps 39:13.
childless. Ge 3:15. +11:30. Le 20:20. 1 S 1:11. Ps +127:3. Pr 13:12. Is 56:5. Je 22:30. Ac +7:5.
the steward. Ge 24:2, 10. 39:4-6, 9. 43:19. 44:1. Pr 17:2.
Eliezer. i.e. *God of help*, **S#461h**. Ex 18:4. 1 Ch 7:8. 15:24. 23:15, 17. 26:25. 27:16. 2 Ch 20:37. Ezr 8:16. 10:18, 23, 31.

3 Behold. Ge 12:2. 13:16. Pr 13:12. Je 12:1. He 10:35, 36.
born. Ge 14:14. Pr 29:21. 30:23. Ec 2:7.
heir. Heb. inherits me.

4 shall come. Ge 17:16. 21:12. 2 S 7:12. 16:11. 2 Ch 32:21. Ga 4:28. Phm 12.

5 Look. Ge +13:14.
tell the stars. Ge 22:17. 26:4. Ex 32:13. Dt 1:10. 10:22. 28:62. 1 Ch 27:23. Ne 9:23. Ps 147:4. Je 33:22. Na 3:16. Ro 9:7, 8. He 11:12.
So. Ge +12:2. 16:10. Ex 32:13. Dt 10:22. 1 Ch 27:23. Ro *4:18*.

6 believed. Ro *4:3, 6, 22*; Ga *3:6*; Ja *2:23*. Ge 28:20. Ro 4:3-6, 9, 20-25. 10:17. Ga 3:6-14. He 11:8.
he counted. Ps 106:31. Ro 4:9, 11, 22. 2 C 5:19. Ga *3:6*.
righteousness. Ge 6:9 (just). 7:1. Is 64:6. Ro 10:3, 4.

7 brought. Ge 11:28-31. 12:1. Ne 9:7. Ac 7:2-4.
to give. Ge +13:15.

8 whereby. Ge 24:2-4, 13, 14. Jg 6:17-24, 36-40. 1 S 14:9, 10. 2 K 20:8. Ps 86:17. Is 7:11. Lk 1:18, 34.
know. Ml 3:10. 1 J 5:13.

9 Take. Je 34:18, 19. He 6:17, 18.
heifer. Ge 22:13. Le 1:3, 10, 14. 3:1, 6. 9:2, 4. 12:8. 14:22, 30. Ps 50:5. Lk 2:24.
three. Is 15:5.

10 divided them. ver. 17. Je +34:18, 19. 2 T 2:15.
the birds. Le 1:17.

11 fowls. Ezk 17:3, 7. Mt 13:4.
Abram. Ps 119:13.
drove. 2 S 21:10.

12 sun. Ge 19:1. 28:11.
deep. Ge 2:21. 28:11. 1 S 26:12. Jb 4:13, 14. 33:15. Da 10:8, 9. Ac 20:9. 2 C 1:9.
horror. Ps 4:3-5. Ac 9:8, 9.
darkness. Ex +10:22.

13 Know. Ge +2:16; +26:28. 2 P 1:19.
thy. Ge 17:8. 21:12. Ex ch. 1, 2, 5. 22:21. 23:9. Le 19:34. Dt 10:19. Ps 105:11, 12, 23-25. Ac 7:6, 7. He 11:8-13.
land. Ge 46:3. Ac 7:17.

shall serve. Dt 5:15. Ps 105:25.

four hundred. Ex 12:40, 41. Ga 3:17. The four hundred years date from Isaac's birth (Ac 7:6). The 430 from the "promise" or Covenant here made (Ga 3:17), and include the whole "sojourning" (Ex 12:40), *Companion Bible*. Ge 17:7. 21:12. Ex 12:40.

14 **that**. Ge ch. 46. Ex 6:5, 6. ch. 7-14. Dt 4:20. 6:22. 7:18, 19. 11:2-4. Jsh 24:4-7, 17. 1 S 12:8. Ne 9:9-11. Ps 51:4. 78:43-51. 105:27-37. 135:9, 14.

judge. Ex 7:4. 12:12. Nu 33:4.

with great. Ex 3:21, 22. 12:35, 36, 38. Ps 105:37.

15 **And thou**. Ge +25:8. +35:18, 29. 47:30. Nu 20:24. 27:13. Jg 2:10. 2 S 12:23. 1 K 2:10. 11:43. Ec +12:7. Lk 20:37, 38. Ac 13:36.

go to. Ge 25:8. 2 K 22:20. Jb 10:21, 22. 16:22. 18:13, 14. Ec 3:21. 12:5. Is 38:10. Mt 8:11. 11:19. Jn 2:25. 11:11. Ac 2:39. Ph 1:23. 2 P 1:13, 14.

in peace. 2 Ch 34:28. Ps 37:37. Is 57:1, 2. Da 12:13. Mt 22:32. He 6:13-19. 11:13-16.

buried. Ge 23:4, 19. 25:8-10. 35:29. 49:29, 31. 50:13. Ec 6:3. Je 8:1, 2.

good. Ge 25:7, 8. 1 Ch 23:1. 29:28. Jb 5:26. 42:17.

16 **in the**. Ex 12:40, 41.

come hither. Jsh 14:1. Ac 7:7.

Amorites. Ge +10:16.

not yet full. Le 18:24-28. 1 K 21:26. 2 K 21:11. Da 8:23. Zc 5:5-11. Mt 23:32-35. Lk 6:35. 1 Th 2:16. 2 P 3:8, 9. Re 6:11. 14:17-19.

17 **dark**. Jb +38:9.

smoking. Ex 3:2, 3. Jg 6:21. 13:20. 1 Ch 21:26. He 12:29. Re +14:11.

furnace. Dt 4:20. 1 K 8:51. Is 31:9. 48:10. Ezk 22:18-22. Je 11:4.

a burning lamp. Heb. a lamp of fire. 2 S 21:17. 22:9, 29. 1 K 11:36. 15:4. Ps 27:1. 132:17. Is 62:1.

passed. Dt 29:12. Jsh 9:6mg. Je 34:18, 19.

18 **made**. Ge 9:8-17. ch. 17. 24:7. Is +55:3. Ga 3:15-17.

covenant. Ge 6:18. +9:16.

Unto thy. Ge +13:15. Ex 3:8. 6:4. 23:23, 27-31. 34:11. Dt 7:1. 11:24. Jsh 1:3, 4. ch. 12, 19. 1 K 4:21. 2 Ch 9:26.

this land. Ge +13:15.

river of Egypt. Is +27:12.

river Euphrates. Ge +2:14. Ps +72:8.

19 **Kenites**. Nu 24:21, 22. Jg 1:16. 4:11, 17. 5:24. 1 S 15:6. 27:10. 30:29. 1 Ch 2:55.

Kenizzites. i.e. *hunter*, **S#7074h**. Ge 36:11. Nu 32:12. Jsh 14:6, 14.

Kadmonites. i.e. *ancients, easterners*, **S#6935h**.

20 **Hittites**. Dt +20:17.

Perrizzites. Ge +13:7.

Rephaims. Ge +14:5. Is 17:5.

21 **Amorites**. Ge +10:16.

Canaanites. Ge +10:18.

Girgashites. i.e. *dwellers on clay soil; a stranger drawing near*, **S#1622h**. Ge +10:16. Mt 8:28.

Jebusites. Ge +10:16.

GENESIS 16

1 A.M. 2092. B.C. 1912.

bare. Ge +11:30. 21:10, 12.

handmaid. 1 S 25:41.

Egyptian. Ge 12:16. 21:9, 21.

name. Ga 4:24, Agar.

Hagar. i.e. *the sojourner, stranger; southern, flight*, **S#1904h**. Ge 16:1, 3, 4, 8, 15, 16. 21:9, 14, 17. 25:12.

2 **the Lord**. Ge 17:16. 18:10. 20:18. 25:21. 30:2, 3, 9, 22. Ru +1:13. 1 S 1:5. Ps +127:3.

go in. Ge 21:10. 27:8.

obtain children. Heb. be builded. Ge 30:3, 6. Ex 21:4. Ru 4:11.

hearkened. Ge 3:1-6, 12, 17. Ep 5:21. 1 P 3:6.

3 A.M. 2093. B.C. 1911.

after. Ga 3:3.

had. Ge 12:4, 5.

gave. ver. 5. Ge 30:4, 9.

his wife. Ge +4:19. 35:22. Jg 19:1-4. Ga 4:25.

4 **her mistress**. 1 S 1:6-8. 2 S 6:16. Pr 30:20, 21, 23. 1 C 4:6. 13:4, 5.

despised. ver. 5.

5 **My wrong**. Lk 10:40, 41.

despised. ver. 4. Ge +21:9.

the Lord. Ge 31:53. Ex 5:21. 1 S 24:12-15. 2 Ch 24:22. Ps 7:8. 35:23. 43:1.

6 **Abram**. Ge 13:8, 9. Pr 14:29. 15:1, 17, 18. 1 P 3:7.

Sarai. i.e. *my princesses; contentious*, **S#8297h**. Ge 11:29, 30, 31. 12:5, 11, 17. 16:1, 2, 3, 5, 6, 8. 17:15.

in. Ge 24:10. Jb 2:6. Ps 106:41, 42. Je 38:5.

as it pleaseth thee. Heb. that which is good in thine eyes. Jsh +22:30mg.

dealt hardly with her. Heb. afflicted her. Pr 29:19.

fled. Ex 2:15. Pr 15:12. 27:8. Ec 10:4. 1 C 7:10-16. 1 P 2:20.

7 **angel of**. ver. 10. Zc +12:8.

found. Ge 2:17-19. Pr 15:3.

the fountain. Ge 25:18. Ex 15:22. 1 S 15:7.

Shur. i.e. *a wall, rampart, fort*, **S#7793h**. Ge 20:1. 25:18. Ex 15:22. 1 S 15:7. 27:8.

8 **Sarai's maid**. ver. 1, 4. Ep 6:5-8. 1 T 6:1, 2.

whence. Ge 3:9. 4:10. Ec 10:4. Je 2:17, 18.

I flee. 1 S 26:19.

face. Ge +11:8.

9 **Return**. Ps 74:21. Pr 24:10. Je 12:5. Mt 25:21. Mk 5:19. Lk 16:10. 1 C 7:13. T +2:4. Phm 12.

submit. Ec 10:4. Mt 20:27. Ro 12:10. 1 C 11:3. +14:34. Ep 5:21, 22. 6:5, 6. Ph +2:3. Col

2:11. +3:18. T 2:9. Phm 21. He 13:17. 1 P 2:18-25. 5:5, 6.

10 the angel. Ge 22:15-18. 31:11-13. 32:24-30. 48:15, 16. Ex 3:2-6. Jg 2:1-3. 6:11, 16, 21-24. 13:16-22. Is 63:9. Ho 12:3-5. Zc 2:8, 9. Ml 3:1. Jn 1:18. Ac 7:30-38. 1 T 6:16.
I will. Ge 17:20. 21:13, 16. 25:12-18. 1 Ch 1:29. Ps 83:6, 7. Ep 6:8.

11 shalt. Ge 17:19. 29:32-35. Is 7:14. Mt 1:21-23. Lk 1:13, 31, 63.
Ishmael. i.e. *God shall hear*.
because. Ge 41:51, 52. 1 S 1:20.
hath. Ge 29:32, 33. Ex 2:23, 24. 3:7. Jb 38:41. Ps 22:24.
heard. Ge 21:17. Ex 2:24. 3:7. 22:23, 27. Ps +5:1. 65:2. +66:18. 130:2. Is 65:24. 1 J +5:14.

12 be a. Ge 21:20. Jb 11:12. 39:5-8.
wild. **S#6501**. Jb 6:5. 11:12. 24:5. 39:5. Ps 104:11. Is 32:14. Je 2:24. 14:6. Ho 8:9.
his hand. Ge 27:40.
against every. Ge 21:20. Ezr 8:31. Ps 10:8, 9. Is 21:13. Je 3:2.
he shall. Ge 25:18.
brethren. Ge 37:28. Jg 8:22, 24.

13 called. ver. 7, 9, 10. Ge 22:14. 28:17, 19. 32:30. Jg 6:24.
Lord that. Ge +12:7. 17:1. 18:1.
Thou God. Ex 34:5-7. Ps 139:1-12. Pr 15:3.
seest. 2 Ch 16:9. Jb 31:4. Ps 139:7. Pr 5:21. Je 16:17. Zc 4:10. He 4:13.
looked. Ge +32:30. 1 T 6:16. 1 J 4:12.
him that. Ge 31:42.

14 well. Heb. *be-er*, a dug well, **S#875h**. Ge 14:10. 16:14. 21:19, 25, 30. 24:11, 20. 26:15, 18-22, 25, 32. 29:2, 3, 8, 10. Ex 2:15. Nu 20:17. 21:16-18, 22. 2 S 17:18, 19, 21. Pr 5:15. SS 4:15.
Beer-lahai-roi. *That is*, The well of him that liveth and seeth me. **S#883h**. Ge 21:31. 24:62. 25:11.
Kadesh. Ge +14:7.
Bered. i.e. *hail; seed place*.

15 A.M. 2094. B.C. 1910.
Hagar. ver. 11. Ge 25:12. 1 Ch 1:28. Ga 4:22, 23.
Ishmael. Ge 17:18, 20, 25, 26. 21:9-21. 25:9, 12. 28:9. 37:27, 28. 39:1.

16 years old. Ge 12:4. 17:1, 17, 24. 21:5.
Hagar. ver. 1. Ge 21:14. 25:12.
Ishmael. Ge 17:18, 20. 21:10, 20. 25:12.

GENESIS 17

1 A.M. 2107. B.C. 1897.
was. Ge 16:16.
the Lord. Ge 12:1.
appeared. Ge +12:7. 16:13. 19:24. +35:9. 1 K 3:5. Jn 1:18.
I am. Ge +18:14. Jn 1:3. 8:56. Ac 7:38. He 7:25. Re +1:8. 15:3. 16:7.

Almighty God. Heb. *El Shaddai*. **S#7706h**. Ge +49:25. Ex +6:3. Jb +5:17. Ezk 10:5. 2 C 6:18. Re 19:15.
walk. Ge +5:22. 1 K 8:23, 25. Ps 15:2. Is 38:3. Mi +6:8. Ac 23:1. 24:16. Col +1:10. He 12:28. 1 J 2:6.
perfect. *or*, upright, *or* sincere. 2 S 22:33. Ps 18:23. Mt +5:48. Ep 1:4. 3:20. 5:27. Ph 2:15. 3:6, 12. Col 3:22. 1 Th 2:10. 3:13. 5:23. He 8:7. 9:14. 12:14. Ja 3:2, 8. 1 P 1:19. 2 P 3:14. Ju 24. Re 14:5.

2 And I. ver. 4-6. Ge 9:9. 15:18. Ps 105:8-11. Ga 3:17, 18.
multiply. Ge 12:2. 13:16. 22:17. Dt 1:10. He 11:12.
exceedingly. Ge +7:19.

3 fell. ver. 17. Ge +18:2. Ex 3:6. 18:7. Le 9:23, 24. Nu 14:5. 16:4, 22, 45. 20:6. 22:31. 24:4. Dt 9:18, 25. Jsh 5:14. 7:6, +10mg. Jg 13:20. 1 K 18:39. 1 Ch 21:16. Jb 1:20. Ezk +1:28. Da 8:17, 18. 10:9, 15, 16. Mt 2:11. +14:33. 17:6. 26:39. Mk 3:11. 5:22, 33. 7:25. 14:35. Lk 5:8, 12. 8:28, 41. 17:16. Jn 11:32. Ac 9:4. 10:10, 25. 22:7. 26:14. 1 C 14:25. Re 1:17. 4:10. 5:8, +12, 14. 7:11. 11:16. 19:4, 10. 22:8.
talked. Ex +33:9.

4 a father. Ge 12:2. 13:16. 16:10. 22:17. 25:1-18. 32:12. 35:11. ch. 36. Nu ch. 1, 26. Ro 4:11-18. Ga 3:28, 29.
many nations. Heb. multitude of nations. Ge 48:19.

5 but thy name. ver. 15. Ge 25:26. 27:36. 32:28. Nu 13:16. Ru 1:20. 2 S 12:25. Ne 9:7. Is 62:2-4. 65:15. Je 20:3. 23:6. 33:16. Ezk 48:35. Mt 1:21-23. 16:18. Jn 1:42. Re 2:17.
Abraham. i.e. *father of a great multitude*, **S#85h**. ver. 9. 15-18, 22-26. Ge 18:6-13, 16-23, 27, 33. 19:27, 29. 20:1, 2, 9-11, 14-18. 21:2-14, 22-29, 34. 22:1-15, 19-23. 23:2-7, 10-20. 24:1-9, 12, 15, 27, 34, 42, 48, 52, 59. 25:1, 5-12, 19. 26:1-5, 15, 18, 24. 28:4, 9, 13. 31:42, 53. 32:9. 35:12, 27. 48:15, 16. 49:30, 31, 50:13, 24. Ex 2:24. 3:6, 15, 16. 4:5. 6:3, 8. 32:13. 33:1. Le 26:42. Nu 32:11. Dt 1:8. 6:10. 9:5, 27. 29:13. 30:20. 34:4. Jsh 24:2, 3. 1 K 18:36. 2 K 13:23. 1 Ch 1:27, 28, 32, 34. 16:16. 29:18. 2 Ch 20:7. 30:6. Ne 9:7. Ps 47:9. 105:6, 9, 42. Is 29:22. 41:8. 51:2. 63:16. Je 33:26. Ezk 33:24. Mi 7:20.
for. Ro 4:17.

6 exceedingly. ver. 2.
nations. ver. 4, 20. Ge 35:11.
kings. ver. 16, 19. Ge 35:11. 36:31. Ex +19:6. Ezr 4:20. Mt 1:6-11. Ro +4:13. Re 1:5, 6. 5:9, +10. 20:6.

7 And I. Ge 15:18. 26:24. Ex 6:4. Mi +7:20. Ro 9:4, 8, 9. Ga 3:17. Ep 2:2.
thy seed. Here, the collective noun *zer'a* is shown to be plural by the words "after thee" (compare verses 8, 9), and by the plural pro-

noun "their generations" (verses 7, 9). This is not the verse referred to in Galatians 3:16, but Ge 21:12.

generations. Ge +9:12.

everlasting. ver. 13, 19. Ge +9:16. Jg 2:1. Ps 111:5. Is 44:7mg. 1 P 1:20. Heb. *olam*, **S#5769h**: Ge 9:16. 17:7, 8, 13, 19. 21:33. 48:4. 49:26. Ex 40:15. 2 S 23:5. Ps 24:7, 9. 93:2. 139:24. Pr 8:23. Is 33:14. 35:10. 40:28. 55:3. 56:5. 60:19, 20. Je 32:40. Ezk 37:26. Da 4:3, 34. 7:14, 27. 12:2. Mi 5:2. For passages where *olam* is rendered *for ever*, see Ex +12:24.

to be a God. ver. 8. Ge 24:12. 26:24. 28:13. 31:5, 42, 53. 32:9. 46:3. Ex 3:6, 15, 16. 20:2. 29:45. Le 11:45. 26:12, 45. 1 K 18:36. 2 K 2:14. 1 Ch 29:18. 2 Ch 20:6, 7. Ps 47:9. 81:10. Is 41:10. Je 11:4. 24:7. 30:22. 31:1, 33. 32:38. Ezk 11:20. 14:11. 28:26. 34:24, 30, 31. 36:28. 37:23, 27. 39:22, 28. Zc 8:8. +13:9. Mt 22:32. Mk 12:26. Lk 20:37. Jn +20:17. Ac 7:32. 2 C 6:16. He 8:10. 11:16. Re 21:3, 7.

and to. Ex 19:5, 6. Dt +29:11. Lk 1:54, 55. Ac +2:39. Ro 9:7-9. 1 C 7:14.

8 **And I**. Ge +13:15. Ac +7:5.
thy seed. ver. +7.
the land. Is +60:21. 63:18.
wherein thou art a stranger. Heb. of thy sojournings. Ge 23:4. 28:4.
everlasting. Heb. *olam*, ver. +7. Ge +8:22. +13:15. 48:4. Ex 21:6. 31:16, 17. 40:15. Le 16:34. Nu 25:13. Dt 32:8. 2 S +23:5. Ps 103:17. He 9:15. 1 P 1:4. 2 P 1:11.
their God. ver. +7. Ex 6:7. Le 26:12. Dt 4:37. 14:2. 26:18. 29:13.

9 **keep**. Ge +4:7. Ps 25:10. 103:17, 18. Is 56:4, 5.

10 **Every**. ver. 11. Ge 34:15. Ex 4:25. 12:48. Dt 10:16. 30:6. Jsh 5:2, 4. Je 4:4. 9:25, 26. Ac 7:8. Ro 2:25, 28, 29. 3:1, 25, 28, 30. 4:9-11. 1 C 7:18, 19. Ga 3:28. 5:3-6. 6:12. Ep 2:11. Ph 3:3. Col 2:11, 12.

11 **circumcise**. Ro 2:28, 29. 1 C 7:19. Ga 5:6. Ph 3:3. Col 2:11.
the flesh. Ex 4:25. Jsh 5:3. 1 S 18:25-27. 2 S 3:14.
a token. Ezk +9:4. Ac 7:8. He 11:28.

12 **he that is eight days old**. Heb. a son of eight days. ver. 25. Ge 21:4. Le 12:3. Jon 4:10mg. Lk 1:59. 2:21. Jn 7:22, 23. Ac 7:8. Ro 2:28. Ph 3:5.
is born. ver. 23. Ex 12:48, 49.
stranger. ver. 27. Ge 35:2, 4. Ex +12:43 (**S#5236h**).

13 **born**. Ge 14:14. 15:3. Ex 12:44. 21:4.
bought. Ge 37:27, 36. 39:1. Ex 21:2, 16. Ne 5:5, 8. Mt 18:25.
everlasting. Heb. *olam*, ver. +7. Ge +9:16.

14 **is not**. Ex 4:24-26. Jsh 5:2.
soul. Heb. *nephesh*, used here as being "cut off" by God. Ge +12:5. Ex 12:15, 19. 31:14. Le

7:20, 21, 25, 27. 17:10. 18:29. 19:8. 20:6. 22:3. 23:29, 30. Nu 9:13. 15:30, 31. 19:13, 20. Ezk 18:4, 20. For the other uses of *nephesh* see Ge +2:7.
cut off. Ge 9:11. Ex 4:24-26. 31:14. Le 7:27. Ps 101:5. Is 53:8. Da 9:26.
broken. Ps 55:20. Is 24:5. 33:8. Je 11:10. 31:32. 1 C 11:27, 29.

15 **As**. ver. 5. Ge 32:28. 2 S 12:25.
Sarah. i.e. *princess*. **S#8283h**. Ge 17:15, 17, 19, 21. 18:6, 9-15. 20:2, 14, 16, 18. 21:1-3, 6, 7, 9, 12. 23:1, 2, 19. 24:36, 67. 25:10, 12. 49:31. Is 51:2.

16 **And I**. Ge 1:28. 12:2. 24:60. Ro 9:9.
give. Ge 18:10-14.
be a mother of nations. Heb. become nations. Ge 35:11. Ga 4:26-31. 1 P 3:6.
kings. ver. +6. Is 49:23.

17 **fell**. ver. +3.
laughed. Ge 18:12. 21:6. Ps 4:7. Jn 8:56. Ro 4:19, 20.

18 **O that**. Ge 21:11. Je 32:39. Ac 2:39.
might live. Dt 33:6.
before. Ge 4:12, 14. Ps 4:6. 41:12. Is 59:2.

19 **Sarah**. ver. 21. Ge 18:10-14. 21:2, 3, 6. 2 K 4:16, 17. Lk 1:13-20. Ro 9:6-9. Ga 4:28-31.
Isaac. Yitzchak, which we change into Isaac, signifies *laughter*; in allusion to Abraham's laughing, ver. 17. By this Abraham did not express his unbelief or weakness of faith, but his joy at the prospect of the fulfillment of so glorious a promise; and to this our Lord evidently alludes, Jn 8:56.
everlasting. Heb. *olam*, ver. +7. Ge +9:12, +16.
his seed. Ge 21:12. 26:2-5. Mt 1:2. Lk +3:23, 24. Ro 9:6-8. He 11:17-19.

20 **heard thee**. Ge +18:32. Ps +27:7. +99:6.
blessed him. Ge 16:10-12.
twelve. Ge 25:12-18.
and I. Ge 21:13, 18.

21 **my**. Ge 21:10-12. 26:2-5. 46:1. 48:15. Ex 2:24. 3:6. Lk 1:55, 72. Ro 9:5, 6, 9. Ga 3:29. He 11:9.
at. Ge 18:10. 21:2, 3. Jb 14:13. Ac +1:7. Ga 4:4.
set time. Ex 27:21. Le 23:2. Nu 28:2. 1 Ch 23:31. 2 Ch 31:3. Ezr 3:5. Jb 30:23. Ps 102:13. Da 8:19. 11:27, 29, 35. 12:7. Hab 2:3. Mt +24:45.

22 **talking**. ver. +3. Ge 35:9-15. Jg 6:21. 13:20. Jn +1:18. 10:30.
went. ver. +1.

23 **circumcised**. ver. 10-14, 26, 27. Ge +18:19. 34:24. Jsh 5:2-9. Ps 119:60. Pr 27:1. Ec 9:10. Ac 16:3. Ro 2:25-29. 4:9-12. 1 C 7:18, 19. Ga 5:6. 6:15.
selfsame. Dt +32:48.

24 **Abraham was**. ver. 1, 17. Ge 12:4. Ro 4:11, 19, 20.

25 **thirteen**. ver. 12. Ge +14:4.
26 **In the**. Ge 12:4. 22:3, 4. Ps 119:60.
 selfsame. ver. +23.
27 **stranger**. ver. +12.
 circumcised. Ge 18:19. Ex 12:44.

GENESIS 18

1 **appeared**. ver. 2, 13, 14, 17, 19, 22, 33. Ge
 15:1. 16:7. +17:1-3, 22. +35:9. Ex 3:2, 4. 4:1,
 5. Jg 13:21. 2 Ch 1:7. Pr 8:22-31. Ml 3:1, 2. Jn
 8:56. Ac 7:2.
 Mamre. Ge +13:18.
 heat. Ge 15:12. 19:1. 31:40. Mt 20:12. Lk
 12:55. Ja 1:11.
2 **And he**. Ge 22:4. Jg 13:3, 9. He 13:2.
 looked. Ge +13:14.
 three. ver. 22. Ge +1:26. 19:1. He 13:2. 1 P
 4:9.
 men. Ge 32:24. Jn 1:14.
 he ran. Ge 24:29. 29:13. Ro 12:13.
 bowed. Ge +17:3. 19:1. 23:7. +24:26. 33:3-7.
 42:6. 43:26, 28. 44:14. 50:18. Ex 18:7. Ru
 2:10. 1 S 24:8. 2 K 2:15.
3 **favor**. Ge 19:19. 32:5. 39:4. Ru 2:2, 10, 13.
 pass not. Ac +16:15.
 servant. Ge 33:5.
4 **wash your feet**. Ge 19:2. 24:32. 43:24. Jg
 19:21. 1 S 25:41. 2 S 11:8. SS 5:3. Lk 7:38, 44.
 Jn 13:5-15. 1 T 5:10.
 rest. Mk 6:31. Jn 6:10.
5 **And I**. Jg 6:18. 13:15. Mt 6:11.
 comfort. Heb. stay. Jg 19:5. Ps 104:15. Is 3:1.
 are ye come. Heb. ye have passed. Ge 19:8.
 33:10.
6 **hastened**. Ge 22:3.
 Make ready quickly. Heb. hasten.
 three. Nu 15:9. Is 32:8. Mt +13:33. Lk 10:38-
 40. Ac 16:15. Ro 12:13. Ga 5:13. He 13:2. 1 P
 4:9.
 measures. 1 S 25:18. 2 K 7:1, 16. Ps 80:5. Is
 40:12. Mt 13:33. Lk 13:21.
 cakes. Ge 19:3. Ex 12:39. Le 7:12. 24:5. Nu
 11:8. 1 K 17:13. Je 7:18. Ezk 4:12. Ho 7:8.
7 **ran**. Ge 19:3. 22:3. Jg 13:15, 16. Am 6:4. Ml
 1:14. Mt 22:4. Lk 15:23, 27, 30.
 calf. Le 3:1.
8 **he took**. Ge 19:3.
 butter. Dt 32:14. Jg 5:25. Pr 30:33. Is 7:15.
 stood. 1 K 10:8. Ne 12:44. Lk 12:37. 17:8. Jn
 12:2. Ro 12:13. Ga 5:13. Re 3:20.
 and they. Ge 19:3. Ex 24:11. Jg 13:15. Ps
 78:25. Lk 22:16, 18, 30. 24:30, 43. Ac 10:41.
9 **Where**. Ge 4:9.
 in. Ge 24:67. 31:33. T 2:5.
10 **he said**. ver. 13, 14. Ge 16:10. 22:15, 16.
 certainly. Ge +2:16. +26:28.
 according. Ge 17:21. 21:2. 2 K 4:16, 17.
 Sarah thy. Ge 17:16, 19, 21. 21:2. Jg 13:3-5.
 Mt 3:9. Lk 1:13. Ro 9:8, 9. Ga 4:23, 28.

heard. Ge 27:5, 6. 37:17, 21. 42:23. Jg 7:11.
Mt 10:27. Lk 12:2, 3. Jn 7:12, 13. Ac 23:16.
Ep 5:11, 12.
11 **old**. Ge 17:17, 24. Lk 1:7, 18, 36. Ro 4:18-21.
 He 11:11, 12, 19.
 ceased. Ge +11:30.
 the manner. Ge 31:35. Le 15:19. Ro 4:19.
 S#734h. Frequently translated path or way. Ge
 49:17. Jg 5:6. Jb 16:22. Ps 16:11. 25:4, 10.
 119:9, 15, 101, 104, 128. Pr 3:6. 12:28. 15:10,
 19, 24. Mi 4:2.
12 **laughed**. ver. 13. Ge 17:17. 21:6, 7. Ps 126:2.
 Lk 1:18-20, 34, 35. He 11:11, 12.
 old. Jb 13:28. Ps 32:3.
 pleasure. **S#5730h**. 2 S 1:24 (delights). Ps 36:8.
 Je 51:34 (delicates).
 my. Ep 5:33. 1 P 3:6.
13 **Wherefore**. Jn 2:25.
 old. Ge 17:17.
14 **Is**. 1 S 14:6. Jb +42:2. Mi 7:18. Mt 3:9. 14:31.
 Ep 3:20. Ph 4:13.
 I will. ver. 10. Ge 17:21. Dt 30:3. 2 K 4:16.
 Mi 7:18. Lk 1:13, 18. Ro 9:9.
15 **denied**. Ge 4:9. 12:13. 27:20. 31:35. Jb 2:10.
 Pr 28:13. Jn 18:17, 25-27. Col 3:9. 1 J 1:8.
 Nay. Ps 44:21. Pr 12:19. Mk 2:8. Jn +2:25. He
 4:13.
16 **looked**. Ge 13:10.
 to bring. 2 S 19:31. Ac 15:3. 20:38. 21:5. Ro
 15:24. 3 J 6.
17 **Shall**. 2 K 4:27. 2 Ch 20:7. Ps 25:14. Am
 +3:7. Jn 15:15. Ja 2:23.
18 **become**. Ge +12:2. Ga 3:8, 14.
 blessed. Ge +12:3. Ps 51:18, 19. 122:6.
19 **For I**. 2 S 7:20. Ps 1:6. 34:15. 40:17. Jn 10:14.
 21:17. 2 T 2:19.
 command. Ge 17:23-27. 26:5. 35:2. Ex
 +13:8. Dt 4:9, 10. 6:6, 7, +20. 11:19-21.
 32:46. Jsh 24:15. 1 S 3:13. 1 Ch +28:9. Est
 1:22n. Jb +1:5. 4:3, 4. Ps 78:2-8. 101:2. 119:9.
 Pr 6:20-22. +22:6. Is 38:19. Ml +4:6. Ep +6:4.
 1 T 3:4, 5, 12. 2 T 1:5. +3:15.
 justice and. Ps 15:2. Pr 2:9. 21:3. Ezk 18:5.
 Mi +6:8.
 that the. Ge +22:18. 1 S 2:30, 31. Ac 27:23,
 24, 31.
20 **the cry**. Ge 19:13. Ex +22:23. Is 3:9. Je 14:7.
 2 P 2:8.
 Sodom and. Dt 32:32. Is 1:10. Je 23:14. Ezk
 16:46. Mt 11:23, 24. Re 11:8.
 sin. Ge 13:13.
 grievous. Ge 13:13. Is 3:9. Ju 7.
21 **I will go down**. Ge 11:5, 7. Ex 3:8. 33:5. Mi
 1:3. Jn 6:38. 1 Th 4:16.
 see. Jb 34:22. Ps 14:2. 90:8. Je 17:1, 10. Zp
 1:12. He 4:13.
 cry. Ge 19:13. La 4:6. Ezk 16:49, 50.
 I will know. Ge 22:12. Ex 33:5. Dt 8:2. 13:3.
 Jsh 22:22. Ps 14:2. 53:2. 139. Lk 16:15. 2 C
 11:11.

22 the men. ver. 2. Ge 19:1.
stood. The two, whom we suppose to have been created angels, departed at this time; and accordingly two entered Sodom at evening: while the one, called Jehovah throughout the chapter, continued with Abraham, who "stood yet before the Lord."—Scott. ver. 1. Ge 19:27. Ex 32:31. Ps 106:23. Je 15:1. 18:20. Ezk 22:30. Ac 7:55. 1 T 2:1. Ja 5:16.
Lord. Ge +17:1. 31:11. 32:30. Jg 6:11.

23 drew. Ja +4:8.
Wilt. ver. 25. Ge 20:4. Ex 23:7. Nu 16:22. 2 S 24:17. Jb 8:3. 34:17. Ps 11:4-7. Je 12:1. 15:1. Mt 13:49. Ro 3:5, 6. Ja 5:17.
destroy. S#5595h. Ge 19:15. 1 S 26:10. 1 Ch 21:12, 13.
the righteous. Ge 20:3, 4. Nu 16:22. 2 S 24:17. S#6662h. Ge 6:9. 2 S 23:3. Jb 12:4. Ps 5:13. 145:17. Pr 29:7. Ec 7:16, 20.
with. Jb 9:22. Ezk 21:3. Mt 5:45.
wicked. S#7563h. Ex 23:7. Jb 3:17. Ps 1:6. 119:155. Pr 5:22. 10:28, 30. Is 53:9. 57:20, 21.

24 there. ver. 32. Is 1:9. Je 5:1. Ezk 14:14. 22:30. Mt 7:13, 14. 2 P 2:8.
spare. Ac 27:24.

25 be far. Je 12:1.
with the wicked. Ps 37:10. Pr 29:16.
righteous should. Jb 8:20. 9:22, 23. Ec 7:15. 8:12, 13. Is 3:10, 11. 57:1, 2. Ml 3:18.
as the wicked. Ex 23:7. Dt 1:16, 17.
Shall. Dt +32:4. Jb 8:3. 34:12, 17-19. Ps 145:9. Ezk +18:25. Zc +7:9. Lk +6:35.
Judge. Ps +7:8.
earth. Ps +94:2.
do right. Ps 9:4mg, 8. +33:5. +145:17. Is 11:4. 2 T +4:8.

26 If. ver. 24. Is 6:13. 10:22. 19:24. 65:8. Je 5:1. Ezk 22:30. Mt 24:22.

27 I have. ver. 30-32. Ezr 9:6. Jb 42:6-8. Is 6:5. Lk 18:1.
dust. Ge +2:7. 3:19. Jb 30:19. Ps 8:4. 113:7. 144:3. Is 6:5. Lk 5:8. 1 C 15:47, 48. 2 C 5:1, 2.

28 wilt. Nu 14:17-19. 1 K 20:32, 33. Jb 23:3, 4.
If I. ver. 26, 29. Ps 78:38. Is 65:8.

29 yet again. Ge 22:15. 1 S +23:4. Lk 18:1, 5, 7. Ep 6:18. He 4:16.

30 Oh. Ge 44:18. Jg 6:39. Es 4:11-16. Jb 40:4. Ps 9:12. 10:17. 89:7. Is 6:5. 55:8, 9. He 12:28, 29.
I will. Ex 34:6. Ezr 5:12. Ps 86:15.

31 Behold. ver. 27. Mt 7:7, 11. Lk 11:8. 18:1. Ep 6:18. He 4:16. 10:20-22.
speak. Jb 40:4. Ps 9:12.

32 Oh. ver. 30. Ge +17:20. 20:7, 17. 47:7. ch. 49. Ex 32:10-14, 31, 32. 34:9. Nu +12:13. 14:11-21. 16:20-22. Dt 1:11. 9:18-20. 33:6-17. Jg 6:39. Ru 1:8, 9. 1 S 12:23. 2 S 12:16. 2 Ch 30:18-20. Ezr 9:3-15. Ne 1:4-9. Jb 1:5. 42:7-10. Ps 106:23. Pr 15:8. Is 62:6, 7. Ezk 22:30. Am 7:1-3. Ja +5:14-17. 1 J +5:15, 16.

speak. Jg 6:39. Ps 86:6.
I will not. Ex 32:9, 10, 14. 33:13, 14. +34:6, 7, 9, 10. Nu 14:11-20. Jb 33:23. Ps 86:5. Is 1:9. 65:8. Ezk 14:16. Mi 7:18. Mt 7:7. Ac 27:24. Ep 3:20. He 7:25. Ja 5:16.

33 And the. ver. 16, 22. Ge 32:26.
communing. Ex +33:9.
and Abraham. Ge 31:55.

GENESIS 19

1 And there came two angels. Ge 18:1-3, 16, 22.
sat. Ps 1:1. Pr 1:14. Jn 18:18.
gate. Ge +14:7. Est 2:19. Pr 31:23.
rose. Ge 18:1-5. Jb 31:32. He 13:2.
bowed. Ge +18:2.

2 turn. Jb 31:32. Lk 24:29. He +13:2.
tarry. or, lodge. Ru 3:13.
wash. Ge +18:4.
rise. Jg 19:9. 1 S 29:10.
Nay. Jg 19:17-21. Je 14:8. Lk 19:5. 24:28, 29. Ac 16:15. Ep 5:11.
street. or, broad place. Jg 19:15.

3 pressed. Ac +16:15.
a feast. Ge 18:6-8. 21:8. 26:30. 29:22. 31:54. 40:20. Jg 14:10, 12. 19:22. 1 S 25:36. 2 S 3:20. 1 K 3:15. 2 K 6:23. Est 1:3, 7. Ec 10:19. Mt 22:2-4. Lk 5:29. Jn 2:9. 12:2. He 13:2. Re 19:9.
unleavened. Ge 18:6. Ex 12:15, 33, 34, 39. Jg 6:19. 1 S 28:24. 1 C 5:8, 11.

4 But. Pr 4:16. 6:18. Mi 7:3. Ro 3:15.
men of. Ge 13:13. 18:20. Ex 32:22. Jg 19:22. Ep 4:19.
all. Ge +7:19. Ex 16:2. 23:2. Je 5:1-6, 31. Mt 27:20-25. Mk 1:33.

5 Where. Le +18:22. Is 1:9. 3:9. Je 3:3. 6:15. Ezk +16:49, 51. Mt 11:23, 24. Ro 1:23, 24, 26, 27. 1 C +6:9. 2 T 3:13. Ju 7.
know. Ge +4:1. Ex +34:15. Mt 1:25.

6 Lot. Jg 19:23.
door. Ex 12:22, 23.
shut the door. ver. 9, 10. Ps 141:3.

7 I pray. Ge 37:21. 42:22. Ex 23:2. Jg 19:23. 1 S 30:23, 24. Pr 1:10. Ac 17:26.
do not. Ex 32:22. Dt 23:17. Ro 1:24. 1 C +6:9-11. Ju 7.

8 I have. Ex 23:32. 34:12, 16. Dt 7:3. Ezr 9:2, 12. 1 C 6:1316-20. 2 C 6:14-18.
known. Ge +4:1. Ge 24:16. Ex +34:15.
let. ver. 31-38. Ge 42:37. Jg 19:24. Mk 9:6. Ro 3:8.
therefore. Ge 18:5. Jg 9:15. Is 58:7.

9 Stand. 1 S 17:44. 25:17. Pr 9:7, 8. Is +65:5. Mt +7:6.
This. Ge 13:12. Ex 2:14. Ac 7:26-28. 2 P 2:7, 8.
pressed. Ge 11:6. 1 S 2:16. Ps 118:13. Pr 14:16. Da 3:19-22.

10 **men**. ver. 1.
    pulled. Dt 33:12. 1 S 2:9. Ps 4:8. 34:7. Is
    63:9. Mt 18:10. Lk 21:18.
11 **with blindness**. Ge 27:1. Dt 28:28, 29. Jg
    16:21. 1 K 14:4. 2 K 6:18-20. 25:7. Is 44:18.
    Mk 14:44. 16:12. Lk +4:30. 24:16, +31. Jn
    20:14. 21:4. Ac 13:11.
    small and. Je 8:10.
    wearied. Ec 10:15. Is 57:10. Je 2:36. Mt 15:14.
12 **Hast**. Ge 7:1. Nu 16:26. Jsh 2:18. 6:22, 23. 1
    S 15:6. Je 51:6. 2 P 2:7, 9.
    son. ver. 14, 17, 22. Re 18:4.
13 **cry**. Ge 13:13. 18:20. Ja +5:4.
    Lord hath. 1 Ch 21:15, 16. Ps 11:5, 6. Ezk
    9:5, 6. Mt 13:41, 42, 49, 50. Ro 3:8, 9. Ju 7.
    Re 16:1-12.
    destroy. Le 26:30-33. Dt 4:26. 28:45.
14 **which**. Mt 1:18.
    Up. ver. 17, 22. Nu 16:21, 26, 45. Je 51:6. Re
    18:4-8.
    as one. Ex 9:21. Pr 29:1. Je 5:12-14. 43:1, 2.
    Mt 9:24. Lk 17:28-30. 24:11. 1 Th 5:3. He
    +11:36. 2 P 3:3, 4.
15 **morning**. Ge 32:24, 26. Jsh 6:15. Jg 19:25.
    hastened. ver. 17, 22. Nu 16:24-27. Pr 6:4, 5.
    Lk 13:24, 25. 2 C +6:2. He 3:7, 8. Re 18:4.
    are here. Heb. are found. Est +1:5mg.
    lest. Lk 17:31.
    iniquity. *or*, punishment. Nu 9:13. Is 53:4.
    Ezk 18:20. Mt 8:17. He 9:28. 1 P 2:24.
16 **lingered**. Ge 22:3. 24:55. Ps 119:60. Jn 6:44.
    Ro +12:11.
    the men. He 1:14.
    laid. ver. 10. Dt 5:15. 6:21. 7:8.
    the Lord. Ex +34:6. Is 63:9. Jl 2:18. Mi 7:18,
    19. Lk +6:35, 36. 18:13. Ro 9:15, 16, 18. 2 C
    1:3. Ep 2:4, 5. T 3:5.
    brought. Jsh 6:22. Ps 34:22. Am 4:11. Zc 3:2.
    2 P 2:9.
17 **he said**. Ge 18:22.
    Escape. ver. 14, 15, 22. Nu 16:26. 1 S 19:11.
    Je 48:6. Mt 3:7. 24:16-18. He 2:3.
    life. Ge +44:30.
    look. ver. 26. Lk 9:62. 17:31, 32. Ph 3:13, 14.
    He 10:38, 39.
    lest. Re 18:14, 15.
18 **Oh**. Ge 32:26. 2 K 5:11, 12. Is 45:11. Mt
    16:22. Jn 13:6-8. Ac 9:13. 10:14.
19 **and thou**. Ps 18:40. 103. 106. 107. 116. 1 T
    1:14-16.
    saving. Ps 41:2. 143:11.
    life. Ge +44:30.
    and. Ge +8:22.
    lest some. Ge 4:14. 12:12, 13. Ex 14:11. 1 S
    27:1. Mt 8:25, 26. Ro 8:31. He +13:6.
20 **this**. ver. 30. Pr 3:5-7. Am 3:6.
    little. *1 S* 15:13-23. 2 K 3:18. Ga 5:9.
    let me. Ps 106:15. Is +66:4.
    and my. Ge 12:13. Ps 119:175. Is 55:3.
    soul. Heb. *nephesh*, Ge +12:13.

21 **See, I**. Ge 4:7. Jb 42:8, 9. Ps 34:15. 102:17.
    145:19. Je 14:10. Mt 12:20. He 4:15, 16.
    accepted. Mt 19:8. Ac 17:30.
    thee. Heb. thy face. Ge +3:19.
    that. Ge 12:2. 18:24.
22 **Haste**. 2 K 10:23. Ezk 9:6. Am 9:9. Re 7:3.
    for. Ge 32:25-28. Ex 32:10. Ps 91:1-10.
    Is 65:8. Mk 6:5. 1 Th 5:9. He 11:40.
    2 P 3:9.
    Zoar. ver. 20, 30. Ge +13:10.
23 **risen**. Heb. gone forth. 1 Th 5:3. 2 P 2:21,
    22.
24 **the Lord**. Dt 29:23. Jb 18:15. Ps 11:6. Is 1:9.
    13:19, 20. Je 20:16. 49:18. 50:40. La 4:6. Ezk
    16:49, 50. Ho 11:8. Am 4:11. Zp 2:9. Zc 2:8, 9.
    Mt 11:23, 24. Lk 17:28, 29. 2 P 2:6. Ju 7.
    Sodom and. Mt 10:15.
    brimstone. Re 21:8.
    and. Ge +1:26.
    Lord. Note the mention here of two
    Jehovahs, one in heaven who sends judg-
    ment upon Sodom and Gomorrah at the bid-
    ding of the Jehovah on earth. This gives
    significant evidence for more than one person
    in the Godhead. The Jehovah upon earth was
    one of the three persons to visit Abraham,
    one of whom stays behind to speak further to
    Abraham and is called Jehovah, Ge 18:13, 14,
    17, 19, 20, 22, 26, 33. Jn 3:13, 31. 6:38, 42.
    8:56, 58. 1 C 2:8. +12:3. Ja 2:1. See also on
    Ge +12:7. +16:13. +17:1. Da +3:28.
25 **overthrew**. Dt 29:23. Is 13:19. La 4:6. 2 P
    2:6.
    plain. Ge 13:10. 14:3. Ps 107:34.
26 **looked back**. ver. 17. Pr 14:14. Lk 9:62. He
    +10:38.
    and. Nu 16:33. Lk 17:31, *32*.
27 **early**. Ge +21:14. 22:3. 28:18. Jg 6:38. 9:33. 2
    S 23:4. 2 K 3:22. Jb 1:5. Ps +5:3. 63:1. Mk
    1:35.
    to the. Ge 18:22-33. Ezk 16:49, 50. Hab 2:1.
    He 2:1.
28 **looked**. Ps 91:8. Is +66:24. Re 3:10.
    smoke. Ge 13:10. Dt 29:23. Ps 107:34. Is 3:9.
    2 P 2:7. Ju 7. Re +14:11. 21:8.
    furnace. Ex 9:8, 10.
29 **God remembered**. Ge +8:1. 12:2. 18:23-33.
    30:22. Dt 9:5. Ne 13:14, 22. Ps 25:7. 105:8,
    42. 145:20.
    sent. Lk +21:36. 2 P 2:6-10.
30 **Lot**. ver. 17-23.
    for he. Ge 49:4. Je 2:36, 37. Ja 1:8.
    feared. Ge +15:1. Dt 33:12. Jb 4:7. 11:18. Ps
    4:8. 16:8. +118:6. Pr 1:33. 3:24. Je 41:17, 18.
    Mt 14:30, 31. 17:6, 7. 25:24, 25. Mk 5:33.
    16:5, 6. Lk 1:12, 13. Ro 8:15. 2 T 1:7.
    Zoar. ver. +22.
    cave. Ge 23:9, 11, 17, 19, 20. 25:9. 49:29, 30,
    32. 50:13. Jsh 10:16, 17, 18, 22, 23, 27. Jg
    6:2. 1 S 13:6. 22:1. 24:3, 7, 8, 10. 2 S 23:13. 1

K 18:4, 13. 19:9. 1 Ch 11:15. Ps 57, title. 142, title. Is 2:19. Ezk 33:27. Jn 11:38. He 11:38.

31 **not**. ver. 28. Mk 9:6.
to come. Ge +4:1. 6:4. 16:2, 4. 38:8, 9, 14-30. Dt 25:5. Is 4:1.
manner. Ge 38:8. Ep 5:7. Col 3:1. Ja 4:4.

32 **Come**. Ge 11:3.
drink. Ge +9:21. Pr 20:1. 23:31-33. Hab 2:15, 16. Ga 5:21. Ep 5:18.
lie. Le 18:6, 7. 20:12. Ga 5:19.
seed. Ge 38:8. Dt 25:5-10. Mk 12:19.

33 **drink**. Pr 20:1. 23:29-35. Hab 2:15, 16.
night. 1 Th 5:7.

34 **I lay**. Is 3:9. Je 3:3. 5:3. 6:15. 8:12.

35 **that night also**. Ps 8:4. Pr 24:16. Ec 7:26. Lk 21:34. Jn +17:6. 1 C 10:11, 12. 1 P 4:7. 2 P 2:7, 8.

36 **were**. ver. 8. Le 18:6, 7. Jg 1:7. 1 S 15:33. Hab 2:15. Mt 7:2.
father. Ezk 22:10.

37 A.M. 2108. B.C. 1896.
Moab. This name is generally interpreted "of the father"; from *mo*, of, and *av*, a father. i.e. *water (seed) of a father*. Ex 15:15. Nu 21:11. Dt 1:5. 2:8. 29:1. Jsh 13:32. 24:9. Jg 3:12-30. 10:6. 11:15-25. Ru 1:1, 2, 6, 22. 2:6. 4:3. 2 K 13:20. Ezk +25:8, 9, 11.
Moabites. Ex 15:15. Nu 21:29. ch. 22-24. 25:1-3. Dt 2:9, 19. 23:3. Jg ch. 3. Ru 2:6. 4:5, 10. 1 S 14:47. 2 S ch. 8. 1 K 11:7. 2 K ch. 3. 4:2. 1 Ch 18:2. Is 15:1. 16:6, 7. Je 27:3. 48:1, 4, 11-18.
unto. ver. +38.

38 **Ben-Ammi**. i.e. *Son of my people*, from *ben*, a son, and *ammi*, my people. **S#1151h**.
children of Ammon. i.e. *unique*, or *great people*, **S#5983h**. Nu 21:24. Dt 2:19. 23:3. Jsh 12:2. 13:10, 25. Jg 3:13. 10:7. 11:15-28. 12:1-3. 1 S 11:1. 12:12. 14:47. 2 S 8:12. 10:1-8. 11:1. 12:9, 26, 31. 17:27. Ne 13:1-3, 23-28. Ps 83:4-8. Is 11:14. Je 9:26. 25:21. 27:3. 40:11, 14. 41:10, 15. 49:1, 2, 6. Ezk 21:20, 28. 25:2, 3, 5, 10. Da 11:41. Am 1:13. Zp 2:8, 9.
unto this day. ver. 37. Ge 26:33. 32:32. 35:20. 47:26. 48:15. 50:20. Ex 10:6. Dt +29:4, 28. Jsh +4:9. Jg +1:21. 1 S +6:18. 1 Ch +4:43.

GENESIS 20

1 A.M. cir. 2107. B.C. cir. 1897.
from. Ge 13:1. 18:1. 24:62.
Kadesh. Ge +14:7. 1 S 15:7.
Gerar. i.e. *sojourning, journeying, lodging*, **S#1642h**. ver. 2. Ge 10:19. 26:1, 6, 17, 20, 26. 2 Ch 14:13, 14.

2 **said**. Ge 12:11-13. 13:15. 26:7. 2 Ch 19:2. 20:37. 32:31. Pr 24:16. 29:25. Ec 7:20. Ga 2:11, 12. Ep 4:25. Col 3:9.
Abimelech. i.e. *father of the king; my father is king*, **S#40h**. Ge 12:15. 26:1, 16.

3 **a dream**. Ge +31:24.
a dead. ver. 7. Ps 105:14. Ezk 33:14, 15. Jon 3:4.
a man's wife. Heb. married to an husband. Dt 21:13. 22:22. 24:1. Is +62:4mg, 5. Ml 2:11. 2 C 11:2.

4 **had**. ver. 6, 18.
near. Le 18:19.
wilt. ver. 17, 18. Ge 18:23-25. 19:24. 2 S 4:11. 1 Ch 21:17.
nation. Ex 5:22, 23. 8:8, 28-30. 14:10. 35:15, 16. Nu 6:22-26. 20:3-6. 27:15-17. Dt 4:17. 26:15. Jsh 7:7-9. Ps 25:22. 60:1-3, 9-11. Ro 10:1.

5 **in the integrity**. *or,* simplicity, *or* sincerity. Ge 17:1. Jsh 22:22. 2 S 15:11. 1 K 9:4. 2 K +20:3. 1 Ch 29:17. Ps 7:8. 25:21. 26:6. 37:14. 78:72. Pr 11:3. 20:7. 2 C 1:12. 1 Th 2:10. 1 T 1:13.
and innocency. Jb 33:9. Ps 24:4. 26:6. 73:13. Da 6:22.

6 **dream**. ver. +3. Dt 13:1-5. Jb 20:8. Ps 126:1. Ec 5:3. Ju 8.
know. 1 S 16:7. Pr 21:1. Je 17:10.
thou didst. Lk 12:48.
withheld. ver. 18. Ge 31:7. 35:5. Ex 34:24. 1 S 25:26, 34. Ps 84:11. Pr 21:1. Ho 2:6, 7. 2 Th 3:3.
sinning. Ge 39:9. Le 6:2. Ps 51:4. 81:12. 2 Th 2:7, 11.
to touch. Ge 3:3. 26:11. Pr 6:29. 1 C 7:1. 2 C 6:17.

7 **a prophet**. Ge 12:1-3. 18:17. 1 Ch 16:22. Ps 25:14. 105:9-15. He 1:1.
pray for. Le 6:4, 7. Dt 9:20. 1 S 7:5, 8. 12:19, 23. 2 S 24:17. 1 K 13:6. 2 K 5:11. 19:2-4. Jb +42:8. Je 14:11. 15:1. 27:18. Ja 5:14-16. 1 J 5:16. Re 11:5, 6.
surely. ver. 18. Ge +2:17. 12:17. Jb 34:19. Ps 105:14. Ezk 3:18. 33:8, 14-16. He 13:4.
all. Ge 12:15. Nu 16:32, 33. 2 S 24:17.

8 **morning**. Ge +21:14. 22:3.
servants. Ge 9:25, 26. 14:14. 16:6. 24:34. 43:18. Le 25:46.
afraid. Ge +19:30. 22:12. Dt 4:10. 10:12. Jb 28:28. Ps 111:10. Pr 1:7. 9:10. 15:33. 2 C 5:11. He 10:31. Ju 23. Re 19:5.

9 **What hast**. Ge 3:13. 4:10. 12:18. 21:25. 26:10. 31:26. Ex 32:21, 35. Jsh 7:25. 1 S 13:11. 26:18, 19. Pr 28:10. Jn 18:35.
a great. Ge 38:24. 39:9. Le 20:10. 2 S 12:5, 10, 11. Ro 2:11. He 13:4.
ought not. Ge 29:26. 34:7. 1 S 26:16. 2 S 13:12. Pr 28:10. T 1:11.

10 **What**. Ge 12:18. 26:10. Ps 15:2, 4. 1 P 3:15.

11 **Surely**. Ge +1:17. Dt +6:2. Ps 36:1-4. Ro 3:18.
slay. Ge 12:12. 26:7.

12 **And yet**. Ge 11:29. 12:13. 1 Th 5:22.
is the. Ge 11:25-29.

13 **God**. Heb. *Elohim*. Ge 12:1, 9, 11. 35:7. 2 Ch 18:31. Is 63:7-14. Ac +7:3-5. He 11:8.

caused. This verb is plural, as is *Elohim*, in harmony with the teaching of three persons in the Godhead. Ge +1:26.

wander. Ho +4:12.

This. 1 S 23:21. Ps 64:5. Ac 5:9.

kindness. Ge 21:23. 24:27. 32:10. 47:29. Ru 3:10. 2 S 9:7. Col 3:10. Mt 6:1. Lk 11:41. Ac 10:2, 4.

say. Ge 12:13. Ep 5:22. 1 P 3:1-6.

14 **And**. Ge +8:22.

took. ver. 11. Ge 12:16.

restored. ver. 2, 7. Ge 12:19, 20.

15 **my land**. Ge 13:9. 34:10. 47:6.

where it pleaseth thee. Heb. as is good in thine eyes. Ge 16:6. 41:37. Pr 16:7.

16 **thy**. ver. 5. Pr 27:5.

thousand. Ge 23:15, 16.

behold. Or, 'behold it (the 1000 shekels) is to thee.' Ge 26:11.

a covering. Ge 24:65. Ru 3:9. Pr 12:16. 1 C 11:5.

thus. Ge 21:25. 1 Ch 21:3-6. Pr 9:8, 9. 12:1. 25:12. 27:5. Jon 1:6. Re 3:19.

17 **prayed**. See on ver. 7. Ge 29:31. Nu 12:13. 21:7. 1 S 5:11, 12. Ezr 6:10. Jb 42:9, 10. Pr 15:8, 29. Is 45:11. Mt 7:7. 21:22. Ac 3:24. Ph 4:6. 1 Th 5:25. Ja 5:16.

18 **closed**. ver. 7. Ge 12:17. 16:2. 30:2. 1 S 1:6. 5:10.

because. Jsh ch. 7. 22:20. Jon 1:12. Mt 5:13. Ac 27:20-25.

GENESIS 21

1 **visited**. Ge 50:24. Ex +3:16. +20:5. 1 S 2:21. Ps 106:4. Lk 1:68. 19:44. Ro 4:17-20.

Sarah as. Ge 17:19. 18:10, 14. Mt 24:35. Ga 4:23, 28. T 1:2.

2 **conceived**. 2 K 4:16, 17. Lk 1:24, 25, 36. Ga 4:22. He 11:11.

at the set. Ge 17:19, 21. 18:10, 14. Ro 9:9.

3 **called**. ver. 6, 12. Ge 17:19. Jsh 24:3. Ro 9:7. He 11:18.

4 **eight days**. Ge 17:10-12. Ex 12:48. Lk 1:6, 59. 2:21. Jn 7:22, 23. Ac 7:8.

5 **an hundred**. Ge 17:1, 17. Ro 4:19. He 6:15.

6 **God**. Ge 17:17. 18:12-15. Ps +113:9. Is +54:1. Lk 1:46-55. Jn 16:21, 22. Ga 4:27, 28. He 11:11.

to laugh. Ge 18:12.

will laugh. Jb 5:22. 8:21. Ps 126:2. Lk 1:14, 58. 6:21. Ro 12:15.

7 **Who**. Dt 4:32-34. Ps 86:8, 10. Is 66:8. 2 Th 1:10.

for I. Ge 18:11, 12.

8 A.M. 2111. B.C. 1893.

and was weaned. 1 S +1:22.

feast. Ge +19:3.

9 **Sarah**. Ge 16:3-6, 15. 17:20.

Egyptian. Ge 16:1, 15.

mocking. or, playing. Ge 16:4, 5. 19:14. 26:8h. 39:14, 17. Ex 32:6. 2 K 2:23, 24. Ne 4:1-5. Jb 30:1. Ps 22:6. Pr 17:5. 20:11. 30:17. La 1:7. Ga 4:22, 29. He 11:36. Ju 18.

10 **Cast out**. Le 21:7. Ge 25:6. 19. 17:19, 21. 36:6, 7. Le 21:7. Pr 22:10. Mt 8:11, 12. 22:13. Jn 8:35. Ga 4:22-31. 1 J 2:19.

heir. Jn 8:35. Ga 3:18. 4:7, *30*. 1 P 1:4.

11 **because**. Ge 17:18. 22:1, 2. 2 S 18:33. Mt 10:37. He 12:11.

12 **hearken**. 1 S 8:7, 9. Is 46:10.

in Isaac. Ge +17:19, 21. Ro *9:7*, 8. He *11:18*.

thy seed. Ga *3:16*.

13 **the son**. ver. 18. Ge +12:2. 16:10.

14 A.M. 2112. B.C. 1892.

rose up. Ge +18:2. +19:27. 24:54. 26:31. 31:55. Jsh 3:1. Ps 119:60. Pr 27:14. Ec 9:10. Je +25:3.

took. Ge 25:6. 36:6, 7.

child. Or, youth, (see ver. 12, 20) as Ishmael was now 16 or 17 years of age. S#3206h, Da +1:4. 2 K 2:23, 24.

sent. Jn 8:35.

wandered. Ge 16:7. 37:15. Ps 107:4. Is 16:8. Ga 4:23-25.

Beer-sheba. ver. +31.

15 **the water**. ver. 14. Ex 15:22-25. 17:1-3. 2 K 3:9. Ps 63:1. Is 44:12. Je 14:3.

16 **Let**. Ge 44:34. 1 K 3:26. Is 49:15. Zc 12:10. Lk 15:20.

lift. Ge +22:13.

wept. Ge +29:11.

17 **heard**. Ge +16:11. 2 K 13:4, 23. Ps 50:15. 91:15. Mt 15:32.

the angel. Ge +16:9, 11.

What. Jg 18:23. 1 S 11:5. Is 22:1.

fear. Ge +15:1. Ps 107:4-6. Mk 5:36.

18 **I will**. ver. 13. Ge 16:10. 17:20. 25:12-18. 1 Ch 1:29-31.

19 **opened**. Ge +3:7. Nu 22:31. 2 K 6:17-20. Ps 119:18. Is 35:5. Lk 24:16, +31.

well. Heb. *beer*, Ge +16:14.

20 **God**. Ge 17:20. +28:15. Jg 6:12. 13:24, 25. Lk 1:80. 2:40.

an archer. Ge +10:9. 16:12. 27:3. 49:23, 24.

21 **Paran**. i.e. *place of caverns; abounding in foliage; their beautifying,* S#6290h. Nu 10:12. 12:16. 13:3, 26. Dt 1:1. +33:2. 1 S 25:1. 1 K 11:18. Hab 3:3.

a wife. Nu +12:1.

22 A.M. 2118. B.C. 1886.

Abimelech. Ge 20:2. 26:26.

Phicol. i.e. *mouth of all,* S#6369h. ver. 32. Ge 26:26.

God. Ge +28:15. 1 C 14:25. Re 3:9.

23 **swear**. ver. 31, 32. Ge 14:22, 23. 24:3. 25:33. 26:28, 31. 31:44, 53. Dt 6:13. 10:20. Jsh 2:12. 1 S 20:3, 16, 17. 24:21, 22. Ps 63:11. Is 19:18. 45:23. 48:1. 65:16. Je 4:2. 12:16. Zp 1:5. Ro 14:11. 2 C 1:23. Ph 2:10, 11. He 6:16.

that thou wilt not deal falsely with me. Heb. if thou shalt lie unto me.
I have. Ge 20:14.
24 **will swear**. Ge 14:13. Ro 12:18. He 6:16.
25 **reproved**. Le +19:17. Pr 17:10. 25:9. 27:5. Mt 18:15-18. Ga 6:1.
because. Ge 26:15-22. 29:8. Ex 2:15-17. Jg 1:15.
well. Heb. *beer*, Ge +16:14.
servants. Ge 13:7. 26:15-22. Ex 2:16, 17.
26 **I wot**. Ge 13:7. 2 K 5:20-24.
27 **took**. Ge 14:22, 23. Pr 17:8.
made. Ge 26:28-31. 31:44, 53. 1 S 18:3. Ga 3:15.
28 **Abraham**. Ge 17:5.
seven. Ge 7:2. 41:26, 27. Le 4:6. Nu 23:1. Jsh 6:4. Ru 4:15. 1 S 2:5. 2 K 5:10. Mi 5:5, 6. Ac 6:3. Re 4:5.
lambs. Ge 22:7, 8. Ex 12:3, 4, 5, 21. Is 53:7. Jn 1:29, 36. Ac 8:32. 1 P 1:19. Re 5:6, 8, 12, 13.
29 **What mean**. Ge 33:8. Ex 12:26. 1 S 15:14.
30 **a witness**. Ge 31:44-48, 52. Jsh 22:27, 28. 24:27.
well. Heb. *beer*, Ge +16:14.
31 **called**. Ge 26:33.
Beer-sheba. i.e. the well of the oath, or the well of seven: alluding to the seven ewe lambs. **S#884h**. ver. 14. Ge 22:19. 26:23, 33. 28:10. 46:1, 5. Jsh 15:28. 19:2. Jg +20:1. 1 S 8:2. 2 S 24:7. 1 K 19:3. 2 K 12:1. 23:8. 1 Ch 4:28. 2 Ch 19:4. 24:1. Ne 11:27, 30. Am 5:5. 8:14.
sware. The verb rendered to *swear* (**S#7650h**) is derived from the word translated *seven* (**S#7651h**). Ge 4:15. Le 26:18. Dt 33:23. 28:7. Pr 6:30, 31.
32 **made a covenant**. ver. +27. Ge 14:13.
the Philistines. Ge 10:14. Je +47:4.
33 **grove**. *or*, tree. Dt 16:21. Jg 3:7. 1 S 22:6. 31:13. Am 8:14.
Beersheba. ver. +31.
called. Ge +4:26. 12:8. 26:23, 25, 33.
Lord. or, Jehovah.
everlasting. Heb. *olam*, Ge +17:7. Ge +14:22. Dt 33:27. Ps 90:2. Is 40:28. +57:15. 63:16. Je 10:10. Da 12:7. Mi 5:2. Jn 8:56-58. Ro 1:20. 16:26. 1 T 1:17.
34 **sojourned**. Ge 20:1. 1 Ch 29:15. Ps 39:12. He 11:9, 13. 1 P 2:11.

GENESIS 22

1 A.M. 2132. B.C. 1872.
God. Ex 15:25, 26. 16:4. Dt 8:2. 13:3. 1 C +10:13. He 11:17. Ja 1:12-14. 2:21. 1 P 1:7.
tempt. Or, *prove*, or *try*, as *tempt* originally signified. Ex 20:20. Dt 8:16. 1 S 17:39. 1 K 10:1. Lk +8:13. Ac 20:19. He 2:18. 4:15. 1 P 1:6.

Behold, here I am. Heb. Behold me. ver. 7, 11. Ex 3:4. Jb 38:35mg. Is 6:8mg.
2 **Take**. Ge 17:19. 21:12. Jn 3:16. Ro 5:8. 8:32. He 11:17. 1 J 4:9, 10.
only. Heb. *yachid*, **S#3173h**, Ps +22:20mg. ver. 12, 16. Dt 6:4. Jg 11:34. Lk +7:12. Jn 3:16. He 11:17. 1 J 4:9.
whom. Pr 4:3. 8:30. Mk 12:6. Jn 3:16. Ro 8:32. Col 1:13. 1 J 4:9, 10.
Moriah. i.e. *chosen of the Lord; my teacher is Jehovah*, **S#4179h**. 1 Ch 21:22. 22:1. 2 Ch 3:1. Mt 27:33.
and offer. Jg 11:31, 39. 2 K 3:27. Mi 6:7. Jn 3:16.
burnt offering. Le +23:12. Ep 5:2.
3 **rose**. Ge 17:23. Is 26:3, 4. Mk 10:28-31. He 11:8, 17-19.
early. Ge +21:14.
place. Dt +12:11.
4 **third**. Ge 31:22. 34:25. +40:20. Ex 5:3. +10:22. 15:22. 19:11, 15. Le 7:17. +19:6. Nu 10:33. 19:12, 19. 31:19. Jsh 1:11. 2 K 20:5. Est 5:1. Ho 6:2. 1 C +15:4.
saw. 1 S 26:13.
5 **Abide**. Ge 45:1. Jn 16:32. He 12:1.
come. He 11:19.
6 **laid it**. Is 53:6. Mt 8:17. Lk 24:26, 27. Jn 19:17. 1 P 2:24. 3:18.
fire. 1 K 18:38. He 12:29.
knife. Zc 13:7.
both. Jn 10:30. 14:10, 11. 16:32.
7 **My father**. Mt 26:39, 42. Jn 18:11. Ro 8:15.
Here am I. Heb. Behold me. ver. 1. Is 58:9. Jn 8:29.
but. Ge 4:2-4. 8:20.
lamb. *or*, **kid**. Ex 12:3mg. 29:38-42. Is 43:23. 53:7. Jn 1:29. 1 P 1:19. Re 5:6. 13:8.
8 **God will**. Ge 18:14. 2 Ch 25:9. Mt 19:26. Jn 1:29, 36. 1 P 1:19, 20. Re 5:6, 12. 7:14. 13:8.
provide. 1 S 16:1. Ro 8:32.
burnt. Ep 5:2. He 10:5.
9 **place**. ver. 2-4. Mt ch. 21, 26, 27.
built. Ge 8:20.
altar. Ge 12:7. Ex 20:25. He 13:10.
bound. Ps 118:27. Is 53:4-10. Mt 27:2. Mk 15:1. Jn 10:17, 18. Ac 8:32. Ga 3:13. Ep 5:2. Ph 2:7, 8. He +9:28. 1 P 2:24.
10 **stretched**. Is 53:6-12. He 11:17-19. Ja 2:21-23.
11 **angel**. ver. 12, 16. Ge 16:7, 9, +10. 21:17. Ps 34:7. 91:11. Mt 17:5.
Abraham. ver. 1. Ex 3:4. 1 S 3:10. Ac 9:4. 26:14.
Abraham. Ge 46:2. Ps 22:1. Mt 7:21, 22. 23:37. 27:46. Mk 15:34. Lk 6:46. 10:41. 13:25, 34. 22:31.
Here. 1 K 19:13.
12 **Lay**. Ge +37:22. 1 S 15:22. Je 19:5. Mi +6:6-8. 1 C +10:13. He 11:19.

neither. Ex 12:46. Nu 9:12. Ps 34:20. Jn 19:36. 1 C 5:7.

now. Ge 26:5. Dt +6:2. 1 S 15:22. Ps 1:6. 25:12, 14. Mal 4:2. Mt 10:37, 38. 19:29. Ep 2:10. He 11:17. 12:28. Ja 2:18, 21, 22. 1 J 5:3. Re 19:5.

know. Ge +18:21.

seeing. Jn 3:16. Ro 5:8. 8:32. 1 J 4:9, 10.

only. ver. 2. Mk +6:3. Lk +7:12. Jn 1:14, 18. +3:16, 18. 1 J 4:9.

13　**lifted**. Ge 13:10, 14. Nu 24:2. Dt 3:27. Jg 9:7. Ru 1:9, 14. 1 S 6:13. 1 Ch 21:16. Jb 2:12. Ps 93:3. 121:1. Is 40:9, 26. Jn 4:35.

looked. Ge +13:14.

behind. ver. 8. Ps 40:6-8. 89:19, 20. Is 30:21. 1 C +10:13. 2 C 1:9, 10.

burnt. ver. 2, 8. Le +23:12.

in the. 1 C 5:7, 8. 1 P 1:19, 20.

stead. Is 53:10, 11. Mt 20:28. Jn 6:51. Ro 4:25. 5:6, 8. 2 C 5:14, 15, 21. Ga 3:13. He 9:28. 10:10.

14　**called**. Ge 16:13, 14. 28:19. 32:30. Ex 17:15. Jg 6:24. 1 S 7:12. Ezk 48:35.

Jehovah-jireh. i.e. The Lord will see, *or* provide. S#3070h, only here. ver. 8, 13. Ex +15:26. 17:15.

day. Ge +19:38.

In. Dt 32:36. Ps 22:4, 5. Da 3:17. Mi 4:10. Jn 1:14. 2 C 1:8-10. 1 T 3:16.

it shall be seen. 2 S 24:25. 1 Ch 21:26. 2 Ch 7:1-3. Jb 11:16. Ps 16:8. 30:5. 112:4. 146:8. Is 25:6. 30:18. 43:2, 3.

15　**angel**. ver. 11. Ge +19:24. 21:17.

second time. Ge 24:44. 41:5, 32. Dt 17:6. Jg 6:39, 40. 1 S 10:22. +23:4. Je 1:13. Jon 3:1. 1 C 2:9.

16　**By myself**. Ps 89:35. 110:4. 132:11. Is 45:23. Je 22:5. 49:13. 51:14. Am 6:8. Mi +7:20. Ac 2:30. Ro 4:13, 14. He 6:13, 14.

sworn. Ge 26:3.

17　**in blessing**. Ge 12:2. 27:28, 29. Ep 1:3.

I will multiply. Ge +13:16. Is +54:1.

as the stars. Ge +15:5.

as the sand. Ge 13:16. 32:12. 41:49. Jsh 11:4. Jg 7:12. 1 S 13:5. 2 S 17:11. 1 K 4:20, 29. Jb 6:3. 29:18. Ps 78:27. 139:18. Is 10:22. 48:19. Je 15:8. 33:22. Ho 1:10. Hab 1:9. Ro 9:27. He 11:12. Re 20:8.

shore. Heb. lip. 1 K 9:26mg.

thy seed. Ge 24:60. Nu 24:17-19. Ps 2:8, 9. 72:8, 9. Je 32:22. Da 2:44. 45. Lk 1:68-75. 1 C 15:57. Re +11:15.

gate. Dt 12:12. 21:19. Ps 87:2. Is 14:31. 24:12. Je 15:7. Mi 1:9.

of his enemies. Dt +28:13. Ps +18:43. 127:5. Ro +11:25.

18　*thy seed*. Ge +12:3. +13:16. Mt 1:1. Lk +3:34. Jn 11:51, 52. Ac 3:25. Ro 1:3. Ga 3:8.

because. ver. 16. Ps +9:10. Is 50:10. Zc 6:15. Mt 7:21, 24-27. Lk 6:46. Jn 3:36. Ac 5:32. Ro

1:5. 2:8. 6:17. 2 C 10:5. 2 Th 1:8. He 5:9. 1 P 1:22.

obeyed. ver. 3, 10. Ge 26:5. Dt +28:1, 2, 15. 1 S 2:30. Je 7:23. He ch. 11.

19　**So Abraham**. ver. 5.

to Beer-sheba. Ge +21:31.

20　A.M. 2142. B.C. 1862.

told. Pr 25:25.

Milcah. Ge +11:29.

Nahor. Ge +11:22.

21　**Huz**. i.e. *the strong; counsellor*, S#5780h. Ge +10:23, Uz.

Buz. i.e. *contempt*, S#938h. 1 Ch 5:14. Jb 32:2, 6. Je 25:23.

Kemuel. Nu 34:24.

Aram. i.e. *high, exalted*, S#758h. Ge 10:22. 24:10. Nu 23:7. Ps 60, title.

22　**Chesed**. i.e. *increase*, S#3777h.

Hazo. i.e. *vision*, S#2375h.

Pildash. i.e. *lamp of fire*, S#6394h.

Jidlaph. i.e. *shedding tears*, S#3044h.

Bethuel. i.e. *man of God; abode of God*, S#1328h. ver. 23. Ge 24:15, 24, 47, 50. 25:20. 28:2, 5. 1 Ch 4:30.

23　**Bethuel**. ver. +22.

Rebekah. i.e. *a rope with a noose*, S#7259h. Ge 24:51, 60, 67. Ro 9:10, Rebecca.

these. Ge 25:13-16. 35:22-26.

24　**concubine**. 1 Ch 1:32. +2:48. Pr 15:25. Da 5:2.

Reumah. i.e. *exalted, high, lofty*, S#7208h.

Tebah. i.e. *confidence; slaughter*, S#2875h.

Gaham. i.e. *having large flaming eyes; sunburnt or swarthy*, S#1514h.

Thahash. i.e. *badger, seal*, S#8477h.

Maachah. Dt 3:14. Jsh 12:5. 2 S 10:6. 1 K +2:39.

GENESIS 23

1　A.M. 2144. B.C. 1860.

Sarah. Ge 17:15.

an. Ge 17:17.

2　**Kirjath-arba**. Jsh +15:54.

Hebron. ver. 19. Nu +13:22.

mourn. Ge +24:67. 27:41. 50:3, 10. Nu 20:29. Dt 34:8. 1 S 28:3. 2 S 1:12, 17. 3:31. 11:27. 2 Ch 35:25. Je 6:26. 22:10, 18. Ezk 24:16-18. Zc 12:10. Jn 11:31, 33, 35. Ac 8:2. 1 Th 5:13.

3　**Heth**. ver. 5, 7. Ge +10:15. 49:30. 1 S 26:6. 2 S 23:39.

4　**stranger**. Ge 17:8. +47:9. Le 25:23. Dt +26:11. Ps +119:19. Ml 3:5. Mt 25:35. Ac +7:5. He 11:9, 13-16.

sojourner. Ex 12:45. Le 25:6, 23, 35, 40, 45, 47. Nu 35:15. 1 K 17:1. Ps 39:12.

burying place. Ge 3:19. 49:30. 50:13. Jb 30:23. Ec 6:3. 12:5, 7. Ac +7:5. S#6913h, *qeber*. Ge 23:4, 6, 9, 20. 1 K 13:22, 30, 31. 2 K

13:21. Jb 5:26. Is 22:16. 53:9. Je 26:23. Ezk 37:12, 13. 39:11. For **S#6900h**, *qeburah*, grave, see Ge +35:20. For **S#7845h**, *shachath*, pit, ditch, destruction, corruption, see Jb +9:31. For **S#7585h**, *sheol*, grave, hell, pit, see Ge +37:35.
bury. ver. 19.

5 **answered**. ver. 14.

6 **my lord**. Ge 18:12. 24:18, 35. 31:35. 32:4, 5, 18. 42:10. 44:5, 8. Ex 32:22. Ru 2:13.
a mighty prince. Heb. a prince of God. Ge 10:9. 30:8. Ex 9:28. 2 S 9:3. Jb +1:16. Ps +36:6mg. Ezk 28:13. Jon 3:3mg. Ac 7:20mg. 1 J 3:1, 2.
prince. Ge 13:2. 14:14. 21:22. 24:35.
choice. Ex 15:4. Dt 12:11. Is 22:7. Ezk 24:5.
sepulchre. Heb. *qeber*, ver. +4.

7 **bowed**. Ge +18:2. Pr 18:24. Ro 12:17, 18. He 12:14. 1 P 3:8.

8 **mind**. Heb. *nephesh*, soul. Dt 18:6. 28:65. 1 S 2:35. 2 S 17:8. 2 K 9:15. 1 Ch 28:9. Je 15:1. Ezk 23:17, 18, 22, 28. 24:25. 36:5. Compare Ge +34:3; Ex +15:9; +23:9. For the other uses of *nephesh* see Ge +2:7. Mt +11:29.
intreat. 1 K 2:17. Lk 7:3, 4. He 7:26. 1 J 2:1, 2.
Ephron. i.e. *fawn-like; strong*. **S#6085h**. ver. 10, 13, 14, 16, 17. 25:9. 49:29, 30. 50:13.

9 **Machpelah**. i.e. *double, folded together*, **S#4375h**. ver. 17, 19. Ge 25:9. 49:30. 50:13.
much money. Heb. full money. Ge 24:22. 1 Ch 21:22, 24. Mt 10:9. Ac 3:6. Ro 12:17. 13:8.
buryingplace. Heb. *qeber*, ver. +4.

10 **dwelt**. Or, sitting. Ge +14:7
audience. Heb. ears.
all that. ver. 18. Ge 34:20, 24. Ru 4:1-4. Jb 29:7. Is 28:6.
his. Ge 24:10. Mt 9:1. Lk 2:3, 4.
gate. Here, "gate" is put for place of legal transactions, Ge +14:7.
his. Ge 24:10. Mt 9:1. Lk 2:3, 4.

11 **my lord**. ver. 6. 2 S 24:20-24. 1 Ch 21:22-24. Is 32:8.
in the. ver. 18. Nu 35:30. Ru 4:1, 4, 9, 11. Lk 19:24. Ac 26:26.

12 **bowed**. See ver. 7. Ge 18:2. 19:1.

13 **I will**. Ge 14:22, 23. 2 S 24:24. Ac 20:35. Ro 13:8. Ph 4:5-8. Col 4:5. He 13:5.

14 **answered**. ver. 5.

15 **shekels**. Ge 17:12, 13. 20:16. Ex 21:32. *30:13*, 15. Jsh 7:21. Ezk 45:12.

16 **weighed**. Ge 43:21. 2 S 24:24. Jb 28:15. Je 32:9. Zc 11:12. Mt 7:12. 26:15. Ro 13:8. Ph 4:8. 1 Th 4:6.
four. ver. 15. Ex 30:13. Ezk 45:12.
merchant. Ge 37:28. 2 S 14:26. 1 K 10:15, 28.

17 **the field**. ver. 20. Ge 25:9. 49:30-32. 50:13. Ac 7:16.
made sure. ver. 20. Ru 4:7-10. Ps 112:5. Je 32:7-14. Mt 10:16. Ep 5:15. Col 4:5.

18 **all**. Ge 34:20. Ru 4:1. Je 32:12.
gate. ver. 10.

19 **buried**. Ge 3:19. 25:9, 10. 35:27-29. 47:30. 49:29-32. 50:13, 25. Jb 30:23. Ec 6:3. 12:5, 7.
Mamre. Ge +13:18.

20 **were**. Ru 4:7-10. 2 S 24:24. Je 32:10, 11.
for a. Ge 25:9. 49:31, 32. 50:5, 13, 24, 25. 2 K 21:18.
buryingplace. Heb. *qeber*, ver. +4.

GENESIS 24

1 **was old**. Ge 18:11. 21:5. 25:20. 1 K 1:1. Lk 1:7.
well stricken in age. Heb. gone into days.
blessed. ver. 35. Ge +12:2. 13:2. 49:25. Ps 112:1-3. Pr +10:22. Is 51:2. Mt 6:33. Ga 3:9. Ep 1:3. 1 T +4:8.

2 **eldest**. Ge 15:2. 1 T 5:17.
ruled. ver. 10. Ge 39:4-6, 8, 9. 44:1.
Put. ver. 9. Ge 47:29. 1 Ch +29:24mg.
thigh. **S#3409h**. Ge +17:11. Ge 24:9. 32:25, 31, 32. 35:11. 46:26mg. 47:29. Ex 1:5mg. 28:42. Nu 5:21, 22, 27. Jg 8:30mg. 1 Ch +29:24mg.

3 **swear**. Ge +21:23. 50:25. Ex 20:7. 23:13. 1 S 20:17.
the God. Ge 14:22. Ne 9:6. Ps 115:15. Je 10:11.
not take. ver. 37. Nu +12:1. Jg +3:6.
Canaanites. Ge +10:18.

4 **to my kindred**. Ge 11:25. 12:1, 7. 28:2. Nu 36:6.

5 **Peradventure**. ver. 39, 58. Ex 20:7. 9:2. Pr 13:16. Ec 5:2. Je 4:2.

6 **Beware**. Ga 5:1. He 10:39. 11:9, 13-16. 2 P 2:20-22.

7 **Lord**. Ezr 1:2. Da 2:44. Jon 1:9. Re 11:13.
took. Ge 12:1-7.
which spake. Ge +13:15. Ac +7:5. Ga *3:16*. He 11:9.
send. Ex 32:34. 33:2. Nu 20:16.
angel. Ex 23:20-23. Ps 32:8. 34:7. Pr 3:5, 6. Is 63:9. He 1:14.

8 **clear**. Nu 30:5, 8. Jsh 2:17-20. Jn 8:32.
only. ver. 4, 5, 6. Ac 7:2.

9 **thigh**. ver. +2.

10 **camels**. Ge 12:16.
for. or, and.
all. ver. 2. Ge +6:12. 39:4-6, 8, 9, 22, 23. +41:56.
hand. Ge +43:26.
Mesopotamia. i.e. *exalted*, **S#763h**. Dt 23:4. Jg 3:8-10. 1 Ch 19:6. Ps 60, title. Ac 2:9.
city. Ge +11:22.

11 **kneel**. Ge 33:13, 14. Pr 12:10.
well. Heb. *beer*, Ge +16:14.
women go out to draw water. Heb. women which draw water go forth. ver. 13-20. Ex 2:16. 1 S 9:11. Jn 4:7.

12 **O Lord**. ver. 27. Ge +17:7, 8.

I pray. Ge 27:10. 43:14. Ne 1:11. 2:4. Ps 37:5. 90:16, 17. 118:25. 122:6. 127:1. Pr 3:6. Ph 4:6. 1 Th 3:10, 11.

13　**Behold**. Ge +3:22.
I stand. ver. 43. Ps 37:5. Pr 3:6.
well. S#5869h, *ayin*, a fountain. Ge 24:13, 16, 29, 30, 42, 43, 45. 49:22. Ex 15:27. Ne 2:13. For **S#875h**, *be-er*, a dug well, see Ge +16:14. For **S#4599h**, *mayan*, a spring or fountain, see Ge +7:11. For **S#4726h**, *maqor*, spring, dug well (even when naturally flowing) see Le +12:7, issue. Pr 10:11. For **S#953h**, *bor* or *bore*, a hewn cistern, well, dungeon, pit, see Ge +37:20.
daughters. ver. 11. Ge 29:9, 10. Ex 2:16. Jg 5:11. 1 S 9:11. Jn 4:7.

14　**And let**. Jg 6:17, 37. 1 S 14:9.
damsel. Heb. *naarah*, **S#5291h**. ver. 16, 28, 55, 57, 61. Ge 34:3, 12. Ex 2:5 (maidens). Dt 22:15, 16, 19-21, 23-29.
pitcher. Jn 4:28.
give. Ge 29:10. Jn 4:9.
she that. ver. 44. Pr 19:14.
thereby. ver. +50. Ge 15:8. Ex 4:1-9. Jg 6:17, 36-40. 7:13-15. 18:5. 1 S 6:7-9. 10:2-10. 14:8, 10. 20:7. 2 S 5:24. 2 K 20:8-11. Is 7:11. Ro 1:10.

15　**before**. ver. 45. Ps 34:15. Is 58:9. +65:24. Da 9:20-23.
Rebekah. ver. 24. Ge 22:20-23.
Milcah. Ge +11:29.
pitcher. Ge 21:14. 29:9. Ex 2:16. Ru 2:2, 17. Pr 31:27.

16　**fair to look upon**. Heb. good of countenance. Ge +29:17.
virgin. Heb. *bethulah*. ver. +43. Le +21:13. **S#1330h**. Dt 22:19, 23, 28. Is 62:5. Jl 1:8.
known. Ge +4:1. Ex +34:15. SS 5:2.
well. Heb. *ayin*, ver. +13.

17　**Let**. 1 K 17:10. Jn 4:7, 9.
water of. Ge ch. 26. Is 21:14. 41:17, 18. 49:10.

18　**Drink**. Pr 31:26. 1 P 3:8. 4:8, 9.

19　**she said**. ver. 14, 45, 46. 1 P 4:9.

20　**hasted**. Ge 18:2. 19:27. 21:14.
well. Heb. *beer*, Ge +16:14.

21　**wondering at**. Ps 34:1-6. Lk 2:19, 51.
to wit. i.e. *to know*, or *to learn*.
the Lord. ver. 12, 56.

22　**took**. ver. 30. Est 5:1. Je 2:32. 1 T 2:9, 10. 1 P 3:8.
earring. *or*, jewel for the forehead. ver. 30, 47. Pr 11:22. Is 3:19-23. Ezk 16:11, +12mg.
of half. Ge 23:15, 16.
gold. Ge +23:9.

23　**Whose**. ver. 47.
room. Jg 19:15. 20:4. Lk 2:7. He 13:2.

24　**I am**. ver. 15. Ge 11:29. 22:20, 23.

25　**We have**. Ge 18:4-8. Jg 19:19-21. Is 32:8. 1 P 4:9.

26　**bowed**. ver. 48, 52. Ge +18:2. 22:5. Ex 4:31.

12:27. 34:8. Nu 22:31. 1 Ch 29:20. 2 Ch 7:3. 20:18. 29:30. Ne 8:6. Ps 22:29. 66:4. 72:9. 95:6. Mi 6:6. Ph 2:10.

27　**Blessed**. ver. 12. Ge 9:26. 14:20. Ex 18:10. 1 S 25:32, 39. Ps 68:19. Lk 1:68. Ep 1:3. 1 T 1:17.
of his. Ge 32:10. Ps 98:3. 100:5. Mi 7:20. Jn 1:17.
mercy. Ge +20:13.
I being in the way. Am +7:15. Mt 4:18. 9:9.
the Lord. ver. 48. Pr 3:6. 4:11-13. 8:20.
of my. ver. 4. Ge 13:8. Ex 2:11, 13.

28　**of**. ver. 48, 55, 67. Ge 29:12. 31:33.

29　**a brother**. ver. 55, 60. Ge 25:20. 27:43. 28:2, 5. 29:5, 12.
Laban. i.e. *white, clean*, **S#3837h**. ver. 50. Ge 25:20. 27:43. 28:2, 5. 29:16. 31:1, 26, 51. 32:4. 46:18, 25. Dt 1:1.
ran. Ge 18:2. 29:13.
well. Heb. *ayin*, ver. +13.

30　**earring**. ver. +22. Ezk 16:11, 12.
well. Heb. *ayin*, ver. +13.

31　**thou**. Ge 26:29. Jg 17:2. Ru 3:10. Ps 115:15. Pr 17:8. 18:16. 19:6.
for I. ver. 25.

32　**he ungirded**. i.e. Laban ungirded.
straw. ver. 25. Jg 19:19.
wash. Ge +18:4.

33　**not eat**. Jb 23:12. Jn 4:14, 31-34.
until. Ps 132:3-5. Pr 22:29. Ec 9:10. Mt 6:33. Ep 6:5-8. 1 T 6:2.

34　**servant**. ver. 2. Ge 15:3.

35　**and**. Ge +8:22.
the Lord. ver. +1. Ge 25:11. 26:12. Ps 18:35. Pr 22:4.
flocks. Ge 12:16. 26:13, 14. Jb 1:3. 42:10-12. Ps 107:38. Mt 6:33.

36　**Sarah**. Ge 11:29, 30. 17:15-19. 18:10-14. 21:1-7. Ro 4:19.
unto. Ge 21:10. 25:5.

37　**And my**. ver. 2-9. Ge 6:2. 27:46. Ezr 9:1-3.
not take. ver. +3. Ne 10:30. 13:25. 2 C +6:14.
Canaanites. Ge +10:18.

38　**But**. ver. 4. Ge 12:1. +21:21.

39　**Peradventure**. ver. 5. Jsh 9:18, 19. Ps 15:4. Je 34:8-21. Ezk 17:14-18. Ga 3:15.

40　**And he**. ver. 7.
before. Ge +5:22.
will. ver. 7. Ex 23:20. 33:2. Ps 1:3. 91:11. Da 3:28. He 1:14. Re 22:8, 16.

41　**clear from**. ver. 8. Dt 29:12. 1 C 7:15, 39.

42　**well**. Heb. *ayin*, ver. +13.
O Lord. ver. 12-14. Ac 10:7, 8, 22.
prosper. ver. 12, 31. Ge 39:3. Ezr 8:21. Ne 1:11. Ps 37:5. 90:17. Ro 1:10.

43　**I stand**. ver. 13, 14.
well. Heb. *ayin*, ver. +13.
virgin. Heb. *almah*. **S#5959h**. Ex 2:8. Ps 68:25. Pr 30:19. SS 1:3. 6:8. Is 7:14.

44 Both. Ge +22:15. Is 32:8. 1 T 2:10. He 13:2. 1 P 3:8.

the woman. ver. 14. Ge 2:22. Pr 16:33. 18:22. 19:14.

appointed. Ge 20:16. 45:8. Jsh +14:2. Ps 37:23. 73:24. Pr 3:5, 6. 16:9, 33. 21:1. Is 28:26. 42:16. 65:11mg.

45 before. ver. 15-20. Is 58:9. +65:24. Da 9:19, 23. Mt 6:8. 7:7. Ac 4:24-33. 10:30. 12:12-17.

speaking. 1 S 1:13-15. 2 S 7:27. Ne 2:4. Ro 8:26.

well. Heb. *ayin*, ver. +13.

46 Drink. ver. +18-20.

47 I put. ver. 22, 53. Ps 45:9, 13, 14. Is 62:3-5. Ezk 16:10-13. Ep 5:26, 27.

48 bowed. ver. 26, 27, 52.

led me. ver. 27, +44. Ge 22:23. Ex 18:20. Ezr 8:21. Ps +32:8. 48:14. 107:7. Pr 3:5, 6. 4:11. Is 48:17.

daughter. Ge +13:8. Here, "daughter" is put for "granddaughter."

49 now if. Ge 47:29. Jsh 2:14.

deal kindly and truly. Heb. do mercy and truth. Ge 32:10. Pr 3:3. Mi +6:8. Mt 23:23.

that I. Nu 20:17. Dt 2:27.

50 Laban. ver. 15, 28, 53, 55, 60.

The thing. ver. +14, 27. 1 S +23:4. 1 K +13:9. Ps 118:23. 126:3. Mt 21:42. Ac 16:10. 15:25, 28.

we. Ge 31:24, 29. 2 S 13:22. Ac 11:17.

51 Rebekah. Ge 20:15.

hath. ver. 15, +44. 2 S 16:10.

52 worshipped. ver. +26, 48. Ps 116:1, 2.

53 jewels. Heb. vessels. Ex 3:22. 11:2. 12:35.

brother. Pr 18:24. Ex 22:22. Dt +10:18. Ps 10:14. Ho 14:3. Ja 1:27.

precious. Dt 33:13-16. 2 Ch 21:3. Ezr 1:6. SS 4:13. Is 39:2.

54 rose. Ge +21:14.

Send me. ver. 56, 59. Ge 28:5, 6. 30:25. 45:24. Lk 8:38, 39.

55 a few days. *or*, a full year, or ten *months*. Ne +13:6mg.

56 Hinder. Ge 45:9-13. Pr 25:25.

prospered. Ps +1:3. Is 48:15.

57 call the damsel. Jg 19:3. 1 S 18:20, 21. 25:40, 41. Jn 9:21, 23.

enquire at. Ex +2:21. Nu +12:1.

58 Wilt thou. Ge 2:24. Ps 45:10, 11. Ru 1:16. Lk 1:38.

I will go. Nu 10:30. 1 C 7:39.

59 their. ver. 50, 53, 60.

nurse. Ge 35:8. Nu 11:12. 1 Th 2:5.

60 they. Ge 1:28. 9:1. 14:19. 17:16. 28:3. 48:15, 16, 20. Ru 4:11, 12.

be thou the mother. *or*, 'be thou for thousands of myriads.' Dt 7:13. Ps 113:9. 127:3-5.

thousands. Ge 17:16. 25:23. Da 7:10.

thy seed. Ge +22:17. Le 25:46. Ps 127:5.

gate. Ge +14:7. Dt 21:19.

61 they rode. Ge 31:34. 1 S 30:17. Est 8:10, 14.

followed. Ge 2:24. Ps 45:10.

62 Lahai-roi. i.e. *the living God looking on me*, **S#883h**. Ge 16:14. 25:11.

south. Ge 12:9.

63 to meditate. *or*, to pray. Jsh 1:8. Ps 1:2. 55:17. 77:11, 12. 119:15, 97, 148. 143:5, 6.

lifted. Ge +22:13.

behold. Ge +3:22.

64 lifted. Ge +22:13.

lighted. Jsh 15:18. Jg 1:14.

65 a vail. Ge 20:16. 38:14. SS 1:7mg. 4:1, 3. 6:7. 1 C 11:5, 6, 10. 1 T 2:9.

66 the servant. Mk 6:30.

67 his mother. Ge 18:6, 9, 10. SS 8:2. Is 54:1-5.

Sarah's tent. Ge 31:33.

and took. Ge 2:22-24. 25:20. 49:31. 2 C 11:1, 2. Ep 5:22-33.

loved her. Ge 26:8. 29:18, 20. 34:3. Jg 16:4. Ep 5:25, 28.

comforted. ver. 63. Ge 23:2, 19. 37:35. 38:12. 2 S 13:39. 1 Th 4:13, 15.

GENESIS 25

1 A.M. cir. 2151. B.C. cir. 1853.

again. Ge +4:19. 23:1, 2. 28:1.

Keturah. i.e. *incense, perfume*, **S#6989h**. ver. 4. 1 Ch 1:32, 33.

2 A.M. cir. 2152. B.C. cir. 1852.

she bare him Zimran. i.e. *musical, psalmody; fine chamois*, **S#2175h**. 1 Ch 1:32, 33. Je 25:25, Zimri.

Jokshan. i.e. *sportsman; a fowler; difficult, their snare*, **S#3370h**. ver. 3. 1 Ch 1:32.

Medan. i.e. *strife, discernment*, **S#4091h**. 1 Ch 1:32.

Midian. i.e. *contention, strife*, **S#4080h**. Ge 36:35. 37:28, 36. Ex 2:15, 16. 3:1. 4:19. 18:1. Nu +10:29. 22:4, 7. 25:15, 18. 31:2, 3, 8, 9. Jg 6:1, 2. 7:8, 13-15, 25. 8:3, 5, 12, 22, 26, 28. 9:17. 1 K 11:18. 1 Ch 1:32, 46. Is 9:4. 10:26. 60:6. Hab 3:7.

Ishbak. i.e. *he will remain*, **S#3435h**. 1 Ch 1:32.

Shuah. i.e. *prostration, depression*, **S#7744h**. 1 Ch 1:32. Jb 2:11. 8:1.

3 A.M. cir. 2180. B.C. cir. 1824.

Sheba. 1 K +10:1.

Dedan. Ge +10:7.

Asshurim. i.e. *steps; going forward*, **S#805h**. 2 S 2:9. Ezk 27:6, 33.

Letushim. i.e. *oppressed; sharpened*, **S#3912h**.

Leummim. i.e. *nations, gatherings*, **S#3817h**.

4 A.M. cir. 2200. B.C. cir. 1804.

Ephah. i.e. *darkness, obscurity*, **S#5891h**. 1 Ch 1:33. 2:46, 47. Is 60:6.

Epher. i.e. *young deer or calf*, **S#6081h**.

Hanoch. i.e. *dedicated*, **S#2585h**. Ge 46:9. Ex 6:14. Nu 26:5. 1 Ch 1:33, Henoch.

Abidah. i.e. *father of knowledge*, S#28h. 1 Ch 1:33.

Eldaah. i.e. *whom God called*, S#420h. 1 Ch 1:33.

5 A.M. cir. 2175. B.C. cir. 1829.
gave. Ge 21:10-12. 24:36. Jg 11:2. Ps 68:18. Mt 11:27. 28:18. Jn 3:35. 17:2. Ro 8:17, 32. 9:7-9. Ga 3:29. 4:28, 30. He 1:2.

6 **concubines**. ver. 1. Ge 30:4, 9. 32:22. Jg 19:1, 2, 4. 1 Ch +2:48.
had. Ge +4:19.
gifts. Ps 17:14, 15. Mt 5:45. Lk 11:11-13. Ac 14:17.
sent. Ge 21:14.
east country. Ge +29:1.

7 A.M. 2183. B.C. 1821.
years. Ge 12:4.

8 **gave up**. ver. 17. Ge 49:33. Jb 3:11. 10:18. 11:20. 13:19. 14:10. Je 15:9. La 1:19. Mt 27:50. Ac 5:5, 10. 7:59. 12:23.
good. Ge 15:15. 35:28, 29. 47:8, 9. Jg 8:32. Pr 9:11. 20:29. Je 6:11. He 12:23.
old man. Ge 43:27. 44:20. Jg 19:16, 17, 20, 22. 1 S 4:18. Lk 1:18.
and full. Ge 35:29. Ex +23:26.
gathered. ver. 17. Ge 15:15. 35:29. 49:29, 33. 50:13. Nu 20:24. 27:13. 31:2. Dt 32:49, 50. Jg 2:10. 2 Ch 34:28. Ac 13:36.

9 **Isaac**. Ge 21:9, 10. 35:29.
in the cave. Ge +49:29.

10 **The field**. Ge 23:16.
there. ver. 8. Ge 49:31. 1 K 2:10. 16:28. 2 K 21:18.

11 **after**. Ge 12:2. 17:19. 22:17. 50:24.
La-hai-roi. Ge 16:14. 24:62.

12 **Now these**. Ge 16:10-15. 17:20. 21:13. Ps 83:6.

13 **the names**. 1 Ch 1:29-31. 5:19, 20.
Nebajoth. i.e. *heights*, S#5032h. Ge 28:9. 36:3. 1 Ch 1:29. Is 60:7.
Kedar. i.e. *darkness; dark skinned*, 1 Ch 1:29. Ps 120:5. SS 1:5. Is 21:16, 17. 42:11. 60:7. Je 2:10. 49:28. Ezk 27:21.
Adbeel. i.e. *disciplined of God*, S#110h. 1 Ch 1:29.
Mibsam. i.e. *fragrant, sweet odor*, S#4017h. 1 Ch 1:29. 4:25.

14 **Mishma**. i.e. *a report, a hearing*, S#4927h.
Dumah. i.e. *silence*, S#1746h. Jsh 15:52. 1 Ch 1:30. Is 21:11.
Massa. i.e. *gift; burden, a prophecy; enduring*, S#4854h. 1 Ch 1:30.

15 **Hadar**. *or*, Hadad. 1 Ch 1:30.
Tema. i.e. *south desert; southerner*, S#8485h. 1 Ch 1:30. Jb 2:11. 6:19. Is 21:14. Je 25:23.
Jetur. i.e. *an enclosure; defence*, S#3195h. 1 Ch 1:31. 5:19. Compare Lk 3:1, Ituraea.
Naphish. i.e. *refreshed; recreation; taking breath*, S#5305h. 1 Ch 1:31. 5:19.
Kedemah. i.e. *eastward*, S#6929h. 1 Ch 1:31.

16 **towns**. or, villages. Is 42:11.
castles. or, encampments. Nu 31:10. Ps 83:6. 1 Ch 6:54. Ne 8:16.
twelve. Ge 17:20, 23.
nations. Nu 25:15. Ps 117:1.

17 A.M. 2231. B.C. 1773.
these are. ver. 7, 8.
gave up. ver. 8. Ac 7:59.
gathered. Ge +15:15. ver. 8. Ge 15:15. 49:29, 33. Dt 32:49, 50.

18 **Havilah**. Ge +10:7. 20:1. 21:14, 21.
as thou. Ge 13:10.
toward. 2 K 23:29. Is 19:23, 24.
died. Heb. fell. Ge 14:10. 16:12. Jsh 23:4. Jg 18:1. 1 Ch 12:20. 26:14. 2 Ch 15:9. Ps 16:6. 78:64. Pr 1:14.
in the. Ge 16:12.

19 A.M. 2108. B.C. 1896.
Abraham. 1 Ch 1:32, 34. Mt 1:2. Lk 3:34. Ac 7:8.

20 A.M. 2148. B.C. 1856.
when he. Ge 22:23. 24:67.
the Syrian. i.e. *sublime, deceiving*, S#761h. Ge 24:29. 28:5. 31:20, 24. Dt 26:5. 2 K 5:20. 8:28, 29. 9:15. Lk 4:27.
Padan-aram. i.e. *table land of Aram*, S#6307h. Ge 28:2, 5, 6, 7. 31:18. 33:18. 35:9, 26. 46:15. 48:7.

21 A.M. 2167. B.C. 1837.
intreated. Ex 8:30. 10:18. Jg 13:8. 1 S 1:11, 27. Ps +50:15. Is 45:11. 58:9. +65:24. Lk 1:13.
because. Ge +11:30. 17:16-19.
and the. 1 Ch 5:20. 2 Ch 33:13. Ezr 8:23. Ps 145:19. Pr 10:24. Mt 7:7.
and Rebekah. Ro 9:10-12.

22 A.M. 2168. B.C. 1836.
struggled. Nu 20:20, 21. 2 S 8:13, 14. Ps 137:7. Jl 3:19. Ml 1:4.
If. Ge 27:46. Jg 5:29, 30. Ps 6:3. Lk 15:21. 19:42.
why am I. Hab 1:12, 13.
she went. 1 S 1:15. 2 K 4:22, 23. 22:14. Est 4:16. Lk 1:25, 38, 46. 2:36. 10:42. Ac 16:14. Ro 16:1, 12.
inquire. Ex 5:22, 23. 18:15. 28:30. 3:7. Le 24:12. Nu 9:6-8. 11:10-15, 21, 22. 15:34. 27:5, 21. Dt 17:9. Jg 1:1, 2. 6:15, 16. 13:8, 9. 18:5. 20:18, 27. 1 S 8:6. 9:9. 10:22. 14:36, 37. 16:1, 2. 22:10, 13, 15. 23:1-4, 10-12. 28:6. 30:6-8. 2 S 2:1. 5:19, 22-24. 21:1. 1 K 14:5. 20:13, 14. 22:5, 7, 8. 2 K 3:11. 8:7, 8. 22:12, 13. 1 Ch 14:14. 2 Ch 18:4, 6. 25:7, 8. 34:21. Ps +25:4. 78:34. Is 30:2. Je 21:1, 2. 37:7, 17. Ezk 14:3, 7, 8. 20:1, 3, 31. 36:37. Zc 7:1-3. Ac 1:6.

23 **Two nations**. Ge 17:16. 24:60.
two manner. ver. +22, 27. Ge 32:6. 33:3. 36:31. Nu 20:14.
the elder. Ge 27:29, 37, 40. +48:14, 18. Nu 24:18. 2 S 8:14. 1 K 22:47. 1 Ch 18:11-13. 2 Ch 25:11, 12. Ps 60:8, 9. 83:5-15. Is ch. 34.

63:1-6. Je 49:7-22. Ezk 25:12-14. ch. 35. Am
1:11, 12. 9:12. Ob 1-16. Ml 1:2-5. Ro *9:10-13*.
Col +1:15.

24 delivered. Lk 1:57. 2:6.
  twins. Ge 38:27. SS 4:2, 5. 6:6. 7:3. Jn 11:16.
  20:24. 21:2. Ac 28:11.
  womb. Ps 139:15. Ec 11:5.
25 all over. Ge 27:11, 16, 23.
  Esau. i.e. *hairy, rough*, **S#6215h**. ver. 26-34. Ge
  26:34. 27:1, 11, 16, 23, 30-38. 28:5-9. 33:9.
  35:1, 29. 36:1. Dt 2:4, 5, 8, 12, 22, 29. Jsh
  24:4. 1 Ch 1:34, 35. Je 49:8, 10. Ob 6, 9, 18,
  19, 21. Ml 1:2, 3. He 12:16, 17.
26 And after. Ge 38:28-30.
  took. Ge 27:36. Ho 12:3.
  Jacob. i.e. *supplanter*, **S#3290h**. ver. 29-34. Ge
  27:6, 18-30, 36. 28:1, 10, 12-22. 29:1, 15-30.
  30:25. 31:3. 32:9, 30. 33:10, 17, 19. 35:1, 29.
  37:3, 28. 42:1, 36. 43:11. 45:26. 46:5. 47:9.
  48:2. 49:33. 50:13. He 11:21.
  Isaac was. ver. 20.
27 a cunning. Ge +10:9.
  a plain man. Ge 6:9. 28:10, 11. 31:39-41.
  46:34. Jb 1:1, 8. 2:3. 8:20. Ps 37:37. 64:4. Pr
  29:10.
  dwelling. He 11:9.
28 loved. Ge +44:30.
  he did eat of his venison. Heb. venison was
  in his mouth. Ge 27:4, 19, 25, 31.
  Rebekah. Ge 27:6.
  loved. Ge +44:30.
29 A.M. 2199. B.C. 1805.
  and he. Jg 8:4, 5. 1 S 14:28, 31. Pr 13:25. Is
  40:30, 31.
30 with that same red pottage. Heb. with that
  red, with that red pottage. ver. 34.
  Edom. i.e. *red*. **S#123h**. Ge 32:3. 36:9, 16, 17,
  19, +21.
31 this day. Ps 122:3. Lk 22:44. Jn 1:14. Ro
  9:32. 2 C 2:17. 3:18.
  birthright. Ge 27:36. 43:33. Dt 21:16, 17. 2
  Ch 21:3.
32 at the point to die. Heb. going to die. Ge 26:1.
  and what. Jb 21:15. 22:17. 34:9. Ml 3:14.
  birthright. Ex 22:9.
33 Swear. Ge +21:23. Mk 6:23.
  this day. ver. 31. Dt +4:26.
  and he sold. Ge 27:36. 36:6, 7. He 12:16.
34 eat. Ec 8:15. Is 22:13. 1 C 15:32.
  thus Esau. Ps 106:24. Zc 11:13. Mt 22:5.
  26:15. Lk 14:18-20. Ac 13:41. Ph +3:18, 19.
  He 12:16, 17.

GENESIS 26

1 A.M. 2200. B.C. 1804.
  the first. Ge +12:10.
  And Isaac. Ge 25:11.
  Abimelech. Ge +20:2. 21:22-32.
2 appeared. Ge +12:7.

dwell. Ge 12:1. Ps 37:3.
3 Sojourn. ver. 12, 14. Ge 20:1. Ps 39:12. He
  11:9, 13-16.
  I will be. Ge 39:2, 21. Ps 32:8. 37:1-6. Is
  +43:2, 5.
  unto thee. Ge +13:15.
  oath. Mi +7:20.
4 multiply. Ge 17:4-8. 18:18.
  as the stars. Ge +15:5.
  seed shall. Ge +12:3. Ac 3:25.
5 obeyed. Ge 12:4. 17:23. +18:19. 22:16, 18. Ps
  112:1, 2. ch. 128. Mt 5:19. 7:24. 1 C 7:19.
  +15:58. Ga 5:6. He 11:8. Ja 2:21, 22.
6 Gerar. ver. 17. Ge +10:19. 20:1.
7 She is my sister. Ge 12:13. 20:2, 5, 12, 13.
  Pr 29:25. Mt 10:28. Ep 5:25. Col 3:9.
  he feared. Pr 29:25. Ec 7:20.
  fair. Ge +29:17.
8 long time. Nu +9:22.
  a window. Jg 5:28. Pr 7:6. SS 2:9.
  sporting. Ge +21:9, **S#6711h**. Ex 32:6. Jg
  16:25. Pr 5:18, 19. Ec 9:9. Is 62:5.
9 Behold. Ge +3:22.
  how. Ge 12:19.
10 What. Ge 12:18, 19. 20:9, 10.
11 toucheth. Ge 20:6. 1 Ch 16:21, 22. Jb +1:11.
  Pr 6:29.
12 sowed. Ge 8:22. 47:23. Ex 23:10, 16. Ec 11:6.
  Is 55:10. 2 C 9:10.
  received. Heb. found. Ge +6:8.
  an hundredfold. Ps 72:16. 126:5, 6. Zc 8:12.
  Mk +10:30. 2 C 9:10, 11. Ga 6:7, 8.
  blessed. ver. 3, 29. Ge 24:1, 35. 30:30. Jb
  42:12. Ps 67:6. Pr 10:22. 1 T +4:8.
13 waxed great. Ge 24:35. Ps 112:3.
  went forward. Heb. went going. Ge 12:9. Ph
  3:13.
14 had possession. Ge 13:2. Jb +1:3. Ps 112:3.
  144:13, 14.
  servants. *or*, husbandry.
  envied. 1 S 18:9. Ps +37:1.
15 wells. Heb. *beer*, Ge +16:14. ver. 18, 19, 20,
  21, 22, 25, 32.
  his father's. Ge 21:30.
  had stopped. 2 Ch 32:3.
16 Go. ver. 27. Jg 11:7. Mk 5:17. Ac 16:39.
  mightier. Ex 1:9. Ps 105:24.
17 Gerar. ver. 6. Ge +10:19. 20:1.
18 wells. ver. +15.
  stopped. 2 Ch 32:3.
  and he. Ge 21:31. Nu 32:38. Ps 16:4. Ho
  2:17. Zc 13:2.
19 well. Heb. *beer*, Ge +16:14. ver. +15.
  springing water. Heb. living. Le +14:5. Nu
  19:17. Je 51:13, 36. Zc 14:8. Jn 3:23. 4:10, 11.
  7:38. Ac 8:36.
20 did strive. Ge 21:25.
  well. ver. +15.
  Esek. i.e. Contention. or, strife. **S#6230h**, only
  here.

21 **well**. ver. +15.
Sitnah. i.e. Hatred. or, accusation. **S#7856h**, only here. Ezr 4:6.

22 **removed**. Mt 5:39. Ro 12:18. 14:19. He 12:14.
well. Heb. *beer*, Ge +16:14. ver. +15.
Rehoboth. i.e. Room.
the Lord. Ps 4:1. 18:19. 118:5.
made room. Ps 4:1.
be fruitful. Ge 17:6. 28:3. 41:52. Ex 1:7.

23 **Beer-sheba**. Ge +21:31.

24 **appeared**. Ge +17:1.
I am the. Ge +17:7.
fear not. Ps +118:6. Is 12:2.
multiply. ver. 3, 4. Ge 13:16.

25 **builded**. Ge +12:7. 35:1. Ex 17:15.
called. Ps 116:17.
well. ver. +15.

26 **Abimelech**. Ge 20:3. 21:22-32.
Ahuzzath. i.e. *possession*, **S#276h**.
Phichol. Ge 21:22, 32. Ps 34, title, note.

27 **seeing**. ver. 14, 16. Jg 11:7. Ac 7:9, 14, 27, 35. Re 3:9.
sent me. ver. 16.

28 **We saw certainly**. Heb. Seeing we saw. Ge +1:29. +2:16. +50:24, 25.
was with. Ge +28:15. 39:5. Is 60:14. 61:6, 9. He 13:5.
Let there. Ge +21:23, 31, 32. Ps 115:13.

29 **That thou wilt**. Heb. If thou shalt. Ge 21:23. 31:29, 52.
not touched. ver. 11, 14, 15. Ge 20:6. Ru 2:9. Jb +1:11. Ezk 17:10.
the blessed. ver. 12. Ge 12:2. 21:22. 22:17. 24:31. Ps 115:15.

30 **made them a feast**. Ge +19:3. Ro 12:18. He 12:14. 1 P 4:9.

31 **betimes**. Ge +21:14.
sware. Ge +21:23. 1 S 14:24. 30:15.
peace. Ro 12:18.

32 **well**. ver. +15.
We have. ver. 25. Pr 2:4, 5. 10:4. 13:4. Mt 7:7.

33 **Shebah**. i.e. *an oath*, **S#7656h**.
Beer-sheba. ver. +23.
unto this day. Ge +19:38.

34 A.M. 2208. B.C. 1796.
And Esau. Ge 36:2, 5, 13.
wife. Ge +4:19.
Judith. i.e. *praised; Jewess*, **S#3067h**, only here. Ge 28:9. +36:2, 3, 5, 14, 25.
the daughter. Nu +12:1. 1 C 7:2. He 12:16.
Beeri. i.e. *spring man; fountained; illustrious; expounder*, **S#882h**. Ge 36:24. Ho 1:1.
Bashemath. Ge 36:2.
Elon. i.e. *mighty oak*, **S#356h**. Ge 36:2. Jsh 19:43. Jg 12:11, 12.

35 **Which**. Ge 6:2. 27:46. 28:1, 2, 8.
grief of. Heb. bitterness of spirit. Put for source of much sorrow.

mind. Mk +2:8. Heb. *ruach*, spirit, **S#7307h**. Pr 29:11. Ezk 11:5. 20:32. Da 5:20. Hab 1:11. The word "spirit" is put for the soul or life in its manifestations. For other examples of this usage see Ge 45:27. Nu 14:24. Jg 8:3. 1 Ch 5:26. 2 Ch 21:16. 36:22. Ezr 1:1. Ps 76:12. 77:3, 6. Pr 1:23. 18:14. 29:11. Ec 7:9. Is 29:10. Je 51:11. Ezk 13:3. Da 2:1, 3. Hg 1:14. Ro 11:8. 1 C 2:12. For the other uses of *ruach*, see Ge +6:3.

GENESIS 27

1 A.M. 2244. B.C. 1760.
dim. Ge 48:10. 1 S 3:2. 4:15. Ec 12:3. Jn 9:3.
eldest son. Ge 25:23-25.

2 **Behold**. Ge +3:22.
I know not. Ge 48:21. 1 S 20:3. Pr 27:1. Ec 9:10. Is 38:1, 3. Mk 13:35. Lk 12:40. Ja 4:14.

3 **take, I**. Ge 10:9. 25:27, 28.
take me. Heb. hunt. ver. 33. Ge 25:27, 28. 1 C 6:12.
venison. Ge +25:28.

4 **that my**. ver. 7, 23, 25, 27. Ge 24:60. 28:3. 48:9, 15-20. 49:28. Le 9:22, 23. Dt 33:1. Jsh 14:13. 22:6. Lk 2:34. 24:51. He 11:20.
soul. Heb. *nephesh*, myself. ver. 19, 25, +31.

5 **Rebekah**. Ge 26:7. 28:5. 29:12. 35:8. 49:31. Ro 9:10.
heard. Ge +18:10.
Esau went. ver. 30.
field. Ge 25:27, 29.

6 **Jacob**. Ge 25:28.
heard. ver. 5. Ge +18:10.

7 **bring me**. ver. 4.
before the. Dt 33:1. Jg 11:11. 1 S 12:7. 23:18. 1 T +5:21.

8 **obey**. ver. 13. Ge 25:23. Lk 16:1-12. Ac 4:19. 5:29. Ep 6:1.

9 **two**. Jg 13:15. 1 S 16:20.
savoury. ver. 4.

10 **thou shalt**. Ro 3:8.
may bless thee. ver. +4, 10, 25, 31.

11 **hairy man**. ver. 23. Ge 25:25.

12 **feel**. ver. 22. Jb 12:16. 2 C 6:8.
a deceiver. ver. 36. Ge 25:27. Je +48:10. 1 Th 5:22.
and I shall. Dt 27:18. Ps 24:5, 6. Je +48:10. Ml 1:14.

13 **upon**. Ge 25:23, 33. 43:9. 1 S 14:24-28, 36-45. 2 S 14:9. Mt 27:25.

14 **mother**. ver. 4, 7, 9, 17, 31. Ge 25:28. Ps 141:4. Pr 23:2, 3. Lk 21:34.

15 **goodly**. Heb. desirable. ver. 27. Is +32:12mg. *Hag 2:7*. 1 J 2:16.
raiment. ver. 27. Ge 37:3. Ex 28:2-4. Lk 15:22. 20:46. He 12:16.

16 **skins**. ver. 22, 23. Ge 38:14. 42:7. Jsh 9:3-21. 1 S 19:13. +21:14. 28:8. 1 K 14:2. 20:38. 22:30, 34. 2 Ch 18:29. 35:22. Ezk 12:6. Mk

14:44. 16:12. Lk +4:30. +24:16.

smooth. ver. 11, 23. Ge 25:25. 2 K 1:8. Zc 13:4.

17 **savoury**. ver. 4, 9. Ex 12:8. Nu 11:5. Lk 11:42.

18 **who art**. ver. 32.

19 **I am**. ver. 21, 24, 25. Ge 3:4. 4:9. 18:15. 29:23-25. 31:35. +34:13. 37:32. 1 K 13:18. 14:2. 2 K 5:25-27. Pr 30:8. Is 28:15. Zc 13:3, 4. Mt 26:70-74. Jn 8:44. Ac 5:4, 5, 8, 10. Ep +4:25.

Esau. Ge 25:25.

that thy. ver. 4.

soul. Heb. *nephesh*, thou. ver. 4, 25, +31.

20 **Because**. Ex 20:7. Jb 13:7.

to me. Heb. before me.

21 **Come**. Ps 73:28. Is 57:19. Ja 4:8.

may feel. ver. 12.

22 **near**. Ge 45:4.

felt. ver. +12.

voice. Jn 10:4, 5, 8, 16, 27. Ro 10:17. 2 C 5:7.

23 **his hands**. ver. 16.

he blessed. Dt 21:16, 17. Ro 9:11, 12. He 11:20.

24 **I am**. 1 S 21:2, 13. 27:10. 2 S 14:5. Jb 13:7, 8. 15:5. Pr 12:19, 22. 30:8. Zc 8:16. Ro 3:7, 8. Ep 4:25. Col 3:9.

25 **my soul**. Heb. *nephesh*. ver. 4, 19, +31.

26 **Come near**. ver. 22. Ge 45:4.

kiss. Ge 48:10.

27 **kissed**. ver. 26. Ge 29:11, 13. 31:28, 55. 33:4. 45:15. 48:10. 50:1. Ex 4:27. 18:7. Ru 1:9, 14. 1 S 10:1. 20:41. 2 S 14:33. 15:5. 19:39. 20:9. 1 K 19:18, 20. Pr 27:6. Mt 26:49. Mk 14:45. Lk 7:38, 45. 15:20. 22:47, 48. Ac 20:37. Ro 16:16. 1 Th 5:26.

blessed. ver. 39. Ge +14:19. 24:60. 28:1-4. 31:55. Ex 39:43. Dt 33:1. He 11:20.

smell. Ex 30:38.

the smell of a field. SS 2:13. Ho 14:6, 7.

which. Ge 26:12. He 6:7.

28 **of the dew**. Dt +33:13. 2 S 1:21. 1 K 17:1. Ps 133:3. He 11:20.

the fatness. Or, fat places. ver. 39. Ge 45:18. 49:20. Nu 13:20. Ps 36:8. Da 11:24. Ro 11:17.

plenty. Dt 7:13. 8:7-9. Jsh 5:6. 2 Ch 2:10. Ps 65:9, 13. Jl 2:19.

corn. Here, "corn" is put for bread or food generally. For other examples of this usage see ver. 37. 42:1, 2. Dt 33:28. 2 K 18:32. Is 36:17. Ho 7:14. Ac 7:12.

wine. Here, "wine" is put for liquid beverage generally. For other examples of this usage see ver. 37. Jg 19:19. Ne 5:15. Ps 4:7. La 2:12.

29 **Let people**. Ge 9:25, 26. 22:17, 18. 1 K +4:21. Ps 2:6-9. Is 9:7. Da 2:44, 45. Re 19:16.

be lord. ver. 37. Ge +25:23, 33.

cursed. Ge +12:3. Nu 22:11, 12. Zp 2:8, 9.

30 **came**. Ge 32:6. Nu 20:18.

hunting. ver. 3-5. Ge +10:9. 21:20. Le 17:13. 1 S 26:20. Jb 10:16. 38:39. Ps 140:11. 141:9, 10. Pr 1:17. 6:5. 12:27. Ec 9:12. Je 50:17. La 3:52. Am 3:5.

31 **eat**. ver. 4.

savoury. ver. 9, +17.

thy soul. Heb. *nephesh*, thou. Used of man as exercising certain powers, or performing certain acts, often rendered by emphatic pronouns. **S#5315h**. ver. 4, 19, 25. Ex 12:16 (man). Le 2:1 (any). 4:2, 27 (one). 5:1, 2, 4, 15, 17. 6:2. 7:18, 20, 21, 27. 11:43, 44 (yourselves). 16:29, 31. 17:12, 15. 20:6, 25. 22:6. 23:27, 30, 32. Nu 5:6 (person). 15:27, 28, 30. 19:22. 29:7. 30:2, 4, 4, 5, 6, 7, 8, 9, 10, 11, 12, 13. Dt 13:6. Jg 5:21. 1 S 1:26. 17:55. 18:1, 3. 20:3, 17. 25:26. 2 S 11:11. 14:19. 2 K 2:2, 4, 6. 4:30. Est 9:31 (themselves). Jb 16:4, 4. 18:4 (himself). 31:30. 32:2 (himself). Ps 35:13. 105:18 (he). 120:6. Pr 6:32. 8:36. 11:17. 13:2. 15:32. 16:17. 19:8, 16. 20:2. 21:23. 22:5. 29:24. Ec 4:8. 6:2. Is 46:2 (themselves). 51:23. 58:3, 5. Je 3:11 (herself). 4:19. 17:21 (yourselves). 51:14 (himself). Ezk 4:14. Am 6:8 (himself). Mi 6:7. For the other uses of *nephesh*, see Ge +2:7. For the equivalent New Testament use of *psyche* to emphasize the personal pronoun in the third person, see 1 P +4:19.

bless. He 7:7.

32 **Who**. ver. 18.

I am. ver. 19.

firstborn. Ge 4:4, 5, 9-16. 17:19-21. 25:31. 48:15-20. 49:3, 4. Dt 21:17. 1 S 16:2-12. 1 K 2:15. 1 Ch 5:1, 2. 26:10.

Esau. Ge 25:25.

33 **trembled very exceedingly**. Heb. trembled with a great trembling greatly. Ge +1:29. Ru 3:8. Jb 21:6. 37:1. Ps 55:5.

taken. Heb. hunted.

thou camest. ver. 25.

yea. Ge 28:3, 4. Jn 10:10, 28, 29. Ro 5:20, 21. +11:29. Ep 1:3. He 11:20.

34 **he cried**. 1 S 30:4. Pr 1:24-28, 31. 19:3. Lk 13:24-28. He 12:17.

cry. Ge 4:10. 41:55. Ex 14:10, 15. 15:25. 17:4. +22:27. Ps 107:6. He 5:7.

35 **Thy brother**. ver. 19-23. Jb 13:7. Ml 2:10. Ro 3:7, 8. 2 C 4:7. 1 Th 4:6.

subtilty. 1 S 23:22. 2 S 13:3. 2 K 10:19. Je 9:4. Mt 26:4. Ac 13:10. 2 C 11:3.

36 **Jacob**. i.e. *a supplanter*. Ge 25:26, 31-34. 32:28. Jn 1:47.

named. Ge +11:9.

he took. Ge 25:26, 33, 34.

37 **Behold**. Ge +3:22.

I have. ver. +29.

with. ver. 28.

corn. ver. 28.

wine. ver. 28.

sustained. or, supported. ver. 28. Dt 34:9 (had laid). Ps 3:5. 51:12. 111:8. 119:116. Is 26:3 (stayed). 59:16.

38 **Hast thou**. ver. 34, 36. Ge 49:28. Pr 1:24-26. Is 32:10-12. 65:14. He 12:17.
lifted. Ge +22:13.
wept. Ge +29:11.

39 **Behold**. Ge +3:22. Ge 36:6-8. Jsh 24:4. He 11:20.
the fatness. or, of the fatness. ver. 28. Nu 20:17. Jsh 24:4.

40 **thy sword**. Ge 32:6. Mt 10:34.
serve. Ge +25:23. 1 S 14:47.
that thou. Nu 20:14, 17. 2 K 8:20-22. 2 Ch 28:17.

41 **hated**. Ge 4:2-8. 37:4, 8. Je +49:7. Ezk 35:5. 1 J 3:12-15.
The days. Ge 35:29.
mourning. Ge +23:2.
then. Ge 32:6. 2 S 13:28, 29. Ps 37:12, 13, 16. 140:4, 5. Ob 10. Ep 4:26, 27. T 1:15, 16. 3:3.

42 **Behold**. Ge +3:22.
comfort himself. Ge 37:18-20. 42:21, 22. Jb 20:12-14. Ps 64:5. Pr 2:14. 4:16, 17.

43 **obey**. ver. 8, 13. Ge 28:7. Pr 30:17. Je 35:14. Ac 5:29.
Haran. Ge +11:26. 24:4.

44 **a few days**. Ge 31:38, 41.
until. Pr 18:19. 20:3. 22:24. 29:22.

45 **then I**. Pr 19:21. La 3:37. Ja 4:13-15.
why. Ge 4:8-16. 9:5, 6. 2 S 14:6, 7. Ac 28:4.
both. Jacob by Esau's hand, and Esau by the avenger of blood, Ge +9:6.

46 **I am**. Nu 11:15. 1 K 19:4. Jb 3:20-22. 7:16. 14:13. Jon 4:3, 9.
because. Nu +12:1.
if Jacob. Ge 24:3.
what. Jb 6:8-11. Ps 118:24. 1 C 15:58.

GENESIS 28

1 **blessed**. ver. 3, 4. Ge 27:4, 27-33. 48:15. 49:28. Dt 33:1. Jsh 22:7.
not take. Nu +12:1.

2 **Arise**. Ho 12:12.
Padan-aram. ver. 5. Ge 22:20-23. 24:10, 15-24. 25:20. 29:1. 31:18. 32:10. 35:9. 46:15.
Laban. Ge 24:29, 50.

3 **God**. Ge 17:1-6. Ex +6:3. Re 21:22.
and make. Ge 1:28. 9:1. 13:16. 22:17, 18. 24:60. 41:52. Ps 127:1, 3-5. 128.
a multitude. Heb. an assembly. Ge 49:6. Ps 22:22, 25.

4 **the blessing**. Ge 12:1-3, 7. 15:5-7. 17:6-8. 22:17, 18. Ps 72:17. Ro 4:7, 8. Ga 3:8, 14. Ep 1:3.
wherein thou art a stranger. Heb. of thy sojournings. Ge 17:8. Ps 39:12.
which. Ge +13:15. Ac +7:5. He 11:9-13.

5 **sent**. Ge 11:31.

he went. Ho 12:12.
Padan-aram. ver. 2.
Bethuel the. Ge 25:20. Dt 26:5.
Rebekah. Ge 24:15.

6 **Esau**. Ge 27:33.
Thou. ver. 1.

7 **obeyed**. Ge 27:43. Ex 20:12. Le 19:3. Pr 1:8. 30:17. Ep +6:1-3. Col 3:20.

8 **the daughters**. ver. 1. Ge 24:3. 26:34, 35.
pleased not. Heb. were evil in the eyes. Nu +22:34mg. Jg +14:3mg.

9 **Then went**. 1 S 15:23.
unto Ishmael. Ge 25:13-17. 36:3, 13, 18.
wives. Ge +4:19.
Mahalath. called also, Bashemath, Ge 36:3.
the sister. Ge 25:13.

10 **Beer-sheba**. Ge +21:31.
went toward. Ge 32:10. Ho 12:12.
Haran. Ge +11:26.

11 **took**. ver. 18. Ge 31:46. Mt 8:20. 2 C 1:5.
put them. ver. 18.

12 **he dreamed**. Ge 15:1, 12. +31:24. He 1:1.
ladder. Ge 32:1, 2. 2 Ch 16:9. Is 41:10. Jn 1:51. 2 T 4:16, 17. He 1:14.
to heaven. Ge 11:4.

13 **the Lord stood**. Ge 35:1, 6, 7. 48:3.
I am. Ge 15:1. +17:7. Mt 22:32. He 11:16.
the land. ver. +4. Ezk 37:24, 25. Ac +7:5.

14 **thy seed**. Ge +13:16. 32:12. 35:11, 12. Ac 3:25. Re 7:4, 9.
spread abroad. Heb. break forth. Ge +30:30mg, 43. Ex 1:12. Pr 3:10.
to the west. Ge 13:14. Dt 12:20. Mt 8:11.
and in thee. Ge +12:3.

15 **with thee**. ver. 20, 21. Ge 21:22. 26:3, 24, 28. 31:3. 32:9. 39:2, 3, 21. 46:4. Ex 3:12. Jsh 3:7. 2 Ch 1:1. Is 7:14. +43:2. 45:14. Je 1:19. Zc 8:23. Mt 18:20. 1 T 4:8. He +13:5.
keep. Ge 48:16. Ps 121:5-8.
bring. Ge 35:6, 7.
for I. Dt 31:6. Jsh 1:5. 1 K 8:57. Jn 10:28, 29. He +13:5, 6. Ju 1.
until. Nu 23:19. Jsh 23:14-16. Mt 24:35.

16 **awaked**. 1 K 3:15. Je 31:26.
And I. Ex 3:5. Jsh 5:15. 1 S 3:4-7. Jb 9:11.

17 **he was**. Ex 3:6. Jg 13:22. Ps 5:7. Mt 17:6. Lk 2:9. 8:35. Re 1:17.
the house. ver. 22. Ge 35:1-13. 2 Ch 5:14. Ec 5:1. 1 T 3:15. He 10:21. 1 P 4:17.

18 **rose up**. Ge +19:27.
set it. Ge 31:13, 45. 35:14, 20. Jsh 4:9, 20. 24:26, 27. 1 S 7:12. 2 S 18:18. Is 19:19.
poured. Le 8:10-12. Nu 7:1.
oil. **S#8081h**. Ge 35:14. Ex 25:6. Le 24:2. Dt 32:13. 33:24. Ja 5:14.

19 **the name**. Ge 48:3. 1 K 12:29. Ho 4:15. 12:4, 5.
Beth-el. Ge +12:8.
Luz. i.e. *almond tree*, **S#3870h**. Ge 35:6. 48:3. Jsh 16:2. 18:13. Jg 1:23, 26.

20 **vowed**. Le ch. 27. Nu 6:1-20. +30:2. Ne ch. 9, 10.
vow. Le +23:38.
If God. ver. +15. Da 3:18.
will keep. Dt 33:7, 12, 24, 25. Ps 17:5-9. 72:12-14. 84:9-12. Jn 17:15.
will give. Ge 48:15. Dt 2:7. 8:3, 4. Pr 27:23-27. 30:8, 9. Ec 2:24-26. 3:12, 13. Mt 6:11, 25-33. 1 T 6:8. He 13:5, 6.
raiment. Mt 6:28-33. 1 T 6:8. He 13:5.

21 **I come**. Jg 11:31. 2 S 19:24, 30.
then. Ex 15:2. Dt 26:17. 2 S 15:8. 2 K 5:17.

22 **pillar**. ver. 18. Le 26:1mg. Dt 16:22mg.
God's. ver. 17. Ge 12:8. 21:33. 33:20. 35:1-15.
I will. Ge 14:20. Le 27:30-33. Dt 14:22, 23.

GENESIS 29

1 **Jacob**. Ps 119:32, 60. Ec 9:7.
went on his journey. Heb. lifted up his feet.
came. Ge 22:20-23. 24:10. 25:20. 28:5-7. Ho 12:12.
people. Heb. children. 1 K 4:30.
east. Ge 10:30. 25:6. Nu 23:7. Jg 6:3, 33. 7:12. 8:10. 1 K 4:30. Jb 1:3. Is 2:6. 11:14. Je 49:28. Ezk 25:4, 10. Mt 2:1.

2 **a well**. Heb. beer, Ge +16:14. Jn 4:6, 14.
there. Ps 23:2. SS 1:6, 7. Is 49:10. Re 7:17.
a great stone. ver. 3, 8, 10. Dt 28:24. Jsh 10:27. Mt 27:60, 66. 28:2. Mk 15:46. 16:3.

3 **all**. Ps 23:2. Ps +149:9. Jn +10:16. 1 C 12:13.
well's. ver. +2.

4 **of Haran**. Ge +11:26.

5 **son of**. Ge 24:24, 29. 31:53. Here, "son" is put for "grandson," 1 K +15:10.

6 **Is he well**. Heb. there peace to him? Jg +18:15mg.

7 **Lo**. Ga 6:9, 10. Ep 5:16.
it is yet high day. Heb. yet the day is great.

8 **until**. ver. 3. Ge 34:14. 43:32.
roll. Mk 16:3. Lk 24:2.
well's. ver. +2.

9 **Rachel**. Ge 24:15. Ex 2:15, 16, 21. SS 1:7, 8.
for she kept them. Ge 24:19. 37:14 with 34:25-30. 1 S 17:14, 15. Pr 31:13. Lk 16:10-12.

10 **Jacob**. Ge 24:19, 20.
rolled. Ex 2:17. Mt 28:2. Mk 16:4.
well's. ver. +2.

11 **kissed**. ver. 13. Ge +27:27.
lifted. Ge +22:13.
and wept. Ge 21:16. +23:2. 27:38. 33:4. +42:24. Nu 14:1. Jg 2:4. Ru 1:9. 1 S 24:16. 30:4. 2 K 13:14. +20:3mg. Ps 30:5. Mk 5:38, 39. Lk 19:41. Jn 11:33-38. Ac 20:19, 31, 37. Ro 12:15. Ph +3:18. 2 T 1:4.

12 **brother**. ver. 5. Ge 13:8. 14:14-16. Here, "brother" put for nephew, see ver. 13. Ge +13:8.
and she. Ge 24:28.

13 **tidings**. Heb. hearing.
he ran. Ge +18:2. 24:29.
and. Ge +8:22.
kissed. ver. +11.
all these. Col 4:5.

14 **my bone**. ver. 12, 15. Ge 2:23. 13:8. Jg 9:2. 2 S 5:1. 19:12, 13. 1 Ch 11:1. Mi 7:5. Ep +5:30.
the space of a month. Heb. a month of days. Ge 47:8mg. Ps 90:10.

15 **brother**. ver. 12.
for nought. Dt 25:4. 1 Ch +21:24. Je 22:13. Lk 10:7. 1 C 9:4-9. Ja +5:4.
tell me. Ge 30:28. 31:7.
wages. Le 19:13. Dt +24:14. Pr +22:23. +23:11. Mal +3:5. Mt 20:1-15. Lk 3:14. 1 T 5:18.

16 **was Leah**. i.e. weary, S#3812h. ver. 17, 23, 25, 30, 31, 32. Ge 30:9-20. 31:4, 14, 33. 33:1, 2, 7. 34:1. 35:23, 26. 46:15, 18. 49:31. Ru 4:11.

17 **Rachel**. ver. +28. Mt 2:18.
beautiful. Ge 6:2. 12:11, 14. 24:16. 26:7. 39:6. 1 S 25:3. 2 S 11:2. 13:1. 14:27. 1 K 1:3, 4. Est 1:11. 2:7. Jb 42:15. Ps 144:12. Pr 6:25. 31:30.

18 **loved**. ver. 20, 30.
I will serve. Ge 31:41. 34:12. Ex 22:16, 17. 2 S 3:14. Ho 3:2. 12:12.

19 **better**. Ps 12:2. Is 6:5, 11.

20 **A.M.** 2251. B.C. 1753.
served. Ge 30:26. Ho 12:12.
seemed. He 12:2.
for the love. Ge 24:67. SS 8:6, 7. 1 C 13:7. 2 C 5:14. Ep 5:2, 25.

21 **Give me**. Mt 1:18.
my days. ver. 18, 20. Ge 31:41.
go in. Ge +4:1. 38:16. Jg 15:1.

22 **and made**. Jg 14:10-18. Ru 4:10-13. Mt 22:2-10. 25:1-10. Jn 2:1-10. Re 19:9.

23 **brought her**. ver. +15. Ge 24:65. 38:14, 15. Mi 7:5.
went in. ver. +21.

24 **Zilpah**. i.e. flippant mouth; to drop, trickle; contempt of the mouth, S#2153h. Ge 30:9, 10, 12. 35:26. 37:2. 46:18.
handmaid. Ge 16:1. 24:59.

25 **in the morning**. 1 C 3:13.
wherefore. Ge 27:35, 36. Jg 1:7. Nu 32:23. Pr 5:22. 11:31. 13:15, 21. 26:27. Mt 7:2, 12. Lk 6:38. Jn 21:17. Ga 6:7. Re 3:19.

26 **must not**. Ge 20:9. 34:7.
country. Heb. place. Mk 7:1-13.
younger before. Jg 15:2. 1 S 18:17.
firstborn. 1 S 14:49.

27 **week**. Ge 2:2, 3. 4:3. 8:10-12. Ex 16:26. Le 18:18. Jg 14:10, 12. Is 58:13. Ml 2:15. Mt 19:5. 1 T 6:10.
we will. ver. 20.

28 **fulfilled her week**. Jg 14:12.
Rachel. i.e. an ewe, S#7354h. ver. 6, 9-18. Ge 30:1, 2, 22, 25. 31:4, 14, 19, 32-34. 33:1, 2, 7.

35:16, 19-25. 46:19-22, 25. 48:7. Ru 4:11. 1 S 10:2. Je 31:15.

wife. Ge +4:19.

29 **Bilhah**. i.e. *tender; alarm; timid*, **S#1090h**. ver. 24. Ge 30:3-7. 35:22, 25. 37:2. 46:25. 1 Ch 4:29. 7:13.

30 **went in**. ver. 23. Ge +4:1.

he loved. ver. 20, 31. Dt 21:15. Pr +13:24. Ml 1:2. Mt 6:24. 10:37. Lk 14:26. Jn 12:25. Ro 9:13.

served. ver. 18. Ge 30:25, 26. 31:15, 41. 1 S 18:17-27. Ho 12:12.

31 **saw**. ver. +32. Ge 31:42. Ex 2:23-25. Ne 9:9. Ac 7:34.

was hated. ver. 30. Ge 27:41. Dt 21:15. Ml 1:3. Mt 6:24. 10:37. 16:25. Lk 14:26. Jn 12:25.

he opened. Ge +11:30. 20:18. Dt 28:4. Ru +4:13. 1 S 1:5, 20, 27. 2:5, 21. Ps +113:9. +127:3. 1 T 2:15. 4:8.

barren. Ge +11:30.

32 A.M. 2252. B.C. 1752.

Reuben. *that is*, See a son. **S#7205h**. Ge 30:14. 35:22, 23. 37:21, 22, 29. 42:22, 37. 46:8, 9. Ge 48:5. 49:3. Ex 1:2. 6:14. Nu +1:5, 20. 16:1. 26:5, +7. Dt 11:6. Jsh 15:6. 18:17. 1 Ch 2:1. 5:1, 3. Re 7:5.

looked. ver. 31. Ex 3:7. 4:31. Dt 26:7. 1 S 1:11, 20. 2 S 16:12. Ps 25:18. Ps 106:44. Lk 1:25.

33 A.M. 2253. B.C. 1751.

Because. Ge 30:6, 8, 18, 20.

Simeon. *that is*, Hearing. **S#8095h**. Ge 34:25, 30. 35:23. 42:24, 36. 43:23. 46:10. 48:5. 49:5. Ex 1:2. 6:15. Nu +1:6. Re 7:7.

34 A.M. 2254. B.C. 1750.

joined. Nu 18:2, 4. Je 50:5.

because. Ge 30:20.

was. Ge 34:25. 35:23. 46:11. 49:5-7. Ex 2:1. 32:26-29. Dt 33:8-10.

Levi. *that is*, Joined. **S#3878h**. Ge 34:25, 30. 35:23. 49:5. Ex 1:2. 6:16. Nu +1:49. 3:17. 16:1. 26:57-59. 1 Ch 6:38, 43, 47. Ezr 8:18.

35 A.M. 2255. B.C. 1749.

Judah. *that is*, Praise. Ge +35:23.

left bearing. Heb. stood from bearing. Ge 49:8. *That is*, for a time; for she had several children afterwards, Ge 30:17.

GENESIS 30

1 **When Rachel**. Ge 29:31.

Rachel envied. Nu 16:3. 1 S 1:4-8. Est 5:13. Ps +37:1.

or else I die. Ge 35:16-19. Nu 11:15, 29. *1 K 19:4. Jb 3:1-3, 11, 20-22. 5:2. 13:19. Je 20:14-18. 2 C 7:10.*

2 **anger**. Ge 31:36. Ex 32:19. Mt 5:22. Mk 3:5. Ep 4:26.

Am I. Ge 50:19. 1 S 1:5. 2:5, 6. 2 K 5:7.

withheld. Ge +11:30. Dt 7:13, 14. Ps +113:9. +127:3. Lk 1:42.

3 **Behold**. ver. 9. Ge 16:2, 3.

Bilhah. Ge +29:29.

she shall. Ge 50:23. Jb 3:12.

have children by her. Heb. be built up by her. Ge 16:2mg. Ru 4:11.

4 **to wife**. Ge 16:3. 21:10. 22:24. 25:1, 6. 33:2. 35:22. 2 S 12:11.

6 A.M. 2256. B.C. 1748.

God. Ge 29:32-35. Ps 35:24. 43:1. La 3:59.

Dan. *that is*, Judging. **S#1835h**. Ge +14:14. 35:25. 46:23. 49:16, 17. Ex 1:4. Nu +1:12. Dt 33:22. Jsh 19:47. Jg +13:2, 24, 25. 15:14-20. 18:29. 1 Ch 2:2. Ezk 27:19.

7 A.M. 2257. B.C. 1747.

Bilhah. ver. 3, 5.

8 **great wrestlings**. Heb. wrestlings of God. Ge +23:6mg.

and she. Ge 35:25. 46:24. 49:21. Dt 33:23.

Naphtali. *that is*, My wrestling. **S#5321h**. Ge 32:24, 25. 35:25. 46:24. 49:21. Ex 1:4. Nu +1:15. 1 Ch 2:2. 7:13. Ezk 48:34. Mt 4:13, Nephthalim. Re 7:6.

9 A.M. 2256. B.C. 1748.

left. ver. 17. Ge 29:35.

gave her. ver. 4. Ge 16:3.

11 **she**. Ge 35:26. 46:16. 49:19. Dt 33:20, 21.

a troop. Ge +24:44.

Gad. *that is*, A troup, or company. i.e. *the seer; fortune*, **S#1410h**. Ge 35:26. 46:16. 49:19. Ex 1:4. Nu +1:14. Dt +3:12. Jsh +11:17. 1 S +22:5. 1 Ch 5:11. Is 65:11mg. Re 7:5.

13 A.M. 2257. B.C. 1747.

Happy am I. Heb. In my happiness.

will call. Pr 31:28. SS 6:9. Lk 1:48.

and she. Dt 33:24, 25.

Asher. *that is*, Happy. **S#836h**. Ge 35:26. 46:17. 49:20. Ex 1:4. Nu +1:13. 26:46. Dt 33:24. 1 Ch 2:2. 7:30, 40. Lk 2:36.

14 A.M. 2256. B.C. 1748.

wheat harvest. Ex 34:22. Jg 15:1. Ru 2:23. 1 S 6:13. 12:17. 1 Ch 21:20. Jl 1:11.

mandrakes. SS 7:13.

give me. Ge 25:30.

15 **Is it**. Nu 16:9, 10, 13. Is 7:13. Ezk 16:47. 34:18. 1 C 4:3.

Therefore. Ge 19:31-36. 38:16. Ezk 16:33. Ho 2:5. 8:9. 9:1.

16 **come in**. Ge +15:15. Ge 29:21, 30.

mandrakes. ver. 14.

And he. 1 C 7:3-5. 1 P 3:7.

lay. Ge 19:33, 34, 35. 34:2. 35:22. He 13:4.

17 A.M. 2257. B.C. 1747.

God hearkened. ver. 6, 22. Ge +29:31. Ex 3:7. 1 S 1:20, 26, 27. Lk 1:13.

18 **and she**. Dt 33:18. 1 Ch 12:32.

Issachar. *that is*, A hire. i.e. *he brings reward or wages*, **S#3485h**. Ge 35:23. 46:13. 49:14. Ex 1:3. Nu +1:29. 1 Ch 2:1. 7:1.

20 A.M. cir. 2258. B.C. cir. 1746.
good dowry. Ge 34:12. Ex 22:16-17. 1 S
18:25. Ru 4:3-9.
now will. ver. 15. Ge 29:34.
and she. Jg 4:10. 5:14. Ps 68:27.
Zebulun. *that is,* Dwelling. **S#2074h**. Ge 35:23.
46:14. 49:13. Ex 1:3. Nu +1:9. 1 Ch 2:1. Mt
4:13.

21 A.M. cir. 2259. B.C. 1745.
Dinah. *that is,* Judgment. i.e. *avenged,* **S#1783h**.
Ge 34:1, 3, 5, 13, 25, 26. 46:15.

22 **remembered**. Ge +8:1. 21:1.
opened. ver. 2. Ge +29:31.

23 **taken away**. Ge +3:15. +11:30. 12:3. +29:31.
Ru +4:13. Lk +1:25.

24 **And she**. Ge 49:22-26. Dt 33:13-17. Ezk
37:16. Ac 7:9-15. He 11:21, 22. Re 7:8.
Joseph. *that is,* Adding. **S#3130h**. ver. 25. Ge
33:2, 7. 35:24. 37:2, 28. 39:1, 2. 40:3, 4.
41:25. 42:6-9. 43:15-17. 44:2, 4, 15. 45:1.
46:4, 29-31. 47:1, 5, 7. 48:1-3. 50:1, 26. Ex
1:5, 6, 8. 13:19. 27:1. 32:33. 34:23. 36:12. Dt
27:12. Jsh 14:4. 16:1, 4. 17:1, 2, 14, 16.
24:32. 1 Ch 2:2. Ps 105:17. Jn 4:5. Ac 7:9, 13,
14, 18. He 11:21, 22.
another son. Ge 35:17, 18.

25 **Send me away**. Ge 24:54, 56.
mine. Ge 18:33. 31:55.
and to. Ge 24:6, 7. 26:3. 27:44, 45. 28:13, 15.
31:13. Ac 7:4, 5. He 11:9, 15, 16.

26 **my wives**. Ge +4:19. 29:19, 20, 30. 31:26,
31, 41. Ho 12:12.
for thou. ver. 29, 30. Ge 31:6, 38-40.

27 **favor**. Ge 18:3. 33:15. 34:11. 47:25. Ex 3:21.
Ru 2:13. Ne 2:5. Da 1:9. Ac 7:10.
learned. Ge 44:15. Nu 23:23. 24:1. 1 K
20:33. Da 4:34, 36, 37. 2 C 5:7.
experience. or, divination. Ge 3:1. Dt
+18:10.
the Lord. ver. 30. Ge 12:3. 39:2-5, 21-23. Ps
1:3. Is 61:9.
for thy. ver. 30. Ge 26:24, 28. 39:3, 23.
41:38, 39. 1 S 18:28. 1 K 3:28. Zc 8:23. Mt
5:16.

28 **wages**. ver. 32. Ge +29:15, 19. 31:7, 41.

29 **Thou knowest**. Ge 31:6, 38-40. Mt 24:45.
Ep 6:5-8. Col 3:22-25. T 2:9, 10. 1 P 2:15, 18.

30 **increased**. Heb. broken forth. ver. 43. 1 Ch
+13:2mg.
and the Lord. ver. +27.
since my coming. Heb. at my foot. 2 K
+3:9mg.
when. 2 C 12:14. 1 T 5:8.

31 **Thou shalt**. 2 S 21:4-6. Ps 118:8. He 13:5.
not give. 2 S 24:24.

32 **of such**. ver. 35. Ge 31:8, 10, 12.

33 **righteousness**. Ge 31:37. 1 S 26:23. 2 S
22:21. Jb 6:29. Ps 37:6.
answer. Is 59:12.
in time to come. Heb. tomorrow. Jsh +4:6.

34 **I would**. Nu 22:29. 1 C 7:7. 14:5. Ga 5:12. Re
3:15.

35 **the hand**. Ge 31:9.

36 **three days**.' Ge +22:4. 31:22. 40:13. Ex 3:18.
8:27. 13:17, 18. 1 C +15:4.
betwixt. Pr 14:7. Mt +15:14.

37 **Jacob**. Ge 31:9-13.
green poplar. Ho 4:13.
hazel. or, almond. Nu 17:8. Ec 12:5. Je 1:11.
chestnut. Ezk 31:8.
pilled. Heb. peeled a peeling.
rods. ver. 41. Nu 21:18. Zc 11:7.

38 **gutters**. ver. 41.
watering troughs. Ge 24:20. Ex 2:16.
conceive. ver. 41. Je 2:24.

39 **brought forth**. Ge 31:9-12, 38, 40, 42. Ex
12:35, 36. Je 27:5, 6.

40 **brown**. ver. 32.

41 **stronger**. Jb 39:4.
conceive. ver. +38.
gutters. ver. 38. Ex 2:16.
rods. ver. +37.

42 **stronger**. Ge 31:1, 9, 16, 43. 32:5.

43 **increased**. ver. 30. Ge 13:2. 24:35. 26:13, 14.
28:15. 31:7, 8, 42. 32:10. 33:11. 36:7. Ec 2:7.
Ezk 39:10.
exceedingly. Heb. greatly, greatly. Ge +6:17.
camels. Ge 12:16. 24:10.

GENESIS 31

1 **Jacob**. ver. 8, 9. Jb 31:31. Ps 17:14. 64:3, 4.
120:3-5. Pr 14:30. 27:4. Ec 4:4. Ezk 16:44. 1 T
6:4. T 3:3.
glory. Glory is here used for wealth, riches,
or property; since those who possess riches,
generally make them the subject of glory. The
original word *cavod,* signifies both glory and
weight. Ge 45:13. Est 5:11. Jb 31:24, 25. Ps
49:16, 17. Is 5:14. 10:3. 60:5mg. +63:15.
66:12. Je 9:23. Mt 4:8. 1 P 1:24.

2 **countenance**. Ge 4:5. Dt 28:54. 1 S 18:9-11.
Da 3:19.
it was. Ge 30:27.
as before. Heb. as yesterday and the day
before. ver. 5. 2 S +3:17mg.

3 **Return**. Ge 28:15, 20, 21, etc. 32:9. 35:1.
50:24. Ps 46:1. 50:15. 90:15.
land. ver. 13, 18. Ge 13:15. 28:13. 30:25.
with thee. Ge +28:15.

5 **I see**. ver. 2, 3.
the God. ver. 3, 13, 42, 53. Ge 32:9. 48:15.
50:17.

6 **with all**. ver. 38-42. Ge 30:29. Ep 6:5-8. Col
3:22-25. T 2:9, 10. 1 P 2:18.

7 **deceived**. Or, mocked. Ge 29:25. 34:13. Ex
8:29. Le 6:2. 19:15, 35, 36. Am 8:5.
changed. ver. 41. Ge +29:15. Le +19:13. Pr
+22:23. +23:11. Mt 20:1-15. Ja +5:4.
ten times. ver. 41. Le 26:26. Nu 14:22. Ne

4:12. Jb 19:3. Zc 8:23. Mt 18:21.
God. ver. 29, 52. Ge +20:6. Jb 1:10. Ps 37:28.
84:11. 105:14, 15. Ec 8:12. Is 54:17. 1 P
3:13.
suffered. Ex +4:21. 5:22. Ps 16:10. Je 4:10.
Ezk 14:9. 20:25. Am +3:6. Mt 6:13. 11:25.
13:11. Ro 9:18. 11:7, 8. 2 Th 2:11.

8 The speckled. Ge 30:32.
9 God hath. ver. 1, 16. Est 8:1, 2. Ps 50:10. Pr
13:22. Mt 20:15.
10 lifted. Ge +22:13.
a dream. ver. +24. Ge 20:6. 28:12. Dt 13:1.
rams. *or*, he-goats.
ringstraked. Ge 30:39.
11 the angel. ver. 5, 13. Ge +16:10. 18:1, 17.
48:15, 16.
Here am I. Ge 22:1. Ex 3:4. 1 S 3:4, 6, 8, 16.
Is 58:9.
12 Lift up. Ge +22:13. Ge 30:37-43.
I have seen. ver. 42. Ex 3:7, 9. Le 19:13. Dt
24:15. Ps 12:5. 139:3. Ec 5:8. Ac 7:34.
Ep 6:9.
13 the God. Ge 28:12-22. 35:7mg.
vow. Le +23:38.
return. ver. 3. Ge 32:9.
14 Rachel. Ru 4:11.
yet any. Ge 2:24. 29:24, 29.
15 strangers. Ex 2:22. Dt 23:20. Ru 2:10. Ps
69:8. Is 28:21.
sold us. ver. 41. Ge 29:15-20, 27-30. 30:26.
Ex 21:7-11. Ne 5:8.
16 which God. ver. 1, 9. Ge 30:35-43.
whatsoever. Ps 45:10.
17 upon camels. Ge 24:10, 61. 1 S 30:17.
18 for to go. Ge 27:1, 2, 41. 28:21. 35:27-29.
19 images. Heb. *teraphim*. ver. 30, 32. Ge
+30:27. 35:2. Jsh 24:2. Jg 17:4, 5. 18:14-24,
31. 1 S 15:23. 19:13, 16. 2 K 23:24mg. Ezk
+21:21mg. Ho 3:4. Zc 10:2.
20 unawares to Laban. Heb. the heart of
Laban. ver. 26mg, 27. 2 S 15:6. Lk 21:34.
21 passed. Ge 2:14. 15:18. Jsh 24:2, 3.
river. The Euphrates is called *the river* on
account of its greatness. For other examples
of this usage see Ps +72:8.
set his. Ge 46:28. Nu 24:1. 2 K 12:17. Je
50:5. Lk 9:51-53.
Gilead. ver. +23. Jsh 13:8, 9.
22 third day. Ge 30:36. Ex 14:5, etc. Jb 5:12,
13.
23 brethren. Ge 13:8. 24:27. Ex 2:11, 13.
mount Gilead. i.e. *perpetual fountain; heap of
witness*, **S#1568h**. ver. 21, 25. Ge +37:25. Dt
3:12. Jg 7:3. SS 4:1.
24 the Syrian. Ge 28:5. Dt 26:5. Ho 12:12.
dream. ver. 10, 11, 29. Ge 20:3. 28:12. 37:5.
40:5. 41:1. Nu 12:6. 22:20, 26. Jg 7:13. 1 K
3:5. Jb 4:13. 33:15-17, 25. Da 2:3. 4:5. 7:1. Mt
1:20. 2:12. 27:19.

Take heed. ver. 42. Ge 24:50. Nu 24:13. 2 S
13:22. Ps 105:14, 15. Is 37:29.
either good or bad. Heb. from good to bad.
25 pitched. Ge 12:8. 33:18. He 11:9.
26 What. ver. 36. Ge 3:13. 4:10. 12:18. 20:9, 10.
26:10. Jsh 7:19. 1 S 13:11. 14:43. 17:29. Jn
18:35.
unawares. Ge +31:20.
carried. ver. 16. Ge 2:24. 34:29. 1 S 30:2.
27 Wherefore. ver. 3-5, 20, 21, 31. Jg 6:27.
secretly. ver. +20.
steal away from me. Heb. hast stolen me.
ver. 20mg.
that I. Pr 26:23-26.
with mirth. Ge 24:59, 60. Jb 21:11-14.
tabret. Ex 15:20.
28 kiss. ver. 55. Ge +27:27.
foolishly. ver. 3, 13, 24. 1 S 13:13. 2 Ch 16:9.
1 C 2:14.
29 the power. Dt 28:32. Ne 5:5. Jb 12:6. Ps
52:1. Pr 3:27. Mi 2:1. Jn 19:10, 11.
the God. ver. 42, 53. Ge 28:13. Jsh 24:2, 3. 2
K 19:10. Da 2:47. 3:28. 6:20, 26. **S#430h**. ver.
30. Ge 1:1.
yesternight. ver. 24.
Take. Ac 5:38, 39. 9:5.
30 my gods. ver. +19. Ex +12:12. 18:11. Nu
33:4. Jg 6:31. 18:24. 1 S 5:2-7. 2 S 5:21. 1 K
18:24. 2 K 18:34. Ps +82:1. 86:8 +138:1. Is
37:19. 46:1, 2. Je 10:11. 43:12. Jn +10:35.
31 Because. ver. 26, 27. Ge 20:11. Pr 29:25.
32 whomsoever. ver. 19, 30. Ge 44:9-12. Jg
11:29-40.
before. ver. 23. Ge 13:8. 19:7. 30:33. 1 S
12:3-5. 2 C 8:20, 21. 12:17-19.
For Jacob. 1 S 14:24-29. 1 C 13:5.
33 Leah's. Ge 24:28, 67.
34 had taken. ver. 17, 19.
furniture. Is 66:20.
searched. Heb. felt.
35 my lord. Heb. the eyes of my lord. Ge 18:12.
45:5mg. Ex +20:12. Le 19:3. Ep +6:1. 1 P
2:18. 3:6.
rise up. Le 19:32. 1 K 2:19.
custom. Ge 18:11. Le 15:19.
36 was wroth. Ge 30:2. 34:7. 49:7. Nu 16:15. 2
K 5:11. 13:19. Pr 28:1. Mk 3:5. Ep 4:26. Ja
1:19, 20.
pursued. 1 S 17:53.
37 set it here. ver. 32. Jsh 7:23. 1 S 12:3, 4. Mt
18:16. 1 C 6:4, 5. 1 Th 2:10. He 13:18. 1 P
2:12. 3:16.
38 twenty. ver. 41.
ewes. Ge 30:27, 30. Ex 23:26. Dt 28:4.
the rams. Ezk 34:2-4.
39 torn of. Ex 22:10, 31. Le 22:8. 1 S 17:34, 35.
Jn 10:12, 13.
I bare. Ex 22:10-13.
or stolen. Ex 22:12. Lk 2:8.

40 **in the day.** Ex 2:19-22. 3:1. Ps 78:70, 71.
Ho 12:12. Lk 2:8. Jn 21:15-17. He 13:7. 1 P
5:2-4.
frost by night. Je 36:30.

41 **fourteen.** ver. 38. Ge 29:18-30. 30:33-40. 1 C
15:10. 2 C 11:26.
ten times. ver. +7.

42 **Except.** ver. 24, 29. Ps 124:1-3.
the fear. ver. 53. Ge 27:33. Ps 53:5. 76:11,
12. 124:1. Pr 1:26, 27. 3:25. Is 8:13. 2 C 5:11.
hath seen. ver. +12. Ge 11:5. 16:11, 13.
29:32. Ex 3:7. 1 Ch 12:17. Ps 31:7.
rebuked. Ju 9.

43 **cattle.** ver. 1. Ge 30:32, 42.
do. Ge 22:12. 27:45. Ex 14:11.

44 **let us.** Ge 15:18. +21:23.
a witness. ver. 48, 52. Ge +21:30. Dt 31:19,
21, 26.

45 **stone.** Ge 28:18-22.

46 **brethren.** ver. 23, 32, 37, 54.
Gather. Jsh 4:5-9, 20-24. 7:26. 2 S 18:17. Ec
3:5.
an heap. Jsh 4:5. Jg 2:1. 3:19. 20. 1 S 7:16.
10:8, 17. 11:15. 13:7. 15:33. 2 S 19:15, 40. 2
K 2:1.

47 **Jegar-sahadutha.** Chald. *that is,* the heap of
witness. **S#3026h.**
Galeed. Heb. *that is,* the heap of witness.
S#1567h. ver. 48. Ps 108:8. He 12:1.

48 **This heap.** Jsh 24:27.
Galeed. *or,* Gilead. ver. 23. Dt 2:36. 3:16. Jsh
13:8, 9.

49 **Mizpah.** i.e. *a beacon,* or *watch-tower,* **S#4708h.**
Jsh +13:26. +15:38, Mizpeh. Jg 11:29. 1 K
15:22. 2 K 25:23, 25. 2 Ch 20:24. Je 40:6, 8,
10, 12, 13. 41:1, 3, 14. Ho 5:1.
watch between. 1 S 12:22-24. 20:42. 2 Ch
16:9. Jb 31:4. 34:21. Pr 5:21. 15:3. Je 16:17.
32:19. Ho 7:2.
when we. Nu 6:24-26. Ac 20:32-38.
2 C 13:11. Ph 1:4, 5. 2 T 1:3, 4. He 13:18-21.
absent. Ge +21:6.

50 **afflict.** Le 18:18. Mt 19:5, 6.
God is witness. Jg 11:10. 1 S 12:5. Je 29:23.
+42:5. Mi 1:2. Ml 2:14. 3:5. 1 Th 2:5.

51 **I have cast.** ver. 45.

52 **heap.** ver. 44, 45, 48.

53 **God of Abraham.** Ge 11:24-29, 31. +17:7.
22:20-24. 24:3, 4.
their father. Jsh 24:2.
judge. Ge 16:5.
sware. Ge +21:23.
fear. ver. +42. Dt 6:13.

54 **offered sacrifice.** *or,* killed beasts. Ge +6:5.
Jg 20:42. 1 S 15:29. Jb 5:16. 31:21. 32:7. Pr
23:21. Ro 8:19. Ph 1:16.
did eat. Ge +19:3. Ex +18:12.

55 **rose.** Ge +21:14.
and kissed. ver. 28. Ge +27:27.

blessed. Ge 24:60. 28:1. Nu 23:5, 8, 11. Dt
23:5. Pr 16:7.
returned. Ge 18:33. 30:25. Nu 24:25.

GENESIS 32

1 **angels.** Ps 91:11. 1 C 3:22. Ep 3:10. He 1:14.

2 **God's.** 2 K 6:17. Ps 34:7. +103:21. Da 10:20.
the name. Jsh 21:38. 2 S 2:8, 12. 17:24, 26,
27. 1 K 2:8. 4:14.
Mahanaim. i.e. *two hosts,* or *camps.* **S#4266h.**
Jsh 13:26, 30. 21:38. 2 S 2:8, 12, 29. 17:24,
27. 19:32. 1 K 2:8. +4:14. 1 Ch 6:80. SS 6:13.

3 **sent.** Ml 3:1. Lk 9:52. 14:31, 32.
Seir. Ge +14:6.
country. Heb. field.
Edom. Ge +25:30.

4 **my lord.** ver. 5, 18. Ge 4:7. 23:6. 27:29, 37.
33:8. Ex 32:22. 1 S 26:17. Pr 6:3. 15:1. Lk
14:11. 1 P 3:6.
servant. 1 K 20:32. Ec 10:4.

5 **have oxen.** Ge 30:43. 31:1, 16. 33:11. Jb
6:22.
may find. Ge 33:8, 15. 47:25. Ru 2:2. 1 S
1:18. 2 S 16:4.

6 **and four.** ver. 8, 11. Ge 27:40, 41. 33:1. Am
5:19.

7 **greatly.** Ex 14:10. Ps 18:4, 5. 31:13. 55:4, 5.
61:2. 142:4. Mt 8:26. Jn 16:33. Ac 14:22. 2 C
1:4, 8-10. 2 T 3:12.
distressed. Ne +9:37.
and he. Ps 112:5. Pr 2:11. Is 28:26. Mt 10:16.

8 **If Esau come.** Ge 33:1-3. Pr +22:3. Mt 10:16.

9 **Jacob.** 1 S 30:6. 2 Ch 20:6, 12. 32:20. Ps
34:4-6. +50:15. 91:15. Ph 4:6, 7.
O God. Ge +17:7.
the Lord. Ge 31:3, 13.

10 **not worthy of the least of all.** Heb. less
than all. Ge 18:27. 2 S 7:18. Jb 42:5, 6. Ps
16:2. Is 6:5. 63:7. Da 9:8, 9. Lk 5:8. 17:10. 2 C
12:11. 1 T 1:12-15. 1 P 5:5. 1 J 1:8-10.
mercies. Ge +20:13. Ge 24:27. Ps 8:5.
truth. Ge 24:27. 28:15. Ps 61:7. 85:10. Mi
7:20.
my staff. Ge 28:10, 11. Jb 8:7. Ps 18:35.
two bands. ver. 5, 7. Ge 30:43. Dt 8:18. Jb
17:9. Ps 18:35. 84:7. Pr 4:18.

11 **Deliverer.** 1 S 12:10. 24:15. Ps 16:1. 25:20.
31:2. 43:1. 59:1, 2. 119:134. 142:6. Pr 18:19.
Da 3:17. Mt 6:13.
the mother. Dt 22:6. Ho 10:14.
with. Heb. upon.

12 **thou.** ver. 6. Ex 32:13. Nu 23:19. 1 S 15:29. 2
S 7:25. 1 K 8:25. Ps 119:58. Is 43:26. Mt
24:35. 2 T 2:13. T 1:2. He 6:17. 10:23.
I will. Ge 28:13-15. 46:3, 4.
as the sand. Ge +22:17.

13 **which.** 1 S 25:8.
to his hand. Or, *under his hand* or power; i.e.

what Providence had put in his power or possession. 1 K 10:14. Ps 90:12.
a present. ver. 20, 21. Jg +3:15.
14 **hundred**. Ge 30:43. 31:9, 16. Dt 8:18. 1 S 25:2. Jb 1:3. 42:12.
16 **space**. ver. 20. Ge 33:8, 9. Ps 112:5. Pr 2:11. Is 28:26. Mt 10:16.
17 **Whose art**. Ge 33:3.
18 **thy servant**. ver. 4, 5.
20 **I will appease**. ver. +13. 1 S 25:17-35. Jb 42:8, 9. Pr 15:18. 16:14.
peradventure. 1 S 6:5. 1 K 20:31. Jon 3:9. 2 T 2:25.
of me. Heb. my face. Ge +3:19. Jb 42:8mg, 9mg. Pr 6:35mg.
22 **his two wives**. Ge +4:19. 30:1-24. 35:18, 22-26. 1 T 5:8.
the ford Jabbok. i.e. *emptying, pouring out, flowing*, **S#2999h**. Nu 21:24. Dt 2:37. 3:16. Jsh 12:2. Jg 11:13, 22.
23 **sent them**. Heb. caused to pass.
24 **left alone**. Ps 127:2. Ac 12:6.
wrestled. Ge 30:8. Lk 13:24. 22:44. Ro 8:26, 27. 15:30. Ep 6:12, 18. Col 2:1. 4:12. He 5:7.
man. ver. 28, 30. Ge 48:16. Is 32:2. Ho 12:3-5. 1 C 15:47.
breaking of the day. Heb. ascending of the morning. ver. 26. Ge 19:15. Ex 14:27. Jg 19:25. Ps +30:5. +46:5mg. SS 2:17.
25 **that he**. Ge 19:22. Nu 14:13, 14. Is 41:14. 45:11. Ho 12:3, 4. Mt 15:22-28. Lk 11:5-8.
touched. ver. 32. Ps 30:6, 7. Mt 26:41, 44. 2 C 12:7-9.
thigh. Ge +24:2.
26 **Let me go**. Ex 32:10. Dt 9:14. SS 7:5. Is 45:11. 64:7. Lk 24:28, 29.
I will not. SS 3:4. Ho 12:4. Mt 15:28. Lk 18:1-7. Ro 8:37. 1 C 15:58. 2 C 12:8, 9. He 5:7.
thou bless. 1 Ch 4:10. Ps 67:1, 6, 7. 115:12, 13.
27 **what**. ver. 29. Ge 27:8.
28 **Thy name**. Ge 17:5, 15. 33:20. 35:10. Nu 13:16. 2 S 12:25. 2 K 17:34. Is 62:2-4. 65:15. Jn 1:42. Re 2:17.
Israel. i.e. *a prince of God; prevailing with God*, **S#3478h**. Ge 35:10, 10, 21, 22, 22. 37:3, 13. 42:5. 43:6, 8, 11. 45:21, 28. 46:1, 2, 5, 8, 29, 30. 47:27, 29, 31. 48:2, 8, 10, 11, 14, 20, 21. 49:2. 50:2. Ex 1:1, 7. 6:14. 32:13. Nu 26:5. Jg 18:29. 1 K 18:31, 36. 2 K 17:34. 1 Ch 1:34. 2:1. 5:1, 1, 3. 6:38. 7:29. 29:10, 18. 2 Ch 30:6. Ezr 8:18.
power. ver. 24. Ho 12:3-5.
with men. Ge 25:31. 27:33-36. 31:24, 36-57. 33:4. 1 S 26:25. Pr 16:7.
prevailed. Ex 32:10. Ps 106:23. Is 1:13. Ezk 23:18.
29 **thy name**. Ex 3:13, 14.
Wherefore. ver. 27. Dt 29:29. Jg 13:16-18. Jb

11:7. Pr 30:4. Is 9:6. Lk 1:19.
blessed. ver. 26. Ge 27:28, 29. 28:3, 4, 13, 14. Ho 6:1.
30 **Jacob**. ver. 31, Penuel. Ge 28:19. Jg 8:8, 17. 1 K 12:25.
Peniel. i.e. *the face of God; divine presence*, **S#6439h**. ver. 31. Jg 8:8, 9, 17. 1 K 12:25. 1 Ch 4:4. 8:25.
I have seen. Ge 16:13. Ex 24:10, 11. 33:14, 18-23. Dt 5:24. Jg 6:22. 13:21, 22. 1 K +22:19. Jb 42:5. Is 6:5. Jn 1:18. 12:41. 14:9. 1 C 13:12. 2 C 3:18. 4:6. Ep 1:17. Col 1:15. 1 T 6:16. 2 T 1:10. He 11:27. 1 J 4:12.
face. Dt +5:4.
life. Heb. *nephesh*, soul. Ge +44:30.
preserved. or, delivered. Ge 16:13. Ex 20:19. 33:18, 20. Dt 5:25. Jg 6:22. 13:22.
31 **rose upon**. Ge 19:15, 23. Ml 4:2.
he halted. ver. 25. Ps 38:17. 2 C 12:7, 9.
thigh. Ge +24:2.
32 **eat not**. 1 S 5:5.
unto this day. Ge +19:38.

GENESIS 33

1 **lifted**. Ge +22:13.
Esau came. Ge 27:41, 42. 32:6.
And he. Ge 32:7, 16.
2 **Rachel**. Ge 29:30. 30:22-24. 37:3. Ml 3:17.
hindermost. Ge +44:30.
3 **passed**. Jn 10:4, 11, 12, 15.
bowed. Ge +18:2. Pr 6:3. Ec 10:4. Lk 14:11.
seven times. 1 S 2:5.
4 **embraced**. Ge 32:28. 43:30, 34. 45:2, 15. Ezr 7:27, 28. Ne 1:11. Jb 2:12. Ps +34:4. Pr +16:7. 21:1.
fell on. Lk +15:20.
wept. Ge +27:27.
5 **lifted**. Ge +22:13.
with. Heb. to.
children. Ge 30:2. 41:52. 48:9. Ru 4:13. 1 S 1:27. 1 Ch 28:5. Ps +127:3. Is 8:18. He 2:13.
8 **What meanest thou by all this drove**? Heb. What is all this band to thee? Ge 32:13-20.
to find. Ge 32:5. 39:5. Est 2:17.
9 **have enough**. Ge 27:39. Pr 30:15. Ec 4:8.
my brother. Ge 4:9. 27:41. Jg 20:23. Pr 16:7. Ac 9:17. 21:20. Phm 7, 16.
keep that thou hast unto thyself. Heb. be that to thee that is thine.
10 **if now**. Ge 19:19. 47:29. 50:4. Ex 33:12, 13. Ru 2:10. 1 S 20:3. Je 31:2.
present. Jg +3:15.
I have seen. Ge 32:30. 43:3. 2 S 3:13. 14:24, 28, 32. Jb 33:26. Ps 41:11. Mt 18:10. Re 22:4.
11 **my blessing**. Jsh 15:19. Jg +3:15. Ro 15:29.
and because. ver. 9. Ph 4:11, 12, 18.
enough. Heb. all things. Ro 8:31, 32. 1 C

3:21. 2 C 6:10. Ph 4:12, 18. 1 T 4:8.
urged him. 2 K 2:17. 5:16, 23. Lk 14:23.
13   **the children**. 1 Ch 22:5. Pr 12:10. Is 40:11.
Ezk 34:15, 16, 23-25. Jn 21:15-17.
14   **according as**, etc. Heb. according to the foot
of the work, etc.; and according to the foot of
the children. Dt +11:6mg.
be able. Is 40:11. Mk 4:33. Ro 15:1. 1 C 3:2.
9:19-22.
unto Seir. Ge +14:6.
15   **leave**. Heb. set, *or* place.
What needeth it? Heb. Wherefore is this?
find grace. Ge 34:11. 47:25. Ru 2:13. 1 S
25:8. 2 S 16:4.
17   **Succoth**. Jsh 13:27. Jg 8:5, 8, 16. 1 K 7:46. Ps
60:6. not Ex 12:37. 13:20.
Succoth. i.e. *Booths*. **S#5523h**. Ex 12:37. 13:20.
Nu 33:5, 6. Jsh 13:27. Jg 8:5, 6, 8, 14, 14, 15,
16. 1 K 7:46. 2 Ch 4:17. Ps 60:6. 108:7.
18   **Shalem**. i.e. *complete, perfect*, **S#8003h**. Ge
14:18. 18:21. 34:2. Ps 76:2. Jn 3:23. 4:5. Ac
7:16.
a city of Shechem. Or, rather, the city of
Shechem. i.e. *shoulder, back, ridge; diligence;
early rising, early in the morning*, **S#7927h**. Ge
12:6, Sichem. 35:4. 37:12-14. Jsh 17:7. 20:7.
21:21. 24:1, 25. Jg 8:31. 9:1-3, 6, 7, 18, 20,
23-26, 31, 34, 39, 41, 46, 47, 49, 57. 21:19. 1
K 12:1, 25. 1 Ch 6:67. 7:28. 2 Ch 10:1. Ps
60:6. 108:7. Je 41:5. Jn 4:5, Sychar. Ac 7:16,
Sychem.
Padan-aram. Ge 25:20. 28:6, 7. 35:9. 46:15.
19   **bought**. Ge 23:17-20. 49:30-32. Jsh 24:32. Jn
4:5. Ac 7:16.
Hamor. i.e. *an ass*, **S#2544h**. Ge 34:2, 4, 6, 8,
13, 18, 20, 24, 26. Jsh 24:32. Jg 9:28. Ac 7:16,
Emmor.
Shechem's. **S#7928h**. Ge 34:2, 4, 6, 8, 11, 13,
18, 20, 24, 26. Jsh 24:32. Jg 9:28.
pieces of money. Jb 42:11. *or*, lambs.
20   **altar**. Ge 8:20. 12:7, 8. 13:18. 21:33.
El-elohe-Israel. i.e. *God, the God of Israel*.
S#415h, only here. Ge 32:28. 35:7.

GENESIS 34
1   A.M. 2272. B.C. 1732.
Dinah. Ge 30:21. 46:15.
the daughters. Ge 26:34. 27:46. 28:6. 30:13.
Je 2:36. 1 T 5:13. T 2:4, 5.
2   **Shechem**. Ge +33:19.
Hivite. Ge +10:17.
saw her. Ge 6:2. 39:6, 7. Jg 14:1. 2 S 11:2. Jb
+31:1, 9. Pr 13:20. Mt 5:28.
took her. Ge 20:2.
defiled her. Heb. humbled her. Dt 21:14.
22:24, 29. Jg 19:24, 25. 20:5. 2 S 13:22. La
5:11. Ezk 22:10, 11.
3   **soul**. Ru 1:14. 1 S 18:1. Ps +84:2. Mt +11:29.
+22:37. Re +18:14. Heb. *nephesh*. **S#5315h**.

"Nephesh" is sometimes used of man manifesting feelings, affections, passions, and exercising mental faculties. In this sense also
rendered "soul" in the following passages: ver.
8. Ge 42:21. 49:6. Le +26:11, 15, 30, 43. Nu
21:4. Dt 4:9, 29. 6:5. 10:12. 11:13, 18. 13:3.
26:16. 30:2, 6, 10. Jsh 22:5. 23:14. Jg 10:16.
16:16. 1 S 1:10, 15. 18:1, 1. 20:4. 23:20. 30:6.
2 S 5:8. 1 K 2:4. 8:48. 11:37. 2 K 4:27. 23:3,
25. 1 Ch 22:19. 2 Ch 6:38. 15:12. 34:31. Jb
3:20. 7:11. 9:21. 10:1, 1. +14:22. 19:2. 21:25.
23:13. 24:12. 27:2. 30:16, 25. Ps 6:3. 11:5.
13:2. 19:7. 24:4. 25:1, 13. 31:7, 9. 33:20. 34:2.
35:9. 42:1, 2, 4, 5, 6, 11. 43:5. 44:25. 49:18.
57:1, 6. 62:1, 5. 63:1, 5, 8. 69:10. 77:2. 84:2.
86:4, 4. 88:3. 94:10. 103:1, 2, 22. 104:1, 35.
107:5, 9, 9, 26. 116:7. 119:20, 25, 28, 81, 129,
167. 123:4. 130:5, 6. 131:2. 138:3. 139:14.
143:6, 8, 11, 12. 146:1. Pr 2:10. 3:22. 13:4, 4,
19. 16:24. 19:2, 18. 21:10. 22:25. 24:14.
25:13. 29:17. Ec 2:24. 6:3. 7:28. SS 1:7. 3:1, 2,
3, 4. 5:6. 6:12. Is 1:14. 26:8, 9. 32:6. 38:15.
42:1. 55:2. 58:10, 10, 11. 61:10. 66:3. Je 4:31.
5:9, 29. 6:8, 16. 9:9. 12:7. 13:17. 14:19. 31:12,
14, 25, 25. 32:41. 50:19. La 3:17, 20, 24. Ezk
7:19. 24:21. Jon 2:7. Hab 2:4. Zc 11:8, 8. For
the other uses of *nephesh* see Ge +2:7.
kindly unto the damsel. Heb. to the heart
of the damsel. Ge 50:21mg. Jg 19:3mg. 2 S
19:7mg. 2 Ch 30:22mg. 32:6mg. Is 40:2mg.
Ho 2:14mg.
4   **Get me**. Nu +12:1. 2 S 13:13.
5   **defiled**. ver. 13, 17. Nu 19:13. 2 K 23:10. Ps
79:1. Ezk 18:6. 22:11. 23:17.
now his. Ge 30:35. 37:13, 14. 1 S 10:27.
16:11. 17:15. 2 S 13:22. Lk 15:25, 29.
held. Le 10:3. Ps 39:9.
7   **were**. Ge 46:7. 2 S 13:21.
wrought folly. Ex 19:5, 6. Ps 93:5. Pr 7:7. Is
+9:17. 1 P 2:9. Ho 2:10.
in Israel. Jg 20:6, 10.
which thing. Ge 20:9. Le 4:2, 13, 27. Ac
+15:20. 1 T 5:13. He 13:4. Ja 3:10.
8   **The soul**. ver. +3. 1 K 11:2. Ps 63:1. 84:2.
119:20.
9   **make ye marriages**. Ge 19:14. Nu +12:1.
10   **and the land**. ver. 21-23. Ge 13:9. 20:15.
42:34. 47:27.
11   **Let me find**. Ge 18:3. 33:15.
12   **dowry**. Ge 24:53. 29:18. 31:41. Ex 22:16, 17.
Dt 22:28, 29. 1 S 18:25-27. 2 S 3:14. Ho 3:2.
Mt 14:17.
13   **deceitfully**. Ge 25:27-34. +27:19. Jg 15:3. 2
S 13:23-29. Jb 13:4, 7. Ps 12:2. Pr 12:13, 18-
20. 24:28, 29. 26:24-26. Is 59:13. Mi 7:2. Mt
28:13. Ro 12:19. Ep 4:25. 1 Th 5:15.
said. 2 Ch 22:10. Ps 137:5-9.
14   **uncircumcised**. Ge 17:11. Jsh 5:2-9. 1 S
14:6. 17:26, 36. 2 S 1:20. 15:7. 1 K 21:9. Mt
2:8, 13. 23. Ro 4:11.

15 If ye. Ga 4:12.

19 because. Ge 29:20. SS 8:6. Is 62:4.
honorable. Ge 41:20. Nu 22:15. 1 S 22:14. 2
K 5:1. 1 Ch 4:9. Is 3:3-5. 5:13. 23:8, 9. Ac
13:50. 17:12.

20 the gate. Ge +14:7. 22:17. 23:10. Dt 17:5.
Ru 4:1. Jb 29:7. Pr 31:23. Am 5:10, 12, 15. Zc
8:16.

22 consent. ver. 15-17.

23 not their. Pr 1:12, 13. 23:4, 5. 28:20. Jn 2:16.
6:26, 27. Ac 19:24-26. 1 T 6:6-10.

24 went out. Ge 23:10, 18.
every male. Ge 17:23. Is 1:10-16. Mt 7:6. Ro
2:28, 29. 1 C 7:19.

25 sore. Jsh 5:6, 8.
Simeon. Ge 29:33, 34. 49:5-7.
took. Ro 12:19. 1 Th 5:15.
slew. Ge 49:6. Nu 31:7, 17. 2 Ch 32:25. Pr
4:16. 6:34, 35.

26 edge. Heb. mouth. Ex 17:13. Nu 21:24. Dt
13:15. Jsh 6:21. 2 S 2:26. 2 K 10:25mg. Is
31:8. Lk 21:24. He 11:34.

27 spoiled. Est 9:10, 16. 1 T 6:10.
they. ver. 2, 31. Ex 2:14. Jsh 7:1, 21. ver.
+13.

28 They took. Nu 31:17. Dt 8:17, 18. Jb 1:15,
16. 20:5.

29 wealth. Heb. strength. *Strength* is put for
wealth. For other examples of this usage see
Dt 8:17. Jb 31:26mg. Pr 5:10. 27:24mg. Is
60:5mg. Jl 2:22. Ro 11:25.
and spoiled. Ge 35:5.

30 Ye have. Ge 49:5-7. Jsh 7:25. 1 K 18:18. 1
Ch 2:7. Pr 11:17, 29. 15:27.
to stink. Ex 5:21. 1 S 13:4. 27:12. 2 S 10:6. 1
Ch 19:6.
Canaanites. Ge +10:18.
Perizzites. Ge +13:7. 15:20, 21.
and I being. Dt 4:27. 7:7. 26:5. 33:6. 1 Ch
16:12, 19. Ps 105:12.
and I shall. Ge 12:2, 12. 28:13, 14. 42:36. 1 S
16:2. 27:1. Ro 4:18-20.

31 Should he. ver. +13. Ge 49:7. Pr 6:34.

GENESIS 35

1 God said. Ge 22:14. Dt 32:36. Ps 46:1.
91:15.
Bethel. ver. 7. Ge +12:8. Ps 47:4. Ec 5:4-6.
Na 1:15.
when thou. Ge 16:8. 27:41-45. Ex 2:15.

2 unto his. Ge +18:19. Jsh 24:15. Ps 101:2-7.
Put away. Ps 101:2-7. Je +4:1. Ezk 20:7, 18.
37:23.
strange gods. ver. 4. Ge 31:19, 34. Ex 20:3,
4. 23:13. Dt 5:7. 6:14. 7:25. 11:28. 32:16. Jsh
23:7. 24:2, 20, 23. Jg 10:16. Ru 1:15. 1 S 7:3.
2 S 7:23. 2 K 17:29. 1 Ch 16:26. Je 5:7. 16:20.
Da 5:4. Ac 19:26. 1 C 10:7. 2 C 6:15-17. Ga
4:8.

clean. ver. 22. Ex 19:10, 14. 2 K 5:10, 12, 13.
Ps 51:2, 7. 119:9-11. Is 1:16. Ezk 18:31.
36:25. Jn 13:10, 11. 2 C 7:1. Ep 5:26. He
10:22. Ja 4:8. 1 P 2:1, 2. Ju 23.
change. Le 14:9. Nu 8:7, 21. 19:19. Zc 3:3-5.
Mt 22:11, 12. Ju 23.

3 who answered. Ge 28:12, 13. 32:7, 24. Ps
46:1. +50:15. 66:13, 14. 91:15. 103:1-5.
107:6, 8, 15. 116:1, 2, 16-18. 118:19-22. Is
30:19.
was with. Ge 28:20. 31:3, 42. Pr 3:6.
Is 43:2.

4 gave. Ac 19:18-20.
strange. ver. +2. Dt 18:10.
earrings. Ex 32:2-4. Jg 8:24-27. Is 3:20. Ho
2:12, 13.
hid them. Ex 32:20. Dt 7:5, 25. Is 2:20.
30:22.
the oak. Ge 12:6, 7. Jsh 24:25, 26. Jg 9:6.

5 terror. Ge 34:30. Ex 15:14-16. 23:27. 34:24.
Le 26:36. Dt 11:25. Jsh 2:9-11, 24. 5:1. 1 S
11:7. 14:15. 2 K 7:6, 7. 2 Ch 14:14. 17:10. Ps
14:5. Ezk 26:17. 32:23. Mi +7:17.

6 Luz. Ge 12:8. +28:19, 22. Jg 1:22-26.

7 built. ver. 1, 3. Ec 5:4, 5.
El-bethel. i.e. *the God of Bethel*. **S#416h**, only
here. Ge 28:12, 13, 19, 22. Ex 17:15. Jg 6:24.
Ezk 48:35.

8 Deborah. i.e. *bee, eloquent*, **S#1683h**.
Rebekah's. Ge 24:59.
under an oak. 1 S 31:13.
Allon-bachuth. i.e. *the oak of weeping*. **S#439h**,
only here. Jg 2:1, 5.

9 God appeared. ver. 1, 7, 11, 15. Ge +12:7.
13:14, 15. 17:1. +18:1. 21:12. 22:1, 15. 26:2,
24. 28:13. 31:3, 11-13. 32:1, 24-30. 46:2, 3.
48:3, 4. Ex 3:16. 1 K 3:5. 9:2. 2 Ch 3:1. Je
31:3. Ezk 40:3. Da 8:15. 10:5, 6, 18. Ho 12:4.
Ac 7:2. Re 1:9-20.

10 thy name shall not. Ge 17:5, 15. 32:27, 28.
1 K 18:31. 2 K 17:34.

11 God Almighty. Ex +6:3.
a nation. Ge +12:2. 18:18. 22:17. 48:4. Ex
1:7. Nu ch. 1-26. 1 S to 2 Ch.
and a company of. Is +54:1.
and kings. Ge +17:6.

12 the land. Ge +13:15. Ex 3:8. Jsh ch. 6-21 to
Ne ch. 13.
thy seed. Nu +24:17.

13 God went. Ge 11:5. 17:22. 18:33. Jg 6:21.
13:20. Lk 24:31.

14 set up. ver. 20. Ge 28:18, 19. Ex 17:15. 1 S
7:12.
drink offering. Le +23:13.

15 Bethel. Ge +12:8. 28:19.

16 a little way to come. Heb. a little piece of
ground. Ge 48:7. 2 K 5:19mg.
Ephrath. Ge +48:7.
hard labor. Ge +3:16. Is 42:14. 66:7. Je 30:6.
Ho 13:13. Mt 24:8. 1 T 2:15.

17 **midwife**. ver. 28. Ex 1:15-21. Ezk 16:4.
Fear not. Ge 30:24. 1 S 4:19-21.

18 A.M. cir. 2275. B.C. cir. 1729.
her soul. Heb. *nephesh*, Ge +44:30. Ge +25:8,
9, 17. 30:1. 1 S 4:20, 21. 1 K 17:22. 2 K 4:32-
37. Jb 14:22. 33:18, 22. Ps +16:10. +31:5.
88:3. Ec 12:7. La 2:12. Mt +10:28. Lk 12:20.
23:46. Ac 7:59. 15:26.
Ben-oni. i.e. *the son of my sorrow*. **S#1126h**, only
here. 1 Ch 4:9.
Benjamin. i.e. *the son of my right hand*. Ge
42:38. 44:20, 27-31. Ps 80:17. **S#1144h**. ver. 24.
Ge 42:4, 36. 43:14, 15, 16, 29. 45:12, 14, 22.
46:19, 21. 49:27. Ex 1:3. Nu +1:37. 1 Ch 2:2.
7:6, 10. 8:1.

19 **Rachel died**. Ge 48:7.
Ephrath. ver. +16.
Bethlehem. Jsh +19:15.

20 **the pillar**. ver. 9, 14. 1 S 10:2. 2 S 18:17, 18.
grave. Heb. *qeburah*, **S#6900h**. Ge 35:20. 47:30.
Dt 34:6. 1 S 10:2. 2 K 9:28. 21:26. 23:30. 2 Ch
26:23. Ec 6:3. Is 14:20. Je 22:19. Ezk 32:23,
24. For **S#6913h**, *qeber*, grave, buryingplace,
sepulchre, see Ge +23:4. For **S#7585h**, *sheol*, see
Ge +37:35.
unto this day. Ge +19:38.

21 **tower**. Mi 4:8. Lk 2:8.
Edar. i.e. *flock*, **S#5740h**. **S#4029h**: ver. 21. Mi
4:8. **S#5740h**: here rendered *Edar*, rendered
Eder, 1 Ch +23:23.

22 **Israel**. Ge 37:3. 45:28. 46:30. 50:2.
lay with. Ge 49:4. Le 18:8. Dt 22:30. 2 S
16:21, 22. 20:3. 1 Ch 5:1. 1 C 5:1.
Now the sons. ver. 18. Ge 29:31-35. 30:5-
24. 46:8-27. 49:1-28. Ex 1:1-5. 6:14-16. Nu
1:5-15, 20-43. 2:3-33. 7:12, etc. 13:4-15.
26:5-51, 57-62. 34:14-28. Dt 27:12, 13. 33:6-
25. Jsh ch. 13-21. Jg 5:14-18. 1 Ch 2:1, 2.
12:23-40. 27:16-22. Ezk ch. 48. Ac 7:8. Re
7:4-8. 21:14.

23 **sons of Leah**. Ge 29:32-35. 30:18-20. 33:2.
46:8-15.
Judah. i.e. *praise, celebrated*, **S#3063h**. Ge
29:35. 37:26. 38:1, 2, 6, 8, 11, 12, 15, 20, 22,
23, 24, 26. 43:3, 8, 14, 16, 18. 44:18. 46:12,
28. 49:8-10. Ex 1:2. Nu +1:27. 26:19. Dt 33:7.
Ru 4:12. 1 Ch 2:1, 3, 4, 10. 4:1, 21, 27. 5:2.
9:4. Ne 11:24. Mi 5:2. Mt 1:2, 3. He 7:14. Re
5:5.

24 **sons of Rachel**. ver. 16-18. Ge 30:22-24.
46:19-22.

25 **sons of Bilhah**. Ge +29:29. 30:4-8. 37:2.
46:23-25.

26 **And the sons**. Ge +29:24.
sons of Jacob. Ge +6:12.
in Padan-aram. Except Benjamin, ver. 18.
Ge 25:20. 28:2. 31:18.

27 **Jacob**. Ge 27:43-45. 28:5.
Mamre. Ge +13:18.
Arbah. i.e. *four sided, square*, **S#704h**. Rendered
Arba: Jsh 15:13. 21:11. Compare Kirjath-
arbah (Jsh +15:54) and Hebron
(Ex +6:18).
Hebron. Nu +13:22.

28 **hundred and fourscore**. Ge 25:7. 47:28.
50:26.

29 A.M. 2288. B.C. 1716.
Isaac. Ge 3:19. 15:15. 25:7, 8, 17. 27:1, 2.
49:33. Jb 5:26. Ec 12:5-7. He 11:13.
gathered. Ge +25:8. +49:33 with 50:13.
full of days. Ge +25:8. Ex +23:26.
his sons. Ge 23:19, 20. 25:9. 27:41. 49:31.

GENESIS 36

1 A.M. 2208. B.C. 1796.
the generations. Ge 22:17. 25:24-34. 27:35-
41. 32:3-7. Nu 20:14-21. Dt 23:7. 1 Ch 1:35.
Is 63:1. Ezk 25:12.

2 **Esau**. Ge 9:25. Nu +12:1.
wives. Ge +4:19.
Adah. *or*, Bashemath, Ge 26:34.
Aholibama. ver. 25. Ge 26:34, Judith.
Hittite. Dt +20:17.
Zibeon. i.e. *many colors, variegated*, **S#6649h**.
ver. 14, 20, 24, 29. 1 Ch 1:38, 40.
Hivite. Ge +10:17.

3 **Bashemath**. i.e. *fragrant*, **S#1315h**. ver. 3, 4,
10, 13, 17. Ge 26:34. 1 K 4:15.
Nebajoth. Ge 25:13. 28:9, Mahalath.

4 **Adah**. 1 Ch 1:35.
Eliphaz. i.e. *God of fine gold; God his strength*,
S#464h. ver. 10-12, 15, 16. 1 Ch 1:35, 36. Jb
2:11. 4:1. 15:1. 22:1. 42:7, 9.
Reuel. i.e. *friend of God*, **S#7467h**. ver. 10, 13,
17. Ex 2:18. Nu 2:14. 10:29. 1 Ch 1:35, 37.
9:8.

5 **Jeush**. i.e. *to whom God hastens; devoured; he
will gather together*, **S#3266h**. ver. 14, 18. 1 Ch
1:35. 7:10. 8:39. 23:10, 11. 2 Ch 11:19.
Jaalam. i.e. *hidden*, **S#3281h**. ver. 14, 18. 1 Ch
1:35.
Korah. i.e. *icy, ice, hail; baldness*, **S#7141h**. ver.
16. Ex 6:21, 24. Nu 16:1, 5, 6, 8, 16, 19, 24,
27, 32, 40, 49. 26:9-11. 27:3. 1 Ch 1:35. 2:43.
6:22, 37. 9:19. Ps ch. 42, 44, 45, 46, 47, 48,
49, 84, 85, 87, 88, titles. Ju 11.
in the land. ver. 6. Ge 35:29.

6 A.M. cir. 2264. B.C. cir. 1740.
persons. Heb. souls. *nephesh*, Ge +12:5. Ezk
27:13. Re 18:13.
went. Ge 13:6, 11. 17:8. 25:23. 28:4. 32:3.

7 **their riches**. Ge 13:6, 11.
the land. Ge 17:8. 28:4.

8 **mount Seir**. ver. 20. Ge +14:6. Ml 1:3.
Esau. ver. 1.

9 **the father of**. Ge 19:37.
the Edomites. Heb. Edom. **S#130h**. ver. 43. Dt
+23:7. 1 K 11:1, 17. 2 K 8:21. 1 Ch 18:12, 13.
2 Ch 21:8, 9, 10. 25:14, 19. 28:17.

10 A.M. cir. 2230. B.C. cir. 1774.
Eliphaz. ver. 3, 4. 1 Ch 1:35, etc.

11 A.M. cir. 2270. B.C. cir. 1734.
Teman. i.e. *southward, the southern country, south desert*, **S#8487h**. ver. 15, 42. Jsh 12:3mg. 13:4. 15:1. 1 Ch 1:36, 53. Jb +2:11. Je 49:7, 20. Ezk 25:13. Am 1:12. Ob 9. Hab 3:3.
Zepho. i.e. *watchtower*, **S#6825h**. ver. 15, 16. 1 Ch 1:35, 36, Zephi.
Gatam. i.e. *great fatigue; their touch; moving to laughter*, **S#1609h**. ver. 16. 1 Ch 1:36.
Kenaz. i.e. *a hunt, hunting; to chase*, **S#7073h**. ver. 15, 42. Ge 15:19. Nu 32:12. Jsh 15:17. Jg 1:13. 3:9, 11. 1 Ch 1:36, 53. 4:13, 15.

12 **Timna**. i.e. *inaccessible; restraint*, **S#8555h**. ver. 22, 40. 1 Ch 1:36, 39, 51.
Amalek. ver. 16. Ex +17:8. Dt 23:7.

13 **these are**. ver. 17. 1 Ch 1:37.
Nahath. i.e. *rest*, **S#5184h**. ver. 17. 1 Ch 1:37. 6:26. 2 Ch 31:13.
Zerah. i.e. *rising of light*, **S#2226h**. ver. 17, 33. Ge 38:30, Zarah. 46:12. Nu 26:13, 20. Jsh 7:1, 18, 24. 22:20. 1 Ch 1:37, 44. 2:4, 6. 4:24. 6:21, 41. 9:6. 2 Ch 14:9. Ne 11:24.
Mizzah. i.e. *dropping; from sprinkling*, **S#4199h**. ver. 17. 1 Ch 1:37.

14 A.M. cir. 2292. B.C. cir. 1712.
Aholibamah. ver. 2, 5, 18. 1 Ch 1:35.

15 First aristocracy of dukes, from A.M. cir. 2429, to A.M. cir. 2471; from B.C. cir. 1575, to B.C. cir. 1533.
dukes. ver. 18. 1 Ch 1:35. Pr 16:28. Je 13:21.
duke Teman. ver. 4, 11, 12. 1 Ch 1:36, 45, 51-54. Jb 2:11. 4:1. Je 49:7, 20. Ezk 25:13. Am 1:12. Ob 9. Hab +3:3.

16 **dukes**. Ex 15:15.

17 **Reuel**. ver. 4, 13. 1 Ch 1:37.

18 **Aholibamah**. ver. 5, 14. 1 Ch 1:35.

19 **who is Edom**. ver. +1.

20 A.M. cir. 2198. B.C. cir. 1806.
Seir. i.e. *shaggy; goat-like; hairy*, **S#8165h**. ver. 2, 22-30. Ge +14:6.
inhabited. Ex 23:31. Nu 32:17. Jg 1:33.
Lotan. i.e. *covering up*, **S#3877h**. ver. 22, 29. 1 Ch 1:38, 39.
Shobal. i.e. *flowing; increasing; waving*, **S#7732h**. ver. 23, 29. 1 Ch 1:38, 40. 2:50, 52. 4:1, 2.
Anah. i.e. *afflicted; answered*, **S#6034h**. ver. 2, 14, 18, 24, 25, 29. 1 Ch 1:38, 40, 41.

21 A.M. cir. 2204. B.C. cir. 1800.
Dishon. i.e. *gazelle, wild goat; a thresher*, **S#1787h**. ver. 25, 30. 1 Ch 1:38, 41.
Ezer. i.e. *union; treasure*, **S#687h**. ver. 27, 30. 1 Ch 1:38, 42.
Dishan. i.e. *antelope; a threshing*, **S#1789h**. ver. 26, 28, 30. 1 Ch 1:38, 42.
Edom. ver. 1, 8, 31, 32, 43. Ge +25:30. Ex 15:15. Nu 33:37. Jsh 15:1, 21. Jg 5:4. 11:17, 18. 1 S 14:47. 1 K 9:26. Is 11:14. Je 9:26. 25:21. 27:3. 40:11. +49:7. Am 2:1.

22 A.M. cir. 2248. B.C. cir. 1756.
Hori. i.e. *cave dweller*, **S#2753h**. ver. 20, 21, 29, 30. Ge 14:6. Nu 13:5. Dt 2:12, 22. 1 Ch 1:39.
Hemam. i.e. *exterminating; raging*, **S#1967h**, only here. 1 Ch 1:39, Homan.
Timna. ver. 12.

23 **Alvan**. i.e. *unrighteous; iniquitous one; their ascent; sublime*, **S#5935h**. 1 Ch 1:40, Alian.
Manahath. i.e. *rest*, **S#4506h**. 1 Ch 1:40. 8:6.
Ebal. i.e. *heap of barrenness; stone*, **S#5858h**. Dt 11:29. 27:4, 13. Jsh 8:30, 33. 1 Ch 1:22, 40.
Shepho. or, Shephi. i.e. *smoothness; barrenness; a naked hill*, **S#8195h**. 1 Ch 1:40.
Onam. i.e. *iniquity; strong*, **S#208h**. 1 Ch 1:40. 2:26, 28.

24 **Ajah**. i.e. *the screamer; a vulture*, **S#345h**. 2 S 3:7. 21:8, 10, 11. 1 Ch 1:40.
found. Le 19:19. Dt 2:10. 2 S 13:29. 18:9. 1 K 1:38, 44. 4:28. Zc 14:15.
mules. or, hot springs. Jsh 15:19.

25 **Dishon**. ver. 21.
Anah. ver. 2, 5, 14, 18. 1 Ch 1:41.

26 **Hemdan**. i.e. *pleasant*, **S#2533h**. 1 Ch 1:41, Amram.
Eshban. i.e. *very red; vigorous*, **S#790h**. 1 Ch 1:41.
Ithran. i.e. *exalted, very eminent; abundance*, **S#3506h**. 1 Ch 1:41. 7:37.
Cheran. i.e. *lyre; lamb*, **S#3763h**. 1 Ch 1:41.

27 **Ezer**. ver. 21. 1 Ch 1:38.
Bilhan. i.e. *tender; timid, fearful*, **S#1092h**. 1 Ch 1:42. 7:10, 10.
Zaavan. i.e. *disquieted*, **S#2190h**. 1 Ch 1:42, Zavan.
Akan. i.e. *acute; tortuous*, **S#6130h**. 1 Ch 1:42, Jakan.

28 **Uz**. Ge +10:23.
Aran. i.e. *wild goat*, **S#765h**. 1 Ch 1:42.

29 **Horites**. ver. 20, 28. 1 Ch 1:41, 42.
duke Lotan. ver. 20. 1 Ch 1:38.

30 From A.M. cir. 2093, to A.M. cir. 2429; from B.C. cir. 1911, to B.C. cir. 1575.
dukes in the. 2 K 11:19. Is 23:15. Da 7:17, 23.

31 **the kings**. Ge 17:6, 16. 25:23. Nu 20:14. 24:17, 18. Dt 17:14-20. 33:5, 29. 1 Ch 1:43-50.
before there. Ge 35:11.

32 **Dinhabah**. i.e. *judgment, concealment*, **S#1838h**. 1 Ch 1:43.

33 A.M. cir. 2135. B.C. cir. 1869.
Bozrah. i.e. *stronghold; sheepfold*, **S#1224h**. 1 Ch 1:44. Is 34:6. 63:1. Je 48:24. 49:13, 22. Am 1:12. Mi 2:12.

34 A.M. cir. 2177. B.C. cir. 1827.
Husham. i.e. *great haste*, **S#2367h**. 1 Ch 1:45, 46.
Temani. i.e. *southward*, **S#8489h**. ver. 11, 15. Jb +2:11.

35 A.M. cir. 2219. B.C. cir. 1785.

Hadad. i.e. *brave, mighty*, **S#1908h**. ver. 36. 1 K 11:14, 17, 19, 21, 21, 25. 1 Ch 1:46, 47, 50, 51.

Bedad. i.e. *solitary*, **S#911h**. 1 Ch 1:46.

Midian. Ge +25:2.

Moab. Ge +19:37.

Avith. i.e. *ruins; subverted; overturning; iniquity*, **S#5762h**. 1 Ch 1:46.

36 A.M. cir. 2261. B.C. cir. 1743.

Samlah. i.e. *peaceable; enwrapping*, **S#8072h**. ver. 37. 1 Ch 1:47, 48.

Masrekah. i.e. *vineyard*, **S#4957h**. 1 Ch 1:47.

37 A.M. cir. 2303. B.C. cir. 1701.

Rehoboth. Ge 10:11. 1 Ch 1:48.

38 A.M. cir. 2315. B.C. cir. 1659.

Baalhanan. i.e. *lord of grace; the lord is gracious*, **S#1177h**. ver. 39. 1 Ch 1:49, 50. 27:28.

Achbor. i.e. *a mouse; agility*, **S#5907h**. ver. 39. 2 K 22:12, 14. 1 Ch 1:49. 2 Ch 34:20, Abdon. Je 26:22. 36:12.

39 A.M. cir. 2387. B.C. cir. 1617.

Hadar. i.e. *honor*, **S#1924h**. 1 Ch 1:50, Hadad. After his death was an aristocracy. Ex 15:15.

Pau. i.e. *sighing*, **S#6464h**. 1 Ch 1:50, Pai.

Mehetabel. i.e. *benefited of God*, **S#4105h**. 1 Ch 1:50. Ne 6:10.

Matred. i.e. *wand of government; causing pursuit; thrusting forward; propelling*, **S#4308h**. 1 Ch 1:50.

Mezahab. i.e. *waters of gold*, **S#4314h**. 1 Ch 1:50.

40 Second aristocracy of dukes, from A.M. cir. 2471, B.C. cir. 1533; to A.M. cir. 2513, B.C. cir. 1491.

And these. ver. 31. 1 Ch 1:51-54.

dukes. ver. 15, 16. Ex 15:15. 1 Ch 1:51-54.

Timnah. i.e. *portion assigned*, **S#8555h**. ver. 12, 22. 1 Ch 1:36, 39, 51.

Alvah. *or*, Aliah. i.e. *iniquity*, **S#5933h**. 1 Ch 1:51.

Jetheth. i.e. *nail; subjugation*, **S#3509h**. 1 Ch 1:51.

41 **Aholibamah**. i.e. *tent of the high place*, **S#173h**. ver. 2, 5, 14, 18, 25. 1 Ch 1:52.

Elah. i.e. *an oak*, **S#425h**. 1 S 17:2, 19. 21:10. 1 K 16:6, 8, 13, 14. 2 K 15:30. 17:1. 18:1, 9. 1 Ch 1:52. 4:15, 15. 9:8.

Pinon. i.e. *perplexity, distraction*, **S#6373h**. 1 Ch 1:52.

42 **Mibzar**. i.e. *fortress, defence*, **S#4014h**. 1 Ch 1:53.

43 **Magdiel**. i.e. *prince of God, declaring of God, praise*, **S#4025h**. 1 Ch 1:54.

Iram. i.e. *belonging to a city; watchful*, **S#5902h**. 1 Ch 1:54.

the dukes. ver. 15, 18, 19, 30, 31. Ex 15:15. Nu 20:14.

their. ver. 7, 8. Ge 25:12. Dt 2:5.

father. Ge 25:30. 45:8. 1 Ch 4:14.

the Edomites. Heb. Edom. ver. 9.

GENESIS 37

1 A.M. 2276. B.C. 1728.

wherein his father was a stranger. Heb. of his father's sojournings. Ge 17:8. 23:4. 28:4mg. 36:7. He 11:9-16.

2 **the generations**. Ge 2:4. 5:1. 6:9. 10:1. 11:10, 27. 25:12, 19. 36:1, 9.

feeding. Jn 10:11, 14.

wives. Ge 30:4, 9. 35:22, 25, 26.

evil report. 1 S 2:22-24. Jn 3:19, 20. 7:7. 1 C 1:11. 5:1. 11:18.

3 **loved**. Jn 3:35. 13:22, 23.

more. Ge +44:30.

son. Ge 44:20-30.

a coat. ver. 23, 32. Ge 27:15. Jg 5:30. 2 S 13:18. Ps 45:13, 14. Ezk 16:16.

colors. *or*, pieces. *Kethoneth passim*, a coat made of stripes of different colored cloth.

4 **more**. Ge +44:30. Ep 6:4.

hated him. ver. 5, 11, 18-24. Ge 4:5. 27:41. 49:23. 1 S 16:12, 13. 17:28. Ps 38:19. 69:4. Jn 7:3-5. 15:18, 19, 24, 25. T 3:3. 1 J 2:11. 3:10, 12. 4:20.

5 **dreamed**. ver. 9. Ge 28:12. +31:24. 42:9. Ps 25:14. Da 2:1. 4:5. Jl 2:28. Am 3:7.

brethren. Jn 7:5.

and they. ver. 4, 8. Ge 49:23. Jn 15:24, 25. 17:14.

6 **Hear**. Ge 44:18. Jg 9:7.

7 **your sheaves**. Ge 42:6, 9. 43:26. 44:14, 19.

obeisance. Ph 2:10. Col 1:18.

8 **reign over us**. ver. 4. Ex 2:14. 1 S 10:27. 17:28. Ps 2:3-6. 118:22. Lk 19:14. 20:17. Ac 4:27, 28. 7:35. He 10:29.

9 **another dream**. ver. 7. Ge 41:25, 32.

the sun. ver. 10. Ge 43:28 44:14, 19. 45:9. 46:29. 47:12. 50:15-21. Ac 7:9-14. Re 12:1.

eleven. 2 K 23:5. Jb 38:22.

stars. Da 8:10. Ph 2:15.

obeisance. Ph 2:10. Col 1:18.

10 **Shall I**. Ge 27:29. Is 60:14. Ph 2:10, 11.

11 **envied**. Ps +37:1. Is 11:13. 26:11.

observed. Ge 24:31. Da 7:28. Lk 2:19, 51.

12 **in Shechem**. ver. 1. Ge +33:18. 34:25-31.

13 **come**. 1 S 17:17-20. Mt 10:16. Lk 20:13.

send. Lk 20:13.

Here am I. Ge 22:1. 27:1, 18. 1 S 3:4-6, 8, 16. Ps 40:7, 8. Ep 6:1-3.

14 **see whether it be well with**. Heb. see the peace of thy brethren, etc. Jg +18:15mg. 1 K 2:33. Ps 125:5. Je 29:7.

bring. Jn 17:3.

out of. Jn 17:5, 24.

vale of Hebron. Nu +13:22.

came to. Jn 4:4, 5.

15 **he was**. Ge 21:14.

wandering. Mt 13:38. Lk 9:58.

What. Jg 4:22. 2 K 6:19. Jn 1:38. 4:27. 18:4, 7. 20:15.

16 **seek**. Lk 19:10.

tell me. SS 1:7.

17 **went after**. Lk 15:4.
Dothan. i.e. *double fountain; two cisterns,*
S#1886h. 2 K 6:13.

18 **came**. Jn 1:11.
conspired. 1 S 19:1. Ps 31:13. 37:12, 32.
109:4. Mt 21:38. 27:1. Jn 11:53. Ac 23:12.

19 **dreamer**. Heb. master of dreams. ver. 5, 11.
Ge +28:12. 49:23mg.

20 **let us**. Ps 64:5. Pr 1:11, 12, 16. 6:17. 27:4. Mk
15:14. T 3:3.
pit. Heb. *bor* or *bore*, a hewn cistern, well,
dungeon, pit. Ps +30:3. Contrast **S#875h**, *be-er*,
a dug well, Ge +16:14.
Some. 1 K 13:24. 2 K 2:24. Pr 10:18. 28:13.
and we. 1 S 24:20. 26:2. Mt 2:2-16. 27:40-
42. Mk 15:14, 29-32. Jn 3:12. 12:10, 11. Ac
4:16-18.

21 **Reuben heard**. Ge 35:22. 42:22.
not kill him. Heb. *nephesh*, Jsh +10:28; Ge
+9:5. Mt +10:28.

22 **Reuben said**. Ge 42:22.
shed. Mt 27:24.
lay. Ge 22:12. Ex 24:11. Dt 13:9. Ac 12:1.

23 **stript**. ver. 3, 31-33. Ge 42:21. Ps 22:18. Mt
27:28.
colors. *or*, pieces. ver. 3mg.

24 **and cast**. Ps 35:7. Is 38:17mg. La 4:20.
the pit. Ps 40:1, 2. 69:2, 14, 15. 88:6, 8.
130:1, 2. Je 38:6. Zc 9:11.

25 **they sat**. Est 3:15. Ps 14:4. Pr 30:20. Am 6:6.
Mt 27:36.
eat. Ex +18:12.
lifted. Ge +22:13.
Ishmeelites. ver. 28, 36. Ge +16:11. 25:1-4,
16-18. 31:23. 1 Ch +27:30.
Gilead. **S#1568h**. Ge 31:21. Nu +26:29. 32:1,
26, 29, 39, 40. Dt 3:10, 13, 15, 16. 34:1. Jsh
13:11, 25, 31. 17:1, 5, 6. 21:38. 22:9, 13, 15,
32. Jg 5:17. 10:4, 8, 17, 18. 2 S 2:9. 17:26.
24:6. 1 K 17:1. 2 K 10:33. 15:29. 1 Ch 5:9, 10,
16. 26:31. Ps 60:7. 108:8. SS 6:5. Je 8:22.
22:6. 46:11. 50:19. Ezk 47:18. Ho 6:8. 12:11.
Am 1:3, 13. Ob 19. Mi 7:14. Zc 10:10.
spicery. or, gum tragacanth or storax. Ge
43:11.
balm. Ge 43:11. Je 8:22. 46:11. 51:8. Ezk
27:17.
myrrh. Ge 43:11.

26 **What profit**. Ge 25:32. Ps 30:9. Je 41:8. Mt
16:26. Ro 6:21.
conceal. ver. 20. Ge 4:10. Dt 17:8. 2 S 1:16.
Jb 16:18. Ezk 24:7.

27 **sell him**. ver. 22. Ex 21:16, 21. Ne 5:8. Mt
16:26. 26:15. 1 T 1:10. Re 18:13.
let not. 1 S 18:17. 2 S 11:14-17. 12:9.
he is our. Ge 29:14. 42:21. Jg 9:2.
were content. Heb. hearkened.

28 **Midianites**. ver. 25, 36. Ge +25:2. 39:1. Ps
83:9.

sold. Ge 45:4, 5. Ps 105:17. Zc 11:12, 13. Mt
26:15. 27:9. Ac 7:9.
twenty pieces. Ge 20:16. 33:19. 45:22. Ex
21:32. Jg 9:4. 16:5. 2 K 5:5.
brought. Mt 2:14.

29 **he rent**. ver. +34.

30 **The child is not**. ver. 20. Ge 42:13, 32, 36.
Je +31:15.

31 **Joseph's coat**. ver. 3, 23. Pr 28:13.

32 **thy son's**. ver. 3. Ge 44:20-23. Lk 15:30.

33 **evil beast**. ver. 20. Ge 44:28. 1 K 13:24. 2 K
2:24. Pr 14:15. Jn 13:7.

34 **Jacob rent**. ver. 29. 2 K +18:37.
sackcloth. Jb +16:15.

35 **his daughters**. Ge 31:43. 35:22-26.
rose up. 2 S 12:17. Jb 2:11. Ps 77:2. Je 31:15.
For I. Ge 42:38. 44:29-31. 45:28.
grave. Heb. *sheol*. Nu 16:30. Dt 32:22. Jb
11:8. 14:3. Pr 30:15, 16. Is 5:14. Hab 2:5.

36 **the Midianites**. ver. +28.
into Egypt. Mt 2:14, 15.
officer. Heb. eunuch. But the word signifies
not only *eunuchs*, but also *chamberlains,*
courtiers, and *officers*. **S#5631h**. Ge 39:1 (officer). 2 K +8:6mg. 18:17, Rabsaris.
+23:11mg. Est 1:10mg. Is 39:7. 56:3, 4. Je
29:2. Da 1:3.
captain. *Or*, chief marshal. Heb. chief of the
slaughtermen, *or* executioners. Ge ch. 39.
40:4. 1 S 9:23. 2 K 25:8mg. Je 39:9mg.

GENESIS 38

1 A.M. 2265. B.C. 1739.
And. Ge +10:5.
it came to pass. ver. 9, 24, 38.
turned. Ge 19:2, 3. Jg 4:18. 2 K 4:8. Pr 9:6.
13:20.
Adullamite. i.e. *a native of Adullam* (i.e. *hid-*
ing place, retreat; justice of the people, Jsh
+12:15), **S#5726h**. ver. 12, 20. Jsh 12:15. 15:35.
1 S 22:1. 2 S 23:13. Mi 1:15.
Hirah. i.e. *liberty; nobility, noble race,* **S#2437h**.
ver. 12.

2 **saw**. Ge 3:6. 6:2. 24:3. 34:2. Jg 14:2. 16:1. 2 S
11:2. 2 C 6:14. 1 J 2:16.
Canaanite. Ge +10:18.
Shuah. Ge 46:12. 1 Ch 2:3, Shua.
took. Ge 6:4. 24:3. 36:2. 46:10. Jg 14:2.
went in. Ge +29:30.

3 A.M. 2266. B.C. 1738.
Er. i.e. *watchful*, **S#6147h**. ver. 6, 7. Ge 46:12.
Nu 26:19. 1 Ch 2:3. 4:21.

4 A.M. 2267. B.C. 1737.
Onan. i.e. *strong; weariness, vanity, iniquity,*
S#209h. ver. 8, 9. Ge 46:12. Nu 26:19, 19. 1 Ch
2:3.

5 A.M. 2268. B.C. 1736.
Shelah. i.e. *petition, a request,* **S#7956h**. ver. 11,
14, 26. Ge 46:12. Nu 26:20, Shelanites. 1 Ch

+1:18 (**S#7974h**). 2:3. 4:21. 9:5, Shilonites. Ne 11:5, Shiloni.

Chezib. i.e. *lying, deceptive*, **S#3580h**. Jsh 15:44, Achzib.

6 **took**. Nu +12:1.

Tamar. i.e. *palm tree*, **S#8559h**. ver. 11, 13, 24. Ru 4:12. 2 S 13:1, 2, 4-8, 10, 19, 20, 22, 32. 14:27. 1 Ch 2:4. 3:9. Mt 1:3.

7 **Er**. Ge 46:12. Nu 26:19.

wicked. Ge 6:8. 13:13. 19:13. 2 Ch 33:6. Jb 34:22. Pr 15:3.

and the. ver. 10. Le 10:2. Nu 26:19. +32:23. 1 Ch 2:3. Jb 15:32. 22:16. Ps 37:22, 38. 55:23. 102:24. Pr 10:27. Ec 7:17. 12:14. Is 40:24.

8 A.M. 2282. B.C. 1722.

Go in. Le 18:16. Nu 36:8, 9. Dt 25:5-10. Ru 1:11, 4:5-11. Mt 22:23-27. Mk 12:19-23. Lk *20:28-33*.

9 **be his**. Dt 25:6. Ru 1:11. 4:10. Jb 5:2. 1 T 1:10. T 3:3.

spilled. ver. 8. Le 15:16-18. 22:4. Dt 23:10. 25:5-10. Ru 3:6-9. 4:5-11. Pr 25:26. Mt 22:24-28.

lest that. Jb 5:2. Pr 27:4. 1 T 1:10. T 3:3. Ja 3:14, 16. 4:5.

give seed. Le +15:16.

10 **displeased**. Heb. was evil in the eyes of. Nu +22:34mg. Je 44:4. Jon 4:1. Hab 1:13.

him also. ver. +7. Ge 46:12. Nu 26:19.

11 **till Shelah**. Ru 1:11, 13.

in her. Le 22:13.

12 **in process of time**. Heb. the days were multiplied. Nu +9:22.

comforted. Ge +24:67.

sheep shearers. Ge 31:19. 1 S 25:4-8, 36. 2 S 13:23-29.

Timnath. i.e. *portion assigned*, **S#8553h**. ver. 13, 14. Jsh 15:10, 35, 57, Timnah. 19:43, Thimnathah. Jg 14:1, 1, 2, 5.

13 **shear**. Ge 31:19. 1 S 25:2, 11.

Timnath. Jg 14:1.

14 **widow's garments off**. Dt 24:17 1 T 5:3-16.

covered. Ge +27:16. Pr 7:10.

vail. Ge 21:16. +24:65.

and sat. Pr 7:12. 9:14, 15. Je 3:2. Ezk 16:25.

an open place. Heb. the door of eyes, *or* of Enajim. Jn +3:23.

Timnath. ver. 12, 13.

that Shelah. ver. 11, 26. Dt 25:5. Ru 1:11. Mt 22:24.

15 **harlot**. ver. 21. Ge 34:31. Le 19:29. 21:14. Nu 25:1, 6. Dt 23:18. Jg 11:1. 16:1. 19:2, 25. 1 K 3:16. Pr 2:18, 19. Am 2:7.

because. 1 Th 5:22. 1 P 3:3-6.

covered. ver. +14.

16 **Go to**. 2 S 13:11.

What wilt. Dt 23:18. Ezk 16:33. Mt 26:15. 1 T 6:10.

17 **I will**. Ezk 16:33.

a kid. Heb. a kid of the goats.

Wilt thou. ver. 20, 24, 25. Pr 20:16. 27:13. Lk 16:8.

18 **Thy signet**. ver. 25, 26. Ge 41:42. Je 22:24. Lk 15:22.

gave it her. ver. 25, 26. Ge 39:12-20. Ho 4:11.

19 **laid by her vail**. ver. 14. 2 S 14:2, 5.

20 **his friend**. Ge 20:9. Le 19:17. Jg 14:20. 2 S 13:3. Lk 23:12.

pledge. Dt 24:10-13, 17.

21 **the harlot**. ver. 15. Dt 22:21. 23:17. 1 K 14:24. 15:12. 22:46. 2 K 23:7. Jb 36:14mg. Pr 2:16. Ho 4:14.

openly by the wayside. *or*, in Enajim. ver. 14.

23 **lest we**. 2 S 12:9. Pr 6:33. Ro 6:21. 2 C 4:2. Ep 5:12. Re 16:15.

be ashamed. Heb. become a contempt.

24 **played the harlot**. ver. 15. Ec 7:26. Je 2:20. 3:1, 6, 8. Ezk 16:15, 28, 41. 23:5, 19, 44. Ho 2:5. 3:3. 4:15.

with child. Ge 16:11. 19:30-38. Ex 21:22. Is 7:14.

let her. Ge 20:3, 7, 9. Le +21:9. Dt 22:21-27. 24:16. 2 S 12:5, 7. Je 29:22, 23. Ezk 16:40. 23:47, 48. Mt 7:1-5. Jn 8:3-11. Ro 2:1, 2. 14:22.

25 **Discern**. ver. 18. Ge 37:32. Ps 50:21. Je 2:26. Ro 2:16. 1 C 4:5. Re 20:12.

26 **acknowledged**. Ge 37:33. Nu +32:23.

She hath. 1 S 24:17. 2 S 24:17. Ezk 16:52. Hab 1:13. Jn 8:9. Ro 3:19.

more righteous. Jb 33:26, 27. Pr 11:6.

because. ver. 14. Dt 25:5. Ru 3:9-12.

And he knew. Ge +4:1. 2 S 16:22. 20:3. Jb 34:31, 32. 40:5. Mt 3:8. Jn 8:11. Ro 13:12. T 2:11, 12. 1 P 4:2, 3.

27 **twins**. Ge +25:24.

28 **travailed**. Ge +35:16.

midwife. Ge +35:17.

scarlet thread. Jsh 2:18.

29 A.M. 2283. B.C. 1721.

his brother. Ge 25:26.

How hast, etc. *or*, Wherefore hast thou made *this* breach against thee?

Pharez. i.e. *a breach*. Ge +46:12.

30 **Zarah**. Ge +36:13. Mt 1:3, Zara.

GENESIS 39

1 A.M. 2276. B.C. 1728.

Joseph. Ge 37:36. 45:4. Ps 105:17. Ac 7:9.

Potiphar. i.e. *priest of the bull; my affliction was broken*, **S#6318h**. Ge 37:36.

officer. Is 49:7.

bought. Ph 2:7.

the Ishmeelites. Ge 37:25, 28.

2 **the Lord**. ver. 21, 22. Ge 21:22. +28:15. 1 S 3:19. 16:18. 18:14, 28. Ps 1:3. 46:7, 11. 91:15. Je 15:20. Mt +28:20. Ac 7:9, 10. Ro 8:31.

with. Jn 16:32.

house. 1 C 7:20-24. 1 T 6:1. T 2:9, 10.

3 **saw that**. ver. 23. Ge 21:22. 26:24, 28.
+30:27, 30. 1 S 18:14, 28. Zc 8:23. Mt 5:16.
Ac 10:38. Ph 2:15, 16. Re 3:9.

prosper. ver. 23. Ge 30:27. Ne 2:20. Ps +1:3.
Is 44:4. 53:10. 1 C 16:2. Col 1:6.

4 **Joseph**. ver. 21. Ge 18:3. 19:19. 32:5. 33:8,
10. 1 S 16:22. Ne 2:4, 5. Pr 16:7. Lk 2:52.

overseer. ver. 22. Ge 15:2. 24:2. 41:40, 41. Pr
14:35. 17:2. 22:29. 27:18. Ac 20:28.

all. Jn 3:35.

5 **blessed**. Ep 1:3. 4:32.

for Joseph's. Ge 12:2. 19:29. 30:27. Dt 28:3-
6. 2 S 6:11, 12. Ps 21:6. 72:17. Mt 24:22. Ac
27:24. Ep 1:3. 2 Th 2:6, 7.

6 **he left**. ver. 4, 8, 23. Lk 16:10. 19:17. 2 T
1:12.

knew. Dt 33:9. Jg 2:10. Ps 37:18. Pr 29:7. Je
1:5. Am 3:2. 1 Th 5:12. 2 T 2:19.

save. Ge 43:32. Pr 31:11.

bread. Ge +3:19.

a goodly person. Ge 12:14, 15. 29:17. 1 S
16:12. 17:42. SS 5:16. Ac 7:20.

well favored. Lk 2:52.

7 A.M. 2285. B.C. 1719.

cast. Ge 6:2. Jb +31:1. Ps 119:37. Ezk 23:5, 6,
12-16. Mt 5:28. 2 P 2:14. 1 J 2:16.

Lie. 2 S 13:11. Pr 2:16. 5:9. 7:13. Je 3:3. Ezk
16:25, 32, 34.

8 **refused**. Est +1:12. Pr 1:10. 2:10, 16-19. 5:3-
8. 6:20-25, 29, 32, 33. 7:5, 25-27. 9:13-18.
22:14. 23:26-28. Is 7:15. Jn 8:46.

my master. Pr 18:24.

all. Jn 3:35.

9 **none**. Ge 24:2. Ne 6:11. Lk 12:48. 1 C 4:2. T
2:10.

how then. Ge 20:3, 6. Le 20:10. 2 S 11:27. Jb
31:9-12, 23. Pr 6:29, 32. Je 5:8, 9. 1 C +6:9,
10. Ga +5:19-21. He 13:4. Re +21:8. 22:15.

sin. Ge 42:18. Le 6:2. Nu +32:23. 2 S 12:13.
Ne 5:15. Ps 51:4. Je 28:16. 50:7. He 4:15. 1 J
3:9.

10 **as she spake**. ver. 8. Pr 2:16. 5:3. 6:25, 26.
7:5, 13. 9:14, 16. 22:14. 23:27.

or to be. Ps 1:1. Pr 1:15. 4:15. 5:8. Mt 6:13. 1
C 6:18. 10:13. 15:33. 1 Th 5:22. 2 Th 3:14. 1 T
5:14. 2 T 2:22. 1 P 2:11.

11 **none of the men**. Jb 24:15. Pr 9:17. Je
23:24. Ml 3:5. Ep 5:3, 12.

12 **caught**. ver. 8, 10, 15. Pr 7:13, etc. Ec 7:26.
Ezk 16:30, 31.

and he left. 1 S 15:27. Pr 1:15. 5:8, 6:5. Ec
7:26. Mk 14:51, 52. 1 C 15:33. 2 T 2:22. 1 P
2:11.

13 **garment in her hand**. Ge 38:25.

14 **an Hebrew**. ver. 17. Ge 10:21. 14:13. 40:15.
Ps 120:3. Ezk 22:5.

mock. Ge +21:9. +26:8.

he came. ver. 7. Ps 35:11. 55:3. Pr 10:18. Is

51:7. 54:17. Mt 5:11. 26:59. Lk 23:2. 2 C 6:8.
1 P 2:20. 3:14-18. 4:14-19.

loud. Heb. great. Dt 22:24, 27.

15 **lifted**. Ge +22:13.

his garment. ver. 12, 13.

16 **laid up**. Je 4:22. 9:3-5. 20:10.

17 **she spake**. Ge +27:19. Ex +20:16. 23:1. Dt
5:20. Ps 120:3. Pr 19:9. Is 54:17. Mt 5:11, 12.
Ja 3:8. 1 P 3:14-17.

Hebrew servant. ver. 14. Ex 20:16. 23:1. 1
K 18:17. 21:9-13. Ps 37:14. 55:3. 120:2-4. Pr
12:19. 19:5, 9. Mt 26:65.

18 **came to pass**. ver. 14. Ex 20:16. 23:1. Le
19:16. Pr 6:19. 12:22. 19:5.

19 **heard**. Jb 29:16. Pr 18:17. +29:12. Ac 25:16.
2 Th 2:11. 1 T +5:19.

his wrath. Ge 4:5, 6. 34:7. Ps 76:10. Pr 6:34,
35. SS 8:16.

20 **into the prison**. or, roundhouse. Ge 40:3, 5,
15. 41:14. Is 53:8. Da 3:21, 22. He +11:36. 1 P
2:19. 3:19.

the king's. Ge 40:1-3, 15. 41:9-14.
Ps 76:10.

bound. Ps 22:16. 105:18, 19. Mt 27:2.

21 **the Lord**. ver. 2. Ge 21:22. 49:23, 24. Ps
91:15. Is 43:2. Da 6:22. Ro 8:31, 32, 37. 1 P
3:13, 14, 17. 4:4-16.

with. Jn 16:32.

showed him mercy. Heb. extended kindness to him.

gave him. Ge 40:3. Ex 3:21. 11:3. 12:36. Ps
37:5, 6. 105:19, 22. 106:46. 112:4. Pr +16:7.
Da 1:9. Ac 7:9, 10.

22 **committed**. ver. 4, 6, 7, 9. Ge 40:3, 4. 1 S
2:30. Ps 37:3, 11. Mt 25:14-30. Lk 12:48.
16:10. 19:17.

23 **keeper**. Ge 40:3, 4.

because. ver. 2, 3. Ge 49:23, 24. 1 S 2:30. Ps
1:3. 37:3-11. Is 43:2. Da 6:22.

with him. ver. +3. Ge +30:27. Ps 91:5. Jn
16:32.

prosper. Ps 1:1-3.

GENESIS 40

1 **it came**. Ge 39:20-23. Est 6:1.

the butler. or, cup-bearer. ver. 13. Ne 1:11.
2:1, 2.

2 **wroth**. Ps 76:10. Pr 16:14. 19:12, 19. 27:4. Ac
12:20.

two. Lk 23:32.

the chief of the butlers. 1 Ch 27:27.

3 **the place**. Ge 39:20, 23. 2 S 20:3mg. Lk
23:32.

4 **the captain**. Ge 37:36. 39:1, 21-23. Ps 37:5.

served. Lk 22:27.

a season. ver. 20. Ge 4:3. 24:55.

5 A.M. 2287. B.C. 1717.

dreamed a dream. ver. 8. Ge 12:1-7.
+31:24. Est 6:1. Da ch. 7, 8.

6 **and, behold**. ver. 8. Ge 41:8. Da 2:1-3. 4:5. 5:6. 7:28. 8:27.

7 **Wherefore**. Jg 18:24. 1 S 1:8. 2 S 13:4. Ne 2:2. Lk 24:17.
   look ye so sadly today. Heb. *are* your faces evil. Lk 24:17.

8 **Do not**, etc. Ge 41:15, 16. Jb 33:15, 16. Ps 25:14. Is 8:19. Da 2:11, 28, 47. 4:8. 5:11-15. Am 3:7. 1 C 12:10, 11.

9 **a vine**. Ge 37:5-10. Jg 7:13-15. Da 2:31. 4:8, 10, etc.

10 **budded**. Nu 13:23. Dt 1:24.
   blossoms. SS 6:11. Is 27:6. 35:1, 2. 37:31. Ho 14:7. Jl 2:22. Zc 8:12.

11 **pressed**. Ge 49:11. Le 10:9. Pr 3:10.
   hand. ver. 21. 1 K 10:5. 2 Ch 9:4. Ne 1:11. 2:1.

12 **This**. ver. 18. Ge 41:12, 25, 26. Jg 7:14. Da 2:36, etc. 4:19, etc.
   The three. Ge 41:26. Jg 7:14. Mt 26:26. 1 C 10:4. Ga 4:25.

13 **Yet**. Lk 23:43.
   within. ver. 7:4.
   three. 1 C +15:4.
   shall. ver. 20-22. 2 K 25:27. Ps 3:3. Je 52:31.
   lift up thine head. *or*, reckon. ver. 19mg, 20mg. 2 K 25:27.

14 **think on me**. Heb. remember me with thee. 1 C 11:24.
   on me. 1 S 25:31. Lk 23:42. 1 C 7:21.
   show kindness. Jsh 2:12. 1 S 20:14, 15. 2 S 9:1. 1 K 2:7. Mt 25:40.
   make mention. Mt 10:32.
   bring. 1 C 7:21.

15 **stolen**. Ge 37:28. Ex 21:16. Dt 24:7. 1 T 1:10.
   the Hebrews. i.e. *descendants of Eber*, **S#5680h**. Ge +14:13. 41:12. 43:32. Ex 2:13. 3:18. 5:3. 7:16. 9:1, 13. 10:3. 1 S 4:6, 9. 13:3, 7, 19. 14:11, 21. 29:3.
   done nothing that. Ge 39:8-12, 20. 1 S 24:11. Ps 59:3, 4. Da 6:22. Lk 23:41. Jn 8:46. 10:32. 15:25. Ac 24:12-21. 25:10, 11. 1 P 3:17, 18.

16 **the chief**. ver. 1, 2.
   white baskets. *or*, baskets full of holes. Am 8:1, 2. Hg 1:6.

17 **bake-meats**. Heb. meat of Pharaoh, the work of a baker, *or* cook. Ge 49:20. 1 Ch 12:20.

18 **This is**. ver. +12. Ge 41:26. 1 C 10:4. 11:24.

19 **within**. ver. 13.
   lift up thy head from off thee. *or*, reckon thee *and take thy office* from thee.
   hang thee. ver. 22. Ge 41:13. Dt 21:22, 23. Jsh 8:29. 10:26. 2 S 21:6. Est 7:9mg, 10. Pr 30:17. Ga 3:13. 1 P 2:24.
   tree. lit. wood. Dt 21:22, 23. Jsh 8:29. 2 S 21:19. Est 7:9mg, 10. Ezk 37:16. Ac 16:24. Ga 3:13. 1 P 2:24.
   and the birds. ver. 17. Dt 28:26. 1 S 17:44,

46. 2 S 21:10. 1 K 14:11. 16:4. 21:24. Ps 79:2. Je 7:33. 12:9mg. 16:4. 34:20. Ezk 39:4. Mt 13:4, 19, 32. Ac 20:27.

20 **third day**. ver. 13, 19. Ge +22:4. Ex +10:22. Jon 1:17. Mt 12:40. 1 C +15:4.
   birthday. Ge +21:8. Jb 3:1. Mt 14:6. Mk 6:21.
   lifted up. *or*, reckoned. ver. 13mg, 19mg. 2 K 25:27. Mt 18:23-25. 25:19. Lk 16:1, 2.

21 **restored**. Je 52:31, 32.
   gave the cup. ver. 13. Ne 2:1.

22 **he hanged**. ver. 8, 19. Ge 41:11-13, 16. Je 23:28. Da 2:19-23, 30. 5:12. Mt 25:19. Ac 5:30.

23 **but forgat him**. Ge 42:21. Jg 8:33. Jb 19:14. Ps 31:12. 105:19. Ec 9:15, 16. Am 6:6. Lk 23:39-43.

GENESIS 41

1 A.M. 2289. B.C. 1715.
   two full years. Heb. *Shenathayim yamim*, two years of days, two complete solar revolutions; as a *month of days* is a full month, Ge 29:14.
   that Pharaoh. Ge +31:24.
   the river. Ge 31:21. Ex 1:22. 4:9. Dt 11:10. Is 19:5. Ezk 29:3, 9.

2 **there came**. ver. 17-27.
   a meadow. Jb 8:11.

3 **ill favored**. ver. 4, 20, 21.

4 **So Pharaoh awoke**. 1 K 3:15.

5 **rank**. Heb. fat. Dt 32:14.

6 **blasted**. Ezk 17:10. 19:12. Ho 13:15.
   east wind. Ge 8:1. **S#6921h**. ver. 23, 27. Ex 10:13. 14:21. Jb 15:2. 27:21. 38:24. Ps 48:7. 78:26. Is 27:8. Je 18:17. Ezk +11:1. 17:10. 19:12. 27:26. Ho 12:1. 13:15. Jon 4:8. Hab 1:9.

7 **a dream**. Ge 20:3. 37:5.

8 **that his**. The use of *spirit* and *soul* are sometimes interchangeable: Ge 41:8 with Ps 42:6. Both depart the body at death: Ge 35:18 with Ps 146:4. 1 S 30:12 with La 1:11mg. Both are affirmed to be within man: Jb 14:22 with Zc 12:1. Mt 20:28 with 27:50. Jn 12:27 with 13:21. He 12:23 with Re 6:9. Both 'soul' (*nephesh*, Ge +23:8) and 'spirit' (*ruach*, Ge +26:35) are rendered *mind*: Ezk 23:18, 28 with Ezk 20:32. Both are used of the departed: 1 P 3:19 with Re 20:4. Both are used of sadness or sorrow: 1 K 21:5 with Ps 62:11. Mt 26:28 with Jn 13:21. Is 26:9a with Is 26:9b. Lk 1:46 with 1:47. Ph 1:27a with Ph 1:27b.
   spirit. Heb. *ruach*, Ge +6:3. Ge 40:6. Da 2:1-3. 4:5, 19. 5:6. 7:28. 8:27. Hab 3:16. Hg 1:14. Mk +2:8. **S#7307h**: The word "spirit" is put for the invisible characteristics of man manifesting his soul or life in states of mind (Ge +26:35) or feeling: Ge +26:35. Ge 45:27. Ex

6:9. 35:21. Nu 5:14, 14, 30. 14:24. Jsh 5:1. Jg
15:19. 1 S 1:15. 30:12. 1 K 10:5. 21:5. 1 Ch
5:26, 26. 2 Ch 9:4. 21:16. 36:22. Ezr 1:1, 5. Jb
6:4. 7:11. 10:12. 15:13. 20:3. 21:4. 32:8, 18.
Ps 32:2. 34:18. 51:10, 11, 12, 17. 76:12. 78:8.
142:3. 143:4, 7. Pr 11:13. 14:29. 15:4, 13.
16:2, 18, 19, 32. 17:22, 27. 18:14, 14. 25:28.
29:23. Ec 1:14, 17. 2:11, 17, 26. 4:4, 6, 16.
6:9. 7:8, 8, 9. 10:4. Is 19:3, 14. 26:9. 29:10,
24. 33:11. 38:16. 54:6. 57:15, 15, 16. 61:3.
65:14. 66:2. Je 51:11. Ezk 13:3, 14b. Da 7:15.
Ho 4:12. 5:4. Mi 2:11 (where by the figure of
speech Hendiadys (Ge +1:26), *ruach* is put for
a false or lying spirit). For the other uses of
ruach, see Ge +6:3.
   troubled. Jb 7:13, 14.
   the magicians of Egypt. Ex 7:11, 22. 8:7,
   18, 19. 9:11. 15:9, 11. Le 19:31. 20:6. Dt 18:9-
   14. Is 8:19. 19:3. 29:14. 47:12, 13. Da 1:20.
   2:2, 10, 27. 4:7, 9. 5:7, 11. Ac 17:18.
   the wise men. Mt 2:1. Ac 7:22.
   but there. Ge 40:8. Jb 5:12, 13. Ps 25:14. Is
   29:14. Da 2:4-11, 27, 28. 5:8. 1 C 1:19. 3:18-
   20.
9 **I do remember**. Ge 40:1-3, 14, 23. Lk 23:41.
10 **Pharaoh**. Ge 39:20. 40:2, 3.
    captain. Ge 37:36.
11 **dreamed**. Ge 40:5-8.
12 **with us**. Lk 23:41.
    Hebrew. Ge +14:13.
    servant. Ge 37:36. 39:1, 20.
    interpreted. Ge 40:12-19.
13 **me he restored**. Ge 40:12, 20-22. Je 1:10.
    Ezk 43:3.
14 **sent**. 1 S 2:7, 8. Ps 105:19-22. 113:7, 8.
    and they brought him hastily. Heb. made
    him run. Ex 10:16. 1 S 2:8. Ps 113:7, 8. Da
    2:25.
    out. Ec 4:14.
    he shaved. 2 S 19:24. 2 K 25:29. Est 4:1-4.
    5:1. Is 61:3, 10. Je 52:32, 33.
15 **I have heard**. ver. 9-13. Ps 25:14. Da 5:12, 16.
    **that thou canst understand a dream to
    interpret it**. *or,* when thou hearest a dream,
    thou canst interpret it. ver. 12, 25. Ge 40:12.
    Jg 7:13, 14. Da 2:36. 4:19.
16 **It is not**. Ge 40:8. Nu 12:6. 2 K 6:27. Da
    2:18-23, 28-30, 47. 4:2. Jn 5:19. Ac 3:7, 12.
    14:14, 15. 1 C 15:10. 2 C 3:5.
    peace. Jg +18:15mg.
17 **In my dream**. ver. 1-7.
18 **fat fleshed**. Je 24:1-3, 5, 8.
19 **poor**. Ru +3:10.
21 **eaten them up**. Heb. come to the inward
    parts of them. Je 9:8mg. Ezk 3:3. Re 10:9, 10.
    still. Ps 37:19. Is 9:20.
23 **withered**. *or,* small.
    thin. ver. 6. 2 K 19:26. Ps 129:6, 7. Ho 8:7.
    9:16. 13:15.
    east wind. ver. +6.

24 **I told this**. ver. 8. Ex 8:19. Da 4:7.
25 **God hath showed**. ver. +16. Ex 9:14. Is
    41:22, 23. 43:9. Da 2:28, 29, 45, 47. Am 3:7.
    Mk 13:23. Jn 5:19. Ep 1:17. Re 4:1.
26 **are**. *or,* signify. ver. 2, 5, 29, 47, 53. Ge 40:18.
    Ex 12:11. 1 C 10:4.
    good ears are seven. Ge +40:12.
    the dream is one. Ge 2:24. Ex 26:6. 1 J 5:7.
27 **seven years of famine**. 2 S 24:13. 2 K 8:1.
28 **What God**. ver. 16, 25. Ge 40:8.
29 **seven years**. ver. 26, 46, 47, 49.
30 **seven years**. ver. 27, 54. 1 K +8:37. Ja 5:17.
    shall be. ver. 21, 51. Pr 31:7. Is 65:16.
    consume. Ge 47:13. Ps 105:16.
    land. Ge +6:11.
31 **grievous**. Heb. heavy. 1 S 5:6. Is 24:20.
32 **dream**. Jl 2:28-32. Ac 2:16-21, 38, 39.
    doubled. Ge 37:7, 9. Jb 33:14, 15. 2 C 13:1.
    twice. Ge +22:15. Pr 14:12. 16:25. Je 1:13.
    it is because. Nu 23:19. Is 14:24-27. 46:10,
    11. Mt 24:35.
    established by. *or,* prepared of. Ps 51:10mg.
    57:7mg. Is 2:2mg. 30:33. Ho +6:3. Mt 25:34,
    41. Mk 10:40. 1 C 2:9. Re 9:15.
33 **therefore**. Da 4:27.
    look out. Ex 18:19-22. Dt 1:13. Ac 6:3.
34 **officers**. *or,* overseers. Nu 31:14. 2 K 11:11,
    12. 2 Ch 34:12. Ne 11:9. 12:42.
    and take. Jb 5:20. Ps 33:19. Pr 6:6-8. +22:3.
    Lk 16:5.
35 **gather**. ver. 48, 49, 56. Ge 45:6, 7.
    under. 2 K 13:5. Is 3:6.
    hand. Ex 4:13.
36 **that the**. Ge 47:13-25.
    perish not. Heb. be not cut off. ver. 30.
37 **the thing**. Ps 105:19. Pr 10:20. 25:11. Ac
    7:10.
    good. Jsh +22:30mg.
38 **we**. Ge +30:27.
    in whom. Nu 27:18. Jb 32:8. Ps 84:11. Pr
    2:6. Da 4:6, 8, 18. 5:11, 14. 6:3. Ac 10:38.
    spirit. Heb. *ruach,* **S#7307h**. Here this word
    represents invisible 'power from on high' (Lk
    24:49) manifesting itself as divine power in
    giving spiritual gifts (Ep 5:18), spoken of as
    coming upon, clothing, falling on, and being
    poured out. Rendered "Spirit," but should be
    "spirit." Ex 28:3. 31:3. 35:31. Nu 11:17, 25,
    25, 26, 29. 24:2. 27:18. Dt 34:9. Jg 3:10. 6:34.
    11:29. 13:25. 14:6, 19. 15:14. 1 S 10:6, 10.
    11:6. 16:13, 14. 19:20, 23. 2 K 2:9, 15. 1 Ch
    12:18. 28:12. 2 Ch 15:1. 20:14. 24:20. Ps
    51:11, 12. 143:10. Pr 1:23. Is 11:2, 2, 2, 2.
    30:1. 32:15. 42:1, 5. 44:3. 59:21. 61:1. 63:11.
    Ezk 2:2. 3:24. 11:5, 19. 36:27. 39:29. Da 4:8,
    9, 18. 5:11, 12, 14. Jl 2:28, 29. Hg 2:5. Zc
    12:10. For the other uses of *ruach,* see Ge
    +6:3.
39 **said**. Ge 30:27.
    God hath. ver. 16, 25, 28, 33. Jn 5:20.

Forasmuch. ver. 32. 1 S 10:6-10. Ac 5:32. 8:15. Ro 5:5. 1 C 13:4-10. Ep 5:18. Col 1:9, 10. Ju 20.

discreet. Is 28:26. Lk 2:47.

40 **Thou shalt**. Ge 39:4-6. 45:8, 9, 26. Ps 105:21, 22. Pr 22:29. Da 2:46-48. 5:29. 6:3. Mt 24:47. He 3:6.

according. Is 9:6, 7.

be ruled. Heb. be armed, *or* kiss. 1 S 10:1. 1 K 19:18. Jb 31:27. Ps 2:12. Ho 13:2.

only. Est 10:3. Ge 44:18 with Jn 14:28.

greater than. Ge 44:18 with Jn 14:28.

41 **See, I have set**. ver. 44. Ge 39:5, 22. Est 10:3. Ps 105:21, 22. Pr 17:2. 22:29. Da 2:7, 8. 4:2, 3. 6:3. Mt 28:18. Ph 2:9-11.

42 **his ring**. Est 3:10, 12. 6:7-12. 8:2, 8, 10, 15. 10:3. Da 2:46, 47. 5:7, 29. Lk 15:22.

fine linen. or, silk. Ezk 27:7.

a gold chain. Pr 1:9. 31:22, 24. SS 1:10. Ezk 16:10, 11. Da 5:7, 16, 29. Lk 19:16-19. Re 1:13.

43 **and they**. Est 6:8, 9.

Bow the knee. *or*, Tender father. Ge 45:8. Heb. Abrech. Ph 2:10.

ruler. Ge 42:6, 30, 33. 45:8, 26. Ac 7:10.

44 **without thee**. Jn 15:5.

lift up his hand . Ex 11:7.

45 **Zaphnath-paaneah**. *or*, prince. i.e. *discovering hidden things*, **S#6847h**, only here. Ex 2:16. 2 S 8:18. Lk 2:1. Ac 11:28.

Asenath. i.e. *fairness; beautiful*, **S#621h**. ver. 50. Ge 46:20.

Potipherah. i.e. *priest of the sun; affliction of the locks (of hair)*, **S#6319h**. ver. 50. Ge 46:20.

priest of. *or*, prince. Ge 14:18. Ex 2:16mg. 2 S 8:18. 20:26. Is +24:2mg.

On. ver. 50. Ge 46:40. Ezk 30:17, Aven.

46 **thirty years**. Ge 37:2. Nu 4:3. 2 S 5:4. Lk 3:23.

he stood. Dt +10:8. Ju 24.

47 From A.M. 2289, B.C. 1715, to A.M. 2296, B.C. 1708.

handfuls. Ge 26:12. Ps 72:16.

48 **he gathered**. ver. 34-36. Ge 47:21.

49 **the sand**. Ge +22:17.

without. Ep 3:8.

50 **unto Joseph**. Ge 46:20. 48:5.

Asenath. ver. 45. Ge 46:20.

priest. *or*, prince. 2 S 8:18. Is +24:2mg.

51 A.M. 2292. B.C. 1712.

called. Ge 48:5, 13, 14, 18-20. Dt 33:17.

firstborn. Ge 48:18. 1 Ch 26:10. Ps 89:27. Je +31:9. Col +1:15.

Manasseh. *i.e.* Forgetting. *causing to forget*, **S#4519h**. ver. 30. Ge 46:20. 48:1, 5, 13, 14, 20. 50:23. Nu +1:10, 34. 26:28, 29. 27:1. 32:39-41. 36:1. Dt 3:14. 33:17. Jsh 4:12. 17:1, 2, 3. 1 K 4:13. 2 K 20:21. 21:1. 1 Ch 3:13. 7:14, 17. 2 Ch 32:33. 33:1. Mt 1:10.

forget. Jb 11:16. Ps 30:5, 11. 45:10. Pr 31:7. Is 57:16. 65:16.

52 A.M. 2293. B.C. 1711.

called he. Ge 29:32-35. 30:6-13. 50:23.

Ephraim. i.e. Fruitful, in Hebrew sounding like the word for *twice fruitful*. Ge 46:20. 48:5, 16, 19. 49:22. Nu +1:33. 2:18. 26:28. Dt 33:17. 1 Ch 7:20, 22. Ps 60:7. 78:9, 10, 67. 80:2. 108:8. Is 7:2. 11:13. 17:3. 28:1, 3. 40:1, 2. Je 31:6, +9, 18, 20. Ezk 37:16, 19. Ho 4:17. 5:3. 6:4. 7:1, 8, 11. 8:11. 11:8, 9. 12:1. 13:1. 14:8. Zc 9:10, 13. 10:7.

fruitful. Jn 12:24.

the land. Ps 105:17, 18. Am 6:6. Ac 7:10.

53 A.M. 2296. B.C. 1708.

years of plenteousness. ver. 29-31. Ps 73:20. Lk 16:25.

54 **the seven**. ver. 3, 4, 6, 7, 27, +30.

according. ver. 30.

as. Jn 2:22.

and the dearth. Ge 45:11.

all. ver. 56, 57. Ge +2:24. +7:19.

but in. Ex 10:23. Ps 37:25. Jn 6:22-59.

55 **famished**. 2 K 6:25-29. Je 14:1-6. La 4:3-10.

Go unto. ver. 40, 41. Ps 105:20-22. Mt 3:17. 17:5. Jn 1:14-16. 2:5. 6:68. Ph 4:19. Col 1:19.

what he. Jn 2:5.

56 **famine**. Am 8:11. Lk 15:14.

over all. Interestingly, the word "all" does not always mean "all." When more is said than is literally meant, this usage is called overstatement or hyperbole (John 21:25), of which 1 K 18:10 is the clearest example. Sometimes "all" means "all" in the purview of the author and his circumstances (ver. 56, 57). Sometimes "all" means every last one without exception (Ec 7:20. Ro 3:23. Col 1:16, 17. He 2:8); sometimes it means every one or kind without distinction, but not without exception (Ge 24:10. Jn 1:9. 2 C 5:19. Re 12:9. Contrast the usage where *many* is put for *all*, Is +53:12); sometimes it means "most" or the majority (Mk 1:33. Lk 3:12 with 7:30 with Mk 1:5), or the greater part (Ex +9:6); sometimes what is said of the whole, collectively, is sometimes said only of a part; and not all of the parts, precisely and singularly (Ge +6:12). Consideration of the context and related passages will usually clarify which sense is to be given to "all" and kindred expressions. For other instances of overstatement see Ge 2:24. +13:16. 19:4. 41:47, 49, 56, 57. Dt 1:28. 2:25. 9:1. 1 S 5:12. 2 S 17:13. 1 K 1:40. 18:10. 2 K 19:24. 20:13. 1 Ch 14:17. Jb 20:17. 29:6. Ps 22:7, 17. 98:3. 139:8. Is 34:3. Ezk 32:4-8. Da 2:37, 38. Am 9:13. Mt 2:3. 3:5, 6. 5:29, 30. 11:23. Lk 2:1. 8:43. Jn 1:9. 3:26. 4:39. 10:8. 12:19. Ac 2:5. Ro 1:8. 8:28. 1 C 13:7. Col 1:6, 23. T 2:11. Re 13:8, 16.

the face . Ge +1:2. Is 23:17. Zc 5:3. Lk 21:35. Ac 17:26.

opened. Ml 3:10. Lk 24:27, 32.

all the storehouses. Heb. all wherein *was*.
sold. Ge 42:6. 47:14-24.
57 **all**. Jg 6:37. 2 S 15:23. Is 13:5.
  countries. Ge 42:1, 5. 50:20. Dt 9:28. Ps
  105:16, 17. Is 49:6.
  famine. Am 8:11.
  in all lands. ver. 54, +56.

GENESIS 42

1 **when Jacob**. Ge 41:54, 57. Ac 7:12.
  saw. ver. 2. Ex 5:19. 20:18. 1 K 19:3. Ho
  5:13. Ga 2:7.
  corn. Ge +27:28.
  Why do ye. Jsh 7:10. 2 K 7:3, 4. Ezr 10:4. Je
  8:14.
2 **get you**. Ge 43:2, 4. 45:9.
  that we. Ge 43:8. Ps 118:17. Is 38:1. Mt 4:4.
3 **ten brethren**. ver. 5, 13. Ge 43:20.
4 **Benjamin**. Ge +35:18.
  Lest. ver. 38. Ge 3:22. 11:4. 43:1, 2. 43:14,
  29. 44:20-22, 27-29, +30, 31-34.
5 **for**. Ge +12:10.
6 **governor**. Ge 41:40, 41. 45:8, 26. Ps 105:16-
  21. Ec 7:19. Da 2:10, 15. 4:17, 25, 26, 32.
  5:21, 29. Ac 7:10.
  he it was. Ge 41:55, 56. Pr 11:26. Ac 4:12.
  bowed. Ge +18:2. 37:7, 9. Re 3:9.
7 **knew**. Jn +2:25.
  made. Ge +27:16. Lk 24:16.
  spake. Jb 36:8-10.
  roughly unto them. Heb. hard things with
  them. ver. 9-12, 14-17, 19, 20. Pr 18:19. Mt
  15:23-26.
8 **Joseph knew**. Jn +2:25.
  they knew not. Lk 24:16. Jn 1:10, 11.
  20:14. 21:4.
9 **remembered**. Ge 37:5-9.
  Ye are spies. ver. 9, 16, 30, 31, 34. Nu 13:2,
  16-20. Jsh 2:1. 6:23. Jg 1:24. 1 S 26:4. Lk
  20:20. He 11:31.
  nakedness. Ge +4:10. Ex 32:25.
10 **my lord**. Ge 27:29, 37. 37:8. 44:9. 1 S 26:17.
  1 K 18:7.
11 **We are**. ver. 31.
  true men. ver. 19, 33, 34. Jn 7:18. 2 C 6:8.
  thy servants. ver. 13. Ge 44:7. 46:34. 47:3.
12 **nakedness**. ver. 9.
13 **Thy servants**. ver. +11, 32. Ge 29:32-35.
  30:6-24. 35:16-26. 43:7. 46:8-27. Ex 1:2-5.
  Nu ch. 1, 10, 26, 34. 1 Ch ch. 2-8.
  youngest. Ge 9:24.
  one is not. ver. 36, 38. Ge 5:24. 37:30. 44:20,
  28. 45:26. Je 31:15. La 5:7. Mt 2:16, 18.
14 **That**. ver. 9-11. Jb 13:24. 19:11. Mt 15:21-
  28.
15 **By the life**. ver. 7, 12, 16, 30. Dt 6:13. 1 S
  1:26. 17:55. 20:3. Je 5:2, 7. Mt 5:33-37.
  23:16-22. Ja 5:12.
  except. ver. 20, 34. Ge 43:3. 44:20-34.

16 **brother**. ver. 15.
  kept in prison. Heb. bound. ver. 19.
  that your. ver. 7, 12, 30.
  truth. ver. 11.
  spies. ver. 9, 11.
17 **put**. Heb. gathered. Ps +27:10mg. Is 24:22.
  +58:8mg. Ac 5:18.
  ward. Ge 40:4, 7. 41:10. Le 24:12. Jb 36:8-
  10. Ps 119:65. Ac 4:3. He 12:10.
18 **I fear God**. Ex +1:17. Lk 18:2, 4.
19 **house**. Ge 40:3. Is 42:7, 22. Je 37:15.
  carry corn. ver. 1, 2, 26. Ge 41:56. 43:1, 2.
  45:23.
20 **bring**. ver. 15, 34. Ge 43:5, 19. 44:23.
  And they. ver. 26. Ge 6:22. Jn 2:5.
21 **they said**. Ge 41:9. Nu +32:23. 2 S 12:13. Jb
  33:27, 28. 34:31, 32. 36:8, 9. Pr 28:13. Ho
  5:15. Mt 27:3, 4. Lk 16:28. Ac 19:18.
  we saw. Ge 37:23-28. Pr 21:13. 24:11, 12. Mt
  7:2. Ja 2:13. 1 J 1:9.
  soul. Heb. *nephesh*, **S#5315h**, Ge +34:3.
  therefore. Ge +6:13. Ps +9:10.
  this distress. Pr 1:27, 28. Je 2:17, 19. 4:18.
  34:17.
22 **Spake I**. Ge 37:21, 22, 29, 30. Lk 23:51. Ro
  2:15.
  his blood. Ge 4:10. Mt 27:25. Lk +11:50, 51.
  Ac 28:4. Re 13:10. 16:9.
23 **understood**. Ge +18:10. Is 11:3.
  he spake unto them by an interpreter.
  Heb. an interpreter was between them. ver.
  24. Ge 43:19. Jn 16:13, 14. 2 C 5:20.
24 **wept**. Ge +29:11. Is 63:9. 1 C 12:26. He 4:15.
  Note the seven times Joseph wept: ver. 24. Ge
  43:30. 45:2, 14. 46:29. 50:1, 17.
  Simeon. Ge +29:33. Ju 22, 23.
25 **commanded**. Ge 44:1, 2. Is 55:1.
  fill. Jn 1:16.
  restore. Is 55:1.
  to give them. Ge 45:21. Mt 6:33.
  provision. Ph 4:19.
  and thus. Jsh 21:45. 23:14. Mt 5:44. Ro
  12:17-21. 1 P 3:9.
26 **laded their asses**. Ge 44:3, 13. 45:17, 23. 1 S
  25:18. 2 S 16:2. 1 Ch 12:40. Ne 13:15. Jb 1:3.
  Is 30:6.
27 **the inn**. Ge 43:21. 44:11. Ex 4:24. Lk 2:7.
  10:34.
28 **their heart**. ver. 36. Ge 27:33. Le 26:36. Dt
  21:26. 28:65. 1 K 10:5. SS 5:6. Lk 21:26.
  failed them. Heb. went forth. Ex 15:15. Jsh
  2:9, 11. 5:1. 7:5. Ps 22:14. Is 13:7. Mk 5:33.
  What is. Is +45:7. La 2:17. 3:37. Am +3:6.
29 **Canaan**. ver. 5, 13. Ge 37:1. 45:17.
  told. Ge 44:24.
30 **roughly to us**. Heb. with us hard things. ver.
  7-20. Pr 13:15. 22:5.
31 **true**. ver. 11.
32 **twelve brethren**. ver. 13.
33 **Hereby**. ver. 15, 19, 20.

34 **traffick**. Ge 34:10, 21. 1 K 10:15. Ezk 17:4.

35 **every man's**. ver. 27, 28. Ge 43:21.

36 **Me have ye**. Ge 37:20-35. 43:14.
all these. Ge 45:28. 47:12. 1 S 27:1. Jb 7:7. 42:10. Ps 34:19. Ec 7:8. Is 38:10. 41:10, 13, 14. Mt 14:31. Ro 8:28, 31. 1 C +10:13. 2 C 4:17. Ja 5:7-11.
against me. Ru +1:13. Je +29:11.

37 **Slay my**. Ge 43:9. 44:32-34. 46:9. Mi 6:7.

38 **his brother**. ver. 13. Ge 30:22-24. +35:18. 37:33, 35.
if mischief. ver. 4. Ge 44:29.
bring down. Ge 37:35. 44:29, 31. 1 K 2:6. Ps 49:14. 71:18. 90:10. Ec 9:10. Is 38:10. 46:4. Ho 13:14. Ac 2:27. Re 20:13.
the grave. Heb. *sheol*, Ge +37:35.

GENESIS 43

1 **the famine**. 1 K +8:37. Ec 9:1, 2.

2 **Go again**. ver. 4, 20. Ge 42:1, 2. Pr 15:16. 16:18. 31:16. 1 T 5:8. 6:6-8.

3 **The man**. Ge 42:15-20, 33, 34. 44:23.
did solemnly protest. Heb. protesting, protested. Ac 7:34.
see my face. ver. 5. 2 S 3:13. 14:24, 28, 32. Est 1:14. Ps 11:7. 16:11. 17:15. Ac 20:25, 38.

5 **will not**. Ge 42:38. 44:26. Ex 20:12.

6 **dealt**. Ge +42:38.

7 **asked us straitly**. Heb. asking asked us. ver. 3mg. Ge +2:16.
tenor. Heb. mouth.
could we certainly know. knowing could we know. ver. 3mg.

8 **lad with me**. Ge 42:38. 44:26. Ex 20:12.
and. Ge +8:22.
that we. Ge 42:2. Dt 33:6. 2 K 7:4, 13. Ps 118:17.
also our. Nu +16:27.

9 **will be**. Ge 42:37. 44:32, 33. 1 K 1:21. Jb 17:3. Ps 119:122. Phm 18, 19. He 7:22.
of my hand. Ge 9:5. 31:39. Ezk 3:18, 20. 33:6, 8. Lk 11:50.

10 **lingered**. Ge 19:16. 45:9.
this second time. *or*, twice by this.

11 **Israel**. Ge 35:22. 37:3. 45:28. 46:30. 50:2.
If it must be. ver. 14. Est 4:16. Ac 21:14.
take. Ge 32:14.
fruits. lit. praise.
land. Je 51:41.
carry down. Dt 33:14. Jg +3:15. 1 K 15:19. 2 K 8:8. 16:8. 20:12. Pr 17:18. Ezk 27:15.
a little balm. Ge +37:25.
honey. Ex +3:8.
spices. 1 K 10:15. 2 Ch 32:27. SS 4:10, 14-16. 5:1. 8:14.
myrrh. Mt +2:11.
nuts. Ge 37:25. 2 Ch 31:5.
almonds. Je 1:11, 12.

12 **double**. ver. 15. Ex 16:5. 22:4, 7, 9. Dt 15:18.

21:17. Jb 11:6. 41:13. 42:10. Is 40:2. 61:7. Je 16:18. 17:18. Zc 9:12. Ro 12:17. 13:8. 2 C 8:21. Ph 4:8. 1 Th 4:6. 5:21. 1 T 5:17. He 13:8. Re 18:6.
mouth. Ge 42:25, 35.

13 **Take also**. Ge 42:38.

14 **God Almighty**. Ex +6:3.
give. Ge 22:14. 32:11-28. 39:21. Ezr 7:27. Ne 1:11. Est 4:16. Ps 37:5-7. 85:7. 100:5. 119:41. Pr 1:1. +16:7. 21:1. Is 49:13. Lk 1:50. Ac 7:10. 21:14. 1 T 1:2, 16. 1 T 1:4. 2 J 3.
If I be, etc. *or*, and I as I have been, etc. ver. 11. Est 4:16.

15 **double money**. ver. +12. Pr 6:31.
went down. Ge 39:1. 46:3, 6.
stood before. Ge 37:7. 47:2, 7. Mt 2:11. Ac 7:13.

16 **the ruler**. ver. 19. Ge 15:2. 24:2-10. 39:4, 5. 44:1.
house. *House* is put for the servants of it.
Bring. Lk 14:23.
slay. Heb. kill a killing. Ge 21:8. 26:30. 31:54. 1 S 25:11mg. Pr 9:2.
make. Mt 22:4.
dine with. Heb. eat.

18 **the men**. Ge 42:21, 28, 35. Jg 13:22. Jb 15:21. Ps 53:5. 73:16. Is 7:2. Mt 14:26, 27. Mk 6:16.
afraid. 1 J 4:18.
seek occasion against us. Heb. Roll himself upon us. Dt 22:14, 17. Jg 14:4. Jb 30:14. 35:9. Lk 3:14. 19:8. Ro 7:8.
bondmen. Ge 44:9, 33. Ex 22:3. 2 K 4:1-7.

19 **steward**. ver. 16, 24. 2 S 19:17. Is 22:15.
communed. Jn 14:26.

20 **we came indeed down**. Heb. coming down we came down. ver. 3, 7. Ge 42:3, 10, 27, 35.

21 **we came**. Ge 42:27-35.
we have. ver. +12. Ro 12:17. 13:8. He 13:5, 18. 1 P 2:12. 3:16.

22 **other money**. Ro 10:3.

23 **Peace**. Nu 6:26. Jg 6:23. 19:20. 1 S 25:6. 1 Ch 12:18. Ezr 4:17. 5:7. Ps 119:165. Is +57:19. Je +29:7. Lk 24:36. Jn 14:27. 20:19, 21, 26. Ro 2:10. 15:13.
I had your money. Heb. Your money came to me.
Simeon. ver. 14. Ge +29:33.

24 **gave them water**. Ge +18:4.

25 **made ready**. ver. 11, 16. Jg +3:15.
bread. Ge +3:19. Ex +18:12.

26 **hand**. Ge 24:10. 35:4. Nu 22:7.
bowed. ver. 28. Ge +18:2. 27:29. 37:7-10, 19, 20. Ps 72:9. Ro 14:11. Ph 2:10, 11. Re 1:17.

27 **welfare**. Heb. peace. Jg +18:15mg.
Is your father well. Heb. *Is there peace* to your father. Jg +18:15mg.
the old. Ge 37:3. 42:11, 13. 44:20. Le +19:32. Jb 32:6. Pr 23:22. 1 T 5:1, 2.

28 **bowed**. ver. +26.

made obeisance. Ex 18:7. 2 S +1:2. 14:4. 1 K 1:16. 2 Ch 24:17.

29 lifted. Ge +22:13.
mother's son. Ge 30:22-24. 35:17, 18.
of whom. Ge 42:11, 13.
God. Ge 45:8. Jsh 7:19. 2 Ch 29:11. Ps 133:1, 2. Mt 9:2, 22. Mk 10:24. 1 T 1:2. He 13:1.
my son. Nu 6:25. Ps 111:4. 112:4. Is 30:19. 33:2. Ml 1:9.

30 his bowels. Is 47:6. +63:15. Am 1:11. Zc 7:9.
chamber. or, inner chamber. Ex 8:3. Dt 32:25. Jg 3:24. 15:1. 16:9, 12. 2 S 4:7. 13:10. 1 K 20:30.
wept there. Ge +42:24.

31 refrained. Ge 45:1. Is 42:14. Je 31:16. 1 P 3:10.
set. Jn 21:12.
bread. ver. 25.

32 eat bread. ver. 16. Ge 31:54.
for that is an abomination. Ge 46:34. Ex 8:26.

33 sat. Ge 42:7. 44:12.
firstborn. Ge 35:23. 46:8. 49:3.
according. Ge 44:5, 12, 15.
birthright. Ge 25:31.

34 messes. 2 S 11:8.
was five. Ge 41:34. 45:22. 47:2, 24. 2 K +7:13. Is 29:18.
times. 1 S 1:5. 9:22-24. Is 19:18.
were merry. Heb. drank largely. Ge 9:21. 1 S 1:14. 2 S 11:13. Pr 31:6. Ec 9:7. 10:19. SS 5:1. Is 29:9. Je 25:27. Hg 1:6. Mt 11:19. Lk 15:24. Jn 2:10.

GENESIS 44

1 the steward. Heb. *him* that *was* over his house. Ge 24:2. 43:16, 19.
Fill the. Ge 42:25. 43:2. Is 3:1.
as much. Jn 6:11.

2 cup. Ge 42:15, 16, 20. 43:32. Dt 8:2, 16. 13:3. Mt 10:16. 2 C 8:8.

4 Up. Dt 2:16.
Wherefore. 1 S 24:17. 2 Ch 20:11. Ps 35:12. 109:5. Pr 17:13. Jn 10:32.

5 divineth. or, maketh trial. lit. divining he divineth. ver. +15mg. 2 K +21:6.

7 Wherefore. Ge 34:25-31. 35:22. 37:18-32. 38:16-18. Jsh 22:22-29. 2 S 20:20. 2 K 8:13. Pr 22:1. Ec 7:1. He 13:18.
forbid. ver. 17. Ge 18:25. Lk +20:16.

8 the money. Ge 42:21, 27, 35. 43:12, 21, 22.
how then. ver. 7. Ex 20:15. Dt 5:19. Mt 19:18. Ro 13:9. Ja 2:10, 11.

9 both. Ge 31:32. Jb 31:38-40. Ps 7:3-5. Ac 25:11.
and we. Ge 43:18.

10 he with whom. ver. 17, 33. Ex 22:3. Mt 18:24, 25.

12 began. Ge 43:33.

and the cup. ver. 26-32. Ge 42:36-38. 43:14.

13 rent their clothes. 2 K +18:37.

14 he was yet. Ge 43:16, 25.
fell. Ge +18:2. 37:7-9. Ph 2:10, 11.

15 What. ver. 4, 5. Ge 3:13. 4:10.
wot ye not. Ge 21:26. 39:8. Ex 32:1.
divine. or, make trial. ver. 5. Ge +30:27.

16 Judah. ver. 32. Ge 43:8, 9.
What shall we say. Dt 25:1. Ezr 9:10, 15. Jb 40:4. Pr 17:15. Is 5:3. Da 9:7. Ac 2:37.
God hath. Ge 37:18-28. 42:21, 22. Nu +32:23. Jsh 7:1, 18. Jg 1:7. Pr 28:17. Mt 7:2. Lk 12:2.
found out. Jn 16:8, 9.
iniquity. Ge 43:9. Is 27:9. Da 9:7.
behold. ver. 9. Ge 37:7, 9.

17 God forbid. ver. +7. Ge +18:25. 42:18. 2 S 23:3. Ps 75:2. Pr 17:15.
he shall. ver. 10.
in peace. Ge 26:29. 37:32, 33.

18 Oh my Lord. ver. 22, 24. Ge 37:8. 43:20.
let thy. Ge 18:30, 32. 2 S 14:12. Jb 33:31. Ac 2:29.
ears. Ge 50:4. 1 S 18:23.
anger. Ex 32:22. Est 1:12. Ps 79:5.
even as. or, as great as (NEB), or, equal to (NASB, NIV). Ge 41:40 with Jn +14:28. Jn 5:18.
Pharaoh. Ge 41:40, 44. Pr 19:12. Da 3:15, 19-23. 5:19. Jn 5:22.

19 asked his servants. Ge 42:7-10. 43:7, 29.

20 we said. Ge 49:8.
a child. Ge 35:18. 37:3, 19. 43:7, 8. 46:21.
little. Ge 43:29. 46:21. 43:8. 44:30-34.
and his brother. Ge 37:33-35. 42:36, 38.
he alone. ver. 27-29. Lk 7:12.

21 Bring. Ge 42:15, 20. 43:29.
that I may. Je 24:6. 40:4. Am 9:4.

22 his father would die. ver. 30. Ge 42:38.

23 Except. Ge 42:15-20. 43:3, 5.

24 we told him. Ge 42:29-34.

25 Go again. Ge 43:2, 5.

26 We cannot. Ge 43:4, 5. Lk 11:7.

27 my wife. Ge 29:18-21, 28. 30:22-25. 35:16-18. 46:19.

28 the one. Ge 37:13, 14.
Surely. Ge 37:33. 42:36, 38.

29 And if. Ge 42:36, 38. 43:14. Ps 88:3, 4.
sorrow. ver. 31. Ge 42:38. Dt 31:17. Ps 88:4.
grave. Heb. *sheol*, S#7585h, Ge +37:35. ver. 31. Ge +37:35. 42:38. Ps 16:10. 88:3. Ec 9:10. Ho 13:14. Mt 11:23. Ac 2:31. Re 20:13.

30 when I. ver. 17, 31, 34.
his life. Heb. his soul is knit with the lad's soul. 1 S 18:1. 25:29. 2 S 18:33. Mt +2:20. Lk 12:22. S#5315h, *nephesh*. *Nephesh* is sometimes used of man as being mortal, subject to death, as here and at ver. 30. Ge 9:5. +12:13. 19:17, 19. 32:30. +35:18.
bound. Ge 25:28. 33:2. 37:3, 4. 42:4. 48:22. 2 S 13:21. 1 Ch 26:10. 1 T 5:21. Ja 2:9. 3:17.

31 when he. 1 S 4:17, 18. 2 C 7:10. 1 Th 4:13.
is not. Ge 37:30. 42:13.
servants shall. ver. 29. Ge 37:26, 27, 35. 1 S 22:22.
grave. ver. +29. Ge +37:35.
32 surety for. Ge 43:8, 9, 16.
33 I pray thee. Ex 32:32. Ro 5:7-10. 9:3.
instead. He 7:22. 1 J 3:16.
34 lest. 1 S 2:33, 34. 2 Ch 34:28. Est 8:6. Je 52:10, 11.
come on. Heb. find. 2 K +9:21mg.

GENESIS 45

1 could not. Ge 43:30, 31. Is 42:14. Je 20:9.
Cause. 2 S 1:20. Mt 18:15. Ac 10:41. 1 C 13:5.
no man. Mt 17:8.
known. Lk 24:31, 35. Ac 7:13.
2 wept. Heb. gave forth his voice in weeping. Ge +42:24.
3 I am Joseph. Mt 14:27. Ac 7:13. 9:5.
doth. ver. 9. Ge 46:29. 48:1, 21. 50:1. Ru 1:8-11, 16-18. 2 K 13:4.
for they. Jb 4:5. 23:15. Zc 12:10. Mt 14:26. Mk 6:50. Lk 5:8. 24:37, 38. Re 1:7.
troubled. *or*, terrified. Ex 15:15. Jg 20:41. Jb 4:5. 21:6. 22:10. 23:15, 16. Zc 12:10. Mt 14:26. Mk 6:50.
4 near. Ep 2:13. Ja +4:8.
I am Joseph. Ge 37:28. 50:18. Mt 14:27. Ac 9:5.
5 be not grieved. Is 40:1, 2. Lk 23:34. 2 C 2:7, 11.
nor angry with yourselves. Heb. neither let there be anger in your eyes. Ge +31:35.
for God. ver. 7, 8. Ge 47:25. 50:20. Ex 9:16. 10:1, 2. 1 S 1:19. 2 S 12:12. 16:10-12. 17:14. Jb 1:21. Ps +46:10. 76:10. 105:16, 17. Mt 18:7. Ac 2:23, 24. 4:24-28. 7:9-15. Ro 3:5-8. 5:20. 6:17. 8:28. 1 C +11:19.
send. 1 J 4:9.
6 two years. Ge 41:29-31, 54-56. 47:18.
in. lit. in the midst. Jsh 3:17. 1 K 3:28mg. Ps 40:8, 10. Hab 3:2. Zc 2:5, 10, 11. Mt 13:25, 49. Lk 17:11. Ac 17:33. 2 C 6:17. He 2:12.
earing. *Earing* means plowing or seed-time. Ge 47:23. Ex 34:21. Dt 21:4. 1 S 8:12. Is 30:24.
7 sent. 1 J 4:9.
to preserve you a posterity. Heb. to put for you a remnant. 2 S 14:7. Je 44:7.
to save. Jg 15:18. 1 Ch 11:14. Ps 18:50. 44:4. Ac 7:35.
great. 2 C 1:10.
8 it was not. ver. 5. Ge +24:44. Jn 15:16. 19:11. Ac 2:23. Ro 9:16.
father. Ge 41:39-48. Jg 17:10. Jb 29:16. Ps 105:21, 22.
lord. He 3:6. 1 P 3:22.

9 and say. Lit. have said. Past tense used for the future tense, "will say." Jb 19:27. Ps 23:5. Pr 1:22. Is 11:1. Jn 3:13. Ro 8:30. 1 C 15:27. Ep 2:6. He 2:7. 3:14. 12:22.
Thus saith. ver. 26-28.
come. ver. 13, 19, 20. Mt 11:30.
tarry not. 2 C 6:2.
10 shalt dwell. lit. hast dwelt. ver. +9.
Goshen. Jsh +10:41.
be near. Jn 14:2, 3. 17:24.
11 nourish. Ge 47:6, 12. Ps 36:7-9. Mt 15:5, 6. Mk 7:9-12. Jn 6:35. 1 T 5:4.
12 your eyes. Ge 42:23. Lk 24:39. Jn 20:27.
my mouth. Not as Ge 42:23.
13 my glory. Jn 17:22, 24. 2 C 4:4. 1 P 1:10-12. Re 21:23.
bring. Ac 7:14.
14 fell. Lk +15:20. Ro 1:31.
wept. Ge +42:24.
15 Moreover. Ge +27:27.
wept. ver. +2.
talked. Ps 77:4. Lk 24:15.
16 it pleased Pharaoh well. Heb. was good in the eyes of Pharaoh. Ge 34:18. 41:37. Dt 1:33. Jsh +22:30mg. Est 2:4. 5:14. Ac 6:5.
17 lade your. Ge 42:25, 26. 44:1, 2.
18 come. Mt 11:28.
the fat. Ge 27:28. 47:6. Nu 18:12, 29. Dt 32:14. Ps 81:16. 147:14. Is 28:1, 4.
19 commanded. Is 49:1, 23. 1 J 3:23, 24.
this do. Mt 7:21. Lk 6:46. Jn 13:17. Ja 1:22. 1 J 2:3, 4.
waggons. ver. 27. Ge 46:5.
for your. Ge 31:17, 18.
come. Mt 11:28. Jn 6:37. 7:37, 38. Re 22:17.
20 regard not. Heb. let not your eye spare, etc. Dt 7:16. 19:13, 21. 2 Ch 25:9. Is 13:18. Ezk 7:4, 9. 9:5. 20:17. Mt 6:19, 20. Ph 3:8, 13, 14. Col 3:1-3. He 10:34.
stuff. Ex 22:7. Jsh 7:11. 1 S 10:22. 25:13. 30:24. Ezk 12:3, 4. Mt 24:17. Lk 17:31.
the good. ver. 18. Ge 20:15. Ezr 9:12. Is 1:19.
21 waggons. ver. 19, 27. Ge 41:43. 46:5, 29. 50:9. Ex 14:6. 15:1, 4, 19. Nu 7:3-9. 1 K 10:28. Is 31:1. 36:9. Ezk 23:24.
commandment. Heb. mouth. ver. 19. Ex 17:1. 38:21. Dt +21:5mg. 2 Ch 8:13. 35:16. Ec 8:2.
22 To all. Ge 24:53. Ex 3:22. 12:35. 2 K 5:5, 22, 23, 26. Zc 3:4.
each. Jg 14:12, 19. 2 K 5:5, 22, 23. Re 6:11.
to Benjamin. Ge 43:34.
five. Ge +43:34.
23 laden with. Heb. carrying. ver. 17.
good things. Ge 24:10. 43:11. Ex 16:3.
24 See that. Ge 37:22. 42:21, 22. Ps ch. 133. Jn 13:34, 35. Ep 4:31, 32. Ph 2:2-5. Col 3:12, 13. 1 Th 5:13.
fall. Pr 29:9. Is 28:21.
26 Joseph. Lk 24:34. Re 1:18, 19.

alive. Ac 25:19.
and he is. ver. 8, 9. Ps 105:21.
And Jacob's. Heb. And his. Ge 37:35. 42:36,
38. 44:28. Jon 2:7.
he believed. Jb 9:16. 29:24. Ps 126:1. Lk
24:11, 41.

27 **the spirit**. Heb. *ruach*, **S#7307h**. Ge +26:35.
+41:8. Jg 15:19. 1 S 30:12. Ps 85:6. Is 57:15.
Ho 6:2. Hab 1:11.

28 **It is enough**. Ge 46:30. Ex 9:28. Nu 16:3, 7.
2 S 24:16. 1 K 19:4. Lk 2:28-30. Jn 16:21, 22.
alive. Ac 25:19.

GENESIS 46

1 A.M. 2298. B.C. 1706.
Beer-sheba. Ge +21:31.
and offered. Ge 4:4. 8:20. 12:8. 22:13.
33:20. 35:3, 7. Jb 1:5. 42:8.
unto. Ge 21:33. 26:23-25. 28:13. 31:42, 53.

2 **in the visions**. Ge 15:1, 13. 22:11. Nu 12:6.
24:4. 2 Ch 26:5. Jb 4:13. 33:14, 15. Da 2:19.
Ac 9:10. 10:3. 16:9.
Jacob. Ge 22:1. Ex 3:3, 4. 1 S 3:4, 10. Ac 9:4.
10:13.

3 **the God**. Ge 28:13.
fear not. Ge +15:1. Je 40:9.
I will. Ge +12:2. 18:18. Ex 12:17, 37. Dt 1:10.
10:22. 26:5. Ac 7:17.

4 **will go**. Ge 28:15. 48:21. Is 43:1, 2.
and I will. Ge 15:14-16. 50:5, 13, 24, 25. Ex
3:8.
and Joseph. Ge 50:1.

5 **Jacob**. Ac 7:15.
in the waggons. Ge 31:17, 18. 45:19, 21, 27.
Ex 10:24, 26.

6 **into Egypt**. Ge 15:13. Nu 20:15. Dt 10:22.
26:5. Jsh 24:4. 1 S 12:8. Ps 105:23. Is 52:4. Ac
7:15.

7 **his daughters**. Ge 37:35. Jsh 24:4. Ps
105:23. Is 52:4. Plural put for the singular, in
reference to his one daughter, Dinah. See
verses 15, 17. For other instances of this
usage see ver. 23. Ge 21:7. 1 Ch 1:41. 2:7.
7:12. 2 Ch 24:25. Mk 1:2. Jn 6:45. Ac 7:42.

8 **the names**. Ge ch. 29, 30. 35:23. ch. 49. Ex
1:1-5. 6:14-18. 1 Ch 2:1, 2. ch. 8. 2 Ch ch. 1,
26.
Reuben. Ge +29:32.

9 **Phallu**. i.e. *wonderful, distinguished*, **S#6396h**.
Ex 6:14, Pallu. Nu 26:5, 8. 1 Ch 5:3.
Hezron. i.e. *blooming; courtyard*, **S#2696h**. ver.
12. Ex 6:14. Nu 26:6, 21. Ru 4:18, 19. 1 Ch
2:5, 9, 18, 21, 24, 25. 4:1. 5:3.

10 **Simeon**. Ge +29:33.
Jemuel. *or*, Nemuel. i.e. *day of God*, **S#3223h**.
Ex 6:15.
Jamin. i.e. *prosperity, right hand; dextrous*,
S#3226h. Ex 6:15. Nu 26:12. 1 Ch 2:27. 4:24.
Ne 8:7.

Ohad. i.e. *union, power*, **S#161h**. Ex 6:15.
Jachin. *or*, Jarib. i.e. *he shall establish*, **S#3199h**.
Ex 6:15. Nu 26:12. 1 K 7:21. 1 Ch 9:10.
24:17. 2 Ch 3:17. Ne 11:10.
Zohar. *or*, Zerah. i.e. *whiteness, dryness*,
S#6714h. Ge 23:8. 25:9. Ex 6:15. 1 Ch 4:7, 24,
Zerah.
Shaul. i.e. *desired; eagerness*, **S#7586h**.
Canaanitish. Ge +10:18. 28:1.

11 **Levi**. Ge +29:34. Nu +1:49. ch. 4, 8. 1 Ch ch.
22-26.
Gershon. *or*, Gershom. i.e. *expulsion; exile*,
S#1648h. Ex 6:16, 17. Nu 3:17, 18, 21, 25.
4:22, 38, 41. 7:7. 10:17. 26:57. Jsh 21:6, 27. 1
Ch 6:1, 16 (Gershom). 15:7 (Gershom). 23:6.
Kohath. i.e. *assembly; obedience*, **S#6955h**. Ex
6:16, 18. Nu 3:17, 27. 26:57, 58. Jsh 21:5, 20,
26. 1 Ch 6:1, 2, 16, 18, 22, 38, 61, 66, 70.
15:5. 23:6, 12. Also **S#6955h**: Nu 3:19, 29. 4:2,
4, 15. 7:9. 16:1.
Merari. i.e. *bitterness*, **S#4847h**. Ex 6:16, 19. Nu
3:17, 20, 33, 35, 36. 4:29, 33, 42, 45. 7:8.
10:17. 26:57. Jsh 21:7, 34, 40. 1 Ch 6:1, 16,
19, 29, 44, 47, 63, 77. 9:14. 15:6, 17. 23:6, 21.
24:26, 27. 26:10, 19. 2 Ch 29:12. 34:12. Ezr
8:19.

12 **Judah**. Ge +35:23.
died in. Ge 38:7-10.
Pharez. i.e. *a breach*, **S#6557h**. Ge 38:29. Nu
26:20, 21. Ru 4:12, 18. 1 Ch 2:4, 5. 4:1. 9:4.
27:3. Ne 11:4, 6, Perez. Mt 1:3, Phares. Lk
3:33.
Hamul. i.e. *pitied*, **S#2538h**. Nu 26:21. 1 Ch
2:5.

13 **Issachar**. Ge +30:18. 1 Ch 12:32.
Tola. i.e. *worm; scarlet*, **S#8439h**. Nu 26:23. Jg
10:1. 1 Ch 7:1, 2.
Phuvah. *or*, Puah. i.e. *mouth; puff, blast*,
S#6312h. Nu 26:23. Jg 10:1, Pua. 1 Ch 7:1,
Puah.
Job. *or*, Jashub. i.e. *desire*, **S#3102h**, only here.
1 Ch 7:1, Jashub.
Shimron. i.e. *watch post; a guardian*, **S#8110h**.

14 **Zebulun**. Ge +30:20.
Jahleel. i.e. *hoping in God*, **S#3177h**. Nu 26:26.

15 **Leah**. Ge 29:32-35. 30:17-21. 35:23. 49:3-15.
Ex 1:2, 3. Nu 1. 10. 26. 1 Ch 2:1.
Padan-aram. Ge 25:20.
with his. Ge 30:21. 34:1, etc.
souls. Heb. *nephesh*, Ge +12:5. ver. 18, 22, 25,
26, 27.

16 **sons of Gad**. Ge +30:11.
Ziphion. *or*, Zephon. i.e. *watchtower*, **S#6837h**.
Haggi. i.e. *festive*, **S#2291h**. Nu 26:15.
Shuni. i.e. *my rest*, **S#7764h**. Nu 26:15.
Ezbon. *or*, Ozni. i.e. *splendor of God*, **S#675h**. 1
Ch 7:7.
Eri. i.e. *watcher of the Lord*, **S#6179h**. Nu 26:16.
Arodi. *or*, Arod. i.e. *my posterity; untamed*,
S#722h. Nu 26:17.

Areli. i.e. *heroic; lion of my God*, **S#692h**. Nu 26:17.

17 **Asher**. Ge +30:13.
Jimnah. i.e. *prosperity; good fortune*, **S#3232h**. Nu 26:44, 44. 1 Ch 7:30, Imnah. 2 Ch 31:14.
Ishuah. i.e. *quiet; he will be even or equal*, **S#3438h**. 1 Ch 7:30, Isuah.
Isui. i.e. *quiet; level*, **S#3438h**. 1 Ch 7:30, Ishuai. See Nu 26:44, Jesui.
Serah. i.e. *princess*, **S#8294h**. Nu 26:46, Sarah. 1 Ch 7:30.
Heber. i.e. *alliance; community*, **S#2268h**. Nu 26:45. Jg 4:11, 17, 21. 5:24. 1 Ch 4:18. 7:31, 32. 8:17.
Malchiel. i.e. *my king is God*, **S#4439h**. Nu 26:45. 1 Ch 7:31.

18 **Zilpah**. Ge +29:24. Ex 1:4.
souls. Heb. *nephesh*, Ge +12:5. ver. 15, 22, 25, 26, 27.

19 **Rachel**. Ge 29:18. 30:24. 35:16-18, 24. 44:27. Ex 1:3, 5. 1 Ch 2:2.
Joseph. Ge ch. 37, 39, 40-45, 47. 49:22-27. 50:1, etc. Nu 1:36, 37. 26:38-41. Dt 33:12-17.

20 **Manasseh**. Ge +41:51.
priest. *or*, prince. Ge 41:45, 50mg.

21 **sons of Benjamin**. Ge +35:18.
Belah. i.e. *consumption; destroying*, **S#1106h**. Ge 14:2, 8. 36:32, 33. Nu 26:38, 40. 1 Ch 1:43, 44. 5:8. 7:6, 7. 8:1, 3.
Becher. i.e. *youth; firstborn; firstfruits*, **S#1071h**. Nu 26:35. 1 Ch 7:6, 8.
Ashbel. i.e. *man of Baal; vain or decaying fire; fire of Bel*, **S#788h**. Nu 26:38. 1 Ch 8:1.
Gera. i.e. *enmity; a grain; sojourning*, **S#1617h**. Jg 3:15. 2 S 16:5. 19:16, 18. 1 K 2:8. 1 Ch 8:3, 5, 7.
Naaman. i.e. *pleasantness*, **S#5283h**. Nu 26:40, 40. 2 K 5:1, 2, 6, 9, 11, 17, 20, 21, 23, 27. 1 Ch 8:4, 7.
Ehi. i.e. *unity; my brother*, **S#278h**. Nu 26:38, Ahiram. Supposed by some to be the same with Ehud, 1 Ch 8:6. See Aharah, 1 Ch +8:1.
Rosh. i.e. *head, chief*, **S#7220h**. Also Ezk 38:2, 3. 39:1, chief.
Muppim. i.e. *anxieties, serpent*, **S#4649h**. Nu 26:39, Shupham. 1 Ch 7:12, Shuppim.
Huppim. i.e. *protection; coverings*, **S#2650h**. Nu 26:39, Hupham. 1 Ch 7:12, 15.
Ard. i.e. *fugitive*, **S#714h**. Nu 26:40. 1 Ch 8:3, Addar.

22 **souls**. Heb. *nephesh*, Ge +12:5. ver. 15, 18, 25, 26, 27.

23 **sons**. ver. 7.
Dan. Ge +30:6.
Hushim. i.e. *hasters; who hasten their birth*, **S#2366h**. Nu 26:42, 43, Shuham. 1 Ch 7:12. 8:8, 11.

24 **Naphtali**. Ge +30:8.
Jahzeel. i.e. *whom God allots*, **S#3183h**. Nu 26:48. 1 Ch 7:13, Jahziel.

Guni. i.e. *protected*, **S#1476h**. Nu 26:48. 1 Ch 5:15. 7:13.
Jezer. i.e. *frame, form; imagination, purpose*, **S#3337h**. Nu 26:49. 1 Ch 7:13.
Shillem. i.e. *requital; recompense*, **S#8006h**. Nu 26:49. Called Shallum, 1 Ch 7:13.

25 **Bilhah**. Ge +29:29. Ex 1:2.
souls. Heb. *nephesh*, Ge +12:5. ver. +15.

26 **souls**. Heb. *nephesh*, Ge +12:5.
loins. Heb. thigh. Ge 24:2. Pr 17:21, 23:24. Is 45:10. He +7:10.
souls. Heb. *nephesh*, Ge +12:5. ver. +15.
three score and. Ex 1:5.

27 **souls**. Heb. *nephesh*, Ge +12:5. ver. +15.
threescore and ten. ver. 15, 18, 22, 25, 26. Ex 1:5. 24:1. Nu 11:16, 24, 25. Dt 10:22. Ezk 8:11. Lk 10:1, 17. Ac 7:14.

28 **Judah**. ver. +12.
to direct. Ge 31:21.
Goshen. ver. 34. Jsh +10:41.

29 **his chariot**. Ge 41:43. 45:19, 21.
presented. Ge +12:7.
fell on. Lk +15:20.
wept. Ge +42:24.

30 **now let**. Ge 45:28. Lk 2:29, 30.

31 **I will**. Ge 45:16-20. 47:1-3. Ac 18:3. He 2:11.
My brethren. He 2:11.

32 **shepherds**. Ge 4:2. 31:18. 37:2. 47:3. Ex 3:1. 1 S 16:11. 17:15. Ps 78:70-72. Is 40:11. Zc 13:5.
their trade hath been to feed cattle. Heb. they are men of cattle. ver. 34. Ge 9:20. 1 K 9:27. 18:5, 6.
and they. Ge 45:10.

33 **What is**. ver. 32. Ge 47:2-4. Jon 1:8.

34 **Thy servants**. ver. 32. Ge 30:35. 32:13-15. 34:5. 37:12.
for every. Ge 43:32. Ex 8:26.

GENESIS 47

1 **Joseph**. Ge 45:16. 46:31.
my brethren. He 2:11.
in the land. Jsh +10:41.

2 **five**. Ge +43:34.
presented. Ac 7:13. 2 C 4:14. Col 1:28. Ju 24.

3 **What is**. Ge 46:33, 34. Am 7:14, 15. Jon 1:8. 2 Th 3:10.
shepherds. Ge 4:2. 46:33, 34.

4 **For to**. Ge 12:10. 15:13. Dt 26:5. Ps 105:23. Is 52:4. Ac 7:6.
for the famine. Ge 43:1. Ac 7:11.
let thy. Ge 46:34.

6 **is**. ver. 11. Ge 13:9. 20:15. 34:10. 45:18-20. Pr 21:1. Jn 17:2.
Goshen. ver. 1, 4, 11.
men of activity. Pr +22:3, 29.
rulers. Ex +18:21. 1 S 21:7. 1 Ch 27:29-31. 2 Ch 26:10. Pr 22:29.

cattle. ver. +16. Ex 9:3-6, 10-21.

7 and Jacob. ver. 10. Ex 12:32. Jsh 14:13. 1 S 2:20. 2 S 16:16. 1 K 1:47. 2 K 4:29. Da 2:4. 5:10. Mt 26:26. Lk 22:19. 1 P 2:17.

8 How old art thou? Heb. How many are the days of the years of thy life? ver. 9. 2 S 19:34.

9 The days. Ge 25:7. 35:28. 1 Ch 29:15. Ps 39:12. 119:19, 54. 2 C 5:6. He 11:9-16. 13:14. 1 P 2:11.
an hundred. Jb 14:1. Ps 39:5. 89:47, 48. 90:3-12. Ja 4:14.
few and evil. Ge 27:42. 31:41. 32:6, 7. 34:2. 35:19, 20, 22. 37:33, 34. 42:36.
have not. ver. 28. Ge 5:27. 11:11, 24, 25. 25:7, 8. 35:28. 50:26. Ex 6:4. 7:7. Dt 34:7. Jsh 24:29. 2 S 19:32-35. Jb 8:8, 9. 42:16, 17. He 11:13. 13:14.

10 blessed. ver. 7. Ge 14:19. Nu 6:23-27. Dt 33:1. Ru 2:4. 2 S 8:10. 19:39. Ps 119:46. 129:8. He 7:7.

11 Rameses. i.e. *son of the sun,* **S#7486h.** ver. 6. Ex 1:11. 12:37. Nu 33:3, 5. Jn 10:10, 28. 14:2, 23. 17:2, 24.

12 nourished. Ru 4:15.
his father. Ex 20:12. Mt 15:4-6. Mk 7:10-13. 1 T 4:8. 5:4, 8.
according to their families. *or,* as a little child is nourished. Heb. according to the little ones. ver. 1, 21, 24. Nu +16:27. Ps 23:1. 1 Th 2:7.

13 A.M. 2300. B.C. 1704.
so that. Ge 41:30, 31. 1 K 18:5. Je 14:1-6. La 2:19, 20. 4:9. Ac 7:11.
fainted. Je 9:12. Jl 1:10-12.

14 the money. Ge 41:56.
Joseph brought. Lk 16:1, 2, 10-12. 1 C 4:2. 1 P 4:10.

15 A.M. 2301. B.C. 1703.
the Egyptians. lit. Egypt. Mt 3:5.
Give us bread. ver. 18, 19, 24. Jg 8:5, 8. 1 S 21:3. 25:8. Ps 37:3. Is 33:16. Mt 6:11.
why. Jn 11:25.

16 Give your cattle. Pr 12:17. Da 6:5-7. 1 C 10:32. Ph 4:8. Col 4:5.

17 for horses. Ex 9:3. 1 K 10:28. Jb 2:4. Is 31:1. Mt 6:24.
fed them. Heb. led them. Ex 15:13. 2 Ch 28:15. 32:22. Ps 23:2. 31:3. Is 40:11. 49:10. 51:8. Jn 21:16.

18 A.M. 2302. B.C. 1702.
We will. 2 K 6:26. Je 38:9.
spent. Mk 5:26. Lk 7:42. 15:14.
bodies. Ro 12:1.

19 die. Jn 11:25.
buy us. Ne 5:2, 3. Jb 2:4. La 1:11. 5:6, 9. Mt 16:26. Ph 3:8, 9.
and give. See on ver. 23.

21 A.M. 2303. B.C. 1701.
And as. Ge 41:48.

removed them. Jb 5:20. Ps 33:19. 37:19. 107:36.
to cities. Ge 41:48.

22 of the priests. *or,* princes. Ge 14:18. 41:45, 50mg. 2 S 8:18.
for the priests. Dt 12:19. Jsh 21. Ezr 7:24. Ne 13:10, 13. Mt 10:10. 1 C 9:13. Ga 6:6. 2 Th 3:10. 1 T 5:17.
portion. lit. statute. Jb 23:12mg. Pr 30:8mg. Ezk 16:27.

23 bought. ver. 19. 1 C 6:20.
here is seed. Ge 41:27. 45:6. Ps 41:1. 107:36, 37. 112:5. Pr 11:26. 12:11. 13:23. Ec 11:6. Is 28:24, 25. 55:10, 11. Mt 24:45. 2 C 9:10.

24 the fifth part. ver. 25. Ge 41:34. Le 27:32. 1 S 8:15-17. Ps 41:1. 112:5.

25 Thou hast. Ge 6:19. 41:45mg. 45:6-8. 50:20. Pr 11:26, 27.
let us. Ge 18:3. 33:15. Ru 2:13.

26 unto this day. Ge +19:38.
except. ver. 22. Ezk 7:24.
priests. *or,* princes. See on ver. 22.

27 dwelt. ver. 11.
grew. Ge 8:7, 9. +12:2. Dt 10:22. Ne 9:23. Ps 105:24. 107:38. Zc 10:8. Ac 7:17.

28 A.M. 2315. B.C. 1689.
seventeen. Ge 37:2.
the whole age. Heb. the days of the years of his life. ver. 8mg, 9. Ps 90:10mg, 12. 119:84. Je +28:3mg.

29 must die. ver. 9. Ge 3:19. 50:24. Dt 31:14. 2 S 7:12. 14:14. 1 K 2:1. Jb 7:1. 14:14. 30:23. Ps 6:5. 23:4. 49:7, 9. 89:48. He +9:27.
put. Ge +24:2.
deal kindly. Ge 24:49.
bury me not. Ge 50:24, 25. Ac 7:15, 16. He 11:22.

30 lie. Ge 23:19. 25:9. 49:29-32. 50:5-14, 25. 2 S 19:37. 1 K 13:22. Ne 2:3, 5.
buryingplace. Heb. *qeburah,* **S#6900h,** Ge +35:20.

31 Swear. Ge 24:3.
And Israel bowed. ver. 29. Ge 24:26. 48:1, 2. 1 K 1:47. He *11:21.*

GENESIS 48

1 thy father. Jn 11:3.
his two sons. Ge 41:50-52. 46:20. 50:23. Jb 42:16. Ps 128:6.

2 strengthened. Dt 3:28. 1 S 23:16. Ne 2:18. Ps 41:3. Pr 23:15. Ep 6:10.

3 God Almighty. Ex +6:3. Re 21:22.
appeared. Ge 28:12-19. +35:9.
Luz. Ge +28:19.
Canaan. Ge 11:31. 12:5. 13:12. 16:3. 17:8. 31:18. 33:18. 35:6. 36:5. 37:1. 42:5. 45:17. 46:6. 47:1. 49:30.

4 Behold, I. Ge +12:2.
will give. Dt 32:8. 2 Ch +20:7. Am +9:14, 15.

everlasting. Heb. *olam*, Ge +17:7. Ge +8:22. +9:16. +13:15. +17:8, 13.

5 **two sons**. Ge 41:50-52. 46:20. Jsh 13:7. 14:4. ch. 16, 17.
 are mine. Le 20:26. Nu 1:10, 32-35. 26:28-37. Is 43:1. Ezk 16:8. Ml 3:17. 2 C 6:18. Ep 1:5.
 Reuben. 1 Ch 5:1, 2. Re 7:6, 7.

6 **and shall be called**. Jsh 13:29. 14:4. 16:5. 1 Ch 5:1, 2. Ps 77:15.

7 **Padan**. i.e. *plain*, **s#6307h**. Ge +25:20.
 Rachel. Ge 35:9, 16-19. 1 S 10:2. Mt 2:18.
 to Ephrath. i.e. *fruitfulness*, **s#672h**. Ge 35:16, 19. Ru +1:2. 1 Ch 2:19. Mi 5:2. Mt 2:1, 16, 18.
 Bethlehem. Jsh +19:15.

9 **my sons**. Ge 30:2. 33:5. Ru 4:11-14. 1 S 1:20, 27. 2:20, 21. 1 ch 25:5. 26:45. Ps +127:3. Is 8:18. 56:3-5.
 bless them. Ge +27:4, 28, 29, 34-40. Dt 33:1. He 11:21.

10 **the eyes**. Ge +27:1.
 dim. Heb. heavy. Is 6:10. 59:1.
 kissed. Ge +27:27.

11 **I had not**. Ge 37:33, 35. 42:36. 45:26.
 God. Ep 3:20.

12 **he bowed himself**. Ge 18:2. 19:1. 23:7. 33:3. 42:6. Ex +20:12. 34:8. Le 19:3, 32. 1 K 2:19. 2 K 4:37. Pr 31:28. 1 C 15:28. Ph 2:5-8. Ep 6:1.

13 **Israel's left**. Ge 41:52. Jg 3:15. +20:16. Ec 10:2. Mt 25:41.
 Israel's right. Ge 41:51. 1 K 2:19. Ps 16:8. +18:35. 45:9. +110:1. Mt 25:33.

14 **right hand**. ver. +13. Ex 15:6. Ps 110:1. 118:16.
 and laid. Ac +8:17.
 guiding. *or*, making his hands wise. ver. 19.
 firstborn. ver. 18. Ge 41:51. 46:20. 1 Ch +26:10. Col +1:15.

15 **blessed**. ver. 16. Ge 27:4. 28:3. 49:28. Dt 33:1. He 11:21.
 Joseph. Ge 49:22. Dt 33:13. Am +5:6.
 did walk. Ge +5:22. Is 30:21. Je 8:2. 1 C 10:31. 2 C 1:12. Col 2:6. 1 Th 2:12.
 fed me. Ge 28:20, 22. +47:17. Ps 23:1. 28:9. 37:3. 103:4, 5. Ec 2:24, 25. 5:12, 18. 6:7. Is 33:16. Mt 6:25-34. 1 T 6:6-10.
 unto. Ge +19:38.

16 **The Angel**. Ge 28:15. Ps 121:7. Is 47:4. Zc +12:8. 1 C 10:4, 9.
 redeemed. Ps +34:2. Mt 6:13. Jn 17:15. Ro 8:23. 2 T 4:18.
 my name. ver. 5. Ge 32:28. Nu +6:27. Dt 28:10. 2 Ch +7:14. Je 14:9. Am 9:12. Ac 15:17.
 grow into. Heb. as fishes do increase. Ge 1:21, 22. Nu 1:46. 26:34, 37.
 a multitude. Ge 49:22. Ex 1:7. Nu 26:28-37. Dt 33:17. Jsh 17:17.

17 **laid his**. ver. 14.
 displeased him. Heb. was evil in his eyes. Nu +22:34mg. 1 S 16:7. 1 K 16:25. Ro 9:7, 8, 11.

18 **Not so**. Ge 19:18. Ex 10:11. Mt 25:9. Ac 10:14. 11:8.
 for this. Ge 27:15. 29:26. 43:33. 49:3.
 firstborn. Ge 41:51. 1 Ch +26:10. Je 31:9. Col +1:15.
 right hand. ver. +13.

19 **said, I know it**. ver. 14. Ge 17:20, 21. 25:23. Nu 1:33-35. 2:19-21. Dt 33:17. Is 7:17. Ezk 37:10. Re 7:6, 8.
 become. Dt 1:10. Ru 4:11, 12.
 multitude. Heb. fulness.

20 **Israel bless**. Ge 24:60. 28:3. Ru 4:11, 12.
 and he set. Nu 2:18-21. 7:48, 54. 10:22, 23. 13:8, 11, 16.

21 **Behold**. Ge 50:24. 1 K 2:2-4. Ps 146:3, 4. Zc 1:5, 6. Lk 2:29. Ac 13:36. 2 T 4:6. He 7:3, 8, 23-25. 2 P 1:14.
 God. Ge 15:14. 46:4. Dt ch. 1. 23:14. Jsh 3:7. 23:14. ch. 24. Ps 18:46.
 land. Ge 12:5. 26:3. 37:1.

22 **given**. Ge 33:19. Dt 21:17. Jsh 24:32. 1 Ch 5:2. Ezk 47:13. Jn 4:5.
 above. Ge +44:30.
 Amorite. Ge +10:16. Jsh 17:14-18.

GENESIS 49

1 **Gather**. Dt 31:12, 28, 29. 33:1, etc. Ps 25:14. 105:15. Is 22:14. 53:1. Da 2:47. 10:1. Am 3:7. Lk 2:26. Ro 1:17, 18. He 10:24, 25. 13:1. Re 4:1.
 last days. Nu 24:14. Dt 4:30. 31:29. Ps +118:24. Is 2:2. +13:6. 39:6. Je 23:20. 30:24. 48:47. 49:39. Ezk 38:8, 16. Da 2:28, 29. 8:17. 10:14. 12:13. Ho 3:5. Jl 2:28. Mi 4:1. Mt 24:6, 14. Jn 6:39, 40, +54. Ac 2:17. 1 C +3:13. 1 T 4:1. 2 T 3:1. He 1:2. Ja 5:3. 1 P 1:5. 2 P 3:3.

2 **hearken**. ver. 29, 33. Ex 18:24-27. 1 S 3:16-18. Ps 34:11. Pr 1:8, 9. 2:1-6. 4:1-4. 5:1. 6:20. 7:1, 24. 8:32. 23:19-22, 26.

3 **my firstborn**. Ge +29:32. 48:18.
 my might. Dt 21:17, 27. Ps 78:51. 105:36.

4 **Unstable**. Jg 5:15, 16. Ja 1:6-8. 2 P 2:14. 3:16.
 thou shalt not excel. Heb. do not thou excel. Ge 46:8. Nu ch. 32. Dt 33:6.
 because. Ge 35:22. Dt 5:21. 27:20. 1 Ch 5:1. 1 C 5:1.
 he went up to my couch. *or*, my couch is gone. 2 K 1:16. Ps 132:3.

5 **Simeon**. Ge +29:33. Pr 18:9.
 instruments, etc. *or*, their swords *are* weapons of violence. Ge 34:25-29, 35.

6 **O my soul**. Heb. *nephesh*, **s#5315h**, Ge +34:3. Jg 5:21. Ps 42:5, 11. 43:5. 103:1. Je 4:19. Lk 12:19.

come. Ge 34:30. Ps 5:10. 26:4, 5. 28:3. 64:2. 94:20, 21. 139:19. Pr 1:11, 15, 16. 12:5.

secret. Dt 27:24. Ps 26:9. 64:2. Pr 11:13. Je 15:17. Ep 5:11.

unto their. Ps 1:1. 26:9. 94:20. 2 C 6:14.

honor. Ps 7:6. +16:9 (glory). +30:12mg. 57:8.

a man. Ge 34:7, 25, 26, 36. Le 19:18. Dt 32:35. 2 S 13:22-39. Ps 94:1. Pr 20:22. Na 1:2. Ro 12:17, 19. He 10:30.

selfwill. Ne 9:24, 37. Is 28:12. 30:15. Da 11:3, 16. Lk 19:14. 2 P 2:10.

digged down a wall. *or*, houghed oxen. Jsh 11:6, 9.

7   **Cursed**. Nu 18:23. Jsh 21:3. 2 S 13:15, 22-28. Pr 26:24, 25. 27:3.

I will divide. Jsh 19:1-9. ch. 21. 1 Ch 4:24-31, 39, 40. 6:65.

8   **shall praise**. Ge +35:23.

thy hand. Nu 1:27. 10:14. 26:22. Jg 1:1, 2. 20:18. 2 S 24:9. 1 K ch. 4. 1 Ch ch. 12. 2 Ch 11:12-17. 14:8. 15:9. 17:2, 14-16. 30:11. Ps 18:40-43. 78:68-71. Is 9:7. Ph 2:10, 11. He 7:14. 10:13. Re 5:5. 11:15.

the neck. Jsh 10:24. 2 S 22:41. Ezk 21:29.

thy father's. Ge 27:29. 37:7-10. 42:6. 2 S 5:3.

9   **is**. Metaphor: a declaration that one thing is (or represents) another. The rest of the verse is Allegory, in the form of extended or continued metaphor. For other instances of the figure Metaphor see Ps 23:1. 109:4. Mt 5:13. 13:38. 26:26. Mk +14:22, 24. Lk 8:14. Jn 6:35. 8:12. 10:9. 15:5.

a lion's. Is +5:29. 1 C 15:24.

prey. ver. 27. Jb 38:39. Ps 17:12. 22:13. 104:21.

gone up. SS 4:8.

he stooped. Nu 23:24. 24:9. Ps 10:10.

rouse. 1 K 4:25.

10   **scepter**. Nu 24:17, 19. 2 S 7:14. 1 Ch 5:2. 28:4. Jb 9:34. Ps 2:9. 45:6. 60:7. 89:32. 110:2. Pr 10:13. Is 2:4. 14:5. Je 30:21. 47:5. Ezk 19:11, 14. Ho 11:12. Am 1:5. Zc 10:11. Mt 23:2. Lk 11:52. Ro 13:4. Re 2:7. 12:5. +19:15.

not depart. Ps 89:39. Ezk 21:26, 27.

from Judah. 2 S 2:4. 1 Ch +5:2. Ps +60:7. Mi +5:2. Mt 1:2. 2:6. He +7:14. Re 5:5.

lawgiver. or, ruler's staff. Nu 21:18. Ezr 1:5, 8. Ps 60:7. 108:8. Is 33:22.

between. Dt +17:15. 28:57. Je 30:21.

feet. Dt +11:6mg. Jg 5:27mg.

until. LXX., until that which is his shall come. Ge +3:15. Ps +16:10. Is +9:6. 11:1-5. 62:11. Je 23:5, 6. Ezk +21:26, 27. Da 9:25, 26. Hg 2:7-9. Mt 1:21. +11:3. 17:5. 21:9. Lk 1:32, 33. Jn 9:7. 18:31. 19:12, 15. 1 C +15:4.

Shiloh. i.e. *a Savior; peace bringer*, **S#7886h**, only here. For **S#7887h**, Shiloh, see Jg +21:19.

unto him. Jn 12:32. 2 C 5:15. Ep 3:21. 2 Th 2:1. He 13:13.

the gathering. or, obedience. Dt 18:15, 18, 19. Ps 2:8. 72:8-11. 98:3. +102:18. Is 2:2. +11:10. 26:18. 45:22. 51:5. 55:4, 5. Ezk +17:23. 21:27. Mi +5:2. Hg 2:7. Zc +14:9, 16. Mt 2:6. 25:32. Mk 16:15. Lk 1:32, 33. Jn 3:17. 11:52. Ro +11:25. 15:12. 2 C 5:10. He 7:14. Re +11:15.

11   **his foal**. Is 63:1-3.

he washed. Dt 33:28. 1 K 4:20, 25. 2 K 18:31, 32. Jl 3:18. Mi 4:4. Re 7:14. 19:18.

12   **red with wine**. Pr 23:29.

with milk. Ex 3:8. SS 5:12.

13   **Zebulun**. Ge +30:20.

Zidon. i.e. *fishery; plenty of fish, hunting*, **S#6721h**. Ge 10:15, +19, Sidon. Jsh 11:8. 19:28. Jg 1:31. 10:6. 18:28. 2 S 24:6. 1 K 17:9. 1 Ch 1:13. Ezr 3:7. Is 23:2, 4, 12. Je 25:22. 27:3. 47:4. Ezk 27:8. 28:21, 22. Jl 3:4. Zc 9:2. Mt 11:21.

14   **Issachar**. Ge +30:18. 1 Ch 12:32.

15   **rest**. Jsh 14:15. Jg 3:11. 2 S 7:1.

bowed. Ps 81:6. Ezk 29:18. Mt 23:4.

16   **shall judge**. Ge +30:6.

17   **shall be**. Jg ch. 14, 15. 16:22-30. 18:22-31. 1 Ch 12:35.

an adder. Heb. an arrow snake. or, horned snake. **S#8207h**, only here. Ps 58:4. 91:13. 140:3. Pr 23:32. Je 8:17.

18   **waited for**. Jb 14:14. Ps 14:7. +25:3. 85:7. 119:41, 166, 174. Is 36:8. Mt 1:21. Mk 15:43. Lk 1:29, 30. 12:35, 36. 23:51. Ro 8:19, 23, 25. 1 C 1:7. Ga 5:5. Ph 1:23. 1 Th 1:10. 2 Th 3:5. He 10:36.

salvation. La 3:26. 2 T 2:10.

19   **Gad**. Ge +30:11. Nu ch. 32. Jg ch. 10, 11.

20   **Asher**. Ge +30:13.

fat. **S#8082h**. Nu 13:20. Jg 3:29. 1 Ch 4:40. Ne 9:25, 35. Is 30:23. 35:2. Ezk 34:14, 16. Hab 1:16.

21   **Naphtali**. Ge +30:8. Ps 18:33, 34.

22   **a fruitful**. Ge 30:22-24. 41:52. 46:27. 48:1, 5, 16, 19, 20. Nu ch. 32. Dt 33:17. Jsh ch. 16. 17:14-17. Ps 1:1-3. 128:1, 3. Ezk 19:11. Jn 15:1.

well. Heb. *ayin*, a fountain. Ge +24:13. Jn 4:14.

branches. Heb. daughters. Nu +21:25mg.

23   **archers**. Ge 37:4, 18, 24, 28. 39:7-20. 42:21. Ps 64:3. 118:13. Jn 16:33. Ac 14:22.

grieved. Is 53:3.

24   **his bow**. Ne 6:9. Jb 29:20. Ps 18:32, 34. 27:14. 28:8. 89:1. Col 1:11. 2 T 4:17.

arms. Jb 22:8mg. Ps 77:15.

were made. Jb 29:20. Ps 18:32-35. 37:14, 15. 44:7. Zc 10:12. Ro 14:4.

strong. Ps 89:19.

the mighty. Ge 35:10, 11. Ex 3:6. Ps 18:1, 30, 32, 34. +132:2.

the shepherd. Ge 45:5, 7, 11. 47:12. 48:15. 50:21. Nu 27:16-18. Dt 34:9. Jsh 1:1-9. ch. 24. Ps 80:1. He 13:20.

the stone. Dt 32:4. Ps 2:12. Is 17:10. 30:29. 63:1-6. Da 2:45. Mt +21:42. 1 C 15:24.

25 **the God**. Ge 28:13, 21. 35:3. 43:23. 48:15, 16. Dt 8:17. 28:12. 33:1, 13-17. He 1:9.
the Almighty. Ge +17:1. Ex +6:3. Nu 24:4, 16. Ru 1:20, 21. Jb +5:17. Ps 68:14. 91:1. Is 13:6. Ezk 1:24. Jl 1:15. Re 1:8.
bless. Ps 45:7.
with blessings. Dt 28:2-12. 33:13. Ps 84:11. 85:12. Mt 6:33. 1 C 3:21, 22. Ep 1:3. Ph 4:19. 1 T +4:8.
of heaven. Ge 27:28, 39. Le 26:4. Dt 28:12. 33:13, 14. Is +26:19. Je 5:24.
of the deep. Ge 1:2. 7:11. Dt 8:7. +33:13. Jon +2:5.
lieth under. Dt +33:13 (**S#8478h**).
womb. Ge +29:31. Ps 128:3.

26 **The blessings**. Dt 33:16.
have prevailed. Ge 27:27-29, 39, 40. 28:3, 4. 37:4. Ep 1:3.
everlasting. Heb. *olam*, Ge +17:7.
hills. Dt 33:15. Ps 89:36. Is 54:10. Ezk 37:25, 26. Jon 2:6. Hab 3:6.
they shall. Dt 33:16. Ps 132:18.
was separate. Ge 37:28. Nu 6:2. Ps 105:17-22. Is 66:5. Ac 7:9. He 7:26.

27 **Benjamin**. Nu +1:37.
ravin. Ge 35:18. 46:21. Dt 33:12.
a wolf. Nu 23:24. Jg 3:15-29. 20:21, 25. 1 S 11:4-11. ch. 14, 15, 17. Ac 8:3. 9:1. Ph 3:5.
morning. Ps 49:14. 55:17. 92:2. Ec 11:6.
the prey. Zp +3:8.
at night. Je 5:6. Ezk 22:25, 27. Ho 13:7, 8. Zp 3:3. Mt 7:15. 10:16. Ac 20:29.

28 **the twelve**. Nu 23:24. Est 8:7, 9, 11. ch. 9, 10. Ezk 39:8-10. Zc 14:1-7. He 12:23.
every one. Ge 35:22. Ex 28:21. 1 K 18:31. Ac 26:7. Ro 12:6. 1 C 12:4, 7, 13. Ja 1:1. 1 P 4:10. Re 7:4.

29 **charged**. Ge 50:16.
gathered. ver. 33. Ge +25:8. He 12:23.
bury me. Ge 15:15. 25:8-17. 35:29. 47:30. 2 S 2:32. 19:37. He 12:23.
in the cave. Ge 23:9, 17, 19. 25:9. 50:13.
Ephron. Ge 50:13.

30 **Abraham bought**. Ge 23:8.
buryingplace. Heb. *qeber*, **S#6913h**, Ge +23:4.

31 **they buried**. Ge 23:3, 16-20. 25:9. 35:29. 47:30. 50:13. Ac 7:16. He 11:13.

32 **The purchase**. Ge 23:17-20.
Heth. Ge +10:15.

33 **had made**. ver. 1, 24-26. Jsh 24:27-29. He 11:22.
and yielded. ver. 29. Ge 15:5. 25:8, 17. 35:29. Jb 3:11. 10:18. 11:20. 13:19. 14:10. Ps 37:37. Je 15:9. La 1:19. Mt 27:50. Mk 15:37, 39. Lk 23:46. Jn 19:30. Ac 5:5, 10. +7:59. 12:23.
ghost. Ac +7:59. Heb. *gava*, **S#1478h**. Ge 6:17 (die). 7:21 (died). 25:8, 17. 35:29. 49:33. Nu

17:12 (die), 13 (dying). 20:3 (died), 3, 29 (dead). Jsh 22:20 (perished). Jb 3:11. 10:18. 13:19. 14:10. 27:5 (die). 29:18 (die). 34:15 (perish). 36:12 (die). Ps 88:15 (die). 104:29 (die). La 1:19. Zc 13:8.
gathered. ver. 29. Ge 25:8, 17. 35:29. Dt 32:49, 50.
unto. Jb 5:26. 30:23. Ec 12:7. Is 57:1, 2. Lk 2:29. He 11:13-16. 12:23.

GENESIS 50

1 **fell**. Ge 46:4. Dt 6:7, 8. Ep 6:4.
wept. Ge +42:24.
kissed. Ge +27:27.

2 **the physicians**. Jb +13:4.
embalmed. ver. 26. 2 Ch 16:14, 18. Mt 26:12. Mk 14:8. 16:1. Lk 24:1. Jn 12:7. 19:39, 40.

3 **forty days**. Ge 8:6. Ex 34:28. Jon +3:4.
mourned. Heb. wept.
threescore. Nu 20:29. Dt 21:13. 34:8.

4 **the days**. ver. 10.
Joseph. Est 4:2.
found grace. Ge 18:3.

5 **made me**. Ge 47:29-31.
Lo, I die. ver. 24. Ge 48:21. 49:29, 30. Dt 4:22. 1 S 14:43.
I have. 2 Ch 16:14. Is 22:16. Mt 27:60.
bury me. Ge 3:19. Jb 30:23. Ps 79:3. Ec 6:3. 12:5, 7.
let me go. Mt 8:21, 22. Lk 9:59, 60.

6 **as he made**. Ge 48:21.

7 **and with him**. Ge 14:16.
elders. Ex +3:16.

8 **only their**. Ex 10:8, 9, 26. Nu 32:24-27.

9 **chariots**. Ge 41:43. 46:29. Ex 14:7, 17, 28. 2 K 18:24. SS 1:9. Ac 8:2.

10 **the threshingfloor**. Nu 15:20. 18:27, 30. Dt 15:14. 16:13mg. Jg 6:37. Ru 3:2. 1 S 23:1. 2 S 6:6. 24:16, 18-21, 24. 1 K 22:10mg. 2 K 6:27. 1 Ch 13:9. 21:15, 28. 2 Ch 3:1. 18:9. Is 21:10. Je 51:33. Da 2:35. Ho 9:2. Mi 4:12. Mt 3:12. Lk 3:17.
beyond Jordan. ver. 11. Dt 1:1.
Atad. i.e. *bramble*, **S#329h**. ver. 11. Jg 9:14mg.
mourned. Ge +23:2.
seven days. ver. 4. Nu 19:11. Dt 34:8. 1 S 31:13. 2 S 1:17. Jb 2:13.

11 **the Canaanites**. Ge +10:18.
Abel-mizraim. i.e. The mourning of the Egyptians. **S#67h**. 1 S 6:18.
beyond Jordan. ver. 10. Dt 3:25, 27. 11:30.

12 **according**. Ge 47:29-31. 49:29-32. Ex 20:12. Ac 7:16. Ep 6:1.

13 **his sons**. Ge 49:29, 30. Ac 7:16.
buried. Ge +15:15. 25:9. +35:29. 49:33.
the cave. Ge 35:27, 29. +49:29. 2 K 21:18.
buryingplace. Heb. *qeber*, Ge +23:4.

15 **their father**. Ge 27:41, 42.

Joseph. Ge 42:17. Le 26:36. Jb 15:21, 22. Ps 14:5. 58:5. Pr 28:1. Ro 2:15.

16 sent. Heb. charged. Pr 29:25.

17 Forgive. Mt 6:12, 14, 15. 18:35. Lk 17:3, 4. Jn 14:9. Ep 4:32. Col 3:12, 13.

they did. ver. 20. Jb 33:27, 28. Ps 21:11. Pr 28:13. Ja 5:16.

servants. Ge 31:42. 49:25. Mt 10:42. 25:40. Mk 10:41. Ga 6:10, 16. Phm 8-20.

wept. Ge +42:24. 45:4, 5, 8.

18 fell. Ge +18:2. 37:7-11. 45:3.

19 fear not. Ge 45:5. Mt 14:27. Lk 24:37, 38.

for am I. Ge 30:2. +49:6. Dt 32:35. 2 K 5:7. Jb 34:19-29. Ro +12:19. He 10:30.

20 ye thought. Ge 37:4, 18-20. Ps 56:5.

evil. Jb 5:9. Ps 12:3. 27:4.

God meant. lit. thought. Ge +45:5-8. Ps 40:5, 17. 76:10. 105:16, 17. 119:71, 91. Pr 19:21. Is 10:5-7, 12. 55:8. Je +29:11. Mk 15:9, 10. Jn 3:16. Ac 2:23, 24. 3:13-15, 26. Ro 8:28. He 2:10.

this day. Ge +19:38.

21 fear. Jn 14:1.

I will nourish. Ge 45:10, 11. 47:12. Mt 5:44. 6:14. Ro 12:20, 21. 1 Th 5:15. 1 P 3:9.

kindly to them. Heb. to their hearts. Ge +34:3mg.

22 an hundred. ver. 26.

23 the children. Ge 48:19. 49:12. Jb 42:16. Ps 128:4, 6.

Machir. i.e. *sold; salesman*, **S#4353h**. Nu 26:29. 27:1. 32:39, 40. 36:1. Dt 3:15. Jsh 13:31. 17:1, 3. Jg 5:14. 2 S 9:4. 1 Ch 2:21, 23. 7:14-17.

brought up. Heb. born.

Joseph's. Ge 30:3.

24 I die. ver. 5. Ge 3:19. Jb 30:23. Ec 12:5, 7. Ro 5:12. He +9:27.

surely. He 11:22.

visit you. Ge 21:1. Ex 4:31. Ezk 25:12mg.

you out. Ge 15:13-16. 26:3. 35:12. 46:4. 48:21. Ex 3:16, 17. He 11:22.

sware. Ge +13:15. 46:4.

to Abraham. Je +33:26.

25 took an. ver. 5. Ge 47:29-31.

and ye. Ex 13:19. Jsh 24:32. Ac 7:15, 16. He 11:22.

26 being an hundred and ten years old. ver. 22. Ge 47:9, 28. Jsh 24:29.

they embalmed. ver. 2, 3.

EXODUS

EXODUS 1

1 A.M. 2299. B.C. 1705.
these are. Ex 6:14-16. Ge 29:31-35. 30:1-21. 35:18, 23-26. 46:8-26. 49:3-27. 1 Ch 2:1, 2. 12:23-40. 27:16-22. Re 7:4-8.
2 Reuben. Ge +29:32. 35:22.
3 Issachar. Ge +30:18.
Benjamin. Ex 28:20.
4 Dan. Ge +30:6.
Gad. Ge +30:11.
Asher. Ge +30:13.
5 loins. Heb. thigh. Ge +24:2.
seventy. ver. 20. Ge +46:27.
souls. Heb. *nephesh*, Ge +12:5.
6 A.M. 2369. B.C. 1635.
Joseph died. Ge 50:24, 26. Ac 7:14-16.
and all. Ec 1:4. He +9:27.
7 And. Ge +8:22.
fruitful. Ex 12:37, 38. Ge 1:20, 28. 9:1. +12:2. 48:4, 16. Dt 10:22. Ne 9:23. Ps 105:24. Ac 7:17, 18.
8 a new king. Dt 32:17. Jg 5:8. Ec 1:9. 2:18, 19. 9:15. Is 42:9. Ezk 11:19.
knew not. Jn 10:4, 5. Ac 7:18. 1 C 2:8. He 6:10.
9 the people. Nu 22:4, 5. Jb 5:2. Ps 105:24, 25. Pr 14:28. 27:4. Ec 4:4. T 3:3. Ja 3:14-16. 4:5.
10 Come on. Ps 2:1-4. 10:2. +83:3, 4. Pr 1:11.
wisely. Nu 22:6. Jb 5:13. Ps 105:25. Pr 16:25. +21:30. Ac 7:19. 23:12. 1 C 3:18-20. Ja 3:15-18.
11 to afflict. Ex 3:7. 5:15. Ge 15:13. Nu 20:15. Dt 26:6.
burdens. Ex 2:11. 5:4, 5. Ps 68:13. 81:6. 105:13.
treasure cities. 1 K 9:19. 2 Ch 8:4, 6. 16:4. 17:12. 32:28.
Pithom. i.e. *a dilation of the mouth; mouth of integrity*, **S#6619h.**
Raamses. i.e. *thunder of the standard*, **S#7486h.** Ge 47:11. Pr 27:4.
12 But the more, etc. Heb. and as they afflicted them, so they multiplied, etc.
multiplied. Ps 105:24. Pr 21:30. Ro 8:28. He 12:6-11.
grieved. ver. 9. Ge 27:46. Le 20:23. Nu 21:5.

22:3. 1 K 11:25. Jb 5:2. Pr 3:11. 27:4. Is 7:6, 16. Jn 12:19. Ac 4:2-4. 5:28-33.
14 their lives. Ex 2:23. 6:9. Ge 15:13. Nu 20:15. Dt 4:20. 26:6. Ru 1:20. Ac 7:19, 34.
in mortar. Ps 68:13. 81:6. Na 3:14.
was with rigour. ver. 13. Ex 5:7-21. 20:2. Le 25:43, 46, 53. Is 14:6. 51:23. 52:5. 58:6. Je 50:33, 34. Mi 3:3.
15 midwives. Ge +35:17. 38:28.
Shiphrah. i.e. *beauty, brightness, fairness,* **S#8236h.**
Puah. i.e. *splendor, splendid; light; displayed; pained in travail,* **S#6326h.**
16 and see them. Jb 10:9. 33:6. Pr 25:11. Is 29:16. 45:9. 64:8. Je 18:6.
then ye shall. ver. 22. Mt 21:38. Re 12:4.
17 feared God. ver. 21. Ex +18:21. Ge 42:18. Le 25:36, 43. Dt +6:2. 25:18. Ne 5:9, 15. Ps 14:4. 31:19. 36:1. Pr 2:5. 8:13. 24:11, 12. Ec 8:12. Da 3:16-18. 6:13. Ho 5:11. Mi 6:16. Mt 10:28. Ac 4:19. 5:29. Ro 3:18. 1 P 2:17.
did not. Da 6:10. Mt 2:12, 13, 14, 16. Ac +4:19. 5:29.
18 Why have. 2 S 13:28. Ec 8:4.
19 midwives said. Jsh 2:4, etc. 1 S 21:2. 2 S 17:19, 20.
20 God. Ps 41:1, 2. 61:5. 85:9. 103:11. 111:5. 145:19. Pr 11:18. 19:17. Ec 8:12. Is 3:10. Mt 10:42. 25:40. Lk 1:50. He +6:10.
the people. ver. 7, 12.
21 made them. 1 S 2:35. 25:28. 2 S 7:11-13, 27-29. 1 K 2:24. 11:38. Ps 37:3. 127:1, 3. Pr 24:3. Ec 8:12. Je 35:2.
houses. Ge +7:1. 24:60. 30:11, 13. Dt 7:14. Ps 128:3.
22 A.M. 2431. B.C. 1573.
Every son. ver. 16. Ex 7:19-21. Ps 105:25. Pr 1:16. 4:16. 27:4. Ac 7:19. Re 16:4-6.
cast. Mt 2:13-16. Ac 7:19.

EXODUS 2

1 A.M. 2432. B.C. 1572.
house. Ge +7:1.
of Levi. Nu +1:49.
2 A.M. 2433. B.C. 1571.
she saw. Ps 112:5. Ac 7:20. He 11:23.

goodly. Lk 2:40, 52. Ac 7:20.
three. He 11:23.

3 **could not**. Ex 1:22. Mt 2:13, 16. Ac 7:19.
an ark. Is 18:2.
bulrushes. Jb 8:11. Is 18:2. 35:7.
with slime. Ge 6:14. 11:3. 14:10.
pitch. Is 34:9.

4 **his sister**. Ex 15:20. Nu 12:1-15. 20:1. 26:59.
Mi 6:4.

5 **daughter**. Ac 7:21.
wash herself. Heb. *rahats*, **S#7364h**, Ex +29:4.
Ex 7:15. 8:20.
when she. 1 K 17:6. Ps 9:9. 12:5. 46:1.
76:10. Pr 21:1. Jon 1:17. 2:10.

6 **she had compassion**. 1 K 8:50. Ne 1:11. Ps
106:46. Pr 21:1. Ac 7:21. 1 P 3:8.

7 **his sister**. ver. 4. Ex 15:20. Nu 12:1. 26:59.

8 **Go**. Ps 27:10. Is 46:3, 4. Ezk 16:8.
mother. Ex 6:20.

9 **take**. Jg 13:8.

10 **and he**. Ge 48:5. Ps 113:7, 8. Ac 7:21, 22. Ga
4:5. He 11:24. 1 J 3:1.
Moses. i.e. *Drawn out*. **S#4872h**. Ex 3:3, 11.
12:21. 14:21. 19:20. 33:11. 34:29. Nu 10:29.
12:3. 20:10. 31:3. Dt 33:1. 34:5. Mt 17:3. Ac
7:22. He 11:24.
Because. Ge 4:25. 16:11. 1 S 1:20. Mt 1:21.

11 A.M. 2473. B.C. 1531.
in. Jg 19:1. Ac 7:23, 25.
Moses. Ac 7:22-24. He 11:24-26.
grown. Ge 21:20.
looked. Mt 11:28.
burdens. Ex 1:11. 3:7. 5:9, 14. Is 58:6. Mt
11:28. Lk 4:18.

12 **looked**. Pr 4:25. Lk 9:62. Ac 7:24-26.
slew. Ge 9:6. Mk 1:25, 26.

13 **strove**. Mt 5:9. Mk 9:33.
and he said. Ac 7:26. 1 C 6:7, 8.
him. Ex 23:1. Dt 25:1.

14 **Who**. Ge 19:9. 37:8-11, 19, 20. Nu 16:3, 13.
Ps 2:2-6. Ml 2:10. Mt 21:23. Lk 12:14. 19:14,
27. Ac 7:26-28, 35.
a prince. Heb. a man, a prince. Ge 13:8mg. Is
+40:13mg.
intendest. 1 S 20:4. 1 K 5:5.
Moses. Pr 19:12. 29:25.
feared. He 11:27.

15 **fled**. Ex 4:19. Ge 28:6, 7. 1 K 19:1-3, 13, 14.
Pr +22:3. Je 26:21-23. Mt 10:23. Ac 7:29. He
11:27.
Midian. Ge +25:2, 4.
sat down. Ge 24:11. 29:2. Jn 4:6.
well. Heb. *be-er*, Ge +16:14.

16 **the priest**. *or*, prince. Ex 3:1. Ge 14:18.
41:45mg. Nu 10:29. Jg 4:11. Is +24:2mg.
they came. Ge 24:11, 14-20. 29:6-10. 1 S 9:11.

17 **shepherds**. Ge 21:25. 26:15-22.
watered. ver. 12. Ge 29:10.

18 **Reul**. Ex 3:1. 4:18. 18:1-12. Jethro, *or* Jether.
Nu 10:29, Raguel.

19 **An Egyptian**. Ge 50:11.
and also. Ge 29:10.

20 **call him**. Ge 24:31-33. 29:13. 31:54. Jb
31:32. Ac +16:15.
eat. Ex +18:12.

21 **content**. ver. 10. Ge 31:38-40. Ph 4:11, 12. 1
T 6:6. He 11:25. 13:5. Ja 1:10.
he gave. Nu +12:1.
Zipporah. i.e. *little bird*; *a sparrow*, **S#6855h**. Ex
4:20-25. 18:2-6. Nu 12:1.

22 **Gershom**. i.e. *a stranger here*; *expulsion*,
S#1647h. Ex 18:3. Jg 18:30. 1 Ch 6:16, 17, 20,
43, 62, 71. 15:7. 23:15, 16. 26:24. Ezr 8:2.
for he said. ver. 10. Ex 18:3. 22:21. 1 Ch
16:20. 29:15. Ps 39:12. 119:19. Ac 7:29. He
11:13, 14.

23 A.M. cir. 2504. B.C. cir. 1500.
in process. Ex 7:7. Ac 7:30.
the king. Ex 4:19. Mt 2:19, 20. Ac 12:23, 24.
sighed. Ge 16:11. Nu 20:16. Dt 26:6, 7. Ps
12:5.
by reason. Dt 4:27-29. Jg 3:9, 14, 15. 4:2, 3.
6:2, 6. 10:7, 10. 2 Ch +6:37. Ezr 9:8, 9. Ne
9:36, 37. Ps +146:7. +119:134.
cry. Ex +22:23. Ne 9:9. Ps +3:4. 81:6, 7.

24 **God heard**. Ex 6:5. +22:23. Ge +16:11. Jg
2:18. Ne 9:27, 28. Ps 22:5, 24. 79:11. 81:7.
102:20. 106:44. 138:3.
remembered. Ge +8:1. 15:14-18. 17:7.
18:18. +19:29. 26:3, 24. 28:12-14. 32:28.
46:2-4. Le +26:42. Ne 9:8, 9.

25 **looked**. Ex 4:31. 1 S 1:11. 2 S 16:12. Jb
33:27. Lk 1:25.
had respect. Heb. knew. Ex 1:8. 3:7, 8. Ge
+39:6. Jb 34:4. Ps 1:6. 55:22. 144:3. Mt 7:23.

EXODUS 3

1 A.M. 2513. B.C. 1491.
kept. Ps 78:70-72. Am 1:1. 7:14, 15. Mt 4:18,
19. Lk 2:8. 1 C 1:27-29. 7:20. Ph 4:11.
flock. Ge 46:34. Is 63:11. Jn 10:11, 14.
Jethro. i.e. *his excellence*. **S#3503h**. ver. 1. Ex
4:18. 18:1, 2, 5, 6, 9, 10, 12.
his father. Ex 2:16, 21. 18:1-6. Nu 10:29. Jg
4:11.
backside. Jsh 8:2. Jg 18:12. 1 K 17:3. Ezk
1:1. Mk +6:31, 32. Ga 1:15-17. He 11:37-40.
Re 1:9.
the mountain. ver. 5. Ex 4:27. 18:5. 19:3,
11. 24:15-17. Nu 10:33. 1 K 19:8.
Horeb. i.e. *desolate*. **S#2722h**. Ex 17:6. 33:6. Dt
1:2, 6, 19. 4:10, 15. 5:2. 9:8. 18:16. 29:1. 1 K
8:9. 19:8. 2 Ch 5:10. Ps 106:19. Ml 4:4.

2 **angel**. ver. 4, 6. Ge 16:7-13. 21:17, 18. 22:11,
12, 15, 16. 31:11, 13. 48:15, 16. Dt 33:16. Jg
6:11-16. 13:20-23. Is 63:9. Ho 12:4, 5. Ml 3:1.
Mk 12:26. Lk 20:37. Ac 7:30-35.
flame. Is 10:17.
bush burned. Ge 15:13-17. Dt 4:11, 20.

5:23. Ps 66:12. Is 43:2. 53:10, 11. Da 3:27. Zc
13:7. Jn 1:14. Ro 8:3. 2 C 1:8-10.
with fire. Ge 15:17. Ex 13:21. 19:18. 24:17.
1 K 19:12. Is 4:5. Ezk 1:27, 28. 8:2. He 10:27.
12:29.
not consumed. Nu 21:28. 26:10. Jb 15:34.
Ps 129:2. Is 43:2.

3 **turn aside**. Jg 14:8. Ru 4:1. Ja 4:8.
and see. Jb 37:14. Ps 107:8. 111:2-4. Da
3:26, 27. Ac 7:31.

4 **unto him**. Dt 33:16.
Moses. Ge 22:1, 11. 46:2. 1 S 3:4, 6, 8, 10. Ps
62:11. Ac 9:4. 10:3, 13.

5 **Draw not**. Ex 19:12, 21. Le 10:3. He 10:22.
12:20.
put off. Ge 28:16, 17. Jsh 5:15. Ec 5:1. Ac
7:33.
holy. Jn 13:10. Ep 2:18. 3:12.

6 **I am**. ver. 14, 15. Ex 4:5. 29:45. Ge 12:1, 7.
+17:7, 8. Ps 132:2. Mt +22:32. Mk *12:26*. Lk
20:37. Ac *3:13. 7:31, 32*.
thy father. Ex 15:2. 18:4. 2 K 20:5. 2 Ch
21:12.
hid. Ge +17:3. Dt 18:16. Jg 13:22. 1 K 19:13.
Ne 9:9. Jb 42:5, 6. Ps 106:44, 45. Is 6:1-5. Da
10:7, 8. Ac 7:34. 22:11. He 12:21.

7 **I have**. Ex +22:23. Ge 29:32. 1 S 9:16. Ne 9:9.
Ps 22:24. 102:20. Is 63:9. He 4:15.
by reason. Ex 1:11.
I know. Ge 18:21. Jb 23:10. Ps 142:3.

8 **I am**. Ge 11:5, 7. 18:21. 50:24. Ps 18:9-19.
12:5. 22:4, 5. 34:8. 91:15. Is 64:1. Jn 3:13.
6:38. Ph 1:6.
come. Mt 5:17. Lk +19:10.
deliver. Ex 6:6-8. 12:51. Ge 15:14. 50:24.
unto a good. ver. 17. Ex 13:5. 33:2, 3. Ge
13:14, 15. 15:18. Le 20:24. Nu 13:19, 27.
14:7, 8. 16:14. Dt 1:7, 25. 3:25. 6:3. 8:7-9.
11:9-24. 26:9-15. 27:3. 28:11. 31:20. Jsh 5:6.
Ne 9:22-25. Je 2:7. 11:5. 32:22. Ezk 20:6, 15.
honey. ver. 17. Ex 13:5. 16:31. 33:3. Ge
43:11. Le 20:24. Nu 13:27. 14:8. 16:13. Dt
6:3. 8:8. 11:9. 26:9, 15. 27:3. 31:20. 32:13.
Jsh 5:6. 2 S 17:29. 2 K 18:32. 2 Ch 31:5. Jb
20:17. Ps 81:16. Is 7:15, 22. Je 11:5. 32:22.
Ezk 16:13, 19. 20:6, 15. 27:17.
unto the place. Ezk 20:5-10.
Canaanites. Ge +10:18.
Hittites. Dt +20:17.
Amorites. Ge +10:16.
Perizzites. Ge +13:7.
Hivites. Ge +10:17.
Jebusites. Ge +10:16.

9 **the cry**. ver. +7. Ge 19:13. Nu 20:16.
and I have. ver. 7. Ex 1:11, 13, 14, 22. Ps
+12:5. Je 50:33, 34. Am 4:1. Mi 2:1-3.

10 **Come now**. Is 1:18. Mt 11:29. Jn 6:37. He
7:25. 11:26.
and I. 1 S 12:6. Ps 77:20. 103:6, 7. 105:26. Is
63:11, 12. Ho 12:13. Mi 6:4. Ac 7:34, 36.

11 **Who am I**. Ex 4:10-13. 6:12. 1 S 18:18. 2 S
7:18. 1 K 3:7, 9. Pr 29:25. Is 6:5-8. Je 1:6. Lk
14:18. Ac 7:23-25. 2 C 2:16. 3:5, 6, 12. Ep
6:10.

12 **Certainly**. Ex 4:12, 15. Ge 15:1. 31:3. Dt
31:8, 23. Jg 6:16. Is 43:2. Mt +28:20. Jn 8:29.
Ac 11:21. Ro 8:31. 2 C 12:9.
token. Ex 4:1-9. Ge 15:8. Jg 6:17, 21, 36-40.
7:11, 13, 14. Ps 86:17. Is 7:14. 37:30. Je 43:9,
10. 51:63, 64.
ye shall. Ex ch. 19-40. Le ch. 1-27. Nu ch. 1-
10.

13 **Moses said**. Ex 4:11. Ps 32:3, 8. Is 58:1. 59:1.
Ezk 3:14, 17. Jn 8:24.
What is his. ver. 14. Ex 15:3. Ge 32:29. Jg
13:6, 17. Pr 30:4. Is +7:14. +9:6. Je 23:6. Mt
1:21, 23.
name. Ex +6:3.

14 **I AM hath**. Ex 6:3. Jb 11:7. Ps +68:4. 90:2. Is
44:6. Mt 18:20. 28:20. Jn 8:58. 2 C 1:20. He
13:8. Re 1:4, 8, 17. 4:8. 16:5.

15 **The Lord**. ver. 6. Ex 4:5. Ge +17:7, 8. Dt
1:11, 35. 4:1. 2 Ch 28:9. Mt *22:32*. Mk *12:26*.
Ac *3:13*. 7:32.
this is my name. Ge 2:2. Ps 72:17, 19. 111:5.
135:13. 145:1, 2. Is 9:6. 63:12.
for ever. Heb. *olam*, Ex +12:24.
my memorial. Ps 102:12. 135:13. Is 42:8. Ho
12:5. Mi 4:5. Ml 3:6. He 13:8.
generations. Ge +9:12.

16 **elders**. Ex 4:29. 12:21. 17:5. 18:12, +21.
19:7. 24:1, 11. Ge 50:7. Nu 11:16, 24, 25. Jsh
+20:4. Mt 26:3. Ac +11:30.
appeared. ver. 2, 4. Ge +35:9.
surely visited. Ex 2:25. 4:31. 13:19. 15:14.
Ge 21:1. 50:24. Ru 1:6. Ps 8:4. Lk 1:68. 19:44.
Ac 15:14. He 2:6, 7. 1 P 2:12.

17 **I will bring**. ver. 9. Ex 2:23-25. Ge 15:13-21.
46:4. 50:24.
unto the land. ver. +8. Ge 15:14, 18-21.
honey. ver. +8.

18 **and they**. ver. 16. Ex 4:31. Jsh 1:17. 2 Ch
30:12. Ps 110:3. Je 26:5.
and thou. Ex 5:1-3.
The Lord. Ex 7:16. 9:1, 13. 10:3.
met. Ex 4:24. 5:3. 25:22. 29:42, 43. 30:6, 36.
Ge 12:1. 15:1. 17:1. 48:3. Nu 17:4. 23:3, 4,
15, 16. Is 64:5.
three days. Ex 8:27. 13:17, 18.
that we may. ver. 12. Ex 7:16. 8:25-28. 9:1.
10:24-26. 19:1. Je 2:2, 6.

19 **will not**. Ex 5:2. 7:4.
no, not by a mighty hand. *or*, but by a
strong hand. Ex 6:1. ch. 7-14. Dt +34:12. Ps
136:11, 12. Is 63:12, 13.

20 **stretch**. Ex +7:5.
smite. Ex 7:3. 11:9. Dt 4:34. 6:22. Ne 9:10.
Ps 105:27. 106:22. 135:8, 9. 136:11, 12. Is
19:22. Je 32:20, 21. Ac 7:36. See Ex ch.
7-13.

after that. Ex 11:8. 12:31, 39. Ge 15:14. Jg 6:8. 8:16. Ps 105:38. Is 26:11.

21 **will give**. Ex 11:3. 12:36. Ge 39:21. Ne 1:11. Ps 106:46. Pr +16:7. Da 1:9. Ac 7:10.

22 **But**. Ex 11:2. 12:35, 36. Ge 15:14. Ps 105:37.
borrow. Ex 22:14. 2 K 4:3. 6:5. *or*, ask. Ex 13:14. 18:7. Jsh 19:50. Jg 5:25. 1 S 1:17, 20. 12:13.
spoil. Jb 27:16, 17. Pr +13:22. Is 33:1. Ezk 39:10.
the Egyptians. *or*, Egypt.

EXODUS 4

1 **will not**. ver. 31. Ex 2:14. 3:18. 1 S 16:2. 1 K 18:14. Je 1:6. Ezk 3:14. Jn 8:47. Ac 7:25. Ro 1:16. 2 C 4:4.

2 **hand**. Ac 28:5, 6.
rod. ver. 17, 20. Ge 30:37. Le 27:32. 1 S 14:27, 43. Ps 110:2. Is 11:4. 28:27. Mi 6:9. 7:14.

3 **it became**. ver. 17. Ex 7:10-15. Am 5:19.

4 **Put forth**. Ge 22:1, 2. Ps 91:13. Mk 16:18. Lk 10:19. Ac 28:3-6.
And he put. Jn 2:5.

5 **That they**. ver. 1. Ex 3:18. 4:31. 19:9. 2 Ch 20:20. Is 7:9. Jn 3:2. 5:36. 11:15, 42. 20:27, 31. Ac 28:5, 6.
the Lord. Ex 3:15. Ge 12:7. 17:1. 18:1. 26:2. 48:3. Je 31:3. Ac 7:2.

6 **leprous as snow**. Nu 12:10. 2 K 5:27.

7 **it was turned**. Nu 12:13, 14. Dt 32:39. 2 K 5:14. Mt 8:3.

8 **if they**. ver. 30, 31. Is 28:10. Jn 12:37.
voice. Jb 12:7. Ps 19:2.
that they. Dt 32:39. 2 K 5:7. Jb 5:18.

9 **the water**. Ex 7:19.
pour. Heb. *shaphak*, **S#8210h**. Le 17:13. Dt 21:7. 1 K 18:28 (gushed. mg, poured). Ps 22:14. 79:3. Is 57:6 (poured). Ezk 20:33, 34. Zp 3:8. Zc 12:10.
shall become. Heb. shall be, and shall be.
blood. Ex 1:22. 7:19-25. Mt 7:2. Jn 2:8-11. Re 16:3-6.

10 **am not**. 1 K 3:7.
eloquent. Heb. a man of words. ver. 1. Jb 12:2. 1 C 2:1-4. 2 C 10:10. 11:6.
heretofore. Heb. since yesterday, nor since the third day. Ex 21:29. 2 S +3:17mg.
slow of speech. Ex 6:12. Je 1:6. Ac 4:13. 7:22.

11 **Who hath**. Ge 18:14. Ps 94:9. 146:8. Is 6:7. 35:5, 6. 42:7. 49:2. 50:4. Je 1:6, 9. Ezk +24:27. Am +3:6. Mt 10:19, 20. Lk 2:14, 15. *Lk 13:1-5*. Jn 9:2, 3. Ja 3:8, 9.

12 **I will**. Ps 25:4, 5. 32:9. 143:10. Is 49:2. 50:4. Je 1:9. Mt 10:19, 20. Mk 13:11. Lk 11:1. 12:11, 12. 21:14, 15. Jn 14:26. Ac 7:22. Ep 6:19.

13 **send**. ver. 1. Ex 23:20. Ge 24:7. 48:16. Jg 2:1.

1 K 19:4. Is 6:8. Je 1:6. 20:9. Ezk 3:14, 15. Jon 1:3, 6. Mt 13:41. Jn 6:29. Ro 12:1.
hand. Hg +1:1mg.
wilt send. *or*, shouldest.

14 **anger**. 2 S 6:7. 1 K 11:9. 1 Ch 21:7. Lk 9:59, 60. Ac 15:38. Ph 2:21.
Aaron. i.e. *teaching*, **S#175h**. Ex 5:20. 6:20. 7:1, 7, 12. 12:1. 16:34. 17:12. 19:24. 24:14. 28:1, 12. 30:10. 32:2-4. Le 10:6. Nu 12:1. 16:11. 17:3. 20:12, 25, 28.
cometh. ver. 27. 1 S 10:1-7. Mk 14:13-15. 2 C 2:13. 7:6, 7. 1 Th 3:6, 7.

15 **and put**. Ex 7:1, 2. 2 S 14:3. Is 51:16. 59:21.
and I. Nu 22:38. 23:5, 12, 16. Dt 18:18. Is 51:16. Je 1:9. Mt 28:20. Lk 21:15. Jn 17:8. 1 C 11:23. 15:1.
will teach. Dt 5:31. 1 S 16:3. Is 50:4.

16 **be to thee**. Ex 7:1, 2. 18:19. Ps +82:6. Jn +10:34, 35.

17 **this rod**. ver. 2. Ex 7:9, 19. 1 C 1:27.

18 **Jethro**. Heb. Jether. Ex +3:1.
Let me go. 1 T 6:1.
and see. Ge 45:3. Ac 15:36.
Go in peace. Lk +7:50.

19 **Midian**. Ge +25:2.
for all. Ex 2:15, 23. Mt 2:20.
life. Heb. *nephesh*, soul. Ge +44:30; Ge +9:5.

20 **his wife**. Ex 2:21, 22. 18:2-4.
an ass. Jsh 15:18. 1 S 25:20. 2 S 17:23. 1 K 13:13.
the rod of God. ver. 2, 17. Ex 17:9. Nu 20:8, 9.

21 **wonders**. Ex 3:20.
I will harden. Ge +31:7. Ex 7:3, +13. 8:15. 9:12, 35. 10:1, 20, 27. 11:10. 14:4, 8. Ge 6:3. Dt 2:30-33, 36. 15:7. Jsh 11:20. 1 S 6:6. 1 K 22:22, 23. 2 Ch 36:13. Jb 9:4. Ps 105:25. Pr 29:1. 6:10. 63:17. Je 5:3. Ezk 33:11. 36:26. Da 5:20. Am +3:6. Zc 7:11, 12. Jn 12:40. Ac 28:26, 27. Ro 1:28. 2:5. 9:18, 22. 11:8-10. 2 C 2:16. 2 Th 2:10-12. He 3:8, 13. Ja 1:13, 14. 1 P 2:8.

22 **Israel**. Ex 19:5, 6. Dt 14:1, 2. 33:6. 2 S 7:14. Is 63:16. Je 31:9. Ho 11:1. Mt 2:15. Ro 9:4. He 12:23. Ja 1:18. 1 J +3:1.
firstborn. Ps 89:27. Je 31:9. Col +1:15.

23 **I will slay**. Ex 11:5. 12:29. Ps 78:51. 105:36. 135:8.

24 **the inn**. Ge +42:27.
the Lord. Ex 3:18. Nu 22:22, 23. 1 Ch 21:16. Ho 13:8.
sought. Ge 17:14. Le 10:3. 1 K 13:24. 1 T 3:4, 5.

25 **a sharp stone**. *or*, knife. Jsh 5:2, 3. Is 5:28. Ezk 3:9.
cast it. Heb. made it touch.
a bloody. 2 S 16:7.

27 **Go into**. ver. 14-16. Ec 4:9. Ac 10:5, 6, 20.
the mount. Ex 3:1. 19:3. 20:18. 24:15-17. 1 K 19:8.
kissed him. Ge +27:27.

28 **told Aaron**. ver. 8, 9, 15, 16. Jon 3:2. Mt 21:29.
   and all. ver. 11-13.
29 **gathered**. Ex +3:16.
30 **And Aaron**. ver. 16.
   did the. ver. 2-9.
31 **believed**. ver. 8, 9. Ex 3:18. Ps 106:12, 13. Lk 8:13.
   visited. Ex +3:16. Lk 1:68.
   looked. Ex 2:25. 3:7.
   bowed. Ge +24:26.

EXODUS 5

1 **and told**. 1 K 21:20. Ps 119:46. Ezk 2:6. Jon 3:3, 4. Mt 10:18, 28. Ac 4:29.
   a feast. Ex 10:9. Is 25:6. 1 C 5:8.
2 **Who**. Ex 3:19. 2 K +18:35. Jb 21:15. Ps 10:4. 12:4. 14:1.
   Israel. Ge +9:27.
   I know not. 1 S 2:12. Jn 16:3. Ro 1:28. 2 Th 1:8.
   neither. Ex 3:19. Je 44:16, 17.
3 **The God**. Ex 3:18.
   lest he. 2 K 17:25. 2 Ch 30:8. Ezr 7:23. Zc 14:16-19.
   with pestilence. Ezk +38:22.
   the sword. Le 26:16. Is 1:20. Je +12:12. Mt 10:34.
4 **Wherefore**. Je 38:4. Am 7:10. Lk 23:2. Ac 16:20, 21. 24:5.
   let. *or*, loose. Ex 32:25.
   burdens. Ex 1:11. 2:11. 6:6.
5 **many**. Ex 1:7-11. Pr 14:28.
   rest. Mt 11:28.
6 **taskmasters**. or, exactors, oppressors. Ex 1:11. Jb 3:18. Pr 12:10. Is 3:12. 60:17. Zc 10:4.
   officers. ver. 10, 13, 14, 15, 19. Ex 2:14. Nu 11:16. 31:14, 48. Dt 1:15. 16:18. 20:5, 8, 9. 29:10. 31:28. Jsh 1:10. 3:2. 8:33. 24:1, 4. 2 Ch 19:11. 26:11.
7 **straw**. Ge 24:25. Jg 19:19.
8 **tale**. Ex 30:32, 37. 2 Ch 24:13. Ezk 45:11.
   heretofore. ver. 7, 14. Ex 4:10mg. Ge 31:2. 1 S 19:7.
   ye shall lay. Ps 106:41.
   idle. ver. 17.
   therefore. Ex 10:11, 25.
9 **Let there more work be laid upon the men**. Heb. Let the work be heavy upon the men. 2 T 3:12.
   vain words. *or*, lying words. 2 K 18:20. Jb 16:3. Je 7:4. 43:2. Zc 1:6. Ml 3:14. Ep 5:6.
10 **taskmasters**. Ex 1:11. Pr 29:12.
11 **not ought**. ver. 13, 14.
12 **stubble**. 1 C +3:12.
13 **hasted**. Jsh 10:15. 17:15. Pr 19:2.
   daily tasks. Heb. a matter of a day in his day. ver. 19. Ex 16:4mg. Le 23:37. 1 K

8:59mg. 2 K 25:30. 1 Ch 16:37. 2 Ch 8:14. 31:16. Ezr 3:4mg. Ne 11:23. 12:47. Je 52:34mg. Da 1:5.
17 **Ye are idle**. Mt 26:8. Jn 6:27. 2 Th 3:10, 11.
18 **yet shall ye deliver**. Ezk 18:18. Da 2:9-13.
19 **evil case**. Dt 32:36. Ec 4:1. 5:8.
21 **The Lord**. Ex 4:31. 6:9. Ge 16:5.
   our savor. Ec 10:1. Jl 2:20. 2 C 2:15, 16.
   to be abhorred. Heb. to stink. Ge +34:30.
   in the eyes. Ex 20:18. Mk 7:21, 22. 1 T 6:19. Re 1:12.
22 **returned**. Ex 17:4. 1 S 30:6. 2 K 19:14. Ps 73:25. Je 12:1.
   evil intreated. Ge +31:7.
   why is it. Nu 11:14, 15. 1 K 19:4, 10. Je 20:7. Hab 2:3.
23 **in thy name**. Ps 118:26. Je 11:21. Jn 5:43.
   neither hast thou delivered. Heb. delivering, thou hast not delivered. Is 26:17, 18. 28:16. He 10:36, 37.

EXODUS 6

1 **Now shalt**. Ex 14:13. Nu 23:23. Dt 32:39. 2 K 7:2, 19. 2 Ch 20:17. Ps 12:5.
   with a strong. Ex 3:19, 20. Dt 4:34. Ps 89:13. 136:12. Is 63:12. Ezk 20:33, 34.
   drive them. Ex 11:1. 12:31, 33, 39.
2 **I am the Lord**. *or*, Jehovah. ver. 6, 8. Ex 14:18. 17:1. 20:2. Ge 15:7. Is 42:8. 43:11, 15. 44:6. Je 9:24. Ml 3:6. Ac 17:24, 25.
3 **name of**. Dt +28:58. Is 12:2. 26:4. Jn 1:3. 8:56. Ac 7:38. Re +1:8. 15:3.
   God Almighty. Heb. *El shaddai*, God Almighty; for *shaddai* means strong, mighty. Ge +17:1. 28:3. 35:11. 43:14. 48:3. +49:25. Jb +5:17. Re 16:14.
   but by my name. Ex 3:13, 14. +15:26. Ge 22:14. 28:13. Ps +9:10. +68:4. +83:18. Is 42:8. Je 10:16. 50:34. 51:19.
   JEHOVAH. i.e. *he will be; self-existent*, **S#3068h**. Ex 3:14. 15:2mg. 17:15. Ge 2:4. 4:1, 3. +12:7, 8. 13:18. +17:1. 19:24. 21:33. 22:14. Jg 6:24. 2 Ch 18:31. Ps 68:4, JAH. +83:18. Is 12:2. 26:4. 42:8. 44:6. 52:5, 6. Jn 8:28, 58. 1 C +12:3. 1 P +2:3. Re 1:4, 8.
4 **established**. Ge 6:18. 15:18. 17:7, 8, 13. 28:4. 2 S 23:5. Is +55:3.
   covenant. Ge 26:3. 35:12.
   the land of their. Ge 15:13. 17:8. 23:4. 26:3. Ps 105:12. Ac 7:5.
5 **the groaning**. Ex 2:24. 3:7. Ps 106:44. Is 63:9.
   I have remembered. Le +26:42.
6 **I am the Lord**. ver. +2, 8, 29. Ezk 20:7-9.
   I will bring. Ex 3:17. 7:4. Dt 26:8. Ps 81:6. 136:11, 12.
   redeem . Ex 15:13. Dt 4:34. 7:8. 15:15. 2 K 17:36. 1 Ch 17:21. Ne 1:10. Is 9:12, 17, 21.
   stretched. Ex 15:12. Dt 4:34. 5:15. 7:19.

9:29. 11:2. 26:8. 1 K 8:42. Ps 136:12. Is 5:25. Je 27:5. 32:21.

judgments. lit. justice. Ex +7:4. Is 5:7. Je 26:11. Jn 3:19.

7 **will take.** Ex 19:5, 6. Ge 17:7, 8. Dt 4:20. 7:6. 14:2. 26:18. 2 S 7:23, 24. Je 31:33. Ho 1:10. 3:3. 1 P 2:9, 10.

I will be. Ex 29:45, 46. Ge +17:7, 8. Dt 29:13. Zc 13:9. Mt 22:32. Ro 8:31. He 11:16. Re 21:3, 7.

from under. Ex 5:4, 5. Ps 81:6.

8 **swear.** Heb. lift up my hand. Ge +14:22.
to give. Ge +13:15. 22:16, 17.
will give. Mt +8:11. Ph 1:6. T 1:2. He 11:39.
I am. ver. +2. Nu 23:19. 1 S 15:29.

9 **hearkened not.** Ex 5:21. 14:12. Jb 21:4. Pr 14:19.

anguish. *or,* impatience. Heb. shortness, *or,* straitness. Jb +21:4mg.
spirit. Heb. *ruach,* Ge +41:8.

11 **speak unto.** ver. 29. Ex 3:10. 5:1, 23. 7:1.

12 **children.** ver. 9. Ex 3:13. 4:29-31. 5:19-21. Ac 7:25.

uncircumcised. ver. 30. Ex 4:10. Le 26:41. Dt 30:6. Is 6:5. Je 1:6. 6:10. 9:26. Ac 7:51.

13 **gave them.** Nu 27:19, 23. Dt 31:14. Ps 91:11. Mt 4:6. 1 T 1:18. 5:21. 6:13, 17. 2 T 2:4. 4:1.

14 **the heads.** ver. 25. Jsh 14:1. 19:51. 1 Ch 5:24. 7:2, 7. 8:6.
The sons. Ge 46:9. 49:3, 4. Nu 26:5, 6. 1 Ch 5:3.
these be. Nu 26:7. Jsh 13:15, 23.

15 **sons.** Ge 46:10. Nu 26:12, 13. 1 Ch 4:24, Nemuel, Jarib, Zerah.
Canaanitish. Ge +10:18.

16 **sons.** Ge +46:11.
according. Ge 10:32. 25:13.
Kohath. Ge +46:11.
an hundred. ver. 18, 20. Ge 35:28. 47:28. 50:26.

17 **sons of Gershon.** Ge 46:11. Nu 3:18, Shimei. 1 Ch 6:17. 23:7, Laadan, Shimei.
Shimi. i.e. *a hearkener,* S#8096h, so rendered only here. 2 S +16:5, Shimei. 1 Ch +8:21, Shimhi.

18 **sons of Kohath.** Nu 3:19, 27. 26:57. 1 Ch 6:2, 18. 15:5.
Amram. i.e. *exalted people,* S#6019h. ver. 20. Nu 3:19. 26:58, 59. 1 Ch 6:2, 3, 18. 23:12, 13. 24:20. Ezr 10:34.
Izhar. i.e. *anointed; oil,* S#3324h. ver. 21. Nu 3:19, Izehar. 16:1. 1 Ch 6:2, 18, 38. 23:12, 18.
Hebron. i.e. *friendship, companionship; confederation, conjunction,* S#2275h. Ge +13:18. Nu +13:22. 1 Ch 2:42, 43. 6:2, 18. 15:9. 23:12, 19. 24:23. 2 Ch 11:10.
Uzziel. i.e. *strength of God,* S#5816h. ver. 22. Le 10:4. Nu 3:19, 30. 1 Ch 4:42. 6:2, 18. 7:7.

15:10. 23:12, 20. 24:24. 25:4. 2 Ch 29:14. Ne 3:8.

and the years. ver. +16.

19 **sons of Merari.** Ge +46:11.
Mahali. i.e. *infirmity, disease; instability,* S#4249h, Nu +3:20, Mahli.
Mushi. i.e. *forsaking; proved of the Lord; sensitive,* S#4187h. Nu 3:20. 1 Ch 6:19, 47. 23:21, 23. 24:26, 30.

20 **Amram.** Ex 2:1, 2. Nu 26:59.
Jochebed. i.e. *whose glory is Jehovah,* S#3115h. Nu 26:59.
his father's sister. Le 18:12, 14. Nu 26:59.
and the years. ver. 16, 18.

21 **Korah.** ver. 24. Ge +36:5.

22 **sons of Uzziel.** ver. +18.
Mishael. i.e. *who is what God is?,* S#4332h. Le 10:4. Ne 8:4. Da 1:6, 7, 11, 19.
Elzaphan. i.e. *whom God protects; God of treasure,* S#469h. Le 10:4. Nu +3:30, Elizaphan.
Zithri. i.e. *protection of the Lord,* S#5644h.

23 **Elisheba.** i.e. *God of the oath,* S#472h. Lk 1:5.
Amminadab. 1 Ch +15:11.
Naashon. i.e. *enchanter,* S#5177h, so rendered only here. See 1 Ch +2:10, Nahshon.
Nadab. i.e. *volunteer, self-impelled,* S#5070h. Ex 24:1, 9. 28:1. Le 10:1, 2. Nu 3:2-4. 20:25. 26:60, 61. 1 K 14:20. 15:25, 27, 31. 1 Ch 2:28, 30. 6:3. 8:30. 9:36. 24:1, 2.
Abihu. i.e. *father of him,* S#30h. Ex 24:1, 9. 28:1. Le 10:1. Nu 3:2, 4. 26:60, 61. 1 Ch 6:3. 24:1, 2.
Eleazar. i.e. *God has helped,* S#499h. ver. 25. Ex 28:1. Le 10:6, 12, 16. Nu 3:2, 4, 32. 4:16. 20:25, 26, 28. 26:60. 27:2, 21, 22. 34:17. Jsh 14:1. 19:51. 21:1. Jg 20:28. 1 Ch 6:3, 4, 50. 9:20. 24:1-6. Ezr 7:5. 8:33.
Ithamar. i.e. *land of palms; he is bitter,* S#385h. Ex 28:1. 38:21. Le 10:6, 12, 16. Nu 3:2, 4. 4:28, 33. 7:8. 26:60. 1 Ch 6:3. 24:1-6. Ezr 8:2.

24 **sons of Korah.** ver. +21.
Assir. i.e. *prisoner,* S#617h. 1 Ch 3:17. 6:22, 23, 37.
Elkanah. i.e. *whom God has redeemed,* S#511h.
Abiasaph. i.e. *gatherer,* S#23h.
Korhites. i.e. *descendants of Korah,* S#7145h. 1 Ch +9:19, Korahites. 12:6. 26:1, 19. 2 Ch 20:19.

25 **Putiel.** i.e. *afflicted of God,* S#6317h.
Phinehas. i.e. *brazen mouth; mouth of pity,* S#6372h. Nu 25:7, 11. 31:6. Jsh 22:13, 30-32. 24:33. Jg 20:28. 1 S 1:3. 2:34. 4:4, 11, 17, 19. 14:3. 1 Ch 6:4, 50. 9:20. Ezr 7:5. 8:2, 33. Ps 106:30, 31.
the heads. ver. 14.

26 **That Aaron.** ver. 13, 20. Jsh 24:5. 1 S 12:6, 8. 1 Ch 6:3. Ps 77:20. 99:6. Mi 6:4.
Bring. ver. 7. Ex 3:10, 11. 20:2. 32:1, 7, 11. Ac 7:35, 36.

armies. Ex 7:4. 12:17, 41, 51. 13:18. Ge 2:1. Nu 1:3, 52. 2:3, 9, 32. 10:14, 18, 22, 28. 33:1.

27 **spake**. Ex 5:1-3. 7:10.
to bring. ver. 13, 26. Ex 32:7. 33:1. Ps 77:20. Mi 6:4.

29 **I am the**. ver. +2, 6, 8.
speak. ver. 11. Ex 7:2. 1 S 3:18. Je 1:7, 8, 17-19. 23:28. 26:2. Ezk 2:6, 7. 3:11, 17. Mt 28:20. Jn 12:49, 50. Ac 20:27.

30 **uncircumcised**. ver. +12. Ex 4:10. 1 C 9:16, 17.

EXODUS 7

1 **See**. Ex 16:29. Ge 19:21. 1 K 17:23. 2 K 6:32. Ec 1:10.
a god. Ex 4:15, 16. 22:9. Ps +82:6. Je 1:10. Lk 21:15. Jn +10:35, 36. Ac 14:11.
thy prophet. Ex 4:15, 30. Ac 14:12.

2 **speak all**. Ex 4:15. 6:29. Dt 4:2. 1 K 22:14. Je 1:7, 17. Ezk 3:10, 17. Mt 28:20. Ac 20:27.

3 **And I**. Ex +4:21, 29.
multiply. Ex 4:7. 9:16. 11:9. Dt 4:34. 7:19. Ne 9:10. Ps 78:43-51. 105:27-36. 135:9. Is 51:9. Je 32:20, 21. Mi 7:15. Jn 4:48. Ac 2:22. 7:36. Ro 15:19.

4 **that I**. Ex +9:3. 10:1. 11:9.
armies. Ex +6:26.
by great. Ex 6:6. Pr 19:29. Is 26:9. Ezk 14:21. 25:11. 30:14, 19. Re 15:4. 16:7. 19:2.

5 **Egyptians**. ver. 17. Ex 8:10, 22. Ezk +6:7.
I stretch. Ex 3:20. +6:6. 9:15. Ps 138:7. Is 5:25. 9:12, 17, 21. 10:4. 14:26, 27. 31:3. Je 6:12. 15:6. 21:5. Ezk 6:14. 14:9. 16:27. 20:33, 34. 25:7. 35:3. Zp 1:4. 2:13.

6 **did as**. ver. 2, 10. Ex 12:28. 39:43. 40:16. Ge 6:22. 22:18. Ps 119:4. Jn 15:10, 14.

7 **fourscore**. Ex 2:23. Ge 41:46. Dt 29:5. 31:2. 34:7. Ps 90:10. Ac 7:23, 30.

9 **Show**. Is 7:11. Mt 12:39. Jn 2:18. 6:30. 10:38.
Take. ver. 10-12. Ex 4:2, 17, 20. 9:23. 10:13.
a serpent. Ps 74:12, 13. Ezk 29:3.

10 **as the Lord**. ver. 9.
it became. Ex 4:3. Am 9:3. Mk 16:18. Lk 10:19.
serpent. S#8577h. Ge 1:21, Heb, sea monster.

11 **wise men**. Ge 41:8, 38, 39. Is 19:11, 12. 47:12, 13. Da 2:2, 27. 4:7-9. 5:7, 11. 2 T 3:8. Re 19:20.
sorcerers. S#3784h. Ex 22:18 (witch). Dt 18:10 (witch). 2 Ch 33:6 (witchcraft). Da 2:2. Ml 3:5. Re +9:21.
magicians. S#2748h. ver. 11, 22. 8:7, 18, 19. 9:11, 11. Ge +41:8. Da 1:20. 2:2.
they also. ver. 22. Ex 8:7, 18. Dt 13:1-3. Mt 24:24. Ga 3:1. Ep 4:14. 2 Th 2:9. Re 13:11-15.

12 **but Aaron's**. Ex 8:18, 19. 9:11. Ac 8:9-13. 13:8-11. 19:19, 20. 1 J 4:4.

13 **hardened**. ver. 4. Ex +4:21. 14:17.

14 **Pharaoh's**. Ex 10:1, 20, 27. Zc 7:12.
heart. ver. 22. Ex +4:21. 8:15, 19, 32. 9:7, 34, 35.
hardened. Heb. heavy. Ge 41:31mg.
he refuseth. Ex 4:23. 8:2. 9:2. 10:4. Is 1:20. Je 8:5. 9:6. He 12:25.

15 **he goeth**. Ex 2:5. 8:20. Ezk 29:3.
the rod. ver. 10. Ex 4:2-4.

16 **The Lord**. Ex 3:18. 5:3. 9:1, 13. 10:3. 1 S 4:6-9.
Let my. Ex 8:1, 20. 13:15. 14:5. Is 45:13. Je 50:33. Ac 4:21-23.
serve. Ex 3:12, 18. 5:1-3. 9:1.

17 **thou shalt**. ver. 5. Ex 5:2. 6:7. 1 S 17:46, 47. 1 K 20:28. 2 K 19:19. Ps 9:16. 83:18. Ezk 29:9. 30:8, 19. 32:15. 38:23. 39:28. Da 4:17, 32, 37. 5:21, 23.
and they. Ex 1:22. 4:9. Ps 78:44. 105:29. Re 8:8. 16:3-6.

18 **the fish**. ver. 21.
shall loathe. Heb. weary themselves. ver. 24. Ge 19:11. Nu 11:20. 21:5. Is 1:14. Je 6:11.

19 **stretch**. Ex 8:5, 6, 16. 9:22, 23, 33. 10:12, 21. 14:21, 26.
their pools. Heb. gathering of their waters. Ge 1:10. Le 11:36.
stone. Dt 25:13. Pr 11:1. Is 34:11. Je 2:27. Zc 4:10.

20 **he lifted**. Ex 17:5, 6, 9-12. Nu 20:8-12.
all the waters. ver. 17, 18. Ps 78:44. 105:29. Jn 2:9-11. Re 8:8.

21 **the fish**. ver. 18. Jn 2:1-10. Re 8:9.

22 **magicians**. ver. +11. Je 27:18. 2 T 3:8.
and Pharaoh's. ver. 13.
as the. ver. 3.

23 **neither**. Ex 9:21. Dt 32:46. 1 S 4:20mg. 2 S 13:20. Jb 7:17. Ps 62:10. Pr 22:17. 24:32mg. 29:1. Is 26:11. Je 5:3. 36:24. Ezk 40:4. Am 4:7-12. Hab 1:5. Ml 2:2.

24 **for they**. ver. 18-21.

25 **seven days**. Ex 8:9, 10. 10:23. 2 S 24:13.

EXODUS 8

1 **Go**. Je 1:17-19. 15:19-21. Ezk 2:6, 7.
Let my. Ex 3:12, 18. 5:1. 7:16.

2 **refuse**. Ex 7:14. 9:2.
frogs. Ps 78:45. 105:30. Re 16:13, 14.

3 **bedchamber**. 2 K 1:16. Ec +10:20.
ovens. Le 2:4. 7:9. 26:26.
kneading troughs. or, dough. Ex 12:34. Ge 40:17.

4 **on thee**. ver. 9, 11, 21. Ex 9:14. 10:6. Ps 107:40. Is 19:11, 22. 23:9. Da 4:37. Ac 12:22, 23.

5 **Stretch forth**. Ex 7:19.

6 **and the frogs**. Le 11:12. Ps 78:45. 105:30. Re 16:13.

7 **magicians did so**. ver. 18. Ex 7:11, 22. Dt 13:1-3. Mt 24:24. 2 Th 2:9-11. 2 T 3:8. Re 13:14.

8 **Intreat**. Ex 5:2. 9:28. 10:17. Nu 21:7. 1 S
12:19. 1 K 13:6. Ac +8:24.
and I will. ver. 25-28. Ex 10:8-11, 24-27.
12:31, 32. 14:5. Ps 66:3mg. 78:34-36. Je 34:8-
16.

9 **Glory over me**. *or*, Have *this* honor over me.
Jg 7:2. 1 K 18:25. Ps 60:8mg. Is 10:15.
when. *or*, against when.
to destroy. Heb. to cut off. ver. 13.

10 **Tomorrow**. *or*, against tomorrow. Pr 27:1. Ja
4:14.
there is none. Ex 9:14, 29. 15:11. Dt 32:31.
33:26. 2 S 7:22. 1 K 8:23. 1 Ch 17:20. Ps 9:16.
35:10. 71:19. 83:18. 86:8. 89:6-8. 113:5. Is
40:18, 25. 46:5, 9. Je 10:6, 7, 16. Mi 7:18.

11 **the frogs**. ver. 3, 9.

12 **cried unto**. ver. 8, 30. Ex 9:33. 10:18. 32:11.
1 S 12:23. Ezk 36:37. Mt 5:44. Ja 5:16-18.

13 **according**. Jn 18:9. Ja +5:16.
word of. Dt 34:10-12.

14 **and the**. ver. 24. Ex 7:21. Is 34:3. Ezk 39:11.
Jl 2:20.

15 **saw**. Ex 14:5. Ec 8:11. Is 26:10. Je 34:7-11.
Ho 6:4.
respite. Est 4:14.
he hardened. Ex +4:21. Re 16:9.

16 **Stretch**. ver. 5, 17.

17 **lice in man**. Ps 105:31. Is 23:9. Ac 12:23.
all. Ex 9:6, 25. 10:12. Ge +7:19.

18 **the magicians**. Ex 7:11.
did so. Dt 28:68. Ezk 24:13. Mt 17:11. Ga
5:4. Ph 3:15. 1 J 1:10. 5:10. 2:26.
they could not. Ex 9:11. Ge 41:8. Is 19:12.
47:12, 13. Da 2:10, 11. 4:7. 5:8. Lk 10:18. 2 T
3:8, 9.

19 **This is**. 1 S 6:3, 9. Da 2:10, 11, 19. Jn 11:47.
Ac 4:16.
the finger. Ex 10:7. +31:18.
and Pharaoh's. ver. +15.

20 **lo**. Ex 7:15.
Let my. ver. 1.

21 **swarms**. Ex 12:38. Ne 13:3. Ps 78:45. 105:31.
Is 7:18.

22 **sever**. Ex 9:4, 6, 26. 10:23. 11:6, 7. 12:13. Ml
3:18.
know. ver. 10. Ex 7:17. Ezk 30:19.
midst. Ps 74:12. 110:2.

23 **put**. Ex 11:7. Ps 50:5.
a division. Heb. a redemption. Ex 33:16. Le
20:24. Nu 23:9. Dt 16:3. 22:15, 17. 33:28. 2 K
13:17. Ps 78:61. 111:9. 130:7. Is 49:6mg, +8.
50:2. Ezk 7:27.
tomorrow. *or*, by tomorrow. ver. 10.
sign. Ex 4:8. +12:13. Jg 6:17, 37.

24 **there**. ver. 21. Ps 78:45. 105:31.
the land. ver. 14.
corrupted. *or*, destroyed. Ge 6:11, 12.

25 **called for**. ver. 8. Ex 9:27. 10:16. 12:31. Re
3:9.
in the land. ver. 11. Ex 10:11, 24.

26 **It is not**. Ex 3:18. 2 C 6:14-17.
we shall. Ge 43:22. 46:34. Dt 7:25, 26. 12:30,
31. Ezr 9:1. Is 44:19.
the abomination. Ex 9:3. 1 K 11:5-7. 2 K
23:13.

27 **three days'**. Ex 3:18. 5:1. 2 C 6:17.
as he shall. Ex 3:12. 10:26. 34:11. Le 10:1.
Mt 28:20.

28 **I will**. Ho 10:2.
only. Ex 8:25. 10:11, 24.
intreat. ver. 8, 29. Ex 9:28. 10:17. 1 K 13:6.
Ezr 6:10. Ec 6:10. Ac 8:24.

29 **tomorrow**. ver. 10.
deal. ver. 8, 15. Ps 66:3mg. 78:34-37. Je
42:20, 21. Ac 5:3, 4. Ga 6:7.

30 **entreated**. ver. 12. Ex 9:33. Ja 5:16.

31 **according**. Ps 65:2.
removed. 1 K 13:6.

32 **hardened**. ver. +15. Ex +4:21. Pr 28:14.

EXODUS 9

1 **Go in**. ver. 13. Ex 3:18. 4:22, 23. 5:1. 8:1, 20.
10:3.
the Lord. Ex 3:18. 5:3. 7:16.

2 **if thou refuse**. Ex 4:23. 8:2. 10:4. Le 26:14-
16, 21, 23, 24, 27, 28. Ps 7:11, 12. 68:21. Is
1:20. Ro 2:8. Re 2:21, 22. 16:9.

3 **the hand**. Ex 8:19. Ru +1:13. 1 S 6:9. 7:13.
12:15. 1 Ch 21:17. Jb 1:11. 2:5. 13:21. 33:7.
Ps 10:12. 17:14. 21:8. 106:26. Is 26:11. La 3:3.
Ezk 39:21. Mi 5:9.
murrain. *or*, pestilence. ver. 15. Ex 5:3. Le
26:25. Ezk 38:22.

4 **sever**. Ex 8:22. 10:23. 12:13. Is 65:13, 14. Ml
3:18.

5 **a set time**. ver. 18. Ex 8:23. 10:4. Nu 16:5.
Jb 24:1. Ec 3:1-11. Je 28:16, 17. Mt 27:63,
64.

6 **all**. ver. 25. Ex 10:12. 32:3, 26. Ge 6:17.
+41:56. Nu 16:32. Dt 28:64. Jsh 6:21. 11:23.
21:43. 2 S 6:5, 15. 16:22. 17:24. 2 K 11:16. 1
Ch 10:6. 14:17. Ps 22:7. 118:10. Is 2:2. Je
26:9. Ho 7:4. Hg 2:7. Mt 3:5. 8:34. 10:22.
16:19. 18:18. 21:26. 24:9. Mk 1:33. 9:23. Lk
2:1, 3. 15:1. Jn 1:16. 10:8. Ro 1:8. 10:18. 1 C
6:2. 9:19, 22. 13:7. Ph 2:21. 4:13. Col 1:23,
28. He 6:16. Re 13:7, 8, 16.
the cattle. ver. 19, 25. Ps 78:48, 50. Mt
10:29. 1 C 9:9, 10.

7 **the heart**. ver. 12. Ex 7:14. 8:32. Jb 9:4. Pr
29:1. Is 48:4. Da 5:20. Ro 9:18.

8 **Take to**. Ex 8:16.
furnace. Ex 19:18. Ge 11:3. 19:28.
toward the heaven. ver. 10.

9 **a boil**. Le 13:18-20. Dt 28:27, 35. 2 K 20:7. Jb
2:7. Is 38:21. Re 16:2.

10 **up toward**. ver. 8.
a boil. ver. +9. Dt 28:27.

11 **magicians**. Ex +7:11. Ge +41:8.

could not. Ex 7:11, 12. 8:18, 19. Is 47:12-14. 2 T 3:8, 9. Re 16:2.

stand. Ps 147:14. Pr 27:7. Da 8:7.

12 the Lord hardened. ver. 35. Ex +4:21. Jg 9:23. 14:4. 1 S 2:25. 16:14. 1 K 12:15. 2 Ch 10:15. 22:7. 25:20. Jb 12:16. Ps 81:11, 12. Pr 21:1. Is 19:2, 14. 29:10. Je 4:10. Ezk 12:2. 14:9. Am +3:6. Mt 13:11, 14. Mk 4:11, 12. Lk 8:10. 2 C 3:14, 15. Re 16:10, 11.

13 rise up early. ver. 1. Ex 7:15. 8:20. Ge +21:14.

the Lord God. Ex 7:16.

Let. Is 61:1.

14 send all. Le 26:18, 21, 28. Dt 28:15-17, 59-61. 29:20-22. 32:39-42. 1 S 4:8. 1 K 8:38. Je 19:8. Mi 6:13. Re 18:8. 22:18.

that thou. Ex +8:10.

15 stretch. ver. 3, 6, 16. Ex +7:5. 11:4-6. 12:29, 30.

cut off. Ex 14:28. 1 K 13:34. Pr 2:22.

16 deed. Ex 14:17. Ps 83:17, 18. Pr 16:4. Ro 9:17, 22. 1 P 2:8, 9. Ju 4.

raised thee up. Heb. made thee stand.

for to. Ex 14:4. 15:11-16. 18:11. Jsh 2:10, 11. 1 S 4:8. Ps 76:10. 136:10-15.

that my. 1 Ch 16:24. Ne 9:10. Ps 64:9. 83:17, 18. Is 63:12-14. Ml 1:11, 14. Ro 9:17.

17 exaltest. Jb 9:4. 15:25, 26. 40:9. Is 10:15. 26:11. 37:23, 24, 29. 45:9. Ac 12:23. 1 C 10:22.

18 tomorrow. 1 K 19:2. 20:6. 2 K 7:1, 18.

I will cause. ver. +12, 22-25. Jb 9:17. Ps 83:15.

rain. ver. 34. Ge 7:4. 1 S 12:17, 18. Ps 77:17.

hail. Is +28:17.

such as. ver. 24. Ex 10:6, 14.

19 and gather. Hab 3:2.

the hail. ver. +18, 25.

20 feared the word. Pr 16:16. +22:3, 23. Jon 3:5, 6. Mk 13:14-16. He 11:7.

21 regarded not. Heb. set not his heart unto. Ex 7:23. 1 S 4:20mg. 2 S 13:26. 1 Ch 22:19. Jb 1:8mg. 7:17. 34:14. Ps +78:43mg. Pr 24:32mg. Ezk 40:4. 44:5mg. Da 10:12.

22 Stretch forth. Ex 7:19. 8:5, 16. 10:12, 21. Re 16:21.

toward heaven. Mt 14:19. Lk 15:18.

23 the Lord sent. Ex 19:16. 20:18. 1 S 7:10. 12:17, 18. 2 S 22:14. Jb 37:1-5. Ps 29:3. 77:18. Re 4:5. 6:1. 8:5. 11:19. 16:18. 19:6.

thunder. Heb. voices. ver. 28. Ps 29:9.

and hail. ver. +18.

24 mingled. Ezk 1:4.

none like. ver. 18, 23. 10:6. Mt 24:21.

25 smote. Ps 105:33.

all. ver. 6.

every. ver. 6. Ex 8:17. 10:12. Ge +7:19.

26 Only in the land. ver. 4, 6. Ex 8:22, etc. 10:23. 11:7. 12:13. Ps 91:7. Is 32:18, 19.

Goshen. Jsh +10:41.

where. Ex 14:29. 15:19. Ps 78:53. Am 4:7.

27 I have. Ex 10:16. Nu 22:34. 1 S 15:24, 30. 26:21. Jb 34:31, 32. Pr 28:13. Mt 27:4.

the Lord. 2 Ch 12:6. Ps 9:16. 129:4. 145:17. La 1:18. Da 9:14. Ro 2:5. 3:19.

28 Intreat. Ex 8:8, 28. 10:17. Ac 8:24.

enough. Ge 45:28. Nu 16:3.

mighty thunderings. Heb. voices of God. Ps 29:3, 4. +36:6mg.

ye shall. Ex 11:1.

29 spread. ver. 33. Ps +88:9.

that the earth. Dt 10:14. Ps 24:1, 2. 50:12. 95:4, 5. 135:6. 1 C 10:26, 28.

30 as for. Pr 16:6. Ec 8:12. Is 26:10. 63:17. Ro 2:4.

I know. Lk +6:35.

not yet fear. Dt 25:18. 2 K 17:25. Jb 6:14mg. Ps 36:1. 55:19. Pr 1:29. Ec 8:13. Is 57:11. Je 2:19. 5:22, 24. 44:10. Ho 10:3. Ml 3:5. Lk 16:31. 18:4.

31 flax. Ru 1:22. 2:23. Am 4:9. Hab 3:17.

barley. Le 27:16.

in the ear. Le 2:14.

bolled. or, in bud.

32 rie. or, spelt. Is 28:25. Ezk 4:9.

not grown up. Heb. hidden, or dark. Ex 10:22.

33 spread. ver. 29. Ex 8:12.

and the thunders. Ex 10:18, 19. Ja 5:17, 18.

34 saw. Ex 8:15. Ec 8:11.

and hardened. Ex +4:21. +7:14. 1 S 6:6. 2 Ch 28:22. 33:23. 36:13. Ro 2:4, 5.

35 was hardened. Ex +7:13.

as the Lord. Ex +4:21.

by Moses. Heb. by the hand of Moses. Hg +1:1mg.

EXODUS 10

1 I have hardened. Ex +4:21. 9:27, 34, 35. Ps 7:11.

that I. Ex 3:20. 7:4. 9:16. 14:17, 18. 15:14, 15. Jsh 2:9, 10. 4:23, 24. 1 S 4:8. Ro 9:17.

2 And that. Ex 13:8, 9, 14. Dt 4:9. 6:20-22. Ps 44:1. 71:18. 78:5, 6. Jl 1:3. Ep 6:4.

wrought. Nu 22:29. 1 S 6:6. 31:4.

may know. Ex 7:17. Ps 58:11. Ezk 20:26, 28.

3 How long. Ex 9:17. Je 13:10. Ezk 5:6. Mt +17:17. He 12:25.

humble. 1 K 21:29. 2 Ch +7:14. 33:12, 19. 34:27. Jb 42:6. Pr 18:12. Is 1:5. 2:11. Je 13:18. Ro 2:4. Ja 4:10. 1 P 5:6.

4 tomorrow. Ex 8:10, 23. 9:5, 18. 11:4, 5.

locusts. Ps +78:46. Pr 30:27.

5 face. Heb. eye. ver. 15. Ge +1:2. Nu 11:7. 22:5, 11.

the residue. Ex 9:32. Jl 1:4. 2:25.

6 fill. Ex 8:3, 21.

which. ver. 14, 15. Ex 9:24. 11:6. Jl 2:2.

unto this day. Ge +19:38.

And he. ver. 11. Ex 11:8. He 11:27.
went out. Mt 10:14.

7 **servants said**. Ex 8:19.
How long. ver. +3.
snare. Ex +23:33. Pr 29:6. Ec 7:26. Is 8:14. 1
C 7:35. 1 P 2:8.
that Egypt. Ps 107:34. Is 14:20. 51:9. Je
48:4. 51:8. Zp 1:18.

8 **brought**. ver. 16, 24. Ex 12:31.
who. Heb. who, and who, etc.

9 **We will go**. Ge 50:8. Dt 31:12, 13. Jsh 24:15.
Ps 148:12, 13. Ec 12:1. Ep 6:4.
our flocks. Pr 3:9.
a feast. Ex 3:18. 5:1, 3. 8:25-28. Nu 29:12. 1
C 5:7, 8.

10 **Let**. ver. 24. Ex 8:25.
be so. Ex 12:30, 31. 13:21.
look to it. 2 Ch 32:15. La 3:37.

11 **Not so**. Ex 8:25, 26. 10:24.
for that. Ps 52:3, 4. 119:69.
And they. ver. 28. Ex 5:4.

12 **Stretch**. Ex 7:19.
eat every. ver. 4, 5.
all that. Ex 9:25. Ge +7:19.

13 **east wind**. Ge +41:6. Ps 107:25-28. 148:8.
Jon 1:4. Mt 8:27.

14 **the locusts**. Ps +78:46.
very grievous. ver. 5. Jl 1:2-4.
before. ver. 6. Ex 11:6. Jl 2:2.
no such. Ex 9:18.

15 **For they**. ver. 5. Jl 1:6, 7. 2:1-11, 25.
face. Ge +1:2.
eat. Ps 78:46. 105:35.

16 **called for**. Heb. hastened to call.
I have. Ex 9:27. Nu 21:7. 22:34. 1 S 15:24,
30. 26:21. 2 S 19:20. Jb 34:31, 32. Pr 28:13.
Mt 27:4.

17 **forgive**. 1 S 15:25. Pr 28:13.
and intreat. Ex +8:8. 9:28. 1 K 13:6. Is
26:16. Ro 15:30. Ac 8:24.
this death. 2 K 4:40. 2 C 1:10.

18 **went**. Ex 8:30.
and intreated. Ex 8:9, 28, 29. Mt 5:44. Lk
6:28.

19 **a mighty**. ver. 13.
cast. Heb. fastened.
the Red sea. Ex 13:18. 15:4. Jl 2:20. He
11:29.

20 **the Lord hardened**. Ex +4:21.

21 **Stretch**. Ex 9:22.
darkness. ver. 22. Ps 35:6. 78:49. Pr 4:19. Ec
2:14. 6:4.
even darkness which may be felt. Heb.
that *one* may feel darkness. Dt 28:29.

22 **thick darkness**. ver. 21. Ex 20:21. Ge 15:12.
Dt +4:11. 5:22. 2 S 22:10, 12. 1 K 8:12. 2 Ch
6:1. Jb 38:9. Ps 18:9, 11. 97:2. 104:20. 105:28.
Pr +20:20. Is 5:30. 8:22. 13:10. 45:7. Je 13:16.
Ezk 32:8. 34:12. Jl 2:2, 10, 31. Am 4:13. 5:8,
20. 8:9. Na 1:8. Zp 1:15. Mt 24:29. 27:45. Mk

13:24-26. 15:33. Lk 21:25, 26. 23:44. He
12:18. 2 P 2:4, 17. Ju 6, 13. Re 16:10.
three days. Ex 3:18. 5:3. Ge +22:4. 30:36.
+40:20. Le +19:6. Jsh 3:11.

23 **but all**. Ex 8:22. 9:4, 26. 14:20. Jsh 24:7. Is
42:16. 60:1-3. 65:13, 14. Ml 3:18. Ep 5:8. Col
1:13. 1 P 2:9.

24 **Go ye**. ver. 8, 9. Ex 8:28. 9:28.
only. Ex 8:25, 28. 10:11.
flocks. Ge 34:23.
little ones. ver. 10. Nu +16:27.

25 **us**. Heb. into our hands.
sacrifices. Ex 29:36-41. Le 9:22. 16:9.

26 **cattle**. Ex 12:32. Is 23:18. 60:5-10. Ho 5:6. Zc
14:20. Ac 2:44, 45. 2 C 8:5.
shall go. Jsh 4:11. 1 C 10:1.
and we. Pr 3:9. He 11:8.

27 **the Lord hardened**. ver. 1, 20. Ex +4:21.
+7:14. Re 9:20. 16:10, 11.

28 **Get thee**. ver. 11.
for in that. 2 Ch 16:10. 25:16. Am 7:13.

29 **I will see**. Ex 11:4-8. 12:30, 31. He 11:27.

EXODUS 11

1 **Yet will**. Ex 9:14. Le 26:21. Dt 4:34. 1 S 6:4.
Jb 10:17. Re 16:9. 22:18.
afterwards. Ex 3:20. Ge 15:14.
thrust you. Ex 12:31-39.

2 **borrow**. Ex +3:22. 12:1, 2, 35, 36. Ge 31:9.
Jb 27:16, 17. Ps 24:1. 105:37. Pr 13:22. Hg
2:8. Mt 20:15.
jewels. Ex 32:2-4, 24. 35:22. Ezk 16:10-13.
Ho 2:8.

3 **the Lord**. Ex 3:21. 12:36. Ge 39:21. Ps
106:46. Ac 7:10.
Moses. Ge 12:2. 2 S 7:9. Est 9:4. Is 60:14. Ac
7:22. Re 3:9.

4 **About**. Ex 12:12, 23, 29. 2 K 19:35. Jb 34:20.
Am 4:10. 5:17. Mt 25:6.
midnight. Mt 25:6.
will I go. 2 S 5:24. Ps 60:10. Is 42:13. Mi
2:13. Zc 14:3.

5 **the firstborn**. Ex 4:23. 12:12, 29. 13:15. Ps
78:51. 105:36. 135:8. 136:10. He 11:28.
behind. Jg 16:21. Is 47:2. La 5:13. Mt
24:41.

6 **a great**. Ex 3:7. 12:30. Pr 21:13. Is 15:4, 5, 8.
Je 31:15. La 3:8. Am 5:17. Zp 1:10. Lk 13:28.
Re 6:16, 17. 18:18, 19.
cry. Mt 25:6.
such as. Ex 8:10. +9:24. 10:6.

7 **dog**. Ps +107:42.
a difference. Ex +7:22. +8:23. 10:23. Le
10:10. Ml 3:18. 1 C 4:7.

8 **And all**. Ex 12:31-33. Is 49:23, 26. Re 3:9.
bow. Ph 2:10.
follow thee. Heb. is at thy feet. Jg 8:5. 2 K
+3:9mg. Da 11:43.
a great anger. Heb. heat of anger. Ex 32:19.

Nu 12:3. Dt 29:24. 32:24. Ps 6:1. Ezk 3:14. Da 3:19. Mk 3:5. Ep 4:26, 27.

9 **Pharaoh**. Ex 3:19. 7:4. 10:1. Ro 9:16-18.
wonders. Ex +7:3.

10 **the Lord**. Ex +4:21.

EXODUS 12

1 A.M. 2513. B.C. 1491.
in. Lk 10:33.

2 **beginning**. 2 C 5:17.
first month. Abib or Nisan. Ex 13:4. 23:15. 34:18. Le 23:5. Nu 28:16. Dt 16:1. Est 3:7.

3 **Speak ye**. Ex 4:30. 6:6. 14:15. 20:19. Le 1:2.
congregation. Le 4:13. 8:3.
tenth. ver. 6. Ps 40:8. Mt 3:17. Jn 12:1, 12. Ga 4:4.
take to. Ge 4:4. 22:8. 1 S 7:9. Jn 1:29, 36. 1 C 5:7. Re 5:6-13. 7:9-14. 13:8.
lamb. *or*, kid. Ex 13:13. 22:1, 9, 10. 34:20. Ge 22:7, 8. Le 5:6. 22:23. Nu 15:11. Dt 17:1. 1 S 14:34. 17:34. 2 Ch 35:7. Is 53:7. 1 C 5:7. 1 P 1:19. Re 5:6. 7:10.
according. Ex 6:11. 2 Ch 25:5. 35:12.
for an. Ge 7:1. 30:30. Pr 31:15. Ac +16:31.
house. Nu ch. 1. Jsh 7:14.

4 **too little**. Jsh 19:9.
souls. Heb. *nephesh*, Ge +12:5.
according to his eating. Ex 16:16.

5 **lamb**. Jn 1:29.
be without. Le +1:3. Dt 17:1. Jn 8:46.
a male. Le 4:28.
of the first year. Heb. son of a year. Le 23:12. 1 S 13:1mg. Ps 102:23, 24. 110:3.

6 **fourteenth**. Le 23:5. Nu 9:3. 28:16, 18. Dt 16:1-6. Jsh 5:10. 2 Ch 30:15. Ezr 6:19. Ezk 45:21.
the whole. 2 Ch 30:15-18. Is 53:6. Mt 27:20, 25. Mk 15:1, 8, 11, 25, 33, 34, 37. Lk 23:1, 18. Jn 11:50. Ac 2:23. 3:14. 4:27. 2 C 5:14. Re 20:6.
assembly. Dt 23:2.
in the evening. Heb. between the two evenings. ver. 18. Ex 16:12. Le 23:5. Nu 9:3. Dt 16:6. Pr 7:9mg. Mt 27:46-50. Mk 15:33. Jn 13:30.

7 **blood**. ver. 13, 22, 23. Le 17:11. Mt 20:28. Ro 5:9. Ep 1:7. He 9:13, 14, +22. 10:14, 29. 11:28. 12:24. 1 P 1:2. 1 J 1:7. Re 13:8.
strike. Ro 4:24, 25. 5:1.

8 **eat the**. Mt 26:26. Jn 6:52-57. 1 J 1:3.
that night. ver. 12, 14, 17. Mt 26:17. Lk 17:34.
roast. Ex 29:31. Dt 16:7. Ps 22:14. Is 53:10. He 12:29.
unleavened. Ex 13:3, 7. 34:25. Nu 9:11. Dt 16:3. 2 Ch 30:2, 5. Ps 32:2, 5. Am 4:5. Mt 16:12. Ac 24:16. 1 C 5:6-8. Ga 5:9.
with bitter. Ex 1:14. Nu 9:11. La 3:15, 19, 20. Zc 12:10. Ep 2:11, 12. 1 Th 1:6. 1 T 1:12-15.

9 **sodden**. Nu 6:19. Dt 16:7.

but roast with fire. ver. 8. Dt 16:7. La 1:13.
head. Col 2:3.
legs. Jn 8:29.
purtenance. Ex 29:13. Le 1:13. Ps 40:8.

10 **let nothing**. Ex 23:18. 29:34. 34:25. Le 7:15-17. 22:30. Dt 16:4, 5.
remain. Ex 16:19. Le 7:15.

11 **loins girded**. Mt 26:19, 20. Lk +12:35. 1 P 2:11.
shoes. Jsh 9:5, 13. Lk 7:38. Ac 12:8. Ep +6:15.
staff. Ge 32:10. 2 K 4:29. Mk 6:8.
haste. Ge 19:15. Dt 20:3. 2 K 7:15. Ps 31:22.
it is the. ver. 27. Le 23:5. Nu 28:16. Dt 16:2-6. 1 C 5:7.
passover. 1 C 11:26.

12 **pass through**. ver. 23. Ex 11:4, 5. Am 5:17.
this night. ver. +8.
will smite. ver. 29, 30. Ex 11:4-6.
against. Nu 33:4. 1 S 5:3. 6:5. 1 Ch 14:12. Is 19:1. Je 43:13. Zp 2:11.
gods. *or*, princes. Ex 15:11. 18:11. +21:6. 22:8, 9, 28mg. Nu 33:4. 1 Ch 16:25. 2 Ch 2:5. Ps 82:1, 6. 86:8. 95:3. 96:4, 5. 97:7, 9. 135:5. 138:1. Is 19:1. Je 43:12. 44:8. 46:25. Ezk 30:13. Zp 2:11. Jn 10:34, 35. Re 12:8.
execute. Ge 15:14. Ac 17:31.
I am the Lord. Ex +6:2. Ezk 12:16. 1 C +8:6.

13 **the blood**. ver. 7, 23. He 11:28.
token. Ge 9:13. +17:11. Jsh +2:12, 21.
and when. 1 Th 1:10. 1 J 1:7.
I see the. Ge 6:5. Ro 3:26. 8:33.
blood. ver. 7. Mt 20:28. Mk 10:45. Col 1:14. He 9:11-14, +22. 1 J 1:7. Re +1:5.
pass over. ver +23:5. Jsh 4:7. Lk 21:36. 1 C 5:7. 1 Th 5:9. Re 3:10.
shall not. Ex 8:22. 9:4, 6. 10:23. 11:6, 7. 14:28, 29. 15:19. Ps 78:53. Ro +5:9. 1 Th +5:9. Re +3:10.
to destroy you. Heb. for a destruction.

14 **this day**. ver. +8.
memorial. Ex 13:9. 17:14. 28:12, 29. 30:16. 39:7. Le +2:2. 24:7. Nu 10:10. 16:40. 31:54. Jsh 4:7. Ne 2:20. Ps 107:1, 2. 111:4. 126:2. 135:13. Is 66:3mg. Zc 6:14. Mt 26:13. Mk 14:9. Lk 22:19. Ac 10:4. 1 C 11:23-26.
a feast. Ex 5:1. Dt 16:11. Ne 8:9-12.
by an ordinance. ver. 17, 24, 43. Ex 13:10. Le 23:4, 5. Nu 10:8. 18:8. Dt 16:1. 1 S 30:25. 2 K 23:21. Ezk 46:14. 1 C 5:7, 8.
for ever. Heb. *olam*, ver. +24.

15 **Seven**. ver. 8. Ex 13:6, 7, etc. 23:15. 34:18, 25. Le 23:5-8. Nu 28:17. Dt 16:3, 5, 8. Mt 16:12. Lk 12:1. Ac 12:3. 1 P 4:2.
unleavened. Le +23:6.
that soul, Heb. *nephesh*, Ge +17:14. ver. 19, 20. Le 17:10, 14. Ga 5:12.
cut off. 1 C 11:30-32.

16 **first day**. Le 23:2, 3, 7, 8, 21, 24, 25, 27, 35. Nu 28:18, 25. 29:1, 12.

no manner. Ex 16:5, 23, 29. 20:10. 35:2, 3. Je 17:21, 22. Ro 4:4, 5.

man. Heb. *nephesh*, soul. Ge +27:31.

17 **unleavened**. Le +23:6.

in this selfsame. Ex 7:5. 13:3, 8. Nu 20:16. Dt +32:48.

this day. ver. +8.

an ordinance. ver. +14.

for ever. Heb. *olam*, ver. +24.

18 **In the first**. ver. +2, 15. Le 23:5, 6. Nu 28:16.

19 **Seven**. Ex 23:15. 34:18. Dt 16:3. 1 C 5:7, 8.

even that. ver. +15. Nu 9:13.

soul. Heb. *nephesh*, Ge +17:14; +12:5.

whether. ver. 43, 48.

born in. ver. +48.

20 **all your habitations**. Ex 10:23. Ge 10:30. Nu 15:2. 1 S 20:18. Ps 1:1. 132:13.

unleavened bread. ver. 15. Ex 13:3, 4, 6, 7. 23:18. Le 23:17. Nu 9:11.

21 **elders**. Ex +3:16.

Draw out. Jg 4:6. 5:14. 20:37. Jb 21:33.

and take. ver. 3. Nu 9:2-5. Jsh 5:10. 2 K 23:21. 2 Ch 30:15-17. 35:5, 6. Ezr 6:20. Mt 26:17-19. Mk 14:12-16. Lk 22:7-13. 1 C 10:4.

lamb. *or*, kid. ver. 3. Ge 4:4. Le 22:21.

the passover. 2 Ch 30:17. Ezr 6:19. Ezk 45:21. Mt 26:17. Mk 14:12, 14. Lk 22:8, 11, 15. 1 C 5:7.

22 **a bunch**. He 9:1, 14, 19. 11:28. 12:24. 1 P 1:2.

hyssop. Ps +51:7. Lk 18:14. Ac 20:21.

dip. Heb. *tabal*, **S#2881h**, 2 K +5:14; 1 Ch 26:11, **S#2882h**. He 11:28.

bason. 2 S 17:28. Je 52:19.

strike. ver. 7.

and none. Jsh 2:18, 19. Is 26:20. Mt 26:30. Jn 15:6. He 6:6.

23 **will pass through**. ver. +12, 13.

pass over. Is 31:5. Mt 26:39.

and will not. 2 S 24:16. Is 37:36. Ezk 9:4, 6. Ro 8:33. 1 C 10:10. 1 Th 1:10. He 11:28. 12:24. Re 7:3. 9:4.

24 **for an**. ver. +14. Ge 17:8-10.

for ever. Ezk 45:17. 46:14. Ep 2:15. Col 2:14. He 8:13. **S#5769h**, *olam*. Rendered "forever" in the following passages: Ex 3:15. 14:13. Ge 3:22. 13:15. Dt 5:29. 2 S 7:13, 16, 24-26, 29. Ps 9:7. 33:11. 37:18, 28. 45:2. 48:8. 49:8, 11. 72:17, 19. 78:69. 89:36, 37. 112:6. 119:89, 111, 152, 160. 146:10. Ec 1:4. Is 9:7. 40:8. 60:21. Je 17:25. Ezk 37:25. Da 2:44. 7:18. Mi 4:7. Also translated "everlasting," Ge +17:7; "perpetual," Ge +9:12; "for evermore," Ps +18:50; "of old" and "ever of old," Ge +6:4; "old" or "ancient," Jb +22:15; "of" or "in old time," Jsh +24:2; "alway" or "always," Ge +6:3; "ever," Ps +5:11. For miscellaneous renderings see Le +25:32; *olam* doubled, rendered "for ever and ever," Da +2:20; "from everlasting to everlasting," Ps +41:13. *olam* in the plu-

ral, Ps +61:4; with *ad*, Ex +15:18. For the Hebrew word *ad*, Nu +24:20. For *nezach*, 2 S +2:26; *kedem*, Mi +5:2; *zmithuth*, Le 25:23; *tamid*, Le +6:13; *dor*, Ps 77:8; *yom*, Ge +43:9. Ps 23:6. For *olam* used in a limited or finite sense see Ps +24:9.

25 **when**. Dt 4:5. 12:8, 9. 16:5-9. Jsh 5:10-12. Ps 105:44, 45.

according. Ex 3:8, 17.

26 **when**. Dt 6:20.

your children. Ex 13:8, 9, 14, 15, 48. Dt 6:7. 11:19. 32:7. Jsh 4:6, 7, 21-24. Ps 78:3-6. 145:4. Is 38:19. Ep 6:4.

27 **It is the sacrifice**. ver. +11, 23. Ex 34:25. 1 C 11:26.

bowed. Ge +24:26.

28 **and did**. ver. 50. Ex 40:16. Ge +6:22. 7:5. He 11:28.

29 **at midnight**. ver. 12. Ex 11:4. 13:15. Jb 34:19, 20. 1 Th 5:2, 3.

the Lord smote. Ge 15:14. Nu 3:13. 8:17. 33:4. 2 Ch 32:21. Ps 78:51. 105:36. 135:8. 136:10. Zc 12:10. Lk 12:20. Ro 6:23. He 11:28. 12:23.

the firstborn of Pharaoh. Ex 4:23. 11:5.

dungeon. Heb. house of the pit, *bor*, Ge +37:20. Ge 40:15. Is 24:22. 51:14. Je 38:6, 13. Zc 9:11.

of cattle. Ex 11:5. Nu 3:13. Ps 135:8.

30 **and there was a great cry**. Ex +11:6. Pr 21:13. Am 5:17. Zc 12:10. Mt 25:6. Ja 2:13.

31 **called**. Ex 10:29.

Rise up. Ex 3:19, 20. 6:1. 11:1, 8. Ps 105:38.

the children. Ex 10:9, 11.

32 **your flocks**. Ex +10:26.

bless me. Ex 8:28. 9:28. Ge 27:34, 38.

33 **urgent**. Ex 10:7. 11:1, 8. Ps 105:38.

We be all. Ge 20:3. Nu 17:12, 13.

34 **kneading troughs**. *or*, dough. Ex 8:3.

before. Ge 19:3. Ac 12:3.

35 **did**. ver. 28.

borrowed. Ex 3:21, +22. 11:2, 3. Ge 15:14. Ps 105:37.

36 **the Lord**. Ex 3:21. 11:3. Ge 39:21. Pr 16:7. Da 1:9. Ac 2:47. 7:10.

lent. 1 S 1:28.

they spoiled. Ex 3:22. Ge 15:14. 31:9, 16. 1 S 30:22. Ps 105:37. 119:43. Is 14:2. Ezk 39:10.

37 **the children**. Nu 33:3, 5.

Rameses. Ex 1:11. Ge 47:11.

six hundred thousand. Ex 38:26. Ge 12:2. 15:5. 46:3. Nu 1:46. 2:32. 11:21. 26:51.

children. Nu +16:27.

38 **mixed**. Ge 12:4. Ne 13:3. Is 51:2. Mt 10:37.

multitude. Ge 17:6. 22:17. 26:4. 28:3, 14. 32:12. 35:11. 46:3 w 47:27. Heb. a great mixture. Nu 11:4. Zc 8:23. Lk 14:25-27.

very much. Ex 17:3. Nu 20:19. 32:1. Dt 3:19.

39 **thrust**. ver. 33. Ex 3:20. 6:1. 11:1.

40 **sojourning**. Ac 13:17. He 11:9.

four hundred and thirty. Ge 12:1-3. 15:13. 17:7. 21:12. Ac 7:6. Ga 3:16, 17.

41 **four hundred and**. ver. 40. Ge 15:16.
selfsame. ver. +17, 51. Ps 102:13. Da 9:24. Hab 2:3. Jn 7:8. Ac 1:7.
hosts. ver. 51. Ex 7:4. Nu 2:32. Jsh 5:14. 1 S 17:26. Ps +24:10.

42 **a night to be much observed**. Heb. a night of observations.
observed. ver. 14. Dt 16:1-6.
in their. Ex 13:10. Le 3:17. Nu 9:3.

43 **passover**. Le +23:5. Jsh 5:10. Mk 14:1. 1 C 5:7.
There shall. ver. 48. Ge 17:12, 27. Le 22:10, 25. Nu 9:14. Ac 2:46. 5:13. 2 C 6:14. Ep 2:12, 19.
stranger. Heb. foreigner. Dt +17:15. **S#5236h**. Ge 17:12, 27. 35:2, 4. Ex 12:43. Le 22:25. Ps 137:4. Is 60:10. For **S#1616h**, see Ge +23:4. ver. +48. For **S#8453h**, see Ge +23:4.

44 **bought**. Ge 17:27. Le 22:11. Ep 2:13.
circumcised. Ge 17:12, 13, 23. Ep 2:19. Col 2:11.

45 **A foreigner**. Ge 23:4. Le 22:10. 25:6. Ps 39:12. Ep 2:12.
hired. Lk 15:19, 29. Ro 4:4, 5.

46 **one house**. 1 C 12:12, 13. Ep 2:19-22. 4:4.
neither. Nu 9:12. Ps 34:20. 51:8. Jn 19:33, 36.

47 **All the**. ver. 3, 6. Nu 9:13. Mt 26:27.
keep it. Heb. do it. ver. 48. Ex 29:36, 38, 39, 41. Is 53:6. Mt 7:21. Lk 11:28.

48 **a stranger**. Heb. sojourner. ver. +43. Dt +26:11. Jsh +20:9. Is 56:6, 7.
let all. Ge 17:12. Ezk 44:9. 47:22.
circumcised. Ph 3:3.
near. He 10:22.
shall be. Ga 3:28. Col 3:11.
born in. ver. 19. Le 16:29. 23:42. 24:22. Ps 37:4. Jn 3:3.

49 **One law**. Le 24:22. Nu 9:14. 15:15. 16, 29. Ga 3:28. Ep 4:4-6. Col 3:11.

50 **as the Lord**. Dt 4:1, 2. 12:32. Mt 7:24, 25. 28:20. Jn 2:5. 13:17. 15:14. Re 22:14.
so did they. ver. 28, 35. Ex 7:6. 39:32. Nu 9:5. Dt 12:32.

51 **selfsame**. ver. +41.
by their armies. ver. 17, 41. Ex +6:26.

EXODUS 13

2 **Sanctify**. ver. 12-15. Ex 4:22. 22:29, 30. 23:19. 34:19, 20. Le 27:26. Nu 3:13. 8:16, 17. 18:15. Dt 15:19. Lk 2:23. 1 C 15:20. Col 1:15. He 12:23.
openeth. ver. 12. Mt 1:25. Lk 2:21.
womb. Nu 3:12. 12:12. Jb 10:18. Ho 9:14.

3 **Remember**. Ex 12:42. 20:8. 23:15. Dt 5:15. 15:15. 16:3, 12. 24:18, 22. 1 Ch 16:12. Ps 105:5. Is 51:1. Lk 22:19. 1 C 11:24. Ep 2:11.

out of the. ver. 14. Ex 20:2. Dt 5:6. 6:12. 8:14. 13:5, 10. Jsh 24:17. Jg 6:8.
house of bondage. Heb. servants. Dt 7:8.
strength. Ex 6:1. Dt 4:34. 11:2, 3. Ne 9:10. Ep 1:19.
there. Ex 12:8, 15. Mt 10:12. 1 C 5:8.

4 **Abib**. i.e. *grean ear of corn*, **S#24h**. Ex 9:31 (in the ear). 23:15. 34:18. Le 2:14 (green ears of corn). Dt 16:1-3. Ezk 3:15.

5 **shall bring**. Ex 3:8, 17. 23:23. 33:2. 34:11. Ge 15:18-21. Dt 7:1. 12:29. 19:1. 20:17. 26:1. Jsh 3:10. 12:8. 24:11. Jg 3:5.
Canaanites. Ge +10:18.
Hittites. Dt +20:17.
Amorites. Ge +10:16.
Hivites. Ge +10:17.
Jebusites. Ge +10:16.
which he sware. Ex 6:8. 33:1. Ge 17:7, 8. 22:16-18. 26:3. 50:24. Nu 14:16, 30. 32:11.
a land. Ex +3:17.
flowing. Ex +3:8.
milk and. Ex 33:3.
honey. Ex +3:8.
thou shalt keep. Ex 12:25, 26.

6 **Seven days**. Ex 12:15-20. 34:18. Le 23:8.

7 **no leavened bread**. Ex 12:19. Mt 16:6, 12. 1 C 5:7. 11:28.

8 **show thy son**. ver. +14. Ex 12:26, 27. Ge +18:19. Dt 4:9, 10. +6:7, 20. 11:19. Jsh 8:35. 24:15. 1 K 2:1-3. 1 Ch 22:11-13. +28:9. Ps 34:11. 44:1. 78:3-8. Pr +19:18. +22:6, 15. 23:13, 14. 29:15, 17. Is 38:19. Ml +4:6. Ep +6:4. Col 3:21. 2 T 1:5. +3:15. He 12:7-10.

9 **a sign**. ver. 16. Nu 15:39. Dt 6:6, 8. 11:18, 19. Pr 1:9. 3:21. 6:20-23. 7:23. SS 8:6. Is 49:16. Je 22:24. Mt 23:5.
memorial. Ex +12:14.
may be. Dt 30:14. Jsh 1:8. Is 59:21. Ro 10:8.
strong hand. ver. 3. Ex 6. Jsh 1:9. Ne 1:10. Ps 89:13. Is 27:1. 40:10. 51:9. Jl 2:11. 1 C 11:26. Re 18:8.

10 **keep**. Ex 12:14, 24. 23:15. Le 23:6. Dt 16:3, 4.
year to. Jg 11:40. 21:19. 1 S 1:3. 2:19.
year. Heb. days. Ge +24:55. +29:14.

11 **Canaanites**. Ge +10:18.
as he sware. ver. +5.

12 **thou shalt**. ver. 2. Ex 22:29. 34:19. Le 27:26. Nu 8:17. 18:15. Dt 15:19. Ezk 44:30.
set apart. Heb. cause to pass over.
openeth. ver. +2. Ex 34:19. Nu 3:12. 18:15.

13 **every firstling of**. Ex 34:20. Nu 18:15-17.
an ass. Ex 34:20.
lamb. *or*, kid. Ex 12:3, 21.
shalt thou. Nu 3:46-51. 18:15, 16. Re 5:9, 12. 14:4.

14 **thy son**. ver. +8. Ex 12:26. Dt 6:20-25. Jsh 4:6, 21-24. Ps 145:4.
in time to come. Heb. tomorrow. Jsh +4:6mg.
By strength. ver. 3.

15 the Lord slew. Ex +12:29.
therefore I. ver. 12.

16 a token upon. ver. 9. Ex +12:13. Pr 3:3.
6:21. 7:3. SS 8:6. Is 49:18. Je 22:24. Hg 2:23.
frontlets. Dt 6:7-9. 11:18. Mt 23:5.
for by. ver. 9, 14. Dt 26:8. Ps 46:1. Is 49:24,
25.

17 God led. Ps 107:7. Pr 16:9. Je 10:23.
the people repent. Ex 14:11, 12. Nu 14:1-4.
Dt 20:8. Jg 7:3. 1 K 8:47. Lk 14:27-32. Ac
15:38. 1 C 10:13.
return. Ex 16:2, 3. Dt 17:16. Ne 9:17. Ac
7:39.

18 led the. Ex 14:2. Nu 33:6-8. Dt 32:10. Ps
107:7.
harnessed. or, by five in a rank. Ex 12:51.
Jsh 1:14. 4:12. Jg 7:11.

19 for he had. Ge 50:24, 25. Jsh 24:32. Ac 7:16.
God. Ex 4:31. Ge 48:21. Lk 1:68. 7:16.

20 they took. Ex 12:37. Nu 33:5, 6.
Etham. i.e. *desolate; limit of habitation*, **S#864h**.
Nu 33:6, 7, 8.

21 the Lord went. Ex 14:19-24. Nu 9:15-23.
10:33. 14:14. Dt 1:33. Ne 9:12, 19. Ps 78:14.
99:7. 105:39. Is 4:5, 6. Ac 7:38. 1 C 10:1, 2.
before. Dt 31:3, 8. 32:10. Jn 10:3.
cloud. Ex 14:19, 20, 24. 16:10. 19:9, 16-18.
24:15-18. 33:9, 10. 40:34, 35, 36, 38. Le 16:2.
Nu 9:15, 17, 19. 10:11, 34. 12:5, 10. 14:14.
16:42. Dt 1:33. 4:11, 12. 31:15. 1 K 8:10, 11. 2
Ch +5:13. 6:1. 7:1-3. Ne 9:12, 19. Ps 18:11-13.
50:3. 78:14. 97:2, 3. 99:7. 104:3, 4. 105:39. Is
4:5. 6:4. 19:1. Ezk 1:4. 10:3, 4. Na 1:3-6. Hab
3:3-5. Zc +2:5. Mt 17:5. +24:30. +25:31. Mk
9:7. Lk 9:34, 35. 1 C 10:1. He 12:29.
light. Ps 119:105.

22 He took. Ne 9:19. Ps 121:4-8.
pillar of fire. Ex 40:38. Re 10:1.

EXODUS 14

1 the Lord spake. Ex 12:1. 13:1.

2 that they. ver. 9. Ex 13:17, 18. Nu 33:7, 8.
Pihahiroth. i.e. *mouth of caves*, **S#6367h**. Nu
33:7.
Migdol. i.e. *a tower*. Ge 11:4. Jsh 15:37. Jg
8:17. Is 5:2. Ezk 29:10. 30:6. **S#4024h**: Nu 33:7.
Je 44:1. 46:14.
Baal-zephon. i.e. *lord of the unknown*, **S#1189h**.
ver. 9. Nu 33:7.

3 Pharaoh. Ex 7:3, 4. Dt 31:21. Ps 139:2, 4.
Ezk 38:10, 11, 17. Ac 4:28.
They are entangled. Jg 16:2. 1 S 23:7, 23.
Ps 3:2. 71:11. Je 20:10, 11.

4 harden. ver. 8, 17. Ex +4:21, etc.
I will be. ver. 18. Ex 9:16. 15:10, 11, 14-16.
18:11. Ne 9:10. Is 2:11, 12. Ezk 20:9. 28:22.
39:13. Da 4:30-37. Ro 9:17, 22, 23. Re 19:1-6.
that the Egyptians. Ex +7:5, 17. Jsh 10:14.
Ezk +6:7.

5 and the heart. Ex 12:33. Ps 105:25.
Why have we. Je 34:10-17. Lk 11:24-26. 2 P
2:20-22.

6 people. ver. 23. Nu 21:23. Dt 2:32. 3:1.

7 six hundred chosen. ver. 23. Ex 15:4. Jsh
17:16-18. Jg 4:3, 15. Ps 20:7. 68:17. Is 37:24.
captains. Ex 15:4.

8 the Lord. ver. +4.
with an high hand. Ex 6:1. 13:9, 16, 18. Nu
33:3. Dt 26:8. 32:27. Jb 38:15. Ps 89:13. Is
26:11. Ac 13:17.

9 the Egyptians. Ex 15:9. Jsh 24:6.
encamping. ver. 2.

10 sore afraid. ver. 30. Ex 15:1. Ps 53:5. Is 7:2.
8:12, 13. 51:12, 13. Mt 8:26. 14:30, 31. 1 J
4:18.
cried out. Jsh 24:7. 2 Ch 18:31. Ne 9:9. Ps
+3:4. 106:44. Is 26:16. Je 22:23. Mt 8:25.

11 Because. Ex 15:23, 24. 16:2, 3. 17:2, 3. Nu
11:1. 14:1-4. 16:41. Ps 106:7, 8.
graves. Heb. *qeber*, Ge +23:4.
wherefore. Ex 5:22. Ge 43:6. Nu 11:15.

12 Is not this. Ex 5:21. 6:9.
Let us alone. Ho 4:17. Mk 1:24. 5:7, 17, 18.
For it had. Jon 4:3, 8.

13 Fear ye not. Ge +15:1. Nu 14:9. Dt 20:3. 2
Ch 20:15, 17. Is 26:3. 30:15.
stand still. Nu 9:8. 1 S 9:27. 12:7. 2 Ch
20:17. Jb 37:14. Ps 46:10. Is 30:7, 15, 18. Mt
8:25, 26.
see the. ver. 30. Ex 15. Ge 49:18. 1 S 12:16. 1
Ch 11:14. Ps 3:8. Is 43:11. Je 3:23. La 3:26.
Ho 13:4, 9. Hab 3:8, 13.
for the Egyptians whom ye have seen
today. or, for whereas ye have seen the
Egyptians today, etc.
ye shall see. ver. 30. Ex 15:4, 5, 10, 19, 21.
Ne 9:9.
for ever. Heb. *olam*, Ex +12:24.

14 the Lord. ver. 25. Ex 15:3. Dt 1:30. 3:22.
20:4. Jsh 10:10, 14, 42. 23:3, 10. Jg 5:20. 2
Ch 20:17, 29. Ne 4:20. Ps 46:10. Is 7:4. 31:4,
5.
hold. Ge 34:5. Ps 50:3. 83:1. Is 30:15.

15 Wherefore. Ex 17:4. Jsh 7:10. Ezr 10:4, 5. Ne
9:9. Is 65:24. Ro 8:26.

16 lift. ver. 21, 26. Ex 4:2, 17, 20. 7:9, 19.
stretch out. Ex 10:12, 21.
and the. ver. 21, 22.

17 I, behold. Ge 6:17. 9:9. Le 26:28. Dt 32:39. Is
48:15. 51:12. Je 23:39. Ezk 5:8. 6:3. 34:11,
20. Ho 5:14.
I will. ver. 8. Ex 4:23. 7:3, 13, 14.
and I will. ver. 4, 18.

18 shall know. ver. 4. Ex 7:5, 17.

19 the angel. ver. 24. Ex 32:34. Nu 20:16. Zc
+12:8.
and the pillar. Ex 13:21, 22.

20 it was a. Jsh 5:13, 14. 1 S 5:11. 1 Ch 21:16.
Ho 14:9. Mt 21:44. 1 P 2:6, 7.

cloud and darkness. Ps 18:11. Pr 4:18, 19. Is 8:14. 2 C 2:15, 16. 4:3. Col 1:12. Ju 13.

21 **stretched**. ver. 16, 26, 27. Ex 7:19. 8:5, 6, 16. 9:22. 10:12, 21. 2 K 5:11. Mt 8:27.
the Lord caused. Ex 15:8. Ps 66:6. Is 14:27. 23:11. Ac 7:36.
go back. *or*, part. Jb 12:17, 19. Ps 125:5. Ezk 32:14.
east wind. Ex 15:8. Ge +41:6. 1 K 19:11. Jb +4:9mg. Ps 18:10, 11. 104:3. Je +23:19.
dry land. Ge 7:22. Jsh 3:17. 4:18. 2 K 2:8. Hg 2:6.
divided. ver. 22, 27, 28. Jsh 3:15, 16. 4:23. Ne 9:11. Jb 26:12. Ps 74:13. 77:16. 78:13. 106:9. 114:3, 5. 136:13. Is 43:16. 51:10, 15. 63:12, 13. Je 31:35. Hab 3:8, 15.

22 **the children**. ver. 29. Ex 15:19. Nu 33:8. 1 C 10:1. He 11:29.
a wall. ver. +21, 29. Zc 2:5.

23 **Egyptians pursued**. ver. 17. Ex 15:9, 19. 1 K 22:20. Ec 9:3. Is 14:24-27.

24 **that in the**. 1 S 11:11.
looked unto. Jb 40:12. Ps 18:13, 14. 77:16-19. 104:32.
through. ver. 19, 20.
and troubled. ver. 25. Jb 22:13. 23:15, 16. 34:20, 29. Ps 48:5.
host. Ge 32:8. 33:8. 50:9.

25 **took off**. Jg 4:15. Ps 46:9. 76:6. Je 51:21.
that they drave them heavily. *or*, and made them go heavily.
Let us flee. Jb 11:20. 20:24. 27:22. Ps 68:12. Am 1:14. 5:19. 9:1.
for the Lord. ver. 14. Dt 3:22. 1 S 4:7, 8.

26 **Stretch out**. ver. 16. Ex 7:19. 8:5. Mt 8:27.
the waters. Ex 1:22. Jg 1:6, 7. Ps 77:16-19. Mt 7:2. Ja 2:13. Re 16:6.

27 **and the sea**. ver. 21, 22. Ex 15:1-21. Jsh 4:18.
Lord. Dt 11:4. Jg 5:20, 21. Ps 78:53.
overthrew. Heb. shook off. Dt 11:4. Ne 5:13. 9:11. Ps 136:15. He 11:29.

28 **the waters**. Ex 15:10. Dt 11:4. Ne 9:11. Ps 78:53. Hab 3:8-10, 13. He 11:29.
remained. ver. 13. Jg 3:29. 2 Ch 20:24. Ps 106:9-11. 136:15. Am 4:6-12.

29 **walked**. ver. 22. Jb 38:8-11. Ps 66:6, 7. 77:19, 20. 78:52, 53. Is 43:2. 51:10, 13. 63:12, 13.
a wall. ver. +22. Jsh 3:16.

30 **the Lord**. ver. 13. 1 S 14:23. 2 Ch 32:22. Ps 44:6, 7. 106:8, 10. Pr 11:8. 21:18. Is 43:3. 63:9. Ho 1:7. Ju 5.
saved. ver. 10. Ex 15:1. Re 5:9. 14:3.
saw. Ps 92:9-11. Is +66:24.

31 **work**. Heb. hand. Jb 27:11. Ps 78:42.
feared. 1 S 12:18. Ps 119:120.
believed. Ex 4:31. 19:9. Ge 15:6. Nu 14:11. 2 Ch +20:20. Ps 95:8. 106:12, 13. Lk +8:13. Jn 2:11, 23-25. 8:30-32. 11:45. Ac 8:13, 18-24. 1 C +15:2. He 2:1. 3:7-12, +14, 15, 18, 19. 4:1, 2, 6. 10:35-39.

EXODUS 15

1 **Then**. Ex 2:23, 24. 14:10, 30. Jg 5:1, etc. 2 S 22:1, etc. Ps 106:12. 107:8, 15, 21, 22. Is 12:1, etc. 51:10, 11. Re 1:5. 5:9. 14:3. 15:3.
hath triumphed. ver. 21. Ex 14:17, 18, 27. 18:11. Col 2:15.

2 **The Lord**. Heb. *Jah*. Ex 17:16. Ps 68:4, 18. 77:11. 89:8. 94:7, 12. 102:18. 104:35. 105:45. 106:1, 48. 111:1. 112:1. 113:1, 9. 115:17, 18, 18. 116:19. 117:2. 118:5, 5, 14, 17, 18, 19. 122:4. 130:3. 135:1, 3, 4, 21. 146:1, 10. 147:1, 20. 148:1, 14. 149:1, 9. 150:1, 6, 6. SS 8:6. Is 12:2. 26:4. 38:11, 11. Re 19:1, 3, 4, 6. Note that "Jah" is explicitly declared to be a name of God at Ps 68:4, thus demonstrating that God has more than one name, Ex +6:3.
my strength. Ps +18:1. 29:1. 59:17. 62:6, 7. 99:4.
song. Dt 10:21. Ps 22:3. 59:17. 109:1. 140:7. Is 25:1. Re 15:3.
my salvation. Ex 14:13. 2 S 22:51. 49:6. Lk 1:77. 2:30. Ac 4:12. Re +7:10.
my. Ex 4:22. Ge 17:7. Ps 22:10. Is 25:1. Je 31:33. 32:38. Zc 13:9.
God. Heb. *El.* ver. 2, +11. Ge 14:18-20, 22. 16:13. 21:33. 31:13. 35:1, 11. 49:25. Ex 6:3. 20:5. 34:6. Nu 12:13. +16:22. Dt 3:24. 4:24, 31. 7:9, 21. 10:17. 32:4. Jsh 3:10. 22:22. 24:19. 1 S 2:3. 2 S 22:31-33, 48. 23:5. Jb 9:2. 13:3. Ps 5:4. 7:11. 16:1. 17:6. 18:2, 30, 32, 47. 19:1. 22:1. 29:3. 31:5. 42:2, +8. 52:1. 68:35. 73:11, 17. 78:7, 8, 18, 19, 34, 35, 41. 85:8. 86:15. 89:7, 26. 90:2. 94:1. 106:14, 21. 107:11. 118:27, 28. 136:26. 139:17, 23. 149:6. 150:1. Is 5:16. 8:10. 9:6. 12:2. 14:13. 31:3. 43:10. 45:20-22. Je +32:18. 51:56. La 3:41. Jon 4:2. Mi 7:18. Ml 1:9. 2:10, 11.
an habitation. Ex 40:34. Ge 28:21, 22. 2 S 7:5. 1 K 8:13, 27. Ps 132:4, 5. Is 57:15. 66:1. Jn 14:23. 2 C 5:19. Ep 2:22. Col 2:9.
my father's. Ex +3:15, 16.
God. Heb. *Elohim.* Ge 1:1. 6:13, 18. 17:3, +7, 8. 19:29. 30:22. 50:24. Ex 2:24. Nu 23:19. 2 S 23:1, 3. 2 Ch 18:31. Is 45:22, 23.
exalt him. Ps 30:1. 145:1. Is +12:4. Jn 5:23. Ph 2:11. He 5:9-14. 19:1, 2.

3 **man of war**. Jsh 17:1. 2 S 17:8. Ps 24:8. 45:3. 46:8, 9. 76:3. Re 19:11-21.
name. Ex +3:13, 15. 6:3, 6. Ps 83:18. Is 42:8.

4 **chariots**. Ex 14:13-28.
chosen. Ex 14:7. Ge +23:6.
captains. Ex 14:7.

5 **depths**. Ex 14:28. Ezk 27:34. Jon 2:2. Mi 7:19. Mt 18:6.
they. Ne 9:11. Je 51:63, 64. Re 18:21.

6 **right hand**. ver. 12. 1 Ch 29:11, 12. Ps +18:35. Is 51:9. 52:10. Mt 6:13.
dashed. Jg 10:8. Ps 2:9. Is 30:14. Je 13:14. Re 2:27.

7 the greatness. Ex 9:16. Dt 33:26. Ps 68:33. 148:13. Is 5:16. Je 10:6.
overthrown. Jg 6:28. 1 K 19:10. 1 Ch 20:1. Ps 28:5. Is 14:17.
them that. Is 37:17, 23, 29, 36, 38. Mi 4:11. Na 1:9-12. Zc 2:8. 14:3, 8. Ac 9:4.
rose up. Ex 32:25. Dt 33:11. Ps 18:40.
sentest forth. Ex 14:24. Ne 1:10. Is 5:24. 9:18. 10:17. Ezk 7:3.
thy wrath. Ps 5:5. Is 1:14, 24. Je 9:9. Na 1:2.
consumed. Ps 59:13. Mt 3:12. 1 C +3:12.

8 blast. Heb. *ruach*, **S#7307h**, used in reference to invisible divine power manifesting itself in executing judgment, rendered *blast*: 2 K 19:7. Is 37:7. Rendered *breath*: Jb +4:9. Rendered *spirit*: Is 4:4. 28:6. 34:16. 40:7. For the other uses of *ruach*, see Ge +6:3.
thy nostrils. Dt 33:10mg. Jb 4:9. Ps 18:15. Ezk 8:17.
waters. Ex +14:21. Ps 78:13, 16. Is 44:3.
the floods. Ex +14:22. Ps 78:13. Hab 3:10.
heap. Jsh 3:13, 16. Ps 33:7. 78:13.
heart. Ps 46:2mg. Pr 23:34mg. 30:19mg. Ezk 27:4mg. Mt 12:40.

9 I will pursue. Ge 49:27. Jg 5:30. 1 K 19:2. 20:10. Is 10:8-13. 17:13, 14. 36:20. 53:12. Hab 3:14. Lk 11:22.
lust. Heb. *nephesh*, soul. Ge 23:8. Dt 12:20. Ec 6:7. Here, *nephesh* is used of man manifesting certain feelings and passions, here strong desire. For other instances of *nephesh* used similarly to express man's exercising various mental faculties and expressing or exercising various feelings, affections, or passions, see Dt 21:14 (she will). Jg 18:25 (angry). 1 S 22:2 (discontented). Est 4:13 (thyself). Ps 27:12 (will). 35:25 (so would we have it). 41:2 (will). 105:22 (pleasure). 131:2 (myself). Pr 6:16 (Him), used of God. 14:10 (his own). 16:26 (he). 27:9 (hearty). Ec 6:9 (desire). Is 5:14 (herself). 49:7 (man). Je 22:27 (desire). 34:16 (pleasure). 37:9 (yourselves). 44:14 (desire). Ezk 16:27 (will). Jon 4:8 (himself). Mi 7:3 (desire). Hab 2:5 (desire). Compare Ex +23:9; Ge +34:3. For the other uses of *nephesh* see Ge +2:7.
destroy. *or*, repossess. Ex 14:5, 9. Nu 14:12. 32:21. Dt 4:38. 1 S 2:7.

10 blow. Ex +14:21. Ge 8:1. Ps 74:13, 14. 135:7. 147:18. Is 11:15. Je 10:13. Am 4:13. Mt 8:27.
the sea. Ex 14:28. Dt 11:4.
they sank. ver. 5.
mighty. Heb. lordly, **S#117h**. Jg 5:25. 1 S 4:8. 2 Ch 23:20. Ne 3:5. Ps 8:1. Is 33:21. Ezk 17:23. Na 2:5. 3:18.

11 like unto thee. Ex +8:10. Dt 3:24. 1 S 2:2. Je 49:19.
gods. *or*, mighty ones. Heb. *El*, **S#410h**. This Hebrew noun emphasizes might. It is used (1)

as a name of God himself, ver. +2; (2) of men, Jb 41:17; Ezk 32:21; (3) of pagan gods or idols, Is 43:10; (4) of angels, Ps 29:1; and (5) of great natural objects, Ps 36:6 (great) mountains; Ps 80:10 (goodly) cedars. Ps 82:1, 2.
glorious. Ps +99:3. Is 30:11. Hab 1:13.
fearful. Ps 2:11. 66:5. 77:14. 90:11. Is 64:2, 3. Je +5:22. He 12:28, 29. Re 19:1-6.

12 stretchedst. ver. 6. Ex +6:6.
right hand. ver. +6.

13 Thou. Ge 19:16. Ep 2:4.
led. Ps 77:14, 15, 20. 73:24. 78:52, 53. 80:1. 106:9. Is 63:12, 13. Je 2:6. 1 P 1:5.
redeemed. Is +43:1.
holy. Ps 78:54. 135:21.

14 hear. Nu 14:14. 22:5. Dt 2:4, 5. Jsh 2:9, 10. 9:24. Ps 48:6.
of Palestina. i.e. *wallowing*, **S#6429h**. ver. 14. Ps 60:8. 83:7. 87:4. 108:9. Is 14:29, 31. Jl 3:4.

15 dukes. Ge 36:40. Nu 20:14-21. Dt 2:4. 1 Ch 1:51-54.
Moab. Nu 22:3-5. Hab 3:7.
melt. Le 26:36. Dt 1:28mg. 20:8. Jsh 2:9mg, 11, 24mg. 5:1. 7:5. 14:8. 1 S 14:16. 2 S 17:10. Ps 22:14. 58:7. 68:2. 112:10. Is 13:7. 19:1. Je 49:23. Ezk 21:7, 12, 15. Na 2:10.

16 Fear. Mi +7:17.
greatness. Ex 18:11. Nu 14:19. Dt +3:24. Da +2:45.
thine arm. Jb 40:9. Ps 71:18mg. 77:15. 79:11mg. 89:10mg, 13. 98:1. 136:12. Is 30:30. 33:2. 40:10. 51:9. 52:10. 53:1. 59:16. 62:8. 63:5. Lk 1:51. Jn 12:38.
still. Ex 11:7. 1 S 2:9. 25:37.
thy people. Ex +19:6. 1 C 6:19, 20.
which thou. Ex 19:5, 6. Dt 32:6, 9. 2 S 7:23. Ps 74:2. Is 43:1-3. 51:10. Je 31:11. Ac 20:28. 1 C 6:19, 20. T 2:14. 1 P 1:18, 19. 2 P 2:1.

17 plant. Ps 78:54, 55. Je +11:17.
mountain. Ex 3:1, 2. Ge 22:2. Nu 22:41. 33:52. Ps 15:1. 78:54, 68, 69. 87:1, 2. Is 57:13. Je 31:23. Mi 4:1, 2. Re 14:1.
place. 1 K 8:13. Is 4:5.
Sanctuary. Ex 25:8. Ps 73:17. 78:69. 107:36. 114:2. Ezk 45:18. Da 8:11. 9:17. 11:31. Ha 2:12.

18 shall reign. Ps 29:10. Is 57:15. Da 4:3. Re +11:15-17.

19 horse. Ex 14:23. Pr 21:31.
brought. Ex 14:28, 29. He 11:29.
sea. Re 15:2.

20 Miriam. i.e. *their rebellion*, **S#4813h**. ver. 21. Nu 12:1, 4, 5, 10, 15. 20:1. 26:59. Dt 24:9. 1 Ch 4:17. 6:3. Mi 6:4.
prophetess. Nu 12:2. Jg 4:4. 2 K 22:14. 2 Ch 34:22. Ne 6:14. Is 8:3. Lk 1:41. 2:36. Ac 21:9. 1 C 11:5. 14:34. Re 2:20.
sister. Ex 2:4. Nu 12:1. 20:1. 26:59. Mi 6:4.
a timbrel. Ge 31:27. Jg 11:34. 1 S 18:6. Ps 68:25. 81:2. 149:3. 150:4. Is 30:32. Re 15:2.

all the women. Jg 11:34. +21:21. 1 S 18:6. 2 S 6:5, 14, 16. 2 K 4:23. 1 Ch 15:20. Ps 68:11, 25. 81:2. 149:3. 150:4.

with dances. Jg 11:34. 21:21. 1 S 18:6. 2 S 6:14, 16. 1 Ch +15:29. Jb 21:11. Ps +30:11. 149:3. Ec 3:4. SS 6:13mg. Je 31:4, 13. La 5:15. Mt 11:17. Lk 15:25.

21 **answered**. 1 S 18:7. 2 Ch 5:13. Ps 24:7-10. ch. 134.

Sing ye. ver. +1. Jg 5:3. Ezr 3:11. Is ch. 5. Re 7:10-12. 5:9. 14:3. 15:3. 19:1-6.

22 **wilderness of Shur**. Ge +16:7.

three days. Ex 3:18. +10:22.

23 **Marah**. i.e. *bitterness; calamity*, **S#4785h**. ver. 23, 23, 23. Nu 33:8, 9. Ru 1:20.

24 **murmured**. Ex 14:11, 12. 16:2, 7-9. 17:3, 4. Nu +11:1-6. 14:1-4, 27, 29. 16:2, 3, 7, 9, 11, 41. 17:5, 10. 20:2-5. 21:5. Ju +16.

What. Ex 17:3. Ps 78:19, 20. Mt 6:25.

25 **cried**. Ex 14:10. 17:4. Ps +50:15. 91:15. 99:6. Je 15:1.

a tree. 2 K 2:21. 4:41. 1 C 1:18.

a statute. Jsh 24:21-25.

proved. Ex 16:4. 20:20. Dt 8:2, 16. 13:3. 33:8. Jg 2:22. 3:1, 4. Ps 66:10. 81:7. Pr 17:3. Je 9:7. 1 P 1:6, 7.

26 **diligently**. Dt 4:9. 6:7, 17. 11:22. 13:14. 24:8. Jsh 22:5. Ps 77:6. 119:4. Pr 11:27. Je 12:16. Zc 6:15. Ro 12:7, 8. Ep 4:3. 1 T 4:15. 5:10. 2 T 2:15. 4:2. T 3:13. He 4:11. 6:11. 1 P 1:10. 3:13. 2 P 1:5, 10. 3:14. Ju +3.

hearken. Dt +15:5.

and wilt. Dt 12:28. 13:18. 1 K 11:33, 38. 2 K 22:2. Ezk 18:5.

put none. Ex +23:25. Ezk 7:9. Ho 6:1.

diseases. Ex 9:10, 11. 12:29. Dt 7:15. 28:27, 60.

for I am. 2 Ch 30:20. Jb 5:18. Ps 6:2. +103:3. Is 57:18. Je 8:22. Ho 6:1. 1 T +4:8.

the Lord that healeth thee. or, *Jehovah-ropheka*, one of the compound names of Jehovah. For other compound names of Jehovah, see (2) *Jehovah-jireh*, the Lord will provide, Ge 22:14. (3) *Jehovah-nissi*, the Lord our banner, Ex 17:15. (4) *Jehovah-mekad-dishkem*, the Lord that doth sanctify you, Ex 31:13; Le 20:8; 21:8; 22:9, 16, 32; Ezk 20:12. (5) *Jehovah-shalom*, the Lord our peace, or the Lord send peace, Jg 6:24. (6) *Jehovah-tsebahoth* (*sabaoth*), Ro 9:29. Ja 5:4, the Lord of hosts, 1 S 1:3. (7) *Jehovah-roi*, the Lord my shepherd, Ps 23:1. (8) *Jehovah-elyon*, the Lord most high, Ps 7:17; 47:2; 97:9. (9) *Jehovah-tsidkenu*, the Lord our righteousness, Je 23:6; 33:16. (10) *Jehovah-shammah*, the Lord is present, or the Lord is there, Ezk 48:35. (11) *Jehovah-hoseenu*, the Lord our maker, Ps 95:6. (12) *Jehovah-elohim*, the eternal creator, Ge 2:4. (13) *Adonai-Jehovah*, the Lord our sovereign, or Master Jehovah, Ge 15:2, 8. (14) *Jehovah-*

eloheenu, the Lord our God, Ps 99:5, 8, 9. (15) *Jehovah-eloheka*, the Lord thy God, Ex 20:2, 5, 7. (16) *Jehovah-elohay*, the Lord my God, Zc 14:5.

27 **Elim**. i.e. *strong ones*, **S#362h**. ver. 27. Ex 16:1. Nu 33:9, 10. Is 12:3. Ezk 47:12. Re 7:17. 22:2.

twelve. Ex 24:4. 28:21. Ge 35:22. Le 24:5. Nu 17:2. 29:17. Dt 1:23. Jsh 4:3. 1 K 4:7. 7:25. 10:20. 18:31. 19:19.

wells. Heb. *ayin*, a fountain, **S#5869h**, Ge +24:13. Ex 2:15. Ge 16:14. 21:30. 24:11. 26:18. 29:2. 1 S 19:22.

palm trees. Le 23:40. Nu 33:9. Dt 34:3. Jg 1:16. 3:13. 2 Ch 28:15.

EXODUS 16

1 A.M. 2513. B.C. 1491.

took. Ex 15:27. Nu 33:10-12.

Sin. 17:1. Nu 33:12. Ezk 30:15, 16.

Sinai. i.e. *bush of the Lord; jagged; my thorns*, **S#5514h**. ver. 1. Ex 19:1, 2, 11, 18, 20, 23. 24:16. 31:18. 34:2, 4, 29, 32. Le 7:38. 25:1. 26:46. 27:34. Nu 1:1, 19. 3:1, 4, 14. 9:1, 5. 10:12. 26:64. 28:6. 33:15, 16. Dt 33:2. Jg 5:5. Ne 9:13. Ps 68:8, 17.

2 **murmured against**. Ex +15:24. Ge 19:4. Ju +16.

3 **Would**. Nu 11:29. 14:2. 20:3-5. Dt 28:67. Jsh 7:7. 2 S 18:33. 2 K 5:3. Ac 26:29. 27:29. 1 C 4:8. 7:7. 14:5. 2 C 11:1. Ga 5:12. Re 3:15.

we had. Nu 11:15. 14:2. Jb 3:1, 10, 20. Je 20:14-18. Jon 4:8, 9.

flesh. Ex 2:23. Nu 11:4, 5.

to kill. Ex 5:21. 17:3. Nu 16:13, 41.

hunger. Dt 8:3. Je 2:6. La 4:9.

4 **I will rain**. Nu 11:7, 8. Ps 78:24, 25. 105:40. Jn 6:31, 32. 1 C 10:3.

a certain rate every day. Heb. the portion of a day in his day. Ex +5:13mg, 19. Pr 30:8. Mt 6:11, 32, 33. Lk 11:3. Jn 6:31.

prove them. Ex +15:25. 20:20. Dt 8:2, 16. 13:3. Jsh 24:15. Jg 3:1.

5 **prepare**. ver. 23. Ex 35:2, 3. Le 25:21, 22.

twice. Ge +43:12.

6 **even**. ver. 8, 12, 13.

the Lord. ver. 3. Ex 6:7. 12:51. 32:1, 7, 11. Nu 16:28, 30. Ps 77:20. Is 63:11, 12.

7 **the morning**. ver. 13.

ye shall. ver. 10. Ex 24:10, +16.

the glory of. Is 6:8-10 with Ac 28:25-27. Ac +5:3, 4. He 3:7-9.

what are we. ver. 2, 3, 8. Nu 16:11.

8 **the Lord heareth**. ver. 9, 12. Nu 14:27. Mt 9:4. Jn 6:41-43. 1 C 10:10.

but against. Nu 21:7. 1 S 8:7. Ps 51:4. Is 32:6. 37:29. Mt 10:40. Lk 10:16. Jn 13:20. Ac 5:4. Ro 13:2. 1 Th 4:8.

9 **Come near**. Nu 16:16.

heard. ver. +2, 8.

10 **that they**. ver. 7. Nu 14:10. 16:19, 42.
appeared. ver. 7. Ex 3:2. 13:21, 22. 14:24.
40:34-38. Le 9:6, 23, 24. Nu 14:10. 16:19, 42.
1 K 8:10, 11. Mt 17:5.
in the cloud. Ex +13:21.

12 **I have**. ver. 8.
At even. ver. 6.
in the morning. ver. 7.
ye shall know. Ex 4:5. 6:7. 7:17. Je 31:34.
Ezk 34:30. 39:22. Jl 3:17. Zc 13:9.

13 **the quails**. Nu 11:31-33. Ps 78:27, 28.
105:40.
the dew. Nu 11:9.

14 **the dew**. Nu 11:7-9. Dt 8:3. Ne 9:15. Ps
78:24. 105:40.
the hoar frost. Jb 38:29. Ps 147:16.

15 **It is manna**. *or*, What is this? *or*, It is a portion. ver. 31, 33, 35. Nu 11:6, 7, 9. Dt 8:3, 16.
Jsh 5:12. Ne 9:15, 20. Ps 78:24. Jn 6:31, 32,
49, 58. 1 C 10:3. He 9:4. Re 2:17.
This is. ver. 4. Nu 21:5. Ps 136:5. Pr 9:5. Lk
12:30. 1 P 2:2.

16 **according**. Ex 12:4.
omer. ver. 18, 33, 36. Le 23:10, 11, 12, 15.
for every man. Heb. by the poll, *or* head. Ex
38:36. Nu 1:2, 18, 20, 22. 3:47. Jg 9:53. 2 K
9:35. 1 Ch 10:10. 23:3, 24.
persons. Heb. *nephesh*, souls, Ge +12:5; Ge
+12:5.
tents. Ex +27:21. 33:7.

17 **more**. Heb, multiplying. ver. 18. Ex 36:5. Le
11:42. 1 Ch 8:40. Ne 6:17. 9:37. Pr 28:8. Ec
6:11. Hab 2:6.
less. Heb. lessening. ver. 18. Nu 11:32.

18 **gathered much**. 2 C 8:14, 15.

19 **leave**. Ex 12:10. 23:18. Mt 6:34.

20 **bred worms**. Mt 6:19. Lk 12:15, 33. He 13:5.
Ja 5:2, 3.
and Moses. Nu 12:3. 16:15. Mk 3:5. 10:14.
Ep 4:26.

21 **every morning**. Pr 6:6-11. Ec 9:10. 12:1. Mt
6:33. Jn 12:35. 2 C 6:2.

22 **on the sixth**. ver. 5, 16. Le 25:12, 22.
rulers. or, princes, elders. Heb, lifted up ones.
Ex 12:21. 17:5. 22:28. 34:31. 35:27. Ge 17:20.

23 **Tomorrow**. Le 10:3.
rest. Ex +20:8-11. 35:3. Lk 23:56. Re 1:10.
bake. Nu 11:8.

24 **did not stink**. ver. 20, 33.

25 **a sabbath**. ver. 23, 29. Ne 9:14.

26 **Six days**. Ex 20:9-11. Dt 5:13. Ezk 46:1. Lk
13:14.
the sabbath. Ge 4:3. 29:27. Is +58:13.

27 **and they found none**. Pr 20:4.

28 **How long**. Nu 20:12. 2 K 17:14. Ps 78:10,
22. 81:13, 14. 106:13. Is 7:9, 13. Je 4:14. 9:6.
Ezk 5:6. 20:13, 16. Mt +17:17.

29 **hath given**. Ex 31:13. Ne 9:14. Is 58:13, 14.
Ezk 20:12.
abide ye. Lk 23:56.

30 **rested**. Le 23:3. Dt 5:12-14. He 4:9.

31 **called the name**. ver. +15.
and it was. Nu 11:6, 7. SS 2:3.
wafers. 1 S 28:11, 12, 16. 1 K 17:12, 14, 16.
19:6.
honey. Ex +3:8. Le 2:11.

32 **Fill**. Ps 103:1, 2. 105:5. 111:4, 5. Lk 22:19. He
2:1.

33 **Take a pot**. He 9:4.

34 **testimony**. Ex 25:16, 21. 26:33, 34. 27:21.
30:6, 26, 36. 31:18. 32:15. 38:21. 40:20. Nu
1:50, 53. 17:10. Dt 10:5. 1 K 8:9. 2 K 11:12.
Ps 19:7. 78:5. 122:4. Is 8:16, 20.

35 **forty years**. Nu 33:38. Dt 8:2, 3. Ne 9:15, 20,
21. Ps 78:24, 25. Mt 5:45. Jn 6:30-58. Re
7:16.
until they came to. Jsh 5:12.
the borders. Nu 33:48-50. Dt 1:8. 34:1-4.

36 **an omer is**. ver. 16, 32, 33.
the tenth part. Le 5:11. 6:20.

EXODUS 17

1 **Sin**. Ex 16:1. Nu 33:12-14.
commandment. lit. mouth. Nu 9:18.
Rephidim. i.e. *supports, props; shrinking of
hands*, **S#7508h**. ver. 8. Ex 19:2. Nu 33:14, 15.

2 **the people**. Ex 5:21. 14:11, 12. 15:24. 16:2,
3. Nu 11:4-6. 14:2. 20:3-5. 21:5.
Give us. Ge 30:1, 2. 1 S 8:6. Lk 15:12.
wherefore. ver. 7. Nu 14:22. Dt 6:16. Ps
78:18, 41, 56. 95:9. 106:14. Is 7:12. Ml 3:15.
Mt 4:7. +16:1-3. Lk 4:12. Ac 5:9. 15:10. 1 C
10:9. He 3:9.

3 **thirsted**. Jn 7:37.
murmured. Ex +15:24. Ju +16.
thou hast. Ex +16:3.

4 **cried**. Ex 14:15. 15:25. Nu 11:11.
almost. Nu 14:10. 16:19. 1 S 30:6. Jn 8:59.
stone. Ex 19:13. 21:28, 29, 32. Le +24:14.

5 **Go on**. Ezk 2:6. Ac 20:23, 24.
thy rod. Ex 7:19, 20. Nu 20:8-11.

6 **I will**. Ex 16:10.
the rock in. Ex 33:22. Is 32:2.
Horeb. Ex 3:1-5.
and thou. Nu 20:9-11. Dt 8:15. Ne 9:15. Ps
78:15, 16, 20. 105:41. 114:8. Is 48:21. 1 C 10:4.
come water. Jn 19:34.
out of. Jg 6:21. Ps 81:16.
that the people. Ps 46:4. Is 41:17, 18. 43:19,
20. 55:1. Jn 4:10, 14. 7:37, 38. Re 22:17.

7 **Massah**. i.e. *Temptation*, **S#4532h**. Nu 20:13. Dt
6:16. 9:22. 33:8.
Meribah. *that is*, Chiding, *or* Strife. **S#4809h**.
ver. 2. Nu 20:13, 24. 27:14. Dt 32:51. Ps 81:7.
chiding. ver. +2.
tempted. Ps 95:8. He 3:8, 9.
Is the Lord. Ex 34:9. Dt 31:17. Jsh 22:31. Is
12:6. Mi 3:11. Jn 1:14. Ac 7:37-39.
among us. Nu 14:42. Dt +23:14.

8 **Amalek**. i.e. *a people that licks up; people lapping*, **S#6002h**. ver. 9-11, 13, 14, 16. Ge 36:12, 16. Nu 13:29. 14:43. 24:20. Dt 25:17, 19. Jg 3:13. 5:14. 6:3, 33. 7:12. 10:12. 1 S 14:48. 15:2, 3, 5-8, 18, 20, 32. 28:18. 30:18. 2 S 1:1. 8:12. 1 Ch 1:36. 4:43. 18:11. Ps 83:7.

9 **unto Joshua**. i.e. *Lord of salvation, the Lord is his salvation*, **S#3091h**. ver. 10, 13, 14. Ex 24:13. 32:17. 33:11. Nu 11:28. 13:16, Oshea, Jehoshua. 14:6, 30, 38. 26:65. 27:18, 22. 32:12, 28. 34:17. Dt 1:38. 3:21, 28. 31:3, 7, 14, 23. 32:44, Hoshea. 34:9. Jsh 1:1, 10, 12, 16. Jg 1:1. 2:6, 7, 8, 21, 23. 1 S 6:14, 18. 1 K 16:34. 2 K 23:8. 1 Ch 7:27. Hg 1:1, 12, 14. 2:2, 4. Zc 3:1, 3, 6, 8, 9. 6:11. Ac 7:45, called Jesus. He 4:8, Jesus.
Choose. Nu 31:3, 4.
will stand. He 2:10. 7:25.
the rod. Ex 4:2, 20.

10 **Joshua**. Jsh 11:15. Mt 28:20. Jn 2:5. 15:14.
and Moses. ver. 9.
Hur. i.e. *a hole or cavern*, **S#2354h**. ver. 12. Ex 24:14. 31:2. 35:30. 38:22. Nu 31:8. Jsh 13:21. 1 K 4:8. 1 Ch 2:19, 20, 50. 4:1, 4. 2 Ch 1:5. Ne 3:9.

11 **Moses held**. 1 S 7:8, 9. Ps 56:9. Lk 18:1. 1 T 2:8. Ja 5:16.
prevailed. Ro 8:37.
let down. Mt 26:41.

12 **Moses'**
hands. Mt 26:40-45. Mk 14:37-40. Ep 6:18. Col 4:2.
stayed up his hands. Ps 35:3. Is 35:3. 2 C 1:11. Ph 1:19. 1 Th 5:25. He 12:12. Ja 1:6.
were steady. He 7:25.

13 **Joshua**. Jsh 10:28, 32, 37, 42. 11:12.
discomfited. Heb. weakened. Jsh 14:10mg. Is 14:12. Jl 3:10.
Amalek. ver. 8.
edge. Ge +34:26.

14 **Write**. This is the first mention of writing in the Bible. Ex +24:4, 7. 34:27. Nu 33:2. 36:13. Dt 28:61. 31:9. Jsh 1:7, 8. Jb 19:23. Hab 2:2, 3.
memorial. Ex +12:14.
for I will. Nu 24:20. Dt 25:17-19. 1 S 14:48. 15:2, 3, 7, 8, 18, 32. 27:8, 9. 30:1, 17. 2 S 1:1, 8-16. 8:12. 1 Ch 4:43. Ezr 9:14.
put out. **S#4229h**. Ge 6:7 (destroy). 7:4, 23. Ex 32:32 (blot), 33. Nu 5:23 (blot out). Dt 9:14. 25:6, 19. 29:20. Ps 51:1, 9. Pr 6:33. Is 43:25.
the remembrance. Ex 3:15 (memorial). Dt 25:19. Jb 18:17. Ps 9:6. 83:4, 7. Pr 10:7. Re 17:14.

15 **altar**. Ge +8:20. 12:7. 26:25. 35:7.
Jehovah-nissi. i.e. *the Lord my banner*, **S#3071h**, only here. Ex +15:26. Ge 22:14. 33:20. Jg 6:24. Ps 20:5. 60:4. Is 11:10.
nissi, **S#5251h**. ver. 15. Nu 21:8 (pole), 9 (pole). 26:10 (sign). Ps 60:4 (banner). Is 5:26

(ensign). 11:10, 12. 13:2. 18:3. 30:17. 31:9. 33:23 (sail). 49:22 (standard). 62:10. Je 4:6, 21. 50:2. 51:12, 27. Ezk 27:7 (sail).
banner. Ps 60:4. SS 2:4. Is 5:26. 11:10. 59:19.

16 **Because**, etc. or, Because the hand of Amalek is against the throne of the Lord, therefore, etc.
the Lord, etc. Heb. the hand upon the throne of the Lord (Heb. *Jah*, Ex +15:2. Ps 68:4. 89:8. Is 26:4), Is 66:1. Ac 7:49.
sworn. Ge 22:16. Nu 32:10. Dt 4:21.
will have war. Nu 24:20. Dt 25:19. 1 S 15:3, 7. 28:18. Ps 21:8-11.
Amalek. Ge +14:7. 36:12.

EXODUS 18

1 **Jethro**. Ex 2:16, 21. 3:1. 4:18. Nu 10:29. Jg 4:11.
heard. Ps 34:2. 44:1. 77:14, 15. 78:4. 105:5, 43. 106:2, 8. Je 33:9. Zc 8:23. Ga 1:23, 24.
God. Ac 7:35, 36. 14:27. 15:12. 21:19, 20. Ro 15:18.
done. Ex 7-15. Jsh 2:10. 9:9. Ne 9:10, 11. Ps 77:14, 15. 78:50-53. 105:36-41. 106:8-11. 136:10-16. Is 63:11-13.

2 **Zipporah**. Ex 2:21. 4:25, 26.

3 **two sons**. Ac 7:29.
Gershom. Ex +2:22. Ps 39:12. He 11:13. 1 P 2:11.

4 **Eliezer**. Ps 46:1. Is 50:7-9. He 13:6.
delivered. Ex 2:15. Ps 18, title, 48. 34:4. Da 6:22. Ac 12:11. 2 C 1:8-10. 2 T 4:17.

5 **came with**. Ex 3:1, 12. 19:11, 20. 24:16, 17. 1 K 19:8.

6 **said**. Mt 12:47.

7 **went**. Ge 14:17. 46:29. Nu 22:36. Jg 11:34. 1 K 2:19. Ac 28:15.
did obeisance. Ge +18:2.
kissed. Ge +27:27. Ps 2:12.
welfare. Heb. peace. Jg +18:15mg.

8 **told**. ver. 1. Ne 9:9-15. Ps 66:16. 71:17-20. 105:1, 2. 145:4-12.
and all the. Ex 15:22-24. 16:3.
come upon them. Heb. found them. 2 K 9:21mg.
how the Lord. Ps 78:42, 43. 81:7. 106:10. 107:2.

9 **rejoiced**. Is 44:23. 66:10. Ro 12:10, 15. 1 C 12:26.
goodness. Ho +3:5.

10 **Blessed be**. Ge 14:20. 2 S 18:28. 1 K 8:15. Ps 41:13. 106:47, 48. Lk 1:68. Ro 12:15. Ep 1:3. 1 Th 3:9. 1 P 1:3. Re 5:11-13. 19:1-6.

11 **Now I know**. Ex 9:16. 1 K 17:24. 2 K 5:15. Pr +19:25.
the Lord. Ex +12:12.
in the thing. Ex 1:10, 16, 22. 5:2, 7. 14:8, 18.
proudly. Ex 10:3. Ne 9:10, 16, 29. Pr +16:5.

12 **took**. Ex 24:5. Ge 4:4. 8:20. 12:7. 26:25. 31:54. Jb 1:5. 42:8.

burnt offering. Le +23:12.

Aaron. Ex 24:11. Le 7:11-17. Dt 12:7. 27:7. 1 Ch 29:21, 22. 2 Ch 30:22. 1 C 10:18, 21, 31.

elders. Ex +3:16.

eat bread. Ex 2:20. Ge +3:19. 31:54. 37:25. 2 S 9:7. Jb 42:11. Ps 14:4. Da 10:3. Lk 14:1, 15.

13 **sat to**. Jg 5:10. Jb 29:7. Is 16:5. Jl 3:12. Mt 23:2. Ro 12:8. 13:6.

judge. Jn 5:27. Ac 17:31.

14 **he said**. Pr 1:5. 9:9. 11:14. 12:15. 19:20. 20:18. 24:6.

What is this. Nu 11:16, 17, 24, 25. Dt 1:9-17. 16:18. 2 K 5:13. 2 Ch 19:5, 8. Ezr 7:10, 25. Ps 9:10. Pr 9:8, 9. Mt 17:27. 21:1-3. Mk 6:31. Lk 10:38-42. Ac 6:2-4. Ro 12:8. 1 T 4:16. 2 T 2:2.

15 **to enquire**. ver. 19, 20. Ge 25:22. Dt 4:29. Le 24:12-14. Nu 15:34. 27:5. 2 K 8:8. 1 Ch 10:14. 2 Ch 14:7. 17:4. 22:9. Ps 34:5. 77:2. 78:34. Is 26:9, 16

16 **a matter**. Ex 23:7. 24:14. Dt 17:8-12. 2 S 15:3. Jb 31:13. Ac 18:14, 15. 1 C 6:1.

one and another. Heb. a man and his fellow. ver. 7. Ex 2:13. 21:18.

make. Le 24:15. Nu 15:35. 27:6, etc. 36:6-9. Dt 4:5. 5:1. 6:1. 1 S 12:23. Mt 28:20. 1 Th 4:1, 2.

17 **not good**. ver. +14. Dt 1:12. 1 K 3:8, 9. 13:18. 2 Ch 19:6. Mt 17:4. Jn 13:6-10.

18 **Thou wilt surely wear away**. Heb. fading thou wilt fade. Jb 14:18mg. Ps 1:3mg. 18:45. 37:2. 90:5, 6. 103:15. Is 40:6, 7, 8. 2 C 12:15. Ph 2:30. 1 Th 2:8, 9.

thou art. Nu 11:14-17. Dt 1:9-12. Ac 6:1-4.

19 **Hearken**. ver. 24. Pr 9:9.

God shall. Ex 3:12. 4:12. Ge 39:2. Dt 20:1. Jsh 1:9. 2 S 14:17. Mt 28:20.

Be thou. ver. +15. Ex 4:16. 20:19. Dt 5:5.

bring. Nu 27:5.

20 **teach**. ver. 16. Dt 4:1, 5. 5:1. 6:1, 2. 7:11. 2 Ch 17:7. Ezr 7:25. Ne 9:13, 14. Ml 2:7. 1 T 3:2. 2 T 2:2. T 1:9mg.

the way. 1 S 12:23. Ps 32:8. 143:8. Is 30:21. Je 6:16. 42:3. Mi 4:2. 1 Th 4:1.

work. Dt 1:18. Ezk 3:17. Mt 28:20. Mk 13:34. 2 Th 3:6-12.

21 **Moreover**. Dt 1:13-17. Ac 6:3.

provide. or, see. i.e. look out for. Ex 24:11. Ge 22:8. Jb 19:26, 27. Ps 11:4, 7. 17:2. Pr 24:32. SS 6:13. Is 30:10 (prophesy). La 2:14. **(S#2372h)**.

able men. ver. 25. Dt 1:13, 15. 16:18. 1 K 3:9-12. 1 Ch 26:8. Pr 28:2. 2 T 2:2. T 1:5-9.

such as fear God. Ex 9:20. 23:2-9. Ge 22:12. 42:18. 2 S 23:3. 1 K 18:3, 12. 2 K 4:1. 2 Ch 19:5-10. Ne 5:9, 15. 7:2. Jb 1:1, 8. 2:3. Pr 1:7. Ec 12:13. Ml 3:16. Mt 10:28. Lk 18:2, 4. Ac 10:2, 35.

men of truth. Jb 29:16. 31:13. Is 16:5. 59:4,

14, 15. Je 5:1. Ezk 18:8. Zc 7:9. 8:16. Ac +6:3.

hating covetousness. Ex 23:8. Dt 16:18, 19. 1 S 8:3. 12:3, 4. 2 K +12:15. Ps 26:9, 10. 119:36. Pr 28:16. Is 33:15. Ezk 22:12. 33:31. Mt 13:22. Mk 7:21, 22. Lk 12:15. Ac +6:3. 20:33. 1 C +4:2. 2 C +7:2. 8:20. 1 T 3:3. 6:5, 9-11. 2 P 2:14, 15.

rulers of thousands. Ex 24:1, 9. Jsh +22:21. Ps 84:10. Mi +5:2. Lk 10:1, 17. Ac 4:32-37.

rulers of hundreds. Jg 7:16. 1 S 25:13. Ac 1:15.

rulers of fifties. Ge 18:24, 26. Mk 6:40. Lk 10:1, 17.

rulers of tens. Ge 18:32. Ru 4:2. 1 S 25:5. Ml 3:16. Mt 10:1. Ac 19:7. Ro +12:5. 1 C 14:26. 2 C 1:4. Ep 5:19-21. 6:4. 1 T +3:5. 4:16. 2 T 2:2. Phm 2. He 3:13. Ja 5:16

22 **at all seasons**. ver. 26. Ro 13:6.

great. Le 24:11. Nu 15:33. 27:2. 36:1. Dt 1:17. 17:8, 9.

they shall. ver. 18. Nu 11:16, 17. Dt 1:9.

23 **do**. 2 Ch 19:6.

and God command thee so. Ge 21:10-12. 1 S 8:6. 7:22. Ac 15:2. Ga 2:2.

able to endure. ver. 14, 18. Ex 21:21.

and all this. Ex 16:29. Ge 18:33. 30:25. 2 S 18:3. 19:39. 21:17. Ph 1:24, 25.

24 **Moses hearkened**. ver. 2-5, 19. Ezr 10:2, 5. Pr +1:5. 1 C 12:21.

25 **chose able**. ver. 21. Dt 1:13-15. Ac 6:5.

26 **at all**. ver. 14, 22.

the hard causes. ver. 15, 22. Dt 17:8. 1 K 3:16-28. 10:1. Jb 29:16.

27 **let his**. Ge 24:59. 31:55. Nu 10:29, 30. Jg 19:9.

his own land. i.e. Midian. Ex 2:15, 16. 3:1. Nu 24:21. Jg 1:16. 4:11. 1 S 15:6. 2 K 10:15. 1 Ch 2:55. Je 35:2.

EXODUS 19

1 A.M. 2513. B.C. 1491.

the third. Ex 12:2, 6. Le 23:16-18.

came. Ex 16:1. Nu 33:15.

2 **Rephidim**. Ex 17:1, 8.

camped. Ex 3:1, 12. 18:5. Ac 7:30, 38. Ga 4:24.

3 **went up**. Ex 20:21. 24:15-18. 34:2. Dt 5:5-31. Ac 7:38.

called. Ex 3:4.

4 **seen**. Ex 7-14. Dt 4:9, 33-36. 29:2. Is 63:9.

I bare you. Dt 32:11, 12. Is 40:31. 63:9. Mt 23:37. Re 12:14.

EAGLES'. Dt 28:49. 2 S 1:23. Jb 9:26. Ps 103:5.

5 **if ye**. Ex 24:7. Ge +4:7. Jsh 24:24. Je +7:23. He 11:8.

keep. Dt 5:2. Ps 25:10. 103:17, 18. Is 56:4. Je 31:31-33.

covenant. Ge 12:1-3. 17:1-14. Dt 29:9. Mt 26:28. Ga 4:24. He 8:9.

a peculiar. Ex 33:16. Le 20:24, 26. 26:12, 18. Nu 23:9. Dt 4:20. 7:6. 14:2, 21. 26:18. 32:8, 9, +43. 1 K 8:53. Ps 135:4. Ec 2:8. SS 8:12. Is 41:8. 43:1. Je 10:16. Ml 3:17. Ac 20:28. 1 C 6:20. 7:23. 2 C 6:16, 17. Ep 1:14. T 2:14. 1 P 2:9.
treasure. 1 Ch 29:3. Ml 3:17.
above all people. Dt 10:15. Ro 11:28, 29.
all the earth. Ex 9:29. Dt 10:14. Jb 41:11. Ps 24:1. 50:12. Da 4:34, 35. 1 C 10:26, 28.

6 **a kingdom**. Lk 22:29.
of priests. Ex 15:16. Dt 26:18. 33:2-4. Ps 122:5. 148:14. Pr 25:5. Is 61:6. 66:21. Ro 12:1. T 2:14. 1 P 2:5, 9. Re 1:5, 6. 5:9, 10. 20:6.
holy nation. Le 10:3. +19:2. Dt 7:6. 26:19. 28:9. Ps 93:5. Is +60:21. 62:12. 1 C 3:17. 1 Th 5:27.

7 **the elders**. Ex +3:16.
and laid. Ex 4:29, 30. 1 C 15:1.

8 **answered**. Ex 20:19. 24:3, 7. Dt 5:27-29. 26:17-19. Jsh 24:24. Ne 10:29.
returned. Ge 37:14. Dt 1:32, 35. Jsh 22:32. Jg 11:11. 1 S 8:21.

9 **Lo**. ver. 16. Ex 20:21. 1 K 8:12. Re 1:7.
thick cloud. Ex +13:21. Is 29:6. Hg 2:7, 9. Re 10:1. 15:8.
that the. Dt 4:12, 36. Jn 12:29, 30.
believe. Ex 14:31. 2 Ch +20:20. Is 7:9. Lk 10:16.
for ever. Heb. *olam*, Ex +12:24.

10 **sanctify**. ver. 15. Le 11:44, 45. 19:2. Jsh 3:5. 7:13. 1 S 16:5. 2 Ch 29:5, 34. 30:17-19. Jb 1:5. 1 C 6:11.
wash. ver. 14. Ge 35:2. Le 11:25. 15:5. Nu 8:7, 21. 31:24. Zc 3:3, 4. He 10:22. 12:28, 29. Re 7:14.

11 **the Lord**. ver. 16, 18, 20. Ex 3:8. 34:5. Nu 11:17. Dt +33:2. Ps 18:9. 144:5. Is 64:1, 2. Hab 3:3-6. Jn 3:13. 6:38.

12 **set bounds**. ver. 21, 23. Jsh 3:4.
Take. Ex 10:28. 34:12. Dt 2:4. 4:9.
or touch. He *12:20, 21*.
surely. Ge +2:16. Ro 3:20.

13 **shall not**. He 12:18, 19.
shot. 1 S 20:36, 37. Ps 11:2.
whether. Ex 21:28, 29. Le 20:15, 16.
when the trumpet. *or*, cornet. ver. 16, 19. 1 C 15:52. 1 Th 4:16.

14 **and sanctified**. ver. +10.

15 **be ready**. Am 4:12. Ml 3:2. Mt 3:10-12. 24:44. 2 P 3:11, 12.
the third. ver. 11, 16. Ex +10:22. Zc 6:3.
come not. 1 S 21:4, 5. Jl 2:16. Zc 7:3. 12:12-14. 1 C 7:5.

16 **thunders**. Ex +9:23, 28, 29. Jb 38:25. Ps 18:11-14. 50:3. 97:4.
thick. ver. +9.
voice. Ezk +10:5. Re 1:10. 4:1.
trumpet. Mt 16:27. 25:31. 1 Th 3:13. 4:16.
all the people. Je 5:22. He 12:21.

17 **Moses brought**. Dt 4:10. 5:5.
nether. Dt +32:22.
meet with. Dt 4:7. Ps 73:28. 145:18. Is 55:6. Jn 14:6. Ep 3:12. He 4:16. 7:19, 25. 10:19, 22. 11:6. Ja 4:8.

18 **mount Sinai**. ver. 13. Ex 20:18. Dt 4:11, 12. 5:22. +33:2. Ps 104:32. Is 6:4.
in fire. Ex 3:2. 24:17. 2 Ch 7:1-3. Je 23:29. 2 Th 1:8. He 12:18-20. 2 P 3:10.
as the smoke. Re +14:11.
mount quaked. Ps 18:7-13. +68:8. He +12:26. Re +6:12.

19 **And when**. ver. 13, 16.
Moses. He 12:21.
God. Ps 81:7.

20 **the Lord came**. ver. +11. Ne 9:13. Ps 81:7.
Moses went up. ver. 3. Ex 24:12, 13, 18. 34:2, 4. Dt 9:9.

21 **charge**. Heb. contest. *or*, protest. ver. 12, 13, 23. Ex 21:29. Ge 43:3. Dt 4:26. 8:19. 30:19. 31:28. 32:46. Je 32:25. Am 3:13.
break. Ex 3:3, 5. 33:20. 1 S 6:19. Ec 5:1. He 12:28, 29.

22 **the priests**. Ex 24:5. Le 10:1-3. Is 52:11.
sanctify. ver. 5, 14, 15.
break. 2 S 6:6-8. 1 Ch 13:9-11. 15:13. 2 Ch 30:3, 15, 18, 19. Ac 5:5, 10. 1 C 11:30-32.

23 **Set bounds**. ver. 12. Jsh 3:4, 5.

24 **and thou**. ver. 20.
but let. ver. 12, 21. Mt 11:12. Lk 13:24. 16:16. Jn 1:17. He 4:16. 10:19-22. 12:18-25, 29.
lest. ver. 22. Ro 4:15. 2 C 3:7-9. Ga 3:10, 11, 19-22.

25 **went down**. ver. 24. Je 26:2. Ac 20:20, 27.

EXODUS 20

1 **God spake**. Dt 4:33, 36. 5:4, 22. Ac 7:38, 53.

2 **I am**. Ex 32:7. 33:1. Dt 5:6. Ps 81:10.
the Lord. Ex +15:26. Ge +17:7, 8. Dt 5:6. 6:4, 5. 2 Ch 28:5. Ps 50:7. Ho 13:4. Ro 3:29. 10:12.
brought. Ex ch. 10-15. Le 19:36. 23:43.
out of the. Ex 13:3. Dt 5:15. 7:8. 13:10. 15:15. 26:6-8.
bondage. Heb. servants. Ex 13:3mg, 14mg.

3 The First Commandment.
Thou shalt have no other gods before me.
shalt. lit. wilt.
have no other. ver. 23. Ex 15:11. 34:14. Dt 5:7. 6:5, 14. +18:10. Jsh 24:18-24. 2 K 17:29-35. 19:17, 18. Ps 29:2. 73:25. 81:9. Is 26:4. 43:10. 44:8. 45:21, 22. 46:9. Je 25:6. 35:15. Ho 13:4. Hab 1:11. Mt 4:10. 6:24. Lk 16:13. 1 C 8:4, 6. Ep 5:5. Ph 3:19. Col 2:18. 3:5. 1 J 5:20, 21. Re 19:10. 22:9.
before. or, beside. Heb. against my face, or presence. ver. 20, with me. Ge 31:50. Dt 19:19. He 3:12. 1 C 8:5. Ep 4:6. Ja 4:4.

4 The Second Commandment.
Thou shalt not make unto thee any graven image. ver. 23. Ex 23:24. 32:1, 8, 23. 34:13, +17. Le 19:4. 26:1. Nu 33:52. Dt 4:15-19, 23-25, +28. 5:8. 7:5, 25. 12:2, 3, 31. 17:2-6. 27:15. Jg 3:19mg. 1 K 12:28. 21:26. 2 K 17:41. 2 Ch 15:8. 33:7, 19, 22. 34:3, 4. Ps 97:7. 115:4-8. 135:15-18. Is 30:22. 40:18-20. 41:24. 42:8, 17. 44:9-20. 45:16. 46:5-8. Je 8:19. 10:3-5, 8, 9, 14-16. 44:4. Ezk 8:10. +14:3. Mi 1:7. +5:13. Na 1:14. Jn 4:24. Ac 14:15. 15:20. 17:29. 19:26-35. Ro 1:23, 25. 2:22. 1 C 5:11. 6:9, 10. 10:7, 14. 2 C 6:16. Ga 5:20. Ep 5:5. 1 P 4:3. 1 J 5:21. Re 9:20. 13:14, 15. 14:9-11. 16:2. +21:8. 22:15.

graven. Ex 34:1, 4. Dt 10:1, 3. Jg 17:3. 1 K 5:18. 2 K 21:7. Ps 97:7. Is 40:19. Hab 2:18. 1 C 8:4.

image. Le 26:1. Dt 4:16, 23, 25. 5:8. 27:15. Jg 17:3.

likeness. Ex 25:18-20, 34. Nu 12:8 (similitude). 21:9. 41:8, 9. Dt 4:12, 15, 16, 23. 5:8. 1 K 7:25. 10:20. Jb 4:16. Ps 17:15.

earth. Ph 2:9, 10. Col 3:5.

5 **not bow down**. Ex 23:24. 34:14. Le 26:1. Jsh 23:7, 16. Jg 2:19. 2 K 17:35, 41. 2 Ch 25:14. Is 44:15, 19. Mt 4:9.

nor serve. Ex 3:12. Ge 35:2. 2 K 10:18. Is 19:21. Je 44:3. 1 C 10:20. 1 J 5:21.

Lord thy God. Ex +15:26.

jealous. Ex 34:14. Nu 25:11. Dt 4:24. 6:15. 29:20. 32:16, 21. Jsh 24:19. 1 K 14:22. Ps 78:58. 79:5. Pr 6:34, 35. Is 42:13. 48:11. Ezk 8:3. 36:5, 6. 38:19. 39:25. Da 1:2. Jl 2:18. Na 1:2. Zp 1:18. 3:8. Zc 1:14. 8:2. Mt 4:10. 1 C 10:22.

God. Heb. *El*, Ex +15:2.

visiting. Ex 34:7. Ge 9:25. Le 20:5. 26:29, 39, 40. Nu 14:18, 33. 1 S +3:13, +14. 15:2, 3. 2 S 21:1, 6. 1 K 21:29. 2 K 23:26. Jb 5:4. 21:19. Ps 79:8. 109:14. Pr 13:21. +17:13. Is 14:20, 21. +24:21mg, 22. 65:6, 7. Je 2:9. +11:22mg. 31:29. 32:18. Ezk 18:1-4. Da 9:6. Ml 4:5, 6. Mt 23:34-36.

of them. Dt 5:9. 7:10. 24:16. 32:41. 2 K 14:5, 6. Ps 81:15. Pr 8:36. Jn 7:7. 15:18, 23, 24. Ro 1:30. 8:7. Ja 4:4.

6 **showing mercy**. or, doing kindness. Dt 4:37. 5:10, 29. 7:9. Ps 89:34. Je 32:39, 40. Mi 7:18. Jn 14:21. Ac 2:39. Ro 11:28, 29.

love me. Jg +5:31. 1 C +2:9. 2 J 6.

keep. Ec 12:13.

7 The Third Commandment.
Thou shalt not take the name of the Lord thy God in vain.
take. Ex +22:11. 23:1. Ge +22:16. Le 18:21. +19:8, 11, 12. 20:3. +21:6. 24:11-16. Nu 23:7. Dt 5:11. +6:13. 23:21-23. Jg 11:35. 2 S 12:14. 1 K 17:1. 22:14. Jb 27:1. Ps +15:4. 50:14-16. 74:10. 81:3. 139:20. Pr 30:8, 9. Ec 5:4-6. Is

29:13. 48:11. Je 4:2. 23:10. 34:16. Ezk 20:9. 36:21. Ho 4:2. Zc 5:3. Mt 5:33-37. 23:16-22. 26:63, 64. Ro +2:24. 2 C 1:23. 11:31. Col +4:5. 1 Th +2:5. 1 T 6:1. He 6:16, 17. Ja 2:7. 5:12. Re 10:5. 13:6. 16:9.

the name. Ps +9:10. Lk 1:49.

Lord. Ex +15:26.

vain. *or*, for vanity *or* falsehood. Ps 12:2. 41:6. 139:20. Is 59:4.

not hold. lit. make.

guiltless. Ex 34:7. Le 24:16, 23. Dt 23:21-23. Jsh 2:12, 17. 9:20. 2 S 21:1, 2. 1 K 2:9. Jb 9:28. 10:14. Ps 19:13. Je 30:11. Ezk 17:13-19. Zc 5:3, 4. or, declare innocent. Nu 14:18. Dt 5:11. Je 46:28. 49:12. Na 1:3.

8 The Fourth Commandment.
Remember the sabbath day, to keep it holy.
Remember. Ex 13:3. 16:23-30. 31:13-15. Ge 2:2, 3. Le 19:3, 30. 23:3. 26:2. Dt 5:12, 13. 2 K 4:22, 23 with He 10:25. Ne 8:9, 10. 9:14. 13:17, 18. Is 1:13. 56:2, 4-6. +58:13. Je 17:21, 27. La 2:6. Ezk 20:12, 13, 16, 20. 22:8, 26, 31. 23:38. 44:24. 46:3. Ho 2:11. Mk 2:27, 28. Lk 4:16. 6:5. +13:14. 14:1. 23:56. Jn 20:1, 19. Ac 20:7. Col 2:16.

the sabbath. Dt 5:14. Ne 13:15-18. Ezk 44:24.

9 **Six days**. Le +23:3.
labor. Ge 3:19. Ro 12:11. Ep 4:28. 2 Th 3:8-10.

10 **the seventh**. Ex 31:13. 34:21. Le 23:3.
sabbath. Ex 16:26. Ezk 20:12. Jn 7:23.
thou shalt. Ex 16:23, 27-29. 34:21. 35:2, 3. Le 23:7. Nu 15:32-36. Ne 10:31. 13:15-17, 19. Je 17:21. Am +8:5. Mt 24:20. Lk 23:56.
any work. Le 23:7, 8. Nu 28:18.
thy manservant. Le 25:6, 7. Dt 5:14, 15.
thy stranger. Ge 17:12, 13, 23. Le 22:25. Nu 15:14-16, 26, 29, 30. Dt 16:11, 12. 24:14-22. +26:11. Ne 10:31. 13:15-21.
within. Ex 16:29. Dt 5:14.
thy gates. Ge +14:7. Dt 6:9. 12:12. 14:27. 17:2. 1 K 8:37. 2 Ch 6:28mg.

11 **six days**. Ex 31:17. Ge 2:1-4. Ps 95:4-7. Mk 2:27, 28. Jn 20:19, 26. Ac 20:7. 1 C 16:2. He 4:2-5, 9-11. Re 1:10.
made. Ge 2:2. Ac 4:24. 14:15. Re 10:6. 14:7.
seventh. Ex 12:15 with Dt 16:8. Le 16:29. 23:32. He 4:4.
sabbath. ver. +8. Ge 2:2, 3.
hallowed it. Le 22:32. Dt 5:12. Je 17:20-27. Ezk 20:20. 44:24. Mt 6:9. Lk 11:2.

12 The Fifth Commandment.
Honor thy father and thy mother.
Honor. Ex 22:28. Ge 9:22, 23. Le 19:3, 32. Dt 5:16. 21:18-21. 27:16. 1 K 2:19. 2 K 2:12. 5:13. 13:14. Pr 1:8, 9. 6:20. 15:5. 19:26. +20:20. 23:22-25. 28:24. 30:11, 17. Is 3:5. Je 35:18, 19. Ezk 22:7. Ml 1:6. 4:6. Mt *19:19*. Mk

10:19. 12:17. Lk 2:51. *18:20*. Jn 19:26, 27. Ro 1:30. 13:7. Ep 5:21. +6:1, *2*, 3. Col +3:20, 21. 1 T 5:1, 2, 4, 17, 19. 6:1, *2*. 2 T 3:2. T 1:6. He 13:7. 1 P 2:17. 3:1-7. 5:5, 6. Ju 8.

father and mother. Ex 21:15, 17. Le 19:3. 20:9. Dt 21:18-21. Pr 10:1. 15:20. 17:25. 19:26. 20:20. 23:22, 24, 25. 28:24. 30:11, 17. Ml 1:6. Ep 6:2. He 12:9.

that thy days. Dt +4:40. 32:47. Pr 3:16. Je 35:18, 19. Ep *6:3*.

long. **S#748h**. Ge 26:8. Ex 20:12. Nu 9:19 (tarried long; mg, prolonged), 22. Dt 4:26 (prolong), 40.

land. Ps 115:16.

13 The Sixth Commandment.
Thou shalt not kill. or, murder. Ex 21:12, 14, 20, 29. 22:2, 3. Ge 4:8-15, 23. 9:5, 6. 27:41, 45. 49:6. Le 24:17, 21. Nu 35:16-21, 31-34. 35:6, 11, 12, 15-31. Dt 4:42. 5:17. 19:11-13. 21:1-9. 22:26. 2 S 12:9, 10. 1 K 2:5, 6. 2 K 21:16. 2 Ch 24:22. Ps 10:8-11. 51:14. Pr 1:11, 18. 28:17. Is 1:15. 26:21. Je 26:15. Mt 5:*21*, 22. 15:19. *19:18*. Mk *10:19*. Lk *18:20*. Jn 8:44. Ac 3:15. 28:4. Ro *13:9*. Ga 5:21. 1 T 1:9. Ja 2:*11*, 13. 4:1, 2. 1 P 4:15. 1 J 3:12-15. Re 16:6. 17:6. 21:8. 22:15.

14 The Seventh Commandment.
Thou shalt not commit adultery. Ge 39:9. Le 18:20. 19:29. 20:10. Dt 5:18. 22:21-24. 2 S 11:4, 5, 27. 12:9-11. Jb 24:15. 31:1, 9, 10. Ps 50:18. Pr 2:15-18. 5:15-20. 6:24-35. 7:18-27. 22:14. 31:3. Je 5:8, 9. 7:9. 13:27. 23:14. 29:22, 23. Ezk 18:6, 11, 15. 22:9-11. Ho 4:11. Ml +3:5. Mt 5:*27*, 28. 19:9, *18*. Mk 10:11, 12, *19*. Lk *18:20*. Jn 8:3-11. Ro 1:24-29. 7:2, 3. *13:9*. 1 C 6:9-11, 18. 7:4. 2 C 11:2. Ga 5:19, 20. Ep 5:3-5. Col 3:5. 1 Th 4:3-7. He 13:4. Ja 2:*11*. 4:4. 2 P 2:14, 18. Ju 7, 10. Re 2:20-22. 17:1-5. +21:8. 22:15.

15 The Eighth Commandment.
Thou shalt not steal. Ex 21:16. 22:1-5, 7-13. Le 6:1-7. +19:11, 13, 35-37. 25:17. Dt 5:19. 19:14. 23:24, 25. 24:7. 25:13-16. 27:17. Jsh 7:24, 25. Jb 20:19-22. 24:2. Ps 37:21. 50:18. 62:10. Pr 1:13-15. 3:27. 6:30, 31. 11:1. 16:11. 20:10, 23. 22:22, 28. 23:10. 28:24. 29:24. 30:8, 9. Is 1:23. 61:8. Je 5:26-29. 7:8-11. 22:13. Ezk 33:15. 45:10. Ho 4:2. 12:7. Am 3:10. 5:11, 12. 8:4-6. Mi 6:10, 11. 7:3. Zc +5:3, 4. Ml 3:5, 8. Mt 15:19. *19:18*. 21:13. 22:21. 23:14, 25. Mk 7:22. *10:19*. 11:17. 12:17, 40. Lk 3:13, 14. 18:11, *20*. +19:8, 46. 20:25, 47. Jn 12:6. Ro 2:21. 13:7, 9. 1 C 5:11. 6:10. Ep 4:28. Col +4:1. 1 Th 4:6. 1 T 1:10. T 2:10. Ja +5:4. 1 P 4:15. Re 9:21.

steal. Ex 21:16. 22:1, 7, 12. Ge 30:33. 31:27. 40:15. 44:8. 2 S 15:6. 19:3. 2 Ch 22:11. Jb 4:12mg. Pr 6:30. 30:9. Zc 5:3.

16 The Ninth Commandment.
Thou shalt not bear false witness.

false. Ex 23:1, 6, 7. Dt 5:20. 1 S 22:8-19. Pr +6:19. 11:13. 20:19. Is 59:3, 4. Ezk 22:9. Mt 5:11. *19:18*. Mk *10:19*. Lk 3:14. *18:20*. Ro 1:30. *13:9*. 1 C 6:10. Ep +4:25, 31. 1 P 4:14.

witness. Dt 17:6. 19:15. Ru 4:9-11. Is 8:2. Mk 14:55, 56.

neighbor. Le 19:18. Dt 5:20. Ep 4:25.

17 The Tenth Commandment.
Thou shalt not covet. Ge 3:6. 14:23. 34:23. Dt 5:21. Jsh 7:21. 1 S 15:19. 1 K 21:6-16. 2 K 5:20. Jb 31:24, 28. Ps +10:3. 119:36. Pr 21:25, 26. 23:4, 5. Ec 4:8. 5:10, 11. Is 5:8. 33:15. 56:11. 57:17. Je 22:17. Ezk +33:31. Am 2:6, 7. Mi 2:2. Hab 2:9. Mt 6:19-24. 13:22. 16:26. Mk 7:21-23. Lk +12:15. 16:14. Jn 12:6. Ac 20:33. Ro 7:7. *13:9*. 1 C 5:10, 11. 6:10. Ep 5:3, 5. Ph 3:19. Col +3:5. 1 T +6:6-10. 2 T 3:2. He 13:5. Ja 4:1, 2. 1 P 5:2. 2 P 2:14, 15. 1 J 2:16.

neighbor's wife. 2 S 11:2-4. Jb 31:1, 9. Pr 4:23. 6:24, 25, 27-29. Je 5:8. Mt 5:28. Ja 1:14, 15. 2 P 2:14.

nor anything that is thy neighbor's. Mt 20:15. Ac 5:4. 2 Th 3:12.

18 And all. Ex 19:16-18. Dt 4:10, 11, 36. 5:22, 23.

saw. Ge 42:1. Is 44:16. Je 33:24. He 12:18.

smoking. Ge 15:17.

they removed. Ps 139:7, 8. Je 23:23, 24. or, were moved (with fear). Is 7:2. 19:1. Ro 4:15.

afar. Ep 2:13.

19 Speak thou. Dt 5:5, 23-28. 18:15, 16. Ac 7:38. Ga 3:19, 20. 1 T 2:5. He 1:2. 12:18, 19.

let not God. Ex 33:20. Ge 32:30. Dt 5:24, 25, 26. He 12:19.

20 Fear not. Ge +15:1. 1 S 12:20, 24.

prove. Ex 15:25, 26. 16:4. Ge 22:1, 12. Dt 8:2, 16. 13:3. Jg 3:1.

his fear. Ge 42:18. Dt +6:2. 28:58. Ne 5:15. Pr 1:7. 3:7. Is 8:13. Mt +10:28. He 12:28.

21 the people. Ex 19:16, 17. Dt 5:5.

thick darkness. Ex +10:22. 19:16. 1 T 6:16.

22 said. Ex 33:1.

I have talked. Ex +33:9. Dt 5:24, 26.

23 not make with me. ver. 3-5. Ex 32:1-4. 1 S 5:4, 5. 2 K 17:33, 41. Je 7:9, 10. Ezk 20:39. 43:8. Da 5:4, 23. Zp 1:5. 1 C 10:21, 22. 2 C 6:14-16. Col 2:18, 19. 1 J 5:20, 21. Re 22:15.

silver. Dt 29:17. Ac 17:29.

24 altar. Ex 27:1-8. 2 K 5:17. Jn 4:24. Ro 10:6-9.

burnt offerings. Le +23:12.

peace offerings. Le +23:19.

in all places. Dt +12:11. 1 K 9:3. 2 Ch 6:6. 7:16. 12:13. Ezr 6:12. Ps 74:7. 76:2. 132:13, 14. Ml 1:11. Mt 28:20. 1 T 2:8.

will bless thee. Ge 12:2. Nu 6:24:27. Dt 7:13. 2 S 6:12. Ps 128:5. 134:3.

25 And. Dt 27:5, 6. Jsh 8:30, 31.

building it of hewn stone. Heb. build them with hewing. 1 K 5:17. Ro 4:4, 5. 1 C 1:17.

lift up. 2 K 5:11mg.

26 **by steps**. Ph 3:3.
  thy nakedness. Ex 28:42, 43. Le 10:3. Ps 89:7. Ec 5:1. He 12:28, 29. 1 P 1:16.

EXODUS 21

1 **the judgments**. Nu 35:24. 36:13. Dt +4:1. 1 K 6:12. 2 Ch 19:10. Ne 9:13, 14. 10:29.
  which. Ex 19:7. 24:3, 4. Dt 4:5, 8, 14, 45. 6:20. Mt 28:20. 1 Th 4:1, 2.

2 **buy**. Le +25:39-43.
  an Hebrew. Ex 12:44. Ge 37:28, 36. Le +25:39-41, 44.
  and in the. Le 25:40-43, 45. Dt 15:1, 12-15, 18. 31:10. Je 34:8-17. Ga 5:1.

3 **by himself**. Heb. with his body. Dt 15:12-14. Ro 12:1. 1 C 6:15. Ja 3:6.

4 **shall be her**. Ex 4:22. Ge 14:14. 15:3. 17:13, 27. 18:19. Ec 2:7. Je 2:14.

5 **And if**. Dt 15:16, 17. Is 26:13. 2 C 5:14, 15.
  shall plainly say. Heb. saying shall say. Ge +2:16.
  master. 1 S 25:10.
  will not. Le 25:47-54. Dt 15:16, 17.

6 **master**. Ge 24:9. Re 22:3.
  the judges. ver. 22. Ex +12:12. 18:21-26. Nu 25:5-8. Dt 1:16. 16:18. 17:9. 19:17, 18. 1 S 8:1; 2. 1 Ch 23:4. 26:29. 2 Ch 19:5. Is 1:26. Zp 3:3.
  bore his ear. Jb 33:16. Ps 40:6-8. Is 48:8. 50:4, 5.
  for ever. Heb. *olam*, Ex +12:24. Le 25:23, 40, 41. Dt 15:17. 1 S 1:11, 22, 28. 27:12. 28:2. 1 K 12:7. Ps 15:4.

7 **sell**. Ne 5:5.
  maidservant. Ge 20:17. 21:10. Jg 9:18.
  go out. ver. 2, 3.

8 **please not**. Heb. be evil in the eyes of, etc. Ge 28:8mg. Jg 14:3. 1 S 8:6. 18:8mg.
  who hath. Dt 20:7. 21:11-14.
  seeing. Ex 8:29. Jg 9:19. Jb 6:15. Ml 2:11-15.
  dealt. Ge 38:14, 26. Je 3:20. Ml 2:14.

9 **betrothed her unto**. Ex 22:17. Ge 38:11. Le 22:13.

10 **her food**. Heb. her flesh. 1 C 7:1-6.
  diminish. or, withdraw. Ex 5:8, 19. Dt 4:2. 12:32. Jb 36:7.

11 **then shall**. ver. +2. Mt 19:8.

12 **smiteth a man**. Ex 20:13. Ge 9:6. Le 24:17. Nu 35:16-24, 30, 31. Dt 19:11-13. 2 S 12:13. Mt 26:52.
  surely. Ge +2:16.

13 **lie not**. Nu 35:11, 22-25. Dt 19:4-6, 11. Mi 7:2.
  God. 1 S 24:4, 9, 10, 17, 18. 2 S 16:10. Is 10:7. Mt 10:29, 30.
  I will appoint. Nu 35:11. Dt 4:41-43. 19:1-3, 9. Jsh 20:2-9.

14 **presumptuously**. Ex 18:11. Nu 15:30, 31. Dt 1:43. 17:12, 13. 18:20, 22. 19:11-13. 1 K

2:28-34. Ps 19:13. He +10:26. 2 P 2:10.
  slay. Nu 35:20, 21. Dt 27:24. 2 S 3:27. 20:9, 10.
  take him. 1 K 1:50, 51. 2:28-34. 2 K 11:15.

15 **father, or his mother**. Ex +20:12. Dt 27:24. 1 T 1:9.
  put to death. Capital crimes under the Mosaic code included: (1) Murder: Nu 35:16. (2) Blasphemy: Le 24:16. Jn 10:32. (3) Manstealing: ver. 16. 1 T 1:10. (4) Idolatry: Ex 22:20. Dt 17:2. (5) Enticement to Idolatry: Dt 13:6, 9. (6) Adultery: Le 20:10. (7) Sodomy and Uncleanness: Le 20:13, 17-20. (8) Incest: Le 20:14, 21. (9) Bestiality: Le 20:15, 16. (10) Witchcraft: Ex 22:18. (11) Smiting Parents: ver. 15. Dt +27:16. (12) Cursing Parents: ver. 17. Le 20:9. (13) Disobeying Parents: Dt 21:20, 21. (14) Sabbath Profanation. Ex 35:2. Nu 15:32. (15) Endangering Human Life: ver. 29.

16 **stealeth**. Ge 40:15. Dt 24:7. 1 T 1:10. Re 18:12.
  selleth him. Ge 37:28. Re 18:12, 13.
  found in. Ex 22:4.

17 **curseth**. *or*, revileth. Ex 22:28. Le 19:14. 24:11. Ec 7:21, 22. Is 8:21. Ac 23:4, 5.
  father, or his mother. ver. 15. Pr +20:20.
  surely. Ge +2:16.

18 **men**. ver. 22. Ex 2:13. Dt 25:11. 2 S 14:6.
  another. *or*, his neighbor. ver. 35. Ex 18:16.
  a stone. ver. 20. Nu 35:16-24.

19 **upon his staff**. 2 S 3:29. Zc 8:4.
  shall pay. ver. 28-34. Le 6:1-5. Nu 5:5-8. Dt 22:13-19, 28, 29.
  the loss. Heb. his ceasing.

20 **smite**. ver. 26, 27. Le 25:45, 46. Dt 19:21. Pr 29:19. Is 58:3, 4. Ep 6:9.
  he shall. Ge 9:6. Nu 35:30-33.
  punished. Heb. avenged. Ge 4:15, 24. Nu 35:19. Ro 13:4.

21 **punished**. or, avenged.
  for. Le 25:45, 46.
  his money. lit. silver.

22 **strive**. ver. 18.
  hurt. **S#5062h**. Ex 8:2 (smite). 12:23, 27. 21:35. 32:35 (plagued). 2 S 12:15 (struck). 2 K 14:12 (put to the worse). Ps 91:12 (dash). Pr 3:23 (stumble).
  fruit depart. Lk +1:44.
  as the judges. ver. +6, 30. Dt 22:18, 19.

23 **life**. Heb. *nephesh*, soul, Ge +44:30.
  for life. Le 24:20. Nu 35:31. Dt 19:21. Mt 5:38.

24 **Eye for eye**. ver. 26, 27. Le 24:19, 20. Dt 19:21. Jg 1:6, 7. 1 S 15:33. Mt 5:38, 39-40. 7:2. Lk 6:38. Re 16:6.

25 **burning**. only here. Pr 6:28. Is 43:2.
  wound for. Ge 4:23. 9:6. Jn 19:11. Ro 13:4.

26 **smite the eye**. ver. 20. Dt 16:19. Ne 5:5. Jb 31:13-15. Ps 9:12. 10:14, 18. 72:12-14. Pr 22:22, 23. Ep 6:9. Col 4:1.

27 **smite**. ver. +19.

28 **the ox**. ver. 32. Ge 9:5, 6. Le 20:15, 16.

29 **his owner also**. Dt 21:1-9.

30 **sum of money**. or, ransom. Ex 30:12.
for the ransom. or, redemption. ver. 22. Ex
30:12. Nu 3:49. 35:31-33. Pr 13:8.
life. Heb. *nephesh*, soul, Ge +44:30.

31 **judgment**. or, sentence.

32 **thirty shekels**. Ge 37:28. Zc 11:12, 13. Mt
26:15. 27:3-9. Ph 2:7.
and the ox. ver. 28, 29.

33 **shall open a**. Ps 9:15. 119:85. Pr 28:10. Ec
10:8. Je 18:20, 22.
pit. Heb. *bor*, Ge +37:20.

34 **owner**. ver. 29, 30. Ex 22:6, 14.
pit. ver. 33. Ge +37:20.

36 **if it be**. ver. 29.
owner hath not kept. Pr +22:3.
surely pay. Le 24:21.

EXODUS 22

1 **sheep**. *or*, goat. ver. 4, 9, 10. Ex 12:3, 5.
he shall restore. Le 6:1-6. Nu 5:7. 2 S 12:6.
Pr 6:31. Lk +19:8.
five oxen. Pr 14:4.

2 **breaking**. Jb 24:14, 16. 30:5. Ho 7:1. Jl 2:9.
Mt 6:19, 20. 24:43. 1 Th 5:2.
no blood. Nu 35:27.

3 **full restitution**. Lk +19:8.
sold for his theft. Ge 44:9. Le +25:39.

4 **found**. Ex 21:16.
he shall restore double. ver. 1, 7, 9. Ge
+43:12. Pr 6:30, 31.

5 **be eaten**. lit. burned or consumed. ver. 6. Jg
15:5. 2 Ch 28:3. Ezk 5:2. Na 2:13.
beast. Ge 45:17. Nu 20:4, 8, 11. Ps 78:48.
feed. lit. burn or consume. Le 6:12. Nu
24:22.
shall he make restitution. ver. 3, 12. Ex
21:34. Jb 20:18.

6 **and catch in**. S#4672h. Ge 2:20 (found).
44:34mg. Ex 18:8. Nu 20:14mg. 32:23 (find).
Jsh 2:23. Jg 6:13. Ps 116:3. 119:143mg.
so that the stacks of corn. Jg 15:4, 5. 2 S
14:30, 31.
he that kindled the fire. ver. 9, 12. Ex
21:33, 34.

7 **if the thief be found**. Je 2:26. Jn 12:6. 1 C
6:10.
let him pay double. ver. +4.

8 **the judges**. ver. 28mg. Ex +12:12. Ge 1:26. 1
Ch 23:4.

9 **for all manner of trespass**. Nu 5:6, 7. 1 K
8:31. Mt 6:14, 15. 18:15, 35. Lk 17:3, 4.
the cause of both parties. Ex 18:21, 22.
23:6-8. Dt 16:18, 19. 25:1. 2 Ch 19:10.
pay double. Ge +43:12.
unto his. ver. 4, 7.

10 **deliver**. Ge 39:8. Lk 12:48. 16:11. 2 T 1:12.

driven. 1 Ch 5:21. 2 Ch 14:15. Jb 1:15, 17. Je
13:17.

11 **an oath of the Lord**. Le 5:1. 6:3. 1 K 2:42,
43. 8:31. Pr 29:24. 30:9. Mt 26:63. He 6:16.
that he hath not. ver. 8. Ex 23:1.

12 **stolen from**. ver. 7. Ge 31:39.
him. i.e. his premises or custody. Ge 30:33.
31:39.

13 **torn in pieces**. Ezk 4:14. Am 3:12. Mi 5:8.
Na 2:12.
let him bring it for witness. Or, rather, "Let
him bring" an evidence of the thing torn,
such as the horns, hoofs, etc.

14 **borrow**. Dt 15:2. 23:19, 20. Ne 5:4. Ps 37:21.
Mt 5:42. Lk 6:35.
make it good. ver. 11. Ex 21:34. Le 24:18.

15 **it came for his hire**. Zc 8:10.

16 **a man entice**. Ge 34:2-4. Dt 22:28, 29.

17 **utterly**. Dt 7:3, 4.
pay. Heb. weigh. Ge 23:16.
dowry of virgins. Ge 34:12. Dt 22:29. 1 S
18:25.

18 **not suffer**. Dt +18:10. Is 19:3. Re +9:21.
witch. Dt 18:10. Ml +3:5 (sorcerers).

19 **lieth with a beast**. Le 18:23, 25. 20:15, 16.
Dt 27:21.

20 **sacrificeth**. Nu 25:2-4, 7, 8. Dt 13:1-15.
17:2-5. 18:20.
unto any god. Dt 8:19. 27:15. 30:17, 18. Jg
2:11-14. 10:6, 7. 1 K 9:6, 7. 2 K 17:9-11, 16,
18-20. 22:17. Ps 78:58, 59. Je 44:2-4. Ezk
36:18, 19.
utterly. Nu 21:3. Jsh 23:15, 16.
destroyed. Heb. devoted. Le +27:21, 28, 29.
Nu 21:2, 3. Dt 3:6. 7:2. 20:17. 1 S 15:3. Ezr
10:8mg. 1 C 16:22.

21 **neither vex**. Ex 12:40. 23:9. Le 19:33, 34.
25:35. Dt 10:19. 24:18, 22. Je 7:6, 7. 22:3. Zc
7:10. Ml +3:5.
a stranger. Dt +26:11.
for ye were strangers. Ex 20:2. 23:9. Dt
10:19. 15:15. 23:7.

22 **not afflict**. 2 K 4:1. Mi 2:9. Mt 23:14.
widow. Is +1:17.
fatherless. Ge +11:28. Dt 10:18. 14:29.
24:17, 19-21. 26:12. 27:19. Jb 6:27. 22:9.
24:3, 9. 29:12, 16. 31:17, 21. Ps 10:14, 18.
68:5. 82:3. 94:6. 146:9. Pr 23:10. Is 1:17, 23.
10:2. Je 5:28. 22:3. 49:11. Ezk 22:7. Ho 14:3.
Zc 7:10. Ml 3:5. Ja 1:27.

23 **they cry at all**. ver. +27. Ex 3:7, 9. Ge 4:10.
18:20, 21. Dt 15:9. 24:14, 15. Jg 10:12. 1 S
25:17, 31. Jb 31:16, 21-23, 38, 39. 34:28.
35:9. Ps +12:5. 34:6, 17. 35:10. 43:1, 2. 68:5.
140:12. 145:19. Pr 21:13. 22:23. 23:11. 30:10.
Is 5:7. 33:10. Je 22:13, 16. Hab 2:9-11. Lk
18:7. Ja +5:4.
I will surely. Ge +6:13. Jb 34:28. Ps 10:17,
18. 18:6. 106:44. 140:12. 145:19. 146:7-9. Pr
22:22, 23. 23:10, 11. Ja +5:4.

24 **my wrath**. Jg +2:14. Jb 20:23. 31:23. Ps 69:24. 76:7. 90:11. Ro 2:5-9. He 10:31.
your wives. Jb 27:13-15. Ps 78:63, 64. 109:9. Is 9:17. Je 15:8. 18:21. La 5:3. Lk 6:38.

25 **lend money**. 2 K 4:1, 7. Is +24:2.
userer. Ps 109:11.
usury. Is +24:2.

26 **to pledge**. Dt 24:6, 10-13, 17. Jb 22:6. 24:3, 9. Pr 20:16. 22:27. Ezk 18:7, 16. 33:15. Am 2:8.

27 **when he crieth**. ver. +23. Ex 2:23, 24. Ps 72:12. Is 19:20.
for I am gracious. Ex +34:6. 2 Ch 30:9. Ps 86:15. 136:10, 11.

28 **the gods**. or, judges. ver. +8, 9. Ps 32:6.
nor curse. Ex 21:17. 1 S 24:6, 10. 26:9. Ec 10:20. Ac 23:3, 5. Ro 13:2-7. T 3:1, 2. 1 P 2:17. 2 P 2:10. Ju 8.

29 **shalt not delay**. Ge 24:56. 34:19. Dt 7:10. 23:21. 26:2-10. Mi 7:1. Ml 3:10. Mt 6:33.
the first of thy ripe fruits. Heb. thy fulness. Le +23:10. Nu 18:29. Dt 22:9.
liquors. Heb. tear. only here; used metaphorically of olives and grapes.
the firstborn. Ex 13:2, 12. 34:19.

30 **Likewise**. Dt 15:19.
seven days. Le 22:27.

31 **holy**. Ex 19:5, 6. Le 11:45. 19:2. Dt 14:21. Ps 93:5. 1 P 1:15, 16. 2:9.
neither. Le 17:15, 16. 20:25. 22:8. Dt 14:21. Ezk 4:14. 44:31. Ac 10:14. 15:20.

EXODUS 23

1 **shalt not**. ver. 7. Ex +20:16. Le +19:16. 2 S 16:3. 19:27. Ps 101:5. 120:3. Pr 10:18. 17:4. 25:23. Je 20:10. Mt 28:14, 15. Ro 3:8.
raise. or, receive. Ps 15:3mg. 1 T +5:19.
an unrighteous witness. Dt 5:20. 19:16-21. 1 K 21:10-13. Pr +6:19. 24:28. Mt 19:18. Lk 3:14. 19:8. Ep 4:25. 2 T 3:3. 1 P 3:16. Re 12:10.

2 **follow**. Ex 32:1-5. Ge 6:12. 7:1. 19:4, 7-9. Nu 14:1-10. Jsh 24:15. 1 S 15:9, 24. 1 K 19:10. Jb 31:34. Pr 1:10, 11, 15. 4:14. Mt +7:13. 27:24-26. Mk 15:15. Lk 23:23, 24, 51. Jn 7:50, 51. Ac 24:27. 25:9. Ro 1:32. Ga 2:11-13.
speak. or, answer.
to decline. ver. 6, 7. Le 19:15. Dt 1:17. Ps 72:2. Je 37:15, 21. 38:5, 6, 9. Ezk 9:9. Hab +1:4.
to wrest. or, incline. Dt 16:19. or, stretch out. Ps 56:5.

3 **countenance**. Ja +2:1.
poor. Ex 30:15. Le 14:21. 19:15. Dt 15:11. Jg 6:15. Ru 3:10. Pr 22:2. Mt 26:11. Mk +14:7. Jn 12:8. 1 J 3:17.

4 **meet thine**. Dt 22:1-4. Jb 31:29, 30. Pr 24:17, 18. Mt +5:44.
ox or. Ex 20:12. 1 S 25:41. Pr 25:21. Lk 3:11. Jn 13:14. Ro 12:20. 1 C 9:9. 1 T 5:10. 6:8.

5 **If thou see**. Dt 22:4.
and wouldest forbear to help him. or, Wilt thou cease to help him? or, wouldest cease to leave thy business for him; thou shalt surely leave it to join with him.

6 **not wrest**. ver. 2, 3. Dt 16:19. 27:19. 2 Ch 19:7. Jb 31:13, 21, 22. Ps 82:3, 4. Ec +5:8. Is 10:1, 2. Je 5:28. 6:28. 7:6. Am 5:11, 12. Mi 3:1-4. Zp 3:1-4. Ml +3:5. Ja 2:5, 6.

7 **far from**. ver. 1. Le 19:11. Dt 19:16-21. Jb 22:23. Pr 4:14, 15. Is 33:15. Lk 3:14. Ep 4:25. 1 Th 5:22.
the innocent. Dt 27:25. Ps 94:21-23. Mt 27:4.
for I will not. Ex 34:7. Pr 17:15. Na 1:3. Ro 1:18. 2:5, 6.

8 **thou shalt take**. Dt 10:17. 16:19. 27:25. 1 S 8:3. 12:3. Ps 26:10. Pr 15:27. 17:8, 23. 19:4. 29:4. Ec 7:7. Is 1:23. 5:23. Ezk 22:12. Ho 4:18. Am 5:12. Mi 7:3. Ac 24:26.
no gift. 2 Ch 19:7. Da 5:17.
the wise. Heb. the seeing. Ex 4:11. Ge +21:19.
perverteth. Pr 27:8, 23.
words. or, cause.

9 **not oppress**. Ex 22:21. Dt 10:19. +24:14-18. 27:19. Ps +12:5. 94:6. Ezk +16:49. 22:7. Ml +3:5.
a stranger. Dt +26:11.
ye know. Mt 18:33. He 2:17, 18.
heart. Heb. nephesh, soul, Ge +34:3; Ge +23:8. Ex +15:9. Le 26:16. Dt 24:15. 1 S 2:33. 2 S 3:21. Ps 10:3. Pr 23:7. 28:25. 31:6. Je 42:20. La 3:51. Ezk 25:6, 15. 27:31. Ho 4:8.

10 **six years**. Le 25:3, 4. Ne 10:31.

11 **the seventh**. Le 25:2-7, 11, 12, 20, 22. 26:34, 35.
let it rest. or, release it. Dt 15:1, 2, 9.
olive-yard. or, olive-trees. Ge 8:11. Dt 6:11.

12 **Six days**. Ex 20:8-11. 31:15, 16. Lk 13:14.
and the son. Dt 5:13-15. Is 58:3.
refreshed. Ex 31:17. 2 S 16:14.

13 **be circumspect**. Dt 4:9, 15. Jsh 22:5. 23:11. 1 Ch 28:7-9. Ps 39:1. Ep 5:15. 1 T 4:16. He 12:15.
make no mention. Nu 32:38. Dt 12:3. Jsh 23:7. Ps 16:4. Je +10:2, 11. Ho 2:17. Zc 13:2. Ep 5:12.

14 **Three**. Ex 34:22, 23. Le 23:4, 5, 16, 34. Dt 16:16.
times. lit. feet. Nu 22:28.

15 **the feast**. Ex 12:14-28, 43-49. 13:6, 7. 34:18. Le 23:5-8. Nu 9:2-14. 28:16-25. Dt 16:1-8. Jsh 5:10, 11. 2 K 23:21-23. Mk 14:12. Lk 22:7. 1 C 5:7, 8.
and none. 1 Ch +21:24.

16 **feast of harvest**. Le 23:9-21. Ac 2:1.
firstfruits. Le +23:10. 27:26. Col 1:15, 18.
in-gathering. Le +23:34-44.
end of. Le 23:36. Dt 16:13.

17 **males shall appear**. Ex 34:23. Dt 12:5. 16:16. 31:11. Ps 84:7. Lk 2:42.

18 **blood**. Ex 12:8, 15. 34:25. Le 2:11. 7:12. Dt 16:4.
sacrifice. *or*, feast. Ps 118:27. Is 29:1. Ml 2:3.
remain. Ex 12:10. Le 7:15.

19 **first of the**. Le 23:10-17. Dt 12:5-7. 14:22.
firstfruits. Le +23:10.
Thou shalt not seethe a kid. Ex 34:26. Dt 14:21. Pr 12:10. Je 10:3.

20 **Angel**. Ex 32:34. 33:2, 14. Nu 20:16. Jsh 6:2. Ps 91:11. Zc +12:8. Mt *11:10*. Mk *1:2*. Lk 7:27. Jn 1:18. 1 C 10:9, 10.
place. Dt +12:11.
prepared. Ge 15:18. Mt 25:34. Jn 14:3.

21 **Beware of him**. Ps 2:12. Mt 17:5. He 12:25.
obey. Je +7:23.
provoke him not. Nu 14:11. Ps 78:40, 56. Ep 4:30. He 3:10, 16.
he will not. Ex 32:34. Nu 14:35. Dt 18:19. Jsh 24:19. Je 5:7. He 3:11. 10:26-29. 12:25. 1 J +5:16.
my name. Ex 3:14. 34:5-7. Ps +9:10. 72:19. 83:18. 91:14. Is 7:14. 9:6. 42:8. 45:6. 57:15. Je 23:6. Mt 1:23. Jn 5:23. 10:30, 38. 14:9, 10. 17:21. Col 2:9. Re 1:8. 2:8, 23. 3:7.

22 **an enemy**. Ge 12:3. Nu 24:9. Dt 30:7. Je 30:20. Zc 2:8. Ac 9:4, 5.
an adversary unto thine adversaries. *or*, I will afflict them that afflict thee. Ex +22:22, 23. Ge +6:13. +12:3. 2 Ch 16:9. Ps 34:7. 91:4. 125:2. Is 41:11. Zc 2:5. Lk 21:18.

23 **mine Angel**. ver. 20. Ex 32:2. Is 5:13.
thee in. Ex 3:17. Ge 15:19-21. 34:2. Jsh 24:8-11.
Amorites. Ge +10:16.
Hittites. Dt +20:17.
Perizzites. Ge +13:7.
Canaanites. Ge +10:18.
Hivites. Ge +10:17.
Jebusites. Ge +10:16.

24 **shalt not**. Ex +20:5.
do after. 2 Ch 33:2, 9. Ps 101:3. Je +10:2. Ezk 16:47.
overthrow. Ex 32:20. 34:13. Nu 33:52. Dt 7:5, 25, 26. 12:2, 3. Jg 2:2. 6:25. 1 K 15:13. 2 K 18:4. 23:4, 6, 14, 15. 1 Ch 14:12. 2 Ch 14:3. 31:1. 34:3-7. Mi 1:7.

25 **And ye**. Dt 6:13. 10:12, 20. 11:13, 14. 13:4. 28:1-6. Jsh 22:5. 24:14, 15, 21, 24. 1 S 7:3. 12:20, 24. Je 8:2. Mt 4:10.
he shall. Dt 7:13. 28:5-8. Is 33:16. Ml 3:10. Mt 6:33. 1 T +4:8.
bread. Is 3:1. 30:20.
take sickness. Le 26:16. Dt 7:15. 28:21. Jb 33:24-26, 28. Ps +103:3.

26 **shall nothing**. Dt 7:14. 28:4. Jb 21:10. Ps 107:38. 144:13. Ml 3:10, 11.
nor be. Ge +11:30. Le 26:9. Dt 28:11. 30:9.

the number. Ge +25:8. 35:29. 1 Ch 23:1. Jb 5:26. 14:5. 15:20. 21:21. 36:26. 42:17. Ps 55:23. 90:10. Ec 2:3mg. 5:18mg. Is 65:20. Ac 1:18.

27 **my fear**. Ge +35:5.
destroy. or, trouble. Ex 14:24. Dt 7:23.
backs. Heb. neck. Ge 49:8. Jsh 7:8mg, 12. 2 S 22:41. 2 Ch 29:6mg. Ps 18:40.

28 **hornets**. lit. hornet. Dt 7:20. Jsh 24:11, 12.
Hivite. Ge +10:17.
Canaanite. Ge +10:18.
Hittite. Dt +20:17.

29 **in one year**. Jsh +15:63. Jg 3:1-4.
lest. Dt 7:22. Ezk +5:17. Jn 15:19. 2 C 12:7-10. Ph 1:24. 1 P 5:10.

30 **By little and little**. Dt 7:22. Ph 3:12-14. 2 P 3:18.
drive them out. Ex 33:2. 34:11. Dt 4:38. 7:1, 22. 9:5. 11:23. Jsh 3:10. 13:6. 23:5. 24:11, 12. Ps 44:2, 3.

31 **I will set**. Nu 34:3-15. Dt 11:24. Jsh 1:4.
the river. Ps +72:8.
deliver the. Nu 21:34. Dt 3:2. Jsh 8:7, 18. 10:8, 19. 21:44. 23:14. 24:8. Jg 1:4. 11:21. 1 S 23:4. 2 S 8:3. 1 K 20:13.

32 **shalt make**. Ex 34:12, 15. Dt 7:2-4, 16, 25, 26. 20:16-18. Jsh 9:6, 14-23. Jg 2:2. 1 S +11:1. 2 S 21:1, 2. Ps 106:35. 2 C 6:14-17.
nor with. Nu 25:1, 2. Dt 7:16.

33 **they make**. 1 K 14:16. 2 Ch 33:9.
snare. Ex 10:7. 34:12. Nu 33:55. Dt 7:16. 12:30. Jsh 23:13. Jg 2:3. 8:27. 1 S 18:21. Jb 40:24. Ps +38:12. 69:22. 106:36. 119:110. Pr 22:25. Ezk 28:24. 2 T 2:26.

EXODUS 24

1 **Come up**. ver. 15. Ex 3:5. 19:9, 20, 24. 20:21. 34:2.
Nadab. Ex +6:23.
seventy. ver. 9. Ex +18:21. Ge +46:27.

2 **alone**. ver. 13, 15, 18. Ex 20:21. Nu 16:5. Je 30:21. 49:19. He 9:24. 10:21, 22.
neither shall. Ex 19:12.

3 **all the judgments**. Ex ch. 21-23. Dt 4:1, 5, 45. 5:1, 31. 6:1. 11:1.
All the words. ver. 7. Ex 19:8. Dt 5:27, 28. Jsh 24:22. Ga 3:19, 20.

4 **Moses wrote**. Ex 34:27, 28. Nu 21:14. 33:2. Dt 17:18, 19. 27:3, 8. 28:58, 61. 29:20, 21, 27. 31:9, 19, 22, 24, 26. Jsh 1:8. 8:31, 34. 23:6. 24:26. 1 S 10:25. 1 K 2:3. 2 K +14:6. 22:8. 23:3, 21, 24. 1 Ch 16:40. 2 Ch 17:9. 25:4. 31:3. +34:14. 35:12. Ezr 3:2. Ne 8:1. 9:3. 13:1. Da 9:11, 13. Mk 12:26. Lk 4:17. 16:31. 20:42. Jn 1:45. 5:45, 46, 47. Ac 1:20. Ga 3:10. He 9:19.
and builded. Ex 20:24-26.
twelve pillars. Ge 28:18, 22. 31:45. Jsh 24:27. Ga 2:9.
according. Ex 28:21. Le 24:5. Nu 17:2. Jsh

4:2, 3, 8, 9, 20. 1 K 11:30. Ezr 6:17. Lk 22:30. Re 21:14.

5 **young men**. Ex 19:22. 33:11. 2 S 18:15. 1 K 20:14. Ac 5:6, 10.
  burnt offerings. Le +23:12.
  peace offerings. Le +23:19.

6 **the blood he**. ver. 8. Ex 12:7, 22. Col 1:20. He 9:18. 12:24. 1 P 1:2, 19.
  on the altar. ver. 8. Le +1:5.

7 **the book**. ver. 4. He 9:18-23.
  read. Dt 31:11-13. Jsh 8:34, 35. 2 K 23:2. Ne 8:3, 8, 18. 13:1. Je 23:22. 36:6, 8. Mt 22:29. Mk 12:24. Lk 4:16. Jn +5:39. Ac 8:30-32. 13:15. Col 4:16. 1 Th 5:27. 1 T 4:13. Re 1:3.
  All that. ver. 3. Jsh 24:24. Je 7:23, 24.

8 **blood**. Mt 26:28. Mk 14:24. Lk 22:30. 1 C 11:25. Ep 1:7. Col 1:20. He 9:18.
  sprinkled. ver. 6. Le +1:5.
  Behold. Zc 9:11. Mt 26:28. Mk 14:24. Lk 22:20. 1 C 11:25. Ep 1:7. He 9:20. 10:4, 5. 13:20. 1 P 1:2.

9 **went up**. ver. +1.

10 **saw**. Ex 3:6. Ge +32:30. Ezk 1:28.
  of a sapphire stone. Ezk 1:26, 27. 10:1. Re 4:3. 21:19-23.
  in his clearness. SS 6:10. Mt 17:2. Re 1:16. 21:11, 18.

11 **nobles**. ver. 1, 9. Nu 21:18. Jg 5:13. 1 K 21:8. 2 Ch 23:20. Ne 2:16. Je 14:3.
  laid not. Ex 19:21. 33:20-23. Ge 32:24-32. Dt 4:33. Jg 13:22.
  they saw. ver. +10.
  eat and drink. Ex 18:12. Ge 18:8. 31:54. Dt 12:7. Jg 13:23. Ec 9:7. Lk 15:23, 24. 1 C 10:16-18.

12 **Come up**. ver. 2, 15, 18. Ex 3:5.
  tables. Ex 31:18. 32:15, 16. 34:1, 4, 28, 29. Dt 4:13. 5:22. 9:9-11. 10:1. Ne 9:13. Je 31:33. 2 C 3:3, 7. He 9:4.
  that thou. Dt 4:14. Ezr 7:10. Mt 5:19.

13 **his minister**. Ex 17:9-14. 32:17. 33:11. Nu 11:28.
  went up. ver. 2.

14 **Tarry ye**. Ex 24:2. 32:1. Ge 22:5. 1 S 10:8. 13:8-13.
  Hur. Ex 17:10, 12.
  if any man. Ex 18:25, 26.

15 **a cloud**. Ex +13:21.

16 **the glory**. ver. 17. Ex 16:7, 10. 40:34, 35. Le 9:6, 23. Nu 14:10, 21. 20:6. 2 Ch 5:14. 7:1. Is +40:5. Ezk +1:28. Jn 11:40. 2 C 4:6. Re 15:8. 21:10, 11, 23.
  seventh day. Ex 19:11. 20:10. Re 1:10.

17 **like a devouring fire**. Ex 3:2. 19:18. Dt 4:24, 36. Ezk 1:27. Na 1:6. Hab 3:4, 5. He 12:18, 29.

18 **went into**. ver. 17. Ex 9:29, 33. 19:20. Pr 28:1.
  forty days. Ex 34:28. Dt 10:10. Jon +3:4. Mk 1:13. Lk 4:2.

EXODUS 25

1 **the Lord spake**. Ex 6:1. 7:1. 8:1. 9:1. 10:1. 11:1. 12:1. 13:1. 14:1. 20:1.

2 **they**. Ex 35:5-29. Nu 7:3-88. Dt 16:16, 17. 1 Ch 29.
  bring me. Heb. take for me.
  offering. or, heave offering. Nu 18:24.
  willingly. Le +23:38. Ne 11:2. Ps 110:3. Ro 12:8.

3 **brass**. rather, copper. Dt 8:9. Jb 28:2.

4 **blue**. Ex 26:1. 2 Ch 3:14. Lk +1:35. Jn 3:13. 1 P 2:22.
  purple. Jg 8:26. Est 1:6. 8:15. Je 10:9. Ezk 27:7, 16. Da 5:7, 16, 29mg. Ac 16:14.
  scarlet. Ge 38:28, 30. Ex 26:1, 31, 36. Le 14:4, 6, 49, 51, 52. Jsh 2:18, 21. Pr 31:21. SS 4:3. Is 1:18.
  fine linen. or, silk. Ex +26:1. Ge 41:42.
  goats' hair. Nu 31:20. 1 S 19:13, 16.

5 **rams' skins**. Ex 26:14. 39:24. He +2:10.
  badgers' skins. Ex 26:14. 39:34. Ps 22:6. Is 53:2, 3. Ezk 16:10. Mk 6:3. Jn 1:10. Ph 2:6, 7. He 7:26.
  shittim wood. Ex 26:15, 26, 37. 27:1. 36:20. Is 41:19.

6 **Oil for**. ver. 37. Ex 27:20. 40:24, 25.
  spices. Ex 30:23-38.

7 **Onyx stones**. Ge +2:12.
  ephod. Ex +28:4, 6, 15.

8 **a sanctuary**. Ex 15:2. 36:1-4. Le 4:6. 10:4. 21:12. He 8:2. 9:1, 2. **S#4720h**, Ex +15:17.
  I may dwell. Ex +29:45. Nu 16:9. He 3:6.

9 **the pattern of the**. ver. +40. Dt 4:17. 2 K 16:10. 1 Ch 28:11-19. Ps 144:12. He 8:5. 9:9.
  tabernacle. Ex 33:7. +38:21.

10 **an ark**. or, chest. or, coffer. Ex 37:1-3. Dt 10:1-3. 2 Ch 8:11. He 9:4. Re 11:19.
  shittim wood. Ex 37:1. He 2:14.

11 **overlay**. ver. 24. Ex 30:3. 1 K 6:20. 2 Ch 3:4.
  pure gold. Jn 1:1, 14. +20:28.
  crown. ver. 24. Ex 30:3. 38:2, 11, 26.

12 **four rings**. ver. 14, 15, 26, 27. Ex 26:29. 27:4, 7. 30:4. 37:5. 38:7.

13 **staves**. ver. 14, 15, 28. Ex 12:11. 27:6. 30:5. 37:4, 5. 40:20. Ge 32:10. Nu 4:6, 8, 11, 14, 15. 21:18. 1 K 8:7, 8. 1 Ch 15:15. 2 Ch 5:8, 9. Mt 10:10. Mk 6:8.

14 **staves**. lit. parts, separated things. **S#905h**. Jb 17:16 (bars). 18:13 (strength; mg, bars), 13. Ezk 17:6 (branches). 19:14. Ho 11:6.

15 **staves**. ver. +13. 1 K 8:8. 2 Ch 5:9.

16 **into**. 2 Ch 6:11. Ps 40:8. He 9:15.
  the testimony. Ex +16:34. 34:29. Nu 17:4. Dt 31:26. 2 Ch 5:10. 34:14, 15. Ac 7:44. Ro 3:2. He 9:4.

17 **mercy seat**. ver. 21. Ex 26:34. 37:6. 40:20. Le 16:2, 12-15. 1 K 6:19. 1 Ch 28:11. 2 Ch

5:7. Lk 18:13. Ro 3:25. He 4:16. 9:5. 10:19-
21. 1 J 2:2.

18 **two cherubims of gold**. Ex 37:7-9. Ge
+3:24. 1 K 8:6, 7. Ezk 41:18, 19. He 9:5.

19 **of the**. *or*, of the matter of the. Jn 17:21, 23.
Ga 2:20. 1 J 1:3, 7.

20 **cherubims shall**. ver. 18. 1 K 8:7. 2 Ch 3:10.
He 9:5.
  covering. Ezk 28:14.
  toward. Ge 28:12. Is 6:1-5. Ezk 1:20. Mt
24:31. Jn 1:51. 1 C 4:9. 11:10. Ep 3:10. Col
2:10. He 1:14. 1 P 1:12. 3:22. Re 5:11, 12.

21 **mercy seat**. ver. +17. Ro 10:4.
  in. ver. 16.
  testimony. ver. 16. Pr 3:3. 7:3. Je 17:1.
31:33. 2 C 3:3, 7. He 8:10. 10:16.

22 **there**. Ex 20:24. Jg 20:26, 27.
  meet. Ex 29:42, 43. 30:6, 36. Nu 17:4. 2 C
5:19. He 4:16.
  commune. Ex +33:9. Le 1:1. 16:2. Dt 5:26-
31.
  from above. Nu 7:89.
  between. Ge +3:24. 2 S 6:2. 2 K 19:15. Ps
80:1. Is 37:16. 1 P 1:12.

23 **a table**. Ex 26:35. 31:8. 35:13. 37:10-16.
39:36. 40:4, 22, 23. Le 24:6. Nu 3:31. 1 K
7:48. 1 Ch 28:16. 2 Ch 4:8, 19. 13:11. Ezk
40:39, 41, 42. 41:22. 44:16. Ml 1:7, 12. 1 C
10:21. He 9:2.
  shittim wood. ver. +5, 10.

24 **overlay**. ver. +11. 1 K 6:20-22.
  crown. ver. +11.

25 **hand breadth**. Ex 37:12. Jg 20:16. 1 K 7:26.
Ps 39:5.
  a golden crown to the border. Ex 30:3.
37:2.

26 **four rings of gold**. ver. +12.

27 **for places of the staves**. ver. 14, 18.

28 **the table**. ver. 14, 27. Nu 10:17. Ac 9:15.

29 **the dishes**. Ex 37:16. Nu 4:7. 7:13, 19, 31,
etc. 1 K 7:50. 2 Ch 4:22. Ezr 1:9-11. Je 52:18,
19.
  covers. Ex 37:16. Nu 4:7. 1 Ch 28:17.
  bowls. Ex 37:16. Nu 4:7. Je 52:19.
  to cover. *or*, to pour out. Le 24:5-9. SS 5:1.
Re 3:20.

30 **showbread**. Heb. bread of faces. Ex 35:13.
39:36. Le 24:5, 6. Nu 4:7. 1 S 21:4, 6. 1 K
7:48. 1 Ch 9:32. 23:29. 2 Ch 2:4. 13:11. Ne
10:33. Ml 1:7, 12. Mt 12:4. He 9:2.
  me. Ps 23:5. 1 C 10:31.

31 **a candlestick**. Ex 26:35. 31:8. 35:14. 37:17-
24. 39:37. 40:24, 25. Le 24:4. Nu 3:31. 4:9.
8:4. 1 K 7:49. 1 Ch 28:15. 2 Ch 4:7, 20. 13:11.
Pr 6:23. Je 52:19. Zc 4:2, 11. Mt 5:15. He 9:2.
2 P 1:19. Re 1:12, 20. 2:1, 5. 4:5. 11:4.
  pure gold. Ex 31:8. 39:37. Le 24:4.
  beaten. Ex +27:20. Is 53:5. He +2:10.
  shaft. or, base. Heb. thigh. Ge +24:2. 41:5. Ex
1:5. 28:42. Nu 5:27. 1 K 14:15.

branches. Ge 41:5 (stalk), 22.
bowls. Ge 44:2. Je 35:5.
his knops. 1 K 6:18. 7:24. Am 9:1. Zp 2:14.
flowers. Nu 17:8. Is 5:24. 18:5. Na 1:4.

33 **like unto**. Nu 17:4-8. Je 1:11, 12.
  and three. Ex 37:19, 20. Zc 4:3.

36 **beaten**. ver. 18, +31. Nu 8:4. 1 K 10:16, 17. 2
Ch 9:15.

37 **seven**. Re +1:12.
  they shall. Ex 27:21. 30:8. Le 24:2-4. 2 Ch
13:11.
  light. *or*, cause to ascend. Ex 27:20. 30:8.
40:4, 25. Le 24:2. Nu 8:2, 3. 1 S 3:3.
  give. Ex 40:24. Nu 8:2. Ps 119:105. Pr 6:23. Is
+8:20. Mt 5:14. Lk 1:79. Jn 1:9. 8:12. 12:35.
Ac 26:18. Re 21:23-25. 22:5.
  it. Heb. the face of it. Nu 8:2.

38 **the tongs**. Ex 37:23. Nu 4:3. 1 K 7:49. 2 Ch
4:21. Is 6:6.
  snuff dishes. Ex 27:3. 37:23. Le 16:12. Nu
4:9. 16:37. 1 K 7:50. 2 K 12:13. 25:14. Je
52:18, 19.

39 **talent**. Ex 37:24. Zc 5:7.

40 **pattern**. ver. 9. Ex 26:30. 27:8. 39:42, 43. Nu
8:4. 1 Ch 28:11, 12, 19. 2 Ch 4:7. Ezk 43:9-
12. Ac 7:44. He 8:5. 9:23.
  was showed thee in the mount. Heb. thou
wast caused to see in the mount.

EXODUS 26

1 **the tabernacle with ten curtains**. Ex
16:16. 33:7. +38:21. 1 Ch 17:1. Jn 1:14. 2:21.
He 9:9, 23, 24.
  fine twined linen. ver. 31, 36. Ex 25:4.
28:5, 6, 15. 35:6, 35. 36:8, 35. 39:3, 8. 1 K
10:28. 1 Ch +4:21. Pr 7:16. 31:22, 24. Ezk
16:10. 27:7, 16. Lk 16:19. Re 18:12. 19:8,
14.
  cherubims. Ex +25:18.
  cunning work. Heb. the work of a cunning
workman, *or*, embroiderer. ver. 31. Ex 28:6,
15. 36:8, 35. 39:3, 8.

2 **curtain**. ver. 7, 8. Nu 4:25. 2 S 7:2. 1 Ch
17:1.

3 **coupled together**. ver. 9. Ex 36:10. Jn
17:21. 1 C 12:4, 12-27. Ep 2:21, 22. 4:3-6, 16.
Col 2:2, 19.

4 **loops of blue**. ver. 5, 10, 11. Ex 36:11, 12,
17.

6 **taches of gold**. ver. 11, 33. Ex 35:11. 36:13,
18. 39:33.
  one tabernacle. Ep 1:22, 23. 4:16. 1 P 2:4, 5.

7 **curtains**. Ex 35:26. 36:14-18. Nu 4:25. Ps
45:13. 1 P 3:4. 5:5.
  goats' hair. Ex 25:4. 35:6, 23. Nu 31:20.
  a covering. ver. 14. Is 4:5mg.
  eleven. ver. 1, 9, 12.

8 **length of one curtain**. ver. 2, 13.

9 **five curtains by themselves**. ver. 3.

10 **fifty loops**. ver. 4-6.

11 **tent**. *or*, covering. ver. 3, 6.

12 **shall hang over**. ver. 9.

13 **a cubit**. ver. 2, 8.
of that which remaineth. Heb. in the remainder, or surplusage.

14 **a covering**. Ex 36:19. Nu 4:5. Ps 27:5. 121:4, 5. Is 4:6. 25:4. 1 C 12:13.
rams' skins dyed red. Ex 25:5. 35:7, 23. 39:34. Nu 4:10. Ezk 16:10.
badgers' skins. Ex 25:5.

15 **boards**. ver. 18, 22-29. Ex 35:11. 36:20-33. 39:33. 40:17, 18. Nu 3:36. 4:31, 32. Ezk 27:5, 6. Ep 2:20, 21.
of shittim. Ex 25:5.

17 **tenons**. or, handles. Heb. hands. ver. 19. Ex 36:22, 24.

19 **forty sockets of silver**. ver. 25, 37. Ex 27:10, 12-18. 36:24-26. 38:27, 30, 31. 40:18. Nu 3:36. 4:31, 32. Jb 38:6mg. SS 5:15.

21 **two sockets under one board**. ver. 19.

23 **corners**. Ex 36:28.

24 **be coupled**. Heb. double; twined. or, twinned. or, paired. Ex 36:29. SS 4:2. 6:6.
and they shall be coupled together above. Ex 36:29, 30. Ps 133:1-3. 1 C 1:10. 3:16. Ep 4:15, 16. 1 P 2:5.
corners. Ex 36:29. 2 Ch 26:9. Ne +3:19. Ezk 41:22. 46:21, 22.

26 **bars**. ver. 27, 28, 29, etc. Dt 3:5. Jg 16:3.
of shittim wood. Ex 36:31-38. Nu 3:36. 4:31. Ro 15:1. 1 C 9:19, 20. Ga 6:1, 2. Ep 4:16. Col 2:19.

28 **reach**. lit. flee. 1 Ch 12:15. Ne 13:28. Jb 41:28. Pr 19:26.

29 **overlay the boards with gold**. Ex +25:11, 12.
places. lit. houses. Ex 23:19. 25:27. 36:34. 37:14, 27. 38:5.

30 **rear up the tabernacle**. Ex +38:21. Dt 27:2. Ep 2:19-22.
according to the. Ex +25:40.
fashion. lit. judgment. Ex 28:15, 29, 30.
showed thee. lit. was caused to see. Ex 25:40mg. Le 13:49. Dt 4:35.

31 **a vail of**. ver. +33, 35. Ex 36:35. 40:3, 21. Le 16:2, 15. 2 Ch 3:14. Mt 27:51. Mk 15:38. Lk 23:45. Jn 1:14. 2 C 3:18. Ep 2:14. 1 T 3:16. 2 T 1:10. He 6:19. 9:3-8. 10:20, 21. 1 J 4:2, 3. 2 J 7.
blue. Ex 25:4. 35:6, 25, 35. 36:8.
purple. Ex +25:4.
scarlet. Ex +25:4. 2 Ch 3:14.
cunning work. ver. *1*. Ex 28:15. 38:23. 2 Ch 2:7-13. Ps 137:5. SS 7:1.
cherubims shall it be made. Ex +25:18.

32 **pillars**. Ex 13:21. 26:37. 27:10-17. Jg 16:25, 26, 29, etc.
of shittim. ver. 37. Ex 36:38. Est 1:6.

their hooks shall be of gold. or, pegs. ver. 37. Ex 27:10, 11, 17. 36:36, 38. 38:10, 11, 12, 17, 19, 28.

33 **vail**. Mt 27:51. Mk 15:38. Lk 4:22. 23:45. Jn 7:46. He +2:10. 10:20.
the taches. Ex 27:10. 36:36.
within the vail. He 9:4, 5.
the ark of the testimony. Ex +16:34. 40:21.
divide. Ro 8:3. 2 C 5:15, 16. He 2:9, 14. 9:8.
the holy place. Le 16:2. 1 K 8:6, 10. 2 Ch 5:7-10. He 9:2, 3.
most holy. Le +2:3.

34 **put the mercy seat**. Ex +25:17.

35 **the table**. Ex +25:23.
the candlestick. Ex +25:31.
side. Heb. rib. ver. 20, 26, 27, 35, etc. Ex 25:12, 14. 30:4mg. 37:27. Ge 2:21, 22.

36 **hanging**. or, covering. Ex 36:37. 40:28. Jg 3:24. Ezk 28:13. Jn 10:9. 14:6. He 9:3.
the tent. Ex 35:11. 39:33. 40:29. Nu 3:25. 9:15. 2 S 7:6. Ps 78:60.
of blue. ver. +31.
wrought with. Ex 27:16. 28:39. 35:35. 36:37. 38:18, 23. 39:29. Jg 5:30.

37 **overlay them with gold**. Ex 36:38.
cast. lit. pour out. Ex 25:12. Ge 28:18. 35:14.

EXODUS 27

1 **altar of shittim wood**. ver. 2. Ex 20:24-26. 24:4. +38:30. 2 S 24:18. 2 Ch +4:1.

2 **horns of it upon the four corners thereof**. Ex 29:12. 30:2, 10. 38:2. Le 4:7, 18, 25, 30, 34. 8:15. 9:9. 16:18. 1 K 1:50, 51. 2:28. Ps 118:27. Ezk 43:15, 20. He 6:18.
overlay it with brass. Nu 16:38, 39. 1 K 8:64.

3 **pans**. or, pots. Ex 16:3. 38:3. 1 K 7:45.
ashes. Le +1:16. Nu 4:13. Ps 20:3mg.
his shovels. Ex 38:3. Le 16:12. Nu 4:14. 1 K 7:40, 45. 2 K 25:14. 2 Ch 4:11, 16. Je 52:18.
basons. or, bowls. 1 K +7:40.
flesh-hooks. or, forks. Ex 38:3. Nu 4:14. 1 S 2:13, 14. 1 Ch 28:17. 2 Ch 4:16.
firepans. Ex 38:3. 1 K 7:45. 2 K 25:15. Je 52:19, 20.

4 **a grate of network**. Ex 35:16. 38:4, 5.
rings in the four corners thereof. Ex +25:12.

5 **compass of the altar**. Ex 38:4.

6 **staves for the altar**. Ex +25:13-15.

7 **bear it**. Ex 25:28. 30:4. Nu 4:13, 14.

8 **as it was showed**. Heb. he showed. Ex +25:40. Mt 15:9. Col 2:20-23.

9 **the court**. Ex 38:9-20. 40:8, 33. 1 K 6:36. 8:64. 2 Ch 33:5. Ps 84:2, 10. 92:13. 100:4. 116:19. Ezk 40:14, 20, 23, 28, 32, 44. 42:3, 19, 20. 46:20-24.

tabernacle. Ex +38:21.
hangings for. Ex 26:31:37. 35:17. 39:40.

10 **sockets shall be of brass**. Ex +26:19-21.
fillets shall be of silver. Ex 36:38. Je 52:21.

14 **hangings of one side**. ver. 9. Ex 26:36.

16 **gate**. Ge +14:7.
of blue. Ex +26:31, 36.
needlework. Ex 28:39. 36:37. 39:29. Jg 5:30. Ps 45:14.

18 **length of the court**. ver. 9-12.
fifty every where. Heb. fifty by fifty.

19 **all the pins thereof**. Ex 35:18. 38:20, 31. 39:40. Nu 3:37. 4:32. Dt 23:13mg. Jg 4:21. 2 Ch 3:9. Ezr 9:8. Ec 12:11. Is 22:23-25. 33:20. 54:2. Ezk 15:3. Zc 10:4.
brass. ver. 3.

20 **pure oil olive**. Ex 39:27. Le 24:2-4. Jg 9:9. Ps 23:5. Zc 4:11-14. Re 11:4.
beaten. Ex 25:31, 36. 29:40. 30:36. 37:7. Le 2:1, 14. 24:5. Nu 8:4. 11:8. Is 28:28. 53:5. He +2:10.
for the light. Ex +25:31-37.
to cause the lamp. Ex 30:8. 1 S 3:3.
to burn. Heb. to ascend up. Ex 25:37. Ps 119:105. Mt 5:16. 1 J 2:20.

21 **the tabernacle of the congregation**. ver. 21. Ex +16:16. +25:9. 28:43. 29:4. Ge +17:21.
without the vail. Ex 26:31-33. 40:3.
testimony. Ex +16:34.
Aaron. Ex 30:8. 1 S 3:3. 2 Ch 13:11. Ml 2:7. Mt 4:16. Lk 12:35. Jn 5:35. 2 C 4:6. Ac 20:27, 28. 2 P 1:19. Re 2:1.
evening to. Ex +30:8. Ge 1:5, 8. Le 24:3. Ps 134:1.
a statute. Ex 28:43. 29:9, 28. Le +3:17. 16:34. 24:9. Nu 18:23. +19:21. 1 S 30:25.
for ever. Heb. olam, Ex +12:24.

EXODUS 28

1 **take**. Le 8:2. Nu 16:9-11. 17:2-9. 2 Ch 26:18-21. He 5:1-5.
with him. Col 2:20. 3:1, 3, 4.
among. ver. 41. Ex 29:1, 9, 44. 30:30. 31:10. 35:19. Nu 18:7. Dt 10:6. 1 Ch 6:10. 2 Ch 11:14. Lk 1:8.
unto me. Jn 14:12. 15:15.
Nadab. Ex +6:23.

2 **holy garments**. Ex 29:5-9, 29, 30. 31:10. 39:1, 2. 40:13. Le 8:7-9, 30. Nu 20:26-28. Ps 132:9, 16. Is 61:3, 10. 64:6. Zc 3:3, 4. Ro 3:22. 13:14. Ga 3:27. He 7:26. Re 19:8.
glory. ver. 40. Ex 19:5, 6. Nu 27:20, 21. Jb 40:10. Ps 90:16, 17. 96:6. 149:4. Is 4:2. Je 9:23, 24. Jn 1:14. 1 C 1:30, 31. He 2:9. 2 P 1:17. 1 J 3:2. Re 5:10. 19:8.

3 **wise hearted**. Ex 31:3-6. 35:30, 35. 36:1, 2. Pr 2:6. Is 28:24-26.
filled. Dt 34:9. Is 11:2. 1 C 12:7-11. Ep 1:17. Ja 1:17.

spirit. Heb. ruach, Ge +41:38.

4 **a breastplate**. ver. 15. Ex +39:8-21.
ephod. ver. 6-15, 28, 31. Ex 25:7. 39:2-5, 21, 22. Le 8:7, 8. Jg 8:27. 17:5. 18:14, 17. 1 S 2:18, 28. 14:3. 21:9. 22:18. 23:6, 9, 10. 28:6. 30:7. 2 S 6:14. Ho 3:4.
a robe. ver. 31-34. Ex 39:25, 26.
broidered. ver. 39, 40. Le 8:7.
a mitre. Ex 39:28. Le 8:9. Zc 3:5.
a girdle. Is 11:5.

5 **gold**. Ex 25:3, 4. 39:2, 3.

6 **ephod**. ver. +4.
linen. Ex +26:1.

7 **shoulderpieces**. Ex 39:4. Ps 55:2. Is 40:11. 63:9. 1 P 5:7.

8 **curious**. or, embroidered. ver. 27, 28. Ex 29:5. 39:20, 21. Le 8:7. Is 11:5. Ep 6:14. 1 P 1:13. Re 1:13.

9 **onyx**. ver. 20. Ge +2:12.
grave. ver. 36. Ex 39:6. 2 Ch 2:7. SS 8:6. Is 49:16.

10 **according to their birth**. Ex 1:1-4. Ge 43:33.

11 **engraver**. Ex 35:35. 38:23. Dt 27:15. 1 S 13:19. 2 S 5:11. 2 K 12:11. 22:6. 24:14, 16.
engravings of a. ver. 21, 36. Je 22:24. Zc 3:9. Ep 1:13. 4:30. 2 T 2:19. Re 7:2.
signet. ver. 21, 36. Ex 39:6, 14, 30. Ge 38:18. 1 K 21:8. Jb 38:14. 41:15. SS 8:6. Je 22:24. Hg 2:23.
ouches of gold. ver. 13, 14, 25. Ex 39:6, 13, 18.

12 **the shoulders**. ver. 7. Ps 89:19. Is 9:6. 12:2. Zc 6:13, 14. He 7:25-28.
Aaron shall bear. ver. 29. Ex 39:6, 7. Ep 5:27. He 7:25.
for a memorial. Ex +12:14. Ge 9:12-17. Is 62:6. Lk 1:54, 72. 2 T 2:19.

14 **chains of**. ver. 24. Ex 39:15.
of wreathen. ver. 22-25. Ex 39:17, 18. 1 K 7:17. 2 K 25:17. 2 Ch 4:12, 13.

15 **the breastplate**. ver. +4, 30.
after. ver. +6. Ex 26:1.

17 **thou shalt**. ver. +9, 11. Ex 39:10, etc. Ml 3:17.
set it in settings of stones. Heb. fill in it fillings of stone. Ex 25:7. 31:5. 35:9, 27, 33. 39:10.
the first row. Ezk 28:13. Re 21:19-21.
a sardius, or, ruby. Ex 39:10. Jb 28:18. Pr 3:15. 8:11. 20:15. 31:10. La 4:7.
a topaz. Jb 28:19. Re 21:20.
a carbuncle. Is 54:11, 12.

18 **emerald**. Ex 39:11. Ezk 27:16.
sapphire. Ex 24:10. Jb 28:6, 16. SS 5:14. Ezk 1:26. 10:1. Re 4:3.
diamond. Je 17:1. Ezk 28:13.

19 **a ligure**. Ex 39:12.
an agate. Is 54:12.

20 **a beryl**. Ezk 1:16. 10:9. Da 10:6. Re 21:20.

an onyx. ver. +9.
a jasper. Re 4:3. 21:11, 18-20.
inclosings. Heb. fillings. ver. 13.

21 **twelve**. ver. 9-11.
every one. Is 43:4. Ml 3:17. Ep 4:7.
according to the twelve. 1 K 18:31. Lk 22:30. Ja 1:1. Re 7:4-8. 21:12.

22 **upon the breastplate**. ver. 14.

23 **two rings**. Ex 25:11-15.

25 **wreathen chains**. ver. 14. Ex 39:15.
on the shoulder pieces. ver. 7.
of the ephod. Ex 39:4.

27 **the curious girdle**. ver. +8.

28 **a lace**. ver. 31, 37. Ex 39:30, 31. Nu 15:38.

29 **in the**. ver. +15, 30.
upon. ver. +12. Je 30:21. Ro 10:1.
a memorial. SS 8:6. Is 49:15, 16.

30 **the Urim**. i.e. *enlightening*, S#224h. Le 8:8. Nu 27:21. Dt 33:8. 1 S 28:6. Ezr 2:63. Ne 7:65. Is 24:15 (fires. mg, valleys). 31:9 (fire). 44:16. 47:14. 50:11. Ezk 5:2.
and Thummim. i.e. *perfections*, S#8550h, plural of S#8537h. Le 8:8. Dt 33:8. Ezr 2:63. Ne 7:65. For S#8537h, see Ge 20:5 (integrity). Le 8:8. Nu 27:21. Dt 33:8. Jg 1:1. 20:18, 23, 27, 28. 1 S 23:9-12. 28:6. 30:7, 8. Ezr 2:63. Ne 7:65. Jn 1:9, 18. 16:13, 14. Ro 12:1, 2. He 1:1, 2.
Aaron's heart. SS 8:6. Re 22:4.
bear the judgment. Zc 6:13. He 9:24.
upon his heart. 2 C 6:11, 12. 7:3. 12:15. Ph 1:7, 8. He 2:17. +4:15. 9:12, 24.

31 **the robe**. ver. 4, 28. Ex 39:22. Le 8:7. Is 61:10. Ro 3:22.

32 **as it were**. Ex 39:28. 2 Ch 26:14. Ne 4:16. Jb 41:26.
that it be not rent. Jn 19:23, 24. Ep 4:3-16.

33 **And**. Ex 39:24-26.
hem, *or*, skirts. ver. 34. Ex 39:24, 25, 26.
pomegranates. 1 K 7:18. 2 K 25:17.
bells. Zc 14:20. Lk 4:22. 11:54. Jn 7:46. He 7:25. 9:24.

34 **golden bell**. Ps 89:15. SS 2:3. 4:3, 13. 6:7, 11. 8:2. Jn 15:4-8, 16. Col 1:5, 6, 10.

35 **goeth in**. Le 16:2. He 9:12.
die not. Ps 2:11.

36 **grave upon it**. ver. +9, 11.
HOLINESS. Ex 39:30. Le 8:9. 10:3, 4. 19:2. 21:1, 7, 8. Ps 93:5. Ezk 43:12. Zc 14:20. 1 C 1:30. He 7:26. 12:14. 1 P 1:15, 16. 2:9. Re 21:27.

37 **blue**. ver. +28, 31. Nu 15:38.
the mitre it. ver. 4. Ex 29:6. 39:30, 31. Le 8:9. Zc 3:5.

38 *forehead*. Re 19:12.
bear the iniquity. ver. 43. Le 10:17. 22:9. Nu 18:1. Is 53:6, 11, 12. Ezk 4:4-6. Jn 1:29. 2 C 5:21. He 9:28. 1 P 2:24. 3:18.
shall hallow. Jn 17:19. He 4:14-16.
gifts. He 13:15.

accepted. Le 1:4. 22:27. 23:11. Is 56:7. 60:7. Ep 1:6. 1 P 2:5.

39 **embroider**. ver. +4.
the girdle. ver. +8. Is 22:21. Mk 10:45. Lk 17:8. Jn 13:2-17. Re 1:13.
needlework. Ps 45:14.

40 **Aaron's**. ver. 4. Ex 39:27, 29, 41. Le 8:13. Ezk 44:17, 18. Mt 22:12, 13. Ep 6:13.
bonnets. Ex 29:9.
glory. ver. +2. 1 T 2:9, 10. 6:9-11. T 2:7, 10. 1 P 3:3, 4. 5:5.

41 **with him**. 1 J 3:2.
anoint them. Ex 29:7, 21. 30:23-30. 40:13, 15. Le +4:3. Nu 35:25. 1 S 9:16. 10:1, 7. 16:1-3, 12, 13. 2 S 2:4. 1 K 1:34. 19:15, 16. 2 K 9:3, 6. 11:12. Ps 45:2, 7. 92:10. 133:2. Is 10:27. 11:2. 61:1. Lk 1:15. 2:11. Jn 3:34. Ac 10:38. 2 C 1:21, 22. 1 J 2:20, 27.
and consecrate them. Heb. fill their hand. Ex 29:9mg, 24, 27, 33, 35. 32:29mg. Le 8:33. 16:32mg. Nu 3:3mg. Jg 17:5mg, 12. 1 K 13:33mg. 1 Ch 29:5mg. 2 Ch 13:9mg. 29:31mg. Ezk 43:26mg. He 5:4. 7:28.
sanctify. 1 Th 5:23.
minister. ver. +1, 4.

42 **breeches**. Ex 20:26. 39:28. Le 6:10. 16:4. Ezk 44:18. Re 3:18. 16:15.
their nakedness. Heb. flesh of their nakedness.
thighs. Ge +24:2.
reach. Heb. be.

43 **unto the altar**. Ex 20:26.
bear not iniquity. Ge +19:15. Le 5:1, 17. 20:19, 20. 22:9. Nu 9:13. 18:22. Mt 22:12, 13.
a statute. Ex 27:21. Le 17:7.
for ever. Heb. *olam*, Ex +12:24.

EXODUS 29

1 **hallow them**. ver. 21. Ex 20:11. 28:41. Le 8:2, etc. Mt 6:9.
to minister. Ex +28:3.
Take. Le 8:2. 9:2. 16:3. 2 Ch 13:9.
without. Le +1:3.

2 **bread**. Ex +12:8. Le 2:4. 6:20-22. 8:2. 1 C 5:7.
tempered. ver. 23. Le 2:4, 5, 15. 7:10. Nu 6:15.
wafers. Le 7:12. 8:26. Nu 6:15, 19.

3 **in the basket**. Le 8:2, 26, 31. Nu 6:17.

4 **unto the door**. Ex 26:36. 40:28. Le 8:3-6.
wash. Heb. *rahats*. ver. 17. Ex 2:5. 30:18-21. 40:12, 30, 31. Ge 18:4. Le 8:6. 14:8, 9. 15:5 (bathe), 13, 16. 16:24. 22:6. Nu 19:19. Dt 21:6. 23:11. Ru 3:3. 2 S 11:2. 1 K 22:38. 2 K 5:10, 12, 13. 2 Ch 4:6. Ps 58:10. SS 5:3. He 9:10.
them with water. Ex 30:18-21. 40:12. Le 8:6. 14:8. Dt 23:11. Ezk 36:25. Jn 13:8-10. 1 C 6:11. Ep 5:26, 27. T 3:5. He +10:22. 1 P 3:21. Re 1:5, 6.

5 garments. Ex +28:2-8.
put upon. Ro 3:22.
curious. Ex 28:8.
6 mitre. Ex 28:36-39. Le 8:9.
7 anointing oil. Ex +28:41. Ps 89:20. He 1:9.
8 his sons. Ex 28:40. Le 8:13.
coats. Ro 13:14.
9 put. Heb. bind. Le 8:13.
on them. Jn 14:6. Ep 1:6. 6:14. Col 3:12, 14. 1 Th 5:8.
the priest's. Ex 28:1. Nu 16:10, 35, 40. 18:7. He 5:4, 5, 10, 7:11-14.
theirs. Re 1:6.
perpetual. Heb. *olam*, Ge +9:12.
consecrate. Heb. fill the hand of. Ex +28:41. Col 2:9, 10. He 7:23-28.
10 cause. ver. 1.
put. ver. 15, 19. Le 1:4. 3:2. 8:14, 18. 16:21. Is 53:6. 2 C 5:21.
11 And. Le 1:4, 5. 8:15. 9:8, 12.
door. ver. 4. Le 1:3.
12 the blood. Le 4:7, 17, 18, 25, 30, 34. 5:9. 8:15. 9:9. 16:14, 18, 19. Ezk 43:20. He 9:13, 14, 22. 10:4.
the horns. Ex +27:2.
thy finger. Mt 12:28. Lk 11:20.
13 all the fat. ver. 22. Le 3:3, 4, 9, 10, 14-16. 4:8, 9, 19, 26, 31, 35. 6:12. 7:3, 31. 8:16, 25. 9:10, 24. 16:25. 17:6. Nu 18:17. Dt 32:14. 2 Ch 7:7. Ps 22:14, 51:17. Pr 23:26. Is 1:11. 34:6, +7. 43:24. 53:10. Ezk 44:7, 15.
and the caul. Le 8:16, 25. 9:10, 19.
burn them. ver. 18, 25. Le 1:9, 15. 3:5. 6:23, 30. 16:25. 17:6. Nu 18:17. 1 S 2:15, 16.
14 flesh. Le 4:11, 12, 21. 8:17. 16:27.
without. Le +4:12.
sin offering. Le +23:19.
15 one. ver. 3, 19. Le 8:18-21.
put. ver. 10. Le 1:4-9.
16 slay the ram. ver. +11, 12.
sprinkle. 1 P 1:2.
17 wash the. Le 1:9, 13. 8:21. 9:14. Je 4:14. Mt 23:26.
unto. *or*, upon. Le 8:20.
18 a burnt offering. Le +23:12. 1 K 18:38. Mk 12:33.
sweet savor. Ge +8:21.
19 other. ver. 3. Le 8:22-29.
Aaron. ver. +10.
20 and put. Le 8:24. 14:14. Is 50:5. Mk 7:33.
tip. Ro 12:1. 1 C 6:19, 20.
sprinkle. Le +1:5.
21 blood. He 9:12. 1 P 2:5. Re 1:5, 6.
the anointing oil. ver. 7. Ex 30:25-31. Le 8:30. 14:15-18, 29. Ps 133:2. Is 11:2-5. 61:1-3.
shall be. ver. 1. Jn 17:19. He 9:22. 10:29.
22 Also thou. ver. 13. Le 8:25-27.
the rump. Le 3:9. 7:3. 9:19.
right shoulder. Nu +18:18.

23 one loaf. ver. 2, 3.
24 put. Le 8:27.
wave them. Heb. shake to and fro. ver. 26, 27. Le 7:30. 8:27, 29. 9:21. 10:15. 14:12. 23:11. Nu 5:25. 6:20. 2 K +5:11mg.
a wave offering. ver. 26, 27. Le +23:15.
before. Dt +12:11.
25 thou. Le 7:29-31. 8:28. Ps 99:6.
for a sweet. ver. +18.
offering. ver. 41. Le 1:9, 13. 2:2, 9, 16. 3:3, 5, 9, 11, 14, 16. 7:5, 25. 10:13. 1 S 2:28.
26 the breast. Nu +18:18.
it shall be thy. Ps 99:6.
27 the breast. ver. 26. Dt 18:3.
the wave offering. Le +23:15.
heave offering. Le +7:14.
the ram of the consecration. ver. 22, 34. Ex +28:41mg. Le 7:37. 8:28-31. He 7:28.
28 Aaron's. Le 7:32-34. 10:14, 15. Dt 18:3.
for ever. Heb. *olam*, Ex +12:24.
is an heave. ver. 27. Le +7:14.
peace offering. Le +23:19.
29 holy. Ex 28:3, 4.
his. Nu 20:26-28.
anointed. ver. 5-7. Ex 30:30. 40:15. Le 8:7-12. Nu 18:8. 35:25.
30 that son. Heb. he of his sons. Nu 20:28. He 7:26.
seven days. ver. 35. Ex 12:15. Ge 8:10, 11. Le 8:33-35. 9:1, 8. 12:2, 3. 13:5. Jsh 6:14, 15. Ezk 43:26. Ac 20:6, 7.
31 the ram. ver. +27.
seethe his flesh. Le 8:31. 1 S 2:13, 15. Ezk 46:20-24.
in the holy place. Le 6:14-16, 26. 7:6. 10:13, 14, 17. 14:13. 24:9. Nu 18:10. Ezk 42:13.
32 Aaron. Ex 24:9-11. Le 10:12-14.
and the bread. ver. 2, 3, 23. Mt 12:4.
33 eat those. Le 10:13-18. Ps 22:26. Jn 6:53-55. 1 C 11:24, 26.
atonement. Jn 6:54-57.
consecrate. Ex +28:41.
a stranger. Le 22:10-13. Nu 1:51. 3:10, 38. 16:40. 18:4, 7.
they are holy. Nu 16:5.
34 flesh. ver. 22, 26, 28.
burn. Ex 12:10. 16:19. Le 7:18, 19. 8:32. 10:16.
35 thus shalt thou do. Ex 40:12-15. Le 8:4, etc.
according. Ex 39:42, 43. 40:16. Jn 15:14.
seven days. ver. 30, 37. Ex 40:12, 13. Le 14:8-11.
consecrate. Ex +28:41.
36 every day. ver. +10-14. Ezk 43:25, 27. 48:18-20. He 10:11.
cleanse. Le 16:16-19, 27. He 9:22, 23.
anoint it. Ex 30:26, 28, 29. 40:9-11. Le 8:10, 11. Nu 7:1.
37 and sanctify it. Ex 40:10. Da 9:24.
it shall be an. Ex 30:29. Mt 23:17, 19.

38 two lambs. Nu 28:3-8. 1 Ch 16:40. 2 Ch 2:4. 13:11. 31:3. Ezr 3:3. Da 9:21, 27. 12:11. Jn 1:29. He 7:27. 1 P 1:19. Re 5:9-12.

39 in the morning. 2 K 16:15. 2 Ch 13:11. Ps 5:3. 55:16, 17. Ezk 46:13-15. Lk 1:10. Ac 26:7.
at even. ver. +41.

40 a tenth. Ex 16:36. Nu 15:4, 9. 28:5, 13.
hin. Ex 30:24. Le 23:13. Nu 15:4. 28:14. Ezk 4:11. 45:24. 46:5, 7, 11, 14.
beaten. Ex +27:20. Is 53:5. He +2:10.
oil. Mt 26:36.
a drink offering. Le +23:13.

41 offer at even. 1 K 18:29, 36. 2 K 16:15. Ezr 9:4, 5. Ps 141:2. Ezk 46:13-15. Da 9:21.
meat offering. Le +23:13.
drink offering. Le +23:13.
for a sweet. ver. 18, 25.

42 continual burnt offering. ver. 38. Ex 30:8. Nu 28:3, 6, 10, 15, 23, 31. 29:2, 8, 11, 13, 16, 19, 22, 25, 31, 34, 38. 1 Ch 16:40. Ezr 3:5. Ne 10:33. Ps 50:8. Da 8:11-13. 12:11.
where. Ex 25:22. 30:6, 36. Le 1:1. Nu 17:4.
meet. Ex 25:22. Le 16:2. 2 C 5:19.
speak. Jn 1:1. 8:26, 43, 47. He 1:2.

43 the tabernacle. *or*, Israel.
sanctified. Ex 40:34. 1 K 8:11. 2 Ch 5:14. 7:1-3. Is 6:1-3. 60:1. Ezk 43:5. Hg 2:7-9. Ml 3:1. 2 C 3:18. 4:6. 1 J 3:2. Re 21:22, 23.

44 sanctify also. Le 21:15. 22:9, 16. Jn 10:36. 17:19. Re 1:5, 6.

45 dwell. Ex 15:17. 25:8. Le 26:12. Nu 5:3. 1 K 6:13. 8:13, 27. Ps 9:11. 68:18. 132:14. Is 12:6. 57:15. Ezk 43:7, 9. Jl 3:17, 21. Zc 2:10. 8:3. Mt 1:23. Jn 14:17, 20, 23. 2 C 6:16. Ep 2:22. Re 21:3.

46 know. Jn 14:7-9.
that I am. Ex +20:2. Je 31:33.
dwell among. Jn 1:14.
them: **I am**. Le 11:44. 18:30. 19:2. Ezk 20:5.

EXODUS 30

1 an altar. ver. 7, 8, 10. Ex 37:25-28. 40:5. Le 4:7, 18. Nu 4:11. 1 K 6:20. 2 Ch 26:16. Re 8:3.
incense. Ps +141:2. Pr 27:9. SS 1:3, +12. Lk 23:44. Jn 16:23, 26. 2 C 2:14, 15. Ph 4:18. He 7:25. 9:24. Re 5:8. 8:3.

2 the horns. Ex +27:2.

3 overlay it. Ex 25:11, 24.
top. Heb. roof.
sides. Heb. walls. Ex 37:26.

4 rings. Ex +25:12.
two corners. Heb. ribs. Ex +26:35.

5 staves. Ex +25:13, 27.

6 vail. Ex 26:31-35. 40:3, 5, 26. Mt 27:51. He 9:3, 4.
mercy seat. Ex 25:21, 22. Le 16:13. 1 Ch 28:11. He 4:16. 9:5.

I will. ver. 36. Ex 29:42, 43. Nu 17:4. He 9:24.

7 sweet incense. Heb. incense of spices. ver. 34-38.
dresseth. Ex 27:20, 21. 1 S 2:28. 3:3. 1 Ch 23:13. Lk 1:9. Ac 6:4.

8 lighteth. *or*, setteth up. Heb. causeth to ascend. Ex 25:37. 27:20, 21. Le 24:2, 3. 1 S 3:3. 2 Ch 13:11.
at even. Heb. between the two evens. Ex 12:6mg.
a perpetual. Ro 8:34. 1 Th 5:17. He 7:25. 9:24.
incense. ver. +1, 34. SS 2:13. 4:13, 14.

9 strange incense. Le 10:1.
meat offering. Le +23:13.
drink offering. Le +23:13.

10 Aaron. Ex 29:36, 37. Le 16:18, 29, 30. 23:27. He 1:3. 9:7, 22, 23, 25.
it once. Le 16:14, 18, 19. Nu 29:7. He +2:10.
sin offering. Le +23:19.
of atonements. Le +23:27.

12 takest. Ex 38:25, 26. Nu 1:2-5. 26:2-4. 2 S 24:2.
their number. Heb. them that are to be numbered.
a ransom. Nu 31:50. 2 Ch 24:6. Jb 33:24. 36:18. Ps 49:7. Mt 20:28. Mk 10:45. 1 T 2:6. 1 P 1:18, 19.
soul. Heb. *nephesh*, Ge +12:13. Jb 32:2mg. 1 P +4:19.
no plague. 2 S 24:2-15. 1 Ch 21:12, 14. 27:24.

13 a shekel is. Ex 38:24. Le 5:15. 27:3, 25. Nu 3:47. 18:16. Ezk 45:12.
an half shekel. Ex 38:26. Ne 10:32. Mt 17:24.

14 from twenty. Nu 1:3, 18, 20. 14:29. 26:2. 32:11.

15 rich. Jb 34:19. Pr 22:2. Ep 6:9. Col 3:25. Ja 2:1.
give more. Heb. multiply.
give less than. Heb. diminish. Je +10:24mg.
an atonement. ver. 12. Le 17:11. Nu 31:50. 2 S 21:3.
souls. Heb. *nephesh*, Ge +12:13.

16 atonement money. Ex 38:25-28. 1 P 1:18, 19.
appoint. Ex 38:25-31. Ne 10:32, 33.
a memorial. Ex +12:14.
souls. Heb. *nephesh*, +Ge 12:13.

18 a laver. Ex 31:9. 38:8. Le 8:11. 1 K 7:23, 38. 2 Ch 4:2, 6, 14, 15. Zc 13:1. Ep 5:26. T 3:5. 1 J 1:7. **S#3595h**: ver. 28. Ex 31:9. 35:16. 38:8. 39:39. 40:7, 11, 30. Le 8:11. 1 S 2:14 (pan). 1 K 7:30, 38, 40, 43. 2 K 16:17. 2 Ch 4:6, 14 (mg. caldrons). 6:13 (scaffold). Zc 12:6 (hearth).
brass. Ex 38:8.
wash. Heb. *rahats*, Ex +29:4. 2 S 22:21, 25. Jb

17:9. Ps 24:3, 4. 26:6. Jn 13:10. Ja 4:8.
put it. Ex 40:7, 30-32.

19 **wash**. Heb. *rahats*, Ex +29:4. 40:31, 32. Ps
26:6. Is 52:11. Jn 13:8-10. 1 C 6:9-11. T 3:5.
He +9:10. +10:22. Ja 3:2. 4:8. Re +1:5, 6.
thereat. or, at it. lit. out of it. Orientals never
put their hands or feet in water to cleanse
them, but pour water upon them (Young).

20 **wash**. Heb. *rahats*, Ex +29:4.
with water. ver. 19. Ac +1:5.
die not. Ex 12:15. Le 10:1-3. 16:1, 2. 1 S
6:19. 1 Ch 13:10. Ps 89:7. Ac 5:5, 10. He
12:28, 29.

21 **wash**. Heb. *rahats*, Ex +29:4.
their hands. ver. 19. Ex 40:12. Le 16:24. 1 K
7:23.
a statute. Ex 28:43.
for ever. Heb. *olam*, Ex +12:24.

23 **principal spices**. ver. 34. Ex 25:6. 37:29. Ge
43:11. 1 K 10:10, 15. 2 Ch 9:1, 9. 32:27. SS
8:14. Je 6:20. Ezk 27:19, 22. There is a nine-
fold enumeration here; so also at SS 4:13, 14;
1 C 12:8-10; 2 C 6:4, 5; Ga 5:22, 23; 2 P 1:5-7.
pure myrrh. Young renders *wild* or *free
honey*. On *free*, see Le 25:10. Is 61:1. Je 34:8,
15, 17. Ezk 46:17. Mt +2:11.
cinnamon. Pr 7:17. SS 4:14, only.
sweet calamus. Young renders *spice-cane*. On
cane, see Ge 41:5. SS 4:14. Is 43:24. Je 6:20.
Ezk 27:19.

24 **cassia**. Ps 45:8.
the shekel. Nu 3:47. Ezk 45:12.
hin. Ex 29:40. Le 19:36. Nu 15:5.

25 **ointment**. SS 1:3.
apothecary. *or*, perfumer. 1 Ch 9:30.
an holy. Ex 37:29. Nu 35:25. Ps 89:20. 133:2.
He 1:9.

26 **anoint**. Ex +28:41. Nu 7:1, 10.

29 **whatsoever**. Ex 29:37. Le 6:18. Mt 23:17,
19.

30 **anoint**. Ex +28:41. Nu 3:3.
consecrate. Ex 28:3. 29:9, 35.
priest's. 1 P 2:5, 9.

31 **an holy**. Ex 37:29. Le 8:12. 21:10. Ps 89:20.
oil. Ro 8:9. 1 C 12:3.

32 **man's**. Le 21:10. Mt 7:6.
flesh. 1 C 2:14.
poured. Heb. *yasak*, **S#3251h**, only here.
composition. ver. 37. Ex +5:8.
it is. ver. 25, 37, 38.

33 **compoundeth**. ver. 38. Lk 12:1, 2. He 10:26-
29.
a stranger. Ex 29:33.
cut off. Ex 12:15, 19. Ge 17:14. Le 7:20, 21.
17:4, 9. 19:8. 23:29. Nu 9:13.

34 **unto thee**. ver. +8, 23. Ex 25:6. 37:29.
stacte. Heb. *nataph*. Jb 36:27 (drops). Je 8:22.
onycha. only here.
galbanum. only here.
frankincense. Mt +2:11.

35 **perfume**. Pr 27:9. SS 1:3. 3:6. Jn 12:3.
after the. ver. 25.
tempered. Heb. salted. Le 2:13. Ezk 16:4.

36 **beat**. Ex +27:20. Is 53:5. He +2:10.
the testimony. Ex +16:34.
where I will. ver. 6. Ex 25:22. 29:42, 43. Le
16:2.

37 **ye shall**. ver. 32, 33.
composition. ver. 32. Ex +5:8. 2 Ch 24:13.
it shall. Ex 29:37. Le 2:3.

38 **to smell**. Ge 8:21. 1 S 16:23.
be cut off. ver. +33.

EXODUS 31

2 **I have**. Ex 33:12, 17. 35:30. 36:1. Is 45:3, 4.
Mk 3:16-19. Jn 3:27.
Bezaleel. i.e. *God is protection; in the shadow of
God, in God's shade*, **S#1212h**. Ex 35:30. 36:1, 2.
37:1. 38:22. 1 Ch 2:20. 2 Ch 1:5. Ezr 10:30.
Uri. i.e. *my light; fiery*, **S#221h**. Ex 35:30. 38:22.
1 K 4:19. 1 Ch 2:20. 2 Ch 1:5. Ezr 10:24.

3 **filled**. Ex 35:31. 36:1. 1 K 3:9. 7:14. Is 28:6,
26. 54:16. Ac 2:4. 1 C 12:4-11. Ja 1:17.
the spirit of God. Heb. *ruach*, Ge +41:38. Is
28:24-29.
workmanship. 1 C 3:10.

4 **devise cunning works**. Ex 25:32-35. 26:1.
28:15. 1 K 7:14. 2 Ch 2:7, 13, 14.

5 **in cutting**. Ex 28:9-21.

6 **I have given**. Ex 4:14, 15. 6:26. Ezr 5:1, 2. Ec
4:9-12. Mt 10:2-4. Lk 10:1. Ac 13:2. 15:39, 40.
Aholiab. i.e. *tent of my father*, **S#171h**. Ex
35:34. 36:1, 2. 38:23.
Ahisamach. i.e. *brother of support*, **S#294h**. Ex
35:34. 38:23.
tribe of Dan. Nu +1:12.
wise hearted. Ex 28:3. 35:10, 25, 26, 35.
36:1, 8. 1 K 3:12. Pr 2:6, 7. Ja 1:5, 16, 17.
that they. Ex ch. 37. 38. Nu ch. 4. 1 K ch. 6.
7. 8. 2 Ch ch. 3. 4. Ezk ch. 43, etc.

7 **tabernacle**. Ex +38:21.
ark. Ex 25:10-22. 37:1-9.
furniture. Heb. vessels. Ex 30:27, 28. 39:33.

8 **the table**. Ex +25:23.
pure candlestick. Ex +25:31.
altar. Ex 30:1-10. 37:25-28.

9 **the altar**. Ex +40:6.
the laver. Ex +30:18.

10 **the cloths**. Ex 28. 39. Le 8:7, 8, 13. Nu 4:5-14.

11 **the anointing**. Ex 30:23-33. 37:29.
sweet incense. Ex +39:38. Ps +141:2.

13 **Verily**. Ex +20:8-11. Le 25:2.
a sign. ver. 17.
that ye may. Le 20:8. 21:8. Ezk 37:28. Jn
17:17, 19. 1 Th 5:23. Ju 1.
Lord. Ex +15:26.
that doth sanctify. lit. Jehovah-
Mekaddishkem. Le 20:8. 21:8. 22:32. Ps 23:5.
Ezk 20:12.

14 **keep**. Ex +20:8.
every one. Is 56:2-6. Ezk 20:13, 16, 21, 24.
surely. Ge +2:16.
doeth. Ex 35:2, 3. Nu 15:35.
soul. Heb. *nephesh*, Ge +17:14.
15 **Six days**. ver. 17. Ex 16:26. 20:9. 34:21. Le
23:3. Ezk 46:1. Lk 13:14.
the sabbath. Ex 16:23. 20:10. Ge 2:2. Le
23:3, 32. Lk 23:56. He 4:9.
holy. Heb. holiness. ver. 10, 14. Ex 16:23.
30:25, 32, 35, 37, etc.
whosoever. Nu 15:32-36. Je 17:24-27.
surely. Ge +2:16.
16 **a perpetual**. Heb. *olam*, Ge +9:12.
covenant. Ge 9:13. 17:11. Je 50:5.
17 **a sign**. ver. 13. Ezk 20:12, 20.
six days. Ge 1:31. 2:2, 3. He 4:3, 4, 10.
for ever. Heb. *olam*, Ex +12:24.
and was refreshed. Ge 1:31. Jb 38:7. Ps
104:31. Je 32:41.
18 **gave**. Ex +24:12. Jn 1:17.
communing. Ex +33:9.
written. Ex 32:16. 34:28. Dt 4:13. 9:10. 10:4.
Is 4:3. Je 31:33. Da 12:1. He 8:10.
the finger. Ex 8:19. Ps 8:3. Is 40:12. 48:13.
Mt 12:28. Lk 11:20. 2 C 3:7, 8.

EXODUS 32

1 A.M. 2513. B.C. 1491.
saw. 1 S 8:5.
delayed. Ex 24:18. Dt 9:9. Mt 24:48, 50, 51.
Lk 12:45. 2 P 3:3, 4.
Up. Ge 19:14. 44:4. Jsh 7:13.
make. Ex +20:4.
which shall. Ex 13:21. 33:3, 14, 15.
the man. ver. 7, 11. Ex 14:11. 16:3. Ho
12:13. Mi 6:4.
we wot. Ge 21:26. 39:8. 44:15. Mt 24:48. Ac
7:40. 2 P 3:4.
2 **golden earrings**. Ex 12:35, 36. Ge 24:22, 47.
Jg 8:24-27. Ezk 16:11, 12, 17. Ho 2:8.
bring. Ex 35:22.
3 **all**. Ex +9:6.
brake off. Jg 17:3, 4. Is 40:19, 20. 46:6. Je 10:9.
4 **fashioned**. Ex 20:23. Dt 9:16. Ps 106:19-21.
Is 44:9, 10. 46:6. Ac 7:41. 17:29.
a graving. Ex 28:9, 11.
molten. ver. 8. Ex +34:17.
calf. ver. 19, 20. Dt 9:16, 21. 1 K 12:28, 32. 2
K 10:29. 17:16. 2 Ch 11:15. 13:8. Ne 9:18. Ps
106:19. Ho 8:5, 6. 10:5. 13:2. Ac 7:41.
These. ver. 8. Jg 17:3, 4. Ne 9:18. Is 40:18,
19. Ro 1:21-23.
which brought. ver. 1, 8. Ex 20:2.
5 **Aaron**. 1 S 14:35. 2 K 16:11. Ho 8:11, 14.
made proclamation. Le 23:2, 4, 21, 37. 1 K
21:9. 2 K 10:20. 2 Ch 30:5.
a feast. ver. 4. Ex 10:9. 12:14. 1 K 12:32, 33.
1 C 5:8.

6 **offered**. Ex 24:4, 5.
sat down. Nu 25:2. Jg 16:23-25. Am 2:8.
8:10. Ac 7:41, 42. 1 C 10:7. Re 11:10.
7 **Go**. Ex 19:24. 33:1. Dt 9:12. Da 9:24.
thy people. ver. 1, 11.
thou broughtest. Ex 20:2. 33:1. Dt 5:6.
corrupted. Ge 6:11, 12. Dt 4:16. 32:5. Jg
2:19. Ho 9:9.
8 **have turned**. Ex 19:8. Dt 9:16. Jg 2:17.
which I. Ex 20:3, 4, 23.
These be. ver. 4. 1 K 12:28.
9 **I have seen**. Ge +16:13. Dt 9:13. Je 13:27.
Ho 6:10.
a stiffnecked. 2 Ch +30:8. Ps 78:8. Pr 29:1.
Zc 7:11, 12. Ac 7:51.
10 **let me alone**. Ge 18:32, 33. 32:26-28. Nu
14:19, 20. 16:22, 45-48. Dt 9:14, 19. Je
+14:11. 15:1. Ja +5:16.
my wrath. ver. 11, 19. Ex 22:24.
and I will. Nu 14:12. Dt 9:14, 19. Mt 3:9.
11 **besought**. Dt 9:18-20, 26-29. Ps 106:23.
the Lord his God. Heb. the face of the Lord.
1 S +13:12mg. 1 K 13:6mg. Jb +11:19mg. Ps
45:12mg. 119:58mg. Pr 19:6. Je +26:19mg.
Da 9:13mg. Zc 7:2mg. Ml 1:9mg.
why doth. Nu 11:11. 16:22. Dt 9:18-29. Ps
74:1, 2. Is 63:17. Je 12:1, 2.
which thou. ver. 7.
12 **Wherefore**. Jsh 7:6, 9. 2 Ch 20:9, 11. Je
14:21.
should. Nu 14:13-16. Dt 9:28. 32:26, 27. Jsh
7:9. Ps 74:18. 79:9, 10. Ezk 20:9, 14, 22.
Turn from. Dt 13:17. Nu 25:4. Jsh 7:26. Ezr
10:14. Ps 78:38. 85:3. Jon 3:9.
repent. ver. 14. Je +18:8. Zc 8:14.
13 **Remember**. Ge 32:12. Le 26:42. Dt 7:8. 9:27.
2 S 7:25. 1 K 8:25. Ps 119:58. Lk 1:54, 55.
to whom. Ge 22:16. 26:3, 4. He 6:13, 14.
I will multiply. Ge +12:2. +28:13, 14. 48:16.
as. Ge +15:5.
for ever. Heb. *olam*, Ex +12:24.
14 **repented**. 1 Ch 21:15. Je +18:8.
15 **turned**. Ex 24:18. Dt 9:15.
the testimony. Ex +16:34. Dt 5:22.
written. Re 5:1.
16 **the tables**. Ex +24:12.
writing. Ex +31:18.
17 **Joshua**. Ex 17:9. 24:13.
they shouted. ver. 18. Ezr 3:11-13. Ps 47:1.
There is a noise. Jsh 6:5, 10, 16, 20. Jg
15:14. 1 S 4:5, 6. 17:20, 52. Jb 39:25. Je
51:14. Am 1:14. 2:2.
18 **being overcome**. Heb. weakness. Jl 3:10.
but the. Ex 15:1, etc. Da 5:4, 23.
19 **he saw**. ver. 4-6. Dt 9:16, 17.
the dancing. Ex 15:20. 2 S 6:14. La 5:15.
anger. ver. 11. Nu 12:3. Mt 5:22. Mk 3:5.
10:14. Ep 4:26.
brake them. Dt 9:17. 27:26. Ps 40:8. Je
31:32. Zc 11:10, 11, 14.

20 **took the calf**. ver. +4.
burnt. Ex +23:24.
made the. Ps 109:18. Pr 1:31. 14:14.
21 **What did**. Ge 20:9. 26:10. Dt 13:6-8. Jsh
7:19-26. 1 S 26:19. 1 K 14:16. 21:22. 2 K
21:9-11.
22 **anger**. Dt 9:20.
knowest. Ex 14:11. 15:24. 16:2-4, 20, 28.
17:2-4. Dt 9:7, 24.
that they are. Dt 31:27. 1 S 15:24. Ps 36:4.
Pr 4:16. Ro 3:10.
23 **they said**. ver. 1-4, 8.
we wot. Ac 7:40.
24 **So they**. ver. 4. Ge 3:12, 13. Lk 10:29. Ro
3:10.
25 **naked**. Is +20:2.
Aaron. Dt 9:20. 2 Ch 28:19.
shame. Ge +2:25.
their enemies. Heb. those that rose up
against them.
26 **camp**. He 13:13.
Who is on. Jsh 5:13. 2 S 20:11. 2 K 9:32. Mt
12:30. Lk 11:23.
come unto. Jsh 24:15.
all. Ex +9:6.
27 **sword**. Ep 6:17.
slay every man. ver. 26, 29. Nu 25:5, 7-12.
Dt 33:8, 9. Lk 14:26. 2 C 5:16.
28 **children**. Dt 33:9. Ml 2:4-6.
there fell. Nu 16:32-35, 41. 1 C 10:8. He 2:2,
3.
29 **For**. *or*, another reading of this verse is: And
Moses said, Consecrate yourselves today to
the Lord; because every man hath been
against his son and against his brother, etc. Ml
4:5, 6.
Moses. Nu 25:11-13. Dt 13:6-11. 33:9, 10. 1
S 15:18-22. Pr 21:3. Jl 2:12-14. Zc 13:3. Mt
10:37.
Consecrate. Heb. fill your hands. Ex +28:41.
30 **Ye have**. ver. 31. 1 S 2:17. 12:20, 23. 2 S
12:9. 2 K 17:21. Ps 25:11. Lk 7:47. 15:18.
peradventure. 2 S 16:12. Am 5:15. Jon 3:9.
2 T 2:25.
an atonement. ver. 32. Le +4:20. Nu 16:44-
47. Jb 42:7, 8. Ro 9:3. Ja +5:16.
31 **returned**. Ex 34:28. Dt 9:18, 19.
sinned. ver. 30. Ezr 9:6, 7, 15. Ne 9:33. Da
9:5, 8, 11.
made. Ex 20:4, 23.
32 **if thou**. Nu 14:19. Da 9:18, 19. Is 1:18. Am
7:2. Lk 23:34.
their sin. Ge 30:27.
blot. ver. 10. Is 4:2. Jn 10:27, 28. Ro 9:3. Re
+3:5.
me. Is 53:4-6. 1 P 2:24.
thy book. ver. 33. Ps 69:28. Da 7:10. Ml
3:16. Re +3:5.
33 **Whosoever**. Ps 49:7, 8. Je 15:1.
sinned. Le 23:30. Ps 69:28. Ezk 18:4.

blot out. ver. 32. Ps 51:1. Is 43:25. 44:22.
my book. ver. +32. Ps 109:13, 14.
34 **mine Angel**. Ex 14:19. 23:20. 33:2, 14, 15.
Nu 20:16. Is 63:9.
the day. Ex +20:5. Nu 14:27-30. Dt 32:35. 2
S 7:14. Ps 89:32. 94:23. 99:8. Je +11:22mg.
43:11. Ho 12:2mg. Am 3:14. Ml +3:5. Mt
23:35. Ro 2:4-6.
35 **they made**. ver. 25. 2 S 12:9, 10. Je 2:19. Mt
27:3-7. Ac 1:18. 7:41.

EXODUS 33

1 **Depart**. Ex 32:24.
thou hast. Ex 17:3. 20:2. 32:1, 7. Dt 5:6.
the land. Ge 22:16-18.
Unto. Ge +13:15. 15:18.
2 **an angel**. Ex +23:20.
drive. Ex +23:20.
the Canaanite. Ge +10:18.
Amorite. Ge +10:16.
Hittite. Dt +20:17.
Perizzite. Ge +13:7.
Hivite. Ge +10:17.
Jebusite. Ge +10:16.
3 **a land**. Ex +3:8.
for I. ver. 15-17. Ex 32:10, 14. Nu 14:12. Dt
32:26, 27. 1 S 2:30. Je 18:7-10. Ezk 3:18, 19.
33:13-16. Jon 3:4, 10.
stiffnecked. 2 Ch +30:8. Ps 78:8. Ac 7:51.
lest I. Ex 23:21. 32:10. Nu 16:21, 45. Am
3:13, 14. Hab 1:13.
4 **they mourned**. Nu 14:1, 39. Ho 7:14. Zc 7:3,
5.
and no. Le 10:6. 2 S 19:24. 1 K 21:27. 2 K
19:1. Ezr 9:3. Est 4:1-4. Jb 1:20. 2:12. Is
32:11. Ezk 24:17, 23. 26:16. Jon 3:6.
5 **Ye are**. ver. 3. Nu 16:45, 46.
in a moment. Nu 16:21, 45. Jb 34:20. Ps
73:19. La 4:6.
put off. Is 22:12.
I may. Ge 18:21. 22:12. Dt 8:2. Ps 139:23.
6 **stripped**. ver. 4. Ex 32:3. Je 2:19.
7 **the tabernacle**. Ex 26:1. Nu 16:24.
afar off. Jsh 3:4. Ps 10:1. 35:22. Pr 15:29. Is
59:2. Ho 9:12.
the Tabernacle of the congregation. Ex
+27:21. +29:42, 43.
sought. Dt 4:29. 2 S 21:1. Ps 27:8. Is 55:6, 7.
Mt 7:7, 8.
unto the. Nu 11:16, 17. 16:19-22. 20:6.
without. Le +4:12.
8 **and stood**. Nu 16:27.
until. 1 T 2:5.
9 **cloudy**. Ex +13:21.
talked. ver. 11. Ex 20:22. 25:22. 31:18. Ge
17:3, 22. 18:33. Nu 7:89. 11:17. 12:8. Dt 4:33,
36. 5:4. Ne 9:13. Ezk 3:22. He 12:25, 26.
10 **worshipped**. Ex 4:31. 1 K 8:14, 22. Lk
18:13.

11 **spake**. ver. +9.
face. Dt +5:4.
his friend. 2 Ch +20:7. Jb 16:21. Is 42:8. Jn 3:29. 11:11. 15:14, 15. Ja 2:23.
his servant. Ex 17:9. 24:13. 32:17.
Nun. i.e. *noon, fish; eternal*. **S#5126h**. ver. 11. Nu 11:28. 13:8, 16. 14:6, 30, 38. 26:65. 27:18. 32:12, 28. 34:17. Dt 1:38. 31:23. 32:44. 34:9. Jsh 1:1. 2:1, 23. 6:6. 14:1. 17:4. 19:49, 51. 21:1. 24:29. Jg 2:8. 1 K 16:34. Ne 8:17.
departed not. Pr 8:34. Lk 2:37.

12 **See**. ver. 1. Ex 32:34.
I know. ver. 17. Ge +18:19. Ps 1:6. +40:17. Is 43:1. Je 1:5. Am 3:2. Jn +10:3, 14, 15. 2 T 2:19.

13 **if**. ver. 15, 17, 18. Ex 34:9. Ps 16:11. 103:7.
show. Ps 25:4. 27:11. 86:11. 119:33. SS 1:7, 8. Is 30:21.
thy way. Nu 12:7, 8. Dt 29:29. Ps 103:7.
know thee. ver. 18. Ps +9:10. Jn 17:3. Ep 1:17. Col +1:10. 2 P +3:18.
consider. Ex 32:7. Dt 9:26, 29. +32:43. Is 63:17, 19. Jl 2:17. Ro 11:28.

14 **My presence**. Ex 13:21. 40:34-38. Jsh 1:5. Ps 32:8. Is 63:9. Mt 28:20.
rest. Dt 3:20. Jsh 21:44. 22:4. 23:1. Ps 95:11. Je 6:16. Mt 11:28. He 4:8, 9.

15 **thy presence**. ver. 3. Ex 34:9. Ge +19:13. Ps 4:6.

16 **wherein**. Ps 73:24.
in that. Nu 14:14. Mt 1:23.
separated. Ex 8:22. +19:5, 6. 34:10. Dt 4:7, 34. 2 S 7:23. Ps 147:20.
face. Ge +1:2.

17 **I will do**. Ge 18:32. 19:21. Is +65:24. Jn 16:23. Ja +5:16. 1 J 5:14, 15.
thou hast. ver. 12. Ge 6:8. 19:19, 21. Mt 17:5.
know thee. ver. +12. Est 2:14. Ps +40:17.

18 **show me**. ver. 20. Ps 4:6. Jn 1:18. 1 T 6:16. T 2:13. 1 J 3:2.
glory. Ex 24:16, 17. Ps 84:11. Is +40:5. Lk 9:32.

19 **all my goodness**. Ne 9:25. Ps 25:13mg. 65:4. Je 31:12, 14. Zc 9:17. Ro 2:4. Ep 1:6-8.
proclaim. Dt +28:58. Is 7:14. 9:6. 12:4.
I will be gracious. Ex +34:6, 7. Ro 9:15, 16-18, 23.
to whom. Dt 7:6, 7. Mt 20:15. Ro 9:10-24. 11:4-6, 23-36. Ep 1:5.

20 **not see**. Ge +32:30. He 1:3. 1 J 3:2. Re 1:16, 17.
face. Ge +19:13.

21 **place by**. Dt 5:31. Jsh 20:4. Is 56:5. Zc 3:7. Lk 15:1.

22 **in a clift**. Ge 49:24. Ps 18:2. 27:5. SS 2:3. Is 2:21. 32:2. 1 C 10:4. 2 C 5:19.
rock. Ex 17:6. 1 K 19:9. Is 32:2. Jn 19:34.
cover thee. Dt 33:12. Ps 91:1, 4. Is 49:2. 51:16.

23 **thou shalt**. ver. +20. Jb 11:7. 26:14.
back parts. Ps +121:5.
face. Ge +19:13. Re 22:4.

EXODUS 34

1 **Hew**. Ex +31:18. 32:16, 19. Dt 10:1, 2. 2 C 3:3.
I will. ver. 28. Dt 10:1-4.
the words. Ps 119:89.
which. Ex 32:19. Dt 9:15-17.

2 **in the morning**. Ge +21:14. 22:3.
in the top. Ex 19:20, 24. 24:12. Dt 9:25.

3 **come**. Ex 19:12, 13, 21. Le 16:17. Mk 9:15. 1 T 2:5. He 12:20.

5 **descended**. Ex 19:18. 33:9. Nu 11:17, 25. 1 K 8:10-12. Lk 9:34, 35.
the name. Nu 14:17. Dt +28:58. Ps +9:10. 102:21.

6 **passed**. Ex 33:20-23. 1 K 19:11.
proclaimed. Nu 14:17-19. Is 12:4.
The Lord. Ex 3:13-16.
God. Heb. *El*. Ex +15:2.
merciful. Ex +20:6. 33:19. Nu 14:18. Dt 4:31. 5:10. 2 S +7:15. 24:14. 1 K 8:23. 1 Ch 16:34. 21:13. 2 Ch 5:13. 7:3, 6. 20:21. 30:9. Ezr 3:11. Ne 1:5. 9:17, 31, 32. Ps +4:1. +5:7. +25:6. 36:7. 57:10. 62:12. 86:5, 15. 89:1. 100:5. 103:8-14, 17. 106:1, 45. 107:1, 43. 109:21. 111:4. 112:4. 118:1. 119:77, 124, 156. 130:7. 136:1. 138:8. 145:8, 9. Is 54:7. 55:7. 63:7, +15. Je +29:11. 33:11. La 3:22, 32. Da 9:9, 18. Jl 2:13. Jon +4:2. Mi 7:18. Mk 5:19. Lk 1:50, 54, 58, 72, 78. 6:36. 8:39. 18:13. Ro +2:4. +12:1. 15:9. 2 C 1:3. Ga 6:16. Ep +2:4. Ph 2:27. T 3:5. He 4:16. Ja 5:11. 1 P 1:3. 2:10.
and gracious. Nu +6:25. 2 S 12:22. 2 K 13:23. Jb 33:24. Ps 77:9. 116:5. Is +30:18. 33:2. Am 5:15. Ml 1:9.
longsuffering. Nu +14:18. Is 48:9. Ezk 20:17. Ro 9:22. 1 P 3:20. 2 P 3:9.
abundant. Ps 31:19. Is 55:7. Mi 7:18. Ro 2:4. 5:20, 21. Ep 1:7, 8.
goodness. Ex 18:9. 33:19. Ge 1:31. 1 K 8:66. 2 Ch 5:13. 7:3. 30:18. Ezr 3:11. 7:9. 8:18. Ne 9:13, 20, 25. Ps 23:6. 25:7. 31:19. 34:8. 65:11. 68:10. 73:1. 86:5. 100:5. 106:1. 107:1. 118:1. 119:39. 135:3. +136:1. 143:10. 145:7, +9. Is 63:7. Je 31:12. 33:11. La 3:25. Ho 3:5. Na 1:7. Mt 7:11. 19:17. 20:15. +28:19. Mk +10:18. Lk +6:35. 11:13. 18:19. Ac 14:17. Ro 2:4. 7:12. 11:22. Ga 5:22. Ja 1:17.
truth. Nu 23:19. Dt 32:4. 1 S 15:29. Ps 19:9. 57:3, 10. 89:14. 91:4. 108:4. 111:8. 117:2. 119:142. 138:2. 146:6. Is 25:1. La 3:23. Da 4:37. Mi 7:20. Mt +28:19. Jn 1:17. 7:28. Ro 3:3, 4. T +1:2. 1 P +4:19. Re 15:3.

7 **Keeping**. Ex 20:6. Dt 5:10. Ne 1:5. 9:32. Ps 86:15. Je 32:18. Da 9:4.
forgiving. Ex 32:32. Ps +32:5. 85:2, 3. 130:4.

Is 33:24. 40:2. Je 50:20. Da 9:9. Mi 7:18. Mt 6:14, 15. 12:31. 18:32-35. Ac 5:31. 13:38. Ro 4:7, 8. Ep 1:7. 1 J 1:9.

that will by no means clear the guilty. Ex 23:7, 21. Nu 14:18-23. Dt 32:35. Jsh 24:19. Jb 10:14. Ps 9:16, 17. 11:5, 6. 58:10, 11. 136:10, 15. Is 45:21. Je 49:12. Mi 6:11. Na 1:2, 3, 6. Ro 2:4-9. 3:19-26. 9:22, 23. He 12:29. Re 20:15. 21:8.

visiting. Ex +20:5.

8 bowed his head. Ge +24:26.

9 If now. Ex 33:13, 17.

let my Lord. Ex 33:14-16. Mt 28:20.

stiffnecked. 2 Ch +30:8.

pardon. Nu 14:19. Ps 25:11.

take us. Ex 19:5. Dt 32:9. Ps 28:9. 33:12. 78:62. +94:14. 135:4. Je 10:16. Zc 2:12.

10 I make. Ex 24:7, 8. Dt 4:13. 5:2, 3. 29:12-14. Jsh 24:25.

I will do marvels. Dt 4:32-37. 32:20. Jsh 6:20. 10:12, 13. 2 S 7:23. Ps 77:14. 78:12. 147:20.

a terrible. Ps +99:3. 106:22. 145:6. Je 32:21.

11 Observe. Dt 4:1, 2, 40. 5:32. 6:3, 25. 12:28, 32. 28:1. Mt 28:20. Jn 14:21.

I drive. Ex 3:8, 17. +23:30. Ge 15:18-21.

Amorite. Ge +10:16.

Canaanite. Ge +10:18.

Hittite. Dt +20:17.

Perizzite. Ge +13:7.

Hivite. Ge +10:17.

Jebusite. Ge +10:16.

12 Take heed. Ex +23:32.

lest. Ex +23:33.

13 ye shall. Ex +23:24.

images. Heb. statues. **S#4676h**. Ex 24:4 (pillars). Ge 28:18 (pillar), 22. 31:13, 45, 51, 52. 2 K +17:10mg. Is 19:19.

groves. 2 K +17:10.

14 worship. Ex +20:3-5. Dt 4:24. 5:7, 9. 6:13. 10:20. 11:16. Jsh 24:14, 19. Ps 29:2. Da 3:5. Na 1:2. Mt 4:9, 10. 6:24. Lk 4:7. Jn 20:28. Re 19:10. 22:9.

whose. ver. 5-7. Ex 33:19. Is 9:6. 57:15.

jealous God. Ex +20:5. Ja 4:4.

15 make. ver. 10, +12.

whoring. Ge +4:1. Le 17:7. 20:5, 6. Nu 15:39. 31:17, 18. Dt 31:16. Jg 2:17. 8:27, 33. 1 K 9:22. 1 Ch 5:25. 2 Ch 21:11, 13. Ps 73:27. 106:39. Is 57:3. Je 3:1, 2, 6, 9. Ezk 6:9. 16:15, 17, 22, 25. 20:30. 23:3, 7, 8, 11, 19, 43. Ho 1:2. 2:2, 5, 13. 4:12. 5:3, 4. 6:10. 9:1. Na 3:4. Ml 2:11. Jn 8:41. 1 C 10:20. Ja 4:4. 2 P 2:14mg. Re 2:14, 20-22. 17:1-5. 18:3, 9. 19:2.

call thee. Nu 25:2. 1 C 10:27.

eat. Ps 106:28. 1 C 8:4, 7, 10. 10:20, 21. Re 2:20.

16 thou take. Nu 25:1, 2. Jg +3:6.

17 no molten gods. Ex 32:4, 8. Le 19:4. Nu 33:52. Dt 9:12, 16. 27:15. Jg 17:4. 1 K 14:9. 2

Ch 34:3. Is 41:29. 42:17. 44:10. 46:6. Je 10:14. 51:17. Ho 13:2. Na 1:14. Hab 2:18. Ac 17:29. 19:26.

18 feast of unleavened. Ex 12:15-20. 13:4, 6, 7. 23:15. Le +23:6. Dt 16:1-4. Mk 14:1. Lk 22:1. Ac 12:3.

19 openeth. Ex 13:2, 12. 22:29. Nu 18:15-17. Ezk 44:30. Lk 2:23.

matrix. **S#7358h**. Ex 13:2 (womb), 12, 15. 34:19. Ge 20:18. 29:31. 30:22. Nu 3:12. 8:16. 12:12. 18:15. 1 S 1:5, 6. Jb 3:11. 10:18. 24:20. 31:15. 38:8. Ps 22:10. 58:3. 110:3. Je 1:5. 20:17, 17, 18. Ho 9:14.

20 firstling. Ex 13:10. Nu 18:15.

ass. Ex +13:13.

lamb. *or*, kid. Ex 12:3.

All the. Ex 13:15. Nu 3:45-51.

none. 1 Ch +21:24.

21 Six. Ex +20:9-11. 23:12. 35:2. Ge 2:3. Dt 5:12-15. Lk +13:14. 23:56.

earing time. Ge 45:6. Dt 21:4. 1 S 8:12. Is 30:24.

22 feast of weeks. Ex 23:16. Nu 28:16-31. 29:12-39. Le +23:15. Dt 16:10-15. Jn 7:2. Ac 2:1.

firstfruits. Le +23:10.

year's end. Heb. revolution of the year. 2 Ch +24:23mg.

23 Thrice. Ex 23:14, 17. Dt 16:16. Ps 84:7.

the God. Ge 32:28. 33:20.

24 I will. ver. 11. Ex 23:27-30. 33:2. Le 18:24. Dt 7:1. Ps 78:55. 80:8.

enlarge. Ex 23:31. Dt 12:20. 19:8. 1 Ch 4:10.

desire. Ge +35:5. Jb 1:10. Pr +16:7. Ac 18:10.

when. 1 S 2:30. Mt 6:33. He 10:25.

25 leaven. Ex 12:20. 23:18. Dt 16:3. 1 C 5:7, 8.

be left. Ex 12:10. 23:18. 29:34. Le 7:15. Nu 9:12.

26 first. Mt 6:33.

firstfruits. Le +23:10.

seeth. Ex 23:19. Dt 14:21.

27 Write. Ex 17:14. 24:4, 7. Dt 31:9.

I have. ver. +10. Dt 4:13. 31:9.

28 forty days. Jon +3:4. Mt 4:2.

he wrote. ver. 1. Ex 31:18. Is 49:8.

commandments. Heb. words. Dt 4:13.

29 A.M. 2513. B.C. 1491.

two tables. Ex +32:15.

wist. Ex 16:15. Jsh 2:4. 8:14. Jg 16:20. Mk 9:6. 14:40. Lk 2:49. Jn 5:13. Ac 12:9. 23:5. Ro 10:4.

the skin. Mt 17:2. Lk 9:29. Ac 6:15. 2 C 3:7-9, 13. Re 1:16. 10:1.

face shone. ver. 30, 35. Ps 67:1. Mt 17:2. Ac 6:15. 2 C 3:7.

30 face. Mt 17:2.

afraid. Nu 12:8. Mk 9:3, 15. Lk 5:8.

31 called. Ex 3:16. 24:1-3.

and Moses talked. Ge 45:3, 15.

32 **he gave**. Ex 21:1. Nu 15:40. 1 K 22:14. Mt 28:20. 1 C 11:23. 15:3.

33 **a vail**. Nu 12:3. Mk 4:33. Ro 10:4. 1 C 2:1-3. 9:22. 2 C 3:13-18. 4:4-6.

34 **he took**. 2 C 3:16. He 4:16. 10:19-22.

35 **saw the face**. ver. 29, 30. Ec 8:1. Da 12:3. Mt 5:16. 13:43. Jn 5:35. Ph 2:15.

EXODUS 35

1 **These**. Ex ch. 25. 31:1-11. 34:32.
do them. Mt 7:21-27. Ro 2:13. Ja 1:22.

2 **Six days**. Ex +20:9, 10. 23:12. 31:13-16. 34:21. Ge 2:3. Le 23:3. Dt 5:12-15. Lk +13:14.
an holy day. Heb. holiness. ver. 19, 21. Ex 26:33. +31:15. 39:1. 40:13. Le 21:6. 22:2, etc.
whosoever doeth work. Nu 15:32-36. Dt 5:12-14. Je 17:27. Ezk 20:15, 16, 20, 21. 22:26, 31. Lk 13:14, 15. Jn 5:16. He 2:2, 3. 10:28, 29.

3 **kindle no fire**. Ex 12:16. 16:23. Nu 15:32, etc. Is +58:13.

4 **This is**. Ex 25:1, 2.

5 **whosoever**. Mk 12:41-44.
willing. Le +23:38.
gold. 1 Ch 22:14, 16. 28:14-18. 2 Ch 4:19-22. Jb 22:25mg. Jn 1:1. 1 C 3:12. 2 P 1:4. Re 3:18. 21:18, 21.

6 **blue**. Ex +25:4. 26:1, 31, 36. 28:5, 6, 15, 33.
goats' hair. Ex +26:7, 8-14.

8 **And oil**. Ex +27:20.
spices. Ex 25:6. 30:23, 28.
sweet incense. Ex +39:38.

9 **onyx stones**. Ge +2:12.

10 **wise hearted**. Ex 31:1-6. 36:1-4. 1 P 4:10.

11 **tabernacle**. Ex +38:21.
taches. Ex +26:6.

12 **ark**. Ex 25:10-22. 37:1-9.
the vail. Ex 26:7, 31-33. 36:35, 36.

13 **The table**. Ex +25:23.
showbread. Ex +25:30.

14 **candlestick**. or, lampstand. Ex +25:31. Ps 148:3.

15 **the incense**. Ex 30:1-10, 22-38. 37:25-28. Ps 141:2.
the hanging. Ex 26:36, 37. 36:37, 38.

16 **The altar**. Ex +40:6.
the laver. Ex +30:18.

17 **The hangings**. Ex 27:9-19. 38:9-20. 2 S 7:2.

18 **The pins**. Ex +27:19.

19 **The cloths**. Ex +31:10. 39:1, 41. Nu 4:5-15.
the holy. Ex 28. 39:1-31.

21 **whose heart**. ver. 5, 22, 26, 29. Ex 25:2. 36:2. Jg 5:3, 9, 12. 2 S 7:27. 1 Ch 28:2, 9. 29:3, 5, 6, 9, 14, 17, 18. Ezr 1:5, 6. 7:27. Ps 110:3. Je 30:21. Pr 4:23. Mt 12:34. 2 C 8:12. 9:7.
spirit. Heb. *ruach*, Ge +41:8.
offering. Le +23:38.

22 **brought**. Ex 32:2, 3.
bracelets. Ex 32:3. 35:11. 2 K 19:28. Is 3:19. 37:29. Ezk 16:11. 19:4, 9. 29:4.
earrings. Ge 24:22.
tablets. Nu 31:50.
every man. 1 Ch 29:6, 7. 2 Ch 24:9-14. Ezr 2:68, 69. Ne 7:70-72. Is 60:9, 13. Mt 2:11. Mk 12:41-44.

23 **blue**. ver. 6-10. Ex 25:2-7. 1 Ch 29:8.

24 **whom**. 2 C 8:12.

25 **wise hearted**. Ex 28:3. 31:6. 36:1. 2 K 23:7. Pr 14:1. 31:19-24. Lk 8:2, 3. Ac 9:39. Ro 16:1-4, 6, 12. Ga 3:28. Ph 4:3.

26 **whose heart**. ver. 21, 29. Ex 36:8.

27 **onyx**. ver. 9. 1 Ch 29:6. Ezr 2:68.

28 **spice**. ver. 8. Ex 30:23-38.

29 **willing offering**. Le +23:38.
whose heart. ver. 21, 22. Jg 5:2, 9. 1 Ch 29:3, 6, 9, 10, 14, 17. 1 C 9:17. 2 C 9:7.
the Lord. ver. 4. Dt 4:2. 11:32. 12:32. Is +8:20. Mt 28:20. 1 C 3:5. Ga 6:16. 2 T 3:15-17. 2 P 1:19.

30 **See**. Ex 31:2-6. 1 K 7:13, 14. Is 28:26. 1 C 3:10. 12:4, 11. Ja 1:17.

31 **And he**. Ex +31:3. Nu 11:25, 26. 27:18. Is 11:2-5. 28:26. 61:1-3. 1 C 12:4-10. Col 2:3. Ja 1:17.
spirit. Heb. *ruach*, Ge +41:38.
workmanship. 2 Ch 2:7, 14.

34 **he hath**. Ex +18:20, 21. Ezr 7:10, 27. Ne 2:12. Ja 1:16, 17.
teach. Ps 94:10.
Aholiab. Ex 31:6. 2 Ch 2:14. Is 28:24-29. 1 C 1:5-7. 12:7.

35 **he filled**. ver. 31. Ex 31:3, 6. 1 K 3:12. 7:14. 2 Ch 2:14. Is 28:26.
the cunning. Ex 26:1. Ac 19:6, 8. 1 C 1:5, 7. 12:4, 8, 12. Ga 3:2, 5. 1 T 3:15. 4:16. 2 T 2:15.
of the weaver. Jb 7:6. Is 38:12.

EXODUS 36

1 **Bezaleel**. Ex +31:2.
wise hearted man. Ex 28:3. 31:6.
for the service. ver. 3, 4. Ex 25:8. Nu 7:9. He 8:2.
according. Ex 23:21, 22. 39:1-43. 40. Ps 119:6. Mt 28:20. Lk 1:6.

2 **in whose**. Ex 28:3. 31:6. 35:10, 21-35. Ac 6:3, 4. 14:23. Col 4:17. He 5:4.
one whose. Ex 35:2, 21, 25, 26. 1 Ch 29:5.

3 **the offering**. Ex 35:5-21, 27, 29.
free offerings. Le +23:38.
every morning. Ps 5:3. 101:8. Pr 8:15. Is 50:4. Je 21:12.

4 **wise men**. 2 Ch 24:13. Mt 24:45. Lk 12:42. 1 C 3:10.

5 **much more**. Ex 32:3. 2 Ch 24:14. 31:6-10. 2 C 8:2, 3. Ph 2:21. +4:17, 18.

6 **gave commandment**. Ex 35:21-29. 38:8. Ge

14:21. 28:22. 45:18-20. Le 26:10. Nu 7:1-88.
31:48-54. 2 S 8:10, 11. 2 Ch 31:10. Pr 11:25.
Ml 3:10. Lk 5:6, 7. 6:38. 12:16, 17. Jn 21:6-
11.

proclaimed. 2 Ch 30:5. 36:22. Ezr 1:1mg.
10:7. Ne 8:15.

restrained. Ge 8:2. Ezk 31:15.

7   **and too much**. ver. +6. 2 Ch 31:10.
Ml 3:10.

8   **wise**. Ex 31:6. 35:10.

made. Ex 26:1-37. 1 Ch 15:1.

cherubims. Ex +25:18, 22. Ge 3:24. 1 K
6:23. 2 Ch 3:10. Ezk 1:5, etc. 10:1-19.

10   **coupled**. Ex 26:3. Ps 122:3. 133:1. Zp 3:9. Ac
2:1. 1 C 1:10. 12:20, 27. Ep 1:23. 2:21, 22.
4:2-6. Ph 2:2. 3:15.

11   **loops**. Ex 26:4.

12   **Fifty loops**. Ex 26:5, 10.

13   **so it became**. 1 C 12:20. Ep 2:20-22. 1 P 2:4,
5.

14   **curtains**. Ex +26:7-13.

19   **covering**. Ex +26:14.

rams' skins dyed red. Ex 25:5.

20   **boards**. Ex +26:15-25. 40:18, 19.

shittim wood. Ex 25:5, 10. Nu 25:1. Dt 10:3.

27   **westward**. Ex 26:22, 27.

29   **coupled**. Heb. twined. Ex 26:24mg. Ps 122:3.
133:1. Ac 2:46. 4:32. 1 C 1:10. 12:13. 2 C
1:10x. Ep 2:15, 19, 21. 3:18, 19. 4:2-6, 15, 16.

30   **under every board two sockets**. Heb. two
sockets, two sockets, under one board. Ex
26:25.

31   **bars**. Ex +25:28. 26:26-29. 30:5.

32   **shittim wood**. Ex 26:26.

the tabernacle. Ex +38:21.

35   **a vail of blue**. Ex +26:31-35. 30:6. 40:21. Mt
27:51. He 10:20.

36   **pillars**. Je 1:18.

37   **an hanging**. Ex 26:36, 37. 40:28.

of needlework. Heb. the work of a needle
worker, or embroiderer. Ex 26:36.

38   **fillets with gold**. Ex 27:10, 11, 17. 38:10,
17, 19, 28.

EXODUS 37

1   **the ark**. Ex 25:10-16. 26:33. 31:7. 40:3, 20,
21. Nu 10:33-36.

2   **he overlaid**. Ex 30:3.

4   **staves**. Ex +25:13. Ac 9:15.

with gold. 1 P 1:7, 18, 19.

5   **the staves**. Nu 1:50. Ex +25:13. 2 S 6:3-7.

6   **mercy seat**. Ex +25:17. Ga 4:4. T 2:14.

pure gold. Jn 1:1, 14. 20:28.

7   **cherubims**. Ex 36:8. 1 K 6:23-29. Ps 80:1.
104:4. Ezk 10:2.

beaten. ver. 22. Ex +27:20. Is 53:5. He +2:10.

8   **on the end**. or, out of, etc.

on the other end. or, out of, etc.

9   **cherubims spread**. Ex 36:8. Ge 3:24. 28:12.

Is 6:2. Ezk 10. Jn 1:51. 2 C 3:18. Ph 3:8. 1 T
3:16. He 1:14.

to the mercy seatward. Ex 25:20. Ep 3:10.
1 P 1:12.

10   **the table**. Ex +25:23. Jn 1:14, 16. Col 1:27.

12   **handbreadth**. Ge +21:16.

16   **dishes**. Ex +25:29. 1 K 7:50. 2 K 12:13. Je
52:18, 19. 2 T 2:20.

cover withal. or, pour out withal.

17   **the candlestick of**. Ex +25:31. Jn 1:4-9.
14:26. Ph 2:15.

20   **almonds**. Ex 25:33. Nu 17:8. Ec 12:5. Je
1:11.

21   **a knop**. Ex 25:35.

22   **were**. Ex 25:31. 1 C 9:27. Col 3:5.

beaten work. ver. +7. Ex +27:20. Ps 51:17.
Is 5:4, 5, 10. 53:5. He +2:10.

23   **seven lamps**. Ex 25:37. Re +1:12. 5:5.

25   **incense altar**. Mt 23:19. Lk +1:11. He 7:25.
13:10. 1 P 2:5.

29   **he made**. Ex +30:23-38. Ps 23:5. 92:10. Is
11:2. 61:1, 3. Jn 3:34. 2 C 1:21, 22. 1 J 2:20,
27.

incense. Ex +39:38. Ps +141:2. He 5:7.
7:25.

sweet spices. 2 C 2:15.

the apothecary. Ex 30:25, 35. Ec 10:1.

EXODUS 38

1   **the altar**. Ex +40:6. Ro 8:3, 4. 12:1. He 3:1.
9:14. 13:10. 1 P 2:5.

**foursquare; and three cubits the height
thereof**. Ezk 43:16. Jn 6:37. He 13:8. Re
21:16.

2   **he made**. Ex +27:2.

brass. Jb 6:12.

3   **he made**. Ex 27:3.

flesh hooks. 1 S 2:13.

5   **the grate**. Ex 27:4.

6   **shittim wood**. Ex 25:6. Dt 10:3.

7   **to bear it withal**. Ac 9:15. 1 C 1:24. 2:2.

8   **the laver**. Ex +30:18-21. Ps 26:6. Jn 13:10. T
3:5, 6. He 9:10. 1 J 3:7. Re 1:5.

looking glasses. or, brazen glasses. Jb 37:18.
Is 3:23mg. 1 C 13:12. Ja 1:23-25.

assembling. Heb. assembling by troops. Nu
4:23. 8:24. 1 S 2:22mg. Ps 84:10. Pr 8:34. Mt
26:69. Lk 2:37. Jn 18:16. Ac 12:13. 1 T 5:5.

9   **the court**. Ex +27:9-19. Ps 89:7. Is 54:2, 3.

14   **hangings**. Ex 27:14.

18   **needlework**. 2 Ch 3:14.

20   **the pins**. ver. 31. Ex +27:19. Ep 2:21, 22. Col
2:19.

21   **sum**. He 8:1, 2.

tabernacle. Ex 25:9. 26:1, 7, 30. 27:9, 19, 21.
30:36. 31:7-9. 35:11, 15, 18. 36:8, 13, 18, 32.
39:32. 40:2, 5, 17, 33, 34. Le 1:1. 8:10. 15:31.
17:4. 26:11. Nu 1:50-53. 3:7, 25, 26, 36, 38.
4:16. 9:15. 10:11, 17, 21. 17:7, 8, 13. 18:2.

Jsh 18:1. 22:19, 29. 2 S 7:6. 1 Ch 6:32, 48. 16:39. 21:29. 23:26. 2 Ch 1:3, 5, 13. 24:6. Ps 78:60. Ezk 37:27. Ac 7:44. He 8:2. 9:11. Re 11:19. 15:5. 21:3.
   of testimony. Ex +16:34.
   by the hand. Nu 4:28-33. Ezr 8:26-30.
   Ithamar. Ex 6:23. 1 Ch 6:3. 24:4.
22 **Bezaleel.** Ex +31:2.
   all that the Lord. Ps 119:6. Je 1:7. Mt 28:20.
23 **Aholiab.** Ex +31:6.
   a cunning. Ex 35:34.
24 **All the gold.** 1 K 6:21, 22, 28, 30. 1 Ch 22:14-16. 29:2-7. Hg 2:8.
   offering. Ex 25:2. 29:24. 35:22.
   the shekel. Ex 30:13, 14, 24. Le 5:15. 27:3, 25. Nu 3:47. 18:16.
26 **bekah.** Ex 30:13. 15, 16. Ge 24:22.
   every man. Heb. a poll. Ex +16:16mg. Nu 1:46.
   every one. Ex 30:11-16. 1 P 1:18, 19.
   six hundred. Ex +12:37.
27 **and the sockets.** Ex 26:19, 21, 25, 32.
28 **and filleted them.** Ex 27:17.
30 **sockets.** Ex 26:37. 27:10, 17.
   the brasen altar. ver. 1-7. Ex 39:39. 2 K 16:14. 2 Ch 1:5. Am +9:1.
31 **And the sockets.** Ex 27:10-12.
   and the sockets. Ex 27:16, 17.
   the pins. ver. +20.

EXODUS 39

1 **the blue.** Ex 25:4. 26:1. 35:23.
   cloths. Ex 31:10. 35:19.
   holy place. Ps 93:5. Ezk 43:12. He 9:12, 25.
   the holy. Ex +28:2-4. Ezk 42:14.
2 **the ephod.** Ex +28:4.
3 **cunning work.** Ex 26:1. 36:8.
5 **curious.** Ex 28:8. 29:5. Le 8:7. 1 S 2:18. Is 11:5. Re 1:13.
   as the Lord. Mt 28:20. 1 C 11:23.
6 **onyx stones.** Ge +2:12.
   ouches. ver. 13, 16, 18. Ex +28:11, 13, 14, 25.
7 **a memorial.** Ex +12:14.
8 **breastplate.** Ex 25:7. 28:4, 13-29. Le 8:8, 9. Ps 89:28. Is 59:17. Ep 6:14. 1 Th 5:8. He 7:24, 25. Re 9:9, 17.
10 **the first row.** Ex 28:16, 17, 21. Re 21:19-21.
   sardius. or, ruby. Ex 28:17. Ezk 28:13.
   topaz. Jb 28:19.
   carbuncle. Ezk 28:13.
11 **emerald.** Ex 28:18. Ezk 27:16.
   sapphire. Jb 28:6, 16.
   diamond. or, sardonyx. Ex 28:18. Ezk 28:13.
12 **ligure.** or, jacinth. Ex 28:19.
   agate. Ex 28:19.
   amethyst. Ex 28:19. Re 21:20.
13 **beryl.** or, chalcedony. Ex 28:20. SS 5:14.
   onyx. ver. 6.

jasper. Ex 28:20. Ezk 28:13. Re 4:3. 21:11, 18, 19.
14 **the names.** Re 21:12.
15 **chains at the ends.** Ex 28:14. 2 Ch 3:5. SS 1:10. Jn 10:28. 17:12. 1 P 1:5. Ju 1.
16 **gold rings.** Ex 25:12.
18 **two wreathen.** Ex 28:14. SS 1:10.
   ephod. ver. 2.
20 **coupling.** Ex 26:3.
21 **as the Lord.** Mt 16:24. 1 C 1:25, 27. 1 P 3:16.
22 **the robe.** Ex 28:31-35.
24 **they made.** Ex 28:33.
   pomegranates. Ga 5:22.
25 **bells.** Ex 28:33, 34. Ps 89:15.
   the pomegranates. SS 4:13.
26 **pomegranate.** Ex 28:34. SS 4:3, 13. 6:7.
   hem. Dt 22:12. Mt 9:20.
27 **coats.** Ex 28:39-42. Le 8:13. Is 61:10. Ezk 44:18. Ro 3:22. 13:14. Ga 3:27. Ph 2:6-8. 1 P 1:13.
   fine. Pr 31:22. Re 19:8.
28 **a mitre.** Ex 28:4, 39. 29:6. Ezk 44:18.
   linen. Ex 28:42.
   bonnets. Ex 29:9. Le 8:13.
   breeches. Ex 28:42. Le 6:10. 16:4. Ezk 44:18.
29 **a girdle.** Ex 28:39. 29:9. Le 8:7, 13. Is 11:5.
   needlework. Ex 38:18, 23.
30 **the plate.** Ex +26:36. 28:36-39. 1 C 1:30. 2 C 5:21. He 1:3. 7:26.
   HOLINESS. Ex 28:36. Zc 14:20. T 2:14. Re 5:10.
32 **all the.** ver. 33, 42. Ex +38:21. Le ch. 8, 9. Nu 4:4-32. Jn 1:14. Col 2:9. 1 J 3:24.
   according. ver. 42, 43. Ex 25:40. 40:32. Dt 12:32. 1 S 15:22. 1 Ch 28:19. Mt 28:20. He 3:2. 8:5.
33 **the tent.** Ex ch. 25-30. 31:7-11. 35:11-19. ch. 36-40.
35 **the mercy seat.** Ex 25:17. He 9:5, 8.
36 **The table.** Ex +25:23.
   the showbread. Ex +25:30.
37 **candlestick.** Ex +25:31.
   even with. Ex 27:21. Mt 5:14-16. Ph 2:15.
38 **golden altar.** Lk +1:11.
   anointing oil. Ex 37:29.
   sweet incense. Heb. the incense of sweet spices. Ex 25:6. 30:7. 31:11. 35:8. 37:29. Le 16:12. Dt +33:10. 2 Ch 2:4.
39 **brasen altar.** Ex +38:30. +40:6.
   laver. Ex +30:18.
40 **court.** Ex 27:9. 35:17. 38:9. 40:7.
   cords. Ex 35:18. Nu 3:26, 37.
   pins. Ex +27:19.
41 **cloths.** ver. 1. Ex 31:10.
   the holy. Ex 28:2.
42 **According.** ver. +32. Ex 23:21, 22. 25-31. 2 T 2:15. 4:7.
   made. Ex 35:10.
43 **did look.** Ex 40:25. Ge 1:31. Ps 104:31.

blessed them. Ge +14:19. Le 9:22, 23. Jsh 22:6. 2 S 6:18. 1 K 8:14. 1 Ch 16:2. 2 Ch 6:3. 30:27. Ne 11:2. Ps 19:11.

EXODUS 40

2 the first month. ver. +17.
tabernacle. ver. 6, 18, 19. Ex +38:21.
3 the ark. ver. 20, 21. Ex 25:10, 22. 26:31, 33, 34. 35:12. 36:35, 36. 37:1-9. Le 16:14. Nu 4:5. Re 11:19. 15:5.
4 the table. ver. 22, 25. Ex 25:23.
the things that, etc. Heb. the order thereof. ver. 23. Ex 39:37. Le 24:5, 6, 8. 2 Ch 2:4. 29:18. Ne 10:33.
the candlestick. ver. 24, 25. Ex +25:31-39. 35:14.
5 the altar. ver. 26, 27. Lk +1:11. Jn 14:6. He 9:24. 10:19-22. 1 J 2:1, 2.
put. ver. 28. Ex 26:36, 37. 36:37, 38.
tabernacle. He 9:11-14.
6 altar of the burnt offering. ver. 10, 29. Ex +27:1-8. 29:12, 13, 16, 44. 30:28. 31:9. 35:16. 38:1-7. Le 4:7, 18. Am +9:1. Ep 1:6, 7. He 13:10. 1 J 2:2. 4:9, 10.
7 the laver. ver. 30-32. Ex +30:18. Ps 26:6. T 3:5. He 10:22. Re 1:5, 6.
8 the court. ver. 33. Ex 27:9-19. 38:9-20. 39:40. Mt 16:18. 1 C 12:28. Ep 4:11, 12.
9 the anointing oil. Ex 30:23-33. 37:29. 39:39. Le 8:10. Nu 7:1. Ps 45:7. Is 11:2. 61:1. Mt 3:16. Jn 3:34. 2 C 1:4, 22. 1 J 2:20, 27.
10 sanctify. Ex 29:36, 37. Le 8:11. Is 11:2. 61:1. Jn 3:34. 17:19.
most holy. Heb. holiness of holinesses. Le +2:3. Lk 1:35. 1 C 1:30. 2 C 5:21. He 7:26.
12 bring Aaron. Ex 29:1-35. Le 8:1-13. 9. Is 11:1-5. 61:1-3. Mt 3:16. Lk 1:35. Jn 3:34. Ro 8:3. Ga 4:4.
unto the door. Ex 30:19, 21. Le 8:4-6. 16:24. 1 K 7:23.
wash. Heb. *rahats*, Ex +29:4.
with water. Ac +1:5.
13 anoint him. Ex +28:41. Jn 17:19. He 10:10, 29.
14 bring his sons. Is 44:3-5. 61:10. Jn 1:16. Ro 8:30. 13:14. 1 C 1:9, 30.
15 as. Jn 3:34. 1 J 2:20.
everlasting. Heb. *olam*, Ex 12:14. +12:24. 30:31, 33. Nu 25:13. Ps 110:4. He ch. 5. 7:3, 7, 17-24. ch. 8-10.
16 according. ver. 19, 21, 23, 25, 27, 32. Ex 23:21, 22. 39:42, 43. Dt 4:2. 12:32. Is +8:20. Mt 28:20. Jn 15:10. 1 C 4:2.

17 the first month. ver. 1, 2. Ex 12:1, 2. 13:4. Nu 7:1. 9:1.
18 reared. ver. 2. Ex 26:15-30. 36:20-34. Le 26:11. Ezk 37:27, 28. Jn 1:14. Ga 4:4. 1 P 1:5. Re 21:3.
and fastened. Is 33:26. Mt 16:18. 1 T 3:15.
19 the tent. Ex 26:1-14. 36:8-19.
20 the testimony. Ex +16:34. Ps 40:8. Mt 3:15.
mercy. ver. 3. Ex +25:17. Ro 10:4.
21 he brought. ver. 3. Ex 26:33. 35:12.
and covered. He 10:19, 20.
22 he put. Jn 6:53-57. Ep 3:8.
northward. ver. 24. Ex 26:35.
23 set. ver. 4. Ex 25:30. Mt 12:4. He 9:2.
bread. Re 2:17.
24 the candlestick. Ex +25:31. Ps 119:105. Jn 1:1, 5, 9. 8:12.
25 he lighted. ver. 4. Ex 25:37. Re 4:5.
26 golden altar. ver. +5. Mt 23:19. Jn 11:42. 17. He 7:25. 10:1. 1 J 2:1.
27 he burnt. Ex 30:7.
28 set up. ver. 5. Ex 26:36, 37. 38:9-19. Jn 10:9. 14:6. Ep 2:18. He 10:19, 20.
29 the altar. ver. +6. Ro 3:24-26. He 9:12. 13:5, 6, 10.
offered. Ex 29:38, etc.
burnt offering. Le +23:12.
meat offering. Le +23:13.
30 laver. ver. 7. Ex +30:18, 19-21. Ezk 36:25. He 10:22.
31 washed. Ps 26:6. 51:6, 7. Jn 13:10. 1 J 1:7, 9.
feet. Jn 13:10.
32 washed. Jn 13:10.
as the Lord. ver. 19. Ex 30:19, 20. Ps 73:19.
33 up the court. ver. 8. Ex 27:9-16. Nu 1:50. Mt 16:8. 1 C 12:12, 28. Ep 4:11-13. He 9:6, 7.
tabernacle. Ex +38:21.
hanging. Jn 10:9. 14:6. Ep 2:18. He 4:14-16.
So Moses. Ex 39:32. 1 K 6:9. Zc 4:9. Jn 4:34. 17:4. 2 T 4:7. He 3:2-5.
34 a cloud. Ex +13:21. 25:8, 21, 22. 29:43. Ezk 43:4-7. Hg 2:7, 9. Re 15:8. 21:3, 23, 24.
35 not able. 2 Ch 5:14. Is 2:10. Re 15:8.
cloud. ver. +34. 2 S 6:2. Ps 80:1. Is 37:16. Ezk 9:3.
glory. Ex +24:16. Zc +2:5. Jn 1:14. Ep 2:21, 22. Col 2:9. He 9:24.
36 when. Ex +13:21, 22. 2 C 5:19, 20.
went onward. Heb. journeyed. ver. 37.
37 if the cloud. Nu 9:19-22. Ps 31:15. Pr 3:5, 6.
38 the cloud. Ex +13:21.
fire. Ps 78:14. 105:39. Is 4:5, 6. He 12:29. 1 J 1:5.
throughout. Ne 9:19.

LEVITICUS

LEVITICUS 1

1 A.M. 2514. B.C. 1490.

called. Ex 19:3. 24:1, 2, 12. 29:42. Jn 1:17. 2 P 1:17.

unto Moses. Nu 12:7, 8. He 3:5.

spake. Ex 29:42. Jn 8:26. He 1:2.

out of. Ex 25:22. 33:7. 39:32. 40:34, 35. Nu 12:4, 5. He 9:11.

2 **If any.** Le 22:18, 19. Ge 4:3-5. 1 Ch 16:29. Ro 12:1, 6. Ep 5:2.

an offering. lit. korban. ver. 3, 10, 14. Le 2:1, 4, 5, 7, 12. Ne 10:34. 13:31. Ezk 20:28. 40:43. Mk 7:11.

3 **a burnt.** Le 8:18, 21. +23:12. Ex 32:6. 38:1. He 10:8-10.

without blemish. ver. 10. Le 3:1. 4:3, 23. 5:15. 6:6. 22:19-25. Ex 12:5. 29:1. Dt 15:21. 17:1. Ezk 43:23. 45:18. Zc 13:7. Ml 1:7, 8, 14. Lk +1:35. Jn 1:36. 8:46. 14:30. Ep 5:27. He +4:15. 7:26. 9:14. 1 P 1:18, 19. 2:22-24. 3:18.

own voluntary will. Le +23:38. Ps 40:8. 110:3. Is 50:6. Jn 10:11, 15, 17, +18. 15:13. Ro 8:32. 2 C 8:12. Ga 2:20. He 9:14. 10:10.

at the. Le 16:7. 17:4. Ex 29:4. Dt 12:5, 6, 13, 14, 27. Ezk 20:40. Jn 10:7, 9. Ep 2:18.

4 **put.** Ex 3:2, 8, 13. 4:4, 15, 24, 29. 8:14, 22. 16:21. Ex 29:10, 15, 19. Nu 8:12. Is 53:4-6. 2 C 5:20, 21.

hand upon. 1 J 1:1.

burnt offering. Le 6:8-13. Ge 8:20. Ezr 3:2. Ps 51:19. Ac 13:39. 2 C 5:19. Ep 2:1-6.

be accepted. Le 22:21, 27. Ps 51:17. Is 56:7. Ro 12:1. Ep 1:6. Ph 4:18. 1 P 2:5.

atonement. Le +4:20. Ro 3:25. He 10:4.

5 **kill.** ver. 11. Le 3:2, 8, 13. 16:15. 2 Ch 29:22-24. Mi 6:6. Col 1:22.

bullock. Pr 14:4.

the priests. ver. 11, 15. 2 Ch 35:11. He 10:11.

sprinkle. ver. 11. Le 8:11, 30. 14:7, 16. Nu +19:13, +21. Is 52:15. He 9:13, 19, 21. 10:22. 11:28. 12:24. 1 P 1:2.

the altar. Le 4:7, 18. Am +9:1.

6 **flay.** Le 7:8. Ge 3:21. 2 Ch 29:34. Ps 2:2. Ac 4:27, 28.

7 **fire.** Le 6:12, 13. 9:24. 10:1. 1 Ch 21:26. 2 Ch 7:1. Ml 1:10.

lay. Ge 22:9. Ne 13:31.

8 **lay the parts.** Le 8:18-21. 9:13, 14. Ex 29:17, 18. 1 K 18:23, 33.

9 **inwards.** ver. 13. Le 8:21. 9:14. Ps 51:6. Je 4:14. Mt 23:25-28.

wash. 1 J 5:8.

burn all. ver. 13, 17. Le 3:11. Ps 66:15. Zc 13:7. He 9:14.

a sweet savor. Ge +8:21.

10 **of the flocks.** ver. 2. Ge 4:4. 8:20. Is 53:6, 7. Jn 1:29. Ac 8:32.

sheep. Ge 22:8. Ex 29:38, 39, 42. Is 53:7.

a male. ver. +3. Jn 6:37.

without blemish. He 9:14.

11 **he shall.** ver. 5. Ex 40:22. Ezk 8:5. Zc 13:7. Lk 24:46.

northward. Le 6:25. 7:2.

and the. ver. 7-9. Le 9:12-14.

12 **shall cut.** ver. 6-8.

13 **shall wash.** ver. 9. Ezk 36:25. Jn 13:10.

the inwards. Mt 23:26. Mk 7:21. Ja 4:8.

14 **of fowls.** Le 5:7. 12:8. Mt 11:29. Lk 2:24. Jn 2:14. 2 C 8:12. He 7:26.

turtledoves. Is 38:14. 59:11. Mt 10:16.

15 **wring off his head.** *or,* pinch off the head with the nail. Le 5:8. Ps 22:1, 21. 69:1-21. Is 53:4, 5, 10. Mt ch. 26, 27. Jn 12:27.

16 **his feathers.** *or,* the filth thereof. Lk 1:35. 1 P 1:2.

east. 2 Ch 5:12. Ps 103:12. Je 31:40. Ezk 43:1, 2, 4. Jn 14:6.

by the place. Le 4:12. 6:10, 11. 16:27. He 13:11-14.

ashes. 2 Ch 5:12. Ps 20:3mg. Pr 30:16. Je 31:40. Ep 1:6.

17 **shall not.** Ge 15:10. Ps 16:10. 22:14. Mt 27:50. Jn 19:30. Ro 4:25. 1 P 1:19-21. 3:18.

it is. ver. 9, 10, 13. Ge +8:21. Ro 12:1. He 10:6-12. 13:15, 16.

LEVITICUS 2

1 **any.** Heb. *nephesh,* soul, Ge +27:31.

meat offering. Le +23:13. Jn 6:35.

fine flour. Ex +27:20. 29:2. Nu 7:13, 19. Is 53:10. Jl 1:9. 2:14. He +2:10.

pour oil. ver. 4-8, 15, 16. Le 7:10-12. Ps

45:7, 8. Is 61:1. 1 J 2:20, 27. Ju 20.
frankincense. Mt +2:11. Lk 1:9, 10. Re 8:3.

2 sons. 1 C 9:13, 14.
the memorial. ver. 9. Le 5:12. 6:15.
Ex +12:14. Nu 5:18. Ne 13:14, 22.
Ep 2:18.

3 the remnant. ver. 10. Le +7:7. Ps 78:24, 25.
He 13:10. Re 2:17.
meat offerings. 1 J 1:3.
most holy. ver. 10. Le 6:17, 25, 29. 7:1, 6.
10:12, 17. 14:13. 21:22. 24:9. 27:28. Ex
26:33. 29:33, 34, 37. 30:10, 29, 36. +40:10.
Nu 18:9, 10. Ezk 42:13. Da 9:24.

4 meat offering. ver. 1. Ps 22:14. Mt 26:38. Jn
12:27.
unleavened cakes. *or*, pierced cakes. Heb.
chaloth, from *chahlal*, to be pierced, or
wounded. ver. 1, 11. Le 6:17. 7:12. 10:12. Ex
12:8. 29:2. Ps 22:16. Jn 19:34, 37. 1 C 5:7, 8.
11:24. He +2:10. 7:26. 1 P 2:1, 22.
wafers. Ex 16:31. 29:2. Is 42:1. 44:3-5. 61:1.
Jn 3:34.

5 in a pan. *or*, on a flat plate, *or* slice. Le 6:21.
7:9. 1 Ch 23:29. Ezk 4:3.

6 part. Le 1:6. Ps 22:1-21. Mk 14. 15. Jn 18.
19. 1 C 11:26. He +2:10.

7 the fryingpan. Le 7:9.
of fine. ver. 1, 2.

9 a memorial. ver. +2.
an offering. ver. 2. Ps 22:13, 14. Is 53:10. Zc
13:7, 9. Ro 12:1. 15:16. Ph 2:17.
sweet savor. Ge +8:21.

10 is left. ver. +3.
meat offering. Jn 6:50, 51.

11 no leaven. Le 6:17. Ex 12:19, 20. Am 4:5. Mt
16:6, 11, 12. Mk 8:15. Lk 12:1. 1 C 5:6-8. Ga
5:9.
honey. Pr 24:13. 25:16, 27. Lk 21:34. Ac
14:22. 1 P 4:2.

12 the oblation. Le 23:10, 11, 17. Ex 22:29.
23:10, 11, 19. Nu 15:20. Dt 26:10. 2 Ch 31:5.
1 C 15:20. Re 14:4.
firstfruits. Le +23:10. Mt 6:33.
be burnt. Heb. ascend, **S#5927h**. Le 19:19
(come). Ge 2:6 (went up). 13:1. 17:22. 19:30.
Ex 2:23 (came up). **S#5927h**.
savor. Ge +8:21.

13 with salt. Ezr 7:22. Ezk 43:24. Mt 5:13. Mk
9:49, 50. Ac 2:27. 3:15. Col 4:6.
the salt. Nu 18:19. 2 Ch 13:5.
with all thine. Ezk 43:24.

14 a meat offering. Le 22:29. +23:13. Ml 1:11.
firstfruits. Le +23:10, 11, 14-17, 20. 1 C
15:20, 23.
corn beaten. Ex +27:20. 2 K 4:42. Is 53:5. He
+2:10.

15 put oil. ver. 1.

16 the memorial. ver. 1, +2, 4-7, 9, 12. Ps
141:2. Is 11:2-4. 61:1. Jn 1:45. 7:41. Ro 8:26,
27. He 5:7.

LEVITICUS 3

1 a sacrifice. Is 9:6. Je +29:11. Mi 5:5. Lk 2:24.
19:38. 1 J 1:3.
peace offering. Le +23:19. Dt 33:27, 28. Jg
+6:24. Is 40:11. Ro 5:1.
without. Le +1:3. Nu 6:14. He +10:22.

2 lay. Le 1:4, 5. 8:22. 16:21, 22. Ex 29:10. Is
53:5, 6. 2 C 5:21. 1 J 1:9, 10.
kill it. Le 1:11. Zc 12:10. Ac 2:36-38. 3:15,
26. 4:10-12, 26-28.

3 the fat. *or*, suet. ver. 16. Ex +29:13, 22. Dt
30:6. Ps 7:9. 119:70. Is 6:10. Ezk 36:26. Mt
13:15. 15:8. Ro 5:5. 6:6. Ep 2:14, 15.

4 caul above the liver, with the kidneys. *or*,
midriff over the liver, and over the kidneys.
ver. 10, 15. Le 4:9. 7:4. 8:16, 25. 9:10, 19. Ex
29:13mg, 22.

5 Aaron's. Ex +29:13. 1 K 8:64. 2 Ch 35:14. He
13:15.
upon the burnt. Le +23:12.

6 a sacrifice. Is 32:17. 42:1. Ga 4:4. Ep 1:10.
2:13-22. He 7:2.
be of. ver. 1. Le 1:2, 10. Is 60:7.
male. Ga 3:28.
he shall. ver. 1, etc. Ac 4:27. Ro 12:1, 2. T
2:11, 12.

7 offer it. ver. 1. 1 K 8:62. Ep 5:2, 12. He 9:14.

8 he shall. ver. 2-5, 13. Le 4:4, 15, 24. Is 53:6,
11, 12. 2 C 5:21. 1 P 2:24.
kill it. Ep 2:18. 3:12. He 10:19-22. Re 5:6.
sprinkle. Le +1:5. Mt 3:17. 2 C 5:19. 1 P
1:19.

9 the fat. ver. 3, 4. Pr 23:26. Is 53:10.
the whole rump. Le 7:3. 8:25. 9:19. Ex
29:22.

10 the caul. ver. +4.

11 burn. ver. 5. Ps 22:14. Is 53:4-10. Ro 8:32.
the food. ver. 16. Le 21:6, 8, 17, 21, 22.
22:25. Nu 28:2. Ezk 44:7. Ml 1:7, 12. 1 C
10:21. 1 J 1:4. Re 3:20.

12 a goat. ver. 1, 7, etc. Le 1:2, 6, 10. 9:3, 15.
10:16. 22:19-27. Is 53:2, 6. Mt 25:32, 33. Ro
8:3. 2 C 5:21.

13 lay his hand. ver. 1-5, 8. Is 53:6, 11, 12. 2 C
5:21. 1 P 2:24. 3:18.
sprinkle. ver. 2, +8. Ro 5:6-11, 15-21.

14 the fat that covereth. ver. 3-5, 9-11. Ex
+29:13. Mt 22:37. 26:38. Ro 12:1, 2.

15 caul above. ver. +4.

16 it is the food. ver. +11.
all the fat. Ex +29:13. Mt 22:37.
savor. Ge +8:21.

17 a perpetual. Heb. *olam*, Ge +9:12. Le 6:18.
7:36. 16:34. 17:7. 23:14. Nu 19:21.
eat neither fat. ver. 16. Ezk +34:3.
blood. Le 7:26, 27. 17:10-14. 19:26. Ge 9:4.
Dt 12:16, 23, 27. 15:23. 1 S 14:32-34. 1 Ch
11:19. Ezk 33:25. 44:7, 15. Mt 16:24. 26:28.
Jn 6:53-56. Ac 15:20, 24, 29. 21:25. Ep 1:7.
5:26. Col 2:16, 20-23. 1 T 4:4. He 10:29.

LEVITICUS 4

2 soul. Heb. *nephesh*, Ge +27:31. ver. 27. Le 5:15, 18. Ex 29:14. Nu 15:22, 27. Ps 19:12.
sin through ignorance. Le 5:15, 17. Nu 15:22-29. Dt 19:4. 1 S 14:27. Jb 10:6. 13:23. 15:15. Ps 19:12. 32:5. Ro 14:23. 1 T 1:13. He 5:2. 9:7. Ja +4:17.
things. or, sins.
which ought. ver. 27. Ge 20:9. Ja 3:10.

3 the priest. Le 7:35. 8:12, 30. 10:7. 21:10, 12. Ex +28:41.
a young bullock. ver. 14. Le 9:2. 16:6, 11. Ezk 43:19.
for a sin offering. Le +23:19. 1 C 3:17. Ga 2:20. Col 2:13, 14. He 1:2, 3. 5:3. 7:27, 28. 9:13, 14. 13:11. 1 P 2:24. 1 J 2:2. Re 1:5, 6.

4 bring. Le 1:3. Ex 29:10, 11.
lay his hand. Le +1:4. 16:21. Is 53:6. Da 9:26. 1 P 3:18.

5 shall take. ver. 16, 17. Le 16:14, 19. Nu 19:4. 1 J 1:7.

6 dip. ver. 17, 25, 30, 34. Le 8:15. 9:9. 16:14, 19. Nu 19:4.
seven times. ver. 17. Le 8:11. 14:16, 18, 27. 16:14, 19. 25:8. 26:18, 24, 28. Nu 19:4. Jsh +6:4, 8.
vail. He 10:20.

7 the horns. Ex +27:2. He 9:21-25.
all the blood. ver. 18, 34. Ex +29:12. Ep 2:13.

8 all the fat. ver. +19, 26, 31, 35. Ex +29:13. Jn 12:27.

10 peace offering. Le +23:19. Ps 32:1. 1 T 2:5, 6.

11 the skin. ver. 21. Le 6:30. 8:14-17. 9:8-11. 16:27. Ex 29:14. Nu 19:5. Ps 103:12. He 13:11-13.

12 without the camp. Heb. to without the camp. ver. 21. Le 6:11. 8:17. 10:4, 5. 13:46. 14:3, 40, 41, 45, 53. 16:27. 24:14, 23. Ex 29:14. 33:7. Nu 5:2-4. 12:12, 14, 15. 15:35, 36. 19:3. 1 K 21:13. Mt 27:31-33. Lk 4:29. Ac 7:58. He 13:11-13.
the ashes. Le 6:10, 11.
burn him. Ex 29:14. Nu 19:5. He 13:11.
where the ashes are poured out. Heb. at the pouring out of the ashes.
poured. Heb. *shephek*, S#8211h, only here.

13 the whole congregation. 1 S 14:32, etc.
through ignorance. ver. 1, +2. Le 5:2-5, 17. 22:14. Nu 15:24-29. Jsh 7:11, 24-26. 1 S 14:33. Ro 3:9-12. 1 T 1:13. He 2:1. 10:26-29.
and are guilty. Le 5:2-5, 17. 6:4. Ezr 10:19. Ho 5:15mg. 1 C 11:27.

14 young bullock. ver. +3. Mk 10:45. 1 P 3:18.

15 the elders. Ex 24:1, 9. Nu 11:16, 25. Dt 21:3-9.
lay. ver. +4. 1 C 15:56, 57.

16 the priest. ver. 5-12. He 9:12-14.

17 the priest. ver. 6, 7. Da 9:24. He 10:10-12. 1 J 1:7. 2:2.

18 upon the. ver. 7.

19 fat. ver. +8-10, 26, 31, 35. Ps 22:14. He 1:3. 9:14.
burn. Le 10:2. Ge 19:24. Ex 9:23, 24. Nu 11:1. 16:35. 26:10. 2 K 1:10-14.

20 with the. ver. 3.
an atonement. ver. 26, 31, +35. Le 1:4. 5:6, 10, 13, 16, 18. 6:7. 9:7. 12:7, 8. 14:18, 20, 29, 53. 16:10, 11, 17, 24. Ex 32:30. Nu 8:12. 15:25, 28. 25:13. 2 S 21:3. 2 Ch 29:24. Da 9:24. Ro 5:11. Ga 3:13. He 1:3. 2:17. 9:14. 10:10-12. 1 J 1:7, 9. 2:1, 2. Re 1:5.
forgiven. ver. 26, 31, 35. Le 5:10, 16, 18. 6:7. Ep 1:7.

21 burn him. Ge 22:8.
as he. ver. 11, 12.
a sin offering. Le +23:19. 1 T 2:5, 6.

22 a ruler. Nu 1:4, 16. 7:2.
hath sinned. Ex 18:21. Nu 16:2. 2 S 21:1-3. 24:10-17.
and done. ver. 2, 13.

23 if his sin. ver. 14. Le 5:4. 2 K 22:10-13.
a kid. Le 9:3. 23:19. Nu 7:16, 22, 28, 34. 15:24. 28:15, 30. 29:5, 11, 16, 19. Ro 8:3.

24 And he. ver. 4, etc. Is 53:6.
in the place. ver. 4, 15, 29, 33. Le 1:3, 5, 11. 3:2, 8, 13. 6:25. 7:2. 14:13. 16:15. Ex 29:11, 38.
burnt offering. Le +23:12.
sin. ver. +3, 21.

25 put. ver. +7, 30. Ex +29:12. Is 40:21. Ro 3:24-26. 8:3, 4. 10:4. He 2:10. 9:22.

26 the fat. ver. +8.
an atonement. ver. +20.
forgiven. Ro 4:7, 8. 2 C 5:21.

27 any one. Heb. any soul, *nephesh*, Ge +27:31. ver. 2. Nu 15:27.
common people. Heb. people of the land. ver. 2, 13. Ex 12:49. Nu 5:6. 15:16, 29.
through ignorance. Pr 20:9. 1 J 1:8-10. 3:4.

28 a kid. ver. 23, 32. Le 5:6. Ge 3:15. Is 7:14. Je 31:22. Ro 8:3. Ga 4:4, 5.
a female. ver. 23. Ga 3:28.

29 lay his hand. ver. +4, 15, 24, 33. He 10:4-14.

30 upon the horns. ver. +7, 25, +34.
pour out. Is 53:12. He 9:22.

31 all the fat. ver. +8.
a sweet. Ge +8:21. Jb 42:8. Ps 40:6, 7. 51:16, 17. 69:30, 31. Is 42:21. 53:10. Mt 3:17. He 1:3. 9:12, 14, 15. 10:12, 14. 1 P 2:4, 5. 1 J 1:7. 4:9, 10. Re 5:9.
and the priest. ver. +20, 35.

32 a lamb. ver. 28. Le 3:6, 7. 5:6. Ex 12:3, 5. Is 53:7. Lk +1:35. Jn 1:29, 36. He 7:26. 1 P 1:18-20. 2:22, 24. 3:18. Re 5:6, 8, 9.
without blemish. ver. 28. Le +1:3.

33 **lay his hand**. ver. +4, 29-31.
34 **the horns of the altar**. ver. 25, 30. Is 42:21.
Jn 17:19. Ro 8:1, 3. 10:4. 2 C 5:21. He 2:10.
10:29. 1 P 1:18-20. 2:24. 3:18.
35 **And he**. ver. +8.
according. Le ch. 1-6.
and the priest shall make. ver. +20. Ro
3:24-26. 4:25. 5:6-11, 15-21. 8:1, 3, 4. 10:4. 2
C 5:21. Ga 1:4. Ep 1:6, 7. 5:2. Col 1:14. He
4:14. 7:26. 9:14, 26-28. 1 P 1:18, 19. 2:22, 24.
3:18. 1 J 4:9, 10.

LEVITICUS 5

1 **a soul**. Heb. *nephesh*, Ge +27:31. ver. 15, 17.
Le 4:2. Ezk +18:4, 20.
hear. Ex 22:11. Jg 17:2. 1 K 8:31. 22:16. 2 Ch
18:15. Pr 29:24. 30:9. Mi +6:8. Mt 26:63.
the voice of swearing. Nu 5:21.
if he do not. Le 19:17. Ep 5:11.
bear. ver. 17. Le 7:18. 17:16. 19:8, 17mg.
20:17. Nu 9:13. Ps 38:4. 90:8. Is 53:11. 1 T
5:22. 1 P 2:24.
iniquity. Ge +19:15mg.
2 **soul**. Heb. *nephesh*, Ge +27:31; Ge +12:5.
touch. Le 7:21. 11:24, 28, 31, 39. Nu 19:11-
16. Dt 14:8. Is 52:11. Da 1:8. Hg 2:13. 2 C 6:17.
hidden. ver. 4, 17. Ps 19:12. Lk 11:44.
and guilty. ver. 17. Le 4:13. 1 J 3:4.
3 **the uncleanness**. Le ch. 12, 13, 15. 22:4-6.
Nu 19:11-16.
when. ver. 4. He 3:13.
4 **if a soul**. Heb. *nephesh*, Ge +27:31; Ge +12:5.
Nu +30:2. Jg +11:30, 31. Pr 10:19.
to do evil. Le 27:2, etc. Jsh 2:14. 9:15. Jg
9:19. 11:31, 34, 35. 21:7, 18. 1 S 1:11. 14:24-
28. 24:21, 22. 25:22. 2 S 21:7. 2 K 6:31. Ps
39:1. 132:2-5. Pr 14:9. Ec 5:2-6. Ezk 17:18,
19. Mt 14:7, 9. Mk 6:23. Ac 23:12.
5 **confess**. Le 16:21. 26:40. Nu 5:7. Jsh 7:19.
Ezr 10:11, 12. Jb 33:27. Ps 32:5. 51:4. Pr
28:13. Je 3:13. Da 9:4. Ro 10:10. 1 J 1:8-10.
6 **trespass offering**. ver. 16, 18, 19. Le 4:28,
32. 6:5, 6, 17. 7:1-7. 14:12, 13, 24, 25. 19:21,
22. Nu 6:12. 18:9. 1 S 6:3, 17. 2 K 12:16. Ezr
10:19. Ps 40:6, 12. Is 53:10. Ezk 40:39. 42:13.
44:29. 46:20. Mt 1:21. 26:28. 1 C 15:3. 2 C
5:19. Ga 1:4. Ep 1:7. Col 1:14. 2:13. He 10:12.
1 P 2:24. 3:18. 1 J 1:9.
a female. Le 4:28, 32.
the priest. ver. 10. Le +4:20.
7 **he be not able to bring a lamb**. Heb. his
hand cannot reach to the sufficiency of a
lamb. ver. 11. Le 12:8. 14:21, 30. 25:26mg. Lk
+11:41. 2 C 8:12. Ja 2:5, 6.
two turtle doves. Le 1:14, 15. Mt 3:16.
10:16. Lk 2:24.
sin. ver. 8, 9. Le +23:19.
burnt. Le +23:12.

8 **wring off**. Le 1:15. Ro 4:25. 1 P 3:18.
9 **sprinkle**. Le +1:5. 4:25, 30, 34. Ex 12:22, 23.
Is 42:21. He 2:10.
the rest. Le +4:7.
10 **burnt**. ver. 7. Le 1:14-17. Ep 5:2.
manner. *or*, ordinance. Le 1:14-17. 9:16. Ge
40:13.
make. ver. 6, 13, 16.
it. Ja 5:15.
11 **But if**. ver. +7. 2 C 8:9.
the tenth part. Ex 16:18, 36.
fine flour. Le 2:1. Nu 7:13, 19, etc. 15:4-9.
He 9:22.
no oil. Le 2:1, 2, 4, 5, 15, 16. Nu 5:15. Ps
22:1-21. 69:1-21. Is 53:2-10.
for it is. ver. 6, 9, 12. 2 C 5:21.
12 **a memorial**. Le +2:2, 9, 16. Nu 5:26.
Ep 5:2.
according. Le 1:9, 13, 17. 2:9. 3:4, 11. 4:35.
13 **the priest**. ver. +6.
shall be. Le 2:3, 10. 7:6. 1 S 2:28. Ho 4:8. 1 C
9:13.
meat offering. Le +23:13.
15 **a soul**. Heb. *nephesh*, Ge +27:31. ver. 1, 2.
trespass. Ec 5:6.
sin through ignorance. Le +4:2. Pr 24:9.
in the holy. ver. 16. Le 7:1, 6. 10:17, 18.
22:1-16. 24:5-9. 27:9-33. Nu 18:9-32. Dt
12:5-12, 26. 15:19, 20. 26:1-15.
then. Le 6:5, 6.
ram. ver. 18. Le 6:6. Ezr 10:19.
thy estimation. Le 27:2-8, 12, 13, 17, 18,
23-27.
the shekel. Ex +30:13. Ps 89:19.
16 **make**. Le 22:14. Ex 22:1, 3, 4. Ps 69:4. Lk
19:8. Ac 26:20.
the fifth. Le 6:4, 5. 27:13, 15, 27, 31. Nu 5:7.
and the priest. ver. +6.
17 **soul**. Heb. *nephesh*, Ge +27:31.
sin. ver. 1. Le 4:2-4, 13, 22, 27.
though. ver. 15. Le +4:2. Ps 19:12. Lk 12:48.
Ro 14:23. 1 T 1:13.
yet is he. ver. 1, 2. Le 4:2, 13, 27.
18 **And he**. ver. +15, 16.
for a trespass. ver. +6. 1 T 2:5, 6.
and the priest. ver. 16. Le 1:4. 4:20. 6:7.
19 **trespassed**. Ezr 10:2. Ps 51:4. Ml 3:8. Ro 7:7-
12. 2 C 5:19-21.

LEVITICUS 6

2 **soul**. Heb. *nephesh*, Ge +27:31.
commit. Le 5:15, 19. Nu 5:6-8. Ps 51:4.
against. Mt 25:40, 45. Ac 9:5.
lie. Le 19:11. Ge 26:7. +43:18. Jn 8:44. Ac
5:4. Ep 4:25. Col 3:9. Re 22:15.
in that. Ex 22:7-10.
in fellowship. *or*, in dealing. Heb. in putting
of the hand. Is 21:2. 24:16. 33:1. Hab 1:13.

deceived. Pr 24:28. 26:19. Is 59:13-15. Je 9:5. Am +8:5. Mi 6:10-12.

3 **have found**. Ex 23:4. Dt 22:1-3.
sweareth. Le 19:12. Ex 22:9-11. Pr 30:9. Je 5:2. 7:9. Zc 5:4. Ml +3:5. Ac 5:3, 4. Col 3:9. 1 J 4:20.

4 **because**. Le 4:13-15. 5:3, 4.
which he. Ge 21:25. Jb 20:19. 24:2. Is 59:6. Ezk 18:7, 12, 18. Am 3:10. Mi 2:2. Zep 1:9.
to keep. Ex 22:7-9.

5 **restore**. Le 5:16. Ex 22:1, 4, 7, 9. Nu 5:7, 8. 1 S 12:3. 2 S 12:6. Ps 69:4. Pr 6:30, 31. Is 58:6, 9. Lk 19:8.
of his trespass offering. *or*, of his being found guilty. Heb. of his trespass. Mt 5:23, 24.

6 **And he shall**. Le 5:15, 16. Mt 5:23, 24.
a ram. Le 5:15, 18. Is 53:10, 11. 2 C 9:15.

7 **make**. Le +4:20. Ex 34:7. Ezk 18:21-23, 26, 27. 33:14-16, 19. Mi 7:18.
it shall be. Is 1:18. Mt 12:31. 1 C 6:9-11.

9 **burnt offering**. Le +23:12.
because of the burning. *or*, for the burning. ver. 12, 13. Ps 66:13-15.

10 **linen garment**. Le 16:4. Ex 28:39-43. 39:27-29. Ps 132:16. Ezk 44:17, 18. Re 7:13. 19:8, 14.
consumed. Le 1:9, 13, 17. Nu 16:21, 35. Ps 20:3mg. 37:20.
beside. Le 1:16.

11 **put off**. Le 16:23. Ezk 44:19. Is 53:9. Jn 19:30.
without. Le +4:12. Jn 19:41, 42.

12 **the fire**. Le 9:24. Nu 4:13, 14. Mk 9:48, 49. He 10:27. 12:29.
burn wood. Le 1:7-9. 3:3-5, 9-11, 14-16. Ex 29:38-42. Ne 13:31.
morning. ver. 9. Ge 22:3.
peace offerings. Le +23:19. 2 Th 3:16.

13 **fire**. Is 6:6, 7. Re 8:5.
ever be burning. Re 4:8.

14 **the meat offering**. Le +23:13. Jn 6:32.

15 **the memorial**. Le +2:2, 9.

16 **the remainder**. Le 2:3, 10. 5:13. Ezk 44:29. 1 C 9:13-15.
his sons. Le 24:9. 1 C 11:24.
unleavened. Ex 12:8. 1 C 5:8.
shall it. ver. 26. Ex +29:31.

17 **baken**. Le 2:11. 1 C 5:6-8. 1 P 2:22.
I have. Le +7:7.
it is most holy. ver. 25. Le +2:3.
sin offering. ver. 25, 30. Le +23:19.
trespass offering. Le +5:6.

18 **the males**. ver. 29. Le 21:21, 22. Nu 18:10.
It shall. Le +3:17.
for ever. Heb. *olam*, Ex +12:24.
every one. Le 22:3-7. Ex 29:37. Ps 89:7. Hg 2:12-14. Zc 14:20, 21. 1 P 1:16. 2:9.

20 **the offering**. Ex 29:2. Nu 18:26-32. He 5:1. 7:27. 8:3, 4.
in the day. ver. 22. He 7:19.

the tenth. Le 5:1. Ex 16:36.
a meat offering. Le +23:13.

21 **a pan**. Le 2:5. 7:9. 1 Ch 9:31.

22 **is anointed**. Le 4:3. Dt 10:6. He 7:23.
for ever. Heb. *olam*, Ex +12:24.
wholly. Le 8:21. Ex 29:22-25. Is 53:10.

23 **shall be**. Ex 29:25. He 7:23.
it shall not be. ver. 16, 17. Le 2:10.

25 **the law**. Le +4:2, 3, etc., 21, 24, 33, 34.
sin offering. ver. +17.
In the place. Le +4:24.
offering. Ge +4:7.
it is. ver. 17. Le +2:3.

26 **priest**. Le +7:7. Ezk 46:20. Ho 4:8. Jn 6:52-57. Ep 5:32.
in the holy. ver. 16.
in the court. Ex 27:9-18. 38:9-19. 40:33. Ezk 42:13.

27 **touch**. ver. 18. Ex 29:37. 30:29. Hg 2:12. Mt 9:21. 14:36.
wash. Heb. *kabas*, Nu +19:21. Le 11:32. 2 C 7:1, 11.

28 **the earthen**. Le 11:33. 15:12. He 9:9, 10.
vessel. Pr 25:4. 2 C 4:10, 11.
brazen pot. Jsh 6:19. Mk 7:4.
and rinsed. Heb. *shatap*, Le +15:11. Le 11:32. T 2:13, 14.

29 **the males**. ver. +18.
it is. ver. 25. Ps 99:1.

30 **no sin offering**. Le +23:19.
holy place. He 9:12. 10:3, 12-14. Re 7:13-15.
burnt. Le +4:12.

LEVITICUS 7

1 **the law**. Le +5:6.
most holy. Le +2:3.

2 **in the place**. Le +4:24. Nu 6:12. Ezk 40:39.
burnt. Le +23:12.
and the. Le +1:5.

3 **all the fat**. Ex +29:13. Ps 51:6, 17.

5 **burn them**. Le 1:9, 13. 2:2, 9, 16. 3:16. Ga 2:20. 5:24. 1 P 4:1, 2.

6 **male**. Le 6:16-18, 29. Nu 18:9, 10.
eaten in. Ex +29:31.
it is most holy. Le +2:3.

7 **sin offering**. Le +23:19.
the trespass. Le +5:6.
have it. Le 2:3. 6:17, 18, 26. 10:13, 14, 17. 14:13. Nu 5:9. 18:9, 11, 19. Dt 18:3, 4. 1 S 2:28. 2 K 12:16. Ezk 44:29. Lk 10:7. 1 C +9:13.

8 **have to himself**. Ezk 44:29. 1 T 5:17, 18.
skin. Le 1:6. 4:11. 15:17. Ge 3:21. Ex 29:14. Nu 19:5. Ro 13:14. Ep 1:6. Ph 3:9. Col 3:12, 14.

9 **the meat offering**. Le +23:13.
in the pan. *or*, on the flat plate, *or* slice. Le 2:5mg. 6:21.
shall be. Le 2:3, 10. 5:13. 6:16-18. Is 33:16. Lk 22:35. 1 C 9:7, 13. Ga 6:6.

10 **all**. Jn 1:16.
   one as much. Ex 16:18. 2 Ch +31:10. 2 C
   8:14. Ph 4:18.
11 **the sacrifice**. He 10:5.
   peace offerings. Le +23:19. Jg +6:24. Ps
   116:17. 119:108. Jn 14:27. Col 1:2.
12 **a thanksgiving**. Le 22:29. 2 Ch 29:31. 33:16.
   Ne 12:43. Ps 50:13, 14, 23. 103:1, 2. 107:8,
   21, 22. 116:17. Je 17:26. 33:11. Ho 14:2. Jon
   2:9. Lk 17:16, 18. Ro 1:21. 2 C 9:11-15. Ep
   5:20. He 13:15. 1 P 2:5.
   unleavened wafers. Le 2:4. 6:16. Nu 6:15.
13 **leavened**. Le 23:17. Am 4:5. Mt +13:33.
   thanksgiving. 1 T 4:4. He 13:15. Ja 3:2, 8, 9.
14 **an heave offering**. ver. 32, 34. Le 10:14, 15.
   Ex +29:27, 28. Nu 5:9mg. 6:20. 15:19-21.
   18:8, 11, 19, 24-30, 32. 31:29, 41, 52mg. Dt
   12:6, 11, 17. Ezr 8:25.Ne 10:37. 12:44. Ezk
   20:40. 44:30mg.
   the priest's. Le 6:26. Nu 18:8-11, 19,
   26-32.
15 **for thanksgiving**. Col 3:15.
   be eaten. Le 22:29, 30. Ex +12:10. 16:19. Ec
   9:10. Jn 9:4. 1 C 10:3. 2 C +6:2. He 3:13-15.
   he shall not. Le 22:30. Ex 12:10. 23:18.
   29:34. 34:25.
16 **be a vow**. Le +23:38.
   a voluntary offering. Le +23:38.
   also the. Le 19:5-8.
17 **the remainder**. Ps 16:10, 11.
   on the third. Le 19:7. Ge +22:4. Ex 19:11.
   Ho 6:2. 1 C +15:4.
   burnt. Le 6:22, 23. 10:16. Ex 12:10. 29:14.
18 **it shall**. Le 10:19. 19:7, 8. 22:23, 25. Je
   14:10, 12. Ho 8:13. Am 5:22. Ml 1:10, 13.
   be imputed. Nu 18:27. Ro 4:11.
   an abomination. Le 11:10, 11, 41. Is 1:11-
   14. 65:4. 66:3. Lk 16:15.
   soul. Heb. *nephesh*, Ge +27:31.
   bear. Le 5:17. 10:17. 17:16. 19:7, 8. 20:17,
   19. 22:16. Is 53:11, 12. Ezk 18:20. He +9:28. 1
   P 2:24.
   iniquity. Ge +19:15mg.
19 **toucheth**. Le 11:24-39. Nu 19:11-16. Hg
   2:13. Lk 11:41. Jn 18:28. Ac 10:15, 16, 28. Ro
   14:14, 20. 2 C 6:17. T 1:15.
   clean shall eat. SS 5:1.
20 **soul**. Heb. *nephesh*, Ge +27:31.
   having. Le 15:2, 3, etc. 1 C 11:28.
   soul. Heb. *nephesh*, Ge +17:14.
   shall be. ver. 21, 25, 27. Ge 17:14. Ex 30:33.
21 **soul**. Heb. *nephesh*, Ge +27:31.
   the uncleanness. Le 5:2, 3. ch. 12, 13, 15.
   22:4. Nu 19:11-16.
   any unclean. Le 11:24-42. Dt 14:7, 8, 10,
   12-20.
   uncleanness of man. Le 15:3. 22:4-9. Ep
   1:4. He 12:10.
   abominable. Le 11:10-13, 20, 41, 42. Dt
   14:3. Ezk 4:14.

22 **soul**. Heb. *nephesh*, Ge +17:14.
   cut off. ver. 20, 25, 27. Le 17:10, 14. 18:29.
   Ge 17:14. Ex 12:15, 19. 30:33-38.
23 **fat**. Ezk +34:3. Ac 28:27. Ro 8:13. 13:13.
24 **beast**. Heb. carcase. Le 11:8. 17:15. 22:8. Ex
   22:31. Dt 14:21. Ezk 4:14. 44:31.
25 **soul**. Heb. *nephesh*, Ge +17:14.
   shall be cut off. ver. +21.
26 **ye shall eat no**. ver. +23. Le 3:17.
27 **soul**. Heb. *nephesh*, Ge +27:31.
   that eateth. Le +3:17. Mt 22:21. Lk 22:17-
   20.
   that soul. Heb. *nephesh*, Ge +17:14. ver. 20,
   21, 25. He 10:29.
   shall be. ver. 21.
29 **He that**. Le +23:19. 1 J 1:7.
30 **own hands**. Le 3:3, 4, 9, 14. Ps 110:3. Jn
   10:18. 2 C 8:12.
   with the breast. Le 8:27. 9:21. Ex 29:24-28.
   Nu 6:20.
   wave offering. Le +23:15.
31 **the priest**. Le 3:5, 11, 16.
   the breast. ver. 34. Le 5:13. 6:16, 26. Nu
   +18:18.
32 **right shoulder**. ver. 34. Le 8:25, 26. 9:21.
   10:14. Nu 6:20. 18:18, 19. Dt 18:3. 1 C 9:13,
   14.
   heave offering. ver. +14.
33 **that offereth**. ver. 3. Le 6:26.
   his part. Ep 1:6.
34 **the wave**. ver. 30-32. Le +23:15.
   breast. Jb 36:5mg. Pr 8:17. Ep 3:17-19.
   heave. ver. +14.
   shoulder. Dt 18:3. 33:12. Pr 8:14. Is 40:11.
   Ep 1:19.
   by a statute. Le +3:17. Ex 29:9.
   for ever. Heb. *olam*, Ex +12:24.
35 **portion**. Ex +28:41.
   he presented. Ex 28:1. 29:1. Nu 18:7-19.
36 **in the day**. Le 8:12, 30. Ex 40:13, 15.
   for ever. Heb. *olam*, Ex +12:24.
37 **the law**. Le +23:12. Mt 20:28. Ro 5:10, 11. 2
   C 5:18, 19. 1 J 2:1, 2.
   meat. Le +23:13.
   sin. Le +23:19.
   trespass. ver. 1-7. Le +5:6.
   consecrations. Le 6:20-23. Ex 29:1.
   sacrifice. ver. 11-21. Le +23:19.
38 **commanded**. Le 1:1, 2. Ml 3:3.

LEVITICUS 8

2 **Aaron**. Ex 29:1-4. Ep 2:18. He 10:5-7.
   garments. Ex 28:2-4, 40-43. 39:1-31, 41.
   anointing. Ex 30:23-37. 40:12-15.
   bullock. Ex 29:1, 2. He 7:27, 28.
3 **gather**. Nu 20:8. 21:16. 1 Ch 13:5. 15:3.
   2 Ch 5:2-6. 30:2, 13, 25. Ne 8:1. Ps 22:25.
   Ac 2:1.
4 **did as**. ver. 9, 13, 17, 29, 35. Ex 39:1, 5, 7,

21, 26, 29, 31, 32, 42, 43. Dt 12:32. Mt 28:20. 1 C 11:23. 15:3.
unto the door. Ex 29:4.

5 **Lord commanded to be done**. Ex 29:4, etc.

6 **washed**. Ex 29:4. 40:12. Ps 51:2, 7. Is 1:16. Ezk 36:25. Zc 13:1. Jn 13:8-10. 1 C 6:11. Ep 5:26. He 9:10. 10:22. Re 1:5, 6. 7:14.

7 **he put**. Ex +28:2.
the ephod. Ex +28:4.

8 **the breastplate**. Ex +39:8. Ps 40:8. SS 8:6.
the Urim. Ex +28:30.

9 **the mitre**. Ex 28:4, 36-38. 29:6. 39:28-30. Zc 3:5. 6:11-14. Ph 2:9-11.
holy crown. Ps 93:5. Col 3:12. Re 4:8.

10 **anointing oil**. Ex 30:23-29. 40:9-11.

11 **he sprinkled**. Le +1:5. T 3:6.
anointed. Le 21:10, 12. Ex 29:7.
laver. Ex 30:18. Pr 27:19. 1 C 6:11. He 10:22. Ja 1:22-24.
sanctify them. Ex 30:29. Ps 45:8.

12 **he poured**. Ex +28:41.
anointing oil. ver. 30. Ps 133:2. 1 J 2:20.

13 **Moses**. Ex 28:40, 41. 29:8, 9. 40:14, 15. 1 Ch 16:29. Ps 30:4. 132:9. Is 61:6, 10. 63:1. 1 P 2:5, 9. Re 1:6. 5:10.
coats. Ex 28:4. Re 1:13.
girded them. Is 11:5.
put. Heb. bound.
bonnets. Ex 39:28, 29.

14 **he brought**. ver. 2. Le 4:3-12. 16:6. Ex 29:10-14. Is 53:10. Ezk 43:19. Ro 8:3. 2 C 5:21. He 7:26-28. 1 P 3:18.
laid. Le 1:4. 4:4. 16:21.

15 **he slew it**. Le 1:5, 11. 3:2, 8. Ex 29:10, 11. Moses. Ex +29:12.
to make. He +2:17.

16 **all the fat**. Le 3:3-5. 4:8, 9. Ex +29:13.

17 **the bullock**. Le 4:11, 12, 21. 6:30. 16:27. Ex 29:14. Ga 3:13. He 13:11-13.
without the camp. Le +4:12. Ps 38:4. 40:12. 69:5.

18 **the ram**. Le 1:4-13. Ex 29:15-18.
burnt offering. Le +23:12.

21 **a sweet savor**. Ge +8:21.
by fire. Le 1:6-8. Ex 29:18.

22 **the ram of consecration**. ver. 2, 29. Le 7:37. Ex 29:19-31. Jn 17:19. 1 C 1:30. 2 C 5:21. Ep 5:25, 27. Re 1:5, 6.

23 **Moses took**. Le 14:14, 17, 28. Ex 29:20. Ro 6:13, 19. 12:1. 1 C 1:2, 30. 6:20. 1 Th 5:22. Ph 1:20. 2:17. He 2:10. 5:8, 9:11, 12. 13:12. Re 7:14, 15.

24 **Moses sprinkled**. He 9:22.

25 *the fat*. ver. +16.

26 **out of**. Ex 29:23. Jn 1:14. Ac 5:12. 1 T 2:5.

27 **upon Aaron's**. Ex 29:24-28. Je 30:21. He 9:14.
and waved. Ex +29:24. 1 P 2:5.
wave offering. Le +23:15.

28 **Moses**. Ex 29:25. Ps 22:13, 14. Zc 13:7. He 3:5. 10:14-22.
they were. ver. +22.

29 **the breast**. Nu +18:18. Is 66:20. 1 C 10:31. 1 P 4:11.
before the Lord. He 13:15.
wave offering. Le +23:15.

30 **the anointing**. Ex +28:41. Ga 5:22-25. He 2:11. 1 P 1:2. Re 7:14.
sprinkled. He 12:24. 1 P 1:2.
his garments. Re 3:4. 6:11. 16:15. 19:8.
and sanctified. Le 10:3. Nu 3:3.

31 **Boil**. Le 6:28. 7:15. Ex 29:31, 32. Dt 12:6, 7. 1 S 2:13-17. Ezk 46:20-24.
eat it. Le 10:17. Jn 6:33, 35, 51, 53-56. Ga 2:20.

32 **remaineth**. Le 7:17. Ex 12:10. 29:34. Pr 27:1. Ec 9:10. 2 C +6:2. He 3:13, 14.

33 **seven days**. Le 14:8. Ex 29:30, 35. Nu 19:12. Ezk 43:25-27.
consecrate. Ex +28:41.

34 **hath done**. He 7:16, 27. 10:11, 12.

35 **abide**. Ps 84:4. Pr 8:34.
the tabernacle. Le 14:8. Ex 29:35. Nu 19:12. Ezk 43:25. 2 C 7:1. Col 2:9, 10. He 7:28. 9:23, 24.
keep. Le 10:1. Ge 26:5. Nu 1:53. 3:7. 9:19. Dt 11:1. 1 K 2:3. Zc 3:7. 1 T 1:3, 4, 18. 5:21. 6:13, 17, 20. 2 T 4:1.

36 **Aaron**. Ex 39:43. 40:16. Dt 4:2. 12:32. 1 S 15:22.
did all. Ge 6:22. Mt 5:48. 7:21. Jn 15:10. He 10:14. 12:23. Ja 1:22. 1 J 4:17.

LEVITICUS 9

1 **the eighth day**. Le 8:33. 12:2, 3. 14:8-10, 23. 15:13, 14, 29. 22:27. Nu 6:9, 10. Ezk 43:26, 27. Mt 28:1. Col 3:4.

2 **a young**. ver. 7, 8. Le 4:3. 8:14. Ex 29:1. 2 C 5:21. He 5:3. 7:27. 10:10-14.
and a ram. Le 8:18.

3 **Take ye**. Le 4:23. 16:5, 15. Ezr 6:17. 10:19. Is 53:10. Ro 8:3. 2 C 5:21. T 2:14. He 9:26-28. 1 P 2:24. 3:18. Re 5:9.
a kid. Le 4:22-24. 10:16.
sin offering. Le +23:19.
a calf. ver. +2.
both. Le 12:6. 14:10.
without blemish. Le +1:3.
burnt. Le +23:12.

4 **a bullock**. Le ch. 3.
peace offerings. Le +23:19.
and a meat offering. Le +23:13.
today. ver. 6, 23. Ex 16:10. 19:11. 24:16. 29:43. 40:34, 35. Nu 14:10. 16:19. 1 K 8:10-12. Ezk 43:2.

5 **and all the congregation**. Ex 19:17. Dt 31:12. 1 Ch 15:3. 2 Ch 5:2, 3. Ne 8:1.

6 **and the glory**. ver. 23. Ex +24:16.

7 **offer thy**. ver. 2. Le 4:3, 20. 8:34. 1 S 3:14. He 5:3. 7:27, 28. 9:7.
atonement. Le +4:20.
offer the. Le 4:16-20. He 5:1.

8 **slew the calf**. Le 1:4, 5. 4:4, 29.

9 **blood**. He 10:19-22.
he dipped. Ex +29:12. He 2:10.

10 **the fat**. Ex +29:12. Is 53:10. 57:15. 66:2.
as the Lord. Le 4:8.

11 **the flesh**. Le 4:11, 12, 21. 8:17. 16:27, 28. He 13:11, 12.

12 **the burnt offering**. Le +23:12. Ep 5:2, 25-27.
sprinkled. He 10:22.

14 **did wash**. Le 8:21.

15 **the goat**. ver. 3. Le 4:27-31. 9:15. Nu ch. 28, 29. Is 53:10. 2 C 5:21. T 2:14. He 2:17. 5:3.

16 **manner**. *or*, ordinance. ver. 12-14. Le 1:3-10. 5:10. 8:18-21. He 10:1-22.

17 **the meat**. ver. 4. Le +23:13. Jn 6:53. Ga 2:20.
took an handful thereof. Heb. filled his hand out of it. Le 2:2.
beside. Ex 29:38-42.

18 **a sacrifice**. Le +23:19. Ro 5:1, 10.

19 **the fat**. ver. 10. Le 3:5, 16.

20 **they put**. Le 7:29-34.
burnt. Le 3:14-17.

21 **the breasts**. Nu +18:18. Is 49:3. Lk 2:14. 1 P 4:11.
wave offering. Le +23:15.

22 **blessed them**. Ge 14:18-20, 22. Nu 6:23-27. Dt 10:8. 21:5. 1 K 8:55. 1 Ch 23:13. 2 Ch 6:3. Ps 28:2. 72:17. 134:2. 141:2. Is 49:22. Mk 10:16. Lk 24:50. Ac 3:26. 2 C 13:14. 1 T 2:8. He 7:6, 7. 1 P 3:9.

23 **came out**. Lk 1:21, 22. He 9:24-28.
the glory. ver. +6. Is +40:5. Mt 17:2. Re 22:5.

24 **there came a fire**. Le 6:13. Ge 4:3, 4. 15:17. Ex 3:2. 2 S 22:9, 13. 2 K 19:15. 1 Ch +21:26. 2 Ch 6:2. Ps 80:1mg.
the fat. Ex +29:13. Ps +20:3mg.
they shouted. Ezr 3:11. He 11:4.
fell. Ge +17:3.

LEVITICUS 10

1 **Nadab**. Le 16:1. 22:9. Ex +6:23.
censer. Le 16:12. Ex 27:3. 38:3. Nu 16:6, 7, 16, 17, 46. He 9:4.
put incense. Ex 31:11. 37:29. 40:27. 1 K 13:1, 2. 2 Ch 26:16-20. Ps +141:2. Je 44:8, 15, 19-21.
strange. Le 9:24. 16:12. Nu 16:18, 46. 2 K 15:1-7. 2 Ch 26:16-23. Ps 50:16. Mk 1:24, 25. Ep 5:18. Ph 3:3.
which. Ex 30:9. Dt 4:2. 12:32. 17:3. Je 7:31. 19:5. 32:35.

2 **fire**. Le 9:24. 16:1. Ex 9:23. Nu 3:3, 4. 16:35. 26:61. 2 S 6:7. 2 K 1:10, 12. 1 Ch 24:2. Jb 37:3. 38:35. Ps 29:7. 77:18. 144:5, 6.
they died. Nu 3:3, 4. 16:32, 33, 49. 26:61. 1

S 6:19. 1 Ch 13:10. 15:13. Is 30:33. Ac 5:5, 10. 1 C 10:11.

3 **said**. ver. 6. 1 S 3:18.
I will be. Le 8:35. 21:6, 8, 15, 17, 21. 22:9. Ex 14:4. 19:22. 29:43, 44. 1 S 6:20. 1 Ch 15:12, 13. 2 Ch 26:16-21. Ps 89:7. 119:120. Is +8:13. 52:11. Ezk 42:13. He 12:28, 29.
before. 1 S 2:30. Is 49:3. Ezk 28:22. Jn 12:28. 13:31, 32. 14:13. Ac 5:11-13. 1 Th 1:10. 1 P 4:17.
Aaron. Ge +18:25. Dt 26:14. 1 S 3:18. Jb 1:20, 21. 2:10. Ps 39:9. 46:10. Is 39:8. Mt 10:37. Ac +21:14.

4 **Uzziel**. Ex +6:18.
carry. Lk 7:12. Ac 5:6, 9, 10. 8:2.

5 **out of the camp**. Le +4:12.

6 **Uncover**. Le 13:45. 21:1-15. Ex 33:5. Nu 5:18. 6:6, 7. 14:6. Dt 33:9. 1 S 16:1. Je 7:29. Ezk 24:16, 17. Mi 1:16.
lest wrath. Nu 16:22, 41-47. Jsh 7:1, 11. 22:18, 20. 2 S 24:1, 15-17.

7 **ye shall**. Le 21:12. Mt 8:21, 22. Lk 9:60.
the anointing. Ex +28:41.

9 **Do not**. Nu 6:3, 20. 1 S 1:13-16. Pr 31:4, 5. Ec 5:1. Is 28:7. Je 35:5, 6. Ezk 44:21. Lk *1*:15. Ac 2:13, 15. 1 C 11:21, 22. Ep 5:18. 1 T 3:3, 8. 5:23. T 1:7. 1 J 2:15-17.
strong drink. Ge +9:21. 1 C 10:12.
it shall be. Le +3:17.
for ever. Heb. *olam*, Ex +12:24.

10 **put difference**. Le 11:47. 20:25, 26. Ex +11:7. Je 15:19. Ezk 22:26. 44:23. Ph 1:10mg. T 1:15. 1 P 1:14-16.

11 **teach**. Dt 24:8. 33:10. 2 Ch 17:9. 30:22. Ne 8:2, 8. 9:13, 14. Je 2:8. 18:18. Ml 2:7. Mt 28:20. Ac 20:27. 1 Th 4:2.

12 **Take**. Le +23:13.
beside the altar. He 13:10.
most holy. Le +2:3.

13 **ye shall**. Ex +29:31.
thy due. 1 C 9:13, 14.
for so I. Le 2:3. 6:16.

14 **wave breast**. Nu +18:18. Jn 4:34.
peace offerings. Le +23:19.

15 **heave shoulder**. Le 7:29, 30, 34.
wave offering. Le +23:15.
for ever. Heb. *olam*, Ex +12:24. Le 7:34. Ge 13:15. 17:8, 13, 17. 1 C 9:13, 14.

16 **the goat**. Le 6:26, 30. 9:3, 15. Ezk 44:29.
angry. Ex 32:19-22. Nu 12:3. Mt 5:22. Mk 3:5. 10:14. Ep 4:26.

17 **Wherefore**. Ex +29:31.
to bear. Le 16:22. 22:16. Ex 28:38, 43. Nu 18:1. Is 53:6-11. Ezk 4:4-6. 18:19, 20. Jn 1:29. 2 C 5:21. He 9:28. 1 P 2:24.
iniquity. Ge +19:15.

18 **the blood**. Le 6:30.
as I commanded. Le 6:26, 30.

19 **this day**. Le 9:8, 12. He 7:27. 9:8.

should. Dt 12:7. 26:14. 1 S 1:7, 8. Is 1:11, 15. Je 6:20. 14:12. Ho 9:4. Ml 1:10, 13. 2:13. Ph 4:4.

20 he was content. 2 Ch 30:18-20. Zc 7:8, 9. Mt 12:3-7, 20.

LEVITICUS 11

2 the beasts. Dt 14:3-8. Ezk 4:14. Da 1:8. Mt 15:11. Mk 7:15-19. Ac 10:12, 14. 15:29. Ro 14:2, 3, 14, 15. Ph 4:8. 1 T 4:4-6. He 9:10. 13:9.

3 parteth. Ps 1:1. Pr 9:6. 2 C 6:17.
cheweth. Dt 6:6, 7. 16:3, etc. Ps 1:2. Pr 2:1, 2, 5, 9, 10. 4:20-22. Ac 17:11. 1 T 4:15. 3 J 2.

4 unclean unto you. Ge 7:1, 2. Dt 14. Is 52:11. 1 C 8:13. 1 Th 5:22. 1 J 3:4.

5 the coney. Ps 104:18. Pr 30:26.
but divideth. Jb 36:14. Mt 7:26. Ro 2:18-24. Ph 3:18, 19. 2 T 3:5. T 1:16.

6 the hare. Dt 14:7.

7 swine. Dt 14:8. Is 65:4. 66:3, 17. Mt 7:6. Lk 8:33. 15:15. Ro 14:14, 17. 1 C 8:8. Col 2:16, 17. 1 T 4:3, 4. He 9:9, 10. 2 P 2:18-22.

8 they are unclean. Le 5:2. Is 52:11. Ho 9:3. Mt 15:11, 20. Mk 7:2, 15, 18. Ac 10:10-15, 28. 15:29. Ro 14:14-17, 21. 1 C 8:8. 2 C 6:17. Ep 5:7, 11. Col 2:16, 21-23. He 9:10.

9 fins and scales. Dt 14:9, 10. Ac 20:21. Ga 5:6. Ja 2:18. 1 J 5:2-5.

10 thing. Heb. *nephesh*, soul, Ge +2:19. Ezk 47:9.
they shall be. Le 7:18. Dt 14:3. Ps 139:21, 22. Pr 13:20. 29:27. Re 21:8.

13 the eagle. Dt 14:12-20. Jb 28:7. 38:41. 39:27-30. Je 4:13, 22. 48:40. La 4:19. Ho 8:1. Hab 1:8. Mt 24:28. Ro 1:28-32. 3:13-17. T 3:3.

15 raven. Ge 8:7. 1 K 17:4, 6. Pr 30:17. Lk 12:24.

16 the owl. Dt 14:15-18. Ps 102:6. Is 13:21, 22. 34:11-15. Jn 3:19-21. Ep 2:2, 3. 4:18, 19. 5:7-11. Ph 3:18, 19. 1 Th 5:5-7. Re 18:2.

19 bat. Is 2:20. 66:17.

20 fowls that creep. ver. 23, 27. Dt 14:19. 2 K 17:28-41. Ps 17:14. Mt 6:24. Ph 3:18, 19. 2 T 4:10. 1 J 2:15-17. Ju 10, 19.

22 the locust. 1 K +8:37. Mt 3:4. Mk 1:6. Ro 14:1. 15:1. He 5:11. 12:12, 13.

24 toucheth the carcass. ver. 8, 27, 28, 31, 38-40. Le 17:15, 16. Is 22:14. 1 C 15:33. 2 C 6:17. Ep 2:1-3. 5:11. Col 2:16, 17, 20. He 9:26. 1 J 1:7.

25 wash his clothes, and be unclean. ver. 28, 40. Le 14:8. 15:5, 7-11, 13. 16:28. Ex 19:10, 14. Nu 19:8, 10, 19, 21, 22. 31:24. Ps 51:2, 7. Zc 13:1. Jn 13:8. Ac 22:16. He 9:10. 10:22. 1 P 3:21. 1 J 1:7. Re 7:14.

27 whatsoever goeth. ver. +20, 23.

28 beareth. ver. 24, 25.
shall wash. ver. 14.
until the even. Ro 13:12.

29 creeping things that creep. ver. 20, 21, 41, 42. Ps 10:3. 17:13, 14. Hab 2:6. Lk 12:15. 16:14. Jn 6:26, 66. Ep 4:14. Ph 3:19. Col 3:5. 2 T 3:2-5. He 13:5.
the mouse. Is 66:17.

31 doth touch. ver. 8, 24, 25.

32 vessel. Dt +23:24.
it must be put into water. Le 6:28. 15:12. Dt 23:11. He 9:10. T 2:14. 3:5.

33 ye shall break it. ver. 35. Le 6:28. 14:45. 15:12. Je 48:38. 2 C 5:1-8. Ph 3:21.

34 all meat. Pr 15:8. 21:4, 27. 28:8. T 1:15.

35 they shall be. ver. 33. Le 6:28. 15:12. 2 C 5:1-7.
broken down. Ps 2:9. Je 48:11.

36 a fountain. Heb. *mayan*, Ge +7:11. Zc 13:1. Jn 4:14.
pit. Heb. *bor*, Ge +37:20.
wherein there is plenty of water. Heb. a gathering together of waters. Ge 1:10. Ex 7:19.

37 sowing seed. Is 61:11. 1 C 15:37. Ph 1:15-18. 1 P 1:23. 1 J 3:9. 5:18.

39 that toucheth. ver. 24, 28, 31, 40. Le 7:24. 15:5, 7. Nu 19:11, 16.

40 eateth. ver. +25. Le 17:15, 16. 22:8. Ex 22:31. Nu 15:30. Dt 14:21. Is 1:16. Ezk 4:14. 36:25. 44:31. Zc 13:1. 1 C 6:11. 10:21. 1 J 1:7.
shall wash. ver. 28. Le 14:8, 9. 15:5-10, 27. 16:26, 28. Nu 19:7, 8, 19.

41 creeping thing. ver. +20, 23, 29.

42 goeth upon the belly. Ge 3:14, 15. Is 65:25. Mi 7:17. Mt 3:7. 23:23. Jn 8:44. 2 C 11:3, 13. T 1:12.
hath more feet. Heb. doth multiply feet.

43 Ye shall. ver. 41, 42. Le 20:25.
yourselves. Heb. *nephesh*, Ge +27:31, your souls. ver. 44. Le 20:25.

44 I am the. Ex +20:2.
ye shall. Le 10:3. +19:2. 1 S 6:20. Ps 99:5, 9. Is 6:3-5. Ezk 4:14. Re 22:11.
yourselves. Heb. *nephesh*, Ge +27:31, your souls. ver. 43.

45 that bringeth. Ex 6:7. 20:2. Ps 105:43-45. Ho 11:1.
be holy. ver. +44.

46 This. Le 7:37. 14:54. 15:32. Ezk 43:12.
creature. Heb. *nephesh*, soul, Ge +2:19. Ge 1:21, 24. 9:10, 12.

47 make a difference. Le 10:10. Ezk 44:23. Ml 3:18. Mt 15:17, 18. 23:23-26. Ac 15:10, 18-20. Ro 14:2, 3, 13-23. 1 C 10:25, 26, 31. Col 2:16, 17. 1 T 4:3-5.

LEVITICUS 12

2 If a woman. Ge 1:28. 3:16. Jb 14:4. 15:14. 25:4. Ps 51:5. Is 43:27. Lk 2:22. Ro 5:12-19.
according. Le 15:19.

3 eighth day. Ge 17:11, 12. Dt 30:6. Lk 1:59.

2:21. Jn 7:22, 23. Ro 3:19. 4:11, 12. 1 C 7:19. Ga 3:17. 5:3, 5, 6. 6:15, 16. Ph 3:3, 5, 7-11. Col 2:11.

4 in the blood. Le 15:25-28. Hag 2:13. Lk 2:22, 23.
nor come. Le 15:31. Ne 12:45.

5 maid child. ver. 2, 4. Ge 3:13, 28. 1 T 2:14, 15.

6 a lamb. ver. +8. Le 1:10-13. 5:6-10. Nu 6:10. Jn 1:29. 2 C 5:21. He 7:26. 1 P 1:18, 19.
of the first year. Heb. a son of his year. Le 14:10. 23:12. Ezk 46:13mg.
burnt. Le +23:12.
sin. Le +23:19.

7 make. Le +4:20. Jb 1:5. 14:4. Ro 3:23, 26. 1 C 7:14.
be cleansed. Le 15:28-30.
issue. Heb. *maqor*, **S#4726h**. Le 20:18. Ps 36:9 (fountain). 68:26. Pr 5:18. 10:11 (well). 13:14. 14:27. 16:22 (wellspring). 18:4. 25:26 (spring). Je 2:13. 9:1. 17:13. 51:36 (springs). Ho 13:15. Zc 13:1. For **S#953h**, *bor*, a hewn cistern, well, etc., see Ge +37:20. For **S#5869h**, *ayin*, a fountain, see Ge +24:13. For **S#4599h**, *mayan*, a spring or fountain, see Ge +7:11.
a male. Ga 3:28.

8 she be not able to bring a lamb. Heb. her hand find not sufficiency of a lamb. Le 1:14. 5:7. 14:22. 15:14, 29. 25:26, 28. Lk 2:22, 24. 2 C 8:9.
make atonement. ver. +7.

LEVITICUS 13

2 skin of. Le 7:8. Is 3:9.
rising. *or*, swelling. ver. 10, 19, 43, etc.
a scab. Le 14:56. Dt 28:27. Is 3:17.
the plague of leprosy. Le 14:3, 35. Ex 4:6, 7. Dt 28:27. 2 K +5:1. Ps 38:5-7. Is 1:5, 6. 1 C 6:11.
he shall. Dt 17:8, 9. 24:8. Ml 2:7. Mk +1:44.
the priest. Ps 19:12. Jn 2:25. He 4:13. Re 1:14.

3 shall look. ver. 2. Le 10:10. Ezk 44:23. Hg 2:11. Ml 2:7. Ac 20:28. Ro 3:19, 20. 7:7. He 13:7. Re 2:23.
turned. ver. 4, 10. Nu 6:5. Ezk 16:30. Ho 7:9.
white. Ex 4:6. Nu 12:10, 12. 2 K 5:27. 2 Ch 26:20.
deeper. Ge 13:3. Je 17:9. Mt 15:19, 20. 2 T 2:16, 17. 3:13.
pronounce. 2 K 5:27. 2 Ch 26:20. Mt 16:19. 18:17, 18. Jn 20:23. Ro 3:19, 20. 1 C 5:4-6. 6:11. 2 Th 3:14, 15. 1 T 1:20.

4 shut up. Le 24:12. Nu 12:15. Dt 13:14. Ezk 44:10. 1 C 4:5. 2 Th 3:14, 15. 1 T 5:24. Ju 22.
plague. ver. 2.

6 look. Is 1:16-18. Jn 15:6. 2 C 2:6, 7. Ga 6:1. Ja 5:19, 20.

pronounce. Is 11:3, 4. 42:3. Ro 14:1. 2 C 2:6, 7. Ju 22, 23.
a scab. ver. 2. Dt 32:5. Ja 3:2.
wash. Le 11:25, 28, 40. 14:8. Ge 35:2. 1 K 8:38, 45. Ps 19:12. Pr 20:9. Ec 7:20. Is 1:16-18. Jn 13:8-10. 15:3. 2 C 7:1. Ga 6:1. He 9:10. 10:22. Ja 5:19, 20. 1 J 1:7-9.

7 the scab. ver. 27, 35, 36. Le 14:4, 10, 21, 22. Ps 38:3. Is 1:5, 6. Lk 5:14. 17:14. Ro 6:12-14. 2 T 2:16, 17.

8 pronounce him. ver. +3. Mt 15:7, 8. Ac 8:21. Ph 3:18, 19. 2 P 2:19.

10 white. ver. 3.
shall see him. ver. 3, 4. Nu 12:10-12. 2 K 5:27. 2 Ch 26:19, 20.
quick raw flesh. Heb. the quickening of living flesh. ver. 14, 15, 24. Pr 12:1. Am 5:10. Jn 3:19, 20. 7:7. T 3:11.

11 old leprosy. Mt 8:2-4. Lk 5:14.

12 cover all. 1 K 8:33. Jb 40:4. 42:6. Is 64:6. Jn 16:8, 9. Ro 7:14. 1 T 1:15. 1 J 1:8-10.

13 covered all. 2 S +12:13. Jb 33:27, 28. 40:4. 42:6. Is 6:5. Lk 5:8, 12. 15:21. 18:13. 23:41. Ro 7:18.
turned white. Nu 12:10.
he is clean. Is 64:6. Jn 9:41.

14 raw flesh. ver. 10.

15 raw flesh. Nu +22:34.

16 turn again. Ro 7:14-24. Ga 1:14-16. Ph 3:6-8. 1 T 1:13-15.

18 a boil. Ex 9:9. +15:26. 2 K 20:7. 2 Ch 16:12. Jb 2:7. Ps 38:3-7. Is 38:21.

20 in sight. ver. +3. Mt 12:45. Jn 5:14. 2 P 2:20.

21 shut him. 1 C 5:5.

22 a plague. i.e. "The plague of the leprosy."

23 stay. Ge 38:26. 2 S 12:13. 2 Ch 19:2, 3. Jb 34:31, 32. 40:4, 5. Pr 28:13. Mt 26:75. 2 C 2:7. Ga 6:1. 1 P 4:2, 3.

24 a hot burning. Heb. a burning of fire. Is 3:24. He 12:5, 11. 1 P 4:12.

25 turned white. ver. 4, 18-20.

26 then the priest. ver. 4, 5, 23.

27 it is the plague of leprosy. ver. +2.

28 And if. Ps 38:3-7, 11. Je 3:12-14. 8:4-6. Re 2:5.

29 upon the head or. 1 K 8:38. 12:28. 2 Ch 6:29. Ps 53:4. Is 1:5. 5:20. 9:15. Mi 3:11. Mt 6:23. 13:14, 15. Jn 16:2, 3. Ac 22:3, 4. 26:9, 10. 2 C 4:3, 4. 11:3. Col 2:18. 2 Th 2:11, 12. T 1:15.

30 scall. ver. 34-37. Le 14:54.
leprosy. Je 14:7-9. Ho 11:7, 8. 14:4.

31 plague. ver. 2.
seven days. ver. 4-6.

32 yellow hair. ver. 30. Mt 23:5. Lk 18:9-12. Ro 2:23.

33 be shaven. 1 P 5:6.

34 the seventh. 1 J 4:1. Ju 22. Re 2:2.
be not. ver. 23.
and he shall. ver. +6.

35 **spread much**. ver. 7, 27. 2 T 2:16, 17. 3:13.

37 **the priest**. Jn 5:22.

39 **if the bright**. Ec 7:20. Ro 7:22-25. Ja 3:2.

40 **hair is fallen off his head**. Heb. head is pilled. ver. 41. SS 5:11. Ro 6:12, 19. 8:10. Ga 4:13.
     bald. Is +3:24.

42 **forehead**. 2 Ch 26:16-20.

44 **utterly unclean**. Jb 36:14. Mt 6:23. 2 P 2:1, 2. 2 J 8-10.
     his plague. Is 1:5.
     head. 2 C 10:5.

45 **his clothes**. Ge 37:29. Jsh 7:6. 2 S 13:19. Jb 1:20. Is 6:5. Je 3:25. 36:24. Jl 2:13.
     and his head. Le 10:6. 21:10.
     bare. Nu 5:18. Ps 140:7. Pr 28:13. Jn 3:36. He 4:13.
     put. Jb 40:4. Ezk 24:17, 22. Mi 3:7.
     Unclean. Jb 42:6. Ps 51:3, 5. Is 6:5. 52:11. 64:6. La 4:15. Lk 5:8. 7:6, 7. 17:12. Ep 5:5.

46 **the days**. Pr 30:12.
     alone. 2 K 7:3. 15:5. Is 59:2. Jn 8:16, 29.
     without. Le +4:12. 2 K +5:1. La 1:1, 8. 4:15. Is 52:11. Ezk 24:17, 22. 1 C 5:5, 9-13. 2 Th 3:6, 14. 1 T 6:5. He 12:15, 16. Re 21:27. 22:15.

47 **The garment**. Ps 109:18. Is 3:16-24. 59:6. 64:6. Ezk 16:16. Ro 13:12. Ep 4:22. Col 3:3. Ju 23. Re 19:8.

48 **thing made of**. Heb. work of. ver. 51. Dt 8:11. Ju 23. Re 3:4.

49 **thing of skin**. Heb. vessel, *or* instrument. ver. 52, 53, 57-59. Le 15:4.
     it is. ver. +2.
     showed unto. Mk +1:44.

50 **look upon**. Ezk 44:23.
     plague. ver. 2.

51 **fretting leprosy**. Le 14:44.

52 **burn**. Le 11:33, 35. Dt 7:25, 26. Is 30:22. Ac 19:19, 20. Col 3:5.
     fretting leprosy. Le 14:44, 45.

54 **wash**. Hg 1:6.

55 **after**. Ezk 24:13. He 6:4-8. 2 P 1:9. 2:20-22.
     not changed. Je 13:23. Lk 13:6-9. 1 C 7:20, 24. T 3:5.
     color. lit. eye. Nu 11:7mg. Ps 112:7. Pr 23:31. Is 28:9mg, 19. 53:1mg. Ezk 1:4. 7:26. Ob 1. Hab 3:2mg. Mt 4:24. 24:6. Jn 12:38. Mk 13:7. Ro 10:16mg. Ga 3:2, 5.
     it be bare within or without. Heb. it *be* bald in the head thereof, or in the forehead thereof. ver. 43.

56 **rend it out**. Ep 4:25.

57 *shalt burn*. Is 33:14. Mt 3:12. 22:7. 25:41. Re 21:8, 27.

58 **be washed**. 2 K 5:10, 14. Ps 51:2. 2 C 7:1. 12:8. He 9:10. Re 1:5. 7:14.
     the second time. Ac 19:1-5.

59 **pronounce**. 1 C 5:3-5. Re 19:8.

LEVITICUS 14

2 **the law**. ver. 54-57. Le 13:59.
     leper. 2 K +5:1. Lk 4:27.
     in the day. Nu 6:9.
     He shall. Mk +1:44.

3 **go forth**. Mt 9:10, 11. 11:19. 21:31, 32. Lk 7:34. 19:10.
     out of. Le +4:12. Lk 10:33. He 13:13.
     be healed. Ex +15:26. 2 K 5:3, 7, 8, 14. Jb 5:18. Mt 10:8. 11:5. Lk 4:27. 7:22. 17:15-19. 1 C 6:9-11.

4 **two**. Le 4:21. Ge 22:8. Mt 10:29.
     birds. *or*, sparrows. ver. 49. Le 1:14. 5:7. 12:8. Mt 10:29, 31. Lk 12:6, 7. Jn 6:38.
     cedar. ver. 6, 49-52. Nu 19:6. 1 K 6:9. Is 2:13.
     scarlet. 2 S 1:24. Is 1:18. He 9:19.
     hyssop. Ps +51:7.

5 **kill one**. Jn 11:49-52. Ac 2:23. Ro 5:6. 2 C 5:21.
     earthen vessel. ver. 50. Nu 5:17. 2 C 4:7. 5:1. 13:4. Ph 2:7, 8. He 2:14.
     running. Ge +26:19. Nu 19:17. SS +4:15. Ezk 34:18, 19. Zc 13:1. Ac 1:5. He 9:14.
     water. 2 K 5:10, 14. Ezk 34:18, 19. Ro 6:3, 4. 8:1, 2, 21. 1 J 5:6, 8.

6 **the living bird**. Jn 14:19. Ro 4:25. 5:10. Ph 2:9-11. He 1:3. Re 1:18.
     dip them. ver. 51-53. Zc 13:1. Ga 6:14. Re 1:5.
     blood. Jn 19:34. He 9:13, 14, 19. 1 J 5:6, 8.
     over. Zp 3:17.

7 **sprinkle**. Le +1:5. Jn 19:34. 1 J 5:6.
     seven times. ver. 51. Le 4:6, 17. 8:11. 16:14, 19. 2 K 5:10, 14. Ps 51:2, 7. Ep 5:26, 27.
     pronounce. Le 13:13, 17. 2 C 5:21.
     let. Le 16:22. Ge 49:21. Da 9:24. Mi 7:19. Ro 4:25. Col 3:1. He 9:26.
     into the open field. Heb. upon the face of the field. ver. 53. Le 17:5. Is 1:18. Zp 3:17. Jn 8:36. 1 C 15:42-44, 54, 55. Ga 5:1, 13.

8 **wash his**. Le 11:25. 13:6, 34. 15:5-8. Ex 19:10, 14. 33:5, 6. Nu 8:7. Jb 19:9. Is 32:11. Re 7:14.
     and shave. Nu 6:9. Jb 1:20. Ps 89:38, 39. Je 48:37.
     wash himself. Le 8:6. 1 P 3:21. Re 1:5, 6.
     come into. Jn 21:15-19. 2 C 2:6, 7. Ep 2:13.
     and shall. Nu 12:15.
     tarry. Mk 5:19. 2 C 5:6.
     seven days. Le 8:33-35. 13:5.

9 **on the seventh**. Nu 19:19.
     shave all his hair. Le 19:27. 21:5. Nu 6:9. 8:7. 2 S 10:4, 5. Ps 69:19, 20. Is 15:2. 50:6. 52:14. Je 41:5. 48:37. He 10:33. 13:13.
     wash his flesh. Nu 19:19. 2 C 7:1.
     clean. Is 44:22.

10 **eighth day**. ver. 23. Le 9:1. 15:13, 14. Mk 16:2-6. Jn 11:25-27. Ac 4:2. Ep 2:4-7. Col 1:21, 22. Re 21:5.

take. Mk +1:44.
he lambs. Le 1:10. Jn 1:29. 1 P 1:19.
ewe lamb. Le 4:32. Nu 6:14.
of the first year. Heb. the daughter of her year. Le 12:6mg.
three tenth. Le 23:13. Ex 29:40. Nu 15:9. 28:20.
a meat offering. Le +23:13.
log of oil. ver. 12, 15, 21, 24.

11 **shall present**. Le 8:3. 13:3. Ex 29:1-4. Nu 8:6-11, 21. Mk +1:44. Ep 5:26, 27. Ju 24.

12 **trespass**. Le +5:6. Ps 51:4.
wave them. Ex +29:24.
wave offering. Le +23:15.

13 **in the place**. Le +4:24.
as the sin. Le +7:7.
it is most holy. Le +2:3.

14 **upon the tip**. Le 8:23, 24. Ex 29:20. Is 50:5. Ro 6:13, 19. 12:1. 1 C 6:20. 2 C 7:1. Ph 1:20. 1 P 1:14, 15. 2:5, 9, 10. Re 1:5, 6.

15 **oil**. Ps 45:7. Jn 3:34. 1 J 2:20.

16 **sprinkle**. Le +1:5.
before the Lord. Le 4:6, 17. Lk 17:18. 1 C 10:31.

17 **the tip**. ver. 14. Le 8:30. Ex 29:20, 21. Ezk 36:27. Jn 1:16. T 3:3-6. 1 P 1:2.

18 **the remnant**. Le 8:12. Ex 29:7. 2 C 1:21, 22. Ep 1:17, 18.
make an atonement. ver. 20, 29, 53. Le +4:20.

19 **sin offering**. ver. 13. Le +23:19.

20 **shall offer**. ver. 10. Ep 5:2.
burnt offering. Le +23:12.

21 **poor**. Le 1:14. 5:7. 12:8. 1 S 2:8. Jb 34:19. Pr 17:5. 22:2. Lk 6:20. 21:2-4. 2 C 8:9, 12-15. Ja 2:5, 6.
cannot. Heb. his hand reach not. ver. 22, 30-32.
one lamb. ver. +10.
to be waved. Heb. for a waving. ver. 12, 24. Ex 29:24.

22 **two turtle doves**. Ps 68:13. SS 2:14. Is 38:14. 59:11. Je 48:28. Ezk 7:16.

23 **he shall bring**. ver. 11.

24 **the priest**. ver. 10-13.
wave offering. Le +23:15.

25 **trespass offering**. ver. 14-20. Le +5:6. Ec 5:1.

29 **make an atonement**. ver. +18, 20. Ex 30:15, 16. Jn 17:19. 1 J 5:6.

30 **turtledoves**. ver. 22. Le 12:8. 15:14, 15. Lk 2:24. Ro 8:3.
such as he can. Le 5:7. Lk +11:41.

32 **the law**. ver. 2, 54-57. Le 13:59.
whose hand. ver. +10, 21. Ps 72:12-14. 136:23. Mt 11:5. 1 C 1:27, 28.

34 **When**. Le 23:10. 25:2. Nu 35:10. Dt 7:2. 12:1, 8. 17:14. 19:1. 26:1. 27:3. Ep 5:3-11.
which I. Ge 12:7. 13:17. 17:8. Nu 32:32. Dt 12:9, 10. 32:49. Jsh 13:1.

I put the plague of leprosy. Ge +24:44. Ex +15:26. Dt 7:15. 1 S 2:6. Pr 3:33. Is 45:7. Am +3:6. 6:11. Mi 6:9.
house. Pr 3:33. 1 C 3:16. 2 T 2:20, 21.

35 **come and tell**. Ps 32:5.
a plague. Dt 7:26. Jsh 7:21. 1 S 3:12-14. 1 K 13:34. Ps 91:10. Pr 3:33. Zc 5:4.

36 **empty**. or, prepare. S#6437h. Ge 24:31. Ps 80:9. Zp 3:15 (cast out). Ml 3:1.
be not made. 1 C 15:33. 2 T 2:17, 18. He 12:15. Re 18:4.
house. Pr 3:33. Zc 5:3, 4.

37 **with hollow streaks**. Le 13:3, 19, 20, 42, 49.

38 **shut**. Le 13:50. 1 C 5:2. 2 C 12:20, 21. 2 P 3:9-11.

39 **come again**. Lk 13:6-9.
spread in. Le 13:7, 8, 22, 27, 36, 51.
house. Jb 19:25-27. Jn 14:2. 1 C 5:5. 15:53. 2 C 5:1-4.

40 **take away**. Ezr 9:2. 10:17. Ps 101:5, 7, 8. Pr 22:10. 25:4, 5. Is 1:25, 26. Mt 18:17. Jn 15:2. 1 C 5:5, 6, 13. T 3:10. 2 J 10, 11. Re 2:2, 6, 14-16, 20.
without the city. Re 22:15.

41 **scraped**. Ne 13:4-10. Ezk 26:4. 2 C 7:11.
into an unclean place. ver. 45. Jb 36:13, 14. Is 65:4. Mt 8:28. 24:51. 1 T 1:20. Re 22:15.

42 **take other stones**. Ge 18:19. Jsh 24:15. 2 Ch 17:7-9. 19:5-7. 29:4, 5. Ps 101:6. Lk 13:6-9. Ac 1:20-26. 1 T 5:9, 10, 21, 22. 2 T 2:2. T 1:5-9.

43 **the plague**. Je 6:28-30. Ezk 24:13. He 6:4-8. 2 P 2:20, 22. Ju 12.

44 **fretting leprosy**. Le 13:51, 52. Pr 4:14, 15. Zc 5:4. 1 C 15:33.

45 **break down**. Le 11:35. 1 K 9:6-9. 2 K 10:27. 17:20-23. 18:4. 25:4-12, 25; 26. Ezr 6:11. Jb 19:25-27. Je 52:13. Ezk 5:4. Mt 22:7. 24:2. Jn 14:2. Ro 11:7-11. 1 C 5:5. 15:53. 2 C 5:1-4. Re 2:5. 11:2.
and the timber. Zc 5:1-4.
into an unclean place. ver. +41.

46 **goeth into**. 2 J 10, 11.
shall be unclean. Le 11:24, 25, 28. 15:5-8, 10. 17:15. 22:6. Nu 19:7-10, 21, 22.

47 **wash his clothes**. ver. +8, 9.

48 **shall come in**. Heb. in coming shall come in, etc.
because. ver. 3. Jb 5:18. Ho 6:1. Mk 5:29, 34. Lk 7:21. 1 C 6:11.

49 **to cleanse**. ver. 4-7.

51 **scarlet**. Jsh 2:18-21.
blood of the. He 9:19.
slain bird. Mk 15:12-20. He 2:14.

53 **let go**. Ps 55:6. 124:7. Is 35:10. Lk 4:18. Jn 18:8. Ro 6:18. 2 C 3:17.
and make. ver. 20.
it shall be clean. Ps 118:15.

54 **the law**. ver. 2, 32. Le 6:9, 14, 25. 7:1, 37.

11:46. 15:32. Nu 5:29. 6:13. 19:14. Dt 24:8.
scall. Le 13:30, 31.

55 **the leprosy**. Le 13:47-59.
of a house. ver. 34.

56 **a rising**. Le 13:2.

57 **teach**. Le 10:10. Je 15:19. Ezk 44:23.
when it is unclean, and when it is clean.
Heb. in the day of the unclean, and in the day
of the clean. Jn 17:15.
this is. Dt 24:8.

LEVITICUS 15

1 **Aaron**. Le 11:1. 13:1. Ps 25:14. Am 3:7. He
1:1.

2 **unto the**. Dt 4:7, 8. Ne 9:13, 14. Ps 78:5.
147:19, 20. Ro 3:2.
when any man. Le 22:4. Nu 5:2. 2 S 3:29.
Mt 9:20. Mk 5:25. 7:20-23. Lk 8:43.
running issue. *or,* running of the reins. Le
22:4mg.

3 **issue**. Le 22:4. Nu 5:2. Mt 9:20. Mk 5:29. Lk
8:43.
flesh run. Le 12:3. Ezk 16:26. 23:20.

4 **thing**. Heb. vessel. ver. 6, 22, 23, 26. Le
13:49.
be unclean. 1 C 15:33. Ep 5:11. T 1:15.

5 **wash his clothes**. Le 11:25, 28, 32. 13:6, 34.
14:8, 9, 27, 46, 47. 16:26, 28. 17:15. Nu
19:10, 22. Ps 26:6. 51:2, 7. Is 1:16. 22:14. Ezk
36:25, 29. He 9:14, 26. 10:22. Ja 4:8. Re 7:14.
and bathe himself. Heb. *rahats,* S#7364h, Ex
+29:4. Le 15:5, 6, 7, 8, 10, 11, 13, 18, 21, 22,
27. 16:26, 28. 17:15, 16. Nu 19:7, 8, 19. 2 K
+5:10. He 9:10.

6 **and bathe**. Heb. *rahats,* S#7364h, Ex +29:4.
ver. +5. Is 1:16. Ja 4:8.

8 **wash his clothes**. Is 1:16. Ga 1:8, 9. 1 T 4:1-
3. T 1:9, 10, 2 P 2:1-3. Ja 4:8. Ju 4.

9 **saddle**. Ge 31:34.

10 **wash his clothes**. ver. +5, 8. Ps 26:6. Ja 4:8.

11 **whomsoever**. Nu 19:19.
rinsed. Heb. *shataph,* S#7857h. Le 6:28. 15:11,
12 (rinsed). 1 K 22:38 (washed). 2 Ch 32:4
(ran. mg, overflowed). Jb 14:19 (washest
away. mg, overflowest). Ps 69:2 (overflow),
15. 78:20. 124:4 (overwhelmed). SS 8:7
(drown). Is 8:8. 10:22. 28:2, 15, 17, 18. 30:28.
43:2. 66:12. Je 8:6. 47:2. Ezk 13:11, 13. 16:9
(throughly washed away). 38:22. Da 11:10,
22 (overflown), 26, 40. He 9:10.

12 **vessel**. Le 6:28. 11:32, 33. Pr 1:21, 23. 3:21. 2
C 5:1. Ph 3:21.
shall be broken. Ps 2:9. 2 P 3:11.

13 **seven days**. ver. 28. Le 8:33. 9:1, 14:8, 10.
Ex 29:35, 37. Nu 12:14. 19:11, 12.
wash. ver. 5, 10, 11. Je 33:8. Ezk 36:25-29. 2
C 7:1. Ja 4:8. Re 1:5.
clean. Ps 51:6.

14 **two turtledoves**. ver. 29, 30. Le 1:14. 12:6,

8 14:22-31. Nu 6:10. 2 C 5:21. He 7:26.
10:10, 12, 14.

15 **the one**. Le 5:7-10. 14:19, 20, 30, 31.
sin offering. Le +23:19.
burnt offering. Le +23:12.
an atonement. Le 4:20, 26, 31, 35. 12:7.
14:18. Nu 15:25. 25:13. Mt 3:17. Ep 1:6. He
1:3.

16 **man's seed**. ver. 5. Le 22:4. Ge +38:9. Dt
23:10, 11. 2 C 7:1. 1 P 2:11. 1 J 1:7.
of copulation. Le 18:6-16, 19, 23. 20:15, 16.
Ge +38:9. Ex 22:19. S#7902h. Ex 16:13 (lay),
14. Le 15:16 (lit. lying), 17, 18, 32. 19:20 (car-
nally; lit., the lying of seed). 22:4. Nu 5:13.

18 **The woman**. ver. 5. Ep 4:17-19. 5:3-11. 2 T
2:22. 1 P 2:11.
unclean. Ex 19:15. 1 S 21:4, 5. Ps 51:5, 6. 1
C 6:12, 18. 2 C 7:1. 1 Th 4:3-5. He +13:4.

19 **and her issue**. Le 12:2, 4. 20:18. La 1:8, 9,
17. Ezk 36:17. Mt 15:19. Mk 5:25.
put apart. Heb. in her separation. ver. 20. Le
12:2, 5.

20 **every thing**. ver. 4-9. Pr 2:16-19. 5:3-13.
6:24, 35. 7:10-27. 9:13-18. 22:27. Ec 7:26. 1 C
15:33.

21 **shall wash**. ver. +5, 6. Is 22:14. 2 C 7:1. He
9:26. Re 7:14.

24 **any man**. ver. 33. Le 20:18. Ezk 18:6. 22:10.
1 Th 5:22. He 13:4. 1 P 2:11.
flowers. *or,* monthly flow. S#5079h. Le 12:2
(separation), 5. 15:19 (put apart; mg, in her
separation), 20, 24 (flowers), 25, 25, 25, 26,
26, 33 (flowers). 18:19 (put apart). 20:21
(unclean thing; mg, a separation). Nu 19:9,
13, 20, 21, 21. 31:23. 2 Ch 29:5 (the filthiness). Ezr 9:11 (unclean with the filthiness).
La 1:17 (menstruous woman). Ezk 7:19
(removed; mg, for a separation, or, uncleanness), 20 (far; mg, unclean thing). 18:6 (menstruous). 22:10. 36:17 (removed woman). Zc
13:1 (uncleanness; mg, separation for
uncleanness). S#2931h, ver. +25.

25 **an issue**. Nu 5:2.
many days. ver. 19-24. Mt 9:20. Mk 5:25.
7:20-23. Lk 8:43.
unclean. S#2931h. Le 5:2. 15:2, 25, 26, 33. Jb
14:4. Is 6:5. 35:8. Is 52:1, 11. 64:6. Je 19:13
(defiled). La 4:15. Ezk 4:13. 22:5 (infamous;
mg, polluted of name), 10 (pollution), 26.
44:23. Ho 9:3. Am 7:17. Hg 2:13, 14. S#5079h,
ver. +24.

27 **shall wash**. ver. 5-8, 13, 21. Le 17:15, 16.
Ezk 36:25, 29. Zc 13:1. He 9:14. +10:22. 1 P
1:18, 19. 1 J 1:7.

28 **number**. ver. 13-15. Mt 1:21. 1 C 1:30. 6:11.
Ga 3:13. 4:4. Ep 1:6, 7.

29 **eighth day**. ver. 14.

30 **sin offering**. Le +23:19.
burnt offering. Le +23:12.
for the issue. Ps 103:3. Ezk 44:23.

31 Thus shall. Le 11:47. 13:59. Nu 5:3. Dt 24:8. Ps 66:18. Ezk 44:23. He 10:29. 12:14, 15. Ju 4.
that they. Le 19:30. 21:23. Nu 5:3. 19:13, 20. Ezk 5:11. 23:38. 44:5-7. Da 9:27. 1 C 3:17.

32 law of him. ver. 1-18. Le 11:46. 13:59. 14:2, 32, 54-57. Nu 5:29. 6:13. 19:14. Ps 119:1, 2, 18, 73, 128, 140. Is 4:4. Ezk 43:12. Zc 13:1. Mt 5:8. Ep 5:25-27. T 1:15. He 9:8-14. 12:28. Re 14:1-5.

33 of her. ver. 19-30.
flowers. ver. +24.
and of him. ver. 24. Le 20:18.

LEVITICUS 16

1 after the death. Le 10:1, 2. 2 C 1:4.

2 he come not. ver. 34. Le 23:27. Ex 26:33, 34. 30:10. 40:20, 21. 1 K 8:6. Ep 2:18. He 9:3, 7, 8. 10:19, 20.
that he die not. ver. 13. Le 8:35. Nu 4:19. 17:10. Mt 27:51. He 4:14-16. 10:19.
in the cloud. ver. 13. Ex +13:21.
the mercy seat. Ex +25:17.

3 Aaron. He 9:7, 12, 24, 25.
a young. Le 4:3. 8:14. Nu 29:7-11.
burnt offering. Le +23:12.

4 holy linen coat. Heb. of holiness. Le 6:10. Ex 28:2, 39-43. 39:27-29. Is 53:2. Ezk 44:17, 18. Lk 1:35. 2 C 8:9. Ph 2:7. He 2:14. 7:26. Re 19:8.
therefore. Le 8:6, 7. Ex 29:4. 30:20. 40:12, 31, 32. He 10:22. Re 1:5, 6.

5 two kids. Le 4:14. 8:2, 14. 9:8-16. Nu 29:11. 2 Ch 29:21. Ezr 6:17. Ezk 45:22, 23. Ro 8:3. He 7:27, 28. 10:5-14.

6 which. Le 8:14-17. He 9:7.
an atonement for himself. Le 9:7. Ezr 10:18, 19. Jb 1:5. Ezk 43:19-27. He 5:2. 7:27, 28. 9:7.
house. Ps 115:12. He 3:6. 1 P 2:5.

7 present them. Le 1:3. 4:4. 12:6, 7. Mt 16:21. Ro 12:1.

8 cast lots. Jsh +14:2.
scape goat. Heb. *Azazel*, that is, the goat gone away. ver. 10, 26. Dt 32:26.

9 upon which. Ac 2:23. 4:27, 28.
fell. Heb. went up. ver. 10.

10 the scape goat. ver. 21, 22.
to make. Le +4:20. Is 53:5, 6, 10, 11. Ro 4:25. 2 C 5:21. He 7:26, 27. 9:23, 24. 1 J 3:16.
let him. Le 14:7.
into. Jn 1:29. 1 J 2:2.

11 the bullock. ver. +3, 6.

12 censer. Nu 16:46. Is 6:6, 7. Re 8:3, 5.
from off. Le 10:1. Nu 16:18, 46. Is 6:6, 7. He 9:14. 1 J 1:7.
before. Dt +16:16.
hands full. Ex 29:24. Dt 16:16. 26:2.
sweet incense. Ex +39:38. Ps +141:2.

beaten. Ex +27:20. Is 53:5. He +2:10.

13 And he. Ex 30:1, 7, 8. Nu 16:7, 18, 46. Re 8:3, 4.
the cloud. Ex 25:21. He 4:14-16. 7:25. 9:24. 1 J 2:1, 2.
cover. Ps 84:11.

14 the blood of. Ro 3:24-26. He 9:7, 13, 25. 10:4, 10-12, 19.
sprinkle. Le +1:5.
eastward. Le +1:16.
blood with. Le 17:11. He 9:22, 25. 10:4. 12:24. 13:20.
seven. ver. 19. Le +4:6.

15 Then shall. ver. 5-9. He 2:17. 5:3. 9:7, 25, 26.
sin offering. Le +23:19.
bring. ver. 2. He 6:19. 9:3, 7, 12.
mercy seat. Ex +25:17. He 2:17. 5:2. 6:19, 20. 9:28.

16 an atonement. ver. 18. Le 8:15. Ex 29:36, 37. Ezk 45:18, 19. Jn 14:3. He 9:22, 23.
all their sins. Ps 69:5. Is 53:4, 6.
remaineth. Heb. dwelleth. Le 15:31.

17 no man. Ex 34:3. Ps 22:1. 69:20. Is 43:11. 45:21. 53:6. 63:3, 5. Da 9:24. Mt 26:56. 27:46. Lk 1:10. Jn 16:32. Ac 4:12. 1 T 2:5. He 1:3. 9:7. 1 P 2:24. 3:18.
and have made. ver. +10, 11. Lk 1:10.

18 go out. ver. 16. Jn 17:19. He 2:11. 5:7, 8. 9:12-14, 22, 23.
horns. Ex +27:2.

19 hallow it. Ezk 43:18-22. Zc 13:1.

20 reconciling. ver. 16. He +2:17.
live goat. Ro 4:25. 8:34. He 7:25. Re 1:18.

21 lay. Le +1:4. Ex 29:10.
confess over. Le 26:40. Ezr 10:1. Ne 1:6, 7. 9:3, etc. Ps 32:5. 51:3. Pr 28:13. Da 9:3-20. Ro 10:10.
putting. Is 53:6. 2 C 5:21.
a fit man. Heb. a man of opportunity. S#6261h, only here.

22 bear upon. Is 53:11, 12. Jn 1:29. Ga 3:13. He 9:28. 1 P 2:24.
not inhabited. Heb. of separation. Ps 103:10, 12. Ezk 18:22. Mi 7:19.
let go. Le 14:7.
in the wilderness. Ps 103:12. Is 38:17. 44:22. Je 31:34. 50:20. Jn 1:29. 1 J 1:7.

23 shall put off. ver. 4. Ezk 42:14. 44:19. Ro 8:3. Ph 2:6-11. He 9:28.

24 wash. Heb. *rahats*, Ex +29:4. ver. 4. Le 8:6. 14:9. 22:6. Ex 29:4. He +9:10. +10:19-22. Re 1:5, 6.
his flesh. He +9:10.
with water. Ex 30:19. Ac +1:5.
in the holy place. Ex 30:19, 21. Lk 7:44. He +9:10.
his garments. Le 8:7-9. Ex 28:4, etc. 29:5.
his burnt. ver. 3, 5.
and make. ver. +17.

25 **the fat**. ver. 6. Le 4:8-10, 19. Ex +29:13.
26 **he that**. ver. 10, 21, 22.
 wash. ver. 28. Le 14:8. 15:5-11, 27. Nu 19:7,
 8, 21. He 7:19. 13:11.
27 **bullock**. Le 4:11, 12, 21. 6:30. 8:17.
 sin. Le +23:19.
 without. Le +4:12.
28 **wash his clothes**. ver. +26.
29 **for ever**. Heb. *olam*, Ex +12:24.
 in the seventh. Le 23:27-32. Ex 30:10. Nu
 29:7. 1 K 8:2. Ezr 3:1. Ga 4:4.
 shall afflict. Nu +29:7. Mt 26:36-39. Lk
 12:50. 1 C 11:31. Ph 2:5-8. He 5:7, 8.
 souls. Heb. *nephesh*, Ge +27:31.
 do no. Le 23:3, 7, 8, 21, 28, 36. Ex 12:16.
 20:10. Is 58:13. He 4:10.
30 **atonement**. Le +23:27. He 9:14.
 to cleanse. Ps 51:2, 7, 10. Je 33:8. Ezk 36:25-
 27. Ep 5:26. T 2:14. He 9:13, 14. 10:1, 2. 1 J
 1:7-9.
 your sins. Mt 26:27, 28. Lk 7:47, 50. 1 C
 15:3. 1 P 2:24. 3:18.
31 **a sabbath**. Le 23:32. 25:4. Ex 31:15. 35:2.
 of rest. He 4:10, 11.
 souls. Heb. *nephesh*, Ge +27:31.
 for ever. Heb. *olam*, Ex +12:24.
32 **the priest**. Le 4:3, 5, 16.
 consecrate. Heb. fill his hand. Ex +28:41mg.
 father's stead. He 5:4, 6. 7:23.
 to minister. Ex 29:29, 30. Nu 20:26-28.
 put on the linen. ver. +4.
 holy garments. Ex 29:29, 30.
33 **an atonement**. ver. 6, 16, 18, 19, 24. Ex
 20:29, 30. He 5:3. 9:14. 1 P 1:19.
 for all. Mk 16:15. Lk 2:10. 2 C 5:15. 1 T 2:6.
 He 2:9. 1 J 2:2.
34 **an everlasting**. Heb. *olam*, Ge +17:7. Le
 23:31. Ex 12:14. Nu 29:7. 2 S 23:5.
 atonement. Le +23:27.
 once a year. Ex 30:10. He 9:7, 25. 10:3, 14.

LEVITICUS 17

3 **be of**. ver. 8, 12, 13, 15.
 that killeth an. Dt 12:5-7, 11-15, 20-22, 26,
 27.
4 **bringeth**. Le 1:3. Dt 12:5, 6, 13, 14. Ezk
 20:40. Jn 10:7, 9. 14:6. Ro 5:13. He 3:12. Ja
 +4:17.
 blood shall. Le 7:18. Ps 32:2. Ro 4:6. 5:13,
 20. Phm 18, 19.
 he hath. Is 66:3.
 be cut off. ver. 10, 14. Le 18:29. 20:3, 16, 18.
 Ge 17:14. Ex 12:15, 19. Nu 15:30, 31.
5 **in the open**. Ge 21:33. 22:2, 13. 31:54. Dt
 12:2. 1 K 14:23. 2 K 16:4. 17:10. 2 Ch 28:4.
 Ps 16:4. Ezk 20:28. 22:9.
 and offer them. Le ch. 3. 7:11-21. Ex 24:5.
 peace offerings. Le +23:19.
6 **sprinkle**. Le 3:2, 8, 13.

the altar of the Lord. Dt 12:27. Jsh 22:29. 2
 Ch +4:1. 33:16. Am +9:1.
 burn the fat. Ex +29:13, 18.
 sweet savor. Ex 29:18.
7 **unto devils**. Dt 32:17. 2 Ch 11:15. 25:14. Ps
 106:37, 39. Jn 12:31. 14:30. 1 C 10:20. 2 C
 4:4. Ep 2:2. Re 9:20.
 gone a whoring. Ex +34:15.
 for ever. Heb. *olam*, Ex +12:24.
8 **that offereth**. ver. 4, 10. Le 1:2, 3. Jg 6:26. 1
 S 7:9. 10:8. 16:2. 2 S 24:25. 1 K 18:30-38. Ml
 1:11.
 burnt offering. Le +23:12.
9 **bringeth**. ver. 4.
10 **soul**. Heb. *nephesh*, Ge +17:14.
 that eateth. ver. 11. Le +3:17.
 I will. Ezk +15:7.
 face. Ge +19:13.
11 **the life**. Heb. *nephesh*, soul, Ge +2:19; Ge
 +9:5. ver. 14. Ge 9:4, +15. Dt 12:23. 2 S 14:7.
 1 Ch 11:19. Est 8:11. Mt +2:20. 27:4, 24. Lk
 12:22.
 flesh. Nu 16:22.
 I have given. Le 8:15. 16:11, 14-19. Mt
 20:28. 26:28. Mk 14:24. Jn 6:53. 19:34. Ro
 3:25. 5:9. Ep 1:7. Col 1:14, 20. He +2:10.
 9:22. 13:12. 1 P 1:2. 1 J 1:7. 2:2. Re 1:5.
 souls. Heb. *nephesh*, Ge +12:13. Le 26:15. 1 S
 1:26. 2 C +12:15mg.
12 **soul**. Heb. *nephesh*, Ge +27:31.
 eat blood. Le +3:17.
 neither. Ex 12:49.
13 **which hunteth**. Le 7:26.
 hunteth. Heb. hunteth any hunting.
 pour out. Dt 12:16, 24. 15:23. 1 S 14:32-34.
 Jb 16:18.
 cover. Ezk 24:7, 8.
14 **life**. Heb. *nephesh*, soul, Ge +2:19. ver. +11,
 +12. Ge 9:4, +15. Dt 12:23.
15 **every**. Le 22:8. Ex 22:31. Dt 14:21. Ezk 4:14.
 44:31.
 soul. Heb. *nephesh*, Ge +27:31.
 that which died of itself. Heb. a carcase. Le
 5:2. 7:24mg. 11:8, 11, 24, 25, 27, 28, 35, 36,
 37, 38, 39, 40, 40. 22:8.
 both wash. S#3526h, Nu +19:21. Le 11:25.
 15:5, 10, 21. Nu 19:8, 19, 21. Re 7:14.
 bathe. S#7364h, Ex +29:4. 2 K 5:10.
 in water. Le 11:32. 16:24. Ex 30:19.
16 **shall bear**. Le 5:1. 7:18. 19:8. 20:17, 19, 20.
 Nu 19:19, 20. Is 53:11. Jn 13:8. Ac 15:20. He
 9:28. 1 P 2:24. Re 2:18. 3:4.

LEVITICUS 18

2 **I am the**. ver. 4. Le 11:44. 19:3, 4, 10, 34.
 20:7. Ge 17:7. Ex 6:7. 20:2. Ps 33:12. Ezk
 20:5, 7, 19, 20.
3 **the doings**. Ezk 20:7, 8. 23:8. Ep 5:7-11. 1 P
 4:2-4.

not do. 2 C 6:17, 18.
and after. Ex 23:24. Je +10:2, 3. Ro 12:2.

4 do my. ver. 26. Dt +4:1.

5 which if a man do. Ge 4:7. Dt 4:1, 2. 6:25. Ne 9:29. Ec 7:20. Ezk 18:9. 20:11, 13, 21. Mt 19:17. Lk 10:28, 29. Ro 3:10. 10:3, *5*, 6. Ga *3:12*. Ja 2:10. 2 P 1:4.
I am the Lord. Ex 6:2, 6, 29. Ml 3:6.

6 near to kin. Heb. remainder of his flesh. Le 20:19. Ge 5:4. Je 51:35mg.
to uncover. ver. 7-19. Le 20:11, 12, 17-21. Mk 7:21, 22. 1 C 5:1. 6:9, 10, 13. Ga 5:19-21. Ep 5:3-7.

7 not uncover. Le 20:11. Ge 19:32. Ezk 22:10.

8 nakedness of. Le 20:11. Ge 35:22. 49:4. Dt 22:30. 27:20. 2 S 16:21, 22. Ezk 22:10. Am 2:7. 1 C 5:1. 7:2.

9 thy sister. Le 20:17. Dt 27:22. 2 S 13:11-14. Ezk 22:11.

11 thy sister. 2 S 13:12. Ezk 22:11.

12 father's sister. Le 20:19. Ex 6:20.

14 father's brother. Le 20:20.

15 daughter in law. Le 20:12. Ge 38:18, 19, 26. Ps 19:12, 13. Ezk 22:11.

16 brother's wife. Le 20:21. Dt 25:5. Mt 14:3, 4. 22:24. Mk 6:17. 12:19. Lk 3:19.

17 a woman. Le 20:14. Dt 27:23. Am 2:7.
it is wickedness. Le 20:14.

18 wife. *or, one* wife to another. Ge +4:19. 29:28. Ex 26:3.
to vex her. Ge 29:21-30. 30:15. 1 S 1:6-8. Ml 2:15.

19 as long. Le 15:19, 24. 20:18. Ezk 18:6. 22:10.

20 shalt not lie. Le 20:10. Ge 38:9. Ex 20:14. Dt 5:18. 22:22, 25. 2 S 11:3, 4, 27. Pr 6:25, 29-33. Ml 3:5. Mt 5:27, 28. Ro 2:22. 1 C 6:9. Ga 5:19. 1 Th 4:3-8. He 13:4.
with. Le 20:13 (both), with Jn 8:5, 6.

21 pass through. Le 20:2. Ex 13:12mg. Dt +18:10.
to Molech. i.e. *king*, **S#4432h**. ver. 21. Le 20:2, 3, 4, 5. 1 K 11:7, 33. 2 K 23:10. Je 32:35. Am 5:26. Ac 7:43, Moloch.
profane. Le 19:12. 20:2-5. 21:6. 22:2, 32. Ezk 36:20-23. Ml 1:12. Ro 1:23. 2:24.

22 lie with mankind. ver. 24. Le 20:13. Ge 19:5, 24. Dt +23:17. Jg 19:22. 2 S +3:29. 2 K +23:7. 2 Ch +19:2. Jb 36:14mg. Ps 9:17. +119:63. Is 3:9. Ro +1:26, 27. 1 C +6:9-11. 2 C 6:17. Ga 5:19-21. Ep 5:5, 7. 1 T 1:10. He 13:4. Ja 5:20. 2 P +2:6. Ju 7, 22, 23.

23 any beast. Le 20:15, 16. Ex 22:19.
confusion. Le 20:12.

24 Defile. ver. 6-23, 30. Je 44:4. Mt 15:18-20. Mk 7:10-23. 1 C 3:17. +6:9-11. 2 C 6:17.
for. Le 20:22, 23. Dt 12:31. 18:12.

25 the land. Nu 35:33, 34. Dt 21:23. Ps 106:38. Is +24:5. Je 2:7. 3:1, 2, 9. 16:18. Ezk 36:17, 18. Mi 2:10. Ro 8:22.
therefore. Ps 89:32. Is 26:21. Je 5:9, 29. 9:9.

14:10. 23:2. Ho 2:13. 8:13. 9:9. Col 3:5-11. Ju 7, 8.
vomiteth. ver. 28. Le 20:22.

26 keep. ver. +4, 5, 30. Dt 12:32. Lk +8:15. +11:28.
nor any stranger. Le 17:8, 10. Je +10:2.

27 abominations. ver. 24. Dt 20:18. 23:18. 25:16. 27:15. 1 K 14:24. 2 K 16:3. 21:2. 2 Ch 36:14. Ezk 16:50. 22:11. Ho 9:10.

28 spew. ver. 25. Le 20:22. Je 9:19. Ezk 36:13, 17. Ro 8:22. Re 2:20, 21. 3:16.

29 souls. Heb. *nephesh*, Ge +17:14.
cut off. Le 17:10. 20:6. Ex +12:15.

30 abominable. ver. 3, 26, 27. Le 20:23. Dt 18:9-12.
that ye defile. ver. 24. Ps 69:5. 106:29-31. Ezk +16:49.
I am. ver. 2, 4. Le 19:4.

LEVITICUS 19

2 Ye shall. Le 11:44, 45. 20:7, 26. 21:8. Ge 5:24. +17:1. Ex 19:6. Dt 14:2, 21. Jb 1:1. Ps 37:31, 37. Am 3:3. Mt +5:48. Jn +17:6. 2 C 6:14-16. 7:1. Ep 1:4. Ph 3:20, 21. Col 1:28. 1 Th 4:7. 1 P 1:15, *16*. 2:5, 9. Ju 24, 25.
am holy. Ps +99:3.

3 fear. Ex +20:12. Mt 15:4-6. Lk 2:51.
keep. ver. 30. Ex +20:8. Is +58:13. Col 2:16.

4 not unto. Ex +20:4. Ezk +39:13.
molten gods. Ex +34:17.

5 peace offerings. Le +23:19.
your own will. Le +23:38. Mk 7:11.

6 shall be eaten. Le 7:11-17.
third. Le 23:11. Ge +22:4. 40:20. Ex 10:22. Lk 24:46. Ro 5:1. 1 C 11:26-28. +15:4. Ep 2:14.

7 abominable. Is 1:13. 65:4. 66:3. Je 16:18.
third day. Lk 24:46. Ro 5:1. Ep 2:14.
it shall. Le +7:18-21. 22:23, 25. 1 C 11:26-28.

8 shall bear. Le 5:1.
profaned. Le 22:2, 32. Ex +20:7. Nu 30:2mg. Ne 13:17. Ps 55:20mg. Je 23:11. Ezk 22:8, 26. 23:38. Am +2:7. Mt 12:5. 1 T 1:9. 4:7. 6:20. 2 T 2:16. He 12:16.
soul. Heb. *nephesh*, Ge +17:14.
cut off. Ex 30:33.

9 ye reap the harvest. Le 23:22. Dt 24:19-21. Ru 2:2, 15, 16. Ps 10:2, 11, 12. Mt 26:11. Ga 2:10.

10 glean. Jg 8:2. Is 17:6. 24:13. Je 49:9. Ob 5. Mi 7:1.
thou shalt leave. Le 25:6.
for the poor. Ps 10:2, 11, 12. Pr 29:8. Ezk +16:49. Mt 26:11. Lk +14:13. Ga 2:10.
stranger. Dt +26:11.

11 not steal. Le 6:2. Ex +20:15, 17. 22:1, 7, 10-12. Dt 5:19. Ps 37:21. Je 6:13. 7:9-11. Zc 5:3, 4. 8:16, 17. 1 C +6:8-10. Ep 4:28.

deal falsely. Am +8:5. Mt 7:15. Ac +6:3.
lie one. Ps 101:7. 116:11. Pr 26:28. Is 32:7. Ro 3:4. Ep +4:25. 2 Th 2:9. Ja 3:14. 1 J 2:21, 22.

12 ye shall. Le 6:3. Ex +20:7. Dt 5:11. Ps 15:4. Je 4:2. 7:9. Zc 5:4. Ml +3:5. Mt 5:33, 34. Ja 5:12.
profane. Le 18:21. 24:11, 15, 16. Ezk 36:20-23.

13 not defraud. Pr 20:10. 22:22. Je 22:3. Ezk 22:29. Mk 10:19. Lk 3:13. 1 Th 4:6.
the wages. lit. work. Dt 24:14, 15. Jb 31:39. Je +22:13. Ml +3:5. Ro 11:6. 1 T +5:18, 19. +Ja 5:4. Re 14:13.

14 not curse. Dt 27:18. Ps 37:28. Ro 12:14. Ja 2:1, 9, 10.
stumblingblock. 1 C 8:9.
fear. ver. 32. Le 25:17. Ge 42:18. Ne 5:15. 1 P 1:17. 2:17.

15 no unrighteousness in. ver. 35. Ex 18:21. 23:2, 3, 7, 8. Dt 25:13-16. Ps 37:28. 82:1-4. Pr 18:5. 29:27. 31:4, 5. Ec 3:16. Hab +1:4. Lk +16:10. Jn +7:24. Ja 2:6-9.
respect the person of the poor. Jb 13:10. Je 22:3. La 3:36. Ro +2:11.
nor honor. Jb 36:19. 1 T +6:5. Ja +2:1.
in righteousness. Dt 16:20. Ps 82:3. Pr +18:13. 21:3. Is 56:1. Mi +6:8. Jn +7:24, 51. 1 T +5:19.

16 talebearer. Ex 23:1. Pr 11:13. 20:19. Ezk 22:9. Ep +4:31. Ja 3:6.
stand. Ex 20:16. 23:1, 7. 1 K 21:10-13. Mt 26:60, 61. 27:4. Ac 6:11-13. 24:4-9.

17 hate. Ge 27:41. Pr 26:24-26. 1 J 2:9, 11. 3:12-15.
rebuke. Ps 141:5. Pr 3:12. 9:8. 27:5, 6. Mt 18:15-17. Lk 17:3. 1 C 13:6. Ga 2:11-14. 4:16. 6:1. Ep 5:11. 1 T 5:20. 2 T 4:2. T 1:13. 2:15. He 3:12, 13. 10:24, 25.
and not suffer sin upon him. or, that thou bear not sin for him. Le 22:9. Ezk 3:17, 18. Ac 20:26, 27. Ro 1:32. 1 C 5:2. 1 T 5:22. Ja 5:19, 20. 1 J 5:16. 2 J 10, 11. Ju 23.

18 not avenge. Ex 23:4, 5. Dt 32:35. 2 S 13:22, 28. Pr 20:22. 24:29. Mt +5:44. Ro 12:17, 19. 13:4. He 10:30.
grudge. Ga 5:20. Ep 4:31. Col 3:8. Ja 5:9. 1 P 2:1.
thou shalt love. Mi +6:8. Mt 5:43. 18:15. 19:19. 22:39, 40. Mk 12:31-34. Lk 10:27-37. 17:3. Ro 13:9. Ga 5:14. 6:1, 2. 1 Th 4:9. Ja 2:8. 1 P 1:22. 3:8-12. 4:15. 1 J 2:9, 11. 3:10-18.
thy neighbor. Ex 20:16. Pr 3:28, 29. 14:21. 16:28, 29. Hab 2:15. Mk 12:31. Lk 10:29-36. Ro +12:5. 13:10. 15:2. Ga +6:10. Ja 2:8, 9.
as thyself. Ps +40:17. Mt 10:31. 16:26. Ro 8:17, 18. Ga 6:4. Ep 5:29. Ph +2:3.

19 thy cattle gender. Ge 36:24. 2 S 13:29. 18:9. 1 K 1:33. Ezr 2:66.
diverse. Mt 6:22, 24. Ga 2:11-18. 4:21-23.

mingled. Dt 22:9-11. Mt 9:16, 17. Ro 11:6. 2 C 6:14-17. Ga 3:9-11.
neither. 1 P 3:3-5.

20 bondmaid. Ge 12:16. 16:1, 2, 3, 5, 6, 8.
betrothed to an husband. or, abused by any.
she. or, they. Le 20:10. Jn 8:5, 6.
shall be scourged. Heb. there shall be a scourging. or, there shall be an investigation.
they shall. Ex 21:20, 21. Dt 22:23, 24. He 7:19.

21 trespass offering. Le +5:6.
22 and the sin. Le +4:20, 26. 1 T 1:8-11.
23 And when. Le +14:34.
fruit. Is 16:8. Ho 9:2. Jl 1:10. Na 1:4. Hab 3:17.
uncircumcised. Le 12:3. 22:27. Ex 6:12, 30. 22:29, 30. Je 6:10. 9:25, 26. Ac 7:51.

24 all the. Nu 18:12, 13. Dt 12:17, 18. 14:28, 29. 18:4. Pr 3:9.
holy to praise the Lord withal. Heb. holiness of praises to the Lord. Ps 50:23. 65:1. Je 17:26.

25 that it may. Le 26:3, 4. Pr 3:9, 10. Ec 11:1, 2. Hg 1:4-6, 9-11. 2:18, 19. Ml 3:8-10.

26 with the blood. Le +3:17.
use. Ex 7:11. 8:7. 1 S +15:23. Je 10:2. Da 2:10. Ml 3:5.
enchantment. 2 K +21:6.
nor. Jg 9:37mg. 2 K 17:17. +21:6.

27 round the corners. Le 21:5. Dt 14:1. Is 15:2. Je 9:26mg. 16:6. 41:5. 48:37. Ezk 7:18. 44:20. 1 C 11:3, 4. Ep 1:22, 23. Col 1:18, 19.

28 cuttings. Le 21:5. Dt 14:1. 1 K 18:28. Je 16:6. 41:5. 47:5. 48:37. Mk 5:5.
for the. Dt 14:1. 1 C 15:29.
dead. Heb. nephesh, soul. Here, nephesh is used of man as actually dead. Nephesh is similarly used elsewhere, rendered the dead at Le 21:1. 22:4. Nu 5:2. 6:11. Rendered dead body at Nu 9:6, 7, 10. Rendered body at Le 21:11. Nu 6:6. 19:11, 13. Hag 2:13. For the other uses of nephesh see Ge +2:7. Mt +10:28.
print. Re 13:16, 17. 14:9, 11. 15:2. 16:2. 19:20. 20:4.

29 prostitute. Heb. profane. S#2490h. Le 18:21. 20:3. 21:9. Is 53:5 (wounded). Ezk 9:6 (begin, began).
to cause. Le 21:7. Ge 18:20, 21. 19:6-8. Dt 23:17. Ho 4:12-14. Mt 18:6, 10, 14. 23:15. Mk 9:42. Lk 17:2. 1 C 6:15.
fall. lit. go a whoring.

30 keep. ver. +3. He 4:3, 10, 11.
reverence. Le 10:3. 15:31. 16:2. Ge 28:16, 17. 2 Ch 33:7. 36:14. Ps 89:7. Ec 5:1. Ezk 9:6. Hab 2:20. Mt 21:13. Jn 2:15, 16. 2 C 6:16. 1 T 3:15. 1 P 4:17.

31 Regard not. lit., turn or look, i.e., turn the face to look. S#6437h, ver. 4, 31. Le +14:36. 20:6. Jb 36:21.

familiar spirits. or, necromancers. **S#178h**. ver. 26. Dt +18:11. 2 K 17:17. Is 47:13. Re +9:21.

wizards. lit., knowing ones. 2 K +21:6.

32 **rise up**. ver. 14. Ge 31:35. +43:27. 1 K 2:19. Jb 32:4, 6. Pr 16:31. 20:29. 23:22. 31:28. Is 3:5. La 5:12. Ro 13:7. Ep 6:1-3. 1 T 5:1. 1 P 2:17.

33 **And if**. Ex 12:48, 49. 22:21. 23:9. Dt 10:18, 19. +24:14. Ml +3:5. Lk 10:29, 30, 36, 37. Jn 4:6, 7, 9.

stranger. ver. 10. Ge +23:4.

vex him. or, oppress him. Le 25:14. Ex 22:21. Ps +12:5. Je 7:6. Ezk 22:7, 29.

34 **the stranger**. ver. +10.

love him as. ver. +18. Ex 12:48, 49. Dt 10:19. Mt 5:43.

35 **no unrighteousness**. ver. +15.

in meteyard. Dt 25:13, 15. Pr 11:1. 16:11. 20:10. Ezk 22:12, 13. Am 8:5, 6. Mi 6:10, 11. Mt 7:2.

36 **Just balances**. Pr 11:1.

weights. Heb. stones. Pr 11:1mg. +16:11mg.

I am. Ex +20:2.

37 **observe all**. Dt +4:1. Mt 3:16, 17. 5:17-19. 7:21. Lk 9:35. 1 J 3:22, 23.

do them. Ro 13:10. 1 C 13:4, 7. 1 J 2:3.

LEVITICUS 20

2 **Again**. Is 28:10, 13.

Whosoever. Le 17:8, 13, 15.

giveth. Dt +18:10. Is 57:5, 6. Ac 7:43, Moloch.

surely. Ge +2:16.

the people. ver. 27. Le +24:14.

3 **I will set**. Pr 29:1. Ezk +15:7.

hath given. ver. 2. 1 K 11:6-13. Is 1:2-4.

to defile. Nu 19:20. Ezk 5:11. 23:38, 39.

profane. Le 18:21. Ezk 20:39. 2 C 6:16.

4 **hide**. 1 S 3:11-13. Ps 50:18. Pr 10:10. 24:24. 28:4. Ho 7:3. Mk 14:11. Lk 11:48. Ac 17:30. 22:20. Ro 1:32mg. Ep 5:11.

and kill. Dt 13:8. 17:2-5. Jsh 7:12. 1 S 3:13, 14. 1 K 20:42. Ho 9:17. Ml 2:11. Re 2:14.

5 **I will**. Le 17:10.

against his. Ex 20:5. Je 32:28-35, 39.

whoring. Ex +34:15.

6 **soul**. Heb. *nephesh*, Ge +27:31.

familiar. ver. 27. Dt +18:11. Ezk 21:21-24.

wizards. 2 K 21:6.

go. Ex +34:15, 16.

I will. Nu 23:19.

soul. Heb. *nephesh*, Ge +17:14.

cut him. 1 Ch 10:13, 14.

7 **Sanctify yourselves**. Le +19:2. Ezk 37:28. Jn 17:17, 19. Ep 5:25-27. Ph 2:12, 13. Col 3:12. 1 Th 4:3, 6, 7. 5:23. He 12:14. 13:12.

8 **And ye**. Dt +4:1. Mt 5:19. 7:24. 12:50. 28:20. Jn 13:17. Ja 1:22. Re 22:14.

Lord. Ex +15:26.

sanctify. Le 21:8. 22:32. Ex +15:26. 28:36. 31:13. Ezk 20:12. 37:28. 1 C 1:30. Ep 4:24. 1 Th 5:23. 2 Th 2:13. 2 T 1:9. He 3:1. 12:14.

9 **curseth**. Pr +20:20. Col 3:20.

surely. Ge +2:16.

his blood. ver. 11-13, 16, 27. Dt +19:10. Jsh 2:19. Jg 9:24. Ac 5:28. +18:6.

10 **the adulterer**. Le 18:20. Dt 22:22-24. 2 S 12:13. Ezk 23:45-47. Jn 8:4, 5.

and the adulteress. Le 19:20mg. Jn 8:5, 6.

surely. Ge +2:16.

11 **lieth with**. Le 18:8. Dt 27:20, 23. Am 2:7. 1 C 5:1.

surely. Ge +2:16.

their. ver. +9.

12 **lie**. Le 18:15. Ge 38:16, 18, 24-26. Dt 27:23.

surely. Ge +2:16.

confusion. Le 18:23.

13 **lie with mankind**. Le +18:22. 1 C +6:9.

surely. Ge +2:16.

14 **a wife**. Le 18:17. Dt 27:23. Am 2:7.

burnt. Le +21:9.

15 **lie with a beast**. Le 18:23. Ex 22:19. Dt 27:21.

surely. Ge +2:16.

16 **And if a woman**. Le 18:24, 25. Ju 17-19.

and the beast. Ex 19:13. 21:28, 32. He 12:20.

surely. Ge +2:16.

17 **sister**. Le 18:9. Ge 20:2, 10-12. Dt 27:22. 2 S 13:12. Ezk 22:11. Ro 5:13.

wicked thing. or, a shame. Job 6:14 (pity). Pr 14:34.

18 **having**. Le 15:24. 18:19. Ezk 18:6. 22:10.

discovered. Heb. made naked. ver. 19. Ps 141:8mg. Is 3:17mg. 22:6mg. La 4:21. Hab 3:13mg. Zp 2:14.

fountain. **S#4726h**, Le 12:7 (issue). Ps 36:9. 68:26. Pr 10:11 (well).

19 **mother's**. Le 18:12, 13, etc. Ex 6:20.

uncovereth. Le 18:6.

20 **uncle's wife**. Le 18:14.

sin. Ge +19:15.

childless. Jb 18:19. Ps 109:13. Je 22:30. Lk 1:7, 25. 23:29.

21 **his brother's**. Le 18:16. Mt 14:3, 4.

an unclean thing. Heb. a separation. Le 12:2, 5, etc.

22 **statutes**. Dt +4:1. Ps 119:80, 145, 171.

judgments. Ex 21:1. Dt 4:45. 5:1. Ps 119:20, 106, 160, 164, 175. Is 26:8, 9.

spue you. Le 18:25-28. 26:33. Dt 28:25, 26.

23 **in the manners**. Dt 9:5. Je +10:2. 1 Th 4:3-7. T 3:3-6.

therefore. Ps +106:40.

24 **But I**. Ex +3:8, 17. 6:8. He 11:16.

a land. Ex 3:17. Dt 32:13, 14. Jg 14:8. 1 S 14:25, 26. Ps 16:11. 81:11-16. Jn 14:2. 1 C 2:9. Re 22:2.

honey. Ex +3:8.

which. ver. 26. Ex 19:5, 6. Ho 11:1-3. Jn 15:19.

25 put a difference. Le ch. 11. Dt 14:3-21. Ac 10:11-15, 28. Ep 5:7-11.

souls. Heb. *nephesh*, Ge +27:31.

abominable. Le 11:43.

creepeth. *or*, moveth. Le 11:44, 46. Ge 1:21. 7:8. Ps 69:34. 104:20.

26 the Lord. ver. +7. Ps 99:5, 9. Is 6:3. 30:11. Re 3:7. 4:8.

severed. ver. +24. Dt 26:18, 19. T 2:14.

27 a familiar. ver. +6. Ex 22:18.

surely. Ge +2:16.

they shall stone. ver. +2.

their blood. ver. +9.

LEVITICUS 21

1 Speak. Ho 5:1. Ml 2:1, 4.

There. ver. 11. Le 10:6, 7. Nu 19:14, 16. Ezk 44:25.

the dead. Heb. *nephesh*, soul, Le +19:28.

2 kin. Le 18:6. Ezk 24:16-18. 1 Th 4:13.

4 he shall. *or*, the verse may be read, *being* an husband among his people, he shall not defile himself *for his wife*, etc. Ezk 24:16, 17.

chief man. ver. 14.

5 not make baldness. Le 10:6. +19:27. Is +3:24. Je 9:26.

cuttings. Le +19:28.

6 holy. ver. 8. Le 10:3. Ex 28:36. 29:44. Ezr 8:28. Ps 132:9, 16. 1 P 2:5, 9. Re 1:6. 20:6.

profane. Le 18:21. +19:8, 12. 22:2, 22. Je 23:11. Ezk 22:26. Ml 1:6, 11, 12.

bread. Le 3:11. Ezk 44:7. Ml 1:7.

therefore. Is 52:11.

7 that is a whore. ver. 8. Ezk 44:22. 1 T 3:11.

put away. Dt 24:1-4. Is 50:1.

for he. 1 T 3:2, 8, 9, 11, 12.

8 sanctify. ver. 6. Ex 19:10, 14. 28:41. 29:1, 43, 44. Jn 17:17, 19.

bread. Ge +3:19.

for I. Le +19:2. Jn 10:36. 17:19. He 7:26. 10:29.

Lord. Ex +15:26.

9 the daughter. 1 S 2:17, 34. 3:13, 14. Ezk 9:6. Ml 2:3. Mt 11:20-24. 1 T 3:4, 5. T 1:6.

she shall be burnt. Le 20:14. Ge 38:24. Jsh 7:15, 25. Is 33:14. Re 17:16. 21:8.

10 high priest among. He 2:17. 3:1. 4:14, 15. 7:26.

upon. Le 16:32. Ex +28:41.

consecrated. Le 8:7-9. Ex 28:2-4.

uncover. Le 10:6, 7. 13:45. 2 S 15:30. Est 6:12.

nor rend. Ge 37:34. Jb 1:20. Mt 26:65.

11 body. Heb. *nephesh*, soul, Le +19:28.

his father. ver. 1, 2. Nu 6:7. 19:14. Dt 33:9. Mt 8:21, 22. 12:46-50. Lk 9:59, 60. 14:26. 2 C 5:16.

12 go out. Le 10:7.

for the crown. ver. +10. Ex 28:36.

13 take a wife. ver. 7. Ezk 44:22. 2 C 11:2. Re 14:4.

virginity. **S#1331h**. Dt 22:14, 15, 17, 20. Jg 11:37, 38. Ezk 23:3, 8. For **S#1330h**, see Ge 24:16. For **S#5959h**, *almah*, see Ge +24:43.

14 take a virgin. Ge +24:16. SS 6:9. 2 C 11:2. Ep 5:27.

15 profane. Ge 18:19. Ezr 2:62. 9:2. Ne 13:23-29. Ml 2:11, 15. Ro 11:16. 1 C 7:14. 2 C 6:14-18.

for I the. ver. 8.

17 blemish. Le 22:20-25. 1 Th 2:10. 1 T 3:2. He 7:26.

let him. ver. 21. Le 10:3. Nu 16:5. Ps 65:4. 1 T 4:12. 1 P 5:3.

bread. *or*, food. Le 3:11, 16.

18 a blind man. Is 56:10. Mt 23:16, 17, 19. 1 T 3:2, 3, 7. T 1:7, 10.

superfluous. Le 22:23.

20 a dwarf. *or*, too slender. **S#1851h**. Ge 41:3 (lean), 4, 6 (thin), 23, 24. Ex 16:14 (small). Le 13:30 (thin). 16:12 (small). 21:20 (dwarf; mg, too slender). 1 K 19:12 (small). Is 29:5. 40:15 (very little thing).

or hath. Dt 23:1.

stones. **S#810h**, only here.

broken. ver. 24. Is 56:3. Mt 19:12.

21 a blemish. Mt 5:48. Lk 6:40. 2 C 13:9. Col 1:28. 2 T 3:17. Ja 1:4. 3:2. 1 P 5:10.

to offer. ver. 6, 8, 17. Jn 6:51. He 7:27.

bread. Ge +3:19.

22 bread. Ge +3:19.

both. Le +2:3.

and of the holy. Le 22:10-13. Nu 18:10, 19.

23 go in. Ex 30:6-8. 40:26, 27. Ezk 44:9-14.

profane. ver. 12. Le 15:31.

for I the Lord. ver. 8. 1 P 1:15, 16.

24 Moses told. He 3:2.

Aaron. Ml 2:1-7. Col 4:17. 1 T 1:18. 2 T 2:2.

LEVITICUS 22

2 separate themselves. ver. 3-6. Le 15:31. Nu 6:3-8.

that they profane not. ver. 32. Le 18:21. 19:12. 20:3. 21:6. Nu 18:32. 1 S 2:12-17. Ezk 44:21.

hallow. Ex 13:12. 28:38. Nu 18:32. Dt 15:19.

3 having his uncleanness upon him. Le 7:20, 21. Ps 89:7.

that soul. Heb. *nephesh*, Ge +17:14.

cut off. Le 10:1, 2. Ex 30:33.

from my. Ex 33:14, 15. Ps 16:11. 51:11. Mt 25:41. 2 Th 1:9.

4 a leper. Le 13:2, 3, 44-46.

running issue. Heb. running of the reins. Le 15:2, 3.

shall not eat. Lk 15:17.

holy things. Le 2:3, 10. 6:25-29. 21:22. Nu 18:9, 19.

until. Le 14:2, etc. 15:13-15.

unclean. Le 21:1. Nu 19:11-16. 1 Th 4:3, 4, 7. Ju 23.

the dead. Heb. *nephesh*, soul, Le +19:28.

whose. Le 15:16.

seed goeth. S#7902h, Le +15:16. Ge +38:9.

5 **whosoever**. Le 11:23, 24, 43, 44.

or a man. Le 15:7, 19.

6 **soul**. Heb. *nephesh*, Ge +27:31.

which hath. Le 11:24, 25. 15:5. 16:24-28. Nu 19:7-10. Hg 2:13. 1 C 6:11. He 7:26. 10:22.

7 **sun is down**. 1 J 1:6, 7.

because it. Le 21:22. Nu 18:11-19. Dt 18:3, 4. 1 C 9:4, 13, 14.

8 **dieth of itself**. Le 17:15. Ex 22:31. Dt 14:21. Ezk 44:31.

9 **bear sin for it**. Le 10:1, 2. 16:2. 19:17mg. Ex 28:43. Nu 18:22, 32.

profane. La 4:13, 14. Ezk 22:26. Mi 3:11, 12. Zp 3:4.

Lord. Ex +15:26.

10 **shall no**. 1 S 21:6. Mt 12:4.

stranger. Ep 2:12, 19.

sojourner. 1 J 2:19.

hired servant. Lk 15:18, 19. Jn 10:12, 13. 15:15.

11 **buy**. Ac 20:28. 1 C 6:20. 1 P 1:18, 19.

soul. Heb. *nephesh*, Ge +12:5.

his money. Heb. the purchase of his money. Ge 17:13. Nu 18:11-13. 1 C 6:19, 20.

born. 2 C 6:18. Ga 6:10. Ep 3:14, 15. 1 P 1:23. 2:2.

eat of. 1 C 9:13, 14.

12 **a stranger**. Heb. a man, a stranger. Le 21:3. Is +40:13mg.

13 **returned unto her father's house**. Ge 38:11.

as in her. Le 10:14. Nu 18:11-19.

14 **eat of**. Le 5:15-19. 27:13, 15.

unwittingly. Nu 15:24-29.

fifth part. Le 6:5. 27:13. Ps 19:12. 139:23, 24.

15 **not profane**. ver. 9. Le 19:8. Nu 18:32. Ezk 22:26.

16 **suffer them to bear the iniquity of trespass**. *or*, lade themselves with the iniquity of trespass in their eating. Le 19:17.

bear. Le 7:18. 1 S 2:12-17. Ps 38:4. Is 53:11, 12. 1 P 2:24.

for I. ver. 9. Le 20:8.

Lord. Ex +15:26.

18 **Whatsoever**. Le 1:2, 10. 17:10, 13.

of the strangers. Nu 15:14-16.

vows. Le +23:38.

freewill offerings. Le +23:38.

burnt offering. Le +23:12.

19 **a male**. Le +1:3. 4:32. Mt 27:4, 19, 24, 54. Lk 23:14, 41, 47. Jn 19:4. 2 C 5:21.

20 **hath a blemish**. ver. 25. Dt 15:21. 17:1. Ml 1:8, 13, 14. Ro 12:1, 2. Ep 5:27. He 9:14. 1 P 1:18, 19.

21 **peace offerings**. Le +23:19.

to accomplish. Le +23:38. Ge 35:1-3.

sheep. *or*, goats. Ge 4:4. Ex 12:3, 21.

it shall be perfect. Le +1:3.

22 **Blind**. ver. 20. Le 21:18-21. Ml 1:8.

an offering. Le 1:9, 13. 3:3, 5.

23 **lamb**. *or*, kid. Ex 12:3.

superfluous. Le 21:18.

vow. Le +23:38.

24 **broken, or cut**. ver. 20. Dt 23:1.

25 **a stranger's**. lit. son of a stranger. Ex +12:43. Nu 15:14-16. 16:40. Dt 31:16. Ezr 6:8-10.

the bread. Le 21:6, 8, 21, 22. Ml 1:7, 8, 12-14.

because. Ep 2:12. 1 J 5:18.

27 **seven days**. Le 12:2, 3. 19:23, 24. Ex 22:30.

28 **ewe**. *or*, she goat. Ex 12:3.

ye shall not kill it. Ex 23:19. 34:26. Dt 14:21. 22:6, 7. Ps 119:156. 145:8, 9. Is 49:15. 66:13. Mt 23:37. Ja 5:11. 1 J 4:16.

29 **sacrifice of thanksgiving**. Le +7:12. Ps 22:25. Am 4:5.

30 **leave none**. Le 7:15-18. 19:6. Ex 16:19, 20. Ac 2:27-32.

31 **keep my commandments**. Nu 15:40. Dt +4:1. 1 Th 4:1, 2.

32 **profane**. ver. +2. Le 18:21.

holy name. Ps 8:9. 9:10. 25:11. 115:1. SS 1:3. Is 26:8. Mt 6:9. Lk 11:2. Jn 17:11. Re 15:3, 4.

I will. Is +8:13.

Lord. Ex +15:26.

hallow you. ver. 16. Le 20:8. 21:8, 15. Ex 19:5, 6. Jn 17:17. 1 C 1:2.

33 **That brought**. Le 11:45. 19:36. 25:38. Ex 6:7. 20:2. Nu 15:41. 24:8, 9. Ps 80:8-11. 81:10. Je 10:7.

LEVITICUS 23

2 **the feasts of the Lord**. ver. 4, 37. Ex 23:14-17. 32:5. 1 S 15:22. Is 1:13, 14. 33:20. La 1:4. Ho 2:11. Na 1:15. Jn 2:13. 5:1. 7:2. Col 2:1, 16.

proclaim. Ex 32:5. Nu 10:2, 3, 10. 2 K 10:20. 2 Ch 30:5. Ps 81:3. Jl 1:14. 2:15. Jon 3:5-9.

convocations. Ge 49:10. Ex 12:16. He 12:23. Re 7:9.

3 **Six days**. Ex +20:8-11. 23:12. 34:21. 35:2, 3. Lk +13:14. Ac 15:21. Col 2:16. Re 1:10.

sabbath of rest. 2 K 4:23. 2 Ch 35:3. Ezk 46:1. Ac 15:21. He 4:3-5, 9.

4 **are the feasts**. or, set feasts. ver. 2, 37. Ex 23:14. Dt 12:14. 16:6. Ps 102:13. Na 1:15. Ro 15:4. Col 2:17.

5 **the fourteenth**. Ex 12:2-14, 18. 13:3-10. 23:15. Nu 9:2-7. 28:16. Dt 16:1-8. Jsh 5:10. 2

Ch 35:18, 19. Mt 26:17. Mk 14:12. Lk 22:7. 1 C 5:7, 8.

at even. Heb. between the two evenings. Ex +12:6. 30:8. Nu 9:3.

passover. Ge 40:20. Ex 12:13, 27, 43-49. 13:10. 34:25. Nu 9:2, 10. 28:16. 33:3. Dt 16:1, 2, 6. 2 K 23:21, 22. 2 Ch 30:1, 13-17. 35:17. Ezr 6:19. Is 31:5. Ezk 45:21. Mt 26:2, 17, 19, 26-29. Mk 14:1, 12. Lk 22:1, 7. Jn 13:1. 19:14. 1 C 5:7. Col 1:14.

6 the feast of unleavened bread. Ex 12:15, 16, 17. 13:6, 7. 23:15. 34:18. Nu 28:17, 18. Dt 16:3, 8, 16. 2 Ch 8:13. 30:13. 35:17. Ezr 6:22. Ezk 45:21. Mt 26:17. Mk 14:1, 2. Lk 22:1, 7. Ac 12:3, 4. 20:6. 1 C 5:7, 8.

seven. Lk 1:74, 75.

eat. Jn 6:50, 51.

7 ye shall have. Nu 28:18-25.

8 by fire. Le 1:9. Nu 28:19-24.

seventh day. Ex 12:16. 14:23-28.

10 When. Le +14:34.

and shall. Le 2:12-16. Ex 22:29. 23:16, 19. 34:22, 26. Nu 15:2, 18-21. 28:26. Dt 16:9. Jsh 3:15.

harvest. Ex 9:31.

sheaf. *or*, handful. Heb. omer. ver. 11, 12, 15. Dt 24:19. Ru 2:7, 15. Jb 24:10. Ps 129:7. Je 9:22. Am 2:13. Zc 12:6.

the firstfruits. ver. 17, 20. Le 2:12, 14. Ge 4:3. Ex 22:29. 23:16, 19. 34:22, 26. Nu 15:20, 21. 18:12. 28:26. Dt 16:10. 18:4. 26:2, 10, 11. 2 K 4:42. 2 Ch 31:5. Ne 10:35-37. 12:44. 13:31. Pr 3:9. Is 4:2. Je 2:3. Ezk 20:40. 44:30. 48:14. Am 6:1mg. Mt 28:5, 6. Jn 12:24. 20:17. Ro 8:23. 11:16. 16:5. 1 C 15:20-23. Col 1:15, 18. 3:3, 4. Ja 1:18. Re 14:4.

11 wave the. ver. +15. Ex +29:24.

sheaf. Ps 22:22. Jn 20:17. He 2:11.

accepted. Ro 4:25. 8:34.

on the morrow after. Ge +22:4. +49:10. Mt 28:1-10. Lk 23:44. 1 C +15:4, 20, 23.

the sabbath. Jn 19:31.

12 an he lamb. Le 1:10. Nu 28:4, 5. Jn 1:29. Ro 6:9, 10. He 9:11, 12, 14, 24. 10:10-12. 1 P 1:19. Re 5:6.

burnt offering. Le +1:3. 3:5. 4:24. 5:7, 10. 6:9-13. 7:2. 8:18, 21. 9:3, 12, 24. 12:6, 8. 14:13, 20. 15:15, 30. 16:3. 17:8, 9. 22:18. Ge 8:20. 22:2, 8, 13. Ex 10:25. 18:12. 20:24. 24:5. 29:18, 42. 40:29. Nu 6:11, 14. 7:15, 16. 8:12. 10:10. 15:3, 5, 8, 24. 28:3, 10, 11, 15, 19, 23, 24, 27, 31. 29:6, 11, 13, 39. Dt 12:6, 27. 27:6. Jsh 8:31. 22:23, 29. Jg 6:26. 13:23. 20:26. 21:4. 1 S 6:14. 7:9. 10:8. 13:9. 15:22. 2 S 6:17, 18. 24:22, 25. 1 K 3:4, 15. 8:64. 9:25. 2 K 16:13, 15. 1 Ch 16:1, 2. 21:23, 26. 2 Ch 2:4. 7:7. 29:24, 31, 32, 35. 33:16. Ezr 3:5, 6. 8:35. Jb 1:5. 42:8. Ps 20:3. 40:6. 50:8. 51:16, 19. 66:13, 15. Is 1:11-15. 50:6. 53:11. 56:7. Je 6:20. 7:21, 22. 14:12. 17:26. 33:18. Ezk 40:38,

39. 43:18, 24, 27. 45:15, 17, 23, 25. 46:2, 4, 12, 13. Ho 6:6. Am 4:4. 5:22. Mt 26:39. Jn 4:34. 10:18. Ac 13:39. Ro 5:19. Ep 1:6. Ph 2:5-8. He 9:14. 10:6, 7. 1 P 2:5.

13 the meat offering. Le 2:1-3, 4-7, 14-16. 5:13. 6:14, 15, 20, 21, 23. 7:9, 10, 37. 9:4, 17. 10:12. 14:10. Ge 4:3. Ex 29:41. 30:9. 40:29. Nu 4:16. 6:15, 17. 7:13. 8:8. 15:3-12, 24. 18:9. 28:2, 5, 12. 29:3, 6, 11, 39. Jsh 22:23, 29. Jg 6:18mg. 13:23. 1 K 8:64. 2 K 3:20. 16:13, 15. 1 Ch 21:23. 23:29. 2 Ch 7:7. Ezr 7:17. Ne 10:33. 13:5, 9. Is 53:5, 10. 57:6. 66:20. Je 17:26. Ezk 42:13. 44:29. 45:15, 17, 24, 25. 46:5, 7, 11, 15, 20. Jl 1:9, 13. 2:14. Am 5:22. Jn 4:34. 6:33, 51. 15:1. He 7:26.

two tenth. Ex 29:40. Nu 28:5.

the drink offering. Ge 35:14. Ex 29:40, 41. 30:9. Nu 6:15, 17. 15:5, 7, 10, 24. 28:7, 10, 14, 15, 24. 29:6, 11, 16, 39. Dt 32:38. 2 K 16:13, 15. 1 Ch 29:21. 2 Ch 29:35. Ezr 7:17. Ps 16:4. 104:15. Is 57:6. 65:11. Je 7:18. 19:13. 32:29. 44:17. Ezk 20:28. 45:17. Jl 1:9, 13. 2:14. Ph 2:17mg.

wine. Le 10:9.

the fourth. Ex 29:40. 30:24. Nu 28:7. Ezk 4:11. 45:24. 46:14.

14 eat. Le 19:23-25. 25:2, 3. Ge 4:4, 5. Ex 22:29. 23:19. Dt 26:2. Jsh 5:11, 12. Mi 7:1.

green ears. or, full ears. Le 2:14.

selfsame. ver. +21. Dt +32:48.

it shall be. Le 3:17. 10:11. Nu 10:8. Dt 16:12. Ne 9:14. Ps 19:8.

forever. Heb. *olam*, Ex +12:24. Ml 3:6.

15 from the morrow. ver. 10, 11. Le 25:8. Ex 34:22. Dt 16:9, 10.

wave offering. ver. 11. Le 7:30, 34. 8:27, 29. 9:21. 10:14, 15. 14:12, 24. Ex 29:24, 26, 27. 35:22. 38:24, 29. Nu 5:25. 6:20, 8:11mg. 18:11, 18. Ro 12:1.

16 fifty days. Ex 23:16. 34:22, 26. Nu 15:19-21. 28:26, 27. Dt 16:9, 10. 2 Ch 8:13. Mt 9:37, 38. Jn 4:35, 36. Ac 2:1-4, 41. 20:16. 1 C 12:13. 16:8. Re 14:1-4.

17 two wave loaves. ver. +15. Nu 28:26, 28. Am 3:3. Mt 18:20. Jn 10:16. Ep 2:14, 15. 1 J 1:3.

fine flour. Le +2:1. Ex +27:20. 29:2. Jn +17:6. He +2:10.

with. Ho 7:4. Am 4:5. Ac 5:1-11. Ro 5:12. 7:18, 23.

leaven. Le 7:13. Mt +13:33.

the firstfruits. ver. +10. Dt 26:1, 2.

18 seven. Ge 4:15. Ps 79:12. Pr 6:31.

lambs. ver. 12, 13. Nu 28:27-31. Ml 1:13, 14. He 10:14.

without blemish. Le 3:1. 2 C 5:21.

burnt offering. Ge 8:20, 21.

with their. ver. +13. Nu 15:4-12.

sweet savor. Ep 5:2.

19 one kid. Le 4:23-28. 16:15. Nu 15:24. 28:30. Ro 8:3. 2 C 5:19, 21.

sin offering. Le 4:3, 21, 24, 25, 29, 32, 33. 5:6-9. 6:17, 25, 30. 7:7, 37. 8:2, 14. 9:2, 3, 7, 8, 10, 15, 22. 10:16, 17. 12:6, 8. 14:13, 19, 22, 31. 15:15, 30. 16:3, 5, 11, 15, 21, 27. Ge 4:7. Ex 29:14. 30:10. Nu 6:11, 14, 16. 7:16, 58. 8:8, 12. 15:24, 27. 18:9. 19:9mg, 17mg. 28:15, 22. 29:5, 11, 19, 22, 25, 28, 31, 34, 38. 2 K 12:16. 2 Ch 29:21, 24. Ezr 6:17. 8:35. Ne 10:33. Ps ch. 22. 40:6. Is 53:6, 10, 12. La 1:12. 3:1-19. Ezk 40:39. 42:13. 43:19. 44:27, 29. 45:17, 19, 22, 23, 25. 46:20. Da 11:31. Ho 4:8. Mt 20:28. Jn 1:29. Ac 13:38. Ro 5:8. 8:3. 2 C 5:21. Ga 3:13. 1 T 1:15. He 9:11-13. 10:11, 18. 13:11-13. 1 J 1:7.

two lambs. Le ch. 3. 7:11-18.

peace offerings. Le 3:1, +11. 4:10. 6:12. +7:11, 15, 29, 37. 9:4, 18. 10:14. 17:5. 19:5. 22:21. Ex 20:24. 24:5. 29:28. Nu 6:14, 17. 7:17. 10:10. 15:8. 29:39. Dt 12:6. 27:7. Jsh 8:31. 22:23. Jg 20:26. 21:4. 1 S 10:8. 11:15. 13:9. 2 S 6:17, 18. 24:25. 1 K 3:15. 8:63, 64. 9:25. 2 K 16:13. 1 Ch 16:1, 2. 21:26. 2 Ch 7:7. 29:35. 30:22. 31:2. 33:16. Ps 50:14. 76:11. 107:22. Pr 7:14. Is 53:5. Ezk 43:27mg. 45:15, 17mg. 46:2, 12. Am 5:22mg. Jon 2:9. Jn 6:51-57. 1 C 10:16. 2 C 9:15. Ep 2:13, 14, 17, 18. Col 1:20. He 13:15.

20 wave them. ver. 17. Le 7:29, 30. Ex 29:24. Lk 2:14. Ep 2:14.
holy to. Le 7:31-34. 8:29. 10:14, 15. Nu 18:8-12. Dt 18:4. Jn 6:57. 1 C 9:11.

21 proclaim. ver. 2, 4. Ex 12:16. Dt 16:11. Is 11:10.
selfsame. ver. +14, 28-30.
convocation. He 10:25.
a statute. ver. 14. Ge 17:7. Ex 12:17. Nu 18:23.
for ever. Heb. *olam*, Ex +12:24.

22 thou shalt not make clean riddance. Le 19:9, 10. Dt 16:11-14. 24:19-21. Ru 2:3-7, 15, 16. Jb 31:16-21. Ps 41:1-3. 112:9. Pr 11:24, 25. Is 58:7, 8, 10. Lk 11:41. Jn 6:12. 12:8. 2 C 8:9. 9:5-12. Ja 1:27.
corners. Mt 24:14. Ac 1:8. Ro 10:12-15.
field. Ps 22:27. 72:11. Mt 13:38.
gather. Is 2:2-4. 25:7. Je 3:17. Zc 2:11. 8:22. Mt 25:32.
gleaning. Is 27:12mg. Re 7:14-17. 20:4.
stranger. Dt +26:11. Mt 25:31-46. Re 7:9.

24 Speak. He 12:25.
In the seventh. Nu 10:10. 29:1-6. 1 Ch 15:28. 2 Ch 5:13. Ezr 3:6. Ne 8:2, 3, 8. Ps 81:1-4. 89:15. 98:6. Is 27:13. 1 C 15:52. 1 Th 4:16. He 12:25.
month. Jn 4:35.
a memorial. Le 25:9. Nu 10:9. 29:1-6. Ne 8:2, 9-12. Is 49:14-16. Ezk 16:60. Ro 11:1, 2.
trumpets. Le 25:9. Nu 10:2, 9. 31:6. 1 K 1:34. 2 K 11:14. 2 Ch 13:12. Ps 72:8. 81:1-3. 89:15 (joyful sound; RV mg, trumpet sound).

98:6. Is 18:3-7. 27:13. 58:1. Je 50:4. Jl 2:1, 12. Zc 10:8. 14:9. Mt 24:31. 1 C 15:51, 52. 1 Th 4:16, 17.

25 offering made by fire. ver. 8. Nu 29:1-6.

27 the tenth. Le 16:29, 30. 25:9. Nu 29:7-11.
day of atonement. Le 16:30, 34. 25:9. Ex 29:36. 30:10. Nu 29:7. Zc 12:10. 13:1. Jn 11:50. He 9:7, 28.
convocation. 2 C 5:10. Re 22:12.
afflict. Nu +29:7. Ps ch. 51. Is 53. Je 31:9, 15-20. La ch. 1-5. Ezk 20:35-38, 43. 36:31. Ho 6:1-3. 14:8. Jon ch. 2. Mi 7:9. Ac 2:37, 38. Ga 2:20. 5:24. Ph 3:10. Ja 4:9. 1 P 4:13.
souls. Heb. *nephesh*, Ge +27:31.
offer. Le 16:11, 15, 24.
offering made by fire. Young renders, "fire offering." Nu 29:8-11.

28 a day of atonement. Le 16:34. Is 53:10. Da 9:24. Zc 3:9. Ro 5:10, 11. He 9:12, 26. 10:10, 14. 1 J 2:2. 4:10. 5:6.

29 soul. Heb. *nephesh*, Ge +17:14.
that shall. ver. +27, 32. Ezk 7:16.
he shall be. Ge 17:14. Ac 3:23.

30 soul. Heb. *nephesh*, Ge +27:31.
the same. Le 20:3, 5, 6. Ge 17:14. Je 15:7. Ezk 14:9. Zp 2:5. 1 C 3:17.
soul. Heb. *nephesh*, Ge +17:14.
from among. Ac 3:23.

31 no manner of work. ver. 28. Mt 12:12. Mk 3:4. Ro 4:4, 5. 11:6. Ep 2:7-10. He 4:8-11.
for ever. Heb. *olam*, Ex +12:24.

32 a sabbath. ver +16:31. Mt 11:28-30. He 4:3, 11.
afflict. ver. +27. Ps 51:17. Is 57:15, 18, 19. 61:3. Je 8:20. Mt +5:4. 1 C 11:31. Re +1:7.
souls. Heb. *nephesh*, Ge +27:31.
celebrate your sabbath. Heb. rest. Le 25:2.

34 The fifteenth. Ex 23:16. 34:22. Nu 29:12. Dt 16:13-15. Ezr 3:4. Ne 8:14. Ezk 45:25. Zc 14:16-19. Jn 1:14. 7:2. He 11:9, 13.
seventh month. 1 K 8:2. Hg 2:1.
the feast. Ex 10:9.
of tabernacles. Ge 30:14. 33:17. Ex 23:16. 34:22. Nu 29:12. Dt 16:13. 26:11. 31:10. Jg 21:19. 2 S 7:6. 1 K 8:2. 2 Ch 5:3. 7:8-10. 8:13. Ezr 3:4. Ne 8:14, 15, 17. Ezk 45:25. Ho 12:9. Zc 8:19, 23. 14:16. Mt 17:4. Jn 7:2, 3, 6, 14, 37-39.
seven days. Ga 4:4. 1 T 3:16. Re 13:8.

35 an holy convocation. ver. 7, 8, 24, 25.

36 Seven. Nu 29:12-38.
the eighth. Nu 29:35, 36. 2 Ch 7:8-11. Ne 8:18. Is 65:17. Jn 7:37. 2 P 3:13. Re 21:1-8.
solemn assembly. Heb. day of restraint. Nu 10:10. 15:3. 29:35. Dt 16:8, 15. 1 K 8:2. 2 K 10:20. 2 Ch 2:4. 7:9. 8:13. Ne 8:18. Ps 81:3. Is 1:13. Je 9:2. La 1:4. 2:6. Jl 1:14. 2:15. Am 5:21. Na 1:15. Zp 3:18. Jn 7:37.

37 the feasts. ver. +2, 4. Dt 16:16, 17.
drink offerings. ver. +13. Ex 29:40. Nu 15:5. 28:7. Ph 2:17mg.

every thing. Ec 3:1. Ga 4:4. 1 T 3:16. Re 13:8.

38　the sabbaths. ver. +3. Le 19:3. Ge 2:2, 3. Ex 20:8-11.

and beside. Nu 29:39. Dt 12:6. 1 Ch 29:3-8. 2 Ch 35:7, 8. Ezr 2:68, 69.

vows. Le 7:16. 22:18, 21, 23. 27:29. Ge 28:20-22. 31:13. Nu 6:21. 15:3, 8. 29:39. Dt 12:6, 11. 23:18, 21-23. Jg 11:30. 1 S 1:11. 2 S 15:7, 8. Jb 22:27. Ps 22:25. 50:14. 56:12. 61:5, 8. 65:1. 66:13, 14. 76:11. 116:14, 18. 132:2. Pr 7:14. Ec 5:4, 5. Is 19:21. Je 44:25. Jon 1:16. 2:9. Na 1:15. Ac 18:18. 21:23, 24.

freewill offerings. Le 1:3. 7:16. 19:5. 22:18, 19, 21, 23, 29. Ex 25:2. 35:5, 21, 29. 36:3. Nu 15:3. 29:39. Dt 12:6, 17. 16:10. 23:23. Jg 5:2, 9. 1 Ch 29:9, 14, 17. 2 Ch 31:14. 35:8. Ezr 1:4, 6. 2:68. 3:5. 7:16. 8:28. Ne 7:70. Ps 54:6mg. 110:3. +119:108. Pr 11:25. Ezk 46:12. Am 4:5. 2 C 8:12. 9:7.

39　when. ver. +34. Ex 23:16. 34:22. Dt 16:13.

feast. Dt 16:13. Zc 14:16. Mt 6:10. 13:39.

gathered in the fruit. Zc 14:5. Mt 1:23. 13:24-30, 34-39. 24:31. 25:10. Mk 13:26, 27. 1 C 2:9, 10. 15:23. 1 Th 4:16-18. Re 7:9-17. 21:3, 4.

on the first. ver. +24, 36.

eighth. Lk 9:28.

40　the boughs. Heb. fruit. Ge 1:11. Ne 8:15. Mt 21:8.

goodly. or, beautiful. Dt 33:17 (glory). Ps 8:5 (honor). 96:6 (majesty). 149:9 (honor). Is 53:2 (comeliness).

of palm trees. Ex 15:27. 1 K 6:29. Ps 92:12. Is 35. 52:1, 2. Ezk 40:16. Jn 12:13. Re 7:9.

boughs. Ps 80:10. Ezk 17:23. 31:3, 10, 14. 36:8. Da 4:12, 14, 21. Ml 4:1.

thick. Ne 8:15. Jb 15:26. Ezk 6:13. 20:28.

willows. Jb 40:22. Ps 137:1, 2. Is 15:7. 40:1, 2. 44:4.

brook. Ge 32:23. Ne 2:15. Jb 6:15. 40:22. Ps 83:9. 110:7. Pr 18:4. Is 15:7. Je 31:40. Jn 18:1.

rejoice. Dt +12:7. 14:26. 28:47. Ps 5:11. 9:2. 66:6. 72:16-19. 96:7-13. 105:43. Is 35:1, 2, 10. 65:13. Jl 2:26. Jn 11:52. 16:22. Ro 5:11. 1 P 1:8.

41　ye shall. Nu 29:12. Ne 8:18.

for ever. Heb. olam, Ex +12:24.

42　dwell in. Ge 33:17. Nu 24:2, 5. Ne 8:14-17. Je 35:10. 2 C 5:1. He 11:13-16.

booths. Ne 8:17. Ho 12:9. Zc 14:16. Mt 17:4. Mk 9:5. Lk 9:27, 33. Jn 7:2, 3, 6, 14, 37-39. 2 P 1:16.

Israelites born. Ex 12:19.

43　your generations. Ex 13:14. Dt 31:10-13. Ps 78:5, 6.

may know. Dt 8:2-9, 14-16. Ps 78:5, 6. Ezk +6:7, 10.

brought them out. Ro 8:22, 23. 2 C 4:17, 18. 2 T 1:12. He 11:14. 12:11. 1 P 5:10.

44　declared. ver. 1, 2. Le 21:24. Mt 28:20.

LEVITICUS 24

2　that they. Ex 27:20, 21. 39:37. 40:24, 25. Nu 8:2-4. 1 S 3:3, 4.

the lamps. 2 Ch 13:11. Ps 119:105, 130, 140. Pr 6:23. Is 8:20. 11:2. Mt 4:16. 5:16. 25:1-8. Lk 1:79. 12:35. Jn 1:4, 9. 5:35. 8:12. Ac 26:18. 2 C 4:6. Ep 1:17, 18. 5:8-14. Ph 2:15, 16.

burn continually. Heb. ascend. Ex 25:37.

3　Without the vail. Ex 27:21. 39:37. Zc 4:2, 3, 10-14. Col 2:9. He 9:2. Re 1:12-14. 2:18. 4:5.

continually. Ex 27:20. Mt 25:1-4. Jn 5:39. 16:13-15. Ac 17:11, 12. 1 J 1:5, 6, 7. 2:27.

forever. Heb. olam, Ex +12:24.

4　the pure. Ex +25:31. Ps 119:105, 130, 140.

5　And thou. Le 24:3, 6, 7. 1 S 21:6.

fine. Ex +27:20. Is 53:5. He +2:10.

twelve cakes. Ex 25:30. 40:23. 1 K 18:31. 1 S 21:4, 5. Mt 12:4. Ac 26:7. Ja 1:1.

6　in two rows. 1 C 14:40.

row. 1 Ch +9:32.

pure table. Ex +25:23.

7　pure. Le 2:2. Ep 1:6. He 7:25. Re 8:3, 4.

the bread. Jn 6:33, 35, 50, 51.

a memorial. Ge 9:16. Ex +12:14.

8　sabbath. Nu 4:7. 1 Ch 9:32. 23:29. 2 Ch 2:4. Ne 10:33. Mt 12:3-5.

everlasting. Heb. olam, Ge +17:7.

covenant. Ge +9:16.

9　Aaron's. Le 8:31. 1 S 21:6. Ml 1:12. Mt 12:4. Mk 2:26. Lk 6:4.

they shall. Le 6:16. 8:3, 31. 10:17. 21:22. Ex 29:32, 33.

eat. Jn 6:50, 51.

in the. Mt 17:5. Jn 19:5.

holy place. Ex +29:31. Ep 2:6.

perpetual. Heb. olam, Ge +9:12.

10　Israelitish. i.e. *a female descendant of Israel*, S#3482h. Le 24:10, 10, 11.

father was. Ex 12:38. Nu 11:4.

11　blasphemed. ver. 15, 16. 2 S 12:14. 1 K 21:10, 13. 2 K 18:30, 35, 37. 19:1-3, 6, 10, 22. 2 Ch 32:14-17. Ps 44:16. 74:10, 18, 22. Is 37:3, 6, 23. 52:5. Mt 12:31. 26:65. Mk 3:28, 29. Lk 12:10. 22:65. Ac 6:11-13. 13:45. 18:6. 26:11. Ro 2:24. 1 T 1:13, +20. 6:1. T 2:5. Ja 2:7. Re 13:5, 6. 16:9, 11, 21.

the name. Heb. hashshem. verse 16. Ex 20:7.

cursed. Jb 1:5, 11, 22. 2:5, 9, 10. Is 8:21.

brought him. Ex 18:22, 26. Nu 15:33-35.

Shelomith. i.e. *peaceable*, S#8019h. 1 Ch 3:19. 23:18. 26:28. 2 Ch 11:20. Ezr 8:10. Also 1 Ch 23:9. 26:25.

Dibri. i.e. *eloquent; promise*, S#1704h.

12　that the mind of the Lord might be showed them. Heb. to expound unto them according to the mouth of the Lord. Ex 18:15, 16, 23. Nu 27:5. 36:5, 6.

14 **without**. Le +4:12.
all that. Dt 13:9. 17:7.
stone. ver. 23. Ex 17:4. Le 20:2, 27. Nu 15:35, 36. Dt 13:10. 17:5. 21:21. 22:21, 24. Jsh 7:25. 1 K 21:10, 13. 2 Ch 24:21. Mt 21:35. 23:37. Mk 12:4. Lk 13:34. Jn 8:59. 10:31-33. 11:8. Ac 7:58, 59. 14:5, 19. 2 C 11:25. He 11:37.

15 **Whosoever curseth**. Ex 20:7. 23:20, 21. Mt 12:31, 32. Ac 7:51. Ep 4:30. 1 Th 5:19.
bear his sin. Le 5:1. 20:16, 17. Nu 9:13.

16 **blasphemeth**. Heb. *nakav*, to express, or distinguish by name. Nu 1:17. 1 Ch 12:31. Is 62:2.
the name. ver. +11. Ps 139:20. Jn 8:58, 59. 10:33-36.
surely. Ge +2:16.
stone him. Jn 10:32.

17 **And he**. Ge 9:5, 6. Ex 21:12-14. Nu 35:31. Dt 19:11, 12. Jn 8:44.
killeth. Heb. smiteth the life of a man. ver. 18.
any man. Heb. *nephesh*, soul. Ge +37:21.
surely. Ge +2:16.

18 **that killeth**. ver. 21.
a beast. Heb. the soul (*nephesh*, Ge +2:19) of a beast. Ex 21:34-36.
beast for beast. Heb. life for life, *nephesh*, Ge +2:19. Re 16:3.

19 **as he**. Dt 19:21. Mt 5:38. 7:2. Ro 5:8. 13:10. 1 J 4:16.

20 **Breach for**. Ex 21:23-25. Dt 19:21. Mt 5:38, 39. 7:1, 2. 1 P 2:19, 21, 22.

21 **a beast**. Heb. *behemah*, no word for "soul" here as there is in ver. 18. Ex 21:33.
a man. ver. 17.

22 **one manner**. Le 17:10. 19:34. Ex 12:49. Nu 9:14. 15:15, 16, 29.

23 **that they**. ver. 14-16. Le +4:12. He 2:2, 3. 10:28-31.
and stone. Jn 10:32.

LEVITICUS 25

1 **the Lord spake**. Ex 19:1. Nu 1:1. 10:11, 12. Ga 4:24, 25.

2 **When ye**. Le +14:34. Dt 32:8, 49. 34:4. Ps 24:1, 2. 115:16. Is 8:8. Je 27:5.
keep. Heb. rest. Le 23:32mg.
a sabbath. Le 26:34, 35. Ex 20:10, 11. 23:10, 11. 2 Ch 36:21.

3 **six years**. Mt 21:33-41. Lk 13:6-9.

4 **in the seventh**. ver. 20-23. Le 26:34, 35, 43. Ex 23:10, 11. 2 Ch 36:21.
sabbath of rest. Ps 96:11, 12. Is 11:6-10. 65:25. He 4:10, 11.

5 **groweth**. 2 K 19:29. Is 37:30.
thy vine undressed. Heb. thy separation. ver. 11.

6 **for thee**. Ex 23:11. Ac 2:44. 4:32, 34, 35.

8 **thou shalt number**. Le 23:15. Ge 2:2.

9 **cause the trumpet**. or, send abroad the loud trumpet. Heb. loud of sound. Nu 10:10. Ps 89:15. Is 27:12, 13. Ac 13:38, 39. Ro 10:18. 15:19. 2 C 5:19-21. 1 Th 1:8.
of the jubilee. ver. 10-12, 52. Le 23:11. 27:17, 24. Nu 10:1-3, 7, 8, 10. 36:4. Dt 16:1. Is 35:1-10. 61:2. 63:4. Lk 23:44. Ac 2:1. 3:21. Re 7:13-17. 21:1.
tenth day of. Le 23:27. Is 27:13. 35:1-10. Re 7:13-17.
the day of atonement. Le 16:20, 30. 23:24, +27.
throughout all. Ps 68:11. Mk 16:15. 2 C +6:2.

10 **proclaim liberty**. Ex 20:2. Ezr 1:3. Ps 146:7. Is 49:9, 24, 25. 61:1-3. 63:4. Je 34:8, 13-17. Zc 9:11, 12. Lk 1:74. 4:16-21. Jn 8:32-36. Ro 6:17, 18. 8:21. 2 C 3:17. Ga 4:25-31. 5:1, 13. 1 P 2:16. 2 P 2:19, 20.
every man. ver. 13, 26-28, 33, 34. Le 27:17-24.
ye shall return. Le 27:24. Nu 36:2-9. Ac +3:21.

11 **A jubilee**. Le 27:17.
ye shall. ver. 5-7.

12 **ye shall**. ver. 6, 7.

13 **In the year of**. ver. 10. Le 27:17-24. Nu 36:4. Is 61:2. 63:4.

14 **not oppress**. ver. 17. Ex +18:21. Le +19:13. Dt 16:19, 20. Jg 4:3. 1 S 12:3, 4. 2 Ch 16:10. Ne 9:36, 37. Jb 20:19, 20. Ps 10:18. Pr 14:31. 21:13. 22:16. 28:3, 8, 15, 16. Ec 5:8. Is 1:17. 3:12-15. 5:7. 33:15. 58:6. Je 22:16, 17. Ezk 22:7, 12, 13. Am 5:11, 12. 8:4-7. Mi 2:2, 3. 6:10-12. 7:3. Lk 3:14. 12:15. 1 C 6:8. He 13:5. Ja 5:1-5. 2 P 2:14.

15 **According to**. Le 27:18-23. Ph 4:5.

17 **shall not**. ver. +14. Ex 18:21. Je 22:16, 17. Lk 12:15. He 13:5. 2 P 2:14.
fear. ver. 43. Ex +1:17. Le 19:14, 32. Ge 39:9. Ex 20:20. Dt 25:18. 1 S 12:24. Ps 19:9. Je 22:16. Ml +3:5. Ac 9:31. Ro 11:20.

18 **Wherefore**. Le 19:37. Ps 103:18.
and ye. Le 26:3-12. Dt 28:1-14. 33:12, 28. Jb 5:22-24. Je 7:3-7. 25:5. Ezk 33:24-26, 29. 36:24-28. Mt 6:33. Ro 8:31, 32. 1 C 3:21-23.
in safety. ver. 19. Dt +12:10. 28:7, 10, 25. 33:27, 28. Ps 127:1. Pr 21:31. +22:3.

19 **the land shall**. Le 26:5. Ps 67:6. 85:12. Is 30:23. 65:21, 22. Ezk 34:25-28. 36:30. Jl 2:24, 26.

20 **What shall**. Nu 11:4, 13. 2 K 6:15-17. 7:2. 2 Ch 25:9. Ps 78:19, 20. Is 1:2. Mt 6:25-34. 8:26. Lk 12:29. Ph 4:6. He 13:5, 6.

21 **I will**. Ge 26:12. 41:47. Ex 16:29. Dt 28:3, 8. Jb 5:22-24. Ps 4:8. 34:10. 133:3. Pr 1:33. 10:22. Je 23:6. Ml 3:10. Mt 6:33. Ro 8:31, 32.

1 C 3:21-23. 2 C 9:10. Ph 4:6, 7. He 11:1. 1 P 5:7.

three years. ver. 4, 8-11.

22　**eighth**. 2 K 19:29. Is 37:30.
　　old fruit. Jsh 5:11, 12.

23　**The land**. ver. +10. 1 K 21:3. Is 62:4. Ezk 48:14. Jl 2:18.
　　for ever. *or*, to be quite cut off. Heb. for cutting off. ver. 30.
　　for the land is mine. Le 27:24. Dt +32:43. Ps 24:1. Is 8:8. 62:4.
　　for ye are. Ge 49:7. 1 Ch 29:15. Ps 39:12. 119:19. He 11:9-13. 1 P 2:11.

24　**redemption**. ver. 26, 27, 29, 31, 32, 48, 51-53. Ru 4:6-8. Ezk 11:15. Jb 19:25. Pr 23:10, 11. Is 47:4. Ro 8:23. 1 C 1:30. Ep 1:7, 13, 14. 4:30. 1 P 1:3-5.

25　**and if**. Ru 2:20. 3:2, 9, 12. 4:4-6. Je 32:7, 8. 2 C 8:9. He 2:13, 14. Re 5:9.
　　his kin. lit. redeemer. ver. 26. Ge 48:16. Nu 5:8. 35:12, 19, 21, 24, 25, 27. Dt 19:6, 12. Jb 19:25.

26　**himself be able to redeem it**. Heb. his hand hath attained, and found sufficiency. ver. 28, 47. Le 5:7mg. Nu 6:21. Jg 9:33mg.

27　**let him count**. ver. 50-53.

28　**and in the**. ver. 13.
　　he shall. Is +35:9, 10. Je 32:15. 1 C 15:52-54. 1 Th 4:13-18. 1 P 1:4, 5.

29　**year**. Heb. days. ver. 30. Ne +13:6mg.

31　**they may be redeemed**. Heb. redemption belongeth unto it. ver. 32, 48. Ps 49:7, 8.

32　**the cities**. Nu 35:2-8. Jsh 21.
　　at any time. Heb. *olam*, **S#5769h**. Rendered "any more," Ezk 27:36. 28:19. "long," Ps 143:3. Ec 12:5. "world," Ps 73:12. Ec 3:11. "continuance," Is 64:5. "eternal," Is 60:15. "lasting," Dt 33:15. "long time," Is 42:14. "at any time," Le 25:32. "since the beginning of the world," Is 64:4.

33　**a man purchase of the Levites**. *or, one* of the Levites redeem them.
　　shall go. ver. 28.
　　for the houses. Nu 18:20-24. Dt 18:1, 2.

34　**the field of**. ver. 23. Ac 4:36, 37.
　　perpetual. Heb. *olam*, Ge +9:12.
　　possession. Nu 35:2, 5. Jn 10:28. 14:2. Ro 6:23. 11:29. 2 C 5:1. He 6:20. 1 P 1:4. 1 J 5:11-13.

35　**thy brother**. ver. 25. Dt 15:7, 8. Pr 14:20, 21. 17:5. 19:17. Mk 14:7. Jn 12:8. 2 C 8:9. Ja 2:5, 6.
　　fallen in decay. Heb. his hand faileth.
　　thou shalt. Ps 37:26. 41:1. 112:5, 9. Pr 14:31. Lk 6:35. Ac 11:29, 30. Ro 12:13, 18, 20. 2 C 9:1, 12-15. Ga 2:10. 1 J 3:17.
　　relieve. Heb. strengthen. Le 19:9, 10. Dt 15:7, 8, 10, 11. Jb +6:14. Pr +21:13. Ezk +16:49. Da 4:27. Mt 10:8. Lk 6:35. Ja 1:27. 2:1-9, 15, 16. 1 J 3:17.

a stranger. Dt +26:11.

36　**usury**. Is +24:2.
　　fear. ver. 17. Ne 5:9, 15.

38　**which**. Ex 20:2.
　　and to be. Le 11:45. 22:32, 33. Nu 15:41. Je 31:1, 33. 32:38. He 11:16.

39　**be sold**. Ex 21:2, 7. 22:3. Dt 15:12-18. 28:68. +32:30. 1 K 9:22. 21:20, 25. 2 K 4:1. 17:17. Ne 5:5. Est 7:4. Is 50:1. Je 34:14. Jl 3:6. Am 2:6. Mt 18:25. Jn 8:35, 36. Ro 6:17-19. 7:14-17, 24. 1 C 6:20.
　　compel him to serve as. Heb. serve thyself with him with the service of, etc. ver. 46mg. Ex 1:14. Je 25:14. 27:7. 30:8.

40　**as an hired**. Ex 21:2, 3.

41　**then shall**. Ex 21:3. Jn 8:32. Ro 6:14. T 2:14.
　　shall return. ver. +10, 28.

42　**my servants**. ver. 55. Ro 6:22. 1 C 7:21-23.
　　as bondmen. Heb. with the sale of a bondman.

43　**not rule**. ver. 46, 53. Ex 1:13, 14. 2:23. 3:7, 9. 5:14. 1 K 9:22. Is 47:6. 58:3. 1 C 6:19, 20. 7:22. Ga 5:1. Ep +6:9. Col +4:1.
　　but shalt. ver. +17. Ex +1:17. Dt 25:18. Ml +3:5.

44　**thy bondmen**. Ex 12:44. Ps 2:8, 9. Is 14:1, 2. Re 2:26, 27.

45　**of the children**. Dt 9:5, 6. Is 14:2. 56:3-6. 61:5.

46　**And ye shall**. Is 14:2.
　　they shall be your bondmen for ever. Heb. ye shall serve yourselves with them. Heb. *olam*, Ex +12:24. ver. +39.
　　ye shall not rule. ver. 43.

47　**sojourner or stranger wax rich**. Heb. the hand of a stranger, etc. obtain, etc. ver. 26. 1 S 2:7, 8. Ja +2:5.

48　**one of his**. ver. +25, 35. Ne 5:5, 8. Ga 4:4, 5. He 2:11-13.

49　**or if he be**. ver. +26. Ps 49:6-8, 14, 15. Is 41:13, 14. 49:24-26. +59:20. Je 50:33, 34. Jn 8:36. Ro +8:16, 17, 23. Ep +5:30.

50　**reckon**. ver. 27.
　　price of his sale. Ne 5:8.
　　according to the time. ver. 40, 53. Dt 15:18. Jb 7:1, 2. 14:6. Is 16:14. 21:16.

52　**jubilee**. ver. 9. Le 26:34, 35. Is 11:11. 27:12, 13. Je 25:11, 12. 29:10. Da 9:2. Am 9:15. Mi 4:6, 7.

53　**shall not**. ver. +43.

54　**in these years**. *or*, by these means.
　　then. ver. 40, 41. Ex 21:2, 3. Is 49:9, 25. 52:3.
　　he shall go. Ps 37:7, 11. Is 26:3, 4. 2 P 3:9, 10, 13-15. Re 22:7, 20.

55　**my servants**. ver. 42. Ex 13:3. 20:2. Ps 116:16. Is 43:3. Lk 1:74, 75. Ro 6:14, 17, 18, 22. 1 C 7:22, 23. 9:19, 21. Ga 5:13. Ep 6:5-8.

LEVITICUS 26

1 **Ye shall**. Ex +20:4. Dt 16:21, 22. 1 K 11:4, 5. Is 2:20. 45:5. 48:5-8. 1 C 10:19, 20.
standing image. *or*, pillar. 2 K +17:10mg.
image of stone. *or*, figured stone. Heb. a stone of picture. Ge 28:18, 22. Nu 33:52.

2 **keep**. Le +19:30. Is 56:4-7.

3 **If**. Ge +4:7.
ye walk. Le 18:4, 5. Dt 11:13-15. 28:1-14. Jsh 23:14, 15. Jg 2:1, 2. Ps 81:12-16. Is 1:19. 48:18, 19. Mt 7:24, 25. Ro 2:7-10. Re 22:14.

4 **Then I**. Dt 28:12. 1 K 17:1. Jb 5:10. 37:11-13. 38:25-28. Ps 65:9-13. 68:9. 104:13. Is 5:6. 30:23. Je 14:22. Ezk 34:26, 27. Jl 2:23, 24. Am 4:7, 8. Mt +5:45. Ac 14:17. Ja 5:7, 17, 18. Re 11:6.
the land. Le 25:21. Ps 67:6. 85:12. Ezk 34:27. 36:30. Hg 2:18, 19. Zc 8:12.

5 **threshing**. Am 9:13. Mt 9:37, 38. Jn 4:35, 36.
eat your. Le 25:19. Ex 16:8. Dt 11:15. Jl 2:19, 26. Ac 14:17. 1 T 6:17.
dwell. Dt +12:10. Jb 11:18, 19. Ps 46:1-7. 90:1. 91:1-14. Pr 18:10. Is 48:17-19. Mt 23:37. 1 P 1:5.

6 **I will**. 1 Ch 22:9. Ps 29:11. 147:14. Is 9:7. 45:7. Je 30:10. Hg 2:9. Zc 9:10. Jn 14:27. Ro 5:1. Ph 4:7-9.
ye shall. ver. +5. Ps 3:5. 121:4-7. 127:1, 2. Pr 3:24. 6:22. Je 30:10. 31:26. Zp 3:13. Ac 12:6.
rid. Heb. cause to cease. Jb 5:22, 23. Is 35:9. Ezk +5:17. Ho 2:18.
shall the sword. i.e. war. Ex +5:3. Je +12:12.

7 **chase**. 1 S 14:6. 2 Ch 20:5-7, 12, 14-17. Zc 12:8.

8 **five of**. Nu 14:9. Dt 28:7. 32:30. Jsh 23:10. Jg 7:19-21. 1 S 14:6-16. 17:45-52. 1 Ch 11:11, 20. Ps 81:14, 15.

9 **For I**. Ex 2:25. 2 K 13:23. Ne 2:20. Ps 89:3. 138:6, 7. Je 33:3. He 8:9.
make you. Ge 17:6, 7, 20. 26:4. 28:3, 14. Ex 1:7. Dt 28:4, 11. Ne 9:23. Ps 107:38.
establish. Ge 6:18. 17:7. Ex 6:4. Is 55:3. Ezk 16:62. Lk 1:72.

10 **eat old**. Le 25:22. Jsh 5:11. 2 K 19:29. Lk 12:17.

11 **tabernacle**. Ex +38:21.
among. Ex 25:8. 29:45. Jsh 22:19. 1 K 8:13, 27. Ps 76:2. 78:68, 69. 132:13, 14. Ezk 37:26-28. Mt 1:23. Jn 1:14. 2 C 6:16. Ep 2:22. Re 21:3.
soul. Heb. *nephesh*, Ge +34:3. ver. 30. Jg 10:16. 1 S 2:35. Jb 23:13. Ps 11:5. 24:4mg. Pr 6:16mg. SS 6:12. Is 1:14. 42:1. Je 5:9, 29. 6:8. 9:9. 12:7. 14:19. 15:1. 32:41. 51:14mg. La 3:20. Ezk 23:18. Am 6:8. Mt 12:18. He 10:38. The preceding references ascribe "soul" to God.
abhor. Ps +106:40.

12 **I will**. Ge 3:8. 5:22, 24. 6:9. Dt 23:14. 2 C 6:16. Re 2:1.

walk. ver. 24, 28. Dt 23:14. 2 C 6:16.
will be. Ge +17:7. Ex 6:7. +19:5, 6. Ps 50:7. 68:18-20. Is 12:2. Je 7:23. 11:4. Jl 2:27.

13 **I am**. Le 25:38, 42, 55. Ex +20:2. Ps 81:6-10. 1 C 6:19, 20.
and I have. Ps 116:16. Is 51:23. Je 2:20. Ezk 34:27. Lk 13:13. Jn 8:36. Ro 8:21. Ga 5:1.

14 **if**. Ge +4:7.
ye will not. ver. 18. Dt 28:15-68. Je 17:27. La 1:18. 2:17. Ml 2:2. Ac 3:23. He 12:25.

15 **if**. Ge +4:7.
despise. ver. 43. Nu 15:31. 2 S 12:9, 10. 2 K 17:15. 2 Ch 36:16. Pr 1:7, 30. Je 6:19. Am 3:1-3. Zc 7:11-13. Ac 13:41. 1 Th 4:8.
soul. Heb. *nephesh*, Ge +34:3. Le 17:11. 1 S 1:26. Ps +50:17. Pr 5:12. Ro 8:7. 2 C +12:15mg.
break. Ge 17:14. Ex 19:5. 24:7. Dt 31:16. Is 24:5. Je 11:10. 31:32. Ezk 16:59. He 8:9.

16 **I will**. Je +11:8.
appoint. Ps 109:6.
over you. Heb. upon you.
terror. Dt 28:65-67. 32:25. Jb 15:20, 21. 18:11. 20:25. Ps 73:19. Is 7:2. Je 15:8. 20:4. He 10:31.
consumption. Ex +15:26. Dt 28:21, 22, 35.
consume. Dt 28:34, 67. 1 S 2:33. Ps +69:3. 78:33. Ezk 33:10. Zc 14:12.
heart. Heb. *nephesh*, soul. Ex +23:9.
and ye shall. Dt 28:33, 51. Jg 6:3-6, 11. Jb 31:8. Is 65:22-24. Je 5:17. 12:13. Mi 6:15. Hg 1:6.
for your. Is 10:4.

17 **set**. Ps 68:1, 2. Ezk +15:7.
ye shall be. Dt 28:25. Jg 2:14. 1 S 4:10. 31:1. Ne 9:27-30. Ps 106:41, 42. Je 19:7. La 1:5. 2:17.
shall flee. ver. 36. Ps 53:5. Pr 28:1.

18 **if**. Ge +4:7.
seven times. ver. 21, 24, 28. 1 S 2:5. Ps 119:164. Pr 24:16. Da 3:19.

19 **will break**. 1 S 4:3, 11. Is 2:12. 25:11. 26:5. Je 13:9. Ezk 7:24. 30:6. Da 4:37. Zp 3:11.
make. Dt 11:16, 17. 28:23. 1 K 17:1. Is 5:1-7. Je 14:1-6. Lk 4:25.

20 **your strength**. Ps 127:1. Is 49:4. Hab 2:13. Ga 4:11.
for your land. ver. +4. Dt 11:17. 28:18, 38-40, 42. Jb 31:40. Ps 107:34. Ho 2:8, 9. Hg 1:9-11. 2:16. 1 C 3:6.

21 **if**. Ge +4:7.
contrary unto me. *or*, at all adventures with me; and so ver. 24.

22 **wild**. ver. +6. 1 K 13:21-24. Je 2:15. 8:17.
rob you. 2 K 2:24. Ezk 5:17.
your high. Jg 5:6. 2 Ch 15:5. Is 24:6. 33:8. La 1:4. Ezk 14:15. 33:28. Mi 3:12. Zc 7:14.

23 **if**. Ge +4:7.
ye will not. Pr 29:1. Is 1:16-20. Je 2:30. 5:3. Ezk 24:13, 14. Am 3:6-12. 4:6-12.

24 **will I also**. 2 S 22:27. Jb 9:4. Ps 18:26. Is 63:10. Ml 2:2. Re ch. 8.
walk. Le +26:12.

25 **will I bring**. Jg 2:14-16. Ps 78:62-64. Je +12:12. La 2:21. Ezk 5:17. 6:3. 21:4-17. 29:8. 33:2. Re 6:3, 4.
covenant. Ps 111:5. Je 31:31-33. 34:13. Ezk 16:8. 17:19.
avenge. Dt 32:35. Ps 94:1. Ezk 20:37. He 10:28-30.
send the pestilence. Ezk +38:22.

26 **I have broken**. 1 K +8:37. Ps 105:16. Is 3:1. 9:20. La 4:3-9. Ezk 4:10, 16. 5:16. 14:13. Ho 4:10. Mi 6:14. Hg 1:6.

27 **if**. Ge +4:7.
ye. ver. 21, 24.

28 **walk**. ver. +12.
in fury. Ex 20:5, 6. Dt +32:22. Is 27:4. +59:18. Je 4:4. 21:5, 12. 23:19. 36:7. 42:18. 44:6. Ezk +7:8. 13:13. 16:38, 42. 21:17. 22:20, 22. 23:25. 24:8, 13. Am 3:2. Zp 2:2. Re 15:1.
I, even I. Ge +6:17.

29 **shall eat**. Dt 28:53, 57. 2 K 6:28, 29. Is 49:15. Je 19:9. La 2:20. 4:10. Ezk 5:10. Mt 24:19. Lk 23:29. He 10:31.

30 **I will destroy**. 1 K 13:2. 2 K 23:8, 16, 20. 2 Ch 14:3-5. 23:17. 31:1. 34:3-7. Is 27:9. Je 8:1-3. Ezk 6:3-6, 13.
high places. 2 K +21:3.
images. lit. sun images. 2 Ch +14:5mg. 34:4mg, 7. Is 17:8mg. 27:9mg. Ezk 6:4mg, 6.
the carcases. Je 16:18.
my soul. Heb. *nephesh*, Ge +34:3. ver. +11, 15.
abhor. Ps +106:40.

31 **And I will make**. 2 K 25:4-10. 2 Ch 36:19. Ne 2:3, 17. Is 1:7. 24:10-12. Je 4:7. 9:11. La 1:1. 2:7. Ezk 6:6. 21:15. Mi 3:12.
and bring. Ps 74:3-8. Je 22:5. 26:6, 9. 52:13. La 1:10. Is 16:12. Ezk 9:6. 21:2. 24:21. Am 7:9. Mt 23:37, 38. 24:1, 2. Lk 21:5, 6, 24. Ac 6:14.
I will not smell. Ge +8:21. Is 1:11-14. 66:3. Am 5:21-23. He 10:26.

32 **And I**. Is 5:6, 9. 24:1. 32:13, 14. Je +18:16. La 5:18. Da 9:2, 18. Hab 3:17. Lk 21:20.
and your. Dt 29:24-28. 2 Ch +29:8. La 4:12.

33 **I will scatter**. Je +9:16. La 1:3. 4:15. Am 9:8, 9. Lk 21:24.

34 **Then shall**. Le 25:2-4, 10. 2 Ch 36:21.

35 **because it**. Is 24:5, 6. Ro 8:22.

36 **I will send**. Ge +35:5. Dt 28:65-67. 1 S 17:24. Jb 15:21, 22. Is 7:2, 4. Am 5:3.
faintness. Ex +15:15.
and the. ver. 7, 8, 17. Dt 1:44. Jb 15:21. Pr 28:1. Is 30:17.
shaken. Heb. driven. **S#5086h**. Jb 13:25. 32:13 (thrusteth him down). Ps 1:4. 68:2, 2. Pr 21:6 (tossed to and fro). Is 19:7. 41:2.
none pursueth. Pr 28:1.

37 **they shall**. Jg 7:22. 1 S 14:15, 16. Is 10:4. Je 37:10.
and ye shall. Nu 14:42. Jsh 7:12, 13. Jg 2:14.

38 **ye shall**. Dt 4:27. 28:48, 68. Is 27:13. Je 42:17, 18, 22. 44:12-14, 27, 28.

39 **shall pine**. Dt 28:65. 30:1. Ne 1:9. Ps 32:3, 4. Je 3:25. 29:12, 13. La 4:9. Ezk 4:17. 6:9. 20:43. 24:23. 33:10. 36:31. Ho 5:15. Zc 10:9.
and also. Ex 20:5. 34:7. Nu 14:18. Dt 5:9. 2 Ch 36:16. Ps 76:7. Je 31:29. Ezk 18:2, 3, 19. Mt 23:35, 36. Ro 11:8-10.

40 **If**. Ge +4:7.
confess. Nu 5:7. Dt 4:29-31. 30:1-3. Jsh 7:19. 2 S 12:13. 1 K 8:33-36, 47. Ne 9:2, etc. Jb 33:27, 28. Ps 32:5. Pr 28:13. Je 3:13. 29:12, 13. 31:18-20. Ezk 36:31. Da 9:3-20. Ho 5:15. 6:1, 2. Zc 10:9. Lk 15:18, 19. 1 J 1:8-10.
and that. ver. 21, 24, 27, 28. Ezk 20:43.

41 **their uncircumcised**. Dt +30:6. Je 4:4. 6:10. 9:25, 26. Ezk 44:7, 9. Ac 7:51. Ro 2:25, 28, 29. Ga 5:6. Ph 3:3. Col 2:11-13.
if then. 1 K 8:47-50. Lk 15:18. 1 J 1:9.
humbled. Ex 10:3. 1 K 21:29. 2 Ch 12:6, 7, 12. 32:26. 33:12, 13, 19, 23. Ezk 6:9. 20:43. Mt 23:12. Lk 14:11. 18:14. Ja 4:6-9. 1 P 5:5, 6.
and they. Ezr 9:4-9, 13, 15. Ne 1:9. 9:33. Ps 39:9. 51:3, 4. 79:1-5. 80:1-7. 85:4-7. Da 9:7-14, 18-25.

42 **remember my covenant**. Ge 9:15. Ex 2:24. 6:5. Dt 4:31. +7:9. Ps +89:34. 105:8, 42. 106:45. 111:5. 136:23. Je 3:13. 14:21. Ezk 16:60. Ho 11:8, 9. Ml +3:6. Lk 1:72.
with Abraham. Ge +15:18. Ac +7:5. Ro +4:13.
remember the land. Ps 85:1, 2. 136:23. Ezk 36:1-15, 33, 34. Jl +2:18.

43 **shall enjoy**. ver. +34, 35. 2 Ch 36:19-21. Je 25:11.
and they. ver. +41. 1 K 8:46-48. 2 Ch 33:12. Jb 5:17. 34:31, 32. Ps 50:15. 119:67, 71, 75. Is 26:16. Je 31:19. Da 9:7-9, 14. He 12:5-11.
they despised. ver. +15. 2 K 17:7-17. 2 Ch 36:14-16.
their soul. Heb. *nephesh*, Ge +34:3. ver. 15, 30. Ps 50:17. Am 5:10. Zc 11:8. Jn 7:7. 15:23, 24. Ro 8:7.

44 **I will not cast**. Dt 4:29-31. 2 S 7:24. 1 K 11:39. 2 K 13:23. 1 Ch 17:22. Ne 9:31. Ps +94:14. 98:2. Is +41:9. Je 4:27. 30:11. 31:35-37. 33:20, 25, 26. 46:28. 51:5. La 3:31. Ezk 14:22, 23. Am 9:9, 11-15. Ro +11:2, 26.
abhor. ver. +11.
break. Ps 89:33. Je 14:21. 33:20, 21. Ezk 16:60.

45 **for their**. Ge 12:2. 15:18. 17:7, 8. Ex 2:24. 19:5, 6. Lk 1:72, 73. Ro 11:12, 23-26, 28, 29. 2 C 3:15, 16.
whom I. Le 22:33. 25:38. Ex 20:2.
in the sight. Ps 98:2, 3. Ezk 20:9, 14, 22.

46 **the statutes**. Dt +4:1. 13:4. Jn 1:17.
    in mount Sinai. Le 25:1. Dt +33:2. Jn 1:17.
    by the hand. Le 8:36. Ex +24:4. Ps 77:20. Hg +1:1mg.

LEVITICUS 27

2 **When**. Nu 6:2. +30:2. 1 S 2:11, 19, 25-28. Ps 4:3. Ro 12:1.
    a singular vow. Le 7:16. Nu ch 6, 30. Ec 5:4, 5.
    for the Lord. Ro 10:2. Ga 4:18. Col 4:13.
    persons. Heb. *nephesh*, Ge +12:5.
    thy estimation. or, thy valuation. lit. arrangement, ordering. ver. 3, 4, 18. Le 5:15, 18. 6:6. Jb 28:13, 17. Ps 55:13. Je 22:13. Lk 10:7.
3 **And thy estimation**. ver. 14. Le 5:15. 6:6. Nu 18:16. 2 K 12:4mg.
    after the. ver. 25. Ex +30:13. 38:24.
    shekel of the sanctuary. or, holy shekel, of unchanging value.
4 **thirty shekels**. Ex 21:32. Zc 11:12, 13. Mt 26:15. 27:9, 10. Ph 2:5-7.
6 **from**. Nu 3:40-43. 18:14-16.
7 **from**. Ps 90:10.
8 **poorer**. Le 5:7. 12:8. 14:21, 22. Mk 14:7. Lk 21:1-4. 2 C 8:9, 12. He 10:5-9.
    according. ver. 16, 18. Le 25:51. Je 5:7.
    his ability. Le 25:26.
10 **He shall not**. ver. 15-33. Ja 1:8.
    alter. Heb. *halaph*, **S#2498h** (change for better): Ge 31:41 (changed); Jb 14:7 (sprout). 29:20 (renewed. mg, changed); Ps 102:26. Is 9:10. 40:31 (renew. mg, change); 41:1. Ge 35:2. Ps 55:19.
    nor change. Heb. *mur*, **S#4171h** (change for worse), Mi +2:4. As in Ge 31:7, 41; an ox for a sheep, or a sheep for an ox.
    the exchange. As in Ps 15:4; 106:20, an old for a young one, or a young one for an old one.
11 **unclean beast**. Dt 23:18. Ml 1:14.
12 **or bad**. Ps 66:13:15. 76:11. Jon 2:9. Ml 1:14.
    as thou valuest it, who art the priest. Heb. according to thy estimation, O priest, etc. ver. 14.
13 **then he shall add**. ver. 10, 15, 19. Le 5:16. 6:4, 5. 22:14.
14 **sanctify**. ver. 21. Le 25:29-31. Nu 18:14. Ps 101:2-7.
    as the priest. ver. 12.
15 **then he shall add**. ver. +13. Dt 23:21-23. Ec 5:4, 5.
16 **of a field**. Ac 4:34-37. 5:4.
    an homer. *or*, the land of an homer. Is 5:10. Ezk 45:11-14. Ho 3:2.
    possession. i.e. derived from his parents, or by marriage, in opposition to "the field of his purchase," noticed in ver. 22 (Young).
    fifty shekels. ver. 3.

18 **after the jubilee**. Le 25:15, 16, 27, 51, 52.
19 **then he shall add**. ver. +13.
    assured to him. He 9:12.
21 **when**. Le 25:10, 28, 31.
    devoted. ver. 28, 29. Ex 22:20. Dt 13:17. Jsh 6:17. 1 S 15:21. Ezr 10:8. Is 44:29mg. Ezk 44:29mg. Ml 4:6.
    priest's. Nu 18:14. Ezk 44:29.
22 **his possessions**. Le 25:10, 25.
23 **thy estimation**. ver. 12, 18.
24 **return**. Le 25:10. Ac 3:21.
    to him. ver. 20. Le 25:28.
    land. Le +25:23. Dt +32:43.
25 **And all**. ver. 3.
    to the shekel. 1 S 2:3. Pr 16:11. Is 26:7. Ac 4:34-37. 5:1-5.
    twenty. Ex +30:13.
26 **the firstling**. Heb. first born, etc. **S#1060h**. Ge 10:15. 22:21. 25:13. +27:19, 32. 35:23. 36:15. 38:6, 7. 41:51. 43:33. +48:14, 18. 49:3. Ex 4:22, 23. 6:14. 11:5. 12:12, 29. 13:2, 13, 15. 22:29. 34:20. Le 27:26 (firstling; mg, firstborn). Nu 1:20 (eldest son): 3:2, 12, 13, 40, 41-43, 45, 46, 50. 8:16-18. 18:15, 17. 26:5. 33:4. Dt 15:19. 21:15, +16, 17. 25:6. 33:17. Jsh 6:26. 17:1. Jg 8:20. 1 S 8:2. 17:13. 2 S 3:2. 1 K 16:34. 2 K 3:27 (eldest). 1 Ch 1:13, 29. 2:3, 13, 25, 27, 42, 50. 3:1, 15. 4:4. 5:1, 3. 6:28. 8:1, 30, 39. 9:5, 31, 36. 26:2, 4, +10. 2 Ch 21:3. Ne 10:36. Jb 1:13, 18 (eldest). 18:13. Ps 78:51. +89:27. 105:36. 135:8. 136:10. Is 14:30. Je +31:9. Mi 6:7. Zc 12:10. Col +1:15. Compare **S#1061h**, firstfruits, Ex +23:16.
    which. Ex 13:2, 12, 13. 22:30. Nu 18:17. Dt 15:19.
27 **and shall add**. ver. 11-13.
28 **no devoted**. ver. +21. Dt +2:34. 25:19. Jsh 6:17-19, 26. Jg 11:30, 31. 21:5, 11, 18. 1 S 14:24-28, 38-45. 15:3, 18, 32, 33. Mt 25:41. Ac 23:12-14. Ro 9:3. 1 C 16:22. Ga 3:10, 13.
    most holy. Le +2:3. 1 Ch 29:1-9. 2 Ch 5:1.
29 **None**. Ex 17:14-16. Nu 21:2, 3. Jsh 6:17-19. 1 S 15:9, 18-23, 26, 33. 1 K 20:42. 1 C 10:2.
    of men. Jg 11:30-40. 21:11.
    surely. Ge +2:16.
30 **all the tithe**. Ge +14:20. 28:22. Nu 18:21-24. Dt 12:5, 6. 14:22, 23. 2 Ch 31:5, 6, 12. Ne 10:37, 38. 12:44. 13:5, 12. Ps 56:12. Ml 3:8-10. Mt +23:23. Lk +11:42. 18:12. He 7:5-9.
31 **at all redeem**. ver. 13.
32 **passeth under the rod**. Je 33:13. Ezk 20:37. Mi 7:14.
    the tenth shall be holy. Nu 18:21. 31:30, 37-41.
33 **neither shall**. ver. 10.
34 **commandments**. Dt +4:1. Jn 1:17.
    Moses. Ps 77:20.
    in mount. Le 25:2. 26:46. Nu 1:1. Ga 4:24, 25. He 12:18-25.

NUMBERS

NUMBERS 1

1 A.M. 2514. B.C. 1490.

wilderness. Nu 10:11, 12, 33. Ex 18:5. 19:1.
Le 27:34. Ac 7:30. Ga 4:25. He 12:18.

tabernacle. Ex 25:22. Le 1:1.

on the first day. Nu 9:1. 10:11. Ex 40:17. 1
K 6:1.

2 **Take ye the sum**. Nu 26:2-4, 63, 64. Ex
30:12. 38:26. 2 S 24:1-3. 1 Ch 21:1, 2. 27:23,
24.

the children. Ge 49:1-3. Ex 1:1-5.

after. ver. 18, 22, 26, etc. Ex 6:14-19.

3 **twenty**. Nu 14:29. 32:11. Ex 30:14.

able. Nu 26:2. Dt 3:18. 24:5. 2 S 24:9. 2 Ch
17:13-18. 26:11-13.

by their. Ex +6:26. Ps 105:37.

4 **every one**. ver. 16. Nu 2:3-31. 7:10-83.
10:14-27. 13:2-15. 17:3. 25:4, 14. 34:18-28.
Ex 18:25, 26. Jsh 22:14. 1 Ch 27:1-22.

5 **stand with**. Ge 29:32-35. 30:5-20. 35:17-26.
46:8-24. ch. 49. Ex 1:2-5. Dt ch. 33. Re 7:4-8.

tribe of Reuben. ver. 21. Nu 2:10, 16. 7:30.
10:18. 13:4. 26:5-7. 32:1, 2, 6, 25, 29, 31, 33,
37. 34:14. Dt 27:13. 33:6. Jsh 4:12. 13:15, 23.
18:7. 20:8. 21:7, 36. 22:9-11, 13, 15, 21, 25,
30-34. Jg 5:15, 16. 1 Ch 5:18. 6:63, 78. Ezk
48:6, 7, 31. Re 7:5.

Elizur. i.e. *my God is a rock*, **S#468h**. Nu 2:10.
7:30, 35. 10:18.

Shedeur. i.e. *the Mighty One is light; spreading
of light*, **S#7707h**. Nu 2:10. 7:30, 35. 10:18.

6 **of Simeon**. ver. 22, 23. Nu 2:12. 7:36. 10:19.
13:5. +25:14. 26:12. 34:20. Dt 27:12. Jsh
19:1, 8, 9. 21:4, 9. Jg 1:3, 17. 1 Ch 2:1. 4:24,
42. 6:65. 12:25. 2 Ch 15:9. 34:6. Ezk 48:24,
25, 33. Re 7:7.

Shelumiel. i.e. *my friend is God; at peace with
God*, **S#8017h**. Nu 2:12. 7:36, 41. 10:19.

Zurishaddai. i.e. *my rock is the Mighty One*,
S#6701h. Nu 2:12. 7:36, 41. 10:19.

7 **Nahshon**. 1 Ch +2:10.

8 **Nethaneel**. i.e. *given by God*, **S#5417h**. Nu 2:5.
7:18, 23. 10:15. 1 Ch 2:14. 15:24. 24:6. 26:4.
2 Ch 17:7. 35:9. Ezr 10:22. Ne 12:21, 36.

Zuar. i.e. *smallness; restraint*, **S#6686h**. Nu 2:5.
7:18, 23. 10:15.

9 **Of Zebulun**. ver. 30, 31. Nu 2:7. 7:24. 10:16.

13:10. 26:26. 34:25. Dt 27:13. 33:18. Jsh
19:10, 16, 27, 34. 21:7, 34. Jg 1:30. 4:6, 10.
5:14, 18. 6:35. 12:12. 1 Ch 6:63, 77. 12:33,
40. 27:19. 2 Ch 30:10, 11, 18. Ps 68:27. Is 9:1.
Ezk 48:26, 27, 33.

Eliab. i.e. *my God is father*, **S#446h**. Nu 2:7.
7:24, 29. 10:16. 16:1, 12. 26:8, 9. Dt 11:6. 1 S
16:6. 17:13, 28. 1 Ch 2:13. 6:27. 12:9. 15:18,
20. 16:5. 2 Ch 11:18.

Helon. i.e. *strong*, **S#2497h**. Nu 2:7. 7:24, 29.
10:16.

10 **of Joseph**. ver. 32. Nu 13:11. 26:28, 37. 36:1,
5. Dt 33:13, 16. Jsh 14:4. 16:1, 4. 17:14, 17.
18:5, 11. 24:32. Jg 1:22, 23, 35. 2 S 19:20. 1 K
11:28. 1 Ch 5:1. 7:29. Ps 77:15. 78:67. 80:1.
81:5. Ezk 37:16, 19. 47:13. 48:32. Am +5:6,
15. 6:6. Ob 18. Zc 10:6. Re 7:8.

Elishama. i.e. *my God hath heard*, **S#476h**. Nu
2:18. 7:48, 53. 10:22. 2 S 5:16. 2 K 25:25. 1
Ch 2:41. 3:6, 8. 7:26. 14:7. 2 Ch 17:8. Je
36:12, 20, 21. 41:1.

Ammihud. 2 S +13:37.

of Manasseh. ver. 34, 35. Nu 2:20. 7:54.
10:23. 13:11. 26:34. 32:33. 34:14, 23. 36:12.
Dt 3:13. 29:8. 33:17. 34:2. Jsh 1:12. 4:12.
12:6. 13:7, 29. 14:4. 16:4, 9. 17:1, 2, 5-9, 11,
12, 17. 18:7. 20:8. 21:5, 6, 25, 27. 22:1, 7, 9-
11, 13, 15, 21, 30, 31. Jg 1:27. 6:15, 35. 7:23.
11:29. 1 Ch 5:18, 23, 26. 6:61, 62, 70, 71.
7:29. 9:3. 12:19, 20, 31, 37. 26:32. 27:20, 21.
2 Ch 15:9. 30:1, 10, 11, 18. 31:1. 34:6, 9. Ps
60:7. 80:2. 108:8. Is 9:21. Ezk 48:4, 5.
Re 7:6.

Gamaliel. i.e. *my rewarder is God*, **S#1583h**. Nu
2:20. 7:54, 59. 10:23.

Pedahzur. i.e. *the ransomed of the Rock*,
S#6301h. Nu 2:20. 7:54, 59. 10:23.

11 **Abidan**. i.e. *father of judgment*, **S#27h**. Nu 2:22.
7:60, 65. 10:24.

Gideoni. i.e. *the cutter down; warlike*, **S#1441h**.
Nu 2:22. 7:60, 65. 10:24.

12 **Of Dan**. ver. 38, 39. Nu 2:25, 31. 7:66. 10:25.
13:12. 26:42. 34:22. Ex 31:6. 35:34. 38:23. Le
24:11. Dt 27:13. 33:22. Jsh 19:40, 47, 48.
21:5, 23. Jg 1:34. 5:17. 13:25. 18:2, 16, 22,
23, 25, 26, 30. 1 Ch 27:22. 2 Ch 2:14.

Ahiezer. 1 Ch +12:3.

Ammishaddai. i.e. *people of the Almighty*, **S#5996h**. Nu 2:25. 7:66, 71. 10:25.

13 Of Asher. ver. 40, 41. Nu 2:27. 7:72. 10:26. 13:13. 26:44, 47. 34:27. Dt 27:13. 33:24. Jsh 19:24, 31, 34. 21:6, 30. Jg 1:31. 5:17. 6:35. 7:23. 1 Ch 6:62, 74. 12:36. 2 Ch 30:11. Ezk 48:2, 3, 34. Re 7:6.

Pagiel. i.e. *he who meeteth me is God; event of God*, **S#6295h**. Nu 2:27. 7:72, 77. 10:26.

Ocran. i.e. *the troubled* or *the troubler; afflicted*, **S#5918h**. Nu 2:27. 7:72, 77. 10:26.

14 Of Gad. ver. 24, 25. Nu 2:14. 7:42. 10:20. 13:15. 26:15, 18. 32:1, 2, 6, 25, 29, 31, 33, 34. 34:14. Ge +30:11. Dt 27:13. 33:20. Jsh 4:12. 13:24, 28. 18:7. 20:8. 21:7, 38. 22:9-11, 13, 15, 21, 25, 30-34. 1 S 13:7. 2 S 24:5. 1 Ch 2:2. 5:11, 26. 6:63, 80. 12:14. Je 49:1. Ezk 48:27, 28, 34. Re 7:5.

Eliasaph. i.e. *my God gathers; protector*, **S#460h**. Nu 7:42, 47. 10:20. Son of Reuel, Nu 2:14.

Deuel. i.e. *known of God; invocation of God*, **S#1845h**. Nu 2:14, Reuel, i.e. *a friend of God*. 7:42, 47. 10:20.

15 Of Naphtali. ver. 42, 43. Nu 2:29. 7:78. 10:27. 13:14. 26:48, 50. 34:28. Dt 27:13. 33:23. 34:2. Jsh 19:32, 39. 20:7. 21:6, 32. Jg 1:33. 4:6, 10. 5:18. 6:35. 7:23. 1 K 4:15. 7:14. 15:20, 29. 1 Ch 6:62, 76. 12:34, 40. 27:19. 2 Ch 16:4. 34:6. Ps 68:27. Is 9:1. Ezk 48:3, 4.

Ahira. i.e. *my brother is evil; brother of evil*, **S#299h**. Nu 2:29. 7:78, 83. 10:27.

Enan. i.e. *having eyes; great fountain*, **S#5881h**. Nu 2:29. 7:78, 83. 10:27.

16 the renowned. Nu 2:3-31. 7:2, 10-83. 10:14-27. 11:17. 16:2. 26:9. Jg 6:15. 1 Ch 27:16-22.

heads. ver. 4. Jsh +22:21.

17 these men. ver. 5-15. Is 43:1. Jn +10:3. Re 7:4, etc.

18 their pedigrees. Ezr 2:59. Ne 7:61. He 7:3mg, 6mg.

by the. ver. +2.

according. ver. 20, etc. Is 43:1. Jn 10:3. Re 7:4.

19 As the. ver. 2. Nu 26:1, 2. 2 S 24:1-10.

20 Reuben, Israel's son. ver. +5. Ge +29:32.

21 were forty and. Nu 2:10, 11. 26:7.

22 Simeon. Ge +29:33.

23 were fifty and. Nu 2:13. 25:8, 9, 14. 26:14.

24 Gad. ver. +14. Ge +30:11.

25 forty and. Nu 2:15. 26:18.

26 Judah. ver. +27. Ge +35:23.

27 tribe of Judah. ver. 7, 26. Nu 2:3, 9. 7:12. 10:14. 13:6. 26:20, 22. 34:19. Ge +49:10. Ex 31:2. 35:30. 38:22. Dt 27:12. 34:2. Jsh 7:1, 16-18. 11:21. 14:6. 15:1, 12, 13, 20, 21, 63. 18:5, 11, 14. 19:1, 9, 34. 20:7. 21:4, 9, 11. Jg 1:2-4, 8-10, 16-19. 10:9. 15:9-11. 17:7. 18:12. 20:18. Ru 1:7. 1 S 11:8. 15:4. 17:1, 52. 18:16. 22:5. 23:3, 23. 27:6, 10. 30:14, 16, 26. 2 S

1:18. 2:1, 4, 7, 10, 11. 3:8, 10. 5:5. 6:2. 11:11. 12:8. 19:11, 14-16, 40-43. 20:2, 4, 5. 21:2. 24:1, 7, 9. 1 K 1:9, 35. 2:32. 4:20, 25. 1 Ch 6:55, 57, 65. 9:3. 12:16, 24. 13:6. 27:18. 28:4. 2 Ch 2:7. 9:11. 17:14. Ezr 1:2, 3, 5, 8. 4:4, 6. 5:1. 7:14. 9:9. 10:7, 9. Ne 1:2. 2:5, 7. 4:10, 16. 5:14. 6:7, 17, 18. 7:6. 11:3, 4, 20, 25, 36. 12:31, 32, 44. 13:12, 15-17. Est 2:6. Ps 48:11. 60:7. 63:t. 68:27. 69:35. 76:1. 78:68. 97:8. 108:8. 114:2. Je 23:6. Ho 4:15. 11:12. He 8:8.

three score and. Nu 2:3, 4. 26:22. 2 S 24:9. 2 Ch 17:14-16.

28 Issachar. ver. 8, +29. Ge +30:18.

29 tribe of Issachar. ver. 8, 28. Nu 2:5. 7:18. 10:15. 13:7. 26:23, 25. 34:26. Dt 27:12. 33:18. Jsh 17:10, 11. 19:17, 23. 21:6, 28. Jg 5:15. 10:1. 1 K 4:17. 15:27. 1 Ch 6:62, 72. 7:5. 12:32, 40. 27:18. 2 Ch 30:18. Ezk 48:25, 26, 33. Re 7:7.

fifty and. Nu 2:6. 26:25.

30 Zebulun. ver. +9. Ge +30:20. Re 7:8.

31 fifty and seven. Nu 2:8. 26:27.

32 Joseph. Nu 2:18, 19. Ge 30:24. ch. 37, 39. 46:20. 48:8-14, 20. 49:22-26.

children of Ephraim. ver. +33. Ge 48:5, 14-20. Dt 33:17.

33 the tribe of Ephraim. ver. 10, 32. Nu 2:18, 24. 7:48. 10:22. 13:8. 26:35, 37. 34:24. Dt 33:17. 34:2. Jsh 14:4. 16:4, 5, 8, 9. 17:8, 9, 17. 21:5, 20. Jg 1:29. 5:14. 7:24. 8:1, 2. 10:9. 12:1, 4, 15. 2 S 2:9. 1 Ch 6:66. 9:3. 12:30. 27:10, 14, 20. 2 Ch 15:9. 17:2. 25:7, 10. 28:7, 12. 30:1, 10, 18. 31:1. 34:6, 9. Ps 60:7. 78:9, 67. 80:2. 108:8. Is 7:2, 5, 8, 9, 17. 9:9, 21. 11:13. 17:3. 28:1, 3. Je 7:15. 31:9, 18, 20. Ezk 37:16, 19. 48:5, 6. Ho 4:17. 5:3, 5, 9, 11-14. 6:4, 10. 7:1, 8, 11. 8:9, 11. 9:3, 8, 11, 13, 16. 10:6, 11. 11:3, 8, 9, 12. 12:1, 8, 14. 13:1, 12. 14:8. Ob 19. Zc 9:10, 13. 10:7.

were forty. Nu 2:19. 26:37.

34 Manasseh. ver. +10. Ge +41:51.

35 thirty and two. Nu 2:21. 26:34. Ge 48:19, 20.

36 Benjamin. Ge +35:18.

37 tribe of Benjamin. ver. 11, 36. Nu 2:22. 7:60. 10:24. 13:9. 26:38, 41. 34:21. Ge 49:27. Dt 27:12. 33:12. Jsh 18:11, 20, 21, 28. 21:4, 17. Jg 1:21. 5:14. 10:9. 19:14. 20:3, 4, 10, 12-15, 17, 18, 20, 21, 23-25, 28, 30-32, 35, 36, 39, 41, 44, 46, 48. 21:1, 6, 13-18, 20, 21, 23. 1 S 4:12. 9:1, 16, 21. 10:2, 20, 21. 13:2, 15, 16. 14:16. 2 S 2:9, 15, 25, 31. 3:19. 4:2. 19:17. 21:14. 23:29. 1 K 4:18. 12:21, 23. 15:22. 1 Ch 6:60, 65. 8:40. 9:3, 7. 11:31. 12:2, 16, 29. 21:6. 27:21. 2 Ch 11:1, 3, 10, 12, 23. 14:8. 15:2, 8, 9. 17:17. 25:5. 31:1. 34:9, 32. Ezr 1:5. 4:1. 10:9. Ne 11:4, 7, 31, 36. Ps 68:27. 80:2. Je 1:1. 6:1. 17:26. 32:8, 44. 33:13. 37:12. 48:22-24, 32. Ho 5:8. Ob 19. Ac 13:21. Ro 11:1. Ph 3:5. Re 7:8.

thirty and five. Nu 2:23. 26:41. Jg 20:44-46. 2 Ch 17:17.

38 **Dan**. ver. +12. Ge +30:6.

39 **threescore and two**. Nu 2:26. 26:43.

40 **Asher**. ver. +13. Ge +30:13.

41 **forty and one**. Nu 2:28. 26:47.

42 **Naphtali**. Ge +30:8. 46:24. 49:21. Re 7:6.

43 **fifty and three**. Nu 2:30. 26:50.

44 **are those**. ver. 2-16. Nu 26:64.

45 **all**. i.e. except the Levites, ver. 47.
house of. Nu 2:32.
twenty years. ver. 3. Nu 14:29.

46 **six hundred thousand**. Nu 23:10. Ge 13:16. 17:6. 22:17. 26:3. 28:14. Ex +12:37. Dt 10:22. 1 K 4:20. 2 S 24:9. 1 Ch 21:5. 2 Ch 13:3. 17:14-19. He 11:11, 12. Re 7:4-9.

47 **the Levites**. ver. 3, 50. Nu 2:33. 3:14-29. ch. 4, 8. 26:57-62. Ge 29:34. 46:11. 1 Ch ch. 6. 21:6.

49 **Only thou**. Nu 2:33. 26:62.
tribe of Levi. Nu 3:6, 15. 4:2. 16:7, 8, 10. 17:3, 8. 18:2, 21. Ge 46:11. Ex 2:1. 6:19. 32:26, 28. Dt 10:8, 9. +12:12. 18:1. 21:5. 27:12. 31:9. 33:8. Jsh 13:14, 33. 14:3. 21:10. 1 K 12:31. 1 Ch 2:1. 6:1, 16. 9:18. 12:26. 21:6. 23:6, 14, 24. 24:20. Ezr 8:15. Ne 10:39. 12:23. Ps 135:20. Ezk 40:46. 48:31. Zc 12:13. Ml 2:4, 8. 3:3. He 7:5, 9. Re 7:7.

50 **thou shalt**. Nu 3:1-10. 4:15, 25-33. Ex 31:18. 32:26-29. 38:21. 1 Ch ch. 23. 25. 26. Ezr 8:25-30, 33, 34. Ne 12:8, 22, 47. 13:5, 10-13, 22.
the tabernacle. ver. 53. Ex +38:21.
of testimony. Ex +16:34.
shall encamp. Nu 2:17. 3:23-38. 10:21.
round about. 1 Ch 9:27. Mt 18:20. Ac 11:23. Re 1:13.

51 **the Levites**. Nu 4:5-33. 10:11, 17-21.
tabernacle. Nu 10:17, 21. Ac 5:42. 1 C 12:4-6, 20, 21.
the stranger. Nu 3:10, 38. 16:40. 18:22. Le 22:10-13. 1 S 6:19. 2 S 6:7.
shall be. Nu 16:23, 24, 31-33, 35. 1 S 6:19. 2 S 6:6, 7.

52 **pitch**. Nu 2:2, 34. ch. 10. 24:2, 5, 6.

53 **shall pitch**. ver. 50. Nu 3:7. 18:3. 1 T 4:13-16. 2 T 4:2.
there be. Nu 8:19. 16:46. 18:5. Le 10:6. 1 S 6:19. Je 5:31. 23:15. Ac 20:28-31.
and the. Nu 3:7, 8. 8:24-26. 18:3-5. 31:30, 47. 1 Ch 23:32. 2 Ch 13:10, 11.

54 **according to**. Nu 2:34. Ezk 23:21, 22. 39:32, 43. 40:16, 32. Dt 32:32. 1 S 15:22. Ps 19:8, 11. Mt 28:20.

NUMBERS 2

2 **shall pitch**. ver. 3, 10. Nu 1:52. 10:14, 18, 22, 25.
the ensign. Is 11:10-12. 18:3. Zc 9:16.

far off. Heb. over against. Jsh 3:3, 4. Pr 14:7. SS 6:4, 10. Je 16:17. Am 9:3.
about the. Nu 1:50, 53. Ps 76:11. Is 12:6. Ezk 43:7. 1 C 14:23, 40. Ph 1:27. Col 2:19. Re 4:2-5.

3 **the standard**. Nu 26:19-22. Ge 49:8-10. Jg 1:1, 2. 1 Ch 5:2.
Nahshon. 1 Ch +2:10.
Judah. Nu +1:27. Re 22:16.

4 **threescore and fourteen**. Nu 1:27. 26:22.

5 **Issachar**. Ge +30:18.
and Nethaneel. Nu +1:8.

6 **fifty and four**. Nu 1:29. 26:25.

7 **Zebulun**. Ge 49:13.
Eliab. Nu +1:9.

8 **fifty and seven**. Nu 1:31. 26:26, 27.

9 **These shall**. Nu 10:14.

10 **camp of Reuben**. Ge 49:3, 4. 1 Ch +5:1, 2.
Elizur. Nu +1:5.

11 **forty and six**. Nu 1:21. 26:7.

12 **Simeon**. Ge +29:33.
Shelumiel. Nu +1:6.

13 **fifty and nine**. Nu 1:23. 26:14.

14 **Gad**. Ge 49:19.
Eliasaph. Nu 1:14. 7:42, 47. 10:20. Son of Deuel.

15 **forty and five**. Nu 1:25. 26:18.

16 **an hundred**. ver. 9, 24, 31.
they shall. Nu 10:18.

17 **tabernacle**. ver. 2. Nu 1:50-53. 3:38. 10:17, 21. 2 S 7:5, 6. Jn 2:21. 1 C 14:40. Col 2:5. Re 21:3.
in the midst. Mt 18:20. Re 1:13.

18 **camp of Ephraim**. Nu +1:33.
Elishama. Nu 1:10.

19 **forty thousand and**. Nu 1:33. 26:37.

20 **Gamaliel**. Nu 1:10. 7:54, 59. 10:23.

21 **his host**. Ge 49:22.
thirty and two. Nu 1:35. 26:34.

22 **Benjamin**. Ge 49:27.
Abidan. Nu +1:11.

23 **thirty and five**. Nu 1:37. 26:41.

24 **Ephraim**. Ge +48:17-19, 20.
an hundred. ver. 9, 16, 31.
And. Nu 10:22.

25 **Dan**. Nu +1:12.
Ahiezer. 1 Ch +12:3.

26 **threescore and**. Nu 1:39. 26:43.

27 **Asher**. Ge 49:20.
Pagiel. Nu 1:13. 7:72, 77. 10:26.

28 **forty**. Nu 1:41. 26:47.

29 **the tribe**. Nu +1:15.
Naphtali. Ge +30:8.
Ahira. Nu +1:15.

30 **fifty and three**. Nu 1:42, 43. 26:50.

31 **Dan**. Nu +1:12.
an hundred. ver. 9, 16, 24.
They. Nu 10:25.

32 **hosts**. Ex +12:41.
six hundred. ver. 9. Ex +12:37.

33 not numbered. Nu 1:47-49.
34 according. Nu 1:54. Ex 39:42. 1 Ch 6:32. Ps
119:6. Lk 1:6. 1 C 14:40. Col 2:5.
so they. ver. 2. Nu 10:28. 23:9, 10, 21. 24:2,
5, 6.

NUMBERS 3

1 generations. Ge 2:4. 5:1. 10:1. Ex 6:16, 20.
Mt 1:1.
spake. Nu 1:1. Le 25:1. 27:34.
2 the names. Ex +6:23.
3 the priests. Ex 28:41. 40:13, 15. Le 8:2, 12,
30.
whom he consecrated. Heb. whose hand
he filled. Ex +28:41. Ex 29:1-37. Le ch. 8, 9.
He 7:28.
4 Nadab. Ex +6:23.
in the sight. 1 Ch 24:1-6. 1 J 3:22.
6 Bring. Nu 1:49-53. 2:17, 33. 8:6-15, 22-26.
16:9-11. 18:2-6. Ex 32:26-29. Dt 33:8, 9. Ps
119:91. Is 42:1. Ml 2:4. Jn 12:26.
near. Ep 2:13.
present. Ep 5:27.
minister unto. Mt 25:40. 27:55. He 6:10.
7 keep. ver. 32. Nu 8:26. 31:30. 1 Ch 23:28-32.
26:20, 22, 26. 2 T 1:14. 4:7.
to do the. Nu 1:50. 8:11, 15, 24-26.
service. Col 3:24.
8 they shall keep. Nu 4:15, 28, 33. 10:17, 21.
1 Ch 26:20-28. Ezr 8:24-30. Is 52:11.
to do the service. Ex 32:26-28. Ps 119:91. Is
42:1. Jn 12:26.
9 thou shalt. Nu 8:19. 18:6, 7. Ep 4:8, 11.
wholly given. Jn 17:24.
10 appoint. Ps 105:26. He 5:4.
they shall. Nu 18:7. 1 Ch 6:49. Ezk 44:8. Ac
6:3, 4. Ro 12:7. 1 T 4:15, 16.
wait. Ex 30:30. Ro 12:7.
priest's office. 1 P 2:5, 9. Re 1:6.
and the stranger. ver. 38. Nu 1:51. 16:35,
40. 18:3. 1 S 6:19. 2 S 6:7. 2 Ch 26:16-21. Ep
2:19. He 8:4. 10:19-22.
12 I have taken. ver. 41, 45. Nu 8:16, 18. 18:6.
firstborn. Le +27:26. He 12:23.
13 Because. Nu 8:16, 17. 18:15. Ex 13:2, 12.
22:29. 34:19. Le 27:26. Ps 89:27. Ezk 44:30.
Lk 2:23. Col +1:13-15. He 12:23. Ja 1:18. Re
1:5.
on the day. Ex 12:29, 30. 13:2, 12, 15. Ps
78:51. 105:36.
15 Number. Ps 147:4. Lk 12:7.
by their families. Dt 32:8, 9.
every male. ver. 22, 28, 34, 39, 40, 43. Nu
18:15, 16. 26:62. Pr 8:17. Je 2:2. 31:3. Mk
10:14. 2 T 3:15.
16 word. Heb. mouth. ver. 39, 51. Dt +21:5.
17 And these. Ge +46:11. Jsh ch. 21. 1 Ch 15:5-
23. 23:6-23. ch. 24-26. Ne 11, 12.
18 Libni. ver. 21. 1 Ch +6:29.

Shimei. 1 Ch 23:7-11. 23:12, 13, 18-20,
Izhar. 25:4. ch. 26. Ne 12:1-26.
19 Amram. ver. 27. Ex +6:18.
Izehar. i.e. *oil,* S#3324h. Ex +6:18, Izhar.
20 Mahli. i.e. *sickly; my sickness, infirmity, disease,*
S#4249h. ver. 33. Ex 6:19, Mahali. 1 Ch 6:19,
29, 47. 15:6. 23:21, 23. 24:26, 28, 30. 25:3.
Ezr 8:18.
21 of the Libnites. ver. +18. S#3846h. Nu 26:58.
Shimites. S#8097h. Zc 12:13, Shimei.
Gershonites. S#1649h. ver. 23, 24. Nu 4:24,
27, 28. 26:57. Jsh 21:33. 1 Ch 23:7. 26:21.
29:8. 2 Ch 29:12.
22 according to. Dt 32:8, 9. Ps 147:4. Lk
12:7.
seven thousand and. Nu 4:38-40.
23 behind. Nu 1:53. 2:17.
24 Lael. i.e. *unto, by, because of God,* S#3815h.
25 the charge. ver. 7. Nu 4:24-28, 44. 7:7.
10:17. 1 Ch 9:14-33. 23:32. 26:21, 22. 2 Ch
31:2, 11-18. Ezr 8:28-30. Mk 13:34. Ro 12:6-
8. 1 C 12:6. Col 4:17. 1 T 1:18.
the tabernacle, and. Ex +38:21.
and the hanging. Ex 26:36, 37. 36:37, 38.
40:28.
26 the hangings. Ex 26:1, 7, 14, 36. 27:9-16.
38:9-16.
the cords. Ex 35:18.
27 of Kohath. ver. 19. Ge +46:11.
Amramites. S#6020h. 1 Ch 26:23.
Izharites. S#3324h. 1 Ch 24:22. 26:23, 29.
Hebronites. S#2276h. Nu 26:58. 1 Ch 26:23,
30, 31.
Uzzielites. S#5817h. 1 Ch 26:23.
Kohathite. S#6956h. Nu 10:21. 2 Ch 29:12.
28 eight thousand. Nu 4:35, 36.
keeping. ver. 7, 31.
29 southward. ver. 23. Nu 1:53. 2:10.
30 Elizaphan. i.e. *God is protector; whom God
hides,* S#469h. Nu 34:25. Ex +6:22, Elzaphan. 1
Ch 15:8. 2 Ch 29:13.
31 the ark. Nu 4:4-16. Ex 25:10-40. ch. 31-35.
37:1-24. 39:33-42. 40:2-16, 30.
the altars. Ex 27:1-8. 30:1-10. 37:25-29.
38:1-7.
and the hanging. Ex 26:31-33. 36:35, 36.
32 Eleazar. Ex +6:23.
chief over. 2 K 25:18. 1 Ch 26:20-24. 1 C
12:18-21.
33 Mahlites. S#4250h. ver. +20. Nu 26:58.
Mushites. S#4188h. Nu 26:58.
34 six thousand and. Nu 5:43, 44.
35 Zuriel. i.e. *my rock is God,* S#6700h.
Abihail. i.e. *father of valor,* S#32h. 1 Ch 2:29.
5:14. 2 Ch 11:18. Est 2:15. 9:29.
shall. ver. 28, 29. Nu 1:53.
northward. Nu 2:25.
36 under the custody and charge. Heb. the
office of the charge. ver. 32. Nu 4:16. 1 C
12:11. 14:33.

the boards. Nu 4:29-33. 7:8. Ex 26:15-29, 32, 37. 27:9-19. 35:11, 18. 36:20-34, 36. 38:17-20. 39:33.

38 **toward**. ver. 23, 29, 35. Nu 1:53. 2:3.
keeping. ver. 10. Nu 18:1-5. 1 Ch 6:48, 49.
for the charge. ver. 7, 8, 10. Ps 93:5.

39 **commandment**. Ge +45:21.
twenty and two thousand. Nu 4:47, 48. 26:62. Mt 7:14.

40 **Number all**. ver. 12, 15, 45. Ex 32:26-29. Ps 87:6. Is 4:3. Lk 10:20. Ph 4:3. 2 T 2:19. He 12:23. Re 3:5. 14:4.

41 **shalt take**. ver. 12, 45. Nu 8:16. 18:15. Ex 24:5, 6. 32:26-29. Mt 20:28. 1 T 2:6.

43 **a month old**. Le 27:6, 25. Ep 1:4-7. 1 P 1:18, 19.
were twenty and two. ver. 39.

45 **the Levites instead**. ver. 12, 40, 41.
be mine. Je 18:1-6. Ro 9:21.

46 **redeemed**. Nu 18:15. Ex 13:13. 1 P 1:18, 19.
which are. ver. 39-43.

47 **five shekels**. Nu 18:16. Le 27:6.
the shekel. ver. 50. Ex +30:13.

50 **a thousand three**. ver. 46, 47. Mt 20:28. Ep 1:4-7. 1 T 2:5, 6. T 2:14. He 9:12. 1 P 1:18. 3:18.

51 **Moses**. ver. 48. Nu 16:15. 1 S 12:3, 4. Ac 20:33. 1 C 9:12. 1 P 5:2.
as the Lord. Le 27:6, 25. Ml 4:4.

NUMBERS 4

2 **Kohath**. Nu +3:19, 27.

3 **thirty years**. Nu 8:24-26. Ge 41:46. 1 Ch 23:3, 24-27. 28:12, 13. Lk 3:23. 1 T 3:6.
enter. 2 K 11:4-12. 2 Ch 23:1-11. 2 C 10:3, 4. Ep 6:10-18. 1 T 1:18.
to do. Nu 3:7, 8. 16:9. 1 Ch 6:48. 23:4, 5, 28-32. 1 T 3:1.

4 **the service**. ver. 15, 19, 24, 30. Nu 3:30, 31. Mk 13:34.

5 **And when**. Nu 2:16, 17. 10:14.
Aaron shall come. ver. 15. Nu 3:27-32.
they shall. Ex 26:31-33. 36:35. 40:3. Is 25:7. Mt 27:51. He 9:3. 10:19, 20, 22.
and cover. Ex 25:10-22. 37:1-9. 2 S 6:2-9.

6 **a cloth**. ver. 7, 8, 11-13. Ex 35:19. 39:1, 41.
the staves. Ex +25:13.

7 **the table**. Ex 25:23-30. 37:10-16. Le 24:5-8.
showbread. Ex +25:30.
cover withal. or, pour out withal. Ge 35:14. Ex 25:29. 29:40. 30:9. 37:16.

8 **cloth of scarlet**. ver. 6, 7, 9, 11-13.

9 **the candlestick**. Ex +25:31. Ps 119:105.

10 **within a covering**. ver. 6, 12.

11 **the golden altar**. Lk +1:11.

12 **the instruments of**. ver. 7, 9, 26, 32. Nu 3:8. 7:1. Ex 25:9. 31:10. 38:17, 21. 2 K 25:14, 15. 1 Ch 9:29. 2 Ch 4:11, 16, 19, 22.

13 **the ashes**. Ex 27:3-5. Le 6:12, 13.

purple cloth. ver. 6-9, 11, 12. Ex 39:1, 41. Ezk 27:7.

14 **all the vessels thereof**. Ex 38:1-7. 2 Ch 4:19.
basons. or, bowls. 1 K +7:40.

15 **after that**. Nu 7:9. 10:21. Dt 31:9. Jsh 4:10. 2 S 6:3. 1 Ch 15:2, 4, 5, 12-15.
come to bear. Nu 10:21. Dt 31:9. Jsh 3:9, 11-13. 1 Ch 13:6-10.
they shall. Nu 3:38. Ex 19:12. 1 S 6:19. 2 S 6:6, 7. 1 Ch 13:9, 10. He 12:18-29.
These things. Nu 3:30, 31.

16 **the office**. ver. 9. Nu 3:32.
the oil. Ex 25:6. 27:20, 21. Le 24:2.
the sweet. Ex 30:34-38. 37:29.
the daily. Ex 29:39-41.
meat offering. Le +23:13.
the anointing. Ex 30:23-33.
the oversight. Lk 4:18. Ac 20:28. 1 C 4:1. 1 T 2:5. He 3:1, 6. 1 P 2:25. 5:2.

18 **Cut ye not off**. ver. 20. Nu 16:32. 17:10. 18:5. Ex 19:21. Le 10:1, 2. 1 S 6:19. 2 S 6:6, 7. Je 38:23.

19 **the most holy**. ver. 4.
appoint. Mk 13:34.

20 **they shall**. ver. 15, 19. Ex 19:21. Le 10:2. 1 S 5:1-3, 6, 10, 11. 6:19. He 10:19, 20. Re 11:19.
the holy things. i.e. the *ark*. 1 K 8:8 with 2 Ch 5:9.

22 **the sum**. Nu +3:18, 21, 24.

23 **thirty years**. ver. +3.
to perform the service. Heb. to war the warfare. ver. 3, 30. Nu 8:24. Ex 38:8. Is 63:1-4. Ro 7:14-24. 1 C 9:7. 2 C 6:7. 10:3-5. Ga 5:17, 24. Ep 6:10-19. 1 T 1:18. 2 T 2:3, 4. 4:7.

24 **burdens**. or, carriage. ver. 15, 19, 27, 31, 32, 47, 49.

25 **the curtains**. Nu +3:25, 26. 7:5-7.
the covering. Ex 26:14.

26 **the hangings**. Ex 27:9.
and their cords. Ex 35:18.

27 **appointment**. Heb. mouth. ver. 37, 41, 45, 49. Dt +21:5mg. Mt 25:14, 15. Mk 13:34. Lk 1:70. 19:12, 13. 1 C 11:2. Ep 2:10. 1 Th 5:18.
burdens. Ga 6:5.

28 **under the hand**. ver. 33. 1 C 12:5, 6.

29 **sons of Merari**. Nu +3:33-35. Ge +46:11.

30 **service**. Heb. warfare. ver. 3, +23mg, 35, 39, 43. Nu 31:3, 4, 5. Ps 110:1-7. 1 T 6:11, 12. 2 T 2:4. 4:7, 8.

31 **the charge**. Nu +3:36, 37. 7:8, 9.
the boards. Ex 26:15.

32 **pins**. Ex +27:19.
and by name. Jn +10:3.
the instruments. ver. +12.

33 **under the hand**. ver. 28. Jsh 3:6. Is 3:6.

34 **Moses and**. ver. 2.

35 **thirty years old**. ver. 3, 23, 30, 39, 43, 47. Nu 8:24-26. 1 Ch 23:3, 24, 26, 27. 28:13. Lk 3:23. 1 T 3:6.

40 two thousand and. Nu 3:32.
41 were numbered. ver. 22.
44 were numbered. ver. 36, 40. Nu 3:22, 23, 24, 25. 1 C 12:8-11.
  three thousand and. Nu 3:34. Dt 33:25. 1 C 10:13. 12:8-12. 2 C 12:9, 10.
45 according. ver. 29.
47 From thirty. ver. 3, 23, 30. 1 Ch 23:3, 27.
  every one. ver. 15, 24, 37. Ro 12:6-8. 1 C 12:4-31. He 2:4. 1 P 4:10.
48 were numbered. ver. 3. 1 Ch 23:27-32.
  were eight thousand and. Nu 3:39. Mt 7:14. 20:16. 22:15.
49 According to the. ver. 37, 41, 45. Nu 1:54. 2:33. 3:51. 7:5, 6. 18:31. 1 C 3:8. He 6:10.
  every one. ver. 15, 24, 31. Is 11:2-4. 42:1-7. 49:1-8. Ro 12:4-8.
  as the Lord. ver. 1, 21. Ps 103:21, 22.

NUMBERS 5

2 put out of the camp. Le +4:12.
  leper. 2 K +5:1.
  and every. Le 15:2-27.
  and whosoever. Nu 9:6-10. 19:11-16. 31:19. Le 21:1.
  the dead. Heb. *nephesh*, soul, Le +19:28. Lk 8:4.
3 without. 2 K 7:3. 1 C 5:7-13. 2 C 6:17. 2 Th 3:6. T 3:10. He 12:15, 16. 2 J 10, 11. Re 21:27.
  defile not. Nu 19:22. Hg 2:13, 14.
  in the midst. Le 26:11, 12. Dt 23:14.
  I dwell. Ex +29:45. 2 C 7:1.
6 When. Le 5:1-4, 17. 6:2, 3.
  person. Heb. *nephesh*, soul, Ge +27:31.
7 confess. Le 5:5. 26:40. Jsh 7:19. Jb 33:27, 28. Ps 32:5. Pr 28:13. Da 9:4. Mt 3:5, 6. 1 J 1:8-10.
  shall recompense. Ex 22:1-3. Le 5:16. 6:4, 5. 2 S 12:6. Pr 6:31. Ezk 33:15, 16. Lk 19:8.
  with the principal. Le 5:15. 6:4-7. 7:7. Lk +19:8.
8 have no. Le 25:25, 26.
  beside the ram. Le 6:6, 7. 7:7.
  an atonement. Le +23:27.
9 offering. *or*, heave offering. Le +7:14. 22:2, 3.
  be his. Le +7:7. Ml 3:8-10.
10 hallowed things. 1 C 3:21-23. 1 P 2:5, 7, 9.
12 If any. ver. 19, 20. Pr 2:16, 17.
13 lie with. Le 18:20. 20:10. Ex +20:14. Pr 7:18, 19. 30:20.
14 spirit. Heb. *ruach*, Ge +41:8. ver. 30. Pr 6:26-35. SS 8:6. Zp 3:8. 1 C 10:22.
15 her offering for her. Le 5:11. Ho 3:2.
  bringing. 1 K 17:18. Ezk 29:16. He 10:3.
16 bring her near. or, rather, *bring it near*; i.e. her offering.
  set her. Rather, *set it*, i.e. the offering; for the

woman is afterwards ordered to be set before the Lord (ver. 18). Le 1:3. Je 17:10. He 13:4. Re 2:22, 23.
17 holy water. Nu 19:2-9, 17. Ex 30:18. 1 Th 5:22.
  of the dust. Jb 2:12. Je 17:13. La 3:29. Jn 8:6, 8.
18 the priest. He 13:4. Re 2:19-23.
  uncover. Le 13:45. 1 C 11:15. He 4:12, 13.
  and put. ver. 15, 25, 26.
  the bitter water. Ge +31:1. ver. 17, 22, 24. Dt 29:18. 1 S 15:32. Pr 5:4. Ec 7:26. Is 38:17. Je 2:19. Re 10:9, 10.
19 charge her. Mt 26:63.
  with another. *or, being* in the power of thy husband. Heb. under thy husband. ver. 20, 29. Nu 3:12, 41, 45. 32:14. Ro 7:2.
21 an oath. Jsh 6:26. 1 S 14:24. Ne 10:29. Mt 26:74.
  The Lord make. Is 65:15. Je 29:22.
  thigh. Ge +24:2.
  rot. Heb. fall. 2 Ch 21:15. Pr 10:7.
22 the curse. He 13:4. Ja 1:14, 15.
  go into. ver. 27. Ps 109:18. Pr 1:31. Ezk 3:3.
  the woman. Dt 27:15-26. Jb 31:21, 22, 39, 40. Ps 7:4, 5.
  Amen. Mt +6:13. Jn +1:51.
23 write these. Ex 17:14. Dt 31:19. 2 Ch 34:24. Jb 31:35. Je 51:60-64. 1 C 16:21, 22. Re 20:12.
  blot. Ps +51:1.
24 the water. Zc 5:3, 4. Ml +3:5. 2 C 5:21. Ga 3:13.
25 priest. ver. 15, 18.
  wave. Ex +29:24. ver +23:15.
26 the memorial. Le 2:2, 9. 5:12. 6:15.
27 if she be defiled. ver. 20. Pr 5:4-11. Ec 7:26. Ro 6:21. 2 C 2:16. He 10:26-30. 2 P 2:10.
  the woman. Ex 34:14. Dt 28:37. Ps 83:9-11. Is 65:15. Je 24:9. 29:18, 22. 42:18. Zc 8:13. 2 C 11:2.
28 And if. ver. 19. Mi 7:7-10. 2 C 4:17. 1 P 1:7.
  and shall. Ps +113:9.
29 the law. Le 7:11. 11:46. 13:59. 14:54-57. 15:32, 33.
  when a wife goeth. ver. 12, 15, 19. Is 5:7, 8.
30 spirit. Heb. *ruach*, Ge +41:8.
31 be guiltless. Ps 37:6.
  bear. Nu 9:13. Le 20:10, 17-20. Ezk 18:4. Ro 2:8, 9.
  iniquity. Ge +19:15.

NUMBERS 6

2 When. ver. 5, 6. Ex 33:16. Le 20:26. Pr 18:1. Ro 1:1. 2 C 6:17. Ga 1:15. He 7:27.
  separate themselves. Le 27:2.
  to vow. Le 27:2. 1 S 1:28. Lk 1:15. Ac 21:23, 24.
  Nazarite. i.e. *separated one*, **S#5139h**. ver. 13,

18, 19, 20, 21. Ge 49:26 (separate from). Le 25:5 (undressed. mg, separation), 11. Dt 33:16 (separated). Jg 13:5, 7. 16:17. La 4:7. Am 2:11, 12.

to separate themselves. *or*, to make *themselves* Nazarites.

3 **from wine**. Le 10:9. Jg 13:4, 5. 14. Pr 31:4, 5. Je 35:6-8. Am 2:12. Lk *1:15*. 7:33, 34. 21:34. Ep 5:18. 1 Th 5:22. 1 T 5:23.

4 **separation**. *or*, Nazariteship. ver. 5, 8, 9, 12, 13, 18, 19, 21.
vine tree. Heb. vine of the wine. Jg 13:14.

5 **razor**. Jg 13:5. 16:17, 19. 1 S 1:11. La 4:7, 8. 1 C 11:10-15.

6 **he shall come**. Nu 19:11-16. Le 19:28. Je 16:5, 6. Ezk 24:16-18. Mt 8:21, 22. Lk 9:59, 60. 2 C 5:16.
dead body. Heb. *nephesh*, soul, Le +19:28.

7 **unclean**. Nu 9:6. Le 21:1, 2, 10-12. Ezk 44:25.
consecration. Heb. separation. ver. 4. Ex 29:6. 39:30. Le 8:9. 1 C 11:10.

8 **All the days**. Jn 17:15-19. Ro 1:1. 2 C 6:17, 18.

9 **and he**. Nu 19:14-19.
shave. ver. 18. Ac 18:18. 21:23, 24. Ph 3:8, 9.

10 **eighth day**. Le 1:14. 5:7-10. 9:1-21. 12:6. 14:22, 23, 31. 15:14, 29. Jn 2:1, 2. Ro 4:25.

11 **offer**. Le 5:8-10. 14:30, 31.
sin offering. Le +23:19.
burnt offering. Le +23:12.
the dead. Heb. *nephesh*, soul, Le +19:28.
and shall. ver. 5. Is 52:11. 2 C 7:1. Re 18:4.

12 **a trespass**. Le +5:6.
but the. Ezk 18:24. Mt 3:15. 24:13. Jn 8:29-31. Ja 2:10. 2 J 8.
lost. Heb. fall. 1 K 20:25. **S#5307h.** Ge 4:5 (fell), 6 (fallen). 15:12 (fell). +25:18 (died; mg, fell). Ex 19:21 (perish). 1 K 1:52 (fall). Ps 5:10. 35:8. 37:24. 91:7. 141:10. Je 6:15.

13 **are fulfilled**. Ac 21:26.
door of. Le 1:2, 3.

14 **one he**. Le 1:4, 10-13. 1 Ch 15:26, 28, 32.
burnt offering. Le +23:12.
one ewe. Le 4:2, 3, 27, 32. Ml 1:13, 14. 1 P 1:19.
sin offering. Le +23:19.
one ram. Le 3:6.
peace offerings. Le +23:19.

15 **a basket**. Le 2:4. 8:2. 9:4. Jn 6:50-59.
anointed. Ex 29:2.
meat offering. Le +23:13.
drink offering. Le +23:13. Is 62:9. 1 C 10:31. 11:26.

16 **sin offering**. Le +23:19.
burnt offering. Le +23:12.

17 **peace offerings**. Le +23:19.
meat offering. Le +23:13.
drink offering. Le +23:13.

18 **shave the head**. ver. 5, 9. Ac 18:18. 21:23, 24, 26.
and put it. Lk 17:10. Ep 1:6.

19 **the sodden**. Le 8:31. 1 S 2:15.
put them. Ex 29:23-28. Le 7:30. 8:27.

20 **priest shall wave**. Ex +29:24.
wave offering. Le +23:15.
with the wave. Nu +18:18.
and after. Ps 16:10, 11. Ec 9:7. Is 25:6. 35:10. 53:10-12. Zc 9:15, 17. 10:7. Mt 26:29. Mk 14:25. Jn 17:4, 5. 19:30. 2 T 4:7, 8.

21 **the law**. Nu +5:29.
beside that. Ezr 2:69. Ga 6:6. He 13:16.

23 **Aaron and**. Le 9:22. 1 Ch 23:13.
ye shall bless. Ge 14:19, 20. 24:60. 27:27-29. 28:3, 4. 47:7, 10. 48:20. Le 9:22, 23. Dt 10:8. 21:5. 33:1. Jsh 8:33. 1 Ch 23:13. Lk 24:50, 51. Ro 1:7. 1 C 1:3. 2 C 13:14. He 7:1, 7. 11:20, 21. 1 P 1:2. 2 P 1:2, 3. 2 J 3.

24 **The Lord**. Ru 2:4. Ps 5:12. 115:12. 133:3. 134:3. Pr +10:22. 1 C 14:16. Ep 6:24. Ph 4:23. Re 1:4, 5.
keep thee. Ps 91:11. 121:3-8. Is 27:3. 42:6. Jn 17:11. Ph 4:7. 1 Th 5:23. 1 P 1:5. Ju 24.

25 **The Lord**. Ps 21:6. 31:16. 67:1. 80:1-3, 7, 19. 119:135. Da 9:17. 2 C 4:4.
face. Ge +19:13.
shine. Ps +27:1.
be gracious. Ge 31:49. 43:29. Ex 33:19. +34:6, 7. Ps 30:7. 77:9. Is 30:19. 33:2. Ml 1:9. Lk 18:13. Jn 1:17. 2 C 13:14. He 13:20, 21.

26 **lift up**. Dt 28:50mg. Ps 4:6. 42:5. 89:15. Ec 8:1mg. Da 8:23. Ac 2:28.
countenance. Ps 21:6. 89:15.
give thee. Ps 16:11. 29:11. Is 26:3, 12. Mi 5:5. Jn 20:21, 26. Ro +5:1. Ep 6:23.
peace. Ge +43:23.

27 **put my name**. Ge 48:16. Ex 3:13-15. 6:3. 34:5-7. Dt 28:10. 1 K 11:36. 14:21. 2 K 21:4. 2 Ch +7:14. Ezr 6:12. Ne 1:9. Ps +9:10. Is 4:1. 43:7. Je 14:9. Da 9:18, 19. Mt +28:19. Jn 17:26. Ac 15:14. Re 3:12. 22:4.
and I will. Nu 23:20. Ge 12:2, 3. 32:26, 29. 1 Ch 4:10. Ps 5:12. 67:7. 115:12, 13. Ga 3:14. Ep 1:3-5. 2:19.

NUMBERS 7

1 **had fully**. Ex 40:2, 17-19.
anointed it. Ex 30:23-30. Le 8:10, 11. ch. 9. He 9:2.
sanctified them. Ge 2:3. Ex 13:2. 1 K 8:64. Mt 23:19.

2 **the princes**. Nu 1:4-16. ch. 2, 10.
and were over, etc. Heb. who stood.
offered. Ex 35:27. 1 Ch 29:6-8. 2 Ch 35:8. Ezr 2:68, 69. Ne 7:70-72.

3 **covered waggons**. or, tilted wagons. Ge 45:19. Is 66:20.

5 **Take it**. Ex 25:1-11. 35:4-10. Ps 16:2, 3. Is 42:1-7. 49:1-8. Ep 4:11-13. T 3:8.
according. Nu 4:9. 18:31. 1 C 3:8. He 6:10.

7 **Two waggons**. Nu 3:25, 26. 4:24-28.
sons of Gershon. Nu 4:25, 40.

8 **four waggons**. Nu 3:36, 37. 4:28-33.
the sons. Nu 4:31, 32, 44, 48.

9 **unto the**. Nu 4:4-15.
because. Nu 3:31. 4:4-16. 2 S 6:6, 13. 1 Ch 15:3, 13. 23:26.
shoulders. Mt 11:29, 30.

10 **dedicating**. Dt 20:5. 1 K 8:63. 2 Ch 2:4. 7:5, 9. Ezr 6:16, 17. Ne 12:27, 43. Ps 30; title. Jn 10:22.

11 **shall offer**. 1 Ch 29:6-10, 13-16.
on his day. 1 C 14:33, 40. Col 2:5.

12 **Nahshon**. 1 Ch +2:10.
Judah. Ge 49:8, 10.

13 **charger**. Ex 25:29. 37:16. 1 K 7:43, 45. 2 K 25:14, 15. Ezr 1:9, 10. 8:25. Je 52:19. Da 5:2. Zc 14:20. Mt 14:8, 11.
the shekel. Ex 30:13. Le 27:3, 25.
a meat offering. Le +23:13.

14 **spoon**. Nu 4:7. Ex 37:16. 1 K 7:50. 2 K 25:14, 15. 2 Ch 4:22. 22:14.
incense. Ex 30:7, 8, 34-38. 35:8.

15 **One young**. Nu ch. 25, 28, 29. Le ch. 1. Is 53:4, 10, 11. Mt 20:28. Jn 17:19. Ro 3:24-26. 5:6-11, 16-21. 8:34. 10:4. 1 T 2:6. T 2:14. He 2:10. 1 P 1:18, 19. 2:24. 3:18.
burnt offering. Le +23:12.

16 **sin offering**. Le +23:19.

17 **peace offerings**. Le +23:19. 2 C 5:19-21.
this was the offering. Nu ch 2, 10. 1 C 14:33.

18 **Nethaneel**. Nu +1:8. 2:5.

19 **He offered**. ver. 12-17.

21 **burnt offering**. Le +23:12. Ro 12:1. Ep 5:2.

23 **peace offerings**. Le +23:19. Mt 10:8.

24 **Eliab**. Nu +1:9. 2:7.

27 **young bullock**. Ps 50:8-14. 51:16. Is 1:11. Je 7:22. Am 5:22.

29 **the offering**. 2 S 24:22, 23. Is 32:8.

30 **Elizur**. Nu +1:5. 2:10.

31 **offering**. ver. 13, etc.
bowl. 1 K +7:40.

32 **spoon**. ver. 14.
incense. Ps 66:15. Ml 1:11. Lk 1:10. Re 8:3.

35 **the offering**. Ac +20:35.

36 **Shelumiel**. Nu 1:6. 2:12.

37 **His offering**. ver. 13, etc.

39 **one lamb**. Ex 12:5. Jn 1:29. Ac 8:32. 1 P 1:19. Re 5:6.

41 **the offering**. 2 C 9:5-7.

42 **Eliasaph**. Nu 1:14. 2:14. Son of Reuel.

43 **offering**. ver. 13, etc.
mingled with oil. Le 2:5. 14:10. He 1:9. 1 J 2:27.

45 **young bullock**. Ps 40:6. Is 53:4. 2 C 5:21.

47 **the offering**. Ex 35:29.

48 **Elishama**. Nu +1:10. 2:18.

49 **His offering**. ver. 13, etc.

53 **the offering**. Ex 35:20-24.

54 **Gamaliel**. Nu 1:10. 2:20.

55 **His offering**. ver. 13, etc.

59 **the offering**. 2 Ch 24:8-11.

60 **Abidan**. ver. 65. Nu +1:11.

61 **His offering**. ver. 13, etc.

62 **incense**. Ps 141:2. Is 66:20. Da 9:27. Ro 15:16. Ph 4:18. He 13:15.

65 **the offering**. Mk 12:41-44.

66 **Ahiezer**. Nu 1:12. 2:25. 10:25. 1 Ch +12:3.

67 **His offering**. ver. 13, etc.

71 **the offering**. 2 C 8:1-4.

72 **Pagiel**. Nu 1:13. 2:27.

73 **His offering**. ver. 13, etc.

77 **the offering**. Ph +4:17, 18.

78 **Ahira**. Nu +1:15. 2:29.

79 **His offering**. ver. 13, etc.

83 **the offering**. Ro 11:35, 36.

84 **the dedication**. ver. +10. 1 Ch 29:6-8. Ezr 2:68, 69. Ne 7:70-72. Is 60:6-10. He 13:10. Re 21:14.
the princes. Jg 5:9. Ne 3:9.

85 **two thousand**. 1 Ch 22:14. 29:4, 7. Ezr 8:25, 26.
after the shekel. ver. +13.

88 **dedication**. 2 Ch 7:5, 9. Ezr 6:16. Ne 12:27.
that it was anointed. ver. 1, 10, 84.

89 **to speak**. Ex +33:9.
him. i.e. God.
he heard. Nu 1:1. Le 1:1. He 4:16.
two cherubims. Ex 25:18-21. 1 S 4:4. 1 K 6:23. Ps 80:1. 1 P 1:12.

NUMBERS 8

2 **lightest**. Ex 40:25. Le 24:1, 2. Ps 119:105, 130. Is +8:20. Mt 5:14. Lk 2:32. Jn 1:9. 3:19. 8:12. 9:5. 2 C 4:6. Ep 5:8. 1 P 2:9. 2 P 1:19. 1 J 1:5. Re +1:12.

3 **as the Lord commanded**. Ps 40:7, 8. Jn 8:28, 29. He 3:1-6.

4 **candlestick**. Ex +25:31.
beaten gold. Ex +27:20. Is 53:5. He +2:10.
beaten work. Ex 25:18. 37:7, 17, 22.
the pattern. Ex +25:40.

6 **cleanse them**. Nu 4:23. 19:17, 18. Ex 19:15. Mt +3:15. 21:23, 24, 25, 27. Mk +1:8. Lk 7:30. Jn 1:28, 29. 3:23, 25. Ac +1:5. 21:24, 25. 1 C 11:28. 2 C 7:1. He 7:13, 14. Ja 4:8.

7 **Sprinkle**. Le +1:5. 8:6. 1 C 6:11. T 3:5, 6. He 9:10.
water. Nu 19:9, 10, 13, 17-19. Ps 51:7. He 9:13. 10:22.
let them shave. Heb. let them cause a razor to pass over, etc. Le 14:8, 9.
wash their. Nu 19:7, 8, 10, 19. 31:20. Ge 35:2. Ex 19:10. Le 15:6, 10, 11, 19, 27. 16:28.

31:20. Ps 51:2. Je 4:14. Mt 23:25, 26. Ep 5:26, 27. Ja 4:8. 1 P 3:21. Re 7:14.

8 **a young**. Ex 29:1, 3. Le 1:3. 8:2.
his meat offering. Le +23:13.
another. Le 4:3, 14. 16:3. Is 53:10. Ro 8:3. 2 C 5:21.
sin offering. Le +23:19.

9 **thou shalt bring**. Ex 29:4, etc. 40:12.
shalt gather the whole. Nu 15:4. 25:7. 35:12.
shalt gather. Le 8:3.
whole. Ge +7:19.

10 **and the children**. Nu 3:45.
hands. Le 1:4. Ac +8:17.

11 **offer**. Heb. wave.
offering. Heb. wave offering. ver. 13, 15, 21. Le +23:15. Ro 12:11. 15:16.
they may execute. Heb. they may be to execute, etc. Nu 1:49-53. 3:5-43. 1 Ch 23:27-32.

12 **Levites**. Ex 29:10. Le 1:4. 8:14. 16:21.
the one. ver. 8. Nu 6:14, 16. Le 5:7, 9, 10. 8:14, 18. 9:7. 14:19, 20, 22. He 10:4-10.
sin offering. Le +23:19. Ga 2:20.
burnt offering. Le +23:12.
atonement. Le 1:4. +4:20. 8:34. He 9:22.

13 **offer them**. ver. 11, 21. Nu 18:6. Ro 12:1. 15:16.

14 **separate**. Nu 6:2. Dt 10:8. Ro 1:1. 2 C 6:17. Ga 1:15. He 7:26.
and the Levites. ver. 17. Nu 3:45. 16:9, 10. 18:6. Ml 3:17.
mine. Jn 17:9, 10.

15 **go in**. ver. 11. Nu 3:23-37. 4:3-32. 1 Ch ch. 23, 25, 26.
and offer. ver. 11, 13. Nu 3:12.

16 **wholly given**. Nu 3:9. Ro 14:8.
instead of such. Nu 3:12, 13, 45.
taken. Ac 15:14.

17 **all the**. Nu 3:13. Ex 13:2, 12-15. Lk 2:23.
on the day. Ex 12:29. Ps 78:51. 105:36. 135:8. He 11:28.
I sanctified. Ex 13:14, 15. 29:44. Le 27:14, 15, 26. Ezk 20:12. Jn 10:36. 17:19. He 10:29. Ja 1:18.

18 **I have taken**. Nu 16:8, 9. Mt 1:23-25. Lk 2:23.

19 **I have given**. Nu 3:6-9. 18:2-6. 1 Ch 23:28-32. Ezk 44:11-14. Jn 17:6, 9, 10, 15.
a gift. Heb. given.
that there. Nu 1:53. 16:46. 18:5. 1 S 6:19. 2 Ch 26:16-20.

21 **were purified**. ver. +7. Nu 19:12, 19. T 2:14.
offered. ver. 11-13, 15. Nu 3:12.
offering. Ju 24.
Aaron made. ver. 12.
atonement. Ro 5:11.

22 **after that**. ver. 15. 2 Ch 30:15-17, 27. 31:2. 35:8-15. Ro 6:18.
before Aaron. Lk 1:74, 75. 1 C 9:19. Ga 1:10.
as the Lord. ver. 5, etc.

24 **from twenty**. Nu 4:3. 1 Ch 23:24.
from twenty and five. Nu 4:3, 23. 1 Ch 23:3, 24-27. 28:12, 13.
wait upon. Heb. war the warfare of, etc. Nu +4:23mg. 1 C 9:7. 2 C 10:4. Ep 6:11-18. Ph 1:17. 1 T 1:18. 6:12. 2 T 2:3-5.
service of. Is 42:1. Ph 2:5-7.

25 **cease waiting upon the service thereof**. Heb. return from the warfare of the service. Nu 4:23. 2 T 4:7.

26 **to keep**. Nu 1:53. 3:32. 18:4. 31:30. 1 Ch 23:32. 26:20-29. Ezk 44:8, 11.
and shall. 1 T 4:15.

NUMBERS 9

1 A.M. 2514. B.C. 1490.
in the first month. Nu +1:1. Ex 40:2.

2 **keep**. Ex 12:1-3, etc.
passover. Le +23:5.
his appointed. Nu 28:16. Ex 12:6, 14. Le 23:5. Dt 16:1, 2. Jsh 5:10. 2 Ch 35:1. Ezr 6:19. Mk 14:12. Lk 22:7. 1 C 5:7, 8.

3 **the fourteenth**. 2 Ch 30:2, 15.
at even. Heb. between the two evenings. Ex 12:6mg. He 9:26.
according to all the rites. ver. 11, 12. Ex +12:7-11.

4 **keep the passover**. Ex 12:1-11. Le 23:5. Dt 16:1. Jsh 5:10.

5 **they kept**. Jsh 5:10.
according. Nu 8:20. 29:40. Ge 6:22. 7:5. Ex 39:32, 42. Dt 1:3. 4:5. Mt 28:20. Jn 15:14. Ac 26:19. He 3:5. 11:8.

6 **defiled**. Nu 5:2. 6:6, 7. 19:11, 16, 18. Le 21:11. Jn 18:28.
dead body. Heb. *nephesh*, soul, Le +19:28. ver. 7, 10.
they came. Nu 15:33. 27:2, 5. Ex 18:15, 19, 26. Le 24:11.

7 **dead body**. Heb. *nephesh*, soul, Le +19:28. ver. 6, 10.
we may not offer. ver. 2. Ex 12:27. Dt 16:2. 2 Ch 30:17-19. 1 C 5:7, 8.

8 **Stand**. Ex 14:13. 1 S 9:27. 12:7. 2 Ch 20:17. Jb 37:14. Ps 46:10. Is 30:18. Je 23:18. Hab 2:1.
I will. Nu 27:5. Ex 18:15, 16. Ps 25:14. 85:8. Pr 3:5, 6. Ezk 2:7. 3:17. Jn 7:17. 17:8. Ac 20:27. 1 C 4:4. 11:23. He 3:5, 6.

10 **be unclean**. ver. 6, 7. Ro 15:8-19. 16:25, 26. 1 C 6:9-11. Ep 2:1, 2, 12, 13. 3:6-9.
dead body. Heb. *nephesh*, soul, Le +19:28. ver. 6, 7.
yet he shall keep. Mt 5:24. Ro 5:8. 1 C 11:28. Ep 2:4, 5.

11 **fourteenth**. ver. 3. Ex 12:2-14, 43-49. 2 Ch 30:2-15. Jn 19:36.
and eat it. Ex 12:8. Ps 69:21. 1 C 5:6-8.

12 **shall leave**. Ex 12:10. Ac 2:30, 31.

break any bone. Ex 12:46. Ps 34:20. Jn 19:36.

according. ver. 3. Ex 12:43.

13 **forbeareth**. Nu 15:30, 31. 19:13. Ge 17:14. Ex 12:15. Le 17:4, 10, 14-16. He 2:3. 6:6. 10:26-29. 12:25.

soul. Heb. *nephesh*, Ge +17:14.

because. ver. +2, 3, 7.

bear his sin. Ge +19:15. Nu 5:31. Le 20:20. 22:9. Ezk 23:49. He +9:28.

14 **if a stranger**. Le 22:25. 24:22. Nu 35:15. Dt +26:11. 29:11. 31:12. Is 56:3-7. Ep 2:19-22.

one ordinance. Ex 12:49. 1 C 12:13. Ep 2:17-19. 4:4. Re 22:17.

15 **on the day**. Ex 40:2, 18.

the cloud. Ex +13:21.

at even. Ex 13:21. 40:38.

16 **alway**. ver. 18-22. Ex 13:21, 22. 14:19, 20. 33:14. 40:38. Dt 1:33. Ne 9:12, 19. Ps 78:14. 80:1. 105:39. Is 4:5, 6. 1 C 10:1. 2 C 5:19. Re 21:3.

17 **when the cloud**. ver. 15. Ex +13:21. Ps 80:1, 2. Is 49:10. Jn 10:3, 4, 9.

and in the. Ex 33:14, 15. Ps 32:8. 73:24. Jn 10:3, 4, 9.

18 **and at the commandment**. ver. 20. Nu 10:13. Ex 17:1. 2 J 6.

as long as. ver. +8. Is 30:18. 1 C 10:1.

19 **tarried long**. Heb. prolonged. ver. 22.

kept the. Nu +1:52, 53. 3:8. Zc 3:7.

20 **few**. Ge 34:30. Is +10:19mg.

21 **abode**. Heb. was. Ne 9:12, 19.

22 **a year**. or, days. Ge 21:34. 26:8. 37:34. 38:12mg. Jg 21:19mg. 1 S 7:2. 29:3.

abode. ver. +17. Nu 1:54. 8:20. 23:21, 22. Ex 13:21, 22. 39:42. 40:16, 36, 37. Dt 1:6, 7. 2:3, 4. Ps 32:8. 48:14. 73:24. 77:20. 78:14. 107:7. 143:10. Pr 3:5, 6. Ac 1:4.

23 **they kept**. ver. 19. Ge 26:5. Jsh 22:3. Ps 77:20. Ezk 44:8. Zc 3:7.

NUMBERS 10

2 **two trumpets**. Le +23:24. 2 K 12:13. 1 Ch 15:28. 2 Ch 5:12.

silver. Ex 30:12-15. 36:24. 1 C 6:20. T 2:14.

of a whole piece. Ex 25:18, 31. Ep 4:5.

the calling. ver. 7. Ps 81:3. 89:15. Is 1:13. Ho 8:1. Jl 1:14.

3 **they shall blow**. Je 4:5. Jl 2:15, 16.

4 **heads of**. Nu 1:4-16. 7:2. Ex +18:21.

5 **blow**. ver. 6, 7. Le 25:8, 9. Is 27:13. 58:1. Jl 2:1.

camps. Nu 2:3-9.

6 **an alarm**. Nu 31:6.

the camps. Nu 2:10-16.

7 **gathered**. Le 25:8, 9. Is 27:13. 1 C 15:51. 1 Th 4:16. 2 Th 2:1.

ye shall blow. ver. 3, 4.

sound. Jl 2:1. 1 Th 1:8.

8 **the sons of**. Nu 31:6. Jsh 6:4-16. 1 Ch 15:24. 16:6. 2 Ch 13:12-15.

trumpets. 1 C 14:8. 1 Th 1:8.

for ever. Heb. *olam*, Ex +12:24. Ge +9:16.

9 **if ye go**. Nu 31:6. Jsh 6:5. 2 Ch 13:14.

war. 1 C 14:8.

oppresseth. Jg 2:18. 3:27. 4:2, 3. 6:9, 34. 7:16-21. 10:8, 12. 1 S 10:18. Ps 106:42.

then ye shall. Ne 4:18-20. Is 18:3. 58:1. Je 4:5, 19, 21. 6:1, 17. Ezk 7:14. 33:3-6. Ho 5:8. Am 3:6. Zp 1:16. 1 C 14:8.

alarm. 1 C 14:8.

remembered. Ge 8:1. Ps 106:4. 136:23. Lk 1:70-74.

10 **in the day**. Nu 29:1. Le 23:24. 25:9, 10. 1 Ch 15:24, 28. 16:42. 2 Ch 5:12, 13. 7:6. 29:26, 28. Ezr 3:10. Ne 12:35. Ps 81:3. 89:15. 98:5, 6. 150:3. Is 27:13. 55:1-4. Mt 11:28. 1 C 15:52. 1 Th 4:16-18. Re 8:2, 6. 22:17.

gladness. Ps +118:24.

solemn. Le +23:36.

beginnings. Col +2:16.

blow with. 1 Ch 15:24.

burnt offerings. Le +23:12.

sacrifices of. Le +7:11.

peace offerings. Le +23:19.

a memorial. ver. 9. Ex +12:14.

11 **on the twentieth**. Nu 1:1. 9:1, 5, 11. Ex 40:2.

the cloud. Nu 9:17-23. Ex 40:36.

12 **took**. Nu 33:16. Ex 13:20. 40:36, 37. Dt 1:19.

out of the. Nu 1:1. 9:1, 5. 33:15. Ex 19:1, 2.

the wilderness. Ge +21:21.

13 **first took**. Nu 2:34. 9:23.

14 **the first**. Nu +1:27.

Nahshon. 1 Ch +2:10.

15 **Issachar**. Nu +1:29.

16 **Zebulun**. Nu +1:9. 7:24.

17 **the tabernacle**. Ex +38:21. He 12:28. 2 P 1:14.

the sons. Nu 3:25, 26, 36, 37. 4:24-33. 7:6-8.

bearing. Nu 1:51. 1 C 11:4-6, 20, 21.

18 **the camp**. Nu +1:5.

Elizur. Nu +1:5. 7:35.

19 **Simeon**. Nu +1:6. 7:36.

20 **Eliasaph**. Nu 1:14. 2:14, a son of Reuel. 7:42.

21 **the Kohathites**. Nu 2:17. +3:27-32.

bearing. Nu 1:51. 1 Ch 15:2, 12-15. Ac 5:42.

the other did. *that is,* the Gershonites and the Merarites. ver. 17. Nu 1:51.

22 **the camp**. Nu 2:18-24. 26:23-41. Ge 48:19. Ps 80:1, 2.

Elishama. Nu +1:10.

23 **Gamaliel**. Nu 1:10. 7:54.

24 **Abidan**. Nu +1:11. 7:60.

25 **the camp**. Nu +1:12.

the rereward. Dt 25:17, 18. Jsh +6:9.

Ahiezer. 1 Ch +12:3.

26 **Pagiel**. Nu 1:13. 7:72.

27 **Ahira**. Nu +1:15. 7:78.

28 Thus were. Heb. These.
according. ver. 35, 36. Nu 2:34. 24:4, 5. SS
6:10. 1 C 14:33, 40. Col 2:5.

29 Hobab. i.e. *loving; cherished*, **S#2246h**. Jg 4:11.
Called Reuel in Ex 2:18.
Raguel. i.e. *friend of God*, **S#7467h**. Nu 2:14. Ge
+36:4, 10, 13, 17, 17. Ex 2:18, Reuel. 3:1.
18:1, 27. 1 Ch 1:35, 37. 9:8.
the Midianite. **S#4084h**. Nu 25:6, 14, 15, 17.
31:2. Ge 37:28.
the Lord. Ge 12:7. 13:15. 15:18. Ac 7:5.
come. Jg 1:16. 4:11. 1 S 15:6. Ps 34:8. Is 2:3.
Je 50:5. Zc 8:21-23. Re 22:17.
for the Lord. Nu 23:19. Ge 32:12. Ex 3:8.
6:7, 8. T 1:2. He 6:18.

30 will not. Ge 24:58. Mt 21:28, 29.
I will depart. Ge 12:1. 31:30. Ru 1:15-17. Ps
45:10. Lk 14:26. 2 C 5:16. He 11:8, 13.

31 instead of eyes. Jb 29:15. Ps 32:8. 1 C
12:14-21. Ga 6:2.

32 what goodness. Ge 12:7. 32:12. Ex 3:8. 6:7,
8. Jg 1:16. 4:11. 1 S 15:6. Mk 16:15. 2 T 4:2. 1
J 1:3.

33 the mount. Ex 3:1. 19:3. 24:17, 18.
the ark. Dt 9:9. 31:26. Jsh 4:7. Jg 20:27. 1 S
4:3. Je 3:16. He 13:20.
went before. Ex 33:14, 15. Dt 1:33. Jsh 3:2-
6, 11-17. Je 31:8, 9. Ezk 20:6. Jn 10:4.
a resting place. Ps 95:11. Is 28:12. 66:1. Je
6:16. Mt 11:28-30. He 4:3-11.

34 the cloud. Ex +13:21.

35 Rise up, Lord. Ps +3:7. 114:1-8.

36 Return, O Lord. Ex 29:45, 46. 33:14-16. Ps
90:13-17. Is 63:8, 9.
many thousands of Israel. Heb. ten thousand thousands. Ge 24:60. Dt 1:10.

NUMBERS 11

1 And when. Nu 10:33. Ex +15:24. 17:2, 3. Dt
9:22. Jb 15:11-13. Ec 7:10. Ro 9:19, 20. Ja
5:9. Ju +16.
complained. *or*, were as it were complainers.
Ru +1:13. Ps +77:3. Ezk +18:25. Pr +19:3. Is
+29:24. Ph +4:11. He +13:5.
it displeased the Lord. Heb. it was evil in
the ears of the Lord. Nu +22:34mg. Ja 5:4.
and the fire. Nu 16:35. Le 10:2. 2 K 1:12. Jb
1:16. Ps 78:21. 79:5. +97:3. 106:18. Is 30:33.
Mk 9:43-49.
the uttermost. Dt 25:18.

2 cried. Nu 21:7. 1 S 7:9. Ps 78:34, 35. Je 15:1.
37:3. 42:2. Ac 8:24.
prayed. Nu 14:13-20. Ge 18:23-33. Ex
32:10-14, 31, 32. 34:9. Dt 9:19, 20. Ps 106:23.
Is 37:4. Je 15:1. Am 7:2-6. Ja +5:16.
1 J 5:16.
the fire. Nu 16:45-48. Ge 19:24. Le 10:2. 1 K
18:38. 2 K 1:12. Jb 1:16. He 7:26. 1 J 2:1, 2.
was quenched. Heb. sunk. Je 51:64.

3 Taberah. *that is*, a burning. **S#8404h**. Dt 9:22.
Is 4:4. 30:27. 33:14. He 12:29.

4 the mixed. Ex 12:38. Le 24:10, 11. Ne 13:3.
fell a lusting. Heb. lusted a lust. ver. 34. Ge
+1:29. Dt 5:21. 2 S 23:15. 1 Ch 11:17. Ps
45:11. 106:14, 15. Pr 13:4. 21:26. 23:3, 6.
24:1. Ec 6:2. Je 17:16. Am 5:18. Ro 1:18. 1 C
10:6. Ep 5:6, 7. Col 3:5, 6. Ja 1:13-15.
the children. 1 C 15:33.
wept again. Heb. returned and wept. Je
18:4mg.
who shall. Ps 78:18-20. 106:14. Ro 13:14. 1
C 10:6.

5 the fish. Ex 16:3. Ps 17:14. Ph 3:19.
cucumbers. Is 1:8.
leeks. lit. grass. **S#2682h**. 1 K 18:5. 2 K 19:26.
Jb 8:12 (herb). 40:15. Ps 37:2. 90:5. 103:15.
104:14. 129:6. 147:8. Pr 27:25 (hay). Is 15:6
(hay). 35:7. 37:27. 40:6, 7, 8. 44:4. 51:12.

6 our. Nu 21:5. Ex 16:3. 2 S 13:4. Ps 81:10-13.
106:21, 22, 25. Ro 3:9, 10, 22, 23. Ro 5:12.
soul. Heb. *nephesh*. Here, *nephesh* is used of
man as possessing animal appetites and
desires, rendered: *soul* (as here) at Nu 21:5. Dt
12:15, 20, 20, 21. 14:26, 26. 1 S 2:16. Jb 6:7.
33:20. Ps 107:18. Pr 6:30. 13:25. Is 29:8, 8. Mi
7:1; *pleasure*, Dt 23:24; *lust*, Ps 78:18; *appetite*,
Pr 23:2. Ec 6:7; *greedy*, Is 56:11. For the other
uses of *nephesh* see Ge +2:7. For the equivalent New Testament use of *psyche*, see Re
+18:14.

7 the manna. Ex 16:14, 15, 31. 1 C 1:23, 24.
Re 2:17.
color thereof as the color of. Heb. eye of it
as the eye of. Le +13:55.
bdellium. Ge 2:12.

8 the people. Ex 16:16-18. Jn 6:27, 33-58.
beat. Ex +27:20. Is 28:28. 53:5. He +2:10.
baked it. Ex 16:23.
taste of it. Ex 16:31.

9 dew fell. Ge 27:28. Ex 16:13, 14. Dt 32:2. Ps
78:23-25. 105:40. 133:3. Ho 14:5. Jn 6:32-35,
48-51.

10 weep throughout. Nu 14:1, 2. 16:27. 21:5.
Ps 106:25.
the anger. ver. 1. Dt 32:22. Ps 78:21, 59.
95:8-11. Is 5:25. Je 17:4.
Moses. Nu 12:3. 20:10-13. Ps 106:32, 33.
139:21. Mk 3:5. 10:14.

11 Wherefore hast thou. ver. 15. Ex 17:4. Dt
1:12. Je 15:10, 18. 20:7-9, 14-18. Ml 3:14. 2 C
11:28.
wherefore have. Jb 10:2. Ps 130:3. 143:2. La
3:22, 23, 39, 40.

12 carry them. Is 40:9, 11. Ezk 34:23. Jn 10:11.
thy bosom. Ps 74:11.
as a nursing. Is 49:15, 23. Ga 4:19. 1 Th 2:7.
the land. Ge 13:15. 22:16, 17. 26:3. 50:24.
Ex 13:5.

13 Whence. Mt 15:33. Mk 8:4. 9:23.

14 **not able**. Ex 18:18. Dt 1:9-12. Jb 5:1. Ps 89:19. Is 9:6. Zc 6:13. 2 C 2:16.

15 **kill me**. 1 K 19:4. Jb 3:20-22. 6:8-10. 7:15. Jon 4:3, 8, 9. Ph 1:20-24. Ja 1:4.
let me not. Je 15:18. 20:18. Zp 3:15.

16 **seventy**. Ge +46:27. Ex 4:29.
officers. Ex +5:6.

17 **I will come**. ver. 25. Nu 12:5. Ge 11:5. 18:21. Ex 19:11, 20. 34:5. Jn 3:13.
talk with. Ex +33:9.
I will take. Nu 27:18. 1 S 10:6. 2 K 2:9, 15. Ne 9:20. Is 44:3. 59:20, 21. Jl 2:28. Jn 7:39. Ro 8:9. 1 C 2:12. 12:4-11. 1 Th 4:8. 1 P 1:22. Ju 19.
spirit. Heb. *ruach*, Ge +41:38. The *Spirit* is put for special operations of the Spirit acting externally in various ways, publicly or privately. For other examples of this use see 2 K 2:9. Da 5:12. 6:3. Lk 1:17, 80. Jn 7:39. Ac 1:5. 7:51. 2 C 3:6.
they shall. Ex 18:22. Dt 16:18. Ac 6:3, 4.

18 **Sanctify**. Ge 35:2. Ex 19:10, 15. Jsh 7:13.
ye have wept. ver. 1, 4-6. Ex 16:3-7. Jg 21:2.
in the ears. Ex 16:7.
flesh to eat. Ps 78:27-29.
it was well. ver. +4, 5. Nu 14:2, 3. Ac 7:39.

20 **whole month**. Heb. month of days. Ex 16:8, 13.
and it. Nu 21:5. Ps 78:27-30. 106:15. Pr 27:7.
despised. 1 S 2:30. 2 S 12:10. Ml 1:6. Ac 7:39. 13:41. 1 Th 4:8.

21 **six hundred thousand footmen**. Ex +12:37.

22 **the flocks**. 2 K 7:2. Mt 15:33. Mk 6:37. 8:4. Lk 1:18, 34. Jn 6:6, 7, 9.

23 **Is the Lord's**. Ge +18:14. Ps 50:10-12. 78:41. Is 50:2. 59:1. Mi 2:7.
hand. Jb 10:8. 12:9, 10. Ps 8:6. 95:5. Is 11:11.
thou shalt. Nu 23:19. 2 K 7:2, 17-19. Je 44:28, 29. Ezk 12:25. 24:14. Mt 24:35.
my word. Ps 119:89-91. 138:2.
shall come. Is 55:8-11.

24 **gathered**. ver. +16, 26.
seventy. Ex +18:21. Lk 10:1.

25 **came down**. ver. 17. Nu 12:5. Ex 34:5. 40:38. Ps 99:7. Lk 9:34, 35.
took. ver. +17. 2 K 2:15. Ja 1:17.
spirit. Heb. *ruach*, Ge +41:38.
gave it. 1 S 10:5, 6, 10. 19:20-24. Je 36:5, 6. Jl 2:28, 29. Ac 2:17, 18. 11:28. 21:9-11. 1 C 11:4, 5. 14:1-3, 31-33. 2 P 1:21.
spirit. Heb. *ruach*, Ge +41:38.

26 **Eldad**. i.e. *God has loved*, **S#419h**. ver. 27.
Medad. i.e. *would be loving*, **S#4312h**. ver. 27.
spirit. Heb. *ruach*, Ge +41:38.
were written. Ex 31:18.
went not out. Ex 3:11. 4:13, 14. 1 S 10:22. 20:26. Je 1:6. 23:24. 36:5.

28 **Joshua**. Ex +17:9.
My lord. Mk 9:38, 39. Lk 9:49, 59. Jn 3:26.

29 **Enviest**. 1 C +4:6. Ph 2:3. Ja 3:14, 15. 4:5. 5:9. 1 P 2:1.
would. Ex +16:3. Ph 1:15-18.
that the. Mt 9:37, 38. Lk 10:2.
spirit. Heb. *ruach*, Ge +41:38.

31 **a wind**. Ex 10:13, 19. 15:10. Ps 135:7.
and brought. Ex 16:13. Ps 78:26-29. 105:40.
quails. Ex 16:13. Ps 78:27, 28.
a day's journey. Heb. the way of a day.
face. Ge +1:2.

32 **homers**. Le 27:16. Is 64:8. Je 18:6. Ezk 45:11.

33 **And while**. Ps 78:30, 31. 106:14, 15. Ho 13:11. Ro 6:23. He 3:17-19.
smote. Nu 16:49. 25:9. Dt 28:27.

34 **Kibroth-hattaavah**. *that is*, the graves of lust. **S#6914h**. ver. 35. Nu 33:16. Dt 9:22. 1 C 10:6.
Kibroth, Heb. *qeber*, Ge +23:4.

35 **journeyed**. Nu 33:17.
Kibroth. Heb. *qeber*, Ge +23:4.
unto Hazeroth. i.e. *yards, enclosures*, **S#2698h**. Nu 12:16. 33:17, 18. Dt 1:1.
abode at. Heb. they were in, etc.

NUMBERS 12

1 **Miriam**. Ex +15:20. Mt 10:36. 12:48. Jn 7:5. 15:20. Ga 4:16.
against. Jn 7:5.
Ethiopian. *or*, Cushite. i.e. *descendants of Cush*, **S#3569h**. Nu 10:29. Ge 25:1-4. Ex 2:16, 21. 3:1. 4:24-26. 18:1-6. Jg 1:16. 4:11. 2 S 18:21-23, 31, 32. 2 K 19:9. 2 Ch 12:3. 14:9, 12, 13. 16:8. 21:16. Je 13:23. 36:14. 38:7, 10, 12. 39:16. Ezk 29:10. 30:8, 9. Da 11:43. Am 9:7. Hab 3:7. Zp 1:1. 2:12. For **S#3568h**, see Ge +2:13.
married. Heb. taken. Nu 36:6. Ge 21:21. 24:3, 4, 37, 51, 57, 58, 60. 26:34, 35. 27:46. 28:1, 2, 6-9. 34:4, 9, 14-16. 36:2. 38:6. 41:45. Ex 2:21. Le 21:14. Jsh 15:16, 17. Jg +3:6. 12:9. 14:2. 1 S 18:27. Je 29:6. 1 C 7:38.

2 **Hath the Lord**. Nu 16:3. Ex 4:30. 5:1. 7:10. 15:20, 21. Mi 6:4.
hath he not. Nu 11:29. Pr 13:10. Ro 12:3, 10. Ph +2:3, 14. 1 P 5:5.
And the. Nu 11:1. Ge 29:33. 2 S 11:27. 2 K 19:4. Ps 94:7-9. Is 37:4. Ezk 35:12, 13. Ro 12:19.

3 **very meek**. Mt +5:5. +11:29. 1 Th 2:7.
above. Nu 11:10-15. 20:10-12. Ps 106:32, 33. 2 C 11:5. 12:11. Ja 3:2, 3.
face. Ge +1:2.

4 **the Lord**. Ps 76:7-9.
Come out. Nu 16:16-21.

5 **in the pillar**. Nu 11:25. 16:19. Ex 34:5. 40:38. Ps 99:7.

6 **a prophet**. Ge 20:7. Ex 7:1. Ps 105:15. Mt

23:31, 34, 37. Lk 20:6. Ep 4:11. Re 11:3, 10.
in a vision. Ge 15:1. 46:2. Jb 4:13. 33:15. Ps
89:19. Ezk 1:1. Da 8:2. 10:8, 16, 17. Lk 1:11,
22. Ac 10:11, 17. 22:17, 18.
a dream. Ge +31:24. Je 23:28.

7 **My servant**. Dt 18:18. Ps 103:7. 105:26. Mt
11:9, 11. Ac 3:22, 23. 7:31.
faithful. 2 Ch 19:9. 34:12. Pr 25:13. 1 C 4:2.
1 T 3:15. He 3:2-6. 1 P 2:4, 5. 3 J 5.

8 **mouth**. Dt +5:4. 8:3. Jsh 9:14. Jb 11:5. Ps
103:7. Is 11:4. 30:27. 55:11. 1 C 13:10. 1 T
6:16.
dark speeches. Ps 49:4. Ezk 17:2. 20:49. Mt
13:35. Jn 15:15. 1 C 13:12. or, riddles.
S#2420h. Jg 14:12-19. 1 K 10:1. 2 Ch 9:1. Ps
49:4. 78:2. Pr 1:6. Ezk 17:2. Da 8:23. Hab 2:6.
similitude. Ex 24:10, 11. 33:19, 23. 34:5-7.
Dt 4:15. Is 40:18. 46:5. Jn 1:18. 14:7-10.
15:24. 2 C 3:18. 4:4-6. Col +1:15. He 1:3.
wherefore. Jn 5:23.
were ye. Ex 34:30. Lk 10:16. 1 Th 4:8. 2 P
2:10. Ju 8.

9 **the anger**. Nu 11:1. Ho 5:15. Na 1:2, 3,
5, 6.

10 **the cloud**. Ex +13:21. Ho 9:12.
behold. Dt 24:9.
leprous. 2 K +5:1.

11 **I beseech thee**. Ex 12:32. 1 S 2:30. 12:19.
15:24, 25. 2 S 24:10. 1 K 13:6. Je 42:2. Ac
8:24. Re 3:9.
lay not. 2 S 19:19. 24:10. 2 Ch 16:9. Ps 38:1-
7. Pr 30:32.
foolishly. 2 S 24:10. Ps 69:5. Pr 24:10.

12 **as one dead**. 2 K +5:1. Ps 88:4, 5. Ep 2:1-5.
Col 2:13. 1 T 5:6.
of whom. Jb 3:16. Ps 58:8. 1 C 15:8.

13 **cried unto**. Nu 14:2, 13-20. 16:41, 46-50. Ex
32:10-14. 1 S 12:23. 15:11. Mt 5:44, 45. Lk
6:28. 23:34. Ac 7:60. Ro 12:21. Ja 5:15, 16.
Heal. Ps +103:3. Mt 8:2, 3.
God. Heb. *El*, Ex +15:2.

14 **spit**. Mt +26:67. He 12:9.
let her be. Le +4:12. 14:8. 2 K +5:1. Ps
103:2-4, 8-14.

15 **shut out**. Dt 24:8, 9. Ro 15:1-4. 2 C 11:29.
Ga 6:1, 2.
and the. Ge 9:21-23. Ex 20:12.
till Miriam. La 3:32. Mi 6:4. 7:8, 9. Hab 3:2.

16 **afterward**. Nu 11:35. 33:18.
Hazeroth. Dt 2:23.
the wilderness. Ge +21:21.

NUMBERS 13

2 **Send thou**. Nu 32:8. Dt 1:22-25. Jsh ch. 2.
of every. Nu 1:4. 34:18.
a ruler. Nu 11:16. Ex 18:25. Dt 1:15.

3 **from the**. Nu 32:8. Ge +21:21. Dt 1:19, 23.
9:23.

4 **Shammua**. i.e. *a rumor; renowned; a*

hearkener, **S#8051h**. 2 S 5:14. 1 Ch 14:4. Ne
11:17. 12:18.
Zaccur. 1 Ch +25:2.

5 **Shaphat**. 1 Ch +3:22.
Hori. Ge +36:22.

6 **Caleb**. i.e. *capable; dog; firmly bound; determi-
nation*, **S#3612h**. ver. 30. Nu 14:6, 24, 30, 38.
26:65. 27:15-23. 33:12. 34:19. Dt 1:36. 31:7-
17. Jsh 14:6, 13, 14. 15:13, 14, 16-18. 21:12.
Jg 1:12-15, 20. 3:9. 1 S 30:14. 1 Ch 2:18, 19,
42, 46, 48-50. 4:15. 6:56.
Jephunneh. i.e. *may he be regarded with favor;
for whom a way is prepared*, **S#3312h**. Nu 14:6,
30, 38. 26:65. 32:12. 34:19. Dt 1:36. Jsh 14:6,
13, 14. 15:13. 21:12. 1 Ch 4:15. 6:56. 7:38.

8 **Oshea**. i.e. *safety*, **S#1954h**. ver. 16, Jehoshua.
Mi 11:28. 27:18-22. Ex 17:9-13. 24:13. 32:17.
Dt 31:7, 8, 14, 23. 34:9. Jsh 1:1-9, 16. 24.

9 **Palti**. i.e. *deliverance of Jehovah; escape of Jah;
my escape*, **S#6406h**. 1 S 25:44.
Raphu. i.e. *healed; comforted*, **S#7505h**.

10 **Gaddiel**. i.e. *troop of God; fortune of God*,
S#1427h.
Sodi. i.e. *counsel of God; my counsel*, **S#5476h**.

11 **Gaddi**. i.e. *troop of Jah; my troop; fortune*,
S#1426h.
Susi. i.e. *horse of Jah; my horse; swallow*,
S#5485h.

12 **Ammiel**. 1 Ch +3:5.
Gemalli. i.e. *deed of Jah; my deed; camel driver*,
S#1582h.

13 **Sethur**. i.e. *hidden, mysterious*, **S#5639h**.

14 **Nahbi**. i.e. *hidden; hidden of the Lord*, **S#5147h**.
Vophsi. i.e. *my addition; addition of Jah; diminished*, **S#2058h**.

15 **Geuel**. i.e. *excellency of God; majesty of God*,
S#1345h.
Machi. i.e. *my lowness; decrease*, **S#4352h**.

16 **Oshea**. Ho 1:1. Ro 9:25.
Jehoshua. i.e. *Jehovah is salvation*, **S#3091h**.
ver. 8. Nu 14:6, 30. Ex 17:9. Mt 1:21-23. Ac
7:45. He 4:8, Jesus.

17 **southward**. ver. 21, 22. Ge +12:9.
the mountain. Nu 14:40. Ge 14:10. Dt 1:44.
Jg 1:9, 19.

18 **the land**. Ex 3:8. Is 64:4. Ezk 34:14. 1 C 2:9,
10.

19 **strong holds**. Jsh 19:29, 35. 2 K 8:12. Ps
89:40. 108:10. Je 6:27. Da 11:15, 24, 39. Am
5:9. Mi 5:11.

20 **whether it be**. Ne 9:25, 35. Ezk 34:14.
good courage. ver. 30, 31. Jsh +1:9. 2:3, 22,
23. 1 Ch 22:11. He 13:6.
the firstripe. ver. 23, 24. Mi 7:1.

21 **from the wilderness of Zin**. i.e. *a thorn;
coldness*, **S#6790h**. Nu 20:1. 27:14, 14. 33:36.
34:3, 4. Dt 32:51. Jsh 15:1, 3. 2 K 3:8.
Rehob. i.e. *a broad place*, **S#7340h**. Jsh 19:28,
30. 21:31. Jg 1:31. 2 S 8:3, 12. 10:8. 1 Ch
6:75. Ne 10:11. Compare Jg 18:28; Am +5:16.

Hamath. i.e. *a walled place; citadel*, **S#2574h**. Nu 34:8. Jsh 13:5. Jg 3:3. 2 S 8:9. 1 K 8:65. 2 K 14:25, 28. 17:24, 30. 18:34. 19:13. 23:33. 25:21. 1 Ch +1:16. 13:5. 18:3, 9. 2 Ch 7:8. 8:3, 4. Is 10:9. 11:11. 36:19. 37:13. Je 39:5. 49:23. 52:9, 27. Ezk 47:16, 17, 20. 48:1. Am 6:2, 14. Zc 9:2.

22 **Ahiman**. Jsh 11:21, 22. 15:13, 14. Jg 1:10. 1 Ch 9:17.
Sheshai. i.e. *whitish*, **S#8344h**. Jsh 15:14. Jg 1:10.
Talmai. i.e. *brotherly; suspending the waters; furrows*, **S#8526h**. Jsh 15:14. Jg 1:10. 2 S 3:3. 13:37. 1 Ch 3:2.
the children. ver. +33.
Hebron. Nu 3:19. Ge +13:18. Jsh 10:36, 39. 11:21, 22. 14:13-15. 15:13, 14, 54. 20:7. 21:11, 13. Jg 1:10, 20. 1 S 30:31. 2 S 2:1, 11. 5:3, 5. 15:7, 10. 1 K 2:11. 1 Ch 6:55, 57. 29:27.
Zoan. i.e. *a low region; removal, motion*, **S#6814h**. Ps 78:12, 43. Is 19:11, 13. 30:4. Ezk 30:14.

23 **brook**. *or*, valley. ver. 24. Nu 21:12. 32:9. Dt 1:24, 25. 2:13mg. Jg 16:4mg. 1 S 17:40mg. 2 S 24:5mg. 1 Ch 11:32. 2 Ch 20:16mg. Pr 30:17mg.
Eschol. i.e. *a cluster; cluster of grapes*, **S#812h**. ver. 24. Nu 32:9. Ge 14:13, 24. Dt 1:24.

24 **brook**. *or*, valley. ver. 23.
Eshcol. *that is*, a cluster of grapes. Ge 14:21-24.

25 **forty days**. Ex 34:28. Jon +3:4.
26 **unto the wilderness**. ver. +3.
Kadesh. Nu +34:4. Ge +14:7.
27 **floweth with**. Dt 1:25, etc.
honey. Ex +3:8.
28 **strong**. Dt 1:28. 2:10, 11, 21. 3:5. 9:1, 2. Pr 26:13.
saw the. ver. 22, +33. Jsh 11:22.
29 **Amalekites**. Nu +14:45. Ps 83:7.
the Hittites. Dt +20:17.
Amorites. Ge +10:16.
30 **Caleb stilled**. Nu 14:6-9, 24. Jsh 14:6-8. Ps 27:1, 2. 60:12. 118:10, 11. Is 41:10-16. Ro 8:31, 37. Ph 4:13. He 11:33.
31 **not able**. Nu 32:9. Dt 1:28. Jsh 14:8. He 3:19.
32 **brought**. Nu 14:36, 37. Dt 1:28. Mt 23:13.
a land. ver. 28. Ezk 36:13. Am 2:9.
men of a great stature. Heb. men of statures. 2 S 21:20. 1 Ch 20:6mg.
33 **saw the giants**. ver. 22. Dt +2:20.
Anak. i.e. *neck chain; long-necked*, **S#6061h**. ver. 22, 28. Dt 9:2. Jsh 15:13, 14. 21:11. Jg 1:20.
and we were. 1 S 17:42. Is 40:22.

NUMBERS 14

1 **lifted up**. Nu 11:1-4. Dt 1:45.
wept. Ge +29:11.

2 **murmured**. Ex +15:24. Ju 16.
Would. ver 28, 29. Nu 11:15. Ex +16:3. 1 K 19:4. Jb 3:11. 7:15, 16. Jon 4:3, 8.
3 **the Lord**. Ps 78:40. Je 9:3.
our wives. ver. 31, 32.
children. Nu +16:27.
4 **Let us make**. Dt 17:16. 28:68. Ne 9:16, 17. Lk 17:32. Ac 7:39. He 10:38, 39. 11:15. 2 P 2:21, 22.
5 **fell on**. Ge +17:3. Ps 105:26.
6 **Joshua**. ver. 24, 30, 38. Nu 13:6, 8, 30.
rent their clothes. 2 K +18:37.
7 **an exceeding good land**. Nu 13:27. Dt 1:25. 6:10, 11. 8:7-9.
8 **bring**. Ge 48:21.
delight. Dt 10:15. 2 S 15:25, 26. 22:20. 1 K 10:9. Ps 22:8. 147:10, 11. Is 62:4. Je 32:41. Zp 3:17. Ro 8:31.
a land which. Nu 13:27.
honey. Ex +3:8.
9 **Only rebel**. Dt 9:7, 23, 24. Is 1:2. 63:10. Da 9:5, 9. Ph 1:27.
neither. Dt 7:18. 20:3.
bread. Nu 24:8. Dt 32:42. Ps 14:4. 74:14.
defence. Heb. shadow. Ps 91:1. 121:5. Is 30:2, 3. 32:2. Je 48:45.
the Lord. Ge 48:21. Ex 33:16. Dt +7:21. Jg 1:22. 1 K 10:9. 2 Ch 15:2. 20:17. Ps 144:1, 2, 15. 146:5. Pr 16:20. Is +43:2.
fear them not. Is 41:14.
10 **But all**. Ex 17:4. 1 S 30:6. Mt 23:37. Ac 7:52, 59.
And the. Ex +24:16, +17.
11 **How long will this**. ver. 27. Mt +17:17.
provoke. ver. 23. Nu 16:30. Dt 9:7, 8, 22, 23. 2 K 19:3mg. Ne 9:18, 26. Ps 78:17, 22, 32, 37-41, 56. 95:8. 106:43. Zc 8:14. He 3:8, 16-19.
believe me. Dt 1:32. Ps 78:22, 32, 41, 42. 106:24. Jn 10:38. 12:37. 15:24. He 3:18.
12 **smite**. Nu 25:9. Ezk +38:22.
will make. Ex +32:10.
13 **Then the**. Ex 32:12. Dt 9:26-28. 32:27. Jsh 7:8, 9. Ps 106:23. Ezk 20:9, 13-15, 17.
from among. lit. out of the midst of them.
14 **they have**. Ex 15:14. Jsh 2:9, 10. 5:1.
among. Dt +23:14.
art seen. Dt +5:4. Jn 1:18. 14:9. 1 C 13:12. 1 J 3:2.
thy cloud. Ex +13:21.
15 **as one**. Jg 6:16.
16 **not able**. Dt 9:28. 32:26, 27. Jsh 7:9.
17 **let the power**. Mi 3:8. Mt 9:6, 8.
18 **longsuffering**. Ex +34:6, 7. Na 1:2, 3. Ro 3:24-26. 5:21. 2 C 5:21. Ep 1:7, 8.
visiting. Je +11:22.
19 **Pardon**. Ex 32:32. 34:9. 1 K 8:34. Ps 51:1, 2. Ezk 20:8, 9. Da 9:16-19.
according. Is 55:7. T 3:4-7.
greatness. Ex +15:16.
and as thou. Ex 32:10-14. 33:17. Ps 78:38.

106:7, 8, 45. Jon 3:10. 4:2. Mi 7:18. Ja 5:15. 1
J 5:14-16.
until now. *or*, hitherto. 1 S 7:12.

20 pardoned. Ps 78:37-43. 106:45. Is 48:9, 11.
Ep 4:32.
according. Ja 5:16. 1 J 5:14, 15.

21 as truly. Dt 32:40. Is 49:18. Je 22:24. Ezk
5:11. 18:3. 33:11, 27. Zp 2:9.
all the. Is +40:5. Mt 6:10.

22 which have. ver. 11. Dt 1:31-35. Ps 95:9-11.
106:26. He 3:17, 18.
tempted. Ex +17:2.
ten times. Ge 31:7, 41. Jb 19:3.

23 Surely they shall not see. Heb. If they see.
Nu 26:64. 32:11. Dt 1:35, etc. Ne 9:23. Ps
95:11. 106:26. Je 15:1. Ezk 20:15. He 3:17,
18. 4:3.

24 But. ver. 30. Jsh 14:1. 22:13.
my servant. ver. 6-9. Nu +13:6.
another. Nu 12:7. 1 K 19:18. Ne 7:2. 1 C
4:17. Col 1:7. 4:9. Re 17:14.
spirit. Heb. *ruach*. Ge +26:35. +41:8. Mt
21:28-32. Mk 10:38, 39. Lk 9:55. 1 C 2:11,
12.
followed me fully. Dt 6:5. Jsh +14:8. 1 Ch
29:9, 18. 2 Ch 25:2. Ps 119:80, 145. Pr 23:26.
Lk 16:10. Ep 6:6, 7. Col 3:23.

25 the Amalekites. ver. +45.
Canaanites. Ge +10:18.
turn you. ver. 4. Dt 1:40. Ps 81:11-13. Pr
1:31.

27 How long. ver. +11.
I have heard. ver. 2. Ex 16:12.

28 As truly. ver. 21, 23. Nu 26:64, 65. 32:11. Dt
1:35. Ps 90:8, 9. He 3:17.
as ye have. ver. 2.

29 carcases. ver. 32, 33. 1 C 10:5. He 3:17. Ju 5.
all that were. Nu 1:45. 26:63-65.

30 sware. Heb. lifted up my hand. Ge +14:22.
save Caleb. ver. +24, 38.

31 little ones. Nu +16:27. 26:4, 64.
ye said. ver. 3.
the land. Ge 25:34. Ps 106:24. Pr 1:25, 30.
Mt 22:5. Ac 13:41. He 12:16, 17.

32 your carcases. ver. +29. 1 C 10:5. He 3:17.

33 shall wander in the wilderness. *or*, feed.
Nu 32:13. Ex 34:7. Jsh 14:10. Ps 107:4, 40.
forty years. Nu 33:38. Dt 1:3. 2:14.
bear. Nu 5:31. Je 3:1, 2. Ezk 23:35, 45-49. Ho
9:1.

34 After. Nu 13:25. 2 Ch 36:21. Jon +3:4.
the number. Ps 95:10. Ezk 4:6. Da 9:24. Re
11:3.
shall ye bear. Nu 18:23. Le 20:19. Ps 38:4.
Ezk 14:10.
ye shall. 1 K 8:56. Ps 77:8. 105:42. Je 18:9,
10. La 3:31-33. He 4:1.
breach of promise. *or*, altering of my purpose. Dt 31:16, 17. 1 S 2:30. Jb 33:10. Zc
11:10.

35 I will surely. Nu 23:19. He 6:13.
this evil. ver. 27-29. Nu 26:65. 1 C 10:5, 11.
He 3:19.

36 the men. Nu 13:31-38. Ml 3:18. 1 C 10:10.

37 died. ver. 12. Nu 16:49. 25:9. Je 28:16, 17.
29:32. 1 C 10:10. He 3:17. Ju 5.

38 Joshua. Nu 26:65. Jsh 14:6-10.

39 mourned greatly. Ex 33:4. Pr 19:3. Is 26:16.
Mt 8:12. He 12:17.

40 rose up. Dt 1:41. Ec 9:3. Mt 7:21-23. 25:11,
12. Lk 13:25.

41 do ye. ver. 25. 2 Ch 24:20.
but it shall. Jb 4:9. Je 2:37. 32:5.

42 Go not. Dt 1:42. Jsh 7:8, 12. 2 Ch 15:2.
24:20. Ps 44:1-11.

43 Amalekites and. ver. +45. Le 26:17. Dt
28:25.
because. Jg 16:20. 1 Ch 28:9. 2 Ch 15:2. Is
63:10. Ho 9:12.

44 they presumed. Nu 15:30. Dt 1:43. Ps 19:13.
2 P 2:9.
the ark. Nu 10:33. 1 S 4:3-11.

45 the Amalekites. S#6003h. ver. 25, 43. Ge
14:7. Ex +17:8, 16. Nu 13:29. Dt 1:44. 32:30.
Jsh 7:5, 11, 12. Jg 6:3. 12:15. 1 S 14:48. 15:6,
7, 15. 27:8. 30:1, 13. 2 S 1:8, 13.
Hormah. i.e. *place desolated*; *destruction*,
S#2767h. Nu 21:3. Dt 1:44. Jsh 12:14. 15:30.
19:4. Jg 1:17. 1 S 30:30. 1 Ch 4:30.

NUMBERS 15

1 It is very probable that the transactions
recorded in this and the four following chapters took place during the time the Israelites
abode in Kadesh (Dt 1:46).

2 When ye be come. ver. 18. Ex 3:17. Le
14:34. 23:10. 25:2. Dt 7:1, 2. 8:7-9. 12:1, 9.

3 will make. Ex 29:18, 25, 41. Le 1:2, 3, 9, 13,
17. 10:13.
a burnt offering. Le +23:12.
a sacrifice. Le +7:11, 16. 22:18-23. +23:38.
Dt 12:11. Pr 7:14.
performing. Heb. separating. ver. 8. Le
22:21. 27:2.
or in a freewill offering. Le +23:38.
in your. Nu 28:16-19, 27. 29:1, 2, 8, 13, etc.
Le 23:8, 12, 36. Dt 16:1-17.
a sweet. Ge +8:21. Mt 3:17.

4 a meat offering. Le +23:13. Ml 1:11. Ro
15:16. He 10:7. 13:16.
the fourth. Nu 28:5, etc. Ex 29:40. Le 2:15.
14:10. 23:13. Jg 9:9. Ezk 46:14. Ro 11:24.

5 the fourth. Nu 28:7, 14.
of wine. Ge 49:11, 12. Jg 9:13. Ne 8:10. Ps
100:2. 104:15. 116:13. SS 1:4. Is 35:10. Zc
9:17. Mt 26:28, 29. Jn 15:1. Ph 2:17.
2 T 4:6.
drink offering. Le +23:13.
burnt offering. Le +23:12.

6 **for a ram**. ver. 4. Nu 28:12-14. Ps 45:7. SS 3:11.

8 **preparest**. Le 22:21.
burnt offering. Le +23:12.
vow. Le +23:38.
peace offerings. Le +23:19.

9 **with a**. Nu 28:12, 14.
a meat. Le +23:13.

10 **drink offering**. ver. +5. Nu 6:15.

11 **Thus shall**. Nu 28.

12 **according to the number**. Mt 9:29. 25:14, 15. 2 C 8:12-15. 9:6, 7.

15 **One**. ver. 29. Nu 9:14. Ex 12:49. Le 24:22. Ga 3:28. Ep 2:11-22. Col 3:11.
an ordinance. Nu 10:8. 18:8. Ex 12:14, 24, 43. 1 S 30:25.
for ever. Heb. *olam*, Ex +12:24.

16 **One law**. Nu 9:14. Ex 12:49. Jn 3:17. 10:16. 14:6. Ac 4:12. Ro 3:29, 30. 1 C 12:13. Ep 2:11-18. +4:4. 1 T 2:3, 4. Re 7:4, 9.

18 **When ye come**. ver. +2. Dt 26:1, etc.

19 **when ye**. Jsh 5:11, 12.
heave offering. Le +7:14.

20 **a cake**. Jsh 5:11, 12. Ne 10:37.
the first. Le +23:10. Mt 6:33.
the heave offering. Le 2:14. +7:14. 23:10, 16, 17.
threshingfloor. Ge +50:10.

21 **an heave offering**. Le +7:14.

22 **if ye have erred**. Le 4:2, 13, 14, 22, 27. 5:13, 15-17. Ps 19:12. Mk +12:24. Lk 12:48. 23:34. Jn 16:3. Ac 2:36-39. 3:17-19. 1 C 2:8.

24 **if ought**. Le +4:13.
without. Heb. from the eyes. Le 4:13.
one young bullock. Le 4:14-21.
burnt offering. Le +23:12.
with his. ver. 8-10.
meat offering. Le +23:13.
drink offering. Le +23:13.
manner. *or*, ordinance. ver. 16.
one kid. Nu 28:15. Le 4:23. 2 Ch 29:21-24. Ezr 6:17. 8:35.
sin offering. Le +23:19.

25 **the priest**. Le +4:20. Ro 3:25.
forgiven them. Lk 23:34. Ac 13:39.

27 **if any**. Le 4:27, 28. Ac 3:17. 17:30. 1 T 1:13.
soul. Heb. *nephesh*, Ge +27:31.

28 **the priest**. Le +4:20.
soul. Heb. *nephesh*, Ge +27:31.

29 **one law**. ver. +15. Nu 9:14. Le 16:29. 17:15. Ro 3:29, 30. 11:13.
sinneth. Heb. doeth. Nu 11:15 (deal).

30 **soul**. Heb. *nephesh*, Ge +27:31.
doeth ought. Nu 9:13. 14:44. Ge 17:14. Ex 21:14. Le 20:3, 6, 10. Dt 1:43. 17:12. 29:19, 20. Ps 19:13. Mt 12:32. He 10:26, 29. 2 P 2:10.
presumptuously. Heb. with a high hand. Ex 14:8. He 10:26.
reproacheth. Ps +31:11.
soul. Heb. *nephesh*, Ge +17:14.

31 **despised**. Le 26:15, 43. 2 S 12:9. 2 Ch 36:16. Ps 119:126. Pr 13:13. Is 30:12. Jn 12:48. 1 Th 4:8. He 4:12, 13. 10:28, 29. Re 19:11-16.
soul. Heb. *nephesh*, Ge +17:14.
his iniquity. Le 5:1. Ps 38:4. Is 53:6. Ezk 18:20. 1 P 2:24. 2 P 2:21.

32 **they found a man**. Ex 16:23, 27, 28. +20:8-10. 31:14, 15. 35:2, 3.

33 **brought him**. Ex 18:19. Jn 8:3, etc.

34 **put him in ward**. Le 24:12.

35 **The man**. Ex 31:14, 15.
surely. Ge +2:16.
stone him. Le +24:14.
without. Le +4:12.

36 **all the congregation**. Jsh 7:25.

38 **fringes in the borders**. Dt 22:12. Mt 9:20. 23:5. Lk 8:44.

39 **remember**. Ex 13:9. Dt 6:6-9. 11:18-21, 28-32. Pr 3:1.
ye seek not. Dt 29:19. Jg 17:5, 6. Jb 31:7. Pr 28:26. Ec 11:9. Je 9:14.
go a whoring. Ex +34:15, 16.

40 **be holy**. Le 11:44, 45. 19:2. Ro 12:1. Ep 1:4. Col 1:2. 1 Th 4:7. 1 P 1:15, 16.

41 **brought you**. Le 11:44, 45. 22:33. 25:38. Ps 105:45. Je 31:31-33. 32:37-41. Ezk 36:25-27. Ro 12:1. 1 Th 4:7. He 11:16. 1 P 1:15, 16. 2:9, 10.

NUMBERS 16

1 **Korah**. Ge +36:5.
Izhar. Ex +6:18.
Kohath. Ge +46:11.
Dathan. i.e. *law; of a fountain*. S#1885h. ver. 1, 12, 24, 25, 27. 26:9. Dt 11:6. Ps 106:17.
Abiram. i.e. *father of elevation*. S#48h. ver. 1, 12, 24, 25, 27. 26:9. Dt 11:6. 1 K 16:34. Ps 106:17.
Eliab. Nu +1:9. 26:5, 8.
On. i.e. *strength; iniquity*. S#203h.
Peleth. i.e. *escape; swiftness*, S#6431h. ver. 1. 1 Ch 2:33.
sons of Reuben. Ge +29:32. 1 Ch 5:1, 2.

2 **famous**. Nu 26:9. Ge 6:4. 1 Ch 5:24. 12:30. Ezk 16:14. 23:10.

3 **gathered**. ver. 11. Nu 12:1, 2. 14:1-4. Ps 106:16. Ac 7:39, 51.
Ye take too much upon you. Heb. It is much for you. ver. 7. Ex 18:13-23.
all the. Ex 19:6. Ezr 9:2. Is 1:11-16. Je 7:3-12. Mt 3:9, 10. Ro 2:28, 29.
the Lord. Ex 29:45, 46. Dt +7:21.

4 **he fell**. ver. 22, 45. Ge +17:3. 2 P 2:9, 10.

5 **the Lord**. Ml 3:18. 2 T *2:19*.
who is holy. ver. 3. Le 21:6-8, 12-15. Is 61:5, 6. 1 P 2:5-9. Re 1:6. 5:9, 10.
will cause. Ex 28:43. Le 10:3. Ps 65:4. Ezk 40:46. 44:15, 16. Ep 2:13. He 10:19-22. 12:14.
even him. Nu 17:5. Ex 28:1. Le 8:2. 21:12. 1

S 2:28. Ps 105:26. Jn 15:16. Ac 1:2, 24. 13:2. 15:7. 22:14. 2 T 2:3, 4, 19.

6 Take. ver. 35-40, 46-48. Le 10:1. 16:12, 13. 1 K 18:21-23.

7 that the man. ver. 3, 5. Ep 1:4. 2 Th 2:13. 1 P 2:9.

too much. ver. 3. 1 K 18:17, 18. Mt 21:23-27.

9 Seemeth it but. ver. 13. Ge 30:15. Jsh 22:17. 1 S 18:23. 2 S 7:19. Jb 15:11. Is 7:13. 29:17. Ezk 16:20. 34:18. 1 C 4:3.

separated. Nu 1:53. 3:10, 38, 41-45. 4:17-20, 49. 8:14-16. 18:2-6. Dt +10:8. 2 Ch 35:3. Ne 12:44. Ezk 44:10, 11. Ac 13:2. 2 C 6:17.

10 near. Ep 2:18.

and seek. Pr 13:10. Mt 20:21, 22. Lk 22:24. Ro 12:10. Ph +2:3. 3 J 9.

11 gathered. Ex 25:22. 29:42, 43. 30:6, 36.

against. ver. 3. 1 S 8:7. Lk 10:16. Jn 12:48. 13:20. Ro 13:2.

what is Aaron. Ex 16:7, 8. 17:2. Ac 5:4. 1 C 3:5.

12 which said. Ex 2:14. Pr 29:9. Is 3:5. Mt 21:29. Lk 19:14, 27. Jn 5:40. Ac 7:35. 1 P 2:13, 14. Ju 8.

13 a small. ver. 9.

out of a. Nu 11:5. Ex 1:11, 22. 2:23.

honey. Ex +3:8.

to kill. Nu 20:3, 4. Ex 16:3. 17:3.

thou make. Ex 2:14. Ps 2:2, 3. Lk 19:14. Ac 7:25-27, 35.

14 Moreover. Nu 45:8-10. Ex 3:8, 17. Le 20:24. 2 P 2:21, 22. 3:3, 4, 9.

put out. Heb. bore out. Jg +16:21. 1 S 11:2. Pr 30:17. Is 51:1.

15 very wroth. Nu 12:3. Ge 4:5, 6. Ex 32:19. Mt 5:22. Mk 3:5. Ep 4:26.

Respect not. ver. 6, 7. Nu 14:25 (turn you). Ge 4:4, 5. 18:22. Is 1:10-15.

I have not. 1 S 12:3, 4. Ac 20:33, 34. 24:16. 1 C 9:15. 2 C 1:12. 7:2. 12:14-17. 1 Th 2:10.

one ass. Jg 15:16.

16 Be thou. ver. 6, 7.

before. Ex 25:22. 1 S 12:3, 7. 2 T 2:14.

17 and bring. 1 S 12:7.

18 every man. 1 C 3:13. Re 8:3-5.

19 Korah. ver. +1.

and the glory. ver. 42. Nu 12:5. Ex +24:16.

21 Separate. 1 Ch 12:8. 23:13. Ezr 6:21. 9:1. 10:8, 11, 16. Ne 9:2. 10:28. Ac 2:40. Ep 5:6, 7. Re +18:4.

that I may. ver. 45. Nu 14:12, 15. Ex 32:10. 33:5. Ps 73:19. Is 37:36. He 12:28, 29.

22 they fell. ver. +4.

the God. Nu 27:16. Jb 12:10. Ec +12:7. Is 57:16. Zc +12:1. He +12:9.

spirits. Heb. *ruach,* **S#7307h.** Here *ruach* has reference to the invisible psychological part of man given to him by God at man's formation at birth, and returning to God at his death. Nu

27:16. Jb 27:3. 34:14. Ps 31:5. 104:30. Ec 3:21, 21. 8:8, 8. 11:5. 12:7. Is 42:5. Ezk 37:9 (wind). Zc 12:1. For the other uses of *ruach,* see Ge +6:3. For the equivalent New Testament Greek category of *pneuma,* see Mt +27:50. He +12:9.

all flesh. Jb 12:10. Ac 17:24-26.

one man sin. Ge 18:23-25, 32. 20:4. Jsh 7:1, etc. 2 S 24:1, 17. Ro 5:18. 1 C 13:7.

wilt thou. Ge 18:23-32. Jsh 7:6, 7. 2 S 24:17. 2 Ch 20:10-12. Ezk 9:8. Jon 1:14.

24 Get you up. ver. 21. Ex 33:7.

25 went unto. 1 T 2:4.

the elders. Nu 11:16, 17, 25, 30.

followed him. Nu 35:30. Jsh 22:13. Mt 18:16. 1 T 5:20.

26 Depart, I pray you. ver. +21-24. Le 27:28, 29. Dt 13:17. Jsh 7:13-15, 23-26. Mt 10:14. Ac 8:20. 13:51. 1 T 5:22.

27 and stood. Ex 32:26-28. 2 K 9:30, 31. Jb 9:4. 40:10, 11. Pr 16:18. 18:12. Is 28:14.

little children. or, infants. **S#2945h.** Nu 14:3, 31. 31:9, 17, 18. 32:16, 17, 24, 26. Ge 34:29. 43:8. 45:19. 46:5. 47:12mg. 50:8, 21. Ex 10:10, 24. 12:37. Dt 1:39. 2:34. 3:6, 19. 20:14. +29:11. 31:12. Jsh 1:14. 8:35. Jg 18:21. 21:10. 2 S 15:22. 2 Ch 20:13. 31:18. Ezr 8:21. Est 3:13. 8:11. Je 40:7. 41:16. 43:6. Ezk 9:6.

28 Hereby. Ex 3:12. 4:1-9. 7:9. Dt 18:22. 1 S 12:15-18. Zc 2:9. 4:9. Jn 5:36. 11:42. 14:11.

of mine. Nu 24:13. 1 K 12:33. 18:36. Ne 6:8. Jb 8:10. Je 14:14. 23:16, 26. Ezk 13:2, 17. Jn 5:30. 6:38.

29 the common, etc. Heb. as every man dieth. Ge 3:19.

visited. Jb 35:15. Is 10:3. Je +11:22. La 4:22.

the Lord. 1 K 22:28. 2 Ch 18:27.

30 make a new thing. Heb. create a creature. Ge +1:29. Jb 31:3. Is 28:21. 43:19. 45:7, 12. Je 31:22.

quick. or, alive. ver. 33. Ps 55:15. Pr 1:12.

pit. Heb. *sheol,* Ge +37:35. *Sheol* is rendered *pit* only here, at ver. 33, and Jb 17:16. Ezk 32:27.

have provoked. Nu +14:11, 23. Dt 31:29. 32:19 (mg. despised).

31 the ground clave. Nu 26:10, 11. 27:3. Dt 11:6. Jb 31:3. Ps 55:15. 106:17, 18. Is 28:21. Ju 11.

32 the earth. ver. 30. Ge 4:11. Is 5:14. Re 12:16.

all. ver. 17. Ex +9:6. Nu 26:11.

33 into the. Ps 9:15. 55:23. 69:15. 143:7. Is 14:9, 15. Ezk 32:18, 30.

pit. Heb. *sheol,* Ge +37:35. ver. +30.

they perished. Ju 11.

34 fled. Is 33:3. Am 1:1. Zc 14:5. He 11:7. Re 6:15-17.

Lest. Nu 17:12, 13.

35 And there. Nu 11:1. 26:10. Ex 22:6. Le 9:24.

10:2. Jb 4:8, 9. Ps 106:18. Is 33:10-12, 14.
two hundred. ver. 2, 17.

37   **the censers**. ver. 7, 18.
hallowed. Le 27:28.

38   **sinners**. 1 K 2:23. Pr 1:18. 8:36. 20:2. Hab
2:10.
souls. Heb. *nephesh*, Ge +12:13.
a sign. ver. 40. Nu 17:10. +26:10.

40   **memorial**. Ex +12:14.
that no. Nu 3:10, 38. 18:4-7. Le 22:10. 2 Ch
26:18-20. Ju 11.
come near. 1 K 13:1-3. 2 Ch 26:16-21.

41   **all the**. ver. 1-7. Nu 14:2. Ps 106:13, 23, 25.
Is 26:11.
Ye have killed. ver. 3. 2 S 16:7, 8. 1 K 18:17.
Je 37:13, 14. 38:4. 43:3. Am +3:6. 7:10. Mt
5:11. Ac 5:28. 21:28. 2 C 6:8.

42   **when the**. ver. 19.
the glory. ver. 19. Ex +24:16.

45   **Get you up**. or, be lifted up. ver. 21, 24, 26.
Jb 24:24. Ps 118:16. Is 33:3, 10. Ezk 10:15,
17, 19.
that. Ex 20:5. 32:34. Je 5:9.
And they. ver. +4. 1 S 12:23-25.

46   **from off**. Le 9:24. 10:1. 16:12, 13. Is 6:6, 7.
Ro 5:9, 10. He 7:25-27. 9:25, 26. Re 8:3-5.
and put. Ps 141:2. Ml 1:11.
an atonement. Ex 30:7-10. Le 16:11-16. 1 J
2:1, 2.
there is wrath. Nu 1:53. 8:19. 11:33. 18:5.
Le 10:6. 1 Ch 27:24. Ps 106:29.
the plague is begun. Nu 11:1, 2. 21:7. Ex
8:12, 29. 9:28. 10:17. Ezk +38:22. Am 7:1-3.

47   **as Moses**. Ps 103:7.
and ran. Mt 5:44. Ro 12:21.
and behold. Ps 106:29.
and he put. ver. 46. Dt 33:10, 11. Is 53:10-
12.

48   **he stood between**. ver. 18, 35. Nu 25:8-11.
2 S 24:16, 17, 25. 1 Ch 21:26, 27. Is 53:12. 1
Th 1:10. 1 T 2:5, 6. He 7:24, 25. Ja 5:16. 1 J
5:14.
was stayed. ver. 50. Nu 25:8. 1 S 21:7. 2 S
24:21, 25. 1 K 8:35. 1 Ch 21:22. 2 Ch 6:26. Ps
106:30.

49   **fourteen thousand**. ver. 32-35. Nu 25:9. 1
Ch 21:14. 27:24. He 2:1-3. 10:28, 29. 12:25.

50   **returned**. ver. 43. 1 Ch 21:26-30. Ps 68:18-
20.

NUMBERS 17

2   **a rod**. Ge 38:18, 25. Ex 4:2.
all their princes. Nu 1:4-16. 2:3-30. 10:14-
27.
twelve rods. Ge 49:10. Ex 4:2, 17. Ps 110:2.
125:3. Ezk 19:14. 21:10, 13. 37:16-20. Mi
7:14.

3   **the head**. Nu 3:2, 3. 18:1, 7. Ex 6:16, 20. 1 C
11:3. Ep 4:15. Col 1:17, 18.

4   **before the**. Ex 25:16-22. 29:42, 43. 30:6, 36.

5   **whom I**. Nu +16:5.
blossom. ver. 8. Is 5:24. 11:1. 27:6. 35:1, 2.
42:1. Ho 14:5. Zc 6:12, 13.
I will. ver. 10. Is 13:11. Ezk 16:41. 23:27.
they murmur. Nu 16:11.

6   **a rod apiece, for each prince one**. Heb. a
rod for one prince, a rod for one prince. ver.
+2.

7   **tabernacle**. Ex +38:21. He 9:23.

8   **budded**. ver. +5. Ge 40:10. Ps 110:2. 132:17,
18. SS 2:3. Is 4:2. Ezk 17:24. 19:12, 14. Jn
12:24. 15:1-6. Ro 1:3, 4. 8:11. 1 C 6:14.
15:20. Ep 1:18-23. Col 3:3, 4. 2 T 1:10.

10   **Bring Aaron's**. He 9:4.
testimony. Ex +16:34.
for a token. Nu 16:38, 40. Ex 16:32. Dt
31:19-26. Ac 17:30, 31. He 9:3, 4.
rebels. Heb. children of rebellion. 1 S 2:12.
30:22. Ps 57:4. Is 1:2. Ho 10:9. Ep 2:2, 3. 5:6.
and thou. ver. 5.

11   **Moses did**. Ge 6:22. 12:4. 18:19. Jsh 11:15.
Mt 7:21. He 5:8, 9.

12   **Behold**. Nu 26:11. Jb 14:1, 2. Ps 90:7. Pr
19:3. Is 57:16. 64:6. Ro 5:12. 6:23. He 12:5. Ja
1:13-15. 4:14.
we die. Ge +49:33. Nu +16:12. Lk 19:14.
perish. Ex 10:7.

13   **Whosoever**. Nu 1:51-53. 18:4-7.
any thing. Ge 3:3. Ex 23:20, 21. 34:14. Le
10:3. 1 S 6:19-21. 2 S 6:6-12. 1 Ch 13:11-13.
15:13. Ps 85:5. 130:3, 4. Is 63:9, 10. Ac 5:5,
11-14. Ep 2:13. He 10:19-22.
consumed. Nu 16:26. 32:13. Dt 2:16. Jb
34:14, 15. Ps 90:7. Is 28:22.
dying. Ge +49:33.

NUMBERS 18

1   **Aaron, Thou**. Nu 17:3, 7, 13. He 4:15.
shall bear. ver. 22. Nu 14:34. Ex 28:38. Le
22:9. Jb 33:24. Ps 89:19. Is 53:6, 11, 12. Ezk
3:18, 19. Ac 20:26, 27. Ro 4:5-8, 23-25. He
7:26-28. 8:1, 2. 13:17. 1 P 2:24.

2   **father**. Jn 20:17. He 2:11.
bring. He 2:10. 1 P 3:18.
joined unto thee. ver. 4. Ge 29:34. 1 C 6:17.
Ep 5:30.
minister. Nu 3:6-9. 8:19, 22.
but thou. Nu 3:10, etc. 4:15. 16:40. 17:7. 1
Ch 16:39, 40. 2 Ch 30:16. Ezk 44:15.

3   **only they**. Nu 3:25, 31, 36. 4:19, 20. 16:40.
neither. Nu 4:15, 17-20.

4   **a stranger**. Nu 1:51. 3:10. 1 S 6:19. 2 S 6:6,
7.

5   **And ye**. Nu 8:2. Ex 27:21. 30:7, etc. Le 24:3.
1 Ch 9:19, 23, 33. 24:5. 1 T 1:18. 3:15. 5:21.
6:20.
no wrath. Nu 8:19. 16:46. Je 23:15. Zc 10:3.

6   **And I**. Ge 6:17. 9:9. Ex 14:17. 31:6. Is 48:15.

51:12. Ezk 34:11, 20.
I have. Nu 3:12, 45.
given. Nu 3:9. 8:16-19.
for the Lord. Jn 17:12.

7 **Therefore thou**. ver. 5. Nu 3:10.
within. Le 16:2, 12-14. He 9:3-6.
as a service. Nu 16:5-7. 1 S 2:28. Ps 65:4. Jn 3:27. Ro 15:15, 16. Ep 3:8. He 5:4.
of gift. Ro 11:29. 1 C 7:7. 12:4-6. 14:1, 12. Ep 4:7, 8, 11, 12. 1 T 4:14. 2 T 1:6. Ja 1:16, 17. 1 P 4:10, 12.
the stranger. ver. 4. Nu 3:38. 16:40.

8 **the charge**. Nu 5:9. Le 6:16, 18, 20, 26. 7:6, 32-34. 10:14, 15. Dt 12:6, 11. 26:13.
heave offerings. ver. 11. Le +7:14.
by reason. Ex 29:21, 29. 40:13, 15. Le 7:35. 8:30. 21:10. Is 10:27. He 1:9. 5:1-6. 7:23, 24. 1 J 2:20, 27.
for ever. Heb. *olam*, Ex +12:24.

9 **every meat offering**. Le +23:13.
sin offering. Le +23:19.
trespass offering. Le +5:6.
most holy. Le +2:3.
for thee. Le +7:7. He 8:3-5.

10 **In the**. Le +2:3.
every male. Le 6:18, 29. 7:6. 21:22.

11 **the heave offering**. Le +7:14.
wave offerings. Le +23:15.
unto thee. Le +7:7.
for ever. Heb. *olam*, Ex +12:24.
every one. Le 22:2, 3, 11-13. 1 P 2:2-5.

12 **best of the oil**. Heb. fat. ver. 29.
the firstfruits. Le +23:10. SS 5:1. Jn 6:48-58.

13 **whatsoever**. Je +24:2.
first ripe. Ro 4:25. 1 C 15:20, 23.
every one. ver. 11.

14 **devoted**. Le 27:28. Ezk 44:29mg. Lk 10:7. 1 C 3:21-23. 9:7-11.

15 **openeth**. Nu 3:13. Ex 13:2, 12. 22:29. 34:20. Le 27:26.
the firstborn. Ex 13:13. 34:20. Le 27:27.

16 **according**. Le 27:2-7.
which is. Ex +30:13. 1 P 1:18, 19.

17 **the firstling**. Dt 15:19-22.
thou shalt. Ex +29:16. Le 3:2-5. Ep 5:2.

18 **as the wave breast**. Nu 6:20. Ex 29:26-28. Le 7:31, 32, 34. 8:29. 9:21. 10:14, 15.

19 **the heave offerings**. ver. 8, 11. Le +7:14. 2 Ch 31:4.
for ever. Heb. *olam*, Ex +12:24.
covenant of salt. Le +2:13.
for ever. Heb. *olam*, Ex +12:24.

20 **no inheritance**. ver. 23, 24. Nu 26:62. Dt 10:9. 12:12. 14:27, 29. Jsh 14:3. 18:7. Col 3:24.
any part. 2 C 6:15.
I am thy part. Ps +16:5. SS 2:16. Ezk 44:28. 1 C 3:21-23. Re 21:3.
inheritance. Dt 14:27. Ezk 44:28. Ro 8:17. Ep 1:11. 1 P 1:4.

21 **the tenth**. ver. 24-26. Le 27:30-32. Dt 12:17-19. 14:22-29. 2 Ch 31:5, 6, 12. Ne 10:37-39. 12:44. 13:12. He 7:5-9.
even the service. ver. 6. Nu 3:7, 8. 1 C 9:13, 14. Ga 6:6.

22 **come nigh**. ver. 7. Nu 1:51. 3:10, 38.
bear sin. Le 20:20. 22:9.
and die. Heb. to die.

23 **do the service**. Nu +3:7.
for ever. Heb. *olam*, Ex +12:24.
among. ver. +20.

24 **the tithes**. Ge +14:20. Le 27:30, 32. Ml 3:8-10. Mt 22:21. +23:23. Ro 13:7. He 7:5.
heave offering. Le +7:14.

26 **then ye shall**. ver. +19.
offer. 1 C 16:1, 2. 2 C 9:7.
heave offering. Le +7:14.
a tenth part. Ne 10:38.

27 **heave offering**. Le +7:14.
as though. Le 6:19-23.
the corn. ver. 30. Ge +50:10.

28 **heave offering**. Le +7:14.
and ye shall. Ge 14:18. He 6:20. 7:1-10.

29 **heave offering**. Le +7:14.
best. Heb. fat. ver. 12.

30 **the best**. ver. 28. Ge 43:11. Dt 6:5. Pr 3:9, 10. Ml 1:8. Mt 6:33. 10:37-39. Ph 3:8, 9.
then it shall. ver. 27.

31 **in every**. Dt 14:22, 23.
your reward. Nu 4:49. 7:5. Je 31:14. Mt 10:10. Lk 10:7. 1 C 3:8. 9:10-14. 2 C 12:13. Ga 6:6. 1 T 5:17, 18. He 6:10.

32 **bear**. ver. 22. Le 19:8.
pollute. Le 22:2, 15. Ml 1:7. Mt 21:33-41. 1 C 11:27, 29.

NUMBERS 19

2 **the ordinance**. Nu 31:21. He 9:10.
a red heifer. ver. 6. Le 14:6. Is 1:18. Re 1:5.
no blemish. Ex +12:5. Le 22:20-25. Ps 45:2. SS 4:7. Ml 1:13, 14. Lk 1:35. He 7:26. 9:13, 14. 1 P 1:19. 2:22.
upon which. Dt 21:3. 1 S 6:7. La 1:14. Mt 17:25, 26. Jn 10:17, 18. Ph 2:6-8.

3 **without the camp**. Le +4:12.

4 **sprinkle**. Le +1:5.
seven. Le +4:6.

5 **her skin**. Ex 29:14. Le 4:11, 12, 21. Ps 22:14. Is 53:10.

6 **cedar wood**. Le 14:4. He 9:19-23.
hyssop. Ps +51:7.
scarlet. Is 1:18.

7 **wash**. ver. 8, 19. Le 11:25, 40. 14:8, 9. 15:5. 16:26-28.
come into. Jn 13:3-10. He 10:22. 1 P 3:21.

9 **clean**. ver. 18. Nu 9:13. 2 C 5:21. He 7:26. 9:13.
lay them up. ver. 17.
a water of separation. ver. 13, 20, 21. Nu

6:12. 31:23, 24. Le 15:20. Zc 13:1. Jn 19:34. 2
C 7:1. He 9:13, 14. 1 J 1:7.
purification for sin. Heb. sin offering. Le
+23:19. Is 52:14, 15. 53:6. Je 33:8.

10 **wash his**. ver. +7, 8, 19. Is 52:11. 1 T 5:22. Ju
23. Re 3:4.
it shall be. Nu 15:15, 16. Ex 12:49. Ro 3:29,
30. Col 3:11.
for ever. Heb. *olam*, Ex +12:24.

11 **toucheth the dead**. ver. 16. Nu 5:2. 9:6, 10.
31:19. Le 11:12, 27, 31, 39. 21:1, 11. La 4:14.
Hg 2:13. Ro 5:12. 2 C 6:17. Ep 2:1. He 9:14.
man. Heb. *nephesh*, soul, Le +19:28. ver. 13.
Nu 6:6. 9:6, 7, 10. Le 21:11. Hg 2:13.

12 **He shall purify**. ver. 17, 18. Ps 51:7. Is 1:16.
Ezk 36:25. Ac 15:9. 24:16. 2 C 1:12. 1 Th 4:3,
4. 1 T 3:9. Ja 1:27. 1 J 3:3. Re 7:14.
third day. Nu 31:19. Ex 19:11, 15. Le 7:17.
Ho 6:2. 1 C +15:3, 4.

13 **dead body**. Heb. *nephesh*, soul, Le +19:28.
purifieth. Nu 15:30. Le 5:3, 6, 17. 15:31. 1 C
3:16, 17. 6:19, 20. He 2:2, 3. 10:29. Re 21:8.
22:11, 15.
soul. Heb. *nephesh*, Ge +17:14. Le 7:20.
the water. ver. 9, 18. Nu 8:7.
sprinkled. Heb. *zaraq*, **S#2236h**. ver. 19, 20.
Nu 18:17. Ex 9:8, 10. 24:6, 8. 29:16, 20. Le
+1:5. 3:2, 8, 13. 7:2, 14. 8:19, 24. 9:12, 18.
17:6. 2 K 16:13, 15. 2 Ch 29:22. 30:16. 34:4.
35:11. Jb 2:12. Is 28:25 (scatter). Ezk 10:2.
36:25. 43:18. Ho 7:9mg. He *9:13, 14.*
his uncleanness. Le 7:20. 22:3. Pr 14:32. Jn
8:24.

14 **unclean**. Jb 15:14-16. Hab 1:13.

15 **open vessel**. Nu 31:20. Le 11:32. 14:36.

16 **toucheth**. ver. 11. Nu 31:19. 1 S 20:25, 26.
a bone. Ezk 39:11-16.
a grave. Heb. *qeber*, Ge +23:4. Mt 23:27. Lk
11:44.

17 **ashes**. Heb. dust. ver. 9, 10.
purification for sin. Heb. sin offering. Le
+23:19.
running water shall be put thereto. Heb.
living waters shall be given. Ge +26:19mg. Le
14:5, 6, 50-52. 15:13. SS +4:15. Is 44:3. Jn
4:10, 11. 7:38. Re 7:17. 22:1.

18 **a clean**. ver. 9. Ps 51:7. Ezk 36:25-27. Jn
15:2, 3. 17:17, 19. 1 C 1:30. He 9:14.
grave. Heb. *qeber*, Ge +23:4.

19 **shall sprinkle**. Ep 5:25-27. T 2:14. 3:3-5. 1 J
1:7. 2:1, 2. Ju 23. Re 1:5, 6.
purify. Nu 31:20, 23. Ps 51:7. Ezk 36:25. 1 C
6:11.
on the seventh day. ver. 12. Nu 31:19. Ge
2:2. Le 14:9.
he shall purify himself. ver. 7, 8, 10.

20 **shall not**. ver. +13. Ge 17:14. Mk 16:16. Ac
13:39-41. Ro 2:4, 5. 2 P 3:14. Re 22:11.
soul. Heb. *nephesh*, Ge +17:14.
water of. Nu 8:5-7. 1 T 1:5, 19.

21 **perpetual**. Heb. *olam*, Ge +9:12. ver. 10, 19.
Ex 12:14, 17. 29:9. 31:16. Le 3:17. 24:3. Nu
18:8, 19.
he that. Le 11:25, 40. 16:26-28. He 7:19.
9:10, 13, 14. 10:4. Ja 1:17.
sprinkleth. Heb. *nazah*, **S#5137h**. ver. 4, 18, 19.
Ex 29:21. Le +1:5. 4:6, 17. 5:9. 6:27. 14:27, 51.
14:7, 16. 16:14, 15, 19. 2 K 9:33. Is 63:3.
wash. Heb. *kabas*, **S#3526h**. ver. 7, 8, 10, 19.
Nu 8:7, 21. 31:24. Ge 49:11. Ex 19:10, 14. Le
6:27. 11:25, 28, 40. 13:6, 34, 54, 55, 56, 58.
14:8, 9, 47. 15:5-8, 10, 11, 13, 17, 21, 22, 27.
16:26, 28. 17:15, 16. 2 S 19:24. 2 K 18:17
(fuller's). Ps 51:2, 7. Is 7:3. 36:2. Je 2:22. 4:14.
Ml 3:2.

22 **whatsoever**. Le 7:19. Ps 19:7-11. 119:140.
Hg 2:13. Ph 4:8. T 1:15. Ja 3:17.
the soul. Heb. *nephesh*, Ge +27:31. Le 15:5.
Mt 15:19, 20. Mk 7:21-23.

NUMBERS 20

1 A.M. 2552. B.C. 1452.
Then. Dt 1:22, 23. 2:14.
into. Nu 13:21. 27:14. 33:36. Dt 32:51.
Kadesh. ver. +22.
Miriam. Ex 2:4, 7. +15:20.

2 **no**. Ex 15:23, 24. 17:1-4.
gathered. Nu 11:1-6. 16:3, 19, 42. 21:5. Ex
16:2, 7, 12. 1 C 10:10, 11.

3 **God**. Nu 14:1, 2. Ex 16:2, 3. 17:2. Jb 3:10, 11.
died. **S#1478h**, Ge +49:33.
when. Nu 11:1, 33, 34. 14:36, 37. 16:31-35,
49. La 4:9.
died. **S#1478h**, Ge +49:33.

4 **why**. Nu 11:5. Ex 5:21. 17:3. Ps 106:21. Ac
7:35, 39, 40.
that we. Nu 16:13, 14, 41. Ex 14:11, 12.
16:3.

5 **this evil**. Nu 16:14. Dt 8:15. Ne 9:21. Je 2:2,
6. Ezk 20:36.
neither. Nu 11:1, 3. 14:2, 37. 16:32, 35, 42,
49. Ex 17:1-3.

6 **they fell**. Ge +17:3. Ex 17:4. Ps 109:3, 4.
the glory. Nu 12:5. Ex +24:16.

8 **the rod**. Nu 21:15, 18. Ex 4:2, 17. 7:20.
14:16. 17:5, 9.
speak. Ge 18:14. Jsh 6:5, 20. Ps 33:9. Mt
21:21. Mk 11:22-24. Lk 11:9, 13. Jn 4:10-14.
16:24. Ac 1:14. 2:1-4. Re 22:1, 17.
bring forth. ver. 11. Ne 9:15. Ps 78:15, 16.
105:41. 114:8. Is 41:17, 18. 43:20. 48:21.

9 **before the Lord**. Nu 17:10.

10 **ye rebels**. Dt 9:24. Ps 106:32, 33. Mt 5:22. Lk
9:54, 55. Ac 23:3-5. Ep 4:26. Ja 3:2.
we fetch. Nu 11:22, 23. Ge 40:8. 41:16. Da
2:28-30. Ac 3:12-16. 14:9-15. Ro 15:17-19. 1
C 3:7.

11 **smote**. ver. 8. Le 10:1. 1 S 15:13, 14, 19, 24.
1 K 13:21-24. 1 Ch 13:9, 10. 15:2, 13. Is 50:5,

6. 53:4, 5, 8, 10. Mt 28:20. Ac 2:23. Ga 3:1. Ja 1:20.

the water. Ex 17:6. Dt 8:15. Is 55:1. Ho 13:5. Jn 4:10. 7:37. 1 C 10:4. Re 22:17.

12 Because ye believed. Nu 11:21, 22. 2 Ch 20:20. Is 7:9. Mt 17:17, 20. Lk 1:20, 45. Ro 4:20.

sanctify. Dt 1:37. Ps 99:8. Is +8:13.

ye shall. ver. 24. Nu 11:15. Dt 3:23-26. 32:49, 50. 34:4. Jsh 1:2. Jn 1:17.

13 the water. Dt 33:8. Ps 81:7. 95:8. 99:5. 106:32, etc.

Meribah. Ex +17:7. Dt 32:51, Meribah-Kadesh.

he was. Is +8:13.

14 Moses. Jg 11:16, 17.

thy brother. Ge 25:29-34. 32:3, 4. 36:40-43. Dt 2:4, etc. 23:7. Ob 10-12. Ml 1:2.

befallen us. Heb. found us. 2 K +9:21mg.

15 our fathers. Ge 46:6. Ac 7:15.

dwelt. Ge 15:13. Ex 12:40.

vexed us. Nu 11:5. 16:13. Ex 1:11-14, 16, 22. 5:14. Dt 26:6. Ac 7:19.

16 we cried. Ex 6:5. +22:23.

sent an. Ex 3:2-6. 14:19. 23:20. 33:2. Is 63:9.

17 through thy. Nu 21:1, 22-24. Dt 2:1-4, 27, 29.

wells. Heb. *be-er*, Ge +16:14.

king's high way. Nu 21:22.

turn to. Dt 2:27. 5:32. Pr 4:27.

19 We will go. Dt 2:6, 28.

20 Thou shalt. ver. 18. Ge 27:41. 32:6. Jg 11:17, 20. Ps 120:7. Ezk 35:5-11. Am 1:11.

And Edom. Ob 10-15.

21 refused. Dt 2:27, 29.

wherefore. Dt 2:4-8. 23:7. Jg 11:18, 24. Lk 9:56.

22 Kadesh. ver. 1, 14, 16. Ge +14:7.

mount Hor. i.e. *who shows*, **S#2023h**. ver. 23, 25, 27. Nu 21:4. 33:37, 38, 39, 41. 34:7, 8. Dt 32:50.

24 gathered. Ge +25:8.

because ye. ver. 11, 12.

word. Heb. mouth. Dt +21:5mg.

25 Take Aaron. Nu 33:38, 39.

26 strip Aaron. Ex 29:29, 30. Is 22:21, 22. He 7:11, 23, 24.

28 Moses. ver. 26. Nu 33:38, etc. Ex 29:29, 30.

put them. Nu 27:16-23. Dt 31:7, 8. 34:9. 1 Ch 22:11, 12, 17. 28:5-9. Ac 20:25-29. 2 P 1:15.

died there. Nu 33:38, 39. Dt 10:6. 32:49, 50. 34:5. He 7:23-25.

29 dead. **S#1478h**, Ge +49:33.

mourned. Ge +23:2. 2 S 3:38.

NUMBERS 21

1 Arad. Nu 33:40. Jsh 12:14. Jg 1:16.

the way of the spies. Nu 13:21, 22. 14:45.

then. Dt 2:32. Jsh 7:5. 11:19, 20. Ps 44:3, 4.

2 vowed. Nu +30:2.

I will. Dt +2:34. 1 C 16:22.

3 hearkened. Ps 10:17. 91:15. 102:17.

Canaanites. Ge +10:18.

and they utterly. Jsh 12:14.

Hormah. *that is,* utter destruction. Nu +14:45.

Chormah, rather a devoting to destruction: so LXX. Anathema.

4 mount Hor. Nu 20:22, 23, 27. 33:41.

by the way. Nu 14:25. Dt 1:40.

compass. Nu 20:18-21. Dt 2:5-8. Jg 11:18.

the soul. Heb. *nephesh*, Ge +34:3. Nu 32:7, 9. Ex 6:9. Dt 11:13. Mt +22:37. Ac 14:22. 1 Th 3:3, 4.

discouraged. or, grieved. Heb. shortened. Nu 11:23. Ex 6:9. Ps 107:4-7. He 12:1-7.

5 spake. Nu 11:1-6. 14:1-4. 16:13, 14, 41. 17:12. Ex 14:11. 15:24. 16:2, 3, 7, 8. 17:2, 3. Ps 68:6. 78:19.

and our soul. Heb. *nephesh*, Nu +11:6. Nu 11:6-9. Ex 16:15, 31. Ps 78:24, 25. Pr 27:7.

6 fiery serpents. Ge 3:14, 15. Dt 8:15. Is 14:29. 30:6. Je 8:17. Am 9:3, 4. 1 C 10:9.

7 We have. Ex 9:27, 28. 1 S 12:19. 15:24, 30. Ps 78:34. Mt 27:4.

pray. Ex 8:8, 28. 1 K 13:6. Je 37:3. Ac 8:24. Ro 8:34. Ja 5:16.

take away. Nu 11:1, 2. Ex 32:11, 12. 2 Ch 20:9. Da 9:18.

And Moses. Nu 11:2. 14:17-20. Ge 20:7. Ex 32:11, 30. Dt 9:20, 26-29. 1 S 12:20-23. Jb 42:8, 10. Ps 106:23. Je 15:1. Ro 10:1.

8 the Lord. Ps 106:43-45. 145:8.

looketh. He +12:2.

9 a serpent of. Ge 3:1-5. 2 K 18:4. Jn 3:14, 15. 8:28. 12:31, 32. Ro 8:3. 2 C 5:21. Re 12:9.

when he. He +12:2. 1 J 3:8.

he lived. Jn 6:40. Ro 1:17. 5:20, 21.

10 set forward. Nu 33:43-45.

Oboth. i.e. *hollow passes*. **S#88h**. ver. 10, 11. 33:43, 44.

11 Ije-abarim. *or,* heaps of Abarim. Nu 33:44, 47, 48. Ps 79:1.

12 the valley of Zared. Dt 2:13, 14, the brook Zered.

Zared. i.e. *the bond subdued*. **S#2218h**. ver. 12. Dt 2:13, 13, 14.

13 on the other side. ver. 14. Nu 22:36. Dt 2:24. Jg 11:18. Is 16:2. Je 48:20.

Arnon. i.e. *a brawling stream*. **S#769h**. ver. 13, 14, 24, 26, 28. 22:36. Dt 2:24, 36. 3:8, 12, 16. 4:48. Jsh 12:1, 2. 13:9, 16. Jg 11:13, 18, 22, 26. 2 K 10:33. Is 16:2. Je 48:20. Called Dibon-Gad (Nu 33:45), whence they removed to Almon-diblathaim (Nu 33:46, 47).

14 in the book. Jsh 10:13. 2 S 1:18. 2 Ch 16:11.

15 stream. or, spring. Compare the plural form in Dt 3:17mg. 4:49. Jsh 10:40. 12:3mg, 8. 13:20mg.

Ar. i.e. *awaking*. **S#6144h**: ver. 28. Dt 2:9, 18, 29. Is 15:1.
lieth. Heb. leaneth.
Moab. 2 K 3:15-27.

16 **Beer**. i.e. *a halting place*. **S#876h**. Jg 9:21.
well. Heb. *be-er*, Ge +16:14.
Gather. Nu 20:8. Ex 17:6. Is 12:3. 41:17, 18. 43:20. 49:10. Jn 4:10, 14. 7:37-39. Re 21:6. 22:1, 17.

17 **sang**. Ex 15:1, 2. Jg 5:1. Ps 105:2. 106:12. Is 12:1, 2, 5. Ja 5:13.
Spring up. Heb. ascend. Jn 4:14.
well. Heb. *be-er*, Ge +16:14.
sing ye. *or*, answer.

18 **princes**. 2 Ch 17:7-9. Ne 3:1, 5. 1 T 6:17, 18.
well. Heb. *be-er*, Ge +16:14.
the lawgiver. Ge 49:10. Dt 5:31. 33:4. Is 33:22. Jn 1:17. Ja 4:12.
And from. Nu 33:45, 47.
Mattanah. i.e. *gift*. **S#4980h**. ver. 18, 19.

19 **Nahaliel**. i.e. *valley* or *stream of God*. **S#5160h**. ver. 19.
Bamoth. i.e. *heights; high places*. **S#1120h**. ver. 19, 20. Compare Nu 22:41.

20 **country**. Heb. field. Nu 22:1. 26:63. 33:49, 50. Dt 1:5.
to the. Nu 23:14. Dt 3:27. 4:49. 34:1.
Pisgah. *or*, the hill. i.e. *a sight*, or *view*. **S#6449h**. ver. 20. 23:14. Dt 3:17, 27. 4:49. 34:1. Jsh 12:3. 13:20.
Jeshimon. *or*, the wilderness. i.e. *the waste*. **S#3452h**, only here. Nu 23:28. Dt 32:10. 1 S 23:19, 24. Ps 68:7. 78:40. 106:14. 107:4. Is 43:19, 20.

21 **sent messengers**. Nu 20:14-19. Dt 2:26-28. Jg 11:19-21.
Sihon. i.e. *a sweeping away; tempestuous*. **S#5511h**. ver. 21, 23, 26-29, 34. 32:33. Dt 1:4. 2:24, 26, 30-32. 3:2, 6. 4:46. 29:7. 31:4. Jsh 2:10. 9:10. 12:2, 5. 13:10, 21, 27. Jg 11:19-21. 1 K 4:19. Ne 9:22. Ps 135:11. 136:19. Je 48:45.

22 **Let**. Nu 20:17.
well. Heb. *be-er*, Ge +16:14.

23 **Sihon would**. Dt 2:30-32. 29:7, 8.
Jahaz. i.e. *a trodden down place*. **S#3096h**. Dt 2:32. Jsh +13:18. Jg 11:20. Is 15:4. Je 48:21, 34.

24 **Israel**. Nu 32:1-4, 33-42. Dt 2:31-37. 29:7. Jsh 9:10. 12:1-3. 13:8-10. 24:8. Jg 11:21-23. 12:1, 2. 24:8. Ne 9:22. Ps 135:10-12. 136:19. Am 2:9.
Arnon. ver. +13.
Jabbok. Ge +32:22.

25 **dwelt**. ver. 31. Nu 32:33-42. Dt 2:12.
in Heshbon. i.e. *intelligence; reason*, or *device*. **S#2809h**: ver. 25-28, 30, 34. 32:3, 37. Dt 1:4. 2:24, 26, 30. 3:2, 6. 4:46. 29:7. Jsh 9:10. 12:2, 5. 13:10, 17, 21, 26, 27. 21:39. Jg 11:19, 26. 1 Ch 6:81. Ne 9:22. SS 7:4. Is 15:4. 16:8, 9. Je 48:2, 34, 45. 49:3.

villages. Heb. daughters. ver. 32. Nu 32:42. Ge 49:22mg. Jsh 15:45, 47. 17:11, 16. Jg 11:26. 2 S 20:19. 1 Ch 7:28mg, 29. 18:1. 2 Ch 13:19. 28:18. Ne 11:25. Ps 45:12. 137:8. SS 7:4. Is 1:8. 10:32. 16:1. 23:12. 37:22. +47:1. Je 4:31. 6:2. 18:13. 31:4, 21. 46:11. +49:2. La 1:6. 2:1, 2, 13. 4:21. Ezk 16:27mg, 46, 49, 53, 55. 26:6. Am 5:2. Zc 9:9. Mt +21:5.

26 **Heshbon**. ver. +25.
Sihon. ver. +21.
Moab. Ezk +25:8.
Arnon. ver. +13.

27 **they that**. ver. 14. Is 14:4. Hab 2:6.
proverbs. or, similes. Dt +28:37. Jb 13:12. 30:19 (become like). Ps 28:1. 49:12, 20. 143:7. Is 14:10. 46:5. Ezk 17:2. 20:49. 24:3.

28 **a fire**. Jg 9:20. Ps 29:7. Is 10:16. Je 48:45, 46. Am 1:4, 7, 10, 12, 14. 2:2, 5.
Ar of Moab. ver. +15. Dt 2:9, 18. Is 15:1, 2.

29 **Moab**. Ezk +25:8.
O people. 1 C 8:4, 5.
Chemosh. i.e. *subduer, vanquisher*. **S#3645h**. Jg 11:24. 1 K 11:7, 33. 2 K 23:13. Je 48:7, 13, 46.

30 **have shot**. Ge 49:23. 2 S 11:24. Ps 18:14.
Dibon. i.e. *pain, grief, waster*. **S#2130h**. Called Dibon-gad in Nu 33:45, because rebuilt by the Gaddites; given to the Reubenites in Jsh 13:9, 17, and afterwards occupied by the Moabites, Is 15:2. Je 48:18, 22. Doubtless it is the same place that is called Dimon in Is 15:19; another town of the same name belonging to Judah is noticed in Ne 11:25, which in Jsh 15:22 is called Dimonah (Young). Nu 32:3, 34. Jsh 13:17. Is 15:2, 9. Je 48:18, 22, 45, 46.
Nophah. i.e. *a gust, blast*. **S#5302h**, only here. Is 15:2, Nebo.
Medeba. i.e. *water of strength; waters of rest*. **S#4311h**: ver. 30. Jsh 13:9, 16. 1 Ch 19:7. Is 15:2.

31 **Israel dwelt**. Nu 32:33-42. Dt 3:16, 17. Jsh 12:1-6. 13:8-32.

32 **Jaazer**. i.e. *helpful*, **S#3270h**. Nu +32:1.
villages. ver. +25.

33 **they turned**. Dt 3:1-6. 29:7. Jsh 13:12.
Bashan. i.e. *light sandy soil*. **S#1316h**. ver. 33. 32:33. Dt 1:4. 3:1, 3, 4, 10, 11, 13, 14. 4:43, 47. 29:7. +32:14. 33:22. Jsh 9:10. 12:4, 5. 13:11, 12, 30, 31. 17:1, 5. 20:8. 21:6, 27. 22:7. 1 K 4:13, 19. 2 K 10:33. 1 Ch 5:11, 12, 16, 23. 6:62, 71. Ne 9:22. Ps 22:12. 68:15, 22. 135:11. 136:20. Is +2:13. 33:9. Je 22:20. 50:19. Ezk 27:6. 39:18. Am 4:1. Mi 7:14. Na 1:4. Zc 11:2.
Og. i.e. *hearth-cake; one who goes in a circle*, or rolls about, from fatness it may be. **S#5747h**. ver. 33. 32:33. Dt 1:4. 3:1, 3, 4, 10, 11, 13. 4:47. 29:7. 31:4. Jsh 2:10. 9:10. 12:4. 13:12, 30, 31. 1 K 4:19. Ne 9:22. Ps 135:11. 136:20.
Edrei. i.e. *goodly pasture; mighty, strong*. **S#154h**. ver. 33. Dt 1:4. 3:1, 10. Jsh 12:4. 13:12, 31. 19:37.

34 **Fear him**. Nu 14:9. Dt 3:2, 11. 20:3. 31:6. Jsh 10:8, 25. Is 41:13.
for I have. Dt 3:3. 7:24. Jsh 8:7. Jg 11:30. 1 S 23:4. 2 S 5:19. 1 K 20:13, 28. 2 K 3:18.
thou shalt. ver. 24. Ps 135:10, 11.
as thou. ver. 24, 25.

35 **smote him**. Dt 3:3-17. 29:7, 8. Jsh 12:4-6. 13:12. Ne 9:22. Ps 135:10-12. 136:17-21. Ro 8:37.

NUMBERS 22

1 **the children**. Nu 21:20. 33:48-50. 36:13. Dt 34:1, 8.
the plains. Heb. Arabah. Nu 26:3, 63. 31:12. 33:48-50. 35:1. 36:13. Dt +11:30. 34:1, 8. Jsh 4:13. 5:10. Je 39:5. 52:8.
on this side. Nu 32:19. 34:15. Dt 1:5. 3:8. Jsh 3:16.
Jericho. i.e. *place of fragrance*, **S#3405h**. Nu 26:3. 31:12. 33:48, 50. 34:15. 35:1. 36:13. Dt 32:49. 34:1, 3. 2 S 10:5. 2 K 25:5. 1 Ch 6:78. 19:5. 2 Ch 28:15. Ezr 2:34. Ne 3:2. 7:36. Je 39:5. 52:8. Also **S#3405h**. Jsh 2:1-3. 3:16. 4:13, 19. 5:10, 13. 6:1, 2, 25, 26. 7:2. 8:2. 9:3. 10:1, 28, 30. 12:9. 13:32. 16:1, 7. 18:12, 21. 20:8. 24:11. 2 K 2:4, 5, 15, 18. Also **S#3405h**. 1 K 16:34.

2 **Balak**. i.e. *a waster*, **S#1111h**. ver. 4, 7, 10, 13-16, 18, 35-41. Nu 23:1-3, 5, 7, 11, 13, 15-18, 25-30. 24:10, 12, 13, 25. Jsh 24:9. Jg 11:25. Mi 6:5.
Zippor. i.e. *bird; hopping*, **S#6834h**. ver. 4, 10, 16. Nu 23:18. Jsh 24:9. Jg 11:25.
saw all. Nu 21:3, 20-35. Jg 11:25.

3 **Moab**. Ge +35:5. Ps 53:5. Is 23:5.

4 **elders**. ver. 7. Nu 25:15-18. 31:8. Ge 25:1, 2. Jsh 13:21, 22.
Now shall. Nu 24:17. Ge 15:2-5. 17:19-21. Je 48:38.
round about. lit. circuit. Ezr 1:6.
And Balak. ver. 2. Jg 11:25.

5 **sent**. Dt 23:4. Jsh 13:22. 24:9. Ne 13:1, 2. Mi 6:5. 2 P 2:15, 16, son of Bosor. Ju 11. Re 2:14.
Balaam. i.e. *destruction of the people; glutton*, **S#1109h**. ver. 7-10, 12-14, 16, 18, 20, 21, 23, 25, 27-31, 34-41. Nu 23:1-5, 11, 16, 25-30. 24:1-3, 10, 12, 15, 25. 31:8, 16. Dt 23:4, 5. Jsh 13:22. 24:9, 10. Ne 13:2. Mi 6:5.
Beor. i.e. *shepherd; burning, torch, fire*, **S#1160h**. Ge 36:32. Nu 24:3, 15. 31:8. Dt 23:4. Jsh 13:22. 24:9. 1 Ch 1:43. Mi 6:5. 2 P 2:15, Bosor.
Pethor. i.e. *interpretation of dreams*, **S#6604h**. Dt 23:4.
his people. or, *Ammon*, Dt 23:4. Nu 23:7. Dt 23:4.
they cover. Ge 13:16. Ex 1:7-10. Ps 105:24.
face. Heb. eye. ver. 11. Ge +1:2.

6 **curse me**. Nu 23:7, 8. 24:9. Ge 12:3. 27:29.

Dt 23:4. Jsh 24:9. 1 S 17:43. Ne 13:2. Ps 109:17, 18. Je 17:5. Mi 6:5.
we. Ge +29:27.
I wot. 1 K 22:6, 8, 13. Ps 109:28. Pr 26:2. Is 47:12, 13. Ezk 13:6. Ac 8:9, 10. 16:16.

7 **rewards of divination**. Dt +18:10. 1 S 6:2. 9:7, 8. Is 56:11. Ezk 13:19. Mi 3:11. Ro 16:18. 2 P +2:15.

8 **this night**. ver. 19, 20. Nu 12:6. 23:12. Je 12:2. Ezk +33:31.

9 **God**. ver. 20. Ge 20:3. 31:24. 41:25. Da 2:45. 4:31, 32. Mt 7:22. 24:24. Jn 11:51.
What men. Ge 3:9-11. 4:9. 16:8. Ex 4:2. 2 K 20:14, 15.

10 **Balak**. ver. +4-6.

11 **face**. Ge +1:2.
able to overcome them. Heb. prevail in fighting against him.

12 **Balaam, Thou shalt**. ver. 20. Jb 33:15-17. Mt 27:19.
thou shalt not curse. ver. 19. Nu 23:3, 13-15, 19, 23. Mi 6:5.
for they. Nu 23:20. Ge 12:2. 22:16-18. Dt 23:5. 33:29. Ps 144:15. 146:3-6. Ro 4:6, 7. 11:29. Ep 1:3.

13 **for the Lord**. ver. 14. Dt 23:5. Ps 29:4.

14 **Balaam refuseth**. ver. 13, 37.

15 **princes**. ver. 7, 8. Ac 10:7, 8.

16 **Let nothing**, etc. Heb. Be not thou letted from, etc.

17 **I will promote**. Nu 24:11. Dt 16:9. Est 5:11. 7:9. Mt 4:8, 9. 16:26.
very great. Ge +2:16.
and I will do. Nu 23:2, 3, 29, 30. Mt 14:7.
come. ver. 6.
curse me. Pr 26:2.

18 **If Balak**. Nu 24:13. T 1:16.
I cannot. Nu 23:26. 24:13. 1 K 22:14. 2 Ch 18:13. Da 5:17. Ac 8:20.
word. Da 4:35. He 4:12, 13.

19 **tarry**. ver. +7, 8. Je 42:4-6, 19-21. 1 T 6:9, 10. 2 P 2:3, 15. Ju 11.

20 **God**. ver. +9.
If the men. 1 S 8:5-9. 12:12-19. Ps 81:12. Ezk 14:2-5. 2 Th 2:9-12.
but yet. ver. 35. Nu 23:12, 26. 24:13. Ps 33:10, 11. 78:30, 31. Is 37:29. 46:9-11. Ho 13:11.

21 **rose up**. Pr 1:15, 16.

22 **God's**. 1 S 2:3. 16:7. 2 K 10:30. Ho 1:4.
and the angel. ver. 35. Ge +48:15, 16. Ex 3:2-6. Ho 12:4, 5.
stood. ver. 32. Ex 4:24. La 2:4. Is 37:28, 29. Ezk 38:3, 4.

23 **the ass saw**. 2 K 6:17. 1 Ch 21:16. Da 10:7. Ac 22:9. 1 C 1:27-29. 2 P 2:16. Ju 11.
the ass turned. Je 8:7.

25 **crushed Balaam's**. Jb 5:13-15. Is 47:12.

26 **where was no way**. Is 26:11. Ho 2:6.

27 **and Balaam's anger**. Pr 12:10. 14:16. 27:3, 4.

28 **the Lord opened**. Ex 4:11. Lk 1:37. 1 C
1:19. 2 P 2:14-16.
What have I. Ro 8:22.

29 **for now would**. Pr 12:10, 16. Ec 9:3.

30 **the ass said**. 2 P 2:16.
upon which thou hast ridden. Heb. who
hast ridden upon me.
ever since I was thine. *or*, ever since thou
wast, unto, etc. 1 C 1:27, 28.

31 **opened**. Nu 24:4mg, 16. Ge 21:19. 1 Ch
21:15, 16, 20. Ps +119:18.
bowed down. Ge +24:26. Ps 9:20. Jn 18:6.
fell flat on his face. *or*, bowed himself.

32 **Wherefore**. ver. 28. Dt 25:4. Ps 36:6. 145:9.
147:9. Jon 4:11.
withstand thee. Heb. be an adversary unto
thee. ver. 22. Zc 3:1mg.
thy way. Dt 23:4. Pr 28:6. Mi 6:5. Ac 13:10.
2 P 2:14, 15.
before me. ver. 20, 22, 35. Ex 3:2-6. Pr 14:2.
28:18.

33 **surely**. Nu 14:37. 16:33-35. 1 K 13:24-28. Re
19:11-15.

34 **I have sinned**. Ex 9:27. 10:16, 17. Jsh 7:20.
1 S 15:24, 30. 24:17. 26:21. 2 S +12:13.
19:20. 1 K 8:38, 39. 1 Ch 28:9. Jb 34:31, 32.
Ps 7:9. 78:34. Je 17:9, 10. Mt 15:7, 8. 27:4, 5.
if it displease thee. Heb. be evil in thine
eyes. ver. +12. Nu 11:1mg. Ge +28:8mg.
38:10mg. 48:17mg. Jsh +22:30mg. 1 S
+8:6mg. 18:8mg. 2 S 11:25mg, 27mg. 1 Ch
21:7mg. Pr 24:18mg. Is 59:15mg.
I will get. Jb 34:31, 32.

35 **Go**. ver. +20. Ps 81:12. 106:15. Is 37:26-29.
Ro 9:17-22. 2 Th 2:9-12.
I shall speak. ver. +20, 21.

36 **went**. Ge 18:2. Ex +18:7. 1 S 13:10.
the border. Nu +21:13.

37 **earnestly send**. Ge +26:28.
am I not able. ver. 16, 17. Nu 24:11. Ps 75:6.
Mt 4:8, 9. Lk 4:6. Jn 5:44.

38 **have I**. ver. 18. Ps 33:10. 76:10. Pr 19:21. Is
44:25. 46:10. 47:12.
the word. Nu 23:16, 26. 24:13. 1 K 22:14. 2
Ch 18:13.

39 **Kirjath-huzoth**. *or*, a city of streets. **S#7155h**,
only here.

40 **offered oxen**. Nu 23:2, 14, 30. Ge 31:54. Pr
1:16. Ezk 21:21-23.

41 **high places**. *Bamoth baal*, "the high places of
Baal." Nu 21:19, 20, Bamoth. 25:2, 3. Dt 12:2.
2 Ch 11:15. Je 48:35.
utmost. Nu 23:13.

NUMBERS 23

1 **Build me**. ver. 29. Ezk 33:31. Ju 11.
seven altars. Ex 20:24. 27:1, etc. 1 S 15:22. 2
K 18:22. Ps 50:8, 9. Pr 15:8. Is 1:11-15. Mt
23:14.

seven oxen. Nu 29:32. 1 Ch 15:26. 2 Ch
29:21. Jb 42:8. Ezk 45:23.

2 **offered**. ver. 14, 30. Ps 50:16, 17.

3 **Stand**. ver. 15.
burnt. Ge 8:20. 22:2, 7, 8, 13. Ex 18:12. Le
ch. 1.
peradventure. ver. 15. Nu 22:8, 9, 31-35.
24:1.
went to a high place. *or*, went solitary. Is
41:18. Je 3:2.

4 **God**. ver. 16. Nu 22:9, 20.
met. ver. 16.
I have prepared. ver. 1. Ps 50:21, 22. Is
58:3, 4. Mt 20:12. Lk 18:12. Jn 16:2. Ro 3:27.
Ep 2:9.

5 **put a word**. ver. 16. Nu 22:35. Dt 18:18. Pr
16:1, 9. Is 51:6. 59:21. Je 1:9. Lk 12:2. Jn
11:51.

6 **he stood**. ver. 3.

7 **he took**. ver. 18. Mt 13:33, 35. Mk 12:12.
parable. ver. 7-12, 18-24. 24:2, 3, 15, 20, 21,
23. Dt +28:37. Jb 27:1. 29:1. Ps 49:4. 78:2. Pr
26:7, 9. Ezk 17:2. 20:49. 24:3. Mi 2:4. Hab
2:6.
Aram. Ge +22:21. 28:2, 7.
Come. Nu 22:5, 6, 11, 17. Pr 26:2.
defy Israel. Dt 23:4. 1 S 17:10, 25, 26, 36,
45. 2 S 21:21. 23:9.

8 **How shall**. ver. 20, 23. Jb 34:29. Is 44:25.
47:12, 13.

9 **the people**. Mt 24:34.
dwell alone. Ex +19:5, 6. 34:12, 13, 15, 16.
Dt 33:28. Est 3:8.
shall not. Ex 8:22, 23. Dt 32:8. 33:28. Ezr
9:2. Je 46:28. Am 9:9. Ro 15:8-10. Ep 2:12-
14.

10 **can count**. Ge 13:16. 22:17. 28:14.
the dust. Ge +13:16.
the fourth. Nu 2:9, 16, 24, 31.
me. Heb. *nephesh*, my soul, or, my life, used
as the idiom for *me, myself, himself*. For other
instances of this use see Jg 16:30mg. Jb 36:14.
Ps 3:2. 16:10. 25:13. 35:13. 103:1. Is 58:5. Lk
12:19. Ac 2:31. Ro 16:4. 1 P 1:9. Here *nephesh*
is used of man as being mortal, subject to
death of various kinds, from which it can be
saved and delivered and life prolonged.
Rendered "me" here, and at Jg 16:30. 1 K
20:32. Rendered "ghost," Jb 11:20; Je 15:9;
"person," 2 S 14:14; "tablets," Is 3:20 (R.V.
perfume boxes), Heb. "houses of the soul,"
i.e. boxes of scent for the nose; "deadly," Ps
17:9 (Heb. "enemies against my *nephesh*");
"himself," 1 K 19:4; Am 2:14, 15; "they," Jb
36:14; "themselves," Is 47:14; "yourselves,"
Dt 4:15; Jsh 23:11. For the rendering "soul,"
see Ge +12:13; for "life, lives," see Ge +44:30.
For *nephesh* used of man as actually dead, see
Le +19:28. For *nephesh* spoken of as going to
sheol, etc., see Ps +30:3. For the equivalent

New Testament use of *psyche* to emphasize the personal pronoun in the first person, see Mt +12:18.

the death. Nu 31:8. Ps 37:37. 116:15. Pr 11:7. 14:32. Is 57:1, 2. Lk 2:29, 30. 1 C 3:21, 22. 15:53-57. 2 C 5:1. Ph 1:21-23. 2 T 4:6-8. 2 P 1:13-15. Re 14:13.

11 I took. ver. 7, 8. Nu 22:11, 17. 24:10. Ge 27:29, 33. Ps 109:17-20.

12 Must. ver. 20, 26. Nu 22:38. 24:13. Pr 26:25. Jn 19:11. Ro 16:18. T 1:16.

13 with me. Jg 17:5, 13.
unto. 1 K 20:23, 28. Mi 6:5.
utmost. Nu 22:41.
and curse me. Jsh 24:9. Ps 109:17. Ja 3:9, 10.

14 Zophim. i.e. *watchers, watchmen*, **S#6839h**, only here.
Pisgah. *or*, the hill. Nu 21:20. Dt 3:27mg. 4:49. 34:1mg.
built seven. ver. 1, 2, 29. Is 1:10, 11. 46:6. Ho 12:11.

15 while I meet. ver. 3. Nu 22:8.

16 met. ver. 4.
put a word. ver. +5. Nu 24:1.

17 What. ver. 26. Jg 3:20. 1 S 3:17. Je 1:9. 37:17.

18 Rise up. Jg 3:20.

19 God. 1 S 15:29. Jb 23:13. Ps 89:35. Hab 2:3. Ml 3:6. Lk 21:33. Ro 11:29. T 1:2. He 6:18. Ja 1:17.
or hath he. Ex 9:16. 1 Ch 17:17. Pr 16:4. Mi 7:20.

20 he hath. Nu 22:12. Ge 12:2. 22:17.
I cannot. Nu 22:18, 38. Jn 10:27-29. Ro 8:38, 39. 1 P 1:5.

21 hath not. Ps 103:12. Is 1:18. 38:17. Je 50:20. Ho 14:2-4. Mi 7:18-20. Jn +17:6. Ro 4:7, 8. 6:14. 8:1. 2 C 5:19.
Jacob. Ge +9:27.
perverseness. Jb 4:8. 15:35. Ps 7:14. 10:7, 14.
Israel. Ge +9:27.
the Lord. Ex 13:21. 29:45, 46. 33:14-16. 34:9. Is 12:6. +43:2. Ezk 48:35. 2 C 6:16.
the shout. Ps 47:5-7. 89:15, 18. 97:1. 118:15. Is 33:22. Lk 19:37, 38. 2 C 2:14.

22 God. Nu 22:5. 24:8. Ex 9:16. 14:18. 20:2. Ps 68:35.
the strength. Dt 33:17. Jb 39:10, 11. Ps 22:21.
unicorn. Ps 29:6. 92:10. Is 34:7.

23 no enchantment. Nu 22:6. Ge 3:15. Ex 7:10-12. 8:16-19. Dt +18:10. 2 K +21:6. Pr 21:30. Mt 12:25, 27. 16:18. Lk 10:18, 19. Ro 16:20. Re 12:9.
against. *or*, in.
according. Ps 44:1-3. 136:13-20. Is 63:9-12. Da 9:15. Mi 6:4, 5. 7:15.
What hath. Ps 31:19. 44:1. 64:9. 126:2, 3. Is 41:4. Jn 11:47. Ac 4:16. 5:12, 14. 10:38. 15:12. Ga 1:23, 24. 1 Th 1:8, 9.

24 as a great. Jg 14:18. Pr 28:1. 30:29, 30. Is +5:29.
he shall. Nu 24:17. Ge 49:27. Da 2:44. Mi 5:8, 9. Zc 10:4, 5. 12:6. Re 19:11-21.

25 Neither curse. Ps 2:1-3.

26 All that. ver. 12, 13. Nu 22:18, 38. 24:12, 13. 1 K 22:14. 2 Ch 18:13. Jl 3:1. Am 3:4-8. Ac 4:19, 20. 5:29.

27 Come. ver. 13.
peradventure. ver. 19, 20. Jb 23:13. Pr 16:25. 19:21. 21:30. 29:1. Is 14:27. 46:10, 11. Ml 3:6. Ro 11:29.

28 Peor. i.e. *cleft, opening*. **S#6465h**. ver. 28. Nu 25:18. 31:16. Jsh 22:17.
Jeshimon. Nu 21:20. 33:49.

29 Build me. ver. 1, 2.

30 every altar. ver. 1, 2.

NUMBERS 24

1 saw. Nu 22:13. 23:20. 31:16. 1 S 24:20. 26:2, 25. Re 2:14.
at other times. Nu 23:3, 15.
to seek for enchantments. Heb. to the meeting of enchantments. 2 K 19:21, 23. +21:6. Is 44:24-26. Ezk 13:22, 23. Ac 16:16-18.

2 lifted. Ge +22:13.
abiding. ver. 5. Nu 2:2, etc. 3:38. 23:9, 10. SS 6:4, 10.
the spirit. Heb. *ruach*, Ge +41:38. Nu 11:25-29. 1 S 10:10. 19:20, 23, 24. 2 Ch 15:1. Mt 7:22. 10:4, 8. Lk 10:20. Jn 11:49-51.

3 he took up. Nu 23:7, 18.
whose eyes are open hath said. Heb. who had his eyes shut, *but now opened*. ver. 4, 16. Nu 22:31.

4 saw. Nu +12:6. Ge 15:12. Ps 89:19. Da 8:26, 27. Ac 10:10, 19. 22:17. 2 C 12:1-4.
Almighty. Ge +49:25.
falling. Ge +17:3. 1 S 19:24.
eyes open. Nu 23:31.

5 How goodly. Mt 8:10. Ro 11:33. Ga 1:6.
tents. Nu 1:52. 2:2. 2 S 20:1. 1 K 12:16. Je 4:20. 30:18. Ml 2:12.
Jacob. Ex 6:3. Ru 1:20, 21.

6 as gardens. Ge 2:8-10. 13:10. 27:27. SS 4:12-15. 6:11. Is 58:11. Je 31:12. Jl 3:18.
as the trees. Ps 1:3. Je 17:8.
which the. Ps 104:16, 17. Is 41:19. 61:3.
as cedar. 1 K 4:33. 2 K 19:23. Ps 29:5. 92:12-14. 104:16. 148:9. Ezk 31:3, 4. 47:12. Am 2:9.

7 pour. Heb. *nazal*, **S#5140h**. Jg 5:5mg. Pr 5:15. Je 18:14.
many waters. Ps 68:26. 93:3, 4. Pr 5:16-18. Is 48:1. Je 51:13. Jn +3:23. Re 17:1, 15.
his king. Ezr 4:20. Ps 2:6-10. 18:43. Jn 1:49. Ph 2:10, 11. Re 19:16.

Agag. i.e. *flame, blazing; sublime*, **S#90h**. Nu 24:7. 1 S 15:8, 9, 20, 32, 33.

his kingdom. Ge 17:4-8, 15, 16. 2 S 5:12. 1 K 4:21. 1 Ch 14:2. Is 2:2. 9:6, 7. Da 2:44. Lk 1:31-33. Ac 5:30, 31. Re 11:15.

8 **God**. Nu 21:5. 23:22.

shall eat. Nu 14:9. 23:24. Dt 7:1.

break. Ps 2:9. 110:2. Is 38:13. Je 50:17. Da 6:24.

pierce. Dt 32:23, 42. Ps 21:12. 45:5. Je 50:9. 1 C 15:25.

9 **couched**. Is +5:29.

who shall. Jb 41:10. Ps 2:12.

Blessed. Ge +12:3. Ac 9:5.

10 **he smote**. Jb 27:23. Ezk 21:14, 17. 22:13.

I called. Nu 22:6, 11, 17. 23:11. Dt 23:4, 5. Jsh 24:9, 10. Ne 13:2.

altogether blessed. Ge +2:16.

11 **I thought**. Nu 22:17, 37.

the Lord. Mt 19:28-30. Ac 8:20. Ph 3:8. He 11:24-26. 1 P 5:2, 3. 2 J 8.

12 **Spake I**. Nu 22:18, 38. Mt 24:25.

13 **If**. Nu 22:18. Is 33:15.

I cannot go. Nu 22:18. 23:26. 1 K 22:14. 2 K 17:13. 2 Ch 18:13.

good or. Ge 24:50. 31:24. 2 S 13:22. Is 41:23. Je 10:5. Zp 1:12.

of mine own mind. Nu 16:28. Jb 38:36. Je 23:16, 26. Ezk 13:2, 17.

but what. Nu 22:18, 20, 38. Je 1:7, 17. 23:13, 18, 21, 22, 28, 29. Ezk 2:7. 3:17. Ac 5:20. 8:18-23. 2 T 4:2. T 2:15. 2 P 2:15, 16. Ju 11.

14 **I will advertise**. ver. 17. Nu 31:7-18. Mi 6:5. Re 2:10, 14.

the latter. Ge +49:1. Is 24:22.

15 **took up**. ver. 3, 4. Nu +23:7, 18. Mt 13:35. Jn 11:51.

16 **which heard**. ver. 4. 2 S 23:1, 2. 1 C 8:1. 13:2.

Almighty. ver. +4.

17 **I shall see him**. Jb 19:25-27. Zc 12:10. Ju 11, 14, 15. Re 1:7.

come. Mt 16:27. 24:30. 26:64. Mk 13:25, 26. Re 6:13-17.

a Star. Da 12:3. Mt 2:2-9. Re +2:28.

out of Jacob. Ge 35:10-12. Mt 1:2. Lk 1:33. 3:23, 34.

a Sceptre. Ge +49:10. Ps 45:6. 78:70-72. 110:2. Is 9:7. Lk 1:32, 33. 24:27. He 1:8.

Israel. Ge +9:27.

smite the corners of Moab. or, smite through the princes of Moab. 1 S 14:38mg. Zc 10:4.

Moab. 2 K 3:5, 26, 27. Ezk +25:8.

all the children. Ps 72:8-11. Re 11:15.

Sheth. i.e. *set, appointed; tumult*, **S#8352h**. ver. 17. Ge 4:25, 26, Seth. 5:3, 4, 6-8. 1 Ch 1:1.

18 **Edom**. Ge +25:23, 30.

Seir. Ge +14:6.

19 **of Jacob**. Ge 49:10. Ps 2:1-12. 72:10, 11. Is 11:10. Mi 5:2, 4. Mt 28:18. 1 C 15:25. Ep 1:20-22. Ph 2:10, 11. He 1:8. 1 P 3:22. Re 19:16.

shall come. ver. +17. Da 7:13, 14.

shall destroy. Ps 21:7-10. Mt 25:46. Lk 19:12, 27.

20 **the first of the nations**. or, the first of the nations that warred against Israel. Ex 17:8, 14-16.

his latter end. Jg 6:3. 1 S 14:48. Est 3:1. 7:9, 10. 9:14.

shall be that he perish for ever. or, shall be even to destruction. Ex +17:14.

21 **the Kenites**. Ge +15:19. Je 35:5-11.

nest. Jb 29:18.

22 **the Kenite**. Heb. Kain. i.e. *a smith; a fabricator; a nest*, **S#7014h**. ver. +21.

until Asshur shall carry thee away captive. or, how long *shall it be ere* Asshur carry thee away captive? Ge +10:22. 2 Ch 36:17-20.

23 **when God**. Nu 23:23. 2 K 5:1. Je 9:1. La 1:15, 16. Ml 3:2.

24 **Chittim**. i.e. *subduers, hidden*, **S#3794h**. Ge +10:4. Da 7:19, 20. 8:5-8, 21. 10:20.

afflict Asshur. Is 10:12.

and shall afflict Eber. Ge +10:24. Da 9:26, 27. Mt 24:15. Lk 20:24. 23:29-31. Jn 11:48.

and he also. Da 2:35, 45. 7:23-26. 11:45. Re 18:2-24.

25 **returned to**. ver. 11. Nu +31:8.

NUMBERS 25

1 **Shittim**. i.e. *thorns; acacias*, **S#7851h**. Nu 33:49. Jsh 2:1. 3:1. Jl 3:18. Mi 6:5.

the people. Nu 31:15, 16. Ec 7:26. 1 C 10:8.

2 **they called**. Ex 34:15, 16. Jsh 22:17. 1 K 11:1-8. Ps 106:28. Ho 9:10. 1 C 10:20, 27, 28. 2 C 6:16, 17. Re 2:14.

bowed. Ex 20:5. 23:24. Jsh 23:7, 16. 1 K 19:18. Ps 16:4.

3 **joined**. ver. 5. Ex 20:5. Dt 4:3, 4. Jsh 22:17. Ps 106:28, 29. Ho 9:10. 1 C 10:20.

unto. Nu 23:28.

Baal-peor. i.e. *lord of the opening*, **S#1187h**. ver. 5. Dt 4:3, 3. Ps 106:28. Ho 9:10.

the anger. Jsh 22:17. Jg 2:14, 20. Ps 90:11. Je 17:4.

4 **all the heads**. ver. 14, 15, 18. Ex 18:25. Dt 4:3. Jsh 22:17. 23:2.

and hang. Dt 13:6-9, 13, 15. 21:22, 23. 2 S 21:6, 9. Est 7:9, 10.

that the fierce. ver. 11. Dt +32:12.

5 **judges**. Ex +21:6.

Slay ye. Ex 22:20. 32:27, 28. Dt 13:6, 9, 13, 15. 17:3-5. 1 K 18:40. Mt 10:37.

6 **a Midianitish**. **S#4084h**. ver. 14, 15. Nu 22:4. 31:2, 9-16.

in the sight of Moses. Nu 15:30, 31. Dt
29:19-21. Je 3:3. 8:12. 36:23. 42:15-18. 43:4-
7. 44:16, 17. 2 P 2:13-15. Ju 13.
weeping. Jg 2:4. Ezr 9:1-4. 10:6-9. Is 22:12.
Ezk 9:4-6. Jl 2:17.

7 **Phinehas**. Ex +6:25.
a javelin. 1 S 18:10, 11. 19:9.

8 **thrust**. ver. 5, 11, 14. Ps 106:29-31.
So the plague. Nu +16:48.

9 **that died**. ver. 4, 5. Nu 16:49, 50. 31:16. Dt
4:3, 4. 1 C 10:8.

11 **turned my**. Jsh 7:25, 26. 2 S 21:14. Ps
106:23. Jn 3:36.
for my sake. Heb. with my zeal. 2 C 11:2.
my jealousy. Ex +20:5. Ezk 16:38.

12 **I give**. Nu 18:1. Ne 13:29. Ml 2:4, 5. 3:1. Ro
5:11. Ep 2:13, 14. He 2:17.

13 **his seed**. 1 S 2:30. 1 K 2:27. 1 Ch 6:4-15, 50-
53.
an everlasting. Heb. *olam*, Ge +17:7. Ex
40:15. Is 61:6. Je 33:17, 22. He 7:11, 17, 18. 1
P 2:5, 9. Re 1:6.
zealous. 1 K 19:10, 14. Ps 69:9. 106:31.
119:139. Jn 2:17. Ac 22:3-5. Ro 10:2-4.
atonement. Le +4:20. Jsh 7:12.

14 **Israelite**. S#3481h. Le 24:10. 2 S 17:25.
Zimri. 1 Ch 2:6.
Salu. i.e. *valued; weighed*, S#5543h. 1 Ch 9:7 &
Ne 11:7, Sallu. Ne 12:7, Sallu. 11:8 & 12:20,
Sallai.
a prince. ver. 4, 5. 2 Ch 19:7.
chief house. Heb. house of a father. ver. 15.
Dt 28:41.
the Simeonites. S#8099h. Nu 1:23. 26:14. Jsh
21:4. 1 Ch 27:16.

15 **Cozbi**. i.e. *lying; false*, S#3579h. ver. 18.
Zur. i.e. *a rock; to besiege*, S#6698h. Nu 31:8. Jsh
13:21. 1 Ch 8:30. 9:36.

17 **Vex**. Nu 31:2. Re 18:6.

18 **vex you**. Nu 31:15, 16. Ge 26:10. Ex 32:21,
35. Re 2:14.
beguiled. Ge 3:13. 2 C 11:3. 2 P 2:14, 15, 18.
which. ver. 8.
Peor's. Nu 23:28.

NUMBERS 26

1 **after the plague**. Nu 25:9.

2 **Take the sum**. Nu 1:2, 3. Ex 30:12. 38:25,
26. Jsh +14:2.

3 **plains of Moab**. ver. 63. Dt 4:46-49. 34:6, 8.
Jericho. Nu +22:1.

4 **commanded**. Nu 1:1-3. Ex 30:12-16. 1 Ch
21:1.

5 **the eldest**. Ge +29:32.
the children. Ge 46:8, 9. Ex 6:14. 1 Ch 5:1-
3.
Hanoch. Ge +25:4.
Hanochites. S#2599h.
Pallu. i.e. *wonderful; distinguished; separated*,

S#6396h. ver. 8. Ge 46:9. Ex 6:14. 1 Ch 5:3.
Palluites. S#6384h.

6 **Hezronites**. S#2697h. ver. 21.
Carmites. S#3757h.

7 **Reubenites**. S#7206h. Nu 34:14. Dt 3:12, 16.
4:43. 29:8. Jsh 1:12. 12:6. 13:8. 22:1. 2 K
10:33. 1 Ch 5:6, 26. 11:42. 12:37. 26:32.
27:16.
forty and three. ver. 1, 21. Nu 2:11. Ge
46:8, 9.

9 **famous**. Nu 1:16. 16:1, 2, etc. Ps 106:17. Ju
11.

10 **earth opened**. Nu 16:2, 31-35, 38. 27:3. Ex
16:35. Ps 106:17, 18.
they became a sign. Nu 16:38. 1 S 2:34. 1 K
13:3. Je 29:22. 44:29. Ezk 14:8. 1 C 10:6-11. 2
P 2:6. Ju 7.

11 **died not**. Nu 16:5, 27, 31-33. Ge +36:5. Ps
ch. 42, 44, 45, etc. Titles.

12 **Nemuel**. i.e. *day of God; circumcised of God*,
S#5241h. ver. 9. Ge 46:10. Ex 6:15, Jemuel. 1
Ch 4:24.
Nemuelites. S#5242h.
Jamin. Ge +46:10.
Jamites. S#3228h.
Jachin. 1 K 7:21. 1 Ch 4:24, Jarib.
Jachinites. S#3200h.

13 **Zerah**. Ge 46:10, Zohar.
Zarhites. S#2227h. ver. 20. Jsh 7:17, 17. 1 Ch
27:11, 13.
Shaulites. S#7587h.

14 **Simeonites**. Nu +1:6. +25:14.

15 **Zephon**. i.e. *watchfulness; watching, looking
out*, S#6827h. Nu 2:14. Ge 46:16, Ziphion,
Haggai, Shuni, Ezbon, Eri, Arodi, Areli.
Zephonites. S#6831h.
Haggites. S#2291h.
Shunites. S#7765h.

16 **Ozni**. *or*, Ezbon. i.e. *hearing; having ears*,
S#244h. Ge 46:16.
Oznites. S#244h.
Erites. S#6180h.

17 **Arod**. i.e. *a wild ass; I shall subdue; I shall roam*,
S#720h. Ge 46:16, Arodi.
Arodites. S#722h. Ge 46:16, Arodi.
Arelites. S#692h. Ge 46:16, Areli.

18 **forty thousand and**. Nu 1:24, 25. 2:14, 15.
1 Ch 5:11-17.

19 **Er and Onan**. Ge 38:1-10. 46:12. 1 Ch 2:3,
etc.

20 **Shelah**. Ge +38:5.
Shelanites. S#8024h.
Pharez. Ge +46:12.
Pharzites. Some editions read *Pharezites*.
S#6558h.
Zerah. Ge +36:13.

21 **Hamulites**. S#2539h.

22 **threescore and**. Nu +1:27. Ge +35:23. Ps
115:14.

23 **sons of Issachar**. Nu +1:29. Ge +30:18.

Tolaites. S#8440h.

Pua. *or*, Phuvah. i.e. *mouth*, S#6312h. Ge 46:13.

Punites. S#6324h.

24 **Jashub**. *or*, Job. i.e. *inhabited; he turns; he will return*, S#3437h. Ge 46:13. 1 Ch 7:1. Ezr 10:29.

Jashubites. S#3432h.

Shimronites. S#8117h.

25 **threescore**. Nu 1:28, 29. 2:5, 6.

26 **sons of Zebulun**. Ge +30:20.

Sered. i.e. *fear, humbling*, S#5624h. Ge 46:14.

Sardites. i.e. *dissension*, S#5625h.

Elonites. S#440h.

Jahleelites. S#3178h.

27 **Zebulunites**. S#2075h. Jg 12:11, 12.

threescore thousand. Nu 1:30, 31. 2:7, 8.

28 **sons of Joseph**. Ge 41:51, 52. 46:20. 48:5, 13-20.

29 **Manasseh**. Ge +41:51.

Machir. Ge +50:23.

Machirites. S#4354h.

Gilead. i.e. *heap of testimony*, S#1568h. ver. 30. Nu 27:1. 36:1. Ge 31:48mg. +37:25. Jsh 17:1, 3. 1 Ch 2:21, 23. 7:14, 17.

Gileadites. S#1569h. Jg 10:3. 11:1, 40. 12:7. 2 S 17:27. 19:31. 1 K 2:7. 2 K 15:25. Ezr 2:61. Ne 7:63.

30 **Jeezer**. i.e. *where is help?* or *there is no help, helpless*, S#372h. called Abiezer. Jsh 17:2. Jg 6:11, 24, 34. 8:2.

Jeezerites. S#373h.

Helek. i.e. *a portion, share*, S#2507h. Jsh 17:2.

Helekites. S#2516h.

31 **Asriel**. i.e. *a binding of God; vow of God*, S#844h. Jsh 17:2. 1 Ch 7:14.

Asrielites. S#845h.

Shechemites. S#7930h.

32 **Shemida**. i.e. *fame of knowledge*, S#8061h. Jsh 17:2. 1 Ch 7:19.

Shemidaites. S#8062h.

Hepher. i.e. *a digging; pit; well*, S#2660h. ver. 33. Nu 27:1. Jsh 17:2, 3. 1 Ch 4:6. 11:36. Also Jsh 12:17. 19:13. 1 K 4:10. 2 K 14:25.

Hepherites. S#2662h.

33 **Zelophehad**. i.e. *first rupture; first breach; being burnt*, S#6765h. Nu 27:1, 7. 36:2, 6, 10, 11. Jsh 17:3. 1 Ch 7:15, 15.

Mahlah. i.e. *disease, sickness*, S#4244h. Nu 27:1. 36:11. Jsh 17:3. 1 Ch 7:18.

Noah. i.e. *wandering*, S#5270h. Nu 27:1. 36:11. Jsh 17:3.

Hoglah. i.e. *a partridge*, S#2295h. Nu 27:1. 36:11. Jsh 17:3.

Milcah. i.e. *queen; counsel*, Ge +11:29.

Tirzah. i.e. *pleasure; charm; she will delight; willing*, S#8656h. Nu 27:1. Jsh 12:24. 17:3. 1 K 14:17. 15:21, 33. 16:6, 8, 15, 17, 23. 2 K 15:14, 16. SS 6:4.

34 **fifty and two thousand**. Nu 1:34, 35. 2:20, 21.

35 **Shuthalhites**. S#8364h.

Becher. Ge +46:21. 1 Ch 7:20, 21. Bered. Tahath. Eladah. Tahath.

Tahan. 1 Ch +7:25.

Tahanites. S#8470h.

36 **Eran**. i.e. *watcher; watchful*, S#6197h.

Eranites. S#6198h.

37 **thirty and two thousand**. Nu 1:32, 33. 2:18, 19.

38 **sons of Benjamin**. Ge 46:21. 1 Ch 7:6-12.

Bela. Ge +46:21.

Belaites. S#1108h.

Ashbel. Ge +46:21.

Ashbelites. S#789h.

Ahiram. i.e. *my brother is high*, S#297h. Ge 46:2.

Ahiramites. S#298h.

Ehi. 1 Ch 8:1, Aharah.

39 **Shupham**. i.e. *serpent-like; bareness*, S#8197h.

Hupham. i.e. *inhabitant of a haven*, S#2349h. Ge 46:21, Muppim, and Huppim.

Huphamites. S#2350h.

40 **Ard**. i.e. *a fugitive*, S#714h. He is called son of Benjamin in Ge +46:21, and grandson of Benjamin in Nu 26:40. In 1 Ch 8:3 he is called Addar.

and Naaman. i.e. *pleasant*. Ge +46:21.

Ardites. S#716h.

Naamites. S#5280h.

41 **forty and five**. Nu 1:36, 37. 2:22, 23. Ge 46:21.

42 **Shuham**. i.e. *pit digger; sink humbly*, S#7748h. Ge 46:23, Hushim.

Shuhamites. S#7749h. ver. 43.

43 **threescore and four**. Nu 1:38, 39. 2:25, 26.

44 **the children of Asher**. Ge 46:17, Jimnah. Ishuah. Isui. 1 Ch 7:30, Imnah. Isuah. Ishuai.

Jimnah. i.e. *prosperity*, S#3232h. Ge 46:17, Jimnah.

Jimnites. S#3232h.

Jesui. i.e. *equal, level*, S#3440h. Ge 46:17. 1 S 14:49. 1 Ch 7:30.

Jesuites. S#3441h.

Beriah. i.e. *in evil*. 1 Ch +7:23.

Beriites. S#1284h.

45 **Heberites**. S#2277h.

Malchielites. S#4440h.

46 **Sarah**. Ge 46:17, Serah.

47 **fifty and three**. Nu 1:40, 41. 2:27, 28.

48 **the sons of Naphtali**. Ge +30:8.

Jahzeel. Ge +46:24.

Jahzeelites. S#3184h.

Guni. Ge +46:24.

Gunites. S#1477h.

49 **Jezer**. Ge +46:24.

Jezerites. S#3340h. 1 Ch 25:11, Izri.

Shillem. Ge +46:24. 1 Ch 7:13, Shallum.

Shillemites. S#8016h.

50 **forty and five**. Nu 1:42, 43. 2:29, 30.

51 **six hundred thousand and**. Ex +12:37. Ge

46:26, 27. Ne 9:23. Jb 12:9, 10, 14, 20-23. Ps 77:20.

53 Unto these. Ge 12:2, 7. Jsh 11:23. 14:4. Ps 49:14. 105:44. Ezk 47:22. Da 7:27. Mt +5:5. Re +5:10. 21:27.

54 many. Nu 32:3, 5. 33:54. Jsh 17:14.
give the more. Heb. multiply his.
give the less. Heb. diminish his. Nu 33:54. 35:8.
according to. Ex 16:18. Jsh 11:23. Mt 25:15-28. Lk 19:13-25. 1 C 15:41. 2 C 8:15.

55 by lot. ver. 56. Jsh 11:23. +14:2. +17:14. 18:6, 10, 11. 19:1, 10, 17, 24, 32, 40. Col 1:12. Re 7:4-8.

56 the lot. lit. mouth of the lot. ver. +55. Jsh 18:10. 21:8. Ro 11:7. 1 C 12:4.

57 these are. Nu 35:2, 3. Ge +46:11.
of Gershon. Nu +3:21.
Merarites. S#4848h.

58 Libnites. Nu 3:17-21. 16:1.
Korathites. S#7145h. 1 Ch +9:19, Korahites.

59 Jochebed. Ex 2:1, 2. 6:20. Le 18:12.

60 unto Aaron. Nu 3:2, 8.

61 Nadab and. Nu 3:4. Le 10:1, 2. 1 Ch 24:1, 2.

62 those that. Nu 1:49. 3:39. 4:47, 48. 18:20-24. 35:2-8. Dt 10:9. 14:27-29. 18:1, 2. Jsh 13:14, 33. 14:3.
they were not. Nu +1:49.
because. Nu 18:20-24. 35:2-8. Dt 10:9. 14:27-29. 18:1, 2. Jsh 13:14, 33. 14:3.

63 numbered by. ver. 3.

64 there was not. Nu ch. 1, 2. Dt 2:14, 15. 4:3, 4. 1 C 10:5.

65 They shall. Nu 14:23, 24, 28-30, 35, 38. Ex 12:37. Dt 2:14, 15. 32:49, 50. Ps 90:3-7. Ro 11:22. 1 C 10:5, 6. He 3:17, 18. Ju 5.
surely. Ge +2:16.
save Caleb. Nu +14:30, 38. Is 46:11. 55:11. Ml 3:18.

NUMBERS 27

1 Zelophehad. Nu 26:33. 36:1-12. Jsh 17:3-6. 1 Ch 7:15. Ga 3:28.
these are the names. Is 49:14-16. Jn 10:3. He 12:23.

2 they stood. Nu 15:33, 34. Ex 18:13, 14, 19-26. 28:29. Dt 17:8-10. He 12:23.

3 died in the. Nu 14:35. 26:64, 65. Ju 5.
in the company. Nu 16:1-3, 19, 32-35, 49. 26:9, 10.
died in his. Ezk 18:4. Jn 8:21, 24. Ro 5:12, 21. 6:23.

4 Why. Ex 32:11. Ps 109:13. Pr 13:9.
done away. Heb. diminished. Nu 36:3.
Give. Jsh 17:4.

5 Moses brought. Nu 15:34. Ex 18:15-19. 25:22. Le 24:12, 13. Jb 23:4. Pr 3:5, 6. 1 J 2:1.

6 the Lord spake. Ps 68:5, 6. Ga 3:28.

7 thou shalt. Nu 36:1, 2. Jsh 17:4. Ps 68:5. Is

56:4-7. Je 49:11. Jn 17:12. Ac 20:32. 26:18. Ga 3:28, 29. Ep 1:9-11, 13, 14. 2:12, 13. Col 1:12. He 9:15. 1 P 1:4, 5.

11 kinsman. Le 25:25, 49. Ru 4:3-6. Je 32:8.
a statute. Nu 35:29. 1 S 30:25.
as the Lord commanded. Ps 2:7, 8. He 1:1, 2.

12 mount. Nu 33:47, 48. Dt 3:27. 32:49. 34:1-4.
Abarim. i.e. *the places beyond; the passages; regions beyond*, S#5682h. Nu 33:47, 48. Dt 32:49. Je 22:20.

13 And when. Dt 31:2. 34:4.
thou also. Nu 31:2. Ge +25:8, 17.
as Aaron. Nu 20:24-28. 33:38. Dt 10:6. 32:50.

14 ye rebelled. Nu 20:8-13. Dt 1:37. 32:51, 52. Ps 106:32, 33.
Mirabah. Nu 20:1, 13, 24. Ex 17:7.

16 the Lord. Nu 16:22. Jb 12:10.
the God. Nu +16:22. Ec +12:7. Zc +12:1. He +12:9.
spirits. Heb. *ruach*, Nu +16:22.
set a man. Nu 13:8, 16. Dt 31:14. 1 S 12:13. 1 K 5:5. Je 3:15. 23:4, 5. Ezk 34:11-16, 23. 37:24. Mt 9:38. Jn 10:11. Jn 14:16-18. Ac 20:28. 1 P 5:2-4.

17 go out. ver. 21. Dt 31:1, 2. 1 S 8:20. 18:13. 2 S 5:2. 1 K 3:7. 2 Ch 1:10. Ps 121:8. Is 37:28. Jn 10:3, 4, 9. Ac 1:21. 2 P 1:14, 15.
lead. Ps 77:20. 78:52. Jn 14:16-18.
as sheep. Ge 49:22-24. 1 K 22:17. 2 Ch 18:16. Ps 80:1. 119:176. Is 40:11. Je 23:1, 2. 50:6, 17. Ezk 34:5. Zc 10:2. 13:7. Mt 9:36. 10:6. 15:24. 18:12. Mk 6:34. Lk 15:4. Jn +10:11-16. He 4:8. 13:20. 1 P 2:24, 25. 5:4.

18 Take thee. Nu +11:28. 13:8, 16. Ex 17:9. Dt 3:28. 31:7, 8, 23. 34:9.
a man. Nu 11:17. Ge 41:38. Jg 3:10. 11:29. 1 S 16:13, 14, 18. Is 63:11. Da 5:14. Jn 3:34. Ac 6:3. 1 C 12:4-11.
spirit. Heb. *ruach*, Ge +41:38.
lay. ver. 23. Ac +8:17.

19 give him. Lk 9:1-5. 10:2-11. Ac 20:28-31. Col 4:17. 1 Th +2:11.

20 put some. Nu 11:17, 28, 29. 1 S 10:6, 9. 2 K 2:9, 10, 15. 1 Ch 29:23, 25.
may be. Jsh 1:16-18.

21 he shall. Jsh 9:14. Jg 1:1. 20:18, 23, 26-28. 1 S 22:10. 23:9. 28:6. 30:7.
Eleazar. Ex +6:23.
shall ask. Jsh 9:14. 1 S 23:9-12. Ps 73:24. Pr 3:5, 6. Is 28:29.
Urim. Ex +28:30.
at his word. ver. 17. Jsh 9:14. 1 S 22:10-15.
go out. ver. +17. Jg 1:1. 20:18, 23.

23 gave. ver. +19. Dt 3:28. Jsh 1:1-9. 3:7.

NUMBERS 28

2 my bread. Ge +3:19. Le 2:1, 2. 3:11. 21:6, 8. Ml 1:7, 12. Jn 6:35, 48.

for a sweet savor unto me. Heb. savor of my rest. Ge +8:21.

in their due season. Nu 9:2, 3, 7, 13. Ge +17:21. Ex 23:15. Ps 81:3. Mt +24:45. Lk 12:42. 1 C 11:20-26. 14:40.

3 **two lambs**. Ge 22:8. Ex 29:38, 39. Le 1:1, 2, 10-13. 6:9. Is 53:7. Ezk 46:13-15. Jn 1:29. Jn 8:46. 14:30. 1 P 1:19, 20. 2:22. He 4:15. 9:14. Re 13:8.

day by day. Heb. in a day. ver. 24. Ex 29:36, 38. Da 8:13. 11:31. 12:11.

4 **one lamb**. Jn 1:29. Re 13:8. 21:23.

and the other. 1 K 18:29, 36. Ezr 9:4, 5. Ps 141:2. Da 9:21.

at even. Heb. between the two evenings. ver. 8. Nu 9:3. Ex 12:6mg. 1 K 18:29, 30. 2 Ch 13:10, 11. Ps 55:17. 141:2.

5 **a tenth**. Nu 15:4, 5. Ex 16:36. 29:38-42. Le 2:1.

meat offering. Le +23:13.

6 **a continual**. ver. 10, 23. Ex +29:42. Le 6:9. 2 Ch 2:4. 31:3. Ezr 3:4. Ezk 46:14. Am 5:25.

was ordained. Ex 24:18. 29:38-42. 31:18.

7 **drink offering**. Le +23:13.

in the holy. Ex 29:42.

to be poured. ver. 14, 31. Le +23:13.

8 **sacrifice**. He 7:24-27. 1 P 1:18, 19.

9 **sabbath**. Ex +20:8-11. 34:21. Le 19:3. 23:3. Ne 13:15-22. Ps 92:1-4. Is 56:2. +58:13, 14. Ezk 20:12. 46:4. Mt 12:5. Mk 2:23-28. He 4:3-5, 9. Re +1:10.

10 **the burnt offering**. Le +23:12.

the continual. ver. +6.

drink offering. Le +23:13.

11 **in the beginnings**. Nu 15:3-11. Ps 40:6-8. Col +2:16.

two young. ver. 19.

12 **three tenth deals**. Nu 15:4-12. 29:10. Ezk 46:5-7.

13 **for a burnt**. ver. 2.

15 **one kid**. ver. 22. Nu 15:24. Le 4:23. 16:15. Ro 8:3. 2 C 5:21.

sin offering. Le +23:19.

beside. ver. 3, 10, 11.

burnt offering. Le +23:12. Zc 13:7. Lk 24:46.

drink offering. Le +23:13.

16 **the fourteenth**. Nu 9:3-5. Ex 12:2-11, 18, 43-49. Le 23:5-8. Dt 16:1-8. Ezk 45:21-24. Mt 26:2, 17. Lk 22:7. Ac 12:3, 4. 1 C 5:7, 8.

passover. Le +23:5.

17 **the fifteenth**. Ex 12:15-17. 13:6. 34:18. Dt 16:1-8.

unleavened. Le +23:6. Mt 26:2, 19, 26-29. 1 C 5:7, 8.

18 **the first**. Ex 12:16. Le 23:7, 8.

holy convocation. Ge 49:10. Le 23:1, 2. He 12:23. Re 7:9.

19 **two young**. Ezk 45:21-25. He 10:10-14.

they shall. ver. 31. Nu 29:8. Le 22:20. Dt 15:21. Ml 1:13, 14. 1 P 1:19.

22 **one goat**. ver. +15.

23 **beside**. ver. 3, 10.

25 **on the seventh**. Ex 12:16. 13:6. Le 23:8.

ye shall do. ver. 18, 26. Nu 29:1, 12, 35. Le 23:3, 8, 21, 25, 35, 36.

26 **in the day**. Ex 23:16. 34:22.

firstfruits. Le +23:10. Ac 2:1, etc.

after your weeks. Le +23:16.

convocation. He 10:25.

27 **two young**. ver. 11, 19. Le 23:18, 19.

sweet savor. Ep 5:2.

seven. Ge 4:15. 8:20, 21. Ps 79:12. Pr 6:31.

30 **one kid**. ver. 15, 22. Nu 15:24. 2 C 5:19, 21. Ga 3:13. 1 P 2:24. 3:18.

31 **without blemish**. ver. 19. Ml 1:13, 14.

NUMBERS 29

1 **the seventh**. Le 23:24, 25. Ezr 3:6. Ne 7:73.

the first day of the month. Col 2:16.

blowing. Nu 10:1-10. 1 Ch 15:28. Ps 81:3. 89:15. Is 27:13. Zc 9:14. Mk 16:15, 16. Ro 10:14-18. 15:16-19. He 12:25.

trumpets. Le +23:24.

2 **sweet savor**. Ge +8:21.

one young. ver. 8, 36. Nu 28:19, 27. Le 1:2-13. He 10:10-14.

lambs. Re 5:6.

without blemish. 1 P 1:19.

3 **meat offering**. Le +23:13.

flour. Nu 28:5.

mingled with oil. Ps 45:7, 8. Ac 10:4. Ep 2:18. He 9:14.

tenth deals. Ex 16:36.

5 **one kid**. Nu 28:15, 22, 30. Le 4:1-12, 22, 23, 27, 28. Zc 13:1. Jn 19:16-18. He 13:11, 12.

6 **the burnt offering**. Le +23:12.

of the month. Nu 28:11-15.

meat offering. Le +23:13.

the daily. Ex +29:42. Le 6:9.

drink offerings. Le +23:13. Ps 104:15. Jn 15:1.

according. ver. 18, 21. Nu 9:14. 15:11, 12, 24. Ezr 3:4.

sweet savor. Ep 5:2.

a sacrifice. He 9:22.

by fire. Nu 28:3-7.

7 **on the tenth**. Le 16:29-31. 23:27.

afflict. Nu 30:13. Le 16:29, 31. 23:27, 29, 32. Ezr 8:21. Ps 35:13mg. 69:10. 126:5, 6. Is 22:12. 53:6. 58:3-5. Da 10:3, 12. Zc 7:3. 12:10. Mt 5:4. Lk 13:3, 5. Ac 27:9. Ro 6:6. 1 C 7:5. 9:27. 15:56, 57. 2 C 7:9-11. Ga 2:20. 5:24. Ph 3:10. Ja 4:8-10. 1 P 4:13. 1 J 2:2.

souls. Heb. *nephesh*, Ge +27:31.

8 **without blemish**. ver. 2, 13. Nu 28:19.

9 **meat offering**. Nu 15:3-12. Le +23:13.

11 **sin offering**. Le +23:19.

beside. Le 16:3, 5, 9. Is 53:10. Da 9:24-26. He 7:27. 9:25-28.

atonement. Le +23:27. Jn 10:18. Ro 8:32. Ga 2:20.
the continual. ver. +6.
burnt offering. Le +23:12.
meat offering. Le +23:13.
drink offerings. Le +23:13.

12 **the fifteenth day**. Le +23:34. Jn 1:14. He 11:9-13.

13 **thirteen young bullocks**. ver. 2, 8. Nu 28:11, 19, 27. Ezr 3:4. He 10:12-14.

14 **oil**. Ezr 3:4. Ezk 45:25. He +2:10.

16 **one kid**. ver. 11.

17 **twelve**. ver. 13, 20, etc. Ps 40:6. 50:8, 9. 51:16, 17. 69:31. Is 1:11. Je 7:22, 23. Ho 6:6. Ro 12:1. He 8:13. 9:3-14.

18 **after the manner**. That is, *after the manner* already prescribed. ver. 3, 4, 6, 9, 10. Nu 15:4-12. 28:7, 14. Ezr 3:4.

19 **sin offering**. ver. 11, 22, 25. Am 8:14. Mk 10:45. 1 P 3:18.
continual. He 13:15.

20 **without blemish**. Jb 33:24. Ro 4:7, 8. 2 C 5:21.

21 **after the manner**. ver. 18.

22 **drink offering**. Ps 16:4. Jl 1:9, 13. 2:14.

23 **without blemish**. Ps 32:1. 1 T 2:5, 6.

25 **continual burnt**. ver. 11. Jn 8:31. Ac 13:43. Ro 2:7. Ga 2:5. 6:9. 2 Th 3:13. He 3:14. 10:39. 13:15.

26 **without spot**. Jb 15:15. He 1:2, 3. 1 J 2:1, 2.

29 **without blemish**. Jn 1:29. Ga 1:4. Ac 4:27, 28.

32 **seven**. Nu +23:1.
without blemish. He 9:26-28.

35 **eighth day**. Le 23:36. 1 S 7:6. Is 12:3. Jn 7:37-39. Ga 4:4. 1 T 3:16. Re 1:5, 6. 7:9-17. 13:8.

39 **do**. *or*, offer. He 9:11-14. 10:10-12. 1 J 1:7.
in your set feasts. Le 23:2. 1 Ch 23:31. 2 Ch 31:3. Ezr 3:5. Ne 10:33. Is 1:14. Da 9:24.
beside your vows. Le +23:38. 1 C 10:31.
freewill offerings. Le +23:38.
burnt offerings. Le +23:12.
meat offerings. Le +23:13.
drink offerings. Le +23:13.
peace offerings. Le +23:19.

40 **Moses told**. Ex 40:16. Dt 4:5. Mt 28:20. Jn 1:17. Ac 20:27. 1 C +15:3. He 3:2, 5.

NUMBERS 30

1 **the heads**. Nu 1:4-16. 7:2. 34:17-28. Ex 18:25. Dt 1:3-17.

2 **If a man**. Le 27:2.
vow a vow. Nu 21:2. Le +23:38. 27:2, etc. Jsh 9:3-6, 14, 15. Jg 11:11, 30, 31, 35, 36, 39. 1 S 14:24-27, 37-44. Ps 15:4. 119:106. Pr 20:25. Mt 14:9. Ac 23:14.
swear. Ex +20:7. Le 5:4. Mt 5:33, 34. 14:7-9. Ac 18:18. +23:12. 2 C 1:23. 9:9-11.

to bind. ver. 3, 4, 10. Mt 23:16, 18. Ac 23:12, 14, 21.
soul. Heb. *nephesh*, Ge +27:31.
break. Heb. profane. Ps 55:20mg.
he shall do. Jb 22:27. Ps 22:25. 50:14. 66:13, 14. 116:14, 18. Ec 5:4, 5. Ezk 17:18. Na 1:15.

3 **woman**. Est 1:17-20. Pr 7:14. 1 C +14:34.

4 **her father**. Ep 6:1-3. Col 3:20. 1 T 3:4. He 12:5, 6.
hear. ver. 2. Le 27:2.
her bond. ver. +2.
soul. Heb. *nephesh*, Ge +27:31.

5 **her father**. Ho 6:6. Mt 15:4-6. Mk 7:10-13. Ep 6:1.
disallow. ver. 8, 12, 15. **S#5106h**. ver. 5, 8, 11. 32:7 (discourage), 7, 9. Ps 33:10 (maketh of none effect). 141:5 (shall break).
soul. Heb. *nephesh*, Ge +27:31.

6 **she vowed**. Heb. her vows *were* upon her. ver. 8. Ps 56:12.
soul. Heb. *nephesh*, Ge +27:31.

7 **held his peace**. 1 S 1:21-23.
soul. Heb. *nephesh*, Ge +27:31.

8 **her husband**. Ge 3:16. 1 C 7:4. 14:34. Ep 5:22-24, 33. Col 3:18. 1 T 2:11-14.
soul. Heb. *nephesh*, Ge +27:31.

9 **a widow**. Le 21:7. Lk 2:37. Ro 7:2.
souls. Heb. *nephesh*, Ge +27:31.

10 **soul**. Heb. *nephesh*, Ge +27:31.

11 **soul**. Heb. *nephesh*, Ge +27:31.

12 **utterly**. Ge +2:16.
her husband hath made. 1 C 11:3.
soul. Heb. *nephesh*, Ge +27:31.
and the Lord. ver. 5, 8. Nu 15:25, 28.

13 **and every**. Ge +3:16. 1 C 11:3, 9. 1 P 3:1-6.
to afflict. Nu +29:7.
soul. Heb. *nephesh*, Ge +27:31.

14 **her husband**. ver. 7.

15 **he shall bear**. ver. 5, 8, 12. Le 5:1, 4-10. Ga 3:28. He 9:22.

16 **the statutes**. Nu 5:29, 30. Le 11:46, 47. 13:59. 14:54-57. 15:32, 33.

NUMBERS 31

2 **Avenge**. ver. 3. Nu 25:17, 18. Dt +32:35. Jg 16:24, 28-30. Ro +12:19.
the Midianites. Ge +25:2.
gathered. Ge +25:8. Ac 7:59. 2 T 4:6, 7.

3 **Arm some**. Ex 17:9-13. Je 25:31. Lk +22:36, 38.
avenge the Lord. Nu 25:11, 13. Ex 17:16. Le 26:25. Jg 5:2, 23. 2 K 9:7. 10:30. Je 46:10. 50:28. Ho 4:1, 2.

4 **Of every tribe a thousand**. Heb. A thousand of a tribe, a thousand of a tribe.
a thousand. Le 26:8. Jg 7:2. 1 S 14:6.

6 **Phinehas**. Ex +6:25.
the holy instruments. Nu 14:44. 33:20-22.

Ex 25:9. Jsh 6:4-6, 13-15. 1 S 4:4, 5, 17. 14:18. 23:9. 2 S 11:11.

to blow. Nu 10:2, 8, 9. 2 Ch 13:12-15.

7 **all.** Dt 20:13, 14. Jg 21:11. 1 S 27:9. 1 K 11:15, 16.

the males. Jg 6:1, 2, 33.

8 **the kings.** Nu 22:4. Jsh 13:21, 22.

Evi. i.e. *desire*, **S#189h.** Jsh 13:21.

Zur. Nu 25:15, 18.

Reba. i.e. *a fourth part*, **S#7254h.** Jsh 13:21.

Balaam. ver. 16. Nu 22:7, 10. 24:25. Dt 23:4, 5. Jsh 13:21, 22. 24:9, 10. Jg 11:25. Ne 13:2. Ps 9:16. 10:2. 34:21. 37:7-10, 12-15, 20, 34-36. 109:28. 119:118, 119. 139:19. Pr 10:25. 11:5-7. Mi 6:5. 1 T 6:9, 10. 2 P +2:15. Ju 11. Re 2:14. 19:20.

9 **the women.** ver. 15, 16. Dt 20:14. 2 Ch 28:5, 8-10.

little ones. ver. 17. Nu +16:27.

10 **burnt all.** Jsh 6:24. 1 S 30:1. 1 K 9:16. Is 1:7. Re 18:8.

11 **took.** Dt 20:10-18. Jsh 8:2.

12 **the plains of Moab.** Nu +22:1.

13 **went forth.** Ge 14:17. 1 S 15:12. 30:21.

without the camp. ver. 12, 22-24. Nu 5:2. 19:11.

14 **wroth.** Nu 12:3. Ex 32:19, 22. Le 10:16. 1 S 15:13, 14. 1 K 20:42. 2 K 13:19. Ep 4:26.

thousands. Jsh +22:21.

battle. Heb. host of war.

15 **Have ye saved.** Dt 2:34. 20:13, 16-18. Jsh 6:21. 8:25. 10:40. 11:14. 1 S 15:3. Ps 137:8, 9. Je 48:10. Ezk 9:6.

16 **these caused.** Nu 24:14. 25:1-3. Pr 23:27. Ec 7:26. 2 P 2:15. Re 2:14.

in the matter. Nu 25:18. Dt 4:3. Jsh 22:17.

and there. Nu 25:9.

17 **kill every male.** Ge 18:25. Jg 21:11, 12.

known. Ge +4:1, 17. Ex +34:15.

him. Heb. a male.

18 **keep alive for yourselves.** Le 25:44. Dt 20:14. 21:10-14. 2 Ch 28:8-10. Is 14:2.

known. Ge +4:1, 17. Ex +34:15.

19 **abide.** Nu 5:2. 19:11-18. 1 Ch 22:8.

any person. Heb. *nephesh*, Jsh +10:28.

20 **raiment.** Nu 19:14-16, 22. Ge 35:2. Ex 19:10.

that is made. Heb. instrument, *or*, vessel.

21 **the ordinance.** Nu +30:16.

23 **abide.** Is 43:2. Zc 13:9. Ml 2:2, 3. Mt 3:11. 1 C 3:13-15. 1 P 1:7. 4:12. 2 P 3:5-7. Re 3:18.

it shall be purified. Nu 8:7. 19:9, 17.

ye shall make. Le 11:32. 15:17. Ep 5:26. T 3:5, 6. 1 P 3:21.

24 **wash.** Nu 19:19, 20. Le 11:25. 14:9. 15:13.

26 **that was taken.** Heb. of the captivity. Is +49:25mg. Am 4:10mg.

27 **two parts.** Jsh 22:8. 1 S 30:4, 24, 25. Ps 68:12.

28 **levy.** Ge 14:20. Jsh 6:19, 24. 2 S 8:11, 12. 1

Ch 18:11. 26:26, 27. Pr 3:9, 10. Is 18:7. 23:18. 60:9. Mt 22:21.

one soul. Heb. *nephesh*, Ge +2:19. ver. 30, 47. Nu 18:26. Ge 1:21, 24. +2:19. 9:4.

29 **an heave offering.** Le +7:14. Dt 12:12, 19.

30 **one portion.** ver. 42-47.

flocks. *or*, goats. ver. 28. Ex 12:21.

and give. ver. 28. Nu 18:24-28. 1 C 9:13, 14.

keep the. Nu 3:7, 8, 25, 31, 36, etc. 18:1-5, 23, 26. 1 Ch 9:27-29. 23:32. 26:20-27. Ac 20:28. 1 C 4:2. Col 4:17. He 13:17.

32 **the prey.** Nu 23:24. Dt 32:35, 39-43. Na 1:2, 3.

35 **persons.** Heb. *nephesh*, souls, Ge +12:5.

40 **the persons.** Heb. *nephesh*, souls, Ge +12:5.

two persons. Heb. *nephesh*, souls, Ge +12:5.

41 **heave offering.** Le +7:14.

Eleazar. ver. 29-31. Nu 18:8, 14, 19, 20. Mt 10:10. 1 C 9:10-14. Ga 6:6. 1 T 5:17. He 7:4-6, 9-12.

46 **persons.** Heb. *nephesh*, souls, Ge +12:5.

47 **the Levites.** Nu 18:21-24. Dt 12:17-19. Lk 10:1-8. 1 Th 5:12, 13.

kept the charge. ver. +30. Ps 134:1. Is 56:10, 11.

49 **charge.** Heb. hand.

lacketh. Nu 23:23. 1 S 30:18, 19. Ps 72:14. Is 49:24, 25. Mi 5:15. Jn 18:9.

50 **therefore brought an oblation.** Ps 107:15, 21, 22. 116:12, 17.

gotten. Heb. found.

an atonement. Ex 30:12, 15, 16. Le 17:11.

souls. Heb. *nephesh*, Ge +12:13.

51 **took the gold.** Nu 7:2-6.

52 **offering.** Heb. heave offering. Le +7:14.

53 **men of war.** Dt 20:14. Jg 8:24-26.

54 **a memorial.** Ex +12:14. Ps 18:49. 103:1, 2. 115:1. 145:7.

NUMBERS 32

1 **the children.** Nu +1:5, 14.

Jazer. i.e. *helpful*, **S#3270h.** ver. 3, 35. Nu 21:32, Jaazer. Jsh 13:25. 21:39. 2 S 24:5. 1 Ch 6:81. 26:31. Is 16:8, 9. Je 48:32.

the place. ver. 26. Ge 13:2, 5, 10, 11. 47:1-4. Ex 9:6, 7. 10:8, 9, 24-26. 12:31, 32. Je 50:19. Mi 7:14. 1 J 2:16.

3 **Ataroth.** i.e. *crowns*, **S#5852h.** ver. 1, 34-38. Jsh 13:17. 16:2, 7. Is 15:2-4. Je 48:22, 23.

Nimrah. i.e. *leopardess*, **S#5247h.** ver. 36, Beth-nimrah. Is 15:6, Nimrim.

Heshbon. Nu +21:25.

Elealeh. i.e. *the exalted God*, **S#500h.** ver. 37. Is 15:4. 16:9. Je 48:34.

Shebam. i.e. *fragrance; their hoar head*, **S#7643h.** ver. 38, Shibmah. Jsh 13:19. Is 16:8, 9. Je 48:32, Sibmah.

Nebo. i.e. *interpreter*, **S#5015h.** ver. 38. Nu 33:47. Dt 32:49. 34:1. 1 Ch 5:8. Ezr 2:29.

10:43. Ne 7:33. Is 15:2. 46:1. Je 48:1, 22.

Beon. i.e. *in the dwelling; indwelling,* **S#1194h.** ver. 38, Baal-meon.

4 **the country.** Nu 21:24, 34. Dt 2:24-35. 1 Ch 5:18-22.

5 **if we have.** Ge 19:19. Ru 2:10. 1 S 20:3. 2 S 14:22. Est 5:2. Je 31:2.
bring us. Dt 1:37. 3:25, 26. Jsh 7:7.

6 **shall ye sit here.** 2 S 11:11. 1 C 13:5. Ph 2:4.

7 **wherefore.** ver. 9. Nu 21:4. Dt 1:28.
discourage. Heb. break. Ac 21:13.

8 **when I sent.** Nu 13:2-26. 14:2. Dt 1:22, 23. Jsh 14:6, 7.

9 **valley of Eschol.** Nu 13:23-33. 14:1-10. Dt 1:24-28.

10 **anger.** Nu 14:11, 21, 23, 29. Dt 1:34-40. Ps 95:11. Ezk 20:15. He 3:8-19.

11 **none.** Nu 26:64, 65. Dt 1:34-36.
from twenty. Nu 14:28, 29. 26:2, 64, 65. Dt 1:35. 2:14, 15.
wholly followed me. Heb. fulfilled after me. ver. 12. Jsh +14:8, 9.

12 **Kenezite.** i.e. *hunter,* **S#7074h.** Ge 15:19. Jsh 14:6, 14.
wholly followed. ver. +11.

13 **wander.** Nu 14:33-35. Dt 2:14. Ps 78:33.
until all. Nu 26:64. Dt 2:15. 1 C 10:5. He 3:16-19.

14 **an increase.** Ge 5:3. 8:21. Ne 9:24-26. Jb 14:4. Ps 51:5. 78:57. Is 1:4. 57:4. Ezk 20:21. Mt 23:31-33. Lk 11:48. Ac 7:51, 52. Ep 2:3.
to augment. Dt 1:34, 35. Ezr 9:13, 14. 10:10. Ne 13:18. Is 65:6, 7.

15 **if ye turn.** Le 26:14-18. Dt 28:15, etc. 30:17-19. Jsh 22:16-18. 2 Ch 7:19-22. 15:2.
he will yet. Nu 14:30-35.
ye shall. Je 38:23. Mt 18:7. Ro 14:15, 20, 21. 1 C 8:11, 12.

16 **and said.** Jg 8:1-3. Pr 15:1, 2. 25:15.
We will. ver. 34-42. Ge 33:17.

17 **we ourselves.** ver. 29-32. Dt 3:18-20. Jsh 4:12, 13.
little ones. Nu +16:27.

18 **not return.** Jsh 22:4, 5.

19 **we will.** Ge 13:10-12. 14:12. 2 K 10:32, 33. 15:29. 1 Ch 5:25, 26. Pr 20:21.
because. ver. 33. Jsh 12:1-6. 13:8.
on this side. ver. 32. Nu 34:15. Jsh 1:14, 15. 22:4, 9.

20 **Moses said.** Dt 3:18-20. Jsh 1:13-15. 4:12, 13. 22:2-4.

22 **land.** Dt 3:20. Jsh 10:30, 42. 11:23. 18:1. Ps 44:1-4. 78:55.
ye shall. Jsh 22:4, 9.
be guiltless. Jsh 2:19. 2 S 3:28.
this land. Dt 3:12-18. Jsh 1:15. 13:8, 29-32. 22:9.

23 **if ye will.** Le 26:14, etc. Dt 28:15, etc.

be sure your sin. Ro 3:23.

will find. Ge 4:7. +6:13. +29:25. 44:16. Ex +22:20. 1 S +3:13. 1 K 13:1-32. 1 Ch +28:9. 2 Ch 28:19. Jb +4:8. 21:17-20. 27:13-17. Ps 1:4-6. +34:16, 21. +37:9. 55:23. 58:8, +11. 73:12, 18, 19. 90:8. 139:11. 140:11. Pr 3:33. 13:5, 15, 21. 15:3. +16:18. +21:7. 26:27. 28:8, 18. 30:17. Ec 10:8. Is 59:1, 2, 12. Je 17:11. +20:11. 22:17-19. Ezk 14:10. 22:12-14. 28:15, 16. +39:23. Zc +10:11. Mt +15:14. +16:27. Ro 1:27. 2:9. 14:12. 1 C 4:5. +6:9, 10. Ga +6:7. Ep +5:5. He 4:12, 13. Ja +1:20. 5:3, 4. 2 P 2:5, 6.

24 **Build.** ver. 16, 34, etc. Jsh 1:13-15.

25 **Thy servants.** Jsh 1:13, 14.

27 **thy servants.** Jsh 4:12, 13.
armed. ver. 17. 2 C 10:4, 5. Ep 6:10-18. 2 T 4:7, 8.
as my lord. Nu 11:28. 12:11. 36:2.

28 **concerning them.** Jsh 1:13.

29 **If the children.** ver. 20-23.

30 **have possessions.** Jsh 11:23. 21:43-45. 22:19.

32 **possession.** Jsh 22:4.

33 **Moses.** ver. +1. Dt 3:12-17. 29:8. Jsh 12:1, 6. 13:8, etc. 22:4.
half the. Nu +1:10.
the kingdom of Sihon. Nu +21:21.

34 **Dibon.** ver. 3. Nu +21:30.
Aroer. i.e. *ruins; destitute,* **S#6177h.** Dt 2:36. 3:12. 4:48. Jsh 12:2. 13:9, 16, 25. Jg 11:33. 1 S 30:28. 2 S 24:5. 2 K 10:33. 1 Ch 5:8. Is 17:2. Je 48:19.

35 **Atroth.** i.e. *crown,* **S#5855h.**
Shophan. *hidden; their bruising,* **S#5855h.**
Jaazer. ver. 1, 3, Jazer.
Jogbehah. i.e. *elevated,* **S#3011h.** Jg 8:11.

36 **Beth-nimrah.** ver. +3, Nimrah. Probably the same as Nimrim in Je 48:34.
Bethharan. i.e. *house of their mount; house of the joyful shouter,* **S#1028h.**

37 **Heshbon.** ver. +3.
Kirjathaim. i.e. *double city,* **S#7156h.** Jsh 13:19. 1 Ch 6:76. Je 48:1, 23. Ezk 25:9.

38 **Nebo.** Is 46:1.
Baal-meon. i.e. *lord of the dwelling,* **S#1186h.** Nu 22:41. Jsh 13:17. 1 Ch 5:8. Je 48:23. Ezk 25:9.
Shibmah. i.e. *spice; why hoary?* **S#7643h.** Jsh 13:19. Is 16:8, 9.
gave other names unto the cities. Heb. they called by names the names of the cities. ver. 3. Ge 26:18. Ex 23:13. Jsh 23:7. Ps 16:4. Is 46:1.

39 **Machir.** Ge +50:23.

40 **gave Gilead.** Dt 3:13-15. Jsh 13:29-31. 17:1. 1 Ch 5:23-26.

41 **Jair.** i.e. *whom Jehovah enlightens; illuminated,* **S#2971h.** Dt 3:14. Jsh 13:30. Jg 10:3, 4, 5. 1 K

4:13. 1 Ch 2:22, 23. Est 2:5.
Havoth-jair. i.e. *villages of Jair*, **S#2334h**. Jg
10:3, 4. 1 K 4:13.

42 **Nobah**. i.e. *a barking*, **S#5025h**. Jg 8:11.
Kenath. i.e. possession, **S#7079h**. 1 Ch 2:23.
villages. Nu +21:25mg.

NUMBERS 33

1 **with their armies**. Ex +6:26.
under the hand. Jsh 24:5. 1 S 12:8. Ps
77:20. Mi 6:4.
2 **Moses wrote**. Ex +24:4.
journeys. Nu 9:17-23. 10:6, 13. Dt 1:2. 8:2.
10:11.
3 **they departed**. Ge 47:11. Ex 1:11. 12:37.
in the first. Ex 12:2. 13:4.
passover. Le +23:5.
with an high. Ex 14:8. Ps 105:38. Is 52:12.
Mi 2:13.
4 **buried**. Ex 12:29, 30. Ps 105:36.
upon their gods. Ex +12:12.
5 **removed**. Ex 12:37.
Rameses. ver. 3. Ex 12:37.
6 **departed**. Ex 13:20, 21.
Succoth. Ex 12:37.
Etham. Ex 13:20.
7 **they removed**. ver. 8. Ex 14:2, 9.
Baal-Zephon. Ex 14:2n, 9.
8 **departed**. Ex 14:21, 22, etc. 15:22-26.
passed. Ex 15:10. Dt 11:4.
three days. Nu 10:33. Ex 15:22. Jon 3:3.
Marah. Ex 15:22, 23.
9 **they removed**. Ex 15:27.
10 **Elim**. Ex 16:1. 17:1.
Red sea. lit. Sea of Suph. Nu 21:4. Ex 10:19.
Dt 1:40.
11 **wilderness of Sin**. Ex 17:1.
12 **Dophkah**. i.e. *beating or knocking*, **S#1850h**.
13 **Allush**. i.e. *mingling together*, **S#442h**.
14 **Rephidim**. Ex 17:1-8, 13. 19:2.
15 **they departed**. Ex 16:1. 19:1, 2.
16 **they removed**. Nu 10:11-13, 33. Dt 1:6.
Kibroth-hattaavah. Heb. *qeber*, Ge +23:4.
That is, the graves of lust. Nu 11:4, 31-34.
17 **Kibroth**. Heb. *qeber*, Ge +23:4.
Hazeroth. Nu 11:35.
18 **they departed**. Nu 12:16.
Rithmah. i.e. *binding; broom copse*, **S#7575h**. Nu
2:16. 13:1, 26. 32:8. Dt 2:19. Jsh 14:7.
19 **Rimmon-parez**. lit. *pomegranate of the breach*,
S#7428h. Jsh 15:32. 19:7.
20 **Libnah**. i.e. *whiteness*, **S#3841h**. ver. 21. Jsh
10:29, 31, 32. 12:15. 15:42. 21:13. 2 K 8:22.
19:8. 23:31. 24:18. 1 Ch 6:57. 2 Ch 21:10. Is
37:8. Je 52:1.
21 **Libnah**. Dt 1:1, Laban.
Rissah, lit. *a drop*, not mentioned
elsewhere.

22 **Kehelathah**. lit. *an assembly*. Not mentioned
elsewhere.
23 **Shapher**. i.e. *beauty; pleasantness*, **S#8234h**. ver.
24.
24 **Shapher**. lit. *beauty*, not mentioned elsewhere.
Haradah. lit. *fear and trembling*, **S#2732h**, not
mentioned elsewhere. ver. 25.
25 **Makheloth**. lit. *assemblies*, **S#4722h**, not mentioned elsewhere. ver. 26.
26 **Tahath**. lit. *place; station; depression,* only here,
S#8480h. 1 Ch 6:24, 37. 7:20, 20.
27 **Tarah**. lit. *delay*, **S#8646h**, only here. ver. 28.
28 **Mithcah**. lit. *sweetness*, **S#4989h**, only here. ver.
29.
29 **Hashmonah**. lit. *fatness*, **S#2832h**, only here.
ver. 30.
30 **Moseroth**. lit. *bonds*, **S#4149h**. ver. 31. Dt 10:6,
Mosera.
31 **Bene-Jaakan**. lit. *sons of Jaakan*, **S#1142h**. ver.
32. In Dt 10:6 more fully "Beeroth (i.e. *wells*)
of the sons of Jaakan." Ge 36:27. Dt 10:6. 1
Ch 1:42, 43.
32 **Hor-hagid-gad**. i.e. *hole of the cleft*, **S#2735h**.
ver. 33. Dt 10:7, Gudgodah.
33 **Jotbathah**. i.e. *goodness*, **S#3193h**. ver. 34. Dt
10:7, Jotbath.
34 **Ebronah**. lit. *a passage, gateway*, **S#5684h**, only
here. ver. 35.
35 **Ezion-gaber**. i.e. *the backbone of man*, **S#6100h**.
Nu 14:25. Dt 2:8. 1 K +9:26, Ezion-geber. 2
Ch 20:36.
36 **wilderness of Zin**. Nu 13:21. 20:1. 27:14.
34:3. Dt 32:51.
37 **Kadesh**. Nu 20:22, 23. 21:4. Ge +14:7.
38 **Aaron**. Nu 20:24-28. Dt 10:6. 32:50.
40 **king Arad**. Nu 21:1-3, etc.
Canaanite. Ge +10:18.
41 **departed**. Nu 21:4.
Zalmonah. i.e. *shady; imagery*, **S#6758h**. ver.
42.
42 **Punon**. lit. *distraction, pining away*, **S#6325h**.
ver. 43.
43 **pitched in Oboth**. lit. *bottles*, see Nu 21:10,
11.
44 **Ije-abarim**. *or,* heaps of Abarim. i.e. *ruins of
further regions*, **S#5863h**. Nu 21:11.
45 **Iim**. lit. *heaps, ruins*, **S#5864h**. Jsh 15:29.
Dibon-gad. lit. *pain or grief of Gad*, **S#1769h**.
ver. 46. Nu 21:30. 32:34.
46 **Dibon-gad**. Nu 32:34. Is 15:2. Je 48:18.
Almon-diblathaim. lit. *a concealment of
branches of figs*, **S#5963h**, only here. ver. 47. Je
48:22, Beth-diblathaim. Ezk 6:14, Diblath.
47 **the mountains of Abarim**. Nu 21:20.
+27:12. Dt 32:49-52.
Nebo. Nu +32:3.
48 **in the plains**. Nu +22:1. 31:12. 35:1.
49 **Beth-jesimoth**. lit. *house of the deserts,*

S#1020h. Jsh 12:3. 13:20. Ezk 25:9.
Abel-shittim. *or*, the plains of Shittim. lit.
*meadow or mount of shittim wood; mourning of
the acacias*, **S#63h**. Nu 25:1-9. Ex 25:5, 10, 23.
Jsh 2:1. Mi 6:5.

50　**in the plains**. ver. 48, 49.

51　**When**. Dt 7:1. 9:1. Jsh 3:17.

52　**drive out**. Ex 23:24, +30-33. 34:12-17. Dt
7:2-5, 25, 26. 12:2, 3, 30, 31. 20:16-18. Jsh
11:11, 12. 23:7.
pictures. *or*, figured stones. Le 26:1. Ezk 8:12.
destroy all. Ex +23:24.
molten images. Ex +34:17.
pluck down. or, lay waste. Le 26:30.

53　**have given**. Ex 23:27-31. Dt 32:8. Ps 24:1, 2.
115:16. 135:12. Je 27:5, 6. Da 4:17, 25, 32.
Mt 20:15.

54　**give the more inheritance**. Heb. multiply
his inheritance. Nu 26:54. 35:8.
give the less inheritance. Heb. diminish his
inheritance. Nu 26:54. 35:8. Ex 30:15.
in the place. Jsh 15:1-12. 16:1, etc. 17:1, etc.
18:11, etc. 19:1-48.
lot falleth. Jsh +14:2.

55　**shall be pricks**. Ex +23:33. Jg 1:21-36.

56　**do unto you**. Le 18:28. 20:23. Dt 28:63.
29:28. Jsh 23:15, 16. 2 Ch 36:17-20. Ezk
12:11. 33:24-29. Zc 1:6. Lk 21:23, 24.

NUMBERS 34

2　**is the land**. Nu 33:51, 53. Ge +13:15. Ps
78:55. 105:11. Ezk 47:14. Ac 17:26.
an inheritance. Ps 16:5, 6. Je 3:19. Ac 26:18.
Ep 1:14, 18. 1 P 1:3, 4.

3　**south quarter**. Ex 23:31. Jsh 15:1-12. Ezk
47:13, 19, etc.
salt sea eastward. Ge +14:3. Ezk 47:8,
18.

4　**Akrabbim**. i.e. *scorpions*, **S#6137h**; **S#4610h**. Jsh
15:3. Jg 1:36.
Zin. ver. 3. Nu 13:21. 20:1. 33:36, 37.
Kadesh-barnea. i.e. *desert of wandering*,
S#6947h. Nu 13:26. 32:8. Dt 1:2, 19. 2:14. 9:23.
Jsh 10:41. 14:6, 7. 15:3.
Hazar-addar. i.e. *village of springs*, **S#2692h**.
Jsh 15:3, 4.
Azmon. i.e. *strong; bone*, **S#6111h**. ver. 5. Jsh
15:4.

5　**the river**. Ps +72:8. Is +27:12.
the sea. ver. 6, 7.

6　**the great sea**. Jsh 1:4. 9:1. 15:12, 47. 23:4.
Ps 104:25. Ezk 47:10, 15, 20. 48:10, 28.

7　**north border**. ver. 3, 6, 9, 10.
mount Hor. Nu 33:37.

8　**the entrance**. Nu +13:21.
Zedad. i.e. *steep place*, **S#6657h**. Ezk 47:15.

9　**Ziphron**. i.e. *sweet smell*, **S#2202h**.
Hazar-enan. Ezk 47:17.

10　**Shepham**. i.e. *high, sticking out; bareness*,
S#8221h. ver. 11.

11　**Riblah**. i.e. *fertility; fruitful*, **S#7247h**. 2 K 23:33.
25:6, 20, 21. Je 39:5, 6. 52:9, 10, 26, 27.
Ain. lit. *eye* or *fountain*, **S#5871h**. Jsh 15:32,
+42, Ashan. 19:7. 21:16. 1 Ch 4:32. 6:59,
Ashan. Jn +3:23.
reach unto. Heb. smitten against. lit. *to wipe
or blot out*, as in Ge 6:7. 7:4, 23, etc.
side. Heb. shoulder. Ex 26:14, 15. 28:7, 12,
etc.
sea of Chinnereth. Jsh +11:2, Chinneroth.
13:27. 19:35. Ezk 47:18, the east sea.

12　**Jordan**. Jsh 3:14-16.
the salt sea. ver. +3. Ge 13:10.

13　**This is the land**. ver. 1.
by lot. Jsh +14:2.

14　**of Reuben**. Nu +26:7. Jsh 14:2, 3.

15　**on this side Jordan**. Nu 32:32.

17　**Eleazar**. Ex +6:23.
Joshua. Nu +13:8, 16.

18　**one prince**. Nu 1:4-16.

19　**Caleb**. Nu +13:6, 30.

20　**tribe of the children of Simeon**.
Nu +1:6.
Shemuel. lit. *heard of God*, **S#8050h**. 1 Ch 6:33.
7:2. See 1 S 1:20.
Ammihud. Nu 1:10.

21　**the tribe of Benjamin**. Nu +1:37.
Elidad. lit. *my God is beloved*, **S#449h**, only
here.
Chislon. lit. *folly, confidence*, **S#3692h**, only
here.

22　**children of Dan**. Nu +1:12.
Bukki. lit. *mouth of Jehovah; my emptiness*,
S#1231h. 1 Ch 6:5, 51. Ezr 7:4.
Jogli. lit. *exiled*, **S#3020h**, only here.

23　**children of Manasseh**. Nu +1:10.
Hanniel. lit. *grace of God*, **S#2592h**. 1 Ch 7:39.
Ephod. lit. *a girdle*, **S#641h**, not mentioned
elsewhere.

24　**children of Ephraim**. Nu +1:33.
Kemuel. lit. *helper; gathered of God*, **S#7055h**.
Ge 22:21. 1 Ch 27:17.
Shiphtan. lit. *judicial*, **S#8204h**, only here.

25　**children of Zebulun**. Nu +1:9.
Elizaphan. Nu +3:30.
Parnach. lit. *delicate*, **S#6535h**, only here.

26　**children of Issachar**. Nu +1:29.
Paltiel. lit. *an escape of God, deliverance of God*,
S#6409h. 2 S 3:15.
Azzan. lit. *strength*, **S#5821h**, only here.

27　**children of Asher**. Ge +30:13.
Ahihud. lit. *my brother is honor, brother of
majesty*, **S#282h**, only here.
Shelomi. lit. *my peaceful one*, **S#8015h**, only
here.

28　**children of Naphtali**. Nu +1:15.
Pedahel. lit. *ransom of God, redeemed of God*,

S#6300h, only here.
Ammihud. ver. 20.
29 **These are**. ver. 18. Jsh 19:51.

NUMBERS 35

1 **the plains**. Nu +22:1.
2 **the children of**. Le 25:32, 33. Jsh 14:3, 4.
21:2, etc. Ezk 45:1-8. 48:8, 22. 1 C 9:10-14.
3 **and the suburbs**. Jsh 21:11. 2 Ch 11:14. Ezk
45:2.
4 **suburbs**. Le 25:34.
5 **to them**. Le 25:32-34.
6 **six cities for refuge**. ver. 13, 14. Dt 4:41-43.
Jsh 20:2-9. 21:3, 13, 21, 27, 32-36, 38. 1 Ch
6:57, 67. Ps 9:9. 62:7, 8. 142:4, 5. Pr 14:26. Is
4:6. Mt 11:28. He 6:8, 18, 19.
to them ye shall add. Heb. above them ye
shall give.
7 **forty and eight**. Jsh 21:3-42. 1 Ch 6:54-81.
8 **possession**. Ge 49:7. Ex 32:28, 29. Dt 33:8-
11. Jsh 21:3.
from them. Nu 26:54. 33:54. Ex 16:18. 2 C
8:13, 14.
he inheriteth. Heb. they inherit.
10 **When ye**. Nu 34:2. Le 14:34. 25:2. Dt 12:9.
19:1, 2.
11 **ye shall appoint**. ver. 6. Jsh 20:2.
refuge. Pr 14:26. He 6:18.
any person. Heb. *nephesh*, Jsh +10:28. ver.
15, 30.
unawares. Heb. by error. ver. 22, 23. Ex
21:13. Dt 4:42. 19:4, 5.
12 **from the avenger**. ver. 19, 25-27. Dt 19:6.
Jsh 20:3-6, 9. 2 S 14:7.
until he stand. ver. 24. Dt 19:11, 12. Jsh
20:4-6.
13 **six cities**. ver. 6.
14 **three cities**. Dt 4:41-43. 19:2, 8-10. Jsh 20:2,
7-9.
15 **both for**. Nu +15:16. Ex 12:49. Le 24:22. Ro
3:29. Ga 3:28.
any person. Heb. *nephesh*, Jsh +10:28. ver.
11, 30.
16 **if he smite**. ver. 22-24. Dt 19:11-13.
the murderer. ver. 30-33. Ge 9:5, 6. Ex
21:12-14. Le 24:17. 1 K 2:29-34.
surely. Ge +2:16.
17 **throwing a stone**. Heb. a stone of the hand.
Ex 21:18.
shall surely. Le 24:17.
18 **surely**. ver. 16.
19 **revenger of blood**. ver. 12, 21, 24, 27. Dt
19:6, 11, 12. Jsh 20:3, 5.
20 **if he thrust**. Ge 4:5, 8. 2 S 3:27. 13:22, 28,
29. 20:10. 1 K 2:5, 6, 31-33. Pr 26:24. 28:17.
Lk 4:29.
by laying. Ex 21:14. Dt 19:11. 1 S 18:10, 11,
25. 19:9-12. 20:1. 23:7-9. 24:11. Ps 10:7-10.

11:2. 35:7, 8. 57:4-6. Pr 1:18, 19. Mk 6:19,
24-26. Ac 20:3. 23:21.
21 **in enmity**. Ge 4:8. 1 J 3:12, 15. Ju 11. Re
22:15.
surely. Ge +2:16.
22 **without enmity**. ver. 11. Ex 21:13. Dt 19:4,
5. Jsh 20:3, 5.
24 **the congregation**. ver. 12. Jsh 20:6.
25 **shall deliver**. Jn 8:36. Ro 8:1. Col 1:21, 22.
abide in it. ver. 28. Jsh 20:6. Ro 3:24-26. Ep
2:16-18. He 4:14-16. 7:25-28. 9:12-15. 10:19-
22.
anointed. Ex +28:41.
26 **come without**. 1 K 2:42-46.
27 **he shall not be guilty of blood**. Heb. no
blood shall be to him. Ex 22:2. Dt 19:6, 10. Jn
8:36. Ro 8:1.
28 **he should**. Jn 15:4-6. Ac 11:23. 27:31. He
3:14. 6:4-8. 10:26-30, 39.
after the death. He 7:22-24. 9:11, 12, 15-17.
29 **a statute**. Nu 27:1, 11.
30 **any person**. Heb. *nephesh*, Jsh +10:28. ver.
11, 15.
the mouth. Dt 17:6, 7. 19:15. Mt 18:16. Jn
8:17, 18. 2 C 13:1. 1 T 5:19. He 10:28. Re
11:3.
any person. Heb. *nephesh*, Jsh +10:28. ver.
11, 15.
31 **Moreover**. Ge 9:5, 6. Ex 21:14. Dt 19:11-13.
2 S 12:13. 1 K 2:28-34. Ps 51:14, 16.
satisfaction. Ex 30:12. 1 S 12:3.
life. Heb. *nephesh*, soul, Ge +44:30.
guilty of death. Heb. faulty to die. Ezk
18:20. Mt 26:66. Mk 14:64.
surely. Ge +2:16.
32 **no satisfaction**. Ac 4:12. Ga 2:21. 3:10-13,
22. He 6:17-20. Re 5:9.
refuge. Ezk 21:19mg.
33 **it defileth**. Le 18:25. Dt 21:1-8, 23. 2 K
23:26. 24:4. Ps 106:38. Is 26:21. Ezk 22:24-27.
Ho 4:2, 3. Mi 4:11. Mt 23:31-35. Lk 11:50, 51.
the land cannot be cleansed. Heb. there
can be no expiation for the land. Dt 32:43. Is
+27:9. Da +9:24. Jl 3:21. Zc 13:1.
but by. Ge 4:9-11. 9:6. Jb 16:18. He 12:22,
24.
34 **Defile not**. Nu 5:3. Le +18:25. 20:24-26. Ps
78:58.
I dwell. Ps 135:21. Is 57:15. Ho 9:3. 2 C 6:16,
17. Re 21:3, 27.
dwell among. Nu 5:3. Ex 25:8. 29:45, 46. 1
K 6:13. Ps 132:14. 135:21. Is 8:18.

NUMBERS 36

1 **Gilead**. Nu 26:29-33. 27:1, 7. Jsh 17:2, 3. 1
Ch 7:14-16.
2 **The Lord commanded**. Nu 27:1-7. Jsh
13:6. +14:2. 17:3.

to give. Nu 27:1, 7. Jsh 17:3-6. Jb 42:15.

3 **whereunto they are received**. Heb. unto whom they shall be.

   the lot of. Jsh +14:2.

4 **the jubilee**. Le 25:10-18, 23. Is 61:2. Lk 4:18, 19.

5 **hath said well**. Nu 27:7. Dt 5:28.

6 **marry**. Heb. be wives. ver. 3, 8, 11, 12. Nu +12:1.

   to whom. 1 C 7:39.

   only to the family. ver. 12. Ge 24:3, 4, 57, 58. 2 C 6:14.

7 **keep himself**. Heb. cleave. ver. 9. 1 K 21:3.

8 **every daughter**. 1 Ch 23:22.

9 **his own**. 1 K 21:3.

10 **as the Lord**. Ex 39:42, 43. Le 24:23. 2 Ch 30:12. Mt 28:20.

11 **Mahlah**. Nu 27:1.

12 **into the families**. Heb. to some that were of the families. 1 Ch 23:22.

13 **the commandments**. Le 7:37, 38. 11:46. 13:59. 14:54-57. 15:32, 33. 27:34. Ps 103:7.

   in the plains of Moab. Nu 26:3. 33:50. 35:1.

DEUTERONOMY

DEUTERONOMY 1

1 **on this**. Nu 32:5, 19, 32. 34:15. Jsh 9:1, 10. 22:4, 7.
the plain. Heb. the Arabah. Dt +11:30mg.
Red sea. *or*, Zuph. Or rather, Suph. Nu 21:14.
Paran. Dt +33:2. Ge +21:21. Hab +3:3.
Tophel. i.e. *quagmire*, **S#8603h**.
Hazeroth. Nu 11:35. 33:17, 18.
Dizahab. i.e. *sufficiency of gold*, **S#1774h**.

2 **eleven days'**. Nu 14:25, 33, 34.
by the way. ver. 44. Dt 2:4, 8. Nu 20:17-21.
Seir. Ge +14:6.
unto. Nu +34:4.

3 **in the fortieth**. Nu 20:1. 33:38.
Moses. Lk 16:31. 24:27. Jn 1:17, 45. 5:39, 45. 9:28, 29.

4 **he had slain**. Nu +21:21-35.
Astaroth. i.e. *accessions*, **S#6252h**. Jsh 9:10. 12:4. 13:12, 31. 21:27. Jg +2:13. 1 Ch 6:71.

5 **to declare**. Dt 4:8. 17:18, 19. 31:9, 11. 32:46.

6 **in Horeb**. Dt 5:2. Ex 3:1. 17:6. 1 K 19:8.
Ye have. Ex 19:1, 2. Nu 10:11-13.

7 **the mount**. Ge 15:16-21. Ex 23:31. Nu 34:3-12. Jsh 24:15. Am 2:9.
Amorites. Ge +10:16.
all the places. Heb. all his neighbors. Dt 12:5.
in the plain. Dt 11:11. Jsh 10:40. 11:16, 17. Zc +7:7.
Canaanites. Ge +10:18.
Lebanon. i.e. *very white*, **S#3844h**. Dt 3:25. 11:24. Jsh 1:4. 9:1. 11:17. 12:7. 13:5, 6. Jg 3:3. 9:15. 1 K 4:33. 5:6, 9, 14. 7:2. 9:19. 10:17, 21. 2 K 14:9. 19:23. 2 Ch 2:8, 16. 8:6. 9:16, 20. 25:18. Ezr 3:7. Ps 29:5, 6. 72:16. 92:12. 104:16. SS 3:9. 4:8, 11, 15. 5:15. 7:4. Is 2:13. 10:34. 14:8. 29:17. 33:9. 35:2. 37:24. 40:16. 60:13. Je 18:14. 22:6, 20, 23. Ezk 17:3. 27:5. 31:3, 15, 16. Ho 14:5, 6, 7. Na 1:4. Hab 2:17. Zc 10:10. 11:1.
the great river. Ge +2:14.

8 **set**. Heb. given.
which. Ge +13:15. 22:16-18.

9 **I am not**. Ex 18:18. Nu 11:11-14, 17.

10 **your God**. Ge 28:14. Ex 12:37. Nu 1:46.
ye are this day. Ge 15:5, 6.
as the stars. Ge +15:5.

11 **make you**. 2 S 24:3. 1 Ch 21:3. Ps 115:14.
and bless you. Dt 33:1, 29. Ge 15:5. 22:17. 26:4. 49:25. Ex 32:13. Nu 6:27. 22:12.

12 **bear your cumbrance**. ver. 9. Ex 18:13-16. Nu 11:11-15. 1 K 3:7-9. Ps 89:19. 2 C 2:16. 3:5.

13 **Take**. Heb. Give. Ex 18:21. Nu 11:16, 17. Ac 1:21-23. 6:2-6.
wise men. 1 K 3:7-9.
rulers. Ex 18:17, 18, 21. Nu 11:16, 17. Ac 6:1-4.

15 **I took**. Dt 16:18. Ex 18:25, 26.
made. Heb. gave. Ep 4:11.
captains over thousands. Jsh +22:21.

16 **charged**. Dt 27:11. 31:14. Nu 27:19. 1 Th 2:11. 1 T 5:21. 6:17.
judges. Ex +21:6.
Hear. Dt 16:18, 19. Ex 23:2, 3, 7, 8. Le 19:15. 2 S 23:3. 2 Ch 19:6-10. Ps 58:1. Jn 7:24.
the stranger. Dt 10:18, 19. 24:14. +26:11. Ge +23:4 (**S#1616h**). Ex 12:48. 22:21. 23:9. Le 24:22. Jsh +20:9. Mt +25:35.

17 **shall not**. Ec 5:8. Jn 7:24. Ro +2:11. Ja +2:1.
respect persons. Heb. acknowledge faces. Jb +19:25. Ps 35:11. Ml 2:9mg.
ye shall hear. Ex 18:22, 26. 23:3, 6, 7. 1 S 12:3, 4. Jb 22:6-9. 29:11-17. 31:13-16. Ps 82:3, 4. Pr 22:22, 23. Je 5:28, 29. Am 5:11, 12. Mi 2:1-3. 3:1-4. 7:3, 4. Ja 2:2-4, 6.
ye shall not. 1 K 21:8-14. Jb 31:34. Pr 29:25. Je 1:17. 1 Th 2:4.
the judgment. 2 Ch 19:6.
the cause. Dt 17:8-10. Ex 18:18, 22, 26.

18 **I commanded**. Dt 4:5, 40. 12:28, 32. Mt 28:20. Ac 20:20, 27.

19 **through**. Dt +8:15. 32:10. Nu 10:12.
Amorites. Ge +10:16.
we came. ver. +2.

20 **the mountain**. ver. 7, 8.

21 **fear not**. Dt 20:1. Nu 13:30. 14:8, 9. Jsh 1:9. Ps +118:6. Lk 12:32.

22 **We will send**. Nu 13:1-20.

23 **I took**. Nu 13:3, etc.
twelve. Mk 3:13, 14.

24 **they turned**. Nu 13:21-27. Jsh 2:1, 2.

25 **good land**. Dt 3:25. Ge +1:22.

26   **ye would not**. Nu 14:1-4. Ps 106:24, 25. Is 63:10. Ac 7:51.
    rebelled. ver. 43. Jsh 1:18. Ps 107:11.
    commandment. Ge +45:21.

27   **the Lord hated us**. Dt 9:28. Ex 16:3, 8. Nu 14:3. 21:5. Mt 25:24. Lk 19:21.

28   **discouraged**. Heb. melted. Ex +15:15.
    The people. Dt 9:1, 2. Nu 13:28-33.
    we have seen. 2 S 21:16-22.
    Anakims. i.e. *descendants of Anak*, **S#6062h**. Dt 1:10, 11, 21. Jsh +11:21.

29   **Dread not**. ver. +21.

30   **he shall**. Dt 20:1-4. Ex 14:14, 25. Jsh 10:42. 1 S 17:45, 46. 2 Ch 14:11, 12. 32:8. Ne 4:20. Ps 46:11. Is 8:9, 10. Ro 8:31, 37.
    according. Ex 7-15. Ps 78:11-13, 43-51. 105:27-36.

31   **in the wilderness**. Ex 16. 17. Ne 9:12-23. Ps 78:14-28. 105:39-41.
    bare thee. Dt 32:11, 12. Ex 19:4. Nu 11:11, 12, 14. Is 40:11. 46:3, 4. 63:9. Ho 11:3, 4. Ac 13:18mg. He 12:5-7.
    all the way. Mt 28:20.

32   **did not believe**. 2 Ch +20:20. Ps 78:22. 106:24. Is 7:9. He 3:12, 18, 19. Ju 5.

33   **Who went**. Ex +13:21. Ps 77:20. Ezk 20:6.
    a cloud. Ex +13:21.

34   **and sware**. Dt 2:14, 15. Nu 14:22-30. 32:8-13. Ps 95:11. Ezk 20:15. He 3:8-11.

35   **Surely**. Nu 14:22, 23, 29. Ps 95:11.

36   **Caleb**. Nu +13:6.
    wholly followed. Heb. fulfilled *to go* after. Jsh +14:8.

37   **the Lord**. Dt 3:23-26. 4:21. 34:4. Nu 20:12. 27:13, 14. Ps 106:32, 33.

38   **Joshua**. Nu 13:8, 16. 14:30, 38. 26:65.
    which standeth. Dt +10:8. Ex 17:9-14. 24:13. 33:11.
    encourage him. Dt 3:28. 31:7, 8, 14, 23. Nu 27:18-23. Jsh 1:1, 6-9.

39   **your little**. Nu +16:27.
    which in. Is 7:15, 16. Jon 4:11. Ro 9:11. Ep 2:3.

40   **turn you**. Nu 14:25.

41   **We have sinned**. Nu 14:39, 40, etc. 22:34. Pr 19:3.

42   **Go not up**. Ex 33:15, 16. Nu 14:41, 42.
    for I am not. Le 26:17. Jsh 7:8-13. 1 S 4:2, 10. Is 30:17. 59:1, 2. Ho 9:12.
    among you. Dt +23:14.

43   **but rebelled against**. 1 S 8:18. 28:4-6. Pr 1:24-28. Is +63:10. Ac 7:51. Ro 8:7, 8.
    commandment. Ge +45:21.
    went presumptuously up. Heb. ye were presumptuous and went up. Nu 14:44.

44   **Amorites**. Ge +10:16.
    chased you. Dt 28:25. 32:30. Ps 118:12. Is 7:18.
    Seir. Ge +14:6.
    unto Hormah. Nu +14:45.

45   **ye returned**. Ps 78:34. He 12:17.
    not hearken. Pr 1:24-31. Zc 7:11, 13.

46   **abode in Kadesh**. Nu 14:25, 34. Ge +14:7.

DEUTERONOMY 2

1   **we turned**. Dt 1:40. Nu 14:25.
    we compassed. Dt 1:2. Nu 21:4. Jg 11:18.

3   **long enough**. ver. 7, 14. Dt 1:6.

4   **Ye are to pass**. Dt 23:7. Nu 20:14-21. Ob 10-13.
    they shall. Ex 15:15. Nu 22:3, 4. 24:14-18.
    take ye. Mt 5:16. Lk 12:15. Ep 5:15. Ph 2:15. Col 4:5.

5   **no, not so much as a foot breadth**. Heb. even to the treading of the sole of the foot. Ac 7:5.
    because. Dt 32:8. Ge 33:16. 36:8. Jsh 24:4. 2 Ch 20:10-12. Je 27:5. Da 4:25, 32. Ac 17:26.

6   **buy meat**. ver. 28, 29. Nu 20:19. Mt 7:12. Ro 12:17. 2 Th 3:7, 8.

7   **blessed**. Ge 12:2. 24:35. 26:12. 30:27. 33:8-11. 39:5. Ps 90:17.
    he knoweth. Dt 8:4. Jb 23:10. Ps 1:6. 31:7. Jn 10:27.
    these forty. Dt 8:2-4. 29:5. Ne 9:21. Lk 22:35.

8   **And when**. Nu 20:20, 21. 21:4. Jg 11:18.
    Seir. Ge +14:6.
    the plain. Heb. the Arabah. Dt +11:30mg.
    Elath. i.e. *palm grove*, **S#359h**. 1 K +9:26, Eloth. 2 K 14:22. 16:6.

9   **Distress not the Moabites**. or, Use no hostility against Moab. Nu 22:4. Jg 11:17. 2 Ch 20:10.
    Ar. ver. 5. Nu 21:15, 28.
    the children. ver. 19. Ge 19:36, 37. Ps 83:8.

10   **The Emims**. Ge 14:5.
    the Anakims. ver. 11, 21.

11   **giants**. ver. +20.
    as the Anakims. Jsh +11:21.

12   **Horims**. i.e. *cave dwellers*, **S#2752h**. ver. 22. Ge 14:6. 36:20-30. 1 Ch 1:38-42.
    succeeded them. Heb. inherited them. ver. 21, 22. Ge 36:31-43. 1 Ch 1:43-54.
    stead. or, room. ver. 21-23.
    as Israel did. ver. 22, 32-37. Dt 3:1-11. Ge 36:20. Nu 21:21, etc.

13   **brook**. or, valley. Nu 13:23mg.
    Zered. i.e. *luxuriant growth of trees*, **S#2218h**. ver. 14. Nu 21:12, Zared.

14   **Kadesh-barnea**. Nu +34:4.
    until all the generation. Dt 1:34, 35. Nu 14:28-35. 26:64, 65. 32:11. Ps 90:3, 9. 95:11. Ezk 20:15. He 3:8-19. Ju 5.

15   **the hand of the**. Ex +9:3. Ps 78:33. 90:7-9. Is 66:14. 1 C 10:5.

18   **pass over**. Nu 21:15, 23. Is 15:1.

19 **distress them not**. ver. 5, +9. Ge 19:36-38. Jg 11:13-27. 2 Ch 20:10.
children of Ammon. Dt 23:3.

20 **land of giants**. Dt 3:13. Jsh 15:8. 17:15. 18:16. 2 S 5:18, 22. 23:13. 1 Ch 11:15. 14:9. Is 17:5.
giants. ver. 11. Dt 3:8-11, 13. Ge 6:4. +14:5. Nu 13:28-33. Jsh 11:21. 12:4. 13:12. 1 S 17:4. 2 S 21:15-22. 1 Ch 11:23. 20:4-6, 8. Jb 16:14. Am 2:9.
Zamzummims. i.e. *noisy tribes*, **S#2157h**. Ge 14:5, Zuzims.

21 **great**. ver. 10, 11. Dt 1:28. 3:11.
but the Lord. ver. 22. Dt 32:7-9. Jg 11:24. Je 27:7, 8. Hab 1:10, 11. Ac 17:26.

22 **Esau**. Ge 36:8.
the Horims. ver. 12. Ge 14:6. 36:20-30. 1 Ch 1:38, etc.
unto this day. Dt +29:4. Ge +19:38.

23 **the Avims**. i.e. *accumulated evils; subverters*, **S#5757h**. Jsh 13:3, Avites. 18:23. 2 K 17:31.
Hazerim. i.e. *inclosures; courts*, **S#2699h**.
Azzah. i.e. *fortified*, **S#5804h**. Ge +10:19, Gaza. 1 K 4:24. Je 25:20.
the Caphtorims which came. Ge +10:14.
dwelt in their stead. Ac 17:26.

24 **the river Arnon**. ver. 36. Nu +21:13-15.
behold. Jsh 6:16. 2 Ch 36:23. Ezr 1:2. Je 27:5. Ezk 29:20. Da 2:38. 4:17.
begin to possess it. Heb. begin, possess. ver. 31.

25 **the dread**. Dt 11:25. 28:10. Ps 105:38. Mi +7:17. Re 3:9.
tremble. Is +64:2.

26 **Kedemoth**. Jsh 13:18. 21:37.
with words. Dt 20:10, 11. Est 9:30. Mt 10:12-15. Lk 10:5, 6, 10-12.

27 **pass through**. ver. 6. Nu 21:21-23. Jg 11:19.

28 **only will I pass**. Nu 20:19.

29 **As the children**. Dt 23:3, 4. Nu 20:18. Jg 11:17, 18.
into the land. Dt 4:1, 21, 40. 5:16. 9:6. 25:15. Ex 20:12. Jsh 1:11-15.

30 **Sihon**. Nu +21:23.
for the Lord. Ex +4:21. Nu 21:23. Jg 11:20.
God hardened. Ex +4:21. Jg 7:22. 2 S 24:1. Jb 17:4. Ps 28:3. +115:3. 119:36. 141:4. Is 19:14. 29:10. 44:18. 45:7. Ezk 14:9. Zc 8:10. Lk 10:21. Re 17:17.
obstinate. Is 48:4.
deliver. Dt 9:3-5. Ge 15:13-16.

31 **give Sihon**. ver. 24. Dt 1:8.

32 **Sihon**. Nu +21:21-30. Ps 120:7.

33 **the Lord**. Dt 3:2, 3. 7:2. 20:16. Ge 14:20. Jsh 21:44. Jg 1:4. 7:2.
we smote. Dt 29:7, 8. Nu 21:23, 24. Jsh 10:30-42. 11:21.

34 **utterly destroyed**. Dt 3:6. 7:2, 26. 13:15. 20:16-18. Le 27:28, 29. Nu 21:2, 3. Jsh 6:21.

7:11. +8:26. 9:24. 10:28, 39, 40. 11:11, 12, 14. 1 S 15:3, 8, 9.
the men, and the women, and the little ones, of every city. Heb. every city of men, and women, and little ones. Nu +16:27.

35 **the cattle**. Dt 3:7. 20:14. Nu 31:9-11. Jsh 8:27.

36 **Aroer**. Nu +32:34.
Arnon. ver. +24.
not. Jsh 1:5. Is 41:15, 16.
God delivered. Nu 14:9. Ps 44:3. 118:6. Ro 8:31.

37 **unto the land**. ver. 5, 9, 19. Dt 3:16. Jg 11:15.
Jabbok. Ge +32:22.

DEUTERONOMY 3

1 **Bashan**. Nu +21:33.
Og. Nu +21:33-35.
Edrei. ver. 10. Nu +21:33.

2 **Fear**. ver. 11. Dt 20:3. Nu 14:9. 2 Ch 20:17. Is 41:10. 43:5. Ac 18:9. 27:24. Re 2:10.
as thou didst. Dt 2:24-37. Nu +21:21-25.

3 **God delivered**. Dt 2:33, 34. Nu 21:35. Jsh 13:12, 30.

4 **all his cities**. Nu 32:33-42. Jsh 12:4. 13:30, 31.
all the region. lit. line. Jsh +17:14. 1 K 4:13.

5 **fenced**. Dt 1:28. Nu 13:28. He 11:30.

6 **we utterly**. Dt +2:34.
as we did. ver. +2.
children. Nu +16:27.

7 **all the cattle**. Dt 2:35. Jsh 8:27. 11:11-14.

8 **the land**. Nu 32:33-42. Jsh 12:2-6. 13:9-12.
Hermon. i.e. *strong fortress*, **S#2768h**. ver. 9. Dt 4:48. Jsh 11:3, 17. 12:1, 5. 13:5, 11. 1 Ch 5:23. Ps 89:12. 133:3. SS 4:8.

9 **Hermon**. ver. +8. Ps 29:6.
Sidonians. **S#6722h**. Ge +10:19, Sidon. +49:13, Zidon. Jsh 13:4, 6. Jg 3:3. +10:12, Zidonians. 1 K 5:6. Mt +11:21.
Sirion. i.e. *coat of mail; breastplate; sheeted with snow*, **S#8303h**. Ps 29:6.
Shenir. i.e. *an apron; bear the lamp*, **S#8149h**. Dt 4:48. 1 Ch 5:23. Ezk 27:5, Senir. SS 4:8.

10 **the cities**. Dt 4:49.
Salchah. i.e. *a walk; firmly bound, straitened basket*, **S#5548h**. Jsh 12:5. 13:11. 1 Ch 5:11.
Edrei. ver. +1.

11 **giants**. Dt +2:20.
Rabbath. i.e. *great or populous place*, **S#7237h**. Jsh +13:25, Rabbah. Ezk 21:20.
nine cubits. 1 S 17:4. Am 2:9.
cubit of a man. Re 21:17.

12 **from Aroer**. Nu +32:34.
Gadites. **S#1425h**. ver. 16. 4:43. 29:8. Nu 34:14. Jsh 1:12. 12:6. 13:8. 22:1. 2 S 23:36. 2 K 10:33. 1 Ch 5:18, 26. 12:8, 37. 26:32.

13 **the rest**. Nu 32:39-42. Jsh 13:29-32. 1 Ch 5:23-26.

which was called. Zc 9:1.
land of giants. ver. 11. Dt +2:20.

14　**Jair**. Nu +32:41.
Argob. ver. 4.
Geshuri. S#1651h. Jsh 13:2. 2 S +3:3. 10:6.
Bashan-havoth-jair. i.e. *Bashan of the villages of Jair*, S#2333h, 2334h. Nu 32:41. Jsh 13:30. Jg 10:4. 1 K 4:13. 1 Ch 2:23.
unto this day. Dt +29:4.

15　**Machir**. Ge +50:23. Jsh 22:7.

16　**Reubenites**. Nu +26:7.
river Jabbok. Ge +32:22.

17　**The plain**. Heb. Arabah. Dt +11:30mg.
Chinnereth. i.e. *a harp*, S#3672h. Nu +34:11. Jsh +11:2.
the sea. Dt 4:49. Ge +14:3.
Ashdoth-pisgah. *or*, the springs of Pisgah, *or*, the hill. S#798h. Dt 4:49. Nu 23:14. Jsh 10:40. 12:3mg, 8. 13:20mg.

18　**I commanded**. Nu 32:20-24. Jsh 1:12-15. 4:12, 13. 22:1-9.
meet for the war. Heb. sons of power. 2 S +2:7mg.

20　**return**. Jsh 22:4, 8.

21　**I commanded**. Nu 27:18-23.
so shall. Jsh 10:25. 1 S 17:36, 37. Ps 9:10. 2 C 1:10. 12:10. Ep 3:20. 2 T 4:17, 18.

22　**shall not**. Is 43:1, 2.
for the Lord. Dt 1:30. 20:4. Ex 14:14. Nu 21:34. Jsh 10:42. 2 Ch 13:12. 20:17, 29. Ps 44:3.

23　**I besought**. 2 C 12:8, 9.

24　**thy greatness**. Dt 5:24. 9:24. 11:2. 1 Ch 29:11. Ps 71:19. 106:2. Da +2:45.
what. Ex 15:11. Ps 35:10. 71:19. 86:8. 89:6, 8. Is 40:18, 25. Da 3:29.
God. Heb. *El*, Ex +15:2.

25　**the good land**. Dt 4:21, 22. Ex +3:8. Nu 32:5.
Lebanon. Dt +1:7.

26　**the Lord**. Dt 1:37. 31:2. 32:51, 52. 34:4. Nu 20:7-12. 27:12-14. Jb 23:13, 14. Ps 106:32, 33. Is 53:5, 6. Mt 26:39.
not hear. Is 59:1, 2. Jn +9:31.
Let it. 1 Ch 17:4, 12, 13. 22:7-9. 28:2-4. Mt 20:22. 2 C 12:8.
speak no more. Ex 32:10. 33:20. 2 S 12:16-23. Je 7:16. 11:14. Ezk 14:3. 20:3. Jn 17:9. 1 J 5:16.

27　**thee up**. Dt 34:1-4. Nu 27:12.
Pisgah. *or*, the hill. ver. 17.
lift up. Ge 13:14, 15. +22:13.
not go. Dt 1:37. 31:2. 32:51, 52. 34:1-4. Ps 106:32. Lk 9:31.

28　*charge Joshua*. *Dt 1:38. 1 Ch 28:9, 10, 20. 1 Th +2:11. 2 T 2:1-3.*
for he shall. Jsh 1:2. 3:7-17. Jn 1:17. Ac 7:45. He 4:8, Jesus.

29　**the valley**. Dt 4:3, 46. 34:6. Nu 25:3. 33:48, 49.

Bethpeor. i.e. *house of the opening*, S#1047h. Dt 4:46. 34:6. Jsh 13:20.

DEUTERONOMY 4

1　**unto the statutes**. ver. 5, 8, 40, 45. Dt 5:1, 31. 6:1, 2, 20. 8:1. 11:1, 32. 12:1. Ex +21:1. Le 18:4, 5, 26. 19:37. 20:8, +22. 22:31. 26:46. 27:34. Ps 19:8, +9. 105:45. 119:4, 5, 7, 160, 164. 147:19, 20. Ezk 11:20. 18:9. 20:11, 19. 36:27. 37:24. Ml 4:4. Mt 28:20. Lk 1:6. Jn 14:21, 24. 15:14. 1 J 2:3-5.
that ye may. Le +18:5.

2　**not add**. Dt 12:32. 18:20. Jsh +1:7. Pr 30:6. Ec 12:13. Je 26:2. Mt 5:18, 43. 15:2-9. Mk 7:1-13. Ga 3:15. Re 22:18, 19.

3　**what the**. Nu 25:1-9. 31:16. Jsh 22:17. Ps 106:28, 29. Ho 9:10.
for all the men. Nu 26:64.

4　**cleave unto**. Dt 10:20. 11:22. 13:4. 30:20. Ge 2:24. Nu 14:30-33. 25:10-13. 26:63-65. Jsh 22:5. 23:8. Ru 1:14-17. 2 K 18:6. Ps 63:8. 119:31. 143:6-11. Is 26:20. Ezk 9:4. Jn 6:67-69. Ac 11:23. Ro 12:9. Re 14:4. 20:4.

5　**I have taught**. ver. +1. Pr 22:19, 20. Mt 28:20. Ac 20:27. 1 C 11:23. 15:3. 1 Th 4:1, 2. 1 T +3:15. He 3:5.

6　**this is your**. Jb 28:28. Ps 19:7. 111:10. 119:98-100. Pr 1:7. 4:5-7. 9:10. 14:8. Je 8:9. Ep 5:17. 2 T 1:13, 14. 3:15. Ja 3:13.
in the sight. Je 20:10, 11. 1 C 4:9.
Surely. 1 K 4:34. 10:6-9. Ps 119:99. Da 1:20. 4:9. 5:11-16. Zc 8:20-23. Ml 3:12.

7　**what nation**. Nu 23:9, 21. 2 S 7:23. Is 43:4.
who hath. Dt 5:26. Ps 46:1. 73:28. 86:5. 145:18. 148:14. Is 55:6. Ep 2:12-22. Ja 4:8.
nigh. Ps 4:5.

8　**statutes**. ver. +1. Dt 10:12, 13. Ps 119:2-8, 86, 96, 127, 128. Ro 7:12-14. 2 T 3:16, 17.

9　**keep thy**. ver. 15, 23. Pr 3:1, 3. 4:20-23. Mt 15:19, 20. Lk 8:18. Ep 5:15. He 2:3. Ja 2:22. 2 P 3:11. 1 J 5:18. Ju 21. Re 16:15.
soul. Heb. *nephesh*, Ge +34:3.
lest they. Jsh 1:18. Ps 119:11. Pr 3:1-3, 21. 4:4. 7:1. He 2:1. Re 3:3.
teach them. Dt 6:7. 11:19. 29:29. 31:19. Ge 18:19. Ex +13:8, 9, 14-16. Jsh 4:6, 7, 21. Ps 34:11-16. 71:18. 78:3-8. Pr 1:8. 4:1-13. +22:6. 23:26. Is 38:19. Ep +6:4. 2 T 1:5. +3:15.

10　**the day**. Dt 5:2. Ex 19:9, 16. 20:18. He 12:18, 19, 25.
fear me. Dt 5:29, 33. +6:2. Lk 1:50. Re 19:5.
all. Dt +12:1.

11　**stood**. Dt 5:23. Ex 19:16-18. 20:18, 19.
midst. Heb. heart. Ex 15:8. 2 S 18:14.
clouds. Ge +9:13.
thick darkness. Ex +10:22.

12　**the Lord**. Dt 5:4, 22, 23. Ex 20:22.
no similitude. ver. 15. Nu 12:8. Is 40:18. Col 1:15.

only ye heard a voice. Heb. save a voice. ver. 33, 36. Ge 4:20. Ex 3:16. 1 K 19:12, 13. Jb 4:10. Is 30:21. 40:3, 6. Ezk +10:5. Mt 3:3, 17. 17:5. Lk 1:64. 2 P 1:17, 18.

13 **And he**. Dt 5:1-21. Ex 19:5. 24:7, 8. He 9:19, 20.
ten. Dt 10:4. Ex 34:28.
he wrote. Ex +31:18. He 9:4.

14 **at that time**. Ex ch. 21-23. Ps 105:44, 45. Is 28:10, 13. Ml 4:4. He 3:5.

15 **Take ye**. ver. +9, 23. Jsh 23:11. 1 Ch 28:9, 10. Ps 119:9. Pr 4:23, 27. Je 17:21. Ml 2:15.
yourselves. Heb. *nephesh*, Nu +23:10.
of similitude. ver. +12. Ex 33:20. Is 40:18. Jn 1:18. Ac 17:29. 2 C 4:4-6. Col 1:15. 1 T 6:16. He 1:3.

16 **corrupt**. Dt 5:9. Ex 20:4, 5. 32:7. Ps 106:19, 20. Je 7:18. Ro 1:22-24.
the likeness. ver. 23. Is 40:18. +66:17. Ezk +16:17. +23:14, 20. Jn 4:24. Ac 17:29. 20:4, 5. 1 T 1:17.

17 **likeness**. Jsh 22:28. Ezk 8:3. Ro 1:22, 23, 25.

19 **when thou**. Ezk +8:16. Am 5:25, 26.
the host. Dt 17:3. Ge 2:1. 2 K 17:16. 21:3. 23:4, 5, 11. 2 Ch 33:3, 5. Ps +24:10. Is 45:12. Je 8:2. 19:13. Zp 1:5. Ac 7:42. Ro 1:25.
which the Lord. Ge 1:16-18. Jsh 10:12, 13. Ne 9:6. Ps 74:16, 17. 136:7-9. 148:3-5. Je 31:35. 33:25. Mt 5:45.
divided. *or*, imparted. Dt 29:26mg.
nations. or, peoples.

20 **the iron**. 1 K 8:51. Je 11:4.
furnace. Ge 15:17.
out of Egypt. Ex 1:11-14. 5:7-9, 18, 19.
a people. Dt 9:26, 29. Ex +19:5, 6. Ps 28:9. 33:12. Is 63:17, 18. Ep 1:18.

21 **angry with me**. Dt +1:37. 3:26. 31:2. Nu 20:12. Ps 106:32, 33.

22 **I must die**. Dt 3:25, 27. 34:4. 1 K 13:21, 22. Am 3:2. He 12:6-10. 2 P 1:13-15.

23 **heed**. ver. +9, 15, 16. Dt 27:9. Jsh 23:11. Mt 24:4. Lk 12:15. 21:8. He 3:12.
lest ye forget. Dt 6:12. 29:25. 31:20. Jsh 23:16. 1 Ch 16:15. Is 24:5. Je 31:32. Ezk 16:59.
make you. ver. +16. Ex 20:4, 5.

24 **thy God**. Ex 24:17. Ps 21:9. Je 21:12-14. Zp +1:18. He 12:29.
consuming. Ml 4:1.
fire. Dt 9:3. 29:20. +32:22. Ps 74:1. 80:4. Is 10:17. 30:27, 30, 33. 33:14. Na 1:5, 6. 2 Th 1:8. He 12:29.
a jealous. Ex +20:5. Is 42:8.
God. Heb. *El*, Ex +15:2.

25 **beget**. Dt 31:16-18. Jg 2:8-15.
corrupt. ver. +16. Dt 31:29. Ex 32:7. Ho 9:9.
do evil. 2 K 17:17-19. 21:2, 14-16. 2 Ch 36:12-16. 1 C 10:22.

26 **I call heaven**. Dt 31:28. 32:1. Ps 50:4. Is 1:2. Je 2:12. 6:19. 22:29. Ezk 36:4. Mi 1:2. 6:2.

this day. ver. 39, 40. Dt 5:1. 6:6. 7:11. 8:1, 11, 19. 9:1, 3. 10:13. 11:2, 8, 13, 26, 27, 28, 32. 13:18. 15:5, 15. 19:9. 26:3, 16, 17, 18. 27:1, 4, 10. 28:1, 13, 14, 15. 30:2, 8, 11, 15, 16, 18, 19. 32:46. Je 42:21. Lk +23:43. Ac 20:26.
ye shall. Dt 29:28. Ge +4:7. Le 18:28. 26:31-35. Jsh 23:16. Is 6:11. 24:1-3. Je 44:22. Ezk 33:28. Lk 21:24.

27 **scatter you**. Je +9:16. Ezk 32:26.
few. Je +42:2.

28 **ye shall**. Dt 28:36, 64. 1 S 26:19. Je 16:13. Ezk 20:32, 39. Da 3:1-7. Ac 7:42.
the work of men's hands. Dt 27:15. Ps 115:4. Is 17:8. 31:7. 40:19. 44:9. 46:6. Ho 13:2. Mi 5:13. Ac 19:26.
neither see. 1 K 18:26. Ps 115:4-7. 135:15, 16. Is 41:22. 44:7, 9, 10. 45:20, 21. 46:6, 7. 48:5. Je 10:3, 9. Hab 2:18. 1 C 12:2. Re 9:20.

29 **But if**. Dt 30:10. Ge +4:7.
seek. 2 Ch 15:4, 15. Ne 1:9. Je 3:12-14. +29:13.
with all. 2 K 10:31. Da 9:3-18. Mt +22:37.
soul. Heb. *nephesh*, Ge +34:3.

30 **in tribulation**. 1 S 26:24. Jb 38:23. Is 2:19. 48:10. Je 23:20. 30:7. Ezk 20:37. Da +12:1. Ho 5:15. Jl 2:11, 31. Na 1:7. Zp +1:15. Zc 10:11. 13:8, 9. Mt 24:8, +21, 29. Re 7:4-8. 12:1, 2, 17.
all these. 1 K 8:46-53. 2 Ch 6:36-39. Da 9:11-19.
are come upon thee. Heb. have found thee. Dt 31:17. Ge 44:34. Ex 18:8mg. Ne 9:32.
in the latter days. Dt 31:29. Ge +49:1. Nu 24:20.
if thou turn. Zc +1:3. Ac +3:19.
obedient. Is 1:19. Je 7:23. Zc 6:15. He 5:9.

31 **the Lord**. Ex +34:6, 7. Ps 78:34-40. Na 1:7. Ml 4:2.
not forsake. Le +26:44. Ro +11:1.
forget. Le +26:42, 45.

32 **ask now**. Dt 32:37. Jb 8:8. Ps 44:1. Is 41:22. Jl 1:2.
the days. Jb 18:20. 24:1. Ps 37:13. 137:7. Is 13:6. Ezk 21:29. 22:4. Ho 1:11. Jl 1:15. Ob 12. Mi 7:4. Lk 17:22, 26. 19:42. 1 C 4:3mg. Ep 5:16.
from the one. Dt 30:4. 2 S +22:8. Mt 24:31. Mk 13:27.

33 **hear the voice**. Dt 5:24-26. 9:10. Ex 19:18, 19. 20:18, 19. 24:11. 33:20. Jg 6:22.

34 **take him**. Ex 1:9. 3:10, 17-20. 6:6.
temptations. Dt 7:19. 29:3. Ex 9:20, 21. 10:7.
by signs. Ex 7:3. Ps 78:12, 48-53. Je 32:21.
by a mighty. Dt 6:21. 7:8, 9. Ex 13:3. 1 P 5:6.
stretched. Ex +6:6.
and by great. Dt 26:8. 34:12. Ex 12:30-33. Je 32:21.

35 showed. Dt 5:24, 26. Ex 24:11. 33:20.
know. 1 S 17:45-47. 1 K 18:36, 37. 2 K 19:19. Ps 58:11. 83:18.
none else. Ex 15:11. 1 S 2:2. 2 S 22:32. Is 44:6, 8. +45:5. Mk 12:29, +32, 43. 1 J 5:20, 21.

36 Out of heaven. ver. 33. Ex 19:9, 19. 24:16. +33:9.

37 because. Dt 9:5. +33:3. Ps 105:6-10. Is 41:8, 9. Lk 1:72, 73. Ro 9:5. 11:28, 29.
and brought. Ex 13:3, 9, 14.
in his sight. 2 Ch 16:9. Ps 32:8. 34:15.
with his. ver. +34. Ps ch. 114. 136:10-15. Is 51:9-11. 63:11, 12.

38 drive. Ex +23:30.
as. Dt 2:31-37. 3:1-16. 8:18.

39 and consider. Dt 32:29. 1 Ch 28:9. Is 1:3. 5:12. Ho 7:2.
the Lord. ver. +35. 1 Ch 29:11. 2 Ch +20:6. Ps 135:6. Da 4:35.
in heaven. Ec 5:2. Mt 3:16, 17. +6:9. Jn 12:28-30. 17:1.
none else. Dt +32:39. Mk +12:32.

40 keep. ver. +1, 6. Dt 28:1-14. Le 22:31. 26:1-13. Je 11:4. Jn 14:15, 21-24.
it may go. Dt 5:16. 6:3, 18. 11:9. 12:25, 28. 22:7. Pr 10:27. Is 38:1-5. Ep 6:3. 1 T 4:8.
prolong. ver. 26. Dt +5:16, 33. 6:2. 11:9. 17:20. 25:15. 30:20. Ex 20:12. 1 K 3:14. Jb 5:26. Ps 21:4. 34:12, 14. +91:16mg. Pr 3:2, 16. 4:10, 20-22. 9:11. 10:27. Ec +8:13. Is 65:20-22. Je 35:7. Ep 6:3. 1 P 3:10.
for ever. or, all the days. i.e. continually. Dt 5:29. 6:24. 11:1. 14:23. 18:5. 19:9. 28:29, 32, 33. 31:13. Ge 6:5. 43:9. 44:32. Jsh 4:24. Jg 16:16. 1 S 2:32.

41 severed three cities. Nu 35:6, 14, 15. Jsh 20:2-9.

42 the slayer. Dt 19:1-10. Ex 21:12, 13. Nu 35:6, 11, 12, 15-28. He 6:18.

43 Bezer. i.e. *gold ore; stronghold; an inaccessible spot*, S#1221h. Ge 36:33. Jsh 20:8. 21:36. 1 Ch 6:78. 7:37.
Ramoth. 1 K +4:13.
Golan. i.e. *great exodus; captive; rejoicing*, S#1474h. Jsh 20:8. 21:27. 1 Ch 6:71.
Bashan. Dt +32:14.
Manassites. S#4520h. Dt 29:8. Jg 12:4. 2 K 10:33. 1 Ch 26:32.

44 this is the law. Dt 1:5. 17:18, 19. 27:3, 8, 26. 33:4. Le 27:34. Nu 36:13. Ml 4:4. Jn 1:17.

45 These. Dt 6:17, 20. 1 K 2:3. Ps 119:2, 14, 22, 24, 111.
statutes. ver. +1. Ps 119:5.
judgments. Ps 119:7.

46 On this side. ver. 47. Dt +1:5. 3:29. Nu 32:19.
over. Dt 3:29.
Beth-peor. Dt 3:29. 34:6. Jsh 13:20.

Moses. Dt 1:4. 2:30-36. 3:8. Nu 21:21-32.
smote. Ps 136:16-22.

47 and of Og. Nu +21:33-35. Ps 68:14, 15.

48 Aroer. Nu +32:34.
even unto. Dt +3:9.
Sion. i.e. *lofty; peak*, S#7865h, only here. Dt 3:9, Shenir. Ps 133:3.
Hermon. Dt +3:8.

49 plain. Heb. Arabah. Dt +11:30mg.
sea. Nu 34:3.
under the springs. or, slopes. Dt 3:17. 34:1. Jsh 10:40. 13:20.

DEUTERONOMY 5

1 all Israel. Dt 1:1. 29:2, 10.
Hear. Dt +4:1. Ps 81:8, 9. 85:8. Is 55:3. Lk 9:35. Re 2:7.
keep, and. Heb. keep to. Mt 23:3.

2 our God. Dt 4:23. Ex 19:5-8. 24:8. He 8:6-13. 9:19-23.

3 made not. Dt 29:10-15. Ge 17:7, 21. Ps 105:8-10. Je 32:38-40. Mt 13:17. Ro 4:23, 24. Ga 3:17-21. He 8:8, 9.

4 The Lord talked. ver. 24-26. Ex 19:9, 18, 19. +33:9.
face. Ge +19:13.
to face. Dt 34:10. Ge 32:30. Ex 33:11. Nu 12:8. 14:14. Jg 6:22. Ezk 20:35. 1 C 13:12. 2 J 12. 3 J 14.

5 stood. ver. 27. Ge 18:22. Ex 19:16. 20:18-21. 24:2, 3. Nu 16:48. Ps 106:23. Je 30:21. Zc 3:1-5. Ga 3:19. He 9:24. 12:18-24.
to show. He 1:2.

6 I am the. Dt +6:4. Ex +20:2-17. 32:7. 33:1. Le 26:1, 2. Is 42:8.
brought. Ps 81:5-10.
bondage. Heb. servants. Dt 6:12. Ex 13:3. 20:2.

7 The First Commandment.
Thou shalt have none other gods before me. Dt 6:4. Ex +20:3. Mt 4:10. Jn 5:23. 1 C 8:5. Col 3:5. 1 J 5:21.

8 The Second Commandment.
Thou shalt not make thee any graven image.
graven image. Ex +20:4.
likeness. Dt 4:12, 15, 16, 23. Ex 20:4. Jb 4:16. Ps 17:15. Is 40:18-25. 46:5-7.

9 shalt not. Ex +20:4-6.
the Lord. Ex 3:15.
a jealous God. Ex +34:14.
visiting. Ex +20:5. Je +11:22. 32:18. Da 9:4-9. Mt 23:35, 36. Ro 11:28, 29.

10 showing. Ex +34:6, 7. Is 1:16-19. Je 32:18. Da 9:4. Mt 7:21-27. Ga 5:6. 1 J 1:7.
love me. Dt 10:12, 13. Jg +5:31. Jn +15:14. Ja 1:25.

11 The Third Commandment.
Thou shalt not take the name of the

Lord thy God in vain. Dt 6:13. Ex +20:7. Le 19:12. 24:10-16. Ps 139:20. Je 4:2. Mt 5:33, 34. Jn 10:30-36. Ja 5:12.

12 The Fourth Commandment.
Keep the sabbath day to sanctify it. Ex +20:8-11.

13 **Six days**. Ex 23:12. 35:2, 3. Ezk 20:12. Lk 13:14-16. 23:56.

14 **the sabbath**. Ge 2:2. Ex 16:29, 30. He 4:4, 9-11.
not do any work. Ex 23:12. 35:2. 2 Th 3:6, 11, 12.
thy stranger. Ne 13:15-21.
thy manservant. Ex 23:12. Le 25:44-46. Ne 5:5.

15 **remember**. Ex +13:3. Is 51:1, 2. Ep 2:11, 12.
the Lord. ver. 6. Ps 116:16. Is 63:9. Lk 1:74, 75. T 2:14.
through. Dt 4:34-37.
stretched. Ex +6:6.

16 The Fifth Commandment.
Honor thy father and thy mother. Ex +20:12. Mt 15:4-6. Mk 7:10-13.
that thy days. ver. 33. Dt +4:40. Zc 8:4. Ep *6:1-3*.

17 The Sixth Commandment.
Thou shalt not kill. Ex +20:13. Ps 51:14. Mt *5:21*, 22. Jn 8:44. Ja *2:11*. 1 J 3:10-12, 15. Re 21:8.

18 The Seventh Commandment.
Neither shalt thou commit adultery. Ex +20:14. Pr 6:32, 33. Mt *5:27, 28*. Lk 18:20. Ja 2:10, 11. He 13:4.

19 The Eighth Commandment.
Neither shalt thou steal. Ex +20:15. Jn 12:4-6. Ro *13:9*. Ep 4:28.

20 The Ninth Commandment.
Neither shalt thou bear false witness against thy neighbor. Dt 19:16-21. Ex +20:16. 23:1. 1 K 21:12, 13. Ps 50:19, 20. Pr 6:19. 19:5, 9. Ml 3:5.
bear. or, answer, in reply to the questions of a judge.
false. or, empty, worthless, testimony.

21 The Tenth Commandment.
Neither shalt thou desire thy neighbor's wife, neither shalt thou covet. Ex +20:17. 1 K 21:1-4. Mi 2:2. Hab 2:9. Lk 12:15. 18:20. Ro *7:7, 8*. 13:9, 10. 1 T 6:9, 10. He 13:5.
desire. Dt 7:25. Ex 20:17. 34:24.
covet. Nu 11:4, 34. 2 S 23:15. 1 Ch 11:17. Ps 45:11. 106:14. Pr 13:4. 21:10, 26. 23:3, 6. 24:1. Ec 6:2. Is 26:9. Je 17:16. Am 5:18.

22 **These words**. ver. +4. Dt 4:12-15, 36. Ex 19:18, 19.
thick darkness. Ex +10:22.
added no more. 1 J 2:7, 8.
he wrote. Ex +24:12.

23 **when ye heard**. Ex 19:19. 20:18, 19. He 12:18-21.

24 **talk**. ver. +4.
he liveth. Dt 4:33. Ge 16:13. +32:30. Ex 3:6. 1 K 19:13. Da 10:9. Re 1:17.

25 **this great**. Dt 18:16. 33:2. 2 C 3:7-9. Ga 3:10, 21, 22. He 12:29.
hear. Heb. add to hear. Is 29:14mg.

26 **who is**. ver. +24. Dt 4:33.
all flesh. Ge 6:12. Is 40:6. Ro 3:20.
living. Je +10:10.

27 **hear all**. Ex 20:19. He 12:19.

28 **they have well said all**. Dt 18:17. Nu 27:7. 36:5. He 1:1-3. 2:1-4. 3:3.

29 **O that there**. Dt 32:29, 30. Ps 55:6. 81:13-15. Is 48:18. 64:1. Je 44:4. Ezk 33:31, 32. Mt 23:37. Lk 19:42. 2 C 5:20. 6:1. Ga 5:12. He 12:25.
keep all. Dt 11:1. Ps 106:3. 119:1-5. Lk 11:28. Jn 15:14. Re 22:14.
that it might. ver. +16. Dt +4:40. 6:3, 18. 12:25, 28. 19:13. 22:7. Ru 3:1. Ps 19:11. Is 3:10. Je 22:14, 15. Ep 6:3. Ja 1:25.
forever. Heb. *olam*, Ex +12:24. Ge +9:12.

31 **by me**. Ex 33:21. Lk 15:1.
I will. ver. +1. Dt +4:1. Ga 3:19.

32 **observe**. Dt 6:3, 25. 8:1. 11:32. 24:8. 2 K 21:8. Ezk 37:24.
ye shall not. Jsh +1:7.

33 **walk**. Dt 10:12. Ps 119:6. Ec 12:13, 14. Je 7:23. Lk 1:6. Ro 2:7.
well. ver. 29. Dt +4:40. Je 7:23. 1 T 4:8.
prolong. ver. +16. Dt +4:40.

DEUTERONOMY 6

1 **the commandments**. Dt +4:1. Nu 36:13.
go to possess it. Heb. pass over. Dt 7:1. Ge 15:7. 28:4. Le 20:24. Ps 37:24.

2 **fear**. ver. 13. Dt +4:10. 10:12, 13, 20. 13:4. 17:13, 19. 28:58. Ge 20:11. 22:12. Ex 20:20. Le 19:32. Jsh 24:14. 1 S 12:23, 24. Ps 145:19. Pr +3:7. Je 32:39, 40. Ml 1:6. Lk 12:5. 1 P 1:17. 2:17.
and thy son. ver. 7. Ge +18:19. Ps 78:4-8.
thy days. Dt +4:40.

3 **and observe**. Dt 4:6. 5:32. Ec 8:12. Is 3:10.
that ye may. Ge 12:2. 13:16. 15:5. 22:17. 26:4. 28:14. Ex 1:7. Ac 7:17.
in the land. Ex 3:8.

4 **the Lord**. Dt 4:35, 36. 5:6. 1 K 18:21. 2 K 19:5. 1 Ch 29:10. Is 42:8. 44:6, 8. 45:5, 6. Je 10:10, 11. Mk *12:29*-32. Jn 17:3. 1 C 8:4-6. 1 T 2:5.
God. Dt 32:39. Ge +1:26. 2:24. Is 45:5. Jn 17:3. 1 C 8:6.
one. Heb. *ehad*, **S#259h**, a compound unity, one made up of others: Ge 1:5, one of seven; 2:11, one of four; 2:21, one of twenty-four; 2:24, one made up of two; 3:22, one of the

three; 49:16, one of twelve; Nu 13:23, one of a cluster; Ps 34:20. Je +10:8mg. Contrast *yahed*, **S#3173h**, unique, a single or only one: Ge 22:2, 12, 16. Jg 11:34. Ps +22:20. 25:16. 35:17. 68:6. Pr 4:3. Je 6:26. Am 8:10. Zc 12:10. See Ps 133:1.

5 thou shalt. Dt 7:9. Jsh 23:11. Jg +5:31. Ps 18:1. 31:23. 145:20. Is 56:6. Mt +22:37. Mk *12:30*, 33. Lk *10:27*. 11:42. Jn 5:42. Ro +8:28. 1 C 2:9. 2 Th 3:5. Ju +21.
God with all. Mt 10:37. Jn 14:20, 21. 2 C 5:14, 15.
soul. Heb. *nephesh*, Ge +34:3.

6 shall be. Dt 11:18. 32:46. 1 Ch 22:19. Jb 22:22. 23:12. Ps 37:31. 40:8. 119:11, 98. Pr 2:1, 10, 11. 3:1-3, 5. 4:4, 20-22. 7:2, 3. Is 51:7. Je 15:16. 31:33. Lk 2:51. 8:15. 2 C 3:3. Col 3:16. 2 J 2.

7 And thou shalt. ver. 2. Dt 4:9, 10. 11:19. Ge +18:19. Ex 12:26, 27. 13:14, 15. Ps 78:4-6. Ep 6:4.
teach. Heb. whet, *or* sharpen. or, repeat. Dt +32:41. Is 28:10.
diligently. Jsh 1:8.
children. Ex +13:8. 2 T +3:15.
shalt talk. Ru 2:4, 12. 4:11. Ps 37:30. 40:9, 10. 107:2. 119:46. 129:8. Pr 6:22. 10:21. 15:2, 7. Ml 3:16. Mt 12:35. Lk 6:45. Ep 4:29. Col 4:6. 1 P 3:15.

8 bind them. Dt 11:18. Ex 13:9, 16. Nu 15:38, 39. Pr 3:3. 6:21. 7:3. Mt 23:5. He 2:1.

9 write them. Dt 11:20. Ex 12:7. Jb 19:23-25. Is 30:8. 57:8. Hab 2:2.

10 land. Ge +13:15.
great. Jsh 24:13. Ne 9:25. Ps 78:55. 105:44.

11 wells. Heb. *bor*, Ge +37:20.
when thou. Dt 7:12-18. 8:10, etc. 32:15. Jg 3:7. Pr 30:8, 9. Je 2:31, 32. Ezk 16:10-20. Mt 19:23, 24.

12 bondage. Heb. bondsmen, *or* servants. Dt 5:6. 7:8. 8:14. 13:5, 10. Ex 13:3mg. 20:2. Jg 6:8.

13 fear. ver. +2. Dt 5:29. 10:12, 20. 13:4. Ex +34:14. Mt *4:10*. Lk *4:8*.
and serve him. Dt +10:12.
shalt swear. Ge +21:23. Le 19:12. Ps 15:4. 63:11. Je 5:2, 7.

14 not go. Dt 8:19. 11:28. Ex 34:14-16. Je 25:6. 1 J 5:21.
of the gods. Dt 13:7.

15 is a jealous. Ex +20:5. Am 3:2.
lest. Dt 7:4. 11:17. Nu 32:10-15. 2 Ch 36:16. Ps 90:7, 11.
destroy. Ge 7:4. Ex 32:12. 1 K 13:34. Am 9:8.
face. Ge +1:2.

16 tempt. Mt *4:7*. Lk *4:12*.
tempted him. Ex +17:2, 7. Nu 20:3, 4, 13. 21:4, 5.

17 diligently. ver. 1, 2. Dt 11:13, 22. Ex +15:26. Ps 119:4. 1 C 15:58. T 3:8. He 6:11. 2 P 1:5-10. 3:14.

18 shalt do. Dt 8:11. 12:25, 28. 13:18. Ex 15:26. Ps 19:11. Is 3:10. Ezk 18:5, 19, 21, 27. 33:14, 16, 19. Ho 14:9. Jn 8:29. Ro 12:2.
that it may. Dt +4:40. +5:16, 29, 33.

19 cast out. Ex 23:28-30. Nu 33:52, 53. Jg 2:1-3. 3:1-4.

20 when thy son. ver. +7. Dt 4:9. 32:7. Ge +18:19. 35:2. Ex 12:26. +13:8, 14. Jsh 4:6, 7, 21-24. 6:13. Jb +1:5. 8:8, 10. 15:18. Ps 44:1. 48:13. 78:3, 5-8. 145:4. Pr +22:6. Ml +4:6. Ep +6:4.
in time to come. Heb. tomorrow. Ex 8:10. Jsh +4:6mg.

21 We were. Dt 5:6, 15. 15:15. 26:5-9. Ex +20:2. Ne 9:9, 10. Ps 136:10-12. Is 51:1. Je 32:20, 21. Ro 6:17, 18. Ep 2:11, 12.
with a mighty. Ex 3:19. 13:3.

22 showed. Dt +4:34. Ex 7-12. 14. Ps 135:9.
sore. Heb. evil. Dt 1:35, 39. 4:25. 24:7. 28:35, 59. Ge 2:9, 17. 3:5, 22. 6:5. Jb 1:1, 8. 2:3. 2:7, 10, 11. 5:19. Ps 23:4. 71:20.
before. Dt 1:30. 3:21. 4:3. 7:19. Ps 58:10, 11. 91:8.

23 to give us. ver. 10, 18. Dt 1:8, 35. Ex +13:5. 2 Ch 20:11.

24 to fear. ver. 2.
for our good. Dt 10:13. Jb 35:7, 8. Pr 9:12. Is 3:10. Je 32:39. Mt 6:33. Ro 6:21, 22.
he might. Dt 4:1, 4. 8:1, 3. Ps 41:2. 66:9. Pr 22:4. Ro 10:5.
at this day. Dt 2:22. +29:4, 28. Ge +19:38.

25 it shall. Dt 24:13. Le +18:5. Ps 106:30, 31. 119:6. Pr 12:28.
righteousness. Ps 71:16. Is 64:6. Je 23:6.
to do. Dt +5:32.

DEUTERONOMY 7

1 the Lord. Dt 6:1, 10, 19, 23. 11:29. 31:3, 20. Ex 6:8. 15:17. +23:30. Nu 14:31. Ps 78:55.
the Hittites. Dt +20:17.
Girgashites. Ge +10:16.
Amorites. Ge +10:16.
Canaanites. Ge +10:18.
Perizzites. Ge +13:7.
Hivites. Ge +10:17.
Jebusites. Ge +10:16.
greater. Dt 4:38. 4:1-3. 20:1.

2 deliver. ver. 23, 24. Dt 3:3. 23:14. Ge 14:20. Jsh 10:24, 25, 30, 32, 42. 21:44. Jg 1:4.
utterly. Dt +2:34. Nu 33:52.
make no. Dt 20:10, 11. Ex +23:32. Jsh 2:14. Jg 1:24.

3 make marriages. Jg +3:6.

4 so will. Dt 6:15. 32:16, 17. Ex 20:5. Jg 2:11, 20. 3:7, 8. 10:6, 7. Pr 29:1.

5 destroy. Ex +23:24.

images. Heb. statues, *or* pillars. 2 K +17:10mg.
and cut. Jg 6:25, 26.
groves. 2 K +17:10.
burn. ver. 25. Dt 9:21. 12:3. Ex 32:20. 2 S 5:21. 1 K 15:13. 2 K 19:18. 23:6. 1 Ch 14:12. Is 37:19. Ac 19:19.

6 **an holy.** Dt 28:9. Ex +33:19. Ps 50:5. Je 2:3.
chosen thee. Ps +33:12.
to be a special. Dt +32:43. Ex +19:5.
face. Ge +1:2.

7 **The Lord.** Ps 115:1. Ro 9:11-15, 18, 21. 11:6. 1 J 3:1. 4:10.
ye were. Dt 10:22. 26:5. Is 51:2. Mt 7:14. Lk 12:32. Ro 9:27-29.

8 **because.** Dt 4:37. 9:4, 5. +33:3. 1 S 12:22. 2 S 22:20. Ps 37:4. 44:3. Is 43:4. Zp 3:17. Mt 11:26. 2 Th 2:13, 14. T 3:3-7.
oath. Ge 22:16-18. Ex 32:13. Ps 105:8-10, 42. Lk 1:55, 72, 73. He 6:13-17.
Lord brought. Dt 4:20, 31. Ex 12:41, 42. 13:3, 14. 20:2.

9 **the faithful.** Ex 34:6, 7. Ps 119:75. 146:6. Is 49:7. La 3:23. 1 C 1:9. 10:13. 2 C 1:18. 1 Th 5:24. 2 Th 3:3. 2 T 2:13. T 1:2. He 6:18. 10:23. 11:11. 1 J 1:9.
God. Heb. *El*, Ex +15:2.
which keepeth. Ge +9:16. 17:7. Le +26:42. Jg 2:1. +5:31. 1 K 8:23. Ne 1:5. 9:32. Da 9:4. Mi 7:18-20.
a thousand. 1 Ch 16:15.

10 **repayeth.** Dt 5:9. 32:35, 41. Ex 23:22. Ps 21:8, 9. Pr 11:31. Is 59:18. 63:3-6. Na 1:2. Ro 12:19.
slack. Dt 32:35. 2 P 3:9, 10.
hateth. Ex 20:5. Jn 15:23, 24.

11 **keep.** Dt 4:1. 5:32. Is 26:9. Jn +14:15.

12 **if.** Heb. because. Dt 8:20. 28:1. Le 26:3. Mt 6:33. Jn 14:21. 1 T 4:8.
hearken. Dt +15:5.
Lord. ver. 9. Ps 105:8-10. Mi 7:20. Lk 1:55, 72, 73.

13 **he will love.** ver. 7. Dt 28:4. Ex 23:25. Ps 1:3. 11:7. 144:12-15. Jn 14:21. 15:10. 16:27.
he will also. Dt 28:3-5, 8, 11, 15-18. Le 26:3-5, 9, 10. Jb 42:12. Ps +127:3. Pr 10:22. Hg 2:15-19. Ml 3:10, 11. Mt 6:33.

14 **blessed.** Dt 33:29. Ge 25:8. 35:29. 1 Ch 23:1. Jb 5:26. 42:17. Ps 55:23. 107:38. 115:15. 147:19, 20. Ml 3:10, 11. Ac 1:18.
male or. Dt 28:4, 11. Ex 23:26, etc. Le 26:9. Ps +127:3.

15 **from thee.** Dt 28:27. Ex 9:11. Le 26:3, 4.
will put none. Dt 28:27, 60. Ex 9:11. 15:26. +23:25. Ps 105:36, 37.
diseases of Egypt. Dt 28:27. 1 S 4:8. 5:10-12.
but will. Dt +30:7.

16 **consume.** ver. 2.
thine eye. Dt 13:8. 19:13, 21. 25:12. Je 21:7.

snare. Ex +23:33. Jg 3:6. 1 C 15:33. 2 C 6:14, 15.

17 **thou shalt.** Dt 8:17. 15:9. 18:21. Is 14:13. 47:8. 49:21. Je 13:22. Zp 1:12. Lk 9:47.
These nations. Nu 13:32. 33:53. Jsh 17:16-18.

18 **shalt not.** Dt 1:29. 3:6. 31:6. Ps 27:1, 2. 46:1, 2. Is 41:10-14.
remember. Ex ch. 8-14. Jg 6:8-10, 13. Ps 77:11. 78:11, 42-51. 105:5, 26-36. 106:7. 111:4. 135:8-10. 136:10-15. 143:5. Is 43:18. 46:9. 51:9, 10. 63:11-15. Mi 6:5. Ep 2:11. 2 P 1:12, 13. 3:1, 2.

19 **great.** Dt 29:3. Ne 9:10, 11. Ezk 20:6-9.
stretched. Ex +6:6.
so shall. Jsh 3:10.

20 **the hornet.** Ex +23:28-30. Jsh 24:12.

21 **not be affrighted.** Jsh 10:8.
the Lord. Dt +23:14. Ex 17:7. Nu 11:20. 14:9, 14, 42. 16:3. 23:21. 35:34. Jsh 3:10. 22:31. Ps 68:17. Is +43:2. Zc 2:10, 11. 1 C 14:25.
a mighty. Dt 2:25. 26:8. Ge 35:5. 1 S 4:8. Ps +99:3. Is +49:26. Zc 12:2-5.
God. Heb. *El*, Ex +15:2.

22 **put out.** Heb. pluck off. ver. 1. Pr 2:22mg.
thou mayest. Ex +23:29, 30. Jg 14:5. Je 49:19.

23 **the Lord.** ver. 2. Jg 1:4. 7:23-25. 11:21.
unto thee. Heb. before thy face. Dt 9:3.
shall destroy. Dt 2:15. 8:20. Is +13:6. Je 17:18. Jl 1:15. 2 Th 1:9.

24 **he shall.** Jsh 10:24, 25, 42. 12:1, etc., 7-24. 21:44.
destroy their name. Dt 9:14. 25:19. 29:20. Ex 17:14. 1 S 24:21. Ps 9:5. 109:13. Pr 10:7. Is 56:5. 65:15. Je 10:11. Zp 1:4.
there shall. Dt 11:25. Jsh 1:5. 10:8. 23:9. 2 S 8:3, 5, 13. 1 K 4:21, 24. Is 54:17. Ro 8:37. 1 C 15:57.

25 **graven.** ver. +5. Jsh 22:5. 24:14, 15, 21. Is 30:22.
thou shalt. Jsh 7:1, 21.
snared. Jg 8:24-27. Zp 1:3. 1 T 6:9, 10.
an abomination. Dt 17:1. 23:18. Re 17:5.

26 **shalt.** Dt 13:17. Le 27:28, 29. Jsh 6:17-24. 7:1, etc., 11-26. Jg 8:27. Ezk 14:7. Hab 2:9-11. Zc 5:4.
but thou shalt. Is 2:20. 30:22. Ezk 11:18. Ho 14:8. Ro 2:22.

DEUTERONOMY 8

1 **observe to do.** Dt +4:1. +5:32, 33. 1 Th 4:1, 2. 1 J 3:21-24. Re 22:14.

2 **remember.** Dt +7:18.
led thee. Dt 1:3, 33. 2:7. 29:5. Ps 136:16. Am 2:10.
to humble. 2 Ch 32:25, 26. 33:12, 19, 23. Jb 33:17. 42:5, 6. Is 2:17. Lk 18:14. Ja 4:6, 10. 1 P 5:5, 6.

prove thee. ver. 16. Dt 13:3. Ge 22:1. Ex 15:25. 16:4. 20:20. Jg 3:1, 4. 2 Ch 32:31. Ps 81:7. 1 P +1:7.
to know. Ge +18:21. Je 17:9, 10. Jn +2:25. Re 2:23.
whether. 2 Ch 33:12, 13. Jb 5:17. 23:10. Ps 78:34, 35. 94:12, 13. 119:67, 71, 75. Pr 3:11, 12. Is 26:9. 27:7, 9. 48:10. Je 24:5. La 3:27. Da 11:35. 12:10. Ho 5:15. Zc 13:9. Jn +10:28. Ro 5:3, 4. 1 C 11:32. 2 C 4:17, 18. 12:10. 2 T +2:12. He 2:10. 12:10, 11. Ja 1:2, 3, 12. 1 P 1:7, 19. Re +3:19.
wouldest keep. Ex 19:8. 32:7, 8.

3 fed thee. Ex 16:2, 3, 12-35. Ps 78:23-25. 105:40. Mt 4:4. Jn 6:30-35, 41, 48-51, 57, 58, 63. 1 C 10:3.
doth. Ps 37:3. 104:27-29. Mt 4:4. Lk 4:4. 12:29, 30. He 13:5, 6.
bread. Ge +3:19.
proceedeth. Je 15:16. Jn 1:1, 14, 45. 6:52-55. 2 T +3:16.
mouth. Nu +12:8.

4 raiment. Ex 3:22. 12:35.
waxed not old. Dt 29:5. Ne 9:21. Mt 6:25-30.

5 consider. Dt 4:9, 23. Is 1:3. Ezk 12:3. 18:28.
as a man. 2 S 7:14. Jb 5:17, 18. Ps 89:32. 94:12. Pr 3:12. 1 C 11:32. He 12:5-11. Re 3:19.

6 walk. Dt 5:33. 10:12, 13. Ex 18:20. 1 S 12:24. 2 Ch 6:31. Ps 128:1. Lk 1:6.
fear him. Ps 111:10. Is 8:13. Ro 13:7. He 12:28.

7 land of brooks. Dt 6:10, 11. 11:10-12. Ex 3:8. Jg 1:12-15. Ne 9:24, 25. Ps 65:9-13. Ezk 20:6. 31:4.

8 land of. Nu 11:5.
wheat. Dt 32:14. Jg 6:11. Ru 2:23. 2 S 4:6. 1 K 5:11. Ps 81:16. 147:14. Ezk 27:17.
barley. 2 Ch 2:10-15. Jn 6:9, 13.
vines. 1 K 4:25. 2 Ch 26:10. SS 2:11-13. Is 7:23. Je 5:17. 31:5. Ho 2:8, 12, 22. Mi 4:4. Hab 3:17.
oil olive. Heb. olive tree of oil. Ex 30:24. Le 24:2.
honey. Ex +3:8. Le 2:11. 20:24.

9 whose stones. Dt 33:25. Jsh 22:8. 1 K 7:9-12. 1 Ch 22:14. Jb 28:2.

10 thou hast. Dt 6:11, 12. Ps 103:1-5, 22. 1 C 10:31. 1 Th 5:18.
then thou. 1 S 1:9, 10. 1 Ch 29:14. Ps 103:2. 106:48. Pr 3:9. Lk +24:30.

11 Beware. Ps 106:21. Pr 1:32. 30:9. Ezk 16:10-15. Ho 2:8, 9.

12 Lest when. Dt 28:47. 31:20. 32:15. Pr 30:9. Ho 13:5, 6.
and hast built. Ec 2:4. Je 22:14, 15. Ezk 11:3. Am 5:11. Hg 1:4. Lk 12:18. 17:28.

13 thy herds. Ge 13:1-5. Jb 1:3. Ps 39:6. Lk 12:13-21.

14 thine heart. Dt +17:20. Je 2:31. 1 C 4:7, 8.
thou forget. ver. +11. Je 2:6.

15 led thee. Dt 1:19. Ps 136:16. Is 63:12-14. Je 2:6.
fiery serpents. Nu 21:6. Ho 13:5.
no water. Je 2:6. Ho 13:5.
who brought. Ex 17:6. Nu 20:11. Ps 78:15, 16. 105:41. 114:8. Is 35:7. 1 C 10:4.
water out. Ps 87:7.

16 fed thee. ver. 3. Ex 16:15.
he might. ver. +2.
to do thee. Je 24:5, 6. La 3:26-33. Ro 8:28. 2 C 4:17. He 12:10, 11. 1 P +1:7.

17 thou say. Dt +7:17.
My power. Dt 9:4. Is 10:8-14. Da 4:30. Ho 12:8. Hab 1:16. Lk 12:19. 2 C 4:7.
wealth. Ge +34:29.

18 he that. Ge 26:12, 13. 1 S 2:7. 1 K 3:13. 1 Ch 29:12. Ps 112:3. 127:1, 2. 128:1-6. 144:1. Pr 8:18. 10:22. Ec 2:24. 5:19. Ho 2:8.
that he may. Dt 7:8, 12.

19 if. Ge +4:7.
I testify against. Dt 4:26. 28:58-68. 29:25-28. 30:18, 19. Jsh 23:13. 1 S 12:25. Da 9:2. Am 3:2. Zp 1:18. 3:6. Lk 12:46-48. 13:3, 5.

20 so shall ye perish. 2 Ch 36:16, 17. Da 9:11, 12. Lk 13:1-5.
obedient. 1 S 15:22, 23. Mt 7:21. Lk 6:46. Jn 3:36. 2 Th 1:7-9. He 5:9. 1 J 2:3.
voice. Dt +13:4. 26:17. 28:2. Jn 10:4, 5, 27.

DEUTERONOMY 9

1 to pass. Dt 3:18. 11:31. 27:2. Jsh 1:11. 3:6, 14, 16. 4:5, 19.
this day. Dt 1:3. +4:26. Jsh 4:19. Jn 8:56. 1 C 4:5. Re 16:14.
nations. Dt +4:38. 7:1. 11:23. 2 S 8:2. Ps 79:7. Mk 5:35.
cities. Dt 1:28. Nu 13:22, 28-33.

2 great. Dt 2:11, 12, 21.
Anakims. Jsh +11:21.
Who can stand. Dt 7:24. Ex 9:11. Jb 11:10. Da 8:4. 11:16. Na 1:6.
Anak. Nu +13:33.

3 Understand. ver. 6. Mt 15:10. Mk 7:14. Ep 5:17.
goeth over. Dt 1:30. 20:4. 31:3-6. Jsh 3:11, 14. Mi 2:13. Re 19:11-16.
a consuming fire. Dt +4:24. Is 27:4.
he shall. Dt 7:1, 2, 16, 23, 24. Ex 23:29-31. Is 41:10-16. Ro 8:31.

4 Speak not. ver. 5. Dt 7:7, 8. 8:17. Ezk 36:22, 32. Ro 10:6. 11:6, 20. 1 C 4:4, 7. Ep 2:4, 5. 2 T 1:9. T 3:3-5.
for the wickedness. Dt 12:31. 18:12. Ge 15:16. Le 18:24, 25. Mt 6:31, 32.

5 Not for. Is +48:9. T 3:5.
that he may. Ge +13:15. Ps 119:89. Is 55:10,

11. Je 1:12. Mi 7:20. Lk 1:54, 55. Jn 17:17. Ac 3:25. 13:32, 33. Ro 11:28. 15:8.

6 Understand. ver. +3, 4. Ezk 20:44.
a stiffnecked. ver. 13. 2 Ch +30:8. Ps 78:8. Ezk 2:4. Zc 7:11, 12. Ac 7:51. Ro 3:9-12. 5:20, 21.

7 Remember. Dt 8:2. Ezk 16:61-63. 20:43. 36:31, 32. 1 C 15:9. Ep 2:11. 1 T 1:13-15.
from the day. Dt 31:27. 32:5, 6. Ex 14:11. 16:2. 17:2. Nu 11:4. 14:1, etc. 16:1, etc. 20:2-5. 21:5. 25:2. Ne 9:16-18. Ps 78:8, etc. 95:8-11. Is 48:8. Da 9:8.

8 Also in Horeb. Ex 32:1-6. Ps 106:19-22.

9 I was. Ex 24:12, 15, 18.
the tables. ver. 15. Ex +24:12. Ga 4:24.
then I. Ex 24:18. 34:28. 1 K 19:8. Mt 4:2.
I neither. ver. 18. 1 K 13:8, 9. 2 K 6:22.

10 written with. Ex +31:18.
all the words. Dt 4:10-15. 5:6-21. 18:16. Ex 19:17-19. 20:1-18. Ac 7:36-38.

11 the tables of the covenant. ver. +9. Nu 10:33. He 8:6-10. 9:4. Ps 40:7, 8.

12 Arise. Ex +32:7, 8.
corrupted. Dt 4:16. 31:29. 32:5. Ge 6:11, 12. Ju 10.
are quickly. ver. 16. Jg 2:17. Ps 78:57. Je 17:9. Ho 6:4. 7:16. Ro 7:18. Ga 1:6.
molten image. Ex +34:17. Is 40:18.

13 I have. Ge 11:5. 18:21. Ex 32:9, 10. Ps 50:7. Je 7:11. 13:27. Ho 6:10. Ml 3:5.
stiffnecked. ver. +6.

14 Let me. Ex 32:10-13. Is 62:6, 7. Je 14:11. 15:1. Lk 11:7-10. 18:1-8. Ac 7:51.
blot. Ps 9:5. Pr 10:7. Re +3:5.
and I will. Nu 14:11, 12. Je 18:7-10. Da 4:34, 35.

15 I turned. Ex 32:14, 15, etc.
the mount. Dt 4:11. 5:23. Ex 9:33. 19:18. He 12:18.

16 I looked. Ex 32:19.
calf. Ex +32:4.

17 cast them. Ex 32:19.
brake. Ps 40:8.

18 I fell down. ver. +9. Ex 32:10-14. 34:28. 2 S 12:16. Ps 106:23.
forty days. ver. 25. Jon +3:4.

19 For I. ver. 8. Ex 32:10, 11. Ne 1:2-7. Lk 12:4, 5. He 12:21.
to destroy. 1 Ch 13:9-12. 21:30. Ps 106:23.
But the. Dt 10:10. Ex 32:14. 33:17. Ps 99:6. 106:23. Am 7:2, 3, 5, 6. Ga 3:19. Ja 5:16, 17.

20 very angry. Ex 32:2-5, 21, 35. He 7:26-28.

21 I took. Is 2:18-21. 30:22. 31:7. 44:22. Je 50:20. Ho 8:11. Mi 7:18, 19. 1 J 1:7.
the calf. Ex +32:4.
burnt. Dt +7:5.
the brook. Ex 17:6. Ps 78:16-20. 105:41.

22 Taberah. Nu 11:1-5.
Massah. Ex 17:7. Ps 78:16-20. 105:41.

Kibroth-hattaavah. Nu 11:4, 34. Heb. *qeber*, Ge +23:4.

23 Likewise. Nu 13:1-3. +34:4.
ye rebelled. Nu 14:1-4, 10-41. Is 63:10.
ye believed. Dt 1:32, 33. 2 K 17:14. Ps 78:22, 32. 106:24, 25. He 3:18, 19. 4:2.

24 rebellious. ver. 6, 7. Dt 31:27. Ex 14:10-12. Ac 7:51.

25 I fell. ver. +16, 18. Ge +17:3.
forty days. Jon +3:4.

26 prayed. Ex 32:11-13. 34:9. Nu 14:13-19. Ps 99:6. 106:23. Je 14:21.
thy people. Ex +32:7. 33:13. 1 S 12:22.
thine inheritance. 1 K 8:51.
which thou hast redeemed. ver. 29. Dt 32:9. Ps 74:1, 2. Is 63:19.
which thou hast brought forth. Dt 7:8. 13:5. 15:15. 21:8. 26:7, 8. Ex 15:13. 2 S 7:23. Ne 1:10. Ps 77:15. 107:2. Is 44:23. Mi 6:4. T 2:14. He 9:12. Re 5:9.

27 Remember. Ex 3:6, 16. 6:3-8. 13:5. 32:13. Je 14:21.
look not. Ex 32:31, 32. 1 S 25:25. Ps 78:8. Pr 21:12. Is 43:24, 25. Je 50:20. Mi 7:18, 19.

28 the land. Ge 41:57. Ex 6:6-8. 1 S 14:25.
Because. Dt 32:26, 27. Ex 32:12. Nu 14:15, 16. Jsh 7:7-9. Ps 115:1, 2. Is 43:25. 48:9-11. Je 14:7-9. Ezk 20:8, 9, 14. Da 9:18, 19.

29 Yet they. ver. 26. Dt 4:20. 1 K 8:51. Ne 1:10. Ps 95:7. 100:3. Is 63:19.
which thou. ver. +26. Dt 4:34. 28:9. Nu +23:21, 22. 1 K 8:51. Je 14:9. 1 J 2:1, 2.

DEUTERONOMY 10

1 Hew. ver. 4. Ex 34:1, 2, 4.
make thee. ver. 3. Ex 25:10-15. He 9:4.

2 thou shalt. ver. 5. Ex +16:34. He 9:4.

3 I made. Ex 25:5, 10. 37:1-9.
hewed. ver. 1. Ex 34:4.

4 he wrote. Ex +31:18.
the ten. Dt 4:13. Ex 34:28.
commandments. Heb. words. Ex 34:28mg.
which. Dt 5:4-21. Ex 20:1-17.
out of the. Dt 4:11-15. 5:22-26. Ex 19:18. He 12:18, 19.
in the day. Dt 9:10. 18:16. Ex 19:17.

5 I turned. Dt 9:15. Ex 32:15. 34:29.
put the. ver. +2.
there they. Jsh 4:9. 1 K 8:8, 9. Ro 3:1, 2. He 9:4.

6 took. Nu 10:6, 12, 13. 33:1, 2.
Beeroth of. i.e. *wells*, **S#885h**, only here. For **S#881h**, Beeroth, see Jsh +9:17.
Jaakan. i.e. *necessity; strait*, **S#3292h**.
Mosera. i.e. *discipline*, **S#4149h**. Nu 33:30, 31, Moseroth. Hor-ha-gid-gad. Jotbatha.
there Aaron. Nu 20:23-28. 33:38.
in his stead. He 7:23-25.

7 From thence. Nu 33:32, 33.

Gudgodah. i.e. *incision*, **S#1412h**.
Jotbath. i.e. *goodness*, **S#3193h**. Nu 33:33, 34.

8 **time the Lord**. Ex 29:1, etc. Le 8:9. Nu 1:47-53. ch. 3, 4, 8. 16:9, 10. 18. Jn 15:16. Ac 13:2. Ro 1:1. 2 C 6:17. Ga 1:15.
separated. Ac 4:13.
bear. Nu 3:31. 4:15. 1 K 8:3, 4, 6. 1 Ch 15:12-15, 26. 23:26. 2 Ch 5:4, 5. Ac 9:15. 2 C 4:10.
to stand. Dt 1:38. 18:5, 7. Ge 41:46. Jg 20:28. 1 S 16:21, 22. 1 K 10:8. 12:6, 8. 17:1. 22:19. 2 Ch 9:7. 29:11. Ps 134:2. 135:2. Ezk 44:11, 15. Da 1:5, 19. Zc +4:14. Lk 1:19. +21:36. Ro 12:7.
unto him. 1 C 7:22. Ep 6:7.
to bless. Dt 21:5. Le 9:22. Nu 6:23-27. 2 Ch 30:27.
his name. Ac 3:16. 4:29, 30.
unto this day. Dt +29:4.

9 **Levi**. Nu +1:49. 26:62. Ezk 44:28.
no part. He 13:14.
Lord. Jsh 13:33.
inheritance. Dt 32:9. Nu 18:20. 35:1-4. Ezk 44:28. Ro 8:17. Ep 1:11. 1 P 1:4.

10 **I stayed**. Dt 9:18, 25. Ex 24:18. 34:28.
first time. *or*, former days.
the Lord hearkened. Dt 3:23-27. 9:19. Ex 32:14, 33, 34. 33:17. Ps 106:23. Mt 27:42.

11 **Arise**. Ex 32:34. 33:1. Mi 2:10.
take thy. Heb. go in.

12 **what doth**. Je 7:22, 23. Mi +6:8. Mt 11:29, 30. 1 J 5:3.
fear. Dt +6:2. Ps 34:9. Ac 9:31.
to walk. Dt +5:33. Jsh 22:5. Ps 81:13. Ezk 11:20. T 2:11, 12. 1 P 1:15, 16.
to love. Dt +6:5. 1 J 2:15.
to serve. Jb 36:11. Zp 3:9. Ro 1:9. He 12:28.
God with all. Mt +22:37.
soul. Heb. *nephesh*, Ge +34:3.

13 **for thy**. Dt 6:24. Pr 9:12. Je 32:39. 1 T 4:8. Ja 1:25.

14 **the heaven**. 1 K 8:27. 2 Ch 2:6. 6:18. Ne 9:6. Ps 68:33. 115:16. 139:7-10. 148:4. Is 66:1. Je 23:24.
heaven of. 2 C +12:2.
the earth. Ge 14:19. Ex 9:29. 19:5. Ps 24:1. 50:12. Je 27:5, 6. 1 C 10:26, 28.

15 **had**. Dt +4:37. +33:3. Nu 14:8.
delight. Dt 7:8. Ps 37:4.
chose. Ps 33:12. 65:4. 106:5. Hg 2:23. Mt 11:27. 24:22, 24, 31. Ro +8:28-30, 33. Col 3:12. T 1:1. 1 P 1:1, 2.

16 **Circumcise**. Dt +30:6.
be no more. Is 30:18, 19. Lk 13:6-9. Ja 5:7. 2 P 3:9, 15.
stiffnecked. 2 Ch +30:8. Pr 29:1. Ja 4:6, 7.

17 **God of gods**. 1 Ch 16:25, 26. Da +2:47.
Lord of lords. Ps 136:3. 1 T 6:15. Re 17:14. 19:16.
a great. Ps +99:3.

God. Heb. *El*, Ex +15:2.
a mighty. Is +10:21. +49:26.
regardeth. Ro +2:11.

18 **doth**. Ps +103:6.
fatherless and. Ge +11:28. 24:53. Ex +22:22-24.
widow. Is +1:17.
loveth. Ps 145:9. Mt 5:45. Ac 14:17.
stranger. ver. 19. Dt +26:11.

19 **Love**. Ex 22:21. 23:9. Le 19:33, 34. Lk 6:35. 10:28-37. 17:18. Ga 6:10. 1 T 6:18. Ja 2:15, 16. 1 J 3:17, 18.
stranger. ver. +18. Ex 12:48, 49.
ye were. 1 C 6:11. Ep 2:19.

20 **fear**. Dt +6:2. Ex +34:14. Mt 4:10. Lk 4:8.
cleave. Dt +4:4.
swear. Ge +21:23. Mt 5:33-37. 23:16-22. Ja 5:12.

21 **thy praise**. Ex 15:2. Ps 22:3. Is 12:2-6. 60:19. Je 17:14. Lk 2:32. Re 21:23.
that hath. Dt 4:32-35. 1 S 12:24. 2 S 7:23. Ps 106:21, 22. Is 64:3. Je 32:20, 21.

22 **with threescore**. Ge +46:27.
persons. Heb. *nephesh*, souls, Ge +12:5.
as the stars. Ge +15:5. Nu 26:51, 62.

DEUTERONOMY 11

1 **thou shalt**. Dt +6:5.
keep. Le 8:35. Zc 3:7. Jn 14:21. 15:8-10. 2 J 6. Re 22:14.
his statutes. Dt +4:1. Lk 1:74, 75.
judgments. Ps 9:16.
commandments. Ps 19:7-10. 112:1.

2 **And know**. Ro 7:1. He 12:5-7.
ye this. Dt 8:19. 29:10. Pr 22:19. Jn 20:29. Ac 1:21, 22. 26:22. 2 P 1:16.
children. ver. 19. Ex +13:8. Dt +6:20.
have not known. Lk 12:47, 48. Jn 20:29. Ro 2:12.
the chastisement. Dt 8:2-5.
his greatness. Dt +3:24.
his mighty. Dt +7:19.
stretched. Ex +6:6.

3 **his miracles**. Dt +4:34. 6:22. 7:8, 19. 26:8. Ex 15:12. Ps 78:12, 13, 43-51. 105:27, etc. 135:9. 136:10-12. Je 32:20, 21.

4 **how he made**. Ex 14:23-31. 15:4, 9, 10, 19. Ps 106:11. He 11:29.
unto this day. Dt +29:4.

5 **what he did**. Ps 77:20. 78:14, etc., 50-53. 105:39-41. 106:12, etc.

6 **he did unto**. Nu 16:1, 31-33. 26:9, 10. 27:3. Ps 106:17. Ju 11.
substance. *or*, living substance which followed them. Ge 7:4, 23.
in their possession. Heb. at their feet. Dt 28:57. 33:3. Ge 33:14mg. 49:10. Jg 5:15mg, 27mg. 2 K +3:9mg.

7 **your eyes**. ver. +2. Dt 5:3. 7:19. Ps 106:2.

145:4-6, 12. 150:2. 1 C 15:5-8. 2 P 1:16. 1 J
1:1.

8 **therefore**. Dt +8:10, 11. 10:12-15. 26:16-19.
28:47. Ps 116:12-16. 119:97-100.
  that ye may. Dt 31:23. Jsh 1:6, 7. Ps 138:3.
  Is 40:31. Da 10:19. 2 C 12:9, 10. Ep 3:16.
  6:10. Ph 4:13. Col 1:11.

9 **prolong**. Dt +4:40. Is 48:18.
  sware. Dt +6:18. 9:5.
  honey. Ex +3:8.

10 **wateredst it with thy foot**. Ps 1:3. Pr 21:1.
  Is 19:7. 37:25. 43:19. Je 17:8. Zc 14:18.

11 **the land**. Dt +8:7-9. Ge 27:28. Ps 65:12, 13.
  104:10-13. Is 28:1. Je 2:7. He 6:7.

12 **careth for**. Heb. seeketh. or searcheth. 1 Ch
  +28:9. Ps +9:10. 14:2. 119:2.
  the eyes. Dt 32:10. 1 K 9:3. Ezr 5:5. Ps +11:4.
  Ezk 5:11. 7:4. 20:17.
  always. Is +58:11.

13 **hearken**. Dt +15:5.
  diligently. ver. 8, 22. Dt +4:29. +6:17. Ps
  119:4, 33-35.
  to love. Dt +6:5.
  with. Mt +22:37.
  soul. Heb. *nephesh*, Ge +34:3.

14 **I will**. Dt 28:12. Le 26:3-5. Jb 5:10, 11.
  37:11-13. Ps 65:9-13. Je 14:22. Ezk 34:26. Jl
  2:22, 23. Mt 5:45. Ja 5:7.
  first rain. Ps 84:6mg. Je 5:24. Ho 6:3. Jl 2:23.
  Zc 10:1.
  latter rain. Jb 29:23. Pr 16:15. Je 3:3. 5:24.
  Ho 6:3. Ac 2:16-18. 3:19-26.

15 **And I will**. 1 K 18:5. Ps 104:14. Je 14:5. Jl
  1:18. 2:22.
  send. Heb. give. Ge 1:29. 3:12. 1 S 12:17. 1 K
  18:1. 2 K 19:7. 2 Ch 6:27. Ps 68:33. Ec 12:7.
  SS 1:12. 2:13. 7:13.
  eat and be full. Dt 6:11. 8:10. Jl 2:19. Hg
  1:6. Ml 3:10, 11.

16 **Take heed**. Dt +4:9, 23. Lk 21:8, 34, 36. He
  2:1. 3:12. 4:1. 12:15.
  your heart. Dt 13:3. 17:20. 29:18. Jb 31:27.
  Is 44:20. Je 17:9. Ja 1:26. 1 J 5:21. Re 12:9.
  13:14. 20:4.
  turn aside. Dt 28:14.
  serve other. Dt 8:19. 30:17. Le 26:1. 1 C 8:5,
  6. 10:14.
  worship. Ex +34:14.

17 **the Lord's wrath**. Dt +6:15. 30:17, 18.
  shut up. Dt 28:23, 24. Le 26:23, 24, 26. 1 K
  8:35. 17:1. 2 Ch 6:26. 7:13, 14. Je 14:1-6. Am
  4:7. Hg 1:9-11. Ja 5:17, 18.
  ye perish. Dt 4:26. 8:19, 20. 30:18. Jsh
  23:13-16.

18 **ye lay up**. Dt +6:6-9. Ex 13:9, 16. Pr 6:20-23.
  He 2:1. 2 P 1:12. 3:1, 2.
  soul. Heb. *nephesh*, Ge +34:3.
  a sign. Mt 23:5.

19 **shall teach**. Dt 4:9, 10. 6:7, +20. Ge 18:19.
  Ex +13:8. 1 Ch 28:9. Ps 34:11. 78:3-6. Pr 1:8,

9. 2:1. 4:1, 10-13. 22:6. Is 38:19. Mt 28:20. Ep
6:4. Col 3:16. 2 T 1:5. +3:15.
  speaking. Ps 119:46-48. Je 23:28.

20 **write**. Dt 6:9. Ha 2:2.

21 **your days**. Dt +4:40. 5:16. 6:2. 32:46, 47. Ps
89:29. Pr 3:2, 16. 4:10. 9:11.
  as the days. Ps 72:5. 89:28, 29. +118:24. Is
  65:20. Re 20:6.
  of heaven upon. Mt 6:10. He +11:13.

22 **if**. Ge +4:7.
  ye shall. ver. +13.
  diligently. Jsh 22:5. Ps 119:4. He 11:6. 2 P
  1:10. 3:14.
  to love. ver. +13. Mt 22:37. 2 T 4:8. 1 J 5:2,
  3.
  to cleave. Dt +4:4. 2 C 11:2, 3.

23 **drive out**. Ex +23:30. Lk 11:21. 1 J 4:4.

24 **Every place**. Nu 34:3, etc. Jsh 14:9. 1 K
  9:17-19.
  the river. Ge +2:14. Ps +72:8.

25 **There shall**. Dt 7:24. 28:10. Ge +35:5. Jsh
  1:5.
  as he hath. Nu 23:19.

26 **I set before**. Dt 30:1, 15-20. Nu 22:6. Ps
  37:22. Ga 3:10, 13, 14.

27 **A blessing**. Dt 28:1-14. Le 26:3-13. Ps 19:11.
  Is 1:19. 3:10. Mt 5:3-12. 25:31, etc. Lk 11:28.
  Jn 13:17. 14:21-23. Ro 2:7. Ja 1:25. Re 22:14.
  if. Ge +4:7.

28 **a curse**. Dt 28:15, etc. 29:19-28. Le 26:14,
  etc. Is 1:20. 3:11. Mt 25:41. Ro 2:8, 9. Ga
  3:10.
  to go after. Dt 6:14.
  other gods. ver. 16. Dt 8:19. 30:17.
  not known. Ga 1:8.

29 **put the blessing**. Dt 27:12-26. Jsh 8:30-35.
  Gerizim. i.e. *the cutters off,* **S#1630h**. Dt 27:12.
  Jsh 8:33. Jg 9:7. Jn 4:20.

30 **Canaanites**. Ge +10:18.
  champaign. Heb. Arabah. Dt 1:1mg. 2:8mg.
  3:17mg. 4:49mg. Nu +22:1mg. Jsh 3:16. 4:13.
  8:14. 11:2, 16. 12:8. 18:18. 1 S 23:24. 2 S
  2:29. 4:7. 15:28. 2 K 14:25. 25:4, 5. Je 39:4.
  52:7, 8. Ezk 47:8. Am +6:14. Zc 14:10.
  Gilgal. Jsh +4:19, 20.
  the plains. or, oaks, or terebinths. Ge 13:18.
  35:4, 8. Jsh 24:26.
  Moreh. Ge 12:6. Jg 7:1.

31 **pass over Jordan**. Dt 9:1. Jsh 1:2, 11. 3:13-
  17. 11:23.

32 **observe to do**. Dt +5:32, 33. 12:32. Mt 7:21-
  27. 28:20. 1 Th 4:1, 2.

DEUTERONOMY 12

1 **the statutes**. Dt +4:1.
  all the days. ver. 19. Dt 4:10. Nu 15:37-41. 1
  K 8:40. Jb 7:1. Ps 104:33. 146:2.

2 **utterly**. Ex +23:24.
  possess. *or,* inherit. Nu 22:41. 2 K 23:13-15.

high mountains. Je 3:6.
the hills. 2 K +17:10.
green tree. Is +57:5.

3 **overthrow**. Heb. break down. Ex +23:24.
and burn. Dt +7:5.
groves. 2 K +17:10.
images. 2 K +17:10mg.
and destroy. Ex +23:13. Re 13:1.

4 **not do so**. ver. 30, 31. Dt 6:13-19. 16:21, 22.
20:18. Le 20:23. Mt 4:10.

5 **But unto**. ver. +11. Dt 16:2. 26:2. Jsh 9:27.
18:1. 1 K 8:16, 20, 29. 14:21. 1 Ch 22:1. 2 Ch
7:12. Ps 78:68. 87:2, 3. Jn 4:20-22. He 12:22.
Re 14:1.
habitation. Ex 15:2. 25:22. Nu 7:89. 1 K
8:27, 29. Ps 132:13, 14. Is 66:1, 2. Ac 7:48-50.
Ep 2:20-22. Col 2:9.

6 **your burnt offerings**. Le +23:12. Ezk 20:40.
sacrifices. Le +7:11. +23:19.
tithes. ver. 11, 17. Dt 14:22-26. 15:19, 20.
26:2. Ge +14:20. Le 27:32, 33. Nu 18:15-17.
Ml 3:8, 10. Mt +23:23. Lk +11:42. 18:12.
heave offerings. Le +7:14.
vows. Le +23:38.
freewill offerings. Le +23:38.

7 **And there**. ver. 18. Dt 14:23, 26. 15:20. 1 K
4:20. Is 23:18.
ye shall rejoice. ver. 12, 18. Dt 14:26. 16:11-
15. 26:11. 27:7. Le 23:40. Ne 8:10. Ps 16:11.
32:11. 68:3. 128:1, 2. Ec 9:7-9. Ml 2:13. Ac
2:46. 16:34. Ph 3:1. 4:4. 1 Th 5:16.
put your hand. Dt 28:8.

8 **every man**. Nu 15:39. Jg 17:6. 21:25. Pr
21:2. Am 5:25. Ac 7:42.
right. Dt 13:18. Jg 21:25. 1 K 12:33. Pr 14:12.

9 **not as yet**. He 2:8. 1 J 3:2.
rest. Dt 25:19. 1 K 8:56. 1 Ch 23:25. Mi 2:10.
He 4:8, 9. 1 P 1:3, 4.

10 **But when**. Dt 3:27. 4:22. +9:1. Jsh 3:17. 4:1,
12.
dwell in safety. Dt 33:12, 28. Le 25:18, 19.
26:5. 1 S 7:12. 1 K 4:25. Ps 4:8. Pr 1:33. Is
11:6-9. Je 23:6. 32:37. 33:11, 16. Ezk 28:26.
34:25, 28. 38:8, 11. 39:26. Ho 2:18. Mi 4:4.
rest from. Jsh 21:43-45.

11 **a place**. ver. 5, +14, 18, 21, 26. Dt 14:23.
15:20. 16:2, 6, 7, 11, 15, +16. 17:8. 18:6.
23:16. 26:2. 31:11. Ge 22:3. Ex 20:24. 23:20.
29:24. 32:34. Jsh 9:27. 18:1. 22:11, 16, 27. 1
K 8:13, 16, 20, 29. 2 Ch 7:12. Ne 1:9. Ps
78:68. Je 7:12. Ezk 48:35. Mt 18:20. Jn 4:20-
23. He 10:25.
burnt offerings. Le +23:12.
sacrifices. Le +7:11. +23:19.
your tithes. ver. +6. Ge +14:20.
heave offering. Le +7:14.
your choice. Heb. the choice of your vows.
vows. Le +23:38.

12 **And ye**. ver. +7. 1 K 8:66. 2 Ch 29:36. 30:21-
26. Ps 100:1, 2. 147:1. 1 J 1:3, 4.

the Levite. ver. 18, 19. Dt 14:27, 29. 16:11,
14. 18:6. 26:12, 13.
gates. Ge +14:7.
forasmuch. Dt 10:9. 18:1, 2. Nu 18:20, 23,
24, 26. Jsh 13:14, 33. 14:4.

13 **Take heed**. ver. 6. Le 17:2-5. 1 K 12:28-32.
15:34. 2 Ch 15:17.
every place. Jsh 22:16, 29.

14 **place**. ver. +11. Le 17:3-9. 23:4. Ps 5:7. 9:11.
2 C 5:19. He 10:19-22, 25. 13:15.

15 **whatsoever**. Dt 14:26.
soul. Heb. nephesh, Nu +11:6.
the unclean. ver. 21, 22. Dt 14:5. 15:22, 23.
Le 17:3-5.

16 **not eat**. ver. 23, 24. Le +3:17.

17 **the tithe**. ver. +6, 11. Dt 14:22-29. 26:12, 14.
Le 27:30-32. Nu 18:21, etc.
thy corn. Ne 10:39.
vows. Le +23:38.
freewill offerings. Le +23:38.
heave offering. Le +7:14.

18 **thou must**. ver. 11, 12, 19. Dt 14:23.
15:20.
rejoice. ver. +7. 1 S 2:1. Pr 3:17. Ec 3:22. Is
12:3. 64:5. 66:10-14. Jl 2:23. Hab 3:18. Ro
5:11. 1 C 10:31. 2 C 6:10. Ga 5:22.

19 **take**. ver. +12. 2 Ch 11:13, 14. 31:4-21. Ne
10:34-39. 1 C 9:10-14.
as long, etc. Heb. all thy days. ver. +1. Jsh
4:24mg.
earth. or, thy ground.

20 **shall**. 1 Ch 4:10.
as he hath. Dt 11:24. 19:8. Ge 15:18-21.
28:14. Ex 23:31. 34:24.
I will. ver. 15. Ge 31:30. Nu 11:4, 20, 34. 2 S
13:39. 23:15. Ps 63:1. 84:2. 107:9. 119:20, 40,
174. 2 C 9:14. Ph 1:8. 2:26.
soul. Heb. nephesh, Nu +11:6.

21 **to put**. ver. +11. 1 K 14:21. 2 Ch 12:13. Ezr
6:12.
soul. Heb. nephesh, Nu +11:6.

22 **roebuck**. ver. 15, 16.

23 **sure**. Heb. strong. Dt 31:6, 7, 23. Jsh 1:6, 7, 9,
18. 10:25. Is 41:6mg.
the blood is. Ge 9:4. Le 3:16, 17. 17:11, 14.
Mt 20:28. Re 5:9.
life. Heb. nephesh, soul, Ge +2:19. Pr 12:10.
not eat. ver. +16.

24 **shalt pour**. ver. 16. Dt 15:23.

25 **that it**. ver. 28. Dt 4:40. 5:16. Ps 112:2. Is
3:10. 48:18, 19. Ezk 33:25.
when. Dt 6:18. 13:18. Ex 15:26. 1 K 11:38.
Ec 2:26. 1 T 4:8.

26 **holy**. ver. 6, 11, 18. Nu 5:9, 10. 18:19.
thy vows. Ge 28:20. Le 22:18, etc. +23:38. 1
S 1:21-24. Ps 66:13-15.

27 **thy burnt**. Le +23:12.
and the blood. Le +3:17. 4:30.
poured out. ver. 16.

28 **Observe**. Dt 24:8. Ex 34:11. Le 19:37. 2 Ch

7:17. Ne 1:5. Ps 105:45. Ezk 37:24. Jn 15:3, 10, 14.

and hear. Is 48:18, 19. Mk 4:24. Lk 8:18.

that it may. ver. 25.

for ever. Heb. *olam*, Ex +12:24.

29 **cut off**. Dt 9:3. 19:1. Ex 23:23. Jsh 23:4. Ps 78:55.

succeedest. Heb. inheritest, *or*, possessest. ver. 2. Dt 19:1.

30 **Take heed**. Ac 20:28.

snared. Ex +23:33. Le 18:3. 2 K 17:15.

by following. Heb. after. Dt 1:4, 8, 36mg. 4:3. Ge 5:4, etc. 6:4. 9:9, 28. Jsh 6:8. Jg 9:3mg. Ps 73:24. Pr 7:22. 24:27. 28:23.

How did. Je +10:2. Ro 12:2. Ep 4:17. 1 P 4:3, 4.

31 **Thou**. ver. 4. Dt 18:9. Ex 23:2. Le 18:3, 26-30. 1 K 21:26. 2 K 17:15-17. 21:2, 11. 2 Ch 33:2, 9. 36:14.

abomination to the. Heb. abomination of the. Dt 7:25. 17:1. 18:12. 22:5. 23:18. 25:16. 27:15.

even their sons. Dt +18:10. Mi 6:7.

32 **observe**. Mt 7:21. 28:20. Lk 6:46. 8:21. Ja 1:22.

thou shalt not. Dt 13:18. Jsh +1:7. 8:30-35. Mt 28:20.

DEUTERONOMY 13

1 **a prophet**. 1 K 13:18. Je 6:13. 23:11. Ezk 13:2, 3, 23. Zc 13:4. Mt +7:15. 24:11.

a dreamer. Je 23:25-28. 27:9. 29:8, 24mg. Zc 10:2.

2 **the sign**. Dt 18:22. Ex 7:22. 1 K 13:3-5, 7-32. Je 28:9. Mt 7:22, 23. 24:24. 2 C 11:13-15. 2 Th 2:9-11. Re 13:13, 14.

3 **hearken**. Is +8:20. Ac +17:11. Ep +4:14. 1 J 4:1.

proveth. Dt +8:2. Ex 16:4. 20:20. Ps 66:10. 81:7. Mt 24:24. 1 C +11:19. 2 Th 2:11. Ja 1:12. 1 J 2:19. 4:4. 1 P 1:6, 7. Re 13:14.

ye love the Lord your God. Dt +6:5. 2 C 8:8.

soul. Heb. *nephesh*, Ge +34:3.

4 **walk**. Ge +5:22. Mi +6:8. Col +1:10.

fear. Dt +6:2.

and obey. Je +7:23. Mt 7:21. Lk 6:46.

his voice. Dt 8:20. 30:20. Jn 10:4, 5, 27.

and cleave. Dt +4:4. Ro 6:13. 1 C 6:17. +15:2mg.

5 **prophet**. Dt 18:20. 1 K 18:40. Is 9:14, 15. 28:17, 18. Je 14:15. 28:15-17. 29:21, 22. Zc 13:3. Re 19:20.

spoken. Heb. spoken a revolt against the Lord. Is 1:5mg. Je +28:16mg.

turn you. ver. 10. Dt 7:4. Je 50:6. Ac 13:8. 2 T 4:4, 5. 2 J 9-11.

put the evil. Dt 17:7, 12. 19:19. 22:21, 22, 24. 24:7. Jg 20:13. 1 C 5:13. He 12:14, 15.

6 **thy brother**. Dt 17:2, 3. 28:54. Ge 16:5. Pr 5:20. 18:24. Mi 7:5-7. Zc 13:2, 3. Mt 12:48-50. 2 C 5:16.

which is. 1 S 18:1, 3. 20:17. 2 S 1:26.

soul. Heb. *nephesh*, Ge +27:31.

entice. Jb 31:27. Ga 2:4. Ep 4:14. Col 2:4. 2 P 2:1. 1 J 2:26, 27. Re 12:9. 13:14. 20:3.

which thou. Dt 32:16-18. Jg 2:13. 5:8. 10:6. 1 K 11:5-7. 2 K 17:30, 31.

7 **gods of the people**. Dt 6:14. 1 Ch 16:26. Is 2:8. Je 2:11, 28. 16:20. Da 5:4. Jn 10:34. 1 C 8:5. 12:2. Ga 4:8.

8 **consent**. Ex 20:3. Pr 1:10. Ga 1:8, 9. 1 J 5:21.

shall thine. Dt +7:16. 19:13. Ezk 5:11. 9:5, 6.

eye. Ge +31:35.

9 **But**. Dt 17:2-7. Ex 22:20. Mt 10:37. Lk 14:26.

thine hand. Dt 17:7. Zc 13:2, 3. Jn 8:7. Ac 7:58.

10 **stone him**. Le +24:14.

which brought. Ex +20:2.

bondage. Heb. bondmen. Dt +6:12.

11 **all Israel**. Dt 17:13. 19:20. Pr 19:25. 21:11. 1 T 5:20.

12 **shalt hear**. Jsh 22:11, etc. Jg 20:1, 2, etc.

13 **the children**. *or*, naughty men. Jg 19:22. 20:13. 1 S 2:12. 10:27. 25:17, 25. 2 S 16:7. 20:1. 23:6. 1 K 21:10, 13. 2 Ch 13:7. Jn 8:44. 2 C 6:15. 1 J 3:10.

Belial. i.e. *wicked; vile; perverse; worthlessness*, S#1100h. Jg 20:13. 1 S 1:16. 10:27. +30:22. 2 S 16:7. 20:1. 2 Ch 13:7. Pr 6:12 (naughty). 16:27mg.

are gone. Dt 4:19. 2 K 17:21. 1 J 2:19. Ju 19. Let us. ver. 2, 6.

14 **inquire**. Dt 17:4. 19:18. Nu 35:30. Is 11:3, 4. Jn 7:24. 1 T 5:19.

15 **edge**. Ge +34:26.

destroying it utterly. Dt +2:34. Ex 22:20. 23:24. Jg 20:48. Re 17:16. 18:18-24. 19:2, 3.

16 **burn with**. Jsh 6:24.

an heap. Nu 21:2, 3. Jsh 6:26. 7:26. 8:28. Is 17:1. 25:2. Je 49:2. Mi 1:6.

for ever. Heb. *olam*, Ex +12:24.

17 **cleave**. Dt +7:26. Jsh 6:18. 7:1.

cursed. *or*, devoted. Le +27:28, 29. 1 C 16:22.

the Lord. Ex +32:12. Jsh 6:26. 22:20.

and show. Ex 20:6. La 3:32.

compassion. Dt 30:3. La 3:32.

and multiply. Ezk 37:26.

as he hath. Ge 22:16, 17. 26:4, 24. 28:14.

18 **to keep**. Dt +12:25, 28, 32. Ps 119:6. Mt 6:33. 7:21, 24.

DEUTERONOMY 14

1 **the children**. Ge 6:2, 4. 1 J +3:1.

ye shall not cut. Le +19:28. Je +10:2. 1 Th 4:13.

baldness. Is +3:24.

2 **For thou**. ver. 21. Dt 28:9. Ex 15:16. +19:5,

6. Le +19:2. 2 S 7:24. Is 6:13. 62:12. Je 31:31-34. Ezk 21:2. Da 8:24. 12:7. Ho 1:10.

3 **not eat**. Le 11:43. 20:25. Is 65:4. Ezk 4:14. Ac 10:12-14. Ro 14:14. 1 C 10:28. 1 T 4:3-5. T 1:15.

4 **the beasts**. Le +11:2-8. 1 K 4:23.

5 **The hart**. Dt 12:15, 22. 15:22. 1 K 4:23. Ps 42:1. SS 2:9, 17. 8:14. Is 35:6. La 1:6.
pygarg. *or*, bison. Heb. *dishon*.
wild ox. or, antelope. Is 51:20mg.
the chamois. or, mountain sheep.

6 **parteth the hoof**. Le +11:3, 4. Ps 1:1, 2. 34:14. Pr 18:1. 2 C 6:17.
and. Dt 17:6. Ge +22:15. 41:32.
cheweth the cud. Jsh 1:8. Ps 1:1, 2. Ph 4:8. 1 T 4:15, 16.

7 **ye shall not eat**. Mt 7:22, 23, 26. 2 T 3:5. T 1:16. 2 P 2:18-22.
unclean. Ge 7:1, 2. Le 11:2-8. Is 52:11. 1 Th 5:22.

8 **the swine**. Is 65:4. 66:3, 17. Lk 15:15, 16. 2 P 2:22.
unclean unto you. ver. 7. Ro 14:14, 17. 1 C 8:8. Col 2:16, 17. 1 T 4:3. He 9:9, 10.
touch. Le 11:26, 27.

9 **shall eat**. Le 11:9-12. Lk 24:42, 43.

10 **hath not fins**. Le 11:10. Da 1:8. Ho 9:3.

11 **clean birds**. Le 14:4. Ezk 22:26. 44:23.

12 **not eat**. Le +11:13-19.

13 **the glede**. Le 11:14.
after his kind. Ge 1:11. 6:20. 7:14. Le 11:14. Ezk 47:10.

14 **raven**. Le +11:15. 1 K 17:4, 6.

15 **the owl**. or, ostrich. Le 11:16. Jb 30:29.
night hawk. Le 11:16.
cuckoo. Le 11:16.
hawk. Le 11:16. Jb 39:26.

16 **little owl**. Le 11:17. Ps 102:6.
great owl. Le 11:17. Is 34:11.
the swan. Le 11:18, 30.

17 **the pelican**. Le 11:18. Ps 102:6.
the cormorant. Is 34:11. Zp 2:13, 14. Re 18:2.

18 **the stork**. Le 11:19. Ps 104:17.
the bat. Le 11:19. Is 2:20.

19 **every creeping**. Le 11:20-23. Ph 3:19.
unclean. ver. 7, 8. 1 C 8:13. 1 J 3:4.

20 **clean fowl**. ver. 11. Ac 15:18-20. Ro 14:2, 3.

21 **any thing**. Le 17:15. 22:8. Ezk 4:14. Ac 15:20.
the stranger. Ex 12:43-45. Le 19:33, 34.
an holy. ver. +2. Da 8:24. 12:7.
Thou shalt. Ex 16:23. 23:19. 34:26. Ps 145:9. Ro 12:2.

22 **truly tithe**. Dt 12:6, 17. 26:12-15. Ge +14:20. Le 27:30-33. Nu 18:21. Ne 10:37.

23 **eat before**. Dt 12:5-7, 17, 18.
place. Dt +12:11.
the firstlings. Dt 15:19, 20.

24 **if the place**. Dt 11:24. 12:21. Ex 23:31.
which. Dt +12:5.

25 **turn**. Mt 21:12. Mk 11:15. Lk 19:45. Jn 2:14.
bind up the money. Ge 23:16. 2 K 5:23. 12:10.

26 **bestow**. Ezr 7:15-17, 22. Mt 21:12. Mk 11:15. Jn 2:14-16.
thy soul. Heb. *nephesh*, Nu +11:6. Dt 12:15, 20, 21. Ps 106:14. 1 C 6:12, 13. 10:6.
soul. Heb. *nephesh*, Nu +11:6.
desireth. Heb. asketh of thee. Dt 6:20. Ge 24:47, 57. Jsh 4:6, 21.
eat. Dt +12:7, 12, 18. 26:11.
rejoice. Ne 8:10. Ps 128:1, 2. Ec 9:7.

27 **the Levite**. Dt +12:12. Ga 6:6. 1 T 5:17.
gates. Ge +14:7.
he hath no. ver. +29.

28 **the end**. ver. +22. Dt 26:12-15. Am 4:4.
thou shalt bring. Ml 3:10. Pr 3:9, 10. 11:24, 25.

29 **he hath**. ver. 27. Dt 12:12. 15:10. 18:1, 2. 26:11. Nu +18:20.
the stranger. Dt 16:11, 14. 24:19-21. +26:11. Ex 22:21-24. Jb 31:16-22. Lk 14:12-14. He 13:2. Ja 1:27.
fatherless. Ex +22:22.
widow. Is +1:17.
that the Lord. Dt 15:10. Ps 41:1. Pr 3:9, 10. 11:24. 14:21. 19:17. Is 58:7-12. Ml 3:10, 11. Lk 6:35. 11:41. 2 C 6:9-11.

DEUTERONOMY 15

1 **seven**. Dt 31:10. Ex 21:2. 23:10, 11. Le 25:2-4. Is 61:1-3. Je 34:8-18. Lk 4:18, 19. Ro 6:17, 18. 1 C 6:20. Ga 5:1.

2 **creditor that lendeth**. Heb. master of the lending of his hand. Ge 37:19.
exact it. Ne 5:7-11. Is 58:3. Am 8:4-6. Mt 6:12, 14, 15. 18:25-35. Lk 6:34-38. 7:42. Ja 2:13.

3 **foreigner**. Dt 23:20. Ex 46:16, 17. Mt 17:25, 26. Jn 8:35. 1 C 6:6, 7. Ga 6:10. Ep 2:19.
brother. 1 Th 4:9. He 13:1.

4 **save**, etc. *or*, To the end that there be no poor among you. ver. 11.
greatly bless. Dt +14:29. 28:1-8, 11. Pr 11:24, 25. 14:21. 28:27. Is 58:10, 11.

5 **Only**. Dt +4:9. Jsh 1:7.
if. Ge +4:7.
hearken. Dt 7:12. 11:13. 13:18. 26:17. 28:1, 2, 15. Ex 15:26. Jg 3:4. 1 K 11:38. Ps 19:11. Ps 81:8. 95:7. Is 55:2, 3. Je 17:24. 26:3.

6 **thou shalt lend**. Dt 28:12, 44. Ps 37:21, 26. 112:5. Pr 22:7. Lk 6:35.
thou shalt reign. Dt 28:13. 1 K 4:21, 24. 2 Ch 9:26. Ezr 4:20. Ne 9:27.

7 **there be**. ver. 11. Mt 26:11.
harden. Dt 2:30. 24:12, 13. Ex 23:6. Pr 22:22. Zc 7:10. 1 J 3:17.
brother. 2 P 1:5, 7.

8 **shalt open**. ver. 9, 11. Le 25:35. Est 9:22. Jb 29:16. Ps 37:21. 41:1. 81:10. 112:5-9. 145:16. Pr 11:24, 25. 19:17. 21:13, 26. 22:9. 28:8, 27. Ec 11:1, 2, 6. Mt 5:42. 18:30. Lk 6:34, 35. Ac 24:17. 2 C 8:7-9. 9:5-13. Ga 2:10. Ja 2:15, 16. 1 J 3:16, 17.
lend. ver. 6. Dt 23:19, 20. Le 25:35-37.
sufficient. Ex 36:6, 7.
his need. Mt +5:42. Lk +6:30. Ja 2:15, 16. 1 J 3:17, 18.
wanteth. Jg 18:10. 19:19, 20. Ps 34:9. Pr 6:11. 11:24. 14:23. 21:5, 17. 22:16. 24:34. 28:27.

9 **Beware**. Pr 4:23. Je 17:10. Mt 15:19. Mk 7:21, 22. Ro 7:8, 9. Ja 4:5.
thought, etc. Heb. word with thine heart of Belial. 1 S 1:16. +30:22mg.
release. Mt 6:12. Lk 11:4.
thine eye. Dt 28:54-56. Pr 23:6. 24:9. 28:22. Mt 20:15. Ja 5:9. 1 P 4:9.
he cry. Ex +22:23. Ps 9:12.
sin unto thee. Mt 25:41-45. Ja 4:17. 1 J 3:15-17.

10 **thine heart**. Mt 25:40. Ac 20:35. Ro 12:8-10. 2 C 9:5-7. Ep 5:3. 1 T 6:18, 19. 1 P 4:11.
because. ver. +4. Dt 14:29. 24:19. Ps 41:1, 2. Pr 11:24, 25. 22:9. Is 32:8. 58:10, 11. Ro 12:13. 2 C 9:8-11. Ph 4:18, 19. He 13:16.

11 **the poor**. Ex +23:3. Pr 22:2. Mt 26:11. Mk 14:7. Jn 12:8.
Thou shalt. ver. +8. Mt +5:42. 25:41, 42. Lk 12:33. Ac 2:45. 4:32-35. 11:28-30. 2 C 8:2-9. 1 J 3:16-18.

12 **if thy brother**. ver. +1. Le +25:39-41.
13 **shalt not**. ver. 14. Ge 31:42. Ex 3:21. 21:2-11. Le 25:42-44. Pr 3:27, 28. Je 22:13. Ml 3:5. Col 4:1.
14 **the Lord**. Ne 8:10. Ps 68:10. Pr 10:22. Ac 20:35. 1 C 16:2. 2 C 9:5-7.
15 **shalt remember**. Ex +13:3. Is 51:1. Mt 6:14, 15. 18:32, 33. Ep 1:7. 4:32. 5:1, 2. T 2:14. 1 J 3:16. 4:9-11.
16 **if he say**. Ex +21:5, 6. Ps 40:6, 8.
17 **ear**. Ex +21:6. Jb 33:16. 36:10, 15. Ps 40:6mg. Is 48:8.
forever. Heb. *olam*, Ex +12:24. Ex +21:6. Le 25:39-42. 1 S 1:22. Ps +24:9.
18 **shall not**. ver. 10.
a double. Ge +43:12. Is 16:14. 21:16. Lk 17:7, 8.
bless. Pr 10:22. 11:24.
19 **the firstling**. Ex 13:2, 12. 22:29, 30. 34:19. Le 27:26. Nu 3:13. 18:17. Lk 2:23. Ro 8:29. 1 C 15:20. Col +1:15. He 12:23.
thou shalt do. Dt 12:5-7, 17. 14:23. 16:11, 14. Nu 18:15.
20 **shalt eat**. Dt +12:5-7, 17.
place. Dt +12:11.
choose. Jsh 18:1. Ps 78:60, 68. 132:13, 14.
21 **if there be**. Le +1:3.

22 **the unclean**. Dt 12:15, 21, 22.
roebuck. Dt 14:5. 2 S 2:18. 1 K 4:23.
hart. Dt +14:5.
23 **not eat the blood**. Le +3:17. Mt 26:28. Mk 14:24. Jn 19:34. Ro 3:25. 5:9. Col 1:14, 20. He 9:22. 1 J 1:7. Re 1:5.
pour. Dt 12:16, 24. Le 17:13.

DEUTERONOMY 16

1 **The month**. Ex 12:2, etc. 13:4. 23:15. 34:18. Le 23:5. Nu 9:2-5. 28:16.
the passover. Le 23:5-8. Nu 28:16-25. 2 K 23:23. 2 Ch 35:13. Mt 26:2, 19, 26-29. Jn 1:29. 1 C 5:7, 8. Ep 1:7.
for in. Ex 12:29-42. 13:4. 23:15. 34:18.
2 **sacrifice**. Ex 12:5-7. Nu 28:16-19. 2 Ch 35:7. Mt 26:2, 17. Mk 14:12. Lk 22:8, 15. 1 C 5:7.
in the place which. ver. 6, 16. Dt +12:11.
3 **eat no**. Ex 12:15, 19, 20, 39. 13:3-7. 34:18. Le +23:6. Nu 9:11. 28:17. 1 C 5:8.
the bread of. Ex +8:23. 1 K 22:27. Ps 102:9. 127:2. Zc 12:10. 2 C 7:10, 11. 1 Th 1:6.
for thou camest. Ex 12:32, 33, 39.
mayest. Ex 12:14, 26, 27. 13:7-9. Ps 111:4. Lk 22:19. 1 C 11:24-26.
4 **there shall**. Ex 12:15. 13:7. 34:25.
neither. Ex +12:10.
5 **sacrifice**. *or*, kill. ver. +2. Dt 12:5, 6.
gates. Ge +14:7.
6 **place**. ver. +16. Dt +12:11.
passover. Le +23:5.
at even. Ex 12:6-9. Nu 9:3, 11. Mt 26:20. Ac 20:7. 1 C 11:20. He 1:2, 3. 9:26. 1 P 1:19, 20.
7 **roast**. lit. cook. Ex 12:8, 9. 2 Ch 35:13. Ps 22:14, 15.
in the place. ver. +2. 2 K 23:23. Jn 2:13, 23. 11:55.
8 **Six days**. Ex 12:15, 16. 13:7, 8. Le 23:6-8. Nu 28:17-19.
unleavened. Le +23:6.
solemn assembly. Heb. restraint. Le +23:36.
9 **Seven weeks**. ver. 10, 16. Le +23:16. He 2:1.
10 **feast of weeks**. Le +23:16.
a tribute. *or*, sufficiency. ver. 16. Le 5:7mg. 12:8mg. 25:26mg. Nu 31:28, 37. Pr 3:9, 10.
freewill offering. Le +23:38.
according. ver. 17. Pr 10:22. Jl 2:14. Hg 2:15-19. Ml 3:10, 11. 1 C 16:2. 2 C 8:10, 12. 9:5-11.
11 **shalt rejoice**. ver. 14. Dt +12:7. Ro 5:11. 2 C 1:24.
and thy. Ge +8:22.
12 **remember**. ver. +15. Dt 15:15. La 3:19, 20. Ro 6:17, 18. Ep 2:1-3, 11.
observe and do. Dt +26:16, 18. Ezr +7:10. Jn +13:17. 1 J +2:3.
13 **shalt observe**. Ps 126. Zc 14:18.

the feast. Le +23:34, 35-36, 42, 43.
gathered. Dt 32:11. Mt 23:37.
corn and thy wine. Heb. floor and thy
winepress. Ge +50:10. Jb 39:12. Jl 2:24. Mt
13:30. Jn 12:24. 1 C 15:23. Re 14:14-16. 20:5.
wine. Re 14:17-20.

14 **rejoice**. ver. +11. Is 25:6-8. 30:29. 35:10.
fatherless. Ex +22:22.
gates. Ge +14:7.

15 **Seven days**. Le 23:36-42. Nu 29:12-38.
because. ver. +10. Dt 7:13. 28:8-12. 30:16.

16 **Three times**. Ex 23:14-17. 34:22, 23. 1 K
9:25. Lk 2:40-42. Jn 2:13. 7:2-10. 11:55.
before. Ex 29:24. Le 16:12.
place. ver. 6. Dt +12:11.
unleavened. Le +23:6.
and they shall. Ex 23:15. 34:20. 1 Ch 29:3-
9, 14-17. Ps 96:8. Pr 3:9, 10. Is 23:18. 60:6-9.
Hg 1:9. Mt 2:11. Mk 12:3.
empty. Dt 26:2. Ex 29:24. Le 16:12. 1 Ch
+21:24.

17 **as he is able**. Heb. according to the gift of his
hand. ver. +10. Le 27:8. Ezr 2:63. Mk 12:41-
44. Lk +11:41mg. 1 C +16:2. 2 C 8:12.
9:6, 7.

18 **Judges**. Dt 21:2. Ex +21:6. Ps 82:2, 3. Ro
13:1-6.
in all thy gates. ver. 14. Dt 17:8. 21:19.
22:15. 25:7. Ge +14:7. 2 S 15:2. Jb 31:21. Is
29:21. Am 5:15. Zc 8:16.
they shall. ver. 19. Dt 1:16, 17. 17:15, 18-20.
19:18, 19. 25:1, 2. Ps 82:2-4. Pr 16:12. 20:28.
29:14. 31:4, 5. Je 22:2, 3, 15, 16. Ezk 45:9,
10. 46:18.

19 **wrest**. or, incline, or, stretch out. Ex 23:2, 6.
Ps 56:5.
judgment. Dt 24:17. 27:19. Ex 23:2, 6-8. 1 S
8:3. 12:3. Jb 31:21, 22. Pr 17:23. 18:5. Ec 7:7.
Is 1:17, 23. 10:2. 33:15. Je 5:28. La 3:35. Ezk
22:12. Mi 7:3. Hab 1:4. Zp 3:3-5. Ac 16:37.
23:3.
respect. Ex 23:7, 8. Pr 24:28. Ro +2:11. Ja
+2:1.
pervert. Ex 23:8. Pr 13:6. 19:3. 21:12. 22:12.
words. or, matters. Pr 22:12mg.

20 **That which**, etc. Heb. Justice, justice. Dt
+25:13-16. Mi +6:8. Ph 4:8.
altogether just. Le +19:15. Ec +5:8. Lk
+16:10. Jn +7:24, 51. 1 T +5:19.
follow. Jg 8:4. Ps 23:6. 34:14. 38:20. Pr
21:21. Is 51:1. Ho 6:3.
live. Dt +4:1. Ezk 18:5, 7-9. Ro 10:5.
inherit. Mt +5:5. Ro +4:13.

21 **plant**. Ge 2:8.
grove. 2 K +17:10.

22 **image**. or, statue, or pillar. Ge 28:18, 22.
31:13. Ex +20:4. 2 K +17:10mg. Ps 10:3. Col
3:5. 1 J 5:21.
which. Dt 12:31. Je 44:4. Zc 8:17. Re 2:6, 15.
hateth. Ps 5:5. 11:5. Pr 6:16.

DEUTERONOMY 17

1 **Thou shalt**. Le +1:3.
sheep. or, goat. Ex 12:3.
any evil favoredness. Ge 41:3, 4, 19.
for that. Dt 23:18. 24:4. 25:16. Pr 6:16. 11:1.
15:8. 20:10.

2 **within any of thy gates**. Dt 13:12. Ge
+14:7.
man. ver. 5. Dt 13:6-14. 29:18.
in transgressing. Dt 4:23. 29:25. 31:20. Le
26:15, 25. Jsh 7:11, 15. 23:16. Jg 2:20. 2 K
18:12. Je 31:32. Ezk 16:38. Ho 6:7. 8:1. He
8:9, 10.
covenant. Ex 34:27.

3 **the sun**. Dt +4:19. Ezk +8:16.
which. Je 7:22, 23, 31. 19:5. 32:35.

4 **enquired**. Dt 13:12-14. 19:18. Pr 25:2. Jn
7:51.

5 **stone them**. Le +24:14.
till they die. 1 K 15:11-13. 2 K 10:23-28.
11:18-20.

6 **the mouth**. Dt 19:15. Nu 35:30. Ho 14:2. Mt
18:16. Jn 8:17, 18. 2 C 13:1. 1 T 5:19. He
10:28.
two. Dt +14:6. Ge +22:15. 41:32. Mt 18:19.

7 **of the witnesses**. Dt 13:9. 1 K 21:12, 13. Ac
7:57- 59.
all the people. Jsh 7:25, 26.
So thou. ver. 12. Dt +13:5.

8 **arise**. Dt 1:17. Ex 18:26. 1 K 3:16-28. 2 Ch
19:8-10. Hg 2:11. Ml 2:7.
between blood. Dt 19:4, 10, 11. Ex 21:12-
14, 20, 22, 28. 22:2. Nu 35:11, 16, 19, etc.
gates. Ge +14:7.
get thee up. Dt +12:5. 16:6, +16. 19:17. Ps
68:16. 122:3-5. 132:13, 14.

9 **the priests**. Nu 27:21. Is +66:21. Je 18:18.
Hg 2:11. Ml 2:7.
the judge. ver. 12. Ex +21:6. The singular is
put for the plural, as at Ge 3:2, 7. 49:6. 1 S
31:1. 1 K 10:22. 2 K 11:10 with 2 Ch 9:21.
23:9. 1 Ch 4:42.
they shall. Dt 19:17-21. Ezk 44:24.

10 **do according**. Mt 22:2, 3.

11 **According to**. Jsh 1:7. 1 K 2:23-25. 3:28. Ml
2:8, 9. Ro 13:1-6. T 3:1. 1 P 2:13-15. 2 P 2:10.
Ju 8.
they shall teach thee. Dt 33:10. Le 10:11. 1
Ch 25:7, 8. 26:32. 2 Ch +15:3. 35:3. Ezr 7:10.
Je 18:18. Hg 2:11, 12. Ml 2:7.
to the right. ver. 20. Jsh +1:7. 2 S 14:19.

12 **will do**. Dt 13:5, 11. Nu 15:30. Ezr 10:8. Ps
19:13. Ho 4:4. Mt 10:14. He 10:26-29.
and will not hearken. Heb. not to hearken.
Je 25:3, etc.
the priest. Dt 10:8. 18:5, 7. Lk 10:16. Jn
12:48. 20:23. 1 Th 4:2, 8.
that man. He 10:28.
thou shalt. ver. +7. Pr 21:11. 1 T 5:20.

13 **shall hear**. Dt +13:11. 19:20.

presumptuously. Nu +15:30, 31. 2 P 2:10.

14 **When thou**. Dt 7:1, 12:9, 10. 18:9. 26:1, 9. Le 14:34. Jsh 1:13.
I will set. 1 S 8:5-7, 10, 19, 20. 12:19.

15 **king**. 1 S 8:18.
whom. 1 S 9:15-17. 10:24, 25. 16:11-13. 2 S 5:2. 1 Ch 12:23. 22:10. 28:5. Ps 2:2, 6. 78:70, 71.
from among. Dt 18:15, 18. Ge +49:10. Ps 89:18-21. Je 30:21. Mt 22:17.
not set. Je 2:25.
stranger. Dt 14:21. +26:11. Ex 12:19, 43mg. 29:33. Le 22:10. Nu 1:51. 3:10, 28. 16:40. 18:4, 7.

16 **multiply horses**. 1 S 8:11. 2 S 8:4. 1 K 4:26. 8:9. 10:26, 28. 2 Ch 9:25. Ps 20:7. Is 30:16. Ho 14:3.
cause. Is 31:1-3. Je 42:14. Ezk 17:15.
Ye shall henceforth. Dt 28:68. Ex 13:17. 14:13. Nu 14:3, 4. Jsh 3:4. Je 42:13-16. Ho 11:5.

17 **multiply wives**. Ge +4:19.
neither shall he. 2 S 8:6, 7, 10, 11. 1 K 10:21, 27. Ps 62:10. Pr 30:8, 9. Is 2:7. Mt 6:19, 20. 13:22. 19:23, 24. Lk 12:15. 1 T 6:9, 17.

18 **that he shall**. 2 K 11:12.
out of that which. Dt 31:9, 25, 26. 2 K 11:12, 17. 22:8, 10, 11, 13. 2 Ch 34:15.

19 **read therein**. Dt 6:6-9. 11:18. Jsh 1:8. Ps 1:2. 119:97-100. Jn 5:39. 2 T +3:15-17.
all the days. Ac 17:11.
fear. Dt +6:2. Pr +1:7. 2 C 5:11. He 10:31. Re 19:5.
keep. Dt 4:10. 14:23. to
do. Dt +26:16, 18.

20 **his heart**. Dt 8:2, 13, 14. 11:16. 2 K 14:10. 2 Ch 25:19. 26:16. 32:25, 26. 33:12, 19, 23. 34:27. Ps 131:1, 2. Pr 16:18. Is 2:12. Ezk 28:2. Da 5:20-23. Hab 2:4. 2 C +1:24. 12:7. 1 T 3:6. Ja 4:6. 1 P 5:5.
he turn. Jsh +1:7.
not aside. Dt 11:16. 28:14.
right hand. ver. +11. 1 S 13:13, 14. 15:23. 1 K 11:12, 13, 34, 36. 2 K 10:30. Ps 19:11. 132:12.
that he. Dt +4:40. Pr 27:24.
in his kingdom. Ge 49:10. 2 S 23:1, 5. Ac 13:32-34.

DEUTERONOMY 18

1 **shall have**. Dt 10:9. 12:19. Nu 18:20. 26:62. Jsh 13:14, 33. 18:7. Ezk 44:28. 1 P 5:2-4.
they shall. Nu 18:8, 9. Jsh 13:14. 1 C 9:13, 14. Ga 6:6.

2 **the Lord**. Ps +16:5. 84:11. Is 61:6. 1 P 2:5, 9. Re 1:5, 6.

3 **due**. Le +7:7. Ml 3:8-10.
offer a sacrifice. Dt 12:27. Le 7:30-34.

4 **firstfruit**. Le +23:10. Ml 3:10.
the fleece. Jb 21:20.

5 **chosen him**. Dt 10:8. 17:12. Ex 28:1, etc. Nu 3:10. 16:5, 9, 10. 17:5-9. 25:13. Jn 15:19.
to stand. Dt +10:8.
in the name. Col 3:17.

6 **come**. Nu 35:2, 3.
and come with. 1 S 1:24-28. 2:18. Ps 26:8. 27:4. 63:1, 2. 84:5, 10. 1 T 3:1. 1 P 5:2.
mind. Heb. *nephesh*, soul, Ge +23:8.
unto the place. Dt +12:11.

7 **as all his brethren**. 2 Ch 31:2-4.

8 **like portions**. Le 7:8, 9, 14. Nu 31:30, 47. Ne 12:44, 47. Lk 10:7. 1 C 9:7-14. 1 T 5:17, 18.
that which cometh of the sale of his patrimony. Heb. his sales by the fathers.

9 **not learn**. Dt +20:18. Le 18:26, 27, 30. Je +10:2.

10 **maketh**. Dt 12:31. Le 18:21. 20:2. 2 K 3:27. 16:3. 17:17. 21:6. 23:10. 2 Ch 28:3. 33:6. Ps 106:37. Is 57:5. Je 7:31. 19:5. 32:35. Ezk 16:21. 20:26, 31. 23:37.
that useth divination. ver. 14. Ge 30:27. Nu 22:7. 23:23. 1 S 15:23mg. 2 K 17:17. Pr 16:10mg. Is 44:25. 47:13. Je 14:14. 27:9. 29:8. Ezk 13:6, 7, 9, 23. 21:21, 22, 29. Ac 8:9-11. 16:16-18. 19:19.
enchanter. 2 K +21:6.
witch. Ex 22:18. Ml +3:5 (sorcerers). Ga 5:20. Re 21:8.

11 **a charmer**. lit. one that charms a charming. Ps 58:5. Is +47:12.
familiar spirits. Le 19:31. 20:6, 27. 1 S 28:3, 7, 9. 2 K 21:6. 23:24. 1 Ch 10:13. 2 Ch 33:6. Is 8:19, 20. 19:3. 29:4. Ac 16:16.
wizard. 2 K +21:6.
or a necromancer. 1 S 28:11-14.

12 **because of**. Dt 9:4, 5. Le 18:24, 25, 27.

13 **Thou shalt**. Mt +5:48. Re 3:2.
perfect. *or*, upright, *or*, sincere. 2 K +20:3.

14 **possess**. *or*, inherit. Dt 12:2mg.
observers of times. ver. 10. 2 K +21:6.
hath not suffered. ver. 10. Ge 20:6. Ps 147:19, 20. Je +10:2. Ezk 21:21, 22. Ac 14:16.

15 **a Prophet**. ver. 18, 19. Mk 9:7. Lk 7:16. Jn 1:25, +45. 6:14. Ac *3:22, 23*. 7:37. He 2:14-17.
midst. Dt +17:15. Ge +49:10.
like unto me. Dt 5:5. Lk 24:19. 1 T 2:5. He 1:1, 2. 2:1-3. 3:2-6.
unto him. Mt 17:5. Lk 9:35. 10:16. Jn 6:29. He 1:2. 2:1-3. 1 J 3:23.
hearken. Mt 11:15. 17:5.

16 **in Horeb**. Dt 9:10.
Let me not hear. Dt 5:24-28. Ex 20:19. He 12:19.

17 **well spoken**. Dt +5:28.

18 **raise them**. ver. 15. Jn 1:45.
Prophet. Dt 32:36. Ps 80:17. +102:16. 118:22, 26. Is 49:5, 6. 63:17, 18. Ezk 34:11, 12. Ho 3:4, 5. Am 9:11. Mi 5:3-7. Mt 13:57,

58. 16:13, 14. 21:10, 11. Jn 1:19, 21. 4:19, 25. 6:14. Ac +3:19-21. 15:16. Ro +11:26.
from among. Dt +17:15.
like unto thee. Dt 5:5. 33:5. 34:10. Ex 32:19, 20, 26, 27. 40:26-29. Nu 12:3, 6-8, 13. Ps 2:6. 110:4. Is 9:6, 7. Zc 6:12, 13. Ml 3:1. Mt 11:29. Lk 24:19. Jn 2:13-17. Ga 3:19, 20. 1 T 2:5. He 3:2-6. 7:22. 12:24, 25.
will put. Is 50:4. 51:16. Jn 17:18.
he shall. Jn 4:25. 8:28. 12:49, 50. 15:15.

19 **whosoever will not**. Mk 16:16. Jn 3:18. 5:45-47. 8:24. 12:44-48. Ac 3:22, 23. He 2:3. 3:7. 10:26. 12:25, 26. Re 19:11-15.
require. Dt 23:21. Jb 3:4. Ezk 20:40. Lk +11:50. 19:27, 44. Ep 6:17. He 4:12.

20 **the prophet**. Dt 13:1-5. Je 2:8. 14:14, 15. 23:13-15, 31. 27:15. Ezk 13:6. Mt 7:15. 2 P 2:12.
in the name. Dt 13:1, 2. 1 K 18:19, 27, 40. Je 2:8. 28:15-17. Zc 13:3. Re 19:20.

21 **How shall we know**. Je 28:9. 1 Th 5:21, 24. 1 J 4:1-3. Re 2:2.

22 **speaketh**. Is 41:22. Je 28:1-14.
if the thing. Dt 13:2. 2 K 20:1. Jon 3:4. 4:2. Zc 1:5, 6.
the Lord hath not spoken. Je 18:7-10. 28:3.
presumptuously. ver. 20. Je 28:15-17. 29:30-32.
shalt not. Pr 26:2. 29:25.

DEUTERONOMY 19

1 **hath cut**. Dt 6:10. 7:1, 2. 12:1, 29. 17:14.
succeedest. Heb. inheritest, or possessest. Dt 12:2, 29. 18:14.

2 **separate three**. Dt 4:41-43. Ex 21:13. Nu 35:10-15. Jsh 20:2-7. He 6:18.

3 **prepare**. Is 35:8. 57:14. 62:10. He 12:13.

4 **the slayer**. Dt 4:42. Nu 35:15-24.
in time past. Heb. from yesterday the third day. ver. 6. 2 S +3:17mg.

5 **As when**. Jb 9:5. Ps 112:5. Pr 20:10. 27:14. Je 15:10. Zc 5:3. Mt 5:22. 6:1, 5, 16. Mk 11:23. He 13:9.
head. Heb. iron. 2 K 6:5-7.
helve. Heb. wood.
lighteth. Heb. findeth.
he shall flee. Nu 35:25. Pr 27:12. Is 32:2.

6 **the avenger**. Nu 35:12. Jsh 20:5. 2 S 14:7.
slay him. Heb. smite him in life. Heb. nephesh, Jsh +10:28. Je +40:14mg.
not worthy. Dt 21:22. 1 S 24:4, 9, 10, 17, 18. Je 26:15, 16. Mt 10:29, 30.
in time past. Heb. from yesterday the third day. ver. +4.

8 **enlarge**. Dt 11:24, 25. 12:20. Ge 15:18-21. 26:3. 28:13, 14. Ex 23:31. 34:24. 1 K 4:21. Ezr 4:20.

9 **If**. Ge +4:7.

thou shalt. Dt +11:22-25. 12:32.
then shalt thou. Jsh 20:7, 8.

10 **innocent blood**. ver. 13. Dt 21:8, 9. 1 K 2:31. 2 K 21:16. 24:3, 4. Ps 51:14. 94:21. 106:37, 38. Pr 6:17. Is 1:15. 59:7. Je 7:6. Jl 3:19. Jon 1:14. Mt 27:4.
blood. Le +20:9.

11 **But if any**. Dt 27:24. Ge 9:6. Ex 21:12-14. Nu 35:16-21, 24. Pr 28:17. Mt 26:52.
mortally. Heb. in life. Heb. nephesh, Jsh +10:28. Dt 22:26.

12 **fetch him**. 1 K 2:5, 6, 28-34.
avenger. Jsh 20:3.
of blood. Ps 9:12. Ho 1:4. Mt 23:35. 27:24.

13 **Thine eye**. Dt 7:16. 13:8. 25:12. Ezk 16:5.
but thou. Dt 21:9. Ge 9:6. Le 24:17, 21. Nu 35:33, 34. 2 S 21:1, 14. 1 K 2:31.

14 **shalt not remove**. Pr +23:10. Ho 5:10.

15 **at the mouth**. Dt 17:6. Nu 35:30. 1 K 21:10, 13. Mt 18:16. 26:60, 61. Jn 8:17. 2 C 13:1. 1 T 5:19. He 10:28. Re 11:3-7.
two. Dt +14:6. +17:6. Ge +22:15. 41:32.

16 **a false witness**. Pr +6:19. Mk 14:55-59.
that which is wrong. or, falling away. Dt 13:5.

17 **before the priests**. Dt 17:9. 21:5. Ml 2:7. Mt 23:2, 3.
judges. Ex +21:6.

18 **diligent**. Dt +13:14. 17:4. 2 Ch 19:6, 7. Jb 29:16.

19 **Then shall**. Pr 19:5, 9. Je 14:15. Da 6:24.
so shalt. Dt +13:5.

20 **shall hear**. Dt 13:11. 17:7, 13. 21:21. Pr 21:11. Ro 13:3, 4. 1 T 5:20.
commit no more. Ge 2:17. Pr 19:25. 21:11. 26:3. Ec 8:11. Is 26:9. 1 T +5:20.

21 **thine eye**. ver. +13.
life shall. Ex 21:23-25. Le 24:17-21. Mt 5:38, 39.
life. Heb. nephesh, soul. Ge +44:30.

DEUTERONOMY 20

1 **goest out**. Dt 3:21, 22. 7:1.
horses. Jsh 10:5-8. 11:4-6, 9. Jg 4:3-9. 2 Ch 14:11. 20:12. Ps 20:7. 33:16, 17. Is 31:1. 37:24, 25.
the Lord. Dt 2:7. Ps 118:6. Is 7:14. +43:2.

2 **the priest**. Nu 10:8, 9. 31:6. Jg 20:27, 28. 1 S 14:18. 30:7, 8. 2 Ch 13:12.

3 **let not**. Ps 27:1-3. Is 35:3, 4. 41:10-14. Mt 10:16, 28, 31. Ep 6:11-18. 1 Th 5:14. He 12:12, 13. Re 2:10.
faint. Heb. be tender. ver. 8.
tremble. Heb. make haste. Jb 40:23. Is 28:16.
be ye terrified. Ps 3:6. Is 8:12, 13. 57:7, 8. Mt 8:26. Mk 16:6, 18. Ac 18:9, 10. 27:24. 1 T 6:12. He 13:6.

4 **to fight**. Dt 1:30. 3:22. 11:25. 32:30. Ex

14:14. Jsh 10:42. 23:10. 2 Ch 13:12. 32:7, 8. Ps 144:1, 2. Ro 8:37.

5 **the officers**. Ex +5:6. 1 S 17:18.
dedicated. Nu +7:10.

6 **eaten of it**. Heb. made it common. Dt 28:30. Le 19:23-25. Je 31:5.
lest he die. Is 65:22. Zp 1:13.

7 **betrothed a wife**. Dt 22:23-25. 24:5. Mt 1:18. Lk 14:20.
lest he die. Dt 28:30. Lk 14:18-20. 2 T 2:4.

8 **fearful**. Dt 1:28. 23:9. Jg 7:3. Lk 9:62. Ac 15:37, 38. Re 3:16. 21:8.
lest his brethren's. Nu 13:31-33. 14:1-3. 32:9. 1 C 15:33.
faint. Heb. melt. Ex +15:15. Jg 15:14mg. Is 40:30, 31. Ml 1:13. Ro 2:7. 1 C 15:58. Ga 6:9. 2 Th 3:13.

9 **to lead the people**. Heb. to be in the head of the people. 1 S 23:8-29.

10 **then proclaim**. 2 S 20:18-22. Is 57:19. Zc 9:10. Lk 10:5, 6. Ac 10:36. 2 C 5:18-21. 6:1. Ep 2:17.

11 **tributaries**. Le 25:42-46. Jsh 9:22, 23, 27. 11:19, 20. 16:10. Jg 1:28, 30-35. 1 K 9:21, 22. Ps 120:7. Lk 19:14.

12 **And if**. Nu 21:21-24.

13 **thou shalt smite**. Nu 31:7-9, 17, 18. 1 K 11:15, 16. Ps 2:6-12. 21:8, 9. 110:1. Lk 19:27. 2 Th 1:7-9.

14 **the women**. Nu 31:9, 12, 18, 35, etc.
little ones. Nu +16:27.
spoil. Ge 49:27. Jsh 8:2. 11:14. 2 Ch 14:13-15. 20:25. Ps 68:12. Ro 8:27.
take unto thyself. Heb. spoil. Ge 34:27.
thou shalt eat. Jsh 22:8.

15 **Thus shalt**. Nu 21:33-35.

16 **the cities**. Dt +2:34. Nu 33:52. Jsh 8:1, 2.
breatheth. Heb. *nephesh*, soul. Ge +2:7.

17 **thou shalt**. Jsh 17:13. Is 34:5, 6. Je 48:10. 50:35-40. Ezk 38:21-23. Re 19:18.
Hittites. i.e. *descendants of Heth*, S#2850h. Dt 7:1. Ge +15:20. 23:10. 25:9. 26:34. 36:2. 49:29, 30. 50:13. Ex 3:8, 17. 13:5. 23:23, 28. 33:2. 34:11. Nu 13:29. Jsh 1:4. 3:10. 9:1. 11:3. 12:8. 24:11. Jg 1:26. 3:5. 1 S 26:6. 2 S 11:3, 6, 17, 21, 24. 12:9, 10. 23:39. 1 K 9:20. 10:29. 11:1. 15:5. 2 K 7:6. 1 Ch 11:41. 2 Ch 1:17. 8:7. Ezr 9:1. Ne 9:8. Ezk 16:3, 45.
Amorites. Ge +10:16.
Canaanites. Ge +10:18.
Perizzites. Ge +13:7.
Hivites. Ge +10:17.
Jebusites. Ge +10:16.

18 **teach**. Dt 7:4, 5. 18:9. Ex 23:33. 34:11-17. Jsh 23:13. Jg 2:3. Je +10:2. 1 C 15:33. 2 C 6:17. Ep 5:11. 2 Th 3:14. 1 T 6:5. 2 T 2:17, 18. Re 18:3-5.

19 **not destroy the trees**. Mt 3:10. 7:15-20. 21:19. Lk 13:7-9. Jn 15:2-8. Re 6:6.
for the tree, etc. *or*, for, O man, the tree of

the field is to be employed in the siege. Dt 26:6. Le 27:12. Mt 5:45. 10:29. Lk 6:35. 1 P 5:7.
to employ, etc. Heb. to go from before thee. Dt 8:7, 8. Ge 2:9.
siege. 2 K 24:20. 25:2.

20 **thou shalt build**. Dt 1:28. 2 Ch 26:15. Ec 9:14. Is 37:33. Je 6:6. 33:4. Ezk 17:17.
be subdued. Heb. come down.

DEUTERONOMY 21

1 **found slain**. Ps 5:6. 9:12. Pr 28:17. Is 26:21. Ac 28:4.

2 **thy elders**. Dt +16:18, 19. Ro 13:3, 4.

3 **an heifer**. Nu 19:2. Je 31:18. Mt 11:28-30. Ph 2:8.

4 **a rough valley**. or, valley with ever-running water. Ex 14:27. Am 5:24. Ac 8:26, 36, 38, 39.
shall strike. or, break. ver. 6. Ex 13:13. 34:20. Is 53:6. 66:3. Ep 1:7. He 9:22. 1 P 2:21-24. 3:18.

5 **for them**. Dt +10:8. 18:5. Nu 6:22-27. 1 Ch 23:13.
chosen to minister. 1 P 2:9.
to bless. Dt 10:8.
by their. Dt +17:8-12. 19:17. Ml 2:7.
word. Heb. mouth. i.e. decision. Dt 34:5. Ge +45:21mg. Nu +3:16mg. 4:27mg. 20:24mg. 27:21. Jsh 9:2mg. 1 S 12:14mg. 2 S 13:32mg. 17:5mg. 1 K 13:21. 2 Ch 18:12mg. Ezr 8:17mg. Jb 33:6mg. 39:27mg. Ps 49:13mg. Ec 10:13mg. La 1:18mg. Ob 12mg.
tried. or, settled and decided.

6 **wash their hands**. Jb 9:30. Ps 19:12. 26:6. 51:2, 7, 14. 73:13. Is 1:15, 16. Je 2:22. Mt 27:24, 25. He 9:10.

7 **Our hands**. Nu 5:19-28. 2 S 16:8. Jb 21:21-23, 37-40. Ps 7:3, 4.

8 **Be merciful**. or, forgive. Heb. cover. Dt 32:43. Ex 29:33. Ezk 16:63mg.
lay not. Nu 35:33. 2 S 3:28. Ps 19:12. Je 26:15. Ezk 22:3, 24, 25. Mt 23:35. 27:25. Lk 11:50. Ac 5:28. 1 Th 2:15, 16. Re 18:24.
unto thy people. Heb. in the midst.
blood. Le +20:9.

9 **shalt thou**. Dt +19:12, 13.
innocent blood. Dt +19:10.
when thou shalt. Dt 13:18. 2 K 10:30, 31.

10 **thou goest**. Dt 20:10-16.

11 **desire**. Ge 6:2. 12:14, 15. 29:18-20. 34:3, 8. Jg 14:2, 3. Pr 6:25. 31:10, 30.
that. Nu 31:18.

12 **and she shall**. 1 C 11:6. Ep 4:22.
pare her nails. *or*, suffer to grow. Heb. make, *or* dress. 2 S 19:24.

13 **shall remain**. Ps 45:10.
and bewail. Ps 45:10, 11. Lk 14:26, 27.

14 **she will**. Heb. *nephesh*, Ex +15:9.

thou shalt. Ex 21:7-11.
because thou. Dt 22:19, 24, 29. Ge 34:2. Jg 19:24. 1 C 7:3. Ep 5:25.

15 **two wives.** Ge +4:19.
hated. Ge 29:31, 33. Lk +14:26.
firstborn. Ge +27:32. +41:51. Le +27:26. Jb 18:13. Col +1:15.

16 **when.** Ge 43:33. 1 Ch 5:2. 26:10. 2 Ch 11:19-22. 21:3. Ro 8:29. Ph 4:8. He 12:16, 17.
make. Ge 48:14-19. 1 Ch 26:10.

17 **by giving.** Ge 25:5, 6, 32, 34. 1 Ch 5:1, 2.
double portion. Ge +43:12. 1 S 1:2, 4, 5mg. 2 K 2:9.
that he hath. Heb. that is found with him.
the beginning. Ge 49:3. Ps 78:51. 105:36.
the right. Ge 25:31-34.

18 **have a stubborn.** or, apostatizing. lit. turning aside, as in ver. 20. **S#5637h.** Ho +9:15. Ne 9:29. Ps 66:7. 68:6, 18. 78:8. Pr 7:11. Is 1:23. 30:1. 65:2. Je 5:23. 6:28. Ho 4:16. 9:15. Zc 7:11.
rebellious son. ver. +20. 1 S 15:23. Pr 28:24. 30:11, 17. Is 1:2.
obey the voice. Ex +20:12. Le 21:9.
when they. Dt 8:5. 2 S 7:14. Pr 13:24. 19:18. 22:15. 23:13, 14. 29:17. He 12:9-11.
will not hearken. Pr 1:8. Is 1:5. Je 5:3. 31:18. Ezk 24:13. Am 4:11, 12. Zc 7:11.

19 **Then.** Ec 8:11.
lay hold. Dt 22:28. Ge 4:21. 39:12.
and bring. ver. 2. Dt 16:18. 25:7. Zc 13:3.
gate. Ge +14:7. 19:1. 23:10, 18.

20 **rebellious. S#4784h.** ver. 18. Nu 20:10. 2 K 14:26 (bitter). Ps 78:8. Je 5:23. Ho +13:16.
he will not obey. Pr 29:17.
he is a glutton. Nu 11:32. Pr 19:26. 20:1. 23:1-3, 19-21, 29-35. 28:7mg. Ph +3:19.
a drunkard. Pr 23:20, 21. Ezk 23:42mg. 1 C 6:9, 10.

21 **all the men.** Le +24:14.
so shalt thou. Dt 13:5, 11. 19:19, 20. 22:21, 24.
all Israel. Dt 13:11. +19:20. Ro 6:23. He 12:9.

22 **worthy of death.** Heb. of the judgment of death. Nu 25:4. Dt 19:6. 22:26. Jsh 8:29. 10:26. 1 S 26:16. 2 S 4:12. Mt 26:66. Ac 23:29. 25:11, 25. 26:31.
thou hang. 2 S 21:6, 9. Lk 23:33. Jn 19:31-38.
tree. Ge 40:19.

23 **tree.** Ge +40:19.
he that is hanged. 2 C 5:21. Ga 3:13.
is accursed of God. Heb. the curse of God. Dt 7:26. Nu 5:21. 25:4. Jsh 7:12. 2 S 21:6. Ps 102:8mg. Je 29:22. Jn 19:31. Ro 9:3. 1 C 16:22. 2 C 5:21. Ga 3:13.
thy land. Le +18:25.
defiled. Ge 34:5.

DEUTERONOMY 22

1 **Thou shalt.** Ex 23:4. Ezk 34:4, 16. Mt 10:6. 15:24. 18:12, 13. Lk 15:4-6. Ja 5:19, 20. 1 P 2:25.
hide thyself. ver. 3, 4. Le 20:4. Pr 24:11. 28:27. Is 8:17. 58:7. Lk 10:31, 32. Ja 2:8.

2 **thou shalt restore.** Mt 7:12. Ga 5:14. 1 Th 4:6. He 10:24. 13:1. Ja 2:8. 1 J 3:11, 18.

3 **ass.** Ex 23:4.
lost things. Ex 22:9. Le 6:3, 4.
hide thyself. ver. 1. Jb 6:16. Ps 55:1. Is 58:7.

4 **thou shalt surely.** Ex 23:4, 5. Mt 5:44. Lk 10:29-37. Ro 15:1. 2 C 12:15. Ga 6:1, 2. 1 Th 5:14. He 12:12, 13.

5 **woman shall not.** Je +10:2. 1 C 11:4-15. 1 T 2:9. T 2:4, 5. 1 P 3:3-5.
abomination. Dt 18:12.

6 **young ones.** Lk 12:6.
thou shalt not. Ge 8:17. 32:11. Le 22:28. Pr 12:10. Ho 10:14.

7 **But thou shalt.** Ge 1:22. Ps 145:9. Mt 23:37. Lk 12:6, 7. 16:10.
that it may. Dt +4:40.
thou mayest. Pr 22:4.

8 **then thou shalt.** Ex 21:28-36. 22:6. Ro 14:13. 1 C 10:32. Ph 1:10. 1 Th 5:22.
thy roof. Jsh 2:6, 8. Jg 16:27. 1 S 9:25. 2 S 11:2. 16:22. 2 K 23:12. Ne 8:16. Is 15:3. 22:1. Je 19:13. 32:29. 48:38. Zp 1:5. Mt 10:27. 24:17. Mk 2:4. 13:15. Lk 5:19. 12:3. 17:31. Ac 10:9.
thou bring. Ge 9:5. Ps 119:156. Ezk 3:18, 20. 32:2-9. Mt 18:6, 7. Ac 20:26, 27. Ja 5:11. 1 J 4:16.

9 **shalt not sow.** Ge 1:11. Le 19:19. Mt 6:24. 9:16. 13:24, 25. Ro 11:6. 2 C 1:12. 6:14-16. 11:3. Ja 1:6-8. 3:10.
fruit of thy seed. Heb. fulness of thy seed. Ex 22:29mg. Nu 18:27.

10 **together.** 2 Ch 18:1. 2 C 6:14.

11 **not wear.** Le 19:19. Mt 6:22, 24. Ga 2:17, 18. 4:21-23.

12 **fringes.** Nu 15:38, 39. 1 K 7:17. Mt 23:5.
quarters. Heb. wings. ver. 30.
coverest. Ge 20:16. Ex 21:10. 22:27.

13 **go in.** Ge +4:1. 6:4. 29:21, 23, 31. Jg 15:1, 2.
and hate. ver. 16. Dt +21:15. 24:3. 2 S 13:15. Ml 2:14-16. Ep 5:28, 29, 33.

14 **give occasions.** ver. 19. Ex 20:16. 23:1. Pr 18:8, 21. 1 T 5:14. or, ascribed or laid actions. ver. 17. 1 S 2:3. 1 Ch 16:8. Ps 9:11.
of speech. Heb. of words. i.e. of discourses or defamations.
evil name. ver. 19. Ne 6:13. Lk 6:22.
found. Ps 26:1, 2, 6.
a maid. S#1331h, Le +21:13. Ge 24:14, +16 **(S#1330h),** 28. Ru 2:6. 4:12.

15 **tokens of ... virginity.** ver. 16, 17, 20. Le

+21:13. Jg 11:37, 38. Ezk 23:3, 8. Lk 15:8-10.
  elders. Dt 21:2.
  gate. Dt 21:19. Ge +14:7.
16 **hateth**. ver. +13. Ml 2:15, 16.
17 **occasions of**. ver. 14. Ge 38:24. Ps 141:4. Ho 1:2.
  spread. Nu 4:7, 11.
  tokens. ver. 15.
  the cloth. or, the garment.
18 **the elders**. Dt 1:13. 16:18. Ex 18:21, 22.
  chastise. Dt 25:2. Pr 10:13. 19:29. 20:30.
19 **amerce**. or, fine. Ex 21:22. 2 Ch 36:3. Pr 17:26. 21:11. 22:3. 27:12. Am 2:8mg.
  because. Ex 23:7. Jb 22:19.
  he may not put. ver. 29. Dt 24:1-4. Mt 19:8, 9.
20 **this thing**. Dt 17:4.
  tokens of virginity. ver. +15.
21 **stone her**. ver. 22, 24. Le +24:14.
  she hath wrought. Le 21:9. Is +9:17.
  to play. Le 19:29. Dt 23:17. He +13:4.
  shalt thou. Dt +13:5.
22 **a man**. Ex 20:14. Le 20:10. Nu 5:22-27. Pr 6:27-29. Ezk 23:45-47. Jn 8:4, 5. He +13:4.
23 **betrothed**. Dt +20:7. Mt 1:18, 19.
24 **both**. Nu 32:23. Ps 34:15-17. 2 C 5:10.
  and ye shall stone. Le 20:10.
  he hath humbled. Dt 21:14. Ge 29:21. Mt 1:20, 24.
  so shalt thou put. ver. +21, 22, 24.
25 **force her**. or, take strong hold of her. 2 S 13:14.
26 **no sin**. Dt +21:22.
  slayeth him. Heb. *nephesh*, Jsh +10:28.
27 **cried**. 1 C 13:7.
  none. Nu 32:23. 1 S 2:3. 2 Ch 16:9. Pr 15:3.
28 **a damsel**. Ex +22:16, 17.
29 **shall give**. Ge 34:12. Ex 22:16, 17.
  because he hath humbled. ver. 19, 24. Dt 21:14.
30 **a man shall**. Dt 27:20. Ge 35:22. 49:3, 4. Le 18:8. 20:11. 1 Ch 5:1. 1 C 5:1, 13.
  discover. Ru 3:9. Ezk 16:8.
  skirt. Heb. wing. ver. 12mg.

DEUTERONOMY 23

1 **wounded**. **S#1795h**, only here. lit. wounded by bruising. See **S#1794h**, Ps +10:10. Le 21:17-21. 22:22-24. 1 K 20:37. Ps 10:10mg. 38:8. 44:19. 51:8, 17. SS 5:7. Ga 3:28.
  stones. Dt 25:11. Jb 40:17.
  member. **S#8212h**, only here. Ho 2:10 **S#5040h**.
  cut. Le 22:24. 1 S 5:4. Ga 5:12.
  shall not enter. Le 21:17, 23. 2 K 20:17, 18. Da 1:3-7.
  shall not. ver. 2, 3, 8. Ne 13:1-3. Ps 65:4. Is 56:3, 4. La 1:10. Mt 19:12. Ac 8:27, 38, 39. 2 C 13:9.

congregation of the Lord. Nu 35:12, 24, 25. Jsh 20:6, 9. 1 K 8:1-3, 5. 1 Ch 13:1, 2, 4. 29:1, 10, 20. 28:1. 29:6. Ps 82:1.
2 **bastard**. Ex 34:6, 7. Is 57:3. Je 31:29, 30. Ezk 18:1-4. Zc 9:6. Jn 8:41. He 12:8.
  tenth generation. ver. 3. Ge 31:7, 41. Ne 13:1.
3 **Ammonite**. ver. 4, 5. Ex 12:48. Le 22:18. Nu 9:14. 15:15. Ru 4:6, 10-22. 1 S +11:11. Is 56:3.
  Moabite. **S#4125h**. Dt 2:11, 29. Ru 1:4, 22. 2:2, 6, 21. 4:5, 10. 1 K 11:1. 1 Ch 11:46. 2 Ch 24:26. Ezr 9:1. Ne 13:1, 23.
  tenth generation. ver. 2.
  for ever. lit. to the age. Heb. *olam*, Ex +12:24. 2 S 5:14. 7:12-16. 1 Ch 3:17, 18. Je 22:24-30. Mt. 1:6, 11, 12. Lk 3:23-28.
4 **Because they met**. Dt 2:28, 29. Ge 14:17, 18. 1 S 25:11. 1 K 18:4. Is 63:9. Zc 2:8. Mt 25:45. Ac 9:4.
  because they hired. Nu 22:5, 7, 17. +31:8.
5 **Nevertheless**. Nu 22:35. 23:5-12, 16-26. 24:9. Mi 6:5. Ro 8:31. 2 C 4:17.
  turned. Pr 26:2. Ro 8:28.
  because the. Dt 7:7, 8. 33:3. Ps 73:1. Je 31:3. Ezk 16:8. Ml 1:2. Ro 9:13. 11:28. Ep 2:4, 5.
6 **Thou shalt**. 2 S 8:2. 12:31. Ezr 9:12. Ne 13:23-25.
  prosperity. Heb. good. ver. 16mg. Jg 9:2mg. 1 S 9:10mg. 1 S 12:23. 15:22.
  for ever. Heb. *olam*, Ex +12:24.
7 **Edomite**. Ge +36:9. 1 S 21:7. 22:9, 18, 22. 1 K 11:14. Ps 52:t.
  he is thy. Ge 25:24-26, 30. Nu 20:14. Ob 10-12. Ml 1:2.
  because thou. Dt 10:19. Ge 45:17, 18. 46:7. 47:6, 12, 27. Ex 22:21. 23:9. Le 19:34. Jb 31:32. Ps 105:23. Mt 25:34, 35. Ac 7:10-18.
8 **enter into**. ver. 1. Ro 3:29, 30. Ep 2:12, 13.
  third generation. ver. 2, 3. Ex 20:5, 6.
9 **keep thee**. Jsh 6:10, 18, 19. 7:11-13. Jg 20:26. 2 Ch 19:4. 20:3-13. 31:20, 21. 32:1-22. Lk 3:14. Re 19:11-14.
10 **that is**. Le 15:16. Nu 5:2, 3. 1 C 5:11-13. 2 C 7:1.
11 **when evening**. Le 11:25. 15:17-23.
  cometh on. Heb. turneth toward. Ge 24:63.
  wash himself. Le +11:32. 14:9. 15:5, 11, 13. 22:6. Ps 51:2, 7. Ezk 36:25. Mt 3:11. Mk 7:2-5. Lk 11:38, 39. Ep 5:26, 27. He 9:9, 10. 10:22. 1 P 3:21. Re 1:5.
12 **a place**. lit. hand. Nu 2:17. Ezk 21:19mg.
13 **paddle**. Heb. nail *or* pin *or*, shovel. Ex +27:19.
  wilt
  ease thyself. Heb. sittest down. Jg 3:24mg. 1 S 24:3.
  dig. Ge 21:30.
  cover. Ezk 24:6-8.
  which cometh. Ezk 4:12.

14 walketh. Ge 3:8. 17:1. Le 26:11, 12. 2 C 6:16. 1 P 5:8.
in the midst. Dt 1:42. 6:15. +7:21. 31:17. Ex 33:3. 34:9.
to deliver. Ex 3:8.
to give. Dt 7:2, 23.
unclean thing. Heb. nakedness of any thing. Dt 24:1mg.
turn away. Le 26:17. 2 P 3:14.

15 shalt not. 1 S 23:11, 12. 30:15. Ob 14. Phm 10-19.
escaped. Ge 32:30. 2 K 19:11.

16 shall dwell. Is 16:3, 4. Lk 15:15-24. T 3:2, 3.
gates. Ge +14:7.
liketh him best. Heb. is good for him. Est 1:19mg.
thou shalt not. Ex 22:21. 23:9. Le 19:33. 25:14, 17. Je 7:6. Zc 7:10. Ml 3:5. Ja 2:6.

17 There shall be, etc. Dt 22:21, 29. Ge 38:21. Le 18:22. 19:29. Pr 2:16.
whore. or, sodomitess. Ge 38:21, 22. Ho 4:14. Ro 1:26.
sodomite. Ge 34:7. Le 18:9, 11. 20:13, 17. Jg 19:22, 23. 20:6. 2 S 13:12. 2 K +23:7. Jb 36:14mg. 1 C 6:9, 10. 1 T 1:9, 10.

18 hire. Ps 93:5. Is 23:17, 18. Ezk 16:31, 33, 34, 41. Ho 9:1. Mi 1:5, 7.
dog. Ps 22:16. Pr 26:11. Is 56:10, 11. Mt 7:6. Ph 3:2. 2 P 2:22. Re 22:15.
any vow. ver. 21. Le +23:38. Ps 5:4-6. Is 61:8. Hab 1:13. Ml 1:14.

19 shalt not. Dt 15:7, 8. 24:10-13. 28:12, 44.
lend upon usury. Is +24:2.
usury of. Is +24:2.

20 a stranger. Heb. nokri, Ge +31:15. Dt 14:21. 15:3. Le 19:33, 34.
mayest lend. Ge 31:15. Ex 23:9.
may bless. Dt +15:10. Pr 19:17. Is 1:19. Lk +6:34-36. +14:14. 1 C 15:58.

21 When. ver. 18. Ge 35:1-3. Nu +30:2.
vow. Le +23:38.
slack. or, delay or be behind. Ge 32:4. 34:19. Ex 22:29. Ec 5:4. 2 P 3:9.

22 forbear. Ge 11:8. 18:11. 41:49.
to vow. Le +23:38. 27:2.
no sin. Ac 5:1-4.

23 That which. Nu +30:2.
freewill offering. Le +23:38.
hast vowed. 1 S 14:24. Je 44:25-27. Mk 6:22, 23. Ac 23:12, 21.

24 thou mayest. Ro 12:13. 1 C 10:26. He 13:5.
grapes. Ge 40:10.
thy fill. or, sufficiency. Ex 16:3. Le 25:19. 26:5.
pleasure. or, desire. Heb. nephesh, soul, Nu +11:6; Ge +23:8. Ps 105:22. Je 2:24.
vessel. Dt 28:5. Le 11:32. 1 S 17:40mg. Mt +10:10.

25 standing corn. Dt 16:9. Ex 22:6.

then thou mayest. Mt 12:1, 2. Mk 2:23. Lk 6:1, 2.
pluck. Jb 8:12. 30:4. Ezk 17:4, 22.
move. or, wave. Dt 27:5. Ex 20:25. Jsh 8:31.
sickle. Dt 16:9.

DEUTERONOMY 24

1 hath taken. Dt 21:15. 22:13. Ex 21:10.
uncleanness. Heb. matter of nakedness. Dt 23:14.
then let him. ver. 3. Ezr 10:3. Je 3:8. Mt 5:31, 32. 19:7-9. Mk 10:4-12.
divorcement. Heb. cutting off. Is 50:1.
send her. Dt 22:19, 29. Ml 2:16. Mt 1:19. Lk 16:18. 1 C 7:11, 12.

2 she may go. Le 21:7, 14. 22:13. Nu 30:9. Ezk 44:22. Mt 5:32. Mk 10:11. 1 C 7:15.

3 hate. Dt +21:15. 22:13, 16. 2 S 13:15. Lk 14:26.
bill of. Mt 19:7. Mk 10:4.
die. Ro 7:2.

4 Her former. Ps 107:33, 34. Je 3:1. Ml 2:14-16.
after that she is defiled. Jg 13:7.
thou shalt. Le 18:24-28. Jsh 22:17, 18.

5 a man. Dt +20:7. Ge 2:24. Mt 19:4-6. Mk 10:6-9. 1 C 7:10-15. Ep 5:28, 29. T 2:4, 5.
neither, etc. Heb. not any thing shall pass upon him.
cheer up. Pr 5:18. Ec 9:9. 1 C 7:29.

6 shall take. Ex 22:26, 27. Re 18:22.
the nether. Ex 11:5. Nu 11:8. Is 47:2. Je 25:10.
upper. Jg 9:53. 2 S 11:21. Mt 18:6. Mk 9:42. Lk 17:2. Re 18:21, 22.
to pledge. Ge 47:19. Ex 22:26. Ne 5:3. Jb 22:6. 24:9. Pr 20:16. 22:27. Am 2:8. Ja 2:5-8.
life. Dt 20:19. Ge 44:30. Lk 12:15.
a man's life. Heb. nephesh, soul, Ge +44:30. Dt 20:19. Ge 44:30. Lk 12:15.

7 found. Ge 37:28. 44:16. Ex 21:16. Ezk 27:13. 1 T 1:10. Re 18:13.
any. Heb. nephesh, soul, Ge +12:5.
then that. Ex +21:16. 22:1-4.
maketh merchandise. Dt 21:14.
and thou shalt. Dt +13:5.

8 the plague of. Le ch. 13, 14. 2 K +5:1.
shall observe. Mk +1:44.

9 remember. Lk 17:32. 1 C 10:6, 11.
Miriam. Nu 12:10-15. 2 K +5:1.

10 When. Dt +15:8.
lend thy brother anything. Heb. lend the loan of anything to thy brother. Dt 15:2.
loan. or debt, or burden. Pr 22:26.
pledge. ver. 11-13.

12 man be poor. ver. 17. Jb 22:6. 24:3, 9.

13 deliver. Ex 22:26, 27. Jb 24:7, 8. 29:11-13. 31:16-20. Ezk 18:7, 12, 16. 33:15. Am 2:8. 2 T 1:16-18.

the sun. ver. 15. 2 C 9:13, 14. Ep 4:26.

in his own raiment. Jb 31:19.

shall be. Dt 6:25. 15:9, 10. Ge 15:6. Ps 106:30, 31. 112:9. Is 58:8. Da 4:27. Ja 1:27. 2:13-23.

14 **not oppress**. Ge +43:18mg. Le 25:40-43. Jb 24:10, 11. 31:13-15. Ps +12:5. Am 2:7. 4:1. Ml +3:5. Lk 10:7.

15 **At his**. Le +19:13. Pr 3:27, 28. Je 22:13. Mt 20:8. Mk 10:19. Ja 5:4.

setteth his heart upon it. Heb. lifteth his soul (Heb. *nephesh*, Ex +23:9) unto it. Ps 24:4. 25:1. 86:4.

lest he cry. Ex +22:23, 24. Ep 6:9.

16 **fathers**. Ex 20:5. 2 K 14:5, 6. 2 Ch 25:4. Je 31:29, 30. Ezk 18:20.

his own. Ezk 18:4.

17 **pervert**. Dt 16:19. Ex 23:2, 6, 9. Le 25:35. 1 S 12:3, 4. Ps 94:20, 21. Pr 22:22, 23. 31:5. Ec 5:8. Is 3:15. 33:15. Ezk 22:29. Am 5:7-12. Mi 2:1, 2. 7:3. Ml 3:5. Lk 3:14. Ja 2:6.

stranger. Dt 10:19. Le 25:35.

fatherless. Ex +22:22.

nor take. Ex +22:26. Jb 24:3.

18 **thou shalt**. ver. +22. Ex +13:3.

19 **When thou**. Le 19:9, 10. 23:22. Ru 2:16. Ps 41:1.

harvest. Is 17:5. Jl 3:13.

it shall be. ver. 20, 21. Dt +14:29. 26:13.

may bless. Dt 15:10. Jb 31:16-22. 42:12. Ps 41:1-3. 112:9. Pr 11:24, 25. 14:21. 19:17. Is 32:8. 58:7-11. Lk 6:35, 38. 14:13, 14. 2 C 9:6-8. 1 J 3:17-19.

20 **beatest**. Jg 6:11. Ru 2:17. Pr 19:17. Is 27:12. 28:27.

go over the boughs again. Heb. bough it after thee. Is 10:33. Ezk 17:6. 31:5, 6, 8, 12, 13.

21 **gatherest**. ver. +19. Le 19:9, 10. 25:5.

afterward. Heb. after thee. Dt 15:10. Ps 41:1.

22 **thou shalt remember**. ver. +18. Dt 7:8. 2 C 8:8, 9. Ep 5:1, 2. 1 J 4:10, 11.

DEUTERONOMY 25

1 **a controversy**. Dt 16:18-20. 17:8, 9. 19:17-19. Ex 23:6, 7. 2 S 23:3. 2 Ch 19:6-10. Jb 29:7-17. Ps 58:1, 2. 82:2-4. Pr 17:15. 31:8, 9. Is 1:17, 23. 5:23. 11:4. 32:1, 2. Je 21:12. Ezk 44:24. Mi 3:1, 2. Hab 1:4, 13. Ml 3:18. Mt 3:10.

2 **worthy**. Mt +10:17. Lk 12:47, 48. 1 P 2:20, 24.

3 **Forty**. Jon +3:4.

not exceed. 2 C 11:24, 25.

vile unto thee. Dt 27:16. Jb 18:3. Pr 12:9. 17:10. 19:25. 27:22. Is 3:5. 16:14. 52:14, 15. 53:3. Lk 15:30. 18:9-12. 1 C 4:9, 11-13. Ja 2:2, 3.

4 **muzzle**. or, stop. Pr 12:10. Ezk 39:11. 1 C 9:9, 10. 1 T 5:17, 18.

treadeth out. Heb. thresheth. Is 28:27. Ho 10:11.

5 **If**. Heb, when. Dt 21:1, 18, 22. 22:6, 8, 13, 22, 23. 23:9, 10.

brethren. Mt *22:24*. Mk *12:19*. Lk 20:28.

husband's brother. *or*, next kinsman. Ge 38:8, 9. Ru 1:12, 13. 3:9, 10. 4:5.

6 **the firstborn**. Ge 38:8-10.

that his name. Dt 9:14. 29:20. Ru 4:10, etc. Ps 9:5. 109:13.

7 **brother's wife**. *or*, next kinsman's wife. Ru 1:15.

go up. Dt 21:19. Ru 4:1-7.

gate. Ge +14:7.

8 **I like not**. Ru 4:6.

9 **loose his shoe**. Ru 4:7, 8, 11. Is 20:2. Mk 1:7. Jn 1:27.

spit. Mt +26:67.

So shall. Ge 38:8-10. Ru 4:10, 11. 1 S 2:30.

build up. Ge 16:2. Ex 1:21. 1 K 11:38. 1 Ch 17:25.

10 **his name**. Ac +1:15.

11 **strive**. 2 T 2:5.

to deliver her husband. Ro 3:8. 1 T 2:9.

secrets. lit. shameful things, only here. Dt 23:1. Ge 17:11. 24:2. Ex 21:22-25. Jb 40:17. Ezk 16:26. Ho 2:10.

12 **thine eye**. Dt +19:13, 21.

13 **in thy bag**. Le 19:35, 36. Pr 1:14. 11:1. 16:11. 20:10. Is 46:6. Ezk 45:10, 11. Ho 12:7, 8. Am 8:5. Mi 6:11, 12. 1 Th 4:3, 6.

divers weights. Heb. a stone and a stone. Pr 11:1.

14 **divers measures**. Heb. an ephah and an ephah. Ex 16:36. Le 19:35, 36. Pr 11:1. 16:11. Ezk 45:10. Ho 12:7, 8. Mk 10:19. 1 Th 4:3, 6.

15 **that thy days**. Dt +4:40.

16 **all that do**. Dt 18:12. 22:5. Pr 11:1. 20:23. Am 8:5-7. 1 C 6:9-11. 1 Th 4:6. Re 21:27.

17 **what Amalek**. Ex +17:8.

18 **feared**. Ex +1:17.

19 **when the**. Jsh 23:1.

thou shalt. Ex +17:14, 16. Est 3:1. 7:10. 9:7-10, 12, 13.

DEUTERONOMY 26

1 **when**. Dt 5:31. 6:1, 10. 7:1. 12:1, 9. 17:14. 18:9. Nu 15:2, 8.

2 **That thou shalt**. 1 C 16:2.

first. Le +23:10.

go unto. 2 Ch 6:6.

place. Dt +12:11. Le 16:12.

3 **the priest**. Dt 19:17. He 7:26. 10:21. 13:15. 1 P 2:5.

which the. Ge +13:15. Lk 1:72, 73. He 6:16-18.

4 **before the**. Mt 5:23, 24. 23:19. He 13:10-12.

5 **A Syrian**. Ge 24:4. 25:20. 28:5. 31:20, 24. Ho 12:12, 13.

ready. Ge 27:41. 31:40. 43:1, 2, 12. 45:7, 11. Is 51:1, 2.

he went down. Ge 42:1, 2. 46:1-7. 47:11. Ps 105:23, 24. Ac 7:15.

a few. Dt 7:7. Ge 46:27. Ex 1:5.

became. Dt +10:22. Ge 47:27. Ex 1:7, 12. Nu 23:10.

6 **the Egyptians**. Dt 4:20. Ex 1:11, 14, 16, 22. 5:9, 19, 23.

7 **we cried**. Ex 2:23-25. 3:9. 4:31. 6:5. Ps 50:15. 103:1, 2. 116:1-4. Je 33:3. Ep 3:20, 21.

looked. Ex 4:31. 1 S 9:16. 2 S 16:12. Ps 102:19, 20. 119:132.

8 **the Lord**. Ex 12:37, 41, 51. 13:3, 16. 14:16, etc. Nu 23:22. Ps 78:12, 13. 105:27-38. 106:7-10. Is 63:12.

outstretched. Ex +6:6.

with great. Dt 4:34.

9 **he hath**. Jsh 23:14. 1 S 7:12. Ps 78:52-54. 105:44. 107:7, 8. Ac 26:22.

a land. Ex +3:8. 1 C 2:9, 10.

10 **I have**. ver. +2. Dt 16:17. 1 Ch 29:14. Ro 12:1. 1 P 4:10, 11.

And thou. ver. 4. Dt 18:4. Ex 22:29. Nu 18:11-13.

and worship. Dt 6:10-13. Ps 22:27, 29. 86:9. 95:6. 115:1. Pr 3:9. Is 66:23. 1 C 10:31. Re 5:13, 14. 22:9.

11 **rejoice**. Dt +12:7. 28:47. Ps 63:3-5. 96:7-9. Is 65:14. Zc 9:17. 1 T 6:17, 18.

the Levite. Dt 18:6. 1 C 9:11.

the stranger. Dt 10:18, 19. 14:29. +17:15. Ex 12:19, 43mg, 48mg, 49. 20:10. 22:21. 23:9, 12. Le 16:29. 17:8. 18:26. 19:10, 34. 23:22. 24:22. 25:35. Nu 9:14. Jsh 8:33. +20:9. Jb 31:32. Mt +25:35. 1 T 5:10. He 13:2. 3 J 5.

12 **the tithes**. Ge +14:20. Le 27:30. Nu 18:24.

the third. Dt +14:22-29.

hast given it. Dt 12:17-19. 16:14. Pr 14:21. Ph 4:18, 19.

13 **Levite**. ver. 12. Dt +12:12. 24:19-21. Jb 31:16-20.

I have not. Ps 18:21-24. 26:1-3, 6. Ac 24:16. 2 C 1:12. 11:31. 1 Th 2:10. 1 J 3:17-22.

forgotten. 2 K 20:1-3. Ps 119:93, 139, 141, 153, 176. Pr 3:1.

14 **eaten**. Is +58:7. Ml 2:13.

the dead. Le 7:20. 21:1, 11. Ps 106:28. Ezk 24:17.

hearkened. ver. 16, +17. Ne 5:13, 19.

15 **Look down**. ver. +7. Ex 14:24. 1 K 8:27, 43. Ps 14:2. 53:2. 85:11. 102:19, 20. Is 57:15. 61:1. 63:15. 66:1, 2. La 3:50. Zc 2:13. Mt 6:9. Ac 7:49.

habitation. 2 Ch 30:27mg. Ps 68:5. Je 25:30. Zc 2:13mg.

bless thy. Nu 6:22-27. Ps 28:9. 51:18. 90:17. 115:12-15. 137:5, 6. Pr 10:22. Je 31:23.

as thou. Jsh 21:45. 1 C 1:9. He 6:13-18. 10:23.

16 **This day**. Dt +4:26.

statutes. Dt +4:1-6. 6:1. 11:1, 8. 12:1, 32. Mt 28:20.

keep. Dt 6:5, 17. 8:2. 13:3, 4. Lk 11:28. Jn 14:15, 21-24. 1 J 5:2, 3.

and do. Ezr +7:10. Mt 5:19. Ja 1:22.

with all. Mt +22:37.

soul. Heb. *nephesh*, Ge +34:3.

17 **avouched**. Dt 5:2, 3. Ex 15:2. 20:19. 24:7. 2 Ch 34:31. Is 12:2. 44:5. Zc 13:9. Ac 27:23. Ro 6:13. 1 C 6:19, 20. 2 C 8:5.

and to. Dt +10:12, 13. 13:4, 5. 30:16. Jsh 22:5. 1 K 2:3, 4. Col +1:10.

to keep. Dt 13:18. Ps 147:19, 20. Lk 11:28.

hearken. Dt +15:5. Mk 4:24. Lk 8:18.

voice. Dt 8:20. Jn 10:3, 4, 5, 27.

18 **And the**. Dt 28:9. Ex 6:7. +19:5, 6. Je 31:32-34. Ezk 36:25-27.

keep. ver. +17. Ps 119:6. Mt 5:19. Jn 14:15. Ro 16:26. 1 J 2:3.

19 **high above**. Dt 4:7, 8. 28:1. Ps 148:14. Is 62:12. 66:20, 21. Je 13:11. 33:9. Ezk 16:12-14. Zp 3:19. 1 P 2:5. Re 1:5, 6.

an holy. Dt 7:6. 28:9. Ex 19:6. 1 P 2:9.

DEUTERONOMY 27

1 **Keep all**. Dt 4:1-3. 11:32. 26:16. Lk 11:28. Jn 15:14. 1 Th 4:1, 2. Ja 2:10.

2 **on the day**. Dt 6:1. 9:1. 11:31. Jsh 1:11. 4:1, 5, etc.

unto the. ver. 3. Dt 26:1.

great stones. Ezk 11:19. 36:26.

and plaister. Is 33:12. Am 2:1.

3 **thou shalt**. Jsh 8:32. Je 31:31-33. 2 C 3:2, 3. He 8:6-10. 10:16.

this law. Dt +6:3.

a land. Ex +3:8.

honey. Ex +3:8.

4 **in mount Ebal**. Ge +36:23. Jg 9:7. Jn 4:9, 20.

5 **And there**. Ex 24:4. Jsh 8:30, 31. 1 K 18:31, 32.

thou shalt not. Ex 20:25.

6 **burnt offerings**. Le +23:12. Ep 5:2.

7 **peace offerings**. Le +23:19. Ac 10:36. Ro 5:1, 10. He 13:20, 21.

rejoice. Dt +12:7. Is 61:3, 10.

8 **thou shalt**. ver. +3. Jsh 8:34, 35.

very plainly. Ps 119:130. Pr +8:9. Is 35:8. Hab 2:2. Jn 7:17. 16:25. 2 C 3:12. 2 P 3:16. 1 J 2:20, 27.

9 **this day**. Dt 26:16-18. Ro 6:17, 18, 22. 1 C 6:9-11. Ep 5:8, 9. 1 P 2:10, 11. 2 P 3:11, 14.

art become. 1 C 6:20. 15:57, 58.

10 **obey**. Dt +10:12, 13. 11:1, 7, 8. +26:16. Le 19:2. Mi 4:5. +6:8. Mt 5:48. Ep 4:17-24. 1 P 1:14-16. 4:1-3.

voice. Dt +26:17. Jn 10:27.

12 **upon mount Gerizim**. Dt +11:29.
Simeon. Ge +29:33.
13 **mount Ebal**. ver. +4.
to curse. Heb. for a cursing.
Reuben. Ge +29:32.
14 **the Levites**. Dt 33:9, 10. Jsh 8:33. Ne 8:7, 8.
Da 9:11. Ml 2:7-9.
15 **Cursed be**. Dt 28:16-19. Ge 9:25. 1 S 26:19.
Je 11:3.
maketh. Ex 32:1-4.
graven. Ex +20:4.
molten. Ex +34:17.
an abomination. Dt 29:17. 1 K 11:5-7. 2 K
23:13. 2 Ch 33:2. Is 44:19. Ezk 7:20. Da
11:31. Mt 24:15. Re 17:4, 5.
and putteth. Ge 31:19, 34. 2 K 17:19. Ps
44:20, 21. Je 23:24. Ezk 8:7-12. 14:4.
And all. Je 11:5. Mt +6:13.
Amen. Le 19:17. Ne 10:29. Je 11:5.
16 **setteth light**. Ml +4:6. Mt 15:4, 6.
father or. Ex +20:12.
Amen. ver. 15.
17 **removeth**. Dt 19:14. Pr +23:10.
18 **the blind**. Le +19:14. Jb 29:15. Pr 28:10. Is
56:10. Mt 15:14. Re 2:14.
19 **perverteth the judgment**. Ex 23:2, 8, 9. Pr
17:23. 31:5. Mi 3:9. Ml +3:5.
fatherless. Ex +22:22.
widow. Is +1:17.
20 **lieth with**. Dt 22:30. Ge 35:22. 49:4. Le 18:8.
20:11. 2 S 16:22. 1 Ch 5:1. Ezk 22:10. Am
2:7. 1 C 5:1.
21 **of beast**. Ex 22:19. Le 18:23. 20:15.
22 **his sister**. Le 18:9. 20:17. 2 S 13:1, 8-14. Ezk
22:11.
23 **lieth with**. Le 18:17. 20:14.
24 **smiteth**. Dt 19:11, 12. Ge 9:5, 6. Ex 20:13.
21:12-14. Le 24:17. Nu 35:31. 2 S 3:27-30.
11:15-17. 12:9-12. 13:28. 20:9, 10. 1 K 2:5, 6.
Ps 51:14.
25 **taketh reward**. Dt 10:17. 16:19. Ex 23:7, 8.
Ps 15:5. Pr 1:11-29. Ezk 22:12, 13. Da 9:11.
Mi 3:10, 11. 7:2, 3. Mt 26:15. 27:3, 4. Ac
1:18.
person. Heb. *nephesh*, Jsh +10:28.
26 **Cursed**. ver. +15. Mt +25:41.
confirmeth. Je 11:3-5. Ezk 18:24. Ro 3:19,
20. 10:5. Ga *3:10*.
all. Ja 2:10.
words. 2 K 22:13.

DEUTERONOMY 28

1 **If**. ver. 15. Ge +4:7. Je +7:5. 2 P +1:10.
thou shalt. Dt +15:5. 27:1. Le 26:3, etc. Ps
106:3. Is 1:19. 3:10. 34:16. Je 11:4. 12:16. Lk
11:28.
to do all. Ps 111:10. 119:6, 128. Lk 1:6. Jn
15:14. Ga 3:10. Ja 2:10, 11.
will set. Dt +26:19. Ps 91:14. 148:14. Is

33:16. Lk 9:48. Ro 2:7.
2 **these blessings**. Ge 22:18. Ps 128:1, 4. Pr
10:22. 1 T 4:8.
come on thee. ver. 15, 45. Zc 1:6. 1 T 4:8.
if. Ge +4:7.
hearken. Dt +15:5. Mk 4:24. Lk 8:18.
voice. Dt +26:17. Jn +10:27.
3 **Blessed**. Ge 1:22, 28. 2:3. Ps +1:1. Ec 10:17.
Is +30:18. Ep 1:3. Re 1:3. 14:13. 16:15. 19:9.
20:6. 22:7, 14.
in the city. Ps 107:36, 37. 128:1-5. 144:12-
15. Is 65:21-23. Zc 8:3-5.
in the field. Ge 26:12. 39:5. Le 26:3. Am
9:13, 14. Hg 2:19. Ml 3:10, 11.
4 **fruit of thy body**. ver. 11, +18. Dt 7:13. Ge
22:17. +29:31. 49:25. Le 26:9. Ps 107:38.
128:3. Pr 10:22. 13:22. 20:7. 1 T 2:15.
4:8.
5 **Blessed**. Ex 23:25. Is 55:2.
thy basket. Dt 26:2, 4.
store. *or*, dough, *or* kneading troughs. ver. 17.
Ex 8:3. 12:34.
6 **Blessed**. Ge 49:28.
comest in. Dt 31:2. Nu 27:17. 2 S 3:25. 2 Ch
1:10. Ps 121:8. Pr 3:33.
7 **shall cause**. ver. 25. Dt 32:30. Le 26:7, 8. 2 S
22:38-41. Ps 89:23. Pr +16:7.
one way. Jsh 23:10. 1 S 14:6.
flee before. Jsh 8:22. 10:10, 11, 42. Jg 7:22.
1 S 7:3, 4, 10, 11. 2 Ch 14:2-6, 9-15. 19:4.
20:22-25. 31:20, 21. 32:21, 22. Zc 12:8.
8 **command**. ver. 45. Le 25:21. Ps 42:8. 44:4.
133:3.
storehouses. *or*, barns. Le 26:4, 5, 10. 2 K
6:27. Ps 144:13. Pr 3:9, 10. Hg 2:19. Ml 3:10,
11. Mt 6:26. 13:30. Lk 12:18, 24, 25.
in all. 2 C 8:9. 9:8.
settest thine hand. Dt 15:7, 10.
9 **establish**. Dt 7:6. 26:18, 19. 29:13. Ge 17:7.
Ex +19:5, 6. Ps 87:5. Is 1:26. 62:12. 2 Th 3:3.
T 2:14. 1 P 2:9-11. 5:10.
sworn. Dt +7:8. 13:17. 29:12. Ex 19:5, 6. Je
11:5. He 6:13-18.
10 **And all**. Ml 3:12.
called. Nu 6:27. 2 Ch 7:14. Is 4:1. 63:19. Da
9:18, 19.
and they shall. Dt 4:6-8. 11:25. Ex 12:33.
14:25. 23:22. Jsh 2:10, 11. 5:1. 1 S 18:12-15,
28, 29. 1 Ch 14:17. Je 33:9. Re 3:9.
11 **plenteous**. ver. +4. Dt 30:9. Le 26:9. Pr
10:22.
in goods. *or*, for good.
fruit of thy. Ge +29:31.
body. Heb. belly. ver. 4, 18, 53. Dt 30:9. Jb
19:17mg. Ps 132:11mg. Mi 6:7mg.
the Lord sware unto. Ex 2:25. 2 K 13:23.
Ne 9:23.
12 **open**. Ps +78:23. Dt 11:14. Le 26:4. Jb 38:22.
Ps 65:9-13. 135:7. Jl 2:23, 24.
treasure. i.e. of rain. Dt 32:34. Le 26:4. Jb

38:22. Ps 33:7. 135:7. Is 33:6. Je 10:13. 50:25. 51:16. Mt 6:20. 19:21. Mk 10:21. Lk 12:33. 18:22. Ro 2:5, 9, 10. 2 C 4:7.

season. Ps 67:6. Ezk 34:26. Zc 8:12.

to bless all. Dt 14:29. 15:10. Is 48:17-19.

shalt lend. ver. 44. Dt 15:6. Is +58:7.

unto many nations. Ezr 4:20. Ro +11:25.

not borrow. 2 K 4:7. 2 Ch 26:5. Ps 37:21. Pr 17:18. +22:7. 27:23, 24. Lk 14:28. Ro +13:8.

13 **the head**. Ge +22:17. Nu 24:18, 19. Ps +18:43. Is 9:14, 15. Ro +11:25.

if. ver. +1.

thou hearken. ver. +1. Dt 4:6-9. Lk +8:18. Ph 1:27.

14 **thou shalt**. Dt 11:16, 26-28. Jsh +1:7.

the right. Is 30:21.

other gods. Dt 6:14, 15. Ex 20:3-5. 34:17. Le 19:4. 26:1.

15 **But**. ver. 1.

if thou wilt. La 2:17. Da 9:11-13. Ml 2:2. Ro 2:8, 9.

not hearken. Le 26:14, 18. Je +7:26. Lk +8:18.

all these curses. ver. +2. Dt 29:20. Ps +9:17. Is 3:11. Je 11:3-5. Mt +25:41. Ac 10:34. Ro +15:4. 2 T 2:15. +3:15-17.

shall come. Je +11:8.

16 **Cursed**. Ezk +34:2.

in the city. ver. 3, etc. Pr 3:33. Is 24:6-12. 43:28. Je 9:11. 26:6. 44:22. La 1:1. 2:11-22. 4:1-13. Ml 2:2. 4:6.

in the field. ver. 55. Ge 3:17, 18. 4:11, 12. 5:29. 8:21, 22. 1 K 17:1, 5, 12. Je 14:2-5, 18. La 5:10. Jl 1:4, 8-18. 2:3. Am 4:6-9. Hg 1:9-11. 2:16, 17. Ml 3:9-12.

17 **thy basket**. ver. 5. Ps 69:22. Pr 1:32. Hg 1:6. Zc 5:3, 4. Ml 2:2. Lk 16:25.

18 **the fruit of thy body**. ver. +4. Ge +11:30. Dt 5:9. Jb 18:16-19. Ps 109:9-15. La 2:11, 12, 20. Ho 9:11-14. Ml 2:3. Lk 23:29, 30.

thy land. ver. +16. Le 26:19, 20, 26. Hab 3:17.

19 **comest in**. ver. 6. Jg 5:6, 7. 2 Ch 15:5.

20 **send**. Ps 7:11.

cursing. or, the curse. Pr 28:27. Mt +25:41.

vexation. or, the trouble. 1 S 14:20. Ps 80:4-16. Is 28:19. 30:17. 51:20. 66:15. Zc 14:12, 13. Jn 3:36. 1 Th 2:16.

rebuke. or, the rebuke. 2 S 22:16. Ps 80:16.

for to do. Heb. which thou wouldest do.

until thou be. Dt 4:26. 7:23. 12:30. 32:30. Le 26:31-33, 38. Jsh 23:16. Ps 92:7.

quickly. Ex 32:8.

forsaken me. Je +1:16.

21 **pestilence**. Ex 9:3, 15. Nu 25:9. Ps 73:27. Je 15:2. 16:4. Ezk +38:22. Ro +1:27.

22 **a consumption**. Le +26:16. 2 Ch 6:28.

sword. or, drought. Dt 32:24. Ge 3:24. Je +12:12. Hg 1:11.

blasting. 1 K 8:37. 2 K 19:26. 2 Ch 6:28. Am 4:9. Hg 2:17.

mildew. S#3420h. 1 K 8:37. 2 Ch 6:28. Je 30:6 (paleness). Am 4:9. Hg 2:17.

perish. Je 44:7, 8.

23 **thy heaven**. Ge +9:13. Le 26:19. 1 K 17:1. 18:2. Je 14:1-6. Am 4:6-8. Ja 5:17, 18.

24 **make the rain**. ver. 12. Ge 19:24. 29:2. Jb 18:15-21. Is 5:24. Am 4:11.

25 **cause thee**. ver. +7. Dt 32:30. Le 26:17, 25, 36, 37. Is 30:1, 17.

removed. Heb. for a removing. Je +15:4mg. Lk 21:24.

26 **thy carcass**. Je +7:33.

27 **the botch**. ver. 35. Ex 9:9, 11. 15:26.

emerods. 1 S 5:6, 9, 12. Ps 78:66.

scab. Le 13:2-8. 21:20. Is 3:17.

canst not be healed. Ezk 24:16. Ro +1:27.

28 **with madness**. 1 S 16:14. 2 K 9:20mg. Ps 60:3. Is 6:9, 10. 19:11-17. 42:19. Je 4:9. Ezk 4:17. Zc 12:4. Lk 21:25, 26. Ac 13:41. 2 Th 2:9-11. 2 T 1:7.

29 **grope**. Ge 27:12, 22. 31:34, 37. Ex 10:21. Jb 5:14. 12:25. Ps 69:23, 24. Is 59:10. La 5:17. Zp 1:17. Ro 11:7-10, 25. 2 C 4:3, 4.

darkness. Ex 10:22.

not prosper. 2 Ch 13:12. Pr 28:13. Is 51:17-20. Je 2:37. 32:5.

thou shalt be. Jg 3:14. 4:2, 3. 6:1-6. 10:8. 13:1. 1 S 13:5-7, 19-22. Ne 9:26-29, 37. Ps 106:40-42. La 5:8. Lk 21:24.

oppressed. ver. 33. Ps 103:6. 146:7. Pr 28:17. Ec 4:1. Je 50:33. Ho 5:11.

spoiled. ver. 31. Je 21:12. 22:3. Ml 1:3.

save. Dt 22:27.

30 **betroth**. Dt 20:6, 7. 2 Ch 29:8, 9. Jb 31:10. Je 8:10. Ho 4:2.

build. Jb 31:8. Is 5:9, 10. 65:21, 22. Je 12:13. La 5:2. Am 5:11. Mi 6:15. Zp 1:13.

gather. Heb. profane, *or*, use it as common meat. Dt 20:6mg. Am 4:9, 10.

31 **ox**. Jg 6:4. Jb 1:14, 15.

be restored to thee. Heb. return to thee.

32 **sons and**. ver. 18, 41. Nu 21:29. 2 Ch 29:9. Ne 5:2-5. Ps +127:3. Je 5:17. 15:7-9. 16:2-4. Ezk 24:25. Jl 3:6. Am 5:27. Mi 4:10.

given. Le +25:39.

fail. ver. 65. Ps +69:3. Je 24:8-10.

no might in thine hand. Ge 31:29. Ex 32:10. Ne 5:5. Pr 3:27. Je 7:16. 11:14. Mi 2:1. Jn 17:9. 1 J 5:16.

33 **The fruit**. ver. 30, 51. Le 26:16. Ne 9:36, 37. Is 1:7. Je 5:17. 8:16. 32:2.

labors. Ps 78:46. 105:44. 109:11. 128:2. Pr 5:10. Ec 2:19. Is 45:14. 65:22. Je 3:24. 20:5. Ezk 23:29. Mt 26:9.

thou shalt be. ver. +29. Je 4:17.

crushed. or, bruised. Jg +10:8mg. Is 36:6. Ho 5:11.

34 mad. ver. +28. 1 S 21:15. 2 K 9:11. Is 33:14. Je 25:15, 16. 29:26. Ho 9:7. Re 16:10, 11.

35 botch. or, ulcer. ver. 27. Jb 2:6, 7. Is 1:6. 3:17, 24.

the sole. 2 S 14:25. Jb 2:7. Is 1:6. Lk 16:20, 21.

36 bring thee. 2 K 17:4-6. 24:12-15. 25:6, 7, 11. 2 Ch 33:11. 36:6, 17, 20. Is 39:7. Je 22:11, 12, 24-27. 24:8-10. 39:5-7. 52:8-11. La 4:20. Ezk 12:12, 13.

there shalt thou. ver. 64. Dt +4:28. Je 16:13. Ezk 20:32, 33, 39.

37 become. ver. 28. Dt 4:30, 31. 29:22-28. Zc 8:13. 12:10. Ro 11:26.

astonishment. 2 Ch +29:8.

a proverb. or, simile. Nu +21:27. +23:7. 1 S 10:12. 24:13. 1 K 4:32. 9:7, 8. 2 Ch 7:20, etc. Je 24:9. Ezk 12:23. 14:8. 16:44. 18:2, 3.

byword. 1 K 9:7. 2 Ch 7:20. Jb 17:6. 30:9. Ps 44:14. Jl 2:17mg.

among. Is 18:2, 7.

lead. i.e. captive.

38 shalt carry. Le +26:26. Is 5:10.

for the locust. Ps +78:46.

39 wine. Ho 2:8, 9.

for the worms. Jl 1:4-7. 2:2-4. Jon 4:7.

40 but. Hg 1:5, 6.

anoint thyself. Ps 23:5. 104:15. Mi 6:15.

41 but. Ge 18:19. Ml 4:5, 6.

thou shalt not enjoy them. Heb. they shall not be thine.

for. ver. 32. 1 K 24:14. La 1:5.

42 thy trees. ver. 38, 39. Am 7:1, 2.

consume. *or*, possess. Jg 14:15.

43 shall get. Jg 2:3, 11-15. 4:2, 3. 10:7-10. 14:4. 15:11, 12. 1 S 13:3-7, 19-23. 2 K 17:20, 23. 24:14-16. Jn 18:31. 19:15.

44 lend to thee. ver. +12.

not lend. ver. 48. Hg 1:6.

be the tail. ver. 13. Ps +18:43. La 1:5.

45 Moreover. ver. 5, 15. Dt 29:20, 21. Le 26:28. 2 K 17:20. Pr 13:21. Is 1:20. 65:14, 15. Je 24:9, 10. 26:2-7. La 2:15-17. Ezk 7:15. 14:21.

all. ver. 8. 2 C 8:9. 9:8.

shall come. Ps 37:22. Pr 26:2. Mt 25:41. Ga 3:10, 13. Re 22:3.

because. Dt 11:27, 28. Ps 119:21. Je 7:22-25.

hearkenedst. ver. +2. Dt +26:17.

voice. ver. +2.

to keep. Dt +26:16.

46 a sign. ver. 37, 59. Dt 29:20, 28. Is 8:18. Je 19:8. 25:18. Ezk 14:8. 23:32, 33. 36:20. 1 C 10:11.

for ever. Heb. *olam*, Ex +12:24.

47 servedst not. Dt 12:7-12. 16:11. 32:13-15. Ne 9:35. 1 T 6:17-19.

with joyfulness. Ne 8:10. Ps 100:2. Lk 1:74.

48 serve. 2 Ch 12:8. Ne 9:35-37. Je 5:19. 17:4. Ezk 17:3, 7, 12. Ro 1:20, 21. 2 P 2:13, 14.

in hunger. Je 44:17, 18, 22, 27. La 5:2-6. Ezk 4:16, 17.

in want of all things. This might well be termed the "poverty curse," which Christ exhausted on the Cross for us. Many of the following references contain significant cause/effect relationships pertaining to poverty (Ps +9:10). 2 Ch 26:5. Jb 15:23. 30:3. Pr 6:10, 11. 11:24. 13:4. 19:15. 20:4. 21:17. 23:21. 24:33, 34. 28:19. 2 C 8:9. 9:8. Ga 3:10, 13. Re 22:3.

a yoke. Is 47:6. Je 27:12, 13. 28:13, 14. Mt 11:29.

49 a nation. Nu 24:24. Is 5:26-30. Je 5:15-17. 6:22, 23. Da 9:26. Hab 1:6, 7. Lk 19:43, 44. Jn 11:48.

as the eagle. Je 4:13. 48:40. 49:22. La 4:19. Ezk 17:3, 12. Da 7:2-4. Ho 8:1. Mt 24:28.

a nation whose. Is 28:11-13. Je 5:15. Ezk 3:6. 1 C 14:21.

understand. Heb. hear.

50 of fierce countenance. Heb. strong of face. Nu +6:26. Pr 7:13mg. Ec 8:1mg. Da 7:7. 8:23.

shall not. 2 Ch 36:17. Is 47:6. Ho 13:16. Lk 19:44. 21:23, 24.

51 the fruit. ver. 33. Is 1:7. 12:8. 62:8.

which also. Le 26:26. Je 15:13. 17:3. Ezk 12:19. Hab 3:16, 17.

not leave. Dt 2:34. 3:3.

corn. Ge 27:28, 37.

wine. or, new wine. Ge 27:28, 37.

oil. Nu 18:12.

increase of. Je 28:14.

52 besiege. Le 26:25. 2 K 17:1-6. 18:13. 24:10, 11. 25:1-4. Is 1:7. 62:8. Je 21:4-7. 37:8. 39:1-3. 52:4-7. Ezk 4:1-8. Da 9:26. Zc 12:2. 14:2. Mt 22:7. 24:15, 16. Lk 19:43, 44. 21:20-24. Re 6:7, 8.

53 eat the fruit. ver. 18, 55, 57. Le +26:29.

body. Heb. belly. ver. 4, 11, 18.

straitness. ver. 55, 57. 1 S 22:2. Ps 119:143. Je 19:9.

54 tender. 1 Ch 22:5. 29:1. 2 Ch 13:7. Pr 4:3.

his eye. Dt 15:9. Pr 23:6. 28:22. Mt 20:15.

and toward. Dt 13:6. 2 S 12:3. Mi 7:5.

his children. Ps 103:13. Is 49:15. Mt 7:9-11. Lk 11:11-13.

55 in the siege. Je 5:10. 34:2. 52:6.

56 tender. ver. 54.

and delicate. Is 3:16. La 4:3-6.

her eye shall be evil. ver. 54.

57 young one. Heb. after-birth. or, her seed. Ge 49:10.

cometh out. Ge 49:10. Is 49:15.

feet. Ezk 16:25.

for she shall. ver. 53.

58 If thou wilt. ver. 15. Le 26:14, 15. 2 K 17:15. Je 7:9, 10, 26-28. Ja 2:10.

book. ver. +61. Dt 31:26. Ex 24:7. Le 26:15.

fear this. Ex 3:14, 15. 6:2, 3. 20:2. 34:5-7. Ps

18:26. 50:7. 72:19. 83:18. Ps 99:1-3. Ec
+12:13. Is 41:10. 42:8. Je 5:12. Am 3:1-3. Mt
10:28. He 10:30, 31.

glorious. or, honored. Ge 34:19. Ex 14:4. Le
10:3. Nu 22:15. Ps 72:19.

fearful. Ge 28:17. Ex 15:11. Ps +99:3. Is
29:23.

name. Dt 32:3. Ex +6:3. 33:19. Nu +6:27. Ps
9:10. 20:1, 7. 89:24. 91:14. 99:3. 113:1, 3.
115:1. Pr 18:10. SS 1:3. Is 30:27. 50:10. Je
10:25. 44:26. Mi 5:4. Jn +1:12. 3:18. 17:6.
20:31. Ac 3:16. 4:12. 5:41. 10:43. Ph 2:9-11. 1
J 2:12.

the Lord. Ex +6:3. 20:2. Ml 2:2.

59 **thy plagues**. ver. 46. Dt 29:20-28. 31:17, 18.
32:22, 26. 1 K 9:7-9. 16:3, 4. La 1:9, 12. 4:12.
Da 9:12. Ho 3:4. Mk 13:19.

wonderful. Le 27:2 (singular). Nu 6:2. Jg
13:19.

long continuance. Ho 3:4, 5. Mt +25:19.

60 **all the diseases**. Dt +7:15. Ex 15:26.

61 **book of this law**. ver. 58. Dt 17:18, 19.
29:21. 30:10. 31:10, 11, 26. Jsh 1:8. 8:34.
23:6. 24:26. 2 K 14:6. 22:8. 23:2. 2 Ch 17:9.
25:4. 34:14. Ne 8:1, 3, 18. Ml 4:4.

bring upon thee. Heb. cause to ascend.

destroyed. Dt 4:25, 26. He 10:31.

62 **few in number**. Dt 26:5. 2 K 13:7. 24:14. Ne
7:4. Is +24:6. Je +42:2. 52:28-30. Am 5:3. Mk
13:20. Ro 9:27-29.

as the stars. Ge +15:5.

63 **rejoiced over**. Dt +30:9. Mi 7:18.

will rejoice over. Pr 1:26. Is 1:24. Ezk 5:13.
33:11.

bring you. Ezk 21:7. 24:23. Am 5:3.

plucked from. Dt 7:22mg. Ps 52:5. Pr
2:22mg. 15:25. Je 12:14, 15. 18:7. 24:6.
31:28, 40. 42:10. Da 7:8.

64 **scatter**. Je +9:16. 16:13. 50:17. Am 9:4. Lk
21:24.

all. Ex +9:6.

there thou shalt. ver. 36. Je 16:13.

65 **shalt thou**. Ge 8:9. Jg 2:14. 2 Ch 36:16. Ps
76:7. Pr 29:1. Is 57:21. Je 2:30. 5:3. Ezk 5:12-
17. 20:32-35. Am 3:6-12. 9:4, 9, 10.

the Lord. Le 26:36. Is 51:17. Ezk 12:18, 19.
Ho 11:10, 11. Hab 3:16. Lk 21:26.

trembling. or, raging. Dt 2:25. Ge 45:24.

failing of eyes. or, consumption of eyes. Le
26:16. Is 10:22 (consumption). 65:14. Ro
11:10.

sorrow. or, grief. Jb 41:22. La 3:65. Mt 24:8.

mind. Heb. *nephesh*, soul. Ge +23:8.

66 **hang in doubt**. 2 S 21:12. Ho 11:7.

thou shalt fear. *ver. 67*. Pr +34:4. La 1:13.
He 10:27. Re 6:15-17.

67 **the morning**. ver. 34. Jb 7:3, 4. Pr 28:1. Re 9:6.

Would God. Ex +16:3. Ps 118:25.

68 **bring thee into Egypt**. Dt 17:16. Je 43:7.
44:12, 14. Ho 8:13. 9:3.

with ships. Ge 49:13.

there ye shall. Ex 20:2. Ne 5:8. Lk 21:24.

be sold. Le +25:39.

DEUTERONOMY 29

1 **the words**. ver. 12, 21-25. Le 26:44, 45. 2 K
23:3. Je 11:2, 6. 34:18. Ac 3:25.

beside the. Dt 4:10-13, 23. 5:2, 3. Ex 19:3-5.
24:2-8. Je 31:32. He 8:9.

2 **Ye have seen all**. Ex +8:12. 19:4. Jsh 24:5, 6.
Ps 78:43-51. 105:27-36. Ac 1:21, 22. 2 P 1:16.
1 J 1:1-3.

3 **temptations**. Dt +4:32-35. 7:18, 19. Ne 9:9-
11.

4 **not given**. Dt +2:30. Is 63:17. Ezk 36:26. Lk
+8:10. Jn 8:43. Ro *11*:7-10. 2 C 3:15. 2 Th
2:10-12. 2 T +2:25. Ja 1:13-17.

unto this day. ver. +28. Dt 34:6. Ge +19:38.
Jsh +4:9.

5 **I have led**. Dt 1:3. 8:2.

your clothes. Dt +8:4. Ne 9:21. Mt 6:31, 32.

and thy shoe. Jsh 9:5, 13. Mt 10:10.

6 **eaten bread**. Dt 8:3. Ex +16:12, 35. Ne 9:15.
Ps 78:24, 25.

neither have. Nu 16:14. 20:8, 11. Ps 78:15,
16. 1 C 9:25. 10:4. Ep 5:18.

7 **Sihon**. Nu +21:21-35.

8 **and gave**. Dt 3:12, 13. Nu 32:33.

9 **Keep**. ver. +1. Dt 4:6. +26:16. Jsh 1:7. 1 K
2:3. Ps 25:10. 103:17, 18. Is 56:1, 2, 4-7. Je
50:5. Lk 11:28. He 13:20, 21.

and do. Dt +26:16. Lk 6:46. Ja 1:22.

prosper. Heb. deal wisely. Ps +1:3. 32:8.
101:2. Is 44:4. 52:13mg. Col 1:6.

10 **stand**. Dt 4:10. 31:12, 13. 2 Ch 23:16. 34:29-
32. Ne 8:2. 9:1, 2, 38. 10:28. Jl 2:16, 17. Re
6:15. 20:12.

11 **little ones**. i.e. infants. ver. +29. Ge 6:18.
12:7. 13:15. 17:7, 8. 21:13. 26:3-5, 24. Le
26:44, 45. Nu +16:27. Ne 12:43. Jb 5:25. Ps
25:13. 37:25, 26. 69:36. 102:28. 112:2. Pr
11:21. 14:26. 20:7. Is 54:13. 65:23. Je 32:39.
Jl 2:16. Mt 14:21. 15:38. 19:13-15. Mk 9:36,
37. 10:14. Lk +18:15. Ac 2:39. +16:15. 1 C
7:14.

wives. Jsh +8:35.

stranger. Dt 5:14. Ex 12:38, 48, 49. Nu 11:4.

the hewer. Jsh 9:21-27. Ga 3:28.
Col 3:11.

12 **thou shouldest**. Dt 5:2, 3. Ex 19:5, 6. Jsh
24:25. 2 K 11:17. 2 Ch 15:12-15.

enter. Heb. pass. Ge 15:17. Jsh 9:6. Ezr 10:3.
Je +34:18, 19.

into his oath. ver. 14. 2 Ch 15:12-15. Ne
10:28, 29.

13 **establish**. Dt +7:6. 26:18, 19. 28:9.

he may be. Ge +17:7. 26:3, 4. 28:13-15. Ex
6:7. Je 31:31-33. 32:38. He 11:16.

14 **do I make**. Je 31:31-34. Ac 2:39. He 8:7-12.

15 **also with him**. Dt +5:3. Je 32:39. 50:5. Mt 13:17. Jn 17:20. 20:29. Ac 2:39. 1 C 7:14.

16 **through the nations**. Dt 2:4, 9, 19, 24. 3:1, 2. Ex 12:12.

17 **abominations**. Heb. detestable things. 1 K 11:5, 7.
idols. Heb. dungy gods. Nu 25:2. 2 K +23:24.
wood and. Dt 4:28. 28:64. 2 K 18:34, 35.
silver and gold. Ex 20:23.

18 **among you man**. Dt 11:16, 17. 13:1-15. 17:2-7. He 3:12.
heart turneth away. Lk 8:13. Ac 8:20-23. He 3:12-14. He 12:15.
among you a root. Je 9:15. Ho 10:4. Am 6:12. Ac 8:23. He 12:15.
gall. *or*, a poisonful herb. Heb. *rosh*. Dt 32:32, 33. Jb 20:16. Ps 69:21. Je 8:14. 9:15. 23:15. La 3:5, 15, 19. Ho 10:4. Am 6:12. Mt 27:34. Ac 8:23.
wormwood. Pr 5:4. Je 9:15. 23:15. La 3:15, 19. Am 5:7. 6:12. Re 8:11.

19 **this curse**. ver. 12. Ge 2:17.
that he bless. Dt 17:2. Ge 22:18. 26:4. Nu 15:30, 39. Ps 10:4-6, 11. 49:18. 72:17. 94:6, 7. Pr 29:1. Is 65:16. Je 4:2. 5:12, 13. 7:3-11. 28:15-17. 44:16, 17, 27. Ezk 13:16, 22. Ep 5:6.
I shall. Ge 3:4. Is 48:22. Ezk +13:22. Re 14:13.
though I walk. Nu 15:30. Ec 11:9. Ro 1:21. 2 C 10:5. Ep 4:17.
imagination. *or*, stubbornness. Je +3:17mg.
to add. Jb 15:16. 34:7. Is 30:1. 56:12. Ro 2:5. Ep 4:19.
drunkenness. or, fullness. Ps 36:8. 65:10. Pr 5:19. 7:18. 11:25.
to thirst. Heb. the drunken to thirsty. 2 S 17:29. Ps 107:5. Pr 25:21. Is 21:14. 29:8. 32:6. 44:3. 55:1. Je 2:25.

20 **will not spare**. 2 K 24:4. Ps 52:5. 78:50. Pr 2:22. 6:34. Is 27:11. Je 13:14. Ezk 5:11. 7:4, 9. 8:18. 9:10. 14:7, 8. 24:14. Ro 8:32. 11:21. 2 P 2:4, 5.
the anger. Jg +2:14.
his jealousy. Ex +20:5. SS 8:6. Ezk 23:25.
smoke. Dt +4:24. Ps 18:8. 74:1. 80:4mg. He 12:29.
all the curses. Dt 27:15-26. 28:15-68.
blot out. Ezk 14:7, 8. Re +3:5.

21 **separate**. Jsh ch. 7. Ezk 13:9. 14:7, 8. Ml 3:18. Mt 24:51. 25:32, 41, 46.
according. Je +11:8.
are written. Heb. is written. Dt 30:10.

22 **shall say**. ver. 24.
sicknesses. 2 Ch 21:19. Ps 103:3. Je 14:18. 16:4.
which the Lord hath laid upon it. Heb. wherewith the Lord hath made it sick. Dt 28:59. Je 19:8. 49:17. 50:13.

23 **brimstone**. Re +9:17.

salt. Jg 9:45. Jb 39:6mg. Ps 107:34mg. Je 17:6. Ezk 47:11. Zp 2:9. Mk 9:49. Lk 14:34, 35.
nor beareth. Ps 107:33, 34.
like the. Ge 14:2. +19:24.

24 **Wherefore**. 1 K 9:8, 9. 2 Ch 7:21, 22. Je 5:19. 13:22. 22:8, 9. La 2:15-17. 4:12. Ezk 14:23. Ro 2:5.

25 **Because**. Is 47:6. Je 40:2, 3. 50:7.
they have forsaken. 1 K 19:10-14. Is 24:1-6. Je 22:9. 31:32. Da 9:11, 13, 14. He 8:9.

26 **they went**. Jg 2:12, 13. 5:8. 2 K 17:7-18. 2 Ch 36:12-17. Je 19:3-13. 44:2-6.
gods whom. Dt 28:64.
whom he had, etc. or, who had not given to them any portion.
given. Heb. divided. or, apportioned. Dt 4:19. Jg 11:24. 1 K 20:23. Is 36:18. Ac 17:26, 29-31.

27 **kindled**. Dt 6:15. 7:4. 11:17. Ps 79:5.
all the curses. ver. 20, 21. Dt 27:15, etc. 28:15, etc. Le 26:14, etc. Je +26:6. Mk 11:20-22. 2 C 5:11.

28 **rooted them**. Dt 28:25, 36, 64. 1 K 14:15. 2 K 17:18, 23. 2 Ch 7:20. Ps 52:5. Pr 2:22. Je 42:10. Lk 21:23, 24.
cast. Dt 28:64. 30:1, 3. Ps 74:1. Is 22:17, 18. Je 7:15. 22:26.
as it is this day. ver. +4. Dt 6:24. 8:18. Ge +19:38. Ezr 9:7. Da 9:7.

29 **secret**. Jb 11:6, 7. 28:28. Ps 25:14. Pr 3:32. Is 48:8. Je 23:18. Da 2:18, 19, 22, 27-30. 4:9. Am 3:7. Mt 13:35. Jn 15:15. 21:22. Ac 1:7. Ro 11:33, 34. 16:25, 26. 1 C 2:10, 16.
things. Dt 30:11-14.
revealed. Ge 18:17-19. Ex 33:13. Nu 12:7, 8. Ps +19:7. +36:9. 78:2-7. 103:7. Is +8:20. Am 3:7. Mt 11:27-30. 13:11. Lk +16:31. Jn 15:15. 20:31. Ro 11:33. 16:26. 2 T 1:5. +3:16, 17. Re 22:18, 19.
and to our. ver. +11. Dt +6:7. 30:2.
for ever. Heb. *olam*, Ex +12:24.

DEUTERONOMY 30

1 **And**. Ezk +37:26. The several great covenants of Scripture may be found at the following passages: (1) Edenic, Ge 1:28. (2) Adamic, Ge 3:14, 15. (3) Noahic, Ge 8:21. 9:11-15. (4) Abrahamic, Ge 15:18. (5) Mosaic, Ex 19:5, 6. (6) Palestinian, Dt 30:1. (7) Davidic, 2 S 7:10, 12, 15, 16. Is +55:3. (8) New, He 8:8.
it shall come. Dt +4:30. Le 26:40-46.
these things. Dt 28:2. Ne 9:36. Da 9:13.
the blessing. ver. 15, 19. Dt 11:26-28. ch. 27, 28. 29:18-23. Le ch. 26.
the curse. Dt 11:28. 28:15-45.
thou shalt call. Dt 4:29. 1 K 8:47, 48. Is 46:8. Ezk 18:28. Lk 15:17.
mind. Dt 4:29-31.

whither. Ge 4:14. Je 8:3.

2 **return unto**. Je 29:12, 13. 30:8-10. Ho 3:5. Zc +1:3. 12:10. Ro 11:23, 24. 2 C 3:16. 1 J 1:9.
obey. 1 S 12:14. Jb 36:11. Is 1:19. Je +7:23. **with all thine heart**. 2 S +7:3. 1 Ch 29:9, 17. Ps 41:12. 119:80. Je 4:14. +29:13. Ep 6:24.
soul. Heb. *nephesh*, Ge +34:3.

3 **That then**. Ps 106:44-46. 126:1-4. Ac +3:19-21.
will turn. Ge 28:15. 48:21. Jb 42:10. Ps 126:1-4. Is 56:8. Je +23:3. La 3:22, 32. Ezk 16:53. 39:25. Zp 2:7. Ro 11:23, 26, 31. Ep 4:8.
have compassion. Dt 13:17. La 3:32. Jl 2:25. Mi +7:20. Zc 10:6.
return and. Ps 2:9. 24:10. 50:3. 96:13. 110:1. Is 9:7. 11:10-12. Je 23:5, 6. Ezk 37:21, 22. Da 7:13, 14, 22. Ho 3:4, 5. Am +9:11. Mi +4:7. Zc 2:10-12. 6:12, 13. 12:10. 13:6. 14:4, 5. Mt 19:28. +23:39. 24:30, 39. +25:31. Mk 13:26. Lk 12:40. 17:30. +18:8. 21:27. 24:25, 26. Jn 14:2, 3. Ac 1:11. 15:14-17. Ro +11:25, 26. 1 C 15:23, 51, 52. Ph 3:20, 21. 1 Th 1:9, 10. 2:19. 3:13. 4:14-17. 2 Th 1:7-10. 2:8. 1 T 6:14, 15. T +2:13. He 10:37. Ja 5:7, 8. 2 P 3:3, 4. 1 J 3:2. Ju 14, 15. Re 1:7, 8. 2:25. 16:15. 19:11. 20:4. 22:7, 12, 20.
gather thee. Ge 15:16. 48:21. 1 Ch 16:35. Ezr 1:1-4. Ne 1:9. Is 52:12mg. Je 12:15. 16:15. +23:3. 24:6. 48:47. 49:6. 50:19, 20. Ezk 20:33-37. Ho 11:11. Jl 3:1. Ob 17-21. Zc 8:7, 8. 10:6-12. Jn 11:51, 52. Ro 11:1-32.
scattered. Ge 11:4. 1 K 22:17. Je +9:16. 31:10. Jl 3:2. Mt 9:36.

4 **driven out**. 2 S 14:13, 14. Ne 1:9. Is 16:3, 4. 27:13. Je 30:17. 49:36. Ezk 34:4, 16. Mi 4:6. Zp 3:19.
unto. Dt 28:64. Ne 1:9. Ps 19:6. Is 11:11-16. 62:11. Ezk 39:25-29. Zp 3:19, 20. Re 7:1-3. 20:7-10.
of heaven. 2 S +22:8.
thence will the. Ne 1:9. Is +11:11. 43:6. 48:20. Je 31:8, 10. Am 9:9. Zp 3:20. Zc 8:7.
gather thee. Is 40:11. 49:5mg. 56:8. Je +23:3. Ezk 20:34, 41. 28:25.

5 **bring thee**. Ne 1:9. Je 29:14. 30:3.
possess it. Is 11:11, 12. Je 23:3-8. 32:6-15, 44. Ezk 37:21-25. Ho 11:10, 11. Mi 4:4.
he will do thee good. ver. 9. Dt 8:16. 28:63. Ezk 34:24-31. Zc 8:13-15.
multiply thee. ver. 16. Dt 1:11. 7:13. 13:17. 28:63. Ge 17:6. Ex 1:7. Le 26:9. 2 S 24:3. Ne 9:23. Ps 107:38. Is 27:6.
fathers. Ho 1:10, 11.

6 **And**. or, For (denoting the reason of a thing). 1 K 1:21. 18:3, 4. Ps 1:3. 5:12. Is 16:2. 64:5.
God will. Ps 51:10. Je 24:7. 31:33. Ezk 11:19, 20. 36:25-27. Jn 1:12, 13. Ro 9:15, 16. 15:16. 1 C 3:5-7. 4:7. Ga +4:6. Ep 2:4, 5, 8, 10. 4:24.

Col 1:12, 13. 2 Th 2:13. 2 T +2:25. T 3:5. He 13:20, 21. Ja 1:18.
circumcise thine heart. Dt 10:16. Le +26:41. Is +60:21. Je 4:4. 9:26. 31:33. 32:39, 40. 50:20. Ezk 11:19, 20. 36:26, 27. 44:7. Ho 2:14-16. Jn 3:3-7, 10. Ro 2:28, 29. 11:26. 2 C 5:17. Col 2:11.
to love the Lord. Dt +6:5.
with. ver. +2.
soul. Heb. *nephesh*, Ge +34:3.

7 **put all**. Dt 7:15. 33:11. Ge 12:3. 22:17. 24:60. Nu 24:14. Jb 8:22. Ps 35:26. 71:13. 109:29. 137:7-9. Is 10:12. 11:14. 14:1-27. 19:1. 34:1, 2. 54:15-17. Je 25:12-16, 29. 30:16, 20. 46:1, 2. 47:1. 50:33, 34. 51:24-26, 34-37. La 3:54-66. 4:21, 22. Ezk 25:3, 6; 8, 12, 15. 38:1. 39:1. Da 12:1. Jl 3:1-8. Am 1:3, 6, 9, 11, 13. Ob 10. Zp 2:8, 9. 3:19. Zc 12:3. Mt 25:31-46.

8 **thou shalt return**. ver. +2. Pr 16:1. Is 1:25, 26. Je 31:33. 32:39, 40. Ezk 11:19, 20. 36:27. 37:24. Ho 6:1. 14:1. Zp 3:20. Ro 11:26, 27. Ep 2:16. Ph 2:13.

9 **make thee**. Dt 28:4, 11-14. Le 26:4-6, 9, 10. Ps 37:25. Je 31:27, 28. Am 9:13-15.
every work. Is 65:21. Ml 3:10. Mt 6:33. Ph 4:19.
thy body. Ge +29:31. Ps +127:3.
thy cattle. Dt 7:14. 28:4. Ps 107:38.
thy land. Le 26:4. Ps 67:6. Je 1:10. 31:28. Ro 8:19-23. 2 C 9:10.
for good. Dt 15:4. 1 K 10:7. Pr 10:22. Je 24:5-7. Ezk 34:27. Ml 3:10-12.
rejoice over thee. Dt 28:63. Ps +104:31. Is 62:5. 65:19. Je 24:6. 32:41. 33:9. Zp 3:17. Lk 15:6-10, 32. Jn 15:11.

10 **If**. Ge +4:7.
hearken unto. ver. +2, 8. Is 55:2, 3. 1 C 7:19.
to keep. Dt 26:16, 17. 30:2. 1 C 7:19. Re 22:14.
book of. Dt 29:21. Ex 17:14. 2 K 22:8. 23:25.
law. Dt 33:4. Pr 3:1, 2.
turn unto. ver. +2. Is 55:2. Ezk 18:21. 33:11, 14, 19.
with all. Mt +22:37.
soul. Heb. *nephesh*, Ge +34:3.

11 **it is not hidden**. Dt 10:12. 17:8. 29:29. Ps 119:11, 50, 105, 162, 172. 147:19, 20. Pr 6:22, 23. +8:9. 30:18. Is +8:20. 30:21. 45:19. 48:16. Je 15:16. 32:17mg. Ro 16:25, 26. Ga 1:8. Col 1:26, 27.
far off. Ec 7:24.

12 **not in heaven**. Pr 30:4. Jn 3:13. Ro *10:6*, 7.

13 **sea**. Jb 28:14.
Who shall. Ac 10:22, 33. 16:9. Ro 10:14, 15.
go over the sea. Pr 2:1-5. 3:13-18. 8:11. 16:6. Mt 12:42. Jn 6:27. Ac 8:27, etc.

14 **the word**. Ps 138:2. Pr 8:22. Is 55:10, 11. Jn 1:1, 14.
very nigh. Dt 4:7, 8. Is 51:5. Ezk 2:5. 33:33.

Lk 10:11, 12. Jn 5:46. Ac 13:26, 38-41. 28:23-28. He 2:1-3.

mouth. Jsh 1:8. Je 12:2. Ezk 33:31. Mt 7:21. Ro 10:8-10. 1 Th 1:8.

heart. He 8:10.

do. Dt 26:16. Mt 7:21. Ja 1:22, 25.

15 I have set. ver. 1, 19. Dt 11:26. 28:1, etc. 32:47. Ps 1:6. Je 21:8. Mk 16:16. Jn 3:16. Ga 3:13, 14. 5:6. 6:8. 1 J 3:23. 5:11, 12.

life. Dt 11:26. 32:47. Ne 9:29. Pr 4:22. 10:16. 11:19. 12:28. Je 21:8.

good. Dt 28:11mg. Jb 7:7. 36:11. Ps 4:6. 25:13mg. 106:5. 128:5. Ec 2:24. 4:8. 6:3.

death. Ge +2:17.

evil. Dt 11:26. Am 5:14.

16 to love. ver. +6. 1 C 13:4.

to keep. Pr 19:16. Jn 14:21. 1 C 7:19.

judgments. Dt 4:45. Le 25:18. Ps 19:9.

live. ver. 19. Dt 32:47. Le +18:5. Ro 7:10. 2 C 3:7.

possess. ver. 5.

17 if. Ge +4:7.

thine. Dt 29:18-28. 31:29. Jg 2:17. 1 S 12:25. Ml 2:8. Jn 3:19-21.

heart turn away. Dt 17:17. 1 K 11:2. Pr 1:32. 14:14. Lk +8:13. 2 T 4:4. He 3:12. 12:25.

not hear. Mt 13:11-17. 2 Th 2:10-12.

drawn away. Dt 31:29.

other gods. Dt 5:9. 6:14. 12:30. 16:22. 28:14. 29:18. Ex +20:5. 23:24. 34:14-16. Jsh 23:7. Jg 6:10. 1 K 11:2, 10. 2 K 17:35, 38. Ps 81:9. 96:5. Je 7:6. 25:6. 35:15. Ezk 20:7, 18. 1 C 8:4-7. 10:7. 1 J 5:21.

serve. Dt 4:19. Jsh 24:16-22. Mt 4:10.

18 denounce. or, declare. Dt 4:26. 8:19, 20. 29:27. 1 K 9:7. 14:15. 2 K 24:3. Is 63:17, 18. Je 10:18. +11:8. 25:9. 44:11.

perish. Dt 4:26.

prolong. Dt 4:26, +40.

passest. Dt 9:1. 11:31. 12:10. 27:2. 31:13. Nu 33:51. 35:10.

Jordan. Jsh 1:14.

19 I call heaven. Dt +4:26. 31:28. 32:1. Ps 50:4. Is 1:2. Je 2:12, 13. 6:19. 22:21, 29, 30. Ezk 36:4. Mi 1:2. 6:1, 2. 1 T 5:21.

record. Jsh 24:27.

that I have. ver. +15. Dt 11:26.

life. Dt 32:47. Pr 8:35. Jn 14:6. Ro 6:23.

death. Ezk 18:31, 32. 33:11. 2 P 3:9.

blessing. Dt 11:26. 28:2.

cursing. Dt 27:26. 28:15, 20.

choose. Ex 8:32. 9:27. 10:16, 17. Jsh 24:15. 2 S +15:6. 24:1, 10. Ps +58:5. +119:59. Pr 1:29-31. 16:9. 23:26. SS 1:4. Is 66:3. Ho 13:9. Mt 13:15. +16:27. 18:7. Lk 22:22. Jn 5:40. Ac +3:19. 4:27, 28. Ro 2:15. +3:19. Ph 2:12, 13.

life. Jsh 24:15-22. 1 K 18:21. Ps 119:30, 111, 173. Pr 1:29. 8:36. Is 56:4. Lk 10:42. Jn 5:40. Re 3:20.

that both thou. Dt 6:2. Je 32:39. Ac 2:39.

20 love. ver. +6, 16.

obey. ver. +2.

cleave. Dt +4:4.

thy life. Dt 4:1. 8:3. 32:47. Ps 27:1. 30:5. 36:9. 66:9. 133:3. Pr 3:22. Jn 5:26. 11:25, 26. 14:6. 17:3. Ac 17:25, 28. Ga 2:20. Col 3:3, 4. Re 21:6. 22:1, 17.

length of thy days. Dt +4:40. 32:47. Ps 61:6.

thou mayest. Dt +4:40. 12:10.

land. Ps 37:3.

sware unto. Dt 10:11. 11:9, 21. 13:17. 28:11. Ge +13:15. Jsh 5:6. Jg 2:1. 2 K 13:23. Ps 106:45. 136:23. Ro +11:1, 2, 28, 29.

DEUTERONOMY 31

2 I am an. Dt 34:7. Ex 7:7. Jsh 14:10, 11. Ps 90:10. Ac 7:20, 23, 29, 30.

I can no more. Dt +34:7. Nu 27:15-17. 2 S 21:17. 1 K 3:7.

Thou shalt not. Dt 3:26, 27. 4:21, 22. 32:48-52. Nu 20:12. 27:13, 14. Ac 20:25. 2 P 1:13, 14.

3 thy God. Dt +9:3. Ge 48:21. Ps 44:2, 3. 146:3-6.

and Joshua. ver. 7, 8, 14, 23. Dt 3:28. 34:9. Nu 27:18-21. Jsh 1:2. 3:7. 4:14. Ac 7:45. He 4:8, Jesus.

4 shall do. Dt 2:33. 3:3-11, 21. 7:2, 16. Ex 23:28-31. Nu 21:24-35.

5 And the Lord. Dt 3:21. 7:2, 18.

according. Dt 7:23-25. 20:16, 17. Ex 23:32, 33. 34:12-16. Nu 33:52-56.

6 Be strong. ver. 7, 23. Dt 20:4. Jsh +1:6.

fear not. Dt 1:29. 7:18. 20:1, 3, 4. Nu 14:9. Ps +118:6. Is 43:1-5. Zc 8:13. Re 21:8.

with thee. Ex 13:21, 22. 33:14. He 13:5.

he will not fail. Dt 4:31. Jsh 1:5. 1 Ch 28:20. Is 41:13-17. He *13:5*.

7 Be strong. ver. +6, 23.

for thou must. ver. +3. Dt 1:38. 3:28. Jn 1:17.

8 he it is that. ver. 3. Dt 9:3. Ex 13:21, 22. 33:14.

before. Jsh 3:11.

he will be. ver. 6. 1 Ch 28:20. Is +43:2. Ro 8:31.

he will not. He *13:5*.

neither forsake. ver. +17.

fear not. Jsh 1:6, 7, 9.

9 Moses wrote. ver. 22-24, 28. Ex +24:4. Nu 33:2. Da 9:13. Ml 4:4. Mk 10:4, 5. 12:19. Lk 20:28. Jn 1:17, 45. 5:46.

delivered. ver. 24-26. Dt 17:18.

the priests. Ho 4:6. Ml 2:7.

which bare. Nu 4:15. Jsh 3:3, 14-17. 6:12. 1 K 8:3. 1 Ch 15:2, 12-15.

10 at the end. Dt 15:1, 2.

feast. Le +23:34-43.

11 to appear. Dt 16:16, 17. Ex 23:16, 17. 34:24. Ps 84:7.

in the place. Dt +12:11.
thou shalt read. Jsh 8:34, 35. 2 K 23:2. Ne 8:1-8, 13, 18. 9:3. Lk 4:16, 17. Ac 13:15. 15:21. Ph 2:16. 2 T 4:2.

12 Gather. ver. 28. Dt +4:10. Le 8:3. 20:8. Jsh 8:34, 35. Ne 8:1-3. 2 K 23:2.
men. Dt 6:6, 7. Ezr 10:1. Ps 19:7-11. Jn 5:39. 2 T 3:15-17.
women and children. Their presence was not generally required at the three great festivals in the other six years (Young). Nu +16:27.
that they may. Dt 29:29. Ps 34:11-14. 78:6, 7.
hear...learn. Ro 10:17.
fear...observe to do. Reverence to God is the basis of obedience.
this law. Evidently the Scriptures do not regard ignorance as the mother of devotion (Young).

13 their children. Dt +6:7. 11:2. Ps 78:4-8. Pr 22:6. Ep 6:4.

14 that thou must die. ver. +2. Dt 34:5. Ge 3:19. Nu 27:13. Jsh 23:14. 2 K 1:4. Ec 9:5. Is 38:1.
I may give. Ac 20:28-31. 2 Th +2:11.
presented. Ex 8:20. 9:13. 14:13. 34:2. Jsh 24:1. 1 S 10:19. Jb 1:6. 2:1. Ro 12:1. Ju 24.
tabernacle of. Ex 27:21, etc.

15 cloud. Ex +13:21.

16 thou shalt. Dt 34:5. Ge +25:8. Nu 27:13. 2 S 7:12. Is 57:2. Ac 13:36. 15:18.
sleep. Heb. lie down. 2 S 7:12. 1 K +11:43. Jb 20:11. Ps 76:5. Da +12:2. 1 Th 4:13. 2 P 3:4.
whoring. Ex 32:6. +34:15. Is +32:9. Ac 20:29, 30.
strangers. Dt 32:12. Ex 12:43. Le 22:25. Jsh 24:20, 23.
forsake me. Je +1:16.
break my. Le 26:15. Jg 2:20. Ps 89:34. Je 31:32.

17 my anger. Jg +2:14. Ps 2:12. 90:11.
I will forsake. ver. +8. Jsh 24:20. Ezr 8:22. Ps +9:10. Is +54:7. Je +11:8. 2 T 2:12. He 12:25. 13:5, 6.
hide my face. Dt 32:20. Jb 13:24. 23:9. 34:29. Ps 10:1. 13:1. 27:9. 30:7. 44:24. 54:8. 69:17. 88:14. 89:46. 102:2. 104:29. 143:7. Is 1:15, 16. 8:17. 59:2. 64:7. Je 18:17. 21:10. 33:5. Ezk 39:23, 24, 29. Mi 3:4.
befall them. Heb. find them. ver. 21. Dt 4:30. Ge 44:34. Jsh 2:23. Jg 6:13. Ne 9:32mg. Jb 34:11.
Are not these. Dt 29:24-27. Jg 6:13. Is 63:17.
among. Dt +7:21.

18 surely hide. ver. 16, +17. Nu 14:42. Jg 6:13. Ps 73:27.

19 this song. ver. 22, 30. Dt 32:1, etc., 44, 45.

and teach it. Dt +4:9, 10. 6:7. 11:19.
put it in their. Ex 4:15. 2 S 14:3. Is 51:16. 59:21. Je 1:9.
a witness. ver. 21, 26. Ex 3:15-17. Ne 9:20. Ezk 2:5. Mt 10:18. 24:14. Lk 2:26. 12:11, 12. Jn 12:48. 14:26. Ac 11:28. 1 J 5:8, 9.

20 when. Dt +6:10-12. 7:1. 8:7.
floweth. Ex +3:8, 17.
eaten. Dt 8:10-14. Ne 9:25, 26.
waxen fat. Dt 32:15. Ne 9:25, 26, 35. Jb 15:27. Ps 17:10. 73:7, 12. 78:31. 119:70. Is 5:17. 6:10. 10:16. +34:7. Je 5:28. 46:21. 50:11. Ezk 34:16, 20. 39:18. Ho 13:6. Mt 13:15. Ac 28:27. Ph 3:19. T 1:12.
then. ver. 16, 17. Dt +30:17. Jg 2:17.

21 this song. ver. +19.
testify. Je +42:19.
against. Heb. before.
I know. Ge 6:5. 8:21. Ps 14:2, 3. 139:2. Is 46:10. Ezk 38:10, 11. Ho 5:3. 13:5, 6. Am 5:25, 26. Jn 2:24, +25. Ac 2:23. 4:28. 7:43.
go about. Heb. do.

22 Moses therefore wrote. ver. +9, 19. Ex +24:4.

23 he gave Joshua. ver. 7, 8, 14. Jsh 1:5-9.
shalt bring. ver. +3. Dt 3:28. Ac 7:45.

24 writing the words. ver. +9. Dt 17:18. Ex +24:4.

25 bare the ark. ver. +9.

26 in the side. Ex +16:34. 2 K 22:8-11. 2 Ch 34:14, 15.
a witness. ver. +19. 2 K 22:8, 13-19. Ro 3:19, 20. Ga 2:19.

27 I know. ver. 21. Dt 32:20.
stiff neck. 2 Ch +30:8.
ye have been. Dt +9:6, 24.

28 Gather unto me. ver. +12. Ge 49:1, 2. Ex +5:6. 18:25.
call heaven. Dt 4:26. Dt +30:19. 32:1. Is 1:2. Lk 19:40.

29 after. Ac 20:29.
corrupt yourselves. Dt 32:5. Jg 2:19. Ps 106:34, 35, 43. Is 1:4. Ho 9:9. Ac 20:30. 2 T 3:1-6. 2 P 1:14, 15. 2:1, 2.
and evil. Dt 28:15, etc. 29:18-28. Le 26:14, etc. 2 Ch 34:24. Lk 19:42-44. 21:24.
the latter days. Ge +49:1. Jb 19:25. Ezk +38:8.

30 Moses spake. Dt +4:5. Jn 12:49. Ac 20:27. He 3:2, 5.

DEUTERONOMY 32

1 Give ear. Dt 4:26. +30:19. 31:28. Ps 49:1, 2. 50:4. Is 1:2. Je 2:12. 6:19. 22:29.
heavens. 2 S 1:21. 1 K 13:2. Ps 114:5. 148:3-5. Is 1:2. Je 2:12. 22:29. 47:6. Ezk 13:11. 36:4, 8. Ho 13:14. Jl 2:21. Mi 6:2. Zc 11:1, 2.

2 doctrine. Jb 11:4. Pr 1:5. 4:2. 9:9. 16:21, 23. Is 29:24.

drop. Dt 33:28. 2 S 23:4. Jb 29:22, 23. Ps 72:6. Is 55:10, 11. Ho 6:4. 14:5. 1 C 3:6-8. He 6:7.

rain. Dt 11:11, 14, 17. Is 44:10, 11.

distil. Nu 24:7. Jg 5:5mg. Jb 36:28. Ps 147:18. SS 4:16. Is 45:8. Je 9:18.

dew. Dt +33:13. Ps 133:3. Is +26:19.

small rain. or, storms. Ho 6:3.

tender herb. Ge 1:11, 12. Ps 72:6.

as the showers. Ps 65:10. 72:6. Je 3:3. 14:22. Ezk 34:26. Mi 5:7. Zc 10:1.

grass. Ge 1:11, 12, 29, 30.

3 **Because**. Ex 3:13-16. 6:3. 20:24. 34:5-7. Ps 29:1, 2. 89:16-18. 105:1-5. 145:1-10. Je 10:6. 23:6. Mt 1:23. 6:9. Jn 17:6, 26.

publish. Ps 22:22. Jn 17:26.

name. Dt +28:58. Re 19:11-13.

greatness. Dt 9:26. 11:2.

ascribe. Dt 5:24. 1 Ch 17:19. 29:11. Ps 29:1, 2. 96:2-8. 145:3. 150:2. Je 10:6. Ep 1:19.

4 **the Rock**. ver. 15, 18, 30, 31. 1 S 2:2. 2 S 22:2, 3, 32, 47. 23:3. Ps 18:2, 31, 46. 61:2-4. 92:15. Is 17:10. 26:4mg. 28:16. 32:2. Hab 1:12. Mt 16:16-18. 1 C 10:4. He 13:8. 1 P 2:6.

his work. Ge 1:31. 2 S 22:31. Ps 18:30, 31. 19:7. 138:8. Ec 3:14. Mt 5:48. Jn 17:4. Ep +3:11. Ja 1:17.

all his. Dt 10:18. Ge +18:25. 1 S 2:3. Jb 8:3. 35:14. Ps 9:16. 77:13, 19. 97:2. 99:4. 103:6. Is 30:18. Je 9:24. Da 4:37. Jn 5:22. Ro 1:32. 2:2, 5. Ja 4:12. Re 15:3, 4.

judgment. Ps 33:5. 67:4. Ne 9:33.

a God. Heb. *El*, Ex +15:2.

of truth. Ex +34:6. Ps 31:5. 61:7. 85:10. 98:3. 100:5. 146:6. Is 25:1. Je 10:10. Jn 1:14, 17. 14:6. T 1:2. or, stedfastness. Ex 17:12. 1 S 26:23. 2 K 12:15. 22:7. Ps 89:1, 2, 5, 8, 24, 33. or, faithfulness. Dt 7:9. He 10:23. 1 P 4:19.

without. Dt 25:16. Jb 34:10-12. Ps 92:15. Hab 1:12, 13. Ro 3:5.

right. Ge +18:25. Ps 25:8. 92:15. 99:4. Ho 14:9.

5 **They have corrupted themselves**. Heb. He hath corrupted to himself. Dt 4:16. 9:12. 31:29. Ge 6:12. Ex 32:7. Jg 2:19. Ps 14:1. Is 1:4. Ho 9:9. Zp 3:7. Mt 7:16-18. 2 C 11:3. Re 14:1.

their spot, etc. *or*, that they are not his children, that is their blot. Jn 8:41, 44. 2 C 7:1. 1 J 3:8-10. Ju 23.

a perverse. Dt 9:24. 2 S 22:27. Ps 18:26. 78:8. 101:4. 125:5. Pr 2:15. 8:8. 11:20. 17:20. 19:1. 22:5. 28:6. Is 1:4. Mt 3:7. 16:4. 17:17. Lk 9:41. Ac 7:51. Ph 2:15.

crooked. Jb 5:13. Pr 8:8. Is 42:16.

generation. Ps 95:10. Ph 2:15.

6 **requite**. ver. 18. Ge 50:15, 17. Ps 116:12. Is 1:2. 2 C 5:14, 15. T 2:11-14.

O foolish. Ps 74:18. Je 4:22. 5:21. Ga 3:1-3.

thy father. ver. 18. Ex 4:22. Is 63:16. Ml 1:6.

Lk 15:18-20. Jn 8:41. Ro 8:15. 1 C 1:21. Ga 3:26. 4:6. 1 J 3:1.

hath bought. Ex 15:16. Ps 74:2. 78:54. Is 43:3, 4. Ac +20:28. 1 C 6:19, 20. 7:23. 2 P 2:1.

made thee. ver. 15. Jb 10:8. Ps 95:6. 100:3. 149:2. Is 27:11. 43:7. 44:2. or, advanced. 1 S 12:6. Est 6:6.

established. Ps 55:22.

7 **Remember**. Ex 13:14. Jb 20:4. Ps 44:1. 77:5. 119:52. Is 51:1-3. 63:11. La 5:21.

days. Is 63:9. Je 2:20. Am 9:11. Mi 5:2. 7:14. Ml 3:4.

of old. Heb. *olam*, Ge +6:4.

many generations. Heb. generation and generation. Ps +33:11mg.

ask. Dt 4:32. Ex 12:26. 13:14. Jg 6:13. Jb 8:8-10. Ps 44:1. 77:5, 6, 11, 12. 78:3, 4. Is 46:9.

8 **most High**. Nu 24:16. Ps +7:17. Is 14:14.

divided. Dt 2:5, 9. 21:16. Ge 10:5, 25, 32. 11:9. Ps 115:16. Pr 16:33. Am 9:7. Zc 9:2. Ac 15:18. 17:26.

inheritance. Ps 115:16.

separated. Ge 11:8, 9. Ex 33:16. Nu 23:9.

he set. Ge 10:15-19. 15:18-21.

bounds. Dt 2:5, 19. Ps 48:2. 100:1. Ro 11:12-16.

according to. Ge 15:18. Ex 23:31. Ps 105:44.

9 **the Lord's**. Ex 15:16. +19:5, 6. 1 S 10:1. Ps 78:71. Is 43:21. Je 10:16. 51:19. Am 3:2. Ep 1:18.

portion. Ex 34:9. 1 K 8:51, 53. Ps +16:5. Is 19:24, 25.

his people. ver. +43. Ps +33:12.

lot. Heb. cord. or, line. Jsh 2:15. 17:5 (portion), +14. 1 Ch 16:18mg. Jb 36:8. Ps 78:55. Pr 5:22. Is 66:7 (pain). Mi 2:5, 10 (destruction). Zc 2:1.

his inheritance. Dt 10:9. Ex 19:5. Jsh 13:33. 1 S +10:1. Ps 47:4. 74:2. 78:71. Lk +1:32, 33.

10 **found**. Dt 8:15, 16. 2 S 9:4. Ne 9:19-21. Ps 107:4, 5. SS 8:5. Je 2:6. Ho 13:5. Jn 15:16.

desert. Dt 26:5. Ps 107:4. SS 3:6. 8:5. Je 2:6. Ezk 16:4. Ho 9:10. 13:9.

waste. or, void. Ge 1:2.

howling. Is 15:8. 43:20. Mi 1:8.

wilderness. Dt 8:15. Nu 21:20mg. Jb 12:24. Je 2:6. Ho 13:5. Ac 7:38.

led him. *or*, compassed him. S#5437h. Ex 13:18. Jsh 6:3. Ne 9:19. Ps 7:7. 26:6. 32:7, 10. 55:10. 59:6, 14. SS 3:2. Je 31:22. Jon 2:3, 5. Ezk 47:2.

about. Ex 13:21, 22. Ps 32:7, 8. 107:7.

he instructed. Dt 4:36. Ne 9:20. Ps 32:7-10. 147:19, 20. Ro 2:18. 3:2.

he kept. Ps 17:8. Pr 7:2. Is 26:3. Zc 2:8. Ph 4:7. 1 P 5:7.

apple. lit. little man. Ps 17:8. Pr 7:2, 9. 20:20.

11 **an eagle**. Is 31:5. +40:31. 46:4. 63:9. Ho 11:3. Re 12:14.

stirreth. Dt 1:6, 7. 1 Ch 5:26.

fluttereth. Ge 1:2. Mt 23:37.
beareth. Ex 19:4. Is 31:5. 40:31. 46:4. 63:9. Ho 11:3.
wings. Jb 39:13. Ps 68:13. +91:4.

12 **the Lord**. Dt 1:31. Ne 9:12. Ps 27:11. 78:14, 52, 53. 80:1. 103:13, 14. 136:16. Is 46:4. 63:9-13.
lead him. ver. 10. Dt 1:31. Ex 13:17, 21. 15:13. 33:13-15. Ps +23:3. Is 48:17.
no strange. Dt 31:16. Ex 12:43 (S#5236h). Le 22:25. Jsh 24:20, 23.
god. Ps 81:9, 10. Is 43:11, 12. 44:7, 8.

13 **ride on**. Dt 33:26, 29. Ex 14:8. Is 58:14. Ezk 36:2. Ho 10:11. i.e. subdue or conquer. Ps 45:4. 66:12. Re 6:2. 19:11, 14.
high. Ps 18:33. Ep 2:6.
places. Dt 1:28. 2:36. 33:29. Is 58:14. Hab 3:19.
eat. Dt 8:8. Ps 81:16.
honey. Ex +3:8. Ps 81:16.
and oil. Dt 8:8. 28:40. 33:24. Ge +28:18. Jb 29:6.
flinty. Dt 8:15. Jb 28:9. Ps 114:8. Is 48:21. 50:7.

14 **Butter**. Ge 18:8. Jg 5:25. 2 S 17:29. Jb 20:17. 29:6. Is 7:15, 22.
kine. Ge 12:6.
sheep. Ge 4:2.
fat of lambs. Le 3:9, 10.
of Bashan. Nu +21:33. 32:4, 33. Jsh 12:4. 1 K 4:13. Ne 9:22. Ps 22:12. Ezk 39:18. Am 4:1. Mi 7:14.
goats. Ge 31:10, 12.
the fat of kidneys of wheat. Ps 81:16. 147:14.
blood. Ge 49:10-12. Ps 75:8. 104:15. Is 27:2. Mt 26:28, 29. Lk 22:18. Jn 6:55, 56.

15 **Jeshurun**. i.e. *upright*, S#3484h. Dt 33:5, 26. Is 44:2.
kicked. 1 S 2:29. Ac 9:5.
waxen fat. Dt +31:20. Ro 2:4, 5.
thick. 1 K 12:10. 2 Ch 10:10. 26:15.
covered with. Jb 15:27. Ps 17:10. 73:7. 119:70.
forsook God. Dt 6:10-12. 8:10-14. Ne 9:25, 26. Je +1:16. Ho 13:6.
made him. ver. 6. Is 51:13.
lightly esteemed. Je 14:21. Mi 7:6. Na 3:6.
the Rock. ver. +4. 2 S 22:47. Ps 18:46. 89:26. 95:1.

16 **provoked**. Dt 5:9.
to jealousy. Ex +20:5. SS 8:6, 7.
with strange. Jg 2:12.
abominations. Dt 7:25. Le 18:27. 2 K 23:13. Ezk 8:17.
anger. Ps 106:29.

17 **sacrificed unto devils**. Le +17:7. Ps 106:37, 38. 1 C 10:20. 1 T 4:1. Re 9:20.
not to God. Ps 90:2. *or*, which were not God. ver. 21. Je 10:15. 1 C 8:4. 10:19.

to gods. Dt 28:64. Is 44:8. Je 2:26-28.
knew not. Ps 1:6. Ho 13:5.
to new gods. Jg 5:8. Da 7:9. Mt 19:8. Ac 7:42, 43.

18 **the Rock**. ver. 4, 15. Is 17:10. 44:8mg.
unmindful. Dt 8:19. Is 17:10. Je 2:32.
forgotten. Dt 6:12. 8:11, 14, 19. Ps 9:17. 44:20-22. 106:21. Is 17:10. 22:10, 11. Je 2:32. 3:21. Ho 8:14.
formed thee. Dt 4:34. Mt 24:8.

19 **And when**. Jg 2:14. Ps 5:4, 5. Am 3:2, 3. Re 3:16.
abhorred them. *or*, despised. Ps +106:40. La 2:6.
provoking. Je 44:21-23.
of his sons. Ps 82:6, 7. Is 1:2. Je 11:15.

20 **I will hide**. Dt +31:17. Ho 5:15. 9:12. Ro 11:20. He 3:19.
their end. Dt 31:29.
a very. ver. +5. Is 65:2-5. Mt 11:16, 17. Lk 7:31, 32.
froward. Pr 2:12, 14. 6:14. 8:13. 10:31, 32. 16:28, 30. 23:33.
children. 2 Ch 20:20. Pr 13:17. 14:5. 20:6. Is 7:9. 26:2. 30:9. Mt 17:17. Mk 9:19. Lk 18:8. 2 Th 3:2. He 11:6.
no faith. Is 30:9. Lk 18:8.

21 **moved me**. ver. +16. Je 8:19.
jealousy. Ex +20:5.
not God. ver. 17mg. Ps 96:5. Is 44:10. 1 C 8:4. 10:20. or, no gods. Ac 19:26. Ga 4:8.
with their vanities. 1 S 12:21. 1 K 16:13, 26. 2 K 17:15. Ps 31:6. Is 41:29. 44:9. Je 2:5. 8:19. 10:3, 8, 15. 14:22. 16:19. 51:18. Jon 2:8. Zc 10:2. Ac 14:15. Ro 1:21. Ep 4:17.
I will. Ho 1:10. 2:23. Ro 9:25. *10:19*. 11:11-14, 25. 1 P 2:9, 10.
move them. Mt 21:43-46. Ac 11:2, 3. 22:21-23. 1 Th 2:15, 16.
foolish nation. Ps 74:18. Je 10:8. Ro 1:22. 1 C 12:2.

22 **For a fire**. Dt +4:24. 29:23. Nu 16:35. Ps 79:5. 83:14. 89:46. +97:3. Is +24:6. Je 4:4. 7:20. 9:10, 11. +17:27. La 2:3. Ezk 20:47, 48. 30:8. 36:5. 38:18, 19. Am 5:6. Mk 9:43-48. Ju 7.
mine anger. Ps 7:11.
shall burn. *or*, hath burned.
lowest. Ps 63:9. 86:13. 88:6. Is 30:33. Am 9:2. Zp 3:8. Mt +10:28. 18:9. 23:33. Ep 4:9.
hell. Heb. *sheol*, Ge +37:35. 2 S 22:6. Jb 11:8. +26:6. Ps +16:10. Is +66:24.
shall consume. *or*, hath consumed. Dt 29:23. Le 26:20. Is 24:6, 19, 20. Am 7:4. Zp 3:8.
foundations. Jb 9:5, 6. Ps 46:2. 144:5. Is 54:10. Mi 1:4. Na 1:5. Hab 3:6, 10, 13.
mountains. Ps 83:14.

23 **heap mischiefs**. Dt 28:15. Le 26:18, 24. Is 24:17, 18. 26:15. 40:2. Je 15:2, 3. Ezk 14:21. Mt 24:7, 8. 1 Th 2:16.

spend. Ezk 5:16.
arrows. ver. 42. Nu 24:8. 2 S 22:15. Jb 6:4. 41:28. Ps 7:12, 13. 18:14. 21:12. 38:2. 45:5. 64:7. 77:17. 91:5. 144:6. La 2:4. 3:12, 13. Hab 3:11. Zc 9:14.

24 **burnt**. 1 K +8:37.
burning heat. Heb. burning coals. Dt 28:22. Jb 5:7. Ps 18:12-14. 76:3. 78:48. 120:4. SS 8:6. Hab 3:5.
destruction. Ps 91:6. Is 28:2. Ho 13:14.
the teeth. Je 16:4. Ezk +5:17.
of beasts. Ps 80:13.
poison. ver. 33. Jb 6:4.
serpents. Ge 3:14. 49:15, 17. Nu 21:6. Is 65:25. Je 8:17. Am 9:3. or, fearful things. Jb 32:6. Mi 7:17.

25 **sword**. 1 Ch 21:11, 12. Ezr 9:7. Is 30:16. Je +12:12. 2 C 7:5.
within. Heb. from the chambers. Ge 43:30. Je 9:21. Ezk 7:15.
destroy. Heb. bereave. Ge 27:45. 42:36. 43:14. 1 S 15:33. Je 50:9mg. Ezk 14:15mg. Ho 9:14mg.
the young. 2 Ch 36:17. Ps 78:62, 63. Je 9:21. La 2:19-22. 4:4. Am 4:10.
virgin. S#1330h, Ge +24:16.
suckling. Dt +29:11. S#3243h. 33:19. Nu 11:12. 1 S 15:3. 22:19. Ps 8:2. SS 8:1. Is 11:8. Je 44:7. La 2:11. 4:4. Jl 2:16.
gray hairs. S#7872h. Ge 15:15 (old age). 25:8. Ge 42:38. 44:29, 31. Le 19:32 (hoary head). Jg 8:32. Ru 4:15. 1 K 2:6, 9. 1 Ch 29:28. Jb 41:32. Ps 71:18 (greyheaded). 92:14. Pr 16:31. 20:29. Is 46:4. Ho 7:9.

26 **scatter**. Is 63:16. Je +9:16. Lk 21:24.
cease. Dt 9:14. Jb 18:17. Ps 34:16.

27 **not**. Ps 115:1.
I feared. Dt 1:17. 18:22. Is +48:9.
wrath. Is 37:28, 29.
lest their. 1 S 12:22. Is 37:28, 29, 35. 47:7. Je 19:4. La 1:9. Ezk 20:13, 14, 20-22. Zc 1:14, 15.
they should. Dt 9:28. Ex 32:12. Nu 14:15, 16. Jsh 7:9. Ps 115:1, 2. 140:8. Is 10:8-15. 37:10, 12-23. Da 4:30-37.
Our hand, etc. or, Our high hand and not the Lord hath done all this.
high. Ps 44:3. 115:2. 137:7-9. 140:8. Je 50:17, 18.
hath not. Is 10:13. Je 40:2, 3.

28 **a nation**. ver. 6. Jb 28:28. Ps 81:12. Pr 1:7. Is 27:11. 29:14. Je 4:22. 8:9. Ho 4:6. Mt 13:14, 15. Ro 11:25. 1 C 3:19.
counsel. Ps 106:13. 107:11. Lk 7:30.
neither. Is 6:10. Mt 13:15.
understanding. ver. 6. Is 1:3. 1 C 2:14.

29 **O that**. Ps 81:13. 107:15, 43. Is 48:18, 19. Ho 14:9. Lk 19:41, 42. 20:41-44. Ro 16:19.
wise. Ps 107:43. Pr 1:5. 27:11. Lk 19:42.
understood. Dt +29:9. Ps 47:7. 101:2.

they would consider. Pr +6:6. Is 10:3. 47:7. Je 5:31. 17:11. La 1:9. Lk 12:20. 16:19-25. 1 T 4:15.

30 **one chase**. Le 26:8. Jsh 23:10. Jg 7:22, 23. 1 S 14:15-17. 2 Ch 24:24. Is 30:17.
sold them. Jg 2:14. 3:8. 4:2. 10:7. Le +25:39. 1 S 12:9. Ps 44:12. Is 52:3. Je 15:13. 1 P 1:18, 19.
shut them. Jg 6:1. Jb 11:10. 16:11. Ps 31:8. Je 21:7.

31 **their rock**. Ex 14:25. Nu 23:8, 23. Jsh 5:1. 1 S 2:2. 4:8. Ezr 1:3. 6:9-12. 7:20, 21. Je 40:3. Da 2:47. 3:29. 6:26, 27.
our Rock. Ps 18:2. 31:2mg, 3. 42:9. 73:26mg. Is 26:4mg. Mt 16:18.
our enemies. 1 S 4:8. Je 40:3. Mk 1:24, +25.

32 **of the vine of Sodom**. Is 5:1, 2. or, worse than the vine of Sodom, etc. Ge +18:20. Je 2:21. La 4:6.
fields of Gomorrah. Is 1:9.
grapes of gall. Dt +29:18. Is 5:4.

33 **the poison**. ver. 24. Jb 20:14-16. Ps 58:4. 140:3. Je 8:14mg. Ro 3:13.
dragons. Ge 1:21. Ex 7:9, 10, 12. Ps 74:13.
venom. Dt 29:18.
asps. Jb 20:14, 16. Ps 58:4.

34 **laid up**. Jb 14:17. Je 2:22. Ho 13:12. Ro 2:5. 1 C 4:5. Re 20:12, 13.
treasures. Dt +28:12.

35 **To me**. ver. 41, 43. Nu 31:2. Ps 94:1. Pr 24:29. Is 1:24. 34:8. 35:4. 47:3. 59:18. 63:4. 66:6. Je +50:15, 28. Ezk 25:14, 17. Mi 5:15. Na 1:2, 6. Lk 18:7, 8. 21:22. Ro 3:5, 6. +12:19, 21. 13:4. 1 Th 4:6. He +10:30. Re 6:10. 18:20. 19:2.
their foot. Ps 9:15. 73:17-19. Pr 4:19. Is 8:15. Je 6:21. 13:16. 1 P 2:8.
shall slide. Ps 38:16. 94:18.
for the day. 2 P 2:3.
calamity. 2 S 22:19. Jb 18:12. 21:17. Is 2:10-21. Je 10:15. Lk 19:44. Re 22:10, 11.
the things. Is 5:19. 30:12, 13. 60:22. Hab 2:3. Lk 18:7, 8. 2 P 2:3. 3:8-10.
that shall come. or, prepared. S#6264h. Est 3:14 (ready). 8:13. Jb 3:8. 15:24. Is 10:13 (treasures).
haste. Nu 32:17 (ready). Jb 20:2.

36 **shall judge**. i.e. shall plead their cause. Dt 10:18. Ps +7:8. 10:18. 50:4-6. 72:4. 82:3mg. 96:13. 103:6. 135:14. 146:7. Is 1:17. 11:4. Je 5:28. +22:16.
repent. Ge 27:42 (comfort himself). 37:35 (comforted). Nu 23:19. Jg 10:15, 16. Ps 85:1-3. 119:52 (comforted). Je +18:8. 31:20.
power. Heb. hand. 1 S 22:17. 2 S 3:12. 14:19. 1 K 10:29mg. Jb 1:12mg. Ps 7:3. 79:8. 85:25. 88:3, 4. Is 1:15. 57:10. 2 C 12:10.
shut up. 1 K 14:10. 21:21. 2 K 9:8. 14:26.
left. 2 K 25:12.

37 **Where**. Jg 10:14. 2 K 3:13. Je 2:28.
rock. ver. 31.

38 **Which**. Ex 34:13. Ps 106:28. 1 C 10:20.
eat the fat. Ge 4:4. Ex 23:18. Le 21:21. Ps
50:13. Ezk 16:18, 19. Ho 2:2. Zp 2:11.
wine. Ho 2:8. 1 C 10:21.
drink offerings. Le +23:13.
let them. Jg 10:14. Je 2:28.
your protection. Heb. an hiding for you. lit.
secret place. Am 9:2.

39 **I, even I**. Ps 102:27. Ge +6:17. Is 41:4. 45:5,
18, 22. 46:4. 48:12. Zp 2:15. He 1:12. Re 1:11.
2:8.
am he. Compare LXX (*ego eimi*) with Jn 8:24,
58. Jn 13:19 with Is 43:10. 46:4. 44:6, 8. 47:8.
no god. Dt 4:35. +6:4. Is +45:5, 18, 22.
with me. Jn 1:1.
I kill. 1 S 2:6. 2 K 5:7. Jb 5:18. Ps 68:20. Is
43:13. Ho 6:1. Am +3:6. Jn 8:24. Re 1:17, 18.
make alive. 1 S +2:6. Is +26:19. Je 31:17.
I wound. 2 Ch 21:18. Ps 51:8. Je 8:11. Ho
6:1.
I heal. Ps +103:3. Ho 6:1.
neither. Jb 10:7. Ps 50:22. Is 43:13. Mi 5:8.
deliver. Is 43:13. Jn 10:28.

40 **I lift**. Ge +14:22. Is 45:23. Je 4:2. He 6:13, 17,
18.
live. Nu 14:28. Ps 90:2. Is 49:18. Je 22:24.
46:18. Ezk 5:11. 14:16. 16:48. 17:16, 19. 18:3.
20:3, 33. 33:11. 34:8. 35:6, 11. Zp 2:9. Jn
14:19. Ro 14:11. 1 T 1:17. 6:15, 16. He 6:13-
18. Re 10:5, 6.
for ever. Heb. *olam*, Ex +12:24.

41 **whet**. or, sharpen. Dt 6:7mg. Ps 7:12. 45:5.
64:3. 120:4. 140:3. Pr 25:18. Is 5:28. 27:1.
34:5, 6. 66:16. Ezk 21:9-15, 20. Zp 2:12. Re
19:11-19.
glittering. or, brightness of. *or*, lightning. Ex
19:16. 2 S 22:15.
sword. Jg 7:20. Ps 17:13. Is 27:1. 34:5, 6. Ezk
21:9. Zc 13:7. Re 19:15.
on judgment. Na 1:3.
render vengeance. ver. +35. Is +61:2.
them that hate. Dt 5:9. 7:10. Ex +20:5. 2 Ch
19:2. Ps 68:1. 81:15. 83:2. 139:21. Jn 15:23,
24. Ro 1:30. 8:7. 2 T 3:4.

42 **make mine**. ver. 23. Ps 68:23. Is 34:6-8. Je
46:10. Ezk 35:6-8. 38:21, 22.
arrows. ver. +23.
drunk. or, merry. Ge 43:34.
my sword. Je +12:12.
devour. 2 S 2:26. 11:25. 18:8. Is 1:20. Je
2:30. Ezk 36:14. Na 2:13. 3:15. Zc 11:1.
slain. or, pierced. Ge 34:27.
revenges. Jsh 10:17, 26. 1 S 15:33. Ps 68:21.

43 **Rejoice**. *or*, Praise his people, ye nations; *or*,
Sing ye. Ex 18:9. Ps 67:3-7. ch. 100. Is 2:2-4.
+35:10. Ro *15:10*.
O ye nations. Ge 12:3. 1 K 8:43. Ps 22:27. Is
11:10. 19:23, 25. Lk 2:10, 11, 32. Ac 13:47,
48. Ro 3:29. 15:9-13. Re 5:9, 10.
with. Le 26:42. Ro 12:15.

for he. Ps +28:4, 5. 48:11. 58:9, 10. 97:8.
136:1, 10, 11. Je 11:19, +20. Ezk 5:13. Zp
+3:14. Lk +23:41.
avenge. ver. +35. 2 K 9:7. Jb 13:24. Je 13:14.
La 2:5. Lk 18:7, 8. 19:27, 43, 44. 21:22-24. Ro
12:19. Re 6:10. 15:2, 4. 18:2, 20. 19:2.
render vengeance. ver. +35, 41.
will be merciful. Dt 21:8mg. Ex 29:33. Nu
+35:33. 2 Ch 30:18. Ps 65:3. 79:9. 85:7. Is 6:7.
+27:9. +41:9. 54:7, 8. +55:3. Da +9:24. Jl
3:21. Mi +7:18, 20. Hab 3:2. Zc 10:6. 13:1.
unto his land. Dt 11:12. Le 25:23. Jsh 22:19.
2 Ch 7:20. Ps 85:1. Is 19:25. 60:21. Je 2:7.
16:18. Ezk 38:16. Ho 9:3. Jl 2:18. 3:2. Zc 9:16.
his people. ver. 9. Dt 7:6. 14:2. 26:18. Ex
15:16. 19:5, 6. 2 Ch 20:7. Ps 83:3. Is 1:24-27.
25:8. Ezk 38:14. Jl 2:18. 3:2. Am 3:2. Lk 2:32.
Ro 11:15, 26.

44 **spake**. Dt 31:22, 30. Re 15:3.
Hoshea. *or*, Joshua. Dt 31:23. Nu 11:28. 13:8,
16.

46 **Set your hearts**. Dt +6:6, 7. Ezk 40:4. 44:5.
Lk 9:44. He 2:1.
words. Jsh 1:8. Ps 32:8. Mt 4:4. Jn 5:24.
+5:39. 6:63. 15:3. Ac 17:11, 12. Ro 1:16.
10:17. Col 1:5, 6. 3:16. 1 Th 1:5. 2:13. 2 T
2:15. +3:15, 16. 4:2. He 11:6. Ja 1:18.
command your children. Dt 4:9. 6:7.
11:19. Jsh 24:15. Ps 78:1-8. Pr 22:6.
Ep 6:4.

47 **not a vain**. Dt +30:19. Le 18:5. Pr 3:1, 2, 18,
22. 4:22. Is 45:19. Mt 6:33. Ro 10:5, 6. 1 T
4:8. 6:6-8. 2 T 3:16. He 4:12. 1 P 3:10-12. 2 P
1:3, 16. Re 22:14.
your life. Dt 5:16, 33. 8:3. 30:20. Le 18:5. Ga
3:12.
prolong. Dt +4:40. 33:25.
go over Jordan. Dt +30:19. 31:13.

48 **the Lord spake**. A.M. 2553. B.C. 1451. An.
Ex. Is. 40. Adar. Nu 27:12, 13.
selfsame. Ge 7:13. 17:23, 26. Ex 12:17, 41,
51. Le 23:14. Jsh 5:11. 10:27. Ezk 40:1.

49 **mountain Abarim**. Dt 34:1. Nu 21:11.
27:12, 13. 33:47, 48.
Nebo. Dt 3:27. Nu +32:3.
and behold. Dt 34:2-5. Is 33:17. 2 C 5:1.
possession. Ge 10:19. 15:18. Jsh 1:3.

50 **And die**. Dt 34:5.
gathered unto. Dt +31:16. Ge +25:8. Da
12:13.
as Aaron. Nu 20:24-29. 33:38.

51 **ye trespassed**. Dt 3:23-27. Nu 20:11, 12, 24.
27:14. Ps 106:32, 33.
Meribah-Kadesh. *or*, strife at Kadesh. Nu
20:13, 14.
Zin. Nu 13:21.
because ye. 1 K 13:21-26. Is 6:3. +8:13. 1 P
4:17.

52 **thou shalt see**. ver. 49. Dt 3:27. 34:1-4. Nu
27:12. He 11:13, 39.

DEUTERONOMY 33

1 **the blessing**. Ge +14:19. Lk 24:50, 51. Jn
14:27. 16:33. ch. 17.
the man. Jsh 14:6. Jg 13:6. 1 S 2:27. 9:6. 1 K
12:22. 13:1. 17:18, 24. 2 K 4:9. 6:6. 8:7, 11.
23:17. Ps 90, title,mg. 1 T +6:11. 2 T 3:17. 2 P
1:21.

2 **The Lord came**. Ps +68:7. Is 63:1-4. Hab
+3:3. Ac +1:11.
from Sinai. Ex 19:18-20. Jg 5:4, 5. Ps 68:7-
10, 21, 23. Je +31:2. Hab +3:3.
rose up. 1 C 15:20.
from Seir. Jg 5:4, 5.
from mount Paran. Hab +3:3.
came with. Zc +14:5. Mk +8:38. Jn +14:2, 3.
Ro +8:19. 1 Th +4:16, 17. 2 Th +2:1.
ten thousands. Ps 68:7, 17. Da 7:9, 10. Ac
7:53. Ga 3:19. 2 Th 1:7. He 2:2. Ju +14. Re
5:11.
saints. Ps +149:5-9. Zc +14:5.
a fiery law. Heb. a fire of law. Dt 5:22. Da
7:9, 10. Mt +3:11, 12. 2 C 3:7, 9. Ga 3:10, 19.
He 2:2. 12:20, 29. 2 P +3:7.
for. Jn 15:14.

3 **he loved**. Dt 7:7, 8. 10:15. Ex 19:5, 6. Ps
47:4. 147:19, 20. Je 31:3. Ho 11:1. Ml 1:2. Jn
13:1. Ro 9:11-13. Ep 2:4, 5. 1 J 4:19.
all his saints. Dt 7:6. 1 S 2:9. Ps 31:15. 50:5.
148:14. +149:9. Je 32:40. Jn 10:28, 29. 17:11-
15. Ro 8:35-39. Col 3:3, 4. 1 P 1:5.
they sat. 2 S 7:18-27. SS 2:3. Is 30:7. Lk
2:46. 8:35. +10:39. Ac 22:3. Ep 2:6.
shall receive. Ps 106:12. Pr 2:1. Lk +11:28.
Jn 8:47. 17:8. Ac 13:7. Ro 10:17. 1 Th 1:6.
4:1.

4 **Moses**. Jn 1:17. 7:19. Ro 3:1, 2.
the inheritance. Dt 9:26-29. Ps 119:72, 111.
Ac +20:32.

5 **king**. Ge 36:31. Ex 18:16, 19. Nu 16:13-15.
Jg 8:22. 9:2. 17:6. Ps 45:1. 72:1. Ac 7:35.
Jeshurun. Dt 32:15.
gathered. Ac 17:7.

6 **Reuben live**. Ge 17:18. 49:3, 4, 8. Nu 32:31,
32. Jsh 22:1-9. Is 6:13.
few. Is +10:19mg. Je 23:3. Ezk 5:3. Ro 9:27.

7 **Judah**. Ge +35:23. Jsh 19:1. Jg 1:3.
Re 22:16.
and bring. Ge 49:8-12. Jg 1:1, etc. Ps 78:68,
70. Is 11:12-14. Je 3:18. 30:3. Ezk 37:15-22.
Ho 1:11. Mi 5:2. Ml 3:1. He 7:14.
let his hands. 2 S 3:1. 5:1, 19, 24. 1 Ch 5:2.
12:22. 2 Ch 17:12-19. Is 9:7. Re 19:13-16.
and be thou. 2 S 7:9-12. Ps 2. 20:2. 21:1, 8.
110:1, 2. 146:5. Lk 19:27. 1 C 15:25. Re
20:10-15.

8 **Levi**. Ge 49:5-7.
Let thy. Ex +28:30.
Thummim. Jn 8:12. Col 2:3.
with thy. Le 21:7. Nu 16:5. 2 Ch 23:6. Ezr
8:28. Ps +16:10. 106:16.

prove at. Dt 6:16. 8:2, 3, 16. Ex 17:7. 32:26.
Nu 20:13. Ps 81:7.

9 **Who said**. Ex 32:25-29. Le 10:6. 21:11. Nu
25:11-13. Ml 2:5. Mt 10:37. 12:48. 22:16. Lk
14:26. 2 C 5:16. Ga 1:10. 1 Th 2:4. 1 T 5:21.
I have not. Ge 29:32. 1 Ch 17:17. Jb 37:24.
neither. Mt 19:29. Lk 14:26.
acknowledge his brethren. Ex 32:29. Mt
10:37. 3 J 9.
for they have. Nu 23:21. Jb 7:17. +36:7. Ps
50:2. +119:1. SS 4:7. Is 43:4. 46:13. 62:3, 5.
Je 18:18. Ml 2:5-7. Mt 13:43. Lk 7:42, 43, 47.
15:7, 22. Jn +1:12. 14:21-23. 15:9, 15. +17:6.
20:17. Ro 8:29. 1 C +2:9. 6:3. 2 C 8:23. Ep
+5:25, 26, 27. Col 1:21, 22. He 12:23. Re 1:6.
14:3. 21:9.
observed. Ml 2:4-6. Mt 28:20. Re 3:8.
kept. Jn 14:23. +17:6.

10 **They shall teach**. *or,* Let them teach, etc. Dt
17:9-11. 24:8. Le 10:11. 2 Ch 17:8-10. 30:22.
Ne 8:1-9, 13-15, 18. 9:4, etc. Je 18:18. Ezk
44:23, 24. Ho 4:6. Ml 2:6-8. Mt 23:2, 3. Jn
21:15, 16.
they shall put incense. *or,* let them put
incense. Ex +39:38. Nu 16:6, 7, 40, 46. 1 S
2:28. 2 Ch 26:18. Ps +141:2. Je +17:26. He
7:25. 9:24.
before thee. Heb. at thy nose. Ex +15:8.
whole. Le 1:9, 13, 17. 9:12, 13. 2 Ch 29:20-
35. Ps 51:19. Ezk 43:27. Ro 12:1. 2 P 2:5.

11 **his substance**. Dt 18:1-5. Nu 18:8-20. 35:2-
8. Mt 6:33. Ro 8:32.
accept. 2 S 24:23. Ps 20:3. 90:17. Ezk 20:40,
41. 43:27. Ml 1:8-10. Ro 14:18. 2 C 5:9. Ph
4:18.
smite. Is 29:21. Je 15:10. Am 5:10. Mt 10:14,
15. Lk 10:10-12, 16. Ro 8:37. 1 C 15:57. 1 Th
4:8.
rise not. Ps 18:37, 38.

12 **Benjamin**. Ge 49:27.
The beloved. ver. 27-29. Jsh 18:11-28. Jg
1:21. 1 K 12:21. 2 Ch 11:1. 15:2. 17:17-19. Ps
45:1. 60:5. 108:6. 127:2. 132:14. Is 5:1. 37:22,
35. 62:4, 5. Je 11:15. Ezk 48:35.
dwell. ver. +28. Is 32:18.
in safety. Ge +19:30.
cover him. Ps 91:4. Is 51:16. Mt 3:16, 17.
23:37.

13 **Joseph**. Ge 48:5, 9, 15-20. 49:22-26.
Blessed. Ps 45:7.
his land. Dt 8:7-10. +32:43. Ps 65:9-13.
heaven. Ge 27:28. 49:25.
the dew. ver. 28. Dt 32:2. Ge 27:28, 29. 2 S
23:3, 4. Jb 29:19. Ps 72:6. 110:3. Pr 3:20.
19:12. Is 18:4. Ezk 34:26. Ho 14:5. Mi 5:7. Zc
8:12.
deep. S#8415h. Jon +2:5. Ge 49:25. Hab 3:10.
coucheth. S#7257h. Ge 4:7 (lieth). 29:2. 49:14,
25 (lieth). Ex 23:5. Dt 22:6 (sitting). Ezk 29:3.
beneath. S#8478h. Ge 35:8. Ex 20:4. 32:19. Dt

4:18, 39. 5:8, 8. Jsh 2:11. Jg 7:8. 1 K 4:12. 7:29. 8:23. Jb 18:16. Is 14:9. 51:6. Am 2:9.

14 **precious things**. ver. 14-16. Dt 28:8. Le 26:4. 2 S 23:4. Ps 65:9-13. 74:16. 84:11. SS 4:13, 16. 7:13. Ml 4:2. Mt 5:45. Ac 14:17. 1 T 6:17.
put forth. Heb. thrust forth.
moon. Heb. moons. Ps 8:3. 104:19. Re 22:2.

15 **ancient**. Heb. *kedem*, Mi +5:2.
chief things. Ge 49:26. Hab 3:6. Ja 5:7.
lasting. Le +25:32.

16 **the earth**. Dt 28:3-5. Ps 24:1. 50:12. 89:11. Je 8:16mg. 1 C 10:26, 28. Ep 1:3.
the good. Ex 3:2-4. Mk 12:26. Lk 2:14. Ac 7:30-33, 35. 2 C 12:7-10.
and upon the top. Ge 37:28, 36. 39:2, 3. 43:32. 45:9-11. Ge 49:26.
separated. He 7:26.

17 **the firstling**. Ge 48:14, 18-20. 1 Ch +5:1.
his horns. Nu 23:22. 24:8. Jb 39:9, 10. Ps 22:21. 29:6. 89:17, 24. 92:10. Is 34:7. Mi 4:13.
unicorns. Heb. an unicorn.
he shall push. 1 K 22:11. 2 Ch 18:10. Ps 44:5.
the ten thousands. Ge 48:19. Nu 26:34, 37. Ho 5:3. 6:4. 7:1.
of Ephraim. Nu +1:33.

18 **Zebulun**. Ge +30:20.
Rejoice. Ge 49:13-15. Jsh 19:10, 11, 17, 22. Jg 4:10. 5:14. 1 Ch 12:32, 33. Ps 89:12. Je 46:18.
going out. Dt 28:6. Ps 121:8.
Issachar. Nu +1:29.

19 **call the people**. Is 2:3. Je 50:4, 5. Mi 4:2. Zc 14:16.
they shall. Ps 4:5. 50:13-15. 51:16, 17. 107:22. He 13:15, 16. 1 P 2:5.
suck of. Dt 32:13. Is 44:22, 23. 60:3-5, 16. 66:11, 12.
in the sand. ver. 24. Jsh 7:21, 22.

20 **Blessed**. Ge 9:26, 27. Jsh 13:8, 10, 24-28. 1 Ch 4:10. 12:8, 37, 38. Ps 18:19, 36.
he dwelleth. 1 Ch 5:18-21. 12:8-14.
lion. Is +5:29.
teareth. Ge 49:27. Ps 149:6-9.

21 **Gad**. Jsh 13:24. 1 Ch 5:18, 20, 21. 12:8.
the first part. Nu 32:1-6, 16, 17, etc.
a portion. Nu 32:33. Jsh 1:14. 22:4.
lawgiver. Ge +49:10. Nu 21:18. Jg 5:14. Ps 60:7. 108:8. Is 33:22.
seated. Heb. cieled. or, covered. 1 K 6:9. 7:3, 7. Je 22:14. Hg 1:4.
he came. Nu 32:16, 21. Jsh 4:12, 13. Jg 5:2, 11.

22 **Dan is**. Ge +30:6. Jg 14:5, 6, 19.
leap. Jsh 19:47. Jg 18:27.

23 **O Naphtali**. Ge 49:21. Ps 36:8. 90:14. Is 9:1, 2. Je 31:14. Mt 4:13, 16. 11:28.
satisfied. Ps 22:26. 36:8. Je 50:19, 20.

with favor. Ps 5:12.
possess. Jsh 19:32-39. Ph 3:12, 13. 2 P 3:18.

24 **Asher be blessed with children**. Ge +30:13. Ps 115:15. 128:3, 6. Lk 2:36-38.
let him be. Pr 3:3, 4. Ec 12:10. Ac 7:10. Ro 14:18. 15:31.
let him dip. ver. 19. Dt +32:13. 1 K 17:12. Jb 29:6.
oil. S#8081h. Ge +28:18. 35:14. Ex 25:6. 27:20. Dt 8:8. 28:40. 32:13. Jb 29:6. Is +1:6mg. 5:1mg. Ezk 32:14. Ho 2:5. 12:1. Am 6:6. Mi 6:7, 15. Hg 2:12. Mt 26:23, 26.

25 **Thy shoes**, etc. or, Under thy shoes shall be iron. Dt 8:9. Jg 5:21. Ro 16:20. Ep +6:15.
and as thy. 1 K 8:59. 2 Ch 16:9. Ne 6:11. Ps 138:3. Is 27:8. 40:29. 41:10. Mk 13:11. 1 C 10:13. 2 C 12:9, 10. Ep 6:10. Ph 4:13. Col 1:11. He 13:5, 6.

26 **none like**. Ex +8:10. Is 43:11-13.
Jeshurun. Dt 32:15.
rideth. 2 S 22:11. Ps 18:10. 68:4, 33, 34. 104:3. Is 19:1. Na 1:3. Hab 3:8.

27 **eternal**. Heb. *kedem*, Mi +5:2. Dt 32:40. Ge +21:33. Ex 15:18. 1 S 15:29. 1 Ch 16:36. Ne 9:5. Ps 9:7. 90:1, 2. 93:2. 102:24-27. Is 9:6. 40:28. 44:6. 48:12. 57:15. 63:16. Je 10:10. La 5:19. Da 4:3, 34. Mi 4:7. 5:2. Hab 1:12. Ro 1:20. +16:26. 1 T 1:17. 6:15, 16. He 1:20-12. 9:14. 13:8. 2 P 3:8. Re 1:11.
refuge. Ps +9:9. 27:5. 36:7. 57:1, 2. 59:16, 17. 71:3, 7. Ph 3:9.
underneath. Ge 49:24. Ex 17:12. Pr 10:25. SS 2:6. Is 26:4. He 13:5. 1 P 1:5. Ju 24.
everlasting. Heb. *olam*, Ge +17:7.
arms. Ps 103:17. Is 26:4. 40:28, 29. Je 31:3. 1 Th 2:16, 17.
thrust. Dt 9:3-5. Ex 23:28. Ps 80:8. Jn 10:28, 29. Ro 8:2. 16:20. Re 20:2, 3, 10.

28 **dwell in safety**. Dt +12:10. Ex 33:16. Re 21:27. 22:14, 15.
the fountain. Dt 8:7, 8. Ps 68:26. Pr 5:15-18. Is 48:1.
corn. Ge +27:28.
and. Ge 27:28. Ps 65:9. 104:16. Ho 2:22. Jl 2:19.
his. ver. 13. Dt 8:7, 8. 11:11. 32:2. Ge 27:28.
dew. Ps 133:3. Ho 14:5.

29 **Happy**. Dt 4:7, 8. Nu 23:20-24. 24:5. 2 S 7:23. 1 K 10:8. Ps +1:1. 148:14. Ep 1:3.
who. Dt 4:7. 2 S 7:23. Ps 147:20.
saved. Is 12:2. 45:17. 1 T 4:10.
the shield. Ps 35:1, 2. +84:11.
the sword. Jg 7:20. Ps 7:12. 45:3. Is 27:1. 34:5, 6. 41:2-4. 66:16. Je 12:12. 47:6. Ep 6:17. He 4:12. Re 1:13, 16. 19:21.
found liars. or, subdued. Ge 22:17. Ps 47:3. +66:3mg. 1 C 15:25, 26.
thou shalt. Dt 9:3. 32:13. Jsh 10:24, 25. Hab 3:19.

DEUTERONOMY 34

1 Moab. Ps 108:8.

the mountain. Dt +32:49. Nu 27:12. 33:47.

Pisgah. *or,* the hill. Nu +21:20mg.

showed him. ver. 4. Dt 3:27. Nu 32:33-40. Ezk 40:2. Re 21:10.

Gilead. Ge +37:25.

Dan. Ge +14:14.

2 unto the utmost sea. Dt 11:24. Ex 23:31. Nu 34:6. Jsh 15:12.

3 the south. Nu 34:3.

the city of palm. Jg 1:16. 3:13. 2 Ch 28:15.

Zoar. Ge +13:10.

4 This is the land. Ge +13:15.

I have caused. Dt 3:26, 27. 32:52. Nu 20:12. Jn 1:17.

5 So Moses. Jsh 1:1. Ps 90 title, mg. Ml 4:4. Jn 8:35, 36. 2 T 2:24, 25. He 3:3-6. 2 P 1:1. Re 15:3.

died there. Dt 31:14. 32:50. Jsh 1:1, 2.

the word. Dt +21:5mg.

6 he buried him. Ju 9.

Moab. Ezk +25:8.

Beth-peor. Dt +3:29.

no man knoweth. Ac 2:29.

sepulchre. S#6900h, *qeburah,* Ge +35:20.

unto this day. Dt +29:4.

7 And Moses. 1 S 4:18. 1 K 1:1. 11:4.

an hundred and twenty. Dt 31:2. Ps 90:10. Ac 7:23, 30, 36.

his eye. Ge 27:1. 48:10. Jsh 14:10, 11. Jb 17:7.

natural force. Heb. moisture. or, freshness, greenness. 1 K 1:1. Is 40:30, 31.

abated. Heb. fled. Jg 6:11mg. Ps 104:7. 114:3, 5. SS 2:17. 4:6. Is 35:10. 51:11.

8 wept for Moses. 1 S 25:1. 2 S 3:35, 38. Is 57:1.

mourning. Ge +23:2.

9 full of the spirit. Heb. *ruach,* Ge +41:38. Ex 31:3. Nu 11:17. 1 K 3:9, 12. 2 K 2:9, 15. Is 11:2. Da 6:3. Jn 3:34. Col 2:3.

Moses. Ac +8:17.

the children. Jsh 1:16-18. 3:7. 4:14.

10 there arose. Dt 18:15-18. Mt 17:1-8. Lk 16:29-31. Ac 3:22, 23. 7:37. He 3:5, 6.

knew. Jn 10:15.

face to face. Dt +5:4. Ex 24:9-11.

11 In all the signs. Rather, "with respect to all the signs and wonders," etc. Dt 4:34. 7:19. Ne 9:6-10. Ps 78:43-58. 105:26-38. Jn 15:24.

to Pharaoh. Ex 11:3.

12 mighty hand. Ex 3:19. 6:1. 13:3, 9, 14, 16. Jsh 4:24. 1 K 8:42. 2 Ch 6:32. Ne 1:10. Ps 136:12. Is 40:10. Je 21:5. 32:21. Ezk 20:33. Da 9:15. Lk 24:19.

great terror. Dt 4:34. 26:8. Je 32:21. 2 C 5:11.

JOSHUA

JOSHUA 1

1 **the death**. Jsh 12:6. Dt +33:1. 34:5. Ac 13:36, 37. Ro 1:1. T 1:1. Ja 1:1. Re 1:18.
Joshua. Ex 17:9-13. Nu +13:8, 16. 27:18-20. Dt 1:38. 31:3, 23. 34:9. Ac 7:45, Jesus.
Moses' minister. Ex 24:13. Nu 11:28. 1 K 19:16. 2 K 3:11. 4:27-29. 5:25-27. Mt 20:26, 27. Lk 16:10.

2 **Moses**. ver. +1. Is 42:1. He 3:5, 6. 7:23, 24.
servant. Re 1:1.
arise. Nu 27:15-21. Dt 3:28. 31:7.

3 **Every**. 1 C 3:22.
the sole. Jsh 14:9. Dt 11:24, 25. T 1:2.

4 **From the wilderness**. Ge 12:7. 13:14-17. 17:8. Ex 6:4. 32:13. Nu 34:2-18. Dt 3:25. 32:8, 9. 1 K +4:21.
the river. Ge +2:14.
Hittites. Dt +20:17.
sea. Nu +34:6.

5 **There shall**. Dt 7:24. 20:4. Ro 8:31, 37.
as I was. ver. 9, 17. Jsh 3:7. 6:27. Dt 31:8, 23. Mt +28:20.
be with. ver. 17. Jsh 3:7. 4:14. Dt 31:6. 1 Ch 28:20.
I will not. Dt 31:6-8. Is 41:10-16. 43:2-5. Ro 8:31, 37. He 13:5.

6 **Be strong**. ver. 7, 9. Jsh 10:25. Dt 31:6, 8, 23. 1 S 4:9. 1 K 2:2. 1 Ch 22:13. 28:10, 20. 2 Ch 15:7. 32:7, 8. Ps 27:14. Is 35:3, 4. Da 10:19. Hg 2:4. Zc 8:9. 1 C 16:13. Ep 3:16. 6:10. Col 1:11. 2 T 2:1.
good courage. 2 Ch 19:11.
unto this people, etc. *or,* thou shalt cause this people to inherit the land.
divide. Nu 34:17-29.
which I sware. Ge 26:3.

7 **which Moses**. ver. 1. Jsh 11:15. Nu 27:23. Dt 31:7.
turn not. Jsh 23:6. Dt +4:2. 5:32. 17:11, 20. 28:14. 1 K 15:5. 2 K 22:2. 2 Ch 34:2. Ps 125:5. Pr 4:27. 8:20. 19:27. Is 30:21. 2 P 2:21.
prosper. *or,* do wisely. ver. +8mg.

8 **book**. Dt 6:6-9. 11:18, 19. 17:18, 19. 30:14. 31:11. Ps 37:30, 31. 40:10. 119:11, 42, 43. Is 59:21. Mt 12:35. Ep 4:29.
not depart. Dt 6:7.

thou shalt meditate. Dt 11:18-21. Ps +1:2, 3. 19:14. 37:31. 63:5, 6. 103:17, 18. 119:11, 15, 97, 99. Pr 2:1-5. 3:1. 4:13, 20, 21, 22, 26. 14:22. Is 64:5. Jn +5:39. Ac +17:11. Ro +15:4. Col 3:16. 1 Th 5:27. 1 T 4:14-16. He 2:1. 1 P 2:2. Re 1:3.
observe. Dt +5:29, 32, 33. 6:1-3. Mt 7:21, 24. 28:20. Lk 11:28. Jn 13:17. 14:21. Ja 1:22-25. Re 22:14.
to do. Jsh 22:5. Dt 30:6.
thy way. Pr 2:6, 7.
prosperous. Ps +1:3. Is 44:4. Col 1:6.
have good success. *or,* do wisely. ver. 7mg.

9 **Have**. Dt 31:7, 8, 23. Jg 6:14. 2 S 13:28. Ac 4:19.
Be strong. ver. 6, 7. Ps 71:16.
courage. ver. 18. Nu 13:20. Dt 31:6, 7, 23. 2 S 10:12. 1 Ch 28:20. 2 Ch 19:11. Ezr 10:2-5. Ne 6:11. Ps 27:14. 31:24. Ph +1:20.
be not afraid. Jsh 8:1. Ge +28:15. Dt 20:1. Ps 27:1, 2. Je 1:7, 8.
for the Lord. Ps 46:7. Is 43:1, 5.
with thee. Ge 28:15. Mt +28:20.

10 **the officers of the people**. Ex +5:6, 10, 14, 15, 19.

11 **three days**. Jsh 3:2. Ex 19:11. 2 K 20:5. Ho 6:2.
ye shall. Dt 9:1, 5. 11:31.
pass over. Is 43:1-3.

12 **Reubenites**. Nu +26:7. Re 22:1-4.

13 **Remember**. Jsh 22:1-4. Nu 32:20-28. Dt 3:18.

14 **little ones**. Dt +29:11.
armed. Heb. marshalled by five. Ex 13:18.
the mighty. Dt 20:8. Re 17:4.

15 **Until**. Nu 32:17-22. Ga 5:13, 14. 6:2. Ph 1:21-26. 2:4.
then ye shall. Jsh 22:4, etc. 1 C 12:26. 13:5.

16 **All that**. Nu 32:25. Dt 5:27. 2 S 15:15. Ro 13:1-5. T 3:1. 1 P 2:13-15.
whithersoever. Mt 8:19. Re 14:4.
will go. Nu 32:17, 18. 1 S 15:22.

17 **as we hearkened**. ver. 5. Jsh 3:7. 4:14.
only the Lord. ver. 5. 1 S 20:13. 1 K 1:37. 1 Ch 28:20, 21. Ps 20:1, 4, 9. 118:25, 26. Mt 21:9. 1 T 2:1, 2.

18 that doth rebel. Dt 17:12. 1 S 11:12. Ps 2:1-6. Lk 19:27. He 10:28, 29, 31. 12:25.
he shall be. Ro 13:1-5.
only be. ver. 6, 7, 9. Ezr 10:4. 1 C 16:13. Ep 6:10.

JOSHUA 2

1 sent. or, had sent.
Shittim. Nu 25:1. 33:49.
to spy secretly. Nu 13:2, 17-21. Jg 18:2, 14, 17. Mt 10:16. Ep 5:15.
even Jericho. Jsh 5:10. 6:1-24.
harlot's house. or, innkeeper, or hostess. Jsh 6:17, 25. Jg 11:1. 16:1. 1 K 3:16. Mt 1:5, Rachab. 20:16. 21:31. He 11:31. Ja 2:25.
Rahab. i.e. spacious, wide; breadth, **S#7343h**. ver. 3. Jsh 6:17, 23, 25.
lodged. Heb. lay. ver. 8.
2 told the king. Ps 127:1. Pr 21:30, 31. Is 43:13. Da 4:35.
3 Bring. Jsh 10:23. Ge 38:24. Le 24:14. Jb 21:30. Jn 19:4. Ac 12:4, 6.
to search. Ge 42:9-12, 31. 2 S 10:3. 1 Ch 19:3.
4 took. Ex 1:19. 2 S 16:18, 19. 17:19, 20. 2 K 6:19.
5 of shutting. ver. 7. Ne 13:19. Is 60:11. Ezk 46:1, 2, 12. Re 21:25.
the men went out. Je 50:20. Ro 3:7, 8.
6 to the roof. ver. 8. Ex 1:15-21. Dt +22:8.
hid them. Ex 2:2. 2 S 17:19. 1 K 18:4, 13. 2 K 11:2. Je 36:26. Col 3:3. He 11:23.
7 Jordan. i.e. descending, **S#3383h**. ver. 10. Jsh 1:2, 11, 14, 15. 3:1, 8, 11, 13-17. Ge 32:10. Nu 32:5, 19, 21, 29, 32. Dt 4:22. Jg 8:4. 2 S 17:22, 24. 2 K 2:6, 7, 13. 5:10, 14. 6:2, 4. Jb 40:23. Ps 42:6. 114:3, 5. Is 9:1. Je 12:5. 49:19. 50:44. Ezk 47:18. Zc 11:3. Mt 3:6.
the fords. Jg 3:28. 12:5.
they shut. ver. 5. Ac 5:23.
9 I know. Ex 18:11. 2 K 5:15. Jb 19:25. Ec 8:12. He 11:1, 2.
that the Lord. Ge 13:14-17. 15:18-21. Ex 3:6-8. Dt 32:8. Ps 115:16. Je 27:5. Mt 20:15.
your terror. Ge +35:5. Dt 28:7, 10. Jg 7:14.
faint. Heb. melt. ver. 11, 24mg. Ex +15:15.
10 For we. Jsh 4:24. Ex 14:21-31. 15:14-16.
what ye did. Nu +21:21-35.
11 had heard. Ex 15:14.
our hearts. ver. +9.
did there remain. Heb. rose up. Re 6:16.
courage. Heb. ruach, spirit, Ge +26:35.
for the Lord. Dt 4:39. 1 K 8:60. 1 Ch 16:31. Ps 83:18. 99:1. 102:15. Je 16:19-21. Da 4:34, 35. 6:25-27. Zc 8:20-23. 2 P 3:10. Re 19:6.
12 swear. Jsh 9:15, 18-20. Ge +21:23. 1 S 30:15. 2 Ch 36:13.
that ye will. Est 8:6. 2 T 1:16-18. Ja 2:13.

my father's. ver. 13. Ge 24:3, 9. Ro 1:31. 1 T 5:8.
give me a true token. ver. 18. Ge +17:11. Ezk +9:4. Mk 14:44. Ro 4:11.
13 lives. Heb. nephesh, souls, Ge +44:30.
14 life. Heb. nephesh, soul. Ge +44:30.
for your's. Heb. instead of you to die. 1 K 20:39.
when the Lord. Jsh 6:17, 25. Ge 24:49. Nu 10:29-32. Jg 1:24, 25. 1 S 20:8. 2 S 9:1. Pr 18:24. Mt 5:7.
15 she let them. 1 S 19:12-17. Ac 9:25. 2 C 11:32, 33.
for her house. Jsh 6:20.
16 Get you. ver. 22. 1 S 23:14, 29. Ps 11:1.
17 We will be. ver. 20. Ge 24:3-8. Ex 20:7. Le 19:11, 12. Nu 30:2. 2 S 21:1, 2, 7.
18 scarlet. ver. 21. Le 14:4. Nu 4:8. 19:6. He 9:19.
thread. Ezk 9:4, 6. Ro 4:11. 2 T 2:19. He 11:28. 12:24.
bring. Heb. gather.
thy father. ver. 13. Jsh 6:23. Ge 7:1. 12:2. 19:12-17. Ex 20:12. Est 8:6. Lk 19:9. Ac 10:27, 33. 11:14. 2 T 1:16.
all thy. Ge 7:1. Ex 12:22. 1 K 17:15. Ac 11:14. 16:15, 31.
19 whosoever. Ex 12:13, 23. Nu 35:26-28. 1 K 2:36-42. Ezk 33:4, 5. Mt 24:17. Ac 27:31. Ph 3:9. He 10:29, 31. 1 J 2:27, 28.
go out. Ex 12:22.
street, his blood. Le 20:9-11. 2 S 1:16. 3:28, 29. Ezk 33:4, 5. Mt 27:24. Ac 18:6. 20:26.
in the house. ver. 13. Jsh 6:23. Ge 7:1. 12:2. 19:12-17. Est 8:6. Lk 19:9. Ac 10:27, 33. 11:14. 16:31. 2 T 1:16.
his blood. ver. 14. 2 S 4:11. 1 K 2:32. Mt 27:25.
20 And if thou. Pr 11:13.
we will be quit. ver. 17.
21 According. 2 Ch 32:8.
and she bound. ver. 18. Ex 12:13. Mt 7:24. Jn 2:5.
22 found them not. 1 S 19:10-12. 2 S 17:20. Ps 32:6, 7, 10.
23 told him. Pr 25:13.
24 Truly the Lord. Jsh 1:8. 21:44, 45. Ex 23:31. Nu 13:32, 33. Pr 25:13.
all the inhabitants. ver. 9-11. Ps 48:5, 6. Re 6:16, 17.
faint. Heb. melt. ver. +9, 11.

JOSHUA 3

1 A.M. 2553. B.C. 1451. An. Ex. Is. 40.
rose early. Ge +21:14.
Shittim. Jsh 2:1. Nu 25:1. Mi 6:5.
Jordan. Dt 32:47.
2 three days. Jsh +1:10, 11.
3 When ye see. ver. 11. Nu +10:33.

the priests. ver. 6, 8, 14-17. Jsh 4:10. 6:6. Nu 4:15. Dt 31:9, 25. 2 S 6:3, 13. 1 Ch 15:11, 12.

ye shall remove. Ex 13:21, 22. Mt 8:19. 16:24. Re 14:4.

go after it. He 12:1, 2.

4 **a space**. Ex 3:5. 19:12. 33:7. Ps 89:7. He 12:28, 29.

have not passed. Dt 17:16.

heretofore. Heb. since yesterday and the third day. 2 S +3:17mg.

5 **Sanctify**. Jsh 7:13. Ex 19:10-15. Le 10:3. 20:7, 8. Nu 11:18. 1 S 16:5. Jb 1:5. Jl 2:16. Jn 17:19.

the Lord. ver. 13, 15. Ps 86:10. 114:1-7.

6 **Take up**. ver. +3. Nu 4:15. 10:33. Mi 2:13. Jn 14:2, 3. He 6:20.

7 **magnify thee**. Jsh 4:14. 1 Ch 29:25. 2 Ch 1:1. Jb 7:17. Ps 18:35. Lk 1:32. Jn 17:1. Ac 5:31. Ph 1:20. 2:9-11.

that, as I was. Jsh +1:5, 17. 4:14.

8 **to the brink**. Heb. to the extremity. i.e. so far as the river then spread itself, which was now more than ordinary, ver. 15.

command. ver. 3. 1 Ch 15:11, 12. 2 Ch 17:8, 9. 29:4-11, 15, 27, 30. 30:12. 31:9, 10. 35:2-6. Ne 12:24-28. 13:22, 28.

ye shall stand. ver. 17. Ex 14:13. La 3:26.

in. ver. 17. Jsh 7:13. 10:13. Ge 45:6. Ex 8:22. 24:18. Pr 30:19.

9 **Come hither**. 1 S 9:27. 12:7.

hear the words. Dt 4:1. 5:26. 12:8.

10 **Hereby ye**. Nu 16:28-30. 1 K 18:36, 37. 22:28. Ps 9:16. Is 7:14. 2 C 13:2, 3. He 11:6.

living. Je +10:10.

God. Heb. *El*, Ex +15:2.

among. Jsh 22:31. Ex 17:7. Dt 31:17. Jg 6:12, 13.

drive out from. Jsh +21:45. Ge 15:15-18. Ex 3:8. +23:30.

Canaanites. Ge +10:18.

Hittites. Dt +20:17.

Hivites. Ge +10:17.

Perizzites. Ge +13:7.

Amorites. Ge +10:16.

Jebusites. Ge +10:16.

Girgashites. Ge +10:16.

11 **the Lord**. ver. 13. Ps 24:1. 47:2. Is 54:5. Je 10:7. Mi 4:13. Zp 2:11. Zc 4:14. 6:5. 14:9.

passeth. ver. 3-6. Is 3:12.

over before. Dt 31:8. Ps 23:4. Lk 19:28. Jn 10:4.

12 **take you twelve**. Jsh 4:2, 9.

13 **the soles**. ver. 15, 16. Ex 14:19-22.

in the waters. Ro 6:3, 4. Col 3:1-4.

of the Lord. *ver. 11*.

stand upon. ver. 16. Ex 15:8. Ps 33:7. 78:13. 114:3-5. Hab 3:15.

14 **bearing the ark**. ver. +3, 6. Jsh 6:6. Nu 10:35. Dt 31:26. Je 3:16. Ac 7:44, 45. 1 C 1:24, 25. He 9:4.

15 **the feet**. ver. 13. Is 26:6.

Jordan overfloweth. Jsh 4:18. 1 Ch 12:15. Je 12:5. 49:19. Mk 1:5.

all the time. Jsh 5:10-12. Le 23:10-16. Dt 16:1-9.

16 **rose up**. ver. +13. Ps 29:10. 77:19. 114:3. Mt 8:26, 27. 14:24-33.

Adam. i.e. *red earth*, **S#121h**. 1 Ch 1:1.

Zaretan. i.e. *narrowness of dwelling place; their distress*, **S#6891h**. 1 K 4:12, Zartanah. 7:46, Zarthan.

the plain. Dt +11:30. 1 K 7:46.

the salt sea. Ge +14:3. Ex 14:19-31. Mt 26:55. Ac 26:26.

against Jericho. Jsh 5:10, 12.

17 **the priests**. ver. 3, 6.

stood firm. Jsh 4:3. 2 K 2:8.

in the midst. Jsh 4:3, 8, 16. Ge +45:6.

all the Israelites. Ex 14:22, 29. Ps 66:6. Is 25:8. He 11:29.

JOSHUA 4

1 **were clean passed**. Jsh 3:17. Dt 27:2.

2 **twelve men**. Jsh 3:12. Nu 1:4-15. 13:2. 34:18. Dt 1:23. 1 K 18:31. Mt 10:1-5.

3 **the priest's feet**. Jsh +3:13.

twelve stones. Jsh 24:27. Ge 28:22. Dt 27. 1 S 7:12. Ps 103:2. 111:4. Lk 19:40.

leave them. ver. 8, 19, 20.

4 **prepared**. ver. 2. Mk 3:14-19.

6 **a sign**. Jsh 22:27. 24:27. Ge 31:51, 52. Ex +12:14. Nu 16:38. Is 55:13. Ezk 20:12, 20.

when your. ver. 21. Ex 12:26, 27. 13:14. Dt 6:20, 21. 11:19. Ps 44:1. 71:18. 78:3-8. Is 38:19. Ac 2:39.

in time to come. Heb. tomorrow. ver. 21. Jsh 3:5. 22:24mg. Ge 30:33mg. Ex 13:14mg. Dt +6:20mg. 1 S 25:31. Ne 2:12. Pr 27:1mg.

7 **the waters**. Jsh 3:13-16.

passed over. Ex 12:13.

memorial. ver. +6. Ex +12:14.

for ever. Heb. *olam*, Ex +12:24.

8 **did as Joshua**. ver. 2-5. Jsh 1:16-18.

9 **set up twelve**. Ex 24:12. 28:21. 1 K 18:31. Ps 111:2-4.

in the midst. Jsh 3:8, 17.

and they are there. ver. 20. 2 P 1:16. 1 J 1:1-3.

unto this day. Jsh 7:26. 8:28, 29. 9:27. 10:27. 13:13. 14:14. 15:63. Ge +19:38. Ep 4:8-10. 1 C 3:21-23.

10 **the ark**. Ac 7:44, 45.

stood in the midst. Jsh +3:8, 13, 16, 17. Is 28:16.

Moses. Nu 27:21-23. Dt 31:9.

hasted. Ex 12:39. Ps 119:60. Pr 27:1. Ec 9:10. 2 C 6:2. He 3:7, 8.

11 **clean passed over**. Ex 10:26. 1 C 10:1. He 1:3.

that the ark. ver. 18. Jsh 3:8, 17.

12 **the children**. Jsh 1:14. Nu 32:20-32.

13 **prepared for war**. *or*, ready armed. Jsh 6:7, 9, 13. Nu 31:5. 32:27. Ep 6:11.
passed over. Ps 116:9.
to the plains. Jsh 5:10. Dt +11:30.

14 **magnified**. Jsh 1:16-18. Jsh +3:7. 1 C 10:2.
they feared him. Ex 14:31. 1 S 12:18. 1 K 3:28. 2 Ch 30:12. Pr 24:21. Ro 13:4.
as they. Jsh 1:5, 17. 3:7.

16 **the priests**. Jsh +3:3-6. Ex 25:16-22. Re 11:19.
come up out of Jordan. Jsh 3:8, 17. Mt 3:11, 16. Mk 1:9, 10. Lk 3:16, 21. Jn 1:28, 31-33. 3:23. 10:40.

17 **Come ye up**. Ge 8:16-18. Da 3:26. Ac 16:23, 35-39.

18 **the soles**. Jsh +3:13, 15.
lifted up. Heb. plucked up. Jsh 8:6, 16.
that the waters. Ex 14:26-28.
and flowed. Heb. went.
over all. Jsh 3:15. 1 Ch 12:15. Is 8:8. Je 12:5.
before. Heb. yesterday, the third day. S#8543h. Jsh 20:5. Ex 5:7, 8, 14. 21:29, 36. Dt 4:42. 1 S 20:27. 21:5. 2 S +3:17mg. 15:20. Jb 8:9.

19 **first month**. Ex 12:2, 3.
Gilgal. i.e. *rolled; rolling; a wheel*, S#1537h. ver. 20. Jsh 5:9, 10. 9:6. 10:6, 7, 9, 15, 43. 12:23. 14:6. 15:7. Dt 11:30. Jg 2:1. 3:19. 1 S 7:16. 10:8. 11:14, 15. 13:4, 7, 8, 12, 15. 15:12, 21, 33. 2 S 19:15, 40. 2 K 2:1. 4:38. Ne 12:29mg. Ho 4:15. 9:15. 12:11. Am 4:4. 5:5. Mi 6:5.

20 **those twelve**. ver. +3, 8.

21 **When your**. ver. +6. Ps 105:2-5. 145:4-7.
in time to come. Heb. tomorrow. ver. 6.

22 **saying**. Jsh +3:17. Ex 14:29. 15:19. Ps 66:5, 6. Is 11:15, 16. 44:27. 51:10. Re 16:12.

23 **as the Lord**. Ps 78:3-8.
which he dried. Ex +14:21.
until we. Jn 8:51. 11:26. 1 C 15:54, 55, 57.

24 **That**. Jn +11:42.
all the people. Ex 9:16. Dt 28:10. 1 S 17:46. 1 K 8:42, 43. 2 K 5:15. 19:19. 1 Ch 5:25. 2 Ch 6:33. 13:9. 32:19. Ezr 3:3. 9:1, 2, 11. 10:11. Ps 106:7, 8. Da 3:26-29. 4:34, 35. 6:26, 27.
that it is. Ex 15:16. 1 Ch 29:12. Ps 89:13.
mighty. Ps 89:19. Is 63:1. Zp 3:17. Ep 1:18-20.
ye might. Ex 14:31. 20:20. Dt 6:2. Ps 76:6-8. 89:7. Je 10:6, 7. 32:40. Re 15:4.
forever. Heb. all days. Dt 12:19mg.

JOSHUA 5

1 **all the kings**. Jsh 12:9-24. 24:15. Ge 10:15, +16, 17-19. 15:18-21. 48:22. Nu 13:29. Jg 11:23. 2 S 21:2. Ezk 16:3. Am 2:9.
Canaanites. Ge +10:18. Ps 135:11.
which were by. Nu 13:29. Jg 3:3. Zp 2:4-6.
heard. Jsh 2:9-11. Ex 15:14, 15. Ps 48:4-6. Lk 21:25, 26. Re 18:10.

melted. Ex +15:15.
neither was. 1 S 25:37. 1 K 10:5. Is 13:6-8. Ezk 21:7. Da 5:6.
spirit. Heb. *ruach*, Ge +41:8.

2 **sharp knives**. *or*, knives of flints. Ex +4:25.
circumcise. Ge 17:10-14. Dt 10:16. 30:6. Ro 2:29. 4:11. Col 2:11.

3 **Joshua**. Ge 17:23-27. Ex 12:48. Mt 16:24.
the hill of the foreskins. *or*, Gibeah haar-aloth.
hill. Ge 49:26. Ex 17:6.
foreskins. S#6190h. Ge 17:11, 14, 23, 24, 25. 34:14. Ex 4:25. Le 12:3. 19:23. Dt 10:16. 1 S 18:25, 27. 2 S 3:14. Je 4:4. 9:25.

4 **All the**. Nu 14:29. 26:64, 65. Dt 2:16. Ps 95:10, 11. 1 C 10:5. He 3:17-19.

5 **they had not**. Dt 12:8, 9. Ho 6:6, 7. Mt 12:7. Ro 2:26. 1 C 7:19. Ga 5:6. 6:15.

6 **walked**. Nu 14:32-34. Dt 1:3. 2:7, 14. 8:4. Ps 95:10, 11. Je 2:2.
because they obeyed not. Dt +26:17. 28:45.
sware that. Nu 14:22, 23. He 3:11.
a land. Jl 3:18.
milk and. Je 11:5.
honey. Ex +3:8.

7 **their children**. Nu 14:31. Dt 1:39.
had not. Ex 4:25. Lk 7:30. Ac 16:3. 19:1-7.

8 **when they**, etc. Heb. when the people had made an end to be circumcised. Ga 5:1. Ph 3:3.
till they were whole. Ge 34:25.

9 **I rolled away**. Jsh 10:18. 24:14. Le 24:14. 1 S 14:6. Je 9:25. Ezk 20:7, 8. 23:3, 8. Ep 2:11, 12.
reproach. Ge 30:23. 34:14. Ex 6:5, 6. 13:3. 15:26. Dt 5:6. 28:27. 1 S 11:2. +17:26, 36. Ps 119:22, 39.
Gilgal. *That is*, rolling. Jsh +4:19.

10 **kept the passover**. Ex 12:3, 6, etc. Nu 9:1-5.

11 **old corn**. Jn 12:24.
on the morrow after the passover. Le 23:10, +11, 14.
unleavened cakes. Ex 12:18-20. 13:6, 7. Le 23:6, 14.
parched. or, roasted. Le 2:14.
in the selfsame day. Dt +32:48.

12 **the manna**. Ex 16:35. Ne 9:20, 21. Re 7:16, 17.
ceased. Ph 4:19.
but they did eat. Dt 6:10, 11. Pr 13:22. Is 65:13, 14. Jn 4:38.

13 **he lifted**. Ge 33:1, 5. Ps 121:1. 123:1. Da 8:3. 10:5.
a man. Jsh 6:2. Ge 18:2. 32:24-30. Ex 23:23. Jg 13:8, 9, 11, 22. Da 10:5. Ho 12:3-5. Zc 1:8. Ac 1:10. Ro 8:31. Re 1:13.
his sword. Nu 22:23, 31. 1 Ch 21:16, 17, 27, 30.
Art thou for us. 1 Ch 12:17, 18.

14 **but as the captain**. *or*, Prince. Ex 23:20-22.

Ps +103:21. Is 55:4. Da 10:13, 21. 12:1. He 2:10. 12:2. Re 12:7. 19:11-14.
the host. Ex +12:41.
fell on his. Ge +17:3. Mt 8:2.
What saith. 1 S 3:9, 10. Is 6:8. Ac 9:6.
my lord. Ex 4:10, 13. Ps 110:1. Mt 22:44. Lk 1:43. 20:42. Jn +20:28. Ph 3:8.
15 **Loose.** Ex 3:5. Ac 7:32, 33. 2 P 1:18.

JOSHUA 6

1 **was straitly.** Heb. did shut up, and was shut up. Jsh 2:7. 2 K 17:4.
because. Jsh 2:9-14, 24. Ps 127:1.
2 **the Lord.** Jsh 5:13-15.
See, I have. ver. 9:24. Jsh 2:9, 24. 8:1. 11:6-8. Jg 11:21. 2 S 5:19. Ne 9:24. Da 2:21, 44. 4:17, 35. 5:18.
the king. Dt 7:24. Jg 11:24.
3 **ye shall.** ver. 7, 14. Nu 14:9. 1 C 1:18, 21-25, 27, 28. 2 C 4:7. 12:9.
six days. Jn 11:39.
4 **trumpets of rams'.** or, jubilee trumpets. Le 25:9, 11. Nu 10:1-10. Jg 7:7, 8, 15-22. 2 Ch 13:12. 20:17, 19, 21. Is 27:13. Zc 4:6.
seven times. Ge 2:3. 7:2, 3. Le +4:6. Nu 23:1. 1 K 18:43. 2 K 5:10. Jb 42:8. Zc 4:2. Re 1:4, 20. 5:1, 6. 8:2, 6. 10:3. 15:1, 7. 16:1.
5 **make a long.** ver. 16, 20. Ex 19:19. 2 Ch 20:21, 22.
the people. Jg 7:20-22. 1 S 4:5. 17:20, 52. 2 Ch 13:14, 15. Je 50:15.
and the wall. Is 25:12. 30:25. 2 C 10:4, 5. He 11:30.
flat. Heb. under it. ver. 20.
6 **Take up the ark.** ver. 8, 13. Jsh +3:3, 6. Ex 25:14. Dt 20:2-4. Ac 9:1.
7 **that is armed.** ver. 3. Jsh 1:14. 4:13.
8 **before the Lord.** ver. 3, 4. Nu 32:20.
9 **and the rereward.** Heb. gathering host. ver. 13. Nu 10:14, 18, 21, 22, 25. Is 52:11, 12. 58:8.
10 **not shout.** Ps 4:4, 5. 46:10, 11. Is 30:15. La 3:26.
any noise with your voice. Heb. your voice to be heard. Is 42:2. Mt 12:19.
until the day. 2 S 5:23, 24. Is 28:16. Lk 24:49. Ac 1:7.
12 **Joshua rose.** Jsh +3:1. Ge 22:3. 28:18. Ex 24:4. Ps 57:8. Pr 8:17. Mk 1:35.
the priests. ver. 6-8. Dt 31:25. Jn 2:5-8. 6:10, 11. 9:6, 7. He 11:7, 8.
13 **went on.** 1 Ch 15:26. Mt 24:13. Ga 6:9.
14 **the second.** ver. 3, 11, 15.
15 **about the dawning.** Ps 119:147. Mt 28:1. 2 P 1:19.
only on that day. ver. 4.
16 **Shout.** ver. 5. Jg 7:20-22. 2 Ch 13:15. 20:22, 23.
hath given. 2 C 10:5. Ph 3:21. 1 J 5:5.
17 **accursed.** or, devoted. Jsh 7:1. Le 27:28, 29.

Nu 21:2, 3. Dt 2:34. 1 Ch 2:7. Ezr 10:8mg. Is 34:6. Je 46:10. Ezk 39:17. Mi 4:13. 1 C 16:22. Ga 3:10, 13.
only Rahab. Jsh +2:1.
because. ver. 22, 23. Jsh 2:4-6, 22. Ge 12:3. 1 S 15:6. Mt 10:41, 42. 25:40. He 6:10. 11:31. Ja 2:25.
18 **in any wise.** Ro 12:9. 2 C 6:17. Ep 5:11. Ja 1:27. 1 J 5:21.
lest ye make. Jsh 7:1, 11, 12, 15. Dt 7:26. 13:15-17.
make the camp. Jsh 7:11, 12. 22:18-20. 1 S 14:28-42. Ec 9:18. Jon 1:12.
and trouble it. Jsh 7:25. 2 S 21:1. 1 K 18:17, 18. Ga 5:12.
19 **all the silver.** 2 S 8:11. 1 Ch 18:11. 26:20, 26, 28. 28:12. 2 Ch 15:18. 31:12. Is 23:17, 18. Mi 4:13.
consecrated. Heb. holiness. Le 19:24mg. Zc 14:20, 21.
the treasury. 1 K 7:51. 14:26. 2 K 24:13. 1 Ch 26:20. Ne 7:70, 71. 10:38. Je 38:11. Mt 27:6. Mk 12:41.
20 **the sound of the trumpet.** 1 Th 4:16.
the wall. ver. +5. Is 2:12, 15. 2 C 10:4, 5. He 11:30. Re 14:8. 18:21.
flat. Heb. under it. ver. 5.
21 **And they.** Am +3:6.
utterly. Dt +2:34. 1 K 20:42. Ps 137:8, 9. Je 48:18. 2 C 7:11. Col 3:5, 6. Re 18:21.
all. Ex +9:6.
22 **Joshua.** ver. 17. Jsh 2:1, etc.
as ye sware unto her. Jsh 2:12-14, 17-20. 9:15, 18-20. 2 S 21:2, 7. Ps 15:4. Ezk 17:13, 16, 18, 19. He 11:31.
23 **out Rahab.** Jsh 2:18. Ge 12:2. 18:24. 19:29. Ac 27:24. He 11:7.
kindred. Heb. families.
left them. Nu 5:2, 3. 31:19. Ac 10:28. 1 C 5:12. Ep 2:12.
24 **burnt.** Jsh 8:28. Dt 13:16. Nu 31:10. 2 K 25:9. Re 17:16. 18:8, 9.
only the silver. ver. +19.
the treasury. ver. 19.
25 **saved.** Lk 5:32.
Rahab. Jsh 11:19, 20. Jg 1:24, 25. Ac 2:21. He 11:31.
she dwelleth. Mt 1:5. Lk 3:32.
unto. Jsh +4:9.
because. Ja 2:25.
26 **adjured.** Nu 5:19-21. 1 S 14:24, etc. 1 K 22:16. Mt 26:63. Ac 19:13.
Cursed. 1 K 16:34. Ml 1:4.
27 **the Lord.** Is +43:2. 2 C 13:14.
his fame. Jsh 9:1, 3, 9. 1 S 2:30. Mt +4:24.

JOSHUA 7

1 **committed.** ver. 20, 21. Jsh 22:16. 2 Ch 24:18. Ezr 9:6. Da 9:7.

for Achan. i.e. *a troubler*, **S#5912h**. ver. 18, 19, 20, 24. Jsh 22:20. 1 Ch 2:6, 7, Achar, Zimri. Ho 2:15.

Zabdi. i.e. *gift of Jehovah; my dowry; giving*, S#2067. ver. 17, 18. 1 Ch 8:19. 27:27. Ne 11:17.

took. Jsh +6:17, 18.

the anger. Jsh 22:18. 2 S 24:1. 1 Ch 21:7. Ec 9:18. Jon 1:7. 1 C 5:1-6. He 12:15, 16.

2 **to Ai**. i.e. *a heap of ruins*, **S#5857h**. ver. 3, 4, 5. Jsh 8:1-3, 9-12, 14, 16-18, 20, 21, 23-26, 28, 29. 9:3. 10:1, 2. 12:9. Ge 12:8, Hai. Ezr 2:28. Ne 7:32. 11:31, Aija. Je 49:3.

Beth-aven. i.e. *house of iniquity, vanity, sorrow*, **S#1007h**. Jsh 18:12. Ge 28:19. 1 S 13:5. 14:23. Ho 4:15. 5:8. 10:5.

Go up. Jsh 2:1. Pr 20:18. 24:6. Mt 10:16. Ep 5:15.

3 **about two**. Heb. about 2000 men, or about 3000 men.

labor. Pr 13:4. 21:25. Lk 13:24. He 4:11. 6:11, 12. 2 P 1:5, 10.

few. 1 K 20:11. Ps 34:2.

4 **fled**. Le 26:14, 17. Dt 28:15, 25. 32:30. Is 30:17. 59:2.

5 **for they**. Dt 1:44.

Shebarim. i.e. *broken places, fractures, terrors*, **S#7671h**.

the going down. *or*, Morad.

melted. Ex +15:15.

6 **rent**. 2 K +18:37.

fell. ver. +10. 2 S 12:16.

before the ark. He 4:16.

until the eventide. Jg 20:23, 26. 21:2. 2 S 1:12.

put dust. 1 S 4:12. 2 S 1:2. 13:19. 15:32. Ne 9:1. Est +4:1. Jb 2:12. La 2:10. Ezk 27:30. Mi 1:10. Re 18:19.

7 **wherefore**. Ex 5:22, 23. 32:12. Nu 14:3. 2 K 3:10. 2 Ch 20:9, 11. Ps 116:11. Je 12:1, 2. He 12:5.

to deliver. Ex 14:11, 12. 17:3. Nu 20:4, 5. Mt 17:17, 20. Mk 8:17, 18.

would to. Ex +16:3.

and dwelt. Jsh 1:2-4. He 10:38. 11:15.

8 **what shall**. Ezr 9:10. Hab 2:1. Ro 3:5, 6.

backs. Heb. necks. ver. 12. Ge 49:8. Ex 23:27.

9 **Canaanites**. Ge +10:18.

shall hear. Ex 32:12. Nu 14:13, 15, 16. 2 Ch 20:9, 11.

environ. Ps 83:4. 124:2, 3.

what wilt thou. Is +48:9. Jl 2:17. Jn 12:28.

10 **wherefore**. Ex 14:15. 1 S 15:22. 16:1. 1 Ch 22:16.

liest. Heb. fallest. ver. 6. Ge +17:3. 1 S 5:3, 4.

11 **Israel**. ver. 1, 20, 21.

and. Ge +8:22.

transgressed. Jsh 23:16. Dt 17:2. Jg 2:20. 2 K 18:12. Is 24:5. 50:1, 2. Je 31:32. Ho 6:7.

the accursed. ver. 21. Jsh 6:17-19.

stolen. Ml 3:8, 9. Mt 22:21.

dissembled. 2 K 5:25, 26. Jn 12:5, 6. Ac 5:1, 2, 9. He 4:13.

among. Le 5:15. Hab 2:6. Zc +5:3, 4.

12 **the children**. Jsh 22:18-20. Nu 14:45. Jg 2:14. Ps 5:4, 5. Pr 28:1. Is 59:2. Hab 1:13.

they were. Jsh 6:18. Dt 7:26. Hg 2:13, 14. 1 J 5:21.

neither. Je 6:8. 23:33. Ho 9:12.

13 **sanctify**. Jsh 3:5. Ex 19:10-15. La 3:40, 41. Jl 2:16, 17. Zp 2:1, 2.

an accursed. ver. +11. 2 Ch 28:10. Mt 7:5.

take away. 1 C 5:1-6, 11-13.

14 **the tribe**. ver. 17, 18. Jsh +14:2.

15 **he that is**. ver. 25, 26. Dt 13:15, 16. 1 S 14:38, 39. 1 C 3:16, 17.

he hath. ver. +11.

wrought. 1 S 26:21.

folly. *or*, wickedness. Is +9:17.

16 **rose up**. Jsh +3:1. Ge +22:3. Ps 119:60. Ec 9:10.

and brought. ver. +14.

17 **the family of**. Ge 38:30, Zarah. Nu 26:20. 1 Ch 2:4-7.

18 **was taken**. Ge +24:44. Nu 32:23. 1 S 14:42. Pr 13:21. 16:33. Je 2:26. Ac 5:1-10.

19 **My son**. 2 T 2:25. T 2:2. Ja 1:20. 1 P 3:8, 9.

give. Re +11:13.

make. Nu 5:6, 7. 2 Ch 30:22. 33:12, 13. Ezr 10:10, 11. Ps 32:5. 51:3. Pr 28:13. Je 3:12, 13. Da 9:4. Ro 10:10. Ja 5:16. 1 J 1:8-10.

tell me. 1 S 14:43. Jon 1:8-10.

20 **Indeed**. Ge 42:21. Ex 9:27. 10:16. Nu 22:34. 1 S 15:24, 30. Jb 7:20. 33:27. Ps 38:18. Mt 27:4.

21 **I saw**. Ge 3:6. 6:2. 2 S 11:2. Jb 31:1. Ps 119:18, 37. Pr 23:31. 28:22. Mt 5:28, 29. 1 J 2:15, 16.

Babylonish garment. **S#8152h**. ver. 24. Ge +10:10.

wedge. Heb. tongue.

I coveted. Ge 2:9. 3:6. Ex +20:17. Dt 7:25. 1 K 21:1, 2. 2 K 5:20-27. Ps 119:36. Hab 2:9. Lk +12:15. Ro 7:7, 8. Ep 5:3. Col +3:5. 1 T +6:9, 10. He 13:5. 2 P 2:15.

took them. Pr +4:23. Mi 2:1, 2. Ja 1:15.

they are hid. ver. 22. Dt 33:19. 2 S 11:6-17. 2 K 5:24, 25. Jb 3:16. 18:10. Is 28:15. 29:15. Lk 12:2.

23 **laid them out**. Heb. poured. 2 S 15:24. Ps 45:2.

24 **And**. Ge +8:22.

took Achan. ver. +1. Jb 20:15. Pr 15:27. Ec 5:13. Ezk 22:13, 14. 1 T 6:9, 10.

his sons, and his daughters. Jsh 6:18, 21. Ge +18:25. Ex 20:5. Nu 16:27-31. Dt 24:16. Jb 20:23-28.

and all that he had. Ge 20:7. Nu 16:32, 33. Ezk 32:27. Da 6:24.

the valley. ver. 26. Jsh 15:7. Is 65:10. Ho 2:15.

Achor. i.e. *troubled*, **S#5911h**. ver. 26. Jsh 15:7. Is 65:10. Ho 2:15.

25 **Why hast**. ver. 11-13. Jsh 6:18. Ge 34:30. 1 K 18:17, 18. 1 Ch 2:7. Hab 2:6-9. Ga 5:12. 2 Th 1:6. He +12:15.

all Israel. Le +24:14.

burned. ver. 15, 24. Le +21:9. Dt 24:16. 1 S 31:12. 2 K 23:20. 2 Ch 34:5. Am 2:1. 6:10.

them. Ep 5:11. 1 T 5:22. 2 J 11.

26 **raised**. Jsh 8:29. 10:27. 2 S 18:17. La 3:53.

So the Lord. Ex +32:12. 2 S 21:14. Is 40:2. Jl 2:13, 18. Zc 6:8.

The valley. ver. 24. Jg 14:14. Is 65:10. Ho 2:15.

Achor. *that is*, Trouble. ver. +25. Jsh 15:7.

unto this day. Jsh +4:9.

JOSHUA 8

1 **Fear not**. Jsh +1:9. 7:6, 7, 9. Dt 1:21. 7:18. 31:8. Ps 46:11. +118:6. Is 12:2. Mt 8:26.

see, I have. Jsh +6:2. Ps 44:3. Da 2:21, 37, 38. 4:25, 35.

2 **do to Ai**. ver. 24, 28, 29. Jsh +6:21. 10:1, 28. Dt 3:2.

only the spoil. ver. 27. Dt 20:13, 14. Jb 27:16, 17. Ps 39:6. Pr 13:22. 28:20. Je 17:11. Lk 12:20, 21.

lay thee. ver. 7, 9, 12, 14, 19. Jg 20:29-33. 2 Ch 13:13. 20:22. Je 51:12.

behind. Ex 3:1.

3 **by night**. Mt 24:39, 50. 25:6. 1 Th 5:2. 2 P 3:10.

4 **lie in wait**. ver. 16. Jg 9:25. 20:29, 33, 36. 1 S 15:2, 5. Ac 23:21.

go not. Ec 7:19. 9:16.

all ready. 2 T 2:21.

5 **as at**. Jsh 7:5.

that we will. Jg 20:31-33. Mt 10:16.

6 **drawn**. Heb. pulled. ver. 16.

They flee. Ex 14:3. 15:9. Jg 20:32. Ec 8:11. 9:12.

7 **for the Lord**. ver. +1. 2 K 5:1. Pr 21:30, 31.

will deliver. 1 C 15:57.

8 **set the city**. ver. 28. Jg 6:24.

see , I have. Jsh 1:9, 16. Jg 4:6. 2 S 13:28.

9 **between**. ver. 12. Jg 7:2. Ge 12:8, Hai. Ezr 2:28. Ne 7:32.

lodged. Ge 32:21.

10 **rose up**. Jsh +3:1. 6:12. 7:16. Ps 119:60.

11 **all the**. ver. 1-5.

12 **five thousand**. ver. 2, 3.

of the city. *or*, of Ai.

13 **liers in wait**. Heb. lying in wait. ver. 4. Jg 20:29.

on the west. ver. 8, 12.

14 **Ai saw it**. ver. 5, 16.

he wist not. Jg 20:34, etc. Ec 9:11, 12. Is 19:11, 13. Da 4:31. Mt 24:39, 50. 1 Th 5:1-3. 2 P 2:3.

15 **by the way**. Jsh 18:12.

16 **called together**. Jg 20:36-39.

drawn away. ver. 5, 6. Jg 20:31. Ps 9:16. Ezk 38:11-22. Re 16:14. 19:19-21.

17 **a man**. ver. 3, 24, 25. Jsh 11:20. Dt 2:30. Jb 5:13. Is 19:11-13.

18 **Stretch**. ver. 7, 26. Ex 8:5. 17:11. Jb 15:25.

the spear. 1 S 17:6, 41, 45. Jb 39:23.

19 **the ambush**. ver. 6-8.

20 **the smoke**. Re +14:11.

and they had. Jb 11:20. Ps 48:5, 6. 76:5. Am 2:14-16.

power. Heb. hand. Jg 18:10.

this way or. 1 K 20:40.

22 **let none**. Jsh 6:21. 10:28. 11:11, 12. Dt 7:2. Jg 20:36-43. Jb 20:5. Is 8:15. 28:13. Lk 17:26-30. 21:34, 35. 1 Th 5:3.

23 **the king**. ver. 29. Jsh 10:17. 1 S 15:8. Re 19:20.

24 **returned unto Ai**. ver. 16. Jsh 10:30-41. 11:10-14. Nu 21:24.

smote it. Dt 13:16. Re 18:19, 21-23.

26 **Joshua**. ver. 18. Ex 17:11.

drew not. ver. 18. Ex 17:11, 12.

utterly destroyed. Jsh 2:10. 10:1. Dt +2:34. Jg 1:17. 21:11. 1 K 9:21. 2 K 19:11. 1 Ch 4:41. 2 Ch 20:23. 32:14. Is 11:15. 34:2. 37:11. Je 25:9. 44:11.

27 **the cattle**. ver. 2. Jsh 11:14. Nu 31:22, 26. Ps 50:10. Mt 20:15.

he commanded. ver. 2.

28 **an heap**. Dt 13:16. 2 K 19:25. Is 17:1. 25:2. Je 9:11. 49:2. 50:26. Mi 3:12. Re 18:19, 21-23.

for ever. Heb. *olam*, Ex +12:24.

unto this day. Jsh +4:9.

29 **the king**. Jsh 10:26-28, 30, 33. Dt 21:22, 23. Est 7:10. Ps 107:40. 110:5. 149:7-9. Ac 12:23. Re 19:17, 18.

hanged on a tree. Jsh 10:26. Dt 21:22, 23.

until eventide. Dt 21:23.

as soon. Jsh 10:27.

a great heap. Jsh 7:26. 2 S 18:17.

unto this day. Jsh +4:9.

30 **built an altar**. Ge +8:20. 12:7, 8. +13:18.

in mount Ebal. ver. 33. Dt 11:29, 30.

31 **as it is**. ver. 34, 35. Jsh 1:8. 2 K 14:6. 22:8. 2 Ch 25:4. 35:12. Ezr 6:18. Ne 13:1. Mk 12:26.

altar. Ex 20:24, 25. Dt 27:5, 6. 1 K 18:31, 32.

and they offered. Ex 18:12. 24:5. Dt 27:6, 7.

burnt offerings. Le +23:12.

peace offerings. Le +23:19.

32 **wrote**. Dt 27:2, 3, 8. Jg 9:6, 7.

copy. or, duplicate. Dt 17:18.

33 **all Israel**. Jsh 23:2. 24:1. Dt 27:12, 13. 29:10, 11.

priests. Jsh 3:3, 6, 14. 4:10, 18. 6:6. Dt 31:9, 25. 1 Ch 15:11-15.

stranger. ver. 35. Nu 15:16, 29. Dt +26:11. 31:12.

Gerizim. Dt +11:29.
Ebal. Dt 27:13-15.
Moses. ver. 30-32. Dt 11:29. 27:12.
34 **he read**. Dt 31:10-12. Ne 8:2, 3. 9:3. 13:1.
blessings. Le ch. 26. Dt 11:26-30. 27:14-26.
28:1-3, etc. 29:20, 21. 30:15-20.
cursings. Dt 27:13-15. 28:15, 16, 45. 29:20,
21. 30:19.
35 **was not**. Dt 4:2. Je 23:22. 26:2. Ac 20:26, 27.
Moses commanded. Dt 31:9-13.
women. Ex 15:20. 35:22. Dt +29:11. 31:12.
Ezr 10:1. Ne 8:2. Jl 2:16. Mk 10:14. Ac 21:5.
little ones. or, infants. Dt +29:11.
strangers. ver. +33.
were. Heb. walked.

JOSHUA 9

1 **all the kings**. Jsh 10:2-5, 23, 28-39. 11:1-5,
10, 11. 12:7-24.
on this. Jsh 1:15. 3:17. 5:1. 22:4, 7. Dt 4:49.
of the great. Ge 15:18-21. Nu +34:6.
Lebanon. Dt +1:7.
Hittite. Dt +20:17.
Amorite. Ge +10:16.
Canaanite. Ge +10:18.
Perizzite. Ge +13:7.
Hivite. Ge +10:17.
Jebusite. Ge +10:16.
2 **gathered**. 2 Ch 20:1, etc. Ps 2:1, 2. 83:2-8. Pr
11:21. Is 8:9, 10, 12. 54:15. Jl 3:9-13. Ac
4:26-28. Re 16:14. 20:8, 9.
accord. Heb. mouth. Dt +21:5mg.
3 **Gibeon**. ver. 17. Jsh +10:2. 2 S 21:1, 2.
Jericho. Jsh ch. 6, 8.
4 **work wilily**. Ge 34:18. Ex 21:14. 1 K 20:31-
33. Pr 1:4. 8:5, 12mg. Mt 10:16. Lk 16:8.
as if. Ge +27:16.
ambassadors. Pr 13:17. 25:13.
wine bottles. S#4997h. ver. 13. Jg 4:19. 1 S
16:20. Ps 56:8. 119:83. Mt 9:17. Mk 2:22. Lk
5:37, 38.
bound up. Ex 12:34. 1 S 25:29. 2 S 20:3mg.
Ho 13:12.
5 **old shoes**. ver. 13. Dt 29:5. 33:25. Lk 15:22.
clouted. or, patched. lit. spotted. Ge 30:32.
provision. lit. hunting. Ge 25:28.
mouldy. or, crumbs. ver. 12. 1 K 14:3.
6 **the camp**. Jsh 5:10. 10:43.
We be. ver. 9. Dt 20:11-15. 1 K 8:41. 2 K
20:14. Lk 14:32.
make ye. Dt 29:12.
7 **Hivites**. Ge +10:17.
how shall. Ex 23:31-33. 34:12. Nu 33:52. Dt
7:2, 3. 20:16, 17. Jg 2:2. 2 C 6:14. Ep 5:11.
8 **We are**. ver. 11, 23, 25, 27. Ge 9:25, 26. Dt
20:11. 1 K 9:20, 21. 2 K 10:5.
Who are. Ge 27:18-26.
9 **From a**. Dt 20:15.
because. 1 K 8:41. 2 Ch 6:32, 33. Ne 9:5. Ps

72:19. 83:18. 148:13. Is 55:5. Ac 8:7.
we have. ver. 24. Jsh 2:9, 10. Ex 9:16. 15:14.
Nu 14:15. 21:33, 34. Is 66:19.
10 **two kings**. Nu +21:21-35.
Ashtaroth. Dt +1:4.
11 **our elders**. Est 8:17.
Take. Jsh 1:11. Mt 10:9, 10. Lk 9:3.
with you. Heb. in your hand. Ge 43:12.
We are your. ver. 8. Est 8:17.
12 **our bread**. ver. 4, 5.
13 **bottles of wine**. rather, wine bottles.
14 **the men took of their victuals**. or, they
received the men by reason of their victuals.
asked not. Ex 28:30. Nu 27:21. Jg 1:1. 20:18,
28. 1 S 14:18, 19. 22:10. 23:9-12. 30:7, 8. 2 S
2:1. 5:19. 1 Ch 10:13, 14. 15:13. +28:9. 2 Ch
15:1, 2. 16:12, 13. Ezr 8:21, 22. Jb 36:13, 14.
Ps 9:17. Pr 1:24-28. 3:5, 6. Is 30:1, 2. 31:1. Je
+10:25. Ja 1:5. +4:2, 3.
mouth. Nu +12:8.
15 **made peace**. Jsh 2:12-19. 6:22-25. 11:19. Dt
20:10, 11. 2 S 21:2. Je 18:7, 8.
and the. 2 S 21:2.
16 **that they heard**. Pr 12:19.
neighbors. Ge 45:10.
17 **Gibeon**. ver. +3.
Chephirah. i.e. *a village; a young lioness; covert,*
S#3716h. Jsh 18:26. Ezr 2:25. Ne 7:29.
Beeroth. Heb. wells. S#881h. Jsh 18:25. Ge
+16:14. 2 S 4:2. Ezr 2:25. Ne 7:29. Compare
S#885h, Dt 10:6.
Kirjath-jearim. i.e. *city of forests*. S#7157h. Jsh
15:9, 60. 18:14, 15. Jg 18:12. 1 S 6:21. 7:1, 2.
1 Ch 2:50, 52, 53. 13:5, 6. 2 Ch 1:4. Ezr 2:25,
Kirjath-arim. Ne 7:29. Je 26:20.
18 **had sworn**. 2 S 21:7. Ps 15:4. 24:4. Ec 5:2, 6.
9:2. Ezk 17:18.
19 **We have**. ver. 20. Ec 8:2. 9:2. Je 4:2.
we may not touch them. Jg +11:35. 2 S
21:1-3. Ezk 17:18. Ro 11:29. Ga 3:15.
20 **lest wrath**. 2 S 21:1-6. 2 Ch 36:13. Pr 20:25.
Ezk 17:12-21. Zc +5:3, 4. Ml +3:5. Ro 1:31. 1
T 1:10.
21 **let them**. ver. 23, 27. Dt 29:11, 12. 2 Ch
2:17, 18. Is +61:5.
as the princes. ver. 15.
22 **Wherefore**. Ge 3:13, 14. 27:35, 36, 41-45.
29:25. 2 C 11:3.
We are. ver. 6, 9, 10.
ye dwell. ver. 16.
23 **cursed**. Ge 9:25, 26. Le 27:28, 29.
none of you be freed. Heb. not be cut off
from you.
hewers. ver. 21, 27. 2 S 3:29. 1 Ch 9:2
(Nethinims). Ezr 2:43. 8:20.
water. Jn 4:7.
24 **the Lord**. Ex 23:31-33. Nu 33:51, 52, 55, 56.
Dt +2:34.
sore afraid. Jb 2:4. Mi +7:17. Mt +10:28.
lives. Heb. *nephesh*, our souls, Ge +44:30.

25 we are. Ge 16:6. Jg 8:15. 2 S 24:14. Is 47:6.
Je 26:14. 38:5.
  as it seemeth. Jg +10:15. Mt 11:26.
  good and right. 2 Ch 14:2. 31:20.
26 delivered. Jsh 24:10.
27 made them. Heb. gave, or, delivered to be.
ver. 21, 23. 1 Ch 9:2. Ezr 2:43. 8:20. Ne 7:60.
11:3, Nethinim.
  for the altar. Ps 84:10. Lk 15:19. Ga 4:1, 3.
  unto this day. Jsh +4:9.
  in the place. Dt +12:11. 2 Ch 6:6. Ps 132:13,
14. Is 14:32.

JOSHUA 10

1 Adoni-zedec. i.e. lord of righteousness. S#139h.
Ge 14:18. He 7:1, 2.
  Jerusalem. i.e. possession or foundation of peace;
the abode of harmony, S#3389h. ver. 3, 5, 23.
12:10. 15:8, 63. 18:28. Ps 51:18. 122:2, 3, 6.
Zc 14:2, 4, 8, 10-12, 14, 16, 17, 21. Ml 2:11.
3:4.
  as he had. Jsh 6:21. 8:2, 22-29.
  how the. Jsh 9:15-27. 11:19, 20. 1 Th 1:8-10.
2 they feared. Jsh 2:9-13, 24. Ex 15:14-16. Dt
11:25. 28:10. Ps 48:4-6. Pr 1:26, 27. 10:24. Ac
5:11. He 10:27, 31. Re 6:15-17.
  Gibeon. i.e. hilly; high hill; little hill, S#1391h.
ver. 1, 4-6, 10, 12, 41. Jsh 9:3, 17. 11:19.
18:25. 21:17. 2 S 2:12, 13, 16, 24. 3:30. 5:25,
Geba. 20:8. 1 K 3:4, 5. 9:2. 1 Ch 8:29. 9:35.
14:16. 16:39. 21:29. 2 Ch 1:3, 13. Ne 3:7.
7:25. Is 28:21. Je 28:1. 41:12, 16.
  the royal cities. Heb. cities of the kingdom.
1 S 27:5. 2 S 12:26.
3 king of Jerusalem. ver. 1, 5. Jsh 12:10-13.
15:35, 39, 54, 63. 18:28.
  Hoham. i.e. he impels, S#1944h.
  Hebron. Jsh 14:15. Ge 23:2. 37:14. Nu 13:22.
2 S 2:11.
  Piram. i.e. a wild ass; indomitable, S#6502h.
  Japhia. i.e. beautiful; splendid; illustrious,
S#3309h. Jsh 19:12. 2 S 5:15. 1 Ch 3:7. 14:6.
  Lachish. i.e. captured; invincible, S#3923h. ver.
5, 23, 31-35. Jsh 12:11. 15:39. 2 K 14:19.
18:14, 17. 19:8. 2 Ch 11:9. 25:27, 32:9. Ne
11:30. Is 36:2. 37:8. Je 34:7. Mi 1:13.
  Debir. i.e. sanctuary; oracle, S#1688h. ver. 38,
39. Jsh 11:21. 12:13. 13:26. 15:7, 15, 49.
21:15. Jg 1:11. 1 Ch 6:58.
4 and help. Is 8:9-13. 41:5-7. Ac 19:24-27.
21:28. Re 16:14. 20:8-10.
  we may. ver. 1. Jsh 9:15. Mt 16:24. Jn 15:19.
16:2, 3. Ac 9:23. 2 T 3:12. Ja 4:4. 1 P 4:4.
  for it. Ps 120:6, 7. Pr 11:21.
5 five kings of. ver. 6. Jsh +9:1, 2. Ge 15:16. Is
8:9, 10.
6 to the camp. Jsh 5:10. 9:6.
  Slack. 2 K 4:24.
  from thy. Jsh 9:15, 24, 25. Is 33:22.

mountains. Jsh 21:11. Dt 1:15. Ps 125:2. Lk
1:39.
7 Joshua ascended. Is 8:12, 13.
8 Fear them not. Jsh 1:5-9. 8:1. 11:6. Dt 1:29.
3:2. 20:1-4. Jg 4:14, 15. Ps 27:1, 2. Is 41:10-
15. Ro 8:31.
9 all night. 1 S 11:9-11. Pr 22:29. 24:11, 12. Ec
9:10. 2 T 2:3. 4:2.
10 the Lord. Jsh 11:8. Ex 14:14. Dt 1:30. 3:22.
Jg 4:15. 1 S 7:10-12. 2 Ch 14:12. Ps 18:13, 14.
44:3. 78:55.
  at Gibeon. Is 28:21.
  Beth-horon. i.e. house of the little cave, S#1032h.
ver. 11. Jsh 16:3, 5. 18:13, 14. 21:22. 1 S
13:18. 1 K 9:17. 1 Ch 6:68. 7:24. 2 Ch 8:5.
25:13. Young notes there are two places of
the same name, the upper (Jsh 16:5; 21:22)
and the lower (Jsh 16:3; 18:13; 2 Ch 25:13).
  Azekah. i.e. a fenced place. S#5825h. ver. 11.
Jsh 15:35. 2 Ch 11:9. Ne 11:30. Je 34:7.
  Makkedah. i.e. place of shepherds, S#4719h. ver.
16, 17, 21, 28, 29. Jsh 12:16. 15:41.
11 the Lord. Ge 19:24. Jg 5:20. Ps 11:6. 77:17,
18. Is +28:17.
12 Sun. ver. 13. Dt 4:19. 17:3. Jb 9:7. 31:26, 27.
Ps 19:4. 74:16. 148:3. Is 28:21. 38:8. 60:20.
Am 8:9. Hab 3:11.
  stand thou. Heb. be silent. Ps +37:7mg. Hab
2:20mg. Zc 2:13.
  Ajalon. i.e. a little hind; deer field. S#357h. Jsh
19:42. 21:24, Aijalon. Jg 1:35. 12:12. 1 S
14:31. 1 Ch 6:69. 8:13. 2 Ch 11:10. 28:18.
13 stood still. Heb. was silent. i.e. still, as this
phrase is commonly used, as 1 S 14:9. Ps 4:4.
Jon 1:12.
  until. Nu 31:2. Jg 5:2. 16:28. Est 8:13. Lk
18:7. Re 6:10.
  Jasher. or, the upright. i.e. straight, S#3477h.
Nu 21:14. 2 S 1:18. 2 Ch 16:11.
  So the sun. ver. 11, 14. Ps 19:4. 74:16, 17.
136:7-9. 148:3. Is 24:23. 38:8. Jl 2:10, 31.
3:15. Mt 5:45. 24:29. Ac 2:20. Re 6:12. 8:12.
16:8, 9. 21:23.
14 there was. 2 K 20:10, 11. Is 38:8. Zc 14:7.
  the Lord. Zc 4:6, 7. Mt 21:21, 22. Mk 11:22-
24. Lk 17:6.
  hearkened. Jg 13:9.
  for the Lord. ver. 42. Jsh 23:3. Ex 14:4. Dt
1:30.
15 Joshua returned. ver. 6, 43. Jn 17:4.
16 and hid. Ps 48:4-6. 139:7-10. Is 2:10-12. Am
9:2, 3. Re 6:15.
  in a cave. Ge +19:30. Is 24:21, 22.
Mi 7:17.
17 found hid. Nu 32:23. He 11:38. Re 6:15, 16.
18 Roll. ver. 22. Jg 9:46-49. Jb 21:30. Am 5:19.
9:1. Mt 27:66.
19 stay ye. Ps 18:37-41. Je 48:10.
  smite. Heb. cut off the tail. Dt 25:18. Is 9:14,
15.

suffer them. ver. 20. 2 S 17:13. 20:6. Je 8:14.

20 had made. ver. 10. Jsh 8:24. 2 Ch 13:17.
fenced cities. 2 S 20:6. Je 8:14.

21 to the camp. ver. 15-17.
none. Ps +107:42. Is 54:7. 57:4.

22 Open. ver. 16-18. 1 S 15:32.

23 the king of. ver. 1, 3, 5.

24 put your feet. Dt 33:29. Jg 8:20. 2 S 22:43.
Ps 2:8-12. 18:40. 91:13. 107:40. 110:1, 5.
149:8, 9. Pr 16:5. Is 26:5, 6. 28:18. 60:11, 12.
Ezk 21:28, 29. Ml 4:3. Ro 16:20. Re 2:26, 27.

25 Fear not. Jsh +1:9. Dt 31:6-8. 1 S 17:37. Ps
63:9. 77:11. Lk 12:32. 2 C 1:10. 2 T 4:17, 18.
be strong. Ep 6:10.
thus shall. Dt 3:21, 22. 7:19. Ro 8:37.

26 Joshua. Jg 8:21. 1 S 15:33.
hanged. Jsh 8:29. Nu 25:4. Dt 21:22, 23. 2 S
21:6, 9. Est 2:23. 7:9, 10. Mt 27:25. Ga 3:13.

27 they took. Jsh 8:29. Dt 21:23. 2 S 18:17.
until this very day. Jsh +4:9. 7:26. Ge
+19:38. Dt +29:4. +32:48.

28 Makkedah. Jsh 15:21, 41, 42.
them. ver. 32, 35, 37, 39. Dt +2:34. Ps 21:8,
9. 110:1. Lk 19:27. 1 C 15:25.
souls. Heb. plural of *nephesh*. Here, *nephesh* is
used of man being slain or killed by man. In
this use *nephesh* may be rendered *everyone,
individuals, persons, person,* as it has no essential reference to soul as a separate, immaterial, conscious constituent part of man which
survives the dissolution of the body (Mt
+10:28). ver. 30, 32, 35, 37, 37, 39. Jsh 11:11.
Je 2:34. Ezk 13:19. 22:25, 27. Rendered (1)
person, Jsh 20:3, 9. Dt 27:25. 1 S 22:22. Pr
28:17. Ezk 17:17. (2) *any,* Le 24:17. (3) *any
person,* Nu 31:19. 35:11, 15, 30, 30. Ezk 33:6.
(4) *him,* Ge +37:21. Dt 19:6. 22:26. (5) *mortally,* Dt 19:11. (6) *life,* 2 S 14:7. (7) *thee,* Je
40:14, 15. Compare Ge +17:14, where *nephesh*
is used of man as being cut off by God. For
the other uses of *nephesh* see Ge +2:7.
and he did. ver. 30. Jsh 8:2.
as he did. Jsh 6:2, 21.

29 Libnah. Nu +33:20.

30 all the souls. Heb. plural of *nephesh.* ver. +28.
Jsh 6:21. 8:2, 29.
as he did. ver. 28. Jsh 6:21. 8:2, 29.

31 Lachish. ver. +3.

32 souls. Heb. *nephesh,* ver. +28.
to Libnah. ver. +29.

33 Horam. i.e. *height; very high,* S#2036h.
Gezer. 1 K +9:16, 17. 1 Ch 14:16.

34 Eglon. ver. 3. Jg +3:12.

35 on that day. ver. 32.
souls. Heb. *nephesh,* ver. +28.
utterly. ver. 37. Jsh +8:26. Le 26:44. Jb
19:10.

36 Hebron. ver. 3, 5. Nu +13:22. 1 Ch 12:23, 28.

37 the king. ver. 23.

souls. Heb. *nephesh,* ver. +28.
according. ver. 35.
utterly. Jsh +8:26.
souls. Heb. *nephesh,* ver. +28.

38 Debir. Jsh 12:13. 15:15-17, 49. 21:15. Jg
1:11-15.

39 souls. Heb. *nephesh,* ver. +28.
he left none. ver. 33, 37, 40. Jsh 11:8. Dt
3:3. 2 K 10:11. Ob 18.

40 all the country. Jsh 15:21-63. 18:21-28.
19:1-8, 40-48.
springs. Jsh 12:3, 8. Dt 3:17. 4:49. 8:7.
utterly. ver. 35, 37. Dt +2:34. 1 K 15:29. Ps
9:17. 2 Th 1:7-9.
all that breathed. Jsh 11:11, 14. Ge +2:7
(S#5397h). 7:22. Dt 20:16.
as the Lord God of Israel commanded.
Jsh 6:17. 8:2, 27. 9:24. Ex 23:31-33. 34:12. Dt
7:2, 16. 20:16, 17. Am +3:6.

41 Kadesh-barnea. Nu +34:4.
Gaza. Ge +10:19.
all the country of Goshen. i.e. *drawing near,*
S#1657h. Jsh 11:16. 15:51. Ge 45:10. 46:28, 29,
34. 47:1, 4, 6, 27. 50:8. Ex 8:22. 9:26.
Gibeon. ver. +2.

42 because. ver. 14. Ex 14:14, 25. Dt 20:4. Ps
44:3-8. 46:1, 7, 11. 80:3. 118:6. Is 8:9, 10.
43:4. Ro 8:31-37. Ep 6:10-12. Ph 4:13. Col
2:15. 1 T 6:12.

43 unto the camp. ver. 15. Jsh +4:19. 1 S
11:14.

JOSHUA 11

1 Jabin. i.e. *whom God observes; he understands,*
S#2985h. ver. 10. Jsh 12:19. 19:36. Jg 4:2, 7,
17, 23, 24. Ps 83:9.
he sent. Jsh 10:3, 4. Ps 2:1-4. 83:1-3. Is
26:11. 43:2, 5-7.
Madon. i.e. *contention,* S#4068h. Jsh 12:19, 20.
19:15, 25.
Shimron. Ge 46:13.
Achshaph. i.e. *enchantment,* S#407h. Jsh
12:20. 19:25.

2 on the north. ver. 21. Jsh 10:6, 40. Lk 1:39.
Chinneroth. i.e. *harps,* S#3672h. Jsh 12:3. Nu
+34:11, Chinnereth, 12. Dt 3:16, 17. 1 K
15:20. Mt 14:34. Lk 5:1, Gennesaret. Jn 6:1,
Sea of Tiberias.
Dor. Jsh 12:23. 17:11. Jg 1:27. 1 K 4:11.

3 Canaanite. Ge +10:18.
Amorite. Ge +10:16.
Hittite. Dt +20:17.
Perizzite. Ge +13:7.
the Jebusite. Ge +10:16.
Hivite. ver. 19. Ge +10:17. Jg 3:3.
Hermon. Dt +3:8.
land of Mizpeh. Jsh +15:38. Ge +31:49.

4 as the sand. Ge +22:17. 2 Ch 20:15.

5 all these. Ps 3:1. 118:10-12. Is 8:9. Re 16:14.

met together. Heb. assembled by appointment. Ec +3:8.
Merom. i.e. *high place*, **S#4792h**. ver. 7.

6 **Be not**. Jsh +10:8. Ps 20:7, 8. 27:1, 2. 33:16, 17. 46:11. Is 8:12, 13.
tomorrow. Jsh 3:5. Jg 20:28. 1 S 11:9. 2 Ch 20:16.
hough. ver. 9. 2 S 8:4.
horses. Dt 17:16. Ps 20:7, 8. 46:9. 147:10, 11. Pr 20:7. Is 30:16. 31:1. Ho 14:3.

7 **suddenly**. Jsh 10:9. Pr 6:15. Is 29:5. 1 Th 5:2, 3.

8 **the Lord**. Jsh 21:44.
great Zidon. *or*, Zidon-rabbah. Ge +49:13.
Misrephoth-maim. *or*, salt pits. Heb. burning of waters. i.e. *boilings*. **S#4956h**. Jsh 13:6. Lk 4:26, Sarepta.
Mizpeh. ver. +3.

9 **he houghed**. ver. 6. 2 S 8:4. Ps 46:9. Ezk 39:9, 10.

10 **Hazor**. ver. 1. Jg 4:2.
the head of all those kingdoms. Ge 41:57; 1 K 18:10.

11 **smote**. Jsh 10:32. Ezk +18:4.
souls. Heb. plural of *nephesh*. Jsh +10:28. Mt +10:28.
edge of. 2 C 10:4. He 4:12.
not any. i.e. no human person. ver. +10.
any left to breathe. Heb. any breath. ver. +14. Ge +2:7 (**S#5397h**). Jsh +10:40. Jb 7:15.

12 **all the**. Jsh 10:28, 30, 32, 35, 37, 39, 40.
utterly destroyed. Dt +2:34.
as Moses. ver. 15. Jsh 8:8, 31. Nu 33:52, 53.

13 **in their**. Heb. on their heap. Je 30:18.

14 **the spoil**. Jsh 8:27. Nu 31:9. Dt 6:10, 11. 20:14.
neither. ver. 11. Ge +2:7 (**S#5397h**). Jsh +10:40.

15 **the Lord**. ver. +12. Ex 34:11-13.
so did Moses. Ex 34:11, 12. Dt 7:2. 31:7.
and so did Joshua. Jsh 1:7. Ex 39:42, 43. Dt 4:5. 2 Ch 30:12.
he left nothing undone. Heb. removed nothing. Dt 4:2. 12:32. 1 S 15:1-3, 8, 9, 11, 19-22. Mt 23:23. Lk 11:42. Ac 20:20, 27.

16 **all that land**. Ge 15:18-21. Nu 34:2-13. Dt 34:2, 3.
hills. Jsh 9:1. 12:8.
the south. Jsh 10:40. 12:8. 18:5. Nu 13:22, 29. 21:1.
the land. Jsh +10:41.
the mountain. ver. 21. Ezk 17:23. 36:1-3, 8.

17 **the mount Halak**. *or*, the smooth mountain. i.e. *smooth, bare*, **S#2510h**. Jsh 12:7.
that goeth. Ge 32:3. Dt 2:1. 33:2.
Seir. Ge +14:6.
Baalgad. i.e. *lord of a troop* or *fortune*, **S#1171h**. Jsh 12:7. 13:5.
all their. Jsh 12:7-24. Dt 7:24. Ep 6:12. Col 2:15.

18 **a long time**. ver. 23. Jsh 14:7-10. Dt 7:22.

19 **the Hivites**. ver. 3. Jsh 9:3-27.

20 **it was**. Ex +4:21. 14:17. Jg 14:4. 1 S 2:25. 1 K 12:15. 2 Ch 25:16.
as the Lord. ver. 12-15. Dt 20:16, 17.

21 **the Anakims**. Jsh 14:12-14. 15:13, 14. Nu 13:22, 28, +33. Dt +1:28. 2:10, 11, 20, 21. 9:2. Jg 1:10, 11, 20. Je 3:23. 9:23. Am 2:9.
Anab. i.e. *a grape*, **S#6024h**. Jsh 15:50.
from the mountains. Heb. mountain. or, hill country.
Joshua destroyed. Jsh +8:26. 10:40, 42. 24:11, 12. Ps 110:5, 6. 149:6-9. Re 6:2. 19:11-21.
Judah, and from. Jsh 15:1. 19:9. Ge 49:9. 1 K 11:1. Ps 18, title. Mk 16:7.

22 **only**. Jsh 23:13. Nu 33:55.
in Gaza. Ge +10:19.
Gath. i.e. *a wine trough; winepress*, **S#1661h**. Jsh 19:13. 1 S 5:8. 6:17. 7:14. 17:4, 23, 52. 21:10, 12. 27:2-4, 11. 2 S 1:20. 15:18. 21:20, 22. 1 K 2:39-41. 2 K 12:17. 14:25. 1 Ch 7:21. 8:13. 18:1. 20:6, 8. 2 Ch 11:8. 26:6. Ps 56:t. Am 6:2. Mi 1:10.
Ashdod. i.e. *fortified*, **S#795h**. Jsh 15:46, 47. 1 S 5:1, 5-7. 6:17. 2 Ch 26:6. Ne 13:23, 24. Is 20:1. Je 25:20. Am 1:8. 3:9. Zp 2:4. Zc 9:6. Ac 8:40, Azotus.

23 **the whole land**. Ex 9:6.
according to all. Ex 23:27-31. 34:11. Nu 34:2-13. Dt 11:23-25. 34:1-4.
according to their. Jsh 14-19. Nu 26:52-55.
And the land. ver. 18. Jsh 14:15. 21:44, 45. 22:4. 23:1. Ps 46:9. 2 T 4:7, 8. He 4:8, 9.

JOSHUA 12

1 **on the other**. Jsh 1:15. 22:4.
from the. Nu +21:13.
unto mount Hermon. Dt +3:8.

2 **Sihon**. Nu +21:21-30.
Jabbok. Ge +32:22.

3 **sea of Chinneroth**. Jsh +11:2.
the sea. Ge +14:3.
Beth-jeshimoth. Nu +33:49.
the south. *or*, Teman. Jsh 11:16. 13:4. Jb 9:9. Ezk 47:19mg. Hab 3:3mg.
Ashdoth-pisgah. *or*, the springs of Pisgah, *or*, the hill. Nu 21:20mg. Dt 3:17mg. 4:49.

4 **the coast**. Nu 21:33-35. Dt 3:1-7, 10, 11, 13. **Bashan**. Dt +32:14.
the remnant. Dt +2:20.
dwelt. Dt +1:4.

5 **Hermon**. ver. +1.
Salcah. Jsh 13:11. Dt 3:10.
unto the border. 2 S 23:34. 2 K 25:23.
Geshurites. **S#1651h**. Jsh 13:11, 13. 1 S 27:8. 2 S +3:3.

6 **did Moses**. Nu 21:24-35.
gave it. Jsh 13:8-32. Nu 32:29-42. Dt 3:11-17.

7 **on this side**. ver. 1. Dt 3:17. 9:1.
Baal-gad. Jsh 11:17. 13:5.
Seir. Ge +14:6.
Joshua gave. Jsh 1:3, 4. 11:23. 13-19. Dt 11:23, 24.

8 **the mountains**. Jsh 10:40. 11:16.
the wilderness. 1 K 2:34. 9:18. Mt 3:1, 3.
the Hittites. Dt 9:1. +20:17.
Amorites. Ge +10:16.
Canaanites. Ge +10:18.
Perizzites. Ge +13:7.
Hivites. Ge +10:17.
Jebusites. Ge +10:16.

9 **Jericho**. Jsh 6:2-21.
Ai. Jsh 8:1, 17, 29, etc.
which is beside Bethel. This is added to distinguish it from Ai of the Ammonites, Je 49:3. Similarly, at Mi 5:2, Bethlehem Ephratah (Ge 35:19) is to be distinguished from Bethlehem in Zebulun, Jsh 19:15.

10 **Jerusalem**. Jsh +10:23.
Hebron. Jsh 10:3, 23, 36, 37.

11 **Jarmuth**. Jsh +21:29.
Lachish. Jsh +10:3.

12 **Eglon**. Jg +3:12.
Gezer. 1 K +9:16.

13 **Debir**. Jsh +10:3.
Geder. i.e. *a wall*, s#1445h. Jsh 15:36.

14 **Hormah**. Nu +14:45.
Arad. Nu 21:1.

15 **Libnah**. Nu +33:20.
Adullam. i.e. *justice of the people; a testimony to them; retreat; hiding place*, s#5725h. Jsh 15:35. 1 S 22:1. 2 S 23:13. 1 Ch 11:15. 2 Ch 11:7. Ne 11:30. Mi 1:15.

16 **Makkedah**. Jsh +10:10.
Bethel. Jsh 8:17. Ge 12:8. 28:19. Jg 1:22.

17 **Tappuah**. Jsh 15:34.
Hepher. Jsh 19:13. 1 K 4:10.

18 **Aphek**. i.e. *strength; strong or fortified place*, s#663h. Jsh 13:4. 19:30. Jg +1:31. 1 S 4:1. 29:1. 1 K 20:26, 30. 2 K 13:17.
Lasharon. or, Sharon. s#8289h. Is +35:2.

19 **Madon**. Jsh 11:1.
Hazor. Jsh +15:23.

20 **Shimron-meron**. i.e. *guardian of arrogance; guard of lashing*, s#8112h, only here. Jsh 11:1. 19:15.
Achshaph. Jsh 11:1. 19:25, 31.

21 **Taanach**. Jsh +17:11.
Migiddo. i.e. *gathering; place of multitudes*, s#4023h. Jsh +17:11. Jg 1:27. 5:19. 1 K 4:12. 9:15. 2 K 9:27. 23:29, 30. 1 Ch 7:29. 2 Ch 35:22. Zc 12:11, Megiddon. Re 16:16.

22 **Kedesh**. Jsh +15:23.
Jokneam. i.e. *possessed by the people*, s#3362h. Jsh 19:11. 21:34.
Carmel. Jsh +15:55.

23 **Dor**. i.e. *habitation, circuit, circle; generation; dwelling*, s#1756h. Jsh 11:2. 17:11. Jg 1:27. 1 K

4:11. 1 Ch 7:29.
the nations. Ge 14:1, 2. Is 9:1.
Gilgal. Jsh +4:19.

24 **Tirzah**. Nu +26:33.

JOSHUA 13

1 A.M. 2560. B.C. 1444. An. Ex. Is. 47.
Joshua. Jsh 14:10. 23:1, 2. 24:29. Ge 18:11. 1 K 1:1. Lk 1:7.
there remaineth. Ph 3:13.
land. Dt 32:9. Ps 16:5.
to be possessed. Heb. to possess it. Dt 31:3.

2 **the land**. Ex 23:29-31. Dt 11:23, 24. Jg 3:1. Am 9:7.
borders. Ge 10:14. 26:1. Jl 3:4.
Geshuri. ver. 11, 13. Dt +3:14.

3 **Sihor**. i.e. *black; turbid*, s#7883h. 1 Ch +13:5, Shihor. Is 23:3. Je 2:18.
Ekron. i.e. *uprooting*, s#6138h. Jsh 15:11, 45, 46. 19:43. Jg 1:18. 1 S 5:10. 6:16, 17. 7:14. 17:52. 2 K 1:2, 3, 6, 16. Je 25:20. Am 1:8. Zp 2:4. Zc 9:5, 7.
which is counted. Ge 10:15-19. Nu 34:2-14. Dt 2:23. Am 9:7.
five lords. Jg 3:3. 1 S 6:4, 16, 17. Zp 2:4, 5.
Gazathites. s#5841h. Jg 16:2, Gazites.
Ashdothites. s#796h. 1 S 5:3, 6. Ne 4:7. 13:23.
Eshkalonites. s#832h. Jg +1:18 (Askelon).
Gitites. s#1663h. 2 S +6:10. 15:18.
Ekronites. s#6139h. 1 S 5:10.
Avites. Dt 2:23, Avims.

4 **the land of**. Jsh 10:40. 11:3. 12:7, 8.
Canaanites. Ge +10:18.
Mearah. or, the cave. s#4632h.
Aphek. This is not the Aphek of Judah of Jsh 15:53, but the Aphek in the tribe of Asher, Jsh +12:18.
the Amorites. Ge +10:16. Jg 1:34-36.

5 **Giblites**. i.e. *stone-squarer*, see 1 K 5:18mg. Ps 83:7. Ezk 27:9. s#1382h. 1 K 5:18.
Lebanon. Dt +1:7.
Baal-gad. Jsh 12:7.
Hermon. Dt +3:8.
Hamath. Nu +13:21.

6 **hill country**. lit. mountain. Jg 3:27. 7:24.
Misrephoth-maim. Jsh 11:8.
them. Jsh 23:11-13. Ge 15:18-21. Ex 23:30, 31. Jg 2:21-23.
by lot. Jsh +14:2.

7 **this land**. Nu 26:53-56. 33:54. 34:2-14. Ezk 47:13-23. 48:23-29.

8 **Moses gave**. Jsh 4:12. 22:4. Nu 32:33-42. Dt 3:12-17.

9 **Aroer**. ver. 16. Nu +32:34.
all the plain. Nu 21:30. 33:45, 46. Is 15:2. Je 48:18, 22.

10 **the cities of**. Nu 21:24-26. Ps 136:19.

11 **Gilead**. Jsh 12:2-5. Dt 3:12, 13. 4:47, 48. 1 Ch 2:23.
Salchah. i.e. *extension; straitened basket*, **S#5548h**. Jsh 12:5. Dt 3:10. 1 Ch 5:11.

12 **Og**. Nu +21:33.
these did. ver. 13. Jsh 11:23. 14:3, 4. Nu 21:23-35.

13 **expelled**. ver. 11. Jsh 23:12, 13. Nu 33:55. Jg 2:1-3. 2 S 3:3. 13:37, 38.
until this day. Jsh +4:9.

14 **Levi**. ver. 33. Nu +1:49.
Sacrifices of the Lord...
made by fire. ver. 33.

16 **from Aroer**. ver. +9.

17 **Heshbon**. Nu +21:25.
Dibon. Nu +21:30.
Bamoth-baal. *or*, the high places of Baal, and the house of Baal-meon. **S#1120h**. Nu 21:19, 20. 22:41. 32:37, 38.
Beth-baal-meon. i.e. *house of habitation of Baal*, **S#1010h**.

18 **Jahaza**. i.e. *trodden down*, **S#3096h**. Jsh 21:36. Nu +21:23, Jahaz. 1 Ch 6:78, 79, Jahzah. Je 48:21.
Kedemoth. i.e. *beginnings*, **S#6932h**. Jsh 21:37. Dt 2:26. 1 Ch 6:79.
Mephaath. i.e. *beauty; splendor*, **S#4158h**. Jsh 21:36, 37. 1 Ch 6:79. Je 48:21.

19 **And Kirjathaim**. Nu 32:37, 38.
Sibmah. Nu 32:38, Shibmah. Is 16:8, 9. Je 48:32.
Zareth-shahar. i.e. *the beauty of dawn, brightness of the dawn*, **S#6890h**.

20 **Beth-peor**. Nu 25:3. Dt 4:46.
Ashdoth-pisgah. *or*, springs of Pisgah, *or*, the hill. Jsh 12:3mg. Dt 3:17.
Beth-jeshimoth. Nu +33:49.

21 **And all**. "All" put for the greater part. Jsh 11:23. 13:12. Ex +9:6. Mt 3:5. 4:23.
the kingdom of Sihon. Dt 3:10.
whom Moses. Nu 21:24-35. Dt 2:30-36.
with the. Nu 31:8.

22 **Balaam**. Nu 22:5-7. 24:1. +31:8.
soothsayer. *or*, diviner. Je +27:9.

23 **and the border thereof**. i.e. those cities or places which bordered upon Jordan. ver. 28.

24 **Gad**. Nu +1:14. 32:34-36.

25 **their coast**. Nu 32:35.
Jazer. Nu +32:1.
and all the cities of Gilead. ver. 31. Jsh 11:23. 13:12. Ex +9:6.
half. Nu 21:26-30. Dt 2:19. Jg 11:13-27.
Rabbah. i.e. *contentious; populous*, **S#7237h**. Jsh 15:60. Dt +3:11, Rabbath. 2 S 11:1. 12:26, 27, 29. 17:27. 1 Ch 20:1. Je 49:2, 3. Ezk 21:20, Rabbath. 25:5. Am 1:14.

26 **Ramath-mizpeh**. i.e. *the watchtower height*, **S#7434h**, only here. Jsh +15:38. 20:8, Ramath-Gilead. Ge +31:49. 1 K 22:3.
Betonim. i.e. *nuts*, **S#993h**.

Mahanaim. Ge +32:2.
Debir. Jsh 10:38, 39. 2 S 9:5. 17:27, 30, Lodebar.

27 **Beth-aram**. i.e. *mountain house*, **S#1027h**, only here. Nu 32:34, 36, Beth-haran.
Beth-nimrah. i.e. *house of the leopardess*, **S#1039h**. Nu 32:3, 36. Is 15:6.
Succoth. Ge 33:17. Jg 8:5, 6, 14-16. 1 K 7:46.
Zaphon. i.e. *north*, **S#6829h**.
Chinnereth. Jsh 11:2. 12:3, Chimneroth. Nu 34:11. Dt 3:17. Lk 5:1, Gennesaret.

30 **their coast**. ver. 26. Nu 32:39-41. Dt 3:13-15. 1 Ch 2:21-23.
Jair. Nu +32:41.
Bashan. Dt +32:14.

31 **Ashtaroth**. Dt +1:4.
Og. Jsh 12:4.
the children of Machir by. Ge +50:23.

33 **gave not**. ver. +14. Nu 18:20.
God. ver. 14. Dt 10:9. 18:2.
their inheritance. Dt 32:9. Ps 16:5. 33:12. 47:4.
as he said. Jsh 18:7. Dt 10:9. 18:1, 2.

JOSHUA 14

1 **which Eleazar**. Ex +6:23. Mt 25:34. 1 P 1:4.

2 **lot**. Jsh 7:14. 13:6. 15:1. +17:14. 18:6, 8, 10. Ge 24:44. Le 16:8. Nu 26:2, 55, 56. 33:54. 34:13. 36:3. Jg 20:9. 1 S 10:20. 14:41. 1 Ch 24:5, 31. 25:8. Ne 10:34. 11:1. Est 3:7. 9:24. Ps 16:5, 6. 22:18. Pr 16:33. 18:18. Ezk 45:1. 47:22. 48:29. Jon 1:7. Mt 27:35. Mk 15:24. Lk 23:34. Jn 19:24. Ac 1:26. 13:19.

3 **Moses**. Jsh 13:8. Nu 32:29-42. Dt 3:12-17.
but unto. Jsh 13:14, 32, 33.

4 **the children**. Ge 48:5, 22. 1 Ch +5:1, 2.
save cities. Jsh 21:2-42. Nu 35:2-8. 1 Ch 6:54-81.

6 **Judah**. Jsh 15:17. Nu 13:6. 32:12. The fourth son of Jacob, but now reckoned the "firstborn," as in 1 Ch +5:2.
Gilgal. Jsh +4:19.
Caleb. Nu +13:6.
Kenezite. ver. 14. Jsh 15:17. Nu 32:12.
Thou knowest. Nu 14:24, 30. Dt 1:36-38.
the man. Nu 12:7, 8. Dt +33:1. 34:5, 10.
concerning me. Nu 14:24.
Kadesh-barnea. Nu +34:4.

7 **sent me**. Nu 13:6, 16-20.
I brought. Nu 13:26-33. 14:6-10. Ps 112:7, 8. Pr 16:23.

8 **made the heart**. Ex +15:15. Nu 13:31.
wholly followed. ver. 14. Nu +14:24. 32:11, 12. Dt 1:36. 2 K 23:3, 25. 1 Ch +22:16. 2 Ch 15:15. 17:3-6. Ps 37:18. 119:69. Pr 20:6. 25:13. 28:20. Mt 7:21. Lk 6:46. 18:28-30. Jn 8:31. Ac 11:23. 13:43. 14:22. Ro 10:9, 10. 12:1, 2, 11. 1 C 7:35. 12:3. 15:58. Ph 3:7, 8,

13, 14. Col +1:23. 1 Th 5:23. 1 T +4:15. 2 T
4:7. He 3:14. 5:9. 6:12. 10:39. +11:6. 2 P 1:3-
10. Re 14:4.

9 **Surely**. Jsh 1:3. Nu 13:22. 14:22-24.
   for ever. Heb. *olam*, Ex +12:24.
   because. ver. +8, 14. Nu 14:24. Dt 1:34, 36.
   Pr 12:14. Je 51:56. Ga 6:7. He 10:35.
10 **hath kept**. Jsh 23:14. 1 Th 5:24.
   forty. Jsh 11:18. Nu 14:33, 34.
   wandered. Heb. walked. Nu 14:33. Dt 1:3.
   2:1. Ps 95:10, 11.
11 **As yet**. Dt 31:2. 34:7. Ps 90:10. 102:27, 28.
   103:5. Mt 28:20.
   go out. Nu 27:16, 17.
12 **this mountain**. Jsh 20:7. Nu 13:22, 28, 30.
   14:8.
   the Anakims. Jsh +11:21.
   if so be. Nu 14:8, 9. 21:34. 1 S 14:6. 2 Ch
   14:11. Ps 18:32-34. 27:1-3. 44:3. 60:12.
   118:10-12. Ro 8:31. 1 C 15:57. Ph 4:13. He
   11:33.
   I shall. Jsh 15:14. Jg 1:20.
   drive them out. Jsh 17:12.
13 **blessed**. Jsh 22:6. Ge 47:7, 10. 1 S 1:17. SS
   6:9.
   gave unto. Jsh 10:36, 37. 15:13, 14. 21:11,
   12. Jg 1:20. 1 Ch 6:55, 56.
14 **Hebron**. Nu +13:22.
   unto this day. Jsh +4:9.
   because. ver. +8, 9. 1 C 15:58.
15 **And the name**. Jsh +21:11.
   And the land. Jsh 11:23. Jg 3:11, 30. 5:31.
   8:28.

JOSHUA 15

1 A.M. 2561. B.C. 1443. An. Ex. Is. 48.
   This then was the lot. Jsh +14:2.
   children of Judah. Jsh 14:6. 18:5.
   even to the. Nu 33:36, 37. 34:3-5. Ezk
   47:19.
   wilderness of Zin. Dt 32:51.
2 **south border**. Nu 34:3. Ezk 47:19.
   the salt sea. Ge +14:3. Ezk 47:8, 18.
   bay. Heb. tongue. ver. 5. Jsh 7:21mg, 24mg.
   10:21. 18:19mg. Is 11:15.
3 **Maaleh-acrabbim**. i.e. *ascent of scorpions. or,*
   the going up to Acrabim. **S#4610h**. Nu 34:4. Jg
   1:36.
   Zin. Ge 14:7. Nu +13:21. 20:1. 32:8.
   Kadesh-barnea. Nu +34:4. Jg 11:16, 17.
   Hezron. Ge +46:9. Nu 34:4.
   Adar. i.e. *exceeding glorious*. **S#146h**. 1 Ch 8:3.
   Nu 34:4, Hazar-addar.
   Karkaa. i.e. *floor, bottom*, **S#7173h**.
4 **Azmon**. Nu +34:4, 5.
   river. ver. 47. Ps +72:8.
5 **the east border**. Nu 34:10, 12. Ezk 47:18.
6 **Beth-hogla**. i.e. *house of a partridge*, **S#1031h**.
   Jsh 18:19, 21.

Beth-arabah. ver. 61. Jsh 18:18, 22.
   the stone. Jsh 18:17.
   Bohan. i.e. *thumb*. **S#932h**. Jsh 18:17.
   the son of. Dt 11:6. 1 Ch 5:3.
7 **Debir**. ver. 15. Jsh +10:3.
   the valley. Jsh 7:26. Is 65:10. Ho 2:15.
   Gilgal. Jsh +4:19. 18:17, Geliloth.
   Adummim. i.e. *ruddy; quieted ones*. **S#131h**.
   Jsh 18:17.
   En-shemesh. i.e. *fountain of the sun*, **S#5885h**.
   Jsh 18:17.
   En-rogel. i.e. *fountain of the spy*, **S#5883h**. Jsh
   18:16. 2 S 17:17. 1 K 1:9. 2 K 18:17. Jn 9:7,
   11, Siloam.
8 **valley of the son of Hinnom**. i.e. *to make
   drowsy; behold them; full of goodness*, **S#2011h**. Jsh
   18:16. 2 K 23:10. 2 Ch 28:3. 33:6. Ne 11:30.
   Je 7:31, 32. 19:2, 6, 11, 14. 31:40. 32:35.
   the Jebusite. ver. 63. Ge +10:16.
   the same is Jerusalem. Jsh 18:28. Dt 33:12.
   Jg 1:21. 1 S 27:6.
   valley of the giants. Dt +2:20.
9 **drawn**. or, marked out. ver. 11. Jsh 18:14,
   17. Is 44:13.
   fountain. Heb. *mayan*, **S#4599h**, Ge +7:11.
   Nephtoah. i.e. *waters of the opening*. **S#5318h**.
   Jsh 18:15.
   Ephron. Ge +23:8.
   Baalah. i.e. *mistress*. **S#1173h**. ver. 10, 11, 29. 2
   S 6:2. 1 Ch 13:6.
   Kirjath-jearim. ver. 60. Jsh +9:17.
10 **mount Seir**. Ge +14:6.
   Jearim. i.e. *forests*. **S#3297h**.
   Chesalon. i.e. *confidence, hope*, **S#3693h**.
   Beth-shemesh. 1 S 6:12-21. There were sev-
   eral cities of this name; this in Judah here,
   and Jsh 21:13, 16; 2 K 14:11, another in
   Issachar, and a third in Naphtali, Jsh 19:22,
   38 (Matthew Poole). Je +43:13.
   Timnah. ver. +57. Ge 38:12, 13. Jg 14:1, 5.
11 **Ekron**. ver. 45. Jsh +13:3.
   Shicron. i.e. *merriment; drunkenness*,
   S#7942h.
   mount Baalah. ver. 9. Jsh 19:44.
   Jabneel. i.e. *built of God*. **S#2995h**. Jsh 19:33.
12 **west border**. Nu 34:6. Ezk 47:20.
   the great sea. ver. 47. Nu +34:6. Dt 11:24.
13 **Caleb**. Nu +13:6.
   Arba. i.e. *four*, **S#704h**. Jsh 21:11. *or*, Kirjath-
   arba. ver. +54. Jsh 21:13.
   Hebron. Nu +13:22.
14 **thence**. Jsh 14:12.
   the three sons. Jsh 10:36, 37. 11:21. Nu
   13:22, 33. Jg 1:10, 20.
15 **went up**. Jsh 10:3, 38. Jg 1:11-13.
   Kirjath-sepher. i.e. *city of books*, compare ver.
   49. **S#7158h**. ver. 16. Jg 1:11, 12. 2 T 4:13.
16 **He that**. Jg 1:6, 12, 13.
   will I give. 1 S 17:25.
   Achsah. i.e. *tinkling ornament*, **S#5915h**. ver.

17. Jg 1:12, 13. 1 Ch 2:49.

my daughter. 1 Ch 2:48, 49.

17 **Othniel**. i.e. *lion of God; force of God*, **S#6274h**. Jg 1:13. 3:9, 11. 1 Ch 4:13. 27:15.

Kenaz. Ge +36:11.

Achsah. 1 Ch 2:49.

18 **she came**. Jg 1:14. Mt 1:18.

to ask. Ex 22:17. Jg 1:14, 15.

she lighted. Ge 24:64. 1 S 25:23.

19 **Give me**. Jg 1:14, 15. Mt 7:7, 8. 1 C 12:31.

a blessing. Ge 33:11. Dt 33:7. 1 S 25:27. Jn 4:10, 14. 2 C 9:5mg. Re 7:17. *or,* "*pool,*" as in 2 S 2:13.

springs of waters. Jn 3:23.

nether springs. Jg 1:15.

20 **the inheritance**. Ge 49:8-12. Dt 33:7.

21 **southward**. Dt 1:7. Jg 1:9.

Kabzeel. i.e. *gathering of God*, **S#6909h**. 2 S 23:20. Ne 11:25. 1 Ch 11:22.

Eder. Ge 35:21.

Jagur. i.e. *a lodging*, **S#3017h**, only here.

22 **Kinah**. i.e. *lamentation*, **S#7016h**.

Dimonah. i.e. *the quieter: silence; sufficient numbering*. **S#1776h**. i.e. Dibon, Ne 11:25.

Adadah. i.e. *a great company*. **S#5735h**.

23 **Kedesh**. i.e. *a sanctuary*, **S#6943h**. Jsh 12:22. 19:37. 20:7. 21:32. Nu 33:37. Dt 1:19. Jg 4:6, 9, 10, 11. 2 K 15:29. 1 Ch 6:72, 76.

Hazor. i.e. *enclosed; castle*. **S#2674h**. ver. 25. Jsh 11:1, 10, 11, 13. 12:19. 19:36. Jg 4:2, 17. 1 S 12:9. 1 K 9:15. 2 K 15:29. Ne 11:33. Je 49:28, 30, 33.

Ithnan. i.e. *a gift*, **S#3497h**.

24 **Ziph**. i.e. *a flowing*, **S#2128h**. ver. 55. 1 S 23:14, 15, 24. 26:2. 1 Ch 2:42. 4:16. 2 Ch 11:8. Ps 54, title.

Telem. Ezr +10:24.

Bealoth. i.e. *mistresses*, **S#1175h**. 1 K 4:10.

25 **Hazor**. Or rather, Hazar-hadattah. i.e. *enclosure of rejoicing: new enclosure, trumpeting of joy, trumpeting anew*.

Kerioth. i.e. *cities*, **S#7152h**. Je 48:24, 41. Am 2:2. Or, rather, Kerioth-Hezron, "the cities of Hezron." Kerioth is supposed to be the birth place of Judas Iscariot, i.e. *the man of Kerioth* (Young).

26 **Amam**. *their mother; metropolis*. **S#538h**.

Shema. i.e. *rumor*. **S#8090h**. Compare **S#8087h**, 1 Ch +2:43, also rendered Shema.

Moladah. i.e. *birth; birthplace; lineage*, as in Jsh 19:2. **S#4137h**. Jsh 19:2. 1 Ch 4:28. Ne 11:26.

27 **Hazar-gaddah**. i.e. *village of the troop or fortune*, **S#2693h**.

Heshmon. i.e. *little fertile place*, **S#2829h**.

Beth-palet. i.e. *house of escape*, **S#1046h**. Ne 11:26.

28 **Hazar-shual**. i.e. *village of a fox*, **S#2705h**. Jsh 19:3. 1 Ch 4:28. Ne 11:27.

Beer-sheba. Ge +21:31.

Bizjoth-jah. i.e. *contempt of Jah*, **S#964h**. not mentioned elsewhere.

29 **Baalah**. Jsh 19:3. 1 Ch 4:29. ver. 9-11. Jsh 19:3.

Iim. Nu 33:45.

Azem. i.e. *strength*, **S#6107h**. Jsh 19:3. 1 Ch 4:29.

30 **Eltolad**. i.e. *the generation*, in 1 Ch 4:29, Tolad. **S#513h**. Jsh 19:4.

Chesil. i.e. *confidence*, **S#3686h**, only here; LXX., Baithel, see Jsh 19:4; 1 Ch 4:30.

Hormah. Nu +14:45.

31 **Ziklag**. i.e. *outpouring of a spring; winding; enveloped in grief*, **S#6860h**. Jsh 19:5. 1 S 27:6. 30:1, 14, 26. 2 S 1:1. 4:10. 1 Ch 4:30. 12:1, 20. Ne 11:28.

Madmannah. i.e. *dung hill*, **S#4089h**. 1 Ch 2:48, 49. Is 10:31, Madmenah. Compare the similar meaning of Dimnah, Jsh 21:35.

Sansannah. i.e. *bushes* or *boughs*. **S#5578h**.

32 **Lebaoth**. i.e. *lionesses*, **S#3822h**, perhaps the same as Beth-lebaoth in Jsh 19:6.

Shilhim. i.e. *presents*, **S#7978h**, only here.

Ain. Nu 34:11.

Rimmon. i.e. *pomegranate*, **S#7417h**. Jg 20:45, 47. 21:13. Ne 11:29, Enrimmon. 1 Ch 4:32. 6:77. Zc 14:10.

33 **Eshtaol**. i.e. *request*, **S#847h**. Jsh 19:41. Nu 13:23. Jg 13:25. 16:31. 18:2, 8, 11.

Zoreah. i.e. *hornet*, **S#6881h**. Jsh +19:41, Zorah. Ne 11:29, Zareah.

Ashnah. i.e. *fortification; strong, mighty*, **S#823h**, only here. ver. 43.

34 **Zanoah**. i.e. *marsh; a rejected place*, **S#2182h**, only here. ver. 56. 1 Ch 4:18. Ne 3:13. 11:30.

En-gannim. Jsh 19:21.

Tappuah. ver. 53. Jsh 12:17. 16:8. 17:8.

Enam. i.e. *fountains; double fountain*, **S#5879h**.

35 **Jarmuth**. Jsh +21:29.

Adullam. Jsh +12:15.

Socoh. i.e. *bough*, **S#7755h**. ver. 48. 1 S 17:1. 1 K 4:10. 1 Ch 4:18. 2 Ch 11:7. 28:18.

Azekah. Jsh +10:10. 1 S 17:1.

36 **Sharaim**. i.e. *two gates*, **S#8189h**. 1 S 17:52. 1 Ch 4:31, Shaaraim.

Adithaim. i.e. *two ornaments; double prey*, **S#5723h**.

Gederah. i.e. *the fence*, **S#1449h**. Jsh 12:13. Perhaps the same as the next mentioned place.

and. *or*, or.

Gederothaim. i.e. *two fences; two sheepfolds*, **S#1453h**.

fourteen cities. There are fifteen in all; but the two last seem to be only two names of the same city.

37 **Zenan**. i.e. *a thorn*, **S#6799h**, perhaps the same as Zaanan, in Mi 1:11.

Hadashah. i.e. *the new one; new city*, **S#2322h**, only here.

Migdal-gad. i.e. *tower of Gad*, **S#4028h**, only here.

38 **Dilean**. i.e. *brought low in affliction; large gourd*, **S#1810h**.

Mizpeh. i.e. *the watchtower*, **S#4708h**. Jsh 11:3. 18:26. Ge +31:49, Mizpah. Jg 10:17. 11:11, 29, 34. 20:1. 21:1, 5. 1 S 7:5, 6, 16. 10:17. 22:3.

Joktheel. i.e. *subdued of God; obedient to God; subdued*, **S#3371h**. 2 K 14:7.

39 **Lachish**. Jsh +10:3.
Bozkath. i.e. *a swelling*, **S#1218h**. 2 K 22:1.
Eglon. Jg +3:12.

40 **Cabbon**. i.e. *to heap up; cake*, **S#3522h**.
Lahmam. i.e. *bread*, **S#3903h**.
Kithlish. i.e. *wall of a man*, **S#3798h**.

41 **Gederoth**. i.e. *fences*, **S#1450h**. 2 Ch 28:18.
Beth-dagon. i.e. *house of Dagon*, **S#1016h**. Jsh 19:37. 1 S 5:2.
Naamah. Ge 4:22.
Makkedah. Jsh +10:10.

42 **Libnah**. Nu +33:20.
Ether. Jsh 19:7.
Ashan. i.e. *smoke; anger*, **S#6228h**. Jsh 19:7. 1 Ch 4:32. 6:59.

43 **Jiphtah**. i.e. *he opens*, **S#3316h**, only here.
Ashnah. ver. 33.
Nezib. i.e. *a pillar; a garrison*, **S#5334h**.

44 **Keilah**. i.e. *a fortress; voice of God*, **S#7084h**. 1 S 23:1-8, 10-13. 1 Ch 4:19. Ne 3:17, 18.
Achzib. i.e. *a lie*, **S#392h**. Jsh 19:29. Ge 38:5, Chezib. Jg 1:31. Mi 1:14.
Mareshah. i.e. *the chief place; summit*, **S#4762h**. 1 Ch 2:42. 4:21. 2 Ch 11:8. 14:9, 10. 20:37. Mi 1:15.

45 **Ekron**. Jsh +13:3.
villages. Nu +21:25.

46 **near**. Heb. by the place of.
Ashdod. Jsh +11:22. Ac 8:40, Azotus.

47 **villages**. Nu +21:25.
Gaza. Ge +10:19.
the river. ver. +4.
great sea. ver. +12.

48 **Shamir**. i.e. *a brier, diamond*, **S#8069h**. LXX. Sophir.
Jattir. i.e. *excellent, abundant*, **S#3492h**. Jsh 21:14. 1 S 30:27. 1 Ch 6:57.
Socoh. i.e. *hedge, fence*. Different from that in ver. 35.

49 **Dannah**. i.e. *a low place*, or *judgment*, **S#1837h**, only here.
Kirjath-sannah. i.e. *city of the bush*, or *study*, which agrees with its other name, ver. 15. **S#7158h**. ver. 15, 16. Jg 1:11, 12. 1 T 4:13. 2 T 2:15. 4:13.
Debir. Jsh +10:3. 11:21.

50 **Anab**. Jsh +11:21.
Eshtemoh. i.e. *obedience*, **S#851h**. Jsh 21:14. 1 S 30:28. 1 Ch 4:17, 19. 6:57, Eshtemoa.
Anim. i.e. *fountains*, **S#6044h**, only here.

51 **Goshen**. Jsh +10:41.
Holon. i.e. *sandy*, **S#2473h**. Jsh 21:15. Je 48:21. Perhaps the same as Hilen in 1 Ch 6:58.
Giloh. i.e. *exile*, **S#1542h**. 2 S 15:12.

52 **Arab**. i.e. *ambush*, **S#694h**, only here.
Dumah. Ge +25:14. Is 21:11.
Eshean. i.e. *a prop, support*, **S#824h**, only here.

53 **Janum**. i.e. *sleep*, **S#3241h**. *or*, Janus. i.e. *slight*. only here.
Beth-taphuah. i.e. *house of the apple*, **S#1054h**.
Aphekah. i.e. *restraint*, **S#664h**, only here. For places with the same name see Jsh 12:18. 13:4.

54 **Humtah**. i.e. *place of lizards*, **S#2547h**, only here.
Kirjath-arba. i.e. *city of four*, **S#7153h**. ver. 13. Jsh 14:15. 20:7. 21:11. Ge 23:2. 35:27. Jg 1:10. Ne 11:25.
Zior. i.e. *a little one*, **S#6730h**.

55 **Maon**. i.e. *habitation*, **S#4584h**. Jg 10:12. 1 S 23:24, 25. 25:2, 7. 1 Ch 2:45. 2 Ch 26:10. Is 35:2.
Carmel. i.e. *fruitful place; fruitful field*, **S#3760h**. Jsh 12:22. +19:26.
Ziph. ver. +24.
Juttah. i.e. *stretched out*, **S#3194h**. Jsh 21:16.

56 **Jezreel**. 1 Ch +4:3.
Jokdeam. i.e. *burning of the people: let the people kindle*, **S#3347h**.
Zanoah. Different from that in ver. 34.

57 **Cain**. Ge +4:1.
Gibeah. Jg +19:12.
Timnah. ver. +10. 2 Ch 28:18.

58 **Halhul**. i.e. *very sandy* or *very painful; travail-pain*, **S#2478h**.
Beth-zur. i.e. *house of a rock*, **S#1049h**. 1 Ch 2:45. 2 Ch 11:7. Ne 3:16.
Gedor. i.e. *hedge, fence*, **S#1446h**. Jsh 12:13. 1 Ch 4:39. 12:7.

59 **Maarath**. i.e. *a cave* or *naked place; treeless place*, **S#4638h**.
Beth-anoth. i.e. *house of answers*, **S#1042h**, a reference to echoes. Compare Jsh 19:38, Beth-anath.
Eltekon. i.e. *the straight* or *right place*, **S#515h**. Compare Elteken, Jsh 19:44.

60 **Kirjath-baal**. i.e. *city of Baal*, **S#7154h**. ver. 9. Jsh 18:14. 1 S 7:1, 2.
Kirjath-jearim. Jsh +9:17.
Rabbah. Jsh +13:25.

61 **wilderness**. or pasture land of Judea.
Beth-arabah. i.e. *house of the desert*, **S#1026h**. ver. 6. Jsh 18:18, 22.
Middin. i.e. *measures; judging*, **S#4081h**.
Secacah. i.e. *enclosure*, **S#5527h**.

62 **Nibshan**. i.e. *soft or sandy soil; level soft soil*, **S#5044h**.
the city of Salt. Ge 19:22.
En-gedi. i.e. *fountain of the kid*, **S#5872h**. Ge 14:7. 1 S 23:29. 24:1. 2 Ch 20:2. SS 1:14. Ezk 47:10.

63 the Jebusites. Ge +10:16. Ro 7:14-21.
 could not drive them out. Jsh 7:12. 13:13.
 16:10. 17:12, 13. Ex 23:29-33. Le 26:37. Dt
 28:32. Jg 1:19, 21, 28, 29. 2:14. 16:17. 1 S
 17:24. 1 K 9:16, 21. Je 51:30. Mt 13:58. Mk
 6:5, 6. 9:18. Jn 15:5. Ro 6:12-14.
 dwell with. Jg 1:21.
 unto this day. Jsh +4:9.

JOSHUA 16

1 fell. Heb. went forth.
 the water. Jsh 8:15. 15:61. 18:12. 2 K 2:19-
 21.
 the wilderness. Jsh 18:12.
2 Bethel. Ge +12:8.
 Archi. i.e. *lengthy*, S#757h. 2 S 15:32. 16:16.
 17:5, 14. 1 Ch 27:33.
3 Japhleti. i.e. *it frees; delivered*, S#3311h. 1 Ch
 7:32, 33.
 Beth-horon. Jsh +10:10, 11.
 Gezer. 1 K +9:16.
 the sea. Jsh 17:9. Nu 34:6.
4 the children of Joseph. Nu +1:10.
 Manasseh. Jsh 14:4.
 Ephraim. Nu +1:33.
5 Ataroth-addar. ver. 2. Jsh 18:13.
6 Michmethah. i.e. *hiding place*, S#4366h. Jsh
 17:7.
 Taanath-shiloh. i.e. *meeting of Shiloh*, S#8387h.
 Jsh 18:1.
 Janohah. i.e. *rest*, S#3239h. ver. 7.
7 Ataroth. ver. 5. 1 Ch 7:28.
 Naarath. i.e. *damsel; maiden place*, S#5292h. 1
 Ch 4:5, 6, Naarah. 7:28, Naaran.
 Jericho. Nu +22:1.
8 Tappuah. Jsh 12:17. 15:34. 17:8.
 river Kanah. i.e. *reed*, S#7071h. Jsh 17:9.
 19:28.
 the sea. ver. 3-6. Nu 34:6.
9 separate cities. Jsh 17:9.
10 they drave not. Jsh +15:63. Dt 7:2. Jg 1:29.
 the Canaanites dwell. Ge +10:18. Nu
 33:52-55.
 Ephraimites. S#669h. Jg 12:4, 5, 5, 6.
 unto this day. Jsh +4:9.
 under tribute. or, task work. Ge 9:26. 49:15.
 Dt 20:11. Jsh 17:13. Jg 1:28, 30, 33, 35. 1 K
 9:16.

JOSHUA 17

1 the firstborn. Ge +41:51. 46:20. 48:18. Dt
 21:17. Col +1:15.
 Machir. Ge +50:23.
 Gilead. Ge +37:25.
 man of war. or, of battle. Ex 15:3. Nu 31:21,
 28, 49.
 Bashan. Jsh 12:4. Nu +21:33. Ps 22:12.
2 the rest. Nu 26:29-32.

the children. Jg 6:11. 8:2. 1 Ch 7:18.
 Abiezer. i.e. *father of help*, S#44h. Nu 26:30,
 Jeezer. Jg 6:34. 8:2. 2 S 23:27. 1 Ch 7:18.
 11:28. 27:12.
 Helek. Nu +26:30.
 children of Asriel. Nu +26:31. 1 Ch 7:14,
 Ashriel.
 Shechem. Ge +33:18.
 children of Hepher. Nu +26:32. 27:1.
 Shemida. Nu +26:32. 1 Ch 7:19.
3 Zelophehad. Nu +26:33. 27:1. 36:2-11.
 Mahlah. Nu +26:33.
 Noah. Nu +26:33.
 Hoglah. Nu +26:33.
 Milcah. Ge +11:29.
 Tirzah. Nu +26:33.
4 Eleazar. Ex +6:23.
 the Lord commanded Moses. Nu 27:6, 7.
 Ga 3:28.
5 ten portions. ver. 2, 3, 14.
 beside. Jsh 13:29-31. Nu 32:30-42.
6 the daughters. Nu 27:8.
 sons. i.e. the Machirites and the Gileadites.
 Nu 26:29.
7 Asher. i.e. *happy*. A city not mentioned elsewhere.
 Michmethah. Jsh +16:6.
 Shechem. ver. 2. Ge +33:18.
 En-tappuah. i.e. *fountain of the apple*, S#5887h.
8 of Tappuah. Jsh 12:17. 15:34, 53. 16:8.
9 river Kanah. or, brook of reeds. Jsh 16:8.
 these cities. Jsh 16:9.
 the outgoings. Jsh 16:3, 8. 19:29.
 the sea. The Mediterranean. Jsh 15:47. Nu
 +34:6.
11 Manasseh. Jsh 16:9. 1 Ch 7:29.
 Beth-shean. i.e. *house of rest; house of quiet*,
 S#1052h. ver. 16. Jg 1:27. 1 S 31:10, 12, Beth-
 shan. 2 S 21:12. 1 K 4:12. 1 Ch 7:29. Mt 4:25.
 Mk 5:20. 7:31.
 and her towns. Heb. daughters. Nu +21:25.
 Ibleam. Jg +1:27. 2 K 9:27. 1 Ch 6:70,
 Bileam.
 Dor. Jsh +12:23. Jg 1:27. 1 K 4:11.
 Endor. i.e. *fountain of Dor* or *habitation*,
 S#5874h. 1 S 28:7. Ps 83:10.
 Taanach. i.e. *wandering through; she will afflict
 thee; humbling thee; sandy*, S#8590h. Jsh 12:21.
 21:25, Tanach. Jg 1:27. 5:19. 1 K 4:12. 1 Ch
 7:29.
 Megiddo. Jsh +12:21. 2 Ch 22:9mg.
12 could not drive out. Jsh 14:12. +15:63. Nu
 33:52-56.
 would dwell. Jg 1:27, 35.
13 waxen strong. Jg 1:28. 2 S 3:1. 2 Ch 26:15.
 Ep 6:10. Ph 4:13. 2 P 3:18.
 put the. Jsh 16:10. Dt 20:11-18. Jg 1:30, 33,
 35. 2 Ch 8:7, 8.
 utterly drive. Dt 20:17.
14 one lot. Jsh 16:4. Ge 48:22. Nu 26:34-37. Dt

3:4. 32:8, 9. 33:13-17. Ps 16:6. 19:4.
105:11mg. Am 7:17. Mi 2:5. 2 C 10:13, 16mg.
a great. Ge 48:19. 49:22-26.
the Lord hath. 1 S 7:12. Ps 115:12.
blessed. Ge 48:19. Nu 26:34, 37. Ep 1:3.

15 **If thou be**. Lk 12:48. 16:10.
the Perizzites. Jsh 3:10. 9:1. 11:3. 12:8. Ge
+13:7. Ex 33:2. Ezr 9:1.
giants. *or*, Rephaims. **S#7497h**. Ge +14:5. Dt
+2:20. 2 S 21:16, 18.
Ephraim. **S#669h**. Jsh 19:50. 20:7. 21:21.
24:30, 33. Jg 2:9. 3:27. 4:5. 7:24. 10:1. 17:1,
8. 18:2, 13. 19:1, 16, 18. 1 S 1:1. 9:4. 14:22. 2
S 20:21. 1 K 4:8. 12:25. 2 K 5:22. 1 Ch 6:67. 2
Ch 13:4. 15:8. 19:4. Je 4:15. 31:6. 50:19.

16 **chariots of iron**. ver. 18. Jg 1:19. 4:3.
Beth-shean. ver. 11.
towns. Nu +21:25.
valley of Jezreel. 1 Ch +4:3.

17 **Thou art a great**. ver. +14.
great power. Ph 4:13.

18 **the mountain shall be thine**. ver. 15. Jsh
15:9. 20:7. Mt 17:20.
for thou shalt. Jsh 11:4-6. 13:6. Nu 14:6-9.
Dt 20:1-4. Ps 27:1, 2. Is 41:10-16. 51:12, 13.
Ro 8:31, 37. 1 C 15:57. Ph 4:13. He 13:6.
iron chariots. ver. 16. Jg 1:19.
strong. Dt 20:1.

JOSHUA 18

1 **assembled**. Dt 12:5.
Shiloh. Jg +21:19.
tabernacle. Ex +38:21.

3 **How long are**. Jg 18:9. Pr 2:2-6. 10:4. 13:4.
15:19. Ec 9:10. Zp 3:16. Mt 20:6. Jn 6:27. Ph
3:13, 14. 2 P 1:10, 11.
slack. *or*, remiss. lit. show yourselves feeble.
Pr 12:27. 18:9. 24:10. He 6:12.

4 **three**. ver. 3. Jsh 3:12. 4:2. Nu 1:4. 13:2. Ec
4:12.
describe. ver. 6, 9.

5 **Judah shall**. Jsh 15:1, etc. 19:1-9.
the house. Jsh ch. 16, 17.
abide. Jn 15:4.

6 **that I may cast**. ver. 8, 10. Jsh +14:2.

7 **the Levites**. Jsh 13:14, 33. Nu 18:20, 23. Dt
10:9. 18:1, 2.
and Gad. Ge +30:11.

8 **Go**. Ge +13:17.
that I may here. ver. 6, 10. Jsh 7:16-18.
13:7. 14:1, +2. Ro 14:19.

9 **described**. Pr 23:10.
into seven. Ac 13:19.
in a book. *or*, on a book. Jsh 10:13. Dt 17:18.
31:24. 1 P 1:4.

10 **cast lots**. ver. +6.
before the Lord. Ps 47:4. 61:5. Jn 17:2. Ac
26:18. Col 1:12.

11 **of Benjamin**. Nu +1:37.

came up. Jsh 14:2. 19:1 (came forth), 17
(came out). Le 16:9mg.
came forth. Jsh 19:1 (came forth), 17 (came
out). Pr 16:33.
between the children. Jsh 15:1-8. 16:1-10.
Dt ch. 10. 13:12.

12 **Jericho**. Nu +22:1.
the wilderness. Jsh +7:2. 8:20.
Beth-haven. Jsh +7:2.

13 **side of Luz**. Ge +28:19.
Atroth-addar. i.e. *crowns of glory*, **S#5853h**. Jsh
16:2, 5. 1 Ch 2:54.
nether Beth-horon. Jsh +10:10.

14 **was drawn**. ver. 17. Jsh 15:9.
corner of the sea. or, west corner.
Kirjath-baal. Jsh +9:17. 15:9, 60. 2 S 6:2.

15 **well**. Heb. *mayan*, **S#4599h**, Ge +7:11.
Nephtoah. Jsh 15:9.

16 **valley of the son of Hinnom**. Jsh +15:8. Is
30:33.
the valley of the giants. Dt +2:20.
Jebusi. i.e. *threshing floor*, **S#2983h**. Mount
Zion, south of Jerusalem; for Jebusi or Jebus
was the ancient name of that city. ver. 28. Jsh
+15:63. Jg 1:8, 21. 19:10.
En-rogel. Jsh +15:7.

17 **En-shemesh**. Jsh 15:7.
Geliloth. i.e. *borders*, **S#1553h**. Jsh 15:7.
the stone. Jsh 15:6.

18 **Arabah**. *or*, the plain. **S#6160h**. Jsh 15:6, 61.
Dt +11:30mg.

19 **Bethhogla**. i.e. *house of a partridge*, **S#1031h**.
ver. 21. Jsh 15:6.
bay. Heb. tongue. Jsh +15:2mg. Is 11:15.
the salt sea. Ge +14:3.

20 **the inheritance**. ver. 11.

21 **Jericho**. ver. +12. Lk 10:30. 19:1.
Beth-hoglah. ver. +19.
Keziz. i.e. *cuttings off; extremity*, **S#7104h**.

22 **Beth-arabah**. ver. 18. Jsh 15:6.
Zemaraim. i.e. *two cuttings off; double woolens;
double fleece; cold; double mountain forest*,
S#6787h. Ge 10:18. 2 Ch 13:4.
Beth-el. Jsh 15:6. 1 K 12:29-32.

23 **Avim**. i.e. *perverse places; perverters; villagers*,
S#5761h. Jsh 13:3, Avites. Dt 2:23, Avims. 2 K
17:31, Avites.
Parah. i.e. *the cow*, **S#6511h**.
Ophrah. 1 S 13:17. Mi 1:10, Beth-ophrah.

24 **Chepher-haammoni**. i.e. *village of the
Ammonites*, **S#3726h**.
Ophni. i.e. *becoming moldy; flying; darkness;
folding together; weariness*, **S#6078h**.
Gaba. i.e. *hill, gently rising; elevation; hillock*,
S#1387h. Jg 19:12. 1 S +13:3, Geba. Ho 5:8.

25 **Gibeon**. Jsh +10:2.
Ramah. Je 31:15.
Beeroth. Jsh +9:17.

26 **Mizpeh**. Jsh +15:38.
Chephirah. Jsh +9:17.

Mozah. i.e. *an outlet; bubbling waters; a spring; fountain, the place from which one goes forth,* **S#4681h**.

27 **Rekem**. 1 Ch +2:43.
Irpeel. i.e. *God heals; God will restore; the health, medicine, or exalting of God,* **S#3416h**. Ps 103:3. Pr 4:22mg.
Taralah. i.e. *a reeling; trembling; release the curse; searching out of a slander; his increase,* **S#8634h**.

28 **Zelah**. i.e. *a rib; limping; one-sided,* **S#6762h**. 2 S 21:14.
Eleph. i.e. *the thousand or chief; learning,* **S#507h**.
Jebusi. ver. 16. Jsh +15:8, 63. 2 S 5:8.
Jerusalem. Jsh 15:63.
Gibeath. i.e. *a high place,* **S#1394h**. Jg +19:12, Gibeah. 1 Ch 12:3.
Kirjath. i.e. *a city,* **S#7157h**.
according. Nu 26:54. 33:54.

JOSHUA 19

1 **second lot**. Jsh 18:6-11.
within the. ver. 9. Ge 49:5-7. Jg 1:3.
2 **Beer-sheba**. Ge +21:31.
Sheba. 1 Ch 4:28.
and Moladah. Jsh +15:26.
3 **Hazar-shual**. Jsh 15:28; 29.
Balah. i.e. *decayed; worn out,* **S#1088h**, only here. Jsh 15:29, Baalah.
Azem. Jsh 15:29, i.e. Ezem.
4 **Eltolad**. Jsh 15:30. 1 Ch 4:29.
Bethul. i.e. *separated,* **S#1329h**, only here. Jsh 15:30, Chesil. 1 Ch 4:29, 30, Bethuel.
Hormah. Nu +14:45.
5 **Ziklag**. Jsh +15:31.
Beth-marcaboth. 1 Ch +4:31.
Hazar-susah. i.e. *a house of horses,* **S#2701h**. 2 K 23:11. 1 Ch 4:31, Hazar-susim.
6 **Beth-lebaoth**. i.e. *house of lions,* **S#1034h**. Jsh 15:32.
Sharuhen. i.e. *a beginning of grace; gracious house,* **S#8287h**.
7 **Ain**. Jsh 15:32.
Remmon. i.e. *elevation; pomegranate,* **S#7417h**, so rendered only here. Jsh 15:32. Nu 33:19, 20. 1 Ch 4:32, Rimmon.
Ether. i.e. *abundance,* **S#6281h**. Jsh 15:42.
Ashan. Jsh +15:42.
8 **Baalath-beer**. i.e. *mistress of a well,* **S#1192h**. 1 Ch 4:33.
Ramath of the south. i.e. *the height; height of the south,* **S#7418h**, only here. 1 S 30:27, Ramoth.
9 **too much**. Ex 16:18. 2 C 8:14, 15.
therefore. ver. 1.
10 **third**. Jsh 18:6, 11.
Zebulun. Ge 49:13. Dt 33:18, 19.
Sarid. i.e. *a remnant; survivor,* **S#8301h**. ver. 12.

11 **toward the sea**. ver. 13, 14. Ge 49:13.
Maralah. i.e. *earthquake,* **S#4831h**.
Dabbasheth. i.e. *a hump of a camel; flowing with honey,* **S#1708h**.
the river. Jg 5:21.
Jokneam. Jsh +12:22. 1 K 4:12. 1 Ch 6:68, Jokmeam.

12 **Chisloth-tabor**. i.e. "*confidence of Tabor (i.e. choice, purity),*" **S#3696h**. ver. 22. Jg 4:6, 12. Ps 89:12.
Daberath. i.e. *led, submissive, obedient,* **S#1705h**. Jsh 21:28, Dabareh. 1 Ch 6:72.
Japhia. i.e. *beautiful.* Jsh 10:3.

13 **Gittah-hepher**. i.e. *wine press of the well,* **S#1662h**. 2 K 14:25, Gath-hepher.
Ittah Kazin. i.e. *time of the captain,* **S#6278h**.
-methoar. *or, which is drawn.* 1 Ch 6:77. i.e. *the marked out pomegranate,* **S#7417h**.
Neah. i.e. *moving, shaking,* **S#5269h**.

14 **Hannathon**. i.e. *gracious,* **S#2615h**.
Jiphthah-el. i.e. *God opens,* **S#3317h**. ver. 27.

15 **Kattath**. **S#7005h**, only here. i.e. *very small; littleness. Kitron, a bond,* as in Jg 1:30. Jsh 21:34, 35.
Nahallal. i.e. *pasture land,* **S#5096h**. Jsh 21:35. Jg 1:30, Nahalol.
Shimron. i.e. *a little watchtower.* Jsh 11:1. 12:20.
Idalah. i.e. *what God exalts,* **S#3030h**.
Beth-lehem. i.e. *house of bread,* **S#1035h**. Different from that in Judah (see Jsh 12:9). Ge 35:19. 48:7. Jg +17:7. Ru 1:19, 22. 2:4. 4:11. 1 S 16:4. 17:15. 20:6, 28. 2 S 2:32. 23:14-16, 24. 1 Ch 2:51. 11:16-18, 26. 2 Ch 11:6. Ezr 2:21. Ne 7:26. Mi 5:2. Mt 2:1, 6. Jn 7:42.

17 **Issachar**. Ge 49:14, 15.

18 **Jezreel**. 1 Ch +4:3.
Chesulloth. i.e. *foolish confidences,* **S#3694h**. ver. 12.
Shunem. i.e. *resting places,* **S#7766h**. 1 S 28:4. 1 K 1:3. 2:17, 21. 2 K 4:8, 12.

19 **Haphraim**. i.e. *two pits,* **S#2663h**.
Shihon. i.e. *wall of strength; a waste; a ruin,* **S#7866h**.
Anaharath. i.e. *groaning, roaring; the groaning of fear,* **S#588h**.

20 **Rabbith**. i.e. *multitude,* **S#7245h**.
Kishion. i.e. *sharpness* or *hardness,* **S#7191h**. Jsh 21:28.
Abez. i.e. *tin,* **S#77h**.

21 **Remeth**. i.e. *a high place,* **S#7432h**, only here. Jsh +21:29.
En-gannim. i.e. *fountain of gardens,* **S#5873h**. Jsh 15:34. 21:29. Different from that in Jsh 15:34.
En-haddah. i.e. *fountain of sharpness,* **S#5876h**.
Beth-pazzez. i.e. *house of dispersion,* **S#1048h**.

22 **Tabor**. ver. 12. Jg +4:6.
Shahazimah. i.e. *to strut proudly,* **S#7831h**.
Beth-shemesh. ver. 38. Je +43:13.

239

24 Asher. Ge +30:13. Nu +1:13. Lk 2:36-38.

25 Helkath. i.e. *a portion, field*, **S#2520h**. Jsh 21:31. 2 S 2:16.

Hali. i.e. *ornament*, **S#2482h**.

Beten. i.e. *belly or womb; valley*, **S#991h**.

Achsaph. i.e. *enchantment; sorcery*. Jsh 11:1. 12:20.

26 Alammelech. i.e. *the king's oak*, **S#487h**.

Amad. i.e. *people of old; eternal people*, **S#6008h**.

Misheal. i.e. *a request*, **S#4861h**. Jsh 21:30. 1 Ch 6:74, Mashal.

Carmel. Different from that in Jsh +15:55. 1 S 15:12. 25:2, 5, 7, 40. 1 K 18:19, 20, 42. 2 K 2:25. 4:25. SS 7:5. Is 33:9. 35:2. 37:24. Je 46:18. 50:19. Am 1:2. 9:3. Mi 7:14. Na 1:4.

Shihor-libnath. i.e. *blackness of whiteness*, **S#7884h**.

27 Beth-dagon. Jsh 15:41. 1 S 5:2.

Zebulun. Ge +30:20.

valley of. ver. 14.

Beth-emek. i.e. *house of the valley*, **S#1025h**.

Neiel. i.e. *motion of God; we shall be shaken of God; the moving of God*, **S#5272h**.

Cabul. i.e. *sandy; a border*, **S#3521h**. 1 K 9:13.

28 Hebron. Jsh 15:54. 21:30. 1 Ch 6:74.

Rehob. ver. 30.

Hammon. i.e. *warm, sunny; hot spring*, **S#2540h**. 1 Ch 6:76.

Kanah. Jsh 16:8. Jn 2:1, 11. 4:46, Cana.

great Zidon. Ge +49:13.

29 Ramah. ver. 36.

strong city. or, fenced city. Nu 13:19. 2 S 24:7.

Tyre. Heb. Tzor. 1 K +7:13. Is ch. 23. Ezk ch. 26-28.

Hosah. 1 Ch +16:38.

Achzib. Jg 1:31. Different from Jsh +15:44; Mi 1:14. Ge 38:5.

30 Ummah. i.e. *association*, **S#5981h**.

Aphek. Jsh +12:18.

Rehob. ver. 28. Nu +13:21.

31 the inheritance. Ge 49:20. Dt 33:24, 25.

33 Heleph. i.e. *an exchange*, **S#2501h**.

Allon. 1 Ch +4:37.

Zaanannim. i.e. *wanderings*, **S#6815h**. Jg 4:11, Zaanaim.

Adami. i.e. *human*. Jsh 3:16.

Nekeb. i.e. *a cavern*, **S#5346h**.

Jabneel. Jsh 15:11.

Lakum. i.e. *fortified place*, **S#3946h**.

34 turneth. Dt 33:23.

Aznoth-tabor. i.e. *ears (summits) of Tabor*, **S#243h**. ver. 12, 22.

Hukkok. i.e. *things decreed; appointed portion*, **S#2712h**. Jsh 21:31, Helkath. 1 Ch 6:75.

south side. Dt 33:23.

Judah. Ge +35:23.

35 Ziddim. i.e. *the sides*, **S#6661h**.

Zer. i.e. *strait; flint*, **S#6863h**.

Hammath. i.e. *warm baths; warm springs*,

S#2575h. 1 Ch 2:55. For other places with the same name see Jsh 19:35. 21:32. Ge 10:18. Nu 13:21. 34:8. 1 K 8:65, Hamath.

Rakkath. i.e. *a shore or river bank; leanness; her spitting; empty; vain*, **S#7557h**.

Chinnereth. Jsh 11:2, Chinneroth. 12:3. 13:27. Nu 34:11. Dt 3:17. Ezk 47:18, the east sea. Mt 14:34, sea of Gennesaret. Mk 6:53. Lk 5:1. Jn 6:1, 23, sea of Tiberias. 21:1.

36 Adamah. i.e. *earth*, **S#128h**. ver. 33.

Ramah. ver. 29.

Hazor. Jsh +15:23.

37 Kedesh. Jsh +15:23.

Edrei. Nu 21:23.

En-hazor. i.e. *fountain of the village*, **S#5877h**.

38 Iron. i.e. *the little fearful one*, **S#3375h**.

Migdal-el. i.e. *tower of God*, **S#4027h**. Mt 15:39, Magdala.

Horem. i.e. *devoted; banned; separated; dedication*, **S#2765h**.

Beth-anath. i.e. *the house of answers, responses, replies, echoes*, **S#1043h**. Jsh 15:59. Jg 1:33, 33.

Beth-shemesh. ver. 22. Jsh 21:16. Jg 1:33.

40 Dan. Dt 33:22.

41 Zorah. i.e. *leprosy*, **S#6881h**. Jsh +15:33, Zoreah. Jg 13:2, 25. 16:31. 18:2, 8, 11. 1 Ch 2:53. 2 Ch 11:10.

Eshtaol. Jsh +15:33.

Ir-shemesh. i.e. *city of the sun*, **S#5905h**. Jsh 21:16. Lk 24:13.

42 Shaalabbin. i.e. *place of foxes*, **S#8169h**. Jg 1:35, Shaalbim. 1 K 4:9, Shaalbim.

Ajalon. Jsh +10:12.

Jethlah. i.e. *lofty place*, **S#3494h**.

43 Elon. Ge +26:34.

Thimnathah. i.e. *portion assigned, divided allotment; a portion there*, **S#8553h**. Ge 38:12. Jg 14:1, 2, Timnath. 2 Ch 28:18, Timnah.

Ekron. Jsh +13:3.

44 Eltekah. Jsh 15:59. 21:23.

Gibbethon. i.e. *a lofty place*, **S#1405h**. Jsh 21:23. 1 K 15:27. 16:15, 17.

Baalath. i.e. *mistress*, **S#1191h**. Jsh 15:29. 1 K 9:18. 2 Ch 8:6.

45 Jehud. i.e. *praised*, **S#3055h**.

Bene-berak. i.e. *sons of lightning*, **S#1139h**.

Gath-rimmon. Jsh +21:25. 1 Ch 6:69.

46 Me-jarkon. i.e. *waters of paleness; yellow water; water of great greenness*, **S#4313h**.

Rakkon. i.e. *thinness*, **S#7542h**.

before. or, over against.

Japho. or, Joppa. i.e. *beauty*, **S#3305h**. 2 Ch 2:16, Joppa. Ezr 3:7. Jon 1:3. Ac 9:36, 38, 43. 10:8.

47 the coast. Jg 1:34, 35. 18:1-29.

called Leshem. i.e. *unto desolation; precious stone; fortress*, **S#3959h**, only here. Jg 18:7, 27, 29, Laish (i.e. *a lion; strong; crushing*).

49 gave. Ezk 45:7, 8.

50 Timnath-serah. i.e. *outspread portion; fruitful*

portion, **s#8556h**. Jsh 24:30. Jg 2:9, Timnath-
heres. 1 Ch 7:24.

51　These are. Jsh 14:1. Nu 34:17-29. Ps 47:3, 4.
Mt 20:23. 25:34. Jn 14:2, 3. 17:2. He 4:8, 9.
in Shiloh. Ge 49:10. Jg +21:19.

JOSHUA 20

1　spake. Jsh 5:14. 6:2. 7:10. 13:1-7.
saying. Ex 21:13. Nu 35:6, 11, 14. Dt 19:2, 9.

2　Appoint. Ex 21:13, 14. Nu 35:6, 11-14. Dt
4:41-43. 19:2-13. Ro 8:1, 33, 34. He 6:18, 19.

3　person. Heb. *nephesh*, Jsh +10:28; Ge +12:5.
unawares *and*
unwittingly. Heb. through ignorance, or
error, or mistake, and without knowledge. Ex
21:14. Le 4:2, 13, 22, 27. 5:15, 18. Dt 4:42.
19:4, 5. 1 K 2:28-31, 34.
your refuge. Nu 35:15-24. Dt 19:5, 6. He
6:18.
avenger of blood. Nu 35:12, 19, 25. Dt 19:6,
12, 13. 2 S 14:11.

4　shall stand. Ex 33:21. Nu 35:12, 14.
at the entering. Ru 4:1, 2. Jb 5:4. 29:7. Pr
31:23. Je 38:7.
the gate. Ge +14:7. Dt 25:7.
shall declare. Is 1:18. 41:21. 56:5.
the elders. Jsh 23:2. 24:1. Ex +3:16. +18:21.
Dt 5:23. 31:28. Jg 21:16. Ru 4:2. 1 S 4:3. 8:4.
15:30. 30:26. 2 S 3:17. 5:3. 17:4, 15. 19:11. 1
K 8:1, 3. 20:7. 2 K 6:32. 23:1. 1 Ch 11:3.
15:25. 21:16. 2 Ch 5:2, 4. 34:29. Je 19:1.
26:17. 29:1. Ezk 8:1, 12. 14:1. 20:1, 3. Jl 1:14.
2:16. Lk 22:66. Ac 4:5. 15:6. 22:5. 23:14.
24:1. 25:15.
take. Jsh 2:18mg. 24:1. Ps 26:9.
a place. Zc 3:7.
that he may. Ep 2:13, 19. He 6:18.

5　if the avenger. Nu 35:12, 25.
shall not deliver. Jb 33:24, 28. Ps 46:1. 48:3.
57:1. Jn 10:28.

6　until. Nu 35:12, 24, 25, 28. 2 K 12:10. He
5:1. 7:27, 28. 8:3. 9:7, 25, 26. 13:11.
he stand. Ex 18:13. Is 50:8. Zc 3:1.
before the congregation. ver. 4. Nu 35:25.
until the death of the high priest. Nu
35:25. Ps 1:5. He 7:23-25.

7　appointed. Heb. sanctified. Nu 16:37, 38. Dt
19:3. Jg 17:3.
Kedesh. Jsh +15:23.
Galilee. i.e. *a circuit*, **s#1551h**. Jsh 21:32. 1 K
9:11. 2 K 15:29. 1 Ch 6:76. Is 9:1. Mt +2:22.
Shechem. Jsh 21:21. Ge 12:6, Sichem.
+33:18.
Kirjath-arba. Jsh +15:54. Jg 21:31.
which is Hebron. Nu +13:22.
mountain of Judah. Mt 5:14. Lk 1:39, 65.

8　the other side Jordan. Dt 19:9.
assigned. Dt 4:41.
Bezer. Dt +4:43.

Ramoth. 1 K +4:13.
Golan. Dt +4:43.

9　the cities. Nu 35:15.
and for the stranger. Jsh 8:33, 35. Le 20:2.
22:18. 24:16. 25:6. Nu 15:14, 30. 19:10.
35:15. Dt 1:16. 5:14. 16:11. +26:11. 29:11.
31:12. 2 Ch 30:25. Ep 2:19.
person. Heb. *nephesh*, Jsh +10:28.
until he stood. ver. +4, 6.

JOSHUA 21

1　the heads. Jsh 19:51. Ex 6:14, 25.
Eleazar. Jsh 14:1. 17:4. Nu 34:17-29.

2　Shiloh. Jg +21:19.
The Lord. Nu 35:2-8. Ezk 48:9-18. Mt 10:10.
Ga 6:6. 1 T 5:17, 18.

3　unto the Levites. Ge 49:7. Dt 33:8-10. 1 Ch
6:54-81.

4　Kohathites. Ex 6:18. Nu 3:17, 27.
the children. ver. 8-19. Jsh 24:33. Ex 6:20.
Nu 3:2-4, 19. 1 Ch 6:54-60.
the tribe. Nu 35:8.

5　the rest. ver. 20-26. Ge +46:11.

6　of Gershon. ver. 27-33. Ge +46:11. Nu
+3:21. 1 Ch 6:62, 71-76.

7　of Merari. ver. 34-40. Ge +46:11.

8　by lot. ver. 3. Jsh +14:2. 18:6. Ge +24:44. Nu
33:54. 35:3. Pr +16:33. 18:18.
as the Lord. Nu 35:2.

9　of Simeon. Jsh 19:1.
these cities. ver. 13-18. 1 Ch 6:65.
mentioned. Heb. called.

10　of Aaron. ver. +4. Ex 6:18, 20-26. Nu 3:2-4,
19, 27. 4:2.

11　And they. 1 Ch 6:55.
the city of Arba. *or*, Kirjath-arba. Jsh
+15:54.
Anak. Nu +13:33.
is Hebron. Nu +13:22.
in the hill. Jsh 20:7, etc. Lk 1:39.

12　fields of. Jsh 14:13-15. 1 Ch 6:55-57. Ne
12:44.
the city. Jsh 20:7.
his possession. Jsh 14:6, 13, +14. 15:13.

13　they gave. 1 Ch 6:56.
Hebron. ver. +11.
a city. Jsh 20:7. Nu 35:6.
Libnah. Nu +33:20.

14　Jattir. Jsh 15:48. 1 S 30:27, 28.
Eshtemoa. Jsh 15:50, Eshtemoh. 1 S 30:26,
28. 1 Ch 4:17, Eshtemoa. 6:57.

15　Holon. Jsh 15:51. 1 Ch 6:58, Hilen.
Debir. Jsh +10:3.

16　Ain. Nu +34:11.
Juttah. Jsh 15:55.
Beth-shemesh. Je +43:13.

17　Gibeon. Jsh +10:2.
Geba. 1 S +13:3. Ne 11:31. Is 10:29.

18　Anathoth. 2 S 23:27. 1 Ch +7:8.

Almon. i.e. *hidden*, **S#5960h**. 1 Ch 6:60, Alemeth.

19 **cities of**. 1 Ch 6:54, 60.
20 **the families**. ver. 5. 1 Ch 6:66.
21 **Shechem**. Ge +33:18.
   Gezer. 1 K +9:16.
22 **Kibzaim**. i.e. *two gatherings*, **S#6911h**. 1 Ch 6:68, Jokdeam.
   Beth-horon. Jsh +10:10.
23 **Dan**. ver. 5. Nu +1:12.
   Eltekeh. i.e. *God-fearing*, **S#514h**. Jsh 19:44, 45.
   Gibbethon. Jsh 19:44.
24 **Aijalon**. i.e. *a large stag*, **S#357h**. Jsh 10:12, Ajalon.
   Gathrimmon. Jsh 19:45.
25 **Tanach**. i.e. *afflicting thee*, **S#8590h**. Jsh +17:11.
   Gath-rimmon. i.e. *winepress of the pomegranate*, **S#1667h**. ver. 24. Jsh 19:45. 21:25. 1 Ch 6:69, 70, Bileam.
26 **children of Kohath**. ver. 5.
27 **And unto**. ver. 6.
   Golan. Dt +4:43.
   in Bashan. Nu +21:33.
   Beesh-terah. i.e. *house or temple of Ashtoreth*, **S#1203h**. Dt +1:4. 1 Ch 6:71.
28 **Kishon**. Jsh 19:20, Kishion. Jg +5:21. 1 Ch 6:72, Kedesh.
   Dabareh. i.e. *manner of speech*, **S#1705h**. Jsh 19:12, Daberath. 1 Ch 6:72, 73.
29 **Jarmuth**. i.e. *height; elevated, high; he will be lifted up; casting down death*, **S#3412h**. Jsh 10:3, 5, 23. 12:11. 15:35. 19:19, 21, Remeth. Ne 11:29. 1 Ch 6:73, Ramoth.
   En-gannim. Jsh 19:21. 1 Ch 6:73, Anem.
30 **Mishal**. i.e. *prayer, sentence, similitude; inquiry; request*, **S#4861h**. Jsh 19:26. Jsh 19:25-28, Misheal (i.e. *who is that which God is?*). 1 Ch 6:74, 75, Mashal (i.e. *a parable, a parabolist; intreaty*).
   Abdon. Jsh 19:28. Jg +12:13.
31 **Helkath**. Jsh 19:25, 34, Hukkok. 1 Ch 6:75, Hukok.
   Rehob. Nu +13:21.
32 **Kedesh**. Jsh +15:23.
   Hammoth-dor. i.e. *hot places of the dwelling*, **S#2576h**. Jsh 19:35, Hammath. Nu 13:21, Hamath. 1 Ch 6:76, Hammon.
   Kartan. i.e. *two cities; their hap; their meeting place*, **S#7178h**. 1 Ch 6:76, Kirjathaim. Different from Nu 32:37.
33 **Gershonites**. ver. 6. Nu +3:21.
34 **And unto**. ver. 7. 1 Ch 6:77.
   Jokneam. Jsh 12:22. 19:11, 15.
   Kartah. i.e. *city; meeting; her hap; her meeting place*, **S#7177h**. Jsh 19:15, Kattah.
35 **Dimnah**. i.e. *dunghill*, **S#1829h**. For similar meaning see Madmannah, Jsh 15:31. 1 Ch 6:77, Rimmon.
   Nahalal. i.e. *pasture, place of leading out*,

S#5096h. Jsh 19:15, Nahallal. Jg 1:30, Nahalol.
36 **Bezer**. Dt +4:43.
   Jahazah. i.e. *strife*, **S#3096h**. Jsh +13:18. Nu +21:23, Jahaz.
37 **Kedemoth**. Jsh +13:18. Dt 2:26. 1 Ch 6:79.
   Mephaath. Jsh +13:18. Je 48:21.
38 **Ramoth**. 1 K +4:13.
   Mahanaim. Ge +32:2.
39 **Heshbon**. Nu +21:25.
   Jazer. Nu +32:1.
40 **of Merari**. ver. 7.
41 **within**. Ge 49:7. Nu 35:1-8. Dt 33:10.
   forty and eight. Nu 36:62.
42 **These cities**. Nu 35:3, 4.
43 **gave unto**. Ge +13:15. Ex 3:8, 17. 23:27-31. Ps 44:3. 106:42-45.
   all the land. Jsh 11:23. 23:14. Ex +9:6. 23:29, 30. 1 K 4:21. 2 Ch 9:26. Ac +7:5. He 11:10. 13, 39. Mt +5:17, 18. +8:11. Ro 15:4, +8.
44 **gave them rest**. Jsh 1:15. 11:23. 22:4, 9. Dt 7:22-24. 31:3-5. He 4:8-10.
   delivered all. Dt 7:24. Ps 78:55.
45 **failed not**. Jsh +23:14, 15. Ps 16:5, 6. 34:10. 1 C 1:9. T 1:2. He 6:18.

JOSHUA 22

1 **Joshua**. Nu 32:18-33.
   Reubenites. Nu +26:7.
2 **Ye have**. Nu 32:20-29. Dt 3:18-20.
   obeyed. Jsh 1:12-18.
3 **have not left**. Ph 1:23-27.
4 **given rest**. Jsh +21:43, 44. Dt 12:9.
   as he promised. Ro 4:21.
   get. Jsh 13:8, 15-33. 14:1-5. Nu 32:33-42. Dt 3:1-17. 29:8.
5 **take**. Ex +15:26. Dt 4:1, 2, 6, 9. 6:6-9, 17. 11:22. 1 Ch 28:7, 8. Ps 106:3. 119:4-6. Pr 4:23. Is 55:2. Je 12:16. He +6:11, 12. 12:15. 2 P 1:5-10.
   love. Dt +6:5. Jn 21:15-17.
   cleave. Dt +4:4.
   serve. Jsh 24:14, 15, 19, 20. 1 S 12:20, 24. Mt +4:10. 6:24. Lk 1:74. 4:8. Jn 12:26. Ac 27:23. Ro 1:9.
   with. Mt +22:37.
   soul. Heb. *nephesh*, Ge +34:3.
6 **blessed them**. ver. 7, 8. Jsh 14:13. Ge 14:19. +31:49. 47:7, 10. Ex 39:43. 1 S 2:20. 2 S 6:18, 20. 2 Ch 30:18. Lk 2:34. 24:50, 51. He 7:6, 7.
7 **Now to**. Jsh 13:29-31. 17:1-12. Nu 32:33.
8 **Return**. Dt 8:9-14, 17, 18. 2 Ch 17:5. 32:27. Pr 3:16. 10:4, 22. 1 C 15:58. He 11:26.
   divide. Nu 31:27. 1 S 30:24. Ps 68:12. Ro 8:37.
9 **the country of Gilead**. Ge +37:25.
   according. Nu 32:20, 22.
10 **built**. ver. 25-28. Jsh 4:5-9. 24:26, 27. Ge 28:18. 31:46-52.

11 **heard**. Le 17:8, 9. Dt 12:5-7. 13:12-14. Jn 20:1, 12.
at the passage. Jsh 2:7. 3:14-16. Jg 12:5. Jn 1:28.

12 **the whole**. Dt 13:15. Jg 20:1-11. Ac 11:2, 3. Ro 10:2. Ga 4:17, 18.

13 **sent**. Nu 16:25. Jg +20:12. Pr 20:18. Mt 18:15.
Phinehas. Ex +6:25. Pr 25:9-13.

14 **with him**. Dt 17:6. Mt 18:16. 2 C 13:1.
chief house. Heb. house of the father.
an head. Ex 18:25. Nu 1:4. 13:2.
among the thousands. ver. +21.

16 **the whole**. ver. 12. Jsh 18:1. Mt +18:17. 1 C 1:10. 5:4. Ga 1:1, 2.
trespass. Le 5:19. 26:40. Nu 5:6. 1 Ch 21:3. 2 Ch 26:18. 28:13. Ezr 9:2, 15. Mt 6:14, 15.
to turn. ver. 18. Ex 32:8. Nu 14:43. 32:15. Dt 7:4. 30:17. 2 Ch 10:19. 25:27. He 12:25.
rebel. Le 17:8, 9. Dt 12:4-6, 13, 14. 1 S 15:23. Ps 78:8. Is 63:10.

17 **Is the iniquity**. Nu 25:3, 4, etc. Dt 4:3, 4. Ps 106:28, 29.
Peor. Nu 23:28. 31:16.
from which. Jsh 24:23. Ezr 9:13, 14. Ac 20:29, 30. 1 C 10:8, 11.
not cleansed. or, have not cleansed ourselves. Nu 8:7, 21. 2 K 5:14. 2 Ch 30:18. Ezr 6:20. Ne 12:30.

18 **following**. ver. +16. Dt 7:4. 1 S 12:14, 20. 1 K 9:6. 2 K 17:21. 2 Ch 25:27. 34:33.
and it will. Ezr 9:13, 14.
he will be. ver. 20. Jsh 7:1, 11, 12. Nu 16:22. 2 S 24:1. 1 Ch 21:1, 14, 17. 1 C 12:26.

19 **unclean**. Ex 15:17. Le 18:25-28. Am 7:17. Ac 10:14, 15. 11:8, 9.
the land of the possession of the Lord. Le 25:23. Dt +32:43. Mi 2:10.
wherein. Jsh 18:1. Le 17:8, 9. Dt 12:5, 6. 2 Ch 11:13, 16, 17.

20 **Did not Achan**. Jsh 7:1, 5, 18, 24. 1 C 10:6. 2 P 2:6. Ju 5, 6.
perished. **S#1478h**, Ge +49:33.

21 **Then the children**. 1 S +25:17. Pr 18:13.
answered. Pr 15:1. 16:1. 18:13. 24:26. Ac 11:4. Ja 1:19. 1 P 3:15.
heads. ver. 14. Ex +18:21-25. Nu 1:16. 10:4. 31:14. Dt 1:15. Jg 6:15. 12:6mg. 15:15. 1 S 6:19. 8:12. 10:19. 17:18. 22:7. 23:23. 2 S 18:1. 1 K 20:30. 1 Ch 12:14, 20. 13:1. 15:25. 26:26. 27:1. 28:1. 29:6. 2 Ch 1:2. 17:14. 25:5. Mi 5:2.

22 **The Lord God of gods**. *El Elohim Yehowah*, literally, The strong God, Elohim Jehovah.
God. Heb. *El*, Ex +15:2. Ex 18:11. Ps +82:1. 95:3. 97:7. *Da +2:47.* Jn +10:33-36. 1 T 6:16. Re 19:16.
he knoweth. 1 K 8:39. Jb 10:7. 23:10. Ps 7:3. 44:20, 21. 139:1-12. Je 12:3. 17:10. Jn +2:24, 25. 21:17. Ac 1:24. 2 C 11:11, 31. He 4:13. Re 2:18, 19, 23.

Israel. Ps 37:6. Mi 7:9. Ml 3:18. Ac 11:2-18. 2 C 5:11.
if it be. 1 S 15:23. Jb 31:5-8, 38-40. Ps 7:3-5. Ac 25:11.

23 **burnt offering**. Le +23:12.
meat offering. Le +23:13.
peace offering. Le +23:19.
let the Lord. 1 S 20:16. Lk +11:50, 51.

24 **for fear**. Ge +18:19.
In time to come. Heb. Tomorrow. Jsh +4:6mg.
What have. Jg +11:12.

25 **ye have no part**. ver. 27. 2 S 20:1. 1 K 12:16. Ezr 4:2, 3. Ne 2:20. Ac 8:21.
make. 1 S 26:19. 1 K 12:27-30. 14:16. 15:30. Mt 18:6.

27 **a witness**. ver. 10, 34. Jsh 24:27. Ge 31:48, 52. Dt 4:26. 1 S 7:12.
that we. Dt +12:11.

28 **Behold**. Ex 25:40. 2 K 16:10. Ezk 43:10, 11. He 8:5.

29 **God forbid**. Lk +20:16.
to build. ver. 23, 26. Dt 12:13, 14. 2 K 18:22. 2 Ch 32:12.
for burnt offerings. ver. +23. Ex 40:6, 9.

30 **it pleased them**. Heb. it was good in their eyes. ver. 33. Ge 16:6mg. 20:15mg. 28:8mg. 41:37. +45:16mg. Jg 8:3. +14:3mg. 1 S 8:6mg. 18:20mg. 25:32, 33. 29:6mg. 2 S 3:36mg. 17:4mg. 19:18mg. 1 K 3:10. 21:2mg. 1 Ch 13:4. 2 Ch 30:4mg. Est 1:21mg. Pr 15:1. Zc 11:12mg. Ac 11:18.

31 **the Lord is**. Le 26:11, 12. Dt +7:21. 2 Ch 15:2. Is 12:6. Zc 8:23. Mt 1:23.
not committed. 1 C 11:31. 2 C 7:11.
now. Heb. then.

32 **and brought**. ver. 12-14. Pr 25:13.

33 **the thing**. ver. +30. Ac 15:12, 31. 2 C 7:7. 1 Th 3:6-8.
blessed. 1 S 25:32, 33. 1 Ch 29:20. Ne 8:5, 6. Ps 68:35. Da 2:19. Lk 2:28. Ep 1:3.

34 **Ed**. i.e. *a witness*. **S#5707h**. ver. 27. Jsh 24:27. 1 K 18:39. Is 43:10. Mt 4:10.

JOSHUA 23

1 **the Lord**. Jsh 11:23. 21:44. 22:4. Ps 46:9. He 4:8, 9.
waxed old. Jsh 13:1. Ge 25:8. Dt 31:2. Phm 9.
stricken in age. Heb. come into days.

2 **Joshua called**. Ge 49:1.
all Israel. Jsh 24:1. Dt 31:28. 1 Ch 28:1. Ac 20:17-35.
and for their elders. Jsh +20:4. Nu 10:4. 1 Ch 28:1. Ps 40:9. 1 C 5:4.

3 **And ye**. Dt 4:9. Ps 44:1, 2. Mal 1:5.
for the. Jsh 10:14, 42. Ex 14:14. Dt 20:4. 2 Ch 20:17. Ps 44:3. 2 C 15:57.

4 **Behold**. Jsh 13:2, 6, 7. 18:10.

by lot. Jsh +14:2.

westward. Heb. at the sunset. Nu +34:6. Ps 80:11.

5　**he shall**. ver. 12, 13. Ex +23:30.

as the Lord. Nu 33:52, 53.

6　**very**. Jsh 1:7-9. Je 9:3. 1 C 16:13. Ep 6:10-19. He 12:4. Re 21:8.

that ye. Jsh +1:7.

7　**That ye come**. ver. 12. Ex 23:33. Dt 7:2, 3. Ps 119:115. Pr 4:14, 15. 1 C 15:33. 2 C 6:14-17. Ep 5:11.

neither. Ex +23:13.

to swear. Je 5:7. Zp 1:5.

8　**But cleave**. *or*, For if ye will cleave, etc. Dt +4:4.

9　**For the Lord**. *or*, Then the Lord will drive. ver. 5. Jsh 21:43, 44. Dt 11:23. Ps 44:2.

no man. Jsh 1:5, 8, 9. 15:14.

10　**One man**. Le 26:8. Dt 28:7. 32:30. Jg 3:31. 7:19-22. 15:15. 1 S 14:6, 12-16. 2 S 23:8. He 11:32-34.

Lord. Jsh 10:42. Ex 14:14. 23:27, etc. Dt 3:22. 20:4. Ps 35:1. 44:4, 5. 46:7. Ro 8:31.

11　**Take good heed**. Jsh 22:5. Dt 2:4. 4:9. 6:5-12. Pr 4:23. Lk 21:34. 1 C 16:22. Ep 5:15. He 12:15. Ju 21.

yourselves. Heb. your souls. Heb. *nephesh*, Nu +23:10. Dt 4:15.

love. Dt +6:5. 1 C 16:22.

12　**go back**. Ps 36:3. 125:5. Is 1:4. Ezk 18:24. Zp 1:6. Mt 12:45. Jn 6:66. He 3:12. 10:38, 39. 2 P 2:18-22. 1 J 2:19.

cleave. Ge 2:24. 34:3. 1 S 18:1-3. 1 K 11:2. Lk 12:52. Ro 12:9.

shall make. Ge 34:9. Jg +3:6.

13　**drive**. Jg 2:2, 3.

snares. Ex +23:33. 1 K 11:4. Re 2:20. or, gins. Jb 18:9. 22:10. Ps 11:6.

traps. or, snares.

scourges. 1 K 12:11, 14. 2 Ch 10:11, 14. Jb 5:21. 9:23. Pr 26:3. Is 10:26. 28:15, 18. Na 3:2.

your sides. Nu 33:55.

until ye perish. Le 26:31-35. Dt 4:26. 28:63-68. 29:28. 30:18. 2 K 17:22, 23. 25:21, 26. Lk 21:24.

14　**I am going**. 1 K 2:2. Jb 30:23. Ec 9:10. 12:5. Ro 5:17. 2 T 4:6. He 9:27. 2 P 1:13, 14.

souls. Heb. *nephesh*, Ge +34:3.

not one thing. Jsh 14:10. 21:43-45. Ex 3:8. 23:27-30. Le 26:3-13. Nu 33:19. Dt 28:1-14. 1 S 3:19. 1 K 8:56. Lk 16:17. 21:33. 1 Th 5:24. He 10:23.

15　**so shall**. Jg 3:8, 12. 4:1, 2. 6:1. 10:6, 7. 13:1. 2 Ch 36:16, 17. Je +11:8. Lk 21:22-24. 1 Th 2:16.

16　**and bowed**. Nu 25:2.

then shall. 2 K 24:20. Is 6:11, 12. Je 4:25-27.

perish. ver. 13. Ps 2:12.

JOSHUA 24

1　**Shechem**. Jsh 8:30, 31. Ge 12:6. +33:18, 19. Jn 4:5, 20.

called. Jsh 23:2. Ex 18:25, 26.

presented. 1 S 10:19. Ac 10:33.

2　**Your fathers**. Ge 11:26, 31. 12:1. 31:53. Dt 26:5. Is 51:2. Ezk 16:3.

the flood. Ps +72:8.

in old time. Heb. *olam*, Ex +12:24. **S#5769h**. Je 2:20. Ezk 26:20.

Nachor. i.e. *snorter*, **S#5152h**. Ge +11:22, Nahor.

served other gods. ver. 15. Ge 31:19, 30, 32, 53. 35:4.

3　**I took**. Ge 12:1-4. Ne 9:7, 8. Ac 7:2-4. He 11:8, 9.

gave. Ge 21:2, 3. Ps +127:3. He 11:11, 12.

4　**unto Isaac**. Ge 25:21, 24-26.

unto Esau. Ge 32:3. 36:8. Dt 2:5.

Jacob. Ge 46:1-7. Ps 105:23. Ac 7:15.

5　**sent**. Ex 3:10. 4:12, 13, 28, 5:1. Ps 105:26.

plagued. Ex ch. 7-12. Ps 78:43-51. 105:27-36. 135:8, 9. 136:10.

6　**I brought**. Ex 12:37, 41, 51. Mi 6:4.

Egyptians. Ex ch. 14, 15. Ne 9:11. Ps 77:15-20. 78:13. 136:13-15. Is 63:12, 13. Ac 7:36. He 11:29.

7　**And when**. Ex 14:10.

he put. Ex 14:20.

brought. Ex 14:27, 28.

your eyes. Ex 14:31. Dt 4:34. 29:2.

ye dwelt. Jsh 5:6. Nu 14:33, 34. Ne 9:12-21. Ps 95:9, 10. Ac 13:17, 18. He 3:17.

8　**I brought**. Jsh 13:10. Nu 21:21-35. Dt 2:32-37. 3:1-8. Ne 9:22. Ps 135:10, 11. 136:17-22.

9　**Then Balak**. Nu 22:5, 6, etc. +31:8.

10　**I would not**. Nu 22:11, 12, 20, 35. 23:3-12, 15-26. 24:5-10. Dt 23:5. Is 54:17.

blessed. Ge +2:16.

11　**And ye**. Jsh 3:14-17. 4:10-12, 19, 23. Ps 114:3, 5.

the men. Jsh ch. 6, 10, 11. Ne 9:24, 25. Ps 78:54, 55. 105:44. Ac 7:45. 13:19.

the Amorites. Ge +10:16.

Perizzites. Ge +13:7.

Canaanites. Ge +10:18.

Hittites. Dt +20:17.

Girgashites. Ge +10:16.

Hivites. Ge +10:17.

Jebusites. Ge +10:16.

12　**I sent**. Ex +23:28.

not. Ps 44:3-6.

13　**And I**. Jsh 21:45.

for which. Jn 4:38.

cities. Jsh 11:13. Dt 6:10-12. 8:7. Pr 13:22.

14　**fear**. Dt +6:2. Jb 1:1. Ps 130:4. Ho 3:5. Ac 9:31.

serve him. ver. 23. Ge 17:1. 20:5, 6. Ex +34:14. Dt 18:13. 2 K 20:3. Ps 119:1, 80. Lk 8:15. Jn 4:23, 24. +10:28. 2 C 1:12. Ep 6:24. Ph 1:10.

in sincerity. Ps +37:18. 1 C 5:8. 2 C 1:12.
2:17. 8:8. Ph 1:10.
in truth. Ps +15:2. Jn 4:23.
put. ver. 2, 23. Ge 35:2. Ex 20:3, 4. Le 17:7.
Ezr 9:11. Ezk 20:18. Am 5:25, 26.
in Egypt. Ezk 20:7, 8. 23:3.

15 choose. Dt +30:19. Ru 1:15, 16. 1 K 18:21.
Ezk 20:39. Mt 6:24. Lk 16:13. Jn 1:12. 6:67.
Ro 6:16. 2 C +6:2. He 2:3. Re 3:20.
whether the gods. ver. 14.
or the gods. Ex 23:24, 32, 33. 34:15. Dt 13:7.
29:18. Jg 6:10.
as for me. Ge +18:19. Ps 101:2. 119:106,
111, 112. Mt 26:33, 35. Jn 6:68. Ac 11:23.
my house. Ex +13:8. Ac +16:31.

16 God forbid. Lk +20:16. He 10:38, 39.

17 that brought. ver. 5-14. Ex 19:4. Dt 32:11,
12. Is 46:4. 63:7-14. Am 2:9, 10.
house of bondage. Ex +13:3. 20:2. Jg 6:8.
great signs. Ps 78:12, 43, 52, 55. 105:44.
in our sight. Ac 26:26. 2 P 1:16. 1 J 1:1.

18 drave out. Ps 105:44.
will we also. Ex 10:2. 15:2. Ps 116:16. Mi
4:2. Zc 8:23. Lk 1:73-75.
our God. Ps 48:14.

19 Ye cannot. ver. 23. Ru 1:15. Mt 6:24. Lk
14:25-33.
holy. Le 10:3. 1 S 6:20. Ps +99:3. Hab 1:13.
a jealous. Ex +20:5. He 12:29.
God. Heb. *El*, Ex +15:2.
he will not. Ex 23:21. 34:7. 1 S 3:14. 2 Ch
36:16. Is 27:11.

20 If. Ge +4:7.
forsake. Je +1:16.
strange. ver. 23. Ex 12:43. Dt 32:12. Jg
10:16mg.
he will turn. Jsh 23:12-15. 1 Ch 28:9. 2 Ch
15:2. Ezr 8:22. Is 1:28. 63:10. 65:11, 12. Je
17:13. Ezk 18:24. Ac 7:42. He 10:26, 27, 38.
after that. Jsh 23:15. Ps 78:58-60, 62, 63.

21 Nay. Ex 19:8. 20:19. 24:3, 7. Dt 5:27, 28.
26:17. Is 44:5.

22 Ye are witnesses. Dt 26:17. Jb 15:6. Lk 19:22.
ye have. Ps 119:111, 173. Lk 10:42. Jn 15:16.

23 put away. ver. 14. Ge 35:2-4. Ex 20:23. Jg
10:15, 16. 1 S 7:3, 4. Ho 14:2, 3, 8. 1 C 10:19-
21. 2 C 6:16-18.
strange. ver. 20.
incline. Ps 119:36. Pr 2:2. He 12:28, 29.

24 people said. ver. 21. Dt 5:28, 29. 23:21-23.
Ec 5:4-7. Jn 15:5. Ph 4:13.

25 made. Ex 15:25. 24:3, 7, 8. Dt 5:2, 3. 29:1,
10-15. 2 K 11:17. 2 Ch 15:12, 15. 23:16.
29:10. 34:29-32. Ne 9:38. 10:28, 29.
in Shechem. ver. 1, 26.

26 Joshua wrote. Ex 24:4. 34:27. Dt 31:24-26.
Is 30:8. Ezk 43:11.
took. Jg 9:6.
great stone. Ge 28:18. 1 S 7:12. Zc 3:9.
set it. Jsh 4:3-9, 20-24. Ge 28:18-22.
under. Ge 35:4, 8. Jg 9:6.

27 this stone. Jsh 22:27, 28, 34. Ge 31:44-52.
Dt 4:26. 30:19. 31:19, 21, 26. 1 S 7:12.
it hath. Dt 32:1. Is 1:2. Je 22:29. Hab 2:11.
Lk 19:40.
deny. Jb 31:23. Pr 30:9. Mt 10:33. 2 T 2:12,
13. T 1:16. Re 3:8.

28 Joshua let. Jg 2:6.

29 After these. Dt 34:5. Jg 2:8. Ps 115:17. 2 T
4:7, 8. Re 14:13.
an hundred and ten. Ge 50:22, 26.

30 Timnath-serah. Jsh 19:50. Jg 2:9.
Gaash. i.e. *shaking*, **S#1608h**. Jg 2:9. 2 S 23:30.
1 Ch 11:32.

31 served. Dt 31:29. Jg 2:7. 2 Ch 24:2, 17, 18.
Ac 20:29. Ph 2:12.
overlived Joshua. Heb. prolonged their days
after Joshua.
which had. Dt 11:2, 3, 7. 31:13.

32 bones. Ge 50:25. Ex 13:19. Ac 7:16. He
11:22.
buried. Ge 33:19, 20. 48:22.
pieces of silver. *or*, lambs.

33 Eleazar. Ex +6:23.
died. Jb 30:23. Ps 49:10. Is 57:1, 2. Zc 1:5. Ac
13:36. He 7:24. 9:26, 27.
Phinehas. Jg 20:28.
mount Ephraim. Jsh +17:15.

JUDGES

JUDGES 1

1 **Now**. Jsh 24:29, 30.
asked. Jg 20:18, 28. Ex 28:30. Nu 27:21. 1 S 22:9, 10. 23:9, 10.
Canaanites. Ge +10:18.

2 **Judah shall**. Ge 49:8-10. Nu +1:27. Re 19:11-16.

3 **Simeon**. Ge +29:33.
I likewise. ver. 17. 2 S 10:11. Ph 1:27, 30.

4 **Lord**. Ex 23:28, 29. Dt 7:2. 9:3. Jsh 10:8-10. 11:6-8. 1 S 14:6, 10. 17:46, 47. 1 K 22:6, 15.
Perizzites. Ge 13:7.
Bezek. i.e. *a flash of lightning*, S#966h. ver. 5. 1 S 11:8.

5 **Adoni-bezek**. i.e. *lord of Bezek*, S#137h. ver. 6, 7.

6 **cut off**. ver. 7. Dt 25:12. 2 S 4:12.
thumbs, etc. lit. "thumbs of his hands and of his feet." Ex 29:20. Le 8:23, 24. 14:14, 17, 25, 28.

7 **their thumbs**. Heb. the thumbs of their hands and of their feet. ver. 6.
gathered. *or*, gleaned. Ru 2:2, 7. Lk 16:21.
as I have. Ex 21:23-25. Le 24:19-21. Dt 19:19. Est 9:25. Ps 7:16. Is +33:1. Je +50:15. 51:56. Da 6:24. Lk 6:37, 38. Ro 2:15. Ga 6:7.

8 **children of Judah**. ver. 21. Jsh +15:63.
set the city. Jg 20:48.

9 **afterward**. Jsh 10:36, 37. 11:21. 15:13-20.
valley. *or*, low country. Dt 1:7. Jsh 9:1. 10:40. 11:2, 16. 12:8. 15:33. Zc +7:7.

10 **Kirjath-arba**. Jsh +15:54.
Sheshai. ver. 20. Nu +13:22, 33. Ps 33:16, 17. Ec 9:11. Je 9:23.

11 **Debir**. Jsh +10:3.
Kirjath-sepher. Jsh +15:15, 16.

12 **And Caleb**. Jsh 15:16, 17. 1 S 17:25. 18:23.
Achsah. Jsh 15:16.

13 **Othniel**. Jsh +15:17.
Kenaz. Ge +36:11.

14 **And it came**. Jsh 15:18, 19.
moved him. Dt 13:6.
and she lighted. Ge 24:64. 1 S 25:23. Jsh 15:18.
ass. Jg 19:28. Ex 4:20. Jsh 15:18.

15 **a blessing**. Jg +3:15. Pr 10:22. 1 C 12:31. He 6:7. 1 P 3:9. or, pool. Ps 84:6. Ec 2:6.

a south land. Ge +12:9.
give me also springs of water. Is 58:11.

16 **the Kenite**. Ge +15:19. Je 35:2.
Moses. Ex 3:1. 4:18. 18:1, 7, 12, 14-17, 27. Nu 10:29.
city of palm. Jg 3:13. Dt 34:3. 2 Ch 28:16.
which. Nu 21:1. Jsh 12:14.
Arad. Nu 21:1. 33:40. Jsh 12:14. 1 Ch +8:15.
they went. Nu 10:29-32. 1 S 15:6.

17 **And Judah**. ver. 3.
Zephath. i.e. *a watchtower*, S#6857h. 2 Ch 14:10, Zephathah.
Hormah. Nu +14:45.

18 **Also Judah**. Jg 3:3. Ex 23:31.
Gaza. Ge +10:19.
Askelon. i.e. *migration* or *a weighing out*, S#831h. Jg +14:19. Jsh 13:3. 1 S 6:17. 2 S 1:20.
Ekron. Jsh +13:3.

19 **the Lord**. ver. 2. Jsh 14:12. Ps 60:12. Ec 9:11. Is 7:14. +43:2.
he drave, etc. *or*, he possessed the mountain.
mountain. Jsh 17:18.
but could. ver. 27-32. Jsh +15:63. Mt 14:30, 31. 17:19, 20. Ph 4:13.
chariots. Ex 14:7, etc. Jsh 11:1-9. 17:16-18. Ps 46:9.

20 **they gave**. Nu +13:6.
the three sons. ver. 10. Nu 13:22.
Anak. Nu +13:33.

21 **Benjamin**. Nu +1:37.
not drive. Jsh +15:63.
Jebusites. Ge +10:16.
unto this day. ver. 26. Jg 6:24. 15:19. 18:12. Ge +19:38.

22 **the house**. Nu +1:10. Am +5:6.
Bethel. Ge +12:8.
the Lord. ver. +19. Ge 49:24.

23 **sent**. Jg 18:2. Jsh 2:1. 7:2.
Luz. Ge +28:19.

24 **we will**. Jsh 2:12-14. 1 S 30:15.

25 **they smote**. Jsh 6:22-25.

26 **the land**. 2 K 7:6. 2 Ch 1:17.
unto this day. ver. +21.

27 **Manasseh**. Jsh 17:11-13.
Beth-shean. Jsh +17:11.
Taanach. Jsh +17:11. 1 S 15:9. Ps 106:34, 35. Je 48:10.

Ibleam. i.e. *swallowing up a people*, **S#2991h**. Jsh 17:11. 2 K 9:27.

Megiddo. Jsh +12:21.

would dwell. ver. 35. Jsh 17:12.

28 **when Israel**. Ex 23:32. Dt 7:2. 1 S 15:9. Ps 106:34, 35. Je 48:10.

29 **Neither did Ephraim**. Jsh 10:33. +15:63.

Gezer. 1 K +9:16.

30 **Zebulun**. Nu +1:9.

Kitron. i.e. *knotty*, **S#7003h**. Jsh 19:15, Kattah. 21:34, Kartah.

Nahalol. i.e. *pasture*, **S#5096h**. Jsh 19:15, Nahalal. 21:35.

31 **Asher**. Jsh 19:24-30.

Accho. i.e. *sand-heated*, **S#5910h**. Ac 21:7, Ptolemais.

Zidon. Ge +49:13.

Ahlab. i.e. *fertility; fatness, fat*, **S#303h**.

Achzib. *or*, **Ecdippa**. Ge 38:5, Chezib. Jsh +15:44. 19:29. Mi 1:14.

Helbah. i.e. *fat, fatness*, **S#2462h**.

Aphik. i.e. *strength*, **S#663h**. Jsh +12:18, Aphek. 15:53, Aphekah.

Rehob. Nu +13:21.

32 **Asherites**. **S#843h**.

dwelt among. Ps 106:34, 35.

33 **Naphtali**. Jsh 19:32-38.

Beth-shemesh. Je +43:13.

Beth-anath. Jsh 19:38.

he dwelt. ver. 29, 30, 32.

became. ver. 30, 35. Ps 18:24.

34 **the Amorites forced**. Jg 18:1. Jsh 19:47.

children of Dan. Jsh 19:40-42.

the mountain. Seir or Baalah: see Jsh 15:10, 11.

35 **would dwell**. ver. 27. Jsh 17:12.

Heres. i.e. *heat* or *the sun*, **S#2776h**, only here. Jg 2:9. Jsh 19:41.

Aijalon. Jsh +10:12.

Shaalbim. i.e. *place of foxes*, **S#8169h**. Jsh 19:42. 1 K 4:9.

prevailed. Heb. was heavy.

36 **from the going**. *or*, Maaleh-akrabbim. Nu 34:4. Jsh 15:3.

the rock. Possibly Petra in Edumea. 2 K +14:7.

JUDGES 2

1 **And an angel**. *or*, messenger. Ex 33:14. Ec 5:6. Is 42:19. Hg 1:13. Zc +12:8. Ml 2:7.

Bochim. i.e. *weepers*, **S#1066h**. ver. 5.

I made. Ex 3:7, 8. 14:14. 20:2. Dt 4:34. Ps 78:51-53. 105:36-38. 1 P 2:9.

have brought. Ge 12:7. 22:16, 17. 26:3, 4. Jsh 3:10. Ps 105:44, 45.

I will never. Ge +17:7, 8. Le +26:42. Je +33:20, 21. Zc 11:10. Ro 11:29.

2 **And ye shall**. Ex +23:32.

throw down. Ex +23:24.

but ye have. ver. 20. Ezr 9:1-3, 10-13. Ps 78:55-58. 106:34-40. Je 7:23-28. 2 Th 1:8. 1 P 4:17.

why have. Ge 3:11, 12. 4:10. Ex 32:21. Je 2:5, 18, 31-33, 36.

3 **I also said**. ver. +21.

their gods. Jg 3:6. Ex +23:33. 1 K 11:1-7.

4 **the people**. 1 S 7:6. Pr 17:10. Je 31:9. Zc 12:10. Lk +6:21. 7:38. 2 C 7:10. Ja 4:9.

5 **Bochim**. *that is*, Weepers. Ge 35:8. Jsh 7:26.

they sacrificed. Jg 6:24. 13:19. 1 S 7:9.

6 **Joshua**. Jsh 22:6. 24:28, etc.

7 **the people**. Jsh 24:31. 2 K 12:2. 2 Ch 24:2, 14-22. Ac 20:29. Ph 2:12.

outlived. Heb. prolonged days after.

8 **Joshua**. Jsh 24:29, 30.

9 **Timnath-heres**. i.e. *image of the sun*, **S#8556h**. Jsh 19:50. 24:30, Timnath-serah.

Gaash. Jsh 24:30.

10 A.M. cir. 2590. B.C. cir. 1414. An. Ex. Is. cir. 77.

gathered. Ge 15:15. +25:8. Dt 31:16. 2 S 7:12. Ac 13:36.

knew not. Ge +39:6. Ex 1:8. 5:2. 1 S 2:12. 1 Ch 28:9. Jb 21:14. Ps 92:5, 6. Is 5:12. Je 9:3. 22:16. 31:34. Ga 4:8, 9. 2 Th 1:8. T 1:16. 1 J 5:21.

11 **did evil**. Jg 4:1. 6:1. 13:1. Ge 13:13. 38:7. 2 Ch 33:2, 6. Ezr 8:12.

and served Baalim. i.e. *the lords (idols)*, **S#1168h**. Jg 3:7. 8:33. 10:6, 10. 1 S 7:4. 12:10. 1 K 18:18. 2 Ch 17:3. 24:7. 28:2. 33:3. 34:4. Je 2:23. 9:14. Ho 2:13, 17. 11:2.

12 **forsook**. Dt 13:5. 29:18, 25. 33:17. Je +1:16.

other gods. Jg 5:8. Dt 6:14, 15.

bowed. Ex 20:5. Dt 5:9.

13 **forsook the Lord**. 2 Ch 27:2. 30:1-12. Je +1:16. Ho 11:7. Jn 6:66. 1 C 10:11, 12. 2 C 12:20, 21. Ga 4:9-11. 5:7. 1 T 1:19. 6:21. He 3:12, 13. 4:11. 12:15.

served. ver. 11. Jg 3:7. 10:6. 1 S 31:10. 1 K 11:5, 33. 2 K 23:13. Ps 78:58. 106:36. 1 C 8:5. 10:20-22.

Baal. Jg +6:25.

Ashtaroth. **S#6252h**. Jg 10:6. Dt +1:4. 1 S 7:3, 4. 12:10. 31:10. 1 K 11:5. 2 K 23:13.

14 **the anger**. ver. 20. Jg 3:7, 8. 10:7. Ex 22:24. 32:10, 11. Le 26:28. Nu 32:14. Dt 28:20, 58. 29:19, 20. 31:17, 18. 32:22. Jsh 23:16. 2 Ch 36:16. Ps 74:1. 78:59. 106:40-42. Na 1:2, 6.

he delivered. 2 K 17:20. 2 Ch 15:5.

spoilers. 1 S 17:53. Ps 89:41. Is 13:16. Je 30:16. Zc 14:2.

sold them. Dt +32:30.

could not. Jsh +15:63. Ps 44:9, 10. Je 37:10.

15 **hand**. Ex +9:3.

against. Je 18:8. 21:10. 44:11, 27. Mi 2:3.

had said. Le 26:15, etc. Dt 4:25-28. 28:15, etc. Jsh 23:15, 16. Ps 78:62-64.

had sworn. Dt 32:40, 41.

greatly. Jg 10:9. Ge 32:7. 1 S 13:6. 14:24. 30:6. 2 C 4:8.

16 A.M. 2591-2909. B.C. 1413-1095.
the Lord. Jg 3:9, 10, 15. 4:5. 6:14. 1 S 12:10, 11. Ac 13:20.
delivered. Heb. saved. ver. 18. Jg 10:1mg. Ne +9:27. Ps 106:43-45.

17 **they would**. 1 S 8:5-8. 12:12, 17, 19. 2 Ch 36:15, 16. Ps 106:43.
whoring. Ex +34:15, 16.
quickly. Ex 32:8. Dt 9:12, 16. Ga 1:6.
which their. ver. 7. Jsh 24:24, 31.

18 **then the Lord**. Ex 3:12. Jsh 1:5. Ac 18:9, 10.
it repented. Jg 10:16. 2 Ch 7:14. Je +18:8.
their groanings. Ex 2:24. 6:5. 2 K 13:4, 22, 23. Ps 12:5. Ezk 30:24.
oppressed. Jg 6:9. Ex 3:9. 1 S 10:18. Is 19:20. Je 30:20.
vexed. Jl 2:8 (thrust).

19 **when the**. ver. 7. Jg 3:11, 12. 4:1. 8:33. Jsh 24:31. 2 Ch 24:17, 18.
corrupted. or, were corrupt. Dt 31:29.
more. Je 16:12. Mt 23:32. 2 T 3:13.
ceased not from. Heb. let nothing fall of. Is 1:16.
stubborn. 1 S 15:23. Je +3:17mg.

20 **the anger**. ver. +14.
transgressed. Ex 24:3-8. Dt 29:10-13. Jsh 23:16. 24:21-25. Je 31:32. Ezk 20:37.

21 **will not**. ver. 3. Jg 3:3. Jsh 23:12, 13. Ezk 20:24-26.

22 **through**. Jg 3:1-4.
prove. Ge 22:1. Dt 8:2, 16. 13:3. 2 Ch 32:31. Jb 23:10. Ps 66:10. Pr 17:3. Ml 3:2, 3.

23 **left**. or, suffered. Jg 3:1. 1 P 1:7. 4:12.

JUDGES 3

1 A.M. 2561. B.C. 1443. An. Ex. Is. 48.
the nations. Jg 2:21, 22. Dt 7:22.
prove. Ex 15:25. 16:4. 20:20. Dt 8:2, 16. 2 Ch 32:31. Jb 23:10. Pr 17:3. Je 6:27. 17:9, 10. Zc 13:9. Jn 2:24. 1 P 1:7. 4:12. Re 2:23.
as had not. Jg 2:10.

2 **might know**. Ge 2:17. 3:5, 7. 2 Ch 12:8. Mt 10:34-39. Jn 16:33. 1 C 9:26, 27. Ep 6:11-18. 1 T 6:12. 2 T 2:3. 4:7.
to teach. 2 S 22:35. Ps 144:1. Lk 22:36.

3 **five lords**. Je +47:4.
Canaanites. Jg 4:2, 23, 24. Ge +10:18.
Sidonians. Dt +3:9.
Hivites. Ge +10:17.
in mount. Nu 34:8. Dt 1:7. 3:9. Jsh 11:3. 13:5.
Baal-hermon. i.e. *place of the nose; having a fortress*, **S#1179h**. 1 Ch 5:23.
Hamath. Nu +13:21.

4 **to prove**. ver. +1. Jg 2:22. Dt 33:8. 1 C 11:19. 2 Th 2:9-12.
hearken. Dt +15:5.

5 **dwelt among**. Jg 1:29-32. Ps 106:34-38.
Canaanites. Ge +10:18.
Hittites. Dt +20:17.
Amorites. Ge +10:16.
Perizzites. Ge +13:7.
Hivites. ver. 3. Ge +10:17.
Jebusites. Ge +10:16.

6 **took their daughters**. Ge 6:2. Ex 34:16. Nu +12:1. Dt 7:3, 4. Jsh 23:12. 1 K 11:1-5. Ezr 9:2, 11, 12. Ne 10:30. 13:23-27. Ezk 16:3. Ml 2:11, 15. 1 C 7:39. 2 C 6:14-17.

7 **did evil**. or, the evil thing; a reference to idolatry. ver. 12. Jg 2:11-13.
and served. Jg 2:13.
Baalim. Jg +2:11.
the groves. 2 K +17:10.

8 A.M. 2591. B.C. 1413. An. Ex. Is. 78.
was hot. Jg +2:14. Ps 6:1. 85:3.
he sold. Dt +32:30.
Chushan-rishathaim. i.e. *a Cushite most wicked or of double wickedness*, **S#3573h**. ver. 10. Hab 3:7.

9 A.M. 2599. B.C. 1405. An. Ex. Is. 86.
cried. ver. 15. Ps +3:4. 106:41-44.
raised up. Jg +2:16.
deliverer. Heb. savior. ver. 15. Dt 22:27. 28:29. 1 S 11:3. Ne +9:27.
who delivered. Ex 2:17.
Othniel. Jsh +15:17.

10 **the Spirit**. Heb. *ruach*, Ge +41:38. Jg 6:34. 11:29. 13:25. 14:6, 19. 15:14. Nu 11:17. 27:18. 1 S 10:6. 11:6. 16:3, 13, 16. 2 Ch 15:1. 20:14. Ps 51:11. Is 61:1. 1 C 12:4-11. He 6:4.
came. Heb. was. Nu 24:2. 1 S 4:1mg. 10:11.
Mesopotamia. Heb. Aram. Ge 11:2. 14:1. Dt 23:4. 1 Ch 19:6, 7.

11 **the land**. ver. 30. Jg 5:31. 8:28. Jsh 11:23. Est 9:22.
Othniel. ver. +9.

12 A.M. 2662. B.C. 1342. An. Ex. Is. 148.
did evil. ver. 7. Jg 2:19. Ho 6:4.
and the Lord. Ex 9:16. 2 K 5:1. Is 10:15. 37:26. 45:1-4. Ezk 38:16. Da 4:22. 5:18. Jn 19:11.
Eglon. i.e. *a little calf*, **S#5700h**. ver. 14, 15, 17. Jsh 10:3, 5, 23, 34, 36, 37. 12:12. 15:39.
the king. 1 S 12:9.

13 **Ammon**. Jg 5:14. Ps 83:6-8.
the city. Jg 1:16. Dt 34:3. Ps 83:7.

14 **served**. Le 26:23-25. Dt 28:40, 47, 48.

15 A.M. 2679. B.C. 1325. An. Ex. Is. 166.
cried unto. ver. +9. Ps 78:34. Je 33:3.
Ehud. 1 Ch 8:6.
Gera. Ge 46:21.
a Benjamite. or, the son of Jemini. 1 S 9:1mg. 2 S 16:1. 19:16. 1 K 2:8.
left-handed. Heb. shut of his right hand. or, restrained, as in Jg 20:16; Ps 69:15 (shut). Ge +48:13. 1 Ch 12:2. Ps 44:3.
sent a present. Jg 1:15. Ge 4:5. 32:13, 18,

20, 21. 33:10, 11. 43:11, 15, 25, 26. 1 S 9:7.
10:27. 16:20. 25:18, 27mg, 35. 30:26mg. 2 S
8:2, 6. 1 K 4:21. 9:14. 10:10, 25. 2 K 5:15.
17:3. 18:31. 2 Ch 9:9, 14, 24. 17:5, 11. 26:8.
32:22, 23. Jb 42:11. Ps 45:12. 68:29. 72:10,
15. 76:11. Pr 17:8. 18:16. 19:6. 21:14. Is 18:7.
36:16. Mt 2:11. 2 C 9:5.

16 **two edges**. Heb. mouths. Ps 149:6. Is
41:15mg. He 4:12. Re 1:16. 2:12.
raiment. or, long robe. Le 6:10.
upon. ver. 21. Ps 45:3. SS 3:8.

17 **a very fat**. ver. 29mg. Ge 41:2, etc. 1 S 2:29.
Jb 15:27. Ps 73:4mg, 7, 19. Je 5:28. 50:11.
Ezk 34:20.

19 **quarries**. or, graven images. ver. 26. Ex
+20:4. Jsh 4:20.
a secret. ver. 20. 2 K 9:5, 6. Ac 23:18, 19.
Keep silence. Am 6:10. 8:3. Hab +2:20.
And all that. Ge 45:1.

20 **a summer parlor**. Heb. a parlor of cooling.
or, upper chamber. ver. 23, 24, 25. Jsh 2:6. 2
S 18:33. 1 K 17:19, 23. 2 K 1:2. 4:10, 11.
23:12. 1 Ch 28:11. 2 Ch 3:9. 9:4. Ne 3:31, 32.
Ps 104:3, 13. Je 22:13, 14. Am 3:15. Mk 2:4.
14:15. Lk 17:31. 22:12. Ac 1:13. 9:37, 39.
10:9. 20:8, 9.
I have. ver. 19. 2 S 12:1, etc. 24:12. Mi 6:9.
he arose. Ps 29:1. Je 10:7.
seat. or, throne. Ge 41:40. Ex 11:5. 12:29. Dt
17:18. 1 S 1:9. 2:8. 4:13, 18.

21 **thrust it**. Nu 25:7, 8. 1 S 15:33. Jb 20:25. Zc
13:3. 2 C 5:16.

22 **blade**. lit. flame. Jg 13:20. Jb 39:23. 41:21. Is
13:8. 29:6. 30:30. 66:15. Jl 2:5.
the dirt came out. or, it came out at the
fundament.

23 **shut the doors**. Jg 9:51. Ge 7:16. Jn 20:19,
26.
locked them. 2 S 13:17, 18. Ne 3:3. SS 4:12.

24 **covereth**, etc. or, doeth his easement. 1 S
24:3. 2 K 18:27mg.

25 **ashamed**. 2 K 2:17. 8:11. Je 6:15. 8:12.
key. 1 Ch +9:27. Pr 8:6. Is 22:22.

26 **escaped**. 1 S 23:13.
tarried. Jg 19:18. Ge 19:16. 43:10. Ex 12:39.
2 S 15:28. Ps 119:60. Is 29:9. Hab 2:3.
the quarries. ver. 19.
Seirath. lit. a hairy or rough place; the hairy she-
goat, **S#8167h**.

27 **he blew**. Jg 5:14. 6:34. 1 S 13:3. 2 S 20:22. 2
K 9:13. Jl 2:1, 15. 1 C 14:8.
mountain. Jsh +17:15, 18.

28 **Follow**. Jg 4:10. 7:17.
the Lord. Jg 7:9, 15. 1 S 17:47.
the fords. Jg 12:5, 6. Jsh 2:7.

29 **lusty**. Heb. fat. or, robust. lit. oily, fat, shining. ver. +17. Ge 49:20. Dt 32:15. Ne 9:25, 35.
Ps 17:10. Is 30:23. Ezk 34:14, 16. Hab 1:16.
valor. Ge 47:6. Ex 18:21, 25. Jsh 1:14. 6:2.
8:3. 10:7.

30 **subdued**. or, humbled. Jg 8:28. 11:23.
And the land. ver. 11. Jg 5:31.

31 **Shamgar**. i.e. destroyer, **S#8044h**. Jg 5:6.
Anath. i.e. afflicted; answered, **S#6067h**. Jg 5:6.
an ox goad. Jg 15:15. 1 S 13:19-22. 17:47,
50. Zc 4:6. 1 C 1:27.
also. Jg 2:16.
Israel. Jg 2:16. 4:1, 3, etc. 5:6, 8. 10:7, 17.
11:4, etc. 1 S 4:1. 13:19, 22.

JUDGES 4

1 A.M. 2699. B.C. 1305. An. Ex. Is. 186.
did evil. Jg 2:11, 19, 20. 3:7, 12. 6:1. 10:6. Le
26:23-25. Ne 9:23-30. Ps 78:56, 57. 106:43-
45. Je 5:3.
dead. Jg 2:9, 10, 19. 3:11, 12.

2 **sold**. Dt +32:30.
Jabin. Jsh +11:1.
Hazor. Jsh +15:23.
Sisera. i.e. battle-array; binding in chains,
S#5516h. ver. 7, 9, 12-18, 22. Jg 5:20, 26, 28,
30. 1 S 12:9. Ezr 2:53. Ne 7:55. Ps 83:9.
Harosheth. i.e. carving; city of crafts, **S#2800h**.
ver. 13, 16.

3 **cried**. 1 S 7:8. Ps +3:4. 78:34. Je 2:27, 28.
chariots of iron. Jg 1:19. Jsh 17:16.
mightily. Jg 5:8. Dt 28:29, 33, 47, 48. Ps
106:42. 107:10-13, 39.

4 A.M. 2719. B.C. 1285. An. Ex. Is 206.
Deborah. Ge +35:8.
prophetess. Ex +15:20. Jl 2:28, 29.
Ga 3:28.
Lapidoth. i.e. lamps; enlightened, **S#3941h**.

5 **the palm**. Ge 35:8.
between Ramah. Je +31:15.
Bethel. Ge +12:8.
in mount Ephraim. Jsh +17:15.
came up. Ex 18:13, 16, 19, 26. Dt 17:8-12. 2
S 15:2-6.

6 **Barak**. i.e. lightning, **S#1301h**. ver. 8-10, 12,
14-16, 22. Jg 5:1, 12, 15. He 11:32.
Abinoam. i.e. my father is pleasant, or father of
pleasantness, **S#42h**. ver. 12. Jg 5:1, 12.
Kedesh-naphtali. i.e. my wrestling, **S#5321h**.
Jsh 19:32, 37. 20:7. 21:32.
Hath. Jsh 1:9. Ps 7:6. Is 13:2-5. Ac 13:47.
Tabor. i.e. mound, height; thou wilt purge;
purity, **S#8396h**. ver. 12, 14. Jg 8:18. Jsh 19:22.
1 S 10:3. 1 Ch 6:77. Ps 89:12. Je 46:18. Ho
5:1.
ten thousand. ver. 10. Jg 5:14-18.

7 **And I will draw**. Ex +4:21. 14:4. Jsh 11:20.
Ezk 38:10-16. Jl 3:11-14.
Kishon. Jg +5:21. 1 K 18:40. Ps 83:9, 10.
deliverer. ver. 14. Ex 21:13. Jsh 8:7. 10:8.
11:6. 1 S 24:10, 18.

8 **If thou**. Ex 4:10-14. Mt 14:30, 31.
wilt go. Is 31:1.

9 **notwithstanding**. 1 S 2:30. 2 Ch 26:18.

not be. Ps 115:1. Je 17:5.
sell Sisera. Jg +2:14.
into the hand of a woman. ver. 17-22. Jg 5:24-27. 9:54. 2 S 20:21, 22.

10 **called**. ver. 13mg.
Zebulun. ver. 6. Jg 5:18.
at his. Jg 5:15mg, 27mg. 2 K +3:9mg.

11 **Heber**. ver. 17. Ge +46:17.
Kenite. Jg 1:16. Nu 24:21.
Hobab. Ex 2:18. 3:1. 18:1. Nu +10:29.
Zaanaim. i.e. *changing; wandering*, **S#6815h**. Jsh 19:33, 37, Zaanannim.
Kedesh. ver. 6. Jsh +15:23.

12 **mount Tabor**. ver. +6. Jsh 19:12, 34.

13 **gathered**. Heb. gathered by cry, or proclamation. Jg 6:34. 1 S 10:17. 2 S 20:4, 5. Jb 35:9. Jon 3:7. Zc 6:8.
chariots. ver. 13. Jsh 11:6.
nine hundred. ver. 2, 3, 7.
chariots of iron. ver. 3.

14 **Up**. Jg 19:28. Ge 19:14. 44:4. Jsh 7:13. 1 S 9:26.
is not. Dt 9:3. 2 S 5:24. Ps 68:7, 8. Is 52:12. Mi 2:13. Zc 14:3.
mount Tabor. Jsh 19:12.

15 **the Lord discomfited**. Jg 5:20, 21. Jsh 10:10. 2 K 7:6. 2 Ch 13:15-17. Ps 20:7, 8. 33:16, 17. 83:9, 10. Pr 21:31. He 11:32.

16 **pursued**. Le 26:7, 8. Jsh 10:19, 20. 11:8. Ps 104:35. Ro 2:12. Ja 2:13.
there. Is 43:17.
a man left. Heb. unto one.

17 **fled**. Jb 12:19-21. 18:7-12. 40:11, 12. Ps 37:35, 36. 107:40. Pr 29:23. Am 5:19, 20.
Jael. i.e. *a roe*, **S#3278h**. ver. 18, 21, 22. Jg 5:6, 24.
peace. Ps 69:22. Is 57:21.

18 **Jael**. 2 K 6:19.
mantle. *or*, rug *or* blanket.

19 **Give me**. Jg 5:25, 26. Ge 24:43. 1 K 17:10. Is 41:17. Jn 4:7.
a bottle. Jsh 9:4, 13. 1 S 16:20. Ps 56:8. 119:83.

20 **Is there**. Jsh 2:3-5. 2 S 17:20.

21 **took**. Jg 3:21, 31. 5:26. 15:15. 1 S 17:43, 49, 50. 1 C 1:19, 27.
a nail. Jg 16:14. Ex +27:19.
and took. Heb. and put.
hammer. 1 K 6:7. Is 44:12. Je 10:4.
went softly. 2 S 18:5 (gently). 1 K 21:27. Jb 15:11 (secret thing. or, gentle word). Is 8:6.
smote. Ps 3:7.
temples. ver. 22. Jg 5:26. SS 4:3. 6:7.
fast asleep. Ps 76:6. Pr 10:5. Da 8:18. 10:9. Jon 1:5, 6.
weary. 1 S 14:28mg.
he died. Jg 5:27.

22 **and I will**. 2 S 17:3, 10-15.

23 **God subdued**. 1 Ch 22:18. Ne 9:24. Ps 18:39, 47. 47:3. 81:14. 1 C 15:28. He 11:33.

24 **prospered**, etc. Heb. going, went and was hard against. 1 S 3:12.

JUDGES 5

1 **sang Deborah**. Ex 15:1, 21. Nu 21:17. 1 S 2:1. 2 Ch 20:21, 27. Jb 38:7. Ps 18, title. Is 12:1-6. 25:1. 26:1. Lk 1:46, 67, 68. Re 15:3, 4. 19:1-3.

2 **for the avenging** Dt 32:43. 2 S 22:47, 48. Ps 18:47. 48:11. 94:1. 97:8. 136:15, 19, 20. 149:6-9. Re 6:10. 16:5, 6. 18:20. 19:2.
when. ver. 9. Jg 5:18. 2 Ch 17:16. Ne 11:2. Ps 110:3. 1 C 9:17. 15:57. 2 C 8:5, 12. 9:7. Ph 2:13. Phm 14.

3 **O ye kings**. Dt 32:1, 3. Ps 2:10-12. 49:1, 2. 119:46. 138:4, 5.
I, even I. ver. 7. Ge 6:17. 9:9. Ex 31:6. Le 26:28. 1 K 18:22. 19:10, 14. Ezr 7:21.
will sing. 2 S +22:50.

4 **Lord**. Dt +33:2.
Seir. Ge +14:6.
the earth trembled. Dt 2:25. Jsh 5:1. +97:4.
the clouds. Ge +9:13. Ex 19:9. 2 S 22:12.
dropped. Ps 68:8. 77:17. SS 5:5.

5 **mountains**. Dt 4:11. Ps +97:5. 114:4.
melted. Heb. flowed. Dt 32:2. Ps 147:18. SS 4:16. Is 64:1, 3.
that Sinai. Ex 19:18. 20:18. Dt 4:11, 12. 5:22-25. He 12:18.

6 **Shamgar**. Jg 3:31.
Jael. Jg 4:17, 18.
the highways. Le 26:22. 2 Ch 15:5. Is 33:8. La 1:4. 4:18. Mi 3:12. Zc 7:14.
travelers. Heb. walkers of paths. Jb 19:8.
byways. Heb. crooked ways. Ps 125:5.

7 **the villages**. Est 9:19.
a mother in Israel. Jg 4:4-6. 2 S 20:19. Is 49:23. Ro 16:13.

8 **new gods**. Jg 2:12, 17. Dt 32:16, 17. Je 2:11, 13.
was there. Jg 4:3. 1 S 13:19-22.

9 **offered**. ver. +2. 1 Ch 29:9. 2 C 8:3, 4, 12, 17. 9:5.

10 **Speak**. *or*, Meditate. 1 Ch 16:9. Jb 12:8. Ps 105:1, 2. 145:5, 6, 11. Is 12:4.
ride. Jg 10:3, 4. 12:13, 14. Zc 9:9. Mt 21:5.
ye that sit. Ps 107:32. Is 28:6. Jl 3:12.

11 **the noise**. La 5:4, 9.
in the places. Ge 24:11, 13, 19, 20, 43-45. 26:20-22. Ex 2:17-19. Is 12:3.
rehearse. 1 S 12:7.
righteous acts. Heb. righteousnesses. 1 S 12:7mg. Ps 145:7. Is 33:15mg. 45:24mg. Mi 6:5.
villages. ver. 7.
go down. Dt 22:24. Jb 29:7. Is 28:6. Je 7:2.

12 **awake, Deborah**. Ps 57:8. 103:1, 2. 108:2. Is 26:19. 51:9, 17. 52:1, 2. 60:1. Je 31:26. 1 C 15:34. Ep 5:14.

utter a song. Ep 5:19. Re 15:3.
lead. Ps 68:18. Is 14:2. 33:1. 49:24-26. Ep 4:8. 2 T 2:26.

13 he made. Ps 49:14. 149:8. Is 41:15, 16. Ezk 17:24. Da 7:18-27. Ro 8:37. Re 2:26, 27. 3:9.
the Lord. Ps 75:7.

14 of Ephraim. Jg 3:15, 26, 27. 4:5, 6.
Amalek. Ex +17:8.
after. Jg 4:10, 14.
Machir. Ge +50:23.
Zebulun. Jg 4:6.
handle the pen. Heb. draw with the pen. Ps 45:1.

15 the princes. 1 Ch +12:32.
Barak. Jg 4:6, 14.
foot. Heb. his feet. Ac 20:13.
For the. *or*, In the divisions, etc. 2 Ch 35:5. Ac 15:39.
thoughts. Heb. impressions. Pr 22:13. 2 C 11:2.

16 sheepfolds. Nu 32:1-5, 24. Ph 2:21. 3:19.
For. *or*, In. ver. 15mg.
great. Ps 4:4. 77:6. La 3:40, 41.
Reuben. Ge 49:4.
searchings. Jb 5:9. 8:8. 9:10. 11:7. 36:26. 38:16. Ps 145:3. Pr 25:3mg, 27. Is 40:28.

17 Gilead. Ge +37:25.
Dan. Nu +1:12.
Asher. Nu +1:13.
sea shore. *or*, sea port.
breaches. *or*, creeks.

18 Zebulun. Nu +1:9.
jeoparded. Heb. exposed to reproach.
their. Est 4:16. 1 J 3:16. Re +12:11.
lives. Heb. *nephesh*, souls, Ge +44:30.
in the high. Jg 4:6, 10, 14.

19 kings. Jsh 10:22-27. 11:1, etc. Ps 48:4-6. 68:12-14. 118:8-12. Re 17:12-14. 19:19.
Taanach. Jsh +17:11.
waters of Megiddo. Jsh +12:21.
they took. ver. 30. Ge 14:22. 4:16. Ps 44:12.

20 fought. Jsh 10:11. 1 S 7:10. Ps 18:12-14. 77:17, 18.
the stars. Jg 4:15.
courses. Heb. paths. Nu 20:19 (high way).
fought. Ge +4:10.

21 Kishon. i.e. *winding; ensnarer*, S#7191h. Jg 4:7, 13. 1 K 18:40. Ps 83:9, 10.
O my soul. Heb. *nephesh*, Ge +27:31. Ge 49:18. Ps 44:5. Is 25:10. Mi 7:10.
trodden. Dt 33:29. Ps 91:13.

22 horsehoofs. Ge 49:17. Ps 20:7. 33:17. 147:10, 11. Is 5:28. Je 47:3. Mi 4:13.
broken. or, hammered. ver. 26. 1 S 14:16. Ps 74:6. 141:5. Pr 23:35. Is 16:8. 28:1mg. 41:7.
pransings. *or*, tramplings, *or* plungings. Na 3:2.
mighty ones. 1 S 21:7. Jb 24:22. 34:20. Ps 22:12. 76:5. 78:25mg. 103:20mg. Is 10:13. 46:12. Je 8:16. 46:12, 15. 47:3. 50:11. La 1:15.

23 Curse ye. 1 S 26:19. Je 48:10. 1 C 16:22.
Meroz. i.e. *leanness*, S#4789h. Mt 21:19.
the angel. Jg 2:1. 4:6. 6:11. 13:3. Mt 25:41.
they came. Jg 21:9, 10. Ne 3:5. Ps 78:9.
to the help. 1 S 17:47. 18:17. 25:28. Ro 15:18. 1 C 3:9. 2 C 6:1.

24 Blessed above women. Jg 4:17. Ge 14:19. Pr 31:31. Lk 1:28, 42. 11:27, 28.

25 asked. Jg 4:19-21.
butter. Ge 18:8. Dt 32:14. 2 S 17:29. Jb 20:17. Pr 30:33. Is 7:15, 22.
dish. Jg 6:38.

26 nail. Jg 4:21.
workmen's. Jb 3:20. 20:22. Pr 16:26. Ec 2:18, 22. 3:9. 4:8. 9:9.
with the. Heb. she hammered.
she smote off. 1 S 17:49-51. 2 S 20:22.

27 At. Heb. Between. Ge 49:10. Dt +11:6mg.
where. Ps 52:7. Mt 7:2. Ja 2:13.
dead. Heb. destroyed. Ps 137:8. Is 33:1. Je 4:30.

28 looked out. 2 S 6:16. 2 K 9:30. 1 Ch 15:29. Pr 7:6.
through. 2 K 1:2. SS 2:9.
Why is. Jg 4:15. SS 8:14. Ja 5:7.

29 wise ladies. 2 S 20:16. 1 K 11:3. Est 1:18. Is 49:23mg. La 1:1.
answer. Heb. her words. Pr 7:5.

30 Have they not sped. Ex 15:9. Jb 20:5.
every man. Heb. the head of a man. 2 S 1:16. 1 K 2:37. 2 K 2:3. Ps 3:3. 7:16. 66:12. Pr 10:6. Is 35:10. Ezk 33:4. Mt 27:25. Ac 18:6.
a damsel. or, female. lit. a womb. Ge 49:25. Pr 30:16. Is 46:3. Ezk 20:26.
of divers. Ge 37:3. 2 S 13:18. 1 Ch 29:2. Ezk 17:3.
needlework. Ps 45:14. Ezk 16:10, 13, 18. 26:16. 27:7, 16, 24.

31 So let. Ps 48:4, 5. +58:10, 11. 83:9-18. 92:9. 97:8. Re 6:10.
O Lord. Ps 2:12. 3:8. 14:7. 134:21. Jon 2:9. Mt 11:15. 17:5. 20:16. 22:14. 24:28. Re 22:20.
that love. Ex 20:6. Dt 5:10. +6:5. Ps 69:36. 91:14. 97:10. 116:1. 122:6. Jn 14:15, 21, 23. 1 C 8:3. Ep 6:24. Ja 1:12. 2:5. 1 P 1:8. 1 J 4:19-21. 5:2, 3.
the sun. Ps 19:4, 5. 37:6. Da 12:3. Ml +4:2.
And the land. Jg 3:11, 30.

JUDGES 6

1 did evil. Jg 2:13, 14, 19, 20. Le 26:14, etc. Dt 28:15, etc. Ne 9:26-29. Ps 106:34-42.
Midian. Ge +25:2.

2 the hand. Le 26:17. Dt 28:47, 48.
prevailed. Heb. was strong.
caves. Ge +19:30. 1 S 14:11. Re 6:15.
strongholds. 1 S 23:14, 19, 29. 24:22. 1 Ch 11:7, 16. 12:8, 16. Is 33:16. Je 48:41. 51:30. Ezk 33:27.

3 **when Israel**. Le 26:16. Dt 28:30-33, 51. Jb 31:8. Is 65:21, 22. Mi 6:15.
  Amalekites. Nu +14:45.
  children. ver. 33. Ge +29:1.
4 **destroyed**. Le 26:16. Dt 28:30, 33, 51. Mi 6:15.
  till thou come. Ge 10:19. 13:10.
  left no. Pr 28:3. Je 49:9, 10. Ob 5.
  sustenance. Jg 17:10.
  sheep. or, goat. Ex 12:3.
5 **tents**. SS 1:5. Is 13:20.
  as grasshoppers. Jg 7:12. 8:10. Je 46:23.
  their camels. Jg 8:21. 1 S 30:17. Is 60:6. Je 49:29, 32.
  to destroy. Ps 83:4-12.
6 **impoverished**. Ps 79:8. 106:43mg. Is 17:4. Je 5:17. Ml 1:4.
  cried. Ps +3:4. 78:34. 106:44. Is 26:16. Ho 5:15.
8 A.M. 2759. B.C. 1245. An. Ex. Is. 246.
  a prophet. Heb. a man, a prophet. Is +40:13mg.
  Thus saith. Jg 2:1-3. Ne 9:9-12. Ps 136:10-16. Is 63:9-14. Ezk 20:5, etc.
9 **drave them**. Ps 44:2, 3.
10 **I am the**. Ex 20:2, 3.
  fear not. 2 K 17:33, 35-39. Je +10:2.
  ye have. Jg 2:2. Pr 5:13. Je 3:13, 25. 9:13. 42:21. 43:4, 7. Zp 3:2. Ro 10:16. He 5:9.
11 **an angel of**. ver. 14-16. Jg 5:23. Jsh 18:23. Zc +12:8.
  an oak. ver. 19. 1 K 13:14.
  in Ophrah. Jg 8:27. 9:5.
  Joash. i.e. *Jehovah has become man; whom Jehovah bestowed*, **S#3101h**. ver. 29, 30, 31. Jg 7:14. 8:13, 29, 32. 2 K 11:2, 21. 12:1. 13:10. 14:1. 1 Ch 3:11. 4:22. +7:8. 12:3. 2 Ch 24:1, 2. 25:25. Ho 1:1. Am 1:1.
  Abi-ezrite. **S#33h**. ver. 24. Jg 8:2, 32. Nu 26:30. Jsh 17:2. 1 Ch 7:17, 18.
  Gideon. i.e. *a cutter down*, **S#1439h**. ver. 13, 19, 22, 24, 27, 29, 39. Jg 7:1, 2, 5, 19, 25. 8:13, 22, 30, 32. He 11:32, Gedeon.
  threshed. or, beating out. Dt 24:20. Ru 2:17. Is 27:12. 28:27.
  wheat. 1 Ch 21:20.
  winepress. **S#1660h**. Ne 13:15. Is 63:2 (wine-fat), 3. La 1:15. Jl 3:13. Mt 26:26. Re 14:19. 19:15.
  hide it. Heb. cause it to flee. Jg 7:21. Ex 9:20. Dt 32:30. +34:6.
12 **the angel**. Jg 13:3. Lk 1:11, 28.
  The Lord. Jg 2:18. Ex 3:12. Ru 2:4.
  with thee. Jsh 1:5.
  valor. Jg 11:1. Jsh 1:14. 6:2. 8:3. 10:7. 1 S 16:18. 2 S +2:7mg.
13 **if the Lord**. Ge 25:22. Ex 34:14-16. Nu 14:14, 15. Ro 8:31.
  why then. Dt 29:24. 30:17, 18. Ps 77:7-9. 89:49. Is 59:1, 2. 63:15.

our fathers. Ps 13:1. 44:1. 78:3, 4, 12. 89:49.
from Egypt. Ps 80:8, 12-14.
forsaken us. Dt 31:17. 2 Ch 15:2. Ps 27:9. Is 41:17. Je 23:33.
14 **the Lord**. ver. +11.
  Go in. Jg 4:6. Jsh 1:5-9. 1 S 12:11. 1 Ch 14:9, 10. He 11:32, 34.
  have not I. Jg 4:6. Jsh 1:9.
15 **wherewith**. Ex 3:11. 4:10. Je 1:6. Lk 1:34.
  my family is poor. Heb. my thousand is the meanest. Ex 18:21-25. 1 S 9:21. 18:23. Mi +5:2.
  the least. Ge 32:10. Ps 68:27. Je 50:45. 1 C 15:9. Ep 3:8.
16 **Surely**. ver. 12. Ex 3:12. Jsh 1:5. Is 41:10, 14-16. Mt 28:20. Mk 16:20. Ac 11:21.
17 **If now**. Ex 33:13, 16.
  sight. Ge 18:3.
  show. ver. 36-40. Ge 15:8-17. Ex 4:1-9. 2 K 20:8-11. Ps 86:17. Is 7:11.
  sign. or, token. Jsh +2:12. Lk 11:29. 2 C 5:7.
18 **Depart not**. Ge 18:3. Nu 14:44.
  bring. Jg 13:15. Ge 18:3, 5. 19:3.
  present. or, meat offering. Le +23:13.
19 **and made**. Jg 13:15-19. Ge 18:6-8.
  a kid. Heb. a kid of the goats. Jg 13:15, 19. 15:1.
  unleavened cakes. Le 2:4.
  an ephah of flour. 1 S 1:24.
  basket. Ge 40:16-18. Ex 29:3, 23, 32. Le 8:2, 26, 31. Nu 6:15, 17, 19.
  broth. ver. 20. Is 65:4.
  pot. Nu 11:8. 1 S 2:14.
20 **lay them**. Jg 13:19.
  pour out. Ex 4:9. Le 14:41. 1 K 18:33, 34.
21 **rose up**. 1 Ch +21:26.
  out of. Jb 29:6. Ps 81:16.
  rock. Ex 17:6.
22 **perceived**. Jg 13:21. Lk 24:31.
  Alas. Jg 11:35. Jsh 7:7. 2 K 3:10. 6:5, 15. Je 1:6. 4:10. 14:13. 30:7. 32:17. Ezk 4:14. 9:8. 11:13. 20:49. Jl 1:15.
  O Lord. 1 S 20:12. Jn 20:28.
  God. Jg 16:28. Ge 15:2, 8. Dt 3:24. 9:26. Jsh 7:7. 2 S 7:18.
  because. Ge +32:30. Jn 12:41.
  face to face. Dt +5:4.
23 **Peace be**. Ge 32:30. +43:23. Ps 85:8. Da 10:19. Ro 1:7.
24 **built**. Jg 21:4. Ge 33:20. Jsh 22:10, 26-28.
  altar. Ge +8:20. +13:18.
  Jehovah-shalom. **S#3073h**. only here. Ex +15:26. that is, *the Lord send peace*. Ge 22:14. Ex 17:15. Je 23:6. 33:16. Ezk 48:35.
  Shalom. Le 3:1. 7:11. Is 9:6. 26:3. Lk 2:14. Jn 14:27. 16:33. Ro 5:1. 15:13. Ph 4:7. Ep 2:14, 15, 17. Col 1:20. He 7:1, 2.
  unto this day. Jg 1:21. Ge +19:38. Dt +29:4. Jsh +4:9.
  Ophrah. Jg 8:32.

25 Take thy father's. Ge 35:2. Jb 22:23. Ps 101:2.

even. *or*, and.

throw. 1 K 18:21, 30. 19:10, 14. Mt 6:24. 2 C 6:15-17.

Baal. i.e. *possessor, owner*, **S#1168h**. ver. 28, 30, 31, 32. Jg 2:11, 13. 8:33. 10:6, 10. 1 S 7:4. 12:10. 1 K 16:31, 32. 18:18, 19, 26, 40. 19:18. 2 K 3:2. 10:18, 22, 28. 11:18. 17:16. 21:3. 23:4. 1 Ch 4:33. 5:5. 8:30. 9:36. 2 Ch 24:7. Je 2:8, 23. 7:9. 9:14. 11:13, 17. 12:16. 19:5. 23:13, 27. 32:29, 35. Ho 2:8, 13, 17. 11:2. 13:1. Zp 1:4.

thy father. Mt 10:37. Ac 4:19. 5:29.

cut down. Ex +23:24.

grove. 2 K +17:10.

26 build. 2 S 24:18.

altar. Ge +13:18.

rock. Heb. strong place. Da 11:7, 10, 31. Na 1:7.

the ordered place. *or*, an orderly manner. Ex 39:37. Le 24:6. 1 S 4:2. 1 Ch 12:38. 1 C 14:33, 40.

27 and did. Dt 4:1, 2. Mt 16:24. Jn 2:5. 15:14. Ga 1:16. 1 Th 2:4.

he did it. Ps 112:5. Jn 3:2.

28 cast down. ver. 30, 31, 32.

29 they said, Gideon. i.e. *they*, some of the people who may have noticed the operations.

30 Bring. Je 26:11. 50:38. Jn 16:2. Ac 26:9. Ph 3:6.

31 Will ye plead. Ex 23:2. Nu 14:6. Ep 5:11.

let him be. Dt 13:5, etc. 17:2-7. 1 K 18:40.

if he be. 1 K 18:27, 29. Ps 115:4-7. Is 41:23. 46:1, 7. Je 10:5, 11. 1 C 8:4.

32 Jerubbaal. *that is*, Let Baal plead. **S#3378h**. Jg 7:1. 8:29, 35. 9:1, 2, 5, 16, 19, 24, 28, 57. 1 S 12:11. 2 S 11:21, Jerubbesheth: that is, Let the shameful *thing* plead. Je 11:13. Ho 9:10.

33 Then all. Ps 3:1. 27:2, 3. 118:10-12. Is 8:9, 10. Ro 8:35-39.

children. ver. +3. 1 Ch 5:19, 20.

went over. Jg 7:24. Jsh 3:16, 17.

the valley. 1 Ch +4:3.

34 the Spirit. Heb. *ruach*, Ge +41:38. Jg 3:10. 13:25. 14:19. 15:14. 1 S 10:6. 11:6. 16:14. 1 Ch 12:18. 2 Ch 24:20. Ps 51:11. 1 C 12:8-11.

came upon. Heb. clothed. 1 Ch 12:18. 2 Ch 24:20. Ro 13:14. Ga 3:27.

blew. Jg 3:27. Nu 10:3.

Abiezer. ver. 11. Jg 8:2. Jsh 17:2.

was gathered. Heb. was called. Jg 4:13. 7:23, 24. 18:22, 23. 1 S 14:20.

35 messengers. 2 Ch 30:6-12.

Manasseh. *Nu* +1:10.

Naphtali. Nu +1:15.

36 If thou wilt. ver. 14, 17-20. Ex 4:1-9. 2 K 20:8, 9. Ps 103:13, 14. Mt 16:1. or, art savior of Israel. 1 S 14:39. 2 K 13:5. Is 43:3. 45:15.

37 Behold. Dt 32:2. Ps 72:6. Ho 6:3, 4. 14:5.

floor. or, threshing floor. Ge +50:10.

dew. Ge 27:28, 39.

only. Ps 147:19, 20. Mt 10:5, 6. 15:24.

dry. or, drought. Ge 31:40.

then shall I know. 1 S 14:8-10. Lk 2:12. 11:29.

38 early. Ge +19:27.

thrust. or, presseth. Jb 39:15. Is 1:6.

wringed. Ps 75:8. Is 51:17. Ezk 23:34.

a bowl. Jg 5:25. Is 35:7.

39 Let not thine. Ge 18:32. Ex 32:22.

prove. Ge 22:1. Ec 2:1.

let it now. Ge +22:15. 1 S 10:22.

dry. Ps 107:33-35. Is 35:6, 7. 43:19, 20. 50:2. Mt 8:12. 21:43. Ac 13:46. 22:21. 28:28. Ro 11:12-22.

40 did so. 2 K 12:7, 10. 13:9, 18. Ps 119:105. Pr 1:4. 3:5, 6. Je 10:23. Ro 10:17. 2 C 5:7. 2 T 3:16, 17.

JUDGES 7

1 Jerubbaal. It appears that Jerubbaal had now become the surname of Gideon. Jg +6:32.

rose up. Ge 22:3. Jsh 3:1. 6:12. Ec 9:10.

Harod. i.e. *trembling*, **S#5878h**, only here. 2 S 23:8, 25.

Midianites. Jg 6:33.

Moreh. Ge 12:6. Dt 11:29, 30.

2 too many. 1 S 14:6. 2 Ch 14:11. Is 40:29. Zc 4:6. 12:7. 1 C 1:27-29. 2:4, 5. 2 C 4:7. 10:4, 5. 12:10.

Israel. Dt 32:27. Is 2:11, 17. Je 9:23. Ro 3:27. 11:18. 1 C 1:29. 2 C 4:7. Ep 2:9. Ja 4:6.

Mine own. Dt 8:17. Is 10:13. Ezk 28:2, 17. Da 4:30. Hab 1:16. Zc 4:6.

3 Whosoever. Dt 20:8. Mt 13:21. Lk 14:25-33. Re 17:14. 21:8.

mount Gilead. 1 S 31:1. 2 S 1:21.

twenty. Mt 20:16.

4 people. Ps 33:16.

I will. Ge 22:1. 1 S 16:7. Jb 23:10. Ps 7:9. 66:10. Je 6:27-30. Ml 3:2, 3.

5 lappeth. Lk 16:10.

7 By the. ver. 18-22. 1 S 14:6. Is 41:14-16.

8 trumpets. Jg 3:27. Le 23:24. +25:9. Nu 10:9. Jsh 6:4, 20. Is 27:13. 1 C 15:52.

unto his tent. Jg 19:9mg.

in the valley. Jg 6:32.

9 the same. Ge 46:2, 3. Jb 4:13. 33:15, 16. Mt 1:20. 2:13. Ac 18:9, 10. 27:23.

Arise. Jsh 1:5-9. Is 41:10-16. 43:1, 2.

I have delivered. Jg 3:10, 28. 4:14, 15. 2 Ch 16:8, 9. 20:17.

10 if thou fear. Jg 4:8, 9. Ex 4:10-14.

Phurah. i.e. *a branch or bough; fruitful, foliage*, **S#6513h**. ver. 11.

thy servant. ver. 13. Jg 6:27.

11 thou shalt. ver. 13-15. Ge +18:10. 24:14. 27:5, 6. 1 S 14:8-12.

thine hands. 1 S 23:16. Ezr 6:22. Ne 6:9. Is 35:3, 4. 2 C 12:9, 10. Ep 3:16. 6:10. Ph 4:13.

armed men. *or*, ranks by five. Ex 13:18mg.

12　**the Midianites**. Jg 6:3, 5, 33. 1 K 4:30.

grasshoppers. Jg 8:10. 2 Ch 14:9-12. Ps 3:1. 33:16. 118:10-12. Is 8:9, 10.

for multitude. Is 60:6.

as the sand. Ge +22:17.

13　**lo, a cake**. Jg 3:15, 31. 4:9, 21. 6:15. Is 41:14, 15. Ho 12:10. 1 C 1:27.

14　**his fellow**. Nu 22:38. 23:5, 20. 24:10-13. Jb 1:10.

into his hand. Ex 15:14, 15. Jsh 2:9, 24. 5:1. 2 K 7:6, 7.

15　**interpretation thereof**. Heb. breaking thereof. Ge 40:8. 41:11. **S#7667h**. Le 21:19 (broken). 24:20 (breach). Jb 41:25 (breakings). Pr 15:4. 16:18 (destruction). Is +51:19mg.

worshipped. Ge 24:26, 27, 48. Ex 4:30, 31. 2 Ch 20:18, 19.

Arise. Jg 4:14. 2 C 10:4-6.

16　**a trumpet**. Heb. trumpets in the hand of all of them.

empty. 1 C 1:27, 28. 2 C 4:7.

lamps. *or*, fire-brands, *or* torches. Jg 15:4, 5. Ge 15:17. Jb 12:5.

17　**Look on**. Jg 9:48. Mt 16:24. 1 C 11:1. He 13:7. 1 P 5:3.

do likewise. Jn 13:15.

18　**blow ye**. ver. 20.

The sword. 1 S 17:47. 2 Ch 20:15-17.

19　**in the beginning**. Ex 14:24. Mt 25:6. 1 Th 5:2, 3. Re 16:15.

they blew. ver. 8.

brake. ver. 16. Ps 2:9. Je 13:13, 14. 19:1-11.

20　**blew**. Nu 10:1-10. Jsh 6:4, 16, 20. Is 27:13. 1 C 15:52. 1 Th 4:16.

brake. 2 C 4:7. He 11:4. 2 P 1:15.

sword. Dt +32:41.

21　**stood**. Ex 14:13, 14. 2 Ch 20:17. Is 30:7, 15.

all the host. Ex 14:25. 2 K 7:6, 7. Jb 15:21, 22. Pr 28:1.

22　**blew**. Jsh 6:4, 16, 20. 2 C 4:7.

the Lord. 1 S 14:16-20. 2 Ch 20:22, 23. Ps 83:9. Is 9:4, 19. 19:2. Je 51:46. Ezk 38:21. Hg 2:22. Zc 14:13. Mt 24:7. Re 6:4.

against his. Zc 14:13.

Bethshittah. i.e. *house (or place) of shittim wood; the acacia house; house of the scourge*, **S#1029h**.

in. *or*, toward.

Zererath. i.e. *cooling; straitness*, **S#6888h**. Probably the same as Zartanah, 1 K 4:12.

border. Heb. lip. Ge 11:1mg. Ex 39:19. 1 K 9:26mg. 2 K +2:13mg. Jb 2:10. 11:2mg. Pr 10:8mg, 10mg. 17:7mg, 28. Is 19:18mg. 36:5mg. 57:19. Ezk 3:5mg. 47:7mg. Da 12:5mg. Zp 3:9mg.

Abelmeholah. i.e. *a meadow of dancing;*

mourning of dancing, **S#65h**. 1 K 4:12. 19:16.

Tabbath. i.e. *good*, **S#2888h**.

23　**gathered**. Jg 6:35. 1 S 14:21, 22.

24　**sent**. Jg 3:27. Ro 15:30. Ph 1:27.

mount. Jsh +13:6. +17:15.

take before. Jg 3:28. 12:5.

Beth-barah. i.e. *house or place of passage*, **S#1012h**. Jn 1:28, Bethabara.

25　**two princes**. Jg 8:3. Ps 83:11, 12.

rock. Jsh 7:26. Is 10:26.

Oreb. i.e. *a raven*, **S#6159h**. Jg 8:3. Ps 83:11. Is 10:26.

Zeeb. i.e. *a wolf*, **S#2062h**. Jg 8:3. Ps 83:11.

the rock. Jg 6:21.

winepress. Jg 6:11. Nu 18:27, 30. Dt 16:13. 2 K 6:27.

and brought. 1 S 17:51, 54. 2 K 10:6, 7. Mt 14:8, 11.

on the other side. Jg 8:4.

JUDGES 8

1　**the men**. Jg 12:1-6. 2 S 19:41. Jb 5:2. Ec 4:4. Ja 4:5, 6.

Why, etc. Heb. What thing is this thou hast done unto us?

sharply. Heb. strongly. Pr 15:1. 25:15.

2　**What**. 1 C 13:4-7. Ga 5:14, 15. Ph 2:2, 3. Ja 1:19, 20. 3:13-18.

Is not the. Jg 6:15.

Abi-ezer. Jg 6:11, 34.

3　**God**. Jg 7:24, 25. Ps 44:3. 115:1. 118:14-16. Jn 4:37. Ro 12:3, 6. 15:18, 19. 1 C 4:7. Ph +2:3.

Then. Pr 15:1. 16:32. 25:11, 15.

anger. Heb. spirit. Heb. *ruach*, Ge +26:35.

4　**faint**. 1 S 14:28, 29, 31, 32. 30:10. 2 C 4:8, 9, 16. Ga 6:9. He 12:1-4.

5　**Succoth**. Ge 33:17. Ps 60:6.

loaves. Ge 14:18. Dt 23:4. 1 S 25:5, 8, 18. 2 S 17:28, 29. 3 J 6-8.

Zebah. i.e. *a sacrifice*, **S#2078h**. ver. 6, 7, 10, 12, 15, 18, 21. Ps 83:11.

Zalmunna. i.e. *a shadow withheld; shelter is denied*, **S#6759h**. ver. 6, 7, 10, 12, 15, 18, 21. Ps 83:11.

6　**Are the**. Jg 5:23. Ge 25:13. 37:25, 28. 1 S 25:10, 11. 1 K 20:11. 2 K 14:9. Pr 18:23. Ph 2:21.

7　**tear**. Heb. thresh. ver. 16.

8　**Penuel**. Ge 32:30, 31. 1 K 12:25.

9　**I come**. 1 K 22:27, 28.

I will break. ver. 17.

10　**Karkor**. i.e. *soft, level ground; battering down; excavation*, **S#7174h**. If this were the name of a place, it is no where else mentioned.

children. Jg 7:12.

fell an hundred, etc. *or*, an hundred and twenty thousand, every one drawing a sword. Jg 7:22. 20:2, 15, 17, 25, 35, 46. 2 K 3:26. 2 Ch 13:17. 28:6, 8. Is 37:36.

11 **Nobah**. 1 Ch 2:23.
Jogbehah. Nu +32:35, 42.
secure. Jg 18:27. 1 S 15:32. 30:16. 1 Th 5:3.

12 **took**. Jsh 10:16-18, 22-25. Jb 12:16-21.
34:19. Ps 83:11. Am 2:14. Re 6:15, 16. 19:19-21.
discomfited. Heb. terrified. 2 S 17:2.

14 **caught**. Jg 1:24, 25. 1 S 30:11-15.
described. Heb. writ.

15 **upbraid**. ver. 6, 7. Is 32:5, 6. 58:10.

16 **the elders**. ver. 7. Pr 10:13. 19:29. Ezr 2:6.
thorns. Mi 7:4.
taught. Heb. made to know. 1 S 14:12. 16:3.
Pr 26:3. Ro 13:4.

17 **he beat**. ver. 9. 1 K 12:25. Pr 16:18.

18 **Tabor**. Jg +4:6.
As thou art. Ps 12:2. Ju 16.
resembled. Heb. according to the form of,
etc. 1 S 16:18.

19 **sons of my mother**. Ge 27:29. Ps 69:8. SS
1:6.
as the Lord liveth. 1 K +17:1.

20 **Up and slay**. Jsh 10:24, 25. 1 S 15:33. Ps
149:9.

21 **Rise thou**. Jg 9:54. 1 S 31:3, 5. Re 9:6.
his strength. Dt 33:25. Ps 83:11, 12.
slew. Ps 83:1.
ornaments. *or*, ornaments like the moon.
ver. 26. Is 3:18.

22 **Rule thou**. Jg 9:8-15. Dt 17:14, 15. 1 S 8:5,
7. 10:19. 12:12. Jn 6:15.

23 **I will**. Jg 2:18. 10:18. 11:9-11. Lk 22:24-27. 2
C 1:24. 1 P 5:3.
the Lord. 1 S 8:6, 7. 10:19. 12:12. Is 33:22.
63:19.

24 **give me**. Ge 24:22, 53. Ex 12:35. 32:3. 1 P
3:3-5.
because. Ge 16:10, 11. 25:13. 37:25, 28. 1 S
25:11. 1 K 20:11.

26 **collars**. *or*, sweet jewels.
purple. Est 8:15. Je 10:9. Ezk 27:7. Lk 16:19.
Jn 19:2, 5. Re 17:4. 18:12, 16.
chains. ver. 21.

27 **an ephod**. Ex +28:4. Is 8:20.
Ophrah. ver. 32. Jg 6:11, 24. Dt 12:5.
a whoring. ver. 33. Ex +34:15.
a snare. Ex +23:33.

28 **was Midian**. ver +25:2. Ps 83:9-12.
lifted. Ps 83:2. Lk 21:28.
forty years. Jg 3:11, 30. 5:31.

29 **Jerubbaal**. Jg +6:32.
in his own house. Ne 5:14, 15.

30 **threescore**. Jg 9:2, 5. 10:4. 12:9, 14. Ge
46:26. Ex 1:5. 2 K 10:1.
of his body begotten. Heb. going out of his
thigh. Ge +24:2.
many wives. Ge +4:19. Ep 5:31-33.

31 **concubine**. Jg 9:1-5. Ge 16:15. 22:24.
Shechem. Ge 12:6. +33:18.
called. Heb. set. Da 1:7.

Abimelech. Jg 9:18. Ge +20:2.

32 **died in**. Ge 15:15. 25:8. Jsh 24:29, 30. 1 Ch
29:28. Jb 5:26. 42:17.
sepulchre. Heb. *qeber*, Ge +23:4.
Ophrah. ver. 27. Jg 6:24.

33 **as soon**. Jg 2:7-10, 17, 19. Ge +40:23. Jsh
24:31. 2 K 12:2. 2 Ch 24:17, 18. Ps 31:12.
went. ver. 27. Jg 2:17. Ex 34:15, 16. Je 3:9.
Baal-berith. Literally, *the lord of the covenant*,
S#1170h. Jg 9:4, 46.

34 **remembered**. Ps 78:11, 42. 106:13, 21. Ec
12:1. Je 2:32.

35 **showed**. Jg 9:5, 16-19. Ec 9:14, 15.
Jerubbaal. Rather, *Jerubbaal Gideon*; as we
say, Simon Peter, or call a person by his
Christian and surname.

JUDGES 9

1 **Abimelech**. Jg 8:31. 2 S 11:21.
Shechem. Ge +33:18.
brethren. Ge +13:8.
communed. 2 S 15:6. 1 K 12:3, 20. Ps 83:2-
4. Je 18:18.

2 **Whether**, etc. Heb. What *is* good? whether,
etc.
threescore. Jg 8:30.
your bone. Ge +29:14.

3 **spake**. Ps 10:3. Pr 1:11-14.
to follow. Heb. after.
our brother. Ge 29:15.

4 **house**. ver. 46-49. Jg 8:33.
vain. Jg 11:3. 1 S 22:2. 2 Ch 13:7. Jb 30:8. Pr
12:11. Ac 17:5.

5 **at Ophrah**. Jg 6:24.
slew. 2 K 10:17. 11:1, 2. 2 Ch 21:4. Mt 2:16,
20.
Jotham. i.e. *Jehovah is perfect*, **S#3147h**. ver. 7,
21, 57. 2 K 15:5, 7, 30, 32, 36, 38. 16:1. 1 Ch
2:47. 3:12. 5:17. 2 Ch 26:21, 23. 27:1, 6, 7, 9.
Is 1:1. 7:1. Ho 1:1. Mi 1:1. Mt 1:9.

6 **the house**. 2 S 5:9. 2 K 12:20.
plain. *or*, oak. Jsh 24:26. 1 K 12:1, 20, 25.

7 **mount Girizim**. Dt +11:29.
Hearken. Ps 18:40, 41. 50:15-21. Pr 1:28, 29.
21:13. 28:9. Is 1:15. 58:6-10. Mt 18:26-34. Ja
2:13.

8 **The trees**. 2 K 14:9. Ezk 17:3, etc. Da 4:10,
etc.
Reign. Jg 8:22, 23.

9 **fatness**. Ps 23:5. Ro 11:17.
wherewith. Ex 29:2, 7, 40. 35:5, 8, 14. Le
2:1. 1 K 19:15, 16. Ps 89:20. 104:15. Ac 4:27.
10:38. 1 J 2:20.
God. Heb. *elohim*, rather *gods*.
to be promoted over the trees. Heb. up
and down for other trees. Jb 1:7. 2:2.

11 **Should I**. Lk 13:6, 7.

13 **cheereth**. Nu 15:5, 7, 10. 28:7. Ps 104:15. Pr
31:6, 7. Ec 10:19. SS 1:2. Is 55:1. Zc 10:7.

14 bramble. *or*, thistle. 2 K 14:9.

15 shadow. Ps +91:1. Da 4:12. Mt 13:32.
let fire. ver. 20, 49. Nu 21:28. Is 1:31. Ezk 19:14. Ga 5:15.
the cedars. 2 K 14:9. Ps 104:16. Is 2:13. 37:24. Ezk 31:3.

16 according. Jg 8:35.

17 fought. Jg 7:20. 8:4-10.
adventured his life. Heb. cast his life. Heb. *nephesh*, soul. Ge +44:30; Ge +9:5. Jg 5:18. 12:3. Est 4:16. Ro 5:8. 16:4. Re 12:11.

18 are risen. ver. 5, 6. Jg 8:35. Ps 109:4.
Abimelech. ver. 6, 14. Jg 8:31.

19 rejoice. Is 8:6. Ph 3:3. Ja 4:16.

20 let fire come out. ver. 15, 23, 56, 57. Jg 7:22. 2 Ch 20:22, 23. Ps 21:9, 10. 28:4. 52:1-5. 120:3, 4. 140:10.

21 Beer. Nu 21:16. Jsh 19:8. 2 S 20:14.

23 A.M. 2771. B.C. 1233. An. Ex. Is. 258.
God sent. ver. 15, 20. 1 S 16:14-16. 18:9, 10. 1 K 12:15. 22:22, 23. 2 Ch 10:15. 18:19-22. Is 19:2, 14. Am +3:6. 2 Th 2:11, 12. Ja 1:13, 14.
dealt. ver. 16. Is 33:1. Mt 7:2.
evil spirit. Heb. *ruach*, used here of an evil spirit being, whether evil angel or demon. For the other uses of *ruach*, see Ge 6:3. 1 S 16:14-16, 23. 18:10. 19:9. 1 K 22:21-23. 2 Ch 18:20-22. Mt +8:16.

24 That the. 1 S 15:33. 1 K 2:32. Est 9:25. Ps 7:15, 16. Pr 26:27. Je 51:56. Mt 7:2. 23:34-36.
aided him in the killing of. Heb. strengthened his hands to kill. Ge +6:13.

25 set liers. Jsh 8:4, 12, 13. Pr 1:11, 13.

26 Gaal. i.e. *a loathing*, **S#1603h**. ver. 28, 30, 31, 35, 36, 37, 39, 41.
brethren. Ge 13:8. 19:7.

27 merry. *or*, songs. Ps 4:7. Is 16:9, 10. 24:7-9. Je 25:30. Am 6:3-6.
the house. ver. 4. Jg 16:23. Ex 32:6, 19. Da 5:1-4, 23.
did eat. Is 22:12-14. Lk 12:19, 20. 17:26-29.
cursed. Le 24:11. 1 S 17:43. Ps 109:17.

28 Who is Abimelech. 1 S 25:10. 2 S 20:1. 1 K 12:16.
Zebul. i.e. *habitation; abiding*, **S#2083h**. ver. 30, 36, 38, 41.
Hamor. Ge 34:2, 6.

29 would to God. 2 S 15:4. 1 K 20:11. Ps 10:3. Ro 1:30, 31.
Increase thine army. 2 S 2:14-17. 2 K 14:8. 18:23. Is 36:8, 9.

30 kindled. *or*, hot. Jg 10:7.

31 privily. Heb. craftily, *or*, to Tormah. ver. 41. Ps 119:118.

32 by night. Jb 24:14-17. Ps 36:4. Pr 1:11-16. 4:16. Ro 3:15.

33 early. Ge +19:27.
as thou shalt find. Heb. as thine hand shall find. Le 25:26mg. 1 S 10:7. 25:8. Ec 9:10.

35 Gaal. ver. 26.
the people. ver. 44.

36 seest the shadow. Ezk 7:7. Mk 8:24.

37 middle. Heb. navel. Ezk 38:12mg.
Meonenim. *or*, the regarders of the times. Dt 18:14. i.e. *observers of clouds*, **S#6049h** (2 K +21:6), not mentioned elsewhere. 1 Ch +12:32. Ps 74:9.

38 Where is. ver. 28, 29. 2 S 2:26, 27. 2 K 14:8-14. Je 2:28.

39 Shechem. 1 K 12:25.

40 he fled before. 1 K 20:18-21, 30.

41 Arumah. i.e. *a high place; exalted*, **S#725h**. ver. 31. 2 K 23:36.
Zebul. ver. 28, 30.

44 rushed forward. ver. 15, 20. Ga 5:15.

45 he took. ver. 20.
beat. 2 K 3:25. Ja 2:13.
with salt. Dt +29:23.

46 tower. Ge 11:4, 5.
an hold. or, high place. ver. 4, 27, 49. Jg 8:33. 1 S 13:6. 1 K 18:26. 2 K 1:2-4. Ps 115:8. Is 28:15-18. 37:38. 42:13. Zp 1:14.
Berith. i.e. *covenant; to eat together*, **S#1286h**, only here. ver. 4. Jg 8:33.

48 Zalmon. i.e. *a great shade*. Ps 68:14.
What ye. Jg 7:17, 18. Pr 1:11, 12.
me do. Heb. I have done.

49 put them. ver. 15, 20. Ga 5:15. Ja 3:16.

50 Thebez. i.e. *brilliancy; he gushed out*, **S#8405h**. 2 S 11:21.

52 Abimelech came. ver. 48, 49. 2 K 14:10. 15:16.

53 woman. ver. 15, 20. 2 S 11:21. 20:21. Jb 31:3. Je 49:20.
brake. Jg +10:8mg.

54 Draw thy. 1 S 31:4, 5.
And his young man. Jg 8:21.

55 when the men. 2 S 18:16. 20:21, 22. 1 K 22:35, 36. Pr 22:10.

56 God rendered. ver. 24. Ge +6:13. Jb 31:3. Ps 9:12. 11:6. 58:10, 11. 94:23. Pr 5:22. Mt 7:2. Ac 28:4. Ga 6:7. Re 19:20, 21.

57 upon them. ver. 20, 24, 45. Jsh 6:26. 1 K 16:34. Jb 31:3. Ps 94:23. Pr 5:22.

JUDGES 10

1 A.M. 2772. B.C. 1232. An. Ex. Is. 259.
arose. Jg 2:16. 3:9.
defend. *or*, deliver. Heb. save. ver. 12, 13. Jg 2:16.
Shamir. Jsh 15:48. 1 K 16:23, 24, Shemer.

3 A.M. 2795. B.C. 1209. An. Ex. Is. 282.
a Gileadite. Nu +26:29.

4 rode. Jg 5:10. 12:14.
called. Nu 32:41. Dt 3:14.
Havoth-jair. *or*, the villages of Jair.

5 Camon. i.e. *abounding in stalks; an elevation; standing*, **S#7056h**.

6 A.M. 2817. B.C. 1187. An. Ex. Is. 304.
did evil. Jg 2:11-13. 4:1. 6:1. 13:1. 1 S 12:10.
A.M. 2799. B.C. 1205. An. Ex. Is. 286.
Baalim. Jg +2:11-14. 2 Ch 28:23. Ps 106:36.
Ashtaroth. Jg +2:13.
the gods of Zidon. 1 K 11:5, 7, 33. 16:31. 2
K 17:16, 29-31. 23:13.
the gods of the Philistines. Jg 16:23. 1 S
5:2. 2 K 1:2, 3. Je 2:13. Ezk 16:25, 26.
forsook. ver. 10, 13. Je +1:16.

7 **was hot**. Jg +2:14.
he sold. Dt +32:30.

8 **that year**. ver. 5. Is 30:13. 1 Th 5:3.
vexed. **S#7492h**. Ex 15:6 (dashed in pieces).
oppressed. Heb. crushed. **S#7533h**. Jg 9:53. Dt
+28:33. 1 S 12:3, 4. 2 K 18:21. 2 Ch 16:10. Jb
20:19mg. Is 42:3 (bruised). 51:23. 58:6. Je
51:34. La 1:15. 3:34. Am +4:1.

9 **passed**. Jg 3:12, 13. 6:3-5. 2 Ch 14:9. 20:1, 2.
distressed. Dt 28:65. 1 S 28:15. 2 Ch 15:5.

10 **cried**. Ps +3:4. 106:43, 44.
forsaken. ver. 6.

11 **did not I**. Jg 2:1-3.
Egyptians. Ex 14:30. 1 S 12:8. Ne 9:9-11. Ps
78:51-53. 106:8-11. He 11:29.
Amorites. Nu 21:21-25, 35. Ps 135:10, 11.
children. Jg 3:11-15.
Philistines. Jg 3:31.

12 **Zidonians**. **S#6722h**. Jg 5:19, etc. 18:7. 1 K
11:1, 5, 33. 16:31. 2 K 23:13. 1 Ch 22:4. Ezk
32:30.
Amalekites. Nu +14:45.
the Maonites. Jsh +15:55. 2 Ch 26:6, 7. Ps
106:42, 43.
ye cried. Ex +22:23.

13 **have forsaken me**. Je +1:16. Jon 2:8.

14 **cry unto**. Dt 32:26-28, 37, 38. 1 K 18:27, 28.
2 K 3:13. Jb 12:1. Pr 1:25-27. Ec 11:9. Is 10:3.
Je 2:28.

15 **We have sinned**. 2 S 12:13. 24:10. Jb 33:27.
Pr 28:13. 1 J 1:8-10.
do thou. Jsh 9:25. 1 S 24:17. Jb 1:21. 2:10.
Jon 2:4. 3:9. Lk 15:18, 19. 23:40, 41.
seemeth, etc. Heb. is good in thine eyes. 1 S
1:23. 3:18. 2 S 10:12. 15:25, 26. 2 K 20:19. 1
Ch 19:13. Ps 39:9. Is 39:8. Ac 21:14. 1 J +5:14.
deliver. 2 S 24:14. Jb 34:31, 32.

16 **they put**. 2 Ch 7:14. 15:8. 33:15. Je 18:7, 8.
Ezk 18:30-32. Ho 14:1-3, 8.
strange gods. Heb. gods of strangers (**S#5236h**,
Ex 12:43mg. Dt +17:15). Ge 35:2, 4. Jsh
24:20. 1 S 7:3.
his soul. Heb. *nephesh*, Ge +34:3; Le +26:11.
Ge 6:6. Ps 78:38, 39. 106:44, 45. Is 63:9, +10.
Je 31:20. Ho 11:8. Lk 15:20. 19:41. Jn 11:34.
Ep 4:30. He 3:10. 4:15.
grieved. Heb. shortened. Ge +6:6. Jb +21:4.
Pr 14:17, 29.

17 **gathered together**. Heb. cried together. Jg
7:23.

Mizpeh. Ge +31:49.

18 **What man**. Jg 1:1. 11:5-8. Is 3:1-8. 34:12.
he shall be. Jg 11:11. 12:7. 1 S 17:25.

JUDGES 11

1 **Jephthah**. i.e. *he opens; whom God sets free,*
S#3316h. ver. 2, 3, 5-15, 28-30, 32, 34, 40.
12:1, 2, 4, 7. Jsh 15:43, Jiphtah. 1 S 12:11. He
11:32, called Jephthae.
a mighty. Jg +6:12. 2 K 5:1.
son of. Dt 23:2.
an harlot. Heb. *zonah*. a woman, an harlot.
or, hostess or inn-keeper. Jg 16:1. Ge 38:21. 1
K 3:16. Is +40:13mg. Je 3:3.

2 **thrust out**. Ge 21:10. Dt 23:2. Ga 4:30.
a strange. Pr 2:16. 5:3, 20. 6:24-26.

3 **from his brethren**. Heb. from the face of.
Tob. i.e. *good; goodness*, **S#2897h**. ver. 5. 2 S
10:6, 8.
vain men. Jg 9:4. 1 S 22:2. 27:2. 30:22-24. Jb
30:1-10. Ac 17:5.

4 A.M. 2817. B.C. 1187. An. Ex. Is. 304.
in process of time. Heb. after days. Jg 10:8.
1 K 18:1. 2 Ch 21:19.

5 **made war**. Jg 10:9, 17, 18.
to fetch. 1 S 10:27. 11:6, 7, 12. Ps 118:22,
23. Ac 7:35-39. 1 C 1:27-29.

7 **Did ye not hate**. Ge 26:27. 37:27. 45:4, 5. Pr
17:17. Is 60:14. Mt 23:37-39. Lk 13:25. Ac
7:9-14. Re 3:9.

8 **the elders**. Ex 8:8, 28. 9:28. 10:17. Jsh
+20:4. 1 K 13:6. Lk 17:3, 4.
we turn. Jg 10:18.

9 **If ye bring**. Nu 32:20-29.

10 **The Lord**. Ge 21:23. 31:50. 1 S 12:5. Je
29:23. 42:5. Ro 1:9. 2 C 11:31.
be witness. Heb. be the hearer between us.
Ge 16:5. 31:48, 50, 52, 53. Dt 1:16. 1 S 24:12.
Je 42:5.
if we do. Ex 20:7. Zc 5:4. Ml +3:5.

11 **head**. ver. 8.
uttered. 1 S 23:9-12. 1 K 3:7-9. 2 C 3:5. Ja
1:5, 17.
Jephthah uttered. Ex +19:8. Jsh 1:8. Pr 3:5,
6. Ph 4:6, 7.
before. Jg 10:17. 20:1. 1 S 10:17. 11:15.
Mizpeh. ver. 29, 34. Jg 10:17. Ge +31:49. Jsh
+15:38.

12 **sent messengers**. Nu 20:14. 21:21. Dt 2:26.
20:10, 11. 2 K 14:8-12. Pr 25:8, 9. Mt 18:15,
16.
What hast. Jsh 22:24. 2 S 16:10. 19:22. 1 K
17:18. 2 K 3:13. 9:18. 2 Ch 35:21. Jb 3:6. Ho
14:8. Jl 3:4. Am 3:6. Mt 8:29. Mk 1:24. 5:7.
Lk 4:34. 5:8. 8:28. Jn +2:4.

13 **Ammon**. Jsh 13:25.
Because Israel. Nu 21:24-26. Pr 19:5, 9.
from Arnon. ver. 18. Nu +21:13.
Jabbok. Ge +32:22.

14 **again unto**. Ps 120:7. Ro 12:18. He 12:14. 1 P 3:11.

15 **Israel took not**. Nu 21:13-15, 27-30. Dt 2:9, 19. 2 Ch 20:10. Ac 17:2. 24:12, 13. 28:23, 30, 31.

16 **walked**. Nu 14:25. Dt 1:40. Jsh 5:6.
came to Kadesh. Ge +14:7.

17 **sent messengers**. Nu 20:14-21. Dt 2:4-8, 29.
the king. Dt 2:9.
abode. Nu 20:1, 16.

18 **went**. Nu 20:22. 21:10-13. 33:37-44. Dt 2:1-8.
compassed. Nu 21:4, etc.
came by. Nu 21:11.
pitched. Nu 21:13. 22:36.

19 **Israel sent**. Nu 21:21-35. Dt 2:26-34. 3:1-17. Jsh 13:8-12.

20 **Sihon trusted not**. Nu 21:23. Dt 2:32.

21 **Lord God**. Ne 9:22. Ps 135:10-12. 136:17-21.
they smote. Nu 21:24, 25. Dt 2:33, 34.
so Israel. Jsh 13:15-32.

22 **And they**. Dt 2:36.
from the wilderness. From Arabia Deserta on the east, to Jordan on the west.

23 **dispossessed**. Ex 34:24. Le 18:24. 20:23. Dt 18:12. Jsh 13:12.

24 **Wilt not thou possess**. 1 K 20:23. 2 K 17:26. Is 36:18.
Chemosh. Nu +21:29.
whomsoever. Dt 9:4, 5. Jsh 3:10. Ps 44:2. 78:55. Mi 4:5.

25 **Balak**. Nu 22:2, etc. +31:8.

26 **Heshbon**. Nu +21:25.
her towns. Heb. daughters. Nu +21:25.
Aroer. Dt 2:36.
three hundred. Jg 3:11, 30. 5:31. 8:28. 9:22. 10:2, 3, 8. 20:46. Nu 1:46. 2:32. 11:21. Jsh 11:18. 23:1.

27 **the Judge**. Ge +18:25. 1 S 2:10. Jb 9:15. 23:7. Ps 7:11. 50:6. 75:7. 82:8. 94:2. 98:9. Ec 11:9. 12:14. Jn 5:22, 23. Ro 14:10-12. 2 C 5:10. 2 T 4:8. He 12:23.
be judge. Ge 16:5. 31:53. 1 S 24:12, 15. Ps 7:8, 9. 2 C 11:11.

28 **hearkened not**. 1 S +25:17. 2 K 14:11. Pr 16:18.

29 **the Spirit**. Heb. *ruach*, Ge +41:38. Jg 3:10. 6:34. 13:25. Nu 11:25. 1 S 10:10. 16:13-15. 1 Ch 12:18.
Jephthah. "Jephthah seems to have been judge only of northeast Israel."
over Mizpeh. ver. +11.

30 **Jephthah vowed a vow**. Ge 31:32. Le +23:38. Nu +30:2. Ezk +17:18. Ac +23:12.

31 **whatsoever**, etc. Heb. that which cometh forth, which shall come forth. Ge 14:17. 18:2. 24:17. Lk 15:20.
shall surely. Le 27:2, 3, 28, 29. 1 S 1:11, 28. 2:18. 14:24, 44. Ps 68:13, 14.
and I will. *or*, or I will, etc. ver. 14-16. Le

32 27:2-5, 11, 12, 28, 29. Nu 30:2. Dt 23:18. Ps 66:13. Is 66:3. Mt 5:29. Mk 12:24. Ac 8:30, 31. 18:24-26. 2 P 3:16.

32 **the Lord**. Jg 1:4. 2:18. 3:10.

33 **Aroer**. Nu +32:34.
Minnith. i.e. *allotment*, S#4511h. Ezk 27:17.
the plain. *or*, Abel. 1 S +6:18.

34 **Mizpeh**. ver. +11.
his daughter. Jg 5:1, etc. Ex +15:20. Ps 148:11, 12.
beside her. *or*, he had not of his own either son or daughter. Heb. of himself.
neither. Zc 12:10. Lk 7:12. 8:42. 9:38.

35 **rent his clothes**. Ge 42:36-38. 2 S 18:33. 2 K +18:37.
Alas. Jg +6:22.
have opened. Jb 3:1. 33:2. Ps +38:13. 49:4. 51:15. 78:2. Pr 8:6. 31:8, 9, 26. Ezk 24:27. Da 10:16. Mt 5:2. 13:35. Lk 1:64. Ac 8:35. 10:34. 18:14. 2 C 6:11. Re 13:6.
my mouth. Le 27:28, 29. Nu 30:2-5. Ps 15:4. Ec 5:2-6. Mt 5:33.
I cannot. Jg 21:1-7, 18. Jsh +9:19. 1 S 14:44, 45. Ps +15:4. Ezk +17:18. Mt 14:7-9. Ac 23:14. Ro 11:29. Ga 3:15.

36 **according to**. Ps 22:25. 76:11.
forasmuch. Jg 16:28-30. 2 S 18:19, 31. 19:30. Ac 20:24. 21:13. Ro 16:4. Ph 2:30.

37 **go up and down**. Heb. go and go down.
bewail. 1 S 1:6. Lk 1:25.
virginity. Ge +11:30. +29:31. 30:23. Ps 127:3. 1 C 7:32. 2 C 11:2.

39 **did with**. ver. 31. Le 27:28, 29. Dt 12:31. Is 66:3.
to his vow. 1 S 1:11, 22, 24, 28. 2:18.
knew no man. Ge +4:1. 19:8.
custom. *or*, ordinance. Le 18:30. 2 Ch 35:25. Je 10:3mg. 32:11.

40 **yearly**. Heb. from year to year. Jg 17:10. +21:19mg. 1 S 1:3mg. Ne +13:6mg.
lament. *or*, to talk with. Jg 5:11.
four. 1 K 9:25.

JUDGES 12

1 **gathered**. Heb. were called. Jg +6:34, 35. 7:23. 10:17.
Wherefore. Jg 8:1. 2 S 19:41-43. Ps 109:4. Ec 4:4. Jn 10:32.
we will burn. Jg 14:15. 15:6. Pr 27:3, 4. Ja 3:16. 4:1, 2.

2 **I and my**. Jg 11:12, etc.

3 **put my life**. Heb. *nephesh*, soul, Ge +44:30. Jg 9:17. 1 S 19:5. 28:21. Jb 13:14. Ps 119:109. Ro 16:4. Re 12:11.
wherefore. Jg 11:27. 2 Ch 13:12.

4 **and the men**. Jg 11:10. Nu 32:39, 40. Dt 3:12-17.
fugitives. 1 S 25:10. Ne 4:4. Ps 78:9. Pr 12:13. 15:1.

5 **the passages**. Jg 3:28. 7:24. Jsh 2:7. 22:11.
6 **Say now**. Jg 18:3. Ne 13:24. Zp 3:9. Mt 26:73. Mk 14:70.
  Shibboleth. **S#7641h**. Ge 41:5 (ears of corn), 6, 7, 22, 23, 24, 26, 27; Ru 2:2; Jb 24:24; Ps 69:2 (floods), 15; Is 17:5, 5; 27:12; Zc 4:12. Jg 18:3. 2 K 8:21. 1 Ch 6:36. Ne 13:24. Mt 26:73. Mk 14:70. Ac 2:6, 7.
  sibboleth. i.e. *a burden; old age*, **S#5451h**, only here.
  there fell. Pr 17:14. 18:19. Ec 10:12. Mt 12:25. Ga 5:15.
  forty and two. Nu 26:37.
  thousand. or, chiefs. Jsh +22:21.
7 **Jephthah**. He 11:32.
  Giliadite. Nu +26:29.
8 **Ibzan**. i.e. *tin; great fatigue; beautiful*, **S#78h**. ver. 10. A.M. 2823. B.C. 1181. An. Ex. Is. 310. "He seems to have been only a civil judge to do justice in North-east Israel."
  Bethlehem. Ge 35:19. 1 S 16:1. Mi 5:2. Mt 2:1.
9 **thirty sons**. ver. 14. Jg 10:4.
11 A.M. 2830. B.C. 1174. An. Ex. Is. 317.
  Elon. Ge +26:34. "A civil judge in North-east Israel."
  Zebulonite. **S#2075h**. ver. 12. Nu 26:27.
12 **Aijalon**. Jsh +10:12. A city different from that in Jg 1:35 (Young).
13 A.M. 2840. B.C. 1164. An. Ex. Is. 327.
  Abdon. i.e. *servile; service; servitude*, **S#5658h**. ver. 15. 1 Ch 8:23, 30. 9:36. 2 Ch 34:20. "A civil judge also in North-east Israel."
  Hillel. i.e. *praising*, **S#1985h**. ver. 15.
14 **nephews**. Heb. sons' sons. Ge 21:23. Jb 18:19. Is 14:22. 1 T 5:4.
  rode. Jg 5:10. 10:4.
15 A.M. 2848. B.C. 1156. An. Ex. Is. 335.
  Pirathonite. **S#6553h**. ver. 13. 2 S 23:30. 1 Ch 11:31. 27:14.
  Pirathon. i.e. *just revenge*, **S#6552h**.
  in the mount. Nu +14:45.

JUDGES 13

1 **did**. Heb. added to commit, etc. Jg 2:11. 3:7. 4:1. 6:1. 10:6. Ro 2:6.
  in the sight. Je 13:23.
  delivered. "This seems a partial captivity." **into the**. 1 S 12:9.
2 **Zorah**. Jsh +19:41.
  Danites. **S#1839h**. Jg 18:1, 11, 30. Ge %49:16. 1 Ch 12:35.
  Manoah. i.e. *rest*, **S#4495h**. ver. 8, 9, 11-13, 15-17, 19-22. Jg 16:31.
  barren. Ge +11:30.
3 **the angel**. Zc +12:8. Lk 1:11, 28, etc.
  but thou. Ge 17:16. 18:10. 1 S 1:20. 2 K 4:16. Lk 1:13, 31.
4 **drink not**. ver. 14. Nu 6:2, 3. Lk 1:15.

  eat not. Le 11:27, 47. Ac 10:14.
5 **no razor**. Nu 6:2, 3, 5. 1 S 1:11. La 4:7. Am 2:11. Mt 2:23.
  begin. 1 S 7:13. 2 S 8:1. 1 Ch 18:1.
6 **A man**. ver. 8. Dt +33:1.
  countenance was. Mt 28:3, 4. Lk 9:29. Ac 6:15. Re 1:16.
  terrible. ver. 22. Ge 28:16, 17. Ex 3:2-6. Da 8:17. 10:5-11. Jl 2:11. Mt 28:4. Re 1:17.
  his name. ver. 17, 18. Ge 32:29. Lk 1:19.
7 **conceive**. Ge 16:11.
  wine. ver. 4.
  strong drink. or, sweet drink.
  womb. *or*, belly. ver. 5.
8 **intreated**. Ge 25:21.
  my Lord. Ge 15:2, 8.
  man of God. ver. 6.
  teach us. Ge 46:28 (direct). Ex +13:8. Jb 34:32. Pr 3:5, 6. Ac 9:6. Ep +6:4. 2 T +3:15.
  what we shall. Ex 2:9.
9 **hearkened**. Ge 30:17. Jsh 10:14. Ps 65:2. Mt 7:7-11.
10 **Behold**. Jn 1:41, 42. 4:28, 29.
12 **How shall we order the child**. Heb. what shall be the manner of the child? Ge +18:19. 40:13 (manner). Pr 4:4. 22:6. Ep 6:4.
  how shall we do unto him. or, what shall he do? Heb. what shall be his work? Ge 5:29.
14 **neither**. ver. 4. Nu 6:3-5.
  all that I. Dt 12:32. Mt 28:20. Jn 2:5. 15:14. 2 Th 3:4.
15 **let us**. Jg 6:18, 19. Ge 18:3-5.
  a kid. Ge 27:9, 16.
  for thee. Heb. before thee.
16 **I will not**. 1 S 28:23.
  bread. Ge +3:19.
  and if, etc. Rather, "but if thou wilt offer," etc.
  unto the. ver. 23. Jg 6:26.
17 **thy name**. ver. 6. Ge 32:27. Ex 3:13.
  do thee honor. 1 S 9:7, 8. 1 K 14:3. Jn 5:23.
18 **Why askest**. ver. 6. Ge 32:29.
  secret. *or*, wonderful. Ex 15:11. Dt 29:29. Ps 77:11, 14. 88:10, 12. 119:129. 139:6. Pr 30:4. Is 9:6. Da +8:13mg.
19 **took**. Jg 6:19, 20. 1 K 18:30-38.
  did wonderously. 1 Ch 21:26.
20 **when the flame**. 2 K 2:11. 1 Ch +21:26. Ps 47:5. He 1:3.
  fell on. Ge +17:3.
21 **knew**. Jg 6:22. Ho 12:4, 5.
22 **We shall**. Ge +32:30. Dt 4:33. 5:26.
  surely. Ge +2:16.
  we have. Jn +1:18.
23 **his wife**. Ec 4:9, 10. 1 C 12:21.
  were pleased to. Jsh 11:20. 1 S 2:25. 2 S 15:26.
  he would not. Ge 4:4, 5. Ps 86:17.
  burnt offering. Le +23:12.
  meat offering. Le +23:13.

he have showed. Ps 25:14. 27:13. Pr 3:32. Jn 14:20, 23. 15:15.

24 A.M. 2849. B.C. 1155. An. Ex. Is. 336. **Samson**. i.e. *a little sun* or *servant*, **S#8123h**. Jg ch 14, 15, 16. He 11:32.

the child. 1 S 3:19. Lk 1:80. 2:52.

25 **the Spirit**. Heb. *ruach*, Ge +41:38. Jg 3:10. 6:34. 11:29. 1 S 11:6. Mt 4:1. Jn 3:34.

move. Ge 41:8. Ps 77:4 (troubled).

the camp of Dan. Heb. Mahaneh-dan, as Jg 18:12.

between. Jg 18:11. Jsh 15:33.

Eshtaol. Jsh +15:33.

JUDGES 14

1 **Timnath**. Ge +38:12, 13. Jsh 15:10. 19:43. 2 Ch 28:18.

saw. Ge 6:2. 34:1, 2. 2 S 11:2. Jb 31:1. Ps 119:37. 1 J 2:16.

2 **get her**. Nu +12:1. 2 K 14:9.

3 **thy brethren**. Ge 13:8. 24:3, 4, 27. 27:46. Dt 7:3. 2 C 6:14.

uncircumcised. Jg 15:18. Ge 34:14. Ex 34:12-16. Dt 7:2, 3. 1 S 14:6. 16:26, 36. 31:4. 2 S 1:20.

she pleaseth me well. Heb. she is right in mine eyes. ver. 7. Nu 23:27. Jsh +22:30mg. 1 S 18:20, 26. 2 S 19:6. 1 K 9:12.

4 **it was of the Lord**. Jsh 11:20. 1 K 12:15. 2 K 6:33. 2 Ch 10:15. 22:7. 25:20. Ps 115:3. Am +3:6.

had dominion. Jg 13:1. 15:11. Dt 28:47, 48.

5 **lion roared**. 1 P 5:8.

against him. Heb. in meeting him. Jg 15:14.

6 **the Spirit**. Heb. *ruach*, Ge +41:38. Jg 3:10. 11:29. 13:25. 1 S 11:6.

came mightily. 2 C 10:4.

rent him. Jg 15:8, 15. 16:30. 1 S 17:34-37, 46. Zc 4:6. 1 J 3:8.

he told. Is 42:2. Mt 11:29.

8 **to take her**. Ge 29:21. Mt 1:20.

9 **he took**. 1 S 14:25-30. Pr 25:15.

10 **made there**. Ge +19:3.

11 **saw him**. 1 S 10:23. 16:6.

thirty. Mt 9:15. Jn 3:29.

12 **a riddle**. 1 K 10:1. Ps +78:2. Ezk 17:2. 20:49. Lk 14:7. Jn 16:29. 1 C 13:12mg.

the seven. Ge 29:27, 28. 2 Ch 7:8.

sheets. *or*, shirts. Pr 31:24. Is 3:23. Mt 27:28. Mk 14:51, 52.

change. ver. 19. Ge 45:22. 2 K 5:5, 22. Mt 6:19. Ja 5:2.

14 **Out of the eater**. Ge 3:15. Dt 8:15, 16. 1 K 17:6. 2 Ch 20:2, 25. Is 53:10-12. Ro 5:3-5. 8:37. 2 C 4:17. 12:9, 10. Ph 1:12-20. He 2:14, 15. 12:10, 11. Ja 1:2-4. 1 P 2:24.

came forth. Is 55:10.

they could. Pr 24:7. Mt 13:11. Ac 8:31.

15 **Entice**. Jg 16:5. Ge 3:1-6. Pr 1:11. 5:3. 6:26. Mi 7:5.

lest we burn. Jg 12:1. 15:6.

take that we have. Heb. possess us, *or*, impoverish us. Dt 28:42mg.

16 **Thou dost**. Jg 16:15.

I have not. Ge 2:24. Mi 7:5.

17 **the seven**. *or*, the rest of the seven days.

he told. Jg 16:16, 17.

she lay. Jg 16:6, 13, 16. Ge 3:6. Jb 2:9. Pr 7:21. Lk 11:8. 18:4, 5.

and she told. Pr 2:16, 17.

18 **What is**. Mt 21:23-26. Ro 9:19, 20.

19 **the Spirit**. Heb. *ruach*, Ge +41:38. ver. 6. Jg 3:10. 13:25. 15:14. 1 S 11:6.

Ashkelon. i.e. *weight; balance*, **S#831h**. Je 25:20. 47:5, 7. Am 1:8. Zp 2:4, 7. Zc 9:5.

spoil. *or*, apparel. 2 S 2:21.

change of garments. ver. 13. Ge 45:22. 2 K 5:5, 22, 23.

20 **given to**. Jg 15:2.

his friend. Ps 55:12, 13. SS 5:1. Je 9:5. Mi 7:5. Mt 26:49, 50. Jn 3:29. 13:18.

JUDGES 15

1 **a kid**. Ge 38:17. Lk 15:29.

I will go. Ge 6:4. 29:21.

suffer. Ge +31:7.

2 **I verily**. Jg 14:16, 20. Ac 26:9.

I gave. Jg 14:20. Ge 38:14.

take her. Heb. let her be thine.

3 **Now shall**, etc. *or*, Now shall I be blameless from the Philistines, though, etc. Jg 14:15.

4 **caught three hundred**. Ps 63:10. SS 2:15. La 5:18.

firebrands. *or*, torches. Jg 7:16mg.

5 **he let them go**. Ex 22:6. 2 S 14:30.

6 **Timnite**. i.e. *one from Timnah*, **S#8554h**.

and burnt. Jg 12:1. 14:15. Pr 10:24. 22:8. Ho 8:7. 1 Th 4:6.

7 **Though**. Jg 14:4, 19. Ro 12:19.

8 **smote them**. Is 25:10. 63:3, 6.

Etam. 2 Ch 11:5, 6.

9 **Lehi**. i.e. *a jawbone*, **S#3896h**. ver. 14, 17mg, 19.

11 **went**. Heb. went down.

the rock Etam. 1 Ch 4:32.

Philistines. Jg 13:1. 14:4. Dt 28:13, 47, 48. Ps 106:41.

12 **to bind thee**. Mt 27:2. Ac 7:25.

fall. Jg 8:21. 1 K 2:25, 34.

13 **surely**. Ge +2:16.

bound him. Ac +21:33.

14 **the Philistines**. Jg 5:30. 16:24. Ex 14:3, 5. 1 S 4:5. Jb 20:5. Mi 7:8.

the Spirit. Heb. *ruach*, Ge +41:38. Jg 3:10. 14:6, 19. Zc 4:6.

came mightily. Jg 16:20. Ac 5:3, 4.

the cords. Jg 16:9, 12. 1 S 17:35. Ps 18:34. 118:11. Ph 4:13.

loosed. Heb. were melted. Dt +20:8mg.

15 **new**. Heb. moist. Is 1:6.

jawbone. Dt 18:3. 1 K 22:24.

slew. or, smiteth. ver. 16. Jg 3:31. 4:21. 7:16. Le 26:8. Jsh 23:10. 1 S 14:6, 14. 17:49, 50. 1 C 1:27, 28.

a thousand. Jg 3:31. 12:6mg. 1 Ch 11:11.

16 **with the jawbone**. Nu 16:15.

heaps upon heaps. Heb. an heap, two heaps.

17 **Ramath-lehi**. i.e. *the high place of the jawbone*. *that is*, the lifting up of the jawbone, *or*, the casting away of the jawbone, **S#7437h**.

18 **he was sore**. Jg 8:4. Ge 21:17, +19. Ps 22:14, 15. Is 40:29, 31. Jn 19:28. 2 C 4:8, 9.

Thou hast given. Ps 3:7, 8. 18:31-40.

shall. Ge 32:31. 2 C 12:7, 8.

and fall. Ge 12:12, 13. 20:11. 1 S 27:1. 2 S 24:14. 2 C 1:8, 9. He 11:32.

the uncircumcised. 1 S 17:26, 36. 2 S 1:20.

19 **the jaw**. *or*, Lehi.

there came. Is 44:3.

his spirit. Heb. *ruach*, Ge +41:8. 45:27. 1 S 30:12. Is 40:26.

En-hakkore. i.e. *fountain of the calling* or *the called* or *of him that called*, as upon God in distress, **S#5875h**. Is 41:17, 18.

called the name. Ge 16:13. 22:14. 28:19. 32:30. Ex 17:15. Ps 34:6. 120:1.

unto this day. Jg 1:26. Jsh +4:9.

20 **he judged**. Jg 13:1, 5. 16:31. "He seems to have judged South-west Israel during twenty years of their servitude of the Philistines."

JUDGES 16

1 **Gaza**. Ge +10:19.

an harlot. Heb. a woman an harlot. or, innkeeper. Jg 11:1. Jsh 2:1. 6:22. 1 K 3:16. Is +40:13mg. Je 3:3.

and went. Ge 38:16-18. Ezr 9:1, 2.

2 **Gazites**. i.e. *inhabitants of Gaza*, **S#5841h**. Jsh 13:3, Gazahtites.

compassed. 1 S 19:11. 23:26. Ps 118:10-12. Ac 9:23, 24. 2 C 11:32, 33.

quiet. Heb. silent. Jg 18:19. Ge 24:21. 1 S 10:27mg. 2 S 19:10mg. 1 K 20:2mg. Pr 17:28.

kill him. Jg 15:18. Mt 21:38. 27:1. Ac 23:15.

3 **took**. Ps 107:16. Is 63:1-5. Mi 2:13. Ac 2:24.

doors. 1 S 21:13. 1 Ch 22:3. Ezk 8:3, 14. 11:1. Ac 12:13.

gate. Ge +14:7.

posts. Dt 11:20. 1 S 1:9. 1 K 6:31, 33.

bar and all. Heb. with the bar. Dt 3:5. 1 S 23:7. 1 K 4:13. 2 Ch 8:5. 14:7. Ne 3:3, 6, 13-15. Jb 38:10. Ps 107:16. 147:13. Pr 18:19. Is

45:2. Je 49:31. 51:30. La 2:9. Ezk 38:11. Am 1:5. Jon 2:6. Na 3:13.

Hebron. Jsh 14:14.

4 **he loved**. 1 K 11:1. Ne 13:26. Pr 22:14. 23:27. 26:11. 27:22. 1 C 10:6.

in the valley. or, by the brook. Ge 32:23. Nu +13:23.

Sorek. i.e. *a hisser*, **S#7796h**.

Delilah. i.e. *lean, poor, weak; delicate; languishing*, **S#1807h**. ver. 6, 10, 12, 13, 18.

5 **the lords**. Jg 3:3. Jsh 13:3. 1 S 29:6.

Entice. Jg 14:15. Pr 2:16-19. 5:3-11, 20. 6:24-26. 7:21-27. 1 C 6:15-18.

afflict. or, humble. ver. 6, 19.

we will. Jg 17:2. Ge 38:16. Nu 22:17, 18. Mi 7:3. Mt 26:15. 1 T 6:9, 10.

6 **Tell me**. Ps 12:2. Pr 6:26. 7:21. 22:14. 26:28. Je 9:2-5. Mi 7:2, 5.

7 **If they bind**. ver. 10. 1 S 19:17. 21:2, 3. 27:10. Pr 12:19. 17:7. Ro 3:8. Ga 6:7. Col 3:9.

green withs. *or*, new cords. Jb 30:11. Ps 11:2. Heb. moist. Ge 30:37. Ezk 17:24. 20:47.

another. Heb. one. ver. 11.

8 **bound him**. Ec 7:26. Ac +21:33.

9 **broken**. Jg 15:14.

toucheth. Heb. smelleth. Ps 58:9.

10 **now tell me**. ver. 7, 13, 15-17. Pr 23:7, 8. 24:28. Ezk 33:31. Lk 22:48.

11 **If they bind me**. Pr 13:3, 5. 29:25. Ep 4:25.

that never, etc. Heb. wherewith work hath not been done.

13 **with the web**. ver. 14.

14 **went away**. Ezr 9:13, 14. Ps 106:43.

15 **How canst**. Jg 14:16. Pr 2:16. 5:3-14.

when thine. Ge 29:20. Dt 6:5. 1 S 15:13, 14. 2 S 16:17. Pr 23:26. SS 8:6, 7. Jn 14:15, 21-24. 15:10. 2 C 5:14, 15. 1 J 2:15, 16. 5:3.

16 **she pressed**. Pr 7:21-23, 26, 27. Lk 11:8. 18:5.

soul. Heb. *nephesh*, Ge +34:3.

vexed. Heb. shortened. Jb 21:4mg. Jon 4:9. Mk 14:34.

17 **all his heart**. Pr 12:23. 29:11. Mi 7:5.

There hath. Jg 13:5. Nu 6:5. Ac 18:18.

from my. Ps 22:10.

18 **Come up**. Ps 62:9. Pr 18:8. Je 9:4-6.

brought money. ver. 5. Nu 22:7. 1 K 21:20. Mt 26:15. Ep 5:5. 1 T 6:10.

19 **she made**. Pr 7:21-23, 26, 27. 23:33, 34. Ec 7:26.

20 **I will go**. ver. 3, 9, 14. Dt 32:30. Is 42:25. Ho 7:9.

as at other times. Jg 20:30, 31. Nu 24:1. 1 S 20:25.

shake myself. Ex 14:27. Ne 5:13. Jb 38:13. Ps 109:23. 136:15mg. Is 33:9, 15. 52:2. Je 51:38mg.

the Lord. Nu 14:9, 42, 43. Jsh 7:12. 1 S

16:14. 18:12. 28:14-16. 2 Ch 15:2. Is 59:1, 2.
Je 9:23, 24. Mt 17:16, 20. 2 C 3:5.
was departed. Jg 15:14. Ac 5:3, 4. 7:9.

21 **and put out**. Heb. and bored out. Nu
16:14mg. 1 S 11:2. Pr 5:22. 14:14. 30:17. Is
51:1. Je 2:19.
bound him. 2 Ch +33:11. Ac +21:33.
fetters of brass. lit. two brasses. 2 S 3:34. La
3:7.
grind. Ex 11:5. Is 47:2. Mt 24:41.

22 **the hair**. Le 26:44. Dt 32:26. Ps 106:44, 45.
107:13, 14.
after he was shaven. *or*, as when he was
shaven.

23 **Dagon**. Jsh 15:41. 19:27. 1 S 5:2-5, 7. 1 Ch
10:10. Je 2:11. Mi 4:5. Ro 1:23-25. 1 C 8:4, 5.
10:20.
to rejoice. Jb 30:9, 10. Ps 35:15, 16. Pr 24:17.
Is 7:1. Mk 12:38.

24 **praised**. Dt 32:27. Is 37:20. Ezk 20:14. Da
5:4, 23. Hab 1:16. Re 11:10.
which slew many of us. Heb. and who
multiplied our slain. Jg 15:8, 16.

25 **their hearts**. Jg 9:27. 18:20. 19:6, 9. 2 S
13:28. 1 K 20:12. Est 3:15. Is 22:13. Da 5:2, 3.
Mt 14:6, 7.
them. Heb. before them.
sport. 2 S 2:14. Pr 24:17, 18. Mi 7:8-10. Mt
26:67, 68. He +11:36.

27 **was full**. 2 K 10:21mg.
the roof. Jg 9:51. Dt +22:8.

28 **called**. 2 Ch 20:12. Ps 50:15. 91:15. 116:4. La
3:31, 32. He 11:32.
remember me. Ps 74:18-23. Jon 2:1, 2, 27.
that I may. Jg 5:31. Ps 58:10, 11. Je +10:25.

29 **took hold**. Ru 3:8mg. Jb 6:18 (turned
aside).
on which it was borne up. *or*, he leaned on
them. 2 K 18:21. Is 36:6.

30 **me**. Heb. my soul, *nephesh*, Nu +23:10. 1 K
20:32. Mt +12:18.
die. Mt 16:25. Ac 20:24. 21:13. Ph 2:17, 30.
He 12:1-4.
and the house. Jb 20:5. 31:3. Ps 62:3. Ec
9:12. Mt 24:38, 39. 1 Th 5:2.
So the dead. Jg 14:19. 15:8, 15. Ge 3:15. Ph
2:8. Col 2:15. He 2:14, 15.

31 **his brethren**. Jn 19:39-42.
between Zorah. Jsh +19:41.
Eshtaol. Jsh +15:33.
buryingplace. Heb. *qeber*, Ge +23:4.
And he judged. Jg 13:25. 15:20.

JUDGES 17

1 A.M. 2585. B.C. 1419. An. Ex. Is. 72.
mount. Jsh +17:15.
Micah. i.e. *who is like Jah?*, S#4319h. ver. 4.

2 **eleven hundred**. Jg 16:5.
cursedst. Jg 5:23. Dt 27:16. 1 S 14:24, 28.

26:19. Ne 13:25. Je 48:10. Ho 4:2. 10:4. Mt
26:74. Ro 9:3. 1 C 16:22.
I took it. Pr 28:24.
Blessed. Ge 14:19. 24:30, 31. Ex 20:7. Ru
3:10. 1 S 23:21. Ne 13:25. Ps 10:3. 2 J 11.

3 **I had wholly**. ver. 13. Jg 18:5. Is 66:3.
a graven image. Ex 20:4, 23. 32:4, 5. Le
19:4. Dt 12:3. Ps 115:4-8. Is 40:18-25. 44:9-
20. Je 10:3-5, 8. Hab 2:18, 19. Jn 16:2.

4 **two hundred**. Is 46:6, 7. Je 10:9, 10.
the founder. or, a refiner. Is 40:19. 41:7mg.
46:6.
molten. Ex +34:16.

5 **an house of gods**. *or*, as *baith Elohim* may
also signify, "a house of God." Jg 18:24. Ge
31:30. Ezr 1:7. Ho 8:14.
ephod. Ex +28:4.
teraphim. Ge +31:19mg.
consecrated. Heb. filled the hand. Ex
+28:41mg. 1 K 13:33, 34. He 5:4.
his sons. Ex 24:5.

6 **no king**. Jg 18:1. 19:1. 21:3, 25. Ge 36:31. Dt
33:5. 1 S 12:12.
right. Dt 12:8. Ps 12:4. Pr 12:15. 14:12. 16:2.
Ec 11:9. Je 44:16, 17.

7 **Beth-lehem-judah**. ver. 8, 9. Jg 19:1, 2, 18.
Jsh +19:15. Ru 1:1, 2. 1 S 17:12. Mi +5:2. Mt
2:1, 5, 6.

8 **departed**. ver. 11. Ne 13:10, 11.
as he journeyed. Heb. in making his way.

10 **a father**. ver. 11. Jg 18:19. Ge 45:8. 2 K 6:21.
8:8, 9. 13:14. Jb 29:16. Is 22:21.
I will give. Jg 18:20. 1 S 2:36. Ezk 13:19. Mt
26:15. Jn 12:6. 1 T 6:10. 1 P 5:2.
year. Jg +11:40mg.
a suit of apparel. *or*, a double suit, etc. Heb.
an order of garments.

12 **consecrated**. ver. 5. Ex +28:41.
his priest. Jg 18:30. Nu 16:5, 8-10. 1 K
12:31. 13:33, 34.

13 **Now know**. Pr 14:12. Is 44:20. 66:3, 4. Mt
15:9, 13. Jn 16:2. Ac 26:9. Ro 10:2, 3.

JUDGES 18

1 **no king**. Jg 17:6. 19:1. 21:25. Ge 36:31. Dt
33:5.
the tribe. Jsh 19:40-48.
for unto. Jg 1:34.

2 **men**. Heb. sons. 2 S +2:7mg.
Zorah. ver. 8, 11. Jsh +19:41.
to spy. Ge 42:9. Nu 13:17. Jsh 2:1. Pr 20:18.
Lk 14:31.
mount. Jsh +17:15.

3 **they knew**. Jg +12:6. Ge 27:22. Mt 26:73.
and what hast. Is 22:16.

4 **hired me**. Jg 17:10. Pr 28:21. Is 56:11. Ezk
13:19. Ho 4:8, 9. Ml 1:10. Jn 10:12, 13. Ac
8:18-21. 20:33. 1 T 3:3. T 1:11. 2 P 2:3, 14,
15.

5 **Ask counsel**. Jg 20:18, 23, 26-28. 1 S 8:21, 22. 14:36, 37. 1 K 22:5. 2 K 16:15. Is 30:1. Ezk 21:21. Ho 4:12. Ac 8:10.
of God. ver. 14. Jg 17:5, 13.

6 **Go in peace**. 1 K 22:6, 12, 15. Je 23:21, 22, 32.
before. Dt 11:12. Ps 33:18. 1 Th 3:11.

7 **Laish**. Jsh 19:47, Leshem.
how they . ver. 27, 28. Re 18:7.
magistrate. Heb. possessor, or, heir, of restraint. ver. 28. 1 S 3:13. 1 K 1:6. Ro 13:3. 1 P 2:14.

8 **Zorah**. ver. +2.
and Eshtaol. Jsh +15:33.

9 **Arise**. Nu 13:30. 14:7-9. Jsh 2:23, 24.
are ye still. 1 K 22:3.
be not. Jsh 18:3. 1 S 4:9. 2 S 10:12. Jn 6:27. He 6:11, 12. 2 P 1:10, 11.

10 **secure**. ver. 7, 27.
God hath. Dt 2:29. 4:1. Jsh 6:16.
where there. Ex 3:8. Dt 8:7-9. 11:11, 12. Ezk 20:6. 1 T 6:17.

11 **appointed**. Heb. girded. ver. 16. Ex 12:11.

12 **Kirjath-jearim**. Jsh +9:17.
Mahaneh-dan. i.e. *camp of Dan*, **S#4265h**, only here. Jg 13:25mg.
unto this day. Jg +1:21.
behind. Ex +3:1.

13 **mount Ephraim**. ver. +2, 3. Jg 17:1. 19:1.

14 **Then**. 1 S 14:28.
in these. ver. 3, 4. Jg 17:5.
now therefore. Pr 19:27. Is 8:19, 20.

15 **saluted him**. Heb. asked him of peace. Ge +29:6mg. 37:14mg. 41:16. 43:23, 27mg. Ex 18:7mg. 1 S 10:4mg. 17:22mg. 25:5mg. 2 S 8:10mg. 11:7mg. 20:9. 2 K 4:23mg, 26. 5:21mg. 9:11, 17. 10:13mg. 1 Ch 18:10mg. Est 2:11mg. Je 15:5mg. 38:4mg. Mt 10:12, 13. Lk 10:4-6. 19:42. Jn 14:27.

16 **six hundred**. ver. 11.

17 **five men**. ver. 2, 14.
the graven. Jg 6:31. 17:4, 5. Ex 32:20. 1 S 4:11. 6:2-9. 2 K 19:18, 19. Is 46:1, 2, 7.

19 **lay thine hand**. or, keep silent. Heb. be deaf. Jg 16:2. 1 S 10:27mg. Jb 21:5. 29:9. 40:4, 5. Pr 30:32. Mi 7:16.
a father. Jg 17:10. 2 K 6:21. 8:8, 9. 13:14. Mt 23:9.

20 **heart**. Jg 17:10. Pr 30:15. Is 56:11. Ezk 13:19. Ho 4:8. Ac 20:33. Ph 3:19. 2 P 2:3, 15, 16.
went. Lk +4:30. Jn 10:12, 13.

21 **little ones**. Nu +16:27.
the carriage. or, goods. 1 S 17:22.

23 **What aileth**. Ge 21:17. 1 S 11:5. 2 S 14:5. 2 K 6:28. Ps 114:5. Is 22:1.
comest. Heb. art gathered together.

24 **what have**. Jg 17:13. Ps 115:8. Is 44:18-20. Je 50:38. 51:17. Ezk 23:5. Hab 2:18, 19. Ac 19:26. Re 17:2.

25 **angry**. Heb. bitter of soul. Heb. *nephesh*, Ex

+15:9. 1 S +30:6mg. He 12:15.
life. Heb. *nephesh*, soul, Ge +44:30.
lives. Heb. *nephesh*, or, souls. Ge +44:30.

27 **Laish**. ver. 7, 10.
quiet and secure. 1 Th 5:3.
they smote. Ge 49:17. Dt 33:22. Jsh 19:47.
burnt. Jsh 11:11.

28 **And there**. 2 S 14:6mg. Ps 7:2. 50:22. Da 3:15-17.
far from. ver. 1, 7. Ge +49:13.
Beth-rehob. Nu 13:21, Rehob. 2 S 10:6.

29 **Dan**. Ge +14:14.
who was. Ge 30:6. 32:28.

30 **set up**. Ex 20:4. Le 26:1. Dt 17:2-7. 27:15. 31:16, 29. Jsh 19:40-48. Ps 78:58-61. 105:44, 45.
Gershom. Ex 2:21, 22.
until. Jg 13:1. 1 S 4:2, 3, 10, 11. Ps 78:60-62.
the land. or, the ark. 1 S 4:5.

31 **all the time**. Jg 19:18. +21:19.

JUDGES 19

1 **when there**. Jg 17:6. 18:1, 7. 21:25.
mount Ephraim. Jsh +17:15.
a concubine. Heb. a woman, a concubine, or, a wife, a concubine. Is +40:13mg. Ml 2:15.
Beth-lehem-judah. Jg +17:7.

2 **played**. Le 21:9. Dt 22:21. Ezk 16:28.
four whole months. or, a year and four months. Heb. days, four months. Jg 11:40. Ge +29:14.

3 **went**. Jg 15:1.
speak. Ge 50:21. Le 19:17. 20:10. Ho 2:14. Mt 1:19. Jn 8:4, 5, 11. Ga 6:1.
friendly unto her. Heb. to her heart. Ge 34:3mg.
to bring. Je 3:1.
his servant. Nu 22:22.

5 **Comfort**. Heb. Strengthen. ver. 8. Ge 18:5. 1 S 14:27-29. 30:12. 1 K 13:7. Ps 104:15. Jn 4:34. Ac 9:19.
with a morsel. ver. 22.

6 **let thine heart**. ver. 9, 21. Jg 9:27. 16:25. Ru 3:7. 1 S 25:36. Est 1:10. Ps 104:15. Lk 12:19. 1 Th 5:3. Re 11:10, 13.

8 **until afternoon**. Heb. till the day declined. 2 K 20:10. Ps 109:23.

9 **the day**. Lk 24:29.
draweth, etc. Heb. is weak.
the day groweth to an end. Heb. it is the pitching time of the day, Je 6:4. Nu 1:51. 10:31, 33. Dt 1:33. Ezk 20:6.
tomorrow. Pr 27:1. Ja 4:13, 14.
home. Heb. to thy tent. Jg 7:8. 20:8.

10 **over against**. Heb. to over against.
Jebus. i.e. *threshing floor*, **S#2982h**. Jg 1:8. 1 Ch 11:4, 5.

11 **the Jebusites**. ver. 10. Ge +10:16.

12 **Gibeah**. i.e. *height; a hill*, **S#1390h**. ver. 13-16. Jg 20:4, 5, 9, 10, 13-15, 19-21, 25, 29-31, 33, 34, 36, 37, 43. Jsh 15:57. 18:25, 28, Gibeath. 21:17. 1 S 10:26. 11:4. 13:2, 15, 16. 14:2, 5, 16. 15:34. 22:6. 23:19. 26:1. 2 S 6:3, 4. 21:6. 23:29. 1 Ch 11:31. 2 Ch 13:2. Is 10:29. Ho 5:8. 9:9. 10:9.

13 **Gibeah**. ver. +12.
Ramah. Je +31:15.

15 **no man**. ver. 18. Ge 18:2-8. 19:2, 3. Mt 25:35, 43. Ro 15:7. He 13:2. 1 P 4:9, 10.

16 **his work**. Ge 3:19. Ps 104:23. 128:2. Pr 13:11. 14:23. 24:27. Ec 1:13. 5:12. Ep 4:28. 1 Th 4:11, 12. 2 Th 3:10.

17 **lifted**. Ge +22:13.
wayfaring man. 2 S 12:4. Je 14:8.
Whither. Ge 16:8. 32:17.
in the street. ver. 15. Ge 19:2.

18 **the house**. Jg 18:31. 20:18. Jsh 18:1. 1 S 1:3, 7.
receiveth. Heb. gathereth. ver. 5. Ps 26:9. Jn 15:6. 3 J 9, 10.

19 **straw and provender**. Ge 24:25, 32.
bread. Ge +3:19.
wine. Ge 14:18. +27:28.

20 **Peace be**. Ge +43:23. 1 C 1:3.
let all thy wants. Ac +16:15. Ro +15:7. Ga 6:6. Ja 2:15, 16. 1 J 3:18.
lodge not. Ge 19:2, 3. 24:31-33.

21 **So he brought**. Ge 24:32. 43:24.
they washed. Ge +18:4.

22 **they were**. ver. 6, 7. Jg 16:25.
the men. Jg 20:5. Ge 19:4. Ho 9:9. 10:9. Ro 1:24.
sons of Belial. 1 S 1:16. 10:27. +30:22. 2 C 6:15.
Bring forth. Ge 19:5. Ro 1:26, 27. 1 C 6:9. Ju 7.

23 **the man**. Ge 19:6, 7.
do not this folly. Is +9:17.

24 **them**. Ge 19:8. Ro 3:8.
humble ye. Ge +34:2mg. Dt 21:14.
so vile a thing. Heb. the matter of this folly. ver. 23. Is +9:17.

25 **knew her**. Ge +4:1.
and abused. Nu 22:29. 1 S 31:4. Je 5:7, 8. Ho 7:4-7. 9:9. 10:9. Ep 4:19.
the day began. Ge 19:15. +32:24mg.

26 **the dawning**. Ex 14:27.
where her lord was. ver. 3, 27. Ge 18:12. 1 P 3:6.

27 **to go**. Jb 24:4, 7, 10. Am 1:11. Lk 10:31, 32.
threshold. 2 K +12:9mg.

28 **But none answered**. Jg 20:5. 1 K 18:26, 29. Is 50:2. 66:4.

29 **knife**. Ge 22:6, 10. Pr 30:14.
divided her. Jg 20:6, 7. 1 S 11:7. Ro 10:2.
with her bones. Dt 21:22, 23.

30 **consider**. Jg 20:7. Pr 11:14. 13:10. 15:22. 20:18. 24:6. Is 8:10. He +13:4.

JUDGES 20

1 **Then all**. ver. 2, 8, 11. Jg 21:5. Dt 13:12, etc. Jsh 22:12.
as one man. 1 S 11:7, 8. 2 S 19:14. Ezr 3:1. Ne 8:1.
from Dan. Ge +14:14.
to Beer-sheba. 1 S 3:20. 2 S 3:10. 17:11. 24:2, 15. 1 K 4:25. 1 Ch 21:2. 2 Ch 30:5.
with the. Nu 32:1, 40. Jsh 17:1. 2 S 2:9.
unto the. ver. 18, 26. Jg 11:11.
in Mizpeh. Jsh +15:38.

2 **chief**. Heb. corners. Dt 1:15. 1 S 14:38. Is 19:13. Zc 10:4.
presented themselves. Jg 5:10. 12:14.
drew sword. ver. 15, 17. Jg 8:10. 2 S 24:9. 2 K 3:26.

3 **the children of Benjamin**. Pr 22:3. Mt 5:25. Lk 12:58, 59. 14:31, 32.
how was. Jg 19:22-27.

4 **the Levite**. Heb. the man the Levite. Ex 2:14.
I came. Jg 19:15-28.

5 **And the men**. or, masters. Jg 9:2, 6, 7, 18, 20, 23, 24, 25, 26, 39. 19:22. Jsh 24:11.
beset. Ge 19:4-8.
and my concubine. Jg 19:25, 26.
forced. Heb. humbled. Jg 19:24. Dt 22:24. Ezk 22:10, 11.

6 **cut her**. Jg 19:29.
folly in Israel. ver. 10. Is +9:17.

7 **ye are all**. Ex 19:5, 6. Dt 4:6. 14:1, 2. 1 C 5:1, 6, 10-12.
give here. Jg 19:30. Jsh 9:14. Pr 20:18. 24:6. Ja 1:5.
counsel. Pr 8:14. Is 8:10.

8 **as one man**. ver. +1, 11.
We will not. Jg 21:1, 5. Pr 21:3. Ec 9:10.

9 **by lot against it**. Jsh +14:2.

10 **ten thousand**. or, myriad. Ge 24:60.

11 **knit**. 1 S 18:1. 1 Ch 12:17. 2 Ch 5:13.
together as one man. Heb. fellows. or, companions. Ps 45:7. +119:63. Pr 28:24. Ec 4:10. SS 1:7. 8:13. Is 1:23. 44:11. Ezk 37:16, 19.

12 **sent men**. Dt 13:14-16. 20:10, 12. Jsh 22:13-16. Mt 18:15-18. Ro 12:18.

13 **deliver**. 2 S 20:21, 22.
children of Belial. Jg +19:22. Dt 13:13. +15:9. 1 S 30:22. 2 S 20:1. 23:6. 1 K 21:13. 2 Ch 13:7.
put away. Dt +13:5. Ec 11:10.
would not. 1 S 2:25. 2 Ch 25:16, 20. Pr 29:1. Ho 9:9. 10:9. Ro 1:32. Re 18:4, 5.

14 **to go**. Nu 20:20. 21:23. 2 Ch 13:13. Jb 15:25, 26.

15 **twenty and six thousand**. ver. 25, 35, 46, 47. Nu 26:41.

16 **left-handed**. Jg 3:15. Ge +48:13. 1 Ch 12:2.
sling stones. 1 S 17:40, 49, 50. 25:29. 2 Ch 26:14. Je 10:18.
hair. 1 S 14:45.
not miss. or, err. lit. sin, by missing the mark.

17 **four hundred thousand**. ver. 2. Nu 1:46. 26:51. 1 S 11:8. 15:4. 1 Ch 21:5. 2 Ch 17:14-18.

18 **house of God**. Jg 18:31. 19:18. Jsh 18:1. Jl 1:14.
asked counsel. ver. 7, 23, 26, 27. Jg 1:1. Nu 27:5, 21. Jsh 9:14.
Judah. Jg 1:1, 2. Ge 49:8-10. Nu 10:14.

19 **rose up**. Jsh 3:1. 6:12. 7:16.

21 **the children of Benjamin**. Ge 49:27. Ho 10:9.
destroyed. Dt 23:9. 2 Ch 28:10. Ps 33:16. 73:18, 19. 77:19. Ec 9:1-3. Je 12:1. Ga 5:15.

22 **encouraged**. Heb. strengthened. ver. 15, 17. Ge 48:2. 1 S 30:6. 2 S 11:25. Ps 64:5.
in the place. Jsh 14:2. 1 K 20:23, 28.

23 **wept**. ver. 26, 27. Ps 78:34-36. Ho 5:15.
asked counsel. Is 1:12, 16. Ho 7:14.
And the. Ja 4:2.

25 **destroyed**. ver. 21. Ge 18:25. Jb 9:12, 13. Ps 97:2. Ro 2:5. 3:5. 11:33.

26 **all the children of Israel**. ver. 18, 23.
wept. 1 S 7:6. 2 Ch 20:3. Ezr 8:21. 9:4, 5. Ps +56:8. Jl 1:14. 2:12-18. Jon 3:5-10.
and sat. Jg 21:2. 2 S 7:18. 1 K 19:4. 1 Ch 17:16. Ne 1:4. Ezk 14:1-3. 20:1.
and fasted. Mt +4:2. +6:16. Lk +18:12.
until even. ver. 23. Jg 21:2. Jsh 7:6.
burnt offerings. Le +23:12.
peace offerings. Le +23:19.

27 **enquired**. ver. 18, 23. Nu 27:21.
the ark. Jsh 18:1. 1 S 4:3, 4. Ps 78:60, 61. Is 59:1. Je 7:12.

28 **Phinehas**. Ex +6:25.
stood. Dt +10:8.
Shall I yet. Jsh 7:7. 1 S 14:37. 23:4-12. 30:8. 2 S 5:19-24. 6:3, 7-12. Pr 3:5, 6. Je 10:23.
Go up. Jg 1:2. 7:9. 2 Ch 20:17.

29 **liers**. ver. 34. Jsh 8:4. 2 S 5:23.

31 **drawn**. Jsh 8:14-16.
smite of the people, and kill, as at. Heb. smite of the people wounded as at, etc. ver. 39.
the house of God. or, Bethel. ver. 18, 26, 27. Jg 18:31. 21:2, 12, 19. 1 S 10:3.
Gibeah. Jg 19:12.
in the field. ver. 23, 30. Jsh 18:24, 28.
thirty men. Jsh 7:5.

32 **Let us flee**. Jsh 8:15, 16.

33 **rose up**. Jsh 8:18-22.
Baal-tamar. i.e. *possessing palms; lord of the palm*, S#1193h.
meadows. lit. a naked place, *or* perhaps *cave*, as in 1 S 13:6.

34 **ten thousand**. ver. 29.
knew not. Jsh 8:14. Jb 21:13. Pr 4:19. 29:6. Ec 8:11, 12. 9:12. Is 3:10, 11. 47:11. Mt 24:44. Lk 21:34. 1 Th 5:3.

35 **the Lord smote**. Dt 32:35.
twenty and five thousand and. ver. 15, 44-46. Jb 20:5.

36 **for the men**. Jsh 8:15, etc.

37 **the liers in wait hasted**. Jsh 8:15, 19.
drew themselves along. or, made a long sound with the trumpets. Ex 19:13. Jsh 6:5. or, marched or went. Heb. drew their feet. Ge 37:28. Ex 12:21. Jg 4:6. Jb 21:33.

38 **Now there**. From this verse to the end of the chapter, we have the details of the same operations which are mentioned, in a general way, in the preceding verses of this chapter.
sign. or, time. Ge +17:21. 2 K 4:16mg.
and. Heb. with.
flame. Heb. elevation.

39 **And when**. ver. 31.
smite and kill. Heb. smite the wounded.

40 **a pillar**. SS 3:6. Re +14:11.
looked. Jsh 8:20.
flame. Heb. whole consumption.

41 **were amazed**. Ge +45:3mg. Ex 15:9, 10. Is 13:8, 9. 33:14. Lk 17:27, 28. 21:26. 1 Th 5:3. 2 P 2:12. Re 6:15-17. 18:8-10.
was come upon them. Heb. touched them.

42 **the battle**. La 1:3. Ho 9:9. 10:9. i.e. the men of battle or war; the abstract for the concrete, as poverty, 2 K 24:14; pride, Ps 36:11; deceit, Pr 12:5; dreams, Je 27:9; election, Ro 11:7, are put for persons that are poor, proud, deceitful, dreamers, elect. Ge +31:54.

43 **inclosed**. Jsh 8:20-22.
with ease. or, from Menuchah, etc. Nu 10:33. 1 Ch 2:52. Je 51:59mg. Mi 2:10.
over against. Heb. unto over against.

45 **Rimmon**. Jsh +15:32.
gleaned. Dt 24:21.
Gidom. i.e. *a cutting down*, S#1440h.

46 **twenty and five thousand**. ver. 15, 35. Jg 11:26. 2 S 5:5.

47 **six hundred**. Jg 21:13. Ps 103:9, 10. Is 1:9. Je 14:7. La 3:32. Hab 3:2.
rock of Rimmon. ver. 45.

48 **smote them**. Dt 13:15-17. 2 Ch 25:13. 28:6-9. Pr 18:19.
the men. Jg 21:5, 10. Ge +6:5. Nu 31:17. Dt 13:15, 16. Jsh 7:15. 1 S 15:3.
came to hand. Heb. was found. 2 K 19:4mg. 2 Ch 29:29mg.
they came to. Heb. were found. Ge 19:15mg. 1 S 9:8. 1 Ch 29:17. Ezr 8:25. Est +1:5mg.

JUDGES 21

1 **had sworn**. Jg 20:1, 8, 10. Je 4:2.
There. ver. 5. Jg 11:30, 31. 1 S 14:24, 28, 29. Ec 5:2. Mk 6:23. Ac 23:12. Ro 10:2.
his daughter. Ex 34:12-16. Dt 7:2, 3.

2 **the house of God**. ver. 12. Jg 20:18, 23, 26. Jsh 18:1.
abode there. or, sat (in prayer). Jg +20:26.

lifted. Jg 2:4. Ge +22:13. 27:38. 1 S 30:4.
wept sore. 2 K +20:3mg.

3 why is. Dt 29:24. Jsh 7:7-9. Ps 74:1. 80:12. Pr 19:3. Is 63:17. Je 12:1.

4 rose early. Ps 78:34, 35. Ho 5:15.
built there. Jg 6:26. Ex 20:24, 25. 1 S 7:9, 17. 11:15. 16:2, 5. 2 S 24:18, 25. 1 K 8:64. He 13:10.
an altar. Ge +13:18.
burnt offerings. Le +23:12.
peace offerings. Le +23:19.

5 came not. ver. 8. Jg 5:23.
a great oath. ver. 1, 18. Jg 5:23. Le 27:28, 29. 1 S 11:7. Je 48:10.
to Mizpeh. Jsh +15:38.
surely. Ge +2:16.

6 repented them. ver. 15. Jg 11:35. 20:23. 2 S 2:26. Ho 11:8. Lk 19:41, 42.

7 sworn. ver. 1, 18. 1 S 14:28, 29, 45.

8 came not up. ver. 5. 1 S 11:7.
Jabesh-gilead. i.e. "Jabesh in the territory of Gilead," **S#1568h.** 1 S 11:1-3. 31:11-13. 2 S 2:5, 6.

10 go and smite. ver. 5. Jg 5:23. 1 S 11:7. 15:3.
women and. Dt 13:15. Jsh 7:24, etc.
the children. Nu +16:27.

11 utterly destroy. or, devote. Le 27:29.
every male. Nu 31:17, 18. Dt 2:34.
hath lain by man. Heb. knoweth the lying with man. ver. 12. Ge +4:1. Nu 31:17, 18.

12 virgins. Heb. women, virgins. Ge +24:16. Is +40:13mg.
Shiloh. Jg 20:18, 23. Jsh 18:1. Ps 78:60. Je 7:12.
Canaan. West of Jordan (Young).

13 to speak. Heb. and spake and called.
the rock Rimmon. Jg 20:47. Jsh +15:32.
call peaceably. or, proclaim peace. Dt 20:10. Is 57:19. Lk 10:5. Ep 2:17.

14 sufficed them not. ver. 12. Jg 20:47. 1 C 7:2.

15 repented. ver. +6, 17.

the Lord had made. Am +3:6.
a breach. 1 Ch 13:11. 15:13. Is 30:13. 58:12.

16 the elders. Ex +18:21. Jsh +20:4.
How. ver. 7.

17 an inheritance. Nu 26:55. 36:7. Jsh 12:6, 7.
be escaped. Ex 10:5.
destroyed. or, blotted out. Ge 6:7.

18 not give. Jg +11:35.
sworn. ver. +1. Jg 11:35.

19 a feast. Le +23:34. Nu 10:10. 28:16, 26. Ps 81:3. Jn 5:1. 7:2.
Shiloh. i.e. his peace, prosperity, **S#7887h.** ver. 12, 21. Jsh 18:1, 8-10. 19:51. 21:2. 22:9, 12. Jg 18:31. 1 S 1:3, 9, 24. 2:14. 3:21. 4:3, 4, 12. 14:3. 1 K 2:27. +11:29. 14:2, 4. Ps 78:60. Je 7:12, 14. 26:6, 9. 41:5.
yearly. Heb. from year to year. lit. from days to days. **S#3117h.** Jg +11:40mg. Nu +9:22.
the east side. or, toward the sun-rising. Jg 20:43.
of the highway. or, on.
Lebonah. i.e. frankincense, **S#3829h.**

21 daughters of Shiloh come. 1 S 1:7, 21, 22, 24; 1 Ch 15:20. Lk 2:22, 23, 41-43.
dance. Ex +15:20.
catch you. ver. 23.

22 Be favorable unto them. or, Gratify us in them. Ps 123:3. Is 33:2. Phm 9-12.
each man. ver. 14. Ge 1:27. 7:13. Mk 10:6-8. 1 C 7:2.
give unto. ver. 1, 7, 18. Pr 20:25.

23 according to their number. ver. 22.
they caught. or, took violently away. ver. 21.
and they went. Jg 2:6.
repaired. Jg 20:48.

24 departed thence. Dt 33:4, 5. Nu 27:15-17. 1 K 22:17.

25 no king. Jg 17:6. 18:1. 19:1.
did. lit. will do. Ex 15:5.
right. Jg 18:7. Dt 12:8. Ps 12:4. Pr 3:5. 14:12. 16:2. 23:4. 26:12. Ec 11:9. Is 5:21. Mi 2:1, 2.

RUTH

RUTH 1

1 the judges. Jg 2:16. 12:8. Ac 13:20.
ruled. Heb. judged. Jg 2:16.
a famine. Ge +12:10. 43:1. Le 26:19. Dt
28:23, 24, 38. Jg 6:3, 4. Ps 107:33, 34. Jl 1:10,
11, 16-20.
Beth-lehem-judah. Jg +17:7.

2 Elimelech. i.e. *my God is king*, **S#458h**. ver. 3.
Ru 2:1, 3. 4:3, 9.
Naomi. i.e. *my pleasant one*, **S#5281h**. ver. 3, 8,
11, 20, 21, 22. 2:1, 2, 6, 20, 22. 3:1. 4:3, 5, 9,
14, 16, 17.
Mahlon. i.e. *sickness*, **S#4248h**. ver. 5. Ru 4:9,
10.
Chilion. i.e. *consumption*, **S#3630h**. ver. 5. Ru
4:9. 1 Ch 4:22.
Ephrathites. **S#673h**. Ge +48:7. Jg 12:5. 1 S
1:1. 17:12. 1 K 11:26. Mi 5:2.
continued. Heb. were.

3 husband died. Ge 11:32. Ac 7:4.
and she was. 2 K 4:1. Ps 34:19. He 12:6, 10,
11.
left. ver. 4. Ge 7:23.

4 wives. Dt 7:3. 23:3. 1 K 11:1, 2.
Orpah. i.e. *a neck* or *hind*, **S#6204h**. ver. 14.
Ruth. i.e. *appearance* or *friend; beauty*, **S#7327h**.
ver. 14, 16, 22. 2:2, 8, 21, 22. 3:9. 4:5, 10, 13.
Mt 1:5.

5 A.M. 2696. B.C. 1308. An. Ex. Is. 183.
Mahlon. Dt 32:39. Ps 89:30-32. Je 2:19.
and the woman. Is 49:21. Mt 22:25-27. Lk
7:12.

6 visited. or, looked after. Ge 21:1. 50:25. Ex
+3:16. 4:31. 13:19. 1 S 2:21. Jb 10:12. Ps 65:9.
107:35-37. Is 24:22. Lk 1:68. 19:44. 1 P 2:12.
in giving. Ge 28:20. 48:15. Ex 16:4-6. Ps
37:25. 104:14, 15. 111:5. 132:15. 145:15.
146:7. 147:14. Pr 30:8. Is 55:10. Mt 6:11. 1 T
6:8.

7 she went. 2 K 8:3.
they went. ver. 10, 14. Ex 18:27.

8 Go. *Jsh* 24:15, etc. Lk 14:25, etc.
the Lord. Ph 4:18, 19. 2 T 1:16-18.
the dead. ver. 5. Ru 2:20. Ep 5:22. 6:2, 3. Col
3:18, 24.

9 rest. Ru 3:1.
she kissed. Ge +27:27.

lifted. Ge +22:13.
wept. Ge +29:11.

10 Surely. Ps 16:3. +119:63. Zc 8:23.

11 are there. Ge 38:8-11. Mt 22:23-28.
womb. or, bowels. Ps 71:6.
that they. Ge 38:8, 11. Dt 25:5.

12 too old. Ge 17:17. 1 T 5:9.
to have an husband. Ex 12:48. Ga 4:5, 7.
I should have. *or*, I were with.

13 tarry. Heb. hope. Ge 38:8, 11.
it grieveth me much. Heb. I have much bitterness. ver. 20. 1 S 30:6mg. 2 K 4:27mg. He
+12:15. **S#4843h**: 2 K 4:27mg. Ru 1:20. Zc
12:10.
for your sakes. ver. 8. 1 J 4:7.
the hand. Ex 7:4, 5. +9:3. Dt 2:15. Jg 2:15. 1
S 5:6, 11. Jb +2:10. 19:21. 30:20, 21. Ps 32:4.
+37:24. 38:2. 39:9, 10. +77:3. Is 29:24. Ezk
+18:25. Mt +5:45. Lk +6:35. Ac 13:11. Ja
+1:13, 17.
against me. Ge 42:36. 2 K +6:33. Pr +19:3.
Je +29:11.

14 lifted. Ge +22:13.
Orpah. Ge +27:27. 1 K 19:20. Mt 10:37.
19:22. Mk 10:21, 22. 2 T 4:10.
but Ruth. Dt +4:4. Pr 17:17. 18:24. Is 14:1.
Zc 8:23. Mt 16:24. Jn 6:66-69. Ac 17:34. He
10:39.

15 gone back. Ps 36:3. 125:5. Zp 1:6. Mt 13:20,
21. He 10:38. 1 J 2:19.
her gods. Nu 21:29. 25:3. Jsh 24:15. Jg
11:24. 2 K 5:18, 19. Mi 4:5.
return. Jsh 24:15, 19. 2 S 15:19, 20. 2 K 2:2.
Lk 14:26-33. 24:28.

16 Intreat me not. *or*, Be not against me. Ru
2:22. Jg 15:12. 18:25.
to leave. 2 K 2:2-6. Lk 5:28. 24:28, 29. Jn
1:38, 39. Ac 21:13.
whither. 2 S 15:21. Mt 8:19. Jn 13:37. Re
14:4.
will lodge. Ru 2:12. Ps 91:1.
thy people. Ru 2:11, 12. Ps 45:10. Is 14:1.
thy God. Jsh 24:18. Da 2:47. 3:29. 4:37. Ho
13:4. 2 C 6:16-18. 1 Th 1:9.
my God. Ru 2:11, 12.

17 the Lord. 1 S 3:17. 14:44. 20:13. 25:22. 2 S
3:9, 35. 19:13. 1 K 2:23. 19:2. 20:10. 2 K 6:31.

do so. Ezk +34:2.
but death. Ac 11:23. 20:24.
part. 2 K 2:11. Pr 18:18. Ro 8:35, 38, 39.

18 **When**. Ac 21:14.
was stedfastly minded. Heb. strengthened herself. 1 K 12:18. 2 Ch 10:18. 13:7. Ac 2:42. Ep 6:10. Ja 1:6, 8.

19 **all the city**. Mt 21:10.
was moved. or, sounded, as in 1 S 4:5. 1 K 1:45. Mt 21:10.
Is this Naomi. Is 23:7. La 2:15.

20 **Naomi**. *that is*, Pleasant. 2 S 1:26. SS 7:6.
Mara. *that is*, Bitter. **S#4755h**, only here. Ex 15:23. Jb 13:26.
the Almighty. Ge +49:25.
dealt. Jb 6:4. 19:6. 27:2mg. Ps 73:14. 88:15. Is 38:13. La 3:1-20. He 12:11.
very bitterly. ver. +13. Pr +19:3.
with me. Ps +40:17. 103:14. Is +29:24. Je +29:11. 1 C +10:13. 2 C 1:3, 4.

21 **and the**. 1 S 2:7, 8. Jb 1:21.
the Lord. Jb 10:17. 13:26. 16:8. Ml +3:5.
empty. Jb 1:21.
hath afflicted. or, done evil. Jb 10:17mg. 16:8. Je +29:11. Am +3:6.

22 **Moabitess**. **S#4125h**. Ru 2:2, 21. 4:5, 10. 2 Ch 24:26.
in the beginning. Ru 2:23. Ex 9:31, 32. Le 23:10, 14. 2 S 21:9. 2 Ch 30:21. Lk 15:23.

RUTH 2

1 **kinsman**. Ru 3:2, 12. Pr 7:4.
a mighty. Dt 8:17, 18. Jb 1:3. 31:25. Ep 3:16.
Boaz. i.e. *fleetness, strength*, **S#1162h**. ver. 3. Ru 3:2, 7. 4:21. Jg 12:8-10. 1 K 7:21. 1 Ch 2:10-12. 2 Ch 3:17. Mt 1:5. Lk 3:32, Booz.

2 **glean ears**. Le 19:9, 10, 16. 23:22. Dt 24:19-21.
find grace. Ge 6:8.

3 **gleaned**. 1 Th 4:11, 12. 2 Th 3:12.
reapers. ver. 4, 5, 6, 7, 14. 1 S 6:13. 2 K 4:18. Ps 129:7. Je 9:22. Am 9:13.
hap was. Heb. hap happened. 1 S 6:9. 20:26. 2 K 8:5. Est 6:1, 2. Ec 2:14, 15mg. 3:19. 9:2, 3. Mt 10:29. Lk 10:31.
part. Ru 4:3.

4 **The Lord**. Ps 118:26. 129:7, 8. Lk 1:28. 2 Th 3:16. 2 T 4:22. 2 J 10, 11.
And they. Ru 4:11. Ge 18:19. Jsh 24:15. Ps 133:1-3. 1 T 6:2.

5 **Boaz**. Ru 4:21. 1 Ch 2:11, 12.

6 **the servant**. Ge 15:2. 24:2. 39:4. Mt 20:8. 24:45.
It is the. Ru 1:16, 19, 22.
Moabitish. **S#4125h**, so rendered only here.

7 **I pray**. Pr 15:33. 18:23. Mt 5:3. Ep 5:21. 1 P 5:5, 6.
sheaves. ver. 15. Dt 24:19. Jb 24:10.
continued. Pr 13:4. 22:29. Ec 9:10. Ro 12:11. Ga 6:9.

8 **my daughter**. 1 S 3:6, 16. 2 K 5:13. Mt 9:2, 22.
neither. SS 1:7, 8.
abide. Mt 10:7-11. Ph 4:8.

9 **not touch thee**. Jb +1:11. Pr 6:29. 1 C 7:1.
go. Ge 24:18-20. Mt 10:42. Jn 4:7-11.

10 **fell**. Ge +18:2. 1 S 25:23, 24. Mt 2:11. 8:2.
Why have. ver. 2, 13. 2 S 9:8. 19:28. Lk 1:43, 48. Ro 12:10.
seeing. Is 56:3-8. Mt 15:22-28. 25:35. Lk 7:6, 7. 17:16-18.

11 **all that**. Ru 1:11, 14-24. Ps 37:5, 6.
and how. Ps 45:10. Lk 5:11, 28. 14:33. 18:29, 30. He 11:8, 9, 24-26.
heretofore. Heb. yesterday, third day. Ex 5:7, 8, 14. 2 S +3:17mg.

12 **recompense**. 1 S 24:19. Pr 23:18mg. Mt +5:12. Lk 6:35. 14:12-14. Col 2:18. 2 T 1:18.
under. Ps 91:1. Mt 11:28. Lk 10:42.
wings. Ru 1:16. Ex 25:20. Ps +91:4.
trust. Ps 91:4. 118:9, 10. Is 30:2.

13 **Let me find**. *or*, I find favor. Ge 33:8, 10, 15. 43:14. 1 S 1:18. 2 S 16:4.
comforted. Is 40:1, 2.
friendly. Heb. to the heart. Ge 34:3. Jg 19:3.
not like. 1 S 25:41. Pr 15:33. SS 1:5, 6. Ph 2:3.

14 **At meal-time**. Jb 31:16-22. Pr 11:24, 25. Is 32:8. 58:7, 10, 11. Lk 14:12-14.
dip. 1 S 14:27.
thy morsel. Pr 17:1.
vinegar. Nu 6:3. Ps 69:21.
parched corn. Le 2:14. 23:14. 1 S 17:17. 25:18. 2 S 17:27, 28.
she did. Dt 8:10. 11:15. 2 K 4:43, 44. Mt 14:20.
was sufficed. ver. 18. Ps 23:5.

15 **reproach**. Heb. shame. Ja 1:5. or, cause to blush. Jg 18:7. 1 S 20:34.

16 **let fall**. Dt 24:19-21. Ps 112:9. Pr 19:17. Mt 25:40. Ro 12:13. 2 C 8:5-11. Phm 7. He 6:10. 1 J 3:17, 18.
rebuke. Ge 37:10.

17 **she gleaned**. Pr 31:27. 2 Th 3:10.
beat out. Dt 24:20. Jg 6:11. Is 27:12. 28:27.
ephah. Ex 16:36. Le 5:11. Jg 6:19. Ezk 45:11, 12.

18 **she had reserved**. ver. 14. Jn 6:12, 13. 1 T 5:4.

19 **blessed**. ver. 10. Ps 41:1. Pr 22:9. 2 C 9:13-15.
Boaz. 1 K 7:21.

20 **Blessed**. Ru 3:10. 2 S 2:5. Jb 29:12, 13. 2 T 1:16-18.
hath not. 2 S 9:1. Pr 17:17. Ph 4:10.
one of our. *or*, one that hath right to redeem. Ru 3:9. 4:6. Le 25:25. Dt 25:5-7. Jb 19:25.

21 **Thou shalt**. ver. 7, 8, 22. SS 1:7, 8.
young men. ver. 8, 22, 23.

22 **It is good**. Pr 27:10. SS 1:8.
meet. *or*, fall not upon thee. Ru 1:16.

23 kept fast by. Pr 6:6-8. 13:1, 20. 1 C 15:33. Ep 6:1-3.
wheat harvest. Ge 30:14.
dwelt with. Pr 7:11, 12.

RUTH 3

1 shall I not. Ru 1:9. 1 C 7:36. 1 T 5:8, 14.
may be. Ge 40:14. Dt +4:40. Ps 128:2. Je 22:15, 16.
2 is not Boaz. Ru 2:20-23. Dt 25:5, 6. He 2:11-14.
kindred. Ru 2:1.
with whose. Ru 2:8, 23.
he winnoweth. Mt 3:12.
threshingfloor. Ge +50:10.
3 anoint thee. Lk +7:46.
put thy. Est 5:1. Is 49:18. 52:1. Je 2:32. 1 T 2:9, 10. Re 19:7. 21:2.
the floor. ver. 2.
4 uncover his feet. *or*, lift up the clothes that are on his feet. ver. 7, 8, 14. Da 10:6. 1 Th 5:22.
6 the floor. ver. +2, 3.
and did. Ex 20:12. Pr 1:8. Jn 2:5. 15:14.
7 eaten and drunk. Jg 9:27. Ps 4:7. Is 9:3.
his heart. Ge 43:34. Jg 16:25. 19:6, 9, 22. 2 S 13:28. Est 1:10. Ps 104:15. Ec 2:24. 3:12, 13. 8:15. 9:7. 10:19. 1 C 10:31. Ep 5:18.
came softly. Jg 4:21. 1 S 18:22. 24:4.
8 afraid. Ge +27:33mg.
turned. or, took hold on. Jg 16:29. Jb 6:18.
9 Ruth. Ru 2:10-13. 1 S 25:41. Lk 14:11.
handmaid. Ru 2:13.
spread therefore. Heb. spread thy wing. Ru 2:12. Ge 20:16. Dt 22:30. 27:20. Ezk 16:8. 1 C 11:5, 6, 10.
a near kinsman. *or*, one that has right to redeem. ver. 12. Ru 2:20.
10 Blessed. Ru 2:4, 20. 1 C 13:4, 5.
at the beginning. Ru 1:8.
followedst not. Dt 25:5. 2 C 6:14. 1 T 5:11, 12.
poor. lit. lean, thin. Ge 41:19. Ex 23:3. 30:15. Le 14:21. 19:15. Jg 6:15. 1 S 2:8. Jb 5:16. 20:10, 19. 31:16. 34:19, 28. Ps 41:1. 72:13. 82:3, 4. 113:7. Pr 10:15. 14:31. 19:4, 17. 21:13. 22:9, 16, 22. 28:3, 6, 8, 11, 15. 29:7. 29:14. Is 11:4. 14:30. 25:4. Je 5:4. 39:10. Am 2:7. 4:1. 5:11. 8:6. Zp 3:12.
rich. Pr 10:15. 14:20. 18:11, 23. 22:2.
11 fear not. Mt 9:22. Mk 5:34. Lk 8:48.
city. Heb. gate. Ru 4:1. Ge +14:7.
virtuous woman. Pr 12:4. 31:10, 29-31.
12 there is. Ru 4:1. Mt 7:12. 1 Th 4:6.
13 Tarry. Ge 19:2.
if he will. Ru 2:20. 4:5. Dt 25:5-9. Mt 22:24-27. Mt 22:24.
the Lord liveth. 1 K +17:1. 2 C 1:23. He 6:16.
the morning. Ps 30:5. 46:5. 143:8.

14 could know. Ge +4:1.
Let it not. Ec 7:1. Ac 24:16. Ro 12:17. 14:16. 1 C 10:32. 2 C 8:21. 1 Th 5:22. 1 P 2:12.
15 vail. *or*, sheet, *or* apron. ver. 9. Is 3:22. 1 C 11:5, 6, 10.
he measured. Is 32:8. Ga 6:10.
16 mother in law. Ru 1:6.
Who art thou. or, How hast thou fared.
18 Sit still. Ps 4:4. 37:3-5. 46:10. Is 23:2. 28:16. 30:7. 50:10.
thou know. Ph 1:6.

RUTH 4

1 to the gate. Ge +14:7. 23:10, 18. Dt 16:18. 17:5. 21:19. 25:7. Jb 29:7. 31:21. Pr 24:7. 31:23. Am 5:10-12, 15.
and sat. Pr 31:23.
the kinsman. Ru 3:12.
of whom. Ru 3:11, 12.
Ho, such. 1 S 21:2. 2 K 6:8. Is 55:1. Zc 2:6.
2 ten men. 1 K 21:8.
the elders. Ex +18:21, 22. 21:8. Dt 29:10. Jsh +20:4. 1 K 21:8. Pr 31:23. La 5:14.
3 he said. Ps 112:5. Pr 13:10.
selleth a parcel. Le 25:25.
4 I thought. Heb. I said I will reveal *in* thine ear. 1 S 9:15mg. 20:2mg, 12mg, 13. 22:8mg, 17. 2 S 7:27mg. 1 Ch 17:25mg. Jb 33:16mg.
Buy it. Je 32:7-9, 25. Ro 12:17. 2 C 8:21. Ph 4:8.
before the inhabitants. Ge 23:17, 18. Je 32:10-12.
for there is none. Le 25:25-29.
5 to raise up. Ru 3:12, 13. Ge 38:8. Dt 25:5, 6. Mt 22:24. Lk 20:28.
6 mar. or, destroy.
7 changing. Le 27:10, 13.
a man plucked off. Dt 25:7-10. Ps 60:8.
testimony. Is 8:16, 20.
9 Ye are witnesses. Ge 23:16-18. Je 32:10-12.
10 have I. Ge 29:18, 19, 27. Pr 18:22. 19:14. 31:10, 11. Ho 3:2. 12:12. Ep 5:25.
the name. Dt 25:6. Jsh 7:9. Ps 34:16. 109:15. Is 48:19. Zc 13:2.
gate. Ge +14:7.
ye are witnesses. Is 8:2, 3. Je 32:25. Ml 2:14. He 13:4.
11 The Lord. Ge 24:60. Ps 127:3-5. 128:3-6.
Rachel. Ge 29:32-35. 30:1-24. 35:16-20. 46:8-27. Nu ch. 26.
build. Dt 25:9. Pr 14:1.
two. Ge +4:19.
did build. Ge 16:2mg. Ex 1:21. Ps 127:1, +3. 128:3.
do thou worthily. *or*, get thee riches, *or* power. Ru 2:1. 1 S 9:1.
Ephratah. Ru +1:2. 1 Ch +2:50. Mi +5:2. Mt 2:6.

be famous. Heb. proclaim *thy* name. ver. 14. Le 24:11, 16. Dt 28:58.

Bethlehem. Ge 35:19. Mi +5:2.

12   **the house**. Ge +46:12.

whom Tamar. Ge +38:6, 29. Lk 3:33.

of the seed. 1 S 2:20. Ga 3:16.

13   A.M. 2697. B.C. 1307. An. Ex. Is. 184.

Boaz took. Ru 3:11.

went in. Ge 6:4. 16:2. 30:3, 9. Jg 15:2.

the Lord. ver. 12. Ge +11:30. +29:31. 33:5. Dt 7:14.

14   **the women**. Lk 1:58. Ro 12:15. 1 C 12:26.

Blessed. Ge 29:35. Ps 34:1-3. 103:1, 2. 1 Th 5:18. 2 Th 1:3.

which hath. Ge 24:27.

not left thee. Heb. caused to cease unto thee.

kinsman. *or,* redeemer. Ru 2:20.

that his. ver. 21, 22. Ge 12:2. Is 11:1-4. Mt 1:5-20.

15   **restorer**. 1 S 2:6. La 1:16mg. Is 58:12.

life. Heb. *nephesh*, soul. Ge +44:30.

a nourisher, etc. Heb. to nourish thy grey hairs. Ge 45:11. 47:12. 1 K 17:4, 9. Ps 55:22. Is 46:4.

for thy. Ru 1:16-18.

better. 1 S 1:8. Pr 18:24.

seven sons. 1 S 2:5. Jb 1:2. Je 15:9.

born him. or, to wit, a son. Jsh 15:19. 1 K 19:21. Jb 31:37. Ezk 29:3.

16   **child**. Ex 2:9.

bosom. 1 K 3:20.

nurse. lit. supporter. Nu 11:12. 2 S 4:4. 2 K 10:1mg, 5. Est 2:7mg. Is 49:23mg.

17   **the women**. Lk 1:58-63.

Obed. i.e. *serving; servant,* **S#5744h**. ver. 15, 21, 22. 1 Ch 2:12, 37, 38. 11:47. 26:7. 2 Ch 33:1. Lk 3:32.

Jesse. 1 Ch +2:12.

David. 1 S +16:19.

18   **the generations**. Ge 2:4. Nu 3:1. Ezr 7:2 with 1 Ch 6:3 with Mt 1:1, 8.

Pharez. Ge +48:12.

Hezron. Ge 46:12. Mt 1:3. Lk 3:33, Esrom.

19   **begat Ram**. 1 Ch 2:9, 10. Mt 1:4, Aram. Lk 3:33.

Amminadab. 1 Ch +15:11.

20   **Nahshon**. 1 Ch +2:10.

Salmon. *or,* Salmah. i.e. *garment; peaceable,* **S#8009h**, only here. 1 Ch 2:11.

21   **Salmon**. 1 Ch 2:11, Salma. Mt 1:5. Lk 3:32.

and Boaz. Ru +2:1.

22   **Jesse**. 1 S 16:1. Is 11:1.

David. 1 Ch 2:15. Mt 1:6. Lk 3:31.

1 SAMUEL

1 SAMUEL 1

1 **Ramathaim-zophim**. i.e. *the two high places of the watchers*, **S#7436h**. ver. 19. Je +31:15.
mount Ephraim. Jsh +17:15.
Elkanah. 1 Ch 6:25-27, 34.
Jeroham. i.e. *he is loved; who finds mercy*, **S#3395h**. 1 Ch 6:27, 34. 8:27. 9:8, 12. 12:7. 27:22. 2 Ch 23:1. Ne 11:12.
Elihu. i.e. *my God is he*, **S#453h**. 1 Ch 6:26, Eliab. 12:20. 26:7. 27:18. Jb 32:2, 4, 5, 6. 34:1. 35:1. 36:1.
Tohu. i.e. *they sank down*, **S#8459h**. 1 Ch 6:26, Nahath. 6:34, Toah.
Zuph. i.e. *dropping of honey; honeycomb*, **S#6689h**. 1 S 9:5. 1 Ch 6:26, Zophai, 6:35, Zuph, or Ziph.
Ephrathite. Ru +1:2.
2 **two wives**. Ge +4:19.
Hannah. i.e. *gracious*, **S#2584h**. ver. 5, 8, 9, 13, 15, 19, 20, 22. 1 S 2:1, 21.
Peninnah. i.e. *pearl* or *coral*, **S#6444h**. ver. 4.
no children. Ge +11:30.
3 **yearly**. Heb. from year to year. Ex 23:14, 17. 34:23. Dt 16:16. Jg +11:40mg. Lk 2:41.
to worship. Dt 12:5-7, 11-14.
Lord of hosts. Ex +15:26. Ps +24:10. Ro 9:29. Ja 5:4.
Shiloh. ver. 9. Jg +21:19.
And the. ver. 9. 1 S 2:12-17, 34. 3:13. 4:4, 11, 17, 18.
Eli. i.e. *going up* or *pestle*, **S#5941h**. ver. 9, 12-14, 17, 25. 1 S 2:11, 12, 20, 22, 27. 3:1, 2, 5, 6, 8, 9, 12, 14-16. 4:4, 11, 13, 14-16. 14:3. 1 K 2:27.
Hophni. i.e. *a boxer; fighter*, **S#2652h**. 1 S 2:34. 4:4, 11, 17.
4 **offered**. Le 3:4. 7:15. Dt 12:5-7, 17. 16:11. 2 S 6:18, 19.
5 **a worthy portion**. *or*, a double portion. Ge 43:34. 45:22.
he loved. Ge 29:30, 31. Dt 21:15.
shut up. Ge +11:30. 20:18.
6 **adversary**. Le 18:18. Jb 6:14. *or*, adversity. Ge 35:3.
provoked her. Heb. angered her. Dt 31:29. 32:21.
had shut. ver. +5. Jb 24:21. Ps +127:3.

7 **year**. 1 S 2:19.
when she. *or*, from the time that she. Heb. from her going up.
not eat. Ps 42:3.
8 **why weepest**. 2 S 12:16, 17. 2 K 8:12. Jb 6:14. Jn 20:13, 15. 1 Th 5:14.
am not. Ru 4:15. Ps 43:4. Is 54:1, 6.
ten sons. Ru 4:15. Ne 4:12. Jb 19:3.
9 **the temple**. 1 S 3:3, 15. 2 S 7:2. Ps +5:7.
10 **in bitterness of soul**. Heb. bitter of soul. Heb. *nephesh*, 1 S +30:6mg. Ru 1:20. Jb 7:11. 9:18. 10:1. Is 38:15. 54:6. La 3:15.
prayed. Ps 50:15. 91:15. Lk 22:44. He 5:7.
wept sore. Ge 50:10. 2 K +20:3.
11 **vowed**. Le +23:38. Nu +30:2-8.
look. Ge +29:32.
remember. Ge +8:1. ver. 19. Ge 8:1. 30:22. Ps 132:1, 2. 136:23.
a man child. Heb. seed of men. A phrase not found elsewhere. Ge 3:15.
there. Nu 6:5. Jg 13:5. 16:17.
12 **continued praying**. Heb. multiplied to pray. Lk 11:8-10. 18:1. Ro 15:30. Ep 6:18. Col 4:2, 12. 1 Th 5:17. Ja 5:16.
13 **spake**. Ge 24:42-45. Ne 2:4. Ps 25:1. Ro 8:26.
not heard. Ge 24:42-45. Ne 2:4, 5. Ro 8:26.
she had. Zc 9:15. Ac 2:13. 1 C 13:7.
drunken. 1 S 25:36. 1 K 16:9. 20:16. Jb 12:25. Ps 107:27. Pr 26:9. Is 19:14. 24:20. 28:1, 3. Je 23:9. Jl 1:5.
14 **How long**. Jsh 22:12-20. Jb 8:2. Ps 62:3. Pr 6:9. Mt 7:1-3.
put away. 1 S 7:3. Ge 35:2. Jsh 24:14, 23. 1 K 20:24. Jb 11:14. 22:23. Ps 39:10. 119:29. Pr 4:24, 27. Ec 11:10. Ep 4:25, 31.
15 **No, my lord**. Pr 15:1. 25:15.
of a sorrowful spirit. Heb. hard of spirit. Heb. *ruach*, Ge +41:8.
poured. Ps 42:4. 62:8. 142:2, 3. 143:6. La 2:19.
soul. *nephesh*, Ge +34:3.
16 **a daughter of Belial**. 1 S 2:12. 10:27. 25:25. Dt +13:13. +15:9. Jg +19:22. 2 C 6:15.
out of. Jb 6:2, 3. 10:1, 2. Mt 12:34, 35.
complaint. *or*, meditation. **S#7879h**. 1 S 1:16. 1 K 18:27mg. 2 K 9:11. Jb 7:13. 9:27. 10:1. 21:4. 23:2. Ps 55:2. 64:1. 102:title. 104:34.

142:2. Pr 23:29 (babbling).
grief. Dt 32:19 (provoking).

17 **Go in peace**. Lk +7:50.
the God. Nu 6:24-26. Ps 20:1, 3-5. Is +29:23.

18 **Let thine**. Ge 32:5. 33:8, 15. Ru 2:13. 1 Th
1:3, 10. 1 P 5:7.
find grace. Ge 6:8. 18:3.
went her way. Ec 9:7. Jn 16:24. Ro 15:13.
Ph 4:6, 7.
countenance. Ps 34:5.

19 **they rose**. 1 S 9:26. Ps 5:3. 55:17. 119:147.
Mk +1:35.
knew. Ge +4:1.
and the Lord. ver. 11. Ge 8:1. 21:1. 30:22. Ps
25:7. +113:9. 136:23. Lk 23:42.

20 **when the time was come about**. Heb. in
revolution of days. 2 Ch +24:23mg.
Samuel. i.e. *God hath heard. that is,* Asked of
God. 1 S ch. 2, 3, 7, 8. 9:9, 14. ch. 10-13, 15,
16. 1 Ch 6:28. 9:22. 11:3. 26:28. 29:29. 2 Ch
35:18. Ps 99:6. Je 15:1.
Because. Ge 4:25. 5:29. 16:11. 20:32-35.
30:6-21. 41:51, 52. Ex 2:10, 22. Mt 1:21.

21 **and all**. Ge 18:19. Jsh 24:15. Ps 101:2. Ac
+16:31.
went up. ver. 3.

22 **then**. Dt 16:16. Lk 2:22, 41, 42.
be weaned. Ge 21:8. 1 K 11:20. Ps 131:2. Is
11:8. 28:9. Ho 1:8.
and there. ver. 11, 28. 1 S 2:11, 18. 3:1. Ps
23:6. 27:4.
for ever. Heb. *olam,* Ex +12:24. Ge +9:16. Ex
21:6. Le 25:23. Jsh 4:7. 2 S 7:29. 22:51. Ps
110:4. Is 9:7.

23 **Do what**. Nu 30:6-11.
the Lord. 2 S 7:25. Is 44:26.
son suck. Ge 21:7, 8. Ex 2:7. Ps 22:9. Mt
24:19. Lk 11:27.

24 A.M. 2839. B.C. 1165. An. Ex. Is. 326.
she took. Nu 15:9, 10. Dt 12:5, 6, 11. 16:16.
three bullocks. ver. 25.
bottle. 1 S 10:3. 25:18. 2 S 16:1. Je +13:12.
house of the Lord. 1 S 4:3, 4. Jsh 18:1.

25 **brought**. Ex 13:2. Lk 2:22, 23. 18:15, 16.

26 **as thy soul**. 1 S 17:55. 20:3. Ge 42:15. Le
17:11. 26:15. 2 S 11:11. 14:19. 2 K 2:2, 4, 6.
4:30. 2 C +12:15mg. Heb. *nephesh,* Ge +27:31.

27 **For this**. ver. 11-13. Mt 7:7.
and the Lord. Ps 66:19. 116:1-5. 118:5. 1 J
5:15.

28 **lent him**. *or,* returned him, whom I have
obtained by petition, to the Lord. Ex 12:36.
he shall be. *or,* he whom I have obtained by
petition shall be returned. Ex 3:22. 2 K 6:5.
he worshipped. Ge 24:26, 48, 52. 2 T 3:15.

1 SAMUEL 2

1 **prayed**. Ne 11:17. Hab 3:1. Ph 4:6.
My heart. Ex 15:2. Jb +13:15. Ps 16:5, 8.

18:2. +23:4. 33:22. 34:2. 38:15, 21. 39:7.
42:1, 2. 43:4. 51:11. 63:1-3, 8. 73:25. 119:57.
Is 12:2. 26:8, 9. 61:10. Je 14:8, 9. La 3:24. Lk
1:46, 47, etc. 1 C 1:9. 1 P 1:8.
mine horn. ver. 10. Ps +92:10.
my mouth. Ex 15:1, 21. Jg 5:1, 2. Ps 51:15.
71:8. Re 18:20.
I rejoice. Ps 9:14. 13:5. 20:5. 34:2. 35:9.
118:14. Dt +12:7.

2 **none holy**. Ps +99:3.
none beside. Dt 4:35. 2 S 22:32. Ps 73:25. Is
43:10, 11. 44:6, 8.
rock. Dt 3:24. 32:4, 30, 31, 39. Ps 18:2. 71:3,
19. 86:8. 89:6, 8. Is 40:18. Je 10:6.

3 **Talk no more**. Ps 12:3, 4.
arrogancy. Heb. hard. Ps 94:4. Pr +16:5. Is
37:23. Ml 3:13. Ju 15, 16.
a God. Heb. *El,* Ex +15:2.
of knowledge. 1 K 8:39. Ps 44:21. 94:7-10.
147:5. Je 17:10. He 4:12. Re 2:23.
by him. Jb 31:6. Pr 16:2. Is 26:7. Da 5:27.

4 **The bows**. Ps 37:15, 17. 46:9. 76:3.
stumbled. Ps 37:24. 145:14. Is 10:4. Je
37:10. Mi 7:8. 2 C 4:9, 10. 12:9, 10. Ep 6:14.
Ph 4:13. He 11:34.
girded with strength. Is +40:29. Zc 12:8.

5 **full**. Ps 34:10. Lk 1:53. 16:25.
the barren. 1 S 1:20. Ps 68:6. 107:41.
+113:9. Is +54:1.
borne seven. Ru 4:15. Jb 1:2. Je 15:9.
waxed feeble. 1 S 1:6. Is 54:1. Je 15:9. Ga
4:27.

6 **killeth**. ver. 7. Dt +32:39. 2 K 5:7. Jb 5:18. Ps
68:20. Da 5:23. Ho 6:1, 2. Jn 5:25-29. 11:25.
Re 1:18.
grave. Heb. *sheol,* Ge +37:35.
he bringeth up. 1 S 20:3. Jb +33:28. Ps
27:13. 41:8, 10. 56:13. +71:20. 116:3, 8, 9,
16. 118:17, 18. 142:5, 7. Is +26:19. Je +31:17.
Ezk 37:12. Jon 2:2-6. Zc 9:11, 12. Mt 12:40.
27:52. Jn 6:54, 58. 11:41, 44. Ro 6:5. +8:11,
23. 1 C 6:14. 15:42-44. 2 C 1:9, 10. Ph 3:21. 2
T 2:18.

7 **maketh poor**. ver. +6. Dt 8:17, 18. Ru 1:21.
Jb 1:21. 5:6, 11, 18. Ps 39:9. 66:11. 89:30-32.
102:10, 23. 2 C 12:7. Ep +1:11.
bringeth. Ps 75:7. Is 2:12. Ja 1:9, 10. 4:10.

8 **the poor**. Jb 2:8. 42:10-12. Ps +113:7, 8. Da
4:17. Lk 1:51, 52. Ja +2:5.
set them. 1 S 15:17. Ge 41:14, 40. 2 S 7:8. Jb
36:6, 7. Ps 45:7, 16. Ec 4:14. Da 2:48. 6:3. Ja
+2:5. Re 1:6. 3:21. +5:10. 22:5.
inherit the throne. Da +7:14, 22, 27. Mt
+19:28. 1 C +6:2.
the pillars. Jb 38:4-6. Ps 24:2. 102:25. 104:5.
He 1:3.

9 **will keep**. Jb 5:24. Ps 37:23, 24. 56:13.
91:11, 12. 94:18. 116:8. 119:105. 121:3, 5, 8.
Pr 16:9. 1 P 1:5.
the feet. Ps 31:8. 56:13.

his saints. Dt 33:3. Ps 37:28. 97:10. Pr 2:8. Is +26:19. Ju 1, +3.

the wicked. Jb +21:30. Pr 20:20.

be silent. Jb 27:19. 40:12, 13. Ps 31:17. 52:5. +107:42. +115:17. +146:4. 147:6. Pr 12:7. Ec 5:17. Is +24:22. 26:14. Je 8:14. Zp 1:15. Mt 8:12. 22:12, 13. 25:30. Ro 3:19. 2 P 2:17. Ju 13.

in darkness. Ps 49:19. Col +1:13. Ju 6, 13.

by strength. 1 S 17:49, 50. Ps 33:16, 17. +49:14mg. +146:3. Ec 9:11. Je 9:23. Zc 4:6.

10 **adversaries.** Ex 15:16. Jg 5:31. Ps 2:9. 21:8, 9. 68:1, 2. 92:9. Lk 19:27.

he thunder. 1 S 7:10. 12:18. Jb 40:9. Ps 18:13, 14.

judge. Ps +7:8.

he shall. 1 S 12:13. 15:28. 16:1. 2 S 7:8, 13. Ps 2:6. 21:1, 7. Is 32:1. 45:24. Mt 25:34. 28:18. Lk 1:51.

the horn. ver. +1.

anointed. 1 S 12:3. Ps 2:2. 18:50. 20:6. 28:8. 45:7. Ac 4:27. 10:38.

11 **minister.** ver. 18. 1 S 1:28. 3:1, 15.

12 **the sons.** Ho 4:6-9. Ml 2:1-9.

sons of Belial. 1 S 10:27. +30:22mg. 2 C 6:15.

knew not the Lord. 1 S 3:7. Jg 2:10. Je 2:8. 22:16. Jn 8:55. 16:3. 17:3. Ro 1:21, 28-30. T 1:16. 1 J 2:4.

14 **all that the flesh-hook.** ver. 29. Ex 29:27, 28. Le 7:31-35. Is 56:11. Ml 1:10. 2 P 2:13-15.

15 **before they.** Le 3:3-5, 16, 17. 7:23, 25, 30, 31. Ro 16:18. Ph 3:19. Ju 12.

16 **presently.** Heb. as on the day. Le 3:16. 7:23-25.

soul. Heb. *nephesh,* Nu +11:6.

I will take. Jg 18:25. Ne 5:15. Ezk +13:19.

17 **before.** Ge 6:11. 10:9. 13:13. 2 K 21:6. Ps 51:4. Is 3:8.

abhorred. Ezk 22:8. Ml 1:6. 2:8, 13. Mt 18:7.

18 **ministered.** ver. 11. 1 S 3:1.

a linen ephod. Ex +28:4.

19 **a little coat.** Ex 28:4.

from year to year. 1 S +1:3, 21. Ex 23:14.

20 **blessed.** Ge 14:19. 27:27-29. Nu 6:23-27. Ru 2:12. 4:11.

loan. *or,* petition which she asked, etc. 1 S 1:27, 28.

21 **visited.** 1 S 1:19, 20. Ge 21:1. Lk 1:68.

grew. ver. 26. 1 S 3:19. Jg 13:24. Lk 1:80. 2:40, 52.

22 **Now.** 1 S 8:1.

did unto. ver. 13-17. Je 7:9, 10. Ezk 22:26. Ho 4:9-11.

women. Ex 38:8.

assembled. assembled by troops. Ex 38:8.

23 **Why.** 1 K 1:6. Ac 9:4. 14:15.

I hear, etc. *or,* I hear evil words of you.

by all. Is 3:9. Je 3:3. 8:12. Ph 3:19.

24 **no good.** Ac 6:3. 2 C 6:8. 1 T 3:7. 3 J 12.

ye make. ver. 17, 22. Ex 32:21. 1 K 13:18-21. 15:30. 2 K 10:31. Ml 2:8. Mt 18:6. 2 P 2:18. Re 2:20.

transgress. *or,* cry out.

25 **sin against.** Dt 17:8-12. 25:1-3.

if a man. 1 S 3:14. Nu 15:30, 31. Ps 51:4, 16. He 10:26.

but if. 1 J 2:1.

who shall. 1 T 2:5. He 7:25.

hearkened. Dt 2:30. Jsh 11:20. 2 Ch 25:16. Pr 15:10. 29:1. Jn 12:39, 40. Ro 9:22.

26 **grew on.** ver. 21.

was in favor. Pr 3:3, 4. Is 40:5. Lk 1:80. 2:40, +52. Ac 2:47. Ro 14:18.

27 **a man.** Dt +33:1. Jg 6:8.

Did I. Ex 4:14, 27.

28 **And did I.** Ex 28:1, 4, 6-30. 29:4, etc. 39:1, etc. Le 8:7, 8. Nu 16:5. 17:5-8. 18:1-7. 2 S 12:7, 2 Ch 29:11.

did I give. Le +7:7.

29 **kick ye.** ver. 13, 17. Dt 32:15. Ml 1:12, 13.

and at mine. ver. 13-16.

habitation. Dt 12:5, 6. Jsh 18:1.

and honorest. Le 19:15. Dt 33:9. Mt 10:37. 22:16. Lk 14:26. 2 C 5:16. Ja 3:17.

make. ver. 13-16. Ezk +13:19. 34:2.

30 **I said.** Ex 28:43. 29:9. Nu 25:11-13.

for ever. Heb. *olam,* Ex +12:24.

Be it far. Nu 22:34mg. Ge +18:25.

them that honor me. Ex +20:12. Jg 9:9. 2 Ch 15:2. Est 6:9, 10. 8:15. Ps 50:23. Pr 3:9, 10. Is 29:13. Je 18:9, 10. Da 4:34. Ml 1:6. Jn 5:23. 8:49. 13:31, 32. 17:4, 5.

I will honor. Ps 18:20. 91:14. Ml 1:6. Mt 6:33. Jn 5:44. 12:26. 1 C 4:5. 1 P 1:7.

that despise. Nu 11:20. 2 S 12:9, 10. Ml 2:8, 9.

lightly esteemed. Lk 16:15.

31 **I will cut.** lit. have cut. 1 S 4:2, 11, 17-20. 14:3. 22:17-20. 1 K 2:26, 27, 35. Jb 22:9. Ps 37:17. Ezk 30:21-24. 44:10.

32 **an enemy,** etc. *or,* the affliction of the tabernacle. 1 S 4:4, 11, 22. Ps 78:59-64.

an old man. Zc 8:4.

33 **to consume.** 1 S 22:21-23. 1 K 1:7, 19. 2:26, 27. Mt 2:16-18.

heart. Heb. *nephesh,* Ex +23:9.

in the flower, etc. Heb. men.

34 **a sign.** 1 S 3:12. Nu +26:10. 1 K 14:12.

in one day. 1 S 4:11, 17.

35 **I will raise.** 1 K 1:8, 45. 2:35. 1 Ch 29:22. Ezk 34:23. 44:15, 16. He 2:17. 7:26-28.

mind. Heb. *nephesh,* soul, Ge +23:8. Le +26:11.

I will build. 1 S 25:28. Ex 1:21. Nu 25:13. 2 S 7:11, 27. 1 K 11:38. 1 Ch 6:8-15. Ne 12:10, 11.

mine. Ps 2:2. 18:50.

36 **is left.** 1 K 2:27. Ezk 44:10-12.

Put. Heb. Join. Or, admit. 1 S 26:19. Jb 30:7. Is 14:1. Hab 2:15.

one of the priest's offices. Heb. somewhat about the priesthood. Ex 29:9.

eat. ver. 29, 30. Ml 1:13.

1 SAMUEL 3

1 **the child**. ver. 15. 1 S 2:11, 18.

the word. ver. 21. Ps 74:9. Is 13:12. Ezk 7:26. Am 8:11, 12.

precious. S#3368h. 2 S 12:30. 1 K 5:17 (costly). 7:9, 10, 11. 10:2, 10, 11. 1 Ch 20:2. 29:2. 2 Ch 3:6. 9:1, 9, 10. 32:27. Jb 28:16. 31:26 (brightness). Ps 36:7mg. 37:20 (fat). 45:9 (honorable). 116:15. Pr 1:13. 3:15. 6:26. 12:27. 17:27. 24:4. Ec 10:1 (reputation). Is 28:16. Je 15:19. La 4:2. Ezk 27:22. 28:13. Da 11:38. Zc 14:6mg.

2 **his eyes**. 1 S 2:22. 4:14. Ge 27:1. 48:10. Ps 90:10. Ec 12:3.

3 **the lamp**. Ex 27:20, 21. 30:7, 8. Le 24:2-4. 2 Ch 13:11.

went out. Ex +30:8.

the temple. 1 S 1:9. Ps 5:7. 27:4. 29:9.

4 **called Samuel**. Ge 22:1. Ex 3:4. Ps 99:6. Ac 9:4. 1 C 12:6-11, 28. Ga 1:15, 16.

6 **my son**. 1 S 4:16. Ge 43:29. 2 S 18:22. Mt 9:2.

7 **Now Samuel**. or, Thus did Samuel before he knew the Lord, and before the word of the Lord was revealed unto him.

did not yet. Je 9:24. Am 3:7. Ac 19:2.

8 **the third**. Jb 33:14, 15. 1 C 13:11, 12.

child. 2 Ch 34:1, 3. Pr 8:17. +22:6. Ec 12:1. Is 28:9. 2 T 3:15.

9 **Speak**. Ex 20:19. Ps 85:8. Is 6:8. Da 10:19. Ac 9:6.

10 **the Lord came**. Ge 32:30.

as at other. ver. 4-6, 8.

11 **I will do**. Is 29:14. Am 3:6, 7. Hab 1:5. Ac 13:41.

both the ears. 2 K 21:12. Is 28:19. Je 19:3. Lk 21:26.

12 **I will perform**. 1 S 2:27-36. Nu 23:19. Jsh 23:15. Zc 1:6. Lk 21:33.

when I begin. etc. Heb. beginning and ending.

13 **For I have told him**. or, And I will tell him, etc. 1 S 2:27-30, etc.

I will judge. 2 Ch 20:12. Ezk 7:3. 18:30. Jl 3:12.

his house. Ge 18:19.

for ever. Heb. olam, Ex +12:24.

which he knoweth. 1 K 2:44. Ec 7:22. 1 J 3:20.

his sons. 1 S 2:12, 17, 22, 23, etc.

vile. or, accursed.

restrained them not. Heb. frowned not upon them. Ex +20:5. Nu 14:33. Nu +32:23. 1 S 2:23-25. 1 K 1:6. 2:24. 16:3. 21:21. Jb 17:5. 21:17-19. Pr +19:18. 22:15. +23:13, 14.

29:15, 17. Is 14:21. Je 32:18. Ho 4:6. Mt 10:37.

14 **the iniquity**. Ex 17:16. 20:5. 1 S 2:25. Nu 15:30, 31. Ps 51:16. Is 22:14. 48:22. Je 7:16. 15:1. Ezk 24:13. He 10:4-10, 26-31.

for ever. Heb. olam, Ex +12:24.

15 **opened**. 1 S 1:9. Ps 84:10. Ml 1:10.

feared. Je 1:6-8. 1 C 16:10, 11.

17 **I pray thee**. Ps 141:5. Da 4:19. Mi 2:7.

God. 1 S 20:13. Ru 1:17. 2 S 3:35. 19:13. 1 K 22:16. Mt 26:63.

more also. Heb. so add. Ru 1:17.

thing. or, word.

18 **Samuel told**. Mt 26:62-64.

every whit. Heb. all the things, or words. Ac +20:20.

It is the Lord. Ge 18:25. Le 10:3. Jg 10:15. 2 S 16:10-12. Is 39:8. La 3:39. 1 P 5:6.

let him. Jg +10:15. Jn 18:11. Ac +21:14.

19 **grew**. 1 S 2:21. Jg 13:24. Lk 1:80. 2:40, 52.

the Lord. 1 S 18:14. Ge 39:2, 21-23. Is 43:2. Mt 1:23. Lk 1:28. 2 C 13:11, 14. 2 T 4:22.

let none. 1 S 9:6. 1 K 8:56. Est 6:10. Is 44:26. 55:11.

20 **Dan**. Jg +20:1.

established. or, faithful. 1 T 1:12.

prophet. Dt 18:22. Ac 3:24. He 11:32.

21 **appeared**. Ge 12:7. 15:1. Nu 12:6. Am 3:7. He 1:1.

the word. ver. 1, 4.

1 SAMUEL 4

1 A.M. 2863. B.C. 1141. An. Ex. Is. 350.

came. or, came to pass. Heb. was. 1 S 3:11. Jg 3:10. 1 K 6:11.

Ebenezer. i.e. stone of help, S#72h. 1 S 5:1. 7:12.

Aphek. Jsh +12:18. 15:53, Aphekah.

2 **put**. 1 S 17:8, 21.

they joined battle. Heb. the battle was spread. or is left. 1 S 10:2. 12:22. 17:20, 22, 28. 30:16.

Israel. Jsh 7:5-8, 12. Ps 44:9, 10.

and they. Ps 79:7, 8. 106:40, 41. La 3:40.

the army. Heb. the array. ver. 12, 16. 1 S 17:20mg. Jg +6:26.

3 **the elders**. Jsh +20:4.

Wherefore. Dt 29:24. Ps 74:1, 11. 78:56. Is 50:1. 58:3.

Let us. 1 S 14:18. Nu 31:6. Jsh 6:4, 5. 2 S 15:25. 1 K +20:23. Is 1:11-15. 55:8. Je 7:4, 8-15. Mt 3:9, 10.

fetch. Heb. take unto us.

the ark. Nu 10:33. Dt 31:26. Jsh 4:7. 1 Ch 17:1. Je 3:16. He 9:4.

it may save. Je 7:8-11. Am 5:21, 22. Mt 23:25-28. Ro 2:28, 29. 1 C 10:1-5. 2 T 3:5. 1 P 3:21. Ju 5.

4 **Lord of hosts**. Jb 25:3. Ps +24:10.

which dwelleth. 2 S 6:2. 2 K 19:15. Ps 80:1. 99:1.
the cherubims. Ge +3:24.
Zophni. 1 S 2:12-17, 22. Ps 50:16, 17. Ml 1:9. Ac 19:15, 16.
with the ark. Nu 4:5, 15.

5 **all Israel**. Jg 15:14. Jb 20:5. Je 7:4. Am 6:3. Mi 2:11.
shouted. Ps 47:1-3.

6 **What meaneth**. Ex 32:17, 18.

7 **were afraid**. Ex 14:25. 15:14-16. Dt 32:30.
heretofore. Heb. yesterday *or* the third day. 1 S 14:21. 21:5. 2 S +3:17mg.

8 **smote**. Ex 7:5. 9:14. 14:27. Ps 78:43-51.
wilderness. Ex 13:20.

9 **Be strong**. Jsh +1:6. 2 S 10:12. Lk 16:8.
as they have. Dt 28:47, 48. Jg 10:7. 13:1. Is 14:2. 33:1.
quit yourselves like men. Heb. be men. 1 K 2:2.

10 **Israel**. ver. 2. Le 26:17. Dt 28:25. Ps 78:9, 60-64.
fled. Mk 14:50.
every man. 2 S 20:1. 1 K 12:16. 22:36. 2 K 14:12.
a very great. 2 S 18:7. 2 Ch 13:17. 28:5, 6. Is 10:3-6.

11 **the ark**. 1 S 2:32. Ps 78:61.
was taken. 1 S 2:32mg. Ps 78:60, 61. Mk 14:46. Ac 2:23.
the two sons. 1 S 2:34. Ps 78:64. Is 3:11.
were slain. Heb. died.

12 **with his clothes rent**. 2 K +18:37.
with earth. Jsh +7:6.

13 **sat upon**. 1 S 1:9.
his heart. Jsh 7:9. Ne 1:3, 4. Ps 26:8. 79:1-8. 137:4-6.

14 **What meaneth**. ver. 6.

15 **ninety**. 1 S 3:2. Ps 90:10.
and his eyes. Ge +27:1.
were dim. Heb. stood. 1 K 14:4mg.

16 **What is there done**. Heb. What is the thing. 2 S 1:4.
my son. 1 S +3:6. Jsh 7:19.

17 **Israel**. ver. 10, 11. 1 S 3:11.

18 **when he made**. ver. 21, 22. Ps 26:8. 42:3, 10. 69:9. La 2:15-19.
his neck. 1 S 2:31, 32. 3:12, 13. Le 10:3. 1 C 11:30-32. 1 P 4:17, 18.

19 **with child**. **S#2030h**: Ge 16:11. 38:24, 25. Ex 21:22. Jg 13:5, 7. 2 S 11:5. 2 K 8:12. 15:16. Is 7:14. 26:17. Je 20:17. 31:8. Am 1:13.
be delivered. *or*, cry out.
bowed herself. Ge 4:7. 49:9. 1 K 8:54. Is 45:23.
travailed. Je 30:6. 50:43. Ho 13:13. Mi 4:9, 10.
pains. Is 21:3.
came upon her. Heb. were turned. 1 S 10:6. Da 10:16.

20 **Fear not**. Ge 35:17, 18. Jn 16:21.
neither did she regard it . Heb. and set not her heart. 1 S 9:20. 25:25. Ex 7:23. 2 S 13:20mg. Ps 48:13mg. 62:10. 77:2. Pr 22:15, 17. 24:32mg. 27:23mg.

21 **Ichabod**. *that is*, Where is the glory? *or*, There is no glory. **S#350h**. 1 S 14:3.
The glory. Ps 26:8. 63:1, 2. 78:61, 64. 106:20. Je 2:11. Ho 9:12.

22 **The glory**. Nu 12:10. Ps 137:5, 6. Ezk 10:18. 11:23. Jn 2:17.

1 SAMUEL 5

1 **took**. 1 S 4:11, 17, 18, 22. Ps 78:61.
Ebenezer. 1 S 4:1. 7:12.
Ashdod. Jsh +11:22.

2 **of Dagon**. Jg 16:23. 1 Ch 10:10. Da 5:2, 23. Hab 1:11, 16.

3 **Dagon was**. Ex 12:12. Ps 97:7. Is 19:1. 46:1, 2. Zp 2:11. Mk 3:11. Lk 10:18-20. 2 C 6:14-16.
fallen. Lk 11:22. Jn 18:6. 1 J 5;21.
set him. Is 19:1. 40:20. 41:7. 44:17-20. 46:1, 2, 7. Je 10:8.

4 **fallen**. ver. +3.
the head. Is 2:18, 19. 27:9. Je 10:11. 50:2. Ezk 6:4-6. Da 11:8. Mi 1:7.
the stump. *or*, the fishy part. Jg 16:23.

5 **neither**. Ps 115:4-7. 135:15-18.
tread. Jsh 5:15. Zp 1:9.

6 **the hand**. ver. 7, 9, 11. Ex +9:3.
emerods. ver. 9, 11. 1 S 6:5. Dt 28:27. Jb 31:3. Ps 78:66.
thereof. 1 S 6:4, 5.

7 **saw**. 1 S 4:8. Ex 8:8, 28. 9:28. 10:7. 12:33.
The ark. 1 S 6:20. 2 S 6:9. 1 Ch 13:11-13. 15:13.
sore. or, hard. Ge 49:7. Dt 1:17. 15:18. 2 S 8:1. 19:43.
upon Dagon our god. ver. 3, 4. Je 46:25. 48:7.

8 **What shall**. Zc 12:3.
Gath. Jsh +11:22.

9 **the hand**. ver. +6. Am 5:19. 9:1-4.
with a very. ver. 11.
and they had emerods. ver. 6. 1 S 6:4, 5, 11. Ps 78:66.

10 **God to Ekron**. Jsh +13:3.
us, to slay us and our people. Heb. me, to slay me and my people. 1 S 7:13.

11 **that it slay**. Ex 14:20. Ho 14:9. Mt 21:44. 1 P 2:6-8.
us not, and our people. Heb. me not, and my people.
a deadly. 2 S 6:11. Is 13:7-9. Je 48:42-44. 2 C 2:15, 16.
the hand. ver. +6, 9.

12 **died**. 1 K 19:17. Am 5:19.
the cry. 1 S 9:16. Ex 12:30. Is 15:3-5. Je 14:2. 25:34. 48:3.

1 SAMUEL 6

1 A.M. 2864. B.C. 1140. An. Ex. Is. 351.
the ark. 1 S 5:1, 3, 10, 11. Ps 78:61.

2 **called**. Ge 41:8. Ex 7:11. Is 47:12, 13. Da 2:2.
5:7. Mt 2:3, 4.
wherewith. Mi 6:6-9.

3 **empty**. Ex 23:15. 34:20. Dt 16:16.
a trespass offering. Le +5:6.
known. ver. 9. 1 S 5:7, 9, 11. Jb 10:2. 34:31,
32.

4 **Five golden**. ver. 5, 17, 18. 1 S 5:6, 9. Ex
12:35. Jsh 13:3. Jg 3:1, 3.
you all. Heb. them.

5 **mice**. Ex 8:5, 17, 24. 10:14, 15. Jl 1:4-7. 2:25.
give glory. Ps 18:44. 66:3mg. Je 3:13. Re
+11:13.
lighten. 1 S 5:6, 11. Ps 32:4. 39:10.
off your. 1 S 5:3, 4, 7. Ex 12:12. Nu 33:4. Is
19:1.

6 **harden**. Jb 9:4. Ps 95:8. Ro 2:5. He 3:13.
the Egyptians. Ex 7:13. 8:15. 9:16, 34. 10:3.
14:17, 23. 15:14-16.
wonderfully. *or,* reproachfully. Ex 10:2.
did they not. Ex 12:31-33.
the people. Heb. them.

7 **new cart**. Ge 45:19. 2 S 6:3. 1 Ch 13:7.
milch. or, suckling. ver. 10. Ge 33:13. Ps
78:71. Is 40:11mg.
on which. Nu 19:2.

8 **jewels**. ver. 4, 5.

9 **Beth-shemesh**. Je +43:13.
he. *or,* it. Am 3:6.
we shall. ver. 3.
not his hand. Ex +9:3.
a chance. 2 S 1:6. Ec 9:11. Lk 10:31. or, accident. Ru 2:3. 1 S 20:26. Ec 2:14, 15. 3:9. 9:2,
3.

11 **they laid**. 2 S 6:3. 1 Ch 13:7. 15:13-15.

13 **lifted**. Ge +22:13.

14 **Bethshemite**. S#1030h. ver. 18.
offered. 1 S 11:5. 20:29. 1 K 18:30-38. 19:21.
burnt offering. Le +23:12.

16 **the five**. ver. 4, 12. Jsh 13:3. Jg 3:3. 16:5, 23-
30.
they returned. 1 S 5:10.

17 **these**. ver. 4.
Ashdod. Jsh +11:22.
Gaza. Ge +10:19.
Askelon. Jg +1:18.
Gath. Jsh +11:22.
Ekron. Jsh +13:3.

18 **the five lords**. ver. 16. Jsh 13:3.
great stone of. *or,* great stone.
Abel. i.e. *meadow,* S#59h. Nu 33:49. Jg
11:33mg. 2 S 20:14, 15, 18. 1 K 15:20. 2 K
15:29.
unto this day. 1 S 27:6. 30:25. Ge +19:38. 2
S 4:3. 6:8. 1 K 8:8. 12:19. 2 K 2:22. 8:22.
14:7. 16:6. 17:41.

19 **he smote**. Ex 19:21. Le 10:1-3. Nu 4:4, 5, 15,

20. Dt 29:29. 2 S 6:7. 1 Ch 13:9, 10. Col 2:18.
1 P 4:17.
looked into. 2 S 6:6, 7. Mt 11:27. Col 2:18.
the ark. Ex 25:21. 40:20. 2 C 3:7.
fifty thousand. or, fifty chief men, as the
original word *eleph* means in Mi +5:2 with Mt
2:6.
lamented. Ge 37:34.
a great slaughter. Le 26:21.

20 **Who is able**. Nu 17:12, 13. 2 S 6:7, 9. 1 Ch
13:11-13. Ps 76:7. Ml 3:2. Mt 8:34. Mk 10:32.
Lk 5:8. 8:37.
whom shall. 1 S 5:8-12.

21 **Kirjath-jearim**. or Kirjath-Baal, Jsh +15:9.
Ps 78:60. Je 7:12, 14.

1 SAMUEL 7

1 **Kirjath-jearim**. Jsh +9:17. Ps 132:6.
Abinadab. 1 S +16:8. Is 52:11.
Eleazar. Ex +6:23.

2 **lamented**. Jg 2:4. Je 3:13, 22-25. 31:9. Zc
12:10, 11. Mt 5:4. 2 C 7:10, 11.

3 A.M. 2884. B.C. 1120. An. Ex. Is. 371.
If. Ge +4:7.
return. 2 K +17:13. Jb 22:23. Is 44:22. Ezk
14:6. 18:30. Zc +1:3.
put away. Ge 35:2. Jsh 24:14, 23.
strange. Ex 12:43. Jg 10:16mg. 2 S 22:45, 46.
Ashtaroth. Jg +2:13.
prepare. Dt 30:6. 1 Ch 22:19. 28:9. 29:16. 2
Ch +12:14mg. Pr 16:1. Je 4:3, 4. Ezk 18:31.
Mt 15:8. Jn 4:24.
serve him. Mt +4:10.

4 **Baalim**. Jg +2:11, 13. 10:15, 16. 1 K 11:33.
Ho 14:3, 8.

5 **Gather**. Ne 9:1. Jl 2:16.
Mizpeh. ver. 12, 16. Jsh +15:38.
I will pray. 1 S 12:23.

6 **drew water**. 1 S 1:15. Nu 29:35. 2 S 14:14.
Jb 16:20. Ps 6:6. 42:3. 119:136. Je 9:1. La
2:11, 18. 3:49.
poured. 2 S 14:14. 23:16, 17. 1 Ch 11:18. Ps
22:14.
fasted. Jon ch. 3. Mt +6:16.
We have sinned. Le 26:40. Jg 10:10. 1 K
8:47. Ezr 9:5-10. Jb 33:27. 40:4. 42:6. Ps 38:3-
8. 106:6. Je 3:13, 14. 31:19. Da 9:3-5. Jl 2:12.
Lk 15:18.
judged. Jg 3:10. Ne 9:27. Ezk 20:4.

7 **afraid**. 1 S 13:6. 17:11. Ex 14:10. 2 Ch 20:3.

8 **Cease**, etc. Heb. Be not silent from us from
crying. 1 S 12:19-24. Ge 18:32. 1 S +23:4. Jb
13:13mg. Ps +3:4. 35:22. 50:3. 83:1. 109:1.
+119:145-147. Is 37:4. Je 38:27mg. Ho 12:4.
Lk 11:5-9. +18:1-6. Ac 12:5. Ja +5:16.

9 **a sucking lamb**. ver. 17. 1 S 6:14, 15. 9:12.
10:8. 16:2. Jg 6:26, 28. 1 K 18:30-38. Is 65:25.
burnt offering. Le +23:12.
cried unto. Ps +3:4. 99:6. Je 15:1. Ja 5:16.

heard. *or,* answered. 1 S 8:18. Ps 20:1, 3, 5, 6. 99:6. Je 15:1. Mi 3:4.

10 thundered. 1 S 2:10. Ex +9:23-25. Jg 5:8, 20. Ps 18:11-14. 81:7. 97:3, 4.
discomfited. Dt 20:3, 4. Jsh 10:10. Jg 4:15. 5:20. Zc 4:6.

11 Beth-car. i.e. *house of Car* or *a lamb,* **S#1033h.**

12 took a stone. Ge 28:18, 19. 31:45-52. 35:14. Jsh 4:9, 20-24. 24:26, 27. Is 19:19. 28:16.
Mizpeh. ver. 5, 6. Jsh 11:3.
Shen. i.e. *a tooth,* **S#8129h.**
Ebenezer. *that is,* The stone of help. 1 S 4:1. 5:1. Ge 22:14. Ex 17:15.
Hitherto. Ps 71:6, 17. Is 46:3, 4. Ac 26:22. 2 C 1:10.

13 subdued. Jg 13:1.
came no more. 1 S 13:1-5.
hand. Ex +9:3.
against. 1 S 14:6-16, 20-23. 17:49-53. 28:3-5. 31:1-7.

14 peace. 1 S 12:11. Dt 7:2, 16. Jg 4:17. Ps 106:34.

15 A.M. 2873-2947. B.C. 1131-1057.
judged. ver. 6. 1 S 12:1. 25:1. Jg 2:16. 3:10, 11. Ac 13:20, 21.

16 year to year. 1 S 1:7. 1 K 5:11. 10:25.
in circuit. Heb. and he circuited. 1 S 9:6, 11, 12. Jg 5:10. 10:4. 12:14. Ps 75:2. 82:3, 4.

17 his return. 1 S 1:1, 19. 8:4. 19:18-23.
he built. 1 S 11:15. Ge +13:18.

1 SAMUEL 8

1 A.M. 2892. B.C. 1112. An. Ex. Is. 379.
made his. Ex +21:6. Jg 8:22, 23. Ne 7:2. 1 T 5:21.
sons judges. Jg 5:10. 10:4. 12:14.

2 Joel. i.e. *the Lord is God,* **S#3100h.** 1 Ch 4:35. 5:4, 8, 12. 6:28, 33, 36, 38, Vashni. 7:3. 11:38. 15:7, 11, 17. 23:8. 26:22. 27:20. 2 Ch 29:12. Ezr 10:43. Ne 11:9. Jl 1:1.
Abiah. i.e. *the Lord is my father,* **S#29h.** 1 Ch 2:24. 6:28. 7:8.

3 his sons. 2 S 15:4. 1 K 12:6-11. 2 K 21:1-3. Ec 2:19. Je 22:15-17.
but turned. Ex 18:21, 22. Dt 16:19. Ps 15:5. 26:10. Is 33:15. Je 22:15-17. 1 T 3:3. 6:10.

4 the elders. Ex 3:16. +18:21. Jsh +20:4.

5 now make. ver. 6-8, 19, 20. 1 S 12:17. Ex 32:1. Nu 23:9. Dt 17:14, 15. Ho 13:10, 11. Ac 13:21.

6 displeased. Heb. was evil in the eyes of. 1 S 12:17. Nu +22:34mg. Jon 4:1.
prayed. 1 S 15:11. Ex 32:31, 32. Nu 16:15, 22, 46. Ezr 9:3-5. Ps 109:4. Lk 6:11, 12. Ph 4:6. Ja 1:5.

7 Hearken. Nu 22:20. Ps 81:11, 12. Is 66:4. Ho 13:9-11.
they have not. 1 S 10:19. 12:17-19. Ex 16:8.

Mt 10:24, 25, 40. Lk 10:16. 19:14, 27. Jn 5:23. 13:16. 15:20, 21.
rejected me. Ex 16:8. Ps 51:4. Ac 5:4.

8 to all. Ex 14:11, 12. 16:3. 17:2. 32:1. Nu 14:2-4. 16:2, 3, 41. Dt 9:24. Jg 2:2, 3, 20. 4:1. 6:1. 13:1. Ps 78:56-59. 95:10. 106:14-21, 34-40. Ac 7:51-53.
forsaken me. Is 1:4. Je 2:13.

9 hearken unto. *or,* obey. ver. 7, 22.
howbeit, etc. *or,* notwithstanding when thou hast solemnly protested against them, then thou shalt show, etc. Ezk 3:18.
the manner. ver. 11-18. 1 S 2:13. 10:25. 14:52. Ezk 45:7, 8. 46:18.

11 This will. 1 S 10:25. Dt 17:14-20.
He will take. 1 S 14:52. 1 K 9:22, 23. 10:26. 12:4, 10. 2 Ch 26:10-15.
his chariots. 1 K 4:26.
run. 2 S 15:1. 1 K 1:5. 18:46.

12 appoint. 1 Ch 27:1-22.
and will set. 1 K 4:7, 22, 23, 27, 28. 2 Ch 32:28, 29.

14 will take. 1 S 22:7. 1 K 21:7, 19. Ezk 46:18.

15 give to. 1 K 4:7, 22, 23.
officers. Heb. eunuchs. 2 K +8:6mg.

18 cry out. Is 8:21.
your king. Dt 17:15. 1 K 12:4, 14, 15.
will not hear. Jb 27:9. Ps 18:41. Pr 1:24-28. 21:13. Is 1:15. Mi 3:4. Lk 13:25.

19 refused to obey. Ps 81:11. Je 7:13. 44:16. Ezk 33:31.

20 we also. ver. 5. Ex 33:16. Le 20:24-26. Nu 23:9. Dt 7:6. Ps 106:35. Je +10:2. Jn 15:19. Ro 12:2. 2 C 6:17. Ph 3:20. 1 P 2:9.
fight our. 2 Ch 32:8.

21 he rehearsed. Ex +19:8. Jg 11:11.

22 Hearken. ver. 7. Ps 106:15. Ho 4:17. 13:11.

1 SAMUEL 9

1 Kish. i.e. *laying a snare* or *bending; a bow,* **S#7027h.** ver. 3. 1 S 10:11, 21. 14:51. 2 S 21:14. 1 Ch 8:30, 33, 33. 9:36, 39, 39. 12:1. 23:21, 22. 24:29, 29. 26:28. 1 Ch 29:12. Est 2:5. Ac 13:21, Cis.
Abiel. i.e. *my father is strong* or *is God,* **S#22h.** 1 S 14:51. 1 Ch 11:32.
Zeror. i.e. *a bundle* or *bag,* **S#6872h.**
Bechorath. i.e. *a first-born,* **S#1064h.**
Aphiah. i.e. *blown* or *inflamed; rekindled, refreshed,* **S#647h.**
a Benjamite. *or,* the son of a man of Jemini.
power. *or,* substance. 1 S 25:2. 2 S 19:32. Jb 1:3.

2 Saul. i.e. *asked; prayed for; desired,* **S#7586h.**
choice. Ex 14:7. Jg 20:15, 16, 34. 1 S 16:7. Ge 6:2. 2 S 14:25, 26. Je 9:23.
from his shoulders. 1 S 10:23. 17:4. Nu 13:33.

3 **the asses**. 1 S 10:2. Ge 12:16. 32:15. 45:23. 49:11. Nu 22:21-33. Jg 5:10. 10:4.

4 **mount**. Jsh +17:15.
Shalisha. i.e. *triangular; a third*, **S#8031h**. 2 K 4:42, Baal-shalisha.
Shalim. i.e. *place of foxes*, **S#8171h**, only here. Ge 33:18. Jn 3:23.

5 **Zuph**. 1 S 1:1.
leave. or, cease. Ge 11:8. 18:11.
take thought. or, sorrow. **S#1672h**. 1 S 10:2. Ps 38:18. Is 57:10, 11. Je 17:8. 38:19. 42:16. Mt 6:25, 28, 34. Lk 12:11, 22.

6 **man of God**. Dt +33:1.
an honorable. 1 Th 2:10. 5:13.
all that he saith. 1 S 3:19, 20. Is 44:26. Zc 1:5, 6. Mt 24:35.

7 **what shall**. Jg 6:18. 13:15-17. 1 K 14:3. 2 K 4:42. 5:5. 8:8. 1 Ch +21:24.
spent in. Heb. gone out of, etc.
there is not. Is 57:9.
present. Jg +3:15.
bring to. Ga 6:6. 1 T 5:17. He 13:16.
have we. Heb. is with us.

8 **I have here at hand**. Heb. there is found in my hand.

9 **enquire**. Ge 25:22. Jg 1:1.
Prophet. Nu 12:6. 24:4.
a Seer. 2 S +24:11. 2 K 17:13. 1 Ch 26:28. 29:29. 2 Ch 16:7, 10. Is 29:10. 30:10. Am 7:12.

10 **Well said**. Heb. Thy word is good. 2 K 5:13, 14.

11 **the hill to the city**. Heb. in the ascent of the city.
found. Ge 24:11, 18-20. Ex 2:16. Jg 5:11.

12 **he is**. 1 S 7:17.
sacrifice. or, feast. lit. the sacrifice of the day. 1 S 16:2. Ge 31:54. Dt 12:6, 7. 1 C 5:7, 8.
the high place. 1 S 10:5, 13. 1 K 3:2-4. 1 Ch 16:39.

13 **he doth bless**. Ex 23:25. Ps 132:15. Lk +24:30.
this time. Heb. today. ver. 27mg.

15 **the Lord**. ver. 17. 1 S 15:1. Ps 25:14. Am 3:7. Mk 11:2-4. 14:13-16. Ac 13:21. 27:23.
told Samuel in his ear. Heb. revealed the ear of Samuel. ver. 17. 1 S 15:22. Ge 18:17. Ru +4:4. Ps 78:1. Is 50:4.

16 **thou shalt**. 1 S 15:1. Ex +28:41.
captain. **S#5057h**: 1 S 10:1. 13:14. 25:30 (ruler). 2 S 5:2. 1 Ch 13:1. Jb 31:37. Ps 76:12. Is 55:4. Ezk 28:2. Da 9:25, 26. 11:22.
save. 1 S 14:23. 18:7.
looked upon. Ex 2:23-25. 3:7-9. Ps 25:18. 106:44.

17 **Behold**. 1 S 16:6-12. Ho 13:11.
reign over. Heb. restrain in. 1 S 3:13. 2 S 23:6, 7. Ne 13:19, 25. Jb 29:9. Ac 13:21. Ro 13:3, 4.

18 **gate**. or, city. ver. 14. Ge +14:7.

19 **the Seer**. Nu 24:4, 16. Je 14:4.
and will tell. Jn 4:29. 1 C 14:25.

20 **three days ago**. Heb. today three days. ver. 3.
set not. 1 S +4:20mg. 1 Ch 29:3. Ps 62:10. Col 3:2.
on whom. 1 S 8:5, 19. 12:13, 15.
desire. Ge +27:15.

21 **a Benjamite**. Jg 20:46-48. Ps 68:27.
the smallest. Mi 5:2.
my family. 1 S 10:27. 15:17. 18:18, 23. Jg 6:14, 15. Ho 13:1. Lk 14:11. Ep 3:8.
so to me. Heb. according to this word.

22 **the parlor**. 2 K 23:11. 1 Ch 9:26, 33. 23:28. 28:12. 2 Ch 31:11. Ezr 8:29.
in the chiefest. Ge 43:32. Lk 14:10.

23 **cook**. lit. slaughter man. Ge 37:36mg. Je 39:9mg.
Bring. 1 S 1:5. Ge 43:34.
portion. Ex 29:26.

24 **cook**. ver. +23.
the shoulder. Le 7:32, 33. Is 9:6. Ezk 24:4.
left. *or*, reserved. Ge 14:10 (remained).
this time. or, appointed season. Ex 13:10.

25 **And when**. ver. 13.
the top. ver. 26. Dt +22:8.

26 **top of the house**. ver. +25.
Up. Ge 19:14. 44:4. 35:7:13. Jg 19:28.

27 **Bid the servant**. 1 S 20:38, 39. Jn 15:14, 15.
but stand. 1 S 12:7. 23:16. Da 10:19.
a while. Heb. today. ver. 13.
that I may. 1 S 15:16. 2 K 9:5, 6. Da 10:21.

1 SAMUEL 10

1 **a vial**. 1 S 2:10. 24:6. 26:11. Ex +28:41. Ac 13:21. Re 5:8.
kissed him. Ps +2:12.
captain. 1 S 8:9, 19. 13:14. Jsh 5:14, 15. 2 S 5:2. 2 K 20:5. He 2:10.
his inheritance. 1 S 26:19. Ex 19:5, 6. Dt +32:9. 2 S 20:19. 21:3. 1 K 8:51, 53. 2 K 21:14. Ps 2:8. 28:9. 78:71. +94:14. 132:11, 13. 135:4. Is 63:17. 65:9. Je 10:16. Zc 2:12. Lk +1:32, 33. Ep 1:18. Col +3:24. He 1:2.

2 **Rachel's**. Ge 35:19, 20. Je 31:15.
sepulchre. **S#6900h**, *qeburah*, Ge +35:20.
Zelzah. i.e. *shade from heat; a clear shadow*, **S#6766h**. Jsh 18:28.
The asses. ver. 16. 1 S 9:3-5.
care. Heb. business.

3 **Tabor**. Jg +4:6.
Bethel. Ge +12:8.
three kids. Le 1:10. 3:6, 12. 7:13. 23:13. Nu 15:5-12.
a bottle. 1 S 1:24. Je +13:12.

4 **salute thee**. Heb. ask thee of peace. Jg +18:15mg.

5 **hill of God**. ver. 10. 1 S 13:3.
garrison. 1 S 13:3. 2 S 5:7. Ps 2:6. 68:15, 16.

a company. 1 S 19:20. 2 K 2:3, 5, 15. 4:38. 6:1. Ps 119:61mg.
high place. 1 S 9:12, 13.
a psaltery. Ex 15:20, 21. 2 S 6:5. 1 K 10:12. 2 K 3:15. 1 Ch 13:8. 15:16, 19-21, 27, 28. 16:5, 42. 25:1-6. 2 Ch 5:12. 9:11. 20:28. 29:25-27. Ps 49:4. 150:3-6.
tabret. Ge 31:27. Ex 15:20. 2 K 3:15.
pipe. 1 K 1:40. Is 5:12. 30:29. Je 48:36.
harp. Re +5:8.
prophesy. 1 C 14:1.
6 Spirit. Heb. *ruach*, Ge +41:38. ver. 10. 1 S 16:13. 19:23, 24. Nu 11:25. Jg 3:10. Jl 2:28. Mt 7:22.
another man. ver. 9-12.
7 let it be. Heb. it shall come to pass that, etc.
signs. Ex 4:8. Lk 2:12. Jn 16:4.
that thou do as occasion, etc. Heb. do for thee as thine hand shall find. 1 S 18:14. Jg +9:33.
God. Ge 21:20. Dt 20:1. Jg 6:12. Is 7:14. 45:1, 2. Mt 1:23. 28:20. Ac 18:10.
8 to Gilgal. Jsh +4:19.
burnt offerings. Le +23:12.
sacrifices of. Le +7:11.
peace offerings. Le +23:19.
9 back. Heb. shoulder. 1 S 9:2. Ge 49:15. Ps 21:12.
gave. Heb. turned.
another heart. ver. 6. Nu 14:24.
and all those signs. ver. 2-5. Jg 6:21, 36-40. 7:11. Is 38:7, 8. Mk 14:16.
10 they came. ver. 5. 1 S 19:20-24.
Spirit. Heb. *ruach*, Ge +41:38.
came upon. Lk 1:67. Ac 2:4. 10:45, 46. 11:15.
11 when all. Jb 42:11. Jn 9:8, 9. Ac 3:10.
beforetime. lit. from yesterday, third day. 2 S +3:17mg.
one to another. Heb. a man to his neighbor. Je 13:14mg.
What is this. Mt 13:54, 55. Ac 2:7, 8. 4:13. 9:21.
Is Saul. 1 S 19:24. Mt 13:54, 55. Jn 7:15. Ga 1:23.
12 of the same place. Heb. from thence.
who is their. Is 54:13. Jn 6:45. 7:16. Ja 1:17.
proverb. Dt +28:37.
14 And he said. 1 S 9:3-10.
no where. 2 K 5:25.
16 matter. 1 S 9:27. Ex 4:18. Jg 14:6. Pr 29:11.
17 unto the Lord. 1 S 7:5, 6. Jg 20:1.
18 Thus saith. Jg 2:1. 6:8, 9. Ne 9:9-12, 27, 28.
brought up. Ge 50:24. Ex 17:3.
and delivered. Ex 18:8. Jsh 24:10.
19 And ye have. 1 S 8:7-9, 19. 12:12, 17-19.
saved you. Jg 3:9mg, 15. 6:36.
present yourselves. 1 S 12:7, 16. Jsh 24:1.
by your tribes. Nu 17:2. Jsh 7:14, etc.
your thousands. Mi +5:2.

20 caused. Jsh 7:16-18.
was taken. Jsh +14:2.
21 Matri. i.e. *rainy; rain of Jehovah*, **S#4309h**.
22 enquired. 1 S 23:2-4, 11, 12. Nu 27:21. Jg 1:1. 20:18, 23, 28.
further. 1 S 16:11. 23:4.
hid. 1 S 9:21. 15:17. Jsh 2:6. Lk 14:11.
23 he was higher. 1 S 9:2. 16:7. 17:4.
24 See ye him. Dt 17:15. 2 S 21:6.
God save the king. Heb. Let the king live. 1 S 25:6. 2 S 16:16mg. 1 K 1:25, 31, 34, 39. 2 K 11:12mg. 2 Ch 23:11mg. Ps 22:26. 34:12. 69:32. Ec 6:8. Mt 21:9. Mk 11:9, 10. Lk 19:38. 1 Th 3:8. 1 T +2:2. 1 P 3:10.
25 the manner. 1 S 8:11-18. Dt 17:14-20. Ezk 45:9, 10. 46:16-18. Ro 13:1-7. 1 T 2:1, 2. T 3:1. 1 P 2:13, 14.
wrote. Dt 17:18, 19.
26 Gibeah. Jg +19:12.
band. Ex 14:4, 9, 28.
whose hearts. Ezr 1:5. Ps 110:3. Ac 7:10. 13:48. 16:14.
27 children of Belial. 1 S 2:12. 11:12. Dt 13:13. +15:9. Jg +19:22. 2 S 20:1. 2 Ch 13:7. Ac 7:35, 51, 52.
brought him. Jg +3:15.
he held his peace. *or*, he was as though he had been deaf. Ps 38:13. Is 36:21. Mt 27:12-14.

1 SAMUEL 11

1 Nahash. i.e. *a serpent*, as in Ge 3:1. **S#5176h**.
ver. 2. 1 S 12:12. Jg 10:7. 11:8, etc. 2 S 10:2. 17:25, 27. 1 Ch 19:1, 2.
the Ammonite. ver. +11. Ge +19:38.
Jabesh-gilead. 1 S 31:11-13. Jg 21:8, 10, etc.
Make. Ge 26:28. Ex +23:32. Dt 23:3. 1 K 20:34. Jb 41:4. Is 36:16. Ezk 17:13.
2 On this. 2 K 18:31.
thrust. Nu 16:14mg. Jg 16:21. Est 3:6. Jb 30:17. Pr 12:10. 30:17. Is 51:1. Je 39:7.
reproach. 1 S +17:26. Ge 34:14.
3 elders. Jsh +20:4.
Give us. Heb. Forbear us.
4 to Gibeah. Jg +19:12.
lifted up. 1 S 30:4. Jg 2:4. 21:2. Ro 12:15. 1 C 12:26. Ga 6:2. He 13:3.
5 after the herd. 1 S 9:1. 1 K 19:19. Ps 78:71.
What aileth. Ge 21:17. Jg 18:23. Is 22:1.
6 Spirit of God. Heb. *ruach*, Ge +41:38. 1 S 10:10. 16:13. Jg 3:10. 6:34. 11:29. 13:25. 14:6.
his anger. Ex 32:19. Nu 12:3. Mk 3:5. Ep 4:26. Ja 1:20.
7 he took. Jg 19:29.
hewed. Jg 19:29. 20:6.
Whosoever. Jg 21:5-11.
the fear. Ge +35:5. Jg 5:23.
with one consent. Heb. as one man. Jg 20:1.

8 **he numbered**. Nu 31:48, 49. Jg 21:5-11. 1 S
14:17. 2 S 18:1, 2. 20:4. 24:1-9. 1 K 20:15, 26.
2 K 25:19. 1 Ch 21:5, 6. 2 Ch 25:5. Is 13:4.
Bezek. Jg 1:4, 5.
the children. 1 S 13:15. 15:4. 2 S 24:9. 2 Ch
17:12-19.
9 **help**. *or*, deliverance. Ps 18:17.
10 **Tomorrow**. ver. 2, 3.
11 **on the morrow**. Ge 22:14. Ps 46:1.
in three. Jg 7:16. 9:43.
morning. Ex 14:24.
slew. ver. 2. Jg 1:7. Mt 7:2. Ja 2:13.
Ammonites. S#5984h. ver. 1, 2. Dt 2:20. 23:3.
2 S 23:37. 1 K 11:1, 5. 14:21, 31. 1 Ch 11:39. 2
Ch 12:13. 20:1. 24:26. 26:8. Ezr 9:1. Ne 2:10,
19. 4:3, 7. 13:1, 23. Je 40:14. Ezk 25:2, 3.
so that two. 1 S 30:17, 18. Jg 4:16.
12 **Who is he**. 1 S 10:27. Ps 21:8. Lk 19:27.
13 **There shall**. 1 S 14:45. 2 S 19:22.
the Lord. 1 S 19:5. Ex 14:13, 30. Ps 44:4-8.
Is 59:16. 1 C 15:10.
wrought salvation. 1 S 14:45.
14 **let us go**. 1 S 7:16. 10:8.
renew. 1 S 10:24. 2 S 5:3. 1 Ch 12:38, 39.
15 **king**. 1 Ch 11:3.
before the Lord. 1 S 10:17.
sacrificed. 1 S 10:8. Ex 24:5. 1 Ch 29:21-24.
sacrifices. Le +7:11.
peace offerings. Le +23:19.
rejoiced greatly. 1 S 8:19. 12:13-15, 17. Ho
13:10, 11. Ja 4:16.

1 SAMUEL 12

1 **Behold**. 1 S 8:5-8, 19-22.
have made. 1 S 10:1, 24. 11:14, 15.
2 **walketh**. 1 S 8:20. Nu 27:17.
I am old. 1 S 8:1, 5. Ps 71:18. Is 46:3, 4. 2 T
4:6. 2 P 1:14.
grayheaded. Jb 15:10.
my sons. 1 S 2:22, 29. 3:13, 16. 8:3.
I have walked. 1 S 3:19, 20.
3 **his anointed**. ver. 5. 1 S 10:1. 24:6. 2 S 1:14-
16. Mt 22:21. Ro 13:1-7.
whose ox. Nu 16:15. Jg 15:16. Ac 20:33.
24:16. 2 C 12:14. 1 Th 2:5, 10. 1 P 5:2.
bribe. Dt 16:19. Heb. ransom. lit. a covering.
S#3724h: Ge 6:14 (with pitch). Ex 24:30 (sum
of money). 30:12. Nu 35:31, 32 (satisfaction).
1 S 6:18 (villages). 12:3. Jb 33:24 (ransom;
mg, or, atonement). 36:18. Ps 49:7. Pr 6:35.
13:8. 21:18. SS 1:14 (camphire). 4:13. Is 48:3.
Am 5:12.
blind mine eyes. *or*, that I should hide mine
eyes at him. Ex 23:8. Le 20:4. Dt 16:19. Pr
28:27. Is 1:15. Ezk 22:26.
I will. Ex 22:4. Le 6:4. Lk 19:8.
4 **hast not**. Ps 37:5, 6. Da 6:4. 3 J 12.
5 **The Lord**. Jb 31:35-40. 42:7.
his anointed. 1 S 26:9.

ye have. Jn 18:38. Ac 23:9. 24:16, 20. 1 C
4:4. 2 C 1:12. 1 Th 2:10.
in my hand. Ex 22:4. Ps 17:3.
6 **It is the Lord**. Ex 6:26. Ne 9:9-14. Ps 77:19,
20. 78:12, etc. 99:6. 105:26, 41. Is 63:7-14.
Ho 12:13. Mi 6:4.
advanced. *or*, made.
7 **stand still**. 1 S 9:27.
reason. Is 1:18. 5:3, 4. Ezk 18:25-30. Mi 6:2,
3. Ac 17:3.
righteous acts. Heb. righteousness, *or* benefits. Jg +5:11.
to. Heb. with.
8 **Jacob**. Ge 46:5-7. Nu 20:15. Ac 7:15.
cried. Ex 2:23, 24. 3:9.
sent Moses. ver. 6. Ex 3:10. 4:14-16, 27-31.
6:26. Ps 77:20.
brought. Ex 12:51. 14:30, 31.
made them. Jsh 1:2-4, 6. 3:10-13. Ps 44:1-3.
78:54, 55. 105:44.
9 **forgat**. Dt 32:18. Jg 3:7. Ps 10:4. 106:21. Je
2:32.
he sold. Dt +32:30.
of the Philistines. Jg 10:7. 13:1.
into the. Jg 3:12. Is 63:10.
10 **And they**. 1 S 7:2. Ps +3:4. 78:34, 35.
106:44. Is 26:16.
forsaken. Je +1:16.
Baalim. Jg +2:11.
Ashtaroth. Jg +2:13.
deliver. Jg 10:15, 16. Is 33:22. Lk 1:74, 75. 2
C 5:14, 15.
11 **Jerubbaal**. Jg +6:32.
Bedan. He 11:32. Jg ch. 13-16.
Jepthah. Jg 11:1, etc.
Samuel. 1 S 7:13.
12 **Nahash**. 1 S 11:1, 2.
Nay. 1 S 8:3, 5, 6, 19, 20. Jg 9:18, 56, 57.
when the Lord. 1 S 8:7. 10:19. Ge 17:7. Ex
19:5, 6. Nu 23:21. Jg 8:23. Ps 74:12. Is 33:22.
Ho 13:10.
13 **behold**. 1 S 10:24. 11:15.
whom ye. 1 S 8:5. 9:20.
have desired. Ps 78:29-31. 106:15. Ho
13:11. Ac 13:21.
14 **If**. Ge +4:7.
ye will. Le 26:1-13. Dt 28:1-14. Jsh 24:14,
20. Ps 81:12-15. Is 3:10. Ro 2:7.
commandment. Heb. mouth. Dt +21:5mg.
continue. Heb. be after.
15 **But if ye**. Le 26:14-30. Dt 28:15-68. Jsh
24:20. Is 1:20. 3:11. Ro 2:8, 9.
hand. Ex +9:3.
against. ver. 9.
16 **stand**. ver. 7. 1 S 15:16. Ex 14:13, 31.
17 **Is it**. ver. 16. Pr 26:1.
wheat harvest. 1 S 6:13. Ru 2:23.
I will call. 1 S 7:9, 10. Jsh 10:12. Ps 99:6. Je
15:1. Ja 5:16-18.
your wickedness. 1 S +8:7.

18 sent thunder. Ex 9:23-25. Re 11:5, 6.
feared. Ex 14:31. Ezr 10:9. Ps 106:12, 13.
19 Pray for thy. 1 S 7:5, 8. Ge 20:7. Ex 9:28.
10:17. 1 K 13:6. Jb 42:8. Ps 78:34, 35. Is
26:16. Ml 1:9. Ac 8:24. Ja 5:15. 1 J 5:16.
20 Fear not. Ex 20:19, 20. 1 P 3:16.
turn not. Dt 11:16. 31:29. Jsh 23:6. Ps 40:4.
101:3. 125:5. Je 3:1.
21 vain things. Dt +32:21. Hab 2:18. 1 C 8:4.
cannot profit. Ps 115:4-8. Is 41:23, 24. 44:9,
10. 45:20. 46:7. Je 10:5. 16:19. Hab 2:18. 1 C
8:4.
nor deliver. Dt 32:30.
22 not forsake. Le 26:44. Dt 31:17. 2 S +7:15. 1
K 6:13. 2 K 21:14. 1 Ch +28:9. 2 Ch 15:2. Is
+41:9, 17. +54:7. +55:3. Ro +11:2. He +13:5.
for his great. Ex 32:12. Nu 14:13-19. Is
+48:9.
it hath. Dt 9:5. 14:2. +33:3. Mt 11:26. Jn
15:16. Ro 11:29. 1 C 4:7. Ep 1:3. Ph 1:6. T 3:5.
23 God forbid. Ge 18:25. Lk +20:16.
in ceasing. Heb. from ceasing. Je 44:18 (left
off). Ac 12:5. Ro 1:9. Col 1:9. 1 Th 3:10. 2 T 1:3.
pray for. Ge 20:7, 17. Jb 42:8-10. Ps 2:8. Je
42:4. Mt 5:44. 18:18, 19. Jn 17:9, 20, 21. Ep
6:18, 19. Col 4:2, 3. 2 Th 1:11, 12. 1 T 2:1-4.
Ja 5:14, 15. 1 J 5:16.
I will teach. Ps 34:11. Pr 4:11. Ec 12:10. Ac
20:20. Col 1:28.
the good. 1 K 8:36. 2 Ch 6:27. Je 6:16.
24 fear the Lord. Dt +6:2. He 12:29.
in truth. Ps 119:80. Jn 1:47.
consider. Ezr 9:13, 14. Is 5:12. Ro 12:1.
how great things. or, what a great *thing*, etc.
Dt 10:21. Ps 126:2, 3.
25 But if. Dt 32:15, etc. Jsh 24:20. Is 3:11.
ye and. 1 S 31:1-5. Dt 28:36. Ho 10:3.

1 SAMUEL 13

1 A.M. 2911. B.C. 1093. An. Ex. Is. 398.
reigned one year. Heb. the son of one year
in his reigning. Ex 12:5. Mi 6:6mg.
2 chose. 1 S 8:11. 14:52.
Michmash. i.e. *treasure*, **S#4363h**. ver. 5, 11,
16, 23. 1 S 14:5, 31. Ne 11:31. Is 10:28.
Bethel. Ge +12:8.
Jonathan. i.e. *Jah hath given*, **S#3129h**. ver. 3,
16, 22. 14:1, 3, 4, 12-14, 17, 21, 27, 29, 39,
40-45, 49. 19:1. 1 K 1:42, 43. 1 Ch 2:32, 33.
10:2. 11:34. Ezr 8:6. 10:15. Ne 12:11, 14, 35.
Je 40:8. For **S#3083h**, see 1 S +14:6.
in Gibeah. Jg +19:12.
3 the garrison. 1 S 10:5. 14:1-6. 2 S 23:14.
Geba. or, the hill. i.e. *a height*, **S#1387h**. ver. 16.
Jsh +18:24, Gaba. 21:17. Jg 20:10, 33. 2 S
5:25. 1 K 15:22. 2 K 23:8. 1 Ch 6:60. 8:6. 2
Ch 16:6. Ezr 2:26. Ne 7:30. 11:31. 12:29. Is
10:29. Zc 14:10.
blew. Jg 3:27. 6:34. 2 S 2:28. 20:1.

4 was had in abomination. Heb. did stink. Ge
+34:30. 46:34. Zc 11:8.
to Gilgal. Jsh +4:19.
5 thirty thousand chariots. Young notes "or
charioteers, as in 2 S 10:18; 1 K 20:21; 1 Ch
19:18; or thirty chief chariots; Syr. and Ar.
read '3000 chariots,' but even Pharaoh had
only 600 (Ex 14:7); Jabin 900 (Jg 4:3); Zerah
300 (2 Ch 14:9)."
as the sand. Ge +22:17.
Beth-aven. Jsh +7:2.
6 in a strait. Ex 14:10-12. Jsh 8:20. Jg 10:9.
20:41. 2 S 24:14. Ph 1:23.
in caves. 1 S 14:11. 23:19. Ge +19:30. Is
42:22.
pits. Heb. *bor*, Ge +37:20.
7 the Hebrews. Le 26:17, 36, 37. Dt 28:25.
Gad. Ge +30:11.
followed him trembling. Heb. trembled
after him. Dt 20:8. Jg 7:3. Ho 11:10, 11.
8 tarried. 1 S 10:8.
9 burnt offering. Le +23:12.
peace offerings. Le +23:19.
he offered. ver. 12, 13. 1 S 14:18. 15:21, 22.
Dt 12:6. 1 K 3:4. Ps 37:7. Pr 15:8. 20:22. 21:3,
27. Is 66:3.
10 Saul. 1 S 15:13.
salute him. Heb. bless him. 1 S 15:13. Ru
2:4. Ps 129:8.
11 What hast. Ge 3:13. 4:10. 20:9. 31:26. Jsh
7:19. 2 S 3:24. 2 K 5:25. Jn 18:35.
Michmash. ver. 2, 5, 16, 23. 1 S 14:5. Is 10:28.
12 said I. 1 K 12:26, 27.
made supplication unto. Heb. intreated the
face of, etc. Ex +32:11mg.
I forced. 1 S 21:7. Ps 66:3. Am 8:5. 2 C 9:7.
13 Thou hast done. 2 S 12:7-9. 1 K 18:18.
21:20. 2 Ch 16:9. 19:2. 25:15, 16. Jb 34:18. Pr
19:3. Mt 14:3, 4.
hast not kept. 1 S 15:11, 22, 28. Ps 50:8-15.
2 T 2:13.
for ever. Heb. *olam*, Ex +12:24.
14 But now. 1 S 2:30. 15:28.
the Lord. 1 S 16:1, 12. 2 S 7:15, 16. Ps 78:70.
84:2. 89:19, 20, etc. Ac 13:22.
heart. Ge 6:6.
captain over. 1 S 9:16. 2 S 5:2. 2 K 20:5. He
2:10.
not kept. Jn 14:15. Re 22:14.
15 present. Heb. found. Est +1:5mg. Lk 9:36. Ro
7:18. Ph 2:8. 3:9. He 11:5.
about six. ver. 2, 6, 7. 1 S 14:2.
16 Gibeah. Heb. Gebah. ver. +3.
17 in three companies. 1 S 11:11.
Ophrah. Jsh 18:23.
Shual. Jsh 19:3.
18 Beth-horon. Jsh +10:10.
Zeboim. Ge 14:2. Ne 11:34. Ho 11:8.
19 there was no. Jg 5:8. 2 K 24:14. Is 54:16. Je
24:1.

21 **a file**. Heb. a file with mouths.
    sharpen. Heb. set.
22 **there was neither**. 1 S 17:47, 50. Jg 5:8. Zc
    4:6. 1 C 1:27-29. 2 C 4:7.
23 **garrison**. *or*, standing camp. ver. 3. 1 S 14:4.
    passage. ver. 2, 5. 1 S 14:1, 4, 5. Is 10:28.

1 SAMUEL 14

1 A.M. 2917. B.C. 1087. An. Ex. Is. 404.
    it came to pass upon a day. *or*, there was a
    day.
    Jonathan. ver. 39-45. 1 S 13:2, 22. 18:1-4. 2
    S 1:4, 5, 25, 26.
    he told not. 1 S 25:19. Jg 6:27. 14:6. Mi 7:5.
2 **in the uttermost**. Jg +19:12.
    a pomegranate. Jg 4:5. 20:45, 47.
    Migron. i.e. *place of great conflict; precipice*,
    S#4051h. Is 10:28.
3 **Ahiah**. 1 S 22:9-12, 20, called Ahimelech. 1
    Ch +8:7.
    Ahitub. i.e. *brother of goodness*, **S#285h**. 1 S
    22:9, 11, 12, 20. 2 S 8:17. 1 Ch 6:7, 8, 11, 12,
    52. 9:11. 18:16. Ezr 7:2. Ne 11:11.
    Ichabod's. 1 S 4:21.
    wearing. Ex +28:4.
4 **the passages**. 1 S 13:23.
    Bozez. i.e. *shining; white*, **S#949h**.
    Seneh. i.e. *bush* or *tooth; bramble*, **S#5573h**.
5 **forefront**. Heb. tooth. ver. 4.
6 **Jonathan**. i.e. *whom Jehovah gave*, **S#3083h**.
    ver. 8. 1 S 18:1, 3, 4. 19:1, 2, 4, 6, 7. 20:1, 3-
    5, 9-13, 16-18, 25, 27, 28, 30, 32-35, 37-40,
    42. 23:16, 18. 31:2. Jg 18:30. 2 S 1:4, 5, 12,
    17, 22, 23, 25, 26. 4:4. 9:1, 3, 6, 7. 15:27, 36.
    17:17, 20. 21:7, 12-14, 21. 23:32. 1 Ch 8:33,
    34. 9:39, 40. 20:7. 27:25, 32. 2 Ch 17:8. Ne
    12:18. Je 37:15, 20. 38:26. For **S#3129h**, see 1 S
    +13:2.
    Come. Dt 31:6. 2 Ch 32:7. Ph 1:28.
    uncircumcised. 1 S 17:26, 36. 31:4. Ge 17:7-
    11. Le +26:41. Jg 15:18. 2 S 1:20. Je 9:23-26.
    Ezk +28:10. Ep 2:11, 12. Ph 3:3.
    it may be. 2 S 16:12. 2 K 19:4. Am 5:15. Zp
    2:3.
    for there is no restraint. Dt 32:30. Jsh
    14:12. Jg 7:4-7. 2 Ch 14:11. Ps 115:1-3. Zc
    4:6. Mt 19:26. Ro 8:31.
7 **Do all**. 1 S 10:7. 2 S 7:3. Ps 46:7. Zc 8:23.
8 **we will pass**. Jg 7:9-14.
9 **they**. Ge 24:13, 14. Jg 6:36-40.
    Tarry. Heb. Be still. Jsh 10:12.
10 **this shall be a sign**. 1 S 10:7. Ge 24:14. Jg
    7:11. Is 7:11-14.
11 **out of the holes**. ver. 22. 1 S 13:6. Jg 6:2.
12 **Come up to us**. ver. 10. 1 S 17:43, 44. 2 S
    2:14-17. 2 K 14:8.
    Come up after me. Ge 24:26, 27, 42, 48. Jg
    4:14. 7:15. 2 S 5:24.
13 **climbed up**. Ps 18:29. He 11:34.

fell. Le 26:7, 8. Dt 28:7. 32:30. Jsh 23:10. Ro
8:31.
14 **an half acre of land**. *or*, half a furrow of an
    acre of land. Ps 129:3.
15 **there was trembling**. Jg 7:21. Jb 18:11.
    the spoilers. 1 S 13:17, 23.
    the earth quaked. Ex 19:18. Mt 24:7. 27:50,
    51.
    very great trembling. Heb. trembling of
    God. Ge +35:5. Le 26:36, 37. 2 S 5:24. 1 Ch
    12:22. Ps +36:6mg. Da 5:6.
16 **melted away**. Ex +15:15. Is 40:15.
    beating down. ver. 20. Jg +7:22.
17 **Number**. 1 S +11:8.
18 **Bring hither**. 1 S 4:3-5. 30:8. Nu 27:21. Jg
    20:18, 23, 28. 2 S 11:11. 15:24-26.
    For the ark. 1 S 5:2. 7:1.
19 **talked unto**. Nu 27:21.
    noise. *or*, tumult.
    Withdraw. ver. 24. 1 S 13:11. Jsh 9:14. Ps
    106:13. Is 28:16.
20 **assembled themselves**. Heb. were cried
    together.
    every man's. ver. +16.
21 **the Hebrews**. 1 S 29:4. Jg 7:23.
22 **hid themselves**. 1 S 13:6. 31:7.
23 **the Lord**. Ex 14:30. Jg 2:18. 2 K 14:27. Ps
    44:6-8. Ho 1:7.
    Beth-aven. Jsh +7:2.
24 **Cursed**. ver. 27-30. Le 27:29. Nu +30:2. Dt
    27:15-26. Jsh 6:17-19, 26. Jg 21:1-5. Pr 11:9.
    Ro 10:2. 1 C 16:22.
    I may be. Jg 5:2. 16:28. Ps 18:47.
25 **all they**. Dt 9:28. Mt 3:5.
    honey. Ex 3:8. Nu 13:27. Mt 3:4.
26 **the people**. Ec 9:2.
27 **his eyes**. ver. 29. 1 S 30:12. Pr 25:26.
28 **adjured**. Jsh 6:26.
    Cursed. ver. +24, 43.
    faint. *or*, weary.
29 **My father**. Jsh 7:25. 1 K 18:18.
    land. Ge +6:11.
    see. Ge 44:3. Pr 4:18. Is 7:15, 22.
30 **had there**. Ec 9:18.
31 **from Michmash**. 1 S +13:2.
    Aijalon. Jsh +10:12.
32 **flew**. 1 S 15:19.
    did eat. Le +3:17.
33 **transgressed**. *or*, dealt treacherously. Mt 7:5.
    Ro 2:1.
34 **with him**. Heb. in his hand.
35 **built**. 1 S 7:9, 17. Jg 21:4. Ho 8:14. 2 T 3:5.
    Ju 12.
    the same, etc. Heb. that altar he began to
    build unto the Lord.
    altar. Ge +13:18.
36 **Let us go**. Jsh 10:9-14, 19. Je 6:5.
    let us not leave. 1 S 11:11. Jsh 11:14.
    Then said the priest. Nu 27:21. Ps 73:28. Is
    48:1, 2. 58:2. Ho +6:1. Ml 2:7. Ja 4:8.

37 Shall I go. 1 S 23:4, 9-12. 30:7, 8. Jg 1:1. 20:18, 28. 2 S 5:19, 23. 1 K 22:5, 6, 15.

he answered him not. 1 S 28:6. Dt 1:45. Ezk 14:3-5. 20:3.

38 Draw ye near. 1 S 10:19, 20. Jsh 7:14, etc.

chief. Heb. corners. Nu 24:17. Jg 20:2. 2 S 18:3. Ps 47:9. Is 19:13mg. Zc 10:4. Mt 21:42. Ep 2:20.

39 the Lord liveth. ver. 24, 44. 1 K +17:10. Ec 9:2.

surely. Ge +2:16.

40 Do what seemeth. ver. 7, 36. 2 S 15:15.

41 Give a perfect lot. or, Show the innocent. Jsh +14:2.

And Saul. 1 S 10:20, 21. Jsh 7:16-18. Jon 1:7.

escaped. Heb. went forth.

43 Tell me. Jsh 7:19. Jon 1:7-10.

I did but. ver. 27.

44 God. 1 S 25:22. Ru 1:17. 2 S 3:9, 35. 19:13.

thou shalt. ver. +39. Ge 38:24. 2 S 12:5, 31. Pr 25:16.

surely. Ge +2:16. 1 S 20:31. 22:16.

45 who hath wrought. ver. 23. 1 S 11:13. 19:5. Ne 9:27.

God forbid. Lk +20:16.

there shall not. 2 S 14:11. 1 K 1:52. Mt 10:30. Lk 21:18. Ac 27:34.

he hath. 2 Ch 19:11. Is 13:3. Ac 14:27. 15:12. 21:19. Ro 15:18. 1 C 3:9. 2 C 6:1. Ph 2:12, 13. Re 17:14. 19:14.

the people. Is 29:20, 21.

47 Saul. 1 S 12:2. 13:1.

fought. 2 K 14:27.

Ammon. 1 S 11:11.

Zobah. i.e. depression; standing, **S#6678h.** 2 S 8:3, 5, 12. 10:6, 8, Zoba. 23:36. 1 K 11:23. 1 Ch 18:3, 5, 9. 19:6. 2 Ch 8:3. Ps 60, title, Aram-Zobah.

48 gathered an host. or, wrought mightily. Ge +34:29.

smote. Ex +17:14.

49 Jonathan. 1 S +13:2. 31:2. 1 Ch 8:33. 9:39.

Ishui. i.e. he is equal, **S#3440h,** so rendered only here. Nu 26:44, Jesui. 1 Ch 7:30, Ishuai. The same as Abinadab in 1 Ch 8:33; 9:39.

Melchishua. i.e. my king is rich; king of wealth, **S#4444h.** 1 S 31:2. Ishbosheth (or Eshbaal) in 2 S 2:18; 1 Ch 8:33, was probably not then born; see also 2 S 21:8.

name of the firstborn. 1 S 18:7-21. 25:44. 2 S 3:13-16. 6:20-23.

Merab. i.e. multiplication, **S#4764h.** 1 S 18:17, 19.

Michal. i.e. a brook, who afterwards became wife of David, as in 1 S 18:27. **S#4324h.** 1 S 18:20, 27, 28. 19:11-13, 17. 25:44. 2 S 3:13, 14. 6:16, 20, 21, 23. 21:8. 1 Ch 15:29.

50 Ahinoam. i.e. brother of grace, **S#293h.** 1 S 25:43. 27:3. 30:5. 2 S 2:2. 3:2. 1 Ch 3:1.

Ahimaaz. i.e. powerful brother, **S#290h.** 2 S 15:27, 36. 17:17, 20. 18:19, 22, 23, 27-29. 1 K 4:15. 1 Ch 6:8, 9, 53.

the name of the captain. 1 S 17:55. 2 S 2:8. 3:27.

Abner. Heb. Abiner. i.e. father of light, **S#74h.** 1 S 17:55, 57. 20:25. 26:5, 7, 14, 15. 2 S 2:8, 12, 14, 17, 19-26, 29-31. 3:6-9, 11, 12, 16, 17, 19-28, 30-33, 37. 4:1, 12. 1 K 2:5, 32. 1 Ch 26:28. 27:21.

Ner. 1 Ch +9:36.

51 Kish. 1 S 9:1, 21.

Abiel. 1 S +9:1.

52 sore. 2 S 11:15.

strong. 1 S 9:1.

valiant. 2 S +2:7mg.

when Saul. 1 S 8:1, 11.

1 SAMUEL 15

1 A.M. 2925. B.C. 1079. An. Ex. Is. 412.

The Lord. ver. 17, 18. 1 S 9:16. 10:1.

hearken. ver. 16. 1 S 12:14. 13:13. 2 S 23:2, 3. 1 Ch 22:12, 13. Ps 2:10, 11.

2 Lord of hosts. Ps +24:10.

I remember. Je 31:34. Ho 7:2. Am 8:7.

Amalek. Ge 36:1, 2, 4. Ex +17:8, 14.

3 Now go. Ge +18:25.

utterly destroy. ver. 8. Ge 22:2. Nu 24:20. Dt +2:34.

slay. Ex 20:5. Nu 31:17. Is 14:21, 22.

ox and sheep. Ge 3:17, 18. Ro 8:20-22.

4 Telaim. i.e. young lambs, **S#2923h.** Jsh 15:24, Telem.

two. 1 S 11:8. 13:15.

5 laid wait. or, fought.

6 the Kenites. Ge +15:19. Ex 18:10, 19. Nu 10:29, 32.

Go, depart. Ge 18:25. 19:12-16. Nu 16:26, 27, 34. Pr 9:6. Is 52:11. Ac 2:40. 2 C 6:17. Re 18:4.

ye showed. Ex 18:9, 10, 19. Nu 10:29-32. 2 T 1:16.

7 smote. 1 S 14:48. Jb 21:30. Ec 8:13.

Havilah. Ge +10:7.

Shur. Ge +16:7.

8 Agag. ver. 3. Nu 24:7. 1 K 20:30, 34-42. Est 3:1.

utterly. ver. +3. 1 S 27:8. 30:1.

9 the best. ver. 3, 15, 19. Jsh 7:21.

the fatlings. or, the second sort. 2 S 6:13.

11 repenteth me. ver. 35. Ps 110:4. Je +18:8. Ro 11:29.

turned back. Jsh 22:16. 1 K 9:6, 7. 11:4. 1 Ch 28:9. Ps 18:21. 36:3. 78:41, 56, 57. 125:5. Ezk 3:20. 13:18. 18:10-13, 24. Ho 6:4. Zp 1:6. Mt 24:13. 25:8. Lk 9:62. Jn 6:66. Ga 5:4. 1 T +1:19. +4:1. 2 T 1:15. He 10:38. 2 P 2:20-22.

hath not performed. ver. 3, 9. 1 S 13:13.

it grieved. ver. 35. 1 S 16:1. Ps +119:136.

he cried. 1 S 12:23. Ps 109:4. Mt 5:44. Lk 6:12.

12 Carmel. Jsh +19:26.
he set him. 1 S 7:12. Jsh 4:8, 9. 2 S 18:18.
a place. 2 S 18:18. Is 56:5.

13 Blessed. 1 S 13:10. Ge 14:19. Jg 17:2. Ru 3:10.
I have performed. ver. 9, 11. Ge 3:12. Nu +32:23. Pr 27:2. 28:13. 30:13. 31:31. Lk 17:10. 18:11, 12.

14 What meaneth. Ps 36:2. 50:16-21. Je 2:18, 19, 22, 23, 34-37. Ml 3:13-15. Lk 19:22. Ro 3:19. 1 C 4:5.

15 for. ver. 9, 21. Ge 3:12, 13. Ex 32:22, 23. Jb 31:33. Pr 28:13.
to. Mt 2:8. Lk 10:29.

16 Stay. 1 S 9:27. 12:7. 1 K 22:16.

17 When thou. 1 S 9:21. 10:22. Jg 6:15. Ho 13:1. Mt 18:4.
the Lord. ver. 1-3. 1 S 10:1.

18 the sinners. Ge 13:13. 15:16. Nu 16:38. Jb 31:3. Pr 10:29. 13:21.
they be consumed. Heb. they consume them.

19 fly upon. Pr 15:27. Je 7:11. Hab 2:9-12. 2 T 4:10.
didst evil. 2 Ch 33:2, 6. 36:12.

20 Yea. ver. 13. Jb 33:9. 34:5. 35:2. 40:8. Mt 19:20. Lk 10:29. 18:11. Ro 10:3. 2 C 10:18.
have brought. ver. 3, 8.

21 the people. ver. +15. Ge 3:12, 13. Ex 32:22, 23.

22 Samuel said. 1 S 9:15, 17. Ps 78:1. Is 50:4.
Hath the Lord. Le +23:12. Pr 15:8. 21:3. Is 66:3. Mi 6:6-8. Mt 9:13. 12:7. 23:23. He 10:4-10.
to obey. Ec 5:1. Je +7:23. Ezk +33:31, 32. Ho 6:6. Mt 5:24. 7:21. Mk 12:33. Lk +6:46. Jn 14:15. 2 C 8:5. 1 J +2:3.
to hearken. Dt +15:5. Lk +8:18. +11:28.

23 rebellion. 1 S 8:7. 12:14, 15. Nu 14:9, 41-45. Dt 9:7, 24. 21:20, 21. Jsh 22:16-19. Jg 6:10. Ne 9:16, 17, 26. Jb +21:14, 15. 34:37. Ps 66:7. 68:6, 18. 78:5-8. 107:11. Pr 17:11. Is 1:5. 7:13. 30:1. 59:12, 13. 63:10. 65:2. Je 5:5. 28:16. 29:32. 44:24-30. Ezk 2:5-8. 11:15. 12:2. Ho 7:14. Zc 7:11, 12. Col 1:21. 2 Th 3:14, 15.
sin. Ge 4:7. 2 S 12:13. Pr 20:9. Da 9:20, 24. Mi 7:19. Zc 14:19mg.
witchcraft. Heb. divination. Ex 22:18. Le 20:6, 27. Dt +18:10. 2 Ch +33:6. Is 8:19. 19:3. Ga 3:1. Re 22:15.
stubbornness. Dt 21:20. Ps 32:9. 58:3-5. 78:8. Pr 29:1. Is 46:12. Je 4:3. 32:33. 44:16. Ezk 33:31, 32. Zc 7:11, 12. Ml +2:2. Mt 21:28-32. Ac 7:51. 2 C 6:16. Ga 5:20. 2 P 2:10. Re 21:8.
iniquity. Ps 5:5. 14:4. 36:3, 4mg. 66:18. 119:133. Is 55:7mg.

idolatry. Ezk +14:3. Col 3:5. 1 J 5:21.
thou hast rejected. 1 S 2:30. 8:7. 13:14. 16:1. 2 K 17:15-20. 1 Ch +28:9. 2 Ch 36:16. Pr 1:7. 5:12.
rejected thee. 2 K 17:20. Mt 7:21-23. 25:12. Lk 13:27. He 3:12, 13, 19. 12:17.

24 I have sinned. ver. 30. Ex 9:27. 10:16. Nu +22:34. 2 S 12:13. Mt 27:4. Ac 8:24.
I feared. ver. 9, 15. Ex 23:2. Jb 31:34. Pr 29:25. Is 51:12, 13. Lk 23:20-25. Ga 1:10. Re 21:8.
obeyed. 1 S 2:29. Ge 3:12, 17. Je 38:5.

25 pardon. Ex 10:17. Ac 8:24.

26 I will not. ver. 31. Ge 42:38. 43:11-14. Lk 24:28, 29. 2 J 11.
for thou. ver. +23. 1 S 2:30. 13:14. 16:1. Je 6:19. Ho 4:6.

27 he laid hold. 1 K 11:30, 31.

28 The Lord. 1 S 28:17, 18. 1 K 11:30, 31.
hath given. 1 S 2:7, 8. Je 27:5, 6. Da 4:17, 32. Jn 19:11. Ro 13:1.
a neighbor. 1 S 13:14. 16:12. Ac 13:22.

29 Strength. *or*, Eternity, *or*, Victory. Dt 33:27. Jb 4:20 **(S#5331h)**. Ps 29:11. 68:35. Is 25:8. 45:24. Jl 3:16. 2 C 12:9. Ph 4:13.
will not lie. Nu 14:28, 29. 23:19. Ps 95:11. Ezk 24:14. 2 T 2:13. T 1:2. He 6:18.
nor repent. Nu 23:19. Ezk 24:14. He 13:8. Ja 1:17.

30 honor me now. Hab 2:4. Jn 5:44. 12:43.
that I may worship. Is 29:13. Lk 18:9-14. 2 T 3:5.

32 Agag said. Je 48:44. 1 Th 5:3. Re 18:7.

33 As thy sword. Ge 9:6. Ex 17:11. Nu 14:45. Je +50:15. Mt 26:52.
Samuel hewed. Nu 25:7, 8. 1 K 18:40. Is 34:6. Je 48:10.

34 Ramah. Je +31:15.
Gibeah. 1 S 11:4.

35 Samuel. 1 S 19:24.
Samuel mourned. ver. 11. 1 S 16:1. Ps 119:136, 158. Je 9:1, 2. Ro 9:2, 3. Ph 3:18.
repented. ver. +11.

1 SAMUEL 16

1 A.M. 2941. B.C. 1063. An. Ex. Is. 428.
How long. 1 S 15:11, 35. Je 7:16. 11:14.
thou mourn. Le 10:3, 6.
seeing. ver. 15, 23. 1 S 13:13, 14. 15:23, 26. Je 6:30. 14:11, 12. 15:1. 1 J 5:16.
horn with oil. Ex +28:41.
Jesse. Ge 49:8-10. 1 Ch +2:12. Ps 78:68-71. 89:19, 20. Is 55:4.
Bethlehemite. **S#1022h**. ver. 18. 1 S 17:58. 2 S 21:19.
I have. Ge 22:8.

2 How can I go. Ex 3:11. 4:1. 1 K 18:9-14. Je 1:6. Mt 10:16. Lk 1:34.

kill me. 1 K 18:14.
Take an heifer. 1 S 21:2. Pr 29:11. Je 38:24-28.
with thee. Heb. in thine hand. 1 S 9:12.
I am come. 1 S 9:12. 20:29. Je 38:26, 27.

3 **call Jesse**. 1 S 9:12, 13. 20:29. 2 S 15:11. Mt 22:1-4.
and I will show. Ex 4:15. Ac 9:6.
anoint. ver. 12, 13. 1 S 9:16. Dt 17:14.

4 **trembled**. 1 S 21:1. 2 S 6:9. 1 K 17:18. Ho 6:5. 11:10. Lk 5:8. 8:37.
coming. Heb. meeting.
Comest. 1 K 2:13. 2 K 9:22. 1 Ch 12:17, 18.

5 **sanctify yourselves**. Ex 19:10, 14, 15. Le 20:7, 8. Nu 11:18. Jsh 3:5. 7:13. 2 Ch 30:17-20. Jb 1:5. Ps 26:2-6. Jl 2:16. 1 C 11:28.

6 **Eliab**. Nu +1:9. 1 Ch 27:18, Elihu.
Surely. Jg 8:18. 1 K 12:26.

7 **Look not**. 1 S 9:2. 10:23, 24. 2 S 14:25. 2 K 5:1. Ps 147:10, 11. Pr 31:30. Is 55:8. 2 C 10:7.
refused him. Ps 75:6, 7.
seeth not. Jb 10:4. Is 55:8, 9. Mt 7:21, 23. Lk 16:15. 1 P 2:4. 3:4.
looketh. Jn 7:24. 2 C 10:7, 10.
outward appearance. Heb. eyes.
on the heart. Dt 26:16. 1 K 8:39. 2 Ch 6:8. 16:9. Ps 66:18. 145:18. Pr 15:11. 16:2. Je 17:10. 29:13. Mt 22:37. 23:26. Lk 16:15. Jn 4:24. Ac 1:24. 8:21, 37. Ro 2:28, 29. 10:10. Col 3:16. 1 T 1:5. He 4:13.

8 **Abinadab**. i.e. *my father is noble; source of liberality*, **S#41h**. 1 S 7:1. 17:13. 31:2. 2 S 6:3, 3, 4. 1 K 4:11. 1 Ch 2:13. 8:33. 9:39. 10:2. 13:7.
chosen. Ge +16:13.

9 **Shammah**. i.e. *desolation* or *hearkening*, **S#8048h**. 1 S 17:13. Ge 36:13, 17. 2 S 13:3, Shimeah. 23:11, 25, 33. 1 Ch 1:37. 2:13, Shimma.

10 **seven**. 1 S 17:12. 1 Ch 2:13-15. Seven in all, including Nathanael, Raddai, and Ozem (1 Ch 2:14, 15); the seventh is not mentioned by name (Young).

11 **Are here all**. 1 S 10:22.
There remaineth. 1 S 17:12-15, 28. Ge 4:2. 2 S 7:8. 1 Ch 17:7. Ps 78:70, 71.
down. Heb. round.

12 **ruddy**. 1 S 17:42. SS 5:10. La 4:7. Ac 7:20. He 11:23.
of a beautiful countenance. Heb. fair of eyes. ver. 7. Ps 45:2. Da 1:15.
And the Lord. 1 S 9:17.
anoint him. Ps 2:2, 6. 89:19, 20. Ac 4:27.

13 **anointed**. Ex +28:41. Ps 89:20.
the Spirit. Heb. *ruach*, Ge +41:38. ver. 18. 1 S 10:6, 9, 10. Nu 11:17. 27:18. Jg 3:10. 11:29. 13:25. 14:6. Is 11:1-3. Jn 3:34. He 1:9.

14 **the Spirit**. Heb. *ruach*, Ge +41:38. 1 S 11:6. Jg 16:29. Ho 9:12.
departed. 1 S 18:12. 28:15. Ps +51:11.
evil spirit. Heb. *ruach*, Jg +9:23; Mt +8:16. 1

S 16:23. 18:10. 19:9, 10. Jg 9:23. 1 K 22:22. Ac 19:15, 16.
from the Lord. 1 S 18:10. Je +29:11. Am +3:6.
troubled. *or*, terrified. ver. 15. 2 S 22:5. Jb 3:5. 7:14. 9:34.

15 **evil spirit**. Heb. *ruach*, Jg +9:23. Mt +8:16.

16 **before thee**. ver. 21, 22. Ge 41:46. 1 K 10:8.
evil spirit. Heb. *ruach*, Jg +9:23. Mt +8:16.
play. ver. 23. 1 S 10:5. 16:23. 2 K 3:15.

18 **playing**. **S#5059h**. 1 S 18:10. 19:9. 2 K 3:15. Ps 33:3. 68:25. Is 23:16. 38:20.
a mighty. 1 S 17:32-36. Jg +6:12. 2 S 17:8, 10.
and prudent. 2 S 14:20.
matters. *or*, speech. Jb 29:22. Col 4:6. T 2:8.
a comely. ver. 12.
the Lord. 1 S 3:19. 10:7. 18:12-14. Ge 39:2, 23. Mt 1:23. 28:20.

19 **David**. i.e. *beloved*, **S#1732h**.
with the sheep. ver. 11. 1 S 17:15, 33, 34. Ex 3:1-10. 1 K 19:19. Ps 78:70-72. 113:8. Am 1:1. 7:14, 15. Mt 4:18-22.

20 **an ass laden**. 1 S 17:18. Jg +3:15. 2 S 16:1, 2.

21 **stood before him**. Dt +10:8.
loved him. Ps 62:9. 118:9. 146:3.

23 **the evil spirit**. Heb. *ruach*, Jg +9:23. ver. +14, 16. Mt +8:16.
Saul. 1 S 18:10, 11. Mt 12:43-45. Lk 11:24-26.
evil spirit. Heb. *ruach*, Jg +9:23; Mt +8:16.

1 SAMUEL 17

1 **gathered**. 1 S 7:7. 13:5. 14:46, 52. Jg 3:3.
Shochoh. Jsh +15:35.
Azekah. Jsh 10:10, 11. 15:35. Je 34:7.
Ephes-dammim. *or*, the coast of Dammim. i.e. *extremity of Dannim; limit of bloods*, **S#658h**. 1 Ch 11:13, Pas-dammim.

2 **the valley**. ver. 19. 1 S 21:9.
set the battle in array. Heb. ranged the battle.

4 **Goliath**. i.e. *an exile*, **S#1555h**. ver. 23. 1 S 21:9, 10. 2 S 21:19. 1 Ch 20:5.
of Gath. Jsh +11:22.
whose height. Dt 3:11. 1 Ch 11:23. Am 2:9.

5 **armed**. Heb. clothed. ver. 38.

6 **target of brass**. *or*, gorget. 1 K 10:16. 2 Ch 9:15.

7 **the staff**. 2 S 21:19. 1 Ch 11:23. 20:5.
and one. Is 2:3, 4. 4:1. 49:20, 21. Mt 10:30. 24:20. Lk 7:44. 1 C 11:6. 2 Th 3:10.

8 **servants to Saul**. ver. 26. 1 S 8:17. 2 S 11:11. 1 Ch 21:3.

9 **and serve us**. 1 S 11:1. Ro 6:16.

10 **I defy**. ver. 25, 26, 36, 45. Nu 23:7, 8. 2 S 21:21. 23:9. Ne 2:9.
give me. Jb 40:9-12. Ps 9:4, 5. Pr 16:18. Je 9:23. Da 4:37.

11 dismayed. Dt 31:8. Jsh 1:9. Ps 27:1. Pr 28:1. Is 51:12, 13. 57:11.

12 David. ver. 58. 1 Ch +2:12.
Ephrathite. Ru +1:2.
eight sons. 1 S +16:10, 11.

13 the names. ver. 28. 1 S 16:6-9. 1 Ch 2:13.
Shammah. 2 S +21:21, Shimeah.

14 the youngest. lit. the small one. 1 S 16:11. Ge 25:23. 2 Ch 21:17. Jon 3:5. Mt 5:19. He 10:21. 13:20.

15 returned. 1 S 16:11, 19-23.

16 forty days. Jon +3:4. Lk 4:2.

17 Take now. Mt 7:11. Lk 11:13.
an ephah. Ex 16:16, 36.
parched corn. 1 S 25:18. Ru 2:14. 2 S 17:28.

18 carry. 1 S 16:20.
cheeses. Heb. cheeses of milk. 2 S 17:29. Jb 10:10.
captain of. Jg 6:15. Mi 5:2.
their thousand. Heb. a thousand.
look. Ge 37:14. Ac 15:36. 1 Th 3:5, 6.

19 the valley. ver. 2.

20 left the sheep. ver. 28. Ep 6:1, 2.
trench. or, place of the carriage. 1 S 26:5. Lk 19:43.
fight. or, battle array, or place of fight.

22 his carriage. Heb. the vessels from upon him. Jg 18:21.
saluted his brethren. Heb. asked his brethren of peace; as Jg +18:15mg.

23 according. ver. 4-10.

24 him. Heb. his face. 1 S 13:6, 7.
sore afraid. ver. 11. Le 26:36. Nu 13:33. Dt 32:30. Is 7:2. 30:17.

25 the king. 1 S 18:17-27. Jsh 15:16. Re 2:7, 17. 3:5, 12, 21.
free in Israel. Ezr 7:24. Mt 17:26.

26 reproach. 1 S 11:2. Jsh +5:9. 7:8, 9. 2 K 19:4, 22. Ne 5:9. Ps +31:11. Da +9:16. Jl 2:17, 19. Ro 8:33.
uncircumcised. ver. 36. 1 S +14:6.
defy. ver. 10. Is 31:3.
the armies. Ex +12:41.
the living God. ver. 36. Je +10:10.

27 So shall it. ver. 25.

28 Eliab's anger. 1 S 16:13. Ge 37:4, 8, 11. Pr 18:19. 27:4. Ec 4:4. Mt 10:36. 27:18. Mk 3:21.
with. ver. 20.
I know. 1 S 16:7. Ps 35:11. Ju 10.

29 What have. Pr 15:1. Ac 11:2-4. 1 C 2:15. 1 P 3:9.
Is there not. Ps 74:10.

30 manner. Heb. word. ver. 26, 27.

31 sent for him. Heb. took him. Pr 22:29.

32 Let. Nu 13:30. 14:9. Dt 20:1-4. Is 35:3. He 12:12.
thy. 1 S 14:6. 16:18. Jsh 14:12. Ps 3:6. 27:1-3.

33 Thou art not. Nu 13:31. Dt 9:2. Ps 11:1. Re 13:4.
for thou art but. ver. 42, 56.

34 and. Ge +8:22.
lamb. or, kid. Ex 12:3.

35 smote him. Jg 14:5, 6. 2 S 23:20. Ps 91:13. Da 6:22. Am 3:12. Ac 28:4-6. 2 T 4:17, 18.

36 this. ver. 26. Ezk 32:19, 27-32. Ro 2:28, 29.
seeing. ver. 10. Is 10:15. 36:8-10, 15, 18. 37:22, 23, 28, 29. Zc 2:8. 12:3. Ac 5:38, 39. 9:4, 5. 12:1, 2, 22, 23.

37 The Lord. 1 S 7:12. Ps 11:1. 18:16, 17. 22:21. 63:7. 77:11. 138:3, 7, 8. Da 6:22. 2 C 1:9, 10. 2 T 4:17, 18.
paw. lit. hand. Ge +9:5.
will deliver. Ps 91:13, 14. 2 C 1:10.
Go. 1 S 24:19. 26:25. 2 S 10:12.
with. 1 S 20:13. 1 Ch 22:11, 16.

38 armed David with his armor. Heb. clothed David with his clothes, ver. 5.

39 I cannot go. Is 31:1.
put them off. Ps 44:5, 6. Ho 1:7. Zc 4:6. Ro 13:12. 2 C 10:4, 5.

40 staff. Jg 3:31. 7:16-20. 15:15, 16. 20:16. Ps 144:1. 1 C 1:27-29.
brook. or, valley. Nu +13:23.
bag. Heb. vessel. ver. 49. Dt 23:24.
scrip. Mt 10:10. Mk 6:8. Lk 22:35, 36.

41 the man. ver. 7. Ge 15:1. Ps 3:3. 144:2.

42 and saw. Ne 4:2, 6.
disdained. 1 K 20:18. 2 K 18:23, 24. Ne 4:2-4. Ps 123:4, 5. 2 C 1:27-29.
a youth. ver. 33. 1 S 16:12.

43 Am I a dog. 1 S 24:14. 2 S 3:8. 9:8. 16:9. 2 K 8:13.
cursed. Ge 27:29. Nu 22:6, 11, 12. Jg 9:27. Ps 10:7. Pr 26:2.

44 Come to me. 1 K 20:10, 11. Ps 10:5. Pr 18:12. Ec 9:11, 12. Je 9:23. Ezk 28:2, 9, 10. 39:17-20.
unto the fowls. Ezk 39:4, 17. Mt +24:28. Lk +17:37.

45 thou comest. Ps 44:6.
in the name. 2 S 22:33-35. 2 Ch 32:8. Ps 3:8. 18:2. 20:5-7. 44:6. 116:4. 118:10, 11. 124:8. 125:1. Pr 18:10. 2 C 3:5. 10:4. Ph 4:13. He 11:33, 34.
defied. ver. 10, 26, 36. Is 37:23, 28.

46 will the Lord. Dt 7:2, 23. 9:2, 3. Jsh 10:8.
deliver thee. Heb. shut thee up. 1 S 23:11, 12, 20. 24:18. 26:8. 2 S 18:28. Ps 31:8.
take thine. ver. 51.
carcases. ver. 44. Is 56:9. Je +7:33. Mt +24:28. Lk +17:37.
fowls of the air. ver. +44.
all the earth. Ex 9:16. 15:14, 15. Jsh 4:24. Ps 46:10. 58:10, 11. Is 52:10. Ezk +6:10. Da 2:47. 3:29. 6:26, 27.

47 the Lord. Ps 46:11.
saveth not. Ps 33:16, 17. 44:6, 7. Pr 21:30, 31. Ho 1:7.
the battle. 1 S 14:6. Ex 15:3. 2 Ch 20:15-17. Ps 46:11. Is 9:7. Zc 4:6. Ro 8:31, 37.

48 **David hasted**. Ps 27:1. Pr 28:1.

49 **smote**. 1 K 22:34. 2 K 9:24. 1 C 1:27, 28.

50 **So David prevailed**. 1 S 21:9. 23:21. Jg 3:31. 15:15. 2 C 12:9.
but there was. ver. 39. 1 S 13:22.

51 **his sword**. 1 S 21:9. 2 S 23:21. Est 7:10. Ps 7:15, 16. He 2:14.
cut off. ver. 46.
head. Jg +7:25.
fled. He 11:34.

52 **the men of Israel**. 1 S 14:21, 22. Jg 7:23. 2 S 23:10.
valley. Jsh 15:33-36, 45, 46.
Shaaraim. i.e. *double gate; goats; demons*, **S#8189h**. Jsh 15:36. 1 Ch 4:31.

53 **they spoiled**. 2 K 7:7-16. Je 4:20. 30:16.

54 **took the head**. 1 S 21:9. Ex 16:33. Jsh 4:7, 8. Jg +7:25. Col 2:15.

55 **whose son**. ver. 58. 1 S 16:21, 22. Ec 2:16. 9:15.
soul. Heb. *nephesh*, Ge +27:31.

56 **stripling**. 1 S 20:22.

57 **the head**. ver. 54.

58 **I am the son**. ver. 12. 1 S 16:18, 19.

1 SAMUEL 18

1 **the soul**. Heb. *nephesh*, Ge +34:3.
of Jonathan. 1 S 14:1-14, 45. Ge 44:30. Jg 20:11. 1 Ch 12:17. Ps 86:11. Col 2:2.
was knit. Jg 20:11. 1 Ch 12:17. 2 Ch 5:13.
the soul. Heb. *nephesh*, Ge +34:3.
loved him. ver. 3. 1 S 19:2. 20:17. Dt 13:6. 2 S 1:26. Pr 18:24.
own soul. Heb. *nephesh*, Ge +27:31.

2 **took him**. 1 S 16:21-23. 17:15.

3 **made a covenant**. 1 S 20:8-17, 42. 23:18. 2 S 9:1-3. 21:7.
soul. Heb. *nephesh*, Ge +27:31.

4 **stripped himself**. Ge 41:42. Est 6:8, 9. Is 61:10. Lk 15:22. 2 C 5:21. Ph 2:7, 8.

5 **behaved**. *or*, prospered. ver. 14, 15, 30. Ge 39:2, 3, 23. Ps 1:3. Ac 7:10.
wisely. Mt 10:16. Ep 5:17. Col 4:5.
the men of war. 1 S 13:2. 14:52.

6 **Philistine**. *or*, Philistines.
the women. Ex +15:20.
instruments of music. Heb. three stringed instruments.

7 **answered**. Ex 15:21. Ps 24:7, 8.
Saul. 1 S 21:11. 29:5. Ex +12:40.
David. Ex +12:40.

8 **the saying**. Est 3:5. Pr 13:10. 27:4. Ec 4:4. Ja 4:5.
displeased him. Heb. *was evil in his eyes*. 1 S 15:11. Nu +22:34mg.
and what. 1 S 13:14. 15:28. 16:13. 20:31. 1 K 2:22.

9 **eyed David**. Ge 4:5, 6. 31:2. Pr 23:6-8. Mt 20:15. Mk 7:22. Ep 4:27. Ja 5:9.

10 **the evil spirit**. Heb. *ruach*, Jg +9:23. 1 S 16:14, 15. 19:9. 26:19. Mt +8:16.
from God. 1 S 16:14. 19:9. Dt +2:30. Jg 9:23. Am +3:6. Ep +1:11.
and he prophesied. 1 S 19:24. 1 K 18:29. 22:12, 20-23. Je 28:2-4, 11. 29:26, 27. Zc 13:2-5. Ac 16:16. 2 Th 2:11.
played. 1 S 16:16, 23.
and there was. 1 S 19:9.

11 **cast the javelin**. 1 S 19:9, 10. 20:33. Pr 27:4. Is 54:17.
And David. Ps 37:32, 33. Is 54:17. Lk 4:30. Jn 8:59. 10:39.

12 **afraid**. ver. 15, 20, 29. 1 S 16:4. Ps 14:5. 48:3-6. 53:5. Mk 6:20. Lk 8:37. Ac 24:25.
the Lord. 1 S 16:13, 18. 22:13. Ac 7:9.
departed. 1 S 16:14. 28:15. Ps 51:11. Ho 9:12. Mt 25:41.

13 **removed**. ver. 17, 25. 1 S 8:12. 22:7.
thousand. 1 S 6:19. 10:19. Mi +5:2.
he went out. ver. 16. Nu 27:16, 17. 2 S 5:2. Ps 121:8.

14 **behaved**. *or*, prospered. ver. +5. Mk 6:20. Lk 8:37. Ac 24:25.
the Lord. 1 S 10:7. 16:18. Is +43:2. Ac 18:10.

15 **wisely**. Ps 112:5. Da 6:4, 5. Col 4:5. Ja 1:5. 3:17.

16 **all Israel**. ver. 5. Lk 19:48. 20:19.
he went. Nu 27:17. 2 S 5:2. 1 K 3:7.

17 **her will I give**. 1 S 17:25. Ps 12:2. 55:21.
valiant. Heb. a son of valor. 2 S +2:7mg.
the Lord's. 1 S 17:47. 25:28. Nu 32:20, 27, 29.
Let not mine. ver. 21, 25. Dt 17:7. 2 S 11:15. 12:9.

18 **Who am I**. ver. 23. 1 S 9:21. Ex 3:11. Ru 2:10. 2 S 7:18. Pr 15:33. 18:12. Je 1:6.

19 **was given**. Jg 14:20.
Adriel. lit. *drove of God; flock of God*, **S#5741h**. 2 S 21:8.
Meholathite. i.e. *mirth; dancing; writhing*, **S#4259h**. Jg 7:22. 2 S 21:8.

20 **loved David**. ver. 28. Ge 29:18, 20. 34:3. Jg 16:4, 15. 2 S 13:1. 1 K 11:1, 2. Ho 3:1.
they told. Ge +24:57.
pleased him. Heb. *was right in his eyes*. ver. 26. Jsh +22:30mg.

21 **a snare**. Ex +23:33. Ps 7:14-16. 38:12. 140:5. 142:3. Pr 26:24-26. 29:5. Je 5:26. 9:8.
the hand. ver. 17. 1 S 19:11, 12.
this day. ver. 26.

22 **commanded**. Ps 36:1-3. 55:21.
servants. 2 S 13:28, 29. Pr 29:12.

23 **a light**. 1 J 3:1.
a poor man. 1 S 9:21. Pr 14:20. 19:6, 7. Ec 9:15, 16.
and lightly. Ps 119:141.

24 **On this manner**. Heb. According to these words.

25 **dowry**. Ge 29:18. 34:12. Ex 22:16, 17.

foreskins. 1 S 17:26, 36. Ge 17:11-14. Jsh 5:3.

to be avenged. 1 S 14:24.

thought. ver. 17. 2 S 17:8-11.

26 **the days**. ver. 21.

expired. Heb. fulfilled. 1 Ch 17:11.

27 **his men**. ver. 13.

slew. Jg 14:19. 2 S 3:14. Is 43:1, 4.

two hundred men. ver. 25. 2 S 3:14.

28 **Saul saw**. 1 S 24:20. 26:25. Ge 30:27. 37:8-11. 39:3. Re 3:9.

29 **yet the**. ver. 12, 15. Ps 37:12-14. Ec 4:4. Ja 2:19.

Saul became. Ge 4:4-8. Jn 11:53. 1 J 3:12-15.

30 **went forth**. 2 S 11:1.

behaved himself. ver. 5. Ps 119:99. Da 1:20. Lk 21:15. Ep 5:15. Ph 1:9.

his name. SS 1:3. Ph 2:9.

set by. Heb. precious. 1 S 2:30. 26:21. 2 K 1:13. Ps 72:14. 116:15. Is 43:4. 1 P 2:4, 7.

1 SAMUEL 19

1 **And Saul**. 1 S 18:8, 9. Pr 27:4. Ec 9:3. Je 9:3. 2 T 3:13.

2 **delighted**. 1 S 18:1-3. Ps 16:3. Jn 15:17-19. 1 J 3:12-14.

Jonathan. 1 S 20:2. Pr 17:17.

hide. Pr +22:3.

3 **and what**. 1 S 20:9, 13.

4 **spake good**. 1 S 20:32. 22:14. Pr 24:11, 12. 31:8, 9. Je 18:20.

sin against. 1 S 2:25. Ge 9:6. 42:22. 2 Ch 6:22. 1 C 8:12. 1 J 3:15.

because his works. Ps 35:12. 109:4, 5. Pr 17:13. Je 18:20. Jn 10:32.

5 **put his**. 1 S 28:21. Jg 9:17. 12:3. Ps 119:109. Ac 20:24. Ph 2:30.

life. Heb. *nephesh*, Ge +44:30.

slew. 1 S 17:49-51.

wrought. 1 S 11:13. 14:45. 17:52, 53. Ex 14:13. 1 Ch 11:14. He 2:3.

sin against innocent. 1 S 20:32. Je 26:15. Mt 27:4, 24.

without a cause. Ps 25:3. 35:19. 69:4. 119:161. Jn 15:25.

6 **sware**. 1 K +17:1. Ps 15:4. Pr 26:24, 25.

he shall not. ver. 10, 11.

7 **in times past**. Heb. yesterday, third day. 1 S 16:21. 18:2, 10, 13. 2 S +3:17mg.

8 **David**. Ps 18:32, etc. 27:3.

him. Heb. his face.

9 **the evil spirit**. Heb. *ruach*, Jg +9:23. 1 S 16:14. +18:10, 11. Mt +8:16.

from the Lord. 1 S +18:10.

10 **sought**. ver. 6. Ho 6:4. Mt 12:43-45. Lk 11:24-26. 2 P 2:20-22.

he slipped. 1 S 20:33. Jb 5:14, 15. Ps 18:17. 34:19. Pr 21:30. Is 54:17. Lk 4:30. Jn 10:39.

and escaped. Ps 124:7. Mt 10:23.

11 **sent messengers**. Ps 59, title, 3, 4, 6, 15, 16.

to watch him. Jg 16:2. Ps 37:32. Mk 6:20. Lk 20:20.

life. Heb. *nephesh*, Ge +44:30.

12 **Michal**. Ps 34:19.

let David. Jsh 2:15. Ac 9:24, 25. 2 C 11:32, 33.

13 **took**. Ge 27:16.

an image. Heb. *teraphim*. Ge +31:19mg.

a pillow. 2 K 8:15.

14 **she said**. Jsh 2:5. 2 S 16:17-19. 17:20.

15 **Bring him**. ver. 6. Jb 31:31. Ps 37:12. Pr 27:3, 4. Ro 3:15.

16 **And when**. Ge 24:67.

17 **Why hast**. 1 S 22:17. 28:12. Mt 2:16.

mine enemy. 1 K 21:20. Ga 4:16.

And Michal. 2 S 17:20.

He said. ver. 14. Ex 1:17-19.

why should. 2 S 2:22.

18 **and escaped**. Ps 35:27. 52:6, 7. 59:16, 17.

to Samuel. 1 S 7:17. 15:34. 28:3. Ps 116:11. Ja 5:16.

Naioth. i.e. *habitations; dwellings*, **S#5121h**. ver. 19, 22, 23. 1 S 20:1.

19 **it was told**. 1 S 22:9, 10. 23:19. 26:1. Pr 29:12.

20 **sent messengers**. ver. 11, 14. Jn 7:32, 45.

when they. 1 S 10:5, 6, 10. Nu 11:25, 26. Jl 2:28. Jn 7:32, 45, 46, etc. 1 C 14:3, 24, 25.

and Samuel. Ps 14:5. 125:2, 3.

Spirit. Heb. *ruach*, Ge +41:38.

21 **sent messengers**. 2 K 1:9-13. Pr 27:22. Je 13:23.

prophesied also. Jl 2:28.

22 **went he also**. Pr 21:1.

well. Heb. *bor*, Ge +37:20.

Sechu. i.e. *watchtower; an observatory; they hedged up; a bough*, **S#7906h**.

23 **the Spirit**. Heb. *ruach*, Ge +41:38. ver. 20. 1 S 10:16. Nu 23:5. 24:2. Mt 7:22. Jn 11:51. 1 C 13:2.

until he came. Pr 16:9. 21:1.

24 **stripped**. Mi 1:8.

lay. Heb. fell. Nu 24:4.

naked. Is +20:2.

Is Saul. 1 S 10:10-12. Mt 7:22, 23. Ac 9:21.

1 SAMUEL 20

1 **fled**. 1 S 19:19-24. 23:26-28. Ps 124:6-8. 2 P 2:9.

What have. 1 S 12:3. 24:11, 17. Ps 7:3-5. 18:20-24. 2 C 1:12. 1 J 3:21.

life. Heb. *nephesh*, soul, Ge +44:20.

2 **God forbid**. Lk +20:16.

show it me. Heb. uncover mine ear. ver. 12. Ru +4:4mg. Ps 40:6. Is 50:5. Jn 15:15. 17:8.

3 **sware**. Ge +21:23.

but truly. 1 S 25:26. 27:1. 2 S 15:21. 2 K 2:2, 4, 6.

and as thy. 1 S 1:26. 17:55. Je 38:16.
 soul. Heb. *nephesh*, Ge +27:31.
 but a step. 1 S 27:1. Dt 28:66. Ps 88:3, 4.
 116:3. 143:7. Is 27:4. Ac 12:4, 6. 1 C 15:30,
 31. 2 C 1:9, 10.
4 Whatsoever, etc. *or*, Say what is thy mind,
 and I will do, etc.
 soul. Heb. *nephesh*, Ge +34:3.
 desireth. Heb. speaketh, *or* thinketh. Jn
 14:13.
5 the new moon. ver. 6. Col +2:16.
 that I may. ver. 19. Pr +22:3.
6 at all miss. lit. missing shall miss.
 Bethlehem. 1 S 17:58. Jn 7:42.
 sacrifice. *or*, feast. 1 S 9:12. 16:2-5.
7 It is well. Dt 1:23. 2 S 17:4.
 evil. ver. 9. 1 S 25:17. Est 7:7.
8 deal kindly. Ge 24:49. 47:29. Jsh 2:14. Ru
 1:8. Pr 3:3.
 thou hast. ver. 16. 1 S 18:3. 23:18.
 if there be. Jsh 22:22. 2 S 14:32. Ps 7:4, 5.
 Ac 25:11.
 why shouldest. 1 Ch 12:17. Ps 116:11.
9 then would. ver. 38, 42. 1 S 19:2.
10 answer thee. ver. 30-34. 1 S 25:10, 14, 17.
 Ge 42:7, 30. 1 K 12:13. Pr 18:23.
12 O Lord. Jsh 22:22. Jg 6:22. Jb 31:4. Ps 17:3.
 139:1-4. Jn 20:28.
 sounded. Heb. searched. Pr 20:5. 25:2, 3.
 show it thee. Heb. uncover thine ear. ver. 2.
 Ru +4:4mg.
13 The Lord do. 1 S 3:17. 25:22. Ru 1:17. 2 S
 3:35. 19:13. 1 K 19:2. 20:10.
 I will show. ver. 2, 12. Ru +4:4mg.
 go. Lk +7:50.
 the Lord be. 1 K +1:37.
 he hath been with my father. 1 S 10:7.
 11:6-13. 14:47. 2 S 7:15.
14 the kindness. 2 S 9:3. Ep 5:1, 2.
15 thou shalt. 1 S 24:21. 2 S 9:1-7. 21:7.
 for ever. Heb. *olam*, Ex +12:24.
 face of. Ge +1:2.
16 made. Heb. cut. 1 S 18:3. Ge 15:18.
 Let the Lord. 1 S 25:22. 31:2. 2 S 4:7, 8.
 21:8. Je 51:56.
17 because he loved him. *or*, by his love
 toward him.
 for he loved. 1 S 18:1, 3. Dt 13:6. 2 S 1:26.
 Pr 18:24. SS 2:14.
 soul. Heb. *nephesh*, Ge +27:31.
18 new moon. ver. +5.
 empty. Heb. missed. ver. 6, 25, 27. 1 S 25:7,
 15, 21. Is 34:16.
19 quickly. *or*, diligently. Heb. greatly.
 hide thyself. ver. 5. 1 S 19:2.
 when the business. Heb. in the day of business.
 Ezel. *or*, that showeth the way. ver. 41.
21 no. Heb. not any thing.
 as the. 1 K +17:1. Am 8:14.

23 the matter. ver. 14, 15.
 the Lord. ver. 42. Ge 16:5. 31:49, 50, 53.
 for ever. Heb. *olam*, Ex +12:24.
24 the king. Ps 50:16-21. Pr 4:17. 15:17. 17:1.
 21:3, 27. Is 1:11-15. Zc 7:6. Jn 18:28.
 meat. Ge +3:19.
25 as at other times. Jg 16:20.
26 not anything. Ex +20:10.
 he is not clean. Le 7:21. 11:24, 27, 31, 40.
 15:5, 16, 17, 19-21. Nu 19:16.
27 Wherefore. 1 S 18:11. 19:9, 10, 15.
 the son. 1 S 22:7-9, 13, 14. 25:10. Is 11:1, 2.
 Mt 13:55. 1 P 2:4.
 meat. Ge +3:19.
28 answered Saul. ver. 6.
29 my brother. 1 S 17:28.
30 Saul's. Jb 5:2. Pr 14:29. 19:12, 19. 21:24.
 25:28. 27:3. Ja 1:19, 20.
 Thou, etc. *or*, Thou perverse rebel. Heb. Son
 of perverse rebellion. Pr 15:2. 21:24. Mt 5:22.
 Ep 4:31. 6:4.
31 send. ver. 8. 1 S 19:6, 11-15.
 shall surely die. Heb. is the son of death. 1 S
 26:16mg. 2 S 12:5mg. 19:28mg. 1 K 2:26mg.
 Ps 79:11mg. 102:20mg. Pr 31:8mg. Jon
 4:10mg. Mt 9:15. 13:38. 23:15. Lk 5:34. Jn
 17:12. Ac 13:10. Ep 2:2, 3. 5:6. 2 Th 2:3.
32 Wherefore. 1 S 19:5. Pr 24:11, 12. 31:8, 9. Jn
 7:51.
 what hath. Mt 27:23. Lk 23:22.
33 cast. 1 S 18:11. 19:10, 11. Pr 22:24. Ec 9:3. Je
 17:9.
 whereby. ver. 7. Ec 7:9.
34 in fierce. Ec 7:20. Ep 4:26.
 he was grieved. Mk 3:5.
35 at the time. ver. 19. 2 S 20:5.
36 Run. ver. 20, 21.
 beyond him. Heb. to pass over him. ver. 21,
 22.
38 Make speed. Ps 55:6-9. Pr 6:4, 5. Mt 24:16-
 18. Mk 13:14-16. Lk 17:31, 32.
39 knew not. 2 S 15:11. Ec 9:5.
40 artillery. Heb. instruments. 1 S 21:8.
 his lad. Heb. the lad that was his. 1 S 24:4.
41 and fell. 1 S 25:23. Ge 43:28. 2 S 9:6.
 and they kissed. Ge +27:27.
 and wept. Ps 6:6, 7. 39:12. 56:8.
 David exceeded. 1 S 18:3. 2 S 1:26.
42 Go in peace. ver. 22. Lk +7:50.
 forasmuch as. *or*, The Lord be witness of
 that which, etc. ver. 23.
 The Lord be between. Ge 31:49.
 And he arose. 1 S 23:18. ver. 23. Ge 31:49.
 for ever. Heb. *olam*, Ex +12:24.

1 SAMUEL 21

1 Nob. 1 S 22:19. Ne 11:32. Is 10:24, 32.
 to Ahimelech. 1 S 14:3, Ahiah. 1 S 22:9-19.
 2 S 8:17. Mk 2:26, Abiathar.

afraid. 1 S 16:4.

2 **The king**. 1 S 16:2. 19:17. 22:22. Ge 27:20, 24. 1 K 13:18. Ps 119:28, 29. Ga 2:12. Col 3:9.

3 **under thine**. ver. 4. Jg 9:29. Is 3:6.
present. Heb. found. Est +1:5mg.

4 **hallowed bread**. ver. 6. Ex +25:30. Mt 12:3, 4.
if the young. Ex 19:15. Le 15:18. Zc 7:3. 1 C 7:5.

5 **the vessels**. Ac 9:15. 2 C 4:7. 1 Th 4:3, 4. 2 T 2:20, 21. 1 P 3:7.
in a manner. Le 24:9.
yea, though it were sanctified this day in the vessel. or, especially when this day there is other sanctified in the vessel. Le 8:26.

6 **gave him**. Mt 12:3, 4. Mk 2:25-27. Lk 6:3, 4.
hot bread. Le 24:5-9.

7 **detained**. Je 7:9-11. Ezk 33:31. Am 8:5. Mt 15:8. Ac 21:26, 27.
Doeg. i.e. *sorrowful, fearful*, **S#1673h**. 1 S 22:9, 18, 22. Ps 52, title.
an Edomite. Dt 23:7, 8.
herdmen. 1 S 11:5. Ge 13:7, 8. 26:20. 1 Ch 27:29. 2 Ch 26:10.

8 **business**. Lk 2:49. Jn 9:4.

9 **The sword**. 1 S 17:51-54. Mk 4:4-10. Ep 6:17. He 4:12. Re 19:15.
the valley. 1 S 17:2, 50.
behold. 1 S 31:10.
behind. Ex +28:4.

10 **fled**. Pr +22:3. Je 26:21.
Achish. or, Abimelech. i.e. *object of fear or reverence*, **S#397h**. ver. 11, 12, 14. 1 S 27:2, 3, 5, 6, 9, 10, 12. 28:1, 2. 29:2, 3, 6, 8, 9. 1 K 2:39, 40. Ps 34, title,mg.
Gath. Jsh +11:22.

11 **the servants**. Ps 56, title.
the king. 1 S 16:1. 18:7, 8. 29:5.

12 **laid up**. Ps 119:11. Lk 2:19, 51.
sore. ver. 10. Ge 12:11-13. 26:7. Ps 34:4. 56:3.

13 **changed**. Jb 14:20. Ps 34, title. Pr 29:25. Ec 7:7.
behavior. lit. taste, as in Ex 16:31. Nu 11:8. 1 S 25:33. Jb 6:6. 12:20. Ps 34:1. 119:66. Pr 11:22. 26:16. Je 48:11. Jon 3:7.
scrabbled. or, made marks. Ezk 9:4.
spittle. Jb 6:6.
fall down. Ps 78:16. La 2:18.

14 **is mad**. or, playeth the madman. Ge +27:16. 1 S 16:2. 2 K 9:11. Ps 34:6, 17-19. Pr +22:3. Ec 7:7. Is 59:15mg.

15 **need**. or, lack. **S#2638h**. 2 S 3:29. 1 K 11:22. 17:16. Pr 6:32. 7:7. 9:4, 16. 10:13, 21. 11:12. 12:9, 11. 15:21. 17:18. 24:30. 28:16. Ec 6:2. 10:3.

1 SAMUEL 22

1 **David**. 1 S 21:10-15. Ps 34 and 57, titles.
the cave Adullam. Jsh +12:15. Ps 142, title.

He 11:38.
they went. Ps 42:1.

2 **distress**. Jg 11:3. Mt 11:12, 28.
was in debt. Heb. had a creditor. Mt 18:25-34.
discontented. Heb. bitter of soul. Heb. *nephesh*, Ex +15:9. 1 S +30:6.
a captain. 1 S 9:16. 25:15, 16. 30:22-24. 2 S 5:2. 2 K 20:5. 1 Ch 11:15-19. Ps 72:12-14. Mt 9:12, 13. 11:19. Lk 15:2. He 2:10.

3 **Mizpeh**. Jsh +15:38.
the king. 1 S 14:47. Ru 1:1-4. 4:10, 17.
Let my father. Ge 47:11. Ex 20:12. Mt 15:4-6. 1 T 5:4.
till I know. 1 S 3:18. 2 S 15:25, 26. Ph 2:23, 24.

4 **Moab**. Is 16:4.
in the hold. 2 S 23:13, 14. 1 Ch 12:16.

5 **Gad**. 2 S 24:11, 13, 14, 18, 19. Ge +30:11. 1 Ch 21:9, 11, 13, 18, 19. 29:29. 2 Ch 29:25.
depart. 1 S 23:1-6. Ne 6:11. Ps 11:1. Is 8:12-14.
David departed. Mt 10:23.
Hareth. i.e. *forest; cutting of wood; engraving*, **S#2802h**.

6 **tree**. or, grove in a high place. 1 S 31:13. Ge 21:33. 35:8. 1 Ch 10:12.
spear. 1 S 18:10. 19:9. 20:33.

7 **the son of Jesse**. ver. 9, 13. 1 S 18:14. 1 Ch +2:12.
give. 1 S 8:14, 15.
captains. Jsh +22:21.

8 **showeth me**. Heb. uncovereth mine ear. ver. 17. Ru +4:4mg.
that my son. 1 S 18:3. 20:8, 13-17, 30-34, 42. 23:16-18.

9 **Doeg**. 1 S 21:7. Ps 52, title, 1-5. Pr 19:5. 29:12. Ezk 22:9. Mt 26:59-61.
the Edomite. 1 S 21:7.
Ahimelech. 1 S 21:1, etc.
Ahitub. 1 S 14:3.

10 **he enquired**. ver. 13, 15. 1 S 21:6, 9. 23:2, 4, 12. 30:8. Nu 27:21. Ps 52:2-4.
him victuals. 1 S 21:6-9.

11 **sent to call**. Ro 3:15.
Nob. i.e. *fruit; high place*, **S#5011h**. ver. 9, 19. 1 S 21:1. Ne 11:32. Is 10:32.

12 **thou son**. ver. 7, 13.
Here I am. Heb. Behold me. 1 S 3:4-6. 2 S 9:6. Is 65:1.

13 **Why have**. ver. 8. Ps 119:69. Am 7:10. Lk 23:2-5.

14 **And who**. 1 S 19:4, 5. 20:32. 24:11. 26:23. 2 S 22:23-25. Pr 24:11, 12. 31:8, 9.
the king's. ver. 13. 1 S 17:25. 18:27.
goeth. 1 S 18:13. 21:2.

15 **thy servant**. Ge 20:5, 6. 2 S 15:11. 2 C 1:12. 1 P 3:16, 17.
less or more. Heb. little or great. 1 S 25:36.

16 **Thou shalt**. 1 S 14:44. 20:31. 1 K 18:4. 19:2.

Pr 28:15. Da 2:5, 12. 3:19, 20. Ac 12:19.
surely. Ge +2:16.
thou, and. Dt 24:16. Est 3:6. Mt 2:16.

17 **footmen**. *or*, guard. Heb. runners. 1 S 8:11.
20:36. 2 S 15:1. 18:22, 24, 26. 1 K 1:5.
14:27mg, 28. 2 K 10:25. 11:4, 6. 2 Ch 12:10.
+30:6.
slay the priests. ver. 13. 1 S 20:33. 25:17. 1
K 18:4.
hand. Dt 32:36.
show. ver. 8. Ru +4:4mg.
would not. 1 S 14:45. Ex +1:17. 2 K 1:13,
14. Ac +4:19. +5:29.

18 **Doeg**. ver. +9.
he fell. 2 Ch 24:21. Ho 5:11. 7:3. Mi 6:16. Zp
3:3. Ac 26:10, 11.
fourscore. 1 S 2:30-33, 36. 3:12-14.
a linen ephod. Ex +28:4, 40. 39:27.

19 **Nob**. ver. 9, 11. 1 S 21:1. Ne 11:32. Is 10:32.
the city. Is 14:31. Je 4:29. 26:2. 48:8. 49:23.
Mi 6:9. Mt 11:21, 23. 23:37. Mk 1:5, 33. Ac
8:25.
men. 1 S 2:33. 4:11, 12. 15:3, 9. Jsh 6:17, 21.
2 S 21:1. Ps 53:4. 137:7. Ho 10:14. Ja 2:13.

20 **one**. 1 S 23:6. 30:7. 2 S 20:25. 1 K 2:26, 27.
Abiathar. i.e. *father of abundance*, **S#54h**. ver.
21, 22. 1 S 23:6, 9. 30:7. 2 S 8:17. 15:24, 27,
29, 35, 36. 17:15. 19:11. 20:25. 1 K 1:7, 19,
25, 42. 2:22, 26, 27, 35. 4:4. 1 Ch 15:11.
18:16. 24:6. 27:34. Mk 2:26.
escaped. 1 S 2:33. 4:12. Jb 1:15-17, 17, 19.

22 **I have occasioned**. 1 S 21:1-9. Ps 44:22.
persons. Heb. *nephesh*, Jsh +10:28.

23 **with me**. Jn 14:19. Col 3:2.
he that seeketh. 1 K 2:26. Mt 24:9. Jn
15:20. 16:2, 3. He 12:1-3.
life. Heb. *nephesh*, soul, Ge +44:30.
but with me. Jn 10:28-30. 17:12. 18:9.

1 SAMUEL 23

1 **Keilah**. Jsh +15:44.
rob the. Le 26:16. Dt 28:33, 51. Jg 6:4, 11.
Mi 6:15.
threshingfloors. Ge +50:10, 11.

2 **enquired**. ver. 4, 6, 9-12. 1 S 30:8. Nu 27:21.
Jsh 9:14. Jg 1:1. 20:18. 2 S 5:19, 23. 1 Ch
14:10. Ps 32:8. Pr 3:5, 6. Je 10:23.

3 **Behold**. ver. 15, 23, 26. Ps 11:1. Je 12:5. Jn
11:8.

4 **inquired**. Is 37:14.
yet again. 1 S 10:22. 16:11. 28:6. Ge 18:29.
+22:15. Jg 6:39. 2 K 13:18, 19. Ec +5:2. Mt
26:42, 44. Lk +11:9. 18:1-8.
for I will. Jsh 8:7. Jg 7:7. 2 S 5:19. 2 K 3:18.

6 *when Abiathar*. 1 S +22:20.
an ephod. Ex +28:4.

7 A.M. 2943. B.C. 1061. An. Ex. Is. 430.
God hath. ver. 14. 1 S 24:4-6. 26:8, 9. Ps
71:10, 11.

he is shut. Ex 14:3. 15:9. Jg 16:2, 3. Jb 10:5.
Lk 19:43, 44.

9 **David**. Ps 10:9. 37:12, 13. Je 11:18, 19. Ac
9:24. 14:6. 23:16-18.
Bring. ver. +6. Nu 27:21. Je 33:3.

10 **destroy the city**. ver. 8. 1 S 22:19, 22. Ge
18:24. Est 3:6. Ps 69:6. Pr 28:15. Jn 18:8. Ro
3:15, 16.

11 **And the Lord**. Ps 50:15. Je 33:3. Mt 7:7, 8.

12 **deliver**. Heb. shut up. ver. 7, 11, 20. 1 S
17:46. +24:18mg. 30:15. Dt 32:30. Jsh 20:5.
Ps 31:8.
They will. ver. 7. Ps 35:12. 41:9. 62:1. 118:8.
Ec 9:14, 15. Is 29:15. Mi 7:5. He 4:13.

13 **six hundred**. 1 S 22:2. 25:13. 30:9, 10.

14 **a mountain**. 1 S 26:20. Jsh 15:48, 55. Ps
11:1-3. 54:3, 4. 124:7.
the wilderness. Jsh +15:24.
Saul. 1 S 27:1. Ps 54:3, 4. Pr 1:16. 4:16.
but God. ver. 7. Ps 32:7. 37:32, 33. 54:3, 4.
Pr 21:30. Je 36:26. Ro 8:31. 2 T 3:11. 4:17,
18.

15 **life**. Heb. *nephesh*, soul. Ge +44:30.

16 **strengthened**. 1 S +9:27. Dt 3:28. Ne 2:18.
Jb 4:3, 4. 16:5. Pr 27:9, 17. Ec 4:9-12. Is 35:3,
4. Ezk 13:22. Da 10:19, 21. Lk 22:32, 43. Ac
13:43. Ep 6:10. 2 T 2:1. He 10:24, 25. 12:12,
13.

17 **Fear not**. Is 41:10, 14. He 13:6.
shall not. Jb 5:11-15. Ps 27:1-3. 46:1, 2.
91:1, 2. Pr 14:26. Is 54:17.
thou shalt be. 1 S 15:28. Lk 12:32.
I shall be. Pr 19:21. Ac 28:16. Ro 15:24.
that also Saul. 1 S 20:31. 24:20. Ac 5:39.

18 **they two**. 1 S 18:3. 20:12-17, 42. 2 S 9:1.
21:7.

19 **the Ziphites**. i.e. *smelters*, **S#2130h**. 1 S 22:7, 8.
26:1. Jsh 15:24. Ps 54, title, 3, 4. Pr 29:12.
Gibeah. Jg +19:12.
hide himself. Ps 54:1. Pr +22:3. Is 45:15.
strong holds. ver. 14, 29. 1 S 22:4. 24:22.
Hachilah. i.e. *red; darksome*, **S#2444h**. 1 S 26:1,
3. 1 S 26:1, 3.
on the south. Heb. on the right hand. Ge
14:15.
Jeshimon. *or*, the wilderness. ver. 24. Nu
21:20. Ps 63, title.

20 **all the desire**. Dt 18:6. 2 S 3:21. Ps 112:10.
Pr 11:23.
soul. Heb. *nephesh*, Ge +34:3.
our part. 1 K 21:11-14. 2 K 10:5-7. Ps 54:3.
Pr 29:26.

21 **Saul said, Blessed**. 1 S 22:8. Jg 17:2. Ps
10:3. Is 66:5. Mi 3:11.

22 **haunt is**. Heb. foot shall be. Jb 5:13.

23 **take knowledge**. Mk 14:1, 10, 11. Jn 18:2,
3.
I will search. 2 S 17:11-13. 1 K +18:10. Pr
1:16. Ro 3:15, 16.
the thousands. Nu 10:36. Jsh +22:21.

24 Ziph. ver. +14.
the wilderness. 1 S 25:2.
Maon. Jsh +15:55.
the south. ver. 19.

25 into a rock. *or*, from the rock. ver. 28. Jg 15:8.

26 David made haste. 1 S 19:12. 20:38. 2 S 15:14. 17:21, 22. Ps 31:22.
away. 2 Ch 20:12. Ps 17:8, 9, 11. 22:12, 16. 31:2-4, 15. 32:7. 118:11-13. 140:1-9. 2 C 1:8. Re 20:9.

27 there came. Ge 22:14. Dt 32:36. 2 K 19:9. Ps 116:3.
the Philistines. 2 K 19:9. Re 12:16.
invaded. Heb. spread themselves upon. 1 S 27:8, 10. 30:1, 14. Jg 9:44. 1 Ch 14:13.

28 Sela-hammahlekoth. *that is*, the rock of divisions. **S#5555h.**

29 strong holds. ver. 14, 19. Ps 63.
En-gedi. Jsh +15:62.

1 SAMUEL 24

1 when Saul. 1 S 23:28, 29.
following. Heb. after.
it was told. 1 S 23:19. Pr 25:5. 29:12. Ezk 22:9. Ho 7:3.
the wilderness. 1 S 23:29.

2 Saul took. 1 S 13:2.
and went. Ps 18:36, 43, 48. 37:32. 38:12.
the rocks. Ps 104:18. 141:6.

3 and Saul. Ps 141:6.
to cover. Jg 3:24mg. 2 K 18:27mg.
David. Ps 57, 142, titles.

4 the men. 1 S 26:8-11. Nu 31:16. 2 S 4:8. 1 K 12:10, 28. 2 Ch 10:10. 22:3. Jb 2:9. 31:31.
I will deliver. ver. 10, 18. 1 S 23:7. 26:23. 1 K +13:18.
Saul's robe. Heb. the robe which was Saul's. ver. 5. 1 S 20:40. 1 K 1:33.

5 David's heart. 2 S 12:9. 24:10. 2 K 22:19. 1 J 3:20, 21.
cut off. 2 S 10:4.

6 The Lord forbid. Lk +20:16.
do. Jb 31:29, 30. Mt 5:44. Ro 12:14-21. 13:1, 2. 1 Th 5:15.
Lord's anointed. 1 S 26:9-11. 2 S 1:14. Ps 105:15.

7 stayed. Heb. cut off. Le 1:17. Jg 14:16. Ps 7:3-5. Pr 31:8. Mt 5:44. Ro 12:17-21.
suffered. 1 S 25:33. Ge +31:7.

8 My lord. 1 S 26:17.
David stooped. 1 S 20:41. 25:23, 24. Ge +18:2. Ex 20:12. Ro 13:7. 1 P 2:17.

9 Wherefore hearest. 1 S 26:19. Le 19:16. Ps 101:5. 141:6. Pr 16:28. 17:4, 9. 18:8. 25:23. 26:20-22, 28. 29:12. Ec 7:21, 22. Ja 3:6.

10 bade me. ver. 4. 1 S 26:8.
not put forth. 1 T 5:19, 20.
the Lord's. ver. +6.

11 my father. 1 S 18:27. 2 K 5:13. Pr 15:1.
neither evil. 1 S 26:18. Ps 7:3, 4. 35:7. Jn 15:25.
thou huntest. 1 S 23:14, 23. 26:20. Jb 10:16. Ps 109:2-5. 140:11. La 4:18. Ezk 13:18. Mi 7:2.
soul. Heb. *nephesh*, Ge +12:13.

12 Lord judge between. 1 S 26:10, 23. Ge 16:5. 31:48-53. Jg 11:27. Jb 5:8. Ps 7:8, 9. 35:1. 43:1. 94:1. Ro 12:19. 1 P 2:23. Re 6:10.
but mine hand. 1 S 26:10, 11.

13 proverb. or, simile. Dt +28:37.
ancients. or "eastern," as in Jb 18:20 (went before). Is 43:18. Ezk 10:19. 11:1. 38:17. 47:18. Jl 2:20. Zc 14:8. Ml 3:4 **(S#6931h).**
Wickedness. Mt 7:16-18. 12:33, 34. 15:19.

14 the king. 2 S 6:20. 1 K 21:7.
a dead dog. 1 S 17:43. 2 S 3:8. 9:8. 16:9.
a flea. 1 S 26:20. Jg 8:1-3.

15 be judge. ver. +12. 2 Ch 24:22. Mi 1:2.
plead. Ps 35:1. 43:1. 119:154. Mi 7:9.
deliver. Heb. judge. 1 S 26:4.

16 Is this. 1 S 26:17. Jb 6:25. Pr 15:1. 25:11. Lk 21:15. Ac 6:10.
Saul lifted. Ge +22:13. 33:4.

17 Thou art. 1 S 26:21. Ge 38:26. Ex 9:27. Ps 37:6. Mt 5:20. 27:4.
thou hast. Mt 5:44. Ro 12:20, 21.
rewarded. 1 S +1:22 **(S#1580h).**

18 Lord. ver. 10. 1 S 23:7. 26:23.
delivered me. Heb. shut me up. 1 S +17:46mg. 23:12mg. 26:8mg. Jb 16:11mg. Ps 31:8.

19 the Lord. 1 S 23:21. 26:25. Jg 17:2. Ps 18:20. Pr 25:21, 22.

20 I know well. 1 S 20:30, 31. 23:17. 2 S 3:17, 18. Jb 15:25. Mt 2:3-6, 13, 16.

21 Swear. Ge +21:23.
that thou. 2 S 21:6-8.

22 David and. Pr 26:24, 25. Mt 10:16, 17. Jn 2:24.
the hold. 1 S 23:29.

1 SAMUEL 25

1 A.M. 2944. B.C. 1060. An. Ex. Is. 431.
Samuel. 1 S 28:3.
lamented. Ge 50:11. Nu 20:29. Dt 34:8. Ac 8:2.
in his house. 1 S 7:17. 1 K 2:34. 2 Ch 33:20. Is 14:18.
at Ramah. 1 S 1:19.
the wilderness. Ge 14:6. +21:21. Ps 63:1. 120:5. 143:6.

2 Maon. Jsh +15:55.
possessions were. *or*, business *was*. Ge 47:3.
Carmel. Jsh +19:26.
man. Ge 26:13. 2 S 19:32. Ps 17:14. 73:3-7. Lk 16:19-25.
three thousand. Ge 13:2. Jb 1:3. 42:12.

shearing. Ge 38:13. 2 S 13:23, 24.
Carmel. 1 S 30:5. Jsh 15:55.

3 Nabal. i.e. *folly; foolish*, **S#5037h**. ver. 4, 5, 9,
10, 14, 19, 25, 26, 34, 36-39. 27:3. 30:5. 2 S
2:2. 3:3.
Abigail. i.e. *cause of delight; father of joy; source
of joy*, **S#26h**. ver. 14, 18, 23, 32, 36, 39, 40, 42.
27:3. 30:5. 2 S 2:2. 3:3. 17:25. 1 Ch 2:16, 17.
3:1.
good. Pr 14:1. 31:26, 30, 31.
understanding. **S#7922h**. 1 S 25:3. 1 Ch
22:12. 26:14. 2 Ch 2:12. 30:22. Ezr 8:18. Ne
8:8. Jb 17:4. Ps 111:10. Pr 3:4. 12:8. 13:15.
16:22. 19:11. 23:9. Da 8:25.
beautiful countenance. Ge 29:17.
was churlish. ver. 10, 11, 17. Ps 10:3. Is
32:5-7.
and he was. 1 S 17:43. 30:14. Jsh 15:13. 2 P
2:22.

4 did shear. Ge 38:13. 2 S 13:23.

5 greet him, etc. Heb. ask him in my name of
peace. Jg +18:15mg.

6 liveth. 1 S +10:24. 1 T 5:6.
Peace be both. Ge +43:23. 2 S 18:28mg. Je
+29:7.

7 thy shepherds. ver. 2.
we hurt. Heb. we shamed. ver. 15, 16, 21. 1
S 20:34. 22:2. Is 11:6-9. Lk 3:14. Ph 2:15. 4:8.

8 a good day. Ne 8:10-12. Est 9:19. Ec 11:2.
Mt 5:42. Lk 11:41. 14:12-14.
thy son. 1 S 3:6. 24:11.

9 ceased. Heb. rested. or, became quiet. Ge 8:4.
2 K 2:15. 2 Ch 14:7.

10 Who is David. 1 S 20:30. 22:7, 8. Ex 5:2. Jg
9:28. 2 S 20:1. 1 K 12:16. Ps 14:1, 6. 73:7, 8.
123:3, 4. Is 32:5, 7.
there be. 1 S 22:2. Ec 7:10.
many servants. Ex 21:5.

11 Shall I then. ver. 3. 1 S 24:13. Dt 8:17. Jg
8:6. Jb 31:17. Ps 73:7, 8. 1 P 4:9.
flesh. Heb. slaughter. Ge 43:16.
give it. Ec 11:1, 2. Ga 6:10.
whom. ver. 14, 15. Jn 9:29, 30. 2 C 6:9.

12 came. 2 S 24:13. Is 36:21, 22. He 13:17.

13 Gird ye. Jsh 9:14. Pr 14:29. 16:32. 19:2, 11.
25:8. Ja 1:19, 20.
David also. 1 S 24:5, 6. Ro 12:19-21.
two hundred. 1 S 30:9, 10, 21-24.

14 railed on them. Heb. flew upon them. 1 S
14:32. 15:19. Mk 15:29.

15 very good. ver. 7, 21. Ph 2:15.
hurt. Heb. shamed. ver. 7.

16 a wall. Ex 14:22. Jb 1:10. Je 15:20. Zc 2:5.

17 evil. 1 S 20:7, 9, 33. 2 Ch 25:16. Est 7:7.
a son of Belial. ver. 25. 1 S +30:22. 2 Ch
13:7.
that a man cannot speak to him. ver. 33. 1
S 20:32, 33. Jsh 22:21. Jg 11:28. 2 S 19:8. 1 K
12:8, 13. 2 K 5:13, 14. 2 Ch 10:8, 13. +25:16.
Jb 31:13. Ps 25:9, 12. Pr 1:5. 8:33. 9:8, 9.

12:15. +13:1, 10. 15:22. 17:10. 18:13. +19:20.
21:29. Ec 4:13. Je 36:25. Zp +3:2. Mt +7:6.
18:17. T 3:10, 11.

18 made haste. ver. 34. Nu 16:46-48. Jg +3:15.
Pr 6:4, 5. Mt 5:25.
took two hundred loaves. 2 S 17:28, 29.
two bottles. 1 S 1:24. Je 13:12.
clusters. Heb. lumps. 1 S 30:12. 2 S 16:1. 1
Ch 12:40.
cakes of figs. 1 S 30:12. 2 K 20:7. 1 Ch
12:40. Is 38:21.

19 Go. Ge 32:16, 20.
But. Pr 31:11, 12, 27.

20 rode. 2 K 4:24.

21 Surely. ver. 13. Jb 30:8. Ps 37:8. Ep 4:26, 31.
1 Th 5:15. 1 P 2:21-23. 3:9.
he hath requited. Ge 44:4. Ps 35:12. 38:20.
109:3-5. Pr 17:13. Je 18:20. Ro 12:21. 1 P
2:20. 3:17.

22 So and more. ver. 32-34. 1 S 3:17. 14:44.
20:13, 16. Ru 1:17.
if I leave. ver. 34.
any that pisseth, etc. ver. 34. 1 K 14:10.
16:11. 21:21. 2 K 9:8.

23 lighted. Jsh 15:18. Jg 1:14.
fell. 1 S 20:41. 24:8.

24 fell. 2 K 4:37. Est 8:3. Mt 18:29.
Upon. ver. 28. Ge 44:33, 34. 2 S 14:9. Phm
18, 19.
let thine. Ge 44:18. 2 S 14:9, 12.
audience. Heb. ears.

25 regard. Heb. lay it to his heart. 1 S +4:20mg.
2 S 13:33. Is 42:25. Ml 2:2.
man of Belial. ver. +17, 26.
Nabal. *that is*, fool.
folly. Pr 12:15. Ec 10:2, 3. Is +9:17.

26 as the Lord liveth. ver. 34. 1 K +17:1.
and as thy. 1 S +1:26.
soul. Heb. *nephesh*, Ge +27:31.
the Lord hath withholden. ver. 33. Ge
20:6.
from. Ro 12:19, 20.
avenging thyself. Heb. saving thyself. ver.
31, 33. Ps 18:47, 48. 44:3. Is 59:16. 63:5. Ro
12:19.
now let. 2 S 18:32. Je 29:22. Da 4:19.

27 blessing. *or*, present. Jg +3:15. 2 S 16:2. 2 K
18:31.
follow. Heb. walk at the feet of. ver. 42mg. 2
K +3:9mg.

28 forgive. ver. 24.
the Lord. 1 S 15:28. 2 S 7:11, 16, 27. 1 K
9:5. 1 Ch 17:10, 25. Ps 89:29.
fighteth. 1 S 17:47. 18:17. 2 S 5:2. 2 Ch
20:15. Ep 6:10, 11.
evil hath. 1 S 24:6, 7, 11, 17. 1 K 15:5. Ps
119:1-3. Mt 5:16. Lk 23:41, 47.

29 to pursue. Ac 9:4.
soul. Heb. *nephesh*, Ge +12:13.
bound. 1 S 2:9. Ge 15:1. Dt 33:29. Ps 66:9.

116:15. Ml 3:17. Mt 10:29, 30.

bundle. Ge 42:35. Mt 13:30.

with the Lord. Jn 10:27-30. 14:19. 17:21, 23. Col 3:3, 4. 1 P 1:5. 1 J 5:20.

souls. Ge +12:13.

sling out. Je 10:18.

as out of the middle of a sling. Heb. in the midst of the bow of a sling.

30 **according**. 1 S 13:14. 15:28. 23:17. Ps 89:20.

31 **grief**. Heb. staggering, or stumbling. Pr 5:12, 13. Ro 14:21. 2 C 1:12.

avenged. ver. 33. 1 S 24:15. 26:23. 2 S 22:48. Ps 94:1. Ro 12:19.

remember. ver. 40. Ge 40:14. Lk 23:42.

32 **Blessed**. Ge 24:27. Ex 18:10. Ezr 7:27. Ps 41:12, 13. 72:18. Lk 1:68. 2 C 8:16.

33 **blessed**. Ps 141:5. Pr 9:9. 17:10. 25:12. 27:21. 28:23.

which hast. ver. 26.

avenging. ver. +26, 31. 1 S 24:19. 26:9, 10. Le 19:18. Pr 20:22.

34 **kept me back**. ver. 26.

hasted. ver. 18. 1 S 11:11. Jsh 10:6, 9.

there had. ver. +22.

35 **received**. Ro +15:7.

brought. Jg +3:15.

Go up. Lk +7:50.

I have hearkened. Pr 16:32. 1 C 13:4, 5, 7. Ja 3:17.

accepted. Ge 19:21. Jb 34:19. Ec 9:7. Ep 1:6.

36 **a feast**. 2 S 13:23. Est 1:3-7. Lk 14:12.

merry. 2 S 13:28. 1 K 20:16. Pr 20:1. 23:29-35. Ec 2:2, 3. 10:19. Is 28:3, 7, 8. Je 51:57. Da 5:1-5. Na 1:10. Hab 2:15, 16. Lk 21:34. Ro 13:13. Ep 5:18. 1 Th 5:7, 8.

very drunken. or, drunk unto excess. lit. unto might, as in 2 Ch 16:14. Ps 119:107. La 5:22. Da 8:8.

she told him. ver. 19. Ps 112:5. Mt 10:16. Ep 5:15.

37 **had told him**. ver. 22, 34.

his heart died. Dt 28:28. Jb 15:21, 22. Pr 23:29-35.

as a stone. lit. hath become a stone. Ge 19:26. Ex 4:3. 7:9-12.

38 **the Lord**. ver. 33. 1 S 6:9. Ex 12:29. 2 K 15:5. 19:35. 2 Ch 10:15. Lk 12:20, 21. Ac 12:23.

39 **Blessed**. ver. 32. Jg 5:2. 2 S 22:47-49. Ps 58:10, 11. Re 19:1-4.

pleaded. Pr 22:23. La 3:58-60. Mi 7:9.

kept his servant. ver. 26, 34. Ho 2:6, 7. 2 C 13:7. 1 Th 5:23. 2 T 4:18.

hath returned. 2 S 3:28, 29. 1 K 2:44. Est 7:10. Ps 7:16. Ezk 17:19.

to take her. Pr 18:22. 19:14. 31:10, 30.

40 **spake**. Ge +24:57.

David sent. Ge 24:37, 38, 51.

41 **thine**. Ru 2:10, 13. Pr 15:33. 18:12.

to wash. Ge +18:4. 2 K 3:11.

42 **Abigail**. Ge 24:61-67. Ps 45:10, 11, 14.

after her. Heb. at her feet. ver. 27.

43 **Ahinoam**. 1 S +14:50.

Jezreel. 1 Ch +4:3.

both. Ge +4:19.

his wives. 1 S 27:3. 30:5. 2 S 5:13-16.

44 **Michal**. 1 S 18:20, 27.

Phalti. i.e. escape of God, **S#6406h**. Nu +13:9, Palti. 2 S 3:14, 15, Phaltiel.

Laish. i.e. a lion, **S#3919h**. Jg 18:7, 14, 27, 29. 2 S 3:15. Is 10:30.

Gallim. i.e. billows, **S#1554h**. Is 10:30.

1 SAMUEL 26

1 **Ziphites**. Jsh 15:24, 55.

Doth not. ver. 3. 1 S 23:19. Ps 54, title.

2 **Saul arose**. 1 S 23:23-25. 24:17. Ps 38:12. 140:4-9.

three thousand. 1 S 24:2.

3 **Hachilah**. ver. 1. 1 S 23:19.

4 **sent out spies**. Jsh 2:1. Mt 10:16.

5 **Abner**. 1 S 9:1. +14:50.

trench. or, midst of his carriages. ver. 7. 1 S 17:20.

6 **Ahimelech**. 2 S +8:17.

Hittite. Ge 10:15. Dt +20:17.

to Abishai. i.e. father of presents; generous, **S#52h**. ver. 7-9. 2 S 2:18, 24. 3:30. 10:10, 14. 16:9, 11. 18:2, 5, 12. 19:21. 20:6, 10. 21:17. 23:18. 1 Ch 2:16. 11:20. 18:12, 19:11, 15.

Zeruiah. 1 Ch +2:16.

Joab. i.e. whose father is Jehovah, **S#3097h**. 2 S 2:13, 14, 18, 22, 24, 26-28, 30, 32. 3:22-24, 26, 27, 29-31. 8:16. 10:7, 9, 13, 14. 11:1, 6, 7, 11, 14, 16-18, 22, 25. 12:26, 27. 14:1-3, 19-23, 29, 30-33. 17:25. 18:2, 5, 10-12, 14-16, 20-22, 29. 19:1, 5, 13. 20:7, 8-11, 13, 15-17, 20-23. 23:18, 24, 37. 24:2-4, 9. 1 K 1:7, 19, 41. 2:5, 22, 28-31, 33. 11:15, 16, 21. 1 Ch 2:16. 4:14. 11:6, 8, 20, 26, 39. 18:15. 19:8, 10, 15. 20:1. 21:2-6. 26:28. 27:7, 24, 34. Ezr 2:6. 8:9. Ne 7:11. Ps 60:t.

Who will go. 1 S 14:6, 7. Jg 7:10, 11.

7 **sleeping**. 1 Th 5:2, 3.

bolster. or, pillow. ver. 11, 16. 1 S 19:13, 16. Ge 28:11, 18. 1 K 19:6mg.

8 **God**. ver. 23. 1 S 23:14. 24:4, 18, 19. Jsh 21:44. Jg 1:4. 1 K 13:18.

delivered. Heb. shut up. 1 S +17:46mg. 24:18. Dt 32:30. Ps 31:8. Ro 11:32mg. Ga 3:22, 23.

the second time. Na 1:9.

9 **who can stretch**. 1 S 24:6, 7. 2 S 1:14, 16. Ps 105:15.

anointed. 1 S 24:6, +10. 1 T 5:19, 20.

10 **the Lord liveth**. 1 S 24:15. 25:26, 38. Ps 94:1, 2, 23. Lk 18:7. Ro 12:19. Re 18:8.

shall smite. 1 S 25:38. Ps 10:15, 17, 18. 140:9-11.

his day. Ge 47:29. Dt 31:14. Jb 7:1. 14:5, 14. Ps 37:10, 13. Ec 3:2. He 9:27.

he shall descend. 1 S 31:6. Dt 32:35.

11 **forbid.** Lk +20:16.

    that I should. 1 S 24:6, 12. 2 S 1:14, 16.

12 **So David.** ver. 7. 1 S 24:4.

    a deep sleep. Ge 2:21. 15:12. Est 6:1. Is 29:10.

13 **the top.** 1 S 24:8. Jg 9:7.

15 **Art.** Ge +20:16.

    there came. ver. 8.

16 **worthy to die.** Heb. the sons of death. 1 S +20:31mg.

    Lord's anointed. ver. 9, 11.

17 **Is this thy.** 1 S 24:8, 16.

18 **Wherefore.** 1 S 24:9, 11-14. Ps 7:3-5. 35:7. 69:4.

    what have I. 1 S 17:29. Jn 8:46. 10:32. 18:23.

19 **let my lord.** 1 S 25:24. Ge 44:18.

    stirred. 1 S 16:14-23. 18:10. 2 S 16:11. 24:1. 1 K 22:22. 1 Ch 21:1.

    accept. Heb. smell. Ge 8:21. Le 26:31. Ps 119:1-8.

    cursed. Pr 6:16-19. 30:10. Je +10:25. Ga 5:12.

    they have driven. Dt 4:27, 28. Jsh 22:25-27. Ps 42:1, 2. 120:5. Is 60:5. Ro 14:15.

    abiding. Heb. cleaving. 1 S 2:36.

    the inheritance. Dt 32:9. 2 S 14:16. 20:19. Ps 42:2. 84:1, 2.

20 **let not my.** 1 S 2:9. 25:29. Ge 4:10.

    the king. 1 S 24:14. Mt 26:47, 55.

    a flea. 1 S 24:14.

    a partridge. Je 17:11.

21 **I have sinned.** 1 S 15:24, 30. 24:17. Ex 9:27. Nu 22:34. Mt 27:4.

    I will no. 1 S 27:4.

    my soul. Heb. *nephesh*, Ge +12:13; Ge +9:5.

    was precious. ver. 24. 1 S 18:30. 2 K 1:13, 14. Ps 49:8. 72:14. 116:15. 139:17.

    played the fool. Ge 31:28.

    have erred. Le 4:13. Mk 12:24, 27.

23 **render.** 1 K 8:32. Ne 13:14. Ps 7:8, 9. 18:20-26.

    I would not. ver. 9, 11.

24 **as thy life.** Heb. *nephesh*, soul, Ge +44:30. Ps 18:25. Mt 5:7. 7:2.

    mine eyes. Ps 17:8. 33:18, 19.

    my life. Heb. *nephesh*, soul, Ge +44:30.

    let him deliver. Ge 48:16. Dt 4:29-31. Ps 18, title, 48. 25:20-22. 34:17, 18. 144:2. Ac 14:22. 2 C 1:9, 10. 2 Th 3:2. *Re 7:14.*

25 *Blessed. 1 S 24:19.* Nu 24:9, 10.

    prevail. Ge 32:28. Is 54:17. Ho 12:4. Ro 8:35, 37.

So David. 1 S 24:22. Pr 26:25.

1 SAMUEL 27

1 A.M. 2946. B.C. 1058. An. Ex. Is. 433.

    And David. 1 S 16:1, 13. 23:17. 25:30. Ps 116:11. Pr 13:12. Is 40:27-31. 51:12. Mt 14:31. Mk 4:40. 2 C 7:5.

    I shall. 2 S 22:1.

    perish. Heb. be consumed. 1 S 26:10.

    there is nothing. 1 S 22:5. Ex 14:12. Nu 14:3. Pr 3:5, 6. Is 30:15, 16. La 3:26, 27.

    into the land. ver. 10, 11. 1 S 21:10-15. 28:1, 2. 29:2-11. 30:1-3.

    despair. Jb 6:26. Ec 2:20. Is 57:10. Je 2:25mg. 18:12.

    so shall. 1 K 19:2, 3. Ps +34:4. Pr +22:3. 29:25. He 13:5, 6.

2 **the six hundred.** 1 S 25:13. 30:8.

    Achish. 1 S +21:10.

    Maoch. i.e. *bruising; breast band*, **S#4582h.**

3 **with his two.** Ge +4:19.

    Jezreelitess. S#3159h. 1 S 30:5. 2 S 2:2. 3:2. 1 Ch 3:1.

    Carmelitess. S#3762h. 1 Ch 3:1.

4 **he sought.** 1 S 26:21.

5 **some town.** Ge 46:34. 2 C 6:17.

6 **Ziklag.** Jsh +15:31.

    unto this day. 1 S +6:18.

7 **the time.** Heb. the number of days. Ps 94:14, 17, 18. Is +10:19mg.

    country. Ge +14:7.

    a full year. Heb. a year of days. 1 S 29:3. Ge +24:55mg.

8 A.M. 2948. B.C. 1056. An. Ex. Is. 435.

    the Geshurites. Jsh +12:5.

    Gezrites. *or,* Gerzites. **S#1511h,** only here. Jsh 10:33. 12:12. 16:3, 10. 21:21. Jg 1:29. 2 S 5:25. 1 K 9:15-17. 1 Ch 6:67. 7:28. 14:16. 20:4.

    the Amalekites. Nu +14:45.

    of old. Heb. *olam*, Ge +6:4.

    as thou goest. 1 S 30:1. Ex 17:14-16.

    Shur. Ge +16:7.

9 **left neither.** Ge 16:7. 25:18. Ex 15:22. +17:14. Le 27:28. Dt 7:2. Ps 139:21, 22.

    and the camels. 1 S 15:3. Jsh 6:21.

10 **Whither,** etc. *or,* Did you not make a road. 1 S 23:27.

    And David. 1 S 21:2. Ge 27:19, 20, 24. Jsh 2:4-6. 2 S 17:20. Ps 119:29, 163. Pr 29:25. Ga 2:11-13. Ep 4:25.

    the Jerahmeelites. S#3397h. 1 S 30:29. 1 Ch 2:9, 25.

    Kenites. Ge +15:19.

11 **Lest.** 1 S 22:22. Pr 12:19. 29:25.

12 **believed.** or, remained stedfast. Ge 15:6.

    utterly to abhor. Heb. to stink. Ge +34:30.

    for ever. Heb. *olam*, Ex +12:24. or, age-during. That is, during his life-time, as in Dt 15:17. Ps +24:9.

1 SAMUEL 28

1 **that the**. 1 S 7:7. 13:5. 17:1. 29:1.
Philistines. Jg 3:1-4.
thou shalt go. 1 S 27:12. 29:2, 3.

2 **Surely**. 1 S 27:10. 2 S 16:16-19. Ro 12:9.

3 **Samuel**. 1 S 25:1. Is 57:1, 2.
Ramah. Je +31:15.
put away. ver. 9. Ex 22:18.
familiar spirits. ver. 7. Dt +18:11.
wizards. ver. 9. 2 K +21:6.

4 **Shunem**. Jsh 19:18. 1 K 1:3. 2 K 4:8.
Gilboa. i.e. *bubbling up of a fountain*, **S#1533h**. 1 S 31:1, 8. 2 S 1:6, 21. 21:12. 1 Ch 10:1, 8.

5 **he was afraid**. 1 S 17:11. Jb 15:21. 18:11. Ps 48:5, 6. 73:19. Pr 10:24. Is 7:2. 21:3, 4. 24:17. 57:20, 21. Da 5:6.
trembled. 1 S 4:13. 14:15. Ge 27:33mg. Jb 37:1.

6 **enquired**. 1 S 14:37. 1 Ch 10:14. Pr 1:27, 28. La 2:9. Ezk 20:1-3, 31. Jn 9:31. Ja 4:3.
by dreams. ver. 15. Ge 20:5-7. 28:12-15. 46:2-4. Nu 12:6. 1 K 3:11-15. 2 K 9:1-3. Jb 33:14-16. Je +23:28. Mt 1:20.
by Urim. Ex +28:30.
by prophets. ver. 15. Nu 12:6. 2 K 19:15, 16, 20. 20:2-5. 2 Ch 20:3-6, 14, 15. Ps 74:9. La 2:9. Ezk 20:1-3. Mi 3:6, 7.

7 **Seek me**. 2 K 1:2, 3. 6:33. Is 8:19, 20. La 3:25, 26. Hab 2:3.
a familiar spirit. ver. +3.
that I may. 1 Ch 10:13.
En-dor. Jsh 17:11. Ps 83:10.

8 **disguised**. Ge +27:16. Jb 24:13-15. 30:18. Je 23:24. Jn 3:19, 20.
by night. 1 S 14:36. 26:7. 31:12.
I pray thee, divine. Dt 18:10, 11, 14. 1 Ch 10:13, 14. Is 8:19. Ezk 21:21, 23, 29.
bring me. ver. 15.

9 **how he hath**. ver. +3.
wherefore. 2 S 18:13. 2 K 5:7.
snare. Dt 12:30. Ps 9:16. 38:12. 109:11.
life. Heb. *nephesh*, soul, Ge +44:30.

10 **sware**. 1 S 14:39. 19:6. Ge 3:5. Ex 20:7. Dt 18:10-12. 2 S 14:11. Mt 26:72. Mk 6:23.
As. 1 K +17:1.
no punishment. lit. *iniquity*. Ge 4:13. 15:15. 19:15. 44:16. 2 K 7:9.

11 **bring up**. Out of Sheol, the state of the dead, supposed to be beneath the ground (Young).

12 **the woman saw**. Before she had time to commence her incantations (Young).
loud voice. Is 14:9. Ezk 32:21. Mt 12:40. Lk +16:23.
deceived me. **S#7411h**: 1 S 19:17. Ge 29:25.

Jsh 9:22. 2 S 19:26. 1 Ch 12:17 (betray). Pr 26:19. La 1:19.
thou art Saul. ver. 3. 1 K 14:5.

13 **gods ascending**. Ex 4:16. 22:28. Ps 82:6, 7. Jn 10:34, 35.

14 **What form is he of**? Heb. What is his form? Jg 8:18mg. Is 52:14. 53:2. La 4:8.
cometh up. Ec 12:7. Is 57:2. Lk 16:22. Re 14:13.
a mantle. or, upper robe. 1 S 15:27. 24:4, 11. 2 K 2:8, 13, 14. Zc 13:4.
and bowed himself. Re 19:10. 22:8, 9.

15 **Why hast**. ver. 8, 11.
disquieted. Jb 9:6. 12:6 (provoke). Is 13:13 (shake). 14:16. 23:11. Je 50:34.
I am sore. Pr 5:11-13. 14:14. Je 2:17, 18.
distressed. 2 S 24:14.
the Philistines. ver. 4.
God. 1 S 16:13, 14. 18:12. Jg 16:20. Ps 51:11. Ho 9:12. Mt 25:41.
answereth. ver. 6. 1 S 23:2, 4, 9, 10.
prophets. Heb. the hand of prophets. ver. 17.
therefore. Lk 16:23-26.

16 **Wherefore**. Jg 5:31. 2 K 6:27. Ps 68:1-3. Re 18:20, 24. 19:1-6.
and is become. Ps 139:20. La 2:5. Mi 5:14.

17 **to him**. *or*, for himself. Pr 16:4.
as he spake. 1 S 13:13, 14. 15:27-29.
me. Heb. mine hand. ver. 15.
thy neighbor. 1 S 15:28. 16:13. 24:20.
hath rent. 1 S 15:28. 1 K 11:31.

18 **obeyedst**. 1 S 13:9. 15:9, 23-26. 1 K 20:42. 1 Ch 10:13. Je 48:10.
wrath. Ps +79:6.
hath the Lord. Ps 50:21, 22.

19 **the Lord**. 1 S 12:25. 31:1-6. 1 K 22:20, 28.
and tomorrow. Ex 9:18. 13:14mg. Dt 6:20mg. Jsh 4:6mg, 21mg. Je 28:16, 17. Da 5:25-28. Mt 26:24. Ac 5:5, 9, 10.
with me. 2 S 7:14, 15. +12:23. Is 14:9-11. Lk 23:43.
deliver. Da 5:25-28.

20 **fell straightway**. Heb. made haste and fell with the fulness of his stature. 1 S 9:2. 10:23. Ge 48:19. 2 S 8:2.
sore afraid. ver. 5. 1 S 25:37. Jb 15:20-24. 26:2. Ps 50:21, 22.
no strength. 1 S 30:4. Le 26:20. 2 K 19:3. 2 Ch 14:11. 20:12.
bread. Ge +3:19.

21 **I have put**. 1 S 19:5. Jg 12:3. Jb 13:14.
life. Heb. *nephesh*, soul, Ge +44:30.
hand. 1 S 19:5. Jg 12:3. Jb 13:14. 1 C 15:30, 31.

22 **morsel of bread**. 1 S 2:36. *Ge 18:5*. Jg 19:5. 2 S 12:3mg. 1 K 17:11. Jb 31:17. Pr 17:1. 23:8. 28:21. Ezk 13:19.

23 **I will**. 1 K 21:4. Pr 25:20.

compelled him. 2 S 13:25, 27. 2 K 5:23. Ac +16:15.

bed. 1 S 19:13, 15, 16. Est 1:6.

24 **a fat calf**. Ge 18:7, 8. Je 46:21. Am 6:4. Ml 4:2. Lk 15:23.

flour. 1 S 1:24. Ge 18:6. Nu 5:15. Jg 6:19. 2 S 17:28. 1 K 4:22. 17:12, 14, 16. 2 K 4:41. 1 Ch 12:40. Is 47:2. Ho 8:7.

kneaded. Ge 18:6. 2 S 13:8. Je 7:18. Ho 7:4.

25 **that night**. ver. 8.

1 SAMUEL 29

1 **the Philistines**. 1 S 28:1, 2, 4.
Aphek. Jsh +12:18.
Jezreel. 1 Ch +4:3.

2 **the lords**. ver. 6, 7. 1 S 5:8-11. 6:4. Jsh 13:3. Jg 16:5, 30.
but David. 1 S 28:1, 2.

3 **these days**. 1 S 27:7.
found. 1 S 25:28. Da 6:5. Jn 19:6. Ro 12:17. 1 P 3:16.

4 **Make this fellow**. 1 S 14:21. 1 Ch 12:19. Lk 16:8.

5 **Is not**. 1 S 18:6, 7. 21:11. Pr 27:14.

6 **the Lord**. Dt 10:20. 1 K +17:1. Is 65:16.
thou hast. Mt 5:16. 1 P 2:12. 3:16.
thy going. Nu 27:17. 2 S 3:25. 2 K 19:27. Ps 121:8.
I have not. ver. 3.
the lords favor, etc. Heb. thou art not good in the eyes of the lords. Jsh +22:30mg.

7 **displease**. Heb. do not evil in the eyes of the lords. Nu 22:34.

8 **But what have**. 1 S 12:3. 17:29. 20:8. 26:18.
with. Heb. before.
that I may not. 1 S 28:2. 2 S 16:18, 19. Ps 34:13, 14. Mt 6:13.

9 **as an angel**. 2 S 14:17, 20. 19:27. Ga 4:14.
the princes. ver. 4.

10 **now rise**. 1 S 30:1, 2. Ge 22:14. Ps 37:23, 24. 1 C 10:13. 2 P 2:9.

11 **And the Philistines**. ver. +1. Jsh 19:18. 2 S 4:4.
Jezreel. ver. +1.

1 SAMUEL 30

1 **were come**. 1 S 29:11. 2 S 1:2.
the Amalekites. Ge 24:62. Ex +17:14. Jsh 11:6.

2 **slew not**. ver. 19. 1 S 27:11. Jb 38:11. Ps 76:10. Is 27:8, 9.

3 **burned**. Ps 34:19. He 12:6. 1 P 1:6, 7. Re 3:9.

4 **lifted up**. 1 S 4:13. 11:4. Ge +22:13. 37:33-35. Nu 14:1, 39. Jg 2:4. 21:2. Ezr 10:1.

5 **two wives**. Ge +4:19.
Carmelite. s#376th. 2 S 2:2. 3:3. 23:35. 1 Ch 11:37.

6 **was greatly**. Ne +9:27. Ps 42:7. 116:3, 4, 10.

2 C 1:8, 9. 7:5.

the people. Ex 17:4. Nu 14:10. Ps 62:9. Mt 21:9. 27:22.

soul. Heb. *nephesh*, Ge +34:3.

grieved. Heb. bitter. 1 S 1:10mg. 22:2mg. Jg 18:25mg. 1 S 22:2mg. 2 S 17:8mg. 2 K 4:27mg. Jb 3:5mg. 27:2mg. Pr 31:6mg.

David. Jb 13:15. Ps 18:6. 26:1, 2. 27:1-3. 34:1-8. 40:1, 2. 42:5, 10, 11. 56:3, 4, 11. 62:1, 5, 8. 0:4, 5. 118:8-13. Pr 18:10. Is 25:4. 37:14-20. Je 16:19. Hab 3:17, 18. Ro 4:18. 8:31. 2 C 1:6, 9, 10. 2 T 1:15. 4:16, 17. He 13:6.

7 **Abiathar**. 1 S +22:20.
bring me hither the ephod. 1 S 23:9-12. 28:6. Ex +28:4. Nu 27:21.

8 **enquired**. 1 S 23:2, 4, 10-12. Jg 20:18, 23, 28. 2 S 5:19, 23. Pr 3:5, 6.
he answered him. 1 S 14:37. 28:6, 15, 16. Nu 27:21. Ps 50:15. 91:15.

9 **the six hundred**. 1 S 25:13. 1 Ch 12:21.
brook Besor. i.e. *cold water; tidings*, s#1308h. ver. 10, 21. Nu 13:23.

10 **for two hundred**. ver. 21.
so faint. 1 S 14:30, 31. Jg 8:4, 5.
the brook Besor. Jsh 15:4. Am 6:14.

11 **gave him**. Dt 15:7-11. 23:7. Pr 25:21. Mt 5:44. 25:35. Lk 10:33, 36, 37. Ro 12:20, 21.

12 **cake of figs**. 1 S 25:18. 2 K 20:7. 1 Ch 12:40. Is 38:21.
his spirit. Heb. *ruach*, Ge +41:8. 1 S 14:27. Jg 15:19. Is 40:29-31.
came again. Ge +2:7. La 1:11.
three days. ver. 13. 1 K 2:11. Est 4:16. Jon 1:17. Mt 12:40. 27:63. Lk 24:21. Jn 2:19. 1 C 15:4.

13 **my master**. Jb 31:13-15. Pr 12:10. Ja 2:13.

14 **the Cherethites**. ver. 16. 2 S +8:18.
Caleb. Jsh 14:13. 15:13.
we burned. ver. 1-3.

15 **Swear**. 1 S 29:6. Jsh 2:12. 9:15, 19, 20. Ezk 17:13, 16, 19.
nor deliver. Dt 23:15, 16.

16 **when he**. Jg 1:24, 25.
spread abroad. Jg 7:12. 1 Th 5:3.
eating. 1 S 25:36-38. Ex 32:6, 17-19, 27, 28. Jg 16:23-30. 2 S 13:28. Is 22:13. Da 5:1-4, 30. Lk 12:19, 20. 17:27-29. 21:34, 35. 1 Th 5:3. Re 11:10-13.
because of all. Jb 20:5.

17 **twilight**. 2 K 7:5, 7. Jb 3:9. 7:4. 24:15. Ps 119:147. Pr 7:9. Is 5:11. 21:4. 59:10. Je 13:16.
the next day. Heb. their morrow.
and there. 1 S 11:11. Jg 4:16. 1 K 20:29, 30. Ps 18:42.
camels. 1 S 15:3. 27:9.

18 **recovered**. ver. 8.
had carried away. ver. 2.
two wives. ver. 5. Ge +4:19.

19 **nothing lacking**. ver. 8. Ge 14:14-16. Nu 31:49. 2 S 17:22. 1 K 4:27. Jb 1:10. Ps 34:9,

10. 91:9, 10. Is 34:16. 40:26. 59:15. Zp 3:5.
Mt 6:33. Ro 8:37.

20 **drave**. Ge 31:18.
This is David's spoil. ver. 26. Ge 49:27. Nu
31:9-12. 2 Ch 20:25. Is 53:12. Ro 8:37.

21 **two hundred men**. ver. 10.
came near. He 13:1. 1 P 3:8.
saluted them. Heb. asked them how they
did. Jg +18:15mg.

22 **wicked**. 1 S 22:2. 25:17, 25.
men of Belial. 1 S 2:12. 25:17, 25. Dt 13:13.
+15:9mg. Jg +19:22. 2 S 20:1. 22:5mg. 23:6. 1
K 21:10, 13. Jb 34:18. Ps 18:4mg. 41:8mg.
101:3mg. Pr 19:28mg. Na 1:11mg, 15mg.
those. Heb. the men.
Because. Mt 7:12.
not give. 1 S 25:11. Est 6:6. Is 56:11. Mk
10:37. Lk 10:31, 32. Ph 2:21. Ja 2:16.

23 **my brethren**. Ge 19:7. Jg 19:23. Ac 7:2.
22:1.
which the Lord. ver. 8. 1 S 2:7. Nu 31:49-
54. Dt 8:10, 18. 1 Ch 29:12-14. Hab 1:16.
who hath. Ps 44:2-7. 121:7, 8.

24 **but as his part**. Nu 31:27. Jsh 22:8. Ps 68:12.
1 C 12:26.
tarrieth. 1 S 25:13. 3 J 8.
part alike. 2 S 8:15. Ps 149:9. Ph +4:17.

25 **forward**. Heb. and forward. 1 S 16:13.
unto this day. 1 S +6:18.

26 **to his friends**. 1 Ch 12:1, etc. Ps 35:27.
68:18. Pr 18:16, 24. Is 32:8.
present. Heb. blessing. Jg +3:15.

27 **Beth-el**. Ge +12:8. Jsh 15:9, Baalah. 16:2.
19:4, Bethul. 1 S 7:1. 9:3.
south Ramoth. Jsh 19:8, Ramath.
Jattir. A city in Judah. Jsh 15:48. 21:14.

28 **Aroer**. Nu +32:34.
Siphmoth. i.e. *coverings*, S#8224h. Nu 34:10,
Shepham.
Eshtemoa. i.e. *obedience*, S#851h. Jsh 15:50,
Eshtemoh. 21:14. 1 Ch 4:17, 19. 6:57.

29 **Rachal**. i.e. *traffic*, S#7403h. 1 S 23:19,
Hachilah.
Jerahmeelites. 1 S 27:10. 1 Ch 2:9, 25-27.
Kenites. Ge +15:19.

30 **Hormah**. Nu +14:45.
Chorashan. i.e. *smoking furnace; anger*, S#3565h.
Jsh 15:42, Ashan. 19:7. 1 Ch 4:32. 6:59.

Athach. i.e. *a lodging place; thy due season*,
S#6269h.

31 **Hebron**. Nu +13:22.

1 SAMUEL 31

1 **the Philistines**. 1 S 28:1, 4, 15. 29:1.
fled. Le 26:36. Dt 28:25.
fell down. 1 S 12:25. 1 Ch 10:1-12.
slain. Heb. wounded. ver. 8. 2 S 1:19, 22, 25.
23:8, 18.
Gilboa. 1 S 28:4. 2 S 1:21.

2 **followed**. 1 S 14:22. 2 S 1:6.
Jonathan. 1 S 13:2, 16. 14:1-14, 49. 18:1-4.
23:17. 1 Ch 8:33. 9:39.
Saul's sons. Ex 20:5. 2 K 25:7.

3 **went sore**. 2 S 1:4, 6. Am 2:14.
archers hit him. Heb. shooters, men with
bows, found him. Ge 49:23. 1 K 22:34.

4 **Draw**. Jg 9:54. 1 Ch 10:4. Je +31:10.
uncircumcised. 1 S +14:6.
abuse me. *or*, mock me. Je +38:19.
he was sore. 2 S 1:14.
Saul. 2 S 1:9, 10. 17:23. 1 K 16:18. 1 Ch
10:13, 14. Mt 27:4, 5. Ac 1:18. 16:27.
a sword. 1 S 22:9, 18.
fell upon. 2 S 1:10. +3:29.

5 **when his**. 1 Ch 10:5.

6 **Saul died**. 1 S 4:10, 11. 11:15. 12:17, 25.
28:19. 1 Ch 10:6, 13, 14. Ec 9:1, 2. Ho 13:10,
11.

7 **they forsook the cities**. 1 S 13:6. Le 26:32,
36. Dt 28:33. Jg 6:2.

8 **to strip**. 1 Ch 10:8. 2 Ch 20:25.

9 **cut off**. ver. 4. 1 S 17:51, 54. 1 Ch 10:9, 10.
to publish. Jg 16:23, 24. 2 S 1:20.

10 **they put**. 1 S 5:2. 21:9.
Ashtaroth. Jg +2:13.
Bethshan. ver. 12. Jsh +17:11.

11 **Jabesh-gilead**. 1 S 11:1. 2 S 2:4.
of that. *or*, concerning him, that which, etc.

12 **valiant**. Jsh 1:14. Jg +6:12.
burnt them there. 2 Ch 16:14. Je 34:5. Am
6:10.

13 **their bones**. Ge 35:8. 2 S 2:4, 5. 21:12-14.
a tree. 1 S 22:6. Ge 21:33. 1 Ch 10:12.
fasted. 2 S 12:16.
seven. Ge 50:10.

2 SAMUEL

2 SAMUEL 1

1 A.M. 2949. B.C. 1055. An. Ex. Is. 436.
   when David. 1 S 30:17-26.
   Ziklag. Jsh +15:31.
2 **the third**. Ge 22:4. Jsh 5:11. 1 S 30:12. Est
   4:16. 5:1. Ho 6:2. Mt 12:40. 16:21.
   a man. 2 S 4:10.
   clothes. 2 K +18:37.
   and earth. Jsh +7:6.
   he fell. Ge 37:7-10. +43:28. 1 S 20:41. 24:8.
   25:23. Ps 66:3. Re 3:9.
3 **From**. 2 K 5:25.
   am I. Jb 1:15-19.
4 **How went**. Heb. What was, etc. 1 S 4:16mg.
   the people. 1 S 31:1-6. 1 Ch 10:1-6.
5 **How knowest**. Pr 14:15. 25:2.
6 **As I happened**. lit. "meeting I met." 2 S
   18:9. 20:1. Ex 5:3. Dt 22:6. 1 S +6:9. Je 32:23
   (hast caused to come).
   by chance. Ge 24:44. Jsh +14:2. Jg 20:22. Ru
   2:3. 1 S +6:9. Je 44:23. Lk 10:31.
   mount. ver. 21. 1 S 28:4. 31:1.
   Saul. 1 S 31:2-7.
7 **Here am I**. Heb. Behold me. 2 S 9:6. Jg 9:54.
   1 S 22:12. Is 6:8mg. 65:1.
8 **an Amalekite**. Ex +17:14. Nu +14:45.
9 **anguish**, etc. *or*, my coat of mail, *or* my
   embroidered coat hindereth me, that my, etc.
   Ex 28:20, 39.
   life. Heb. *nephesh*, soul, Ge +44:30.
10 **slew**. Jg 1:7. 9:54. 1 S 22:18. 31:4, 5. Mt 7:2.
   crown. 2 S 12:30. La 5:16.
   bracelet. Nu 31:50.
11 **rent**. 2 K +18:37.
   likewise. Ro 12:15.
12 **mourned**. Ps 35:13, 14. Pr 24:17. Je 9:1. Am
   6:6. Mt 5:44. 2 C 11:29. 1 P 3:8.
13 **Whence art**. ver. 8.
   stranger. Ge 23:4. Ex 12:48mg. Dt +26:11.
   Jsh +20:9. Mt +25:35.
   an Amalekite. Dt 25:19.
14 **How**. Nu 12:8. 1 S 31:4. 2 P 2:10.
   stretch forth. 1 S 24:6. 26:9. Ps *105:15*.
   to destroy. *2 S 14:11. 24:16*.
   anointed. *Heb*. Messiah, as in ver. 16, 21.
15 *Go near*. 2 S 4:10-12. Jg 8:20. 1 S 22:17, 18.
   1 K 2:25, 34, 46. Jb 5:12. Pr 11:18.

16 **Thy blood**. Ge 9:5, 6. Jsh 2:19. Jg 9:24. 1 S
   26:9. Ac +18:6.
   head. Jg +5:30.
   mouth. ver. 10. Jb 15:6. Pr 6:2. Lk 19:22. Ro
   3:19.
17 **lamented**. ver. 19. 2 S 3:33. Ge 50:11. 2 Ch
   35:25. Je 9:17-21. Ezk 27:32. 32:16.
18 **teach**. Ge 49:8. 1 S 11:3. 31:3.
   bow. 1 S 20:6.
   written in. Nu 21:14. Jsh 10:13. 2 Ch 16:11.
   the book. Jsh 10:13, 33.
   Jasher. *or*, the upright.
19 **beauty**. ver. 23. Dt 4:7, 8. 1 S 31:8. Is 4:2.
   53:2. La 2:1. Zc 11:7, 10.
   how are. ver. 25, 27. La 5:16.
20 **Tell**. Dt 32:26, 27. Jg 14:19. 16:23, 24. 1 S
   17:4. 31:9. Mi 1:10.
   Askelon. Jg +1:18.
   Philistines. Ex 15:20, 21. Jg 11:34. 1 S 18:6.
   Ezk 16:27, 57.
   uncircumcised. 1 S +14:6.
   triumph. Ps 28:7 (rejoiceth). 60:6 (rejoice).
   68:4. 94:3. 96:12 (joyful). 108:7. 149:5. Pr
   23:16. Is 23:12. Je 11:15. 15:17. 50:11. 51:39.
   Hab 3:18. Zp 3:14.
21 **mountains**. 1 S 31:1. 1 Ch 10:1, 8.
   no dew. Jg 5:23. Jb 3:3-10. Is 5:6. Je 20:14-
   16.
   offerings. Ex 29:27, 28. Le +23:15. Ezr
   +8:25. Jl 1:9. 2:14.
   anointed. 1 S 10:1. Is 21:5.
22 **the bow**. 1 S 14:6-14. 18:4. Is 34:6, 7.
23 **lovely**. 1 S 9:2.
   pleasant. *or*, sweet. 2 S 23:1. 1 S 18:1. 20:2.
   Jb 36:11. Ps 16:6, 11. 81:2. 133:1. 135:3.
   147:1. Pr 22:18. 23:8. 24:4. SS 1:16.
   they were. 1 S 31:1-5.
   swifter. 2 S 2:18. Dt 28:49. 1 Ch 12:8. Jb
   9:26. Je 4:13. La 4:19. Hab 1:8.
   stronger. 2 S 23:20. Jg 14:18. Pr 30:30.
24 **Ye daughters**. *Jg 5:30*. Ps 68:12. Pr 31:21. Is
   3:16-26. Je 2:32. 1 T 2:9, 10. 1 P 3:3-5.
25 **How are**. ver. 19, 27. La 5:16.
   thou wast. Jg 5:18. 1 S 14:13-15.
26 **my brother**. Pr 27:10.
   thy love. 1 S 18:1-4. 19:2. 20:17, 41. 23:16.
   Pr 5:19.

27 **How are**. ver. 19, 25.
   weapons. 2 K 2:12. 13:14. Ps 46:9. 76:6. Ezk 39:9, 10.

2 SAMUEL 2

1 **enquired**. 2 S 5:19, 23. Nu 27:21. Jg 1:1. 1 S 23:2, 4, 9-12. 30:7, 8. Ps 25:4, 5. 27:4. 143:8. Pr 3:5, 6. Ezk 36:37.
   Hebron. ver. 11. Nu +13:22.
2 **his two wives**. Ge +4:19. Lk 22:28, 29.
3 **his men**. 1 S 22:2. 27:2, 3. 30:1, 9, 10. 1 Ch 12:1, 22, etc.
   the cities. Jsh 21:11, 12.
4 **the men of Judah**. ver. 11. 2 S 19:11, 42. Ge 49:8-10.
   anointed. ver. 7. 2 S 5:3, 5, 17. Ex +28:41. 1 Ch 11:3.
   the men of Jabesh-gilead. 1 S 31:11-13.
5 **Blessed**. Ru 1:8. 2:20. 3:10. 1 S 23:21. 24:19. 25:32, 33. Ps 115:15.
6 **the Lord**. 2 S 15:20. Ps 57:3. Pr 14:22. Mt 5:7. 2 T 1:16-18.
   I also. 2 S 9:3, 7. 10:2. Mt 5:44. 10:16. Phm 18, 19.
7 **let your**. 2 S 10:12. Ge 15:1. 1 S 4:9. 31:7, 12. 1 C 16:13. Ep 6:10.
   valiant. Heb. the sons of valor. 2 S 13:28mg. 17:10mg. Dt 3:18mg. Jg +6:12. 18:2mg. 21:10. 1 S 14:52. 18:17mg. 2 K 2:16mg. 1 Ch 5:18mg. 9:13mg. 26:6. 2 Ch 26:17. 28:6mg.
8 **Abner**. 1 S +14:50.
   Saul's host. Heb. the host which was Saul's. Ge 32:1, 2. 1 S 24:4.
   Ish-bosheth. 2 S 3:7, 8. 4:5, 6. 1 Ch 8:33. 9:39, Esh-baal.
   Mahanaim. Ge +32:2.
9 **Gilead**. Ge +37:25.
   Ashurites. i.e. *guided, blessed*, **S#843h**. Jg 1:32, Asherites; Ezk 27:6. Ge 30:13. Nu 1:40.
   over Jezreel. 1 Ch +4:3.
10 **Judah followed**. 1 K 12:20.
11 **time**. Heb. number of days. 2 S 5:4, 5. 1 K 2:11. 1 Ch 3:4. 29:27. Is +10:19mg.
12 A.M. 2951. B.C. 1053. An. Ex. Is. 438.
   Mahanaim. ver. +8.
   Gibeon. Jsh +10:3.
13 **Joab**. ver. 18. 1 S +26:6.
   together. Heb. them together.
   pool. Je 41:12.
14 **play before**. ver. 17, 26, 27. Pr 10:23. 17:14. 20:18. 25:8. 26:18, 19.
16 **caught**. Ge 19:16.
   sword. Jg 3:21.
   Helkath-hazzurim. *that is*, the field of strong men. i.e. *portion* or *place of the sharp weapons*, **S#2521h**.
17 **Abner**. 2 S 3:1.
18 **three**. 1 Ch 2:15, 16. 11:26.
   was as light. 2 S 1:23. 22:34. 1 Ch 12:8. Ps

147:10, 11. Ec 9:11. Am 2:14.
   foot. Heb. his feet.
   a wild roe. Heb. one of the roes that is in the field. 1 K 4:23. Ps 18:33. SS 2:17. 8:14. Hab 3:19.
19 **turned**. ver. 21. Jsh 1:7. 23:6. 2 K 22:2. Pr 4:27.
   following Abner. Heb. after Abner.
21 **armor**. *or*, spoil. Jg 14:19.
22 **wherefore**. 1 S 19:17. 2 K 14:10-12. Pr 29:1. Ec 6:10.
   how then. 2 S 3:27.
23 **the fifth rib**. 2 S 3:27. 4:6. 5:6. 20:10.
   stood still. 2 S 20:12, 13.
24 **Ammah**. i.e. *cubit* or *pedestal; beginning; head*, **S#522h**. 2 S 8:1.
   Giah. i.e. *breaking forth of a fountain*, **S#1520h**.
26 **Shall**. ver. 14. Ac 7:26.
   sword. 2 S 11:25. Is 1:20. Je 2:30. 12:12. 46:10, 14. Ho 11:6.
   for ever. Jb +4:20 (**S#5331h**).
   it will be. ver. 16. Pr 17:14.
   how long. Mt +17:17.
27 **As God**. ver. 14. 1 S 25:26. Jb 27:2.
   unless. ver. 14. Pr 15:1. 17:14. 20:18. 25:8. Is 47:7. Lk 14:31, 32.
   in the morning. Heb. from the morning.
   gone up. *or*, gone away.
29 **the plain**. lit. the Arabah. Dt +11:30.
   Bithron. i.e. *separation*, **S#1338h**. SS 2:17, Bether.
   Mahanaim. ver. +8.
30 **nineteen**. ver. 16.
31 **three hundred**. 1 S 3:1. 1 K 20:11.
32 **buried**. 1 S 17:58. 1 Ch 2:13-16. 2 Ch 16:14. 21:1.
   sepulchre. Heb. *qeber*, Ge +23:4.
   went. 2 S 5:1. Pr 22:29.

2 SAMUEL 3

1 **long war**. 1 K 14:30. 15:16, 32.
   between. Ge 3:15. Ps 45:3-5. Mt 10:35, 36. Ga 5:17. Ep 6:12.
   David waxed. 2 S 2:17. Est 6:13. Jb 8:7. 17:9. Ps 84:5, 7. Pr +4:18, 19. 10:29, 30. 24:3, 5. Da 2:34, 35, 44, 45. Re 6:2.
2 **sons born**. 1 Ch 3:1-4.
   Amnon. i.e. *stedfast*, **S#550h**. 2 S 13:1-4, 6-10, 15, 22, 26-29, 32, 33, 39. 2 S 13:20, Aminon. Ge 49:3, 4. 1 Ch 3:1. 4:20.
   Ahinoam. 1 S 25:43.
3 **Chileab**. i.e. *the father hath completed*, **S#3609h**. 1 Ch 3:1, Daniel.
   Abigail. 2 S 2:2. 1 S 25:3, 42.
   Absalom. 2 S 13:20-28. 14:24-33. 15:1-18. 17:1-14. 18:9-18, 33.
   Maacah. i.e. *oppression*, **S#4601h**, 1 K +2:39, Maachah.
   Talmai. 2 S 13:37, 38.

Geshur. i.e. *expulsion; proud beholder; a bridge*, **S#1650h**. 2 S 13:37, 38. 14:23, 32. 15:8. Dt +3:14. Jsh +12:5. 13:13. 1 S 27:8. 1 Ch 2:23. 3:2.

4 **Adonijah**. 1 K 1:5, etc. 2:13-25.
Haggith. i.e. *festive*, **S#2294h**. 1 K 1:5, 11. 2:13. 1 Ch 3:2.
Shephatiah. i.e. *Jah hath judged*, **S#8203h**. 1 Ch 3:3. 9:8, Shephathiah. Ezr 2:4, 57. 8:8. Ne 7:9, 59. 11:4. Je 38:1. Also 1 Ch 12:5. 27:16. 2 Ch 21:2.
Abital. i.e. *father of dew*, **S#37h**. 1 Ch 3:3.

5 **Ithream**. i.e. *abundance* or *remnant of a people*, **S#3507h**. 1 Ch 3:3.
Eglah. i.e. *a calf*, **S#5698h**. 1 Ch 3:3.

6 **Abner**. 2 S 2:8, 9. 2 K 10:23. 2 Ch 25:8. Pr 21:30. Is 8:9, 10. Jl 3:9-13. Mt 12:30.
himself strong. 1 Ch 11:10. Da 10:21mg.
for. or, in.

7 **had**. Ge +4:19.
concubine. 2 S 21:8, 11. Ge 22:24.
Rizpah. i.e. *a burning coal*, **S#7532h**. 2 S 21:8, 10, 11.
Aiah. i.e. *kite* or *vulture*, **S#345h**. 2 S 21:8, 10, 11. 1 Ch 1:40.
gone in. 2 S 12:8. 16:21, 22. Ge 6:4. 1 K 2:17, 21, 22.

8 **Abner**. Ps 76:10. Mk 6:18, 19.
Ishbosheth. i.e. *man of shame*, **S#378h**. ver. 10, 12, 15. 2 S 3:8, 14, 15. 4:5, 8, 12.
Am I a dog's head. 2 S 9:8. 16:9. Dt 23:18. 1 S 24:14, 15. 2 K 8:13.
do show. ver. 9, 18. 2 S 5:2. 1 S 15:28. Ps 2:1-4. Is 37:23. Ac 9:4, 5.

9 **So do God**. ver. 35. 2 S 19:13. Ru 1:17. 1 S 3:17. 14:44. 25:22. 1 K 19:2. 2 K 6:31.
as the Lord. 1 S 15:28. 16:1-13. 28:17. 1 Ch 12:23. Ps 89:3, 4, 19, 20, 35-37. 132:11.

10 **translate the kingdom from**. 1 Ch 12:23.
from Dan. Jg +20:1.

11 **because**. ver. 39.

12 **Whose**. 2 S 19:6. 20:1-13.
Make. Ps 62:9. Lk 16:5-8.
my hand. ver. 21, 27. 2 S 5:1-3. 19:14, 41-43. 20:1, 2. Dt +32:36. 1 Ch 11:1-3. 12:38-40. Mt 21:8-10.

13 **that is**. Heb. saying.
Thou shalt. Ge 43:3. 44:23, 26.
Michal. ver. 20-23. 1 S 18:20-28. 19:11-17. 1 Ch 15:29.

14 **Ish-bosheth**. 2 S 2:10.
an hundred. 1 S 18:25, 27.

15 **Phaltiel**. i.e. *escape of God; deliverance of God*, **S#6409h**. Nu 34:26. 1 S 25:44, Phalti.

16 **along weeping**. Heb. going and weeping. Pr 9:17, 18.
Bahurim. i.e. *choice youths*, **S#980h**. 2 S 16:5. 17:18. 19:16. 1 K 2:8.

17 **Ye sought**. 2 S 5:1, 2. Ezk 21:27. 1 P 4:3.
in times past. Heb. both yesterday and the

third day. 2 S 5:2mg. Ge +31:2mg. Ex +4:10mg. Dt 19:4mg. Jsh 3:4mg. +4:18mg. Ru 2:11mg. 1 S 4:7mg. 10:11mg. +19:7mg. 2 K 13:5mg. 1 Ch 11:2mg. Is 30:33mg.

18 **for the Lord**. ver. 9. 1 S 13:14. 15:28. 16:1, 12, 13. Jn 12:42, 43.
By the hand. Ps 89:3, 4, 19-23. 132:17, 18.

19 **Benjamin**. 1 S 10:20, 21. 1 Ch 12:29. Ps 68:27.

20 **David**. Ge +19:3. 31:44, 46, 54.

21 **will gather**. ver. 10, 12. 2 S 2:9. Ph 2:21.
reign over. 1 K 11:37. Ps 20:4.
heart. Heb. *nephesh*, Ex +23:9.

24 **What hast**. ver. 8, 39. 2 S 19:5-7. Nu 23:11. Jn 18:35.

25 **that he came**. ver. 27. 2 K 18:32mg. Jn 7:12, 47. Ro 2:1.
and to know. 2 S 10:3. Ge 42:9, 12, 16. Nu 27:17. Dt 28:6. 1 S 29:4-6. Ps 121:8. Is 37:28.

26 **he sent**. Pr 26:23-26. 27:4-6.
well. Heb. *bor*, Ge +37:20.
Sirah. i.e. *the turning aside; departure; a pot, hook*, **S#5626h**.

27 **took him**. 2 S 20:9, 10. Dt 27:24. 1 K 2:5, 32.
quietly. *or*, peaceably. Je 41:2, 6, 7.
and smote. ver. 6-10. 2 S 4:6.
fifth rib. 2 S 2:23.
for the blood. 2 S 2:19-23.

28 **guiltless**. Ge 9:6. Ex 21:12. Nu 35:33. Dt 21:1-9. Mt 27:24.
for ever. Heb. *olam*, Ex +12:24.
blood. Heb. bloods. 2 K +9:26mg.

29 **rest**. 2 S 1:16. Jg 9:24, 56, 57. 1 K 2:31-34. Pr 6:16, 17. Is 24:16-18. Ac 28:4. Re 16:6.
and let there. 1 S 2:32-36. 2 K 1:10. 5:27. Ne 4:5. Ps 10:15. 55:15. 58:6. 68:2. 69:22. 83:11. 109:6, 8-19. 137:7. Je +10:25. Ac 23:3. Ga 1:9.
fail. Heb. be cut off. Je 30:23mg.
an issue. Le 15:2.
leper. 2 K +5:1.
leaneth on a staff. Ex 21:19. Le 21:18. Dt 22:5. 23:1. Jsh 9:23. Pr 31:19. Is 56:3-5. 1 C +6:9.
falleth on. 1 S 31:4, 5. Est 2:23. Ac 1:18.
the sword. Le 26:25, 33. Dt 28:22. 32:25.
lacketh bread. Ps 37:25. 109:10.

30 **slew Abner**. Dt 27:24. Pr 28:17. Ac 28:4.
because. 2 S 2:19-23.

31 **Rend**. 2 K +18:37.
sackcloth. Jb +16:15.
mourn. Ge +23:2.
bier. Heb. bed. Lk 7:14.

32 **lifted**. 2 S 1:12. 18:33. 1 S 30:4. Jb 31:29. Pr 24:17. Lk 19:41, 42.
grave. Heb. *qeber*, Ge +23:4.

33 **as a fool dieth**. 2 S 13:12, 13, 28, 29. Jb 5:2. Pr 18:7. Ec 2:15, 16. Je 17:11. Lk 12:19, 20.

34 **hands**. Ps +107:10, 11.
fetters. lit. brasses. 2 Ch +33:11.

wicked men. Heb. children of iniquity. 2 S 7:10. 1 Ch 17:9. Jb 24:14. Ps 89:22. Ho 6:9.
wept. 2 S 1:12.

35 **cause**. 2 S 12:17. Je 16:7. Ezk 24:17, 22.
So do. ver. 9. Ru 1:17.
till the. 2 S 1:12. Jg 20:26.

36 **took notice**. Mk 7:37.
pleased them. Heb. was good in their eyes. Jsh +22:30mg.
as. 2 S 15:6, 13. Ps 62:9. Mk 7:37. 15:11-13.

38 **a prince**. ver. 12. 2 S 2:8. 1 S 14:50; 51. Jb 32:9.

39 **I am**. Ex 21:12. 2 Ch 19:6, 7. Ps 75:10. 101:8. Pr 20:8. 25:5.
weak. Heb. tender. 1 Ch 22:5. Is 7:4mg. Ro 13:4.
the sons. 1 Ch +2:16.
too hard. 2 S 19:6, 7, 13.
the Lord. Ge +6:13. 1 K 2:5, 6, 33, 34. Ps 7:16. 28:4. 62:12. 2 T +4:14.

2 SAMUEL 4

1 **his hands**. 2 S 17:2. Ezr 4:4. Ne 6:9. Is 13:7. 35:3. Je 6:24. 50:43. Zp 3:16.
and all. Mt 2:2, 3.

2 **captains**. 2 S 3:22. 2 K 5:2. 6:23.
Baanah. ver. 5.
other. Heb. second.
Rechab. i.e. *a rider; horseman; charioteer,* **S#7394h**. ver. 5, 6, 9. 2 K 10:15, 23. 1 Ch 2:55. Ne 3:14. Je 35:6, 8, 14, 16, 19.
Rimmon. 2 K +5:18.
Beerothite. **S#886h**. ver. 3, 5, 9. 2 S 23:37.
Beeroth. Jsh +9:17.

3 **fled**. 1 S 31:7. Ne 11:33.
Gittaim. i.e. *two wine-fats; double winepress,* **S#1664h**. 2 S 6:10, 11. Ne 11:33.
until this day. 1 S 6:18.

4 **Jonathan**. 2 S 9:3.
when the tidings. 1 S 29:1, 11. 31:1-10.
Mephibosheth. 1 Ch 8:34. 9:40, Meribaal.

5 **Baanah**. i.e. *son of response; answering; affliction; son of grief,* **S#1196h**. ver. 2, 6, 9. 2 S 23:29. 1 Ch 11:30. Ezr 2:2. Ne 7:7. 10:27.
went. 2 Ch 24:25. 25:27. 33:24.
lay on a bed. 2 S 11:2. 1 K 16:9. Pr 24:33, 34. *1 Th 5:3-7*.

6 **as though**. 2 S 11:15. 13:28. 15:6. 1 K 21:8. 2 K 9:23. Ne 6:2. Est 3:8. Je +9:8.
under. 2 S 2:23. 3:27. 20:10.

7 **took his head**. 1 S 17:54. 31:9. 2 K 10:6, 7. Mt 14:11. Mk 6:28, 29.

8 **sought**. 1 S 18:11. 19:2-11, 15. 20:1. 23:15. 25:29. Ps 63:9, 10. 71:24. Mt 2:20.
life. Heb. *nephesh,* soul, Ge +44:30.
the Lord. 2 S 18:19, 31. 22:48. 1 S +24:4. Lk 18:7, 8. Re 6:10. 18:20.

9 **As the Lord liveth**. Ru 3:13.
who hath. Ps +34:22. 2 T 4:17, 18.
soul. Heb. *nephesh,* Ge +12:13.

10 **one**. 2 S 1:2-16.
thinking, etc. Heb. he was in his own eyes, as a bringer, etc.
who thought, etc. *or,* which was the reward I gave him for his tidings.

11 **when wicked**. Dt 27:24. 1 K 2:32. Pr 25:26. Hab 1:4, 12. 1 J 3:12.
require. 2 S 3:27, 39. Ex 21:12. Nu 35:31-34. Lk +11:50.
from. Ge 4:11. 6:13. 7:23. Ex 9:15. Ps 109:15. Pr 2:22. Je 10:11.

12 **slew them**. 2 S 1:15. Ps 55:23. Mt 7:2.
hanged. 2 S 21:9. Dt 21:22, 23.
in the sepulchre. Heb. *qeber,* Ge +23:4.
of Abner. 2 S 3:32.

2 SAMUEL 5

1 **came**. 1 Ch 11:1-3. 12:23-40.
we are. 2 S 3:17, 18. 19:13. Ge 29:14. Dt 17:15. Jg 9:2. Ezk 21:27. Ep 5:30. He 2:14. 1 P 4:3.

2 **time past**. lit. yesterday, the third day. 2 S +3:17mg.
leddest out. ver. 24. Nu 27:17. 1 S 18:13, 16. 25:28. Is 55:4. Jn 10:4.
feed. 1 S 16:1, 12, 13. 25:30. Is +40:11. Ezk 37:24, 25. Jn 10:3, 4, 11.
a captain. 1 S 9:16. 13:14. 18:13. 2 K 20:5. Is 55:4. He 2:10.

3 **So all**. Ex 3:16. Jsh +20:4.
made. 1 S 11:15. 2 K 11:17. 2 Ch 23:16. Ne 9:38.
before. Jg 11:11. 1 S 23:18.
anointed. 2 S 2:4. 1 S 16:13.

4 **thirty**. Nu 4:43. Lk 3:23.
forty. 1 Ch 26:31. 29:27. 2 Ch 9:30. Ac 13:21.

5 **seven years**. 2 S 2:11. 1 K 2:11. 1 Ch 3:4.

6 **Jerusalem**. Ge 14:18. Jsh 10:3. Jg 1:8. He 7:1.
the Jebusites. Ge +10:16.
which spake. ver. 8.
Except. Je 37:10.
thinking, David cannot. *or,* saying, David shall not, etc.

7 **David took**. 1 Ch 11:5.
Zion. i.e. *the dry or sunny part of Jerusalem, at the south; spiritual illumination,* **S#6726h**. Ps 2:6. 9:11, 14. 14:7. 48:2, 11, 12. 51:18. 69:35. 102:13, 16, 21. 110:2. 137:1, 3. 146:10. 149:2. Is 12:6. 14:32. 16:1. 24:23. 28:16. 29:8. 33: 20. 34:8. 51:3, 11, 16. 59:20. Je 26:18. Jl 2:32. Mi 4:2. Zc 9:9, 13. Ro 9:33. He 12:22. Re 14:1.
the same. ver. 9. 2 S 6:10. 1 K 2:10. 3:1. 8:1. 1 Ch 11:7. 2 Ch 5:2. 24:16.

8 **Whosoever**. Jsh 15:16, 17. 1 S 17:25.

the gutter. Ps 42:7. 84:6.
Jebusites. Ge +10:16.
soul. Heb. *nephesh*, Ge +34:3.
he shall be. 1 Ch 11:6-9.
Wherefore, etc. *or*, Because they had said,
even the blind and the lame, he shall not
come into the house. Ac 3:2, 8.

9 **city**. ver. 7.
   Millo. i.e. *a bastion; a filling up; a rampart,
mound*, **S#4407h**. Jg 9:6, 20. 1 K 9:15, 24.
11:27. 2 K 12:20. 1 Ch 11:8. 2 Ch 32:5.

10 **went on, and grew great**. Heb. went going
and growing. 2 S 3:1. 1 Ch 11:9. Jb 17:9. Pr
4:18. Is 9:7. Da 2:44, 45. Lk 2:52.
   the Lord. Ge 21:22. Ps 46:7, 11. Is 8:9, 10.
Ro 8:31.

11 **Hiram**. i.e. *noble; freeman; height of life*,
S#2438h. 1 K 5:1, 10. 7:13, 40, 45. 9:11. 10:11.
1 Ch +8:5, Huram. 14:1.
   Tyre. 1 K +7:13.
   masons. Heb. hewers of stone of the wall.
   they built. 2 S 7:2. 1 K 7:1-12. Ec 2:4-11. Je
22:14-16.

12 **David**. 2 S 7:16. 1 Ch 14:2.
   his people. 1 K 10:9. 2 Ch 2:11. Est 4:14. Is
1:25-27. Da 2:30.

13 **David took**. Ge 25:5, 6. Le 18:18mg. Dt
17:17. 1 Ch 3:9. 14:3-7. 2 Ch 11:18-21.
13:21.
   more concubines. 2 S 16:21.
   and wives. Ge +4:19.

14 **the names**. 1 Ch 3:5-9. 14:4.
   Shammuah. i.e. *rumor; a hearkener; heard*,
S#8051h. Nu 13:4. 1 Ch 14:4. Ne 11:17. 12:18.
or, Shimea, as 1 Ch 3:5.
   Shobab. 1 Ch +2:18.
   Nathan. 2 Ch +9:29.
   Solomon. i.e. *peace*, **S#8010h**. 2 S 12:24, 25. Mt
1:6.

15 **Ibhar**. i.e. *he chooses; whom God chooses*,
S#2984h. 1 Ch 3:6. 14:5.
   Elishua. i.e. *my God saves; God of supplication
or riches*, **S#474h**. *or*, Elishama, as 1 Ch 3:6. 1
Ch 14:5.
   Nepheg. i.e. *a going forth; sprout*, **S#5298h**. Ex
6:21. 1 Ch 3:7. 14:6.
   Japhia. Jsh +10:3.

16 **Elishama**. Nu +1:10.
   Eliada. i.e. *God knows*, **S#450h**. 1 K 11:23.
1 Ch 3:8. 2 Ch 17:17. *or*, Beeliada, as
1 Ch 14:7.
   Eliphalet. i.e. *God escapes; God of salvation*,
S#467h. 1 Ch 3:6, 8, Eliphelet. 14:5, 7.

17 **But when**. 1 Ch 14:8, 9. Ps 2:1-5. Re 11:15-
18.
   the hold. 2 S 23:14. 1 Ch 11:16.
18 **the valley**. 2 S 23:13, 15, 16.
   Rephaim. Ge +14:5. Dt +2:20.

19 **enquired**. 2 S 2:1. 1 S 23:2, 4. 30:7, 8. 1 Ch
14:10. Ja 4:15.

And the Lord. ver. 23. Jg 20:28. 1 S 28:6.
30:8. 1 K 22:6, 15-23. Pr 3:6.

20 **Baal-perazim**. *that is*, The plain of breaches.
i.e. *lord of breaches*, **S#1188h**. 1 Ch 14:11mg. Is
28:21. La 2:13.
   broken forth. 2 S 6:8mg. 2 Ch 20:37. 24:7.

21 **David**. 1 S 5:2-6.
   burned them. *or*, took them away. or, lifted
them up. Dt +7:5. Is 46:1, 2. Je 43:12.

22 **came up**. 1 K 20:22. 1 Ch 14:13.
   spread themselves. Jg 15:9.
   valley of Rephaim. ver. 18. Jsh 15:8.

23 **enquired**. ver. 19.
   fetch. Jsh 8:2, 7. 1 Ch 14:14. Mt 9:29, 30. Mk
8:23-25. Jn 9:6, 7.
   the mulberry trees. Rather, an under-
ground aqueduct. ver. 8, 24. 2 S 23:13, 15,
16. 1 Ch 14:14, 15. Ps 84:6.

24 **sound**. 2 K 7:6. 19:7.
   a going. or, a stepping. **S#6807h**. 1 Ch 14:15. Is
3:20.
   thou shalt bestir. Ex 11:7. Jg 4:14. 7:15. 1 S
14:9-12. 1 Ch 14:15. Ph 2:11, 12.
   go out before. ver. +2. Jg 4:14. Ps 60:12. Ezk
46:10. Jn 10:4.

25 **Geba**. 1 Ch 14:16, Gibeon.
   Gazer. i.e. *a portion*, **S#1507h**. Jsh 16:10. 1 Ch
14:16.

2 SAMUEL 6

1 **gathered**. 2 S 5:1. 1 K 8:1. 1 Ch 13:1-4. Ps
132:1-6.

2 **Baale of Judah**. i.e. *possessors of Judah*,
S#1184h, called Baalah in Jsh 15:9, 10, and
Kirjath-Jearim in 1 Ch 13:6; and Kirjath-Baal
in Jsh 15:60. 1 S 7:1. 1 Ch 13:5, 6.
   whose name, etc., *or*, at which the name,
even the name of the Lord of hosts, was
called upon. Le 24:11-16.
   hosts. Ps +24:10.
   dwelleth. Ge +3:24. 1 S +4:4. 1 P 1:12.

3 **set**, etc. Heb. made the ark of God to ride. Nu
4:5-12, 15. 7:9. 10:21. 1 S 6:7, 8, 14.
   Gibeah. *or*, the hill. 1 S 7:1.
   Uzzah. i.e. *strength*, **S#5798h**. 2 K 21:18, 26. 1
Ch 8:7. 13:7, 9, 10, 11. Ezr 2:49. Ne 7:51.
Also ver. 6, 7, 8. 1 Ch 6:29.
   Ahio. i.e. *his brother; brotherly*, **S#283h**. ver. 4. 1
Ch 8:14, 31. 9:37. 13:7.

4 **the house**. 1 S 7:1, 2. 1 Ch 13:7.
   accompanying. Heb. with.

5 **David**. 1 S 10:5. 16:16. 2 K 3:15. 1 Ch 13:8.
15:10-24. Ps 47:5. 68:25-27. 150:3-5. Da 3:5,
7, 10, 15. Am 5:23. 6:5.
   all. Ex +9:6.
   played. 1 S 18:7. 1 Ch 13:8. 15:29.
   on all manner. 1 Ch 13:8.
   fir wood. Na 2:3.
   harps. Re +5:8.

psalteries. 1 S 10:5.
timbrels. Ge 31:27.
cymbals. Ps 150:5.

6 **Nachon's**. i.e. *smitten; established*, **S#5225h**. 1 Ch 13:9, Chidon.
threshingfloor. Ge +50:10.
put forth. Nu 4:15, 19, 20. 1 S 6:19. Mt 11:27. Col 2:18.
his hand. 1 Ch 13:9. 16:7. Jb 24:6. Ps 119:126.
shook it. *or*, stumbled. 2 K 9:33.

7 **God smote**. Le 10:1-3. 1 S 6:19. 1 Ch 13:10. 15:2, 13. 1 C 11:30-32.
error. *or*, rashness.

8 **displeased**. 1 Ch 13:11, 12. Jon 4:1, 9.
made. Heb. broken. 2 S 5:20.
a breach. 2 S +5:20.
Perez-uzzah. *that is*, The breach of Uzzah. **S#6560h**. 1 Ch 13:11.
to this day. 1 S +6:18.

9 **afraid**. Nu 17:12, 13. 1 S 5:10, 11. 6:20. Ps 76:7. 119:120. Is 6:5. Lk 5:8, 9. 1 P 3:6.
How shall. 1 K 8:27. 1 Ch 13:11, 12. Jb 25:5, 6.

10 **Obed-edom**. i.e. *servant of Edom*, **S#5654h**. ver. 11, 12. 1 Ch 13:13, 14. 15:18, 21, 24, 25. 16:5, 38. 26:4, 8, 15. 2 Ch 25:24.
Gittite. i.e. *winepress*, **S#1663h**. ver. 11. Jsh +13:3. 2 S 4:3. 15:19, 22. 18:2. 21:19. 1 Ch 13:13. 15:18, 21, 24. 16:5, 6. 20:5.

11 **the Lord blessed**. Ge 30:27. 39:5, 23. 1 Ch 13:14. Pr 3:9, 10. 10:22. Ml 3:10. Jn 14:23. 2 C 2:15, 16.

12 **because**. Mt 10:42.
So David. 1 Ch 15:1-4, 11-14, 16, 25. Ps 24:7-10. 68:24-27. 132:6-8.

13 **when they**. Nu 4:15. 7:9. Jsh 3:3. 1 Ch 15:2, 15, 25, 26.
oxen. 1 K 8:5. 2 Ch 5:6.

14 **danced**. Ex +15:20.
with all his. Dt 6:5. Ec 9:10. Col 3:23.
girded. Ex +28:4. 1 Ch 15:27. Ps 110:4. Zc 6:13.

15 **David**. Ps 132:28.
all. Ex +9:6.
with shouting. 1 Ch 15:16, 24, 25, 28. Ezr 3:10, 11. Ps 47:1, 5, 6. 68:24-27. 1 Th 4:16.
the sound. Nu 10:1-10. Jsh 6:4, 5. Ps 150:3. 1 Th 4:16.

16 **And as**. 1 Ch 15:29.
Michal. 2 S +3:14.
looked through. Jg 5:28. 2 K 9:30.
despised. 1 Ch 15:29. Ps 69:7. Is 53:2, 3. Ac 2:13. 1 C 1:28. 2:14.

17 **they brought**. 1 Ch 15:1. 16:1. 2 Ch 1:4. Ps 132:1-8.
pitched. Heb. stretched. Ge 12:8. 26:25.
offered. 1 K 8:5, 62-65. 2 Ch 5:6. 7:5-7. Ezr 6:16, 17.

burnt offerings. Le +23:12.
peace offerings. Le +23:19.

18 **as soon**. 1 K 8:55. 1 Ch 16:2. 2 Ch 6:3. 30:18, 19, 27. Ac 3:26.
burnt offerings. Le +23:12.
peace offerings. Le +23:19.
he blessed. Ge 14:19. Ex 39:43. Le 9:22, 23. 2 Ch 30:27. He 7:1-7.

19 **he dealt**. 1 Ch 16:3. 2 Ch 30:24. 35:7, 8, 12, 13. Ne 8:10. Ezk 45:17. Ac 20:35. Ep 4:8.
So all the. 1 K 8:66. 2 Ch 7:10.

20 **bless**. ver. 18. Ge 18:19. Jsh 24:15. 1 Ch 16:43. Ps 30, title. 101:2.
Michal. ver. 16. Ps 69:7-9. Mk 3:21.
How. Ge +37:19. Jb 26:2. Je 22:23.
glorious. Ne 4:3, 4. Is 53:2, 3. Jn 13:6. 1 C 4:10-13. Ph 2:7, 8.
uncovered. ver. 14, 16. Is +20:2.
vain fellows. Jg 9:4. Jb 30:8.
shamelessly. *or*, openly. 1 P 4:14.

21 **before**. ver. 14, 16. 1 C 10:31. Col 3:23. 2 T 1:7.
chose. 1 S 13:14. 15:28. 16:1, 12. Ps 78:70-72. 89:19, 20. Ac 13:22.
play. ver. 5. 1 Ch 15:29. Ps 69:7-9. 123:4.

22 **more vile**. Ps 51:5. 69:5. Is 50:6. 51:7. Mt 5:11, 12. Ac 5:41, 42. He 12:2. 1 P 4:14.
in mine. Ge 32:10. Jb 40:4. 42:6. 1 T 1:15. 1 P 5:6.
maid-servants. *or*, handmaids.
I be had. 1 S 2:30.

23 **Michal**. 1 S 1:6-8. Is 4:1. Ho 9:11. Lk 1:25.
no child. Ge +11:30. Le 20:20. Ps +127:3. Je 22:30.
unto the day. 1 S 15:35. Is 22:14. Mt 1:25.

2 SAMUEL 7

1 **the king**. 1 Ch 17:1, etc. Da 4:29, 30.
the Lord. Jsh 21:44. 23:1. 1 K 5:4. 2 Ch 14:6. Ps 18, title. Pr 16:7. Lk 1:74, 75.

2 **Nathan**. 2 Ch +9:29.
I dwell. 2 S 5:11. 1 Ch 14:1. 17:1. Je 22:13-15. Hg 1:4.
the ark. Ps 132:5. Jn 2:17. Ac 7:46.
curtains. 2 S 6:17. Ex 26:1-14. 40:21. 1 Ch 16:1. 2 Ch 1:4. Je 4:20. Hab 3:7.

3 **Go, do**. 2 K 4:27.
all that. 1 S +16:7. 1 K 8:17, 18. 10:24. 1 Ch 22:7. 28:2. Ps 20:4. 37:4.
for the. 1 S 10:7. 1 J 2:27.

4 **that night**. Nu 12:6. 1 Ch 17:3. Am 3:7.

5 **my servant David**. Heb. to my servant, to David. 1 Ch 17:7.
Shalt. 1 K 5:3. 8:16-19. 1 Ch 17:4. 22:7, 8. 28:3, etc.

6 **I have not**. Jsh 18:1. 1 K 8:16. 1 Ch 17:5, 6.
walked. Ex 33:14, 15. 40:35-38. Le 26:23, 24, 27, 28. Nu 10:33-36. Dt 23:14. 2 C 6:16. Re 2:1.

tent. Ex 40:18, 19, 34.
tabernacle. Ex +38:21.

7 walked. Le 26:11, 12. Dt 23:14. 2 C 6:16.
any of the tribes. 1 Ch 17:6, any of the judges.
feed. Is +40:11.

8 the Lord. 2 C *6:18*.
I took thee. 1 S 16:11, 12. 1 Ch 17:7. Ps 78:70.
following. Heb. after. Je +17:16mg.
ruler. 2 S 6:21. 12:7. 1 S 9:16. 10:1.

9 And I was. 2 S 8:6, 14. 22:30, 34-38. Is +43:2.
cut off. 2 S 22:1. 1 S 31:6. Ps 18:37-42. 89:23. 132:18.
out of thy sight. Heb. from thy face. Is 5:21mg.
a great name. 2 S 8:13. Ge 12:2. 1 S 2:8. 1 Ch 17:8. Ps 113:7, 8. Lk 1:52.
like unto. Ps 87:3-6.

10 I will. Ps 89:3, 4.
plant them. Je +11:17. Ezk 37:25-27. Am 9:15.
a place. Jn 14:2, 3. 1 P 1:4. Re 3:12.
neither. Ps 89:22, 23. Is 60:18. Ezk 28:24. Ho 2:18. Re 21:4.
move no more. 2 K 21:8. Is 60:21. Je 24:6. 32:41. 33:19-22. Ezk 34:28. 37:25. Jl 3:20. Am +9:15. Mi 4:4.
children of wickedness. 2 S 3:34mg. Ps 89:22.
as beforetime. Ex 1:13, 14, 22. Jg 4:3. 6:2-6. 1 S 13:17.

11 since. Jg 2:14-16. 1 S 12:9-11. Ps 106:42.
have caused. ver. 1. Jb 5:18, 19. 34:29. Ps 46:9.
he will make. ver. 27. Ex 1:21. 1 K 2:24. 11:38. 1 Ch 17:10. 22:10. Ps 89:3, 4. 127:1. Pr 14:1. He 3:6.
house. Ge +7:1.

12 And when. 1 K 2:1. 8:20. Jb 7:1.
sleep. Ge +25:8. Dt 31:16. 1 K +11:43. Da +12:2. Ac 13:36. 1 C 15:51. 1 Th 4:14.
I will set. Ge 15:4. Jsh 17:14. 1 K 8:20. 1 Ch 17:11. Ps 89:29. 115:12. 132:11, 12. Is 9:7. 11:1-3, 10. Mt 22:42-44. Ac 2:30. Ro 1:3. 2 T 2:8.
thy seed. Ps 16:8-10. 89:3, 4, 35-37. Is +9:6, 7. +55:3, 4. Am 9:11, 12. Mt +1:1. Lk 1:32, 69. Ac 2:25-28. +13:23. 15:15-18.

13 He shall. 1 K 5:5. 6:12. 8:19. 1 Ch 17:11, 12. 22:9, 10. 28:6, 10. Zc 6:13. Mt 16:18. Lk 1:31-33. He 3:3. 1 P 2:5.
an house. 1 K 11:38, 39. Am 9:11. Ac +15:16.
I will stablish. ver. +16. 1 K 2:45. 8:25. 9:5. 1 Ch 22:10. 28:7. Ps 21:4, 7. 89:4, 21, 27-29, 35-37. 132:11-18. Is 9:7. 49:8. +55:3. Lk 1:32, 33.
the throne. He +1:8.

his kingdom. Da +7:14. He +1:8.
for ever. Heb. *olam*, Ex +12:24. Ge +9:16. Da +7:14. He +1:8. Re 11:15.

14 I will be. 1 Ch 17:13. 28:6. Ps 89:20-37. Mt 3:17. 2 C 6:16, 18. He *1:5*. Re *21:7*.
If he. Ps 89:30-35.
I will. Dt 8:5. Jb 5:17. Ps 94:12, 13. Pr 3:11, 12. Je 30:11. 1 C 11:32. He 12:5-11. Re 3:19.
with the rod. 2 K 5:1. 1 Ch 6:15. Jb 1:15, 17, 21. Ps 17:13, 14. +39:9. Is 10:5-7, 12, 15. 13:5. 37:7. Je 27:8. 50:9. Ezk 25:14. Hab 1:6, 12.

15 But my mercy. ver. 14, 16. 1 S 19:24. Is 38:5. +55:3.
not depart. 1 S +28:19. 1 K +11:39. 1 Ch 28:9. Ps 89:28, 33, 37. +132:11.
as I took. 1 S 15:23, 28. 16:14. 1 K 11:13, 34-36. Is 9:7. 37:35.

16 thine house. ver. +13. Ge 49:10. 1 K 1:48. 2 K 19:34. 1 Ch 17:13, 14. Ps 45:6. 72:5, 8, 17-19. 89:36, 37. Is 9:7. Da 2:44. +7:14. Mt 16:18. Lk *1:32, 33*. Jn 12:34.
for ever. Heb. *olam*, Ex +12:24. Ps 145:13. Da 7:14. Jn 12:34.
thy throne. He 1:8. Re 11:15.
for ever. Heb. *olam*, Ex +12:24.

17 According to. 1 Ch 17:15. Ac 20:20, 27. 1 C 15:3.

18 sat. Jg +20:26. 1 Ch 17:16. Is 37:14.
Who am I. Ge 32:10. Ex 3:11. Jg 6:15. 1 S 9:21. 15:17. 18:18. Ps 8:4. Ep 3:8.

19 And this. 2 S 12:8. Nu 16:9, 13.
but thou. ver. 11-16. 1 Ch 17:17. Ps 103:17.
And is this. Ps 36:7. Is 55:8, 9. Ep 2:7. 3:19, 20.
manner. Heb. law. 1 Ch 17:17.

20 knowest. Ge 18:19. 1 S 16:7. 1 Ch 17:19. Ps 139:1. Jn +2:25. 21:17. He 4:13. Re 2:23.

21 thy word's. Nu 23:19. Dt 9:5. Jsh 23:14, 15. Ps 115:1. 138:2. Is 43:25. Je 14:7. Ezk 36:22. Mt 24:35. Lk 1:54, 55, 72.
according. Mt 11:26. Lk 10:21. 12:32. 1 C 1:1. Ep 1:9. 3:11.

22 Wherefore. Dt 3:24. Ps 86:10. Ezk 36:22, 32. Da +2:45.
none. Ex +8:10. Dt 4:35. 1 S 2:2. Is 45:5, 18, 22.

23 what one. Dt 4:7, 8, 32-34. 33:29. Ps 147:20. Ro 3:1, 2.
went. Ex 3:7, 8. 19:5, 6. Nu 14:13, 14. Ps 111:9. Is 63:7-14. T 2:14. 1 P 2:9. Re 5:9.
make him. Ex 9:16. Jsh 7:9. 1 Ch 17:21. Is 63:12, 14. Ezk 20:9. Ep 1:6.
great things. Dt 10:21. Ps 40:5. 65:5. 66:3. 106:22. 145:6.
thy people. Dt 9:26. 15:15. Ne 1:10.
nations and their gods. Ex 12:12.

24 confirmed. Ge 17:7. Dt 26:18.
for ever. Heb. *olam*, Ex +12:24. Ge +9:12. Je +31:36. Ro +11:1.

art become. ver. 23. Ex 15:2. Dt 27:9. 1 Ch 17:22. Ps 48:14. Is 12:2. Je 31:1, 33. 32:38. Ho 1:10. Zc 13:9. Jn 1:12. Ro 9:25, 26. 1 P 2:10.

25 **his house**. 2 S 12:15, 16. 1 K 8:25, 26. 2 K 4:1. 1 Ch 22:11, 12. La 2:19-21. Mt 9:18. 15:22. 19:13-15. Lk 16:27-30. Jn 4:46, 47.
    establish it. Ps 119:49. Je 11:4, 5. Ezk 36:37.
    for ever. Heb. *olam*, Ex +12:24. Ge +9:12.
    and do. Ge 32:12. Ex 32:13. 1 K 8:25. Ps 119:58.

26 **let thy**. 1 Ch 17:23, 24. 29:10-13. Ps 72:18, 19. 115:1. Mt 6:9. Jn 12:28.
    for ever. Heb. *olam*, Ex +12:24.
    before thee. Ge 17:18. 1 Ch 17:23, 24. Ps 89:36.

27 **revealed**. Heb. opened the ear. Ru +4:4mg. Ps 40:6.
    I will. ver. 11.
    found. 1 Ch 17:25, 26. Ps 10:17.

28 **thy words**. Nu +23:19. Jn 17:17. 2 C 1:20. T +1:2.

29 **let it please thee to bless**. Heb. be thou pleased and bless. Nu 6:24-26. 2 K 5:23. 1 Ch 17:27. Ps 115:12-15.
    for ever. Heb. *olam*, Ex +12:24. 2 S 22:51.

2 SAMUEL 8

1 A.M. 2964. B.C. 1040. An. Ex. Is 451.
    And after. 2 S 7:9. 21:15-22.
    Metheg-ammah. *or*, the bridle of Ammah. i.e. *the bridle of the arm*, S#4965h, only here. 2 S 2:24. 1 Ch 18:1, etc., Gath.

2 **he smote**. Jg 3:29, 30. 1 S 14:47. Ezk +25:8.
    measured. 2 S 12:31. Is 18:2. 28:17.
    And so. ver. 6, 12-14. 2 K 1:1. 3:4-27. 1 Ch 18:2.
    brought gifts. Jg +3:15.

3 **Hadadezer**. i.e. *Hadad is help; noisy helper*, S#1909h. ver. 5, 7-10, 12. 1 K 11:23. 1 Ch 18:3, Hadarezer.
    Rehob. ver. 12. 2 S 10:8. Nu +13:21.
    Compare S#7339h, Am +5:16.
    Zobah. 1 S +14:47.
    at the river. Ge +2:14.

4 **from him**. *or*, of his.
    chariots. As 1 Ch 18:4. See another elipsis supplied from Chronicles at 2 S 5:8.
    seven hundred. In the parallel place in *Chronicles* it is "seven thousand horsemen," 1 Ch 18:4.
    David houghed. Dt 17:16. Jsh 11:6, 9. Ps 20:7. 33:16, 17.
    reserved. 1 K 10:26.

5 **And when**. 1 K 11:23-25. 1 Ch 18:5, 6. 1 7:8.
    came. Jb 9:13. Ps 83:4-8. Is 8:9, 10. 31:3.
    Zobah. 2 Ch 8:3.

6 **garrisons**. ver. 14. 2 S 23:14. 1 S 13:3. 14:1, 6, 15. 2 Ch 17:2. Ps 18:34-46.

became. ver. 2.
    the Lord. ver. 14. 2 S 7:9. 1 Ch 18:13. Ps 5:11, 12. 121:7, 8. 140:7. 144:1, 2. Pr 21:31.

7 **shields**. 1 K 10:16, 17. 14:26, 27. 1 Ch 18:7. 2 Ch 9:15, 16.

8 **Betah**. i.e. *confidence; security; refuge*, S#984h, only here. In 1 Ch 18:8 it is called Tibhath. 1 Ch 18:8, Tibhath.
    Berothai. i.e. *my wells*, S#1268h. 1 Ch 18:8, Chun. Ezk 47:16, Berothah.
    exceeding. 1 Ch 22:14, 16. 29:7. 2 Ch 4:1-18.

9 **Toi**. i.e. *erring; wandering*, S#8583h. ver. 10. 1 Ch 18:9, Tou.
    Hamath. Nu +13:21.

10 **Joram**. 1 Ch +26:25.
    salute him. Heb. ask him of peace. Jg +18:15mg. Is 39:1.
    to bless him. 1 S 13:10mg. 1 K 1:47. Ps 129:8.
    had wars. Heb. was a man of wars. 1 Ch 18:10mg. Is 42:13.
    brought with him. Heb. in his hand were.

11 **Which**. 1 K 7:51. 1 Ch 18:11. 22:14-16. 26:26-28. 29:2. Mi 4:13.

12 **Syria**. 2 S 10:11, 14. 12:26-31. 1 Ch 18:11.

13 **gat him**. 2 S 7:9.
    smiting. Heb. his smiting.
    the valley of salt. 2 K 14:7. 1 Ch 18:12. 2 Ch 25:11. Ps 60, title.
    being. *or*, slaying. 1 Ch 18:12.

14 **all they**. Ge +25:23. Ps 108:9, 10.
    the Lord. ver. +6. Ps 121:4-8. Pr 20:26, 28.

15 **over all Israel**. 2 S 3:12. 5:5.
    David executed. Ps 75:2. 78:71, 72. 89:14. 101:1-8. 119:121. Pr 8:15. Is 9:7. Je +21:12. Am 5:15, 24.

16 **Joab**. 1 S +26:6.
    Jehoshaphat. i.e. *whom Jehovah judges; Jehovah is judge*, S#3092h. 2 S 20:24. 1 K 4:3, 17. 15:24. 22:2, 4, 5, 7, 8, 10, 18, 29, 30, 32, 41, 42, 44, 45, 48-51. 2 K 1:17. 3:1, 7, 11, 12, 14. 8:16. 9:2, 14. 12:18. 1 Ch 3:10. 18:15. 2 Ch 17:1, 3, 5, 10-12. 18:1, 3, 4, 6, 7, 9, 17, 28, 29, 31. 19:1, 2, 4, 8. 20:1-3, 5, 15, 18, 20, 25, 27, 30, 31, 34, 35, 37. 21:1, 2, 12. 22:9. Jl 3:2, 12. Mt 1:8.
    Ahilud. i.e. *brother of one born*, S#286h. 2 S 20:24. 1 K 4:8, 12. 1 Ch 18:15.
    recorder. *or*, remembrancer, *or* writer of chronicles. Ge 41:9. Nu 5:15. 2 S 20:24mg. 1 K 4:3mg. 2 K 18:18, 37. 1 Ch 18:15mg. 2 Ch 34:8. Is 36:3mg, 22. 62:6mg. 66:3mg. Ezk 21:23. 29:16.

17 **Zadok**. i.e. *just*, S#6659h. 2 S 15:24, 25, 27, 29, 35, 36. 17:15. 18:19, 22, 27. 19:11. 20:25. 1 K 1:8, 26, 32, 34, 38, 39, 44, 45. 2:35. 4:2, 4. 2 K 15:33. 1 Ch 6:8, 12, 53. 9:11. 12:28. 15:11. 16:39. 18:16. 24:3, 6, 31. 27:17. 29:22. 2 Ch 27:1. 31:10. Ezr 7:2. Ne 3:4, 29. 10:21. 11:11.

13:13. Ezk 40:46. 43:19. 44:15. 48:11.

Ahitub. 1 S 14:3.

Ahimelech. i.e. *brother of the king*, **S#288h**. 1 S 21:1, 2, 8. 22:9, 11, 14, 16, 20. 23:6. 26:6. 30:7. 1 Ch 24:3, 6, 31. Ps 52:t.

Abiathar. 1 S +22:20.

and Seraiah. i.e. *Jah's prince; warrior of Jehovah*, **S#8304h**. 2 S +20:25, Sheva. 1 K +4:3, Shisha. 2 K 25:18, 23. 1 Ch 4:13, 14, 35. 6:14. +18:16, Shavsha. Ezr 2:2. 7:1. Ne 10:2. 11:11. 12:1, 12. Je 40:8. 51:59, 61. 52:24.

scribe. *or*, secretary. That is, writer, as in Jg 5:14. 2 S 20:25. 1 K 4:3mg. 2 K 12:10mg. 18:18mg, 37. 19:2. Est 3:12mg. Je 36:10. 52:25.

18 **Benaiah**. 1 Ch +15:24.

Jehoiada. 1 Ch 18:17.

the Cherethites. i.e. *cutters off*, that is, *executioners*. **S#3774h**. 2 S 15:18. 20:7, 23. 1 S 30:14. 1 K 1:38, 44. 1 Ch 18:17. Ezk 25:16. Zp 2:5.

Pelethites. i.e. *runners*, **S#6432h**, as in 2 S 15:18; 20:7, 23. 1 K 1:38.

chief rulers. *or*, princes. 2 S 20:26. Is +24:2mg.

2 SAMUEL 9

1 **show him**. 2 S 1:26. 1 S 18:1-4. 20:14-17, 42. 23:16-18. 1 K 2:7. Ps 24:3, 4. Pr 27:10. Mt 10:42. 25:40. Mk 9:41. Jn 19:26, 27. Phm 9-12. 1 P 3:8.

2 **a servant**. Ge 15:2, 3. 24:2. 39:6.

was Ziba. i.e. *a thing planted*, **S#6717h**. ver. 3, 4, 9, 10, 11, 12. 2 S 16:1-4. 19:17, 29.

3 **the kindness of God**. Ge +6:2. +23:6. Dt 4:37. 10:15. 1 S 20:14-17. Mt 5:44, 45. Lk 6:36. T 3:3, 4.

yet a son. 2 S 4:4. 19:26.

4 **Where**. Dt 32:10.

Machir. 2 S 17:27-29. Ge +50:23.

Ammiel. ver. 5. 2 S 17:27. Nu 13:12.

Lo-debar. 2 S 17:27. Jsh 13:26.

5 **sent, and**. Ps 63:1. 68:9.

6 **Mephibosheth**. 1 Ch 8:34. 9:40, called Merib-baal.

he fell. Ge 18:2. 33:3. 1 S 20:41. 25:23.

7 **Fear not**. Ge 43:18, 23. 50:18-21. 1 S 12:19, 20, 24. Is 35:3, 4. Mk 5:33, 34. Lk 1:12, 13, 29, 30.

for I will. ver. +1, 3. Ru 2:11, 12. 2 T 1:16-18.

kindness. 2 S 19:32, 33. Mt 25:34-36.

father. Here, father is put for grandfather. 1 K +15:10.

eat bread. ver. 11. 2 S 19:28, 33. 1 K 2:7. Ps 41:9. Je 52:33, 34. Mt 6:11. Lk 22:30. Re 3:20.

8 **a dead dog**. 2 S 3:8. 16:9. 1 S 24:14, 15. 26:20. Mt 15:26, 27.

9 **I have given**. 2 S 16:4. 19:29. 1 S 9:1. Is 32:8.

10 **shall eat bread**. ver. 7, 11-13. 2 S 19:28. 1 K 2:7. 2 K 25:29. Lk 14:15.

11 **Ziba**. 2 S 19:17.

According. 2 S 16:1-4. 19:26.

said the king. Ex 18:4.

12 **son**. 1 Ch 8:8, 34-40. 9:40-44, Micah.

Micha. i.e. *humble*, **S#4316h**. 1 Ch 9:15. Ne 10:11. 11:17, 22.

servants. Mi 7:5, 6.

13 **he did eat**. ver. 7, 10, 11.

was lame. ver. 3.

2 SAMUEL 10

1 A.M. 2967. B.C. 1037. An. Ex. Is. 454.

king. Jg 10:7-9. 11:12-28. 1 S 11:1-3. 1 Ch 19:1-3.

Hanun. i.e. *gracious; favored*, **S#2586h**. ver. 2-4. 1 Ch 19:2-4, 6. Ne 3:13, 30.

2 **show kindness**. Dt 23:3-6. Ne 4:3-7. 13:1-3.

Nahash. 1 S 11:1.

as his father. 1 S 22:3, 4.

3 **Thinkest thou that David doth**. Heb. In thine eyes doth David.

not. Ge 42:9, 16. 1 C 13:5, 7.

4 **and shaved**. 2 S 19:24. Le +19:27. 1 Ch 19:3, 4. Ezr 9:3. Ps 109:4, 5. Is 50:6. Lk 22:64. Jn 18:22.

cut off. Is 20:4. 47:2, 3. Je 41:5. Re 3:18.

5 **Jericho**. Nu +22:1.

6 **stank**. Ge +34:30. Is 65:5.

Syrians of Beth-rehob. i.e. *house of the broad way*, **S#1050h**. Jg 18:28. Pr 25:8. Is 8:9, 10.

Zobah. ver. 8. 1 S +14:47.

Maacah. Jsh 13:11-13.

Ish-tob. *or*, the men of Tob. Jg 11:3, 5.

7 **all the host**. 2 S 23:8, etc. 1 Ch 19:8, etc.

8 **at the entering**. 1 Ch 19:7.

Rehob. ver. 6. Nu +13:21.

Ishtob. **S#382h**. i.e. *good man*, **S#382h**. ver. 6.

9 **the front**. Jsh 8:21, 22. Jg 20:42, 43.

11 **If**. 1 Ch 19:9-12. Ne 4:20. Lk 22:32. Ro 15:1. Ga 6:2. Ph 1:27, 28.

12 **Be of good**. Jsh +1:9. 1 S 14:6, 12. 17:32. 2 Ch 32:7. Ne 4:14. He 13:6.

play. 1 S 4:9. 1 Ch 19:13. 1 C 16:13.

the Lord. 2 S 16:10, 11. Jg +10:15.

13 **they fled**. 1 K 20:13-21, 28-30. 1 Ch 19:14, 15. 2 Ch 13:5-16.

14 **Abishai**. 1 S +26:6.

15 A.M. 2968. B.C. 1036. An. Ex. Is. 455.

gathered. Ps 2:1. Is 8:9, 10. Mi 4:11, 12. Zc 14:2, 3. Re 19:19-21.

16 **Hadarezer**. i.e. *majesty of help*, **S#1928h**. ver. 19. 2 S 8:3-8. 1 Ch 18:3, 5, 7-10. 19:16, 19.

the river. 2 S 8:3.

Helam. i.e. *fortress*, **S#2431h**.

Shobach. i.e. *enlarging; turning back*, **S#7731h**. ver. 18. *or*, Shophach. i.e. *pouring out*. 1 Ch 19:16.

17 he gathered. 1 Ch 19:17.
18 fled. 2 S 8:4. Ps 18:38. 46:11.
  horsemen. 1 Ch 19:18, footmen.
  Shobach. Jg 4:2, 22. 5:26.
19 servants. Ge 14:1-5. Jsh 11:10. Jg 1:7. 1 K
  20:1. Da 2:37.
  and served. By paying a tribute, so that Ge
  15:18 was now fulfilled (Young).
  feared. 2 S 8:6. 1 Ch 19:19. Ps 18:37, 38.
  48:4, 5. Is 26:11. Re 18:10.

2 SAMUEL 11

1 A.M. 2969. B.C. 1035. An. Ex. Is. 456.
  after the year, etc. Heb. at the return of the
  year. 2 Ch +24:23mg.
  at the time. 1 Ch +20:1.
  David sent. 1 Ch 20:1. Zc 14:3.
  Rabbah. Jsh +13:25.
  David tarried. Ro 12:11. He 6:11, 12. 1 P
  5:8.
2 arose from. 2 S 4:5, 7. Pr 19:15. 24:33, 34.
  Ezk 16:49. Mt 26:40, 41. 1 Th 5:6, 7. 1 P 4:7.
  the roof of. Dt +22:8.
  he saw. Ge 3:6. 6:2. 34:2. Jb 31:1. Ps +101:3.
  119:37. Mt 5:28. 1 J 2:16.
  washing. Heb. *rahats*, Ex +29:4.
  very beautiful. Ge +29:17.
3 sent. Je 5:8. Ho 7:6, 7. Ja 1:14, 15.
  Bath-sheba. *or*, Bath-shua. i.e. *daughter of an*
  oath, **S#1339h**. 2 S 12:24. 1 K 1:11, 15, 16, 28,
  31. 2:13, 18, 19. 1 Ch 3:5, Bath-shua. Ps 51:t.
  Eliam. i.e. *God is gatherer*, **S#463h**. 2 S 23:34.
  or, Ammiel. 1 Ch 3:5.
  Uriah. i.e. *light of Jah*, **S#223h**. 2 S 12:9, 10.
  23:8, 39. 1 K 15:5. 1 Ch 11:41. Ne 3:4, Urijah.
4 sent messengers. Ge 39:7. Jb 31:9-11. Ps
  50:18.
  he lay. Ps 51, title. Ga 5:19, 21. Ja 1:14, 15.
  she was, etc. *or*, and when she had purified
  herself, etc., she returned. Pr 30:20. Is 66:17.
  purified. Le 12:2-5. 15:19-28, etc. 18:19.
5 I am with child. Dt 22:22. Nu +32:23. Pr
  6:34. 7:23.
6 Send me. Ge 4:7. 38:18-23. 1 S 15:30. Jb
  20:12-14. Pr 28:13. Is 29:13. Mt 26:70, 72, 74.
7 how Joab did. Heb. of the peace of Joab. Jg
  +18:15mg.
8 go down. Ps 44:21. Is 29:15. Lk 12:2. He
  4:13.
  wash. Ge +18:4.
  there followed him. Heb. there went out
  after him. Ps 12:2. 55:21.
  a mess. or, gift. A token of respect. Ge 43:34.
  2 Ch 24:6, 9. Est 2:18.
9 Uriah slept. Jb 5:12-14. Pr 21:30.
11 The ark. 2 S 7:2, 6. 1 S 4:4. 14:18.
  my lord. 2 S 20:6. Mt 10:24, 25. Jn 13:14. 1
  C 9:25-27. 2 T 2:3, 4, 12. He 12:1, 2.
  shall I then. Is 22:12-14.

as thou livest. 2 S 14:19. 1 S 1:26. 17:55.
  20:3. 25:26.
  soul. Heb. *nephesh*, Ge +27:31.
  I will not. ver. 1.
12 Tarry. Je 2:22, 23, 37.
13 made him drunk. lit. made him merry. Ge
  9:21. 19:32-35. 43:34. Ex 32:21. SS 5:1. Hab
  2:15.
  with the servants. ver. 9.
14 wrote a letter. 1 K 21:8-10. Ps 19:13. 52:2.
  62:9. Je 9:1-4. 17:9. Mi 7:3-5.
15 Set ye. ver. 17. 1 S 18:17, 21, 25. Ps 51:4, 14.
  Je 20:23.
  hottest. Heb. strong.
  from him. Heb. from after him.
  and die. 2 S 12:9.
16 he assigned. ver. 21. 2 S 3:27. 20:9, 10. 1 S
  22:17-19. 1 K 2:5, 31-34. 21:12-14. 2 K 10:6.
  Pr 29:12. Ho 5:11. Ac 5:29.
17 there fell. 2 S 12:9. Ps 51:14.
21 Abimelech. Jg 9:53.
  Jerubbesheth. i.e. *he will contend with shame*,
  S#3380h, only here. Jg +6:32, Jerubbaal.
  Thy servant. 2 S 3:27, 34. Ps 39:8. Is 14:10.
  Ezk 16:51, 52.
22 the messenger. Pr 25:13.
25 displease thee. Heb. be evil in thine eyes.
  Nu +22:34mg.
  for the sword. Jsh 7:8, 9. 1 S 6:9. Ec 9:1-3,
  11, 12.
  one. Heb. so and such.
  make. 2 S 12:26.
26 she mourned. 2 S 3:31. 14:2. Ge 27:41.
27 fetched her. 2 S 3:2-5. 5:13-16. 12:9. Dt
  22:29.
  But the thing. Ge 38:10. 1 Ch 21:7.
  displeased. Heb. was evil in the eyes of. ver.
  25. Le 20:10. Ps 5:6. 50:18, 19, 21, 22. 51:4,
  5. Pr 24:18mg. He 13:4.

2 SAMUEL 12

1 A.M. 2970. B.C. 1034. An. Ex. Is. 457.
  the Lord. 2 S 7:1-5. 24:11-13. 1 K 13:1. 18:1.
  2 K 1:3.
  unto David. 2 S 11:10-17, 25. 14:14. Is
  57:17, 18.
  he came. Ps 51, title.
  There were. 2 S 14:5-11. Jg 9:7-15. 1 K
  20:35-41. Is 5:1-7. Mt 21:33-45. Lk 15:11, etc.
  16:19, etc.
2 exceeding. ver. 8. 2 S 3:2-5. 5:13-16. 15:16.
  Jb 1:3.
3 one little. 2 S 11:3. Pr 5:18, 19.
  meat. Heb. morsel. Ge 18:5.
  lay in his. Dt 13:6. Mi 7:5.
4 a traveller. Ge 18:2-7. Ja 1:14.
  took the. 2 S 11:3, 4.
5 David's. 2 S 24:14. Ge 38:24. 1 S 25:22. Lk
  6:41, 42. 9:55. Ro +2:1.

As the Lord. 1 K +17:1.
shall surely die. or, is worthy to die. Heb. is a son of death. 1 S +20:31.

6 **restore**. Ex 22:1. Pr 6:31. Lk 19:8.
because. Ja 2:13.

7 **Thou art**. 1 S 13:13. 1 K 18:18. 21:19, 20. Mt 14:4.
I anointed. 2 S 7:8. 1 S 15:17. 16:13.
I delivered. 2 S 22:1, 49. 1 S 18:11, 21. 19:10-15. 23:7, 14, 26-28. Ps 18, title.

8 **thy master's wives**. ver. 11. Ge +4:19. 1 K 2:22.
gave thee. 2 S 2:4. 5:5. 1 S 15:19.
I would. 2 S 7:19. Ps 37:4. 84:11. 86:15. Ro 8:32.

9 **despised**. ver. 10. 2 S 11:4, 14-17. Ge 9:5, 6. Ex 20:13, 14. Nu 15:30, 31. 1 S 15:19, 23. Pr 5:21. 13:13. 19:16. Is 5:24. Am 2:4. He 10:28, 29.
to do evil. 2 Ch 33:6. Ps 51:4. 90:8. 139:1, 2. Je 18:10.
thou hast. 2 S 11:15-27.

10 **the sword**. 2 S 13:28, 29. 18:14, 15, 33. 1 K 2:23-25. Am 7:9. Mt 26:52.
never depart. Pr +17:13.
because. Nu 11:20. 1 S 2:30. Ml 1:6, 7. Mt 6:24. Ro 2:4. 1 Th 4:8.
hast taken. Ge 20:3. Pr 6:32, 33.

11 **I will raise**. 2 S 13:1-14, 28, 29. 15:6, 10. 16:11.
I will take. 2 S 16:21, 22. Dt 28:30. 1 S +18:10. 1 K 1:5. Je +29:11. Ezk 14:9. 20:25, 26. Ho 4:13, 14. Am +3:6.

12 **secretly**. 2 S 11:4, 8, 13, 15. Jb 24:15. Ec 12:14. Mk 4:22. Lk 12:1, 2. 1 C 4:5.

13 **David**. 1 S 15:20, 24. 1 K 13:4. 21:20. 22:8. 2 K 1:9. 2 Ch 16:10. 24:20-22. 25:16. Mt 14:3-5, 10.
I have sinned. 2 S 24:10. Ge 39:9. Le 26:40, 42. Nu +22:34. 1 S 15:24, 25, 30. Ne 9:33. Jb 7:20. 33:27. 40:4. 42:6. Ps 32:3-5. 51:4. Pr 25:12. 28:13. Is 6:5. Je 3:13. 14:7, 20. Da 9:5. Mi 7:9. Lk 15:21. 23:41. Ac 2:37. 1 J 1:8-10.
The Lord. 2 S 24:10. Jb 7:21. Ps 32:1, 2. 51:9. 130:3, 4. Is 6:5-7. 38:17. 43:25. 44:22. La 3:32. Mi 7:18, 19. Zc 3:4. Jn 8:11. He 9:26. 1 J 1:7, 9. 2:1. Re 1:5.
thou. Le 20:10. Nu 35:31-33. Ps 51:16. Ac 13:38, 39. Ro 8:33, 34.
not die. Ge +2:17. Le 20:10. Ps 51:6. Pr 14:12. 16:25. Ezk 18:4. Ac 13:38, 39. Ro 8:33, 34. 1 J +5:16.

14 **by this deed**. Ne 5:9. Ps 74:10. Is 52:5. Ezk 36:20-23. Mt 18:7. Ro 2:24.
given great. 2 Ch +19:2.
occasion. Ps 39:1. Pr +25:26.
blaspheme. Le +24:11.
the child. Ps 89:31-33. 94:12. Pr 3:11, 12. Am 3:2. 1 C 11:32. He 12:6. Re 3:19.

15 **struck the child**. Dt 32:29. 1 S 25:38. 26:10. 2 K 15:5. 2 Ch 13:20. Ps 104:29. Ac 12:23.

16 **besought**. ver. 22. Ps 50:15. Is 26:16. Jl 2:12-14. Jon 3:9.
fasted. Heb. fasted a fast. 1 S 31:13. 1 K 21:27. Mt +6:16. Ac 9:9.
lay all night. 2 S 13:31. Jb 20:12-14. Ps 32:4. 88:1, 2.

17 **the elders**. 2 S 3:35. Jsh +20:4. 1 S 28:23. 1 K 12:6.

18 **seventh day**. Jb 2:13.
vex. Heb. do hurt to. Nu 20:15.

20 **arose**. Jb 1:20. 2:10. Ps 39:9. La 3:39-41.
and washed. Ru 3:3.
anointed. Lk +7:46.
and changed. Ps 51:12, 14, 15.
the house. 2 S 6:17. 7:18. Jb 1:20.

21 **What thing**. 1 C 2:15.

22 **I fasted**. Ps 107:17-20. Is 38:1-3, 5. Jl 1:14. 2:14. Am 5:15. Jon 1:6. 3:9, 10. Ja 4:9, 10.

23 **I shall go**. Ge +37:35. 1 S 28:19. Jb 30:23. Je 31:15-17. Am +9:2. Lk 23:43. 2 C +5:8.
he shall not. Jb 7:8-10. +16:22. Jn 11:25, 26. He +9:27.

24 A.M. 2971. B.C. 1033. An. Ex. Is. 458.
she bare. 2 S 7:12. 1 Ch 3:5. 22:9, 10. 28:5, 6. 29:1. Mt 1:6.
Solomon. in Heb. Shelomoh, as in 2 S 5:14.

25 **Nathan**. ver. 1-14. 2 Ch +9:29.
Jedidiah. that is, Beloved of the Lord. i.e. dearly beloved of Jah, **S#3041h**, only here. Ne 13:26. Mt 3:17. 17:5.

26 **Joab**. 2 S 11:25. 1 Ch 20:1.
Rabbah. Jsh +13:25.

27 **Rabbah**. 2 S 11:1. Dt 3:11. Ezk 21:20.

28 **it be called after my name**. Heb. my name be called upon it. Je +14:9mg. Jn 7:18.

30 **took**. 1 Ch 20:2.
their king's. or, Malcam. 2 K +23:13. Je 49:1mg. Zp 1:5.
in great abundance. Heb. very great. ver. 2. 2 S 8:8. Ps 21:3.

31 **and put them**. 1 Ch 20:3. 2 S 8:2. Ps 21:8, 9. Am 1:3.
pass through. Je 43:11. Mt 25:32.
brickkiln. or, platform. Je 43:9. Mt 25:31-33.

2 SAMUEL 13

1 A.M. 2972. B.C. 1032. An. Ex. Is. 459.
Absalom. **S#53h**. ver. 4, 20. 2 S 3:3. 14:1, 21, 23. 15:1-4. 16:8, 15-23. 17:1. 18:5. 19:1. 20:6. 1 K 1:6. 2:7, 28. 15:2, 10. 1 Ch 3:2. 2 Ch 11:20, 21. Ps 3, title.
a fair sister. 2 S 11:2. Ge +29:17.
Tamar. Ge +38:6.
Amnon. 2 S 3:2, 3.
loved her. ver. 15. Ge 29:18, 20. 34:3. 1 K 11:1.

2 **vexed**. 1 K 21:4. SS 5:8. 2 C 7:10.

Amnon, etc. Heb. it was marvellous, *or* hidden, in the eyes of Amnon. Zc 8:6.

hard. Ge 18:14.

3 **a friend**. Ge 38:1, 20. Jg 14:20. Est 5:10, 14. 6:13. Pr 19:6.

Jonadab. Je +35:6.

Shimeah. S#8093h. ver. 32. 1 S 16:9, Shammah. 1 S 17:13.

subtil man. 2 S 14:2, 19, 20. Ge 3:1. Pr 19:27. Je 4:22. Ro 16:19. 1 C 3:19. Ja 3:15.

4 **Why art**. 1 K 21:7. Est 5:13, 14. Lk 12:32.

lean. Heb. thin. 2 S 3:1.

from day to day. Heb. morning by morning. Ex 16:21. 30:7. 36:3. Le 6:12. 1 Ch 9:27. 23:30. 2 Ch 13:11. Is 28:19. 50:4. Ezk 46:13mg, 14, 15. Zp 3:5mg.

I love. Is 3:9. Je 8:12. Mi 7:3.

my brother. Le 18:9. 20:17.

5 **Lay thee**. 2 S 16:21-23. 17:1-4. Ps 50:18, 19. Pr 19:27. Mk 6:24, 25. Ac 23:15.

6 **make me**. Ge 18:6. Mt 13:33.

cakes. ver. 8.

8 **flour**. *or*, paste. Ex 12:34, 39. Je 7:18. Ho 7:4.

9 **And Amnon**. 2 S 12:12. Ge 45:1. Jg 3:19. Jn 3:20. Ep 5:12.

11 **Come lie**. Ge 39:7, 12.

12 **force me**. Heb. humble me. ver. 14, 22, 32. Ge 34:2. Dt 21:14. 22:29.

no such thing ought. Heb. it ought not so. Le 18:9, 11. 20:17.

folly. Pr 5:22, 23. 7:7. Is +9:17.

13 **shame**. Ge 30:23.

fools. Dt 32:6, 21.

Now therefore. Ge 19:8. Jg 19:24.

14 **forced her**. 2 S 12:11. Dt 22:25-27. Jg 20:5. Est 7:8.

15 **hated her**. Ezk 23:17.

exceedingly. Heb. with great hatred greatly. ver. 36mg.

16 **cause**. Ge 21:11, 25. Je 3:8.

would not hearken. Dt 22:28, 29. 1 S +25:17.

17 **bolt**. Jg 3:23.

18 **a garment**. Ge 37:3, 23, 32. Jg 5:30. Ps 45:13, 14.

robes. Ex 28:4, 31, 34. Ps 45:14. Ezk 16:10, 13.

virgins. Ge 24:16 (S#1330h).

19 **put ashes**. Jsh +7:6.

rent. 2 K +18:37.

laid her hand. Je 2:37.

20 **Amnon**. Heb. Aminon.

but hold. Pr 26:24. Ro 12:19.

regard not. Heb. set not thine heart on. 2 S 18:3mg. Ex 7:23. 1 S +4:20mg.

desolate. Heb. and desolate. Ge 34:2. 46:15. Without society; as in Is 49:8, 19. 54:1. 61:4. La 1:4, 13, 16. 3:11. Ezk 36:4. Da 8:13. 9:18, 26, 27. 12:11.

21 **heard**. Ge 35:22.

he was very wroth. 2 S 3:28, 29. 12:5, 10,

11. Ge 4:5. 34:7. +44:30. 1 S 2:22-25, 29. Ps 101:8. Pr 17:25. 19:13.

22 **spake**. Le 19:17, 18. Pr 25:9. Mt 18:15.

neither good. Ge 24:50. 31:24, 29.

hated. Le 19:17, 18. Pr 10:18. 26:24. 27:4-6. Ec 7:9. Ep 4:26, 31. 1 J 3:15.

23 A.M. 2974. B.C. 1030. An. Ex. Is. 461.

sheepshearers. Ge 38:12, 13. 1 S 25:2, 4, 36. 2 K 3:4. 2 Ch 26:10. Is 53:7.

Baal-hazor. i.e. *possessor of Hazor; having a village*, S#1178h, only here. Jsh 15:25.

invited. 1 K 1:9, 19, 25.

24 **let the king**. 2 S 11:8-15. Ps 12:2. 55:21. Je 41:6, 7.

25 **pressed**. Ge 19:2, 3. Jg 19:7-10. 1 S 28:23. 2 K 5:23. Lk 14:23. 24:29. Ac 16:15.

blessed. 2 S 14:22mg. Ru 2:4.

26 **let my brother**. 2 S 3:27. 11:13-15. 20:9. Ps 55:21.

27 **Absalom**. Pr 26:24-26.

28 **commanded**. 2 S 11:15. Ex 1:16, 17. 1 S 22:17, 18. Ac 5:29.

heart is merry. 2 S 11:13. Ge 9:21. 19:32-35. Jg 19:6, 9, 22. Ru 3:7. 1 S 25:36-38. 1 K 20:16. Est 1:10. Ps 104:15. Ec 9:7. 10:19. Da 5:2-6, 30. Na 1:10. Lk 21:34. Ep 5:18. Ja 5:13.

fear not. Nu 22:16, 17. 1 S 28:10, 13.

have not I. *or*, Will you not, since I have, etc. Jsh 1:9.

valiant. Heb. sons of valor. 2 S +2:7mg.

29 **servants**. 1 S 22:18, 19. 1 K 21:11-13. 2 K 1:9-12. Pr 29:12. Mi 7:3.

gat him up. Heb. rode.

mule. 2 S 18:9. Ge 36:24. Le 19:19. 1 K 1:33. 10:25. 18:5. 2 K 5:17. 1 Ch 12:40. 2 Ch 9:24. Ezr 2:66. Ne 7:68. Ps 32:9. Is 66:20. Ezk 27:14. Zc 14:15.

30 **tidings**. 2 S 4:4, 10. 18:19. Ex 33:4. 1 S 4:19. 11:4, 5. 27:9-11. Ps 112:7.

slain all. 2 S 12:10. Jg 9:5.

31 **arose**. 2 S 12:16.

tare. 2 K +18:37.

all his servants. 2 S 1:11. 3:31.

32 **Jonadab**. ver. 3-5.

Shimeah. 1 S 16:9, Shammah.

appointment. Heb. mouth. Dt +21:5mg.

determined. *or*, settled. Ge 27:41. Ps 7:14. Pr 24:11, 12.

33 **let not my lord**. 2 S 19:19.

34 **Absalom fled**. ver. 38. Ge 4:8-14. Pr 28:17. Je 47:44. Am 5:19.

35 **as thy servant said**. Heb. according to the word of thy servant.

36 **very sore**. Heb. with a great weeping greatly. ver. 15mg. 2 K +20:3mg.

37 **Talmai**. 2 S 3:3. 1 Ch 3:2.

Ammihud. i.e. *my people is honorable; people of majesty*, S#5989h. *or*, Ammihur. Nu 1:10. 2:18. 7:48, 53. 10:22. 34:20, 28. 2 S 13:37. 1 Ch 7:26. 9:4.

38 A.M. 2974-2977. B.C. 1030-1027. An. Ex. Is. 461-464.
Geshur. 2 S +3:3.
three years. 2 S 14:23.

39 **the soul of.** Ge 31:30. Dt 28:32. Ph 2:26.
longed. *or,* was consumed. Ps 84:2. 119:20.
comforted. 2 S 12:23. Ge +24:67.

2 SAMUEL 14

1 A.M. 2977. B.C. 1027. An. Ex. Is. 464.
Joab. 2 S 2:18. 1 Ch 2:16.
toward Absalom. 2 S 13:39. 18:33. 19:2, 4.
Pr 29:26.

2 **to Tekoah.** i.e. *a trumpet blast,* **S#8620h.** 1 Ch +2:24, Tekoa. Ne 3:5, 27.
mourning. 2 S 11:26.
anoint. Lk +7:46.

3 **put the words.** ver. 19. Ex 4:15. Nu 23:5. Dt 18:18. Is 51:16. 59:21. Je 1:9.

4 **fell on her.** 2 S +1:2.
Help. Heb. Save. 2 K 6:26-28. Jb 29:12-14. Lk 18:3-5.

5 **I am indeed.** 2 S 12:1-3. Jg 9:8-15.

6 **and they two.** Ge 4:8. Ex 2:13. Dt 22:26, 27.
none to part. Heb. no deliverer between. Dt 32:39. Jg 8:34. 18:28. Jb 5:4. 10:7. Ps 7:2. 35:10. 50:22. 71:11. Pr 14:25. Is 5:29. 42:22. 43:13. Da 8:4, 7. Ho 5:14. Mi 5:8.

7 **the whole.** Ge 4:14. Nu 35:19. Dt 19:12.
the life. Heb. *nephesh,* Jsh +10:28. Le 17:11. Est 8:11. Mt +2:20. Lk 12:22.
so they. Ge 27:45. Dt 25:6.
quench. 2 S 21:17.
upon the earth. Heb. upon the face of the earth.

8 **I will give.** 2 S 12:5, 6. 16:4. Jb 29:16. Pr 18:13. Is 11:3, 4.

9 **the iniquity.** Ge 27:13. 1 S 25:24. Mt 27:25.
and the king. 2 S 3:28, 29. Nu 35:33. Dt 21:1-9. 1 K 2:33.

11 **let the king.** Ge 14:22. 24:2, 3. 31:50. 1 S 20:42.
thou, etc. Heb. the revenger of blood do not multiply to destroy.
the revengers. Nu 35:19, 27. Dt 19:4-10. Jsh 20:3-6.
As the Lord. 1 S 14:45. 28:10. Je 4:2.
not one hair. 1 K 1:52. Mt 10:30. Lk 21:18. Ac 27:34.

12 **Let thine.** 1 S 25:24.
speak one word. Ge 18:27, 32. 44:18. Je 12:1.
Say on. Ac 26:1.

13 **Wherefore.** 2 S 12:7. 1 K 20:40-42. Lk 7:42-44.
people. 2 S 7:8. Jg 20:2. He 11:25.
in that the king. 2 S 13:37, 38.

14 **we must.** 2 S 11:25. Jb 30:23. 34:15. Ps 90:3, 10. Ec 3:19, 20. 9:5. He 9:27.

as water spilt. 1 S 7:6. Jb 14:7-12, 14. Ps 22:14. 79:3.
neither, etc. *or,* because God hath not taken away his life, he hath also devised means, etc.
person. Heb. *nephesh,* soul, Nu +23:10.
God. Ro +2:11.
he devise. Ex 21:13. Le 26:40. Nu 35:15, 25, 28. Is 50:1, 2. Ml 2:16.

16 **hand.** Ge 20:5.
the inheritance. 2 S 20:19. 1 S 26:19.

17 **comfortable.** Heb. for rest.
as an angel. ver. 20. 2 S 19:27. Ge +17:1. 1 S 29:9. Pr 27:21. 29:5.
to discern. Heb. to hear. 1 K 3:9, 28. Jb 6:30. 1 C 2:14, 15mg. He 5:14.

18 **Hide not.** 1 S 3:17, 18. Je 38:14, 25.

19 **the hand.** Dt +32:36.
of Joab. 1 S +26:6.
As thy soul. Heb. *nephesh,* Ge +27:31. 2 S 11:11. 1 S 1:26. 17:55. 20:3. 25:26. 2 K 2:2.
turn. Nu 20:17. Dt 5:32. 28:14. Jsh 1:7. Pr 4:27.
he put. ver. +3. Ex 4:15. Lk 21:15.

20 **fetch.** 2 S 5:23.
according. ver. 17. 2 S 19:27. Jb 32:21, 22. Pr 26:28. 29:5.
to know. Ge 3:5. Jb 38:16, etc. 1 C 8:1, 2.

21 **I have done.** ver. 11. 1 S 14:39. Mk 6:26.

22 **thanked.** Heb. blessed. 2 S 19:39. Ne 11:2. Jb 29:11. 31:20. Pr 31:28.
I have found. Ge 6:8. Ex 33:16, 17. Ru 2:2. 1 S 20:3.
his. *or,* thy.

23 **Geshur.** 2 S +3:3. 13:37.

24 **let him not.** ver. 28. 2 S 3:13. Ge 43:3. Ex 10:28. Pr 16:15. Re 22:4.

25 **But in all Israel,** etc. Heb. And as Absalom there was not a beautiful man in all Israel to praise greatly. 1 S 9:2. 16:7. Pr 31:30. Mt 23:27.
from the sole. Dt 28:35. Jb 2:7. Is 1:6. Ep 5:27.

26 **when he polled.** 2 S 18:9. Is 3:24. 1 C 11:14. Re 9:8.
two hundred shekels. Ge 23:16. Le 19:36. Ezk 45:9-14.

27 **born.** 2 S 18:18. Jb 18:16-19. Is 14:22. Je 22:30.
one daughter. 1 K 15:22. 2 Ch 11:20.
Tamar. Ge +38:6.
fair countenance. 2 S 11:2. Ge +29:17.

28 A.M. 2977-2979. B.C. 1027-1025. An. Ex. Is. 464-466.
and saw not. ver. 24.

29 **but he would.** ver. 30, 31. Est 1:12. Mt 22:3.

30 **near mine.** Heb. near my place. 2 S 19:43.
go and set. 2 S 13:28, 29. Jg 15:4, 5.
And Absalom's. 1 K 21:9-14. 2 K 9:33. 10:6, 7.

32 **it had been.** Ex 14:12. 16:3. 17:3.

if there. Ge 3:12. 1 S 15:13. Ps 36:2. Pr
28:13. Je 2:22, 23. 8:12. Mt 25:44. Ro 3:19.
33 A.M. 2979. B.C. 1025. An. Ex. Is. 466.
kissed Absalom. Ge +27:27. Ps +2:12.

2 SAMUEL 15

1 A.M. 2980. B.C. 1024.
Absalom. 2 S 12:11. Dt 17:16. 1 S 8:11. 1 K
1:5, 33. 10:26-29. Ps 20:7. Pr 11:2. 16:18.
17:19. Je 22:14-16.
2 **rose up**. Jb 24:14. Pr 4:16. Mt 27:1.
gate. Ge +14:7.
came. Heb. to come. Ex 18:14, 16, 26. 1 K
3:16-28.
3 **thy matters**. Nu 16:3, 13, 14. Ps 12:2. Da
11:21. 2 P 2:10.
there is, etc. *or*, none will hear thee from the
king downward. 2 S 8:15. Ex 20:12. 21:17. Pr
30:11, 17. Ezk 22:7. Mt 15:4. Ac 23:5. 1 P
2:17.
4 **Oh that I.** Jg 9:1-5, 29. Pr 25:6. Lk 14:8-11.
I would do. Pr 24:15, 16. 27:2. 2 P 2:19.
5 **took him**. Ps 10:9, 10. 55:21. Pr 26:25.
and kissed. 2 S 14:33.
6 **stole**. 1 Ch 12:32. Pr +4:23. 11:9. Ro 16:18.
Ep +4:14. 2 P 2:3.
hearts. Ge +31:20mg. Pr +4:23.
7 A.M. 2983. B.C. 1021. An. Ex. Is. 470.
forty years. 2 S 13:38. 1 S 16:1, 13.
let me go. 2 S 13:24-27.
pay. 1 S 16:2. Pr 21:27. Is 58:4. Mt 2:8.
23:14.
vow. Le +23:38.
8 **thy servant**. Nu 30:2. 1 S 16:2. Pr 21:27.
vowed. Le +23:38.
Geshur. 2 S +3:3.
If. Ge +28:20.
I will serve. Jsh 24:15. Is 28:15. Je 9:3-5.
42:20.
10 **spies**. 2 S 13:28. 14:30.
reigneth. 2 S 19:10. Jb 20:5, etc. Ps 73:18,
19.
Hebron. 2 S 2:1, 11. 3:2, 3. 5:5. 1 Ch 11:3.
12:23, 38.
11 **called**. 1 S 9:13. 16:3-5.
their simplicity. Ge 20:5. 1 S 22:15. Pr
14:15. 22:3. Mt 10:16. Ro 16:18, 19.
knew not. 1 S 20:39. Ec 9:5.
12 **Ahithophel**. i.e. *brother of folly*, S#302h. ver.
31, 34. 2 S 16:15, 20-23. 17:1, 6, 7, 14, 15,
21, 23. 23:34. 1 Ch 27:33, 34.
Gilonite. S#1526h. 2 S 23:34.
David's. Ps 41:9. 55:12-14. Mi 7:5, 6. Jn
13:18.
Giloh. Jsh 15:51.
while he offered. Nu 23:1, 14, 30. 1 S 16:3,
5. 1 K 21:9, 12. Ps 50:16-21. Pr 21:27. Is 1:10-
16. T 1:16.
the people. Ps 3:1, 2. 43:1, 2.

13 **The hearts**. ver. 6. 2 S 3:36. Jg 9:3. Ps 62:9.
Mt 21:9. 27:22.
14 **Arise**. 2 S 19:9. 1 S 27:1. Ps 3, title.
bring. Heb. thrust. 2 S 14:14. Ezk 46:18. Mt
11:12mg. Lk 10:15.
and smite. 2 S 23:16, 17. Ps 51:18. 55:3-11.
137:5, 6.
15 **Behold**. Pr 18:24. Lk 22:28, 29. Jn 6:66-69.
15:14.
are ready. Jsh 1:16. 2 Ch 34:16. Mt 8:19. Lk
22:23. Jn 2:5. Re 14:4.
appoint. Heb. choose.
16 **the king**. Ps 3, title.
after him. Heb. at his feet. Jg 4:10. 1 S 25:27,
42mg.
ten women. 2 S 12:11. 16:21, 22. 20:3. Ro
12:2.
17 **went forth**. Ps 3, title, 2. 66:12. Ec 10:7.
18 **Cherethites**. 2 S +8:18.
Gittites. ver. 19-22. 2 S +6:10. Jsh +13:3. 1 S
27:3.
19 **Ittai**. i.e. *living being*, S#863h. ver. 21, 22. 2 S
18:2, 5, 12. 23:29. Ru 1:11-13. 1 Ch 11:31,
Ithai.
20 **go up and down**. Heb. wander in going. Ps
56:8. 59:15. Am 8:12. Mt 8:19, 20. He 11:37,
38.
seeing. 1 S 23:13.
mercy. 2 S 2:6. Ps 25:10. 57:3. 61:7. 85:10.
89:14. Pr 14:22. Jn 1:17. 2 T 1:16-18.
21 **As the Lord**. 1 K +17:1.
surely. Ru 1:16, 17. Pr 17:17. 18:24. Mk
8:19, 20. Jn 6:66-69. Ac 11:23. 21:13. 2 C 7:3.
there also. Jn 12:26.
22 **and all the little**. Ge 33:1, 2. Nu +16:27.
23 **all**. Ge +41:57.
the country. Ge +6:11.
wept. Ro 12:15.
the brook Kidron. i.e. *gloomy, full of
darkness*, S#6939h. 1 K 2:37. 15:13. 2 K 23:4, 6,
12. 2 Ch 15:16. 29:16. 30:14. Je 31:40. Jn
18:1, Cedron.
the wilderness. 2 S 16:2. Mt 3:1, 3. Lk 1:80.
24 **Zadok**. ver. 27, 35. 2 S +8:17.
bearing. 2 S 6:13. Nu 4:15. 7:9. Jsh 3:3, 6, 15-
17. 4:16-18. 6:4, 6. 1 S 4:3-5, 11. 1 Ch 15:2.
25 **Carry back**. 2 S 12:10, 11. 1 S 4:3-11. Je 7:4.
if I shall. 2 S 6:22.
he will bring. Ps 26:8. 27:4, 5. 42:1, 2. 43:3,
4. 62:5. 63:1, 2. 84:1-3, 10. 122:1, 9. Is 38:22.
habitation. 2 S 6:17. 7:2.
26 **I have no**. 2 S 22:20. Nu 14:8. 1 K 10:9. 2 Ch
9:8. Ps 18:19. Is 42:1. 62:4. Je 22:28. 32:41.
Ml 1:10.
let him. Jg +10:15. Ac +21:14.
27 **a seer**. 2 S 24:11. 1 S 9:9. 1 Ch 25:5.
return. ver. 34, 36. 2 S 17:17.
28 **I will tarry**. ver. 23. 2 S 16:2. 17:1, 16.
in the plain. Heb. arabah. Dt +11:30. Jsh
5:10.

30 **the ascent**. Zc 14:4. Lk 19:29, 37. 21:37. 22:39. Ac 1:12.
mount Olivet. i.e. *olive yard*, **S#2132h**. Mt +21:1.
and wept as he went up. Heb. going up and weeping. Ps 43:1, 2, 5.
his head covered. Est +6:12.
barefoot. Is 20:2, 4. Ezk 24:17, 23.
covered. Est 7:8.
weeping. Ps 51:17. Mt +5:4. 1 C 12:26. 1 P 5:6.

31 **Ahithophel**. ver. 12. Ps 3:1, 2. 37:12, 13. 41:9. 55:12, 14, 21, 23. Mt 26:14, 15. Jn 13:18.
O Lord. Ps 55:15-17. 109:3, 4.
turn the counsel. 2 S 16:23. Je +19:7. Ja 3:15.

32 **the top**. ver. 30. 1 K 11:7. Lk 19:29. Jn 8:1.
he worshipped. 1 K 8:44, 45. Jb 1:20, 21. Ps 3:3-5, 7. 4:1-3. 50:15. 91:15.
Hushai. i.e. *hastening of the Lord*, **S#2365h**. ver. 37. 2 S 16:16-18. 17:5-8, 14, 15. 1 K 4:16. 1 Ch 27:33.
Archite. **S#757h**. 2 S 16:16. 17:5, 14. Jsh 16:2. 1 Ch 27:33.
coat rent. 2 K +18:37.
earth. Jsh +7:6.

33 **then thou**. 2 S 19:35.

34 **return**. ver. 20. Jsh 8:2. Mt 10:6.
as I have been. 2 S 16:16-19.
mayest. 2 S 17:5-14.

35 **thou shalt tell**. 2 S 17:15, 16.

36 **their two sons**. ver. 27. 2 S 17:17. 18:19, etc.

37 **friend**. 2 S 16:16. 1 Ch 27:33.
Absalom. 2 S 16:15.

2 SAMUEL 16

1 **little past**. 2 S 15:30, 32.
Ziba. 2 S 9:2, 9-12.
with a couple. 2 S 17:27-29. 19:32. 1 S 17:17, 18.
raisins. 1 S 25:18. 30:12. 1 Ch 12:40. Pr 18:16. 29:4, 5.
summer. Is +16:9.
a bottle. 1 S 1:24. 10:3. 16:20. Je +13:12.
wine. 1 S 1:24. 10:3. 25:18.

2 **What meanest**. Ge 21:29. 33:8. Ezk 37:18.
The asses. 2 S 15:1. 19:26. Jg 5:10. 10:4.
for the young. 1 S 25:27.
that such. 2 S 15:23. 17:29. Jg 8:4, 5. 1 S 14:28. Pr 17:23. 31:6, 7.

3 **where is**. 2 S 9:9, 10. Ps 88:18. Mi 7:5.
Today. 2 S 19:24-30. Ex 20:16. Dt 19:18, 19. *Ps 15:3. 101:5.* Pr 1:19. 21:28. 1 T 6:9, 10. Ju 11.

4 **Behold**. 2 S 14:10, 11. Ex 23:8. Dt 19:15. Pr 18:13, 17. 19:2.
I humbly beseech thee. Heb. I do obeisance. 2 S 14:4, 22.

5 **Bahurim**. ver. 14. 2 S +3:16. Jsh 21:18. 1 Ch 6:60.
whose name. 2 S 19:16, etc. 1 K 2:8, 9, 36-44, etc.
Shimei. i.e. *famous, heard of*, **S#8096h**. ver. 7, 13. Ex 6:17. Nu 3:18. 2 S 19:16, 18, 21, 23. 1 K 1:8. 2:8, 36, 38-42, 44. 4:18. 1 Ch 3:19. 4:26, 27. 5:4. 6:17, 29, 42. 8:21. 23:7, 9, 10. 25:17. 27:27. 2 Ch 29:14. 31:12, 13. Ezr 10:23, 33, 38. Est 2:5. Zc 12:13.
he came, etc. *or*, he still came forth and cursed.
cursed. Ex 22:28. 1 S 17:43. Ps 69:26. 109:16-19, 28. Pr 26:2. Ec 10:20. Is 8:21. Mt 5:11, 12.

7 **bloody man**. Heb. man of blood. 2 S 3:37. 11:15-17. 12:9. Ps 5:6. 26:9mg. 51:14. 55:23mg.
man of Belial. 1 S +30:22mg.

8 **returned**. Jg 9:24, 56, 57. 1 K 2:32, 33. Ac 28:4, 5. Re 16:6.
the blood. 2 S 1:16. 3:28, 29. 4:8-12. Ps 3:2. 4:2.
thou, etc. *or*, thee in thy evil.

9 **Abishai**. 1 S +26:6.
dead dog. 2 S 3:8. 9:8. 1 S 24:14.
curse. Ex +22:28. Ac 23:5. 1 P 2:17.
let me go. 1 S 26:6-11. Jb 31:30, 31. Je 40:13-16.

10 **What have**. 2 S 3:39. Jg +11:12. 1 K 2:5. Mt 16:23. Lk 9:54-56. 1 P 2:23.
so let him. Ge 50:20. 1 K 22:21-23. 2 K 18:25. La 3:38, 39. Jn 18:11.
Who shall. 1 S +18:10. Jb 2:10. 9:12. Ec 8:4. Da 4:35. Am +3:6. Ro 9:20. Ep +1:11.

11 **Behold**. 2 S 12:11, 12.
came forth. 2 S 7:12. Ge 15:4.
seeketh. 2 S 17:1-4. 2 K 19:37. 2 Ch 32:21. Mt 10:21.
life. Heb. *nephesh*, soul, Ge +44:30.
the Lord. Is 10:5-7. Ezk 14:9. 20:25.

12 **the Lord**. Ge +29:32.
affliction. *or*, tears. Heb. eye. Lk +6:21.
requite. Dt 23:5. Is 27:7. Mt 5:11, 12. Ro 8:28. 2 C 4:17. 2 Th 1:7. He 12:10. 1 P 4:12-19.

13 **cursed**. ver. 5, 6. Ps 109:17, 18, 26-28.
cast dust. Heb. dusted him with dust. Ac 22:23.

14 **there**. ver. 5. Ps 3:5. 4:8.

15 **Absalom**. 2 S 15:37.

16 **David's friend**. 2 S 15:37.
God save the king. Heb. Let the king live. 1 S 10:24. 1 K 1:25, 34. 2 K 11:12. Pr 27:14. Da 2:4. 5:10. 6:6, 21. Mt 21:9.

17 **Is this thy**. Dt 32:6.
why wentest. 2 S 15:32-37. 19:25. Pr 17:17. 18:24.

18 **whom the Lord**. 2 S 5:1-3. 1 S 16:13.

19 **should I not serve**. 2 S 15:34. 1 S 28:2. 29:8. Ps 55:21. Ga 2:13.

20 Give counsel. Ex 1:10. Ps 2:2. 37:12, 13. Pr +21:30. Is 8:10. 29:15. Mt 27:1. Ac 4:23-28.

21 Go in. Ge 6:4. 38:16.
  unto thy. 2 S 12:11. Le 18:8. 20:11. 1 K 2:17, 22. 1 Ch +2:48. 1 C 5:1.
  abhorred. Ge 34:30. 1 S 13:4.
  thy father. Ge 49:3, 4.
  then shall. 1 S 27:12.
  the hands. 2 S 2:7. Zc 8:13.

22 the top. Dt +22:8.
  went in. 2 S 12:11, 12. Nu 25:6. Is 3:9. Je 3:3. 8:12. Ezk 24:7. Ph 3:19.
  concubines. 1 Ch +2:48.
  in the sight. 2 S 12:11, 12. Zc 2:8.
  of all. Ex +9:6.

23 the counsel. 1 Ch 27:33.
  as if. Nu 27:21. 1 S 30:8. Ps 28:2. 1 P 4:11.
  oracle of God. Heb. word of God. Ps 19:7.
  all the counsel. 2 S 17:14, 23. Jb 28:28. Je 4:22. +19:7. Mt 11:25. Lk 16:8. Ro 1:22. Ja 3:13-18.
  both. 2 S 15:12. Ec 10:1.

2 SAMUEL 17

1 I will arise. Pr 1:16. 4:16. Is 59:7, 8.
  this night. Ps 3:3-5. 4:8. 109:2-4.

2 weary. 2 S 16:14. Dt 25:18.
  I will smite. 1 K 22:31. Zc 13:7. Mt 21:38. 26:31. Jn 7:7. 11:50. 18:4-8.

3 I will bring. 2 S 3:21.
  shall be. Is 48:22. 57:21. 1 Th 5:3.

4 the saying. 1 S 18:20, 21. 23:21. Est 5:14. Ro 1:32.
  pleased Absalom well. Heb. was right in the eyes of Absalom. Jsh +22:30mg.

5 Hushai. 2 S 15:32-37. 16:16-19.
  he saith. Heb. is in his mouth. Dt +21:5mg.

6 saying. Heb. word.

7 given. Heb. counselled.
  not good. Pr 31:8.

8 mighty men. 2 S 15:18. 21:18-22. 23:8, 9, 16, 18, 20-22. Ge 6:4. 10:8, 9. Dt 10:17. Jsh 1:14. 1 S 16:18. 17:34-36, 50. 1 Ch 11:25-47. He 11:32-34.
  chafed in their minds. Heb. bitter of soul. Heb. *nephesh*, Ge +23:8. 1 S +30:6mg.
  as a bear. 2 K 2:24. Pr 17:12. 28:15. Da 7:5. Ho 13:8.
  thy father is. Ex 15:3. 1 S 23:23.

9 he is hid. Jg 20:33. 1 S 22:1. 24:3.
  some. Jsh 7:5. 8:6. Jg 20:32. 1 S 14:14, 15.
  pit. Heb. *pachath*, **S#6354h**. 2 S 18:17. Is 24:17, 18. Je 48:28, 43, 44. La 3:47.
  overthrown. Heb. fallen.

10 valiant. or, son of valor. 2 S +2:7mg.
  heart. 2 S 1:23. 23:20. Ge 49:9. Nu 24:8, 9. Pr 28:1.
  utterly melt. Ex +15:15.

thy father. 1 S 18:17. He 11:34.
  and they which. SS 3:7.

11 all Israel. 2 S 24:2.
  from Dan to. Jg +20:1.
  as the sand. Ge +22:17. 1 K 20:10.
  thou go. Heb. thy face, *or* presence, go, etc.
  in thine. 2 S 12:28. Ps 7:15, 16. 9:16.

12 in some place. 1 S 23:23.
  we will. Ps 12:2. 2 P 2:18.
  light upon. 1 K 20:10. 2 K 18:23. 19:24. Is 10:13, 14. Ob 3.
  dew. Dt 32:2. Ps 133:3. Pr 19:12. Is 18:4. Ho 14:5. Mi 5:7.

13 bring ropes. 2 S 8:2. Jsh 2:15. 1 K 20:31, 32. Est 1:8. Jb 41:1.
  draw. or, tear. Je 15:3. 22:19. 49:20. 50:45.
  river. or, brook *or* valley. Ge 26:17, 19. Nu +13:23mg.
  small stone. Am 9:9. Mt 24:2.

14 the Lord. Ge 32:28. Ex 9:16. Dt 2:30. 2 Ch 25:16, 20.
  appointed. Heb. commanded. Ps 7:6. 33:9, 10. La 3:37. Am 9:3.
  to defeat. 2 S 15:31, 34. 16:23. Pr 19:21. Je +19:7.
  good counsel. Lk 16:8.
  the Lord. Am +3:6.
  bring evil. Is +45:7.

15 Zadok. 2 S +8:17. 15:35.

16 Lodge. 2 S 15:28.
  but speedily. ver. 21, 22. 2 S 15:14, 28. 1 S 20:38. Ps 55:8. Pr 6:4, 5. Mt 24:16-18.
  be swallowed. Ps +35:25.

17 Jonathan. 2 S 15:27, 36.
  stayed. Jsh 2:4, etc.
  En-rogel. Jsh +15:7.
  wench. or, the maid servant.

18 Bahurim. 2 S +3:16.
  well. Heb. *be-er*, Ge +16:14.
  court. Ge 25:16. 1 S 6:26.

19 spread a covering. Nu 4:6, 7, etc. Jsh 2:4-6, etc. Ps 105:39. Is 22:8.
  well's. Heb. *be-er*, Ge +16:14.
  spread. Nu 11:32. Jb 12:23. Ps 88:9. Je 8:9.
  ground corn. Pr 27:22.
  the thing. Ex 1:19.

20 They be gone. 2 S 15:34. Ex 1:19. Jsh 2:4, 5. 1 S 19:14-17. 21:2. 27:11, 12.
  when they had sought. Jsh 2:22, 23.

21 well. Heb. *be-er*, Ge +16:14.
  Arise. ver. 15, 16.
  thus hath Ahithophel. ver. 1-3.

22 and they passed. ver. 24. Pr 27:12. Mt 10:16.
  there lacked. Nu 31:49. Jn 18:9.

23 saw. Pr 16:18. 19:3.
  followed. Heb. done.
  his city. 2 S 15:12.
  put his household in order. Heb. gave

charge concerning his house. 2 K 20:1mg. Is 38:1mg.

and hanged himself. 2 S 15:31. 1 S 31:4, 5. 1 K 16:18. +19:4. Jb 31:3. Ps 5:10. 35:8. 37:7, 35, 36. 55:23. Mt 27:5. Ac 1:18. or, strangled. Na 2:12.

buried. 2 S 2:32. Jg 8:32.

sepulchre. Heb. *qeber*, Ge +23:4.

24 Mahanaim. Ge +32:2.
all. Ex +9:6.

25 Amasa. i.e. *a load, burden; burden bearer*, **S#6021h**. 2 S 19:13. 20:4, 5, 8, 9, 10, 12. 1 K 2:5, 32. 1 Ch 2:17. 2 Ch 28:12.
Ithra. i.e. *super-abundance*, **S#3501h**. 1 K 2:5, Jether. 1 Ch 2:16, 17, Jether the Ishmaelite.
Abigail. Heb. Abigal. i.e. *father of joy*.
Nahash. or, Jesse. 1 S +11:1. 1 Ch 2:13, 16.
Zeruiah. 1 Ch +2:16.

26 land of Gilead. Ge +37:25.

27 Shobi. i.e. *one leading away captive*, **S#7629h**.
the son of Nahash. 2 S 10:1, 2. 1 S 11:1.
Rabbah. Jsh +13:25.
Machir. 2 S 9:4. Ge +50:23.
Ammiel. 1 Ch +3:5.
Lo-debar. i.e. *barren*, **S#3810h**. 2 S 9:4, 5.
Barzillai. 2 S 19:31, 32. +21:8. 1 K 2:7. Ezr 2:61.
Rogelim. i.e. *footmen; treaders; fullers*, **S#7274h**. 2 S 19:31.

28 beds. 2 S 16:1, 2. Ge 49:4. 1 S 25:18. Is 32:8.
basons. or, cups. Ex 12:22.
earthen vessels. Ps 2:9. Is 29:16. 30:14. Je 19:1, 11.
wheat. Ge 30:14.
barley. Ex 9:31.
flour. Ge 18:6.
parched. or, roasted. Le 23:14.
beans. Ezk 4:9.
lentiles. Ge 25:34.

29 honey. Ge 43:11.
butter. Ge 18:8.
sheep. Ge 4:2, 4.
cheese of kine. 1 S 17:18.
for David. Lk 8:3. Ph 4:15-19.
to eat. 2 S 17:2. Ps 34:8-10. 84:11.
The people. Jg 8:4-6. Ec 11:1, 2. Is 21:14. 58:7.
in the wilderness. 2 S 16:2, 14. Ps 107:4-6.

2 SAMUEL 18

1 numbered. Ex 17:9. Jsh 8:10. 1 S +11:8.
captains of thousands. Jsh +22:21.

2 a third part. Jg 7:16, 19. 9:43.
the hand of Joab. 2 S 10:7-10.
Ittai. 2 S 15:19-22.
I will surely. 2 S 17:11. Ps 3:6. 27:1-3. 118:6-8.

3 Thou shalt. 2 S 21:17.
if we flee. 2 S 17:2. 1 K 22:31. Zc 13:7.

care for us. Heb. set their heart on us. 2 S 13:20.
worth, etc. Heb. as ten thousand of us. SS 5:10. La 4:20.
succor. Heb. be to succor. 2 S 10:11. 11:1. Ex 17:10-12.

4 by the gate. ver. 24. Is 28:6.
by hundreds. ver. 1. 1 S 29:2.

5 Deal gently. 2 S 16:11. 17:1-4, 14. Dt 21:18-21. Ps 103:13. Lk 23:34.
all the people. ver. 12.

6 wood of Ephraim. Jsh 17:15, 18. Jg 12:4-6.

7 the people. 2 S 2:17. 15:6. 19:41-43.
a great. Pr 11:21. 24:21, 22.
twenty thousand men. 2 S 2:26, 31. 2 Ch 13:16, 17. 28:6.

8 the wood. Ex 15:10. Jsh 10:11. Jg 5:20, 21. 1 K 20:30. Ps 3:7. 43:1.
devoured more. Heb. multiplied to devour. lit. eat. Ge 31:15. Nu 26:10. 2 Ch 7:13.

9 his head. ver. 14. 2 S 14:26. 17:23. Mt 27:5.
taken up. Dt 21:23. 27:16, 20. Jb 18:8-10. 31:3. Ps 63:9, 10. Pr 20:20. 30:17. Je 48:44. Mk 7:10. Ga 3:13.

12 receive, etc. Heb. weigh upon mine hand.
in our hearing. ver. 5.
Beware, etc. Heb. Beware, whosoever *ye be*, of the, etc.

13 wrought. 2 S 1:15, 16. 4:10-12.
life. Heb. *nephesh*, soul, Ge +44:30.
for there is no. 2 S 14:19, 20. He 4:13.

14 with thee. Heb. before thee.
thrust them. ver. 5. Jg 4:21. 5:26, 31. Ps 45:5. 1 Th 5:3.
midst. Heb. heart. Dt 4:11. Ps 46:2. Jon 2:3. Mt 12:40.

15 and slew. Ps 109:6, 12.

16 blew the trumpet. 2 S 2:28. 20:22. Nu 10:2-10. 1 C 14:8.

17 heap. properly a "round heap," as in Ge 31:46-52. Jsh 7:26. 8:29. 10:27. Pr 10:7. Je 22:18, 19.
fled. 2 S 19:8. 20:22. 1 S 4:10. 13:2. 1 K 8:66. 2 K 8:21. 13:5.
tent. 2 S 19:8. 1 S 4:10.

18 reared up. 1 S 15:12.
pillar. Ge 28:18. 35:14, 20.
the king's. Ge 14:17. Jl 3:2.
I have no son. 2 S 14:27. Jb 18:16, 17. Ps 109:13. Je 22:30.
he called. Ge 11:4. 1 S 15:12. Ps 49:11. Da 4:30.
unto this day. Jsh +4:9.
Absalom's place. or, monument. lit. "hand," as in 1 S 15:12. Ge 11:9. Is 56:5. Ac 1:18, 19.

19 Ahimaaz. ver. 23, 27-29. 1 S +14:50.
avenged him. Heb. judged him from the hand, etc. Ps 7:6, 8, 9. 9:4, 16. 10:14, 18. Ro 12:19.

20 **bear tidings**. Heb. be a man of tidings. 2 S 17:16-21.
because. ver. 5, 27, 29, 33.
22 **howsoever**. Heb. be what may. ver. 23.
ready. *or*, convenient. Ro 1:15, 28. Ep 5:4.
23 **overran Cushi**. Jn 20:4.
24 **between**. ver. 4. 1 S 4:13.
the watchman. 2 K 9:17-20. Is 21:6-9, 11, 12. Ezk 33:2-7.
lifted. Ge +22:13.
26 **porter**. 1 Ch +23:5.
27 **Methinketh**. Heb. I see. 2 K 9:20.
He is a good. 1 K 1:42. Pr 25:13, 25. Is 52:7. Ro 10:15.
28 **All is well**. *or*, Peace be to thee. Heb. Peace. Je +29:7.
he fell down upon his face. 2 S 1:2. 14:4. 1 S 25:6.
Blessed. 2 S 22:47. Ge 14:20. 24:27. 2 Ch 20:26. Ps 115:1. 124:6. 144:1, 2. Re 19:1-3.
delivered up. Heb. shut up. 1 S 17:46. 24:18. 26:8. Ps 31:8.
29 **Is the young man Absalom safe?** Heb. is there peace to, etc.? ver. 32. 2 S 20:9.
I saw a great. ver. 19, 20, 22.
31 **Tidings**. Heb. Tidings is brought.
the Lord. ver. 19, 28. 2 S 22:48, 49. Dt 32:35, 36. Jg 5:31. Ps 18:47, 48. 58:10. 94:1-4. 124:2, 3. Lk 18:7, 8.
32 **The enemies**. Jg 5:31. Ps 68:1, 2. Da 4:19.
33 **much moved**. or, troubled *or* angry. 2 S 7:10. 22:8. Ge 45:24.
the chamber over the gate. Jg 3:20, 23, 24, 25. 1 K 17:19, 23. 2 K 1:2. 4:10, 11. 23:12. 1 Ch 28:11.
O my son. 2 S 19:4.
would God. 2 S 12:10-23. Ex +16:3. Ps 103:13. Pr 10:1. 17:25. Zc 12:10. Ja 5:17.

2 SAMUEL 19

1 **it was told**. 2 S 18:5, 12, 14, 20, 33. Pr 17:25.
2 **victory**. Heb. salvation, *or*, deliverance. 2 S 23:10, 12. 1 S 11:9, 13. 1 Ch 11:14.
turned. Pr 16:15. 19:12.
3 **into the city**. ver. 32. 2 S 17:24.
steal. Ge 31:27.
4 **covered**. Est +6:12. Ps 69:7.
O my son. 2 S 18:33.
5 **saved**. Ne 9:27. Ps 3:8. 18:47, 48.
life. Heb. *nephesh*, soul, Ge +44:30.
lives. Heb. *nephesh*, Ge +44:30.
6 **In that**, etc. Heb. By loving, etc. Jn 3:16. Ro 5:8, 10. 8:32.
thou regardest, etc. Heb. princes or servants *are* not to thee. 1 C 1:28.
then it had. 2 S 3:24, 25. Jb 34:18. Pr 19:9, 10. Ac 23:5.
7 **arise**. Pr +19:15.

comfortably unto thy. Heb. to the heart of thy. Ge +34:3mg.
there. Pr 14:28.
all the evil. Ps 71:4-6, 9-11, 18-20. 129:1, 2. Mt 27:64.
8 **sat in the gate**. 2 S 15:2. 18:6-8. Ge +14:7. 1 S +25:17. 2 K +5:13. 7:1. Je 38:7. 39:3.
for Israel. ver. 3. 2 S 18:6-8. 1 K 22:36. 2 K 14:12.
9 **strife**. Ge 3:12, 13. Ex 32:24. Ja 3:14-16.
The king. 2 S 8:10. 1 S 17:50. 18:5-7, 25. 19:5.
he is fled. 2 S 15:14.
10 **whom**. 2 S 15:12, 13. Ho 8:4.
is dead. 2 S 18:14.
speak ye not a word. Heb. are ye silent? Jg +16:2mg. 18:9. 1 K 20:2mg.
11 **sent**. 2 S 15:29, 35, 36. 1 K 2:25, 26, 35.
Speak. 2 C 5:20.
Why are. Mt 5:16. 2 Th 3:9.
12 **my bones**. Ge +29:14.
13 **Amasa**. 2 S 17:25. 1 Ch 2:16, 17. 12:18.
God. 2 S 3:39. Ru 1:17. 1 K 19:2.
room of Joab. ver. 5-7. 1 S +26:6.
14 **even**. Jg 20:1. Ps 110:2, 3. Je 32:39. Ezk 11:19. Ac 4:32.
15 **Gilgal**. Jsh +4:19.
16 **Shimei**. 2 S +16:5.
hasted. Jb 2:4. Pr 6:4, 5. Mt 5:25.
17 **Ziba**. ver. 26, 27. 2 S 9:2, 10. 16:1-4.
18 **what he thought good**. Heb. the good in his eyes. ver. 27, 37, 38. 2 S 24:22. Jsh +22:30mg.
fell down. Ps 66:3. 81:15. Re 3:9.
19 **And said**. Ec 10:4.
Let not. 1 S 22:15. Ps 32:2. Ro 4:6-8. 2 C 5:19.
remember. Ps 79:8. Is 43:25. Je 31:34.
did perversely. 2 S 16:5-9, etc. Ex 10:16, 17. 1 S 26:21. Mt 27:4.
take it. 2 S 13:20, 33. 1 S 25:25.
20 **I am come**. Ps 78:34-37. Je 22:23. Ho 5:15.
Joseph. ver. 9. 2 S 16:5. 19:16. Ge 46:19. 48:14, 20. 1 K 12:20, 25. Ho 4:15-17. 5:3. Am +5:6.
21 **Shall not**. Ex 22:28. 1 K 21:10, 11. Ec 10:20.
cursed. 2 S 16:5, 7, 9, 13. 1 S 24:6. 26:9.
22 **What have**. Jg +11:12.
shall there any man. 1 S 11:13. 25:32, 33. 26:8. 2 S +3:39. Is 16:5. Lk 9:54-56.
23 **Thou shalt**. 1 K 2:8, 9, 37, 46.
sware. 1 S 28:10. 30:15. He 6:16.
24 **Mephibosheth**. 2 S 9:3, 6. 16:3.
the son. *or*, grandson. 1 K +15:10.
dressed his feet. 2 S 15:30. Dt 21:12. Is 15:2. Je 41:5. Mt 6:16. Ro 12:15. He 13:3.
25 **Wherefore**. 2 S 16:17.
26 **I will saddle**. 2 S 16:2, 3.
thy servant. 2 S 4:4.

27 **slandered**. 2 S 16:3. Ex 20:16. Ep +4:31.
as an angel. 2 S 14:17, 20. 1 S 29:9.
28 **father's**. 1 K +15:10mg.
were. Ge 32:10.
dead men. Heb. men of death. 1 S
+20:31mg.
didst thou. 2 S 9:7, 8, 10, 13.
to cry. 2 K 8:3.
29 **Why speakest**. Jb 19:16, 17. Pr 18:13. Ac
18:15.
Thou. 2 S 16:4. Dt 19:17-19. Ps 82:2. 101:5.
30 **Yea**. 2 S 1:26. Ac 20:24. Ph 1:20.
31 **Barzillai came**. 1 K 2:7. Ezr 2:61. Ne 7:63.
32 **fourscore**. Ge 5:27. 9:29. 25:7. 47:28. 50:26.
Dt 34:7. Ps 90:3-10. Pr 16:31.
provided. 2 S 17:27. 1 P 4:9.
for he was. 1 S 25:2. Jb 1:3.
33 **Come thou**. 2 S 9:11. Mt 25:34-40. Lk
22:28-30. 2 Th 1:7.
34 **How long have I to live?** Heb. How many
days *are* the years of my life? Ge +29:14. Ge
47:8mg, 9. Jb 14:14. Ps 39:5, 6. 1 C 7:29. Ja
4:14.
35 **can I discern**. Jb 6:30. 12:11. He 5:14. 1 P
2:3.
taste. Ec 12:1-5.
I hear. Ezr 2:65. Ne 7:67. Ec 2:8. 12:4.
a burden. 2 S 13:25. 15:33.
36 **the king**. Lk 6:38.
37 **I may die**. Ge 48:21. Jsh 23:14. Lk 2:29, 30.
2 T 4:6. 2 P 1:14.
by the grave. Heb. *qeber*, Ge +23:4. 47:30.
49:29-31. 50:13. 1 K 13:22.
Chimham. i.e. *a longing*. ver. 38. It is spelled
Chimhan in ver. 40. 1 K 2:7. Je 41:17.
38 **require**. Heb. choose.
39 **kissed Barzillai**. Ge +27:27.
blessed. 2 S 6:18, 20. 13:25. Ge 14:19. 28:3.
47:7, 10. Lk 2:34.
returned. Ge 31:55. Nu 24:25.
1 S 24:22.
40 **Chimham**. Heb. Chimhan. i.e. *longing, pining*,
S#3643h. ver. 37, 38. Je 41:17.
all the people. ver. 11-15. Ge 49:10. Mt
21:9. Mk 11:9, 10. 15:14.
41 **Why have**. Jg 8:1. 12:1. Jn 7:5, 6.
stolen. ver. 3. Ge 31:26, 27.
42 **Because**. ver. 12. 2 S 5:1. 1 Ch 2:3-17.
43 **We have**. 2 S 20:1, 2, 6. 1 K 12:16.
ten parts. 2 S 5:1. Ge 47:24. Pr 13:10.
despise us. Heb. set us at light. Ge 16:4, 5. Is
9:1. 23:9. Ezk 22:7.
our advice. ver. 9, 14. Ga 5:20, 26.
Ph +2:3.
the words. Jg 8:1. 9:23. 12:1-6. Pr 15:1.
17:14. 18:19. Ro 12:21. Ga 5:15, 20. Ja 1:20.
3:2-10, 14-16. 4:1-5.
Judah. Jg 8:1. 12:1. Is 9:21. 11:13.
were fiercer. or, harder. Ge 49:7. Dt 1:17.
15:18. 1 S 5:7.

2 SAMUEL 20

1 **And there**. 2 S 19:41-43. Ps 34:19.
happened. 2 S +1:6.
a man of Belial. 1 S +30:22. Ps 17:13. Pr
26:21. Hab 1:12, 13.
Sheba. i.e. *an oath*, **S#7652h**. ver. 2, 6, 7, 10,
13, 21, 22. 1 Ch 5:13. Also Jsh 19:2.
Bichri. i.e. *first fruits; youthful*, **S#1075h**. ver. 2,
6, 7, 10, 13, 21, 22.
he blew. 2 S 15:10. Jg 3:27. Pr 24:21, 22.
25:8.
We have. 2 S 19:43. 1 K 12:16. 2 Ch 10:16.
Lk 19:14, 27. Ac 8:21.
every man to. ver. 22. 1 S 4:10. 1 K 12:16. 2
Ch 10:16.
2 **every man**. 2 S 19:41. Ps 62:9. 118:8-10. Pr
17:14.
the men. Jn 6:66-68. Ac 11:23.
from Jordan. 2 S 19:15, 40, 41. 2 Ch 10:17.
3 **ten women**. 2 S 15:16. 16:21, 22.
ward. Heb. an house of ward. Ge 40:3.
shut. Heb. bound.
living in widowhood. Heb. in widowhood
of life.
4 **Amasa**. 2 S 17:25. 19:13. 1 Ch 2:17.
Assemble. Heb. Call. ver. 5. Jg 4:13. 1 S
+11:8.
5 **So Amasa**. 2 S 19:13.
tarried. 1 S 13:8.
6 **Abishai**. 1 S +26:6.
do us. 2 S 19:7.
thy lord's. 2 S 11:11. 1 K 1:33.
escape us. Heb. deliver himself from our
eyes.
7 **Joab's men**. ver. 23. 2 S 8:16. 1 K 1:44.
Cherithites. 2 S +8:18. 2 K 11:4.
8 **in Gibeon**. Jsh +10:2.
Amasa. ver. 4, 5.
9 **Art thou**. Ps 55:21. Pr 26:24-26. Mi 7:2.
took Amasa. 2 S 10:4.
to kiss him. Pr 6:34. 27:4. Mt 26:48, 49. Lk
22:47, 48.
10 **in Joab's**. ver. 9. Jg 3:21. 1 Ch 12:2.
he smote. 2 S 2:23. 3:27. 4:6. Ge 4:8. 1 K
2:5, 6, 31-34.
and shed. Ac 1:18, 19.
struck him not again. Heb. doubled not his
stroke. 1 S 26:8.
11 **He that**. ver. 6, 7, 13, 21.
for David. ver. 4. 2 K 9:32.
12 **Amasa wallowed**. 2 S 17:25. Ps 9:16. 55:23.
Pr 24:21, 22.
13 **the highway**. Nu 20:19.
14 **Abel**. Jsh 18:21, 25. 2 S +6:18. 2 Ch 16:4.
Bethmaachah. i.e. *house of oppression*,
S#1038h. ver. 15. 2 K 15:29.
Berites. **S#1276h**, only here. Jsh 18:25,
Beeroth.
15 **cast up**. 2 K 19:32. Is 29:3. 37:33. Je 6:6.
32:24. 33:4. Ezk 4:2. 26:8. Lk 19:43.

a bank. Je 32:24.

it stood in the trench. *or*, it stood against the outmost wall. 1 K 21:23. Is 26:1. La 2:8. Na 3:8.

battered, etc. Heb. marred to throw down.

16 **wise woman**. ver. 22. 2 S 14:2. Jg +5:29. 1 S 19:11-18. 25:3, 18, 23-25, 32, 33. 1 K 12:7. Pr 11:16. 12:4. 14:1. 31:10, 30. Ec 9:14-18. Ac 18:26. 23:16. Ro 16:3, 4.

17 **Hear the words**. 2 S 14:12. 1 S 25:24.

18 **They were wont**, etc. *or*, They plainly spake in the beginning, saying, Surely they will ask of Abel, and so make an end. 2 S 2:1. 16:23. Dt 20:10, 11. 1 S 23:2. 30:8. Pr 12:15.

at Abel. ver. +14.

19 **peaceable**. Ge 18:23. Ro 13:3, 4. 1 T +2:2.

a mother. Nu +21:25, 32. Jg 5:7. Is 50:1. Ezk 16:45-49. 23:2. Ho 2:2. Ga 4:26.

swallow. Ps +35:25.

the inheritance. 2 S 21:3. Ex 19:5, 6. Dt 32:9. 1 S 26:19.

20 **Far be it**. 2 S 23:17. Jb 21:16. 22:18.

that I should. ver. 10. Pr 28:13. Je 17:9. Lk 10:29.

21 **a man**. ver. 1. Jg 2:9. 7:24. 2 K 5:22. Je 4:15. 50:19.

by name. Heb. by his name.

lifted. 2 S 23:18. 1 S 24:6. 26:9.

his head. 2 S 17:2, 3. 2 K 10:7. Jn 18:4-8.

22 **in her wisdom**. ver. +16. Ec 7:19. 9:14-18.

he blew. ver. 1. 2 S 2:28. 18:16.

retired. Heb. were scattered.

every man to. ver. 1. 1 S 4:10.

And Joab. 2 S 3:28-39. 11:6-21. Ec 8:11.

23 **Now Joab**. 2 S 8:16-18. 1 Ch 18:15-17.

Benaiah. ver. 7.

Cherethites. ver. +7.

24 **Adoram**. i.e. *high honor; their glory*, **S#151h**. 1 K 4:6. 12:18.

tribute. 1 K 4:6.

Jehoshaphat. 2 S +8:16.

recorder. *or*, remembrancer. 2 S +8:16mg.

25 **Sheva**. i.e. *Jehovah contends; habitation; vanity; guile*, **S#7724h**. 2 S 8:17, Seraiah. 1 K 4:4. 1 Ch 2:49. 18:16, Shavsha.

26 **Ira**. i.e. *stirring; watchfulness*, **S#5896h**. 2 S 23:26, 38. 1 Ch 11:28, 40, Ithrite. 27:9.

Jairite. **S#2972h**, only here. Nu 32:41. Jg 10:4, 5.

chief ruler. *or*, prince. 2 S 8:18. 24:11. Ge 41:43, 45. Ex 2:14, 16. 2 Ch 35:15. Is +24:2mg.

2 SAMUEL 21

1 A.M. 2986. B.C. 1018. An. Ex. Is. 473.

a famine. Ge +12:10.

enquired. Heb. sought the face, etc. Ge +19:13. Nu 27:21.

of the Lord. 2 S 5:19, 23. Nu 27:21. 1 S 23:2,

4, 11. Jb 5:8-10. 10:2. Ps 50:15. 91:15.

It is. Jsh 7:1, 11, 12.

Saul. 1 S 22:17-19.

Gibeonites. **S#1393h**. ver. 2, 3, 4, 9. 1 Ch 12:4. Ne 3:7.

2 **now the**. Jsh 9:3-21.

the Amorites. Ge +15:16. Jsh 6:19. Am 2:9, 10.

in his zeal. Dt 7:16. 1 S 14:44. 15:8, 9, 22, 23. 2 K 10:16, 31. Lk 9:54, 55. Jn 12:43. 16:2. Ro 10:2. Ga 4:17, 18.

3 **wherewith**. Ge 32:20. Le +4:20. 1 S 2:25. Mi 6:6, 7. He 9:22. 10:4-12.

bless. 2 S 20:19.

4 **We will**, etc. *or*, It is not silver nor gold that we have to do with Saul, or his house; neither pertains it to us to kill, etc.

no silver. Ps 49:6-8. 1 P 1:18, 19.

5 **The man**. ver. 1. Est 9:24, 25. Mt 7:2.

devised. *or*, cut us off. Jg 20:5. Ps 50:21. Da 9:26. Ho 4:5, 6.

6 **hang**. 2 S 17:23. 18:10. Ge 40:19, 22. Nu 25:4, 5. Dt 21:22, 23. Jsh 8:29. 10:26. Ezr 6:11. Est 9:10, 13, 14. Mt 27:5.

in Gibeah. 1 S 10:26. 11:4.

whom the Lord did choose. *or*, the chosen of the Lord. 1 S 9:16, 17. 10:1, 24. Am 3:2. Ac 13:21.

7 **Mephibosheth**. 2 S 4:4. 9:10. 16:4. 19:25.

because. 1 S 18:3. 20:8, 15, 17, 42. 23:18.

8 **Rizpah**. 2 S 3:7.

Armoni. i.e. *palatial; my palace*, **S#764h**.

Mephibosheth. i.e. *exterminating the idol or shame; idol breaker*, **S#4648h**. ver. 7. 2 S 4:4. 9:6, 10-13. 16:1, 4. 19:24, 25, 30.

Michal. *or*, Michal's sister. 1 S 18:19.

brought up for. Heb. bare to. Ge 50:23. 1 S 18:19.

Barzillai. i.e. *strong; iron of the Lord; he is iron*, **S#1271h**. 2 S 17:27. 19:32-34, 39. 1 K 2:7. Ezr 2:61. Ne 7:63, 63.

the Meholathite. Jg 7:22. 1 K 4:12.

9 **before the Lord**. ver. 6. 2 S 6:17, 21. Ex 20:5. Nu 35:31-34. Dt 21:1-9. 1 S 15:33. 2 K 24:3, 4.

in the beginning. Ru 1:22.

barley harvest. Le 23:10, 11.

10 **Rizpah**. ver. 8. 2 S 3:7.

took sackcloth. Jb +16:15.

from the. ver. 9. Dt 21:13, 23.

until water. Dt 11:14. 1 K 18:41-45. Je 5:24, 25. 14:22. Ho 6:3. Jl 2:23. Zc 10:1.

suffered. Ge 31:7.

the birds. Ge 40:19. Ezk 39:4.

11 **told David**. 2 S 2:4. Ru 2:11, 12.

concubine. 1 Ch +2:48.

12 **the bones of Saul**. 2 S 2:5-7. 1 S 31:11-13.

Beth-shan. Jsh 17:11.

when. Ge +2:17.

in Gilboa. 2 S 1:6, 21. 1 S 28:4. 31:1. 1 Ch 10:1, 8.

14　buried. 2 S 3:32. 4:12.
Zelah. Jsh 18:28. 1 S 10:2, Zelzah.
sepulchre. Heb. *qeber*, Ge +23:4.
God. 2 S 24:25. Ex 32:27-29. Nu 25:13. Jsh 7:26. 1 K 18:40, 41. Je 14:1-7. Jl 2:18, 19. Am 7:1-6. Jon 1:15. Zc 6:8.

15　the Philistines. 2 S 5:17, 22. 1 Ch 20:4.
and David waxed faint. Jsh 14:10, 11. Jg 4:21. 1 S 14:28mg, 31. Ps 71:9, 18. 73:26. Ec 12:3. Is 40:28-30. Je 9:23, 24. 1 P 1:24, 25.

16　Ishbi-benob. i.e. *whose seat is in Nob* or *on high*, **S#3430h**.
of the sons. Nu +13:33. Dt 1:28.
the giant. *or*, Rapha. ver. 18, 20mg, 22. Dt +2:20.
whose spear. Heb. the staff, *or* the head.
brass. 1 S 17:7.
thought. 1 S 17:45-51.

17　Abishai. 1 S 26:6.
succored. 2 S 22:19. Ps 46:1. 144:10.
Thou shalt. 2 S 18:3.
quench. 2 S 14:7. 1 K 11:36. 15:4. Ps 132:17. Jn 1:8, 9. 5:35.
light. Heb. candle, *or* lamp. Ex 25:37. Ps +18:28mg. Jn 8:12.

18　And it came. 1 Ch 20:4-8.
Gob. i.e. *a pit*, **S#1359h**. ver. 19. In 1 Ch 20:4, it is Gezer.
Sibbechai. i.e. *thicket of Jehovah; my thicket*, **S#5444h**. 2 S 23:27, Mebunnai. 1 Ch 11:29. 20:4. 27:11.
Hushathite. 2 S 23:27. 1 Ch 4:4. 11:29. 20:4.
Saph. i.e. *bason; threshold*, **S#5593h**. 1 Ch 20:4, Sippai.
the giant. *or*, Rapha. ver. 16mg, 20mg.

19　Elhanan. i.e. *God is kind*, **S#445h**. 2 S 23:24. 1 Ch 11:26. 20:5.
Jaare-oregim. i.e. *forest of the weavers*, **S#3296h**. *or*, Jair. 1 Ch 20:5, Jair.
Goliath. 1 S 17:4, etc.
staff. lit. wood. Ge +40:19.
beam. 1 S 17:7. 1 Ch 11:23. 20:5.

20　yet a battle. 1 Ch 20:6.
Gath. 1 S 17:4.
stature. or, of contention. Nu 13:32mg. 1 Ch 20:6mg. Pr 26:21. Je 15:10.
toes. lit. "fingers," as in Ex 8:19. 1 Ch 20:6.
the giant. *or*, Rapha. ver. 16mg, 18mg.

21　defied. *or*, reproached. Jg 8:15. 1 S 17:10, 25, 26, 36, 45. 2 K 19:13.
Jonathan. Brother of Jonadab, 2 S 13:3. 1 Ch 27:32.
Shimeah. i.e. *the hearing-that is, answering-prayer; astonishment; desolation*, **S#8092h**. 2 S 13:3, 32. 1 S 16:9. 17:13, Shammah. 1 Ch 2:13, Shimma.

22　the giant. ver. 16, 18, 20mg.
four. 1 Ch 20:8.

fell by. Jsh 14:12. Ps 60:12. 108:13. 118:15. Ec 9:11. Je 9:23. Ro 8:31, 37.

2 SAMUEL 22

1　David. Ps 50:14. 103:1-6. 116:1, etc.
words. Ex 15:1. Jg 5:1.
in the day. ver. 49. Ps 18, title. 34:19. Is 12:1, etc. 2 C 1:10. 2 T 4:18. Re 7:9-17.
and out. 1 S 23:14. 24:15. 25:29. 26:24. 27:1.

2　The Lord. Dt 32:4. 1 S 2:2. Ps 18:2, etc. 31:3. 42:9. 71:3. 91:2. 144:2. Mt 16:18.

3　in him. Ps 18:2. Is 8:17. 12:2. He *2:13a*.
shield. Ps +84:11.
the horn. Ps +92:10.
my high. ver. 51. Ps 61:3. 144:2. Pr 18:10.
my refuge. Ps 9:9. 14:6. 18:2. 27:5. 32:7. 46:1, 7, 11. 59:16. 71:7. 142:4. Is 32:2. Je 16:19.
my savior. Is 12:2. 45:21. Lk 1:47, 71. T 3:4, 6.
thou savest. ver. 49. Ps 55:9. 72:14. 86:14. 140:1, 4, 11.

4　I will. Ps 116:2, 4, 13, 17.
worthy. Ps +18:3. 66:2. 106:2. 148:1-4. Re 5:12.
so shall. Ps 34:6. 55:16. 56:9. 57:1-3. Ro 10:13.

5　waves. or, pangs. Ps 42:7. 88:7. 93:4. Jon 2:3. 1 Th 5:3.
the floods. Ps +93:3, 4.
ungodly men. Heb. Belial. 1 S +30:22.

6　sorrows. *or*, cords. Jb 36:8. Ps +18:5. 116:3. 140:5. Pr 5:22. Jon 2:2.
hell. Heb. *sheol*, Ge +37:35.
the snares. Pr 14:27.

7　my distress. Ps 116:4. Ne +9:37. Mt 26:38, 39. Lk 22:44. He 5:7.
did hear. Ex 3:7. Ps 34:6, 15-17.
out. 1 K 8:28-30. Ps 18:6. 27:4. Jon 2:4, 7. Hab 2:20.
my cry. Ja +5:4.

8　the earth. Ps +97:4.
foundations. 2 S 22:16. Dt 4:32. 30:4. +32:22. Ne 1:9. Jb +26:11. 38:4. Ps 72:9. 82:5. Pr 8:29. Is 13:5. Mt 24:31.

9　went. ver. 16. Ex 15:7, 8. 19:18. 24:17. Dt 32:22. Jb 4:9. 41:20, 21. Ps 18:8, 15. 97:3-5. Is 30:27, 33. Je 5:14. 15:14. Da 7:9, 10. He 12:29.
out of his. Heb. by his, etc.
coals. Hab 3:5.

10　bowed. Is 64:1-3.
darkness. ver. 12. Ex +10:22.

11　rode. Dt +33:26.
a cherub. Ge +3:24. Ps 68:17.
did fly. Ps +18:10.
upon the. Ps 139:9.

12　made. ver. 10. Ps 18:11, 12. 27:5. 97:2.
darkness. ver. +10.

dark waters. Heb. binding of waters.
thick clouds. Ex 19:9. Jg 5:4. Ps +18:11.
skies. Dt 33:26.

13 **brightness**. 2 S 23:4. Ps 18:12. Pr 4:18. Is 4:5.
50:10. 60:3, 19. 62:1. Ezk 1:4, 13, 27, 28.
10:4. Jl 2:10. 3:15. Am 5:20.
coals of fire. ver. 9. Le 16:5. Ps 18:12, 13.
Ezk 1:13. 10:2.
kindled. ver. 9. Ex 3:2, 3.

14 **thundered**. Ex +9:23. Jg 5:20. 1 S 2:10. Ps
+18:13.

15 **arrows**. Dt +32:23. Ps +18:14.

16 **the channels**. Ex 14:21-27. 15:8-10. Ps
18:15-17. 114:3-7. Ezk +31:12 (**S#650h**).
rebuking. Ex 15:8. Jb 38:11. Ps 106:9. Na
1:4. Hab 3:8-10. Mt 8:26, 27.
blast. Heb. *neshamah*, Ge +2:7.
breath. Heb. *ruach*, Ex +15:8.
nostrils. *or*, anger. ver. 9. Ps 74:1.

17 **sent**. Ps +18:16.
he drew. Ps +18:16. 32:6. 59:1, 2. 93:3, 4.
124:4, 5. 130:1. Is 43:2. La 3:54. Jon 2:3.
many. *or*, great. Ps 42:7. 69:1, 2.

18 **delivered**. ver. 1. Ps 3:7. 56:9. 2 C 1:10. 2 T
4:17.

19 **prevented**. 2 S 15:10-13. 1 S 19:11-17.
23:26, 27. Ps 18:18, 19. 118:10-13. Mt 27:39-
44.
the Lord. Ps 71:20, 21. Is 26:34. 50:10.

20 **brought**. Ge 26:22. 1 Ch 4:10. Ho 4:16.
delighted. 2 S 15:26. Ps 22:8. 147:11. 149:4.
Is 42:1. Mt 3:17. 17:5. 27:43. Ac 2:32-36.

21 **rewarded**. ver. 25. 1 S 26:23. 1 K 8:32. Ps
7:3, 4, 8. 18:20-25. 19:11. 1 C 15:58.
cleanness. Ex 30:18. Jb 17:9. Ja 4:8.
hands. Jb 17:9. Ps 24:3, 4. 26:6. Ja 4:8.

22 **I have kept**. Nu 16:15. 1 S 12:3. Jb 23:10-12.
2 C 1:12.
the ways. Ge 18:19. Ps 119:1, 3. 128:1. Pr
8:32.
have not. Ps 36:3. 125:5. Zp 1:6. Jn 15:10.
He 10:38, 39.

23 **For all**. Ps 119:6, 86, 128. Lk 1:6. Jn 15:14.
judgments. Dt 6:1, 2. 7:12. Ps 19:8, 9.
119:13, 30, 102.
I did not. Dt 8:11.

24 **upright**. Ge 6:9. 17:1. Jb 1:1. Ps 51:6. 84:11.
Jn 1:47. 2 C 5:11.
before him. Heb. to him. Ps 18:23.
kept. 1 S 24:11. Pr 4:23. He 12:1.

25 **recompensed**. ver. 21. Is 3:10. Ro 2:7, 8. 2 C
5:10.
cleanness. ver. +21.
in his eye sight. Heb. before his eyes. Pr
5:21.

26 **the merciful**. Mt 5:7. Ja 2:13.

27 **the pure**. Mt 5:8.
froward. Le 26:23-28. Dt 28:58-61. Ps 125:5.
show thyself unsavory. *or*, wrestle. Ex
18:11. Ps 18:26. Is 45:9.

28 **afflicted**. Ex 3:7, 8. Ps 12:5. 18:27. 72:12, 13.
113:7, 8. 140:12. Is 61:1-3. 63:9. Mt 5:3.
but thine. Ex 10:3. Pr +16:5. Is 37:23, 28, 29.
haughty. Jb 9:4. Da 5:20.

29 **lamp**. *or*, candle. Ps +18:28. 27:1. 84:11. Jn
8:12. 2 P 1:19. Re 21:23.
lighten. Ps 4:6. 18:28. 97:11. 112:4. Is 50:10.
60:19, 20. Mi 7:9. Ml 4:2. Jn 12:46. Ep 5:8.

30 **run through**. *or*, broken. Ps 18:29. 118:10-
12. Ro 8:37. Ph 4:13.

31 **God**. Heb. *El*, Ex +15:2.
his way. Mt 5:48. Re 15:3.
the word. Ps +18:30.
tried. *or*, refined. Ps 12:6.
a buckler. ver. 3. Ge 15:1. Dt 33:29. Ps 35:2.
91:4.
that trust. Ps 5:11. 18:30. Pr 14:32. Is +26:3.
Na 1:7.

32 **For who**. Is 42:8. 44:6, 8. Je 10:6, 7, 16.
God. Heb. *El*, Ex +15:2.
a rock. ver. 2, 3.

33 **God**. Heb. *El*, Ex +15:2.
strength. Ex 15:2. Ps 18:32. 27:1. 28:7, 8.
31:4. 46:1. Is 41:10. Zc 10:12. 2 C 12:9. Ep
6:10. Ph 4:13.
maketh. Heb. riddeth, *or* looseth.
my way. He 13:21.
perfect. Jb 22:3. Ps 119:1. Mt +5:48.

34 **maketh**. Heb. equalleth to. Pr 26:7.
like hinds'. 2 S 2:18. Dt 33:25. Hab 3:19.
setteth. Is 33:16. 58:14.

35 **teacheth**. Ps +18:34.
to war. Heb. for the war. 2 C 10:4, 5. Ep
6:13.
a bow. Ezk 39:3, 9, 10.

36 **the shield**. Ge 15:1. Ps 84:11. Ep 6:16.
gentleness. Ps 18:35.
made me great. Heb. multiplied me. Ps
12:2. 22:17. Ps 115:14.

37 **enlarged**. Ps +18:36. Pr 4:12.
feet. Heb. ankles. 1 S 2:9. Ps 17:5. 94:18.
119:117. 121:3.

38 **pursued**. 2 S 5:18-25. 8:1, 2, 13, 14. 10:14.
Ps 18:37. 21:8, 9. Ro 8:37.

39 **consumed**. Ps 18:37, 38. 110:1, 5, 6. 118:10-
12. Ml 4:1, 3. Ro 16:20.

40 **girded**. 1 S 17:49-51. 23:5. Ps 18:32, 39. Is
45:5. Col 1:11.
them. Ps 44:5. 144:2.
subdued. Heb. caused to bow. Is 60:14. Re
3:9.

41 **necks**. Ge 49:8. Ex 23:7. Jsh 10:24. 11:23. Ps
18:40, 41. 1 C 15:25.
I might. Ps 21:8, 9. Lk 19:14, 27. 2 Th 1:8, 9.

42 **unto the Lord**. 1 S 28:6. Jb 27:9. Ezk 20:3.
Mi 3:4. Mt 7:22, 23.
answered them not. ver. 41. Ps +18:41. Pr
+1:28. 15:29. 21:13. Is 8:21. Je 7:16. 11:14.
14:11.

43 **as small**. 2 K 13:7. Ps 35:5. Da 2:35. Ml 4:1.

as the mire. Ps 18:42. Is 10:6. Mi 7:10. Zc 10:5.

did spread. Dt 32:26. Is 26:15. Zc 2:6. Lk 21:24.

44 **delivered**. 2 S 18:6-8. 19:9, 14. 20:1, 2, 22. Ps 2:1-6. 18:43. Ac 4:25-28.

head. 2 S 8:1-14. Ps 2:8. 60:8, 9. 72:8, 9. 110:6. Is 60:12. Da 7:14. Ro 15:12. Re 11:15. 19:16.

a people. Is 65:1. Ho 2:23. Ro 9:25.

45 **Strangers**. Heb. Sons of the stranger. ver. 46. Ge 17:12, 27. 35:2, 4. 1 S 7:3. 2 Ch 14:3. Is 56:3, 6.

submit themselves. *or*, yield feigned obedience. Heb. lie. Ps +66:3mg. Ezk 33:31, 32. Ac 8:13, 21-23.

46 **fade away**. Ps 1:3. Is 64:6. Ja 1:11.

out. Is 2:19, 21. Am 9:3. Mi 7:17. Re 6:15, 16.

47 **Lord**. Dt 32:39, 40. Jb 19:25.

exalted. Is +12:4.

the rock of. Ps +89:26. Lk 1:47.

48 **God**. Heb. *El*, Ex +15:2.

avengeth me. Heb. giveth avengement for me. 2 S 18:19, 31. 1 S 25:30. Ps 18:47. 94:1.

that bringeth. Ps 110:1. 144:2. 1 C 15:25.

49 **thou also**. 2 S 5:12. 7:8, 9. Nu 24:7, 17-19. 1 S 2:8. Ps +18:48.

the violent. Ps 52:1.

50 **Therefore**. Ps 18:49. Ro *15:9*.

among. Ro 15:9.

I will sing. Ps 7:17. 18:49. 103:1. 138:1. 145:1, 2. 146:1, 2. Is 12:1-6.

51 **the tower**. ver. 2. Ps 3:3. 21:1. 48:3. +61:3. 89:26. 91:2. 144:10.

his anointed. Ps +18:50.

seed. 2 S 7:12, 13. Ps 18:50. 89:29, 36. Is 8:18. Je 30:9. Lk +1:31-33. Ac 4:27. He 2:13. Re +11:15.

evermore. Ps +18:50.

2 SAMUEL 23

1 A.M. 2989. B.C. 1015. An. Ex. Is. 476.

the last. Ge 49:1. Dt 33:1. Jsh ch. 23. 24. Ps 72:20. 2 P 1:13-15.

raised. 2 S 7:8, 9. Ps 78:70, 71. 89:27.

the anointed. 1 S 2:10. 16:12, 13. 24:6. Ps +2:2, 6mg. 89:20. La 4:20.

sweet psalmist. 1 Ch 16:4, 5, 7, 9. Am 6:5. Lk 20:42. 24:44. Ep 5:19, 20. Col 3:16. Ja 5:13.

2 **The Spirit**. Heb. *ruach*, Is +48:16. Mt 22:43. Mk 12:36. Lk 24:44. Ac 2:25-31. 4:25. 5:3, 4. He 3:7, 8. 2 P 1:21.

3 **God**. Ex 3:15. 19:5, 6. 20:2. Is +29:23.

the Rock. 2 S 22:2, 32. Dt 32:4, 30, 31. Ps 42:9.

He that ruleth. *or*, Be thou ruler, etc. Ps 110:2.

must be just. Ex 23:6-8. Dt 16:18-20. Pr 31:9. Is +11:4, 5. Zc 9:9. He 1:8.

ruling. Ex +18:21. 2 Ch 19:7-9. Ne 5:15.

4 **he shall**. Is 11:4.

as the light. Ge +19:27. Ps 89:36. Jn 1:7.

morning. Re +2:28.

clouds. Ge +9:13.

tender. Dt 32:2. Ps 72:6. Is 4:2. Mi 5:7.

5 **Although**. 2 S 7:18. 12:10. 13:14, 15, 28. 18:14, 15. 1 K 1:5. 2:24, 25. 11:6-8. 12:14.

God. Heb. *El*, Ex +15:2.

he hath made. 1 Ch 17:11-14. Is +55:3. Ro 3:3, 4.

everlasting. Ge +9:16.

covenant. Is +55:3. Ho 2:19, 20.

ordered. or, arranged. Jsh 2:6. Is 30:33. Je 6:23. 50:42. Ezk 23:41. Jl 2:5. 1 C 14:33, 40.

and sure. 1 S 2:35. 25:28. 1 K 11:38. Is +55:3. He 6:19.

all my salvation. Ps 62:2. 119:81.

desire. Ps 27:4. 63:1-3. 73:25, 26.

to grow. Is 4:2. 7:14. 9:6, 7. 11:1. 27:6. Am 9:11. 1 C 3:6, 7.

6 **the sons of Belial**. 2 S 20:1. 1 S +30:22.

thorns. Ge 3:18. SS 2:2. Is 9:18. 33:12. Ezk 2:6. Mi 7:4.

thrust away. Jb 20:8. Ps 64:8.

7 **fenced**. Heb. filled.

and they shall be. 2 S 22:8-10. Is 27:4. Mt 3:10-12. 13:42. Lk 19:14, 27. Jn 15:6. 2 Th 1:8. 2:8. He 6:8.

utterly burned. Is 9:5. Re 19:20.

8 A.M. 2949-2989. B.C. 1055-1015. An. Ex. Is. 436-476.

The Tachmonite. i.e. *wise*, S#8461h. *or*, Josheb-basebet, the Tachmonite, head of the three. 1 Ch +11:11, 12. 27:2, 32.

chief among. Je +13:18mg.

Adino. i.e. *a spear; his delight*, S#5722h.

Eznite. i.e. *sharp or strong*, S#6112h.

he lift up. 1 Ch 11:11.

whom he slew. Heb. slain.

9 **Eleazar**. 1 Ch 11:12-14. 27:4, Dodai.

Ahohite. i.e. *descendant of Ahoah* (i.e. *brother of the Lord*, 1 Ch +8:4), S#266h. ver. 28. 1 Ch 8:1, 3, +4. 11:12, 29. 27:4.

defied. Nu 23:7, 8. 1 S 17:10, 26, 36, 45, 46. 1 S 63:3, 5. Mk 14:50.

the men. Is 63:3, 5. Mk 14:50.

10 **and smote**. 1 Ch 11:13, 14.

the Lord. Jsh 10:10, 42. 11:8. Jg 15:14, 18. 1 S 11:13. 14:6, 23. 19:5. 2 K 5:1. Ps 108:13. 144:10. Ro 15:18. 2 C 4:5. Ep 6:10-18.

and the people. Ps 68:12. Is 53:12.

11 **Shammah**. 1 Ch 11:27, Shammoth the Harorite.

Agee. i.e. *fugitive*, S#89h.

Hararite. i.e. *mountaineer; the curser*, S#2043h. ver. 33. 1 Ch 11:34, 35.

the Philistines. 1 Ch 11:13, 14.

into a troop. *or*, for foraging. Heb. *chay*, ver. 13.

12 **the Lord**. ver. +10. Ps 3:8. 44:2. Pr 21:31.

13 **three**, etc. *or*, the three captains over the thirty. ver. 8. Ex 14:7. 1 Ch 11:15-19.
   the cave. Jsh +12:15.
   troop. Heb. *chay*, ver. 11mg.
   the valley. Dt +2:20.

14 **an hold**. 2 S 5:17. 1 S 22:1, 4, 5. 24:22. 1 Ch 12:16.
   garrison. 1 S 10:5. 13:4, 23. 14:1, 6.

15 **longed**. Nu 11:4, 5. Ps 42:1, 2. 63:1. 119:81. Is 41:17, 18. 44:3. Jn 4:10, 14. 7:37, 38.
   well. Heb. *bor*, Ge +37:20.
   Bethlehem. Jsh +19:15. Jn 4:14.

16 **the three**. ver. 9. 1 S 19:5. Ac 20:24. Ro 5:7. 2 C 5:14.
   well. Heb. *bor*, Ge +37:20.
   poured. Heb. *nasak*, S#5258h. 1 Ch 11:18. Nu 28:7. Ge 35:14.
   it unto. Nu 28:7. 1 S 7:6. La 2:19. Ph 2:17.

17 **Be it far**. 2 S 20:20. Ge 44:17. 1 S 2:30. 26:11. 1 K 21:3. 1 Ch 11:19.
   the blood. Ge 9:4. Le 17:10. Ps 72:14. Mt 26:28. Mk 14:24. Jn 6:52-54. 2 C 5:14.
   jeopardy. Jg 5:18. 1 C 15:30.
   lives. Heb. *nephesh*, souls, Ge +44:30.

18 **Abishai**. 1 S +26:6.
   and slew them. Heb. slain.

19 **he attained**. ver. 9, 13, 16. 1 Ch 11:25. Mt 13:8, 23. 1 C 15:41.

20 **Benaiah**. 1 Ch +15:24.
   Kabzeel. Jsh 15:21.
   who had done many acts. Heb. great of acts.
   he slew. Ex 15:15.
   lion-like men. Heb. lions of God. 2 S 1:23. 1 Ch 11:22-24. 12:8. Is 29:1, 2, 7. Ezk 43:15.
   slew a lion. Jg 14:5, 6. 1 S 17:34-37.
   pit. Heb. *bor*, Ge +37:20.
   snow. 1 Ch 11:22. Jb 6:16. 37:6. 38:22. Ps 68:14. 147:16. 148:8. Pr 25:13. 26:1. 31:21. Je 18:14.

21 **a goodly man**. Heb. a man of countenance, *or* sight, *called*, 1 Ch 11:23, a man of great stature.
   slew him. 1 S 17:51. Col 2:15.

23 **more honorable**. *or*, honorable among the thirty. 1 Ch 27:6.
   over his guard. *or*, over his council. Heb. at his command. *or*, listeners. 2 S 8:18. 20:23. 1 S 22:14. Is 11:14.

24 **Asahel**. 1 Ch +2:16.
   Dodo. i.e. *his love or uncle; amatory; his beloved*, S#1734h. ver. 9. Jg 10:1. 1 Ch 11:12, 26.

25 **Shammah**. 1 Ch 11:27, 28, Shammoth the Harorite.
   Harodite. i.e. *trembling, terror*, S#2733h. Jg 7:1.
   Elika. i.e. *God of the congregation* or *rejected*, S#470h.

26 **Paltite**. i.e. *my escape*, S#6407h. 1 Ch 11:27. 27:10, Pelonite.
   Ira. i.e. *watchful*. ver. 38. 1 Ch 11:28. 27:9.
   Ikkesh. i.e. *perverse*, S#6142h. 1 Ch 11:28. 27:9.
   Tekoite. S#8621h. 2 S +14:2, 4, 9. 1 Ch 11:28. 27:9. Ne 3:5, 27.

27 **Abiezer**. Jsh +17:2. 1 Ch 11:28, Antothite. 27:12, Anetothite.
   Anethothite. S#6069h, so rendered only here. Jsh 21:18. 1 Ch 11:28. 12:3. 27:12, Anetothite. Je 29:27.
   Mebunnai. i.e. *built up; buildings of the Lord*, S#4012h, only here. 2 S 21:18. 1 Ch 11:29, Sibbecai. 27:11.
   Hushathite. i.e. *sensuality*, S#2843h. 2 S 21:18. 1 Ch 4:4. A descendant of Judah. 11:29. 20:4. 27:11.

28 **Zalmon**. i.e. *shady; his image*, S#6756h. 1 Ch 11:29, Ilai.
   Ahohite. ver. 9. 1 Ch 8:4. 11:12.
   Maharai. i.e. *hasting*, S#4121h. 1 Ch 11:30. 27:13.
   Netophathite. i.e. *distillation; an inhabitant of Netophah* (Ezr 2:22), a city of Judah, S#5200h. ver. 29. 2 K 25:23. 1 Ch 2:54. 9:16. 11:30. 27:13, 15. Ne 7:26. 12:28. Je 40:8.

29 **Heleb**. i.e. *fatness*, S#2460h. 1 Ch 11:30, Heled. 27:15, Heldai.
   Baanah. 2 S +4:5. 1 Ch 11:30.
   Ittai. 1 Ch 11:31, Ithai. Not the Gittite in 2 S 15:19.
   Ribai. i.e. *my striving*, S#7380h. 1 Ch 11:31.
   Gibeah. Jg +19:12.

30 **Benaiah**. ver. +20.
   Pirathonite. Jg +12:15.
   Hiddai. i.e. *echo; chief*, S#1914h. 1 Ch 11:32, Hurai.
   brooks, *or*, valleys. Dt 1:24. Jg 2:9. +16:4.
   Gaash. Jsh 24:30. Jg 2:9.

31 **Abi-albon**. i.e. *valiant*, S#45h. 1 Ch 11:32, Abiel.
   Arbathite. S#6164h. Jsh 15:6, 7. Jsh 18:18, 22. 1 Ch 11:32.
   Azmaveth. i.e. *strong to death; strength of death*, S#5820h. 1 Ch 8:36. 9:42. 11:33. 12:3. 27:25. Ezr 2:24. Ne 12:29.
   Barhumite. i.e. *son of the blackened; a native of Bahurim*, S#1273h. 2 S 16:5. 19:16. 1 Ch 11:33, Baharumite.

32 **Eliahba**. i.e. *God hides*, S#455h. 1 Ch 11:33.
   Shaalbonite. S#8170h. Jsh 19:42. 1 K 4:9. 1 Ch 11:33.
   Jashen. i.e. *sleepy; ancient*, S#3464h. 1 Ch 11:34, Hashem, the Gizonite.

33 **Shammah**. 1 S +16:9. 1 Ch 11:27.
   Hararite. ver. +11.
   Ahiam. i.e. *brother of a mother*, S#279h. 1 Ch 11:35.
   Sharar. i.e. *hostile; an observer*, S#8325h. 1 Ch 11:35, Sacar.

34 Eliphelet. 1 Ch 11:35, Eliphal son of Ur.
Ahasbai. i.e. *brother of my encompassers; I will take refuge in my arms; I flee to the Lord*, **S#308h**.
Maachathite. **S#4602h**. 2 S 10:6, 8. Dt 3:14. Jsh 12:5. 13:11, 13. 2 K 25:23. 1 Ch 4:19. Je 40:8.
Eliam. 2 S +11:3. 1 Ch 11:36, Ahijah the Pelonite.
Ahithophel. 2 S +15:12.

35 Hezrai. i.e. *my court* or *village*, **S#2695h**. 1 Ch 11:37, Hezro.
Carmelite. Jsh 15:55. 1 S 25:2.
Paarai. i.e. *my openings*, **S#6474h**. 1 Ch 11:37, Naarai.
Arbite. **S#701h**. Jsh 15:52.

36 Igal. i.e. *whom God redeems; God will revenge*, **S#3008h**. Nu 13:7. 1 Ch 3:22. 11:38, Joel.
Nathan. 2 Ch +9:29.
Zobah. 1 S +14:47.
Bani. 1 Ch 11:38, Mibhar, son of Haggeri.

37 Zelek. i.e. *a cleft*, **S#6768h**. 1 Ch 11:39.
Nahari. i.e. *my snorting; snorer*, **S#5171h**. 1 Ch 11:37, 39.
Beerothite. 2 S 4:2. Jsh 18:25.
armorbearer. 2 S 18:15.

38 Ira. 2 S +20:26.
Ithrite. i.e. *remaining*, **S#3505h**. 1 Ch 2:50, 53. 4:15, 17. 11:40.
Gareb. i.e. *reviler; scrabby; scabby; leprous*, **S#1619h**. 1 Ch 11:40. Je 31:39.

39 Uriah. 2 S +11:3, 6, etc. Mt 1:6.
thirty and seven in all. ver. 13, 16-17, 19, 23. [3]; ver. 18-19, 22-23 [3]; ver. 24-39 [31] gives 37.

2 SAMUEL 24

1 A.M. 2987. B.C. 1017. An. Ex. Is. 474.
again. 2 S 21:1, etc.
he. That is, Satan, 1 Ch 21:1. Ja 1:13, 14.
moved. 2 S 12:11. 16:10. Ge 45:5. 50:20. Ex 7:3. Dt +2:30. 1 S 18:10. 26:19. 1 K 22:20-23. Ezk 14:9. 20:25. Am +3:6. Ac 4:28. 2 Th 2:11.
Go, number. 1 S +11:8. 1 Ch 27:23, 24.

2 Joab. 1 S +26:6.
Go now, etc. *or*, Compass now all. 1 Ch 21:2.
from Dan. ver. 15. Jg +20:1.
that I may. Dt 8:13, 14. 2 Ch 32:25, 26, 31. Pr 29:23. Je 17:5. 2 C 12:7.

3 Now the Lord. 2 S 10:12. 1 Ch 21:3, 4. 27:23. Ps 115:14. Pr 14:28. Is 60:5.

4 the king's. 1 S +25:17. 1 Ch 21:4. Ec 8:4.
went out. Ex 1:17. Ac +5:29.
to number. Nu 1:2-4. 1 Ch 27:1.

5 Aroer. Nu +32:34.
river. *or*, valley. Nu +13:23mg.
Jazer. Nu +32:1.

6 Gilead. Ge +37:25.
land of Tahtim-hodshi. *or*, nether land newly inhabited. i.e. *my new places; under the*

new moon, **S#8483h**.
Dan-jaan. i.e. *judge of purpose*, **S#1842h**. Jsh 19:47. Jg 18:29.
Zidon. Ge +49:13.

7 Tyre. 1 K +7:13.
to Beer-sheba. ver. 2. Ge +21:31-33.
the Hivites. Ge +10:17.
the Canaanites. Ge +10:18.

8 Jerusalem. 1 Ch 21:4.

9 eight hundred thousand. Nu 1:45, 46. 26:51. 1 Ch 21:5, 6. 27:23, 24.

10 David's heart. 1 S 24:5. Jn 8:9. 1 J 3:20, 21.
I have sinned. 2 S 12:13. 1 Ch 21:8. 2 Ch 32:26. Jb 33:27, 28. Ps 32:5. Pr 28:13. Mi 7:8, 9, 18, 19. 1 J 1:9.
take away. Jb 7:21. Ho 14:2. Jn 1:29.
foolishly. 2 S 12:13. Dt 32:6. 1 S 13:13. 26:21. 1 Ch 21:7, 8. 2 Ch 16:9. Pr 24:9. Mk 7:22. T 3:3.

11 Gad. 1 S +22:5.
seer. 1 S 9:9. 2 K 17:13. 1 Ch 21:9. 25:5. 26:28. 29:29. 2 Ch 9:29. 12:15. 16:7, 10. 19:2. 29:25, 30. Is 29:10. 30:10. Am 7:12.

12 I offer. 1 Ch 21:10, 11.
that I may. 2 S 12:9, 10, 14. Le 26:41, 43. Jb 5:17, 18. Pr 3:12. He 12:6-10. Re 3:19.

13 seven. Le 26:20. 1 K +8:37.
flee. Le 26:17, 36, 37. Dt 28:25, 52.
three days. Ps 91:6. Ezk +38:22.

14 I am in. 1 S 13:6. 2 K 6:15. 1 Ch 21:13. Jn 12:27. Ph +1:23.
let us fall. Ex +34:6, 7. Is +55:3. Je +29:11.
for his. Ex +34:6, 7. Ps ch. 136. Ja 2:13.
great. *or*, many. Ps 119:156.
let me not. 2 K 13:3-7. 2 Ch 28:5-9. Ps 106:41, 42. Pr 12:10. Is 47:6. Zc 1:15.

15 the Lord. ver. +13. Ex 30:12. Nu 25:9. 1 S 6:19. 1 Ch 27:24.
from Dan. ver. +2.
seventy thousand men. Is 37:36.

16 the angel. Ex 12:23. 2 K 19:35. 1 Ch 21:15, 16. 2 Ch 32:21. Jb 38:7. Ps 35:6. 91:11, 12. Da 6:22. 9:21, 22. Mt 13:39, 41. 18:10. Lk 16:22. Ac 12:23. He 1:14.
the Lord repented. 1 S 15:11. Ps 78:38. Je +18:8. Hab 3:2.
It is enough. Ex 9:28. 1 K 19:4. Is 27:8. 40:1, 2. 57:16. Jl 2:13, 14. Mk 14:41. 2 C 2:6.
Araunah. i.e. *make ye to shine; I shall shout for joy*, **S#728h**. ver. 18, 20-24. 1 Ch 21:15. 2 Ch 3:1, Ornan.
the Jebusite. Ge +10:16.

17 spake. 1 Ch 21:16, 17.
Lo, I have sinned. ver. 10. Jb 7:20. 42:6. Ps 51:2-5. Is 6:5.
these sheep. 1 K 22:17. Ps 44:11. 74:1. Ezk 34:2-6, 23, 24. Zc 13:7.
let thine. Ge 44:33. Jn 10:11, 12. 1 P 2:24, 25.

18 Gad. ver. +11.
threshingfloor. Ge +50:10.

Araunah. Heb. Araniah. ver. +16.
Jebusite. Ge +10:16.

19 as the Lord. Ge 6:22. 1 Ch 21:19. 2 Ch 20:20. 36:16. Ne 9:26. He 11:8.

20 bowed. 2 S 9:8. Ge 18:2. Ru 2:10. 1 Ch 21:20, 21.

21 Wherefore. ver. 3, 18.
To buy. Ge 23:8-16. 1 Ch 21:22. Je 32:6-14.
the plague. 2 S 21:3-14. Nu +16:48.

22 Araunah. ver. 16.
Let my lord. Ge 23:11. 1 Ch 21:22.
be oxen. 1 S 6:14. 1 K 19:21.

23 as a king. Ps 45:16. Is 32:8.
give unto. Ge 23:11. 1 Ch 21:23.
The Lord. Jb 42:8, 9. Ps 20:3, 4. Is 60:7. Ezk 20:40, 41. Ho 8:13. Ro 15:30, 31. 1 T 2:1, 2.

He 7:7. 1 P 2:5.

24 Nay. Ge 23:13. 29:15. 1 Ch 21:24. Is 43:23, 24. Ml 1:12-14. Ro 12:17.
that which. Ex 23:15. Dt 16:16. Pr 3:9. Mt 19:27. Mk +10:28-30. Lk 5:28. 21:4. Jn 12:3. Ac 20:24. Ph 3:7, 8.
doth cost me nothing. 1 Ch +21:24.
So David. 1 Ch 21:25. 22:1.

25 built there. Ge +8:20. +13:18. 22:9. 1 S 7:9, 17. 1 Ch 21:26-30.
and offered. Jg 20:26. 21:4.
burnt offerings. Le +23:12.
peace offerings. Le +23:19.
So the Lord. ver. 14. 2 S 21:14. 1 Ch 21:26, 27. La 3:32, 33.
the plague. ver. +21.

1 KINGS

1 KINGS 1

1 A.M. 2989. B.C. 1015. An. Ex. Is. 476.
old. 2 S 5:4. 1 Ch 23:1. 29:27, 28. Ps 90:10. Ec 12:1.
and stricken in years. Heb. and entered into days. Ge 18:11. 24:1. Jsh 23:1, 2. Lk 1:7.
clothes. Ge 24:53. 27:15, 27.
heat. Dt 19:6. Ec 4:11. Ezk 24:11.

2 **Let there be sought**. Heb. Let them seek.
a young virgin. Heb. a damsel, a virgin. Jg 21:12.
stand. Dt 10:8. 1 S 16:21, 22. 2 Ch 29:11.
cherish him. Heb. be a cherisher unto him. or, companion. ver. 4. Ps 139:3 (acquaint).
lie. Ge 16:5. Dt 13:6. 2 S 12:3. Mi 7:5.
get heat. Ec 4:11.

3 **So**. Est 2:2-4.
coasts. Jg 19:29. 1 S 11:7. 2 S 21:5.
Abishag. i.e. *father of error*, **S#49h**. ver. 15. 1 K 2:17, 21, 22.
Shunamite. i.e. *perfect*, **S#7767h**. ver. 15. 2 K 2:17, 21, 22. Jsh 19:18. 1 S 28:4. 2 K 4:8, 12, 25, 36.

4 **very**. lit. "unto might." 1 S 25:36.
fair. Ge +29:17.
knew. Ge +4:1. Mt 1:25.

5 **Adonijah**. i.e. *Jehovah is my Lord*, **S#138h**. ver. 7, 18. 1 K 2:28. 2 S 3:4. 1 Ch 3:2. Ne 10:16.
Haggith. 2 S +3:4.
exalted. ver. 11. 1 K 2:24. Ex 9:17. Pr 16:18. 18:12. Lk 14:11. 18:14.
I will. Dt 17:15. Jg 9:2. 1 Ch 22:5-11. 28:5. 29:1.
be king. Heb. reign.
and he. Dt 17:16. 2 S 12:10. 15:1. Is 2:7.

6 **his father**. Ge +44:30. 2 S 13:21.
had not. 1 S +3:13mg. Pr +19:18. 22:15. +23:13, 14. 29:15. He 12:5, 6.
at any time. Heb. from his days.
very goodly. 1 S 9:2. 10:23. 2 S 14:25.
his mother. or, Haggith.
bare him. 2 S 3:3, 4. 1 Ch 3:2.

7 **And he conferred**. Heb. his words were. 2 S 15:12. Ps 2:2.
Joab. 1 S +26:6.
Abiathar. 1 S +22:20.

following Adonijah helped him. Heb. helped after Adonijah. 1 K 2:22, 26-35.

8 **Zadok**. 2 S +8:17.
Benaiah. 1 Ch +15:24.
Nathan. 2 Ch +9:29.
Shimei. 2 S +16:5.
Rei. i.e. *my friend*, **S#7472h**.
the mighty. 2 S 23:8-39. 1 Ch 11:10-47.

9 **slew**. 2 S 15:12. Pr 15:8.
Zoheleth. i.e. *fearful, creeping thing*, **S#2120h**.
En-rogel. *or*, the well Rogel. Jsh 15:7.
called. 2 S 13:23-27. 15:11.

10 **But Nathan**. ver. 8, 19. 2 S 12:1, etc.

11 **Nathan**. 2 S 7:12-17. 12:24, 25. 1 Ch 22:9, 10. 28:4, 5. 29:1.
Adonijah. ver. +5.
Haggith. 2 S 3:4.

12 **let me**. Pr 11:14. 20:18. 27:9. Je 38:15.
save. ver. 21. Ge 19:17. Ac 27:31.
the life. Heb. *nephesh*, soul, Ge +44:30. Jg 9:5. 2 K 11:1. 2 Ch 21:4. 22:10. Mt 21:38.

13 **Assuredly**. ver. 11, 17, 30. 1 Ch 22:6-13. 28:5. 29:1. Ps 2:6, 7.
sit. ver. 17, 24, 30, 35, 48. 1 K 2:12. Dt 17:18. 1 Ch 29:23. Ps 132:11, 12. Is 9:7. Je 33:21. Lk 1:32, 33.

14 **I also**. ver. 17-27. 2 C 13:1.
confirm. Heb. fill up.

15 **very old**. ver. 2-4.

16 **bowed**. ver. 23. Ge +43:28.
And the. 1 K 2:20. Est 7:2. Mt 20:21, 32.
What wouldest thou? Heb. What to thee? Est 5:2, 3.

17 **My lord**. Ge 18:12. 1 P 3:6.
thou swarest. ver. 13, 30.

18 **Adonijah**. ver. 5, 24. 2 S 15:10.
thou knowest. ver. 11, 24, 27. Ac 3:17.

19 **he hath slain**. ver. 7-10, 25.

20 **the eyes**. 2 Ch 20:12. Ps 25:15. 123:1, 2. Zc 3:9.
that thou. 2 S 23:2. 1 Ch 22:8-10. 28:5, 6, 10. 29:1.

21 **sleep**. 1 K +11:43. Ge 15:15.
offenders. Heb. sinners. 1 K 2:15, 22-24.

22 **while she**. Ge 24:15. Jb 1:16-18. Da 9:20.

23 **he bowed**. ver. +16. Ro 13:7. 1 P 2:17.

24 **hast thou**. ver. 14, 18.
reign. ver. 5, 13, 17.

25 **slain**. ver. 9, 19. 1 S 11:14, 15. 1 Ch 29:21-23.
God save king Adonijah. Heb. Let king Adonijah live. ver. 34. 1 S +10:24mg.

26 **me thy**. ver. 8, 19. 2 S 7:2, 12-17. 12:25.

27 **and thou**. ver. 24. 2 K 4:27. Jn 15:15.

28 **into the king's presence**. Heb. before the king.

29 **As the**. 1 K +17:1.
hath. Ps +34:22. 138:7.
soul. Heb. *nephesh*, Ge +12:13.

30 **Even as I sware**. ver. 13, 17.

31 **did reverence**. 2 S 9:6. Est 3:2. Mt 21:37. Ep 5:33. He 12:9.
Let my. ver. 25. Ne +2:3.
for ever. Heb. *olam*, Ex +12:24.

32 **Zadok**. ver. 8, 26, 38.

33 **Take**. 2 S 20:6.
to ride. ver. 5, 38, 44. Ge 41:43. Est 6:6-11.
mine own mule. Heb. the mule which belongeth to me. Le 19:19.
Gihon. ver. 38, 45. 2 Ch 32:30. 33:14.

34 **Zadok**. Ex +28:41. 2 S 5:3. 2 Ch 23:11. Ps 89:20, 36. Is 45:1.
blow ye. 2 S 15:10. 2 K 9:13. 11:14. Ps 98:5-7.
God. ver. +25.

35 **sit**. ver. +13, 17.
I have. 1 K 2:15. 1 Ch 23:1. 28:4, 5. Ps 2:6. 72, title, 1, 2.

36 **Amen**. Je 11:5. Mt +6:13.
the Lord. 1 S 25:29. 1 Ch 17:27. Ps 18:2. 63:1. 89:20, 26.

37 **As the**. 1 K 3:7-9. Ge +28:15. 1 S 17:37. 20:13. 2 S 7:9. 1 Ch 17:8. 22:11, 16. 28:20. Is +43:2, 5. Mt +28:20. Ro 15:33.
and make. ver. 47. 2 S 24:3. 2 K 2:9. Ps 72:8, 17-19. 89:27. Da 7:14.

38 **Zadok**. ver. 8, 26.
the Cherethites. 2 S +8:18.
king David's. ver. 33.

39 **an horn**. 1 S 16:3.
out. Ex 30:23-33. Ps 89:20.
anointed. 1 Ch 29:22.
all the people. ver. +25.

40 **pipes**. *or*, flutes. Da 3:5.
rejoiced. 1 S 11:15. 2 K 11:14, 20. 1 Ch 12:38-40. Ps 97:1. Zc 9:9. Lk 19:37. Re 11:15-18.

41 **as they**. Jb 20:5. Pr 14:13. Ec 7:4-6. Mt 24:38, 39. Lk 17:26-29.
Wherefore. Ex 32:17. Jb 15:21, 22. Ps 73:18-20.
the city. Mt 21:9-11, 15. Ac 21:31.

42 **Jonathan**. 2 S 15:36. 17:17.
a valiant. 1 K 22:18. 2 S 18:27. 2 K 9:22. Is 57:21. 1 Th 5:2, 3.

43 **Verily**. ver. 32-40.

44 **Cherethites**. ver. 38.
ride upon. ver. 32, 33, 38.

45 **Gihon**. 2 S 5:23. 2 Ch 32:30.
the city. ver. 40. 1 S 4:5. Ezr 3:13.
This is. 1 K 14:6. 1 S 28:29. Da 5:26-28.

46 **Solomon sitteth**. ver. 13. 1 Ch 29:23. Ps 132:11. Hag 2:22.

47 **bless**. Ex 12:32. 2 S 8:10. 21:3. Ezr 6:10. Ps 20:1-4.
God. ver. 37. Lk 19:38.
bowed. Ge 47:31. He 11:21.

48 **Blessed**. Ge 14:20. 1 Ch 29:10, 20. Ne 9:5. Ps 34:1. 41:13. 72:17-19. 103:1, 2. 145:2. Da 4:34. Lk 1:46, 47, 68, 69. Ep 1:3. 1 P 1:3.
which. 1 K 3:6. 1 Ch 17:11-14, 17. Ps 132:11, 12. Pr 17:6.
mine eyes. 2 S 24:3. Ps 128:5, 6.

49 **all the guests**. Pr 28:1. Is 21:4, 5. Da 5:4-6.

50 **caught**. 1 K 2:28. Ex 21:14. +27:2.

52 **there shall**. 1 S 14:45. 2 S 14:11. Mt 10:29, 30. Lk 21:18. Ac 27:34.
wickedness. 1 K 2:21-25. Jb 15:22. Pr 13:6. 21:12.

53 **bowed himself**. ver. 16, 31. 2 S 1:2.
Go to. 1 K 2:36. 2 S 14:24, 28. Pr 24:21.

1 KINGS 2

1 **the days**. Ge 47:29. Dt 31:14. 33:1. 2 T 4:6. 2 P 1:13-15.
charged. Nu 27:19. Dt 3:28. 31:23. Ac 20:28-31. 1 T 1:18. 6:13. 2 T 4:1.

2 **I go**. Jsh 23:14. Jb 16:22. 30:23. Ps 89:48. He 9:27.
be thou. Dt 17:19, 20. Jsh +1:6. 1 P 1:13. 2 P 1:5.
and show. 1 K 3:7. 2 S 10:12. Ec 12:13. 1 C 16:13. 1 T 4:12.

3 **And keep**. Dt 29:9. Jsh +1:7. 22:5. 1 Ch 22:12, 13. 28:8, 9. 29:19.
statutes. Dt +4:1, 5, 8. 5:1. 6:1, 2.
testimonies. Dt 4:45. Ps 19:7. 119:2, 111, 138.
written. Dt 17:18-20. Ml 4:4.
that thou. Dt 29:9.
prosper. *or*, do wisely. 1 S 18:5, 14, 30. Ps +1:3. 119:98-100. Pr 3:1-4.
whithersoever. 2 S 8:6, 14. 2 K 18:7.

4 **That the Lord**. Ge 18:19. Dt 7:12. 1 Ch 28:9. Jn 15:9, 10. Ju 20, 21, 24.
his word. 2 S 7:11-16, 25. 1 Ch 17:11-15. 22:9-11. 28:5-7. Ps 89:29-37. 132:11, 12.
walk. Ge +5:22. Le 26:3. 2 Ch 17:3.
with all their heart. Mt +22:37.
soul. Heb. *nephesh*, Ge +34:3.
fail, etc. Heb. be cut off from thee from the throne. 1 K 8:25. 2 S 7:12, 13, 16. Ps 37:9, 22. Zc 14:2.

5 **Joab**. 1 S +26:6.
Abner. 2 S 3:27.

Amasa. 2 S 20:10.
Jether. 2 S 17:25, Ithra.
shed. Heb. put. Je 2:34. 6:15. Ezk 24:7, 8.

6 **according**. ver. 9. Pr 20:26.
let. ver. 28-34. Ge 9:6. Nu 35:33. Pr 28:17. Ec 8:11. Is 65:20.
grave. Heb. *sheol*, Ge +37:35.
in. Ge 42:38. 2 K 22:20. Ps 37:37. Is 48:22. 57:2, 21.

7 **Barzillai**. 2 S 17:27-29. 19:31-40. Pr 27:10.
eat. 2 S 9:7, 10. 19:28. Lk 12:37. 22:28-30. Re 3:20, 21.
when I fled. 2 S 15:13-15.

8 **Shimei**. ver. 36-46. 2 S +16:5.
grievous. Heb. strong. Jb 6:25. Mi 2:10.
he came. 2 S 19:16-23. Je 4:2.

9 **hold him**. Ex 20:7. 22:28. Jb 9:28.
wise. 1 K 3:12, 28. Mt 5:43, 44.
his. ver. 6. Ge 42:38. 44:31.
grave. Heb. *sheol*, Ge +37:35.
with. Nu 32:23.

10 **So David**. 1 K +11:43. 1 Ch 29:28. Ac 2:29. 13:36.
the city. 1 K 3:1. 11:43. 2 S 5:7. 1 Ch 11:7.

11 **reigned over**. 2 S 5:4. 1 Ch 29:26, 27.
seven years. 2 S 2:11. 2 K 24:8.

12 A.M. 2990. B.C. 1014. An. Ex. Is. 477.
sat Solomon. 1 K 1:46. 1 Ch 29:23-25. 2 Ch 1:1. Ps 132:12.
his kingdom. 2 S 7:12, 13, 29. Ps 72:8, etc. 89:36, 37.

13 **Adonijah**. 1 K +1:5-10, 50-53.
Comest. 1 S 16:4, 5. 2 K 9:18-22. 1 Ch 12:17, 18. Lk 10:5, 6.

14 **I have**. 2 S 14:12. Lk 7:40.

15 **Thou knowest**. 1 K 1:5, 25. 2 S 15:6, 13. 16:18.
for it was. 2 S 7:12. 12:24. 1 Ch 22:9, 10. 28:5-7. Pr 21:30. Je 27:5-8. Da 2:22.

16 **deny me not**. Heb. turn not away my face. ver. 17, 20. 2 Ch 6:42. Ps 132:10. Pr 30:7.

17 **Abishag**. 1 K 1:2-4. 2 S 3:7. 12:8.

18 **Well**. Pr 14:15.

19 **rose up**. Ex +20:12.
she sat. Ps 45:9. 110:1. Mt 25:33.

20 **I desire**. Mt 20:20, 21. Jn 2:3, 4.
Ask on. Mt 7:7-11. 18:19. Mk 10:35, 36. 11:24. Lk 11:9, 10. Jn 14:13, 14. 15:16.

21 **Let Abishag**. Ge 49:3. 2 S 16:21, 22.

22 **why dost**. Mt 20:22. Mk 10:38. Ja 4:3.
the kingdom. 1 K 1:5-7, 11, 24, 25.

23 **God**. 1 K 20:10. Ru 1:17. 1 S 14:44. 2 S 3:9, 35. 19:13. 2 K 6:31.
if Adonijah. 2 S 16:23.
spoken. Ps 64:8. 140:9. Pr 18:6, 7. Ec 10:12. Lk 19:22.
life. Heb. *nephesh*, soul, Ge +44:30; Ge +9:5.

24 **as the Lord**. 1 K +17:1.
set me. 1 K 3:6, 7. 10:9. 1 Ch 29:23. 2 Ch 1:8, 9.

made me. Ex 1:21. 1 S 25:28. 2 S 7:11-13, 27. 1 Ch 17:10, 17, 23. Ps 127:1.
as he promised. 1 Ch 22:10.
put. 1 K 1:52. Ec 8:11-13.

25 **he fell**. ver. 31, 34, 46. Jg 8:20, 21. 1 S 15:33. 2 S 1:15. 4:12.

26 **Abiathar**. ver. 35. 1 K 1:7, 25.
Anathoth. 1 Ch +7:8.
worthy of death. Heb. a man of death. 1 S +20:31mg.
barest. 1 S 22:20-23. 23:6-9. 2 S 15:24, 29. 1 Ch 15:11, 12.
hast been. 2 S 15:24-29. Mt 10:42. Lk 22:28. Ga 3:4.

27 **So Solomon**. 1 S 2:30-36.
that he. 1 S 2:30-36. 3:12-14. Mt 26:56. Jn 12:38. 19:24, 28, 36, 37.
Shiloh. Jg +21:19.

28 **Joab had**. 1 K 1:7. Dt 32:35. 2 S 18:2, 14, 15.
caught. 1 K +1:50. Ex +27:2.

29 **he is by**. Ex 21:14. Ezk 9:6. 1 P 4:17.
Go. ver. 25, 31, 46.

31 **Do**. Ex 21:14.
that thou. Ge 9:5, 6. Nu 35:33. Dt 19:10. 2 K 9:26. Pr 28:17. Ac 28:4.
which. ver. 5.
and from. 2 S 3:28.

32 **return**. ver. 44. Ge 4:11. Jg 9:24, 57. Ps 7:16.
two men. 2 S 3:27. 20:10.
more righteous. 1 S 15:28. 2 S 4:11. 2 Ch 21:13. Est 1:19.
my father. 2 S 3:26, 37.
Abner. ver. 5. 1 S +14:50.
Amasa. 2 S 20:10.
Jether. ver. 5. 2 S 17:25, Ithra.

33 **return upon**. ver. +32. 2 S 3:29. 2 K 5:27. Ps 101:8. 109:6-15. Mt 27:25.
for ever. Heb. *olam*, Ex +12:24.
upon David. 2 S 3:28. Pr 25:5.
his house. Ps 89:29, 36, 37. 132:12. Is 9:6, 7. 11:1-9. Lk 1:31-33. 2:14.
for ever. Heb. *olam*, Ex +12:24.

34 **Benaiah**. ver. 25, 31, 46.
and fell. Ex 24:14.
buried. 2 K 21:18. 2 Ch 33:20.
in the. Jsh 15:61. Mt 3:1.

35 **in his room**. Jb 34:24.
Zadok. ver. +27. Nu 25:11-13. 1 S 2:35. 1 Ch 6:4-15, 50-53. 24:3. 29:22. Ps 109:8. Ac 1:20.

36 **Shimei**. ver. +8, 9. Pr 20:8, 26.
Build. 1 K 1:53. 2 S 14:24, 28.

37 **on the day**. Ge +2:17.
over the. 2 S +15:23.
surely die. Ge +2:16.
thy blood. ver. 31, 33. Jsh 2:19. Ac +18:6.
head. Jg +5:30.

38 **The saying**. 1 K 20:4. 2 K 20:19.

39 A.M. 2993. B.C. 1011. An. Ex. Is. 480.
Achish. 1 S +21:10.
Maachah. i.e. *oppression*, **S#4601h**. 1 K 15:2,

10, 13. Ge 22:24. Jsh 13:13. 2 S 3:3. 10:6, 8. 1 Ch 2:48. 3:2. 7:15, 16. 8:29. 9:35. 11:43. 19:6, 7. 27:16. 2 Ch 11:20-22. 15:16.

40 arose. Pr 15:27. Lk 12:15. 1 T +6:10.

42 Did I not. ver. 36-38. Ps 15:4. Lk 19:22.
  on the day. Ge +2:17.
  surely die. Ge +2:16.
  and thou saidst. Lk 15:22.

43 Why. 2 S 21:2. Ezk 17:18, 19.
  commandment. 2 Ch 30:12. Ec 8:2. Ro 13:5.

44 Thou knowest. 2 S 16:5-13. Jn 8:9. Ro 2:15. 1 J 3:20.
  return. ver. +32, 33. Ps 7:16. Pr 5:22. Ezk 17:19. Ho 4:9mg.

45 blessed. Ps 21:6. 72:17.
  the throne. ver. +24, 33, 34. Pr 25:5. Is 9:6, 7.
  for ever. Heb. *olam*, Ex +12:24.

46 the kingdom. ver. 12, 45. 2 Ch 1:1. Pr 29:4.

1 KINGS 3

1 A.M. 2990. B.C. 1014. An. Ex. Is. 477.
  affinity. 2 Ch 18:1. Ezr 9:14.
  and took. 1 K 7:8. 9:24. 11:1.
  the city. 2 S 5:7. 1 Ch 11:7.
  his own. 1 K 7:1-12.
  the house. 1 K ch. 6. 7:13-51. 2 Ch ch. 2-4. Ezr 5:11.
  the wall. 1 K 9:15-19.

2 the people. Le 17:3-6. Dt 12:2-5. 2 K +21:3.
  was no. 1 K 5:3. 1 Ch 17:4-6. 28:3-6. Ac 7:47-49.

3 loved. Dt 6:5. 10:12. 30:6, 16, 20. 2 S 12:24, 25. Ps 31:23. Mt 22:36, 37. Mk 12:29, 30. Ro 8:28. 13:10. 1 C 8:3. 2 C 5:14. Ja 1:12. 2:5. 1 J 4:19, 20. 5:2, 3.
  walking. ver. +6, +14. 1 K 2:3, 4. 11:34. 15:3. 1 Ch 28:8, 9. 2 Ch 17:3-5. Jn 14:15, 21.
  only he. 2 K +21:3.

4 Gibeon. Jsh +10:2.
  a thousand. 1 K +8:63. 2 Ch 7:5. Is 40:16.

5 the Lord. 1 K 9:2.
  in a dream. Ge +31:24.
  Ask what. 2 Ch 1:7-12. Mt 7:7, 8. Mk 10:36-38, 51. 11:24. Lk 11:9. Jn 14:13, 14. 15:16. 16:23, 24. Ja 1:5, 6. 1 J 5:14, 15.

6 thy servant. Nu 12:7. 2 S 7:5.
  great. 2 S 7:8-12. 12:7, 8. 22:47-51. 1 Ch 29:12-14. Ps 78:70-72. Is +55:3.
  mercy. *or*, bounty. Ps 13:6. 116:7. 119:17. 2 C 9:5, 11.
  according. 1 K 9:4. 15:5. Ge +17:1. Ps 18:20-24.
  that. 1 K +1:48.

7 thou hast. Da 2:21. 4:25, 32. 5:18, 21.
  a little. Ex 4:10. 1 Ch 29:1. 2 Ch 1:8, 9. Jb 32:6-8. Ec 10:16. Je 1:6. Mt 18:3, 4.
  know not. Ps 32:8.

to go. Nu 27:15-17. Dt 31:2. 1 S 18:16. 2 S 5:2. Ps 121:8. Jn 10:3, 4, 9.

8 thy people. Ex 19:5, 6. Dt 7:6-8. 1 S 12:22. Ps 78:71.
  cannot. Ge 13:16. 15:5. 22:17. 1 Ch 21:2, 5, 6. 27:23, 24.

9 Give therefore. 1 Ch 22:12. 29:19. 2 Ch 1:10. Ps 119:34, 73, 144. Pr 2:3-9. 3:13-18. 16:16. Ja 1:5. 3:17.
  understanding. Heb. hearing. Pr 20:12.
  to judge. ver. 28. Ps 72:1, 2. Pr 14:8. Ec 7:11, 19. 9:15-18. Jn 5:30.
  discern. 2 S 14:17. Is 11:2-4. 1 C 2:14, 15. Ep 5:17. Ph 1:10g. He +5:14.
  who is able. Ex 3:11, 12. 4:10-13. Je 1:6. Mt 3:11, 14. 2 C 2:16. 3:5.

10 pleased. Pr 15:8.

11 hast not. Ps 4:6. Pr 16:31. Mt 20:21, 22. Ro 8:26. Ja 4:2, 3.
  long life. Heb. many days. 2 Ch 1:11.
  the life. Heb. *nephesh*, soul, Ge +44:30.
  discern. Heb. hear. ver. 9mg.

12 I have done. Ps 10:17. Pr 2:1-9. Is 65:24. Ro 8:26, 27. 1 J 5:14, 15.
  I have given. ver. 28. 1 K 2:6, 9. 4:29-34. 5:12. 10:3-8, 23, 24. 1 Ch 29:25. 2 Ch 1:11, 12. 2:12. 9:5-8, 22. Ec 1:13, 16. 2:9. Lk 21:15.
  neither. Mt 12:42. Col 2:3.
  thee. 1 K 10:23.

13 And I. Ps 84:11, 12. Mt 6:33. Ro 8:32. 1 C 3:22, 23. Ep 3:20.
  riches. 1 K 4:21-24. 10:23-29. Pr 3:13, 16.
  shall not be. *or*, hath not been.

14 if thou. 1 K 2:3, 4. 1 Ch 22:12, 13. 28:9. 2 Ch 7:17-19. Ps 132:12. Zc 3:7.
  as thy. ver. +3. 1 K 9:4, 5. 15:5. 2 Ch 17:3, 4. 29:2. 34:2. Jn +17:6. Ac 13:22.
  I will lengthen. Dt +4:40. 1 T +4:8.

15 awoke. Ge 41:7. Je 31:26.
  before. 2 S 6:17. 1 Ch 16:1, 2.
  burnt offerings. Le +23:12.
  peace offerings. Le +23:19.
  a feast. Ge +19:3. Da 5:1. Mk 6:21.

16 two women. Le 19:29. Dt 23:17. Jsh 2:1.
  harlots. or, tavern-keepers. Jsh 2:1. Jg 11:1.
  stood. Ex 18:13, 16. Nu 27:2.

17 O my Lord. Ge 43:20. Ro 13:7.

20 midnight. Jb 24:13-17. Ps 139:11. Mt 13:25. Jn 3:20.
  took. ver. 21.

21 give. Ge 21:7. 1 S 1:23. La 4:3, 4.

22 Nay. ver. 23, 24.

25 Divide. ver. 28. Pr 25:8.

26 her bowels. Is +63:15.
  yearned. Heb. were hot. Ps 39:3.
  give her. Ro +1:31.

28 feared. Ex 14:31. Jsh 4:14. 1 S 12:18. 1 Ch 29:24. Pr 24:21.
  saw. Ge 30:27.
  the wisdom. ver. 9-12. Ezr 7:25. Ec 7:19. Da

2:21, 47. 5:11. 1 C 1:24, 30. Col 2:3.
in him. Heb. in the midst of him. Ge +45:6.
to do. Ps 72:2, 4.

1 KINGS 4

1 **over all Israel**. 1 K 11:13, 35, 36. 12:19, 20.
2 S 5:5. 1 Ch 12:38. 2 Ch 9:30. Ec 1:12.

2 **the princes**. Ex +18:21. 2 S 8:15-18. 20:23-
26. 1 C 12:28.
 Azariah. 1 Ch +6:36. 27:17.
 priest. or, chief officer. Ge 41:45. 1 Ch 6:10.

3 **Elihoreph**. i.e. God of my maturity; God of
autumn, **S#456h**.
 Shisha. i.e. whiteness, **S#7894h**, only here. 2 S
8:17, Seraiah. 20:25, Sheva. 1 Ch 18:16,
Shavsha.
 scribes. or, secretaries. 2 S +8:17mg.
 recorder. or, remembrancer. 2 S +8:16mg.

4 **Benaiah**. 1 Ch +15:24.
 Zadok. 1 K 2:26, 27, 35. 2 S +8:17.

5 **son of Nathan**. 1 K 1:10, etc. 2 S 7:2. 12:1-
15, 25.
 the officers. ver. 7.
 Zabud. i.e. endowed, **S#2071h**.
 the principal. 2 S 8:18. 20:26.
 the king's. 2 S 15:37. 16:16. 19:37, 38. 1 Ch
27:33. Pr 22:11. Lk 22:29. Jn 13:23. 15:14,
15. Ja 2:23.

6 **Ahishar**. i.e. brother of a singer or of the
upright, **S#301h**.
 household. 2 S 20:24.
 Adoniram. i.e. Lord of height, **S#141h**. 1 K
5:14. 12:18. 2 S 20:24, Adoram. 2 Ch 10:18,
Hadoram.
 Abda. i.e. servant.
 tribute. or, levy. 1 K 5:13, 14. 9:15, 21.

7 **officers**. ver. 5, 27. 1 K 5:16. 9:23. 2 Ch 8:10.
 each man. 1 Ch 27:1-15.

8 **The son of Hur**. or, Ben-hur. i.e. son of whiteness. Jg 17:1. 19:1.

9 **The son of Dekar**. or, Ben-dekar. i.e. son of
piercing through, **S#1857h**.
 Makaz. i.e. extremity; end, **S#4739h**.
 Shaalbim. Jsh 19:42, Shaalabbin.
 Beth-shemesh. Je +43:13.
 Elon-beth-hanan. i.e. oak of the house of grace,
S#358h. Jsh 19:43.

10 **The son of Hesed**. or, Ben-hesed. i.e. son of
kindness, **S#2618h**.
 Aruboth. i.e. windows, **S#700h**.
 Sochoh. Jsh +15:35.
 Hepher. Jsh 12:17. 17:2.

11 **The son of Abinadab**. or, Ben-abinadab.
 Dor. Jsh 12:23. 17:11. Jg 1:27.
 Taphath. i.e. a drop or dropping, **S#2955h**.

12 **Baana**. i.e. son of affliction, **S#1195h**. ver. 16. Ne
3:4.
 Taanach. Jsh +17:11.
 Megiddo. Jsh +12:21.

 Beth-shean. Jsh +17:11.
 Zartanah. i.e. perplexity; their distress, **S#6891h**.
1 K 7:46, Zarthan. Jsh 3:16, Zaretan.
 Jezreel. 1 Ch +4:3.
 Abel-meholah. 1 K 19:16. Jg 7:22.
 Jokneam. Jsh 19:11. 1 Ch 6:68.

13 **The son of Geber**. or, Ben-geber. i.e. the son
of a mighty one.
 Ramoth-gilead. i.e. perpetual spring, **S#7433h**.
1 K 22:4, 6, 12, 15, 20, 29. Dt 4:43. Jsh 20:8.
21:38. 2 K 8:28. 9:1, 4, 14. 1 Ch 6:80. 2 Ch
18:2, 3, 5, 11, 14, 19, 28. 22:5.
 the towns. Nu +32:41.
 Argob. i.e. stony; lion's den, **S#709h**. Dt 3:4, 8,
13, 14. 2 K 15:25. Ps 22:12. 68:15.
 Bashan. Dt +32:14.
 with walls. Dt 3:4. 2 Ch 8:5.
 brasen bars. 2 Ch +8:5.

14 **Ahinadab**. i.e. brother of liberality, **S#292h**.
 Mahanaim. or, to Mahanaim. Ge +32:2.

15 **Ahimaaz**. 2 S 15:27.
 Naphtali. Jsh 19:32-39.
 Basmath. i.e. spicy, **S#1315h**. Ge +36:3,
Bashemath.
 the daughter. ver. 11. 1 S 18:18.

16 **Hushai**. 2 S 15:32, 37.
 Asher. Jsh 19:24-31.
 Aloth. i.e. ascents, **S#1175h**. Jsh 15:24.

17 **Paruah**. i.e. flourishing, **S#6515h**.
 Issachar. Nu +1:29. Jsh 19:17-23.

18 **Shimei**. 2 S +16:5.
 Elah. Ge +36:41.
 Benjamin. Jsh 18:20-28.

19 **Geber**. i.e. strong; a valiant man, **S#1398h**.
 Uri. Ex +31:2.
 the country of Sihon. Nu +21:21-35.
 Bashan. ver. +13.

20 **many**. Zc 10:8.
 as the sand. 1 K 3:8. Ge 15:5. +22:17. Pr
14:28.
 eating. 1 S 30:16. 1 Ch 12:39. Jb 1:18. Ps
72:3-7. Ec 2:24. Is 22:13. Mi 4:4. Zc 3:10.
9:15. Ac 2:46.

21 **Solomon reigned**. ver. 24. Dt 11:24. Jsh 1:4.
21:43. Ezr 4:20. Ps 72:8-11.
 over all kingdoms. Is +26:15. Je +7:7.
33:21. Ac +3:19-21. 7:5. He 11:13, 39.
 from the river. Ps +72:8.
 brought. Jg +3:15.

22 **provision**. Heb. bread.
 measures. Heb. cors. 1 K 5:11. 2 Ch 2:10.
27:5. Ezk 45:14.

23 **Ten fat**. Ne 5:17, 18.
 roebucks. Dt 15:22. 2 S 2:18.

24 **the river**. Ps +72:8.
 Tiphsah. i.e. a passage over. 2 K 15:16.
 Azzah. Ge +10:19.
 all the kings. ver. 21. Ps 68:29. 72:8, 10, 11.
 had peace. 1 K 5:4. 1 Ch 22:9. Ps 72:3, 7. Is
9:7. Lk 2:14. He 7:1, 2.

25 **safely**. Heb. confidently. Dt +12:10. Is 60:18.
every man. 2 K 18:31. Mi 4:4. Zc 3:10.
from Dan. Jg +20:1.

26 **forty thousand**. 1 K 10:25, 26. Dt 17:16. 2 S
8:4. 2 Ch 1:14. 9:25. Ps 20:7.

27 **those officers**. ver. 7-19.
lacked nothing. Ne 9:21. Lk 22:35.

28 **dromedaries**. *or*, mules, *or* swift beasts. Est
8:10, 14. Mi 1:13.

29 **God**. 1 K 3:12, 28. 10:23, 24. 2 Ch 1:10-12. Ps
119:34. Pr 2:6. Ec 1:16. 2:26. Ja 1:5, 17. 3:17.
largeness. Is 60:5.
as the sand. ver. +20.

30 **the children**. Ge +29:1. Da 1:20. 4:7. 5:11,
12. Mt 2:1, 16.
east. Is 2:6.
the wisdom of Egypt. Is 19:11, 12. Ac 7:22.

31 **wiser**. 1 K +3:12. Mt 12:42. Lk 11:31. Col
2:3.
Ethan. 1 Ch 15:19. Ps 89, title.
Ezrahite. i.e. *sprung up*, **S#250h**. Ps 88, title.
89, title.
Heman. 1 Ch +2:6.
Chalcol. i.e. *nourished; comprehended*, **S#3633h**.
1 Ch 2:6.
Darda. i.e. *pearl of knowledge; bearer*, **S#1862h**. 1
Ch 2:6, Dara.
Mahol. i.e. *a dance*, **S#4235h**. 1 Ch 2:6, Zerah.
his fame. 1 K 5:7. 10:1, 6. 2 Ch 9:23. Mt
+4:24.

32 **he spake**. Pr ch. 1, etc. Ec 12:9. Mt 13:35.
proverbs. or, similes. Dt +28:37. Pr +1:1.
songs. Ps ch 72, 127. SS 1:1, etc.

33 **the cedar tree**. Nu +24:6.
the hyssop. Ps +51:7.
of beasts. Ge 1:20-25.

34 **there came**. 1 K 10:1. 2 Ch 9:1, 23. Is 2:2. Zc
8:23.

1 KINGS 5

1 A.M. 2990. B.C. 1014. An. Ex. Is. 477.
Hiram. ver. 10, 13. 1 K 9:12-14.
sent. 2 S 8:10. 10:1, 2. Ps 45:12.
for Hiram. 2 S +5:11. Pr 27:10. Am 1:9.

2 **Solomon sent**. 2 Ch 2:3.

3 **could not**. 2 S 7:5-11. 1 Ch 22:4-6. 2 Ch 6:6-
8.
the wars. 1 Ch 22:8. 28:3. 2 Ch 2:3.
put. Jsh 10:24. Ps 8:6. 110:1. Ml 4:3. 1 C
15:25. Ep 1:22.

4 **hath given**. 1 K +4:24. 1 Ch 22:9. Ps 72:7. Is
9:7. Ac 9:31.

5 **behold**. 2 Ch 2:1-4, etc.
purpose. Heb. say. 2 Ch 2:1.
as the Lord. 2 S 7:12, 13. 1 Ch 17:12. 22:10.
28:6, 10. Zc 6:12, 13.

6 **cedar trees**. 1 K 6:9, 10, 16, 20. 2 Ch 2:8, 10,
16. Ps 29:5.
will I give hire. Ro 12:17. Ph 4:8.

appoint. Heb. say. 1 K 11:18.
that there is not. 1 C 12:14-21. Ep 4:7.
Sidonians. Ge 10:15. Ezr 3:7. 1 Ch 22:4.

7 **Blessed**. 1 K 10:9. 2 Ch 2:11, 12. 9:7, 8. Ps
122:6, 7. 137:6.
which hath. 1 K 1:48. Ge 33:5. Is 8:18. 9:6.
a wise son. 1 K +3:9. 2 Ch 2:11. Pr 10:1.
13:1. 15:20. 23:24.

8 **considered**. Heb. heard.
timber of fir. 1 K 6:15, 34. 2 S 6:5. 2 Ch 3:5.

9 **Lebanon**. Dt +1:7.
and I will. 2 Ch 2:16.
appoint. Heb. send.
in giving food. 2 Ch 2:15. Ezr 3:7. Ezk
27:17. Ac 12:20.

11 **measures**. Heb. *cors*. 1 K +4:22mg. 2 Ch 2:10.

12 **as he promised him**. 1 K 3:12. 4:29. 2 Ch
1:12. He 10:23. Ja 1:5.
they two. 1 K 15:19. Ge 21:32. Am 1:9.

13 **levy**. Heb. tribute of men. 1 K 4:6.
the levy. 1 K 9:15.

14 **a month**. 1 K 4:7-19. 1 Ch 27:1-15.
Adoniram. 1 K +4:6.

15 **threescore and ten thousand**. 1 K 9:20-22.
2 Ch 2:17, 18. 8:7-9. Ezr 2:58. Ne 7:57, 60.

16 **three thousand three hundred**. 1 K 9:23.
2 Ch 2:2.

17 **costly stones**. 1 K 6:7. 7:9. 1 Ch 22:2. Ps
144:12. Is 28:16. 1 C 3:11, 12. 1 P 2:6, 7. Re
21:14-21.

18 **the stone-squarers**. or, Giblites. Jsh 13:5. Ps
83:7. Ezk 27:9.

1 KINGS 6

1 A.M. 2993. B.C. 1011. An. Ex. Is. 480.
And it came. Jg 11:26. 2 Ch 3:1, 2.
in the month Zif. i.e. *brightness, beauty*,
S#2099h. ver. 37. Nu 1:1.
began. Heb. built. Ac 7:47.
build. 1 Ch 29:19. Zc 6:12, 13, 15. Jn 2:19-
21. 1 C 6:19. 2 C 6:16. Ep 2:20-22. Col 2:7.
He 3:6. 9:11. 11:10. 1 P 2:5.

2 **the house**. Ezk ch. 40. 41.
threescore. Ezr 6:3, 4. Ezk 41:1, etc. Re
21:16, 17.

3 **the porch**. 1 Ch 28:11. 2 Ch 3:3, 4. Ezk
41:15. Mt 4:5. Jn 10:23. Ac 3:10, 11.

4 **windows of narrow lights**. or, windows
broad within, and narrow without; or, skewed
and closed. 1 K 6:4. SS 2:9. Ezk 40:16. 41:16,
26.

5 **against**. or, upon, or joining to.
built. 1 Ch 9:26. 23:28. 28:11. 2 Ch 31:11.
Ne 10:37. 12:44. 13:5-9. SS 1:4. Je 35:4. Ezk
40:44. 41:5-11. 42:3-12.
chambers. Heb. floors.
oracle. ver. 16, 19-23, 31. 1 K 7:49. 8:6, 8. Ex
25:22. Le 16:2. Nu 7:89. 2 Ch 3:16. 4:20. 5:7,
9. Ps 28:2.

chambers. Heb. ribs. ver. 8. 1 K 7:3. Ezk 41:5-9, 11, 26.

6   **narrowed rests**. *or*, narrowings, *or* rebatements.
the beams. Ezk 41:6.

7   **built of stone**. 1 K 5:17, 18. Dt 27:5, 6. Pr 24:27. Ro 9:23. 2 C 5:5. Col 1:12. 1 P 2:5.
neither hammer. Is 42:2. Ac 9:31. Ja 1:20. 3:17, 18.

8   **side**. Heb. shoulder.
went up. Ezk 41:6, 7.

9   **he built**. ver. 14, 38.
with beams and boards of cedar. *or*, the vault beams and the ceilings with cedar.

12   **if thou**. Ge +4:7.
wilt walk. 1 K 2:3, 4. 3:14. 8:23. 9:3-6. 2 K 20:3. 1 Ch 28:9. 2 Ch 7:17, 18. 17:3. Zc 3:7. Col 1:23.
and keep. 1 K 8:25. 1 S 12:14, 15. 13:13, 14. Ps 132:12.
then will I perform. 2 S 7:13. 1 Ch 22:10.

13   **I will dwell**. Ex +29:45. Le 26:11. Ezk 37:26-28.
will not forsake. Dt +31:6, 8. 1 S 12:22. 1 Ch 28:9, 20. He +13:5.

14   A.M. 2993-3000. B.C. 1011-1004.
Solomon built. ver. 9, 38. Ac 7:47, 48.

15   **both the floors of the house, and the walls**. *or*, from the floor of the house, unto the walls, etc. and so ver. 16.

16   **built them**. ver. 5, 19, 20. 1 K 8:6. Ex 25:21, 22. 26:23. Le 16:2. 2 Ch 3:8. Ezk 45:3. He 9:3, 8, 11, 24.
the oracle. ver. +5.

18   **knops**. *or*, gourds. 2 K 4:39.
open flowers. *or*, openings of flowers.
no stone. 1 P 2:5.

19   **the oracle**. ver. +5, 16.
to set. 1 K 8:6-10. Ex 40:20, 21. 2 Ch 5:7. He 9:3, 4.

20   **twenty cubits**. ver. 2, 3.
pure. Heb. shut up. 2 Ch +9:20.
the altar. ver. +22.

21   **overlaid**. Ex 26:29, 32. 36:34. 2 Ch 3:7-9.
by the chains. ver. 5. Ex 26:32, 33. 2 Ch 3:14-16.

22   **also**. ver. 20. Ex 30:1, 3, 5, 6. 36:34. 2 Ch 3:7, etc.
the whole altar. Lk +1:11.

23   **two cherubims**. Ge +3:24. 1 P 1:12.
olive trees. *or*, oily trees. Heb. trees of oil. ver. 31-33. Ne 8:15. Is 41:19.

27   **they stretched forth the wings of the cherubims**. *or*, the cherubims stretched forth their wings. Ge +3:24.

29   **carved figures**. Ex 36:8. 2 Ch 3:14. 4:2-5. Ps 103:20. 148:2. Lk 2:13, 14. Ep 3:10. Re 5:11-14.
palm trees. Ps 92:12-15. Re 7:9.

open flowers. Heb. openings of flowers. ver. 18, 32.

30   **the floor**. Is 54:11, 12. 60:17. Re 20:18-21. 21:18.

31   **doors**. Jn 10:9. 14:1, 6. Ep 2:18. He 10:19, 20.
a fifth part. *or*, five square.

32   **two doors**. *or*, leaves of the doors. Ge +19:6. Ezk 41:23-25.
olive tree. Ge 8:11. Lk 3:22.
open flowers. Heb. openings of flowers. ver. 18, 29.

33   **a fourth part**. *or*, four square.

34   **fir tree**. 1 K 5:8.
the two leaves. Ezk 41:23-25.

36   **the inner**. Ex 27:9-19. 38:9-20. 2 Ch 4:9. 7:7. Re 11:2.

37   **the fourth year**. ver. 1. 2 Ch 3:2.

38   **Bul**. i.e. *changeable*, **S#945h**, only here.
finished. Ezr 6:14, 15. Zc 4:9. 6:13-15.
throughout, etc. *or*, with all the appurtenances thereof, and with all the ordinances thereof.
finished. Is 66:9. Ph 1:6.
seven years. ver. 1, 9. 1 K 7:1. Ezr 3:8-13. 6:15. Jn 2:20.

1 KINGS 7

1   **thirteen years**. 1 K 9:10. 2 Ch 8:1. Ec 2:4, 5. Mt 6:33.

2   **the house**. 1 K 9:19. 10:17. 2 Ch 9:16. SS 7:4.

3   **beams**. Heb. ribs. 1 K 6:5mg.

4   **windows**. ver. 5. 1 K 6:4. Is 54:12. Ezk 40:16, 22, 25, 29, 33, 36. 41:26.
light was against light. Heb. sight against sight.

5   **doors and posts were square, with the windows**. *or*, spaces and pillars *were* square in prospect. Ex 27:1. Ezk 41:21. 43:16.

6   **before them**. *or*, according to them. Ezk 41:25, 26.
thick. 2 Ch 4:17. Ezk 41:25.
before them. *or*, according to them.

7   **a porch**. 1 K 6:3.
for the throne. 1 K 10:18-20. Ps 122:5. Is 9:7.
of judgment. 1 K 3:9, 28. Pr 20:8.
from one side of the floor to the other. Heb. from floor to floor.

8   **another court**. 2 K 20:4.
an house. 1 K 3:1. 9:24. 2 Ch 8:11.

9   **costly stones**. ver. 10, 11. 1 K 5:17.
saw. 2 S 12:31. 1 Ch 20:3.
coping. lit. hand-breadth. Heb. spans. ver. 26. 2 Ch 4:5. Ps 39:5.

10   **the foundations**. Is 28:16. 54:11. 1 C 3:10, 11. Re 21:19, 20.

11   **above were**. Ep 2:20-22. 1 P 2:5.

12 **three rows**. 1 K 6:36.
the porch. Jn 10:23. Ac 3:11. 5:12.

13 **Hiram**. ver. 40. 2 S +5:11.
Tyre. i.e. *rock, strength*, **S#6865h**. 1 K 5:1. 9:11, 12. Jsh 19:29. 2 S 5:11. 24:7. 1 Ch 14:1. 2 Ch 2:3, 11. Ps 45:12. 83:7. 87:4. Is 23:1, 5, 8, 15, 17. Je +25:22, Tyrus. Mt +11:21.

14 **a widow's son**. Heb. the son of a widow woman.
tribe. 2 Ch 2:14.
Naphtali. 2 Ch 2:14.
his father. 2 Ch 4:16.
worker. or, plower, graver. 1 K 19:19. Jb 1:14.
in brass. Ezk 27:13.
he was filled. Ex 31:2-6. 35:30-35. 36:1, 2, 8. 2 Ch 2:13, 14. 4:11. Is 28:26. Da 1:17.

15 **cast**. Heb. fashioned. Ex 32:4.
two pillars. ver. 21. 2 K 25:13, 16, 17. 2 Ch 3:15-17. 4:12, etc. Je 52:21-23.
eighteen cubits. 2 Ch 3:15.
line. or, cord. Ge 14:23. Jsh 2:18. Jg 16:12. Ec 4:12. SS 4:3. Je 52:21.

16 **two chapiters**. or, crowns. ver. 17, 18, 19, 20, 31, 41, 42. Ex 36:38. 38:17, 19, 28. 2 K 25:17. 2 Ch 4:12, 13. Je 52:22.
molten. or, cast. ver. 23, 33. 2 K 4:5h (poured out). 2 Ch 4:2. Jb 11:15h (stedfast). 37:18.

17 **checker work**. ver. 18, 20, 41, 42. 2 K 1:2. 25:17. 2 Ch 4:12, 13. Jb 18:8. Je 52:22, 23.
wreaths. Ex 28:14, 22, 24, 25. 39:15-18. Dt 22:12. 2 K 25:17.
chainwork. Ex 28:14. 39:15. 2 Ch 3:5, 16.

19 **lily work**. ver. 22, 26. 1 K 6:18, 32-35. Ps 45, title (Shoshannim). 69:t. 80:t. SS 2:16. 4:5. 5:13. 6:2, 3. 7:2.

20 **and the pomegranates**. 2 K 25:17. 2 Ch 3:16. 4:13. Je 52:22, 23.

21 **And he set the pillars**. Ex 36:38. 38:17, 19, 28. 2 Ch 3:17. Je 52:17. Ga 2:9. Re 3:12.
the porch. ver. 12. 1 K 6:3. Ezk 40:48, 49.
Jachin. Ge +46:10. 2 S 7:12. Is 9:7.
Boaz. Ru +2:1. Is 45:24. Mt 16:18.

23 **he made**. Ex 30:18.
a molten sea. 2 K 25:13. 2 Ch 4:2. Je 52:17, 20.
the one brim to the other. Heb. his brim to his brim. Ex 30:19, 21. 40:12. Le 11:29-36. Nu 8:7, LXX. 19:21, 22. 31:23, 24. 2 Ch 4:3. Jb 9:30. Mt 26:6-12. Jn 2:6. 13:5-10.

24 **knops**. 1 K 6:18. Ex 25:31-36. 37:17-22.
compassing the sea. 2 Ch 4:3.

25 **upon twelve**. 2 Ch 4:4, 5. Je 52:20. Ezk 1:10. Mt 28:19. Mk 16:15, 16. Lk 24:47. 1 C 9:9. Re 4:6, 7.

26 **an hand breadth**. Je 52:21.
with flowers. ver. 19. 1 K 6:18, 32, 35.
cup. Ge 40:11. 2 Ch 4:5.
it contained. 2 Ch 4:3, 6.
two thousand. ver. 38. 2 K 4:5. Ezk 45:14.

27 **ten bases**. 2 K 25:13, 16. 2 Ch 4:14. Je 52:17, 20.

28 **borders**. Ex 25:25, 27. 37:12, 14. 2 S 22:46. 2 K 16:17. Ps 18:45. Mi 7:17 (out of their holes).

29 **lions**. ver. 25. 1 K 6:27. Ezk 1:10. 10:14. 41:18, 19. Ho 5:14. Re 4:6, 7. 5:5.
cherubims. Ge 3:34. Ex 25:18. 37:7. He 9:5.
certain additions. 1 P 2:5.

30 **wheels**. Ex 14:25. Pr 20:26. 25:11mg. Is 28:27. Ezk 1:15-21. 3:13. 10:10-13. Na 3:2.

31 **gravings**. or, carvings. 1 K 6:18, 29, 32.

32 **joined to the base**. Heb. in the base.

33 **And the work**. Ezk 1:16, 18.

36 **plates**. or, tablets. Ex 24:12.
graved cherubims. ver. 29. 1 K 6:29, 32, 35. Ezk 40:31, 37. 41:18-20, 25, 26.
proportion. Heb. nakedness. Na 2:5.

37 **casting**. ver. 16, 23.
measure. Ex 26:2.
one size. 1 K 6:25.

38 **ten lavers**. Ex +30:18. He 9:10. 10:22. 1 J 1:7. Re 7:14.
baths. ver. 26. 2 Ch 2:10. 4:5. Is 5:10. Ezk 45:10. 11, 14.

39 **side**. Heb. shoulder. 1 K 6:8.
he set. 2 Ch 4:6, 10.
the sea. Zc 13:1. Lk 24:47. Jn 13:8. T 3:5, 6. He 9:10. +10:22. Re 7:13, 14.

40 **Hiram**. Heb. Hirom. ver. 13.
the lavers. ver. 38. 2 K 25:14, 15. 2 Ch 4:6, 11-16. Je 52:18, 19.
the shovels. ver. 45.
the basons. or, sprinkling bowls. ver. 45, 50. Ex 24:6. **S#4219h**: Ex 27:3. 38:3. Nu 4:14. 7:13, 19, 25, 31, 37, 43, 49, 55, 61, 67, 73, 79, 84, 85. 2 K 12:13. 25:15. 1 Ch 28:17. 2 Ch 4:8, 11, 22. Ne 7:70. Je 52:18, 19. Am 6:6. Zc 9:15. 14:20.
So Hiram. Ex 39:32-43.

41 **two pillars**. ver. 15-22. 2 Ch 4:12.
bowls. ver. 42. 2 Ch 4:12, 13. Ec 12:6. Zc 4:3.
two networks. ver. 17, 18.

42 **the pillars**. Heb. the face of the pillars.

43 **ten bases**. ver. 27-39.

44 **one sea**. ver. 23-26.

45 **the pots**. Ex 27:3. 38:3. Le 8:31. 1 S 2:13, 14. 2 Ch 4:16. Ezk 46:20-24. Zc 14:20, 21.
bright brass. Heb. brass made bright, or scoured. Is 18:2 (peeled), 7. Ezk 21:10 (furbished), 11.

46 **plain**. or, circuit. Ge 13:10, 11.
the clay ground. Heb. the thickness of the ground.
Succoth. Ge 33:17.
Zarthan. i.e. *narrowness of dwelling place; their distress*, **S#6891h**. 1 K 4:12, Zartanah. Jsh 3:16, Zaretan. 2 Ch 4:17, Zeredathah.

47 **because they were exceeding many**. Heb.

for the exceeding multitude. 2 Ch 4:18. Jn
14:2. Ro 9:23, 24.

found out. Heb. searched. 1 Ch 22:3, 14, 16.
Je +31:37. 46:23.

48　**the altar**. Lk +1:11.

of gold. That is, covered with it. 1 K 6:20. Re
8:3.

the table. Ex +25:23.

the showbread. Ex +25:30.

49　**the candlesticks**. Ex +25:31.

pure gold. 2 Ch +9:20.

before the oracle. 1 K +6:5.

the tongs. Ex 25:38. Nu 4:9. 2 Ch 4:21. Is
6:6.

50　**bowls**. Ex 12:22. 2 S 17:28.

snuffers. 2 K 12:13. 25:14. 2 Ch 4:22. Je
52:18.

basons. or, sprinkling bowls. ver. +40, 45.

spoons. Ex 25:29. Nu 7:86.

censers. Heb. ash pans. Ex 25:38. Le 16:12. 2
Ch 4:21, 22.

the temple. Ex 25:29, 38. 2 Ch 4:21, 22. 1 C
12:4-7.

51　**was ended**. Ex 40:33. Ezr 6:15. Zc 4:9.

**things which David his father had dedi-
cated**. Heb. holy things of David. 2 S 8:7-11.
1 Ch 18:7, 8, 10, 11. 26:26-28. 28:11-18.
29:2-8. 2 Ch 5:1.

treasures. Dt 28:12. 32:34.

1 KINGS 8

1　A.M. 3000. B.C. 1004.

Solomon. 2 Ch 5:2, etc.

assembled. Jsh 23:2. 24:1. 1 Ch 28:1. 2 Ch
30:1. Ezr 3:1.

elders. Ex +18:21. Jsh +20:4.

chief of the fathers. Heb. princes. Nu +1:16.
7:3.

that they might bring. 2 S 6:1, 2, 6, 12. 1
Ch 13:1-5. 15:3, 25.

out of the city. 1 K 3:15. 2 S 5:7-9. 6:12-17.
1 Ch 11:7. 15:29. 16:1. Ps 9:11. 102:21. Is
28:16. 46:13. 1 P 2:6.

Zion. 2 S +5:7. 2 K 19:21, 31. 1 Ch +11:5. 1 P
2:5, 7, 9.

2　**at the feast**. Le +23:34.

Ethanim. i.e. *perennial streams*, **S#388h**, only
here, the same as Tisri, part of September and
October (Young).

3　**came**. 2 S 6:17.

the priests took up. Nu 4:15. Dt 31:9. Jsh
3:3, 6, 14, 15. 4:9. 6:6. 1 Ch 15:2, 11-15. 2 Ch
5:4-8. Is 52:11.

4　*and the*. 1 K 3:4. 2 Ch 1:3.

tabernacle of the congregation. Ex +25:9.
26:1. 27:21. 33:7. 40:2-33.

holy vessels. Nu 31:6.

5　**assembled unto**. Nu 14:35. 16:11. 27:3. 2
Ch 5:6.

sacrificing sheep. ver. 62, 63. 2 S 6:13. 1 Ch
16:1. He 9:28. 10:14.

could not be told. 1 K 3:8. Ge 16:10. 32:12.
1 Ch 23:3. 2 Ch 5:6. Je 33:22. Ho 1:10.

6　**And the priests**. ver. 4. 2 S 6:17. 2 Ch 5:7.

his place. 1 K 6:19. Ex 26:33, 34. 40:20, 21.

the oracle. ver. 8. 1 K +6:5.

under the wings. ver. 7. Ge +3:24. Ru 2:12.

7　**two wings**. Ps 80:1. 99:1. He 9:5, 24.

8　**drew out the staves**. Ex +25:13.

ends. Heb. heads.

holy place. *or*, ark, as 2 Ch 5:9.

unto this day. ver. +24. 1 S +6:18.

9　**nothing**. Ex 25:21. Dt 10:2. 2 Ch 5:10.

in the ark. Ex 16:33. He 9:3, 4.

put there at Horeb. Ex +16:34. Dt 31:26.

when. *or*, where. ver. 21. Ex 24:8. 34:27, 28.
Dt 4:13.

10　**the cloud**. Ex +13:21. Re 15:8.

filled. Ezk 10:3, 4.

11　**for the glory**. Ex +24:16. Is +40:5. Ac 7:55.

filled. 2 Ch +5:14.

12　**The Lord**. Le 16:2.

the thick. Ps 139:12. Is 45:15.

darkness. Ex +10:22. Jb 22:13. Is 60:2.

13　**surely built**. 2 S 7:13. 1 Ch 17:12. 22:10, 11.
28:6, 10, 20. 2 Ch 6:2. Ps 49:14. Is 63:15. Hab
3:11.

a settled. Ex 15:17. Ps 78:68, 69. 132:13, 14.
Jn 4:21-23. Ac 6:14. He 8:5-13. 9:11, 12, 24.

for ever. Heb. *olam*, plural, Ps +61:4.

14　**blessed all**. ver. 55, 56. Jsh 22:6. 2 S 6:18. 1
Ch 16:2. 2 Ch 6:3. 30:18-20. Ps 118:26. Lk
24:50, 51.

all the congregation. 2 Ch 7:6. Ne 8:7. 9:2.
Mt 13:2.

15　**Blessed**. 1 Ch 29:10, 20. 2 Ch 6:4. 20:26. Ne
9:5. Ps 41:13. 72:18, 19. 115:18. 117:1, 2. Lk
1:68. Ep 1:3. 1 P 1:3.

which spake. 2 S 7:5, 25, 28, 29. 1 Ch
17:12. Is 1:20. Lk 1:70.

hath. Jsh 21:45. 23:15, 16. Ps 138:2. Mt
24:35. Lk 1:54, 55, 72.

16　**since**. 2 S +7:6, 7. 2 Ch 6:5, etc.

I chose. 1 Ch 17:5, 6. Ps 132:13.

my name. ver. +29. 1 K 11:36. Dt 12:11. 2 K
23:27. Ne 1:9. Je 7:12. Da 9:19.

I chose David. 1 S 16:1. 2 S 7:8. 1 Ch 28:4.
Ps 78:70. 89:19, 20.

17　**it was**. 2 S 7:2, 3. 1 Ch 17:1, 2, etc. 22:7. 28:2.

18　**Whereas**. 2 Ch 6:7-9. 2 C 8:12.

in thine heart. 2 Ch 32:26. Ps 55:21. 78:72.
95:10. Pr 6:14. 23:7. Ec 9:3. Is 10:7. Je 48:29.
Mt 5:8. 15:18, 19. Ro 10:10. He 3:12.

19　**shalt not**. 1 K 5:3-5. 2 S 7:5, 12, 13. 1 Ch
17:4, 11, 12. 22:8-10. 28:6.

20　**hath performed**. ver. +15. Ne 9:8. Is 9:7. Je
29:10, 11, 29. Ezk 12:25. 37:14. Mi 7:20. Ro
4:21. Ph 1:6.

as the Lord. 1 Ch 28:5, 6.

21 And I have. ver. 5, 6.
the covenant. ver. 9. Ex 34:28. Dt 9:9, 11. 31:26. Ro 9:4.

22 stood. 2 K 11:14. 23:3. 2 Ch 6:12, 13, etc.
the altar. ver. +64.
spread forth. ver. 54. Ps +88:9.

23 Lord God. Ge 33:20. Ex 3:15.
no God. Ex +8:10. 1 S 2:2.
who keepest. Dt +7:9. Ps 36:5. 89:3-5. Mi 7:19, 20.
mercy. Ex +34:6.
walk before. 1 K 6:12. Ge +17:1.

24 thou spakest. ver. +15. 2 S 7:12, 16. 2 Ch 6:14, 15.
as it is. ver. +8. Ezr 9:7. Je +25:18. 44:22.

25 keep with thy. 1 K 2:4. Ge 32:12. Ex 32:13. 2 S 7:25, 27-29. 1 Ch 17:23-27. Ps 119:58. Lk 1:68-72.
There shall not, etc. Heb. There shall not be cut off unto thee a man from my sight. 2 S 7:25. 2 Ch 21:7. Ps 89:33-37. 132:12. Je 33:17-26. Lk 1:32, 33.
so that. Heb. only if.
thy children. 1 K 2:4. 9:4-6. 1 Ch 28:9. 2 Ch 6:16, 17. Ps 132:12.

26 And now. ver. 23. Is +29:23.
let thy word. 2 S 7:25-29. 2 Ch 1:9. Ps 119:49. Je 11:5. Ezk 36:36, 37.

27 But will. Ge 18:13. Nu 22:32. 2 Ch 6:18. Ps 58:1. Is 66:1. Jn 1:14. Ac 7:48, 49. 17:24. 2 C 6:16. 1 J 3:1.
dwell. Ps 139:7, 12. Je 23:23, 24. Am 9:2.
the heaven. Dt +10:14. Ps 113:4.

28 Yet have thou. 2 Ch 6:19. Ps 141:2. Da 9:17-19. Lk 18:1, 7.
respect. Ge 18:22.
prayer. ver. 29, 38, 45, 49, 54. 1 K 9:3. 2 S 7:27. 2 K 19:4. 20:5. 2 Ch 6:19, 20, 29, 35, 39, 40.
supplication. Jsh 11:20. Ezr 9:8.
hearken. Ps 4:1. 5:1. 86:3, 6, 7. 88:1, 2.
cry. 2 Ch 6:19. Ps 17:1. 30:5 (joy). 61:1. 119:169. 126:2 (singing), 5 (joy), 6 (rejoicing). Is 35:10 (songs). 51:11. 54:1. Je 7:16. Zp 3:17.

29 That thine. ver. 52. 2 Ch 16:9.
open. Zc +12:4.
My name. ver. 16, 43mg. 1 K 11:36. Ex 20:24. Dt 12:11. 16:2, 6. 26:2. 2 K 21:4, 7. 23:27. 2 Ch 6:5, 6, 20. 7:16. 20:8. 33:4, 7. Ne 1:9. Jn 14:13, 14.
toward this place. or, in this place. Da +6:10.

30 when they shall. 2 Ch 20:8, 9. Ne 1:5, 6.
toward this place. or, in this place. ver. 29. Da +6:10. Jon 2:4.
and hear. ver. 34, 36, 39, 43, 49. 2 Ch 6:21. Ps 33:13, 14. 113:5, 6. 123:1. Ec 5:2. Is 57:15. Mt 6:9.
forgive. ver. 34, 36, 39. 2 Ch +7:14. Ps 130:3, 4. Da 9:19. Mt 6:12.

31 If. Ge +4:7.
trespass. 2 Ch 6:22, 23.
an oath be laid upon him. Heb. he require an oath of him. Ex 22:8-11. Le 5:1. Pr 30:9.
the oath. Ge 24:41. Nu 5:16-22. Mt 23:18.

32 hear thou. ver. +30.
condemning the wicked. Ex 22:9. 34:7. Nu 5:27. Dt 25:1. Ne 13:28, 29. Ps 10:13-15. 28:4, 5. 31:17, 18. 40:14, 15. 59:12-15. 79:6-12. 109:4-13. 140:8-11. 144:5-8. Pr 1:31. Is 3:10, 11. Je +10:25. 17:18. Ezk 18:13, 30. Ro 2:6-10.
his way. Ge +6:13. Nu +32:23. 2 Ch 6:23.
justifying. Ex 23:7. Pr 17:15. Is 3:10. Ezk 18:20. Ro 2:13. 7:9.
to give. 1 T +4:8.

33 smitten down. Le 26:17, 25. Dt 28:25, 48. Jsh 7:8. 2 Ch 6:24, 25. Ps 44:10.
because they have. Jsh 7:11, 12. Jg 6:1, 2. 2 K 17:7-18. 18:11, 12. 2 Ch 36:14-17.
turn again. Le 26:39-42. Ne 1:8, 9. Jon 3:10.
pray. Ezr 9:5, etc. Ne 9:1-3, etc. Is 63:15-19. ch. 64, etc. Da 9:3, etc.
in. or, toward. ver. 30.

34 forgive the sin. ver. 30, 44-53. Jg 20:26. Ezr 1:1-6. Ps 106:47. Je 31:4-9, 27. 32:37. 33:10-13. Da 9:2, 16-19, 25. Ho +3:4, 5. Am 7:2. Zc 1:12. 12:10-14. 13:8, 9.
which thou gavest. Ge 13:15. Ex 6:8. Jsh 21:43.

35 heaven. 1 K 17:1. Le 26:19. Dt 11:17. 28:12, 23, 24. 2 S 24:13. Je 14:1-7. Ezk 14:13. Ml 3:10. Lk 4:25. Re 11:6.
if they pray. ver. 33. 2 Ch 6:24, 26. Ro 10:9. 15:9.
confess. ver. 29, 30. Jl 1:13-20. 2:15-17.
and turn. ver. 33. Is 1:15, 16. 9:13. Ezk 18:30-32. Ho 14:1.

36 thou teach. Ps 25:4, 5, 8, 9, 12. 27:11. 32:8. 94:12. 119:33. 143:8. Is 35:8. Mi 4:2.
the good way. 1 S 12:23, 24. 2 Ch 6:26, 27. Is 30:21. Je 6:16. 42:3. Mt 22:16.
give rain. 1 K 18:1, 27-40, 45. Ps 68:9. 147:8. Je 14:22. Ja 5:17, 18.

37 in the land famine. Ge +12:10. 26:1. 41:30, 31, 54, 57. 42:5. 43:1. Le 26:16, 25, +26. Dt 28:21, 22-25, 38-42, 52-61. 32:24. Ru 1:1. 2 S 21:1. 24:13. 1 K 18:2. 2 K 4:38. 6:25-29. 8:1. 25:3. 1 Ch 21:12. 2 Ch 6:28-31. 20:9. Ps 105:16, 34, 35. Je 14:12, 15, 18. 32:2, 24. 38:9. 52:6. La 5:10. Ezk 5:12, 16. 7:15. 14:13, 21. Jl 1:4-7, 15-20. 2:25, 26. Am 4:6. Mt 24:7. Lk 4:25. 15:14. 21:11. Ac 7:11. 11:28. Re 6:5, 6, 8. 18:8.
pestilence. Ex 5:3. 9:3, 15.
blasting. Dt 28:22. 2 Ch 6:28. Am 4:9. Hg 2:17.
mildew. Dt +28:22.
locust. Le 11:22. Dt 28:38, 42. Jg 6:5. 7:12. 2

Ch 6:28. 7:13. Jb 39:20. Ps +78:46. Pr 30:27. Je 46:23.

caterpiller. Ps +78:46. Je 51:14, 27.

cities. *or*, jurisdiction. or, gates. Ge +14:7. 19:1. 2 Ch +6:28mg.

sickness. Ex 15:26. +23:25. 2 Ch 6:28.

38 **prayer**. 2 Ch 20:5-13. Ps 50:15. 91:15. Is 37:4, 15-21. Jl 2:17. Am 7:1-6.

the plague. 2 Ch 6:29. Jb 7:11. Ps 32:3, 4. 42:6, 9, 11. 73:21, 22. 142:3-5. Pr 14:10. Ro 7:24. Ph 4:6.

spread forth. ver. +22.

39 **Then hear**. ver. +30, 32, 36. Ps 94:9. 139:2, 4. Is 40:13, 14.

in heaven. Ps 2:4. 24:3. Is 26:21. Mi 1:3.

give to every man. Ps 18:20-26. 28:4. Je 17:10. 32:19. Ezk 18:30. Re 22:12.

knowest. Ps 11:4, 5. Je +17:10. Jn +2:25.

children. Ge 11:5.

40 **fear thee**. Ge 22:12. Ex 20:20. Dt 6:2, 13. 1 S 12:24. Ps 115:13. 130:4. Je 32:39, 40. Ho 3:5. Ac 9:31. 10:2. He 12:28. Re 15:4. 19:5.

all. Dt +12:1.

41 **a stranger**. 1 K 10:1, 2. Ge 31:15. Ru 1:16. 2:11. 2 Ch 6:32. Is 56:3-7. Mt 8:5, 10, 11. 15:22-28. Lk 17:18. Jn 12:20. Ac 10:1-4.

cometh out. 1 K 10:1, 2. Ex 18:8-12. 2 K 5:1-7, 16, 17. Is 60:1-10. Mt 2:1. 12:42. Ac 8:27, etc.

42 **For they shall**. Ex 15:14. Dt 4:6. Jsh 2:10, 11. 9:9, 10. 2 Ch 32:31. Da 2:47. 3:28. 4:37.

great name. Ex 3:13-16. 34:5-7. Jsh 7:9. Ps 86:8, 9. Ezk 20:9.

thy strong hand. Ex 3:19. 9:15. 13:14. Dt 3:24. 2 K 17:36. Ps 89:13. Is 51:9. 63:12. Je 31:11. 32:17.

stretched. Ex +6:6.

when he shall. Ps 2:8. Is 66:19, 20. Je 3:19. Zc 14:16. Ac 8:27.

43 **in heaven**. ver. +39.

thy dwelling place. *or*, settled place of thy dwelling. Ex 15:17.

that all the people. 2 Ch 6:33. Ps 22:27. 67:2. 72:10, 11. 86:9. Is 11:9, 10. Ezk +6:7, 10. Re 11:15.

fear thee. Ps 102:15. ch. 117.

this house. Heb. thy name is called upon this house. ver. 29. 2 Ch 6:33. Je +14:9mg. 32:34. 34:15.

44 **go out to battle**. Dt 20:1-4. 31:3-6. Jsh 1:2-5. 2 Ch 6:34.

whithersoever. Nu 31:1, etc. Jsh 6:2-5. 8:1, 2. Jg 1:1, 2. 4:6. 6:14. 1 S 15:3, 18. 30:8. 2 S 5:19, 23.

shall pray. 2 Ch 14:9-12. 18:31. 20:6-13. 32:20.

toward the city. Heb. the way of the city. ver. +16. Ps 78:67-69. 132:13, 14. Da 6:10. 9:17-19.

45 **cause**. *or*, right. lit. done their judgment. ver.

49, 59. Ge +18:25. 2 Ch 6:35, 39. Ps 9:4. Je 5:28.

46 **If**. Ge +4:7.

they sin. Ph 3:12.

there is no man. Ps 19:12. Pr +20:9.

angry. 2 Ch 6:36. Ezr 9:14. Ps 2:12. 60:1. 79:5. 85:5. Is 12:1.

deliver them to the enemy. Le 26:34, 44. Dt 28:36, 64. 2 Ch 28:8. Je 40:1.

captives. Ge 34:29. Dt 21:10. 2 Ch 6:36. 28:11. Ps 68:18.

unto the land. Le 26:34-39. Dt 4:26, 27. 28:36, 64-68. 29:28. 2 K 17:6, 18, 23. 25:21. Da 9:7-14. Lk 21:24.

47 **Yet if they**. Le 26:40-45. Dt 4:29-31. 30:1, 2. 2 Ch 6:37. 33:12, 13. Ezk 16:61, 63. 18:28. Hg 1:7. Lk 15:17.

bethink themselves. Heb. bring back to their heart. Dt 4:39. 30:1.

saying. Ezr 9:6, 7. Ne 1:6, etc. 9:26-30. Ps 106:6. Is 64:6-12. Da 9:5-11. Zc 12:10.

done perversely. Jb 33:27, 28. Je 31:18-20. Lk 15:18.

48 **And so return**. Jg 10:15, 16. Pr 23:26. Je +29:13. Zc +1:3. Ro 10:10.

soul. Heb. *nephesh*, Ge +34:3.

pray unto. ver. 29, 30. Da 6:10.

the city. ver. +44.

49 **Then hear**. ver. +30.

cause. *or*, right. ver. 45. 2 K 19:19. Zc 1:15, 16.

50 **and give them**. 2 Ch 30:9. Ezr 7:6, 27, 28. Ne 1:11. 2:4-8. Ps 106:46. Pr 16:7. Da 1:9, 10. Ac 7:9, 10.

51 **thy people**. ver. 53. Ex 32:11, 12. Nu 14:13-19. Dt 9:26-29. 2 Ch 6:39. Ne 1:10. Is 63:16-18. 64:9. Je 51:19.

the furnace. Dt 4:20. Pr 17:3. 27:21. Is 48:10. Je 11:4. Ezk 22:18, 20, 22.

52 **That thine**. ver. +29.

in all that. Ps 86:5. 145:18.

53 **separate**. Ex +19:5, 6. Dt 4:34. 9:26, 29. 10:15.

thine inheritance. Dt +32:9. 1 S +10:1. Ne 1:10. Je 10:16. Ep 1:18. 1 P 2:9, 10.

as thou spakest. Ex 19:5, 6. 33:16. Dt 9:26, 29. 14:2. 33:1-3, 26-29.

by the hand. Hg +1:1mg.

54 **when Solomon**. Lk 11:1. 22:45.

kneeling. 2 Ch +6:13. Ps 95:6. Lk 22:41, 45. Ac 20:36. 21:5.

with his hands. ver. +22.

55 **blessed**. ver. +14. Nu 6:23-26. 2 S 6:18. 1 Ch 16:2.

56 **Blessed be**. ver. 15.

hath given rest. Dt 3:20. 12:10, 12. Jsh 21:44. 2 Ch 14:6. He 4:3-9.

there. Jsh 21:45. 23:14, 15. Lk 1:54, 55, 72, 73. 21:33.

failed. Heb. fallen. Jsh 21:45. 23:14. 1 S 3:19. 2 K 10:10.

57 The Lord. Dt 31:6, 8. Jsh 1:5, 9. 1 Ch 28:9. 2
Ch 32:7, 8. Ps 46:7, 11. Is 8:10. 41:10. Mt
1:23. 28:20. Ro 8:31. He +13:5.
58 incline. Jsh 24:23. 2 S 19:14. Ps 110:3.
119:36. 141:4. Pr 2:2. 21:1. SS 1:4. Je +31:33.
Ezk 36:26, 27. Ph 2:13. He 13:21.
his commandments. Dt 4:1, 45. 6:1. 1 J 2:3.
59 let these my words. 2 Ch 6:41, 42.
nigh. Ps 102:1, 2. 141:2. Jn 17:9, 20-24. 1 J
2:2.
at all times. Heb. the thing of a day in his
day. Ex +5:13mg. Lk 11:3.
as the matter. Ex 5:11. 16:4. Dt 33:25. 2 Ch
8:13. Ezr 3:4.
60 That all. ver. +43. Jsh 4:24. 1 S 17:46. 2 K
19:19.
the Lord. 1 K 18:39. Dt 4:35, 39. Is 44:6, 8,
24. 45:5, 6, 22. Je 10:10-12. Jl 2:27.
God. 1 K 18:21. Ge 5:22. 6:9, 11. 17:18. 20:6,
7. Dt 4:35. Da 9:11.
none else. Is +45:5.
61 perfect. 2 K +20:3. Mt +5:48. Ju 24, 25.
62 the king. 2 S 6:17-19. 2 Ch 7:4-7.
63 a sacrifice. Le ch. 3. +7:11. 1 Ch 29:21. 2 Ch
1:6. 15:11. 29:32-35. 30:24. 35:7-9. Ezr 6:16,
17. Ezk 45:17. Mi 6:7.
peace offerings. Le +23:19.
dedicated. Nu +7:10, 11, 84-88. Pr 22:6. Jn
10:22.
64 hallow. Nu 16:37, 38. 2 Ch 7:7. 36:14. He
13:10-12.
burnt offerings. Le +23:12.
meat offerings. Le +23:13.
peace offerings. Le +23:19.
the brazen. 2 Ch +4:1.
65 held. ver. 2. Le 23:34-43. 2 Ch 7:8, 9.
a great. 2 Ch 30:13. Ps 40:9, 10.
from the entering. Nu +13:21.
the river. Ps +72:8.
seven days. 2 Ch 7:8, 9. 30:23.
66 the eighth day. ver. 1. 2 Ch 7:10. 31:1.
blessed. or, thanked. ver. 1, 47.
joyful. Dt +12:7. Ps 81:1. 95:1, 2. 106:4, 5.
122:6, 9. 149:2, 5. Is 61:9, 10. 66:13, 14. Je
31:12-14. Zp 3:14. Zc 9:9, 17.
tents. 2 S 18:17.
glad of heart. 1 S 25:36. 2 S 13:28. 2 Ch
7:10.
David. 1 K 10:9. 2 Ch 7:10.

1 KINGS 9

1 A.M. 3013. B.C. 991.
it came. 1 K 6:37, 38. 7:1, 51. 2 Ch 7:11, etc.
the house. 2 Ch 8:1-6. Ec 2:4.
all Solomon's desire. ver. 11, 19. 2 Ch 8:6.
Ec 2:10. 6:9. Is 21:4.
pleased. Ge 34:19. 2 Ch 7:11. Ec 2:4-6.
2 appeared. Ge +35:9.
as he. 1 K 3:5. 11:9. 2 Ch 1:7-12. 7:12.

3 I have heard. 2 K 20:5. Ps 10:17. 66:19.
116:1. Da 9:23. Jn 11:42. Ac 10:31. 1 J 5:14.
I have hallowed. 1 K 8:10, 11. Ex 20:11. Nu
16:38. Mt 6:9.
to put. 1 K 8:29. Dt 12:5, 11, 21. 16:11.
for ever. Heb. olam, Ex +12:24.
mine eyes. Dt 11:12. 2 Ch 6:40. 7:15, 16. Ps
132:13, 14. SS 4:9, 10. Is 3:8. Je 15:1.
4 And if. Ge +4:7.
thou wilt walk. 1 K 3:14. 8:25. 11:4, 6, 38.
14:8. 15:5. Ge 17:1. Dt 28:1. 2 Ch 7:17, 18. Jb
23:11, 12. Ps 15:2. 26:1, 11. Pr 20:7. Zc 3:7.
Lk 1:6. 1 Th 4:1, 2.
in integrity. Ge 20:5, 6. Ps 78:72. 101:2. Pr
10:9. 28:18.
5 I will establish. 1 K 2:4. 6:12. 8:15, 20. 2 S
7:12, 16. 1 Ch 22:9, 10. Ps 89:28-39. 132:11,
12.
for ever. Heb. olam, Ex +12:24.
6 if ye. 1 S 2:30. 2 S 7:14-16. 1 Ch 28:9. 2 Ch
7:19-22. 15:2. Ps 89:30-37.
go. 1 K 11:4-10. Jsh 23:15, 16.
7 I will cut. Le 18:24-28. Dt 4:26. 29:26-28. 2
K 17:20-23. 25:9, 21. Je 7:15. 24:9. Ezk
33:27-29. Lk 21:24.
this house. ver. +3. 2 K 25:9. 2 Ch 7:20.
36:19. Je 7:4-14. 26:6, 18. 52:13. La 2:6, 7.
Ezk 24:21. Mi 3:12. Mt 24:2. Lk 21:24.
name. Dt 12:11.
and Israel. Dt +28:37. Ne 4:1-4.
proverb. Dt +28:37.
byword. Dt +28:37.
8 at. 2 Ch +29:8. Is 64:11. Da 9:12.
hiss. 2 Ch +29:8.
Why. Dt 29:24-26. Je 2:11. 22:8, 9, 28.
9 Because. Dt 29:25-28. 2 Ch 7:22. Je 2:10-13,
19. 5:19. 16:10-13. 50:7. La 2:16, 17. 4:13-15.
Ezk 36:17-20. Zp 1:4, 5.
therefore. Je 12:7, 8.
10 at the end of twenty. ver. 1. 1 K 6:37, 38.
7:1. 2 Ch 8:1, etc.
11 Now Hiram. 1 K 5:6-10. 2 Ch 2:8-10, 16.
king Solomon. 2 Ch 8:2.
of Galilee. Jsh +20:7.
12 they pleased him not. Heb. were not right
in his eyes. Nu 22:34mg. Jg 14:3mg.
13 What cities. Is 2:22.
my brother. 1 K 5:1, 2. Am 1:9.
Cabul. that is, Displeasing, or dirty. Jsh 19:27.
14 Hiram sent. ver. 11, 28. Jg +3:15. 1 K 10:10,
14, 21.
15 A.M. 2989-3029. B.C. 1015-975.
the reason. ver. 21. 1 K +5:13.
to build. ver. 10. 1 K 6:38. 7:1. 2 Ch 8:1.
Millo. ver. 24. 2 S +5:9.
the wall. Ps 51:18.
Hazor. Jsh +15:23.
Megiddo. Jsh +12:21.
Gezer. ver. +16, 17.
16 Gezer. i.e. precipice, **S#1507h**. ver. 15, 17. Jsh

10:33. 12:12. 16:3, 10. 21:21. Jg 1:29. 1 Ch 6:67. 7:28. 20:4.

Canaanites. Ge +10:18.

daughter. ver. +24. 1 K 3:1.

17 **Gezer**. ver. +16. 1 S 27:8.

Beth-horon. Jsh +10:10.

18 **Baalath**. Jsh 19:44.

Tadmor. 2 Ch 8:3, 4. Ezk 47:19.

19 **the cities of store**. 1 K 4:26-28. Ex 1:11. 2 Ch 8:4, 6. 16:4. 17:12. 32:28.

chariots. 1 K 4:26. 10:26. 2 Ch 1:14. 8:6. 9:25.

that which Solomon desired. Heb. the desire of Solomon which he desired. ver. +1. Ec 2:10. 6:9.

Lebanon. Dt +1:7.

20 **left**. 2 Ch 8:7, 8, etc.

Amorites. Ge +10:16.

Hittites. Dt +20:17.

Perizzites. Ge +13:7.

Hivites. Ge +10:17.

Jebusites. Ge +10:16.

21 **left**. Jg 1:21, 27-35. 2:20-23. 3:1-4. Ps 106:34-36.

not. Jsh +15:63.

levy. ver. 15. 1 K 5:13. Jg 1:28, 35.

tribute. Ge 9:25, 26. Le 25:39. Jg 1:28.

bondservice. Ge 9:25, 26. 49:15. 2 S 12:31. 2 Ch 8:7, 8. Ezr 2:55-58. Ne 7:57. 11:3.

22 **of the children**. Le +25:39.

but they were men. 1 K 4:1-27. 1 S 8:11, 12. 2 Ch 8:9, 10.

23 **chief**. 1 K 5:16. 2 Ch 2:18. 8:10.

24 **Pharaoh's**. ver. 16. 1 K 3:1. 7:8. 2 Ch 8:11.

the city of David. 2 S 5:9.

Millo. ver. +15.

25 **three times**. Ex 23:14-17. 34:23. Dt 16:16. 2 Ch 8:12, 13. At the Passover, Pentecost, and Tabernacle festivals (Young).

burnt offerings. Le +23:12.

peace offerings. Le +23:19.

he burnt incense. Ex 30:7. 1 Ch 23:13. 2 Ch 26:16-21. 29:11. 34:25.

upon the altar that was before. Heb. upon it which was before. Am +9:1.

So he finished the house. 1 K 6:38. 2 Ch 8:16.

26 **made a navy**. ver. 27. 1 K 10:11, 22. 2 Ch 8:12, 17, 18, etc. Is 33:21.

Ezion-geber. i.e. *the giant's backbone*, **S#6100h**. 1 K 22:48. Nu +33:35, 36. 2 Ch 8:17.

Eloth. i.e. *grove*, **S#359h**. Dt +2:8, Elath. 2 Ch 8:17. 26:2.

shore. Heb. lip. Jg +7:22mg.

27 **his servants**. 1 K 5:6, 9. 22:49. 2 Ch 20:36, 37.

28 **Ophir**. 1 K 10:11. 22:48. Ge 10:29. 1 Ch 1:23. 29:4. 2 Ch 8:18. 9:10. Jb 22:24. 28:16. Ps 45:9. Is 13:12.

four hundred and twenty. In 2 Ch 8:18, it is 450.

1 KINGS 10

1 A.M. 3014. B.C. 990.

And when. 2 Ch 9:1, etc. Mt 12:42. Lk 11:31.

Sheba. i.e. *seven; oath*, **S#7614h**. ver. 4, 10, 13. Ge 10:7, 28. 25:3. 1 Ch 1:9, 22, 32. 2 Ch 9:1, 3, 9, 12. Jb 1:15. 6:19. Ps 72:10, 15. Is 60:6. Je 6:20. Ezk 27:22, 23. 38:13.

heard. 1 K 4:31, 34.

concerning. Jb 28:28. Pr 2:3-6. Jn 17:3. 1 C 1:20, 21.

prove him. Jg 14:12-14. Ps 49:4. Pr 1:5, 6. Mt 13:11, 35. Mk 4:34.

hard questions. Nu +12:8. Da 8:23.

2 **a very great train**. 2 K 5:5, 9. Is 60:6-9. Ac 25:23.

spices. Ex 25:6. 2 K 20:13.

communed. Ge 18:33. Jb 4:2. Ps 4:4. 62:8. Da 1:19. Lk 24:15. Jn 1:39.

3 **told her**. 2 Ch 9:2. Pr 1:5, 6. 13:20. Is 42:16. Mt 13:11. Jn 7:17. 15:15. 1 C 1:30. Col 2:3.

questions. Heb. words.

hid from the king. ver. 1. 1 K 3:12. 2 S 14:17, 20. Da 2:20-23. Jn +2:24, 25. Col 2:2, 3. He 4:12, 13.

4 **Solomon's**. 1 K 3:28. 4:29-31. 2 Ch 9:3, 4. Ec 12:9. Mt 12:42.

the house. 1 K ch. 6. 7.

5 **the meat**. 1 K 4:22, 23.

attendance. Heb. standing.

cupbearers. *or*, butlers. Ge 40:1.

ascent. 2 K 16:18. 1 Ch 9:18. 26:16. 2 Ch 23:13. Ezk 44:3. 46:2.

there was no. Ge +2:24. Jsh 5:1. 2 Ch 9:4.

spirit. Heb. *ruach*, Ge +41:8.

6 **report**. Heb. word. 2 Ch 9:5, 6mg.

acts. *or*, sayings.

7 **I believed not**. Is 64:4. Zc 9:17. Mk 16:11. Jn 20:25-29. 1 C 2:9. 1 J 3:2.

came. Jn 1:39.

thy wisdom and prosperity exceeded the fame. Heb. thou hast added wisdom and goodness to the fame.

8 **happy are these**. 2 Ch 9:7, 8. Pr 3:13, 14. 8:34. 10:21. 13:20. Mt 13:16, 17. Lk 10:23, 24, 39-42. 11:28, 31.

continually. Is 40:31. +58:11. Ho 12:6.

9 **Blessed**. 1 K +5:7. Ps 72:17-19.

delighteth. Ps 18:19. 22:8. Is 42:1. 62:4.

to set thee. Pr 8:15.

because the. Dt 7:8. 1 Ch 17:22. 2 Ch 2:11.

for ever. Heb. *olam*, Ex +12:24.

to do. Pr 8:15, 16. Is 9:7. +11:4, 5. Je +21:12. Ro 13:3, 4.

10 **she gave**. ver. 2, +25.

spices. Ex +30:23.

and precious. Pr 3:13-15. 20:15. Re 21:11.

11 **Hiram**. 1 K 9:26, 27.

Ophir. 1 K +9:28.

almug. 2 Ch 2:8. 9:10, 11, algum trees.

12 **pillars**. *or,* rails. Heb. a prop. 2 Ch 9:11.
    harps. 1 Ch 23:5. 25:1, etc. Ps 92:1-3. 150:3-5. Re 14:2, 3.

13 **all her desire**. ver. 2. 1 K 9:1. Ps 20:4. 37:4. Ml 3:10. Mt 15:28. Jn 14:13, 14. Ep 3:20.
    which Solomon gave her of his royal bounty. Heb. which he gave her, according to the hand of king Solomon.

14 A.M. 2989-3029. B.C. 1015-975.
    was six hundred threescore and six. ver. 14. 1 K 9:28. Re 13:18.

15 **kings of Arabia**. 1 Ch 9:24. 2 Ch +9:14. 17:11. Ps 72:10.
    governors. *or,* captains. 1 K 20:24. 2 K 18:24. 2 Ch 9:14. Ezr 5:14. 8:36. Ne 2:7, 9. 3:7. 5:14, 15, 18. 12:26. Est 3:12. 8:9. 9:3. Is 36:9. Je 51:23, 28, 57. Ezk 23:6, 12, 23. Hg 1:1, 14. 2:2, 21. Ml 1:8.

16 **two hundred**. 1 K 14:26-28. 2 Ch 9:15, 16. 12:9, 10.

17 **three hundred shields**. 1 K 14:26.
    in the house. 1 K +7:2.

18 **a great throne**. 2 Ch 9:17-19. Ps 45:6. 110:1. 122:5. He 1:3, 8. Re 20:11.
    ivory. ver. 22. 1 K 22:39. Ps 45:8. Ezk 27:6. Am 6:4. Re 18:12.

19 **behind**. Heb. on the hinder part thereof.
    stays. Heb. hands.

20 **lions**. Ge 49:9. Nu 23:24. 24:9. Re 5:5.
    the like made. Heb. so made.

21 **drinking**. 2 Ch 9:20-22.
    the house. ver. 17. 1 K 7:2.
    none were of silver. *or,* there was no silver in them.

22 **Tharshish**. Ge +10:4.
    ivory. *or,* elephants' teeth. ver. 18. Am 3:15.
    apes. rather, monkeys.
    peacocks. Jb 39:13.

23 **exceeded**. 1 K 3:12, 13. 4:29-34. 2 Ch 9:22, 23. Ps 89:27. Ep 3:8. Col 1:18, 19. 2:2, 3.

24 **sought to**. Heb. sought the face of.
    which God. 1 K 3:9, 12, 28. Pr 2:6. Da 1:17. 2:21, 23. 5:11. Ja 1:5.

25 **every man**. ver. 10. Jg +3:15.
    and mules. 1 K 1:33. 18:5. Ge 36:24. Ezr 2:66. Est 8:10, 14. Is 66:20. Ezk 27:14.
    a rate. 2 K 17:4. 2 Ch 9:24.

26 **Solomon**. 1 K +4:26. Dt 17:16. 2 Ch 1:14. 9:25. Is 2:7.
    in the cities. 2 Ch 9:25.

27 **the king**. 2 Ch 1:15-17. 9:27. Jb 22:24, 25.
    made. Heb. gave.
    as stones. Ge +41:56. 2 Ch 1:9, 15. 9:27.

28 **Solomon**, etc. Heb. the going forth of the horses which was Solomon's.
    horses brought. Dt 17:16. 2 Ch 1:16, 17. 9:28. Is 31:1-3. 36:9. Ho 14:3.
    and linen yarn. Ge 41:42. Ex +26:1. Is 19:9.

29 **the kings**. Jsh 1:4. 2 K 7:6.
    Hittites. Dt +20:17.

their means. Heb. their hand. Dt +32:36. Nu 15:23. 2 Ch 7:6mg. 8:18. Ho 12:10mg. Ml +1:1mg, 9mg.

1 KINGS 11

1 A.M. 3020-3029. B.C. 984-975.
    loved. ver. 8. Ge 6:2-5. Dt 17:17. Pr +2:16. 23:33.
    together with. *or,* beside. 1 K 3:1. Le 18:18.
    Moabites. Ezk +25:8.
    Ammonites. 1 S +11:11.
    Edomites. Ge +36:21.
    Zidonians. Jg +10:12.
    Hittites. Dt +20:17.

2 **Ye shall not go in**. Ex 23:32, 33. Jg +3:6. Ezr 10:2, etc.
    surely. 1 K 16:31-33. Nu 25:1-3. 2 Ch 21:6.
    Solomon. Ge 2:24. 34:3. Jg 16:4-21. 2 Ch 19:2. Ps 139:21. Ro 1:32. 12:9. 1 C 15:33. Re 2:4.

3 **seven hundred**. Ge +4:19. Jg 9:5. Ec 7:28.

4 **when Solomon**. ver. 42. 1 K 6:1. 9:10. 14:21.
    his wives. ver. 2. Ge +4:19. Dt 7:4.
    turned away. Ex 32:1-6. 1 S 15:11. 2 S 12:7. 2 Ch 16:7-10. Je 8:5. Ho 11:7. Mt 16:6. Lk 19:14.
    his heart. ver. 6, 38. 6:12, 13. 9:4. 2 K +20:3. 2 Ch 17:3. 31:20, 21. 34:2.

5 **Ashtoreth**. i.e. *queen of heaven,* **S#6253h**. ver. 33. Jg +2:13. Je 2:10-13. Je 7:18.
    Milcom. i.e. *high king,* **S#4445h**. ver. 7, 33. Le 18:21. 20:2-5, Molech. 2 K 23:13. Zp 1:5, Malcham.

6 **went not fully after**. Heb. fulfilled not after. Nu 14:24. Jsh 14:8, 14.

7 **build an high**. 2 K +21:3.
    Chemosh. Nu +21:29.
    Molech. Le +18:21.
    abomination. Dt 13:14. 17:3, 4. 27:15. Is 44:19. Ezk 18:12. Da 11:31. 12:11. Re 17:4, 5.
    the hill. Ge 33:2. 2 S 15:30. 2 K 23:13. Zc 14:4. Mt 26:30. Ac 1:9, 12.

8 **all his strange wives**. ver. 1. Ezk 16:22-29. Ho 4:11, 12. 1 C 10:11, 12, 20-22.

9 **angry**. Ex 4:14. Nu 12:9. Dt 3:26. 9:8, 20. 2 S 6:7. 11:27. 1 Ch 21:7. Ps 78:58-60. 90:7, 8.
    his heart. ver. 2, 3. Dt 7:4. Pr +4:23. Is 29:13, 14. Ho 4:11. 2 T 4:10.
    which had appeared. 1 K 3:5. 9:2.
    twice. T 3:10.

10 **commanded**. 1 K 6:12, 13. 9:4-7. 2 Ch 7:17-22.

11 **is done of thee**. Heb. is with thee.
    thou hast not. Is 29:13, 14.
    I will surely. ver. 31. 1 K 12:15, 16, 20. Nu 14:23, 35. 1 S 2:30-32. 13:13, 14. 15:26-28. 2 S 12:9-12.

12 **in the days**. 1 K 21:29. 2 K 20:17, 19. 22:19, 20.

for David. 1 K 9:4, 5. Ge 12:2. 19:29.
I will rend it out. Ex +20:5.
the hand. Ge +9:5.

13 **Howbeit.** ver. 39. 2 S 7:15, 16. 1 Ch 17:13,
14. 2 Ch 6:6. Ps 89:33-37.
one tribe. ver. 35, 36. 1 K 12:20.
for David. 1 K 11:12, 32. Dt 9:5. 2 K 13:23.
19:34. Ps 89:49. 132:1, 17. Is 9:7. Je 33:17-26.
Lk 1:32, 33.
for Jerusalem's. Dt 12:5, 11. 2 K 21:4.
23:27. Ps 132:13, 14. Is 14:32. 62:1, 7. Je
33:15, 16.

14 **the Lord.** 1 K 12:15. 1 S 26:19. 2 S 24:1. 1
Ch 5:26. Is 10:5, 26. 13:17. Am +3:6.
an adversary. lit. "a satan." ver. 23, 25. 1 K
5:4. Nu 22:22. 1 S 29:4. 2 S 7:14. Ps 89:30-34.
1 P 5:8.
Edom. Am 1:11.

15 **when David.** 2 S 8:14. 1 Ch 18:12, 13. Ps 60,
title. 108:10.
after he had. Ge 25:23. 27:40. Nu 24:18, 19.
Dt 20:13. Ml 1:2, 3.
every male. Nu 31:17.

16 **Joab remain.** 1 Ch 11:6.

17 **Hadad.** Ex 2:1-10. 2 S 4:4. 2 K 11:2. Mt 2:13,
14.
a little child. 1 K 3:7. 1 S 20:35. 2 K 2:23.
5:14. Is 11:6.

18 **Midian.** Ge +25:2, 4.
Paran. Ge 14:6. +21:21.

19 **found.** Ge 39:4, 21. Ac 7:10, 21.
that he gave. Ge 41:45.
Tahpenes. i.e. *head of the age*, according to
Gesenius. **S#8472h.** ver. 20, 20. Je 43:7-9.
queen. 1 K 15:13. 2 K 10:13. 2 Ch 15:16. Je
13:18. 29:2.

20 **Genubath.** i.e. *theft*, **S#1592h.**
weaned. 1 S +1:22, 24.

21 **Hadad.** 1 K 2:10, 34. Ex 4:19. Mt 2:20.
Let me depart. Heb. Send me away. Ge
45:24. Jsh 2:21. 1 S 9:26. 2 S 3:21.

22 **But.** Je 2:31. Lk 22:35.
Nothing. Heb. Not.
let me go. 2 S 18:22, 23. Ps 37:8. Mk 14:31.

23 **God.** ver. +14. 2 S 16:11. Ezr 1:1. Is 13:17.
37:26. 45:5. Ezk 38:16.
Rezon. i.e. *to wax lean; a prince*, **S#7331h.**
Eliadah. i.e. *God knows*, **S#450h.** 2 S 5:16. 1 Ch
3:8. 2 Ch 17:17.
Hadadezer. 2 S +8:3. +10:16, Hadarezer. Ps
60, title.

24 **to Damascus.** Ge +14:15.

25 **an adversary.** ver. 14.
all the days. 1 K 5:4. 2 Ch 15:2.
abhorred. Ge 34:30. Dt 23:7. 2 S 16:21. Ps
106:40. Zc 11:8.

26 **Jeroboam.** i.e. *the people will contend*, **S#3379h.**
ver. 11, 28. 1 K 12:2, 20, 32. 13:1. 14:16.
15:30. 16:3. 21:22. 22:52. 2 K 3:3. 13:13.
14:16, 23, 28. 1 Ch 5:17. 2 Ch 9:29. 10:2.

11:4, 14. 13:1-4. Ho 1:1. Am 1:1. 7:10, 11.
Nebat. i.e. *regard*, **S#5028h.** 1 K 12:2, 15. 15:1.
16:3, 26, 31. 21:22. 22:52. 2 K 3:3. 9:9. 10:29.
13:2, 11. 14:24. 15:9, 18, 24, 28. 17:21. 23:15.
2 Ch 9:29. 10:2, 15. 13:6.
an Ephrathite. Ru +1:2.
Solomon's servant. 1 K 9:22. 2 Ch 13:6.
Zeruah. i.e. *a hornet*, **S#6871h.**

27 **lifted up.** 2 S 20:21. Pr 30:32. Is 26:11.
Solomon. 1 K 9:15, 24.
repaired. Heb. closed. Ge 2:21. 7:16. 19:6,
10. Am 9:11.
the breaches. Ne 4:7. Ps 60:2. Is 22:9. Ezk
13:5.
the city. 2 S +5:7.

28 **was industrious.** Heb. did work. Pr 22:29.
he made. 1 K 5:16.
charge. Heb. burden. Dt 1:12. Is 14:25. Mt
11:30.
the house. Am +5:6.

29 **Ahijah.** 1 K +14:6.
Shilonite. **S#7888h.** 1 K 12:15. 15:29. Jg
+21:19. 1 Ch 9:5. 2 Ch 9:29. 10:15.
and they two. Ge 4:8. 2 S 14:6.

30 **rent it.** 1 S 15:27, 28. 24:4, 5.
twelve pieces. 1 K 18:31. Ex 24:4.

31 **thus saith.** ver. 11, 12. 1 K 14:2.

32 **he shall.** 1 K +12:20.
one tribe. 1 K 12:20, 23. 2 Ch 11:13. 15:9.
for Jerusalem's sake. ver. +13.

33 **they have forsaken.** ver. 9. 1 K 3:14. 6:12,
13. 9:5-7. 1 Ch 28:9. 2 Ch 15:2. Je 2:13. Ho
4:17.
Ashtoreth. ver. 5-8.

34 **Howbeit.** ver. 12, 13, 31. Jb 11:6. Ps 103:10.
Hab 3:2.
for David. Is 55:3.
he kept. Jn +17:6. Ja 4:11. 1 J 2:3.

35 **I will take.** Ex 20:5, 6.
will give. 1 K 12:15-17, 20. 2 Ch 10:15-17.

36 **one tribe.** 1 K 12:16, 17. 2 K 8:19.
David. 1 K 15:4. 2 S 7:16, 29. 21:17. 2 K
8:19. 2 Ch 21:7. Ps 132:17. Je +33:17-21. Am
9:11, 12. Lk 1:69, 70, 78, 79. Ac 15:16, 17.
light. Heb. lamp, *or* candle. Ps +18:28mg.
the city. ver. +13. 1 K 9:3. Ga 4:25, 26. He
12:22. Re 21:10.

37 **according.** ver. 26. Dt 14:26. 2 S 3:21.
soul. Heb. *nephesh*, Ge +34:3.

38 **if thou wilt.** 1 K 3:14. 6:12. 9:4, 5. Ex 19:5.
Zc 3:7.
hearken. Dt +15:5.
that I will. Dt +31:8. Jsh 1:5.
build thee. 1 K 14:7-14. 2 S 7:11, 16, 26-29.
1 Ch 17:10, 24-27.
sure house. Is +55:3. Am +9:11. Ac 1:6.
15:16.

39 **afflict.** 1 K 12:16. 14:8, 25, 26. Ps 89:38-45,
49-51.
not for ever. ver. +36. Le +26:44. Ps 89:30-

34. Is 7:14. 9:7. 11:1-10. +41:9. 60:20. Je 23:5, 6. Zc 10:6. Ml +3:6. Lk 1:32, 33. 2:4, 11. Ro +11:1, 2, 29.

40 Solomon sought. 2 Ch 16:10. Pr 21:30. Is 14:24-27. 46:10. La 3:37.
Shishak. i.e. *greedy of fine linen; he who will give drink*, **S#7895h**. A.M. 3026. B.C. 978. 1 K 14:25. 2 Ch 12:2, 5, 9.

41 rest. 2 Ch 9:29-31.
acts. *or*, words, *or* things. 2 Ch +16:11.

42 time. Heb. days.
forty years. 1 K 2:11.

43 A.M. 3029. B.C. 975.
slept with. ver. 21. 1 K 1:21. 2:10. +14:20, 31. 15:8, 24. 16:6, 28. 22:40. Ge +25:8. 35:29. +49:33 with 50:13. Dt 31:16. 2 S 7:12. 2 K 8:24. 10:35. 13:13. 14:16, 29. 16:20. 20:21. 21:18. 24:6. 2 Ch 27:9. 28:27. 32:33.
buried. 1 K 2:10. 14:31. 2 K 8:24. 9:28. 12:21. 14:20. 21:18, 26. 2 Ch 21:20. 24:16, 25. 26:23. 28:27. 32:33. 33:20. Je 22:19.
Rehoboam. 1 K +14:21.

1 KINGS 12

1 A.M. 3029. B.C. 975.
Rehoboam. 1 K +14:21.
Shechem. Ge 12:6, Sichem. +33:18.

2 Jeroboam the son of Nebat. 1 K +11:26.

4 our yoke. 1 K 4:7, 20, 22, 23, 25. 9:15, 22, 23. 1 S 8:11-18. 2 Ch 10:4, 5. Mt 11:29, 30. 23:4. 1 J 5:3.

6 consulted with. 2 S 16:20. 17:5. Jb 12:12. 32:7. Pr 11:14. 12:15. 13:10. 15:22. 20:18. 24:6. 27:10. Je 42:2-5. 43:2.
old men. or, elders. Ge 50:7. 2 S 12:17.

7 they spake. ver. +10. Ex 18:19. 1 S 19:11. 2 S 20:16-22. 25:33. Da 4:27. Mt 27:19. Ac 5:35. Re 3:18. Sources of wise counsel: (1) The Lord, Pr 16:9. (2) God's written word, Ps 119:105. (3) Pastors and elders, He 13:7, 17. (4) Mature men, 1 K +12:7. (5) Parents, Col 3:20. (6) Wise women, 2 S +20:16. (7) Wife, 1 S 19:11. 25:33. (8) Servants or employees, 2 K +5:13. (9) The lowliest servants of Christ, 1 C 6:4. (10) Individuals faithful in the smallest of matters, Lk +16:10. Pr 20:6. (11) Individuals well grounded in Bible doctrine, 1 T +4:16. (12) Those God has placed in authority over us, Ge +16:9. (13) Believers who manifest the Biblical pattern of relationships to others, Ro +12:3; 15:7; Ph +2:3; 1 P 5:5. (14) Individuals that demonstrate the qualities of character and special talent in the area of needed advice, Pr 13:20; Lk 16:8; Ac +6:3. See sources of true guidance (1 K +13:9).
If thou wilt. 2 Ch 10:6, 7. Mk 10:43, 44. Ph 2:7-11.
be a servant. Ex +18:21. Mt 20:25-27. 23:11. Mk 9:35. Lk 22:24-27. 2 C +1:24.

serve them. Ro +12:3, 16. Ga 5:13. Ph +2:3.
answer them. 1 S +25:17. 2 K +5:13. 2 Ch +#10:7. Pr 15:1. 25:15. Ep +6:9. Col +4:1. 1 T 5:19.
speak good. ver. 13. 2 S 15:3-6. Ec 10:4. Zc 1:13.

8 forsook the counsel. ver. 13. 1 K 13:15-22. 1 S +25:17. 2 Ch +#10:8. 25:15, 16. Pr 1:2-5, 25, 30. 19:20. 25:12. Ec 10:2, 3.
consulted with. Pr 29:12. 1 T 5:19.
young men that. 2 Ch +10:8. 13:7.

9 What counsel. 1 K 22:6-8. 2 S 17:5, 6. 2 Ch 10:9. 18:5-7. 2 T 4:3.

10 spake unto. ver. +7, 28. Nu 31:16. 2 Ch 10:10. 22:3. Jb 2:9. Sources of unwise counsel: (1) Immature advisors, often young, lacking in judgment and experience, 1 K 12:10. (2) Our peer group, 2 Ch 13:7. (3) Individuals who offer advice contrary to the will of God revealed in the Bible, 1 K 13:18. (4) Individuals prompted by false spiritual gifts, Je +23:28. (5) False teachers, Ezk 14:10. (6) Those of unstable character, Pr 22:24. (7) Unfaithful individuals, Pr 25:19. (8) The proud and boastful, Pr 20:6. (9) Those who lack integrity, or compromise justice, Lk +16:10. (10) Those who compromise the truth and receive falsehood, Pr 29:12. (11) The generality of opinion expressed by the crowd, or majority opinion, when not in accordance with the principles of God's word, Ex 23:2. (12) Feelings and emotions, Ge 49:4; Je 23:17; 2 C 5:7; Ja 1:6, 8; 2 P 2:14. (13) Conscience uninformed by the Bible, Pr 14:12; Ac 24:16. (14) The occult, Is +8:19, 20. (15) Misunderstood or misapplied Scripture, Jg 6:40; 11:39; Mt 4:6; 2 T 2:15; 2 P 3:16. See sources of false guidance (1 K +13:18).
Thus shalt thou. 2 S 17:7-13.
My little finger. 2 Ch 10:10, 11. Pr 10:14. 18:6, 7. 28:25. 29:23. Is 47:6.

11 I will add. Ex 1:13, 14. 5:5-9, 18. 1 S 8:18. 2 Ch 16:10. Is 58:6. Je 27:11. 28:13, 14.
but I will chastise. Le 26:18, 28. Dt 8:5.
scorpions. ver. 14. Ezk 2:6. Re 9:3-10.

12 Come to me again. ver. 5. 2 Ch 10:12-14.

13 answered. 1 K 20:6-11. Ge 42:7, 30. Ex 5:2. 10:28. Jg 12:1-6. 1 S 20:10, 30, 31. 25:10, 11. 2 S 19:43. Pr 10:11, 32. 15:1. 18:6, 7, 23. Ec 10:12. Ja 3:17.
roughly. Heb. hardly. Ge 16:6. 1 S 20:10.
forsook. ver. +8. Pr 13:20. 22:28. 23:10.

14 the counsel. 2 Ch 22:4, 5. Est 1:16-21. 2:2-4. Pr 12:5. Is 19:11-13. Da 6:7.
My father made. ver. 10, 11. Pr 13:10. 16:18. 17:14. Ec 7:8. Ja 3:14-18. 4:1, 2.

15 the cause. ver. 24. 1 K 22:23. Dt 2:30. Jg 14:4. 2 S 24:1. 2 Ch 10:15. 22:7. 25:16, 20. Ps 5:10. Am +3:6. Ac 2:23. 4:28.

that he might. 1 K +11:11, 29-38. 1 S 15:29. 2 S 17:14. 2 K 9:36. 10:10. Is 14:13-17. 46:10, 11. Da 4:35. Jn 19:23, 24, 28, 29, 32-37. Ac 3:17. 13:27-29.

16 **What portion**. 2 S +20:1. 2 Ch 10:16.
to your tents. 1 K 22:17, 36. 2 S 20:1.
now see. 1 K 11:13, 34, 36, 39. 2 S 7:15, 16. Ps 2:1-6. 76:10. 89:29-37. 132:17. Is 7:2, 6, 7. 9:6, 7. Je 23:5, 6. 33:15, 16, 21. Lk 19:14, 27.
So Israel. Jg 8:35. 2 S 15:13. 16:11.

17 **the children**. 1 K 11:13, 36. 2 Ch 10:17. 11:13-17.

18 **Adoram**. 1 K 4:6. 5:14, Adoniram. 2 S 20:24. 2 Ch 10:18, Hadoram.
all Israel. Ex 17:4. Nu 14:10. 2 Ch 24:21. Ac 5:26. 7:57, 58.
made speed. Heb. strengthened himself. Ru 1:18. 2 Ch 10:18mg. 13:7.
flee to Jerusalem. 1 K 20:18-20. Pr 28:1, 2. Am 2:16.

19 **Israel**. 1 S 10:19. 2 K 17:21. 2 Ch 10:19. 13:5-7, 17. Is 7:17.
rebelled. or, fell away. 2 K 1:1. 3:5, 7. He 6:6.
unto this day. 1 S +6:18.

20 **and made him**. 1 S 10:24. Ho 8:4.
none that followed. ver. +17. 1 K 11:13, 32. Ho 11:12.
Judah. 1 K 11:32. Ex +12:40.
only. ver. 21, 23. 1 K 11:13, 32, 36.

21 **when Rehoboam**. 2 Ch 11:1-3.
an hundred. 1 Ch 21:5. 2 Ch 14:8, 11. 17:14-19. Pr 21:30, 31.

22 **Shemaiah**. 1 Ch +9:16.
the man. Dt +33:1.

24 **Ye shall not go up**. Nu 14:42. 2 Ch 11:4. 25:7, 8. 28:9-13.
for this thing. ver. +15. 1 K 11:29-38. Ho 8:4.
They hearkened. 2 Ch 25:10. 28:13-15.

25 **built**. 1 K 9:15, 17, 18. 15:17. 16:24. 2 Ch 11:5-12.
Shechem. ver. +1.
Penuel. Ge 32:30, 31. Jg 8:8, 17.

26 **said in his heart**. Ps 14:1. Mk 2:6-8. Lk 7:39.
Now shall. 1 K 11:38. 1 S 27:1. 2 Ch +20:20. Is 7:9. Je 38:18-21. Jn 11:47-50. 12:10, 11, 19. Ac 4:16, 17.

27 **go up**. 1 K 8:29, 30, 44. 11:32. Dt 12:5-7, 14. 16:2, 6.
and they shall. Ge 12:12, 13. 26:7. Pr 29:25. 1 C 1:19, 20.

28 **took counsel**. ver. +8, 9. Ex 1:10. Is 30:1.
two calves of gold. Ex +20:4. +32:4.
It is too much. Is 30:10. 2 P 2:19.
behold. Ex +32:4, 8. Ps 106:20.

29 **Bethel**. Ge +12:8. Ho 4:15.
Dan. Ge +14:14.

30 **became a sin**. 1 K 13:34. 2 K 10:31. 17:21.

31 **an house**. 1 K 13:24, 32. Dt 24:15. Ezk 16:25. Ho 12:11.
high. 2 K +21:3.

priests. 1 K 13:33. Nu 3:6, 10. 2 K 17:32. 2 Ch 11:14. 15. 13:9. Ezk 44:6-8.

32 **like unto**. 1 K 8:2, 5. Le 23:33, 34, etc. Nu 29:12, etc. Ezk 43:8. Da 7:25. Mt 15:8, 9.
offered upon the altar. or, went up to the altar. ver. 33. 1 K 13:1.
sacrificing. or, to sacrifice.
he placed. Am 7:10-13.

33 **offered upon the altar**. or, went up to the altar, etc. ver. 32.
in the month. Nu 15:39. Ps 106:39. Is 29:13. Da 7:25. Mt 15:6. Mk 7:13.
own heart. Nu +16:28. Dt 12:8.
he offered. 1 K 13:1. 1 S 13:12. 2 Ch 26:16.
and burnt incense. Heb. to burn incense. 1 K 13:1.

1 KINGS 13

1 **there came**. ver. 5, 6, 11, 14, 26. Dt +33:1. 2 K 23:17. 2 Ch 9:29. Je 25:4.
by the word. ver. 5, 9, 26, 32. 1 K 20:35. Je 25:3. 1 Th 4:15.
Jeroboam. 1 K 12:32, 33. 2 Ch 26:18.
burn. or, offer. Nu 16:40. Je 11:12. 32:29. Ml 1:11. Re 8:3.

2 **O altar**. Dt +32:1. Is 1:2. 58:1. Je 22:29. Ezk 36:1, 4. 38:4. Lk 19:40.
a child shall. 2 K 4:16. Is 9:6. Mt 1:21.
Josiah. i.e. sustained of Jehovah, **s#2977h**. 2 K 21:24, 26. 22:1, 3. 23:16, 19, 23, 24, 28-30, 34. 1 Ch 3:14, 15. 2 Ch 33:25. 34:1, 33. 35:1, 7, 16, 18-20, 22-26. 36:1. Je 1:2, 3. 3:6. 22:11, 18. 25:1, 3. 26:1. 27:1. 35:1. 36:1, 2, 9. 37:1. 45:1. 46:2. Zp 1:1. Zc 6:10. Mt 1:10, 11, Josias.
by name. 2 K 22:1, 2. 23:15-18. 2 Ch 34:1, 4-7. Is 42:9. 44:26-28. 45:1. 46:10. 48:5-7.
offer. 2 K 23:15-17.

3 **he gave**. Ex 4:3-5, 8, 9. 7:10. Nu +26:10. Dt 13:1-3. 2 K 20:8. Is 7:11-14. 38:6-8, 22. Mt 12:38-40. Jn 2:18. 1 C 1:22.

4 **Lay hold**. 2 Ch 16:10. 18:25, etc. 25:15, 16. Ps 105:14, 15. Je 20:2-4. 26:8-11, 20-23. 38:4-6. Am 7:10-17. Mt 25:40. 26:57. Mk 14:44-46. Jn 13:20. Ac 6:12-14.
his hand. Ge 19:11. 2 K 6:18-20. Je 20:4-6. Lk 3:19, 20. 6:10. Jn 18:6. Ac 9:4, 5. 13:8-11. Re 11:5.

5 **according to**. ver. 3. 1 K 22:28, 35. Ex 9:18-25. Nu 16:23-35. Dt 18:22. Je 28:16, 17. Mk 16:20. Ac 5:1-10.

6 **now**. Ex 8:8, 28. 9:28. 10:17. 12:32. Nu 21:7. 1 S 12:19. Je 37:3. 42:2-4. Ac 8:24. Ja 5:16. Re 3:9.
besought. Ex 8:12, 13. Nu 12:13. 1 S 12:23. Mt 5:44. Lk 6:27, 28. 23:34. Ac 7:60. Ro 12:14, 21. Ja 5:16-18. 1 J 2:1.
Lord. Heb. face of the Lord. Ex 32:11mg.

7 **refresh**. Ge 18:5. Jg 13:15. 19:21.

I will give. 1 S 9:7, 8. 2 K 5:15. Je 40:5. Ml 1:10. Ac 8:18-20. 1 P 5:2.

8 If. Nu 22:18. 24:13. Est 5:3, 6. 7:2. Mk 6:23. **go.** 2 K 5:16, 26, 27. Mk 6:11. 2 C 11:9, 10.

9 For. ver. +1, 21, 22. 1 S 15:22. Jb 23:12. Jn 13:17. 15:9, 10, 14.

by the word. ver. +18. Sources of true guidance: (1) The Bible, Ps 119:105; Is +8:20. (2) Our thoughts, 1 K 8:18; Pr +4:23; 16:3, 9. Test their source, 1 K 8:17, 18; 10:24; Je 23:16; Ac 5:3. May be correct and good, 1 K 8:18; 2 Ch 31:20, 21; Da 1:8; Ac 7:60; 26:29. May be evil, Dt 15:9; Pr 23:7; 1 T 4:1, 2; Ja 1:14, 15. Diet may affect judgment, Is 7:15, 22. (3) Circumstances, 1 S 14:15; Pr 16:33. Interpret circumstances carefully, 1 S 24:4. (4) The already revealed will of God, Ro 12:1, 2; 2 C 6:14. (5) Understanding enlightened by the study God's word, Ep 1:18, 19; 5:17; Col 1:9. (6) Obedience to the direct commands of Scripture, 1 S +15:22. (7) Needs, Ac 15:36. (8) Checks in the way, Ge 24:27; Nu 22:22, 26; Pr 30:19; Ac 16:6; Ro 1:13; 15:22; 1 Th 2:18. (9) By faith and bridle, Ps 32:8, 9. (10) Wise counsel, 1 S 9:27; 1 K +12:7; Pr 11:14; 15:22; 24:6; 27:17. (11) God's peace, wrought by the Holy Spirit, Jn 14:27; Ro 15:13; Ph 4:6, 7; Col 3:15. False peace can mislead, ver. +18; Ezk +13:10. (12) The church, Ac 13:1-3; 1 T +4:16. He 13:7, 17. (13) Chastening, He 12:6. (14) Pastors and elders, He 13:7, 17. (15) Parents, Pr 12:15; 13:10; 1 C 7:37, 38; Col 3:20. (16) Wife or husband, 1 S 19:11; 25:33; Mt 27:19; Ep 5:22, 23; 1 P 3:7, 8. See sources of wise counsel (1 K +12:7).

Eat no bread. Nu 16:26. Dt 13:13-18. Ps 141:4. Ro 16:17. 1 C 5:11. Ep 5:11. 2 J 10, 11. Re 18:4.

11 an old prophet. ver. 20, 21. Nu 23:4, 5. 24:2. 1 S 10:11. 2 K 23:18. Ezk 13:2, 16. Mt 7:22. 2 P 2:16.

sons. Heb. son.

came. 1 T 3:5.

13 Saddle me. ver. 27. Nu 22:21. Jg 5:10. 10:4. 2 S 19:26.

14 sitting. 1 K 19:4. Jn 4:6, 34. 1 C 4:11, 12. 2 C 11:27. Ph 4:12, 13.

Art thou. ver. +1.

16 I may not. ver. 8, 9. Ge 3:1-3. Nu 22:13, 19. Mt 4:10. 16:23.

17 It was. Heb. a word was.

by the word. ver. +1. 1 K 20:35. 1 Th 4:15.

18 a prophet also. ver. +9. Sources of false guidance: (1) Mishandling God's written word, Jg 6:40; 11:35. Mk 9:43; 2 T 2:15; 2 P 3:17. (2) Heeding only what you want to hear, 1 K +12:9; 2 T 4:3. (3) Wrong friends, 2 Ch 13:7; 1 C 15:33. (4) Inexperienced or unqualified individuals, often young, who lack the necessary discernment, 1 K +12:10; 2 T 3:14; He 5:14;

13:7. (5) Requiring God to specially engineer circumstances or signs, Jg 6:40. True signs or circumstances cannot confirm what is contrary to God's word, 2 C 6:14. (6) Thinking based on artificial categories imposed upon Scripture or Christian experience but not taught in the word of God, 2 T 2:15. (7) Wrongly weighting factors like circumstances, 1 S 24:4; 2 S 4:8; the feeling of peace (ver. +9. Ezk +13:10), which can be affected by our present physical state of health, Pr 17:22; Ro 15:13; 2 C 5:7. Supposed need for haste, Pr 19:2; 28:22; Col 1:10; Ja 1:5. (8) Occult practices, Is 8:19. (9) Dreams, Je +23:28. (10) Understanding uninformed by books and Bible study tools, Da 9:2; Jn 5:39; 2 T 3:16, 17; 4:13. (11) Resolutely holding to a favorite set of prooftexts from Scripture, rather than adhering to the whole counsel of God, 2 K 22:8; Mk 12:24; 2 P 1:20. (12) Not making the Bible our final authority, Pr +8:9; 18:1; Is +8:20; Je +23:28; Ac 17:11; Ga 1:8; 2 T +3:15-17. (13) False teachers, cults, and religions, Je 14:14; Ezk 14:10. (14) Anything that lacks good judgment, Pr +22:3; Lk 14:28-32. (15) Guidance from an individual who falsely claims a spiritual gift, or possesses a false gift, ver. 18. (16) Guidance which conflicts with genuine guidance previously received, ver. 18. See sources of unwise counsel (1 K +12:10).

an angel. Nu 22:35. Jg 6:11, 12. 13:3. 2 C 11:14. Ga 1:8.

But. Ge 3:4, 5. Is 9:15, 16. Je 5:12, 31. 23:14, 16, 17, 32. 28:15, 16. Ezk 13:6, 7, 9, 10, 22. Mt 7:15. 24:24. Ro 16:18. 2 C 11:3, 13-15. Ga 1:8. 2 P 2:1. 1 J 4:1. Re 19:20.

19 he went back. ver. 9. Ge 3:6. Dt 13:1, 3, 5. 18:20. Ac 4:19. 2 P 2:18, 19.

20 the word of the Lord. Nu 23:5, 16. 24:4, 16-24. Ps +50:16. Mt 7:22. Jn 11:51. 1 C 13:2.

21 Thus saith. ver. 17. Ge 3:7. Est 6:13. Je 2:19. Ga 1:8, 9.

thou hast disobeyed. Le 10:3. Nu 20:12, 24. 1 S 4:18. 13:13, 14. 15:19, 22-24. 2 S 6:7. 12:9-11. 24:13. Re 3:19.

22 camest back. Jb 23:12. Jn 13:17.

eaten. ver. 19.

of the. ver. 9.

carcase. ver. 30. 1 K 14:13. 2 Ch 21:19, 20. Is 14:18-20. Je 22:18, 19.

not come. Nu 20:12, 24. Dt 32:50, 51.

sepulchre. Heb. *qeber*, Ge +23:4.

24 a lion. 1 K 20:36. 2 K 2:24. Pr 22:13. 26:13. Am 5:19. 1 C 11:31, 32. 1 P 4:17, 18.

slew him. 2 S 6:7. Pr 11:31.

26 the man. Le 10:3. 2 S 12:10, 14. Ps 119:120. Pr 11:31. Ezk 9:6. 1 C 11:30. He 12:28, 29. 1 P 4:17.

torn. Heb. broken. ver. 28.

which he spake. ver. 9.

28 **the lion had**. 1 K 17:4, 6. Le 10:2, 5. Jb 38:11. Ps 148:7, 8. Je 5:22, 23. Da 3:22, 27, 28. 6:22-24. Ac 16:26. He 11:33, 34.

torn. Heb. broken. ver. 26.

30 **grave**. Heb. *qeber*, Ge +23:4.

mourned over. 1 K 14:13. Je 22:18. Ac 8:2.

31 **sepulchre**. Heb. *qeber*, Ge +23:4.

lay my bones. Nu 23:10. Ps 26:9. Ec 8:10. Lk 16:22, 23.

32 **the saying**. ver. 2. 2 K 23:16-19.

the houses. 1 K 12:29, 31. Le 26:30.

in the cities. 1 K +16:24.

33 A.M. 3030-3050. B.C. 974-954.

Jeroboam. 1 K 12:31-33. 2 Ch 11:15. 13:9. Am 4:6-11.

made again. Heb. returned and made. Ne 9:28. Ps 78:34. Je 18:4mg. 2 T 3:13.

high places. 2 K +21:3.

whosoever. Nu 1:51. 3:10. 17:5, 12, 13.

consecrated him. Heb. filled his hand. Ex +28:41mg.

34 **became sin**. 1 K 12:30. 2 K 10:31. 17:21. Ps 78:32. 2 T 3:13.

to cut it off. 1 K 12:26. 14:10. 15:29, 30. Pr 13:6.

the face. Ge +1:2.

1 KINGS 14

1 **Abijah**. i.e. *my father is Jah*, **S#29h**. 1 Ch 24:10. 2 Ch 11:20, 22. 12:16. 13:1-4, 15, 17, 19-22. 14:1. 29:1. Ne 10:7. 12:4, 17. Lk 1:5.

that time. 1 K 13:33, 34.

the son. ver. 12, 13. Ex 20:5. 1 S 4:19, 20. 31:2. 2 S 12:15.

2 **disguise thyself**. ver. 5, 6. 22:30. Ge +27:16. 2 S 14:2, 3. Lk 12:2.

Ahijah. ver. 6.

3 **And take**. 1 K 13:7. 1 S 9:7, 8. 2 K 4:42. 5:5, 15. 8:7-9.

with thee. Heb. in thine hand. Ge 24:10.

cracknels. *or*, cakes. Jsh 9:5. 2 S 13:6.

cruse. *or*, bottle. Je 19:1, 10.

he shall tell. 2 K 1:2. 8:8. Lk 7:2, 3. Jn 4:47, 48, 50. 11:3.

4 **Shiloh**. Jg +21:19.

for his eyes. Ge 27:1. 48:10. Dt 34:7. 1 S 3:2. 4:15. Ps 90:10. Ec 12:3.

were set by reason of his age. Heb. stood for his hoariness. 1 S 4:15.

5 **the Lord**. 2 K 4:27. 6:8-12. Ps 139:1-4. Pr 21:30. Am 3:7. Ac 10:19, 20.

6 **Ahijah**. i.e. *Jehovah is brother*, **S#281h**. ver. 2, 18. 1 K 11:29, 30. 12:15. 15:29. 2 Ch 9:29. *10:15*.

sound of her feet. 2 K 6:32.

thou wife. Jb 5:13. Ps 33:10.

why feignest. ver. 2, 5. Ps 139:1-6. Pr 21:30. Ezk 14:3-5, 7, 8. Lk 12:2. 20:20-23. Ac 5:3-5, 9, 10. He 4:13.

for I am. ver. 10, 11. 13:20-22. 20:42. 21:18-24. 22:8. 1 S 15:16, 26. 28:18. Je 21:2-7. Ezk 2:4, 5. Da 4:19-25. 5:17-28. Mk 14:21.

heavy. Heb. hard. 1 K 12:4, 13.

7 **Forasmuch**. 1 K 12:24. 16:2. 1 S 2:27-30. 15:16. 2 S 12:7, 8.

8 **rent**. 1 K 11:30, 31.

my servant David. 1 K 3:14. 11:33-38. 15:5. 2 Ch 17:3. 28:1. Ac 13:22, 36.

9 **hast done**. ver. 16. 1 K 12:28. 13:33, 34. 15:34. 16:31.

thou hast gone. Dt 32:16, 17, 21. Jg 5:8. 2 Ch 11:15. Ps 106:19, 20. 115:4-8. Is 44:9-20. Je 10:14-16.

to provoke. ver. 15, 22. Dt 9:8-16, 24. 29:28. 2 K 21:3. 23:26. 2 Ch 33:6. Ps 78:40, 56. 106:29. Is 65:3, 4. Je 7:9, 10. Ezk 8:3, 17. 1 C 10:22.

cast me. Ne 9:26. Ps 50:17. Ezk 23:35.

10 **I will bring**. 1 K 15:25-30. Am 3:6.

him that pisseth. 1 S +25:22.

him that is shut up. Dt +32:36.

as a man taketh. 1 S 2:30. 2 K 21:13. Is 14:19, 23. Je +16:4. Ezk 26:4. Lk 14:34, 35.

11 **that dieth**. 1 K 16:4. 21:19, 23, 24. Is 56:9. Je +7:33. 15:3. Ezk 29:5. 32:4.

12 **when thy feet**. ver. 3, 16, 17. 2 K 1:6, 16. Jn 4:50-52.

13 **shall mourn**. Nu 20:29. Je 22:10, 18.

grave. Heb. *qeber*, Ge +23:4.

there is found. 1 K 19:18. 2 Ch 12:12. 19:3. Jb 19:28. Ezk 18:14, etc. Phm 6. 2 P 2:8, 9.

14 **the Lord**. 1 K 15:27-29.

but what. 1 C 11:22.

even now. Ec 8:11. Ezk 7:2-7. 12:22-28. Ja 5:9. 2 P 2:3.

15 **the Lord**. 1 S 12:25. 2 K 17:6, 7.

as a reed. Mt 11:7. Lk 7:24.

root up Israel. Dt 29:28. Ps 52:5. Pr 2:22. Am 2:9. Zp 2:4. Mt 15:13.

this good land. Le 26:32-34, 43. Dt 4:26, 27. 28:36, 63-68. 29:24-28. Jsh 23:15, 16.

shall scatter. 2 K 15:29. 17:6, 23. 18:11, 12. Am 5:27. Ac 7:43.

beyond the river. i.e. *beyond the river Euphrates*. 2 K 15:29. 17:6, Gozan.

because. Is 1:28, 29.

groves. 2 K +17:10.

provoking. ver. +9. 1 K 16:33.

16 **he shall give Israel**. Jsh 23:15, 16. Ps 52:5. 81:12. Is 40:24. Ho 9:11, 12, 16, 17.

who did sin. 1 K 12:30. 13:34. 15:30, 34. 16:2. Ex 32:21, 35. 2 K 15:29. 17:6. Je 5:31. Ho 5:11, 12. Mi 6:16. Mt 18:7. Ro 14:13.

who made. 1 K 15:26. 2 K 3:3. 10:29. 13:2.

17 **Tirzah**. Nu +26:33.

when she came. ver. 12, 13. 1 S 2:30-34. 4:18-20.

threshold. Jg 19:27.

the child died. Jn 4:51.

19 A.M. 3029-3050. B.C. 975-954.
how he warred. ver. 30. 2 Ch 13:2-20.
book. ver. 29. 1 K 15:31. 16:5, 15, 20, 27.
22:39. 1 Ch 27:24. Est 6:1.

20 **slept**. Heb. lay down. ver. 31. 1 K +11:43.
22:40, 50. 2 K 10:35. 13:9, 13. 14:16, 29.
15:7, 22, 38. 2 Ch 9:31. 12:16. 14:1, etc. Jb
7:21. 11:18. 14:12. Ps 3:5. 4:8.
Nadab. 1 K 15:25-31. Ex +6:23.

21 **Rehoboam**. i.e. *enlargement of the people*,
S#7346h. 1 K 11:43. 12:1, 21. 1 Ch 3:10. 2 Ch
9:31. 10:1, 6. 11:1, 5, 17. 12:1, 13, 16. 13:7.
Mt 1:7.
forty and one years. 2 Ch 22:13.
the city. 1 K +8:16, 44. 11:36. Ps 78:68, 69.
87:1, 2. 132:13, 14. Is 12:6.
to put his name. Ex +20:24. Dt 12:5, 21.
Naamah. ver. 31. Ge +4:32. 2 Ch 22:3.
Ammonitess. 1 S +11:11.

22 **Judah**. Jg 3:7, 12. 4:1. 2 K 17:19. 2 Ch 12:1.
Je 3:7-11.
they provoked. ver. +9.
to jealousy. Ex +20:5.
above all. 1 K 16:30. 2 K 21:11. Ezk 16:47,
48.

23 **they also**. 2 Ch 14:3. Pr 16:7.
built. 2 K +21:3.
images. *or*, standing images, *or* statues. 2 K
+17:10.
groves. 2 K +17:10.
high hill. 2 K +17:10.
green tree. Is +57:5.

24 **And there**. Le +18:22. 2 K +23:7. 1 C 5:1.
6:9, 10.

25 A.M. 3034. B.C. 970.
Shishak. 1 K 11:40. 2 Ch 12:2-4.

26 **he took away**. 1 K +7:51. 15:18. 2 K 24:13.
2 Ch 12:9-11. Ps 39:6. 89:35-45.
the shields of gold. 1 K 10:16, 17. 2 Ch
9:15, 16. Pr 23:5. Ec 2:18, 19.

27 **made**. La 4:1, 2.
guard. Heb. runners. ver. 1, 5. 1 K 18:46. 1 S
8:11. 22:17. 2 S 15:1.

28 **the guard chamber**. 2 Ch 12:11. Ezk 40:7.

29 A.M. 3029-3046. B.C. 975-958.
are they not written. ver. +19. 1 K 11:41.
15:23. 22:45. 2 Ch 12:15.

30 **there was war**. 1 K 12:24. 15:6, 7. 2 Ch
12:15.

31 A.M. 3046. B.C. 958.
Rehoboam. ver. +21. 1 K 15:3, 24. 22:50.
his mother's. ver. +21.
Abijam. 1 Ch 3:10, Abia. 2 Ch 12:16, Abijah.
Mt 1:7, Abia.

1 KINGS 15

1 **Now in the**. 1 K 14:31. 2 Ch 13:1, 2, etc.
Abijam. i.e. *father of the sea; seaman*, **S#38h**.
ver. 7, 8. 1 K 14:31.

2 **his mother's**. or, grandmother's. ver. +10,
13. 2 Ch 11:20-22.
Maachah. 1 K +2:39. 2 Ch 13:2, Michaiah
the daughter of Uriel.
Abishalom. i.e. *father of peace*, **S#53h**. ver. 10.
2 Ch 11:21, Absalom.

3 **all the sins**. 1 K 14:21, 22.
and his heart. 1 K +3:14. 2 K +20:3. 2 Ch
31:20, 21. Ps 119:80.

4 **for David's**. 1 K 11:12, 32. Ge 12:2. 19:29.
26:5. Dt 4:37. 2 S 7:12-16. Is 37:35. Je 33:20-
26. Ro 11:28.
give him. 1 K 11:36. 2 Ch 21:7. Ps 132:17.
Lk 1:69-79. 2:32. Jn 8:12. Re 22:16.
lamp. *or*, candle. 1 K 11:36. 2 S 21:17. Ps
18:28.
and to establish. Ps 87:5. Is 9:7. 14:32. 62:7.
Je 33:2. Mi 4:1, 2. Mt 16:18.

5 **David**. ver. +3. 1 K +3:14. 11:4, +34. 14:8.
Jsh +1:7. Ps 119:6. Lk 1:6. Ac 13:22, 36.
save only. 2 S 11:4, 15-17. 12:9, 10. Ps 51,
title.

6 **there was war**. 1 K +14:30. 2 Ch 13:3.

7 **the rest**. 1 K +14:29. 2 Ch 13:2, 21, 22.
there was war. 2 Ch 13:3-20.

8 A.M. 3049. B.C. 955.
Abijam. 1 K 14:1, 31. 2 Ch 14:1.
Asa. 1 Ch +9:16.

10 A.M. 3049-3090. B.C. 955-914.
mother's. *that is*, grandmother's. ver. 2, 13.
Ge 28:13. 2 S 9:7. 19:28. 2 K 8:26mg. 14:3. 1
Ch 7:6, 13, 14, 24. 2 Ch 11:18, 20, 21. 13:2.
15:16mg. 34:1, 2. Je 27:7. Da 5:2mg, 11.

11 **Asa**. ver. 3. 2 Ch 14:2, 11. 15:17. 16:7-10.

12 **the sodomites**. 2 K +23:7. Ju 7.
all the idols. ver. 3. 1 K 11:7, 8. 14:23. 2 K
+23:24. 2 Ch 14:2-5. Zc 1:2-6. 1 P 1:18.

13 **Maachah**. ver. +2, 10.
his mother. or, grandmother. ver. +10. Dt
13:6-11. 33:9. Zc 13:3. Mt 10:37. 12:46-50. 2
C 5:16. Ga 2:5, 6, 14.
grove. 2 K +17:10.
destroyed. Heb. cut off. Le 26:30. Ex +23:24.
and burnt. Dt +7:5. Jsh 6:24.
the brook. 2 S +15:23.

14 **the high places**. 2 K +21:3.
was perfect. ver. 3. 2 K +20:3. 2 Ch
+12:14mg. 27:6. Ps 7:9. 66:18.

15 **he brought**. 1 K +7:51. 1 Ch 26:26-28. 2 Ch
14:13. 15:18.
things. Heb. holy. 2 K 12:4. 1 Ch 26:20. 2 Ch
5:1.

16 **there was war**. ver. 6, 7, 32. 1 K 14:30. 2 Ch
16:1, etc.
Baasha. i.e. *evil; offensive*, **S#1201h**. ver. 17, 19,
21, 22, 27, 28, 32, 33. 16:1, 3-8, 11, 12, 13.
21:22. 2 K 9:9. 2 Ch 16:1, 3, 5, 6. Je 41:9.

17 A.M. 3074. B.C. 930.
Baasha. ver. 27. 2 Ch 16:1, etc.
Ramah. ver. 21. Je +31:15.

he might not suffer. 1 K 12:27. 2 Ch 11:13-17.

18　**Asa.** ver. +8, 15. 1 K 14:26. 2 K 12:18. 18:15, 16. 2 Ch 15:18. 16:2-6.
Ben-hadad. i.e. *son of shouting*, **S#1130h.** ver. 20. 1 K 20:1, 2, 5, 9, 10, 16, 20, 26, 30, 32, 33. 2 K 6:24. 8:7, 9. 13:3, 24, 25. 2 Ch 16:2, 4. Je 49:27. Am 1:4.
Tabrimon. i.e. *good is the pomegranate*, or *good is Rimmon*, the Syrian deity. **S#2886h.**
Hezion. i.e. *vision*, **S#2383h.** 1 K 11:25, Rezon.
Damascus. Ge +14:15.

19　**There is a league.** 2 Ch 19:2. Is 31:1.
break thy league. 2 S 21:2. 2 Ch 16:3. Ezk 17:13-16. Ro 1:31. 3:8.
depart. Heb. go up. 2 Ch 16:3.

20　**Ijon.** i.e. *ruin*, **S#5859h.** 2 K 15:29. 2 Ch 16:4. Ezk 48:1, Hazar-enan.
Dan. Ge +14:14.
Abel-beth-maachah. i.e. *mourning of the house of oppression*, **S#62h.** 1 S +6:18. 2 S 20:14, 15. 2 K 15:29. 2 Ch 16:4.
Cinneroth. i.e. *lyres*, **S#3672h.** Jsh +11:2.

21　**when Baasha.** 2 Ch 16:5.
Tirzah. Nu +26:33.

22　**made a proclamation.** 2 Ch 16:6.
exempted. Heb. free.
Geba. 1 S +13:3.
Mizpah. Ge +31:49.

23　**The rest of all.** ver. 7, 8. 1 K 14:29-31.
in the time. 2 Ch 16:12-14. Ps 90:10.

24　A.M. 3090. B.C. 914.
was buried. 2 Ch 16:14.
Jehoshaphat. 2 S +8:16.

25　A.M. 3050-3051. B.C. 954-953.
Nadab. Ex +6:23.
began to reign. Heb. reigned. ver. 33. 1 K 14:21. 16:8, 11, 23, 29. 22:41. 2 K 8:16.
two years. ver. 28, 33.

26　**he did evil.** 1 K 16:7, 25, 30.
walked. ver. 34. 1 K 12:28-33. 13:33, 34. 22:52. 2 Ch 22:3. Je 9:14. Ezk 20:18. Am 2:4. Mt 14:8.
in his sin. ver. 30, 34. 1 K 14:16. 16:19, 26. 21:22. 22:52. Ge 20:9. Ex 32:21. 1 S 2:24. 2 K 3:3. 21:11. 23:15. Je 32:35. Ro 14:15. 1 C 8:10-13.

27　**Baasha the son.** ver. 16, 17. 1 K 14:14.
conspired. 1 K 16:9. 1 S 22:8. 2 K 12:20.
Gibbethon. Jsh +19:44.

28　**in the third year.** ver. 25, 33. Dt 32:35.

29　**he left not.** 1 K 14:9-16. 2 K 9:7-10, 36, 37. 10:10, 11, 31. 19:25.
any that. Dt 20:16. Jsh 10:40. 11:11.
breathed. Heb. *neshamah*, Ge +2:7.

30　**the sins.** ver. +26. 1 K 14:9-16.
by his provocation. 1 K 14:22.

31　A.M. 3050-51. B.C. 954-953.
are they not written. 1 K 14:19. 16:5, 14, 20, 27.

32　A.M. 3051-3074. B.C. 953-930.
there was war. ver. +16. 1 K 16:8-10. 2 Ch 15:19. 16:1.

33　**twenty and four years.** 1 K 16:8.

34　**he did evil.** ver. 26.
walked. ver. +26. 1 K 14:16. Is 1:4.

1 KINGS 16

1　A.M. 3073. B.C. 931.
the word of the Lord. 1 K 13:1, 20.
Jehu. ver. 7. 2 Ch 19:2. 20:34.
Hanani. 1 K 15:33. 2 Ch 16:7-10.

2　**I exalted thee.** 1 K 14:7. 1 S 2:8, 27, 28. 15:17-19. 2 S 12:7-11. Ps 113:7, 8. Lk 1:52.
dust. Ge +18:27.
thou hast walked. 1 K +13:33, 34. 15:34.
hast made my people. 1 K +14:16. 15:26. Ex 32:21. 1 S 2:24. 26:19. Mt 5:19.

3　**will make thy house.** ver. 11, 12. 1 K 14:10. 15:29, 30. 21:21-24. Is 66:24. Je 22:19.

4　**shall the dogs eat.** 1 K +14:11.

5　A.M. 3051-3074. B.C. 953-930.
the rest. 1 K +14:19. 15:31. 2 Ch 16:1, etc.

6　A.M. 3074. B.C. 930.
Baasha slept with. 1 K +11:43.
Tirzah. Nu +26:33.
Elah. ver. 8, 13, 14.

7　**the hand.** ver. +1, 2.
and against his house. Ex 20:5.
in provoking. ver. 13.
with the work. Ps 115:4. Is 2:8. 44:9-20.
because he killed him. 1 K 14:14. 15:27-29. 2 K 10:30, 31. Is 10:6, 7. Ho 1:4. Ac 2:23. 4:27, 28.

8　A.M. 3075. B.C. 929.
In the twenty and sixth year. 1 K 2:11. 15:25. Jsh 5:11. 1 S 30:12.

9　**his servant.** 2 K 9:31.
conspired. 1 K 15:27. 2 K 9:14. 12:20. 15:10, 25, 30.
drinking. 1 K 20:16. 1 S 25:36-38. 2 S 13:28, 29. Pr 23:29-35. Je 51:57. Da 5:1-4, 30. Na 1:10. Hab 2:15, 16. Mt 24:49-51. Lk 21:34.
Arza. i.e. *earth; earthiness*, **S#777h.**
steward of. Heb. which *was* over. 1 K 18:3. Ge 15:2. 24:2, 10. 39:4, 9. 43:16.

10　**Zimri.** 2 K 9:31.
reigned. ver. 15.

11　**he slew.** 1 K 15:29. Jg 1:7.
he left him. 1 S +25:22.
neither of his kinsfolks, nor of his friends. or, both his kinsmen and his friends. kinsmen, or redeemers. Ge 48:16. Ex 6:6. Le 25:25.

12　**according.** ver. +1-4.
by Jehu the prophet. Heb. by the hand of Jehu the prophet. ver. 1, 7, 34. 14:18. 15:29. 17:16. Le 8:36. 2 S 12:25. 2 K 9:36mg. 10:10mg. 14:25. 17:13mg. 19:23mg. 24:2mg.

1 Ch 11:3mg. 25:2mg. 29:8. 2 Ch 10:15. 23:18mg. 29:25mg. 33:8. 34:14mg. Ezr 9:11mg. Ps 63:10mg. 77:2mg. Pr 26:6. Hg +1:1mg.

13   **in provoking**. 1 K 15:30.
vanities. Dt +32:21. Je 18:15. 1 C 8:4. 10:19, 20.

14   **they not written**. ver. +5.

15   **seven**. ver. 8. 2 K 9:31. Jb 20:5. Ps 9:16. 37:35.
And the people were encamped. Jsh +19:44.

16   **Omri**. i.e. *my sheaf; servant of the Lord; pupil of Jehovah*, **S#6018h**. ver. 17, 21-23, 25, 27-30. 2 K 8:26. 1 Ch 7:8. 9:4. 27:18. 2 Ch 22:2. Mi 6:16.

17   **besieged Tirzah**. Jg 9:45, 50, 56, 57. 2 K 6:24, 25. 18:9-12. 25:1-4. Lk 19:43, 44.

18   **palace**. **S#759h**. 2 K 15:25. 2 Ch 36:19. Ps 48:3, 13. 122:7. Pr 18:19 (castle). Is 23:13. 25:2. 32:14. 34:13. Je 6:5. 9:21. 17:27. 30:18. 49:27. La 2:5, 7. Ho 8:14. Am 1:4, 7, 10, 12, 14. 2:2, 5. 3:9, 10, 11. 6:8. Mi 5:5.
and burnt the king's house. Jg 9:54. 1 S 31:4, 5. 2 S +17:23. Jb 2:9, 10. Mt 27:5.

19   **in doing**. ver. 7, 13. 1 K 15:30. Ps 9:16. 58:9-11.
in his. 1 K +12:28. 14:16. 15:26, 34.

20   **the rest**. ver. 5, 14, 27. 1 K 14:19. 15:31. 22:39.
treason. 2 K 11:14. 2 Ch 23:13.

21   **divided**. ver. 8, 29. 1 K 15:25, 28. Pr 28:2. Is 9:18-21. 19:2. Mt 12:25. 1 C 1:12, 13. Ep 4:3-5.
Tibni. i.e. *my structure; building of Jah*, **S#8402h**. ver. 22, 22.
Ginath. i.e. *a garden; protection*, **S#1527h**. ver. 22.

23   A.M. 3079-3086. B.C. 925-918.
the thirty and first. ver. 10, 15. 2 Ch 22:2.
began Omri. Mi 6:16.
twelve years. ver. 8, 29.

24   **the name of the city**. Jn 4:4, 5. Ac 8:5-8.
Samaria. Heb. Shomeron, from Shemer, i.e. *dregs*. i.e. *an adamant stone; guardianship*, **S#8111h**. ver. 28, 29, 32. 1 K 13:32. 18:2. 20:1, 10, 17, 24, 43. 21:1, 18. 22:10, 37, 38, 51. 2 K 1:2, 3. 2:25. 3:1, 6. 5:3. 6:19, 20. 15:27. 17:1, 6, 24. 18:9, 10. 2 Ch 18:2, 9. 22:9. 25:13, 24. 28:8, 9, 15. Ezr 4:10. Ne 4:2. Is 7:9. 8:4. 9:9. 10:9, 10, 11. 36:19. Je 23:13. 31:5. 41:5. Ezk 16:46, 51, 53, 55. 23:4, 33. Ho 7:1. 8:5, 6. 10:5, 7. 13:16. Am 3:9, 12. 4:1. 6:1. 8:14. Ob 19. Mi 1:1, 5, 6.
Shemer. i.e. *dregs; a thorn; guardianship*, **S#8106h**.

25   **did worse**. ver. 30, 31, 33. 1 K 14:9. Mi 6:16.

26   **he walked**. ver. 2, 7, 19. 1 K 12:26-36. 13:33, 34.
their vanities. ver. +13.

27   **the rest**. ver. 5, 14, 20. 1 K 15:31.

28   **So Omri slept**. ver. +6.
Ahab. i.e. *father's brother; uncle*, **S#256h**. ver. 29, 30, 33. 1 K 17:1. 18:1-3, 5, 6, 9, 12, 16, 17, 20, 41, 42, 44-46. 19:1. 20:2, 13, 14. 21:1-4, 8, 15, 16, 18, 20, 21, 24, 25, 27, 29. 22:20, 39-41, 49, 51. 2 K 1:3:1, 5. 8:16, 18, 25, 27-29. 9:7-9, 25, 29. 10:1, 10, 11, 17, 18, 30. 21:3, 13. 2 Ch 18:1-3, 19. 21:6, 13. 22:3-8. Je 29:21, 22. Mi 6:16.

29   A.M. 3086-3107. B.C. 918-897.
Samaria. ver. +24.

30   **above**. ver. 25, 31, 33. 1 K 14:9. 21:25. 2 K 3:2.

31   **as if it had been a light thing**. Heb. was it a light thing. Ge 30:15. Nu 16:9. Is 7:13. Ezk 8:17. 16:20, 47. 34:18.
took to wife. Ge 6:2. Dt 7:3, 4. Jsh 23:12, 13. Ne 13:23-29.
Jezebel. i.e. *without habitation; a dunghill; without cohabitation; unchaste*, **S#348h**. 1 K 18:4, 13, 19. 19:1, 2. 21:5, 7, 11, 14, 15, 23, 25. 2 K 9:7, 10, 22, 30, 36, 37. Re 2:20.
Ethbaal. i.e. *with Baal*, **S#856h**.
the Zidonians. Jg +10:12.
and went. 1 K +11:4, 8.
served Baal. 1 K 21:25, 26. Jg +2:11. +6:25. 2 K 17:16.

32   **the house of Baal**. 2 K 10:21, 26, 27.

33   **made a grove**. 2 K +17:10.
did more to provoke. ver. 30. 1 K 21:19, 25. 22:6, 8.

34   **Hiel**. i.e. *God liveth*, **S#2419h**.
Bethelite. **S#1017h**.
build Jericho. 2 K 2:4, 19-22.
Abiram. Nu +16:1.
Segub. 1 Ch +2:21. Je 52:10.
according to. Jsh 6:26. 23:14, 15. Zc 1:5. Mt 24:35.

1 KINGS 17

1   A.M. 3094. B.C. 910.
Elijah. Heb. Elijahu. i.e. *My God is He*, **S#452h**. ver. 13, 15, 16, 18, 22-24. 1 K 18:1, 2, 7, 8, 11, 14-17, 21-23, 25, 27, 30, 31, 36, 40-42, 46. 19:1, 2, 9, 13, 19-21. 21:17, 20, 28. 2 K 1:10, 13, 15, 17. 2:1, 2, 4, 6, 9, 11, 13-15. 3:11. 9:36. 10:10, 17. 2 Ch 21:12. Mt 11:14. 16:14. 17:3, 4, 10, 11, 12. 27:47, 49. Lk 1:17. 4:25, 26. 9:30, 33, 54. Jn 1:21, 25. Ro 11:2, Elias.
the Tishbite. i.e. *captivity; recourse*, **S#8664h**. 1 K 21:17, 28. 2 K 1:3, 8. 9:36. In Galilee, Jn 7:52.
inhabitants. Ge 23:4 (**S#8453h**). Nu 35:15. 1 Ch 29:15.
As the Lord God. ver. 12. 1 K 1:29. 2:24. 18:10, 15. 22:14. Jg 8:19. Ru 3:13. 1 S 14:39, 45. 19:6. 20:3, 21. 25:26. 26:10. 28:10. 29:6. 2

S 12:5. 15:21. 2 K 2:2, 4, 6. 3:14. 4:30. 5:16, 20. Is 49:18. Je 4:2. 5:2. 12:16. Mt 7:29. Lk 1:17.

before whom. Dt +10:8. Pr 8:34. Ac 27:23.

dew nor rain. Lk 4:25. Ja 5:17. Re 11:6.

2 **the word**. 1 K 12:22. 1 Ch 17:3. Je 7:1. 11:1. 18:1. Ho 1:1, 2.

3 **hide thyself**. 1 K 22:25. Ps 31:20. +83:3. Pr +22:3. He 11:38. Re 12:6, 14.

Cherith. i.e. *a cutting off; piercing; slaying*, **S#3747h**. ver. 5.

4 **I have commanded**. ver. 9. 1 K 19:5-8. Nu 20:8. Jb 34:29. 38:8-13, 41. Ps 33:8, 9. 147:9. Am 9:3, 4. Mt 4:4, 11.

feed. Ru +4:15.

5 **did according**. 1 K 19:9. Pr 3:5, 6. Mt 16:24. Jn 15:14.

6 **the ravens**. Ex 16:35. Nu 11:23. Jg 14:14. 15:18, 19. Ps 34:9, 10. 37:3, 19. 78:15, 16, 23, 24. Is 33:16. Je 37:21. 40:4. Hab 3:17, 18. Mt 4:4. 6:31-33. 14:19-21. 19:26. Lk 22:35. He 6:18. 13:5, 6.

he drank. Ps 110:7.

7 A.M. 3095. B.C. 909.

after a while. Heb. at the end of days. ver. 15. Ne +13:6mg.

the brook. Is 40:30, 31. 54:10.

8 **the word**. ver. 2. Ge 22:14. Is 41:17. He 13:6.

9 **Zarephath**. i.e. *a refining place; smelting house*, **S#6886h**. ver. 10. Ob 20. Lk 4:26, Sarepta.

Zidon. Ge +49:13.

widow woman. ver. 4. Jg 7:2, 4. 2 S 14:5. Ro 4:17-21. 2 C 4:7.

sustain. Ge 45:11. Ru +4:15. Is 54:10. Mt 15:21, 22. Lk 4:25, 26.

10 **he arose**. Ro 4:20, 21.

the gate. Ge +14:7. 2 S 19:8.

Fetch me. Ge 21:15. 24:17. Jn 4:7. 2 C 11:27. He 11:37.

11 **as she was going**. Ge 24:18, 19. Mt 10:41, 42. 25:35-40. He 13:2.

a morsel. ver. 9. 1 K 18:4. Ge 18:5.

12 **As the Lord**. ver. +1.

liveth. Jg 8:19.

have not. Mk 12:44.

cake. Ps 35:16.

but an handful. Ex 9:8. Le 2:2. 2 K 4:2-7. Mt 15:33, 34.

meal. Ge 18:6.

barrel. or, pitcher. ver. 14, 16. 18:33. Ge 24:14, 15, 16, 17, 18, 20, 43, 45, 46. Jg 7:16, 19, 20. Ec 12:6.

oil. Ge 28:18. Ge 49:20. Dt 33:24. Jsh 19:24-28.

cruse. or, dish. ver. 14, 16. 1 K 19:6. 1 S 26:11, 12, 16.

gathering. Nu 15:32, 33.

two sticks. Is 17:6. Je 3:14.

that we may eat it. Ge 21:16. Je 14:18. La 4:9. Ezk 12:18, 19. Jl 1:15, 16.

13 **Elijah**. Lk 4:26.

Fear not. Ge +15:1. 2 Ch 20:17.

make me thereof. Ge 22:1, 2. Jg 7:5-7. Mt 19:21, 22. He 11:17. 1 P 1:7.

first. Pr 3:9, 10. Ml 3:10. Mt 6:33. 10:37. 15:33-38.

14 **thus saith**. 2 K 3:16. 7:1. 9:6.

The barrel of meal. ver. 4. 2 K 4:2-7, 42-44. Mt 14:17-20. 15:36-38.

sendeth. Heb. giveth.

15 **did according**. Ge 6:22. 12:4. 22:3. 2 Ch 20:20. Mt 15:28. Mk 12:43. Jn 11:40. Ro 4:19, 20. He 11:7, 8, 17.

many days. or, a full year. ver. 7.

16 **the barrel**. Mt 9:28-30. 15:28. 19:26. Lk 1:37, 45. Jn 4:50, 51. 11:40.

according. 1 K 13:5.

by Elijah. Heb. by the hand of Elijah. 1 K +16:12mg.

17 A.M. 3096. B.C. 908.

the son of the woman. Ge 22:1, 2. 2 K 4:18-20. Zc 12:10. Jn 11:3, 4, 14. Ja 1:2-4, 12. 1 P 1:7. 4:12.

mistress. lit. "lady," as in 1 S 28:7. Na 3:4.

that there was. Jb 12:10. 34:14. Ps 104:29. Da 5:23. Ja 2:26mg.

breath. Heb. neshamah, Ge +2:7.

18 **What have I**. Dt 32:39. Jg +11:12.

O thou man. Dt +33:1.

art thou come. 1 K 18:9. Ge 42:21, 22. 50:15, 17. 1 S 16:4. Jb 13:23, 26. Ezk 21:23, 24. Mk 5:7, 15-17. 6:16.

to call. Nu 5:15. Ezk 29:16. Lk 5:8.

19 **into a loft**. or, chamber. ver. 23. Jg 3:20. 2 S +18:33. 2 K 4:10, 21, 32. Ac 9:37.

20 **he cried**. 1 K 18:36, 37. Ex 17:4. 1 S 7:8, 9. 2 K 19:4, 15. Ps 99:6. Mt 21:22. Ja 5:15-18.

hast thou also. Ge 18:23-25. Jsh 7:8, 9. Ps 73:13, 14. Je 12:1.

21 **stretched himself**. Heb. measured himself. 2 K 4:33-35. Ac 20:10.

O Lord my God. Ac 9:40. He 11:19.

soul. Heb. nephesh, Ge +12:13. Mt +10:28. Ac 2:27.

into him. Heb. into his inward parts.

22 **soul**. Heb. nephesh, Ge +12:13. +25:8, 9, 17. 35:18. Jb 14:22. 33:18, 22. Ps 88:3. Mt +10:28. Ac 2:37. +7:59.

into him. Heb. into his inward parts. Ge 18:12 (within), 24 (within).

and he revived. Dt 32:39. 1 S 2:6. 2 K 13:21. Lk 7:14, 15. 8:54-56. Jn 5:28, 29. 11:43, 44. Ac 9:40. 20:12. Ro 14:9. He 11:35. Re 11:11.

23 **chamber**. ver. 23. 2 S +18:33.

See, thy son liveth. 2 K 4:36, 37. Lk 7:15. Ac 9:41. He 11:35.

24 **Now by this**. Jn 2:11. 3:2. 4:42-48. 11:15, 42. 15:24. 16:30.

the word. Ec 12:10. 1 Th 2:13. 1 J 2:21.

1 KINGS 18

1 A.M. 3098. B.C. 906.
after many days. 1 K 17:1. Ne 13:6mg. Lk 4:25. Ja 5:17. Re 11:2, 6.
in the third year. 1 K 17:1, 7, 15. Lk 4:25. Ja 5:17.
Go. ver. 2, 15, etc.
I will send rain. Le 26:4. Dt 28:12. Ps 65:9-13. Is 5:6. Je 10:13. 14:22. Jl 2:23. Am 4:7.

2 **went to show**. Ps 27:1. 56:4. Pr 28:1. Is 51:12. He 13:5, 6.
a sore. 1 K +8:37.

3 **Obadiah**. Heb. Obadiahu.
the governor of his house. Heb. over *his* house. Ge 24:2, 10. 39:4, 5, 9. +41:40, 41.
feared the Lord. ver. 12. Ex +18:21. Pr 14:26, 27.

4 **Jezebel**. Heb. Izabel. ver. 13, 19. 1 K 16:31.
cut off the prophets. 1 K 19:18. Ne 9:26. Mt 21:35. Re 17:4-6.
hid. Jsh 6:17.
in a cave. He 11:38.
fed them. ver. 13. 2 K 6:22, 23. Mt 10:40-42. 25:35, 40.
bread and water. 1 K 13:8, 9, 16.

5 **fountains**. Heb. *mayan*, Ge +7:11.
grass. Ps 104:14. Je 14:5, 6. Jl 1:18, 20. 2:22. Hab 3:17. Ro 8:20-22.
we lose not all the beasts. Heb. we cut not off *ourselves* from the beasts.

6 **Ahab went**. Je 14:3.

7 **was in the way**. 1 K 11:29.
he knew. 2 K 1:6-8. Mt 3:4. 11:8.
fell on. Ge 18:2. 50:18. 1 S 20:41. 2 S 19:18. Is 60:14.
my lord Elijah. Ge 18:12. 44:16, 20, 33. Nu 12:11.

8 **thy lord**. ver. 3. Ro 13:7. 1 P 2:17, 18.

9 **What have I sinned**. ver. 12. 1 K +17:18. Ex 5:21.

10 **the Lord**. ver. 15. 1 K +17:1.
no nation or kingdom. Ge +41:56. 2 K 20:13. Mt 5:29.
whither my lord. Ps 10:2. Je 26:20-23.
they found thee not. 1 K 17:5, 9. Ps 12:7, 8. 31:20. 91:1. Je 36:26. Jn 8:59.

11 **Go, tell thy lord**. ver. 8, 14.

12 **the Spirit**. Heb. *ruach*, Is +48:16.
carry. Ezk +8:3. Mt 4:1.
he shall slay me. 1 S 22:11-19. Da 2:5-13. Mt 2:16. Ac 12:19.
from my youth. 1 S 2:18, 26. 3:19, 20. 2 Ch 34:3. Ps 71:17, 18. Pr 8:13. Ec 7:18. Is 50:10. Lk 1:15. 2 T 3:15.

13 **what I did**. ver. 4. Ge 20:4, 5. Ps 18:21-24. Ac 20:34. 1 Th 2:9, 10.
I hid an hundred. Mt 10:41, 42.
fed them. Mt 25:35.

14 **tell**. Ex 4:1. 1 S 16:2. Je 1:6.
and he shall slay me. Mt 10:28.

15 **As the Lord**. ver. +10. He 6:16, 17.
of hosts liveth. Ps +24:10.
before whom I. Dt 1:38. +10:8.
I will surely. Ps 27:1. Pr 28:1. Is 51:7, 8. He 13:5, 6.

17 **he that troubleth**. 1 K 21:20. Jsh 7:25. Je 26:8, 9. 38:4. Am 7:10. Ac 16:20. 17:6. 24:5.

18 **I have not**. Ezk 3:8. Mt 14:4. Ac 24:13, 20.
but thou. Ge 3:12, 13. 2 K 9:19. Ro 7:14.
in that ye have. 1 K 9:9. 2 Ch 15:2. Pr 11:19. 13:21. Is 3:11. Je 2:13, 19. Ro 2:8, 9.

19 **mount Carmel**. ver. 42, 43. Jsh +19:26.
the prophets of Baal. 1 K 22:6. 2 P 2:1. Re 19:20.
prophets of the groves. 2 K +17:10.
eat at Jezebel's table. 1 K 19:1, 2. 2 K 9:22. Re 2:20.

20 **gathered**. 1 K 22:9.

21 **How long**. Mt +17:17.
halt ye. Dt 4:35. Jsh 24:15. 2 K 17:41. Zp 1:5. Mt 6:24. Lk 16:13. Jn 1:12. Ro 6:16-22. 1 C 10:21, 22. 2 C 6:14-16. He 2:3. Re 3:15, 16, 20.
opinions. *or*, thoughts. Ps 119:113.
if the Lord. ver. 39. Ex 5:1, 2. Jsh 24:15, 23, 24. 1 S 7:3. 1 Ch 17:26. 2 Ch 33:13. Ps 100:3.
answered. Ge 24:50. 44:16. Jb 40:4, 5. Mt 22:12, 34, 36. Ro 3:19. 6:21.

22 **I only**. 1 K 19:10, 14. 20:13, 22, 35, 38. 22:6-8. Ro 11:3.
Baal's prophets. ver. 19, 20. Mt 7:13-15. 2 T 4:3, 4. 2 P 2:1-3.

24 **answereth by fire**. ver. 38. 1 Ch +21:26. Is 31:9.
and said. 2 S 14:19.
It is well spoken. Heb. The word is good. Is 39:8.

26 **from morning**. Mt 6:7.
saying. Ac 19:34.
hear. *or*, answer. ver. 37.
no voice. ver. 24. Ps 115:4-8. 135:15-20. Is 37:38. 44:17. 45:20. Je 10:5. Da 5:23. Hab 2:18. 1 C 8:4. 10:19, 20. 12:2.
answered. *or*, heard.
leaped upon the altar. *or*, leaped up and down at the altar. Zp 1:9.

27 **Elijah**. 1 K 22:15. 2 Ch 25:8. Ec 11:9. Is 8:9, 10. 44:15-17. Ezk 20:39. Am 4:4, 5. Mt 26:45. Mk 7:9. 14:41.
Cry aloud. Heb. with a great voice.
for he is a god. Is 41:23.
he is talking. *or*, he meditateth. 1 S +1:16. 2 K 9:11. Jb 7:13. 9:27. 10:1. 21:4. 23:2. Ps 55:2. 64:1. 102, title. 104:34. 142:3. Ps 23:29.
is pursuing. Heb. hath a pursuit.
must be awaked. Ps 44:23. 78:65, 66. 121:4. Is 51:9. Mk 4:38, 39.

28 **cut themselves**. Le +19:28. Mk 9:22.
the blood gushed out upon them. Heb. they poured out blood upon them. 1 S 25:31.

Pr 1:16. Is 59:7. Je 6:11. 22:17. Ezk 9:8. 17:17 (casting up). 20:8, 13, 21. 21:22. 22:6, 9, 12, 27. Zp 3:8.

29 **prophesied.** 1 K 22:10, 12. 1 S 18:10. Je 28:6-9. Ac 16:16, 17. 1 C 11:4, 5.
offering. Heb. ascending. ver. +36.
voice. ver. +26. Ga 4:8. 2 T 3:8, 9.
that regarded. Heb. attention. 2 K 4:31. Is 21:7. 1 C 8:4. Ga 4:8.

30 **he repaired.** 1 K 19:10, 14. 2 Ch 33:16. Ro 11:3.
the altar of the Lord. Ge 12:7.

31 **twelve stones.** Ex 24:4. Jsh 4:3, 4, 20. Ezr 6:17. Je 31:1. Ezk 37:16-22. 47:13. Ep 2:20. 4:4-6. Re 7:4-8. 21:12.
saying. Ge 32:28. 33:20. 35:10. 2 K 17:34. Is 48:1.

32 **And with.** Ex 20:24, 25. Jg 6:26. 21:4. 1 S 7:9, 17.
an altar. Ge +8:20. +13:18.
in the name. 1 C 10:31. Col 3:17.

33 **he put.** Ge 22:9. Le 1:6-8.
Fill four. Da 3:19-25. Jn 11:39, 40. 19:33, 34.
pour it. Jg 6:20.

34 **Do it the second.** 2 C 4:2. 8:21.

35 **ran.** Heb. went.
the trench. ver. 32, 38.

36 **at the time.** ver. 29. Ex 29:39-41. Ezr 9:4, 5. Ps 141:2. Da 8:13. 9:21. 12:11. Ac 3:1. 10:30.
Lord God of Abraham. ver. 21. Ge +17:7. Ex 32:13. Ep 1:17. 3:14.
let it. 1 K 8:43. 1 S 17:46, 47. 2 K 1:3, 6. 5:15. 19:19. Ps 67:1, 2. 83:18. Ezk 36:23. 39:7.
and that I have. 1 K 22:28. Nu 16:28-30. Jn 11:42. 1 C 10:31. Col 3:17.

37 **Hear me.** ver. 24, 29, 36. Ge 32:24, 26, 28. 2 Ch 14:11. 32:19, 20. Is 37:17-20. Da 9:17-19. Lk 11:8. Ja 5:16, 17.
may know. Ezk +6:7, 10. Jn +11:42.
thou hast turned. Je 31:18, 19. Ezk 36:25-27. Ml 4:5, 6. Lk 1:16, 17.

38 **Then the.** Ge 15:17. 1 Ch +21:26.
fire. ver. 24. Le 10:2. 2 K 1:12. Jb 1:16. Is 31:9.

39 **they fell.** Ge +17:3.
The Lord. ver. 21, 24. Jn 5:35. 20:28. Ac 2:37. 4:16.

40 **Take.** or, Apprehend. 2 K 10:25.
Kishon. Jg +5:21.
slew them there. Dt 13:5. 18:20. Je 48:10. Zc 13:2, 3. Re 19:20. 20:10.

41 **Get.** Ec 9:7. Ac 27:34.
a sound, etc. or, a sound of a noise of rain. ver. +1. 1 K 17:1.

42 **Elijah.** ver. 19. Mt 14:23. Lk 6:12. Ac 10:9.
he cast himself. Ge 24:52. Jsh 7:6. 2 S 12:16. Da 9:3. Mk 14:35. Ja 5:16-18.
put his face. 1 K 19:13. Ezr 9:6. Ps 89:7. Is 6:2. 38:2. Da 9:7.

43 **Go up.** Ps 5:3. Lk 18:1.
Go again. Ge 32:26. Ezk 36:37. Hab 2:3. Lk 18:7. Ep 6:18. He 10:36, 37.
seven. Jsh +6:4.

44 **a little cloud.** Ge +9:14. Jb 8:7. Zc 4:10.
Prepare. Heb. Tie, or, Bind. 1 S 6:7, 10. 2 K +9:21mg.

45 **black.** Je 4:28.
clouds. Ge +9:13.
there was. ver. 39, 40. Nu 25:8. 2 S 21:14. Ezk 36:37. Ja 5:18.
Jezreel. 1 Ch +4:3.

46 **the hand.** 2 K 3:15. Is 8:11. Ezk 1:3. 3:14, 22. 8:1. 33:22. 37:1. 40:1. Ac 11:21.
he girded. Lk +12:35.
ran before. Mt 22:21. 1 P 2:17.
to the entrance of. Heb. till thou come to.
Jezreel. Jsh 17:16.

1 KINGS 19

1 **Ahab.** 1 K 16:31. 21:5-7, 25.
how he had slain. 1 K 18:40.

2 **So let.** 1 K 2:28. 20:10. Ru 1:17. 2 K 6:31.
if I. Ex 10:28. 15:9. 2 K 19:10-12, 22, 27, 28. Da 3:15.
life. Heb. nephesh, soul, Ge +44:30.
tomorrow. Pr 27:1. Ac 12-4-6. Ja 4:13, 14.

3 **saw.** Ge +42:1.
he arose. Ge 12:12, 13. Ex 2:15. 1 S 27:1. Is 51:12, 13. Mt 26:56, 70-74. 2 C 12:7.
and went. Pr +22:3.
life. Heb. nephesh, soul, Ge +44:30; +23:8.
Beer-sheba. Ge +21:31. Am 7:12, 13.

4 **sat down.** 1 K 13:14. Ge 21:15, 16. Jg +20:26. Jn 4:6.
juniper tree. Jb 30:4. Ps 120:4.
he requested. ver. 3. Ge 42:36. Nu 11:15. 2 K 2:11. Jb 3:1, 20-22. 7:15. Pr 12:25. Is 49:14. Je 20:14-18. Jon 4:1-4, 8. Ph 1:21-24. Ju +16. Re 9:6.
for himself. Heb. for his life. Heb. nephesh, soul, Nu +23:10.
life. Heb. nephesh, soul, Ge +44:30.
might die. Jb +6:9.
take away. Nu 11:11, 14, 15. Jg 16:28-30. Jb 6:8, 9. 14:13. Jon 4:1-3. Lk 2:25-30.
better. Am 6:2. Na 3:8. Mt 6:26. Ro 3:9.

5 **as he lay.** Ge 28:11-15.
an angel. Ps 34:7, 10. Da 8:19. 9:21. 10:9, 10. Ac 12:7. He 1:14. 13:5.
Arise. Pr 20:13.

6 **cake.** 1 K 17:6, 9-15. Ge 18:6. Ex 12:39. Nu 11:8. Ps 37:3. Is 33:16. Ezk 4:12. Ho 7:8. Mt 4:11. 6:32. Mk 8:2, 3. Jn 21:5, 9.
the coals. or, burning stones. Is 6:6.
cruse. 1 K 17:12, 14, 16. 1 S 26:11, 12, 16.
head. Heb. bolster. Ge 28:11, 18. 1 S 19:13, 16. +26:7, 11, 16.

7 **the angel.** ver. +5. Lk 22:43.

because the journey. Dt 33:25. Ps 103:13, 14. Mk 8:2, 3.

8 **in the strength**. Da 1:15. 2 C 12:9.
forty days. Ex 34:28. Jon +3:4. Mk 1:13. Lk 4:2.
Horeb. Ex +3:1. 19:18. Ml 4:4, 5.

9 **unto a cave**. Ge +19:30. Ex 33:21, 22. Je 9:2. He 11:38.
What doest thou. ver. 13. Ge 3:9. 16:8. Je 2:18. Jon 1:3, 4.

10 **very jealous**. Ex 20:5. 34:14. Nu 25:11, 13. Dt 5:9, 10. 2 S 21:2 (zeal). Ps 69:9. 119:139. Jn 2:17.
thrown down. ver. 14. 1 K 18:4, 30. Je 2:30. Ho 5:11. Mi 6:16. 7:2. Ro *11:3*.
I only. 1 K 18:4, 20, 22. 20:13, 22, 35, 41, 42. 22:8. Ro 11:2-4.
they seek my. ver. 2. 1 K 18:10, 17.
life. Heb. *nephesh*, soul, Ge +44:30.

11 **stand upon the mount**. Ex 19:20. 24:12, 18. 34:2. Mt 17:1-3. 2 P 1:17, 18.
the Lord passed. Ex 33:21-23. 34:6. Hab 3:3-5.
wind rent. Jb +38:1. Ps 50:3. Is 30:30. Ezk 37:7. Re 20:11.
the mountains. Ex 19:16. 20:18.
but the Lord was not in the wind. Zc 4:6.
an earthquake. S#7494h. 1 S 14:15. Ps 68:8. He +12:26. Re +6:12.

12 **a fire**. 1 K 18:38. Ge 15:17. Ex 3:2. Dt 4:11, 12, 33. 2 K 1:10. 2:11. He 12:29.
a still. Ex 34:6. Jb 4:16. 33:7. Zc 4:6. Ac 2:2, 36, 37.

13 **he wrapped his face**. 1 K +18:42. Ex 3:5, 6. 33:18, 19, 23. 1 S 21:9. Is 6:2, 5. 25:7 (cast).
mantle. or, robe. Ge 25:25 (garment). Jsh 7:21, 24. 2 K 2:8, 13, 14. Ezk 17:8 (goodly; lit. a vine of magnificence). Jon 3:6. Zc 11:3 (glory). 13:4 (garment).
What doest. ver. 9. Ge +3:9. 16:8. Jn 21:15-17.

14 **I have been**. ver. 9, 10. Is 62:1, 6, 7.
forsaken. Dt 29:25. 31:20. Ps 78:37. Is 1:4. Je 22:9. Da 11:30. Ho 6:7. He 8:9.
thrown down. Ro *11:3*.

15 **wilderness of Damascus**. Ge +14:15.
anoint. Is 45:1. Je 1:10. 27:2, etc.
Hazael. 2 K +8:8.

16 **Jehu**. i.e. he is. 2 K +9:1-3, 6-14.
Nimshi. i.e. *drawn out, saved*, S#5250h. 2 K 9:2, 14, 20. 2 Ch 22:7.
Elisha. i.e. *God of safety; thy God is salvation*, S#477h. ver. 17. ver. +19-21. 2 K 2:1-5, 9, 12, 14, 15, 19, 22. 3:11, 13, 14. 4:1, 2, 8, 17, 32, 38. 5:8-10, 20, 25. 6:1, 12, 17-21, 31, 32. 7:1. 8:1, 4, 5, 7, 10, 13, 14. 9:1. 13:14, 15, 16, 17, 20, 21. Lk 4:27, Eliseus.
Shaphat. 1 Ch +3:22.
Abel-meholah. 1 K 4:12. Jg 7:22.

17 **him that escapeth**. 2 K 9:24, 33. 10:1-7, 23, 33. Is 24:17, 18. Am 2:14. 5:19.

the sword of Hazael. 2 K 8:12, 13. 10:32. 13:3, 22.
the sword of Jehu. 2 K 9:14, 24. 10:6, 7, 9, 10.
Elisha slay. 2 K 2:23, 24. 6:11, 12. Is 11:4. Je 1:10. Ho 6:5. Re 19:21.

18 **Yet I have left**. *or*, Yet will I leave. Is 1:9. 10:20-22. Ro 11:4, 5.
the knees. Ex 20:5. Ps 95:6. Is 49:23. Ro 14:10-12. Ph 2:10.
every mouth. Ge +41:40mg. Jb 31:27. Ps 2:12. Ho 13:2.
kissed. Ge +27:27.

19 **Elisha**. ver. +16.
he with. Ex 3:1. Jg 6:11. Ps 78:70-72. Am 7:14. Zc 13:5. Mt 4:18, 19.
his mantle. ver. 13. 1 S 28:14. 2 K 2:8, 13, 14.

20 **he left**. Mt 4:20, 22. 9:9. 19:27-29.
Let me, I pray. Mt 8:21, 22. Lk 9:61, 62. Ac 20:37.
Go back again. Heb. Go, return.

21 **boiled their flesh**. 2 S 24:22.
gave unto. Lk 5:28, 29.
ministered. 1 K 18:43. Ex 24:13. Nu 27:18-20. 2 K 2:3. 3:11. Ac 13:5. 2 T 4:11. Phm 13.

1 KINGS 20

1 A.M. 3103. B.C. 901.
Ben-hadad. 1 K +15:18.
thirty and two. ver. 16, 24. Ge 14:1-5. Jg 1:7. Ezr 7:12. Is 10:8. Ezk 26:7. Da 2:37.
and horses. Ex 14:7. Dt 20:1. Jg 4:3. 1 S 13:5. Is 37:24.
besieged. Le 26:25. Dt 28:52. 2 K 6:24-29. 17:5, 6.

2 **he sent**. 2 K 19:9. Is 36:2, etc. 37:9, 10.

3 **Thy silver and**. Ex 15:9. Is 10:13, 14.

4 **I am thine**. Le 26:36. Dt 28:48. Jg 15:11-13. 1 S 13:6, 7. 2 K 18:14-16.

6 **and they shall search**. 1 S 13:19-21. 2 S 24:14. 2 K 18:31, 32.
pleasant. Heb. desirable. Is +32:12mg. 1 J 2:16.
and take. Ex 15:9. Is 10:13, 14.

7 **all the elders**. Jsh +20:4. 2 K 5:7. 1 Ch 13:1. 28:1. Pr 11:14.
Mark. 2 K 5:7.
seeketh mischief. Jb 15:35. Ps 7:14. 36:4. 62:3. 140:2. Pr 6:14. 11:27. 24:2. Da 11:27. Ro 3:13-18.
denied him not. Heb. kept not back from him. ver. 4.

8 **the elders**. 1 K 8:1. Jsh +20:4.
Hearken not. Pr 11:14.

10 **and said**. Mt +5:29.
The gods. 1 K 19:2. Ac 23:12.
if the dust. 2 S 17:12, 13. 2 K 19:23, 24. Is 10:13, 14. 37:24, 25.

handfuls. Is 40:12.
follow me. Heb. *are* at my feet. 2 K +3:9mg.

11 Let not him, etc. 1 S 14:6, 12, 13. 17:44-47. Pr 27:1. Ec 9:11. Is 10:15, 16. Mt 26:33-35, 75.
harness. Ex 13:18.

12 message. Heb. word.
drinking. ver. 16. 1 K 16:9. 1 S 25:36. 2 S 13:28. Pr 31:4, 5. Da 5:2, 30. Lk 21:34. Ep 5:18.
pavilions. *or*, tents. Je 43:10.
Set yourselves in array.
And they set, etc. *or*, Place *the engines*. And they placed *engines*. 1 S 15:2.

13 came. Heb. approached.
Hast thou. 2 K 6:8-12. 7:1. 13:23. Is 7:1-9. Ezk 20:14, 22.
and thou shalt. ver. 28. 1 K 18:37. Ex 16:12. Is 37:20. Ezk +6:7.

14 young men. *or*, servants. Ge 14:14-16. Jg 7:16-20. 1 S 17:50. 1 C 1:27-29.
order. Heb. bind, *or* tie. 2 K +9:21mg.

15 numbered. 1 S +11:8.
two hundred and. Jg 7:7, 16. 1 S 14:6. 2 Ch 14:11.
seven thousand. 1 K 19:18. 1 S 14:2. 2 K 13:7. Ps 106:40-43.

16 Ben-hadad. ver. +11, 12. 1 K 16:9. Pr 23:29-32. 31:4, 5. Ec 10:16, 17. Ho 4:11.
the thirty and two. Is 54:15.

17 the young men. ver. 14, 15, 19.

18 Whether they. 1 S 2:3, 4. 14:11, 12. 17:44. 2 K 14:8-12. Pr 18:12.

20 they slew. 2 S 2:16. Ec 9:11.
the Syrians. Le 26:8. Jg 7:20-22. 1 S 14:13-15. 2 K 7:6, 7. Ps 33:16. 46:6.
escaped. 1 S 30:16, 17. 2 K 19:36.

21 went out. Jg 3:28. 7:23-25. 1 S 14:20-22. 17:52. 2 K 3:18, 24.

22 the prophet. ver. 13, 38. 1 K 19:10. 22:8. 2 K 6:12.
strengthen. 2 Ch 25:8, 11. Ps 27:14. Pr 18:10. 20:18. Is 8:9. Jl 3:9, 10. Ep 6:10.
at the return. ver. 26. 2 Ch +24:23mg. Ps 115:2, 3. Is 26:11. 42:8.

23 Their gods. ver. 28. 1 K 14:23. Jg 11:24. 1 S 4:8. 2 K +17:25, 26. 19:12. 2 Ch 32:13-19. Ps 50:21, 22. 121:1, 2. Is 42:8.

24 Take the. ver. 1, 16. 1 K 22:31. Pr +21:30.

25 thou hast lost. Heb. was fallen.
and surely. Ps 10:3.

26 return of the year. ver. 22.
numbered. 1 S +11:8.
Aphek. ver. 30. Jsh +12:18.
to fight against Israel. *Heb. to the war with Israel.*

27 were all present. *or*, were victualled. 1 K 4:7, 27. Jsh 1:11. Jg 7:8.
like two. Dt 32:30. Jg 6:5. 1 S 13:5-8. 14:2. 2 Ch 14:11. 32:7, 8. Ec 9:11.

28 there came. ver. 13, 22. 1 K 13:1. 17:18. 2 Ch 20:14-20.
Because. ver. +23. Is 37:29-37.
therefore will. ver. 13. Dt 32:27. Jsh 7:8, 9. Jb 12:16-19. Ps 58:10, 11. 79:10. Is 37:29, 35. Je 14:7. Ezk 20:9, 14. 36:21-23, 32.
ye shall know. ver. +13. Ex 6:7. 8:22. Dt 29:6. Ezk +6:7.

29 seven days. Jsh 6:15. 1 S 17:16. Ps 10:16.
an hundred thousand. Dt 32:30. 2 S 10:18. 2 Ch 13:17. 20:23-25. 28:6. Is 37:36.

30 the rest. Ps 18:25.
a wall. Is 24:18. Je 48:44. Am 2:14, 15. 5:19. 9:3. Lk 13:4.
thousand. Jsh +22:21.
fled. ver. 10, 20. Da 4:37.
into an inner chamber. *or*, from chamber to chamber. Heb. into a chamber within a chamber. 1 K 22:25mg. Ge 43:30. 2 K 9:2. 2 Ch 18:24.

31 his servants. ver. 23. 2 K 5:13.
merciful kings. Pr 20:28. Is 16:5. Ep 1:7, 8.
put sackcloth. Jb +16:15.
peradventure. 2 K 7:4. Est 4:16. Jb 2:4. Mt +10:28.
life. Heb. *nephesh*, soul, Ge +44:30.

32 Thy servant. ver. 3-6. Jb 12:17, 18. 40:11, 12. Is 2:11, 12. 10:12. Da 5:20-23. Ob 3, 4.
me. Heb. *nephesh*, soul, Nu +23:10.
he is my brother. ver. 42. 1 S 15:8-20.

33 the men. Pr 25:13. Lk 16:8.
diligently observe. lit. divined and hasted. Ge 30:27 (S#5172h, "divine").
and he caused. 2 K 10:15. Ac 8:31.

34 The cities. 1 K 15:20. 2 Ch 16:4.
So he made a covenant. ver. 42. 1 K 22:31. 2 Ch 18:30. Is 8:12. 26:10.

35 of the sons. ver. 38. 1 S 10:12. 2 K 2:3, 5, 7, 15. 4:1, 38. Am 7:14.
in the word. 1 K 13:1, 2, 17, 18.
smite me. ver. 37. Is 8:18. 20:2, 3. Je 27:2, 3. Ezk 4:3. Mt 16:24.

36 Because thou. 1 K 13:21-24, 26. 1 S 15:22, 23.

37 Smite me. ver. 35. Ex 21:12.
so that , etc. Heb. smiting and wounding.

38 the prophet. Is 8:18. 20:2, 3. Je 27:2, 3. Ezk 4:3.
disguised. Ge +27:16. 2 S 14:2. Mt 6:16.

39 Thy servant. Jg 9:7-20. 2 S 12:1-7. 2 S 12:1-7. 14:5-7. Mk 12:1-12.
thy life. Heb. *nephesh*, soul, Ge +44:30. ver. 42. 2 K 10:24.
or else. Ex 21:30. Jb 36:18. Ps 49:7, 8. Pr 6:35. 13:8. 1 P 1:18, 19.
pay. Heb. weigh. Ex 22:17. Est 3:9. 4:7.

40 he was gone. Heb. he *was* not. Je 31:15.
So shall thy judgment be. 2 S 12:5-7. Jb 15:6. Mt 21:41-43. 25:24-27. Lk 19:22.

41 the ashes away. ver. 38. 2 S 13:19. Jb 2:8. Je 6:26.

42 Because. ver. 34. 1 K 22:31-37. 1 S 15:9-11.
let go. Is 26:10.
thy life. Heb. *nephesh*, soul, Ge +44:30.
shall go. 1 K 22:31-37. 2 K 6:24. 8:12. 2 Ch 18:33, 34.
43 went. 1 K 21:4. 22:8. Est 5:13. 6:12, 13. Jb 5:2. Pr +19:3.

1 KINGS 21

1 A.M. 3105. B.C. 899.
after. 1 K 20:35-43. 2 Ch 28:22. Ezr 9:13, 14. Is 9:13. Je 5:3.
Naboth. i.e. *increase, produce*, **S#5022h**. ver. 2-4, 6-9, 12-16, 18, 19. 2 K 9:21, 25, 26.
Jezreelite. **S#3158h**. ver. 4, 6, 7, 15, 16. 2 K 9:21, 25.
Jezreel. 1 Ch +4:3.
2 Give me. Ge 3:6. Ex 20:17. Le 25:14-28. Dt 5:21. 1 S 8:14. Je 22:17. Hab 2:9-11. Lk 12:15. 1 T 6:9. Ja 1:14, 15.
a garden of herbs. 2 K 9:27. Dt 11:10. Ec 2:5. SS 4:15.
seem good to thee. Heb. be good in thine eyes. Jsh +22:30mg.
3 The Lord forbid. Lk +20:16.
I should give. Le 25:23. Nu 36:7. Ezk 46:18.
4 heavy. 1 K 20:43. Jb 5:2. Pr 14:30. +19:3. Is 57:20, 21. Jon 4:1, 9. Hab 2:9-12.
I will not. ver. 3. Nu 22:13, 14.
And he laid him. Ge 4:5-8. 2 S 13:2, 4. Ec 6:9. 7:8, 9. Ep 4:27. Ja 1:14, 15.
5 Jezebel. ver. 25. 1 K 16:31. 18:4. 19:2. Ge 3:6.
Why is thy. 2 S 13:4. Ne 2:2. Est 4:5.
spirit. Heb. *ruach*, Ge +41:8.
6 Because. ver. 2. Est 5:9-14. 6:12. Pr 14:30. 1 T 6:9, 10. Ja 4:2-7.
I will not give. ver. 3, 4.
7 Dost thou now. 1 S 8:14. 2 S 13:4. Pr 30:31. Ec 4:1. 8:4. Da 5:19-21.
I will give thee. ver. 15, 16. Mi 2:1, 2. 7:3.
8 she wrote. 2 S 11:14, 15. 2 Ch 32:17. Ezr 4:7, 8, 11. Ne 6:5. Est 3:12-15. 8:8-13.
the elders. Nu 11:16. Dt 16:18, 19. 21:1-9.
the nobles. ver. 1. 2 K 10:1-7, 11.
9 Proclaim a fast. Ge 34:13-17. Is 58:4. Mt 2:8. 23:14. Lk 20:47. Jn 18:28.
on high among. Heb. in the top of. ver. 12. Je 13:18mg.
10 two men. Dt 19:15. Mt 26:59, 60. Ac 6:11.
sons of Belial. 1 S +30:22. 2 S +16:7.
Thou didst blaspheme. Ex 22:28. Mk +14:64.
11 did as Jezebel. Ex 1:17, 21. 23:1, 2. Le 19:15. 1 S 22:17. 23:20. 2 K 10:6, 7. 2 Ch 24:21. Pr 29:12, 26. Da 3:18-25. Ho 5:11. Mi 6:16. Mt 2:12, 16. Ac 4:19. 5:29.
12 proclaimed a fast. ver. 8-10. Is 58:4.
13 children of Belial. 1 S +30:22. 2 S +16:7.

the men of Belial. Ex 20:16. Dt 5:20. 19:16-21. Ps 27:12. 35:11. Pr 6:16, 19. 19:5, 9. 25:18. Ml 3:5. Mk 14:56-59.
blaspheme God. ver. +10. Jb 1:5, 11. 2:9. Ac 7:57-59.
the king. Ec 10:20. Is 8:21. Am 7:10. Lk 23:2. Jn 19:12. Ac 24:5.
they carried him. Le +4:12.
stoned. Le +24:14. 2 K 9:26. Ec 4:1.
14 Naboth is stoned. 2 S 11:14-24. Ec 5:8. 8:14.
15 Arise. ver.+7. Pr 1:10-16. 4:17.
16 Ahab rose up. 2 S 1:13-16. 4:9-12. 11:25-27. 23:15-17. Ps 50:18. Is 33:15. Ob 12-14. Ro 1:32. 2 P 2:15.
17 the word. 2 K 1:15, 16. 5:26. Ps 9:12. Is 26:21.
18 which is in Samaria. 1 K 13:32. 2 Ch 22:9.
19 Hast thou killed. Ge 3:11. 4:9, 10. 2 S 12:9. Mi 3:1-4. Hab 2:9, 12.
In the place. 1 K 22:38. Jg 1:7. 2 S 12:11. 2 K 9:25, 26, 36. Est 7:10. Ps 7:15, 16. 9:16. 58:10, 11. Mt 7:2.
20 Hast thou found me. 1 K 18:17. 22:8. 2 Ch 18:7, 17. Ps 10:8. Pr 1:18. Am 5:10. Mk 12:12. Ga 4:16. Re 11:10.
thou hast sold. ver. 25. Le +25:39.
to work. 1 K 16:30. Nu 32:13. 2 K 21:2. 2 Ch 33:6. Ro 7:14. Ep 4:19.
21 Behold. 1 K +14:10. Ex 20:5, 6. 2 K 9:7-9. 10:1-7, 11-14, 17, 30.
him that pisseth. 1 S +25:22.
him that is shut up. Dt +32:36.
22 make thine. 1 K 15:29. 16:3, 4, 11.
made Israel to sin. 1 K +14:16. 15:30, 34. 16:26.
23 Jezebel. ver. +25. 2 K 9:10, 30-37.
wall. *or*, ditch. 2 S 20:15. 2 K 9:36. Ps 122:7. Is 26:1. La 2:8. Na 3:8.
24 that dieth. 1 K 14:11. 16:4. Is 14:19. Je 15:3. Ezk 32:4, 5. 39:18-20. Re 19:18.
25 But there. ver. 20. 1 K 16:30-33. 2 K 23:25.
sell himself. ver. +20.
whom Jezebel. ver. 7. 1 K 11:1-4. 16:31. 18:4. 19:2. Pr 22:14. Ec 7:26. Mk 6:17-27. Ac 6:12. 14:2.
stirred up. *or*, incited. Dt 13:6. Jsh 15:18. Jg 1:14. 1 S 26:19. 2 S 24:1. 1 Ch 21:1. 2 Ch 18:2, 31.
26 very abominably. 2 Ch 15:8. Is 65:4. Je 16:18. 44:4. Ezk 18:12. 1 P 4:3. Re 21:8.
following idols. 2 K +23:24.
according to. Ge 15:16. Le 20:22, 23. Dt +12:31. 2 K 16:3. Ezr 9:11-14. Ps 106:35-39. Ezk 16:47.
Amorites. Ge +10:16.
27 that he. 2 Ch 12:7. Ja 4:10. 1 P 5:6.
rent. 2 K +18:37.
lay in sackcloth. Jb +16:15.
went softly. Is 38:15.

29 **Seest thou**. Je 7:17. Lk 7:44.
Ahab. Ex 10:3. Ps 18:44. 66:3. 78:34-37.
I will not. Ps 86:15. Ezk 33:10, 11. Mi 7:18.
Ro 2:4. 2 P 3:9.
the evil in. ver. +21-23.
in his son's days. 2 K 9:25, 26, 33-37. 10:1-
7, 11.

1 KINGS 22

1 A.M. 3104-3107. B.C. 900-897.
they continued. 1 K +20:34.
2 A.M. 3107. B.C. 897.
in the third. ver. 1. Mt 12:40. 16:21.
Jehoshaphat. ver. 41, 44. 2 S +8:16. 2 K
8:18.
3 **Ramoth**. 1 K 4:13. Dt 4:41-43. Jsh 20:7, 8.
still. Heb. silent from taking it. Jsh 18:3. Jg
16:2mg. 18:9. 2 S 19:10mg.
4 **Wilt thou go**. 2 K 3:7. 2 Ch 18:3.
with me. Ec 4:9, 10.
I am as thou. 2 Ch 19:2. Ps 139:21, 22. Pr
13:20. 1 C 15:33. 2 C 6:16, 17. Ep 5:11. 2 J
11. Re 2:2, 6.
5 **Enquire**. Nu 27:21. Jsh 9:14. Jg 1:1. 20:18,
23, 28. 1 S 14:18, 19. 23:2, 4, 9-12. 30:8. 2 K
1:3. 3:11. 1 Ch 10:13. 2 Ch 18:4, 5. Pr 3:5, 6.
Je 21:2. 42:2-6. Ezk 14:3. 20:1-3.
6 **the prophets together**. 1 K 18:19. 2 T 4:3.
Go up. ver. 15, 22, 23. 2 Ch 18:14. Je 5:31.
8:10, 11. 14:13, 14. 23:14-17. 28:1-9. Ezk
13:7-16, 22. Mt 7:15. 2 P 2:1-3. Re 19:20.
the Lord. Na 3:18.
7 **Is there not**. 2 K 3:11-13. 2 Ch 18:6, 7.
8 **yet one man**. 1 K 18:4. 19:10, 14. 20:41, 42.
Micaiah. i.e. *who is like God?*, **S#4321h**. ver. 9,
13, 14, 15, 24, 25, 26, 28. 2 Ch 18:7, 8, 12,
13, 14, 23, 24, 25, 27.
Imlah. i.e. *he fills*, **S#3229h**. ver. 9. 2 Ch 18:7,
8, Imla.
but I hate him. ver. 27. 1 K 20:43. 21:20. Ge
37:8. 2 Ch 36:16. Ps 34:21. Pr 9:8. 15:12. Is
49:7. Je 18:18. 20:10. 43:3, 4. Am 5:10. Zc
11:8. Mt 10:22. Jn 3:19-21. 7:7. 15:18, 19.
17:14. Ga 4:16. Re 11:7-10.
good. ver. 13. Is 30:10. Je 38:4. Mi 2:11.
concerning me. 1 K 20:35-42. 2 K 9:22. Is
3:11. 57:19-21.
Let not the. 1 K 21:27-29. Pr 5:12-14. Mi
2:7.
9 **officer**. *or*, eunuch. 2 K +8:6mg.
Hasten. ver. 26, 27.
10 **having put**. ver. 30. Est 5:1. 6:8, 9. Mt 6:20.
11:8. Ac 12:21. 25:23.
void place. Heb. floor. Ge +50:10, 11.
gate. Ge +14:7.
of Samaria. 1 K +16:24.
all the prophets. 1 K 18:29. 2 Ch 18:9-11.
Je 27:14-16. Ezk 13:1-9.
11 **Zedekiah**. i.e. *justice or righteousness of*

Jehovah, **S#6667h**. ver. 24. 2 K 24:17, 18, 20.
25:2, 7. 1 Ch 3:15, 16. 2 Ch 18:10, 23. 36:10,
11. Ne 10:1. Je 37:1, 3, 17, 18, 21.
horns of iron. Je 27:2. 28:10-14. Zc 1:18-21.
Ac 19:13-16. 2 C 11:13-15. 2 T 3:8.
Thus saith. Je 23:17, 25, 31. 28:2, 3. 29:21.
Ezk 13:6-9. 22:27, 28. Mi 3:11.
12 **Go up**. ver. 6-15, 32-36. 2 Ch 35:22.
13 **Behold now**. Ps 10:11. 11:1. 14:1. 50:21. Is
30:10, 11. Ho 7:3. Am 7:13-17. Mi 2:6, 7, 11.
1 C 2:14-16.
14 **what the Lord**. Nu 22:38. 24:13. 2 Ch
18:12, 13. Je 23:28. 26:2, 3. 42:4. Ezk 2:4-8.
3:17-19. Ac 20:20, 26, 27. 2 C 2:17. 4:1, 2. Ga
1:10.
15 **shall we go**. ver. +6.
Go, and prosper. ver. 6. 1 K 18:27. Jg 10:14.
2 K 3:13. 2 Ch 18:14. Ec 11:9. Na 3:18. Mt
26:45.
for. Ec 11:9. Je 2:28. Am 4:4, 5. Mt 23:32. Jn
13:27. Ro 11:19, 20.
16 **shall I adjure**. Jsh 6:26. 1 S 14:24. 2 Ch
18:15. Mt 26:63. Mk 5:7. Ac 19:13.
that thou tell. Je 42:3-6. Mt 22:16, 17.
17 **I saw**. 1 S 9:9. Je 1:11-16. Ezk 1:4. Ac 10:11-
17.
as sheep. ver. 34-36. Nu +27:17.
18 **Did I not tell**. ver. +8. Pr 10:24. 27:22. 29:1.
Lk 11:45.
19 **Hear thou**. Je +7:2.
I saw the Lord. 1 K 19:11-18. Ge 17:22.
18:1, 2, 22. 19:1. 26:2-4, 24. 28:12-15 with
35:1. 32:24-32. 35:9-15. Ex 3:1-4. 19:11-24.
24:12-18. 33:11, 23. 34:5. Le 9:23, 24. 10:1,
2. Nu 12:4, 5. 22:20, 34, 35. Dt 5:4, 22-29.
31:2, 15, 16. Jsh 5:13-15. Jg 2:1-5. 6:11, 14,
16. 13:3-7, 22. 1 S 3:10, 21. 1 Ch 21:16, 17
with 2 Ch 3:1. 2 Ch 18:18-22. Jb 42:5. Is 6:1-
3. Ezk 1:26-28. Da 7:9, 10. Ac 7:55, 56. Re
4:2, 3.
all the host. Jb 1:6. 2:1. Ps +103:21. Is 6:2, 3.
Da 7:10. Zc 1:10. Mt 18:10. 25:31. He 1:7, 14.
12:22. Re 5:11.
standing by. Zc +3:7.
20 **persuade**. *or*, deceive. ver. 21, 22. Ex 22:16.
Jb 12:16. Pr 25:15. Je 4:10. 20:7mg. Ezk 14:9.
And one. Zc 1:10. He 1:7, 14.
21 **there came**. ver. 23. Jb 1:6, 7. 2:1.
a spirit. Heb. *ruach*, Jg +9:23.
22 **a lying spirit**. Heb. *ruach*, Jg +9:23. Jb 1:8-
11. 2:4-6. 12:16. Jn 8:44. Ac 5:3, 4. 2 Th 2:9,
10. 1 T 4:1, 2. 1 J 4:6. Re 12:9, 10. 13:14.
16:13, 14. 20:3, 7, 8, 10.
Thou shalt. ver. 20. Jg 9:23. Jb 12:16. Ps
109:17. 2 Th 2:10-12. Re 17:17.
23 **behold, the Lord**. Ex +4:21. 2 Ch 25:16. Is
44:20. Ezk 14:3-5, Mt 13:13-15. 24:24, 25.
spirit. Heb. *ruach*, Jg +9:23.
and the Lord. ver. 8-11. 1 K 20:42. 21:19.
Nu 23:19, 20. 24:13. Is 3:11.

24 Zedekiah. ver. 11.
smote Micaiah. Mt +27:30. Jn 15:18, 20.
Which way. Je 28:10, 11. 29:26, 27. Mt
26:68. 27:42, 43.
Spirit. Is +48:16.
25 Behold. Nu 31:8. Is 9:14-16. Je 23:15. 28:16,
17. 29:21, 22, 32. Am 7:17. 2 P 2:1. Re 19:20.
into an inner chamber. *or*, from chamber to
chamber. Heb. a chamber in a chamber. 1 K
+20:30mg.
26 the king of Israel said. Pr 29:1.
carry him back. ver. 9.
27 Put this fellow. He +11:36.
bread of affliction. Dt 16:3. Ps 80:5. 102:9.
127:2. Is 30:20.
until I come in peace. Lk 12:45, 46. 1 Th
5:2, 3. Ja 4:13, 14.
28 If thou return. Nu 16:29. Dt 18:20-22. 2 K
1:10, 12. Is 44:25, 26. Je 28:8, 9. Ac 13:10, 11.
Hearken. 1 K 18:21-24, 36, 37. 2 Ch 18:27.
Am 3:1. Mi 1:2. Mk 7:14-16. 12:37.
29 the king. ver. 2-6. 2 Ch 18:28.
30 I will, etc. *or*, when he was to disguise himself, and enter into battle.
put thou on. ver. 10. Ps 12:2.
disguised himself. Ge +27:16. 2 S 14:2. Pr
+21:30. Je 23:24.
31 thirty and two. 1 K 20:24. 2 Ch 18:30.
Fight. 1 K 20:33-42.
small or great. Ge +19:11. 1 S 30:2. Je 16:6.
32 they turned. Pr 13:20.
Jehoshaphat. Ex 14:10. 2 Ch 18:31. Ps
50:15. 76:10. 91:15. 116:1, 2. 130:1-4. Jon
2:1, 2.
33 that they turned. ver. 31. Ps 76:10.
34 at a venture. Heb. in his simplicity. 2 S 15:11.
and smote. 1 S 17:49. 2 K 9:24.
joints of the harness. Heb. joints and the
breastplate. 1 K 20:11. Re 9:9.
wounded. Heb. made sick. 2 K 8:29mg. 2 Ch
18:33mg. 35:23mg. Mi 6:13.
35 increased. Heb. ascended. Ezk 41:7.
died at even. ver. 28. 1 K 20:42.
midst. Heb. bosom.
36 there went. ver. 17, 31. 1 K 12:16. 2 K
14:12.
Every man. 1 K 12:24. Jg 7:7, 8. 21:24. 1 S
4:10. 2 S 19:8. 2 K 14:12.
37 was brought. Heb. came.
38 and the dogs. 1 K +21:19. Jsh 23:14, 15. Is
44:25, 26. 48:3-5. Je 44:21-23. Zc 1:4-6. Mt
24:35.
39 A.M. 3086-3107. B.C. 918-897.
the rest. 1 K 14:19. 15:23, 31. 16:5, 20, 27.
the ivory house. 1 K 10:18, 22. Ps 45:8. Ezk
27:6, 15. Am 3:15. 6:4.

40 slept. 1 K +11:43.
Ahaziah. i.e. *possessed of Jehovah*, s#274h. ver.
49, 51. 2 K 1:2, 17, 18. 8:24, 25, 29. 9:16, 27,
29. 1 Ch 3:11. 2 Ch 20:35, 37. 22:1, 6,
Azariah. 25:23, Jehoahaz.
41 A.M. 3090. B.C. 914.
Jehoshaphat. ver. +2.
began to reign. *"Began to reign alone, ver. 51."*
42 thirty and five. 2 K 1:17. 8:16.
And his mother's. 1 K 14:21. 15:2, 10.
Azubah. i.e. *a forsaken woman*, s#5806h. 2 Ch
20:31.
Shilhi. i.e. *armed*, s#7977h. 2 Ch 20:31.
43 he walked. 1 K 15:11, 14. 2 Ch 14:2-5, 11.
15:8, 17. 17:3.
he turned. 1 K 15:5. Ex 32:8. 1 S 12:20, 21.
2 Ch 16:7-12. Ps 40:4. 101:3. 125:5. Pr 4:27.
doing. 2 Ch 17:3-6. 19:3, 4. 20:3, etc.
the high. 2 K +21:3.
44 made peace. ver. 2. 2 K 8:18. 2 Ch 19:2.
21:6. 2 C 6:14.
45 Now. ver. 39.
are they not written. 1 K 11:41. 14:29.
the chronicles. 2 Ch 20:34.
46 the remnant. Jg 19:22. 2 K +23:7. 1 C 6:9. 1
T 1:10. Ju 7.
47 no king. Ge +25:23. 36:31, etc. 2 K 3:9. 8:20.
Ps 108:9, 10.
Edom. 2 S 8:14. 2 K 8:20.
a deputy. 1 K 4:5.
48 Jehoshaphat. 2 Ch 20:35, 36, etc.
made ships. *or*, *had* ten ships. 1 K 10:22. 2
Ch 9:21. Ps 48:7. Is 2:16. 60:9. Jon 1:3.
Tharshish. Ge +10:4.
to Ophir. 1 K +9:28.
they went not. 2 Ch 20:37. 25:7.
Ezion-geber. 1 K +9:26.
50 A.M. 3115. B.C. 889.
slept with his fathers. ver. +40. 1 K 2:10. 2
Ch 21:1.
in the city. 1 K +11:43. 14:31. 15:24.
Jehoram. 2 K +1:17.
51 A.M. 3107-3108. B.C. 897-896.
began. *"Now he begins to reign alone, ver. 40."*
two years. 1 K 15:25. 16:8. 2 K 1:17. 3:1.
52 he did evil. 1 K +15:26. 16:30-33.
2 K 1:2-7.
in the way. 1 K 21:25. 2 K 8:27. 9:22. 2 Ch
22:3. Mk 6:24. Re 3:20.
and in the way. 1 K 12:28-33. 14:9-16.
15:34. 2 K 3:3.
53 he served Baal. 1 K 16:31. Jg 2:1-11. 2 K
1:2. 3:2.
provoked. 1 K 16:7. Ps 106:29. Is 65:3. Ezk
8:3.
according to all. 1 K 21:29. Ezk 18:14-18.

2 KINGS

2 KINGS 1

1 A.M. 3108. B.C. 896.
Moab. Ezk +25:8.
after the. 2 K 3:4, 5. 8:20, 22.

2 **a lattice**. Dt 22:8. Jg 3:20. 5:28. SS 2:9. Ac 20:9.
upper chamber. 2 S 18:33.
was sick. 1 K 22:34mg. 2 Ch 21:14, 15. Jb 31:3.
Baal-zebub. i.e. lord of the fly, **S#1176h**. ver. 3, 6, 16. Mt 10:25. 12:24-27. Mk 3:22. Lk 11:15, Beelzebub.
god. Jg 11:24. 1 S 5:10. 1 K 11:33. Is 37:12, 19.
whether. 2 K 8:7-10. 1 K 14:3.

3 **angel**. ver. 15. 1 K 19:5, 7. Ac 8:26. 12:7-11.
Elijah. ver. 8. 1 K 17:1.
Arise. 1 K 18:1.
Is it not. ver. 6, 16. 2 K 5:8, 15. 1 S 17:46. 1 K 18:36. Ps 76:1.
ye go. Je 2:11-13. Jon 2:8. Mk 3:22.

4 **Thou shalt**, etc. Heb. The bed whither thou art gone up, thou shalt not come down from it. ver. 6, 16.
but shalt. Ge 2:17. 3:4. Nu 26:65. 1 S 28:19. 1 K 14:12. Pr 11:19. 14:32. Ezk 18:4. Jon 2:8.

6 **Thus saith**. Is 41:22, 23.
therefore. ver. 3, 4. 1 Ch 10:13, 14. Ps 16:4.

7 **What manner of man was he**? Heb. What *was* the manner of the man? Jg 8:18. 1 S 28:14.

8 **an hairy man**. Is 20:2. Zc 13:4mg. Mt 3:4. 11:8. Lk 1:17. Re 11:3.

9 **sent unto**. 2 K 6:13, 14. 1 K 18:4, 10. 19:2. 22:8, 26, 27. Mt 14:3.
he sat. 1 K 18:42. Lk 6:11, 12.
Thou man of God. Am 7:12. Mt 26:68. 27:29, 41-43. Mk 15:29, 32. He 11:36.

10 **If I be a man of God**. 2 K 2:23, 24. Nu 16:28-30. 1 K 18:36-38. 22:28. 2 Ch 36:16. Ps 105:15. Mt 21:41. 23:34-37. Ac 5:3-10.
let fire. Nu 11:1. 16:35. Jb 1:16. Ps 106:18. Je +10:25. Lk 9:54. He 12:29. *Re 11:5*.
consumed. Da 3:22, 25. 6:24. Ac 12:19.

11 **Again**. Nu 16:41. 1 S 6:9. Is 26:11. Je 5:3. Jn 18:5-12. Ac 4:16, 17.
O man. 1 S 22:17-19. Pr 29:12. Is 32:7. Mt 2:16. Lk 22:63, 64.

12 **If I**. ver. 9, 10.
let fire. ver. 10.

13 **he sent again**. Jb 15:25, 26. Pr 27:22. Ec 9:3. Is 1:5.
fell on. Heb. bowed. 1 K 19:18. Is 66:2.
besought. Ex 11:8. Nu 12:11-13. 1 K 13:6. Is 60:14. Re 3:9.
O man of God. Ps 102:17. Ja 4:7.
life. Heb. *nephesh*, soul, Ge +44:30.
be precious. ver. 14. 1 S 18:30. 26:21. Ps 72:14.

14 **Behold**. ver. 10, 11.
let my. 1 S 26:21, 24. Ps 49:8. 72:14. 116:15. Pr 6:26. Mt 16:25, 26. Ac 20:24.
life. Heb. *nephesh*, soul, Ge +44:30.

15 **be not afraid of him**. Ge 15:1. 1 K 18:15. Ps 27:1. Is 51:12, 13. Je 1:17. 15:20. Ezk 2:6. Mt +10:28. He 11:27.

16 **Forasmuch**. ver. 3, 4, 6. Ex 4:22, 23. 1 K 14:6-13. 21:18-24. 22:28.
Baal-zebub. Literally, "the lord of flies;" or, "Baal the fly god." Ex 8:24. Mt +10:25.
on which thou art gone up. Ge 49:4. 2 K 5:21, 34. Ps 132:3.
surely. Ge +2:16.

17 **Jehoram**. i.e. *the Lord exalts*, **S#3088h**. 2 K 3:1, 6. 8:16, 25, 29. 9:24. 12:18. 1 K 22:50. 2 Ch 17:8. 21:1, 3, 4, 5, 9, 16. 22:1, 5, 6, 7, 11.
in the second. 2 K 3:1. 8:16, 17. 1 K 22:51.

18 **in the book**. 1 K +14:19. 22:39.

2 KINGS 2

1 **take up**. Ge 5:24. 1 K 19:4. Lk 9:51. Ac 1:9. He 11:5. Re 11:12.
by a whirlwind. ver. 11. 1 K 18:12. 19:11. Jb 38:1. 40:6. Ps 107:25, 29. 148:8. Is 21:1. 29:6. 40:24. 41:16. Je 23:19. 25:32. 30:23. Ezk 1:4. 13:11, 13. Zc 9:14.
Elisha. 1 K 19:16-21.
Gilgal. Jsh +4:19.

2 **Tarry here**. Ru 1:15, 16. 2 S 15:19, 20. Jn 6:67, 68.
As the Lord. ver. 4, 6. 1 S 1:26. 17:55. 1 K +17:1. Ac 2:42. 11:23.
soul. Heb. *nephesh*, Ge +27:31.

I will not. Ru 1:16-18. 2 S 15:21. 1 J 2:19.
Bethel. Ge +12:8.

3   **And the sons**. ver. 5, 7, 15. 2 K 4:1, 38. 9:1.
1 S 10:10-12. 19:20. 1 K 18:4. 20:35. Is 8:18.
thy master. Dt 33:3. Ac 22:3.
thy head. Jg +5:30.
hold. Ec 3:7.

4   **Jericho**. Nu +22:1. Lk 19:1.
As the Lord. ver. +2.
soul. Heb. *nephesh*, Ge +27:31.

5   **the sons**. i.e. disciples. ver. 5, 7, 15. 2 K 4:1, 38.
5:22. 6:1. 9:1, 4. 1 S 10:10. 19:20. 1 K 20:35.
thy master. ver. +3. Jsh 1:1, 2. Lk 24:51. Jn
17:5-7. Ac 1:2, 11. 20:25.
Yea, I know it. Ge 48:19. Ec 3:7. Is 41:1. Hab
2:20.

6   **As the Lord**. ver. 4. 1 S 20:3.
soul. Heb. *nephesh*, Ge +27:31.

7   **fifty men**. ver. 17. 1 K 18:4, 13.
to view afar off. Heb. in sight, *or* over
against. ver. 15. 2 K 4:25.

8   **his mantle**. 2 K 1:8. 1 K 19:13, 19. or, robe.
S#155h: ver. 13, 14. Ge 25:25. Jsh 7:21, 24. 1 K
19:13, 19.
were. ver. 14. Ex 14:21, 22. Jsh 3:14-17. Ps
114:5-7. Is 11:15. He 11:29. Re 16:12.

9   **Ask what**. 2 K 13:14-19. Nu 27:16-23. Dt
34:9. 1 Ch 29:18, 19. Ps 72:1, 20. Lk 24:45-
51. Jn 17:9-13. Ac 1:8. 8:17. 20:25, 36.
before. Is +63:16.
Elisha said. Nu 11:17, 25. 1 K 3:9. 2 Ch 1:9,
10. Jn 14:12-14. 16:7. 1 C 12:31.
a double portion. lit. "two mouths," as in Dt
+21:17; Zc 13:8. Nu 27:20. Dt 21:17. Zc 9:12.
12:8. 1 T 5:17.
spirit. Heb. *ruach*, Ge +41:38; Nu +11:17.

10   **Thou hast**. Mk 11:22-24. Jn 16:24.
asked a hard thing. Heb. done hard in asking. Lk 21:36. Ac 1:6, 7.
if thou see. ver. 12. Ac 1:9, 10.
it shall be. Zc 12:8. Mk 11:22-24. Jn 16:24. 1
C 12:31. 14:12.

11   **a chariot**. Ps +68:17. Ezk 1:4, etc. 10:9, etc.
Zc 6:1-8. He 1:14.
parted. Ge 30:40 (separate). Dt 32:8 (separated). Ru 1:17. Pr 16:28. 17:9. 18:18.
by a whirlwind. ver. +1.
into heaven. Mk +16:19.

12   **And**. Ge +8:22.
saw it. ver. 10.
My father. 2 K 13:14. Jb 22:30. Pr 11:11. Ec
7:19. 9:16-18. Is 37:4, 15, 21. Ac 27:24.
he saw him. Pr 30:4. Mk 16:19. Lk 2:15.
24:51. Jn 3:13. Ac 1:9. 2 C 5:2, 4. Ep 4:8. Re
11:12.
rent them. Ge 37:29, 34. Jb 1:20, 21. Is 57:1,
2. Ac 8:2.

13   **the mantle**. ver. +8. 1 K +19:13, 19.
bank. Heb. lip. Ge 41:17. Dt 4:48. Jsh 13:9,
16. Jg +7:22mg.

14   **And**. Ge +8:22.
smote. ver. +8-10. Jsh 1:1-9. Mk 16:20. Jn
14:12. Ac 2:33. 3:12, 13.
Where is. Jg 6:13. 1 K 18:36-39. Ps 42:2, 10.
115:2. Jl 2:17.

15   **to view**. ver. +7.
The spirit. Heb. *ruach*, Ge +41:38. Nu 11:25-
29. 27:20. Jsh 3:7. Is 11:2. 59:21. Jn 15:26,
27. Ac 1:8. 2 C 12:9. 1 P 4:14.
bowed. ver. 19. 2 K 4:1-4, 37. 6:1-7. Jsh
4:14.

16   **strong men**. Heb. sons of strength. 2 S
+2:7mg. 1 Ch 26:7, 9.
the Spirit. Heb. *ruach*, Ge +41:38; Nu
+11:17.
taken. Ezk +8:3.
some mountain. Heb. one of the mountains.

17   **they urged**. 2 K 5:16. Ge 19:3 (pressed), 9.
33:11. Jg 19:7. 2 S 18:22, 23. Lk 11:8. Ro
10:2.
ashamed. 2 K 8:11. Jg 3:25.
found him not. He 11:5.

18   **Go not**. Ro 10:2.

19   **my lord seeth**. Nu 12:11. 1 K 18:7, 13. 1 T
5:17.
the water. Ex 7:19. 15:23. Jsh 6:17, 26. 1 K
16:34.
barren. Heb. causing to miscarry. ver. 21. Ge
31:38. Ex 23:26. Dt 28:2-4, 11, 15-18. Jb
21:10. Ho 9:14. Ml 3:11.

20   **cruse**. 2 K 21:13. 2 Ch +35:13. Pr 19:24.
26:15.
salt therein. Jg 9:45. Ezk 47:11. Zp 2:9.

21   **spring**. or, source. 2 Ch 32:20 (cause). Ps
107:33, 35. Is 41:18. 58:11.
cast. 2 K 4:41. 5:10. 6:6. Ex 7:19. 15:25, 26.
Le 2:13. Mt 5:11, 13. Mk 7:33. 8:23. 9:50. Jn
9:6.
I have healed. Ezk 47:8-11. 1 C 1:18-28. Re
22:2, 3.
there shall. Ps 107:33-38. Re 21:4.

22   **healed**. Ex 15:23-25.
unto this day. 1 S +6:18.

23   **Bethel**. Ge +12:8.
little. Ge 44:20. 1 S 20:35.
children. or, young men. ver. +24. Ge 22:5,
12. 41:12. 43:8. Ru 2:15. 2 S 18:5. 2 Ch 12:13
with 13:7. Jb +19:18. 30:1, 8, etc. Ps 148:12.
Pr 20:11. 22:6, 15. Ec 11:10. Is 1:4. 3:5. Je
7:18.
mocked. Ge +21:9. Pr 17:5. 30:17. Is 57:3, 4.
Ezk 22:5. Hab 1:10. Ga 4:29. 6:7. He +11:36.
Go up. ver. 11. Mt 27:29-31, 40-43.
baldhead. Le 13:40. Is +3:24.

24   **cursed them**. 2 K 1:10-12. Ge 8:21. 12:3.
9:25. Ex 21:17mg. 22:28. Dt 28:15-26. Jg
9:20, 57. Ne 13:25. Je 28:16. 29:21-23. La
3:65. Am 7:17. Mk 11:14, 21. Ac 5:5, 9. 8:20.
13:9-11. 2 C 10:6.
she bears. 1 S 17:34, 36, 37. 2 S 17:8. Pr

17:12. 28:15. Is 11:7. 59:11. La 3:10. Ho 13:8. Am 5:19.

and tare. 2 K 8:12 (ripped). 15:16. Ge 22:3 (clave). 1 S 6:14. Jb 28:10. Ps 78:15. Is 59:5. Ezk 13:11, 13. Ho 13:8. Hab 3:9.

children. S#3206h. Da +1:4. Ge 21:14, 15, 16.

of them. Ge 4:23. Ex 20:5. 1 K 13:24. 19:17. 20:36.

25 **mount Carmel**. Jsh +19:26.

2 KINGS 3

1 **Jehoram**. 2 K +1:17. 1 K 22:51.

2 **wrought evil**. 2 K 6:31, 32. 21:6, 20. 1 S +15:19. 1 K 16:19.

but not. 1 K 16:33. 21:20, 25.

and like. 2 K 9:22, 34. 1 K 21:5-15, 25.

image. Heb. statue. 2 K +17:10mg. Ge 28:18, 22.

Baal. Jg +6:25.

3 **he cleaved**. 2 K 10:20-31. 1 K 12:28-33.

which made. 1 K +14:16. 15:26, 34. 16:31.

he departed. 2 K 13:2, 6, 11. 14:24. 15:9, 18. 17:22. 1 K 12:26-28. 13:33. 1 C 1:19, 20.

4 **Mesha**. i.e. *safety*, S#4337h.

Moab. Ezk +25:8.

a sheepmaster. Ge 13:2. 26:13, 14. 2 Ch 26:10. Jb 1:3. 42:12.

lambs. Is 16:1.

5 **that the king**. 2 K +1:1. 8:20. 2 Ch 21:8-10.

6 A.M. 3109. B.C. 895.

numbered. 1 S 11:8. 15:4. 2 S 24:1, etc. 1 K 20:27.

7 **wilt thou go**. 1 K +22:4, 32, 33. 2 Ch 18:3, 29-32. 19:2. 21:4-7. 22:3, 4, 10-12.

8 **wilderness of Edom**. Nu 13:21. Nu 21:4, 5. Ml 1:2, 3.

9 **Edom**. 1 K 22:47.

no water. Ex 15:22. 17:1. Nu 20:2, 4. 21:5. 33:14.

that followed them. Heb. at their feet. Ge 30:30mg. Ex 11:8mg. Dt 11:6mg. Jg 4:10. 1 S 25:27mg, 42mg. 1 K 20:10mg.

10 **the Lord**. 2 K 6:33. Ge 4:13. Ps 78:34-36. Pr 19:3. Is 8:21. 51:20.

11 **Is there not here**. 1 K 22:7. Ps 74:9. Am 3:7.

that we may. ver. 1, 3. Jsh 9:14. Jg 20:8-11, 18, 23, 26-28. 1 Ch 10:13. 14:10, 14. 15:13.

poured. Heb. *yatsaq*, S#3332h. To "pour water on the hands" is put for serving.

water. Ge 18:4. Ex 30:19. Jsh 1:1. 1 K 19:21. Is 44:3. Lk 7:44. 22:26, 27. Jn 13:4, 5, 13, 14. Ph 2:22. 1 T 5:10.

12 **The word**. 2 K 2:14, 15, 21, 24. 1 S 3:19-21.

Israel. 2 K 2:25. 5:8, 9, 15. Is 49:23. 60:14. Re 3:9.

13 **What have**. Jg +11:12. Ezk 14:3-5. 2 C 5:16. 6:15.

get. Jg 10:14. Ru 1:15. Pr 1:28-30. Je 2:27, 28. Ezk 14:3.

the prophets. 1 K 18:19. 22:6, 10, 11, 22-25.

Nay. ver. 10. Dt 32:37-39. Ho 6:1.

14 **As the Lord**. 1 K +17:1.

I regard. Ge 19:21. 2 Ch 17:3-9. 19:3, 4. Ps 15:4.

I would not look. 1 S 15:26-31. 1 K 14:5, etc. 21:20. Je 1:18. Da 5:17-23. Mt 22:16.

15 **bring me**. 1 S 10:5, 6. 16:23. 18:10. 1 Ch 25:1-3. Ep 5:18, 19.

the hand. 1 K +18:46.

16 **make this valley**. 2 K 4:3. Nu 21:8, 16-18.

ditches. lit. ditches ditches. Is 10:31 (Gebim. or, the ditches). Je 14:3 (pits).

17 **Ye shall not**. 1 K 18:36-39. Ps 84:6. 107:35. Is 41:17, 18. 43:19, 20. 48:21.

that ye may. Ex 17:6. Nu 20:8-11.

18 **And this**. 1 K 3:13. Je 32:17, 27. Lk 1:27. Ep 3:20.

a light thing. 2 K 20:10. 1 K 16:31. Is 7:13. 49:6. Ezk 8:17.

he will. 1 K 20:13, 28. Is 7:1-9.

19 **And ye**. 2 K 13:17. Nu 24:17. Jg 6:16. 1 S 15:3. 23:2.

fenced city. Nu 13:19. 32:17, 36. Jsh 10:20. 19:29, 35. 1 S 6:18. 2 S 24:7.

choice. 2 K 19:23.

fell. 2 K 6:5. Dt 20:19, 20.

stop. With dust and stones, as in ver. 25. 2 Ch 32:3, 4, 30.

wells. Heb. *mayan*, Ge +7:11 (S#4599h). Ge 8:2. Le 11:36. Jsh 15:9. 18:15. 1 K 18:5.

mar. Heb. grieve. lit. pain. ver. 25. Jb 5:18 (sore). Is 5:2. Ezk 13:22 (sad). 28:24.

20 **when the meat offering**. Ex 29:39, 40. Le +23:13. 1 K 18:36. Da 9:21.

there came water. This supply was altogether miraculous; for there was neither wind nor rain, nor any other natural means to furnish it.

filled. Ps 78:15, 16, 20. Is 35:6, 7.

21 **gathered**. Heb. were cried together. Jsh 8:16. Jg 7:23.

put on armor. Heb. gird himself with a girdle. Ex 12:11. 1 K 20:11. Ep 6:14.

22 **early**. Ge +19:27.

shone. lit. "arisen." Ge 32:31.

red. Ge 25:30. Nu 19:2. SS 5:10. Is 63:2. Zc 1:8. 6:2.

23 **This is blood**. 2 K 6:18-20. 7:6.

surely. Ge +2:16.

slain. Heb. destroyed. lit. "dried up." Ge 8:13. Ezk 26:19. 30:7.

now therefore. Ex 15:9. Jg 5:30. 2 Ch 20:25. Is 10:14.

spoil. Ge 49:27.

24 **smote the**. Jsh 8:20-22. Jg 20:40-46. Is 16:7, 11. 1 Th 5:3, 4.

went forward. or, smote it in even smiting.

25 **beat down**. ver. 19. Jg 9:45. 2 S 8:2. Is 37:26, 27.

stopped. ver. 19. Ge 26:15, 18. 2 Ch 32:4.
wells. Heb. *mayan*, Ge +7:11. ver. 19.
and felled. Dt 20:19, 20.
only in, etc. Heb. until he left the stones
thereof in Kir-haraseth.
Kir-haraseth. i.e. *wall of clay*, **S#7025h**. Dt 2:9.
Is 15:1. 16:7, 11. Je 48:31, 36, Kir-heres.
slingers. 1 S 17:40, 50. 25:29. 2 Ch 26:14mg.
Jb 41:28. Je 10:18. Zc 9:15mg.

26 **that drew swords**. Jg 8:10. 20:2.
break through. Is 7:6. Je 39:2.
unto the king of Edom. ver. 9. Am 2:1.

27 **eldest son**. or, first born. Dt 12:31. 21:15-17.
Mi 6:7.
offered him. Ge 22:2, 13. Dt +18:10, Jg
11:31, 39. Mi 6:7.
burnt offering. Jg 11:31, 39.
upon the wall. 2 K 9:33. 1 S 31:10, 12.
they departed. 1 S 14:36-46. 1 K 20:13, 28,
43.
returned. 2 Ch 20:1, 22, 23.

2 KINGS 4

1 A.M. 3110. B.C. 894.
sons. ver. 38. 2 K +2:3, 5. 1 K 20:35.
thy servant did fear. Ex +18:21. Ps 103:11,
17. 112:1, 2. 115:13. 147:11. Ec 8:12. Ml 4:2.
Ac 13:26. Re 15:4. 19:5.
the creditor. Le +25:39, 40, 48. Ne 10:31.
Mt 18:25, 30, 35. Ja 2:13.
to take. Dt 24:14. Pr 14:31. Ml 3:5.

2 **What shall I**. 2 K 2:9. 6:26, 27. Ps 81:10. Mt
15:34. Jn 6:5-7. 16:24. Ac 3:6. 2 C 6:10.
save a pot of oil. 1 K 17:12. Ja 2:5.

3 **empty vessels**. 2 K 3:16. Jn 2:7.
borrow not a few. Heb. scant not. 2 K
13:18, 19. Ps 81:10. Jn 16:24.

4 **thou shalt shut**. ver. 32, 33. 1 K 17:19, 20.
Is 26:20. Mt 6:6. Mk 5:40. Ac 9:40.
and shalt pour. Mk 6:37-44. 8:5-9. Jn 2:7-9.
6:11. Ep 3:20.

5 **she went**. 2 K 5:11. 1 K 17:15, 16. Lk 1:45.
He 11:7, 8.

6 **when the vessels**. ver. 43, 44. Mt 9:29.
13:58. +14:20. Lk 6:19. 2 C 6:12, 13.
And the oil. 2 K 13:19. Ex 16:18. Jsh 5:12. 1
K 17:14. Jn 6:12.

7 **pay**. Ps +37:21. Ro 12:17. 13:8. Ph 4:8. 1 Th
2:9, 10. 4:12. 2 Th 3:7-12.
debt, *or*, creditor. Ex 22:25.
thy children. Is +58:7. 1 T +5:8.

8 **it fell on**. Heb. there was. ver. 11, 18. Jb 1:6,
13. 2:1.
Shunem. ver. 12. Jsh 19:18. 1 S 28:4. 1 K
1:3.
a great woman. 2 S 19:32. Jb 1:3. 32:9. Lk
1:15.
she constrained him. she laid hold on him.
Pr 7:21. Ac +16:15.

9 **she said**. Pr 31:10, 11. 1 P 3:1.
this is. Mt 5:16. 1 Th 2:10. T 1:8. 2 P 1:21.
3:2.
man of God. ver. 16, 22, 25, 27, 42. Dt
+33:1.

10 **Let us**. Is 32:8. Mt 10:41, 42. 25:40. Mk 9:41.
Lk 8:3. Ro 12:13. He 10:24. 13:2. 1 P 4:9, 10.
a little chamber. ver. 11. Jg 3:20. 2 S 18:33.
1 K 17:19.
bed. lit. "a thing stretched out." Ge 47:31.
table. Ex 25:23.
stool. or, high seat. lit. "a throne." Ge 41:40.
Ex 11:5. 12:29. Dt 17:18. Jg 3:20. 1 S 1:9. 2:8.
4:13, 18.

11 **it fell on a day**. Jb 1:6, 13.
chamber. ver. 10. Jg 3:20. 2 S 18:33.

12 **Gehazi**. i.e. *valley of vision*, **S#1522h**. ver. 12,
14, 25, 27, 29, 31, 36. 2 K 5:20, 21, 25. 8:4, 5.
servant. 2 K 3:11. 1 K 18:43. 19:3. Ac 13:5.

13 **thou hast**. Mt 10:40-42. Lk 9:3-5. Ro 16:2, 6.
Ph 4:18, 19. 1 Th 5:12, 13. 2 T 1:16-18. He
6:10.
careful. 1 S 16:4.
to the king. 2 K 3:15-18. 8:3-6. Ge 14:24. 2
S 19:32-38.
to the captain. 2 K 9:5. 2 S 19:13. 1 K 2:32.
I dwell. Je 6:2mg. 1 T 6:6-8. He 13:5.
among. lit. in the midst. Ge +45:6.
mine own. 2 K 8:1. Ru 1:1-4. Ps 37:3.

14 **she hath no child**. Ge +11:30. 17:17.

16 **About this**. Ge 17:21. 18:10, 14.
season. Heb. set time. ver. 17. Ge +17:21. Jg
20:38mg.
thou shalt. Ge 17:16, 17. Lk 1:13, 30, 31.
my lord. 2 K +2:19.
do not lie. ver. 28. 2 K 5:10, 11. Ge 18:12-
15. 1 K 17:18. 18:9. Ps 116:11. Lk 1:18-20.

17 **the woman**. Ge 21:1. 1 S 1:19, 20. Ps
+113:9. Lk 1:24, 25, 36. He 11:11.

18 **to the reapers**. Ru 2:4.

19 **My head**. Jb 14:1, 2. Je 4:19.

20 **his mother**. Is 49:15. 66:13. Lk 7:12.
and then died. Ge 22:2. 37:3, 35. 1 K 17:17.
Ezk 24:16-18. Lk 2:35. Jn 11:3, 5, 14.

21 **went up**. 2 K 1:16.
the bed. ver. 10. 1 K 17:19.
of the man of God. Jg 13:6. 1 K 17:16.
and shut. or, made secure.
the door. ver. 4, 5, 33.

22 **I may run**. ver. 24, 26. Jn 11:3. Ac 9:38.

23 **go to him**. Jg 13:8. 2 Ch 17:9.
new moon. Col +2:16.
nor sabbath. 2 Ch 15:3. 35:3. Mk 6:2.
she said. Ex +15:20. Jg +21:21. 1 Ch 15:20.
well. Heb. peace. ver. 26. Jg +18:15mg.

24 **Then she**. Ex 4:20. 1 S 25:20. 1 K 13:13, 23.
an ass. 1 S 25:18-20.
Drive. 1 S 25:19.
slack not thy riding for me. Heb. restrain
not for me to ride.

25 to mount Carmel. Jsh +19:26.
26 Run now. Zc 2:4.
Is it well with thee. Jg +18:15mg. Ac 15:36.
It is well. ver. 23. Le 10:3. 1 S 3:18. Jb 1:21,
22. Ps 39:9.
27 him by the feet. Heb. by his feet. Mt 28:9.
Lk 7:38.
thrust. Mt 15:23. 20:31. Mk 10:13. Jn 4:27.
12:4-6.
Let her alone. Mk 14:6. Jn 12:7.
soul. Heb. *nephesh*, Ge +34:3. Ge 35:18. Jb
+14:22. Mt +10:28. 1 Th 5:23.
vexed. Heb. bitter. 1 S +30:6. Jb 3:20. 7:11.
10:1. Pr 14:10mg. 18:14.
hid it from me. 2 K 6:12. Ge 18:17. 2 S 7:3.
Am 3:7. Jn 15:15.
28 Did I desire. Ge 30:1.
Do not. ver. +16.
29 said to. Is 2:4. Je 9:17, 18. 10:18. Ezk 39:9,
10. Am 5:16. Mt 24:20. Lk 22:36.
Gird up thy loins. Lk +12:35.
take my. 2 K 2:14. Ex 4:17.
salute him not. 1 S 13:10mg. Lk 10:4. Ac
18:22. 21:7, 19. 25:13.
lay my staff. 2 K 2:8, 14. Ex 7:19, 20. 14:16.
Jsh 6:4, 5. Ac 3:16. 19:12.
30 As the Lord. 1 K +17:1.
as. 1 S +1:26.
soul. Heb. *nephesh*, Ge +27:31.
I will not. Ex 33:12-16. Ru 1:16-18.
31 neither voice. 1 S 14:37. 28:6. Ezk 14:3. Mt
17:16-21. Mk 9:19-29. Ac 19:13-17.
hearing. Heb. attention. 1 K 18:26, 29. Is
21:7.
not awaked. 1 S 26:12. Jb 14:12. Ps 3:5.
17:15. 35:23. 44:23. 59:4, 5. 73:20. 139:18. Pr
6:22. 23:35. Is 26:19. 29:8. Je 31:26. 51:39,
57. Ezk 7:6mg. Da 12:2. Jl 1:5. Hab 2:19. Mk
5:39. Jn 11:11, 43, 44. Ep 5:14.
32 the child. 1 K 17:17. Lk 8:52, 53. Jn 11:17.
33 shut the door. ver. 4. Mt 6:6.
prayed. 2 K 5:11. 6:17, 18, 20. 1 K 17:20, 21.
18:26, 27. Jn 11:41, 42. Ac 9:40. Ja 5:13-18.
34 went up. 2 K 1:16.
lay upon. 1 K 17:21. Ac 20:10.
stretched himself. ver. 35. 1 K 18:42.
waxed warm. Ex 16:21. 1 K 1:2. Ps 39:3. Ec
4:11. Is 44:15, 16. 47:14.
35 to and fro. Heb. once hither and once
thither.
and the child opened. 2 K 8:1, 5. 13:21. 1 K
17:22. Lk 7:14, 15. 8:55. Jn 11:43, 44. Ac 9:40.
eyes. Ge +21:19.
36 Call this Shunammite. ver. 12.
Take up. 1 K 17:23. Lk 7:15. He 11:35.
37 fell at his feet. ver. 27. 2 K 2:15. 1 K 17:24.
took up her son. 2 K 8:1, 5. 1 K 17:23. He
11:35.
38 Elisha. 2 K 2:1. 1 S 7:16, 17. Ac 10:38. 15:36.
Gilgal. 2 K 2:1.

a dearth. 1 K +8:37.
the sons. 2 K 2:3. 1 S 19:20.
were sitting. Dt 33:3. Pr 8:34. Lk 2:46. 8:35,
38. 10:39. Ac 22:3.
Set on the great pot. Ex 16:3. Ezk 24:3. Mk
6:37. 8:2-6. Lk 9:13. Jn 21:5, 9.
pottage. Ge 25:29, 34. Hg 2:12.
39 herbs. Is 26:19.
a wild vine. Is 5:4. Je 2:21. Mt 15:13. He
12:15.
40 O thou. ver. 9. 2 K 1:9, 11, 13. Dt 33:1. 1 K
17:18.
death. Ex 10:17. 15:23. Mk 16:18.
41 he cast. 2 K 2:21. 5:10. 6:6. Ex 15:25. Jn 9:6.
1 C 1:25.
meal. Ge 18:6.
there. Ac 28:5.
harm. Heb. evil thing.
42 Baal-shalisha. i.e. *lord of the third part*,
S#1190h, only here. 1 S 9:4, 7.
bread. ver. 38. Le +23:10. Dt 12:6. 1 S 9:7. 2
Ch 11:13, 14. 1 C 9:11. Ga 6:6.
of barley. 2 K 7:1, 16-18. Dt 8:8. 32:14. Jn
6:9, 13.
the husk thereof. *or*, his scrip, *or* garment.
43 his servitor. ver. +12. 2 K 6:15mg.
Ex 24:13.
What. Mt +14:17.
They shall eat. Mt +14:20. 16:8-10. Mk
8:20.
shall leave. Ex 36:7. Ru 2:14. 2 Ch 31:10. Je
44:7.
44 and left. ver. 43.

2 KINGS 5

1 A.M. 3110. B.C. 894.
Naaman. Ge +46:21. Nu 26:40. Lk 4:27.
a great. 2 K 4:8. Ex 11:3. 1 S 16:7. Est 9:4.
10:3.
with. Heb. before. ver. 3.
honorable. *or*, gracious. Heb. lifted up, *or*
accepted in countenance. 2 K 3:14. Jb
22:8mg. Is 3:3mg. 9:15.
by him. Pr 21:31. Is 10:5, 6. Je 27:5, 6. Da
2:37, 38. Jn 19:11. Ro 15:18.
deliverance. *or*, victory.
a leper. ver. 27. 2 K 7:3. 8:4. 15:5. Le 13:2, 3,
44-46. 14:2, 34. Nu 5:2. 12:10-12, 14. Dt
24:8, 9. 2 S 3:29. 2 Ch 26:19-23. Mt 8:2, 3.
10:8. 11:5. 26:6. Mk 1:40-42. Lk 4:27. 5:12.
7:22. 17:12. 2 C 12:7.
2 by companies. 2 K 6:23. 13:20. Jg 9:34. 1 S
13:17, 18.
waited on. Heb. was before. Ps 123:2.
3 mistress. Ge 16:4, 8, 9.
Would God. Ex +16:3.
with. Heb. before. ver. 1.
he would. ver. 8. Mt 8:2, 3. 11:5. Lk 17:12-14.
recover him of. Heb. gather in. ver. 6, 7, 11.

4 **and told his lord**. 2 K 7:9-11. Mk 5:19. 16:9, 10. Jn 1:42-46. 4:28, 29. 1 C 1:26, 27.

5 **Go to, go**. Ge 11:3, 7. Ec 2:1. Is 5:5. Ja 4:13. 5:1.

and took. 2 K 8:8, 9. Nu 22:7, 17, 18. 24:11-13. 1 S 9:8. 1 K 13:7. 45:3. Ac 8:18-20.

with him. Heb. in his hand. 2 K 8:8, 9.

ten talents of silver. Ten talents at $1,920 each would be $19,200.

six thousand. At $9.69 1/2 each would be $58,170.

gold. Ge +23:9.

ten changes. Ge 45:22. Jg 14:12. Ja 5:2, 3.

6 **the king of Israel**. 1 K 20:7.

7 **that he rent**. 2 K +18:37.

Am I God. Ge 30:2. Dt 32:39. 1 S 2:6. Da 2:11. Ho 6:1.

see how. 1 K 20:7. Lk 11:54.

8 **rent his clothes**. ver. +7.

let him come. ver. 3, 15. 2 K 1:6. 1 K 17:24. 18:36, 37.

and he shall. Ex 11:8. Ro 11:13. Ezk 2:5. Ho 12:13.

9 **Naaman came**. 2 K 3:12. 6:32. Is 60:14. Ac 16:29, 30, 37-39.

10 **sent a messenger**. Mt 15:23-26.

wash. Heb. *rahats*, Ex +29:4. ver. 12, 13. 2 K 2:21. 3:11, 16. 4:41.

seven times. Le 14:7, 16, 51. Jsh +6:4.

thy flesh. ver. 14. Ex 4:6, 7.

11 **Naaman**. Pr 13:10. Mt 8:8. 15:27. Lk 14:11.

wroth. Ge 40:2. Ac 26:9.

went away. Pr 1:32. Mt 19:22. Jn 6:66-69. 13:20. He 12:25.

Behold. Pr 3:7. Is 55:8, 9. Jn 4:48. 1 C 1:21-25. 2:14-16. 3:18-20.

I thought, etc. Heb. I said, etc. *or*, I said with myself, He will surely come out, etc.

strike. Heb. move up and down. Ex 20:25. 29:24mg, 26, 27. 35:22. Jb 31:21. Is 11:15.

12 **Abana**. i.e. *a stone; constancy; a sure ordinance*, **S#71h**. SS 4:8, Amana.

and Pharpar. i.e. *swift; producing fruit*, **S#6554h**, only here. *or*, Amana.

rivers. **S#5104h**. Heb. *nahar*, a perennial river. Used of the Euphrates (Ge +15:18. 2 Ch +9:26. Is +27:12) and the great rivers of Mesopotamia (Ge 2:10, 13, 14. Ps 137:1), but it is not used of the river Jordan (unless it, or the Dead Sea is intended in Ps 56:6. 74:15. Hab 3:8, 9). Ezk +32:2.

better. ver. 17. 2 K 2:8, 14. Jsh 3:15-17. Ezk 47:1-8. Zc 13:1. 14:8. Mk 1:9.

waters. Heb. *mayim*, **S#4325h**. Natural use: Ge 1:2. Jsh 3:13. 11:5. Da 12:6, 7. Ritual use: Nu 8:7. 19:7, 17. Ezk 36:25. Metaphorical use: Ps 1:3. Is 58:11. Je 2:13. Eschatalogical use: Ezk 47:1. Zc 14:8.

rage. Ge 27:44.

13 **his servants**. ver. 3. Jsh 22:21. 1 S +25:17. 2

S 19:8. 1 K 12:7. 20:24, 31. Jb 31:13. 32:8, 9. Pr 18:13. Je 38:7-10. Mt +18:31. Lk 22:26. 1 C 6:4, 5.

and spake. Pr +9:8, 9. +13:18. 1 T +5:19.

My father. 2 K 2:12. 6:21. 13:14. Ge 41:43. Ml 1:6. Mt 23:9. 1 C 4:15.

how much rather. Pr 3:7. 1 C 1:21, 27.

Wash. ver. +10. Ps 51:2, 7. Is 1:16. Jn 13:8. Ac 22:16. Ep 5:26, 27. T 3:5. He +10:22. 1 P 3:21. Re 7:14.

14 **Then**. Pr 17:10.

went he down. Jb 31:13. Pr 9:9. 25:11, 12. Ezk 47:1-9. Zc 13:1. 14:8. Jn 5:4. Ac 8:38.

and dipped. Heb. *tabal*, **S#2881h**. 2 K 8:15. Ge 37:31. Ex 12:22. Le 4:6, 17. 9:9. 14:6, 7, 16, 51. Nu 19:13, 18. Dt 33:24. Jsh 3:15. 1 S 14:27. Ru 2:12. Jb +9:31. See **S#2882h**, 1 Ch 26:11. The Hebrew *tabal* is rendered by *baptidzo* by the Septuagint in this place only.

seven times. Ps 12:6.

in Jordan. Mt 3:6. Mk +1:5, 9.

according to. ver. 10. 2 Ch 20:20. Jn 2:5. He 11:7, 8.

his flesh. ver. 10. Jb 33:25.

and he was clean. Lk 4:27. 5:13. T 2:14.

15 **he returned**. Lk 17:15-18.

now I know. ver. 8. Jsh 2:9-11. 9:9, 24. 1 S 17:46, 47. 1 K 18:36. Is 43:10, 11. 44:6, 8. 45:6. Je 10:10, 11. 16:19-21. Da 2:47. 3:29. 4:34, 35. 6:26, 27. Ro 10:10.

a blessing. Jg +3:15.

16 **As the Lord**. 1 K +17:1.

I will receive none. ver. 20, 26. Ge 14:22, 23. 1 K 13:8. Da 5:17. Mt 10:8. Ac 8:18-20. 20:33-35. 1 C 6:12. 10:32, 33. 2 C 11:9, 10. 12:14.

he urged. 2 K 2:17. Ge 19:3, 9, 11. Jg 19:7.

he refused. Ge 37:35. 39:8. 48:19.

17 **two mules'**. 2 K 9:25. Jg 19:3, 10. 1 S 11:7. 14:14. 2 S 16:1. 1 K 19:19, 21. Jb 1:3. 42:12. Is 5:10. 21:7, 9. Je 51:23.

of earth. ver. 12. Ex 20:24. Ro 14:1.

will henceforth. 1 K 18:21. Ac 26:18. 1 Th 1:9. 1 P 4:3.

18 **Rimmon**. i.e. *pomegranate*, **S#7417h**. Ac 7:43.

and he leaneth. 2 K 7:2, 17.

on my hand. 1 K 7:2.

and I bow. 2 K 17:35. Ex 20:5. 1 K 19:18.

when I bow. Ru 1:15. Mi 4:5.

the Lord pardon. Ru 1:15. 2 Ch 30:18, 19. Je +10:2. 50:20. Am 4:5. Ro 14:1, 3, 4, 10-14. Ga 6:1.

19 **he said**. Mt 9:16, 17. Jn 16:12. 1 C 3:2. He 5:13, 14.

Go. Ezk 12:13. Jn 19:22. Ac 17:22.

in peace. Lk +7:50.

little way. Heb. a little piece of ground. Ge 35:16mg. 48:7.

20 **Gehazi**. 2 K 4:12, 31, 36. Mt 10:4. Jn 6:70. 12:6. 13:2. Ac 8:18, 19.

my master. Pr 26:16. Lk 16:8. Jn 12:5, 6. Ac 5:2.
as the Lord liveth. ver. +16. 2 K 6:31. Ex 20:7. **and take**. Ex 20:17. Ps 10:3. Je 22:17. Hab 2:9. Lk 12:15. 1 T 6:9-11. 2 T 4:10. T 1:7. 1 P 5:2. 2 P 2:14, 15.

21 **he lighted**. Lk 7:6, 7. Ac 8:31. 10:25, 26.
Is all well. Heb. Is there peace? ver. 22. Jg +18:15mg.

22 **My master**. 1 K 13:18. Is 59:3. Je 9:3, 5. Jn 8:44. Ac 5:3, 4. Re +21:8.
the sons. 2 K +2:3. 1 K 20:35.
give them. 2 C 12:16-18.
a talent. ver. +5. Ex 38:24-28. 1 K 20:39.

23 **Be content**. 2 K 6:3. Jg 19:6. 2 S 7:29mg. 1 K 20:7. 2 Ch 17:27mg. Jb 6:28. Lk 11:54.
And he urged him. ver. 16. 2 K 2:17. 1 S 28:23. 2 S 13:25, 27.
bound. 2 K 12:10mg. Dt 14:25.
bags. or, purses. Is 3:22.
and they bare. Is 30:6.

24 **tower**. or, secret place. Heb. *Ophel*. Nu 14:14. 2 Ch 27:3mg. 33:14mg. Ne 3:26mg, 27. 11:21mg. Is 32:14mg. Mi 4:8. Hab 2:4.
and bestowed. Jsh 7:1, 11, 12, 21. 1 K 21:16. Is 29:15. Hab 2:6. Zc 5:3, 4.

25 **stood before**. Pr 30:20. Ezk 33:31. Mt 26:15, 16, 21-25. Jn 13:2, 26-30.
Whence. 2 K 20:14. Ge 3:8, 9. 4:9. 16:8.
Thy servant. ver. 22. Ac 5:3, 4.
no whither. Heb. not hither or thither.

26 **he said**. Ps 63:11. Pr 12:19, 22. Ac 5:9.
Went. 2 K 6:12. 1 C 5:3. Col 2:5.
Is it a time. ver. 16. Ge 14:23. Ec 3:1-8. Mt 10:8. Ac 20:33, 35. 1 C 9:11, 12. 2 C 11:8-12. 2 Th 3:8, 9.
and. Ge +8:22.

27 **leprosy**. ver. +1. Jsh 7:25. Is 59:2, 3. Ho 10:13. Ml 2:3, 4, 8, 9. Mt 27:3-5. Ac 5:5, 10. 8:20. 1 T 6:10. 2 P 2:3.
cleave. Ge 2:24.
unto thy seed. 1 S 2:30-36. 2 S 3:29.
for ever. Heb. *olam*, Ex +12:24.
a leper. 2 K 15:5. Ex 4:6. Nu 12:10.
as snow. Ex 4:6. Nu 12:10. 2 S 23:20. 1 Ch 11:22. Jb 6:16. 9:30. 24:19. 37:6. 38:22. Ps 51:7. 147:16. 148:8. Pr 25:13. 26:1. 31:21. Is 1:18. 55:10. Je 18:14. La 4:7.

2 KINGS 6

1 **the sons**. 2 K +2:3. 4:1. 1 K 20:35.
the place. 2 K 4:38. 1 S 19:20.
too strait for us. Jsh 17:14. 19:47. Jb 36:16. Is 49:19, 20. 54:2, 3.

2 **and take thence**. Jn 21:3. Ac 18:3. 20:34, 35. 1 C 9:6. 1 Th 2:9. 2 Th 3:8. 1 T 6:6.

3 **Be content**. 2 K 5:23. Jg 19:6. Jb 6:28.
go with thy. Jg 4:8.

4 **they cut down wood**. Dt 19:5. 29:11.

5 **ax head**. Heb. iron. Ps 105:18. Ec 10:10. Is 10:34.
Alas, master. ver. 15. 2 K 3:10. Re 18:10, 16, 19.
for it was borrowed. 2 K 4:7. Ex 22:14, 15. Ps 37:21.

6 **he cut down**. 2 K 2:21. 4:41. Ex 15:25. Mk 7:33, 34. 8:23-25. Jn 9:6, 7.

7 **Take it up**. 2 K 4:7, 36. 2 Ch 20:20. Lk 7:15. Ac 9:41.
put out. Ex 4:4.

8 **the king**. ver. 24. 1 K 20:1, 34. 22:31.
took. 1 K 20:23. Jb 5:12, 13. Pr 20:18. +21:30. Is 7:5-7. 8:10. Je 23:23, 24.
camp. or, encamping.

9 **Beware**. 2 K 3:17-19. 1 K 20:13, 28.
thither the Syrians. 2 K 4:27. Am 3:7. Re 1:1.

10 **sent to the place**. 2 K 5:14. Ex 9:20, 21. 1 K 20:15. Pr 27:12. Mt 24:15-17.
warned him. Ezk 3:18-21. Mt 2:12. 3:7. He 11:7.
saved. 2 K 2:12. 13:14. 2 Ch 20:20. Am 7:1-6. Ac 27:24.

11 **Therefore**. 1 S 28:21. Jb 18:7-11. Ps 48:4, 5. Is 57:20, 21. Mt 2:3, etc.
Will ye not. 1 S 22:8.

12 **None**. Heb. No.
Elisha. 2 K 5:3, 8, 13-15. Am 3:7.
telleth. ver. 9, 10. Is 29:15. Je 23:23, 24. Da 2:22, 23, 28-30, 47. 4:9-18.
thy bedchamber. 2 K 1:16. Ps 139:1-4. Ec 10:20.

13 **spy where**. 1 S 23:22, 23. Ps 10:8-10. 37:12-14, 32, 33. Je 36:26. Mt 2:4-8. Jn 11:47-53. Ac 23:12-27.
Dothan. Ge 37:17.

14 **sent he thither horses**. 2 K 1:9-13. 1 S 23:26. 24:2. Mt 26:47, 55. Jn 18:3-6.
great. Heb. heavy. 2 K 18:17mg. Ge 50:9. 1 K 3:9. 10:2. 2 Ch 9:1. Is 36:2.

15 **servant**. or, minister. 2 K +3:11. 4:43mg. 5:20, 27. Ex 24:13. 1 K 19:21. Mt 20:26-28. Ac 13:5.
Alas. ver. 5. 2 Ch 20:12. Ps 53:5. Mt 8:26.

16 **Fear not**. Ps 11:1. +118:6, 11, 12. Is 8:12, 13. Ph 1:28.
they that be. 2 Ch 16:9. Ps 55:18. Is +43:2. Mt 26:53. 1 J 4:4.

17 **prayed**. Ps 91:15. Ja 5:16-18.
open his eyes. ver. 18-20. Ps +119:18. Re 3:7.
full of horses. Ps 34:7. 91:11. Ezk 1:13-16. Zc 1:8. 6:1-7. Mt 26:53. He 1:14. Re 19:11, 14.
chariots. Ps +68:17.

18 **Smite this people**. Ge +19:11. Dt 28:28. Jb 5:14. Zc 12:4. Jn 9:39. 12:40. Ac 13:11. Ro 11:7.

19 **follow me**. Heb. come ye after me. ver. 32. Mt 16:24. Mk 8:34. Lk 9:23.
I will bring. 2 S 16:18, 19. Lk 24:16.

20 **open the eyes**. ver. +17. Lk 24:31.
opened. Jg 20:40-42. Lk 16:23.

21 **My father**. 2 K 2:12. 5:13. 8:9. 13:14.
shall. 1 S 24:4, 19. 26:8. Lk 9:54-56. 22:49.
Ro 12:21.

22 **shalt not**. Ro 12:21.
wouldest. Dt 20:11-16. 2 Ch 28:8-13.
thy sword and. Ge 48:22. Jsh 24:12. Ps 44:6.
Ho 1:7. 2:18.
set bread. Pr 25:21, 22. Mt 5:44. Ro 12:20,
21.

23 **he prepared**. 1 S 24:17, 18. 2 Ch 28:15. Pr
25:21, 22. Mt 5:47. Lk 6:35. 10:29-37.
So the bands. ver. 8, 9. 2 K 5:2. 13:20. 24:2. 2
Ch 22:1. 25:9, 10, 13. 26:11. Mt 4:11. Lk 4:13.

24 **gathered**. 2 K 17:5. 18:9. 25:1. Dt 28:52. 1 K
20:1. 22:31. Ec 9:14.

25 **a great famine**. ver. 28, 29. 2 K 7:4. 1 K
+8:37.
an ass's head. Ezk 4:13-16.

26 **Help, my lord**. 2 S 14:4. Is 10:3. Lk 18:3. Ac
21:28.

27 **If the Lord**, etc. or, Let not the Lord save
thee. 2 K 7:2.
whence. Ps +60:11. 62:8.
barnfloor. Ge +50:10.
winepress. Jg 7:25. Jb 24:11.

28 **What aileth thee**. Ge 21:17. Jg 18:23. 1 S
1:8. 2 S 14:5. Ps 114:5. Is 22:1.
Give thy son. Le +26:29. Is 9:20, 21.

29 **next**. Heb. other. Ge 17:21.
she hath hid. 1 K 3:26. Is 49:15. 66:13.

30 **he rent his clothes**. 2 K +18:37.
sackcloth. Jb +16:15.

31 **God do so**. Ru 1:17. 1 S 3:17. 14:44. 25:22. 2
S 3:9, 35. 19:13. 1 K 2:23.
if the head. 1 K 18:17. 19:2. 22:8. Je 37:15,
16. 38:4. Jn 11:50. Ac 23:12, 13.

32 **the elders**. Ezk 33:31. Jsh +20:4.
ere the messenger. ver. 12. 2 K 5:26.
See ye how. Lk 13:32.
son of a murderer. 1 K 18:4, 13, 14. 21:10,
13. Is 1:21.
the sound. 2 K 7:17. 1 K 14:6.

33 **this evil is of the Lord**. Ge 4:13. Ex 16:6-8.
Dt +2:30. Ru +1:13. 1 S 28:6-8. 31:4. Jb 1:11,
21. 2:5, 9. Pr 19:3. Is 8:21. 29:24. +45:7. Je
2:25. Ezk +18:25. 33:10. Am +3:6. Mt 27:4,
5. Ro +9:14. 2 C 2:7, 11. Ja +1:13, 17. Re
16:9-11.
wait for the. Ps 27:14. +37:7, 9. 62:5. Is
8:17. 26:3. 29:24. 50:10. La 3:25, 26. Hab 2:3.
Lk 18:1.

2 KINGS 7

1 **Elisha said**. 2 K +6:33. 20:16. 1 K 22:19. Is
1:10. Ezk 37:4.
Tomorrow. ver. 18, 19. Ex 8:23. 9:5, 6.
14:13. 16:12. Jsh 3:5. 1 S 11:9. Ps 46:5.

a measure of fine flour. 2 K 6:25. Re 6:6.
of barley. 2 K 4:42. Jn 6:9.
in the gate of Samaria. ver. 18. Ge +14:7. 2
S 19:8.

2 **a lord**, etc. or, a lord which belonged to the
king, leaning on his hand. 2 K 5:18.
if the Lord. Ge 18:12-14. Nu 11:21-23. Ps
78:19-21, 41.
windows. Ge 7:11. Ml 3:10.
might this. Mt 19:26. Mk 11:23.
thou shalt see it. ver. 17-20. Dt 3:27. 2 Ch
20:20. Is 7:9. Ro 3:3. 2 T 2:13. He 3:17-19.

3 **four leprous**. 2 K +5:1.
Why. ver. 4. Je 8:14. 27:13.

4 **we will enter**. Je 14:18.
let us fall. 1 Ch 12:19. Je 37:13, 14.
if they save us. Est 4:16. Je 8:14. Jon 3:9. Lk
15:17-19.
we shall but die. 2 S 14:14. He +9:27.

5 **in the twilight**. 1 S 30:17. Ezk 12:6, 7, 12.
behold. Le 27:8, 36. Dt 28:7. 32:25, 30.

6 **the Lord**. 2 K 3:22, 23, etc. 2 S 5:24. Je 20:3,
4. +49:14. Ezk 10:5. Re 9:9.
the kings of the Hittites. Dt +20:17.
the kings of the Egyptians. 2 Ch 12:2, 3. Is
31:1. 36:9.

7 **they arose**. Jb 18:11. Ps 48:4-6. 68:12. Pr
21:1. 28:1. Je 20:4. 48:8, 9.
and fled. Ps 53:5.
their horses. Ps 20:7, 8. 33:17. Am 2:14-16.
and fled for their. Nu 35:11, 12. Pr 6:5. Is
2:20, 21. Mt 24:16-18. He 6:18.
life. Heb. nephesh, soul, Ge +44:30.

8 **hid it**. 2 K 5:24. Jsh 7:21. Je 41:8. Mt 13:44.
25:18.

9 **they said one**. ver. 3. Hg 1:4, 5.
this day. ver. 6. Is 41:27. 52:7. Na 1:15. Lk
2:10. Ph 2:4.
some mischief will come upon us. Heb.
we shall find punishment. 2 K 5:26, 27. Ge
4:13. Nu +32:23. Pr 24:16.
go and tell. Is 52:7. Jn 1:41, 45. 4:29. Re
22:17.

10 **the porter**. ver. 11. 2 S 18:26. Ps 127:1. Mk
13:34, 35.
no man there. ver. 6, 7.
as they were. Jn 4:6.

12 **unto his servants**. 2 K 6:8. Ge 20:8. 41:38. 1
K 20:7, 23.
I will now. ver. 1. 2 K 5:7.
They know that we be hungry. 2 K 6:25-
29.
hide themselves. Jsh 8:4-12. Jg 20:29-37.

13 **And one**. 2 K +5:13.
Let some take. Ex +18:17, 23. 1 S 25:17-25.
Pr 13:16. 14:8, 15. 18:15. 22:3. 27:12. Ho
14:9. Mt +7:6.
five. Ge 43:34. 1 S 1:8. Is 4:1. 19:18. Am 1:3,
6, 9, 11. Zc 8:23.
in the city. Heb. in it.

they are even. ver. 4. 2 K 6:33. Je 14:18. La 4:9.

15 **vessels**. Est 1:7. Is 22:24.
had cast away. Jb 2:4. Is 2:20. 10:3. 31:7. Ezk 18:31. Mt 16:26. 24:16-18. Ph 3:7, 8. He 12:1.

16 **spoiled the tents**. 1 S 17:53. 2 Ch 14:12-15. 20:25. Jb 27:16, 17. Ps 68:12. Is 33:1, 4, 23.
according to. ver. 1. Nu 23:19. Is 44:26. Mt 24:35.

17 **the lord**. ver. 2.
the people trode upon him. 2 K 9:33. Jg 20:43. Is 25:10. Mi 7:10. He 10:29.

18 **as the man**. ver. 1, 2. 2 K 6:32. Ge 18:14.
in the gate. ver. 1. Ge +14:7. 2 S 19:8.

19 **that lord answered**. ver. 2.

20 **so it fell**. Nu 20:12. 2 Ch +20:20. Jb 20:23. Is 7:9. Je 17:5, 6. He 3:18, 19.

2 KINGS 8

1 A.M. 3113. B.C. 891.
whose son. 2 K +4:18, 31-35.
sojourn. Ge 12:10. 26:1. 47:4. Ru 1:1.
the Lord. 1 K +8:37. Ps 107:34. Hg 1:11.
called for a famine. Je 25:29.
seven years. Ge 41:27. 2 S 21:1. 24:13. Lk 4:25.

2 **with**. 1 T 5:8.
land. Jg 3:3. 1 S 27:1-3.

3 A.M. 3119. B.C. 885.
she went forth. ver. 6. 2 K 4:13. 6:26. 2 S 14:4. Ps 82:3, 4. Je 22:16. Lk 18:3-5.

4 **the king**. Mt 2:7, 8. 14:1. Lk 23:8, 9. Ac 24:24-26.
Gehazi. 2 K 5:20-27. 7:3, 10.
Tell. Mt 2:8. Lk 9:9. 23:8. Jn 9:27. Ac 24:24.
all the great. 2 K 2:14, 20-22, 24. 3:14-16. 4:3-6, 16, 17. 5:14, 27. 6:6, 9-12, 17-20, 32. 7:1, 16-20.

5 **he had restored**. 2 K 4:35.
behold, the woman. Ru 2:3. Est 5:14. 6:11, 12. Pr 16:9. Ec 9:11. Mt 10:29, 30. Ac 8:27, etc. Ro 8:31.
My lord. 2 K 6:12, 26. 1 S 26:17. Ps 145:1.

6 **officer**. or, eunuch. 2 K 9:32mg. 20:18. 23:11mg. 24:12mg, 15mg. 25:19mg. Ge +37:36mg. 39:1. 40:2, 7. 1 S 8:15mg. 1 K 22:9mg. 1 Ch 28:1mg. 2 Ch 18:8mg. Est 1:10mg. 2:15, 21. Is 39:7. Je +29:2mg. 52:25. Da 1:3, 7, 18.
Restore all. Dt 22:2. Jg 11:13. 2 S 9:7. Pr 16:7. 21:1.

7 **Damascus**. Ge +14:15.
Ben-hadad. 1 K +15:18. 22:31.
The man of God. 2 K 1:9, 10. 2:15. 6:12. Dt +33:1.
is come. Jg 16:2. Ac 17:6.

8 **Hazael**. i.e. *God has seen*, **S#2371h**. ver. 9, 12, 13, 15, 28, 29. 2 K 9:14, 15. 10:32. 12:17, 18.

13:3, 22, 24, 25. 1 K 19:15, 17. 2 Ch 22:5, 6. Am 1:4.
Take. 2 K +5:5. 1 S 9:7. 1 K 14:3.
enquire. 2 K 1:2, 6. 3:11-13. 1 K 14:1-4. Lk 13:23. Ac 16:30.

9 **Hazael**. ver. +8.
with him. Heb. in his hand. 2 K 5:5.
Thy son Ben-hadad. 2 K 6:21. 13:14. 16:7. 1 S 25:8. Phm 10.

10 **Thou mayest**. 1 K 22:15.
the Lord. ver. 13. Ge 41:39. Je 38:21. Ezk 11:25. Am 3:7. 7:1, 4, 7. 8:1. Zc 1:20. Re 22:1.
he shall surely die. ver. 15. 2 K 1:4, 16. Ge +2:16, 17. Ezk 18:13.

11 **stedfastly**. Heb. and set *it*. 2 K 12:17. Lk 9:51.
wept. Ge 45:2. Ps 119:136. Je 4:19. 9:1, 18. 13:17. 14:17. Lk 19:41. Jn 11:35. Ac 20:19, 31. Ro 9:2. Ph 3:18.

12 **my lord**. 2 K +4:28. 1 K 18:13.
the evil. 2 K 10:32, 33. 12:17. 13:3, 7. Am 1:3, 4.
strongholds. Nu 13:19.
set on fire. Jsh 8:8.
wilt dash. Ps +137:9.
children. or, sucklings. 1 S 15:3. 22:19. Jb 3:16. Ps 8:2. 17:14. 137:9.
rip up. 2 K 15:16. Ho 13:16. Am 1:13.
with child. Ge 16:11. 38:24, 25.

13 **a dog**. 1 S 17:43. 2 S 9:8. Ps 22:16, 20. Is 56:10, 11. Mt 7:6. Ph 3:2. Re 22:15.
he should do. Je 17:9. Mt 26:33-35.
The Lord. ver. +10. 1 K 19:15. Mi 2:1.

14 **He told me**. ver. 10. 2 K 5:25. Mt 26:16.

15 **And it came**. ver. 13. 1 S 16:12, 13. 24:4-7, 13. 26:9-11. 1 K 11:26-37.
on the morrow. Ps 36:4. Mi 2:1.
that he took a thick cloth. 1 S 19:13.
so that he died. 2 K 9:24. 15:10-14, 25, 30. 1 K 15:28. 16:10, 18. Is 33:1.
Hazael. ver. 13. 1 K 19:15.

16 A.M. 3112. B.C. 892.
Jehoram. 2 K +1:17.
began to reign. Heb. reigned. 1 K 15:25. "Began to reign in concert with his father."

17 A.M. 3112-3119. B.C. 892-885.
Thirty and two. 2 Ch 21:5-10.

18 **in the way**. 2 K 3:2, 3. 1 K 22:52, 53.
the house. 2 K 9:7, 8. 21:3, 13. 2 Ch 21:13. Mi 6:16.
the daughter. ver. 26. 1 K 21:25. 2 Ch 18:1. 19:2. 21:6. 22:1-4.
his wife. Ge 6:1-5. Dt 7:3, 4. 1 K +11:1-5. Ne 13:25, 26.

19 **for David**. 2 K 19:34. 2 S 7:12, 13, 15. 1 K 11:36. 15:4, 5. 2 Ch 21:7. Is 7:14. 37:35. Je 33:25, 26. Ho 11:9. Lk 1:32, 33.
light. Heb. candle, *or* lamp. Ps +18:28mg.

20 **Edom**. ver. 22. 2 K 3:9, 27. Ge 27:40. 2 Ch 21:8-10.
made a king. 2 S 8:14. 1 K 22:47.

21 Zair. i.e. *little, small; in tribulation*, **S#6811h**. Jg 12:6. Ne 13:24. Mt 26:73. Mk 14:70. Ac 2:6, 7.

22 Yet. "And so fulfilled Ge 27:40." ver. +20.
Edom. 1 K 22:47.
unto this day. 1 S +6:18.
Libnah. Nu +33:20.

23 the rest of. 2 K 15:6, 36. 1 K +11:41. 14:29. 15:23. 2 Ch 21:11-20.

24 slept with his fathers. 1 K +11:43.
Ahaziah. 1 K +22:40.

25 A.M. 3119-3120. B.C. 885-884.
In the twelfth year. ver. 16, 17. 2 K 9:29. 2 Ch 21:20.
Ahaziah. Ahaziah, Joash, and Amaziah are all omitted in Mt 1:8; all died violent deaths. 2 K 9:27. 12:20. 14:19.

26 Two and twenty. ver. 17. 2 Ch 22:2.
one year. 2 K 9:21-27. 2 Ch 22:5-8.
Athaliah. 2 K 11:1, 2, 13-16. 1 Ch +8:26.
daughter. *or*, grand-daughter. ver. 18. 1 K +15:10.

27 he walked. ver. +18.
the son in law. ver. 18. 2 Ch 22:3, 4. Ec 7:26. 2 C 6:14-17.

28 A.M. 3120. B.C. 884.
he went. 2 K 3:7. 9:15. 1 K 22:4. 2 Ch 18:2, 3, 31. 19:2. 22:5.
Hazael. ver. 12, 13. 1 K 19:17.
Ramoth-gilead. 1 K +4:13.

29 Joram. 2 K 9:15.
which the Syrians had given. Heb. wherewith the Syrians had wounded.
Ramah. "*Called* Ramoth, ver. 28."
Ahaziah. 2 K 9:16. 2 Ch 22:6, 7.
sick. Heb. wounded. 1 K +22:34mg.

2 KINGS 9

1 the children. 2 K 2:3. 4:1. 6:1-3. 1 K +20:35.
Gird up thy loins. Lk +12:35-37.
box of oil. ver. 3. 1 S 10:1. 16:1. 1 K 1:39.
Ramoth-gilead. 1 K +4:13.

2 Jehu. i.e. *he is; Jehovah is he*, **S#3058h**. ver. 5, 11, 13-22, 24, 27, 30, 31. 2 K 10:1, 5, 11, 13, 18-21, 23-25, 28-31, 34-36. 12:1. 13:1. 14:8. 15:12. 1 K 19:16, 17. 1 Ch 2:38, 38. 4:35. 12:3. 2 Ch 19:2. 20:34. 22:7, 8, 9. 25:17. Ho 1:4.
among his brethren. ver. 5, 11.
inner chamber. Heb. chamber in a chamber. 1 K 20:30mg. 22:25mg.

3 pour it. Ex +28:41.
I have anointed. 2 K 8:13. 1 S 15:1, 17. 1 K 1:39. Ps 75:6, 7. Pr 8:15, 16. Je 27:5-7. Da 2:21. 4:35. 5:18. Jn 19:10, 11.
and flee. 1 S 16:2. Mt 2:13. 10:16.

4 the young man. Is +40:13mg.
the prophet. 2 K 2:3.

5 I have an errand. Jg 3:19.

6 he arose. Ac 23:18, 19.
I have anointed. ver. +3. 2 Ch 22:7. Ps 2:6mg. 75:6. Is 45:1. Da 2:21. 4:17, 32. 5:20, 21.
over the people. 1 K 3:8. 10:9. 14:7. 16:2.

7 I may avenge. Dt 32:35, 43. Ps 94:1-7. 116:15. Mt 23:35. Lk 18:7, 8. Ro 12:19. 13:4. He 10:30. Re 6:9, 10. 18:20. 19:2.
at the hand. ver. 32-37. 1 K 18:4. 21:15, 21, 25.

8 I will cut off. 1 K +14:10, 11. 21:21, 22.
him that pisseth. 1 S +25:22.
him that is shut up. Dt +32:36.

9 like the house. 1 K 14:10, 11. 15:29. 21:22.
and like the house. 1 K 16:3-5, 11, 12.

10 the dogs. ver. 35, 36. 1 K 21:23. Je 22:19.
he opened. ver. 3. Jg 3:26.

11 all is well. ver. 17, 19, 22. Jg +18:15mg.
this mad fellow. Dt 28:34. 1 S 21:14mg, 15. Is 59:15mg. Je 29:26. Ho 9:7. Mk 3:21. Jn 10:20. Ac 17:18. 26:24. 1 C 4:10. 2 C 5:13.
communication. 1 S 1:16. 1 K 18:27mg. Jb 7:13. 9:27. 10:1. 21:4. 23:2. Ps 55:2. 64:1. 102:1. 104:34. 142:2. Pr 23:29.

12 false. Je 37:14. 40:16.
thus and thus. ver. +6-10.

13 and took every. Mt 21:7, 8. Mk 11:7, 8.
on the top. lit. "bone." Jg 9:46, 51. Ne 3:15. **S#1634h**, 1635h. Ge 49:14 (strong). 2 K 9:13 (top). Jb 40:18. Pr 17:22. 25:15. Da 6:24.
blew with trumpets. 2 S 15:10. 1 K 1:34, 39. Ps 47:5-7. 98:6.
is king. Heb. reigneth.

14 conspired. ver. 31. 2 K 8:12-15. 10:9. 15:30. 1 K 15:27. 16:7, 9, 16.
kept Ramoth-gilead. ver. +1.

15 Joram. Heb. Jehoram.
returned. 2 K 8:29. 2 Ch 22:6.
had given. Heb. smote.
minds. Heb. *nephesh*, soul, Ge +23:8.
none go forth. Heb. no escaper go forth. 1 S 27:9-11.

16 And Ahaziah. 1 K +22:40.

17 a watchman. 2 S 13:34. 18:24. Is 21:6-9, 11, 12. 56:10. 62:6. Ezk 33:2-9. Ac 20:26-31.
Take an horseman. 2 K 7:14.
Is it peace. ver. 19. Jg +18:15mg. 1 S 16:4. 1 K 2:13.

18 What hast. 1 K +18:18. Jg +11:12.
thou to do. ver. 19, 22. Is 48:22. 59:8. Je 16:5. Ro 3:17.

20 driving. *or*, marching. Hab 1:6. 3:12.
for he driveth. 2 K 10:16. Ec 9:10. Is 54:16. Da 11:44.
furiously. Heb. in madness. ver. 11. Dt 28:28. Zc 12:4.

21 Make ready. Heb. bind. 1 K 18:44mg. 20:14mg. 2 Ch 13:3mg. Ps 118:27. Je 46:4. Mi 1:13.
Joram. 2 Ch 22:7.

met. Heb. found. 2 K 10:13mg, 15mg. Ge 44:34mg. Ex 18:8mg. Nu 20:14mg. Ne 9:32mg. Jb 31:29. Ps 116:3mg. 119:143mg.
the portion of Naboth. ver. 25. 1 K 21:1-7, 15, 18, 19.

22 **Is it peace**. ver. 11, 17.
What peace. ver. 18. Is 48:22. 57:19-21. 59:8. Je 16:5. Ro 3:17.
the whoredoms. Ex 7:11. +34:15. 1 K 16:30-33. 18:4. 19:1, 2. 21:8-10, 25.
witchcrafts. 2 Ch +33:6. Re +9:21.

23 **There is treachery**. 2 K 11:14. 2 Ch 23:13.

24 **drew a bow with his full strength**. Heb. filled his hand with a bow.
smote. 1 K 22:34. Jb 20:23-25. Ps 50:22. Pr 21:30. Ec 8:12, 13. 1 Th 5:3.
sunk. Heb. bowed. Ge 49:9.

25 **Bidkar**. i.e. *son of piercing through; stabber; assassin*, **S#920h**.
the Lord. 1 K 21:19, 24-29. Is 13:1. Je 23:33-38. Na 1:1. Ml 1:1. Mt 11:30.

26 **blood of Naboth**. Heb. bloods. Ge 4:10mg. 2 S 3:28mg. 1 Ch 28:3mg. Ps 5:6mg. 51:14mg. 55:23mg. Is 1:15mg. 26:21mg. Ezk 16:9mg. 18:13mg. 22:2mg. Ho 4:2mg. 12:14mg. Mi 3:10mg. Na 3:1mg. Hab 2:8mg, 12mg, 17. Zc 9:7mg.
of his sons. Dt 24:16. 2 Ch 24:25. 25:4.
I will requite. Ex 20:5. Dt 5:9. Ezk 18:19.
plat. *or*, portion. ver. 21, 25. 1 K 21:19.

27 **Ahaziah**. 2 K 8:29. Nu 16:26. 2 Ch 22:7-9. Pr 13:20. 2 C 6:17.
garden house. 1 K 21:2.
And they did. 2 Ch 22:9.
Gur. i.e. *a whelp* or *sojourner*, **S#1483h**.
Ibleam. Jsh 17:11. Jg 1:27.
Megiddo. "In the kingdom of Samaria." Jsh +12:21. 2 Ch 22:9.

28 **his servants carried**. 2 K 12:21. 14:19, 20. 23:30. 2 Ch 25:28. 35:24.
sepulchre. Heb. *qeburah*, Ge +35:20 **(S#6900h)**.

29 **in the eleventh**. 2 K 8:16, 24, 25. 2 Ch 21:18, 19. 22:1, 2.
began Ahaziah. "Then he began to reign as viceroy to his father in his sickness, 2 Ch 21:18, 19. But in Joram's twelfth year, he began to reign alone. 2 K 8:25."

30 **Jezebel**. 1 K 19:1, 2.
painted her face. Heb. put her eyes in painting. Pr 6:25. Je 4:30mg. Ezk 23:40.
tired her head. Is 3:18-24. Je 13:18mg. Ezk 24:17. 1 T 2:9, 10. 1 P 3:3.
looked out. Jg +5:28.

31 **Zimri**. 1 K 16:9-20.
peace. ver. +18-22.

32 **Who is on my side**? Ex 32:26. 1 Ch 12:18. 2 Ch 11:12. Ps 118:6. 124:1, 2.
eunuchs. *or*, chamberlains. 2 K +8:6mg. Ac 12:20.

33 **Throw her down**. 1 K +21:11.
sprinkled. Le 6:27. Is 63:3.
and he trode. ver. 26. 2 K 7:20. Is 25:10. La 1:15. Mi 7:10. Ml 4:3. Mt 5:13. He 10:29.

34 **he did eat**. 1 K 18:41. Est 3:15. Am 6:4.
this cursed woman. 1 K 21:25. Pr 10:7. Is 65:15. Mt 25:41.
she is a king's daughter. 1 K 16:31.

35 **but they found**. Jb 31:3. Ec 6:3. Is 14:18-20. Je 22:19. 36:30. Ac 12:23.
skull. Ex 16:16. 38:26. Nu 1:2, 18, 20, 22. 3:47. Jg 9:53. 1 Ch 10:10. 23:3, 24.
the palms. Le 14:15, 26. 1 S 5:4.

36 **This is**. 1 K +21:23.
by his. Heb. by the hand of his. 1 K +16:12mg.

37 **the carcase**. Ec 6:3. Je +7:33. Ezk 32:23-30.
as dung. Je +16:4.

2 KINGS 10

1 **seventy sons**. Ge +13:8. Jg 8:30. 10:4. 12:14. 16:28. 2 Ch 22:9.
in Samaria. 2 K 5:3. 1 K 13:32. +15:10.
the rulers. Dt +16:18. 1 K 21:8-14.
them. Heb. nourishers. ver. 5. Est 2:7.

2 **as soon**. 2 K +5:6.

3 **Look even**. Dt 17:14, 15. 1 S 10:24. 11:15. 2 S 2:8, 9. 1 K 1:24, 25. 12:20.
fight for. 2 S 2:12-17. 1 K 12:21. Jn 18:36.

4 **Behold**. 2 K 9:24, 27.
how then shall. Is 27:4. Je 49:19. Na 1:6. Lk 14:31.

5 **We are thy servants**. 2 K 18:14. Jsh 9:11, 24, 25. 1 K 20:4, 32. Je 27:7, 8, 17. Jn 12:26.

6 **If ye be mine**. Heb. If ye *be* for me. 2 K +9:32. Mt 12:30. Lk 9:50.
take ye. Nu 25:4. 1 K +21:8-11.
your master's sons. Dt 5:9. Jsh 7:24, 25. Jb 21:19. Is 14:21, 22. Re 2:20-23.

7 **slew**. Ge 22:10. 37:31. Ex 12:6.
seventy men. ver. 9. 2 K 11:1. Jg 9:5, etc. 1 K 21:21. 2 Ch 21:4. Mt 14:8-11.
heads. Jg +7:25.
baskets. **S#1731h**. 1 S 2:14 (kettle). 2 Ch 35:13 (cauldrons). Jb 41:20 (pot). Ps 81:6mg. Je 24:2.

8 **there came**. 2 S 11:18-21. 1 K 21:14. Mk 6:28.
until the morning. Dt 21:23.

9 **Ye be righteous**. 1 S 12:3. Is 5:3.
I conspired. 2 K +9:14-24. Ho 1:4.

10 **fall unto the earth**. 1 S 3:19. 15:29. Je 44:28, 29. Zc 1:6. Mk 13:31.
the Lord hath done. 2 K 9:7-10. 1 K 21:19, 21-24, 29.
by. Heb. by the hand of. 1 K +16:12mg.

11 **and**. Ps 125:5. Pr 13:20.
kinsfolks. *or*, acquaintance. Ru 2:1. Jb 19:14. Ps 31:11. 55:13. 88:8, 18. Is 12:5 (known).

his priests. 2 K 23:30. 2 S 20:26. 1 K 18:19, 40. 22:6. Re 19:20. 20:10.
he left. Jsh 10:30. 11:8. 1 K 14:10. 15:29. 16:11. 21:21, 22. Jb 18:19. Ps 109:13. Is 14:21, 22. Jn 10:35.

12 **shearing house**. Heb. house of shepherds binding *sheep*. ver. 14.

13 **met with**. Heb. found. ver. 15. 2 K +9:21mg.
the brethren. 2 K 8:24, 29. 9:21-27. 2 Ch 21:17. 22:1-10.
salute. Heb. the peace of, etc. Jg +18:15mg.
queen. 1 K 11:19. 15:13. 2 Ch 15:16. Je 13:18. 29:2.

14 **Take them alive**. ver. 6, 10, 11. Ge 39:12 (caught). 1 K 20:18.
pit. Heb. *bor*, Ge +37:20.
neither left. 2 K 8:18. 11:1. 2 Ch 22:8, 10.

15 **lighted on**. Heb. found. ver. 13mg. 2 K +9:21mg.
Jehonadab. i.e. *The Lord gave freely*, S#3082h. ver. 23. Je +35:6, 8, 14, 16, 18, 19, Jonadab.
Rechab. 2 S +4:2.
saluted. Heb. blessed. 2 K 4:29. Ge +31:55. 47:7, 10. 1 S 13:10mg.
Is thine heart right. 1 Ch 12:17, 18. Jn 21:15-17. Ga 4:12.
give me. Ezr 10:19. Ezk 17:18. Ga 2:9.
he took him. Ac 8:31.

16 **Come with me**. ver. 31. 2 K 9:7-9. Nu 23:4. 24:13-16. 1 K 19:10, 14, 17. Pr 27:2. Ezk 33:31. Mt 6:2, 5. Ro 10:2.

17 **he slew**. ver. +11. 2 K 9:8. 2 Ch 22:8. Ps 109:8, 9. Ml 4:1.
according. ver. +10. 2 K 9:25, 26. 1 K 21:21.

18 **Ahab served Baal**. 2 K 3:2. 1 K 16:31, 32. 18:19, 22, 40.
Jehu. Jb 13:7. Ro 3:8. Ph 4:8.

19 **all the prophets of Baal**. 2 K 3:13. 1 K 22:6.
all his servants. ver. 21.
all his priests. ver. 11.
But Jehu. ver. +18. Jb 13:7. Pr 29:5. 2 C 4:2. 11:3, 13-15. 12:16-18. 1 Th 2:3.

20 **Proclaim**. Heb. Sanctify. 1 K 18:19, 20. 21:12. Jl 1:14.
solemn assembly. Le 23:36.
they proclaimed. Ex 32:5.

21 **And they came**. Jl 3:2, 11-14. Re 16:16.
the house of Baal. 1 K 16:32.
full from one end to another. or, so full *that they stood* mouth to mouth. Jg 16:27.

22 **vestments**. Ex 28:2. Mt 22:11, 12.

23 **Jehonadab**. ver. 15.
Search. Ge 31:35. 44:12. 1 S 23:23. 1 K 20:6, etc.
none of. Ge 19:22. Ezk 9:6. Am 9:9. Re 7:3.
the worshippers. Mt 13:30, 41. 25:32, 33.

24 **If any of the men**. 1 K 20:30-42.
his life. Heb. *nephesh*, soul, Ge +44:30. 1 K 20:39.

25 **Go in**. Ex 32:27. Dt 13:6-11. Ezk 9:5-7.

guard. or, runners. 1 S 22:17mg.
let. Dt 13:9-11. Ezk 22:21, 22. Re 16:6, 7.
edge. Heb. mouth. Ge +34:26mg.

26 **images**. Heb. statues. or, standing pillars. 2 K +17:10mg. Ge 28:18, 22. 31:13, 45, 51, 52. Ex 24:4.
and burned them. 2 K 19:18. 2 S 5:21.

27 **brake down the image**. 2 K 18:4. 23:7-14. Le 26:30. Dt 7:5, 25. 1 K 16:32. 2 Ch 34:3-7.
made it a draught house. or, latrine. Ezr 6:11. Da 2:5. 3:29.

29 A.M. 3120-3148. B.C. 884-856.
the sins. 2 K 13:2, 11. 14:24. 15:9, 18, 24, 28. 17:22. 1 K 12:28-30. 13:33, 34. 14:16.
who made Israel to sin. Ge 20:9. Ex 32:21. 1 S 2:24. Mk 6:24-26. 1 C 8:9-13. Ga 2:12, 13.
the golden calves. Ex +32:4.
in Beth-el. 1 K 12:29.

30 **Because thou hast**. 1 K 21:29. Ezk 29:18-20. Ho 1:4.
according to all that. 1 S 15:18-24. 1 K 20:42. 21:22.
thy children. ver. 35. 2 K 13:1, 10. 14:23. 15:8-12.
fourth. 2 K 15:12. Ge 15:16.

31 **took no heed**. Heb. observed not. Nu 23:12. Dt 4:15, 23. 1 K 2:4. Ps 39:1. 119:9. Pr 4:23. He 2:1. 12:15.
walk. Dt 5:33. 10:12, 13. 2 Ch 6:16. Ne 10:29. Ps 78:10. Ezk 36:27. Da 9:10.
he departed. ver. 29. 2 K 3:3. 1 K 14:16.

32 **cut**. Heb. cut off the ends of. Pr 26:6. Hab 2:10.
Hazael. 2 K 8:12. 13:22. 1 K 19:17.

33 **eastward**. Heb. toward the rising of the sun.
the land of Gilead. Ge +37:25.
even. or, even to. Am 1:3, 4.
Bashan. Dt +32:14.

34 **the rest of**. 2 K 12:19. 13:8. 1 K +11:41. 14:19, 29.

35 A.M. 3148. B.C. 856.
Jehu slept. 1 K +11:43.
Jehoahaz. i.e. *Jah has taken hold; whom Jehovah holds*, S#3059h. 2 K 13:1, 4, 7-10, 22, 25. 14:8, 17. 23:30, 31, 34. 2 Ch 21:17. 25:17, 23, 25. 36:1. Reigned 17 years, as 2 K 13:1.

36 **the time**. Heb. the days *were*.
twenty and eight years. Thus Jehu's reign was longer than any other king of Israel.

2 KINGS 11

1 A.M. 3120. B.C. 884.
Athaliah. 2 Ch 22:10. 24:7.
the mother. 2 K 8:18, 26. 9:27.
and destroyed. Mt 2:13, 16. 21:38, 39.
seed royal. Heb. seed of the kingdom. 2 K 25:25mg. Jsh 10:2. 1 S 27:5. 1 K 11:14. 2 Ch 22:10. Est 1:7. Je 41:1. Ezk 17:13. Da 1:3.

2 **Jehosheba**. i.e. *sworn of Jehovah*, S#3089h. 2 Ch 22:11, Jehoshabeath.

Joram. 2 K 8:16, Jehoram. 1 Ch +26:25.

Joash. 2 K 12:1, 2, Jehoash. Jg +6:11.

stole him. 2 Ch 22:11.

they hid him. 2 K 8:19. Pr 21:30. Is 7:6, 7. 37:35. 65:8, 9. Je 33:17, 21, 26.

his nurse. Ge 24:59. 32:15 (milch). 35:8. Ex 2:7. 2 Ch 22:11. Is 49:23.

in the bedchamber. 1 K 6:5, 6, 8, 10. Je 35:2. Ezk 40:45.

3 A.M. 3120-3126. B.C. 884-878.

hid. 1 S 14:22. 1 Ch 21:20. 2 Ch 22:9, 12. Pr +22:3. Col 3:3.

And Athaliah. 2 Ch 22:12. Ps 12:8. Ml 3:15.

4 A.M. 3126. B.C. 878.

the seventh. 2 Ch 23:1, etc.

Jehoiada. i.e. *Jehovah hath known; whom Jehovah knows,* **S#3077h.** ver. 4, 9, 15, 17. 12:2, 7, 9. 2 Ch 22:11. 23:1, 8, 9, 11, 14, 16, 18. 24:2, 3, 6, 12, 14, 15, 17, 20, 22, 25.

rulers. ver. 9. 1 Ch 9:13.

over hundreds. Ex 18:21, 25.

the captains. or, executioners. ver. 19. 2 S 20:23 (Cherethites). Ac 5:24, 26.

guards. or, runners. ver. 13mg. 1 S 22:17mg. 1 K 14:27mg.

made a covenant. ver. 17. 2 K 23:3. Jsh 24:25. 1 S 18:3. 23:18. 2 Ch 15:12. 29:10. 34:31, 32. Ne 9:38.

took an oath. Ge 50:25. 1 K 18:10. Ne 5:12. 10:29.

5 **that enter.** 1 Ch 9:25. 23:3-6, 32. 24:3-6. Lk 1:8, 9.

the watch. ver. 19. 2 K 16:18. 1 K 10:5. Je 26:10. Ezk 44:2, 3. 46:2, 3.

6 **the gate of Sur.** i.e. *turning aside; deteriorated,* **S#5495h,** only here. 1 Ch 26:13-19. 2 Ch 23:4, 5. In 2 Ch 23:5 it is "the foundation," by changing a Hebrew letter (Young).

the guard. or, runners. In 2 Ch 23:4mg, called "of the thresholds" (Young).

that it be not broken down. *or,* from breaking up.

7 **parts.** *or,* companies. Heb. hands. Ge 47:24. 2 S 19:43. Ne 11:1. Da 1:20.

go forth. ver. 5. 2 Ch 23:6.

8 **compass.** 2 K 6:14. Jsh 6:3, 11.

he that cometh. ver. 15. Ex 21:14. 1 K 2:28-31. 2 Ch 23:7.

the ranges. ver. 15. 1 K 6:9. 2 Ch 23:14.

9 **the captains.** ver. 4. 1 Ch 26:26. 2 Ch 23:8.

10 **king David's spears.** 1 S 21:9. 2 S 8:7. 1 Ch 26:26, 27. 2 Ch 5:1. 23:9, 10.

11 **every man.** ver. 8, 10.

corner. Heb. shoulder. Ex 26:14, 15. 28:7, 12, 25, 27.

by the altar. Ex 40:6. 2 Ch 6:12. Ezk 8:16. Jl 2:17. Mt 23:35. Lk 11:51.

12 **he brought.** ver. 2, 4. 2 Ch 23:11.

put the crown. 2 S 1:10. 12:30. Est 2:17.

6:8. Ps 21:3. 89:39. 132:18. Mt 27:29. He 2:9. Re 19:12.

the testimony. 2 K +14:6. Ex +16:34. Dt 17:18-20. Ps 78:5. Is 8:16, 20.

anointed him. 2 K 9:3. 1 S 10:1. 16:13. 2 S 2:4, 7. 5:3. 1 K 1:39. La 4:20. Ac 4:27. 2 C 1:21. He 1:9.

and they clapped. Nu 24:10. Jb 27:23. Ps 47:1. 98:8. Is 55:12.

and said. Ne +2:3. Ps 72:15-17. Pr 29:2.

God save the king. Heb. Let the king live. 1 S +10:24mg.

13 **when Athaliah.** 2 Ch 23:12-15.

14 **a pillar.** 2 K 23:3. 2 Ch 34:31. Called "his pillar" in 2 Ch 23:13 (Young).

trumpeters. or, trumpets. 2 K 12:13. Nu 10:2, 8, 9, 10. 31:6. 1 Ch 13:8. 15:24, 28. 16:6, 42.

the princes. ver. 10, 11. Nu 10:1-10.

all the people. 1 K 1:39, 40. 1 Ch 12:40. Pr 29:2. Lk 19:37. Re 19:1-7.

rent. 2 K +18:37.

Treason. ver. 1, 2. 2 K 9:23. 1 K 18:17, 18. or, Conspiracy. 2 K 12:20. 14:19. 15:15, 30. 17:4. 1 K 16:20. 2 Ch 15:12. 23:13mg. 25:27. Is 8:12. Je 11:9. Ezk 22:25.

15 **captains.** ver. 4, 9, 10. 2 Ch 23:9, 14.

officers. or, inspectors. Nu 31:14, 48. 2 Ch 23:14.

Have. Ge 9:6. Ex 21:14. Mt 7:2. Ja 2:13.

followeth. ver. +8.

Let. Ezk 9:7.

16 **by the which.** 2 Ch 23:15.

there was she slain. Ge 9:6. Jg 1:7. Mt 7:2. Ja 2:13. Re 16:5-7.

17 **made a covenant.** ver. +4. Dt 5:2, 3. 29:1-15. Jsh 24:25. 2 Ch 15:12-14. 29:10. 34:31. Ezr 10:3. Ne 5:12, 13. 9:38. 10:28, 29. 2 C 8:5.

between the king. 1 S 10:25. 2 S 5:3. 1 Ch 11:3. 2 Ch 23:16. Ro 13:1-6.

18 **went.** 2 K 9:25-28. 10:26. 18:4. 23:4-6, 10, 14. 2 Ch 23:17. 34:4, 7.

brake they. 2 K 18:4. Ex 32:20. Dt 12:3. 2 Ch 12:17. Is 2:18. Zc 13:2.

images. Nu 33:52. 1 S 6:5, 11. 2 Ch 23:17.

and slew. Dt 13:5, 9. 1 K 18:40. 2 Ch 23:17. Zc 13:2, 3.

Mattan. i.e. *a gift,* **S#4977h.** 2 Ch 23:17. Je 38:1.

appointed. 2 Ch 23:18-20.

officers. Heb. offices. 1 Ch 26:30. 2 Ch 24:11.

19 **took.** ver. 4-11. 2 Ch 23:20.

by the way. ver. +5. 2 Ch 23:5, 19.

he sat. 1 K 1:13. 1 Ch 29:23. Je 17:25. 22:4, 30. Mt 19:28. 25:31.

20 **rejoiced.** ver. +14. 2 Ch 23:21. Pr 11:10. 29:2.

slew Athaliah. ver. +15.

21 **Seven years old.** ver. 4. 2 K 22:1. 2 Ch 24:1, etc.

2 KINGS 12

1 **the seventh**. 2 K 9:27. 11:1, 3, 4, 21. 2 Ch 24:1, etc.
Jehoash. i.e. *whom Jehovah bestowed; Jehovah is foundation,* S#3060h. ver. 2, 4, 6, 7, 18. 2 K 11:2mg, 21. 13:10, 25. 14:8, 9, 11, 13-17. 1 Ch 3:11, Joash. +7:8.
forty years. 2 S 5:4. 1 K 11:42.
Zibiah. i.e. *a roe,* S#6645h. 2 Ch 24:1.
Beer-sheba. Ge +21:31.
2 **Jehoash did**. 2 K 14:3. 2 Ch 24:2, 17-22. 25:2. 26:4.
instructed. or, directed. Ge 46:28. Ex 4:12, 15.
3 **high places**. 2 K +21:3. Je 2:20.
4 A.M. 3148. B.C. 856.
said to the priests. 2 K 22:4. 2 Ch 29:4-11. 35:2.
the money. ver. 18. Ge 23:16. 1 K 7:51. 1 Ch 18:11. 2 Ch 15:18. 31:12.
dedicated things. or, holy things. Heb. holinesses. Le 5:15, 16. 27:12-27, 31.
even the money. 2 K 22:4. Ex 30:12-16. 2 Ch 24:9, 10.
that every man is set at. Heb. of the souls of his estimation.
man, Heb. *nephesh,* soul, Ge +12:5. Le 27:2-8.
and all the money. Ex 25:1, 2. 35:5, 22, 29. 36:3. 1 Ch 29:3-9, 17. Ezr 1:6. 2:69. 7:16. 8:25-28. Lk 21:4.
cometh, etc. Heb. ascendeth upon the heart of a man. Ex 35:5. 1 Ch 29:9. Je +3:16mg. 1 C 2:9.
5 **Let the priests**. 2 Ch 24:5.
let them repair. ver. 12. 2 K 22:5, 6. 1 K 11:27. 2 Ch 24:7. Is 58:12.
6 **three and twentieth year**. Heb. twentieth year and third year.
the priests. 1 S 2:29, 30. 2 Ch 29:24. Is 56:10-12. Ml 1:10. Ph 2:21. 1 P 5:2.
7 **king Jehoash**. 2 Ch 24:5, 6, etc.
Jehoiada. ver. 2. 2 K 11:4. 2 Ch 23:1. 24:16.
Why repair ye. 1 Ch 21:3.
8 **consented**. Ge 34:15, 22, 23.
9 **took a chest**. Ge 50:26. Ex 25:10. 2 Ch 24:8, 10, 11. Mk 12:41.
bored. Ex 18:21.
hole. 1 S 14:11.
beside. 2 Ch 24:10.
the priests. 2 Ch 22:4. 23:4. 25:18. 1 Ch 15:18, 24. Je 35:4. 52:24.
door. Heb. threshold. 2 K 22:4mg. 23:4. 25:18mg. Jg 19:27. 1 K +14:17. 1 Ch 9:19mg. 2 Ch 34:9. Est 2:21mg. 6:2mg. Ps 84:10mg. Is 6:4mg. Je 35:4mg. 52:24mg.
10 **the king's**. 2 K 19:2. 22:3, 12. 2 S 8:17. 20:25.
scribe. or, secretary. 2 S +8:17mg.
put up. Heb. bound up. 2 K 5:23. Dt 14:25.
in bags. 2 K 5:23.
and told. Ge 13:16.

11 **gave the money**. 2 K 22:5, 6. 2 Ch 24:11, 12. 34:9-11.
being told. or, weighed. Jb 28:25. Ps 75:3. Is 40:12.
laid it out. Heb. brought it forth.
carpenters. 2 S 5:11.
12 **masons**. 1 K 5:17, 18. Ezr 3:7. 5:8. Lk 21:5.
was laid out. Heb. went forth.
13 **there were not**. 2 Ch 24:14.
bowls. Ex 12:22. Nu +7:13, 14. 1 K 7:48-50. Ezr 1:9-11.
snuffers. 1 K 7:50.
basons. 1 K +7:40.
trumpets. Nu +10:2.
15 **they reckoned not**. 2 K 22:7.
for they dealt. Ex 18:21. 2 Ch 34:12. Ne 7:2. Pr 28:20. Is 52:11. Mt +24:45. 25:21. Lk 16:1, 10, 11. Ac +6:3. 1 C +4:2, 3. 2 C 7:2. 8:20, 21. Ph +2:12. 2 T 2:2. 3 J 5.
faithfully. S#530h. 2 K 22:7. Ex 17:12 (steady). +18:21. Dt 32:4 (truth). 1 S 26:23. 2 Ch 31:12. Ne 5:15. Pr 28:20. La 3:23. Hab 2:4 (by his faith).
16 **trespass money**. Le +5:6. Nu 5:8-10.
sin money. or, sin offering money. Le +23:19.
it was. Le +7:7.
17 A.M. 3164. B.C. 840.
Hazael. 2 K +8:8.
against Gath. Jsh +11:22.
set his face. Ge 31:21. Je 42:15. Lk 9:51, 53.
to Jerusalem. 2 Ch 24:23, 24.
18 **took all the hallowed**. 2 K 16:8. 18:15, 16. 1 K 15:18. 2 Ch 16:2.
went away. Heb. went up.
19 **the rest of the acts**. 2 K 8:23. 1 K 11:41. 14:19, 29.
20 **his servants**. 2 K 14:5. 2 Ch 24:24, 25. 25:27. 33:24.
conspiracy. 2 K +11:14. 1 K 15:27. 2 Ch 24:21.
the house of Millo. or, Beth-millo. 2 S +5:9.
Silla. i.e. *a basket; weighing place,* S#5538h, only here. 2 Ch 26:16.
21 **Jozachar**. i.e. *Jehovah has remembered,* S#3108h. 2 Ch 24:26, Zabad.
Shimeath. i.e. *hearing; fame, report,* S#8100h. 2 Ch 24:6.
Jehozabad. 1 Ch +26:4.
Shomer. i.e. *a keeper; guarding,* S#7763h. 2 Ch 24:26, Shimrith.
Amaziah his son. 1 Ch +4:34. 2 Ch 24:27.

2 KINGS 13

1 **three and twentieth year**. Heb. twentieth year, and third year. 2 K 8:26. 10:36. 11:4, 21. 12:6mg.
Jehoahaz. 2 K 10:35.
2 A.M. 3148-3165. B.C. 856-839.

followed. Heb. walked after. ver. 11. 2 K +10:29. 1 S 17:13, 14. 2 S 3:31. 1 K 12:26-33. 14:8, 16. Ho 5:11.

3 and he delivered. Le +26:17. Dt 4:24-27. Jg 3:7, 8. 10:7-14. Is 10:5, 6. He 12:29.
Hazael. ver. 22. 2 K +8:8.
Ben-hadad. ver. +24, 25.
all their days. ver. 22-25.

4 Jehoahaz. Nu 21:7. Jg 6:6, 7. 10:10. Ps 78:34. Is 26:16. Je 2:27.
the Lord. 2 K 14:26. Ge 21:17. Ex 3:7. Jg 10:15, 16. 2 Ch 33:12, 13, 19. Ps 50:15. 106:43, 44. Je 33:3.
he saw. Ge 31:42. Ex 3:9. Is 63:9.
because the king. ver. 22. 2 K 14:26.

5 a savior. ver. 25. Ne +9:27.
beforetime. Heb. yesterday *and* third day. 2 S +3:17mg.

6 departed. ver. +2. 2 K 17:20-23. Dt 32:15-18.
walked. Heb. he walked. 1 K 15:3. 16:26.
and there remained. Heb. and there stood. 1 K 16:33. Ec 2:9.
grove. or, shrine. 2 K +17:10.

7 fifty horsemen. 1 S 13:6, 7, 15, 19-23. 1 K 20:15, 27. Is 36:8.
the king. 2 K 8:12. 10:32.
like the dust. Ps 18:42.
threshing. Is +21:10.

8 the rest of the acts. 2 K 10:34, 35. 1 K +11:4. 14:19, 20, 29, 31.

9 A.M. 3165. B.C. 839.
slept with. 1 K +11:43.
buried him. ver. 13. 2 K 10:35. 1 K 14:13.
Joash. ver. 10. 2 K 14:8, Jehoash.
reigned in his stead. "Alone."

10 began Jehoash. "In consort with his father, 2 K 14:1."

11 he departed. ver. +2, 6. 2 K 3:3. 10:29.

12 A.M. 3163-3179. B.C. 841-825.
the rest. ver. 14-25. 2 K 14:15, 25.
his might. 2 K 14:8-16. 2 Ch 25:17-24.

13 slept with his fathers. 1 K +11:43.
Jeroboam. 1 K +11:26.
buried. ver. +9.

14 A.M. 3166. B.C. 838.
fallen sick. 2 K 20:1. Ge 48:1. Is +38:1. Jn 11:3. Ph 2:26, 27. 2 T 4:20.
sickness. Dt 7:15.
he died. Ps 12:1. Is 57:1. Zc 1:5. Ac 13:36.
O my father. 2 K 2:12. 6:21. Pr 11:11. Ezk 14:14. 22:30. Mk 6:20.
the chariot. ver. +2:11.

16 Put thine hand. Heb. make thine hand to ride. 2 S 6:3.
Elisha. 2 K 4:34. Ge 49:24. Ps 144:1.

17 Open. 2 K 5:10-14. Jn 2:5-8. 11:39-41.
eastward. Ge 13:14.
The arrow. Ex 4:2, 17. +8:23. Jg 7:9-20. 2 S 5:24. Ps 144:1. 1 C 1:18.
Aphek. Jsh +12:18.

18 Smite. Is 20:2-4. Ezk 4:1-10. 5:1-4. 12:1-7.
he smote thrice. 2 K 4:6. Ex 17:11.
and stayed. Lk +11:9. Ja 1:6, 7. 4:2.

19 the man of God. 2 K 1:9-15. 4:16, 40. 6:9. 10:14.
was wroth. Le 10:16. Nu 16:15. Mk 3:5.
shouldest have. 1 S +23:4. Is 62:6, 7. Lk +11:9.
then hadst. Mt 11:23. Lk 19:42. Jn 4:10. Ep +3:20.
now thou shalt. ver. 25. Mk 6:5.

20 A.M. 3167. B.C. 837.
buried him. 2 Ch 24:16. Ac 8:2.
the bands. 2 K 5:2. 6:23. 24:2.
the Moabites. 2 K 3:5, 24-27. Jg 3:12. 6:3-6.

21 sepulchre. Heb. *qeber*, Ge +23:4.
was let down. Heb. went *down*.
touched. 2 K 4:35. Is 26:19. Ezk 37:1-10. Mt 27:52, 53. Jn +5:25, 28, 29. 11:44. Ac 5:15, 16. 19:12. Re 11:11.

22 A.M. 3148-3165. B.C. 856-839.
Hazael. ver. 3-7. 2 K 8:12. Ps 106:40-42.

23 the Lord. 2 K 14:27. Ex 33:19. 34:6, 7. Jg 10:16. Ps 86:15. Is 30:18, 19. Je 12:15. Mi 7:18, 19.
had respect. Ex 2:24, 25. 1 K 8:28.
because of his covenant. Ge 13:16, 17. 17:2-5, 7, 8. Ex 3:6, 7. 32:13, 14. Le +26:42. Dt 32:36. Mi 7:18-20.
neither cast he. Le +26:44. Ps +51:11. Mt 25:41.
presence. Heb. face. Ge 3:8. 6:3.
as yet. Is +54:7.

24 Hazael. Ps 125:3. Lk 18:7.
Ben-hadad. ver. 3. 1 K +15:18.

25 A.M. 3168. B.C. 836.
took again. Heb. returned and took. 2 Ch 19:4.
Three times. ver. 18, 19. Am 1:4.

2 KINGS 14

1 A.M. 3165. B.C. 839.
Joash. ver. 15. Jg +6:11.
reigned Amaziah. 1 Ch +4:34.

2 Jehoaddan. i.e. *Lord of pleasure*, **S#3086h**. 2 Ch 25:1.

3 A.M. 3165-3194. B.C. 839-810.
he did. 2 K 12:2. 1 K 11:4. 15:3. 2 Ch 25:2, 3.
he did according. 2 Ch 24:2, 17. 25:14-16. Je 16:19. Zc 1:4-6. 1 P 1:18.

4 the high places. 2 K +21:3.

5 A.M. 3166. B.C. 838.
that he slew. Ge 9:6. Ex 21:12-14. Nu 35:33.
his servants. 2 K 12:20, 21. 2 Ch 25:3, 4.

6 The fathers. Dt *24:16*. Je 2:8. 2 K 11:12. 2 Ch 14:4. 17:9. 25:4. 34:14. Ezk +18:4, 20.
for his own sin. Dt 24:16. 2 Ch 25:4. Jb 19:4. Ezk 18:2, 20. Is 3:11. Je 31:29, 30. Ga 6:5,

7 A.M. 3177. B.C. 827.
slew. 2 K 8:20-22. 2 Ch 25:11, 12.
the valley of salt. 2 S +8:13.
Selah. *or*, the rock (**S#5554h**). i.e. Petra. Jsh 15:38. Jg 1:36. 2 Ch 25:12. Is 16:1. Ob +3.
Joktheel. Jsh 15:38.
unto this day. 1 S +6:18.

8 A.M. 3178. B.C. 826.
Amaziah. 2 Ch 25:17-24.
Come. ver. 11. 2 S 2:14-17. Pr 13:10. 17:14. 18:6. 20:18. 25:8.
look. ver. 11. 2 K 23:29.

9 **The thistle**. Jg 9:8-15. 2 S 12:1-4. 1 K 4:33. Ezk 20:49. The word *choach* is rendered here, and in 2 Ch 25:18. Jb 31:18, thistle, in 1 S 13:6, thicket, in Is 34:13, bramble, and in 2 Ch 33:11. Pr 26:9. SS 2:2. Ho 9:6, thorn, is probably the black thorn.

10 **thine heart**. Dt +17:20.
glory of this. Ex 8:9. Je 9:23, 24. Ja 1:9.
home. Heb. thy house.
why shouldest. 2 Ch 35:21. Pr 3:30. 15:18. 20:3. +25:8. 26:17.

11 **Amaziah**. 2 Ch 25:16, 20.
looked. ver. 8.
Beth-shemesh. Je +43:13.

12 **was put to the worse**. Heb. was smitten. 1 S 4:10. Pr 16:18. 29:23.
they fled. 1 S 4:10. 2 S 18:17. 1 K 22:36.

13 **took Amaziah**. 2 K 25:6. 2 Ch 33:11. 36:6, 10. Jb 40:11, 12. Pr 16:18. 29:23. Is 2:11, 12. Da 4:37. Lk 14:11.
the gate of Ephraim. 2 Ch 25:23, 24. Ne 8:16. 12:39.
the corner. 2 Ch 26:9. Ne 3:13. Je 31:38. Zc 14:10.

14 **all the gold**. 2 K 24:13. 25:15. 1 K 7:51. 14:26. 15:18.
and hostages. 2 K 18:23mg. 2 Ch 25:4.

15 A.M. 3163-3179. B.C. 841-825.
the rest. 2 K 10:34, 35. 13:12. 1 K 14:19, 20.

16 A.M. 3179. B.C. 825.
Jehoash slept with. 1 K +11:43.
was buried. 2 K +13:9.
Jeroboam. 1 K +11:26.

17 A.M. 3779-3194. B.C. 825-810.
Amaziah. ver. +1, 2, 23. 2 K 13:10.

18 **the rest**. 2 K 13:8, 12. 1 K 11:41. 14:29.

19 A.M. 3194. B.C. 810.
they made. 2 K 12:20, 21. 15:10, 14, 25, 30. 21:23. 2 Ch 25:27, 28.
conspiracy. 2 K +11:14.
fled to Lachish. Jsh +10:3.

20 **he was buried**. 1 K +11:43.

21 **Azariah**. 2 K 15:13. 2 Ch 26:1, Uzziah. Is 1:1. 6:1. Mt 1:8, 9, Ozias.
made him king. 2 Ch 21:24. 1 Ch 3:12.

22 **Elath**. Dt +2:8.

23 A.M. 3179-3220. B.C. 825-784.
the fifteenth. ver. 17.

Jeroboam. ver. +16, 27.
began to reign. "Now he begins to reign alone."

24 **in the sight**. 2 K 21:6. Ge 38:7. Dt 9:18. 1 K 21:25.
he departed. 2 K 13:2, 6, 11. 1 K 12:28, etc. Ps 106:20.
who made. 1 K 14:16.

25 **from the entering of Hamath**. Nu +13:21.
unto the sea. Ge 14:3. Dt 3:17.
of the plain. Dt +11:30.
by the hand. 1 K +16:12mg.
Jonah. Jon 1:1. Mt 12:39, 40. 16:4, Jonas.
Amittai. i.e. *true, steadfast*. **S#573h**: Jon 1:1.
Gath-hepher. i.e. *wine-press of the well*. **S#1662h**. Jsh 19:13, Gittah-hepher. Jn 7:52. In Zebulun, in Galilee.

26 **saw the affliction**. 2 K 13:4. Ex 3:7, 9. Jg 10:16. Ps 106:43-45. Is 63:9.
bitter. lit. "rebellious." Nu 20:10. Dt 21:18, 20. Ps 78:8. Je 5:23.
not any shut. Dt +32:36.
any helper. Jb 29:12. 30:13. Ps 22:11mg. 72:12. Is 63:5. La 1:7. Da 11:45.

27 **said not**. 2 K 13:23. Ho 1:6.
blot out. Ex 32:32, 33. Dt 9:14. 25:19. 29:20. Ps 69:28. Ro +11:1, 2, etc. Re 3:5.
he saved. 2 K 5:1. 13:5. Ho 1:7. T 3:4-6.

28 **the rest**. ver. +15.
Damascus. Ge +14:15.
Hamath. Nu +13:21.
which belonged to Judah. 2 S 3:11.

29 A.M. 3220. B.C. 784.
Jeroboam slept with. 1 K +11:43.
Zachariah. i.e. *remembered by Jah*. **S#2148h**: rendered "Zachariah," "Zechariah." 2 K 15:11. 1 Ch 9:21, 37. 15:20. 16:5. 2 Ch 17:7. 24:20. 34:12. Ezr 8:3, 11, 16. 10:26. Ne 8:4. 11:4, 5, 12. 12:16, 35, 41. Zc 1:1, 7. 7:1, 8.
reigned. "After an interregnum of eleven years."

2 KINGS 15

1 A.M. 3194. B.C. 810.
In the. ver. 8. 2 K 14:16, 17.
twenty and seventh. "This is the twenty-seventh year of Jeroboam's partnership in the kingdom with his father, who made him consort at his going to the Syrian wars. It is the sixteenth year of Jeroboam's monarchy."
Azariah. ver. 13, 30, etc. 2 K 14:21. 2 Ch +26:1, Uzziah.

2 **Sixteen years old**. 2 Ch 26:3, 4.

3 **he did that which was right**. 2 K 12:2, 3. 14:3, 4. 2 Ch 26:4.

4 **the high places**. ver. 35. 2 K +21:3.

5 A.M. 3239-3246. B.C. 765-758.
the Lord. Jb 34:19.
so that. 2 K +5:1.

and dwelt. Le +13:46.
Jotham. Jg +9:5.
judging. 2 S 8:15. 15:2-4. 1 K 3:9, 28. Ps 72:1.

6   **the rest**. 2 Ch 26:22, 23.
Azariah. ver. 32, 34. Mt 1:8.
they not written. 2 K 14:18. 2 Ch 26:5-15.

7   A.M. 3246. B.C. 758.
Azariah. 2 Ch +26:1, Uzziah.
slept with. 1 K +11:43.

8   A.M. 3231. B.C. 773.
the thirty. "There having been an interregnum for eleven years." ver. 1. 2 K 14:16, 17, 21.
Zachariah. 2 K 14:29.

9   **as his**. 2 K 10:29, 31. 13:2, 11. 14:24.

10   A.M. 3232. B.C. 772.
Shallum. i.e. *restitution; retribution*, **S#7967h**. ver. 13-15. Je 22:11.
Jabesh. i.e. *dry; shame*, **S#3003h**. ver. 13, 14.
smote him. "As prophesied, Am 7:9."
slew him. ver. 14, 25, 30. 2 K 9:24, 31. 1 K 15:28. 16:9, 10. Ho 1:4, 5.

11   **the rest**. 2 K +14:15.

12   A.M. 3120. B.C. 884.
the word. 2 K 10:30.
Thy son. 2 K 13:1, 10, 13. 14:29.
And so. 2 K 9:25, 26, 36, 37. 10:10. Nu 23:19. Zc 1:6. Mk 13:31. Jn 10:35. 19:24, 36, 37. Ac 1:16.

13   A.M. 3232. B.C. 772.
Uzziah. ver. +1, Azariah.
a full month. Heb. a month of days. Ge 41:1. Dt 21:13. 1 K 16:15. Jb 20:15. Ps 55:23. Pr 28:2, 17. Da 10:2.

14   **Menahem**. i.e. *a comforter*, **S#4505h**. ver. 16, 17, 19, 20, 21, 22, 23.
Gadi. i.e. *a Gadite; troop of God*, **S#1424h**. ver. 17.
Tirzah. Nu +26:33.
and smote. ver. +10.

15   **the rest**. ver. +11. 1 K 14:19, 29. 22:39.

16   **Tiphsah**. i.e. *ford*, **S#8607h**. 1 K 4:24.
all the women. 2 K +8:12.

17   A.M. 3232-3243. B.C. 772-761.
nine and thirtieth. ver. 13.

18   **evil in the sight**. ver. +9.
who made Israel. 1 K 14:16.

19   A.M. 3233. B.C. 771.
Pul. i.e. *a lord, elephant*, or *bean*, **S#6322h**. 1 Ch 5:25, 26. Is 9:1. 66:19.
Menahem. 2 K 12:18. 16:8. 17:3, 4. 18:16. Ho 5:13. 8:9, 10. 10:6.
to confirm. 2 K 14:5. Je 17:5.

20   *Menahem*. 2 K 23:35.
exacted. Heb. caused to come forth.
the mighty. Ru 2:1. 2 S 19:32. Jb 1:3.
stayed not. ver. 29. 2 K 17:3, 4. 2 K 18:14-17.

21   A.M. 3232-3243. B.C. 772-761.
the rest. ver. +15.

22   **Menahem slept with**. 1 K +11:43.
Pekahiah. i.e. *opened by Jah*, **S#6494h**. ver. 23, 26.

23   A.M. 3243. B.C. 761.
and reigned two years. 2 K 21:19. 1 K 15:25. 16:8. 22:51. Jb 20:5.

24   A.M. 3243-3245. B.C. 761-759.
evil in. ver. 9, 18.

25   A.M. 3245. B.C. 759.
Pekah. i.e. *opening; open-eyed*, **S#6492h**. ver. 27, 29, 30, 31, 32, 37. 2 K 16:1, 5. 2 Ch 28:6. Is 7:1.
Remaliah. i.e. *whom Jehovah adores*, **S#7425h**. ver. 27, 30, 32, 37. 2 K 16:1, 5. 2 Ch 28:6. Is 7:1, 4, 5, 9. 8:6.
a captain. 2 K 9:5. 1 K 16:9.
conspired. ver. 10. 2 K 9:14.
in the palace of. 1 K 16:18. 2 Ch 36:19.
with Argob. 1 K +4:13.
Arieh. i.e. *the lion*, **S#745h**.

26   **the rest**. ver. +15.

27   A.M. 3245-3265. B.C. 750-739.
the two and fiftieth. ver. 2, 8, 13, 23.
Pekah. ver. 25, 37. Is 7:1, 4, 9.

28   **evil**. or, the evil thing. That is, idolatry. ver. 9, 18. 2 K 13:2, 6. 21:2.

29   **Tiglath-pileser**. i.e. *lord of the Tigris*, **S#8407h**. 2 K 16:7, 10. 1 Ch 5:6, 26. 2 Ch 28:20, 21, Tiglath-pilneser. Is 9:1.
Ijon. 1 K 15:20. 2 Ch 16:4.
Abel-beth-maachah. 1 S +6:18.
Janoah. i.e. *rest*, **S#3239h**. Jsh 16:6, 7, Janohah.
Kedesh. Jsh +15:23.
Hazor. Jsh +15:23.
Gilead. Ge +37:25.
Galilee. Jsh +20:7.
carried them. 2 K 17:6, 23. Le 26:32, 38, 39. Dt 4:26, 27. 28:25, 64, 65. Is 1:7. 7:20.

30   A.M. 3265. B.C. 739.
Hoshea. i.e. *ease, safety*, **S#1954h**. 2 K 17:1, 3, 4, 6. 18:1, 9, 10.
Elah. Ge +36:41.
made. ver. 10, 25.
conspiracy. 2 K +11:14.
and smote. Ho 10:3, 7, 15.
reigned. "After an anarchy for some years, 2 K 17:1. Ho 10:3, 7, 15."
in the twentieth. "In the fourth year of Ahaz, in the twentieth year after Jotham had begun to reign: Usher." ver. 32, 33. 2 K 16:1. 17:1. 2 Ch 27:1. 28:4-6, 16. Is 7:1-9. 8:6.

32   A.M. 3246. B.C. 758.
Jotham. ver. +5, 7.
Uzziah. ver. +1, Azariah.

33   A.M. 3246-3262. B.C. 758-742.
Jerusha. i.e. *a possession*, **S#3387h**. 2 Ch 27:1, Jerushah.
Zadok. 2 S +8:17.

34   **according**. ver. 3, 4. 2 Ch 26:4, 5. 27:2.

35 Howbeit. ver. +4.
    the higher gate. 2 Ch 23:20. 27:3.
36 **the rest**. ver. 6, 7. 2 Ch 27:4-9.
37 A.M. 3262. B.C. 742.
    In those days. 2 K 16:3. Is ch. 38.
    began. 2 K 10:32. 1 S 3:12. Je 25:29. Lk
    21:28.
    to send. Dt 28:48. Ps 78:49. Is 10:5-7. Je
    16:16. 43:10.
    Rezin. i.e. *a prince; stable, firm,* **S#7526h**. 2 K
    16:5, 6, 9. 2 Ch 28:6. Ezr 2:48. Ne 7:50. Is 7:1,
    4, 8. 8:6. 9:11. Ho 5:12, 13.
    Pekah. ver. +27.
38 **Jotham**. 1 K +11:43.
    Ahaz. 1 Ch +8:35.

2 KINGS 16

1 **seventeenth**. 2 K 15:27-30, 32, 33.
    Ahaz. 1 Ch +8:35.
2 **did not**. 2 K 14:3. 15:3, 34. 18:3. 22:2. 1 K
    3:14. 9:4. 11:4-8. 15:3. 2 Ch 17:3. 29:2. 34:2,
    3.
3 **he walked**. 2 K 8:18. 1 K 12:28-30. 16:31-
    33. 21:25, 26. 22:52, 53. 2 Ch 22:3. 28:2-4.
    Ro 1:21-24, 29-31. Ep 4:17-19.
    made his son. Dt +18:10.
    according. 2 K 21:2, 11. Dt 12:31. 1 K 14:24.
    2 Ch 33:2. Ps 106:35. Ezk 16:47.
    abominations. Ge 43:32. 46:34. Ex 8:26.
    cast out. Ex 34:24.
4 **he sacrificed**. 2 K 14:4.
    high places. 2 K +21:3.
    on the hills. 2 K +17:10. Is 65:4. 66:17.
    green tree. Is +57:5.
5 A.M. 3262. B.C. 742.
    Rezin. 2 K 15:37. 2 Ch 28:5-15. Is 7:1, 2, etc.
    but could not. 1 K 11:36. 15:4. Is 7:4-6, 14.
    8:6, 9, 10. 9:6, 7.
6 **recovered**. 2 K 14:22. Dt 2:8.
    and drave. Ex 3:5. Dt 7:1, 22. 28:40.
    Elath. Heb. Eloth. Dt +2:8.
    unto this day. 1 S +6:18.
7 **Tiglath-pileser**. Heb. Tilgath-pileser. 2 K
    15:29. 1 Ch 5:26, etc. 2 Ch 28:20, Tilgath-pil-
    neser.
    I am thy servant. 1 K 20:4, 32, 33.
    and save. Ps 146:3-5. Je 17:5. La 4:17. Ho
    5:13. 7:11. 8:9. 11:5. 12:1. 14:3.
8 **the silver**. ver. 17, 18. 2 K 12:17, 18. 18:15,
    16. 2 Ch 16:2. 28:20, 21.
    to the king. Ps 7:15, 16. Is 7:17. 8:7, 8.
    for a present. or, bribe. Ex 23:8. 1 K 15:19.
9 A.M. 3264. B.C. 740.
    went up. 2 Ch 28:5. Foretold Am 1:3-5.
    Damascus. Heb. Dammesek. ver. 10, 11. Ge
    +14:15.
    Kir. Is 22:6. Am 1:5. 9:7.
    slew Rezin. Is 7:16. 9:11.
10 **saw an altar**. Dt 12:30. 2 Ch 28:23-25. Je

    +10:2. Ezk 23:16, 17. Ro 12:2. 1 P 1:18.
    Urijah. Is 8:2.
    the pattern. Ex 24:4. 39:43. 1 Ch 28:11, 12,
    19. Ps 106:39. Ezk 43:8, 11. Mt 15:6, 9.
11 **built an altar**. 1 K 21:11-13. 2 Ch 26:17, 18.
    Je 23:11. Ezk 22:26. Da 3:7. Ho 4:6. 5:11. Ml
    2:7-9. Ga 1:10.
    Urijah. Is 8:2.
12 **approached**. 1 K 13:1. 2 Ch 26:16-19. 28:23,
    25.
    offered thereon. Nu 18:4-7.
13 **he burnt**. Le ch. 1-3.
    burnt offering. Le +23:12.
    meat offering. Le +23:13.
    drink offering. Le +23:13.
    sprinkled. Le +1:5.
    of his peace offerings. Heb. of the peace
    offerings which were his. Le +23:19. 1 S 24:4.
14 **the brasen**. Ex +38:30.
    from. ver. 10-12.
    on the north side. Out of view (Young).
15 **the morning**. 2 K 3:20. Ex 29:39-41. Nu
    28:2-10. Da 9:21, 27. 11:31. 12:11.
    the king's burnt offering. Le +23:12.
    meat offering. Le +23:13.
    drink offerings. Le +23:13.
    brasen altar. 2 Ch 4:1.
    for me to enquire by. 2 K 18:4. Ge 44:5. 2
    Ch 33:6. Is 2:6. Ho 4:12.
16 **Thus did Urijah**. ver. 11. Ac 4:19. 5:29. 1 Th
    2:4. Ju 11.
17 A.M. 3265. B.C. 739.
    cut off. 2 Ch 28:24. 29:19.
    borders. 1 K 7:23, 27-39. 2 Ch 4:14.
    sea. 2 K 25:13-16. 1 K 7:23-26. 2 Ch 4:15. Je
    52:20.
18 **the covert**. 2 K 11:5. 1 K 10:5. Ezk 46:2.
19 A.M. 3262-3278. B.C. 742-726. 2 K 15:6, 7,
    36, 38. 20:20, 21. 1 K 14:29.
20 A.M. 3278. B.C. 726.
    Ahaz slept with. 1 K +11:43.
    buried. 2 K 21:18, 26. 2 Ch 28:27.
    Hezekiah. i.e. *the might of Jehovah,* **S#2396h**. 2
    K 18:1. 19:1, 14. 20:1. 1 Ch 3:13. 2 Ch 28:27.
    29:1. Pr 25:1. Is 1:1. 37:14. Ho 1:1. Mi 1:1. Zp
    1:1. Mt 1:9, 10, Ezekias.

2 KINGS 17

1 A.M. 3274. B.C. 730.
    In the twelfth year. 2 K 15:30. 18:9.
    Hoshea. "After an interregnum, 2 K 15:30.
    18:9."
2 **but not as the kings**. 2 K 3:2. 10:31. 13:2,
    11. 15:9, 18, 24. 2 Ch 30:5-11.
3 **Shalmaneser**. i.e. *retribution; their peace offer-*
    ing of bondage, **S#8022h**. 2 K 18:9. Ho 10:14,
    Shalman.
    king of Assyria. 2 K 15:19, 29. 16:7. 18:13.
    19:36, 37. Is 7:7, 8. 10:5, 6, 11, 12.

and Hoshea. 2 K +15:30. 16:8. 18:14-16, 31.
gave. Heb. rendered.
presents. or, tribute. Jg +3:15.

4 A.M. 3279. B.C. 725.
found conspiracy. 2 K +11:14. 24:1, 20. Ezk 17:13-19.
So. i.e. conspicuous; lifted up, **S#5471h**.
king of Egypt. 2 K 18:21. Is 30:1-4. 31:1-3. Ezk 17:15.
brought. 2 K 18:14, 15.
bound him. 2 K 25:7. 2 Ch 32:11. Ps 149:7, 8.

5 A.M. 3281-3283. B.C. 723-721.
the king. 2 K 18:9.
three years. 2 K 25:1-3. Je 52:4, 5.

6 A.M. 3283. B.C. 721.
the king of Assyria. 2 K 18:10, 11. Ho 1:6, 9. 13:16, foretold.
carried. Le 26:32, 33, 38. Dt 4:25-28. 28:36, 64. 29:27, 28. 30:18. 1 K 14:15, 16. Am 5:27.
Halah. i.e. painful; fresh anguish, **S#2477h**. 2 K 18:12. 19:12. 1 Ch 5:26. Is 37:12, 13.
Habor. i.e. a joining together, **S#2249h**. 2 K 18:11. 1 Ch 5:26.
Gozan. i.e. cut off; quarry, **S#1470h**. 2 K 18:11. 19:12. 1 Ch 5:26. Is 37:12.
Medes. 1 Ch 5:26. Is 13:17. 21:2. Da 5:28.

7 **sinned.** Dt 31:16, 17, 29. 32:15, etc. Jsh 23:16. Jg 2:14-17. 2 Ch 36:14-16. Ne 9:26. Ps 106:35-41. Ezk 23:2, etc. Ho 4:1-3. 8:5-14.
the Lord. 2 K 16:2. 1 K 11:4. 15:3. 2 Ch 36:5.
which had. Ex +20:2.
and had feared. ver. 35. Je 10:5.

8 **walked.** 2 K 16:3, 10. 21:2. Le 18:3, 27-30. Dt 12:30, 31. 18:9. 1 K 12:28. 16:31-33. 21:26. 106:35. Je +10:2.
of the kings of Israel. Ho 5:11. Mi 6:16.

9 **secretly.** Dt 13:6. 27:15. Jb 31:27. Ezk 8:12. Mt 6:4, 18.
high places. 2 K +21:3.
from the tower. 2 K 18:8. Ho 12:11.

10 **they set.** 2 K 16:4. Ex 34:13. Le 26:1. 1 K 14:23. Is 57:5.
images. Heb. statues. or, standing pillars. 2 K 3:2mg. 10:26mg, 27. 18:4mg. 23:14mg. Ge 35:14, 20. Ex 23:24. 34:13mg. Le 26:1mg. Dt 7:5mg. 12:3. 16:22mg. 1 K 14:23mg. 2 Ch 14:3mg. 31:1mg. Je 43:13mg. Ezk 26:11. Ho 3:4mg. 10:1mg, 2. Mi 5:13mg.
groves. ver. 16. 2 K 13:6. 18:4. 21:3. 23:6, 14. Ex 34:13. Dt 7:5. 12:3. 16:21. Jg 3:7. 6:25. 1 K 14:15, 23. 15:13. 16:33. 18:19. 2 Ch 14:3. 15:16. 17:6. 19:3. 24:18. 33:3, 19. 34:3, 7. Is 17:8. 27:9. Je 17:2. Mi 5:14.
high hill. 2 K 16:4. Dt 12:2. 1 K 14:23. 2 Ch 28:4. Is 57:5, 7. 65:7. Je 2:20. 3:6, 9. 12:12. 13:27. 17:2. Ezk 6:13. 20:28. Ho 4:13.
green tree. Is +57:5.

11 **burnt.** 1 K 13:1. 2 Ch 28:25. Je 44:17.
to provoke. 2 K 21:6. Ps 78:56-58.

12 **whereof.** Ex 20:3-5. 34:14. Le 26:1. Dt 4:19. 5:7-9.
Ye shall not. Dt 4:15-19, 23-25. 12:4.

13 **testified.** Dt 8:19. Je +42:19.
and against Judah. 2 Ch 36:15, 16. Je 3:8-11. 42:19. Ho 4:15.
all. Heb. the hand of all. ver. 23. 2 K 24:2. Dt 4:26. Jsh 23:16. Jg 6:10. 10:11-14. 1 S 12:7-15. 1 K +16:12mg. Is 1:5-15, 21-24. Je 5:29-31. 35:15. Zc 1:3-6.
seers. 1 S +9:9. 1 Ch 29:29.
Turn ye. 2 Ch 7:14. Is 1:16-20. 55:6, 7. Je 7:3-7. 18:11. 25:4, 5. 35:15. Ezk 18:31. Ho 14:1. 2 P 3:9.
keep. Je 7:22, 23. 26:4-6.

14 **would not hear.** 1 S +25:17. Je +7:26.
but hardened. 2 Ch +30:8. Pr 29:1.
and did not believe. Dt 1:32. Ps 78:22, 32. 106:24. He 3:12.

15 **they rejected.** Je 8:9.
his covenant. Ex 24:6-8. Dt 29:10-15, 25, 26. Je 31:32.
testimonies. Dt 6:17, 18. 2 Ch 36:15, 16. Ne 9:26, 29, 30. Je 44:4, 23.
vanity. Dt +32:21, 31.
became vain. Ps 115:8. 1 C 8:4.
concerning whom. ver. 8, 11, 12. Dt 12:30, 31. 2 Ch 33:2, 9. Je +10:2.
not do like them. Ex +23:2. Je +10:2. Mt 6:8.

16 **molten images.** Ex +34:17.
calves. Ex +32:4.
a grove. ver. +10.
worshipped. Dt +4:19.
Baal. Jg +6:25.

17 **they caused.** Dt +18:10.
used divination. Dt +18:10. Is 8:19. 47:9, 12, 13. Mi 5:12. Ga 5:20.
enchantments. 2 K +21:6. Le 19:26.
sold. Le +25:39.
in the sight. ver. 11. 2 K 21:6.

18 **removed.** Dt 29:20-28. 32:21-26. Jsh 23:13, 15. Ps +51:11. Ho 9:3.
the tribe. 1 K 11:13, 32, 36. 12:20. Ho 11:12.
Judah. 1 K 11:32.

19 **Also Judah.** 1 K 14:22, 23. 2 Ch 21:11, 13. Je 2:28. 3:8-11. Ezk 16:51, 52. 22:2-16. 23:4-13.
walked. 2 K 8:18, 27. 16:3.

20 **rejected.** ver. 15. 1 S 15:23, 26. 16:1. Je 6:30. Ro +11:1, 2.
all the seed. 1 Ch 16:13. Ne 9:2. Is 45:25. Je +31:36, 37. 33:24-26. 46:28.
delivered. 2 K 13:3, 7. 15:18-20, 29. 18:9. 2 Ch 28:5, 6. Ne 9:27, 28.
cast. ver. +18. Dt 11:12. Jon 1:3, 10. Mt 25:41.

21 **For he rent.** 1 K 11:11, 31. 14:8. Is 7:17.
they made. 1 K 12:19, 20. 2 Ch 10:15-19.

Jeroboam drave. Dt 13:13. 1 K 12:20, 28-30. 14:16. 2 Ch 11:14, 15.

a great sin. Ge 20:9. Ex 32:21. 1 S 2:17, 24. Ps 25:11. Jn 19:11.

22 walked in all the sins. 2 K +3:3. 10:29, 31. 13:2, 6, 11. 15:9.

23 the Lord. ver. 18, 20.

as he had said. ver. 13. 1 K 13:2. 14:16. Ho 1:4-9. Am 5:27. Mi 1:6.

So was Israel. ver. 6. 2 K 18:11, 12.

24 A.M. 3326. B.C. 678.

the king. Ezr 4:2-10.

Babylon. i.e. *confusion*, **S#894h**. ver. 30. 2 Ch 33:11.

Cutha. i.e. *place of crushing*, **S#3575h**. Ge 10:6. 2 K 17:30.

Ava. i.e. *perverted*, **S#5755h**. ver. 31. 2 K 18:34. 19:13. Dt 2:23. Is 37:13, Ivah.

Hamath. Nu +13:21.

Sepharvaim. i.e. *city of the sun; two-fold enumeration*, **S#5617h**. ver. 31. 2 K 18:34. 19:13. Is 36:19. 37:13.

in the cities thereof. ver. 6. Mt 10:5.

25 they feared. ver. 28, 32, 34, 41. Jsh 22:25. Je 10:7. Da 6:26. Jon 1:9.

the Lord sent. Jg 14:5. 1 S 17:34. 1 K 13:24. Je 5:6. Ezk +5:17. Am 3:12.

26 and placed. ver. 24.

know not. ver. 27. 1 S 8:9. 10:25. Am 3:14.

God of the land. Jg 11:24. 1 K 20:23.

27 one of the priests. Jg 17:13. 1 K 12:31. 13:2. 2 Ch 11:15.

28 in Bethel. 1 K 12:29-32.

taught them. Is 29:13. Mt 15:14.

29 made gods. Ps 115:4-8. 135:15-18. Is 44:9-20. Je 2:28. 10:2-5. Ho 8:5, 6. Mi 4:5. Ro 1:23.

the houses. ver. 32. 2 K 23:19. 1 K 12:31. 13:32.

high places. Le 26:30. 1 K 12:31. 13:32.

in their cities. Je 11:13.

30 Babylon. ver. 24.

Succoth-benoth. i.e. *booths of daughters*. Literally, "the tents of the daughters," **S#5524h**, only here. 2 K 5:18. 19:37. 21:7. Ge 24:67.

Cuth. i.e. *burning, crushing*, **S#3575h**, only here.

Nergal. i.e. *the lamp rolled*, **S#5370h**, only here.

Ashima. i.e. *guiltiness*, **S#807h**, only here.

31 the Avites. ver. 24. Ezr 4:9.

Nibhaz. i.e. *to speak*, **S#5026h**, only here.

Tartak. i.e. *intense darkness; a flat basket*, **S#8662h**, only here.

Sepharvites. i.e. *inhabitants of Sepharvaim*, **S#5616h**, only here.

burnt their children. ver. 17. Le 18:21. Dt 12:30, 31.

Adrammelech. i.e. *honor of the king*. 2 K 19:37.

Anammelech. i.e. *the affliction of the king*, **S#6048h**.

32 made unto themselves. 1 K 12:31. 13:33.

the lowest. 1 K 12:31. 13:33.

the houses. ver. 29. 2 K 23:19. 1 K 13:32.

33 They feared. ver. 41. 1 K 18:21. Ho 10:2. Zp 1:5. Mt 6:24. Lk 16:13.

34 fear not. ver. 25, 27, 28, 33.

whom he named Israel. Ge 32:28. 33:20. 35:10. 1 K 11:31. 18:31. Is 48:1.

35 With whom. ver. 15. Ex 19:5, 6. 24:6-8. Dt 29:10-15. Je 31:31-34. He 8:6-13.

charged them. Ex 20:4, 5. 34:12-17. Dt 4:23-27. 13:1, etc. Jsh 23:7, 16.

not fear other gods. Jg 6:10. Je 10:5.

nor bow. Mt 28:9. Col 3:24.

36 a stretched. Ex +6:6. 9:15. Dt 5:15. Je 32:21. Ac 4:30.

him shall ye fear. Dt +6:2. 12:5, 6, 11, 12. Mt +10:28.

37 the statutes. Le 19:37. Dt 4:44, 45. 5:31-33. 6:1, 2. 12:32. 1 Ch 29:19. Ps 19:8-11. 105:44, 45.

wrote for you. Ex +24:4. Dt 31:9, 11. Ne 9:13, 14. 2 T 3:16.

and ye shall not. ver. +35.

38 the covenant. 1 K 8:9.

ye shall not forget. Dt 4:23. 6:12. 8:11, 14-18.

neither shall. ver. 35. Jg 6:10.

39 the Lord. ver. +36. 1 S 12:24. Is 8:12-14. Je 10:7. Lk 1:50.

he shall deliver. Ne 9:27. Lk 1:71, 74, 75.

40 they did not. Je 13:23.

but they did. ver. 8, 12, 34. Dt 4:28.

41 these nations. ver. 32, 33. Jsh 24:14-20. 1 K 18:21. Zp 1:5. Mt 6:24. Re 3:15, 16.

graven. Ex +20:4.

unto this day. 1 S +6:18. Ezr 4:1-3.

2 KINGS 18

1 A.M. 3278. B.C. 726.

in the third. ver. 9. 2 K 15:30. 17:1.

Hezekiah. 2 K +16:20.

2 Twenty and five years old. A.M. 3278-3306. B.C. 726-698.

Abi. i.e. *my father*, **S#21h**. 2 Ch 29:1, Abijah.

3 right in the sight. 2 K 20:3. Ex 15:26. Dt 6:18. 2 Ch 31:20, 21. Jb 33:27. Ps 119:128. Ro 7:12. Ep 6:1.

according. 2 K 22:2. 1 K 3:14. 11:4, 38. 15:5, 11. 2 Ch 29:2.

4 removed. 2 K +21:3.

brake. Ex +23:24.

images. Heb. statues. 2 K +17:10.

groves. 2 K +17:10.

the brasen serpent. Nu 21:8, 9. Jn 3:14, 15.

unto those days. 2 K 16:15.

Nehushtan. *that is*, a piece of brass (**S#5180h**).

5 trusted. 2 K 19:10. 2 Ch 32:7, 8. Jb 13:15. Ps 13:5. 27:1, 2. 46:1, 2. 84:12. 146:5, 6. Je 17:7, 8. Mt 27:43. Ep 1:12.

after him. 2 K 19:15-19. 23:25. 2 Ch 14:11.
16:7-9. 20:20, 35.

6 he clave. Dt +4:4.
from following him. Heb. from after him. 2
K 17:21.
kept. 2 K 17:13, 16, 19. Je 11:4. Jn 14:15,
21. 15:10, 14. 1 J 2:3. 5:3.

7 And the Lord. 1 S 18:14. 2 Ch 15:2. Is
+43:2. Ac 7:9, 10.
he prospered. 1 S 18:5, 14mg. 2 S 8:6, 14. 2
Ch 31:21. 32:30. Ps +1:3. 60:12.
rebelled. ver. 20. 2 K 16:7.

8 the Philistines. 1 Ch 4:41. 2 Ch 28:18. Is
14:29.
Gaza. Heb. Azzah. Ge +10:19mg.
from the tower. 2 K 17:9. 2 Ch 26:10. Is
5:2.

9 A.M. 3281. B.C. 723.
the fourth year. ver. 1. 2 K 17:4-6.
Shalmaneser. 2 K 17:3, etc. Ho 10:14,
Shalman.

10 A.M. 3283. B.C. 721.
they took it. Ho 13:16. Am 3:11-15. 4:1-3.
6:7. 9:1-4. Mi 1:6-9. 6:16. 7:13.
the king. 2 K 17:6. 19:11. Is 7:8. 8:4. 9:9-21.
10:5, 11. Ho 8:8, 9. 9:3. Am 5:1-3, 6, 25-27.
Ac 7:43.
Halah. 2 K +17:6.
Gozan. 2 K +17:6.

12 they obeyed not. 2 K 17:7-23. Dt 8:20.
11:28. 29:24-28. 31:17. Ne 9:17, 26, 27. Ps
107:17. Is 1:19. Je 3:8. Da 9:6-11. Mi 3:4. 2
Th 1:8. 1 P 2:8. 4:17.
Moses. Nu 12:7. Dt 34:5. Jsh 1:1. 2 T 2:24.
He 3:5, 6.

13 A.M. 3291. B.C. 713.
the fourteenth. 2 Ch 32:1, etc. Is 36:1, etc.
Sennacherib. Heb. Sanherib. i.e. *the thorn
laid waste*. Is 20:1. S#5576h. 2 K 19:16, 20, 36. 2
Ch 32:1, 2, 9, 10, 22. Is 36:1. 37:17, 21, 37.
come up. Is 7:17, etc. 8:7, 8. 10:5. Ho 12:1,
2.

14 I have offended. ver. 7. 1 K 20:4. Pr 29:25.
Lk 14:31, 32.

15 Hezekiah gave. 2 K 12:18. 16:8. 1 K 15:15,
18, 19. 2 Ch 16:2.

16 gold. 1 K 6:31-35. 2 Ch 29:3.
it. Heb. them.

17 A.M. 3294. B.C. 710.
the king. 2 Ch 32:9. Is 20:1. 36:2.
Tartan. i.e. *commander-in-chief; release the
dragon*. S#8661h: ver. 17. Is 20:1. Calmet
remarks, that these are not the names of persons, but of offices: Tartan signifies "he who
presides over gifts or tribute;" Rabsaris, "the
chief of the eunuchs;" and Rabshakeh, "the
chief cup-bearer."
Rabshakeh. S#7262h: ver. 17, 19, 26, 27, 28, 37.
2 K 19:4, 8. Is 36:2, 4, 11, 12, 13, 22. 37:4, 8.
great. Heb. heavy. 2 K 6:14mg.

the conduit of the upper pool. 2 K 20:20.
Jsh +15:7 (En-Rogel). 2 S 5:23. Is 7:3. 22:9-
11. 36:2. Ezk +47:1.

18 Eliakim. i.e. *God raises up*, S#471h. ver. 26, 37.
2 K 19:2. 23:34. 2 Ch 36:4. Ne 12:41. Is
22:20-24. 36:3, 11, 22. 37:2. Mt 1:13. Lk 3:30.
Hilkiah. i.e. *the Lord is my portion*, S#2518h. ver.
26. 2 K 22:4, 8, 14. 23:4, 24. 1 Ch 6:13. 9:11.
26:11. 2 Ch 34:9, 14, 15, 18, 20, 22. 35:8. Ezr
7:1. Is 22:20. 36:3, 22. Je 1:1.
Shebna. i.e. *youth, tenderness*, or *tender age*,
S#7644h. ver. 26, 37. Is 22:15-19. 36:22.
the scribe. *or*, secretary. ver. 37. 2 S
+8:17mg.
Joah. 2 Ch 34:8. Is 36:3.
Asaph. i.e. *a gatherer; collector*, S#623h. ver. 37.
1 Ch 6:39. 9:15. 15:17, 19. 16:5, 7, 37. 25:1,
2, 6, 9. 26:1. 2 Ch 5:12. 20:14. 29:13, 30.
35:15. Ezr 2:41. 3:10. Ne 2:8. 7:44. 11:17, 22.
12:35, 46. Ps 50, title. ch 73-83, titles. Is 36:3,
22.
the recorder. 2 S +8:16mg.

19 Rab-shakeh. ver. 17. Is 36:2.
Thus saith. 2 Ch 32:10. Is 10:8-14. 36:4.
37:13. Da 4:30.
What confidence. ver. 22, 29, 30. 2 K 19:10.
2 Ch 32:7, 8, 10, 11, 14-16. Ps 4:2. Is 36:4, 7.
37:10.

20 sayest. *or*, talkest.
vain words. Heb. word of the lips.
I have counsel and strength for the war.
or, but counsel and strength *are* for the war.
Pr +21:30, 31.
rebellest. ver. 14.

21 trustest. Heb. trustest thee. ver. 24.
the staff. Is 36:6. Ezk 29:6, 7.
bruised. Jg +10:8mg.
upon Egypt. Is 30:2, 7. 31:1-3.
so is Pharaoh. 2 K 17:4. Je 46:17.

22 We trust. ver. 5. Da 3:15. Mt 27:43.
whose high places. ver. +4. 1 C 2:15.

23 pledges. Heb. hostages. 2 K 14:14.
I will deliver. 1 S 17:42-44. 1 K 20:10, 18.
Ne 4:2-5. Ps 123:3, 4. Is 10:13, 14. 36:8, 9.

24 How then. Is 10:8. Da 2:37, 38. 4:22, 37.
thy trust. ver. 21. Dt 17:16. Is 31:1, 3. 36:6,
9. Je 37:7. 42:14-18. Ezk 17:15, 17.
chariots. Ps 20:7, 8.

25 Am I now. 2 K 19:6, 22, etc. 1 K 13:18. 2 Ch
35:21. Is 10:5, 6. Am +3:6. Jn 19:10, 11.

26 in the Syrian language. Ezr 4:7. Is 36:11,
12. Da 2:4.
on the wall. Ge +18:10.

27 eat. 2 K 6:25. Dt 28:53-57. Ps 73:8. La 4:5.
Ezk 4:13, 15.
their own piss. Heb. the water of their feet.
Jg 3:24mg. 1 S 24:3.

28 Rab-shakeh. 2 Ch 32:18. Is 36:13-18.
the king of Assyria. ver. 19. Ezr 7:12. Ps
47:2. Is 10:8-13. Ezk 29:3. 31:3-10. Re 19:16.

29 **saith**. Ps 73:8, 9.
Let not. 2 Ch 32:11, 15. Da 3:15-17. 6:16. Jn 19:10, 11. 2 Th 2:4, 8.
deceive you. ver. 32mg. 2 K 19:10. Ge 3:13.

30 **make you**. ver. 22. 2 K 19:10, 22. Ps 4:2. 11:1. 22:7, 8. 71:9, 11. 125:1, 2. Mt 27:43. Lk 23:35.
this city. 2 K 19:32-34.

31 **Make an agreement with me**. or, Seek my favor. Heb. Make with me a blessing. Jg +3:15.
eat ye. 1 K 4:20, 25. Zc 3:10.
cistern. or, pit. Heb. bor, Ge +37:20. Pr +5:15.

32 **I come**. ver. 11. 2 K 17:6, 23. 24:14-16. 25:11. Pr 18:16.
like your own. Dt 11:12.
corn. Ge +27:28.
honey. Ex +3:8.
persuadeth. or, deceiveth. ver. 29. 2 Ch 32:11, 15.

33 **Hath any**. 2 K 19:12, 13, 17, 18. 2 Ch 32:14-17, 19. Is 10:10, 11. 36:18-20. Da 3:15.
gods of the nations. 2 K 17:26. Jg 11:24. 1 K 20:23.

34 **the gods**. 2 K 19:13. Nu 13:21. 2 S 8:9. Je 49:23.
Hamath. Nu +13:21.
Arpad. i.e. spread out or supported, **S#774h**. 2 K 19:13. Is 10:9. 36:19. 37:13. Je 49:23. Ezk 27:8, 11.
the gods. ver. +33.
Sepharvaim. 2 K 17:24. 19:13.
Hena. 2 K 19:13.
Ivah. i.e. overturning, **S#5755h**. 2 K 17:24-33, Ava. 19:13. Is 36:18, 19. 37:11-13, 18, 19.
have they delivered. 2 K 17:6, 23, 24, 30, 31. 19:12, 13.

35 **Who are**. 2 K 19:17. Da 3:15.
that the Lord. Ex 5:2. 2 Ch 32:15, 19. Jb 15:25, 26. Is 10:15. 37:23-29.

36 **held their peace**. Ge 34:5. Ps +38:13, 14. Pr 9:7. 26:4. Mt 7:6.

37 **Eliakim**. ver. +18.
the scribe. ver. 18mg. 2 S +8:17mg.
the recorder. 2 S +8:16mg.
with their clothes rent. 2 K 5:7. 11:14. 19:1. 22:11, 19. Ge 37:29, 34. 44:13. Le 10:6. 21:10. Nu 14:6. Jsh 7:6. Jg 11:35. 1 S 4:12, 16. 2 S 1:2, 11, 12. 3:31. 13:19, 31. 15:32. 1 K 21:27. 2 K 5:7. 6:30. 2 Ch 34:19. Ezr 9:3, 5. Est 4:1. Jb 1:20. 2:12. Is 33:7. 36:21, 22. 37:1. Je 36:24. Jl 2:13. Mt 26:65. Mk 14:63. Ac 14:14.

2 KINGS 19

1 A.M. 3294. B.C. 710. This chapter is nearly identical to Isaiah 37.
when king. Is 37:1, etc.
he rent. 2 K +18:37.

covered. Jb +16:15.
went into. 2 Ch 7:15, 16. Jb 1:20, 21.

2 **he sent Eliakim**. 2 K +18:18. 22:13, 14.
the elders of the priests. Is 37:2. Je 19:1.
covered with sackcloth. 1 K 20:31.
to Isaiah. 2 Ch 26:22. Mt 4:14. Lk 3:4, Esaias.
the son of Amoz. i.e. a strong one, **S#531h**. ver. 20. 2 K 20:1. 2 Ch 26:22. 32:20, 32. Is 1:1. 2:1. 13:1. 20:2. 37:2, 21. 38:1.

3 **This day**. 2 K 18:29. Ps 39:11. 123:3, 4. Je 30:5-7. Ho 5:15. 6:1.
blasphemy. or, provocation. Nu +14:11. Ezk 35:12.
for the children. Is 26:17, 18. 66:9. Ho 13:13.

4 **the Lord**. Ge 22:14. Dt 32:36. Jsh 14:12. 1 S 14:6. 2 S 16:12.
whom the king. 2 K 18:17-35.
reprove. ver. 22. 1 S 17:45. Ps 50:21. 74:18.
lift up. 2 Ch 32:20. Ps 50:15. Je 33:3. Ezk 36:37. Ro 9:27. Ja 5:16, 17.
the remnant. 2 K 17:5, 6. 18:13. 2 Ch 28:5, 6. Is 8:7, 8. 10:6. Mi +4:7.
left. Heb. found. Est +1:5mg.

6 **Isaiah**. Is 37:6, 7, etc.
Be not afraid. 2 K 6:16. Ex 14:13. Le 26:8. Dt 20:1, 3, 4. Jsh 11:6. 2 Ch 20:15, 17. Is 41:10-14. 51:7, 12, 13.
the servants. 2 K 18:17, 35. Ps 74:18, 23. Re 13:6.

7 **a blast**. Heb. ruach, Ex +15:8. ver. 35-37. Jb +4:9. Ps 11:6. 50:3. Is 10:16-18. Je 51:1.
hear a rumor. Je +49:14.
I will cause. ver. 36, 37. 2 Ch 32:21.

8 **returned**. 1 S 23:27.
Libnah. Nu +33:20.
Lachish. Jsh +10:3.

9 **when he heard**. 1 S 23:27, 28. Is 37:9.
Tirhakah. i.e. inquirer; beholder, **S#8640h**. Is 37:9.
Ethiopia. Ge +2:13.
sent. 2 K 18:17.

10 **Let not**. 2 K 18:5, 29, 30. 2 Ch 32:15-19. Is 37:10-14.

11 **thou hast heard**. ver. 17, 18. 2 K 17:5, etc. 2 Ch 32:13, 14. Is 10:8-11.

12 **Have the gods**. 2 K 18:33, 34.
Gozan. 2 K +17:6.
Haran. Ge +11:26.
Rezeph. i.e. heated stone, **S#7530h**. Is 37:12.
Eden. Ge 2:8. Am +1:5.
Thelasar. i.e. hill of Assur; weariness of the prince, **S#8515h**. Is 37:12, Telassar.

13 **the king**. Nu +13:21.
Arpad. 2 K 18:34. Is 37:13, etc., Arphad.

14 **Hezekiah**. Is 37:14.
spread it. 1 K 8:28-30. Ezr 9:5. Ps 74:10, 11. 91:1, 2. 123:1-4.

15 **prayed**. 2 S 7:18, etc. 2 Ch 14:11. 20:6. 32:20. Da 9:3, 4.

O Lord God. Ge 32:28. 33:20. 1 K 8:23. 1 Ch 4:10. Is 41:17.

dwellest. Ge +3:24. 1 S +4:4.

thou art the God. 2 K 5:15. 1 K 18:39. Is 43:10. 44:6, 8. 45:22. Da 4:34, 35.

thou alone. Is +37:16.

of all. Jg 11:24. 1 K 20:23. Is 36:18.

thou hast made. Ge 1:1. 2:4. Jn +1:3.

16 **bow down**. Ps 31:2. Is 37:17.

open. Zc +12:4.

which hath sent. ver. 4. Ps 79:12. Is 37:4, 17. He 11:26.

17 **Of a truth**. Jb 9:2. Is 5:9. Je 26:15. Da 2:47. Mt 14:33. Lk 22:59. Ac 4:27. 1 C 14:25.

the kings. 2 K 16:9. 17:6, 24. 1 Ch 5:26. Is 7:17, 18. 10:9-11.

18 **have cast**. Heb. have given. Dt +7:5. Is 46:1, 2.

no gods. Is +37:19.

the work. Ps +115:8.

19 **O Lord**. Ex 9:15, 16. Jsh 7:9. 1 S 17:45-47. 1 K 8:43. 18:36, 37. 20:28. Ps 67:1, 2. 83:18. Da 4:34-37.

that thou art. 1 K 18:39.

thou only. Is +37:20. 44:6.

20 **which thou hast**. 2 S 15:31. 17:23.

I have heard. 2 K 20:5. 2 Ch 32:20, 21. Jb 22:27. Ps 50:15. 65:2. Is 58:9. 65:24. Je 33:3. Da 9:20-23. Jn 11:42. Ac 10:4, 31. 1 J 5:14, 15.

21 **the word**. Ps 126:1-3.

The virgin. Je +18:13.

the daughter. Mt +21:5.

shaken her head. Je +18:16.

22 **Whom**. 2 K 18:28-35. Ex 5:2. Ps +31:11. 73:9.

exalted thy voice. Ex 9:17. Pr 30:13. Is 10:15. 14:13, 14. Ezk 28:2-9. Da 5:20-23. 2 C 10:5. 2 Th 2:3, 4.

the Holy One. Is +1:4.

23 **By**. Heb. By the hand of. 2 K 14:25. 1 K +16:12mg.

messengers. 2 K 18:17. 2 Ch 32:17.

With the multitude. 2 K 18:23, 33, 34. Ps 20:7. Is 10:7-11, 14. 37:24, 25. Ezk 31:3, etc. Am 9:3.

tall cedar trees thereof. Heb. tallness of the cedar trees thereof. Nu +24:6.

the forest of his Carmel. or, the forest, and his fruitful field. Is 10:18.

24 **with the sole**. Ex 15:9. 2 S 17:13. 1 K 20:10. Da 4:30.

besieged places. or, fenced places. Is +37:25mg.

25 **Hast thou not**, etc. or, Hast thou not heard how I have made it long ago, and formed it of ancient times? should I now bring it to be laid waste, and fenced cities to be ruinous heaps?

I have done it. Ps 33:11. 76:10. Is 10:5, 6, 15. 37:26, 27. +45:7. 46:10, 11. 54:16. Ac 4:27, 28.

ancient times. Heb. kedem, Mi +5:2.

26 **of small power**. Heb. short of hand. Nu 11:23. 14:9. Ps 48:4-7. 127:1. Je 37:10. 50:36, 37. 51:30, 32.

they were. 1 P +1:24.

the grass. Ps 129:6-8.

27 **I know**. Ps 139:1-11. Je 23:23, 24.

abode. or, sitting. Ex 15:17.

thy going out. Dt 28:6, 19. Ps 121:8. Is 37:28, 29.

28 **thy rage**. Ps 2:1-5. 7:6. 10:13, 14. 46:6. 93:3, 4. Lk 6:11. Jn 15:18, 23, 24. Ac 7:51.

thy tumult. Ps 65:7. 74:4, 23. 83:2.

I will put. Jb 41:2. Ps 32:9. Ezk 29:4. 38:4. Am 4:2. Ja 3:3.

by the way. ver. 33, 36, 37.

29 **a sign**. ver. 21, 31-34. 2 K 20:8, 9. Ex 3:12. 1 S 2:34. Is 7:11-14. Lk 2:12.

Ye shall eat. Le 25:4, 5, 20-22. Is 37:30.

30 **the remnant that**, etc. Heb. the escaping of the house of Judah that remaineth. ver. +4. 2 Ch 32:22, 23.

shall yet again. Ps 80:9. Is 27:6. 37:31, 32.

31 **For**. ver. 4. Je 44:14. Ro 9:27. 11:5.

they that escape. Heb. the escaping. Ge 32:8. 45:7.

the zeal. Is +9:7. Ezk 5:13. 20:9. Zc 1:14. Jn 2:17.

32 **He shall not come**. Is 8:7-10. 10:24, 25, 28-32. 37:33-35.

cast a bank. 2 S 20:15. Ezk 21:22. Lk 19:43, 44.

33 **By the way**. ver. 28, 36.

34 **I will defend**. 2 K 20:6. Ps 46:5, 6. 48:2-8. Is 31:5. 38:6.

for mine. Dt 32:27. Is 43:25. 48:9, 11. Ezk 36:22. Ep 1:6, 14.

my servant. 1 K 11:12, 13. 15:4. Is 9:7. Je 23:5, 6. 33:20, +21, +25, 26.

35 **that night**. Ex 12:29. Da 5:30. 1 Th 5:2, 3.

the angel. Ex 12:29, 30. 2 S 24:16. 1 Ch 21:12, 16. 2 Ch 32:21, 22. Ps 35:5, 6. Ac 12:23.

and smote. Is 10:16-19, 33. 30:30-33. 37:36. Ho 1:7.

when they arose. Ex 12:30. Ps 76:5-7, 10.

36 **Sennacherib**. ver. 7, 28, 33.

Nineveh. Ge +10:11.

37 **Nisroch**. i.e. great eagle, **S#5268h**. ver. 10. 2 K 18:5, 30. Dt 32:31. 2 Ch 32:14, 19. Is 37:37, 38.

Adrammelech. i.e. honor of the king; splendor, **S#152h**. 2 K 17:31. Is 37:38.

Sharezer. i.e. prince of fire, **S#8272h**. Is 37:38. Zc 7:2.

his sons smote. ver. 7. 2 Ch 32:21.

Armenia. Heb. Ararat. **S#780h**. Ge 8:4. Is 37:38. Je 51:27.

Esarhaddon. i.e. gift of fire, **S#634h**. Ezr 4:2. Is 37:38.

2 KINGS 20

1 A.M. 3291. B.C. 713.
In those days. Ge +2:17.
was Hezekiah sick. 2 K 13:14. 2 Ch 32:24, etc. Is 38:1, etc. Jn 11:1-5. Ph 2:27, 30. 2 T +4:20.
the prophet. 2 K 19:2, 20.
Set thine house in order. Heb. Give charge concerning thine house. 2 S 17:23mg. Is 38:1mg.
thou shalt die. Je 18:7-10. Jon 3:4-10.

2 **he turned**. 1 K 8:30. 1 S 20:25. Ps 50:15. Is 38:2, 3. Mt 6:6.

3 **remember**. Ge 8:1. Ne 5:19. 13:14, 22, 31. Ps 25:7. 89:47, 50. 119:49. Is 63:11.
I have walked. 2 K 18:3-6. Ge +5:22. Jb 1:1, 8.
in truth. 2 Ch 31:20, 21. Ps 32:2. 145:18. Je 4:2. Jn 1:47. 2 C 1:12. 1 J 3:21, 22.
perfect. Ru 2:12 (full). 1 K 8:61. 11:4. 15:3, 14. 1 Ch 28:9. 29:9, 19. 2 Ch 16:9. 19:9. 25:2. Ps 37:18. 101:2. Pr 11:1mg. Is 38:3. Mt +5:48.
heart. Jsh 14:8, 9, 14. 1 Ch 12:38. 2 Ch 15:17. 16:9. Ps 119:2, 34. Pr 3:5. Is 38:3. Je 29:13. Jl 2:12. Mt 5:8. 22:37. Ac 8:37. 16:14.
have done. Jb 23:11. He 6:10.
wept sore. Heb. wept with a great weeping. Jg 21:2. 1 S 1:10mg. 2 S 12:21, 22. 13:36mg. 18:33. Ezr 10:1mg. Ps 6:6, 8. 102:9. Is 38:3mg, 14. Je 13:17. 22:10. He 5:7.

4 **afore**. Ge 21:16, 17. 24:12-15. Nu 16:28-33. Jg 15:18, 19. 16:28-30. 1 K 13:6. 18:36-38. 2 Ch 13:14-16. 14:10-12. 20:3-7, 12-17. Ne 2:4-8. Ps +40:17. 138:3. Is 65:24. Da 9:20-23. 10:2-6, 11, 12. Jon 1:13-15. Zc 1:12, 13. Mt 8:5-7, 24-26. 9:18, 19, 23-25, 27-29. 17:14-18. 20:30-34. Mk 1:40-42. 7:32-34. 8:22-25. 10:46-52. Lk 3:21, 22. 17:12-14. Jn 4:49-53. Ac 9:39, 40.
court. or, city. 2 K 22:14. 1 K 7:8.

5 **Turn again**. 2 S 7:3-5. 1 Ch 17:2-4.
the captain. Jsh 5:14, 15. 1 S 9:16. 10:1. 2 S 5:2. 2 Ch 13:12. He 2:10.
the God. 2 Ch 34:3. Is 38:5. 55:3. Mt 22:32.
I have heard. 2 K 19:20. Ps 65:2. 66:19, 20. Lk 1:13.
I have seen. Ps +56:8.
I will heal. ver. 7. Dt 32:39. Jb 33:19, 26. Ps +103:3. Mt 8:2, 3, 17. Ph 2:27.
thou shalt go. ver. 8. Ps 66:13-15, 19, 20. 116:12-14. 118:17-19. Is 38:22. Jn 5:14.

6 **I will add**. Jb 14:5, 6. Ps 116:15. Ac 27:24.
I will defend. 2 K +19:34. 2 Ch 32:22. Is 10:24.

7 **Take a lump**. 2 K 2:20-22. 4:41. Is 38:21. Jn 9:6.
the boil. Ex 9:9. Jb 2:7.

8 **What shall be**. ver. 5. 2 K 19:29. Jg 6:17, 37-40. Is 7:11, 14. 38:22. Ho 6:2.

9 **This sign**. Is 38:7, 8. Mt 16:1-4. Mk 8:11, 12. Lk 11:29, 30.
shadow. Jb 7:2. Is 38:8.

10 **It is a light**. 2 K 2:10. 3:18. Is 49:6. Mk 9:28, 29. Jn 14:12.
go down. Jg 19:8mg. Ps 109:23.
backward. Ge 9:23.

11 **cried unto**. Ex 14:15. 1 K 17:20, 21. 18:36-38. Ac 9:40.
he brought. Jsh 10:12-14. 2 Ch 32:24, 31. Is 38:8.
dial. Heb. degrees. lit. goings up or steps, as in Ex 20:26; 1 K 10:19, 20.

12 A.M. 3292. B.C. 712.
Berodach-baladan. Is 39:1, etc.; Merodach-baladan. i.e. *the mighty lord*, **S#1255h**.
Baladan. i.e. *having power and riches*, **S#1081h**. Is 39:1.
king. 2 Ch 32:31.
Babylon. Ge 10:10. 11:9. Is 13:1, 19. 14:4.
sent letters. 2 S 8:10. 10:2.
for he had heard. Is 39:1.

13 **hearkened**. Dt 7:25. Pr 1:10. 4:14, 15. Is 33:15, 16. Mt 26:41. 1 C 10:13. Ep 6:11-18. Ja 1:12. 4:7. 1 P 5:8, 9.
showed. 2 K 5:11. Ex 5:2. 2 Ch 26:16. 32:25, 27. Est 3:5. Pr 11:2. 15:33. 16:18. 18:12. Is 10:13. 14:13. 39:2. 47:10. Da 4:30. 5:23. Ob 3. Lk 12:15-21.
precious things. or, spicery. Ge 37:25. 43:11. 1 K 10:2, 10, 15, 25.
armor. or, jewels. Heb. vessels. 2 Ch 32:27. Is 39:2mg.
there was nothing. 2 Ch 32:25, 26. Pr 23:5. Ec 7:20.
nor in all. Ge +7:19. 1 K 18:10. Mt 5:29.
dominion. ver. 13. 2 Ch 8:6.

14 **came Isaiah**. Is 39:3-8.
What said. 2 K 5:25, 26. 2 S 12:7, etc. 2 Ch 16:7-10. 25:7-9, 15, 16. Ps 141:5. Pr 25:12. Je 26:18, 19. Am 7:12, 13. Mk 6:18, 19.
a far country. Dt 28:49. Jsh 9:6, 9. Is 13:5.

15 **All the things**. ver. 13. Nu +32:23. Jsh 7:19. Jb 31:33. Pr 28:13. 1 J 1:8-10.

16 **Hear**. 2 K 7:1. 1 K 22:19. Is 1:10. Am 7:16.

17 **shall be carried**. Le 26:19. Is +39:6.

18 **thy sons**. 2 K 24:12. 25:6. 2 Ch 33:11.
they shall be. "Fulfilled, Da 1:3-7." 2 K +8:6mg.

19 **Good**. Le 10:3. Jg +10:15. La 3:22, 31-33, 39.
Is it not good, etc. or, Shall there not be peace and truth, etc.
peace and truth. Est 9:30. Je 33:6. Zc 8:19. Lk 2:10, 14. 1 T 2:1, +2.

20 **he made a pool**. 2 Ch 32:4, 30, 32. Ne 3:16. Is 22:9-11.
a conduit. 2 K 18:17. 2 S 5:23.
the book. 2 K 8:23. 15:6, 26. 16:19. 1 K 14:19. 15:7, 23.

21 A.M. 3306. B.C. 698.

slept with his fathers. 1 K +11:43. 2 Ch 26:23. 32:33.

Manasseh. 2 K 21:1. Ge +41:51mg. Is 38:19.

2 KINGS 21

1 A.M. 3306-3361. B.C. 698-643.

was twelve. 2 K 20:21. 1 Ch 3:13. 2 Ch 32:33. 33:1, etc. Mt 1:10, Manasses.

Hephzibah. Pr 5:19. Is +62:4mg.

2 **And he did**. ver. 7, 16. 2 K 16:2-4. 22:17. 2 Ch 33:2-4.

after the abominations. Le 18:25-29. Dt 12:31. 2 Ch 36:14. Ezk 16:51.

3 **high places**. 2 K 12:3. 14:4. 15:4, 35. 16:4. 17:9. 18:4, 22. 23:13, 20. Le 26:30. Nu 21:28. 22:41. 33:52. Dt 12:13, 14. 1 K 3:2, 3, 4. 11:7. 12:31, 32. 13:33. 14:23. 15:14. 22:43. 2 Ch 11:15. 14:3, 5. 15:17. 17:6. 20:33. 21:11. 28:4. 31:1. 32:12. 33:3, 17. 34:3. Ps 78:58. Is 15:2. 16:12. 36:7. Je 7:31. 12:12. 17:3. 19:5. 32:35. Ezk 6:3, 6. 16:16, 24, 25, 39. 20:29. 36:2. 43:7. Ho 10:8. Mi 1:5.

which. 2 K 18:4, 22. 2 Ch 32:12. 34:3.

he reared. 2 K 10:18-20. 1 K 16:31-33. 18:21, 26.

a grove. i.e. Asherah or Astarte. 2 K +17:10. Is +66:17.

Ahab. 2 K 8:18, 27. Mi 6:16.

the host of heaven. Dt +4:19. Jb 31:26, 28. Je 7:18. 44:17, 19. Ezk 8:15, 16.

4 **he built**. 2 K 16:10-16. Je 32:34.

In Jerusalem. Ex 20:24. Dt 12:5. 2 S 7:13. 1 K 8:29. 9:3. Ps 78:68, 69. 132:13, 14.

5 **in the two courts**. 2 K 23:4, 6. 1 K 6:36. 7:12. 2 Ch 33:5, 15. Ezk 40:28, 32, 37, 47. 42:3. 43:5. 44:19.

6 A.M. 3321. B.C. 683.

pass through the fire. Dt +18:10. Is 65:3. Mi 6:7.

observed times. or, observed clouds. **S#6049h**: Ge 9:14 (bring a cloud). Le 19:26, 31. Dt +18:10, 14. Jg 9:37mg. 2 Ch 33:6. Is 2:6 (soothsayers). 57:3 (sorceress). Je 27:9 (enchanters). Mi 5:12 (soothsayers).

enchantments. **S#5172h**. 2 K 17:17. Ge +30:27 (learned by experience). 44:5, 15. Le 19:26. Nu 23:23. 24:1. Dt +18:10. 1 K 20:33 (observe). 2 Ch 33:6.

familiar spirits. Dt +18:11.

wizards. **S#3049h**. 2 K 23:24. Le 19:31. 20:6, 27. Dt 18:11. 1 S 28:3, 9. 2 Ch 33:6. Is 8:19. 19:3.

wrought. 2 K 24:3, 4. Ge 13:13.

7 A.M. 3306-3327. B.C. 698-677.

he set. 2 K 23:6. 2 Ch 33:7, 15.

graven image. Ex +20:4.

In this house. ver. 4. 2 K 23:27. 2 S 7:13. 1 K 8:29, 44. 9:3, 7. 2 Ch 7:12, 16, 20. Ne 1:9. Ps 74:2. 78:68, 69. 132:13, 14. Je 32:34.

for ever. Heb. *olam*, Ex +12:24.

8 **will I make**. 2 K 18:11. 2 S 7:10. 1 Ch 17:9. 2 Ch 33:8.

only if they. Le 26:3, etc. Dt 5:28, 29. 28:1, etc. Jsh 23:11-13. Ps 37:3. 81:11-16. Is 1:19. Je 7:3-7, 23. 17:20-27. Ezk 22:2-16. 33:25-29.

9 **they hearkened not**. 2 Ch 36:16. Ezr 9:10, 11. Ne 9:26, 29, 30. Ps 81:11. Da 9:6, 10, 11. Lk 13:34. Jn 15:22. Ja 4:17.

seduced. 1 K 14:16. 2 Ch 33:9. Ps 12:8. Pr 29:12. Ho 5:11. Re 2:20.

more evil. Je 2:10, 11. Ezk 16:47, 51, 52.

10 **the Lord spake by**. 2 Ch 33:10. 36:15. Ne 9:26, 30. Mt 23:34-37.

11 **Because**. 2 K 23:26, 27. 24:3, 4. Je 15:4.

above all. ver. 9. 1 K 21:26. Ezk 16:3, 45.

Amorites. Ge +10:16.

made Judah. ver. 9. 1 K 14:16. 15:30. 16:19.

12 **I am bringing**. 2 K 22:16. Da 9:12. Mi 3:12.

whosoever. 1 S 3:11. Is 28:16. Je 19:3. Am 3:2. Mt 24:21, 22. Lk 23:28, 29. Re 6:15-17.

13 **I will stretch**. 2 K 17:6. Is 10:22. 28:17. 34:11. La 2:8. Ezk 23:31-34. Am 7:7, 8. Zc 1:16.

the plummet. 2 K 10:11. 1 K 21:21-24.

I will wipe. 1 K 14:10. Is 14:23. Je 25:9. Ezk 24:10, 11. Re 18:21-23.

wiping it, and turning it upside down. Heb. he wipeth and turneth it upon the face thereof.

14 **And I will**. Ps 37:28. 89:38, etc. Is +54:7.

the remnant. 2 K 19:4, 30, 31. 24:2. 2 Ch 36:16, 17. 23:33.

deliver. Le 26:17, 36-38. Dt 4:26, 27. 28:25, 31-33, 48. Jg 2:14, 15. Ne 9:27-37. Ps 71:1-7. 106:40-43. Is 10:6. La 1:5, 10.

15 **have provoked**. Is 65:3.

since the day. Dt 9:24. 31:27, 29. Jg 2:11-13. Ps 106:34-40. Ezk 16:15, etc. 20:4, 13, 21, 23, 30. 23:3, 8, etc. Da 9:5-11.

16 **Manasseh**. Nu 35:33. Dt +19:10. Je 2:34. 15:4. 19:4. Mt 23:30, 31. Lk 13:34. He 11:37.

one end to another. Heb. mouth to mouth. 2 K +10:21mg.

beside his sin. ver. 7, 11. Ex 32:31. 1 K 14:15, 16. 2 Ch 33:9.

17 **the rest**. 2 K +20:20, 21. 2 Ch 33:1-20.

18 A.M. 3361. B.C. 643.

slept with his fathers. 2 K 24:6. 1 K +11:43.

and was buried. 1 K +11:43.

the garden. Jn 19:41.

Uzza. ver. 26. 2 S +6:3.

Amon. Ne +7:59.

19 A.M. 3361-3363. B.C. 643-641.

Amon. Ne +7:59.

two years. 2 K 15:23, 25. 16:8. 22:51.

Meshullemeth. i.e. *one recompensed*, **S#4922h**.

Haruz. i.e. *sharp pointed, diligent*, **S#2743h**.

Jotbah. i.e. *goodness; pleasantness*, **S#3192h**. See **S#3193h**: Nu 33:33, 34. Dt 10:7.

20 **as his father**. ver. 2-7. Nu 32:14. 2 Ch 33:22, 23. Mt 23:32. Ac 7:51.

22 **he forsook**. 2 K 22:17. Dt 32:15. 1 K 11:33. 1 Ch 28:9. Je 2:13. Jon 2:8.

23 A.M. 3363. B.C. 641.
the servants. 2 K 12:20. 14:19. 15:25, 30. 1 K 15:27. 16:9. 2 Ch 33:24, 25.

24 **the people of the land slew**. 2 K 14:5.
made Josiah. 2 K 11:17. 14:21. 1 S 11:15. 2 S 5:3. 1 K 12:1, 20. 2 Ch 22:1. 26:1. 33:25.

25 **the rest**. ver. 17. 2 K 20:20.

26 **sepulchre**. Heb. qeburah, Ge +35:20.
in the garden. ver. +18. 2 S 6:6-8.
Josiah. 1 K +13:2.

2 KINGS 22

1 A.M. 3363-3394. B.C. 641-610.
Josiah. 1 K +13:2.
eight years old. 2 K 11:21. 21:1. Ps 8:2. Ec 10:16. Is 3:4.
Jedidah. i.e. beloved; amiable, **S#3040h**.
Adaiah. Ne +11:5.
Boskath. i.e. loftiness; stony region, **S#1218h**. Jsh 15:39, Bozkath.

2 **right**. 2 K 16:2. 18:3. 2 Ch 29:2. Pr 20:11.
walked. Ge +5:22. 1 K 11:38. 2 Ch 17:3.
turned. Jsh +1:7. Ezk 18:14-17.

3 A.M. 3380. B.C. 642.
in the. 2 Ch 34:3-8, etc.
Shaphan. i.e. a coney, S#8227. ver. 8, 9, 10, 12, 14. 2 K 25:22. 2 Ch 34:8, 15, 16, 18, 20. Je 26:24. 29:3. 36:10-12. 39:14. 40:5, 9, 11. 41:2. 43:6. Ezk 8:11.
Azaliah. 2 Ch +34:8.
Meshullam. 1 Ch +9:12.

4 **Hilkiah**. 2 K +18:18.
sum the silver. 2 K 12:4, 8-11. 2 Ch 24:8-12. Mk 12:41, 42.
the keepers. 1 Ch 9:19. 26:13-19. 2 Ch 8:14. Ne 11:19. Ps 84:10.
door. Heb. threshold. 2 K +12:9mg.

5 **deliver**. 2 K 12:11-14.
to repair. 2 K 12:5. 2 Ch 24:7, 12, 13, 27. Ezr 3:7.
the breaches. 2 K 12:8, 12.

6 **carpenters**. or, artificers. Ex 28:11. 35:35. 38:23.
builders. 2 K 12:11. Ge 4:17. 1 K 5:18. 6:12.
masons. or, repairers of the wall. 2 K 12:12. Is 58:12. Ezk 22:30.

7 **Howbeit**. 2 K 12:15. 2 Ch 24:14.
they dealt faithfully. 2 K +12:15. Ex 36:5, 6.

8 **I have found**. 2 K 14:6. Dt 31:24-26. 2 Ch 34:14, 15, etc. Je 2:8. 2 T 3:16.

9 **Shaphan**. ver. +3, 12.
the scribe. 2 K +18:18.
gathered. Heb. melted. Ezk 22:20. or, poured out. 2 Ch 34:17. Jb 10:10.

10 **Shaphan**. Dt 31:9-13. 2 Ch 34:18. Ne 8:1-7, 14, 15, 18. 13:1. Je 36:6, 15, 21.
the king. Dt 17:18-20. Je 13:18. 22:1, 2.

11 **that he rent**. ver. 19. 2 K +18:37. Jon 3:6, 7.

12 **the king**. 2 K 19:2, 3. 2 Ch 34:19-21. Is 37:1-4.
Ahikam. i.e. brother of a withstander or the enemy, **S#296h**. ver. 9, 14. 2 K 25:22. 2 Ch 34:20. Je 26:22, 24. 39:14. 40:5. 41:1. 43:6.
Achbor. Ge +36:38. 2 Ch 34:20, Abdon.
Michaiah. i.e. who is like Jah, **S#4320h**. or, Micah. Jg 17:1. 2 Ch 34:20. Ne 12:35, 41. Je 26:18.
Asahiah. ver. 14.

13 **enquire**. 2 K 3:11. 1 K 22:7, 8. 1 Ch 10:13, 14. Ps 25:14. Pr 3:6. Je 21:1, 2. 37:17. Ezk 14:3, 4. 20:1-3. Am 3:7.
great. Ex 20:5. Dt 4:23-27. 17:18. 29:23-28. 31:9-13, 17, 18. Ne 8:8, 9. 9:3. Ps 76:7. Da 9:5, 6. Na 1:6. Ro 3:20. 4:15. 7:9. Re 6:17.
because our fathers. 2 Ch 29:6. 34:21. Ps 106:6. Je 16:12. 44:17. La 5:7. Da 9:8, 10. Ja 1:22-25.
not hearkened. Dt 27:26. Ja 2:10.

14 **Asahia**. i.e. wrought of Jah, **S#6222h**. ver. 12. 2 Ch +34:20, Asaiah.
Huldah. i.e. a mole or weasel, **S#2468h**. 2 Ch 34:22.
prophetess. Ex +15:20.
Shallum. 2 K +15:10.
Tikvah. i.e. expectation; hope, **S#8616h**. 2 Ch 34:22, Tikvath. Ezr 10:15.
Harhas. i.e. extremely poor; glittering, **S#2745h**. 2 Ch 34:22, Hasrah.
wardrobe. Heb. garments. 2 K 10:22. Ne 7:72.
college. or, second part. 2 Ch 34:22mg. Ne 11:9. Zp 1:10.

15 **Thus saith**. 2 K 1:6, 16. Je 23:28.

16 **Behold**. 2 K 20:17. 21:12, 13. 2 Ch 34:24, 25.
all the words. 2 K 25:1-4. Le 26:15, etc. Dt 28:15, etc. 29:18-23. 30:17, 18. 31:16-18. 32:15-26. Jsh 23:13, 15. Da 9:11-14.

17 **have forsaken**. 2 K 12:15. Ex 32:34. Dt 29:24-28. Jg 3:7, 8. 1 K 9:6-9. 2 Ch 31:12. Ne 9:26, 27. Ps 106:35-42. Je +1:16. Da 9:11-14. Lk 16:10. 1 C 4:2. 3 J 5.
the works. Ps 115:4-8. Is 2:8, 9. 44:17-20. 46:5-8. Mi 5:13.
therefore. 1 Th 2:16.
shall not be. Dt 32:22. 2 Ch 36:16. Zp 1:18. Mt +3:12. +25:41.

18 **the king**. 2 Ch 34:26-28.
thus shall ye. Is 3:10. Ml 3:16, 17.

19 **heart was tender**. 1 S 24:5. Ps +51:17. 119:120. Is 46:12. Je 36:24, 29-32. Ro 2:4, 5. Ja 4:6-10.
humbled. Ex 10:3. Le 26:40, 41. 1 K 21:29. 2 Ch 33:12, 19, 23. Mi 6:8. 1 P 5:5, 6.
a desolation. Le 26:31, 32. Dt 29:23.

curse. Je +26:6.

hast rent. ver. +11.

wept. Nu 25:6. Ezr 9:3, 4. Ne 8:9. Ps +119:136.

I also have. 2 K 19:20. 20:5.

20 **I will gather**. Ge +25:8. Dt 31:16. 1 Ch 17:11. 2 Ch 34:28.

thou shalt. 2 Ch 35:22-24. Is 57:1.

be gathered. 2 K 23:29, 30. Ps 37:37. Is 57:1, 2. Je 22:10, 15, 16.

grave. Heb. *qeber*, Ge +23:4.

2 KINGS 23

1 **the king sent**. 2 S 6:1. 2 Ch 29:20. 30:2.

elders. Jsh +20:4.

2 **both small and great**. Heb. from small even unto great. Ge 19:11. 1 S 5:9. 30:2. 2 Ch 15:13. Est 1:5. Jb 3:19. Ps 115:13. Ac +8:10. 26:22. Re 11:18. 19:5. 20:12.

he read. Dt 31:10-13, 28. 2 Ch 17:9. Ne 8:1-8. 9:3. 13:1.

the book. 2 K 22:8. Dt 31:26. 1 K 8:9.

3 **stood**. 2 K 11:14, 17. 2 Ch 23:13. 34:31, 32.

made a covenant. Ex 24:7, 8. Dt 5:1-3. 29:1, 20-15. Jsh 24:25. 2 Ch 15:12-14. 23:16. 29:19. Ezr 10:3. Ne 9:38. 10:28, etc. Je 50:5. He 8:8-13. 12:24. 13:20.

to walk. Ge +5:22. Dt 8:19.

his commandments. Dt 4:45. 5:1. 6:1. Ps 19:7-9.

with all their heart. Mt +22:37.

And all. Ex 24:3. Jsh 24:24. 2 Ch 34:32, 33. Ec 8:2. Je 4:2.

soul. Heb. *nephesh*, Ge +34:3.

4 **priests of the second order**. 1 Ch 24:14-19. Mt 26:3. 27:1.

the keepers. 2 K +22:4. 1 Ch 26:1-19.

door. 2 K +12:9mg.

to bring. 2 K 21:3, 7. 2 Ch 33:3, 7. 34:3, 4.

Baal. Jg +6:25. Is 27:9.

Kidron. 2 S +15:23.

Bethel. Ge +12:8. Ho 4:15.

5 **put down**. Heb. caused to cease.

the idolatrous priests. Heb. Chemarim. Ho 10:5mg. "Foretold, Zp 1:4, 5."

planets. *or*, twelve signs, *or* constellations. Jb 38:32mg.

all the host. Dt +4:19. Ezk +8:16.

6 **the grove**. Or rather, *Ashera*, or Astarte. 2 K +17:10.

to powder. Ex 32:20.

and burned. Dt +7:5.

the graves. Heb. *qeber*, Ge +23:4. 2 K 10:27. 2 Ch 34:4.

7 **the sodomites**. Ge 19:4, 5. Dt +23:17mg. 1 K 14:24. 15:12. 22:46. Jb 36:14mg. Ro 1:26, 27.

where. Ex 35:25, 26. Ezk 8:14. 16:16. Ho 2:13.

hangings. Heb. houses.

8 **Geba**. 1 S +13:3.

Beer-sheba. Ge +21:31.

9 **the priests**. Ezk 44:10-44. Ml 2:8, 9.

but they did. 1 S 2:36. Ezk 44:29-31.

10 **Topheth**. i.e. *the wonder*, S#8612h. Le +18:21. 1 K 11:7, 33. Ps 106:37, 38. Je +7:31. Ezk 20:31. 23:37. Am 5:26. Ac 7:43.

the valley of the children of Hinnom. Jsh +15:8. Mt 5:22.

might make. Dt +18:10.

to Molech. ver. 13, Milcom. Le +18:21.

11 **the sun**. ver. 5. 2 Ch 34:4. Ezk +8:16.

chamber. 1 S 9:22. 1 Ch 9:26, 33. 2 Ch 31:11. Ezr 8:29. 10:6. Ne 10:37-39.

Nathan-melech. i.e. *ruled by conscience*, S#5419h.

chamberlain. *or*, eunuch, *or* officer. 2 K +8:6mg.

12 **on the top**. Dt +22:8.

upper chamber. Jg +3:20. 2 S 18:33.

which Manasseh. 2 K 21:5, 21, 22. 2 Ch 33:5, 15.

brake them down from thence. *or*, ran from thence.

cast. ver. +6.

13 **the mount of corruption**. *that is*, the mount of Olives. 1 K 11:7.

Solomon. 1 K 11:7. Ne 13:26.

Ashtoreth. S#6252h. Jg +2:13.

Chemosh. Nu +21:29.

Milcom. S#4445h. 2 S 12:30rmg. 1 K 11:5, 33. 1 Ch 8:9. Je 49:1mg. Zp 1:5, Malcham.

14 **he brake**. Ex +23:24.

images. Heb. statutes. 2 K +17:10mg.

groves. Dt 7:5.

the bones of men. ver. 16. Nu 19:11, 16, 18. Je 8:1, 2. Ezk 39:12-16. Mt 23:27, 28.

15 **the altar**. 2 K 10:31. 1 K 12:28-38. 14:16. 15:30. 21:22.

stamped. ver. +6.

16 **sepulchres**. Heb. *qeber*, Ge +23:4.

in the mount. Jsh 24:30, 33.

burned. 1 K 13:1, 2, 32. Mt 24:35. Jn +10:35.

who proclaimed. 2 K 21:19-22, 24.

17 **What title**. Je 31:21. Ezk 39:15.

It is the sepulchre. Heb. *qeber*, Ge +23:4.

of the man of God. Dt +33:1. 1 K 13:1, 30, 31.

18 **alone**. Heb. to escape. 1 S 20:29.

the bones of the prophet. 1 K 13:1-22, 31.

19 **the houses**. 2 K 17:9. 1 K 12:31. 13:32.

the cities. 2 Ch 30:6-11. 31:1. 34:6, 7.

the kings. 2 K 8:18. 1 K 16:33. Mi 6:16.

to provoke the Lord. 2 K 17:16-18. 21:6. Ps 78:58. Je 7:18, 19. Ezk 8:17, 18.

20 **he slew**. *or*, he sacrificed. 2 K 10:25. 11:18. Ex 22:20. Dt 13:5. 1 K 13:2. 18:40. Is 34:6. Zc 13:2, 3.

burned. 2 Ch 34:5.

21 **Keep**. 2 Ch 35:1, etc.
passover. Le +23:5.
as it is written. Ex 12:3, etc. Le 23:5-8. Nu 9:2-5. 28:16-25. Dt 16:1-8.
22 **Surely**. 2 Ch 35:18, 19.
passover. Le +23:5.
of the kings. 2 Ch 30:1-3, 13-20. 35:3-17.
24 A.M. 3381. B.C. 623.
Moreover. "His eighteenth year ending."
familiar spirits. Dt +18:11. Re 22:15.
wizards. 2 K +21:6.
images. or, teraphim. Ge +31:19mg.
idols. 2 K 17:12. 21:11, 21. Le 26:30. Dt 29:17. 1 K 15:12. 21:26. Je 50:2. Ezk 6:4. 20:8, 18. 22:3. 30:13.
abominations. Dt 29:17.
that he might. Le 19:31. 20:27. Dt 18:10-12. Is 8:20. Ro 3:20. Ja 1:25.
the book. 2 K +22:8-13. 2 Ch +34:14-19.
25 A.M. 3363-3394. B.C. 641-610.
unto him. 2 K 18:5.
that turned. ver. +3. 1 K 15:5.
soul. Heb. nephesh, Ge +34:3.
according. Ne 10:29. Ml 4:4. Jn 1:17. 7:19.
26 **Notwithstanding**. 2 K 21:11-13. 22:16, 17. 24:2, 4. Ex 32:34. 2 Ch 36:16. Je 3:7-10. 15:1-4.
fierceness. 2 Ch +24:18. 30:8.
provocations. Heb. angers. 1 K 21:22.
27 **I will remove**. 2 K 18:11. 21:13. 24:3. 25:11. Dt 29:27, 28. Je 2:19. 3:11. Ezk 23:32-35.
out of my sight. Ps +51:11. La 2:7.
My name. 2 K 21:4, 7. 1 K 8:29. 9:3.
28 **the rest**. 2 K +20:20. 2 Ch 35:26, 27.
29 A.M. 3394. B.C. 610.
Pharaoh-nechoh. S#6549h. ver. 33, 34, 35. 2 Ch 35:20-24. Je 46:2.
Euphrates. Ge +2:14.
Josiah went. 2 Ch 35:20-23.
slew him. 2 K 22:20. Ec 8:14. 9:1, 2. Is 57:1, 2. Ro 11:33.
Migiddo. Jsh +12:21.
he had seen him. 2 K 14:8, 11.
30 **servants**. 2 K 9:28. 1 K 22:33-38. 2 Ch 35:24.
sepulchre. Heb. qeburah, Ge +35:20 (S#6900h).
the people. 2 K 14:21. 21:24. 2 Ch 36:1, 2, etc.
Jehoahaz. 1 K 13:3, etc. 1 Ch 3:15, Shallum. Je 22:11, Shallum.
anointed. 1 S 9:14-16.
31 **Jehoahaz**. 1 Ch 3:15. Je 22:11, Shallum.
Hamutal. i.e. kinsman of the dew, S#2537h. 2 K 24:18. Je 52:1.
Libnah. Nu +33:20.
32 **he did**. 2 K 21:2-7, 21, 22.
33 **put him**. 2 Ch 36:3, 4. Ezk 19:3, 4.
Riblah. 2 K 25:6. Nu 34:11. Je 39:5, 6. 52:9, 10, 26, 27.
Hamath. Nu +13:21.

that he might not reign. or, because he reigned.
put, etc. Heb. set a mulct upon the land. or, a fine. 2 K 18:14. Ex 21:22. 2 Ch 36:3. Pr 19:19.
34 **Eliakim**. 2 K +18:18.
the son. 1 Ch 3:15.
turned. 2 K 24:17. Ge 41:45. Da 1:7.
Jehoiakim. 1 Ch +3:15. Mt 1:11, Jakim.
he came. Je 22:11, 12. Ezk 19:3, 4.
35 **the silver**. ver. 33.
taxed. 2 K 15:19, 20. Le 27:8, 12, 14.
exacted. Ex 3:7.
36 A.M. 3394-3405. B.C. 610-599.
Jehoiakim. 1 Ch +3:15.
twenty and five years old. ver. 31.
Zebudah. i.e. endowed, S#2080h.
Pedaiah. i.e. whom Jehovah delivers; ransomed; whom Jehovah redeemed. S#6305h: ver. 36. 1 Ch 3:18, 19. 27:20. Ne 3:25. 8:4. 11:7. 13:13.
Rumah. i.e. height, S#7316h.
37 **he did**. Je 22:13-17. 26:20-23. 36:23-26, 31. Ezk 19:5-9.
all that. 2 Ch 28:22-25. 33:4-10, 22, 23.

2 KINGS 24

1 **his days**. 2 K 17:5. 2 Ch 36:6, etc. Je 25:1, 9. 46:2. Da 1:1.
Nebuchadnezzar. i.e. Nebo is prince of gods, or god of fire, or prince of the god Mercury. Je 39:1, 11, Nebuchadrezzer. 43:10. Ezk 29:18. S#5019A: ver. 1, 10, 11. 2 K 25:1, 8, 22. 1 Ch 6:15. 2 Ch 36:6, 7, 10, 13. Ezr 2:1. Je 27:6, 8, 20. 28:3, 11, 14. 29:1, 3. 34:1. 39:5. Da 1:1. See also S#5019B: Ezr 1:7. Ne 7:6. Est 2:6. Da 1:18. 2:1. Also S#5019C: Je 21:2, 7. 22:25. 24:1. 25:1, 9. 29:21. 32:1, 28. 35:11. 37:1. 39:1, 11. 43:10. 44:30. 46:2, 13, 26. 49:28, 30. 50:17. 51:34. 52:4, 12, 28, 29, 30. Ezk 26:7. 29:18, 19. 30:10. See also S#5020h: Ezr 5:12, 14. 6:5. Da 2:28, 46. 3:1-3, 5, 7, 9, 13, 14, 16, 19, 24, 26, 28. 4:1, 4, 18, 28, 31, 33, 34, 37. 5:2, 11, 18.
2 **the Lord**. 2 K 6:23. 13:20, 21. Dt 28:49, 50. 2 Ch 33:11. Jb 1:17. Is 7:17. 13:5. Je 35:11. Ezk 19:8.
bands. or, troops. Ge 49:19.
Chaldees. 2 K 25:4. Ge 11:31. 15:7. Je 35:11.
Syrians. 2 K 6:23. Je 35:11.
Ammon. 1 S 11:1.
according. 2 K 20:17. 21:12-14. 23:27. Is 6:11, 12. Je 25:9. 26:6, 20. 32:28. Mi 3:12.
his. Heb. the hand of his. 1 K +16:12mg.
3 **Surely**. 2 K 18:25. Ge 50:20. 2 Ch 24:24. 25:16. Is 10:5, 6. 45:7. 46:10, 11. Am +3:6.
remove them. 2 K 23:26, 27. Le 26:33-35. Dt 4:26, 27. 28:63. 29:28. Jsh 23:15. Je 15:1-4. Mi 2:10.
for the sins. 2 K 21:2-11. Ex 20:5.
4 **for the innocent**. Nu 35:33. Dt +19:10. Je 2:34. 19:4.

he filled. Ps 106:38.
blood. Le +20:9.
which. Je 15:1, 2. La 3:42. Ezk 33:25.
5 **the rest**. 2 Ch 36:8. Je 22:13-17. ch. 26. 36.
6 A.M. 3405. B.C. 599.
slept. 2 K 9:35. 1 K +11:43. 2 Ch 36:6, 8. Je 22:18, 19. 36:30. Ro 6:4.
Jehoiachin. ver. +8. Je 22:30.
7 **the king**. Je 37:5-7. 46:2.
river of Egypt. Ge +15:18.
Euphrates. Ge +2:14.
8 **Jehoiachin**. i.e. *the Lord will establish.* Je +24:1, Jeconiah. Je +22:24, Coniah. Mt 1:11, 12, Jechonias. **S#3078h**: 2 K 24:6, 12, 15. 25:27. 2 Ch 36:8, 9. Je 52:31.
eighteen years. ver. 15. 2 Ch 36:9.
three months. 1 K +2:11. 2 Ch 36:9.
Nehushta. i.e. *brass,* **S#5179h**. ver. 15.
Elnathan. i.e. *God hath given,* **S#494h**. Ezr 8:16. Je 26:22. 36:12, 25.
9 **evil**. 1 K 15:26.
according. ver. 19. 2 Ch 36:12.
10 **At that time**. Da 1:1, 2.
was besieged. Heb. came into siege. Dt +20:19.
12 **Jehoiachin**. ver. +8. Je 38:17, 18. Ezk 17:12.
officers. *or,* eunuchs. 2 K +8:6mg.
took him. 2 K 25:27. Je 52:28, 31.
eighth year. "Nebuchadnezzar's eighth year." Je 25:1. 52:28.
13 **he carried**. Is +39:6, 7.
and cut. 2 K 16:17. 2 Ch +4:19.
which Solomon. 1 K 7:48-50. 2 Ch 4:7-22.
as the Lord had said. 2 K 20:17. Je 20:5.
14 **all**. Ge +7:19.
Jerusalem. 2 Ch 39:9, 10. Je 24:1-5. 52:28. Ezk 1:1, 2.
ten thousand. Je 52:28.
craftsmen. Ex 28:11. 1 S 13:19-22. Je 24:1.
and smiths. ver. 16. Je 24:1. 29:2.
the poorest sort. 2 K 25:12. Je 39:10. 40:7. 52:16. Ezk 17:14.
15 **he carried**. ver. +8. 2 Ch 36:10. Est 2:6. Je 22:24-28.
officers. *or,* eunuchs. 2 K +8:6mg.
16 **seven thousand**. Je 29:2. 52:28.
apt for war. Dt 20:20. 1 K 12:21.
brought captive to Babylon. Je 24:1. 29:1, 2. 52:28. Ezk 17:12.
17 **the king**. 2 Ch 36:10, 11. Je 37:1. 52:1.
Mattaniah. i.e. *gift of Jah,* **S#4983h**. 1 Ch 9:15. 25:4, 16. 2 Ch 20:14. 29:13. Ezr 10:26, 27, 30, 37. Ne 11:17, 22. 12:8, 25, 35. 13:13.
his father's brother. Le 10:4. 1 Ch 3:15, 16. 2 Ch 36:10.
changed. 2 K 23:34. Ge 41:45. 2 Ch 36:4. Da 1:7.
18 A.M. 3405-3416. B.C. 599-588.
Zedekiah. 1 K +22:11.

Hamutal. 2 K 23:31.
Libnah. 2 K 23:31.
19 **And he did**. 2 K 23:37. 2 Ch 36:12. Je 24:8. ch. 37; 38. Ezk 21:25.
20 **through**. 2 K 22:17. Ex 9:14-17. Dt +2:30. Is 19:11-14. 1 C 1:20. 2 Th 2:9-11.
cast. Ps +51:11.
Zedekiah. 2 Ch 36:13. Je 27:12-15. 38:17-21. Ezk 17:15-20.

2 KINGS 25

1 A.M. 3414. B.C. 590.
in the ninth. 2 Ch 36:17, etc. Je 34:2, 3, 8-10. 39:1, etc. 52:4, 5, etc. Ezk 24:1, 2, etc.
Nebuchadnezzar. 2 K +24:1, 10. 1 Ch 6:15. Je 27:8. 32:28. 43:10. 51:34. Ezk 26:7, Nebuchadrezzar. Da 4:1, etc.
pitched. Is 29:3. Je 32:24. Ezk 4:1-8. 21:22-24. Lk 19:43, 44.
3 A.M. 3416. B.C. 588.
the ninth day. Je 39:2. 52:6. Zc 8:19.
fourth. Je 39:2.
the famine. 1 K +8:37.
there was no. Je 37:21. 38:2.
4 **the city**. Je 5:10. 39:2, 3. 52:6, 7, etc. Ezk 33:21.
fled. Le 26:17, 36. Dt 28:25. 32:24, 25, 30. Je 39:4-7.
and the king. ver. 5. Ex 12:12.
5 **Chaldees pursued**. 2 Ch 36:17.
and overtook. Is 30:16. Je 24:8. 39:5. 52:8. Am 2:14-16.
6 **they took**. 2 Ch 33:11. Je +21:7.
Riblah. 2 K 23:33. Je 52:9.
gave judgment upon him. Heb. spake judgment with him. Je +4:12mg.
7 **they slew**. Ge 21:16. 44:34. Dt 28:34. Je 22:30. 39:6, 7. 52:10, 11.
and put out. Heb. and made blind. Je 32:4, 5. 34:3. Ezk 12:13, etc.
bound him. 2 Ch +33:11. Ezk 7:27. 17:16-20.
8 **in the fifth month**. Je 52:12-14. Zc 7:3. 8:19.
the nineteenth. ver. 27. 2 K 24:12.
Nebuzar-adan. i.e. *whom Nebo favors.* ver. 11, 20. Je 39:9-14. 40:1-4. 43:6. 52:12-16. La 4:12. **S#5018h**: ver. 8, 11, 20. Je 39:9, 10, 11, 13. 40:1. 41:10. 43:6. 52:12, 15, 16, 26, 30.
captain. *or,* chief marshal. *or,* executioner. Ge 37:36mg.
9 **he burnt**. 1 K 9:8. Je 7:14. 26:9. La 1:10. 2:7. Mi 3:12. Lk 21:5, 6. Ac 6:13, 14.
the king's. Je +17:27.
10 **brake**. Je 5:10. +39:8.
11 **the rest**. Je 15:1, 2. 39:9. 52:15. Ezk 5:2. 12:15, 16. 22:15, 16.
fugitives. Heb. fallen away.
12 **left of the poor**. 2 K 24:44. Je 39:10. 40:7. 52:16. Ezk 33:24. Mt 26:11.

13 **the**. 2 Ch +4:19. Is +39:6. La 1:10.
pillars. Ex 27:3. 1 K 7:15, 27. 2 Ch 4:12, 13.
bases. 1 K 7:23-45. 2 Ch 4:2-6, 14-16.

14 **the pots**. Ex 27:3. 38:3. 1 K 7:47-50. 2 Ch
4:20-22. 24:14.
the shovels. Ex 27:3.
the snuffers. 1 K 7:50.
the spoons. 1 K 7:50.

15 **firepans**. Ex 27:3. 1 K 7:45.
bowls. 1 K +7:40.
and such things. Ex 37:23. Nu 7:13, 14. 2
Ch +4:19. 24:14.

16 **one sea**. Heb. the one sea.
the brass. 1 K 7:47.
without weight. 1 K 7:47.

17 **one pillar**. 1 K 7:15, 16. 2 Ch 36:18. Je
27:19, 22. 52:21-23.

18 **captain**. ver. 24, 25, etc.
Seraiah. 2 S +8:17.
Zephaniah. Zp +1:1.
the second priest. Je 52:24.
door. Heb. threshold. 2 K +12:9mg.

19 **officer**. *or*, eunuch. 2 K +8:6mg.
was set. **S#6496h**, Ge +41:34mg.
were in the king's presence. Heb. saw the
king's face. Est 1:14.
principal. *or*, scribe of the captain of the
host.
mustered. 1 S +11:8.

20 **and brought**. Je 52:26, 27. La 4:16.

21 **the king**. Je 34:21.
So Judah. 2 K 17:20. 23:27. Le 26:33-35. Dt
4:26. 28:36, 64. Je 24:9, 10. 25:9-11. Ezk
12:25-28. 24:14. Am 5:27. +9:14, 15.

22 **the people**. Je 40:5, 6, etc.
Gedaliah. ver. 25. 1 Ch +25:3.
Ahikam. 2 K +22:12.
Shaphan. 2 K +22:3.

23 **And when**. Je 40:7-9, 11, 12.
Mizpah. Ge +31:49.
Ishmael. Ge +16:11.
Nethaniah. 1 Ch +25:12.
Johanan. i.e. *Jah is gracious*, **S#3110h**. 1 Ch
3:15, 24. 6:9, 10. 12:4, 12. Ezr 8:12. 10:6. Ne
12:22, 23. Je 40:8, 13, 15, 16. 41:11, 13-16.
42:1, 8. 43:2, 4, 5.
Careah. i.e. *bald*. **S#7143h**: ver. 23. Je 40:8, 13,
15, 16. 41:11, 13, 14, 16. 42:1, 8. 43:2, 4, 5.
Seraiah. ver. 18.
Tanhumeth. i.e. *consolation*, **S#8576h**: ver. 23.
Je 40:8.
the. Je 40:8.

24 **Netophathite**. 2 S +23:28, 29.
Jaazaniah. i.e. *Jah gives ear*, **S#2970h**. Je 35:3.
Ezk 8:11. 11:1.
Maachathite. Dt 3:14. 2 S 20:14.

24 **sware to them**. 2 S 14:11. 19:23. Je 40:9,
10. Ezk 33:24-29.
and it shall be. Je 27:5, 6, 11. 31:2. 40:9.
42:6.

25 **seventh**. Zc 7:5. 8:19.
Ishmael. ver. 23. Je 40:15, 16. 41:1-15.
Elishama. Nu +1:10.
royal. Heb. of the kingdom. 2 K 11:1. 2 S
12:26. Est 1:7. Is 62:3. Je 41:1. Ezk 17:13. Da
1:3.
Mizpah. ver. +23. Jsh 18:25.

26 **all the people**. Je 41:16-18. 42:14-22. 43:4-
7.
Chaldees. **S#3778h**. ver. 4, Ge 11:28, 31. 2 K
24:2. 5, 10, 13, 24-26. 2 Ch 36:17. Ne 9:7. Jb
1:17. Is 13:19. 23:13. 43:14. 47:1, 5. 48:14,
20. Je 21:4, 9. 22:25. 24:5. 25:12. 32:4, 5, 24,
25, 28, 29, 43. 33:5. 35:11. 37:5, 8, 9-11, 13,
14. 38:2, 18, 19, 23. 39:5, 8. 40:9, 10. 41:3,
18. 43:3. 50:1, 8, 10, 25, 35, 45. 51:4, 24, 35,
54. 52:7, 8, 14, 17. Ezk 1:3. 12:13. 23:14, 15,
23. Da 1:4. 2:2, 4. 5:30. 9:1. Hab 1:6. Also Ezk
11:24. 16:29. 23:16.

27 A.M. 3442. B.C. 562.
it came to pass. Je 24:5, 6. 52:31-34.
the captivity of Jehoiachin. 2 K 24:12, 15.
seven and twentieth day. Je 52:31.
Evil-merodach. i.e. *the fool of Merodach*,
S#192h: Je 52:31.
king of Babylon. Pr 21:1.
lift up the head. Ge 40:13, 20.
prison. or, house of restraint. ver. 29. 2 K
17:4. 1 K 22:27. 2 Ch 18:26. Is 42:7, 22. Je
37:15, 18. 52:33.

28 **kindly to him**. Heb. good things with him.
Nu 10:29. 1 K 12:7. Ps 78:38, 39. 106:46. Je
12:6mg. Da 11:34.
the throne. Je 27:6-11. Da 2:37. 5:18, 19.

29 **changed**. 2 K 24:12. Ge 41:14, 42. Est 4:4.
8:15. Is 61:3. Zc 3:4. Lk 15:22.
he did eat bread. 2 S 9:7.
continually. Is +58:11.

30 **continual**. Is +58:11.
a daily rate. Ne 11:23. 12:47. Pr 15:17 (dinner). Je 40:5. 52:34. Da 1:5. Mt 6:11. Lk 11:3.
Ac 6:1.
every day. or, a day in its day. Ex +5:13mg.
all the days of his life. Ge 48:15, 16.

1 CHRONICLES

1 CHRONICLES 1

1 **Adam**. Ge 2:19.
Sheth. Ge +4:25, 26. 5:3, 8. Lk 3:38, Seth.
Enosh. i.e. *a mortal*, **S#583h**. Ge 4:26. 5:6, 7, 9, 10, 11. Lk 3:38, Enos.

2 **Kenan**. i.e. *owner; fixed*, **S#7018h**. Ge 5:9, 10-14. Lk 3:37, Cainan.
Mahalaleel. Ge +5:12. Lk 3:37, Maleleel.
Jered. i.e. *a descent*, **S#3382h**. Ge 5:15, 16, 18-20. 1 Ch 4:18. Lk 3:37, Jared.

3 **Henoch**. i.e. *disciplined; initiated*, **S#2585h**. ver. 3, Ge 4:17, 18. 5:18-24. 25:4. 46:9. Ex 6:14. Nu 26:5. 33. 1 Ch 5:3. He 11:5. Ju 14, Enoch.
Methuselah. Ge +5:21, 25-27. Lk 3:37, Mathusala.
Lamech. Ge +4:18. 5:28-31. Lk 3:36.

4 **Noah**. Ge +5:29, 32. Mt 24:37, 38. Lk +3:36, Noe.
Shem. Ge +5:32.

5 **the sons of Japheth**. Ge 10:1-5. Ezk 27:13. 38:2, 3, 6. 39:1.
Gomer. Ge +10:2.
Magog. Ge +10:2.
Madai. Ge +10:2.
Javan. Ge +10:2.
Tubal. Ge +10:2.
Meshech. Ge +10:2.
Tiras. Ge +10:2.

6 **Ashchenaz**. Ge +10:3, Ashkenaz.
Riphath. *or*, Diphath, as it is in some copies. Ge +10:3.

7 **Tarshish**. Ge +10:4.
Kittim. Ge +10:4.
Dodanim. *or*, Rodanim, according to some copies. Ge +10:4.

8 **sons of Ham**. Ge 10:6, 7.
Put. Ge 10:6, Phut.

9 **Sabta**. i.e. *he compassed the chamber; to surround*, **S#5454h**. Ge 10:7.
Sabtechah. i.e. *terror*, **S#5455h**. Ge 10:7.

10 **Cush**. Ge +10:6.
begat Nimrod. Ge +10:8-12. Mi 5:6.

11 **Mizraim**. Ge +10:6.
Ludim. Ge +10:13.
Anamim. Ge +10:13.

Lehabim. Ge +10:13.
Naphtuhim. Ge +10:13.

12 **Pathrusim**. Ge +10:14.
Caphthorim. i.e. *a native of Caphtor*, **S#3732h**. Ge +10:14.

13 **Canaan**. Ge 9:22, 25, 26. 10:15-19, Sidon.
Heth. Ge +10:15. Dt +20:17.

14 **Jebusite**. Ge +10:16.
Amorite. Ge +10:16.
Girgashite. Ge +10:16.

15 **Hivite**. Ge +10:17.

16 **Arvadite**. i.e. *a refuge for the roving*, **S#721h**. Ge 10:18.
Zemarite. **S#6786h**. Ge 10:18.
Hamathite. i.e. *one from Hamath* (Nu +13:21), **S#2577h**. Ge 10:18.

17 **sons of Shem**. Ge 10:22-32. 11:10.
Elam. Ge +10:22.
Asshur. Ge +10:22.
Lud. Ge +10:22.
Aram. Ge +22:21.
Uz. Ge +10:23.
Meshech. Ge +10:2, 23, Mash.

18 **Shelah**. ver. 24. Ge +10:24, Salah.

19 **Eber**. Ge +10: 24.
Peleg. *that is*, Division. Ge +10:25.

20 **Joktan**. Ge +10:25.
Hazarmaveth. Ge +10:26, 27.

21 **Hadoram**. Ge +10:27.

22 **Ebal**. Ge 10:28, Obal. +36:23.

23 **Ophir**. Ge 10:29. 1 K +9:28.
Havilah. Ge +10:7.

24 **Shem**. Ge +5:32. 11:10-26.
Shelah. ver. +18.

25 **Eber**. Lk 3:35, Heber.
Peleg. Lk 3:35, Phalec.
Reu. Ge +11:18. Lk 3:35, Ragau.

26 **Serug**. Ge +11:20.
Nahor. Ge +11:22.
Terah. Ge +11:26. Lk 3:34, Thara.

27 **Abram**. Ge +11:26, 27-32. 17:5. Jsh 24:2. Ne 9:7.

28 **Isaac**. Ge +17:19, 20, 21. 21:2-5, 12.
Ishmael. Ge +16:11, 12-16. 21:9, 10.

29 **The firstborn**. Ge 25:12-16.
Nebaioth. Ge +25:13.
Kedar. Ge +25:13.

30 **Dumah**. Ge +25:14. Is 21:11.
Hadad. or, Hadar. Ge 25:15.
Tema. Ge +25:15.
31 **Jetur**. Ge +25:15.
32 A.M. 2151. B.C. 1853.
the sons. Ge 25:1-4.
Midian. Ge +25:2.
Sheba. 1 K +10:1.
Dedan. Ge +10:7.
33 **Ephah**. Ge +25:4. Is 60:6.
Abida. i.e. *father of knowledge*, **S#28h**. Ge 25:4.
34 **Abraham**. Ge 21:2, 3. Mt 1:2. Lk 3:34. Ac 7:8.
The sons of Isaac. Ge 25:24-28. Ml 1:2-4. Ro 9:10-13.
Israel. Ge +32:28.
35 **sons of Esau**. Ge 36:4, 5, 9, 10.
36 **Teman**. ver. 53. Ge +36:11.
Omar. i.e. *eloquent*, **S#201h**. Ge 36:11, 15.
Zephi. i.e. *expectation; watch thou*, **S#6825h**. Ge 36:11, 15, Zepho.
37 **Reuel**. Ge +36:4.
38 **the sons of Seir**. Ge 36:20, 29, 30.
Dishon. i.e. *a thresher; antelope*, **S#1787h**. ver. 38, 41, 41. Ge 36:21, 25, 30.
Ezar. i.e. *treasure*, **S#687h**. ver. 38, 42. Ge +36:21, 27, 30, Ezer.
39 **Hori**. Ge +36:22. Dt 2:12, 22.
Homam. i.e. *destruction*, **S#1950h**. Ge 36:22, Hemam.
40 **Alian**. i.e. *lofty*, **S#5935h**. Ge 36:23, Alvan, Shepho.
Shephi. i.e. *my bareness; my prominence*, **S#8195h**.
Aiyah. Ge 36:24, Ajah.
41 **The sons**. Ge +46:7.
Dishon. ver. +38. Ge 36:25.
Amram. Ge 36:26, Hemdan.
42 **Zavan**. i.e. *disquiet*, **S#2190h**. Ge 36:27, Zaavan, Achan.
Jakan. i.e. *let him oppress them*, **S#3292h**.
Uz. Ge +10:23.
43 **the kings**. Ge 36:31-39. 49:10. Nu 24:17-19.
44 **Bozrah**. Ge +36:33.
45 **Jobab**. Ge +10:29.
Husham. Ge 36:34.
Temanites. ver. 36, 53. Jb +2:11.
46 **Hadad**. Ge +36:35.
Bedad. Ge +36:35.
Midian. Ge +25:2.
Avith. Ge +36:35.
47 **Samlah**. Ge +36:36.
Masrekah. Ge +36:36.
48 **Shaul**. Ge 36:37, Saul.
49 **Baal-hanan**. Ge +36:38.
Achbor. Ge +36:38.
50 **Hadad**. Ge 36:39, Hadar.
Pai. i.e. *sighing*, **S#6464h**. Ge 36:39, Pau.
51 **Aliah**. i.e. *moral perverseness*, **S#5933h**. Ge 36:40, Alvah.

52 **Duke Aholibamah**. Ge +36:41.
53 **Kenaz**. Ge +36:11.
Teman. Ge +36:11.
Mibzar. Ge +36:42.
54 **Magdiel**. Ge +36:43.
These are. Ge 36:41-43.

1 CHRONICLES 2

1 A.M. 2252, etc. B.C. 1752, etc.
Israel. or, Jacob. Ge +25:26. +32:28. 49:2.
Reuben. Ge +29:32.
Simeon. Ge +29:33.
Levi. Ge +29:34.
Judah. Ge +35:23.
Issachar. Ge +30:18.
Zebulun. Ge +30:20.
2 **Dan**. Ge +30:6.
Joseph. Ge +30:24.
Benjamin. Ge +35:18.
Naphtali. Ge +30:8.
Gad. Ge +30:11.
Asher. Ge +30:13.
3 **Er, and**. 1 Ch 9:5. Ge 38:2-10. 46:12. Nu 26:19.
Onan. Ge +38:4.
Shelah. Ge +38:5.
Shua. i.e. *riches; a cry; salvation*, **S#7770h**. Ge 38:2.
Canaanitess. Ge +10:18.
firstborn. Le +27:26.
4 **Tamar**. Ge +38:6.
Pharez. Ge +46:12.
Zerah. Ge +36:13. Mt 1:3, Zara.
5 **Hezron**. Ge +46:9, 12. Nu 26:21. Ru 4:18. Mt 1:3. Lk 3:33, Esrom.
6 **Zimri**. i.e. *praised; snug; my song; my field*, **S#2174h**. 1 Ch 8:36. 9:42. Nu 25:14. 1 K 16:9, 10, 12, 15, 16, 18, 20. 2 K 9:31. Je 25:25.
Ethan. i.e. *perennial, constant; ancient*, **S#387h**. ver. 8. 1 Ch 6:42, 44. 15:17, 19. 1 K 4:31. Ps 89, title.
Heman. i.e. *faithful*, **S#1968h**. 1 Ch 6:33. 15:17, 19. 16:41, 42. 25:1, 4-6. 1 K 4:31. 2 Ch 5:12. 29:14. 35:15. Ps 88, title.
Calcol. i.e. *sustenance; comprehended*, **S#3633h**. 1 K 4:31.
Dara. i.e. *pearl of wisdom*, **S#1873h**. 1 K +4:31, Darda.
7 **Carmi**. 1 Ch +4:1.
Achar. i.e. *troublesome*, **S#5917h**. Jsh 7:1-5, Achan.
accursed. Dt 7:26. 13:17. Jsh 6:18. 7:11-15, 25. 22:20.
8 **Ethan**. ver. +6.
Azariah. 1 Ch +6:36.
9 **Jerahmeel**. i.e. *on whom God has mercy*, **S#3396h**. ver. 25-27, 33, 42. 1 Ch 24:29. Je 36:26.
Ram. Ru 4:19. Jb +32:2. Mt 1:3. Lk 3:33, Aram.

Chelubai. i.e. *the bold, the valiant*, S#3621h. ver. 18, 19, 24, 42, Caleb.

10 **Amminadab**. 1 Ch +15:11.
Nahshon. i.e. *a diviner*, S#5177h. ver. 11. Ex 6:23. Nu 1:7. 2:3. 7:12, 17. 10:14. Ru 4:20. Mt 1:4. Lk 3:32, Naasson.

11 **Salma**. i.e. *clothed, a garment; raiment*, S#8007h. ver. 51, 54. Ru 4:21. Mt 1:4, 5. Lk 3:32, Salmon.
Boaz. Ru +2:1. Lk 3:32, Booz.

12 **Jesse**. i.e. *wealthy; firm; extant*, S#3448h. 1 Ch 10:14. Ru 4:17, 22. 1 S 16:1, 12, 18. 17:12, 58. 20:27, 30, 31. 22:7, 8. 25:10. 2 S 20:1. 23:1. 1 K 12:16. Ps 72:20. Is 11:1, 10. Mt 1:5, 6. Lk 3:32. Ac 13:22. Ro 15:12.

13 **his firstborn**. 1 S 16:6, etc. 17:13, 28.
Eliab. 1 Ch 27:18, Elihu. Nu +1:9.
Shimma. i.e. *annunciation*, S#8092h. 1 Ch 3:5. 6:30, 39. 20:7, Shimea. 1 S 16:9, Shammah. 2 S 21:21.

14 **Nethaneel**. Nu +1:8.
Raddai. i.e. *subduing; trodden down*, S#7288h.

15 **Ozem**. i.e. *strength; eagerness*, S#684h. ver. 25. 1 S 16:10, 11. 17:12-14.

16 **Zeruiah**. i.e. *pierce ye Jah; tribulation; cleft*, S#6870h. 1 Ch 11:6, 39. 18:12, 15. 26:28. 27:24. 1 S 26:6. 2 S 2:13, 18. 3:39. 8:16. 14:1. 16:9, 10. 17:25. 18:2. 19:21, 22. 21:17. 23:18, 37. 1 K 1:7. 2:5, 22.
Abigail. 1 S +25:3.
the sons of. 1 S 26:6. 2 S 2:18-23. 3:39. 16:9-11. 19:22.
Abishai. 1 S +26:6.
Joab. 1 S +26:6.
Asahel. i.e. *God is doer; wrought of God, whom God created*, S#6214h. 1 Ch 11:26. 27:7. 2 S 2:18-23, 30, 32. 3:27, 30. 23:24. 2 Ch 17:8. 31:13. Ezr 10:15.

17 **Amasa**. 2 S +17:25. 19:13. 20:4-12. 1 K 2:5, 32.
Jether. 2 S 17:25, Ithra an Israelite.
Ishmeelite. S#3459, a descendant of Ishmael.

18 A.M. 2534, etc. B.C. 1470, etc.
Caleb. ver. 9, Chelubai, 42.
Hezron. Ge +46:9.
Azubah. 1 K +22:42.
Jerioth. i.e. *breaking asunder*, S#3408h.
Jesher. i.e. *righteous*, S#3475h.
Shobab. i.e. *apostate; backsliding, rebellious*, S#7727h. 1 Ch 3:5. 14:4. 2 S 5:14.
Ardon. i.e. *fugitive*, S#715h.

19 **Ephrath**. ver. 24, +50. Ge +48:7.
Hur. Ex +17:10.

20 **Uri**. Ex +31:2.
Bezaleel. Ex +31:2.

21 **Hezron**. Ge +46:9.
Machir. Ge +50:23.
married. Heb. took. 1 Ch 4:18.

Segub. i.e. *elevated; exalted; made strong*, S#7687h. ver. 22. 1 K 16:34.

22 **Jair**. Nu +32:41. Dt 3:14. Jsh 13:30.

23 **Geshur**. 2 S +3:3.
Kenath. Nu +32:42. Jg 8:11.

24 **Caleb-ephratah**. i.e. *fruitfulness*, S#3613h. ver. 9, 18, 19. 1 S 30:14.
Ashur. i.e. *noble and happy; black*, S#804h. 1 Ch 4:5.
Tekoa. i.e. *sound of the trumpet*, S#8620h. 1 Ch 4:5. 2 S 14:2. 2 Ch 11:6. 20:20. Je 6:1. Am 1:1.

25 **Jerahmeel**. ver. 9.
firstborn. Le 27:26.
Hezron. Ge +46:9.
Ram. Jb +32:2.
Bunah. i.e. *understanding, discretion*, S#946h.
Oren. i.e. *a pine; tall and strong*, S#767h.
Ozem. ver. 15.
Ahijah. 1 K +14:6.

26 **another wife**. 1 Ch 4:5. Ge +4:19.
Atarah. i.e. *a crown*, S#5851h.
Onam. Ge +36:23.

27 **Ram**. ver. 25.
Maaz. i.e. *anger; closure*, S#4619h.
Jamin. Ge +46:10.
Eker. i.e. *offshoot; eradication*, S#6134h.

28 **Onam**. ver. 26.
Shammai. i.e. *my desolations; destructive*, S#8060h. ver. 32, 44, 45. 1 Ch 4:17.
Jada. i.e. *knowing*, S#3047h. ver. 32.
Nadab. Ex +6:23.
Abishur. i.e. *uprightness*, S#51h. ver. 29.

29 **Abihail**. Nu +3:35.
Ahban. i.e. *brother of understanding*, S#257h.
Molid. i.e. *begetter*, S#4140h.

30 **Nadab**. ver. 28.
Seled. i.e. *exaltation; recoil*, S#5540h.
Appaim. i.e. *double-nosed*, S#649h. ver. 31.
died without children. ver. 32. Ge +11:30. 2 K 4:14. Lk 20:29.

31 **Ishi**. i.e. *salutary*, S#3469h. 1 Ch 4:20, 42. 5:24.
Sheshan. i.e. *lily; fine linen*, S#8348h. ver. 34, 35.
children of Sheshan. ver. 34, 35.
Ahlai. ver. 35. 1 Ch +11:41.

32 **Jada**. ver. 28.
Jether. i.e. *excellence, superiority*, S#3500h. ver. 17. 1 Ch 4:17. 7:38. Ex 4:18. Jg 8:20. 1 K 2:5, 32.
Jonathan. 1 S +13:2.
died without children. ver. +30.

33 **Peleth**. Nu +16:1.
Zaza. i.e. *going back; brightness; fulness*, S#2117h.

34 **no sons**. Nu 27:3, 4, 8.
but daughters. Nu 36:2, 10, 11.
Jarha. i.e. *increasing moon*, S#3398h. ver. 35.

35 **his daughter**. ver. 31.
Attai. i.e. *opportune*, S#6262h. ver. 36. 1 Ch 12:11. 2 Ch 11:20.

36 **Zabad**. i.e. *gift; endowed*, **S#2066h**. ver. 37. 1 Ch 7:21. 11:41. 2 Ch 24:26. Ezr 10:27, 33, 43.

37 **Ephlal**. i.e. *intercession*, **S#654h**.
Obed. Ru +4:17.

38 **Jehu**. 2 K +9:2.
Azariah. 1 Ch +6:36. 2 Ch 23:1.

39 **Helez**. i.e. *strength*, **S#2503h**. 1 Ch 11:27. 27:10. 2 S 23:26.
Eleasah. i.e. *God has wrought*, **S#501h**. ver. 40. 1 Ch 8:37. 9:43. Ezr 10:22. Je 29:3.

40 **Sisamai**. i.e. *distinguished one; swallow*, **S#5581h**.
Shallum. 2 K +15:10.

41 **Jekamiah**. i.e. *let Jah arise*, **S#3359h**. 1 Ch 3:18.
Elishama. Nu +1:10.

42 **Caleb**. ver. 9, Chelubai, 18, 19, 24.
Mesha. i.e. *safety*, **S#4338h**, only here. Ge +10:30.
his firstborn. Ge 49:3. Ex 4:22, 23. Ro 8:29. He 12:23.
the father. i.e. the founder.
Ziph. Jsh +15:24. 1 S +23:19.
Mareshah. Jsh +15:44.
the father of. ver. 23, 24, 45, 49, 52. 1 Ch 8:29. Ezr 2:21-35. Ne 7:25-38.
Hebron. Ex +6:18.

43 **Korah**. Ge +36:5.
Tappuah. i.e. *bearing* or *fruitful in apples; thou wilt cause to breathe*, **S#8599h**.
Rekem. i.e. *flower garden; embroidery; variegation*, **S#7552h**. ver. 44. 1 Ch 7:16. Nu 31:8. Jsh 13:21.
Shema. i.e. *rumor*, **S#8087h**. ver. 44. 1 Ch 5:8. 8:13. Jsh +15:26. Ne 8:4.

44 **Raham**. i.e. *compassionate*, **S#7357h**.
Jorkoam. i.e. *paleness* or *spreading of the people*, **S#3421h**.

45 **Beth-zur**. Jsh +15:58. 2 Ch 11:7.

46 **Ephah**. Ge +25:4.
Caleb's. ver. 18, 19, 48.
Haran. i.e. *very dry*, **S#2771h**. ver. 47. Ge 11:31, 32. 12:4, 5. 27:43. 28:10. 29:4. 2 K 19:12. Is 37:12. Ezk 27:23.
Moza. 1 Ch +8:36.
Gazez. i.e. *shearer*, **S#1495h**.

47 **Jahdai**. i.e. *the Lord directs*, **S#3056h**.
Regem. i.e. *stoning; friend*, **S#7276h**.
Gesham. i.e. *large clod*, **S#1529h**.
Pelet. 1 Ch +12:3. Jsh 15:27.
Ephah. Ge +25:4.
Shaaph. i.e. *division; fleeing*, **S#8174h**. ver. 49.

48 **Maachah**. 1 K +2:39.
concubine. ver. 46. 1 Ch 7:14. Ge 16:2, 3. 21:10. 22:24. 25:5, 6. 29:24, 29. 35:22. 36:12. Ex 21:7-11. Le 19:20. Dt 21:10-14. Jg 8:31. 9:18. 19:1. 2 S 3:7, 8. 5:13. 15:16. 16:21, 22. 19:5. 20:3. 21:11. 1 K 11:3. 2 Ch 11:21. 13:21. Est 2:14. SS 6:8, 9. Da 5:2, 3. Mt 19:5. 1 C 7:2.

Sheber. i.e. *hope; a breach*, **S#7669h**.
Tirhanah. i.e. *a camp-spy; inclination*, **S#8647h**.

49 **the father of Madmannah**. ver. 42. Jsh +15:31. Is 10:31, Madmenah.
Sheva. 2 S +20:25.
Macbenah. i.e. *poverty of the son*, **S#4343h**.
Gibea. i.e. *a hill*, **S#1388h**. Jsh 15:57. 2 S 21:6, Gibeah.
Achsa. i.e. *anklet*, **S#5915h**. Not as Jsh 15:16, 17. Jg 1:12, 13.

50 **Ephratah**. i.e. *fruitfulness; land, region*, **S#672h**. ver. 19, 24, Ephrath. 1 Ch 4:4. Ge +48:7. Ru 4:11. Ps 132:6. Mi 5:2.
Kirjath-jearim. ver. 53. Jsh +9:17.

51 **Salma**. ver. +11. 1 Ch 4:4.
Beth-lehem. Jsh +19:15.
Hareph. i.e. *reproachful*, **S#2780h**.
Beth-gader. i.e. *house of the wall*, **S#1013h**.

52 **Shobal**. Ge +36:20.
Haroeh. i.e. *vision; prophet*, **S#7204h**. or, Reaiah, 1 Ch 4:2.
half of the Manahethites. i.e. *midst of the resting places*, **S#2679h**. or, half of the Menuchites, or, Hatsiham-menuchoth.

53 **Ithrites**. 2 S +23:38.
Puhites. i.e. *a hinge; openness; simplicity*, **S#6336h**.
Shumathites. i.e. *the exalted; garlic*, **S#8126h**.
Mishraites. i.e. *a shepherd*, **S#4954h**.
Zareathites. i.e. *dwellers in Zareah or Zorah*, **S#6882h**. ver. 54 (Zorites). 4:2. Jsh +19:41.
Eshtaulites. i.e. *descendants of Eshtaol*, **S#848h**.

54 **Salma**. ver. 51.
Bethlehem. ver. 51. Ge 35:19.
Netophathites. 2 S +23:28.
Ataroth. or, Atarites, or, crowns of the house of Joab. Nu +32:3. Jsh 16:2.
Manahethites. ver. 52.
Zorites. i.e. *descendants of Zorah*, **S#6882h**. Jsh 15:33.

55 **the scribes**. Ezr 7:6. Je 8:8.
Jabez. 1 Ch 4:9, +10.
Tirathites. i.e. *nourishers*, **S#8654h**.
Shimeathites. i.e. *descendants of Shimeah*, **S#8101h**.
Suchathites. i.e. *bushmen; hedges*, **S#7756h**.
Kenites. Ge +15:19.
Hemath. i.e. *a wall*, **S#2575h**. Jsh 19:35.
Rechab. 2 S +4:2.

1 CHRONICLES 3

1 A.M. 2951, etc. B.C. 1053, etc.
the sons of David. 2 S 3:2-5.
Amnon. 2 S +3:2. 13:1, 29.
Ahinoam. 1 S +14:50. 25:42, 43. 27:3.
Jezreelitess. Jsh 15:56.
Daniel. 2 S 3:3.
of Abigail. 1 S 25:39-42.

2 **Absalom**. 2 S +13:1, 20-28, 38. 18:14, 18, 33. 19:4-10.
Geshur. 2 S +3:3.
Adonijah. 2 S 3:4. 1 K +1:5. 2:24, 25.
3 **Eglah**. 2 S +3:5. 6:23.
4 **there he reigned**. 2 S 2:11. 5:4, 5. 1 K 2:11.
and in Jerusalem. 2 S 5:4, 14, etc.
5 **Shimea**. i.e. *a report; fame*, **S#8092h**. 1 Ch 14:4. 2 S 5:14, Shammuah. **S#8092h**: 1 Ch 2:13. 6:30, 39. 20:7. 2 S 21:21.
Nathan. 2 Ch +9:29.
Solomon. 1 Ch 28:5, 6. 2 S +5:14. 12:24, 25.
Bath-shua. i.e. *daughter of the oath*. 2 S 11:3, Bath-sheba. Mt 1:6. **S#1340h**. 1 Ch 2:3. Ge 38:12.
Ammiel. i.e. *my people are of God; one of the family of God*, **S#5988h**. 1 Ch 26:5. Nu 13:12. 2 S 9:4, 5. 11:3, Eliam. 17:27.
6 **Ibhar**. 2 S +5:15.
Elishama. 1 Ch 14:5. Nu +1:10. 2 S +5:15, Elishua.
Eliphelet. i.e. *God his deliverance; God of escape*, **S#467h**. ver. 8. 1 Ch 8:39. 11:35, Eliphal. 14:5, Elpalet, 7. 2 S 5:16, Eliphalet. 23:34. Ezr 8:13. 10:33.
7 **Nogah**. i.e. *brightness*, **S#5052h**. 1 Ch 14:6. 2 S 5:15, 16.
8 **Eliada**. 1 Ch 14:7, Beeliada. 1 K +11:23.
Eliphelet. ver. +6.
9 **of the concubines**. 2 S 5:13.
Tamar. Ge +38:6.
10 **Rehoboam**. 1 K +14:21.
Abia. i.e. *whose father is Jah*. 1 K 15:1, Abijam. 2 Ch 13:1, Abijah. **S#29h**. 1 Ch 2:24. 6:28. 7:8. 24:10. 2 K 18:2, Abi. 2 Ch 11:20, 22. 14:1. 29:1. Ne 10:7. 12:4, 17. Mt 1:7. Lk 1:5.
Asa. 1 Ch +9:16.
Jehoshaphat. 2 S +8:16.
11 **Joram**. 1 Ch +26:25.
Ahaziah. 1 K +22:40.
Joash. Jg +6:11.
12 **Amaziah**. 1 Ch +4:34.
Azariah. 1 Ch +6:36. 2 Ch +26:1, Uzziah.
Jotham. Jg +9:5.
13 **Ahaz**. 1 Ch +8:35.
Hezekiah. 2 K +16:20.
Manasseh. Ge +41:51.
14 **Amon**. Ne +7:59.
Josiah. 1 K +13:2.
15 **Johanan**. *or*, Jehoahaz. 2 K +10:35. 23:30. +25:23.
Jehoiakim. i.e. *Jehovah will raise*. **S#3079h**. ver. 16. 2 K 23:34, Eliakim, 35, 36. 24:1, 5, 6, 19. 2 Ch 36:4, 5, 8. Je 1:3. 22:18, 24. 24:1. 25:1. *26:1, 21-23*. 27:1, 20. 28:4. 35:1. 36:1, 9, 28-30, 32. 37:1. 45:1. 46:2. 52:2. Da 1:1, 2. Mt 1:11.
Zedekiah. 1 K +22:11.
Shallum. 2 K +15:10. 2 K 23:30. 2 Ch 36:1, Jehoahaz. Je 22:11.

16 **Jeconiah**. Je +24:1.
Zedekiah. ver. +15.
his son. 2 K 24:17, being his uncle. Nu 27:8-10. 1 K +15:10.
17 **Assir**. Ex +6:24.
Salathiel. i.e. *asked of God*. Ezr 5:2, Shealtiel. Mt 1:12. **S#7597h**. ver. 17. Ezr 3:2, 8. Ne 12:1. Hg 1:1. 2:23. See **S#7597h**: Hg 1:12, 14. 2:2.
18 **Malchiram**. i.e. *king of altitude*, **S#4443h**.
Pedaiah. 2 K +23:36.
Shenazar. i.e. *light of splendor; tribulation*, **S#8137h**.
Jecamiah. i.e. *Jah will rise*, **S#3359h**. ver. 18. 1 Ch 2:41, 41.
Hoshama. i.e. *Jehovah hears*, **S#1953h**.
Nedabiah. i.e. *Jah impels*, **S#5072h**.
19 **the sons of Pedaiah**. 1 K 15:10. Mt 1:12.
Zerubbabel. Hg +1:1.
Meshullam. 1 Ch +9:12.
Hananiah. 1 Ch +25:23.
Shelomith. Le +24:11.
their sister. ver. 20.
20 **Hashubah**. i.e. *esteemed*, **S#2807h**.
Ohel. i.e. *a tent*, **S#169h**.
Berechiah. Zc +1:7.
Hasadiah. i.e. *love or mercy of the Lord*, **S#2619h**.
Jushab-hesed. i.e. *mercy restored*, **S#3142h**.
21 **Hananiah**. 1 Ch +25:23.
Pelatiah. i.e. *deliverance of the Lord*, **S#6410h**. 1 Ch 4:42. Ne 10:22. Ezk 11:1, 13.
Jesaiah. i.e. *Jah has saved*, **S#3470h**. Ne 11:7.
Rephaiah. 1 Ch +9:43.
Arnan. i.e. *lion of perpetuity*, **S#770h**.
Obadiah. Ob +1.
Shechaniah. ver. +22.
22 **Shechaniah**. i.e. *intimate with Jehovah; dwelling of Jehovah*, **S#7935h**. ver. 21. Ezr 8:3, 5. 10:2. Ne 3:29. 6:18. 12:3, 14, Shebaniah. Also **S#7935h**: 1 Ch 24:11. 2 Ch 31:15.
Shemiah. 1 Ch +9:16.
Hattush. Ezr +8:2.
Igeal. i.e. *he will redeem*, **S#3008h**. ver. 22. Nu 13:7. 2 S 23:36.
Bariah. i.e. *fugitive*, **S#1282h**.
Neariah. i.e. *servant of Jah*, **S#5294h**. ver. 23. 1 Ch 4:42.
Shaphat. i.e. *judge*, **S#8202h**. 1 Ch 5:12. 27:29. Nu 13:5. 1 K 19:16, 19. 2 K 3:11. 6:31.
23 **Elioenai**. 1 Ch +26:3.
Hezekiah. Heb. Hiskijah. *or*, Hiskijahu. **S#2396h**, 1 K +16:20.
Azrikam. i.e. *help against an enemy; my help has arisen*, **S#5840h**. 1 Ch 8:38. 9:14, 44. 2 Ch 28:7. Ne 11:15.
24 **Hodaiah**. i.e. *majesty of Jah*, **S#1939h**.
Eliashib. i.e. *God will restore*, **S#475h**. 1 Ch 24:12. Ezr 10:6, 24, 27, 36. Ne 3:1, 20, 21. 12:10, 22, 23. 13:4, 7, 28.
Pelaiah. Ne +8:7.

Akkub. i.e. *lain in wait; insidious*, **S#6126h**. 1 Ch 9:17. Ezr 2:42, 45. Ne 7:45. 8:7. 11:19. 12:25.

Johanan. 2 K +25:23.

Dalaiah. i.e. *drawn of Jah, delivered*, **S#1806h**. Je +36:12, Delaiah, 25.

Anani. i.e. *my cloud*, **S#6054h**.

1 CHRONICLES 4

1   A.M. 2283, etc. B.C. 1721, etc.

Pharez. Ge +46:12.

Hezron. Ge +46:9. Lk 3:33, Esrom.

Carmi. i.e. *my vineyard*, **S#3756h**. Ge 46:9. Ex 6:14. Nu 26:6. Jsh 7:1, 18. 1 Ch 2:7. 5:3. *or*, Chelubai, 1 Ch 2:9. *or*, Caleb, 1 Ch 2:18.

2   **Reaiah**. i.e. *whom Jehovah cares for*. 1 Ch 2:52, Haroeh. **S#7211h**. 1 Ch 5:5. Ezr 2:47. Ne 7:50.

Shobal. Ge +36:20.

Jahath. i.e. *comfort; union*, **S#3189h**. 1 Ch 6:20, 43. 23:10, 11. 24:22. 2 Ch 34:12.

Ahumai. i.e. *dweller near waters*, **S#267h**.

Lahad. i.e. *oppressed; in triumph or joy*, **S#3855h**.

Zorathites. i.e. *inhabitants of Zorah*, **S#6882h**. 2 Ch 2:53, 54. Jsh 15:33. Jg 13:25. For Zorah, see Jsh +19:41.

3   **Etam**. Jg 15:11. 2 Ch 11:6.

Jezreel. i.e. *God soweth*, **S#3157h**. Jsh 15:56. 17:16. 19:18. Jg 6:33. 1 S 25:43. 29:1, 11. 2 S 2:9. 4:4. 1 K 4:12. 18:45, 46. 21:1, 23. 2 K 8:29. 9:10, 15-17, 30, 36, 37. 10:1, 6, 7, 11. 2 Ch 22:6. Ho 1:4, 5, 11. 2:22.

Ishma. i.e. *desolation*, **S#3457h**.

Idbash. i.e. *honeyed; fat one*, **S#3031h**.

Hazelelponi. i.e. *the shadow turned towards me*, **S#6753h**.

4   **Penuel**. i.e. *the face of God*, **S#6439h**. 1 Ch 8:25. Also Ge 32:31, Peniel. Also Ge 32:30. Jg 8:8, 8, 9, 17. 1 K 12:25.

Gedor. ver. 18, 39. Jsh 15:36, +58.

Ezer. i.e. *help*, **S#5829h**. 1 Ch 12:9. Ne 3:19. 12:42. Compare Ge +36:21.

Hushah. i.e. *haste*, **S#2364h**.

Hur. ver. 1. 1 Ch 2:19, 50. Ex +17:10.

firstborn. Le +27:26.

Ephratah. 1 Ch +2:50.

the father. 1 Ch 2:19, 42.

5   **Ashur**. 1 Ch +2:24.

Tekoa. 1 Ch +2:24.

two wives. Ge +4:19.

Helah. i.e. *scum*, **S#2458h**. ver. 7.

Naarah. i.e. *a maiden*, **S#5292h**. ver. 6. Also, Jsh 16:7.

6   **Ahuzam**. i.e. *their possession*, **S#275h**.

Hepher. Nu +26:32.

Temeni. i.e. *ordained; my right hand*, **S#8488h**.

Haahashtari. i.e. *muleteer; courier; I will diligently observe the searching*, **S#326h**.

7   **Helah**. ver. 5.

Zereth. i.e. *splendor*, **S#6889h**.

Jezoar. i.e. *whiteness; he will shine*, **S#3328h**.

Ethnan. i.e. *hire*, **S#869h**.

8   **Coz**. i.e. *thorn; trouble*, **S#6976h**. 1 Ch +24:10, Hakoz. Ezr +2:61, Koz. Ne 3:4, 21. 7:63.

Anub. i.e. *clustered*, **S#6036h**.

Zobebah. i.e. *sluggish; an army*, **S#6637h**.

Aharhel. i.e. *behind the breastwork*, **S#316h**.

Harum. i.e. *high*, **S#2037h**. Probably *Jabez* should be mentioned here; as otherwise he is as a *consequent* without an antecedent.

9   **more honorable**. Ge 34:19. Is 43:4. Ac 17:11.

Jabez. *That is*, Sorrowful. ver. +10.

I bare him. 1 Ch 7:23. Ge 3:16. 35:18. 1 S 4:21. Is 53:3.

10   **Jabez**. i.e. *trouble; he will cause pain*, **S#3258h**. ver. 9. 1 Ch 2:55.

called on. 1 Ch 16:8. Ge 12:8. Jb 12:4. Ps 55:16. 99:6. 116:2-4. Je 33:3. Ro 10:12-14. 1 C 1:2.

the God. Ge 32:28. Is +29:23.

Oh that , etc. Heb. If thou wilt, etc. Lk 19:42.

bless me. Ge 12:2. 32:26. Ps 72:17. Ac 3:26. Ep 1:3.

enlarge. Jsh 17:14-18. Jg 1:27-36. Pr 10:22.

thine hand. Ps 119:173. Is 41:10. Jn 10:28.

that thou. Ge 48:16. Pr 30:8, 9. Mt 6:13. Ro 12:9. 16:19. 2 T 4:18.

keep me. Heb. do *me*.

from evil. Ps 121:7. Jn 17:15.

that it may. Ps 32:3, 4. 51:8, 12. Mt 26:75. Jn 21:17. 2 C 2:1-7. Ep 4:30. Re 3:19.

grieve me. Ex +32:32.

God granted. 1 K 3:7-13. Jb 22:27, 28. Ps 21:4. 65:2. 66:19, 20. 116:1, 2. Mt 7:7-11. Ep 3:20.

11   **Chelub**. i.e. *basket; coop*, **S#3620h**. 1 Ch 27:26.

Shuah. Ge +25:2.

Mehir. i.e. *price; ability*, **S#4243h**.

Eshton. i.e. *effeminate; womanly*, **S#850h**. ver. 12.

12   **Bethrapha**. i.e. *house of the healer* or *giants* or *feeble*, **S#1051h**.

Paseah. i.e. *lame, limping*, **S#6454h**. Ezr 2:49. Ne 3:6. 7:51.

Tehinnah. i.e. *graciousness*, **S#8468h**.

Irnahash. *or*, the city of Nahash. i.e. *city of the serpent*, **S#5904h**.

Rechah. i.e. *tenderness*, **S#7397h**.

13   **Kenaz**. Ge +36:11.

Othniel. Jsh +15:17.

Seraiah. 2 S +8:17.

Hathath. i.e. *casting down*, **S#2867h**. *or*, Hathath *and* Meonathai, *who begat*, etc.

14   **Meonothai**. i.e. *my dwellings*, **S#4587h**.

Ophrah. i.e. *dustiness; fawn-like*, **S#6084h**. Jsh 18:23. Jg 6:11, 24. 1 S 13:17.

Seraiah. 2 S +8:17.

Joab. 1 S +26:6.

valley. Ne 11:35. *or*, *inhabitants* of the valley. Ge 41:57. 1 K 10:24. 2 K 16:9.

Charashim. i.e. *craftsmen*, **S#2798h**. Ne 11:35.
for they were craftsmen. 2 K 24:14. Ne 11:35.

15 **Caleb**. Nu +13:6.
Jephunneh. Nu +13:6.
Iru. i.e. *city-wise*, **S#5900h**.
Elah. Ge +36:41.
Naam. i.e. *pleasantness*, **S#5277h**.
Kenaz. or, Uknaz. Ge +36:11.

16 **Jehaleleel**. i.e. *he praises God*, **S#3094h**. 2 Ch 29:12, Jehalelel.
Ziph. Jsh +15:24.
Ziphah. i.e. *flowing; refinery*, **S#2129h**.
Tiria. i.e. *fear; beholding*, **S#8493h**.
Asareel. i.e. *right of God*, **S#840h**.

17 **Ezra**. Ezr +7:12. ver. 16, Asareel.
Jether. 1 Ch +2:32.
Mered. i.e. *rebellion*, **S#4778h**. ver. 18.
Epher. Ge +25:4.
Jalon. i.e. *lodging*, **S#3210h**.
and she bare. ver. 18. Ps +127:3.
Miriam. Ex +15:20.
Shammai. 1 Ch +2:28.
Ishbah. i.e. *he will praise*, **S#3431h**.
Eshtemoa. ver. 19. 1 Ch 6:57. Jsh 15:50, Eshtemoh. 21:14. 1 S +30:28.

18 **Jehudijah**. i.e. *Jewess*, **S#3057h**. ver. +19.
Jered. 1 Ch +1:2.
the father of. ver. 4, 39. 1 Ch 2:42. Jsh 15:58.
Gedor. Jsh +15:58.
Heber. Ge +46:17.
Socho. Jsh +15:35.
Jekuthiel. i.e. *the fear* or *veneration* or *preservation of God; God is almightiness*, **S#3354h**.
Zanoah. Jsh +15:34.
Bithiah. i.e. *worshiper of Jah; daughter of Jah*, **S#1332h**.
daughter of Pharaoh. 1 K 3:1, 6. 7:8. 9:16, 24. 2 Ch 8:11.
Mered. ver. 17.

19 **Hodiah**. i.e. *my glory is Jah*, **S#1940h**. or, Jehudijah, *mentioned before*, ver. 18.
Naham. i.e. *comforter*, **S#5163h**.
Keilah. Jsh +15:44.
Garmite. i.e. *bony, strong*, **S#1636h**.
Eshtemoa. 1 S +30:28.
Maachathite. 2 S 10:6. +23:34.

20 **Shimon**. i.e. *waste*, **S#7889h**.
Amnon. 2 S +3:2.
Rinnah. i.e. *a joyful shout*, **S#7441h**.
Ben-hanan. i.e. *son graciously given*, **S#1135h**.
Tilon. i.e. *suspension; thou shalt abide*, **S#8436h**.
Ishi. Ho +2:16.
Zoheth. i.e. *releasing; strong*, **S#2105h**.
Ben-zoheth. i.e. *son of releasing* or *violent removal*, **S#1132h**.

21 **Shelah**. Ge +38:5.
Judah. Ge +35:23.
Er. Ge +38:3.

Lecah. i.e. *journey*, **S#3922h**.
Laadah. i.e. *order*, **S#3935h**.
Mareshah. Jsh +15:44.
fine linen. 1 Ch 15:27. 2 Ch 2:14. 3:14. 5:12. Est 1:6. 8:15. Ezk 27:16.
Ashbea. i.e. *adjurer*, **S#791h**.

22 **Jokim**. i.e. *Jah will rise*, **S#3137h**.
Chozeba. i.e. *falsehood*, **S#3578h**.
Joash. 1 Ch +7:8. Jsh +6:11.
Saraph. i.e. *fiery serpent*, **S#8315h**.
Moab. Ge +19:37.
Jashubi-lehem. i.e. *restorer of bread*, **S#3433h**.
things. or, records.

23 **the potters**. ver. 14. Ps 81:6.
dwelt with. Mk 3:14.

24 **The sons of Simeon**. Jsh 19:2-10.
Simeon. Ge +29:33.
Nemuel. Nu +26:12. or, Jemuel. Ge 46:10. Ex 6:15.
Jamin. Ge +46:10.
Jarib. i.e. *an adversary*, **S#3402h**. Ezr 8:16. 10:18. or, Jachin. Ge +46:10. Nu 26:12-14.
Zerah. Ge +36:13. +46:10, Zohar.

25 **Shallum**. 2 K +15:10.
Mibsam. Ge +25:13.
Mishma. Ge +25:14.

26 **Hamuel**. i.e. *God is sun; heat of God; they were heated of God*, **S#2536h**.
Zacchur. i.e. *remembered; mindful*, **S#2139h**.
Shimei. 2 S +16:5.

27 **sixteen sons and six daughters**. Ps +127:3.
like to. Heb. unto. Nu 2:4, 13. 26:14, 22.
multiply. ver. 38. Ge 49:7. Nu 2:4.

28 **they dwelt**. Jsh 19:2-8.
Beer-sheba. Ge +21:31.
Moladah. Jsh +15:26.
Hazar-shual. Jsh +15:28.

29 **Bilhah**. Ge +29:29. or, Balah, Jsh 19:3.
Ezem. i.e. *bone*, **S#6107h**. Jsh +15:29, Azem. 19:3.
Tolad. i.e. *posterity*, **S#8434h**. Jsh 19:4, Eltolad.

30 **Bethuel**. Ge +22:22. Jsh 19:4, Bethul.
Hormah. Nu +14:45.
Ziklag. Jsh +15:31.

31 **Beth-marcaboth**. i.e. *the chariot-house*, **S#1024h**. Jsh 19:5.
Hazar-susim. i.e. *court of the horses*, **S#2702h**. or, Hazar-susah, Jsh 19:5, 6.
Beth-birei. i.e. *house of creation*, **S#1011h**. Jsh 19:6, Beth-lebaoth.
Shaaraim. Jsh +15:36. 19:6, Sharuhen.

32 **Etam**. i.e. *ravenous creatures*, **S#5862h**. ver. 3. Jg 15:8, 11. 2 Ch 11:6.
Ain. Nu +34:11.
Rimmon. Jsh 19:7, Remmon. 2 K +5:18.
Tochen. i.e. *measurement; portion cut out; task assigned*, **S#8507h**.
Ashan. Jsh +15:42.

33 **Baal**. Jsh 19:8, Baalath-beer. Jg +6:25.

their genealogy. *or,* as they divided them-selves by nations among them.

34 **Meshobab**. i.e. *returned; restored; backsliding,* S#4877h.

Jamlech. i.e. *let him reign,* S#3230h.

Joshah. i.e. *aid; setting upright; Jah a gift; he will be prospered,* S#3144h.

Amaziah. i.e. *whom Jehovah strengthened,* S#558h. 1 Ch 6:45. 2 K 12:21. 13:12. 14:8. 15:1. Am 7:10, 12, 14. Also S#558h: 1 Ch 3:12. 2 K 14:1, 9, 11, 13, 15, 17, 18, 21, 23. 15:3. 2 Ch 24:27. 25:1, 5, 9-11, 13-15, 17, 18, 20, 21, 23, 25-27. 26:1, 4.

35 **Joel**. 1 S +8:2.

Jehu. 2 K +9:2.

Josibiah. i.e. *Jehovah will cause to dwell; will be made to sit down of the Lord,* S#3143h.

Seraiah. 2 S +8:17.

Asiel. i.e. *wrought of God,* S#6221h.

36 **Elioenai**. 1 Ch +26:3.

Jaakobah. i.e. *supplanter, deceiver,* S#3291h.

Jeshohaiah. i.e. *Jah will empty; depression of the Lord,* S#3439h.

Asaiah. 2 Ch +34:20.

Adiel. i.e. *witness of God; ornament of God,* S#5717h. 1 Ch 9:12. 27:25.

Jesimiel. i.e. *naming of God; he will be placed of God,* S#3450h.

Benaiah. 1 Ch +15:24.

37 **Ziza**. i.e. *abundance,* S#2124h. 2 Ch 11:20.

Shiphi. i.e. *my abundance; bald, naked, eminent,* S#8230h.

Allon. i.e. *an oak; thick through,* S#438h. Jsh 19:33. See Ge 35:8.

Jedaiah. Ne +3:10.

Shimri. i.e. *watchful; vigilant,* S#8113h. 1 Ch 11:45. +26:10, Simri. 2 Ch 29:13.

Shemaiah. 1 Ch +9:16.

38 **mentioned by their names**. Heb. coming by names. ver. 41. 1 Ch 5:24. Ge 6:4. Jb 3:6.

the house. ver. 27.

increased greatly. 1 Ch +13:2mg.

39 **Gedor**. ver. 4, 18. Jsh 12:13, Geder. 15:58.

40 **fat pasture**. Nu 13:20. Ne 9:25, 35.

the land. Jg 18:7-10.

wide. Ps 104:25.

quiet. Jg 18:7, 27.

peaceable. 1 T 2:1, 2.

Ham. Ge +5:32. Ge 9:22, etc. 10:6. Ps 78:51. 105:23.

41 **these written**. ver. 33-38.

Hezekiah. 2 K +16:20. 18:8, etc. Is 14:28-32.

the habitations. Or, the *Meunnim,* or Maonites. Jg +10:12. 2 Ch 26:27.

destroyed them utterly. 2 K 19:11. 2 Ch 20:23.

rooms. 1 Ch 5:22.

pasture. Nu 32:1-4.

42 **mount Seir**. Ge +14:6.

43 **the rest**. Ex +17:14.

unto this day. 1 Ch 5:26. 13:11. Ge +19:38. 2 Ch 5:9. Ne 9:32. Je 25:18. 44:6, 22. Mt 27:8. 28:15.

1 CHRONICLES 5

1 A.M. 2294, etc. B.C. 1710, etc.

he was. Ge +29:32. 46:8. 49:3. Ex 6:14.

forasmuch. Ge 35:22. 49:4. Le 18:8. 20:11. Dt 27:20. 1 C 5:1.

birthright. 1 Ch 26:10. Ge 48:15-22. Dt 21:17. Col +1:15.

and. Ge 25:23. 1 S 16:6-11.

reckoned. Jsh 14:6.

2 **Judah**. Ge +35:23. +49:8-10. Mi +5:2. Mt 2:6. He 7:14. Re 5:5.

the chief ruler. *or,* the prince. Ge 49:10. 1 S 16:1, 10, 12. 2 S 8:15. Ps 78:68-71. Je 23:5, 6. Mi +5:2. Mt 2:6. He 7:14.

birthright was. Ge 49:26. Ro 8:29.

3 **sons**. Ge 46:9. Ex 6:14. Nu 26:5-9.

Hanoch. Ge +25:4.

Pallu. Ge 46:9, Phallu. Nu +26:5.

Hezron. Ge +46:9.

Carmi. 1 Ch +4:1.

4 **Joel**. 1 S +8:2.

Shemaiah. 1 Ch +9:16.

Gog. i.e. *to cover; surmount; top; roof; extension; mountain,* S#1463h. Ezk 38:2, 3, 14, 16, 18. 39:1, 11, 15.

Shimei. 2 S +16:5.

5 **Micah**. Mi +1:1.

Reaia. i.e. *seen of Jah,* S#7211h. 1 Ch 4:2, Reaiah. Ezr 2:47. Ne 7:50.

Baal. Jg +6:25.

6 **Beerah**. i.e. *a well,* S#880h.

Tilgath-pilneser. ver. 26. 2 K +15:29. 16:7, Tiglath-pileser.

Reubenites. Nu +26:7.

7 **when the genealogy**. ver. 17.

Jeiel. i.e. *treasure of God,* S#3273h. 1 Ch +9:35, Jehiel. 11:44. 15:18, 21. 16:5. 2 Ch 20:14. 26:11. 29:13. 35:9. Ezr 8:13. 10:43.

Zechariah. Zc +1:1.

8 **Bela**. Ge +14:2.

Azaz. i.e. *the strong one,* S#5811h.

Shema. Jsh +15:26. *or,* Shemaiah, ver. 4.

Aroer. Nu +32:34.

Nebo. Nu +32:3.

Baal-meon. Nu +32:38.

9 **Euphrates**. Ge +2:14.

Gilead. ver. 16. Ge +37:25.

because. Jsh 22:8, 9.

10 A.M. 2944. B.C. 1060.

the Hagarites. i.e. *fugitives,* S#1905h. ver. 19, 20. Ge 21:9. 25:12. 2 S 24:6. Ps +83:6, Hagarenes. Also 1 Ch +11:38, Haggeri. +27:31.

throughout, etc. Heb. upon all the face of the East.

11 **Gad**. Ge +30:11.
  in the land of Bashan. Dt +32:14.
  Salcah. Jsh +13:11.
12 **Joel**. 1 S +8:2.
  Shapham. i.e. *bald*, **S#8223h**.
  Jaanai. i.e. *responsive*, **S#3285h**.
  Shaphat. 1 Ch +3:22.
  Bashan. ver. 11. Nu +21:33.
13 **Michael**. Da +12:1.
  Meshullam. 1 Ch +9:12.
  Sheba. 1 K +10:1.
  Jorai. i.e. *rainy*, **S#3140h**.
  Jachan. i.e. *afflicted*, **S#3275h**.
  Zia. i.e. *trembling; smelling*, **S#2127h**.
  Heber. Ge +46:17.
14 **Abihail**. Nu +3:35.
  Huri. i.e. *nobleman*, **S#2359h**.
  Jaroah. i.e. *making a sweet odor*, **S#3386h**.
  Gilead. Ge +31:23.
  Michael. Da +12:1.
  Jeshishai. i.e. *aged*, **S#3454h**.
  Jahdo. i.e. *together*, **S#3163h**.
  Buz. Ge +22:21.
15 **Ahi**. i.e. *brotherly*, **S#277h**. 1 Ch 7:34.
  Abdiel. i.e. *servant of God*, **S#5661h**.
  Guni. Ge +46:24.
16 **Gilead**. Ge +31:23.
  Bashan. ver. 11.
  Sharon. Is +35:2.
  their borders. Heb. goings forth.
17 **reckoned by genealogies**. ver. 7.
  Jotham. Jg +9:5.
  Jeroboam. 1 K +11:26.
18 **Reuben**. Ge +29:32.
  Gadites. Dt +3:12.
  Manasseh. Ge +41:51.
  valiant men. Heb. sons of valor. ver. 24. 2 S +2:7mg.
  to shoot. 1 Ch 8:40. 2 Ch 14:8. Ps 7:13.
  four and forty. Jsh 4:12, 13.
  that went. Nu 1:3.
19 **made war**. ver. +10.
  the Hagarites. ver. +10.
  Jetur. 1 Ch 1:31. Ge +25:15.
  Nephish. i.e. *pleasure; refreshment; respiration*, **S#5305h**. 1 Ch 1:31. Ge +25:15, Naphish.
  Nodab. i.e. *nobility; liberal*, **S#5114h**.
20 **And they**. ver. 22. Ex 17:11. Jsh 10:14, 42. 1 S 7:12. 19:5. Ps 46:1. 146:5, 6.
  for they cried. 1 K 8:44, 45. 2 Ch 13:14, 15. 14:11-13. 18:31. 20:12. 32:20, 21.
  in the battle. 1 K 22:32. 2 Ch 13:13, 14. 14:10, 11. 18:31.
  because. Ps 9:10. 20:7, 8. 22:4, 5. 84:11, 12. Je 17:7, 8. Na 1:7. Ep 1:12.
21 **took away**. Heb. led captive. 2 Ch 14:15.
  camels. Ge 24:61. 37:25. Jg 5:10.
  men. Heb. souls of men. Nu 31:35. Ezk 27:13. Re 18:13.
  souls. Heb. *nephesh*, Ge +12:5.

22 **the war was of God**. Ex 14:14. Jsh 23:10. Jg 3:2. 2 Ch 32:8. Ne 4:20. Ps 24:8. Pr +22:3. Zc 14:3. Lk 14:31, 32. +22:36. Ro 8:31.
  they dwelt. Nu 32:33.
  steads. 1 Ch 4:41.
  until the captivity. ver. 6, 26. 2 K 15:29. 17:6.
23 **Manasseh**. Ge +41:51.
  Bashan. Dt +32:14.
  Baal-hermon. Jsh 13:29-31. Jg +3:3.
  Senir. i.e. *coat of mail; bear the lamp; pointed*, **S#8149h**. Ezk 27:5. Also Dt 3:9. SS 4:8, Shenir.
  mount Hermon. Dt +3:8.
24 **Epher**. Ge +25:4.
  Ishi. 1 Ch +2:31.
  Eliel. 1 Ch +8:20.
  Azriel. i.e. *help of God*, **S#5837h**. 1 Ch 27:19. Je 36:26.
  Jeremiah. Je +1:1.
  Hodaviah. i.e. *majesty of God*, **S#1938h**. 1 Ch 9:7. Ezr 2:40. Ne 7:43, Hodevah.
  Jahdiel. i.e. *he will be gladdened of God*, **S#3164h**.
  mighty men of valor. ver. +18mg.
  famous men. Heb. men of names. 1 Ch 4:38. 12:30mg.
25 **a whoring**. Ex +34:15. 2 K 17:7-18.
  after the gods. Jg 2:12. 2 Ch 25:14, 15. Ps 106:34-39.
26 **stirred up**. 2 S 24:1. 2 Ch 33:11. Ezr 1:5. Is 10:5, 6. 13:2-5.
  the spirit. Heb. *ruach*, Ge +41:8; +26:35.
  Pul. 2 K +15:19.
  Tilgath-pilneser. i.e. *lord of the Tigris*, **S#8407h**. ver. 6. 2 Ch 28:20. Also 2 K +15:29, Tiglath-pilneser. 16:7, 10.
  Reubenites. Nu +26:7.
  Gadites. ver. 18.
  and brought them. 2 K 17:6. 18:11. 19:12. Is 37:12.
  Halah. 2 K +17:6.
  Habor. 2 K +17:6.
  Hara. i.e. *mountainous*, **S#2024h**.
  Gozan. 2 K +17:6.
  unto this day. 1 Ch +4:43.

1 CHRONICLES 6

1 A.M. 2304, etc. B.C. 1700, etc.
  sons of Levi. Ge +29:34.
  Gershon. Ge +46:11. or, Gershom. ver. 16, 17, 20. Ex +2:22.
  Kohath. Ge +46:11.
  Merari. Ge +46:11.
2 **the sons of Kohath**. 1 Ch 23:12. Ex 6:18, 21-24.
  Amram. ver. 22, Amminadab. Ex +6:18.
  Izhar. ver. 22. Ex +6:18.
  Hebron. Ex +6:18.
  Uzziel. Ex +6:18.

3 Aaron. 1 Ch 23:13. Ex +4:14. 6:20.
Miriam. Ex 2:4, 7. +15:20.
Nadab. Ex +6:23.
Abihu. Ex +6:23.
Eleazar. Ex +6:23.
4 Phinehas. ver. 50. Ex +6:25.
Abishua. i.e. *prosperous; father of welfare* or
help or *riches* or *salvation* or *success*, S#50. ver.
5, 50. 1 Ch 8:4. Ezr 7:5.
5 Bukki. Nu +34:22.
Uzzi. i.e. *my strength*, **S#5813h**. ver. 6, 51. 1 Ch
7:2, 3, 7. 9:8. Ezr 7:4. Ne 11:22. 12:19, 42.
6 Zerahiah. Ezr +7:4.
Meraioth. Ne +12:15.
7 Amariah. Ezr +7:3.
Ahitub. 1 S +14:3.
8 Ahitub. 2 S 8:17.
Zadok. 2 S +8:17.
Ahimaaz. 1 S +14:50.
9 Azariah. ver. +36.
Johanan. 2 K +25:23.
10 A.M. 3244. B.C. 760.
executed. 2 Ch 26:17-20.
the temple. Heb. the house.
Solomon built. 1 K ch. 6, 7. 2 Ch 3:4.
11 Azariah. ver. 9, +36.
Amariah. 2 Ch 19:11. Ezr +7:3.
Ahitub. 1 S +14:3.
12 Zadok. 2 S +8:17.
Shallum. 1 Ch 9:11. 2 K +15:10. Ne 11:11,
Meshullam.
13 Hilkiah. 2 K +18:18.
Azariah. ver. +36.
14 A.M. 3416. B.C. 588.
Seraiah. 2 S +8:17. Zc 6:11.
15 Jehozadak. i.e. *whom Jehovah has made just;*
Jehovah is the righteous one. Ezr +3:2, Jozadak.
5:2. Hg +1:1, 12, 14. 2:2, Josedech. **S#3087h**.
ver. 14. Hg 1:1, 12, 14. 2:2, 4. Zc 6:11.
when the Lord. 2 K 25:18, 21. 2 Ch 36:17-
21. Je 39:9. 52:12-15, 28.
by the hand. Ex 4:13. 2 S +7:14. 2 K 14:27.
25:21. Ac 14:27. Ro 15:18.
16 A.M. 2304, etc. B.C. 1700, etc.
Gershom. ver. 1. Ex 6:16, Gershon.
17 the sons of Gershom. Nu +3:21.
Libni. ver. +29.
Shimei. 2 S +16:5.
18 sons of Kohath. Ge +46:11.
Amram. ver. 2, 3. Ex +6:18.
19 Merari. Ge +46:11.
Mahli. Nu +3:20.
Mushi. Ex +6:19.
20 Libni. ver. 17, +29.
Jahath. 1 Ch +4:2.
Zimmah. ver. 42. 2 Ch +29:12.
his son. or, grandson. ver. 42, 43. 1 Ch 3:19.
1 K +15:10.
21 Joah. Is +36:3. *or*, Ethan, ver. 42.
Iddo. Ezr +5:1. *or*, Adaiah, Ne +11:5.

Zerah. ver. 41. Ge +36:13.
Jeaterai. i.e. *my steps*, **S#2979h**. ver. 41, Ethni.
22 Amminadab. ver. 2, 18. 1 Ch +15:11. Ex
+6:18, 21, 24, Izhar.
Korah. Ge +36:5.
Assir. Ex +6:24. Nu 26:11.
23 Elkanah. Ex +6:24.
Ebiasaph. i.e. *father of increase*, **S#43h**. ver. 37.
1 Ch 9:19. Ex +6:24, Abiasaph.
Assir. Ex +6:24.
24 Tahath. Nu 33:26.
Uriel. 1 Ch +15:5. *or*, Zephaniah, ver. 36.
Uzziah. *or*, Azariah, ver. +36. 2 Ch +26:1.
Shaul. Ge +46:10. *or*, Joel, ver. 36.
25 A.M. 2904, etc. B.C. 1100, etc.
Elkanah. ver. 22, 35, 36. Ex +6:24.
Amasai. 2 Ch +29:12.
Ahimoth. i.e. *brother of death*, **S#287h**.
26 Zophai. i.e. *my overflows; honey of the Lord*,
S#6689h. ver. 35, Zuph. 1 S 1:1, Zuph. Also 1 S
9:5, Zuph.
Nahath. ver. 34, Toah. Ge +36:13. 1 S 1:1,
Tohu.
27 Eliab. ver. 34, Eliel. Nu +1:9. 1 S 1:1, Elihu.
Jeroham. 1 S +1:1.
Elkanah. Ex +6:24. 1 S 1:1, 19, 20.
28 firstborn. 1 Ch +5:1. Le +27:26.
Vashni. i.e. *Jah is strong; wherefore, sleep thou;*
changed; my year; second; liberal gift of the Lord,
S#2059h. ver. 33. 1 S 8:2, Joel.
29 Merari. Ge +46:11.
Mahli. ver. +19.
Libni. i.e. *white, transparent*, **S#3845h**. ver. 17,
20. Ex 6:17. Nu 3:18. 1 Ch 6:17, 20.
Shimei. ver. 17.
Uzza. 2 K +21:18.
30 Haggiah. i.e. *festival of Jah*, **S#2293h**.
Asaiah. 2 Ch +34:20.
31 A.M. 2962. B.C. 1042.
whom David. 1 Ch 15:16-22, 27. 25:1-31.
after that. 1 Ch 16:1. 2 S 6:17. Ps 132:8, 14.
had rest. He 4:9. Re 14:13.
32 they ministered. 1 Ch 16:4-6, 37-42. Ps
68:24, 25.
with singing. Ep 5:19.
until Solomon. ver. 10. 1 K 8:6-13.
and then. 1 Ch 9:33. 25:8-31. 2 Ch 29:25-
30. 31:2. 35:15. Ezr 3:10, 11. 6:18. Ne 11:17-
23. 12:27, 28, 45-47. Ps 134:1, 2. 135:1-3.
waited. Heb. stood. ver. 33. 1 K 12:6, 8.
according to their order. 1 C 12:11.
33 waited. Heb. stood. ver. 32. Dt +10:8. Pr
8:34. Ep 6:13.
Heman. 1 Ch +2:6.
Joel. ver. 28, Vashni. 1 S +8:2.
Shemuel. ver. 28. Nu +34:20.
34 Elkanah. Ex +6:24.
Jeroham. 1 S +1:1.
Eliel. ver. 27, Eliab. 1 Ch +8:20.

Toah. i.e. *depressing; inclination; sinking, prostration*, **S#8430h**. ver. 26, Nathah.

35 **Zuph**. ver. +26, Zophai. 1 S +1:1.
Elkanah. ver. 25.

36 **Joel**. ver. 24, Shaul, 28.
Azariah. i.e. *whom Jehovah aids; Jah has helped*, **S#5838h**. ver. 9-11, 13, 14. 1 Ch 2:8, 38, 39. 3:12. 9:11. 2 Ch 21:2. 23:1. Ezr 7:1, 3. Ne 3:23, 24. 7:7. 8:7. 10:2. 12:33. Je 43:2. Da 1:6, 7, 11, 19. Also **S#5838h**: 1 K 4:2, 5. 2 K 14:21. 15:6, 8. 2 Ch 15:1. 21:2. 22:6. 23:1. 26:17, 20. 28:12. 29:12. 31:10, 13.
Zephaniah. ver. 24, Shaul, Uzziah, Uriel. Zp +1:1.

37 **Tahath**. Nu +33:26.
Assir. Ex +6:24.
Ebiasaph. ver. +23.
Korah. Ge +36:5.

38 **Izhar**. Ex +6:18.
Kohath. Ge +46:11.
Levi. Ge +29:34.
Israel. Ge +32:28.

39 **Asaph**. 2 K +18:18.
on his right hand. ver. 31. 1 Ch 25:3.
Berachiah. i.e. *blessed of Jehovah*, **S#1296h**. 15:17. 2 Ch 28:12. Zc 1:7. Also **S#1296h**: 1 Ch 3:20. 9:16. 15:23. Ne 3:4, 30. 6:18. Zc 1:1.
Shimea. 1 Ch 3:5.

40 **Michael**. Da +12:1.
Baaseiah. i.e. *work of the Lord*, **S#1202h**.
Malchiah. Je +38:1.

41 **Ethni**. i.e. *Jehovah's reward; my hire*, **S#867h**. ver. 21, Jeaterai.
Zerah. ver. +21.
Adaiah. ver. 21, Iddo. Ne +11:5.

42 **Ethan**. ver. 21, Joah. 1 Ch +2:6.
Zimmah. ver. 20.
Shimei. 2 S +16:5.

43 **Jahath**. ver. 20.
Gershom. ver. 1, 16, 17, 20. Ge +46:11, Gershon. Ex +2:22.

44 **stood**. ver. 32, 39.
on the left hand. Ge +48:13. Jg +20:16.
Ethan. 1 Ch +2:6. 25:1, 3, 6, Jeduthun. Ps 89, title.
Kishi. i.e. *sharing of the Lord*, **S#7029h**. 1 Ch +15:17, Kushaiah. 2 Ch 29:12.
Abdi. i.e. *servant of Jehovah*, **S#5660h**. 2 Ch 29:12. Ezr 10:26.

45 **Hashabiah**. 1 Ch +9:14.
Amaziah. 1 Ch +4:34.
Hilkiah. 2 K +18:18.

46 **Amzi**. Ne 11:12.
Bani. Ezr +2:10.
Shamer. i.e. *guardian; prison; the lees, or crust of wine*, **S#8106h**. 1 Ch 7:34. 8:12.

47 **Mahli**. Nu +3:20.
Mushi. Nu +3:33.
Merari. Ge +46:11.
Levi. Ge +29:34.

48 **brethren**. 1 Ch 23:2, etc. ch. 25. 26. Nu ch. 3. 4. 8:5-26. 16:9, 10. ch. 18.
appointed. 1 C 12:28.

49 A.M. 2513. B.C. 1491.
Aaron. Ex 27:1-8. 30:1-7. Le 1:5, 7-9. ch. 8-10, 21, 22. Nu 16:16-50. ch. 17. Dt 18:1-8. He 7:11-14.
make an atonement. Ex 29:33, 36, 37. 30:10-16. Le 4:20. Nu 15:25. 16:46. Jb 33:24mg.
Moses. Dt 34:5. Jsh 1:1.

50 **Eleazar**. ver. 3-9. Ex +6:23.
Phinehas. ver. +4.

51 **Bukki**. ver. 5.

52 **Meraioth**. ver. 6, 7.

53 **Zadok**. ver. +8. 1 S 2:35.

54 A.M. 2561. B.C. 1443.
these are. Nu 35:1-8. Jsh 21:3-8.
castles. Ge 25:16. Nu 31:10. Ps 69:25. Pr 18:10, 11. Ep 3:8.
of the families. Jsh 21:4, 5.
for their's. Jsh 21:4.

55 **Hebron**. Nu +13:22.

56 **the fields**. Jsh 14:13. 15:13.
Caleb. Nu +13:6.

57 **they gave**. 1 S 22:10. 2 Ch 31:15.
the city of refuge. Nu 35:13-15. Jsh +20:7-9.
Libnah. Nu +33:20.
Jattir. 1 Ch +4:17. Jsh 15:48.

58 **Hilen**. i.e. *fortress*, **S#2432h**. *or*, Holon. Jsh 15:51. 21:15.
Debir. Jsh +10:3.

59 **Ashan**. Nu +34:11, Ain. Jsh +15:42.
Beth-shemesh. Je +43:13.

60 **Geba**. 1 S +13:3.
Alemeth. i.e. *covering; a hiding place*, **S#5954h**. Jsh 21:18, Almon. 1 Ch 7:8.
Anathoth. 1 Ch +7:8.
thirteen cities. Jsh +10:2. +15:55. 21:16, 17. 1 Ch +14:16.

61 **And unto**. ver. 1, 2, 18, 33.
left. ver. 66. Jsh 21:4, 5, 20-26.
by lot. Jsh 14:2.
ten cities. Jsh 21:26.

62 **Gershom**. ver. 71-76. Ex +2:22. Jsh 21:27-33.

63 **Merari**. ver. 77-81. Ge +46:11.
by lot. Jsh +14:2.

64 **the children**. Jsh 21:41, 42.
with their. Nu 35:2-5.

65 **these cities**. ver. 57-60.

66 **the residue**. ver. 61. Jsh 21:20-26.

67 **Shechem**. Ge +33:18.
Gezer. 1 K +9:16.

68 **Jokmeam**. i.e. *gathered of the people; he will establish the people*, **S#3361h**. 1 K 4:12. See Jsh 21:22, Kibzaim.
Beth-horon. Jsh +10:10.

69 **Aijalon**. Jsh +10:12, Ajalon.
Gath-rimmon. Jsh 21:24, +25.

70 **Aner**. Jsh 21:25, Tanach, Gath-rimmon.
Bileam. i.e. *devouring; foreigner*, **S#1109h**.
Compare the same Hebrew word, rendered
Balaam, Nu +22:5. Jsh 17:11, Ibleam. Jg
+1:27.

71 **Golan**. Dt +4:43.
Bashan. Dt +32:14.
Ashtaroth. Dt +1:4.

72 **Kedesh**. Jsh +15:23.
Daberath. Jsh +19:12. 21:28, 29, Kishon,
Daberah, Jarmuth, En-gannim.

73 **Ramoth**. i.e. *heights; coral*, **S#7216h**. ver. 80. Dt
4:43. Jsh 20:8.
Anem. i.e. *double fountain; two eyes*, **S#6046h**.

74 **Mashal**. i.e. *entreaty*, **S#4913h**. Jsh 19:26.
+21:30, Mishal.

75 **Hukok**. i.e. *a ditch; appointed portion; the
engraving*, **S#2712h**. Jsh 19:34. Compare Jsh
+19:25, 26. 21:31, Helkath.

76 **Kedesh**. ver. +72.
Hammon. Jsh 19:35, 37. 21:32, Hammoth-
dor, Kartan.
Kirjathaim. Nu +32:37.

77 **Unto**. Jsh 21:34-39.
Rimmon. Jsh 19:12, 13. 21:34, 35, Jokneam,
Kartah, Dimnah, Nahalal. 2 K +5:18.
Tabor. Jg +4:6.

78 **Bezer**. Dt +4:43.
Jahzah. i.e. *threshing-floor*, **S#3096h**. Jsh
+13:18.

79 **Kedemoth**. Jsh +13:18.
Mephaath. Jsh +13:18.

80 **Ramoth**. ver. +73. 1 K +4:13.
Mahanaim. Ge +32:2.

81 **Heshbon**. Nu +21:25.
Jazer. Nu +32:1.

1 CHRONICLES 7

1 **the sons of Issachar**. Ge +30:18.
Tola. Ge +46:13.
Puah. Ge +46:13, Phuvah. Ex +1:15. Nu
26:23, 24, Pua.
Jashub. Ge 46:13, Job. Nu +26:24.
Shimrom. i.e. *vigilant guardian*, **S#8110h**. Ge
+46:13, Shimron. Nu 26:24. Also Jsh 11:1.
19:15.

2 **Uzzi**. 1 Ch +6:5.
Rephaiah. 1 Ch +9:43.
Jeriel. i.e. *founded of God*, **S#3400h**.
Jahmai. i.e. *guarded of the Lord*, **S#3181h**.
Jibsam. i.e. *pleasant*, **S#3005h**.
Shemuel. Nu +34:20.
valiant men. Jg +6:12. 2 S +2:7mg.
whose number. ver. 4, 5. 1 Ch 21:1-5. 27:1,
23, 24. 2 S 24:1-9.

3 **Izrahiah**. i.e. *whom Jehovah brought to light;
whom Jah brings forth*, **S#3156h**. Ne 12:42,
Jezrahiah.
Michael. Da +12:1.

Obadiah. Ob +1.
Joel. 1 S +8:2.
Ishiah. i.e. *gift of the Lord*, **S#3449h**. 1 Ch 23:20.
24:21, 25, 25. Ezr +10:31, Ishijah.

4 **with them**. 1 Ch 12:32.

6 **the sons**. 1 K +15:10mg.
of Benjamin. 1 Ch 8:1, etc. Ge 46:21. Nu
26:38-41.
Jediael. i.e. *known of God*, **S#3043h**. ver. 10, 11.
1 Ch 11:45. 12:20. 26:2.

7 **Bela**. Ge +14:2.
Ezbon. Ge +46:16.
Uzzi. 1 Ch +6:5.
Uzziel. Ex +6:18.
Jerimoth. i.e. *he who fears*, **S#3406h**. 1 Ch
12:5. 24:30. 25:4. 27:19. 2 Ch 11:18.
31:13.
Iri. i.e. *urbane; my city*, **S#5901h**.
mighty men. Jg +6:12. 2 S +2:7mg.
were reckoned. 1 Ch 21:1-5. 2 Ch 17:17,
18.

8 **Becher**. Ge +46:21.
Zemira. i.e. *palm; causing singing; song, dance*;
S#2160h.
Joash. i.e. *Jehovah has helped; Jehovah-fired*,
S#3135h. 1 Ch 27:28.
Eliezer. Ge +15:2.
Elioenai. 1 Ch 26:3.
Omri. 1 K +16:16.
Jerimoth. Ezr +10:26, Jeremoth.
Abiah. 1 S +8:2.
Anathoth. i.e. *answers to prayers; affliction;
answers*, **S#6068h**. Jsh 21:18. 1 K 2:26. 1 Ch
6:60. Ezr 2:23. Ne 7:27. 10:19. 11:32. Is
10:30. Je 1:1. 11:21, 23. 32:7-9.
Alameth. i.e. *concealment; covering*, **S#5964h**. 1
Ch +6:60, Alemeth. 8:36. 9:42.

9 **mighty men**. ver. 7.

10 **Jediael**. ver. +6.
Bilhan. Ge +36:27.
Jeush. Ge +36:5.
Benjamin. Ge +35:18.
Ehud. 1 Ch +8:6. Jg 3:15, etc.
Chenaanah. i.e. *submissive; humiliation; one
who bends the knee or merchant; traffic*, **S#3668h**.
1 K 22:11, 24. 2 Ch 18:10.
Zethan. i.e. *olive tree*, **S#2133h**.
Tharshish. i.e. *a precious stone; will cause
poverty; breaking*, **S#8659h**. Ge +10:4. Est 1:14.
Ahishahar. i.e. *brother of the morning*, **S#300h**.

11 **mighty men**. 2 Ch 17:13, etc.

12 **Shuppim**. i.e. *serpents*, **S#8206h**. ver. 15. 1 Ch
26:16. Ge 46:21, Muppim, Huppim. Nu 26:39,
Shupham, Hupham.
Huppim. Ge +46:21.
Ir. i.e. *a city*, **S#5893h**. ver. 7, Iri.
Hushim. Ge +46:23.
the sons. Ge +46:7. Plural put for singular
(Ge +46:7). Ge 46:23. Jg ch. 18. Re ch 7.
Aher. i.e. *another; following*, **S#313h**. Ge 46:23.

Jg 18:30. 20:35. 1 K 12:29, 30. 2 K 10:29. Am 8:14. 1 Ch 8:1, Aharah. Nu 26:38, Ahiram.

13 Jahziel. i.e. *allotted of God*, **S#3185h**. Ge +46:24. Nu 26:48, Jahzeel.
  Guni. Ge +46:24.
  Jezer. Ge +46:24.
  Shallum. Ge +46:24. Nu 26:49, Shillem. 2 K +15:10.
  the sons of. or, grandchildren. Ge 30:3-8. 35:22. 46:25. 1 K +15:10.
  Bilhah. Ge +29:29.

14 The sons of. or, grandchildren. ver. 13. Nu 26:29-33. 27:1.
  Ashriel. i.e. *vow of, or bound of God*, **S#844h**. Nu +26:31, Asriel. Jsh 17:2.
  concubine. 1 Ch +2:48.
  Aramitess. i.e. *highlandress; exalted of Jah*, **S#761h**. Elsewhere rendered *Syrian*, Ge +25:20.
  Machir. Ge +50:23.
  Gilead. ver. 17. Ge +31:23. Nu 26:29.

15 the sister. ver. 16.
  Huppim. ver. 12.
  Maachah. 1 K +2:39.
  the second. Nu 26:29, etc.
  and Zelophehad. Nu +26:33. 27:1-11. 36:1-12.
  had daughters. 1 Ch 2:34.

16 Peresh. i.e. *excrement, dung*, **S#6570h**.
  Sheresh. i.e. *a root*, **S#8329h**.
  Ulam. i.e. *their strength; first of all, portico, vestibule*, **S#198h**. ver. 17. 1 Ch 8:39, 40.
  Rakem. i.e. *embroidery; versicolor*, **S#7552h**. 1 Ch +2:43, 44. 7:16. Nu 31:8. Jsh 13:21.

17 Bedan. i.e. *son of judgment; fat, robust*, **S#917h**. 1 S 12:11.
  These. ver. 14, 15.

18 Hammoleketh. i.e. *queen*, **S#4447h**.
  Ishod. i.e. *man of renown*, **S#379h**.
  Abiezer. Nu 26:30, Jeezer. Jsh +17:2. Jg 6:11, 24, 34. 8:2.
  Mahalah. i.e. *disease, infirmity, sickness*, **S#4244h**. Nu +26:33, Mahlah. 27:1. 36:11. Jsh 17:3.

19 Shemidah. i.e. *fame of wisdom; my name he knows*, **S#8061h**. Nu +26:32, Shemida. Jsh 17:2.
  Ahian. i.e. *brotherly; firmly bound*, **S#291h**.
  Shechem. Ge +33:18.
  Likhi. i.e. *learned; my doctrine*, **S#3949h**.
  Aniam. i.e. *lament of the people*, **S#593h**.

20 And the sons. Nu 26:35, 36.
  Ephraim. Ge +41:52.
  Shuthelah. ver. +21.
  Bered. Ge +16:14.
  Tahath. Nu +33:26.
  Eladah. i.e. *God's ornament*, **S#497h**.

21 Zabad. 1 Ch +2:36.
  Shuthelah. i.e. *freshly appointed; resembling rejuvenation*, **S#7803h**. ver. 20. Nu 26:35, 36.
  Ezer. **S#5827h**. 1 Ch +4:4. Ge +36:21.
  Elead. i.e. *God is witness*, **S#496h**.

Gath. Jsh +11:22.
  because they came. or, when.

22 mourned. Ge 37:34.
  and his brethren. or, kinsmen. 1 Ch +15:5. Jb 2:11.

23 Beriah. i.e. *in evil; gift, or calamity*, **S#1283h**. ver. 30, 31. 1 Ch 8:13, 16. 23:10, 11. Ge 46:17. Nu 26:44.
  because. 1 Ch 4:9 with 2 S 23:5. Ge 35:18. 1 S 4:21.

24 his daughter. i.e. his grandchild, or great-grandchild. 1 K +15:10. 2 K 8:26.
  Sherah. i.e. *kinswoman; near kinship*, **S#7609h**.
  Beth-horon. Jsh +10:10.
  Uzzen-sherah. i.e. *heard by near kinship; ear of Sherah*, **S#242h**.

25 Rephah. i.e. *healing; to sustain; riches, wealth; healing or enfeebling of the breath*, **S#7506h**.
  Resheph. i.e. *lightning; a flame*, **S#7566h**.
  Telah. i.e. *making green; invigorator*, **S#8520h**.
  Tahan. i.e. *thou wilt encamp*, **S#8465h**. Nu 26:35.

26 Laadan. 1 Ch +23:7.
  Ammihud. 2 S +13:37.
  Elishama. Nu +1:10. 7:48.

27 Non. i.e. *perpetuity*, **S#5126h**. Nu 13:8, 16, Nun.
  Jehoshuah. i.e. *Jehovah is salvation*, **S#3091h**. Ex 17:9-14. 24:13. 32:17. Nu 11:28, Joshua. 13:8, 16, Oshea. 14:6. 27:18. Dt 31:23, Joshua. Ac 7:45. He 4:8, Jesus.

28 Bethel. Ge +12:8.
  Naaran. i.e. *juvenile; handmaid; damsel*, **S#5295h**. Jsh 16:17, Naarath.
  Gezer. 1 K +9:16.
  Shechem. Ge +33:18.
  Gaza. Ge +10:19.
  towns. Heb. daughters. Nu +21:25mg.

29 Manasseh. Jsh 17:7-11.
  Beth-shean. Jsh +17:11.
  Taanach. Jsh +17:11.
  Megiddo. Jsh +12:21.
  towns. Heb. daughters. Nu +21:25.
  dwelt. Jsh ch. 16, 17. Jg 1:22-29.

30 Asher. Ge +30:13.
  Imnah. i.e. *good fortune; dexterity; prosperity; right-handed; the right side; he will number; he allotteth*, **S#3232h**. 2 Ch 31:14. Ge 46:17. Nu +26:44, Jimnah, +44, Jimnites.
  Isuah. i.e. *likeness; even, level*, **S#3438h**. Ge +46:17, Ishua.
  Ishuai. i.e. *Jah is self satisfying; he will justify me*, **S#3440h**. Ge +46:17, Isui. Nu +26:44, Jesui. 1 S +14:49, Ishui.
  Beriah. ver. +23.
  Serah. Ge +46:17.

31 Heber. Ge +46:17.
  Malchiel. Ge +46:17.
  Birzavith. i.e. *in leanness; choice olive*, **S#1269h**.

32 Japhlet. i.e. *he will set free*, **S#3310h**. ver. 33.
  Shomer. ver. 34, Shamer. 2 K +12:21.

Hotham. i.e. *a seal; signet-ring*, S#2369h. 1 Ch 11:44.

Shua. 1 Ch +2:3.

33 **Pasach**. i.e. *to divide; torn asunder*, S#6457h.

Bimhal. i.e. *in circumcision; son of mixture or corruption*, S#1118h.

Ashvath. i.e. *made; the joy of reward*, S#6220h.

34 **Shamer**. ver. 32, Shomer.

Ahi. 1 Ch +5:15.

Rohgah. i.e. *agitation; copious rain*, S#7303h.

Jehubbah. i.e. *binding; he will be hidden*, S#3160h.

Aram. Ge +22:21.

35 **Helem**. i.e. *strength; smiter*, S#1987h. For S#2494h, Helem, see Zc 6:14.

Zophah. i.e. *expanding; a vial*, S#6690h. ver. 36.

Imna. i.e. *he will restrain; he will keep back, or deny himself*, S#3234h.

Shelesh. i.e. *triplicate, triad, third, triplet; strength*, S#8028h.

Amal. i.e. *perverseness; wearisome labor, troublesome*, S#6000h.

36 **Suah**. i.e. *offal; filth; sweepings*, S#5477h.

Harnepher. i.e. *roaring of breath; the frustrator burnt; snorting or panting*, S#2774h.

Shual. i.e. *a fox; a jackal; a burrower*, S#7777h. 1 S 13:17.

Beri. i.e. *my well; of the well; well of God*, S#1275h.

Imrah. i.e. *a rebel; he will extol himself*, S#3236h.

37 **Bezer**. Dt +4:43.

Hod. i.e. *glory, majesty; confession*, S#1936h.

Shamma. i.e. *destruction, desolation; astonishment*, S#8037h.

Shilshah. i.e. *triplication, triad, the third*, S#8030h.

Ithran. ver. 38, Jether. Ge +36:26.

Beera. i.e. *a well*, S#878h.

38 **Jether**. 1 Ch +2:32.

Jephunneh. Nu +13:6.

Pispah. i.e. *disappearance; dispersion*, S#6462h.

Ara. i.e. *I shall see; herd or assembly; a lion; cursing*, S#690h.

39 **Ulla**. i.e. *burden; sacrifice killed on the altar; he was taken up; yoke*, S#5925h.

Arah. i.e. *a wayfarer; wandering, traveling*, S#733h. Ezr 2:5. Ne 6:18. 7:10.

Haniel. i.e. *favor of God*, S#2592h. Nu 34:23.

Rezia. i.e. *delight, satisfaction; haste*, S#7525h.

40 **the number**. 1 Ch 21:1-5. 2 S 24:1-9.

1 CHRONICLES 8

1 **Bela**. 1 Ch 7:6-12. Ge +14:2. 46:21.

his firstborn. Le +27:26.

Ashbel. Ge +46:21.

the second. ver. +39. 1 Ch 7:15.

Aharah. i.e. *after his brother*, S#315h. Nu 26:38, Ahiram.

2 **Nohah**. i.e. *quietude*, S#5119h.

Rapha. i.e. *he healed; the giant; the shrunken*, S#7498h. ver. 37. 1 Ch 20:4, 6, 8. Also 2 S 21:16, 18, 20, 22.

3 **Addar**. i.e. *mighty one; honorable, great*, S#146h. Ge +46:21. Nu 26:40, Ard.

Gera. Ge +46:21.

Abihud. i.e. *father of majesty; father of praise*, S#31h.

4 **Abishua**. 1 Ch +6:4.

Naaman. Ge +46:21. Nu 26:40.

Ahoah. i.e. *brotherly; brother of the Lord; brother of rest*, S#265h. 2 S 23:28.

5 **Gera**. ver. 3. Ge +46:21. Jg 3:15.

Shephuphan. i.e. *serpent-like*, S#8197h. 1 Ch 7:12, Shuppim. Nu 26:39, Shupham.

Huram. i.e. *noble, ingenuous*, S#2361h. 2 S +5:11, Hiram. 2 Ch 2:3, 11-13. 4:11, 16. 8:2, 18. 9:10, 21.

6 **Ehud**. i.e. *strong; undivided; union; joining together*, S#261. 1 Ch 7:10. Jg 3:20, etc. 4:1.

Geba. 1 S +13:3.

Manahath. 1 Ch 2:52, 54. Ge +36:23.

7 **Naaman**. ver. 4.

Ahiah. i.e. *friend of Jehovah*, S#281h. 1 S 14:3, 18. 1 K 4:3.

Gera. Ge +46:21.

Uzza. 2 K +21:18.

Ahihud. i.e. *my brother is united*, S#284h.

8 **Shaharaim**. i.e. *double-dawn*, S#7842h.

in the. Ru 1:1.

Hushim. Ge +46:23.

Baara. i.e. *kindling of the moon*, S#1199h.

after he had sent them away. ver. 9. Ge 25:6. Mt 19:3-9. 2 T 3:3.

wives. 1 Ch 4:5. Ge +4:19.

9 **Hodesh**. i.e. *the new moon*, S#2321h.

Jobab. Ge +10:29.

Zibia. i.e. *a gazelle; honorable chief*, S#6644h.

Mesha. i.e. *waters of devastation; making to forget*, S#4331h, only here. 1 Ch 2:42. 2 K 3:4.

Malcham. i.e. *most high king*, S#4445h.

10 **Jeuz**. i.e. *counselor*, S#3263h.

Shachia. i.e. *captivation; captive of the Lord; the return of Jah*, S#7634h.

Mirma. i.e. *deceit, guile, fraud*, S#4821h.

11 **Hushim**. Ge +46:23.

Abitub. i.e. *good; father of goodness*, S#36h.

Elpaal. i.e. *God the maker; God the reward*, S#508h. ver. 12, 18.

12 **Eber**. Ge +10:24.

Misham. i.e. *their cleansing or regarding*, S#4936h.

Shamed. i.e. *destruction; exterminator; persecution; guardian*, S#8106h. 1 Ch 6:46, Shamer. 1 K 16:24, Shemer.

Ono. Ezr +2:33.

Lod. Ne +7:37. Ac 9:32, 35, 38.

13 **Beriah**. 1 Ch +7:23.

Shema. ver. 21, Shimhi. Jsh +15:26.

the fathers. 1 Ch 2:42, 49, 50, 52. 4:4.

Aijalon. Jsh +10:12.
Gath. Jsh +11:22.

14 **Ahio**. 2 S +6:3.
Shashak. i.e. *the longed-for*, **S#8349h**. ver. 25.
Jeremoth. Ezr +10:26.

15 **Zebadiah**. 1 Ch +26:2.
Arad. i.e. *an ambush*, **S#6166h**. Nu 21:1. 33:40. Jsh 12:14. Jg 1:16.
Ader. i.e. *a flock*, **S#5738h**.

16 **Michael**. Da +12:1.
Ispah. i.e. *prominent*, **S#3472h**.
Joha. i.e. *lead thou, Jehovah*, **S#3109h**. 1 Ch 11:45.
Beriah. ver. 13. 1 Ch +7:23.

17 **Zebadiah**. 1 Ch +26:2.
Meshullam. 1 Ch +9:12.
Hezeki. i.e. *my strong one; strength of the Lord*, **S#2395h**.
Heber. Ge +46:17.

18 **Ishmerai**. i.e. *preservative; will be kept of the Lord*, **S#3461h**.
Jezliah. i.e. *Jah preserves; he shall pour out suitably*; **S#3152h**.
Jobab. Ge +10:29.
Elpaal. ver. +11.

19 **Jakim**. i.e. *God sets up*, **S#3356h**. 1 Ch 24:12.
Zichri. 1 Ch +9:15.
Zabdi. Jsh +7:1.

20 **Elienai**. i.e. *God of my eyes*, **S#462h**.
Zilthai. i.e. *protection*, **S#6769h**. 1 Ch 12:20.
Eliel. i.e. *God of might*, **S#447h**. ver. 22. 1 Ch 5:24. 6:34. 11:46, 47. 12:11. 15:9, 11. 2 Ch 31:13.

21 **Adaiah**. Ne +11:5.
Beraiah. i.e. *created of Jah*, **S#1256h**.
Shimrath. i.e. *guardianship; ward*, **S#8119h**.
Shimhi. i.e. *renowned, famous, heard of*, **S#8096h**. 2 S +16:5, Shimei; Ex +6:17, Shimi. See ver. 13, Shema.

22 **Ishpan**. i.e. *strong one*, **S#3473h**.
Heber. Ge +46:17.
Eliel. ver. +20.

23 **Abdon**. Jg +12:13.
Zichri. 1 Ch +9:15.
Hanan. 1 Ch +9:44.

24 **Hananiah**. 1 Ch +25:23.
Elam. Ge +10:22.
Antothijah. i.e. *answer of the Lord; answers or afflictions of Jah*, **S#6070h**.

25 **Iphedeiah**. i.e. *the Lord will redeem*, **S#3301h**.
Penuel. 1 Ch +4:4.
Shashak. ver. +14.

26 **Shamsherai**. i.e. *sun-like*, **S#8125h**.
Shehariah. i.e. *sought of the Lord*, **S#7841h**.
Athaliah. i.e. *afflicted of the Lord*, **S#6271h**. 2 K 11:1, 3, 13, 14. 2 Ch 22:12. Ezr 8:7. Also **S#6271h**: 2 K 8:26. 11:2, 20. 2 Ch 22:2, 10, 11. 23:12, 13, 21. 24:7.

27 **Jaresiah**. i.e. *nourished of the Lord; honey which is of Jah*, **S#3298h**.

Eliah. i.e. *my God is Jah*, **S#452h**. 2 K 1:3, 4, 8, 12. Ezr 10:21, 26. Ml 4:5.

28 **dwelt**. Jsh 15:63. 18:28. Jg 1:21. Ne 11:1, 7-9.
Jerusalem. 1 Ch 9:34.

29 **And**. 1 Ch 9:35-38.
Gibeon. Jsh +10:2.
the father. 1 Ch 9:35, 36, Jehiel.
Maachah. 1 K +2:39.

30 **Abdon**. ver. +23.
Zur. Nu +25:15.
Kish. 1 S +9:1.
Baal. 1 Ch +5:5.
Nadab. Ex +6:23.

31 **Gedor**. Jsh +15:58.
Ahio. 2 S +6:3.
Zacher. i.e. *memorial; remembrance*, **S#2144h**. 1 Ch 9:37, Zechariah.

32 **Mikloth**. 1 Ch +27:4.
Shimeah. **S#8039h**, only here. 1 Ch 9:38, Shimeam. 2 S +21:21.

33 **And**. 1 Ch 9:39-44.
Ner. 1 Ch +9:36.
Kish. 1 S +9:1. Ac 13:21, Cis.
Saul. 1 S +9:2. 14:49. 31:2.
Jonathan. 1 S +13:2.
Malchishua. i.e. *my king is salvation*, **S#4444h**. 1 Ch 9:39. 10:2. 1 S +14:49. 31:2, Melchishua.
Abinadab. 1 S 14:49, Ishui. +16:8.
Esh-baal. i.e. *fire of Baal*, **S#792h**. 1 Ch 9:39. 2 S 2:8. 4:12, Ish-bosheth.

34 **Merib-baal**. 1 Ch +9:40. 2 S 4:4, Mephibosheth. 9:6, 10. 19:24-30.
Micah. 2 S 9:12, Micha.

35 **Pithon**. i.e. *mouth of a monster*, **S#6377h**. 1 Ch 9:41.
Melech. i.e. *king; counselor*, **S#4429h**. 1 Ch 9:41.
Tarea. i.e. *chamber of guile*, **S#8390h**. 1 Ch +9:41, Tahrea.
Ahaz. i.e. *possessor*, **S#271h**. ver. 36. 1 Ch 3:13. 9:42. 2 K 15:38. 16:1, 2, 5, 7, 8, 10, 11, 15-17, 19, 20. 17:1. 18:1. 20:11. 23:12. 2 Ch 27:9. 28:1, 16, 19, 21, 22, 24, 27. 29:19. Is 1:1. 7:1, 3, 10, 12. 14:28. 38:8. Ho 1:1. Mi 1:1. Mt 1:9, Achaz.

36 **Jehoadah**. i.e. *Jehovah adorned*, **S#3085h**. 1 Ch 9:42, Jarah.
Alemeth. 1 Ch +6:60.
Azmaveth. 2 S +23:31.
Zimri. 1 Ch +2:6.
Moza. i.e. *fountain; the place from which one goes forth*, **S#4162h**. ver. 37. 1 Ch 2:46. 9:42, 43.

37 **Binea**. i.e. *a gushing forth*, **S#1150h**.
Rapha. ver. +2. 1 Ch 9:43, Rephaiah.
Eleasah. 1 Ch +2:39.
Azel. i.e. *reserved*, **S#682h**. ver. 38. 1 Ch 9:43, 44. Mi +1:11, Beth-ezel.

38 **Azrikam**. 1 Ch +3:23.

Bocheru. i.e. *his first born; the first-born is he,* **S#1074h.** ver. 38. 1 Ch 9:44. Here is a case of a son being given a name which literally means "firstborn," but he was not born first, but second. This is another evidence that "firstborn" does not mean born first, but has primary reference to certain legal privileges pertaining to the birthright. The eldest son succeeded to his father's rank and position as head of the family or tribe, and as representative of its prerogatives. He also inherited a double portion of his father's property, a right guaranteed even when his mother was the less loved of two wives (Dt 21:17; 2 K 2:9). A birthright might be sold to a younger brother, as Esau sold his birthright to Jacob (Ge 25:29, 34; He 12:16). It might also be forfeited on account of misconduct (1 Ch +5:1). 1 Ch +26:10. Ge +41:51. 48:18. Le +23:10. 2 Ch 21:3. Jb 18:13. Ps 89:20, 27. Je +31:9. Col +1:15.

Ishmael. Ge +16:11.

Sheariah. i.e. *gate of Jah,* **S#8187h.** 1 Ch 9:44.

Obadiah. Ob +1.

Hanan. 1 Ch +9:44.

39 Eshek. i.e. *oppression,* **S#6232h.**

Ulam. 1 Ch +7:16.

Jehush. i.e. *whom God hastens,* **S#3266h.** 1 Ch 1:35. 7:10. 23:10, 11. Ge +36:5, Jeush, 14, 18. 2 Ch 11:19.

the second. 1 Ch 2:13. 3:1, 15. +7:12, Aher, 15.

Eliphelet. 1 Ch +3:6.

40 archers. 1 Ch 12:2. 2 Ch 14:8.

many sons. Ps 127:3-5. 128:3-6.

1 CHRONICLES 9

1 A.M. 2804, etc. B.C. 1200, etc.

all Israel. Ezr 2:59, 62, 63. Ne 7:5, 64. Mt 1:1-16. Lk 3:28-38.

carried. 2 Ch 33:11. 36:9, 10, 18-20. Je 39:9. 52:14, 15. Da 1:2.

transgression. 1 Ch 5:25.

2 A.M. 3468. B.C. 536.

the first. Ezr 2:70. Ne 7:73. 11:3.

the Nethinims. i.e. *dedicated; given, offered; given ones,* **S#5411h.** Le 27:2-8. Jsh 9:21-27. Ezr 2:43, 58, 70. 7:7, 24 (S5412h). 8:17, 20. Ne 3:26, 31. 7:46, 60, 73. 10:28. 11:3, 21.

3 Jerusalem. Ne 11:1, 4-9.

of the children of Ephraim. 2 Ch 11:16. 30:11, 18.

4 Uthai. i.e. *whom Jehovah succors; mine helper (by teaching); mine iniquity,* **S#5793h.** Ezr 8:14.

Ammihud. 2 S +13:37.

Omri. 1 K +16:16.

Imri. i.e. *eloquent; promise of the lord,* **S#566h.** Ne 3:2.

Bani. Ezr +2:10.

Pharez. Ge +46:12.

5 Shilonites. Ge +38:5. 1 K +11:29.

Asaiah. 2 Ch +34:20.

firstborn. 1 Ch +8:38.

6 Zerah. Ge +36:13.

Jeuel. i.e. *swept away of God; God has taken away,* **S#3262h.**

7 Sallu. i.e. *elevation; measured,* **S#5543h.** Ne 11:7.

Meshullam. ver. +12.

Hodaviah. 1 Ch +5:24.

Hasenuah. i.e. *the hated bristling,* **S#5574h.** Ne 11:9.

8 Ibneiah. i.e. *Jehovah will build,* **S#2997h.**

Jeroham. 1 S +1:1.

Elah. Ge +36:41.

Uzzi. 1 Ch +6:5.

Michri. i.e. *bought of the Lord,* **S#4381h.**

Meshullam. ver. +12.

Shephathiah. i.e. *whom Jehovah defends; judged of Jehovah,* **S#8203h.** 2 S +3:4, Shephatiah.

Reuel. Ge +36:4.

Ibnijah. i.e. *building of Jah,* **S#2998h.**

9 nine hundred and fifty-six. Ne 11:8.

in the house. 2 Ch 35:4.

10 And of. 1 Ch 24:7, 17. Ne 11:10-14.

Jedaiah. i.e. *for whom Jehovah cares; Jehovah has been kind,* **S#3048h.** 1 Ch 24:7. Ezr 2:36. Ne 7:39. 11:10. 12:6, 7, 19, 21. Zc 6:10, 14.

Jehoiarib. 1 Ch +24:7. Ne 11:10, etc. 12:19, Joiarib.

Jachin. Ge +46:10.

11 Azariah. 1 Ch +6:36. Ne 11:11, Seraiah.

Hilkiah. 2 K +18:18.

Meshullam. ver. +12.

Zadok. 2 S +8:17.

Meraioth. Ne +12:15.

Ahitub. 1 S +14:3.

the ruler. 1 Ch 24:5. Nu 4:15, 16, 28, 33. 2 K 23:4. 25:18. Ne 11:11. Ac 4:1. 5:24, 26.

12 And. Ne 11:12.

Adaiah. Ne +11:5.

Jeroham. 1 S +1:1.

Pashur. Je +20:1.

Malchijah. i.e. *my king is Jehovah,* **S#4441h.** 1 Ch 24:9. Ezr 10:25. Ne 3:11. 10:3. 12:42.

Maasiai. i.e. *work of the Lord,* **S#4640h.**

Adiel. 1 Ch +4:36.

Jahzerah. i.e. *protection; he will be narrow-eyed,* **S#3170h.**

Meshullam. i.e. *friend; recompensed,* **S#4918h.** ver. 7, 8, 11. 1 Ch 3:19. 5:13. 8:17. 2 K 22:3. 2 Ch 34:12. Ezr 8:16. 10:15, 29. Ne 3:4, 6, 30. 6:18. 8:4. 10:7, 20. 11:7, 11. 12:13, 16, 25, 33.

Meshillemith. i.e. *reconciliation; those who repay,* **S#4921h.**

Immer. i.e. *talking; loquacious; promise,* **S#564h.** 1 Ch 24:14. Ezr 2:37, 59. 10:20. Ne 3:29. 7:40, 61. 11:13. Je 20:1.

13 very able men. Heb. *mighty men of valor.* 2 S +2:7mg. Ne 11:14. Is +10:21 (**S#1368h**).

14 And. Ne 11:15-19.
Shemiah. ver. +16.
Hasshub. i.e. *considerate,* **S#2815h.** Ne +3:11, Hashub, 23. 10:23. 11:15.
Azrikam. 1 Ch +3:23.
Hashabiah. i.e. *esteemed of the Lord,* **S#2811h.** 1 Ch 6:45. 25:3, 19. 26:30. 27:17. Ezr 8:19, 24. Ne 3:17. 10:11. 11:15, 22. 12:21, 24.
Merari. Ge +46:11.
15 Bakbakkar. i.e. *diligent investigator,* **S#1230h.**
Heresh. i.e. *an artificer; engrave, scratch; silence, dumb,* **S#2792h.**
Galal. i.e. *worthy; a roller, as e.g. the rolling of one's way upon the Lord* (Ps 37:5mg); *because of,* **S#1559h.** ver. 16. Ne 11:17.
Mattaniah. 2 K +24:17.
Micah. **S#4316h.** Mi +1:1.
Zichri. i.e. *memorable; remembered of the Lord,* **S#2147h.** 1 Ch 8:19, 23, 27. 26:25. 27:16. Ex 6:21. 2 Ch 17:16. 23:1. 28:7. Ne 11:9. 12:17.
Asaph. 2 K +18:18.
16 Obadiah. Ne +11:17, Abda. Ob +1:1.
Shemaiah. i.e. *whom Jehovah heard and answered; obeying Jah.* Ne 11:17, Shammua. **S#8098h:** ver. 14. 1 Ch 3:22. 4:37. 5:4. 15:8, 11. 24:6. 26:4, 6, 7. 2 Ch 12:5, 7, 15. 29:14. Ezr 8:13, 16. 10:21, 31. Ne 3:29. 6:10. 10:8. 11:15. 12:6, 18, 34-36, 42. Je 29:31, 32. Also **S#8098h:** 1 K 12:22. 2 Ch 11:2. 17:8. 31:15. 35:9. Je 26:20. 29:24. 36:12.
Galal. ver. +15.
the son of. 1 Ch 25:1, 3, 6. 2 Ch 35:15.
Jeduthun. i.e. *let them give praise,* **S#3038h.** 1 Ch 16:41, 42. 25:1, 3, 6. 2 Ch 5:12. 29:14. 35:15. Ne 11:17. Ps 39:t. 62:t. 77:t. Also **S#3038h:** 1 Ch 16:38. Ne 11:17. Ps 30:t.
Berechiah. Zc +1:7.
Asa. i.e. *healer; physician,* **S#609h.** 1 Ch 3:10. 1 K 15:8, 9, 11, 13, 14, 16-18, 20, 22-24, 25, 28, 32, 33. 16:8, 10, 15, 23, 29. 22:41, 43, 46. 2 Ch 14:1, 2, 8, 10-13. 15:2, 8, 10, 16, 17, 19. 16:1, 2, 4, 6, 7, 10-13. 17:2. 20:32. 21:12. Je 41:9. Mt 1:7, 8.
Elkanah. Ex +6:24.
Netophathites. 2 S +23:28.
17 the porters. 1 Ch +23:5. ch. 26. Ne 11:19. 12:45.
Shallum. ver. 19. 1 Ch 26:1, 14. 2 K +15:10. Ezr 2:42.
Akkub. 1 Ch +3:24.
Talmon. i.e. *great or injurious oppression; captive; outcast,* **S#2929h.** Ezr 2:42. Ne 7:45. 11:19. 12:25.
Ahiman. i.e. *brother of a portion* or *gift; brother of whom?,* **S#289h.** Nu 13:22. Jsh 15:14. Jg 1:10.
18 the king's. 1 K 10:5. 2 K 11:19. 15:35. Ezr 44:2, 3. 46:1, 2. Ac 3:11.
they. 1 Ch 26:12-19.
19 Shallum. ver. 17.

Kore. i.e. *partridge; calling; happening,* **S#6981h.** 1 Ch 26:1. 2 Ch 31:14.
Ebiasaph. 1 Ch +6:23.
Korah. Ge +36:5.
Korahites. i.e. *descendants of Korah.* **S#7145h.** ver. 31. Ex +6:24, Korhites. Nu 26:58, Korathites. 2 Ch 20:19.
keepers. ver. 22. Mk 13:34. Lk 12:36-38.
gates. Heb. thresholds. 2 K +12:9mg.
over the host. 2 K 11:9, 15. 2 Ch 23:4-10.
keepers of the entry. 1 Ch 26:7, 8, 13-19.
20 Phinehas. Ex +6:25.
Eleazar. Ex +6:23.
the Lord. Nu 25:11-13. 1 S 16:18. Ac 7:9, 10.
21 Zechariah. 1 Ch 26:14. Zc +1:1.
Meshelemiah. i.e. *whom the Lord repays; bringing peace-offering of Jah,* **S#4920h.** 1 Ch 26:1, 2, 9. In 1 Ch 26:14, Shelemiah.
22 chosen to be. 1 Ch 7:40.
porters. Mk 13:34.
gates. ver. 19.
in their. ver. 16, 25. Ne 11:25-30, 36. 12:28, 29, 44.
David. 1 Ch ch. 23, 25, 26. 28:13, 21.
Samuel. 1 S 9:9.
did ordain. Heb. founded. Ps 8:2.
set office. or, trust. ver. 26, 31. 2 Ch 31:15mg.
23 the oversight. 1 Ch 23:32. 2 Ch 23:19. Ne 12:45. Ezk 44:10, 11, 14.
24 four. 1 Ch 26:14-18.
25 in their villages. ver. 16.
seven days. 2 K 11:5, 7. 2 Ch 23:8.
time to time. Ezk 4:10, 11.
26 set office. or, trust. ver. 22. 1 T 1:11.
chambers. or, storehouses. ver. 33. 2 K 23:11.
treasuries. 1 Ch 26:20-27. 2 Ch 31:5-12. Ne 10:38, 39. 13:5. Mt 13:52.
27 round about. Nu 1:50. Mt 18:20. Ac 11:23. Re 1:13.
the charge. 1 Ch 23:32. Ro 12:7.
the opening. Jg 3:25 (key). 1 S 3:15. Is 22:22 (key). Ml 1:10. Lk +11:52. 14:23.
morning. 2 S 13:4mg.
28 the charge. 1 Ch 26:22-26. Nu 3:25-37. Ezr 8:25-30. Ne 12:44. 13:4, 5.
ministering vessels. 2 T 2:20, 21.
bring them in and out. Heb. bring them in by tale, and carry them out.
29 oversee. 1 Th 5:12, 13. He 13:17.
vessels. 2 T 2:20, 21.
instruments. or, vessels. Ge 49:5.
the oil. Ex 27:20.
the frankincense. Mt +2:11.
spices. Ga 5:22, 23.
30 of the sons. Ex 30:25, 33, 35-38. 37:29.
ointment. SS 1:3, 12. 4:10. Mt 26:7. Jn 16:23.
31 Shallum. ver. 17, 19.

set office. *or*, trust. ver. 22, 26.

in the pans. *or*, on flat plates, *or* slices. 1 Ch 23:29. Le 2:5, 7. 6:21. 7:9.

32   the sons. 1 Ch 6:33, etc.

showbread. Heb. bread of ordering. 1 Ch 23:29. 28:16. Le 24:6 (row), 7 (row). 2 Ch 2:4. 13:11. 29:18. Ne 10:33.

to prepare. Ex +25:30.

33   the singers. 1 Ch +6:31-33. 15:16-22. 16:4-6. 25:1, etc. Ezr 7:24.

chambers. SS 2:4.

were free. Ne 11:17, 22, 23. Jn 8:36. Ro 6:22.

they, etc. Heb. upon them.

employed. Ps 134:1, 2. 135:1-3. Ac 20:18, 31. 1 C 15:58. Re 7:15.

34   chief fathers. ver. 13. Ne 11:1-15.

dwelt. Jn 15:4. 16:33.

Jerusalem. 1 Ch 8:28.

35   A.M. 2804, etc. B.C. 1200, etc.

in Gibeon. Jsh +10:2.

the father. 1 Ch 2:23, 24, 45, 50-52.

Jehiel. i.e. *treasured; hidden of God*, **S#3273h**.

whose wife's. 1 Ch 8:29.

36   firstborn. 1 Ch +8:38.

Abdon. Jg +12:13.

Zur. Nu +25:15.

Kish. ver. 39. 1 Ch +8:33. 1 S +9:1.

Baal. 1 Ch +5:5.

Ner. i.e. *a light*, **S#5369h**. ver. 39. 1 Ch 8:33. 26:28. 1 S 14:50, 51. 26:5, 14. 2 S 2:8, 12. 3:23, 25, 28, 37. 1 K 2:5, 32.

Nadab. Ex +6:23.

37   Gedor. Jsh +15:58.

Ahio. 2 S +6:3.

Zechariah. 1 Ch +8:31, Zacher.

Mikloth. 1 Ch +27:4.

38   Shimeam. i.e. *their desolation; rumor; fame*, **S#8043h**. 1 Ch 8:32, Shimeah.

39   Ner. ver. +36.

Kish. 1 S +9:1.

Saul. 1 S +9:2.

and Saul. 1 Ch 10:2. 1 S 13:22. 14:1, 49, Ishui. 31:2.

Esh-baal. 1 Ch +8:33.

40   Merib-baal. i.e. *Baal is contentious*, **S#4807h**. 1 Ch 8:34.

Merib-baal. i.e. *rebellion of Baal; contender against Baal*, **S#4810h**. 1 Ch +8:34-36.

Micah. Mi +1:1.

41   Pithon. 1 Ch +8:35.

Melech. 1 Ch +8:35.

Tahrea. i.e. *cunning; delaying cries; separate the friend*, **S#8475h**.

and Ahaz. 1 Ch 8:35.

42   Ahaz. 1 Ch +8:35.

Jarah. i.e. *honeycomb; honey-wood*, **S#3294h**. 1 Ch 8:36, Jehoadah.

Alemeth. 1 Ch +6:60. 8:36.

43   Rephaiah. i.e. *enfeebled of Jah; healed of the Lord*, **S#7509h**. 1 Ch 3:21. 4:42. 7:2. Ne 3:9.

Eleasah. 1 Ch +2:39.

Azel. 1 Ch +8:37.

44   Azrikam. 1 Ch 8:38.

Hanan. i.e. *compassionate; a gracious giver*, **S#2605h**. 1 Ch 8:23, 38. 11:43. Ezr 2:46. Ne 7:49. 8:7. 10:10, 22, 26. 13:13. Je 35:4.

1 CHRONICLES 10

1   A.M. 2948. B.C. 1056.

Now. 1 S 31:1-13.

the Philistines fought. 1 S 28:1. 29:1, 2. 31:1, 2, etc.

slain. *or*, wounded.

mount Gilboa. ver. 8. 1 S +28:4. 31:1. 2 S 1:6, 21. 21:12.

2   Jonathan. 1 Ch 8:33. 9:39. 1 S +13:2. 14:6, 39, 40. 2 K 23:29. Is 57:1, 2.

Abinadab. 1 S 14:49, Ishui. +16:8.

the sons. Ex 20:5. 2 K 25:7.

3   went sore. 1 S 31:3-6. 2 S 1:4-10. Am 2:14.

archers. Heb. shooters with bows. 1 S 31:3.

hit. Heb. found.

he was wounded. Ge 49:23, 24.

4   Draw. Jg 9:54.

thrust. Je +37:10.

uncircumcised. Jg 15:18. 1 S 14:6. 17:26, 36. 2 S 1:20.

abuse. *or*, mock. Jg 16:21, 23-25.

he was. 1 S 31:4. 2 S 1:14-16.

Saul took. ver. 5. 2 S 1:9, 10. 17:23. 1 K 16:18. Mt 27:4, 5. Ac 1:18. 16:27.

6   Saul. 1 S 4:10, 11, 18. 12:25. Ec 9:1, 2. Ho 13:10, 11.

and all. Ex +9:6. 1 S 31:6.

his house. Ge +7:1.

7   then they. Le 26:31, 36. Dt 28:33, 43. Jg 6:2. 1 S 13:6. 31:7.

8   to strip. 1 S 31:8. 2 K 3:23. 2 Ch 20:25.

9   took. ver. 4. 1 S 31:9, 10. 2 S 1:20. Mt 14:11.

tidings. Jg 16:23, 24. Da 5:2-4, 23.

10   their gods. 1 S 31:10, Ashtaroth.

in the temple. 1 S 5:2-7.

Dagon. i.e. *fish-god* (from its *fecundity*); *honored fish*, **S#1712h**. ver. 10. Jg 16:23. 1 S 5:2, 2, 3, 3, 4, 4, 4, 5, 5, 5, 7. Note thirteen occurrences of this word. Ge +14:4.

11   when. 1 S 11:1-11. 31:11-13. 2 S 2:4-7.

12   the oak. Ge 35:8. 2 S 21:12-14. 31:13.

fasted. Ge 50:10. 2 S 3:35.

13   committed. Heb. transgressed. 2 Ch 28:19. 36:14.

even against. 1 S 13:13, 14. 15:3, 23, 28.

for asking. 1 S 28:7-20.

a familiar spirit. Dt +18:11. Re +9:21.

14   enquired not. Jg 10:11-16. 1 S 28:6. Ps 106:13. Ezk 14:3-6.

he slew. Ps 17:13. Is 10:7, 15.

turned. 1 S 13:14. 15:28. 16:1, 11-13. 28:17. 2 S 3:9, 10. 5:3.

David. 1 S +16:19.
Jesse. Heb. Isai. 1 Ch +2:12.

1 CHRONICLES 11

1 A.M. 2956. B.C. 1048. An. Ex. Is. 443.
all Israel. 1 Ch 12:23-40. 2 S 5:1, etc.
Hebron. Ex +6:18. Nu 13:22. 2 S 2:1. 15:10.
1 K 2:11.
Behold. Ge +29:14. Dt 17:15.

2 **in time past**. Heb. both yesterday and the
third day. 2 S +3:17mg.
that leddest. Nu 27:17. 1 S 18:13. Is 55:4. Jn
+10:4.
Thou shalt. 1 S 16:1, 13. Is +40:11.
feed. or, rule. Ezk 34:23.
ruler. 2 S 5:2. 1 K 3:9. 14:7.

3 **elders**. Jsh +20:4.
David made. 1 S 11:15. 2 K 11:17. 2 Ch
23:3.
before. Jg 11:11. 1 S 23:18.
anointed. 1 S 16:1, 12, 13. 2 S 2:4. 2 K
23:30.
according. 1 S 15:28. 28:17.
by. Heb. by the hand of. 1 K +16:12mg. 2 K
24:2. 2 Ch 34:14mg.

4 **David**. 2 S 5:6-10.
Jebus. ver. 5. Jg +19:10.
Jebusites. Ge +10:16.
the inhabitants. Ge +10:16. 15:21. Ex 3:17.

5 **Thou shalt**. 1 S 17:9, 10, 26, 36.
the castle of Zion. 2 S +5:7. 1 K 8:1. 2 Ch
5:2. Ps 2:6. 9:11. 48:2, 12, 13. 78:68. 87:2, 5.
125:1, 2. 132:13. La 4:11, 12. Ro 9:33. He
12:22. Re 14:1.
the city. ver. 7. 2 S 5:9. 6:10, 12. Ps 122:5.

6 **Whosoever**. Jsh 15:16, 17. 1 S +17:25.
chief. Heb. head. ver. 10, 11, 20. 1 Ch 12:18,
23.
Joab. 1 S +26:6.

7 **David dwelt**. Ps 2:6.
the city of David. *that is*, Zion. ver. 5. 2 S
5:7.

8 **Millo**. 2 S +5:9.
repaired. Heb. revived. Ne 4:2.

9 **waxed greater and greater**. Heb. went in
going and increasing. 2 S 3:1. 5:10. Est 9:4. Jb
17:9. Pr 4:18. Is 9:7.
for. 1 Ch 9:20. Ps 46:7, 11. Is 8:9, 10. 41:10,
14. Ro 8:31.

10 A.M. 2949-89. B.C. 1055-1015. An. Ex. Is.
436-476.
the chief. 2 S 23:8.
strengthened themselves with. *or*, held
strongly with. Ge 48:2. 2 S 3:6. Da 10:21mg.
to make. 1 Ch 12:38. 2 S 3:17, 18, 21.
according. 1 S 16:1, 12-14.

11 **Jashobeam**. i.e. *to whom the people turn*. 2 S
23:8, The Tachmonite, Adino, the Eznite.
S#3434h: 1 Ch 12:6. 27:2.

an Hachmonite. i.e. *wise; very wise*, **S#2453h**. 1
Ch 27:32. *or*, son of Hachmoni. ver. 38. 1 Ch
27:32.
the chief. 1 Ch 12:18.

12 **Eleazar**. 1 Ch +27:4, Dodai. Ex +6:23. 2 S
23:9.
Dodo. 2 S +23:24.
Ahohite. 1 Ch 8:4. 2 S +23:9.
the three. ver. 19, 21. 2 S 23:17-19, 23.

13 **Pas-dammim**. i.e. *dell of bloodshed; vanishing
of bloods*, **S#6450h**. 1 S 17:1.

14 **set**. *or*, stood. 2 S 23:12.
and the Lord. 1 S 14:23. 19:5. 2 S 23:10. 2 K
5:1. Ps 18:50.
deliverance. *or*, salvation. 2 S 19:2. Ps
144:10. Pr 21:31.

15 **of the thirty captains**. *or*, captains over the
thirty. 2 S 23:13, etc.
the cave. Jsh +12:15.
Rephaim. Dt +2:20.

16 **in the hold**. 1 S 22:1. 23:25. Ps 142, title.
the Philistines'. 1 S 10:5. 13:4, 23.

17 **longed**. Nu 11:4, 5. 2 S 23:15, 16. Ps 143:6.
of the water. Ps 42:1, 2. 63:1. Is 12:3. Jn
4:10, 14.
well. Heb. *bor*, Ge +37:20.
of Bethlehem. 2 S 5:23. 23:15.

18 **brake**. 1 S 19:5. SS 8:6. Ac 20:24. 21:13. 2 C
5:14, 15.
well. Heb. *bor*, Ge +37:20.
poured. 1 S 7:6.

19 **My God**. 2 S 23:17.
forbid. Lk +20:16.
shall I. Le +17:10. Jb 31:31. Ps 72:14. Mk
14:24. Jn 6:55.
that have put their lives. Heb. with their
lives. Ro 16:4.
lives. Heb. *nephesh*, souls, Ge +44:30.
in jeopardy. Jg 5:18. 9:17. 1 S 19:5. 1 C
15:30.
These. ver. +12.

20 **Abishai**. 1 S +26:6.

21 **howbeit**. Mt 13:8. 1 C 15:41.
honorable . 2 S 23:19.

22 **Benaiah**. 1 Ch +15:24. 27:5, 6. 2 S 8:18.
20:23. 23:20-23. 1 K 1:8, 38. 2:30, 34, 35.
Jehoiada. 2 K +11:4.
Kabzeel. Jsh +15:21.
who had done many acts. Heb. great of
deeds.
lion-like. 1 Ch 12:8. 2 S 1:23. 23:20.
slew a. Jg 14:5, 6. 1 S 17:34-36.

23 **a man of great stature**. Heb. a man of
measure. Nu 13:32. 2 S 21:20. 23:21. Is 45:14.
five cubits. Dt 3:11. 1 S 17:4. That is, about
seven and a half feet.
a spear. 1 Ch 20:5.
like a weaver's beam. 1 Ch 20:5. 1 S 17:7. 2
S 21:19.
slew him. 1 S 17:51.

24 **the three**. 2 S 23:18.
25 **but attained**. ver. 21.
David. 2 S 20:23.
26 **the valiant men**. 2 S 23:24. or, mighty ones.
1 Ch 9:13mg.
Asahel. 1 Ch +2:16.
Elhanan. 2 S +21:19.
27 **Shammoth**. i.e. *desolations*, S#8054h. 1 Ch 27:8,
Shamhuth. 2 S 23:25, Shammah the Harodite.
Harorite. i.e. *the mountaineer*, S#2033h.
Helez. 1 Ch +2:39.
Pelonite. i.e. *nameless; such an one; a certain
unnamed one*, S#6397h. 1 Ch 11:27, 36. 27:10.
In 2 S +23:26 he is called a Paltite.
28 **Ira**. 2 S +20:26.
Ikkesh. 2 S +23:26.
Tekoite. 2 S +23:26.
Abi-ezer. Jsh +17:2.
Antothite. i.e. *a native of Anathoth* (i.e.
answers; songs, 1 Ch +7:8), S#6069h. 1 Ch
11:28. 12:3. +27:12, Anetothite. 2 S +23:27,
Anethothite. Je 29:27.
29 **Sibbecai**. i.e. *thicket of Jah; my thickets*, S#5444h.
1 Ch 11:29. 20:4. 27:11. 2 S 21:18. 1 Ch
27:11. 2 S +23:27, Mebunnai.
Ilai. i.e. *supreme; most high; my elevations; my
sucklings*, S#5866h. 2 S +23:28, Zalmon.
Ahohite. ver. 12.
30 **Maharai**. 1 Ch 27:13. 2 S +23:28.
Netophathite. 2 S +23:28.
Heled. i.e. *the world is transient; the age* (see
Heldai, i.e. *life, age, duration*, 1 Ch +27:15),
S#2466h. 1 Ch 27:15, Heldai. 2 S 23:29, Heleb.
Baanah. 2 S +4:5.
31 **Ithai**. i.e. *there is; my sign; with me*, S#863h.
S#2833h. 2 S 23:29, Ittai (2 S +15:19).
Ribai. 2 S +23:29.
Gibeah. Jg +19:12.
Benaiah. 1 Ch +15:24.
Pirathonite. Jg +12:15.
32 **Hurai**. i.e. *linen worker; of fine linen; my caves;
my white (stuffs)*, S#2360h. 2 S +23:30, Hiddai.
Abiel. 1 S +9:1. 2 S +23:31, Abi-albon.
Arbathite. 2 S +23:31.
33 **Azmaveth**. 2 S +23:31. or, Armaveth. i.e.
strength of death.
Baharumite. i.e. *inhabitant of Bahurim* (i.e.
chosen, proved, or *beloved; the young; choice
youths*, 2 S +3:16), S#978h. 2 S +23:31,
Barhumite.
Eliahba. 2 S +23:32.
Shaalbonite. 2 S +23:32.
34 **Hashem**. i.e. *dull, sleepy; to make desolate*,
S#2044h. 2 S 23:32, Jashen.
Gizonite. i.e. *shearer; quarryman; stone-quar-
rier*, S#1493h.
Jonathan. 1 S +13:2.
Shage. i.e. *wandering, erring; touching softly*,
S#7681h.
Hararite. 2 S +23:11.

35 **Ahiam**. 2 S +23:33.
Sacar. i.e. *recompense; wages; hire; a hireling*,
S#7940h. 1 Ch 11:35. 26:4.
Hararite. ver. 34.
Eliphal. i.e. *God is the judge; my God has judged*,
S#465h. 2 S 23:34, Eliphelet.
Ur. 2 S 23:34, Ahasbai.
36 **Hepher**. Nu +26:32.
Mecherathite. i.e. *inhabitant of Mecherah; he
of the dugout; he of the digging tool; swordite (sol-
dier); wicked counsels*, S#4382h. 2 S 23:34.
Ahijah. 1 K +14:6.
Pelonite. ver. +27. 1 Ch 27:10.
37 **Hezro**. i.e. *his court; bulwark of the Lord*,
S#2695h. 2 S 23:35. Also 2 S +23:35, Hezrai.
Carmelite. 1 S 30:5.
Naarai. i.e. *child of the Lord; my shakings; my
roarings*, S#5293h. 2 S 23:35, Paarai the Arbite.
Ezbai. i.e. *spoil; my humblings*, S#229h.
38 **Joel**. 1 S +8:2. 2 S 23:36, Igal the son of
Nathan.
Nathan. 2 Ch +9:29.
Mibhar. i.e. *choicest; most choice*, S#4006h.
Haggeri. i.e. *wanderer; fugitive; ensnaring; the
sojourner*, S#1905h. 1 Ch 11:38. +27:31,
Hagerite. Also 1 Ch +5:10, Hagarites, 19, 20.
Ps 83:6, Hagarenes. or, the Haggerite.
39 **Zelek**. 2 S +23:37.
Ammonite. 1 S +11:11.
Naharai. i.e. *snorer; snorter; neigher*, S#5171h. 2
S 23:37.
Berothite. i.e. *inhabitant of Berothai* (i.e. *wells
of the Lord*, 2 S +8:8); *my wells*, S#1307h.
Joab. 1 S +26:6.
Zeruiah. 1 Ch +2:16.
40 **Ira**. ver. +28.
Ithrite. 2 S +23:38. 2 S 20:26, Jairite.
Gareb. 2 S +23:38.
41 **Uriah**. 2 S +11:3.
Zabad. i.e. *dowry*. 1 Ch 2:31, +36.
Ahlai. i.e. *Jehovah is staying; wishful; would to
God!; O, would that*, S#304h. 1 Ch 2:31.
42 **Adina**. i.e. *luxuriant; effeminate; soft, pliant,
pleasant; voluptuous*, S#5721h.
Shiza. i.e. *raising up; who sprinkled; brightness*,
S#7877h.
43 **Hanan**. 1 Ch +9:44.
Maachah. 1 K +2:39.
Joshaphat. i.e. *Jehovah is judge*, S#3146h. 1 Ch
11:43. 15:24.
Mithnite. i.e. *slenderness; strength; an athlete*
(literally, *he of loins*); *a giver*, S#4981h.
44 **Uzzia**. i.e. *strength of God; power of God*,
S#5814h.
Ashterathite. i.e. *a native of Ashtaroth* (i.e.
queen of heaven; thought searching). Jsh 9:10.
Shama. i.e. *a hearkener; hearing*, S#8091h.
Jehiel. 1 Ch +9:35.
Hothan. i.e. *signet-ring*, S#2369h. 1 Ch +7:32,
Hotham. 11:44.

Aroerite. i.e. *gentilic of Aroer* (i.e. *destitute; naked; a naked tree,* or *heath,* Nu 32:34); *a native or inhabitant of Aroer* (1 S 30:28), **S#6200h**.

45 **Jediael**. 1 Ch +7:6.
the son of Shimri. 1 Ch +4:37. *or*, the Shimrite.
Joha. 1 Ch +8:16.
Tizite. i.e. *going forth; thou shalt go forth,* **S#8491h**.

46 **Eliel**. 1 Ch +8:20.
Mahavite. i.e. *assemblers; places of assembly; declarers,* **S#4233h**.
Jeribai. i.e. *my contender; defended; he will contend,* **S#3403h**.
Joshaviah. i.e. *set upright of the Lord; he will be prospered of Jah; may Jah sustain him,* **S#3145h**.
Elnaam. i.e. *God is delight; God of pleasantness,* **S#493h**.
Ithmah. i.e. *orphanage; bereavedness, loneliness; orphanhood,* **S#3495h**.
Moabite. Dt +23:3.

47 **Eliel**. ver. 46.
Obed. Ru +4:17.
Jasiel. i.e. *made by God,* **S#3300h**. 1 Ch 27:21, Jaasiel.
Mesobaite. i.e. *found of Jah; congregation of the Lord,* **S#4677h**.

1 CHRONICLES 12

1 **these are**. 1 S 27:2, 6. 2 S 1:1. 4:10.
while he yet, etc. Heb. *being* yet shut up. Dt 32:36. 1 K 14:10. 21:21. 2 K 9:8. 14:26.
Saul. 1 Ch 8:33. 9:39.
the mighty men. 1 Ch 11:10, 19, 24, 25.

2 **armed with bows**. 2 Ch 17:17. Ps 78:9.
could use both. Jg 3:15. 20:15, 16. Jb 36:32.
in hurling. 1 S 17:49.

3 **Ahiezer**. i.e. *brother of help,* **S#295h**. Nu 1:12. 2:25. 7:66, 71. 10:25.
Joash. 1 Ch +7:8.
Shemaah. i.e. *obeying; hearing, fame, report; the hearkener,* **S#8094h**. *or*, Hasmaah.
Gibeathite. i.e. *inhabitant of Gibeah* (i.e. *the hill,* Jg +19:12), **S#1395h**. 1 S 11:4. 2 S 21:6.
Jeziel. i.e. *sprinkled of God; assembly of God; let him be sprinkled of God,* **S#3149h**.
Pelet. i.e. *liberation; escape; deliverance,* **S#6404h**. 1 Ch 2:47.
Azmaveth. 1 Ch 11:33. 2 S +23:31.
Berachah. i.e. *blessing; prosperity; benediction,* **S#1294h**.
Jehu. 2 K +9:2.
Antothite. 1 Ch +11:28. 27:12. Jsh 21:18.

4 **Ismaiah**. i.e. *whom Jehovah hears; he will hear the Lord,* **S#3460h**. 1 Ch 27:19.
the Gibeonite. Jsh 9:3, 17-23.
a mighty man. 1 Ch 11:15.
Jeremiah. Je +1:1.

Jahaziel. 1 Ch +24:33.
Johanan. 2 K +25:23.
Josabad. i.e. *God has endowed,* **S#3107h**. ver. 20. 2 Ch +31:13, Jozabad. 35:9.
Gederathite. i.e. *inhabitant of Gederah* (i.e. *a wall or fence,* Jsh +15:36), **S#1452h**. Jsh 15:36.

5 **Eluzai**. i.e. *God is my refuge* or *strength; God of my gathering; God is my praise,* **S#498h**.
Jerimoth. 1 Ch +7:7.
Bealiah. i.e. *mastered of Jah; possession of the Lord,* **S#1183h**.
Shemariah. i.e. *guarded of Jehovah; kept by Jah,* **S#8114h**. Ezr 10:32, 41.
Shephatiah. 2 S +3:4.
Haruphite. i.e. *descendants of Haruph* or *Hariph* (i.e. *maturity; time of fruit,* Ne +7:24); *matured,* **S#2741h**.

6 **Elkanah**. Ex +6:24.
Jesiah. i.e. *Jah will lend,* **S#3449h**. 1 Ch 23:20. 26:25, Jeshaiah.
Azareel. i.e. *whom God helps; helped by God,* **S#5832h**. 1 Ch 25:18. 27:22. Ezr 10:41. Ne 11:13. +12:36, Azarael.
Joezer. i.e. *Jah is help; he that aids or assists; Lord of help,* **S#3134h**.
Jashobeam. 1 Ch +11:11.
Korhites. Ex +6:24.

7 **Joelah**. i.e. *Jah helps; removing of oaks; let him be profitable,* **S#3132h**.
Zebadiah. 1 Ch 26:2.
Jeroham. 1 S +1:1.
Gedor. 1 Ch 4:18, 39. Jsh +15:58.

8 **into the hold**. ver. 16. Jg +6:2.
men of might. lit. mighty men of valor. 1 Ch +9:13mg. Is +10:21 (**S#1308h**).
of war. Heb. of the host.
handle. 2 Ch 25:5. Je 46:9.
whose faces. 1 Ch 11:22. 2 S 1:23. 17:10. 23:20. Pr 28:1.
as swift as the roes upon the mountains. Heb. as the roes upon the mountains to make haste. 2 S 2:18. Pr 6:5. SS 8:14.

9 **Ezer**. Ge +36:21.
Obadiah. Ob +1.
Eliab. Nu +1:9.

10 **Mishmannah**. i.e. *fatness; fattening,* **S#4925h**.
Jeremiah. ver. 4, 13.

11 **Attai**. 1 Ch +2:35.
Eliel. 1 Ch +8:20.

12 **Johanan**. 2 K +25:23.
Elzabad. 1 Ch +26:7.

13 **Jeremiah**. ver. 4, 10.
Machbanai. i.e. *bond of the Lord; he brought low my sons,* **S#4344h**.

14 **one of the least**, etc. *or*, one that was least *could resist* an hundred, and the greatest a thousand. Le 26:8. Dt 32:30.

15 **the first month**. Ex 12:2. Jsh 3:15.
it had overflown. Heb. it had filled over. Jsh 3:15. 4:18. Je 12:5. 49:19.

16 **the children**. ver. 2.
the hold. ver. +8.
17 **to meet them**. Heb. before them.
If ye be come. 1 S 16:4. 2 S 3:20-25. 1 K 2:13. 2 K 9:22. Ps 12:1, 2.
heart. 1 S 18:1, 3. 2 K 10:15. Ps 86:11. 2 C 13:11. Ph 1:27.
knit. Heb. be one. Jg 20:1. 1 S 18:1. 2 Ch 5:13. Je 32:39. Ac 4:32. 1 C 1:10.
betray. or, deceive. Ge 29:25. Jsh 9:22. 1 S 19:17. 28:12. 2 S 19:26. Pr 26:19. La 1:19.
wrong. or, violence. Ge 16:5. Jb 16:17. 19:7mg. Is 53:9.
God. Ge 31:42, 53. 1 S 24:11-17. 26:23, 24. Ps 7:6. 1 P 2:23.
rebuke it. Ge 20:16. 21:25. 31:42. Zc 3:2. Ju 9.
18 **the spirit**. Heb. *ruach*, Ge +41:38. Jg 6:34. 13:25. Is 59:17.
came upon. Heb. clothed. Jg 6:34mg.
Amasai. 1 Ch 2:17. 2 S +17:25. 19:13. 20:4, etc., Amasa. 2 Ch +29:12.
and on thy side. Ru 1:16. 2 S 15:21. 2 K 9:32. Mt 12:30.
peace. Ge +43:23. Ga 6:16. Ep 6:23, 24.
thy God. 1 S 25:28, 29. 2 S 5:2. Zc 8:23. Jn 6:67, 68.
captains of the band. 1 S 8:12. 22:7. 1 K 9:22.
19 **when he came**. 1 S 29:2-4.
to the jeopardy of our heads. Heb. on our heads. 1 S 29:4.
20 **As he went**. 1 S 29:11.
Adnah. i.e. *resting forever; time* or *pleasure*, **S#5734h**. 2 Ch 17:14.
Jozabad. 2 Ch +31:13.
Jediael. 1 Ch +7:6.
Michael. Da +12:1.
Elihu. 1 S +1:1.
Zilthai. 1 Ch +8:20.
captains of the thousands. Jsh +22:21.
21 **against the band**. or, with a band. 1 S 30:1-17.
mighty men. ver. 20. 1 Ch 5:24. 9:13mg. 11:10, 21, 22. Jg +6:12. 2 S +2:7mg.
22 **day by day**. 2 S 2:2-4. 3:1. Jb 17:9.
like the host. Ge 32:2. Jsh 5:14. Ps 148:2.
of God. Ge +23:6mg. 1 S 14:15mg. Jb 1:16mg.
23 A.M. 2956. B.C. 1048. An. Ex. Is. 433.
the numbers. 1 Ch 11:1-3. 2 S 2:3, 4. 5:1-3.
bands. or, captains, or men. Heb. heads. Jb 1:17.
came to David. 2 S 2:3, 4.
to turn. 1 Ch 10:14.
according. 1 Ch 11:10. 1 S 16:1, 3, 12, 13. 2 S 3:18. Ps 2:6. 89:19, 20.
24 **spear**. 2 Ch 25:5.
armed. or, prepared. Nu 31:5.
25 **children of Simeon**. Nu +1:6.
26 **children of Levi**. ver. 6. Ge +29:34. Nu 1:47.
27 **Jehoiada**. 2 K +11:4.
the leader. 1 Ch 9:20. 2 K 11:4, 9. 25:18.

Aaronites. i.e. *descendants of Aaron* (i.e. *very high*, Ex +4:14), **S#175h**. 1 Ch 6:49-57. 27:17.
28 **Zadok**. 2 S +8:17.
29 **kindred**. Heb. brethren. ver. 2. Ge 31:23.
the greatest part of them. Heb. a multitude of them. 2 S 2:8, 9. 2 Ch 30:18.
30 **famous**. Heb. men of names. 1 Ch 5:24mg. Ge 6:4.
31 **the half tribe**. Nu +1:10. Jsh ch. 17.
32 **Issachar**. Nu +1:29.
had understanding. 2 Ch 11:23. Jg +9:37mg. Ezr 8:16. Ps 74:9. Je +8:7. Da 12:4, 9, 10. Mt +24:45. Lk 3:14. +11:52. Ac 1:7.
the times. Ge 49:14. Est 1:13. Jb 11:17. Ps 31:15. Is 22:12-14. 33:6. Mi 6:9. Mt 16:3. Lk 12:56, 57. 2 T 3:1.
to know. Pr 14:8. Ep 5:17.
all their. Pr 24:5. Ec 7:19. 9:18.
33 **expert in war**. or, rangers of battle, or ranged in battle. ver. 35.
keep rank. or, set the battle in array.
they were not of double heart. Heb. they were without a heart and a heart. Ps 12:2. Jn 1:47.
34 **Naphtali**. Ge +30:8.
35 **Danites**. Jg +13:2.
36 **Asher**. Ge +30:13.
expert in war. or, keeping their rank. ver. 33. Jl 2:7.
37 **the other side**. Nu +26:7. Jsh 13:7-32.
38 **came with**. Ps 12:3. 28:3.
a perfect heart. 2 K +20:3. Ps 101:2.
all the rest. ver. 17, 18. Ge 49:8-10. 2 Ch 30:12. Ps 110:3. Ezk 11:19.
one. Heb. *yahad*. Dt +6:4. 2 S 19:14. 2 Ch 30:12. Ps 133:1. Ac 4:32.
heart. Ps 12:2. 1 T 3:8. Ja 1:8.
39 **eating and drinking**. Ge 26:30. 31:54. 2 S 6:19. 19:42.
40 **brought**. 2 S 16:1. 17:27-29.
camels. 1 S 27:9. 2 K 8:9. 2 Ch 9:1.
meat, meal. or, victual of meal. or, fine flour. Ge 18:6. Nu 5:15. Jg 6:19. 1 S 1:24. 28:24. 2 S 17:28. 1 K 4:22. 17:12, 14, 16.
cakes of figs. 1 S 25:18. 30:12. 2 K 20:7. Ne 13:15. Is 38:21.
bunches of raisins. 1 S 25:18. 30:12. 2 S 16:1.
wine. Ge 9:21. 2 S 6:17-19.
oil. Dt 12:17. 1 K 17:12.
sheep. Dt 14:4. 23:14.
there was joy. 1 K 1:40. 2 K 11:20. 2 Ch 30:22-26. Pr 11:10. 29:2. Je 23:5, 6. Lk 19:37, 38. Re 19:5-7.

1 CHRONICLES 13

1 **consulted**. Jsh +20:4. +22:21.
2 **If it seem**. 1 K 12:7. 2 K 9:15. Pr 15:22. Phm 8, 9.

and that it be. Ex 18:23. 2 S 7:2-5.

send abroad. Heb. break forth, and send. 1 Ch 4:38. Ge +28:14mg. 30:30mg. 2 Ch 31:5mg.

left. 1 Ch 10:7. 1 S 31:1. Is 37:4.

the priests. 1 Ch 15:2-14. Nu 4:44, etc. 2 Ch 31:4, etc.

their cities and suburbs. Heb. the cities of their suburbs. 1 Ch 6:54-81. Nu 35:2-9.

3 **bring again.** Heb. bring about.

the ark. 1 S 7:1, 2. Ps 132:6.

we enquired. 1 S 14:18, 36. 22:10, 15. 23:2, 9-12.

4 **the thing.** Jsh +22:30mg. Est 8:5.

5 **David.** 1 S 7:1. 2 S 6:1.

Shihor. i.e. *turbid, very black, breaking forth,* **S#7883h.** Nu 34:5-8. Jsh +13:3, Sihor. 1 K 4:21.

Hemath. 1 Ch +2:55. Nu +13:21, Hamath.

Kirjath-jearim. Jsh +9:17.

6 **Baalah.** Jsh +15:9, 60. 2 S 6:2, Baale.

that dwelleth. Ge +3:24. 1 S +4:4.

whose name. Ex 20:24. 23:21. Nu 6:27. 1 K 8:16.

7 **carried the ark.** Heb. made the ark to ride. ver. 9, 10. Nu 3:10, 38. 4:15. Hab 2:20.

in a new cart. 1 Ch 15:2, 13. Nu 4:15. 1 S 6:7. 2 S 6:3.

out of the house. 1 S 7:1, 2.

8 **David.** 1 Ch 15:10-24. 1 S 10:5. 2 S 6:5, etc. 2 K 3:15. Ps 47:5. 68:25-27. 150:3-5.

singing. Heb. songs. Ge 31:27. Jg 5:12. 1 K 4:32.

with harps. 1 Ch 23:5. Am 5:23. 6:5. Re +5:8.

psalteries. 1 S 10:5.

timbrels. Ge 31:27.

cymbals. 1 Ch 15:16, 19, 28. 16:5, 42. 25:1, 6. 2 Ch 5:12, 13. 29:25. Ezr 3:10. Ne 12:27.

trumpets. Nu 10:2, 8, 9, 10. 2 K +11:14.

9 **threshingfloor.** Ge +50:10.

Chidon. i.e. *a spear, shield, dart; great destruction,* **S#3592h.** 2 S +6:6, Nachon.

stumbled. or, shook it. or, were released. Ex 23:11. Dt 15:2, 3. 2 S 6:6. 2 K 9:33. Ps 141:6. Je 17:4.

10 **he put.** 1 Ch 15:13, 15. Nu 4:15. Jsh 6:6.

there he died. Le 10:1-3. Nu 16:35. 1 S 6:19. 2 Ch 26:16-20. Ps 89:7. 1 C 11:30-32.

11 **displeased.** Ge 4:5. 2 S 6:7-9. Jon 4:4, 9.

breach. 1 Ch 14:11mg. Ge 38:29. Jg 21:15. 2 S 5:20. 1 K 11:27. Ne 6:1. Jb 16:14. 30:14.

Perez-uzza. *that is,* The breach of Uzza. i.e. *the breach was strengthened,* **S#6560h.** 1 Ch 16:11. 2 S 6:8.

to this day. 1 Ch +4:43.

12 **afraid of God.** Nu 17:12, 13. 1 S 5:10, 11. 6:20. Ps 119:120. Is 6:5. Lk 5:8, 9.

How. 1 K 8:27. Jb 25:5, 6. Mt 25:24.

13 **brought.** Heb. removed. 2 S 6:10.

Obed-edom. i.e. servant of Edom. 2 S +6:10.

the Gittite. Jsh 21:24. 2 S 4:3. +6:10.

14 **the Lord blessed.** 1 Ch 26:5. Ge 30:27. 39:5. 2 Ch 25:24. Pr 3:9, 10. 10:22. Ml 3:10, 11.

1 CHRONICLES 14

1 A.M. 2961. B.C. 1043. An. Ex. Is. 448.

Hiram. 2 S +5:11.

and timber. 1 Ch 22:2. 1 K 5:6, 9, 10, 18. 2 Ch 2:3, 8-10. Ezr 3:7.

to build him. 1 Ch 17:1. 2 S 7:2. 1 K 7:1-12. Je 22:13-15.

2 **the Lord.** 1 Ch 17:17. 2 S 7:16. Ps 89:20-37.

his kingdom. Nu 24:7. 2 S 7:8.

because. 1 K 10:9. 2 Ch 2:11. Est 4:14. Is 1:25-27. Da 2:30.

3 **took.** 1 Ch 3:1-4. Ge +4:19. Pr 5:18, 19. Ec 7:26-29. 9:9.

more. Heb. yet.

wives. Ge +4:19.

4 **Shammua.** 1 Ch 3:5, etc., Shimea. Nu +13:4. 2 S +5:14, Shammuah.

Shobab. 1 Ch +2:18.

Nathan. 2 Ch +9:29.

Solomon. 1 Ch 22:9-12. 28:5, 6. 2 S +5:14. 12:24, 25. 1 K 1:13, 17. 2:15. 3:3, 5-11. Mt 1:6.

5 **Ibhar.** 2 S +5:15.

Elishua. 1 Ch 3:6, Elishama. 2 S +5:15.

Elpalet. i.e. *God has escaped; God is escape,* **S#467h.** 1 Ch +3:6, Eliphelet. 2 S +5:16, Eliphalet.

6 **Nogah.** 1 Ch +3:7.

Nepheg. 2 S +5:15.

Japhia. Jsh +10:3.

7 **Elishama.** Nu +1:10.

Beeliada. i.e. *the Lord has known; lord of knowledge,* **S#1182h.** 1 Ch 3:8. 2 S 5:16, Eliada.

and Eliphalet. 1 Ch 3:8, Eliphelet. 2 S +5:16.

8 A.M. 2957. B.C. 1047. An. Ex. Is. 444.

And when. 1 S 21:11. 2 S 5:17-25.

anointed. 1 Ch 11:3. 2 S 5:3.

all the Philistines. Ps 2:1-6. Re 11:15-18.

9 **the valley.** Dt +2:20.

10 **enquired.** ver. 14, 15. 1 Ch 13:3. 1 S 7:8. 14:36, 37. 23:2-4, 9-12. 2 S 2:1. 5:19, 23, 24. 2 Ch 20:2-4.

Shall I go. 1 S 30:8. Pr 3:6.

Go up. Jg 4:6, 7. 1 K 22:6, 15-17.

11 **Baal-perazim.** 2 S +5:20mg. Is 28:21.

God. Ps 18:13-15. 44:3. 144:1, 10.

like the breaking. Ex 14:28. Jb 30:14. Mt 7:27.

Baal-perazim. *that is,* a place of breaches.

12 **were burned.** Ex 12:12. Dt +7:5. 1 S 5:2-6.

13 **yet again.** ver. 9. 2 S 5:22-25. 1 K 20:22.

14 **enquired again.** ver. 10. Ps 27:4.

turn away. Jsh 8:2-7. Jn 9:6, 7.

mulberry trees. 2 S 5:23. Ps 84:6mg. 2 K 18:17.

15 **when thou shalt hear**. Le 26:36. 2 S 5:23. 2
K 7:6. 19:7. Ac 2:2.
then thou. Jg 4:14. 7:9, 15. 1 S 14:9-22. Ph
2:12, 13.
for God. Is 13:4. 45:1, 2. Mi 2:12, 13.
16 **did as God**. Ge 6:22. Ex 39:42, 43. Jn 2:5.
13:17. 15:14.
Gibeon. Jsh +10:2.
Gazer. 1 Ch 6:67. Jsh 16:10, Gezer. 2 S
+5:25.
17 **fame of David**. Jsh 6:27. 2 Ch 26:8. Ps
18:44.
all lands. Ex +9:6.
the fear of him. Ex 15:14-16. Dt 2:25.
11:25. Jsh 2:9-11. 9:24.
all nations. Ex +9:6.

1 CHRONICLES 15

1 A.M. 2962. B.C. 1042.
And. 1 S 6:12-23.
houses. 2 S 5:9. 13:7, 8. 14:24.
and prepared. ver. 3. 1 Ch 16:1. 17:1-5. Ps
132:5. Ac 7:46.
2 **None ought to**, etc. Heb. *It is* not to carry the
ark of God, but for the Levites. Jn 3:7. Ro 8:8.
them hath. Nu 4:2-15, 19, 20. 7:9. Dt 10:8.
31:9. Jsh 3:3. 6:6. 2 Ch 35:3.
chosen. Ac 9:15.
to minister. Nu 8:13, 14, 24-26. 18:1-8. Is
66:21. Je 33:17-22.
for ever. Ex +12:24.
3 **gathered**. 1 Ch 13:5. 1 K 8:1.
to bring up. ver. 1. 2 S 6:12.
4 **the children of Aaron**. 1 Ch 6:16-20, 49,
50. 12:26-28. Ex 6:16-22. Nu 3:4.
5 **Uriel**. i.e. *flame of God; light* or *fire of God; my
light is God*, **S#222h**. ver. 11. 1 Ch 6:24. 2 Ch
13:2.
brethren. *or*, kinsmen. ver. 6-10, 12, 16-18.
1 Ch 7:22. 16:7.
6 **Merari**. Ge +46:11.
Asaiah. 2 Ch +34:20.
7 **Gershom**. Ex +2:22.
Joel. ver. 11. 1 Ch 23:8.
8 **Elizaphan**. Nu +3:30.
Shemaiah. ver. 11. 1 Ch +9:16.
9 **Hebron**. Ex +6:18.
Eliel. 1 Ch +8:20.
10 **Uzziel**. Ex +6:18.
Amminadab. 1 Ch 6:22.
11 **Zadok**. 2 S +8:17.
Abiathar. 1 S +22:20.
Uriel. ver. 5-10.
Amminadab. i.e. *kindred of the prince; my people is willing; people of liberality*, **S#5992h**. ver. 10.
1 Ch 2:10. 6:22. Ex 6:23. Nu 1:7. 2:3. 7:12,
17. 10:14. Ru 4:19, 20. Mt 1:4. Lk 3:33.
12 **Ye are the chief**. 1 Ch 9:34. 24:31.
sanctify. ver. 14. Ex 19:14, 15. 2 Ch 5:11.

29:4, 5. 30:15. 35:6. Ezk 48:11. Jn 17:17. Ro
12:1, 2. Re 5:9, 10.
13 **ye did it**. 1 Ch 13:7-9. 2 S 6:3.
the Lord. 1 Ch 13:10, 11. 2 S 6:7, 8.
for that. ver. 2. Nu 4:15. 7:9. Dt 31:9. 2 Ch
30:17-20. Pr 28:13. 1 J 1:8-10.
due order. Ge 22:3. Dt +16:16. Jsh 22:11,
16, 21, 22-30. 1 C 11:2. 14:40.
14 **sanctified**. Le 10:3. 2 Ch 29:15, 34. Jl 2:16,
17.
15 **bare the ark**. Nu 7:9.
staves. Ex +25:12.
16 **And David**. 2 Ch 30:12. Ezr 7:24-28. Is
49:23.
chief. ver. 12. Ac 14:23. 1 T 3:1-15. 2 T 2:2. T
1:5.
the singers. ver. 27, 28. 1 Ch 6:31-38. 13:8.
16:42. 23:5. 25:1-6. 2 Ch 29:28-30. Ne 12:36,
46. Ps 87:7. 149:3. 150:3, 4.
instruments. 1 Ch 16:42.
psalteries. Ps 92:1-3. 144:9.
lifting up. 2 Ch 5:13. Ezr 3:10, 11. Ne 12:43.
Ps 81:1. 92:1-3. 95:1. 100:1. Je 33:11.
with joy. Ep 5:19. Ph 4:4. Col 3:16.
17 **Heman**. 1 Ch +2:6.
Joel. 1 Ch 6:33. 1 S +8:2.
Asaph. 2 K +18:18.
Berachiah. 1 Ch +6:39.
Merari. ver. 6.
Ethan. ver. 19. 1 Ch +2:6. 6:44, son of Kishi.
Kushaiah. i.e. *bow* or *snare of Jah; entrapped of
Jah*, **S#6984h**.
18 **the second degree**. 1 Ch 25:2-6, 9-31.
Zechariah. 1 Ch 16:5, 6. Zc +1:1.
Ben. i.e. *son*, **S#1122h**.
Jaaziel. i.e. *comforted of God*, **S#3268h**. ver. 20,
Aziel.
Shemiramoth. i.e. *most high name* or *heaven*,
S#8070h. 1 Ch 15:18, 20. 16:5. 2 Ch 17:8.
Jehiel. Ezr +8:9.
Unni. i.e. *depressed; afflicted song*, **S#6042h**. ver.
20. Ne 12:9.
Eliab. Nu +1:9.
Benaiah. ver. +24.
Maaseiah. Je +21:1.
Mattithiah. Ezr +10:43.
Elipheleh. i.e. *who exalts God*, **S#466h**.
Mikneiah. i.e. *possession of the Lord*, **S#4737h**.
ver. 21.
Obed-edom. 2 S +6:10.
Jeiel. 1 Ch +5:7.
porters. or, gate keepers. 2 S 18:26.
Ps 84:10.
19 **Heman**. ver. 17.
cymbals of brass. ver. 16. 1 Ch 13:8. 16:5,
42. 25:1, 6. Ps 150:5.
20 **Aziel**. i.e. *strength of God; comforted of God*,
S#5815h. ver. 18, Jaaziel.
psalteries. ver. 16. 1 S +10:5.
Alamoth. i.e. *hiding places; virgins* (as *covered*,

veiled, or *private*); girls, i.e. *the soprano or female voice*, **S#5961h**. Ps 46:title. or, virgins. Virgins joined in the triumphal processions, Young notes, as Ex +15:20. Jg +21:21. 2 K 4:23. For the related **S#5959h** (*almah*, virgin), see Ge +24:43.

21 Mattithiah. ver. 18. 1 Ch 16:5. Ezr +10:43.
harps. ver. 16. Re +5:8.
Sheminith. i.e. *octave*; *eighth*, **S#8067h**. Ps ch. 6, 12, titles.
to excell. or, to oversee. 1 Ch 23:4. 2 Ch 34:12. Ezr 3:8, 9.

22 Chenaniah. i.e. *perfected* or *established of God*; *covered by Jah*; *as perpetuated of Jah*, **S#3663h**. 1 Ch 26:29. Also ver. 27.
for, etc. or, for the carriage: he instructed about the carriage. For "carriage," Young renders "burden," noting, "of the song."
song. Heb. lifting up. ver. 16, 27. 1 Ch 6:32. 25:7. 2 Ch 23:13.
he instructed about. 1 Ch 16:42. 25:7, 8. Ep 5:19. Col 3:16.
skilful. or, intelligent. 1 Ch 25:7, 8 (teacher). 27:32. 28:9. 2 Ch 26:5. 34:12. 35:3. Ezr 8:16. Ne 8:2, 3, 7, 9. 10:28. Ps 119:130. Pr 8:9. 17:10, 24. 28:2, 7, 11. Is 57:1. Da 1:4. 8:5, 23, 27.

23 Berechiah. ver. 17.
Elkanah. Ex +6:24.
doorkeepers. 1 Ch 9:21-23. 2 K 22:4. 25:18. Ps 84:10.

24 Shebaniah. i.e. *Jehovah hath dealt tenderly*, **S#7645h**. Ne 9:4, 5. 10:4, 10, 12. 12:14.
Jehoshaphat. 2 S +8:16.
Nethaneel. Nu +1:8.
Amasai. 2 Ch +29:12.
Zechariah. ver. 18.
Benaiah. i.e. *built up of the Lord*, **S#1141h**. ver. 18, 20. 1 Ch 11:24, 31. 16:5, 6. 18:17. 27:5, 6, 14, 34. 2 S 8:18. 20:23. 23:20, 22, 30. 1 K 1:8, 10, 26, 32, 36, 38, 44. 2:25, 29, 30, 34, 35, 46. 4:4. 2 Ch 31:13. Ezk 11:1.
Eliezer. Ge +15:2.
the priests. 1 Ch 16:6. Nu 10:8. 2 Ch 5:12, 13. Ps 81:3. Jl 2:1, 15.
trumpets. Nu 10:5, 6.
Jehiah. i.e. *Jah will live*, **S#3174h**.
Obed-edom. ver. 18, 23.
doorkeepers. ver. 18. Ps 84:10.

25 David. 2 S 6:12, 13, etc. 1 K 8:1.
captains over thousands. Jsh +22:21.
Obed-edom. 1 Ch 13:14.
with joy. 1 Ch 13:11, 12. Dt 12:7, 18. 16:11, 15. 2 Ch 20:27, 28. Ezr 6:16. Ps 95:1, 2. *100:1, 2. Ph 3:3. 4:4.*

26 God helped. 1 Ch 29:14. 1 S 7:12. Ac 26:22, 23. 2 C 2:16. 3:5.
they. 2 S 6:13. Ps 66:13-15.
bullocks. Nu +23:1, 2, 4, 29.

27 a robe. Mt 27:28. Jn 19:23. 1 J 3:2. Re 1:13.

Chenaniah. ver. +22.
song. or, carriage. ver. 22.
ephod. Ex +28:4.

28 brought up. 2 S 6:15. Mt 21:1-11. Lk 19:29-38. Jn 12:12-15.
with shouting. ver. 16. 1 Ch 13:8. 2 Ch 5:12, 13. Ezr 3:10, 11. Ps 47:1-5. 68:25. 98:4-6. 150:3-5.
the cornet. Ex 19:16.

29 as the ark. 1 Ch 17:1. Nu 10:33. Dt 31:26. Jsh 4:7. Jg 20:27. 1 S 4:3. Je 3:16. He 9:4.
Lord. 2 S 6:16.
Michal. 1 S 18:27, 28. 19:11-17. 25:44. 2 S 3:13, 14.
window. 2 S 6:16.
dancing. Ex +15:20. or, skipping. Ps 29:6. 114:4. Is 13:21. Jl 2:5. Na 3:2.
playing. 1 S 18:7. 2 S 6:5.
she despised. 2 S 6:20-23. Ps 69:7-9. Ac 2:13. 1 C 2:14. 2 C 5:13.

1 CHRONICLES 16

1 they brought. 2 S 6:17-19. 1 K 8:6. 2 Ch 5:7.
in the midst. 1 Ch 15:1, 12. 2 Ch 1:4. Ps 132:8.
they offered. 1 K 8:5. 2 Ch 5:6. Ezr 6:16-18.
burnt sacrifices. Le +23:12.
peace offerings. Le +23:19.

2 the burnt offerings. Le +23:12.
peace offerings. Le +23:19.
he blessed. Ge 14:19. 20:7. 47:7, 10. Nu 6:23-27. Jsh 22:6. 2 S 6:18. 1 K 8:55, 56. 2 Ch 29:29. 30:18-20, 27. Lk 24:50, 51. He 7:7.

3 to every one. 2 Ch 30:24. 35:7, 8. Ne 8:10. Ezk 45:17. 1 P 4:9.

4 he appointed. 1 Ch 15:16. 23:2-6. 24:3.
minister. ver. 37-42. 1 Ch 23:27-32. Nu 18:1-6.
to record. ver. 8. Ps ch. 37-70, titles. 103:2. 105:5. Is 62:6, 7. Ac 14:27. Re 1:2.
the Lord God. Ge 17:7. 32:28. 33:20mg. 1 K 8:15. Ps 72:18. 106:48.

5 Asaph. 2 K +18:18.
psalteries and with harps. Heb. instruments of psalteries and harps. 1 Ch 15:20, 21. Re +5:8.

6 with trumpets. Nu 10:8. 2 Ch 5:12, 13. 13:12. 29:26-28.

7 on that day. 2 S 22:1. 23:1, 2. 2 Ch 29:30. Ne 12:24.
into the hand. Ps ch. 12-18, titles.

8 Give thanks. This beautiful hymn, to the 22nd verse, is nearly the same as Ps 105:1-15; from the 23rd to the 33rd it accords with Ps 96; and the conclusion agrees with Ps 106, with the addition of ver. 34-36. Ps 105:1-15.
call. Is 12:4. Ac 9:14. 1 C 1:2.
make. 1 K 8:43. 2 K 19:19. Ps 67:2-4. 78:3-6. 145:5, 6.

9 **Sing unto**. Ps 95:1, 2. 96:1, 2. 98:1-4. Ml 3:16.
psalms. Mt 26:30. Ep 5:19. Col 3:16. Ja 5:13.
talk ye. Ps 40:10. 71:17. 96:3. 145:4-6, 12.

10 **Glory**. Ps 34:2. Is 45:25. Je 9:23, 24. 1 C 1:30, 31, Gr.
let the heart. 1 Ch 28:9. Pr 8:17. Is 45:19. 55:6, 7. Je 29:13. Mt 7:7, 8.

11 **Seek**. Am 5:6. Zp 2:2, 3.
his strength. 2 Ch 6:41. Ps 68:35. 78:61. +86:16. Ps 105:4 with Ps 132:8.
seek his. Ps 4:6. 27:8, 9. 67:1.
continually. Ps 72:15. Is 62:6. Ho 12:6. Re 4:8.

12 **Remember**. ver. 8, 9. Ps 103:2. 111:4.
the judgments. Ps 19:9. 119:13, 20, 75, 137. Ro 11:33. Re 16:7. 19:2.

13 **ye seed**. Ge 17:7. 28:13, 14. 35:10-12.
his chosen. Ex 19:5, 6. Dt 7:6. Ps 135:4. 1 P 2:9.

14 **the Lord**. Ex 15:2. Ps 63:1. 95:7. 100:3. 118:28.
his judgments. ver. 12. Ps 48:10, 11. 97:8, 9.

15 **ye mindful**. Ps 25:10. 44:17. 105:8. Ml 4:4.
always. Heb. *olam*, Ge +6:3.
a thousand generations. Dt 7:9.

16 **which he made**. Ge 15:18. 17:2. 26:3. 28:13, 14. 35:11. Ex 3:15. Ne 9:8. Lk 1:72, 73. Ac 3:25. Ga 3:15-17. He 6:13-18.

17 **for a law**. Ps 78:10.
an everlasting. Ge +9:16. +17:7, 8. Ex 3:17. Jsh 24:11-13. 2 S 23:5. Is 55:3. Je 11:2. He 13:20.

18 **Unto thee**. Ge 12:7. 13:15. 17:8. 28:13, 14. 35:11, 12.
lot. Heb. cord. Dt +32:9mg. 2 S 8:2. Mi 2:5.
inheritance. Nu 26:53-56. Dt 32:8.

19 **but few**. Heb. but men of number. Ge 34:30. Is +10:19mg.
a few. Ge 34:30. Dt 7:7. 26:5. Ac 7:5. He 11:13.

20 **they went**. Ge 12:10. 20:1. 46:3, 6.
one kingdom. Ps 105:13.

21 **He suffered**. Ge 31:24, 29, 42.
he reproved. Ge 12:17. 20:3. Ex 7:15-18. 9:13-18.

22 **Touch**. 1 K 19:16. Ps 105:15. 1 J 2:27.
prophets. Ge 20:7. 27:39, 40. 48:19, 20. 49:8-10.

23 **Sing**. ver. +9. Ex 15:21. Ps 30:4. 96:1-13. Is 12:5.
show forth. Ps 40:10. 71:15. Is 51:6-8.

24 **Declare**. 2 K 19:19. Ps 22:27. Is 12:2-6. Da 4:1-3.

25 **great**. Ps 89:7. 144:3-6. Is 40:12-17. Re 15:3, 4.
feared. Ps 66:3-5. 76:7. Je +5:22.
all gods. Ex +12:12.

26 **all the gods**. Le 19:4. Ps 115:4-8. Is 44:9, etc. Je 10:10-14. Ac 19:26. 1 C +8:4.

the Lord. Ps 102:25. Is 40:26. 42:5. 44:24. Je 10:11, 12. Re 14:7.

27 **Glory**. Ps 8:1. 16:11. 63:2, 3. Jn 17:24.
strength. Ps 27:4-6. 28:7, 8. 43:2-4.
place. Ps 96:6.

28 **Give**. Ps 29:1, 2. 68:34.
ye kindreds. Ps 66:1, 2. 67:4, 7. 86:8-10. 98:4. 100:1, 2. Is 11:10.
glory. 1 Ch 29:10-14. Ps 115:1, 2. 1 C 15:10. 2 C 12:9, 10. Ep 1:6, 17-19. Ph 4:13. 1 T +1:17.

29 **the glory**. Ps 89:5-8. 108:3-5. 148:13, 14. Is 6:3. Re 4:9-11. 5:12-14. 7:12.
bring. 1 K 8:41-43. Ps 68:30, 31. 72:10, 15. Is 60:6, 7.
an offering. Dt 16:16. Jg 20:26, 27. Jb 42:8. Ps 20:1-4. Is 56:7. Mi 6:6, 7.
come. Ps 95:2. 100:4.
the beauty. 2 Ch 20:21. Ps 29:2. 50:2. 96:6, 9. 110:3. Ezk 7:20. 24:25.

30 **before him**. ver. 23, 25. Ps 96:9. Re 11:15.
stable. Ps 33:9. 93:1. 104:5. 148:5, 6. Ec +1:4. Is 49:8. Je 10:12. Col 1:17. He 1:3. 2 P 3:10.
not moved. Ps 104:5.

31 **Let the heavens**. Ps 19:1. 89:5. 148:1-4. Lk 2:13, 14. 15:10.
let the earth. Ps 97:1. 98:4. Lk 2:10.
The Lord. Ps +93:1, 2. 145:1. Is 33:22. Mt 6:13.

32 **the sea**. Ps 93:4. 98:7.
fields. Ps 98:8. 148:9, 10. Is 44:23.

33 **the trees**. Ps 96:12, 13. Ezk 17:22-24.
because. Ps 98:9. 2 Th 1:8, 10. 2 P 3:14. Re 11:17, 18.

34 **give thanks**. Ps +136:1.
mercy. Ex +34:6.
for ever. Heb. *olam*, Ex +12:24.

35 **Save us**. Ps 14:7. 53:6. 106:17, 48.
O God. Ps +88:1.
give. Ps 35:27, 28. 51:13-15. 105:45. Is 43:21. Ep 1:12. 1 P 2:5, 9.
glory. ver. 9, 10. Ps 44:8. Is 45:25. 1 C 1:31.

36 **Blessed**. 1 K 8:15, 56. Ps 72:18, 19. 106:48. Ep 1:3. 1 P 1:3.
for ever and ever. Heb. *olam* doubled, Da +2:20. 1 Ch 29:10. Ne 9:5. Ps 41:13.
all the people said. Dt 27:15-26.
Amen. i.e. *so it is*. Je +11:5mg. Mt +6:13.

37 **minister before**. Ep 6:7. Col 3:24.
the ark. ver. 4-6. 1 Ch 15:17-24. 25:1-6.
as every day's. 2 Ch 8:14. Ezr 3:4. Ac 2:46, 47.

38 **Obed-edom**. 2 S +6:10.
Jeduthun. 1 Ch +9:16.
Hosah. i.e. *fleeing for refuge; place of refuge; trusting*, **S#2621h**. 1 Ch 16:38. 26:10, 11, 16. Jsh 19:29.

39 **Zadok**. 1 Ch 12:28. 2 S +8:17.
before. Ex +38:21.
in the high. 1 K 3:4.

40 **To offer**. Ex +29:42. 1 K 18:29. 2 Ch 2:4. 31:3. Ezr 3:3. Ezk 46:13-15. Da 9:21. Am 4:4.
morning and evening. Heb. in the morning and in the evening.

41 **Heman**. ver. 37. 1 Ch +2:6.
chosen. or, choice. 1 Ch 7:40. 9:22. Zp 3:9 (pure). Mk 7:13, 14.
expressed. 1 Ch 12:31. Nu 1:17. Ezr 8:20.
by name. Jn 10:3.
to give. ver. +34. 2 Ch 5:13. 7:3. 20:21. Ps 103:17. Lk 1:50.
for ever. Heb. *olam*, Ex +12:24.

42 **trumpets**. 2 Ch 29:25-28. Ps 150:3-6.
musical instruments. 1 Ch 15:16, 22. 25:6. 2 Ch 5:13. Ps 84:10. Jn 14:2. Ro 15:4. 1 C 14:26. Ep 5:19. Col 3:16. 2 T 3:16, 17.
of God. 1 Ch 12:22. 2 Ch 30:21mg. Ge +23:6mg. Jb +1:16mg. Ac 7:20mg. 1 Th 4:16.
porters. Heb. for the gate. 1 Ch +23:5. Ne 11:19mg.

43 **all the people**. 2 S 6:19, +20. 1 K 8:66.
to bless. Ge 18:19. Jsh 24:15. Ps 101:2.

1 CHRONICLES 17

1 **as David**. 2 S 7:1, 2, etc. 2 Ch 6:7-9. Da 4:4, 29, 30.
Nathan. 2 Ch +9:29.
I dwell. 1 Ch 14:1. Je 22:15. Hg 1:4, 9.
the ark. Ps 132:5. Ac 7:46.
under curtains. ver. 5. 1 Ch 15:1. 16:1. Ex 40:19-21. 2 S 6:17. 2 Ch 1:4.

2 **Do all**. 1 Ch 22:7. 28:2. Jsh 9:14. 1 S 16:7. Ps 20:4. 1 C 13:9.
for God. 1 S 10:7. 2 S 7:3. Zc 8:23. Lk 1:28.

3 **word**. Nu 12:6. 2 K 20:1-5. Is 30:21. Am 3:7.

4 **tell**. Is 55:8, 9. Ro 11:33, 34.
Thou shalt not. 1 Ch 22:7, 8. 28:2, 3. 2 S 7:4, 5. 1 K 8:19. 2 Ch 6:8, 9.

5 **dwelt**. 2 S 7:6. 1 K 8:27. 2 Ch 2:6. 6:18. Is 66:1, 2. Ac 7:44-50.
gone. Heb. been.
from tent to tent. Ex 40:2, 3. 2 S 6:17. 1 K 8:4, 16.

6 **walked**. Ex 33:14, 15. 40:35-38. Le 26:11, 12. Nu 10:33-36. Dt 23:14. 2 C 6:16. Re 2:1.
the judges. Jg 2:16-18. 1 S 12:11. 2 S 7:7, tribes. Ac 13:20.
feed. 1 Ch 11:2. Ps 78:71, 72. Je 23:4. Ezk 34:2. Mi 5:4. Mt 2:6mg.

7 **I took thee**. Ex 3:1-10. 1 S 16:11, 12. 17:15. 2 S 7:8. Ps 78:70, 71. Am 7:14, 15. Mt 4:18-22. Lk 5:10.
from following. Heb. from after.
ruler. 2 S 6:21. Mt 2:6.

8 **I have been**. ver. 2. Ge +28:15.
have cut off. 1 S 26:10. 31:1-6. 2 S 22:1, 38-41. Ps 18, title.
made thee. ver. 17. 2 S 8:13. Ezr 4:20. Ps 71:21. 75:7. 113:7, 8. Lk 1:52.

9 **I will**. Je 31:3-12. Ezk 34:13.
plant. Ps 92:13. Je +11:17.
and shall be. Ezk 28:4. 36:14, 15. 37:25. Am 9:15. Re 21:4.
the children of. 2 S +3:34mg. 7:10. Ps 89:22. Ep 2:2, 3. 5:6.
waste. Is 49:17. 60:18.
as at the. Ex 1:13, 14. 2:23.

10 **And since**. Jg 2:14-18. 3:8. 4:3. 6:3-6. 1 S 13:5, 6, 19, 20.
Moreover. Ps 18:40, etc. 21:8, 9. 89:23. 110:1. 1 C 15:25.
subdue. Mi 7:19.
the Lord. Ex 1:21. 2 S 7:11. Ps 127:1.

11 **when thy**. 1 Ch 29:15, 28. Ac 13:36.
go to be. Ge 15:15. Dt 31:16. 1 K 1:21. 2:10. Ac 2:29.
I will raise. 1 Ch 28:5. 2 S 7:12, 13. 12:24, 25. 1 K 8:20. Ps 132:11. Je 23:5, 6. Ro 1:3, 4.

12 **He shall**. 1 Ch 22:9, 10. 28:6-10. 1 K 5:5. 2 Ch ch. 3, 4. Ezr 5:11. Zc 6:12, 13. Jn 2:19-21. Ac 7:47, 48. Col 2:9.
I will. Ps 89:4, 29, 36, 37. Is 9:7. Da 2:44. 1 C 15:25. Re 11:15.
for ever. Heb. *olam*, Ex +12:24.

13 **I will be**. 2 S 7:14. Ps 89:26-28, etc. Is 55:3. 2 C 6:18. He 1:5. Re 21:7.
my son. Ps 2:7, 12. Lk 9:35. Jn 3:35.
I will not. 2 S 7:15, 16. 1 K 11:12, 13, 36.
as I took. ver. 12. 1 Ch 10:14. 1 S 15:28.

14 **in mine**. Ps 2:6. 72:17. 89:36. Lk 1:32, 33. He 3:6.
for ever. Ex +12:24.
for evermore. Ps +18:50.

15 **According**. 2 S 7:17. Je 23:28. Ac 20:27.

16 **sat before**. Jg +20:26, 27. 21:2. 2 S 7:18. 1 K 19:4. 2 K 19:14. Ne 1:4. Ezk 14:1-3. 20:1.
Who am I. Ge 32:10. Ps 144:3. Ep 3:8.
what is. Jg 6:15. 1 S 9:21.
that thou hast. Ge 48:15, 16. 1 S 7:12. Ac 26:22. 2 C 1:10.

17 **a small thing**. ver. 7, 8. 2 S 7:19. 12:8. 2 K 3:18. Is 49:6.
thou hast. ver. 11-15. Ep 3:20.
hast regarded. ver. 8. 1 K 3:13. Ps 78:70-72. 89:19, etc. Ph 2:8-11.

18 **the honor**. 1 S 2:30. 2 S 7:20-24.
thou knowest. Ge +39:6. 1 S 16:7. Ps 139:1. Jn 21:17. Re 2:23.

19 **thy servants**. Is 37:35. 42:1. 49:3, 5, 6. Da 9:17.
according. Mt 11:26. Ep 1:9-11. 3:11.
great things. Heb. greatnesses. 1 Ch 29:11, 12. Ps 111:3, 6.

20 **none**. Ex +8:10. 18:11. Dt 3:24. Ep 3:20.
beside thee. Dt 4:35, 39. 1 S 2:2. Is 43:10. 44:6. 45:5, 22.
according. Ps 44:1. 78:3, 4. Is 63:12.

21 **what one**. Dt 4:7, 32-34. 33:26-29. Ps 147:20.

redeem. Ex 3:7, 8. 19:4-6. Dt 15:15. Ps 77:15. 107:2. 111:9. Is 63:9. T 2:14.

make thee. Ne 9:10. Is 48:9. 63:12. Ezk 20:9, 10.

greatness. Dt 4:34. Ps +99:3. 114:3-8.

by driving. Dt 7:1, 2. Jsh 10:42. 21:43-45. 24:11, 12. Ps 44:2, 3.

22 **thy people**. Ge 17:7. Ex 19:5, 6. Dt 7:6-8. 26:18, 19. 1 S 12:22. Je 31:31-34. Zc 13:9. Ro 9:4-6, 25, 26. +11:1, 2, etc. 1 P 2:9.

for ever. Heb. *olam*, Ex +12:24. Jn 10:28. Ro +11:1.

23 **let the thing**. Ge 32:12. 2 S 7:25-29. Ps 119:49. Je 11:5. Lk 1:38.

for ever. Heb. *olam*, Ex +12:24.

24 **that thy name**. 2 Ch 6:33. Ps 21:13. 72:19. Mt 6:9, 13. Jn 12:28. 17:1. Ph 2:11. 1 P 4:11.

for ever. Heb. *olam*, Ex +12:24.

a God. Je 31:1. He 8:10. 11:16. Re 21:3.

and let. Ps 90:17.

25 **told thy servant**. Heb. revealed the ear of thy servant. Ru +4:4mg.

that thou. ver. +10.

found. Ps 10:17. Ezk 36:37. 1 J 5:14, 15.

26 **thou art God**. Ex 34:6, 7. T 1:2. He 6:18.

27 **let it please**. *or*, it hath pleased. 2 S 7:29mg. 2 K 5:23.

blessest. Ge 27:33. Ps 72:17. Ro 11:29. Ep 1:3.

for ever. Heb. *olam*, Ex +12:24.

1 CHRONICLES 18

1 A.M. 2964. B.C. 1040. An. Ex. Is. 451.

after this. 2 S 8:1, 2, etc.

Gath. Jsh +11:22. 2 S 8:1, Metheg-ammah.

towns. Nu +21:25.

2 **he smote**. Jg 3:29, 30. Ezk +25:8.

brought gifts. 1 S 10:27. 1 K 10:2, 25. 2 K 3:4, 5. Ps 68:29, 30. 72:8-10. Is 16:1.

3 **Hadarezer**. 2 S 8:3, Hadadezer.

Zobah. 1 S +14:47.

by the river. Ps +72:8.

4 **seven thousand**. 2 S 8:4, seven hundred.

houghed. Dt 17:16. Jsh 11:6, 9. Ps 20:7. 33:16, 17.

an hundred chariots. 1 K 4:26. 10:26.

5 **the Syrians**. 2 S 8:5, 6. 1 K 11:23, 24.

Damascus. Heb. Darmesek. Ge +14:15.

to help. Is 8:9, 10.

Zobah. ver. +3.

6 **Syria-damascus**. S#758h. A place where David put garrisons.

became David's. ver. +2. Ps 18:43, 44.

Thus the Lord. 1 Ch 17:8. Ps 121:8. Pr 21:31.

7 **shields**. 1 K 10:16, 17. 14:26-28. 2 Ch 9:15, 16. 12:9, 10.

8 **Tibhath**. i.e. *slaughter; confidence, security; the slaughter-place*, S#2880h. 2 S 8:8, Betah, Berothai.

Chun. i.e. *established; firm, choice; to stand upright*, S#3560h.

wherewith. 1 Ch 22:14. 1 K 7:15-47. 2 Ch 4:2-6, 12-18. Je 52:17-23.

9 **Tou**. i.e. *who wanders; error, going astray; do ye mock; do ye stray away*, S#8583h. ver. 9, 10. Also 2 S 8:9, 10, Toi.

10 **Hadoram**. *or*, Joram. 2 S 8:10. Joram, in the parallel text, seems a mistake for "Hadoram," or "Idoram," for the LXX. have here Ieddouram.

enquire. *or*, salute him. Jg +18:15mg.

congratulate him. Heb. bless him.

had war. Heb. was the man of wars. Is 41:12.

with him. 2 S 8:10.

all manner. 2 Ch 9:1, 23, 24. Is 39:1.

11 **dedicated**. 1 Ch 22:14. 26:20, 26, 27. 29:14. Ex 35:5, 21-24. Jsh 6:19. 2 S 8:11, 12. 1 K 7:51. 2 K 12:18. 2 Ch 5:1. Mi 4:13.

the children. 1 Ch 20:1, 2.

Amalek. Ex +17:8.

12 **Abishai**. Heb. Abshai. 1 Ch 19:11mg. 1 S +26:6.

Zeruiah. 1 Ch +2:16.

slew of the Edomites. ver. +13. 2 S 7:13.

the valley of Salt. 2 S +8:13.

13 **garrisons**. ver. 6. 1 S 10:5. 13:3. 14:1. 2 S 7:14, etc. 23:14. 2 C 11:32.

all the Edomites. Ge +25:23.

Thus the Lord. ver. 6. Ps 18:48-50. 121:7. 144:10.

14 **David**. 1 Ch 12:38.

executed. Ps 78:71, 72. 89:14. Is 9:7. Je +21:12.

15 **Joab**. 1 S +26:6.

Jehoshaphat. 2 S +8:16.

recorder. *or*, remembrancer. 2 S +8:16mg.

16 **Abimelech**. 2 S 8:17, Ahimelech.

Abiathar. 1 S +22:20.

Shavsha. i.e. *God's warrior; habitation; plain*, S#7798h. 2 S 8:17, Seraiah. 20:25, Sheva. 1 K 4:3, Shisha.

17 **Benaiah**. 1 Ch +15:24.

Cherethites. 2 S +8:18.

about the king. Heb. at the hand of the king. 1 Ch 23:28mg.

1 CHRONICLES 19

1 **Nahash**. 1 S 11:1, 2. 12:12. 2 S 10:1-3.

2 **I will show**. 1 S 30:26. 2 S 9:1, 7. 2 K 4:13. Est 6:3. Ec 9:15.

the children. Ge 19:37, 38. Dt 23:3-6. Ne 4:3, 7. 13:1.

3 **the princes**. 1 S 29:4, 9. 1 K 12:8-11.

Thinkest thou that David. Heb. In thine eyes doth David. 1 C 13:5-7.

to search. Ge 42:9-18. Jsh 2:1-3. Jg 1:23, 24. 18:2, 8-10.

4 **took David's**. Ps 35:12. 109:4, 5.

shaved them. Le 19:27. Is 15:2. Je 41:5. 48:37.
and cut. Is 20:4. 47:2, 3.
sent them. 2 S 10:4, 5. 2 Ch 36:16. Mk 12:4.
Lk 20:10, 11.

5 **and told David**. Mt 18:31.
at Jericho. Jsh 6:24-26. 1 K 16:34.
your beards. Jg 16:22.

6 **had made**. Lk 10:16. 1 Th 4:8.
odious. Heb. to stink. Ge +34:30.
a thousand. 2 Ch 16:2, 3. 25:6. 27:5. Ps 46:9.
Syria-maachah. **S#758h**. 2 S 10:6.
Zobah. 1 Ch 18:3, 5, 9. 1 S +14:47. 2 S 8:3. 1
K 11:23, 24.

7 **hired**. 1 Ch 18:4. Ex 14:9. Jg 4:3. 1 S 13:5. 2
Ch 14:9. Ps 20:7-9.
thirty and two thousand chariots. 2 S
10:6.
the king of Maachah. 2 S 10:6, king
Maachah.
Medeba. Nu 21:30. Jsh 13:9. Is 15:2.

8 **Joab**. 1 Ch 11:6, 10, etc. 1 S +26:6. 2 S 23:8,
etc.

9 **put the battle**. 1 S 17:2. 1 S 18:4. 2 Ch 13:3.
14:10. Is 28:6. Je 50:42. Jl 2:5.
the kings. 2 S 10:8. 1 K 20:1, 24.

10 **when Joab**. 2 S 10:9-14.
battle. Heb. face of the battle.
set against. Jsh 8:22. Jg 20:42, 43.
choice. *or*, young men. 1 S 8:16. 9:2.

11 **Abishai**. Heb. Abshai. ver. 15. 1 S +26:6.
and they set. ver. +9.

12 **If the Syrians**. Ne 4:20. Ec 4:9-12. Ga 6:2. Ph
1:27, 28.

13 **of good**. Dt 31:6, 7. Jsh 1:7. 10:25. 1 S 4:9.
14:6-12. 17:32. 2 S 10:12. Ezr 10:4. Ne 4:14.
Ps 27:14. 1 C 16:13.
let the Lord. Jg +10:15. 2 S 16:10, 11.

14 **they fled**. 1 K 20:13, 19-21, 28-30. 2 Ch
13:5-16. Je 46:15, 16.

15 **they likewise**. Le 26:7. Ro 8:31.

16 A.M. 2968. B.C. 1036. An. Ex. Is. 455.
and drew. Ps 2:1. Is 8:9. Mi 4:11, 12. Zc
14:1-3.
river. *that is*, Euphrates. ver. 6. Ps +72:8.
Shophach. i.e. *poured forth; pouring out*,
S#7780h. ver. 16, 18. 2 S 10:16, Shobach.

17 **upon them**. 2 S 10:17.
and set. ver. 9. Is 22:6, 7.

18 **fled before Israel**. ver. 13, 14. Ps 18:32.
33:16. 46:11.
seven thousand. 2 S 10:18.
footmen. 2 S 10:18, horsemen.

19 **the servants**. Ge 14:4, 5. Jsh 9:9-11. 2 S
10:19. 1 K 20:1, 12. Ps 18:39, 44. Is 10:8.
would. 1 Ch 14:17. Ps 48:3-6.

1 CHRONICLES 20

1 A.M. 2969. B.C. 1035. An. Ex. Is. 456.
And it came. 2 S 11:1.

after the year was expired. Heb. at the
return of the year. 2 K 13:20. 2 Ch +24:23mg.
at the time. 2 S 11:1. 1 K 20:22, 26. Jb
7:1mg. Ec +3:8. Is 40:2mg.
wasted. Is 6:11. 54:16.
Rabbah. Jsh +13:25.
Joab smote. 2 S 11:16-25. 12:26-31.

2 **it**. Heb. the weight of it.
and he brought. 1 Ch 18:11. 2 S 8:11, 12.

3 **And he**. 1 Ch 19:2-5. Ps 21:8, 9.
with saws. Ex 1:14. Jsh 9:23. Jg 8:6, 7, 16,
17. 1 K 9:21.

4 A.M. 2986. B.C. 1018. An. Ex. Is. 473.
there arose. *or*, there continued. Heb. there
stood. 2 S 21:15.
Gezer. *or*, Gob. 2 S 21:18, etc. 1 K +9:16.
Sibbechai. 1 Ch 11:29, Sibbecai.
Sippai. i.e. *threshold; my basins*, **S#5598h**. 2 S
21:18, Saph.
the giant. *or*, Rapha. Dt +2:20.

5 **Jair**. 2 S 21:19, Jaare-oregim.
Lahmi. i.e. *my bread; a warrior; an eater*,
S#3902h.
Goliath. 1 S 17:4. 21:9. 22:10. 2 S 21:19.
weaver's beam. 1 Ch 11:23. 1 S 17:7.

6 **of great stature**. Heb. a man of measure. Nu
13:32mg. 2 S 21:20.
toes. lit. fingers. 2 S 21:20.
the son of the giant. Heb. born to the giant,
or Rapha.

7 **defied**. *or*, reproached. 1 S 17:10, 26, 36. Is
27:33.
Shimea. 1 Ch 2:13, Shimma. 1 S 16:9,
Shammah.

8 **they fell**. Jsh 14:12. Ec 9:11. Je 9:23. Ro
8:31.

1 CHRONICLES 21

1 A.M. 2987. B.C. 1017. An. Ex. Is. 474.
Satan. Ge 3:13. 2 S 24:1. 1 K 22:20-22. Jb
1:6-12. 2:1, 4-6. Ps +5:9. Zc 3:1. Mt 4:3.
+7:15. Lk 22:31. Jn 13:2. Ac 5:3. 2 C 11:3, 14.
2 Th 2:9. 1 T 4:1. 2 T 2:26. Ja 1:13. Re 12:10.
16:13, 14.
provoked David. Lk 11:53. Ga 5:26. He
10:24.

2 **Joab**. 2 S 24:2-4.
Beer-sheba. Jg +20:1.
bring. 1 Ch 27:23, 24.
that I may. Dt 8:13-17. 2 Ch 32:25, 26. Pr
29:23. 2 C 12:7.

3 **The Lord**. 1 Ch 19:13. Ps 115:14. Pr 14:28. Is
26:15. 48:19.
why will. Ge 20:9. Ex 32:21. Nu 32:9, 10. 1
S 2:24. 1 K 14:16.

4 **the king's**. Ec 8:4.
Wherefore. Ex 1:17. Da 3:18. Ac 5:29.
and went. 2 S 24:3-8.

5 **number**. 1 S +11:8.

a thousand thousand and. The Syriac has 800,000, as in the parallel passage of Samuel. 1 Ch 27:23. 2 S 24:9.

6 **Levi**. Nu +1:49.
Joab. 2 S 3:27. 11:15-21. 20:9, 10.

7 **And God was displeased with this thing**. Heb. And it was evil in the eyes of God concerning this thing. Nu +22:34mg. 2 S 11:27. 1 K 15:5.
he smote. ver. 14. Jsh 7:1, 5, 13. 22:16-26. 2 S 21:1, 14. 24:1.

8 **I have sinned**. 2 S 12:13. 24:10. Ps 25:11. 32:5. Je 3:13. Lk 15:18, 19. 1 J 1:9.
do away. Ps 51:1-3. Ho 14:2. Jn 1:29.
I have done. Ge 34:7. 1 S 13:13. 26:21. 2 S 13:13. 2 Ch 16:9.

9 **Gad**. 1 S +22:5.
seer. 1 S 9:9.

10 **offer thee**. Heb. stretch out. Jb 9:8. 26:7. Ps 104:2. Is 40:22. 42:5. 44:24. 51:13. 66:12. Je 10:20. Ezk 25:16. Zc 12:1.
choose. Jsh 24:15. Pr 1:29-31.
that I may. Nu 20:12. 2 S 12:10-12. 1 K 13:21, 22. Pr 3:12. Re 3:19.

11 **Choose thee**. Heb. Take to thee. Pr 19:20.

12 **three years' famine**. 1 K +8:37.
to be destroyed. Le 26:17, 36, 37. Dt 28:15, 25, 51, 52. Je 42:16.
the sword. ver. 16. Je +12:12.
even the pestilence. Ps 91:6. Ezk +38:22.
the angel. ver. 15, 16. Ex 12:23. 2 K 19:35. Mt 13:49, 50. Ac 12:23. Re 7:1-3.
Now therefore. 2 S 24:13, 14.

13 **I am in**. 2 K 6:15. 7:4. Est 4:11, 16. Jn 12:27. Ph 1:23.
let me fall. He 10:31.
great. *or*, many. Ex +34:6, 7. Jon 3:9. Hab 3:2.
but let me. 2 Ch 28:9. Pr 12:10. Is 46:7. 47:6.

14 **the Lord**. ver. +12.
seventy. Ex 12:30. Nu 25:9. 1 S 6:19. 2 K 19:35.

15 **unto Jerusalem**. 2 S 24:16. Je 7:12. 26:9, 18. Mt 23:37, 38.
repented him. Jg 10:16. Ps 78:38. Je +18:8.
It is enough. Ex 9:28. 1 K 19:4. Ps 90:13. Mk 14:41.
Ornan. i.e. *strong one; large pine, tall as a great pine*. 2 S 24:18, Araunah. **S#771h:** ver. 15, 18, 20-25, 28. 2 Ch 3:1.

16 **lifted**. Ge +22:13.
and saw. Ge +3:7.
the angel. Ge 3:24. Ex 14:19, 20. Nu 22:31. Jsh 5:13, 14. 2 K 6:17.
clothed. Jb +16:15.
fell upon. Ge +17:3.

17 **Is it not I**. ver. 8. 2 S 24:17. Ps 51:4. Ezk 16:63.
even I it is. Gr. *ego eimi*. Is +41:4. Jn +8:28, 58.

these sheep. 1 K 22:17. Ps 44:11.
what have. 2 S 24:1.
hand. Ex +9:3.
be on me. Ge 44:33. Ex 32:32, 33. Jn 10:11, 12. Ro 9:3. 1 J 3:16.
on my father's. Ex 20:5. 2 S 12:10. Ps 51:14. Is 39:7, 8.
that they should. Jsh 22:18.

18 **the angel**. ver. 11. Ac 8:26, etc.
that David. ver. 15. 2 S 24:18. 2 Ch 3:1.
set up. 1 K 18:31, 32, 36, 37.
in the. Jg 6:11-16. 2 S 24:18, 19, 25.

19 **went up**. 2 K 5:10-14. Jn 2:5. Ac 9:6.

20 **And Ornan**, etc. *or*, When Ornan turned back and saw the angel, *then he*, and his four sons with him, hid themselves. Jg 6:11.

21 **bowed himself**. 1 S 25:23. 2 S 24:18-20.

22 **Grant**. Heb. Give. 1 K 21:2.
thou shalt grant. 2 S 24:21.
price. Ge +23:9.
that the plague. Nu +16:48.

23 **Take it**. Ge 23:4-6. 2 S 24:22, 23. Je 32:8.
the oxen. 1 S 6:14. 1 K 19:21. Is 28:27, 28.
burnt offerings. Le +23:12.
meat offering. Le +23:13.

24 **Nay**. Ge 14:23. 23:13. Dt 16:16, 17. Ml 1:12-14. Ro 12:17.
price. Ge +23:9.
for I will not. 2 S 24:24. Pr 3:9.
burnt offerings. Le +23:12.
without cost. Ge 29:15. Ex 23:15. 34:20. Dt 16:16. 1 S 9:7, 8. 2 S 24:24. Lk 21:4. 1 C +16:2. Ph 3:8.

25 **David gave**. 2 S 24:24, 25.

26 **built there**. Ex 20:24, 25. 24:4, 5.
burnt offerings. Le +23:12.
peace offerings. Le +23:19.
and called. 1 S 7:8, 9. Ps 51:15. 91:15. 99:6. Pr 15:8. Is 65:24. Je 33:3.
answered him. Nu 16:28-35. 1 K 18:36-38.
by fire. Le 9:24. Jg 6:21. 13:20. 1 K 18:24, 38. 2 Ch 7:1. Ps 20:3mg.

27 **the Lord**. ver. 15, 16. 2 S 24:16. Ps 103:20. La 3:31-33. He 1:14.
he put. ver. 12, 20. Je 47:6. Ezk 21:30. Mt 26:52. Jn 18:11.

28 **threshingfloor**. Ge +50:10.

29 **the tabernacle**. Ex +38:21.
Gibeon. Jsh +10:2.

30 **he was afraid**. ver. 16. 1 Ch 13:12. Dt 10:12. 2 S 6:9. Jb 13:21. 21:6. 23:15. Ps 90:11. 119:120. Je 5:22. 10:7. He 12:28, 29. Re 1:17. 15:4.

1 CHRONICLES 22

1 **This is the house**. 1 Ch 21:18-28. Ge 28:17. Dt 12:5-7, 11. 2 S 24:18. 2 Ch 3:1. 6:5, 6. Ps 78:60, 67-69. 132:13, 14. Jn 4:20-22.
and this is the altar. 2 K 18:22. 2 Ch 32:12.

2 **the strangers**. Ge +23:4. Ex 12:48mg. Dt +26:11. Jsh +20:9. 1 K 9:20, 21. 2 Ch 2:17. 8:7, 8. Is 61:5, 6. Mt +25:35. Ep 2:12, 19-22.
masons. 1 Ch 14:1. 2 S 5:11. 1 K 5:17, 18. 6:7. 7:9-12. 2 K 12:12. 22:6. Ezr 3:7.

3 **prepared iron**. 1 Ch 29:2, 7.
without weight. ver. 14. 1 K 7:47. 2 Ch 4:18. Je 52:20.

4 **cedar trees**. 2 S 5:11. 1 K 5:6-10. 2 Ch 2:3. Ezr 3:7.

5 **Solomon**. 1 Ch 29:1. 1 K 3:7. 2 Ch 13:7.
exceeding. 1 K 9:8. 2 Ch 2:5. 7:21. Ezr 3:12. Is 64:11. Ezr 7:20. Hg 2:3, 9. Lk 21:5.
David prepared. Dt 31:2-7. Ec 9:10. Jn 3:30. 4:37, 38. 9:4. 13:1. 2 P 1:13-15.

6 **charged him**. Mt 28:18-20. Ac 1:2. 20:25-31. 1 Th +2:11.

7 **it was in**. 1 Ch 17:1, etc. 28:2, etc. 29:3. 2 S 7:2. 1 K 8:17-19. 2 Ch 6:7-9. Ps 132:5. Ac 6:46.
unto the name. Dt 12:5, 11, 21. 1 K 8:16, 20, 29. 9:3. 2 Ch 2:4. Ezr 6:12.

8 **Thou hast shed**. 1 Ch 28:3. Nu 31:20, 24. 1 K 5:3.
thou shalt not. 1 Ch 17:4-10. 2 S 7:5-11.

9 **a son**. 1 Ch 17:11. 28:5-7. 2 S 7:12, 13.
man of rest. Ge 5:29.
I will give. 1 K 4:20, 25. 5:4. Ps 72:7. Is 9:6, 7.
Solomon. *that is,* Peaceable. 2 S 12:24, 25.
I will give peace. Jg 6:24mg. Jb 34:29. Is 26:12. 45:7. 57:19. 66:12. Hg 2:9.

10 **He shall build**. 1 Ch 17:12, 13. 28:6. 2 S 7:13. 1 K 5:5. 8:19, 20. Zc 6:12, 13.
he shall be. Ps 89:26, 27. He 1:5.
I will establish. 1 Ch 17:14. 28:7. Ps 89:36, 37. Is 9:7.
for ever. Heb. *olam,* Ex +12:24.

11 **the Lord**. ver. 16. 1 K +1:37. Is 26:12. +43:2.

12 **Only the**. 1 K 3:9-12. 2 Ch 1:10. Ps 72:1. Pr 2:6, 7. Lk 21:15. Ja 1:5.
give thee. Jsh 1:5, 6. 2 Ch 19:11.
that thou mayest. Dt 4:6. 1 K 11:1-10. Pr 14:8. Jn +13:17. 1 J 2:3.

13 **Then shalt**. 1 Ch 28:7. Ps +1:3. 119:6. Je 22:3, 4.
to fulfill. Mt 3:15. Ac 13:22. Ga 6:2. Ja 2:8.
be strong. Jsh +1:6.

14 **trouble**. *or,* poverty. 2 C 8:2.
hundred thousand talents. 1 Ch 29:4-7. 1 K 10:14.
without weight. ver. +3. 2 K 25:16. Je 52:20.

15 **hewers and workers of stone and timber**. *that is,* masons and carpenters. ver. 2-4.
all manner. Ex 28:6. 31:3-5. 35:32-35. 1 K 7:14.

16 **the gold**. ver. 3, 14.
Arise. Jsh 1:2, 5, 9. 7:10. Jg 4:14. 18:9, 10. 2 Ch 20:17. Ep 5:14. Ph 2:12, 13. 4:13.

be doing. Ge 3:19. Ex 20:9. Jsh +14:8. Jg 5:23. Pr 10:4, 5. 12:24. 13:4. 22:29. 27:23, 24. 28:19. Ec 5:12. 9:10. Is 52:1. Am 6:1. Lk +12:37. 16:10. Jn +5:17. Ro 13:11. Ga +4:18. Ep 4:28. 6:7. Col 3:23-25. 1 Th 4:11, 12. 1 T +5:13.
and the Lord. ver. +11.

17 **all the princes**. 1 Ch 28:21. 29:6. Ro 16:2, 3. Ph 4:3. 3 J 8.

18 **Is not**. Jg 6:12-14. Ro 8:31.
and hath. ver. +9. 1 Ch 23:25. Dt 12:10, 11. Jsh 22:4. 23:1. 2 S 7:1. Ac 9:31.
before the Lord. Dt 20:4. Jsh 10:42. 1 S 25:28. 2 S 5:19, 20. Ps 44:1-5.

19 **set your**. 1 Ch 16:11. 28:9. Dt 4:29. 32:46, 47. Ps 27:4. 2 Ch 20:3. Da 9:3. Hg 1:5mg. Ac 11:23.
soul. Heb. *nephesh,* Ge +34:3.
arise. ver. +16. Is 60:1. Ac 22:16.
to bring. 1 K 8:6, 21. 2 Ch 5:7. 6:11.
to the name. ver. +7. 1 K 5:3.

1 CHRONICLES 23

1 A.M. 2989. B.C. 1015. An. Ex. Is. 476.
old. 1 Ch 29:28. Ge 25:8. 35:29. 1 K 1:1. Jb 5:26.
he made. 1 Ch 28:5. 29:22-25. 1 K 1:33-39.

2 **he gathered**. 1 Ch 13:1. 28:1. Jsh 23:2. 24:1. 2 Ch 34:29, 30.

3 **the Levites**. Nu 4:2, 3, 23, 30, 35, 43, 47.
thirty and eight. Nu 4:48.

4 **twenty**. ver. 28-32. 1 Ch 6:48. 9:28-32. 26:20-27.
set forward. *or,* oversee. 1 Ch 15:21. 2 Ch 2:2, 18. 34:12. Ezr 3:8, 9. Ne 11:9, 22. Ac 20:28.
officers and judges. Ex +21:6. 2 Ch 19:8. Ml 2:7.

5 **porters**. 1 Ch 9:17-27. 15:23, 24. 16:38, 42. 26:1-12. 2 S 18:26. 2 Ch 8:14. 35:15. Ezr 7:7. Ne 7:73. 11:19. 12:45.
praised. 1 Ch 6:31-48. 9:33. 15:16-22. 16:41, 42. 25:1-7. 2 Ch 20:19-21. Ps 87:7.
the instruments. 1 K 10:12. 2 Ch 29:25, 26. Am +6:5.

6 **divided**. 2 Ch 8:14. 29:25. 31:2. 35:10. Ezr 6:18.
courses. Heb. divisions. 1 Ch 24:1. 26:1.
Gershon. Ge +46:11.

7 **Gershonites**. Nu +3:21.
Laadan. i.e. *put in order; for their adornment,* S#3936h. ver. 8, 9. 1 Ch 7:26. 26:21.

8 **Jehiel**. Ezr +8:9.
Zetham. i.e. *olive tree,* S#2241h. 1 Ch 26:22.
Joel. 1 S +8:2.

9 **Shelomith**. Le +24:11.
Haziel. i.e. *seen of God; vision of God,* S#2381h.
Haran. Ge +11:26.

10 **Zina**. i.e. *nourishing; fruitful,* S#2126h. ver. 11, Ziza.

Jeush. Ge +36:5, 18. 2 Ch 11:18.
Beriah. 1 Ch +8:21.

11 **Zizah**. i.e. *full breast; abundance; exuberance*, **S#2125h**. ver. 10, Zina.
had not many sons. Heb. did not multiply sons.

12 **sons of Kohath**. Ge +46:11.
Izhar. Ex +6:18.
Hebron. Ex +6:18.
Uzziel. Ex +6:18.

13 **The sons**. Ex +6:18.
Aaron. Ex +4:14.
Moses. Ex +2:10.
separated. Ex 28:1, etc. Nu 18:1. Ps 99:6. 106:16. Ac 13:2. Ro 1:1. Ga 1:15. He 5:4.
sanctify. Ex 29:33-37, 44. 49:9-15. Le 10:10, 17, 18. 16:11-19, 32, 33. 17:2-6. Nu 18:3-8.
to burn incense. Ex 30:6-10, 34-38. Le 10:1, 2. 16:12, 13. Nu 16:16-18, 35-40, 46, 47. 1 S 2:28. 2 Ch 26:18-21. Lk 1:9. Re 8:3.
to bless. Le 9:22, 23. Nu 6:23-27. Dt 21:5.

14 **the man**. Dt +33:1. 1 T +6:11.
his sons. 1 Ch 26:23-25.

15 **Gershom**. Ex +2:22. 4:20. 18:3, 4.

16 **Shebuel**. i.e. *captive of God; abide ye with God*, **S#7619h**. 1 Ch 25:4. 26:24. Also 1 Ch 24:20. 25:20, Shubael.

17 **Rehabiah**. i.e. *breadth of Jah; enlarging of the Lord*, **S#7345h**. 1 Ch 24:21. 26:25.
the chief. *or*, the first. 1 Ch 26:25.
were very many. Heb. were highly multiplied.

18 **Shelomith**. 1 Ch 24:22, Shelomoth. 26:26.

19 **Hebron**. ver. +12.
Jeriah. i.e. *Jehovah will teach*, **S#3404h**. 1 Ch 24:23. 26:31, Jerijah.
Amariah. Ezr +7:3.
Jahaziel. 1 Ch +24:23.
Jekameam. 1 Ch +24:23.

21 **Merari**. ver. 6. Ge +46:11.
Mahli. Nu +3:20.
Mushi. Ex +6:19.
Eleazar. Ex +6:23.
Kish. 1 Ch 24:29. 1 S +9:1.

22 **had no sons**. 1 Ch +2:34. 24:28.
but daughters. 1 Ch +2:34.
brethren. *or*, kinsmen. 1 Ch 7:22. +15:5.
took them. Nu 36:6-8.

23 **Eder**. i.e. *a flock*, **S#5740h**. 1 Ch 24:30. Jsh 15:21.
Jeremoth. 1 Ch 24:30, Jerimoth.

24 **the sons of Levi**. Nu 10:17, 21.
after the house. Nu 1:4. 2:32. 3:15, 20. 4:34-49.
by their polls. Nu 1:2, 18, 22. 3:47.
twenty. ver. 3, 27. Nu 1:3. 4:3. 8:24. Ezr 3:8.

25 **The Lord**. 1 Ch +22:18. 2 S 7:1, 11.
given rest. 1 T 2:1, 2. He 4:9. Re 14:13.
that they may dwell in Jerusalem. *or*, and he dwelleth in Jerusalem. 1 K 8:13, 27. Ps

9:11. 68:16, 18. 132:13, 14. 135:21. Is 8:18. Jl 3:21. Zc 8:3. 2 C 6:16. Col 2:9.
for ever. Ge +9:12. Ex +12:24.

26 **no more carry**. Nu 4:5, 49. 7:9. 2 T 4:7, 8. Re 3:12. 7:15, 16. 14:13.

27 **by the last**. ver. 3, 24. 2 S 23:1. Ps 72:20.
numbered. Heb. number.

28 **office was to wait**, etc. Heb. station was at the hand of Aaron. 1 Ch 18:17mg. Ne 11:24. Ps 123:2. 2 C 4:5.
for the service. ver. 4. 1 Ch 28:13. Nu 3:6-9. 8:11-22, 26. 18:2-6.
in the chambers. 1 Ch 9:26. 1 K 6:5. 2 Ch 31:11. Ezr 8:29. Ne 13:4, 5, 9. Je 35:4. Ezk 41:6-11, 26. 42:3, 13.
purifying. 1 Ch 9:28, 29. 2 Ch 29:5, 18, 19. 35:3-6, 11-14.

29 **for the showbread**. Ex +25:30. 2 Ch 29:18.
the fine flour. 1 Ch 9:29, etc. Le 6:20-23.
meat offering. Le +23:13.
unleavened. Le 2:4-7. 7:9.
pan. *or*, flat plate.
for all manner of measure. Le 19:35, 36. Nu 3:50.

30 **stand**. 1 Ch 6:31-33. 9:33. 16:37-42. 25:1-7. 2 Ch 29:25-28. 31:2. Ezr 3:10, 11. Ps 135:1-3, 19, 20. 137:2-4. Re 5:8-14. 14:3.
every morning. Ex 29:39-42. 2 S 13:4mg. Ps +5:3. 92:1-3. 134:1, 2.
thank. 1 Th 5:18.
at even. Mt +14:23.

31 **in the sabbaths**. Le 23:24, 39. Col +2:16.
set feasts. Ge +17:21. Le ch. 23. Nu ch. 28, 29.
the order. 1 Ch 15:11-13. Ne 11:17.
before. Ep 1:4.

32 **keep**. 1 Ch 9:27. Nu 1:53. 1 K 8:4.
the charge of the sons. Nu 3:6-8, 38.

1 CHRONICLES 24

1 **the divisions**. 1 Ch 23:6mg.
The sons. Ex +6:23.

2 **Nadab**. Ex +6:23.
Abihu. Ex +6:23.
died. Le 10:2. Nu 3:4. 16:39, 40. 18:7. 26:61.
Eleazar. Ex +6:23. 29:9. Nu 18:7.
Ithamar. Ex +6:23.

3 **Zadok**. ver. 6, 31. 2 S +8:17.
Ahimelech. This was Abiathar, who appears to have had the name of Ahimelech, as well as his father. 1 S 21:1. 22:9, etc. 2 S 8:17. Mk 2:26.

4 **more**. 1 Ch 15:6-12, 16.
sons of Eleazar. Nu 25:11-13. 1 S 2:30-38.
according. 1 Ch +23:24.

5 **they divided by lot**. Jsh +14:2.
the governors. 1 Ch 9:11. 2 Ch 35:8. Ne 11:11. Mt 26:3. 27:1. Ac 4:1, 6. 5:24.

6 **Shemaiah**. 1 Ch +9:16.

Nethaneel. Nu +1:8.
the scribe. 1 K 4:3. 2 Ch 34:13. Ezr 7:6. Ne 8:1. Mt 8:19. 13:52. 23:1, 2.
principal household. Heb. house of the father. ver. 4. 1 Ch 23:24.

7 **Jehoiarib**. i.e. *Jehovah defended; the Lord will contend*, **S#3080h**. 1 Ch 9:10. Ne 12:19, Joiarib.
to Jedaiah. 1 Ch +9:10. Ezr 2:36. Ne 7:39. 11:10.

8 **Harim**. i.e. *flat-nosed; compressed; bent upward*, **S#2766h**. Ezr 2:32, 39. 10:21, 31. Ne 3:11. 7:35, 42. 10:5, 27. 12:15.
Seorim. i.e. *barley; bearded ones*, **S#8188h**.

9 **Malchijah**. 1 Ch +9:12.
Mijamin. i.e. *from the right hand*, **S#4326h**. Ne 10:7. +12:5, Miamin, 17, 41, Miniamin.

10 **Hakkoz**. i.e. *the thorn*, **S#6976h**.
Abijah. 1 K +14:1.

11 **Jeshuah**. i.e. *a savior*, **S#3442h**. Ne +8:17, Jeshua.
Shecaniah. i.e. *habitation of the Lord*, **S#7935h**. 1 Ch 3:21, 22. Ezr 8:3, 5. 10:2. Ne 3:29. 6:18. 12:3.

12 **Eliashib**. 1 Ch +3:24.
Jakim. 1 Ch +8:19.

13 **Huppah**. i.e. *a covering; nuptial bed; chamber*, **S#2647h**.
Jeshebeab. i.e. *seat or habitation of his father; father's dwelling*, **S#3428h**.

14 **Bilgah**. Ne +12:5.
Immer. 1 Ch +9:12.

15 **Hezir**. i.e. *protected*, **S#2387h**. Ne 10:20.
Aphses. i.e. *dispersion*, **S#6483h**.

16 **Pethahiah**. Ne +11:24.
Jehezekel. i.e. *God will strengthen*, **S#3168h**.

17 **Jachin**. Ge +46:10.
Gamul. i.e. *weaned; deed; recompensed*, **S#1577h**.

18 **Delaiah**. Je +36:12.
Maaziah. i.e. *strengthened of Jehovah*, **S#4590h**. Ne 10:8.

19 **the orderings**. 1 Ch 9:25. 2 Ch 23:4, 8. 1 C +14:40.
under Aaron. ver. 1. He 7:11.

20 **Amram**. Ex +6:18.
Shubael. i.e. *captive; the return of God*, **S#7619h**. 1 Ch 23:16. 25:4, 20. 26:24, Shebuel.
Jehdeiah. i.e. *unity of Jah*, **S#3165h**. 1 Ch 27:30.

21 **Rehabiah**. 1 Ch 23:17.
Isshiah. i.e. *forgotten of Jah*, **S#3449h**. ver. 25. 1 Ch 26:25, Jeshaiah.

22 **Izharites**. i.e. *descendants of Izhar* (i.e. *anointed; oil*, Ex +6:18), **S#3325h**. 1 Ch 26:23, 29. Nu 3:27. The original is uniformly Izharites. 1 Ch 23:18. Ex 6:21. Nu 3:19, 27, Izeharites.
Shelomoth. i.e. *peaceful; pacifications; retributions*, **S#8013h**. 1 Ch 23:9. 26:25, 26. The variation of "Shelomith" and "Shelomoth" arises from the mutation of *wav* and *yood*. 1 Ch

23:18. 26:26, Shelomith.
Jahath. 1 Ch +4:2.

23 **Jeriah**. 1 Ch +23:19.
Jahaziel. i.e. *beheld of God*, **S#3166h**. 1 Ch 12:4. 16:6. 23:19. 2 Ch 20:14. Ezr 8:5.
Jekameam. i.e. *the people will rise*, **S#3360h**. 1 Ch 23:19.

24 **Uzziel**. Ex +6:18.
Michah. i.e. *who is like Jehovah?*, **S#4318h**. ver. 25. 1 Ch 23:20, Micah.
Shamir. i.e. *guarding; a thorn*, **S#8053h**. Jsh 15:48. Jg 10:1, 2.

25 **Isshiah**. 1 Ch 23:20, Jesiah.
Zechariah. 1 Ch 15:18, 20.

26 **Jaaziah**. i.e. *comforted of the Lord*, **S#3269h**. ver. 27.
Beno. i.e. *son of him*, **S#1121h**. ver. 27.

27 **sons**. Ge +46:11.
Shoham. i.e. *an onyx stone*, **S#7719h**.
Zaccur. 1 Ch +25:2.
Ibri. i.e. *born beyond the river*, **S#5681h**.

28 **who had no sons**. 1 Ch +2:34. 23:22.

29 **Jerahmeel**. 1 Ch +2:9.

30 **Mushri**. 1 Ch 6:47. 23:23.
Jerimoth. 1 Ch +7:7.

31 **lots**. ver. 5, 6. Nu 26:56.
even the principal. 1 Ch 25:8. 26:13.

1 CHRONICLES 25

1 **the captains**. 1 Ch 12:28. 23:2. 24:5, 6. 2 Ch 23:1, 9.
Asaph. 2 K +18:18.
prophesy. ver. 3. 1 S 10:5. 2 K 3:15. 1 C 14:24-26.
harps. 1 Ch +13:8. 15:16-21. 16:4, 5, 42. 23:5-7. 2 Ch 23:13. 29:25, 26. 31:2. 34:12. Ezr 3:10, 11. Ne 12:24, 27, 43-46. Ps 81:2. 92:1-3. 150:3-5. Re 15:2-4.
psalteries. 1 S +10:5.
cymbals. 1 Ch +13:8.

2 **Asaph**. ver. +1.
Zaccur. i.e. *remembered; mindful*, **S#2139h**. ver. 10. 1 Ch +4:26, Zacchur. 24:27. Nu 13:4. Ezr +8:14, Zabbud. Ne 3:2. 10:12. 12:35. 13:13.
Joseph. Ge +30:24.
Nethaniah. ver. +12.
Asarelah. i.e. *upright toward God; an upright or straight oak; guided towards God*, **S#841h**. "Otherwise called Jesharelah, ver. 14."
under the hands. ver. 3, 6. Is 3:6.
according to the order of the king. Heb. by the hands of the king. ver. 6mg. 1 Ch 11:3mg, 2 Ch 23:18mg. 34:14mg. 1 K +16:12mg. Ezr 3:10.

3 **Jeduthun**. 1 Ch +9:16.
Gedaliah. i.e. *greatness of Jah*, **S#1436h**. ver. 9. 2 K 25:22-25. Je 38:1. 39:14. 40:6, 7, 9, 11-16. 41:1-4, 6, 9, 10, 18. 43:6. Also Ezr 10:18. Je 40:5, 8. 41:16. Zp 1:1.

Zeri. i.e. *distillation; balm*, **S#6874h**. ver. 11, Izri.

Jeshaiah. i.e. *the salvation of Jehovah*, **S#3470h**. ver. 15. 1 Ch 26:25. Ezr 8:7, 19.

Hashabiah. 1 Ch +9:14.

Mattithiah. ver. 21. 1 Ch 15:18, 21. Ezr +10:43.

six. "With Shimei, mentioned ver. 17." or, "Shishah." i.e. "six." Perhaps the same as "Shimea" in ver. 17 (Young).

to give thanks. 1 Ch 23:30. Ps +136:1. Je 33:11.

4 **Heman**. 1 Ch +2:6.

Bukkiah. ver. +13.

Mattaniah. ver. 16. 2 K +24:17.

Uzziel. ver. 18, Azareel. 1 Ch 24:24.

Shebuel. ver. 20. 1 Ch 24:20, Shubael.

Jerimoth. ver. 22. 1 Ch 24:30.

Hananiah. ver. +23.

Hanani. i.e. *favorable*, **S#2607h**. ver. 25. 1 K 16:1, 7. 2 Ch 16:7. 19:2. 20:34. Ezr 10:20. Ne 1:2. 7:2. 12:36.

Eliathah. i.e. *my God hath come*, **S#448h**. ver. 27.

Giddalti. i.e. *I have magnified*, **S#1437h**. ver. 29.

Romamti-eser. i.e. *exultation of help*, **S#7320h**. ver. 31.

Joshbekashah. i.e. *a hard or sharp seat*, **S#3436h**. ver. 24.

Mallothi. i.e. *I have spoken*, **S#4413h**. ver. 26.

Hothir. i.e. *undaunted*, **S#1956h**. ver. 28.

Mahazioth. i.e. *visions; seeing a sign*, **S#4238h**. ver. 30.

5 **the king's seer**. 1 Ch 21:9. 1 S 9:9. 2 S +24:11.

words. or, matters.

God gave. 1 Ch 4:27. 28:5. Ge +29:31. 33:5. Ps +127:3. Is 8:18.

6 **under the hands**. ver. 2, 3.

for song. ver. 1-3. 1 Ch 15:22. 23:5. Ps 68:25. Ep 5:19. Col 3:16.

according to the king's order. Heb. by the hands of the king. ver. +2mg.

Asaph. ver. +1-4.

7 **two hundred**. 1 Ch 23:5.

instructed. or, taught. SS 3:8. Is 29:13. Ho 10:11.

cunning. or, intelligent. In music, etc. 1 Ch +15:22.

8 **cast lots**. Jsh +14:2.

ward against ward. 1 Ch 24:31. 26:13, 16. Ne 12:24.

the teacher. 1 Ch 15:22. 2 Ch 23:13.

9 **Joseph**. ver. 2.

the second. Dr. Geddes, chiefly on the authority of the Arabic, adds, "who with his sons and brethren were twelve."

10 **Zaccur**. ver. 2.

11 **Izri**. i.e. *created*, **S#3339h**. ver. 3, Zeri.

12 **Nethaniah**. i.e. *given of the Lord*, **S#5418h**. ver. 2. 2 Ch 17:8. Je 36:14. 40:8. 41:9. 2 K 25:23, 25. Je 40:14, 15. 41:1, 2, 6, 7, 10-12, 15, 16, 18.

13 **Bukkiah**. i.e. *emptying of the Lord*, **S#1232h**. ver. 4.

14 **Jesharelah**. i.e. *right towards God*, **S#3480h**. ver. 2, Asarelah.

15 **Jeshaiah**. ver. +3.

16 **Mattaniah**. ver. 4.

17 **Shimei**. 2 S +16:5.

18 **Azareel**. ver. 4, Uzziel.

19 **Hashabiah**. ver. 3.

20 **Shubael**. ver. 4, Shebuel. 1 Ch +24:20.

21 **Mattithiah**. ver. 3.

22 **Jerimoth**. ver. 4. 1 Ch 23:23. 24:30.

23 **Hananiah**. i.e. *whom Jehovah gave*, **S#2608h**. ver. 4. 2 Ch 26:11. Je 36:12. Also 1 Ch 3:19, 21. 8:24. Ezr 10:28. Ne 3:8, 30. 7:2. 10:23. 12:12, 41. Je 28:1, 5, 10, 11-13, 15, 17. 37:13. Da 1:6, 7, 11, 19. 2:17.

25 **Hanani**. ver. 4.

26 **Mallothi**. ver. 4.

27 **Eliathah**. ver. 4.

28 **Hothir**. ver. 4.

29 **Giddalti**. ver. 4.

30 **Mahazioth**. ver. 4.

31 **Romamti-ezer**. ver. 4.

1 CHRONICLES 26

1 **the divisions**. 1 Ch 23:5.

the porters. 1 Ch 9:17-27. 15:18, 23, 24. 2 Ch 23:19.

Korhites. Nu 26:9-11. Ps 44-49, titles.

Meshelemiah. ver. 14, Shelemiah.

Kore. 1 Ch +9:19.

Asaph. 1 Ch 9:19, Ebiasaph. 2 K +18:18.

2 **Zechariah**. Zc +1:1.

Jediael. 1 Ch +7:6.

Zebadiah. i.e. *the gift of Jehovah*, **S#2069h**. 2 Ch 17:8. 19:11. Also 1 Ch 8:15, 17. 12:7. 27:7. Ezr 8:8. 10:20.

Jathniel. i.e. *given of God*, **S#3496h**.

3 **Elam**. Ge +10:22.

Jehohanan. 2 Ch +17:15.

Elioenai. i.e. *God the Lord of my eyes*, **S#454h**. Ezr 8:4, Elihoenai. Also 1 Ch 3:23, 24. 4:36. 7:8. Ezr 10:22, 27. Ne 12:41.

4 **Obed-edom**. 2 S +6:10.

Shemaiah. 1 Ch +9:16.

Jehozabad. i.e. *the Lord gave*, **S#3075h**. 2 K 12:21. 2 Ch 17:18. 24:26.

Joah. Is +36:3.

Sacar. 1 Ch +11:35.

Nethaneel. Nu +1:8.

5 **Ammiel**. 1 Ch +3:5.

Issachar. Ge +30:18.

Peulthai. i.e. *my wages*, **S#6469h**.

him. "That is, Obed-edom, as 1 Ch 13:14." 1 Ch 15:24. 16:38. 2 S 6:11. Ps 128:1.

6 **mighty men of valor**. ver. 8, 30, 32. 1 Ch 12:28. 2 S +2:7mg. Ne 11:14. 1 T 6:12. 2 T 2:3.

7 **Othni**. i.e. *lion of the Lord*, **S#6273h**.
  Rephael. i.e. *healed of God*, **S#7501h**.
  Obed. Ru +4:17.
  Elzabad. i.e. *God gave*, **S#443h**. 1 Ch 12:12.
  strong men. ver. 9. 2 K 2:16.
  Elihu. 1 S +1:1.
  Semachiah. i.e. *sustained of the Lord*, **S#5565h**.

8 **able men**. Ex +18:21, 25. Mt 25:15. 1 C
  12:4-11. 2 C 3:6. 2 T 2:2. 1 P 4:11.
  strength. Ep 6:10.

9 **Meshelemiah**. ver. 1, 14.

10 **Hosah**. 1 Ch +16:38.
  Simri. i.e. *watchful*, **S#8113h**.
  not the firstborn. 1 Ch +5:1, 2. Ge 48:14,
  19. Jsh 14:6. 2 Ch 21:3. Je +31:9. Col +1:15.
  yet. Ge +44:30.
  his father. 1 Ch +5:1, 2.
  made him. 2 Ch 11:22.

11 **Hilkiah**. 2 K +18:18.
  Tebaliah. i.e. *dipped of Jehovah; whom Jehovah
  has purified*, **S#2882h**. Ex 12:22, **S#2881h**, *tabal,
  dip*; 2 K 5:14.
  Zechariah. Zc +1:1.

12 **wards**. 1 Ch +25:8.

13 **as well the small as the great**. Heb. *or*, as
  well for the small as for the great. 1 Ch 24:31.
  25:8.

14 **Shelemiah**. i.e. *repaid of the Lord*. ver. 1,
  Meshelemiah. **S#8018h**: Ezr 10:41. Je 36:14,
  26. 38:1. Also Ezr 10:39. Ne 3:30. 13:13. Je
  37:3, 13.
  Zechariah. ver. 2.
  wise. or, understanding. 1 Ch 22:12. 1 S
  25:3.
  counsellor. 2 S 15:12.

15 **Asuppim**. Heb. gatherings. **S#624h**. ver. 17. 2
  Ch 25:24. Ne 12:25. Ec 12:11.

16 **Shupphim**. 1 Ch +7:12.
  Hosah. ver. 10, 11.
  Shallecheth. i.e. *casting forth*, **S#7996h**.
  causeway. Nu 20:19. Jg 5:20mg. 1 K 10:5. 2
  Ch 9:4.
  going up. 1 K 10:5. 2 Ch 9:4. Ne 3:31.
  ward against ward. That is, their stations
  were opposite to each other; as the north to
  the south, and the east to the west. ver. 12. 1
  Ch 25:8. Ne 12:24.

17 **Eastward**. 1 Ch 9:24. 2 Ch 8:14.
  Asuppim. ver. 15.

18 **Parbar**. i.e. *a quarter of Jerusalem* (Strong),
  S#6503h. 2 K 23:11.

19 **Kore**. Nu 16:11, Korah.

20 **Ahijah**. 1 K +14:4.
  treasures. ver. 22. 1 Ch 9:26-30. 22:3, 4, 14-
  16. 28:12-19. 29:2-8. 1 K 14:26. 15:18. Ml 3:10.
  dedicated things. Heb. holy things. ver. 26-
  28. 1 Ch 18:11. 1 K 7:51. 15:15. 2 Ch 31:11,
  12.

21 **Laaden**. 1 Ch 6:17, Libni. 23:7.
  Jehieli. i.e. *my God lives*, **S#3172h**. ver. 22.

22 **Jehieli**. 1 Ch 23:8. 29:8, Jehiel.
  over the treasures. ver. 20. Ne 10:38.

23 **Amramites**. 1 Ch 23:12. Nu 3:19, 27.

24 **Shebuel**. 1 Ch 23:15, +16. 24:20, Shubael.
  Gershom. Ex +2:22.
  Moses. Ex +2:10.

25 **Eliezer**. 1 Ch 23:15. Ex 18:4.
  Rehabiah. 1 Ch +23:17.
  Jeshaiah. 1 Ch +25:3.
  Joram. i.e. *height; Jehovah has or is exalted*,
  S#3141h. 1 Ch 3:11. 18:10, Hadoram. 2 S 8:10.
  1 K 22:50, Jehoram. 2 K 8:16, 21, 23-25, 28,
  29. 9:14, 16, 29. 11:2. 2 Ch 22:5, 7. Mt 1:8.
  Zichri. 1 Ch +9:15.
  Shelomith. 1 Ch 23:18. Le +24:11.

26 **over all the treasures**. 1 Ch 18:11. 22:14.
  29:2-9. Nu 31:30-52.

27 **Out**. Jsh 6:19.
  spoils won in battles. Heb. battles and spoils.
  to maintain. 2 K 12:14. Ne 10:32-34.

28 **Samuel**. 1 S 9:9.
  Kish. 1 S +9:1.
  Abner. 1 S +14:50.
  Ner. 1 Ch +9:36.
  Joab. 1 S +26:6.
  Zeruiah. 1 Ch +2:16.

29 **Izharites**. ver. 23. 1 Ch 23:12, 18.
  Chenaniah. 1 Ch +15:22.
  the outward. 2 Ch 34:13. Ne 11:16.
  officers. 2 Ch 19:8-11.
  judges. Ex +21:6.

30 **the Hebronites**. 1 Ch 23:12, 19. Nu +3:27.
  Hashabiah. 1 Ch +9:14.
  men of valor. ver. +6.
  officers. Heb. over the charge.

31 **Jerijah**. i.e. *shot by Jah*, **S#3404h**. 1 Ch +23:19,
  Jeriah.
  fortieth. 1 Ch 29:27. 1 K 2:11.
  sought for. Ge 42:22. Is 65:1. Ezk 14:3. 20:3,
  31. 36:37.
  Jazer. Nu +32:1.

32 **men of valor**. ver. 6-9.
  chief fathers. 1 Ch 15:12. 23:24. 24:31.
  Reubenites. Nu +26:7.
  and affairs. Heb. and thing. 1 Ch 27:1. 2 Ch
  19:11.

1 CHRONICLES 27

1 **the chief fathers**. 1 Ch 26:26.
  captains of thousands. Jsh +22:21.
  served. 1 Ch 28:1. 2 Ch 17:12-19. 26:11-13.
  any matter. 1 K 5:14.
  month. 1 K 4:7, 27.

2 **first month**. called Nisan *or* Abib.
  Jashobeam. 1 Ch +11:11.
  Zabdiel. Ne +11:14.

3 **Perez**. i.e. *rupture; breach; division*, **S#6557h**. Ge
  +46:12, Pharez.
  the chief. Ge 49:8-10. Nu 7:12. 10:14.

4 **second month**. called Ziv or Ijar.
Dodai. i.e. *beloved of the Lord*; *amatory*; *my beloved*, **S#1737h**. 1 Ch 11:12. 2 S 23:9, Dodo.
Mikloth. i.e. *lots*; *sprouts*; *triflings*; *staves*, **S#4732h**. 1 Ch 8:32. 9:37, 38.

5 **third month**. called Sivan.
Benaiah. 1 Ch +15:24. Or, "Benaiah, the son of Jehoiada the chief priest:" it was Jehoiada, and not Benaiah, who was a priest.
Jehoiada. 2 K +11:4.
chief priest. *or*, principal officer. Ge 41:45. 1 K 4:5.

6 **mighty**. 1 Ch 11:22-25. 2 S 22:20-23. 23:20-23.
Ammizabad. i.e. *people of the endower* or *bountiful giver*, **S#5990h**.

7 **fourth month**. called Tammuz.
Asahel. 1 Ch +2:16.
Zebadiah. 1 Ch +26:2.

8 **fifth month**. called Ab.
Shamhuth. i.e. *desolation, astonishment; exaltation; destruction*, **S#8049h**. 1 Ch 11:27, Shammoth the Hararite. 26:29. 2 S 23:25, Shammah the Harodite.
Izrahite. i.e. *he will arise; he will be bright*, **S#3155h**.

9 **sixth month**. called Elul. 1 Ch 11:28.
Ira. 2 S +20:26.
Ikkesh. 2 S +23:26.

10 **seventh month**. called Tizri.
Helez. 1 Ch +2:39.
Pelonite. 2 S 23:26, Paltite.

11 **eighth month**. called Marchesvan or Bul.
Sibbecai. 1 Ch +11:29. 2 S 21:18.
Zarhites. Nu 26:20.

12 **ninth month**. called Cisleu.
Abiezer. Jsh +17:2.
Anetothite. i.e. *an inhabitant of Anathoth* (i.e. *answers, songs*, 1 Ch +7:8), **S#6069h**. 1 Ch +11:28, Antothite. 2 S 23:27, Anethothite.

13 **tenth month**. called Tebet.
Maharai. 1 Ch 11:30. 2 S +23:28.
Zarhites. ver. 11.

14 **eleventh month**. called Shebet.
Benaiah. 1 Ch +15:24.

15 **twelfth month**. called Adar.
Heldai. i.e. *worldly; vital; long-lived*, **S#2469h**. 1 Ch 11:30, Heled. 2 S 23:29, Heleb. Zc 6:10.
Othniel. Jsh +15:17.

16 **Furthermore**. ver. 22. 1 Ch 28:1.
Eliezar. Ge +15:2.
Shephatiah. 2 S +3:4.

17 **Hashabiah**. 1 Ch +9:14.
of the Aaronites. 1 Ch +12:27, 28.
Zadok. 2 S +8:17.

18 **Elihu**. 1 S +1:1. 16:6. 17:13, 29, Eliab.
Omri. 1 K +16:16.

19 **Ishmaiah**. i.e. *Jehovah will hear*, **S#3460h**.
Jerimoth. 1 Ch +7:7.

20 **Azaziah**. i.e. *strengthened of the Lord*, **S#5812h**. 1 Ch 15:21. 2 Ch 31:13.
Pedaiah. 2 K +23:36.

21 **Iddo**. i.e. *casting*. **S#3035h**. 1 K 4:14. 2 Ch 9:29. 12:15. 13:22. Ezr +10:43, Jadau.
Jaasiel. i.e. *made of God*, **S#3300h**. 1 Ch +11:47, Jasiel.
Abner. 1 S +14:50.

23 **from twenty**. Nu 1:18.
he would increase. Ge +15:5.

24 **began to number**. 1 Ch 21:1-17. 2 S 24:1-15.
finished not. Levi and Benjamin being omitted. 1 Ch 21:6, 7. 2 S 24:15.
was the number put. Heb. ascended the number.
account. Ge 34:30 (number). 41:49.
chronicles. lit. "words or matters of the days," as in 1 K 14:19.

25 **the king's**. 2 K 18:15. 2 Ch 16:2.
Azmaveth. 2 S +23:31.
the storehouses. Ge 41:48. Ex 1:11. 2 Ch 26:10. Je 41:8.
fields. Ge 27:27.
cities. Ge 41:35, 48.
villages. lit. "coverings," as in Jsh 18:24. 1 S 6:18. Ne 6:2. SS 7:11.
castles. or, towers. lit. "great places." **S#4026h**. Ge 11:4, 5. 35:21. Jsh 15:37. 19:38. Jg 8:9, 17. 9:46, 47, 49, 51, 52. 2 K 9:17. 17:9. 18:8. 2 Ch 14:7. 26:9, 10, 15. 27:4. 32:5. Ne 3:1, 11, 25-27. 8:4mg. 12:38, 39. Ps 48:12. 61:3. Pr 18:10. SS 4:4. 5:13mg. 7:4. 8:10. Is 2:15. 5:2. 30:25. 33:18. Je 31:38. Ezk 26:4, 9. 27:11. Mi 4:8. Zc 14:10.
Jehonathan. i.e. *Jehovah-given; Jehovah is giver*, **S#3083h**. 2 Ch 17:8. Ne 12:18.

26 **Ezri**. i.e. *helpful; my help; help of the Lord*, **S#5836h**.

27 **Shimei**. 2 S +16:5.
the increase of the vineyards. Heb. that which was of the vineyards.
Ramathite. i.e. *citizen of Ramath* (i.e. *lofty place*, Jsh +19:8), **S#7435h**.
Shiphmite. i.e. *native of Shepham* (i.e. *bare, bald*, Nu +34:10), **S#8225h**.

28 **And over**. 1 K 4:7.
the sycamore trees. 1 K 20:27.
Baal-hanan. Ge +36:38.
Gederite. i.e. *inhabitants of Geder or Gederah* (i.e. *a wall or fence*, Jsh +12:13; +15:36), **S#1451h**.
Joash. 1 Ch +7:8.

29 **Sharon**. Is +35:2.
Shitrai. i.e. *Jah is arbitrator*, **S#7861h**.
Sharonite. i.e. *inhabitant of Sharon*, **S#8290h**.
Adlai. i.e. *my ornament*, **S#5724h**.

30 **the camels**. Jb 1:3.
Obil. i.e. *mournful; overseer of camels*, **S#179h**.
the Ishmaelite. i.e. *descendant of Ishmael,*

S#3459h. 1 Ch +2:17, Ishmeelite. Ge 37:25. Ps 83:6.

the asses. Ge 36:24. Nu 31:34. Ne 7:69.

Jehdeiah. 1 Ch +24:20.

Meronothite. i.e. *inhabitant of Meronoth* (i.e. *sharp tempestuous sea*), **S#4824h**. Ne 3:7.

31　**Jaziz**. i.e. *gives life and motion*, **S#3151h**.

Hagerite. i.e. *fugitive*, **S#1905h**. 1 Ch +11:38, Haggeri.

32　**uncle**. 2 S 13:3. 21:21, nephew.

counsellor. 1 Ch 26:14. 2 S 15:12.

wise. or, understanding. Pr 28:2.

scribe. *or*, secretary. Jg 5:14.

Jehiel. Ezr +8:9.

son of Hachmoni. i.e. *very wise*, **S#2453h**. *or*, Hachmonite. 1 Ch 11:11.

33　**Ahithophel**. 2 S +15:12.

Hushai. 2 S 15:32, 37. 16:16.

Archite. Jsh 16:2.

companion. 2 S 15:37. 16:16, 17. Ps 55:13. Zc 13:7.

34　**Jehoiada**. 2 K +11:4.

Benaiah. ver. 5.

Abiathar. 1 S +22:20.

the general. 1 Ch 11:6.

Joab. 1 S +26:6.

1 CHRONICLES 28

1　**assembled**. 1 Ch 23:2. Jsh 23:2. 24:1.

the princes. 1 Ch 27:16-22.

the captains of the companies. 1 Ch 27:1-15, 25.

thousands. Jsh +22:21.

the stewards. 1 Ch 27:25-31.

substance. *or*, cattle.

and of his sons. *or*, and his sons.

officers. *or*, eunuchs. 1 Ch 27:32-34. 2 K +8:6mg.

the mighty men. 1 Ch 11:10.

2　**stood up**. Ge 48:2. 1 K 1:47.

my brethren. 1 Ch 11:1-3. Dt 17:15, 20. Ps 22:22. He 2:11, 12.

I had in mine heart. 1 Ch 17:1, 2. 2 S 7:1, 2. 1 K 8:17, 18.

rest. 1 Ch 6:31. Ps 132:3-8, 14.

the footstool. Is +66:1.

had made ready. 1 Ch 18:7-11. 22:2-5, 14.

3　**Thou shalt**. 1 Ch 17:4. 22:8. 2 S 7:5-13. 1 K 5:3. 2 Ch 6:8, 9.

blood. Heb. bloods. 2 K +9:26mg.

4　**chose me**. 1 S 16:6-13. 2 S 7:7-16. Ps 78:68-72. 89:16-27.

for ever. Heb. *olam*, Ex +12:24. 1 Ch 29:27. Ps +24:9.

chosen Judah. 1 Ch 5:2. Ge +35:23. 49:8-10.

the house of Judah. 1 S 16:1.

the house of my father. 1 S 26:1.

among the sons. 1 S 16:12, 13. Ps 18:19. 147:10, 11.

5　**all my sons**. 1 Ch 3:1-9. 14:4-7.

he hath chosen. 1 Ch 22:9, 10. 23:1. 29:1.

to sit. 1 Ch 17:14. 29:23. 2 Ch 1:8, 9. Ps 72, title, 1, etc. Is 9:6, 7.

6　**he shall**. 1 Ch 17:11-14. 22:9, 10. 2 S 7:13, 14. 2 Ch 1:9. Zc 6:12, 13. He 3:3, 6.

I have. He 4:5.

7　**Moreover**. Ps 89:28-37. 132:12. Da 2:44.

if. 1 Ch 22:13. 1 K 6:12, 13. 9:4, 5. 11:9-13.

for ever. Heb. *olam*, Ex +12:24. ver. 7, 8. 1 Ch 17:23, 27.

constant. Heb. strong. ver. 10. Jsh 1:6, 7. 1 K 2:2-4.

as at this day. 1 K 8:61. 11:4.

8　**in the sight**. Dt 4:6. Mt 5:14-16. Ph 2:15, 16. He 12:1, 2.

in the audience. Dt 4:26. 29:10, 15. Ac 10:33.

keep. Ps 119:4, 10, 11, 27, 33, 34, 44. Pr 2:1-5. 3:1. Is 34:16. Ac 17:11.

that ye may. Dt 4:1. 5:32, 33. 6:1-3.

leave it. Ezr 9:12. Pr 13:22.

for ever. Heb. *olam*, Ex +12:24.

9　**know thou**. Dt 4:35. 1 K 8:43. Ps +9:10. Je 9:24. 22:16. 24:7. 31:34. Ho 4:16. Jn 8:55. 17:3. Ac 17:23, 30. Ro 1:28. 1 C 15:34. 2 C 4:6.

the God. Ge 28:13. Ex 3:16. 15:2. 1 K 3:6. Ps 18:2. 89:26.

serve him. 2 K +20:3. 22:2. Jb 36:11, 12. Ps 101:2. Jn 1:47. 4:24. Ro 1:9. He 12:28.

a willing. 2 C 8:12. 9:7. 1 P 5:2.

mind. Heb. *nephesh*, Ge +23:8.

the Lord searcheth. Je +17:10. Jn +2:25.

the imaginations. Ge 6:5. 8:21. Dt 31:21. Ps 139:2. Ezk 38:10.

if thou seek him. Pr 1:28. 2:1-6. Je +29:13.

but if. Ge +4:7. Pr 1:29-32. 8:36. 9:12. 11:19. Mt 5:25, 26. 7:13, 14. 25:1-13, 14-30, +46. Mk 16:16. Lk 19:12-27. Ro 2:5-10. Ga 6:7, 8. Re 22:19.

thou forsake him. 1 K 9:6-9. Je +1:16.

he will. 2 S 7:15. Ps +44:9. Is +54:7.

10　**Take heed now**. ver. 6. 1 Ch 22:16-19. 1 K 2:3, 4. 1 T 4:16.

11　**the pattern**. ver. 19. Ex +25:40. 2 Ch 3:3.

the porch. 1 K 6:3. 2 Ch 3:4. Ezk 40:8, 9, 15, 48, 49.

the houses. 1 K 6:16-20. 2 Ch 3:5-10. Ezk 41:13, etc. He 9:2-8.

the treasuries. 1 Ch 9:26-29. 26:20-27. Lk 21:1.

upper chambers. 2 S 18:33. 1 K 6:5, 6, 10. 2 Ch 3:9. Ne 10:38, 39. 13:5. Je 35:2. Ezk 41:6, etc.

the place. Ex +25:17.

12　**the pattern**. Ex 31:2. Jn 13:15. Ep 4:11-13.

that he had by. Heb. that was with him by.

the spirit. Heb. *ruach*, Ge +41:38. Ex 25:40. He 8:5.

the treasuries. 1 Ch 26:20, 26-28. 1 K 14:26. 15:15, 18. 2 K 16:8. 18:15.

13 **the courses**. 1 Ch 24:1, etc. 25:1, etc.
the vessels. 1 Ch 9:29. 1 K ch. 7. Ezr 8:25-30, 33.

14 **of gold**. 1 K 7:48, 49.

15 **the candlesticks**. Ex +25:31.

16 **tables**. Ex +25:23.
of showbread. Ex +25:30.

17 **pure gold**. 1 S 2:13, 14. 2 Ch 4:20-22.
the bowls. 1 K +7:40, 48-50. 10:21.

18 **the altar**. Lk +1:11.
chariot. Ps +68:17.
cherubims. Ge +3:24. Ezk 1:4, 15-24.

19 **the Lord**. ver. 11, 12.
understand in writing. Is 8:20. Mk 12:24.
by his hand upon me. Ezk 1:3. 3:14, 22.
pattern. Ex +25:40. Jn 13:15. Ep 4:11-17.

20 **Be strong**. ver. 10. Jsh +1:6.
fear not. Ps 27:1, 2. Is 41:10, 13. Ro 8:31.
with. 1 K +1:37.
he will not fail thee. Jsh 1:5. He +13:5.

21 **the courses**. 1 Ch ch. 24-26.
with thee...service. Mt 28:20. Mk 16:20.
all manner. Ex 31:3.
willing. Ex 35:25, 26, 35. 36:1-4. Ps 110:3. Ro 13:1.
also the princes. 1 Ch 22:17, 18. T 3:1.
at thy. Ne 11:23.

1 CHRONICLES 29

1 **said unto**. 1 Ch 28:1, 8.
whom. 1 Ch 28:5, 6. 1 K 8:19, 20.
young. 1 Ch 22:5. 1 K 3:7. 2 Ch 13:7. Pr 4:3. Je 1:6, 7.
palace. 1 Ch 28:10. 2 Ch 2:4, 5.

2 **I have prepared**. 1 Ch 22:3-5, 14-16.
with all. 2 Ch 31:20, 21. Ec 9:10. 2 C 8:3. Col 3:23. 1 P 4:10, 11.
the gold. Ge +23:9. 1 Ch 28:14-18.
onyx stones. Ge +2:12. Is 54:11, 12. Re 21:18-21.

3 **I have set**. Ps 26:8. 27:4. 84:1-10. 122:1-9.
I have. 1 Ch 21:24. Pr 3:9, 10.
over and above. 1 Ch 22:4, 5, 14-16.

4 **gold of Ophir**. 1 K +9:28.

5 **who then**. Ex 25:2-9. 35:5, etc. Nu 7:2, 3, 10-14, etc. Ezr 1:4-6. 2:68, 69. 7:15, 16.
consecrate his service. Heb. to fill his hand. Ex +28:41mg.

6 **the chief**. 1 Ch 27:1, etc. Is 60:3-10.
the rulers. 1 Ch 27:25, etc. 2 C 9:7.

7 **drams**. Ezr 2:69. 8:7. Ne 7:70-72.

8 **by the hand**. 1 Ch 25:2mg.
Jehiel the Gershonite. 1 Ch 23:8. 26:21, 22.

9 **they offered willingly**. Ex 25:2. Le +23:38. Dt 16:10, 11. Jg 5:9. Ps 110:3. 2 C 8:3, 12. 9:7, 8.

perfect heart. ver. 17, 19. 2 K +20:3.
David. Pr 23:15, 16. Lk 15:6. Jn 15:11. Ph 2:15-17. 4:1, 10. 1 Th 3:6-9.

10 **David blessed**. ver. 20. 2 Ch 20:26-28. Ps 103:1, 2. 138:1. 146:2.
Blessed be thou. 1 K 8:15. 2 Ch 6:4. Ps 72:18, 19. 89:52. Ezk 3:12. Ep 1:3. 1 T 1:17. 1 P 1:3. Re 5:12.
Lord God. Ge 32:28. Is +29:23.
our father. Is 63:16. Mt 6:9. Lk 11:2. Ro 1:7. 8:15. Ph 4:20. 2 Th 2:16.
for ever and ever. Heb. *olam* doubled, Da +2:20.

11 **is the greatness**. Dt 10:17. Ne 9:6. Jb 11:7-9. 26:14. 36:26. 37:22, 23. Ps 47:7. Is 40:12-18. Da 2:37, +45. 4:30, 34, 35. Na 1:3-6. Mt 6:13. 1 T 1:17. 6:15, 16. Ju 25. Re 4:10, 11. 5:12, 13. 7:9-12. 19:1.
and. Ge +8:22.
the victory. 1 S 15:29. Jb +4:20 (**S#5331h**). Ps 98:1.
majesty. Jb 37:22. 40:10. Ps 21:5. 29:4. 45:3, 4. 93:1. 96:6. +104:1. 145:5, 12. Is 2:10, 19. 24:14. +57:15. Mi 5:4. He 1:3. 8:1. 2 P 1:16. Ju 25.
for all that. Ge 1:1. 14:19, 22. Ps 115:15, 16. Is 42:5. 66:1. Je 10:10-12. 27:5. Da 4:32, 34, 35. Ro +14:8.
thine is the. Ps 97:1. 99:1. 145:1, 12, 13. Da 4:3. Re 11:15.
exalted. Is +12:4.

12 **riches**. Dt 8:18. 1 S 2:7, 8. Jb 42:10. Ps 75:6, 7. 113:7, 8. Pr 8:18. 10:22. Ec 5:19. Lk 1:51-53. Ro 11:35, 36.
reignest over all. Da 6:26. Ep +1:11.
power. Jb 9:19. Ps 62:11. Is 43:13. 46:10. Je 32:17. Da 5:18-21. Mt 28:18. Jn 19:11. Ep 3:20. Re 11:17.
to make great. Ps +115:3. Da 2:37.
give strength. 2 Ch 16:9. Ps 18:31, 32. 28:8. 29:1, 11. 68:28, 34, 35. 144:1, 2. Is 40:29. 45:24. Ep 3:16. Ph 4:13. Col 1:11.

13 **we thank**. Ps +136:1. Da 2:23. 2 C 2:14. 8:16. 9:15. 1 Th 2:13.

14 **who am I**. Ge 32:10. 2 S 7:18. Da 4:30. 1 C 15:9, 10. 2 C 3:5. 12:9-11.
that we should. Ps 115:1. Re 4:10.
be able. Heb. retain, *or* obtain strength. 2 Ch 2:6mg. 13:20. 14:11. 20:37. 22:9. Da 10:8, 16. 11:6.
willingly. ver. 9. Ph 2:13. Ja 1:17.
all things. Ge 28:22. Ps 50:10-12. Ro 11:36. 1 C 16:2.
of thine own. Heb. of thine hand. ver. 16. Dt 26:10.
given thee. Pr 23:26.

15 **For we**. Ge +47:9.
strangers. Ge +23:4. Ex 12:48mg. Dt +26:11. Jsh +20:9. Mt +25:35.
sojourners. Ge 23:4. 1 K 17:1. Ps 39:12. He 11:13.

our days. Jb 14:2. Ps 90:9. 102:11. 144:4. Ec 6:12. Is 40:6-8. Ja 4:14.

abiding. Heb. expectation. Ezr 10:2. Je 14:8. 17:13. 50:7.

16 **all this store**. ver. 14. 2 Ch 31:10. Ps 24:1. Ho 2:8. Lk 19:16.

17 **triest the heart**. Dt 8:2. Ps 51:6. Pr 16:2. 21:2. Je +17:10.

hast pleasure. Pr 11:20. 15:8, 9. Jn 1:47.

in uprightness. 2 Ch 16:9. Jb 8:6. Ps 11:7. 15:1, 2. 18:25. 37:18. 125:4. 119:80. Pr 2:7, 21. 10:29. 11:3, 6, 20. 12:22. 13:6. 15:8. 21:18. 28:10, 18, 20. Mi 1:7. Ro 14:22.

in the uprightness. Ac 24:16. 2 C 1:12. 1 Th 2:10.

with joy thy people. ver. 9. Phm 7, 20.

present. Heb. found. Jg +20:48mg.

18 **Lord God of**. Ex 3:6, 15. 4:5. Mt +22:32. Ac +3:13.

keep. Dt 30:6. Ps 51:10. 119:116, 117. Je 10:23. 32:39, 40. Ph 1:6, 9-11. 1 Th 3:11, 12. He 13:21.

for ever. Heb. *olam*, Ex +12:24.

in the imagination. 1 Ch 28:9. Ge 6:5. Ps 119:113. Is 26:3mg.

prepare. Heb. stablish. 1 Ch 17:12. 2 Ch +12:14mg. 2 Th 2:16, 17. 1 P 5:10.

19 **And give**. 1 Ch 28:9. Ps 72:1. 119:80. Ja 1:17.

perfect heart. 2 K +20:3. 1 Ch 12:38. Ps +37:18.

the which. ver. 2. 1 Ch 22:14.

20 **Now bless**. 1 Ch 16:36. 2 Ch 20:21. Ps 134:2. 135:19-21. ch. 145. 146:1, 2. 148:13, 14, etc.

bowed down. Ge +24:26. Ps 29:1, 2.

worshipped. Ex 14:31. 1 S 12:18. Pr 24:21. 1 P 2:17.

21 **sacrificed**. 1 K 8:62-65. 2 Ch 7:4-9. Ezr 6:17.

burnt offerings. Le +23:12.

drink offerings. Le +23:13.

22 **eat and drink**. Ex 24:11. Dt 12:7, 11, 12. 16:14-17. 2 Ch 7:10. Ne 8:12. Ec 2:24. 3:12, 13. 8:15. 9:7. 1 T 6:17, 18.

the second time. 1 Ch 23:1. Ac 19:3, 5.

and anointed. 1 K 1:31, 34-39.

Zadok. 1 K 2:35.

23 **sat on the throne**. 1 Ch 17:11, 12. 28:5. Ps 132:11. Is 9:6, 7.

prospered. 1 Ch 22:11.

all Israel. Ec 8:2-5. Ro 13:1.

24 **all the princes**. 1 Ch 22:17. 28:21.

all the sons. 1 Ch 3:39. 1 K 1:50-53. 2:24, 25.

submitted themselves unto. Heb. gave the hand under. Ge +24:2. 2 K 10:15. 2 Ch 30:8mg. Ezr 10:19. Je 50:15. La 5:6. Ezk 17:18. 27:21mg. Ga 2:9.

25 **magnified Solomon**. Jsh 3:7. 4:14. 2 Ch 1:1. Jb 7:17. Ac 19:17.

bestowed. 1 K 3:13. 2 Ch 1:12. Ec 2:9. Da 5:18, 19. He 2:9.

26 **over all Israel**. 1 Ch 18:14. Ps 78:71, 72.

27 **forty years**. 1 Ch 3:4. 2 S 5:4, 5. 1 K 2:11.

28 **a good old age**. Ge 15:15. +25:8. Jb 5:26. Pr 16:31. Ac 13:36.

full of days. 1 Ch 23:1. Ge 35:29. Jb 5:26.

29 **the acts**. 1 K 11:41. 14:29. He 11:32, 33.

book. *or*, history. Heb. words.

Samuel. 1 S 9:9.

Nathan. 2 Ch +9:29.

Gad the seer. 1 S +22:5.

30 **his might**. 2 K 10:34. 14:28.

the times. Da 2:21. 4:23, 25.

2 CHRONICLES

2 CHRONICLES 1

1 A.M. 2989. B.C. 1015. An. Ex. Is. 476.
was strengthened. 1 K 2:12, 46.
the Lord. Ge +28:15. 1 Ch 17:8. 22:11.
magnified. 1 Ch 29:25. Ph 2:9-11.

2 **to the captains**. 2 Ch 29:20. 30:2. 34:29, 30.
Jsh +22:21.
the chief. 1 Ch 15:12. 24:4, 31.

3 **Gibeon**. Jsh +10:2.
the tabernacle. Ex +38:21.
the servant. Dt 34:5.

4 **the ark**. 2 S 6:2, 17. 1 Ch 13:5, 6. 15:1, 25-28.
for he had pitched. 1 Ch 16:1. Ps 132:5, 6.

5 **the brasen**. Ex +38:30. +40:6.
Bezaleel. Ex +31:2.
he put. *or, was* there. ver. 3.
sought unto it. went to seek the Lord there.
1 Ch 13:3.

6 **a thousand**. 1 K 3:4. 8:63. 1 Ch 29:21. Is
40:16.

7 **In that night**. 1 K 3:5-15.
appear. Ge +35:9.
Ask. Pr 3:5, 6. Mt 7:7, 8. Mk 10:36. Lk 11:9.
Jn 16:23. 1 J 5:14, 15.

8 **Thou hast showed**. 2 S 7:8, 9. 12:7, 8.
22:51. 23:1. Ps 86:13. 89:20-28, 49. Is 55:3.
to reign. 1 Ch 28:5. 29:23.

9 **let thy promise**. 2 Ch 6:16, 17. Ge 32:11,
12. 2 S 7:12-16, 25-29. 1 Ch 17:11-14, 23-27.
28:6, 7. Ne 1:8-10. Ps 89:35-37. 119:38, 41,
49, 58. 132:11, 12.
for thou hast. 1 K 3:7, 8.
like the dust. Heb. much as the dust. Ge
13:16. 22:17. Nu 23:10.

10 **Give me**. 1 K 3:9. Jb 28:28. Ps +32:8. 119:34,
73. Pr 2:2-6. 3:13-18. 4:7. 9:10. 23:12. Ho 6:3.
Mt 7:7. Lk 11:9. Jn 17:3. Ja 1:5.
go out. Nu +27:17. Dt 31:2. 2 S 5:2.
for who can. 2 C 2:16. 3:5.

11 **this was**. 1 S 16:7. 1 K 3:11-13. 8:18. 1 Ch
28:2. 29:17, 18. Pr 23:7. Ac 5:4. He 4:12.
the life. Heb. *nephesh*, soul, Ge +44:30.
that thou mayest. 1 K 3:28. Pr 14:8. Ja
3:13, 17.

12 **I will give**. Mt 6:33. Ep 3:20.
such as none. 2 Ch 9:22. 1 Ch 29:25. Ec 2:9.
Ja 1:5.

13 **at Gibeon**. ver. +3.
reigned. 1 K 4:24, 25.

14 **Solomon**. 2 Ch 9:25. Dt 17:16. 1 K 4:26.
10:16, 26, etc.

15 **the king**. ver. 12. 2 Ch 9:27. 1 K 10:27, etc.
Jb 22:24, 25. Is 60:17.
made. Heb. gave. Ge 9:12.
sycamore trees. 2 Ch 9:27. 1 Ch 27:28. Is
9:10. Am 7:14.

16 **Solomon**. Heb. the going forth of the horses
which *was* Solomon's. 2 Ch 9:28. 1 K 10:28, 29.

17 **the kings**. 2 K 7:6. 10:29.
Hittites. Dt +20:17.
means. Heb. hand.

2 CHRONICLES 2

1 **determined**. 1 K 5:5.
for the name. Dt 12:5, 11. 28:58. 1 K 8:18,
20. 1 Ch 22:10. Mt 6:9, 10.
an house. 1 K 7:1. 9:1.

2 **told out threescore**. ver. 18. 1 K 5:15, 16.

3 **Huram**. 1 K 5:1, Hiram. 1 Ch +8:5.
As thou didst. 2 S +5:11.

4 **build**. ver. 1. 1 K 8:18.
to dedicate. 1 K 8:63.
to burn. Ex 30:7.
sweet incense. Heb. incense of spices. Ex
25:6. +39:38.
the continual. Ex +25:30.
the burnt. Le +23:12.
new moons. Col +2:16.
the solemn feasts. or, set feasts. Ge +17:21.
Le 23:2, 36. Nu ch. 28, 29.
for ever. Heb. *olam*, Ex +12:24.

5 **great**. ver. +9. 1 Ch 29:1. Ezk 7:20.
great is our God. Ex +12:12. Da +2:45. 1 T
6:15.

6 **But who**. 2 Ch 6:18. 1 K 8:27. Is 66:1. Ac
7:48, 49.
is able. Heb. hath retained, or obtained
strength. 1 Ch +29:14mg.
who am I then. 2 Ch 1:10. Ex 3:11. 2 S 7:18.
1 Ch 29:14. 2 C 2:16. Ep 3:8.
save only. Dt 12:5, 6, 11, 14, 26.

7 **cunning**. Ex 31:3-5. 1 K 7:14. Is 28:26, 29.
60:10.

to grave. Heb. to grave gravings. ver. 14. Ex 39:6.

whom David. 1 Ch 22:15, 16.

8 **Send me also**. 1 K 5:6.

algum trees. *or*, algummim. 1 K 10:11, almug trees.

9 **wonderful great**. Heb. great and wonderful. ver. 5. 2 Ch 7:21. 1 K 9:8. Jl 2:26.

10 **I will give**. 1 K 5:11. Lk 10:7. Ro 13:7, 8.

measures. 1 K +4:22mg. Ezr 7:22mg.

baths of wine. 1 K 7:26, 38. Ezr 7:22.

11 **Because**. 2 Ch 9:8. Dt 7:7, 8. 1 K 10:9. Ps 72:17.

12 **Huram**. 1 K 5:7. 1 Ch 29:20. Ps 72:18, 19. Lk 1:68. 1 P 1:3.

that made heaven. Ge ch. 1, 2. Ps 33:6. 102:25. 124:8. 136:5, 6. 146:5, 6. Je 10:10. Ac 4:24. 14:15. Col 1:16, 17. Re 4:11. 10:6.

endued, etc. Heb. knowing prudence and understanding. 2 Ch 1:10-12.

an house. ver. 1.

13 **of Huram**. 2 Ch 4:16.

14 **The son**. 1 K 7:13, 14.

skilful. ver. 7. Ex 31:3, 4.

15 **which my lord**. ver. 10. 1 K 5:11.

16 **we will cut**. 1 K 5:8, 9.

as much as thou shalt need. Heb. according to all thy need.

Joppa. i.e. *lovely; fair to him*, **S#3305h**. ver. 16. Jsh 19:46. Ezr 3:7. Jon 1:3. Ac 9:36. 10:32.

17 **numbered**. ver. 2. 2 Ch 8:7, 8. 1 K 5:13-16. 9:20, 21.

the strangers.

Heb. the men the strangers. Ge 13:8mg.

after the numbering. 1 Ch 22:2.

18 **threescore**. "As it is ver. 2."

2 CHRONICLES 3

1 A.M. 2993. B.C. 1011. An. Ex. Is. 480.

Solomon. 1 K 6:1, etc.

in mount Moriah. Ge 22:2, 14.

where the Lord appeared unto David. *or*, which was seen of David.

Ornan. 2 S 24:18-25, Araunah. 1 Ch 21:18. 22:1.

2 **in the second**. 1 K 6:1.

3 A.M. 2993-3000. B.C. 1011-1004.

Solomon. 1 Ch 28:11-19.

instructed. Heb. founded. Ezr 3:11.

The length. 1 K 6:2, 3.

4 **the porch**. Jn 10:23. Ac 3:11. 5:12.

5 **the greater**. 1 K 6:15-17, 21, 22.

6 **garnished**. Heb. covered. ver. 4, 10.

precious. 1 Ch 29:2, 8. Is 54:11, 12. Re 21:18-21.

Parvaim. i.e. *Oriental regions; he broke their hooks*, **S#6516h**.

7 **overlaid**. Ex 26:29. 1 K 6:20-22, 30. Ezk 7:20.

beams. 2 K 6:2, 5. SS 1:17.

posts. 1 K +14:17 (**S#5592h**). Is 6:4.

graved cherubims. Ex 26:1. 1 K 6:35.

8 **the most holy**. Ex 26:33. 1 K 6:19, 20. He 9:3, 9. 10:19.

9 **nails**. Ex +27:19.

upper chambers. 1 Ch 28:11.

10 **two cherubims**. 1 K 6:23-28.

image work. *or*, *as some think*, of moveable work.

13 **inward**. *or*, toward the house. 2 Ch 4:4. Ex 25:20. 28:26. 39:19. 2 S 5:9. 1 K 7:25. Ezk 40:9.

14 **the vail**. Ex 26:31-35. Mt 27:51. He 9:3. 10:20.

blue. Ex 26:31. 36:35.

purple. Ex +25:4. 26:31. 36:35.

wrought. Heb. caused to ascend.

15 **two pillars**. 1 K 7:15-24. Je 52:20-23.

thirty. 1 K 7:15.

high. Heb. long.

16 **chains**. ver. 5. Ex 28:14. 39:15. 1 K 6:21. 7:17. Ezk 7:23.

the oracle. 1 K +6:5.

an hundred. 1 K 7:20.

17 **reared up**. 1 K 7:21.

Jachin. *that is*, He shall establish.

Boaz. *that is*, In it *is* strength. Ru +2:1.

2 CHRONICLES 4

1 **an altar of brass**. 2 Ch 7:7. 8:12. 15:8. 29:18. 33:16. 35:16. Ex +38:30. +40:6. 1 K 8:22, 54, 64. 9:25. 2 K 18:22. Ezr 3:3. Ne 10:34. Ezk 43:13-17. Am +9:1. Mt +5:23.

2 **a molten sea**. Ex 30:18-21. 1 K 7:23. Zc 13:1. T 3:5. Re 7:14.

brim to brim. Heb. his brim to his brim. lit. lip. ver. 5. Jg +7:22mg. 1 K 9:26.

3 **And under**. 1 K 7:24-26. Ezk 1:10. 10:14. 1 C 9:9, 10. Re 4:7.

Oxen. 1 K 6:18. 2 K 4:39.

round. Ezk 37:2. 40:5, 14, 16, 17, 25, 29, 30, 33, 36, 43. 41:5-8, 10-12, 16, 17, 19. 42:15, 20. 43:12.

4 **It stood**. Mt 16:18. Ep 2:20. Re 21:14.

three. Mt 28:19, 20. Mk 16:15. Lk 24:46, 47. Ac 9:15.

5 **thickness**. 1 K 7:26. Je 52:21.

handbreadth. Ex 25:25. 37:12. 1 K 7:26. Ps 39:5. Ezk 40:5, 43. 43:13.

brim. ver. 2.

cup. Ge 40:11, 13, 21. 1 K 7:26.

with flowers. ver. 21. Ex 25:31, 33, 34. 37:17, 19, 20. Nu 8:4. 17:8. 1 K 7:26, 49. Is 5:24. 18:5. Na 1:4.

of lilies. *or*, like a lily flower. SS 2:1, 2. Ho 14:5.

three thousand baths. 1 K 7:26.

6 **ten lavers**. Ex +30:18. Ps 51:2. 1 C 6:11.

such things as they offered for the burnt **offering**. Heb. the work of the burnt offering. Le 1:9, 13. Ezk 40:38.

but the sea. ver. 2. Ex 29:4. He 9:14, 23. Re 1:5, 6. 7:14.

7 **ten candlesticks**. Ex +25:31. Jn 8:12.
according to. Ex +25:40.

8 **ten tables**. Ex +25:23. Is 25:6.
basons. or, bowls. 1 K +7:40.

9 **the court**. 1 K 6:36. 7:12.

10 **he set**. 1 K 7:39.

11 **the pots**. 1 K 7:40, 45.
basons. or, bowls. 1 K +7:40.
finished. Heb. finished to make.

12 **To wit**. 2 Ch 3:15-17.
the pommels. 1 K 7:41.

13 **four hundred**. Ex 28:33, 34. 1 K 7:20, 42. SS 4:13. Je 52:23.
pillars. Heb. face of the pillars.

14 **made also**. Ga 4:25.
bases. 1 K 7:27-43.
lavers. or, caldrons. ver. 6.

15 **One sea**. ver. 2-5.

16 **pots also**. ver. 11. Ex 27:3. 38:3. Zc 14:20, 21.
flesh-hooks. 1 S 2:13, 14. 1 Ch 28:17.
Huram. 1 K 7:13, 14, 45, Hiram.
his father. 2 Ch 2:13.
bright. Heb. made bright, or, scoured. or, purified. Le 6:28. Je 46:4 (furbish).

17 **clay ground**. Heb. thicknesses of the ground. Ex 19:9. Jg 5:4. 1 K 7:46.
Zeredathah. i.e. *puncture; scene of the adversary's rule; cooling*, **S#6868h**. 1 K 7:46, Zarthan.

18 **the weight**. 1 K 7:47. 1 Ch 22:3, 14. Je 52:20.

19 **all the vessels**. 2 Ch 36:7, 10, 18. 1 K 7:48-50. 2 K 24:13. 25:13-15. Ezr 1:7-11. Je 27:16-22. 28:3, 6. 52:18, 19. Da 1:2. 5:2, 3, 23.
the golden. Lk +1:11.
the tables. Ex +25:23.

20 **the candlesticks**. ver. +7.
burn after. Ex 27:20, 21.
the oracle. 1 K +6:5.

21 **the flowers**. ver. 5. Ex 25:31, etc. 37:20. 1 K 6:18, 29, 35.
perfect gold. Heb. perfections of gold. That is, the purest and best gold.

22 **snuffers**. Ex 37:23. 1 K 7:50. 2 K 12:18. 25:14. Je 52:18.
basons. or, bowls. ver. 8, 11. 1 K +7:40.
the entry. 1 K 6:31, 32. 7:50.

2 CHRONICLES 5

1 A.M. 3000. B.C. 1004.
finished. Ep 5:27. 2 Th 1:10.
brought in all. 1 K 7:51. 1 Ch 22:14. 26:26-28.

2 **Then Solomon**. ver. 1, 12. 1 K 8:1-11. 1 Ch 28:1.
the chief. 1 Ch 15:12. 24:6, 31. 26:26.

the ark. Nu 10:33, 36.
out. 2 Ch 1:4. 2 S 6:12. 1 Ch 16:1.
the city. 2 S 5:7.
which is Zion. 1 Ch +11:5.

3 **Wherefore**. 1 K 8:2.
in the feast. Le +23:34-36.

4 **the Levites**. Nu 4:15. Jsh 3:6. 6:6. 1 K 8:3. 1 Ch 15:2, 12-14.

5 **the tabernacle**. 2 Ch 1:3. 1 K 8:4, 6.

6 **king Solomon**. 2 S 6:13. 1 K 8:5. 1 Ch 16:1, 2. 29:21.

7 **the priests**. Ps 132:8.
his place. 2 Ch 35:3. He 1:3. Re 21:3.
to the oracle. Ex 37:6-9. 1 K +6:5. He 9:4, 5.

8 **the staves**. Ex +25:13.

9 **the ends**. 1 K 8:8, 9.
there it is. or, they are there: as 1 K 8:8.
unto this day. 1 Ch +4:43.

10 **save**. 2 Ch 6:11. Ex 31:18. 32:15, 16, 19. 34:1. 40:20. Dt 10:2-5. He 9:4.
when. or, where.
the Lord. Ex 19:5. 24:7, 8. Dt 29:1, 10-14. Je 31:31-34. He 8:6-13.

11 **priests**. Re 5:9, 10.
present. Heb. found. Est +1:5mg.
sanctified. 2 Ch 29:5, 15, 34. 30:15, 17-20. Ex 19:10, 14, 15. Jb 1:5.
by course. 2 Ch 35:4. 1 Ch ch. 24.

12 **the Levites**. 2 Ch 29:25. 1 Ch 15:16-22. 16:4-6, 41, 42. 23:5, 30. 25:1-7. Ezr 3:10, 11.
singers. ver. 13. 1 K 10:12. 1 Ch 9:33. 15:16, 19, 27.
Asaph. 2 K 18:18.
arrayed. 1 Ch 15:27. Re 15:6. 19:8.
white linen. 1 Ch +4:21.
cymbals. 1 Ch +13:8. Ps 92:3. 149:3. 150:3-5.
psalteries. 1 S +10:5. 2 S 6:5.
harps. Re +5:8.
stood. Le 1:16. Ps 20:3mg. Ep 1:6.
an hundred. Nu 10:1-5. Jsh 6:6-20. 1 Ch 15:24. 16:6. Ps 68:25.
trumpets. 2 Ch 13:12, 14. 29:26. Nu 10:2. 1 Ch 15:24. 16:6. Ezr 3:10. Ne 12:35, 41.

13 **as one**. Jg 20:11. 1 S 18:1. 1 Ch 12:17. Ps 95:1, 2. 100:1, 2. Is 52:8. Je 32:39. Ac 4:32. Ro 15:6. Re 5:8-14.
one sound. Re 5:9.
praising. 1 Ch 16:4, 36. 23:5, 30. 25:3.
thanking. or, confessing. 1 Ch 16:4, 7, 35, 41. 23:30. 25:3.
lifted. Ge +22:13.
with the trumpets. ver. +12. Ps 68:25, 26.
instruments of music. 1 Ch 16:42.
he is good. Ex +34:6. Ps ch. 136.
for ever. Heb. *olam*, Ex +12:24.
then the house. Ex 40:34, 35. 1 K 8:10-12.
was filled. Is 6:4. Re 15:8.
with a cloud. Ex +13:21. Da 7:13. Mt 26:64. Mk 13:26. 14:62. Lk 21:27. Ac 1:9. 1 Th 4:17. Re 1:7. 14:14.

14 **the priests**. 2 Ch 7:2. 1 T 6:16.
the glory. Ex +24:16. Is 6:1-4. Hg 2:9. Re 15:8.
filled. ver. 13. 2 Ch 7:1, 2. Ex 40:34, 35. 1 K 8:10, 11.

2 CHRONICLES 6

1 **The Lord**. Ex +10:22. +13:21.
2 **I have built**. 2 Ch 2:4-6. 2 S 7:13. 1 K 8:13. 1 Ch 17:12. 22:10, 11. 28:6, 20. Ps 132:5, 13, 14. Jn 4:21-23. He 9:11, 12. Re 21:3.
for ever. Heb. *olam*, plural, Ps +61:4.
3 **turned his face**. 1 K 8:14.
blessed. 2 Ch 29:29. Nu 6:23-27. Jsh 22:6. 1 K 8:55-61. 1 Ch 16:2. Lk 24:50, 51.
all the congregation. 1 K 8:14. Ne 8:5-7. Mt 13:2.
4 **Blessed**. 1 K 8:15. 1 Ch 29:10, 20. Ps 41:13. 68:4, 32-35. 72:18, 19. Lk 1:68, 69. Ep 1:3.
who hath with. 1 Ch 17:12. Ps 138:1, 2. Mt 24:35. Lk 1:70.
5 **Since the day**. 2 S 7:6, 7. 1 K 8:16.
my name. Ex 20:24. 23:21. Dt 12:5, 11. Da 9:19.
neither chose. 1 S 10:24. 13:13, 14. 15:23. 2 S 7:15, 16.
6 **But I have chosen Jerusalem**. 2 Ch 12:13. Dt 12:5-7, 11. Ps 48:1. 78:68-70. 132:13. Is 14:32.
chosen David. 1 S 16:1. 1 Ch 28:4. Ps 89:19, 20.
7 **it was**. 2 S 7:2, 3. 1 K 5:3. 8:17. 1 Ch 17:1. 22:7. 28:2, etc.
8 **Forasmuch**. 1 S 30:24.
heart. 1 S 16:7.
thou didst well. 1 K 8:18-21. Mk 14:8. 2 C 8:12.
9 **thy son**. 2 S 7:12, 13. 1 Ch 17:4, 11, 12.
10 **performed his word**. ver. 4.
I am risen. 2 Ch 1:1. 1 K 2:12. 3:6, 7. 1 Ch 29:15, 23. Ec 1:4. 2:18, 19.
as the Lord. 1 Ch 17:11. 28:5.
11 **I put the ark**. 2 Ch 5:7, 10. Ex 40:20. 1 K 8:9, 21. He 9:4.
the covenant. Ge +49:10.
12 **he stood**. 1 K 8:22, etc. 2 K 11:14. 23:3. Ps 29:1, 2.
spread forth. Ps +88:9.
13 **scaffold**. Ne 8:4.
long. Heb. the length thereof, etc.
the court. 2 Ch 4:9. 1 K 6:36. 7:12.
kneeled down. 1 K 8:54. Ezr 9:5. Ps 95:6. Da 6:10. Lk 22:41. Ac 20:36. 21:5.
14 **O Lord God**. Ge 33:20. 35:10. Ex 3:15. 1 K 8:23. 18:36. 1 Ch 29:10, 20.
no God. Ex 15:11. Dt 4:39. 2 S 7:22. Ps 86:8. 89:6, 8. Je 10:6, 16.
keepest covenant. Dt 7:9. Ne 1:5. Ps 89:28. Da 9:4. Mi 7:18-20. Lk 1:72.

mercy. Ps 103:17, 18. Lk 1:50, 54, 55.
walk before. Ge 5:24. 17:1. 1 K 3:6. 6:12. Lk 1:6. 1 Th 2:12.
15 **and spakest**. 2 S 7:12. 1 K 8:24. 1 Ch 22:9, 10.
hast fulfilled. ver. 4. Jsh 21:45.
16 **keep**. Ezk 36:37. Jn 15:14, 15.
hast promised. ver. 17, 42. Ge 32:9, 12. Ex 32:13. 1 K 8:26. Ne 1:8-10. 9:32. Ps 105:42. 119:41, 49, 58, 76, 154, 169. Je 14:21. Lk 2:29.
saying. 2 Ch 7:18. 2 S 7:12-16. 1 K 2:4. 6:12. Ps 132:12.
There shall not fail thee a man. Heb. There shall not a man be cut off. 2 Ch 7:18.
to walk. Ps 26:3. 119:1.
17 **O Lord**. ver. 4, 14. Ex 24:10. Is 41:17. 45:3.
let thy. 2 S 7:25-29. Je 11:5.
verified. Ps 89:49. Je 15:15-18.
18 **But will**. Ex 29:45, 46. 1 K 8:27. Ps 68:18. 113:5, 6. Is 57:15. 66:1. Ac 7:48, 49. 17:24.
heaven. Dt +10:14.
how much. 2 Ch 32:15. Jb 4:19. 9:14. 25:4-6. Mt 7:11.
19 **Have respect**. 1 K 8:28. Ps 74:20. 130:2. Da 9:17-19. Lk 18:1-7.
to hearken. Ps 4:1. 5:1, 2. 20:1-3. Jn 17:20.
20 **thine eyes**. 2 Ch 16:9. Ps 121:5. Zc +12:4.
put thy name. ver. 6. Dt 26:2. Col 2:9.
toward this place. *or*, in this place. Ps 132:7. Da +6:10.
21 **make**. Heb. pray. 1 K 8:29.
thy dwelling place. ver. 39. 2 Ch 30:27. Jb 22:12-14. Ps 123:1. Ec 5:2. Is 57:15. Mt 6:9.
forgive. Ps 85:2, 3. 130:3, 4. Is 43:25. Da 9:19. Mi 7:18. Mt 6:12.
22 **sin**. 1 K 8:31, 32.
and an oath, etc. Heb. and he require an oath of him. Ex 22:11. Le 5:1. Pr 30:9.
the oath. Nu 5:19-22. Mt 23:18.
23 **from heaven**. ver. 21.
and judge. Ezk 33:20.
requiting. Nu 5:27. 2 K 9:26. Ps 10:14. Pr 1:31. Is 3:11. Je 28:16, 17. 51:56. Ro 2:9.
justifying. Dt 25:1. Pr 17:15. Is 3:10. Ezk 18:20. Ro 2:10.
24 **put to the worse**. *or*, be smitten. Le 26:17, 37. Dt 28:25, 48. Jsh 7:8. 1 K 8:33, 34. Ps 44:10.
because. Jsh 7:11, 12. Jg 2:11, 14, 15. 2 K 17:7-18.
shall return. Le 26:40-42. Dt 4:29-31. 30:1-6. Ne 1:8, 9. Pr 28:13. Je 3:12, 13.
pray. Ezr 9:5, etc. Ne 9:1, etc. Is ch. 63, 64. Da 9:3, etc.
in. *or*, toward. ver. 20.
25 **forgive the sin**. Ezr 1:1-6. Ps 106:40-47. Je 33:6-13.
which thou. Ge 13:15. Ex 6:8. Jsh 21:43.
26 **the heaven**. Le 26:19. Dt 11:17. 28:23. 1 K ch. 17, 18. Lk 4:25.

there is no rain. Is 5:6. 50:1, 2. Ezk 14:13. Am 4:4-9. Re 11:6.

if they pray. Je 14:1-9. Jl 1:13-20. 2:15-17.

turn from. Ps 28:13. Ezk 18:27-32.

thou dost. 2 Ch 33:12, 13. Is 26:16. Ho 5:15. 6:1.

27 **when thou hast**. 1 K 8:35, 36. Ps 25:4, 5, 8, 12. 94:12. 119:33. Mi 4:2. Jn 6:45.

good way. Is 30:21. Je 6:16. 42:3.

send rain. 1 K 18:40-45. Jb 37:11-14. Ps 68:9. Je 5:24. 14:22. Ezk 34:26. Ho 2:21, 22. Jl 2:23. Zc 10:1. Ja 5:17, 18.

28 **if there be dearth**. 1 K +8:37.

locusts. Ps +78:46.

their enemies. 2 Ch 12:2-5. 20:9-13. 32:1. Le 26:25. Dt 28:52-57.

cities of their land. Heb. land of their gates. Ge +14:7. 2 S 19:8. 1 K 8:37. 2 K 7:1.

whatsoever. 2 Ch 32:24. 1 K 8:37, 38. Ja 5:13.

29 **what prayer**. Ps 33:12, 13. 50:15. 91:15.

know. Ps 32:2-6. 142:1, 2. Pr 14:10.

spread forth. ver. 12, 13. Is 1:15.

in. or, toward. ver. +20.

30 **render**. Ps 18:20-26. Je +17:10. Ezk 18:30.

thou only. Ps 11:4, 5. Jn +2:25.

31 **fear thee**. Ex 20:20. 1 S 12:24. Jb 28:28. Ps 128:1. 130:4. Ac 9:31.

so long, etc. Heb. all the days which they live upon the face of the land.

32 **the stranger**. Ex +12:48mg, 49. Ru 1:16. 2:11, 12. 1 K 8:41-43. 10:1, 2. Is 56:3-7. Mt 2:1. 8:10, 11. Jn 10:16. 12:20. Ac 8:27-39. 10:1-4. Ep 2:12, 13.

is come. Ex 18:8-12. Jsh 2:9. 9:9. 2 K 5:3, 8, 15. Is 60:1-10. Zc 8:22. Mt 12:42.

thy mighty. Ex 3:19, 20. 13:14. Ps 89:13.

if they come. Is 66:20. Zc 14:16, 17. Ac 2:10.

33 **that all people**. Ps 46:10. 137:4, 5. 1 K +8:43. Is 49:6. 54:1-3.

fear thee. Je 10:7.

this house, etc. Heb. thy name is called upon this house. Nu 6:27. 1 K 8:16. Je +14:9mg.

34 **thy people**. 2 Ch 14:11, 12. 20:4. Dt 20:1-4. Jsh 1:2-5. 1 K 8:44, 45.

to war. Nu 21:1, 2. 1 Ch +5:20. +14:10. Ps 60:9, 10.

by the way. Nu 31:2-6. Jsh 8:1-8. Jg 1:1, 2. 1 S 15:3, 18.

they pray. 2 Ch 14:9-12. 18:31. 20:6-13. 32:20, 21.

toward. ver. 6, +20. 1 K 8:13. Is 14:32. Da 6:10.

35 **hear thou**. Da 9:17-19.

maintain. Is 37:21-36.

cause. or, right. Ps 9:3, 4. Je 5:28.

36 **they sin**. 1 K 8:46, 50.

for there is no man. Pr +20:9. Ro 3:23.

thou be angry. Le 26:34-44. Dt 4:26, 27. 28:36, 64-68. 29:24-28. 2 K 17:6, 18, 23. 15:21. Da 9:7-14. Lk 21:24.

they carry away captives. Heb. they that take them captives carry them away. 1 K 8:46.

37 **Yet if**. Le 26:40-45. Dt 4:29, 30. 30:1-3. Lk 15:17.

bethink themselves. Heb. bring back to their heart.

and pray. Ex +2:23. Dt 4:27-29. Ps +119:134. Je 29:12-14. 31:8, 9. La 5:1-8. Da 9:1-3.

We have sinned. Ezr 9:6, 7. Ne 1:6. 9:26-30. Jb 33:27, 28. Ps 106:6. Is 64:6-12. Je 3:12-14. 31:18-20. Da 9:5-11. Lk 15:18, 19.

38 **return**. Je 29:12-14. Zc +1:3.

soul. Heb. nephesh, Ge +34:3.

pray toward. ver. +20. 2 Ch 33:11-13. Da 9:3, 4.

the city. ver. 34. Da 6:10.

39 **cause**. or, right. ver. 35. Zc 1:15, 16.

forgive. Ps 25:18. Mi 7:18-20.

40 **my God**. Ps 7:3. 13:3. 22:1, 2. 88:1.

thine eyes. ver. +20.

thine ears. Ps 17:1. 31:2. 116:2.

that is made in this place. Heb. of this place. 2 Ch 7:15mg.

41 **arise**. Ps +3:7.

thy resting. 1 Ch 28:2. Is 66:1.

the ark. Jsh 3:13. 6:4, 5. Ps 110:2. Ro 1:16.

thy priests. Ex +28:2. Is 59:16-18. 61:3, 6, 10. Ep 4:22-24. 1 Th +5:25.

thy saints. Ne 9:25. Ps 65:4, 11. Is 65:18, 19. Zc 9:17. Ph 3:3. 4:4.

42 **turn not**. 1 K 2:16.

thine anointed. 1 K 1:34. Ps 2:2. Is 61:1.

remember. Ps 132:1. Is 55:3. Ac 13:34.

the mercies. Is +55:3.

2 CHRONICLES 7

1 **when Solomon**. 1 K 8:54, etc. Is 65:24. Da 9:20. Ac 4:31. 16:25, 26.

the fire. Ge 15:17. Ex 29:43. 1 Ch +21:26. Ml 3:1, 2.

the glory. Ex +24:16. Is 6:1-4. Hg 2:7-9.

2 **the priests**. 2 Ch 5:14. Ex 24:17. Is 6:5. Re 15:8.

3 **they bowed**. Ge +24:26.

For he is. Ex +34:6.

for ever. Heb. olam, Ex +12:24.

4 **Then the king**. 1 K 8:62-66.

5 **a sacrifice**. 2 Ch 1:6. 5:6. 15:11. 29:32, 33. 30:24. 35:7-9. 1 K 8:62, 63. 1 Ch 29:21. Ezr 6:16, 17. Ezk 45:17. Mi 6:7.

dedicated. Nu +7:10.

6 **the priests**. 1 Ch 16:39, 40. 24:1-3.

the Levites. 2 Ch 29:25. 1 Ch 6:31, 32. 15:16-21. 16:4-6, 41, 42. 25:1-7. Ps 87:7.

which David. Am 6:5.

because his mercy. ver. +3.

for ever. Heb. olam, Ex +12:24.

ministry. Heb. hand. 2 Ch 8:18. Nu 15:23. Is 52:6.

the priests. 2 Ch 5:12. Nu 10:1-10. Jsh 6:4. 1 Ch 13:8. 15:24. 16:6, 42.

7 **hallowed**. 1 K +8:64.
burnt offerings. Le +23:12.
peace offerings. Le +23:19.
the brazen. 2 Ch +4:1.
meat offerings. Le +23:13.
fat. Ex +29:13.

8 **kept**. Le +23:34-43. 1 K 8:65.
a very great. 2 Ch 30:13.
from the entering. Ge 15:18. Nu +13:21.
unto. 1 K 4:21-25.

9 **solemn assembly**. Heb. restraint. Le +23:36.
seven days. 2 Ch 30:23. 1 K 8:65.

10 **three and twentieth**. 1 K 8:66.
glad. Dt +12:7. Ps 33:1. 92:4. 105:3. 106:5. Ac 16:34.
goodness. 2 Ch 6:41. Ex 18:1.

11 **Solomon**. 2 Ch 2:1. 1 K 9:1, etc.
all that came. Ec 2:4, 10, 11.

12 **the Lord**. 2 Ch 1:7. Ge 17:1. 1 K 9:2.
I have heard. 2 K 20:5. Ps 10:17. 66:19. Lk 1:13. Ac 10:31. 1 J 5:14, 15.
have chosen. ver. 16. Dt 12:5, 11. Ps 78:68, 69. 132:13, 14.
an house of sacrifice. 2 Ch 2:6. Dt 12:6.

13 **If I shut up heaven**. 2 Ch 6:26-28. Dt 11:17. Jb 11:10. 12:14. Ps 107:34. Lk 4:25. Re 3:7. 11:6.
I command. Ps +78:46.
devour. 2 S 18:8mg.
I send. Nu 14:12. 16:46, 47. 2 S 24:13-15. Ezk 14:19-21.

14 **If**. Ge +4:7.
my people. Is 63:19.
which are called by my name. Heb. upon whom my name is called. 2 Ch 6:33mg. Nu +6:27. Is 63:19mg. Lk 15:16mg.
humble. 2 Ch 6:37-39. 33:12, 13, 18, 19. Le 26:40, 41. Dt 4:29, 30. 30:1-6. Ps 25:9. +35:13. Ezk 33:11. Da +10:12. Mi +6:8. Lk 18:13. Ja 4:9, 10.
and pray. Ps 145:18, 19. Is 26:8, 9. Je 29:13. Mk 11:23, 24. Ac 9:11. 1 T 2:1-4.
seek my face. 1 Ch 28:9. Ps +9:10. Is 26:9. 45:19. 55:6, 7. La 3:40, 41. Ho 5:6, 7, 15. Lk 11:9, 10. He 11:6.
turn from. Pr 28:13. Is 59:20. 66:2. Je +35:15. Ho 6:1-3. Lk +13:3. 15:21-23.
then will I hear. 2 Ch 6:27, 30, 39. Ps 91:15. Is 30:18. +65:24. Je 33:3. Zc 13:9. Jn 15:7. Re 3:20.
forgive their sin. Ex 34:7. Is 1:18. 43:25. 44:22. 59:1, 2. Je +31:34. Ho 5:15. 6:1. Zp 3:15. Lk 24:47. Ac +3:19-21. +10:36, 43. Ja 5:15. 1 J 1:7, 9.
heal their land. 2 Ch 6:28-31. Nu 14:11-13, 19. 2 S 24:15-17. Ps 60:2. Is 11:6. 27:6. 35:1. Je 8:22. 33:6. 51:9. Am +9:13-15. Mt +19:28. Ac +3:19. Ro +8:19, 21. Re +22:3.

15 **mine eyes**. Zc +12:4.
that is made in this place. Heb. of this place. 2 Ch 6:40.

16 **have I chosen**. Dt 12:21. 16:11. 1 K 8:16, 44, 48. Ps 132:14. Zc 3:2.
my name. 2 Ch +6:5, 6, 20. 33:4-7. 1 K 8:35. 9:3. 2 K 21:4, 7, 8.
for ever. Heb. *olam*, Ex +12:24.
eyes. ver. +15. Mt 3:17. Jn +2:19-21. Col 2:9.

17 **if thou wilt**. Dt 28:1, etc. 1 K 2:3. 3:14. 8:25. 9:4, etc. 11:38. 1 Ch +28:9. Zc 3:7.
observe. Dt 4:40. Ps 105:45. Ezk 36:27. Jn 14:21. 15:10. 1 J 2:3.

18 **stablish**. 2 S 7:13-16.
as I have. Ps 89:28-40. 132:11, 12.
shall not. 1 K 9:5. Je +33:20, 21, 25, 26.
fail thee. Heb. be cut off to thee: 2 Ch 6:16mg. 1 K 8:25.

19 **if ye turn away**. Le 26:14, 33, etc. Dt 28:15, 36, 37, etc. 1 S 12:25. Je +1:16.
shall go. Dt +4:23-27. Jsh 23:15, 16. 1 K 9:6, 7. 11:4-8.

20 **I pluck**. 2 K 17:20. Ps 52:5. Je +12:17. Ju 12.
my land. Dt +32:43.
a proverb. Dt +28:37. Ne 4:1-4. La 2:15, 16.

21 **this house**. 1 K 9:8.
astonishment. 2 Ch +29:8.
Why. Dt 29:24-28. 1 K 9:8, 9. Je 5:19. 13:22. 16:10-12. 22:8, 9, 28.

22 **Because they forsook**. Je +1:16. La 2:16, 17. 4:13-15. Ezk 14:23. 36:17-20.
therefore. 2 Ch 36:17. Da 9:12.

2 CHRONICLES 8

1 **at the end**. 1 K +9:10.

2 **the cities**. 1 K 9:11-13.

3 **Hamath-zobah**. i.e. *the swelling host's enclosure of wrath; fortress of Zobah* (i.e. *depression*, 1 S +14:47), **S#2578h**. Nu +13:21. 2 S 8:3. 1 K 11:23-25. 1 Ch 18:3.

4 **he built**. 1 K 9:17-19.
Tadmor. i.e. *thou wilt scatter myrrh; wonder, admiration; palm city*, **S#8412h**. ver. 4. 1 K 9:18.

5 **Beth-horon**. Jsh +10:10.
with walls. 2 Ch 14:7. Dt 3:5. 1 S 23:7. 1 K 4:13.

6 **Baalath**. Jsh 19:44. 1 K 9:18.
the store cities. ver. 4. 2 Ch 17:12. 1 K 9:19.
chariot cities. 2 Ch 1:14. 1 K 10:26.
all that Solomon desired to build. Heb. all the desire of Solomon which he desired to build. 1 K 9:19. Ec 2:4, 10, etc.
and in Lebanon. 1 K 7:2. SS 4:8.

7 **As for all**. 1 K 9:20-22.
the Hittites. Dt +20:17.
Amorites. Ge +10:16.
Perizzites. Ge +13:7.

Hivites. Ge +10:17.
Jebusites. Ge +10:16.

8 **whom the children**. Jg 1:21-36. Ps 106:34.
to pay. 2 Ch 2:17, 18. Jsh 16:10. 17:13. 1 K 5:13, 14.

9 **But of the**. Ex 19:5, 6. Le 25:39-46. Ga 4:26, 31.
they were men. 1 S 8:11, 12.

10 **two hundred**. 2 Ch 2:18. 1 K 5:16. 9:23.

11 **brought up**. 1 K 3:1. 7:8. 9:24.
holy. Heb. holiness. Ex 3:5. 29:43. 35:2. Ezk 21:2. 2 P 1:18.

12 **altar**. 2 Ch +4:1.
before the porch. 1 Ch 28:11. Ezk 8:16. Jl 2:17. Jn 10:23.

13 **every day**. Ex 29:38-42. Le ch. 23. Nu ch. 28, 29. Ezk 45:17. 46:3-15.
new moons. Col +2:16.
solemn. Le +23:36.
three times. Ex 23:14-17. Dt 16:16. 1 K 9:25.
unleavened. Le 23:6.
weeks. Le +23:16.
booths. Le +23:34.

14 **the courses**. 2 Ch 5:11. 23:4. 31:2. 1 Ch 24:1-19. Lk 1:5, 8.
the Levites. 2 Ch 35:10. 1 Ch 6:31, 32, etc. 15:16-22. 16:4-6, 42. ch. 23. 24:20-31. ch. 25. Ezr 6:18.
the porters. 1 Ch 9:17. +23:5. 26:1-19.
so had David the man of God commanded. Heb. so *was* the commandment of David the man of God. Dt +33:1. 2 S 23:2. 1 Ch 28:19. Ac 13:22, 36. 1 T +6:11.

15 **they departed not**. 2 Ch 30:12. Ex 39:42, 43.
commandment of. 2 Ch 29:25. Jn 14:21. 15:14. 1 C 12:18. 1 J 2:3.
the treasures. 1 K 7:51. 1 Ch 9:29. 26:20-26.

16 **all the work**. 1 K 5:18. 6:7.

17 **Ezion-geber**. 1 K +9:26.
Eloth. 1 K +9:26.

18 **Huram**. 1 Ch +8:5.
Ophir. 1 K +9:28.
took thence. 1 K 9:28. Ec 2:8.

2 CHRONICLES 9

1 A.M. 3014. B.C. 990.
And when. 1 K +10:1, 2, etc. Mt 12:42. Lk 11:31.
Sheba. 1 K +10:1.
fame. 2 Ch 1:1, 12. 1 K 4:31.
hard questions. Nu +12:8. Jg 14:12-19. 1 K 10:1. Ps 49:4. 78:2. Pr 1:6. Mt 13:11, 35.
great. 2 K 6:14mg. 7:6.
camels. Ps 72:10, 15. Is 60:6.
spices. ver. 9. Ex 25:6. 30:23. 35:8. Mt 2:11.
precious stones. 2 S 12:30.
communed. 1 S 1:15. Ps 142:2. Mt 12:34.

2 **all**. Pr 13:20. 18:4. Mk 4:11, 34. Jn 15:15. Ja 1:5.
there. 1 K 3:12. 4:29. Col 2:3. He 4:12.

3 **seen the wisdom**. 1 K 10:3, 4. Ac 11:23.
the house. 2 Ch ch. 3, 4. 1 K ch. 6, 7.

4 **the meat**. 1 K 4:22, 23. Pr 9:5. Jn 6:53-57.
the sitting. Ge 10:30 (dwelling). 1 K 10:5. Lk 12:37. Re 3:20.
cupbearers. *or*, butlers. Ge 40:1-23. 1 K 10:5. Ne 1:11.
ascent. 2 Ch 23:13. 2 K 16:18. 1 Ch 9:18. Ezk 44:3. 46:2.
there was. Ps 119:81. 143:7. SS 5:8. Da 10:17. Re 1:17.
spirit. Heb. *ruach*, Ge +41:8.

5 **report**. Heb. word. 1 K +10:6.
acts. *or*, sayings.

6 **I believed not**. Jn 20:25-29.
the one half. 1 K +10:7. Ps 31:19. Zc 9:17. 1 C 2:9. 1 J 3:2.
for thou. Jn 1:45-49.
exceedest. ver. 5. 1 K 4:31, 34. SS 5:9-16. Jn 7:46.

7 **Happy are**. Dt 33:29. 1 K 10:8. Ps 27:4. 84:10-12. Pr 3:3, 14. 8:34. 10:21. 13:20. Mt 13:16, 17. Lk 10:39-42. 11:28.

8 **Blessed**. 1 Ch 29:10, 20. Ps 72:18, 19. 2 C 9:12-15.
which delighted. 2 S 15:25, 26. 1 K +10:9. Ps 18:19. 22:8. Is 42:1. 62:4.
because thy God. 2 Ch 2:11. Dt 7:8. 1 Ch 17:22.
establish them. Ro +11:1.
for ever. Heb. *olam*, Ex +12:24.
to do judgment. 2 S 8:15. 23:3. 1 K 3:28. Ps 72:2. 99:4. Pr 21:3. Is 9:7. 11:1-5. 32:1, 2. Je 33:15, 16. He +1:8, 9.

9 **she gave**. ver. 24. Jg +3:15.
of spices. ver. 1. Ge 43:11. Ex 30:34.

10 **brought gold**. 2 Ch +8:18. 1 K 9:27, +28. 10:22.
algum trees. 2 Ch 2:8. 1 K 10:11, almug trees.

11 **terraces**. *or*, stays. Heb. highways. Nu 20:19. 1 K 10:22. Ps 84:6. Pr 16:17.
harps. 1 K 10:12. 1 Ch +13:8. 23:5. 25:1. Ps 92:1-3. 150:3-5. Re 5:8.

12 **all her desire**. 1 K 10:13. Ps 20:4. Ep 3:20.

13 **the weight**. 1 K 10:14, 15. Ps 68:29. 72:10, 15.

14 **chapmen**. or, tourists. Nu 14:6 (spies).
merchants. Ge 23:16. 37:28.
Arabia. i.e. *dusky; mixed; desert or sterile*, S#6152h. 2 Ch 17:11. 26:7. 1 K 10:15. Is 13:20. 21:13. Je 3:2. 25:24. Ezk 27:21. Ac 2:11. Ga 1:17. 4:25.
governors. or, captains. 1 K 10:15.

15 **two**. 2 Ch 12:9, 10. 1 K +10:16, 17.

16 **in the house**. 1 K 7:2.

17 **a great throne**. 1 K +10:18-20. Ps 45:8. Re 20:11.

pure. ver. 17. 2 Ch 3:4. 13:11. 30:17 (clean). Jb 14:4. 28:19. Ps 12:6. 19:9. 51:10. Pr 15:26. Ezk 36:25. 44:23. Hab 1:13. Ml 1:11.

18 **stays**. Heb. hands. 1 K 7:35, 36.
   two lions. Ge 49:9, 10. Nu 23:24. 24:9. Re 5:5.

19 **twelve lions**. Mt 19:28. Re 21:12.

20 **drinking**. 1 K 10:21. Est 1:7. Da 5:2, 3.
   pure. Heb. shut up. or, refined. ver. +17.
   S#5462h. 2 Ch 4:20, 22. 1 K 6:20, 21. 7:49, 50. 10:21. Jb 41:15 (shut up). Ezk 44:1, 2. 46:1.
   none were of silver. or, there was no silver in them.
   it was. ver. 27. Is 2:22. Je 31:5.
   not. 1 K 10:21.

21 **Tarshish**. Ge +10:4.
   ivory. or elephant's teeth.
   peacocks. Jb 39:13.

22 **passed all the kings**. 2 Ch 1:12. 1 K 3:12, 13. 4:30, 31. 10:23, 24. Ps 89:27. Mt 12:42. Col 2:2, 3.

23 **sought**. ver. 6, 7. 1 K 4:34. Is 11:2, 10.
   God. 2 Ch 1:10-12. 1 K +3:28. Pr 2:6. Da 1:17. 2:21-23. 5:11. Lk 21:15. 1 C 1:30. 12:8. Ep 1:17. Ja 1:5, 16, 17. 3:17.

24 **every man**. ver. +9.

25 **four thousand stalls**. 2 Ch 1:14. Dt 17:16. 1 K 4:26. 10:26.

26 **reigned over**. Jsh 21:43. 1 K 4:21, 24. Ps 72:8-11. Da 7:14. Ac 7:5. Re 19:16.
   river. That is, Euphrates. Ge 2:14. Jsh 13:2-7. Ezr 4:20. 7:25. Ps +72:8.

27 **the king**. ver. 20. 2 Ch 1:15-17. 1 K 10:27, etc. Jb 22:24, 25.
   made. Heb. gave. 1 Ch 27:28. Ps 78:47. Is 9:10. Am 7:14. Lk 19:4.

28 **brought**. ver. 25. 2 Ch 1:16. Dt 17:16. 1 K 4:26. 10:18. 11:1. Is 2:7, 8. 31:1.

29 **the rest**. 1 K 11:41-43.
   book. Heb. words.
   Nathan. i.e. given, placed; a giver, **S#5416h**. ver. 29. 2 Ch 29:25. 2 S 5:14. 7:2-4, 17. 12:1, 5, 7, 13, 15, 25. 23:36. 1 K 1:8, 10, 11, 22-24, 32, 34, 38, 44, 45. 4:5. 1 Ch 2:36. 3:5. 11:38. 14:4. 17:1-3, 15. 29:29. Ezr 8:16. 10:39. Ps 51, title. Zc 12:12. Lk 3:31.
   Ahijah. 1 K +14:6.
   Iddo. 1 Ch +27:21.

30 **Solomon**. 1 K 11:42, 43.

31 A.M. 3029. B.C. 975.
   slept with. 1 K +11:43.

2 CHRONICLES 10

1 **Rehoboam**. 1 K +14:21.
   Shechem. Ge +33:18.
   all. 1 K 4:1. 1 Ch 12:38.

2 **Jeroboam**. 1 K +11:26. 1 Ch 11:26, 28, 40. 12:2.

3 **they sent**. 1 K 12:3.

4 **Thy father**. 1 S 8:11-18. 1 K 12:4. Is 47:6. Mt 11:29, 30. 23:4. 1 J 5:3.
   grievous. Ex 1:13, 14. 2:23. 1 K 4:20, 25. 9:22.
   ease thou. Mt 11:28.

5 **Come again**. 1 K 12:5. Pr 3:28.

6 **took counsel**. Jb 12:12, 13. 32:7. Pr 12:15. 19:20. 27:10. Je 42:2-5, 20.
   What counsel. 2 S 16:20. 17:5, 6.

7 **If thou be kind**. 1 K 12:7. Pr 15:1.
   speak good. Ge 49:21. 2 S 15:2-6.

8 **he forsook**. 2 Ch 25:15, 16. 1 S +25:17. 2 S 17:14. 1 K +12:8. Pr 1:25. 9:9. 19:20. 25:12. Ec 10:2, 3, 16. Is 30:1.
   the young men. 2 Ch 13:7. 1 T 5:1, 2, 10, 14. T 2:1-5. 1 P 5:5.

9 **What advice**. ver. 6. 2 S 17:5, 6. 1 K 22:6-8.
   Ease. ver. +4. 1 K +12:9. Pr 24:6. 2 T 3:14. 2 T 4:3.

10 **Thus shalt**. 2 S 17:7-13. Pr +21:30. Is 19:11-13.
   My little finger. 1 K 12:10, 11. Pr 10:14. 13:16. 14:16. 18:6, 7. 28:25. 29:23.

11 **my father**. ver. +4.
   put. Heb. laded.
   I will put. Ex 1:13, 14. 5:5-9, 18. 1 S 8:18. Is 47:6. 58:6. Je 28:13, 14. Mt 11:29.
   scorpions. ver. 14. Dt 8:15. Ezk 2:6. Lk 10:19. Re 9:3, 5, 10.

12 **Come**. ver. 5. 1 K 12:12-15.

13 **answered**. Ge 42:7, 30. Ex 10:28. 1 S 25:10, 11. 1 K 20:6-11. Pr 15:1.
   forsook. ver. 8. Pr 19:27.

14 **the advice**. 2 Ch 22:4, 5. Pr 12:5. Da 6:7.
   My father. ver. +10, 11. Pr 17:14. Ec 2:19. 7:8. 10:16. Ja 3:14-18. 4:1, 2.

15 **the king**. Is 30:12, 13.
   the cause. 2 Ch 25:16-20. Dt +2:30. Jg 14:4. 1 S 2:25. 1 K 12:15, 24. 22:20. Is 19:14. Ac 2:23. 4:28.
   that the Lord. 1 K 11:29-39. Jn 12:37-39. 19:24, 32-36.
   by the hand. 1 K +16:12mg.
   Ahijah. 1 K +14:6.

16 **What portion**. 2 S 20:1. 1 K 12:16, 17.
   the son. 1 S 20:27, 30, 31. 22:7, 9, 13.
   David. 2 S 7:15, 16. 1 K 11:13, 34-39. 1 Ch 17:14. Ps 2:1-6. 76:10. 89:29-37. 132:17. Is 9:6, 7. 11:1. Je +33:20, 21, 25, 26. Ezk 37:24, 25. Am 9:11. Lk 1:32, 33. 19:14, 27. Ac 2:30. 1 C 15:25. Re 22:16.
   So all Israel. ver. 19. Jg 8:35. 2 S 15:13. 16:11. Jn 6:66. 7:53.

17 **But as for**. 2 Ch 11:1. 1 K 11:36. 12:17.

18 **Hadoram**. 1 K 4:6. 5:14, Adoniram. 12:18, Adoram.
   stoned him. 2 Ch 24:21. Ac 7:57, 58.
   made speed. Heb. strengthened himself. 2 Ch 13:7. Ru 1:18mg. 1 K 12:18mg.
   chariot. 1 K 12:18.

19 **Israel**. ver. 16. 2 Ch 13:5-7. 1 K 12:19, 20. 2 K 17:21-23. Ps 89:30.
  unto this day. 2 Ch +5:9. Jsh +4:9. Ezr 9:7.

2 CHRONICLES 11

1 **when Rehoboam**. 1 K 12:21.
  an hundred and. Ps 33:10, 16. Pr 21:30, 31.
2 **to Shemaiah**. 1 Ch +9:16.
  the man. 2 Ch 8:14. Dt 33:1. 1 S 2:27. 1 T 6:11.
3 **to all Israel**. Ge 49:28. Ex 24:4. 2 K 17:34. Ph 3:5. Re 7:4-8.
4 **against**. Ge 13:8. 2 S 2:26. Ac 7:26. 1 C 6:5-8. He 13:1. 1 P 3:8. 1 J 3:11-13.
  return. 2 Ch 10:16. 1 K 22:36.
  for this thing. 2 Ch +10:15. Ge 50:20. 1 K 11:29-38. Ps 33:11. Ho 8:4.
  they obeyed. 2 Ch 25:7-10. 28:9-15.
5 A.M. 3029-3032. B.C. 975-972.
  built. 2 Ch 8:2-6. 14:6, 7. 16:6. 17:12. 26:6. 27:4. Is 22:8-11.
6 **Beth-lehem**. Jsh +19:15.
  Etam. Jg 15:8. 1 Ch 4:32.
  Tekoa. 1 Ch +2:24. Ne 3:5, 27.
7 **Beth-zur**. Jsh +15:58.
  Shoco. Jsh +15:35, Socoh, 48.
  Adullam. Jsh +12:15.
8 **Gath**. 1 Ch 18:1.
  Mareshah. Jsh +15:44.
  Ziph. Jsh +15:24.
9 **Adoraim**. i.e. *double mound; double glory*, **S#115h**.
  Lachish. Jsh +10:3.
10 **Zorah**. Jsh +19:41.
  Hebron. Nu +13:22. Jsh +20:7.
11 **he fortified**. Is 22:10, 11.
  captains. ver. 23. 2 Ch 17:19.
12 **he put shields**. 2 Ch 26:14, 15. 32:5. 2 S 13:19, 22.
  having Judah. ver. +1.
13 A.M. 3030. B.C. 974.
  resorted to him. Heb. presented themselves to him.
14 **suburbs**. Nu 35:2-5. Jsh 21:20-42. 1 Ch 6:66-81.
  their possession. Le 27:30-34. Nu 18:21-28.
  Jeroboam. 2 Ch 13:9. 1 K 12:28-33. 13:33.
15 **high places**. 2 K +21:3.
  for the devils. Le 17:7. Dt 32:17. 1 C 10:20, 21. 1 T 4:1. Re 16:14.
  for the calves. Ex +32:4.
16 **And after**. 2 Ch 15:9. 30:11, 18, 19. Jsh 22:19. Ps 84:5-7.
  set. Ex 9:21mg. Dt 32:46. 1 Ch 22:19. 2 Ch +12:14mg. Jb 34:14. Ps 62:10. 108:1. Da 6:14. Ho 4:8. Ac 11:23.
  to sacrifice. Dt 12:5, 6, 11, 13, 14. 1 Ch 16:29. 22:1.
17 A.M. 3029-3032. B.C. 975-972.

strengthened. 2 Ch 12:1.
  three years. 2 Ch 1:1-12. 7:17-19. 8:13-16. Ho 6:4. Mt 13:20, 21.
18 A.M. 3029-3046. B.C. 975-958.
  Mahalath. i.e. *sickness; harp, wind instrument; appeasing*, **S#4258h**. ver. 18. Ge 28:9.
  daughter. or, granddaughter. 1 K +15:10.
  to wife. Ge +4:19.
  Eliab. Nu +1:9. 1 Ch 27:18, Elihu.
19 **Jeush**. Ge +36:5.
  Shamariah. i.e. *preserved* or *guarded of Jah*, **S#8114h**.
  Zaham. i.e. *loathing, disgust; fat*, **S#2093h**.
20 **Maachah**. ver. 21. 2 Ch 13:2, Michaiah the daughter of Uriel.
  Absalom. 1 K 15:2, Abishalom.
  Abijah. 1 K +14:1. 1 K 15:1, Abijam. Mt 1:7, Abia.
21 **eighteen wives**. ver. 23. Ge +4:19. 1 Ch 3:1-9.
  concubines. 1 Ch +2:48.
22 **made Abijah**. Dt 21:15-17. 1 Ch +5:1, 2. 26:10. 29:1.
23 **he dealt**. 2 Ch 10:8-15. Lk 16:8.
  wisely. 1 Ch +12:32.
  dispersed. 2 Ch 21:3. Ge 25:6. 1 K 1:5, 6.
  every fenced city. ver. 11.
  desired. Dt 14:26.
  many wives. Heb. a multitude of wives. ver. +21.

2 CHRONICLES 12

1 A.M. 3032. B.C. 972.
  when Rehoboam. ver. +13. 2 Ch 11:17.
  had strengthened. Ps 118:8, 9. Is 30:2, 3. Je 17:5-8.
  he forsook. 2 Ch 26:13-16. Dt 6:10-12. 8:10-14. 32:15, 18. 1 K 9:9. Je +1:16. Ho 13:1, 6-8.
  all Israel. 2 Ch 11:3. 1 K 12:17. 14:22-24. 2 K 17:19. Ho 5:10, 11. Mi 6:16.
2 A.M. 3034. B.C. 970.
  Shishak. 1 K +11:40. 14:24-26.
  because. 2 Ch 7:19, 20. 36:14-19. Jg 2:13-15. 1 Ch +28:9. Ne 9:26, 27. Ps 106:43, 44. Is 63:10. Je 2:19. 44:22, 23. La 5:15, 16. Ga 6:7.
3 **twelve hundred**. Jg 4:13. 1 S 13:5. 2 S 10:18.
  without number. 2 Ch 14:9. Jg 6:5. Re 9:16.
  Lubims. i.e. *inhabitants of the interior of Africa; dwellers in a thirsty land*, **S#3864h**. ver. 3. 2 Ch 16:8. Ge 10:13. Ezk 30:5. Da 11:43, Libyans. Na 3:9. Ac 2:10.
  the Sukkims. i.e. *dwelling in booths; thicket men*, **S#5525h**.
  Ethiopians. Ge +10:6-8.
4 **the fenced**. 2 Ch 11:5-12. Is 36:1. Je 5:10.
  came. 2 K 18:17. Is 8:8. 10:11.
5 **Shemaiah**. 1 Ch +9:16.
  Ye have forsaken me. ver. +1, 2. Dt 28:15,

etc. Jg 10:9-14. Je 2:19. 4:18. 5:19.

left you. 2 S 24:14. Ps 37:33. Is +54:7.

6 **humbled**. 2 Ch 32:26. 33:12, 19, 23. Ex 10:3. Le 26:40, 41. 1 K 8:37-39. Ps 78:34, 35. Je 13:15, 18. 44:10. Da 5:22. Ho 5:15. Lk 18:14. Ja 4:6, 10.

The Lord. Ex 9:27. Jg 1:7. Jb 33:27. Ps 129:4. La 1:18. Da 9:14. Ro 10:3.

7 **the Lord**. Jg 10:15, 16. 1 K 21:28, 29. Je 3:13. Lk 15:18-21.

humbled themselves. 2 Ch +7:14. 1 K 21:27. Ja 4:10. 1 P 5:6.

therefore. Le 26:41, 42.

some deliverance. *or*, a little while. Ex 33:18-23. Nu 21:6-9. Dt 3:23-27. 2 K 13:4-7, 23. 1 Ch 16:19. Is 1:9. Je 21:1-9. Ezk 14:13-20. Am 7:6-8. Mk 10:35-40. Lk 22:41-43.

and my wrath. 2 Ch 34:21, 25. Ps 79:6. Is 42:25. Je 7:20. Re 14:10. 16:2-17.

8 **Nevertheless**. Ne 9:36. Is 26:13.

his servants. Ps 40:17. 44:4. Is 43:15. Ac 27:23.

that they may. Dt 28:47, 48. Jg 3:1, 2. Je 10:24. Ho 8:10.

9 **Shishak**. 1 K 14:25, 26.

took away. 1 K 15:18. 2 K 16:8. 18:15, 16. La 1:10.

the shields. 2 Ch 9:15, 16. 1 K 10:16, 17.

10 **shields of brass**. 1 K 14:27. La 4:1.

the chief. 2 S 8:18. 23:23. 1 Ch 11:25. SS 3:7, 8.

guard. 2 K 10:25mg.

11 **chamber**. 1 K 14:28. Ezk 40:7, 10, 12, 13, 16, 21, 29, 33, 36.

12 **when**. ver. +6, 7. 2 Ch 19:3. Is 57:15. La 3:22, 33, 42. 1 P 5:6.

also in Judah things went well. *or*, yet in Judah there were good things. 2 Ch 19:3. Ge 18:24. 1 K 14:13. Is 6:13.

13 A.M. 3029-3046. B.C. 975-958.

for Rehoboam. 1 K +14:21.

the city. 2 Ch +6:6. Ps 48:1-3. 78:68, 69.

to put. Dt +12:11.

an Ammonitess. 1 S +11:11.

14 **he did evil**. 2 Ch 19:3. 1 K 14:22.

he prepared. Heb. he fixed. ver. 1. 2 Ch 11:16. 19:3. 20:33. 27:6mg. 30:19. 1 S 7:3. 1 K 15:14. 1 Ch 29:18mg. Ezr 7:10. Jb 11:13. Ps 10:17mg. 57:7mg. 78:8, 37. 112:7. Ho 6:3mg. Hg 1:5mg. 1 C 15:58. 16:13.

to seek. Dt 5:29. Ps 105:3, 4. Je +29:13. Ezk 33:31.

15 **first and last**. 2 Ch 9:29.

book. Heb. words.

Shemaiah. ver. 5. 1 K 12:22.

Iddo. 1 Ch +27:21.

wars. 1 K 14:30.

16 **slept**. 1 K +11:43.

Abijah. 1 K +14:1, 31, Abijam. 1 Ch 3:10. Mt 1:7, Abia.

2 CHRONICLES 13

1 A.M. 3046-3049. B.C. 958-955.

in the eighteenth. 2 Ch +12:16. 1 K 15:1, etc.

2 **Michaiah**. 2 Ch 11:20, Maachah the daughter of Absalom. 1 K 15:2, Abishalom.

Gibeah. Jg +19:12. A.M. 3047. B.C. 957.

And there was. 1 K 15:6, 7.

3 **set**. Heb. bound together. 1 S 17:1-3. 2 K +9:21mg.

four hundred thousand. 2 Ch 11:1. 14:8. 17:14-18. 26:12, 13. 1 Ch 21:5.

eight hundred thousand. 2 Ch 14:9.

mighty men. Jg +6:12.

4 **Zemaraim**. Ge 10:18. Jsh 18:22.

Hear me. 2 Ch 15:2. Jg 9:7.

5 **Ought ye not**. Ne 5:9. Pr 1:29. Mk 12:24. 2 P 3:5.

the Lord. Jg 11:21-24. Je 27:5-7. Da 4:25-32. 5:18.

to David. 1 S 16:1, 12. 2 S 7:12-16. 1 K 8:20. 1 Ch 17:11, 14. 28:4, 5. Ps 89:19-37. Je +33:21, 22, 25, 26. Lk 1:31-33.

for ever. Heb. *olam*, Ex +12:24.

a covenant of salt. Le +2:13.

6 **rebelled**. 2 Ch 10:19. 1 K 11:26. 12:20, 27.

7 **vain men**. or, "empty ones." Ge 37:24. 41:27. Jg 9:4. 11:3. 1 S 22:2. Jb 30:8. Ps 26:4. Pr +12:11. 13:20. 28:19. Ac 17:5. T 1:10.

the children of Belial. Dt +13:13. +15:9. Jg +19:22. 1 K 21:10, 13.

young. 2 Ch 10:8, 14, 16. 12:13. Ec 10:16. Is 3:4. 1 C 14:20. He 5:12.

could not. 2 Ch 10:1-4, 8. 1 K +12:7, 10. Ps +119:63. Pr 1:10. +19:27. 1 C 10:13. +15:33.

8 **the kingdom**. 2 Ch 9:8. Ps 2:1-6. Is 7:6, 7. 9:6, 7. Lk 19:14, 27.

a great multitude. 2 Ch 14:9-11. 20:6, 12. Ps 33:16.

with you golden. Ex +32:4.

9 **cast out**. 2 Ch 11:14, 15. Lk 6:22, 23. 20:15. Jn 9:34, 35.

made you priests. 1 K 12:31-33. 12:13. 13:33.

consecrate himself. Heb. fill his hand. Ex +28:41mg.

young. Ex 29:1, 35. Le 8:2.

no gods. Dt 32:17. 2 K 19:18. Je 2:11. Ho 8:6. Ac 19:26. Ga 4:8.

10 **the Lord**. 2 Ch 11:16, 17. Ex 19:5, 6. Zc 13:9.

the priests. Ex 29:1, etc. Nu 16:40. 18:1-7.

business. Nu 3:7. Ne 11:22. Ro 12:11. Col 3:24.

11 **they burn**. 2 Ch 2:4. Ex 29:38-42.

morning. 2 S 13:4mg.

sweet incense. Ex +39:38. Le 2:1-3. Ps +141:2.

showbread. Ex +25:30.

table. Ex +25:23.

the candlestick. Ex +25:31.

every evening. Ex +30:8.
we keep. Ge 26:5. Nu 9:19, 23. Ezk 44:8, 15. 48:11.

12 God. 1 S 4:5-7. Zc 10:5.
with us. Is +43:2. 1 J 4:4.
for our captain. Dt 20:4. Jsh 5:13-15. Ps 20:7. He 2:10.
his priests. Nu 10:8, 9. 31:6. Jsh 6:13-20.
fight ye. Jb 15:25, 26. 40:9. Is 45:9. Je 50:24. Ac 5:39. 9:4, 5.
ye shall not. 2 Ch 24:20. Nu 14:41. Dt 28:29. Jb 9:4. Is 54:17. Je 2:37. Ezk 17:9.

13 an ambushment. 2 Ch 20:22. Jsh 8:4. Pr 21:30. Je 4:22.

14 looked back. Ex 14:10. Jsh 8:20. Jg 20:33-43. 2 S 10:8-14.
cried. 2 Ch 14:10, 11. 18:31. Ps 50:15. 91:5.
the priests. ver. +12.

15 as the men. 2 Ch 20:21. Jsh 6:16, 20. Jg 7:18-22. Ps 47:1-5.
God smote. 2 Ch 14:12. Nu 32:4. Jsh 11:8. Jg 4:15. 2 K 5:1. Ps 118:4-7. Is 37:36.

16 God delivered. Ge 14:20. Dt 2:36. 3:3. Jsh 10:12. 21:44. Jg 1:4. 11:21. 1 S 23:7.

17 five hundred thousand. ver. 3, 12. 2 Ch 28:6. Is 10:16-19. 37:36. Na 1:5. 1 C 10:22.

18 relied. 2 Ch 16:8, 9. 20:20. 2 K 18:5. 1 Ch 5:20. Ps 22:4, 5. 146:5. Da 3:28. Na 1:7. Ep 1:12.

19 took cities. Jsh 10:19, 39. 11:12. 1 S 31:7.
Jeshanah. i.e. *old, ancient*, **S#3466h.**
Ephrain. i.e. *the two fawns; doubly dust,* **S#6085h.** 2 Ch 15:8. Ge +23:8, Ephron. Jsh 15:9, Ephron. Jn 11:54.
towns. lit. daughters. Nu +21:25mg.

20 did. Ps 18:37, 38.
the Lord struck. 1 S 25:38. 26:10. Ezk 26:14. Ac 12:23.
he died. 1 K 14:20. 15:9.

21 waxed. 2 S 5:12, 13.
fourteen wives. 2 Ch +11:21. Ge +4:19.
begat. Jg 8:30, 31. 9:5. 10:4.

22 the rest. 1 K 15:7.
story. or, commentary. 2 Ch 24:27mg.
Iddo. 1 Ch +27:21.

2 CHRONICLES 14

1 A.M. 3049. B.C. 955.
slept with his fathers. 1 K +11:43.
Asa. 1 Ch +9:16.

2 A.M. 3063-3073. B.C. 941-931.
good and right. 2 Ch 31:20. 1 K 15:11, 14. Lk 1:75.

3 For he took. 2 Ch +17:3. Dt +7:5. 1 K 11:7, 8. 14:22-24. Pr 16:7.
strange. 2 Ch 33:15. Ex +12:43. 2 S 22:45, 46.
the high places. 2 K +21:3.
brake. Ex +23:24.

images. Heb. statues. 2 K +17:10mg.
cut down. Ex +23:24. 1 K 11:7.
groves. 2 K +17:10.

4 commanded. 2 Ch 29:21, 27, 30. 30:12. 33:16. 34:32, 33. Ge 18:19. Jsh 24:15. 1 S 3:13. Ezr 10:7-12. Ne 13:9, 19-22. Ps 101:2-8.
seek. 2 Ch +11:16. 30:19. Is 55:6, 7. Am 5:4.
to do. Ne 10:29-39. Ps 119:10. Jn 13:17.
law and. 2 Ch +34:14.

5 images. Heb. sun-images. Le +26:30mg.

6 And he built. 2 Ch 8:2-6. 11:5-12.
for the land. Jg 3:11, 30. 5:31. 1 K 5:4. 1 Ch 22:9.
the Lord. 2 Ch 15:15. Jsh 23:1. Jb 34:29. Ps 46:9.

7 Therefore. 2 Ch 32:5. Ac 9:31.
while the land. Jn 9:4. 12:35, 36. He 3:13-15.
because we have sought. ver. 4. 2 Ch 31:21. Dt 4:7, 29-31. 1 Ch +28:9. Jb 33:26-29. 42:10. Ps 37:4, 5. 50:14. 55:16-18, 22. 105:3, 4. 138:3. Pr 15:8. Is 41:17, 18. 45:22-24. 55:1, 6, 7. La 3:25, 26, 54-58. Jl 2:15-19, 32. Mi 7:7, 8. Mt 6:33. 18:19, 20. Lk 11:9-13. Ro 8:26, 27. 10:13. Ph 4:6, 7. 1 P 3:12. 1 J +5:14-16. Re 3:20.
and he hath given. ver. 6. Jsh 23:1. Mt 11:28, 29. 1 T 2:1, 2.
prospered. Ps +1:3.

8 out of Judah. 2 Ch 11:1. 13:3. 17:14-19. 25:5.

9 A.M. 3063. B.C. 941.
Zerah. Ge +36:13.
with. 2 Ch 12:2, 3. 16:8. 2 K 19:9. Is 8:9, 10. Ezk 30:5. Re 16:14.
Mareshah. Jsh +15:44.

10 Zephathah. i.e. *watch tower*, **S#6859h.** Jsh 19:4. Jg 1:17, Zephath.

11 cried unto. 2 Ch 13:14. 18:31. 32:20. Ex 14:10. 1 Ch 5:20. Ps 18:6. 22:5. 34:6. 50:15. 91:15. 120:1. Ac 2:21.
nothing. 2 Ch 16:8. Le 26:8. Dt 32:30. Jg 7:7. 1 S 14:6. 1 K 20:27-30. Am 5:9. 2 C 12:9, 10.
them that. 2 Ch 20:12. Dt 32:36. 1 K 20:27. Is 40:29-31.
rest on thee. 2 Ch 32:8. 1 S 17:35, 36. Ps 37:5. Pr 18:10. Is 26:3, 4. 41:10-14. Jn 14:1, 27. Ro 8:31.
in thy name. 2 Ch 13:12, 18. 1 S 17:45, 46. Ps 20:5, 7. Is 26:13. Ac 3:16.
man. or, mortal man. Ge 13:8mg. Dt 32:27. Jsh 7:8, 9. 1 S 2:9. Jb 4:17. Ps 9:19. 79:9, 10. Is 2:22. Je 1:19. Zc 2:8. Mt 16:18. Ac 9:4.

12 the Lord smote. 2 Ch 13:15. 20:22. Ex 14:25. Dt 28:7. 32:39. Jsh 10:10. Ps 60:12. 136:17, 18. 1 C 9:26. 15:57.

13 Gerar. ver. 14. Ge 10:1, 19. 20:1. 26:1.
destroyed. Heb. broken. lit. "shivered," ver. 3. 2 Ch 20:37. Ex 22:10, 14. Le 6:28. 15:12.
before the Lord. Jb 6:9. 9:4. 2 Th 1:9.

his host. Jsh 5:14. 1 S 25:28. 1 Ch 12:22. Ps 108:11.

14 **the fear**. 2 Ch 20:29. Ge +35:5. Jb 15:21. Ps 48:5, 6. Is 31:9.
exceeding. 2 Ch 20:25. Jg 14:19. 2 K 7:7, 8, 16. Ps 68:12. Is 33:23. Ro 8:37.

15 **the tents of cattle**. 1 Ch 4:41.
carried away. Nu 31:9, 30-47. 1 S 30:20. 1 Ch 5:21.

2 CHRONICLES 15

1 **the Spirit**. Heb. *ruach*, Ge +41:38. 2 Ch 20:14. 24:20. Nu 24:2. Jg 3:10. 2 S 23:2. 2 P 1:21.
Azariah. 1 Ch +6:36.
Oded. i.e. *causing to stand; reiteration; restoration; surrounding; established, setting up*, **S#5752h**. 2 Ch 15:1, 8. 28:9.

2 **to meet Asa**. Heb. before Asa.
Hear ye me. 2 Ch 13:4. 20:15, 20. Jg 9:7. Ps 49:1, 2. Is 7:13. Mt 13:9. Re 2:7, 11, 17, 29. 3:6, 13, 22.
The Lord. Is +43:2. Ja 4:8.
if. Ge +4:7.
ye seek him. ver. 4, 15. 2 Ch 33:12, 13. Je +29:13.
if ye forsake. Je +1:16. Ro +11:1, 2. Col +1:23. He 12:25. 2 P 1:10.
he will forsake. Is +54:7.

3 **a long**. 1 K 12:28-33. Ho 3:4.
true God. Je 10:10. Jn 17:3. 1 Th 1:9. 1 J 5:20.
a teaching priest. 2 Ch 17:8, 9. Le 10:11. Dt +17:11. 33:10. Ne 8:9. Je 23:22. Ezk 44:21-23. Am 8:11. Mi 3:11. Ml 2:7. Mt 2:4, 5. Ro 12:7. Ep 4:11. 1 T 3:2. 2 T 2:24.
without law. Ro 2:12. 7:8, 9. 1 C 9:21.

4 **in their trouble**. Jg 3:9, 10. 10:10-16. Ps 106:44. Zc +1:3.
found of them. ver. 15. Is 55:6. 65:1, 2. Ro 10:20.

5 **no peace**. Jg 5:6. 1 S 13:6. Ps 121:8.
great vexations. Mt 24:6, 7. Lk 21:25.

6 **nation**. 2 Ch 12:15. 13:17. Mk 13:8. Lk 21:9, 10.
destroyed. Heb. beaten in pieces. Jb 4:20mg. Is 30:14.
God. 2 Ch 33:11. 36:17. Jg 2:14. Ps 106:41. Is 10:6. Am 3:6. Lk 21:22-24.

7 **Be ye strong**. Jsh +1:6.
your work. Ge 15:1. Ru 2:12. Ps 19:11. 58:11. Mt 5:12, 46. 6:1, 4, 6, 18. 10:41, 42. Lk 6:35. Ro 4:4, 5. 1 C 3:8, 14. 9:17, 18. 15:58. Ga 6:9. Col 3:24. He 6:10. 10:35. 2 J 8.

8 **Oded**. ver. 1.
took courage. 2 Ch 19:11mg. Is 44:14mg. Ac 28:15.
abominable idols. Heb. abominations. Le 18:30. Dt 27:15. 1 K 11:5, 7. 2 K 23:13. Is 65:4. Je 16:18. Ezk 8:10. 1 P 4:3. Re 17:4, 5.

the cities. 2 Ch 13:19.
the altar of the Lord. 2 Ch +4:1.

9 **the strangers**. 2 Ch 11:16. 30:1-11, 25.
they fell. 1 K 12:19. 1 Ch 12:19.
they saw. Ge 39:3. 1 S 18:28. 1 K 3:28. Zc 8:21-23. Ac 7:9, 10. 9:31.

10 **the third month**. Est 8:9. That is, Sivan, about the time of pentecost, or feast of weeks; so Targum (Young).

11 **offered**. 2 Ch 14:13-15. Nu 31:28, 29, 50. 1 S 15:15, 21. 1 Ch 26:26, 27.
the same time. Heb. in that day.
seven hundred. 2 Ch 1:6. 7:5.

12 **they entered**. 2 Ch 23:16. 29:10. 34:31, 32. Dt 29:1, 12. 2 K 23:3. Ne 9:38. 10:29. Je 50:5. 2 C 8:5.
covenant. 2 K 11:14. 23:3. Ezr 10:3. Ne 9:36-38. Je 50:4, 5.
seek. ver. +4. 2 Ch 7:14. Je 29:12, 13. Ac 24:14. He 11:6.
with all their heart. 1 Ch 22:19. Ps 42:1. Je +29:13. La 2:19. Ho 7:14.
soul. Heb. *nephesh*, Ge +34:3.

13 **whosoever**. Ex 22:20. Dt 13:5-15. 17:2-5. 1 K 18:40. Jn 1:17. 3:18, 36.
whether small. Ex 12:29. Dt 29:18. 2 K +23:2. Jb 34:19. Re 6:15.

14 **sware**. Ne 5:13. 10:29.
trumpets. Ps 81:1-4.

15 **rejoiced**. 2 Ch 23:16-21. Dt +12:7. Ps 119:111. 2 C 1:12.
sworn. Ps 119:106.
sought him. ver. +2, 4, 12. Is 26:8. 45:19. Ph 1:23.
and he was. ver. +4. Lk 11:9, 10.
the Lord gave. ver. 6. Jsh 23:1. Jb 34:29. 1 T 2:1, 2.

16 **Maachah**. 1 K +2:39.
the mother. *that is*, grandmother. 1 K +15:10.
he removed. 2 Ch 14:3-5. Ex 32:27, 28. Dt 13:6-8. 33:9. Zc 13:3. Mk 3:21, 31-35. 2 C 5:16.
idol. Heb. horror. 1 K 15:13.
grove. 2 K +17:10.
cut down. 2 Ch 14:3-5. 34:7. Le 26:30. Dt +7:5. 1 K 15:14.

17 **the high places**. 2 K +21:3.
nevertheless. Re +2:6.
the heart of Asa. 2 Ch 16:7-12. 1 K 11:4, +34. Jn +17:6.

18 **brought**. 1 K 7:51. 15:14, 15. 1 Ch 26:20-26.

19 A.M. 3063-73. B.C. 941-931.
five and thirtieth. 2 Ch 16:1. 1 K 15:16, 17, 32, 33.

2 CHRONICLES 16

1 A.M. 3074. B.C. 930.
In the sixth and thirtieth year. 1 K 15:16-22 with 16:6, 8.

of the reign. or, kingdom. 2 Ch 15:19. Nu 24:7. 1 S 20:31. 1 K 2:12. 1 Ch 11:10. 14:2. 17:14. 22:10. 28:5.

to the intent. 2 Ch 11:13-17. 15:5, 9. 1 K 12:27.

2 **brought out**. 2 Ch 28:21. 2 K 12:18. 16:8. 18:15.

Damascus. Heb. Darmesek. 1 Ch 18:5mg.

3 **a league**. 2 Ch 18:3. 19:2. Jg 2:2. Is 31:1-3. 2 C 6:16.

break. Ge 20:9, 10. Ex 32:21. Jsh 9:19, 20. 2 S 21:2. Ps 15:4. Ezk 17:18, 19. Ro 1:31, 32. 2 T 3:3.

4 **hearkened**. 1 T 6:10. 2 P 2:15.

his armies. Heb. armies which were his. 1 K 15:20.

Ijon. 1 K +15:20.

Dan. Ge +14:14.

Abel-maim. i.e. *mourning of the waters* or *meadow*, **S#66h**. 1 K 15:20, Abel-beth-maachah.

the store cities. 2 Ch 8:6. 17:12. 1 K 9:19.

5 **that he left off**. ver. 1.

6 **they carried**. 1 K 15:22.

Geba. 1 S +13:3.

Mizpah. Ge +31:49.

7 **Hanani**. 2 Ch 19:2. 20:34. 1 K 16:1.

Because. Ps 146:3-6. Is 31:1. 32:2. Je 17:5, 6. Ep 1:12, 13.

relied on. 2 Ch 13:18. 32:7, 8. 2 K 18:5. 1 Ch 5:20.

the host. ver. 3.

8 **the Ethiopians**. Ge +10:6.

the Lubims. 2 Ch 12:3.

a huge host. Heb. in abundance.

because. ver. 7. Ps 9:9, 10. 37:39, 40.

9 **the eyes**. Ps +11:4. 113:6. Pr 5:21. Je 16:17. 32:19. Zc 4:10. 1 P 5:8.

to show himself, etc. *or*, strongly to hold with *them*, etc.

whose heart. 2 K +20:3. Ps 37:37.

Herein. 1 S 13:13. 2 S 12:7-12. 1 Ch 21:8. Jb 34:18, 19. Je 5:21. Mt 5:22. Lk 12:20. 1 C 15:36. Ga 3:1.

henceforth. 1 K 15:32.

10 **wroth**. 2 Ch 25:16. 26:19. 2 S 12:13. 24:10-14. Ps 141:5. Pr 9:7-9.

put him. He +11:36.

oppressed. Heb. crushed. Jg +10:8mg.

the same time. 2 S 11:4. 12:31.

11 A.M. 3049-3090. B.C. 955-914.

the acts of Asa. 2 Ch 9:29. 12:15. 20:34. 26:22.

in the book. Nu 21:14. Jsh 10:13. 2 S 1:18.

Judah. 2 Ch 25:26. 27:7. 32:32. 33:18. 35:27. 1 K 15:23.

12 A.M. 3088. B.C. 916.

diseased. Mt 7:2. Lk 6:37, 38. Re 3:19.

in his disease. ver. +9. 2 Ch 28:22. 1 Ch 10:14. Je 17:5.

physicians. Jb +13:4.

13 A.M. 3090. B.C. 914.

slept with. 1 K +11:43. 15:24. 2 K 24:6.

14 **his own**. 2 Ch 35:24. Is 22:16. Jn 19:41, 42.

sepulchres. Heb. *qeber*, Ge +23:4.

made. Heb. digged. Ge 50:5.

sweet odors. Ge 50:2. Mk 16:1. Jn 19:39, 40.

the apothecaries' art. Ex 30:25-37. Ec 10:1.

a very great burning. ver. 14. 2 Ch 21:19. 34:5. Ge 11:3mg. Jsh +7:25. Je 34:5.

2 CHRONICLES 17

1 **Jehoshaphat**. 2 S +8:16.

and strengthened. 2 Ch 12:1. 26:8. 32:5. 1 S 23:16. Ezk 7:28. Ep 6:10.

2 **placed forces**. 2 Ch +11:11, 12.

in the cities. 2 Ch 11:5. 15:8.

3 **the Lord**. 2 Ch 15:2, 9. Ge 39:2, 3, 21. Ex 3:12. 4:12. Jsh 1:5, 9. Jg 2:18. 6:12. 2 S 5:10. 1 Ch 22:18. Ps 46:7, 11. Is 8:10. 41:10. Mt 1:23. 18:20. 28:20. 2 T 4:22.

he walked. 2 S 8:15. 1 K 11:6. 15:3, 4. 2 K 14:3. 16:2. 18:3. 22:2. Ps 132:1-5.

first ways. Re 2:4.

his father David. *or*, his father, and of David. 2 Ch 14:2-5, 11. 15:8-13.

sought not. Jg +2:11.

Baalim. 1 K 16:32.

4 **walked**. Lk 1:6. 1 Th 2:12. 4:1.

not after. 1 K 12:28, 30, 33. 13:33, 34. 16:31-33. 2 K 8:18. 17:19. Je 3:7, 8. Ho 4:15.

5 A.M. 3091. B.C. 913.

the Lord. 2 S 7:25, 26. 1 K 9:4, 5. Ps 127:1. 132:12. 1 P 5:10.

brought. Heb. gave.

presents. Jg +3:15.

he had riches. 2 Ch 1:15. 9:27. 18:1. 32:27-29. Ge 13:2. 26:13, 14. Dt 8:13, 14. 1 K 10:27. Jb 42:12. Mt 6:33.

6 **his heart**. Dt 28:47. Jb 22:26.

lifted up. *that is*, was encouraged.

in the ways. 1 K 22:43. Ps 18:21, 22. 119:1. 138:5. Ho 14:9. Ac 13:10.

he took away. 2 Ch 14:3. 15:17. 19:3. 20:33. 31:1. 34:3-7. 1 K 22:43.

high places. 2 K +21:3.

groves. 2 K +17:10.

7 A.M. 3092. B.C. 912.

he sent. Dt 4:5. Ps 34:11. 51:13. Ec 1:12. 12:9, 10. Is 49:23.

Ben-hail. i.e. *son of strength or valor, might or worth*, **S#1134h**.

Obadiah. Ob +1.

Zechariah. Zc +1:1.

Nethaneel. Nu +1:8.

Michaiah. 2 K +22:12.

to teach. 2 Ch 15:3. 30:22. 35:3. Dt 33:10.

Ne 8:7, 8, 13, 14. 9:3. Mt 4:23. Mk 4:2. Lk 4:43, 44. Ac 1:1.

8 Shemaiah. 1 Ch 9:16.
Nethaniah. 1 Ch +25:12.
Zebadiah. 1 Ch +26:2.
Asahel. 1 Ch +2:16.
Shemiramoth. 1 Ch +15:18, 20. 16:5.
Jehonathan. 1 Ch +27:25.
Adonijah. 1 K +1:5.
Tobijah. i.e. *goodness of Jehovah*, **S#2900h**. Zc 6:10, 14.
Tob-adonijah. i.e. *good is my God; distinguished of my Lord Jehovah*, **S#2899h**.
Elishama. Nu +1:10.
Jehoram. 2 K +1:17.
priests. Ezr 7:1-6. Ml 2:7.

9 they taught. 2 Ch +15:3. 35:3. Jg 13:8. 2 K 4:23. Ne 8:7, 8. 1 T 5:17.
the book. 2 Ch +34:14. Dt 6:6-9. 17:18. 31:9, 11-13. Jsh 1:7, 8. Is 8:20. Mt 15:2-9. 28:19, 20. Lk 4:17-19. Jn 5:39, 46. Ac 13:15. 15:21. 28:23. Ro 3:2. 2 C 5:19. Col 3:16. 1 Th 2:4. 1 P 4:11.
throughout. Mt 10:23. 11:1. Ac 8:40.

10 the fear. Ge +35:5.
fell. Heb. was.
so that. 2 Ch 16:9. Ex 34:24. Pr 16:7.

11 brought. ver. +5. 2 K 3:4.

12 A.M. 3092-3115. B.C. 912-889.
waxed great. 2 Ch 18:1. 1 Ch 29:25.
in Judah. 2 Ch 8:2-6. 11:5-12. 14:6, 7. 26:6-9. 27:4. 32:5, 27-29.
castles. *or*, palaces. 2 Ch 27:4. 1 Ch 29:1, 19. Ezr 6:2.
cities of store. 2 Ch 8:4, 6. 16:4. 32:28. Ex 1:11. 1 K 9:19.

13 much business. 2 Ch 26:10-15. 1 Ch 27:25-31.
mighty men of valor. 2 Ch 13:3. Jg +6:12.

14 the numbers. Ge 12:2. 13:16. 15:5.
to the house. Nu 1:2, 18.
Adnah. 1 Ch +12:20.
three hundred. 2 Ch 11:1. 13:3. 14:8. 26:13.
thousand. or, chiefs. Jsh +22:21. Jb 33:23. SS 4:4. Is 60:22.

15 next to him. Heb. at his hand. ver. 16, 18. 2 Ch 23:18mg. 29:27mg. 31:15mg. Jsh 15:46mg. 1 Ch 25:2mg, 6mg. Ne 3:2mg. 13:13mg.
Jehohanan. i.e. *Jehovah is a gracious giver; the Lord gave in grace*, **S#3076h**. ver. 17:15. 2 Ch 23:1. 1 Ch 26:3. Ezr 10:28. Ne 12:13, 42.
thousand. or, chiefs. ver. +14.

16 Amasiah. i.e. *lord of Jah; laden of Jah; lifted up, or borne of the Lord*, **S#6007h**.
Zichri. 1 Ch +9:15.
willingly. Jg 5:2, 9. 1 Ch 29:9, 14, 17. Ps 110:3. 2 C 8:3-5, 12.
thousand. or, chiefs. ver. +14.
mighty men. ver. 13.

17 Eliada. 2 S +5:16.
mighty man of. Jg +6:12.
armed men. 2 Ch 14:8. 2 S 1:21, 22.
thousand. or, chiefs. ver. +14.

18 Jehozabad. 1 Ch +26:4.
thousand. or, chiefs. ver. +14.

19 put in. ver. 2, 12. 2 Ch 11:12, 23.
fenced cities. or, cities of fortress. Nu 13:19. 32:17, 36. Jsh 10:20.

2 CHRONICLES 18

1 A.M. 3107. B.C. 897.
riches. 2 Ch 1:11-15. 17:5, 12. Mt 6:33.
joined affinity. ver. 31. 2 Ch 19:2. 21:6. 22:2, 3. Dt 22:10. 1 K 16:31-33. 21:25. 2 K 8:18, 26, 27. 11:1. 2 C 6:14.

2 after certain years. Heb. at the end of years. 2 Ch 8:1. 1 K 17:7mg. Ne 13:6mg.
he went. 2 Ch 19:2. 1 K 22:2, etc.
Ahab. 1 K 1:9. Is 22:12, 13. Lk 17:27-29.
persuaded. 1 K 22:4, 20-22. Pr 23:7.
Ramoth-gilead. 1 K +4:13.

3 I am as thou. 1 K +22:4. 2 K 3:7. Ps 139:21. Am 3:3. Ep 5:11. 2 J 10, 11.

4 Enquire. 2 Ch 34:26. 1 S 23:2, 4, 9-12. 2 S 2:1. 5:19, 23. 1 K 22:5, 6. Ps 27:4. Je 21:2. Ezk 20:3.

5 prophets. 1 K 18:19. 2 K 3:13. 2 T 4:3.
Shall we go. Je 38:14, etc. 42:2, 3, 20.
Go up. ver. 14, 20, 21. Je 8:10, 11. 23:14, 17. 28:1, etc. Ezk 13:3-16, 22. Mi 2:11. 3:11. Re 19:20.

6 Is there not. 1 K 22:7-9. 2 K 3:11-13.
besides. Heb. yet, or more. ver. 7.

7 one man. 1 K 18:4. 19:10.
I hate him. 1 K 18:17. 20:42, 43. 21:20. Ps 34:21. 55:3. 69:14. Pr 9:8. 29:10. Je 18:18. Am 5:10. Mk 6:18, 19, 27. Lk 6:22. Jn 7:7. 15:18, 19, 24. Ga 4:16.
good. Is 30:10. Je 38:4.
me. ver. 13. 2 K 9:22. Ezk 3:17-19. Ac 20:26, 27.
Micaiah. i.e. *like him; who is like Jah?*, **S#4319h**, so rendered only here. ver. 14. 1 K +22:8, 14.
Imla. i.e. *he fills; he will fulfill*, **S#3229h**. 2 Ch 18:7, 8. 1 K 22:8, 9.
Let not the. Pr 25:12. Mi 2:7.

8 officers. *or*, eunuchs. 2 K +8:6mg.
Fetch quickly. Heb. Hasten. ver. 25, 26. Ge 18:6. 19:22. 45:9. Jg 9:48. 1 S 9:12. 23:27. 2 S 15:14. 1 K 22:9. Est 5:5. 6:10.

9 sat either. 1 K 22:10-12. Is 14:9. Ezk 26:16. Da 7:6. Mt 19:28.
clothed. ver. 29. Mt 6:29. 11:8.
void place. *or*, floor. i.e. threshingfloor. Ge +50:10.
gate. Ge +14:7. 2 S 19:8. 2 K 7:1.
all the prophets. Je 27:14-16.

10 Zedekiah. 1 K +22:11.

Chenaanah. i.e. *a Canaanitess*. 1 Ch +7:10.
horns of iron. Je 27:2. 28:10-14. Zc 1:18-21.
2 T 3:8.
Thus. Je 23:17, 21, 25, 31. 28:2, 3. 29:21. Ezk
13:7. 22:28.
they be consumed. Heb. *thou* consume
them. 1 K 22:11.

11 **all the prophets**. ver. 5, 12, 33, 34. Pr 24:24,
25. Mi 3:5. 2 P 2:1-3. Ju 16. Re 16:13, 14.
19:20.

12 **Behold**. Jb 22:13. Ps 10:11. Is 30:10. Ho 7:3.
Am 7:12, 13. Mi 2:6, 11. 1 C 2:14-16.
assent. Heb. mouth. Dt +21:5mg. 1 K 22:13.

13 **even what my God**. Nu 22:18-20, 35.
23:12, 26. 24:13. 1 K 22:14. Je 23:28. 42:4.
Ezk 2:7. Mi 2:6, 7. Ac 20:27. 1 C 11:23. 2 C
2:17. Ga 1:10. 1 Th 2:4.

14 **Micaiah**. S#4318h, so rendered only here.
Go ye up. 1 K 18:27. 22:15. Ec 11:1. La 4:21.
Am 4:4, 5. Mt 26:45.

15 **shall I adjure**. 1 S 14:24. 1 K 22:16. Mt
26:63. Mk 5:7. Ac 19:13.

16 **he said**. Mt 26:64.
as sheep. ver. 33, 34. Nu +27:17.
master. 2 S 2:7. 5:2. 2 K 10:3.

17 **Did I not tell**. ver. 7. 1 K 22:18. Pr 29:1. Je
43:2, 3.
but evil. *or*, but for evil.

18 **hear the word**. Is 1:10. 28:14. 39:5. Je 2:4.
19:3. 34:4. Am 7:16.
I saw. 1 K 22:19-23. Is 6:1-5. Da 7:9, 10. Ac
7:55, 56.
all the host. Ps +103:21. Zc 1:10.

19 **Who shall entice**. 1 K 22:20. Jb 12:16. Is
6:9, 10. 54:16. Ezk 14:9. 2 Th 2:11, 12. Ja
1:13, 14.
go up. 2 Ch 25:8, 19. Pr 11:5.

20 **there came**. Jb 1:6. 2:1. 2 C 11:3, 13-15.
spirit. Heb. *ruach*, Jg +9:23.

21 **a lying**. ver. 22. Ge 3:4, 5. 1 K +22:21, 22. Jn
8:44. 1 J 4:6. Re 12:9. 13:14. 20:8.
spirit. Heb. *ruach*, Jg +9:23.
Thou shalt. ver. +19. Jg +9:23. Jb 1:12. 2:6.
Ps 109:17.

22 **the Lord hath**. Ex 4:21. 1 S 18:10. 2 S 12:11.
24:1. Jb 12:16. Is 19:14. Ezk 14:3-5, 9. Mt
24:24, 25. 2 C 11:11-13. 2 Th 2:9-11. 1 T 4:1,
2.
spirit. Heb. *ruach*, Jg +9:23.
and the Lord. ver. 7, 17. 2 C 25:18. Is 3:11.
Je 18:11. Mi 2:3. Mt 26:24, 25. Mk 14:20, 21.

23 **Zedekiah**. ver. +10. Mt +27:30.
Which way. Je 29:26, 27. Mt 26:67, 68. Jn
9:40, 41.
Spirit. Is +48:16.

24 **Behold**. Is 26:11. Je 28:16, 17. 29:21, 22, 32.
into an inner chamber. *or*, from chamber to
chamber. Heb. into a chamber in a chamber. 1
S 19:16. 1 K 20:30mg. 22:25mg. 2 K 9:2mg. Is
26:20.

25 **and carry him back**. ver. 8. Je 37:15-21.
38:6, 7. Ac 24:25-27.

26 **Put**. ver. +15. Mt 5:12. He +11:36. Re 11:10.
this fellow. 1 S 25:21. Mt 12:24. Lk 23:2. Ac
22:22.
prison. 1 K 22:27. 2 K 17:4. 25:27, 29. Is
42:7, 22. Je 37:15, 18. 52:33.
bread of affliction. Ps 80:5. 102:9. Is 30:20.
until I return. Dt 29:19. Ps 10:5. Pr 14:16. 1
Th 5:2, 3.

27 **If**. Nu 16:29. Am 9:10. Ac 13:10, 11.
Hearken. Mt 13:9. 15:10. Mk 7:14. Lk 20:45,
46.

28 **the king**. 1 K 22:29-33.

29 **I will disguise**. Ge +27:16. Jb 24:15. 30:18.
Je 23:24.
put thou on thy robes. Ps 12:2. Pr 26:25.
the king. 2 Ch 35:22, 23.

30 **Fight ye**. 1 K 20:33, 34, 42.
small or great. 2 Ch +15:13. Ge 19:11. Dt
1:17.

31 **but**. 2 Ch 20:37.
Jehoshaphat. 2 Ch 13:14. 14:11. Ex 14:10.
Ps 116:1, 2. 2 C 1:9, 10.
the Lord. 2 Ch 26:7. Ps 34:7. 46:1, 11. 94:17.
118:13.
God moved them. 1 Ch 5:26. Ezr 1:1. 6:22.
7:27. Ne 1:11. Pr 16:1, 7, 9. 21:1. Is 64:8. Zc
12:1. Ac 16:14.

32 **from pursuing him**. Heb. from after him. 1
K 22:33.

33 **a certain man**. 1 K +22:34.
at a venture. Heb. in his simplicity. 2 S
15:11. 1 K 9:4. 22:34.
between the, etc. Heb. between the joints
and between the breastplate. 1 K 22:34, 35. Is
41:7.
harness. or, coat of mail. 2 Ch 26:14. 1 S
17:5. 1 K 22:34. Ne 4:16. Is 59:17.
wounded. Heb. made sick. 2 Ch 35:23mg. 1
K 22:34mg. 2 K 8:25mg.

34 **he died**. ver. 16, 19, 27. Nu +32:23. Pr 13:21.
28:17.

2 CHRONICLES 19

1 A.M. 3108. B.C. 896.
in peace. 2 Ch 18:31, 32.

2 **And Jehu**. 2 Ch 20:34. 1 K 16:1, 7, 12.
Hanani. 2 Ch 16:7.
the seer. 1 S +9:9.
help the ungodly. 2 Ch 18:3, 28. 2 S 12:14.
1 K 21:25. Jb 8:20. Ps 15:4. 139:21, 22. Pr
1:10-19. Mk +1:25. Ro 1:32. 16:17. 2 C 6:14-
17. Ep 5:11. 2 J 10, 11. Ju 3.
love them that. Mt 10:11-14. 1 C 5:9-11.
10:20. Ep 5:11. 2 Th 3:6, 14, 15. 2 T 3:5. 2 J
9-11.
hate the Lord. 2 Ch 18:7. Ex 20:5. Dt 5:9.
7:10. 32:41. 33:11. Ps 21:8. 68:1. 71:15. Pr

13:20. Jn 15:18, 23. Ro 1:30. 8:7. 1 C 15:33. Ja 4:4.

is wrath. 2 Ch +24:18. 32:25. Ps 90:7, 8. Ro 1:18. 1 C 11:31, 32.

3 **Nevertheless**. Re +2:6.
good things. 2 Ch 12:12mg, 14. 17:3-6. 1 K 14:13. Ro 7:18.
taken away. 2 Ch +17:6.
groves. 2 K +17:10.
prepared. 2 Ch +12:14.

4 **went out again**. Heb. returned and went out. 1 S 7:15-17.
Beer-sheba. Ge +21:31.
mount Ephraim. Jsh 17:15.
brought them back. 2 Ch 15:8-13. 17:7-9. 29:10, 11. 1 S 7:3, 4. Ml 4:6. Lk 1:17.

5 **he set**. ver. 8. Ex +21:6. Ro 13:1-5. 1 P 2:13, 14.
fenced cities. 2 Ch 17:2.

6 **Take**. Jsh 22:5. 1 Ch 28:10. Lk 12:15. 21:8. Ac 5:35. 22:26.
ye judge. Dt 1:17. Ps 82:1-6. Ec 5:8.
not for. Ex 18:17, 23. Ep 6:6, 7. Col 3:23.
judgment. Heb. matter of judgment. Ec 5:8.

7 **let the**. Ge 42:18. Ex +18:21, 22, 25, 26. Ne 5:15. Is 1:23-26.
no iniquity. Ge +18:25. Dt 32:4. Ps 92:15. Zp 3:5. Ml 2:6. Ro 3:5, 6. 9:14.
respect of persons. Ro +2:11.
taking of gifts. Ex 23:8. Dt 16:18, 19. Is 1:23. 33:15. Mi 7:3.

8 **Levites**. 2 Ch 17:8.
the judgment. ver. +5. Dt 21:5. 25:1. Ps 19:9. Is 58:2. Je 5:4, 5. +8:7.

9 **in the fear**. ver. +7. Dt 1:16, 17. 2 S 23:3. Is 11:3-5. 32:1.
faithfully. 2 Ch 34:12. Ex 17:12. Nu 12:7. Dt 32:4. Pr 25:13. Lk 16:10. 3 J 5.
perfect heart. 2 K +20:3.

10 **between blood**. Dt 17:8-13.
law and commandment. Ex 24:12.
statutes and judgments. Ex 15:25. Dt +4:1.
warn them. Ezk 3:18-21. 33:6. Ac 20:20, 31. 1 Th 5:14.
wrath come. Nu 16:46. Jsh 22:18-20.

11 **Amariah**. 1 Ch 6:11.
all matters. ver. 8. 1 Ch 26:30. Ml 2:7.
officers. Ex +5:6, 10, 14, 15, 19.
Deal courageously. Heb. Take courage and do. Jsh +1:6, +9.
the Lord. ver. 6. 2 Ch 15:2. Ps 18:25, 26. Jn 14:23, 24. Ro 2:4-13. Ph 4:8, 9.
the good. Ps 37:23. 112:5. Pr 2:20. Ec 2:26. Lk 23:50. Ac 11:24.

2 CHRONICLES 20

1 **after this also**. 2 Ch 19:5, 11. 32:1.
the children of Moab. Ezk +25:8.
Ammonites. 1 S +11:11.

came against. 2 Ch 19:2. Is 7:1. 8:9, 10. Je 10:24. Re 3:19.

2 **beyond the sea**. Ge 14:3. Nu 34:12. Jsh 3:16.
Hazazon-tamar. i.e. *pruning of the palm; division of the palm*, **S#2688h**. ver. 2. Ge 14:7.
En-gedi. Jsh +15:62.

3 **feared**. Ge 28:20-22. 32:7-11, 24-28. Ex 14:10. Ne 2:2-4. Ps 27:12, 13. 31:22. +34:4. 56:1-4. 69:14-18. 141:8, 9. Pr 30:7-9. Is 37:3-6. Je 26:19. Jon 1:16. 3:5. Mt +10:28.
himself. Heb. his face.
seek the Lord. 2 Ch +11:16. 19:3. Ps +9:10. +34:4. Is 55:6.
proclaimed. Mt +6:16.

4 **gathered**. Ps 42:4. Is 2:3. Ac 4:31, 32.
ask help of the Lord. Ps 34:5, 6. 50:15. 60:10-12.
the cities. 2 Ch 19:5. Ps 69:35.

5 **Jehoshaphat**. 2 Ch +6:12, 13. 34:31. 1 K 8:22. 2 K 19:14-19.
in the house. 2 K 19:14, 15. Ac 3:1. 22:17.

6 **O Lord**. Ge +17:7.
God in heaven. Dt 4:39. Jsh 2:11. 1 K 8:23. Ps 115:3. Is 57:15, 16. 66:1. Mt +6:9.
rulest not. 1 Ch 29:11, 12. Jb 25:2. Ps 47:2, 8. Je 27:5-8. Da 4:17, 25, 32-35. Mt 28:18.
in thine hand. 1 Ch 29:11, 12. Ps 62:11. Mt 6:13.
none is able. Ac 11:17.

7 **our God**. 2 Ch 14:11. Ge 15:7, 18. +17:7. Ex 6:7. 19:5-7. 20:2. 1 Ch 17:21-24.
who. Heb. thou.
drive out. Ex +33:2. Ps 44:2.
thy people. Dt +32:43.
gavest. Ge +13:15. Jsh 24:3, 13. 1 K +4:21.
Abraham. Ac +7:5. Ro +4:13.
thy friend. Ge 18:19. Is 41:8. Jn 11:11. 15:15. Ja 2:23.
for ever. Heb. *olam*, Ex +12:24. Is +41:9. +54:7-10. +55:3. Je 32:40, 41. 33:20, 21, 25, 26. Mi 7:20. Ml 3:6.

8 **built thee**. 2 Ch +2:4. 6:10.

9 **If, when evil**. Ex 32:12. Jsh 7:6, 9. 1 K 8:33, +37.
we stand. 1 Ch +17:16. Lk +18:13.
and in thy presence. Mt 18:20.
thy name. 2 Ch +6:20. Ex 20:24. 23:21.

10 **whom thou**. Nu 20:17-21. Dt 2:4, 5, 9, 19. Jg 11:15-18.

11 **how they reward us**. Ge 44:4. Ex 32:12. Jsh 7:6, 9. Ps 7:4. 35:12. Pr 17:13. Je 18:20.
to cast us. Jg 11:23, 24. Ps 83:3-12.
hast given. Dt 6:23.

12 **wilt**. Dt 32:36. Jg 11:27. 1 S 3:13. Ps 7:6, 8. 9:19. 43:1. 83:11, 12. Is 2:4. 72:4. Jl 3:12. Re 19:11.
judge. Ge +15:14.
we have. 2 Ch +14:11. 1 S 14:6. 2 C 1:8, 9.
neither. 2 K 6:15.

our eyes. Ps 25:15. 121:1, 2. 123:1, 2. 141:8. Jon 2:4.

13 **all Judah**. Dt 29:10, 11. Ezr 10:1. Jon 3:5. Ac 21:5.

stood. Lk +18:13.

with their little ones. Dt +29:11. 1 C 7:14.

14 **Then upon**. Is 58:9. 65:24. Da 9:20, 21. Ac 10:4, 31.

came the Spirit. Heb. *ruach*, Ge +41:38. 2 Ch 15:1. 24:20. Nu 11:25, 26. 24:2.

15 **Be not afraid**. 2 Ch 32:7, 8. Ex 14:13, 14. Dt 1:29, 30. 20:1, 4. 31:6, 8. Jsh 11:6. Ne 4:14. Ps 27:1, 2. Is 41:10-16. 43:1, 2.

the battle. 2 Ch 32:8. 1 S 17:47. Ps 35:1.

16 **cliff**. Heb. ascent. 1 S 9:11.

Ziz. i.e. *blossom, fringe; wing; branch,* **S#6732h**.

brook. *or,* valley. Ge 26:17, 19. 32:23. Nu +13:23mg.

the wilderness. ver. 20.

Jeruel. i.e. *foundation of God; founded of God; fear ye God; taught of God,* **S#3385h**.

17 **not need**. ver. 22, 23. Ex 14:13, 14, 25.

stand ye still. Ps 46:10, 11. Is 30:7, 15. La 3:26.

for the Lord. Is +43:2. Am 5:14.

18 **bowed his head**. Ge +24:26.

fell before. Jb 1:20.

19 **Levites**. 1 Ch 15:16-22. 16:5, 42. 23:5. 25:1-7.

Korhites. Ps ch. 44, 49, titles.

stood. Lk +18:13.

a loud. 2 Ch 5:13. Ezr 3:12, 13. Ne 12:42, 43. Ps 81:1. 95:1, 2.

20 **rose early**. Ge +21:14.

Tekoa. 1 Ch +2:24.

Hear me. ver. +15.

Believe in the Lord. Ps 106:12. Is 7:9mg. 26:3. +50:10. Jn 11:40. 14:1. Ro 8:31. He 6:12. 11:6. or, remain stedfast in Jehovah. Ge 15:6. 45:26.

be established. Col +1:23. or, become sted-fast. 2 Ch 1:9. 6:17. Ge 42:20. 2 S 7:16. 1 K 8:26. 1 Ch 17:23, 24. 1 C +15:58. 2 P 1:3-10.

believe his prophets. Ex 14:31. Lk +16:31. 24:25. Jn 5:46, 47. 13:20. Ac 10:43. 13:27, 40. 15:15. 24:14. 26:22, 27. 28:23. Ro 1:2.

prosper. Ps +1:3.

21 **consulted**. 1 Ch 13:1, 2. Pr 11:14.

appointed. 2 Ch 29:25-30. 30:21. Ezr 3:10, 11. Ne 12:27.

that should praise. Heb. praisers of.

the beauty. 1 Ch 16:29. Ps 29:2. 50:2. 90:17. 96:9.

his mercy. Ex +34:6.

for ever. Heb. *olam*, Ex +12:24.

22 **when they**. Heb. in the time that they, etc.

to sing and to. Heb. in singing and.

the Lord set ambushments. Jg +7:22. 2 K 6:17. Ps 35:5, 6.

were smitten. *or,* smote one another.

23 **mount Seir**. Ge +14:6.

to destroy another. Heb. for the destruction. Jg +7:22.

24 **they were dead**. Ex 14:30. 1 Ch 5:22. Ps 110:6. Is 37:36. Je 33:5.

none escaped. Heb. *there was* not an escaping. 2 Ch 12:7. Jg 21:17. Ezr 9:8, 14.

25 **they found**. Ex 12:35, 36. 1 S 30:19, 20. 2 K 7:9-16. Ps 68:12. Ro 8:37.

precious jewels. Ex 3:22. Nu 31:51. Jg 8:24-26. Pr 3:15.

it was so much. Ezk 39:8, 9.

26 **Berachah**. *that is,* Blessing.

blessed. Ex 15:1-19. 2 S 22:1. Ps 103:1, 2. 107:21, 22. Lk 1:68. Re 19:1-6.

the name. Ge 28:19. 32:30. Ex 17:15. 1 S 7:12. Is 62:4. Ac 1:19.

unto this day. 2 Ch 5:9. 10:19. Jsh +4:9. 1 Ch +4:43.

27 **forefront**. Heb. head. 2 S 6:14, 15. Mi 2:13. He 6:20.

the Lord. 1 S 2:1. Ne 12:43. Ps 20:5. 30:1. Is 35:10. 51:11. Re 18:20.

28 **with**. 2 S 6:5. 1 Ch 13:8. 16:42. 23:5. 25:6. Ps 57:8. 92:3. 149:3. 150:3-5. Re 14:2, 3.

psalteries. 1 S +10:5.

harps. 1 Ch +13:8.

trumpets. 2 Ch +5:12.

29 **the fear**. 2 Ch 17:10. Ge 35:5. Ex 23:27. Jsh 5:1. 2 K 7:6.

they had heard. Ex 15:14-16. Jsh 2:9-11. 9:9-11.

30 **was quiet**. Jb 34:29. 1 T +2:1, 2.

his God. 2 Ch 14:6, 7. 15:15. Jsh 23:1. 2 S 7:1. Jb 34:29. Pr 16:7. Jn 14:27.

31 A.M. 3090-3115. B.C. 914-889.

Jehoshaphat reigned. 1 K 22:41-44.

32 **he walked**. 2 Ch +17:3-6.

the way. 2 Ch +14:2-4, 11-13. 1 K 15:11.

departed not. 2 Ch 16:7-12. Ps 18:21. 36:3.

33 **the high places**. 2 Ch 19:3. 2 K +21:3.

had not. 2 Ch +12:14. Dt 29:4.

34 **the rest**. 2 Ch +12:15. 13:22. 16:11.

book. Heb. words.

Jehu the son of Hanani. 2 Ch 19:2. 1 K 16:1, 7.

is mentioned. Heb. was made to ascend. 2 Ch 3:14. 1 Ch 27:24.

35 A.M. 3108. B.C. 896.

did Jehoshaphat join. 1 K 22:48, 49.

who did very wickedly. 2 K 1:2-16.

36 **And he joined**. 2 Ch 18:1. Lk 15:15.

make ships. 1 K 22:48, 49.

Tarshish. 1 K +10:22, Tharshish.

Ezion-gaber. Nu +33:35.

37 **Eliezer**. Ge +15:2.

Dodavah. i.e. *beloved of Jehovah; love of the Lord,* **S#1735h**.

Mareshah. Jsh +15:44.

Because. 2 Ch 18:31. +19:2. Jsh 7:11, 12. Pr 13:20.
the Lord. 2 Ch 16:9. Pr 9:6. 13:20. He 12:6. Re 3:19.
And the ships. 1 K 22:48. 1 Ch 29:14.
broken. Ps 48:7.
to Tarshish. 2 Ch 9:21.

2 CHRONICLES 21

1 A.M. 3115. B.C. 889.
Jehoshaphat. 2 S +8:16.
was buried. ver. +20. 2 Ch 9:31. 12:16.
Jehoram. 2 K +1:17.
reigned. "Alone." 1 K 22:50.
2 **Israel**. ver. 4. 2 Ch 12:6. 23:2. 24:5, 16. 28:19, 23, 27. 33:18. 35:18.
3 **gave them**. 2 Ch 11:23. Ge 25:6. Dt 21:15-17.
Jehoram. "Jehoram made partner of the kingdom with his father, 1 K 8:16."
firstborn. 1 Ch +26:10.
4 **slew all**. ver. 17. 2 Ch 22:8, 10. Ge 4:8. Jg 9:5, 56, 57. 1 J 3:12.
5 A.M. 3112-3119. B.C. 892-885.
Jehoram. "In consort, 2 K 8:16, 17."
6 **in the way**. 1 K 16:25-33.
he had. 2 Ch 18:1. 22:2. 2 K 8:18. Ne 13:25, 26.
7 **Howbeit**. 2 Ch 22:11. Is 7:6, 7.
because. 2 S 23:5. Ps 89:28-34, 39. Je 33:20-26.
as he promised. 2 S 7:12-17. 1 K 11:13, 36. 2 K 8:19. Ps 132:11, 17, 18, etc. Lk 1:69, 79.
light. Heb. lamp, or candle. 1 K 11:36mg. 15:4mg. 2 K 8:19mg.
8 A.M. 3115. B.C. 889.
the Edomites. Ge 27:40. 2 K 8:20-22.
dominion. Heb. hand. 2 K 8:20.
and made. 1 K 22:47. 2 K 3:9.
9 **with his**. 2 K 8:21.
10 **unto this day**. 2 Ch 5:9. 10:19. 20:26.
Libnah. Nu +33:20.
because. 2 Ch 13:10. 15:2. Dt 32:21. 1 K 11:31-33. Je 2:13.
11 **Moreover**. Dt 12:2-4. 2 K +21:3.
caused. 1 K 14:9, 16. 2 K 21:11. Hab 2:15. Re 2:20.
fornication. ver. 13.
compelled. 2 Ch 33:9. 2 K 17:21. Da 3:5, 6, 15. Re 13:15-17. 17:5, 6.
12 A.M. 3116. B.C. 888.
there came. 2 K 2:11, 12.
a writing. "Which was writ before his assumption, 2 K 2:1." Je 36:2, 23, 28-32. Ezk 2:9, 10. Da 5:5, 25-29.
Elijah the prophet. 2 K 2:11.
in the ways of Jehoshaphat. 2 Ch 17:3, 4. 1 K 22:43.
nor in the ways of Asa. 2 Ch 14:2-5. 1 K 15:11.

13 **in the way**. 1 K 16:25, 30-33.
a whoring. ver. 11. Ex +34:15.
of Ahab. 1 K 16:33.
hast slain. ver. 4. Ge 4:10-12. 42:21, 22. Jg 9:56, 57. 1 K 2:31-33. Is 26:21. Hab 2:12. 1 J 3:12.
better than. 1 K 2:32.
14 **plague**. Heb. stroke. Le 26:21.
thy people. Ho 5:11. Mi 6:16.
thy children. Ex 20:5.
15 **by disease**. ver. 18, 19. Nu 5:27. Dt 28:61. Ac 12:23.
thy bowels fall. Ps 109:18. Ac 1:18.
the sickness. ver. 18. Dt 28:27, 35, 59, 67.
16 A.M. 3117. B.C. 887.
the Lord stirred. 2 Ch 33:11. 1 S 26:19. 2 S 24:1. 1 K 11:11, 14, 23. Ezr 1:1, 5. Is 10:5, 6. 45:5-7. Am 3:6.
spirit. Heb. ruach, Ge +41:8; Ge +26:35.
Philistines. 2 Ch 17:11.
17 **carried away**. Heb. carried captive. Jb 5:3, 4.
his sons also. 2 Ch 22:1. 24:7.
Jehoahaz. 2 Ch 22:1, Ahaziah. 22:6, Azariah.
youngest. lit. the small one.
18 A.M. 3117-3119. B.C. 887-885.
And after all. "His son Ahaziah Prorex, 2 K 9:29, soon after."
an incurable disease. ver. +15. 2 Ch +36:16mg. 2 K 9:29. Ac 12:23.
19 **made no**. 2 Ch 16:14. Je 34:5.
20 A.M. 3119. B.C. 885.
Thirty and two. ver. 5.
without being desired. Heb. without desire. 2 Ch 23:21. 1 S 9:20. Pr 10:7. Je 22:18, 28. Hg 2:7.
but not. 2 Ch 24:25. 28:27. Je 22:18.
sepulchres. Heb. qeber, Ge +23:4.

2 CHRONICLES 22

1 **the inhabitants**. 2 Ch 23:3. 26:1. 33:25. 36:1.
Ahaziah. ver. 6, Azariah. 2 Ch 21:17, Jehoahaz. 1 K +22:40.
slain. 2 Ch 21:16, 17.
2 A.M. 3119, 3120. B.C. 885, 884.
Forty and two. 2 K 8:26.
Athaliah. 2 Ch 21:6. 1 K 16:28.
3 **his mother**. Ge 6:4, 5. Dt 7:3, 4. 13:6-10. Jg 17:4, 5. Ne 13:23-27. Ml 2:15. Mt 14:8-11.
his counseller. Ge 27:12, 13. Mt 10:37. Ac 4:19.
4 **they were his**. 2 Ch 24:17, 18. Pr 1:10. 12:5. 13:20. 19:27.
5 **He walked**. Ps 1:1. Mi 6:16.
went with. 2 K 8:28, 29, etc.
Ramoth-gilead. 1 K +4:13. Da 5:22.
6 **And he returned**. 2 K 9:15.
which were given him. Heb. wherewith they wounded him.

Azariah. ver. 1, 7, Ahaziah. 2 Ch 21:17, Jehoahaz. 1 Ch +6:36.

to see Jehoram. 2 K 8:29. 10:13, 14.

7 **destruction**. Heb. treading down. Ml 4:3.

was of God. 2 Ch 10:15. Dt 32:35. Jg 14:4. 1 K 12:15. 22:20. Ps 9:16. Is 46:10. Ho 14:9.

he went out. 2 K 9:21.

the Lord had. 1 K 19:16. 2 K 9:1-7.

8 **when Jehu**. 2 K 10:10-14.

9 **he sought Ahaziah**. "2 K 9:27, at Megiddo, in the kingdom of Samaria."

in Samaria. 1 K 13:32.

Because. 1 K 14:13. 2 K 9:28, 34.

the son of Jehoshaphat. 2 Ch 17:3, 4. 21:20.

the house. ver. 1, 8. 2 Ch 21:4, 17.

10 **Athaliah**. ver. 2-4. 2 K 11:1.

11 **Jehoshabeath**. i.e. *Jehovah's oath*. **S#3090h**. 2 K 11:2, Jehosheba.

bedchamber. Ezk 40:45, 46.

Jehoiada. 2 Ch 23:1.

she slew him not. 2 Ch 21:7. 2 S 7:13. 1 K 15:4. Ps 33:10. 76:10. Pr 21:30. Is 65:8. Ac 4:28.

12 A.M. 3120-3126. B.C. 884-878.

hid in the house. Ps 27:5.

Athaliah. Ps 12:8. 73:14, 18, 19. Je 12:1. Hab 1:12.

2 CHRONICLES 23

1 **seventh year**. 2 K 11:4, etc.

Elishaphat. i.e. *God of judgment; God of defence*, **S#478h**.

covenant with him. 2 Ch 15:12. 1 S 18:3. Ne 9:38.

2 **went about**. Ps 112:5. Mt 10:16. Ep 5:15.

the chief of. 2 Ch 11:13-17. 1 Ch 15:12. 24:6.

3 **made a covenant**. ver. 16. 2 S 5:3. 2 K 11:17. 1 Ch 11:3.

as the Lord. 2 Ch 6:16. 7:18. 21:7. 2 S 7:12, 16. 1 K 2:4. 9:5. 1 Ch 9:9-27. Ps 89:29, 36.

4 **entering**. 1 Ch 23:3-6. 24:3-6. Lk 1:8, 9.

porters. 1 Ch 26:13-16.

doors. Heb. thresholds. 1 K +14:17. Is 6:4.

5 **the king's house**. 2 K 11:5, 6. Ezk 44:2, 3. 46:2, 3.

the gate. Ac 3:2.

of the foundation. 2 K 11:6.

6 **they that minister**. 2 K 11:6, 7. 1 Ch 23:28-32.

7 **the Levites**. 2 K 11:8, 9.

whosoever. Ex 19:12, 13. 21:14. Nu 3:10, 38.

8 **the Levites**. 2 K 11:9.

the courses. 1 Ch ch. 24-26.

9 **spears**. 1 S 21:9. 2 S 8:7.

10 **side of the temple**. Heb. shoulder of the house. Ex 27:14, 15. 38:14, 15. 1 K 6:8mg. 2 K 11:11. Ezk 25:9mg.

along by. 2 Ch 6:12. Ex 40:6.

11 **they brought**. 2 Ch 22:11. 2 K 11:12.

put upon. 2 S 1:10. Ps 21:3. 89:39. 132:18. He 2:9. Ja 1:12. 2:5. Re 4:4, 10. 5:10. 19:12.

the testimony. Ex 25:16. 31:18. Dt 17:18-20. Ps 2:10-12. 78:5. Is 8:16, 20. 49:23.

anointed him. 1 S 10:1. 2 S 5:3. 1 K 1:39. Ps 89:20. Ac 4:26, 27.

God save the king. Heb. Let the king live. 1 S +10:24.

12 **Now when**. 2 K 11:13-16.

she came. 2 K 9:32-37.

13 **she looked**. Ps 14:5.

the king. 2 Ch 34:31. 2 K 23:3.

his pillar. 2 K 11:14.

and the princes. Nu 10:1-10. 1 Ch 15:24.

all the people. 1 K 1:39, 40. 1 Ch 12:40. Pr 11:10. 29:2.

sounded. Jg 7:8, 18-22. 2 K 9:13.

the singers. 1 Ch 15:16-22, 27. 25:1-8.

instruments of music. 1 Ch 16:42.

taught to sing. 1 Ch 6:32. 15:22. 25:7. Ep 5:19. Col 3:16.

Then Athaliah. Ec 9:12.

Treason. Heb. Conspiracy. 1 K 16:20. 18:17, 18. 2 K 9:23. 11:14. Ro 2:1, 2.

14 **captains**. 2 K 11:15.

Have her forth. Ex 21:14.

whoso followeth her. 2 K 10:25. 11:8, 15.

Slay her not in. Ezk 9:7.

15 **the horse gate**. Ne 3:28. Je 31:40.

they slew her there. 2 Ch 22:10. Jg 1:7. Ps 5:6. 55:23. Mt 7:2. Ja 2:13. Re 16:5-7.

16 **made a covenant**. 2 Ch 15:12, 14. 29:10. 34:31, 32. Dt 5:2, 3. 29:1-15. 2 K 11:17. Ezr 10:3. Ne 5:12, 13. 9:38. 10:29, etc.

that they should. Dt 26:17-19. Jsh 24:21-25. Is 44:5.

17 **the house of Baal**. 2 Ch 34:4, 7. 2 K 10:25-28. 11:18. 18:4.

brake his altars. Dt 12:3. Is 2:18. Zc 13:2, 3.

slew Mattan. Dt 13:5, 9. 1 K 18:40. 2 K 11:18, 19.

18 **whom David**. 1 Ch ch. 23, 24.

as it is written. Nu ch. 28.

by David. Heb. by the hands of David. 2 Ch 29:25mg. 34:14mg. 1 K +16:12mg. 1 Ch 25:2mg, etc.

19 **porters**. 1 Ch 9:23, 24. ch. 26.

that none. Is 52:1. Re 21:27.

unclean. 2 C 6:16-18. Zc 14:21.

20 **the captains**. 2 K 11:9, 10, 19.

21 **all the people**. 2 K 11:20. Ps 58:10, 11. Pr 11:10. Re 18:20. 19:1-4.

2 CHRONICLES 24

1 A.M. 3126-3165. B.C. 878-839.

Joash. Jg +6:11.

seven years old. 2 K 11:2, 21.

Zibiah. 2 K 12:1.
Beer-sheba. Ge +21:31.

2 A.M. 3126-3162. B.C. 878-842.
Joash. 2 Ch 25:2. 26:4, 5. 2 K 12:2. Ps 78:36, 37. 106:12, 13. Mk 4:16, 17.
all the days of Jehoiada. ver. 17-22. Is 29:13.

3 **took for him**. ver. 15. Ge 21:21. 24:4.
two wives. Ge +4:19.

4 A.M. 3148. B.C. 856.
repair. Heb. renew. ver. 5-7, 12. Is 61:4.

5 **gather of all Israel**. 2 Ch 29:3. 34:8, 9. 2 K 12:4, 5. 1 C 16:1, 2. 2 C 8:19, 20, 23, 24. 9:7.
Howbeit. 2 K 12:6, 7.

6 **Why hast thou**. 2 S 24:3.
the collection. Ex 30:12-16.
tabernacle. Ex +38:21.

7 **the sons of Athaliah**. 2 Ch 21:17. 22:1.
that wicked. 2 Ch 28:22-24. Est 7:6. Pr 10:7. 2 Th 2:8. Re 2:20.
the dedicated. 2 K 12:4.
did they bestow. Dt 32:15-17. Ezk 16:17-21. Da 5:2-4, 23. Ho 2:8, 9, 13.

8 **at the king's**. 2 K 12:8, 9. Mk 12:41.

9 **proclamation**. Heb. voice. Ezr 1:1.
collection. ver. 6. Mt 17:24-27.

10 **rejoiced**. 1 Ch 29:9. Is 64:5. Ac 2:45-47. 2 C 8:2. 9:7.

11 **at what time**. 2 K 12:10-12.
the king's scribe. 2 K 12:10.
Thus they did. 1 C 16:2.

12 **gave it to such**. 2 Ch 34:9-11.
masons. 1 K 5:15.

13 **the work was perfected by them**. Heb. the healing went up upon the work by their hand. Ne 4:7. Je +8:22.
in his state. Ex +5:8. 1 Ch 22:5. Ezk 45:11. Hg 2:3. Mk 13:1, 2.

14 **vessels of the house**. 2 K 12:13, 14.
vessels to minister. 1 K 7:50.
to offer withal. or, pestils. Le 16:12. Pr 27:22.
And they offered. Ex 29:38-42. Nu 28:2, etc.
all the days. ver. 2.

15 A.M. 3162. B.C. 842.
and was full of days. Ge 15:15. +25:8. 1 Ch 23:1. Jb 5:26. Ps 91:16mg.
an hundred and thirty. Ge 47:9. Ps 90:10.

16 **in the city**. 1 S 2:30. 1 K 2:10. Ac 2:29.
because. 2 Ch ch. 23. 31:20. Ne 13:14. He 6:10.

17 A.M. 3162-3165. B.C. 842-839.
Now after. Dt 31:27. Ac 20:29, 30. 2 P 1:15.
the princes of Judah. 2 Ch 10:8-10. 22:3, 4. Pr 7:21-23. 20:19. 26:8, 28. 29:5. Da 11:32.
Then the king. Pr 29:12.

18 **And they left**. ver. 4. 2 Ch 21:13. 33:3-7. 1 K 11:4, 5. 14:9, 23.
served groves. 2 K +17:10.

wrath. 2 Ch 19:2. 28:13. 29:8. 30:8. 32:25. 36:14-16. Jsh 22:20. Jg 5:8. 2 S 24:1. Ho 5:10, 11, 14. Zp 1:4-6. Ep 5:6.

19 **Yet he sent**. 2 Ch 36:15, 16. Je 7:25, 26. 25:3-5. 26:5. 35:15. 44:4, 5. Zc 7:12. Mt 21:34-46. 23:34. Mk 12:2-5. Lk 11:47-51. 16:31. 20:9-15.
testified. Je +42:19.
but they would. Ps 95:7, 8. Is 28:23. 42:23. 51:4. 55:3. Mt 13:9, 15, 16.

20 **And the Spirit**. Heb. ruach, Ge +41:38. 2 Ch 15:1. 20:14.
came upon. Heb. clothed. Jg 6:34. 1 Ch 12:18.
the son. 2 Ch 23:11.
transgress. Nu 14:41. 1 S 13:13, 14. 2 S 12:9, 10. Zc 7:11-14.
cannot prosper. 2 Ch 13:12. Ge 24:21. Nu 14:41. Dt 28:29. Ps +1:3. Pr 28:13. Is 54:17. Je 2:37. 22:30. 32:5. Ezk 17:9. Da 11:27.
because. Dt 29:25, 26. Je +1:16. 4:18. 5:25.
forsaken you. Is +54:7.

21 **conspired**. Je 11:19. 18:18. 38:4-6.
stoned him. Le +24:14.

22 **remembered not**. Ps 109:4. Lk 17:15-18. Jn 10:32.
but slew his son. Pr 17:13.
he said. Lk 23:34. Ac 7:60. 2 T 4:16.
The Lord. Je +10:25. 26:14, 15. Re 18:20. 19:2.
and require it. Je 51:56. Lk +11:50, 51.

23 A.M. 3165. B.C. 839.
at the end, etc. Heb. in the revolution of the year. 2 Ch 36:10mg. Ex 34:22mg. 1 S +1:20mg. 2 S 11:1mg. 1 K 20:22, 26. 1 Ch 20:1mg. Ps 19:6.
the host. Dt 32:35. 2 K 12:17, 18.
princes. ver. 17, 18. Ps 2:10, 11. 58:10, 11. 82:6, 7.
Damascus. Heb. Darmesek. 1 Ch 18:5mg.

24 **came**. Le 26:8, 37. Dt 32:30. Is 30:17. Je 37:10.
delivered. 2 Ch 16:8, 9. 20:11, 12. Le 26:25. Dt 28:25, 48.
So. 2 Ch 22:8. Is 10:5, 6. 13:5. Hab 1:12.

25 **great diseases**. 2 Ch 21:16, 18, 19. 22:6.
his own servants. 2 K 12:20. 14:19, 20.
for the blood. ver. 21, 22. Ps 10:14. Re 16:6.
the sons of Jehoiada. Ge +46:7.
not. ver. 16. 2 Ch 21:20. 28:27.
sepulchres. Heb. qeber, Ge +23:4.

26 **Zabad**. or, Jozachar. 2 K 12:21.
Shimrith. i.e. female guard; a guardian, S#8116h. or, Shomer. 2 K 12:21.

27 **burdens**. 2 K 12:18.
repairing. Heb. founding. ver. 13. 2 Ch 23:5.
story. or, commentary. 2 Ch 9:29. 13:22mg. 16:11. 20:34.
Amaziah. 1 Ch +4:34.

2 CHRONICLES 25

1 **twenty and five**. 2 K 14:1-3.
2 **but not**. ver. 14. 2 Ch 24:2. 26:4. 1 S 16:7. 2
K 14:4. Ps 78:37. Is 29:13. Ho 10:2. Ac 8:21.
Ja 1:8. 4:8.
3 A.M. 3166. B.C. 838.
Now it came. 2 K 14:5, etc.
established to him. Heb. confirmed upon
him. 2 K 14:5. 15:19.
he slew. 2 Ch 24:25, 26. Ge 9:5, 6. Ex 21:14.
Nu 35:31-33.
4 **as it is written**. 2 Ch 34:14. Dt 24:16. 2 K
14:5, +6. Je 31:29, 30. Ezk 18:4, 20.
of Moses. Ex +24:4.
5 A.M. 3177. B.C. 827.
captains over thousands. Jsh +22:21.
numbered. 1 S +11:8.
from twenty. Nu 1:3.
three. 2 Ch 11:1. 14:8. 17:14-18.
6 **mighty men of valor**. 2 Ch 13:3. 17:13. Jg
+6:12.
an hundred talents of silver. Ex 38:25, 25.
7 **a man of God**. 2 S 12:1. 1 K 13:1. 1 T 6:11. 2
T 3:17.
for the Lord. 2 Ch 13:12. 19:2. 1 K 12:28. Is
28:1-3. Ho 5:13-15. 9:13.
8 **be strong**. 2 Ch 18:14. Ec 11:9. Is 8:9, 10. Jl
3:9-14. Mt 26:45.
God hath power. 2 Ch 14:11. 20:6. Jg 7:7. 1
S 14:6. Jb 5:18. 9:13. Ps 20:7. 33:16-20.
62:11. Ec 9:11.
cast down. 2 Ch 28:23.
9 **army**. Heb. band. ver. 10, 13. 2 K 6:23.
The Lord. 2 Ch 1:12. Ge 45:20. Dt 8:18. Ps
24:1. Pr 10:22. Hg 2:8. Lk 18:29, 30. Ep 3:20.
Ph 3:8. 4:19.
10 **Amaziah**. 1 K 12:24.
home. Heb. to their place. 1 S 2:20.
great anger. 2 Ch 28:11, 13. 29:10. 30:8. Ex
11:8. 2 S 19:43. Pr 29:22.
11 **valley of salt**. 2 S +8:13.
children of Seir. ver. 14. Ge +14:6.
12 **the rock**. Heb. "Selah," as in 2 K 14:7. The
same with Petra (Young).
cast them. 2 S 12:31. 1 Ch 20:3.
broken in pieces. 2 Ch 20:10. 21:8-10. Ge
7:11.
13 **soldiers of the army**. Heb. sons of the band.
ver. 9.
Samaria. 1 K +16:24, 29.
Beth-horon. Jsh +10:10.
14 **he brought**. 2 Ch 28:23. Is 44:19.
his gods. Ex 20:3-5. Dt 7:5, 25. 2 S 5:21.
15 **a prophet**. ver. 7. 2 Ch 16:7-9. 19:2. 20:37. 2
S 12:1-6.
Why hast thou sought. 2 Ch 24:20. Jg 2:2.
Je 2:5.
the gods. 2 Ch 13:9. 32:19. Ps 96:5.
which could not. ver. 11, 12. Ps 115:4-8. Is
44:9, 10. 46:1, 2. Je 10:7. 1 C 8:4. 10:20.

16 **Art thou made**. 2 Ch 16:10. 18:25. 24:21.
Am 7:10-13. Mt 21:23.
forbear. 2 Ch 35:21. Ex 14:12. 1 S +25:17. Pr
9:7, 8. Is 30:10, 11. Je 29:26. 2 T 4:2, 3. Re
11:10.
determined. Heb. counselled. 2 Ch 18:20,
21. Ex 9:16. Dt +2:30. 1 S 2:25. Is 19:17.
46:10. Ac 4:28. Ro 9:22. Ep 1:11.
hast not hearkened. Dt 28:1, 2, 15. 1 S
+25:17. Ps 81:11. 107:11. 119:24mg. Pr 1:25,
26, 30. Lk 7:30.
17 A.M. 3178. B.C. 826.
Amaziah. ver. 13. 1 Ch +4:34.
let us see. 2 S 2:14. Pr 20:3.
in the face. ver. 21. Ge 42:1. 2 K 14:8, 11.
18 **thistle**. *or,* furze-bush, *or* thorn. 2 Ch 33:11.
Jg 9:8-15. 1 S 13:6. 1 K 4:33. 2 K 14:9. Jb
31:40. 41:2. Pr 26:9. SS 2:2. Is 34:13. Ho 9:6.
a wild beast. Heb. a beast of the field. Le
26:22. 2 S 2:18. 2 K 4:39. Jb 39:15. Ps 80:13.
Ho 13:8.
19 **heart**. Dt +17:20. Pr 13:10. 28:25.
to boast. Je 9:23. 1 C 1:29.
why shouldest. 2 Ch 35:21. Pr 18:6. 20:3.
26:17. Lk 14:31.
20 **it came of God**. ver. 16. 2 Ch 22:7. 1 K
12:15. Ps 81:11, 12. Ac 28:25-27. 2 Th 2:9-11.
1 P 2:8.
sought after. ver. 14, 15.
21 **they saw one another**. ver. 17.
Beth-shemesh. Je +43:13.
22 **put to the worse**. Heb. smitten. 2 Ch 28:5,
6.
fled. 1 S 4:10. 1 K 22:36.
23 **took Amaziah**. 2 Ch 33:11. 36:6, 10. Pr
16:18. 29:23. Da 4:37. Ob 3. Lk 14:11.
Jehoahaz. 2 Ch 21:17. 22:1, Ahaziah. 22:6,
Azariah.
gate of Ephraim. Ne 8:16. 12:39.
corner gate. Heb. the gate of it that looketh.
2 Ch 26:9. 2 K 14:13. Je 31:38.
24 **all the gold**. 2 Ch 12:9. 2 K 14:14.
25 A.M. 3179-3194. B.C. 825-810.
Joash. Jg +6:11. 2 K 14:17, etc., Jehoash.
26 **rest of the acts**. 2 Ch 20:34. 2 K 14:15.
27 A.M. 3194. B.C. 810.
after the time. 2 Ch 15:2.
from following. Heb. from after. 2 Ch 34:33.
Ex 7:2.
made. Heb. conspired a conspiracy. 2 Ch
24:25. 2 K 12:20. +14:11, 19. 15:15, 30.
Lachish. Jsh +10:3.
28 **the city of Judah**. *that is,* the city of David,
as it is 2 K 14:20.

2 CHRONICLES 26

1 **all the**. 2 Ch 22:1. 33:25.
Uzziah. i.e. *power of Jehovah; strength of God;
my strength is Jehovah*. 2 K 14:21. 15:1, etc. 1

Ch 3:12, Azariah. Mt 1:8, 9, Ozias. **S#5818h:**
ver. 3, 8, 9, 11, 14, 18, 19, 21-23. 2 Ch 27:2. 2
K 15:1, 7, 13, 17, 20, 23, 27, 32, 34. 1 Ch
6:24. 27:25. Ezr 10:21. Ne 11:4. Is 1:1. 6:1.
7:1. Ho 1:1. Am 1:1. Zc 14:5.

2 Eloth. 1 K +9:26.
  restored. 2 Ch 25:23, 28.

3 A.M. 3194-3246. B.C. 810-758.
  Uzziah. ver. 1.
  Jecoliah. i.e. *able through Jehovah; made strong
  of the Lord*, **S#3203h**. 2 K 15:2.

4 he did. 2 T +3:15.
  in the sight. Ac +10:31.
  according to all. 2 Ch 25:2.
  his father. 2 Ch 17:3. 1 K 9:4. Ep +6:4.

5 as long. Notice the explicit cause/effect relationship stated to exist between seeking God
(the cause), and prosperity, the effect (Ps
+9:10).
  he sought the Lord. 2 Ch 24:2. Jg 2:7. Ho
  6:4. Mk 4:16, 17. Ac 20:30.
  had. Ge 41:15, 38. Da 1:17. 2:19. 5:16. 10:1.
  visions. Heb. seeing.
  and as long. 2 Ch 15:2. 25:8. 1 Ch 22:11, 13.
  prosper. Dt +28:12, 44, +48. Ps +1:3.

6 warred against. 2 Ch 21:16. Is 14:29.
  the wall of Gath. 2 S 8:1. 1 Ch 18:1.
  Jabneh. i.e. *God lets build*, **S#2996h**.
  about. or, in *the country of*. 1 S 5:1, 6.

7 God helped. 2 Ch 14:11. 1 Ch 5:20. 12:18.
  Ps 18:29, 34, 35. Is 14:29. Ac 26:22.
  the Arabians. 2 Ch 17:11. 21:16.
  Gur-baal. i.e. *sojourn of Baal* or *the possessor*,
  S#1485h.
  Mehunims. i.e. *dwellings, habitations*, **S#4586h**.
  Ezr 2:50. Ne 7:52. Compare **S#4584h**, Maon,
  Maonites, Jsh +15:55; Jg +10:12.

8 the Ammonites. Ge +19:38. 1 S +11:11.
  gave. Jg +3:15.
  his name. Ge 12:2. 2 S 8:13. 1 K 4:31. Mt
  4:24.
  spread. Heb. went. ver. 15. Ho 14:6mg.

9 the corner gate. 2 Ch 25:23mg. 2 K 14:13.
  Je 31:38. Zc 14:10.
  the valley gate. Ne 2:13. 3:13, 19, 32. Je
  31:40.
  the turning. Ne 3:20, 24.
  fortified. or, repaired.

10 digged many wells. or, cut out many cisterns. Heb. *bor*, Ge +37:20. Ge 21:30. 26:15,
18-21, 32. Ne 9:25.
  he had much cattle. 2 K 3:4. 1 Ch 27:26-31.
  husbandmen. Jl 1:11.
  Carmel. or, fruitful fields. 2 K 19:23.
  Is 29:17.
  husbandry. Heb. ground. Ge 4:2.

11 went out. 2 K 5:2.

13 an army. Heb. the power of an army.
  three hundred. 2 Ch 11:1. 13:3. 14:8.
  17:14-19.

14 slings to cast stones. Heb. stones of slings.
  Jg 20:16. 1 S 17:49. 2 K +3:25mg. Zc 9:15mg.

15 cunning men. 2 Ch 2:7, 14. Ex 31:4.
  spread far. Heb. went forth. Mt 4:24.
  strong. Dt 32:15. Jsh 17:13. 1 C 10:12.

16 when he was. Dt +17:20. Mk +4:19. 1 C
  10:12. Col 2:18.
  went into. 2 K 16:12, 13.
  to burn incense. Nu 16:1, 7, 18, 35. 1 K
  +12:33.
  the altar of incense. Lk +1:11.

17 Azariah. 1 Ch +6:36.
  valiant men. 2 S +2:7mg. 1 Ch 12:28.

18 withstood Uzziah. 2 Ch 16:7-9. 19:2. Je
  13:18. Mt 10:18, 28. 14:4. 2 C 5:16. Ga 2:11.
  not unto thee. Nu 16:40, 46-48. 18:6, 7.
  incense. 2 Ch 13:10, 11. Ex +30:1. +39:38.
  Jn 9:31.
  but to the priests. Ex 30:7, 8. 1 Ch 6:49.
  9:30. 1 C +14:40. He 5:4.
  go out. 1 C 5:5.
  thou hast trespassed. 1 Ch 15:13.
  neither shall it be. 1 S 2:30. Da 4:37. Jn
  5:44. Ja 2:1.

19 while he was wroth. 2 Ch 16:10. 25:16.
  the leprosy. 2 K +5:1.

20 hasted also. Est 6:12.
  the Lord. Le 14:34. Dt 28:22, 35.

21 A.M. 3239-3246. B.C. 765-758.
  Uzziah. 2 K 15:5.
  dwelt. Le 13:46. Nu 5:2, 3. 12:15. 2 K 7:3.
  several. Heb. free. 2 K 15:5. or, separate. Lk
  17:12.

22 first. 2 Ch 9:29. 12:15. 1 Ch 29:29.
  Isaiah. Is 1:1. 6:1.

23 A.M. 3246. B.C. 758.
  slept with. 2 Ch +28:27. 1 K +11:43. +14:20.
  2 K 15:6, 7. 24:6.
  they buried him. ver. 18. 1 K +11:43.
  the burial. Heb. *qeburah*, Ge +35:20.

2 CHRONICLES 27

1 A.M. 3246-3262. B.C. 758-742.
  Jotham. Jg +9:5.
  twenty and five. 2 K 15:32, 33, etc.
  Jerushah. i.e. *possessed; possession*, **S#3388h**.

2 And he did. 2 Ch 26:4. 2 K 15:34.
  he entered not. 2 Ch 26:16-21. Ps 119:120.
  Ac 5:13.
  the people. 2 K 15:35.

3 high gate. 2 Ch 23:20. Je 20:2.
  Ophel. i.e. *a height; mound; hill; swelling;
  tumor; darkness*, **S#6077h**. or, the tower. 2 K
  +5:24mg.

4 he built cities. 2 Ch 11:5-10. 14:7. 26:9, 10.
  the mountains. Jsh 14:12, 13. Lk 1:39.
  castles and towers. lit. "great places." Ge
  11:4, 5. 35:21. 1 Ch +27:25.

5 the king of the Ammonites. 2 Ch 20:1. Jg

11:4, etc. 2 S 10:1-14. Je 49:1-6.

ten thousand. Rather, "ten thousand *cors* (*korim*) of wheat." The *cor* was the same as the *homer*, and contained about 32 pecks 1 pint. 1 K +4:22mg.

So much. Heb. This.

6 **Jotham**. 2 Ch 26:5.

prepared. *or*, established. 2 Ch +12:14mg. 1 Ch 17:11.

7 **Now the rest**. 2 Ch 20:34. 26:22, 23. 32:32, 33. A.M. 3262. B.C. 742.

they are written. There is not so much found in the book of Kings, which we have now, as here: in both places we have abridged accounts; the larger histories having been lost.

8 **He was**. ver. 1. 2 K 15:33.

9 **Jotham**. 2 K 15:38.

2 CHRONICLES 28

1 A.M. 3262-3278. B.C. 742-726.

Ahaz. 1 Ch +8:35.

David his father. 2 Ch 17:3.

2 **For he walked**. 2 Ch 21:6. 22:3, 4. 1 K 16:31-33. 2 K 10:26-28.

molten images. Ex 34:17. Le 19:4.

Baalim. Jg +2:11-13.

3 **burnt incense**. *or*, offered sacrifice. ver. 4, 25. 2 Ch 29:11. 2 K 16:13, 15.

the valley of the son of Hinnom. Jsh +15:8.

burnt. Dt +18:10. Je 2:34. Mi 6:7.

after the abominations. 2 Ch 33:2. Dt 12:31.

4 **He sacrificed**. Le 26:30. 2 K 16:4.

high places. 2 K +21:3.

the hills. 2 K +17:10.

green tree. Is +57:5.

5 **his God**. 2 Ch 36:5. Ex 20:2, 3.

delivered him. 2 Ch 24:24. 33:11. 36:17. Jg 2:14. 2 K 16:5, 6. Is 7:1, 6.

Damascus. Heb. Darmesek. ver. 23. 1 Ch 18:5.

6 **Pekah**. 2 K 15:27, 37. Is 7:4, 5, 9. 9:21.

an hundred and twenty thousand. 2 Ch 13:17.

valiant men. Heb. sons of valor. 2 S +2:7mg.

because. 2 Ch 15:2. Dt 6:14, 15. 28:15, 25. 29:24-26. 31:16, 17. 32:30. Jsh 23:16. 24:20. Is 1:28. 24:5, 6. Je 2:19. 15:6.

7 **next to the king**. Heb. the second to the king. Ge 41:43. 43:12, 15. Est 10:3.

8 **carried**. Dt 28:25, 41.

brethren. 2 Ch 11:4. Ac 7:26. 13:26.

9 **he went out**. 2 Ch 19:1, 2. 25:15, 16. 1 K 20:13, 22, 42. 2 K 20:14, 15.

because the Lord God. ver. 5. Jg 3:8. Ps 69:26. Is 10:5-7. 47:6. Je 15:17, 18. Ezk 25:12-17. 26:2, 3. Ob 10-16. Zc 1:15.

reacheth. Ge 4:10. 11:4. Ezr 9:6. Re 18:5.

10 **keep under**. Le 25:39-46. or, subdue. Ge 1:28. Ne 5:5. Est 7:8. Je 34:11, 16. Mi 7:19. Zc 9:15.

not with. Je 25:29. Mt 7:2-4. Ro 12:20, 21. 1 P 4:17, 18.

sins against. 2 Ch 24:18. 33:23. Le 4:3. 6:5, 7. 22:16. 1 Ch 21:3. Ezr 9:6. Pr 20:9. Ec 7:20.

the Lord. ver. 5.

11 **deliver**. Is 58:6. Je 34:14, 15. He 13:1-3.

the fierce wrath. Ex 32:12. Nu 25:4. 32:14. Dt 13:17. Ezr 10:14. Mt 5:7. 7:2. Ja 2:13.

12 **the heads**. 1 Ch 28:1.

Azariah. 1 Ch +6:36.

Johanan. 2 K +25:23.

Berechiah. Zc +1:7.

Meshillemoth. i.e. *recompenses; reconciliation; those who repay*, **S#4919h**. ver. 12. Ne 11:13.

Jehizkiah. i.e. *strengthened by Jah*, **S#3169h**.

Shallum. 2 K +15:10.

Amasa. 2 S +17:25.

Hadlai. i.e. *ceasing; worldly; forsaken of the Lord; my forbearings*, **S#2311h**.

stood up. Je 26:6.

13 **add more**. Nu 32:14. Jsh 22:17, 18. Mt 23:32, 35. Ro 2:5.

14 **the armed men**. 2 Ch 20:21. 1 Ch 12:23.

15 **expressed by name**. ver. 12.

clothed. Jb 31:15-23. Is 58:7. Mt 25:35-45. Ac 9:39. 1 T 5:10. Ja 2:15, 16. 1 J 3:17, 18.

gave them. 2 K 6:22. Pr 25:21, 22. Lk 6:27. 8:27, 35. Ro 12:20, 21.

carried. Ro 15:1.

the city. Dt 34:3. Jg 1:16.

16 **did king**. 2 K 16:5-7. Is 7:1-9, 17.

17 **the Edomites**. 2 Ch 25:11, 12. Le 26:18. Ob 10, 13, 14.

captives. Heb. a captivity. ver. 11, 13, 14, 15. Is 49:25mg. Am +1:6mg.

18 **Philistines**. Ezk 16:27, 57.

Beth-shemesh. Je +43:13.

Ajalon. Jsh +10:12.

Gederoth. Jsh 15:41.

Shocho. Jsh +15:35.

Timnah. Jg 14:1, Timnath.

Gimzo. i.e. *producing sycamores*, **S#1579h**.

villages. Nu +21:25mg.

19 **the Lord**. Dt 28:43. 1 S 2:7. Jb 40:12. Ps 106:41-43. Pr 29:23.

because of Ahaz. Ho 5:11. Mi 6:16.

Israel. 2 Ch 21:2.

made Judah. Is +20:2.

20 A.M. 3264. B.C. 740.

Tilgath-pilneser. 2 K 15:29. 16:7-10, Tiglath-pileser. 1 Ch 5:26. Ho 5:13.

distressed him. 2 K 17:5. Is 7:20. 30:3, 16. Je 2:37.

21 **took away**. 2 Ch 12:9. 2 K 18:15, 16. Pr 20:25.

22 **in the**. 2 Ch 33:12. Ps 50:15. Is 1:5. Ezk 21:13. Ho 5:15. Re 16:9-11.

this is. Est 7:6. Ps 52:7.

23 **For he sacrificed**. 2 Ch 25:14. 2 K 16:12, 13.
Damascus. Heb. Darmesek. ver. 5mg.
Because the gods. Hab 1:1.
sacrifice to them. Je 10:5. 44:15-18.
But they were. Is 1:28. Je 44:20-28. Ho 13:9.

24 **cut in pieces**. 2 K 16:17, 18. 25:13, etc.
shut up. 2 Ch 29:3, 7.
he made. 2 Ch 33:3-5. Je 2:28. Ho 12:11. Ac 17:16, 23.

25 **burn**. or, offer. ver. 3mg.
God. Ac +3:13.

26 **the rest**. 2 Ch 20:34. 27:7-9. 2 K 16:19, 20.

27 A.M. 3278. B.C. 726.
slept with. 1 K +11:43.
they brought. 1 K +11:43. 1 S 2:30. Pr 10:7.
sepulchres. Heb. qeber, Ge +23:4.
the kings of Israel. 2 Ch 21:2.

2 CHRONICLES 29

1 A.M. 3278-3306. B.C. 726-698.
Hezekiah. 2 K +16:20.
Abijah. 1 K +14:1.
Zechariah. 2 Ch 26:5. Is 8:2. Zc +1:1.

2 **he did**. 2 Ch 28:1. 34:2. 2 K 18:3.

3 A.M. 3278. B.C. 726.
He in the first. 2 Ch 34:3. Ps 101:3. Ec 9:10. Mt 6:33. Ga 1:16.
opened. ver. 7. 2 Ch 28:24. 2 K 16:14-18.

4 **east street**. 2 Ch 32:6. Ne 3:29. Je 19:2.

5 **sanctify now**. 2 Ch 35:6. Ex 19:10, 15. 1 Ch 15:12.
sanctify the house. ver. 16. 2 Ch 34:3-8. Ezk 36:25. Mt 21:12, 13. 1 C 3:16, 17. 2 C 6:16. 7:1. Ep 5:26, 27.
carry forth. Ezk 8:3, 9, etc.

6 **For our fathers**. 2 Ch 28:2-4, 23-25. 34:21. Ezr 5:12. 9:7. Ne 9:16, 32. Je 16:19. 44:21. La 5:7. Da 9:8, 16. Mt 10:37. 23:30-32.
have forsaken him. Je 2:13, 17.
turned away. Je 2:27. Ezk 8:16.
turned their backs. Heb. given the neck. Ex 23:27mg. Ps 18:40.

7 **they have shut**. ver. 3. 2 Ch 28:24. Le 24:2-8. 2 K 16:17, 18. Ps 119:105. Ml 1:10. Re 8:4.
nor offered. Ne 13:10. Pr +11:24. Is 43:23, 24. Ml 3:8. Ac 5:1, 2.

8 **Wherefore**. ver. 10. 2 Ch +24:18. 34:24, 25. 36:14-16. Le 10:6. Nu 1:53. 16:46. 18:5. Dt 28:15-20. Jsh 7:1. 22:18, 20. 1 S 6:19. 2 S 24:1. 1 Ch 27:24. Ps 106:29.
he hath delivered. 2 Ch 28:6-8.
trouble. Heb. commotion. Dt 28:25. Is 28:19. Je 15:4. 24:9. 29:18, 19. 34:17.
to astonishment. Le 26:32. Dt 28:37, 59. 1 K 9:8. 2 K 22:19. 2 Ch 7:21. Je 18:15, 16. 19:8. 25:9, 11, 18. 29:18. 42:18. 44:12, 22. 49:17. 51:37. Ezk 5:15.
hissing. 1 K 9:8. Jb 27:23. Is 5:26. 7:18. Je

18:16. 19:8. 25:9, 18. 29:18. 49:17. 50:13. 51:37. La 2:15, 16. Ezk 27:36. Mi 6:16..Zp 2:15. Zc 10:8.

9 **our fathers**. 2 Ch 28:5-8, 17. Le 26:17. La 5:7.

10 **Now it is**. 2 Ch 6:7, 8.
to make a covenant. 2 Ch 15:12, 13. 23:16. 34:30-32. Ezr 10:3. Ne 9:38. 10:1, etc. Je 34:15, 18. 50:5. 2 C 8:5.
that his fierce. ver. 8. 2 Ch 19:2, 10. +24:18. 2 K 23:3, 26. Ex 32:12. Nu 25:4.

11 **negligent**. or, deceived. 2 K 4:28. Ga 6:7, 8.
the Lord. Nu 3:6-9. 8:6-14. 18:2-6. Dt +10:8.
chosen. Ep 1:4.
burn incense. or, offer sacrifice. 2 Ch 28:3mg. Nu 16:35-40. 18:7.

12 **Mahath**. i.e. snatching, S#4287h. 2 Ch 31:13. 1 Ch 6:35.
Amasai. i.e. burdensome, S#6022h. 1 Ch 6:25, 35. 12:18. 15:24.
Joel. 1 S +8:2.
Azariah. 1 Ch +6:36.
Kohathites. Ge +46:11. Nu +3:27. 4:2, etc.
Merari. Ge +46:11.
Kish. 1 S +9:1.
Abdi. 1 Ch +6:44.
Jehalelel. i.e. he praises God, S#3094h. 1 Ch +4:16, Jehaleleel.
of the Gershonites. Nu +3:21.
Joah. Is +36:3.
Zimmah. i.e. bad counsel; lewdness, S#2155h. 1 Ch 6:20, 42.
Eden. Ge +2:8.

13 **Elizaphan**. Nu +3:30.
Asaph. 2 K +18:18.

14 **Heman**. 1 Ch +2:6.
Jeduthun. 1 Ch 25:1, 3, 6.

15 **sanctified themselves**. ver. 5.
by the words of the Lord. or, in the business of the Lord. ver. 30. 2 Ch 30:12.
to cleanse. 1 Ch 23:28.

16 **the inner part**. 2 Ch 3:8. 5:7. Ex 26:33, 34. 1 K 6:19, 20. He 9:2-8, 23, 24.
to cleanse. 2 C 6:16-18.
all the uncleanness. Ezk 36:29. Mt 21:12, 13. 23:27.
Kidron. 2 S +15:23.

17 **the porch**. ver. 7. 2 Ch 3:4. 1 K 6:3. 1 Ch 28:11.
the sixteenth. Ex 12:2-8.

18 **the altar**. 2 Ch +4:1, 7.
the showbread. 2 Ch 4:8. 13:11.

19 **all the vessels**. 2 Ch 28:24.
did cast away. 2 Ch 11:14. 28:9. Is 19:6.

20 **rose**. Ge 22:3. Ex 24:4. Jsh 6:12. Je 25:4.

21 **seven**. Nu 23:1, 14, 29. 1 Ch 15:26. Ezr 8:35. Jb 42:8. Ezk 45:23.
a sin offering. Le +23:19. 2 C 5:21.

22 **sprinkled**. Le +1:5.

23 **forth**. Heb. near. ver. 31.
they laid. Le 1:4. 4:15, 24.

24 **reconciliation**. He +2:17.
 to make. Le +4:20.
 burnt. Le +23:12.
 sin offering. Le +23:19.
25 **And he set**. 1 Ch 9:33. 15:16-22. 16:4, 5, 42.
 25:1-7.
 cymbals. 1 Ch +13:8.
 psalteries. 1 S +10:5.
 harps. Re +5:8.
 according. 2 Ch 8:14. 35:15. 1 Ch 23:5.
 28:12, 19.
 Gad. 1 S +22:5.
 Nathan. 2 Ch +9:29.
 for so was. 2 Ch 30:12.
 of the Lord by his prophets. Heb. by the
 hand of the Lord, by the hand of his prophets.
 1 K +16:12mg.
26 **the instruments**. 1 Ch 23:5. Ps 87:7. 150:3-
 5. Is 38:20. Am 6:5.
 the priests. 2 Ch 5:12, 13. Nu 10:8, 10. Jsh
 6:4-9. 1 Ch 15:24. 16:6. Ps 81:3. 98:5, 6. 150:3.
27 **when**. Heb. in the time.
 the song of. 2 Ch 7:3. 20:21. 23:18. 1 Ch
 25:7. Ps 136:1. 137:3, 4.
 the instruments. Heb. hands of instruments.
 2 Ch 23:18mg.
28 **And all the congregation**. Ps 68:24-26. Re
 5:8-14.
 worshipped. or, did obeisance. Ge 37:9. 2 K
 19:37. Ne 9:3, 6. Est 3:2, 5. Is 37:38. Ezk 8:16.
 Zp 1:5.
 the singers sang. Heb. song. Ps 89:15.
29 **present**. Heb. found. Est +1:5mg.
 bowed themselves. 2 Ch 20:18. 1 Ch 29:20.
 Ps 72:11. Ro 14:11. Ph 2:10, 11.
30 **with the words**. 2 S 23:1, 2. 1 Ch 16:7-36.
 they sang. Ps 33:1. 95:1, 2, 6. 149:2.
 with gladness. Dt +12:7.
 bowed. Ge +24:26.
31 **consecrated yourselves**. or, filled your
 hand. Ex +28:41mg. Le 21:10.
 sacrifices. Le ch. 1, 3.
 thank. Le +7:12.
 and as many, etc. Le 1:3. 23:38. Ezr 1:4.
32 **the number**. 1 K 3:4. 8:63. 1 Ch 29:21. Ezr
 6:17.
33 **the consecrated things**. ver. 31.
34 **the priests**. ver. 5. 2 Ch 30:16, 17.
 their brethren. 2 Ch 35:11. Nu 8:15, 19.
 18:3, 6, 7.
 did help them. Heb. strengthened them. Jb
 8:20mg. Ro 16:3.
 for the Levites. 2 Ch 30:3.
 upright. 1 Ch 29:17. Ps 7:10. 26:6. 94:15. 1 C
 5:8. Ph 1:10.
35 **the burnt offerings**. ver. 32. Le +23:12.
 the fat. Ex 29:13. Le 3:15, 16.
 peace offerings. Le +23:19.
 the drink offerings. Le +23:13.
 So the. 1 Ch 16:37-42. Ezr 6:18. 1 C +14:40.

36 **Hezekiah rejoiced**. 1 Ch 29:9, 17. Ezr 6:22.
 1 Th 3:8, 9.
 and all. Mt 3:5.
 God. 2 Ch 30:12. 1 Ch 29:18. Ps 10:17. Pr
 16:1. Lk 1:17.
 the thing. Ac 2:41.

2 CHRONICLES 30

1 **Israel**. 2 Ch 11:13, 16.
 Ephraim. ver. 10, 11. Nu +1:33.
 to the house. Dt 16:2-6.
 to keep. Ex 12:3-20. Le +23:5. 1 C 5:7, 8.
2 **the king**. 1 Ch 13:1-3. Pr 11:14. 15:22. Ec
 4:13.
 in the second month. Nu 9:10, 11.
3 **at that time**. Ex 12:6, 18.
 because. 2 Ch 29:34.
4 **pleased the king**. Heb. was right in the eyes
 of the king. Jsh +22:30mg.
5 **established**. Ezr 6:8-12. Est 3:12-15. 8:8-10.
 9:20, 21. Da 6:8.
 to make proclamation. 2 Ch 24:9. 36:22.
 Le +23:2, 4. Da 4:1, etc.
 from Beer-sheba. Jg +20:1.
 for they. 2 Ch 35:18. Dt 12:32. 1 C 11:2.
6 **the posts went**. 1 S 22:17mg. Jb 9:25. Est
 3:13, 15. 8:10, 14. Je 51:31.
 the king. Heb. the hand of the king. 2 Ch
 31:13mg.
 turn again. La 5:21. Ezk +33:11.
 and he will. Is 6:13.
 escaped. 2 Ch 28:20. 1 K 15:19, 29. 1 Ch
 5:26. Is 1:9.
7 **like**. Ezk 20:13-18. Zc 1:3, 4.
 as. 2 Ch 29:8.
8 **be ye not stiffnecked**. Heb. harden not
 your necks. 2 Ch 36:13. Ex 32:9. 33:3, 5.
 34:9. Dt 9:6, 13. 10:16. 31:27. 2 K 17:14. Ne
 9:16, 17, 29. Ps 78:8. Is 48:4. Je 7:26. 17:23.
 19:15. Ac 7:51. Ro 10:21.
 yield yourselves. Heb. give the hand. 1 Ch
 +29:24mg. Ps 68:31. Ro 6:13-19.
 enter into. Ps 63:2. 68:24. 73:17.
 which he hath. Ps 132:13, 14.
 for ever. Heb. olam, Ex +12:24.
 serve. Dt 6:13, 17. Jsh 24:15. Mt +4:10. Jn
 12:26. Ro 6:22. Col 3:22-24. Re 7:15.
 the fierceness. 2 Ch +24:18. 28:11, 13.
 29:10. 2 K 23:26. Ps 78:49.
9 **if**. Ge +4:7.
 ye turn. 2 Ch +7:14. Le 26:40-42. Dt 30:2-4.
 1 K 8:50. Ps 106:46.
 so that they shall. Je 29:12-14. 31:27, 28.
 the Lord. Ex +34:6, 7.
 will not. 2 Ch 15:2. Pr 28:13. Is 55:7. Ezk
 18:30-32.
 turn away. Je 18:17.
10 **the posts**. ver. +6. Est 3:13, 15. 8:10, 14. Jb
 9:25.

they laughed. Pr +1:26. Lk +8:53.
mocked. He +11:36.

11 **divers of Asher**. ver. 18, 21. 2 Ch 11:16. Ac 17:34.
humbled themselves. 2 Ch 12:6, 7, 12. 33:12, 19, 23. 34:27. Ex 10:3. Le 26:41. Da 5:22. Lk 14:11. 18:14. Ja 4:10. 1 P 5:6.

12 **the hand of God**. 2 Ch 29:36. 1 Ch 29:18, 19. Ezr 7:27. Ps 110:3. Je 24:7. 32:39. Ezk 36:26. Ph 2:13. 2 Th 2:13, 14.
the commandment. Dt 4:2, 5, 6. 1 Th 4:2.
by the word. 2 Ch 29:25. Ac 4:19.

13 **there assembled**. Ps 84:7.
feast of unleavened. Le +23:6.
the second month. ver. 2.

14 **altars**. 2 Ch 28:24. 34:4, 7. 2 K 18:22. 23:12, 13. Is 2:18-20.
the brook. 2 S +15:23.

15 **passover**. Le +23:5.
were ashamed. 2 Ch 29:34. Ezk 16:61-63. 43:10, 11.
and sanctified. ver. 24. 2 Ch 5:11. 29:15, 34. 31:18. Ex 19:10, 22.

16 **they stood**. 2 Ch 35:10, 15.
place. Heb. standing. 2 Ch 34:31. 1 K 10:5. Ne 8:7. 9:3. 13:11.
after their manner. 2 K 11:14.
Moses. Dt +33:1.
the priests. Le +1:5.

17 **the Levites**. 2 Ch 29:34. 35:3-6.
the killing. Ex 12:6.
passovers. Ex +12:21.

18 **many of Ephraim**. ver. +11.
had not cleansed. Nu 9:10, etc. 19:20. 1 C 11:28.
the passover. Ex 12:43, etc.
prayed. Ge 20:7, 17. Jb 42:8, 9. Ja 5:15, 16. 1 J 5:16.
The good. 2 Ch 6:21. Ex 34:6-9. Nu 14:18-20. Ps 25:8. 86:5. 119:68. Da 9:19.

19 **prepareth**. 2 Ch +12:14mg. Pr 23:26.
though he be not. Le 12:4. 15:31-33. 21:17-23. 22:3-6. Nu 9:6. 19:13-20.

20 **healed**. Ex 15:26. Ps +103:3. Ja 5:15, 16.

21 **present**. Heb. found. Est +1:5mg.
the feast. Ex 12:15. 13:6. Le 23:6. Ru 1:22. Lk 15:23. 22:1, 7. 1 C 5:7, 8.
great gladness. ver. 26. 2 Ch 7:10. 29:30. Dt +12:7.
the priests. 2 Ch +20:21. 29:25-27.
day by day. Ac 2:46, 47.
loud instruments. Heb. instruments of strength. 1 Ch 16:42. Ps 68:33. 150:3-5.

22 **comfortably unto all**. Heb. to the heart of all. Ge +34:3mg.
taught. 2 Ch 15:3. 17:9. 35:3. Le 10:11. Dt 33:10. Ezr 7:10, 25. Ne 8:7, 8, 18. 9:3. Hg 2:11. Ml 2:7. Ga 6:6. 2 T 2:2. 4:2.
the good knowledge. Pr 2:6, 7. 8:6. Je 23:28. Jn 17:3. 2 C 2:14. 4:6. Ph 3:8.

feast. Ge +17:21. Le 23:2.
peace offerings. Le +23:19.
and making. Dt 26:3-11. Ezr 10:11. Ne 9:3.
confession. 1 J 1:9.

23 **took counsel**. ver. 2.
to keep. 2 Ch 7:9. 1 K 8:65.
they kept. 2 Ch 35:18. Ne 8:17.

24 **did give**. Heb. lifted up, or, offered. 2 Ch 35:7, 8. 1 Ch 29:3-9. Ezk 45:17. Ep 4:8.
a great. 2 Ch 29:34.

25 **the strangers**. ver. +11, 18. Ge +23:4. Ex 12:43-47, +48mg, 49. Dt +26:11.
rejoiced. 1 Ch 16:10, 11. Ps 92:4. 104:34.

26 **since the time**. 2 Ch 7:9, 10.

27 **the priests**. Nu +6:23-26. Dt 10:8.
their prayer. 1 K +8:30, 39. Ac 10:4. 1 J 5:14, 15.
his holy dwelling place. Heb. the habitation of his holiness. Dt +26:15. Ps 68:5. Is +57:15. 63:15. 66:1. Je 25:30. Zc 2:13mg.

2 CHRONICLES 31

1 **Now when**. 2 Ch ch. 30.
all Israel. 1 K 18:38-40. 2 K 23:2-20.
present. Heb. found. Est +1:5mg.
brake. 2 Ch 23:17. 32:12. Ex +23:24.
images. Heb. statues. 2 K +17:10mg.
groves. 2 K +17:10. 21:3. 23:6.
high places. 2 K +21:3.
in Ephraim. 2 Ch 30:1, 18. 34:6, 7. 2 K 17:2. 18:4. 23:15.
until, etc. Heb. until to make an end.
possession. Ge 17:8. 23:4.

2 **the courses**. 2 Ch 5:11. 8:14. 23:8. 1 Ch 16:37, 40. ch. 23-26. Ezr 6:18. Lk 1:5.
to give thanks. 2 Ch 29:24-26. 1 Ch 16:4-6, 41. 23:30. 25:1-3. Ne 11:17. Ps 134:1-3. 135:1-3, 26. Je 33:11.
burnt offerings. Le +23:12.
peace offerings. Le +23:19.
in the gates of the tents of the Lord. 1 Ch 23:32.

3 **the king's**. 2 Ch 30:24. 1 Ch 26:26. Ezk 45:17. 46:4-7, 12-18.
for the morning. Ex +29:38-42. Nu 28:3-8.
the burnt. Nu +28:9, 10.
for the new moons. Nu +28:11-31. ch. 29. Dt 16:1-17. 2 K 4:23. 2 Ch +2:4. Ps 81:1-4. Col 2:16, 17.
the set feasts. Ge +17:21. Le 23:2.

4 **the portion**. ver. 16. Le 27:30-33. Nu 18:8-21, 26-28. Ml 3:8-10.
that they might. 2 Ch 17:9. Ne 13:10-13. Ro 15:4. 1 C 9:9-14. Ga 6:6.
the law. Ml 2:7.

5 **as soon**. 2 Ch 24:10, 11. Ex 22:29. 35:5, 20-29. 36:5, 6. 2 C 8:2-5.
came abroad. Heb. brake forth. 1 Ch +13:2mg.

the firstfruits. Le +23:10.
honey. *or*, dates. Ge 43:11.
tithe of all. Le 27:30. Ne 13:12. Mt 23:23. Lk 18:12.

6 **the children**. 2 Ch 11:16, 17.
the tithe. Le 27:30. Dt 14:28.
by heaps. Heb. heaps, heaps. Ex 8:14. 2 K 3:16. Ru 3:7. Ne 4:2. 13:15 (sheaves). SS 7:2. Je 50:26. Hg 2:16.

7 **the third month**. Le 23:16-24. That is, Sivan.

8 **blessed**. Jl 2:13.
the Lord. Ge 14:20. Jg 5:9. 1 K 8:14, 15. 1 Ch 29:10-20. Ezr 7:27. 2 C 8:16. Ep 1:3. Ph 4:10, 19. 1 Th 3:9. 1 P 1:3.
and his people. 2 Ch 6:3. Ge 14:19. 2 S 6:18. 1 K 8:55.

10 **Azariah**. 1 Ch +6:36.
Zadok. 2 S +8:17.
Since. Pr 3:9, 10. Hg 2:18, 19. Ml 3:10. 1 T +4:8.
we have had. 2 K 4:43, 44. Mt 15:37. Ph 4:18.
left plenty. Ex +36:6. Le 7:10. Ml +3:10. Mt 14:20. Lk 15:17. Ph 4:18.
the Lord. Ge 26:12. 30:27-30. 39:5, 23. Le 25:21. 26:4, 5. Dt 28:8. Pr 10:22. 2 C 9:8-11.

11 **chambers**. *or*, storehouses. 1 S 9:22. 2 K 23:11. 1 Ch 9:26, 33. 23:28. 28:12. Ezr 8:29. 10:6. Ne 10:37, 38, 39. 13:5, 12, 13.

12 **the offerings**. ver. 14. Ne 10:39. or, heave offering. Ex 29:27.
the dedicated. 2 K 12:15.
faithfully. 2 K 12:15. 22:17. Lk 16:10. 1 C 4:2. 3 J 5.
over which. 1 Ch 26:20-26.
Cononiah. i.e. *prepared of Jah*, S#3562h. ver. 13. 2 Ch 35:9.
Shimei. 2 S +16:5.

13 **Jehiel**. Ezr +8:9.
Azaziah. 1 Ch +27:20.
Nahath. Ge +36:13.
Asahel. 1 Ch +2:16.
Jerimoth. 1 Ch +7:7.
Jozabad. i.e. *the Lord gave*, S#3107h. 2 Ch 35:9. 1 Ch 12:4, 20. Ezr 8:33. 10:22, 23. Ne 8:7. 11:16.
Eliel. 1 Ch +8:20.
Ismachiah. i.e. *supported of Jah*, S#3253h.
Mahath. 2 Ch +29:12.
Benaiah. 1 Ch +15:24.
under, etc. Heb. at the hand. ver. 15. 2 Ch 30:6mg.
at the commandment. ver. 4, 11. 2 Ch +30:12.
Azariah. ver. +10.

14 **the porter**. 1 Ch 26:12, 14, 17.
the freewill offerings. Le +23:38.
to distribute. Ne 13:13. Lk 12:42.
the most. Le 2:10. 6:16, 17. 7:1-6. 10:12, 13. 27:28.

15 **next him**. Heb. at his hand. ver. 13mg. 2 Ch +17:15mg.
the cities. Jsh 21:9-19. 1 Ch 6:54-60.
set office. *or*, trust. 1 Ch 9:22mg.
as well. 1 Ch 25:8.

16 **his daily**. Ex +5:13mg. Le 21:22, 23. Lk 12:42.

17 **genealogy**. Nu 3:15, 20. 4:38, 42, 46. 17:2, 3. Ezr 2:59.
twenty. Nu 4:3. 8:24. 1 Ch 23:24, 27.
by their courses. ver. +2. 1 Ch 24:20-31. ch. 25, 26.

18 **set office**. *or*, trust. ver. 15mg. 1 Ch 9:22mg.
they sanctified. Is 5:16. Ro 15:16.
holiness. 2 C 7:1. He 12:14.

19 **the fields**. ver. 15. Le 25:34. Nu 35:2-5. 1 Ch 6:54, 60.
the men. ver. 12-15. 2 Ch 28:15.

20 **wrought**. 1 K 15:5. 2 K 20:3. 22:2. Jn 1:47. Ac 24:16. 1 Th 2:10. 3 J 5.

21 **work**. Ec 9:10. Col 3:23.
in the law. Ps 1:2, 3.
to seek. Je +29:13.
he did it. 1 Ch 22:19. Ec 9:10. Mt +22:37.
prospered. Ps +1:3. Mt 7:24-27.

2 CHRONICLES 32

1 **these things**. 2 Ch 20:1, 2. 2 K 18:13, etc. Is 36:1, etc.
king of Assyria. 2 K 15:19. 17:6. 18:11, 19, 20. Is 7:17, 18. 8:6-8. 10:5, 6. Ho 11:5.
win them. Heb. break them up. Is 10:7-11. 37:24, 25. Mi 2:13.

2 **he was purposed to fight**. Heb. his face *was* to war. 2 K 12:17. Lk 9:51, 52.

3 **took counsel**. 2 Ch 30:2. 2 K 18:20. Pr 15:22. 20:18. 24:6. Is 40:13. Ro 11:34.
to stop. Ge 26:15, 18. 2 K 20:20. Is 22:8-11.

4 **who stopped**. ver. 3, 30.
fountains. Heb. *mayan*, Ge +7:11.
the brook. ver. 30. 2 Ch 30:14.
ran through the midst of. Heb. overflowed. Jb 14:19. Is 10:22. 28:2.
kings. ver. +1. 2 K 18:9, 13. 19:17. Is 10:8.
find. 2 K 3:9, 16, 17. 19:21.

5 **he strengthened**. 2 Ch 12:1. 14:5-7. 17:1, 2. 23:1. 26:8. Is 22:9, 10.
that was broken. 2 Ch 25:23.
another wall. 2 K 25:4. Je 39:4.
Millo. 2 S +5:9.
darts. *or*, swords, *or* weapons. 2 Ch 23:10. 26:14, 15. Ne 4:17. Jl 2:8mg.

6 **he set captains**. 2 Ch 17:14-19. 1 Ch 27:3, 4, etc.
in the street. Ezr 10:9. Ne 8:1-3, 16.
gate. Ge +14:7.
comfortably to them. Heb. to their heart. Ge +34:3mg.

7 **strong**. Jsh +1:6.

be not afraid. 2 Ch 20:15. 2 K 18:30. 19:6, 7.
with us. Is +43:2.

8 **an arm**. Jb 26:2. 40:9. Je 17:5. 1 C 1:29.
with us. 2 Ch 14:11. 1 S 8:20. 17:45. Ps 20:7.
44:6. 125:1. Is +43:2.
to fight. 2 Ch 20:15. Dt 20:1, 4. Jsh 10:42.
rested. Heb. leaned. ver. 15. 2 Ch 20:20. Ps
71:6. SS 8:5. Is 36:18. 48:2.
upon the words. Pr 12:25. Jn 4:50.

9 A.M. 3294. B.C. 710.
Sennacherib. 2 K +18:17. Is 36:2.
Lachish. Jsh +10:3.
power. Heb. dominion. 1 K 9:19. 2 K 20:13.

10 **Thus saith**. 2 K +18:19. Is 36:4.
siege. Heb. stronghold. 2 Ch 8:5. 11:5. Dt
20:19, 20. 2 K 24:10mg. Is +37:25mg. Hab
2:1.

11 **to give over**. 2 K +18:27. Is 36:12, 18.
The Lord our God. ver. 15. 2 K 18:30.
19:10. Ps 3:2. 11:1-3. 22:8. 42:10. 71:11. Mt
27:43.

12 **Hath not**. 2 K +21:3.
taken away. 2 Ch 20:33. 31:1.
Ye shall worship. Dt +12:13, 14, 26, 27.
one altar. 2 Ch 4:1. Ex 27:1-8. 30:1-6. 40:26-
29. 1 K 7:48.

13 **I and my**. 2 K 15:29. 17:5, 6. 19:11-13, 17,
18. Is 10:9, 10, 14. 37:12, 13, 18-20. Da 4:30,
37. 5:19.
were the gods. ver. +19. 2 K 18:33-35.
19:18, 19. 20:23. Ps 115:3-8. Is 44:8-10. Je
10:11, 12, 16. Ac 19:26. 1 C 8:4.

14 **among**. Is +10:11, 12.
your God. Ex 14:3. 15:9-11. Is 42:8.

15 **deceive**. 2 K +18:29. 19:10.
persuade. ver. 11. Dt 13:6. Jsh 15:18. 1 K
22:22. Is 36:18. Ac 19:26. Ga 1:10.
much less. Ex 5:2. Da 3:15. Jn 19:10, 11.

16 **yet**. Jb 15:25, 26. Ps 73:9.
against. Jn 15:21.

17 **He wrote**. 2 K +19:9, 14. Ne 6:5. Is 37:14.
to rail. 2 K 19:22, 28. Is 10:15. 37:23, 24, 28,
29. Re 13:6.
As the gods. 2 K 19:12.

18 **they cried**. 2 K +#18:26-28. Is 36:13.
to affright. 1 S 17:10, 26. Ne 6:9.

19 **spake**. ver. +13-17. 1 S 17:36. Jb 15:25, 26.
Ps 10:13, 14. 73:8-11. 139:19, 20.
the God. 2 Ch 6:6. Ps 76:1, 2. 78:68. 87:1-3.
132:13, 14. Is 14:32. He 12:22.
the gods of. ver. 13. Jg 11:24. 1 K 20:23. 2 K
17:26. 18:33.
the work. Dt 4:28. 27:15. 2 K 19:18. Ps
135:15-18. Is 2:8. 37:19. 44:16-20. Je 1:16.
10:3, 9. 32:30. Ho 8:5, 6.

20 **Hezekiah**. 2 K +19:14-19. Is 37:1, 14-20.
the prophet. 2 K 19:2-4. Is 37:2-4.
prayed. 2 Ch 14:11. 20:6-12. Ps 50:15.
+91:14, 15.
to heaven. Ps +73:9.

21 **the Lord**. 2 K +19:20, 35, etc. Is 10:16-18.
37:21, 36, 37. 42:8.
angel. 2 S 24:16. Ps 18:50. Da 3:28. 6:22. Mt
13:49, 50. Ac 12:23.
cut off all. Ex 12:29. Jb 9:4. Ps 76:5, 7, 12.
mighty men of. 2 Ch 13:3. 17:13. 25:6. Jg
+6:12.
the leaders. Is 10:8, 16-19, 34. 17:12-14.
29:5-8. 30:30-33. 33:10-12. 36:9. Re 6:15, 16.
19:17, 18.
with shame. Ps 132:18. Pr 11:2. 16:18.
he was come. 2 K +19:36, 37. Is 37:37, 38.
slew him. Heb. made him fall. 2 K 19:7.

22 **Lord**. Ps 18:48-50. 37:39, 40. 144:10. Is
10:24, 25. 31:4, 5. 31:4, 5. 33:22. Ho 1:7.
guided. 2 Ch 28:15. Ge 47:17. Ex 15:13. Ps
48:14. 71:20, 21. 73:24. Is 58:11. Jn 16:13. 2
Th 3:5.

23 **gifts**. 2 S 8:10, 11. Ezr 7:15-22, 27. Is 60:7-9.
presents. Heb. precious things. Jg +3:15.
he was magnified. 2 Ch 1:1. 1 Ch 29:25.

24 **Hezekiah**. 2 K +20:1-3. Is 38:1-3.
gave him a sign. or, wrought a miracle for
him. 2 K 20:4-11. Is 38:4-8, 21, 22.

25 **rendered not again**. Dt 32:6. Ps 116:12, 13.
Ho 14:2. Lk 17:17, 18.
his heart. ver. 31. Dt +17:20. 2 K 20:13.
therefore. 2 Ch 24:18. 2 S 24:1, 10-17. 1 Ch
21:1, 12-17. Ps +9:10. 115:1.
wrath upon. 2 Ch +24:18.

26 **Hezekiah**. 2 Ch 33:12, 19, 23. 34:27. Le
26:40, 41. 2 K 20:19. Je 26:18, 19. Ja 4:10.
pride. Heb. lifting up. Ps 10:4.
so. 1 K 21:19.
came not. Ps 115:1.
days. 2 Ch 34:27, 28. 1 K 21:29. 2 K 20:16-
19. Is 39:6-8.

27 A.M. 3278-3306. B.C. 726-698.
exceeding much. 2 Ch 1:12. 9:27. 17:5. Pr
10:22.
treasuries. 1 Ch 27:25, etc.
precious stones. 2 S 12:30. 1 K 5:17.
pleasant jewels. Heb. instruments of desire.
2 Ch 20:25. 2 K 20:13. Je +25:34mg.

28 **Storehouses**. 2 Ch 26:10.
stalls. 1 K 4:26.
cotes. 2 S 7:8.

29 **possessions**. 2 Ch 26:10. Ge 13:2-6. 1 Ch
27:29-31. Jb 1:3, 9. 42:12.
God. 2 Ch 25:9. Dt 8:18. 1 S 2:7. 1 Ch 29:12.
Pr 10:22. 1 T 6:17, 18.

30 **Hezekiah**. Or, "Hezekiah stopped the upper
going out (*motza*, i.e. the egress into the open
air) of the waters of Gihon, and brought them
underneath (*lemattah*, by a subterraneous
course) to the west of the city of David." 2 S
5:23. 1 K 1:45. 2 K 18:17. 20:20.
stopped. ver. +4. Is 22:9-11.
Gihon. 1 K 1:33, 38, 45.
And Hezekiah. Ps +1:3.

31 A.M. 3292. B.C. 712.
in the business. 2 K 20:12, 13. Is 39:1, 2, etc.
ambassadors. Heb. interpreters. Ge 42:23. Jb 16:20 (scorn). 33:23. Is 43:27mg.
the wonder. ver. 24. 2 K 20:8-11. Is 38:8.
God left him. Jg 16:20. Ps 27:9. 51:11, 12. 119:116, 117. Jn 15:5.
to try him. Ge 22:1. Ex 15:25. Dt 8:2, 16. Jb 1:11, 12. 2:3-6. Ps 139:1, 2, 23, 24. Pr 17:3. Da 11:35. Zc 13:9. Mt 3:2, 3. Ja 1:13. 1 P 1:7.
that he might. Dt 8:2. 13:3.

32 A.M. 3278-3306. B.C. 726-698.
goodness. Heb. kindnesses. 2 Ch 31:20, 21. 35:26. Ne 13:14.
in the vision. Is ch. 36-39.
in the book. 2 K ch. 18-20.

33 **slept.** 1 K +11:43.
chiefest. or, highest. 2 S 15:30.
sepulchres. Heb. qeber, Ge +23:4.
did him. 2 Ch 16:14. Ge 50:10, 11. Nu 20:29. Dt 34:8. 1 S 2:30. 25:1. Pr 10:7.
And Manasseh. 2 Ch +33:1, etc.

2 CHRONICLES 33

1 A.M. 3306-3361. B.C. 698-643.
Manasseh. Ge +41:51.
twelve. 2 Ch 34:1, 2. Ec 10:16. Is 3:4, 12.

2 **like unto.** 2 Ch 28:3. 36:14. Le 18:24-30. 20:22, 23. Dt 12:31. 18:9-14. 2 K 17:11, 15. 21:2, 9. Ezr 9:14. Ps 106:35-40. Ezk 11:12.

3 **he built again.** Heb. he returned and built. 2 Ch 19:4. Ec 2:19. 9:18.
which Hezekiah. 2 K +21:3.
he reared. 2 Ch 28:2-4. Jg 2:11-13.
made groves. 2 K +17:10.
the host. Dt +4:19.

4 **he built.** ver. 15. 2 Ch 34:3, 4. 2 K 21:4, 5. Je 7:30.
In Jerusalem. 2 Ch 6:6. 7:16. 32:19. Dt 12:11. 1 K 8:29. 9:3.
for ever. Heb. olam, Ex +12:24.

5 **the host.** Dt +4:19.
in the two. 2 Ch 4:9. Je 32:34, 35. Ezk 8:7-18.

6 **caused.** Dt +18:10.
he observed times. 2 K +21:6.
enchantments. 2 K +21:6. Is 47:9, 12.
witchcraft. Dt 18:10. 1 S 15:23. 2 K 9:22. Mi 5:12. Na 3:4. Ga 5:20.
familiar spirit. Dt +18:11.
wizards. 2 K +21:6.
anger. Dt 4:25. 9:18. 31:29. 32:16, 21.

7 **he set a carved image.** Ex +20:4. 2 K 21:7.
in the house. 2 K 21:7, 8. 23:6.
God had said. ver. +4. 1 K 8:29. Ps 132:13, 14.
which I have. 2 Ch 6:6. 1 K 8:44, 48. 11:13, 32. Ps 78:68.
for ever. Heb. olam, Ex +12:24.

8 **will I.** 2 S +7:10. 1 Ch 17:9.
so that they. 2 Ch 7:17-22. Dt 28:1-14. 30:15-20. Is 1:19, 20. Ezk 33:25, 26.
to do all. Dt 4:40. 5:1, 31-33. 6:1. 8:1. 27:26. Lk 1:6. Ga 3:10-13.
by the hand. 2 Ch 34:14mg. Le 8:36. 10:11.

9 **made Judah.** 1 K 14:16. 15:26. 2 K 21:16. 23:26. 24:3, 4. Pr 29:12. Mi 6:16.
to err. 2 K 21:9. Jb 12:24, 25. Ps 119:21, 118. Ho +4:12. Mk 12:24, 27.
to do worse. ver. +2. 2 K 21:9-11. Ezk 16:45-47. Ps 86:13. Mt 11:22. Lk +12:48. Ro +2:12.
the heathen. Le 18:24. Dt 2:21. Jsh 24:8. 2 K 17:8-11.

10 **the Lord spake.** 2 Ch 36:15, 16. Je +25:4.

11 A.M. 3327. B.C. 677.
the Lord. Dt 28:36. Jb 36:8.
the captains. Is 10:8. 36:9.
of the king. Heb. which were the king's. 1 S 24:4. 2 K 16:13. Ne 9:32, 37. Is 5:26-30. 7:18-20.
among the thorns. 1 S 13:6. La 3:7. Ezk 19:4, 6.
bound him. 2 K 23:33. 25:6. Ps +107:10.
fetters. or, chains. 2 Ch 36:6. Jg 16:21. 2 S 3:34. 2 K 25:7. Ps 149:8. Je 39:7. 40:1. 52:11.

12 **And when.** 2 Ch 28:22. Le 26:39-42. Dt 4:30, 31. Je 31:18-20. Ho 5:15. Mi 6:9. Lk 15:16-18.
affliction. Ps 106:43, 44.
he besought. ver. 18, 19. Ps 50:15. Ac 9:11.
the Lord. 2 Ch +28:5.
humbled. ver. 19, 23. 2 Ch 32:26. Ex 10:3. Lk 18:14, 15. Ja 4:10. 1 P 5:5, 6.

13 **he was intreated.** 1 Ch 5:20. Ezr 8:23. Jb 22:23, 27. 33:16-30. 36:8-10. Ps 32:3-5. 86:5. Is 55:6-9. Je 29:12, 13. Mt 7:7, 8. Lk 23:42, 43. Jn 4:10.
brought him. Ezr 7:27. Pr 16:7. 21:1. Mt 6:33.
knew. Dt 29:6. Ps 9:16. 46:10. Je 24:7. Da 4:25, 34, 35. Jn 17:3. He 8:11.

14 A.M. 3327-3361. B.C. 677-643.
he built. 2 Ch 32:5.
Gihon. 2 Ch 32:30. 1 K 1:33, 45.
fish gate. Ne 3:3. 12:39. Zp 1:10.
Ophel. or, the tower. 2 K +5:24mg.
put. 2 Ch 11:11, 12. 17:19.

15 **he took.** ver. 3-7. 2 K 21:7. Is 2:17-21. Ezk 18:20-22. Ho 14:1-3. Mt 3:8.
strange. 2 Ch 14:3. Ex 12:43 (S#5236h). Ne 9:2.

16 **repaired.** 2 Ch 29:18. 1 K 18:30.
altar. 2 Ch +4:1. Le +17:6.
peace. Le +23:19.
thank. Le +7:12-18.
commanded. ver. 9. 2 Ch 14:4. 2 Ch +30:12. Ge 18:19. Lk 22:32.

17 **people.** 2 K +21:3.

18 A.M. 3306-3361. B.C. 698-643.
the rest. 2 Ch 20:34. 32:32. 1 K +11:41.
his prayer. ver. 12, 13, 19.
the seers. ver. 10. 1 S 9:9. 2 K 17:13. Is 29:10. 30:10. Am 7:12. Mi 3:7.
in the book. 1 K 14:19. 15:31.

19 **his prayer also**. ver. 11, 12, 19. Pr 15:8. Ac 9:11. 1 J 1:9.
all his sins. ver. 1-10. Ro 5:16.
groves. 2 K +17:10.
graven. Ex +20:4.
before he. ver. +12. 2 Ch 30:11. 36:12. Ps 119:67, 71, 75. Je 44:10. Da 5:22.
the seers. or, Hosai.

20 **Manasseh**. 2 Ch +32:33. 2 K 21:18.
Amon. Ne +7:59.

21 A.M. 3361-3363. B.C. 643-641.
two years. ver. 1. Lk 12:19, 20. Ja 4:13-15.

22 **as did Manasseh**. ver. 1-10. 2 K 21:1-11, 20. Ezk 20:18.
for Amon sacrificed. Dt 7:5. Is 44:13, etc. Ac 19:19.

23 **humbled not**. ver. 1, 12, 19. Je 8:12.
trespassed more and more. Heb. multiplied trespass. ver. 6. 2 Ch 28:22. 36:14. Ex 36:5. Le 11:42. Je 7:26. 2 T 3:13.

24 A.M. 3363. B.C. 641.
conspired. 2 Ch 24:25, 26. 25:27, 28. 2 S 4:5-12. 2 K 21:23-26. Ps 55:23. Ro 11:22.

25 **slew**. Ge 9:5, 6. Nu 35:31, 33.
the people. 2 Ch 26:1. 36:1.
Josiah. 2 Ch 34:1.

2 CHRONICLES 34

1 A.M. 3363-3394. B.C. 641-610.
Josiah. 1 K +13:2.
eight years. 2 Ch 24:1. 26:1. 33:1. 1 S 2:18, 26. 1 K 3:7-9. Ec 4:13.

2 **right in the sight**. 2 Ch 14:2. 17:3. 29:2. 1 K 14:8. 2 K 22:2.
declined. Jsh +1:7.

3 A.M. 3370. B.C. 634.
while he. 1 K 22:5. 29:1. Ps 119:9. Ec 12:1. 2 T 3:15.
to seek. 2 Ch +15:2. 1 Ch 28:9. Pr 8:17. Mt 6:33.
purge. 2 Ch +33:17, 22. Le 26:30. 2 K 23:4, 14.
the high places. 2 K +21:3.
the groves. Heb. Asherim. or, Asherah poles. 2 K +17:10.
carved images. ver. 4, 7. Ex +20:4.
molten images. Ex +34:17.

4 **brake down**. 2 Ch 33:3. Ex +23:24. Le 26:30.
images. or, sun images. Le +26:30mg. 2 K 23:4, 5, 11.
made dust. ver. 7. 33:22. Ex 32:20. Dt 9:21. 2 K 23:12. Ps 18:42. Is 27:9.

graves. Heb. face of the graves. Heb. qeber. Ge +23:4. Dt +7:5.

5 **he burnt the bones**. 1 K 13:2. 2 K +23:16. Is 65:4. Ezk 24:10, 12. 43:7.
cleansed. ver. 7. Nu 35:33. Je 3:10. 4:14. Ezk 22:24.

6 **in**. 2 Ch 30:1, 10, 11. 31:1. 2 K 23:15-20.
mattocks. or, mauls. 1 S 13:20, 21. Pr 25:18. Is 7:25.

7 **beaten**. ver. +4.
into powder. Heb. to make powder. ver. 4.
he returned. 2 Ch 31:1.

8 A.M. 3380. B.C. 624.
the eighteenth. Je 1:2, 3.
sent Shaphan. 2 K +22:3.
Azaliah. i.e. kept back by Jah; Jah has reserved, **S#683h**. ver. 8. 2 K 22:3.
Maaseiah. Je +21:1.
governor. 2 Ch 18:25.
Joah. Is +36:3.
Joahaz. i.e. whom the Lord holds fast, **S#3099h**. 2 Ch 34:8. 36:2, 4. 2 K 14:1.
recorder. 2 S +8:16mg.

9 **Hilkiah**. ver. 14, 15, 18, 20, 22. 2 K +18:18.
they delivered. 2 Ch 24:11-14. 2 K 22:5-7. Ph 4:8.
doors. 2 K +12:9mg.
Manasseh. 2 Ch 30:10, 18. 31:1.
and they returned. or, and the inhabitants of. ver. 7.

10 **in the hand**. 2 K 12:11, 12, 14. 22:5, 6. Ezr 3:7.

11 **floor**. or, rafter. Ne 2:8. 3:3, 6.
the kings. 2 Ch 33:4-7, 22.

12 **faithfully**. 2 Ch 19:9. 31:12. Nu 12:7. 2 K 12:15. 22:7. Ne 7:2. Pr 25:13. 28:20. 1 C 4:2. 3 J 5.
overseers. 1 Ch 9:29. 1 Th 5:12, 13. He 13:17.
all. 1 Ch 6:31, etc. 15:16-22. 16:4, 5, 41, 42. 23:5. 25:1, etc.

13 **over**. 1 Th 5:12, 13. He 13:17.
the bearers. 2 Ch 2:10, 18. Ne 4:10. Ga 6:2, 5.
overseers. 1 Ch 9:28, 29. 1 Th 5:12, 13. He 13:17.
and of the Levites. 1 Ch 23:4, 5.
scribes. Ezr 7:6. Je 8:8. Mt 26:3. 2 C 3:2, 3.
officers. 2 Ch 19:11. 1 Ch 23:4. 26:29, 30.
porters. 2 Ch 8:14. 1 Ch 9:17. 15:18. 16:38, 42. 26:1, etc. Ezr 7:7.

14 **Hilkiah**. 2 K +22:8, etc. Dt 31:24-26.
found. 2 Ch 17:9. 25:4. 2 K 11:12. 14:6. 22:8.
the law. 2 Ch 12:1. 31:4. 35:26. Dt 17:18, 19. Jsh 1:8. Ezr 7:10. Ps 1:2. Is 5:24. 30:9. Je 8:8. Lk 2:39.
by Moses. Heb. by the hand of Moses. 2 Ch 35:6. Ex +24:4. Le 8:36. 10:11. 26:46. 1 K +16:12mg. 2 K 14:6. 22:8.

15 **answered**. Jg 18:14. 1 S 9:17.

Shaphan. 2 K 22:10.
the book. 2 K 22:8. Ezr 7:6. Ne 8:1.

16 Shaphan. 2 K +22:9, 10. Je 36:20, 21.
thy servants. Heb. the hand of thy servants.
they do. 2 S 15:15. Jn 2:5.

17 And they. ver. +8-10.
gathered together. Heb. poured out, or
melted. ver. 21, 25. 2 K 22:9. Jb 10:10.

18 And Shaphan read. Dt 17:19. Jsh 1:8. Ps
119:46, 97-99. Je 36:20, 21. Re 1:3.
it. Heb. in it. 2 K 22:10.

19 the words. Ro 3:20. 7:7-11. Ga 2:19. 3:10-
13.
that he rent. 2 K +18:37. Lk 14:11.

20 Ahikam. 2 K +22:12.
Abdon. Jg +12:13. 2 K 22:12, Achbor. Je
26:22.
Micah. Mi +1:1.
Asaiah. i.e. the Lord has wrought, S#6222h. 2 K
+22:14, Asahiah. 1 Ch 4:36. 6:30. 9:5. 15:6,
11.

21 enquire. Ex 18:15. 1 S 9:9. 1 K 22:5-7. Je
21:2. Ezk 14:1, etc. 20:1-7.
that are left. 2 Ch 28:6. 33:11. 2 K 17:6, 7.
22:13. Is 37:2-4. Je 42:2.
great. Le 26:14, etc. Dt 28:15. 29:18-28.
30:17-19. 31:16-22. 32:15-25. Ro 1:18. 2:8-
12. 4:15.
poured. Ezk +7:8.

22 the prophetess. Ex +15:20.
Tikvath. i.e. expectation; shall be gathered; hope,
S#8616h. 2 K +22:14, Tikvah.
Hasrah. i.e. extreme poverty; she was lacking,
S#2641h. 2 K +22:14, Harhas.
wardrobe. Heb. garments.
college. or, school, or second part. 2 K
22:14mg. Ne 11:9. Zp 1:10.

23 Tell ye the man. 2 K +22:15-20. Je 21:3-7.
37:7-10.

24 I will bring. 2 Ch 36:14-20. Jsh 23:16. 2 K
21:12. 23:26, 27. Is 5:4-6. Je 6:19. 11:11.
19:3, 15. 35:17. 36:31.
all the curses. ver. +21.

25 Because. 2 Ch 33:3-9. 2 K 24:3, 4. Is 2:8, 9.
Je +1:16. 15:1-4.
my wrath. Ezk +7:8.
shall not. 2 K 22:17. Je +4:4. 7:20. Ezk
20:48. Mk 9:43-48.

26 as for. ver. 21, 23.

27 Because. Ps 9:10.
thine heart. 2 Ch +32:12, 13. 2 K 22:18, 19.
Ps 34:18. 51:17. Is 57:15. +66:2. Ezk 36:26.
humble. 2 Ch +32:26. 33:12, 19. Ja 4:6-10.
didst rend. ver. +19.
I have even. 2 Ch +7:14. Ps 10:17. Is 65:24.

28 I will gather. 2 Ch 35:24. 2 K +22:20. Is
57:1, 2. Je 15:1. Ezk 14:14-21.
grave. Heb. qeber, Ge +23:4.
in peace. Ps 37:37.
neither. 1 K 21:29. 2 K 20:19. Is 39:8.

29 the king. 1 S 12:23. 1 Ch 29:2, etc. Mk 14:8.
gathered. 2 Ch 30:2. 2 K 23:1-3.

30 great and small. Heb. from great even to
small. 2 Ch 15:12, 13. 18:30. Dt 1:17. Jb 3:19.
he read. 2 Ch 6:1, etc. 17:7-9. Dt 17:18-20.
Ne 8:2-5. Ec 1:12. 12:9, 10.
their ears. Jn 8:47. Ja 1:19-22.
the book. ver. 15, 18, 19, 24. Ex 24:7. 2 K
23:2, 21. Je 31:31, 32.

31 in his place. 2 Ch 6:13. 2 K 11:14. 23:3. Ezk
46:2.
made a covenant. 2 Ch 23:16. 29:10. Ex
24:6-8. Dt 29:1, 10-15. Jsh 24:25. Ne 9:38.
10:29. Je 50:5. He 8:6-13.
and his testimonies. Ps 119:111, 112.
with all his heart. Mt +22:37.
soul. Heb. nephesh, Ge +34:3.
to perform. Ps 119:106.

32 caused. 2 Ch 14:4. 30:12. 33:16. Ge 18:19. Ec
8:2.
present. Heb. found. Est +1:5mg.
did. Je 3:10.

33 took away. ver. +3-7. 2 K 23:4-20.
the abominations. Ge 43:32. 46:34. Ex 8:26.
1 K 11:5-7.
all his days. Jsh 24:31. Je 3:10. Ho 6:4.
from following. Heb. from after. 2 Ch
25:27mg.

2 CHRONICLES 35

1 Josiah. 2 Ch ch. 30. 2 K 23:21-23.
the fourteenth. Ex 12:6. Nu 9:3. Dt 16:1-8.
Ezr 6:19. Ezk 45:21.

2 charges. 2 Ch 23:8, 18. 31:2. Nu 18:5-7. 1 Ch
ch. 24. Ezr 6:18.
encouraged. 2 Ch 29:5-11. 31:2. 1 Ch 22:19.
1 C 15:58.

3 the Levites that taught. 2 Ch +15:3. 17:8,
9. 30:22. Le 10:11. 23:3. Dt 17:9. 33:10. 2 K
+4:22, 23. 1 Ch 25:7, 8. 26:32. Ezr 7:10, 25.
Ne 8:7, 8. Ml 2:7. Mt 23:2, 3. 1 C 14:34. T 2:2.
Put. 2 Ch 5:7. 8:11. 34:14. He 1:3. Re 21:3.
in the house. 2 Ch +5:7.
not be. Nu 4:15-49. 1 Ch 23:26. He 4:9. Re
7:15, 16. 14:13.
serve now. Nu 8:19. 16:9, 10. 2 C 4:5. Re
7:15.

4 the houses. 1 Ch 9:10-34. Ne 11:10-20.
after your courses. 1 Ch ch. 23-26.
and according. 2 Ch 8:14.

5 And stand. Ps 134:1. 135:2.
divisions. Ezr 6:18.
families of the fathers. Heb. house of the
fathers.
the people. Heb. the sons of the people. ver.
7, 12. Ex 12:3.

6 So kill. 2 Ch 30:15-17. Ex 12:6, 21, 22. Ezr
6:20, 21.
sanctify. 2 Ch 29:5, 15, 34. 30:3, 15-19. Ge

35:2. Ex 19:10, 15. Nu 19:11-20. Jb 1:5. Ps 51:7. Jl 2:16. He 9:13, 14.

7 Josiah. 2 Ch 7:8-10. 30:24. Is 32:8. Ezk 45:17.
gave. Heb. offered. ver. 8mg, 9mg. 2 Ch 30:24mg. 1 K 8:63.
passover offerings. 2 Ch 30:17.
present. 2 Ch +29:29mg. Jg +20:48mg.
the king's substance. 1 K 8:63. 1 Ch 29:3.

8 his princes. 2 Ch 29:31-33. 1 Ch 29:6-9, 17. Ezr 1:6. 2:68, 69. 7:16. 8:25-35. Ne 7:70-72. Ps 45:12. Ac 2:44, 45. 4:34, 35.
gave. Heb. offered. ver. +7mg.
willingly. Le +23:38.
Hilkiah. 2 Ch 34:14-20.
rulers. 1 Ch 9:20. 24:4, 5. Je 29:25, 26. Ac 4:1. 5:26.

9 Conaniah. i.e. *prepared of Jah; established of Jehovah*, **S#3562h**. 2 Ch 31:12, 13. 35:9.
gave. Heb. offered. ver. +7mg. Is 1:10-15. Je 3:10. 7:21-28. Mi 6:6-8.

10 the priests. ver. 4, 5. 2 Ch 30:16. Ezr 6:18.
king's. 1 C 12:18.
commandment. Jn 14:21. 15:14.

11 passover. 1 C 5:7, 8.
the priests. Le +1:5.
flayed them. 2 Ch 29:34.

12 as it is written. Le 3:3, 5, 9-11, 14-16.

13 roasted. Ex 12:8, 9. Dt 16:7. Ps 22:14. La 1:12, 13.
sod. Le 6:28. Nu 6:19. 1 S 2:13-15. Ezk 46:20-24.
pots. Ex 16:3. 27:3. 38:3. 1 K 7:45.
caldrons. 1 S 2:14. 2 K 10:7. Jb 41:20. Ps 81:6. Je 24:2.
pans. 2 K 2:20 (cruse). 21:13 (dish).
divided them speedily. Heb. made *them* run. 2 K 23:12. Ro 12:11.

14 because the priests. Ac 6:2-4.
busied. 2 Ch 13:10. Ne 11:22. Ro 12:11.

15 singers. 2 Ch 5:12, 13. 20:21. 29:28.
place. Heb. station. ver. 10. 1 Ch 23:28.
according. 2 Ch 29:25, 26. 1 Ch 16:41, 42. 23:5. 25:1-7. Ps ch. 77-79, titles.
the porters. 1 Ch 9:17-19. +23:5. 26:14-19.
not depart. Mt 24:46.

17 present. Heb. found. Est +1:5mg.
passover. Le +23:5.
the feast. 2 Ch 30:21-23. Ex 12:15-20. 13:6, 7. 23:15. 34:18. Le 23:5-8. Nu 28:16-25. Dt 16:3, 4, 8. 1 C 5:7, 8.
unleavened. Le +23:6.

18 there was no passover. 2 Ch 30:5, 23. 2 K 23:21-23. Ne 8:17.
neither did. 2 Ch 30:26, 27.
present. Heb. found. 2 Ch +29:29mg. Jg +20:48mg.

20 A.M. 3394. B.C. 610.
After. 2 K 23:29.
temple. Heb. house. 2 Ch 34:8, 10.

Necho. i.e. *the smitten* or *lame*, **S#5224h**. ver. 20, 22. 2 Ch 36:4. 2 K 23:29, etc., Pharaoh-nechoh. Je 46:2, etc.
Charchemish. i.e. *fortified city; fortress of refuge; fortress of Chemosh*, **S#3751h**. ver. 20. Is 10:9. Je 46:2.

21 What have I. Jg +11:12.
to do. Mt 27:19.
house wherewith I have war. Heb. house of my war.
God. 2 K 18:25. Is 36:10.
forbear thee. 2 Ch 25:19.

22 but disguised. Ge +27:16.
the mouth. ver. 21. 2 Ch 18:4-6. Jsh 9:14.
of God. Ex 12:12. 20:23. 1 S 5:7; 1 K 11:5. Ps 96:5. 97:7.
Megiddo. Jsh +12:21.

23 the archers. 2 Ch 18:33. Ge 49:23. 2 K 9:24. La 3:13.
wounded. Heb. made sick. 2 Ch 18:33mg. 1 K 22:34mg. 2 K 8:29.

24 the second. Ge 41:43.
they. 2 K 22:30.
died. Ps 36:6. Ec 8:14. 9:1, 2.
in one of the. or, among the. 2 Ch 34:28.
sepulchres. Heb. *qeber*, Ge +23:4.
Judah. Zc 12:11.

25 Jeremiah. Je 22:10. La 4:20.
lamented. 2 S 1:17. 3:33. Ezk 27:32. 32:16. Mt +9:23.
all the singing. Ec 12:5.
singing women. 2 S 19:35. Ec 2:8. Ezr 2:65. Ne 7:67.
and made them. Je 22:20.
an ordinance. Jg 11:39mg. Je 10:3mg.

26 goodness. Heb. kindnesses. 2 Ch 31:20. 32:32. Ne 13:14.

27 deeds. 2 Ch 20:34. 24:27. 25:26. 26:22. 32:32. 33:19. 2 K 10:34. 16:19. 20:20. 21:25.

2 CHRONICLES 36

1 the people. 2 Ch 26:1. 33:25. 2 K 23:30, etc.
Jehoahaz. 2 K 23:31-34. 1 Ch 3:15. Je 22:11.

3 put him down. Heb. removed him. 2 K 23:33.
condemned. Heb. mulcted. or, fineth. Ex 21:22. Pr 19:19.

4 made Eliakim. 2 K +18:18. 1 Ch +3:15.
Necho. Je 22:10-12. Ezk 19:3, 4.

5 Jehoiakim. 2 K 23:36, 37. Je 22:13-19. 26:21-23. 36:1, 27-32.

6 A.M. 3397. B.C. 607.
came up. 2 K 24:1, 2, 5, 6, 13, etc. Ezk 19:5-9. Da 1:1, 2. Hab 1:5-10.
fetters. or, chains. 2 Ch +33:11.
carry him to. Je +39:7.

7 A.M. 3398. B.C. 606.
the vessels. 2 Ch +4:19.

8 A.M. 3394-3405. B.C. 610-599.

written. 2 K 24:5, 6.
Jehoiachin. 2 K +24:8.

9 A.M. 3405. B.C. 599.
eight years old. rather, eighteen years. 2 K 24:8, 9.

10 **when the year was expired**. Heb. at the return of the year. 2 Ch +24:23mg.
king Nebuchadnezzar. 2 K 24:10-17. 25:27-30. Je 29:2. Ezk 1:2.
goodly vessels. Heb. vessels of desire. ver. +7. Je +25:34mg.
Zedekiah. 1 K +22:11.

11 A.M. 3405-3416. B.C. 599-588.
one and twenty. 2 K 24:18-20. Je 52:1-3.

12 **humbled**. 2 Ch 32:26. 33:12, 19, 23. Ex 10:3. Da 5:22, 23. Ja 4:10. 1 P 5:6.
before Jeremiah. Je 21:1, etc. 27:12, etc. 28:1, etc. 34:2, etc. 37:2, etc. 38:14, etc.
the mouth. 2 Ch 35:22.

13 **rebelled**. Jsh 9:15, 19, 20. 2 S 21:2. Ezk 17:11-20.
who had. Jsh 9:15, 19, 20. 2 S 21:2.
stiffened. 2 Ch +30:8.
hardened. Ex +4:21. 9:17. Ne 9:29.

14 **all the chief**. 2 K 16:10-16. Ezr 9:7. Je 5:5. 37:13-15. 38:4. Ezk 22:6, 26-28. Da 9:6, 8. Mi 3:1-4, 9-11. 7:2. Zp 3:3, 4.
very much. 2 Ch 28:3. 33:9.
polluted. 2 Ch 33:4-7. Ezk 8:5-16.

15 **the Lord**. 2 Ch 33:10. 2 K 17:13.
sent. 2 Ch +24:19.
by his messengers. Heb. by the hand of his messengers.
betimes. i.e. continually and carefully.
because. Jg 10:16. 2 K 13:23. Ho 11:8. Lk 19:41-44.

16 **mocked**. Je 5:12, 13. Ac 2:13. He +11:36.
despised. Pr 1:24-30. Lk 16:14. Ac 13:41. 1 Th 4:8.
misused. Je 32:3. 38:6. Mt 5:12. 21:33-41. 23:34-47. Ac 7:52.
the wrath. Ps 74:1. 79:1-5.
till. Pr 6:15. 29:1.
remedy. Heb. healing. 2 Ch 21:18. Pr 4:22. 6:15. 12:18. 13:17. 16:24. 29:1. Je 8:15. 14:19. 33:6. Ml 4:2.

17 **he brought**. 2 Ch 33:11. Dt 28:49. 2 K 24:2, 3. Ezr 9:7. Je 15:8. 32:42. 40:3. Da 9:14.
the king. 2 K 25:1, etc. Je 39:1, etc. 52:1, etc.
who slew. Le 26:14, etc. Dt 28:15, etc. 29:18-28. 30:18. 31:16-18. 32:15-28. Ps 74:20. 79:2, 3. Je +11:22. 15:9. 18:21. La 2:21, 22.
in the house. 2 Ch 24:21. La 2:20. Ezk 9:5-7. Lk 13:1, 2.
no compassion. Dt 28:50. Ps 74:20.
or maiden. or, virgin. Ge +24:16. Ex 22:16, 17.

18 A.M. 3416. B.C. 588.
all the vessels. ver. +7, 10.
treasures. Is +39:6. Zc 1:6.

19 **they burnt**. Je 7:4, 14. +17:27. La 4:1. Mi 3:12. Lk 21:6.
brake down. Je +39:8.

20 A.M. 3416-3468. B.C. 588-536.
And them that had escaped from. Heb. And the remainder from. 2 K 25:11.
they were servants. Dt 28:47, 48. Je 27:7.
until the reign. ver. 22. Ezr 1:1, etc.

21 **To fulfil**. Je 25:9, 12. 26:6, 7. 27:12, 13. 29:10. Da 9:2. Zc 1:4-6.
until the land. Le 25:4-6. 26:34, 35, 43. Zc 1:12.
desolate. Je +18:16.

22 A.M. 3468. B.C. 536.
in the first. Ezr 1:1-3.
Cyrus. Is +45:1. 44:28. Da 10:1.
Persia. i.e. *he divided*, **S#6539h**. ver. 20, 22, 23. Ezr 1:1, 2, 8. 3:7. 4:3, 5, 7. 7:1. 9:9. Est 1:3, 14, 18, 19. 10:2. Ezk 27:10. 38:5. Da 8:20. 10:1, 13, 13, 20. 11:2.
that the word. ver. 21. Je 25:12, 14. 29:10. 32:42-44. 33:10-14. He 10:23.
the Lord stirred. 2 Ch 21:16. 1 S 26:19. 1 K 11:14, 23. 1 Ch 5:26. Ezr 1:5. Is 13:3-5, 17, 18. 44:28. 45:1-5. Hg 1:14.
spirit. Heb. *ruach*, Ge +41:8; +26:35.
a proclamation. 2 Ch 24:9. 30:5.

23 **All the kingdoms**. Ps 75:5-7. Da 2:21, 37. 4:35. 5:18, 23.
he hath charged. Is 44:26-28.
Who is there. 1 Ch 22:16. 29:5. Ezr 7:13. Zc 2:6, 7. Ro 8:31.

EZRA

EZRA 1

1 A.M. 3468. B.C. 536.
Now in the. 2 Ch 36:22, 23.
Cyrus. Is +45:1.
by the mouth. Je 25:12-14. 29:10. 33:7-13. Da 9:2.
the Lord. Ezr 5:13-15. 6:22. 7:27. Ps 106:46. Pr 21:1. Da 2:1.
stirred up. 2 Ch 36:21. Je 51:11. Hg 1:14.
spirit. Heb. *ruach*, Ge +41:8; +26:35.
made a proclamation. Heb. caused a voice to pass. Ezr 10:7. Ex 36:6. Le 25:9. 2 Ch 30:5. Ne 8:15. Da 9:25. Mt 3:1-3. Jn 1:23.

2 **Lord God**. 1 K 8:27. 2 Ch 2:12. Is 66:1. Je 10:11. Da 2:21, 28. 5:23.
hath given. 2 Ch 36:23. Je 27:6, 7. Da 2:37, 38. 4:25, 32. 5:19-21. 7:5, 15.
all the kingdoms. 1 K 18:10.
he hath charged. Is 44:26-28. 45:1, 12, 13.

3 **all his people**. 2 Ch 36:23. 1 K 18:39.
his God. Jsh 1:9. 1 Ch 28:20. Mt 28:20.
he is the God. Dt 32:31. Ps 83:18. Is 45:5. Je 10:10. Da 2:47. 6:26. Ac 10:36.

4 **let the men**. Ezr 7:16-18. Ac 24:17. 3 J 6-8.
help him. Heb. lift him up. Ezr 8:36. 1 K 9:11. Est 9:3. Ps 28:9. Ec 4:9, 10. Ga 6:2.
the freewill. Le +23:38. Ezr 2:68-70.

5 **with all whose**. ver. 1. 2 Ch 36:22. Ne 2:12. Pr 16:1. 2 C 8:16. Ph 2:13. Ja 1:16, 17. 3 J 11.
spirit. Heb. *ruach*, Ge +41:8. Ps 78:8. Da 5:12. 2 C +12:8.

6 **strengthened their hands**. *that is*, helped them. Ezr 4:4. 7:15, 16. 8:25-28, 33. Je 38:4.
willingly offered. ver. +4.

7 **Also Cyrus**. Ezr 5:14. 6:5.
brought forth the vessels. 2 K 24:13. Je +3:16.
Nebuchadnezzar. 2 Ch +4:19.

8 **Mithredath**. i.e. *given by Mithras; searching out of law; given by the genius of the sun*, **S#4990h**. Ezr 1:8. 4:7.
Sheshbazzar. i.e. *joy in tribulation; worshipper of fire; deliverance of brightness; fine linen in the tribulation*, **S#8339h**. ver. 11. Ezr 5:14, 16. Hg 1:1, 14. 2:2-4. Zc 4:6-10.

9 **chargers of gold**. Nu 7:13, 19, etc. 1 K 7:50.

2 Ch 4:8, 11, 21, 22. 24:14. Mt 14:8.
nine. Mt 10:29-31.

11 **the vessels**. ver. 6. 2 K 25:15. Ro 9:23. 2 T 2:19-21.
captivity. Heb. transportation. Ezr 4:1mg. Mt 1:11, 12.

EZRA 2

1 **the children**. Ezr 5:8. 6:2. Ne 7:6, etc. Est 1:1. 3:8, 11. 8:9. Ac 23:34.
whom Nebuchadnezzar. 2 K 24:14-16. 25:11. 2 Ch ch. 36. Je 39:52. La 1:3, 5. 4:22. Zp 2:7.

2 **Zerubbabel**. Ezr 1:11, Sheshbazzar. Hg +1:1.
Jeshua. Ne +8:17. Hg 1:12, 14. 2:4. Zc 3:1, 3, 8, 9, Joshua.
Nehemiah. Ne +1:1.
Seraiah. 2 S +8:17. Ne 7:7, Azariah, Raamiah, Nahamani, Mispereth, Nehum.
Reelaiah. i.e. *trembling of the Lord*, **S#7480h**.
Mordecai. Est +2:5.
Bilshan. i.e. *son of the tongue, i.e. loquacious or eloquent*, **S#1114h**. Ne 7:7.
Mizpar. i.e. *number*, **S#4558h**.
Bigvai. i.e. *happy; a gardener; in my bodies*, **S#902h**. ver. 14. Ezr 8:14. Ne 7:7, 19. 10:16.
Rehum. Ne +12:3.

3 **Parosh**. i.e. *a flea*, **S#6551h**. Ezr 8:3, Pharosh. 10:25. Ne 3:25. 7:8. 10:14.

4 **Shephatiah**. Ezr 8:8. 2 S +3:4. Ne 7:9.

5 **Arah**. 1 Ch +7:39. Ne 6:18. 7:10, six hundred fifty-two.

6 **Pahath-moab**. i.e. *pit, snare*, or *governor of Moab*, **S#6355h**. Ezr 8:4. 10:30. Ne 3:11. 7:11, 2818. 10:14.
Joab. Ezr 8:9. 1 S +26:6.

7 **Elam**. ver. 31. Ge +10:22.

8 **Zattu**. i.e. *ornament; beauty*, **S#2240h**. Ezr 10:27. Ne 7:13, 845. 10:14.

9 **Zaccai**. Ne +7:14.

10 **Bani**. i.e. *built up*, **S#1137h**. Ezr 10:29, 34, 38. 2 S 23:36. 1 Ch 6:46. 9:4. Ne 3:17. 8:7. 9:4, 5. 10:13, 14. 11:22. The variation of *Bani* and *Binnui* arises from the elision of *wav*; but the LXX. have here *Banoui*, as in the parallel place. Ezr 10:34. Ne 7:15, Binnui, 648.

11 **Bebai**. i.e. *fatherly; my cavities*, **S#893h**. Ezr 8:11. 10:28. Ne 7:16, 628. 10:15.

12 **Azgad**. i.e. *the god Gad is strong*, **S#5803h**. Ezr 8:12. Ne 7:17, 2322. 10:15.

13 **Adonikim**. Ezr 8:13. Ne +7:18, 667.

14 **Bigvai**. ver. +2. Ezr 8:14. Ne 7:19, 2067.

15 **Adin**. i.e. *luxuriant*, **S#5720h**. Ezr 8:6. Ne 7:20, 655. 10:16.

16 **Ater**. i.e. *left handed (i.e., shut as to the right hand); dumb*, **S#333h**. Ne 7:21.

17 **Bezai**. Ne +7:23, 324.

18 **Jorah**. i.e. *shooting, sprinkling; autumnal rain*, **S#3139h**. Ne 7:24, Hariph.

19 **Hashum**. i.e. *rich, wealthy*, **S#2828h**. Ezr 10:33. Ne 7:22, 328. 8:4. 10:18.

20 **Gibbar**. i.e. *a mighty one, a hero*, **S#1402h**. Ne 7:25, Gibeon.

21 **Beth-lehem**. Jsh +19:15.

22 **Netophah**. i.e. *distillation*, **S#5199h**. 2 S 23:28. 1 Ch 2:54. Ne 7:26, 188. Je 40:8.

23 **Anathoth**. 1 Ch +7:8.

24 **Azmaveth**. 2 S +23:31. Ne 7:28, Beth-azmaveth.

25 **Kirjath-arim**. i.e. *city of forests* or *enemies* or *cities*, **S#7157h**. Jsh 18:28. Also Jsh +9:17, Kirjath-jearim.
     Chephirah. Jsh +9:17.
     Beeroth. Jsh +9:17.

26 **Ramah**. Je +31:15.
     Gaba. Jsh +18:24.

27 **Michmas**. i.e. *a treasure*, **S#4363h**. 1 S +13:2, Michmash, 5, 11, 16, 23. 14:5, 31. Ne 7:31. 11:31. Is 10:28, Michmash.

28 **Bethel**. Ge +12:8.
     Ai. Ge 12:8, Hai. Jsh +7:2. 8:9, 17. Ne 7:32, 123.

29 **Nebo**. Nu +32:3.

30 **Magbish**. i.e. *congregating; crystallizing*, **S#4019h**.

31 **Elam**. ver. 7. Ge +10:22. Ne 7:34.

32 **Harim**. 1 Ch +24:8.

33 **Lod**. Ne +7:37.
     Hadid. or, Hadrid, as in some copies. i.e. *sharp*, **S#2307h**. Ne 7:37. 11:34.
     Ono. i.e. *strong; gain-bringing*, **S#207h**. 1 Ch 8:12. Ne 6:2. 7:37. 11:35.

34 **Jericho**. Nu +22:1. 1 K 16:34. Ne 7:36.

35 **Senaah**. i.e. *thorny, bushy; high; hatred*, **S#5570h**. Ne 3:3. 7:38, 3930.

36 **Jedaiah**. 1 Ch +9:10. 24:7.
     Jeshua. Ne +8:17.

37 **Immer**. 1 Ch +9:12.

38 **Pashur**. Je +20:1.

39 **Harim**. ver. +32.

40 **Kadmiel**. i.e. *servant of God; going before God*, **S#6934h**. Ezr 3:9. Ne 7:43. 9:4, 5. 10:9. 12:8, 24.
     Hodaviah. Ezr 3:9, Judah. 1 Ch +5:24. Ne 7:43, Hodevah.

41 **singers**. 2 Ch 35:15.
     Asaph. 2 K +18:18. Ne 7:44, 148.

42 **the porters**. 1 Ch 26:1, etc. Ne 7:45, 138.
     Shallum. 2 K +15:10.
     Ater. ver. +16.
     Talmon. 1 Ch +9:17.
     Akkub. 1 Ch +3:24.
     Hatita. i.e. *my sin removed*, **S#2410h**. Ne 7:45.
     Shobai. i.e. *a captor*, **S#7630h**. Ne 7:45.

43 **Nethinims**. ver. 58. 1 Ch +9:2.
     Ziha. i.e. *drought*, **S#6727h**. Ne 7:46. 11:21.
     Hasupha. i.e. *made bare*, **S#2817h**. Ne 7:46, Hashupha.
     Tabbaoth. Ne +7:46.

44 **Keros**. i.e. *stooping*, **S#7026h**. Ne 7:47.
     Siaha. i.e. *departing*, **S#5517h**. Ne 7:47, Sia.
     Padon. i.e. *liberation, redemption; ransom*, **S#6303h**. Ne 7:47.

45 **Lebanah**. i.e. *white, the moon*, **S#3838h**. Ne 7:48, Lebana, Hagaba.
     Hagabah. i.e. *a locust; grasshopper, leaper*, **S#2286h**. Ne 7:48.
     Akkub. 1 Ch +3:24.

46 **Hagab**. i.e. *a locust; grasshopper*, **S#2285h**.
     Shalmai. or, Shamlai. i.e. *peaceable; my peace-offerings; my garment*, **S#8073h**.
     Hanan. 1 Ch +9:44.

47 **Giddel**. i.e. *too great*, **S#1435h**. ver. 56. Ne 7:49, 58.
     Gahar. i.e. *hiding place; lurking place; the valley burned*, **S#1515h**. Ne 7:49.
     Reaiah. 1 Ch +4:2.

48 **Rezin**. 2 K +15:37.
     Nekoda. i.e. *speckled, spotted*, **S#5353h**. ver. 60. Ne 7:50, 62.
     Gazzam. i.e. *palmer-worm*, **S#1502h**. Ne 7:51.

49 **Uzza**. 2 K +21:18.
     Paseah. 1 Ch +4:12. Ne 7:51, Phaseah.
     Besai. i.e. *a sword; domineering; victory; trodden down of the Lord*, **S#1153h**. Ne 7:52.

50 **Asnah**. i.e. *storehouse*, **S#619h**.
     Mehunim. i.e. *dwellings*, **S#4586h**. Ne 7:52, Meunim, Nephisheshim.
     Nephusim. i.e. *expansions*, **S#5304h**. Ne 7:52.

51 **Bakbuk**. i.e. *a bottle*, **S#1227h**. Ne 7:53.
     Hakupha. i.e. *bent, bowed*, **S#2709h**. Ne 7:53.
     Harhur. i.e. *inflammation*, **S#2744h**. Ne 7:53.

52 **Bazluth**. i.e. *stripping*, **S#1213h**. Ne 7:54, Bazlith.
     Mehida. i.e. *junction*, **S#4240h**. Ne 7:54.
     Harsha. i.e. *secret work*, **S#2797h**. Ne 7:54.

53 **Barkos**. i.e. *a painter*, **S#1302h**. Ne 7:55.
     Sisera. Jg +4:2.
     Thamah. i.e. *laughter*, **S#8547h**. Ne 7:55, Tamah.

54 **Neziah**. i.e. *pure, sincere*, **S#5335h**. Ne 7:56.
     Hatipha. i.e. *captive*, **S#2412h**. Ne 7:56.

55 **Solomon's**. 1 K 9:21.
     Sotai. i.e. *drawing back*, **S#5479h**. Ne 7:57.
     Sophereth. Ne +7:57.
     Peruda. i.e. *kernel*, **S#6514h**. Ne 7:57, Perida.

56 **Jaalah**. i.e. *female ibex*, **S#3279h**. Ne 7:58, Jaala.

Darkon. i.e. *scatterer*, **S#1874h**. Ne 7:58.

Giddel. ver. +47.

57 Shephatiah. 2 S +3:4.

Hattil. i.e. *fluctuating*, **S#2411h**. Ne 7:59.

Pochereth. i.e. *a snaring*, **S#6380h**. Ne 7:59.

Zebaim. i.e. *gazelles*, **S#6380h**.

Ami. i.e. *bond-servant*, **S#532h**. Ne +7:59, Amon.

58 Nethinims. 1 Ch +9:2.

Solomon's. 1 K 9:21.

59 Tel-harsa. i.e. *hill* or *heap of salt*, **S#8528h**. Ne 7:61, Tel-haresha, Addon.

Tel-harsa. i.e. *mound of workmanship*, **S#8521h**. Ne 7:61.

Cherub. i.e. *celestial*; *guard*, **S#3743h**. Ne 7:61.

Addan. i.e. *lord, judge*, **S#135h**.

Immer. 1 Ch +9:12.

seed. *or*, pedigree.

60 of Delaiah. Ne 7:62, 642. Je +36:12.

Tobiah. i.e. *pleasing to Jehovah*, **S#2900h**. Ne 2:10, 19. 4:3, 7. 6:1, 12, 14, 17, 19. 7:62. 13:4, 7, 8. Zc 6:14. Also 2 Ch 17:8. Zc 6:10, Tobijah.

61 the children. Ne 7:63, 64.

Habaiah. i.e. *hidden of Jah*, **S#2252h**. Ne 7:63.

Koz. i.e. *the thorn; a trouble*, **S#6976h**. 1 Ch +4:8, Coz. +24:10, Hakkoz. Ne 3:4, 21. 7:63.

Barzillai. 2 S 17:27. 19:31-39. +21:8. 1 K 2:7.

62 therefore. Le 21:21-23. Nu 3:10. 16:40. 18:7.

not found. Lk 10:20. 2 T 2:19.

were they, as polluted, put from the priesthood. Heb. they were polluted from the priesthood. Ezk 44:10-14.

63 Tirshatha. *or*, governor. i.e. *severity*, **S#8660h**. Ne 7:65, 70. 8:9. 10:1.

should not. Le 2:3, 10. 6:17, 29. 7:16. 10:17, 18. Nu 18:9-11, 19, 32.

Urim. Ex +28:30.

64 forty and two thousand three. Ezr 9:8. Ne 7:66-69. Is 10:20-22. Je 23:3.

65 servants. Is 14:1, 2.

two hundred. Ps +68:25. Ec 2:8. Mt +9:23.

68 offered freely. Le +23:38. Nu 7:3, etc. Lk 21:1-4.

in his place. Ezr 3:3. 1 Ch 21:18. 22:1. 2 Ch 3:1.

69 the treasure. Ezr 8:25-34. 1 K 7:51. 1 Ch 22:14. 26:20-28. Ne 7:71, 72.

70 the priests. Ezr 6:16, 17. 1 Ch 11:2. Ne 7:73. 11:3.

EZRA 3

1 the seventh month. That is, *Tisri*. Ex 23:14-17. Le 16:29. 23:24, 27, etc. Nu 29:1, etc. Dt 16:16. Ne 8:2, 14.

as one. Jg 20:1. Ne 8:1. Zp 3:9. Ac 2:46. 4:32. 1 C 1:10.

2 Jeshua. Hg 1:1, 12, 14. 2:2-4. Zc 3:1, 8. 6:11, Joshua the son of Josedech.

Jozadak. i.e. *Jah is just*, **S#3136h**. ver. 8. Ezr 5:2. 10:18. Ne 12:26.

Zerubbabel. Hg +1:1.

as it is written. Ex 20:24, 25. Nu 28:3, etc. Dt 12:5-7, 11. 2 Ch 6:6. Ps 78:68.

3 the altar. 2 Ch +4:1.

for fear. Ezr 4:11-16. 8:21, 22. Ps 27:1, 2. 56:2-4.

even burnt. Ex 29:38-42. Nu 28:2-8.

4 the feast. Le +23:34-36.

the daily. Nu 29:12-38.

as the duty of every day required. Heb. the matter of the day in his day. Ex +5:13mg.

5 the continual. Ex +29:42.

burnt offering. Le +23:12.

new moons. Col +2:16.

set feasts. Ge +17:21.

willingly. 2 Ch 29:31, 32.

freewill offering. Le +23:38.

6 first day of. Le 23:23-25. Ne 8:18.

burnt offerings. Le +23:12.

the foundation of the temple of the Lord was not yet laid. Heb. the temple of the Lord was not yet founded.

7 gave money. 2 K 12:11, 12. 22:5, 6. 2 Ch 24:12, 13.

masons. 1 K 5:15. 2 K 12:12.

carpenters. *or*, workmen. Ex 28:11. 35:35.

meat. 1 K 5:6, 9-11. 2 Ch 2:10-15. Ezk 27:17. Ac 12:20.

Joppa. 2 Ch 2:16. Jon 1:3. Ac 9:36. 10:5, 6.

according. Ezr 6:3-5.

8 Zerubbabel. ver. +2.

twenty years old. Nu 4:3. 1 Ch 23:24-32.

9 Jeshua. Ezr 2:40.

Judah. Ezr 2:40, Hodaviah. Ne 7:43, Hodevah.

together. Heb. as one. Ezr 2:64. 6:20. 2 Ch 5:13.

Henadad. i.e. *grace or favor of Hadad* (i.e. *chief, most high*, Ge +36:35), **S#2582h**. Ne 3:18, 24. 10:9.

10 when the builders. Zc 4:10.

they set. Ex 28:40-42. 1 S 22:18. 1 Ch 15:27. Ne 12:24, etc.

trumpets. Nu 10:1-10. 1 Ch 15:24. 16:5, 6, 42.

the sons of Asaph. 2 K +18:18.

after the ordinance. 1 Ch 6:31, etc. 16:4-7. 23:5. 2 Ch 29:25, 26.

11 they sang. Ex 15:21. Ne 12:24, 40. Ps 24:7-10. 135:3. Is 6:3.

thanks. Ps +136:1.

because. Ex +34:6.

for ever. Heb. *olam*, Ex +12:24.

shouted. Jsh 6:5, 10, 16. Ps 47:1, 5. Is 12:6. 44:23. Zc 9:9.

because. Ps 102:13, 14. Re 21:10-14.

12 many. Hg 2:3.

had seen. 2 K 25:2, 9.

when the foundation. Jb 8:7. 38:4, 6, 7. Is 41:14. 60:22. Da 2:34, 35. Zc 4:10. Mt 13:31, 32.
wept. Ps 126:6. Je 31:8, 9.

13 **So that**. Hg 2:1-9.
the noise. Jg 2:5.
shouted. Ne 12:43. Ps 5:11. Je 33:11. Zc 4:7. Lk 19:37-40.
and the noise. Ex 32:17, 18. 1 S 4:5. 1 K 1:40, 45. Ps 100:1, 2.

EZRA 4

1 **the adversaries**. ver. 7-9. 1 K 5:4, 5. 1 Ch 22:9, 10. Ne 4:1-11. Da 9:25. 1 C 16:9.
children of the captivity. Heb. sons of the transportation. Ezr 1:11mg. 6:16, 19, 20. 10:7, 16. Da 5:13.

2 **Zerubbabel**. Hg +1:1.
Let us. Pr 26:23-26. 2 C 11:13-15. Ga 2:4. 2 T 3:8. 2 P 2:1, 2.
we seek. Dt 27:4. Jn 4:20.
we do. 2 K 17:24, 27-33, 41.
Esar-haddon. ver. 10, Asnapper. 2 K 19:37.
Assur. **S#804h**. Ge +10:22. Ps 73:8. Is 37:37, Assyria.

3 **Ye have nothing**. Ne 2:20. Jn 4:22, 23. Ac 8:21. Ro 9:4, 5. 2 C 6:14-16. 3 J 9, 10.
king Cyrus. Ezr 1:1-3. 6:3-5. 2 Ch 36:22, 23. Is 44:28. 45:1, 4. Mt 10:16.

4 **weakened**. Ezr 3:3. Ne 6:9. Is 35:3, 4. Je 38:4.
troubled. Ne 4:7, 8, 11.

5 **hired**. Ps 2:1, 2. Na 1:11. Ac 24:1, etc.
Darius. i.e. *conservator; a restrainer; investigation; the dwelling will be full of heaviness*. ver. 24. Ezr 5:5, etc. 6:1, etc. **S#1867h**: ver. 5. Ne 12:22. Da 9:1. 11:1. Hg 1:1, 15. 2:10. Zc 1:1, 7. 7:1.
to frustrate. ver. 24.

6 A.M. 3475. B.C. 529.
Ahasuerus. Heb. Ahashverosh. Est 1:1. Da 9:1.
wrote. Mt 27:37. Ac 24:5-9, 13. 25:7. Re 12:10.

7 A.M. 3482. B.C. 522.
Artaxerxes. i.e. *silence of light; great king* or *warrior*, **S#783h**. ver. 7, 8, 11, 23. Ezr 6:14. 7:1, 7, 11, 12, 21. 8:1. Ne 2:1. 5:14. 13:6.
Bishlam. *or*, in peace. ver. 17. i.e. *son of peace*, **S#1312h**.
Mithredath. Ezr +1:8.
Tabeel. i.e. *God is good; goodness of God*, **S#2870h**. Ezr 4:7. Also Is 7:6, Tabeal.
companions. Heb. societies. ver. 9, 17. Ezr 5:6.
the Syrian tongue. 2 K 18:26. Is 36:11. Da 2:4.

8 **Rehum**. Ne +12:3.
chancellor. or, counsellor. lit. "master of taste," that is, discretion, counsel.

Shimshai. i.e. *my minister; sunny; sun of the Lord*, **S#8124h**. ver. 8, 9, 17, 23.
scribe. *or*, secretary. ver. 9. 2 S 8:17. 20:25. 1 K 4:3. 2 K 18:18.

9 **companions**. Chal. societies. ver. 17, 23. Ezr 5:3, 6. 6:6, 13.
the Dinaites. i.e. *a cause; judgment*, **S#1784h**. 2 K 17:24, 30, 31.
Apharsathchites. i.e. *I will divide the deceivers; causers of division*, **S#671h**. Ezr 5:6. 6:6; Apharsachites.
Tarpelites. i.e. *hill of wonder; gate or passage of bulls; they of the fallen* or *wondrous mountain*, **S#2967h**.
Apharsites. i.e. *causers of division*, **S#670h**.
Archevites. i.e. *length*, **S#756h**.
Babylonians. i.e. *inhabitants of Babylon* (i.e. *confusion, mixture*, Da +1:1), **S#896h**.
Susanchites. i.e. *inhabitants of Susa* (Shushan, i.e. *lily*, Da +8:2) or *Susi* (i.e. *horseman*, Nu +13:11), **S#7801h**. Est 1:2. 2:3. Da 8:2.
Dehavites. i.e. *villagers; the sickly*, **S#1723h**.
Elamites. i.e. *original inhabitants of the country of Elam* (i.e. *hidden time; eternity; their heaps; suckling them*, Ge +10:22), **S#5962h**, only here. Ac 2:9.

10 **And the rest**. ver. 1. 2 K 17:24, etc.
noble Asnapper. i.e. *the swift; horned bull; thorn abolished*, **S#620h**. Ro 13:7.
at such a time. Chal. *Cheeneth*. ver. 11, 17. Ezr 7:12.

11 **at such a time**. ver. 15, 19. 2 K 18:20. 24:1. 2 Ch 36:13. Je 52:3. Ezk 17:12-21. Lk 23:2-5. Ac 24:5. 1 Th 5:22. 1 P 2:13-15.
Artaxerxes. ver. 17. Ezr 7:12.

12 **rebellious**. ver. 15, 19. 2 K 18:20. 24:1. 2 Ch 36:13. Je 52:3. Ezk 17:12-21. Lk 23:2-5. Ac 24:5. 1 Th 5:22. 1 P 2:13-15.
bad city. Ps 48:1, 2. Is 1:21-23. Lk 13:34.
set up. *or*, finished. ver. 13, 16. Ezr 5:3, 9, 16. 6:14. Ne 1:3. Da 9:25.
joined. Chal. sewed together.

13 **if this city**. Ne 5:4. Ps 52:2. 119:69.
pay. Chal. give. ver. 20.
not pay toll. Ezr 7:24. Mt 9:9. 17:25. Ro 13:6, 7.
revenue. *or*, strength.

14 **have maintenance**, etc. Chal. are salted with the salt of the palace.
and it was. Ezk 33:31. Jn 12:5, 6. 19:12-15.

15 **this city**. ver. 12. Ne 2:19. 6:6. Est 3:5-8. Da 6:4-13. Ac 17:6, 7.
moved. Chal. made. ver. 19.
within the same. Chal. in the midst thereof. Ezr 5:7. 6:2.
old time. Heb. *olam*, Jb +22:15.
for which. 2 K 24:20. 25:1, 4. 2 Ch 36:13, 19. Je 52:3, etc.

16 **thou shalt have**. ver. 20. 2 S 8:3. 1 K 4:24.

17 **companions**. Chal. societies. ver. 7, 9.

Peace. Ezr 7:12. Ge +43:23. Ac 23:26.
at such a time. ver. 10, 11.

18 **plainly read**. Le 24:12mg. Nu 15:34. Ne 8:8.

19 **I commanded**. Chal. by me a decree is set. ver. 21. Ezr 5:3, 9, 13, 17.
search. ver. 15. Ezr 5:17. 6:1, 2. Dt 13:14. Pr 25:2.
and it is found. 2 K 18:7. 24:20. Ezk 17:13-19.
made insurrection. Chal. lifted up itself. Nu 16:3.

20 **mighty kings**. 1 K 4:21, 24. 1 Ch 18:3. Ps 72:8.
beyond. ver. 16. Ge 15:18. Jsh 1:3, 4. 1 K 4:21. 1 Ch 19:16. 2 Ch +9:26. Ps 72:8.
toll. 1 Ch 18:6, 13. 19:19. 2 Ch 9:14, 23, 24. 17:10, 11. 26:7, 8.

21 **Give ye**, etc. Chal. Make a decree. ver. 19.

22 **why should**. ver. 13. Est 3:8, 9. 7:3, 4.

23 **Rehum**. ver. +8, 9, 17.
they went up. Pr 4:16. Mi 2:1. Ro 3:15.
force. Chal. arm.

24 **So**. Ne 6:3, 9. Jb 20:5. Ps 44:23-26. 1 Th 2:18.
Darius. Ezr 5:5. 6:1. Hg 1:15.

EZRA 5

1 A.M. 3484. B.C. 520.
Haggai. Hg 1:1, etc.
Zechariah. Zc 1:1, etc.
the son of Iddo. That is, "the *grandson* of Iddo;" for Zechariah was the son of Berechiah, the son of Iddo. 1 K +15:10. 1 Ch 6:20. 7:6.
Iddo. i.e. *favorite; due time*, S#5714h. Ezr 6:14. 1 Ch 6:21. +27:21. Ne 12:4, 16. Zc 1:1, 7.
in the name. Mi 5:4. Hg 1:2-8. Zc 1:3, 4. 4:6-10.

2 **rose up**. Ezr 3:2. Hg 1:12-15.
Jeshua. Zc 6:11, Joshua, Josedech.
the prophets. Ezr 6:14. Hg 2:4-9, 20-23. Zc ch. 3, 4. 2 C 1:24.

3 **Tatnai**. i.e. *liberal*, S#8674h. Ezr 5:3, 6. 6:6, 13. 7:21. Ne 2:7-9.
Shetharboznai. i.e. *star of splendor; one that despiseth*, S#8370h. ver. 3, 6. Ezr 6:6, 13.
Who hath commanded you. ver. 9. Ezr 1:3. Mt 21:23. Ac 4:7.

4 **What are**. ver. 10.
make this building. Chal. build this building.

5 **But the eye**. Ezr 7:6, 28. 8:22. Ps +11:4. 76:10. Ph 1:28. 1 P 3:12.
that they. Ps 129:2-5.
then they returned. Ezr 6:6-12.

6 A.M. 3485. B.C. 519.
copy. Ezr 4:11, 23.
Apharsachites. Ezr 4:9, Apharsathchites. 6:6.

7 **wherein**. Chal. in the midst whereof.
all peace. Je +29:7. Da 3:9.

8 **the province**. Ezr 2:1. Ne 7:6. 11:3. Est 1:1, 22.
Judea. i.e. *confession; praised*, S#3061h. ver. 1, 8. Ezr 7:14. Da 2:25. 5:13, 13. 6:13.
the great God. Ezr 1:2, 3. 6:10. 7:23. Dt 32:31. Da +2:45. 3:26. 4:2, 34-37. 6:26.
great stones. Chal. stones of rolling. Ezr 6:4. Mk 13:1, 2.

9 **Who commanded**. ver. 3, 4. 2 Ch 36:23.

10 **asked**. ver. 4.

11 **We are**. Jsh 24:15. Ps 119:46. Da 3:26. Jon 1:9. Mt 10:32. Lk 12:8. Ac 27:23. Ro 1:16. 6:16. Ga 6:14.
which a great. 1 Ch ch. 6, 7. 2 Ch ch. 3-5.

12 A.M. 3408. B.C. 536.
But after. 2 K 21:12-15. 2 Ch 34:24, 25. 36:16, 17. Ne 9:26, 27. Is 59:1, 2. Je 5:29. Da 9:5.
he gave. Dt 28:15, etc. 29:24-28. 31:17. 32:30. Jg 2:14. 4:2. 6:1. 1 K 9:6-9. 2 Ch 7:19-22. Ps 106:40.
into the hand. 2 K 24:2, 10, etc. 25:1, 8-11, etc. 2 Ch 36:6, etc. Je 39:1, etc. 52:1, etc. Da 1:1, 2.
Babylon. S#895h. ver. 12-14, 17. Ezr 6:1, 5. 7:16. Da 2:12, 14, 18, 24, 48, 49. 3:1, 12, 30. 4:6, 29, 30. 5:7. 7:1.

13 **in the first year**. Ezr 1:1-8. 6:3-5. Is 44:28. 45:1.

14 **the vessels**. Ezr 1:7-10. 6:5. 2 Ch 36:7, 18. Je 52:19. Da 5:2, 3.
the king. Ezr 7:27. Pr 21:1.
Sheshbazzar. ver. 16. Ezr 1:11.
whom. Hg 1:1, 14. 2:2, 21.
governor. *or*, deputy. Ac 13:7, 8, 12.

15 **let the house**. Ezr 1:2. 3:3. 6:3.

16 **Sheshbazzar**. ver. 14.
laid. ver. 2. Ezr 3:8, 10. Hg 1:12-14. 2:18. Zc 4:10. A.M. 3468-3485. B.C. 536-519.
it is not finished. Ezr 6:15.

17 A.M. 3485. B.C. 519.
let there be. Ezr 4:15, 19. 6:1, 2. Pr 25:2.
a decree. Ezr 6:3-5.

EZRA 6

1 **and search**. Ezr 4:15, 19. 5:17. Jb 29:16. Pr 25:2.
rolls. Chal. books. Ps 40:7. Je 36:2-4, 20-23, 29, 32. Ezk 2:9. 3:1. Re 5:1.
laid up. Chal. made to descend.

2 **at Achmetha**. *or*, Ecbatana, *or*, in a coffer. i.e. *place of assemblage; brother of death; citadel*, or *summer house*, S#307h.
Medes. i.e. *measure; abounding; garment; extended of the Lord*, S#4075h. Ezr 6:2. Da 5:28. 6:8, 12, 15.

3 **the first year**. Young indicates B.C. 536. Ezr 1:1-4. 5:13-15. 2 Ch 36:22, 23. Is 44:28.
the place. Dt 12:5, 6, 11-14. 2 Ch 2:6. Ps 122:4.

the height. 1 K 6:2, 3. 2 Ch 3:3, 4. Ezk 41:13-15. Re 21:16.

4 three rows. 1 K 6:36.
great stones. Ezr 5:8mg.
the expenses. Ezr 7:20-23. Ps 68:29. 72:10. Is 49:23. 60:6-10. Re 12:16.

5 the golden. Ezr 1:7, 8. 5:14. Je 27:16, 18-22. Da 1:2. 5:2.
which Nebuchadnezzar. 2 K 24:13. 25:14, 15. 2 Ch 36:6, 7, 10, 18. Je 52:19.
brought. Chal. go. Ezr 5:5. 7:13.

6 Tatnai. Ezr 5:3.
your companions. Chal. their societies. ver. 13. Ezr 4:9mg. 5:6.
Apharsachites. i.e. *causers of division; I will divide the deceivers*, S#671h. Ezr 4:9. 5:6. ver. 6.
be ye far. Ge 32:28. 43:14. Ne 1:11. Ps 76:10. Pr 21:1, 30. Is 27:8. Ac 4:26-28. Ro 8:31.

7 Let the work. Ac 5:38, 39.

8 I make a decree. Chal. by me a decree is made. ver. 11, 12, 14. Ezr 7:13, 21, 23.
the king's. ver. 4. Ezr 4:16, 20. 7:15-22. Ps 68:29-31. Hg 2:8.
hindered. Chal. made to cease. Ezr 4:21, 23. 5:5.

9 young bullocks. Le 1:3-5, 10. 9:2. Ps 50:9-13.
lambs. Ex 29:38-42. Nu ch. 28, 29.
wheat. Le 2:1, etc. Nu 15:4, etc. 1 Ch 9:29.
salt. Le 2:13. Mk 9:49.
let it be given. Is 49:23.

10 sweet savors. Chal. rest. Ge +8:21.
pray. 1 T +2:1, 2.

11 whosoever. Ezr 7:26.
timber. Est 5:14. 7:10.
hanged. Chal. destroyed.
his house. 2 K 9:37. 10:27. Da 2:5. 3:29.

12 caused. Ex 20:24. Dt 12:5, 11. 16:2. 1 K 9:3. 2 Ch 7:16. Ps 132:13, 14.
destroy. Ps 5:10. 21:8-10. 137:8, 9. Is 60:12. Ob 10. Zc 12:2-4. Ac 5:38, 39. 9:5. Re 19:14-21.
I Darius. Est 3:14, 15. 8:14.
speed. ver. 13. Ec 9:10.

13 Tatnai. Ezr 4:9, 23. 5:6.
so they did. Est 6:11. Jb 5:12, 13. Pr 29:26.

14 And the elders. Ezr 3:8. 4:3.
prospered. 2 Ch +20:20.
through. Ezr 5:1, 2. Hg 1:12-14. 2:2, etc. Zc ch. 2-4, 6.
finished it. Zc 4:9.
according. Is 44:28. Hg 1:8.
commandment. Chal. decree. ver. 8. Ezr 4:19.
Cyrus. ver. 3. Ezr 1:1-4. 4:24. 5:13.
Artaxerxes. A.M. 3540, B.C. 464. Ez 7:1.

15 A.M. 3489. B.C. 515.
Adar. Est 3:7, 13. 8:12. 9:1, 15, 17, 19, 21.

16 the children. 1 Ch 9:2. Ne 7:73.
children of the captivity. Chal. sons of the transportation. Ezr +4:1mg.
the dedication. Nu +7:10.
with joy. ver. 22. Ezr 3:11, 12. Dt 12:7. 1 Ch 15:28. 2 Ch 7:10. 30:23, 26. Ne 8:10. 12:43. Ps 122:1. Ph 4:4.

17 offered. Ezr 8:35. Nu 7:2, etc. 1 K 8:63, 64. 1 Ch 16:1-3. 2 Ch 7:5. 29:31-35.
a sin offering. Le +23:19.
according to. 1 K 18:31. Lk 22:30. Re 7:4-8. 21:12.

18 the priests. 1 Ch ch. 23-26. 2 Ch 35:4, 5.
as it is written. Chal. according to the writing. Nu 3:6. 8:9, etc.

19 the children. ver. 16.
kept. Ex 12:6, etc. Jsh 5:10. 2 Ch ch. 30-35.
passover. Le +23:5.

20 purified together. 2 Ch 29:34. 30:15-17.
killed. Ex 12:21. 2 Ch 35:11. He 7:27.

21 all such. Ezr 9:11. Nu 9:6, 7, 10-14. 1 Ch 16:10, 11. 2 Ch 30:17. Is 52:11. Ezk 36:25. 2 C 6:17. 7:1.
did eat. Ex 12:47-49. Ps 93:5.

22 the feast. Ex 12:15-20. 13:6, 7. 2 Ch 30:21. 35:17. Mt 26:17. 1 C 5:7, 8.
unleavened. Le +23:6.
with joy. Ga 5:22. Ph 4:4.
turned. Ezr 7:27. Pr 16:7. 21:1. Jn 19:11.
the king. ver. 6, etc. Ezr 1:1. 2 K 23:29. 2 Ch 33:11. Zc 10:10, 11.

EZRA 7

1 A.M. 3547. B.C. 457.
Artaxerxes. ver. 12, 21. Ezr 6:14. Ne 2:1.
Ezra. ver. 10, +12. Ezr ch. 8-10. Ne 8:2-9.
the son. i.e. his grandson; persons omitted for brevity sake may be supplied out of 1 Ch ch. 6-9 (Matthew Poole). Ezr 5:1. 1 K +15:10. 1 Ch 3:19. 6:20. 7:6.
Seraiah. 2 S +8:17. 1 Ch 9:11.
Azariah. 1 Ch +6:36.
Hilkiah. 2 K +18:18.

2 Shallum. 2 K +15:10.
Zadok. 2 S +8:17.
Ahitub. 1 S +14:3.

3 Amariah. i.e. *the saying of Jehovah*, S#568h. Ezr 10:42. 1 Ch 6:7, 11, 52. 23:19. Ne 10:3. 11:4. 12:2, 13. Zp 1:1.
Azariah. ver. +1. Six generations are omitted between him and Meraioth, see 1 Ch 6:7-10.
Meraioth. Ne +12:15.

4 Zerahiah. i.e. *rising of light of the Lord*, S#2228h. Ezr 8:4. 1 Ch 6:6, 51.
Uzzi. 1 Ch +6:5.
Bukki. Nu +34:22.

5 Abishua. 1 Ch 6:4.
Phinehas. Ex +6:25.
Eleazar. Ex +6:23. Nu 31:31, 54. Jsh 24:33.
Aaron. Ex +4:14.
chief priest. 2 Ch 19:11. 26:20. He 5:4.

6 a ready. ver. 11, 12, 21. Ps 45:1. Pr 22:29. Is 16:5. Mt 13:52.

scribe. Ne 8:4, 9, 13. 12:26, 36. Je 8:8. Mt 7:29. 17:10. 22:35, 36. 23:2, 13. Mk 12:28. 1 C 1:20.

the law. Dt 4:5. 28:1. Mt 28:20. 1 C 15:1. 1 Th 4:1, 2.

granted him. ver. 11-26.

according to. ver. 9, 28. Ezr 6:22. 8:18, 22, 31. Ge 32:28. Ne 1:10, 11. 2:8, 12, 18. 4:15. Pr 3:6. Is 50:2. 59:1.

the hand. Ne +2:8.

7 the children. Ezr 8:1-14.

the Levites. Ezr 2:40, 41. 8:15-20.

singers. 1 Ch 6:31, etc. 25:1-8. 2 Ch +35:15.

porters. Ezr 2:42. 1 Ch 9:17, etc. +23:5. Ne 7:45.

Nethinims. ver. 24. 1 Ch +9:2.

Artaxerxes. ver. 11, 12. Ezr 6:14. 8:1. Ne 2:1.

9 began he to go up. Heb. was the foundation of the going up.

according to. ver. 6. Ne 2:8, 18.

hand. Ne +2:8.

10 prepared. or, directed. 2 Ch +12:14mg. Pr 16:1.

to seek the law. ver. 6. Ps 1:2. 19:7. 119:45, 96-100. Jn +5:39. Ac +17:2, 3, 11.

to do it. Dt 16:12. +26:16, 18. Mt 5:19. 7:24. Lk 6:46. 11:28. Jn +13:17. Re 22:14.

and to teach. ver. 25. Dt 33:10. 2 Ch 17:8, 9. +20:20. 30:22. 35:3. Ne 8:1-9. Ml 2:7. Ac 1:1. 1 T 3:2. 2 T +2:2. 4:2. T 2:1, 15.

11 the copy. Ezr 4:11. 5:6.

a scribe. ver. 6. Mt 23:2, 13. Mk 7:1-13.

12 Artaxerxes. 1 K 4:24. 20:1. Is 10:8. Ezk 26:7. Da 2:37, 47. 1 T 6:15. Re 17:14. 19:16.

unto Ezra, etc. or, to Ezra the priest, a perfect scribe of the law of the God of heaven, *peace*, etc.

Ezra. i.e. *help*, S#5830h. ver. 1, 6, 10, 11. Ezr 10:1, 2, 5, 6, 10, 16. Ne 8:1, 2, 4-6, 9, 13. 12:1, 13, 26, 33, 36. Also S#5831h. ver. 12, 21, 25.

and at such a time. Ezr 4:10, 11, 17. 1 Ch 12:32.

13 I make. Ezr 5:13. 6:1. 2 Ch 30:5. Est 3:15. 9:14. Ps 148:6.

minded. Ezr 1:3. Ps 110:3. Ph 2:13. Re 22:17.

14 of the king. Chal. from before the king.

seven counselors. Est 1:14.

according. ver. 25, 26. Dt 17:18, 19. Is 8:20.

thy God. Ezr 1:3. 5:8. 6:12. Da 2:47. 6:20, 26.

15 the silver. Ezr 6:4, 8-10. Ps 68:29, 30. 72:10. 76:11. Is 60:6-9. Re 21:24-26.

whose habitation. Ezr 6:12. 2 Ch 2:6. 6:1, 2, 6. Ps 9:11. 26:8. 76:2. 132:13, 14. 135:21.

16 all the silver. Ezr 8:25-28.

freewill offering. Le +23:38.

17 buy speedily. Ezr +6:9, 10. Dt 14:24-26. Mt 21:12, 13. Jn 2:14.

their meat offerings. Le +23:13.

drink offerings. Le +23:13.

offer them. Dt 12:5-11.

18 whatsoever. 2 K 12:15. 22:7.

that do. ver. 23. Ep 5:17.

after the will. Ezr 5:17. 2 C 1:24.

19 The vessels. Ezr 8:27-30, 33, 34.

the God of Jerusalem. 2 Ch 32:19. Je 3:17.

20 bestow it. Ezr 6:4, 8, etc.

21 Artaxerxes. ver. 12, 13.

beyond the river. Ezr 4:16, 20. 6:6.

Ezra the priest. ver. 6, 10, 11.

22 measures. Chal. *cors*. 1 K +4:22mg. Lk 16:6mg.

baths of wine. Ezk 45:14. Lk 16:6mg.

salt. Le +2:13.

without prescribing. Jn 3:34.

23 Whatsoever is commanded. Chal. Whatsoever is of the decree. ver. 13, 18.

let it be. Dt 6:17. 11:22. Ps 119:4. Ec 9:10.

why should there be wrath. Ezr 6:10-12. 2 Ch +24:18. 30:8. Zc 12:3. 1 T +2:2.

24 touching any. ver. 7. Ezr 2:36-55.

25 the wisdom. ver. 14. 1 K 3:28. 1 Ch 22:12. Ps 19:7. 119:98-100. Pr 2:6. 6:23. Ja 1:5. 3:17, 18.

set magistrates. Ex +18:14-25. Dt 16:18. 1 Ch 23:4. 2 Ch 19:8-10.

beyond. That is, "west of the Euphrates," which was *beyond* with regard to the king of Persia, who was on the east. Ezr 6:6.

the river. Ezr 4:20. 1 Ch 19:16. 2 Ch +9:26.

teach ye. ver. +10. 2 Ch +17:7-9. Ne 8:1-3, 7, 8. 9:3. 13:1-3. Ml 2:7. Mt 13:52. 23:2, 3. 28:19. Mk 6:34. Ro 10:14-17. Ep 4:11. 1 T 4:11-16. 2 T 2:2.

26 whosoever. Ezr 6:11. Da 3:28, 29. 6:26.

the law of thy God. 2 Ch 30:12.

whether it be. Ex ch. 21, 22. Le ch. 20. Dt ch. 13.

banishment. Chal. rooting out. Ps 52:5.

confiscation. 2 K 23:33. Pr 19:19. He 11:37.

imprisonment. Da 4:15, 23.

27 Blessed. Ezr 6:22. 1 Ch 29:10, etc. Ph 4:10.

put such. Ezr 6:22. Ne 2:12. 7:5. 2 C 8:16. He 8:10. 10:16. Ja 1:17. Re 17:17.

in the king's heart. Ne 2:8. Pr 21:1.

to beautify. Is 60:13.

28 extended. Ezr 9:9. Ge 32:28. 43:14. Ne 1:11.

his counsellors. ver. 14. Jon 3:7.

And I was strengthened. Ps 46:1.

as the hand. ver. 6, 9. Ezr 5:5. 8:18. Ne 2:8. 2 T 4:17, 18.

EZRA 8

1 the chief. Ezr 1:5. 1 Ch 9:34. 24:31. 26:32. 2 Ch 26:12. Ne 7:70, 71.

genealogy. Ezr 2:62. 1 Ch 4:33. 9:1.

them that went up. Ezr 7:7, 13.

2 Phinehas. 1 Ch 6:3, 4, etc. 24:1-6.

Gershom. Ex +2:22.

Ithamar. Ex +6:23.

Daniel. Da +1:8.

David. 1 Ch 3:1, 22.
Hattush. i.e. *assembled; sin was hasted*, **S#2407h**. 1 Ch 3:22. Ne 3:10. 10:4. 12:2.

3 **Shechaniah**. 1 Ch +3:22.
Pharosh. i.e. *dancing*, **S#6551h**. Ezr +2:3, Parosh.
Zechariah. Zc +1:1.

4 **Pahath-moab**. Ezr +2:6.
Elihoenai. i.e. *God the Lord of my eyes*, **S#454h**. 1 Ch 26:3, Elioenai.
Zerahiah. Ezr +7:4.

5 **Shechaniah**. ver. 3.
Jahaziel. 1 Ch +24:23.

6 **Adin**. Ezr +2:15.
Ebed. i.e. *servant*, **S#5651h**. Jg 9:26, 28, 30, 31, 35.
Jonathan. 1 S +13:2.

7 **Elam**. Ge +10:22.
Jeshaiah. 1 Ch +25:3.
Athaliah. 1 Ch +8:26.

8 **Shephatiah**. 2 S +3:4.
Zebadiah. 1 Ch +26:2.
Michael. Da +12:1.

9 **Joab**. 1 S +26:6.
Obadiah. Ob +1.
Jehiel. i.e. *God lives*, **S#3171h**. Ezr 10:2, 21, 26. 1 Ch 15:18, 20. 16:5. 23:8. 27:32. 29:8. 2 Ch 21:2. 29:14. 31:13. 35:8. 1 Ch +9:35, Jehiel (**S#3273h**).

10 **Shelomith**. Le +24:11.
Josiphiah. i.e. *added to by Jah*, **S#3131h**.

11 **Bebai**. Ezr +2:11. 10:28. Ne 7:16.

12 **Azgad**. Ezr +2:12. Ne 7:17.
Johanan. 2 K +25:23.
the son of Hakkatan. *or*, the youngest son.
Hakkatan. i.e. *small; son of the little one*, **S#6997h**.

13 **Adonikam**. Ne +7:18.
Eliphelet. 1 Ch +3:6.
Jeiel. 1 Ch +5:7.
Shemaiah. 1 Ch +9:16.

14 **Bigvai**. Ezr +2:2, 14. Ne 7:19.
Uthai. 1 Ch +9:4.
Zabbud. *or*, Zaccur, *as some read*. i.e. *endowed; given*, **S#2072h**. Ne 10:12.

15 **Ahava**. i.e. *continual flowing*, **S#163h**. ver. 21, 31. Ps 137:1. Ezk 1:1. 3:15. Ac 16:13.
abode. Heb. pitched. Nu 9:20, 22. 31:19.
and found. ver. 2. Ezr 7:7, 24.

16 **Eliezer**. Ge +15:2.
Ariel. Is +29:1.
Shemaiah. ver. +13.
Elnathan. 2 K +24:8.
Jarib. 1 Ch +4:24.
Nathan. 2 Ch +9:29.
Zechariah. ver. 11.
Meshullam. 1 Ch +9:12.
chief men. ver. 1.
Joiarib. i.e. *Jah will contend*, **S#3114h**. Ne 11:5, 10. 12:6, 19.
men of understanding. ver. 18. 1 K 3:11. 1

Ch +12:32. 26:14. 2 Ch 2:12. Pr 2:6. 20:5. 28:2. Da 2:21. 2 T 2:7. 1 J 5:20.

17 **Iddo**. i.e. *great calamity; I will praise him*, **S#112h**.
Casiphia. i.e. *silver of the Lord; longing of Jah*, **S#3703h**. ver. 31. Ezr 7:9.
I told them. Heb. I put words in their mouth. Ex 4:15. Dt 18:18. 2 S 14:3, 19. Je 1:9. 15:19.
the Nethinims. 1 Ch +9:2.
ministers. Nu 8:22-26. 18:6. 1 Ch 23:3-6, 26-32. T 1:5.

18 **by the good hand**. ver. 22. Ezr 7:28. Ne 2:8. Pr 3:6.
a man of understanding. ver. +16. 1 S 25:3. 1 Ch 22:12. Pr 24:3. Je 3:15. Da 1:20. 1 C 14:20.
Mahli. Nu +3:20.
Sherebiah. i.e. *set free of Jah*, **S#8274h**. ver. 24. Ne 8:7. 9:4, 5. 10:12. 12:8, 24.

19 **Hashabiah**. 1 Ch +9:14.
Jeshaiah. 1 Ch +25:3.
Merari. Ge +46:11.

20 **Nethinims**. ver. +17.
all of them. Ph 4:3.

21 **I proclaimed**. Mt +6:16.
afflict ourselves. Nu +29:7. Je 31:8, 9.
to seek. 2 Ch +7:14. Je 50:4, 5.
a right way. Ps 5:8. 107:2-8. 143:8-10. Pr 3:6. Is 30:21. 35:8. 42:16. 49:10. Je 10:23.
for our little ones. Nu +16:27. Ps 8:2. Mk 10:13-16. Ac 2:39.

22 **I was ashamed**. 1 C 9:15. 2 C 7:14.
The hand. Ezr 7:6, 9, 28. 2 Ch 16:9. Ps 33:18, 19. 34:15, 22. Is 3:10, 11. Je 17:5, 7. La 3:25. Ro 8:28. 2 C 10:3, 4. 1 P 3:12.
seek. Je +29:13.
his power and his wrath. Jsh 23:16. 2 Ch 15:2. Ps 21:8, 9. 34:16. 90:11. Zp 1:2-6. He 10:38. 1 P 3:12.
against. Ex 32:9, 10. 1 S +15:11. Pr 14:14. Je +1:16. Ho 6:4, 5. Zp 1:4, 6.

23 **we fasted**. Mt +6:16.
besought. Je 29:12, 13. 33:3. 50:4, 5.
and he was intreated. ver. 31. Dt 4:29. 1 Ch 5:20. 2 Ch 33:12, 13. Ps 66:18-20. Is 19:22. Je 29:12, 13. Mt 7:7, 8.

24 **Sherebiah**. ver. 18, 19.

25 **weighed**. ver. 33, 34. Ezr 1:8. 2 C 8:20, 21. Ph 4:8.
the silver. Ezr 7:15, 16.
offering. or, heave-offering. Ex 25:2, 3. Le +7:14. 2 S 1:21.

27 **fine copper**. *or*, yellow *or* shining brass.
precious. Heb. desirable. 2 Ch 20:25. La 4:2. Je +25:34mg.

28 **Ye are holy**. Le 21:6-8. Dt 33:8. Is 52:11.
the vessels. Ezr 1:7-11. Le 22:2, 3. Nu 4:4-15, 19, 20. 7:13, 84-88. 1 K 7:48-51. 1 Ch 23:28. 2 Ch 24:14.

freewill offering. Le +23:38.

29 Watch ye. 1 Ch 26:20-26. Mk 13:34, 35. Ac 20:31. 2 T 4:5.
 until ye weigh them before. ver. 33, 34.
 in the chambers. Ezr 10:6. 2 K 23:11.

30 the house of our God. ver. 22. 1 Ch 29:2, 3. Ps 122:9. Is 60:13.

31 the river of Ahava. ver. 15, 21.
 the hand. ver. 22. Ezr 7:9, 28. Jb 5:19-24. Ps 91:9-14. Is 41:10-14. Ac 25:3. 26:22.
 and he delivered. ver. 22. 2 Ch 16:9. Ps 34:7.
 lay in wait. Jsh 8:2, 4, 7, 12, 14, 19, 21. Jg 16:9, 12. 20:29, 33, 36, 37, 38. 1 S 22:8, 13. Je 51:12. La 3:10.

32 we came. Ezr 7:8, 9. Ne 2:11.

33 weighed. ver. 26, 30. 1 Ch 28:14-18. 2 C 8:20, 21.
 Meremoth. i.e. heights; elevations, S#4822h. Ezr 10:36. Ne 3:4, 21. 10:5. 12:3. See Meraioth, Ne +12:15.
 Uriah. 2 S +11:3.
 Jozabad. 2 Ch +31:13.
 Jeshua. Ne +8:17.
 Binnui. Ezr +10:30.

35 children of, etc. or, sons of the removal. Ezr 4:1. 6:19, 20.
 offered burnt offerings. Le +23:12. Ps 116:12-19. Lk 1:74, 75.
 twelve bullocks. Ezr 6:17. Nu 7:27.
 sin offering. Le +23:19.

36 the king's commissions. Ezr 7:21-24.
 lieutenants. Ezr 4:7, etc. 5:6, etc.
 they furthered. Ezr 6:13. Is 56:6, 7. Ac 18:27. Re 12:16.

EZRA 9

1 the princes. Ezr 10:8. Je 26:10, 16.
 have not separated. Ezr 6:21, 22. 10:10, 11. Ex 33:16. Nu 23:9. Ne 9:2. 13:3. Is 52:11. 2 C 6:14-18.
 doing according. Le 18:3, 24-30. Dt 12:30, 31. 18:9. 2 K 21:2. 2 Ch 33:2. Ps 106:35. Je 10:2. Ro 2:17-25.
 of the Canaanites. Ge +10:18.
 Hittites. Dt +20:17.
 Perizzites. Ge +13:7.
 Jebusites. Ge +10:16.
 Ammonites. 1 S +11:11.
 Moabites. Nu 25:1-3.
 Amorites. Ge +10:16.

2 taken of their. Ezr 10:18-44. Jg +3:6.
 the holy seed. Ex 19:6. 22:31. Dt 7:6. 14:2. Is 6:13. Ml 2:15. 1 C 7:14.
 mingled. Ge 6:2. Ne 13:3, 23, 24. 2 C 6:14.
 the hand. Ezr 10:18-44. Ne 13:4, 17, 28.

3 rent. ver. 5. 2 K +18:37.
 off. Ne 13:25. Is +3:24.
 sat. Ne 1:4. Jb 2:12, 13. Ps 66:3. 119:53. 143:4. Je 8:21. Ezk 3:15. Da 4:19. 8:27.

4 trembled. 2 Ch 34:27. Is +66:2. He 12:28, 29.
 until. Ex 29:39. Da 9:21. Ac 3:1.

5 evening sacrifice. Mt +14:23.
 heaviness. or, affliction.
 rent my garment. ver. 3. 2 K +18:37.
 I fell. 2 Ch 6:13. Ps 95:6. Lk 22:41. Ac 21:5. Ep 3:14.
 spread. Ps +88:9.

6 I am ashamed. Jb 40:4. 42:6. Ps 38:4. 44:15. Je 3:3, 24, 25. 6:15. 8:12. 31:19. Ezk 16:61, 63. Da 9:7-9. Ro 6:21.
 our iniquities. Ge 13:13. Ps 38:4. Is 1:18. 59:12.
 trespass. or, guiltiness. 2 Ch 24:18.
 grown up. Ge +2:24. +41:56. 2 Ch 28:9. Lk 15:21. Re 18:5.

7 Since the days. Nu 32:14. 2 Ch 29:6. 30:7. Ne 9:32-34. Ps 106:6, 7. La 5:7. Da 9:5-8. Zc 1:4, 5. Mt 23:30-33. Ac 7:51, 52.
 for our iniquities. Le 26:14, etc. Dt 4:25-28. 28:15, etc. 29:22-28. 30:17-19. 31:20-22. 32:15-28. 1 S 12:15. 1 K 9:6-9. Ne 9:30.
 into the hand. 2 K 17:5-8. 18:9-12. 24:1-4. 2 Ch 36:16-19. Ne 9:36, 37. Da 9:11-14.
 to confusion. Da 9:7, 8.
 as it is this day. 1 K +8:24.

8 little space. Heb. moment. Nu 16:21. Is 26:20.
 grace hath. ver. 9. Ne 1:11. 9:31. Hab 3:2.
 a remnant. ver. 14. Mi +4:7.
 a nail. or, a pin. i.e. a constant and sure abode. Ex +27:19.
 in his holy place. Is 56:5. Re 3:12.
 lighten. 1 S 14:27, 29. Jb 33:30. Ps 13:3. 34:5.
 reviving. Ps 85:6. 138:7. Is 57:15. Ezk 37:11-14. Ho 6:2.

9 we were bondmen. Ne 9:36, 37.
 yet our God. Ps 106:45, 46. 136:23, 24. Ezk 11:16.
 in the sight. Ezr 1:1-4, 7-11. 6:1-12. 7:6, 8, 11-28.
 to set up. Ezr 6:14, 15. Hg 1:9. Zc 4:6-10.
 repair. Heb. set up. 2 S 22:34.
 a wall. Or rather, a hedge or fence, gader, such as were made for sheep-folds. Is 5:2, 5. La 2:8, 9, 18. Da 9:25. Zc 2:5.

10 what shall we say. Ge 44:16. Jsh 7:8. La 3:22. Da 9:4-16. Ro 3:19.

11 by thy servants. Heb. by the hand of thy servants. 1 K +16:12mg. Ne 9:30. Zc 7:12.
 The land. ver. 1. Le 18:24-30. Dt 12:31. 18:12. 2 Ch 33:2.
 the filthiness. Ezr 6:21. Ezk 36:25-27. 2 C 7:1.
 one end to another. Heb. mouth to mouth. 2 K 10:21mg. 21:16mg.

12 give not. Jg +3:6.
 nor seek their peace. Dt 23:6. 2 Ch 19:2. 2 J 10, 11.
 for ever. Heb. olam, Ex +12:24.

that ye may. Dt 6:1, 2. 28:4. Jsh 1:6-9.
and eat. Is 1:19.
and leave it. Ge 18:18, 19. Ps 112:1, 2. Pr 13:22. 20:7.
for ever. Heb. *olam*, Ex +12:24.

13 **after all**. Ne 9:32. Ezk 24:13, 14. Ga 3:4.
hast punished, etc. Heb. hast withheld beneath our iniquities.
less. Ps 103:10-14. La 3:22, 39, 40. Hab 3:2.
hast given us. Ps 106:45, 46.

14 **we again**. Jn 5:14. Ro 6:1. 2 P 2:20, 21.
join in. ver. 2. Ex 23:32. Jg 2:2. Ne 13:23-27.
wouldst not thou. Ex 32:10. Nu 16:21, 45. Dt 9:8, 14.
no remnant. ver. +8. Dt 32:26, 27. Je 46:28.

15 **thou art righteous**. Ne 9:33, 34. Da 9:7-11, 14. Ro 10:3.
for we remain. La 3:22, 23.
in our trespasses. Is 64:6, 7. Ezk 33:10. Zc 3:3, 4. Jn 8:21, 24. 1 C 15:17.
we cannot. Jb 9:2, 3. Ps 130:3, 4. 143:2. Ro 3:19.

EZRA 10

1 **when Ezra**. Da 9:3, 4, 20. Ac 10:30.
when he had. Le 26:40, 41. Ps 32:5. Ho 14:2. 1 J 1:8-10.
weeping. Ps +119:136.
before the house. 1 K 8:30. 9:3. 2 Ch 7:12. 20:9.
a very great. Dt 31:12. 2 Ch 20:13. Ne 10:28. Jl 2:16-18. Ac 21:5.
very sore. Heb. wept a great weeping. Jg 2:4, 5. Ne 8:9.

2 **Shechaniah**. ver. 26. Ne 3:29.
Elam. Ge +10:22.
We have trespassed. Ex 34:12. Ne 13:27. Ja 2:9.
yet now there is hope. Ex 34:6, 7. Is 55:6, 7. Je 3:12, 13. 1 J 1:7-9.

3 **let us make**. lit. let us cut a covenant. Dt +29:12. Jsh 9:6. 2 K 11:17. 2 Ch 29:10. 34:31, 32. Ne 9:38. 10:29, etc.
put away. Heb. bring forth. ver. 19. Ne 9:2. 13:30.
according to the counsel. 2 Ch 30:12.
of those that. Is +66:2.
at the commandment. Dt 7:2, 3. Jsh 23:12, 13.
let it. Ne 8:14. 13:1-3. Is 8:20. 1 C 7:12, 13, 39. 2 C 6:14.

4 **Arise**. Jsh 7:10, etc. 1 Ch 22:16, 19. Ec 9:10.
for this matter. Ezr 7:23-28. Mk 13:34.
we also will. Jsh 1:16-18. 1 Ch 28:10, 21.
be of good. Jsh +1:9. Is 35:3, 4. He 10:24. 12:12, 13.

5 **arose**. Pr 1:5. 9:9. 15:23. 25:11, 12. 27:9.
made. ver. 3. Ne 5:12. 10:29. 13:25. Mt 26:63.

6 **the chamber**. Ezr 8:29. 1 S 9:22. 2 K 23:11.

1 Ch 9:26. Ne 13:5.
Johanan. Ne 3:1, 20. 12:10, 22. 13:28.
he did eat. Dt 9:18. Jb 23:12. Jn 4:31-34.
he mourned. Ezr 9:4. Is 22:12. Da 9:3.

7 **they made**. Ezr 1:1. 2 Ch 30:5.

8 **And that whatsoever**. Ezr 7:26. Jg 21:5. 1 S 11:7.
forfeited. Heb. devoted. Ex 22:20. Le +27:28, 29. Jsh 6:19.
himself separated. Ne 13:3. Mt 18:17. Jn 9:22, 34. 16:2. 1 C 5:13.

9 **the ninth month**. Ezr 7:8, 9. Est 2:16.
trembling. 1 S 12:17, 18. Je 10:10, 13.
great rain. Heb. showers. ver. 13.

10 **taken**. Heb. caused to dwell, *or*, brought back.
to increase. Ezr 9:6. Nu 32:14. Jsh 22:17, 18. 2 Ch 28:13. Mt 23:32.

11 **make confession**. Le 26:40-42. Jsh 7:19. Ps 32:5. Pr 28:13. Je 3:13. 1 J 1:7-9.
do his. Is 1:16-18. 56:4. Ro 12:2. Col +1:10. He 13:21.
separate. Ezr 9:1. Ne 13:3. 2 C 6:17.
and from the. Dt 7:3, 4. 1 C 2:12-14.

12 **As thou hast said**. Ge 18:25. Lk 6:35.
so must we do. ver. 3, 4. 2 Ch 30:8. Ne 13:23. Ps 78:37, 57.

13 **the people**. ver. 18-44. Mt 7:13, 14.
time of. lit. the season (is) showers. Ge +49:9.
we are many that have transgressed in this thing. *or*, we have greatly offended in this thing.

14 **our rulers**. Dt 17:9, 18, 19. 2 Ch 19:5-7. Ac 5:21. 6:12. 23:1.
the fierce wrath. Ex +32:12. Nu 32:14. 2 Ch +24:18. 29:10. 30:8. Is 12:1.
for this matter be turned from us. *or*, be turned from us, till this matter *be dispatched*.

15 **Jonathan**. 1 S +13:2.
Asahel. 1 Ch +2:16.
Jahaziah. i.e. *he will see the Lord*, **S#3167h**.
Tikvah. 2 K +22:14.
were employed. Heb. stood. or, against.
Meshullam. 1 Ch +9:12.
Shabbethai. i.e. *born on the Sabbath*, **S#7678h**. Ne 8:7. 11:16.

16 **to examine the matter**. Dt 13:14. Jb 29:16. Jn 7:51.

17 A.M. 3548. B.C. 456.
the first day of. i.e. Nisan. Ex 12:2.

18 **the sons**. Ezr 9:1. Le 21:7, 13-15. 1 S 2:22-24. Ne 13:28. Je 23:11, 14. Ezk 44:22. Ml 2:8, 9. 1 T 3:11.
Jeshua. 1 Ch 6:14, 15. Ne +8:17. Hg 1:1. Zc 3:1, Joshua.
Maaseiah. ver. +21.

19 **gave their hands**. Le 5:17-19. 1 Ch +29:24mg.
a ram. Le 5:15, 16. 6:4, 6.
trespass. Le +5:6.

20 **Immer**. 1 Ch +9:12.

Hanani. 1 Ch +25:4.
Zebadiah. 1 Ch +26:2.

21 **Harim**. 1 Ch +24:8.
Maaseiah. Je +21:1.
Elijah. 1 K +17:1.
Shemaiah. 1 Ch +9:16.
Jehiel. Ezr +8:9.
Uzziah. 2 Ch +26:1.

22 **Pashur**. Je +20:1.
Elioenai. 1 Ch +26:3.
Maaseiah. ver. +21.
Ishmael. Ge +16:11.
Nethaneel. Nu +1:8.
Jozabad. 2 Ch +31:13.
Elasah. i.e. *God has made*, **S#501h**. 1 Ch +2:39,
40. 8:37. 9:43, Eleasah. Je 29:3.

23 **Jozabad**. ver. +22.
Shimei. 2 S +16:5.
Kelaiah. i.e. *light or swift one of Jah*, **S#7041h**.
Kelita. i.e. *congregation of the Lord*, **S#7042h**. Ne
8:7. 10:10.
Pethahiah. Ne +11:24.
Judah. Ge +35:23.
Eliezer. Ge +15:2.

24 **singers**. 2 Ch +35:15.
Eliashib. 1 Ch +3:24.
porters. 1 Ch 16:42mg. 23:5. 2 Ch 35:15.
Shallum. 2 K +15:10.
Telem. i.e. *oppression*, **S#2928h**. Jsh 15:24. 1 S
15:4, Telaim.

25 **sons of Parosh**. Ezr +2:3.
Ramiah. i.e. *placed of the Lord*, **S#7422h**.
Jeziah. i.e. *he will be sprinkled of the Lord*,
S#3150h.
Malchiah. Je +38:1.
Miamin. Ne +12:5.
Eleazar. Ex +6:23.
Malchijah. 1 Ch +9:12.
Benaiah. 1 Ch +15:24.

26 **Elam**. ver. +2.
Mattaniah. 2 K +24:17.
Zechariah. Zc +1:1.
Jehiel. ver. 2. Ezr +8:9.
Abdi. 1 Ch +6:44.
Jeremoth. i.e. *heights*, **S#3406h**. ver. 27. 1 Ch
+7:7 (Jerimoth), 8. 8:14. 23:23. 25:22.

27 **Zattu**. Ezr +2:8. Ne 7:13.
Aziza. i.e. *strong; mightiness; fortified*, **S#5819h**.

28 **Bebai**. Ezr 2:11. 8:11. Ne 7:16.
Zabbai. i.e. *pure; portion of God*, **S#2079h**. Ne 3:20.
Athlai. i.e. *my due times*, **S#6270h**.

29 **Bani**. Ezr +2:10.
Malluch. Ne +10:4.
Adaiah. Ne +11:5.
Jashub. Nu +26:24.
Sheal. i.e. *he asked; prayer; petition*, **S#7594h**.
Ramoth. 1 Ch +6:73.

30 **Pahath-moab**. Ezr +2:6.
Adna. i.e. *pleasure*, **S#5733h**. Ne 12:15.

Chelal. i.e. *completion, perfection; finished*,
S#3636h.
Benaiah. 1 Ch +15:24.
Maaseiah. Je +21:1.
Mattaniah. 2 K +24:17.
Bezaleel. Ex +31:2.
Binnui. i.e. *built up; building*, **S#1131h**. ver. 38.
Ezr 8:33. Ne 3:24. 7:15. 10:9. 12:8.
Manasseh. Ge +41:51.

31 **Harim**. ver. +21.
Ishijah. i.e. *forgotten of Jah*, **S#3449h**. 1 Ch
+7:3, Ishiah. +12:6, Jesaiah.
Malchiah. Ne 3:11, Malchijah. Je +38:1.
Shemaiah. 1 Ch +9:16.
Shimeon. i.e. *a hearkener*, **S#8095h**. For
S#8095h, Simeon, see Ge +29:33.

33 **Hashum**. Ezr +2:19.
Mattenai. Ne +12:19.
Mattathah. i.e. *gift of the Lord*, **S#4992h**.
Zabad. 1 Ch +2:36.
Eliphelet. 1 Ch +3:6.
Jeremai. i.e. *dweller on high*, **S#3413h**.

34 **Bani**. ver. 29.
Maadai. i.e. *ornament of the Lord; my unclothings, my slidings*, **S#4572h**.
Amram. Ex +6:18.
Uel. i.e. *desire of God; wish or will of God*,
S#177h.

35 **Benaiah**. 1 Ch +15:24.
Bedeiah. i.e. *servant of Jehovah*, **S#912h**.
Chelluh. i.e. *consumed of the Lord*, **S#3622h**.

36 **Vaniah**. **S#2057h**.
Meremoth. Ezr +8:33.
Eliashib. 1 Ch +3:24.

37 **Mattaniah**. ver. 30.
Mattenai. ver. 33.
Jaasau. i.e. *made by Jah*, **S#3299h**.

40 **Machnadebai**. or, Mabnadebai, *according to
some copies*. i.e. *a bond; what is like the liberality
of the Lord*, **S#4367h**.
Shashai. i.e. *whitish*, or *sixth*, **S#8343h**.
Sharai. i.e. *beginning; liberated of the Lord*,
S#8298h.

41 **Azareel**. 1 Ch +12:6.
Shelemiah. 1 Ch +26:14.
Shemariah. 1 Ch +12:5.

43 **Nebo**. Ezr 2:29. Nu +32:3. Ne 7:33.
Jeiel. 1 Ch +5:7.
Mattithiah. i.e. *gift of Jehovah*, **S#4993h**. 1 Ch
9:31. 16:5. Ne 8:4. Also 1 Ch 15:18, 21. 25:3,
21.
Zabad. ver. 33.
Zebina. i.e. *bought; a precious possession*,
S#2081h.
Jadau. i.e. *loving or judging; praised; beloved
of the Lord*, **S#3035h**. Also 1 Ch +27:21,
Iddo.

44 **strange wives**. Pr 2:16. 5:3, 20.
and some of them. ver. 3.

NEHEMIAH

NEHEMIAH 1

1 **Nehemiah.** i.e. *whom Jehovah comforts; comforted of Jah; comfort of the Lord,* S#5166h. ver. 1. Ne 3:16. 7:7. 8:9. 10:1, 8. 12:26, 47. Ezr 2:2.
Hachaliah. i.e. *reddened* or *dimmed by Jah; whose eyes Jehovah enlivens; dark flashing of the Lord; the waiting on Jah,* S#2446h. ver. 1. Ne 10:1.
in the month. Ezr 10:9. Zc 7:1.
in the twentieth. Ezr 7:7.
Shushan. Da +8:2.

2 **Hanani.** Ne 7:2.
I asked. Ps 122:6-9. 137:5, 6.
that had escaped. Ezr 9:8, 9, 14. Je 44:14. Ezk 6:9. 7:16. 24:26, 27.

3 **the province.** Ne 7:6. 11:3. Ezr 2:1. 5:8. Est 1:1.
in great. Ne 9:36, 37. Ps 44:11-14. 137:1-3. Is 32:9-14. La 1:7. 3:61. 5:1.
reproach. 1 K 9:7. Ps 79:4. Is 43:28. Je 24:9. 29:18. 42:18. 44:8-12.
the wall. Ne 2:17. Is 5:5. 64:10, 11. Je 5:10. +39:8.

4 **I sat down.** Jg +20:26. 1 S 4:17-22. Ps 137:1.
wept. Ps +56:8. Zp 3:18.
mourned. Jl +2:12.
certain days. Da 10:2.
fasted. Mt +6:16.
and prayed. 1 K 8:44, 48. Da 6:10.
the God. Ne 2:4. Ezr 5:11, 12. Da 2:18. Jon 1:9.

5 **beseech.** Ex 32:11. 33:18. Nu 12:13. Ps 80:14. 116:4. 118:25. 119:108. Am 7:2. Jon 1:14. 4:3. Ml 1:9. Mt 8:5. Mk 1:40. Lk 8:28. 9:38.
the great. Ps +99:3.
keepeth. Dt +7:9. He 6:13-18.
and mercy. Ex +34:6. Ps 102:13, 14. Is 55:3.

6 **thine ear.** Ps 130:2.
eyes open. Zc +12:4.
day and night. 1 S 15:11. Ps 55:17. 88:1. Lk 2:37. 18:7. 1 T 5:5. 2 T 1:3.
confess. Ezr 9:6, 7. 10:11. Ps 32:5. Is 64:6, 7. La 3:39-42. Da 9:4, 20. 1 J 1:9.
both I. 2 Ch 28:10. 29:6. Ps 106:6. Is 6:5. La 5:7. Ep 2:3.

7 **dealt.** Ne 9:29-35. Ps 78:56, 57. 106:6. Da 9:5, 6.

corruptly. 2 Ch 27:2. Ho 9:9. Zp 3:7. Re 19:2.
the commandments. Le 27:34. Dt 4:1. 5:1. 6:1. 28:15. 1 K 2:3. Ps 19:8, 9. 119:5-8.
which thou. Dt 4:5. 2 Ch 25:4. Ezr 7:6. Da 9:11, 13. Ml 4:4.

8 **Remember.** Ps 119:49. Lk 1:72.
If. Ge +4:7.
ye transgress. 1 K 9:6, 7. Je +9:16.

9 **if ye turn.** Le 26:39-42. Je 29:11-14. Zc +1:3.
heaven. 2 S +22:8.
yet will I. Dt +30:3. Mt 24:31.
will bring. Je 3:14. Ezk 36:24.
the place. Dt +12:11. 1 K 9:3. Ezr 6:12.

10 **Now these.** Ex 32:11. Dt 9:29. Is 63:16-19. 64:9. Da 9:15, etc.
whom. Ex 15:13. Dt 15:15. Ps 74:2.
thy strong. Ex 6:1. 13:9. Ps 136:12. Da 9:15.

11 **let now.** ver. +6. Ps 86:6. 130:2.
who desire. Pr 1:29. Is 26:8, 9. He 13:18.
grant. Ne 2:8. Ge 32:11, 28. 43:14. Ezr 1:1. 7:6, 27, 28. Pr 21:1. 1 T +2:2.
For I was. Ne 2:1. Ge 40:2, 9-13, 21, 23. 41:9.

NEHEMIAH 2

1 **Nisan.** i.e. *their flight; standard; proving,* S#5212h. Ne 2:1. Est 3:7.
the twentieth. Ne 1:1. Ezr 7:1, 7.
I took up. Ne 1:11. Ge 40:11, 21.

2 **Why is thy.** Ge 40:7.
sorrow. Pr 15:13.

3 **Let the king.** 1 K 1:31. Da 2:4. 3:9. 5:10. 6:6, 21.
for ever. Heb. *olam,* Ex +12:24.
the city. Ne 1:3. Ps 102:14. 137:6. La 2:9.
the place. 2 Ch 21:20. 28:27. 32:33.
sepulchres. Heb. *qeber,* Ge +23:4.

4 **For what.** 1 K 3:5. Est 5:3, 6. 7:2. Mk 10:51.
So I prayed. Ne 1:4, 11. 2 S 12:13-17. 15:31. Pr 3:6. Jon 3:6-9. Ph 4:6. 1 Th 5:17. 1 T 2:8.

5 **If it please.** Ezr 5:17. Est 1:19. 5:8. 7:3. 8:5.
and if thy. Ru 2:13. 2 S 14:22. Pr 3:4.
sepulchres. Heb. *qeber,* Ge +23:4.

6 **the queen.** Heb. the wife. Ps 45:9.
So it pleased. ver. 4. Ne 1:11. Is 58:12. 61:4. 65:24.

I set him a time. Ne 5:14. 13:6.

7 let letters. ver. 9. Ezr 6:6. 7:21.
that they may. Ezr 8:22.

8 forest. Ec 2:5. SS 4:13.
palace. Ne 7:2. 1 Ch 29:1.
the wall. ver. 17. Ne 3:1, etc.
the house. Ne 3:7. 7:2.
the king. ver. 18. Ge 32:28. Ezr 5:5. 6:22.
7:6, 9, 27, 28. Pr 21:1. Is 66:14. Da 1:9. Ac
7:10. 26:22. 2 C 8:16.
hand. ver. 18. Ru +1:13. Ezr 7:6, 9, 28. 8:18.

9 to the governors. ver. 7.
Now the. Ezr 8:22.

10 Sanballat. i.e. *hated in secret; hate in disguise;
hatred* (or *thorn*) *in secret*, **S#5571h**. ver. 19. Ne
4:1-3, 7. 6:1, 2, 5, 12, 14. 13:28.
Horonite. i.e. *one from Horonaim* (i.e. *two caverns*, Is +15:5), **S#2772h**. ver. 10, 19. Ne 13:28.
Is 15:5. Je 48:5, 34.
the servant. Pr 30:22. Ec 10:7.
the Ammonite. 1 S +11:11.
it grieved. Nu 22:3, 4. Ps 112:10. 122:6-9. Pr
27:4. Ezk 25:6-8. Mi 7:9, 10, 16, 17. Ac 4:2.
5:24. 19:26, 27.
there was come. Ezr 4:4, etc.

11 I came. Ezr 8:32.

12 I arose. Ge 32:22-24. Jsh 10:9. Jg 6:27. 9:32.
Mt 2:14. Mk 1:35.
neither. Ec 3:7. Am 5:13. Mi 7:5. Mt 10:16.
my God. Ezr 7:27. Ps 51:18. +122:6. Je
31:33. 32:40. 2 C 8:16. Ja 1:16, 17.
Re 17:17.

13 the gate. ver. 15. Ne 3:13. 2 Ch 26:9.
well. Heb. *ayin*, Ge +24:13.
the dung port. Ne 3:13, 14. 12:31. Jsh 15:8.
the walls. ver. 3, 17. Ne 1:3. Je 5:10.

14 the gate of the fountain. Ne 3:15. 2 K
18:17. 20:20. 2 Ch 32:30.
the king's pool. 2 S 5:23. 1 K 1:45.

15 the brook. 2 S 15:23. Je 31:38-40. Jn 18:1.
the gate. ver. 13.

16 the rulers. ver. 12.

17 Ye see. La 2:2, 8, 9. 3:51.
come. Ezr 5:1, 2. 10:2-4. Is 35:3, 4.
build. Ps 127:1.
a reproach. Ne 1:3. 1 S 11:2. Ps +31:11.

18 I told. 1 J 1:3.
the hand. ver. +8.
So they strengthened. 2 S 2:7. 1 Ch 11:10.
19:13. 2 Ch 32:5. Ezr 6:22. Hg 1:13, 14. Ep
6:10. Ph 2:13. He 12:12.

19 Sanballat. ver. 10. Ne 6:1, 2.
Geshem. Ne 6:6, Gashmu.
laughed. Lk +8:53.
will ye rebel. Ne 6:6. Ezr 4:15, 16. Lk 23:2.
Jn 19:12. Ac 24:5.

20 The God. ver. 4. 2 Ch 26:5. Ps 20:5. 35:27.
102:13, 14. 122:6. Ec 7:18.
ye have no. Ezr 4:3. Ac 8:21.
memorial. Ex +12:14. Is 56:5.

NEHEMIAH 3

1 Eliashib. ver. 20. 1 Ch +3:24.
the sheep gate. Ne 12:39. Jn 5:2.
sanctified it. Ne 12:30. Dt 20:5. Ps 30, title.
Pr 3:6, 9.
the tower. Ne 12:39. Je 31:38. Zc 14:10.
Meah. i.e. *an hundred*, **S#3968h**. Ne 3:1.
12:39.

2 next unto him. Heb. at his hand. 2 Ch
+17:15mg.
the men. Ne 7:36. Ezr 2:34.
Zaccur. Ne 10:12.

3 the fish gate. Ne 12:39. 2 Ch 33:14. Zep
1:10.
Hassenaah. i.e. *thorny place; thorn-bush*,
S#5570h. Ne 3:3. 7:38. Ezr 2:35.
the beams. ver. 6. Ne 2:8.
the doors. Ne 6:1. 7:1.
locks. ver. 6, 13, 14, 15. SS 5:5.
bars. ver. 6, 13, 14, 15. Ex 26:26. Dt 3:5. Jg
16:3.

4 Meremoth. ver. 21. Ne 10:5. Ezr +8:33.
Urijah. Ezr 8:33, Uriah. Je +26:20.
Koz. Ezr +2:61.
Meshullam. 1 Ch +9:12.
Berechiah. Zc +1:7.
Meshezabeel. i.e. *set free of God*, **S#4898h**. Ne
10:21. 11:24.
Zadok. 2 S +8:17.
Baana. 1 K +4:12.

5 the Tekoites. ver. 27. 2 S 14:2.
Am 1:1.
their nobles. Jg 5:23. Je 5:4, 5. 1 C 1:26.
1 T 6:17, 18.
put not. Je 27:2, 8, 12. 30:8, 9. Mt 11:29.
Ac 15:10.

6 the old gate. Ne 12:39.
Jehoiada. i.e. *Jah has known*, **S#3111h**. Ne
+12:10, Joiada. For **S#3077h**, see 2 K +11:4,
Jehoiada.
Paseah. 1 Ch +4:12.
Meshullam. ver. 4.
Besodeiah. i.e. *counsel of Jehovah*, **S#1152h**.

7 Melatiah. i.e. *delivered of the Lord; Jah's (way
of) escape*, **S#4424h**.
the Gibeonite. Jsh +10:2. 2 S 21:2.
Jadon. i.e. *God will judge*, **S#3036h**.
Mizpah. ver. 19. 2 Ch 16:6.
Meronothite. 1 Ch 27:30.
the throne. Ne 2:8. Ge +41:40. Ex 11:5.
12:29. Dt 17:18. Jg 3:20. 1 S 1:9. 2:8. 4:13,
18. 2 S 3:10.

8 Uzziel. Ex +6:18.
Harhaiah. i.e. *burning or anger of the Lord*,
S#2736h.
the goldsmiths. or, refiners. ver. 31, 32. Jg
17:4. Pr 25:4. Is 40:19. 46:6.
Hananiah. 1 Ch +25:23.
of the apothecaries. or, compounders. Ge
50:2. Ex 30:25, 35. 37:29. Ec 10:1.

fortified. *or*, left.

the broad wall. Ne 12:38. 2 Ch 25:23. 26:9.

9 **Rephaiah**. 1 Ch +9:43.

Hur. Ex +17:10.

the ruler. ver. 12, 17.

10 **Jedaiah**. i.e. *he confesses Jah*, **S#3042h**. 1 Ch 4:37. Zc 6:10, 14.

Harumaph. i.e. *snub-nosed*, **S#2739h**.

even. ver. 23, 28-30.

Hattush. Ne 9:38. 10:1, 4. Ezr +8:2.

Hashabniah. i.e. *esteemed of the Lord*, **S#2813h**. ver. 10. Ne 9:5.

11 **Malchijah**. 1 Ch +9:12.

Harim. 1 Ch +24:8.

Hashub. i.e. *much esteemed*, **S#2815h**. ver. 23. 10:23. 11:15. 1 Ch 9:14.

Pahath-moab. Ezr +2:6.

furnaces. Ne 12:38. Ge 15:17.

other piece. Heb. second measure.

the tower. Ne 12:38.

12 **Shallum**. 2 K +15:10.

Halohesh. i.e. *enchanter*, **S#3873h**. Ne 9:38. 10:1, 24.

the ruler. ver. 9, 14-18.

he and his daughters. Ex 35:25. 1 Ch +2:34. Ac 21:8, 9. Ph 4:3.

13 **The valley gate**. Ne 2:13.

Hanun. ver. 30.

Zanoah. Jsh +15:34, 56.

14 **the dung gate**. Ne 2:13. 12:31.

Rechab. 2 S +4:2.

the ruler. ver. 9, 12, 15-18.

Beth-haccerem. Je +6:1.

15 **the gate**. Ne 2:14. 12:37. 2 Ch 32:30.

Shallun. i.e. *retribution*, **S#7968h**.

Col-hozeh. i.e. *all-seer*, **S#3626h**. Ne 11:5.

the ruler. ver. 9, 12, 14.

Mizpah. ver. 7. Jsh 15:38. Jg 20:1, 3, Mizpeh. Je 40:6.

Siloah. i.e. *dart, shoot, sent forth*, **S#7975h**. Is 8:6, Shiloah. Is 8:6, Shiloah. Lk 13:4. Jn 9:7, Siloam.

king's garden. 2 K 25:4.

the stairs. Ne 12:37. Ex 20:26. 2 S 5:6, 7.

16 **Nehemiah**. Ne +1:1.

Azbuk. i.e. *wholly forsaken*, **S#5802h**.

the ruler. ver. 9, 12, 14.

Beth-zur. Jsh +15:58.

the sepulchres. Heb. *qeber*, Ge +23:4.

of David. 2 Ch 16:14. Ac 2:29.

the pool. 2 K 18:17. 20:20. Is 7:3. 22:11.

the house. 1 K 14:27, 28. 2 Ch 12:10, 11. SS 3:7.

17 **repaired**. 1 C 3:10-13.

the ruler. ver. 16. I Ch 23:4.

Keilah. Jsh +15:44.

18 **Bavai**. i.e. *with the desire of God*, **S#942h**.

Henadad. Ezr +3:9.

19 **Ezer**. Ne 12:42.

Jeshua. Ne +8:17.

Mizpah. ver. 15.

another piece. or, a second measure. Ex 26:2, 8. 36:9, 15.

the turning. ver. 20, 24, 25. Ex +26:24.

20 **Zabbai**. *or*, Zaccai.

earnestly. Ec 9:10. Ro +12:11.

Eliashib. ver. +1, 21.

21 **Meremoth**. ver. 4.

Koz. Ne 7:63. Ezr 2:61.

22 **repaired**. 1 C 3:10-13.

the men of the plain. Ne 6:2. 12:28.

23 **over against**. ver. 10, 29, 30.

Azariah. Ne 10:2.

Maaseiah. Je +21:1.

Ananiah. i.e. *Jah's cloud; cloud of the Lord*, **S#6055h**. ver. 23. Ne 11:32.

24 **Binnui**. Ezr +10:30.

another piece. ver. 11, 19, 27.

the turning. ver. 20.

25 **Palal**. i.e. *mediator*, **S#6420h**.

Uzai. i.e. *swiftness of the Lord; I shall have my sprinklings*, **S#186h**.

the king's. Je 22:14. 39:8.

by the court. Ne 12:39. Je 32:2. 33:1. 37:21. 39:15.

Pedaiah. Ne 8:4.

Parosh. Ezr +2:3.

26 **Nethinims**. 1 Ch +9:2.

dwelt. etc. *or, which* dwelt in Ophel, *repaired* unto.

Ophel. *or*, the tower. ver. 27. 2 K +5:24mg.

the water gate. Ne 8:1, 3. 12:37.

27 **the Tekoites**. ver. 5.

the wall. ver. 26.

Ophel. 2 K +5:24mg.

28 **the horse**. 2 K 11:16. 2 Ch 23:15. Je 31:40.

every one. ver. 10, 23.

29 **Zadok**. Ne 13:13.

the son. 1 Ch +9:12.

Shemaiah. Ezr 8:16.

Shechaniah. Ezr 10:2.

the east gate. Je 19:2.

30 **Zalaph**. i.e. *wound*, **S#6764h**.

another piece. ver. 21.

Meshullam. ver. +4.

31 **the goldsmith's**. ver. 8, 32.

Nethinims. ver. +26.

merchants. ver. 32. Ne 13:20. 1 K 10:15. SS 3:6. Ezk 17:4. 27:3, 13, 15, 17, 20, 22, 23, 24. Na 3:16.

Miphkad. i.e. *muster*, **S#4663h**.

going up of the corner. *or*, corner-chamber. 1 K 10:5. 1 Ch 26:16mg. 2 Ch 9:4.

32 **the sheep gate**. ver. 1. Ne 12:39. Jn 5:2.

the goldsmiths. ver. 8, 31.

NEHEMIAH 4

1 **Sanballat**. Ne 2:10, 19. Ezr 4:1-5. Ac 5:17.

mocked. Ps 35:15, 16. 44:13, 14. Mt 27:29. He 11:36.

2 the army. Ezr 4:9, 10.
What do. 1 S 17:42. Ps 123:4.
feeble. 1 S 14:11, 12. 17:43, 44. Zc 12:8. 1 C 1:27.
fortify themselves. Heb. leave to themselves. Ne 3:8.
sacrifice. Ne 12:27, 43.
revive. ver. 10. Ezk 37:3-13. Hab 3:2.

3 Tobiah. Ne 2:10, 19. 6:1. 1 K 20:10, 18. 2 K 18:23.

4 Hear. Ne 6:9. Ps 123:3, 4. Ps 33:22. 82:8. 104:24. 109:21. 123:3, 4.
despised. Heb. despite.
turn. 1 S 17:26. Ps 79:12. Pr 3:34. Ho 12:14.

5 cover not. Ps 59:5-13. 69:27, 28. 109:14, 15. Je +10:25.
their sin. Ps +51:1.
before the builders. Is 36:11, 12.

6 we built. Da 9:25.
had a mind. Ne 6:15. 1 Ch 29:3, 14, 17, 18. 2 Ch 29:36. Ps 110:3. 2 C 8:16, 17. Ph 2:13. He 13:21.

7 Sanballat. ver. 1. Ne 2:10, 19.
the Ammonites. Ge +19:38. 1 S +11:11.
Ashdodites. i.e. *inhabitants of Ashdod* (i.e. *strong to oppress or spoil*, Jsh +11:22), **S#796h**. ver. 7. Ne 13:23, 24. Jsh 13:3. 1 S 5:1-3, 6. 2 Ch 26:6-8. Je 25:20. Am 1:8. 3:9. Zc 9:5, 6.
heard. Ezr 4:4-16. 5:8.
were made up. Heb. ascended. lit. healing went up to the walls. 2 Ch 24:13mg. Je +8:22.
then. Ge 3:15. Ac 4:17, 18. 5:33. Re 12:12, 13, 17.

8 all. Ps 2:1-3. 83:3-11. Is 8:9, 10. Ac 23:12, 13.
hinder it. Heb. make an error to it. Je 20:10. Lk 11:52. 1 Th 2:18.

9 Nevertheless. Ne 1:11. Ge 32:9-12, 28. 2 K 19:14-19. Ps 50:15. 55:16-22. Lk 6:11, 12. Ac 4:24-30.
set a watch. Mt 26:41. Mk 13:33. 14:38. Lk +21:36. Col 4:2. 1 P 5:8.

10 The strength. Nu 13:31. 32:9. Ps 11:1, 2. Hg 1:2.
bearers. 2 Ch 2:18. Ezk 29:18.

11 They shall not. Jg 20:29, etc. 2 S 17:2. Ps 56:6. Is 47:11. Ac 23:12, 21. 1 Th 5:2.

12 ten times. Ge 31:7, 41. Nu 14:22. 1 S +1:8. Jb 19:3.
From all places, etc. *or*, That from all places ye must return to us.

13 Therefore. Ge 32:13-20. 2 Ch 32:2-8. Ps 112:5. Mt 10:16. 1 C 14:20.
in the lower places. Heb. from the lower parts of the place, etc.
their swords. ver. 17, 18. Jg 3:2. 1 Ch +5:22. SS 3:7, 8. Lk +22:36. Ep 6:11-20.

14 Be not ye afraid. Nu 14:9. Dt 1:21, 29, 30. 20:3, 4. Jsh 1:9. 2 Ch 20:15-17. 32:7. Ps 27:1. 46:11. Is 41:10-14. Mt +10:28. He +13:6.

remember. Ps 20:7. 77:10-20. 143:5. Is 51:12, 13. 63:11-13.
the broad wall.
great. Ps +99:3.
fight. Dt 10:18. 2 S 10:12.

15 God. Je +19:7.
every one. Mk 13:34. Ro +12:11. 1 Th 4:11.

16 my servants. ver. 23. Ne 5:15, 16. Ps 101:6.
and the other half. ver. 21. 1 S 30:24. Pr +22:3.
habergeons. **S#8302h**. 1 S 17:5, 38. 1 K 22:34. 2 Ch 18:33. 26:14. Is 59:17.

17 builded. 1 C 3:10-13.
bare burdens. ver. 10.
with one. Da 9:25. 1 C 9:26. 16:9, 13. 2 C 6:7. Ep 6:11, etc. Ph 1:28. 2 T 2:3. 4:7.

18 builders. 1 C 3:10-13.
by his side. Heb. on his loins. Ezk 9:2, 3, 11.
he that sounded. Nu 10:9. 2 Ch 13:12-17. 1 C 14:8.

19 I said. ver. 14. Ne 5:7. 7:5.

20 our God. Ex 14:14, 25. Dt 1:30. 3:22. 20:4. Jsh 23:10. Zc 14:3. Ro 8:31.

21 So we. 1 C 15:10, 58. Ga 6:9. Col 1:29.

22 every one. Ne 11:1, 2.

23 So neither I. Ne 5:16. 7:2. Jg 9:48. 1 C 15:10.
saving that, etc. *or*, every one *went* with his weapon *for* water, Jg 5:11.

NEHEMIAH 5

1 a great cry. Ex 3:7. 22:25-27. Jb 31:38, 39. 34:28. Is 5:7. Lk 18:7. Ja +5:4.
their brethren. Le 25:35-37. Dt 15:7-11. Ac 7:26. 1 C 6:6-8.

2 We, our sons. Ps 127:3-5. 128:2-4. Ml 2:2.
we take up corn. Ge 41:57. 42:2. 43:8.

3 mortgaged. Ge 47:15-25. Le 25:35-39. Dt 15:7.
because. Ml 3:8-11.

4 the king's tribute. Ne 9:37. Dt 28:47, 48. Jsh 16:10. 1 K 9:21. Ezr 4:13, 20.

5 our flesh. Ge 37:27. Pr 11:17. Is 58:6, 7. Ja 2:5, 6.
we. Ex 21:1-11. Le +25:39-43.

6 I was very. Ne 13:8, 25. Ex 11:8. Nu 16:15. Mk 3:5. Ep 4:26.

7 I consulted with myself. Heb. my heart consulted in me. Ps 4:4. 27:8.
I rebuked. Le 19:15, 17. 2 Ch 19:6, 7. Ps 82:1-4. Pr 27:5. 2 C 5:16. Ga 2:11. 1 T 5:20. T 2:15.
Ye exact usury. Dt 24:10-13. Is +24:2. Ezk 45:9.
I set a great assembly. 2 Ch 28:9-13. Mt 18:17.

8 We after. Mt 25:15, 29. 2 C 8:12. Ga 6:10.
redeemed. Le 25:47-49.
sell your. Ex 21:16. Dt 24:7.
shall they. Ro 14:15. 1 C 8:11.
held. Jb 29:10. 32:15. Mt 22:12. Ro 3:19.

9 **It is not.** 1 S 2:24. Pr 16:29. 17:26. 18:5. 19:2. 24:23.
ought ye. Da 6:4, 5. T 2:8. 1 P 2:15.
walk. ver. 15. Ex +1:17. Ac 9:31.
reproach. Ge 13:7, 8. 2 S 12:14. Ezk 36:20. Ro 2:24. 1 T 5:14. T 2:5. 1 P 2:11, 12.

10 **I likewise.** Mi 2:1. Lk 3:13, 14. 1 C 9:12-18.
I pray you. 2 C 5:11, 20. 6:1. Phm 8, 9.
leave. ver. 7. Ex 22:25-27. Ps 15:5. Ezk 18:8, 13.

11 **Restore.** Ex 22:1. Le 6:4, 5. Nu 5:7. 1 S 12:3. 2 S 12:6. Is 58:6. Lk 3:8. 19:8.
their lands. ver. 3, 4.
the hundredth. Is +24:2.

12 **We will restore.** 2 Ch 28:14, 15. Ezr 10:12. Mt 19:21, 22. Lk +19:8.
I called. Ne 10:29. 13:25. 2 K 23:2, 3. 2 Ch 6:22, 23. 15:13, 14. Ezr 10:5. Je 34:8-10. Mt 26:63.

13 **I shook.** Ex 14:27mg. Jg 16:20.
my lap. Ps 129:7. Is 49:22mg. Mt 10:14. Ac 13:51. 18:6.
So God. 1 S 15:28. 1 K 11:29-31. Zc 5:3, 4.
emptied. Heb. empty, or void. **S#7386h.** Ge 37:24. 41:27. Dt 32:47. Jg 7:16. 9:4. 11:3. 2 S 6:20. 2 K 4:3. 2 Ch 13:7. Pr 12:11. 28:19. Is 29:8. Ezk 24:11.
Amen. Mt +6:13.
praised. Ge 12:15. Jg 16:24. 1 Ch 16:36.
the people. 2 K 23:3. Ps 50:14. 76:11. 119:106. Ec 5:5.

14 **from the twentieth.** Ne 2:1. 13:6.
I and my. 1 C 9:4-15, 18. 2 Th 3:8, 9.
the bread. Ezr 4:13, 14. Ro 13:6, 7.

15 **governors.** 1 K 10:15.
bread. Ge +3:19.
and wine. Ge +27:28.
even their. 1 S 2:15-17. 8:15. Pr 29:12.
so did. Mt 5:47. 2 C 11:9. 12:13.
because. ver. 9. Ex +1:17. Jb 31:23. Pr +3:7. Lk 18:2-4.

16 **I continued.** Lk 8:15. Ro 2:7. 1 C 15:58. Ga 6:9.
neither bought. Nu 16:15. Ac 20:33-35. 1 Th 2:5, 6.
all my. 2 C 12:16-18. Ph 2:20, 21.

17 **at my table.** 2 S 9:7, 13. 1 K 18:19.
an hundred and fifty. Is 32:8. Ro 12:13. 1 P 4:9, 10.

18 **Now that.** 1 K 4:22, 23.
required. ver. 14, 15.
because the bondage. Ps 37:21, 26.

19 **Think.** Ne 13:14, 22, 31. Ge 40:14. Ps 25:6, 7. +40:17. 106:4. Je 29:11. Jon 1:6.
according to. Ps 18:23-25. Mt 10:42. 25:34-40. Mk 9:41.
have done. Ne 13:14. Ge 20:5. Dt 26:13-15. 2 K 4:1. 20:3. Ps 7:8, 9. 25:21. 26:1, 3. 40:9, 10. 69:8-10. 119:29, 30, 77, 94, 121, 132, 173.

NEHEMIAH 6

1 **when Sanballat.** Ne 2:10, 19. 4:1, 7.
Geshem. i.e. *shower*, **S#1654h.** ver. 1, 2, 6. Ne 2:19. Gashmu.
no breach. Ne 4:6, 7. Da 9:25.
at that time. Ne 3:1, 3, 6.

2 **Come..** 2 S 3:27. 20:9. Ps 37:12. Pr 26:24-26. Ec 4:4.
Ono. Ezr +2:33.
they thought. Ps 12:2. 37:12, 32. Je 41:2. Ezk 33:31. Mi 7:4, 5. Lk 20:19-21.

3 **And I sent.** Pr 14:15. Mt 10:16.
I am doing. Ec 9:10. Lk 14:30. Jn 9:4. 1 T 4:15, 16.

4 **four times.** Jg 16:6, 10, 15-20. Pr 7:21. Lk 18:5. 1 C 15:58. Ga 2:5.
and I answered. Pr 14:15.

5 **with an open letter.** 2 K 18:26-28. 2 C 2:11. 11:13-15. Ep 6:11. 2 Th 2:10.

6 **It is reported.** Je 9:3-6. 20:10. Mt 5:11. Ro 3:8. 2 C 6:8. 1 P 2:12, 13. 3:16.
Gashmu. i.e. *a shower*, **S#1654h.** ver. +1, 2, Geshem.
that thou and. Ne 2:19. Ezr 4:12, 15.
that thou mayest. Lk 23:2. Jn 19:13.

7 **appointed.** ver. 12, 13.
a king. 2 S 15:10-12. 1 K 1:7, 18, 25, 34. Ac 17:7.
Come now. Pr 26:24-26. Ac 23:15.

8 **There are.** Ac 24:12, 13. 25:7, 10.
thou feignest. Jb 13:4. Ps 36:3. 38:12. 52:2. Is 59:4. Da 11:27. Mt 12:34. Jn 8:44.
own heart. Nu +16:28.

9 **For they.** ver. 14. Ne 4:10-14. 2 Ch 32:18.
Their hands. 2 Ch 15:7. Ezr 4:1-24. Is 35:3, 4. Je 38:4. He 12:12.
Now therefore. 1 S 30:6. Ps 56:3. 68:35. 71:1. 138:3. Is 41:10. Zc 10:12. 2 C 12:9. Ep 3:16. 6:10. Ph 4:13. 1 P 5:10.
O God. ver. 14. Ne 5:19.

10 **Shemaiah.** ver. 12. 1 Ch +9:16. Pr 11:9. Mt 7:15.
Delaiah. Je +36:12.
Mehetabeel. i.e. *done good to by God; God's best; benefited of God*, **S#4105h.** ver. 10. Ge +36:39, Mehetabel. 1 Ch 1:50.
shut up. 2 K 9:8. Je 36:5. Ezk 3:24.
Let us meet. Ps 12:2. 37:12. 120:2, 3.
the house. 1 K 6:5. 2 K 11:3.
let us shut. 2 Ch 28:24. 29:3, 7. Ml 1:10. Ac 21:30.
in the night. Jb 24:13-17. Jn 3:20.

11 **Should such.** ver. 3. 1 S 19:5. Jb 4:3-6. Ps 11:1, 2. 112:6, 8. Pr 28:1. Is 10:18. Lk 13:31-33. Ac 8:1. 20:24. 21:13. He 11:27.
would go. ver. 9. Nu 32:7-9. Ps 56:2, 3. Ec 10:1. Ph 2:17, 30.

12 **I perceived.** Ezk 13:22. 1 C 2:15. 12:10.
God had. Je 14:14. 23:16, 25. 28:15. Ezk 13:7. 1 J 4:1.

hired him. Is 56:11. Ezk 13:19. Mi 3:11. Ac 20:33. 1 T 3:3. T 1:7. 1 P 5:2. 2 P 2:3. Re 18:13.

13 **that I should**. Pr 29:5. Is 51:7, 12, 13. 57:11. Je 1:17. Ezk 2:6. 13:17, etc. Mt 10:28. 2 T 1:7. Re 21:8.

and sin. Ja 4:17.

and that they. ver. 6. Pr 22:1. Ec 7:1.

report, that. Je 18:18. 20:10. Da 6:4, 5. Mt 22:15. 26:59. Ac 6:13. 2 C 11:12. 1 T 5:14. T 2:8.

reproach me. Ne 4:4.

14 **My God**. ver. 19. Ps 22:1. 63:1.

think thou. Ne 13:29. Ps 36:11, 12. Je +10:25. 1 J 5:16.

on the prophetess. Ex +15:20. 1 K 22:22-24. Is 9:14, 15. Je 14:15, 18. 28:1, 10, 15. Ezk 13:16, 17. Mt 7:15. 24:11, 24. 2 T 3:8. Re 19:20.

Noadiah. i.e. *convened of Jah; met by Jah*, **S#5129h**. Ezr 8:33.

put me. Ps 62:4. 2 T 4:14.

15 **wall**. Ezr 6:15. Ps 1:3. Da 9:25.

Elul. i.e. *outcry; nothingness*, **S#435h**. The sixth month of the Hebrew year, part of August and September.

fifty. Ne 4:1, 2.

16 **when all our enemies**. ver. 1, 2. Ne 2:10. 4:1, 7.

for they perceived. Ex 14:25. Nu 23:23. Jsh 5:1. Ps 14:5. 126:2, 3. Ac 5:38.

17 **the nobles**. Ne 3:5. 5:7. 13:28. Mi 7:1-6. Mt 24:10-12.

sent many letters unto Tobiah. Heb. multiplied their letters passing to Tobiah.

18 **Arah**. Ne 7:10. Ezr 2:5.

Meshullam. 1 Ch +9:12.

19 **they reported**. Le 19:16. Pr 20:19. 26:20. 28:4. Jn 7:7. 15:19. 1 J 4:5.

words. *or*, matters.

letters. ver. 5, 17. Ne 2:7, 8, 9. 2 Ch 30:1, 6. Est 9:26, 29.

to put. ver. 9, 13. Is 37:10-14. Ac 4:18-21.

NEHEMIAH 7

1 **the wall**. Ne 3:1, etc. 6:15.

I had set up. Ne 3:3. 6:1.

the porters. Ne 10:39. 11:3. 12:24. 1 Ch ch. 23, 25, 26. 2 Ch 31:2. Ezr 3:8.

2 **my brother**. Ne 1:2.

Hananiah. Ne 10:23.

the ruler. Ne 2:8.

a faithful man. Nu 12:7. Ps 101:6. Da 6:4. Mt 24:45. 25:21. *Lk* 16:10-12. 1 C 4:2. 2 T 2:2.

feared God. Ex +18:21. Is 33:5, 6.

3 **Let not the gates**. Ne 13:19. Ps 127:1. Mt 10:16.

every one to be. Ne 3:23, 28-30.

4 **large and great**. Heb. broad in spaces. Jg 18:10. Ps 119:45mg. Is 22:18mg.

the houses. Is 58:12. Hg 1:4-6. Mt 6:33.

5 **my God**. Ne 5:19. 6:14.

put into mine. Ezr 7:27. 1 C 15:10. 2 C 3:5. 8:16. Ph 2:12, 13. Col 1:29. Ja 1:16.

that. ver. 64. 1 Ch 9:1, etc. Ezr 2:62.

6 **the children**. Ezr ch. 2. 5:8. 6:2.

whom Nebuchadnezzar. 2 K 24:14-16. 25:11. 2 Ch ch. 36. Je ch. 39, 52.

7 **Zerubbabel**. Ezr 1:11, Sheshbazzar. Hg +1:1.

Jeshua. Ne +8:17. Zc 3:1-3, Joshua.

Azariah. Ezr 2:2, Seraiah, Reelaiah.

Raamiah. i.e. *thunder of Jah*, **S#7485h**.

Nahamani. i.e. *comforting; repenting; he comforted me*, **S#5167h**.

Mispereth. i.e. *enumerator; number, a few*, **S#4559h**. Ezr 2:2, Mizpar.

Nehum. i.e. *penitent; merciful; comfort*, **S#5149h**. Ne 12:3. Ezr 2:2, Rehum.

8 **Parosh**. Ezr +2:3.

9 **Shephatiah**. 2 S +3:4. Ezr 2:4. 8:8.

10 **Arah**. Ne 6:18. Ezr 2:5, 755.

11 **Pahath-moab**. Ezr +2:6, 2812.

12 **Elam**. ver. 34. Ge +10:22. Ezr 2:7. 8:7. 10:26.

13 **Zattu**. Ezr 2:8, 945.

14 **Zaccai**. i.e. *pure; just; pure of the Lord*, **S#2140h**. Ezr 2:9. +10:28, Zabbai.

15 **Binnui**. Ezr 2:10, Bani. 642.

16 **Bebai**. Ezr 2:11, 623.

17 **Azgad**. Ezr 2:12, 1222.

18 **Adonikam**. i.e. *my lord has arisen*, **S#140h**. Ezr 2:13, 666. 8:13.

19 **Bigvai**. Ezr 2:14, 2056.

20 **Adin**. Ezr 2:15, 454.

21 **Ater**. Ezr 2:16.

22 **Hashum**. Ezr 2:19, 223.

23 **Bezai**. i.e. *shining*, **S#1209h**. Ne 10:18. Ezr 2:17, 323.

24 **Hariph**. i.e. *reproach*, **S#2756h**. Ne 10:19. Ezr 2:18, Jorah. 2 Ch 34:20.

25 **Gibeon**. Ezr 2:20, Gibbar.

26 **Bethlehem**. Ezr 2:21, 22, 179.

27 **Anathoth**. 1 Ch +7:8.

28 **Beth-azmaveth**. i.e. *house of death's power*, **S#1041h**. Ezr 2:24, Azmaveth.

29 **Kirjath-jearim**. Jsh +9:17. Ezr 2:25, Kirjatharim.

Beeroth. Jsh +9:17.

30 **Ramah**. Jsh 18:24, 25. Ezr 2:26. Je +31:15.

31 **Michmas**. 1 S 13:5, 23. Ezr 2:27. Is 10:28, Michmash.

32 **Bethel**. Jsh 8:9, 17. Ezr 2:28, 223.

33 **Nebo**. Ezr 2:29.

fifty and two. Ezr 2:30.

34 **the other Elam**. ver. 12. Ezr 2:31.

35 **Harim**. 1 Ch +24:8.

36 **Jericho**. Ezr 2:34.

37 **Lod**. i.e. *travail*, **S#3850h**. Ne 6:2. 11:34, 35. 1 Ch 8:12. Ezr 2:33, 725.

38 Senaah. Ezr 2:35, 3630.

39 Jedaiah. 1 Ch 24:7, etc. Ezr 2:36.

40 Immer. 1 Ch +9:12.

41 Pashur. Je +20:1.

42 Harim. 1 Ch +24:8.

43 Hodevah. i.e. *honor of Jah*, **S#1937h**. Ezr 2:40, Hodaviah. 3:9, Judah.

44 The singers. 1 Ch 25:2. Ezr 2:41, 128.

45 The porters. 1 Ch +23:5. ch. 26. Ezr 2:42, 130.

46 Nethinims. 1 Ch +9:2.
Hashupha. i.e. *made bare*, **S#2817h**. Ezr 2:43, Hasupha.
Tabbaoth. i.e. *signets*, **S#2884h**. Ezr 2:43.

47 Sia. i.e. *congregation*, **S#5517h**. Ezr 2:44, Siaha.

48 Lebana. i.e. *the moon*, **S#3838h**. Ezr 2:45.
Hagaba. i.e. *locust*, **S#2286h**. Ezr 2:45, 46, Hagabah, or Hagab.
Shalmai. i.e. *clothed*, **S#8014h**. Ezr 2:46, Shamlai.

51 Phaseah. i.e. *vacillating*, **S#6454h**. Ne 3:6. 1 Ch +4:12, Paseah. Ezr 2:49.

52 Meunim. i.e. *a residence*, **S#4586h**. Ezr 2:50, Mehunim, Nephusim.
Nephishesim. i.e. *refreshed of spices*, **S#5300h**. Ezr 2:50.

54 Bazlith. i.e. *stripping; making naked*, **S#1213h**. Ezr 2:52, Bazluth.

55 Tamah. i.e. *laughter; thou wilt be fat*, **S#8547h**. Ezr 2:53, Thamah.

57 Solomon's. Ne 11:3.
Sophereth. i.e. *female scribe; registrar*, **S#5618h**. Ezr 2:55.
Perida. i.e. *grain, kernel; eminent*, **S#6514h**. Ezr 2:55, Peruda.

58 Jaala. i.e. *a wild goat*, **S#3279h**. Ezr 2:56, Jaalah.

59 Amon. i.e. *architect; to be faithful*, **S#526h**. 1 K 22:26. 2 K 21:18, 19, 23-25. 1 Ch 3:14. 2 Ch 18:25. 33:20, 21-23, 25. Ezr 2:57, Ami. Je 1:2. 25:3. Mt 1:10.

60 the Nethinims. Ezr 2:58.

61 Tel-haresha. i.e. *height of an enchanter*, **S#8521h**. Ezr 2:59, Tel-harsa, Addan.
Addon. i.e. *foundation; depression; calamity*, **S#114h**.
seed. *or*, pedigree.

62 six hundred. Ezr 2:60, 652.

63 of the priests. Ezr 2:61-63.
Barzillai. 2 S 17:27. 19:31-33. 1 K 2:7.

64 These sought. Mt 22:11-13.
those that were. ver. 5. 1 Ch 9:1.
but it was. Mt 25:11, 12.
as polluted. Ne 13:29. Le 4:3.

65 the Tirshatha. *or*, the governor. Ezr +2:63.
that they should. Le 21:21-23.
till there. Ex +28:30.

66 whole congregation. Ezr 2:64.

67 their manservants. Is 45:1, 2. Je 27:7.
two hundred. Ezr 2:65, 200.

68 Their horses. Ezr 2:66, 67.
mules. 2 S 13:29. 18:9.

69 asses. Ge 12:16. 22:3, 5.

70 some. Heb. part. Ezr 2:68-70. Da 1:2.
the chief. Nu 7:2-86. 1 Ch 29:3-9.
gave. Le +23:38.
The Tirshatha. ver. +65.
drams. *Darkemonim*, or *darics*; a Persian gold coin.
basons. Ex 12:22. 1 K +7:40, 45.

71 chief. Jb 34:19. Lk 21:1-4. 2 C 8:12.
pound. *Manim*, manehs or minas. Ezk 45:12.

73 when the seventh. Ezr 2:70. 3:1.

NEHEMIAH 8

1 A.M. 3559. B.C. 445.
all the people. Ezr 3:1, etc.
as one man. Jg 20:1, 8.
before. ver. 16. Ne 3:26. 12:37.
gate. Ge +14:7.
they spake. Jb 23:12.
Ezra. ver. 4-9. Ezr 7:6, 11. Je 8:8, 9. Mt 13:52. 23:2, 13, 34.
bring. Dt 31:11. 2 Ch 34:15. Is 8:20. Ml 4:4.

2 priest. Dt 17:18. 31:9, 10. Ml 2:7.
congregation. Dt 31:11-13. 2 Ch 17:7-9. Ac 15:21.
could hear with understanding. Heb. understood in hearing. Is 28:9.
the first. Le +23:24. Nu 29:1. 1 K 8:2.

3 he read. ver. 8. Dt 31:11-13. Je 36:6. Lk 4:16-20. Ac 13:15, 27. 15:21.
gate. Ge +14:7.
morning. Heb. light. Ac 20:7, 11. 28:23.
could understand. ver. 2. Is 28:9.
ears. Mt 7:28, 29. Mk 12:37. Lk 8:18. 19:48. Ac 16:14. 17:11. 1 Th 2:13. He 2:1-3. Re 2:29. 3:22.

4 pulpit. Heb. tower.
Anaiah. i.e. *answer of the Lord*, **S#6043h**. Ne 10:22.
Maaseiah. Je +21:1.
Malchiah. Je +38:1.
Hashum. Ezr +2:19.
Hashbadana. i.e. *considerate in judging*, **S#2806h**.
Meshullam. 1 Ch +9:12.

5 opened. Lk 4:16, 17.
sight. Heb. eyes. Ge 18:3.
stood up. Ex 15:20. Jg 3:20. 20:26. 1 K 8:14. 2 Ch 7:6.

6 blessed. 1 Ch 29:20. 2 Ch 6:4. Ps 41:13. 72:18, 19. Ep 1:3. 1 P 1:3.
Amen. Mt +6:13.
with lifting. Ge 14:22. Ps 28:2. 63:4. 134:2. 141:2. La 3:41. 1 T 2:8.
bowed. Ge +24:26.
with their faces. Le 9:24. Mt 26:39. Re 7:11.

7 Jeshua. ver. +17.

Bani. Ezr +2:10.

Sherebiah. Ezr +8:18.

Akkub. 1 Ch +3:24.

Hodijah. i.e. *majesty of God*, **S#1941h**. Ne 9:5. 10:10, 13, 18. 1 Ch 4:19.

Maaseiah. ver. +4.

Kelita. Ne 10:10. Ezr 10:23.

Azariah. 1 Ch +6:36.

Jozabad. 2 Ch +31:13.

Hanan. Ne 10:10.

Pelaiah. i.e. *distinguished of the Lord*, **S#6411h**. Ne 10:10. 1 Ch 3:24.

caused. Le 10:11. Dt 33:10. 2 Ch 17:7-9. 30:22. Ml 2:7.

8 **they read**. Is 34:16. Jn +5:39. 1 T 4:13. 2 T +3:15. Re 1:3.

distinctly. or, explaining. lit. "spread out," as in Le 24:12mg. Nu 15:34. Ezr 4:18. Ezk 34:12. Lk 24:32. Ac +17:2, 3.

and gave the sense. 1 S 25:3. 1 Ch 22:12. Hab 2:2. Mt 5:21, 22, 27, 28. Lk 24:27, 32, 45. Ac 8:30-35. +17:2, 3. 28:23.

9 **Nehemiah**. Ne 7:65, 70. 10:1. Ezr 2:63.

Tirshatha. *or*, governor. Ne 12:26. Ezr +2:63.

Ezra. Ezr 7:11.

the Levites. ver. 7, 8. 2 Ch 15:3. 30:22. 35:3. Ho 4:6.

This day. ver. 2. Le 23:24. Nu 29:1-6.

mourn not. Dt 12:7, 12. 16:11, 14, 15. 26:14. Ec 3:4. Is 61:3. Ml 2:13.

all the people. 2 K 22:11, 19. 2 Ch 34:19, 21. Ro 3:20. 7:9. 2 C 7:9-11.

10 **Go your way**. Ec 2:24. 3:13. 5:18. 9:7. 1 T 6:17, 18.

eat. SS 5:1.

send. Dt 26:11-13. Est 9:19, 22. Jb 31:16-18. Ec 11:2. Lk 11:41. Re 11:10.

neither. Dt 28:47. Ps 100:2. Lk 1:74.

the joy. Dt +12:7. Ps 5:11. 21:1. 28:7, 8. 119:80. 149:2. Pr 14:30. 15:13, 15. 17:22. Is 6:7, 8. 35:1-4. 61:10. Jn 16:33. Ro 14:17. 2 C 8:2. 12:8, 9.

11 **stilled**. Nu 13:30. Hab +2:20.

12 **to send**. ver. 10.

to make. Ps 126:1-3.

because. ver. 7, 8. Jb 23:12. Ps 19:8-11. 119:14, 16, 72, 97, 103, 104, 111, 127, 128, 130, 171, 174. Pr 2:10, 11. 24:13, 14. Je 15:16. Lk 24:32. Ro 7:18.

13 **the second**. 2 Ch 30:23. Pr 2:1-6. 8:33, 34. 12:1. Mk 6:33, 34. Lk 19:47, 48. Ac 4:1. 13:42.

to understand the words of the law. *or*, that they might instruct in the words of the law. ver. 7, 8. Lk 24:32. 2 T 2:24, 25.

14 **by**. Heb. by the hand of. 1 K +16:12mg. 2 Ch 34:14mg.

dwell. Le +23:34, 40-43.

booths. Ge 33:17. Mt 17:4.

the feast. Le +23:34, 42.

15 **And that**. Ex 23:14, 17. Le 23:4. Nu 10:10. Ps 81:3.

in Jerusalem. Dt 16:16.

the mount. Jg 9:48, 49. Mt +21:1.

fetch. Le +23:40.

olive. Ge 8:11. Jg 9:8, 9. 1 K 6:23. Ps 52:8. Je 11:16. Ho 14:6. Zc 4:11-14. Ro 11:16-25. He 4:16. Re 11:4.

pine. Mi 4:2.

myrtle. Is 35:10. 55:13.

palm. Jn 12:13. Re 7:9.

16 **the roof**. Dt +22:8.

the courts. 2 Ch 20:5. 33:5.

the street of the water gate. ver. 3. Ne 3:26. 12:37.

gate of Ephraim. Ne 12:37, 39. 2 K 14:13.

17 **sat under**. Jn 1:14. He 11:9, 13.

Jeshua. i.e. *salvation of the Lord*. Jsh 1:1, Joshua. He 4:8; Jesus. **S#3442h**: ver. 7. Ne 3:19. 7:7, 11, 39, 43. 9:4, 5. 10:9. 11:26. 12:1, 7, 8, 10, 24, 26. 1 Ch +24:11. 2 Ch 31:15. Ezr 2:2, 6, 36, 50. 3:2, 8, 9. 4:3. 8:33. 10:18. Also Ezr 5:2.

for since. 2 K 23:22, 23. 2 Ch 30:23. 35:18.

had not. Le +23:34.

done so. 2 Ch 30:26. 35:18.

there was. 1 Ch 29:22. 2 Ch 7:10. 30:21-23.

18 **day by day**. Dt 31:10-13.

a solemn assembly. Heb. a restraint. Le +23:36.

NEHEMIAH 9

1 **twenty**. Le 23:34, 39. 2 Ch 7:10.

of this month. Ne 8:2.

fasting. Mt +6:16.

sackclothes. Jb +16:15.

earth. Jsh +7:6.

2 **the seed**. Ne 13:3, 30. Ezr 9:2. 10:11. 2 C 6:17.

strangers. Heb. strange children. Ne 13:30. Ex +12:43. 2 Ch 33:15. Ps 144:7, 11. Is 2:6. Ho 5:7.

confessed. Ne 1:6. Le 26:39, 40. Ezr 9:6, 7, 15. Ps 106:6, 7. Da 9:3-10, 20. 1 J 1:7-9.

3 **they stood**. Ne 8:4, 7, 8.

one fourth. Ne 8:3.

4 **stood**. Lk +18:13.

stairs. *or*, scaffold. Ne 3:15. Ex 20:26.

Jeshua. ver. 5. Ne +8:17.

Kadmiel. Ezr +2:40.

Shebaniah. 1 Ch +15:24.

Bunni. i.e. *built*, **S#1138h**. Ne 10:15. 11:15.

Sherebiah. Ezr +8:18.

Bani. Ezr +2:10.

Chenani. i.e. *perpetuator; perfector, protector*, **S#3662h**.

cried. 2 Ch 20:19. Ps 3:4. 77:1. 130:1. La 3:8. Jn 11:43. Ac 7:60.

5 **Hashabniah**. Ne +3:10.

Hodijah. Ne +8:7.
Pethahiah. Ne +11:24. Ezr 10:23.
Stand up. 1 K 8:14, 22. 1 Ch +17:16. 2 Ch
20:13, 19. Ps ch. 134. 135:1-3. Lk +18:13.
bless. 1 Ch 29:20. Ezr 3:11. Ps 103:1, 2. ch.
117. 145:2. 146:2. Je 33:10, 11. Mt 11:25. Ep
3:20, 21. 1 P 1:3.
for ever and. Heb. *olam* doubled, Da +2:20.
thy glorious. Ex 15:6, 11. Dt 28:58. 1 Ch
29:13. Ps 72:18, 19, 145:5, 11, 12. 2 C 4:6.
exalted. 2 S 7:26. 1 K 8:27. Ps 16:2. 106:2. Is
+12:4.
6 **even thou**. Dt 6:4. 2 K 19:15, 19. Ps 86:10. Is
37:16, 20. 43:10. 44:6, 8. Mk 12:29, 30. Jn
10:30.
Lord alone. Ps 24:7, 10. 97:9. 102:24-27. Pr
16:4. Ec 12:14. Is 6:1-3. +40:3, 10, 11, 28.
44:6. Je 23:5, 6. Ho 1:7. Zc 13:7. Ml 3:1. Jn
8:24. 1 C 12:3. Col 1:17. He 1:3.
thou hast. Ge 1:1. 2:1. Ex 20:11. Ps 33:6.
136:5-9. 146:6. Je 10:11, 12. Col +1:15, 16.
Re 4:11. 14:7.
the heaven. Dt +10:14.
preservest. Ps +36:6. Col 1:17. He 1:3.
the host. Ps +103:21. Is 6:2, 3. He 1:6. Re
5:11-13.
worshippeth. He 1:6. Re +5:12.
7 **choose**. Ge 12:1, 2. Dt 10:15. Jsh 24:2, 3. Is
41:8, 9. 51:2. Ac 13:17.
Ur. Ge 11:31. 15:7. Ac 7:2-4.
gavest. Ge 17:5.
8 **foundest**. Ge 12:1-3. 15:6, 18. 22:12. Ac
13:22. 1 T 1:12, 13. He 11:8, 17. Ja 2:21-23.
madest. Ge +13:15. 22:16-18. Dt 7:8, 9. Lk
1:72, 73.
the Canaanites. Ge +10:18.
Hittites. Dt +20:17.
Amorites. Ge +10:16.
Perizzites. Ge +13:7.
Jebusites. Ge +10:16.
hast performed. Dt 26:3. Jsh 11:23. 21:43-
45. 23:14. Ps 105:43, 44.
righteous. Nu 23:19. Ps 92:14, 15. T 1:2. He
6:18. 1 J 1:9.
9 **didst see**. Ex 2:25. 3:7, 8, 9, 16. Ac 7:34.
heardest. Ex 14:10-12.
10 **showedst**. Ex ch. 7-10. 12:29, 30. 14:15-31.
Dt 4:34. 11:3, 4. Ps 78:12, 13, 43-53. 105:27-
37. 106:7-11. 135:8, 9. 136:10-15. Ac 7:36.
they. Ex 5:2, 7, 8. 9:17. 10:3. 18:11. Jb 40:11,
12. Da 4:37. 5:23. 1 P 5:5.
didst. Ex 9:16. Jsh 2:10, 11. Ps 83:18. Is
63:12, 14. Je 32:20. Ezk 20:9. Da 9:15. Ro
9:17.
11 **divide**. Ex +14:21.
their persecutors. Ex 15:1-21. Ps 106:9-11.
He 11:29.
as a stone. Ex 15:5, 10. Re 18:21.
12 **thou leddest**. ver. 19. Ex +13:21.
in the way. Ps 107:7. 143:8.

13 **camest**. Ex 19:11, 16-20. Dt 33:2. Is 64:1, 3.
Hab 3:3.
spakest. Ex +33:9.
gavest. Dt 4:8. 10:12, 13. Ps 19:7-11.
119:127, 128. Ezk 20:11-13. Ro 7:12-14, 16.
true laws. Heb. laws of truth. Ps 119:160.
14 **madest**. Ex +20:8-11.
commandest. Ex ch. 21-23. Le 27:34. Dt
4:5, 45. 5:31.
Moses. Ne 1:8. Jn 1:17.
15 **gavest**. Ex 16:4, 14, 15. Dt 8:3, 16. Ps 78:24,
25. 105:40. Jn 6:31-35. 1 C 10:3.
broughtest. ver. 20. Ex 17:6. Nu 20:7-11. Dt
8:15. Ps 78:15-20. 105:41. 114:8. 1 C 10:4.
go. Dt 1:8. Jsh 1:2-4.
sworn. Heb. lift up thine hand. Ge 14:22. Nu
14:30mg. Ezk 20:15.
16 **dealt**. ver. 10, 29. Ex 32:9. Dt 9:6, 13, 23, 24,
27. 32:15. Ps 78:8, etc. 106:6. Is 63:10. Je
2:31. Ac 7:51.
hardened. 2 Ch +30:8. Ps 95:8-10. Pr 29:1.
Ro 2:5. He 3:13, 15.
hearkened not. Ex 15:26. Dt 5:29. Je +7:26.
17 **refused**. Nu 14:3, 4, 11, 41. 16:14. Ps 106:24,
25. Pr 1:24. He 12:25.
mindful. Ps 78:11, 42, 43. 86:5, 15. 106:7,
13. Mt 16:9-11. 2 P 1:12-15.
appointed. Nu 14:4. Ac 7:39.
a God. Ex +34:6.
ready to pardon. Heb. of pardons. Ps 130:4.
Da 9:9.
gracious. Ex +34:6, 7. Ps 78:38. Ro 9:15. Ep
1:6, 7.
forsookest. 1 K 6:13. 8:57. Ps 106:43-46.
18 **when they made**. Ex +32:4. Ezk 20:7, etc.
19 **in thy**. ver. 27. 1 S 12:22. Ps 78:38. 99:8.
106:7, 8, 45. Is 44:21. La 3:22. Ezk 20:14, 22.
Da 9:9, 18. Ml 3:6.
the pillar. ver. +12. Ex +13:21.
20 **gavest**. ver. 30. Nu 11:17, 25-29.
Is 63:11-14.
good. Ps 143:10. Ro 15:30. Ga 5:22, 23. Ep
5:9. 2 P 1:21.
spirit. Is +48:16. 63:10. Hg 2:4, 5.
withheldest. Ex 16:15, 35. Jsh 5:12.
gavest. Ex 17:6. Ps 105:41. Is 41:17, 18.
48:21. 49:10. Jn 4:10, 14. 7:37-39. 1 C 10:4.
21 **forty**. Ex 16:35. Nu 14:33, 34. Dt 2:7. 8:2.
Am 5:25. Ac 13:18.
clothes waxed not old. Dt 8:4. 29:5.
lacked nothing. 1 K 4:27. Lk 22:35.
their. Dt 8:4. 29:5. Ps 34:10.
22 **thou**. Jsh 10:11. Ps 78:65. 105:44.
divide. Dt 32:26. Jsh 11:23.
Sihon. Nu +21:21-35.
Bashan. Dt +32:14.
23 **multipliedst**. Ge 22:17. 1 Ch 27:23.
as the stars. Ge +15:5.
broughtest. Jsh ch. 1, 3, etc.
which thou. Ge +13:15.

24 **So the**. Nu 14:31. Jsh 21:43, 45. 23:4. 24:11, 12.
thou subduest. Jsh 18:1. 1 Ch 22:18. Ps 44:2, 3.
as they would. Heb. according to their will. 2 T 2:26.

25 **strong**. Nu 13:27, 28. Dt 3:5. 6:10-12. 9:1-3.
a fat land. ver. 35. Dt 6:11. 8:7-10. 32:13. Jsh 24:13. Ps 105:44. Ezk 20:6.
wells. or, cisterns. Heb. bor, Ge +37:20.
fruit trees. Heb. trees of food.
did eat. Ezk 16:49.
and became fat. Dt +31:20.
delighted. 1 K 8:66. Je 31:14. Ho 3:5. Ro 2:4.

26 **they were**. Jg 2:11, 12. 3:6, 7. 10:6, 13, 14. Ps 78:56, 57. 106:34-40. Ezk 16:15, etc. 20:21. 23:4, etc.
cast thy law. 1 K 14:9. Ps 50:17. Ezk 33:3-5.
slew. 1 K 18:4, 13. 19:10. 2 Ch 24:20, 21. 36:16. Je 26:20-23. Mt 21:35. 23:34-37. Ac 7:52. 1 Th 2:15.
testified. Je +42:19.
wrought. ver. 18. 2 K 21:11. Ezk 22:25-31.

27 **thou deliveredst**. Dt 31:16-18. Jg 2:14, 15. 3:8, etc. 2 Ch 36:17. Ps 106:41, 42. Da 9:10-14.
in the time. Dt 4:29-31. Ps +3:4. 106:43-45.
manifold. Am 5:12.
saviors. Jg 2:16, 18. 3:9, 15, 31. 1 S 12:10, 11. 2 K 13:5. 14:25, 27. Is 19:20. Ob 21. Lk 2:11.

28 **did evil again**. Heb. returned to do evil. Jg 3:11, 12, 30. 4:1. 5:31. 6:1. Ps 78:34, 36.
heardest. 1 K 8:33, 34, 39. Is 63:15.
many times. Ps 106:43-45.

29 **testifiedst**. ver. 26. Dt 4:26. Je +42:19. Ho 6:5.
yet they. ver. 10, 16. Ex 10:3. Je 13:15-17. 43:2. 44:10, 16, 17. Da 5:20. Ja 4:6-10.
which. Le +18:5.
withdrew the shoulder. Heb. gave a withdrawing shoulder. Zc 7:11, 12.
and hardened. Je +7:26.

30 **many years**. Ps 86:15. Ro 2:4. 2 P 3:9.
forbear them. Heb. protract over them.
testifiedst. ver. 26.
by thy spirit. ver. 20. Is +48:16. 63:10. Ac 7:51. 28:25. 1 P 1:11. 2 P 1:21.
thy prophets. Heb. the hand of thy prophets. Ezr +9:11. 2 Ch 32:15mg. Ho 6:5.
therefore. Is 5:5, 6. 42:24. Je 40:2, 3. 44:22. La 2:17. Zc 7:13.

31 **for thy great**. Je 5:10, 18. Da 9:9.
didst not. Le +26:44. Is 1:9. 57:16. Je 5:18.
gracious. ver. +17.

32 **our God**. Ps +99:3.
keepest. Dt +7:9.
and mercy. Ex 34:7.
trouble. Heb. weariness. or, travail. Ex 18:8. Nu 20:14. La 3:5.

little before thee. Le 26:18, 21, 24, 28. Ezr 9:13.
come upon us. Heb. found us. 2 K +9:21mg.
on our kings. 2 K 23:29, 33, 34. 25:7, 18-21, 25, 26. 2 Ch ch. 36. Je 8:1-3. 22:18, 19. 34:19-22. ch. 39, 52. Da 9:6, 8.
since the time. 2 K 15:19, 29. 17:3. Is 7:17, 18. 8:7, 8. 10:5-7. ch. 36, 37.
unto this day. 1 Ch +4:43.

33 **Howbeit**. Ge 18:25. Jb 34:23. Ps 119:137. 145:17. Je 12:1. La 1:18. Da 9:5-14.
just. Ps 145:17. Da 9:7.
but we. Le 26:40, 41. Jb 33:27. Ps 106:6. Da 9:5-10.

34 **Neither**. Da 9:7.
nor hearkened. Je 29:19.
thy testimonies. ver. 30. 2 K 17:15.
thou didst. Je +42:19.

35 **For they**. Dt 28:47. Je 5:19. Ro 3:4, 5.
thy great. ver. 25.
fat land. Dt 8:7-10. 31:21. 32:12-15.

36 **we are**. Dt 28:48. 2 Ch 12:8. Ezr 9:9.

37 **it yieldeth**. Dt 28:33, 39, 51. Ezr 4:13. 6:8. 7:24.
dominion. Ne 5:8. Le 26:17. Dt 28:48. Jn 8:33.
distress. Ge 32:7, 9-11. 35:2, 3. 1 S 30:6. 2 S 22:7. 2 Ch 20:12, 13. Ps 4:1. 18:6. 25:17. 107:6, 13, 19. 118:5. 120:1. La 1:20. 3:52-58. 5:1-6. Jon 2:2. 2 C 4:8.

38 **we make**. Ne 10:29. 2 K 23:3. 2 Ch 15:12, 13. 23:16. 29:10. 34:31. Ezr 10:3.
seal unto it. Heb. are at the sealing, or sealed. Ne 10:1. Jn 3:33.

NEHEMIAH 10

1 **those that sealed**. Heb. at the sealings. Ne 9:38.
Nehemiah. Ne +1:1. 8:9.
Tirshatha. or, governor. Ezr +2:63.
son of Hachaliah. Ne 1:1.
Zidkijah. i.e. righteousness of Jehovah; justice of the Lord, **S#6667h**. 1 K +22:11, Zedekiah.

2 **Seraiah**. 2 S +8:17.
Azariah. 1 Ch +6:36.

3 **Pashur**. Je +20:1.
Amariah. Ne 12:2, 13.
Malchijah. 1 Ch +9:12.

4 **Hattush**. Ne 3:10. Ezr +8:2.
Shebaniah. Ne 12:14.
Malluch. i.e. reigning; counsellor; kingly, **S#4409h**. ver. 27. Ne 12:2. 1 Ch 6:44. Ezr 10:29, 32.

5 **Harim**. 1 Ch +24:8.
Meremoth. Ne 3:4, 21. 12:3.

6 **Ginnethon**. i.e. gardener, **S#1599h**. Ne 12:4, Ginnetho, 16.
Baruch. Ne 3:20.

7 **Meshullam**. 1 Ch +9:12.

Abijah. Ne 12:4.
Mijamin. 1 Ch +24:9.
8 **Bilgai**. i.e. *consolation of the Lord*, **S#1084h**. Ne 12:5, Bilgah.
Shemaiah. 1 Ch +9:16.
9 **Jeshua**. Ne +8:17.
Azaniah. i.e. *heard of Jah*, **S#245h**.
Henadad. Ezr +3:9.
10 **Shebaniah**. 1 Ch +15:24.
Hodijah. Ne 8:7.
Kelita. Ezr 10:23.
11 **Hashabiah**. 1 Ch +9:14.
12 **Sherebiah**. Ne 8:7. 9:4. 12:8. Ezr +8:18.
13 **Beninu**. i.e. *our son; our edification*, **S#1148h**.
14 **Parosh**. Ezr +2:3.
Zatthu. i.e. *an ornament; sprout*, **S#2240h**. Ne 7:13, Zattu. Ezr +2:8, etc.
Bani. Ne 7:15, Binnui. Ezr +2:10.
15 **Azgad**. Ne 7:16, 17. Ezr 2:11, 12. 8:11, 12. 10:28.
16 **Bigvai**. Ne 7:19-21. Ezr 2:14-16. 8:14.
17 **Ater**. Ezr +2:16.
Hizkijah. i.e. *the strength of God*, **S#2396h**. 2 K +16:20, Hezekiah.
Azzur. i.e. *helped; helpful*, **S#5809h**. Je +28:1, Azur. Ezk 11:1.
18 **Hashum**. Ezr +2:19.
19 **Hariph**. Ne +7:24.
Anathoth. 1 Ch +7:8.
Nebai. i.e. *fruit of the Lord*, **S#5109h**.
20 **Magpiash**. i.e. *killer of moths; collector*, **S#4047h**.
21 **Meshezabeel**. Ne +3:4.
22 **Pelatiah**. 1 Ch +3:21.
23 **Hoshea**. 2 K +15:30.
Hananiah. 1 Ch +25:23.
24 **Hallohesh**. i.e. *the whisperer; enchanter; the charmer*, **S#3873h**. Ne 3:12.
Pileha. i.e. *cleavage; a slice; servitude*, **S#6401h**.
Shobek. i.e. *forsaking*, **S#7733h**.
25 **Rehum**. Ne +12:3.
Hashabnah. i.e. *inventiveness*, **S#2812h**.
26 **Ahijah**. 1 K +14:6.
Hanan. 1 Ch +9:44.
Anan. i.e. *a cloud; covering*, **S#6052h**.
28 **the rest**. Ne 7:72, 73. Ezr 2:36-43, 70.
all they. Ne 9:2. 13:3. Le 20:24. Ezr 9:1, 2. 10:11-19. 2 C 6:14-17.
unto the law. Ro 1:1.
every one. Ne 8:2. Ps 47:7. Ec 5:2. Je 4:2.
29 **clave**. Is 14:1. Ac 11:23. 17:34. Ro 12:9.
entered into. Ne 5:12, 13. 13:25. Dt 27:15, etc. 29:10-14. 2 Ch 15:13, 14. 34:31, 32. Ps 119:106. Ac 23:12-15, 21.
curse. or, *execration*. **S#423h**. Ge 24:41. Dt 29:12, 14, 19, 20, 21. 30:7. 2 Ch 34:24. Jb 31:30. Pr 29:24. Is 24:6. Je 23:10. 29:18. Da 9:11. Zc 5:3.
oath. **S#7621h**. Ge 24:8. 26:3. Ex 22:11. Nu 5:21. 30:2, 10, 13. Jsh 2:17, 20. 2 Ch 15:15. Zc 8:17.

to walk. 2 K 10:31. 23:3. 2 Ch 6:16. 34:31. Je 26:4. Col 1:10. 1 Th 4:1, 2.
given. Dt 33:4. Ml 4:4. Jn 1:17. 7:19.
by. Heb. by the hand of. Ne 8:14mg. 1 K +16:12mg.
to observe and do. Dt 5:1, 32. 26:16, 18. Ezr +7:10. Ps 105:45. Ezk 36:27. Jn 13:17. 15:14. T 2:11-14.
the Lord. Ps 8:1, 9.
30 **not give**. Jg +3:6. Ezr 10:10-12.
31 **the people**. Ne 13:15-22. Ex 20:10. Le 23:3. Dt 5:12-14. Is 58:13, 14. Je 17:21, 22.
on the holy day. Ex 12:16. Le 16:29. 23:21, 35, 36. Col 2:16.
and that we. Ex 23:10, 11. Le 25:4-7. 2 Ch 36:21.
the exaction. Ne 5:1-13. Dt 15:1-3, 7-9. Mt +6:12. 18:27-35. Ja 2:13.
debt. Heb. band. Is 58:6. or, hand. Dt 15:2mg.
32 **to charge**. Ge 28:22. Pr 3:9. Mt 5:17. 17:24-27.
the third part. Ex 30:11-16. Mt 17:24-27. 2 C 8:12.
33 **the showbread**. Ex +25:30.
meat offering. Le +23:13.
the continual burnt offering. Ex +29:42. He 10:11.
sabbaths. Ex 31:13. Le 19:3.
new moons. Col +2:16.
set feasts. Ge +17:21. Le 23:2.
holy things. Le 5:15. 22:14.
sin offerings. Le +23:19.
all the work. 2 Ch 24:5-14.
34 **cast**. Jsh +14:2.
the wood offering. Ne 13:31. Le 6:12. Jsh 9:27. Is 40:16.
at times. He 10:3-7.
altar. Le +17:6.
as it is written. Le 6:12, 13.
35 **the firstfruits**. Le 19:23-26. +23:10. Ml 3:8-12.
36 **the firstborn**. Ex 13:2, 12-15. 34:19. Le 27:26, 27. Nu 18:15, 16. Dt 12:6.
unto. Nu 18:9-19. 1 C 9:6-14. Ga 6:6.
37 **should bring**. Ml 3:8-10. 1 C 9:13.
the firstfruits. Le +23:10.
offerings. or, *heave-offerings*. Le +7:14. 2 S 1:21.
to the chambers. Ne 13:5, 9. 1 K 6:5-10. 2 Ch 31:11, 12.
and the tithes. Le 27:30-33. Nu 18:21, 24-32. 2 Ch 31:6, 11, 12. Ml 3:8, 10.
38 **when the Levites**. Nu 18:26-28.
the tithe. Ge 14:20. Le 27:30. Nu 18:26.
the chambers. 1 S 9:22. 2 K 23:11.
the treasure house. Ne 13:12, 13. 1 Ch 9:26. 2 Ch 31:11, 12. Da 1:2. 1 C 16:1, 2. 2 C 9:7. Ph 4:17, 18.
39 **For the children**. Dt 12:6-11, 17. 14:23-27. 2 Ch 31:12.

the children. Nu 18:30.
we will not. Ne 13:10, 11. Ps 122:9. He 10:25.

NEHEMIAH 11

1 **the rulers**. Ne 7:4, 5. Dt 17:8, 9. Ps 122:5.
cast lots. Jsh +14:2.
one of ten. Jg 20:9, 10.
the holy. ver. 18. Is 48:2. 52:1. Mt 4:5. 27:53.
parts. 2 K 11:7mg.

2 **blessed**. Dt 24:13. Jb 29:13. 31:20.
willingly. Jg 5:9. 2 C 8:5, 16, 17.

3 **Now**. 1 Ch 9:18.
the chief. Ne 7:6. Ezr 2:1.
Israel. Ne 7:73. 1 Ch 9:1-3. Ezr 2:70.
Nethinims. 1 Ch +9:2.
the children. Ne 7:57-60. Ezr 2:55-58.

4 **dwelt**. 1 Ch 9:3, 4, etc.
Athaiah. i.e. *Jah's due season*, S#6265h.
Perez. Ge +48:12.

5 **Col-hozeh**. Ne 3:15.
Hazaiah. i.e. *seen of the Lord*, S#2382h.
Adaiah. i.e. *witness of Jehovah*, S#5718h. ver. 12. 2 K 22:1. 1 Ch 6:41. 8:21. 9:12. Ezr 10:29, 39. Also 2 Ch 23:1.
Shiloni. i.e. *descendants of Shelah*, S#8023h. Ge +38:5, Shelah.

7 **the sons**. 1 Ch 9:7-9.
Joed. i.e. *Jehovah is witness*, S#3133h.
Kolaiah. i.e. *the voice of Jehovah*, S#6964h. Je 29:21.

8 **Gabbai**. i.e. *exactor of tribute; collective*, S#1373h.
Sallai. Ne +12:20.

9 **Judah**. 1 Ch 9:7, Hodaviah, Hasenuah.
Senuah. i.e. *the hatred; pointed; light*, S#5574h. 1 Ch 9:7.
second. 2 K 22:14mg. 2 Ch 34:22mg. Zp 1:10.

10 **Jedaiah**. Ne 7:39. 12:19. 1 Ch 9:10, and Jehoiarib. Ezr 2:36. 8:16.
Joiarib. Ne 12:6.

11 **Seraiah**. 1 Ch 6:7-14. 9:11, Azariah. Ezr 7:1-5.
the ruler. Nu 3:32. 1 Ch 9:1. 2 Ch 19:11. 31:13. Ac 5:24.

12 **Adaiah**. ver. +5. 1 Ch 9:12, 13.
Pelaliah. i.e. *intervention of Jah*, S#6421h.
Amzi. i.e. *strength of God*, S#557h. 1 Ch 6:46.

13 **Amashai**. i.e. *burdensome*, S#6023h.
Ahasai. i.e. *possessor of God*, S#273h.

14 **mighty men**. Jg +6:12.
Zabdiel. i.e. *gift of God*, S#2068h. 1 Ch 27:2.
of one of the great men. *or*, of Haggedolim.

15 **Shemaiah**. 1 Ch +9:16.

16 **Shabbethai**. Ne 8:7.
had the oversight of. Heb. *were* over. 1 Ch 9:28, 29. 26:20. 2 Ch 34:12, 13. 1 Th 5:12, 13.

2 T 2:20, 21. He 13:17.
outward. Ac 6:2, 3.

17 **Zabdi**. Ne 10:12, Zaccur. 1 Ch 9:15, Zichri.
to begin. Ne 12:8, 31. 1 Ch 16:4, 41. 25:1-6.
thanksgiving in prayer. Ph 4:6. 1 Th 5:17, 18.
Bakbukiah. i.e. *emptied of the Lord; Jah's bottle*, S#1229h. Ne 12:9, 25.
Abda. i.e. *service*, S#5653h. 1 K 4:6.

18 **the holy**. ver. 1. 1 K 11:13. Da 9:24. Mt 24:15. 27:53. Re 11:2. 21:2.

19 **Akkub**. 1 Ch +3:24.
that kept. Ps 84:10.
the gates. Heb. at the gates. 1 Ch 16:42mg.

21 **the Nethinims**. ver. +3.
Ophel. *or*, the tower. 2 K +5:24mg.
Gispa. i.e. *soothing; caress; touching gently; the clod breathed*, S#1658h.

22 **overseer**. ver. 9, 14. Ne 12:42. Ac 20:28.
Uzzi. Ne 12:42.
Bani. Ezr +2:10.
Hashabiah. 1 Ch +9:14.
Mattaniah. ver. 17. 2 K +24:17.
Of the sons. ver. 17. Ne +12:46.
were over. ver. 11, 16. 1 Ch 9:16-32.
business. Nu 3:7. 2 Ch 13:10. Ro 12:11. Col 3:24.

23 **the king's commandment**. 1 Ch 9:33. 16:4, 37. 25:6. 28:21. Ezr 6:8, 9. 7:20-24.
a certain portion. *or*, a sure ordinance. Ne 9:38. 1 K 8:59. Je 52:34. Da 1:5.
for every day. Ex +5:13mg, 19. Lk 11:3. 2 C 4:16.

24 **Pethahiah**. i.e. *Jehovah sets free*, S#6611h. Ne 9:5. 1 Ch 24:16. Ezr 10:23.
Meshezabeel. Ne 10:21.
Zerah. Ge +36:13. Mt 1:3, Zara.
at the king's. 1 Ch 18:17mg. 23:28mg.

25 **Kirjath-arba**. Jsh +15:54.
Dibon. Jsh 15:22, Dimonah.
Jekabzeel. i.e. *gathered of God*, S#3343h. Jsh 15:21, Kabzeel.
villages thereof. lit. daughters. Nu +21:25mg.

26 **Moladah**. Jsh 15:26. 19:2.
Beth-phelet. i.e. *house of escape; place of escape*, S#1046h. Jsh 15:27, Beth-palet.

27 **Hazar-shua**. Jsh 15:28. 19:3.
Beer-sheba. Ge +21:31.

28 **Ziklag**. Jsh +15:31.
Mekonah. i.e. *provision; foundation; a settlement*, S#4368h.

29 **En-rimmon**. i.e. *fountain of the pomegranate*, S#5884h. Jsh +15:32, Rimmon.
Zareah. i.e. *a hornet; leprosy*, S#6881h. Jsh +19:41, Zorah.
Jarmuth. Jsh +21:29.

30 **Zanoah**. Jsh +15:34.
Adullam. Jsh 12:15.

Lachish. Jsh +10:3.
Azekah. Jsh 15:35.
the valley of Hinnom. Ne 2:13. Jsh +15:8.

31 **from Geba**. or, of Geba. 1 S +13:3.
at Michmash. or, to Michmash. Ne 7:31, Michmas. 1 S 13:11, 23. Is 10:28.
Aija. i.e. *heap of ruins*, S#5857h. Ne 7:32, Ai. Ge +12:8, Hai. Jsh +7:2, Ai. 8:9. Is +10:28, Aiath.
Beth-el. Ge +12:8.

32 **Anathoth**. 1 Ch +7:8.
Nob. 1 S 21:1. 22:19. Is 10:32.

33 **Ramah**. Je +31:15.
Gittaim. 2 S 4:3.

34 **Zeboim**. 1 S 13:18.
Neballot. i.e. *secret folly*, S#5041h.

35 **Lod**. Ne +7:37.
the valley. 1 Ch 4:14.

36 **And of**. Jsh ch. 21. 1 Ch 6:54-81.
divisions. Ge 49:7.

NEHEMIAH 12

1 **the priests**. Ne 7:7. Ezr 2:1, 2.
Zerubbabel. Hg +1:1.
Jeshua. ver. 10. Zc 3:1-9. 6:11, Joshua.
Seraiah. ver. 12-21. Ne 10:2-8. Ezr 2:2.

2 **Amariah**. Ezr +7:3.
Malluch. ver. +14, Melicu. Ne +10:4.

3 **Shechaniah**. ver. 14, Shebaniah. 1 Ch +3:22.
Rehum. i.e. *merciful*. ver. 15, Harim. S#7348h: Ne 3:17. 10:25. Ezr 2:2. 4:8, 9, 17, 23.
Meremoth. ver. 15, Meraioth.

4 **Iddo**. Ezr +5:1.
Ginnetho. i.e. *gardener; his protection*, S#1599h. ver. 16, Ginnethon.
Abijah. Lk 1:5, Abia.

5 **Miamin**. i.e. *on the right hand*, S#4326h. ver. 17, 41, Miniamin. 1 Ch +24:9, Mijamin. Ezr 10:25. ver. 14, Melicu.
Maadiah. i.e. *pleasantness*, S#4573h. ver. 17, Moadiah.
Bilgah. i.e. *cheerfulness*, S#1083h. ver. 18. 1 Ch 24:14. Ne +10:8, Bilgai.

6 **Shemaiah**. 1 Ch +9:16.
Joiarib. Ne 11:10. 1 Ch 9:10, Jehoiarib. Ezr +8:16.

7 **Sallu**. 1 Ch +9:7. ver. 20, Sallai.
Amok. i.e. *unsearchable*, S#5987h. ver. 20.
the chief. 1 Ch 24:18.
of Jeshua. ver. 1. Ezr 3:2. Hg 1:1. Zc 3:1.

8 **Jeshua**. Ne +8:17.
Mattaniah. 2 K +24:17.
the thanksgiving. *that is*, The psalms of thanksgiving. or, confession. ver. 24. 1 Ch 9:33.

9 **over against**. Ps 134:1-3.
watches. or, charges. 1 Ch 23:6. 26:12.

10 **Jeshua**. ver. 26. 1 Ch 6:3-15. The high-priest.

Joiakim. i.e. *Jehovah will establish,* S#3113h. ver. 12, 26.
Joiada. i.e. *whom Jehovah cares for,* S#3111h. ver. 11, 22. Ne 3:6, Jehoiada. 13:28.
Eliashib. 1 Ch +3:24.

11 **Jonathan**. 1 S +13:2.
Jaddua. i.e. *celebrated,* S#3037h. ver. 22. Ne 10:21.

12 **the chief**. ver. 22. 1 Ch 9:33, 34. 15:12. 24:6-31.
Seraiah. ver. 1. 2 S +8:17.
Meraiah. i.e. *rebellion against Jah; lifted up of the Lord,* S#4811h.

14 **Melicu**. i.e. *my reign* or *counsel; my royalty,* S#4409h. ver. 2, Malluch.
Shebaniah. ver. 3, Shechaniah. 1 Ch +15:24.

15 **Harim**. ver. 3, Rehum.
Meraioth. i.e. *rebellious*. ver. 3, Meremoth. S#4812h. Ne 11:11. 1 Ch 6:6, 7, 52. 9:11. Ezr 7:3.
Helkai. i.e. *portion of the Lord,* S#2517h.

16 **Iddo**. ver. 4.
Ginnethon. ver. 4, Ginnetho.

17 **Miniamin**. i.e. *from* or *on the right hand,* S#4509h. ver. 41. 2 Ch 31:15. ver. 5, Miamin.
Moadiah. i.e. *set time of Jah; assembly or festival of Jah,* S#4153h. ver. 5, Maadiah.
Piltai. i.e. *flight; deliverance of the Lord; my escapes,* S#6408h.

18 **Bilgah**. ver. +5.
Shemaiah. ver. +6.

19 **Joiarib**. Ezr +8:16.
Mattenai. i.e. *gift of the Lord,* S#4982h. Ezr 10:33, 37.

20 **Sallai**. i.e. *lifted up* or *basket weaver,* S#5543h. ver. 7, Sallu. Ne 11:8. Also Nu 25:14, Salu. Also 1 Ch +9:7.
Kallai. i.e. *swift messenger of Jehovah,* S#7040h.

22 **Eliashib**. ver. 10, 11.
recorded. ver. 12, 13.

23 **the book**. 1 Ch 9:14, etc.

24 **Hashabiah**. 1 Ch +9:14.
Sherebiah. ver. 8. Ezr +8:18.
over against. ver. 9.
to praise. 2 S 14:25. 2 Ch 5:13.
to give thanks. ver. 8, 27, 31, 38, 40. Ne 11:17. 1 Ch 16:4, 7, 35.
according. 1 Ch ch. 23, 25, 26.
the man of God. ver. 36. Dt +33:1. 1 T +6:11.
ward. ver. 9. 1 Ch 25:8. 26:16. Ezr 3:10, 11.

25 **Mattaniah**. ver. +8, 9.
keeping. 1 Ch 23:32. 26:12. Is 21:8.
thresholds. or, treasuries, or assemblies. 1 Ch 26:15mg, 17.

26 **Joiakim**. ver. 10.
Nehemiah. Ne 8:9. Ezr 7:6, 11.

27 **A.M.** 3559. **B.C.** 445.
the dedication. Nu +7:10.
out. Ne 11:20. 1 Ch 15:4, 12, 13. 25:6. 26:31,

32. 2 Ch 5:13. 29:4-11, 30. Ezr 8:15-20.

gladness. Ne 8:17. Dt 16:11. 2 S 6:12. 2 Ch 29:22. Ps 98:4-6. 100:1, 2. Ph 4:4.

thanksgivings. 1 Ch 13:8. 15:16, 28. 16:5, 42. 23:5. 25:1-6. 2 Ch 5:13. 7:6. Ezr 3:10, 11. Ps 81:1-4. 92:1-3. 149:3. 150:2-5. Re 5:8.

28 **plain**. Ne 6:2.

Netophathi. 2 S +23:28, Netophathite.

29 **the house**. Or, *Beth-Gilgal*. Jsh +4:19.

Geba. 1 S +13:3.

Azmaveth. Ezr 2:24.

30 **themselves**. Ge 35:2. Ex 19:10, 15. Nu 19:2-20. 2 Ch 29:5, 34. Ezr 6:21. Jb 1:5. He 5:1, 3.

purified. He 9:22, 23.

31 **the princes**. 1 Ch 13:1. 28:1. 2 Ch 5:2.

two great. ver. 38, 40.

thanks. Heb. celebrations.

dung gate. Ne 2:13. 3:13, 14.

32 **Hoshaiah**. i.e. *set free of the Lord*, **S#1955h**. Je 42:1. 43:2.

33 **Azariah**. Ne 10:2-7. 1 Ch +6:36.

35 **with trumpets**. Nu 10:2-10. Jsh 6:4. 2 Ch 5:12. 13:12.

Zechariah. Ne 11:17. 1 Ch 6:39-43. 25:2. 26:10, 11.

36 **Azarael**. i.e. *God helped*, **S#5832h**. 1 Ch +12:6, Azareel.

Milalai. i.e. *eloquent; talkative*, **S#4450h**.

Gilalai. i.e. *rolled off of the Lord; my dung; weighty*, **S#1562h**.

Maai. i.e. *compassionate; my bowels; sympathetic*, **S#4597h**.

musical instruments. 1 Ch 16:42. 23:5. 2 Ch 8:14. Am 6:5.

the man of God. ver. 24.

Ezra. Ezr 7:1. 8:1.

37 **the fountain gate**. Ne 2:14. 3:15, etc.

the stairs. Ne 3:15. 2 S 5:7-9.

water gate. Ne 3:26. 8:1, 3, 16.

38 **other**. ver. 31.

thanks. ver. +31.

tower. Ne 3:11.

broad. Ne 3:8.

39 **the gate of Ephraim**. Ne 8:16. 2 K 14:13.

the old gate. Ne 3:6.

the fish gate. Ne 3:3. Zp 1:10.

the tower. Ne 3:1. Je 31:38.

the sheep gate. Ne 3:32. Jn 5:2.

the prison gate. Ne 3:25, 31. Je 20:1, 2. 32:2.

40 **two companies**. ver. 31, 32. Ps 42:4. 47:6-9. ch. 134.

thanks. ver. 31.

rulers. **S#5461h**. Ne 2:16. 4:14, 19. 5:7, 17. 7:5. 13:11. Ezr 9:2. Is 41:25. Je 51:23, 28, 57. Ezk 23:6, 12, 23.

41 **with trumpets**. ver. 35. 2 Ch +5:12.

42 **sang loud**. Heb. made *their voice* to be heard. Ps 81:1. 95:1. 98:4-9. 100:1, 2. Is 12:5, 6.

Jezrahiah. i.e. *God is risen; brought to the light*

of the Lord, **S#3156h**. 1 Ch +7:3, Izrahiah.

overseer. or, inspector. Ne 11:9, 14, 22. Ge 41:34mg.

43 **offered**. Nu 10:10. Dt 12:11, 12. 1 Ch 29:21, 22. 2 Ch 7:5-7, 10. 29:35, 36. Ps 27:6.

God. 2 Ch 20:27. Jb 34:29. Ps 28:7. 30:11, 12. 92:4. Is 61:3. 66:10-14. Je 33:11. Jn 16:22.

the wives also. Ne 8:2. Ex +15:20, 21. Jg +21:21. 1 S 18:6. 2 S 1:20. 1 K 4:23. 1 Ch 15:20. 2 Ch 20:13. Ps 148:11-13. Je 31:13. Mt 21:9, 15. Ep 5:19. Ja 5:13.

the children. Dt +29:11. Ps 148:12. Mt 21:15. 2 T +3:15.

the joy. 1 S 4:5. Ezr 3:13.

44 **some**. Ne 10:37-39. 13:5, 12, 13. 2 Ch 13:11, 12. 31:11-13.

chambers. 1 Ch 9:26. 26:21-26.

treasures. Ne 7:70, 71. 10:38. 13:12mg.

offerings. or, heave offerings. Ne 13:5. Le +7:14.

firstfruits. Le +23:10.

fields of the cities. Jsh 21:12. 1 Ch 6:56.

of the law. *that is*, appointed by the law.

Judah rejoiced. Heb. the joy of Judah.

Levites. Nu 3:10. 8:24, 25. 1 Ch 23:28. 2 Ch 5:11, 12. Pr 8:34. Is 40:31. Ro 12:7.

waited. Heb. stood.

45 **the singers**. 1 Ch ch. 25, 26. 2 Ch +35:15.

porters. 1 Ch +23:5.

ward of the purification. Le 12:4, 5. 13:8, 35. 15:31. 1 Ch 23:28. 2 Ch 23:6. Is 35:8. Ac 16:3. Ga 2:3.

commandment of. 1 Ch 25:1. 26:1. 2 Ch 8:14.

46 **and Asaph**. 2 K +18:18.

of old. Heb. *kedem*, Mi +5:2.

47 **Zerubbabel**. ver. 1, 12, 26.

gave. Ne 10:35-39. 13:10-12. 2 Ch 31:5, 6. Ml 3:8-10. Ga 6:6.

and they. Nu 18:21-29.

every day. Ge 39:10. Ex +5:13mg.

sanctified. *that is*, set apart. Ne 3:1.

NEHEMIAH 13

1 **they read**. Heb. there was read. Ne 8:3-8. 9:3. Dt 3:11, 12. 2 K 23:2. Is 34:16. Lk 4:16-19. 10:26. Ac 13:15. 15:21.

audience. Heb. ears.

the Ammonite. ver. +23. Dt 23:3-5. 1 S +11:11.

Moabite. Ezk +25:8.

for ever. Heb. *olam*, Ex +12:24.

2 **Because**. Dt 23:4. Mt 25:40.

hired Balaam. Nu 22:3-6. +31:8.

our God. Nu 23:8-11, 18. 24:5-10. +31:8. Ps 109:28.

3 **when they**. Ps 19:7-11. 119:9, 11. Pr 6:23. Ro 3:20.

that they separated. Ne 9:2. 10:28. Ge 12:4.

Ex 12:38. Ezr 10:11. Is 51:2. Mt 10:37. Ja 1:27.

the mixed. Ex 12:38. Nu 11:4.

4 **Eliashib**. ver. 7. 1 Ch +3:24.

having the oversight of. Heb. being set over. Ne 12:44.

the chamber. ver. 5, 9. Ne 10:37-39.

allied. ver. 28. Ne 6:17, 18.

5 **a great**. Ne 10:38. 12:44. 2 Ch 34:11.

meat offering. Le +23:13.

which was commanded to be given to the. Heb. the commandment of the. Nu 18:21-24.

6 **But**. Ex 32:1. 2 Ch 24:17, 18. Mt 13:25.

the two. Ne 2:1. 5:14.

after certain days. Heb. at the end of days. Ne 2:5, 6. Ge +4:3mg. +24:55mg. Le 25:29. Jg +11:40mg. 1 K 17:7mg.

obtained I. or, I earnestly requested. 1 S 20:6, 28.

7 **understood**. Ezr 9:1. 1 C 1:11.

Tobiah. Ne 4:3.

in preparing. ver. 1, 5. La 1:10. Mt 21:12, 13. Ac 21:28, 29.

8 **it grieved**. Ezr 9:3, 4. 10:1. Ps 69:9.

I cast. Mk 11:15-17. Jn 2:13-17.

9 **they cleansed**. Ne 12:45. 2 Ch 29:5, 15-19.

meat offering. Le +23:13.

10 **the portions**. Ne 10:37. 12:47. Ml 1:6-14. 3:8. 1 T 5:17, 18.

to his field. Nu 35:2.

11 **contended**. ver. 17, 25. Ne 5:6-13. Jb 31:34. Pr 28:4. Ep 5:11. Ju 3.

Why is the house. Ne 10:39. 1 S 2:17. Ml 3:8-11.

place. Heb. standing. 2 Ch 30:16mg.

12 **brought**. Ne 10:37-39. 12:44. Le 27:30. Nu 18:20-26. Dt 14:22.

treasuries. or, storehouses. Ml 3:10.

13 **I made**. Ne 12:44. 2 Ch 31:12-15.

Shelemiah. Ne 3:30.

Pedaiah. Ne 8:4.

next to them. Heb. at their hand. Ne 3:2mg. 2 Ch +17:15mg.

Zaccur. Ne 10:12.

Mattaniah. 2 K +24:17.

counted faithful. Ne 7:2. 2 K 12:15. 22:7. Lk +12:42. 16:10-12. Ac 6:3. 1 C 4:1, 2. 1 T 1:12. 3:10. 3 J 5.

their office. Heb. it was upon them.

to distribute. 2 Ch 31:14-16. Lk 12:42, 43. Ac 4:35. 6:1.

14 **Remember me**. ver. 22, 31. Ne 5:19. Ps 122:6-9. He 6:10. Re 3:5.

wipe not. ver. 22.

good deeds. Heb. kindnesses. Ge +20:13. 2 Ch 32:32mg.

house. 1 Ch 29:3. 2 Ch 24:16. 31:20, 21. Ezr 7:20, 24, 27. Ps 122:6-9.

offices. or, observations. 2 Ch 7:6. or, charges. Ne 4:9, 22, 23. 7:3.

15 **treading wine**. Ex 20:8-11. 34:21. 35:2. Is 58:13. Ezk 20:13.

burdens. Ne 10:31. Nu 15:32-36. Je 17:21, 22, 24, 27.

I testified. ver. 21. Je +42:19. Re 22:18, 19.

16 **men of Tyre**. Ex 23:12. Dt 5:14. Ezk 27:3.

17 **I contended**. ver. 11, 25. Ne 5:7. Ps 82:1, 2. Pr 28:4. Is 1:10. Je 5:5. 13:18. 22:2, etc. Mi 3:1, 9. Ju 3.

profane the sabbath day. Ezk 20:12. 22:26, 31. 23:38.

18 **Did not your**. Ezr 9:13-15. Je 17:21-23, 27. 44:9, 22. Ezk 23:8, 26. Zc 1:4-6.

ye bring more. Le 26:18, 28. Nu 32:14. Jsh 22:17, 18.

19 **began to be**. Le 23:32.

I commanded. Ne 7:3. Ex 31:14-17. Je 17:19-22.

21 **I testified**. ver. +15.

about the wall. Heb. before the wall.

I will lay. Ezr 7:26. Ro 13:3, 4. 1 P 2:14.

22 **I commanded**. Ne 7:64, 65. 12:30. 2 K 23:4. 1 Ch 15:12-14. 2 Ch 29:4, 5, 24, 27, 30. Is 49:23.

cleanse. Ne 12:10.

sanctify. Dt 5:12.

Remember. ver. 14, 31. Ne 5:19. Ps 132:1-5. Is 38:3. 2 C 1:12. 2 T 4:7, 8.

spare me. Ps 25:6, 7. 51:1. 130:3, 4, 7. 143:1, 2.

greatness. or, multitude. Ps 5:7. Is 55:7.

thy mercy. Ge 19:19, 20. Nu 14:19. Dt 4:31. 1 K 3:6, 7. Ps 25:6. 31:16. 44:26. 51:1. 69:13, 16. 86:4, 5, 14, 15. 106:44, 45. 109:21, 26. Is 63:15. La 3:22, 23. Da 9:18. Jl 2:13.

23 **married**. Heb. made to dwell with them. Jg +3:6. Ezr 10:10, 44.

Ashdod. Ne 4:7. Jsh +11:22. 13:3.

Ammon. ver. 1-3. Ge +19:38.

24 **could not speak**. Heb. they discerned not to speak.

each people. Heb. people and people. Zp 3:9.

25 **I contended**. ver. 11, 17. Pr 28:4. Je 9:3. Ju +3.

cursed. or, reviled. ver. 2. Ne 5:13. +10:29. Dt 27:14-26. Ps 15:4. Lk 11:45, 46. **S#7043h:** Ge 8:21. Dt 23:4. Jsh 24:9. 2 S 16:7.

smote. Dt 25:2, 3. Ezr 7:26.

plucked. Is 50:6.

made them. Ne +10:29, 30. Dt 6:13. 2 Ch 15:12-15. Ezr 10:5.

Ye shall not. Jg +3:6.

26 **Did not Solomon**. 1 K 11:1-8. Ec 7:26.

yet among. 2 S 12:24, 25. 1 K 3:13. 2 Ch 1:12. 9:22.

who was beloved. 2 S 12:24.

27 **Shall we then**. 1 S 30:24.

to transgress. Ezr 10:2.

28 **And one**. Dt 27:4. Jn 4:20.
Joiada. Ne 12:10, 22.
Eliashib. Ne 3:1.
son in law. ver. 4, 5. Ne 6:17-19.
Sanballat. Ne 2:19.
I chased. ver. 25. Ps 101:8. Pr 20:8, 26. Ro
13:3, 4.

29 **Remember**. Ne 6:14. Ps 59:5-13. 2 T 4:14.
because they have defiled. Heb. for the
defilings of. Le 21:1-7.

the covenant. Nu 16:9, 10. 25:12, 13. 1 S
2:30. Ml 2:4-8, 10-12.

30 **cleansed**. Ne 10:30.
strangers. Ne 9:2. Ex 12:43. Ps 18:44, 45.
appointed. Ne 12:1-26. 1 Ch ch. 23-26.

31 **the wood**. Ne 10:34.
at times appointed. Ezr 10:14.
firstfruits. Le +23:10.
Remember. ver. 14, 22. Ps 25:7. 26:8, 9.
106:4. Lk 23:42.

ESTHER

ESTHER 1

1 A.M. 3540. B.C. 464.

Ahasuerus. i.e. *lion king; a prince clothed with majesty; I will be silent and poor*, **S#325h**. ver. 1, 2, 9, 10, 15-17, 19. Est 2:1, 12, 16, 21. 3:1, 6-8, 12. 6:2. 7:5. 8:1, 7, 10, 12. 9:2, 20, 30. 10:1, 3. Ezr 4:6. 6:14. Da 9:1.

from India. i.e. *praise; murmuring or roaring of the sea; flee ye away; give ye thanks*, **S#1912h**. ver. 1. Est 8:9. Is 18:1. 37:9.

an hundred and. Da 6:1.

2 **sat**. 2 S 7:1. 1 K 1:46. Da 4:4.

Shushan. Da +8:2.

3 A.M. 3542. B.C. 462.

he made. Est 2:18. Ge +19:3. Da 5:1. Mk 6:21.

of Persia. ver. 14. Ezr 1:2. Is 21:2. Je 51:11. Da 5:28. 8:20.

Media. i.e. *a garment; extended of the Lord; measured*, **S#4074h**. ver. 3, 14, 18. Est 10:2. Is 21:2. Da 8:20. For other renderings of **S#4074h**, see *Madai*, Ge +10:2; *Medes*, Ezr +6:2.

the nobles. Da 3:2, 3. 6:1, 6, 7.

4 **When he**. Is 39:2. Ezk 28:5. Da 4:30.

the riches. Ps 76:1-4. 145:5, 12, 13. Da 2:37-44. 7:9-14. Mt 4:8. 6:13. Ro 9:23. Ep 1:18. Col 1:27. Re 4:11.

excellent. 1 Ch 29:11, 12, 25. Jb 40:10. Ps 21:5. 45:3. 93:1. Da 4:36. 5:18. 2 P 1:16, 17.

5 **present**. Heb. found. Est 4:16mg. Ge 19:15mg. Jg +20:48mg. 1 S 13:15mg. 21:3mg. 2 K 19:4mg. 2 Ch 5:11mg. +29:29mg. 30:21mg. 31:1mg. 34:32mg, 33mg. 35:17mg. Is 37:4mg. Zc 11:6mg.

seven days. 2 Ch 7:8, 9. 30:21-25.

6 **white**. Ex 26:1, 31, 32, 36, 37.

blue. *or*, violet. Est 8:15. Ex 25:4.

fastened. 1 Ch 24:6 (taken). Ec 9:12 (caught). SS 3:8 (hold).

cords. Jsh 2:15. 2 S 8:2.

fine linen. Est 8:15. 1 Ch +4:21.

purple. Est 8:15. Ex 25:4.

rings. SS 5:14.

pillars. Ex 13:21, 22. 14:19.

marble. SS 5:15.

the beds. Est 7:8. Ge 47:31. 48:2. SS 3:7-10. Is 57:1. Ezk 23:41. Am 2:8. 6:4.

pavement. 2 Ch 7:3. Ezk 40:17, 18. 42:3.

red, etc. *or*, of porphyre, and marble, and alabaster, and stone of blue color.

7 **vessels of gold**. 1 K 10:21. 2 Ch 9:20. Da 5:2-4.

royal wine. Heb. wine of the kingdom.

state of the king. Heb. hand of the king. 2 Ch 9:3, 4.

8 **none did compel**. Je 35:8. 51:7. Hab 2:15, 16.

the officers. Jn 2:8.

9 **the queen**. Est 5:4, 8.

10 **the heart**. Ge 43:34. Jg 16:25. 1 S 25:36, 37. 2 S 13:28. Pr 20:1. Ec 7:2-4. 10:19. Ep 5:18, 19.

Mehuman. i.e. *stedfast; faithful; their discomfiture*, **S#4104h**.

Biztha. i.e. *a eunuch; despite; unfruitful, gelding; booty*, **S#968h**.

Harbona. i.e. *an ass-driver; warlike; martial*, **S#2726h**. Est 7:9, Harbonah.

Bigtha. i.e. *a gardener; given by fortune*, i.e. *the sun; in the wine-press*, **S#903h**.

Abagtha. i.e. *gardener; father of the wine press; fortune, by fortune*, **S#5h**.

Zethar. i.e. *a star; very great; stair; searcher*, **S#2242h**.

Carcas. i.e. *an eagle; covering of a lamb; severe*, **S#3752h**.

chamberlains. *or*, eunuchs. 2 K +8:6mg.

11 **To bring**. Pr 16:9. 23:29-33. Mk 6:21, 22. 1 C 5:11.

Vashti. i.e. *beautiful woman; drinking; doubling; wherefore waste thou away; wherefore banquet thou*, **S#2060h**. ver. 9, 11, 12, 15, 16, 17, 19. Est 2:1, 4, 17.

beauty. Ps 45:11. 50:2. Pr 6:25. Is +33:17.

fair to look on. Heb. good of countenance. Ge +29:17.

12 **refused**. Ge 3:16. 37:35. 39:8. Ps +101:4. +119:63. Pr 1:10. Da 1:8. 11:17. Ep 5:22, 24. He 11:24-26. 1 P 3:1. 4:3, 4.

by his chamberlains. Heb. which *was* by the hand of *his* eunuchs. 1 K +16:12mg.

was the king. Pr 19:12. 20:2. Da 2:12. 3:13, 19. Na 1:6. Re 6:16, 17.

burned. Ex 32:19, 22. Dt 29:20. Ps 74:1. 79:5.

13 **the wise**. Je 10:7. Da 2:2, 12, 27. 4:6, 7. 5:7. Mt 2:1.
   knew. 1 Ch +12:32. Mt 16:3.
14 **Carshena**. i.e. *spoiling of war*, or *black; distinguished; illustrious; change thou the lamb* (or *head, or pasture*), **S#3771h**.
   Shethar. i.e. *a star; appointed searcher; a remnant*, **S#8369h**.
   Admatha. i.e. *human; having a dark complexion; her earthiness; man's chamber*, **S#133h**.
   Tarshish. Ge +10:4.
   Meres. i.e. *lofty, worthy; elevated; moisture; fractured*, **S#4825h**.
   Marsena. i.e. *lofty, worthy; high; bitter is the thorn bush*, **S#4826h**.
   Memucan. i.e. *established, prepared; strong in authority; their poverty*, **S#4462h**. ver. 14, 16, 21.
   the seven. Ezr 7:14.
   saw. Ge +43:3. 2 K 25:19. Mt 18:10. Re 22:4.
   face. Ge +19:13.
15 **What shall we do**. Heb. What to do. Est 6:6.
16 **done wrong**. Ac 18:14. 25:10. 1 C 6:7, 8.
17 **women**. Nu 30:3-13. 1 C +14:34.
   despise. 2 S 6:16. Ep 5:33.
18 **the ladies**. *Saroth*, the *princesses*: but the meaning is well expressed by our term *ladies*. Jg 5:29. 1 K 11:3.
19 **it please the king**. Heb. it be good with the king. ver. 21mg. Est 3:9. 8:5. Dt 23:16mg. Ne 2:5, 7.
   from him. Heb. from before him.
   Persians. i.e. *inhabitants of Persia* (2 Ch +36:22), **S#6539h**.
   it be not altered. Heb. it pass not away. Est 8:8. Da 6:8-15, 17.
   another. Heb. her companion. Ex 11:2. Is 34:15, 16. Je 9:20. Zc 11:9mg.
   that is better. 1 S 15:28. 1 K 3:32.
20 **throughout**. Dt 17:13. 21:21.
   all the wives. Ep 5:33. Col +3:18. 1 P 3:1-7.
21 **pleased the king**. Heb. was good in the eyes of the king. ver. 19mg. Est 2:4. Nu 24:1. Jsh +22:30mg.
22 **into every province**. Est 3:12. 8:9. Da 3:29. 4:1.
   that every man. Ge +18:19. Ep 5:22-24. 1 T 2:12. 3:3-5. T 2:4, 5.
   it should, etc. Heb. one should publish *it* according to the language of his country. Est 3:12.
   according. Lk 16:8. Ac 2:5-11. 1 C 14:19, 20.

ESTHER 2

1 A.M. 3543. B.C. 461.
   he remembered. Da 6:14-18.
   what was decreed. Est 1:12-21.
2 **king's servants**. Est 1:10, 14. 6:14.
   Let there be. Ge 12:14. 1 K 1:2.
   virgins. ver. 3, 17, 19. Ge +24:16.

3 **in all the provinces**. Est 1:1, 2.
   the custody. Heb. the hand. ver. 8, 14.
   Hege. i.e. *eunuch; brier; venerable; meditation*, **S#1896h**. ver. 8, Hegai.
   their things. ver. 12-14. Pr 20:30. Is 3:18-23.
4 **let the maiden**. Mt 20:16. 22:14.
   the thing. Est 1:21. 3:9, 10. 2 S 13:4-6. 16:21-23. 17:4. Mt 14:6.
5 **Shushan**. ver. 3. Da +8:2.
   a certain. Est 3:2-6. 10:3.
   Jew. i.e. *celebrated; praised*, **S#3064h**. Est 3:4. 5:13. 6:10. 8:7. 9:29, 31. 10:3. Je 34:9. Zc 8:23.
   Mordecai. i.e. *a little man; worshipper of Mars; bitterness of my oppressed*, **S#4782h**. ver. 7, 10, 11, 15, 19, 20-22. Est 3:2-6. 4:1, 4-7, 9, 10, 12, 13, 15, 17. 5:9, 13, 14. 6:2-4, 10-13. 7:9, 10. 8:1, 2, 7, 9, 15. 9:3, 4, 20, 23, 29, 31. 10:2, 3. Ezr 2:2. Ne 7:7.
   the son of Shimei. 1 S 9:1. 2 S +16:5.
   Kish. 1 S 9:1, 2.
6 **Jeconiah**. Je +24:1.
7 **brought up**. Heb. nourished. ver. 20. Nu 11:12. 2 K 10:1mg, 5. Ep 6:4.
   Hadassah. i.e. *a myrtle*, **S#1919h**. Da 1:6, 7.
   his uncle's. ver. 15. Je 32:7-12.
   neither father nor mother. Ge +11:28.
   fair and beautiful. Heb. fair of form and good of countenance. Est 1:11mg. Ge +29:17.
   took. Ge 48:5. 2 C 6:18. 1 J 3:1.
8 **were gathered**. ver. 3.
   Hegai. i.e. *grooming; venerable; an eunuch*, **S#1896h**. ver. 15.
   Esther. i.e. *star; happiness; I will be hidden*, **S#635h**. ver. 7, 10, 11, 15-18, 20, 22. Est 4:4, 5, 8-10, 12, 13, 15, 17. 5:1-7, 12. 6:14. 7:1-3, 5-8. 8:1-4, 7. 9:12, 13, 29, 31, 32.
9 **she obtained kindness**. ver. 15, 17. Est 5:2. Ge 39:21. 1 K 8:50. Ezr 7:6. Ne 2:8. Ps 106:46. Pr 16:7. Da 1:9. Ac 7:10.
   gave her her things. ver. 3, 12.
   such things. Heb. her portions. Est 9:19, 22. Ex 29:26.
   preferred her. Heb. changed her. 1 S 21:13. Ps 34:t.
10 **had not showed**. Est 3:8. 4:13, 14. 7:4. Mt 10:16.
   for Mordecai. ver. 7, 20. Ep 6:1.
11 **walked**. ver. 13, 14.
   how Esther did. Heb. the peace of Esther. Jg +18:15mg.
12 A.M. 3546. B.C. 458.
   to go in. 1 Th 4:4, 5.
   six months. Is 57:9. Lk 7:37, 38.
   myrrh. Mt +2:11.
14 **Shaashgaz**. i.e. *servant of the beautiful; who succored the cut off*, **S#8190h**.
   concubines. 1 Ch +2:48.
   delighted. Est 4:11. Ge 34:19. Dt 21:14. Is 62:4, 5.
   she were called. Ex 33:17. Is 43:1. 45:4.

15 **who had taken**. ver. 7.
chamberlain. 2 K +8:6mg.
Esther. SS 6:9. 8:10. Ac 7:10.

16 **the tenth month**. Est 8:9.
Tebeth. i.e. *goodness*, **S#2887h**.
the seventh year. ver. 1, 3. Ezr 7:8.

17 **favor**. *or*, kindness. ver. 9.
in his sight. Heb. before him. ver. 9. Est 1:19.
so that he set. Est 4:14. 1 S 2:8. Ps 45:14, 15.
75:6, 7. 113:7, 8. Ezk 17:24. Lk 1:48-52.

18 A.M. 3547. B.C. 457.
made a great. Est 1:3-5. Ge 29:22. Jg 14:10-
17. SS 3:11. 5:1. Mt 22:2. Lk 14:8. Re 9:19.
release. Heb. rest.
gave gifts. Est 9:22. Ge 43:34. Jg 20:38
(flame), 40. 1 S 25:8. 2 S 11:8h. Ne 8:11. Re
11:10.

19 **the virgins**. ver. 3, 4.
sat in the king's gate. Ge +14:7. ver. 21. Est
3:2, 3. 5:13.

20 **had not yet showed**. ver. 10.
for Esther. Ep 6:1-3.
brought up. ver. 7.

21 **gate**. Ge +14:7.
chamberlains. 2 K +8:6mg.
Bigthan. i.e. *garden; given of fortune*, i.e. *the
sun*, **S#904h**. Est 6:2, Bigthana.
Teresh. i.e. *severe; austere*, **S#8657h**. Est 6:2.
door. Heb. threshold. 2 K +12:9mg.
and sought. 2 S 4:5, 6. 16:11. 1 K 15:25-27.
16:9. 2 K 9:22-24. 12:20. 21:23.
Ps 144:10.
lay hand. 1 S 24:6. Ro 13:1, 2.

22 **the king**. Ec 10:20. Ac 23:12-22.
and Esther certified. Est 6:1, 2. Ro 11:33.
Mordecai's name. Ph 2:4.

23 **hanged**. Est 5:14. 7:10. Ge 40:19, 22. Dt
21:22, 23. Jsh 8:29.
the book. Est 6:1, 2. Ml 3:16.

ESTHER 3

1 A.M. 3551. B.C. 453.
promote. Est 7:6. Ps 12:8. Pr 29:2.
Haman. i.e. *magnificent, Mercury; solitary; the
rager; their tumult*, **S#2001h**. Est 3:1, 2, 4-8, 10-
12, 15. 4:7. 5:4, 5, 8-12, 14. 6:4-7, 10-14. 7:1,
6-10. 8:1-3, 5, 7. 9:10, 12-14, 24.
Hammedatha. i.e. *a twin; measurement; given
by the god Hom*, **S#4099h**. ver. 1, 10. Est 8:5.
9:10, 24.
Agagite. i.e. *of the royal seed of Agag* (i.e. *blazing, sublime*, Nu +24:7), **S#91h**. ver. 1, 10. Est
8:3, 5. 9:24. For **S#90h**, see Nu +24:7, Agag. 1
S 15:8, 33.
above all princes. Est 1:14. Ge 41:40, 55.
Ezr 7:14. Da 6:2.

2 **the king's servants**. Est 2:19, 21.
gate. Ge +14:7.
bowed. Ge 41:43. Ph 2:10.

bowed not. ver. 1, 5. Ex 17:14, 16.
Dt 25:19. 1 S 15:3. Ps 15:4. 139:21, 22. Re
+22:8, 9.

3 **Why**. ver. 2. Ex 1:17. Mt 15:2, 3.

4 **when they spake**. Ge 39:10.
hearkened not. Ac 4:19. 5:29.
that they told. Da 3:8, 9. 6:13.
he had told. Ezr 1:3. Da 3:12, 16-18, 23-30.
6:20-28. Jon 1:9.

5 **that Mordecai**. ver. 2. Est 5:9.
full of wrath. Est 1:12. Ge 4:5, 6. Jb 5:2. Pr
12:16. 19:19. 21:24. 27:3, 4. Da 3:19.

6 **sought**. Ps 10:2. 83:4. Re 12:12.

7 **the first month**. Ne 2:1.
Nisan. Part of February and March. Ex 12:2.
13:4.
in the twelfth. Est 1:3. 2:16.
they cast Pur. i.e. *a part, a portion; lot; frustration*, **S#6332h**. ver. 7. Est 9:24, 26, 28, 29, 31, 32.
lot. Jsh +14:2.
from day to day. To obtain a lucky day.
month to month. Is 47:13.
Adar. i.e. *glorious; power; fire*, **S#143h**. ver. 7, 13.
Est 8:12. 9:1, 15, 17, 19, 21. Twelfth month of
the Jewish sacred year. Part of January and
February. Est 9:1, 5, 17-19, 21. Ezr 6:15.

8 **scattered abroad**. Je +9:16. 50:17. Jn 7:35.
their laws. Ezr 4:12-15. Ac 16:20, 21. 17:6,
7. 24:5. 28:22.
for the king's profit to. Heb. meet, *or* equal
for the king to, etc.

9 **that they may be destroyed**. Heb. to
destroy them. Ps 37:12-15.
and I will pay. Heb. and I will weigh. Est
4:7. Ge 23:16. 1 K 20:39.
ten thousand. Mt 18:24.

10 **took**. Est 8:2, 8. Ge 41:42.
enemy. *or*, oppressor. Est 7:6. 8:1. 9:10, 24.
Ps 6:7.

11 **to do**. Ps 73:7. Je 26:14. 40:4. Lk 23:25.

12 **then were**. Est 8:9, etc.
scribes. *or*, secretaries. 2 S +8:17mg.
according. Est 1:22. 8:9. 9:27.
in the name. 1 K 21:8. Da 6:8, 12, 15.
sealed. Est 8:2, 8, 10.

13 **by posts**. Est 8:10, 14. 2 Ch 30:6. Jb 9:25. Je
51:31. Ro 3:15.
both young. Ge 19:4. Ex 10:9. 1 S 15:3.
22:19.
in one day. Est 8:12-14. Ja 2:13.
the spoil. Est 8:11. 9:10. Is 10:6.

14 **The copy**. Est 8:13, 14.
published. or, revealed. Est 8:13. Nu 24:4, 6.
Je 32:11, 14.

15 **The posts**. ver. 13.
hastened. Est 6:12. 8:14. 2 Ch 26:20. Pr
1:16. 4:16.
sat down. Ge 37:24, 25. Pr 10:23. Ho 7:5.
Am 6:6. Jn 16:20. Re 11:10.
drink. Ex 32:6. 2 S 11:11.

the city. Est 4:16. 8:15. Pr 29:2.
perplexed. Ex 14:3. Pr 29:2. Jl 1:18.

ESTHER 4

1 **all that**. Est 3:8-13.
rent. 2 K +18:37.
sackcloth. Jb +16:15.
with ashes. ver. 3. Jsh +7:6. Jb 2:8. 42:6. Is
58:5. 61:3. Je 6:26. 25:34. Ezk 27:30, 31. Da
9:3. Jon 3:6. Mt 11:21. Lk 10:13.
and cried. Ge 27:34. Is 15:4. 22:4. Ezk 21:6.
27:31. Mi 1:8. Zp 1:14. Re 18:17-19.
3 **in every province**. Est 1:1. 3:12.
great mourning. 1 S 4:13, 14. 11:4. Is 22:4,
12. 37:1-3.
fasting. Mt +6:16.
weeping. Mt 13:42. 22:13. 25:30.
many lay in sackcloth and ashes. Heb.
sackcloth and ashes were laid under many. Is
58:5. Da 9:3.
4 **chamberlains**. Heb. eunuchs. Est 1:12. 1 S
8:15mg. 2 K 9:32. Is 56:3. Ac 8:27.
sent raiment. Is 52:1, 2. Is 61:3.
but he received it not. Ge 37:35. Ps 77:2. Je
31:15.
5 **Hatach**. i.e. *gift; truth; he that strikes*, **S#2047h**.
ver. 5, 6, 9, 10.
appointed to attend upon her. Heb. set
before her. Est 1:10, 12.
to know. Ro 12:15. 1 C 12:26. Ph 2:4. He
4:15.
7 **all that had**. Est 3:2-15.
8 **the copy**. Est 3:14, 15.
to charge. Est 2:20. 1 T 6:13, 17.
to make supplication. Jb 9:15. Pr 16:14, 15.
Ec 10:4. Ac 12:20.
request. Est 7:3, 4. 8:6. Ne 2:3-5. Pr 21:1.
11 **the inner court**. Est 5:1.
one law. Da 2:9.
the king shall. Est 5:2. 8:4.
but I. Est 1:19. 2:14. 1 P 3:7.
13 **Think not**. Pr 24:10-12. Mt 16:24, 25. Jn
12:25. Ph 2:30. He 12:3.
thyself. Heb. *nephesh*, soul, Ex +15:9.
14 **holdest thy peace**. Pr 31:8, 9.
then shall. Ge 22:14. Nu 23:22-24. Dt 32:26,
27, 36. 1 S 12:22. Is 54:17. Je 30:11. 33:24-
26. 46:28. Am 9:8, 9. Mt 16:18. 24:22.
enlargement. Heb. respiration. Ex 8:15. Ezr
9:9. Jb 9:18.
but thou. Est 2:7, 15. Jg 14:15-18. 15:6.
whether. Ge 45:4-8. Is 45:1-5. 49:23. Ac
7:20-25.
for such a time. 1 S 17:29. 2 K 19:3. Ne
6:11.
16 **present**. Heb. found. Est 1:5mg.
fast. Mt +6:16.
eat nor drink. Ac 9:9. 27:33.
three days. Est 5:1. Jsh 5:11. 1 S 30:12. Mt

+12:40. Young notes, one whole day and part
of two others.
I also. Ge 18:19. Jsh 24:15. Ac 10:7.
if I perish. Ge 43:14. 1 S 19:5. 2 S 10:12. 2 K
7:4. Da 3:17, 18. Lk 9:24. Ac 20:24. 21:13. Ro
16:4. Ph 2:30.
17 **went**. Heb. passed. Ex 17:5. 32:27. 38:26. 1 K
22:24.

ESTHER 5

1 **on the third day**. Est 4:16. Mt 27:64.
royal. Est 1:11. 8:15. Mt 10:16. 11:8. 1 P 3:3-
5.
inner. Est 4:11. 6:4.
sat. 1 K 10:18-20. Lk 22:30. Re 3:21.
2 **she**. Ge 32:28. Ne 1:11. Ps 116:1. Pr 21:1. Ac
7:10. 10:4.
golden sceptre. Est 4:11. 8:4.
3 **What**. ver. 6. 7:2. 9:12. 1 K 2:20. 3:5. Mt
20:20-22. Lk 18:41.
to. ver. 6. Mk 6:23.
4 **If it seem**. ver. 8. Pr 29:11.
the banquet. ver. 8. Est 3:15. Ge 27:25.
32:20. Ps 112:5. 1 C 14:20.
5 **Cause Haman**. Est 6:14.
6 **the king said**. ver. 3. Est 7:2. 9:12.
7 **petition**. ver. 6, 8. Est 7:2, 3. 9:12.
request. ver. 3, 8. Est 7:2, 3. 9:12.
8 **perform**. Heb. do.
tomorrow. Est 6:1, etc. Pr 16:9.
9 **joyful**. Jb 20:5. Am 6:12, 13. Lk 6:25. Jn
16:20. Ja 4:9.
he stood not up. Est 3:2. Ps 15:4. Mt 10:28.
he was full. Est 3:5. 1 K 21:4. Jb 31:31. Ps
27:3. Da 3:13, 16-19. Mt 2:16. Ac 7:54.
10 **refrained**. Ge 43:30, 31. 45:1. 2 S 13:22, 23.
Ps 55:21. Ec 7:9.
called for his friends. Heb. caused his
friends to come.
Zeresh. i.e. *golden; star of adoration; a stranger in
want; misery*, **S#2238h**. ver. 10, 14. Est 6:13, 13.
11 **the glory**. Est 1:4. Ge 31:1. Jb 31:24, 25. Ps
49:6, 16, 17. Is 10:8. Je 9:23, 24. Da 4:30. Mk
10:24. Lk 12:19, 20. 1 T 6:17.
the multitude. Est 9:7-10, 12, 13. Jb 27:14,
15. Ps 17:14. Ho 9:13, 14.
and how he had. Est 3:1.
12 **tomorrow**. Jb 8:12, 13. 20:5-8. Ps 37:35, 36.
Pr 7:22, 23. 27:1. Lk 21:34, 35. 1 Th 5:3.
13 **Yet all this**. 1 K 21:4-6. Jb 15:20. 18:4. Pr
10:2. Ec 1:2, 14. Ph 4:11, 12.
14 **said Zeresh**. 2 S 13:3-5. 1 K 21:7, 25. 2 Ch
22:3, 4. Mk 6:19-24.
Let a gallows. Heb. Let a tree. Est 7:9.
speak thou. Est 3:8, etc. 6:4.
go thou in. Est 3:15. 1 K 21:7. Am 6:4-6. Re
11:10.
the thing. 2 S 16:21-23. 17:1-4. Mk 14:10,
11. Ac 23:14, 15. Ro 1:32.

he caused. Est 7:10. Ps 7:13-16. 9:15. 37:14, 32. Pr 1:18. 4:16. Ro 3:15.

ESTHER 6

1 **that night**. Est 5:8. Ge 22:14. 1 S 23:26, 27. Is 41:17. Ro 11:33.
could not the king sleep. Heb. the king's sleep fled away. Ge 28:16. 31:40. Jg 16:14. Ps 31:11. Da 2:1. 6:18.
the book of records. Est 2:23. Ml 3:16.

2 **Bigthana**. i.e. *given of fortune*, i.e. *of the sun; gardener; in their winepress*, **S#904h**. Est 2:21, Bigthan.
door. Heb. threshold. 2 K +12:9mg.

3 **What honor**. Jg 1:12, 13. 1 S 17:25, 26. 1 Ch 11:6. Da 5:7, 16, 29. Ac 28:8-10.
There is nothing. Ge 40:23. Ps 118:8, 9. Ec 9:15.

4 **Who is in the court**. Pr 3:27, 28. Ec 9:10.
the outward. Est 4:11. 5:1.
to speak. Est 3:8-11. 5:14. 7:9. Jb 5:13. Ps 2:4. 33:19.

6 **whom the king** , etc. Heb. in whose honor the king delighteth. Ps 35:27. Is 42:1. 62:4, 5. Je 32:41. Mt 3:17. Jn 5:23.
To whom. Est 3:2, 3. 5:11. Pr 1:32. +16:5. 1 C 10:12. Ph +2:3.

7 **whom the king**, etc. Heb. in whose honor the king delighteth. ver. 9, 11.

8 **Let the royal apparel**. lit. the clothing of the kingdom. Heb. Let them bring the royal apparel, wherewith the king clotheth himself. 1 S 18:4. Lk 15:22.
the horse. 1 K 1:33.

9 **bring him**. Heb. cause him to ride.
proclaim. Ge 41:43. 1 K 1:33, 34. Zc 9:9.
honor. Est 8:15. 1 S 2:30.

10 **Make haste**. Da 4:37. Lk 14:11. Re 18:7.
let nothing fail. Heb. suffer not a whit to fall. 1 S 3:19. 2 K 10:10.

11 **took Haman**. Ezr 6:13. Is 60:14. Lk 1:52. Re 3:9.
and arrayed. Est 8:15. 9:3. Ps 30:11. Is 61:3.

12 **came again**. Est 2:19. 1 S 3:15. Ps 131:1, 2.
hasted to his house. 2 S 17:23. 1 K +20:43. 2 Ch 26:20. Jb 20:5.
having. Est 7:8. 2 S 15:30. 19:4. Jb 9:24. Is 22:17. Je 14:3, 4.

13 **Zeresh**. Est 5:10-14.
said his wise. Ge 41:8. Da 2:12.
If Mordecai. Ge 40:19. 1 S 28:19, 20. Jb 15:24. Da 5:26-28. Zc 12:2, 3.
but shalt surely. Jg 7:14. Jb 16:2. Pr 28:18. Ho 14:9.

14 **hasted to bring**. Est 5:8, 14. Dt 32:35, 36.

ESTHER 7

1 **banquet**. Heb. drink. Est 3:15. 5:4, 8. Ge 24:19.

2 **the king said**. Est +5:6. Jn 16:24.

3 **let my**. ver. 7. 1 K 20:31. 2 K 1:13. Jb 2:4. Je 38:26.
life. Heb. *nephesh*, soul, Ge +44:30.
my people. Est 4:8. Ps 122:6-9.

4 **we are sold**. Est 3:9. 4:7, 8. Le +25:39. 1 S 22:23.
to be destroyed, etc. Heb. that they should destroy, and kill, and cause to perish. Est 3:13. 8:11. Ps 44:22, 23. Pr 14:28.
But if we. Ge 37:26-28. Jsh 9:23.
the enemy. ver. 6. Est 3:9.

5 **Who is he**. Ge 27:33. Jb 9:24.
that durst, etc. Heb. whose heart hath filled him. Ac 5:3.

6 **The adversary**. Heb. The man adversary. lit. "distresser, straitener." Est 3:10.
enemy. Est 8:13. 9:1, 5, 16, 22.
this wicked. 1 S 24:13. Ps 27:2. 139:19-22. Pr 24:24, 25. Ec 5:8. 1 C 5:13. 2 Th 2:8.
was afraid. Ne 6:16. Jb 15:21, 22. 18:5-12. Ps 73:5-9, 17-20. Pr 16:14. Is 21:4. Da 5:5, 6.
before. *or*, at the presence of. Est 1:19.

7 **in his wrath**. Est 1:12.
. **Haman**. Pr 14:19. Is 60:14. Re 3:9.
life. Heb. *nephesh*, soul, Ge +44:30.
for he saw. 1 S 20:7, 9. 25:17. Ps 112:10. Pr 19:12. Da 3:19.

8 **the bed**. Est 1:6. Is 49:23.
before me. Heb. with me.
they covered Haman's. Est +6:12.

9 **Harbonah**. i.e. *very warlike; martial; droughtiness; his sword*, **S#2726h**. Est 1:10, Harbona.
one of the chamberlains. Est 6:14. 2 K 9:32, 33.
Behold. Est 5:14. Jb 27:20-23. Ps 7:15, 16. 35:8. 141:10. Pr 14:5, 6.
gallows. Heb. tree. Est 5:14. Ge +40:19.
had made. Pr 26:27.
who had spoken. Est 2:21-23. 6:2.
Hang him thereon. Est 9:25. 1 S 17:51. Jb +4:8. Ps 35:8. 37:35, 36. +57:6. 73:19. Pr 11:5, 6. Da 6:7, 24.

10 **gallows**. lit. tree. Ge +40:19.
Then was the king's. Jg 15:7. Ezk 5:13. Zc 6:8.

ESTHER 8

1 **give the house**. Jb 27:16, 17. Ps 39:6. 49:6-13. Pr 13:22. 28:8. Ec 2:18, 19. Lk 12:20.
came before. Est 1:14. 2:7, 15.

2 **his ring**. Est 3:10. Ge 41:42. Is 22:19-22. Lk 15:22.
Esther set. 2 S 9:7-10. Ps 37:34. Ec 2:18-26. 5:13, 14. Da 2:48.

3 **fell**. 1 S 25:24. 2 K 4:27.
besought him with tears. Heb. she wept and besought him. Is 38:3. Ho 12:4. He 5:7.
mischief. Est 3:8-15. 7:4.

4 **held out**. Est 4:11. 5:2.

5 **and if I**. Est 7:3. Ex 33:13, 16. 1 S 20:29.
I be pleasing. Est 2:4, 17.
letters. Heb. device. Est 3:12, 13.
which he wrote. *or*, who wrote.

6 **For how**. Ge 44:34. Je 4:19. 9:1. Lk 19:41,
42. Ro 9:2, 3. 10:1.
endure to see. Heb. be able that I may see.
the evil. Est 7:4. Ne 2:3.

7 **Behold**. ver. 1. Pr 13:22.
him they have hanged. Est 7:10.
Ga 3:13.

8 **as it liketh**. Dt 23:16. Is 45:11. Jn 15:7.
in the king's name. Est 3:12. 1 K 21:8.
may no man reverse. ver. 5. Est 1:19. Da
6:8, 12-15. 2 T 2:19. He 6:17, 18.

9 **the king's**. Est 3:12.
Sivan. i.e. *their covering*, **S#5510h**. The third
month of the Jewish sacred year. Part of May
and June.
and to the lieutenants. Est 1:1, 22. 3:12,
13. Da 6:1.
India. Est 1:1.
and according. Est 1:22. 3:12. 2 K 18:26. Da
4:1. 1 C 14:9-11.

10 **in the king**. 1 K 21:8. Ec 8:4. Da 4:1.
by posts. Est 3:13, 15. 2 Ch 30:6. Jb 9:25. Je
51:21.
young dromedaries. Is 60:6. 66:20.
Je 2:23.

11 **to gather**. Est 9:2-16.
life. Heb. *nephesh*, soul, Ge +44:30; Ge +9:5.
Le 17:11. 2 S 14:7. Mt +2:20. Lk 12:22.
to destroy. Ps 37:14, 15. 68:23. 137:8. 146:6-
9. Ezk 39:10.
little ones. Nu +16:27.
and to take the spoil. Est 3:13. 9:10, 15, 16.
Is 10:6.

12 **one day**. Est 9:1. Ex 15:9, 10. Jg 1:6, 7.
upon the thirteenth. Est 3:13-15.

13 **publish**. Heb. revealed. Est 3:14mg.
avenge themselves. Jg 16:28. Ps 37:14, 15.
68:23. 92:10, 11. +149:6-9. Lk 18:7. Re 6:10.
19:2.

14 **being hastened**. 1 S 21:8. Ec 9:10.
Shushan. Da +8:2.

15 **the presence**. Est 6:9, 10. 1 S 2:30.
royal apparel. Est 5:1. 6:8, 11. Ge 41:42. Mt
6:29. 11:8. Lk 16:19.
blue. *or*, violet. Est 1:6mg.
and with a great crown. Ex 25:4. 39:27.
the city. Est 3:15. Pr 29:2.

16 **Jews**. Est 4:1-3, 16. Ps 30:5-11.
had light. Est 9:17. Ps 18:28. 97:11. Pr 4:18,
19. 11:10. *Is* 30:29, 39. 35:10.

17 **a feast**. Est 9:17, 19, 22. 1 S 25:8. Ne 8:10.
many of the people. Ps 18:43. Zc 8:20-23.
for the fear. Est 9:2. Ge 35:5. Ex 15:16. Dt
2:25. 11:25.

ESTHER 9

1 A.M. 3552. B.C. 452.
in the twelfth. Est 3:7, 13. 8:12.
hoped. Ac 12:11.
though it was turned. Dt 32:36. 2 S 22:41.
Ps 30:11. Is 14:1, 2. 60:14-16. Re 11:18.

2 **gathered**. ver. 10, 16. Est 8:11.
as sought. Dt +2:30. Jsh 11:20. Ps 71:13, 24.
Is 8:9.
the fear. Est 8:17. Ge 35:5. Ex 23:27.
Jsh 2:9.

3 **the rulers**. Est 3:12. 8:9. Ezr 8:36. Da 3:2.
6:1, 2.
officers of the king. Heb. those which did
the business that *belonged* to the king.
the fear. Est 3:2-6. 8:5.

4 **was great**. Ps 18:43.
his fame. Jsh 6:27. 1 S 2:30. 1 Ch 14:17. Zp
3:19. Mt 4:24.
waxed. 2 S 3:1. 1 Ch 11:9. Jb 17:9. Ps 1:3.
84:7. Pr 4:18. Is 9:7.

5 **smote**. Ps 18:34-40, 47, 48. 20:7, 8. 149:6-9.
2 Th 1:6.
the stroke. Je 18:21.
what they would. Heb. according to their
will. Ne 9:24.

6 **Shushan**. Da +8:2.

7 **Parshandatha**. i.e. *given forth to light; revela-*
tion of corporeal; of noble birth; he repeatedly
broke the decree, **S#6577h**.
Dalphon. i.e. *a dropping; strenuous dripping*,
S#1813h.
Aspatha. i.e. *given by the horse; the enticed gath-*
ered, **S#630h**.

8 **Poratha**. i.e. *ornament; fruitful; favored; frustra-*
tion, **S#6334h**.
Adalia. i.e. *fire-god; strong hearted; I shall be*
drawn up of Jah, **S#118h**.
Aridatha. i.e. *strong; the lion of the decree; great*
(noble) birth, **S#743h**.

9 **Parmashta**. i.e. *strong fisted; superior; spoiled is*
the banquet, **S#6534h**.
Arisai. i.e. *lion-like; lion of my banners*, **S#747h**.
Aridai. i.e. *strong; the lion is enough; great, bril-*
liant, **S#742h**.
Vajezatha. i.e. *pure; white; he sprinkled there;*
olive trees; sincere, **S#2055h**.

10 **ten sons**. Est 5:11. Ex 20:5. Jb 18:18, 19.
27:13-15. Ps 21:10. 69:25. 109:12, 13.
enemy. Est 3:1. 7:4, 6. Ex 17:16.
but on the spoil. ver. 15, 16. Est 8:11. Ge
14:23. Ro 12:17. Ph 4:8.

11 **was brought**. Heb. came.

12 **what is thy petition**. Est 5:6. 7:2.

13 **If it please the king**. Est 1:19.
according unto. Est 8:11.
let Haman's ten sons be hanged. Heb. let
men hang Haman's ten sons. Dt 21:23. 2 S
21:6, 9. Ga 3:13.

15 **gathered themselves**. ver. 2, 13. Est 8:11. Ps 118:7-12.
but on the prey. ver. 10, 16. 1 Th 5:22. He 13:5.

16 **gathered themselves**. ver. 2. Est 8:11.
stood. Est 8:11. Le 26:7, 8.
lives. Heb. *nephesh*, souls, Ge +44:30.

17 **of the same**. Heb. in it. ver. 1, 18, 21. Est 3:12. 8:9.

18 **on the thirteenth**. ver. 1, 11, 13, 15.

19 **gladness**. ver. 22. Est 8:17. Dt 16:11, 14. Ne 8:10-12. Ps 118:11-16. Lk 11:41. Re 11:10.
sending portions. ver. 22. Est 2:9. Ex 29:26.

20 **Mordecai wrote these**. Ex 17:14. +24:4. Dt 31:19-22. 1 Ch 16:12. Ps 124:1-3. 145:4-12. 2 C 1:10, 11.
in all the provinces. Est 1:1, 22. 3:12. 8:9.

22 **the days**. Est 3:12, 13. Ex 13:3-8. Ps 103:2. Is 12:1, 2. 14:3.
from sorrow. Ps 30:11. Is 61:3. Je 31:13. Mt 5:4. Jn 16:20-22.
sending portions. ver. 19. Ne 8:10-12. Lk 11:41. Ac 2:44-46. Ga 2:10.

24 **the enemy**. or, adversary. ver. 10. Est 3:5-13. 7:6.
Pur. Est 3:7. Jsh +14:2.
consume. Heb. crush. Ex 14:24 (troubled). 23:27 (destroy). Dt 2:15. Je 51:34.

25 **when Esther came**. Heb. when she came. ver. 13, 14. Est 7:5-10. 8:1-14.
return upon. Nu +32:23. Jg 1:7. Jb +4:8. Ps 109:17, 18. 140:9. 141:10. Ec 10:8. Da 6:24. Mt 21:44.

26 **they called**. Nu 16:40. Ezk 39:11.
Purim. i.e. *lot; frustration*, **S#6332h.** ver. 26, 28, 29, 31, 32.
Pur. *that is*, Lot. ver. 24. Est 3:7.
letter. ver. 20.

27 **and upon their seed**. Dt 5:3. 29:14, 15. Jsh 9:15. 1 S 30:25. 2 S 21:1, 2.

all such. Est 8:17. Is 56:3, 6. Zc 2:11. 8:23.
fail. Heb. pass. ver. 28.

28 **remembered**. Ex 12:17. Ps 78:5-7. 103:2.
fail. Heb. pass. ver. 27.
the memorial. Ex 13:8, 9. Jsh 4:7. Zc 6:14.
perish from their seed. Heb. be ended from their seed. Is 66:17.

29 **the daughter of Abihail**. Est 2:15.
authority. Heb. strength. Est 10:2. Da 2:37. 11:17.
confirm. ver. 20. Est 8:10.

30 **the hundred twenty and**. Est 1:1. 8:9.
words of peace. Is 39:8. Zc 8:19.

31 **themselves**. Heb. their souls. Heb. *nephesh*, Ge +27:31. Le 11:43. Jb 18:4. Ps 131:2. Is ◄46:2. Je 37:9.
and for their seed. ver. 27.
the fastings. Est 4:3, 16. 2 S 12:16. Jon 3:2-9.
their cry. Ps 145:18, 19.

32 **decree**. or, saying. Est 1:15. 2:20. 2 Ch +34:27.
was written. Ex 17:14.

ESTHER 10

1 **laid a tribute**. Est 1:1. 8:9. Lk 2:1.
the isles. Is +11:11.

2 **all the acts**. 1 K 11:41. 22:30.
advanced him. Heb. made him great. Est 8:15. 9:4. Ps 18:35. Da 2:48.
in the book . Est 2:23. 6:1. 1 K 14:19.
Media. Est +1:3.
Persia. 2 Ch +36:22.

3 **Jew**. Est 2:5. 5:13. 6:10.
next unto the king. Ge +41:40. 44. 1 S 23:17. 2 Ch 28:7. Da 5:16, 29.
accepted. Est 3:2. Dt 33:24. Ro 14:18.
seeking. Dt 11:12. Ne 2:10. Ps 122:6-9. Ro 9:2, 3. 10:1.
speaking peace. Ps 28:3. 37:37, 38.

JOB

JOB 1

1 **Uz.** Ge +10:23.
Job. i.e. *the persecuted; the cry of woe; I will exclaim,* **S#347h.** ver. 1, 5, 8, 9, 14, 20, 22. Jb 2:3, 7, 10. 3:1, 2. 6:1. 9:1. 12:1. 16:1. 19:1. 21:1. 23:1. 26:1. 27:1. 29:1. 31:40. 32:1-4, 12. 33:1, 31. 34:5, 7, 35, 36. 35:16. 37:14. 38:1. 40:1, 3, 6. 42:1, 7-10, 12, 15-17. Ezk 14:14, 20. Ja 5:11.
perfect. ver. 8. Jb 23:11, 12. 31:1, etc. 2 Ch 31:20, 21. Mt +5:48. Jn 1:47. Ro 3:23.
upright. ver. 8. Jb 2:3. 4:7. 8:6. 17:8. 23:7. 33:27. Ex 15:26.
feared God. Ex +18:21. Pr 8:13. 16:6. Da 6:20.
eschewed evil. ver. 8. Pr 11:22mg. 14:16. 2 T +2:19.

2 **seven.** Ru 4:15. 1 S 2:5. Je 15:9.
sons. Jb 13:13. Est 5:11. Ps 107:38. +127:3-5. 128:3, 4.
three daughters. Jb 42:13.

3 **substance.** *or,* cattle. Ge 12:5. 13:6. 34:23. 2 Ch 32:29.
seven thousand. Jb 42:12. Ge 12:16. 26:14. Nu 31:32-34. Jg 6:5. 1 S 25:2. 2 K 3:4. Pr 10:22.
household. *or,* husbandry. Ge 26:14. 2 Ch 26:10.
greatest. Jb 29:9, 10, 25. 31:37.
men. Heb. sons. Jg 6:3. 7:12. 8:10. 1 K 4:30.
of the east. Ge +29:1.

4 **feasted.** lit. "drinking." ver. 5. Ge 19:3. Est 5:4.
sent and called. Est 5:12. Ps 133:1. He 13:1.

5 **gone about.** or, gone round. Jb 19:6. Le 19:27.
sanctified. Jb 41:25. Ge 35:2, 3. Ex 19:10, 14. 1 S 16:5. Ne 12:30. Jn 11:55.
rose up. Ge +19:27.
offered burnt. Le +23:12.
according. 1 K 18:31. Ac 21:26.
Job said. *Ge* 18:19. Dt +6:20. 1 S 12:23. 2 S +6:20. Ep 6:18. 1 Th 5:17. Ja 5:16.
It may be. Ge 8:21. Ezk 18:31. 36:26. 2 C 11:2.
cursed. ver. 11. Jb 2:5, 9. Ex 21:17 with Dt 27:16. Le 24:10-16. 1 K 21:10, 13. Ezk 22:7. 2

P 2:10. Ju 8. or, blessed. Lk 12:15-21.
in their hearts. Ge 6:5. Je 4:14. 17:9, 10. Mk 7:21-23. Ac 8:22. 1 C 4:5.
Thus. Jb 27:10.
continually. Heb. all the days. Jb 15:20. Ge 6:5mg. 1 S 18:29. Lk 1:75. 18:7. Ep 6:18.

6 **Now.** Jb 2:1.
the sons. Ge +6:2.
of God. Ge +6:2. Jb 38:7. Ge +6:2. Ps 89:6. Da 3:25. Lk 3:38.
came to. Ps 103:20. Mt 18:10. or, station themselves. Jb 2:1. Ex 8:20. Zc 4:14.
Satan. Heb. the adversary. i.e. *adversary, opposer,* **S#7854h.** ver. 7, 8, 9, 12. 2:1, 2, 3, 4, 6, 7. Nu 22:22, 32mg. 1 S 29:4. 2 S 19:22. 1 K 5:4. 11:14, 23, 25. 22:19. 1 Ch 21:1. Ps 109:6. Zc 3:1, 2. 2 C 11:14. Re 12:9, 10.
came also. 1 K 22:19, 21. Jn 6:70.
among them. Heb. in the midst of them. Jb 2:1, 8. 15:19. 20:13 (within). 42:15. Ge 1:6 (in the midst). 18:24 (within). Ps 22:14, 22. 40:8mg, 10. Pr 1:14. 4:21. Je 44:7mg. Ezk 14:16mg. Zc 2:10.

7 **Satan.** Mt 13:19, 38, 39. Lk 4:5. 8:12. 22:31. Jn 8:44. 13:2. Ac 5:3. 2 C 2:11. 4:4. Ep 2:2. 6:12. 2 T 2:26. 1 P 5:8. Re 2:24. 12:9, 10, 12. 20:7, 8.
Whence. Jb 2:2. 2 K 5:25.
From going. Is 57:20. Zc 1:10, 11. 6:7. Mt 12:43. 1 P 5:8. Re 12:9, 12-17. 20:8.

8 **considered.** Heb. set thy heart on. Jb 2:3. 34:14. Ex +9:21mg. Ps +78:43mg. Ezk 40:4. Lk 22:31, 32.
my servant. Nu 12:7, 8. Ps 89:20. Is 42:1.
none. Nu 12:3. 1 K 4:30, 31. 2 K 23:25. Na 1:7. 2 T 2:19.
a perfect. ver. +1. Jb 8:20. 9:22, 23.
upright. Jb 12:4. 17:8, 9. 23:11, 12. Ps 84:11.
one that feareth. Ne 5:15. Ps 36:1. Pr 8:13. Lk 23:39, 40.
escheweth. ver. 1. Ps 34:14. 37:27. Is 1:16.

9 **Then Satan.** Zc 3:1.
Doth Job. ver. 21. Jb 2:10. 21:14, 15. Ml 1:10. Mt 16:26. 1 T 4:8. 6:6.

10 **an hedge.** Ge 15:1. Dt 33:27-29. 1 S 25:16. Ps 5:12. 34:7. 80:12. Is 5:1, 2, 5. Zc 2:5, 8. 1 P 1:5.

about. Ge 39:5. Dt 28:2-6. Ps 71:21. 128:1-4.
thou hast blessed. Jb 42:12. Ge 26:12.
30:30. 49:25. Dt 7:13. 33:11. Ps 90:17.
107:38. Pr +10:22.
substance. *or*, cattle. Ge 30:43.

11 **But**. ver. 12. Jb 2:5. 19:21. Is 5:25. Ezk 25:7,
13, 16.
put forth. Jb 2:5.
thine hand. Ex +9:3. Ru +1:13.
touch. Jb 2:5. 4:5. 19:21. Ge 26:11, 29. Ru
2:9. Ps 105:15. Je 12:14. Zc 2:8. Lk 22:31. Jn
19:11. He 11:28. 1 J 5:18.
and he will curse thee. Heb. if he curse
thee not. ver. 5, 21. Jb +2:9. Is 8:21. Ml 3:13,
14. Re 16:9, 11, 21.

12 **Behold**. 1 K 22:22, 23. Lk 8:32. 22:31, 32. Jn
19:11. 2 C 12:7.
power. Heb. hand. Ge 16:6. Dt 32:36mg. Je
38:5. Jn 3:35, 36.
only. Jb 2:4-6. Ps 76:10. Is 27:8. 1 C 10:13.
So Satan. Jb 2:7. Lk 8:33.
from the presence. Ge 4:16. Ps 5:4.

13 **there was**. ver. 13. 1 S 1:4. 2 K 4:8. Lk 16:19.
a day. ver. 6. Jb 2:1.
when. ver. 4. Pr 27:1. Ec 9:12. Lk 12:19, 20.
17:27-29. 21:34.
eldest brother's. or, the first-born. ver. 18.
Jb +18:13.

14 **messenger**. 1 S 4:17. 2 S 15:13. Je 51:31.
plowing. Jb 4:8. 1 K 19:19.

15 **Sabeans**. lit. Sheba. i.e. *he who is coming; eminent*, **S#7614h**. Ge 10:7, 28. 25:3. Ps 72:10. Is
45:14. Ezk 23:42. Jl 3:8.
edge. Ge 34:26mg. Ex 17:13.
and I only. ver. 16, 17, 19. 1 S 22:20, 21.

16 **there came**. Ge 19:24. Le 9:24. 1 K 18:38. 2
K 1:10, 12, 14. Am 7:4. Re 13:13.
The fire of God. *or*, A great fire. Ge 19:24.
+23:6mg. Nu 11:1, 3. 1 S 26:12. 1 K 18:38. 2
K 1:12. 1 Ch 12:22. +16:42. Ps +36:6mg. SS
8:6. Ho 13:5. 1 Th 4:6.

17 **The Chaldeans**. Ge 11:28. Is 23:13. Hab 1:6.
fell. Heb. rushed. Jg 9:33, 44. 20:37.
I only am. ver. 15. 2 S 1:3.

18 **there came**. Jb 6:2, 3. 16:14. 19:9, 10. 23:2.
Is 28:19. Je 51:31. La 1:12. Am 4:6-11.
Thy sons. ver. 4, 13. Jb 8:4. 27:14. Ps 34:19.
Ec 9:2.
eating. 2 S 13:28.

19 **a great**. Je 4:11, 12. Ep 2:2.
from. Heb. from aside, etc.
it fell. Jg 16:30. 1 K 20:30. Mt 7:27. Lk 13:1-
5. Ac 28:4.
they are dead. Ge 37:32, 33. 42:36. 2 S
18:33.
to tell thee. Ps 34:19. 36:6. Ec 9:2. Is 21:4.
Lk 13:1-5.

20 **rent**. 2 K +18:37.
mantle. *or*, robe. Jb 2:12. 29:14. Ex 28:4.
shaved. Ge 41:14. Is +3:24.

fell. Ge +17:3. 2 S 12:16-20. 1 P 5:6.
and worshipped. Ps 101:1. Is 24:15. Hab
3:17, 18.

21 **Naked**. Jb 22:6. 24:7, 10. 26:6. Ge 2:25.
came I. Ge 3:19. Ps 49:17. Ec 5:15. 12:7. 1 T
6:7.
the Lord gave. Jb 2:10. Ge 30:2. Ec 5:19. La
+3:38. Ac +21:14. Ja 1:17.
the Lord. Jg +10:15. Ps 89:52.
taken away. Ge 45:5. 2 S 16:12. 1 K 12:15.
Ps 39:9. Is 42:24. +45:7. Am +3:7. Mt 20:15.
Ac 4:28.
blessed. ver. 11. 1 S 3:18. 2 K 20:19. Ps 34:1.
89:38-52. Is 24:15. Ep 5:20. 1 Th 5:18.

22 **In all this**. Jb 2:10. Ja 1:4, 12. 5:11. 1 P 1:7.
charged God foolishly. *or*, attributed folly to
God. Jb +2:10. 24:12. 33:13. 34:10, 18, 19.
40:4-8. Ru +1:13. Ps 74:22. +77:3. Pr +19:3. Is
+29:24. Je 23:13mg. Ezk +18:25. Ro 9:20.

JOB 2

1 **Again**. Jb +1:6. Is 6:1, 2. Lk 1:19. He 1:14.
sons of God. Ge +6:2.

2 **From whence**. Ge 16:8.
From going. Jb 1:7. Jn 14:30. 2 C 4:4. 1 P
5:8.

3 **Hast thou**. Lk 12:8.
none like. Ge 7:1. Ps 1:2, 4. Je 15:19. Ezk
44:23. Jn 15:19. Ac 8:21. 2 C +5:17. T 2:14. 1
P 2:9. 1 J 5:19.
a perfect. Mt +5:48.
an upright. Pr 11:3. 13:6. 14:2. 15:8. 16:17.
Ro 12:12.
holdeth. Jb 1:21, 22. 13:15. 27:5, 6. Ps 26:1.
41:12. Ro 12:12. 2 C 4:9. 1 Th 3:3. Ja 1:12. 1
P 1:7.
thou movedst. Jb 1:11.
destroy him. Heb. swallow him up. Jb 5:5.
7:19. 8:18. 10:8. Ge 41:7. Ps +35:25.
without. Jb 9:17. Jn 9:3.

4 **all that**. Est 7:3, 4. Is 2:20, 21. Je 41:8. Mt
6:25. 16:26. Ac 27:18, 19. Ph 3:8-10.
Skin for skin. Jb 18:13.
life. Heb. *nephesh*, soul, Ge +44:30.

5 **put forth**. Ex +9:3. Mt 10:29-31. Re 12:9, 10.
touch. Jb +1:11. Ps 6:2. 32:3. 51:8.
bone and. Jb 19:20. Lk +24:39.
he will curse. ver. 9. Jb 1:5, 11. Le 24:15. Is
8:21.

6 **Behold**. Jb +1:12.
but. *or*, only.
save. Jb 38:10, 11. Ps 65:7. 72:13. 118:18.
121:3. Lk 8:29-33. 22:31, 32. 1 C 10:13. Re
2:10. 20:1, 2, 7.
his life. Heb. *nephesh*, soul, Ge +44:30.

7 **So went**. 1 K 22:22.
sore boils. Jb 30:17-19, 30. Ex 9:9-11. Dt
28:27, 35. Ps 38:7. Lk 16:20. 1 P 4:12. Re
16:11.

from the sole. Dt 28:35. 2 S 14:25. Is 1:6. 3:17.

8 **took him**. Jb 19:14-17. Ps 38:5, 7. Lk 16:20, 21.
  he sat. Est +4:1. La 4:5.

9 **his wife**. Ge 3:6, 12. 1 K 11:4.
  retain. ver. 3. Jb 21:14, 15. 2 K 6:33. Ml 3:14.
  curse God. ver. 5. Jb 1:11.

10 **Thou speakest**. Ge 3:17. 2 S 19:22. Mt 16:23.
  as one. 2 S 6:20, 21. 13:13. 24:10. 2 Ch 16:9. Pr 9:6, 13. Mt 25:2.
  the foolish. Jb 30:8. Dt 32:6. Pr +19:3.
  women speaketh. 2 S +20:16. 1 T 5:13-15. 2 T 3:6-8.
  receive good. Jb 1:1-3, 10, 21. 2 S 19:28. Ps +37:24. 104:28. +145:9. Je +29:11. La +3:38-41. Mt +5:45. Lk +6:35. Jn 18:11. Ro 12:12. He 12:9-11. Ja +1:17. 5:10, 11.
  not receive. Jb 9:24.
  evil. Ru +1:13. 2 K +6:23. Am +3:6.
  In all this. Jb 1:22. Ps 39:1. 59:12. Mt 12:34-37. Ja 3:2. 5:10.

11 **friends**. Jb 6:14. 16:20. 19:19, 21. 42:7. Pr 17:17. 18:24. 27:10.
  Eliphaz. Jb 42:9. Ge +36:4.
  Temanite. S#8489h. ver. 11. Jb 4:1. 15:1. 22:1. 42:7, 9. Ge 36:34. 1 Ch 1:45. From Teman (i.e. *the southern country; southward*, Ge +36:11), in Edom. Jb 6:19. 15:1. Ge +36:11, 15. Je 49:7.
  Bildad. i.e. *son of contention; confusing (by mingling) love*, S#1085h. ver. 11. Jb 8:1. 18:1. 25:1. 42:9.
  Shuhite. S#7747h. ver. 11. Jb 8:1. 18:1. 25:1. 42:9. Descendant of Shuah (i.e. *depression; prostration*, Ge +25:2), in Arabia Petraea. Jb 8:1. 18:1. Ge 25:2. 1 Ch 1:32.
  Zophar. i.e. *chirper; departing early; insolence; a climber; crown*, S#6691h. ver. 11. Jb 11:1. 20:1. 42:9.
  Naamathite. i.e. *inhabitant of Naamah* (i.e. *pleasantness*, Ge +4:22), in Edom, S#5284h. ver. 11. Jb 11:1. 20:1. 42:9.
  appointment. Ex 25:22. 29:42, 43. 30:6, 36.
  to come. Jb 42:11. Ge 37:35. Is 51:19. Jn 11:19. Ro 12:15. 1 C 12:26. He 13:3.
  to mourn. Pr 17:17. Ec 7:4. Ro 12:15. lit. "nod to him." Jb 42:11.
  to comfort. Jb 13:4. 16:2.

12 **lifted**. Ge +22:13.
  knew him. Jb 19:14. Ru 1:19-21. La 4:7, 8.
  their voice. Ge 27:34. Jg 2:4. 1 S 11:4. 30:4. 2 S 13:36. Est 4:1.
  they rent. Jb +1:20.
  sprinkled. Ex 9:8, 10. 24:6, 8. 29:16, 20.
  dust upon. Jsh +7:6.

13 **they sat**. Ezr 9:3. Ne 1:4. Is 3:26. 47:1. La +2:10.

seven days and. Ge 1:5, 8. 50:10. Ezk 3:15.
none spake. Jb 4:2. Ps 77:4. Ec 3:7.
grief. or, pain. Jb 5:18. 14:22. 16:6. Ps 39:2. Is 17:11. 65:14. Je 15:18. La 1:12.

JOB 3

1 **After**. Jb 1:22. 2:10.
  opened. Jg +11:35. Ps 119:172. Mt 11:25. Mk 11:14.
  his mouth. Jb 35:16. Ps 39:2, 3. 106:33.
  cursed. ver. 3. Jb 1:11. 2:5, 9. Je 20:14, 15. La 4:1. Ja 3:8.
  his day. That is, the day of his birth.

2 **spake**. Heb. answered. Jg 18:14.

3 **Let the day**. Jb 10:18, 19. Je 15:10. 20:14, 15.

4 **darkness**. Ex 10:22, 23. Jl 2:2. Am 5:18. Mt 27:45. Ac 27:20. Re 16:10.
  God regard. Dt 11:12.

5 **the shadow**. Ps +23:4.
  stain it. *or*, challenge it. Nu 35:19. or, redeem. Jb 19:25. Ge 48:16. Ex 6:6.
  let a cloud. Dt 4:11. Ezk 30:3. 34:12. Jl 2:2. He 12:18.
  let the blackness. *or*, let them terrify it, as those *who have* a bitter day. Jg +18:25mg. Je 4:28. Am 8:10.

6 **let it not be joined unto the days**. *or*, let it not rejoice among the days. Is 14:20.
  joined. Ge 49:6. Ps 86:11. Is 14:20.
  months. Jb 7:3. 29:2. 39:2. Ex 2:2.

7 **solitary**. Is 13:20-22. 24:8. Je 7:34. Re 18:22, 23.

8 **Let them curse**. Ge 27:29. Nu 24:9.
  who are ready. Mt +9:23.
  their mourning. *or*, a leviathan. Jb 41:1, 10. Ps 74:14.

9 **for light**. Jb 30:26. Je 8:15. 13:16.
  the dawning of the day. Heb. the eye-lids of the morning. Jb 41:18.

10 **it shut not**. Jb 10:18, 19. Ge 20:18. 29:31, 32. 1 S 1:5. Ec 6:3-5. Je 20:17, 18.
  hid. Jb 6:2, 3. 10:1. 23:2. Ec 11:10.

11 **died I**. Ps 58:8. Je 15:10. Ho 9:14.
  ghost. Heb. *gava*, Ge +49:33 (S#1478h).
  when I came. Ps 22:9, 10. 71:6. 139:13-16. Is 46:3.

12 **the knees**. Ge 30:3. 50:23. Ps 71:6. Is 66:12. Ezk 16:4, 5.

13 **then had I been at rest**. Ec 6:3-5. 9:10.

14 **kings**. Jb 30:23. 1 K 2:10. 11:43. Ps 49:6-10, 14. 89:48. Ec 8:8. Is 14:10-16. Ezk 27:18-32. which built. Jb 15:28. Is 5:8. Ezk 26:20.

15 **who filled their houses**. Jb 22:25. 27:16. Nu 22:18. 1 K 10:27. Is 2:7. Zp 1:18. Zc 9:3.

16 **an hidden**. Ps 58:8. 1 C 15:8.
  untimely birth. or, abortion. Ec 4:3. 6:3. Lk +1:44.
  infants. 1 S 15:3. 22:19.

17 **the wicked**. Jb 14:13. Ps 55:5-8. Mt +10:28. Lk 12:4. 2 Th 1:6, 7. 2 P 2:8.

the weary. Heb. the wearied in strength. Dt 25:18. 2 S 17:2. Ec 1:8.

at rest. Is 57:1, 2. Mt 11:28. He 4:9, 11. Re +14:13.

18 **they**. Jb 39:7. Ex 5:6-8, 15-19. Jg 4:3. Is 14:3, 4.

19 **The small**. Jb 30:23. Ps 49:2, 6-10. Ec 8:8. 12:5, 7. Lk 16:22, 23. He +9:27.

and the servant. Ps 49:14-20.

20 **Wherefore**. Jb 6:9. 7:15, 16. Je 20:18.

light. ver. 16. Jb 33:28, 30.

the bitter. Jb 7:15, 16. 1 S 1:10. 2 K +4:27mg. Pr 31:6.

soul. Heb. *nephesh*, Ge +34:3.

21 **long**. Heb. wait. Nu 11:15. 1 K 19:4. Jon 4:3, 8. Re 9:6.

dig. Pr 2:4.

22 **rejoice exceedingly**. Ps 43:4. 45:15. 65:12. Pr 23:24. Is 16:10. Je 48:33. Da 1:10. Ho 9:1. Jl 1:16.

grave. Heb. *qeber*, Ge +23:4. Jb 5:26. 10:19. 17:1. 21:32.

23 **whose way**. Is 40:27.

hedged in. Jb 12:14. 19:8. Ps 31:8. La 3:7, 9. Ho 2:6.

24 **my sighing**. Jb 7:19. Ps 80:5. 102:9.

I eat. Heb. my meat.

my roarings. Ps +22:1.

25 **the thing**, etc. Heb. I feared a fear and it came upon me. Jb 15:21mg. Ps +34:4. Pr +10:24. Ec 9:12. Is +8:12. Je +10:5. 15:17, 18. Jon 4:2.

come upon. Jb 4:5.

that which. Jb 1:5. 31:23. Pr +10:24.

26 **yet trouble came**. Jb 27:9. Ps 143:11.

JOB 4

1 **Eliphaz**. Jb +2:11.

answered. Jb 3:1, 2. 6:1. 8:1.

2 **to commune**. Heb. a word.

wilt thou. 2 C 2:4-6. 7:8-10.

withhold himself from speaking. Heb. refrain from words. Jb 32:18-20. Je 6:11. 20:9. Ac 4:20.

3 **Behold**. Ge 18:19. Pr 10:21. 15:7. 16:21. Is 50:4. Ep 4:29. Col 4:6.

and thou hast strengthened. Jb 16:5. Dt 3:28. Ezr 6:22. Is 35:3. Ezk 13:22. Lk 22:32, 43. He 10:24.

4 **Thy words**. Ep 4:29. Col 4:6.

upholden. 1 S 23:16. Ps 145:14. Pr 12:18. 16:23, 24. 2 C 1:4. 2:7. 7:6. 1 Th 5:14. He 12:12, 13.

strengthened. 1 S 23:16. 2 C 1:4. He 10:24.

feeble knees. Heb. bowing knees. Is 35:3, 4. Da 5:6. He 12:12.

5 **it is come**. Jb 3:25, 26.

thou faintest. Pr 24:10. Je 12:5. 2 C 4:1, 16. He 12:3, 5.

it toucheth. Jb +1:11.

6 **thy fear**. Jb 1:1, 9, 10. 2 K 20:3.

thy confidence. Jb 13:15. Pr 3:26. 14:26.

thy hope. Jb 17:15. 1 P 1:13, 17.

the uprightness. Jb 1:8. 16:17. 23:11, 12. 27:5, 6. 29:12-17. 31:1, etc.

7 **who ever**. Jb 8:20. 9:22, 23. 36:6, 7. Ge +19:30. Ps 37:25. Ec 7:15. 9:1, 2. Ac 28:4. 2 P 2:9.

8 **they that plow**. Ps 7:14-16. Pr 22:8. Je 4:18. Ho 8:7. 10:12, 13. 2 C 9:6. Ga 6:7, 8.

reap the same. Jb 5:13. 34:11. Ge +6:13. Nu +32:23. Ps 5:10. 7:15, 16. 9:15, 16. +57:6. Pr 1:31. 5:22. 11:5, 6. 12:13, 14. 22:8. 26:27. 28:10. Is 3:10, 11. Je 2:19. 6:19. Ezk 22:31.

9 **the blast**. Heb. *neshamah*, Ge +2:7. Ex 15:8. 2 S 22:16. 2 K 19:7. Ps +18:15.

by the breath. Heb. *ruach*, Ge +6:3. Jb 15:30. Ex +15:8. 2 S 22:16. Ps 18:15. 33:6. Is 11:4. 30:28.

of his nostrils. *that is*, by his anger. Jb 1:19. Ex +15:8. Is 30:33. 2 Th 2:8. Re 2:16.

10 **the teeth**. Jb 29:17. Ps 3:7. 57:4. 58:6. Pr 30:14.

11 **old lion**. Is +5:29.

perisheth. Ps 34:10.

the stout. Jb 1:19. 8:3, 4. 27:14, 15.

12 **a thing**. Ps 62:11.

secretly. Heb. by stealth. Ge 40:15.

a little. 1 C 13:12.

13 **thoughts**. Jb 33:14-16. Ge +31:24. 46:2. Da 2:19, 28, 29.

deep sleep. Ge 2:21. 15:12. Da 8:18. 10:9.

14 **Fear**. Jb 7:14. Ps 119:120. Is 6:5. Da 10:11. Hab 3:16. Lk 1:12, 29. Re 1:17.

came upon. Heb. met. Jb 39:21. Ge 42:38.

all my bones. Heb. the multitude of my bones. Jb 33:19.

15 **a spirit**. Heb. *ruach*, Ps +104:4. Mt 14:26. Lk 24:37-39. He 1:7, 14.

the hair. Is 13:8. 21:3, 4. Da 5:6.

16 **there**, etc. *or*, I heard a still voice. 1 K 19:12. Ps 107:29.

17 **Shall mortal**. Jb 8:3. 9:2. 35:2. 40:8. Ge 18:25. Ps 143:2. 145:17. Ec 7:20. Je 12:1. Ro 2:5. 3:4-7. 9:20. 11:33.

shall a man. Jb 9:30, 31. 14:4. 15:14. 25:4. Je 17:9. Mt 19:17. Mk 7:20-23. Re 4:8.

18 **he put**. Jb 15:15, 16. 25:5, 6. Ps 103:20, 21. 104:4. Is 6:2, 3.

and his angels he charged with folly. *or*, nor in his angels *in whom* he put light. 2 P 2:4. Ju 6.

19 **How much less**. Jb 15:16.

dwell. Jb 10:9. 13:12. 33:6. Ge +2:7. +3:19. 18:27. Ec +12:7. 2 C 4:7. 5:1.

crushed. Jb 13:28. 14:2. Ps 39:4, 5, 11. 90:5-7. 103:15, 16. +146:4. 1 P 1:24.

20 **destroyed**. Heb. beaten in pieces. 2 Ch 15:6mg. Is 24:12. Je 46:5mg. Mi 1:7.
from morning. Is 38:12, 13.
they perish. Jb 14:14. 16:22. Ps 39:13. 90:5, 6. 92:7.
for ever. S#5331h. ver. 20. Jb 14:20. 20:7. 23:7. 34:36 (the end). 36:7. 1 S 15:29 (Strength; mg, or Eternity, or victory). 2 S 2:26. 1 Ch 29:11 (victory). Ps 9:6 (perpetual end; lit. completed for ever), 18 (alway). 10:11 (lit. not for ever). 13:1. 16:11 (evermore). 44:23. 49:9, 19. 52:5. 68:16. 74:1, 3 (perpetual), 10, 19. 77:8. 79:5. 89:46. 103:9 (always). Pr 21:28 (constantly). Is 13:20. 25:8 (victory). 28:28. 33:20. 34:10 (for ever and ever). 57:16 (always). Je 3:5 (the end). 15:18 (perpetual). 50:39. La 3:18 (strength). 5:20. Am 1:11. 8:7. Hab 1:4 (never).
without. Jb 18:17. 20:7. 2 Ch 21:20. Ps 37:36. Pr 10:7.

21 **excellency**. Ps 39:5, 11. 49:14. 146:3, 4. Is 14:16. Lk 16:22, 23. Ja 1:11.
die. Jb 36:12. Ps 49:20. Is 2:22. Lk 12:20.
without wisdom. Pr 5:23. Ho 4:6. Lk +11:52.

JOB 5

1 **and to which**. Jb 15:8-10, 15. Is 41:1, 21-23. He 12:1.
the saints. Jb 4:18. 15:15. Dt 33:2, 3. Ps 16:3. 106:16. Ep 1:1.
turn. or, look. Jb 6:28. 21:5mg. 24:18. 36:21.

2 **wrath**. Jb 18:4. Jon 4:9. Ja +1:20.
the foolish. Ps 14:1. 75:4. 92:6. 94:8. 107:17. Pr 1:22, 23. 8:5. Ec 7:9.
envy. or, indignation. 1 S 18:8, 9. Ps +37:1. Ro 2:8.
one. Ho 7:11. 2 T 3:6.

3 **taking**. Jb 27:8. Ps 37:35, 36. 73:3-9, 18-20. 92:7. Je 12:1-3.
cursed. Dt 27:15, etc. Ps 69:25. Ac 1:20.

4 **children**. Jb 4:10, 11. 8:4. 18:16-19. 27:14. Ex 20:5. Ps 109:9-15. 119:155. 127:5.
they are crushed. Jb 1:19. Lk 13:4, 5.
neither. Jb 10:7. Ps 7:2. 50:22.

5 **harvest**. Dt 28:33, 51. Jg 6:3-6. Is 62:8.
the thorns. Jg 6:11. 2 Ch 33:11.
the robber. Jb 1:15, 17. 12:6. 18:9. Ho 8:7.
swalloweth. Ps +35:25.

6 **affliction**. or, iniquity. Jb 4:8. Pr 14:22. 22:8.
trouble. Jb 34:29. Dt 32:27. 1 S 6:9. Ps 90:7, 8. Is 45:7. La 3:38, 39. Am +3:6.
spring out. Ho 10:4. He 12:15.

7 **man**. Jb 7:17, 18. 14:1. Ge 3:17-19. Ps 90:8, 9. 1 C 10:13.
born. Ge 4:26. 6:1. 10:21.
trouble. or, labor. Jb 14:1. Ec 1:8. 2:22. 5:15-17.
sparks fly upward. Heb. sons of the burning coal lift up to fly. Jb 39:27. Pr 26:2. Ob 4.

8 **seek**. Jb 8:5. 22:21, 27. Ge 32:7-12. 2 Ch 33:12, 13. Ps +50:15. 77:1, 2. 116:3, 4. Jon 2:1-7.
unto God. Ps 37:5. 2 T 1:12. 1 P 2:23. 4:19.

9 **doeth**. Da +4:3.
unsearchable. Heb. there is no search. Jb +11:7.
marvellous. Jb 26:5-14.
without number. Heb. till there be no number. Ps 40:5. 139:18.

10 **giveth**. Jb 28:26. Ps 65:9-11. 104:13. 147:8. Je 5:24. 10:13. 14:22. 51:16. Am 4:7. Mt 5:45. Ac 14:17.
fields. Heb. outplaces. Jb 18:17. 31:32. 38:26-28. Am +5:16.

11 **set up**. 1 S 2:7, 8. Ps 91:14. 107:41. 113:7, 8. Ezk 17:24. Lk 1:52, 53.
those. Lk 6:21. Ja 1:9. 4:6-10. 1 P 5:10.
exalted. Dt 33:27-29. 1 P 1:3.

12 **disappointeth**. Ps 37:17. Je +19:7.
their hands. Ps 21:11. 76:5. Is 37:36. Ac 12:11. 23:12, etc.
their enterprise. or, any thing.

13 **taketh**. Jb +4:8. 2 S 15:31, 34. 17:23. Est 6:4-11. Ps 35:7, 8. 141:10. Da 6:24. Lk 1:51. 1 C *1:19, 20, 27. 3:19, 20.*
of the froward. Ps 18:26. Pr 3:32. 8:13.

14 **meet with**. or, run into. Ge 32:17. 33:8. Ex 4:24.
darkness. Jb 12:25. Dt 28:29. Pr 4:19. Is 59:10. Am 8:9.
grope. Jb 12:25. Ge 27:12, 22. 31:34mg, 37mg. Ex 10:21.

15 **he saveth**. Ps 107:41. +140:12.

16 **the poor**. Ps 9:18. Is 14:32. Zc 9:12. Lk +4:18.
and iniquity. Ps +107:42.

17 **happy**. Jb 34:31, 32. Ps 94:12. 119:75. Pr 3:11, 12. Je 31:18-20. He 12:5-11. Ja 1:12. 5:11. Re 3:19.
despise not. Pr 24:10. He 12:5.
chastening. Jb 34:31, 32.
Almighty. Jb 6:4, 14. 8:3, 5. 11:7. 13:3. 15:25. 21:15, 20. 22:3, 17, 23, 25, 26. 23:16. 24:1. 27:2, 10, 11, 13. 29:5. 31:2, 35. 32:8. 33:4. 34:10, 12. 35:13. 37:23. 40:2. Ge +49:25.

18 **he maketh sore**. Dt +32:39. 1 S 2:6, 7. Ps 147:3. Is 30:26.
bindeth up. Ex 15:26. Ps 147:3. Is 30:26. 61:1. Ho 6:1.
hands. Mk +5:23.
make whole. Ps +103:2, 3. Is 12:3.

19 **deliver thee**. Ps +34:19. 91:3-7. 1 C 10:13.
in seven. Jb 2:13. Pr 24:16. Is 4:1.
no evil. Ps 91:7-10.

20 **famine**. Ge 45:7-11. 1 K 17:6, 9, 14, 15. Ps +37:3. Hab 3:17, 18.
redeem. Ps 49:7, 15. 103:4. Ho 13:14.
in war. Ps 27:3. 60:12. 91:5. Is 41:11, 12. Je 39:17, 18. Mt 24:6.

power. Heb. hands. Ps 63:10mg.
the sword. Le 26:6.

21 **be hid**. Jb 11:15. Ps 31:20. 37:6. 55:21. 57:3,
4. Pr 12:18. Is 54:17. Je 18:18. Ja 3:5-8.
from the scourge. *or*, when the tongue
scourgeth. Jb 9:23. Ps 31:20.
neither. Ps 91:5-7.

22 **famine**. Ge 45:7. 1 K 17:6, 15, 16. Ps 33:18,
19.
laugh. Ge +21:6. 2 K 19:21.
afraid. Le +26:6. Ps 91:5-7. Is 11:9. 65:25. Da
6:22.

23 **thou**. Ps 91:12, 13. Ro 8:38, 39.
beasts. ver. +22.

24 **thou shalt know**. Jb 18:6, 15, 21. 21:7-9. 1
S 30:3. Is 4:5, 6.
thy tabernacle, etc. *or*, peace is thy tabernacle. Ps 25:13mg.
thou shalt visit. Dt 28:6. Ps 91:10. 121:7, 8.
or, inspect. Jb 7:18. 31:14.
sin. *or*, err. Ps 107:4, 40. +130:8.

25 **thy seed**. Jb 42:13-16. Ge 15:5. Le 26:9. Dt
28:4. Ps 112:2. 127:3-5. 128:3-6.
great. *or*, much. or, numerous.
as the grass. Ps 72:16. Is 44:3, 4.

26 **grave**. Heb. *qeber*, Ge +23:4.
in a full age. Jb 42:16, 17. Ge 15:15. +25:8.
Ex +23:26.
cometh. Heb. ascendeth. Jb 36:20. Ge
32:24mg.

27 **we have searched**. Jb 8:8-10. 12:2. 13:2.
15:9, 10, 17. 32:11, 12. Ps 111:2. Pr 2:3-5.
for thy good. Heb. for thyself. Jb 22:2. Dt
10:13. Pr 9:12.

JOB 6

1 **answered**. Jb 4:1.

2 **throughly**. Jb 4:5. 23:2. 31:6.
laid. Heb. lifted up. Is 40:15.

3 **heavier**. Pr 27:3. Mt 11:28.
than. Ge +22:17.
my words are swallowed up. *that is*, I want
words to express my grief. Jb 37:19, 20. Ps
40:5. 77:4.

4 **the arrows**. Jb 16:12-14. Dt +32:23, 42.
drinketh up. Dt 32:24. Ps 143:7. Pr 18:14.
Mk 14:33, 34. 15:34.
spirit. Heb. *ruach*, Ge +41:8.
the terrors. Jb 9:17. 30:15. 31:23. Ps 88:15,
16. 2 C 5:11.

5 **when he hath grass**. Heb. at grass. Ps
104:14.
loweth. Ps 42:1. Je 14:6. Jl 1:18-20.

6 **that which**. ver. 25. Jb 16:2. Le 2:13. Ps
107:18. Lk 14:34. Col 4:6.
without salt. Mt 5:13. Mk 9:50.
taste. ver. 30. Jb 12:11. 34:3. Ps 119:103. He
6:4, 5.

7 **soul**. Heb. *nephesh*, Nu +11:6.

as my sorrowful meat. 1 K 17:12. 22:27. Ps
102:9. Ezk 4:14, 16. 12:18, 19. Da 10:3.

8 **O that**. Jb 14:13.
might have. Ps +27:7. 37:4.
the thing that I long for. Heb. my expectation. ver. 11-13. Jb 17:14-16. Ps 119:81.

9 **that it would**. Jb 3:20-22. 7:15, 16. 14:13.
Nu 11:14, 15. 1 K 19:4. Jon 4:3, 8. Re 9:6.
that he would. Jb 19:21. Ps 32:4. Is 38:10-13.

10 **Then**. Jb 3:22. 21:33.
I would. Jb 9:4.
let him not. Dt 29:20. Ro 8:32. 2 P 2:4, 5.
have not concealed. Jb 23:12. Ps 37:30.
71:17, 18. Ac +20:20.
the Holy One. Ps +99:3. Is +1:4.

11 **What**. Jb 7:5-7. 10:20. 13:25, 28. 17:1, 14-16.
Ps 39:5. 90:5-10. 102:23. 103:14-16.
life. Heb. *nephesh*, soul, Ge +44:30.

12 **of brass**. Heb. brasen. Jb 40:18. 41:24.

13 **Is not my**. Jb 19:28. 2 C 1:12. Ga 6:4.
and is wisdom. Jb 12:2, 3. 13:2.

14 **To him**. Jb 4:3, 4. 16:5. 19:21. Le +25:35. 2 S
16:17. Ps 35:14, 15. Pr 17:17. Ro 12:15. 1 C
12:26. 2 C 11:29. Ga 6:2. Ph 4:14. He 13:3.
is afflicted. Heb. melteth. Dt 20:8.
he forsaketh. Ge 20:11. Ps 36:1-3. Lk 23:40.
He +3:12, 13.

15 **My brethren**. Jb 19:19. Ps 38:11. 41:9.
55:12-14. 88:18. Je 9:4, 5. 30:14. Mi 7:5, 6. Jn
13:18. 16:32.
as the stream. Je 15:18. Ju 12.

16 **blackish**. Jb 5:15 (mourn). 30:28. Ps 35:14
(heavily).
ice. Jb 37:10. 38:29. Ge 31:40. Ps 147:17. Je
36:30. Ezk 1:22.
snow. Jb 37:6. 1 Ch 11:22. Ps 147:18.
is hid. Dt 22:1, 3. Ps 55:1. Is 58:2.

17 **vanish**. Heb. are cut off. Jb 23:17.
when it is hot they are consumed. Heb. in
the heat thereof they are extinguished. Jb
24:19. 1 K 17:1, 7.

18 **The paths**. Is 3:12.
are turned. Jg 16:29. Ru 3:8mg.
nothing. Jb 12:24. 26:7. Ge 1:2. Is 40:23.
perish. Jb 3:3. 4:7, 9, 11, 20. 8:13.

19 **troops**. Jb 31:32.
Tema. Ge +25:15. +47:15.
looked. Jb 28:24. 35:5. 36:25. 39:29.
companies. lit. goings. Jb 29:6. Ps 68:24. Pr
31:27. Na 2:5. Hab 3:6.
Sheba. Jb 1:15. 1 K +10:1.
waited. or, hoped. Jb 3:9. 7:2. 17:13. 30:26.

20 **confounded**. Je 14:3, 4. 17:13. Ro 5:5. 9:33.
ashamed. Ps 34:5.

21 **ye are nothing**. *or*, ye are like to them. Heb.
to it. ver. 15. Jb 13:4. Ps 62:9. Is 2:22. Je 17:5,
6.
nothing. Heb. not. Da 4:35. Ga 2:6.
ye see. Jb 2:11-13. Ps 38:11. Pr 19:7. Je 51:9.
Mt 26:31, 56. 2 T 4:16. Re 18:9, 10, 17, 18.

22 **Bring unto me**. Jb 42:11. 1 S 12:3. Ac 20:33.
reward. Jb 15:34. Ezk 16:33.

23 **Redeem**. Jb 5:20. Le 25:48. Ne 5:8. Ps 49:7, 8, 15. 107:2. Je 15:21.

24 **Teach me**. Jb 5:27. 32:11, 15, 16. 33:1, 31-33. 34:32. Ps +25:9. 32:8. 39:1. Pr 9:9. 25:12. Ja 1:19.
I will. Jb 2:10. 33:3. Ps +39:1, 2. 141:3. Pr 10:19. 11:12. 17:27, 28. Ec +5:2. Mt 6:7. Ja 3:2.
cause me. Jb 10:2. Ps 19:7, 12. 119:11, 99, 104, 105, 130. Pr +8:8, 9. Mk 12:24.
erred. Jb 19:4. Le 4:13. Is +29:24.

25 **forcible**. Jb 4:4. 16:5. Pr 12:18. 16:21-24. 18:21. 25:11. Ec 12:10, 11.
what doth. Jb 13:5. 16:3, 4. 21:34. 24:25. 32:3.

26 **reprove**. Jb 2:10. 3:3, etc. 4:3, 4. 34:3-9. 38:2. 40:5, 8. 42:3, 7. Mt 12:37.
one that. ver. 4, 9. Jb 10:1.
as wind. Jb 8:2. Ho 12:1. Ep 4:14.

27 **overwhelm**. Heb. cause to fall upon. Ge 2:21. 1 Ch 24:31. Est 6:10mg. Ps 22:18. Ezk 47:22. 48:29. Jon 1:7.
the fatherless. Ex +22:22.
ye dig. Ps 7:15. 57:6. Je 18:20, 22.

28 **evident unto you**. Heb. before your face.
if I lie. Jb 11:3. 13:4. 34:6. Nu 23:19.

29 **Return**. Jb 17:10. Ml 3:18.
my righteousness. Jb 27:4-6.
in it. *that is*, in this matter. Jb 13:18. 23:10. 34:5.

30 **iniquity**. Jb 33:8-12. 42:3-6.
cannot. ver. 6. Jb 12:11. 34:3. He 5:14.
taste. Heb. palate. Jb 29:10. +31:30mg.
discern. Ml 3:18.
perverse things. Ps 5:9. La 1:7mg.

JOB 7

1 **Is there**. Jb 14:5, 13, 14. 2 K 8:9, 10. 20:6. Ps 39:4. Is 38:5. Jn 11:9, 10.
an appointed time. *or*, a warfare. Jb 10:17. 14:1, 3, 5, 6, 14. 1 Ch +20:1. Ec 8:8. He 9:27.
like the days. Jb 14:6. Le 25:50. Dt 15:18. Is 21:16. Mt 20:1-15.

2 **earnestly desireth**. Heb. gapeth after. Ps 119:131. 143:6. Ec +2:23. Is +42:14mg. Am 2:7.
the shadow. Je 6:4.
as an hireling. Le +19:13. Dt +24:15. Ml +3:5. Ja +5:4.

3 **months of**. Jb 29:2. Ps 6:6. 39:5. Ec 1:14.
wearisome. Jb 30:17. Dt 28:67. Ps 42:3. Ec +2:23. *La 1:2*, 16.

4 **When**. ver. 13, 14. Jb 17:12. 30:17. Dt 28:67. Ps 6:6. 77:4. 130:6.
night, etc. Heb. evening be measured. Jb 4:12. 28:25. Ro 13:12.
tossings. Jb 15:23. Ps 109:23. Is 54:11.

5 **flesh**. Jb 2:7, 8. 17:14. +19:26. 24:20. 30:18, 19. Ps 38:5-7. Is 1:6. 14:11. Ac 12:23.
loathsome. Jb 9:31. Is +66:24. Ezk 20:43.

6 **swifter**. Jb 9:25. 10:20. 16:22. 17:11. Ps 90:5, 6. 102:11. 103:15, 16. 144:4. Is 38:11-13. 40:6, 7. Ja 1:11. 4:14. 1 P 1:24.
without hope. Jb 6:11. 17:15. Pr 14:32. Is 38:11. Je 2:25. Ep 2:12. 1 Th 4:13. 1 P 1:13.

7 **remember**. Jb 10:9. Ge 42:36. Ne 1:8. Ps 74:18, 22. 89:47, 50. Je 15:15.
my life. Ps 78:39. Ja 4:14.
no more see. Heb. not return to see, *that is*, to enjoy. Jb +10:21, 22. Ps 39:13.

8 **The eye**. Jb 20:9. Ps 37:36.
thine eyes. Jb 13:27. 14:3. Ps 39:11. 90:8, 9.
I am not. *that is*, I can live no longer. ver. +9, 21.

9 **the cloud**. Jb 37:11.
vanisheth. Ja 4:14.
he that. Jb 10:21. 14:10-14. 16:22. 2 S 12:23. 14:14. Ps 39:13. Is 38:11.
goeth down. Ge 37:35.
grave. Heb. *sheol*, Ge +37:35.
come up no more. ver. 8, 10. 10:21. +16:22. Ps 39:13. He +9:27.

10 **shall return**. ver. 8, +9. Jb 8:18. 20:9. Ps 103:16.

11 **I will not**. Jb 6:26. 10:1. 13:13. 16:6. 21:3. Ps 39:3. 40:9.
the anguish. Ge 42:21. 2 K 4:27, 28. Mt 26:37, 38. Lk 22:44. 2 C 2:4.
spirit. Heb. *ruach*, Ge +41:8.
the bitterness. Jb 10:1, 15. 21:25. 1 S +1:10mg. 2 K +4:27mg. Is 38:15, 17.
soul. Heb. *nephesh*, Ge +34:3.

12 **Am I a sea**. ver. 17. Jb 38:6-11. La 3:7.
a whale. Jb 41:1, etc.

13 **My bed**. ver. 3, 4. Jb 9:27, 28. Ps 6:6. 77:4.

14 **thou scarest**. Ge 40:5-7. 41:8. Jg 7:13, 14. Ec +2:23. Da 2:1. Mt 27:19.

15 **soul**. Heb. *nephesh*, Ge +12:13.
chooseth. 2 S 17:23. Na 2:12. Mt 27:5.
death. 1 K 19:4.
life. Heb. bones. Jb 19:20.

16 **I loathe it**. Jb 3:20-22. 6:9. 10:1. Ge 27:46. 1 K 19:4. Jon 4:3, 8.
alway. Heb. *olam*, Ge +6:3.
let me alone. Jb 10:20. 14:6. Ps 39:10, 13.
my days. Ps 62:9. 78:33. 144:4. Ec 6:11, 12.

17 **What is man**. Ps +8:4.
magnify. ver. 12. 1 S 24:14.
set thine. Jb 34:14, 15.

18 **visit**. Ex 20:5. 32:34. Is 26:14. 27:3. 38:12, 13.
every morning. Ps 73:14. 101:8. Ec 11:6. Is 33:2. La 3:23.
try. *Ge* 22:1. Dt 8:16. Je 9:7. Da 12:10. Zc 13:9. 1 P 1:7.

19 **How long**. Jb 9:18. Ps 6:3. 13:1-3. 80:4. 94:3. Re 6:10.

20 **I have sinned**. Jb 9:29-31. 13:26. 14:16, 17.
22:5. 31:33. 33:9, 27. Ps 80:4.
O thou preserver. Ne 9:6. Ps +36:6.
why hast. ver. 12. Jb 6:4. 16:12-14. Ps 21:12.
La 3:12.
I am. ver. 11. Jb 3:24.
21 **why dost**. Jb 9:28. 10:14. 13:23, 24. Is 64:9.
La 3:42-44. 5:20-22.
take away. 2 S 24:10. Ho 14:2. Mi 7:18, 19.
Jn 1:29. T 2:14. 1 J 1:9. 3:5.
sleep. Jb 3:13. 10:9. 17:14. 20:11. 21:26, 32,
33. Ps 104:29. Ec +12:7. Is +26:19. Da +12:2.
seek me. Jb 8:5. 24:5. Pr 1:28.
in the morning. ver. 18. Re +2:28.
but I shall not be. ver. 8, +9. Ps 37:36.
103:15.

JOB 8

1 **Bildad**. Jb +2:11.
2 **How long**. Jb 11:2. 16:3. Mt +17:17.
the words. Jb 6:9, 26. 7:11. 15:2. 1 K 19:11.
3 **God**. Jb 4:17. 9:2. 10:3. 19:7. 34:5, 12, 17-19.
40:8. Ge +18:25. Dt 32:4. 2 Ch 19:7. Ps 89:14.
Ezk +18:25. 33:17, 20. Da 9:14. Ro 2:5. 3:4-6.
or doth. Jb +4:17.
Almighty. Jb +5:17. Ps 99:4. Re 15:3. 16:7.
4 **he have cast**. Jb 1:5, 18, 19. 5:4. 18:16-19.
Ge 13:13. 19:13-25.
for their transgression. Heb. in the hand of
their transgression. Is 64:7mg.
5 **thou wouldest**. Jb 5:8. 11:13. 22:21-23, etc.
2 Ch 33:12, 13. Je +29:13. He 3:7, 8.
betimes. Jb 7:21. Ps 63:1. 78:34. Pr 1:28.
8:17. Is 26:9. Ho 5:15.
supplication. Jb 9:15. 19:16. Ge 42:21.
6 **thou wert**. Jb 1:8. 4:6, 7. 21:14, 15. 16:17. Ps
26:5, 6. Pr 15:8. Is 1:15-19. 1 T 2:8. 1 J 3:19-22.
he would. Ps +3:7.
make. Jb 22:23-30. Is 3:10.
7 **thy beginning**. Jb 42:12, 13. Pr +4:18. Zc
4:10. Mt 13:12, 31, 32.
thy latter. Dt 8:16. Pr 19:20. Zc 14:7. 2 P
2:20.
8 **enquire**. Jb 12:12. 15:10, 18. 32:6, 7. Dt
4:32. 32:7. Ps 44:1. 78:3, 4. Is 38:19. Ro 15:4.
1 C 10:11.
9 **we are but**. Jb 7:6. Ge 47:9. 1 Ch 29:15. Ps
39:5. 90:4. 102:11. 144:4.
nothing. Heb. not.
a shadow. Jb 14:2.
10 **Shall not**. Jb 12:7, 8. 32:7. Dt 6:7. 11:19. Ps
145:4. Is 38:19. He 11:4. 12:1.
utter words. Pr 16:23. 18:15. Mt 12:35.
their heart. Nu +16:28.
11 **the rush**. Ex 2:3. Is 19:5-7.
12 **yet in**. Ps 129:6, 7. Je 17:6. Mt 13:20. Ja 1:10,
11. 1 P 1:24.
13 **that forget God**. Dt 6:12. 8:11, 14, 19. Ps
9:17. 10:4. 50:22. Is 51:13.

the hypocrite's. Jb 13:16. 15:34. 17:8. 20:5.
27:8-10. 34:30. 36:13. Ps 35:16. Pr 11:9. Is
9:17. 10:6. 29:20. 32:6. 33:14. Mt +6:2. 24:51.
Lk +12:1, 2.
hope. Jb 11:20. 18:14. Pr 10:28. 11:7. 12:7. Is
33:14. +38:18. La 3:18, 64, 65. Ezk 22:14. Mt
+25:46. Lk +16:26.
shall perish. Jb +36:18. Ps 36:12. 112:10. Pr
+10:28. He +9:27.
14 **web**. Heb. house. Is 59:5, 6.
15 **it shall not stand**. Jb 18:14. 27:18. Ps 52:5-
7. 112:10. Pr 10:28. Mt 7:24-27. Lk 6:47-49.
16 **green**. Jb 21:7-15. Ps 37:35, 36. 73:3-12.
his branch. Jb 5:3.
17 **roots**. Jb 18:16. 29:19. Is 5:24. 40:24. Je 12:1,
2. Mk 11:20. Ju 12.
18 **he**. Jb 7:10. 20:9. Ps 37:10, 36. 73:18, 19.
92:7.
from his place. Jb 7:8. 27:21.
saying. Jb 15:23. 32:17. Ex 18:4.
19 **this is the joy**. Jb 20:5. Mt 13:20, 21.
out of the earth. 1 S 2:8. Ps 75:7. 113:7. Ezk
17:24. Mt 3:9.
20 **not cast away**. Jb 4:7. 9:22. Ps 37:24, 37.
94:14.
a perfect. Jb +1:1.
help the evil doers. Heb. take the ungodly
by the hand. 2 Ch +19:2. Is 45:1. 51:18.
21 **laughing**. Ge +21:6.
rejoicing. Heb. shouting for joy. Ezr 3:11-13.
Ne 12:43. Ps 32:11. 98:4. 100:1. Is 65:13, 14.
22 **clothed**. Ps 35:26. 109:29. 132:18. 1 P 5:5.
dwelling place. Jb 5:24. 11:14. 12:6. 15:34.
18:14. 21:28.
come to nought. Heb. not be. ver. 18. Jb
7:21. 24:24mg.

JOB 9

2 **it is so**. Jb 8:20.
of a truth. Jb 12:2.
how should. Jb 4:17. 32:2. 33:9. 34:5. Ps
40:12. Pr +20:9. Ro 3:20. 5:1.
with. *or*, before.
God. Heb. *El*, Ex +15:2.
3 **he will contend**. ver. 20, 32, 33. Jb 10:2.
23:3-7. 31:35-37. 33:13. 34:14, 15. 40:2. Is
57:15, 16. Ro 9:20.
he cannot. Ps 19:12. 40:12. 1 J 1:8. 3:20.
thousand. Jb 33:23.
4 **wise in heart**. ver. 19. Jb 36:5. 2 S 22:28. Ps
104:24. 136:5. Pr 16:18. Da 2:20. 4:34-37.
5:20. Ro 11:33. Ep 1:8, 19. 3:10, 20. Ju 24,
25.
who hath hardened. Jb 6:10. 15:23-27.
40:9. Ex 9:14-17. 14:17, 18. Pr 28:14. 29:1.
Da 5:20-30. 1 C 10:22. He 3:7, 12, 13.
5 **removeth**. Jb 28:9. 46:2. 68:8. 114:6. Is
40:12. Hab 3:6, 10. Zc 4:7. Mt 21:21. 1 C 13:2.
Re 6:14. 11:13.

which overturneth. Na 1:5, 6. Zc 14:4, 5. Mt 27:51. Lk 21:11. Re 16:18-20.

6 **shaketh**. He +12:26. Re 20:11.
the pillars. Jb +26:11. 38:4-7. Ps +97:4. Jl 2:10.

7 **commandeth**. Ex 10:21, 22. Jsh 10:12-14. Da 4:35. Am 4:13. 8:9. Mt 24:29.
sealeth. Jb 37:7. 38:12-15, 19, 20. Is 13:10. Ezk 32:7. Lk 21:25, 26.

8 **Which**. Ge 1:6, 7. Ps 33:6. Is +40:22.
treadeth. Jb 38:11. Ps 77:19. 93:3, 4. Mt 14:25-30. Jn 6:19.
waves. Heb. heights. Le 26:30. Nu 21:28. Is 14:14.

9 **maketh**. Jb 38:31, 32, etc. Ge 1:16. Ps 147:4. Am 5:8.
Arcturus. Heb. *Ash*. lit. *moth*. i.e. *consuming; gathering*, **S#5906h**. ver. 9. Jb 38:32.
Orion. Heb. *Cesil*. lit. *fool; burly one*, **S#3685h**. ver. 9. Jb 38:31. Is 13:10 (constellations). Am 5:8.
Pleiades. Heb. *Cimah*. i.e. *to sail; for what*, **S#3598h**. ver. 9. Jb 38:31. Am 5:8 (seven stars).
chambers of. Jb 37:9mg. Ps 104:3, 13. Ac 28:13.

10 **great things**. Ps 71:15. Je 33:3. Ep 3:20.
past. Jb +11:7.
wonders. Da +4:3.
without number. Jb 1:5. 3:6. 5:9. 14:5.

11 **he goeth**. Jb 23:8, 9. 35:14. Ps 77:19. 1 T 6:16.

12 **he taketh**. Jb 34:29. Is +14:27.
hinder him. Heb. turn him away. Jb 11:10.
What. Jb 33:13. Is 45:9. Je 18:6. Mt 11:26. 20:15. Ro 9:18-20. 11:34.

13 **the proud helpers**. Heb. the helpers of pride, *or* strength. Jb 26:12. 40:9-11. Ps 89:10mg. Is 30:7. 31:2, 3. 51:9. Ja 4:6, 7.

14 **How much**. Jb 4:19. 25:6. 1 K 8:27.
shall I. Jb 11:4, 5.
choose. Jb 7:15. 15:5. 23:4, 7. 29:25. 33:5.

15 **though**. Jb 10:15. 1 C 4:4.
I would. Jb 5:8. 8:5. 10:2. 22:27. 34:31, 32. 1 K 8:38, 39. 2 Ch 33:13. Je 31:9. Da 9:3, 18.
my judge. Jb 23:7. 1 P 2:23.

16 **If I had**. Ps 18:6. 66:18-20. 116:1, 2.
would I. Jb 29:24. Ex 6:9. Jg 6:13. Ps 126:1. Lk 24:41. Ac 12:14-16.

17 **For he**. Jb 16:14. Ps 29:5. 42:7. +83:15. Mt 12:20.
multiplieth. Jb 1:14-19. 2:7, 13.
without cause. Jb 2:3. 16:17. 34:6. Ps 25:3. Jn 9:3. 15:25.

18 **will not**. Jb 7:19. Ps 39:13. 88:7, 15-18. La 3:3, 18.
to take. Est 4:14.
breath. Ge +6:17.
filleth me. Jb 3:20. La 3:15, 19. He 12:11.
bitterness. 1 S +1:10mg.

19 **he is strong**. ver. +4. Jb 36:17-19. 40:9, 10.

Ps 62:11. Mt 6:13. 1 C 1:25. 10:22.
who shall. ver. 32, 33. Jb 31:35. 33:5-7.

20 **justify**. ver. 2. Jb 4:17. 32:1, 2. Ps 130:3. 143:2. Lk 10:29. 16:15. 18:14.
mine. Lk 15:5, 6. 34:35. 35:16. Pr 10:19. Is 6:5. Mt 12:36, 37. Ja 3:2.
I am perfect. Mt +5:48. 1 J 1:8, 10.
it shall. Jb 33:8-13. Pr 17:20. 1 T 6:5.

21 **yet would**. Ps 139:23, 24. Pr 28:26. Je 17:9, 10. 1 C 4:4. 1 J 3:20.
soul. Heb. *nephesh*, Ge +34:3.
I would. Jb 7:15, 16, 21.

22 **I said**. Jb 38:2. 40:2. 42:3.
He destroyeth. Jb 10:8. Ge 18:23, 25. Le 26:16. Je 14:12. Mi 1:4. Na 1:5. Zc 14:4. Re 6:14. 16:20.
the perfect. Is 57:1, 2. Ezk 18:9, 19.
and. Jb 3:19. Ps 73:2. Ec 9:1-3. Je 12:1. Ezk 21:3, 4. Am +3:6. Mt 5:45. Lk 13:2-4.
the wicked. Jb 42:7-9. Ezk 33:19. Lk 13:3. Jn 9:3.

23 **If the**. Jb 1:13-19. 2:7.
he will. Jb 4:7. 8:20. 2 S 24:15, 17. Ps 44:22. Ezk 14:19-21. 21:13. He 11:36, 37.

24 **earth**. Jb 12:6-10. 21:7-15. Ps 17:14. 73:3-7. Je 12:1, 2. Dt 4:17. 5:18-21. 7:7, etc. Hab 1:14-17.
is given. Da 4:17.
he covereth. Est +6:12.
if not. Jb 24:25. 32:2.

25 **swifter**. Jb 7:6, 7.
a post. 1 S 20:36. 22:17mg. 2 Ch 30:6. Est 8:14.
they flee away. Ps 39:5, 11. 89:47. 90:9, 10. Ja 4:14.

26 **swift ships**. Heb. ships of desire, *or*, ships of Ebeh. or, reed *or* enmity. Ex 2:3. Is 18:2.
as the eagle. Jb 39:27-30. 2 S 1:23. Pr 23:5. Je 4:13. La 4:19. Hab 1:8.

27 **If I say**. Jb 7:13.
my complaint. Jb 7:11. 10:1. 21:4. 23:2. 1 S 1:10. Ps 77:2, 3.
comfort. Jb 10:20. Ps 39:13. Je 8:18. Am 5:9.

28 **afraid**. Jb 21:6. Ps 88:15, 16. 119:120. Je 8:18.
I know. ver. 2, 20, 21. Jb 14:16, 17. Ex 20:7. Ps 130:3.

29 **be wicked**. ver. +22. Jb 10:7, 14-17. 21:16, 17, 27. 22:5, etc. Ge 15:6. Ps 73:13. Je 2:35.
in vain. Jb 7:16. 21:34. 27:12. 35:16. He 6:10.

30 **wash**. **S#7364h**, +Ex 29:4. Jb 14:4. 1 K 8:36. Ps 26:6. 51:7. Pr 20:9. 28:13. Is 1:16-18. 64:6. Je 2:22. 4:14. Ro 10:3. 1 J 1:8.

31 **shalt**. ver. 20. Jb 15:6.
plunge. or, dip. Heb. *tabal*, **S#2881h**. Ge 37:31. Ex +12:22 (**S#2881h**). Le 9:9. 1 S 14:27. 2 K 5:14. 8:15.
ditch. **S#7845h**. *shachath*, "pit," "ditch," "corruption," "grave." ver. 31. Jb 17:14 (corrup-

tion). 33:18 (pit), 22 (grave), 24, 28, 30. Ps 7:15 (ditch). 9:15. 16:10 (corruption). 30:9. 35:7. 49:9. 55:23 (destruction). 94:13. 103:4. Pr 26:27. Is 38:17 (pit). 51:14. Ezk 19:4, 8. 28:8. Jon 2:6 (corruption; mg, pit). For **S#6900h**, *qeburah*, grave, see Ge +35:20. For **S#6913h**, *qeber*, "grave," "burying place," see Ge +23:4. For **S#7585h**, *sheol*, see Ge +37:35.

mine. Is 59:6. 64:6. Ph 3:8, 9.

abhor me. *or*, make me to be abhorred. Jb 19:19. 30:10. Dt 7:26.

32 not a man. Jb 33:12. 35:5-7. Nu 23:19. 1 S 16:7. Ec 6:10. Is 45:9. Je 49:19. Ro 9:20. 1 J 3:20.

we should. Jb 13:18-23. 23:3-7. Ps 143:2.

33 is there. ver. 19. 1 S 2:25. Ps 106:23. 1 J 2:1, 2.

daysman. Heb. one that should argue, *or*, umpire. lit. a reasoner. Jb 32:12. 40:2. 1 S 2:25. Is 1:18.

that might. 1 K 3:16, etc.

lay. Ps 139:5.

his hand. Jb 13:21.

34 take his rod. La 3:1-8.

let not. Jb 13:11, 20-22. 23:15. 31:23. 33:7. 37:1. Ps 39:10. 90:11.

35 Then would. Jb 13:22.

but it is not so with me. Heb. but I am not so with myself. Jb 29:2, etc.

JOB 10

1 My soul. Heb. *nephesh*, Ge +34:3. Jb 3:20-23. 6:8, 9. 7:15, 16, 20. 9:21. 14:13. Nu 11:15. 1 K 19:4. Jon 4:3, 8.

is weary of my life. *or*, cut off while I live. Jb 8:14. Ps 95:10.

I will leave. Jb 7:11. 19:4. 21:2-4.

upon myself. Jb 30:16.

I will speak. ver. 15, 16. Jb 6:2-4, 26. 7:11. 16:6-16. Ps 32:3-5. Is 38:15, 17.

bitterness. Jb 7:11. 1 S +1:10mg. 2 K +4:27mg.

soul. Heb. *nephesh*, Ge +34:3.

2 Do not. Ps 6:1-4. 25:7. 38:1-8. 109:21. 143:2. Ro 8:1.

show me. Jb 8:5, 6. 34:31, 32. Ps 139:23, 24. La 3:40-42. 5:16, 17. 1 C 11:31, 32.

3 Is it good. Jb 34:5-7, 18, 19. 36:7-9, 17, 18. 40:2, 8. La 3:2-18.

despise. Ps 69:33.

the work. Heb. the labor. Jb 14:15. 34:19. Ps 138:8. Is 64:8. 1 P 4:19.

shine upon. Jb 8:20. Je 12:1-3.

4 seest thou. Jb 9:32. 1 S 16:7. Lk 16:15. Re 1:14.

5 thy days as. Ps 90:2-4. 102:12, 24-27. He 1:12. 2 P 3:8.

6 thou inquirest. ver. 14-17. Ps 10:15. 44:21. Je 2:34. Zp 1:12. Jn +2:24, 25. 1 C 4:5.

7 thou knowest. Heb. It is upon thy knowledge. Jb 23:10. 31:6, 14, 35. 42:7. Ps 1:6. 7:3, 8, 9. 17:3. 26:1-5. 139:1, 2, 21-24. Jn 21:17. 2 C 1:12. 1 Th 2:10.

and there. Jb 23:13, 14. Dt +32:39. Ps 50:22. Da 3:15. Ho 2:10. Jn +10:27-30.

8 hands. Nu +11:23. Ps 119:73. Is 43:7.

have made me. Heb. took pains about me. or, grieved me. Ps 56:5. Is 63:10.

yet thou. ver. 3. Ge 6:6, 7. Je 18:3-10.

9 Remember. Jb 7:7. Ps 25:6, 7, 18. 89:47. 106:4.

thou hast. Ge +2:7. +3:19. Is 45:9. 64:8. Je 18:6.

into dust again. Jb 17:14. Ps 22:15. 90:3. Ec 12:7. Ro 9:21.

10 poured. Jb 3:24. 2 K 22:9. Ps 139:14-16.

11 clothed. 2 C 5:2, 3.

fenced. Heb. hedged. Jb 1:10. 40:17, 18. Ezk 37:4-8. Ho 2:6. Ep 4:16.

12 life and favor. Ge 19:19. Mt 6:25. Ac 17:25, 28.

spirit. Heb. *ruach*, Ge +41:8.

13 hid. Jb 23:9. Ec 8:6, 7. Is 45:15. Ro 11:33.

I know. Jb 23:13. Dt +32:39. Is 45:7. 46:9-11. La 3:37. Ep 3:11.

14 then. Jb 13:26, 27. 14:16, 17. Ps 130:3. 139:1.

thou wilt. Jb 7:21. Ex 34:6, 7. Nu 14:18.

15 If I be wicked. ver. 7. Jb 9:29. 27:7. Ps 9:17. Is 3:11. 6:5. Ml 3:18. Ro 2:8, 9.

righteous. Jb 9:12, 15, 20, 21. Is 64:5, 6. Lk 17:10.

I am full. Jb 21:6. 23:15.

see. Ex 3:7, 8. Ps 25:18. 119:153. La 1:20. 5:1, etc.

16 Thou huntest. Is +5:29.

marvelous. Nu 16:29, 30. Dt 28:59.

17 witnesses. *that is*, plagues. Jb 16:8. Ge 31:44. Ru 1:21. Ml +3:5.

changes. Jb 14:14. Ge 45:22. Jg 14:12. 2 K 5:22. Ps 55:19. Je 48:11. Zp 1:12.

war. Jb +7:1. 14:14. 16:11-16. 19:6-11.

18 hast thou. Jb 3:10, 11. Je 15:10. 20:14-18. Mt 26:24.

given up. Jb 11:20. 14:10.

ghost. Ge +49:33.

19 as though. Ps 58:8.

not been. Ob 16.

womb. Jb 1:21. 3:10, 11. 15:2 (belly), 35.

grave. Heb. *qeber*, Ge +23:4. Jb 3:3. Je 15:10.

20 my days few. Jb 7:6, 7, 16. 8:9. 9:25, 26. 14:1. Ps 39:5. 103:15, 16.

cease. Jb 7:17-21. 13:21. Ps 39:13.

21 I go whence. Jb +7:8-10. 14:10-14. Is 38:11.

not return. Jb +16:22. 2 S 12:23. 14:14.

the land. Ps 88:6, 11, 12. Mt +4:16.

the shadow. Ps +23:4.

22 darkness. or, obscurity. Jb 3:5. Ps 88:6, 11, 12. Pr 1:12. 15:24. Is 14:9. Am 4:13. Lk 16:23.

as darkness. or, thick darkness. Jb 3:6. 23:17. 28:3.

the shadow of death. Ps +23:4. 88:12. Lk 16:26.

without any order. S#5468h. Only here. "arrangement; order;" disorder, confusion, of the dark underworld (Gesenius). Ge 1:2 with Is 45:18. Lk 16:23, 24. 1 C 14:33, 40.

where light is as. Ps 91:6. Mt 6:23. Lk 11:35. 16:27-31.

JOB 11

1 **Zophar**. Jb +2:11. 20:1.

2 **the multitude**. Jb 16:3. 18:2. Ps 140:11. Pr 10:19. Ac 17:18. Ja 1:19.

full of talk. Heb. of lips. Jg +7:22mg.

3 **thy lies**. or, thy devices. Jb 13:4. 15:2, 3. 24:25.

mockest. Jb 34:7. Lk +22:63.

make thee. Ps 83:16. 2 Th 3:14. T 2:8.

4 **For thou**. Jb 6:10. 10:7. 1 P 3:15.

my doctrine. Dt 32:2. Pr 1:5. Is 29:24.

pure. Jb 8:6. 16:17. 33:9.

I am clean. Jb 6:29, 30. 7:20. 9:2, 3. 10:7. 14:4. 34:5, 6. 35:2. Ps 19:9. 24:4. 73:1.

5 **oh that God**. Jb 23:3-7. 31:35. 33:6-18. 38:1, 2. 40:1-5, 8. 42:7.

lips. Nu +12:8.

6 **show thee**. Jb 15:8, 11. 28:28. Dt 29:29. Ps 25:14. Da 2:28, 47. Mt 13:35. Ro 16:25, 26. 1 C 2:9-11. Ep 3:5.

double. Ge +43:12.

God exacteth. Ezr 9:13. Ps +13:1. 103:10. 106:43-46. La 3:22.

7 **Canst**. Jb 5:9. 9:10. 26:14. 37:23. Ps 73:16. 139:6-10. Pr 30:3. Ec 3:11. 7:24. 8:17. 11:5. Is 40:28. Da +4:3. Mt 11:27. Ro 11:33. 1 C 2:10, 16. 13:9. Ep 3:8, 19. He 11:6.

8 **It is as high as heaven**. Heb. the heights of heaven. Ep 3:18. Jb 22:12. 35:5. 2 Ch 6:18. Ps 103:11. 148:13. Pr 25:2, 3. Is 55:9.

deeper. Jb 26:6. Ps 139:6-8. Am +9:2. Ep 3:18, 19.

hell. Heb. *sheol*, Ge +37:35.

what canst. Jb +36:26.

9 **longer**. Jb 28:24, 25. Ps 65:5-8. 139:9, 10.

10 **If he cut off**. or, If he make a change. Jb 5:18. 9:4, 12, 13. 12:14. 34:29. Is 14:27. Da 4:35.

shut up. Jb 38:8. Dt 32:30. Ps 31:8. Re 3:7.

hinder him. Heb. turn him away. Jb 9:12. Is 43:13.

11 **he knoweth**. Ps 94:11. Je 17:9, 10. Jn +2:24, 25. He 4:13. Re 2:23.

vain men. Ps 26:4.

he seeth. Jb 22:13, 14. Ps 10:11, 14. 35:22. Ec 5:8. Ho 7:2. Hab 1:13. He 4:13.

12 **For vain**. Heb. For empty. Ex 27:8. 38:7. Ps 62:9, 10. 73:22. 92:6. Ec 3:18. Je 52:31. Ro 1:22. Ja 2:20.

would. Jb 5:13. 12:2, 3. 28:28. Pr 30:2-4. Ro 12:16. 1 C 3:18-20. Ja 3:13-17.

man be. Jb 15:14. Ps 51:5. Ep 2:3.

a wild. Jb 6:5. 39:5-8. Je 2:24.

13 **prepare**. Jb 5:8. 8:5, 6. 22:21, 22. 2 Ch +12:14mg. Pr 16:1. Lk +12:47.

stretch. Ps +88:9.

14 **iniquity**. Jb 4:7, 8. 22:5. Is 1:15.

put it far. Jb 22:23. 34:32. Is 1:16. Ezk 18:30, 31. Ja 4:8.

let not. Ps 101:2. Zc 5:3, 4.

15 **lift up**. Jb 10:15. 22:26. Ge 4:5, 6. Ps 119:6, 7. 2 C 1:12. 1 T 2:8. 1 J 2:28. 3:19-22.

thou shalt be. Ps 27:1, 2. 46:1, 2. 112:6-8. Pr 14:26. 28:1.

16 **Because**. Ge 41:51. Pr 31:7. Ec 5:20. Is 54:4. 65:16. Jn 16:21. Re 7:14-17.

as waters. Jb 6:15. Ge 9:11. Is 12:1, 2. +54:9.

17 **age**. Jb 42:11-17. 1 Ch +12:32. Ps 92:14. +112:4. Is 58:8-10. Zc 14:6, 7. Lk 2:26-32.

be clearer than. Heb. arise above, etc. or, fli- est. Jb 5:7. 20:8. Dt 4:17.

thou shalt. 1 Ch 29:10. Ho 6:3.

18 **secure**. Ge 19:30. Ps 91:5. 112:7. 125:1. Pr 1:33. 3:24. Is 33:16. 43:2. He 13:6.

because. Jb 6:11. 7:6. 22:27-29. Ps 43:5. Pr 14:32. Ro 5:3-5. Col 1:27.

thou shalt take. Le 26:5, 6. Ps 3:5. 4:8. Pr 3:24-26.

19 **many**. Jb 42:8, 9. Ge 26:26-31. Ps 45:12. Pr 19:6. Is 60:14. Re 3:9.

make suit unto thee. Heb. intreat thy face. Ge +3:19. Ex +32:11mg.

20 **the eyes**. Le 26:16. Ps +69:3.

they shall not escape. Heb. flight shall per- ish from them. Am 2:14. 5:19, 20. 9:1-3. He 2:3. or, refuge shall, etc. 2 S 22:3. Ps 59:16.

their hope. Jb 8:13, 14. 18:14. 27:8. Pr 10:24. 11:7. 20:20. Is +38:18. Lk 16:23-26.

the giving up of the ghost. or, a puff of breath. Heb. *nephesh*, soul, Nu +23:10. Je 15:9.

JOB 12

2 **No doubt**. or, truly. Jb 9:2. 19:4, 5. 34:12.

ye are the people. Jb 6:24, 25. 8:8-10. 11:2, 3, 6, 12. 15:2, 10. 17:4. 20:3. 32:7-13. Pr 28:11. Is 5:21. 1 C 4:10. 1 C 6:5.

wisdom shall die. Jb 15:8. 17:10. Is 5:21. Je 7:4. 1 C 6:5. 13:8. He 8:11.

3 **But I have**. Jb 13:2-5. Pr 26:4. 2 C 11:5, 6, 21-23.

understanding. Heb. an heart. Jb 1:5. 9:4. 10:13. 17:11. 34:34. Je 5:21. Ac 8:22.

I am not inferior to you. Heb. I fall not lower than you. Jb 13:2. 14:18.

who knoweth not such things as these. Heb. with whom are not such as these. Jb 6:6, 7. 15:9. 26:2, 3. Ac 17:28. Ro 1:19. 1 C 10:13.

4 **one mocked**. Lk +22:63.
calleth. Jb 16:20. Ps 91:15. Je 33:3. Mi 7:7.
the just. Pr 14:2.
laughed. Lk +8:53.

5 **ready**. Dt 32:35. Ps 17:5. 94:18. Je 13:16.
a lamp. Jb 18:5. Pr 13:9. 20:20. Mt 25:8.
of him. Jb 6:5. 16:4. Ps 123:3, 4. Am 6:1-6.
Lk 12:19. 16:19, 20.

6 **tabernacles**. Jb 9:24. 21:7-15. Ps 17:14. 37:1,
35. 73:11, 12. 92:7. Je 5:27, 28. Ml 3:15.

7 **But ask**. Jb 21:29, 30. Pr 6:6. Is 1:3. Je +8:7.
Ro 8:20-22.
teach. ver. 8. Jb 6:24. 8:10.
tell. Ge 3:11.

8 **speak**. Jb 7:11. Jg 5:10. 1 Ch 16:9.
teach. ver. 7. Jb 8:10. Is 28:9.
fishes. Ge 9:2.
declare. Jb 15:17. 28:27. 38:37mg.

9 **Who**. ver. 3. Ac 19:35.
the hand. Jb 22:18. Nu +11:23. Dt 8:17, 18.
1 S 2:7. Je 27:5, 6. Da 4:17. 5:18. Ro 11:36. Ja
2:5-7.

10 **whose hand**. Nu +11:23. 16:22. Ps 22:29. Da
5:23. Ac 17:25, 28. 2 C +3:5.
soul. *or*, life. Heb. *nephesh*, Ge +2:19. Jb 2:4,
6. 3:20. Jsh 11:11. 1 Th 5:23. He 4:12.
living thing. Jb 3:20. 5:22, 23. 7:7. 28:21.
the breath. Heb. *ruach*, Ge +6:17. Jb 27:3.
34:14, 15. Ge 2:7. +6:17. Nu +27:16. Ps
104:29. 146:3, +4. Ec +12:7. Zc +12:1.
mankind. Heb. flesh of man. Heb. *ish*. Ge
2:23. 3:22, 24. 4:1. Ps 49:2. 62:9. Is 2:9. 5:15.
31:8. Jn 3:6. Ac 17:26, 31. 1 C 15:39.

11 **Doth**. Jb 34:3. 1 C 10:15. Ph 1:10mg. He
5:14. 1 P 2:3.
mouth. Heb. palate. Jb +31:30mg.

12 **the ancient**. Jb 8:8. 15:10. 29:8. 32:7. 2 Ch
36:17.
length of days. Dt 30:20. Ps 21:4.
understanding. ver. 13. Jb 26:12. 32:11mg.
Pr 16:31.

13 **him**. *that is,* God. Jb 32:6-9.
wisdom. ver. 16. Jb 9:4. 28:20-28. 36:5. Ps
104:24. 147:5. Pr 2:6, 7. 3:19. Je 10:12. Da
2:20. Mt +28:19. Lk 21:15. Ro 11:33. +16:27.
1 C 1:24. 2:7. Ep 1:8. 3:10. Col 2:3. 1 T 1:17.
Ja 1:5.
counsel. Pr 8:14. Is +14:27. 40:13, 14. Ro
11:34.

14 **he breaketh**. Jb 9:12, 13. 11:10. Is 14:23. Je
51:58, 64. Ml 1:4.
he shutteth. Jb 16:11. 1 S 17:46. 24:18.
26:8mg. Is 22:22. Ro 11:32mg. Re 3:7.
up. Heb. upon.

15 **Behold**. ver. 10. Ge 8:1, 2. Dt 11:17. 1 K
8:35, 36. 17:1. Je 14:22. Na 1:4. Lk 4:25. Ja
5:17, 18. Re 11:6.
he sendeth. Ge 6:13, 17. 7:11, 23. Ps 104:7-
9. Am 5:8.

16 **With**. ver. 13. Mt 6:13.

the deceived. Nu 15:28. 1 K 22:22, 23. Ps
119:67. Ezk 14:9. Ga 3:1. Ep 4:14.
the deceiver. Dt 27:18. Pr 28:10. Mt 23:13.
Mk 9:42. Lk +11:52. 2 T 3:13.

17 **He leadeth**. Je +19:7.

18 **He looseth**. 2 Ch 33:11-14. Je 52:31-34. Da
2:21. Re 19:16.

19 **leadeth princes**. Jsh 10:24, 42. 1 S 17:45,
46. Is 37:36-38. 45:1. Re 17:14. 19:19-21.

20 **the speech of the trusty**. Heb. the lip of the
faithful. Pr 10:21. 12:19, 22.
taketh. ver. 24. Jb 17:4. 32:9. 39:17. Is 3:1-3.

21 **poureth**. Ex 8:2, 16, 24. 1 K 21:23, 24. 2 K
9:26, 34-37. Ps 107:40. Is 23:9. 24:21, 22.
37:38. Da 2:21, 22. 4:32, 33. Mt 2:12, 13. Ac
12:23.
weakeneth the strength of the mighty.
or, looseth the girdle of the strong. Is 22:21.
+45:1, 5. Lk +12:35.

22 **discovereth**. Jb 11:6. 28:20-23. 2 K 6:12. Ps
44:21. 139:12. Da 2:22. Mt 10:26. 1 C 2:10.
4:5.
shadow. Ps +23:4.

23 **increaseth**. Ex 1:7, 20. Ps 107:38. Is 9:3.
26:15. 27:6. 51:2. 60:22. Je 30:19. 33:22. Zc
10:8.
straiteneth them again. Heb. leadeth in. Is
3:1-3.

24 **He taketh**. ver. 20. Jb 17:4. Ex 8:2, 6, 16, 24.
Is 6:9, 10. 19:1. 23:9. Da 4:16, 33. Ho 7:11. Ac
12:23.
and causeth. Ps 107:4, 40.
wander. ver. 25. Ge 20:13. 2 K 21:9. 2 Ch
33:9. Ps 107:40. Pr 12:26. Is 63:17. Je 23:13,
32. Am 2:4.
in a wilderness. Jb 6:18. 26:7. Ge 1:2. Dt
32:10.

25 **grope**. Jb 5:14. Ge 19:11. Dt 28:29. Is 59:10.
Ac 13:11. 1 J 2:11.
maketh. Ps 107:27. Is 19:14. 24:20.
stagger. Heb. wander. ver. +24.
like a. Ps 107:27.
drunken. 1 S 1:13. 25:36.

JOB 13

1 **Lo**. Jb 5:9-16. 12:9, etc. 42:3-6.
ear. Jb 4:12. 5:27. 8:8-10. 15:17, 18. Ps 78:3,
4. 1 J 1:3.

2 **ye know**. Jb 12:3. 15:8, 9. 34:35. 35:16. 37:2.
40:4, 5. 42:7. 1 C 8:1, 2. 2 C 11:4, 5, 16-18.
12:11.

3 **Surely**. ver. 22. Jb 9:34, 35. 11:5. 23:3-7.
31:35.
I desire. Jb 9:3, 14, 15. Is 41:21. Je 12:1mg,
2. Mi 6:2.
reason. ver. +15mg. Ps ch. 73. Is 1:18-20.
God. Heb. *El*, Ex +15:2.

4 **ye are forgers**. Jb 4:7-11. 5:1-5. 8:3, 4. 18:5,
etc. 21:27-34. 22:6, etc. Ex 20:16. Ps 119:69.

physicians. Ge 50:2. 2 Ch 16:12. Jb 16:2. Je 6:14. 8:11, 22. 30:13. 46:11. Ezk 34:4. Ho 5:13. Mt 9:12. Mk 2:17. 5:26. Lk 4:23. 5:31. 8:43. Col 4:14.

5 **Oh that ye**. ver. 13. Jb 11:3. 16:3. 18:2. 19:2. 21:2, 3. 32:1.
   and it. Pr 17:28. Ec 5:3. Am 5:13. Ja 1:19.

6 **Hear now**. Jb 21:2, 3. 33:1-3. 34:2. Jg 9:7. Pr 8:6, 7.

7 **speak wickedly for**. Jb 4:7. 11:2-4. 17:5. 32:21, 22. 36:4. Jn 16:2. Ro 3:5-8. 2 C 4:2.

8 **accept**. Ro +2:11. Ja +2:1.

9 **search**. Jb 34:36. Ps 44:21. Je +17:10.
   as one. Is 28:22. Lk +22:63. Ga 6:7, 8.

10 **reprove**. Jb 42:7, 8. Ps 50:21, 22. 82:2. Pr 24:23. Ja 2:9.

11 **Shall**. Ps 119:120. Je 5:22. 10:10. Mt +10:28. Re 15:3, 4.
   his dread. ver. 21. Ex 15:16. Is 8:13.

12 **remembrances**. Jb 18:17. Ex 17:14. Ps 34:16. 102:12. 109:15. Pr 10:7. Is 26:14.
   like. or, similes of. Jb 27:1. 29:1. Nu +21:27. +23:7.
   ashes. Ge 18:27. Is 44:20.
   to bodies. Jb 4:19. Ge +2:7. 2 C 5:1.

13 **Hold your peace**. Heb. Be silent from me. Jb 33:31, 33. 1 S 7:8mg. Is 41:1.
   let me. ver. +5. Jb 7:11. 10:1. 21:3.
   and let come. Jb 6:9, 10. 7:15, 16.

14 **I take**. Jb 18:4. Ec 4:5. Is 9:20. 49:26.
   and put. Jg 12:3. 1 S 19:5. 28:21. Ps 119:109.
   life. Heb. *nephesh*, soul, Ge +44:30. 1 C 15:30, 31.

15 **slay me**. ver. 18. Jb +19:25-27. 23:10. 24:14. Ru +1:13. Ps 23:4. 139:19. Pr 14:32. +19:3. Ro 8:38, 39.
   yet will. Hab +3:17, 18.
   trust. 1 S 17:37. 2 K 18:5-7. Ps 7:1. +9:10. 56:4. 71:5. Is 50:10. Da 3:16-18. Mi 7:8. 1 J 3:21.
   but I will. Jb 10:7. 16:17, 21. 23:4-7. 27:5. 31:31-37. 40:2, 4, 5, 8. 1 J 3:20.
   maintain. Heb. prove, *or* argue. ver. 3. Jb 15:3. Is 1:18.

16 **my salvation**. Ex 15:2. Ps 27:1. 62:6, 7. 118:14, 21. Is 12:2. Je 3:23. Ac 4:12. 13:47.
   for an hypocrite. Jb +8:13.

17 **diligently**. ver. 6. Jb 33:1.

18 **I have ordered**. Jb 16:21. 23:4. 40:7.
   I know. Jb 9:2, 3, 20. 40:7, 8. 42:9. Ps 37:6. Is 43:26. Ro 8:33, 34. 2 C 1:12.

19 **that will plead**. Jb 19:5. 33:5-7, 32. Is 50:7, 8. Ro 8:33.
   if I hold. ver. 13. Jb 7:11. Je 20:9.
   ghost. Ge +49:33 (**S#1478h**).

20 **do not two**. Jb 9:34, 35.
   hide myself. Ge 3:8-10. Ps 139:12. Re 6:15, 16.

21 **Withdraw**. Jb 10:20. 22:15-17. Ex +9:3.
   let not. ver. 11. Jb +33:7. Ps 119:120.

22 **call**. Jb 9:32. 38:3. 40:4, 5. 42:3-6.

23 **many**. Jb 22:5. Ps 44:20, 21.
   make me. Jb 36:8, 9. Ps 139:23, 24.
   to know. Ps 25:8, 9. Pr 20:12. Jn 9:36. Ac 8:31.

24 **hidest thou**. Jb 10:2. 29:2, 3. Dt +31:17. Ps 77:6-9.
   holdest me. Jb 16:9. 19:11. 30:21. 31:35. 33:10. 1 S 28:16. La 2:5. 2 Th 3:15.

25 **break**. Jb 14:3. 1 S 24:14. Is 17:13. Is 42:3. Mt 12:20.
   stubble. 1 C +3:12.

26 **writest**. Jb 3:20. Ru 1:20. Ps 88:3, etc.
   makest. Jb 20:11. Ps 25:7. Pr 5:11-13. Je 31:19. Jn 5:5, 14.

27 **puttest**. Pr +7:22. He +11:36.
   and lookest. Heb. and observest. Jb 10:6, 14. 14:16, 17. 16:9.
   settest. Jb 2:7.
   print. **S#2707h**. 1 K 6:35 (carved work). Ezk 8:10 (portrayed). 23:14.
   heels. Heb. roots. Jb 8:17. 14:8. 18:16. 19:28. 36:30mg.

28 **And he**. Jb 30:17-19, 29, 30. Nu 12:12.
   as a garment. Jb 4:19. Ps 39:11. Ho 5:12.

JOB 14

1 **born**. Jb 15:14. 25:4. Ps 51:5. Mt 11:11.
   of few days. Heb. short of days. Jb 7:1, 6. 9:25. Ge 47:9. Ps 39:5.
   full. ver. 5, 7. Ec +2:17, 23. Jn 15:11. He 12:11.
   trouble. Jb 5:7.

2 **like**. 1 P +1:24.
   fleeth. Jb 8:9. 9:25, 26. 1 Ch 29:15. Ps 102:11. 144:4. Ec 8:13.

3 **And dost**. Jb 7:17, 18. 13:25. Ps 144:3.
   bringest. Jb 9:19, 20, 32. 13:27. Ps 143:2. Ro 3:19.

4 **Who can bring**. Heb. Who will give. Ge 5:3. Ps 14:7. 90:5. Pr +20:9. Je 13:23. Mt 7:16-18. 12:33. Jn 6:44, 65. Ro 5:12. 8:8, 9.
   a clean. Lk +1:35.
   not one. Ps 14:3.

5 **his days**. ver. 14. Pr 7:1. 12:10. Ps 39:4. 139:16mg. Da 5:26, 30. 9:24. 11:36. Lk 12:20. Ac 17:26. He +9:27.
   determined. Ex +26:36. Is 14:26. Ac 17:26. Ep +1:11.
   the number. Ps 90:10, 12. +102:24.
   thou hast. Jb 23:13, 14. Ps 104:9, 29. Da 4:35. Re 1:18. 3:7.
   bounds. ver. 13. Jb 23:12, 14. 26:10.
   cannot pass. Jb 19:8.

6 **Turn**. Jb 7:16, 19. 10:20. Ps 39:13.
   rest. Heb. cease. ver. 7. Jb 3:17. 7:16. 10:20. 16:6.
   accomplish. or, enjoy. Jb 33:26. 34:9. Le 26:43. 2 Ch 36:21.
   as an hireling. Jb 7:1, 2. Mt 20:1-8.

7 **that it will sprout**. ver. 14. Jb 19:10. Is 11:1. 27:6. Da 4:15, 23-25.

8 **die in the ground**. Is +26:19. Jn 12:24. 1 C 15:36.

9 **and bring**. Ezk 17:3-10, 22-24. 19:10, 11. Ro 11:17-24.

10 **wasteth away**. Heb. is weakened, or, cut off. Ex 17:13 (discomfited). Ps 90:10. Is 14:12. Jl 3:10.
man. Jb 3:11. 10:18. 11:20. 17:13-16. Ge 49:33. Mt 27:50. Ac 5:10.
ghost. Jb 3:11. 10:18. 13:19. Ps +146:4.
where is he. ver. 12. Jb 7:7-10. 19:26. Pr 14:32. Lk 16:22, 23.

11 **the flood**. Jb 6:15-18. Je 15:18.

12 **So man**. Jb 10:21, 22. 30:23. Ec 3:19-21. 12:5.
till the heavens. Jb 19:25-27. Ps 102:26. Is 51:6. 65:17. 66:22. Mt 24:35. Ac 3:21. Ro 8:20. 2 P 3:7, 10-13. Re 20:11. 21:1.
awake. Jb 3:13. 7:21. Is +26:19. Da +12:2. Jn 11:11-13, 25. Ep 5:14. 1 Th 4:14-16.

13 **hide me**. Jb 3:17-19. Ps 16:10. 30:3. 139:8. Is 38:10. 57:1, 2.
grave. Heb. sheol, Ge +37:35. Ps 6:5. 16:10. Ec 9:10. Is 38:18, 19.
until. Is 12:1. 26:20, 21.
appoint me. Mk 13:32. Ac 1:7. 17:31.
remember. Ge 8:1. Ps 106:4. Lk 23:42.

14 **shall he live**. Jb 19:25, 26. 1 S +2:6. Ps 89:48. Is +26:19. Ezk 37:1-14. Mt 22:29-32. Jn 5:28, 29. Ac 26:8. 1 C 15:42-44. 1 Th 4:14-16. Re 20:12, 13.
all the days. ver. 5. Jb 7:1. 42:16. Ge 47:8mg. 2 S 19:34mg. Ps 27:14. 40:1, 2. La 3:25, 26. Ja 5:7, 8.
will I wait. Jb 13:15. La 3:26. 1 C 15:51, 52. Ph 1:23-25. 3:21. Ju 21.
change. Jb 10:17. Ge 45:22. Jg 14:12. 2 K 5:22. Pr 31:8. 1 C 15:51, 52. Ph 3:21.

15 **shall call**. Jb 13:22. Ps 50:4, 5. 1 Th 4:16, 17. 1 J 2:28.
thou wilt have. Jb 7:21. 10:3, 8. Ps 138:8. Ph 1:6. 1 P 4:19.

16 **thou numberest**. Jb 10:6, 14. 13:27. 31:4. 33:11. 34:21. Ps 56:6. 139:1-4. Pr 5:21. Je 32:19. Mt 10:30.
watch. Pr 5:21. Je 16:17.

17 **sealed up**. Jb 21:19. 37:7. Dt 32:34. Ne 9:38. Ho 13:12.
bag. or, bundle. Ge 42:35.
iniquity. Je 2:22.

18 **the mountain**. Ps 102:25, 26. Is 40:12. 41:15, 16. 54:10. 64:1. Je 4:24. Re 6:14. 8:8. 20:11.
cometh to nought. Heb. fadeth.
the rock. Jb 18:4. Mt 27:51.

19 **The waters**. 2 S 22:43.
washest. Heb. overflowest. Ge 6:17. 7:21-23. Le 15:11. 1 K 22:38. 2 Ch 32:4mg.

destroyest. Jb 19:10. 27:8. Ps 30:6, 7. Ezk 37:11. Lk 12:19, 20.

20 **prevailest**. Jb 15:24. Ec 4:12. 8:8.
for ever. Heb. netsach, Jb +4:20.
he passeth. Jb 16:22. Ge 25:32mg. 2 S 12:23. 1 K 2:2. Ps 1:1 (walketh). 78:39. 109:23. Pr 4:18 (more and more; lit. going and shineth). Ec 1:4. 3:20 (go). 6:6 (go). 9:10 (goest). 12:5 (goeth). Ho 13:3.
changest. ver. 14. Jb 2:12. La 4:8.

21 **he knoweth it not**. 1 S 4:20. Ps 39:6. Ec 2:18, 19. 9:5. Is 39:7, 8. 63:16.
not. Ps +146:4.

22 **his flesh**. Jb 19:20, 22, 26. 33:19-21. Da +7:15.
pain. Jb 5:18. Ge 34:25.
his soul. Heb. nephesh, Ge +34:3. Pr 14:32. Is 10:18. Lk 16:23, 24.
within him. Jb 33:18, 22. Ge +25:8, 9, 17. 35:18. Nu 27:16. 1 K 17:22. 2 K 4:27. Ps 42:6. 43:5. 63:1. 88:3. Ec +3:21. Ezk +18:20. Da +7:15. Zc +12:1. Mt +10:28. 1 Th 5:23.
mourn. Is 3:26. 19:8. 24:4.

JOB 15

1 **Eliphaz**. Jb +2:11. 4:1. 22:1. 42:7, 9.

2 **a wise man**. Jb 11:2, 3. 13:2. Ja 3:13.
vain knowledge. Heb. knowledge of wind. Jb 6:26. 8:2. 16:3.
fill. Ho 12:1.
east wind. Ge +41:6.

3 **he reason**. Jb 13:4, 5. 16:2, 3. 26:1-3. Ml 3:13-15. Mt 12:36, 37. Col 4:6. 1 T 6:4, 5.

4 **castest off**. Heb. makest void. Jb 4:5, 6. 5:12. 6:14. 40:8. Nu 30:12. Ps 36:1-3. 119:126. Ro 3:31. Ga 2:21.
restrainest. Jb 5:8. 1 Ch 10:13, 14. Je +10:25. Am 6:10. Lk 18:1. Ja 4:2.
prayer. or, speech. or, meditation. Ps 64:1. Ps 119:97, 99.

5 **uttereth**. Heb. teacheth. Jb 9:22-24. 12:6. 33:33. 35:11. Pr 22:25. Mk 7:21, 22. Lk 6:45. Ja 1:26.
thou choosest. Ps 50:19, 20. 52:2-4. 64:3. 120:2, 3. Je 9:3-5, 8. Ja 3:5-8.

6 **own mouth**. Jb 9:20. Ps 64:8. Mt 12:37. 26:65. Lk 19:22.
thine own. Jb 33:8-12. 34:5-9. 35:2, 3. 40:8. 42:3.

7 **the first**. ver. 10. Jb 12:12. Ge 4:1.
or wast thou. Jb 38:4, etc. Ps 90:2. Pr 8:22-25.

8 **the secret**. Jb 11:6. Dt 29:29. Ps 25:14. Pr 3:32. Je 23:18. Am 3:7. Mt 11:25. 13:11, 35. Jn 15:15. Ro 11:34. 16:25, 26. 1 C 2:9-11, 16.
thou restrain. Jb 12:2. 13:5, 6.

9 **knowest**. Jb 13:2. 26:3, 4. 2 C 10:7. 11:5, 21-30.

10 **the gray-headed**. Jb 8:8-10. 12:20. 32:6, 7. Dt 32:7. Pr 16:31.

11 **the consolations**. Jb 5:8-26. 11:13-19. 2 C
1:3-5. 7:6.
is there. ver. 8. Jb 13:2. 1 K 22:24.

12 **thine heart**. Ec 11:9. Mk 7:21, 22. Ac 5:3, 4.
8:22. Ja 1:14, 15.
thy eyes. Jb 17:2. Ps 35:19. Pr 6:13. 10:10.

13 **turnest**. ver. 25-27. Jb 9:4. Ro 8:7, 8.
spirit. Heb. *ruach*, Ge +41:8.
and lettest. Jb 10:3. 12:6. Ps 34:13. Ml 3:13.
Ja 1:26. 3:2-6.

14 **is man**. Ps +8:4.
clean. Pr +20:9.
born of. Jb 25:4.

15 **he putteth**. Jb +4:18. 25:5. Is 6:2-5.

16 **abominable**. Jb 4:19. 42:6. Ps 14:1-3. 53:3.
Ro 1:28-30. 3:9-19. T 3:3.
drinketh. Jb 20:12. 34:7. Pr 19:28.

17 **hear me**. Jb 5:27. 13:5, 6. 33:1. 34:2. 36:2.

18 **from their**. ver. 10. Jb 8:8. Ps 71:18. 78:3-6.
Is 38:19.

19 **Unto whom**. Ge 10:25, 32. Dt 32:8. Jl 3:17.

20 **travaileth**. Ec 9:3. Ro 8:22.
the number. Ps 90:3, 4, 12. Lk 12:19-21. Ja
5:1-6.

21 **dreadful sound**. Heb. sound of fears. Jb
18:11. Ge 3:9, 10. Le 26:36. 2 K 7:6. Pr 1:26,
27.
in prosperity. Jb 1:13-19. 20:5-7, 22-24. Le
26:36. 1 S 25:36-38. Ps 73:18-20. 92:7. Ac
12:21-23. 1 Th 5:3.
the destroyer. 1 C 10:10. Re 9:11.

22 **He believeth not**. Jb 6:11. 9:16. 2 K 6:33. Is
8:21, 22. Mt 27:5.
and he is. Jb 20:24, 25.

23 **wandereth**. Jb 30:3, 4. Ge 4:12. Ps 59:15.
109:10. La 5:6, 9. He 11:37, 38.
the day. Jb 18:5, 6, 12, 18. Ec 11:8. Jl 2:2.
Am 5:20. Zp 1:15. He 10:27.

24 **anguish**. Jb 6:2-4. Ps 119:143. Pr 1:27. Is
13:3. Mt 26:37, 38. Ro 2:9.
as a king. Pr 6:11. 24:34.

25 **he stretcheth**. Le 26:23. Ps 73:9, 11. Is 27:4.
Da 5:23. Ml 3:13. Ac 9:5. 12:1, 23.
strengtheneth. Jb 9:4. 40:9-11. Ex 5:2, 3.
9:17. 1 S 4:7-9. 6:6. Ps 52:7. Is 8:9, 10. 10:12-
14. 41:4-7.

26 **runneth**. 2 Ch 28:22. 32:13-17.
even on. Jb 16:12. Ge 49:8. Ps 18:40.

27 **he covereth**. Jb 17:10.
fatness. Dt +31:20.

28 **desolate**. Jb 3:14. 18:15. Is 5:8-10. Mi 7:13.
which are ready. Je 9:11. 26:18. 51:37. Mi
3:12.

29 **neither shall**. Jb 20:22-28. 22:15-20. 27:16,
17. Ps 49:16, 17. Lk 12:19-21. 16:2, 19-22. Ja
1:11. 5:1-3.

30 **depart**. ver. 22. Jb 10:21, 22. 18:5, 6, 18. Mt
8:12. 22:13. 2 P 2:17. Ju 13.
the flame. Jb 20:26. Ezk 15:4-7. Mt +25:41.
by the breath. Heb. *ruach*, Jb +4:9. Re 19:15.

31 **not him**. Jb 12:16. Is 44:20. Ga 6:3, 7, 8. Ep
5:6.
trust. Ps 62:10. Is 59:4. Jon 2:8.
for vanity. Jb 4:8. Pr 22:8. Is 17:10, 11. Ho
8:7. Ga 6:8.

32 **accomplished**. *or*, cut off.
before his time. Jb 14:5. Ps +102:24.
and his branch. Jb 8:16-19. 14:7-9. 18:16,
17. Ps 52:5-8. Is 27:11. Ezk 17:8-10. Ho 9:16.
14:5-7. Jn 15:6.

33 **shake off**. Is 33:9. Re 6:13.
and. Dt 28:39, 40.

34 **the congregation**. Jb +8:13.
the tabernacles. Jb 11:14. 12:6. 22:5-9.
29:12-17. 1 S 8:3. 12:3. Mi 7:3. Am 5:11, 12.

35 **conceive**. Ho 10:13. Ga 6:7, 8. Ja +1:15.
vanity. *or*, iniquity. Jb 31:5. Ge 27:35.
belly. Pr 18:8. 20:27. 26:22. Jn 7:38.

JOB 16

2 **heard**. Jb 6:6, 25. 11:2, 3. 13:5. 19:2, 3. 26:2,
3. Ja 1:19.
miserable. *or*, troublesome. Jb 13:4. Ps
69:26. Ph 1:16.
comforters. 2 S 10:3. 1 Ch 19:3. Ps 69:20.

3 **vain words**. Heb. words of wind. Jb 6:26.
8:2. 15:2.
what emboldeneth. Jb 20:3. 32:3-6. Mt
22:46. T 1:11. 2:8.

4 **if your soul**. Heb. *nephesh*, Ge +27:31. Jb 6:2-
5, 14. Mt 7:12. Ro 12:15. 1 C 12:26.
soul's. Heb. *nephesh*, Ge +27:31.
up words. Jb 11:2. 35:16. Pr 10:19. Ec 10:14.
shake mine. Nu 32:13 (wander). 2 S 15:20.
Ps 59:15. Je +18:16. Zp 2:15.

5 **But I would**. Jb 4:3, 4. 6:14. 29:25. Ps 27:14.
Pr 27:9, 17. Is 35:3, 4. Ga 6:1.

6 **my grief**. Jb 10:1. Ps 77:1-9. 88:15-18.
what am I eased. Heb. what goeth from me.
Jb +14:20.

7 **he hath**. Jb 3:17. 7:3, 16. 10:1. Ps 6:6, 7. Pr
3:11, 12. Is 50:4. Mi 6:13.
hast made. Jb 1:15-19. 29:5, etc.

8 **is a witness**. Jb 10:17. Ru 1:21. Ep 5:27.
my leanness. Ps 106:15. Is 10:16. 24:16.

9 **teareth me**. Jb 10:16, 17. 18:4. Ps 50:22. La
3:10, 11. Ho 5:14.
he gnasheth. Ps +37:12.
mine. Jb 13:24, 27. 19:11. Mi 7:8.

10 **gaped**. Ps 22:13, 16, 17. 35:21. 69:20. Mt
26:67. Lk 23:35, 36.
they have smitten. Mt +27:30.
gathered. Ps 35:15. 94:21. Ac 4:27.

11 **delivered me**. Heb. shut me up. 1 S
23:12mg. 24:18mg. Ps 27:12. 31:8. Ro
11:32mg.
to the ungodly. Jb 1:13-19. 2:7. Ps 7:14. Jn
19:16. 2 C 12:7.
turned. Ps 27:12.

12 **at ease**. Jb 1:2, 3. 3:26. 29:3, 18, 19.
   broken me. Jb 4:10. Ps 44:19. La 3:4. Mt
   21:44.
   by my neck. Jb 15:26. Ro 16:4.
   shaken. La 3:11. Ezk 29:7.
   set me up. Jb 7:12, 20. La 3:12.
13 **archers**. Jb 6:4. Ge 49:23. Ps 7:12, 13.
   he cleaveth. Jb 19:27. La 3:13.
   doth. Jb 6:10. Dt 29:20. Ezk 5:11. Ro 8:32. 2
   P 2:5.
   poureth. Jb 20:25. La 2:11.
14 **breaketh**. La 2:11. 3:3-5, 11.
   runneth. Jg 15:8. Ps 42:7.
   giant. Dt +2:20.
15 **sewed**. 1 K 21:27. Is 22:12.
   sackcloth. Ge 37:34. 2 S 3:31. 21:10. 1 K
   20:31. 21:27. 2 K 6:30. 19:1, 2. 1 Ch 21:16.
   Ne 9:1. Est 4:1-3. Ps 30:11. 35:13. 69:11. Is
   3:24. 15:3. 20:2. 22:12. 32:11. 37:1, 2. 50:3.
   58:5. Je 4:8. 6:26. 48:37. 49:3. La 2:10. Ezk
   7:18. 27:31. Da 9:3. Jl 1:8, 13. Am 8:10. Jon
   3:5, 6, 8. Mt 11:21. Lk 10:13. Re 6:12. 11:3.
   defiled my horn. Jb 30:19. 1 S 2:10. Ps 7:5.
   75:5, 10.
16 **face**. Ps 31:9. 32:3. Is 52:14. Lk +6:21.
   on my eyelids. Jb 17:7. Ps 116:3. Jon ch. 2.
   Mk 14:34.
   shadow. Ps +23:4.
17 **Not for**. Jb 11:14. 15:20, 34. 21:27, 28. 22:5-
   9. 27:6, 7. 29:12-17. 31:1, etc. Ps 7:3-5.
   44:17-21.
   my prayer is pure. Jb 8:5, 6. 11:13-15. Ps
   66:18, 19. Pr 15:8, 29. 1 T 2:8. 2 T 2:22. Ja
   4:8.
18 **O earth**. Je 22:29.
   cover not. Ge 4:11. Ne 4:5. Is 26:21. Ezk
   24:7.
   let my cry. Jb 27:9. Ps 66:18, 19. Is 1:15.
   58:9, 10. Ja 4:3, 4.
19 **my witness**. 1 S 12:5. Ro 1:9. 9:1. 2 C 1:23.
   11:31. 1 Th 2:10.
   on high. Heb. in the high places. Jb 5:11.
   25:2. 31:2. Ps 113:5.
20 **scorn me**. Heb. are my scorners. ver. 4. Jb
   12:4, 5. 17:2.
   poureth. Ps 109:4. 142:2. Lk 6:11, 12, +21.
21 **plead**. Jb 9:34, 35. 13:3, 22. 23:3-7. 31:35.
   40:1-5. Ec 6:10. Is 43:26. 45:9. Je 2:29. Ro
   9:20.
   neighbor. or, friend.
22 **a few years**. Heb. years of number. Jb 14:5,
   14. Is +10:19mg.
   not return. Jb +7:9, 10. 10:21. 14:10.
   +36:18. 2 S 12:23. Ec 12:5. He +9:27.

JOB 17

1 **breath**. Heb. ruach, Ge +6:17.
   is corrupt. or, spirit is spent. Jb 19:17. Ps
   +146:4.

   my days. Jb 6:11. 42:16. Is 57:16.
   the graves. Heb. qeber, Ge +23:4. ver. 13, 14.
   Ps 88:3-5. Is 38:10-14.
2 **mockers**. Lk +22:63.
   continue. Heb. lodge. Jb 19:4. 29:19. 31:32.
   Ps 25:13mg. 91:1mg.
   provocation. 1 S 1:6, 7.
3 **put me**. Jb 9:33. Ge 43:9. 44:32. Pr 11:15.
   20:16. He 7:22.
   strike. Pr 6:1. 11:15mg. 17:18. 22:26.
4 **thou hast**. 2 S 15:31. 17:14. 2 Ch 25:16. Is
   19:14. Mt 11:25. 13:11. Ro 11:8. 1 C 1:20.
5 **He that**. Ps +12:3. Pr 19:22.
   the eyes. Ps +69:3.
   his children. Ex 20:5. 1 K 11:12.
6 **a by-word**. or, proverb. Jb +13:12. Dt
   +28:37.
   aforetime. or, before them.
   as a tabret. Ge 31:27. Is 5:12.
7 **Mine eye**. ver. +5. Ps +6:7.
   members. or, thoughts. ver. 11.
   shadow. Ps 109:23, 24. Ec 6:12.
8 **astonied**. Le 26:32. 1 K 9:8. Ps 73:12-15. Ec
   5:8. Hab 1:13. Ro 11:33.
   stir up. Jb 29:31. Is 64:7. Ac 13:46.
   hypocrite. Jb +8:13.
9 **hold on**. Jb 16:12. 18:9, 20mg. Ps 84:7, 11.
   Pr 4:18. 14:16. Is 35:8-10. 1 P 1:5. 1 J 2:19.
   clean. Ge 20:5. Ex 30:18. Ps 24:4. 26:6.
   73:13. Is 1:15, 16. Mk 7:2.
   hands. 2 S 22:21, 25. Ps 24:3, 4. 26:6. Ja 4:8.
   be stronger and stronger. Heb. add
   strength. 2 S 3:1. Ec 1:18. Is 40:29-31. 2 C
   12:9, 10.
10 **do ye return**. Jb 6:29. Ml 3:18.
   for I. ver. 4. Jb 15:9. 32:9. 42:7. 1 C 1:20. 6:5.
11 **My days**. Jb 7:6. 9:25, 26. Is 38:10.
   purposes. Pr 16:9. 19:21. Ec 9:10. Is 8:10. La
   3:37. Ro 1:13. 2 C 1:15-17. Ja 4:13-15.
   thoughts. Heb. possessions. Ps +146:4. Is
   14:23. Ob 17.
12 **change**. Jb 7:3, 4, 13, 14. 24:14-16. Dt 28:67.
   short. Heb. near. Jb 19:14. 20:5mg.
13 **If I wait**. Jb 14:14. Ps 27:14. La 3:25, 26.
   the grave. Heb. sheol, Ge +37:25. ver. 1, 16.
   Jb 7:9. 10:21, 22. 11:8. 14:13. 30:23.
   I have made. Jb 41:30 (spreadeth). Ps 139:8.
   SS 2:5 (comfort; mg. straw). Is 57:2.
   bed. or, couch. Ge 49:4. 1 K 6:5 (chambers;
   mg. floors), 6, 10.
14 **said**. Heb. cried, or called.
   corruption. Jb 9:31. 21:32, 33. 33:18, 22, 24.
   Ps 16:10. 49:9. Ac 2:27-31. 13:34-37. 1 C
   15:42, 53, 54.
   to the worm. Jb 7:5. 19:26. 21:26. 24:20.
   25:6. Is 14:11.
15 **my hope**. Jb 4:6. 5:16. 6:8, 11. 7:6. 8:13.
   13:15. 19:10.
16 **the bars of the**. Jb 18:13mg, 14. 33:18-28.
   Ps 88:4-8. 143:7. Is 38:17, 18. Jon 2:6.

pit. Heb. *sheol*, Ge +37:35.
rest. Jb 3:17-19. Ezk 37:11. 2 C 1:9,

JOB 18

1 **Bildad**. Jb +2:11. 8:1. 25:1. 42:7-9.
2 **How long**. Jb 8:2. 11:2. 13:5, 6. 16:2, 3.
  mark. Jb 13:5, 6, 17. 21:2. 33:1. or, set an
  end. Jb 16:3. 28:3.
  afterwards. Pr 18:13. Ja 1:19.
3 **Wherefore**. Jb 12:7, 8. 17:4, 10. Ps 73:22. Ec
  3:18. Ro 12:10.
4 **teareth**. Jb 5:2. 13:14. 16:9. Jon 4:9. Mk
  9:18. Lk 9:39.
  himself. Heb. his soul. Heb. *nephesh*, Ge
  +27:31.
  shall the. Jb 40:8. Ezk 9:9.
  the rock. Jb 14:18. Is 54:10. Mt 24:35.
5 **the light**. Jb 20:5. Ps +112:4. Pr 4:19. 13:9.
  20:20. 24:20.
  spark. Is 50:11.
6 **candle**. or, lamp. Ps +18:28mg. Re 18:23.
  put out. Pr 20:20. 24:20.
7 **steps**. Jb 20:22. 36:16. Ps 18:36. Pr 4:12.
  his own. Jb 5:12, 13. 2 S 15:31. 17:14. Ps
  33:10. Pr 1:30-32. Ho 10:6. 1 C 3:19.
8 **he is cast**. Jb 22:10. Ps +57:6. Pr 29:6. Ezk
  32:3. 1 T 3:7. 6:9. 2 T 2:26.
9 **The gin**. Is 8:14, 15.
  robber. Jb 1:15, 17. 5:5.
10 **snare**. Ps 9:15. 11:6. Ezk 12:13. Ro 11:9.
  laid. Heb. hidden. Jb 3:16. 20:26. 40:13.
11 **Terrors**. Jb 6:4. 15:21. 20:25. Ps 73:19. 91:5.
  Je 6:25. 20:3, 4. 46:5. 49:29. 2 C 5:11. Re
  6:15, 16.
  drive him. Heb. scatter him. Jb 37:11. 38:24.
  Ge 11:8.
  to his feet. Le 26:36. 2 K 7:6, 7. Ps 53:5. Pr
  28:1.
12 **hunger-bitten**. Jb 15:23, 24. 1 S 2:5, 36. Ps
  34:10. 109:10.
  destruction. Ps 7:12-14. 1 Th 5:3. 2 P 2:3.
13 **strength**. Heb. bars. Jb 17:16. Jon 2:6.
  the firstborn. or, chief, worst, or cruelest of
  death. Ge +41:51. 49:3. Is 14:30. Col +1:15.
  Re 6:8.
14 **confidence**. Jb 8:14. 11:20. Ps 112:10. Pr
  10:28. Mt 7:26, 27.
  the king of terrors. Jb 24:17. 41:34. Ps 55:4.
  Pr 14:32. 1 C 15:55, 56. He 2:15.
15 **dwell**. ver. 12, 13. Zc 5:4.
  because. Jb 20:18-21. 31:38, 39. Je 22:13.
  Hab 2:6-11.
  brimstone. Ge +19:24. Re +9:17.
16 **roots**. Jb 29:19. Is 5:24. Ho 9:16. Am 2:9. Ml
  4:1.
  shall his branch. Jb 5:3, 4. 15:30.
17 **remembrance**. Jb 13:12. Ps 34:16. 83:4.
  109:13. Pr 2:22. 10:7.
18 **He shall be driven**. Heb. They shall drive

him. Jb 3:20. 10:22. 11:14. Pr 2:22. Is 8:21,
22. Ju 13.
  chased. Jb 20:8. Pr 14:32. Is 17:13, 14. Da
  4:33. 5:21.
19 **neither**. Jb 1:19. 8:4. 42:13-16. Ps 109:13. Is
  14:21, 22. Je 22:30.
  nor any. Jb 20:26-28. Is 5:8, 9.
20 **come after**. lit. "those behind." or, western.
  Zc 14:8.
  astonied. Dt 29:23, 24. 1 K 9:8. Je 18:16.
  his day. Dt +4:32. Ps 37:13. 137:7. Ezk 21:25.
  Ob 11-15. Lk 19:42, 44.
  went before. or, lived with him. or, easterns.
  Jl 2:10. Zc 14:8mg.
  were affrighted. Heb. laid hold on horror.
  Jb 2:12, 13. 19:13-19. Ezk 27:35. 32:10.
21 **such are**. ver. 14-16. Ex 12:30.
  knoweth. Jb 21:14. Ex 5:2. Jg 2:10. 1 S 2:12.
  1 Ch +28:9. Ps 79:6. Je 9:3. 10:25. Ro 1:28. 1
  Th 4:5. 2 Th 1:8. T 1:16.

JOB 19

2 **How long**. Re +6:10.
  vex. Jb 27:2. Jg 16:16. Ps 6:2, 3. 42:10. 2 P
  2:7, 8.
  soul. Heb. *nephesh*, Ge +34:3.
  break me. Ps 55:21. 59:7. 64:3. Pr 12:18.
  18:21. Ja 3:6-8.
3 **ten times**. Ge 31:7. Le 26:26. Nu 14:22. 1 S
  1:8. Ne 4:12. Da 1:20.
  ye reproached. Jb 4:6-11. 5:3, 4. 8:4-6. 11:3,
  14. 15:4-6, 11, 12. 18:4, etc.
  make yourselves strange to me. or, harden
  yourselves against me. ver. 17. Ge 42:7. Ps
  +69:8.
4 **I have erred**. Jb 11:3-6.
  mine. 2 S 24:17. Pr 9:12. Ezk 18:4. 2 C 5:10.
  Ga 6:5.
5 **magnify**. Ps 35:26. 38:16. 41:11. 55:12. Mi
  7:8. Zp 2:10. Zc 12:7.
  plead. 1 S 1:6. Ne 1:3. Is 4:1. Lk 1:25. 13:2-4.
  Jn 9:2, 34.
6 **God**. Jb 7:20. 16:11-14. Ps 44:9-14. 66:10-12.
  compassed. Jb 18:8-10. La 1:12, 13. Ezk
  12:13. 32:3. Ho 7:12. Mt 13:47.
7 **I cry**. Jb 10:3, 15-17. 16:17-19. 21:27. Ps
  22:2. Je 20:8. La 3:8. Hab 1:2, 3.
  wrong. or, violence. Jb 16:17. Ge 6:11, 13. 1
  Ch 12:17mg.
  no judgment. Jb 9:32. 13:15-23. 16:21.
  23:3-7. 31:35, 36. 34:5. 40:8.
8 **fenced**. Jb 3:23. Ps 88:8. La 3:7, 9. Ho 2:6.
  set. Jsh 24:7. Pr 4:19. Is 50:10. Je 13:16.
  23:12. Jn 8:12.
9 **stripped**. Jb 29:7-14, 20, 21. 30:1. Ps 49:16,
  17. 89:44. Is 61:6. Ho 9:11, 12.
10 **destroyed**. Jb 1:13-19. 2:7. Ps 88:13-18. La
  2:5, 6. 2 C 4:8, 9.
  I am gone. Jb 17:11. Ps 102:11.

mine hope. Jb 6:11. 8:13-18. 17:15. 24:20. Ps 37:35, 36.

11 **kindled**. Dt 32:22. Ps 89:46. 90:7.
he counteth. Jb 13:24. 16:9. 33:10. La 2:5.

12 **His**. Jb 16:11. Is 10:5, 6. 51:23.
raise. Jb 30:12.

13 **put my brethren**. Ps 31:11. 38:11. +69:8, 20. 88:8, 18. Mt 26:56. 2 T 4:16.
estranged. Jb 6:21-23.

14 **kinsfolk**. 2 K 10:11mg. Ps 38:11. Pr 18:24. Mi 7:5, 6. Mt 10:21.
familiar. 2 S 16:23. Ps 55:12-14. Je 20:10. Jn 13:18.

15 **dwell**. ver. 16-19.
count me. Jb 31:31, 32. Ps 123:3, 4.

16 **my servant**. Jb 1:15, 16, 17, 19.

17 **breath**. Heb. *ruach*, spirit, put for manner, Ge +26:35. Jb 1:19. 2:9, 10. 4:9, 15. 6:4, 26. 17:1.
body. Heb. belly. Dt +28:11mg. Ps 132:11mg. Mi 6:7mg.

18 **Yea**. Jb 30:1, 12. 2 K 2:23. Is 3:5.
young children. or, the wicked. Jb 16:11. 21:11. 2 K +2:23.
despised. Jb 5:17. 7:16. 8:20. 9:21.

19 **my inward friends**. Heb. the men of my secret. Ps 41:9mg. 55:12-14, 20.
they whom. Jb 6:14, 15. Ps 109:4, 5. Lk 22:48.

20 **bone**. Jb 30:30. 33:19-22. Ps 22:14-17. 32:3, 4. 38:2. 102:3, 5. La 4:8.
and to. or, as.
and I am. Jb 2:4-6. 7:5. La 3:4. 5:10.

21 **have pity**. Jb 6:14. Ro 12:15. 1 C 12:26. He 13:3.
the hand. Ex +9:3. 6:4.
touched. Jb +1:11.

22 **persecute**. Jb 10:16. 16:13, 14. Ps 69:26.
and are not. Jb 2:5. 31:31. Is 51:23. Mi 3:3.

23 **Oh**. Heb. Who will give, etc.
my words. Jb 31:35. Is 8:1. 30:8.
oh that they were. Jb 13:26.
a book. Je 36:2.

24 **graven**. Ex 28:11, 12, 21. 32:16. Dt 27:2, 3, 8. Je 17:1. 2 C 3:1-6.

25 **I know**. Dt +1:17mg. Ps +9:10. Je 9:24. 22:16. 31:34. Jn 10:27. 17:3. Ro 8:35, 37. 1 C 8:3. 2 T 1:12. 4:6-8. He 6:11, 12, 17-20. 1 J 2:3. 3:18, 19. 5:10, 20.
my redeemer. Jb 33:23, 24. Is +41:14. Ep 1:7.
shall stand. Ge +3:15. 22:18. Jn 5:22-29. Ju 14, 15.
latter day. Ge +49:1.
upon the earth. Ps 37:9. 96:13. 102:13, 16. Is 24:23. Zc 14:4. Mt 5:5. Jn 14:3. 1 Th 4:17. Re 5:10.

26 **And though**, etc. or, After I shall awake, though this *body* be destroyed, yet out of my flesh shall I see God. Ps 17:15.
after. Is +26:19. Da 12:2. Ph 3:21.

destroy. **s#5362h**. Young renders, "compassed," and notes "It never means destroy." ver. 6. Jb 1:5. Le 19:27. Jsh 6:3, 11. 1 K 7:24. 2 K 6:14. 11:8. 2 Ch 4:3. 23:7. Ps 17:9. 22:16. 48:12. 88:17. Is 10:34mg. 15:8. 29:1. La 3:5.
in my flesh. Ps 16:9, 11. Mt 5:8. Jn +5:29. 1 C 13:12. 15:53. Ph 3:21. 1 J 3:2. Re 1:7.
see God. Ps 45:6. Is 25:9. 52:7. Jn 1:1. 20:28. Ac 20:28. Ro 9:5. 2 C 5:19. Col 2:8, 9. 1 T 3:16. T 2:13. He 1:8. 2 P 1:1mg. Ju 4. Re 21:6, 7.

27 **I shall**. Nu 24:17. Is +26:19.
mine eyes. Is 33:17.
shall behold. lit. have beheld. Past tense put for the future tense, as at Ro 8:30. Ep 2:6. He 12:22.
not another. Heb. a stranger. Lk +24:39. Ac +2:36.
though my reins, etc. or, my reins within me are consumed with earnest desire (for that day). Ps 118:24. 119:81. Lk 2:25, 38. Ph 1:23.
within me. Heb. in my bosom. Ge 16:5. Ex 4:6, 7. Pr 22:18mg.

28 **Why**. ver. 22. Ps 69:26.
seeing, etc. or, and what root of matter is found in me?
the root. 1 K 14:13.

29 **ye afraid**. Jb 13:7-11. Ro 13:1-4.
that ye may. Ps 58:10, 11. Ec 11:9. Mt 7:1, 2. Ja 4:11, 12.

JOB 20

1 **Zophar**. Jb +2:11. 11:1. 42:9.

2 **my thoughts**. ver. 3. Jb 4:2. 13:19. 32:13-20. Ps 39:2, 3. Je 20:9. Ro 10:2.
and for. Ps 31:22. 116:11. Pr 14:29. 29:20. Ec 7:9. Mk 6:25. Ja 1:19, 20.
I make haste. Heb. my haste *is* in me.

3 **the check**. Jb 19:29.
the spirit. Heb. *ruach*, Ge +41:8. ver. 2. Jb 27:11. 33:3. Ps 49:3. 78:2-5.

4 **thou not**. Jb 8:8, 9. 15:10. 32:7.
man. Ge 1:28. 9:1-3. Ps 115:16.

5 **the triumphing**. Jb 5:3. 15:29-34. 18:5, 6. 27:13-23. Ex 15:9, 10. Jg 16:21-30. Est 5:11, 12. 7:10. Ps 37:35, 36. 73:18-20. 94:3. Ac 12:22, 23.
short. Heb. from near. Jb 17:12mg. 1 K 16:15. Ezk 7:8.
the joy. Jb 8:19. 27:8. Mt 7:21. 13:20, 21. Ga 6:4. Ja 4:16.
hypocrite. Jb +8:13.

6 **his excellency**. Ge 11:4. Is 14:13, 14. Da 4:11, 22. Am 9:2. Ob 3, 4. Mt 11:23.
clouds. Heb. cloud. Ge 9:13.

7 **perish**. Je +16:4.
for ever. Heb. *netsach*, Jb +4:20.
shall say. Jb 14:10. Ps 37:10.

8 **fly away**. Ps 73:20. 83:10. 90:5. Is 29:7, 8.

9 **The eye**. ver. 7. Jb 7:8, 10. 8:18. 27:23. Ps 37:10, 36. 103:15, 16.

10 **His children**, etc. or, The poor shall oppress his children. Jb 5:4. 27:14. Pr 28:3. Mt 18:28.
   seek. Ps 109:10.
   his hands. ver. 15, 18, 20. Ex 12:36. 22:1, 3, 9. 2 S 12:6. Pr 6:31. Lk +19:8.

11 **bones**. Jb 13:26. 19:20. Ps 25:7. Pr 5:11-13, 22, 23. Ezk 32:27.
   which shall lie. Jb 21:26. Pr 14:32. Ezk 24:13. Jn 8:21, 24. Ac 1:25.

12 **wickedness**. Jb 15:16. Ge 3:6. Pr 9:16-18. 20:17. Ec 11:9.
   he hide. Ps 10:7. 109:17, 18.

13 **spare it**. Mt 5:29, 30. Mk 9:43-49. Ro 8:13.
   within his mouth. Heb. in the midst of his palate. Jb +31:30mg.

14 **his meat**. 2 S 11:2-5. 12:10, 11. Ps 32:3, 4. 38:1-8. 51:8, 9. Pr 1:31. 23:20, 21, 29-35. Je 2:19. Ml 2:2.
   the gall. ver. 16. Dt 32:24. Ro 3:13.

15 **swallowed**. Pr 23:8. Mt 27:3, 4.
   vomit. Pr 26:11. 2 P 2:22.

16 **the poison**. Ro 3:13.
   the viper's. Is 30:6. Mt 3:7. Ac 28:3-6.

17 **shall not see**. Nu 14:23. 2 K 7:2. Je 17:6-8. Lk 16:24.
   the rivers. Jb 29:6. Ps 1:3. 36:8, 9. 46:4. Is 41:17. Je 17:6. Re 22:1.
   floods. or, streaming brooks. or, flowing. Jb 14:11. 22:16. 28:11.
   brooks. Jb 6:15. 21:33. 22:24. Ps 36:8. Is 58:9-11. Jn 7:37.
   of honey. Ex +3:8.

18 **shall he restore**. ver. +10, 15.
   swallow. ver. 15. Ps +35:25. Mt 23:14, 24.
   his substance. Heb. the substance of his exchange. Jb 15:31 (recompence). 28:17. Le 27:10, 33. Ru 4:7.
   and he shall. Jb 31:25, 29. Is 24:7-11. Je 11:15, 16. 22:13, 17. Ezk 7:12. Ho 9:1. Ja 4:8, 9.

19 **Because**. Jb 21:27, 28. 22:6. 24:2-12. 31:13-22, 38, 39. 35:9. 1 S 12:3, 4. Ps 10:18. +12:5. Ezk 22:29. Am 4:1-3. Ja 2:6, 13.
   oppressed. Heb. crushed. Jg +10:8.
   he hath violently. Jb 18:15. 24:2. 1 K 21:19. Is 5:7, 8. Mi 2:2, 9.

20 **Surely**. Ec 5:13, 14. Is 57:20, 21.
   feel. Heb. know. Pr 23:35mg. Ec 8:5mg. Is 59:8.
   that which. Ps 39:11. 1 K 21:19. Is 44:9.

21 **none of his meat be left**. or, be none left for his meat. Jb 18:19. Pr 22:22, 23. Ec 5:13, 14. Je 17:11. Am 4:1, 2. Lk 16:24, 25.

22 **the fulness**. Jb 15:29. 18:7. Ps 39:5. Ec 2:18-20. Re 18:7.
   every hand. Jb 1:15, 17. 16:11. 2 K 24:2. Is 10:6.
   wicked. or, troublesome. Jb 3:17.

23 **he is about**. Nu 11:33. Ps 78:30, 31. Ml 2:2. Lk 12:17-20.
   rain it. Ge 19:24. Ex 9:23. Ps 11:6. 78:30, 31. Is 21:4.

24 **flee from**. 1 K 20:30. Is 24:18. Je 48:43, 44. Am 5:19. 9:1-3.
   the bow. 2 S 22:35.
   strike him. Pr 7:23.

25 **drawn**. Jb 16:13. Dt 32:41. 2 S 18:14. Ps 7:12, 13.
   terrors. Jb 6:4. 15:21. 18:11. 27:20. Ps 73:19. 88:15. Je 20:3, 4. 2 C 5:11.

26 **darkness**. Jb 18:5, 6. Is 8:22. Mt 8:12. Ju 13.
   a fire. Ps 21:9. 120:4. Is +30:33. Mt 3:12.
   it shall go. Jb 18:19. Ps 109:9-15. Is 14:20-22.

27 **heaven**. Ps 44:20, 21. Je 29:23. Ml +3:5. Lk 12:2, 3. Ro 2:16. 1 C 4:5.
   earth. Jb 16:18. 18:18. Is 26:21.

28 **increase**. ver. 10, 18-22. Jb 5:5. 27:14-19. 2 K 20:17. Re 18:17.
   and his goods. Pr +11:4. Zp 1:18. Mt 16:26. Ja 5:1-3.
   day of his wrath. Jb +21:30. Pr +11:4. Zp +1:18. Ro +2:5.

29 **the portion**. Jb 18:21. 27:13. 31:2, 3. Ge +6:13. Dt 29:20-28. Ps 11:5, 6. 17:14. Ec 8:13. Is 3:11. 54:17. Mt 24:51.
   heritage. Ps 16:6.
   appointed unto him by God. Heb. of his decree from God. Jb 2:10. La 3:38. Is 45:7. Da 4:24. Am +3:6.

JOB 21

2 **Hear**. Jb 13:3, 4. 18:2. 33:1, 31-33. 34:2. Jg 9:7. Is 55:2. He 2:1.
   let this be. Jb 15:11. 16:2.

3 **that I may**. Jb 13:13. 33:31-33.
   mock on. Lk +22:63.

4 **is my complaint**. Jb 7:11-21. 10:1, 2. 1 S 1:16. Ps 22:1-3. 77:3-9. 102, title. 142:2, 3. Mt 26:38, 39.
   if it were. 2 K 6:26, 27. Ps 42:11.
   spirit. Heb. ruach, Ge +41:8.
   troubled. Heb. shortened. Ex 6:9mg. Nu 21:4mg. Jg +10:16mg. 16:16mg. Pr 14:29mg. Mi 2:7mg. Zc 11:8mg.

5 **Mark me**. Heb. Look unto me. Jb +5:1mg.
   be astonished. Jb 2:12. 17:8. 19:20, 21.
   lay your. Jb 29:9. 40:4. Jg +18:19. Ps 39:9. Pr 30:32. Am 5:13. Mi 7:16. Ro 11:33.

6 **Even when**. Ps 77:3. 88:15. 119:120. La 3:19, 20. Hab 3:16.

7 **Wherefore**. Jb 12:6. Ps 17:10. 73:3-12. Je 12:1-3. Hab 1:15, 16.
   mighty. Ps 37:35. Da 4:17. Re 13:2-7. 17:2-4.

8 **Their seed**. Jb 5:3, 4. 18:19. 20:10, 28. Pr 17:6.

9 **safe from fear**. Heb. peace from fear. Jb

3:25. 4:14. 13:11. 15:21mg. 18:11. Ps 73:19. Is
57:19-21.
the rod. Jb 9:34. 37:13mg. Ge 49:10. Ps 73:5.
89:32.

10 **their cow**. Ex 23:26. Dt 7:13, 14. 28:11. Ps
144:13, 14. Ec 9:1, 2. Lk 12:16-21. 16:19.

11 **send forth**. Ps 17:14. 107:41. 127:3-5.
dance. Ex +15:20.

12 **They take**. Ge 4:21. 31:27. Is 5:12. 22:13.
Am 6:4-6.
timbrel. Ex +15:20.
harp. Re +5:8.
organ. Jb 30:31. Ge 4:21. Ps 150:4.

13 **They spend**. Jb 36:11. Ps 73:4. Mt 24:38, 39.
Lk 12:19, 20. Lk 16:19, 22. 17:28, 29. or,
wear out. Jb 13:28. Ge 18:12.
wealth. *or*, mirth. 2 S 13:28. Pr 14:13. Lk
16:25.
moment. Jb 7:18. 20:5. 34:20. Lk 16:19, 22.
Mt 8:29.
grave. Heb. *sheol*, Ge +37:35. Jb 7:9. 11:8.
14:13. 17:13.

14 **they say**. Jb 22:17. Ps 10:4, 11. Hab 1:15. Mt
8:29. Lk 8:28, 37. Jn 15-23, 24. Ro 8:7.
for we. Ps 54:3. Pr 1:7, 22, 29. Je 44:16, 17.
Lk 19:14, 27. Jn 3:19, 20. 8:45-47. Ro 1:28.
8:7. 2 Th 2:10-12. 2 T 4:3, 4.
knowledge. Ps 32:9. Pr 13:18. 15:32. 19:2. Is
5:13. Je +44:17. Ezk +39:23. Ho 4:1, 6. Jn
16:2, 3. 17:3. 1 C 2:7, 8. 14:20. 2 Th 1:7, 8.

15 **What is**. Ex 5:2. Ps 12:4. Pr 30:9. Ho 13:6.
Almighty. Jb +5:17.
and what profit. Jb 34:9. 35:3. Nu +32:23.
Ps +37:9. +106:13. Pr +28:16. Is 30:11. Ml
1:13, 14. +18:12. Ph 2:21. 1 T 6:5. 2 T 3:2,
+5.
if we. Is 45:19. Mt 7:7. Jn 16:24. Ja 4:2.

16 **Lo**. Jb 1:21. 12:9, 10. Ps 49:6, 7. 52:5-7. Ec
8:8. Lk 16:2, 25.
the counsel. Jb 22:18. Ge 49:6. Ps 1:1. Pr
1:10. 5:8.

17 **How oft**. Jb 18:5, 6, 18. Pr 13:9. 20:20.
24:20. Mt 25:8.
candle. *or*, lamp. Ps +18:28mg.
cometh. Ro 1:27.
distributeth. Ps 32:10. 90:7-9. Lk 12:46. Ro
2:8, 9.

18 **as stubble**. 1 C +3:12.
wind. Je +23:19.
chaff. Lk +3:17.
carrieth. Heb. stealeth. Jb 27:20.

19 **layeth**. Jb 22:24. Dt 32:34. Mt 6:19, 20. Ro
2:5.
iniquity. *that is*, the punishment of his iniquity. Ge 4:7. Is 53:4-6. 2 C 5:21.
for his children. Ex 20:5. Ps 109:9, etc. Is
14:21. Ezk 18:14, 19, 20. Mt 23:31-35.
he rewardeth. Dt 32:41. 2 S 3:39. Ps 54:5.
Mt 16:27. 2 T 4:14. Re 18:6.
he shall. Ml 3:18.

20 **see**. Jb 27:19. Lk 16:23.
drink. Ps 75:8. Is 51:17. Je 25:15, 16. 51:7.
Re 14:10. 19:15.
Almighty. ver. +15.

21 **For what**. Jb 14:21. Ec 2:18, 19. Lk 16:27,
28.
the number. Ps +102:24.

22 **teach**. Jb 40:2. Is 40:13, 14. 45:9. Ro 11:34. 1
C 2:16.
he judgeth. Jb 34:17-19. Ps 113:5, 6. Ec 5:8.
Is 40:22, 23. 1 C 6:3. 2 P 2:4. Ju 6. Re 20:1-3,
12-15.

23 **in his full strength**. Heb. in his very perfection, *or*, the strength of his perfection. Jb
20:22, 23. Ps 49:17. 73:4, 5. Lk 12:19-21.

24 **His breasts**. *or*, His milk pails. Jb 15:27. Ps
17:10.
moistened. Pr 3:8.

25 **in the bitterness**. Jb 3:20. 7:11. 9:18. 10:1. 2
S 17:8mg. Pr 14:10. Is 38:15-17.
soul. Heb. *nephesh*, Ge +34:3.
never. Jb 20:23. 1 K 17:12. Ec 6:2. Ezk 4:16,
17. 12:18.

26 **alike**. Jb 3:18, 19. 20:11. Ec 9:2.
the worms. Jb 17:14. 19:26. Ps 49:14. Is
14:11.

27 **I know**. Jb 4:8-11. 5:3-5. 8:3-6. 15:20, etc.
20:5, 29. Lk 5:22.
ye wrongfully. Jb 32:3. 42:7. Ps 59:4.
119:86. 1 P 2:19.

28 **Where**. Jb 20:7. Ps 37:36. 52:5, 6. Hab 2:9-
11. Zc 5:4.
dwelling places. Heb. tent of the tabernacles. Jb 8:22. 15:34. 18:14, 21. Nu 16:26-34.

29 **go by**. Ps 129:8.
tokens. Ge 1:14. 4:15. 9:12, 13, 17.

30 **the wicked**. Pr 16:4. Na 1:2. Mt 8:29. 2 P
2:9, 17. 3:7. Ju 13.
reserved. Jb 33:18. Ju 6.
day. Jb 20:28. Ps 110:5. Pr 11:4. Is +2:11. Zp
1:15. Ro 2:5. Re 6:17.
brought forth. ver. 32. Jb 10:19. Ps 45:14.
wrath. Heb. wraths. Jb 20:28. 24:1. Ps 7:6.
110:5. Pr +11:4. La 1:12. 2:1. Is 13:13. Je
+30:7. Ezk +7:19. Zp +1:18. Lk +21:34-36. Ro
+2:5. 5:9. Ep 2:6. 5:6. 1 Th 1:10. 5:9.

31 **declare**. 2 S 12:7-12. 1 K 21:19-24. Ps 50:21.
Is 58:1. Je 2:33-35. Mk 6:18. Lk 16:28. Ac
24:25. Ga 2:11. Ep 5:11.
repay. ver. 19. Jb 41:11. Dt 7:10. Is 59:18. Ro
12:19. Ja 2:13.

32 **he be**. Ps 49:14. Ezk 32:21-32. Lk 16:22.
grave. Heb. graves. *qeber*, Ge +23:4. Jb 3:12.
5:26. 10:19.
remain in the tomb. Heb. watch in the
heap. **S#1430h**. Jb 5:26 (shock). Ex 22:6
(stacks). Jg 15:5 (shocks).

33 **sweet**. Jb 3:17, 18.
every man. Jb 30:23. Ge 3:19. Ec 1:4. 8:8.
12:7. He +9:27.

34 **comfort**. Jb 16:2.
   seeing. Jb 13:4. 32:3. 42:7.
   falsehood. Heb. transgression. Le 5:15. 6:2.
   26:40.

JOB 22

2 **a man**. Jb 35:6-8. Ps 16:2. Lk 17:10.
   as he that, etc. *or*, if he may be profitable,
   doth his good success depend thereon? Jb
   21:15. Dt 10:13. Pr 3:13-18. 4:7-9. 9:12. Ec
   7:11, 12. Mt 5:29. Ga 6:7, 8.

3 **any pleasure**. 1 Ch 29:17. Ps 16:2. 147:10,
   11. Pr 11:1, 20. 12:22. 15:8. Ml 2:17. Ph 4:18.
   thou makest. Jb 23:10-12. Ps 39:1. 119:3-6,
   59. Lk 17:10. Ac 24:16. 2 C 7:1.

4 **reprove**. Ps 39:11. 76:6. 80:16. Re 3:19.
   for fear. Jb 7:12.
   will he enter. Jb 9:19, 32. 14:3. 16:21. 23:6,
   7. 34:23. Ps 130:3, 4. 143:2. Ec 12:14. Is 3:14,
   15.

5 **not thy**. Jb 4:7-11. 11:14. 15:5, 6, 31-34.
   21:27. 32:3.
   thine. Ps 19:12. 40:12.

6 **For thou**. Jb 24:3, 9, 10. Ex +22:26, 27. Dt
   24:10-18. Ezk 18:7, 12, 16. Am 2:8.
   stripped, etc. Heb. stripped the clothes of the
   naked. Jb 19:9. Ge 37:23. Is 58:10. Je 22:19.
   Mt 6:23. 16:25. Ac 5:41. 1 C 1:25, 27-29.
   9:17. 2 C 6:4, 8-10. 8:2. 12:10, 11. Ep 3:8. 1 T
   5:6.
   naked. Jb 31:19, 20. Is +20:2.

7 **not given**. Jb 31:17. Dt 15:7-11. Ps 112:9. Pr
   11:24, 25. 19:17. Is 58:7, 10. Ezk 18:7, 16. Mt
   25:42. Ro 12:20. Ja 2:15, 16.

8 **But as**. Jb 29:7-17. 31:34. 1 K 21:11-15. Ps
   12:8. Mi 7:3.
   mighty man. Heb. man of arm.
   honorable. Heb. eminent, *or*, accepted for
   countenance. Jb 13:8. 2 K +5:1mg.

9 **widows**. Is +1:17.
   arms. Ps 10:15. 37:17. Ezk 30:22.
   fatherless. Ex +22:22.

10 **snares**. Jb 18:8-10. 19:6. Ps 11:6.
   sudden. Jb 6:4. 13:21. Pr 1:27. 3:25, 26. 1 Th
   5:3.

11 **darkness**. Jb 18:6, 18. 19:8. Pr 4:19. Is 8:22.
   La 3:2. Jl 2:2, 3. Mt 8:12.
   abundance. Ps 42:7. 69:1, 2. 124:4. La 3:54.
   Jon 2:3.

12 **not God**. Is +57:15. 66:1. Mt +6:9.
   height. Heb. head. Jb 1:20. 12:24 (chief). Ge
   2:10.
   stars. Jb 3:9. 9:7. 25:5. 38:7. Ps +8:3, 4.

13 **How**. *or*, What.
   doth God know. Ps 10:11. 59:7. 73:11. 94:7-
   9. 139:11, 12. Ezk 8:12. 9:9. Zp 1:12.

14 **Thick clouds**. Jb 20:6. 26:8. 30:15. 34:22. Ge
   +9:13. Ps 33:14. 97:2. 139:1, 2, 11, 12. Je
   23:24. Lk 12:2, 3.

covering. or, secret place. Jb 13:10. 24:15.
31:27.
   circuit. Pr 8:14. Is 40:22.

15 **the old**. Heb. *olam*, **S#5769h**. Ezr 4:15, 19. Pr
   22:28. 23:10. Is 44:7. 58:12. 61:4. Je 5:15.
   6:16. 18:15. Ezk 25:15. 36:2.
   way. Mt +24:37.

16 **cut down**. Ps +102:24.
   whose foundation was overflown with a
   flood. Heb. a flood was poured upon their
   foundation. Ge 7:11, 17-24. Mt +24:37-39.

17 **Depart**. Jb 21:10, +14, 15. Is 30:11. Mt 8:29,
   34. Ro 1:28.
   and what. Ps 4:6. Ml 3:14.
   for them. *or*, to them.

18 **he filled**. Jb 12:6. 1 S 2:7. Ps 17:14. Je 12:2.
   Ac 14:17. 15:16.
   the counsel. Jb 21:16. Ps 1:1.

19 **righteous**. Ps 48:11. +58:10. 97:8.
   see. Is +66:24.
   innocent. Jb 9:23. Ps 52:6.

20 **our substance**. *or*, our estate. Jb 4:7. 8:3, 4.
   15:5, 6. 20:18, 19. 21:27, 28. Lk 13:1-5.
   the remnant. *or*, their excellency. Jb 4:21.
   Ge 49:3. Ps 17:14.
   the fire. Jb 1:16. 20:26. Ge 19:24. Lk 17:29,
   30. 2 P 2:6, 7.

21 **Acquaint**. Jb 27:8-10. 1 Ch +28:9. Ho 6:6. Jn
   17:3. 2 C 4:6. 2 P 1:2.
   him. *that is*, God.
   be at peace. Mt 5:25. Ro +5:1.

22 **receive**. Dt 4:1, 2. Pr 2:1-9. 1 Th 4:1, 2.
   lay up. Dt +6:6-9. Mt 12:35. 13:52. Re 22:18,
   19.

23 **return**. Jb 8:5, 6. 11:13, 14. Is 55:6, 7. Ho
   14:1, 2. Zc 1:3. Ac 26:20.
   built up. Jb 12:14. Je 31:4. Col 2:7. Ju 20.
   thou shalt. Jb 11:14. 18:15. Jsh 7:13-16. Is
   33:15. Zc 5:3, 4.
   put. 2 T 2:19.

24 **lay up**. 1 K 10:21. 2 Ch 1:15. 9:10, 27.
   as dust. *or*, on the dust.
   Ophir. 1 K +9:28.

25 **the Almighty**. Jb +5:17. Ge 15:1. Ps 18:2.
   84:11. Is 41:10. Ro 8:31.
   defence. *or*, gold. Ps 16:5, 6. Is 33:6. 2 C
   6:10. Ja 2:5.
   plenty of silver. Heb. silver of strength. Nu
   23:22. 24:8. Ps 95:4. Ec 7:12.

26 **shalt thou**. Jb 27:10. 34:9. Ps 37:4. SS 2:3. Is
   58:14. Ro 7:22.
   lift up. Jb 11:15. Ps 25:1. 86:4. 143:8. 1 J
   3:20, 21.

27 **make thy**. Ps 66:17-20. 116:1. 1 J +5:14, 15.
   pay thy vows. Le +23:38.

28 **decree**. Ps 20:4. 90:17. Is +45:11. La 3:37. Mt
   21:22. Ja 4:15.
   the light. Jb 29:3. Ps +112:4. Is 30:21.

29 **men**. Jb 5:19, etc. Ps 9:2, 3. 91:14-16. 92:9-
   11.

cast down. Ps 147:6.

he shall. Pr 29:23. Is 57:15. Lk 14:11. 18:9-14. Ja 4:6. 1 P 5:5.

the humble person. Heb. him that hath low eyes. Ps 138:6. Is 66:2. Ezk 21:26, 27. Lk 1:52. 18:13, 14.

30 **He shall deliver the island of the innocent**. *or*, The innocent shall deliver the island. Jb 42:8. Ge 18:26-32. Is 58:12. Je 5:1. Ac 27:24.

pureness. Is 1:15. Ml 1:9. Mt 17:19, 20. Ac 19:15, 16. 1 T 2:8. Ja 5:15, 16.

JOB 23

2 **my complaint**. Jb 6:2. 10:1. La 3:19, 20. Ps 77:2-9.

stroke. Heb. hand. Ps 22:20mg.

heavier. Jb 11:6.

3 **Oh that**. Jb 13:3. 16:21. 40:1-5. Is 26:8, 13. Je 14:7.

where. Is 55:6, 7. 2 C 5:19, 20. He 4:16.

that I might. Jb 31:35-37. Re 3:20.

4 **order**. Jb 13:18. 37:19. Ps 43:1. Is 43:26.

fill my mouth. Ge 18:25-32. 32:12. Ex 32:12, 13. Nu 14:13-19. Jsh 7:8, 9. Ps 25:11. Da 9:18, 19.

5 **know**. Jb 10:2. 13:22, 23. 42:2-6. 1 C 4:3, 4.

6 **plead**. Jb 9:19, 33, 34. 13:21. Ps 78:38. Is 27:4, 8. 57:16. Mi 2:1.

power. Mt 28:18.

but he would. Ps +18:1. 138:3.

7 **There**. Is 1:18. Je 3:5. 12:1.

so should. Jb 9:15. Ro 3:19-22. 8:1, 33, 34.

for ever. Heb. *netsach*, Jb +4:20.

8 **I go**. Jb 9:11. Ps 10:1. 13:1-3. Is 45:15. 1 T 6:16.

9 **he hideth himself**. Ps 89:46. Is 8:17.

10 **he knoweth**. Ge 18:19. 2 K 20:3. Ps 1:6. +40:17. 103:14. 139:1-3. Jn 21:17. 2 T 2:19.

the way that I take. Heb. the way that is with me.

he hath. Jb 1:11, 12. 2:5, 6. Ps 17:3. He 11:17. 1 P +1:7.

I shall. Jb 42:5-8.

11 **My foot**. 1 S 12:2-5. Ps 18:20-24. 44:18. Ac 20:18, 19, 33, 34. 2 C 1:12. 1 Th 2:10.

his way. Jb 17:9. Ps 36:3. 125:5. Zp 1:6. Lk 8:13-15. Ro 2:7. 2 P 2:20-22.

12 **Neither**. Jn 6:66-69. 8:31. Ac 14:22. He 10:38, 39. 1 J 2:19.

I have esteemed. Heb. hid, *or*, laid up. Jb 22:22. Ps 19:9, 10. 119:11, 103, 127. Je 15:16. Jn 4:32, 34. 1 P 2:2.

necessary food. *or*, appointed portion. ver. 14. Jb 14:5, 13. Pr 30:8mg. Ezr 10:6. Lk +12:42, 46.

13 **who can**. Jb 9:12, 13. 11:10. 12:14. 34:29. Nu 23:19, 20. Ec 1:15. 3:14. Ro 9:19. Ja 1:17.

and what. Ps 135:6. Is +14:27. Ro +9:18.

soul. Heb. *nephesh*, Ge +34:3; Le +26:11.

14 **performeth**. Ps 57:2.

appointed. Jb 7:3. Mi 6:9. 1 Th 3:3. 5:9. 1 P 2:8.

many such. Ps 77:19. 97:2. Is 40:27, 28. Ro 11:33.

15 **am I troubled**. ver. 3. Jb 10:15. 31:23. Ps 77:3. 119:120. Hab 3:16.

presence. Ps 9:3.

16 **For God**. Ps 22:14. Is 6:5. 57:16.

Almighty. Jb 27:2. Ru 1:20. Ps 88:16. Jl 1:15.

17 **cut off**. Jb 6:9. 2 K 22:20. Is 57:1.

the darkness from. Jb 15:22. 18:6, 18. 19:8. 22:11.

JOB 24

1 **Why**. Ge 26:27.

seeing. Ps 31:15. Ec 3:17. 8:6, 7. 9:11, 12. Is 60:22. Da 2:21. Lk 21:22-24. Ac 1:7. 17:26. 1 Th 5:1. 1 T 4:1. 6:15. 2 P 2:3. 3:7, 8.

times. Ge 24:11. Ps 31:15. 119:126. Ac +1:6, 7.

hidden. Jb 15:20. Je 16:17.

they that know. Ps +9:10. 36:10. 91:14. Jn 17:3.

not see. Ge 7:4. 18:17, 20, 21. Ps 73:16-19. Je 12:1-3. Mt 24:38. Ro +2:5.

his days. Jb +20:28. Dt +4:32. Pr 6:34. Is +2:12. +13:6, 9. Je 46:10. Jl 1:15. 2:1. Ob 15. Zp 1:7. Ac 2:20. 1 C +3:13. 4:3.

2 **landmarks**. Pr +23:10.

violently. Jb 1:15, 17. 5:5.

feed thereof. *or*, feed them. or, do evil. ver. 9, 19. Jb 20:19. Ge 21:25.

3 **widow's**. Is +1:17.

ox. 1 S 12:3.

pledge. Jb 22:6. Dt 24:6, 10-13, 17.

4 **turn**. ver. 14. Jb 31:16. Ps 109:16. Pr 22:16. 30:14. Is 10:2. Ezk 18:12, 18. 22:29. Am 2:7. 8:4-6. Mi 2:1, 2.

hide. Pr 28:12, 28. Ja 5:4-6.

5 **wild asses**. Jb 39:5-7. Je 2:24. Ho 8:9.

rising. ver. 14. Pr 4:16. Ho 7:6. Mi 2:1. Zp 3:3. Jn 18:28. Ac 23:12.

the wilderness. Jb 5:5. 12:6. Ge 16:12. 27:40.

6 **They reap**. Dt 28:33, 51. Jg 6:3-6. Mi 6:15.

corn. Heb. mingled corn, *or* dredge.

they gather, etc. Heb. the wicked gather the vintage. Am 8:4-6.

7 **the naked**. ver. +10. Jb 31:19, 20. Ex 22:26, 27. Dt 24:11-13. Ac 9:39.

no covering. Ge 31:40. Pr 31:21mg.

8 **are wet**. Jb 8:16. SS 5:2.

showers. *or*, inundation. Is 4:6. 25:4. 28:2. 30:30. 32:2. Hab 3:10.

embrace. Ge 29:13. 48:10. La 4:5. He 11:38.

shelter. *or*, refuge. Ps 14:6. 46:1. 61:3. 62:7, 8. 71:7. 73:28. 91:2, 9. 94:22. 104:18. 142:5.

9 **They pluck**. 2 K 4:1. Ne 5:5.

10 **naked**. ver. +7.

without clothing. Is +20:2.

they take away. Dt 24:19. Am 2:7, 8. 5:11, 12.

11 **make oil**. Dt 25:4. Je +22:13. Ja +5:4.

12 **groan**. Ex 1:13, 14. 2:23, 24. 22:27. Jg 10:16. Ps +12:5. Ec 4:1. Is 52:5.

soul. Heb. *nephesh*, Ge +34:3.

wounded. Ps 69:26. 109:22.

yet God. Ps 50:21. Ec 8:11, 12. Ml 2:17. 3:15. Ro 2:4, 5. 2 P 3:15.

13 **rebel**. Lk 12:47, 48. Jn 3:19, 20. 9:39-41. 15:22-24. Ro 1:32. 2:17-24. Ja 4:17.

they know not. Pr 4:19. Jn 12:35, 40. Ro 3:11-17. 2 Th 2:10-12.

nor abide. Jb 23:11, 12. Jn 8:31, 44. 15:6. 2 P 2:20-22. 1 J 2:19. Ju 6.

14 **murderer**. 2 S 11:14-17. Ps 10:8-10. Mi 2:1, 2. Ep 5:7-11.

in the night. Lk 12:39. 1 Th 5:2. Re 3:3.

15 **eye**. Ex 20:14. 2 S 11:4-13. 12:12. Ps 50:18. Pr 6:32-35. 7:9, 10.

No eye. Jb 22:13, 14. Ps 10:11. 73:11. 94:7. Ezk 8:12. 9:9.

disguiseth his face. Heb. setteth *his* face in secret. Ge +27:16. 38:14, 15.

16 **In the dark**. Ex 22:2, 3. Ezk 12:5-7, 12. Mt 24:43.

they know not. ver. 13. Jb 38:12, 13. Ps 119:105, 130. Is 8:20. Mk 12:24. Jn 3:19-21. 8:12. 2 C 4:3-6. Ep 5:11-13.

17 **in the terrors**. Jb +3:5. Ps 73:18, 19. Je 2:26. 2 C 5:10, 11. Re 6:16, 17.

18 **swift**. Ps 58:7. 73:18-20. Is 23:10.

their portion. Dt 28:16-20. Ps 69:22. Pr 3:33. Ml 2:2.

19 **Drought**. Jb 6:15-17. 30:3. Ps 63:1. 78:17.

consume. Heb. violently take.

snow waters. Jb 9:30.

so doth. Jb 21:23, 32-34. Ps 49:14. 58:8, 9. 68:2. Pr 14:32. Ec 9:4-6. Lk 12:20. 16:22.

20 **the worm**. Jb 17:14. 19:26.

he shall be. Pr 10:7. Ec 8:10. Is 26:14.

wickedness. Jb 14:7-10. 18:16, 17. Da 4:14. Mt 3:10.

21 **evil entreateth**. Ge 30:23. 1 S 1:6, 7. Is 4:1. Lk 1:25. or, devoureth. Jb 1:14. Mt 23:14.

the barren. Ge +11:30.

doeth not. ver. 3. Jb 29:13. 31:16-18.

widow. Is +1:17.

22 **draweth**. Est 3:8-10. Da 6:4-9. Jn 19:12-16. Re 16:13, 14. 17:2.

no man is sure of life. *or*, he trusteth not his own life. Jb 29:24. Dt 28:66. Mt 6:27. Ja 4:14.

23 **it be given**. Ps 73:3-12. Je 12:1-3.

whereon. Ec 8:11. Is 10:8-11. 56:12. Lk 12:16-20, 45. 1 Th 5:3.

yet his eyes. Ps 10:13, 14. 11:4, 5. Pr 5:21. 15:3. 25:21-23. Ec 5:8. Je 16:17. 32:19. Am

8:7. 9:2. Hab 1:13. Re 2:1, 2, 23.

24 **are exalted**. Jb 20:5. Ps 37:10, 35, 36. 73:19. 92:7. Ja 1:11. 5:1-3.

gone. Heb. not. Jb 8:22mg. 27:19.

brought low. Ps 106:43. Ec 10:18.

taken out. Heb. closed up. Jb 5:16. Dt 15:7.

cut off. Jb 14:2. 18:16. Ge 17:11. Ps 37:2.

the ears of corn. Is 17:5, 6. Re 14:14-20.

25 **who will make**. Jb 9:24. 11:2, 3. 15:2.

JOB 25

1 **Bildad**. Jb +2:11.

2 **dominion**. Jb 9:2-10. 26:5-14. 40:9-14. 1 Ch 29:11, 12. 2 Ch 20:6. Ps 99:1-3. Je 10:6, 7. Da 4:34-37. Mt 6:13. 28:18. Ep 1:20, 21. Ju 25. Re 6:16.

he maketh. Is 57:15, 19. Mt 5:9. 2 C 5:18-21. Ep 2:16, 17. Col 1:20.

3 **there**. Ps 103:20, 21. 148:2-4. Is 40:26. Je 31:35. Da 7:10. Mt 26:53. Re 5:11.

upon whom. Jb 38:12, 13. Ge 1:3-5, 14-16. Ps 19:4-6. Mt 5:45. Jn 1:4, 9. Ja 1:17.

4 **How then**. Jb 4:17-19. Pr +20:9. Ac 13:39. Ro 3:19, 20, 26. 5:1. T 3:5.

how can. Jb 14:3, 4. Ps 51:5. Zc 13:1. 1 C 6:11. Ep 2:3. 1 J 1:9. Re 1:5.

born. Jb 14:1.

5 **even to**. Is 24:23. 60:19, 20. 2 C 3:10.

6 **How much less**, etc. Jb 4:19. 17:14. Ge 18:27. Dt 28:39. Ps 22:6. Is 14:11. 41:14. Da 3:1.

man. Ps +8:4.

son of man. Jb 35:8.

worm. Ps 22:6.

JOB 26

2 **How hast thou**. Jb 12:2. 1 K 18:27.

helped. Jb 4:3, 4. 6:25. 16:4, 5. 2 Ch 32:8. Is 35:3, 4. 40:14. 41:5-7.

without. Is 40:29.

no strength. Is 41:1. Ro 5:6.

3 **counselled**. Jb 6:13. 12:3. 13:5. 15:8-10. 17:10. 32:11-13.

plentifully. Jb 33:3, 33. 38:2. Ps 49:1-4. 71:15-18. Pr 8:6-9. Ac 20:20, 27.

4 **and whose**. Jb 20:3. 32:18. 1 K 22:23, 24. Ec 12:7. Lk 9:55. Jn 3:6. 1 C 12:3. 1 J 4:1-3. Re 16:13, 14.

spirit. Heb. *neshamah*, Ge +2:7, breath. Jb 4:9. 27:3. 32:8. 33:4.

5 **Dead things**. Jb 41:1, etc. Ge 6:4. Ps 104:25, 26. Ezk 29:3-5. or, Rephaim. S#7496. Ps 88:10. Pr 2:18. 9:18. 21:16. Is 14:9. +26:14, 19.

formed. ver. 13. Jb 15:7. 35:14. 39:1.

waters. ver. 8, 10. 3:24. 5:10. 8:11.

and. *or*, with.

inhabitants. Jb 4:19. Ge 14:13.

6 Hell. Heb. *sheol*, Ge +37:35. Jb 7:9. 11:8. 14:13. 17:13. 31:12. Dt +32:22. Ps 9:17. 139:8, 11. Pr 15:11. Is 14:9. Am 9:2. He 4:13.
naked. Jb 1:21. 22:6. 24:7, +10.
destruction. Heb. *abaddon*, **S#11h:** ver. 6. Jb 28:22. 31:12. Ps 88:11. Pr 15:11. 27:20.
no covering. Jb 24:7. 31:19. Ge 20:16. Is +66:24.

7 stretcheth. Jb 9:8. Ge 1:1, 2. 1 Ch 21:10. Ps 24:2. 104:2-5. Pr 8:23-27. Is 40:22, 26. 42:5.
the north. Jb 37:22. Ge 13:14. 28:14. Ps 89:12.
hangeth. Ge 40:19, 22. 41:13.
nothing. Jb 38:6. Ps 104:5. Pr 3:19, 20. 8:27. Is 40:22.

8 bindeth up. Jb 36:29. 38:9, 37. Ge 1:6, 7. Ps 135:7. Pr 30:4. Je 10:13.
thick clouds. Jb 37:11-16. Ge +9:13. Ps 18:10, 11.
and the cloud. Is 5:6.

9 holdeth back. Ex 20:21. 33:20-23. 34:3. 1 K 8:12. Ps 97:2. Hab 3:3-5. 1 T 6:16.

10 compassed. Jb 38:8-11. Ps 33:7. 104:6-9. Pr 8:29. Je 5:22.
bounds. Ge 1:9. Ps 104:9.
until. Ge 8:22. Is +54:9, 10.
day and night come to an end. Heb. end of light with darkness.

11 pillars. Jb 9:6. 1 S 2:8. 2 S +22:8. Ps 18:7, 15. 75:3. Hg 2:21. He 12:26, 27. 2 P 3:10. Re 20:11.
are astonished. Jb 15:15.

12 divideth. Ex +14:21. Ps 29:10. 93:3, 4.
he smiteth. Jb 40:11, 12. Is 2:12. Da 4:37. Ja 4:6.
the proud. Heb. pride. Ps 89:9, 10. Is 51:9.

13 his spirit. Heb. *ruach*, Is +48:16. Ge 1:2. Ps 33:6, 7. 51:11. 104:30. 139:7. Is 11:1, 2. +48:16. 57:15. Jn 1:3.
hand. Ps 102:24, 25. Is 64:8.
formed. Ge 1:24, 25.
the crooked serpent. Ge 3:1. Ps 74:13, 14. Is 27:1. 51:9. Re 12:9.

14 how little. Jb +11:7-9. 1 C 13:9-12.
the thunder. Jb 40:9. 1 S 2:10. Ps 29:3.

JOB 27

1 Job. Nu 23:7. 24:3, 15. Ps 49:4. 78:2. Pr 26:7.
continued. Heb. added to take up. Jb 29:1. Nu 23:7.
parable. Jb 13:12. Nu +23:7.

2 God liveth. Nu 14:21. Ru 3:13. 1 S 14:39, 45. 20:21. 25:26, 34. 2 S 2:27. 1 K 17:1. 18:15. Je 4:2. 5:2. 12:16. Ezk 33:11.
taken. Jb 10:3. 34:5. Is 40:27.
vexed my soul. Heb. made my soul bitter. Heb. *nephesh*, Ge +34:3.Ru 1:20, 21. 1 S +30:6mg.

3 breath. Heb. *neshamah*, Ge +2:7. Jb +14:22. 32:8. 33:4. 34:14. Ps +146:4. Ec 3:21. 12:7.

the spirit of God. *that is*, the breath which God gave him. Heb. *ruach*, Nu +16:22; Ge +2:7. Is 2:22. Ac 17:25.

4 My lips. Jb 13:7. 34:6. Jn 8:55. 2 C 11:10.

5 God forbid. Lk +20:16.
justify. Jb 32:3. 42:7. Dt 25:1. Pr 17:15. Ga 2:11.
die. Ge +49:33 **(S#1478h)**.
I will not. Jb 2:9. 13:15. 29:14. 2 C 1:12.

6 righteousness. Mt 5:20. Ph 3:9.
I hold fast. Jb 2:3. Ps 18:20-23. Pr 4:13.
my heart. Ac 24:16. 2 C 12:11. 1 J 3:20, 21.
so long as I live. Heb. from my days.

7 mine enemy. 1 S 25:26. 2 S 18:32. Je +10:25. Da 4:19.

8 what is. Jb 11:20. 22:21-27. 31:3. Mt 16:26. Mk 8:36, 37. Lk 9:25. 12:20, 21. 1 T 6:9, 10. Ja 5:1-3.
hypocrite. Jb +8:13.
when. 1 Ch +28:9. Pr 1:24-32. Is +27:11. Mt +25:46. Lk +9:24. 13:25. 16:24-25, +26. 2 C +6:2.
soul. Heb. *nephesh*, Ge +12:13.

9 Will God. Ps +66:18. 109:7.
his cry. Ho 7:14. Lk 13:25.

10 delight. Jb 22:26, 27. Ps 37:4. 43:4. Hab 3:18.
will he always call upon. Ps +14:1. 78:34-36. Mt 13:21. Lk +18:1.

11 teach. Jb 4:3, 4. 6:10. Is 8:11.
by the hand. *or, being* in the hand, etc. Ps 25:8, 12. 32:8. Pr 4:11.
that which. Jb 32:8-10. Dt 4:5. Ps 71:17, 18. Ac 20:20, 27.
not conceal. Jb 6:10. 15:18.

12 ye yourselves. Jb 21:28-30. Ec 8:14. 9:1-3.
altogether. Jb 6:25-29. 13:4-9. 16:3. 17:2. 19:2, 3. 21:3. 26:2-4.

13 the portion. Jb 20:29. 31:3. Ps 11:6. Ec 8:13. Is 3:11. 2 P 2:9.
the heritage of oppressors. Ps +12:5. Is 61:8. Je 5:27-29. Ezk 22:12-14, 29, 31. Ml +3:5. Ja 2:13.

14 children. Jb 21:11, 12. Dt 28:32, 41. 2 K 9:7, 8. 10:6-10. Est 5:11. 9:5-10. Ps 109:13. Ho 9:13, 14. Lk 23:29.
his offspring. 1 S 2:5.

15 Those. 1 K 14:10, 11. 16:3, 4. 21:21-24.
his widows. 1 S 4:19, 20. Ps 78:64. Je 22:18. Ezk 24:23.

16 heap up. Jb 22:24, 25. 1 K 10:27. Hab 2:6. Zc 9:3.
as the dust. Ge +13:16.
prepare raiment. Mt 6:19. Ja 5:2.

17 but the just. Pr 13:22. 28:8. Ec 2:26.

18 as a moth. Jb 8:14, 15. Is 51:8.
as a booth. Is 1:8. 38:12. La 2:6.

19 shall lie. Jb 14:13-15. 21:23-26, 30. 30:23.
gathered. Ge 49:10. Je 8:2. Mt 3:12. 23:37.
he openeth. Jb 20:7-9. Ps 58:9. 73:19, 20.
he is not. Jb 8:22. 14:10, 12. 24:24mg.

20 **Terrors**. Jb 15:21. 18:11. 22:16. Ps 18:4. 42:7. 69:14, 15. Jon 2:3.
a tempest. Jb 20:23. 21:18. Ex 12:29. 2 K 19:35. Da 5:30.

21 **east wind**. Ge +41:6.
a storm. Ex 9:23-25. Ps +83:15. Na 1:3-8.

22 **For God**. Ex 9:14. Dt 32:23. Jsh 10:11.
not spare. Dt 29:20. Ezk 9:5, 6. Ro 8:32. 2 P 2:4, 5.
he would fain flee. Heb. in fleeing he would flee. Jb 20:24. Ex 14:25-28. Jg 4:17-21. Is 10:3. Am 2:14. 9:1-3.

23 **clap**. Est 9:22-25. Pr 11:10. La 2:15. Na 3:19. Re 18:20.
hiss him. 2 Ch +29:8.

JOB 28

1 **vein**. or, mine. Jb 38:27. Nu 30:12. 1 K 10:28.
the silver. Ge 2:11, 12. 23:15. 24:22. 1 K 7:48-50. 10:21. 1 Ch 29:2-5.
where they fine it. Jb 12:6. Pr 17:3. 27:21. Is 48:10. Zc 13:9. Ml 3:2, 3. 1 P 1:7.

2 **Iron**. Ge 4:22. Nu 31:22. Dt 8:9. 1 Ch 22:14.
earth. or, dust. ver. 6. Jb 2:12. 4:19. 5:6. 7:5, 21. 27:16.

3 **searcheth**. Pr 2:4. Ec 1:13. Hab 2:13. Mt 6:33. Lk 16:8.
the shadow. Ps +23:4.

4 **flood**. or, stream or valley. That is, a mine.
sojourner. Jb 19:15. Ex 3:22. +12:49.
forgotten of the foot. That is, unvisited.
dried up. or, low. Ps 79:8. 116:6. 142:6.
gone away. or, wandered, or moved. Ex 20:18.

5 **out of it**. Ge 1:11, 12, 29. Ps 104:14, 15. Is 28:25-29.
fire. Ezk 28:13, 14.

6 **sapphires**. ver. 16. Ex 24:10. SS 5:14. Is 54:11. Re 21:19.
dust of gold. or, gold ore.

7 **a path**. ver. 21-23. Jb 11:6. 38:19, 24. Ro 11:33.
the vulture's eye. Le 11:14. Dt 14:13.

8 **trodden**. Jg 20:43. Ps 25:5, 9.
lion's whelps. or, sons of pride. Jb 41:34.
fierce lion. Jb 4:10. 10:16. Ps 91:13.

9 **rock**. or, flint. Dt 8:15. 32:13. Ps 114:8. Is 50:7.
he overturneth. Na 1:4-6.

10 **cutteth**. Jb 26:8. Ge 22:3.
rivers. or, brooks. Ge 41:1, 2, 3, 17, 18.
every precious thing. Pr 14:23. 24:4. Is 43:4. Hab 3:9.

11 **bindeth**. Jb 26:8. Is 37:25. 43:2. 44:27.
overflowing. Heb. weeping. Jb 16:16. Ge 45:2mg. 2 S 13:36mg.
and the thing. Is 45:2, 3. 1 C 4:5.

12 **where shall wisdom**. ver. 20, 28. 1 K 3:9. Ps 51:6. Pr 2:4-6. 18:1. Ec 7:23-25. 1 C 1:19, 20, 30. Col 2:3. Ja 1:5, 17.

13 **knoweth**. ver. 15-19. Ps 19:10. 119:72. Pr 3:14, 15. 8:11, 18, 19. 16:16. 23:23. Ec 8:16, 17.
in the land. ver. 21, 22. Ps +27:13.

14 **depth**. Jb 38:16, 30. Ge 1:2. 7:11. Ro 11:33, 34.
the sea. Jb 6:3. 7:12. 9:8. 11:9. 12:8.

15 **It cannot be gotten for gold**. Heb. Fine gold shall not be given for it. ver. 18. Pr 3:13-15. 8:10, 17, 19. 16:16. 23:23. Ac 8:18.

16 **the gold**. 1 Ch 29:4. Ps 45:9. Is 13:12.
Ophir. 1 K +9:28.
onyx. Ge +2:12.

17 **crystal**. Ezk 1:22. Re 4:6. 21:11. 22:1.
jewels. or, vessels. 2 Ch 9:20, 24. Est 1:7. Is 39:2mg.

18 **coral**. or, Ramoth. Ezk 27:16.
pearls. Mt 7:6. 13:45, 46. 1 T 2:9. Re 17:4. 18:12. 21:21.
price of wisdom. Pr 4:7. 17:16. 18:1.
rubies. Pr 3:13-15. 8:11. 31:10. La 4:7.

19 **topaz**. Ex 28:17. 39:10. Ezk 28:13. Re 21:20.

20 **Whence then**. ver. +12. Pr 2:6. Ec 7:23, 24. Is 53:8. 1 C 2:6-15. Ja 1:5, 17.

21 **hid**. Ps 49:3, 4. Mt 11:25. 13:17, 35. 1 C 2:7-10. Col 2:3.
from the fowls. ver. 7.
air. or, heaven. Jb 2:12. 12:7. Ge 1:1, 26, 28.

22 **Destruction**. Heb. abaddon, Jb +26:6. ver. 14. Jb 31:12. Ps 83:10-12.
death. Jb 3:21. 5:20. 7:15. 18:13.

23 **God understandeth**. Ps 19:7. 147:5. Pr 2:6. 8:14. Mt 11:27. Lk 10:21, 22. Ac 15:18. Ro 11:33. 1 C 1:30. Ju 25.
knoweth the place. Pr 15:3.

24 **he looketh**. 2 Ch 16:9. Pr 15:3. Zc 4:10. Re 5:6.

25 **To make the weight**, etc. Ps 135:7. Is 40:12.
he weigheth. Is 40:15.

26 **he made**. Jb 36:26, 32. 38:25. Ps 148:8. Je 14:22. Am 4:7. Zc 10:1.
a way. Jb 37:3-5. Ps 29:3-10.

27 **declare it**. or, number it. Jb 12:8. 15:17. 38:37.
he prepared it. Ps 19:1. Pr 8:22-29.

28 **unto man**. Dt 29:29. Pr 8:4, 5, 32-36.
fear. Dt 4:6. Ps 33:18, 19. 34:7-9. 145:19. Pr 1:7. +3:7. 9:10. Ml 3:16, 17. Ja 3:13-17. Re 11:18.
to depart. Pr 5:7. 13:14. 16:6, 17. Is 1:16. 2 T +2:19.

JOB 29

1 **continued**. Heb. added to take up. Jb 27:1mg.
parable. Jb 13:12. Nu +23:7.

2 **as in months**. Jb 1:1-5. 7:3.
past. Heb. kedem, Mi +5:2.
God. Jb 1:10. Ps 37:28. Ju 1.

3 **candle**. *or*, lamp. Ps +18:28mg. Pr 20:20. 24:20.
by his light. Jb 22:28. Ps 4:6. 23:4. 27:1.
84:11. Is 2:4. Jn 8:12. 12:46. Ep 5:8, 14.

4 **the secret**. Jb 1:10. 15:8. Ps 25:14. 27:5.
91:1. Pr 3:32. Col 3:3.

5 **the Almighty**. Jb +5:17.
with. Jb 23:3, 8-10. Dt 33:27-29. Jsh 1:9. Jg
6:12, 13. Ps 30:7. 43:2. 44:8, 9. SS 2:4. 3:1, 2.
Je 14:8. Mt 9:15.
my children. Jb 1:2-5. 42:13-16. Ps 127:3-5.
128:3. Pr 17:6.

6 **I washed**. Jb 9:30. 20:17. Ge 49:11. Dt 32:13.
33:24.
rock. Ps 81:16. Ac 2:33.
poured. Jb 28:2.
me out. Heb. with me.
rivers. Ps 1:3. 46:4. 65:9. 119:136.
oil. Ge 28:18. 35:14. Ex 25:6. Dt +33:24.

7 **to the gate**. Ge +14:7. Dt 16:18. 21:19. Ru
4:1, 2, 11. Zc 8:16.

8 **young men**. Le 19:32. Pr 16:31. 20:8. Ro
13:3, 4. T 3:1. 1 P 5:5.
the aged. Ro 13:7. 1 P 2:17.

9 **refrained**. Jb 4:2. 7:11. Pr 10:19. Ja 1:19.
laid. Jb 21:5. 40:4. Jg 18:19. Pr 30:32.

10 **nobles held their peace**. Heb. voice of the
nobles was hid.
their tongue. Ps 137:6. Ezk 3:26.

11 **the ear**. Jb 31:20. Pr 29:2. Lk 4:22. 11:27.
blessed. Ge +31:35.

12 **I delivered**. Jb 22:5-9. Ne 5:2-13. Je +22:16.
the fatherless. Ex +22:22.

13 **The blessing**. Dt 24:13. Ac 9:39-41. 2 C
9:12-14. 2 T 1:16-18.
ready. Jb 31:19. Dt 26:5. Pr 31:6-9. Is 27:13.
I caused. Dt 16:11. Ne 8:10-12. Phm 7.
the widow's. Ja 1:27.
sing. Ps 67:4. Is 65:14.

14 **I put**. Ex +28:2. Dt 24:13. Is +59:17.
a diadem. Is 28:5. 62:3.

15 **eyes**. Nu 10:31. Mt +11:5. 1 C 12:12, etc.

16 **a father**. Jb 31:18. Est 2:7. Ps 68:5. Ep 5:1. Ja
1:27.
the cause. Ex 18:26. Dt 13:14. 17:8-10. 1 K
3:16-28. Pr 25:2. 29:7.

17 **I brake**. Ps 3:7. 58:8. Pr 30:14.
jaws. Heb. jaw teeth, *or*, grinders. Pr 30:14. Jl
1:6.
and plucked. Heb. and cast. 1 S 17:35. Ps
124:3, 6.

18 **I shall die**. Ge +49:33 (**S#1478h**). Jb 3:11.
10:18. 13:19. 14:10. Ps 30:6, 7. Je 22:23.
49:16. Ob 4. Hab 2:9.
multiply. Jb 5:26. 42:16, 17. Ps 91:16.
as the sand. Ge +22:17.

19 **root**. Jb 18:16. Ps 1:3. Je 17:8. Ho 14:5-7.
spread out. Heb. opened. Nu 19:15. Jsh
8:17. 1 K 8:29.
dew. Jb 38:28. Dt +33:13.
branch. Jb 5:5. 14:9.

20 **glory**. ver. 14. Jb 19:9. Ge 45:13. Ps 3:3.
fresh. Heb. new. Is 43:19.
my bow. Ge 49:24.
renewed. Heb. changed. Ps 103:5. Is 40:31. 2
C 4:16.

21 **gave ear**. ver. 9, 10. Jb 32:11, 12.

22 **After my**. Jb 32:15, 16. 33:31-33. Is 52:15.
Mt 22:46.
speech. Dt 32:2. SS 4:11. Ezk 20:46. Am
7:16. Mi 2:6mg.

23 **as for the rain**. Ps 72:6.
the latter rain. Dt +11:14. Zc 10:1.

24 **they believed**. Ge 45:26. Ps 126:1. Lk 24:41.
the light. Ps 4:6. 89:15.

25 **chose out**. Ge 41:40. Jg 11:8. 2 S 5:2. 1 Ch
13:1-4.
dwelt. Ge 14:14-17. Dt 33:5.
one that. Jb 4:3, 4. Is 35:3, 4. 61:1-3. 2 C 1:3,
4. 7:5-7. 1 Th 3:2, 3.

JOB 30

1 **they that are**. Jb 19:13-19. 29:8-10. 2 K
+2:23. Is 3:5.
younger than I. Heb. of fewer days than I.
Jb 32:6mg.
derision. Lk +16:14.
whose. Ac 17:5. T 1:12.

2 **strength of**. Is 10:13.
old age. Jb 5:26.

3 **solitary**. *or*, dark as the night. Jb 24:13-16. Is
49:21.
fleeing into. Jb 24:5. He 11:38.
in former time. Heb. yesternight. Ge 19:34.

4 **juniper roots**. 1 K 19:4, 5. Ps 120:4.
for their meat. 2 K 4:38, 39. Am 7:14. Lk
15:16.

5 **driven**. Ge 4:12-14. Ps 109:10. Da 4:25, 32, 33.

6 **dwell**. Jg 6:2. 1 S 22:1, 2. Is 2:19. Re 6:15.
caves. Heb. holes. 1 S 14:11. 2 K 12:9.
the rocks. Je 4:29.

7 **brayed**. Jb 6:5. 11:12. Ge 16:12.
the nettles. Pr 24:31. Is 34:13. Ho 9:6. Zp
2:9.

8 **children**. 2 K 8:18, 27. 2 Ch 22:3. Ps 49:10-
13. Je 7:18. Mk 6:24.
fools. Pr 1:7, 22. 16:22.
base men. Heb. men of no name. Jb 18:17. 1
Ch 11:27.
viler. Jb 40:4. Ps 15:4. Is 32:6.

9 **song**. Ps 35:15, 16. 69:12. La 3:14, 63.
byword. Jb +17:6.

10 **abhor me**. Jb 19:19. 42:6. Ps 88:8. Zc 11:8.
flee far. Jb 19:13, 14. Ps 88:8. Pr 19:7. Mt
26:56.
spare not to spit in my face. Heb. withhold
not spittle from my face. Mt +26:67.

11 **loosed**. Jb 12:18, 21. 2 S 16:5-8.
let loose. Ps 35:21. Mt 26:67, 68. 27:39-44.
Ja 1:26.

12 **rise**. Jb 19:18. Is 3:5.
they raise up. Jb 19:12.
13 **they set forward**. Ps 69:26. Zc 1:15.
14 **as a wide**. Jb 22:16. Ps 18:4. 69:14, 15. Is 8:7, 8.
15 **Terrors**. Jb 6:4. 7:14. 9:27, 28. 10:16. Ps 88:15.
soul. Heb. principal one. Ps 51:12.
as a cloud. Is 44:22. Ho 6:4. 13:3.
16 **my soul**. Heb. *nephesh*, Ge +34:3. Ps 22:14. 42:4. Is 53:12.
have taken hold. Ps 40:12.
17 **My bones**. Jb 33:19-21. Ps 6:2-6. 38:2-8.
in the night season. Jb 7:4. Ps 22:2. Is 38:13.
18 **By the great**. Jb 2:7. 7:5. 19:20. Ps 38:5. Is 1:5, 6.
19 **cast me**. Jb 9:31. Ps 40:2. 69:1, 2. Je 38:6.
become like. Nu +21:27.
dust. Jb 2:8. 42:6. Ge 18:27.
20 **I cry**. Jb 19:7. 27:9. Ps 22:2. 80:4, 5. La 3:8, 44. Mt 15:23.
dost not hear. Jb +35:12.
21 **become cruel**. Heb. turned to be cruel. Jb 7:20, 21. 10:14-17. 13:25-28. 16:9-14. 19:6-9. Ps 77:7-9. Je 30:14.
thy strong hand. Heb. the strength of thy hand. Jb 6:9. 23:6. Ps 89:13. 1 P 5:6.
against me. Ru +1:13.
22 **liftest me**. Jb 21:18. Ps 1:4. Is 17:13. Je 4:11, 12. Ezk 5:2. Ho 4:19. 13:3.
to ride. Ps 18:10. 104:3.
substance. *or*, wisdom. Jb 6:13. 12:16. Pr 2:7.
23 **the house**. Jb 14:5. 21:33. Ge 3:19. 1 S 13:11. 2 S 14:14. Ec 8:8. 9:5. 12:5-7. He +9:27.
appointed. Ge +17:21.
24 **grave**. Heb. heap. **S#1164h**, only here. Ps 79:1. Je 26:18. Mi 1:6. 3:12.
they cry. Jg 5:31. Ps 35:25. Mt 27:39-44.
25 **Did not I**. Ps 35:13, 14. Je 13:17. 18:20. Lk 19:41. Jn 11:35. Ro 12:15.
in trouble. Heb. hard of day. Ge 42:7mg, 30. Ex 1:14. 6:9.
was. Jb 31:16-21. Ps 12:1. Pr 14:21, 31. 17:5. 19:17. 28:8. Is 58:7, 8. Da 4:27. 2 C 9:9.
soul. Heb. *nephesh*, Ge +34:3.
26 **When I looked**. Jb 3:25, 26. 29:18. Je 8:15. 14:19. 15:18. Mi 1:12.
light. Jb 18:6, 18. 23:17. Ps 97:11. Is 50:10.
27 **My bowels**. Ps 22:4. Je 4:19. 31:20. La 1:20. 2:11.
28 **I went**. Is 53:3, 4. La 3:1-3. Mt +5:4.
29 **a brother**. Jb 17:14. Ps 102:6. Is 13:21, 22. 38:14. Mi 1:8. Ml 1:3.
owls. *or*, ostriches. **S#3284h**: Le 11:16. Dt 14:15. Is 13:21. 34:13. 43:20. Je 50:39. Mi 1:8. See also **S#3283h**, La 4:3.
30 **my skin**. Ps 119:83. La 3:4. 4:8. 5:10.

black. Le 13:31., 37. SS 1:5.
my bones. Ps 102:3.
31 **My harp**. Re +5:8.
mourning. Ge 27:41. 50:10, 11. Ps 137:1-4. Ec 3:4. Is 21:4. 22:12. 24:7-9. La 5:15. Da 6:18.
organ. Jb 21:12. Ge 4:21. Ps 150:4.
weep. Ex 2:6.

JOB 31

1 **a covenant**. Ge 6:2. 2 S 11:2-4. Ps +101:3. 119:37. Pr 4:25. 23:31-33. Mt 5:28, 29. 2 P 2:14. 1 J 2:16.
think. Pr 6:25. Ja 1:14, 15.
2 **what portion**. Jb 20:29. 27:13. He 13:4.
3 **destruction**. Jb 21:30. Ps 1:6. 37:20. 55:23. 73:18. 145:20. Pr 1:27. 10:29. 21:15. Mt +7:13. Ro 9:22. 1 Th 5:3. 2 Th 1:9. 2 P 2:1.
a strange. Is 28:21. Ju 7.
4 **Doth not he see**. Jb 14:16. 34:21. Ge 16:13. 2 Ch 16:9. Ps 44:21. 139:1-3. Pr 5:21. 15:3. Je 16:17. 32:19. Jn 1:48. He 4:13.
count. Mt 6:8, 26. 10:29-31.
5 **If**. Ps 7:3-5.
walked. Ps 4:2. 12:2. 44:20, 21. Pr 12:11. Je 2:5. Ezk 13:8.
6 **Let me be weighed in an even balance**. Heb. Let him weigh me in balances of justice. 1 S 2:3. Ps 7:8, 9. 17:2, 3. 26:1. Pr 16:11. Is 26:7. Da 5:27. Mi 6:11.
know. Jsh 22:22. Ps 1:6. 139:23. Mt 7:23. 2 T 2:19.
7 **If my**. Ps 44:20, 21.
mine heart. Nu 15:39. Ec 11:9. Ezk 6:9. 14:3, 7. Mt 5:29. 1 J 2:16.
walked. Ge +31:35.
cleaved. Ps 101:3. Is 33:15.
8 **let me**. Jb 5:5. 24:6. Le 26:16. Dt 28:30-33, 38, 51. Jg 6:3-6. Mi 6:15.
let my. Jb 5:4. 15:30. 18:19. Ps 109:13.
9 **If mine**. Jg 16:5. 1 K 11:4. Ne 13:26. Pr 2:16-19. 5:3, etc. 6:25. 7:21. 22:14. Ec 7:26.
if I. Jb 24:15, 16. Je 5:8. Ho 7:4.
10 **grind**. Ex 11:5. Dt 28:30. Is 47:2. Mt 24:41.
and let. 2 S 12:11. Je 8:10. Ho 4:13, 14.
11 **For this**. Le 20:10. 1 C 7:9. Col 3:5, 6. He 13:4. Re 22:15.
an heinous. Ge 20:9. 26:10. 39:9. Ex 20:14. Pr 6:29-33.
an iniquity. ver. 28. Ge 38:24. Le 20:10. Dt 22:22-24. Ezk 16:38.
12 **a fire**. Pr 3:33. 6:27-29, 32. Je 5:7-9. Ml +3:5. He 13:4.
destruction. Heb. *abaddon*, Jb +26:6. 28:22. Ps 88:1.
13 **the cause**. Ge 14:14. 17:12. 24:2-4, 10. Ex 21:20, 21, 26, 27. Le 25:43, 46. Dt 15:12-15. Je 34:14-17. Ep 6:9. Col 4:1.
when. 1 S +25:17. 2 K 5:13, 16.

14 **What then**. Jb 9:32. 10:2. Ps 7:6. 9:12, 19. 10:12-15. 44:21. 76:9. 143:2. Is 10:3. Zc 2:13.
when he. Ho 9:7. Mi 7:4. Mt 7:2. Ja 2:13.
what shall. Ro 3:19.

15 **Did not he**. Jb 34:19. Ne 5:5. Pr 14:31. 22:2. Is 58:7. Ml 2:10.
did not one fashion us in the womb? *or*, did not he fashion us in one womb? Jb 10:8-12. Ge 3:20. Ps 139:14-16. Ml 2:10. Ac 17:26.

16 **withheld**. Jb 22:7-9. Dt 15:7-10. Ps 112:9. Ezk 18:7, 16. Lk 16:21. Ac 11:29. Ro 12:13. Ga 2:10. Ja 2:15, 16. 1 J 3:17.
the eyes. Ps +69:3.
widow. Is +1:17.

17 **eaten my morsel**. Dt 15:11, 14. Ne 8:10. Is 58:6, 7. Ezk +18:7. Lk 11:41. 14:13, 14. Jn 13:29. Ac 4:32.
the fatherless. Ex +22:22.

18 **youth**. Jb 13:26. Ge 8:21.
guided. Jb 12:23mg. 38:32. Ge 24:48.
her. *that is*, the widow. ver. 16.

19 **perish**. Jb 22:6. 2 Ch 28:15. Is +58:7. Ezk +18:7. Mt 25:36, 43. Lk 3:11. Ac 9:39. Ja 2:16. 1 J 3:18.

20 **his loins**. Jb 29:11. 38:3. 40:7. Ge 35:11. Dt 24:13.

21 **lifted**. 2 K 5:11mg.
fatherless. Ex +22:22.
when. Mi 2:1, 2. 7:3.
help. Le 19:15. Dt 25:1. Pr 18:17. Jn 7:24, 51.
gate. Jb 5:4. 29:7. Ps 69:12. Je 38:7.

22 **let**. ver. 10, 40. Jsh 22:22, 23. Ps 7:4, 5. 137:5.
arm. Je 32:21.
shoulder. Ex 28:7.
blade. ver. 36. Ge 9:23. 21:14.
bone. *or*, chanel bone. Jb 40:21 (reed). Ge 41:5 (stalk). Is 42:3 (reed).

23 **destruction**. Jb 20:23. 21:20. Ge 39:9. Ps 119:120. Is 13:6. Jl 1:15. 2 C 5:11.
by. Jb 13:11. 40:9. 42:5, 6. Ps 76:7.

24 **made gold my hope**. Ge 31:1. Dt 8:12-14. Ps 49:6, 7, 17. 52:7. 62:10. Pr 10:15. 11:28. 30:9. Mk 10:24, 25. Lk +12:15. Col 3:5. 1 T 6:9, 10, 17.

25 **rejoiced**. Est 5:11. Pr 23:5. Je 9:23. Ezk 28:5. Da 4:30. Lk 12:19. 16:19, 25.
because. Dt 8:17, 18. Is 10:13, 14. Da 4:30. Ho 12:8. Hab 1:16.
gotten much. Heb. found much. ver. +29. Jb 11:7. 17:10.

26 **beheld**. Ge 1:16-18. Dt 11:16. Ezk +8:16. Ro 1:20.
sun. Heb. light. Jb 3:9, 16, 20. 12:22, 25.
the moon. Ps 8:3, 4. Je 44:17.
in brightness. Heb. bright.

27 **my heart**. Dt 11:16. 13:6. Is 44:20. Ro 1:21, 28.
my mouth hath kissed my hand. Heb. my hand hath kissed my mouth. Ps +2:12.
kissed. Ge +27:27.

28 **an iniquity**. ver. 11. Jb 9:15. 23:7. Ge 18:25. Dt 17:2-7, 9. Jg 11:27. Ps 50:6. He 12:23.
for. Jsh 24:23, 27. Pr 30:9. T 1:16. 2 P 2:1. 1 J 2:23. Ju 4.

29 **I rejoiced**. 2 S 1:12. 4:10, 11. 16:5-8. Ps 35:13, 14, 25, 26. Pr +17:5.
found. 2 K +9:21mg.

30 **have**. Ex 23:4, 5. Mt 5:43, 44. Ro 12:14. 1 P 2:22, 23. 3:9.
mouth. Heb. palate. Jb 6:30mg. 12:11mg. 20:13mg. 33:2mg. 34:3mg. Ps 119:103mg. Pr 5:3mg. 24:13mg. Ec 5:2, 6. SS 2:3mg. 5:16mg. Ho 8:1mg. Mt 5:22. 12:36. Ja 3:6, 9, 10.
soul. Heb. *nephesh*, Ge +27:31.

31 **the men**. 1 S 24:4, 10. 26:8. 2 S 16:9, 10. 19:21, 22. Je 40:15, 16. Lk 9:54, 55. 22:50, 51.
Oh. Jb 19:22. Ps 27:2. 35:25. Pr 1:11, 12, 18. Mi 3:2, 3.

32 **The stranger**. ver. 17, 18. Ge 19:2, 3. Dt +26:11. Jg 19:15, 20, 21. Is 58:7. Mt +25:35, 40, 44, 45. Ro 12:13. 1 T 5:10. He 13:2. 1 P 4:9.
in the street. lit. outplace. Jb 5:10mg. 18:17 (street). Am +5:16 (**S#2351h**, highways).
opened. Ge 18:2-7. 19:1-3. Ac 28:7. Ro +15:7. 1 P 4:9, 10. 3 J 5, 6.
traveller. *or*, way. Jb 6:18, 19. Is 3:12.

33 **covered**. Ge 3:7, 8, 12. Jsh 7:11. Pr 28:13. Ho 6:7. Ac 5:8. 1 J 1:8-10.
as Adam. *or*, after the manner of men. Ps 82:7. Ho 6:7mg.

34 **Did I**. Ex 23:2. Pr 29:25. Je 38:4, 5, 16, 19. Mt 27:20-26. Ac 24:27.
the contempt. Jb 22:8. 34:19. Ex 32:27. Nu 25:14, 15. Ne 5:7. 13:4-8, 28. 2 C 5:16.
that I. Est 4:11, 14. Pr 24:11, 12. Am 5:11-13. Mi 7:3.

35 **Oh**. Jb 13:3. 17:3. 23:3-7. 33:6. 38:1-3. 40:4, 5.
my desire is, that the Almighty would answer me. *or*, my sign is that the Almighty will answer me. Jb +5:17. 13:21, 22. 38:1. Ps 26:1.
mine. Jb 13:24. 19:11, 23, 24. 33:10, 11. Mt 5:25.

36 **I would**. Ex 28:12. Is 22:22.
a crown. Jb 29:14. Is 62:3. Ph 4:1.

37 **declare**. Jb 9:3. 13:15. 14:16. 42:3-6. Ps 19:12.
as a prince. Ge 32:28. Ep 3:12. He 4:15, 16. 1 J 3:19-21.

38 **cry**. Jb 20:27. Ex +22:23.
complain. Heb. weep. Ps 65:10, 13.

39 **fruits**. Heb. strength. Ge 4:12.
without money. Le +19:13. Dt 24:14, 15. Je 22:13. Ml +3:5. Ja +5:4.
caused the owners thereof to lose their life. Heb. caused the soul of the owners

thereof to expire, or breathe out. 1 K 21:13-16, 19. Pr 1:19. Is 26:21. Ezk 22:6, 12, 13. Ml 1:13.

life. Heb. *nephesh*, soul, Ge +44:30.

40 **thistles**. Ge 3:17, 18. 2 K +14:9. Is 7:23. Zp 2:9. Ml 1:3.

cockle. or, noisome weeds.

The words. Ps 72:20.

JOB 32

1 **to answer**. Heb. from answering.

righteous. Jb 6:29. 10:2, 7. 13:15. 23:7. 27:4-6. 29:11-17. 31:1, etc. 33:9.

2 **kindled**. Ps 69:9. Mk 3:5. Ep 4:26.

Elihu. ver. 5, 6. Jb 34:1. 36:1. 1 S +1:1.

Barachel. i.e. *blessed of God*, S#1292h. ver. 6.

Busite. i.e. *despised one*, S#940h. ver. 6. Ge 22:21. Je 25:23.

kindred. Jb 31:34. Ge 8:19mg. 10:5, 18.

Ram. i.e. *high one; elevated*, S#7410h. Jb 32:2. Ru 4:19, 19. 1 Ch 2:9, 10, 25, 27.

because. Jb 10:3. 27:2. 34:5, 6, 17, 18. 35:2. 40:8. Lk 10:29.

himself. Heb. his soul, *nephesh*, Ge +27:31. Ex 30:12. 1 P +4:19.

3 **because**. ver. 1. Jb 24:25. 25:2-6. 26:2-4.

and yet. Jb 8:6. 15:34. 22:5. Ac 24:5, 13.

4 **waited till Job had spoken**. Heb. expected Job in words. ver. 11, 12. Pr 18:13.

elder. Heb. elder for days.

5 **his wrath**. ver. 2. Ex 32:19.

6 **I am**. Le 19:32. Ro 13:7. 1 T 5:1. T 2:6. 1 P 5:5.

young. Heb. few of days. Jb 30:1mg.

ye are. Jb 15:10.

durst not. Heb. feared. Jb 15:7. 1 S 17:28-30.

7 **should speak**. Jb 8:8-10. 12:12. 1 K 12:6-8. Ps 34:11, 12. Pr 1:1-4. 16:31. He 5:12.

8 **spirit**. Heb. *ruach*, Ge +41:8. Jb +14:22. Ec +3:21. 12:7. Zc 12:1.

the inspiration. Heb. *neshamah*, Ge +2:7. Jb 4:12-21. 33:16. 35:11. 38:36. Ge 41:39. 1 K 3:12, 28. 4:29. Pr 2:6. Ec 2:26. Da 1:17. 2:21. Mt 11:25. 1 C 2:10-12. 12:8. 2 T 3:16. Ja 1:5.

Almighty. Jb +5:17.

giveth them. Ps 32:8. 119:99.

9 **Great**. Je 5:5. Mt 11:25. Jn 7:48. 1 C 1:26, 27. 2:7, 8. Ja 2:6, 7.

neither. Jb 12:20. Ec 4:13.

the aged. Jb 12:12. Ps 119:100.

10 **Hearken**. Ec 3:7. 1 C 7:25, 40.

11 **I waited for**. ver. 4, 16. Jb 29:21, 23. 1 S 10:8. 13:8. Pr 18:13.

reasons. Heb. understandings. Jb 12:12, 13. 26:12. Ex 31:3.

whilst. Jb 5:27. 13:9. 28:27. Pr 18:17. 28:11. Ec 12:9, 10.

what to say. Heb. words. Jb 33:1.

12 **behold**. ver. 3. 1 T 1:7.

13 **Lest**. Ge 14:23. Jg 7:2. Is 48:5, 7. Zc 12:7.

We. Jb 12:2. 15:8-10. Is 5:21. Je 9:23. Ezk 28:3. 1 C 1:19-21, 27-29. 3:18, 19.

God. Jb 1:21. 2:10. 4:9. 6:4. 19:6, 21. Jn 19:11.

14 **directed**. Heb. ordered. or, set in array. Jb 6:4. 13:18. 23:4. 33:5.

speeches. or, sayings. ver. 12. Jb 6:10, 25, 26. 8:2.

15 **amazed**. Jb 6:24, 25. 29:22. 2 K 19:26. Mt 7:28. 22:22, 26, 34, 46.

left off speaking. Heb. removed speeches from themselves. Jb 9:5. Ge 12:8. 26:22.

16 **for they**. Jb 13:5. Pr 17:28. Am 5:13. Ja 1:19.

17 **I will answer**. ver. 10. Jb 33:12. 35:3, 4.

opinion. ver. 6, 10. Jb 36:3. 37:16.

18 **matter**. Heb. words. Jb 4:2mg. 16:4.

the spirit. Heb. *ruach*, Ge +41:8. Ps 39:3. Je 6:11. 20:9. Ezk 3:14, etc. Ac 4:20. 2 C 5:13, 14.

within me. Heb. of my belly. Jb 19:27. Pr 22:18mg.

constraineth. or, distressed. Dt 28:53, 55, 57.

19 **hath no vent**. Heb. is not opened. Jb 12:14. Ge 7:11.

burst. Jb 26:8. Ge 7:11.

new. Mt 9:17.

bottles. Le +19:31. 2 K +21:6 (S#178h).

20 **I will speak**. Jb 13:13, 19. 20:2. 21:3.

be refreshed. Heb. breathe. 1 S 16:23.

I will open. Pr 8:6, 7.

21 **accept**. Ro +2:11. Ja +2:1.

flattering. 2 S 14:17, 20. Ac 12:22, 23. 24:2, 3.

22 **I know not**. That is, *I cannot*. Jb 5:24, 25. 9:2, 5.

flattering titles. Ps +12:3. Mt 23:9. Ga 1:10.

maker. Jb 4:17. 31:15. 35:10. 40:19.

take me away. Jb 21:21. Ps 12:3. 102:23, 24. Is 38:10. 64:6. Ac 12:23. 1 C 11:30. Ja 5:20. 1 J 5:16.

JOB 33

1 **hear**. Jb 13:6. 34:2. Ps 49:1-3. Mk 4:9.

2 **I have opened**. Jg +11:35.

mouth. Heb. palate. Jb +31:30mg.

3 **the uprightness**. Jb 27:4. Pr 8:7, 8. 1 Th 2:3, 4.

my lips. Jb 15:2. 36:3, 4. 38:2. Ps 37:30, 31. Pr 15:2, 7. 20:15. 22:17, 18.

4 **The Spirit**. Heb. *ruach*, Is +48:16. Jb 10:12. 26:13. 27:3. 32:8. Ge 2:7. Ps 33:6. Ac 5:3, 4. Ro 8:2. 1 C 15:45.

God. Heb. *El*, Ex +15:2.

made. Jb 10:9. 12:9. 31:15. 40:15. Lk 1:35.

breath. Heb. *neshamah*, Ge +2:7.

the Almighty. Jb +5:17. Ge +17:1. 2 C 6:18.

5 **If**. ver. 32, 33. Jb 32:1, 12.
set. Jb 23:4, 5. 32:14. Ps 50:21.
stand. Ac 10:26.

6 **I am**. Jb 9:32-35. 13:3, 20-22. 23:3, 4. 31:35.
wish. Heb. mouth. Dt +21:5mg. Zc 1:21.
in. Ge 30:2. Ex 4:16. 2 C 5:20. He 2:14.
I also. Jb 4:19. 10:9. 13:12. Ge 2:7. 3:19. 2 C 5:1.
formed. Heb. cut. lit. "nipped." Ps 35:19. Is 51:1. 2 C 4:7.

7 **my terror**. Jb 9:34. 13:21. Ps 88:16.
my hand. Ps 103:14. Ex +9:3. He 4:15.

8 **hearing**. Heb. ears. Jb 4:12. 12:11. 13:1, 17. Ex 17:14. Dt 13:14. Je 29:23.

9 **clean**. Jb 9:17. 10:7. 11:4. 16:17. 23:11, 12. 27:5, 6. 29:14.
innocent. Jb 9:23, 28. 17:8. Je 2:35.

10 **he findeth**. Jb 9:30, 31. 10:15-17. 13:25, 26. 14:16, 17. 34:5, 6.
he counteth. Jb 6:26. 13:24. 16:9. 19:11. 30:21, 22. 31:35.

11 **putteth**. Pr +7:22.
marketh. Jb 31:4. Da 4:35.

12 **thou**. Jb 1:22. 34:10-12, 17-19, 23. 35:2. 36:22, 23. Je 2:35. Ezk 18:25. Ro 9:19-21.
I will. Jb 32:17. 35:4.
God. Jb 9:4. 26:14. 36:5. 40:2, 8, 9. Je 18:6.

13 **strive**. Jb 9:14. 15:25, 26. Is 45:9. Je 50:24. Ezk 22:14. Ac 5:39. 9:4, 5. 1 C 10:22.
giveth not account. Heb. answereth not. Jb 40:2. Dt 29:29. Ps 62:11. 115:3. Is 44:10. 46:10. Da 4:35. Mt 20:15. Ac 1:7. Ro 11:34.

14 **God**. Jb 40:5. Ps 62:11.
perceiveth. 2 Ch 33:10. Pr 1:24, 29. Is 6:9. Mt 13:14. Mk 8:17, 18. Lk 24:25. Jn 3:19.

15 **a dream**. Jb 4:13. Ge +31:24. Je 23:28. 2 C 3:14-17. He 1:1. 2 P 1:19-21.
deep. Ge 15:12. Da 8:18, 19. 10:9.

16 **openeth**. Heb. revealeth, *or,* uncovereth. Jb 36:10, 15. 2 S 7:27. Ps 40:6. Is 6:10. 48:8. 50:5. Lk 24:45. Ac 16:14.
sealeth. Jb 37:7. Ne 9:38. Ro 15:28.

17 **withdraw**. Jb 17:11. Ge 20:6. Is 23:9. Ho 2:6. Mt 27:19. Ac 9:2-6. 26:10-13.
purpose. Heb. work. Jb 1:10. 14:15. 34:19. 37:7. Ge 5:29.
hide. Dt 8:16. 2 Ch 32:25, 26. Is 2:11. Da 4:30-37. 2 C 12:7. Ja 4:10.

18 **keepeth**. Ac 16:27-33. Ro 2:4. 2 P 3:9, 15.
soul. Heb. *nephesh,* Ps +30:3. Jb +14:22. Ge 25:8, 9, 17. 35:18. 1 K 17:22. Ps 88:3. Mt +10:28.
pit. Heb. *shachath,* Jb +9:31 (**S#7845h**).
Shachath occurs in connection with *nephesh* here and Jb 33:22, 28, 30. Ps 35:7. Is 38:17.
perishing. Heb. passing. ver. 28. 2 K 4:8. 6:9. Pr 10:25. 19:11. La 3:44. Ac 16:27, 28.

19 **chastened**. Jb 5:17, 18. Dt 8:5. Ps 94:12, 13. 119:67, 71. Is 27:9. 1 C 11:32. He 12:5-11. Re 3:19.

pain. Jb 7:4. 20:11. 30:17, 18, 30. 2 Ch 16:10, 12. Ps 38:1-8. Is 38:12, 13.

20 **his life**. Ps 107:17, 18.
soul. Heb. *nephesh,* Nu +11:6.
dainty meat. Heb. meat of desire. Ge 3:6. 49:26. Nu 11:4. Pr 23:3. Je +25:34mg.

21 **His flesh**. Jb 7:5. 13:28. 14:20, 22. 19:20. Ps 32:3, 4. 39:11. 102:3-5. Pr 5:11.
his bones. Ps 22:15-17.

22 **his soul**. Heb. *nephesh,* Ps +30:3. Jb 7:7. +14:22. 17:1, 13-16. 1 S 2:6. Ps 30:3. 88:3-5. Is 38:10. Mt +10:28.
draweth near. Ge 27:41. 47:29. Dt 31:14.
grave. Heb. *shachath,* Jb +9:31. ver. 18.
his life. Jb 15:21. Ex 12:23. 2 S 24:16. Ps 17:4. Ac 12:23. 1 C 10:10. Re 9:11.
the destroyers. 1 S 2:6. 2 K 17:26. Je 26:15. Mt +10:28.

23 **a messenger**. Jg 2:1mg. 2 Ch 36:15, 16. Is 63:9. Hg 1:13. Ml 2:7. 3:1. Ac 10:43. 2 C 5:20.
an interpreter. Jb 34:32. Ge 40:8. Ps 94:12. Is 61:1-3. Ac 8:30, 31. 1 C 11:30-32. Ga 3:19. 1 T 2:5. He 8:6. 9:15. 12:5-12. lit. "sweetener," as in Jb 16:20. 2 Ch 32:31. Ps 119:103. Is 43:27.
one among. Jb 9:3. Ps 12:1. 89:19. Ro 11:13.
a thousand. Dt 33:2. Ec 7:28. SS 5:10. Mi +5:2.
to show. Jb 11:6. 34:10, 12. 35:14. 36:3, 8-13. 37:23. Ne 9:33. Ps 119:75. La 3:22, 23, 32, 39-41. Ezk 18:25-28. Da 9:14.
his uprightness. ver. 3. Jb 6:25. Dt 9:5. Pr 14:2.

24 **Then**. ver. 18. Jb 22:21. Ex 33:19. 34:6, 7. Ps 86:5, 15. Ho 14:2, 4. Mi 7:18-20. Ro 5:20, 21.
Deliver. Jb 36:10, 11. Ex 15:26. Ps 30:9-12. 40:2. 71:3. 86:13. Is 38:17-19. Je 31:20. Zc 9:11.
soul. Heb. *nephesh,* Ps +30:3.
pit. *or,* corruption. ver. +18, 22.
I have found. Jb 36:18. Ps 49:7, 8. 89:19. Mt 20:28. Jn 1:17. Ro 3:24-26. 1 T 2:5, 6. He 9:12. 1 P 1:18, 19.
a ransom. *or,* an atonement. Jb 36:18. 1 S +12:3 (**S#3724h**). Is 53:10, 11. Mt 20:28.

25 **His flesh**. 2 K 5:14.
a child's. Heb. childhood. Jb 36:14. Ps 88:15. Pr 29:21.
return. Jb 42:16. Dt 34:7. Jsh 14:10, 11. Ps 103:5. Is 40:31. Ho 2:15.

26 **pray**. 2 K 20:2-5. 2 Ch 7:14. 33:12, 13, 19. Ps 6:1-9. 28:1, 2, 6. 30:7-11. 41:8-11. 50:15. 91:15. 116:1-6. Is 30:19. Je 33:3. Jon 2:2-7. Mt 7:7, 8. Ac 9:11.
and he shall. Jb 42:8, 9. Nu 6:25, 26. Ps 4:6, 7. 16:11. 30:5. 67:1. Ac 2:28. Ju 24.
he will. Jb 34:11. 1 S 26:23. Ps 18:20. 62:12. Pr 24:12. Mt 10:41, 42. He 11:26.

27 **looketh**, etc. *or,* shall look upon men, and say, I have sinned, etc. Ge 16:13. 2 Ch 16:9.

Ps 11:4. 14:2. 53:2. 139:1-4. Pr 5:21. 15:3. Je 23:24.

I have sinned. Jb 7:20. Nu 12:11. 2 S 12:13. Pr 28:13. Je 3:13. 31:18, 19. Lk 15:18-22. 18:13. 1 J 1:8-10.

perverted. Ec 5:8.

right. Ps 19:7, 8. 119:128. Ro 7:12-14, 16, 22.

it profited. Jb 34:9. Je 2:8. Mt 16:26. Ro 6:21.

28 **will deliver**, etc. *or*, hath delivered my soul, etc. ver. 18, 24. Jb 17:16. Dt +32:39. 1 S 2:6. Ps 9:13. 40:2. 55:23. 66:8, 9. 68:20. 69:15. 91:7. 102:19, 20. 107:18, 19. 116:15. Is 38:17, 18. Re 20:1-3.

soul. Heb. *nephesh*, Ps +30:3.

pit. Heb. *shachath*, ver. +18.

shall see. ver. 20, 22. Jb 3:9, 16, 20. Ps 49:19. Is 9:2. Jn 11:9.

29 **all**. ver. 14-17. 1 C 12:6. 2 C 5:5. Ep +1:11. Ph 2:13. Col 1:29. He 13:21.

worketh. Jb 7:20. 11:8. 22:17. 34:32.

oftentimes. Heb. twice and thrice. ver. 14. Jb 40:5. 2 K 6:10. 2 C 12:8.

30 **To bring**. ver. 24, 28. Ps 40:1, 2. 118:17, 18. Is 51:1.

soul. Heb. *nephesh*, Ps +30:3.

pit. Heb. *shachath*, ver. +18.

enlightened. Ps 56:13. Is 2:5. 38:17. Jn 8:12. Ac 26:18.

31 **Mark well**. Jb 13:6. 18:2. 21:2. 32:11.

32 **I desire**. Jb 9:3. 13:3. 15:4, 5. 21:27. 22:5-9. 27:5.

justify. Jb 32:2. Ezk 16:52. Ro 3:26. 8:33.

33 **hearken**. Ps 34:11. Pr 4:1, 2. 5:1, 2.

I shall teach. ver. 3. Ps 49:3. Pr 8:5.

wisdom. Jb 4:21. 11:6. 12:2. 1 C 1:30.

JOB 34

1 **answered**. Jg 18:14.

2 **wise men**. ver. 34. Jb 5:13. Pr 1:5. 1 C 10:15. 14:20.

have knowledge. Jb 19:13. 24:1. 42:11.

3 **the ear**. Jb 6:30. 12:11. 1 C 2:15. He 5:14.

mouth. Heb. palate. Jb +31:30mg.

4 **choose**. ver. 36. Jg 19:30. 20:7. 1 C 6:2-5. Ga 2:11-14. 1 Th 5:21.

know. Is 11:2-5. Jn 7:24. Ro 12:2.

5 **I am righteous**. Jb 10:7. 11:4. 16:17. 29:14. 32:1. 33:9.

God. Jb 9:17. 27:2.

6 **I lie**. Jb 6:28. 27:4-6.

wound. Heb. arrow. Jb 6:4. 16:13. Ge 49:23. Nu 24:8.

incurable. **S#605h**. 2 S 12:15 (very sick). Is 17:11 (desperate). Je 15:18. 17:9, 16 (woeful). 30:12, 15. Mi 1:9.

without transgression. ver. 37. Jb 7:21. 8:4. 33:9.

7 **drinketh**. Jb 15:16. Dt 29:19. Pr 1:22. 4:17.

8 **Which goeth**. Jb 2:10. 11:3. 15:5. Ps 1:1. 26:4. 50:18. 73:12-15. Pr 1:15. 2:12. 4:14. 13:20. 1 C 15:33.

9 **It profiteth**. Jb 9:22, 23, 29-31. 21:14-16, 30. 22:17. 35:3. Ml 3:14.

delight. Jb 27:10. Ps 37:4.

10 **understanding**. Heb. heart. ver. 2, 3, 34. Jb +12:3. Pr 6:32. 15:32mg. Je 5:21. Ac 8:22.

far be it. Jb 8:3. 36:23. Ge 18:25. Dt 32:4. 2 Ch 19:7. Ps 92:15. Je 12:1. Ro 3:4, 5. 9:14. Ja 1:13.

11 **the work**. Jb 33:26. Ezk 33:17-20. Mt +16:27. 1 C 3:13.

cause. Pr 1:31. Ga 6:7, 8.

12 **surely**. Ps 11:7. 145:17. Hab 1:12, 13.

do wickedly. ver. 17, 29. Jb 9:20.

pervert. Jb 8:3. 19:6. Ps 119:78.

13 **Who hath given**. Jb 36:23. 38:4, etc. 40:8-11. 1 Ch 29:11. Pr 8:23-30. Is 40:13, 14. Da 4:35. Ro 11:34-36.

the whole world. Heb. the world, all of it. Jb 18:18. 37:12.

14 **set**. ver. 23. Jb 7:17. 9:4.

upon man. Heb. upon him.

he gather. Jb 39:12. Ps +36:6. 104:29. Is 24:22.

spirit. Heb. *ruach*, Nu +16:22. Ps 104:29.

breath. Heb. *neshamah*, Ge +2:7. Jb 4:9. 26:4. 27:3. 32:8.

15 **All flesh**. Jb 30:23. Ge 3:19. +6:3. Ps 90:3-10. Ec 12:7. Is 27:4. 57:16.

perish. Jb 3:11. 10:18. 13:19. 14:10. Ge +49:33.

turn again. Jb 10:9, 21. Ge 3:19. Ps 104:29. +146:4. Ec 3:20. 12:7.

16 **thou hast**. Jb 12:3. 13:2-6.

understanding. Jb 20:3. 28:12.

17 **even**. Ge 18:25. 2 S 23:3. Ro 3:5-7.

govern. Heb. bind. Jb 5:18. Jg 18:7.

wilt. Jb 1:22. 40:8. 2 S 19:21. Ro 9:14.

18 **to say**. Ex 22:28. Pr 17:26. Ac 23:3, 5. Ro 13:7. 1 P 2:17. 2 P 2:10. Ju 8.

ungodly. 1 S +30:22.

19 **accepteth**. Jb 13:8. Ro +2:11. He 12:28.

princes. Jb 12:19, 21. Ps 2:2-4. Ec 5:8. Is 3:14.

regardeth. Le +19:15. Ps 49:6, 7. Ja +2:5.

they. Jb 31:15. Pr 14:31. 22:2.

20 **a moment**. Ps 73:19. Is 30:13. 37:38. Da 5:30. Lk 12:20. Ac 12:23. 1 Th 5:2. 2 P 2:3.

troubled. Ex 12:29, 30. Is 37:36. Mt 25:6. Lk 17:26-29.

the mighty shall be taken away. Heb. they shall take away the mighty. Jb 18:18.

without. 1 S 25:37-39. 26:10. Is 10:16-19. 30:30-33. Da 2:34, 44, 45. Zc 4:6.

21 **his eyes**. Jb 31:4. Ge 16:13. Ps +11:4. 139:23. Pr 5:21. Je 16:17. 32:19. Am 9:8.

22 **no darkness**. Ps 139:11, 12. Is 29:15. Je 23:24. Am 9:2, 3. 1 C 4:5. He 4:13. Re 6:15, 16.

nor shadow. Ps +23:4.
the workers. Jb 31:3. Ps 5:5. Pr 10:29. Mt 7:23. Lk 13:27.

23 **he will**. ver. 10-12. Jb 11:6. Ezr 9:13. Ps 119:137. Is 42:3. Da 9:7-9.
that he. Jb 9:32, 33. 16:21. 23:7. Je 2:5. Ro 9:20.
enter. Heb. go. Jb 14:3.

24 **break**. Jb 19:2. Ps 2:9. 72:4. 94:5. Je 51:20-23. Da 2:21, 34, 35, 44, 45. Lk 1:52.
number. Heb. searching out. Jb 5:9. 8:8. 9:10. 11:7. 36:26.
set. 1 S 2:30-36. 15:28. 1 K 14:7, 8, 14. Ps 113:7, 8. Da 5:28-31.

25 **he knoweth**. Ps 33:15. Is 66:18. Ho 7:2. Am 8:7. Re 20:12.
in the night. ver. 20. SS 3:8. Is 15:1. 1 Th 5:2.
destroyed. Heb. crushed. Jb 5:4.

26 **in the**. Ex 14:30. Dt 13:9-11. 21:21. 2 S 12:11, 12. Is +66:24. 1 T 5:20, 24. Re 18:9, 10, 20.
open sight of others. Heb. place of beholders. Lk 12:2, 3. 2 T 3:9.

27 **turned**. 1 S 15:11. Ps 125:5. Zp 1:6. Lk 17:31, 32. Ac 15:38. 2 T 4:10. He 10:39.
from him. Heb. from after him.
would. Ps 28:5. 107:43. Pr 1:29, 30. Is 1:3. 5:12. Hg 2:15-19.

28 **cry of the poor**. Jb 22:9, 10. 24:12. 29:12, 13.
and he heareth. Ex +22:23-27.

29 **When he giveth**. Jb 29:1-3. 2 S 7:1. Is 14:3-8. 26:3. 30:15. Ro +5:1. 8:31-34.
when he hideth. Dt +31:17.
who then can behold. Jb 12:14. 23:13. Pr 16:7.
whether. 2 K 18:9-12. 2 Ch 36:14-17. Je 27:8.

30 **hypocrite**. Jb +8:13.
reign not. ver. 21. 1 K 12:28-30. 2 K 21:9. Ps 12:8. Ec 9:18. Ho 5:11. 13:11. Mi 6:16. 2 Th 2:4-11. Re 13:3, 4, 11-14.

31 **it is meet**. Jb 33:27. 40:3-5. 42:6. Le 26:41. Ezr 9:13, 14. Ne 9:33-38. Je 31:18, 19. Da 9:7-14. Mi 7:9.

32 **which**. Jb 10:2. Ps 19:12. 25:4, 5. 32:8. 119:18. 139:23, 24. 143:8-10.
teach. 2 Ch 1:7-10. Ps 25:9. 119:66. Pr 2:3-6. Is 45:11, 12. Da 2:17-21. Ph 1:9.
if. Pr 28:13. Lk 3:8-14. Ep 4:22, 25-28. 1 P 4:3.

33 **Should**. Jb 9:12. 18:4. Is 45:9. Ro 9:20. 11:35.
according to thy mind. Heb. from with thee. Jb 23:10.
he will. ver. 11. Jb 15:31. Ps 89:30-32. Pr 11:31. 2 Th 1:6, 7. He 2:2. 11:26.
whether thou refuse. Ps 135:6. Mt 20:12-15.
what. Jb 33:5, 32.

34 **understanding**. Heb. heart. ver. 2, 4, +10, 16. 1 C 10:15.

35 **hath spoken**. Jb 13:2. 15:2. 35:16. 38:2. 42:3.

36 **My desire is that Job may be tried**. *or*, My father, let Job be tried. Jb 23:16. Ps 17:3. 26:2. Ja 5:11.
the end. Heb. *netsach*, Jb +4:20.
his answers. ver. 8, 9. Jb 12:6. 21:7. 24:1.

37 **rebellion**. 1 S 15:23. Is 1:19, 20.
he clappeth. Jb 27:23.
multiplieth. Jb 8:2, 3. 11:2, 3. 35:2, 3, 16. 42:7.

JOB 35

2 **Thinkest**. Mt 12:36, 37. Lk 19:22.
My. Jb 9:17. 10:7. 16:17. 19:6, 7. 27:2-6. 34:5. 40:8.

3 **What advantage**. Jb 9:21, 22. 10:15. 21:15. 31:2. 34:9. Ps 73:13. Ml 3:14.
if I be cleansed from my sin. *or, by it* more than my sin.

4 **answer thee**. Heb. return to thee words.
thy. Jb 34:8. Pr 13:20.

5 **Look**. Jb 22:12. 25:5, 6. 36:26-33. 37:1-5, 22, 23. 1 K 8:27. Ps 8:3, 4. Is 40:22, 23. 55:9.
the clouds. Jb 36:29. 37:16. Na 1:3.

6 **what doest**. Pr 8:36. 9:12. Je 7:19.

7 **what givest**. Jb 22:2, 3. 1 Ch 29:14. Ps 16:2, 3. Pr 8:36. Ro 11:35.

8 **may hurt**. Jsh 7:1-5, 24, 25. 22:20. Ec 9:18. Jon 1:12.
may profit. Jb 42:8. Ge 12:2. 18:24, etc. 19:29. Ps 106:23, 30. Ezk 22:30, 31. Ac 27:24. He 11:7.

9 **oppressions**. Ge +43:18.
they make. Jb 24:12. Ex +22:23. Ne 5:1-5. Ps 55:2, 3. 56:1, 2.
the arm. Jb 40:9. Ps 10:15.

10 **none**. Jb 36:13. 2 K 1:2, 3. 1 Ch 10:13, 14. 2 Ch 28:22, 23. Is 8:21.
Where. Ec 12:1. Is 51:13. 1 P 4:19.
my. Jb 32:22. 36:3. Is 54:5.
maker. Heb. makers. Ge +1:26. Ec 12:1. Is 54:5.
who. Ps 42:8. 77:6. 119:62. 149:5. Ac 16:25.

11 **Who teacheth**. Jb 32:8. Ge +1:26. +2:7. Ps 8:5, 6. 94:12.

12 **they cry**. Ps 18:41. Pr 1:28.
none giveth answer. or, he answereth not. Jb 19:7. 30:20. Ps 22:2. +66:18. La 3:8. Hab 1:2.
because. Ps +9:10.
pride. Ps 73:6-8. +119:21. 123:3, 4. Is 14:14-17.

13 **God**. Jb 22:22-27. Ec 5:1-3. Ho 7:14. 8:2, 3. Mt 6:7. 20:21, 22.
not hear. Ps +66:18.
regard. Jb 30:20. Ps 102:17. Am 5:22.

14 thou sayest. Jb 9:11. 23:3, 8-10.
yet. Jb 9:19. 19:7. Ps 77:5-10. 97:2. Is 30:18.
54:17. Mi 7:7-9.
trust. Ps 27:12-14. 37:5, 6. 62:5, 8. Is 50:10.
Ro 8:33, 34.

15 because. Jb 9:14. 13:15. Nu 20:12. Lk 1:20.
he. *that is*, God.
visited. Ps 89:32. Re 3:19.
he. *that is*, Job.
in great. Jb 4:5. 30:15, etc. Ps 88:11-16. Ho
11:8, 9. He 12:11, 12.

16 open. Jb 3:1. 33:2, 8-12. 34:35-37. 38:2.
42:3.

JOB 36

2 Suffer. Jb 21:3. 33:31-33. He 13:22.
I have yet to speak, etc. Heb. there are yet
words for God. Jb 13:7, 8. 33:6. Ex 4:16. Je
15:19. Ezk 2:7. 2 C 5:20.

3 fetch. Jb 28:12, 13, 20-24. 32:8. Pr 2:4, 5. Mt
2:1, 2. 12:42. Ac 8:27, etc. Ro 10:6-8. Ja 1:5,
17. 3:17.
ascribe. Jb 32:2. 34:5, 10-12. Dt 32:4. Ps
11:7. 99:4. 145:17. Je 12:1. Da 9:7, 14. Ro
3:25, 26. 9:14. Re 15:3.

4 my. Jb 13:4, 7. 21:27, 34. 22:6, etc. Pr 8:7, 8.
2 C 2:17. 2 P 1:16.
perfect. Jb 37:16. Lk 1:3. Ac 24:22. 1 C
14:20mg. Col 4:12. 2 T 3:16, 17.
in knowledge. Ps 49:3. Pr 22:20, 21.

5 despiseth. Jb 10:3. 31:13. Ps 22:24. 138:6.
mighty. Jb 9:4, 19. 12:13-16. 26:12-14.
37:23. Ps 99:4. 147:5. Je 10:12. 32:19. 1 C
1:24-28.
wisdom. Heb. heart. Jb 34:10.

6 preserveth. Jb 21:7-9, 30. Ps 55:23. Je 12:1,
2. 2 P 2:9.
giveth right. Jb 29:12-17. Ps 9:12. 10:14, 15.
72:4, 12-14. 82:1-4. Pr 22:22, 23. Is 10:1, 2.
11:4. La 3:35, 36. Am 5:12. Ga 5:13. 1 T
+1:10.
poor. *or*, afflicted. Ex 22:22-24. Ps 140:12.

7 withdraweth not. 2 Ch 16:9. Ps 33:18.
34:15. Is 40:1. 63:9. Zp 3:17. 1 P 3:12.
with. Jb 1:3. 42:12. Ge 23:6. 41:40. 1 S 2:8.
Est 10:3. Ps 78:70-72. 113:7, 8.
he doth. 2 S 7:13-16. Ps 112:7-10. 2 Th 3:3.
for ever. Heb. *netsach*, Jb +4:20.

8 if. Jb 13:27. 19:6. 33:18, 19. Ps 18:5. 107:10.
116:3. La 3:9.
cords. Pr 5:22.

9 he showeth. Jb 10:2. Ge +6:3. Dt 4:21, 22. 2
Ch 33:11-13. Ps 94:12. 119:67, 71. La 3:39,
40. Lk 15:17-19. Jn 16:7, 8. 1 C 11:32.
their. Ps 5:10. Is 59:12. Ezk 18:28-31. Ro
5:20. 1 T 1:15.

10 openeth. ver. 15. Jb 33:16-23. Ps 40:6. Is
48:8, 17. 50:5. Ac 16:14.
commandeth. Dt 4:30, 31. Pr 1:22, 23. 8:4,

5. 9:4-6. Is 1:16-20. 55:6, 7. Je 4:3, 4. 7:3-7.
Ezk 18:30, 31. Ho 14:1. Mt 3:8. Ac 3:19.
17:30. Ja 4:8.

11 If they obey. Jb 22:21. Dt 4:30, 31, +40. Is
1:19, 20. Je 7:23. 26:13. Jn +13:17. Ro 6:17.
He 5:7, 9. 11:8.
spend. Jb 11:13-19. 21:11-13. 22:23-25.
42:12. Ec 9:2, 3. Ja 5:5. Re 18:7.
prosperity. 2 Ch +20:20. Ps 122:6.
pleasures. or, pleasantness. or, pleasant
places. Ps +16:6, 11.

12 if. Dt 18:15, etc. 29:15-20. Is 1:19, 20. 3:11.
Ro 2:8, 9.
perish. Heb. pass away. Jb 6:15. 14:5. 19:8.
34:20. Ps 37:36.
sword. Jb 33:18. 2 Ch 23:10. 32:5mg.
die. Jb 4:21. Ge +49:33 (**S#1478h**).
without knowledge. Ps +49:20. Jn 8:21-24.

13 hypocrites. Jb +8:13.
heap. Nu 32:14. 2 Ch 28:13, 22. Ro 2:5.
they. Jb 15:4. 27:8-10. 35:9, 10. Mt 22:12,
13.
bindeth. ver. 8. Ps 107:10.

14 They. Heb. Their soul. Heb. *nephesh*, Nu
+23:10.
die. Jb 15:32. 21:23-25. 22:16. Ge 38:7-10.
Le 10:1, 2. Ps 55:23.
and. Ps +9:10.
unclean. *or*, sodomites. Ge 19:5, 24, 25. Dt
23:17mg. 2 K +23:7.

15 delivereth. ver. 6.
poor. *or*, afflicted. ver. 6. Jb 34:28. Ps 102:17.
openeth. ver. 10. 2 Ch 12:8.

16 broad place. Jb 19:8. 38:18. 42:10-17. Ps
18:19. 31:7, 8. 40:1-3. 118:5.
that which should be set on thy table.
Heb. the rest of thy table. Jb 17:16. Pr 29:9.
full. Ps 23:5. 36:8. 63:5. Is 25:6. 55:2.

17 fulfilled. Jb 15:5. 34:8, 36. Ps 9:4, 5, 7, 8. Ro
1:32. Re 18:4.
take hold on thee. *or*, should uphold thee.
Ge 48:17. Ex 17:12.

18 Because. Ps 2:5, 12. 110:5. Is 55:6. Mt 3:7. Lk
16:26. Ro 1:18. 2:5. Ep 5:6. He 2:3. 9:27.
wrath. Is 66:16, 24. Jn +3:36.
take thee away. Jb 16:22. Ps 102:24. Ec
+7:17. Is +38:10.
his. Ps 39:10. Is 14:6. Ezk 24:16.
then. Jb 33:24. Ps 49:7, 8. 1 T 2:6. He 2:3.
10:26.
cannot. Jb +8:13. Is +38:18. He +9:27.
deliver thee. Heb. turn thee aside. Jb 23:11
(declined). 24:4. Pr +10:28. 21:1.

19 Will. Pr 10:2. 11:4. Is 2:20. Zp 1:18. Ja +5:3,
4.
nor all. Jb 9:13. 34:20. Ps 33:16, 17. Pr 11:21.
Is 37:36.
forces. Is 60:5.

20 Desire not. Jb 3:20, 21. 6:9. 7:15. +14:13.
34:20. Je 17:16. Am 5:18.

the night. Jb +10:21. 17:13, 14. 27:20. Jn 9:4.

cut off. Ex 12:29. 2 K 19:35. Pr +14:32. Ec 11:3. Da 5:30. Lk 12:20. Ac 1:25. 1 Th 5:2, 3.

21 **regard not iniquity**. Ps 66:18. Ezk 14:4. Mt 5:29, 30.

hast thou chosen. Is +66:4.

affliction. Jb 34:7-9. 35:3. Da 3:16-18. 6:10. Mt 13:21. 16:24. Ac 5:40, 41. He 11:25. 1 P 3:17. 4:15, 16.

22 **God**. 1 S 2:7, 8. Ps 75:7. Is 14:5. Je 27:5-8. Da 4:25, 32. 5:18. Lk 1:52. Ro 13:1.

who teacheth. Jb 32:8, 9. Ps 32:8. 94:10, 12. Pr 4:11. Is 48:17. 54:13. Je 31:33. Jn 6:45.

23 **Who hath**. Jb 34:13-33. Is 40:13, 14. Ro 11:34. 1 C 2:16. Ep +1:11.

Thou. Jb 8:3. 34:10. 40:8. Ro 2:5. 3:5. 9:14.

24 **magnify**. Jb 12:13, etc. 26:5-14. Ps 28:5. 34:3. 72:18. 86:8-10. 92:4, 5. 104:24. 107:8, 15. 111:2-4, 8. 139:5, 6, 14. 145:10-12. Je 10:12, 13. Da 4:3, 37. Lk 1:46-55. 1 T +1:17. Re 15:3-5.

which. Dt 4:19. Ps 19:1-4. Ac 14:17. Ro 1:19-21.

25 **may behold**. Jb 6:19. 28:24. 35:5. 39:29.

26 **God**. Da +2:45.

we. Jb 11:7-9. 26:14. 37:5, 23. 1 K 8:27. Mt +11:27. Jn 17:25, 26. 1 C 13:12.

neither. Ps 90:2. 102:24-27. He 1:12. 2 P 3:8.

27 **he**. Jb 5:9, 10. 38:25-28, 34. Ge 2:5, 6. Ps 65:9-13. 147:8. Is 5:6. Je 14:22.

pour. Heb. *zaqaq*, **S#2212h**. Ml 3:3 (purge). Ps 12:6 (purified). Is 25:6 (well refined).

the vapor. ver. 33. Ps 148:8.

28 **the clouds**. Jb 37:11-13. Ge 7:11, 12. Pr 3:20.

29 **the spreadings**. Jb 37:16. 38:9, 37. 1 K 18:44, 45. Ps 104:3.

the noise. Jb 37:2-5. Ps 18:13. 29:3-10. 77:16-19. 104:7. Na 1:3. Hab 3:10.

30 **he**. Jb 38:25, 34, 35. Lk 17:24.

and. Jb 38:8-11. Ge 1:9. Ex 14:22, 28. 15:4, 5. Ps 18:11-16. 104:5-9.

bottom. Heb. roots. Jb 8:17. 9:8. 13:27mg. 14:8. 18:16. Ge 1:9.

31 **by them**. Jb 37:13. 38:22, 23. Ge 6:17. 7:17-24. 19:24. Ex 9:23-25. 14:26, 27. Dt 8:2, 15. Jsh 10:11. 1 S 2:10. 7:10. 12:18.

he giveth. Jb 38:26, 27. Ps 65:9-13. 104:13-15, 27, 28. 136:25. Pr 31:15. Mt +24:45. Ac 14:17.

32 **With clouds**. Jb 26:9. Ex 10:21-23. *Ps 18:11.* 135:7. 147:8, 9. 148:8. *Ac 27:20.* For "clouds," Young renders *"two palms." Jb 2:7* (sole). 1 K *18:44. 1 Ch 12:2.*

covered. ver. 30. Jb 9:24. 15:27. 16:18. *21:26.*

the light. Jb 31:26. 37:3. Ps 136:7.

commandeth. Jb 37:12. 38:12.

cometh betwixt. lit. striking against. Jb

37:11, 12, 15. Ps 18:14. 29:7. Is 59:16 (intercessor).

33 **noise**. ver. 29. Jb 37:2. 2 S 22:14. 1 K 18:41-45.

the cattle. Je 14:4-6. Jl 1:18. 2:22.

the vapor. Heb. that which goeth up. ver. 27.

JOB 37

1 **my heart**. Jb 4:14. 21:6. 38:1. Ex 19:16. Ps 89:7. 119:120. Je 5:22. Da 10:7, 8. Hab 3:16. Mt 28:2-4. Ac 16:26, 29.

2 **Hear attentively**. Heb. Hear in hearing. Jb 32:10. Ge +2:16. Mt +13:9. Lk +8:18. 16:31.

the noise. ver. 5. Jb 36:29, 33. 38:1. Ps 104:7. Ezk +10:5.

3 **He**. Ps 77:18. 97:4. Mt 24:27. Re 11:19.

lightning. Heb. light. Jb 36:32.

ends. Heb. wings. Jb 38:13mg. Is 11:12mg. +24:16mg.

4 **a voice**. Ps 29:3-9. 68:33.

the voice. Ex 15:7, 8. Dt 33:26.

he will. Jb 36:27-33.

5 **thundereth**. 2 S 22:14, 15. Ps 68:32, 33.

great. Da +4:3.

which. Jb +36:26.

6 **he saith**. Jb 38:22. Ps 147:16-18. 148:8.

likewise to the small, etc. Heb. and to the shower of rain, and to the showers of rain of his strength. Jb 36:27.

great rain. Ge 7:10-12. Ezr 10:9, 13. Pr 28:3. Ezk 13:11, 13. Am 9:6. Mt 7:25-27.

7 **He sealeth**. Jb 5:12. 9:7. 33:16, 17.

that. Jb 36:24. Ps 46:8. 64:9. 92:4. 109:26, 27. 111:2. Ec 8:17. Is 5:12. 26:11.

8 **the beasts**. Ps 104:22.

9 **south**. Heb. chamber. Jb 9:9. Ge 43:30. Ps 104:3.

the whirlwind. Jb 38:1. Je +23:19.

north. Heb. scattering *winds*. Jb 38:32. Ps 18:15. 147:17, 18.

10 **breath**. Heb. *neshamah*, Ge +2:7. Jb 4:9. 32:8. 33:4.

frost. Jb 6:16. 38:29, 30. Ge 31:40. Ps 78:47. 147:16-18.

breadth. Ge 6:15. 13:17. Ex 25:10.

11 **he wearieth**. Jb 36:27, 28.

he scattereth. Jb 36:30, 32. Is 18:4. Mt 17:5.

his bright cloud. Heb. the cloud of his light. Jb 36:32.

12 *it is turned*. Ps 65:9, 10. 104:24. Je 14:22. Jl 2:23. Am 4:7.

that. Ps 148:8. Ja 5:17, 18. Re 11:6.

face. Ge +1:2.

13 **whether**. ver. 6. Jb 36:31. 38:37, 38. Ex 9:18-25. 1 S 12:18, 19. Ezr 10:9.

correction. Heb. a rod. Jb 9:34. 21:9. Ge 49:10.

for his land. Jb 38:26, 27.

for mercy. 2 S 21:10, 14. 1 K 18:45. Jl 2:23.

14 **stand**. Ex 14:13. Hab +2:20.
consider. Jb 26:6-14. 36:24. Ps 111:2. 145:5, 6, 10-12.

15 **Dost**. Jb 28:24-27. 34:14. 38:4, etc. Ps 119:90, 91. Is 40:26.
the light. ver. 11. Jb 36:30-32. 38:24, 25.

16 **the balancings**. Jb 26:8. 36:29. Ps 104:2, 3. Is 40:22. Je 10:13.
clouds. Ge +9:13.
perfect. Jb 36:4. 1 S 2:3. Ps 104:24. 147:5. Pr 3:19, 20. Je 10:12, 13.

17 **he quieteth**. Jb 6:17. 38:31. Ps 94:13. 147:18. Is 30:15. Lk 12:55.
south. Dt 33:23. Ec 1:6. 11:3.

18 **spread**. Ge 1:6-8. Ps 148:4-6. 150:1. Pr 8:27. Is +40:22.
as. Ex 38:8.

19 **Teach**. Jb 12:3. 13:3, 6. Lk 11:1.
we. Jb 26:14. 28:20, 21. 38:2. 42:3. Ps 73:16, 17, 22. 139:6. Pr 30:2-4. Ro 8:26. 1 C 13:12. 1 J 3:2.

20 **Shall it**. Ps 139:4. Mt 12:36, 37.
surely. Jb 6:3. 11:7, 8. Ec 5:2.

21 **see not**. Jb 26:9. 36:32. 38:25.
light. ver. 3, 11, 15.

22 **Fair**. Heb. Gold. Jb 28:1-6.
weather. Ge +9:14. Pr 25:23.
with God. Jb 40:10. 1 Ch 29:11. Ps 29:4. 66:5. 68:7, 8. 76:12. 93:1. 104:1. 145:5. Is 2:10, 19. Mi 5:4. Na 1:3. Hab 3:3, etc. He 1:3. 12:29. Ju 25.

23 **Almighty**. Jb +5:17.
we cannot. ver. 19. Jb +11:7. 23:3. +36:26. Pr 30:3, 4. Lk 10:22. 1 C 2:11. 1 T 6:16.
excellent. Jb 9:4, 19. 12:13. 36:5. Ps 62:11. 65:6. 66:3. 93:1. 99:4. 146:6, 7. Is 28:29. 45:21. Mt 6:13.
in judgment. Ps 36:5-7.
he will. Jb 16:7-17. Ps 30:5. +90:15. +119:75. La 3:32, 33. He 12:10.

24 **fear**. Je +5:22. 32:39. Ro 2:4. 11:20-22.
he respecteth. Jb 5:13. Ec 9:11. Is 5:21. Mt 11:25, 26. Lk 10:21. 1 C 1:26. 3:19.

JOB 38

1 **the Lord**. or, Jehovah. Jb 1:6. 2:1.
out of. Jb 37:1, 2, 9, 14. Ex 19:16-19. Dt 4:11, 12. 5:22-24. 1 K 19:11. 2 K 2:1, 11. Je +23:19. He 12:18.

2 **darkeneth counsel**. Jb 5:13. 12:3, 13. 23:4, 5. 24:25. 26:3. 27:11. 34:35. 35:16. 42:3. Ro 1:22. 1 T 1:7.

3 **Gird**. Lk +12:35.
for. Jb 13:15, 22. 23:3-7. 31:35-37.
answer **thou me**. Heb. make me know. Jb 40:7. 42:4.

4 **Where**. Pr 8:22, 29, 30. 30:4.
when I laid. Ge 1:1. 2:4. Ps 102:25. 104:5. He 1:2, 10.

hast. Heb. knowest.

5 **laid**. Jb 11:9. 28:25. Pr 8:27. Is 40:12, 22.
who hath stretched. Ps 19:4. 78:55. Is 34:11. Zc 2:1, 2. 2 C 10:16.

6 **Whereupon**. Jb 26:7. 1 S 2:8. Ps 24:2. 93:1. 104:5. Zc 12:1. 2 P 3:5.
foundations. Heb. sockets. Ex 26:18-25.
fastened. Heb. made to sink. Pr 8:25. Je 38:22.
or who laid. Ps 118:22. 144:12. Is 28:16. Ep 2:20, 21.

7 **the morning stars**. Jb +22:12. Re +2:28.
sang. Le 9:24. Ps 35:27.
sons. Ge +6:2.
of God. Jb 1:6. 2:1. Ge 6:4. Ps 104:4. Re 5:11.
shouted. Jb 30:5. Ezr 3:11, 12. Zc 4:7.

8 **who**. ver. 10. Ge 1:9. Ps 33:7. 104:9. Pr 8:29. Je 5:22.
out. ver. 29.

9 **thick darkness**. Ge 1:2, 5, 18. 15:12, 17. Ex +10:22. Jb 22:13. Jn 12:35.
swaddlingband. Ezk 16:4.

10 **brake up for it my decreed place**. *or,* established my decree upon it. Jb 26:10. Ge 1:9, 10. 9:15. Ps 104:9. Je 5:22.

11 **Hitherto**. Ps 65:6, 7. 93:3, 4. Pr 8:29. Mk 4:39-41.
but. Jb 1:12. 2:6. Ps 76:10. 89:9. Is 27:8. Lk 8:32, 33. Re 20:2, 3, 7, 8.
thy proud waves. Heb. the pride of thy waves. Jb 35:12. Ps 42:7. Pr 21:24mg.

12 **commanded**. Ge 1:5. Ps 74:16. 136:7, 8. 148:3-5.
since. ver. 4, 21. Jb 8:9. 15:7.
the dayspring. Jb 3:9. 41:18. Ge 19:15. Ps 74:16. Am 5:8. Lk 1:78. 2 P 1:19.

13 **take**. Ps 19:4-6. 139:9-12.
ends. Heb. wings. Jb 37:3mg. 39:13.
the wicked. Jb 24:13-17. Ex 14:27. Ps 104:21, 22, 35.

14 **turned**. Jb 37:12.
clay. Jb 4:19. 10:9. 13:12. 27:16.
seal. Jb 41:15. Ge 38:18. Ex 28:11.
they stand. Jb 1:6. 2:1.
as a garment. Ps 104:2, 6.

15 **from**. Jb 5:14. 18:5, 18. Ex 10:21-23. 2 K 6:18. Pr 4:19. 13:9. Is 8:21, 22. Je 13:16. Ac 13:10, 11.
the high. Ps 10:15. 37:17. Ezk 30:22.

16 **the springs**. Ps 77:19. Pr 8:24. Je 51:36.
walked. Jb 26:5, 6.

17 **the gates**. Ps 9:13. 107:18. 116:3. Is 38:10. Mt 16:18.
opened. Ge 35:7. 1 S 2:27. Re 1:18.
the shadow of death. Ps +23:4.

18 **the breadth**. Ps 74:17. 89:11, 12. Is 40:28. Je 31:37. Re 20:9.

19 **the way**. ver. 12, 13. Ge 1:3, 4. 14-18. Dt 4:19. Is 45:7. Jn 1:9. 8:12.

light. Da 2:22.
darkness. Ps 18:11. 104:20. 105:28. Je 13:16. Ezk 32:8. Am 4:13. Mt 27:45.
20 **it to**. *or*, it at.
the bound. Ge 10:19. 23:17.
21 **because thou**. ver. 4, 12. Jb 11:12. 15:7.
22 **the treasures**. Dt 28:12. 32:34. Jsh 6:19. 1 K 7:51. 14:26. 15:18. Ne 13:12mg. Ps 33:7. 135:7. Je 10:13. Ml 3:10.
snow. Jb 6:16. 9:30. 24:19. 37:6. Ps 33:7. 135:7.
hail. Ps 77:17. Is +28:17.
23 **Which I**. Jb 36:31. 37:13. Ex 9:18, 24. Jsh 10:11. Is 30:30. Ezk 13:11-13. Mt 7:27. Re 16:21.
reserved. Jb 7:11. 16:5, 6.
the time. 2 S +11:1. 1 Ch +12:32. 20:1. Ec +3:8.
of trouble. or, distress. Jb 6:23. 7:11. 15:24. 16:9. Je 30:7.
battle. 2 S 17:11. Ps 55:18.
war. Jb 5:20. 39:25. 41:8.
24 **the light**. ver. 12, 13. Mt 24:27.
east wind. Ge +41:6.
25 **divided**. Jb 28:26. 36:27, 28. 37:3-6. Ps 29:3-10. 55:9.
watercourse. or, conduit. **S#8585h**. 1 K 18:32, 35, 38. 2 K 18:17. 20:20. Is 7:3. 36:2. Je 30:13 (healing). 46:11 (cured). Ezk 31:4mg.
overflowing. Ps 32:6. Pr 27:4mg.
lightning. S#2385h. Jb 28:26. Zc 10:1mg. For **S#1300h**, see on ver. +35. For **S#3940h**, see Jb +41:19.
26 **on the wilderness**. Ps 104:10-14. 107:35. 147:8, 9. Is 35:1, 2. 41:18, 19. 43:19, 20. Je 14:22. He 6:7, 8.
28 **Hath the**. ver. 8. Jb 5:9, 10. 1 S 12:17, 18. Ps 65:9, 10. 147:7, 8. Je 5:24. 10:13. 14:22. Jl 2:23. Am 4:7. Mt 5:45.
dew. Jb 29:19. Ge 27:28, 39. Ex 16:13. Dt 33:13, 28. 2 S 1:21. 1 K 17:1. Pr 3:20. Ho 14:5.
29 **Out of**. ver. 8. Jb 6:16. 37:10. Ge 31:40. Ps 147:16, 17.
hoary frost. Ex 16:14. 1 Ch 28:17 (bason). Ps 147:16.
30 **the face**. Jb 37:10.
frozen. Heb. taken. Jb 41:17.
31 **bind**. Jb 39:10. 41:5. Ge 38:28.
sweet influences. Ge 49:20. 1 S 15:32. Pr 29:17. La 4:5.
Pleiades. *or*, the seven stars. Heb. Cimah. Jb +9:9mg. Am 5:8.
loose. or, open. Jb 12:18. 30:11. 39:5. 41:14.
Orion. *or*, Cesil. Jb +9:9. Am 5:8.
32 **Mazzaroth**. *or*, the twelve signs. Jb 37:9. i.e. *Great Bear*; *scatterings*, **S#4216h**. Probably the same as *mazzaloth*, 2 K 23:5mg.
season. ver. +23.
guide Arcturus. Heb. guide them. Jb +9:9.

33 **the ordinances**. Ge 1:16. 8:22. 26:5. Ex 12:14. Ps 119:90, 91. Pr 3:19. Je +31:35, 36. 33:25, 26.
canst. ver. 12, 13.
34 **Canst thou**. 1 S 12:18. Am 5:8. Zc 10:1. Ja 5:18.
clouds. Jb 20:6. 22:14. Ge +9:13.
abundance. Jb 22:11. 2 K 9:17. Is 60:6. Ezk 26:10.
cover. Jb 9:24. 16:18. 21:26. 22:11. Ps 69:1, 2. 124:4. La 3:54.
35 **Canst**. Ex 9:23-25, 29. Le 10:2. Nu 11:1. 16:35. 2 K 1:10, 14. Re 11:5, 6.
lightnings. S#1300h. Jb 20:25. Ex 19:16. Dt 32:41 (glittering; lit. the lightning). 2 S 22:15. Ps 18:14. 77:18. 97:4. 135:7. 144:6. Je 10:13. 51:16. Ezk 1:13. 21:10 (glitter), 15, 28. Da 10:6. Na 2:4. 3:3mg. Hab 3:11. Zc 9:14. For **S#2385h**, see on ver. +25.
Here we are. Heb. Behold us. Ge 22:1mg. 1 S 22:12. Is 6:8mg. 65:1.
36 **Who hath put**. Jb 32:8. Ps 51:6. Pr 2:6. Ec 2:26. Ja 1:5, 17.
inward parts. Ps 51:6.
who hath given. Ex 31:3. 36:1, 2. Is 28:26.
37 **number**. Jb 12:8. 14:16. 15:17. Ge 15:5. Ps 147:4.
clouds. Ge +9:13.
or who. Ge 8:1, 2. 9:15.
stay. Heb. cause to lie down. 2 S 8:2. 1 K 3:20.
bottles. 1 S 1:24. 10:3. 25:18. Je +13:12.
38 **groweth into hardness**. *or*, is turned into mire. Heb. is poured. Jb 22:16. 1 K 22:35. 2 K 3:11. 4:40. 9:6. Is 44:3.
clods. Jb 21:33.
cleave. Jb 41:17.
39 **Wilt thou**. Ps 104:21. 145:15, 16. Is +5:29.
appetite. Heb. life. or, desire. Jb 3:20. 7:7. 33:20.
40 **they couch**. Jb 9:3. Ps 10:10. Is +5:29.
dens. Jb 37:8. Dt 33:27. Ps 76:2.
covert. or, thicket. Jb 27:18. 36:29. Ge 33:17.
41 **Who provideth**. Jb 11:13. Ps 104:27, 28. 147:9. Mt 6:26. Lk 12:24.
raven. Ge 8:7. Le 11:15. Lk 12:24.
his food. or, provision. lit. "hunting," as in Ge 10:9.
young ones. Jb 21:11. 39:3. Ge 4:23.
cry. Jb 19:7. 24:12. 30:20, 28.
wander. Ge 21:14. 37:15. Ex 23:4.

JOB 39

1 **the wild goats**. 1 S 24:2. Ps 104:18.
when the hinds. Ps 29:9. Je 14:5.
2 **number the months**. Je 2:24.
3 **bow**. Jb 31:10. Ge 49:9.
young ones. Jb 21:11. 38:41. Ge 4:23.
bring forth. lit. "cleave." Jb 16:13. 2 K 4:39.
cast out. Jb 8:4. 12:15. 14:20.

sorrows. or, pangs. Jb 18:10 (snare). 21:17. 36:8 (cords). 41:1 (cord). 2 S 22:6. 1 Ch 16:18mg. Ps 16:6 (lines).

5 the wild ass. Jb 6:5. 11:12. 24:5. Ge 16:12. Ps 104:11. Is 32:14. Je 2:23, 24. 14:6. Da 5:21. Ho 8:9.
who hath loosed. Ge 49:14.

6 barren land. Heb. salt places. Dt +29:23.

7 scorneth. ver. 18. Jb 3:18. Is 31:4.
driver. Heb. exactor. Ex 5:13-16, 18. Is 58:3.

8 The range. Jb 40:15, 20-22. Ge 1:29, 30. Ps 104:27, 28. 145:15, 16.

9 the unicorn. Nu 23:22. Dt 33:17. Ps 22:21. 92:10.
or abide. Is 1:3.

10 bind. ver. 5, 7. Jb 1:14. 41:5. Ps 129:3. Ho 10:10, 11. Mi 1:13.

11 trust. Ps 20:7. 33:16, 17. 147:10. Is 30:16. 31:1-3.
leave. Ge 1:26, 28. 9:2. 42:26. Ps 144:14. Pr 14:4. Is 30:6. 46:1.

12 that he. Ne 13:15. Am 2:13.
gather. Pr 3:10. Hg 2:19. Mt 3:2. 13:30.

13 peacocks. 1 K 10:22. 2 Ch 9:21.
wings and feathers unto the. *or*, the feathers of the stork and. Jb 30:29mg. Le 11:19. Ps 104:17. Je 8:7. Zc 5:9.

14 eggs. Dt 22:6. Is 10:14. 59:5.
in dust. Jb 20:11.

15 crush. Is 59:5.
break them. Da 7:23.

16 hardened. La 4:3.
as though. Dt 28:56, 57. 1 K 3:26, 27. 2 K 6:28, 29. La 2:20. Ro 1:31.
her labor. Ec 10:15. Hab 2:13.

17 deprived. Jb 17:4. 35:11. Dt 2:30. 2 Ch 32:31. Is 19:11-14. 57:17. Je +8:7. Ja 1:17.

18 she scorneth. ver. 7, 22. Jb 5:22. 41:29. 2 K 19:21.

19 the horse. Ex 15:1, 21. Ps 147:10. Pr 21:31.
clothed. Ps 93:1. 104:1.
thunder. ver. 25. Mk 3:17.

20 the glory. Jb 41:20, 21. Je 8:16.
terrible. Heb. terrors. Jb 9:34. 13:21. 18:11. 20:25.

21 He paweth. *or*, His feet dig. Jg 5:22.
and rejoiceth. 1 S 17:4-10, 42. Ps 19:5. Je 9:23.
he goeth. Pr 21:31. Je 8:6.
armed men. Heb. armor. Jb 20:24. 1 K 10:25.

22 mocketh. ver. 16, 18. Jb 41:33. Je 8:6.

23 The quiver. Jb 41:26-29. Ps 127:5. Is 22:6. 49:2. Je 5:16. La 3:13.

24 He swalloweth. Jb 37:20. Hab 1:8, 9.
neither. Jb 9:16. 29:24. Lk 24:41.

25 Ha, ha. Ps 35:21, 25. 40:15. 70:3. Is 44:16. Ezk 25:3. 26:2. 36:2.

26 the hawk. Le 11:16. Dt 14:15.
stretch. SS 2:12. Je 8:7.
south. Jb 9:9. Ex 26:18, 35. 27:9.

27 the eagle. Jb 9:26. Ex 19:4. Le 11:13. Ps 103:5. Pr 23:5. Is 40:31. La 4:19. Ho 8:1.
at thy command. Heb. by thy mouth. Dt +21:5mg.
make. Je 49:16. Ob 4. Hab 2:9.
nest. Jb 29:18. Ge 6:14mg. Nu 24:21.
on high. Jb 38:34. Ge 14:22. 31:45.

28 dwell. Jb 3:5. 4:19.
abideth. Ps 91:1, 2.
rock. ver. 1.
upon. 1 S 14:4.
crag. or, tooth. Jb 4:10. 13:14. 16:9. 19:20. 1 S 14:5mg.
strong place. 1 S 22:4, 5. 24:22.

29 she seeketh. Jb 9:26.
eyes behold. Jb 6:19. 28:24.

30 young ones. or, brood. Dt 22:6. Ps 84:3.
where the slain. Jb 24:12. Ge 34:27. Le 21:7 (profane). Ezk +39:17-19. Mt 24:28. Lk 17:37.

JOB 40

1 the Lord answered. ver. 6. Jb 38:1.

2 Shall. Jb 9:3. 33:13. Ec 6:10. Is 45:9-11. 50:8. 1 C 10:22.
instruct. Is 40:14. 1 C 2:16.
he that reproveth. Jb 3:11, 12, 20, 23. 7:12, 19-21. 9:17, 18, 32-35. 10:3-7, 14-17. 13:21-27. 14:16, 17. 16:11-21. 19:6-11. 27:2. 30:21-23. Ezk 18:2, 25. Mt 20:11-15. Ro 9:19-23. 11:34-36.

4 Behold. Jb 42:6. Ge 18:27. 32:10. 2 S 24:10. 1 K 19:4. Ezr +9:6, 15. Ne 9:33. Ps 51:4, 5. Is 6:5. 53:6. 64:6. Da 9:5, 7. Lk 5:8. 15:18, 19, 21. 18:13. 1 T 1:15.
I am vile. SS 1:15. 4:7.
what. Jb 9:31-35. 16:21. 23:4-7. 31:37.
I will. Jb 21:5. 29:9. Jg 10:15. 18:19. Ps 39:9. 102:3-7. Pr 28:13. 30:32. Mi 7:16. Hab +2:20. 2 C 7:10.
lay. Jg +18:19.

5 once. Jb 5:19. 19:3. 33:14, 29. 1 S 1:8. Ne 4:12. Ps 62:11. Pr 6:16. 30:15, 18, 21, 29. Ec 11:2. Am 1:3, 6, 9, 11, 13. 2:1, 4, 6. Mi 5:5.
but I will not. Jb 34:31, 32. Ro 3:19.
twice. Jb 33:14. 2 K 6:10. Ps 62:11.
but I will proceed. Je 31:18, 19.

6 out of the whirlwind. Jb 38:1. Ps 50:3, 4. He 12:18-20. 2 P 3:10-12.

7 Gird. Lk +12:35.
I will. Jb 13:22. 23:3, 4. 42:4.

8 Wilt. Ps 51:4. Ro 3:4.
disannul. Is 14:27. 28:18. Ga 3:15, 17. He 7:18.
wilt thou condemn. Jb 10:3. 27:2-6. 32:2. 34:5, 6. 35:2, 3.

9 Hast. Jb 9:4. 23:6. 33:12, 13. Ex 15:6. Is 45:9. 1 C 10:22.
arm. Ex +15:16.
canst. Jb 37:4, 5. Ezk 10:5.

10 **Deck**. Jb 39:19. Ps 93:1. 104:1, 2. Is 59:17.
  majesty. 1 Ch 29:11. Ps 21:5. 45:3, 4. Mt
  +6:13. 2 P 1:16, 17. Ju 24, 25.
  glory. Ex 28:2. Ps 50:2. 90:16, 17. 149:4. Is
  4:2mg. 1 C 15:54.

11 **Cast**. Jb 20:23. 27:22. Dt 32:22. Ps 78:49, 50.
  144:6. Ro 2:8, 9.
  behold. Ex 15:6-12. Pr +6:17. Ac 12:22, 23.
  Ja 4:6.

12 **tread**. Ps 60:12. Pr 15:25. Is 10:6. Zc 10:5. Ml
  4:3. Ro 16:20mg.
  in. Jb 36:20. Ec 11:3. Ac 1:25.

13 **Hide**. Jb 14:13. Ps 49:14. Is 2:10.
  bind. Jb 36:13. Est 7:8. Jn 11:44.

14 **that**. Ps 44:3, 6. Is 40:29. Ro 5:6. Ep 2:4-9.

15 **behemoth**. *or*, the elephant, as some think.
  which. Ge 1:24-26.
  he. ver. 20. Jb 39:8. Ps 104:14.

17 **moveth**. *or*, setteth up. lit. delighteth,
  desireth. Jb 9:3.
  tail. Ex 4:4. Dt 28:13, 44.
  cedar. Le 14:4, 6, 49, 51, 52.
  sinews. Jb 10:11. 41:23. Ge 32:32. Is 48:4.
  Ezk 37:6, 8.
  stones. or, thighs. lit. fearful things. Jb 3:25.
  Ge +24:2. Dt 23:1.
  wrapped together. La 1:14.

18 **his bones**. Jb 7:12. Is 48:4. Mi 4:13.

19 **the chief**. Jb 26:13, 14. Ps 104:24.
  he that. Ps 7:12. Is 27:1. 34:6. Lk 2:35.

20 **the mountains**. ver. 15. Ps 147:8, 9.
  where. Ps 104:14, 26.

21 **the reed**. Is 19:6, 7. 35:7.

22 **the willows**. Le 23:40. Is 15:7. Ezk 17:5.

23 **drinketh**. Heb. oppresseth. Jb 10:3. Le 6:2, 4.
  Is 37:25mg.
  hasteth not. Ps 55:8. Is 28:16.
  Jordan. Ge 13:10, 11. 32:10. Jsh 3:15.

24 **He taketh**. *or*, Will any take him in his sight,
  or bore his nose with a gin? Jb 41:1, 2.
  pierceth. Jb 3:8. 5:3.
  snares. Jb 34:30. Ex +23:33.

JOB 41

1 **draw**. Jb 21:33. 24:22. Ex 12:21.
  leviathan. *that is*, a whale, *or* a whirlpool. Jb
  3:8mg. Ps 74:14. 104:26. Is 27:1.
  hook. Is 19:8. Hab 1:15.
  cord. Jb 18:10 (snare). 21:17 (sorrows). 36:8.
  lettest down. Heb. drownest. Ezk 32:14.

2 **put**. Is 30:28. 37:29. Ezk 29:4, 5.

3 **will he**. Ps 55:21. Pr 15:1. 18:23. 25:15. Is
  30:10.

4 **will he make**. 1 K 20:31-34.
  wilt thou. Ge 1:28. 2:19. Ps 8:5, 6.
  a servant. Jb 3:19. Ex 21:6. Dt 15:17.
  for ever. Heb. *olam*, Ex +12:24.

5 **play**. Jg 16:25-30.
  bird. Ge 7:14. 15:10. Le 14:6, 7.

  bind. Jb 28:11. 38:31. 39:10. Ge 38:28.
  maidens. Ge 24:14, 16, 28, 55.

6 **thy companions**. Jb 34:8. Jg 14:11. 20:11.
  make a banquet. 2 K 6:23.
  part him. Ge 32:7. 33:1. Ex 21:35. Jg 7:16.
  merchants. Jg 1:31, 32. Pr 31:24. Is 23:11.
  Ho 12:7. Zp 1:11. Zc 14:21.

7 **fish**. ver. 26-29. Jb 40:24.

8 **Lay thine**. 1 K 20:11. 2 K 10:4. Lk 14:31, 32.

9 **shall**. Dt 28:34. 1 S 3:11. Is 28:19. Lk 21:11.

10 **dare**. Ge 49:9. Nu 24:9. Ps 2:11, 12. Ezk 8:17,
  18.
  who. Jb 9:4. 40:9. Je 12:5. 1 C 10:22.

11 **Who**. Jb 22:2, 3. 35:7. Ps 21:3. Ro 11:34, 35.
  whatsoever. Ex 19:5. Dt 10:14. 1 Ch 29:11-
  14. Ps 24:1. 50:12. 115:16. 1 C 10:26, 28.

12 **conceal**. Jb 6:24. 11:3. 13:5.
  parts. Jb 11:3. 18:13.
  power. Jb 12:13. 26:14. 39:19.
  comely. Ge 1:25. or, grace. Ge 6:8. 18:3. 19:19.
  30:27. Pr 11:16. lit. the grace of his structure.
  proportion. or, arrangement. Jb 28:13. Ex
  40:4.

13 **with**. *or*, within.
  double. Ge +43:12. 2 K 19:28. Ps 32:9. Ja 3:3.

14 **the doors**. Jb 38:10. Ec 12:4.
  his teeth. Ps 57:4. 58:6. Pr 30:14. Da 7:7.

15 **scales**. Heb. strong pieces of shields. Jb 15:26.
  Ge 15:1. Dt 33:29.
  pride. Je 9:23.
  a close. Ezk 44:1, 2. 46:1. Re 5:2, 3, 5.
  seal. Jb 38:14. Ge 38:18. Ex 28:11.

16 **near**. Ge 18:23. 19:9.
  air. or, wind. Jb 1:19. 4:9, 15. 6:4.

17 **joined**. ver. 23. Jb 19:20. 29:10. 31:7.

18 **the eyelids**. Jb 3:9mg. Re 1:14.

19 **Out of his**. Ps 18:8.
  lamps. Jb 12:5. 41:19. Ge 15:17. Ex 20:18
  (lightnings). Jg 7:16, 20. 15:4, 5. Is 62:1. Ezk
  1:13. Da 10:6. Na 2:4. Zc 12:6.

20 **smoke**. Ge 15:17. Ex 19:18.
  seething. or, blown. Jb 20:26. Je 1:13, 14.
  pot. 1 S 2:14. 2 K 10:7.
  cauldron. or, reeds. ver. 2, hook. Is 9:14.
  19:15. 58:5.

21 **breath**. Heb. *nephesh*, soul, Ge +2:19.
  kindleth. Dt 32:22. 2 S 22:13. Ps 18:8, 12.
  57:4. Is 30:33. Hab 3:5.
  flame. S#3851h. Jb 39:23 (glittering). Jg 3:22
  (blade). 13:20. Is 13:8. 29:6. 30:30. 66:15. Jl
  2:5. Na 3:3mg.

22 **In his neck**. Jb 39:19. 40:16.
  is turned into joy. Heb. rejoiceth. Ho 13:14.
  1 C 15:55-57.

23 **flakes**. Heb. fallings. Am 8:6.
  are joined. ver. 17.
  firm. ver. 24. Jb 28:2.
  moved. 1 Ch 16:30. Ps 10:6. 13:4.

24 **as hard**. Is 48:4. Je 5:3. Zc 7:12.

25 **by reason**. Ps 107:28. Jon 1:4-6.

26 **The sword**. Jb 39:21-24. 1 S 13:19, 22. 17:7.
habergeon. *or*, breastplate. 2 Ch 26:14.
27 **esteemeth**. Jb 6:26. 13:24. 19:11.
iron. Jb 19:24. 20:24. 28:2. 40:18.
straw. Jb 21:18. Ge 24:25, 32.
brass. Jb 20:24h. 28:2. 40:18.
rotten wood. Jb 13:28. Pr 10:7.
28 **slingstones**. 2 Ch 26:14. Zc 9:15.
29 **he laugheth**. Jb 39:7. Hab 1:10.
shaking. Jb 39:24 (fierceness). 1 K 19:11, 12.
Ezk 37:7. 38:19. Na 3:2 (rattling).
spear. Jb 39:23. Jsh 8:18, 26.
30 **Sharp stones**. Heb. Sharp pieces of pots-herd.
spreadeth. Jb 17:13.
sharp pointed things. or, gold. Ps 68:13. Pr
3:14. 8:10.
mire. 2 S 22:43. Ps 18:42.
31 **He maketh**. ver. 20.
to boil. Jb 30:27. Ezk 24:5.
pot. Ex 16:3. 27:3. 38:3. 1 K 7:45. 2 K 4:38,
39, 40, 41. 2 Ch 4:16. Ps 58:9. Ec 7:6.
deep. Ps 68:22. 69:2, 15. 107:24.
ointment. Ezk 24:10.
32 **to shine**. Ge 1:15.
deep. Jb 28:14. 38:16, 30. Ge 1:2.
hoary. Ge 15:15 (old age). 25:8. 42:38. Pr
16:31. 20:29.
33 **Upon earth**. Jb 40:19.
is made. Heb. behave themselves. ver. 24.
without fear. or, terror. S#2844h. Ge 9:2
(dread). 1 S 2:4 (broken). Je 46:5 (dismayed).
34 **high things**. Ge 7:19. Dt 3:5.
he is. Jb 26:12. Ex 5:2. Ps 74:13, 14. Is 27:1.
Ezk 29:3. Re 12:1-3. 13:2. 20:2, 3.
children of pride. Jb 28:8.

JOB 42

2 **thou canst do every thing**. Ge 17:1. 18:14.
Ps +115:3. 135:6. Is 40:12. 43:13. Je 32:17,
27. Hab 3:6. Mt 19:26. Mk 10:27. Lk 1:37.
18:27. Ac 26:8. Re 19:6.
no thought. Ps 44:21. Ezk 38:10. Jn +2:25.
can be withholden from thee. *or*, of thine
can be hindered. Jb 23:13. Pr +19:21. +21:30.
Ec 3:14. Is 8:10. 14:27. 46:10. Da 4:35. Ep
+1:11.
3 **Who**. Jb 38:2.
things. Ps 40:5. 131:1. 139:6. Pr 30:2-4.
4 **Hear**. Ge 18:27, 30-32.
I will. Jb 38:3. 40:7.
5 **heard**. Jb 4:12. 28:22. 33:16. Ro 10:17.
mine. Jb 23:8, 9. Nu 12:6-8. Is 6:1. Jn 1:18.
12:41, 45. Ac 7:55, 56.
6 **I abhor**. Jb 9:31. 40:3, 4. Ezr 9:6. Ps 51:17. Is
6:5. *Je* 31:19. Ezk 16:63. 20:43. 36:31. Lk
15:18, 19. 1 C 15:8, 9. 1 T 1:13-16. Ja 4:7-10.

repent. Jb 30:19. 1 K 21:27.
ashes. Est +4:1. La 3:16. Ezk 28:18.
7 **Eliphaz**. Jb +2:11. 8:1. 11:1.
My wrath. Jb 32:2, 3, 5.
ye have. Jb 11:5, 6. Ps 51:4.
8 **seven bullocks**. Nu +23:1, 14, 29. He 10:4,
10-14.
go to. Mt 5:23, 24.
offer. Le +23:12.
my servant Job shall. Ge 20:17. Is 60:14. Je
14:11. 15:1. Ezk 14:14. He 7:25. Ja 5:14-18. 1
J 5:6. Re 3:9.
him. Heb. his face, *or* person. ver. 9. 1 S
25:35. Ml 1:8, 9. Mt 3:17. Ep 1:6.
lest. Ps 103:10. 2 T 4:14.
folly. Is +9:17.
9 **did**. Jb 34:31, 32. Is 60:14. Mt 7:24. Jn 2:5.
Ac 9:6. 10:33. He 11:8.
Job. Heb. the face of Job. ver. 8. Jb 22:27. Pr
3:11, 12. Ec 9:7. Zc 8:23.
10 **turned**. Jb 5:18-20. Dt 30:3. Ps 14:7. 53:6.
126:1, 4.
when. Ge 20:17. Ex 17:3, 4. Nu 12:2, 13.
14:1-4, 10, 13-20. 16:21, 22, 46-48. Dt 9:20.
Pr 11:25. Lk 14:14. 23:34. Ac 7:50, 60.
the Lord. Jb 8:6, 7. 22:24, 25. Dt 8:18. 1 S
2:7. 2 Ch 25:9. Pr 22:4. Hg 2:8.
gave Job twice as much as he had before.
Heb. added all that had been to Job unto the
double. Ge 41:43. +43:12, 15.
11 **all his brethren**. Jb 19:13, 14. Pr 14:20.
16:7.
bread. Ex +18:12. Is +58:7.
they bemoaned. Jb 2:11. 4:4. 16:5. Ge
37:35. Is 35:3, 4. Jn 11:19. Ro 12:15. 1 C
12:26. He 12:12. 13:3.
every man. Jb 6:22, 23. Ge 24:22, 53. Jg +3:15.
12 **So**. Jb 8:7. Dt 8:16. Pr 10:22. Ec 7:8. 1 T 6:17.
Ja 5:11.
he had. Jb 1:3. Ge 24:35. 26:12-14. Ps
107:38. 144:13-15.
13 **seven sons**. Jb 1:2. Ps 107:41. +127:3. Is
49:20.
14 **Jemima**. i.e. *a dove; affectionate*, S#3224h.
Kezia. i.e. *cassia; scraped off*, S#7103h. Ps 45:9.
Keren-happuch. i.e. *horn of painting; flashes
or splendor of color; horn of beauty*, S#7163h.
15 **no women**. Ps 144:12. Ac 7:20.
fair. Ge +29:17.
gave. Nu 27:7. Jsh 15:18, 19. 18:4.
inheritance. Jb 20:29. 27:13. 31:2.
among. Ge 24:3, 4.
16 **an hundred and forty**. Ge 11:32. 25:7. 35:28.
47:28. 50:26. Dt 34:7. Jsh 24:29. Ps 90:10.
and saw. Ge 50:23. Ps 128:6. Pr 17:6.
17 **full of days**. Jb 5:26. Ge 15:15. 25:8. Dt 6:2.
Ps 91:16. Pr 3:16. Jn 11:25. He +9:27.

PSALMS

PSALM 1

1 A.M. 3560. B.C. 444.
Blessed. Ps 2:12. 32:1, 2. 33:12. 34:8. 40:4. 41:1. 65:4. 84:4, 5, 12. 89:15. 94:12. 106:3. 112:1. 115:12-15. 119:1, 2. 127:5. 128:1, 2. 137:8, 9. 144:15. 146:5. Dt +28:3. 33:29. Je 17:7. Mt 16:17. Lk 11:28. Jn 13:17. 20:29. Re 1:3. 14:13. 16:15. 19:9. 20:6. 22:7, 14.
the man. Ps 32:2.
that walketh. Pr 4:14. Ep 4:1. 1 J 2:6.
not in. Ps 81:12. +119:63. Ge 5:24. Le 26:27, 28. 1 K 16:31. Jb 31:5. Pr 1:15. 4:14, 15. 13:20. Is 45:22. Ezk 20:18. Mt +7:13. 2 C 6:17. 1 P 4:3.
counsel. Ps 64:2. Ge 49:6. 2 Ch 22:3-5. Jb 10:3. 21:16. Lk 23:51.
ungodly. or, wicked. ver. 4, 5, 6. Ge 18:23, 25. Ex 2:13. 9:27.
nor. Ps 7:5. 18:37, 38. Is 1:4. 19:8. Ezk 2:6. Da 9:5. Hab 1:5. Zc 7:11. 8:12. 1 C 4:8. 1 J 1:1.
standeth. Ps 26:12. Ro 5:2. Ep 6:13, 14.
way. ver. 6. Ps 36:4. 146:9. Pr 2:12. 4:19. 13:15. Mt 7:13, 14. Jn 18:18.
sitteth. Ps +26:4.
seat. Ex +12:20.
scornful. Pr 1:22. 3:34. 9:12. 19:29. 2 P 3:3.
2 **But his delight**. Ps 40:8. 112:1. 119:11, 35, 47, 48, 70, 72, 92. Jb 23:12. Je 15:16. Ro 7:22. Col 3:16. 1 J 5:3.
meditate. Ps 16:8. 63:5. 77:11, 12. 104:34. 119:11, 15, 23, 24, 87-99, 148. 143:5, 6. Dt 17:18, 19. Jsh 1:8. Da 6:10. Mt +14:23. 1 T 4:15.
day. Ps 88:1. 119:97. Dt 6:6, 7. Lk 2:37. 18:7. 1 Th 2:9. 2 T 1:3.
night. Ps 119:148.
3 **like**. ver. 4. Ps 5:12. 17:8. 131:2. Mt 7:24-27. 9:36. 1 P 2:25.
tree. Jb 14:9. *Is 44:4*. Je 17:8. Ezk 17:8. *19:10*. 47:12. Re 22:2.
planted. Mt 15:13.
rivers. Ps 46:4. 65:9. 119:136. Jb 29:6. Pr 5:16. 21:1. Is 30:25. 32:2. 44:4. La 3:48.
bringeth forth. Ps 92:14. Is 3:10. Mt 21:34, 41. Col 1:6.
shall not. Is 27:11. Mt 13:6. 21:19. Jn 15:6. Ju 12.

wither. Heb. fade. Ps 5:12. 18:45. 32:7, 10. 37:2. 92:12. Ex 18:18.
whatsoever. Ps 37:5. 57:2. 128:2. 129:8. Ge 24:56. 39:3, 23. 1 Ch 22:11, 13. 2 Ch 14:7. 24:20. 31:21. 32:23, 30. Jb 11:15, 17. 22:28. Is 3:10. 65:21-23.
prosper. Ps 122:6. Dt 29:9. Jsh 1:7, 8. 1 K 2:3. 1 Ch 22:13. 2 Ch 20:20. 26:5. Mt 6:33. Ro 8:28. 1 T +4:8. 3 J 2.
4 **not so**. Mt 13:41, 49.
like. ver. +3.
chaff. Ps 35:5. Jb 21:18. Pr 14:32. Is 29:5. Je 23:28. Mt 3:12. 1 J 2:17.
wind. Je +13:24.
5 **shall**. Ps 5:5. 24:3. Ec 12:14. Lk +21:36.
sinners. Ps 26:9. Nu 16:33. Ml 3:18. Mt 13:49. 25:32, 41, 46. Lk 13:28. Ep 6:13.
6 **knoweth**. Ps 34:15. 37:18-24. 142:3. Jb 23:10. Pr 2:8. Jn +2:25.
way. Ps 73:20. 112:10. 146:9. Pr 14:12. 15:9. Mt 7:13. 2 P 2:12.
righteous. ver. 5. Ps 5:12. 34:15. 92:12. Jb 36:7. Is 3:10. Mt 13:43.
ungodly. Ps 37:20. 145:20. Jb 31:3.
perish. Lk 12:20.

PSALM 2

1 A.M. 2962. B.C. 1042.
Why. Mt 17:17.
do the heathen. Ps 18:43. 46:6. 83:4-8. Is 8:9, 10. Lk 18:32. Ac 4:25, 26.
rage. or, tumultuously assemble. Lk 22:1, 2, 5, 22, 23. Ac 16:22. 17:5, 6. 19:28-32. Re +11:18. 19:19.
people. Mt 21:38. Jn 11:49, 50. Ac 5:39. Re 17:14.
imagine. Heb. meditate. Ps 1:2.
a vain. Ps 4:2. 73:13. Le 26:16. Pr 21:30.
2 **kings**. ver. 10. Ps 48:4. 110:5. Mt 2:16. Lk 13:31. 23:11, 12. Ac 12:1-6. Re 17:12-14.
rulers. Mt 26:3, 57, 59. 27:1. Ac 4:5-8, 26, 28.
take counsel. Mt 27:1, 2.
Lord. Ex 16:7. Pr +21:30. Jn 15:23. Ac 9:4.
against his. Is 53:2-4. Mt 10:24, 25. 13:55-57. 26:66-68. 27:29-31, 34. Mk 15:27-32. Lk

4:2, 29. 16:14. Jn 10:20, 31. 15:24. 19:5, 6.

anointed. 2 S +23:1. Lk +23:2. Jn +1:41mg.

3 Let us break. Je 5:5. Mt 11:29, 30. Lk 19:14, 27. Ro 6:18. 1 P 2:7, 8.

4 He that. Ps 68:33. Is 40:22. +57:15.

sitteth. Ml +3:3.

heavens. 1 K +8:39. Mt +6:9.

shall laugh. Ps 37:13. 53:5. 59:8. 2 K 19:21. Pr 1:26.

in derision. Pr 1:24-33. Is 14:4, 12. Mi 2:4.

5 Then. Ps 50:16-22. Is 11:4. 66:6. Mt 22:7. 23:33-36. Lk 19:27, 43, 44. Re 1:16. 19:15.

vex. *or*, trouble. Ps +83:15.

sore. Ps 110:5, 6. Zc 1:15.

6 Yet. Ps 45:6. 89:27, 36, 37. 110:1, 2. Is 9:6, 7. Da 7:13, 14. Mt 28:18. Ac 2:34-36. 5:30, 31. Ep 1:22. Ph 2:9-11.

set. Heb. anointed. lit. "poured out." 2 K 9:6. Is 29:10. Zc 14:4, 5, 8, 9.

my king. Ps 45:6, 7. Je 30:9. Lk +1:32, 33. Jn +1:49. Re 1:5.

my, etc. Heb. Zion, the hill of my holiness. Ps 50:2. 1 Ch +11:5. Is +24:23.

7 the decree. *or*, for a decree. Ps 89:3, 4. 148:6. Jb 23:13. Is 46:10. Ro +1:4.

Thou art. Mt 3:17. 8:29. 16:16. 17:5. Ac 8:37. *13:33*. He *1:5*. 3:6. 5:5, 8.

my Son. Ps 72:1. 110:5-7. Is 7:14. +9:6. 11:1-5. Da +3:25. Mi +5:2. Mk 1:1. Lk +1:35. Jn 1:34-50. 3:16-18. 5:25. 20:31. 1 J 4:14. Re +1:5, 6.

this. Ps 89:26, 27. Jn 1:14, 18. 3:16. He 1:6. Re +3:14.

begotten. Ps 22:31. 87:4-6. Ac 13:33. Col 1:18. He 5:5. 1 J 2:29. 3:9.

8 Ask. Jn 17:4, 5.

I shall give. Ps 22:27, 28. 72:8, 11, 17, 19. 102:15, 16. Is 55:4, 5. 59:19, 20. 66:8, 9, 18-20, 23. Da 2:44. +7:13, 14, 27. Am 9:11, 12. Zc 2:10, 11. 8:21-23. Mt +8:11, 18, 19. Jn 12:32. Re 11:15.

the heathen. Ps 67:2-5. 74:20. Is 22:26. Mt 9:38.

thine inheritance. Ps +82:8.

uttermost parts. Ps 22:27. 67:7. +72:8. Zc 14:9. Mt +5:5. 28:18, 19.

thy possession. Ge 17:8. Dt 32:49.

9 break. Ps 3:7. Is 38:13. 45:2.

them with. Ps 89:23. 110:5, 6. Da +2:44.

rod of iron. Ps 23:4. 45:6. 110:2. He 1:8. Re +2:27.

10 Be wise. Je 6:8. Ho 14:9.

O ye kings. Ps 45:12. Is +49:7.

be *instructed*. Ps 82:1-8.

11 Serve. Ps 89:7. Ph 2:12. He 4:1, 2. 12:25, 28, 29.

rejoice. Ps 95:1-8. 97:1. 99:1. 119:120. 1 C 7:29-31. Ph 2:12. He 4:1, 2. 12:25.

12 Kiss. Ge +27:27. 41:40, 43, 44. 1 S 10:1. 1 K

19:18. Jb 31:27. Ho 13:2. Jn 5:23.

Son. ver. 7. Is 7:14. +9:6.

ye perish. Ps 1:6. Is 24:6. 66:24. Ezk 20:38. Zc 14:3, 12, 13. Ml 4:1, 3. Jn 14:6. Re 6:16, 17.

the way. Ex 33:3.

when. ver. 5. 2 Th 1:8, 9. Re 6:16, 17. 14:9-11.

wrath is kindled. Ex 33:5. Is 26:20.

Blessed. Ps +1:1. Jn 6:47. 14:6. Ro 9:33. 10:11. Ep 1:12. 1 P 1:21. 2:6.

their trust. Ps +9:10. 16:1. 18:2. 37:40. 46:1. 57:1. 91:9, 10. Dt 32:37. Ru 2:12. Is +26:3, 4. Je 17:5. Jn 6:27. He 6:18.

PSALM 3

(*Title*.) A.M. 2983. B.C. 1021.

Psalm. *Mizmor*, from the verb to cut, prune, sing, a poem cut into short sentences, divided into syllables, pruned from every redundancy, and thus adapted for singing.

when. 2 S ch. 15-18.

1 how. 2 S 15:12. 16:15. 17:11-13. Mt 27:25.

many. Ps 17:7. Mt 10:21.

2 my soul. Heb. *nephesh*, Ge +12:13; Nu +23:10.

no. Ps 22:7, 8. 42:3, 10. 71:11. 2 S 16:7, 8. Mt 27:42, 43.

Selah. ver. 4, 8. Ps +9:16. Hab 3:3, 9, 13.

3 a shield. Ps +84:11.

for. *or*, about.

my. Ps 4:2. 62:7. Is 45:25. 60:19. Lk 2:32. Re 21:11, 23.

the lifter. Ps 27:6. 110:7. Ge 40:13. 2 K 25:27.

head. Jg +5:30.

4 I cried. Ps 18:3, 6. 22:2-5. 28:1. 30:2, 8. 31:22. 34:4, 6, 17. 39:12. +50:15. 55:17. 56:9. 57:2. 61:1, 2. 66:17-19. 69:3. 72:12. 77:1. 84:2. 86:3, 4. 88:1. 91:15. 102:1. 107:6, 13, 19, 28. 116:1-4. 130:1, 2. 138:3. 141:1. 142:1-3, 5, 6. Ex 2:23. 3:7. 8:12. 14:10. 17:4. Jsh 24:7. Jg 3:9, 15. 4:3. 6:6. 10:10. 1 S 7:8, 9. 12:10. 15:11. 2 K 20:11. 2 Ch 13:13, 14. Ne 9:9, 27. Is 65:24. Je 29:12, 13. Ezk 8:18. 9:8. 11:13. Ho 8:2. Jl 1:14, 19. 2:1. Jon 2:2. Mt 7:7. 15:22. 20:30, 31. 27:46, 50. Mk 10:46-48. He 5:7. Ja 5:13. Re 6:10. 7:9, 10.

he heard. Ps 34:4.

his. Ps 2:6. 43:3. 99:9. 132:13, 14.

Selah. Ps +9:16.

5 I laid. Ps 4:8. 121:4-7. 127:2. Le 26:6. Jb 11:18, 19. Pr 3:24. 6:22. Ac 12:6.

the Lord. Ps 4:8. 66:9. Pr 14:26. 18:10. Is 26:3.

6 I will. Ps +118:6. Ro 8:31.

ten thousands. 2 S 18:7.

set. Ps 2:2.

7 Arise. Ps 7:6. 9:19. 10:12. 12:5. 35:23. 44:23,

26. 59:4, 5. 68:1. 74:22. 76:9. 78:65. 80:2. 82:8. 102:13. 132:8. Nu 10:35. 2 Ch 6:41. Jb 8:6. Is 2:12, 21. 33:10. 51:9, 17. 52:1. 60:1, 2. Hab 2:19. Zp 3:8. Mk 4:38.

smitten. Jb 16:10.

broken. Ps +2:9. 58:6. Jb 29:17. La 3:30.

8 **Salvation**. Ps 60:11. Pr 21:31. Ac 4:12. Re +7:10.

thy blessing. Ps 29:11. 72:17. Ac 3:26. Ep 1:3. He 6:14. 1 P 3:9.

Selah. Ps +9:16.

PSALM 4

(*Title.*) **chief Musician**. *or*, overseer. Ps 22, 42, 45, titles. 1 Ch 25:1-6.

Neginoth. i.e. *harp songs*, **S#5058h**. Ps 4, 6, 54, 55, 61, 67, titles. 69:12. 76, title. 77:6. Is 38:20. La 3:14. 5:14. Hab 3:19mg.

1 **Hear me**. Ps +5:1-3. 13:3. 20:1, 2. 22:1, 2. 27:7. 28:1, 2. 30:10. 31:2. 69:16, 17. 88:1, 2. 102:1, 2. 119:169, 170. Da 9:18, 19.

O God. Ps 11:7. 24:5. 41:12. Is 45:24. Je 23:6. 1 C 1:30. 2 C 5:20, 21.

thou. Ps 18:18, 19. 31:8. 40:1-3. 116:6, 16. 1 S 17:37. 19:11, 12. 23:26-28. Jb 36:16. 2 C 1:8, 10.

enlarged. Ge +26:22.

have mercy upon me. *or*, be gracious unto me. Ps 6:2. 9:13, 14. 25:10, 16, 17. 26:11. 27:7. 31:9. 33:22. 40:11, 12. 41:4, 10. 51:1. 56:1. 57:1. 61:7. 66:20. 67:1. 77:7-9. 85:7. 86:3-5, 16. 90:14. 119:41, 58, 75-77, 132. 123:3. 143:12. Ex +34:6, 7. Zc 1:12. Mt +9:27. 1 T 1:2. 2 T 1:2, 16-18. T 1:4. He 4:16. 2 J 1:3.

2 **ye sons**. Ps 57:4. 58:1. Ec 8:11. 9:3, 12.

how. Mt +17:17.

my glory. Ps 3:3. 14:6. 106:20. Is 20:5. 45:17. Je 2:11. Ho 4:7. 1 C 1:31.

love. Ps 2:1. 1 S 12:21. Is 59:4. Je 2:5. Jon 2:8.

leasing. Ps 5:6. 58:3. 63:11. Je 9:3. Ep 4:25. Re 21:8.

3 **But know**. Ex 33:16. Ep 2:10. 2 T +1:9. 2 P 2:9.

the Lord. Ps 34:15. 55:16, 17. 56:9. 91:14, 15. Jn 15:16.

set apart. 2 C 6:17. T 2:14.

godly. Ps 1:1, 4, 5.

for. Ps 56:9. T 2:14.

will hear. Ps +3:4. 5:3. 28:6. 99:6-8. Nu 20:15, 16. Dt 4:7, 29. 5:28. Jsh 10:14. 2 K 20:5. 2 Ch 15:2. Jb 33:26. Is 45:11, 19. 55:6, 7. Je 33:3. La 3:57, 58. Da 9:20, 21. 10:12. Ho 14:1, 2. Mi 7:7. Mt 6:6. 18:19, 20. Lk 11:9. 15:20. Jn 15:16. Ac 10:30, 31. Ro 10:12, 13, 20. Ph 4:6. Ja 4:8. 5:4. 1 P 3:12. 1 J +5:14. Re 3:20. 5:8. 8:3, 4.

4 **Stand**. Ps 2:11. +9:10. 33:8. 119:161. Pr 16:6. Je 5:22.

sin. Jb 28:28. Pr 3:7. 16:6, 17. Ep 4:26.

commune. Ps 63:6. 77:6. 2 C 13:5.

upon. Mi 2:1.

bed. 2 K 20:1, 2. Ps 63:5, 6. SS 3:1.

be still. Jsh +10:13. Hab +2:20.

Selah. ver. 2. Ps +9:16.

5 **Offer**. Ps 50:14. 51:17, 19. Dt 33:19. 2 S 15:12. Is 1:11-18. 61:8. Ml 1:8, 11-14. Mt 5:23, 24. He 13:15, 16.

put. Ps 2:12. 26:1. 37:3. 62:8. 84:11, 12. Pr 3:5. Is 26:3, 4. 50:10. 1 P 4:19.

6 **many**. Ps 39:6. 49:16-20. Ec 2:3, etc. Is 55:2. Lk 12:19. 16:19. Ja 4:13. 5:1-5.

lift. Ps 21:6. 42:5. 44:3. 67:1. 80:1-3, 7, 19. 89:15. 119:135. Nu 6:26. 2 C 4:6.

7 **put gladness**. Ps 37:4. 40:3. 43:4. 63:2-5. 92:4. Jb 8:21. Pr 17:22. SS 1:4. Jn 14:7. 1 P 1:8.

the time. Jg 9:27. Pr 14:13. Is 9:3. Je 48:33.

8 **I will**. Ps 3:5. 16:8. +34:4, 7. 112:7. 121:4-7. Le 26:6. Jb 11:18, 19. Pr 3:24. 6:22. Is 41:10. 1 Th 4:13, 14. 5:10. 2 T 1:7. Re 14:13.

sleep. Ps +127:2.

for. Ps 34:7. Jg 9:51. 2 K 20:19. Pr 22:3. Ho 2:18. Ro 8:35-39. 1 T 2:2.

dwell. Ps 23:4. Dt +12:10.

safety. Ps 119:117. Ge 19:30. 1 S 30:6.

PSALM 5

(*Title.*) **Nehiloth**. i.e. *we shall divide the inheritance*, **S#5155h**.

1 **Give**. Ps 17:1. 39:12. 54:2. 55:1, 2. 64:1. 80:1. 84:8. 86:1. 130:2. 141:1. 1 P 3:12. 1 J 5:14, 15.

ear. Ge +16:11.

consider my. Ps 19:14. 37:4. 145:19. 1 S 1:13, 16, mg. Ml 3:16. Ro 8:26.

2 **Hearken**. Ps 17:1. 55:2. 61:1. 86:6.

unto the. Ps 3:4.

my King. Ps 10:16. 24:7, 8. 44:4. 47:6, 7. 74:12. 99:1-4. 145:1. Is 33:22.

unto thee. Ps 65:2.

3 **My voice**. Ps 22:2. 55:17. 59:16. 88:13. Mi 7:7. Hab 2:1. Col 4:2.

morning. Ps 55:17. 88:13. 119:147. 130:6. Ge +19:27. 1 Ch 23:30. Is 26:9. Mk 1:35.

4 **For thou**. He 12:14.

God. Heb. *El*, Ex +15:2. Ps 50:21. 1 Ch 29:17. Hab 1:13. Ml 2:17.

evil. Ps 94:20. 101:7. 140:13. Hab 1:13. Jn 14:23. He 12:14. 2 P 3:13. Re 21:23, 27.

5 **The foolish**. Ps 14:1. 73:3. 92:6. 94:8. Pr 1:7, 22. 8:5. Ec 5:4. Hab 1:13.

stand. Ps +1:5. 130:3.

in thy sight. Heb. before thine eyes. Ps 18:24mg.

thou hatest. Ps 10:3. Ex +15:7. Le 20:23. Pr 6:16-19. Ho 9:15. Zc 11:8. Mt 7:23. 25:41.

6 **destroy**. Ps 4:2. Re 21:8. 22:15.

the bloody, etc. Heb. man of bloods and deceit. Ps 26:8-10. 43:1. Ge 34:14, 25, 26, 28. 2 S +16:7mg, 8. 20:1. 2 K +9:26mg. Ro 1:29.

7 **But**. Ps 55:16. Jsh 24:15. Lk 6:11, 12.
in the. Ps 51:1. 52:8. 69:13, 16. 106:7, 45. 109:26. Ex +34:6. Is 55:7. Ro 5:20, 21.
in thy fear. Ps 25:12-15. 34:9, 10. 130:4. 145:19. Is 50:10. Je 10:6, 7. 26:19. Ho 3:5. Jon 1:16. Hab 3:2. Ac 9:31. 10:2. He 5:7. 12:28, 29. 1 P 1:17-19. Re 15:4.
I worship. Ps 132:7. Da +6:10. He 4:16.
thy holy temple. Heb. the temple of thy holiness. Ps 27:4. 29:9. 48:9. 134:1, 2. 135:1, 2. 1 S 1:9. Is 64:11.

8 **Lead**. Ps 23:3. 25:4, 5. 32:8. 86:11. 119:10, 64. 143:8-10. Pr 3:5, 6. 8:20.
righteousness. Ps 36:10. 118:19. 119:40. 132:9. Ho 10:12. Zp 2:3. Mt 6:33. 2 C 9:10. Ph 1:9-11.
mine. Heb. those which observe me. Ps 27:11mg. 54:5mg. 56:2mg. 59:10mg. 71:10mg. 2 S 12:14.
make. Ps 25:4. 27:11. Pr 4:25. Mt 3:3. He 12:13.
straight. Is 45:2, 13mg.

9 **For**. Ps 36:1-4. 52:2. 58:3. 62:4, 9. 111:1-3. Je 9:3-6. Mi 6:12. Ro 1:29-31. 3:13.
no. Ps +50:16. +66:18. Ge 6:5. Pr 21:4. Ec 8:11. 9:3. 2 Ch 5:14. Jb +21:15. Mt +13:38. Ro +7:18. Ep 2:1-3, 12. Col 2:13.
faithfulness. or, stedfastness. Ps 51:10mg. Jb 42:7, 8.
their mouth. Heb. his mouth, *that is*, the mouth of any of them.
inward part. Ps 51:6. 58:2. 62:4mg. 64:5, 6. Je 4:14. 17:9. Mt +7:15. Mk 7:21, 22. Lk 11:39. +18:12. Jn +8:44. 2 T +3:5. He 3:13. Ja +3:6.
very wickedness. Heb. wickednesses. Ps 38:12. 52:2, 7. 55:11.
throat. Lk 11:44. Ro *3:13*.
sepulchre. Heb. *qeber*, Ge +23:4. Lk 11:44.
they flatter. Ps +12:3.
tongue. Pr 10:20. 25:15. Je 18:18.

10 **Destroy**. or, Make them guilty. Ps 34:21, 22. 35:26. 83:9-11. 137:7. Ge 27:29. Nu 21:1, 2. Jg 5:31. 2 S 15:31. 2 Ch 20:10-13. Is 24:6mg. Je +10:25. Ezk 25:12. Ro 3:19, 20.
let. Ps 17:13. 21:8-10. 31:18. 35:1-8, 26. 64:6-8. 66:7. 83:9-18. 109:6-20. 137:7-9. Dt +2:30. 1 S 25:29, 39. 2 S 15:31. 17:14, 23. 2 Ch 25:16. Jb +4:8. 1 C 3:19.
by. or, from.
the multitude. La 1:5. Ho 9:7.
they. *Is* 1:2, 20. +63:10. Da 9:5, 9.

11 **But**. Ps 35:27. 40:16. 58:10. 68:3. 70:1-4. Jg 5:31. Is 65:13-16. Re 18:20. 19:1-7.
rejoice. 1 Th +5:16.
ever. Heb. *olam*, **s#5769h**; Ps 111:5. 119:98. Jl 2:2.

shout. Ps 32:11. 47:1-5. 65:13. Ezr 3:11-13. Jb 38:7. Zc 4:7. 9:9.
defendest. Heb. coverest over, *or*, protectest. Ps 91:4. Ex 40:21. Jg 3:24.
love. Ps 69:36. Ro 8:28. 1 C 2:9. Ja 1:12. 2:5.

12 **bless**. Ps 1:1-3. 3:8. 29:11. 32:7, 10. 112:1. 115:13. Dt 33:23. Is 3:10.
wilt. Ps 32:10.
compass. Heb. crown. Ps 8:5. 65:11. 103:4.
shield. Ps +84:11.

PSALM 6

(*Title*.) A.M. 2970. B.C. 1034.
Neginoth. Ps +4, title.
Sheminith. or, the eighth. Ps 12, title. 1 Ch 15:21mg.

1 **rebuke**. Ps 2:5. 38:1. Is 54:9. 57:16. Je 10:24. 46:28. 1 C 11:31, 32.
neither chasten. Ps 74:1. Ex 32:11. Is 64:9.

2 **for I**. Ps 38:7, 8. 41:3. 102:23, 24. 103:13-17. 109:22-24.
O Lord, heal. Ps 22:11. 23:4. 27:1. 30:2. 41:4. 46:1. 61:2. 119:151. Ge 20:17. Ex 15:26. Nu 12:13. Dt +32:39. 33:27. Jb 5:17, 18. Is 38:14. 40:29. Je 17:14. La 3:56, 57. Ho 6:1. Mt 4:24. 12:20. 2 Th 2:16, 17.
my. Ps 32:3. 38:3. 51:8. Jb 19:20. 33:19-21.

3 **My**. Ps 22:14. 31:9, 10. 38:8. 42:5, 11. 77:2, 3. Pr 18:14. Mt 26:38.
soul. Heb. *nephesh*, Ge +34:3.
how. Ps 77:7. Pr 13:12. Lk +18:7. Re +6:10.

4 **Return**. Ps 60:1. 69:16, 17. 80:14, 15. 90:13, 14. Is 63:17. Ml 3:7.
deliver. Ps 17:13. 22:20. 86:13. 116:4, 8. 120:2. 121:7. Is 38:17.
soul. Heb. *nephesh*, Ge +12:13.
for. Ps 25:7. 69:13. 79:8, 9. Da 9:18. Ep 1:6. 2:7, 8.

5 **For**. Ps 30:9. 88:10-12. +115:17. 118:17. Is 38:18, 19.
no remembrance. Ps +13:3. +146:4. Ec +9:5.
in the. Ec 9:10. Jn 9:4.
grave. Heb. *sheol*, Ge +37:35.
give thee thanks. He 13:15.

6 **I am**. Ps 38:8, 9. 69:3. 77:2-9. 88:9. 102:3-5. 143:4-7. Jb 7:3. 10:1. 23:2.
all the. *or*, every.
I water. Lk +6:21. 7:38.

7 **Mine**. Ps 31:9, 10. 38:10. +69:3. 88:9. Le 26:16.
it waxeth. Ps 32:3.

8 **Depart**. Ps 119:115. 139:19. Mt 7:23. 25:41. Lk 13:27.
for. ver. +6. Ps 3:4. 145:18.

9 **hath heard**. Ps 3:4. 31:22. 40:1, 2. 66:19, 20. 118:5. 120:1. 138:3. Jon 2:2, 7. Mt 7:7. 2 C 12:8-10. 1 J 5:14, 15.
will receive. Ps 116:1, 2. 145:18. 2 C 1:10, 11.

10 **Let all**. Ps 5:10. 7:6. 25:3. +71:13. 83:16, 17. 86:17. 109:28, 29. 112:10. 132:18. Jb 6:20. Is 26:11.
sore. Ps 2:5. 21:8, 9.
return. Ps 59:14. Jb 6:29. +21:30. Is +24:22. Ml 3:18. Re 20:5.
and be ashamed. Ps 109:28. Pr 29:1. Je 48:1, 20. Hab 1:12. 1 Th 5:3.

PSALM 7

(*Title*.) A.M. 2983. B.C. 1021.
Shiggaion. i.e. *varieties in song; erratic*, **S#7692h**. Hab 3:1. *Shiggaion* probably denotes a *mournful song*, or *elegy*, from the Arabic *shaga*, to be anxious, sorrowful. Hab 3:1.
words. *or*, business. 2 S ch. 16.
Cush. *Cush* signifies black, an epithet, in all languages, when applied to the mind, expressive of moral turpitude; and therefore probably here applied to *Shimei*, denoting that he was a calumniator and villain.

1 **O Lord**. Ps 13:3, 5. 18:28. 30:2, 12. 43:4. 89:26. Jsh 14:8. Je 31:18. Da 9:4, 19, 20. Zc 14:5.
in thee. Ps 11:1. 18:2. 25:2. 26:1. 31:1. 32:10. 146:3-6. Pr 3:5. Is 50:10. 1 P 1:21.
save. Ps 3:7. 17:7-9. 31:15. 35:1-3. Je 15:15. 20:11. 1 P 4:19.
persecute. Ps 31:15. 35:2-4. 119:84-86. 142:6. 143:3, 4. Je 15:15. 17:18.

2 **Lest**. Ps 35:15.
soul. Heb. *nephesh*, Ge +12:13.
like. Ps 10:9. 17:12. 22:13. 34:10. 35:17. 57:4. 58:6. 91:13. Is +5:29.
rending. Ps 50:22.
while. Jg 18:28. 2 S 14:6mg. Jb 10:7.
none to deliver. Heb. not a deliverer.

3 **if I**. Ps 59:3. Jsh 22:22. 1 S 20:8. 22:8, 13. 24:9. 26:18, 19. 2 S 16:7, 8. Jb 16:17-19.
if there. Ps 66:18. 1 S 24:11. Jb 11:14. 2 C 1:12. 1 J 3:21.
hands. Ge +9:5. Dt +32:36.

4 **If I**. Ps 55:20. 109:5. Ge 44:4. Pr 17:13. Je 18:20, 21.
I have delivered. 1 S 24:7, 10, 11. 26:9-17, 24.
without. 1 S 19:4, 5. 20:1. 22:14. 24:11-15, 17-19. 25:28, 29. 26:21.

5 **Let**. Jb 31:5-10, 38-40.
soul. Heb. *nephesh*, Ge +12:13.
tread. Ps 44:5. 60:12. Jb 40:12. Is 10:6. 63:3. Zc 10:5. Ml 4:3.
lay mine. Ps 49:12. Jb 16:15. 40:13. Je 17:13.
honor. Ge +49:6. i.e. myself who gives honor.
Selah. Ps +9:16.

6 **Arise**. Ps +3:7. 80:1, 17. 110:1. Is 3:13.
lift up. Ps 74:3. 94:1, 2. Is 33:10. 37:20.
rage of mine enemies. 2 S 16:7, 8.
awake. Ps 73:20.

to the judgment. Ps 76:8, 9. 103:6. 2 S 17:14mg. Jb +21:30. Na 1:2. 1 Th 1:10. 5:9.

7 **So**. Ps 48:11. 58:10, 11. Re 11:17, 18. 16:5-7. 18:20. 19:2.
congregation. Ac 15:14.
compass thee. Is 57:1. Jl 2:32. Zp +2:3. Ro 5:9. 1 Th 1:10. 4:17. 5:9, 10.
for their sakes. Nu 27:17. Dt 9:29. 1 K 8:51. Ne 1:10. 9:32. Is 63:17-19. 64:8-11.
return. Ps 93:4. 113:5, 6. 138:6. Ec +5:8. Is +57:15. 1 Th 4:17.

8 **The Lord shall judge**. Ps 11:4. 58:11. 67:4. 82:1, 8. +94:2, 15. 98:9. 110:6. Ge 18:25. Dt +32:36. 1 S 2:10. Ec 3:17. 11:9. 12:14. Is 2:4. 9:7. 11:3-5. 16:5. 33:22. +42:1, 4. 51:5. Je 23:5. Ezk 18:30. 33:20. Jl 3:12. Mi 4:3. Mt +10:15. 12:36. 25:31, 32. Jn 5:22, 27. Ac 17:31. Ro 2:5, 6, 16. 3:6. 1 C 4:4, 5. 2 C +5:10. He 9:27. 12:23. Ju 15. Re 19:11.
judge me. Ps 26:1, 2. 35:23, 24. 43:1. 54:1. 119:84. 130:3. 143:2. Ge 31:53. 2 Ch 6:22, 23. 20:12. La 3:59. 1 C 4:3-5. 1 J 3:21. Re 6:10, 11.
according. Ps 17:2, 3. 18:20-24. 35:24-27. 2 C 1:12.
to mine. Ps 25:21. 26:11. 41:12. 78:72. Pr 19:1. 1 Th 2:10.

9 **Oh**. Ps 9:5, 6. 10:15, 18. 58:6. 74:10, 11, 22, 23. Is 37:36-38. Da 11:45. Ac 12:23.
but establish. Ps 37:23mg. 40:2. 1 S 2:9. 2 Ch 6:22, 23. Ro 16:25. 1 Th 3:13. 1 P 5:10. Ju 1.
for. Ps 44:21. Je +17:10.
the hearts. Ps 51:6. 66:18. 73:11. 1 K 15:14.

10 **My**, etc. Heb. My buckler *is* upon God. Ps 3:3. 18:1, 2. 62:7. 84:11. 89:18. Ge 15:1.
which. Ps 112:2. 125:4. Jb 8:6. Pr 2:21. 11:20. 28:18.

11 **God judgeth**, etc. *or*, God *is* a righteous judge. ver. 8. Ps 94:15. 140:12, 13. Ge +18:25.
God. Heb. *El*, Ex +15:2.
is angry. Ps 103:13. 147:11. Ge 6:6. Ho 11:8. Zp 3:17. Mt 3:17. 1 J 4:8.

12 **If**. Ps 85:4. Is 55:6, 7. Je 31:18, 19. Ezk 18:30. 33:11. Mt 3:10. 18:3. Ac 3:19.
he will. Dt 32:41. Is 27:1. 34:5. Ezk 21:9-11, 23.

13 **He hath**. Note repetition used to interpret what has already been said: ver. 13 explains ver. 12. For other examples, see Ps 77:19. Is 1:23. 34:6. 44:3. Is 51:1, 2. Ho 7:8, 9. Am 3:8. Mt 1:23. 6:24. Mk 5:41. 15:22, 34. Lk 16:13. Jn 1:38, 41, 42. 7:39. 9:7. Ac 4:36. 9:36. 13:8. 2 T 4:6. He 7:2.
prepared. Is 33:11.
ordaineth. Ps 11:2. 45:5. 64:3, 7. 144:6. Dt 32:23, 42. Jb 6:4. La 3:12, 13. Hab 3:11, 13.
persecutors. Ac 9:4, 5. 2 Th 1:6. Re 6:10. 16:6.

14 **he travaileth**. Jb 15:20.
conceived. Ja +1:15.

15 made. Heb. hath digged. Ps 119:85. Jb 6:27.
Je 18:20.
pit. Heb. *bor*, Ge +37:20.
and is. Ps 10:2. +57:6. Jb +4:8. Ec 10:8, 9.

16 His mischief. Ps 36:4, 12. 37:12, 13. 1 S
23:9. 24:12, 13. 26:10. 28:19. 31:3, 4. 1 K
2:32. Est 9:25. Mt 27:3-5.
shall return. Jg 1:7. Jb +4:8.
own pate. Jg +5:30mg.

17 according. Ps 35:28. 51:14. 71:15, 16. 98:2.
111:3. 145:7.
Lord most high. Ps 9:2. 21:7. 46:4. 47:2.
50:14. 56:2. 57:2. 73:11. 77:10. 78:17, 35, 56.
82:6. 83:18. 91:1, 9. 92:1, 8. 97:9. 107:11. Ge
14:18. Dt 32:8. La 3:35, 38. Da 3:26. 4:17, 25,
32, 34. 5:18, 21. 7:18. Mk +5:7. Lk 1:76. 8:28.
Ac 7:48. 16:17. He 7:1.

PSALM 8

(Title.) **Gittith**. i.e. *a wine-press*, **S#1665h**. Ps
81, 84, titles.

1 our Lord. ver. 9. Ps 63:1. 145:1. Is 26:13. Mt
22:45. Jn +20:28. Ph 2:9-11. 3:8. Re 19:16.
how excellent. Ps 72:17-19. 113:2-4.
148:13. Ex 15:11. 34:5-7. Dt 28:58. SS 5:16.
thy name. SS 1:3.
thy glory. Ps 36:5. 57:10, 11. 68:4. 108:4, 5.
1 K 8:27. Hab +3:3. Ep 4:10. Ph 2:9, 10. He
7:26.

2 Out. Mt 11:25. *21:16*. Lk 10:21. 1 C 1:27.
12:9.
ordained. Heb. founded. Ps 24:2. 78:69mg.
89:11. 102:25. 1 Ch 9:22. Hab 1:12mg.
strength. Ps +16:19. 84:5-7. Is 40:31. Am
5:9. Mt *21:16*. 2 C 12:9, 10.
still. Ps 4:4. 46:10. Ex 11:7. 15:16. Jsh 2:9-11.
1 S 2:9. Is 37:20-29, 36-38. Hab 2:20.
the enemy. Ps 44:16.

3 When. Ps 19:1. 111:2. Jb 22:12. 36:24. Ro
1:20.
work. Ps 33:6. Ge 1:1.
thy fingers. Ex +31:18.
moon. Ps 104:19. 136:7-9. 148:3. Ge 1:16-18.
Dt 4:19. Jb 25:3, 5. Is 40:26.

4 What. Ps 31:19. 139:17. 2 S 7:18, 19. 2 Ch
6:18.
is man. Ps 144:3. Jb 7:17. 15:14. 25:6. Is
40:17. He *2:6-9*.
mindful. Ps 9:12.
son of man. Ps +4:2. 80:17. 144:3. 146:3. Jb
25:6. 35:8. Is 51:12. 56:2. Ezk +2:1. Da +7:13.
8:17. Mt +8:20.
visitest. Ps 106:4. Ge 21:1. Ex 4:31. Lk 1:68.
7:16. *19:44*. Ac 15:14. 1 P 2:12.

5 For thou. Ps 103:20. Ge 1:26, 27. +2:7. 2 S
14:20. Jb 4:18-20. Ph 2:7, 8. He 2:7, 9, 16.
a little lower. Lk 20:36.
than the angels. or, than God. Heb. *Elohim*.
Ps 29:1mg. 71:19. 89:6. 97:7. 138:1. 139:7. Ge

1:26. Jb 36:26. Is 28:29. 40:12-26. +57:15.
Ezk +28:9. Jn 1:18mg. Ro 9:5. 1 T 6:16.
hast crowned. Ps 21:3-5. 45:1-3, 6. Jn
13:31, 32. Ep 1:21. Ph 2:9-11. He 2:9. 1 P
1:20, 21.
glory. Ps +30:12mg.

6 madest. Ge +1:26, 28. 9:2. 24:36. Mt 28:18.
He +1:2.
hands. Nu +11:23.
thou hast. 1 C *15:27*.
put. Ps 110:1. Is 9:6. 1 C 15:24-27. Ep 1:22.
He 2:8, 9. 1 P 3:22.
under. Ps +110:1.

7 All sheep, etc. Heb. Flocks and oxen, all of
them. Ps 50:10. Ge 2:20. Nu 32:24. Dt 7:13.
28:4, 18, 51.
beasts of. Ps 50:11. 80:13.

8 The fowl. Ps 148:10. Ge 1:20-25. Jb 38:39-
41. 39:1, etc. 40:15-24. 41:1, etc.

9 how excellent. ver. 1. Ps 104:24. Dt 33:26.
Jb 11:7.

PSALM 9

(Title.) A.M. 2941. B.C. 1063.
Muthlabben. i.e. *death of the son*, **S#4192h**. Ps
48:14. Probably "the death of the champion:"
so the Chaldee has, "A Psalm of David, to be
sung concerning the death of the man who
went out between (*mibbeyney*) the camps;"
evidently considering *labben*, of the same
import as *bainayim*, "a middle-man or champion," as Goliath is termed 1 S 17:4, concerning whose defeat this psalm is generally
supposed to have been composed.

1 praise. Ps 7:17. 34:1-4. 103:1, 2. 145:1-3.
146:1, 2. 1 Ch 29:10-13. Is 12:1. He 13:15. Re
5:9-14.
with my. Ps 86:12. 111:1. 138:1. Lk 10:27.
show. ver. 14. Ps 51:15. 106:2. 1 Ch 16:12,
24. Is 43:21. 60:6. Re 15:3.

2 I will be glad. Ps 4:7. 5:11. 27:6. 28:7. 32:11.
43:4. 92:4. 97:11, 12. 104:34. Hab 3:17, 18.
Ph 4:4.
and rejoice. Ps 33:21. 43:4. 1 S 2:1. Is 61:1-
3, 10. Jl 2:21, 23. Lk 1:46, 47. Jn 15:11.
16:22. Ac 2:46, 47. 13:52. Ro 5:2, 11. 14:17.
15:13. Ga 5:22. Ph 3:3. Col 1:11. 1 Th 1:6. 1 P
1:8.
O thou. Ps +7:1.

3 they shall. Ps 68:1, 2. 76:7. 80:16. Is 64:3. 2
Th 1:9. Re 6:12-17. 20:11.
presence. Je 5:22.

4 maintained, etc. Heb. made my judgment.
Ps 16:5. +140:12. 2 S 18:19mg.
throne. Ps +11:4.
right. Heb. in righteousness. Is +11:4. 1 P
2:23.

5 rebuked. Ps 2:1, 8, 9. 78:55. 79:10. 149:7. 1
S 17:45-51. 2 S 5:6, etc. 8:1-15. 10:6-9.

21:15-22. 22:44-46. Re 19:15.

destroyed. Ps 5:6. 1 S 25:39. 31:4. 2 S 17:23. Ml 4:3.

the wicked. ver. 17. Ps 10:2-4, 13, 15. Hab 1:10, 11, 13. 2 Th 2:8.

put out. Ps 109:13. Dt 9:14. 29:20. Jb 20:28. Pr 10:7. 13:9. Ec +9:5. Is 14:22.

for ever. Heb. *olam*, Ps +21:4.

6 **O thou**, etc. *or*, The destructions of the enemy are come to a perpetual end, and their cities hast thou destroyed, etc. Ps 7:5. 8:2. Ex 15:6. Mi 7:8, 10.

perpetual end. Jb +4:20 (**S#5331h**).

destructions. Ps 46:9. Ex 14:13. Is 10:24, 25. 14:6-8. 51:12, 13. Na 1:9-13. 1 C 15:26, 54-57. Re 20:2.

thou hast. 1 S 30:1. 31:7. Is 10:6, 7, 13, 14. 14:17. 37:26. Je 51:25.

memorial. 2 K 19:25. Is 14:22, 23. Je 51:62-64.

7 **But**. Ps 90:2. 102:12, 24-27. He 1:11, 12. 13:8. 2 P 3:8.

for ever. Heb. *olam*, Ex +12:24.

he hath. Ps 50:3-5. 103:19. Re 20:11-13.

8 **he shall judge**. Ps +7:8. 99:4.

world. Ge +6:11.

9 **The Lord**. Ps 14:6. 32:7. 46:1, 11. 48:3. 62:7, 8. 91:1, 2, 9. 94:22. 142:4, 5. Dt 33:27. Pr 18:10. Is 4:5, 6. 8:14. 25:4. 32:2. Je 16:19. Na 1:7. Lk 13:34. He 6:18.

be a refuge. Heb. be a high place. Ps 18:2. 20:1mg. 46:7mg. 59:9mg. 62:2mg. 91:2. 2 S 22:3.

in times. Ps 31:7. 37:24, 39. 46:1-3. 50:15. 55:22. 77:1, 2. 108:12. 112:4. Jb 34:23. Is 25:4. La 3:31-33. Mt 11:28. 2 C 4:8, 9.

10 This verse illustrates two helpful Bible study methods. One method, the "my responsibility/God's responsibility" method applies to many verses: just ask, while reading a verse, "What does this verse say about my responsibility?" and "What does this verse say about God's responsibility?" Two clear examples to try are Pr 3:5, 6. 10:4, 22.

The second method is the "cause/effect relationships" method. As you read a verse, ask "What does this verse say is the cause?" and "What does this verse say is the effect?" You will discover important principles the Bible teaches about root causes and Biblically related solutions to life problems. At Psalm 9:10, these relationships (marked out below) show that the corrective for a lack of trust in God is to know His name, another way of saying get to know His character better to trust Him more. Cause/effect relationship verses are not easy to find, so many are listed here; explore them to discover practical truth to apply to the problems and issues of life.

Cause/effect relationships can be discov-

ered in the following passages: Ps 10:3mg. 18:3. 33:21. 37:31, 40. 66:18. 67:5-7. 69:32. 78:5-8 (correcting stubbornness and rebellion in children). 89:31, 32 (if/then). 106:12 (believed his word/sang his praises). 119:67, 71, 104, 128, 155, 165, 171. Ge 22:18. 30:1 (envy, cause/despair, result). Dt 17:19, 20. Dt +28:3 (most verses which contain the word "blessed" suggest cause/effect relationships). Dt 28:15 (failure to listen to and obey God's word brings a curse). 1 S 12:15. 1 Ch 5:20. 22:13. +28:9. 2 Ch +7:14. 13:18. 20:20. 26:5 (seeking God/prosperity). Many cause/effect relationships pertaining to poverty may be found stated in the references given for the note on the "poverty curse," Dt +28:48. 2 Ch 33:12. Jb 35:12. 36:12-14mg. Pr 1:28, 29. +3:33. 28:5, 9. 29:15. 30:8, 9. Is 26:3 with Ph 4:6-8. Is 3:9. 7:9mg. 26:9. 27:11. +29:24 (erred in spirit/come to understanding; murmured/learn doctrine). 33:15, 16. 58:7, 8, 9-11, 13, 14. 59:2. 66:4. Je 5:25. 6:19. 10:21. 17:24, 25. 23:22. Ezk 12:2 (rebellion blinds and deafens). 16:49. 33:31 (covetousness hinders response and obedience to God's word). Other cause/effect relationships pertaining to covetousness are stated or implied in the following references: Jsh 7:21 (theft); 1 S 15:9 (disobedience); 1 K 20:6 (robbery); 21:2 (meanness); 2 K 5:20 (unscrupulousness); Pr 21:25, 26 (laziness); Lk 16:14 (scoffing or derision). Da 6:23. 9:11, 13. Ho +4:12 (err, **S#8582h**. The context of nearly every occurrence of this Hebrew word contains a cause/effect relationship). 13:6. Am 2:4. 3:10. Mi 3:4. Hab 1:4. Zp 1:17. Zc +5:3, 4. 7:12, 13. Ml 2:13, 14. 3:5, 9-12. Mt 13:22. Lk 7:47. Jn 5:44. 16:27. 1 C 12:25 (lack of care/schism). Ep 6:1-3. 2 T 2:7. 2 P 3:16 (unlearned/unstable) with Col 1:23 (grounded/settled). 1 J 2:14.

they that know. This clause represents "my responsibility." It also reflects the "cause." Ps 91:14. Ex 34:5-7. 1 Ch +28:9. Jb +19:25. Pr 18:10. Jn 17:3. 2 C 4:6. 2 T 1:12. 1 J 2:3, 4. 5:20.

thy name. Ex +15:2. Le +22:32. Dt +28:58. 1 K 18:24. Am 9:12. Mt 10:41. Ac 15:14.

will put their trust. This clause represents "my responsibility." It reflects the "result" or "effect" of knowing God's name, that is, His character. Ps 5:11. +11:1. 57:1. 146:5, 6. Jb +13:15. Is 26:3, 4. 50:10.

hast not forsaken. This clause represents God's responsibility. It reflects the "result" or "effect" of seeking Him. Ps 37:24, 25, 28. 105:3, 4. 1 S 12:22. Is 41:17. 46:3, 4. Jn 6:37. 2 C 1:9, 10. 2 C 4:9. He +13:5. Ju 24.

that seek. This clause represents "my responsibility." It reflects the "cause" which effects the result described in the preceding clause, namely, seeking God results in reaping the benefit of His provision for our security. Ps +34:4. 2 Ch +7:14. 26:5. Je +29:13.

11 **Sing**. Ps 33:1-3. 47:6, 7. 96:1, 2. 148:1-5, 13, 14. He 13:15.
   which. 1 Ch +11:5. Is 12:6. 14:32.
   declare. Ps 66:2, 5. 96:10. 105:1, 2. 107:22. 118:17. Is 12:4-6. Jn 17:26.

12 **When**. Ge 9:5. 2 K 24:4. Is 26:21. Mt 23:35. Lk 11:50, 51. 18:7, 8. Re 6:9, 10. 16:6.
   blood. Dt +19:12.
   he forgetteth. Ps 10:14, 17. 22:24. 34:6. 102:17. Ex 3:7, 9. Lk 18:7, 8.
   humble. *or*, afflicted. Ps 10:12mg. Jg 10:16. Mt 18:4. Lk +18:14.

13 **Have**. Ps +4:1.
   consider. Ps 13:3. 25:19. 31:7. 119:153. 142:6. La 1:9, 11. 2:20. 5:1.
   trouble. Ps +107:6.
   thou. Ps 30:3. 56:13. 86:13. 116:3, 4.
   the gates. Ge +14:7. Ps 68:20. Jb +38:17. Jon 2:6.

14 **That**. Ps 51:15. 79:13. 106:2. 138:1.
   show forth. 1 P 2:9.
   in the gates. Ps 22:22, 25. 35:18. 42:4. 109:30, 31. 116:18, 19. 118:19, 20. 149:1, 2.
   daughter. Mt +21:5.
   I will. Ps 13:5. 20:5. 21:1. 35:9. 51:12. 1 S 2:1. Is 12:3. Hab 3:18. Lk 1:47.

15 **The heathen**. Ps +57:6. Jb +4:8.

16 **known**. Ps 48:11. 58:10, 11. 83:17, 18. Dt 29:22-28. Jsh 2:10, 11. Jg 1:7. 1 S 6:19, 20. 17:46. Ezk +6:7.
   wicked. Ps 11:6. 140:9. Pr 1:32. 6:2. 12:13. Is 8:15. 28:13.
   Higgaion. *that is*, Meditation. **S#1902h**. Ps 5:1. 19:14. 92:3mg. La 3:62 (device).
   Selah. i.e. *make clear; prominent*, **S#5542h**. ver. 16, 20. Ps 3:2, 4, 8. 4:2, 4. 7:5. 20:3. 21:2. 24:6, 10. 32:4, 5, 7. 39:5, 11. 44:8. 46:3, 7, 11. 47:4. 48:8. 49:13, 15. 50:6. 52:3, 5. 54:3. 55:7, 19. 57:3, 6. 59:5, 13. 60:4. 61:4. 62:4, 8. 66:4, 7, 15. 67:1, 4. 68:7, 19, 32. 75:3. 76:3, 9. 77:3, 9, 15. 81:7. 82:2. 83:8. 84:4, 8. 85:2. 87:3, 6. 88:7, 10. 89:4, 37, 45, 48. 140:3, 5, 8. 143:6. Hab 3:3, 9, 13.

17 **The wicked**. Pr 14:32. Is 3:11. 5:14. Mt 25:41-46. Ro 2:8, 9. 2 Th 1:7-9. Re 20:15. 21:8.
   turned. Ge 37:5.
   hell. Heb. *sheol*, Ge +37:35. Ps 1:5. 11:6. +16:10. 18:5. 55:15. 139:8. Dt +32:22, +43. Jb 21:20. 26:6. 31:3. 36:13. Pr 15:24. 27:20. Is 5:14. 33:14. +66:24. Ho 13:9, 14. Ml 4:1. Mt 3:7, 10-12. 7:19, 27. 8:11, 12. 13:40-42, 47-50. 11:23, 24. 23:33. +25:32, 41. Mk 9:43, 44. Lk 16:22, 23, +24. Jn 5:28, 29. 15:6. 17:12. Ro +11:22. 1 C 16:22. Ph 3:18, 19. 2 Th 1:6-9. 2:3, 9-12. He 10:26, 27. Ja +1:15. 2 P 2:4, 9, 10, 17. 3:7. Ju 7. Re 19:20. 20:15. +21:8.

forget. Ps +14:1. 44:17, 20. 50:22. 106:13, 21. Dt 32:18. Jg 3:7. 1 S 12:9. Jb 8:13. Je 2:32. 3:21. 13:25. 18:15. 23:27. Ezk 22:12. Ho 2:13.

18 **For the needy**. ver. 12. Ps +40:17. Lk 1:53. 6:20. Ja 2:5.
   alway. Jb +4:20 (**S#5331h**).
   forgotten. Ps +13:1.
   expectation. Pr 23:17, 18. 24:14. Ph 1:20.
   the poor. Ps 10:17. 74:19.
   for ever. **S#5703h**. Heb. *ad*. ver. 5, 18. Ps 10:16. 19:9. 21:4, 6. 22:26. 37:29. 45:6, 17. 48:14. 52:8. 61:8. 83:17. 89:29. 92:7. 104:5. 111:3, 8, 10. 112:3, 9. 119:44. 132:12 (for evermore), 14. 145:1, 2, 21. 148:6. Ex 15:18. Nu 24:20, 24. 1 Ch 28:9. Jb 19:24. 20:4 (of old). Pr 12:19. 29:14. Is 9:6 (everlasting). 26:4. 30:8. 45:17 (without end). 57:15 (eternity). 64:9. 65:18. Da 12:3. Am 1:11 (perpetually). Mi 4:5. 7:18. Hab 3:6 (everlasting).

19 **Arise**. Ps +3:7.
   let not. Ge 32:28. 1 S 2:8-10. 2 Ch 14:11. Is 42:13, 14.
   let the. Ps 2:1-3. 79:6. 149:7. Je +10:25. Jl 3:12. Mi 5:15. Zc 14:18. Re 19:15.

20 **Put**. Ps 76:12. Ge +35:5. Je 32:40. Ezk 30:13.
   the nations. Ps 67:1-4. 86:8, 9. Is 64:1, 2.
   may. Ps 82:6, 7. Is 31:3. Ezk 28:2, 9. Ac 12:22, 23.

PSALM 10

1 A.M. 3463. B.C. 541.
   standest. Ps 46:1. 109:31. Je 14:8. Mt 27:46.
   afar off. Ps 22:1.
   hidest. Dt +31:17.

2 **The wicked**, etc. Heb. In the pride of the wicked he doth, etc.
   pride. Ps 17:10. 31:18. 36:11. 59:12. 73:6-9. +119:21, 51, 69, 85, 122. 123:4. 140:5. Ge 11:4. Pr +16:5. Is 10:12, 13. 14:13, 16. Je 43:2. Ezk 16:49, 50.
   let. Ps 7:16. 9:15, 16. Pr 5:22.

3 **boasteth**. Ps 35:21. 49:6. 52:1. 73:8, 9. 94:4. Ex 15:9. Is 10:7-11. 37:23, 24. Ja 4:13, 16.
   heart's. Heb. soul's, *nephesh*, Ex +23:9.
   and blesseth, etc. *or*, the covetous blesseth *himself*, he abhorreth the Lord. Ps 49:11-13, 18. 52:1. Dt 29:19. 1 S 23:21. Jb 31:24, 25. Pr 28:4. Ho 12:7, 8. Zc 11:5-8. Lk 12:19. Ro 1:29, 30, 32. 2 T 3:2-4. 1 J +2:15, 16.
   covetous. Ps 112:10. 119:36. Ex +20:17. Pr 28:16. Lk 12:15, 20. 1 C 5:11. Ep 5:3, 5. He 13:5.
   whom. Ps +34:16. Jsh 7:20, 21, 25, 26. Is 57:17. Je 22:17. Mi 6:10-12. Hab 2:9. Mt 26:15, 16. Lk 12:15. 16:14, 15. 1 C +6:10. Ep 5:5. Col 3:5, 6. 1 T 6:9, 10. 2 P 2:3, 14, 15.
   abhorreth. ver. 13. Ps +106:40. Ph 3:19.

4 **the pride**. Pr +6:17. Mt 20:10-15. Lk 15:28-30. Ro 10:3. 1 C 1:18, 23.

will not seek. Ps 14:2. 27:8. 50:21. 94:8. Ex 5:2. Dt 8:14. Jb 22:17. Pr +6:6, 9. 30:9. Is 5:12. Je 2:31. 4:22. 8:7. Ho 7:11. Da 5:22, 23. Zp 2:3. Jn +17:25. 2 P +3:5.
God, etc. *or*, all his thoughts *are*, *There is* no God. Ps +14:1. Is 26:11. 2 C 2:14.
thoughts. Ge 6:5. Is 59:7. 65:2. Je 4:14. Mk 7:21. Ac 8:22. Ro 1:21, 28.

5 **His**. Ge 6:12. Pr 1:19. 2:13-15. Is 10:1. Ho 9:9. Ro 3:16.
thy judgments. Ps 92:5, 6. Pr 15:24. 24:1. Is 5:12. 26:11. 28:15. 42:25. Ho 14:9.
he puffeth. Ps 12:5. Jg 9:27, 28, 38. 2 S 5:6. 1 K 20:10, 11, 13. 2 Ch 32:15-19.

6 **said**. Ps 11:1. 14:1. Mt 24:48.
not . Ps 15:5. 30:6. Ec 8:11. Is 28:15, 16. 47:7. 56:12. Na 1:10. Mt 24:48-51. 1 Th 5:3. Re 18:7.
never. Heb. unto generation and generation. Ps +33:11mg.

7 **full**. Ps 59:12. 62:4. 109:17, 18. Ro 3:*14*.
and deceit. Heb. deceits. Ps 5:9. 7:14. 36:3. 52:4. 55:21. 58:3. 64:3. Is 59:4. Je 9:3, 6. Ro 3:13.
under. Jb 20:12.
mischief. Ps 7:14. 140:9. Jb 15:35. Mt 12:34. Ja 3:6-8.
vanity. *or*, iniquity. Ps 12:2. 41:6. 144:8, 11. Pr 21:6. 30:8. 2 P 2:18.

8 **sitteth**. 1 S 22:18, 19. 23:23. 1 K 21:20. 2 K 21:16. Pr 1:11, 12, 18. Hab 3:14. Lk 8:1. 10:1.
his eyes. Ps 17:11. Pr 6:12, 13. Je 22:17.
are privily set. Heb. hide themselves. Ps 27:5. 31:19, 20. 56:6.

9 **He lieth**. Ps 59:3. Mi 7:2. Ac 23:21.
secretly. Heb. in the secret places. Is +5:29.
to catch. Je 5:26. Ezk 19:3-6. Hab 1:15. Jn 10:12.
poor, when. Ps +12:5. 14:6. 35:10. 37:14. 109:31. Jb 5:15, 16. 20:19. 24:14. Pr 14:31. 22:16. 28:15. Is 3:15. 32:7. Ezk 22:29. Am 2:6, 7. 4:1. 5:11, 12. 8:4, 6. Hab 3:14.

10 **croucheth**. Heb. breaketh himself. **S#1794h**. Ps 38:8. 44:19. 51:8, 17 (contrite). Dt +23:1 (**S#1795h**). 1 S 2:36.
humbleth. 1 S 18:21-26. 23:21, 22. 2 S 15:5.
by his strong ones. Heb. *or*, into his strong parts.

11 **said**. ver. 6. Mk 2:6. Lk 7:39.
God. Ps 64:5. 73:11. 94:7. Jb 22:13, 14. Pr 15:3. Ec 8:11. Ezk 8:12. 9:9.
never. Jb +4:20 (**S#5331h**).

12 **Arise**. Ps +3:7.
lift. Ps 94:2. Is 33:10.
hand. Ex +9:3.
forget. Ps +13:1.
humble. *or*, afflicted. ver. 2, 9, 17. Ps 9:12mg, 18.

13 **contemn**. Ps 74:10, 18. Nu 11:20. 2 S 12:9, 10. Lk 10:16. 1 Th 4:8.
Thou. Lk +11:50, 51.

14 **Thou hast**. Ps 35:22. Pr 15:3. Je 16:17. 23:24. He 4:13.
for thou. Hab 1:13.
to requite. Jg 1:7. 2 K 9:26. 2 Ch 6:23. Je 51:56. Jl 3:4.
thy hand. 2 S 18:19mg.
the poor. Ps 12:5.
committeth. Heb. leaveth. Ps 37:4. 55:22. Is 10:3. Je 49:11. 2 T 1:12. 1 P 2:23. 4:19. 5:7.
fatherless. ver. +18. Ex +22:22.

15 **Break**. Ps 3:7. 37:17. Jb 38:15. Ezk 30:21, 22. Zc 11:17.
seek. Ps 7:9. 2 K 21:12-15. Jb 10:6. 20:27. Je 2:34. Ezk 23:48. Zp 1:12.

16 **The Lord**. Ps 29:10. 146:10. Is 33:22. Je +10:10. La 5:19. Da 6:26. 1 T 1:17.
for ever. Heb. *olam*, Ps +21:4.
and ever. Ps +9:18 (**S#5703h**).
heathen. Ps 9:5, 15. 18:43-45. 44:2, 3. 78:55. 80:8.

17 **Lord**. Ps 9:12, 18. 37:4. Pr 10:24.
heard. 1 J +5:14, 15.
humble. 2 Ch 33:12, 13. 34:27. Pr 15:8. Mt +5:3. 18:4. Lk 18:13, 14. Ja 4:6, 10. 1 P 5:5.
thou wilt prepare. *or*, establish. Ps 65:4. 89:2, 4. 2 Ch +12:14mg. 29:36. 30:12. Pr 16:1. Jn 6:44, 65. Ro 8:26, 27. Ep 2:18. 3:12. 2 Th 3:5. Ja 1:16, 17.
cause. Ps +34:15. 102:17. Is +65:24. Ac 4:24-31. 12:5, etc. Ja 4:3. 1 P 3:12.
thine ear. Ps 31:2. 40:6. 55:1. 71:2. 130:2. Is 50:4, 5. Ezk 8:18. Ja +5:4.
to hear. Ge +16:11.

18 **judge**. ver. 14. Dt +32:36. Lk 18:7, 8.
fatherless. ver. +14. Ml +3:5.
oppressed. or, bruised. Ps 9:9. 74:19-21. Pr 26:28.
the man . Ps 17:14. Lk 16:25. 1 C 15:47, 48. Ph 3:18, 19.
oppress. *or*, terrify. Dt 1:29 (Dread). 7:21. 20:3. 31:6. Jsh 1:9 (afraid). Is 2:19, 21 (shake terribly).

PSALM 11

1 A.M. 2942. B.C. 1062.
In the. Ps 7:1. +9:10. 16:1. 25:2. 31:14. 56:11. 2 Ch 14:11. 16:8. Is 26:3, 4.
my trust. Ps 2:12. 18:30. 20:7. 22:4. 28:7. 31:19. 32:10. 37:5, 40. 40:4. 56:3. 57:1. 112:7. 118:8, 9. 125:1. 1 S 30:6. 2 Ch 13:18. Jb 13:15. Pr 3:5, 6. 16:20. 18:10. 29:25. Is 12:2. 26:3, 4. 50:10. 57:13. Je 17:7. 39:18. Da 3:28. 6:23. Na 1:7. 2 C 1:9, 10. 1 T 4:10. 6:17. 1 P 5:7.
how. 1 S 19:11. 20:38. 21:10-12. 22:3. 23:14. 26:19, 20. 27:1.
soul. Heb. *nephesh*, Ge +12:13.
Flee. Ps 55:6, 7. Pr 6:5. Lk 13:31.

2 **For, lo**. Ps 10:2. 37:14. 64:3, 4. Je 9:3.

make. Ps 21:12.

that. Ps 10:8, 9. 64:5. 142:3. 1 S 18:21. 23:9. Mt 26:4. Ac 23:12-15.

privily. Heb. in darkness. Ps 91:6. Jb 3:6.

the upright. Ps 7:10. 32:11. 64:10. 94:15. 97:11. 125:4.

3 If the foundations. Ps 75:3. 82:5. Is 58:12. 2 T 1:13. 2:19. T 1:13.

what. 1 K 19:13-18. 22:12-14. 2 Ch 32:13-15. Ne 6:10-12. Je 26:11-15. Da 3:15-18. 6:10, etc. Jn 11:8-10. Ac 4:5-12, 24-33.

4 The Lord. Ps 9:11. 18:6. Ex 40:34, 35. 1 Ch 17:5. Hab 2:20. Zc 2:13. 2 Th 2:4.

the Lord's throne. Ps 9:4, 7. +47:8. 89:14. 97:2. 103:19. 1 K 22:19. 2 Ch 18:18. Is 6:1. 66:1. Je 3:17. 14:21. 17:12. Ezk 1:26. 43:7. Mt 5:34. 23:21, 22. 25:31. Ac 7:49. He 8:1. 12:2. Re 3:21. 4:2, 10. 5:1, 7, 13. 6:16. 7:15-17. 12:5. 14:3. 19:4. 20:11. 21:5. 22:1, 3.

in heaven. Mt +6:9.

his eyes. Ps 31:22. 32:8. 33:13, 18. 34:15, 16. 44:21. 66:7. Ge 3:8. Dt 11:12. 2 Ch 16:9. Jb 31:4. 34:21. Pr 15:3. Is 1:16. 65:16. Je 16:17. 17:10. 23:24. 24:6. 32:19. Ho 13:14. Am 9:3. Zc +12:4. He 4:13. 1 P 3:12.

behold. Ge +16:13.

5 trieth. Ps 17:3. 139:1, 23, 24. Ge 22:1. Je 17:10. 20:12. 1 P +1:7.

wicked. Ps 5:4, 5. 10:3. 21:8. Pr 6:16-19. Je 12:8. Zc 11:8.

loveth. Pr 21:17. Mt 6:5. Lk 11:43. Jn 3:19. 2 T 4:8, 10.

his soul. Heb. *nephesh*, Ge +34:3; Le +26:11.

6 Upon the wicked. Ps 105:32. Ge +19:24. Ex 9:23, 24. Jb 20:23. Is 24:17, 18. Ezk 13:13. 38:22. 2 P 3:7.

snares. *or*, quick burning coals. Ps 69:22. 91:3. 119:110. Hab +3:5.

fire. Ps 18:8, 12, 13. 21:9. 2 P +3:7.

brimstone. Re +9:17.

horrible tempest. *or*, a burning tempest. Ps 119:53. La 5:10mg.

portion. Ps 16:5. 17:14. Ge 43:34. 1 S 1:4. 9:23. Jb 20:29. 27:13, etc.

their cup. Ps 16:5. 75:8. Is 51:17, 22. Je 25:15-17. Hab 2:16. Jn 18:11.

7 For. Ps 45:7. 99:4. 146:8. Is 61:8.

his. Ps 5:12. 21:6. 33:18. 34:15. 42:5. Jb 36:7. 1 P 3:12.

PSALM 12

(*Title*.) chief. *or*, overseer. Ps 4, 5, 6, 8, 9, titles.

Sheminith. *or*, The eighth. *or*, octave. Ps 6, title. 1 Ch 15:21.

1 Help. *or*, Save. Ps 3:7. 6:4. 54:1. Mt 8:25. 14:30.

godly. Ge 6:12. Is 1:9, 21, 22. 57:1. 63:5. Je 5:1. Mi 7:1, 2. Mt 24:12. 2 C 5:8.

faithful. Pr 20:6. Is 59:4, 13-15. Lk 18:8.

2 speak vanity. Ps 10:7. 36:3, 4. 38:12. 41:6. 52:1-4. 59:12. 144:8, 11. Is 58:9. Je 9:2-6, 8.

flattering. ver. +3. Ps 28:3. 62:4.

a double heart. Heb. an heart and an heart. Ps 28:3. 86:11. 1 Ch 12:33mg. Ho 10:2. 2 T 3:8. Ja 1:8.

3 cut. Ps 64:8. Jb 32:22. Pr 6:17. 10:31. 18:21. Ec 10:12. Ho 7:16.

flattering. Ps 5:9. 78:36. Jb 17:5. 32:21, 22. Pr 2:16. 6:24. 7:5, 21. 20:19. 24:24. 26:28. 28:23. 29:5. Ezk 12:24. Da 11:21. Ro 16:18. 1 Th 2:5.

tongue. Ps 17:10. 73:8, 9. Ex 15:9. 1 S 2:3. 17:43, 44. 2 K 19:23, 24. Is 10:10. Ezk 28:2, 9. 29:3. Da 4:30, 31. 7:8, 25. Ml 3:13. 2 P 2:18. Ju 16. Re 13:5.

proud. Heb. great. Ps 52:2. Pr 18:21.

4 With. Je 18:18. Ja 3:5, 6.

our own. Heb. with us. 1 C 6:19.

who is. Ps 2:2, 3. Ps +14:1. Ge 3:5. Ex 5:2. Jg 21:25. Jb 21:14, 15. Je 2:31. 44:16, 17. Da 3:15. 11:36. Mt 25:24, 25. Lk +19:14, 27. 2 Th 2:4.

lord. Ps 8:1, 9. 45:11. 97:5.

5 oppression. Ps 10:12, 18. 54:3. 55:3. 72:4. 73:8. 74:21, 22. 79:10, 11. 146:7, 8. Ex 2:23, 24. 3:7-9. 22:21-24. Dt 24:14. Jg 10:16. Jb 20:19. +27:13. Pr 14:31. 21:13. 22:16, 22, 23. 23:10, 11. Ec 4:1. 5:8. Is 3:15. 10:1-3. 19:20. La 3:34-36. Ezk +16:49. 18:12, 13, 18. 22:7. Am 4:1. 8:4-7. Ml +3:5. Ja +5:4.

poor. Ps 9:12mg, 18. 10:2, 9, 12mg, 14. 35:10.

sighing. Ps 79:11. Ex 2:23. +22:23. Je 45:3. La 1:22. Ezk 9:4. Mk 7:34.

now. Is 33:10. Mi 7:8, 9.

arise. Ps +3:7.

puffeth at. *or*, would ensnare. Ps 10:5. Jb 5:15, 21.

6 words. Ps 18:30. 19:8. 119:140. 2 S 22:31. Pr 30:5.

as silver. Ps 66:10.

7 thou shalt keep. Ps 16:1. 37:28, 40. 121:8. 145:20. Dt 33:3. 1 S 2:9. Is 26:3. 27:3. Jn 17:11. 1 P 1:5. Ju 1. Re 3:10.

them, etc. Heb. him, i.e. every one of them. Ps 17:12. 141:10.

this. Ps 10:18. Mt 3:7.

for ever. Heb. *olam*, Ex +12:24.

8 wicked. Pr 29:12. Ho 5:11. Mi 6:16.

when. Jg 9:18, etc. 1 S 18:17, 18. Est 3:6, etc. Is 32:4-6. Mk 14:63-65.

men. Heb. of the sons of men. ver. 1. Ps 8:4. Jb 30:8. Da 11:21.

PSALM 13

(*Title*.) A.M. 3464. B.C. 510.

chief. *or*, overseer. Ps 12, title.

1 How long. Ps 80:4-7. 85:5. 89:46. La 3:7, 8.

Da 10:3, 12, 13. Mt 15:22-28. Lk 18:7, 8. Re +6:10, 11.

forget. Ps 9:18. 10:11, 12. 22:1, 2. 42:9. 44:23, 24. 49:14, 15. 74:19, 23. 77:7-9. Jb 11:6. Is 49:14, 15. Je 23:39. La 5:20, 21. Ho 4:6. Am 8:7. Lk 12:6.

for ever. Jb +4:20.

wilt thou hide. Ps 22:1, 2. Dt +31:17. Is 54:7, 8.

face. Ge +19:13.

2 **take**. Ps 77:2-12. 94:18, 19. 142:4-7. Jb 7:12-15. 9:19-21, 27, 28. 10:15. 23:8-10. Je 15:18.

soul. Heb. *nephesh*, Ge +34:3.

sorrow. Ps 38:17. 116:3. Ne 2:2. Pr 15:13. Ec 5:17. Je 8:18. 45:3. Mt 26:38. Jn 16:6. Ro 9:2. Ph 2:27.

enemy. Ps 7:2, 4, 5. 8:2. 9:6. 10:18. 17:9. 74:10, 18. 1 S 18:29. 24:19. Est 7:6. La 1:9. Mi 7:8-10.

exalted. Ps 22:7, 8. 31:18. 42:10. 44:14-16. 123:3, 4. 143:3, 4. La 1:5. Lk 22:53.

3 **Consider**. Ps +9:13.

lighten. Ps 18:28. 1 S 14:27, 29. Ezr 9:8. Lk 2:32. Re 21:23.

lest. Je 51:39, 57. Ep 5:14.

I sleep. Ps 6:5. 115:17. 146:3, +4. Pr 10:7. Ec 3:19, 20. 9:5, 6, 10. Da +12:2. 1 Th +4:13.

4 **Lest mine enemy**. Ps 10:11. 25:2. 35:19, 25. 38:16. Jsh 7:8, 9. Ezk 35:12-15.

I have. Ps 9:19. Je 1:19. La 1:16.

when. Ps 55:22. 62:2, 6. 112:6. 121:1-3. Pr 12:3.

5 **But**. Ps 32:10. 33:18, 21, 22. 36:7. 52:8. 147:11. Is 12:2. Ju 21.

my heart. Ps 9:14. 20:5. 35:9. 43:4, 5. 51:12. 119:81. 1 S 2:1. Hab 3:18. Lk 1:47. 2:20, 29, 30.

6 **I**. Ps 21:13. 57:9-11. 59:16.

he. Ps 116:7. 119:17.

dealt bountifully. 1 S +1:22.

PSALM 14

1 **fool**. Ps 53:1. 73:3. 92:6. 94:6-8. 107:17. 1 S 25:25. Pr 1:7, 22. 13:19. 27:22. Je 4:22. Zc 11:15. Lk 12:20.

no God. Ps +9:17. 10:4mg. +12:4. 52:1-6. 59:7. Jb 21:14, 15. 22:13. Ex 5:2. Is 22:13. Ezk 8:12. +13:22. Lk +19:14. Ro 1:28. 3:18. Ep 2:12. He +3:12. 2 P 3:3, 4.

are corrupt. Ps 36:1-4. 51:5. 73:8, 9, 11, 12. 94:4-8. Ge 6:5, 11, 12. Is 1:4. 48:8. Jn 3:6. 8:44. Ro 7:23. Ep 4:22.

abominable. Jb 15:14-16. Mt 12:34. 15:19. Jn 3:19, 20. Ro 1:21, etc. Ep 2:1-3. T 1:16. 3:3. 1 P 4:3. Re 21:8.

there is none. Pr +20:9. Ec 7:20, 29. 9:3. Je 17:9. Ac 10:1, 2. Ro 3:10-12. 5:19. 8:7, 8. Ep 2:1-3.

2 **The Lord**. Ps 33:13, 14. 102:19, 20. Ge 6:12.

11:5. 18:21. Is 63:15. 64:1. La 3:50.

see. Ge +18:21.

any. Ps 82:5. 107:43. Pr 2:9. 8:5. 9:4, 16. Is 27:11. Je 4:22. Da 12:10. Mt 13:15. Ro 3:11.

seek God. Ps 69:32. 2 Ch 19:3. 30:19. Is 8:19. 55:6. Ac 2:21. 17:27. He 11:6.

3 **all gone**. Ps 119:176. Pr +20:9. Is 59:7, 8, 13-15. Je 2:13. 2 P 2:13-15.

filthy. Heb. stinking. Ps 38:5. 53:3. Jb 15:16. Is 64:6. Ezk 36:25. 2 C 7:1.

there. ver. 1. Ex 8:31. 12:30. Dt 1:35. Jb 14:4. Ro 3:10. 1 C 6:5.

4 **Have**. Ps 94:8, 9. Pr 1:29. Is 5:13. 27:11. 29:14. 44:19, 20. 45:20. Ho 4:6. Ro 1:21, 22, 28. 2 C 4:3, 4. Ep 4:17, 18.

eat up. Je +10:25.

as. Ex +18:12.

and call not. Je +10:25.

5 **were**, etc. Heb. they feared a fear. Ps 53:5mg. Ge +1:29. +35:5. Est 8:17. Jb 3:25. Pr 1:26-28. 28:1. Is 7:2. +8:12.

God. Ps 46:5, 7, 11. Is 8:10. 12:6. 41:10. 43:1, 2. Mt 1:23.

the generation. Ps 22:30. 24:6. 73:15. 112:2. 1 P 2:9.

6 **Ye**. Ps 3:2. 4:2. 22:7, 8. 42:10. Ne 4:2-4. Is 37:10, 11. Ezk 35:10. Da 3:15. Mt 27:40-43.

Lord. Ps +9:9.

7 **Oh**, etc. Heb. Who will give, etc. Ps 25:22. +53:6. 106:47. 1 Ch 16:35.

the salvation. Ps 51:18. Is 14:32. +25:9. 45:17. 46:13. 59:20. 62:11. Zc +9:9. Lk 2:10, 11. Ro 11:26. 2 T 2:26. He +9:28.

Israel. Ge +9:27.

out of Zion. Is +59:20.

bringeth back. Ps 126:1, 2, 4. Jb 42:10. Je +23:3.

Jacob. Ge +9:27.

shall rejoice. Ps 48:11. 85:6. 149:2. Ne 12:43. Je 33:10, 11. Re 18:20. 19:7.

PSALM 15

1 **Lord**. Ps 1:1-4. 23:6. 24:3-5. 27:4. 61:4. 84:4. 92:13. Mt 5:8. Jn 3:3-5. 14:3. 17:24. Re 7:14-17. 14:4. 21:3, 4, 23, 24.

abide. Heb. sojourn. Ps 5:4. 61:4. 105:12, 23. **holy**. Ps 2:6. 3:4. 43:3, 4. 87:1-3. He 12:22. Re 14:1.

2 **He**. Ps 84:11, 12. Pr 2:7, 8. 28:18. Is 33:15-17. Mi 2:7. Lk 1:6. 1 C 13:5. Ga 2:14. 1 J 2:6.

worketh. Ac 10:35. Ro 2:10. Ga 5:5, 6. Ep 2:10. He 11:6, 33. 1 J 2:29. 3:7. Re 22:14, 15.

speaketh the truth. Ps 34:12, 13. +51:6. Jsh 24:14. Jn 3:21. 4:23. 1 C 5:8. Ep +4:25. 6:14. Ph +4:8. He 10:23. 1 J 1:6. 3:18. 2 J 1.

3 **backbiteth not**. Ps 34:13. Ex +20:16. Le +19:16. Ro +1:30. Ep +4:31.

doeth. 1 S 24:11. Is 56:2. Mt 7:12. Ro 12:17. 13:10. 3 J 11.

taketh up. *or*, receiveth *or*, endureth. Ex 23:1mg. Pr 22:10. 25:23. Ep 5:11. 1 T +5:19.

4   **a vile**. Ps 101:4. 2 K 3:13, 14. Est 3:2. Jb 32:21, 22. Is 32:5, 6. Da 5:17, etc. Ac 24:2, 3, 25. Ja 2:1-9.

but he honoreth. Ps 16:3. 101:6. 119:63. 122:6. Nu 24:9. Mt 12:49, 50. He 6:10. 1 J 3:14, 18, 19. 4:12.

sweareth. Ps 24:4, 5. Le 5:4. 6:2. Nu +30:2. Jsh 9:18-20. Jg +11:31, 35. 21:5. 1 S 20:16. 2 S 21:1, 2. Je 7:9. Ezk 17:12-19. Ho 4:2. 10:4. Am 1:9. Zc 5:4. 8:17. Ml 1:14. +3:5. Mt 5:33-37. 23:16-22. Ro 1:31. Ga 3:15. 1 T 1:10.

changeth not. Jsh +9:19. Jg 11:30, 35. Jn 13:1. He 12:2.

5   **putteth**. Is +24:2.

nor taketh. Ex 23:7, 8. Dt 16:19. Is 33:15. Mi 7:3. Mt 26:15. 27:3-5.

He that doeth. Ps 16:8. 55:22. 106:3. 112:6. Pr 12:3. Ezk 18:27. Mi +6:8. Mt 7:21-25. Jn +13:17. Ja 1:22-25. 2 P +1:10, 11.

PSALM 16

(Title.) A.M. 2962. B.C. 1042.

Michtam. i.e. *secret treasure; golden; a song graven upon stone; the poverty of the perfect; (blood) staining* (i.e. *deep dyeing*), **S#4387h**. Ps 56, 57, 58, 60, titles. *or*, A golden Psalm of David.

1   **Preserve**. Ps 17:5, 8. 31:23. 37:28. 97:10. 116:6. Pr 2:8.

God. Heb. *El*, Ex +15:2.

for. Ps +9:10. +11:1. 22:8. 25:20. 84:12. 125:1. 146:5. Is 26:3, 4. Je 17:7, 8. 2 C 1:9. 2 T 1:12.

2   **thou hast**. Ps 8:1. 27:8. 31:14. 89:26. 91:2. Is 26:13. 44:5. Zc 13:9. Jn +20:28.

my goodness. Ps 50:9, 10. Jb 22:2, 3. 35:7, 8. Lk 17:10. Ro 11:35.

3   **But**. Ga 6:10. T 3:8. He 6:10.

the saints. Ps 30:4. 116:15. 2 Ch 6:41. Mt 25:40. Ac 9:13. Ep 1:1.

the excellent. Pr 12:26. SS 4:1, etc. 6:1, etc. 7:1, etc. Ml 3:17.

in whom. Ps 119:63. Pr 8:31. 13:20. SS 7:10. Is 62:4. Ep 5:25-27. 1 J 3:14-17.

4   **Their**. Ps 32:10. 97:7. Re 14:9-11. 18:4, 5.

hasten, etc. *or*, give gifts to another.

drink offerings. Le +23:13. Is 66:3.

nor take. Ex +23:13. Je +10:2.

5   **The Lord is the portion**. Ps 11:6. 73:26. 119:57. 142:5. Ge 15:1. Nu 18:20. Dt 10:9. 18:1, 2. 32:9. Jsh 13:33. Je 10:16. 51:19. La 3:24.

mine inheritance. Heb. my part. Ps 17:14. 47:4. 50:18. 73:26. Jsh 13:33.

of my cup. Ps 11:6. 23:5. 116:13. Ep 5:18.

thou maintainest. Ps 2:6. 9:4. 21:7-12. 61:6, 7. 89:4, 20-37. 110:1, 2. 132:11, 17, 18. Jsh

13:1. Is 42:1. 53:12. Ac 2:32. 5:31. 1 C 15:25. 2 T 1:12. 1 P 1:5.

my lot. Dt 32:9. Jsh +14:2. 21:45. Da 12:13. Col 1:12.

6   **The lines**. Ps 78:55. Jsh +17:14. 18:9. Am 7:17.

fallen. Jsh 18:11.

in pleasant. Ps 21:1-3. Jsh 15:8. Jb 36:11mg. He 12:2.

places. Consider the literal meanings of the sites in Jsh 15:15, 34, 41 (Naamah, i.e. *pleasantness*.), 49, 51, 55, 60. 19:8, 12, 13, 21, 37, 38. 20:7. Jn 14:2.

I have. Ps 73:24. Je 3:19. Jn 20:17. Ac 26:18. Ro 8:17. 1 C 3:21-23. Ep 1:18. Ph 2:9-11. 2 T 2:12. Re 3:21.

heritage. Dt 32:9. Is 54:17. Ep 1:11. Col 1:12.

7   **who hath**. Ps 73:24. 119:7. Pr 8:14. Is 11:2-4. 48:17. 50:4.

my reins. i.e. my thoughts. Ps 73:21. Je 12:2. 17:10. Re 2:23.

in the night. Ps 17:3. 22:2. 42:8. 63:6. 77:2, 6. 119:55, 148. Jb 33:15, 16. Is 26:9. Lk 6:12.

8   **I have**. Ps 139:18. Ac 2:25-28. He 11:27.

he is. Ps 73:23, 26. 109:31. 110:5. 121:5.

always. Is +58:11.

right hand. Ac 2:25.

I shall. Ps 15:5. 62:6.

not. Ge 19:30.

9   **my heart**. Lk 10:21, 22.

my glory. Here "my glory" is put for "my tongue," confirmed by the New Testament citation (Ac 2:26) which interprets the figure, rather than literally translates it. Other instances of New Testament quotations which interpret a figure rather than literally translate it include Ps 8:2 with Mt 21:16; Ps 40:6 w He 10:5; Is 6:10 w Mt 13:15, but contrast Jn 12:40; Is 65:1 w Ro 10:20; Ho 14:2 w He 13:15. Ps 7:5. +30:12mg. 57:8. +108:1. Ge 49:6. Ac 2:26. Ja 3:5-9.

my flesh. Ps 63:1. 84:2. Jb 14:14, 15, +22. +19:26, 27. Pr 14:32. Is +26:19. Mt 26:41. Mk 14:38. Lk +24:39. Jn +5:29. Ro 2:28. 1 C 5:5. 7:28. 2 C 4:11. 7:5. 12:7. 1 Th 4:13, 14.

shall rest. Heb. dwell confidently. Jb +19:26. Ezk +38:8, 11mg. Ph 1:21. Re +14:13.

in hope. Jb 14:14, 15. 19:26, 27. Is +26:19. Jn +5:29. Ro +15:4. 1 C 15:19. Ga 5:5. Ep 1:18. 4:4. Ph 1:20. 1 Th 4:13. 1 P 3:15.

10   **not leave my**. Ps +9:17. 49:15mg. 71:20. 86:13. 139:8. Le 19:28. Nu 6:6. Dt 32:22. Jb 11:8. Pr 15:11. 27:20. Is 5:14. 14:9. Am 9:2. Lk 16:23. Jn 2:21, 22. Ac 2:24, 31. 3:15. 7:59. 1 C 15:55mg. Re 1:18. 20:13, 14.

soul. Heb. *nephesh*, Ps +30:3; Ge 12:5; Nu 23:10. Ps 49:15. 103:1. Lk 1:46. Ac 2:27, 31. Re +6:9. 20:4.

hell. Heb. *sheol*, Ge +37:35. Ps +30:3. 139:8. Is 14:9. Am 9:2. Mt +10:28.

neither. Ps 49:15. 71:20. Ge +3:15. +49:10. Is +7:14. 35:3-6. ch. 53. Zc 11:12, 13. Ac 2:27-31. *13:35-38*. 1 C 15:42, 50-54.

suffer. Am +3:6.

Holy One. or, saint. Ps 89:18, 19. Dt 33:8. Is +1:4. 10:17. 29:23. Da 9:24. Mk 1:24. Lk +1:35. 4:34. Ac 2:27. 3:14. 4:27. 13:35. He 7:26. 1 J 2:20. Re 3:7.

corruption. Heb. *shachath*, Jb +9:31 (S#7845h). Ps +30:3.

11 **show me**. Ex 33:13, 18.

path. Ps 21:4. Pr 2:19. 4:18. 5:6. 12:28. Is 2:3. Mt 7:14. Ro 8:11. 1 P 1:21.

of life. Jn 3:16. 10:10.

in thy presence. Ps 17:15. 21:5, 6. Ex 33:15. Mt 5:8. Jn 16:24. Ac *2:28*. 1 C 13:12. 2 C 4:17. Ep 3:19. 1 J 3:2. Ju 24. Re 7:15-17. 22:5.

at thy. Mk 16:19. Ac 7:56. He 12:2. 1 P 3:22.

pleasures. Ps +36:8. Jb 36:11. Mt 25:33, 46.

evermore. Jb +4:20 (S#5331h).

PSALM 17

(Title.) A.M. 2942. B.C. 1062. Ps 86, 142, titles.

1 **Hear**. Ps 7:8. 18:20. 43:1. 140:12. 145:18. 1 J 3:21.

the right. Heb. justice. Ps 9:4. 119:75. Dt +16:20mg. Jb 8:3.

attend. Ps 5:2. 55:2, 3. 61:1. 66:19. 142:6. 2 Ch 7:15. Ne 1:6. Da 9:18, 19.

my cry. Ps +30:5mg.

give ear. Ps +5:1.

not out of feigned lips. Heb. without lips of deceit. Ps +66:3. 145:18. Mt 15:8. Jn 1:47.

2 **Let my**. Ps 37:6, 33. 2 Th 1:6-9. Ju 24.

things. Ezk 18:25, 29. 33:17, 20.

3 **proved**. Ps 7:9. 11:5. 26:2. 139:1-4. 1 C 4:4. 1 P +1:7.

night. Ps 16:7. Jb 24:14, 15. Ho 7:6. Mi 2:1. Ac 16:9. 18:9, 10.

tried. Ps +11:5.

shalt. Ps 7:4. 44:17-21. 1 S 24:10, 12. 26:11, 23. 2 C 1:12.

I am. Ps 39:1. 119:106. Pr 13:3. Ac 11:23. Ja 3:2.

4 **works**. Ps 14:1-3. Ge 6:5, 11. Jb 15:16. 31:33. 1 C 3:3, 15. 1 P 4:2, 3, 18.

by the. Ps 119:9-11, 105. Mt 4:4, 6, 7, 10.

word. Ps 119:9-11. Pr 2:10-15. Mt 4:4, 7, 10. Jn 17:17. Ep 6:17. Ja 1:18. Re 12:11.

destroyer. 1 P 5:8. Re 9:11mg.

5 **Hold up**. Ps 51:11, 12. 63:8. 68:35. 119:32, 116, 117, 133. 121:3, 7. 1 S 2:9. SS 1:4. Je 10:23. Jn 15:5. 1 C 15:10. 1 P 1:5.

that my footsteps. Ps 18:36. 38:16. 94:18.

slip not. Heb. be not moved. Ps 10:6. 13:4. 15:5. 16:8.

6 **I have**. Ps 55:16. 66:19, 20. 116:2.

God. Heb. *El*, Ex +15:2.

incline. Ps 13:3, 4. 71:2. 116:2. 130:2. Is 37:17, 20. Da 9:17-19.

7 **Show**. Ps 31:21. 78:12. Ro 5:20, 21. Re 15:3.

lovingkindness. Ps 36:7, 10. 40:11. 89:49. 143:8.

savest, etc. *or*, savest them which trust in thee, from those that rise up against thy right hand. Ps 5:11, 12. 10:12-16. 1 S 17:45-47. 25:28, 29. 2 K 19:22, 34. 2 Ch 16:9.

by thy. Ps +18:35.

8 **Keep me**. Ps 33:18, 19. 140:4. Nu 6:24. Jn 17:11-15.

apple. Dt 32:10. 1 S 26:24. Pr 7:2. Zc 2:8.

hide. Ps +64:2.

shadow. Ps +91:1.

wings. Ps +91:4.

9 **oppress**. Heb. waste. Ps 137:8mg. 1 Ch 17:9. Pr 11:3 (destroy). Ezk 32:12 (spoil).

deadly enemies. Heb. enemies against the soul. Heb. *nephesh*, Nu +23:10. Ps 7:5. 35:4, 7, 12. 1 S 24:11.

10 **They are**. Dt +31:20.

with. Ps +10:2. 12:3, 4. Ex 15:9. Pr +16:5. 2 P 2:18. Re 13:5, 6.

11 **compassed**. 1 S 23:26. 24:2, 3. 26:2, 3.

set. Ps 10:8-10. Pr 6:13, 14.

12 **Like**, etc. Heb. The likeness of him, (*that is*, of every one of them), *is* as a lion *that* desireth to ravin. Is +5:29.

lurking. Heb. sitting. Ps 2:4. 9:11 (dwelleth). 107:10, 34.

13 **Arise**. Ps 3:7. 7:6. 44:23, 26. 119:126. Is 51:9.

disappoint him. Heb. prevent his face. Ps 95:2mg.

soul. Heb. *nephesh*, Ge +12:13.

which is. *or*, by. Ps 7:11-13.

thy. Is 10:5, 15. 13:5. 37:26. 54:16. Hab 1:12. Ac 4:27, 28.

sword. Dt +32:41.

14 **which are**. *or*, by. ver. +13.

thy hand. Ex +9:3.

men of. Lk 16:8. Jn 8:23. 15:19. 17:14. 1 J 4:4, 5.

portion. Ps 11:6. 49:17-19. 73:12, 17, 18. Jb 20:29. Mt 6:2, 5. Lk 12:19-21. 16:25. Ja 5:5.

belly. Jb 12:6, 9. 21:7-15. 22:18.

hid. Pr 2:4. 13:22. Mt 13:44.

they are full, etc. *or*, their children are full. Is 2:7. 57:17.

leave. Ps 39:6. Jb 21:21. 27:14-17. Lk 16:27, 28.

15 **As**. Ps 5:7. Jsh 24:15.

I will. Ps 4:6. 119:111. Jb 19:26, 27. Is 33:15. Mt 5:8. Ac 2:28. He +12:2. Re 6:16.

thy face. Ps 11:7. 16:11. 140:13. Ge +43:3. Re 22:4.

in righteousness. Ge 17:1. Is 61:10. Mt 5:8. Lk 1:6. Ep 5:25-27. 1 J 3:2. Re 21:27.

I shall be. Is 53:11. Mt +5:6. Re 21:3, 4, 23.

I awake. Ps 49:14. Jb 14:12. 19:25, 26. Is +26:19. Mt 27:52, 53.

with thy. Ge +1:26, 27. Ph 3:21. 1 J 3:2, 3.

PSALM 18

(*Title*.) A.M. 2986. B.C. 1018.

the servant. Ps 36, title. 116:16. Ac 13:36. He 3:5.

this song. 2 S 22:1-51.

in the day. Ps 34:19. Ex 15:1, etc. Jg 5:1, etc. 1 S 2:1-10. Is 12:1-6.

1 **I will love**. Ps 144:1, 2. Dt +6:5. Mt 10:37. Lk 7:47. Jn 21:17. Ro 5:5. 1 C 13:13. 16:22. Ga 5:22. He 6:10. 1 P 1:8.

my strength. ver. 32. Ps 19:14. 27:1, 14. 28:7, 8. 29:11. 68:35. 71:3, 16. 84:5, 7. 118:14. Ex 15:2. Is 12:2. 26:4. 27:5. 40:31. 41:10. 45:24. Je 16:19. Hab 3:19. Zc 10:12. 2 C 12:9. Ep +3:16. 6:10. Ph 4:13. Col 1:11. 2 T 4:17.

2 **Lord**. Ps +9:9. 28:1.

rock. Dt +32:31.

fortress. Ps 91:2. 144:2. Je 16:19.

deliverer. Ps 34:4, 7, 17, +19. 91:14. Da 3:17. 6:16. Mt +6:13.

God. Heb. *El*, Ex +15:2.

strength. Heb. rock.

whom. Ps 22:4. Ro 11:29. He 2:13.

buckler. Ps 91:4. Ge +15:1. Pr 2:7.

horn. Ps +92:10.

high. Pr 18:10.

3 **I will**. Ps 5:2, 3. 28:1, 2. 55:16. 62:8. 2 S 22:4. Ph 4:6, 7.

who. Ps 65:1, 2. 76:4. Ne 9:5. Re 4:11. 5:12-14.

so shall. Ps 50:15. 91:15. Lk 1:71. Ac 2:21. Ro 8:31-39.

enemies. Ps 3:1-3. 7:6. 143:3, 4, 9. Ex 14:10. 1 S 7:7, 8. 24:15. 1 K 8:33, 34. 2 K 19:16-19. 2 Ch 14:9-11. Ne 4:7-9. 9:28. Lk 1:74.

4 **sorrows**. Ps 116:3. Is 13:8. 53:3, 4. Mt 26:38, 39. Mk 14:33, 34. 2 C 1:9.

floods. Ps 22:12, 13, 16. +93:3. Jon 2:2-7. Mt 26:47, 55. 27:24, 25, 39-44. Ac 21:30.

ungodly men. Heb. Belial. 1 S +30:22.

5 **The sorrows**. *or*, cords. Ps 86:13. 88:3-8, 15-17. Ac 2:24.

hell. Heb. *sheol*, Ge +37:35.

snares. Pr 13:14. Ec 9:12.

6 **distress**. ver. 3, 4. Ps 50:15. 130:1, 2. Mk 14:36. Ac 12:5.

cried. Ps +3:4.

heard. Ps 5:7. 11:4. 27:4, 5. 2 S 22:7. Hab 2:20. Re 11:19.

my cry. Ex 2:23. 1 K 8:27-30. 2 Ch 30:27.

7 **earth**. Ps +97:4. Ac 4:31. 16:25, 26.

foundations. Dt +32:22. Je +4:24. Ezk 38:19, 20. Zc 14:4. 1 C 13:2.

8 **went**. Ps 11:6. 21:9. 74:1. 104:32. 144:5, 6.

Ge 19:28. Ex 20:18. Le 10:2. Nu 11:1. 16:35. Dt 29:20, 23, 24. 2 Th 1:8.

out of his. Heb. by his.

fire. Ps +97:3. Am 4:11.

9 **He bowed**. Ps 68:4. 144:5, etc. Dt 33:26. Is 51:6. Jl +3:16. He +12:26. 2 P +3:10. Re 20:11.

darkness. Ex +10:22. Jn 13:7.

10 **rode**. Dt +33:26. Ezk 1:5-14. 10:20-22. He 1:7.

cherub. Ge +3:24.

he did fly. 2 S +22:11.

wind. Ps +104:3.

11 **darkness**. ver. +9.

secret. Ps 27:5. 81:7. 91:1.

thick

clouds. Ps +104:3. Ge +9:13.

12 **At the**. Ps 97:3, 4. Hab 3:4, 5, 11. Mt 17:2, 5.

clouds. Ge +9:13.

hail. Is +28:17.

13 **thundered**. Ps 78:48. 104:7. 1 S 7:10. Re 4:5. 8:5. 19:6.

Highest. Ezk +10:5.

hail. ver. +12.

coals. Ps 140:10. Dt +32:24mg.

14 **Yea**. Jsh 10:10. Is 30:30.

his arrows. Dt +32:23.

he shot. Jb +38:35. 40:9-12.

15 **channels**. Ps 74:15. 106:9. Ex 15:8. Jsh 3:13-16. 2 S 22:16.

foundations. Ps 104:5. Jb 38:4-6. Je 31:37. Jon 2:6. Mi 6:2.

O Lord. 2 K 19:7. Is 30:27, 28, 33.

blast. Heb. *neshamah*, Jb +4:9.

breath. Heb. *ruach*, Ge +2:7. Ex +15:8.

nostrils. Ex +15:8.

16 **He sent**. Ps 57:3. 144:7.

drew. ver. 43. Ps 40:1-3. Ex 2:10. 2 S +22:17.

many waters. *or*, great waters. Ps 29:3. Is 43:2. Jon 2:5, 6. Re 17:15.

17 **strong**. Ps 38:19. 2 S 22:1, 18. He 2:14, 15.

them. ver. 40, 41. Ps 9:13. 25:19. 69:4-14. 118:7. Jb 16:9. Lk 19:14.

they were. Ps 35:10. Ep 6:10-12.

18 **prevented me**. ver. 5. Ps 17:13. Mt 17:25.

in the day. Ge +2:17. Dt 32:35. 2 S 22:19. 23:12. Je 18:17. Ob 10-14. Zc 1:15.

but. Ps 46:1, 2, 11. 1 S 30:6.

19 **brought**. ver. 36. Ps 31:8. 40:2. 118:5. Jb 36:16.

because. Ps 37:23. 2 S 22:18-27. 1 K 10:9.

20 **rewarded**. Ps 58:11. 1 S 24:17, 20. Pr 11:18. Is 49:4. 62:11. Mt 6:4. Ro 2:6, 7. 1 C 3:8.

cleanness. ver. 24. Ps 7:3. 24:4. 26:6. 1 S 24:11-13. Ac 24:16. He 7:26.

21 **For I**. Ps 17:4. 26:1. 119:10, 11. Mt 5:29. Ac 24:16. 1 Th 2:10. He 12:1.

have not. Ps 119:102. 1 S 15:11. 1 J 2:19.

22 **For all**. Ps 119:13, 128. Jn 5:14.

I did. Ps 119:112, 117.

23 **upright**. Ps 7:8. 11:7. 17:3. 37:27. 1 S 26:23. 1 Ch 29:17.
before. Heb. with.
I kept. Mt 5:29, 30. 18:8, 9.

24 **the Lord recompensed me**. 1 S 26:23. Ru 2:12. Mt 10:41, 42. 2 Th 1:6, 7. He 6:10.
in his eyesight. Heb. before his eyes. Ps 5:5mg.

25 **With the merciful**. Ps 41:1-4. 112:4-6. 1 K 8:32. Is 57:1, 2. 58:7, 8. Mt 18:33-35. Lk 6:35-38.
thou wilt. Is 26:7. Ezk 18:25-30. Ro 9:14.

26 **pure**. 2 S 22:27. Is 52:11.
froward. Ps 109:17-19. Le 26:23, 24, 27, 28. Pr 3:34. Ro 2:4-6, 9. Ja 2:13.
and with. Lk 19:21, 22.
show thyself froward. or, wrestle. **S#6617h**. Ge 30:8. 2 S 22:27mg. Jb 5:13. Pr 8:8.

27 **save**. Ps 9:18. 34:6, 18, 19. 40:17. 2 S 22:28. Is 57:15. 66:2. Lk 1:52, 53. 2 C 8:9. Ja 2:5.
afflicted people. Je +30:7. Da +12:1.
bring down. Ps 17:10, 13. Is 57:15.
high looks. Heb. soaring eyes. Pr +6:17mg.

28 **thou wilt**. Ps +112:4.
candle. or, lamp. Ps 119:105mg. 132:17mg. 2 S 21:17mg. +22:29mg. 1 K 11:36mg. 2 K 8:19mg. Jb 18:6mg. 21:17mg. 29:3mg. Pr +6:23mg. 13:9mg. 20:20mg, 27mg. 24:20mg. Is 62:1.
my God. Is 42:16. Mt 4:16. Lk 1:79. 1 P 2:9.

29 **by thee**. Ps 44:6, 7. 144:1, 10. 1 S 17:49. 23:2. 30:8. 2 S 5:19, 20, 25. Ep 6:10-13. Col 2:15. Re 3:21.
run. or, broken. 2 K 23:12mg.
by my God. 2 S 22:30. 1 C 15:10. 2 C 12:9, 10.

30 **God**. Heb. El, Ex +15:2.
his way. Ps 19:7. 25:10. Dt 32:4. 2 S 22:31. Da 4:37. Ro 12:2. Re 15:3.
tried. or, refined. Ps 12:6. 19:8-10. 119:140. Pr 30:5.
a buckler. ver. 2. Ps 17:7. 84:11, 12. Pr 2:7.

31 **For who**. Ps 86:8. Dt 32:15, 31, 39. 1 S 2:2. 2 S 22:32. Is 45:5, 21, 22.
a rock. Ps 62:6, 7. Is 26:4mg.

32 **God**. Heb. El, Ex +15:2.
girdeth. Ps 30:11. 45:3. 93:1. Lk +12:35.
with strength. Ps 28:7. 91:1. Is 45:5.
maketh. Mt +5:48. Jn 15:5. 1 C 15:10. 2 C 3:5.

33 **maketh**. 2 S 2:18.
high. Ps 81:16. Dt 32:13. 33:29. 2 S 22:34. Hab 3:19. Ep 2:6.

34 **teacheth**. Ps 144:1. 2 S 22:35. Is 28:6. 45:1. Lk +22:36.
so that. Ps 46:9. Je 49:35. Ho 1:5.

35 **shield**. Ps 5:12. 28:7. Dt 33:29. 2 S 22:36.
right hand. Ps 17:7. 20:6. 44:3. 45:4. 60:5. 63:8. 73:23. 74:11. 77:10. 78:54. 80:15. 89:13. 98:1. +110:1. 118:15, 16. 139:10. Ge 48:13.

Ex 15:6, 12. SS 2:6. Is 41:10, 13. 48:13. 63:12. Ac 2:33. 5:31.
gentleness. or, with thy meekness thou hast multiplied me. Ps 45:4. Is 40:11. 42:3. 2 C 10:1. Ga 5:22, 23. He 12:7-10. Ja 3:17, 18.

36 **enlarged**. Ps 4:1. 37:23. Jb 18:7. 36:16. Lk 12:50. 24:46-48.
feet. Heb. ankles. 2 S 22:37. Pr 4:12.
not slip. Ps 17:5.

37 **pursued**. Ps 3:7. 9:3. 35:2-5. 118:11, 12. Nu 24:17-19. Is 53:10-12. 62:1-6. Re 6:2. 19:19, 20.

38 **wounded**. 1 S 17:49-51. 23:5. 30:17. 2 S ch. 5, 8, 10. 18:7, 8. 21:15-22. 22:39.
under my feet. 1 C 15:25.

39 **For thou**. ver. 32.
girded. ver. 32. Ps 30:11. Ezk 30:24, 25.
subdued. Heb. caused to bow. Ps 34:21. 66:3. 2 S 22:40. 1 Ch 22:18. Is 45:14. 1 C 15:25-28. Ep 1:22. Ph 3:21.
under me. Ro 16:20.

40 **necks**. Jsh 10:24. La 5:5.
that. Ps 34:21. 2 S 22:41. Pr 8:36. Jn 15:23.

41 **but there**. 2 S 22:42, 43. Ho 7:14.
answered them not. Ps +66:18. 145:18.

42 **beat**. Ps 50:22. 2 K 13:7. Is 41:2, 15, 16.
cast. Is 10:6. 25:10. Zc 10:5. Ml 4:3.

43 **from**. 1 S 2:9, 10. 2 S 3:1. 5:1-7. Ac 5:31.
made me. Ps 22:27, 28. 108:9. Dt 28:13. 2 S ch. 5, 8, 10. 22:44-46. Is 49:6, 22, 23. 52:15. Zc +14:9. Ro 15:12, 18. Ep 1:22.
head of the heathen. Ps 110:2. Ge +22:17. Dt +28:13. Je 3:17. Mi 4:7. Zp 3:15. Zc 14:9. Ro +11:25.
a people. Is 52:15. 55:5. Ho 1:10. Ac 13:46, 47. 28:28. Ro 16:26. 1 P 2:10. Re 11:15.

44 **As soon**, etc. Heb. at the hearing of the ear. Ps 150:5 (loud). Ge 29:13mg. Jb 42:5. Hab 3:2mg. Ro 10:16, 17. Ep 2:12.
strangers. Heb. sons of the stranger. ver. 45. Ps 66:3. 81:9, 15. 137:4. 144:7, 11. Ex 12:43 (**S#5236h**). Dt 33:29. 2 S 1:13. Ne 13:30. Is 62:8. Ezk 44:7mg.
shall submit. or, yield feigned obedience. Heb. lie. Ps +66:3mg. 68:30.

45 **strangers**. ver. +44. Is 24:4. Mi 7:17. Ja 1:11.
afraid. Jsh 2:9. Re 6:16.

46 **Lord**. Je 10:10. Jn 14:19. Re 1:18.
blessed. ver. 2. Ps 42:9.
the God. Ps +88:1.
exalted. Is +12:4.

47 **God**. Heb. El, Ex +15:2.
avengeth. Heb. giveth avengements for me. Dt 32:35. 2 S 22:48. Na 1:2. Ro 12:19.
subdueth. or, destroyeth. Ps 47:3.

48 **liftest**. Ps 22:27-30. 59:1, 2. 89:13. Ph 2:9.
violent man. Heb. man of violence. Ps 7:16. 25:19mg. 86:14. 140:1, 4, 11.

49 **Therefore**. 2 S 22:50. Ro 15:9.
will I give thanks. or, confess. Ps 14:7.

30:12. 72:18, 19. 138:4. 2 S 22:50, 51. Ro
15:9. 1 T 6:13.

sing. Ps 108:3. Mt 26:30. Ro 15:9.

50 **Great**. Ps 2:6. 78:71, 72. 89:3, 4. 144:10. 1 S
2:10. 16:1. Ac 2:34-36. Ph 2:9-11.

to his king. Ps 89:20-38. 132:10. 1 S 2:10. 2
S 7:13. 1 Ch 17:11-14, 27. Is 9:6, 7. Lk 1:31-
33, 69. Ro 1:3. 11:29. Ga 3:16.

for evermore. Heb. *olam*, **S#5769h**. Ps 37:27.
86:12. 89:28, 52. 92:8. 106:31. 113:2. 115:18.
121:8. 133:3. 2 S 22:51. 1 Ch 17:14. Ezk
37:26, 28.

PSALM 19

(*Title*.) **A Psalm**. It is uncertain when this
highly finished and beautiful ode was composed; though some think it was written by
David in the wilderness when persecuted by
Saul.

1 **The heavens**. Ps 8:3. 33:6. 115:16. 148:3, 4.
Is 40:22-26. Je 10:11, 12. Ro 1:19, 20. +2:12-
16.

declare. Ps 71:15. 78:4 (showing). Ge 24:66.
Jg 7:13 (told). 2 K 8:5 (telling).

God. Heb. *El*, Ex +15:2.

the firmament. Ps 150:1, 2. Ge 1:6-8, 14,
15. Da 12:3.

showeth. Ps 147:19. Ge 41:24. Jg 14:19
(expounded). 2 S 1:5, 6, 13 (told). Est 2:20. Is
41:26. 42:9. 45:19. 46:10. Je 4:15. Am 4:13.

handywork. Ps 8:6. 28:4, 5.

2 **Day unto**. Ps 24:7-10. 78:3-6. 134:1-3.
148:12. Ex 15:20, 21. Is 38:19.

night unto. Ps 74:16. 136:8, 9. Ge 1:17, 18.
+8:22.

3 **There**. *or*, "They have no speech, nor words,
nor is their voice heard; yet into all the earth
hath gone out their sound, and to the
extremity of the world their words." Dt 4:19.

where. *or*, without *these* their voice is heard.

4 **Their**. Ps 98:3. Is 49:6. Ro 10:18. 2 C 10:13-16.

line. *or*, rule, *or*, direction. Jsh +17:14. Ro
10:18.

In them. Ge 1:14-18. Ml 4:2. Jn 8:12.

5 **bridegroom**. Is 61:10. 62:5. Jn 3:29.

rejoiceth. Ec 1:5. 1 C 9:24-26. Ph 3:13, 14.
He 12:1, 2.

6 **His going**. Ps 139:9. Jb 25:3. Ec 1:5. Col 1:23.

circuit. Jb 22:14.

7 **law**. *or*, doctrine. Ps 78:1-7. 119:72, 96-100,
105, 127, 128. 147:19, 20. Dt 6:6-9. 17:18-20.
Jsh 1:8. Jb 23:12. Ro 3:2. 15:4. Ep 6:17.

perfect. ver. 8, 9. Ps 18:30. 111:7. Dt 32:4. Pr
30:5. Mt +5:48. Ro 12:2. Ja 1:17.

converting. *or*, restoring. Ps 23:3. 119:9, 93,
150. +126:5. Mk +4:14. Jn 5:39. 15:3. 17:17,
19. Ac +27:31. Ro 1:16. 10:17. 1 C +1:17.
+4:15. Ep 6:17. 1 Th 2:13. 2 T 3:15. Ja 1:18,
21-25. 1 P 1:23.

soul. Heb. *nephesh*, Ge +34:3.

testimony. Ps 93:5. 119:14, 24, 111, 152. Is
8:16, 20. Jn 3:32, 33. 5:39. Ac 10:43. 2 T 1:8.
1 J 5:9-12. Re 19:10.

sure. Ps 111:7. 2 S 23:5. 2 T 2:19. He 6:18,
19.

making wise. Ps 119:98-100, 130. Pr 1:4, 5,
22, 23. 8:9. Is 8:20. Lk 10:21. Ro 15:4. Col
3:16. 2 T 3:15-17. 1 P 2:2.

8 **statutes**. Ps 119:12, 16, 80, 171. Ge 26:5. Ex
18:16. Dt +4:1.

right. Ps 119:128. Ne 9:13.

rejoicing the heart. Ps 1:2. 40:8. 119:14, 24,
54, 92, 111, 121, 143. Dt 12:11, 12. 16:11, 14.
Ne 8:12. Is 64:5. Je 15:16. Ro 7:22.

is pure. Ps 12:6. 119:140. Pr 30:5. Da 10:21.
Ro 7:12-14. Ph 4:8.

enlightening. Ps 13:3. 119:98-100, 105, 130.
Pr 2:6. 6:23. 8:9. Is 8:20. Ro 2:17-20. 3:20.
7:7. Ga 2:19. 3:10-13, 21.

9 **The fear**. Ps 36:1. Ge 22:12. 42:18. 1 S 12:24.
1 K 18:3, 4, 12. Pr +3:7. Ro 3:10-18.

is clean. Ps 119:9. Jn 17:17.

enduring. Ps 111:10. 112:1-6. 119:160. Mt
5:17, 18.

for ever. Heb. *ad*, Ps +9:18.

judgments. Ps 10:5. 36:6. 72:1, 2. 119:7, 39,
62, 75, 106, 137, 138, 142, 160, 164. Dt +4:1.
Is 26:8. Ro 2:2. 11:22. Re 15:3. 16:7. 19:2.

true. Heb. truth. Ps 15:2. 25:5. Da 10:21.

10 **desired**. Jb 23:12.

than gold. Ps 119:72, 127. Jb 28:15-17. Pr
3:13-15. 8:10, 11, 19. 16:16.

sweeter. Ps 63:5. 119:103. Jb 23:12. Pr
24:13, 14.

honeycomb. Heb. the dropping of honey-
combs. 1 S 14:26-29.

11 **Moreover**. Ps 119:11. 2 Ch 19:10. Pr 6:22,
23. Ezk 3:17-21. 33:3-9. Mt 3:7. Ac 20:31. 1 C
4:14. 10:11. 1 Th 5:14. He 11:7.

keeping. Pr 3:16-18. 29:18. Lk +11:28. Ja
1:25. Re 14:13. 22:7.

great reward. Ps 25:10. 103:17, 18. Ex 20:6.
Le 18:5. Dt 32:46, 47. Ne 9:29. Pr 3:1, 2. Is
1:19, 20. Ezk 18:5-9. 20:13. Mt +5:12. 7:21,
24, 25. 19:17. Lk 10:27, 28. Jn 12:26. Ro
10:5. Re 22:14.

12 **Who can**. Ps 40:12. 49:11. Le 4:2, 3. Jb 6:24.
34:32. Pr 16:4. Is 40:17. 64:6. Je 17:9. 1 C 4:4.
15:35, 44. 2 T 1:10. He 9:7. 2 P 3:10. 1 J 4:8.
5:7. Re 20:11. 22:16.

cleanse. Ps 51:2, +7, +10. 65:3. 119:9. Mt
8:2, 3. 1 J 1:7.

from secret. Ps 90:8. 139:2, 23, 24. Le 4:2,
etc. Jb 34:32. Je 17:9.

13 **Keep back**. Ps 119:10, 29, 37, 133. 141:3, 4.
Ge 20:6. 1 S 25:32-34, 39. Pr 30:7-9. 2 C 13:7.
Ph 1:9, 10. 1 Th 5:23.

presumptuous. Ex 21:14. Nu 15:30, 31. Dt
17:12, 13. He 10:26. 2 P 2:10.

let. Ps 119:133. Ro 6:12-14, 16-22.
upright. Ps 7:10. 11:7. 84:11. Ac 24:16.
I shall. Ps 18:23. 1 Ch 10:13, 14.
great. Heb. much. ver. 11. Ps 25:11. 29:3mg.
transgression. Ps 5:10. 25:7. 32:1. Mt 12:31,
32. Ja 5:20. 1 J +5:16.

14 **Let**. Ps 5:1, 2. 51:15. 66:18-20. 119:108. Ge
4:4, 5. Pr 15:8. Ro 15:16. He 11:4. 13:15. 1 P
2:5.
 meditation. Ps 5:1. 37:4. 145:19. Ge 24:63.
Ml 3:16.
 strength. Heb. rock. Ps +18:1, 2. 73:26mg.
 redeemer. Jb 19:25. Is +41:14. 1 Th 1:10. T
2:14. 1 P 1:18, 19.

PSALM 20

1 A.M. 2968. B.C. 1036.
 hear. Ps 41:1. 46:1. 50:5. 60:11. 91:15. 138:7.
Je 30:7. Mt 26:38, 39. He 5:7.
 day of. Ps 37:39, 40. +50:15. 2 C 1:3, 4.
 name. i.e. Jacob's God Himself. Ps +9:10. Ex
20:24. Dt +28:58.
 God of Jacob. Ps 46:7, 11. 76:6. +84:8. Ge
32:27-29. 48:15, 16. Ex 3:13-15.
 defend. Heb. set thee on an high place. Ps
+9:9mg. 91:14. 144:2.

2 **thee help**. Heb. thy help.
 from. Ps 73:17. 1 K 6:16. 8:44, 45. 1 Ch
21:26. 2 Ch 20:8, 9.
 strengthen. Heb. support thee.
 out. 2 S 5:7. 6:17. Is 12:6. 14:32. 37:34, 35.

3 **Remember**. Ge 4:4. Is 60:7. Ep 5:2. 1 P 2:5.
 accept. Heb. turn to ashes, *or*, make fat. Le
+1:16. 1 Ch +21:26. 2 Ch 5:12. Ep 1:6.
 burnt. Le +23:12.
 Selah. Ps +9:16.

4 **Grant**. Ps 2:8. 21:2. 37:4. 145:19. Pr 11:23. Is
49:8. 53:11. Mt 21:22. Jn 11:42. 16:23. Ro
8:27, 28. He 7:25. 1 J 5:14, 15.

5 **rejoice**. Ps 13:5. 19:4. 21:1. 35:9. 118:15. Is
12:1-3. 25:9. 61:10. Hab 3:18. Lk 1:47.
 and in. Ps 60:4. Ex +17:15mg. Nu 10:35, 36.
1 S 17:45. Is 11:10. Mi 4:5.

6 **Now**. Ps 2:2. 18:50. 28:8. 89:20-23. Ac 2:36.
4:10.
 he will. 1 K 8:30, 43. Mt 6:9.
 his holy heaven. Heb. the heaven of his
holiness. Is 57:15. 63:15.
 with, etc. Heb. by the strength of the salvation of his right hand. Ps +18:35.

7 **Some trust**. Ps 33:16, 17. 44:6. 125:1. 1 S
13:5. 17:39, 45. 2 S 8:4. 10:18. Pr 21:31. Is
30:16. 31:1. Je 17:5.
 but we. Ps 45:17. 2 Ch 13:10-12, 16. 14:11.
20:12, 20. 32:8.
 the name. Ps +9:10.

8 **They**. Ps 34:21, 22. Jg 5:31.
 but we. Ps 125:1. 146:5-9. Je 17:7, 8. La
4:22.

9 **Save**, etc. or, "O Jehovah, save the king;
answer us when we call upon thee." Ps
118:25, 26. Mt 21:9, 15.
 let. Ps 2:6-10. 5:2. 24:7. 44:4. 74:12.

PSALM 21

(*Title.*) **A Psalm**. This is the people's song of
triumph, after the victory for which they
prayed in the former Psalm.

1 **the king**. Ps 2:6. 20:6, 9. 63:11. 72:1, 2. Is
9:6, 7. Mt 2:2.
 joy. Ps 28:7. 62:7. 95:1. 99:4. Ne 8:10.
 in thy. Ps 20:5. 71:17-24. 118:14, 15. He
12:2.

2 **his heart's**. Ps 2:8, 9. 20:4, 5. 92:11. Is 49:6-
12. He 7:25.
 not withholden. Jn 11:42. He +5:7.
 Selah. Ps +9:16.

3 **preventest**. Ps 18:18. 1 S 16:13. 2 S 2:4. 5:3.
Jb 41:11. Is 65:24. Ro 11:35.
 blessings. Ps 31:19. 2 Ch 6:41. Ro 2:4. Ep 1:3.
 settest. 2 S 12:30. 1 Ch 20:2. He 2:9. Re
19:12.

4 **asked life**. Ps 13:3. 16:10, 11. 30:2, 3. 39:13.
41:10. 61:5, 6. 69:32, 33. 102:24. 107:18, 19.
119:17, 77, 175. 2 S 7:12, 13. Is 9:7. 38:1-3.
Je 15:15. Da 2:17, 18. Jon 1:13, 14. Mt 8:24,
25. 14:30, 31. Jn 14:19. Ro 6:9, 23. He 7:25. 1
J 5:16.
 length of days. Ps 72:17. 89:29, 36, 37. Dt
+4:40. Re 1:18.
 for ever. **S#5769h**, *olam* in conjunction with
ad. Ps 9:5. 10:16. 45:6, 17. 48:14. 52:8. 111:8.
119:44. 145:1, 2, 21. 148:6. Ex 15:18. Is 30:8.
Da 12:3. Mi 4:5.
 and ever. Heb. *ad*, Ps +9:18.

5 **glory**. Ps 3:3. 62:7. 2 S 7:8, 9, 19. Is 49:5-7.
63:1. Jn 13:31, 32. 17:1, 5, 22. Ph 2:9-11. He
8:1. 2 P 1:17. Re 5:8-13.
 honor. Ps 110:1. 1 Ch 17:11-15, 27. Mt
28:18. Ep 1:20-22. 1 P 3:22.

6 **made**. Heb. set him to be blessings. Ps 72:17-
19. Ge 12:2. Lk 2:10, 11, 30-32. Ac 3:26. Ga
3:9, 14. Ep 1:3.
 for ever. Ps +9:18.
 made him exceeding glad. Heb. gladded
him with joy. Ps 4:6, 7. 16:11. 45:7. 63:2-5.
Ac 2:25, 28.
 thy countenance. Nu 6:26.

7 **For the**. Ps 13:5. 18:2. 20:7, 8. 26:1. 61:4, 6,
7. 91:2, 9, 10. 1 S 30:6. Mt 27:43. He 2:13.
 most. Ps +7:17.
 he shall. Ps 16:8. Da 7:14.

8 **Thine hand**. Ps 2:9. 18, title. 72:9. 89:22, 23.
110:1, 2. Ex +9:3. 1 S 25:29. 31:3. 2 S 7:1.
Am 9:2, 3. Lk 19:14, 27. 1 C 15:25. He 10:28,
29. Re 19:15.

9 **Thou**. Ge 19:28. Da 3:20-22. Ml 4:1. Mt
13:42, 50. 25:41, 46. 2 Th 1:8. Re 20:14.

anger. Heb. countenance. or, presence. 2 K 25:19mg. Jb 23:15. Mt 24:3. Ph 2:12. 2 Th 1:9. 2 T 4:1.
the Lord. Ps 56:1, 2. 106:17. Jb 6:3. La 2:2.
in his. Ps 2:5, 12. Mt 22:7. 1 Th 2:16. Re 6:16, 17. 19:15.
the fire shall. Ps +97:3. Dt 9:3. Is +24:6. Mt +25:41, 46. He 10:26, 27. 2 P +3:7, 13.

10 **Their fruit**. Ps 37:28. 109:13. 1 K 13:34. Jb 18:16-19. 20:28. Is 14:20. Ml 4:1.
their seed. Ex +20:5.

11 **intended evil**. Mt 2:13.
against thee. Pr 21:30.
imagined. Ps 2:1. 10:2. 31:13. 35:20. Je 11:18, 19. Ezk 11:2. Mt 21:46. 26:4, 5. Ac 5:27, 28.
are not. Ps 83:4. Is 7:6, 7. 8:9, 10. Mt 2:8, 16. 27:63, 64. 28:2-6. Ac 4:17, 18.

12 **Therefore**. Ps 9:3. 44:10. 56:9.
make , etc. or, set them as a butt. Jb 7:20. 16:12, 13. La 3:12.
back. Heb. shoulder. 1 S 10:9mg.
arrows. Dt +32:23.

13 **Be thou**. Ps 72:18, 19. Jb 9:19. Is +12:4. Mt 6:10, 13. Re 11:16, 17.
so will. Ps 58:10, 11. Re 15:3, 4. 16:5-7. 18:20. 19:1-6.

PSALM 22

(**Title.**) A.M. 2962. B.C. 1042.
Aijeleth. or, the hind of the morning. **S#365h**.
ver. 16. Ps 42:1, 2. Pr 5:19. Je 14:5.

1 **My God**. Heb. *El*, Ex +15:2. Ps 31:14-16. 43:1-5. Mt 27:46. Mk *15:34*. Lk 24:44.
my God. Ge 22:11.
why hast. Ps 26:9. 37:28. 71:11. 1 S 12:22. He +13:5. 1 P 1:11.
far. ver. 11. Ps 46:1.
helping. Heb. my salvation. Is 46:13.
roaring. Ps 32:3, 4. 38:8. Jb 3:24. 4:10. 37:4. Is +5:29. 59:11. La 3:8. Ezk 19:7. Ho 7:14. Am +1:2. Lk 22:44. He 5:7.

2 **I cry**. or, call. Ps 18:3, 6. 42:3. 55:16, 17. 80:18. 86:3, 7. 91:15. 102:2. Jb 14:15. 27:10.
daytime. Ps 42:3. 55:17. 88:1. Lk 18:7. 1 Th 3:10. 2 T 1:3.
but. Ps 80:4. La 3:8, 44.
in the night. Ps +119:55. Lk 6:12. 18:7, 8. 22:41-46.
am not silent. Heb. there is no silence to me. Ps 39:2. 62:1mg. 65:1mg. Mt 26:44.

3 **But**. Ps 145:17-19. Jb 13:15. Is 6:3. Re 4:8.
that. Ps 50:23. 65:1. Dt 10:21.

4 **Our fathers**. Ps 44:1-7. Ge 15:6. 32:9-12, 28. Ex 14:13, 14, 31. 1 S 7:9-12. Ro 4:18-22. He 11:8-32.

5 **cried**. Ps 99:6, 7. 106:44. Jg 4:3. 6:6. 10:10-16.
and were. Ps 25:2, 3. 31:1. 69:6, 7. 71:1. Is 45:17. 49:23. Ro 9:33. 10:11. 1 P 2:6.

6 **I am**. Jb 25:6. Is 41:14.
a reproach. Ps +31:11. 88:8. Is 53:3. Zc 11:8. Mt 11:19. 12:24. 27:20-23. Jn 7:15, 20, 47-49. 8:48.
despised of. Is 49:7. Mt 26:67, 68.

7 **All**. Ex +9:6.
laugh. Lk +8:53. 23:11, 35-39.
shoot out. Heb. open. Ps 31:18. Jb 16:4, 10. 30:9-11. Is 57:4. Mt 26:66-68.
shake. Je +18:16. Mt 27:39, 40.

8 **He trusted**. Heb. rolled himself on. Ps 37:5. 55:22. Pr 16:3mg. Mt 27:42, *43*.
let him. Ps 3:1, 2. 42:10. 71:11. 91:14. Mt 27:41-43. Mk 15:30-32.
seeing, etc. or, if he delight. Ps 18:19. Is 42:1. Mt 3:17. 12:18. 17:5. Lk 23:35.

9 **that took**. Ps 71:6. 139:15, 16. Is 49:1, 2.
thou didst. Ps 71:17. Is 7:14, 15. 9:6.
make me hope. or, keep me in safety. or, trust, or, lean. 2 K 18:30. Is 36:15. Je 28:15. 29:31. Mt 2:13-15. Re 12:4, 5.

10 **cast**. Is 46:3, 4. 49:1. Lk 2:40, 52.
thou. Jn 20:17.
from. Je 1:5. Ga 1:15, 16.

11 **Be not far**. Ps 10:1. 13:1-3. 35:22. 38:21. +51:11. 69:1, 2, 18. 71:12. Je 14:7, 8. Mk 5:18. Lk 24:29. Jn 4:40. 16:32. 17:21. Ep 3:17. 2 T 4:22. He 5:7. Re 3:20.
none to help. Heb. not a helper. Ps 72:12. 142:4-6. Dt 32:36. Mt 26:56, 72-74.

12 **Many**. Ps 68:30. Je 50:11.
strong. Dt 32:14, 15. Is 34:7. Ezk 39:18. Am 4:1-3. Mt 27:1. Ac 4:27.
of Bashan. Ps 68:15, 22. 135:11. Dt +32:14.

13 **gaped**, etc. Heb. opened their mouths against me. ver. 7. Ps 35:21. 66:14mg. Jb 16:10. La 2:16. 3:46. Mt 26:3, 4, 59-65.
as a ravening. ver. 21. Is +5:29. Ezk 22:27, 28.

14 **I am**. Mt 26:38. Lk 22:44. Jn 12:27.
poured out. Dt 12:27. 1 S 7:6. 2 S 14:14.
all my bones. ver. 17. Ps 6:2. 31:10. 32:3. Da 5:6.
out of joint. or, sundered. Ps 92:9. Jb 4:11. 41:17.
my heart. Jb 23:16. Mk 14:33, 34. Jn 19:34.
melted. Ex +15:15.

15 **strength**. Ps 32:3, 4. Pr 17:22.
tongue. Ps 69:3, 21. Jb 29:10. La 4:4. Jn 19:28.
into the dust. Ps 30:9. 104:29. Ge +3:19. 18:27. Jb 7:21. 10:9. 34:15. Is 53:12. Da 12:2. Mt 27:50. 1 C +15:3.

16 **dogs**. Ps 22, title. ver. 20. Ps 59:6, 14. +7:6. Ph 3:2. Re 22:15.
compassed. Je 12:6. Lk 11:53, 54.
assembly. Ps 86:14. Je 12:6. Mt 26:57. Mk 15:16-20. Lk 22:63-71. 23:4, 5, 10, 11, 23, 35.
they pierced. Ps 105:18, 19. Zc 12:10. 13:6. Mt 27:35. Mk 15:24. Lk 23:33. 24:39. Jn 19:23, 37. 20:25, 27.

17 **I may**. Ps 102:3-5. Jb 33:21. Is 52:14.
look. Mt 27:36, 39-41. Mk 15:29-32. Lk 23:27, 35.
stare upon. Lk 23:35.

18 **they part**. Ps 60:6 (divide). 68:12. 108:7. Jsh 18:10. Is 53:12. Mt 27:35. Mk 15:24. Lk 23:34. Jn 19:23, 24.
cast lots. Jsh +14:2. Jn 19:24.

19 **But**. ver. 11. Ps 10:1.
O my. Ps 18:1. 21:1.
haste. Ps +40:17. 49:17. 118:25.

20 **soul**. Heb. *nephesh*, Ge +12:13. Ps 17:13. Zc 13:7.
my darling. Heb. my only one. **S#3173h**. Ps 25:16. 35:17mg. 68:6. Ge 22:2, 12, 16. Jg 11:34. Pr 4:3. Je 6:26. Am 8:10. Zc 12:10. LXX. renders "only begotten." Jn 3:16.
from the power. Heb. from the hand. Ac 4:27. 1 P 5:8.
dog. ver. 16.

21 **Save me from**. Lk 4:13. Ac 5:31. 2 T 4:17.
heard. Ps 118:5. He 5:7.
me from. Lk 22:53. Jn 14:30. 2 T 4:17. 1 P 5:8.
horns. Nu 23:22. Dt 33:17. Jb 39:9, 10. Is 34:7. Jn 8:59. Ac 4:27. 5:30-32.

22 **I will declare**. Ps 40:9. 71:18, 19. Lk 15:6. Jn 7:25, 26. He 2:11, *12*. Ju 24.
my brethren. Mt 12:48, 49. 25:40. 28:10. Jn 20:17. Ro 8:29.
in the midst. ver. 25. Ps 40:9, 10.

23 **Ye that**. Ps 115:11, 13. 135:19, 20. 145:19. 1 Ch 16:8-13. Lk 1:50.
all ye. Ps 105:3-7. 106:5. 107:1, 2. 135:19, 20.
glorify. Ps 50:23. Is 25:3. Mt +9:8. Jn 17:4. 1 C 6:19, 20. 10:31.
all ye the. ver. 30. 1 Ch 16:13.
seed of Israel. Ga 6:16.

24 **For**. ver. 6. Ps +40:17. Is 50:6-9.
neither. Lk 23:46.
but. ver. 2. Ps 116:3-6. 118:5. He 5:7.

25 **My praise**. ver. 22. Ps 35:18. 40:9, 10. 111:1.
vows. Le +23:38.

26 **The meek**. Mt +5:5.
shall eat. ver. 29. Le 7:11-17. Pr 9:5. Is 25:6. 49:9. 55:1, 2. 65:13. Mt 22:4. Lk 14:15. 15:23. Jn 6:48-58.
they. Ps 105:3, 4.
your heart. Ps 69:32. Pr 23:7. Mt 13:15. Jn 4:14. 6:51. Ro 10:10.
live. 1 S +10:24.
for ever. Ps +9:18.

27 **All the ends**. Ps 2:8. 59:13. +86:9. 98:3. Is 45:22. 46:8, 9. 49:6, 12. Je +31:8.
turn. Hg 1:5. Lk 15:17, 18. Ac +9:35. Ro 16:26.
and all. Ps 2:8. +86:9. 96:7. 98:3. 117:1. Is +11:10. Re 7:9-12.

28 **the kingdom**. Mt +6:10.

governor. Ps 47:2, 7, 8. 89:18. 99:1. 103:19. 146:10. Is 33:22. Da 4:34. Re 19:6, 16.

29 **that be**. Ps 73:7. 78:31. Is 10:16.
fat. Ps 92:14. Is 30:23.
shall eat and worship. Ps 113:7. Is 26:19. 29:4. Ph 2:10. Re 20:12-15.
bow. Ps 45:12. 72:11. Is 45:23. 60:3. Ro 14:10-12. Ph 2:10. Re 5:13.
and none. Ps 49:6-9. Jb 12:10. Ho 13:9. Jn 3:36. 11:25, 26. 2 C +3:5.
soul. Heb. *nephesh*, Ge +12:13.

30 **A seed**. Is 53:10. He 2:13.
it shall. Ps 14:5. 24:6. 73:15. 87:6. Mt 3:9. 24:34. Ga 3:26-29. 1 P 2:9.

31 **They**. Ps 78:6. 86:9. 102:18. 145:4-7. Is 44:3-5. 49:21-23. 54:1. 60:4. 66:7-9.
his righteousness. Ro 1:17. 3:21-25. 5:19-21. 2 C 5:21.
unto. Ps 78:6. Jn 20:29. Ro 3:21, 22.
people. Is 28:11. Ho 2:23. Ro 9:24.
born. Ps +2:7.
he hath done. Heb. it is finished. Jn 19:30.

PSALM 23

1 **The Lord**. Ex +15:26.
is. Ge +49:9.
my shepherd. Heb. *Jehovah-roi*. Ps 79:13. 95:7. Mt 26:31. Jn +10:11.
I shall not want. Ps 34:9, 10, 22. 84:11. Ge 22:14 (*Jehovah-jireh*). Mt 6:33. Mk 11:22-24. Lk 11:9-13. Ro 8:32. Ph 4:19. Ja 1:5-8. 1 J 3:20-22. 5:13-15. 3 J 2.

2 **He maketh**. Is 40:11. Je 31:2. Mt 24:45. Jn 6:27.
lie down. Pr +3:24. Mt 11:28.
green pastures. Heb. pastures of tender grass. Ps 37:2. 65:11-13. Is 35:1, 2. Ezk 34:14. Jn 10:9.
he leadeth. ver. +3.
still waters. Heb. waters of quietness. Ps +46:4. Jg 6:24 (*Jehovah-shalom*). Jb 34:29. Is +41:18. 1 T +2:2. Re 21:6.

3 **He restoreth**. Ps 19:7mg. 51:10-12. 119:176. Ex 15:26 (*Jehovah-ropheka*). Je 32:37-42. Mi 7:8, 9, 18, 19. Lk 22:31, 32. Jn 21:15-19. 1 J 2:1. Re 3:19.
soul. Heb. *nephesh*, Ge +12:13.
he leadeth. Ps +32:8. Dt +32:12. 1 K +13:9. 2 Ch 32:22. Pr 3:5, 6. 8:20. Is +42:16. Lk 1:79. Jn 10:4, 13. 16:13. Ph 1:10. Col 1:9, 10. Re 7:17.
paths. Ps 16:11. 85:13. Pr +8:20. Is 42:16.
righteousness. Je 23:6. 33:16 (*Jehovah-tsid-kenu*).
for his. Ps 72:17-19. 1 S +12:22. 1 J 2:12.
name's. Ps +9:10. 1 K 8:41. Is +48:9.

4 **though**. Jsh 3:11.
I walk through. Ps 138:7. Jsh 3:11.
the valley. Jl 3:2, 11.
shadow of death. Ps 44:19. 107:10, 14. Jb

3:5. 10:21, 22. 12:22. 16:16. 24:17. 28:3.
34:22. +38:17. Is 9:2. Je 2:6. 13:16. Am 5:8.
Mt 4:16. Lk 1:79.

I will fear no. Ps +118:6. Zp 3:16. Lk 12:32.
1 C +15:55-57. 2 T 1:7.

for thou. Ps 14:5. 16:8. 31:7, 8. 1 S +2:1. Jb
29:5. Is 25:4. +43:2. 49:13. Je 16:19. Zc 8:23.
Ac 27:20-25. Ro 8:31. 1 C +10:13. 2 C 1:3, 4.

art with me. Ps 40:17. 118:7, 10, 13, 18. Ezk
48:35 (*Jehovah-shammah*). Mi 2:12, 13. Zp
3:17. Zc 9:14-16.

thy rod. Ps 74:2. Ge +49:10. Ex +4:20. Is 9:4.
Je 10:16. Zc 11:10, 14. Re 12:10.

thy staff. Jg 6:21. 2 K 4:29, 31. 18:21. Zc 8:4.

comfort. Ps 119:50. Ro 15:4. 2 C +1:3, 4.

5 **preparest.** Ps 22:26, 29. 31:19, 20. 78:25-28.
Jn 6:53-56. 10:9, 10. 16:22.

a table. Ps 69:22. 78:19. 128:3. Jb 36:16. Lk
+22:29, 30. 1 C 10:21. Re 7:17.

presence. or, over against. Zc 14:1-5. Ph
1:12-18. 1 P +1:7. Re 19:9, 13-21.

enemies. Ps 6:7. 7:4. Ex 17:15 (*Jehovah-nissi*).

anointest. Heb. makest fat. Ps 28:8. Ex 31:13
(*Jehovah-mekadishkem*). Pr 15:30. Mt +6:17.
26:6, 7. Mk 14:8. Lk +7:46. He +1:9.

with oil. Ps +45:7. 55:21. Ja 5:14.

my cup. Ps 16:5. 73:10. 97:10-12. 103:1-5.
116:13. Jn 1:16. 1 C 10:16. Ep 3:17-20.

runneth over. or, is full. Ps 66:12mg (moist).

6 **goodness.** Ps 21:3. 25:7. 84:11. +100:5. 1 Ch
16:34. La 3:22, 23.

mercy. Ps 103:17.

follow. He 13:6.

and I. Ps 15:1. 16:11. 17:15. 27:4-6. 73:24-
26. 84:10. Is 2:2. Jn 14:2, 3. 2 C 5:1. Ph 1:23.
2 T 4:18. He 11:10-16. 13:14. Re 7:15. 21:3.

dwell in. or, return to. Is 35:10. +51:11.

the house. Ac +15:16, 17. He 3:6.

for ever. Heb. to length of days. Ps
+91:16mg. Re 3:12.

PSALM 24

1 A.M. 2962. B.C. 1042.

earth. Ps 50:12. Ex 9:29. 19:5. Dt 10:14. 1 Ch
29:11. Jb 41:11. Da 4:25. Ro +14:8. 1 C 10:26,
28.

world. Ps 89:11. 98:7. Na 1:5.

2 **For.** Ps 33:6, 7. 95:4, 5. 104:5, 6. 136:6. Ge
1:9, 10. Jb 38:4. Je 10:11-16. 2 P 3:5-7.

and. Ps 93:1. 96:10. Ge 8:22. Jb 38:8-11. Je
5:22.

3 **Who.** Ps 15:1-5. 68:18. Ml 3:2. Jn 13:36.
20:17. Ep 4:8-10. Re 22:14.

the hill. Ps 68:15, 16. 78:68, 69. 132:13, 14.
2 S 6:12-17. 1 K +8:39. 1 Ch 15:1, 25-28. He
12:22-24.

stand. Ps +1:5. Le 10:3. Ml 3:1, 2. He 12:28, 29.

4 **He that**, etc. Heb. the clean of hands. Ps
18:20. 26:6. Ex 30:18. 2 S 22:21, 25. Jb 9:30.

17:9. Is 1:15, 16. 33:15, 16. 1 T 2:8. Ja 4:8.

pure. Ps 37:18. 51:10. 73:1. Ge 6:5. Pr 20:9.
Je 4:14. Mt +5:8. Ac 15:9. 2 C 7:1. He 12:14.
Re 21:1-4, 27. 22:14, 15.

heart. Ps 84:2. 1 P 3:4.

lifted. Ps 25:1. 143:8. Dt 4:19. Ezk 18:6, 15.
Ac 14:15.

his. or, my (LXX.).

soul. Heb. *nephesh*, Ge +34:3. Le +26:11.

sworn. Ps 15:4. Je 5:2. 7:9, 10. Zc +5:3, 4. Ml
+3:5. 1 T 1:10.

5 **receive.** Ps 50:23. 67:6, 7. 72:17. 115:12, 13.
128:1-5. Nu 6:24-27. Is 33:15, 17. Mt 5:3-12.
Jn 7:17. Ro 4:6-9. Ga 3:9, 14. Ep 1:3. 1 P 3:9.

righteousness. Is 46:13. 51:5, 6, 8. 54:17.
61:10. Ro 3:21, 22. 5:17, 18. 1 C 1:30. 2 C
5:21. Ga 5:5. Ph 3:9. 2 T 4:8.

God. Ps +88:1. Is 45:17.

6 **This is.** Ps 73:15. Is 53:10. Mt +24:34. Ro
4:16.

that seek. Ps 27:8. 105:4. Jn 1:47-49.

O Jacob. *or*, O God of Jacob.

Selah. ver. 10. Ps +9:16.

7 **Lift.** Ps 118:19, 20. Is 26:2.

everlasting. Heb. *olam*, Ge +17:7. ver. +9.

King. Ps 21:1, 5. 29:3. 97:6. Je 23:5, 6. Hg
2:7, 9. Ml 3:1. Ac 7:2. 1 C 2:8. Ja 2:1. 2 P
3:18. Re 4:11. 17:14, 15.

shall. Ps 68:16-18. 132:8. Nu 10:35, 36. 2 S
6:17. 1 K 8:6, 11. 2 Ch 6:41. Mk 16:19. 2 C
6:16. Ep 4:8-10. He 6:20. 1 P 3:22. Re 3:20.

8 **Who is.** Jb 22:21. Is 63:1-3. Je 23:6. 1 C
15:57.

The Lord strong. Ps 45:3-6. 50:1. 93:1. Is
9:6. 49:24-26. 63:1-6. Col 2:15. Re 6:2. 19:11-
21.

9 **Lift up.** ver. 7.

gates. Ps 122:2.

everlasting. Heb. *olam*, Ge +17:7. The word
"everlasting" is sometimes applied to things of
this age (Mt 12:32) to express very long
though finite duration, either past or future.
Ge 49:26. Ex +21:6. Le 16:34. Dt 15:17. 1 S
27:12. 1 K 8:13. 1 Ch 28:4. Is 32:14. Phm 15.

come in. Ps 68:16.

10 **King of glory.** ver. +7.

The Lord. Ps +103:21. Ex +12:41. Dt +4:19.
Is 6:3-5. Jn 12:40, 41. 14:9.

of hosts. Ps 46:7, 11. Ex +15:26. 1 S 1:3, 11.
4:4. 15:2. 17:45. 2 S 7:26. 1 K 18:15. Is 1:9.
5:16. 6:3, 5. 8:13. 37:16. 44:6. 47:4. 48:2.
51:15. 54:5. Je +10:16. Ho 12:5. Am +4:13. Zc
2:8-11. 3:7. 13:7. Ml 3:1. Ro 9:29. Ja 5:4.

he is. Ps 2:6-12. Mt 25:31, 34. Lk 9:26. T 2:13.

PSALM 25

1 A.M. cir. 3463. B.C. cir. 541.

do I. Ps 24:4. 86:4. 143:8. 1 S 1:15. La 3:41.

soul. Heb. *nephesh*, Ge +34:3.

2 **O my God**. Ps 7:1. 18:2. 22:1, 5, 8. 34:8. 37:40. 71:1. Is 26:3, 4. 28:16. 41:16, 17. 49:23. Ro 5:5. 10:11. 1 P 2:6.

trust. Ps 5:11. 22:4, 5.

not be ashamed. ver. 20. Ps 31:1. 119:116. Is 28:16. Jl +2:26. Ro 9:33. 10:11. 1 P 2:6.

let not. Ps 13:2-4. 35:19-25. 41:11. 56:1. 94:3, 4. 142:6. Is 36:14-20. 37:10, 20, 35.

3 **wait**. ver. 21. Ps 27:14. 33:20. 37:7, 9, 34. 40:1-3. 59:9. 62:1, 5. 123:2. 130:5, 6. Ge 49:18. Pr 20:22. 27:18. Is 8:17. 25:9. 26:8. 30:18. 33:2. 40:31. 64:4. Je 14:22. La 3:25, 26. Ho 12:6. Mi 7:7. Hab 2:3. Zp 3:8. Lk 2:25. Ro 8:25.

be ashamed. Ps 69:6. Pr 3:35. Is 65:13. Da 12:2.

let. Ps 6:10. 31:17. 35:26. 40:14, 15. 70:2, 3. 71:13. 132:18. Je 20:11.

without. Ps 7:4, 5. 59:2-5. 69:4. 109:3, 5. 119:78. Jn 15:25.

4 **Show me**. Ps 5:1, 8. 27:11. 67:2. 86:11. 119:17, 18, 27, 135. 143:8, 10. Ex 33:13. 1 K 18:37. Jb 23:3. 34:32. Pr 2:3-6. 8:20. Is 2:3. Je 6:16. 50:5. Jn 6:28. 17:3. Ep 1:17, 18. 3:17-19. Col 1:9.

thy ways. Ps 86:11. 119:27. Is 53:6. Mt 7:14. Jn 14:6.

teach me. Ps 32:8. 143:8, 10. Jb 36:22. Is 2:3. 48:17. Jn 14:26. 1 J 2:27.

thy paths. Ps 16:11. 23:3. Is 2:3.

5 **Lead me**. ver. 8, 10. Ps 43:3, 4. 107:7. 119:133. Ex 4:1, 10. 33:12, 13. Jsh 7:8. 1 S 28:5, 6. 30:7, 8. 2 S 2:1. Is 30:21. 35:8. 42:16. 49:10. Je 4:16. 31:9. Jn 8:31, 32. 14:26. 16:13. Ac 9:6. Ro 8:14. Ep 4:21. 1 Th 3:11. 1 J 2:27. Re 7:17.

in thy truth. Ps 119:30. Jn 16:13.

teach. Ps 119:26, 33, 66. Ne 9:20. Jb 36:22. Is 54:13. Je 31:33, 34. 50:5. Jn 6:45. Ep 4:20, 21.

God. Ps +88:1.

on thee. Ps 22:2. 86:3. 88:1. 119:97. Pr 8:34. 23:17. Is 30:18. Lk 18:7.

all the day. Ps 32:3. 35:28. 38:6.

6 **Remember**. Ps 98:3. 106:45. 136:23. 2 Ch 6:42. Lk 1:54, 71, 72.

thy. Ps 40:11. 69:13, 16. 103:4.

tender mercies. Heb. bowels. Ps 40:11. 77:9. 79:8. 103:4, 17. Ex +34:6. Is +63:15. Je 16:5. 2 C 1:3.

lovingkindnesses. Ps +5:7. 6:4. 26:3. 36:7. 40:10, 11. 42:8. 48:9. +51:1. 69:16. 88:11. 89:49. 119:88.

for they. Ps 77:7-12. 136:11, etc. Ge 24:27. 32:9, 10. Ex 15:13. +34:6, 7. Ne 9:19, 27, 28.

ever of old. Heb. olam, Ge +6:4.

7 **Remember**. Ps 79:8. 109:14, 16. Is 38:17. 43:25. 64:9. Mt 6:12. He 8:12. 10:16-18.

the sins. Jb 13:26. 20:11. Pr 5:7-14. Je 3:25. Jn 5:5, 14.

according. Ps 51:1. 109:26. 119:124.

for thy. Ps 6:4. 31:16. Ep 1:6, 7. 2:4-8.

goodness' sake. Ps 27:13. 31:19. 86:4, 5.

8 **Good**. Ps 119:68.

upright. Ps 92:15. Is 26:7.

teach. Pr 1:20-23. 2:1-6. 9:4-6. Mi 4:2. Mt 9:13. 11:29, 30. Lk 11:13. Jn 6:44, 45. 2 C 4:6. Ep 1:17, 18. Ja 1:5.

9 **meek**. Mt +5:5.

guide. Ps +23:3. 32:8, 9. 73:24. 119:66. 143:10. Pr 3:5, 6. 8:20. Is 42:1-3. Ezk 11:19, 20. 36:27.

teach. ver. 4. Ps 34:11. 119:12, 26, 64, 68. Jb 34:32.

his way. Ps 119:35. Jn 14:6. Ac 9:2. 13:10. He 10:20.

10 **the paths**. Ps 18:25, 26. 23:4-6. 37:23, 24. 91:14. 119:75, 76. 138:7. Ge 5:24. 17:1. 48:15, 16. Is 43:2. Ho 14:9. Ro 8:28.

mercy. Ps 33:4. 57:3. 85:10. 89:14. 98:3. Ge 24:27. 2 S 15:20. Is 25:1. Jn 1:14, 17. Ja 5:11.

and truth. ver. 5. Ps 15:2. 19:9.

keep. Ps 24:4, 5. 50:23. 103:17, 18. Is 56:1-6. Ho 14:9. Zp 2:3. Ac 10:35. Ro 2:13. He 8:8-12. 12:14. 13:20, 21.

11 **thy name's**. Ps 23:3. 31:3. 63:4. 83:18. 102:15. 109:21. 1 Ch 16:35. Is +48:9. 63:19. 1 J 2:12.

for it. Nu 14:17-19. Ro 5:15, 20, 21.

12 **What**. Ps 34:12, 13. Pr 22:29. 29:20. Je 9:12. Ezk 8:6. Ho 14:9. Mt 11:7, 8, 9.

that feareth. Pr 2:5. +3:7. 15:33.

him. Ps 32:8. 37:23. Is 35:8. Jn 3:20, 21. 7:17. 8:31, 32. Ac 11:14. 2 Th 2:10-12. 1 J 2:27.

13 **His soul**. Heb. nephesh, Ge +34:3; Nu +23:10. Dt 33:12, 26-29. Pr 1:33. 19:23. 29:25. Ezk 34:25-28. Mt 11:28, 29.

dwell at ease. Heb. lodge in goodness. Ps 31:19. 36:8. 63:5. Jb 17:2mg. Is 66:10-14. Je 31:12-14. Zp 3:17. Zc 9:17. Ph 4:19.

his seed. Dt +29:11. 2 K 2:4. Is 44:3. 59:21. Ac +2:39.

inherit. Ezk 33:24-26. Mt +5:5. 1 P 3:10. 2 P 3:13.

14 **secret**. Ps 119:18. Ge 18:17-19. Ex 33:13. Nu 12:7, 8. Jg 13:18. Dt +29:29. Jb 15:8. 29:4. Ps 103:7. Pr 3:32. Je 23:18mg. Am +3:7. Mt 13:11, 12. Jn 7:17. 14:17, 21-23. 15:15. 17:6. 1 C 2:10, 14. Ep 1:9, 18. Col 3:3. Re 2:17.

and he. Jn 7:17. +15:15. 17:26.

will, etc. or, his covenant to make them know it. Ge 17:13. Dt 4:13. 2 Ch +20:7. Ps 89:34. Is 54:7-10. +55:3. Je 31:31-34. 32:36-42. Ac 3:19-21. Ro 11:26, 27, 29. 15:8.

15 **Mine eyes**. Ps 34:15. 121:1, 2. 123:1, 2. 141:8.

pluck. Heb. bring forth. Ps 31:4. Ex 4:7.

my feet. Pr 3:26.

out. Ps 31:4. 124:7, 8. Je 5:26. 2 T 2:25, 26.

16 Turn. Ps 60:1. 69:16. 86:16. Mi +7:19.
for I. Ps 69:14-20. 88:15-18. 143:4. Da 9:17.
Mk 15:33-35.

17 The troubles. Ps +34:19. 38:1-8. 42:7. 77:2-4. Hab 3:17-19. 1 C 4:11-13. 2 C 4:8, 9.
bring. Ps 40:1, 2. 116:3-6. Ne +9:37.

18 Look upon. Ps 80:14, 15. 119:132, 153. 1 S 1:11. 2 S 16:12. 2 Ch 24:22. La 5:1. Lk 1:25.
forgive. Ps 32:1-5. 51:8, 9. Mt 9:2.

19 Consider. Ps +9:13.
enemies. Ps 3:1, 2. +5:8. 27:2, 12. 38:19. 56:2. 57:4. 59:1. 138:7. 143:3. 2 S 16:11. 17:2-4. Lk 22:2. 23:5, 21-23.
cruel hatred. Heb. hatred of violence. Ps 11:5. 18:48mg. 52:2. 74:20. 86:14. 140:1, 4, 11.

20 O keep. Ps 17:8. 22:20, 21. 121:7. Lk 23:46. Ac 7:59.
soul. Heb. *nephesh*, Ge +12:5, 13.
let. Ps 71:1, 2.
ashamed. ver. +2.
for. Ps 16:1.

21 Let integrity. Ps 7:8. 18:20-24. 26:1, 11. 41:12. 1 S 24:11-13. 26:23. Pr 11:3. 20:7. Da 6:22. Ac +6:3. 24:16. 25:10, 11.

22 Redeem. Ps 14:7. 51:18, 19. +122:6. +130:8. 137:5, 6.

PSALM 26

1 Judge. Ps 7:8. 35:24. 43:1. 54:1. 1 S 24:15mg. 1 C 4:3-6.
for. ver. 11. Ps 15:2. 25:21. 2 K 20:3. Pr 20:7. Ac 23:1. 24:16. 2 C 1:12. 1 Th 2:10. 1 J 3:21.
trusted. Ps 4:5. 25:2. 28:7. 31:14. Pr 29:25.
I shall. Ps 21:7. 37:31. 62:2, 6. 94:18. 121:3, 7, 8. 1 S 2:9. 1 T 1:19. 1 P 1:5. 2 P 1:10.

2 Examine. Ps +17:3. Jb 13:23. 31:4-6. Je +17:10.
prove me. Ge 22:1 (tempt). Da 1:12.

3 For. Ps 52:1. 85:10-13. Mt 5:44-48. Lk 6:36. 2 C 3:18. 5:14, 15. 8:9. Ep 4:32. 5:1, 2. Col 3:12, 13. 1 J 4:7-12, 19-21. 3 J 11.
and. Ps 25:5. 101:2. 119:142. 2 K 20:3. Is 2:5. 8:20. Jn 14:6. Ep 4:20-25. 1 J 1:7. 2 J 4. 3 J 3, 4.

4 not sat. ver. 5. Ps 1:1. 101:7. +119:63, 115. 139:19. Pr 1:10-16, 18. 4:14-17. 7:24-27. 9:6. 12:11. 13:20. 14:7. 22:24, 25. 24:1, 2, 21. 28:7, 19. 29:3. Je 15:17. Lk 22:55. 1 C 15:33. 2 C 6:17.
neither will. Ps 141:4.

5 hated. Ps 5:5. Pr +8:13.
will. Ps 1:1. Mt 9:11, 12. 1 C 5:9-11.

6 wash. Ps 24:4. 73:13. Ex 30:18, 19, 20. Is 1:16-18. Ac 22:16. T 3:5. He 10:19-22.
hands. Ps 24:4. 2 S 22:21, 25. Jb 17:9. Ja 4:8.
so will. Ps 43:4. Ml 2:11-13. Mt 5:23, 24. 1 C 11:28, 29. 1 T 2:8.

7 That. Ps 9:14. 66:13-15. 95:2. 100:4, 5.

116:12-14, 18, 19. 118:19, 27. 134:2. Dt 26:2-10. 1 S 1:24, 27. 2 Ch 20:26-29.
tell. Ps 71:17-19. 72:18. 105:2. 119:27. 136:4, 5. 145:5. Lk 19:37-40.

8 Lord. Ps 27:4-6. 42:4. 84:1, 2, 10. 122:1-4, 9. 2 S 15:25. 1 Ch 29:3. Is 38:20, 22. Lk 2:37, 46, 49. 19:45-47. Jn 2:14-17.
where, etc. Heb. of the tabernacle of thine honor. Ps 63:2, 3. Ex 25:21, 22. 40:34, 35. 2 Ch 5:14. 6:1, 2.

9 Gather not. *or,* Take not away. Ps 28:1-3. 1 S 25:29. Ml 3:18. Mt 13:30. 24:51. 25:32, 41, 46. Re 22:14, 15.
soul. Heb. *nephesh*, Ge +12:13.
bloody men. Heb. men of blood. Ps 51:14. 55:23. 139:19. 1 S 22:18, 19. 2 S +16:7mg. 21:1.

10 In. Ps 10:14. 11:2. 36:4. 52:2. 55:9-11. Pr 1:16. 4:16. Mi 2:1-3. Mt 26:3, 4. Ac 23:12.
full of. Heb. filled with.
bribes. Ex 23:8. Dt 16:19. 1 S 8:3. Is 33:15. Ezk 22:12, 13. Am 5:12. Mi 7:3.

11 I will. ver. 1. 1 S 12:2-5. 2 Ch 31:20, 21. Ne 5:15. Jb 1:1. Is 38:3. Lk 1:6. 1 Th 2:10.
redeem. Ps 44:26. 49:7, 15. 69:18. 130:7, 8. Mt 20:28. T 2:14. 1 P 1:18, 19.
and. Ps 130:3, 4, 7, 8. Ne 13:14, 22, 31.

12 My. Ps 27:11. 40:2. 1 S 2:9. Pr 10:9.
in the. ver. 7. Ps 22:22-25. 107:32. 111:1. 122:4. He 2:12.

PSALM 27

1 light. Ps 18:28. 36:9. 43:3. 84:11. Jb 29:3. Is 2:5. 60:1-3, 19, 20. Mi 7:7, 8. Ml 4:2. Jn 1:1-5, 9. 8:12. Ja 1:17. Re 21:23. 22:5.
salvation. Ps 3:8. 18:2, 46. 62:2, 6. 68:19, 20. 118:14, 15, 21. Ex 15:2. Is 12:2. 51:6-8. 61:10. Lk 2:30. 3:6. Ep 6:17. Re 7:10.
fear. Ge 19:30.
strength. Ps +18:1. 43:2.
of whom. Ps 11:1. +118:6. Mt 8:26. Ro 8:31.

2 wicked. Ps 3:7. 18:4. 22:16. 62:3, 4.
came upon. Heb. approached against.
to eat. Jb 19:22. 31:31. Je +10:25.
they. Ps 18:38-42. 118:12. Is 8:9, 15. Jn 18:3-6.

3 host. Ps 3:6. 52:6. 2 K 6:15-17. 2 Ch 20:15. Ph 1:28. 1 P 3:14.
war. 1 S 28:15, 16. Is 41:11, 12. 54:16, 17. Ro 8:35-37. Re 2:10. 12:7-11.
in. 2 C 5:6-8.

4 One thing. Ps 26:8. Ec 3:19. Mk 10:21. Lk 10:42. Jn 9:25. Ph 3:13. 2 P 3:8.
seek. ver. 8. Je 29:13. Da 9:3. Mt 6:33. 7:7, 8. Lk 11:9, 10. 13:24. 18:1. He 11:6.
dwell. Ps 23:6. 26:6. 36:8. 63:1, 2. 65:4. 84:1-4, 10. 87:5, 6. 92:13, 14. 1 S 1:11. Lk 2:37. 1 T 5:5.
behold. Ps 50:2. 63:2. 90:17. Zc 9:17. 2 C 3:18. 4:6.

beauty. Ps 45:11. Zc 9:17. *or,* delight. Ps 63:2-5. **S#5278h**. Ps 90:17. Pr 3:17 (pleasantness). 15:26. 16:24. Zc 11:7, 10.

enquire. 1 S 22:10. 30:8. 2 S 21:1. 1 Ch 10:13, 14.

temple. Ps +5:7.

5 For in. Ps 10:1. 32:6, 7. 46:1. 50:15. 77:2. 91:15. 138:7. Pr 1:24-28. Is 26:16. Je 2:27, 28.

hide me. Ps +64:2. 119:114. Pr 18:10. Mt 23:37. Col 3:3.

secret. Ps 31:20. +91:1. 2 Ch 22:12. Ne 6:10, 11.

set me. Ps 18:33. 40:2. 61:2. Hab 3:18, 19. Mt 7:24, 25. 16:16-18.

6 And now. Ps 3:3. 110:7. Ge 40:13, 20. 2 K 25:27.

above. 2 S 7:9. 22:1, 49. 1 Ch 22:18.

therefore. Ps 22:22-25. 26:6, 7. 43:3, 4. 66:13-16. 107:22. 116:17-19. 2 Ch 30:21-26. Je 33:11. He 13:15. 1 P 2:5.

joy. Heb. shouting. Ps 47:1. Ezr 3:11-13. Is 12:6. Je 31:7. Zp 3:14, 15. Zc 9:9. Lk 19:37, 38.

I will. Ps 21:1, 13. 81:1. 95:1. 100:1, 2. 138:5. Ep 5:19, 20. Re 5:9. 15:3.

7 Hear. Ps +4:1. 5:2. 130:2-4. 143:1, 2.

and answer. Ps 3:4. 6:8, 9. 18:6. 20:1-4. 21:2, 4. 22:4, 5, 24. 28:6. 30:2, 3. 31:22. +34:4-6. 38:1. 40:1. 66:19, 20. 77:1, 2. 81:7. 86:6, 7. 91:14, 15. +99:6. 102:1, 2. 106:44. 107:6. 108:6. 116:1, 2. 118:5, 21. 119:26. 120:1. 138:3. 143:1. 1 K 8:28-30. Jb 6:8. 13:20-22. La 3:57, 58. Ho 12:3, 4. Jon 2:2, 7. Lk 23:42, 43. Ac 4:31. 2 C 12:8, 9. Ja 5:16-18.

8 When, etc. *or,* My heart said unto thee, Let my face seek thy face, etc.

Seek. Ps 24:6. 105:4. Is 45:19. 55:6, 7. Ho +5:15.

Thy. Ps 63:1, 2. 119:58mg. Je 29:12, 13.

9 Hide not. Dt +31:17.

put. Ps 30:5. 51:11. Is 50:1.

thou. Ps 71:5, 6, 17, 18. 1 S 7:12. Is 46:3, 4. 2 C 1:9, 10. 2 T 4:17, 18.

leave me not. Ps 38:21. 119:121. 141:8. 1 K 8:57, 58. 1 Ch +28:9. Je 14:7-9. 32:40. He +13:5.

neither forsake. Ps +9:10. 43:2. 44:23, 24. +51:11. 71:9, 12, 18. 74:1. 77:7. 88:14. 119:8. La 5:20. Mt 27:46. He +13:5.

O God. Ps 38:21, 22. +88:1.

10 When. Ps 10:14. 69:8. 2 S 16:11. Is 49:15. Je 49:11. Ho 14:3. Mt 10:21, 22, 36.

the Lord. Jn 9:35. 16:32. 2 T 4:16, 17.

take me up. Heb. gather me. Ps 26:9. 39:6. 50:5. 85:3. 104:29. Ge 42:17mg. Jb 34:14. 39:12. Is 40:11. 58:8mg.

11 Teach me. Ps +32:8. 86:11. 119:10, 33. Pr 2:6-9. Is 30:20, 21. Je 50:4, 5.

a plain path. Heb. a way of plainness. Ps 26:12. Pr 8:9. 15:19. Is 35:8. Lk 3:4-6.

because of. Ps 69:18.

mine enemies. Heb. those which observe me. Ps +5:8mg. 56:5, 6. 64:6. Je 20:10. Da 6:4, 5. Lk 20:20.

12 will. Heb. *nephesh,* Ex +15:9. Ps 31:8. 35:25. 38:16. 41:11. 140:8.

false. 1 S 22:9, 10. 26:19. 2 S 16:7, 8. Pr +6:19.

breathe. Ps 25:19. Ac 9:1. 26:11.

13 fainted. Ps 42:5. 56:3. 116:9-11. 119:92. 2 C 4:1, 8-14, 16. Ep 2:8.

in the land. Ps 52:5. 56:13. 116:9. 142:5. Jb 28:13. 33:30. Is 38:11, 19. 53:8. Je 11:19. +31:17. Ezk 26:20. 32:23, 26, 27, 32.

of the living. Ps 116:3, 7-9, 15, 16. Je +31:17.

14 Wait. Ps +25:3. 31:24.

be of good courage. Jsh +1:9. Da 6:10. Ac 28:15. 1 C 16:13. 2 T 4:5-8.

and. Ps +18:1. 138:3. Jsh +1:6.

PSALM 28

1 Unto. Ps +3:4. 5:2.

O. Ps 18:2. 42:9. Dt 32:4. Is 26:4mg. 40:31.

be. Ps 35:22. 83:1.

to. Heb. from.

I become like. Ps 30:9. 69:15. 88:4-6. +146:4. Nu +21:27. Jb 33:28. Pr 1:12. Is 38:18. Re 20:3.

pit. Heb. *bor,* Ge +37:20.

2 supplications. Ps 5:7. 1 K 8:28, 29.

when. Ps 125:5.

lift. Ps +88:9.

toward. Da +6:10.

thy holy oracle. *or,* the oracle of thy sanctuary. 1 K +6:5.

3 Draw me not. Ps 26:9. Nu 16:26. Mt 7:23. 25:41, 46. 2 C 6:17. Re 18:4.

speak. Ps 12:2, 3. 55:21. 62:4. Je 9:8, 9. Mi 3:5. Mt 22:15-18.

mischief. Ps 7:14. 10:7, 14. 36:4. 52:1. 1 Ch 12:33. Pr 26:23-26.

4 Give. Je +10:25. Re 18:6.

and. Ps 2:1-5. 21:10, 11. Ezk 38:10.

the work. Ps 62:12. 103:10. 109:17-21. 130:3, 4. Ro 2:6-8. 11:22. Ja 2:13.

render. Ezr 9:13. Jb 11:6.

5 Because. Ps 10:5. 92:4-6. 104:24. 107:31. 111:2-4. Jb 34:26, 27. Is 5:12. 22:11. 26:9-11. Ho 14:9. Jn 10:25. 12:37. Ro 1:20, 28.

operation. Ps 8:3, 4. 19:1, 2. Nu 23:23. Is 5:12. 40:26. 45:8, 12, 18. Je 10:12, 13. Ep 1:19-21.

destroy them. Ps 92:5-7.

not build. Ps 64:7, 9. 2 S 7:13, 27. 1 K 11:38. Pr 21:12. Is 5:14. Je 31:4. 33:20, 21.

6 Blessed. Ps 31:21, 22. 66:19, 20. 69:33, 34. 107:19-22. 116:1, 2. 118:5.

7 strength. ver. 8. Ps +18:1. 46:1.

shield. Ps +84:11.
heart. Ps 13:5. 22:4. 56:3, 4. 118:6-9, 13-15.
therefore. Ps 16:9-11. 21:1. 30:11, 12. 33:21. 68:3, 4. Is 61:10.
with. Ps 96:1-3. Ex 15:1, etc. Jg 5:1, etc. 1 S 2:1, etc. 2 S 22:1, etc. Re 5:9. 15:3.

8 **their**. *or*, his.
strength. ver. +7. Is 49:5. He 11:34.
saving strength. Heb. strength of salvations. Ps 3:2, 8. 9:14. 13:5. 27:1. 31:2, 4. 37:39. Is 33:6mg.
his. Ps 2:2. 20:6. 1 S 16:13. Is 61:1.

9 **Save**. Ps 14:7. 25:22. 80:14-19. Je 31:7.
thy people. Ge +20:4. Ex 32:11, 31, 32. Nu 14:19. 21:7. Dt 9:26. 26:15. 2 S 24:17. 1 K +8:34. 1 Ch 21:17. 2 Ch 30:18, 19. Ne 1:8-10.
bless. Dt 9:29. 2 S 21:3. 1 K 8:51, 53. Je 10:16. Ep 1:18.
feed. *or*, rule. Is +40:11.
lift. Ezr 1:4mg. 1 C 6:14.
for ever. Heb. *olam*, Ex +12:24. 1 P 5:4.

PSALM 29

1 **Give**. Jsh +7:19. Is +42:12.
mighty. Heb. sons of the mighty.
sons. Ps 89:6.
strength. Ps 68:34.

2 **Give**. 1 Ch 16:28, 29.
glory, etc. Heb. honor of his name. Ps 96:6, 8. 97:9. 113:3-6. 145:3-7.
worship. Ps 27:4. 96:9. 2 Ch 20:21.
the beauty of holiness. *or*, his glorious sanctuary. Ps 90:17. 1 Ch 16:29.

3 **The voice**. Ezk +10:5. Mt 8:26, 27. Jn +10:3.
God. Heb. *El*, Ex +15:2. Ps +24:7.
thundereth. Ex +9:23.
many waters. *or*, great waters. Ps 93:3, 4. 104:3.

4 **powerful**. Heb. in power. Ps 33:9. Jb 26:11-14. Je 51:15, 16. Lk 4:36. 8:25.
full of. Heb. in. Jb 40:9-12. Is 66:6. Ezk 10:5.

5 **breaketh**. Is 2:13.
cedars. Nu +24:6.

6 **skip**. Ps 114:4-7.
Lebanon. Je 4:23-25. Hab 3:6-11. Re 20:11.
Sirion. Dt 3:9.
unicorn. Ps 92:10. Nu 23:22.

7 **The voice**. Jb 37:2-5.
divideth. Heb. cutteth out. 1 K 5:15.
flames. Le +10:2.

8 **shaketh**. Ps +97:4. He +12:26.
wilderness. Dt 8:15.
Kadesh. Nu 13:26.

9 **voice**. ver. +3. Ps 68:33.
maketh. Jb 39:1-3.
calve. *or*, be in pain. Pr 25:23mg.
discovereth. Ps 63:2. Is 9:18. 10:18, 19. Ezk 20:46-48.

in his temple. Ps +5:7. 46:2-5.
doth, etc. *or*, every whit of it uttereth.

10 **sitteth**. ver. 3. Ps +65:7. Ge 6:17.
King. Je +10:10.
for ever. Heb. *olam*, Ex +12:24.

11 **give**. Ps +18:1. 138:3. Zc 10:6.
bless. Jn 20:19. Ro +5:1.

PSALM 30

(*Title*.) A.M. 2987. B.C. 1017.
A Psalm. Or, "A Psalm or song of David, at the dedication of the house;" by which is supposed to be meant the place he built on the threshing floor of Araunah, after the grievous plague which had nearly desolated the kingdom. 2 S 24:25, etc. 1 Ch 21:6.
at the. Nu +7:10. 2 S 5:11. 6:20. 7:2. 20:3.

1 **extol**. Ps 34:3, 4. 66:17. 145:1. Da 4:37.
for. Ps 27:6. 28:9.
hast not. Ps 13:4. 25:2. 35:19, 24, 25. 41:11. 79:4, 10. 89:41-46. 140:8. La 2:15.

2 **hast healed**. Ps 6:1, 2. 13:3. 39:10-13. 41:10. 51:8. 77:2. 88:2, 3. +103:3. 118:18. Ge 20:17. 2 S 12:15, 16. 2 K 8:7, 8. 20:1-6. 2 Ch 6:28-31. Mt 8:5-7. 14:35, 36. Mk 5:22, 23. Lk 4:38. Jn 4:46, 47. 11:1-3. Ac 28:8.

3 **brought**. Ps +16:10. 40:1, 2. 56:13. 71:20. 86:13mg. 116:8. 139:8. Jb 14:13. 33:19-22, 28. Is 38:10, 17, 18. Jon 2:4-6.
soul. Heb. *nephesh*, Ge +2:7. The soul spoken of as going to: *sheol* (Ps +16:10. 86:13. 89:48. Pr 23:14); *shachath*, **S#7845h** (Jb +9:31), a pit for taking wild beasts (Ps 35:7. Jb 33:18, 22, 28, 30. Is 38:17); *shuchah*, Je 18:20; silence, Heb. *dumah*, Ps 94:17.
grave. Heb. *sheol*, Ge +37:35. Ps 6:5. 9:17.
down. Ps 28:1.
pit. Heb. *bor*, Ge +37:20 (**S#953h**). Ps 7:15. 28:1. 40:2. 88:4, 6.

4 **Sing**. Ps 32:11. 33:1-3. 71:22. 97:12. 103:20-22. 132:9. 135:19-21. 148:14. 149:1. 1 Ch 16:4. Re 19:5, 6.
at the remembrance. *or*, to the memorial. Ps 97:12mg.
holiness. Ps 5:4, 5. 89:18, 35. 145:17. Ex 15:11. Le 11:44. Jsh 24:19. 1 S 2:2. 6:20. Is 6:3. 43:3, 15. 47:4. Ezk 39:7. Hab 1:13. Jn 17:11. 1 P 1:15. Re 4:8. 15:4.

5 **For**. Ps 103:9, 17. Is 12:1. 26:20. 54:7, 8. 57:15, 16. Je 3:5. 2 C 4:17.
his anger, etc. Heb. there is but a moment in his anger.
in his favor. Ps 16:11. 36:7-9. 63:3. Re 22:1, 17.
weeping. Ps +56:8-11. Mt 2:18. +5:4.
for a night. Heb. in the evening. Ps 55:17. 59:6.
joy. Heb. singing. Ps 17:1 (cry). 107:22mg. 126:2, 5mg, 6. Is 14:7. 51:11. Zp 3:17.

cometh. Ps 4:6. 36:9.

in the morning. Ps 5:3. Ge +32:24mg. Re +2:28.

6 **And**. Jb 29:18-20. Is 47:7. 56:12. Da 4:30. Mk +4:19. Lk 12:19, 20. 2 C 12:7.
I shall. Ps 15:5. 16:8. 119:117.

7 **by thy**. ver. 5. Ps 5:12. 18:35, 36. 44:3. 89:17. Jb 10:12.
made, etc. Heb. settled strength for my mountain. Ps 40:2. 1 Ch 17:26, 27.
thou. Ps 102:10. Dt +31:17. Jb 30:26-31. Is 38:17. Mt 27:46.

8 **unto**. Ps 34:6. 77:1, 2. 130:1, 2. 1 C 12:8, 9. Ph 4:6, 7.

9 **What**. Ps 6:5. 88:10-12. 115:17, 18. 118:17. Ec 9:10. Is 38:18.
Shall the dust. Ps +146:4.

10 **Hear**. Ps 51:1, 2. 143:1, 7-9.
be thou. Ps 28:7. 54:4.

11 **turned**. ver. 5. Ps 126:1, 2. Ge 37:35. 45:28. 2 Ch 20:3, 9, 12, 20, 27, 28. Est 9:22. Mt +5:4.
dancing. Ex +15:20.
sackcloth. Jb +16:15.
girded. Ps +18:32, 39. Ne 8:10. Is 61:3, 10. Lk 15:22.
gladness. Ps 31:7. 40:16. 118:24-26. 122:1. Ep 5:19, 20.

12 **my glory**. *that is, my* tongue, *or, my* soul. Ps 3:3. 4:2. 7:5. 8:5. 16:9. 57:8. 106:20. 108:1, 2. 149:5. Ge +49:6. Ja 3:2-10.
and not. Lk 19:40. Ac 4:20.
I will. Ps 9:1, 2. 13:6. 71:14, 23. 100:4. 145:2. 146:1, 2. Lk +6:35. Ro 1:21, 28. Ep 5:19, 20. Ph 4:6. Col 2:7. 3:15. 4:2. He 13:15. Re 4:8, 9. 7:12.
for ever. Heb. *olam*, Ex +12:24.

PSALM 31

1 A.M. 2943. B.C. 1061.
In thee. Ps 22:4, 5. 25:2. 71:1, 2. Is 49:23. Ro 5:5. 10:11.
ashamed. Ps +25:2.
deliver. Ps 7:8, 9. 43:1. 143:1, 11, 12. Da 9:16.

2 **Bow**. Ps 71:2. 86:1. 130:2. Pr 22:17.
thine ear. Ps +10:17.
deliver. Ps 40:17. 69:17. 70:1. 102:2. 143:7. Jb 7:21. Lk 18:8.
my strong rock. Heb. to me for a rock of strength. Ps +18:1, 2, 31. 62:7. 94:22. Dt +32:31. 2 S 22:3. 23:3.
an house. Ps 71:3. 90:1. 91:9. Is 33:16. Jn 6:56. 1 J 4:12, 15, 16.

3 **rock**. Dt +32:31.
fortress. Ps 71:3. 91:2. 144:2. Je 16:19.
for thy. Ps +25:11. Ep 1:12.
lead. Ps +23:3. +32:8. Ne 9:12, 19.

4 **Pull**. Ps 25:15. 35:7. 57:6. 124:7. 140:5. Pr 29:5. 2 T 2:26.

my strength. Ps 19:14. 2 C 12:9.

5 **Into**. Ps 17:15. Mt 27:50. Mk 15:37. Lk *23:46.* Jn 19:30. Ac 7:59. 2 C 5:1. 2 T 1:12.
thine hand. Ps +37:24. 104:28. 144:7. Jn 10:28, 29. Ac 4:30.
I commit. Ps 4:8. 22:30. 23:4. 73:26. 2 S 23:5. Is 26:3. Mt 27:43. Lk 23:46. Ro 8:38, 39. 2 T 1:12. 1 J 3:2. 5:13.
spirit. Heb. *ruach*, Nu +16:22. Ge +35:18. Lk 23:46. Ac 7:59.
thou hast redeemed. Ps +34:22. Le 25:48. Jb +19:25. SS 2:16. Is 50:2.
God. Heb. *El*, Ex +15:2.
of truth. Dt 32:4. 2 T 2:13. T 1:2. He 6:18.

6 **hated**. Ps 11:5. 24:3, 4. 25:19. Pr +8:13.
regard. or, observe. Ps 34:20. 71:10mg. 97:10 (preserveth). Jsh 1:8.
lying vanities. Ps 24:4. 96:7-9. Dt +32:21. 1 Ch 16:28, 29. 1 C 8:4. 10:19, 20.

7 **I will**. Ps 13:5. Is 49:13. Je 33:11.
considered. Ps +9:13.
trouble. Ps 71:20. +107:6. Jb 10:9. La 3:50.
known. Ps 1:6. 142:3. Jb 23:10. Is 43:2. 63:9, 16. Jn 10:27-30. 1 C 8:3. Ga 4:9. 2 T 2:19.
soul. Heb. *nephesh*, Ge +34:3.

8 **shut me**. Ps 88:8. Dt 32:30. 1 S 17:46. 24:18. 26:8. 2 S 18:28mg. Jb 16:11. Is 19:4mg.
set. Ps 4:1. 18:19. Jb 36:16.

9 **mine**. Ps +6:7.
my soul. Heb. *nephesh*, Ge +34:3. Ps 6:1, 2. 22:14, 15. 38:1-10. 44:25. 73:14, 26. 88:3-5. 102:3-5. 107:10. Jb 33:19-22.

10 **my life**. Ps 78:33. 88:15. 102:3, etc. Jb 3:24. Ro 9:2.
strength. Ps 71:9.
bones. Ps 32:3, 4. 102:3-5.

11 **reproach**. Ps 22:6. 39:8. 42:10. 44:13, 16. 69:7, 9, 19, 20. 74:10, 18, 22. 79:4, 12. 89:41, 50, 51. 102:8. 109:25. 119:39. Nu 15:30. 1 S +17:26. Ne 2:17. Pr 14:31, 34. Is 37:23. 49:7. 51:7. 53:4, 5. Je 6:10. 20:8. 24:9. 29:18. 42:18. 44:8, 12. La 3:30, 61. 5:1. Ezk 5:14, 15. 22:4. 36:15. Da +9:16. Zp 2:8, 10. Mt 27:39-44. Lk 6:22. 11:45. Ro 15:3. 1 C 4:13. 2 C 12:10. He 10:33. 11:26. 13:13. 1 P 4:14.
especially. Ps 38:11. 41:8, 9. 88:8, 18. Jb 19:13, 14. Je 12:6. Mi 7:6. Mt 10:21, 22.
a fear. Ps 64:8. Jb 6:21-23. Mt 26:69-75. 2 T 4:16.
acquaintance. 2 K 10:11mg. Jb 19:13.
fled. Mt 26:56, 74.

12 **forgotten**. Ps 88:4, 5. Jg 8:33. Ec 9:5. Is 38:11, 12.
a broken vessel. Heb. a vessel that perisheth. Ps 2:9. 119:83. Is 30:14. Ro 9:21, 22. Re 2:27.

13 **I have**. Ps 55:10. 101:5. 1 S 22:8-10. 24:9. Je 20:10. Lk 23:1, 2, 5.
fear. Ps 56:1-3. 57:4. Je 6:25. 20:3mg, 4, 10. La 2:22.

while. 1 S 19:10-17. 20:33. 23:19, 20. 2 S 17:1-4. Je 11:19. Mt 26:3, 4, 59. 27:1.
life. Heb. *nephesh*, soul, Ge +44:30.

14 **But I trusted**. Jb 13:15.
Thou. Ps 16:1, 2. 18:2. 22:1, 2. 43:5. 56:3, 4. 63:1. 71:12, 22. Mt 26:39, 42. 27:46. Jn 20:17.

15 **My times**. Ps +90:12. +91:16. 116:15. 1 S 26:10. 2 S 7:12. 1 Ch +12:32. Jb 24:1. Ec 3:1-8. Is +38:10. Lk 9:51. Jn 7:6, 30. 12:27. 13:1. 17:1. Ac 1:7. 23:11. 27:24. 2 T 4:6. 2 P 1:14.
deliver. Ps 17:8, 9, 13. 71:10-12. 142:6. 143:3, 12. Je 15:20, 21.

16 **Make thy face to shine**. Ps 4:6. 30:7. 67:1. 80:3, 7, 19. 119:135. Nu 6:25, 26. Da 9:17.
save me. Ps 2:8. 6:4. 20:9. 28:9. 35:3. 43:3. 51:1, 12. 60:5. 69:29. 85:7. 86:2, 16. 106:45. 119:41, 81, +94, 123, 174. Is 33:2. Je 3:22, 23. 17:14. Da 9:9, 18. Ac 2:21. Ro 9:15, 23. 10:1, 13. Ep 1:6, 7. 2:4-7. Ph 1:19.

17 **Let me**. ver. 1. Ps 34:5. Is 50:6, 7. Jl +2:26, 27.
wicked. Ps +71:13. Is 65:13, 14. Da 12:2.
them. Ps 115:17. 1 S 2:9. Mt 22:12, 13.
silent in the grave. *or*, cut off for the grave.
silent. Ps 4:4. 30:12. 35:15. Re +20:5.
the grave. Heb. *sheol*, Ge +37:35.

18 **the lying**. Ps 12:3. 59:12. 63:11. 140:9-11. 1 S 2:3. Pr 12:19. Is 54:17. Jn 8:44. Re +21:8. 22:15.
speak. Ps 64:3, 4. 123:3, 4. 1 S 2:3. 2 Ch 32:16. Is 37:22-24. Mt 10:25. 12:24. Jn 8:48. Ac 25:7.
grievous things. Heb. a hard thing. Ps 94:4. Mt 10:25. Ac 9:5. Ju 14, 15. or, ancient sayings. Ps 75:5. 94:4.
proudly. Ps +10:2. 46:3.
contemptuously. Ps 107:40. 119:22. 123:3, 4.

19 **how great**. Ps 36:7-10. 73:1, 24-26. 91:1. 145:7-9. Dt 11:11, 12. Jsh 1:3, 5, 9. Is 64:4. La 3:23-25. 1 C 2:9. 3:9. Ep 2:10. 1 J 3:1, 2.
laid up. Ps 16:11. Is 35:10. Col 3:2-4. He 10:34. Ja 2:5. 1 P 1:4, 5.
wrought for. Ps +68:28. 126:2, 3. Nu 23:23. Is 26:12. 64:4. Jn 3:21. Ac 15:12. 1 C 2:9. 2 C 5:5. 1 T 4:8.
before the sons. Ps 36:7-9. Is 35:10. Mt 5:16. 1 P 2:15.

20 **hide**. Ps +64:2. 91:1-4.
from. Ps 10:2. 36:11. 40:4. 86:14. 124:5. 140:5. Ex 18:11. Ja 4:6.
the strife. Ps 64:2-4. 140:3. Jb 5:21. Ro 13:13. 2 C 12:20. Ga 5:20. 1 T 6:4. Ja 3:5, 6, 14-16.

21 **Blessed**. Ps 103:2.
marvelous. Ps 17:7. 98:1. 118:23. 1 P 2:9.
strong city. *or*, fenced city. 1 S 23:7-13. 2 Ch 8:5. 11:5. Is +37:25mg. Je 1:18.

22 **I said**. Ps 116:11. 1 S 23:26. 27:1.

I am. ver. 17mg. Ps 88:16. Jb 35:14. Is 6:5mg. 38:10-12. 49:14. La 3:54, 55. Ezk 37:11. Jon 2:4.
thine eyes. Ps +11:4.
nevertheless. Ps 6:9. 42:5. 2 Ch 33:11-13. La 3:56, 57. Jon 2:7-9. He 5:7.

23 **O love**. Ps 34:9. Dt +6:5. 1 Th 4:1.
saints. Ps 30:4. 89:7. 97:10. 145:10. Re 19:5, 6.
for the. Dt 33:3. 1 S 2:9. Mt 24:13. Jn 10:27-30. Ju 1.
faithful. Ps 12:1. 2 S 20:19. Mt +24:45. Lk 19:17. 1 C +15:58. He 6:10-12. Re 2:10.
plentifully rewardeth. Ps 54:5. 94:2. Ge +6:13. Ro 12:19. Re 18:6.
proud doer. Pr +6:17. 11:2. 13:10. 28:25. Is 16:6, 7. Ro 12:3, 16. 1 J 2:16.

24 **Be of**. Jsh +1:9. Is 35:3, 4. Lk 22:31, 32. He 12:12, 13. Ja 5:10, 11.
shall strengthen. Ps 29:11. 138:3. Lk 22:32. Col 1:11.
all ye. Ps 146:5. Ro 15:12, 13. 1 P 1:21.
that hope. Ps +42:11. 94:19. Col 1:5, 23, 27. 1 P 1:3, 13, 21. 1 J 3:3.

PSALM 32

(*Title*.) A.M. 2970. B.C. 1034.
A Psalm. *or*, A Psalm of David giving instruction.
Maschil. i.e. *with understanding*, **S#7919h**. Ps 32, 41, 42, 44, 45, 52, 53, 54, 74, 88, 89, 142, titles. Ge 3:6 (wise). 1 S 18:14mg, 15. 2 Ch 30:22. Ne 8:13mg. Jb 22:2. Ps 14:2 (understand). 47:7. Pr 10:5.

1 **Blessed**. Ps +1:1, 2. Dt +28:3. Mt 5:3-12. 16:17. Ro 4:7, 8.
transgression. Is 1:18. Ro 4:6-8.
forgiven. Ge 3:7, 21. Pr 28:13. Je +31:34.
covered. Ps 85:2. Ex 34:7. Ne 4:5. Is 61:10. Je 23:6. Mi 7:18. Jn 1:29. Ro 4:9, 23-25. 5:1, 2. Re 3:18. 7:13-17.

2 **Blessed**. Dt +28:3.
the man. Ps 1:1. 112:1. Je 17:5, 7.
the Lord. Le 17:4. Ro 5:13. 8:33. 2 C 5:19-21. 1 P 2:24.
whose. ver. 11. Ps 125:4. Jn 1:47. 2 C 1:12. 1 T 1:5. 1 P 2:1, 2, 22. Re 14:5.
spirit. Heb. *ruach*, Ge +41:8.

3 **When**. Ps 39:3. 107:2. Ge 3:8-19. Ex 3:13. 1 S 31:13. 2 S 11:27. 12:1-12. 21:12-14. Pr 28:13. Is 57:17. Je 20:9. 31:18, 19. Lk 15:15, 16.
bones. "Bones" put for the whole body; see 1 S 31:13; 2 S 21:12-14. Ps 6:2. 31:9, 10. 38:3. 51:8. 102:3-5. Jb 30:17, 30. La 1:13. 3:4.
roaring. "Roaring" put for the pains or pangs which occasion it; as otherwise it would be a contradiction to the silence he maintained. Ps +22:1. Is 51:20.

4 **hand**. Ex +9:3. Ru +1:13.

moisture. Ps 22:15. 90:6, 7. 102:3, 4. Jb 30:30. La 4:8. 5:10.
Selah. Ps +9:16.

5 **acknowledged**. Ps 38:18. 51:3-5. 86:5. Le 26:39, 40. Jsh 7:19. 2 S 12:13. 24:10. Jb 33:27, 28. Pr 28:13. Je 3:13. Lk 15:21-24. I J 1:8-10.
have. Jb 31:33. Pr 30:20. Je 2:23, 35. Lk 16:15.
I said. Is 65:24. Ho 6:1. Lk 15:17-19, 21.
confess. Ps 41:4. 51:3, 4. 106:6, 7. 119:176. Is 64:5. Je 3:25. 14:20. La 1:20. 3:41. Da 9:4-13. Lk 15:18, 19. Ja 5:16.
forgavest. Ps 30:5. 86:5, 15. +103:3, 12. Ex +34:7. 2 S 12:13. Is 44:22. 65:24. Je 31:20, 34. Lk 7:47. 15:20-23. Jn 1:29. Ep 4:32.
iniquity. Ps 51:4. 2 S 12:9, 13. Ml 3:8.
Selah. Ps +9:16.

6 **For this**. Ps 34:2-5. 40:3. 51:12, 13. Is 26:20, 21. 2 C 1:4. 1 T 1:16.
godly. Ps 4:3. 2 C 7:9, 10. T 2:12.
pray. Pr 1:28. Is 49:8. 55:6. Lk 19:42-44. Jn 7:34. 2 C 6:2. Ja 4:3.
a time, etc. Heb. a time of finding. Is 55:6. 1 T 1:16. He 4:16.
in the floods. Ps 42:7. 69:1, 2, 13-15. 124:4, 5. Ge 7:17-22. Is 43:2. Mt 7:24-27. Ac 20:23, 24. Re 12:15, 16.

7 **my hiding place**. Ps 9:9. +64:2. 119:114. Ge 3:8. Dt 32:10. Col 3:3.
preserve. Ps 12:7. 25:21. 40:11. 71:1, 2. La 3:5.
compass. ver. 10. Ps 1:3. 5:12. 18:5. 109:3. La 3:5.
songs. Ps 40:3. 98:1. Ex 15:1-3. Jg 5:1. 2 S 22:1. Re 7:10. 15:2, 3.
Selah. Ps +9:16.

8 **instruct**. Ps 25:8, 12. 34:11. 51:13. 66:16. 94:8. 101:2. Dt +29:9 (**S#7919h**). Pr 3:1. 4:1-13. 8:10, 11. Mt 11:29. Lk 22:32. Jn 7:17.
teach. Jn 14:26. Ja 1:5.
the way. Ps 143:8. Ex 33:14. 1 K 3:7. 2 Ch 20:12. Pr 3:5-7.
I will guide, etc. Heb. I will counsel thee, mine eye shall be upon thee. Ps 5:8. +25:4, 5, 9, 10. 27:11. 31:3-5. 33:18. 43:3. 48:14. 61:2. 73:24. 78:72. 107:4-7. 119:133. 139:23, 24. 143:8, 10. 1 K 3:9. Pr 3:5, 6. Is 30:21. 49:10. Je 3:4. 6:16. 42:2, 3. Mi 7:7, 8. Jn 6:68. Ac 1:24. 9:6. 1 Th 3:10, 11. 2 Th 3:5.
mine eye. Ps +11:4. 123:2.

9 **Be ye**. Pr 26:3. Je 31:18. Ja 3:3. 4:7-10.
no understanding. Jb 35:11. Je 4:22. 8:6, +7.

10 **Many**. Ps 16:4. 34:19-21. 140:11. Pr 13:21. Ec 8:12, 13. Is 3:11. 57:21. Ro 2:8, 9. 1 T 6:10.
but. Ps 147:11. Is 12:2, 3. +26:3.
compass. Ps 1:3. 5:12. La 3:5.

11 **Be glad**. Ps 64:10. Dt +12:7. 1 S 2:1.
shout. Ps +5:11. 98:4.
upright. ver. +2.

PSALM 33

1 **Rejoice**. Dt +12:7. 1 C 1:30, 31.
ye righteous. Ps 118:15. Ro 3:10. 5:19.
praise. Ps 50:14-16. 78:36, 37. 135:3. 147:1. Pr 15:8.

2 **Praise**. Ex 15:20. Re +5:8.
with the psaltery. Ps 144:9. 1 Ch 13:8.

3 **a new**. Ps 40:3. 96:1. 98:1. 144:9. 149:1. Is 42:10. Ep 5:19. Col 3:16. Re 5:9. 14:3.
play. 1 Ch 13:8. 15:22. 25:7. 2 Ch 34:12.

4 **the word**. Ps 12:6. 19:7, 8. 119:75, 128. Pr 30:5. Mi 2:7. Ro 7:12.
all his. Ps 25:10. 36:5, 6. 85:10, 11. 96:13. Ge 24:27. Dt 32:4. Da 4:37. Jn 14:6. Ro 15:8, 9. T 1:2.

5 **He**. Ps 11:7. 45:7. 99:4. He 1:9. Re 15:3, 4.
judgment. Ps 1:5. 7:6. 9:4mg, 7, 16. 48:10. 92:15. 97:2. 111:3. 119:137, 138, 142. 145:17. Ge +18:25. 2 Ch 19:7. Jb 8:3. 34:12. 37:23. Je 9:24. Re 15:3, 4.
earth. Ps 36:6. 104:24. 119:64. 145:15, 16. Mt +5:45. Ac 14:17.
goodness. or, mercy. ver. 18, 22. Ps 5:7. 6:4.

6 **By the**. ver. 9. Ps 148:1-5. Ge 1:1, 6, 7. Jn +1:3. 11:3. 2 P 3:5. Re 19:13.
the host. Ps +103:21. Ro 1:25.
breath. Heb. *ruach*, Ex +15:8. Ps 104:30. Ge 2:7. Jb 26:13. 33:4. Jn 20:22.

7 **He gathereth**. Ps 104:6-9. Ge 1:9, 10. Jb 26:10. 38:8-11. Pr 8:29. Je 5:22.
heap. Ex 15:8. Jsh 3:13, 16. Hab 3:15.

8 **the earth**. Ps 22:27. 96:9, 10. Je 5:22. 10:7-12. Da 6:25, 26. Re 4:11. 14:6, 7. 15:4.
stand. Ps 76:7. He 12:29.

9 **For**. ver. 6. Ps 148:5, 6. Ge 1:3. He +11:3.
and it stood. Ps 93:5. 119:90, 91. Col 1:16, 17. He 1:3. Re 4:11.

10 **The Lord**. Ps 2:1-4. 9:15. 76:10. Ge 50:20. Ex 1:12. Je +19:7. Mt 2:16. Ac 2:36. 8:4. Ph 1:12, 13.
bringeth. Heb. maketh frustrate. Is 44:25. or, maketh void. Ps 89:33mg. Ezk 17:19.
to nought. Ps +146:4.
he maketh. Ps 21:11. 140:8. +146:4.

11 **The counsel**. Is +14:27. Je +19:7. Ezk 38:10, etc. Da 4:37. Ac 4:27, 28.
for ever. Heb. *olam*, Ex +12:24.
thoughts. Ps 92:5. Is 55:8, 9. Je 29:11. Mi 4:12.
all generations. Heb. generation and generation. Ps +10:6mg. 49:11mg. 61:6mg. 77:8mg. +79:13mg. 89:1mg. 90:1mg. 100:5mg. 119:90mg. 135:13mg. Dt 32:7mg. Pr 27:24mg. Jl 2:2mg. Ac 15:18.

12 **Blessed**. Ps +1:1. 147:19, 20. Ex 19:5, 6. Dt 33:29.
chosen. Ps 135:4. Dt 4:20. 7:6-8. +10:15. 32:9, 10. Is 45:4. Jn 15:16. Ro 3:1, 2. 9:4. Ga 3:29.
his own inheritance. Ps 16:5. 28:9. Jsh 13:33. Je 10:16. T 2:14.

13 looketh. Ps +11:4. 14:2. 94:7, 9. 102:19. Ge 6:12. Jb 28:24. Pr 15:3. La 3:50.
beholdeth. Ps 53:2. Je 23:23, 24. He 4:13.

14 the place. Ps 123:1. 1 K 8:27, 30. Is 57:15. 66:1. Lk 11:2. 1 T 6:16.

15 fashioneth. Pr 21:1, 2. 22:2. 27:19. Ec 7:29. Is 64:8. Ac 17:26. 2 T +2:25.
considereth. Ps 44:21. 94:11. Jb 11:11. 34:21, 22. Pr 5:21. 24:12. Je 32:19. Ho 7:2. 1 C 4:5.

16 no king. Ps 20:7, 8. 44:3, 6, 7. Ex 14:17, 18, 28. Jsh 11:4-8. Jg 7:2, 12, etc. 1 S 14:8-16. 1 K 20:10, 27-29. 2 Ch 14:9-13. 20:12, 15, 23. 32:8, 9, 21.
mighty. Jsh 14:12. 1 S 17:4, 45-49. 2 S 21:16-22. Je 9:23.

17 An horse. Ps 20:7. Jg 4:15. 2 K 7:6, 7. Pr 21:31. Ec 9:11. Is 30:16. Ho 14:3.
his great. Ps 147:10. Jb 39:19-25.

18 the eye. Ps +11:4. 17:8. 123:2. 1 S 26:24. Jb 36:7.
hope. Ps 13:5. +42:11. 52:8. Ro 4:4-8.

19 To deliver. Ps 91:3-7, 10. Jn 5:24. 10:28-30.
soul. Heb. *nephesh*, Ge +12:13; +9:5.
in famine. Ps +37:3. Hab 3:17, 18. Zc 10:1. Mt 4:4.

20 soul. Heb. *nephesh*, Ge +34:3.
waiteth. Ps +25:3.
he is. Ps 115:9-12. 144:1, 2. 1 Ch 5:20.

21 For. Ps +13:5. 28:7. 30:10-12. Is 25:9. Zc 10:7. Jn 16:22.
his. 1 Ch 16:10, 35. Lk 1:47-50. Re 4:8.

22 Let thy. Ps 5:11, 12. +13:5. 119:49, 76.
according. Mt 9:29.

PSALM 34

(Title.) A.M. 2942. B.C. 1062.
Abimelech. *or*, Achish. Achish, king of Gath, is probably here called Abimelech, because that was a common name of the Philistine kings (see the parallel texts). This is the second of the alphabetical Psalms (the first being Ps 25); each verse beginning consecutively with a letter of the Hebrew alphabet. The verse, however, which begins with *wav*, and which should come in between the fifth and sixth, is totally wanting; but as the 22nd, which now begins with *pay*, *podeh*, "redeemeth," is entirely out of the series, it is not improbable that it was originally written *oophodeh*, "and redeemeth," and occupied that situation, in which connection it reads admirably. Ge 20:2. 26:1, 26. 1 S 21:13-15. Pr 29:25.

1 bless. Ps 71:8, 14, 15. 145:1, 2. Is 24:15, 16. Ac 5:41. 16:25. Ep 5:20. Col 3:17. 1 Th 5:18. 2 Th 1:3. 2:13. He 13:15.
his praise. Ps 67:5-7. 92:1, 2. 100:4, 5. 119:164. 147:1. Re 4:8.

2 soul. Heb. *nephesh*, Ge +34:3.
make. Ps 44:8. 105:3. Is 45:25. Je 9:24. 1 C 1:31. 2 C 10:17.
the humble. Ps 22:22-24. 32:5, 6. 66:16. 119:74. 142:7. Mt 5:16. 1 T 1:15, 16.

3 magnify. Ps 35:27. 40:16. 69:30. Lk 1:46. Ac 19:17. Ph 1:20.
let us. Ps 33:1, 2. 66:8. 103:20-22. 148:1, etc. 1 Ch 29:20. 2 Ch 29:30. Re 14:7. 19:5, 6.

4 sought. Ps +9:10. 18:6. 22:24. 31:22. 77:1, 2. 116:1-6. 2 Ch 20:3. Jon 2:2. Mt 7:7. Lk 11:9. 2 C 12:8, 9. He 5:7.
he heard. Ps +27:7. +99:6. He 5:7.
delivered. Ps 103:14. 1 C +10:13.
from. Ps +118:6. 1 S 27:1. 2 Ch +20:3. Jb +3:25. Pr +22:3. Is +8:12. +12:2. Je +10:5. 2 C 7:5, 6. 2 T 1:7.

5 They looked. Ps 67:1. 123:1, 2. Jb 6:19, 20. Is 45:22. Jn 1:29. He 12:2. 1 P 5:7.
and were. Ps 13:3. 18:28. 97:11. 1 S 1:18. Est 8:16. Jb 33:30. Mi 7:8, 9. Jn 8:12.
lightened. *or*, flowed unto him.
their. Ps 83:16. 2 S 19:5. Jn 8:12. Ro 5:1.

6 This. Ps +3:4. +40:17.
saved. ver. 17-19. Ge 48:16. 2 S 22:1. Re 7:14-17.

7 The angel. Ps 91:11, 12. 2 K 6:17. 19:35. Da 6:22. Mt 18:10. Lk 16:22. He 1:14.
encampeth. Ge 32:1, 2. Zc 9:8.
delivereth. Ps 7:4. 18:19. 50:15. 81:7. 91:15. 2 S 22:20. Jb 36:15. Is 63:9. Ac 12:7. or, armeth. Jsh 4:13mg. 6:7, 9, 13. 1 Ch 12:23, 24mg.

8 taste. Ps 119:103. SS 5:1. He 5:13, 14. 1 P 2:2, +3. 1 J 1:1-3.
Lord. Ps 36:7, 10. 52:1. Je 31:14. Zc 9:17. Lk +6:35. 1 J 4:7-10.
blessed. Is +26:3.

9 fear. Ps 22:23. 31:23. 89:7. Ge 22:12. Is 8:13, 14. Ho 3:5. He 12:28, 29. Re 15:3, 4.
no want. Ps 23:1, 5. +84:11. Lk 12:30-32. 1 T 6:6, 17.

10 lions. Ps 104:21. Is +5:29. Lk 1:51-53.
but. Ps +84:11. Jsh 21:45. Lk 12:31.

11 Come. Pr 1:8. 4:1. 7:24. 8:17, 32. 22:6. Ec 11:9, 10. 12:1. Is 28:9. Mt 18:2-4. Mk 10:14-16. Jn 13:33. 2 T 3:15.
hearken. ver. 5.
I will teach. Ps 32:8. 66:16-20. Pr 1:7. 2:1-9. +3:7. Is 28:9, 26.

12 What. Dt +4:40. 1 P 3:*10, 11*. Re 22:14.
life. 1 S +10:24.
that he. Ps 4:6. Jb 7:7. Ec 2:3. 12:13. 1 T 4:8. Re 21:4.

13 Keep. Ps 12:3, 4. 39:1. 120:3, 4. 141:3. Pr 12:14. +21:23. Ep 4:29.
speaking. Ps 55:11. Pr 12:17, 19, 22. 19:9. Is 63:8. Col 3:9. 1 P 2:1, 22. Re 14:4, 5.

14 Depart from evil. Pr 4:27. 8:13. 13:14. 28:13. 2 T +2:19. He 12:1. 1 P 3:*11*.

do good. Mi +6:8. Lk +6:9, 35. Ac 10:38. Ga +6:10. T 2:14. He +13:16. Ja +4:17. 3 J 11.

seek peace. Ps 120:7. Pr 16:7. Mt 5:9. Ro 12:10, 18. 14:17, 19. 2 C 13:11. Ga 5:22. 1 Th 4:11. 2 T 2:22, 24, 25. He 12:14. Ja 3:17, 18. 1 P 3:10, 11.

15 **The eyes**. Ps 1:6. +11:4. 25:15. Jb +36:7. 1 P +*3:12*.

ears are open. ver. 6, 17. Ps 130:2. 2 Ch 6:40. Is 37:14-21. Da 9:17-23. 1 J +5:14.

their cry. ver. +17.

16 **face**. Ge +19:13. Ezk +15:7. Am 9:4. 1 P *3:12*.

against them. Ps 37:35, 36. Ge +6:13. Is 1:20. Ml +3:5. Ro 2:7-10.

to cut. Ps 10:16. 37:9, 10, 20, 36, 38. Jb 18:17. Pr 10:7. 11:7. 14:32. Ec 8:10. Je 17:13. 1 C +6:9, 10. Ep +5:5, 6.

17 **cry**. ver. +6, 15, 19. Ex +22:23, 24. 2 Ch 32:20, 21, 24. Ac 12:5-11.

delivereth. Ps 20:1-4. 22:11. 25:22. 31:9, 10. 39:10. 40:1, 2. 50:14, 15. 54:6, 7. 71:20. 77:2. 107:4-6, 11-13, 25-28. 116:3, 4. Is 33:2. Jon 3:5-9. Jn 12:27, 28.

18 **is nigh**. Ps 75:1. 85:9. 119:151. 145:18. Is 55:6.

unto them, etc. Heb. to the broken of heart. Ps 51:15-17. 69:19, 20.

such as, etc. Heb. the contrite of spirit. Heb. *ruach*, Ge +41:8. 2 K 22:19. Is 57:15. 66:2. Ezk 36:26, 31.

19 **Many**. Ps 71:20. +119:75. Jb 5:19. 30:9, etc. 42:12. Pr 24:16. Jn 16:33. Ac +14:22. 2 C 4:7-12, 17. 11:23-27. 1 Th 3:3, 4. 2 T 3:11, 12. He 11:33-38. Ja 1:2. 5:10, 11. 1 P 4:12, 13. Re 7:14-17.

delivereth. ver. 6, 17. Ps 18:2, 3, 27, 28. 25:17. 30:5. 42:11. 54:7. 68:13. 71:20. 107:19. 126:5, 6. 146:8. Jb 5:19. 8:20, 21. 11:16. 36:16. Pr 11:8. 12:13. 24:16. Je 29:11. 31:12, 13. Ho 6:1. 2 C 1:10. 2 T 3:11. 4:17, 18. 2 P 2:9.

20 **He keepeth**. Ps 35:10. 91:12. Da 6:22-24.

broken. Ps 22:14-17. Ex 12:46. Nu 9:12. Jn 19:36.

21 **Evil**. Ps 37:30-40. 94:23. 145:20. Is 3:11.

they. Ps 37:12-15. 40:15. 89:23. 1 S 19:4, 5. 31:4. 1 K 22:8, 37. Lk 19:14, 27, 41-44. Jn 7:7. 15:18-23. 1 Th 2:15, 16. 2 Th 1:6-9.

desolate. *or*, guilty. Ex 20:7.

22 **redeemeth**. Ps 31:5. 71:23. 72:14. 103:4. 106:10. 107:2. 130:8. 136:24. Ge 48:16. 2 S 4:9. 1 K 1:29. La 3:58. T 2:14. 1 P 1:18, 19. Re 5:9.

soul. Heb. *nephesh*, Ge +12:13. Ps 49:15.

none. Ps 9:9, +10. 84:11, 12. Jn 10:27-29. Ro 8:31-39. 1 P 1:5.

PSALM 35

1 A.M. 2942. B.C. 1062.

Plead. Ps 43:1. 119:154. 1 S 24:15. 25:38, 39. Pr 22:23. 23:11. Je 51:36. La 3:58. Mi 7:8, 9.

fight. Ex 14:25. Jsh 10:42. 2 Ch 20:15. Ne 4:20. Ac 5:39. 23:9.

2 **Take hold**. Ps 7:12, 13. Ex 15:3. Dt 32:41, 42. Is 13:5. 42:13.

shield. Is 59:17, 18. Je 50:25. 51:20.

3 **stop**. Ps 27:2. 76:10. 1 S 23:26, 27. Jb 1:10. Is 8:9, 10. 10:12. Ac 4:28.

say. Ps 51:12. 62:7. 85:8, 9. 91:16. Ge 49:18. Is 12:2. Lk 2:30.

soul. Heb. *nephesh*, Ge +12:13.

4 **confounded**. ver. 26. Ps 31:17, 18. +71:13.

that seek. Ps 38:12. 1 S 23:23. 1 K 19:10. Ezk 13:19. Mt 27:1.

soul. Heb. *nephesh*, Ge +12:13.

turned. Ps 129:5. Is 37:29. Je 46:5. Jn 18:6.

5 **as chaff**. Lk +3:17.

and let. ver. 6. Ex 14:19. Is 37:36. Ac 12:23. He 11:28.

6 **their**. Ps 73:18. Pr 4:19. Je 13:16. 23:12.

dark and slippery. Heb. darkness and slipperiness.

and let. ver. 5. 2 K 19:35. Ec +5:6. Ezk 9:1-6. Mt 13:30, 39-43.

7 **without**. Ps 7:3-5. 25:3. 64:4. Jn 15:25.

hid. Ps +57:6. 119:85.

pit. Heb. *shachath*, Jb +9:31 (**S#7845h**). 33:18.

soul. Heb. *nephesh*, Ps +30:3.

8 **Let destruction**. Ps 64:7. +71:13. 73:18-20. Pr 29:1. Lk 21:34. 1 Th 5:3.

at unawares. Heb. which he knoweth not of. ver. 15. Ps 73:22mg.

net. Ps +57:6.

into. 1 S 18:17. 31:2-4. 2 S 17:2-4, 23. 18:14, 15. Mt 27:3-5.

9 **soul**. Heb. *nephesh*, Ge +34:3.

be joyful. Ps 13:5. 21:1. 33:21. 48:11. 58:10, 11. 68:1-3. 1 S 2:1. Is 61:10. Hab 3:18. Lk 1:46, 47. Ga 5:22. Ph 3:1-3.

10 **All**. Ps 22:14. 32:3. 34:20. 38:3. 51:8. 102:3. Jb 33:19-25.

who. Ex +8:10.

which deliverest. Ps +40:17. 79:11. +140:12.

too strong. Ps 18:17.

11 **False witnesses**. Heb. Witnesses of wrong. 1 S 24:9. 25:10. Pr +6:19. Mt 26:59, 60. Ac 24:5, 6, 12, 13.

laid. Heb. asked me.

to my charge. Is 53:8. Mt 26:63-66. 27:23-26. Mk 15:55-59.

12 **They**. Ps 38:20. 109:3-5. 1 S 19:4, 5, 15. 22:13, 14. Pr 17:13. Je 18:20. Jn 10:32.

spoiling. Heb. depriving. 1 S 20:31-33. Is 47:8, 9. Lk 23:21-23.

my soul. Or, "my life," as the word *nephesh* frequently denotes, Ge +12:13.

13 **when**. Jb 30:25. Mt 5:44. Ro 12:14, 15.

sackcloth. Jb +16:15.

humbled. *or*, afflicted. Nu +29:7. 1 K 21:27-29. Mt +6:16.

soul. Heb. *nephesh*, Ge +27:31; Nu +23:10.
my prayer. Mt 10:13. Lk 10:6.

14 **I behaved**, etc. Heb. I walked as a friend, as a brother to me.
I bowed. 2 S 1:11, 12, 17, etc.
as one. *Or*, "as a mourning mother," *kaavel aim*, Ge 24:67. Jl +2:12.

15 **in mine**. ver. 25, 26. Ps 41:8. 71:10, 11. Pr +17:5.
adversity. Heb. halting. Ps 38:17mg. Je 20:10. 1 C 13:6.
the abjects. Ps 22:16. 69:12. Jb 30:1-12. Mt 27:27-30, 39-44. Mk 14:65. Ac 17:5.
I knew. ver. 8mg.
they. Ps 7:2. 57:4. Jb 16:9.

16 **hypocritical**. 1 S 20:24, etc. Jb +8:13. Is 1:14, 15. Jn 18:28. 1 C 5:8.
mockers. Mt 27:27-30.
gnashed. Ps +37:12.

17 **how**. Re +6:10.
look. Ps 10:14. Hab 1:13.
rescue. Ps 22:20, 21. 57:4. 69:14, 15. 142:6, 7.
soul. Heb. *nephesh*, Ge +12:13.
darling. Heb. only one. Ps +22:20mg.
lions. Ps +7:2.

18 **give**. Ps 22:22-25, 31. 40:9, 10. 69:30-34. 111:1. 116:14, 18. He 2:12.
praise. Ps 67:1-4. ch. 117. 138:4, 5. Ro 15:9.
much. Heb. strong. Is 25:3.

19 **Let**. ver. 15. Ps 13:4. 25:2. 38:16. 59:10. Jn 16:20-22. Re 11:7-10.
wrongfully. Heb. falsely. Ps 7:14. 38:19. 109:2, 3. Jb 20:5. Mk 14:55, 56, 59.
wink. Jb 15:12. Pr 6:13. 10:10.
that hate. Ps 69:4. 109:3. 119:161. 1 S 24:11, 12. La 3:52. Jn *15:25*.
without a cause. Ps 69:4. Mk 15:9, 10.

20 **For**. Ps 120:5-7. 140:2. Pr 15:18. 17:19. 18:6. 26:21. Hab 1:3.
but. Ps 31:13. 36:3, 4. 38:12. 52:2. 64:4-6. 140:2-5. Je 11:19. Da 6:5. Mt 12:24. 26:4. Ac 23:15. 25:3.
devise. Ps 10:2. 21:11. 32:2. 36:4. 40:17.
deceitful matters. lit. words of frauds. Ps 36:4. 37:7. 38:12. 55:21. +65:3mg. Pr 6:14. 14:22. 16:30. 24:8. Is 32:7. Je 9:8. 18:12. Ezk 11:2. Mi 2:1. 6:12.
quiet. lit. "shrivelled," i.e. timid. Mt 12:19. Ph 2:15. 1 Th 4:11. 1 T 2:2. 1 P 2:22, 23.

21 **Yea**. Ps 22:13. Is 9:12. Lk 11:53, 54.
Aha. Ps 40:15. 54:7. 70:3.

22 **This**. Ex 3:7. Ac 7:34.
keep. Ps 28:1. 39:12. 50:21. 83:1.
be. Ps 10:1. 22:11, 19. 38:21. 71:12. Is 65:6.

23 **Stir**. Ps +3:7.
my God. Ps 89:26. 142:5. Jn +20:28.

24 **Judge**. Ps 7:8. 18:20-24. 26:1. 43:1. 59:10. 2 Th 1:6. 1 P 2:22.

and let. ver. 19. Jb 20:5.

25 **say**. Ps 27:12. 28:3. 70:3. 74:8. Jb 1:5. Mk 2:6, 8.
Ah. Heb. Ah, ah, our soul. Heb. *nephesh*, Ex +15:9.
so would. Ps 140:8. Ex 15:9. Mt 27:43.
swallowed. Ps 56:1, 2. 57:3. 124:3. Nu 16:32. 26:10. 2 S 17:16. 20:19. Jb 2:3mg. 5:5. 20:15, 18. Pr 1:12. Is 49:19. Je 51:34, 44. La 2:2, 5, 16. Ezk 36:3. Ho 8:8. Am 8:4. 1 C 15:54. 2 C 5:4.

26 **ashamed**. ver. 4. Ps +71:13. 132:18. Is 65:13-15.
clothed. Ps 109:28, 29. 132:18. Jb 8:22. 1 P 5:5.
magnify. Ps 38:16. 55:12. Jb 19:5. Is 10:15. Je 48:26. Da 11:36.

27 **Let them**. Jb 42:7-10.
shout. Ps 40:16. 68:3. 132:9, 16. 142:7. Is 66:10, 11. Jn 16:22. Ro 12:15. 1 C 12:26.
righteous cause. Heb. righteousness. Pr 8:18.
say. Ps 70:4.
which. Ps 149:4. Je 32:40, 41. Zp 3:14, 17.
prosperity. Ps 25:12-14. 37:9, 34. 118:25. Ge 28:20-22. 1 Ch 4:10. 2 Ch 26:5. 31:21. Jb 8:5-7. 22:23-28. Ro 1:10. 1 T 2:1, 2.

28 **my tongue**. Ps 34:1. 50:15. 51:14, 15. 71:24. 104:33, 34. 145:1, 2, 5, 21.

PSALM 36

(*Title*.) A.M. cir. 3463. B.C. cir. 541.
A Psalm. This Psalm is supposed by some to have been composed by David at the beginning of Saul's persecution; but Calmet and others, on good grounds, are of the opinion that it was written during the Babylonian captivity.
servant. Ps 18, 90, titles. Ps 143:12. Dt 34:5. 2 T 2:24. T 1:1. Ja 1:1. 2 P 1:1. Ju 1. Re 1:1.

1 **The transgression**. 1 S 15:13, 14. Pr 20:11. Mt 7:16-20. 12:33, 34. T 1:16.
no. Ps 112:1. Ex +1:17. Ro *3:18*.

2 **For he**. Ps 10:3. 49:18. Dt 29:19. Je 2:23, 34, 35. 17:9. Ho 12:7, 8. Lk 10:29. 16:14, 15. Ro 7:9. 10:3.
until, etc. Heb. to find his iniquity to hate. 1 S 15:18-24. 1 Ch 10:13, 14. Ro 3:9. He 3:13.

3 **The words**. Ps 5:9. 12:2, 3. 55:21. 58:3. 140:3. 1 S 18:21. 19:6, 7. 26:21. Mt 22:15-18, 35.
he hath. Ps 125:5. 1 S 11:6-13. 13:13, 14. 15:26. 16:14. Je 4:22. Zp 1:6. He 10:38, 39. 1 J 2:19.

4 **deviseth**. Ps 38:12. 1 S 19:11. Est 5:14. 6:4. Pr 4:16. Ho 7:6, 7. Mi 2:1. Mt 27:1. Ac 23:12.
mischief. *or*, vanity. ver. 3 (iniquity), 12. Ps 5:5. 6:8. 7:14. 10:7.

setteth. Pr 24:23. Is 65:2. Je 6:16. 8:6. 9:2-9. Mi 6:8.

abhorreth. Jb 15:16. Pr +8:13. Ro 1:32.

5 mercy. Ps 52:1. 57:10. 103:11. 108:4. Ex 34:6. Is 55:7-9.

faithfulness. Ps 89:2, 34. 92:2. 100:5. 111:5. 119:75, 89, 90. Dt 7:9. Nu 23:19. Jsh 23:14. Is 25:1. 49:7. La 3:23. Ho 2:19, 20. Mt 24:35. +28:19. 1 C 1:9. 10:13. 1 Th 5:24. 2 Th 3:3. 2 T 2:13. T 1:2. He +2:17. 6:18-20. 10:23. 1 P 4:19. 1 J 1:9.

clouds. Ps 57:10. 68:34mg. 108:4mg.

6 righteousness. Ps 71:19. 97:2. 145:17. Ge 18:25. Dt 32:4. Is 45:19, 21-24. Ro 3:25.

great mountains. Heb. mountains of God. Ps 80:10mg. Ge +23:6mg. 30:8mg. Ex 9:28mg. 1 S 14:15mg. Jb +1:16mg. Jon 3:3mg.

judgments. Ps 77:19. 92:5. Jb 11:7-9. 37:23. Is 40:28. Je 12:1. Mt 11:25, 26. Ro +11:33. Re 15:3.

thou preservest. Ps 63:8. 66:8, 9. 104:14, etc. 121:7. 145:9. 147:9. Ne 9:6. Jb 7:20. 10:12. 34:14, 15. Pr 24:12. Jon 4:11. Mt 10:29, 30. 1 T 4:10. He 1:3.

7 How. Ps 31:19. 103:4. Ex +34:6. Je 9:24. Jn 3:16. 1 J 3:1. 4:9, 10.

excellent. Heb. precious. Ps +37:20mg. 139:17. 1 P 2:6, 7. 2 P 1:4.

children. Ps 11:4.

under. Ge 45:11.

shadow. Ps +91:1.

wings. Ps +91:4.

8 abundantly. Zc 9:17. Mt +5:6. Jn 7:37.

satisfied. Heb. watered. Ps 65:10. Pr 7:18. Is 58:11.

and thou. Ps 16:11. 46:4. 116:13. Jb 20:17. Is 43:20. 48:21. Re 22:1-17.

river. Ps 78:20. Je +2:13.

9 For. Is 12:3. Je 2:13. Jn 4:10, 14. 7:37-39. Ro 6:23. Re 21:6. 22:17.

fountain. Je +2:13.

in thy light. Ps 27:1. Dt 32:2. Jb 29:3. Pr 4:18. Is 2:5. 60:1, 2, 19. Ml 4:2. Jn 1:8, 9. 8:12. 17:25, 26. 2 C 3:18. 4:6. Ja 1:17. 1 P 2:9. 1 J 1:7. Re 21:23.

see light. Jb 29:3. Is 2:5. Re 21:23. 22:5.

10 continue. Heb. draw out at length. Ps 103:17, 18. Ex 12:21. SS 1:4. Je 31:3. Ezk 32:20. Jn 15:9, 10. 1 P 1:5.

that know. Ps +9:10. Je 22:16. 24:7. Jn 17:3. He 8:11.

and thy. Ps 7:8-10. 18:24, 25. 94:14, 15. 97:10, 11. 143:1, 2. Is 51:6-8. 2 T 4:7, 8.

11 foot. Ps +10:2. 12:3-5. Is 51:23.

hand. Ps 16:8. 17:8-14. 21:7, 8. 62:6. 125:1-3. Ro 8:35-39.

12 There. Ps 9:16. 55:23. 58:10, 11. 64:7-9. Jg 5:31. 2 Th 1:8, 9. Re 15:4. 19:1-6.

shall not. Ps 1:5. 18:38. 112:10. Jb +8:13. Is +38:18. Je 51:64. He +9:27.

PSALM 37

(Title.) This is the third alphabetical psalm. It seems to have been intended as an instructive and consoling ode for the captives in Babylon, who might feel themselves severely tempted when they saw those idolaters in prosperity, and themselves in adversity.

1 Fret. ver. 7. 1 S 1:6-8. Pr 19:3. 24:1, 19, 20.

envious. Ps 73:3. 106:16. Ge 26:14. 30:1. 37:11. Jb 5:2. Pr 3:31. 14:30. 23:17. 24:1, 2, 19, 20. 27:4. +28:16. Ec 4:4. Mt 16:26. 27:17, 18. Mk 15:10. Ac 5:17. 7:9. 13:45. 17:5. Ro 1:29. 13:13. 1 C 3:3. 13:4. Ga 5:21. T 3:3. Ja 3:14-16. 4:5, 6. 1 P 2:1, 2.

2 they shall. ver. 35, 36. Ps 73:17-20. Jb 20:5-9. Lk 12:20. 1 P +1:24.

3 Trust. Ps 4:5. 26:1. Is 1:16-19. 50:10. Je 17:7, 8. 1 C 15:57, 58. He 6:10-12.

so shalt. Ge 26:2. 1 S 26:19. He 11:13-16.

dwell. ver. 27, 29. 2 S 7:10.

land. Dt 30:20.

verily. Heb. in truth, or, stableness. Ps 33:4. 36:5. Is 33:6.

be fed. ver. 19, 25. Ps 33:19. 34:9, 10. 107:9. 111:5. 132:15. 136:25. 146:7. 147:14. Jb 5:19-22. Pr 10:3. 13:25. Is 33:16. 41:17. 65:13. Ezk 36:29, 30. Jl 2:26. Mt 6:31-33. Lk 1:53. +6:38. 12:22-24, 28. 22:35. Ph 4:11, 18, 19.

4 Delight. Ps 43:4. 104:34. Jb 22:26. 27:10. 34:9. SS 2:3. Is 58:2, 14. Ph 4:6, 7. 1 P 1:8.

and. Ps 21:1, 2. 145:19. Dt 7:8. 10:15. Jn 15:7, 16. 1 J 5:14, 15.

desires. Ps 5:1. 19:14. 145:19. 1 K 10:13. Jb 6:8. Ml 3:10. Ep 3:20.

5 Commit. Heb. Roll thy way upon. Ps 10:14. 22:8mg. 55:22. Pr 16:3mg. Mt 6:25. Lk 12:22, 29, 30. Ph 4:6, 7. 1 P 2:23. 5:7.

and. Ps 22:31. 119:126. Jb 22:28. Ec 9:1. La 3:37. Ja 4:15.

6 he shall. Ps 31:20. Is 54:17. 1 C 4:5.

light. Ps +112:4. Ml 3:18.

7 Rest in. Heb. Be silent to. Ps 38:13-15. 62:1mg, 5. 65:1mg. 143:9mg. Ex 14:13, 14. Jsh 10:12mg. 2 Ch 20:17. Is 53:7. La 3:26. Ezk 24:17mg. Jon 1:11mg. Hab +2:20mg.

wait patiently. Ps +25:3. +39:9. Is 41:1. Mt 6:9, 10. 26:39. Lk 22:41, 42. Ac 21:14. Ga 6:9. He 10:36, 37. Ja +4:7. 5:7-11.

fret not. ver. 1, 8. Ps 73:3-14. Je 12:1.

the man. Jb 21:7, 17. Ec 5:8. Is 10:13, 14. Da 11:36. Re 13:3-10.

8 Cease. Jb 18:4. Pr 4:24. 30:33. Mt 5:22. 1 T 2:8. Ja +1:20. 3:14-18.

fret. Ps 31:22. 73:15. 116:11. 1 S 25:21, 22, 33. Je 20:14, 15. Jon 4:1, 9. Lk 9:54, 55.

9 evildoers. ver. 35, 36. Ps +34:16. 55:23. 104:35. Jb 20:23-29. 27:13, 14, etc.

cut off. ver. 22, 23, 34, 38. Ps 2:8, 9. 12:3. +34:16. 82:8. +101:8. Ge 9:11. Jsh 11:21. 23:4. 1 S 2:10. 1 K 9:7. Pr 2:21, 22. Is 1:27,

28. 2:12. 11:1-6. 13:9. 17:14. 24:1, 3-6, 17-20, 23. 26:20, 21. 28:21, 22. 29:7, 8. Je 25:31-33. Ezk 38:21, 22. 39:1-10, 12, 17. Da 12:1. Jl 3:9, 13-17. Zp 1:2, 3, 17, 18. 3:8, 9, 12, 13. Ml 4:1-3. Re 16:17-21. 19:19, 21. 20:1, 2.

but those that wait. Ps 91:13-16. 122:6. 2 Ch 14:7. 15:12-15. 17:3-5. 26:1, 5. 31:21. Jb 8:5-7. Jb 21:15. 22:23-28. 42:10-13. Is 19:19, 20. 41:17, 18. 65:10. Je 14:22. 29:7. Jl 2:17-19. Mt 6:33, 34. 1 T 2:1, 2.

inherit. ver. 11, 22, 29, 34. Is 58:14.

the earth. Dt 30:4, 5. Ps 2:8. 27:13. 115:16-18. 116:8, 9. Pr 10:30. 11:31. 12:7. Ec +1:4. Da 7:27. Mt +5:5.

10 **yet**. Ps 73:18-20. Jb 24:24. Is 10:25. 29:17. He 10:36, 37. 1 P 4:7. Re 6:10, 11.

wicked. ver. 35, 36. Ps 49:10. 103:16. Jb 7:10, 21. 14:10. 20:8, 9. Lk 12:20, 21. 16:27, 28.

thou. Ps 52:5-7. 58:10, 11. 107:42, 43. 1 S 25:38, 39. 2 K 9:25, 34-37. Est 7:10. 8:1. Is 14:16-19.

11 **the meek**. Mt +5:5.

inherit. ver. +9. Ps 2:8. Mt +5:5. 2 P 3:13.

delight. Ps 36:8. 72:7. 119:165. Is 26:3. 48:18. 57:18-21. Jn 14:27. Ph 4:7.

abundance. Is 55:7.

peace. Ps 72:3, 7. Is 2:4. 52:8. 57:21. 60:17, 18. 66:12. Mi 4:3, 4.

12 **The wicked**. ver. 32. 1 S 18:21. 23:7-9. 2 S 15:10-12. Est 3:6. Mt 26:4, 16.

plotteth. *or*, practiseth. Da 8:12, 24. Mi 2:1.

gnasheth. **S#2786h**. Ps 35:16. 112:10. Jb 16:9. La 2:16. Mt +25:30. Ac 7:54.

13 **laugh**. Ps 2:4. Pr 1:26.

his day. 1 S 26:10. Je 50:27. Ezk 21:25, 29. Da 5:26.

14 **wicked**. Ps 64:2-6. Ac 12:2, 3, 11, 23.

slay. 1 S 24:11, 17. Pr 29:10, 27. Hab 1:13. Mt 23:30-34. Ac 7:52. 1 J 3:12, 13.

such as, etc. Heb. the upright of way. Ps 7:10. 125:4.

15 **sword**. Ps +57:6. 1 S 31:4. 2 S 17:23. Is 37:38. Mi 5:6. Mt 27:4, 5.

bows. Ps 46:9. 76:3-6. Je 51:56. Ho 1:5. 2:18.

16 **A little**. Pr 3:33. 10:22. 13:25. 15:16, 17. 16:8. 30:8, 9. Ec 2:26. 4:6. Mt 6:11. 1 T 6:6, 8-10.

the riches. Ps 39:6. Is 60:5.

17 **arms**. Ps 10:15. Jb 38:15. Ezk 30:21-25.

Lord. ver. 24. Ps 41:12. 51:12. 63:8. 119:116, 117. 145:14. 1 S 2:9. Is 41:10, 11. 42:1. Ro 8:31. Ju 24.

18 **knoweth**. Ps 1:6. 31:7. Nu 16:5. *Na* 1:7. Mt 6:32. 2 T 2:19.

the days. ver. 13. Ps 31:15. 49:5. Dt 33:25. Mt 24:21-24. 2 T 3:1-5. 4:2-4. Re 11:3-5.

upright. Ps 119:1, 80. Jsh +14:8. 2 K +20:3.

inheritance. Ps 16:11. 21:4. 73:24. 103:17. Is

+60:21. Ac +20:32. Ro 5:21. 6:23. 1 J 2:25.

for ever. Heb. *olam*, Ex +12:24.

19 **not be ashamed**. Jl +2:26.

in the evil time. Ec 9:12. Am 5:13. Mi 2:3. Ep 5:16.

days of famine. ver. +3. Ps 33:18, 19. Jb 5:20-22. 15:20. Pr 10:3. Is 33:16.

20 **But the wicked**. Ps 1:6. 34:16. 68:2. 92:9. Jg 5:31. Lk 13:3, 5. 2 P 2:12.

shall perish. ver. 22, 28, 34. Ps 52:5. 1 S 2:9. Pr 21:16. Re 20:5.

as the fat of lambs. Heb. preciousness. Ps 36:7mg. 45:9 (honorable). 72:14. 116:15. 1 S +3:1. Dt 33:14-16. Zc 14:6mg.

smoke. Ps 18:8. 68:2. 102:3. Ge 19:28. Le 3:3-11, 16. Dt 29:20. He 12:29.

21 **borroweth**. Dt 15:6. 28:12, 43, 44. 2 K 4:1-5. Ne 5:1-5. Pr 11:15. 17:18. 22:7, 26. Ro 13:8. 1 C 5:11.

payeth not again. Ps 112:5. Le +19:13. 2 K 4:7. Ezk 18:7-9. Ml +3:5. Lk 16:10. 1 C 10:32.

righteous. Ps 112:5, 9. Dt 15:9-11. Jb 31:16-20. Is 32:8. 58:7-10. Lk 6:30, 34. Ac 11:29. 20:35. 2 C 8:9. 9:6, etc. He 6:10. 13:16.

showeth mercy. Mi +6:8. Mt +23:23.

and giveth. Pr 11:24-26. Lk +6:35, 38. Ac +20:35.

22 **blessed**. ver. 11, 18. Ps 32:1. 115:15. 128:1. Pr 3:33.

inherit. Mt +5:5.

cursed. Mt +25:41.

cut off. ver. 9, 28. Zc +5:3, 4.

23 **steps**. Ps 17:5. 85:13. 119:133. 121:3, 8. 1 S 2:9. Jb 23:11, 12. Pr 16:9. 20:24. Is 30:21. Je 10:23.

ordered. *or*, established. Ps 7:9. 40:2. Pr 4:26.

delighteth. Ps 147:10, 11. Pr 11:1, 20. Je 9:24. He 13:16.

24 **Though**. Ps 34:19, 20. 40:2. 91:12. 94:18. 145:14. Pr 24:16. Mi 7:7, 8. Lk 2:34. 22:31, 32, 60-62. 2 C 4:9.

shall not. Pr 24:16. 2 P +1:10. Ju 24.

for. ver. 17. Ps 145:14. Jn 10:27-30.

his hand. Ps 104:28. Ru +1:13. 2 Ch 30:12. Ezr 7:9. 8:18. Ne 2:18. Jn +10:28. Ja +1:13, 17.

25 **I have**. Ps 71:9, 18. Jb 32:6, 7. Ac 21:16. Phm 8, 9.

yet. ver. 28. Ps 94:14. Jsh 1:5. 1 S 12:22. Is 33:16. 2 C 4:9. He 12:5, 6. +13:5.

nor his seed. Ps 59:15. 109:10. Dt +29:11. 1 S 2:7, 8. 21:3. 25:4-11. Jb 15:23. Pr 13:22. Lk 1:53-55. 2 C 11:27. Ph 4:12.

begging bread. Ps 34:10. Ge 41:54. Dt 15:7-11. Mt 26:11. Lk 16:20, 21.

26 **ever**. Heb. all the day.

merciful. ver. 21. Ps 112:5, 9. Dt 15:8-10. Mt 5:7. Lk 6:35-38.

lendeth. Lk +6:38.

his seed. ver. +25.

27 **Depart**. 2 T +2:19.
do good. ver. 3. 1 Th 5:15. T 3:8, 14. He 13:16, 21. 1 J 2:16, 17.
dwell. Ps 102:28.
for evermore. Ps +18:50.

28 **loveth**. Ps 11:7. 45:6, 7. 99:4. Is 30:18. 61:8. Je 9:24.
judgment. Heb. *mishpat*, justice, equity. ver. 6, 30.
forsaketh not. ver. 25, 40. Ps 92:13-15. Is 59:21. Je 32:40, 41. Jn 5:24. 6:39, 40. 10:28-30. 15:9. He +13:5. 1 J 2:19. 1 P 1:5. Ju 1.
for ever. Heb. *olam*, Ex +12:24.
but. Ps 21:10. Ex +20:5. Jb 18:19. 27:14. Pr 2:22. Is 14:20, 21.

29 **The righteous**. ver. 9, 11, 18, 27. Dt 30:20. Pr 2:21. 2 P 3:13. Re 21:3, 4, 7.
for ever. Ps +9:18 (**S#5703h**).

30 **The mouth**. Ps 71:15, 24. Dt 6:7-9. Jb 6:25. Pr 10:21, 31. 12:18. 15:2, 7, 23, 28. 25:11-13. 26:4, 5. 27:9. 29:11, 20. Ec 3:7. 10:12. Mt 12:35. Ep 4:29. Col 4:6.
his tongue. Ps 17:3. 71:15. 119:43, 46, 172. Is 50:4. Ml 3:16. Lk 4:22. Ep 5:19. 1 Th 5:11.

31 **law**. Ps 1:2. 119:11. Dt +6:6. He 8:10.
none. ver. 23. Ps 121:3.
steps. *or*, goings. Ps 17:5. 40:2. 44:18mg. 73:2. Jb 23:11. Pr 14:15. Ezk 27:6mg.

32 **watcheth**. ver. 12. Ps 10:8-10. 1 S 19:11. Je 20:10. Da 6:4. Mk 6:20. Lk 6:7. 11:54. 14:1. 19:47, 48. 20:20. Ac 9:24.

33 **will not**. Ps 31:7, 8. 124:6, 7. 1 S 23:26-28. 2 T 4:17. 2 P 2:9.
condemn. Ps 109:31. Ro 8:1, 33, 34.

34 **Wait**. ver. 3, 7, 9. Ps +25:3. 69:6. 145:15. Is 49:23.
keep. Ps 18:21. Jb 17:9. 23:10-12. Pr 4:25-27. 16:17. Mt 24:13.
exalt. Ps 92:10. 112:9. Lk 14:11. He 10:36. 1 P 1:7. 5:6.
when. Ps 52:5, 6.
thou shalt see. Is +66:24.

35 **I have**. Ps 73:3-11. Est 5:11. Jb 5:3. 21:7-17. Is 14:14-19.
spreading. Col 2:7.
a green bay tree. *or*, a green tree that groweth in his own soil. Jb 8:13-19. Ezk 31:6-10, 18. Da 4:20, etc.

36 **he passed away**. ver. +10. Ex 15:9, 10, 19. 1 S 31:6. 2 S 17:23. Jb 20:5-9. Is 10:16-19, 33, 34. Da 4:25. Ac 12:22, 23. or, But one passed by. Pr 24:30.

37 **Mark**. ver. 34.
the perfect. Jb 42:12-17. Pr 14:32. Is 32:17. 57:2. Mt +5:48. Lk 2:25-29. Ac 7:59, 60. 2 T 4:6-8. 2 P 1:14.
the end. Heb. *Acharith*, sequel, after-life, after-history, issue, progeny. ver. 38. Ps 73:17. 109:13. Nu 23:10. Dt 8:16. 32:29. Pr 23:17,

18. 24:14, 20. 1 C +15:55.
peace. Mt +5:9.

38 **the transgressors**. Ps 1:4-6. 9:17. 52:5. 104:35. Pr 14:32. Is +24:22. Mt 13:30, 49, 50. 25:46. Ro 6:23. 2 Th 1:8, 9.
the end. ver. +37. Nu 24:20. Pr 3:25.

39 **salvation**. Ps +42:5mg. 98:2. Is 61:10. 63:5. He +9:28. Re +7:10.
strength. Ps 9:9. 46:1. 91:15. Is 33:2. Col 1:11. 2 T 4:17.

40 **the Lord**. Is 31:5. 46:4. Da 3:17, 28. 6:23.
from. Ps 17:13. 27:2. 1 J 2:13, 14. 5:18.
and save. Ps 32:6, 7. Pr 3:26.
because. Ps 22:4, 5. 36:7. 1 Ch 5:20.

PSALM 38

(Title). This deeply penitential Psalm is supposed to have been composed by David under some grievous affliction, either bodily or mental, or both, after his illicit intercourse with Bathsheba.
to bring. Ps 70, title.

1 **rebuke**. Ps 6:1. 88:7, 15, 16. Is 27:8. 54:8. Je 10:24. 30:11. Hab 3:2. He 12:5-11.
hot. Dt 9:19.

2 **arrows**. Dt +32:23.
thy hand. Ex +9:3. Ru +1:13.

3 **soundness**. Ps 31:9. 2 Ch 26:19. Jb 2:7, 8. 33:19-22. Is 1:5, 6.
neither. Ps 6:2. 51:8. 102:3, 5.
rest. Heb. peace, or, health. Ge 15:15 (peace). 29:6 (well). 43:27 (well, mg. peace), 28 (good health).
because. Ps 51:8. 90:7, 8. La 3:40-42.

4 **mine**. Ps 40:12. Ezr +9:6. Ro 7:24.
gone over. Ps 42:7.
as an. Le 7:18. Is 53:11. La 1:14. Mt 11:28. He 12-1. 1 P 2:24.

5 **My wounds**. ver. 7. Ps 32:3. Is 1:5, 6. Je 8:22.

6 **troubled**. Heb. wearied. Is 21:3.
bowed. Ps +145:14.
mourning. Mt +5:4.

7 **my loins**. Ps 41:8. 2 Ch 21:18, 19. Jb 7:5. 30:18. Ac 12:23.
no soundness. ver. 3. Is 1:6. Lk 16:20.

8 **roared**. Ps +22:1, 2. Jb 30:28.

9 **Lord**. Instead of *adonay*, "Lord," several MSS. read *yehowah*, "Jehovah."
groaning. Ps 102:5, 20. Jn 1:48. Ro 8:22, 23, 26, 27. 2 C 5:2.

10 **heart panteth**. Ps 42:1. 143:4-7. Is 21:4.
the light. Ps +6:7. 1 S 14:27-29.
gone from. Heb. not with.

11 **lovers**. Ps 31:11. Jb 6:21-23. 19:13-17. Mt 26:56. Lk 23:49. Jn 16:32.
friends. Ps 55:12-14. Jb 19:14, 19. Mt 26:56. 2 T 4:16.
stand aloof. Ps 88:8. Is 63:3. Lk 10:31, 32. 23:49.

sore. Heb. stroke. or, plague. Ps 39:10. 89:32. 91:10.

kinsmen. or, neighbors. Ps 15:3. Ge 19:20 (near). Ex 32:37. Dt 4:7 (nigh). Jsh 9:16. Jb 19:14.

afar off. Lk 22:54. 23:49.

12 **life**. Heb. nephesh, soul, Ge +44:30; Ge +9:5.

lay snares. Ps 10:9. 64:2-5. +141:9. Ex +23:33. 2 S 17:1-3.

speak. Ps 35:20. 62:3, 4. 2 S 16:7, 8. Lk 20:21, 22.

13 **But I**. 2 S 16:10-12. 1 P 2:23.

openeth not. Ps 39:1, 9. 141:3. Jg +11:35. 2 K 18:36. Pr 13:3. 24:7. Ec 3:7. Is 36:21. 53:7. Am 5:13. Mt +26:63. 27:12. Ac 8:32.

14 **that heareth**. Am 5:13. Mi 7:5. Mk 15:3-5. Jn 8:6.

in whose mouth. Is 53:7. Mt +26:63. 1 P 2:23.

15 **in thee**, etc. or, thee do I wait for.

do. Ps +42:11. 123:1-3. 2 S 16:12.

hear. or, answer. Ps 91:15. 138:3. Is 30:19. 65:24.

Lord. Here also, instead of adonay, one hundred and two MSS. read yehowah, "Jehovah."

16 **For I said**. Ps 13:3, 4. 35:24-26.

rejoice over. Dt 32:35. Pr 24:17, 18.

foot. Ps 94:18. Dt 32:35.

magnify. Ps 35:26.

17 **to halt**. Heb. for halting. Ps 35:15mg. Je 20:10. Mi 4:6, 7.

sorrow. ver. 6. Ps 6:6. 77:2, 3. Is 53:3-5.

18 **For**. Ps 32:5. 51:3. Jb 31:33. 33:27. Pr 28:13.

sorry. Ps 119:136. 1 S +9:5. Ezr 10:1. Jb 42:6. Ezk 9:4. Da 9:3. Jl 2:12. Mt 26:75. Lk 15:18, 19. 18:13. 2 C 7:7-11.

19 **But**. Ps +25:19.

are lively, etc. Heb. being living are strong. or, without cause. Ps 35:19. 79:5.

they that. Ps 35:19. 69:4. Mt 10:22. Jn 15:18-25. Ac 4:25-28.

20 **render**. Ps 7:4. 35:12. 109:3-5. 1 S 19:4-6. 23:5, 12. 25:16, 21. Je 18:20.

because. Mt 5:10. Jn 10:31, 32. 1 P 3:13, 17, 18. 4:14-16. 1 J 3:12.

21 **Forsake**. He +13:5.

O my God. Ps 22:1, 11, 19, 24. 35:21, 22.

22 **Make**. Ps +40:17.

to help me. Heb. for my help. Ps 27:9. 35:2. 146:5.

O Lord. Ps 27:1. 62:2, 6. Is 12:2.

PSALM 39

(Title.) A.M. 2970. B.C. 1034.

Jeduthun. Jeduthun, probably the same as Ethan, 1 Ch 6:44, was one of the sons of Merari; and is supposed to have been one of the four masters of music, or leaders of bands, belonging to the temple service. It is therefore probable that David, having composed this Psalm, gave it to Jeduthun and his company to sing; and it is very likely, that it was written on the same occasion as the preceding. Ps 62, 77, titles. 1 Ch +9:16. 16:41. 25:1-6.

1 **I said**. Ps 119:9. 1 K 2:4. 2 K 10:31. Pr 4:26, 27. He 2:1.

that I. Ps 12:4. 73:8, 9. 141:3. Pr 18:21. 21:23.

will keep. Ps +38:13, 14. Jb +6:24. Ec +5:2.

my mouth, etc. Heb. a bridle, or, muzzle, for my mouth. Ja 1:26. 3:2-8.

while. 2 S 12:14. Pr +25:26. Am 5:13. Mi 7:5, 6. Mt +7:6. Col 4:5.

2 **I was**. Ps 38:13, 14. Is 53:7. Mt 27:12-14.

silence. Ps 32:3. Je 20:9.

even. Mt +7:6.

my sorrow. Jb 32:19, 20. Ac 4:20.

stirred. Heb. troubled. Ge 34:30. Pr 15:6.

3 **My heart**. Je 20:9. Ezk 3:14. Lk 24:32. Ac 4:20.

fire. Ps 11:6. 18:8, 12. 21:9. 29:7.

4 **make me**. Ps 90:12. 119:84. Nu 23:10. Jb 14:13.

how frail I am. or, what time I have here. Ps 78:39. 89:47. 90:9. 102:11. 103:14-16. 144:4. Jb 14:1. Ec 6:12. Is 53:3. Ezk 3:27. Ja 4:14.

5 **Behold**. Ps 90:4, 5, 9, 10. Ge 47:9. 2 S 19:34. Jb 7:6. 9:25, 26. 14:1, 2. Ja 4:14.

handbreadth. 1 K 7:26. 2 Ch 4:5.

mine age. S#2465h. Ps 17:14 (world). 49:1 (world). 89:47 (short time; lit. transitory). Jb 11:17.

as nothing. Ps 89:47. 2 C 4:18. 2 P 3:8.

verily. ver. 11. Ps 62:9. 144:4. Ec 1:2. 2:11. Is 40:17.

at his best state. Heb. settled. Ps 82:1. 119:89.

Selah. ver. 11. Ps +9:16.

6 **vain show**. Heb. an image. Ps 73:20. 1 C 7:31. Ja 4:14.

surely. Ec 1:14. 2:17, 18, 20, 21. 4:7, 8. 6:11, 12. 12:8, 13. Is 55:2. Lk 10:40-42. 12:20, 21. 29. 1 P 5:7.

he heapeth. Ps 49:10, 11. Jb 27:16, 17. Pr 13:22. 23:5. 27:24. Ec 2:8, 18-21, 26. 5:14. Lk 12:20, 21. Ja 5:3.

7 **what wait**. Ps 33:18-20. 130:5-7. Ge 49:18. Lk 2:25.

hope. Ps +42:11. Jb 13:15. Je 3:23. Ro 8:24, 25. 15:13. He 11:13, 16. 1 P 1:13.

8 **Deliver**. Ps 25:11, 18. 51:7-10, 14. 65:3. 119:133. 130:8. Mi 7:19. Mt 1:21. +6:13. T 2:14.

make. Ps +31:11. 35:21. 57:3. 2 S 12:13, 14. 16:7, 8. Jl 2:17, 19. Ro 2:23, 24.

9 **dumb**. Ps 38:13. 46:10. Le 10:3. 1 S 3:18. Jb 40:4, 5. Mi 7:9.

opened not. Ps +38:13.

because thou didst it. Ps 97:1. +119:75. Jg

+10:15. 2 S 16:10, 11. Ne 9:33. Jb 34:31, 32.
Is 38:15. 52:7. Ezk 14:23. Da 4:35. Am +3:6.
Mt 6:10. Mk 7:37. Jn 12:17, 28. 13:7. 18:11.
Ac +21:14. He 12:9. Ja 4:7. 1 P 4:19.

10 Remove. Ps 25:16, 17. 1 S 6:5. Jb 9:34.
13:21. Mt 26:39.
I am consumed. Ps 38:3, 4.
blow. Heb. conflict. Jb 40:8.
hand. Ex +9:3.

11 When. Ps 38:1-8. 90:7-10. 1 C 5:5. 11:30-32.
He 12:6. Re 3:19.
his beauty, etc. Heb. that which is to be
desired in him to melt away. Ps 102:10, 11. Jb
4:19. 13:28. 30:30. Is 50:9. Ho 5:12.
surely. ver. 5. Ps 144:4.
Selah. ver. +5.

12 hold. Ps 116:3.
tears. Ps +56:8.
for I am. Ps 119:19, 54. Le 25:23. 1 Ch 29:15.
2 C 5:6. He 11:13. 1 P 1:17. 2:11.
stranger. Ps 94:6. 119:19. 146:9. Ge +23:4.
Ex 12:48mg. Le 25:23. He 11:13.
sojourner. Ge +23:4. Ex 12:45. 1 Ch 29:15. 2
C 5:6. 1 P 1:17. 2:11.
as all. Ge 47:9. 1 Ch 29:15.

13 spare. 1 Ch 29:28. Jb 10:20, 21. 14:5, 6.
be no. Ps 71:20. Ge 5:24. 42:36. Jb 14:10-12.
16:22. 17:13. 1 C 15:55.

PSALM 40

(Title.) A.M. 2970. B.C. 1034. This psalm is
supposed to have been composed by David
about the same time, and on the same occasion, as the two preceding; with this difference, that here he magnifies God for having
obtained the mercy which he sought there. It
also contains a remarkable prophecy of the
incarnation and sacrifice of Jesus Christ.

1 I waited. Heb. In waiting I waited. Ps +25:3.
Mt 21:28. Lk 12:37. Ja 5:7-11.
inclined. Ps 116:2. 130:2. Da 9:18.

2 brought. Ps 18:16, 17. 71:20. +86:13. 116:3.
142:6, 7. 143:3. Jb 33:28mg. SS 2:4. Is
+24:22. 38:17. Je 38:6. Jon 2:5, 6. Zc 9:11. Ac
2:24, 27-31.
horrible. Ps 65:7. 74:23.
pit. Heb. pit of noise. Heb. *bor*, Ge +37:20. Ps
7:15. 28:1. 30:3. 88:4. Ge 37:24. Zc 9:11. Mt
13:50.
the miry. Ps 69:2, 14, 15. Je 38:6-12. La
3:53-55.
set. Ps 27:5. 61:2. Mt 7:24, 25.
established. Ps 17:5. 18:36. 37:23. 119:133.
Ac 5:30, 31.

3 And he. Ps 4:7. 33:3. 144:9. Re 5:9, 10. 14:3.
praise. Ps 103:1-5. Is 12:1-4.
many. Ps 34:1-6. 35:27. 52:6. 64:9, 10. 142:7.
Ac 2:31-41. 4:4.
and fear. Lk +1:65.

4 Blessed. Ps 2:12. 34:8. 84:11, 12. 118:8, 9. Dt
+28:3. Je 17:7, 8. Ro 15:12, 13.
respecteth. Ps 15:4. 101:3-7. 119:21. Ja 2:1-
4.
as turn. Ps 125:5. Is 44:18-20. Je 10:14, 15.
Jon 2:8. 2 Th 2:9-11.

5 Many. Jb 26:14. Da +4:3.
thoughts. Ps 71:15. 92:5. 139:6, 17, 18. Ge
+50:20. Is 55:8, 9. Je 29:11.
they cannot, etc. *or*, none can order them
unto thee. Jb 37:19, 20.

6 Sacrifice. Ps 50:8. 51:16. 1 S 15:22. Is 1:11.
66:3. Je 7:21-23. Ho 6:6. Mt 9:13. 12:7. He
10:5-7, 8-12.
mine ears. The writer of Hebrews interprets
"ear" to represent the whole body of the lis-
tening and obedient servant of Jehovah at He
10:5. Ps +10:17. +16:9. Ex 21:6. Jb 33:16.
36:10. Is 50:4, 5.
opened. Heb. digged. or, prepared. Ps 7:15.
22:16. 57:6. 119:85. Dt 15:17. 2 K 6:23. Jb
41:6.
burnt offering. Le +23:12.
sin offering. Le +23:19.

7 Lo. He *10:7-9*.
I come. Ge 37:13.
in the. Ge +3:15. Lk 24:27, 44. Jn +5:39. Ac
10:43. 1 C +15:3, 4. 1 P 1:10, 11. Re 19:10.
volume. Je 36:2.
written of me. Lk +24:44.

8 I delight. Ps 22:29. 112:1. 119:16, 24, 47, 92.
Jb 23:12. Is 53:12. Je 15:16. Jn 4:34. 5:30.
6:38. 10:11-18. Ro 7:22. 8:29. Ga 2:20. Ph
2:8. He 9:25, 26. 10:5-10. 12:2.
yea. Dt +6:6.
within my heart. Heb. in the midst of my
bowels. Ex 32:19. Dt 9:17. Pr 4:21.

9 preached. Ps 22:22, 25. 35:18. 71:15-18. Mk
16:15, 16. Lk 4:16-22. He 2:12.
righteousness. Ro 3:21, 22.
congregation. Ps 22:22.
not. Ps 119:13, 171, 172. He 2:3.
thou knowest. Ps 139:2. Jn 21:17.

10 not hid. Ezk 2:7. 3:17, 18. Ac +20:20, 21, 26,
27. Ro 10:9, 10. 1 Th 1:8. Re 22:17.
righteousness. Ro 1:16, 17. 3:22-26. 10:3.
Ph 3:9.
within. lit. in the midst.
faithfulness. Ac 13:32, 33. Ro 15:8, 9. 2 Th
3:3.
salvation. Is 49:6. Lk 2:30-32. 3:6. 1 T 1:15.
lovingkindness. Ps +25:6, 10. 34:6. Mi 7:20.
Jn 1:17. 3:16, 17.

11 Withhold. Ps +51:1.
let thy. Ps 23:6. 43:3. 57:3. 61:7. 85:10. He
5:7.
continually. Is +58:11.

12 innumerable. Ps 22:11-19. He 4:15.
mine iniquities. Ps 38:4. Le +5:6. Is 53:6. Lk
18:13, 14. 1 P 3:18.

look up. Lk +18:13.
they are. Ps 19:12. 69:4.
heart. Ps 73:26. Ge 42:28. Lk 21:26.
faileth. Heb. forsaketh. Ps 9:10. 22:1. 38:10.
Is 42:4.

13 **Be pleased**. Ps 25:17, 18. Mt 26:36-44.
make. ver. +17.

14 **Let them be ashamed**. Ps +71:13. Is 45:24.
that. Mt 21:38-41.
soul. Heb. *nephesh*, Ge +12:13.
driven. Ps 9:3. Jn 18:6. Ac 9:4-6. 12:23, 24.

15 **desolate**. Ps 69:24, 25. 70:3. 73:19. 109:6-20.
Lk 19:43, 44. 21:23, 24.
say. Ps 35:21, 25. 70:3, 4.

16 **all**. Ps 22:26. 35:27. 68:3. 70:4. 105:3. Is
65:13, 14.
rejoice. Ps 21:1, 2. 28:7. 31:7. 33:20, 21.
35:9. 63:5. 1 Ch 16:10. 2 Ch 30:26, 27. Is
12:3. 56:7. Hab 3:17, 18. Mt 13:44. Ac 16:25.
1 Th 5:16, 17.
love. Ps 119:81, 111, 123, 166, 167. Mt
13:45, 46. Ph 3:7-9.
say. Ps 35:27. Lk 1:46, 47. Ac 19:17.

17 **I am poor**. Ps 34:6. 69:29, 33. 70:5. 72:4, 12,
13. 86:1. +102:17. 109:22, 31. Is 41:17. Mt
8:20. 2 C 8:9. Ja +2:5.
needy. Ps 9:18. +12:5. 35:10. 37:14. +72:12.
86:1. 109:21, 22. Is 41:17.
the Lord. 1 P 5:7.
thinketh. ver. 5. Ps 32:8mg. +35:20 (devise).
92:5. 104:34. Ne 5:19.
upon me. Ps +1:6. 139:1, 2. Ex +33:12, 17. 1
Ch 16:41. 2 Ch +12:8. Je +29:11. Na 1:7. Ml
3:16. Mt 6:26, 32. 10:29-31. Jn 10:3, 14. Ac
27:23. 1 C +8:3. Ga 4:9. 2 T 2:19.
my help. ver. 13. Ps 54:4. Is 50:7-9. He
+13:6.
my deliverer. Ps 18:2, 48. +34:17, 19. 70:5.
144:2.
make. ver. 13. Ps 22:19. 38:22. 69:17mg.
70:1, 5. 71:12. 102:2. 141:1. 143:7, 8. Ge
24:56. 2 K +20:4. Is 30:19. 62:6, 7. +65:24. Da
10:12, 13. Mt 6:8. Lk +11:9. Re 22:20.

PSALM 41

(Title.) This Psalm is supposed to have been
written on the same occasion as the three former; and to relate to David's affliction, and
the evil treatment he received from his enemies during its continuance.

1 **Blessed**. Ps 112:9. Dt 15:7-11. +28:3. Jb
29:12-16. 31:16-20. Pr 14:21. 19:17. 28:27. Ec
11:1, 2. Is 58:7-11. Mt 25:40. Mk 14:7. Lk
14:13, 14. 2 C 8:9. 9:8-14. Ga 2:10.
the poor. *or*, the weak, *or* sick. Ps 72:13.
82:3, 4. 113:7. Ex 23:3. 2 S 3:1. Mt 25:34-39.
Ac 20:35. 1 Th 5:14.
Lord. Ps 34:19. 37:26, 39, 40. He 6:10. Ja
2:13.

time of trouble. Heb. the day of evil. Ps
37:19. Pr 16:4. Ec 12:1. Re 3:10.

2 **preserve**. Ps 33:19. 91:3-7. Je 45:4, 5.
blessed. Ps 128:1-6. 1 T 4:8.
thou wilt not. *or*, do not thou. Ps 27:12.
37:32, 33. 140:8, 9.
the will. Heb. *nephesh*, Ex +15:9.

3 **strengthen**. Ps 73:26. 116:6. Ge 49:25. Dt
7:13. 2 K 1:6, 16. 20:5, 6. 2 C 4:16, 17. Ph
2:26, 27. 1 T 2:15.
the bed. or, couch. Ps 6:6. 132:3.
make. Heb. turn. Ps 30:11. 66:6. 78:9.
his bed. Ps 4:4. 36:4. 149:5.
sickness. Dt 7:15. 28:59, 61.

4 **Lord**. Ps 32:5. 51:1-3.
be merciful. Lk 18:13.
heal. Ps 6:2-4. +103:3. 147:3. 2 Ch 30:18-20.
Ho 6:1. Ja 5:15, 16.
soul. Heb. *nephesh*, Ge +12:13.

5 **Mine**. Ps 22:6-8. 102:8.
his name. Jb 18:17. 20:7. Pr 10:7.

6 **speaketh**. Ps 12:2. 26:24, 25. Ne 6:1-14. Pr
26:24-26. Da 11:27. Mi 7:5-7. Lk 11:53, 54.
20:20-23. 2 C 11:26.
when. Je 20:10.

7 **whisper**. 2 S 12:19. Ro +1:29.
against. Ps 31:13. 56:5, 6. Mt 22:15.
26:3, 4.
my hurt. Heb. evil to me. ver. 1mg.

8 **An evil disease**. Heb. A thing of Belial. Ps
38:3-7. 1 S +30:22. Jb 2:7, 8. Lk 13:16. Ac
10:38.
and now. Ps 3:2. 71:11. Mt 27:41-43,
63, 64.

9 **Yea**. Ps 55:12-14, 20-22. 2 S 15:12. Jb 19:19.
Je 20:10.
mine own familiar friend. Heb. the man of
my peace. Je 20:10mg. 38:22mg. Ob 7. Lk
22:3.
which did eat. Dt 32:15. Ob 7. Mt 26:20-23.
Jn 13:*18*, 26, 27.
bread. Ge +3:19. Ob 7.
lifted up. Heb. magnified. Ps 35:26. 38:16.
55:12. +126:2mg. Jl 2:20mg.
heel. Ps 49:5. 56:6. 77:19. 89:51.
against. Lk 22:48.

10 **be merciful**. Ps 57:1. 109:21.
that. Ps 18:37-42. 21:8-10. 69:22-28. 109:6-
20. Lk 19:27.

11 **because**. Ps 13:4. 31:8. 35:25. 86:17. 124:6.
Je 20:13. Col 2:15.

12 **thou**. Ps 25:21. 42:5. 94:18.
settest. Ps 16:11. 17:15. 34:15. 73:23, 24. Jb
36:7. Jn 17:24. 2 T 4:18.
for ever. Heb. *olam*, Ex +12:24.

13 **Blessed**. Ps 89:52. Is +29:23. Ep 1:3. Re 4:8.
5:9-14. 7:12. 11:17.
everlasting, and to everlasting. Heb. *olam*
doubled, Da +2:20. Ps 90:2. 103:17. 106:48.
Amen. Mt +6:13.

PSALM 42

(Title.) A.M. 2983. B.C. 1021.
Maschil. *or, a Psalm* giving instruction, of the sons, etc. Or, 'An instructive Psalm,' or didactic ode, 'for the sons of Korah.' It is generally supposed to have been written by David when driven from Jerusalem and beyond Jordan, by Absalom's rebellion.
the sons. Ps 44-49, 84, 85, titles. Ge +36:5. 1 Ch 25:1-5.

1 **panteth.** Heb. brayeth. Jl 1:20.
so panteth. Ps 63:1, 2. 84:2. 119:131. 143:6, 7. 2 S 15:14, 29, 30. SS 5:5. Is 26:8, 9.
soul. Heb. *nephesh*, Ge +34:3.

2 **soul.** Heb. *nephesh*, Ge +34:3.
thirsteth. Ps 27:8. 36:8, 9. 63:1, 2. 143:5, 6. Is 44:3. 63:1. Jn 7:37. Re 22:1.
living. Jb 23:3. Je 2:13. +10:10. Jn 5:26.
God. Heb. *El*, Ex +15:2.
when shall. Ps 27:4. 84:4, 10. Jb 23:3.

3 **tears.** Ps +56:8. 80:5. 102:9.
while. ver. 10. Ps 3:2. 22:8. 79:10, 12. 115:2.

4 **When.** Ru 1:21. Jb 29:2, etc. 30:1, etc. La 4:1. Lk 16:25.
I pour out. Ps 62:8. 1 S 1:15, 16. Jb 30:16.
soul. Heb. *nephesh*, Ge +34:3.
for I. 1 Ch 15:15-28. ch. 16.
with the voice. Ps 81:1-3. 122:1. Dt 16:11, 14, 15. 2 Ch 7:10. 30:23-26. Is 30:29. Na 1:15.
kept holyday. Ps 84:7. 122:1. Ex 23:14. Dt 16:13.

5 **Why art thou cast down.** Heb. Why art thou bowed down. ver. 11. Ps 41:12. 43:5. 55:4, 5. 61:2. 142:2, 3. 143:3, 4. +145:14. 1 S 30:6. Mt *26:38.* Mk 14:33, 34.
O my. Ps 103:1, 22. 104:1. 146:1.
soul. Heb. *nephesh*, Ge +34:3.
hope. Ps 27:13, 14. 37:7. 56:3, 11. 71:14. Jb 13:15. Is 50:10. La 3:24-26. Ro 4:18-20. 5:3-5. 1 Th 1:3. He 10:36, 37.
praise him. *or,* give thanks. Ps 18:49.
yet praise. Jb 13:15.
for the help, etc. *or,* his presence is salvation. Ps 14:7. 44:3. 91:15, 16. +102:16. Nu 6:26. Is +25:9. +59:19, 20. Mt 1:23. 28:20. He +9:28. Re 11:17.

6 **my God.** Ps 22:1. 43:4. 88:1-3. Mt 26:39. 27:46.
soul. Heb. *nephesh*, Ge +34:3.
within me. Ps 43:5. 88:3. Jb +14:22.
therefore. Ps 77:6-11. Jon 2:7.
from the. Ps 61:2. 2 S 17:22, 27.
Hermonites. i.e. *devoted, banned; nose, strong fortress*, **S#2769h,** only here. Dt 3:8, 9. 4:47, 48.
the hill Mizar. *or,* the little hill. **S#4706h.** Ps 133:3.

7 **Deep calleth.** Ge +1:2. Jb 1:14-19. 10:17. Je 4:20. Ezk 7:26.
waterspouts. 2 S 5:8 (the gutter).

all thy. Ps 69:14, 15. 88:7, 15-17. La 3:53-55. Jon 2:3.

8 **command.** Ps 44:4. 133:3. Le 25:21. Dt 28:8. Mt 8:8.
in the night. Ps 32:7. 63:5, 6. +119:55. 149:5. Jb 35:10. Is 30:29. Ac 16:25.
the God. Heb. *El*, Ex +15:2. Ps 27:1. Ac 17:28. Col 3:3.

9 **God.** Ps 18:2. 28:1. 62:2, 6, 7. 78:35.
rock. Dt +32:31.
forgotten. Ps +13:1. Is 40:27.
why go. Mt +5:4.
because. Ps 55:3. Ec 4:1. La 5:1-16.

10 **As with.** ver. 3. Pr 12:18. Lk 2:35.
sword. *or,* killing. Ezk 21:22.
bones. Pr 16:24.
reproach. Ps 14:4. +31:11. 35:15. 44:22. 64:2-4. Ne 4:4. Jb 16:10. Da 7:25. Jn 10:20. He 11:36-38. Re 7:14.
while. ver. 3. Jl 2:17. Mi 7:10.

11 **Why art.** Mt *26:38.* Mk 14:34.
cast down. ver. 5. Ps 43:5.
O my. ver. +5.
soul. Heb. *nephesh*, Ge +34:3.
hope. Ps 31:24. 33:18, 22. 38:15. 39:7. 43:5. 71:5, 14. 119:49, 74, 81, 114, 147, 166. 130:5, 7. 131:3. 146:5. 147:11. Je 14:8. 17:7, 13, 17. 50:7. La 3:21, 24, 26. Jl 3:16. He 6:18, 19.
the health. Je +33:6. Mt 9:12.
countenance. ver. 5.

PSALM 43

(Title.) A.M. 2983. B.C. 1021.

1 **Judge.** Ps 7:8. 26:1. 35:24. 75:7. 1 C 4:4. 1 P 2:23.
plead. Ps 35:1. 1 S 24:15. Pr 22:23. 23:11. Mi 7:9.
ungodly. *or,* unmerciful. Ps 4:3. 18:25. 145:17mg. Mi 7:2mg.
the deceitful. Heb. a man of deceit and iniquity. Ps 71:4. 2 S 15:31. 16:20-23. 17:1-4.

2 **the God.** Ps +18:1. 140:7. Zc 10:12.
why dost. Ps +77:7.
why go. Ps 42:9.

3 **send.** Ps 40:11. 57:3. 97:11. 119:105. 2 S 15:20. Mi 7:8, 20. Jn 1:4, 17.
light. Ps +27:1.
truth. Jn 15:3. 17:17.
lead. Ps +32:8. 119:9, 11, 105. Pr 3:5, 6.
thy holy. Ps 2:6. 3:4. 23:3, 6. 68:15, 16. 78:68. 132:13, 14.
tabernacles. 1 Ch 16:1, 39. 21:29.

4 **Then.** Ps 66:13-15. 116:12-19. Is 38:22.
I go unto. Ju 24.
my exceeding joy. Heb. the gladness of my joy. Ps 71:23. Is 61:10. Hab 3:17, 18. Ro 5:11.
upon. Re +5:8.
O God. Ps 42:6.

5 **Why.** Mt 26:38. Mk *14:34.*

cast down. Ps 42:5, 11.
soul. Heb. *nephesh*, Ge +34:3. Ps 63:1. 88:3.
within me. Jb +14:22. Ps 42:6.
health. *Yeshuoth*, "salvations," or deliverances: see Ps 44:4. Ps 3:2, 8. 42:5.
countenance. Ps 42:5.

PSALM 44

(*Title*.) A.M. 3294. B.C. 710.
for the sons. Ps 42, title.

1 **have heard**. Ps 22:31. 71:18. 78:3-7. 105:1, 2. 145:4. Ex 12:24-27. 13:14, 15. Is 38:19. Jl 1:3.
in the times. Nu 21:14-16, 27-30. Jb 8:8, 9. 15:17-19.
of old. Mi +5:2.

2 **drive out**. Ps 78:55. 80:8. 105:44. 135:10-12. 136:17-22. Ex 15:17, 19. +23:30. Jsh 10:42. 21:43. Ne 9:22-27.
plantedst. Je +11:17.
how thou didst afflict. Ps 89:9. Ex 23:28. Nu 13:32. Jsh 10:11. 24:12. 1 S 5:6, 7. Je 17:8. Ezk 17:6.

3 **For**. Dt 4:37, 38. 8:11, 12, 14, 17, 18. 9:5, 6. Jsh 24:12. Zc 4:6. 2 C 4:7.
thy right hand. Ps +18:35.
light. Ps 42:5, 11. 80:16.
because. Nu 14:8. Dt 7:7, 8. 1 S 12:22. Ml 1:2, 3. Ro 9:10-15.

4 **my King**. Ps 74:12. 89:18. 149:2. 2 Ch 12:8. Is 33:22. 43:15. Ac 27:23.
command. Ps 42:8. Mk 1:25, 26, 31, 41. 9:25.
deliverances. Ps 3:2, 8. 9:14. 13:5. 43:5.

5 **Through thee**. Ps 18:39-42. 118:10-13. Is 41:14-16. Ph 4:13.
push. Dt 33:17. 1 K 22:11. Da 8:4.
tread. Ps 60:12. 91:13. 108:13. Is 41:14, 15. Zc 10:5. Ro 16:20mg.

6 **not trust**. Ps 20:7. 33:16, 17. 125:1. 1 S 17:39, 45. 2 Ch 32:8. Ho 1:7.
bow. Ps 46:9. Ge +49:10. Zc 10:4.

7 **But**. Ps 140:7. 144:10. Jsh 1:5. 10:8-10, 42. 11:6. 23:9, 10. Jg 2:18. 7:4-7. 1 S 7:8-12. 14:6-10. 17:47. 2 S 7:10.
put them. Ps 40:14. 83:1-18. 132:18.

8 **In God**. Ps 34:2. Is 45:25. Je 9:24. Ro 2:17. 15:17. 1 C 1:29-31.
praise. Ps 115:1, 18.
for ever. Heb. *olam*, Ex +12:24.
Selah. Ps +9:16.

9 **thou hast**. ver. 23. Ps 43:2. +51:11. 60:1, 10. 74:1. +77:7. 80:12, 13. 88:14. 89:38-45. +94:14. 108:11. 2 K 17:19, 20. 1 Ch 28:9. Je 6:30. 7:15. 14:19. 15:1. 23:39. 33:24-26. La 5:22. Ho 1:4, 6, 9. 9:17. Ro +11:1-6.
goest not. Nu 14:42.

10 **Thou**. Ps 78:9. Le 26:14, 17, 36, 37. Dt 28:25. Jsh 7:8, 12. 1 S 4:17. 31:1-7.
spoil. Ps 89:41. Is 10:6, 14. Je 15:13. 20:8.

11 **given**. Je 12:3. Ro 8:36.
like sheep appointed for meat. Heb. as sheep of meat. Ps 14:4.
scattered. Ps 60:1. 2 K 17:6. Is 11:11, 12. Je +9:16. 32:37. Ezk 34:12. Lk 21:24.

12 **sellest**. Dt +32:30.
for nought. Heb. without riches. Ps 112:3. 119:14.
increase. Ne 5:8-12. Re 18:13.

13 **makest**. Ps +31:11. 80:6. Ezk 36:19-23.
scorn. Ps 123:3, 4.
derision. Lk +16:14.

14 **byword**. Dt +28:37.
shaking. Je +18:16.

15 **confusion**. Jsh 7:7-9. Ezr +9:6.
covered. Ps 69:7. 71:13. 89:45. Je 51:51.

16 **reproacheth**. Ps +31:11. 119:42. 1 S 11:2. Pr 27:11.
blasphemeth. Le +24:11.
enemy. Ps 8:2.
avenger. Ps 8:2. Je 5:9, 29.

17 **All this**. Da 9:13.
yet. ver. 20. Ps 9:17. Dt 6:12. 8:14. Is 17:10. Je 2:32.
dealt. Je 31:32. Ezk 16:59. 20:37. Ac 24:16.

18 **heart**. Ps 119:2. Pr +4:23.
turned back. Ps 78:57. 125:5. 1 K 15:5. Jb 34:27. Je 11:10. Zp 1:6. Lk +8:13. 17:32. He 10:39.
steps. *or*, goings. Ps +37:31mg. 119:3.
declined. Ps 119:51, 157. Jb 23:11, 12. Pr 4:23. 1 C 15:58. 1 Th 2:10.

19 **Though**. Ps 38:8. 60:1-3. Je 14:17.
in the. Ps 74:13, 14. Is 27:1. 34:13, 14. 35:7. Ezk 29:3. Re 12:9. 13:2, 11-13. 16:10.
shadow of death. Ps +23:4.

20 **If we**. ver. 17. Ps 7:3-5. Jb 31:5, etc.
stretched. Ps +88:9.

21 **Shall**. Ps +11:4. 139:1, etc. Jb 31:4, 14.
knoweth. Ps 90:8. Jsh 22:22, 23. 1 S 2:3. Pr 5:21. 15:11. Ec 12:14. Jn +2:25. Ro 2:16. 1 C 4:5.

22 **Yea**. Ro *8:36*.
killed. ver. 11. Ps 79:2, 3. 1 S 22:17-19. 1 K 19:10. Mt 5:10-12. Jn 15:21. 16:2, 3. Ro 8:35, 37. 1 C 4:9. 15:30, 31. 1 P 4:14. Re 11:3-9. 17:6.

23 **Awake**. Ps +3:7. 121:3, 4. Is 40:27, 28. Mk 8:24-26.
cast. ver. +9.
for ever. Jb +4:20.

24 **Wherefore**. Ps 43:1-4. Dt +31:17.
forgettest. Ps +13:1. Ex 2:23, 24. Is 40:27, 28. Re 6:9, 10.
affliction. Ps 9:13. 25:8. 31:17. Ex 3:7.
oppression. Ps 17:8, 9. 42:9. 119:121, 122, +134. Ex 3:9. Dt 26:7. Is 19:19, 20. 38:14.

25 **For our**. Ps 66:11, 12. La 4:5.
soul. Heb. *nephesh*, Ge +34:3.
bowed down. Pr 2:8. Is 51:23. La 3:20mg.
to the dust. Ps 7:5. 18:42. 22:15, 29. 119:25.

26 Arise. ver. +23.

for our help. Heb. a help for us. Ps 63:7.

redeem. Ps 26:11. 130:7, 8.

PSALM 45

(*Title*.) **To the chief**. Or, rather, "To the chief musician upon the hexachords, a didactic ode for the sons of Korah, and a song of loves." *Shoshannim* most probably denotes hexachords, or six-stringed instruments, from *shesh*, "six;" hence the Persian *shashta*, a six-stringed lute. This Psalm is supposed by some to be an epithalamium, or nuptial song, on the marriage of Solomon with Pharaoh's daughter; but with what propriety could Solomon be described as "fairer than the children of men, a mighty warrior, a victorious conqueror," and a prince whose "throne is for ever and ever"? A greater than Solomon is here; and the person described is none other than the Messiah, as is acknowledged by many Jewish writers. The Targum on ver. 3 says, "Thy beauty, *malka mesheecha*, O King Messiah, is greater than the children of men;" and the Apostle expressly quotes it as such, He 1:8, 9. It was probably written by David after Nathan's prophetic address, 1 Ch 17:27.

Shoshanim. Ps 69, 80, titles.

Maschil. *or*, of instruction.

A Song. SS 1:1, 2, etc. Is 5:1. Ep 5:32.

1 is inditing. Heb.

boileth, *or*, bubbleth up. Jb 32:18-20. Pr 16:23. Mt 12:35.

a good. Ps 49:3. Jb 33:3. 34:4. Pr 8:6-9.

touching. Ps 2:6. 24:7-10. 110:1, 2. SS 1:12. Is 32:1, 2. Mt 25:34. 27:37.

tongue. 2 S 23:2. 2 P 1:21.

2 fairer. 1 S 16:12. SS 2:3. 5:10-16. Is 33:17. Da 1:15. Zc 9:17. Mt 17:2. Jn 1:14. Col 1:15-18. He 1:3, 4. 7:26. Re 1:13-18.

grace. Pr 22:11. Is 50:4. Lk 4:22. Jn 1:16. 7:46. He 12:27, 28.

thy lips. Jn 7:46.

God. Ps 21:6. 72:17-19. Ph 2:9-11.

for ever. Heb. *olam*, Ex +12:24.

3 Gird. Ps +18:32. Is 49:2. 63:1-6. He 4:12. Re 1:16. 19:15, 21.

O most mighty. Ex +15:3. Is +9:6, 7. Ac +10:36. Ro 14:9.

glory. Ps 21:5. 96:6. 104:1. 145:5, 12. He 1:3. 8:1. Ju 25.

4 ride, etc. Heb. prosper thou, ride thou. Re 6:2. 19:11.

prosperously. Ps 110:2, 3. Is 53:10. 1 Th 1:5. 2:13. 2 Th 3:1.

because. Ps 60:4. Jn 1:17. 14:6.

meekness. Zp +2:3. Mt +11:29.

right. Ps +18:35.

terrible. Ps 2:9. 21:8, 9. 65:5. 110:5, 6. Is

59:17, 18. 63:1-6. Lk 19:27. 2 Th 1:8, 9. Re 6:16, 17. +11:18. 19:17-21. 20:15.

5 Thine. Dt +32:23.

sharp. Ps 2:1-9. Is 49:2. Lk 19:42-44. 20:18, 19. Ac 2:37, 41. 5:33. 7:54.

people. Ps 22:27. 66:3, 4. Lk 19:27. Ac 4:4. 5:14. 6:7. Ro 15:18, 19. 2 C 10:4.

6 throne. Ps 47:8. +89:3, 4, 14, 29, 36, 37. 93:2. 145:13. Is 16:5. Da 2:44. 7:14, 27. Mt +19:28. Lk 1:32, 33. He +1:8. 4:16. 8:1. Re 3:21.

O God. Heb. *Elohim*, **S#430h**. ver. 2, 7. Ge 1:1. 6:13, 18. 17:1-8. +19:29. 50:24. Ex +2:24. Nu 23:19. 2 S 23:1-5. Jb +19:26. Is 9:6, 7. 40:9, 10. 45:22, 23. Je 23:5, 6. Jn 1:1. 1 T 3:16. He 6:17, 18.

for ever. Heb. *olam*, Ps +21:4. Ps 10:16. +72:5, 7, 17. 89:4. 110:4. 2 S 7:13, 16. Is 9:7. Lk 1:33. Re 11:15.

and ever. Ps +9:18 (**S#5703h**).

the sceptre. Ps +2:9. Is +11:4.

kingdom. Ps 47:7. 1 C 15:24, 25. Re 19:16.

7 Thou. Ps 33:5. 99:4. Mt 3:15. Lk 23:47. 2 C 5:21. He 1:9. 7:26. 1 J 3:5.

hatest. Pr +8:13. Mt 7:23. Lk 13:27. Re 21:27.

God. *or*, O God. Heb. *Elohim*, **S#430h**. ver. 6.

thy God. Heb. *Elohim*, **S#430h**. ver. 6. Ps 89:26. Is 61:1. Jn 20:17. Ep 1:3.

hath. Ps 89:20. Ge 49:25, 26. Lk 3:22. 4:18-21.

anointed. Ex +28:41. Jn +1:41mg.

oil. Ps 21:6. 23:5. 89:20. 1 K 1:39, 40. Ac 2:28.

gladness. Ps 21:6. Is 53:10, 11. Lk 15:10.

above. Jn 1:16. Ro 8:29. Ep 4:7. Ph 2:9. Col 1:18, 19. He 2:14.

8 All. Pr 27:9. 2 C 2:14-16.

garments. Ps 133:1, 2. SS 4:16.

smell of. or, are.

myrrh. Jn 19:39.

cassia. Ex 30:23, 24.

ivory. ver. 15. 1 K 22:39. Am 3:15. Jn 14:2.

whereby. Ps 16:11. He 12:2.

9 Kings. ver. 13. Ps 72:10. SS 6:8, 9. 7:1. Is 49:23. 60:10, 11. 2 C 6:18. Re 21:24.

upon. 1 K 2:9, 19.

queen. SS 4:8-11. Jn 3:29. Ep 5:26, 27. Re 19:7, 8. 21:2, 9.

gold of Ophir. 1 K +9:28.

10 Hearken. SS 2:10-13. Is 55:1-3. 2 C 6:17, 18. 7:1.

forget. Ge 2:24. 12:1. Dt 21:13. 33:9. Mt 10:37. 19:29. Lk 14:26. 2 C 5:16. 6:17.

11 So shall. SS 1:8, 12-16. 2:2, 14. 4:1-5, 7, 9, 10. 6:4. 7:1-10. Is 62:4, 5. Zp 3:17. Ep 5:26, 27.

desire. Ps 27:4. 73:25. SS 7:10. Is 62:5. 1 P 1:8.

Lord. ver. 6. Is 54:5. Je 23:5, 6. Jn +20:28. Ac 10:36. Ro 14:9. Ph 2:10, 11. 3:8.

worship. Ps 2:12. 95:6. Is 54:5. Lk 24:52. Jn 4:21, 22. 5:23. Re 5:8-14.

12 **And the**. Is 23:17, 18. Ac 21:3-6.

daughter. Nu +21:25.

with. Jg +3:15. Is 60:6, 7.

rich. Ps 22:29. Is 49:23. 60:3, 10, 11.

favor. Heb. face. Ex +32:11mg.

13 **king's**. ver. 9, 10. SS 7:1. Is 61:10. 1 P 2:9. Re 19:7, 8.

all glorious. 1 S 16:7. Lk 11:40. Ro 2:29. 2 C 5:17. 1 P 3:3, 4.

within. Le 10:18. Mt 23:26-28. Lk 11:40. Ro 2:29.

her clothing. ver. 9. Pr 31:22. Mt 5:16. 22:11, 12. Ro 3:22. 13:14. Re 3:18.

14 **She**. SS 1:4. Jn 17:24. 2 C 11:2.

be brought. Ps 43:4. SS 3:11. Ju 24.

raiment. Ex 28:39. Jg 5:30. Mt 22:11.

virgins. Ge 24:16. SS 1:3, 5. 2:7, 5:8, 9. 6:1, 8, 13. 8:13. Re 14:1-4.

15 **With gladness**. Is +35:10. +51:11. +55:12, 13. +60:19, 20. 61:10. Lk 15:32. Ju 24. Re 7:15-17.

they shall. Is 56:5. Jn +14:3. Re 3:12, 21.

16 **Instead**. Ps 22:30. Mt +19:29. Mk +10:29, 30. Ph 3:7, 8.

children. Is 49:21, 22. +54:1-5. 60:1-5. Ro 11:19. Ga 4:26, 27.

princes. 1 P 2:9. Re 1:6. +5:10. 20:6.

in all the earth. Mt +5:5.

17 **I will**. Ps 22:30, 31. 72:17-19. 145:4-7. Is 59:21. Ml 1:11. Mt 26:13. 1 C 11:26.

generations. Ge +9:12.

therefore. Ps 72:17. SS 6:9. Is 61:9. 62:1-3.

the people. Is 41:9. Zc 10:6. Ro +11:1, 2.

for ever. Heb. olam, Ps +21:4.

and ever. Heb. ad, Ps +9:18.

PSALM 46

(*Title*.) A.M. 3108. B.C. 896.

for. or, of.

the sons. Ps 84, 85, 87, titles.

Alamoth. or, virgins. 1 Ch 15:20.

1 **refuge**. ver. 7, 11. Ps +9:9. Pr 14:26.

a very. Ps 145:18. Ge 22:14. Dt 4:7. 2 S 22:17-20.

in trouble. Ps 60:11.

2 **will**. Ps 23:4. +118:6. Mt 7:24, 25. 8:24-26. Ro 8:31.

though. Ge 7:11, 12. Lk 21:9-11, 25-28, 33. 2 P 3:10-14.

mountains. Mt 21:21.

midst of the sea. Heb. heart of the seas. Ex 15:8. Ezk 27:4mg.

3 **the waters**. Ps 18:4. 65:7. 93:3, 4. Jb 38:11. Is 5:30. 17:12, 13. Je 5:22. Mt 7:25. Re 17:15.

mountains. Ps 114:4-7. Jg 5:4, 5. 1 K 19:11.

Jb 9:5, 6. Je 4:24. Mi 1:4. Na 1:5. Re 16:20.

Selah. ver. 7, 11. Ps +9:16.

4 **a river**. Ps 23:2. 36:8, 9. Is 8:6, 7. 48:18. Ezk 47:1-12. Jn 7:37-39. Re 22:1-3.

city. Ps 48:1, 8. 87:3. 2 Ch 6:6. Is 37:35, 36. 60:14. He 12:22. Re 21:2, 3, 10.

holy. Dt 12:11, 12.

most. Ps +7:17. Ec 5:8. Mi 6:6.

5 **God is**. Ps 68:18. Dt 23:14. Is 12:6. Ezk 43:7, 9. Ho 11:9. Jl 2:27. Zp 3:15. Zc 2:5, 10, 11. 8:3. Mt 18:20. Re 2:1.

she. Ps 62:2, 6. 112:6. 125:1. Mt 16:16, 18.

God shall help. Zc +12:8. +14:3.

and that, etc. Heb. when the morning appeareth. Ex 14:24, 27. Re +2:28.

6 **heathen**. Ps +2:1-4. 76:3. 83:2-8. 2 Ch 14:9-13. 20:1, 20-24. Is 10:26-34. 37:21-36.

kingdoms. Is 14:12-16.

voice. Ezk +10:5.

earth. Ps 68:8. Jsh 2:9, 11, 24. Hab 3:5, 6, 10, 11. 2 P +3:10-12. Re 6:13, 14. 14:6-8. 20:11.

7 **Lord of hosts**. ver. 11. Ps +24:10.

with us. Ex 33:14, 15. Nu 14:9. 2 Ch 13:12. Is +43:2.

Jacob. Ps +20:1.

our refuge. Heb. an high place for us. Ps +9:9mg.

8 **Come**. Ps 66:5. 92:4-6. 111:2, 3. Nu 23:23.

desolations. Ps 66:3. Ex 10:7. 12:30. 14:30, 31. Jsh 11:20. 2 Ch 20:23, 24. Is 24:1. 34:2, etc. 45:7. Am +3:6. Na 1:4, 5, 8.

9 **maketh**. Is 2:4. 11:9. 60:18. Mi 4:3, 4.

breaketh. Ps 76:3-6. Ex +15:3. Ezk 39:3, 9, 10.

bow. Ps +44:6.

burneth. Jsh 11:6, 9. Mi 5:10.

10 **Be still**. Ex 14:13. Is 30:7, 15. Hab +2:20.

know. Ps 83:18. 100:3. Ex 18:11. 1 S 17:46. 1 K 18:36. 2 K 19:19.

I will be. Ps 86:9. 104:31. 145:10-12. Nu 14:20, 21. Is +12:4. Ezk 38:23. Lk 10:18. Jn 11:40. 1 J 3:8. Re 15:3, 4.

11 **with us**. 1 S 17:47.

refuge. ver. +1, 7.

PSALM 47

(*Title*.) A Psalm. This Psalm is supposed to have been composed by Solomon on the removal of the ark into the temple, 2 Ch ch. 7.

for. or, of. Ps 46, title.

1 **clap**. Ps 98:8. 2 K 11:12. Is 55:12.

shout. ver. 5. Ps 98:4. 1 S 10:24. 2 S 6:15. 2 Ch 13:15. Ezr 3:11-13. Je 31:7. Zp 3:14. Zc 4:7. 9:9. Lk 19:37-40. Re 19:1, 2.

2 **Lord most high**. Ex +15:26.

is terrible. Ps +99:3. 145:6.

a great King. ver. 7. Ps 22:27-29. 48:2. 95:3. 102:16. Ne +9:6. Is +33:22. 40:3. Je 23:5, 6. Da +2:45. 7:13, 14. Zp +3:15. Zc 2:10. 12:10. 14:9. Ml 1:14. Mt 5:35. 28:18. Ph 2:9-11.

3 **subdue**. Ps 18:47. 81:14. Dt +33:29mg. Jsh 21:44. Je +20:11. Ph 3:21. 1 P 2:25.
our feet. Ps 110:1-3. Jsh 10:24, 25. Is 49:23. 1 C 15:25. Re 2:27.

4 **choose**. Dt 11:12. Je 3:19. Ezk 20:6. Mt 25:34. 1 C 3:22, 23.
inheritance. Ps +16:5, 6. Dt 32:9. Jsh 13:33. Ep 1:18. 1 P 1:4.
excellency. Ps 16:3. Is 60:15. Am 6:8. 8:7. Na 2:2.
whom. Dt +33:3. Ho 14:4. 1 J 4:9, 10.
Selah. Ps +9:16.

5 **God**. Ps 24:7-10. 68:17-19, 24, 25, 33. Lk 24:51-53. Ac 1:5-11. Ep 4:8-10. 1 T 3:16. He 9:24.
gone up. 1 Th 4:16.
with a shout. Ps 78:65. Nu 23:21. 2 S 6:15. 1 Ch 15:28.
sound. Ps 81:3. 150:3. Nu 10:1-10. Jsh 6:5. 1 Ch 15:24. 16:42. 1 C 15:52. 1 Th 4:16. Re 8:6, etc. 11:15.

6 **to God**. Ps 96:1, 2. ch. 117. 149:1-3. Ex 15:21. 1 Ch 16:9. 29:20. Is 12:4-6. Ep 5:18-20.
our King. Ps 145:1. Is 33:22. Zc 9:9. Mt 25:34. 27:37.

7 **King**. ver. 2, 8. Zc 14:9. Re 11:15.
sing. 1 C 14:14, 15. Col 3:16.
with understanding. or, every one that hath understanding. Ps 107:43. Dt 32:29. Lk 19:42.

8 **reigneth**. Ps 22:27-29. 93:1. 96:10. 97:1. 99:1. 110:6. 1 Ch 16:31. Is 40:9, 10. 1 C +15:24, 25. Re 11:15. 19:6.
God sitteth. Ps +45:6. He +1:8.
throne. Ps +11:4. +45:6, 7. 48:1. 94:20. He 4:16.

9 **The princes**, etc. or, The voluntary of the people are gathered unto the people of, etc. Ps 72:7-9. 110:2, 3. Ge +49:10. Is 11:10. 60:4, 5. 66:19, 20. Ro 11:25.
the God. Ge +17:7, 8. Ro 4:11, 12. Ga 3:29.
shields. Ps 89:18mg. Pr 30:5.
he is. Is +12:4. Re 21:24.

PSALM 48

(*Title*.) A.M. 3489. B.C. 515.
Song. 2 Ch ch. 20. Ps 30, title.
for. or, of. Ps 46, title.

1 **Great**. Ps 86:10. 87:3. Da +2:45.
greatly. Ps 89:1-7. Ne 9:5. He 2:12. Re 15:3, 4. 19:5.
city. Ps 46:4. 65:1. 78:68. 87:3. 102:13, 16. Zc 14:8, 9, 11. He 12:22. Re 21:2, 10-22.
mountain. Ps 47:8. 99:9. Is 2:2, 3. 27:13. Je 31:23. Ob 17. Mi 4:1. Zc 8:3. Mt 24:15.

2 **Beautiful**. Ps 50:2. Je +3:19mg. La 2:15.
joy. Is 60:15-20. 66:10. Ezk 20:6. Ml 3:12. He 12:22.
on the sides. Is 14:13.

the city. Ps 47:7, 8. Ml 1:14. Mt 5:35.

3 **God is known**. Ps 76:1-5. 125:1. 2 Ch 12:7. 14:9-15. 20:1, etc. Is 4:5, 6. 37:33-36. Zc 2:4, 5.

4 **lo**. Ps 83:2-8. 2 S 10:6, 14, 16-19. Is 7:1. 8:8-10. 10:8. 29:5-8. Re 17:12-14. 19:19, 20. 20:8, 9.
they passed. Re 21:24.

5 **were**. Ex 14:25. 2 K 7:6, 7. 19:35-37.

6 **Fear**. Ex 15:15, 16. Is 13:6-8. Da 5:6.
pain. Je +4:31.
travail. Ge 16:11. Mt +24:8.

7 **breakest**. Ezk 27:25, 26.
ships. 1 K 22:48. 2 Ch 20:36. Is 2:16.
Tarshish. Ge +10:4.
east. Ge +41:6.

8 **As we**. Ps 44:1, 2. 78:3-6. Is 38:19.
city of the Lord. ver. 1, 2. Ps +101:8. Is 60:21. Zc 2:12.
God. Ps 46:5. 87:5. Is 2:2. 14:32. Mi 4:1. Mt 16:18.
for ever. Heb. *olam*, Ex +12:24.
Selah. Ps +9:16.

9 **thought**. Ps 26:3. 77:10, 11. 104:34. 105:5, 6.
lovingkindness. Ps 40:10. 63:3. SS 1:4. Lk 22:19, 20.
in the midst. Ps 63:2. 77:12-14. 2 Ch 20:5-13. Is 26:8.

10 **According**. Ps 67:2. 113:3. 138:2-4. Ex 3:13-15. 34:5-7. Dt 28:58. Jsh 7:9. Ml 1:11, 14.
thy right. Ps 11:7. 45:7. 99:4. 145:17. Re 19:2, 11.

11 **rejoice**. Ps 149:2.
daughters. Ps 97:8. SS +1:5. Is 37:22. Je 49:2. Zc 9:9. Lk 23:28.
because. Ps +58:10. 137:8, 9. 2 Ch 20:26, 27. Re 15:4. 16:5-7.

12 **Walk**. Ne 12:31-40. Mt 24:1, 2.
tell. Ps 78:4, 6, 7. Is 33:18-20. He 12:22.

13 **Mark ye well**. Heb. Set your heart to. Ps 62:10. Ex 7:23. 1 S +4:20mg. 2 S 13:20mg. Jb 7:17. Pr 22:17. 24:32mg. 27:23mg.
her bulwarks. Ps 10:10mg. 122:7. Is 26:1. 59:19.
consider. or, raise up. Is 58:12. Am 9:11. Ac 15:14-16.
that ye. Ps 71:18. 78:4. Dt 11:19. Jl 1:3.

14 **this God**. Ps 16:2. 31:14. 73:24, 26. La 3:24.
our God. Ps 118:28. Ge 17:7. Jsh 24:18. Ro 8:15. Ga 4:6. Re 21:3.
for ever. Heb. *olam*, Ps +21:4.
and ever. Ps +9:18 (S#5703h).
guide. Ps +32:8. Ge 48:15. Is 58:11.
unto death. 1 C +15:55.

PSALM 49

(*Title*.) A.M. cir. 3464. B.C. cir. 540.
A Psalm. This Psalm was probably written by one of the descendants of the sons of Korah, during the Babylonian captivity.
for. or, of. Ps 46, 48, titles.

1 **Hear**. Ps 34:11. 78:1. Pr 1:20-23. Mt 11:15. 13:9. Re 2:7, 11, 17, 29.
  inhabitants. Ps 50:1. Is 49:6. Ml 1:11. Mt 28:19, 20. Ro 3:29. 10:18.

2 **Both low**. Ps 62:9. 1 S 2:7, 8. Jb 34:19. Pr 22:2. Je 5:4, 5. Ja 1:9-11. 2:1-7. Re 6:15-17.

3 **mouth**. Dt 32:2. Jb 33:3, 33. Pr 4:1, 2. 8:6-11. 22:17, 20, 21. Lk 4:22. 2 T 3:15-17.
  meditation. Ps 19:14. 45:1. 104:34. Mt 12:34, 35.

4 **incline**. Ps 78:2. Mt 13:34, 35.
  parable. Nu +23:7. Mt 13:11-15.
  will open. Jg +11:35. Da +12:4, 9.
  dark saying. Ps +78:2. Lk 12:3. 2 C 3:12.

5 **Wherefore**. Ps 27:1, 2. 46:1, 2. Is 41:10, 11. Ac 27:24. Ro 8:33, 34. Ph 1:28.
  days. Pr 24:10. Am 5:13. Ep 5:16.
  iniquity. Ps 38:4. Pr 5:22. Ho 7:2.
  heels. Ps 22:16. 56:6, 7. Ge 49:17. 1 S 26:20.

6 **trust**. Ps 52:7. 62:10. Jb 31:24, 25, 28. Pr 10:15. 23:5. Mk 10:24. 1 T 6:17.
  boast. Est 5:11. Je 9:23. Ezk 28:4, 5. Ho 12:8. Lk 12:19.

7 **None**. Ex 32:33.
  give. Mt 16:26. 20:28. 1 T 2:6. 1 P 1:18.
  ransom. 1 S +12:3.

8 **the redemption**. Ex 21:30. Jb 36:18, 19.
  soul. Heb. *nephesh*, Ge +12:13. ver. 15, 18.
  is precious. Ps 72:14. 116:15. 139:17. 1 S 18:30mg. Jb 36:18, 19. Is 28:16. 1 P 1:18, 19. 2:7. 2 P 1:1, 4.
  it ceaseth. Ps 36:3. Ge 11:8. 18:11. 41:49. Dt 32:22.
  for ever. Heb. *olam*, Ex +12:24.

9 **That he**. Ps 89:48. Pr 10:2. 11:4. Ec 8:8. Zc 1:5. Lk 16:22, 23.
  for ever. Jb +4:20 (S#5331h).
  not see. Ps +16:10. 49:15. Jn 8:51, 52. Ac 2:27, 31. 13:33, 35-37.

10 **wise**. Ec 2:16-21. 9:1, 2. Ro 5:12-14. He +9:27.
   fool. Ps 73:22. 92:6, 7. 94:8. Pr 12:1. 30:2. Je 10:8.
   leave. ver. 17. Ps 17:14. 39:6. Pr 11:4. Ec 2:18, 19, 21, 26. 5:13-16. Je 17:11. Lk 12:20. 1 T +6:6-10.

11 **Their inward**, etc. Or, "Their grave is their house for ever, their dwelling place through all generations, though their names are celebrated over countries." Ps 5:9. 64:6. Ezk 38:10. Lk 11:39. Ac 8:22.
   thought. Ps +89:47. +90:12. Pr +14:13. 24:33. Is 28:15. 56:12. Am 6:3. Lk 12:19. Ac 24:25.
   for ever. Heb. *olam*, Ex +12:24.
   all generations. Heb. generation and generation. Ps +33:11mg. 45:17.
   they call. Ge 4:17. 1 S 15:12. 2 S 18:18.
   lands. Ps 83:10. 104:30. 105:35.
   names. Ge 4:17. 11:4. Jsh 19:47. 2 S 18:18.

12 **man**. Heb. *adam*. ver. 20. Ps 8:4. 11:4. 12:1.

in honor. ver. 20. Ps 37:35, 36. 39:5. 82:7. Est 1:4, 20. 6:3. Ja 1:10, 11. 1 P 1:24.
abideth. Ps 25:13mg. 30:5. 55:7 (remain). 91:1mg. Ge 19:2. 32:13. Is 1:21. He +9:27. 1 J 2:17.
like. ver. 20. Nu +21:27.
beasts. ver. 20. Ps 8:7. 36:6. 50:10. Ec 3:18-21. 9:12.
perish. *or*, cut off. ver. 20. Is 6:5mg.

13 **folly**. Lk 12:20. 1 C 3:19.
   approve their sayings. Heb. delight in their mouth. Ps 50:18. 51:16. 62:4. Dt +21:5mg. Je 44:17. Lk 11:47, 48. 16:27, 28.
   Selah. Ps +9:16.

14 **Like sheep**. Ps 44:11. Je 12:3. Ro 8:36.
   they. Jb 17:13, 14. 21:13, 26. 30:23. Ec 12:7. Is 38:10, 11.
   grave. Heb. *sheol*, Ge +37:35.
   death. Jb 24:19, 20.
   upright. Ps 47:3. Da 7:22. Ml 4:3. Lk 22:30. 1 C 6:2. Re 2:26, 27. 20:4, 5.
   have dominion. Ps +145:13. 149:4-9. Ge +1:26. Lk 19:17.
   in the morning. Ml 3:17. Re +2:28.
   their. Ps 39:11. Jb 4:21.
   beauty. *or*, strength. Is 45:16.
   in the grave, etc. *or*, the grave being an habitation to every one of them. Jb 30:23. Pr 10:28. 14:32. Is +24:21, 22. Re +20:5.
   grave. Heb. *sheol*, Ge +37:35.
   dwelling. 1 K 8:13. 2 Ch 6:2. Is 63:15. Hab 3:11.

15 **God**. Ps 31:5. 56:13. 73:24. Ho 13:14. Re 5:9. 14:13.
   soul. Heb. *nephesh*, Ge +12:13; Ps +16:10.
   from. 1 C +15:55.
   power. Heb. hand. Ps 89:48. Ge +9:5.
   the grave. *or*, hell. Heb. *sheol*, Ge +37:35. Ps +16:10. 86:13. 89:48.
   shall receive me. Ps 31:5. 73:24. Lk 23:46. Jn 14:3. Ac 7:59.
   Selah. Ps +9:16.

16 **Be not**. ver. 5. Ps 37:1, 7. Est 3:1-6. Pr 28:12.
   made rich. Lk 12:20.
   glory. Ge 31:1. Est 5:11. Re 21:24, 26.

17 **he shall**. Jb 1:21. 27:19. Ec 5:15. Lk 12:20. 16:24. 1 T 6:7.
   his. Is 5:14. 10:3. 1 C 15:43.

18 **while he lived**. Heb. in his life. Ps 7:5. 16:11. 17:14. 18:46.
   blessed. Dt 29:19. Ho 12:8. Lk 12:19.
   soul. Heb. *nephesh*, Ge +34:3.
   praise. 1 S 25:6. Est 3:2. Ac 12:20-22. Re 13:3, 4.

19 **He**. Heb. The soul. lit. It, i.e. *nephesh* (ver. 18), Ge +12:5. Ec 3:21. 12:7. Lk 12:20. 16:22, 23.
   to the generation. Ge 15:15. 1 K 16:6.
   never. Ps 56:13. Jb +4:20 (S#5331h). 33:30. Mt 8:12. 22:13. Ju 13.
   see light. Ps 36:9.

20 Man. ver. 12. Est 5:11-14. 7:10.
   honor. Pr 16:31.
   understandeth not. Ps 119:155. Jb 4:21.
   36:12. Pr 21:30. Is 8:20. 27:11. Mk 12:24. Lk
   +11:52.
   is like. ver. 12. Ps 32:9. 73:18, 19, 22. Nu
   +21:27. Ec 3:18, 19.

PSALM 50

(*Title*.) of Asaph. *or*, for Asaph. Ps 73-83,
titles. 2 K +18:18.
1 mighty God. Heb. *El, Elohim, Jehovah*. Ps
   145:3-6. Ge 17:1. Jsh 22:22. Ne 9:6, 32. Is
   +9:6. Je 10:6. 32:18, 19.
   even. 1 K 18:21, 36, 37. Is 37:20. 54:5.
   hath spoken. Is 1:2. Am 3:8.
   called. Ps 49:1, 2. 113:3. Ml 1:11. Mt 25:31,
   32. He 1:1, 2.
2 Out of Zion. Ps 68:24. +102:16. Is 12:6.
   +26:21. Ho +5:15. Hab 2:20. He 12:22-26.
   perfection. Ps 48:2. 87:2, 3. 90:17. SS 5:16.
   Zc 9:17.
   God. Ps 80:1. Dt +33:2. Hab 3:3, 4. 2 C 4:6.
   Re 1:16. 21:23.
3 Our God. Ps 48:14. 68:20.
   shall come. Is +35:4.
   keep. ver. 21. Ps 83:1. Is 42:13, 14. 65:6, 7.
   a fire. Ps +97:3. Ex 19:18. Le 10:2. Nu 16:35.
   Dt 9:3. 1 K 19:11, 12. Ml 3:2, 3. Mt 3:12. 1 Th
   2:16. He 2:3. 10:28, 29.
   it shall. Ps 18:7-15. 97:4, 5.
4 call. ver. 6. Dt 4:36. 30:19. 31:28. 32:1. Is 1:2.
   Mi 6:1, 2.
   judge. Dt +32:36. Lk +12:47. Jn 5:22, 23. 2 C
   5:10. 1 P 4:17. Ju 14, 15.
5 Gather. Mt 24:31. Jn 11:52. 1 Th 4:16, 17. 2
   Th 2:1.
   my saints. Ps 97:10. Ex 8:23. Dt +33:2, 3. Pr
   2:8. Is 13:3. Jl 3:11. Zc +14:5. Ml 3:16, 17. 1 C
   +6:2, 3. 1 Th +3:13. Ju 14.
   made. Ex 24:3-8. Dt 26:17-19. Je 31:32. Mt
   26:28. He 9:10-23. 12:22, 24. 13:20.
   by sacrifice. Je +34:18.
6 heavens. Ps 97:6. Ro 2:5. Re 16:5-7. 19:2.
   God is judge. Ps +94:2.
   Selah. Ps +9:16.
7 Hear. Ps 81:8. Is 1:18. Je 2:4, 5, 9. Mi 6:1-8.
   O my. Ps 81:10-12. Ex 19:5, 6. Dt 26:17, 18.
   1 S 12:22-25.
   testify. Je +42:19. Ml +3:5.
   I am. Ex 20:2. 2 Ch 28:5. Ezk 20:5, 7, 19, 20.
   Zc 13:9.
8 I will not. Ro 2:25.
   burnt. Le +23:12.
9 take no. Is 43:23, 24. Mi 6:6-8. Ac 17:25. He
   10:4-6.
10 every. Ps 8:6-8. 104:24, 25. Ge 1:24, 25. 2:19.
   8:17. 9:2, 3. 1 Ch 29:14-16. Jb 40:15, etc. Je
   27:5, 6. Da 2:38.

   cattle. Ps 104:14. Ge 31:9. Jon 4:11.
11 know. Ps 104:12. 147:9. Ge 1:20-22. Jb
   38:41. 39:13-18, 26-30. Mt 6:26. 10:29-31. Lk
   12:24.
   wild. Is 56:9. Ezk 14:15, 16.
   mine. Heb. with me.
12 world. Ps 24:1, 2. 115:15, 16. Ex 19:5. Dt
   10:14. Jb 41:11. 1 C 10:26-28.
   mine. Ro +14:8.
   fulness. Ps 104:24. 145:15, 16. Ge 1:11, 12,
   28-30. 8:17. 1 Ch 29:14.
13 eat. ver. 3.
   flesh. Ps 16:9. 27:2. 38:3. 56:4.
   bulls. lit. "mighty ones." Ps 22:12. 68:30.
   76:5. 78:25mg.
   drink. Ps 75:8. 78:44. 110:7.
   blood. Ps 5:6. 9:12. 16:4. 26:9.
   goats. ver. 9.
14 Offer. ver. 23. Ps 69:30, 31. 147:1.
   Le +23:19.
   thanksgiving. Le +7:12. Pr 7:14. Am 4:5. 1
   Th 5:18. Ja 5:13.
   pay thy vows. Le +23:38. Nu +30:2.
15 call. Ps +3:4. 2 Ch 33:12, 13. Jb 22:27. Pr
   1:28. Is 58:9. Zc 13:9. Lk 22:44. Ac 16:25. Ja
   5:13.
   day of trouble. Ps 20:1. 77:2. 86:7. 107:6. 2
   K 19:3, 4. Je +30:7.
   deliver. Ps 34:3, 4. 54:6, 7. 66:13-20. Lk
   17:15-18.
   glorify. ver. +23.
16 But unto. Is 1:12-15. Je 9:2. Mt 4:10. 16:23.
   Ac 8:20-23.
   wicked. Is 1:11-15. 48:22. 55:6, 7. Ezk 18:27.
   Am 5:21-23. Mt 15:7, 8. 18:3. 23:25, 26. Jn
   3:3, 5, 7. He 11:6.
   What hast. 2 Ch +19:2. Pr 26:7. Is 1:11-15.
   48:1, 2. 58:1-7. Je 7:4-7. 23:38. Mt 7:3-5, 22,
   23. Mk +1:25. +3:12. Lk 5:14. Jn 4:24. Ac
   19:13-16. Ro 2:17-24. 1 C 9:27. 2 P 2:15.
   thou shouldest. Ps 25:14. 78:35-38. Ezk
   20:37, 38. He 8:9.
17 hatest. Pr 1:7, 28, 29. 5:12, 13. 8:36. 12:1. Jn
   3:20. Ro 1:28. 2:21, 23. 2 Th 2:10-12. 2 T 4:3,
   4.
   castest. Ne 9:26. Is 5:24. Je 8:9. 18:12. 36:23,
   etc.
18 consentedst. Pr 1:10-19. Is 5:23. Mi 7:3. Ro
   1:32. Ep 5:11-13.
   hast been partaker. Heb. thy portion was.
   Le 20:10. Jb 31:9-11. Pr 2:16-19. 7:19-23. Je
   5:8, 9. Mt 23:30. 1 T 5:22. He 13:4.
19 givest. Heb. sendest. Ps 52:2-4. 55:20. 78:25.
   Je 9:5, 9.
   tongue. Ps 5:9. 10:7. 12:2, 3. 36:3, 4. 52:2.
   55:12, 21. 64:3-5. Jb 27:4. Is 59:3, 4. Ho 4:2.
   Ro 3:13, 14. Ja 3:5-9. Re +21:8.
20 speakest. Ps 31:18. Mt 5:11. Lk 22:65.
   slanderest. Le +19:16. Ep +4:31.
   thine own. Mt 10:21.

21 **I kept**. ver. 3. Ps 109:1-3. Ec 8:11, 12. Is
26:10. 57:11. Ro 2:4, 5. 2 P 3:9.
thoughtest. Ps 73:11. 94:7-11. Nu 23:19. Is
40:15-18.
**that I was altogether such an one as thy-
self**. Or, as Bishop Horsley renders, "that I
AM (*eheyeh*) is such an one as thyself." Ex
+3:14.
will. ver. 8. Pr 29:1. Re 3:19.
set. Ps 90:8. Ec 12:14. Am 8:7. 1 C 4:5.
22 **consider**. Dt 32:18. Ec 7:14. Ezk 18:28. Hg
1:5. Lk 15:17.
forget. Ps +9:17. 10:4. Jb 8:13. Is 51:13. Je
2:32. Ho 4:6.
I tear. Ho 5:14. 13:8. Re 6:16, 17.
none. Ps 7:2. 2 S 22:42. Is 42:22. Am 2:14.
Mi 5:8.
23 **Whoso**. ver. 14, 15. Ps 27:6. Ro 12:1. He
13:15. 1 P 2:9.
glorifieth. Mt +9:8.
to him. Ps 24:4, 5. 25:14. 85:9. 119:166. Jn
7:17. 8:31, 32. Ac 10:2-4. 11:14. 13:26. Ga
6:16.
ordereth his conversation. Heb. disposeth
his way. Ps 66:18. 119:166. Is +66:4. Lk
+21:36. Jn +9:31. Ph 1:27. 2:12, 13. Col
+1:10. 3:1-3. 1 Th 4:1. Ja 3:13. 1 P 1:15. 2 P
3:11. 1 J 3:3.
salvation. Ps 91:16. Is 12:2. 45:17. 49:6.
51:5, 6. Lk 2:25, 29, 30. He +9:28. 1 P 1:13.

PSALM 51

(Title.) A.M. 2970. B.C. 1034.
chief. Ps 4, 5, 6, 8, 9, etc., titles.
when. 2 S 12:1-13.
Nathan. 2 S 11:2, etc.
Bathsheba. 2 S 11:3. 12:24. 1 K 15:5. 1 Ch
3:5. Mt 1:6.
1 **Have mercy**. Ps +4:1. Ezk 18:23, 31. Lk 15:7,
10, 32. 18:13. Jn 8:11. Ro 11:32. 2 P 3:9.
O God. Ex +34:6, 7. Jn 1:17. Ep 1:6-8.
lovingkindness. Ps 13:5. 17:7.
multitude. Ps +5:7. Ne 9:19.
tender. Ps 40:11. 69:16. 77:9. 79:8. 145:9.
blot. ver. 9. Ps 25:11, 18. Nu 5:23. 2 K 21:13.
Ne 4:5. Is 1:16-20. 43:25. 44:22. 55:7. 59:1, 2.
Je 18:23. Ho 14:2. Mt 4:17. Lk +13:3, 5.
24:47. Ac +3:19. 26:18. Ro 2:4-7. 3:24-31.
6:23. 8:1-13. Ep 1:6. Col 2:14. 1 J 1:7-9. 3:5-
10. Re 2:5. +3:5.
transgressions. ver. 3. Ps 5:10. 19:13. 32:1.
Jb 34:37. Pr 10:19.
2 **Wash**. ver. 7. Ps 65:3. Ex 19:10. Is 1:16. 4:4.
Je 2:22. 4:14. Ezk 36:25. Zc 13:1. Ml 3:2, 3.
Mt 3:11. 20:22. Lk 12:50. Jn 3:5. Ac 1:5.
+22:16. Ro 2:28, 29. 6:3-5. 1 C 6:11. 10:1, 2.
12:13. Ga 3:27. Col 2:11-13. T 3:5, 6. He 9:13,
14. 10:21, 22. 1 J 1:7-9. Ju 23. Re 1:5. 7:14.
iniquity. ver. 5, 9. Ps 18:23. 25:11.

cleanse. ver. 7. Ps 19:12. Le 13:6, 13, 17, 23,
34. Je 33:8. Ezk 36:33. Zc 3:3, 4. 1 J 1:7.
sin. ver. 3. Ps 25:7, 18. 32:5. 38:3.
3 **For I**. Ps 32:5. 38:17, 18. 41:4. Le 26:40, 41.
Nu 5:7. Dt 4:29-31. 30:1-3. 1 K 8:33-36, 47.
Ne 9:2. Jb 33:27, 28. Pr 28:13. Je 3:13. 31:18-
20. Ezk 6:9. Da 9:3-20. Ho 5:15. Lk 15:18-21.
1 J 1:9.
acknowledge. Ps 1:6. 4:3. +9:10. 36:10. 39:4.
44:21. 46:10. Pr 3:6. Is 61:9. Je 3:13. 14:20.
my sin. Ps 40:12. Ge 42:21. Is 59:12. Je 3:25.
Da 9:5, 6.
ever. Ps 16:8. 25:15. 34:1. 38:3. Is +58:11
(continually).
4 **Against thee**. Ps 41:4. Ge 9:6. 20:6. 39:9. Ex
16:8. Le 5:19. 6:2-7. 1 S 8:7. 2 S 12:9, 10, 13,
14. 24:10. Pr 8:36. Is 59:2. Lk 15:21. Ac 5:4.
Ja 2:9-11.
sinned. Ps 78:32. 106:6.
evil. Ge 38:7. Nu 32:13. 2 K 17:17. 21:6. Lk
15:21.
that. Ge 18:19.
thou. Ps 50:4, 6. Ru 3:19. Lk 7:29. Ro 3:4.
justified. or, righteous. Ps 143:2. Ge 38:26.
when. Ac 17:31. Ro 2:5. Re 15:3, 4. 16:5.
19:11.
clear. or, pure. Jb 15:14. 25:4. Mi 6:11.
judgest. Ps 10:18. 96:13.
5 **shapen**. Ps 58:3. Ge 5:3. 8:21. Jn 8:44. Ro
2:12-16. 5:12-21. 1 J 3:8.
iniquity. Ro 7:17.
in sin. ver. 9. Ps 103:10. Ge 41:9. Pr +20:9.
mother. Ps 139:13.
conceive. Heb. warm. Ge 30:38, 39, 41.
31:10. 1 K 1:1h (heat). 8:46. Jb 14:1, 4.
15:14, 16. 25:4, 5. Ec 4:11h (warm). Is 48:8.
Lk +1:35.
6 **Behold**. Ps 26:2. Ge 20:5, 6. 2 K 20:3. 1 Ch
29:17. 2 Ch 31:20, 21. Jb 4:18. 15:15. 25:5. Pr
2:21. 11:20. Je 5:3. Jn 4:23, 24. 2 C 1:12. Ja
4:8.
desirest. Ps 40:6, 8. Jb 33:32.
truth. Ps 15:2. 19:9. 25:5, 10. 145:18. Jsh
24:14. 1 K 2:4. 3:6. 2 K 20:3. Pr 12:17, 19. Mt
23:25. Jn 3:21. Ja 4:8. 1 J 2:4. 3 J 3.
inward. Ps 5:9. 125:4. 1 S 16:7. Jb 38:36. Je
31:33. Mk 7:20-23. Lk 11:39. Ro 1:18-32.
2:29. 7:22. 1 C 6:9-11. 2 C 5:17, 18. Ga 5:19-
21. Col 3:5-10.
in the hidden. Ps 26:2. 2 K 20:3. Jb 32:8. Je
17:9. 32:40. Ezk 28:3. Da 12:9. Lk 11:39. Jn
1:47. 2 C 1:12. 1 P 3:4.
make. Jb 28:28. 33:27, 28. 34:31. 35:11.
38:36. 39:17. Pr 2:6. Ec 2:26. Mt 11:19. Lk
7:35. 2 T 3:15. Ja 1:5.
to know. Ps 16:11. 89:1.
wisdom. Ps 19:12. 37:30. 90:12. 104:24. Ex
4:10. 1 Ch 22:11, 12. 2 Ch 1:8-10. Jb 11:6.
34:32. 35:10, 11. Pr 28:5. Je 33:3. Da 2:20-23.
1 C 1:22-24. Ep 1:17, 18. Col 1:9, 10. Ja 1:5.

7 Purge. Ex 29:36. Le 8:15. 14:4-7, 49-52. Nu 19:18-20. Jb 9:30. Ezk 36:25. Ml 3:3. He 1:3. 9:14, 19.

hyssop. Ex 12:22. Le 14:4, 6, 49. Nu 19:6, 18. 1 K 4:33. Jn 19:29. He 9:19.

and. He 9:13, 14. 1 J 1:7. Re 1:5.

clean. Le 11:32. 12:7, 8. 13:6. Mt 26:28. Col 1:20. He 9:12, 14, 22. 13:12, 20. 1 J 5:8-10.

wash me. ver. +2. Ps +19:12. Jn 13:8, 9. Ac 15:8, 9. 22:16. T 3:5, 6.

whiter. Jb 38:22. Is 1:18. Da 11:35. Jl 1:7. Jn 13:10. 15:3. 17:17. Ep 5:26, 27. 1 Th 4:3. 5:23. Re 7:13, 14.

snow. Ps 147:16. 148:8. Ex 4:6.

8 Make. Ps 13:5. 30:11. 119:81, 82. 126:5, 6. Mt +5:4.

hear. Ps 66:8. 76:8. Ac 16:14.

joy. ver. 12. Ps 32:11. 45:7. 67:4. 70:4. 85:6. 86:4. 90:14, 15. 105:43. 106:5. 109:28. 119:111. Is 35:10. Jl 1:16. Col 1:10, 11.

gladness. Ps 4:7. 16:11. 21:6. 30:11.

bones. Ps 6:2, 3. 22:14, 17. 31:10. 32:3. 34:20. 35:10. 38:3. Jb 5:17, 18. Pr 16:24. Is 57:15-18. Ho 6:1, 2. Lk 4:18. Ac 2:37-41. 16:29-34.

broken. or, bruised. ver. 17. Ps 44:19.

rejoice. Ps 9:14. 13:4, 5. Mt 5:4.

9 Hide. Ps 10:11. 13:1. 17:8. 22:24. Is 38:17. Je 16:17. Mi 7:18, 19.

face. Nu 23:21. 2 C 3:18.

blot. ver. +1.

10 Create. or, Prepare. ver. +7. Ps 57:7mg. Ge 41:32mg. Is 65:17. Ho +6:3. Jn 3:6-8. 2 C 5:17. Ga 6:15. Ep 2:10.

clean. Ps 12:6. 19:9. 24:4. 73:1. 1 S 10:9. Pr 15:26. 20:9. Je 13:27. 24:7. 31:21, 22, 33. 32:39, 40. Ezk 11:19. 18:31. 36:25-27, 37. Hab 1:13. Mt 5:8. Ac 15:9. 1 P 1:22.

heart. Je 4:4. Zc 7:12.

renew. Ps 104:30. La 5:21. Lk 22:32. Ro 12:2. Ep 4:22-24. Col 3:10. T 3:5.

right. or, constant. or, stedfast. Ps 5:9mg. 57:7. 78:8, 37. 86:11. 108:1. 112:7. Jsh 14:14. 1 K 15:3-5. Jb 42:7. Ac 11:23. 1 C 15:58. Ja 1:8.

spirit. Heb. *ruach*, Ge +41:8. Is +29:24. ver. 17. Is 26:9. Ezk 11:19. 18:31. Mt +5:3. 26:41. Jn 3:6. Ac 17:16. 19:21. 20:22. Ro 1:9. +8:1. 8:2. 1 C 5:3, 4, 5. 6:20. Ep 4:23. 1 P 3:4.

within. Ps 5:9. 49:11.

11 Cast me not. Ps +27:9. +44:9. 102:10. Ge 4:14. 37:24. Ex 1:22. Le 13:46. 1 S 16:13, 14. 2 K 13:23. 17:18-23. 23:27. 24:20. Est 4:15-17. 5:1, 2. Je +7:15. 52:3. 2 Th 1:9. He 10:14, 19.

thy presence. Ps 6:3, 4. 10:1. 13:1, 2. 22:1-6, +11. 25:16. 27:8-10. 31:16. 35:22, 23. 60:1. 63:1, 2. 69:16-19. 80:14-19. 88:14, 15. 91:15, 16. 144:5-8. Is 63:15-19. 64:1-4. Je 14:8, 9. 15:15. 31:18. La 5:20, 21. Mk 5:18. 15:34. Lk

24:28, 29. Jn 4:40. 11:32. 17:20-23. 2 C 13:14. Ep 3:16-19. 2 T 4:22. Re 3:20.

take not. Ge 6:3. Jg 13:25. 15:14. 16:20. 1 S 10:10. 16:14. 2 S 7:15. Is 63:10, 11. Jn 14:16. Ep 1:13. 4:30.

holy. ver. 12. Ps 143:10. Ge +41:38. Ne 9:20. Is 63:10-12. Ezk 36:27. Hg 2:5. Lk 11:13. Jn 14:16, 17, 26. Ro 1:4. 8:9. Ep 4:30.

spirit. Heb. *ruach*, Ge +41:8.

12 Restore. Ps 54:7. 85:6-8. Ge 20:7. 2 K 8:6. Jb 20:10, 18. 29:2, 3. Is 41:13. 42:22. 57:17, 18. Je 31:9-14.

joy. ver. 8. Ps 13:5. 21:1. 35:9. Is 49:13. 61:10. Mt 26:75. Lk 1:47. Jn 21:15-17. Ro 5:2-11. 1 P 1:8.

salvation. Ps 18:2, 35, 46. 20:6.

uphold. Ps 3:5. 17:5. 19:13. 37:17, 24. 41:3, 12. 54:4. 63:8. 119:116, 117, 133. Is 41:10. Je 10:23. Ro 14:4. 1 P 1:5. Ju 24.

free. or, willing. Ps 54:6. 110:3. Ex 35:5, 22. 2 Ch 29:31. Mt 26:41. Ro 7:25. 8:2, 15. 2 C 3:17. Ga 4:6, 7. 2 T 1:7.

spirit. Heb. *ruach*, Ge +41:8.

13 Then. Ps 18:26. 32:5, 8-10. 119:37. 2 Ch 6:27. Zc 3:1-8. Mk 5:19. Lk 22:32. Jn 21:15-17. Ac 2:38-41. 9:19-22. 2 C 5:8-20.

teach. Ps 19:7, 8. 25:9. 34:11. 94:12. 126:1-3. Pr 11:30. 1 T 1:12-16.

transgressors. Ps 37:38. Is 1:28.

ways. Ps 5:8. 18:21, 30. 25:4, 8, 9. 32:8. Is 2:3. Ac 13:10.

sinners. Ps 1:1, 5. 25:8. 26:9. 104:35.

converted. or, turned. Ps 6:10. 19:7. 22:27. Is 1:27. 6:10. Je 31:18. Mk 4:12. Ac +3:19. Ja +5:19, 20.

14 Deliver. Ps 7:1. 22:20. 25:20. 26:9. 39:8. 55:23. Ge 9:6. 44:22. Dt 21:7, 8. 2 S 3:28. 11:15-17. 12:9. 21:1. Ezk 3:21. Jon 1:14.

bloodguiltiness. Heb. bloods. Ps 9:12. 16:4. 26:9. Ge 9:5, 6. Le +20:9. 2 S 11:14-21. 12:9. 16:7mg. 2 K +9:26mg. Jon 1:14. Zc 12:10. Ac +18:6.

thou God. Ps +88:1. Re 7:10.

salvation. Ps 33:17. 37:39. 38:22. 40:10, 16. Pr 11:14. 21:31. 24:6. Is 45:17. Je 3:23. La 3:26.

tongue. Ps 35:28. 40:9, 10. 71:15-24. 86:12, 13.

sing. Ps 5:11. 20:5. 32:11. 59:16. 63:7. Is 53:4-6. 54:1.

righteousness. Ps 145:1, 17. Ezr 9:13. Ne 9:33. Da 9:7, 16. Ro 10:3. Ph 3:9.

15 O Lord. Ge 44:16. 1 S 2:9. Ezk 16:63. Mt 22:12. Ro 3:19.

open. Ex 4:11, 15. Jg +11:35. Is 6:5-7. 32:4. 35:6. Ezk 3:27. 29:21. Mk 7:34.

mouth. Ps 63:3-5. 119:13. He 13:15.

show forth. or, declare. Ps 9:14. 19:1. 22:31. 30:9. 38:18.

praise. Ps 9:14. 22:3, 25. 33:1. 34:1. 50:14, 23.

16 **desirest**. ver. 6, 19. Ps 40:6. 50:8, 13. 69:31.
Ex 21:14. Nu 15:27, 30, 31. 35:31. Dt 22:22. 1
S 15:22. Ho 6:6. Mi 6:6-8.
sacrifice. ver. 17, 19. Ps 4:5. 27:6.
else would I. *or*, that I should.
delightest. or, acceptest. Ps 40:6. 50:8, 18.
69:30, 31. Pr 15:8. 21:27. Is 1:11-15. Je 7:22,
23, 27. Am 5:21-23. He 10:5, 6.
burnt offering. ver. 19. Le +23:12. Ep 5:2.

17 **sacrifices**. Ps 107:22. Ho 6:6. Mk 12:33. Jn
6:28. Ro 12:1. Ph 4:18. He 13:16. 1 P 2:5.
a broken. Ps 34:18. 147:3. 2 K 22:13, 19, 20.
Is 57:15. 60:1. 61:1-3. 66:2. Ezk 9:3, 4, 6. Mt
+5:3. Lk 18:11-14.
spirit. Heb. *ruach*, Ge +41:8; ver. 10.
contrite. or, bruised. ver. 8. Ps 34:18. 131:1,
2. Is 57:15. 61:1. 66:2.
heart. Ps 38:8.
thou. Ps 22:24. 69:33. 73:20. 102:17. 2 Ch
33:12, 13. Am 5:21. Lk 7:39-50. 15:2-7, 10,
21-32. 18:9-14.

18 **Do good**. Ps 25:22. 36:3. 49:18. 69:35, 36.
102:16. 122:6-9. 137:5, 6. Ex 20:24. Dt 30:1-
10. Is 51:3. 62:1, 6, 7. Je 51:50. 2 C 11:28, 29.
thy. Lk 12:32. Ep 1:5, 9, +11. Ph 2:13. 2 Th
1:11.
Zion. Ps 2:6. 9:11, 14. 14:7. 20:2. 50:2. 74:2.
102:13-17. 122:6, 7. Is +24:23.
build. Ps 28:5. 78:69. 89:40. +102:16. 127:1.
2 S 5:9. 1 K 3:1. Ne 2:17. Is 58:12. Ezk 36:33.
Da 9:25. Mi 7:11. Zc 2:5. Ac 15:15, 16.
walls. Ps 55:10. Ne 12:27. Is 22:10. 26:1.
60:10, 18. Re 21:14.

19 **pleased**. Ps 66:13-15. 118:27. Ep 1:6. 5:2.
sacrifices. Ps 4:5. 27:6. Le 26:31. Dt 33:19.
Ml 3:3. Ro 12:1.
burnt offering. ver. 16. Le +23:12.
whole burnt. Le 6:22, 23. Dt 33:10. 1 S 7:9.
they. Is 60:7. Zc 8:20-23.
bullocks. Ps 22:12. 50:9. 69:31.
altar. Ps 26:6. 43:4. 84:3. He 13:10.

PSALM 52

(*Title*.) A.M. 2942. B.C. 1062.
Doeg. Ps 54:3. 1 S 21:7. 22:9-19.
told. Ps 59:7. Je 9:8. Ex 22:9.

1 **boastest**. Ps 10:2, 3. 94:4, 22, 23. Ro 1:30. 2
T 3:2.
mischief. Ps 7:14. 10:7. 36:3-6. Pr 6:14, 18. Is
59:4. Mi 7:3.
O mighty. Ge 6:4, 5. 10:8, 9. 1 S 21:7.
goodness. Ps 37:32, 33. 103:17. 107:1. 137:1,
2. 140:11, 12. 1 J 4:7, 8.
God. Heb. *El*, Ex +15:2.

2 **Thy**. Ps 50:19. 64:2-6. 140:2, 3. Pr 6:16-*19.*
30:14. Je 9:3, 4. 18:18. *Mt 26:59.* Ac 6:11-13.
24:1, 5. *Re 12:10.*
like. *Ps 57*:4. 59:7. Pr 12:18. 18:21.
working. Ps 109:2. 120:2. 2 C 4:2. 11:13.

3 **lovest**. Je 4:22. Mi 3:2. Ro 1:25. 2 T 3:4.
lying. Mt 26:59. Ep +4:25.
Selah. Ps +9:16.

4 **devouring**. 1 S 22:18, 19. Ja 3:6-9.
O thou. *or, and* the.

5 **God**. Ps 7:14-16. 55:23. 64:7-10. 120:2-4.
140:9-11. Pr 12:19. 19:5, 9. Re 21:8.
destroy thee. Heb. beat thee down. Ps 58:6.
Ex 34:13. Pr 2:22. 19:9.
for ever. Jb +4:20. Mt +25:46.
pluck. Ps 37:35, 36. Jb 18:14. 20:6, 7. Lk
16:27, 28.
root. Pr 2:22.
the land. Ps +27:13.
Selah. Ps +9:16.

6 **righteous**. Ps 97:8. Ml 1:5. Re 15:4.
16:5-7.
shall see. Is +66:24.
and fear. Ps 40:3. 119:120.
laugh. Jb 22:19. Is 37:22. +58:10.

7 **Lo**. Is 14:16, 17. Jn 19:5.
made. Ps 146:3-5. Je 17:5.
trusted. Ps 49:6, etc. 62:9, 10. Jb 31:24, 25. 1
T 6:17.
strengthened. Ps 73:7-11, 18-20. Ec 8:8. Ho
12:7, 8.
wickedness. *or*, substance. ver. 2. Ps 5:9.
38:12.

8 **like**. Ps 1:3. 92:12-14. Je 11:16. Ho 14:6-8.
Ro 11:24.
I trust. Ps +13:5.
for ever. Heb. *olam*, Ps +21:4.
and ever. Ps +9:18.

9 **praise**. Ps 145:1, 2. 146:2. Ep 3:20, 21.
for ever. Heb. *olam*, Ex +12:24.
wait. Ps 27:14. 40:1. 48:9, 10. 62:1, 5. 123:2,
3. 130:5, 6. Pr 18:10. La 3:25, 26.
for it is. Ps 54:6. 73:25, 26, 28.

PSALM 53

(*Title*.) A.M. cir. 3464. B.C. cir. 540.
Mahalath. i.e. *sickness*, **S#4257h**. Ps 88, title.

1 **fool**. Ps +14:1, etc. Mt 5:22.
said. Ps 10:4, 6, 11, 13. 50:21, 22. 1 K 12:26.
Ro 1:21, 28.
Corrupt. Jb 14:4. 15:16.
have done. Le 18:24-30. Dt 12:31. 1 K
14:24. Ezk 16:47, 51. Ep 5:12.
there is. Ro 3:10-12.

2 **God looked down**. Ps 11:4. +14:2. Jb 33:27.
Je 16:17. 23:24.
to see. Ge +18:21.
any that. Ps 111:10. Dt 4:6. Jb 28:28.
seek. *Ps* 10:4. 27:8. Pr 2:1-5. Je +29:13. Jn
3:19.

3 **Every**. Ps 14:3. 2 S 20:2. Is 53:6. 64:6. Je 8:5,
6. Zp 1:6.
filthy. Ps +14:3. Re 22:11, 12.
none. Ro 3:12. 1 J 2:29. 3 J 11.

10 **In God**. ver. +4. Ps 60:6. Ge 32:11. Mt 24:35.
He 6:18. 2 P 1:4.
11 **I will not**. ver. 4. Ps 112:7, 8.
12 **Thy vows**. Ge 35:1-3. Nu +30:2.
I will. Ps 9:1-3. 21:13. 59:16, 17. Is 12:1.
13 **For**. Ps 86:12, 13. 116:8. 2 C 1:10. 1 Th 1:10.
He 2:15. Ja 5:20.
soul. Heb. *nephesh*, Ge +12:13; +9:5.
wilt not thou. Is 51:19. Lk 14:5.
deliver my feet. Ps 17:5. 94:18. 145:14. 1 S
2:9.
falling. Ps 17:5. 2 P +1:10.
walk. Ps 116:9. Ge 17:1. Is 2:5. 38:3.
the light. Jb 33:30. Jn 8:12. 12:35, 36. Ep
5:8-14. Re 21:23, 24.

PSALM 57

(*Title*.) A.M. 2943. B.C. 1061.
Al-taschith. *or*, destroy not. A golden Psalm.
This Psalm is supposed to have been called *al
tashcheth*, or "destroy not," because David
thus addressed one of his followers when
about to kill Saul in the cave; and *michtam*, or
"golden," because written, or worthy to be
written, in gold. Ps 58, 59, titles.
when. Ps 142, title. 1 S 22:1. 24:3, 8.
1 **be merciful**. Ps +56:1.
soul. Heb. *nephesh*, Ge +34:3.
trusteth. Ps +9:10. 13:5. 125:1. Is 50:10.
shadow. Ps +91:1.
wings. Ps +91:4.
refuge. Ps 9:9, 10. 11:1. 62:8. 71:3-7. 142:3-
5.
until. Is 10:25. 26:20. Mt 23:37. 24:22. Jn
16:20. Ja 5:10, 11. Re 7:14. 21:4.
2 **God most**. Ps +7:17. 136:2, 3. Is 57:15.
that performeth. Ps 138:8. Jb 23:14. Is
26:12. Ph 1:6. 2:12, 13. He 13:21.
3 **send**. Ps 18:6, etc. 144:5-7. Mt 28:2-6. Ac
12:11.
from the reproach of him. *or*, he reproacheth him, etc.
swallow. Ps +35:25. 61:7. Nu 23:24. Jb
31:31. Mi 3:2, 3.
Selah. Ps +9:16.
send. Ps 40:11. 43:3. Jn 1:17.
4 **soul**. Heb. *nephesh*, Ge +12:13.
among. Is +5:29.
set. Jg 9:20. Ja 3:6.
sons. Ps +4:2.
whose. Pr 30:14.
tongue. Ps 52:2. 55:21. 64:3. Pr 12:18. 25:18.
Re 19:15.
5 **Be thou**. ver. 11. Is +12:4. 37:20. Mt 6:9, 10.
above. Ps 8:1. 113:4-6.
thy glory. Ps 72:19. 148:13. Nu 14:21. Is 6:3.
Hab 2:14. 3:3.
6 **a net**. Ps 9:15, 16. 35:7, 8. 140:5, 9. 141:10. 1
S 23:22-26. Jb 18:8. Pr 1:17. 29:5. Mi 7:2.

my soul. Heb. *nephesh*, Ge +34:3. Ps 42:6.
142:3. 143:4. Mt 26:37, 38.
pit. Ps 7:15, 16.
they are fallen. Ps 37:15. 94:23. Est 3:9.
5:14. 6:13. 7:5, 10. 9:25. Jb +4:8. Da 6:24.
Selah. Ps +9:16.
7 **My**. Ps 108:1, 2. 112:7.
fixed. *or*, prepared. Ps 5:9. 38:17. 51:10mg.
108:1. Ge 41:32mg. 2 Ch +12:14mg.
I will. Ps 34:1, 4. Is 24:15. Ro 5:3. Ep 5:20.
8 **Awake**. Jg 5:12. Is 52:1, 9.
my glory. Ps 16:9. +30:12. 108:1-3. Ge
+49:6. Ac 2:26.
I myself will awake early. or, morning
dawn. Ps 59:4. 108:2. 139:9. Ge 19:15.
9 **I will**. Ps 2:1. 18:49. 22:22, 23. 96:3. 138:1, 4,
5. 145:10-12. Ro 15:9.
10 **For**. Ps 36:5. 71:19. 85:10, 11. 89:1, 2.
103:11. 108:4.
truth. Ge 9:9-17. Is 54:7-10. He 6:17, 18.
11 **Be thou exalted**. ver. +5. Ps 8:1, 9. Re 15:3,
4.

PSALM 58

(*Title*.) **Al-taschith**. *or*, Destroy not, A golden
Psalm. Ps 57, 59, titles.
1 **Do**. Ps 72:1-4. Dt 16:18, 19. 2 S 23:3. 2 Ch
19:6, 7. Is 11:3-5. 32:1. Je 23:5, 6.
O congregation. Ps 82:1, 2. Nu 11:16. Dt
1:15, 16. 2 S 5:3. Mt 26:3. 27:1. Lk 23:50, 51.
Ac 5:21.
O ye. Ps +4:2. 82:6, 7.
2 **in heart**. Ps 21:11. Ec 3:16. Is 59:4-6. Je
22:16, 17. Ezk 22:12, 27. Mi 3:1-3, 9-12. Jn
11:47-53.
weigh. Ps 94:20. Is 10:1. 26:7.
3 **estranged**, etc. Ps 51:5. Jb 15:14. Pr 22:15. Is
48:8. Ep 2:3, 12. 4:18.
as soon, etc. Heb. from the belly. Ps 22:10. Is
46:3. 48:8.
4 **poison**. Ps 140:3. Ec 10:11. Ro 3:13. Ja 3:8.
like. Heb. according to the likeness of.
serpent. Mt +3:7.
the deaf. Je 8:17. Ac 7:57.
adder. *or*, asp. Ps 91:13. Dt 32:33. Jb 20:14,
16. Is 11:8.
5 **will not hearken**. Pr 1:24, 25. Zc 7:11-13.
Mt 22:2-6. Lk 14:17-20.
charming never so wisely. *or*, *be* the
charmer never so cunning. Dt 18:11. Pr 21:9.
25:24. Is 19:3. 47:9, +12. Ho 6:9.
so wisely. Pr 30:24.
6 **Break their**. Ps 3:7. 10:15. Jb 29:17. Ezk
30:21, etc.
young. Is +5:29.
7 **melt**. Ex +15:15.
8 **a snail**. Nu +32:23.
pass. Ps 37:35, 36. Mt 24:35. Ja 1:10.
untimely. Jb 3:16. Ec 6:3.

9 **thorns**. Ps 118:12. Ec 7:6.
take them away. Ps 37:10, 36, 38. 55:23.
73:18-20. Jb 18:18. 20:5, 7-9, 26-29. Pr
+14:32. Mt 13:30, 41, 42. Lk 17:34-37.
as. Je +23:19.
both living, etc. Heb. as living as wrath. Nu
16:30.

10 **rejoice when**. Ps 48:11. 52:6. 64:10. 68:1-3.
107:42. Dt +32:43. Jg 5:31. Jb 22:19. Pr
11:10. Re 11:17, 18. 18:20. 19:1-7.
seeth. Is +66:24. Jn +18:36.
the vengeance. Ps 49:14, 15. 101:8. Ge
+6:13. Dt +32:35. Is +24:6. 61:2. Je 20:12. Ml
+4:3. Re 6:10.
wash. Ps 68:23. Jb 29:6. Re 14:20.

11 **Verily there is**. Ps 73:13-15. 92:15. Ml 3:14.
a reward for. Heb. fruit of the, etc. Ps 1:1-3.
4:3. 15:1-5. 37:3, 9, 10, 17-20, 25, 26. +84:11.
92:12, 13. 112:1-3. Ge 19:15, 22. 2 Ch 16:9.
Pr 14:34. 16:8. 20:7. 28:16, 18. Is 33:15, 16.
58:6-8. Da 3:18, 30. 6:21, 22, 28. Mt +5:12.
Ro 6:21, 22. 8:28. 1 T 6:6. 1 P 3:10-13.
verily he. Ps +7:8. 64:9. 83:18. Ml 2:17. 2 P
3:4-10.

PSALM 59

(Title.) A.M. 2942. B.C. 1062.
Al-taschith. _or_, destroy not. A golden Psalm.
Ps 57, 58, titles.
Michtam. The seven poems of the celebrated
Arabian poets who flourished before the time
of Mohammed, called _Moallakat_, from being
suspended on the walls of the temple of
Mecca, were also called _Modhabat_, "golden,"
because they were written in letters of gold
on the papyrus; and probably this is another
reason why the six poems of David were
called _golden_.
when. Jg 16:2, 3. 1 S 19:11, etc. 2 C 11:32, 33.

1 **Deliver**. Ps 7:1, 2. 18:48. 71:4. 143:12. Lk
1:74, 75. 2 T 4:17, 18.
from mine enemies. Ps 7:1. 17:8, 9. +18:3.
25:19, 20. 44:4, 5. 60:11, 12. 80:6, 7. 1 S
12:10. 2 S 22:3, 4. La 3:52-58.
defend me. Heb. set me on high. Ps 12:5.
91:14. Is 33:16.

2 **save**. Ps 26:9. 27:2. 55:23. 139:19.

3 **they**. Ps 10:9, 10. 37:32, 33. 38:12. 56:6. 1 S
19:1. Pr 12:6. Mi 7:2. Ac 23:21.
my soul. Heb. _nephesh_, Ge +12:13.
the mighty. Ps 2:2. Ac 4:26, 27.
not. Ps 7:3-6. 69:4. 1 S 24:11, 17. 26:18. Jn
15:25.

4 **run**. 1 S 19:12-24. Pr 1:16. Is 59:7. Ac 23:15.
Ro 3:15.
without. Ps 109:3. 1 S 24:11. Da 6:4. Jn
15:24, 25. 19:6.
awake. Ps +3:7.
help me. Heb. meet me. Ps 35:2.

5 **the God**. Ge 33:20. Ex 3:15.
visit. Ex 20:5.
the heathen. Ps 9:15. 54:3. Is 1:10. Am 9:7.
Ro 2:28, 29. 9:6.
be not. Ps 7:12, 13. +9:17. Is 27:11. Je 7:16.
+10:25. Ezk 18:27, 28. Ro 2:5. Ja 2:13. 1 J
5:16.
Selah. ver. 13. Ps +9:16.

6 **return**. ver. 14. 1 S 19:11. Jn 18:3.

7 **belch**. Pr 15:2mg. Mt 12:34.
swords. Ps 55:21. 57:4. 64:3-5. 109:2, 3. Pr
12:18.
who. Ps 10:11, 13. 73:11. 94:7-10. Jb 22:12,
13. Je 33:24.

8 **thou**. Ps 2:4. 37:13. 1 S 19:15, 16. Pr 1:26.
heathen. ver. 5. Mt 18:17.

9 **his strength**. Instead of _uzzo_, "his strength,"
fourteen MSS. and all the ancient versions,
read _uzzee_, "my strength:" "O my Strength, I
will wait upon thee." Ps 18:1, 2. +25:3. 38:19.
46:1. Is 12:2. 26:3, 4. Mt 6:13.
God. ver. 17. Ps 62:2.
defence. Heb. high place. Ps +9:9mg. 94:22.
144:2. Pr 2:8. Is 58:14. Hab 3:19. 2 T 4:18.

10 **The God**. ver. 17. 2 C 1:3. Ep 2:4, 5. 1 P 5:10.
prevent. Ps 21:3. 79:8. Is +65:24. 1 Th 4:15.
let me see. 1 S 26:10. 2 S 1:11, 12, 17. Is
+66:24. Je 17:16, 18. Lk 19:41-44. Ro 10:2, 3.
enemies. Heb. observers. Ps +5:8mg.
56:2, 6.

11 **Slay**. Ge 4:12-15. Jg 1:6, 7. Ec 9:5. Je 30:11.
Ezk 12:15, 16. 14:22, 23. Re 9:6.
scatter. Ps 44:11. 52:5. Le 26:33. Dt 4:27.
28:64. 30:3, 4. Ezk 12:15. Lk 1:51, 52. 21:24.
bring. Jb 40:12.
our shield. Ps 3:3. 84:11.

12 **For the**. Ps 64:7, 8. 79:12. 120:3, 4. 140:9,
10. Pr 12:13. 18:7. Mt 12:36, 37. 27:25, 63.
taken. Ps +10:2. Pr 6:2. 11:6.
cursing. Ps 109:17, 18. Ho 4:2. Lk 23:5.

13 **Consume**. ver. 11. Ps 7:9. Nu 14:34, 35.
32:13. Dt 2:14-16. 7:22, 23. Hab 1:12.
not be. Ps +115:17. +146:4.
let them know. Ps 46:10, 11. 102:15. 135:5,
6. Is +24:21. Ezk +6:7, 10.
God ruleth. Ps 102:16. Is 54:5. Zc +14:9.
Selah. Ps +9:16.

14 **at evening**. ver. 6, 16. Ps 22:16. Is 65:14.
return. Ps +6:10. Is +24:22. Re +20:5.
go around. Re 20:9.
like a dog. Re 22:15.

15 **wander**. Ps 109:10. Jb 15:23. 30:1-7. Is 8:21.
for meat. Heb. to eat. Dt 28:48, 53-58. 2 K
6:25-29. La 4:4, 5, 9, 10. 5:9, 10. Mt 24:7, 8.
grudge, etc. _or_, if they be not satisfied, then
they will stay all night. Ps +49:12. Pr 19:23.
if. Is 56:11. Mi 8:5.

16 **But**. ver. 9, 10. Ps 21:13. 106:8. 145:11. Ex
15:6. Jb 37:23.
sing aloud. Ps 31:7. 36:5. 86:13. 89:1. 101:1.

Is 24:14, 16. +51:11. Zc +2:10. Ro 15:9. Ep 1:6, 7.

in the morning. ver. 14. Ps 5:3. 1 S 19:11, 12. Re +2:28.

for thou. Ps 4:1. 61:2, 3. 1 S 17:37. 2 C 1:10. Ep 3:20.

day. Ps 77:2. 116:1-5. 138:7. Je 30:7. He 5:7.

17 **O my**. Ps 18:1, 2. 46:1.

for. ver. 9, 10.

PSALM 60

(Title.) A.M. 2964. B.C. 1040.

Shushan-eduth. Probably a hexachord harp, or lute; for *aiduth* appears to be the same as the Arabic *ood*, a harp or lute: concerning *shushan*, Ps 45, 80, titles. i.e. *lily of testimony*, **S#7802h**.

Michtam. *or*, a golden *Psalm*. Ps 59, title.

when he strove. 2 S 8:3, 12, 13. 10:16. 1 Ch 18:3, 12, 13. 19:16-19.

Aramnaharaim. i.e. *highland of two rivers*, **S#763h**. Ge 24:10 (Mesopotamia). Dt 23:4. Jg 3:8. 1 Ch 19:6.

Aramzobah. i.e. *exalted station; exalted conflict*, **S#760h**.

valley. 2 S +8:13.

1 **O God**. ver. 10. Ps +44:9.

scattered. Heb. broken. Ps 59:11. 80:12. 89:40. 1 S 4:10, 11, 17. 13:6, 7, 11, 19-22. 31:7. 33:1-7. 2 S 5:20.

O turn. Ps 79:9. 80:3, 7, 19. 85:4. 90:13. Is 30:19. La 3:31, 32. Ho +14:2. Zc 10:6.

2 **made**. Ps 104:32. 114:7. 2 S 22:8. Jb 9:6. Is 5:25. Je 4:24. 10:10. Am 8:8. Hab 3:10. Mt 27:51.

broken. Ps 89:40. 2 S 2:8, etc. 3:11-14. Is 7:8. Je 14:17. 48:38. Hg 2:6, 7.

heal. 2 Ch +7:14. Jb 5:18. Is 30:26. Je 30:17. La 2:13. Ezk 34:16. Ho 6:1.

3 **showed**. Ps 71:20. Dt 28:28, 34. Ne 9:32. Da 9:12.

hard things. Je +30:7. Da +12:1.

to drink. Ps 75:8. Is 51:17, 22. Je 25:15. La 4:21. Ezk 23:31, 32. Hab 2:16. Re 16:19. 18:6.

4 **a banner**. Ps 20:5. Ex +17:15. SS 2:4. Is 11:12. 49:22. 59:19. Jn 12:32.

because. Ps 12:1, 2. 45:4. Is 59:14, 15. Je 5:1-3.

Selah. Ps +9:16.

5 **That**. ver. 12. Ps 22:8. 108:6, etc. Dt 7:7, 8. 33:3. Is 41:8. Mt 3:17. 17:5.

save. He 7:25.

right hand. Ps +18:35.

6 **God hath**. Ps 89:19, 35. 108:7-13. 132:11. 1 S 16:1. 2 S 3:18. 5:2. Je 23:9. Am 4:2.

rejoice. Ps 56:4. 119:162. 2 S 7:18-20. Lk 1:45-47.

divide. Jsh 1:6. 2 S 2:8, 9. 5:1-3.

Shechem. Ge +33:18.

valley. Jsh 13:27.

7 **Gilead**. Ge +37:25.

strength. Dt 33:17. 1 S 28:2.

Judah. Ps 76:1. 108:8. 114:2. Mt 1:2. He 7:14. Re 5:5.

lawgiver. Ps 108:8. Ge +49:10. Nu 21:18. Is 33:22.

8 **Moab**. Ezk +25:8.

washpot. or, pot for washing.

wash. or, washing. **S#7366h**. Ps 108:9. Ge 18:4. From **S#7364h**, Ex +29:4. 2 K 3:11.

pot. **S#5518h**. Ps 58:9. 108:9. Ex 16:3. 27:3.

over Edom. Ge +25:23.

cast. Ps 2:3. 50:17. 51:11. 71:9.

shoe. Ps 108:9. Ge 14:23. Ex 3:5. Jsh 10:24. Ru 4:7. Mt 10:14. Lk 10:11. Jn 1:27. 3:30. Ac 13:51.

triumph. *or*, triumph thou over me (by an irony). Ps 108:9, 10. Ex 8:9mg. 2 S 5:17. 8:1. 21:15-22.

9 **Who**. Jg 1:12, 24, 25. 1 Ch 11:6, 17-19.

strong city. Heb. city of strength. 2 S 11:1. 12:26, etc. Is +37:25mg.

10 **Wilt**. Ps 20:7. 44:5-9. 118:9, 10. Is 8:17. 12:1, 2.

hadst. ver. +1.

didst. Dt 1:42. 20:4. Jsh 7:12. 10:42. 1 S 4:6, 7, 10, 11. 1 Ch 10:1, etc.

11 **Give us help**. Ps 25:22. 30:8-10. 40:17. 44:23-26. 54:1-3. 59:2-4. 61:2. 69:1-3. 70:1, 2. 77:1, 2. 81:7. 86:6, 7. 88:1-3. 102:1, 2. 109:21-26. 130:8. Ge 4:13, 14. 19:18-22. 28:20-22. 32:9-12. Ex 17:3, 4. 2 Ch 20:3, 4. Ne 2:2-4. 9:27. Is 33:2. 41:10. Je 17:17, 18. 26:19. La 2:18, 19. 5:1, 2, 4-6. Jl 1:19, 20. Hab 3:2. Ja +5:4.

from trouble. Ps 46:1.

vain. Ps 108:12. 118:8, 9. 124:1-3. 127:1. 146:3. 2 K 6:27. Is 2:22. 30:7. 31:3. Je 17:5. La 4:17.

help. Heb. salvation. Ps 62:1. 146:3mg.

12 **Through God**. Ro 8:37. 1 C 15:57. Ep 6:10. Ph 4:13.

we shall. Ps 18:32-42. 144:1. Nu 24:18, 19. Jsh 1:9. 14:12. 2 S 10:12. 1 Ch 19:13.

tread. Ps 44:5. Is 10:6. 63:3. Zc 10:5. Ml 4:3. 1 C 15:25. Re 19:15.

PSALM 61

(Title.) **Neginah**. i.e. *a harp song*, **S#5058h**. Instead of *neginath*, many MSS. have *neginoth*; and two MSS. supply *mizmor*, a Psalm. Some suppose this Psalm was composed when David was driven by Absalom's rebellion beyond Jordan, and from the sanctuary of God. Ps 4, 6, 54, 55, 67, titles. 69:12 (song). 76, title. 77:6 (song). Is 38:20. La 3:14. 5:14. Hab 3:19mg.

1 **Hear**. Ps 5:1-3. 17:1. 28:2. 55:1, 2. 130:2. Ph 4:6.
2 **From the end**. Ps 42:6. 139:9, 10. Dt 4:27, 29. Jon 2:2-4.
   when my heart. Ps 43:5. 55:5. 77:3. 142:3. 143:4. Is 54:11. Mk 14:33, 34. Lk 22:44.
   overwhelmed. Ps +77:3. Ge 30:42 (feeble). La 2:19.
   the rock. Ps 18:46. 27:5. 40:2. 62:2, 6. 2 S 15:14, 17. Is 32:2.
3 **thou**. Ps 4:6, 7. 116:2. 140:7. 1 S 17:37. Is 46:3, 4. 2 C 1:10.
   strong. Ps 18:2. Pr 18:10.
   tower. 2 S 22:51. Pr 18:10.
4 **abide**. ver. 7. Ps 15:1. 23:6. 27:4. 90:1. 91:1. 92:13. Re 3:12.
   for ever. Heb. *olam* plural, **S#5769h**. Rendered (1) *for ever*: Ps 61:4. 77:7. 1 K 8:13. 2 Ch 6:2; (2) *everlasting*: Ps 145:13. Is 26:4. 45:17a. Da 9:24; (3) *of ancient times* or *old time*: Ps 77:5. Ec 1:10; (4) *of old*: Is 51:9.
   trust. *or*, make my refuge. Ps 62:7. 142:4, 5. He 6:18.
   wings. Ps +91:4.
   Selah. Ps +9:16.
5 **hast heard**. Ps 56:12. 65:1. 66:19.
   vows. Le +23:38.
   heritage. Ps 16:5, 6. 115:13. 119:111. Is 54:17. Ml 3:16-18. Ac 10:35.
6 **wilt prolong the king's life**. Heb. shalt add days to the days of the king. Ps 21:4, 6. 72:15-17. 2 S 7:16. Is 53:10.
   many generations. Heb. generation and generation. Ps +33:11mg. 89:36, 37.
7 **abide**. Ps 41:12. Is 9:6, 7. Lk 1:32, 33. He 7:21-25. 9:24.
   for ever. Heb. *olam*, Ex +12:24.
   prepare. Ps 40:11. 43:3. 57:3. 85:10. Ge 24:27. 32:10. Pr 20:28. Mi 7:20. Lk 1:54, 55. Jn 1:17. 2 C 1:20.
8 **sing**. Ps 30:12. 79:13. 145:1, 2. 146:2.
   for ever. Ps +9:18.
   vows. Le +23:38.

PSALM 62

(*Title*.) **Jeduthun**. Ps 39, 77, titles. 1 Ch +9:16.
1 **Truly**. *or*, Only. ver. 2, 5, 6, 9.
   my soul. Heb. *nephesh*, Ge +34:3. Ps +25:3. Ja 5:7.
   waiteth. Heb. is silent. Ps +37:7mg. 65:1mg. 131:2.
   from. Ps 37:39. 68:19, 20. 121:2. Is 12:2. Je 3:23. Lk 2:30-32.
2 **He only**. ver. 6. Ps 18:2. 21:1. 27:1. 73:25, 26. Dt 32:30, 31. Is 26:4. 32:2.
   defence. Heb. high place. Ps +9:9mg.
   I shall. Ps +37:24. Mi 7:8, 9. 1 C 10:13. 2 C 4:8, 9.

3 **How**. Mt +17:17.
   imagine. Ps 21:11. 38:12. 140:2. Ho 7:15.
   ye shall. Ps 73:18-20. 1 S 26:10.
   bowing. Is 30:13, 14.
4 **consult**. Ps 2:1-3. Mt 2:3, 4, 16. 22:15, 23, 34, 35. 26:3, 4. 27:1. Jn 11:47-50. Ac 4:16, 17, 25-28.
   delight. Ho 7:3. Ro 1:32. Ep +4:25.
   bless. Ps 28:3. 55:21. Lk 20:20, 21.
   inwardly. Heb. in their inward parts. Ps 5:9. 51:6. Lk 11:39. Ro 7:22.
   Selah. Ps +9:16.
5 **soul**. Heb. *nephesh*, Ge +34:3. Ps 42:5, 11. 43:5. 103:1, 2. 104:1, 35. 146:1.
   wait. ver. 1, 2. Ps +25:3. Lk 11:6. Jn 6:67-69.
   my. Ps 39:7. 71:5. 81:10. Je 17:17. Ml 3:10. Ph 1:20.
6 **rock**. ver. 2. Ps 18:31, 32. Is 45:17. Ho 1:7.
   I shall. Ps 16:8. 112:6. Pr 10:30. 12:7.
7 **In God**. Is 45:25. Je 3:23. 9:23, 24. 1 C 1:30, 31. Ga 6:14.
   glory. Ps 3:3. 4:2.
   rock. Ps 18:2, 31, 32, 46. 94:22. 95:1. Is 26:4.
8 **Trust**. Ps 22:4, 5. 34:1, 2. 46:1-3. Jb 13:15. Is 26:4. 50:10. 1 J 2:28.
   pour out. Ps 42:4. 102, title. 142:2. 1 S 1:15. 1 K 10:2. Is 26:16. La 2:19. Jon 3:8. Ph 4:6. Ja +5:16.
   God. Ps +9:9. Pr 14:26.
   Selah. Ps +9:16.
9 **Surely**. Ps 39:5, 11. 1 S 18:5-7. 23:12, 19, 20. 2 S 15:6. Mt 21:9. Jn 19:15.
   of high. Ps 55:13, 14. 118:8, 9. 1 S 18:21-26. 26:21-25. 2 S 15:31. Ro 3:4.
   laid. Da 5:27.
   altogether. *or*, alike.
   lighter. Is 40:15, 17.
   vanity. Ps 31:6. 39:5, 6, 11. 78:33.
10 **Trust not**. Jb 20:19-29. Is 28:15. 30:12. 47:10. 59:4. Je 13:25. 17:11.
   in oppression. Ps +12:5. Dt +24:14. Ezk +16:49.
   riches. Ps 39:6. 49:6, 7, 16, 17. 52:7. Dt 6:10-12. 8:12-14. Jb 27:16, etc. 31:24, 25. Pr 11:4, 28. 28:22. Mk 8:36, 37. 10:23, 24. Lk 12:15-21. 2 C 8:9. 9:8. 1 T +6:9, 10, 17. Re 3:17.
   set not. Ps 91:14. Pr 23:5. Mt 6:19-21. Col 3:2. 1 T +6:9.
11 **spoken once**. Jb 33:14. 40:5.
   power. *or*, strength. Ps 24:8. 68:34, 35. 89:8. Ge 17:1. 18:14. 49:24. Dt 3:24. Is 26:4. 63:1. Da 2:20. Zp 3:17. Mt 6:13. 28:18, 19. Mk 10:27. Jn 19:11. 1 C 10:22. Ep 3:20, 21. 1 P 5:6. Re 18:8. 19:1, 6.
12 **Lord**. Ps +24:10.
   mercy. Ex +34:6, 7.
   thou renderest. Ezk 7:27. 18:30. 33:20. Mt +16:27. 1 C 3:8. Ep 6:8. Col 3:25.
   his work. Ec 9:5. Mk 13:34.

PSALM 63

(Title.) A.M. 2913. B.C. 1061.
when. 1 S 22:5. 23:14-16, 23-25. 26:1-3. 2 S 15:28.

1 **thou.** Ps 31:14. 42:11. 91:2. 118:28. 143:10. Ex 15:2. Je 31:1, 33. Zc 13:9. Jn 20:17.
early. Ps 5:3. 78:34. Jb 8:5. Pr 1:27, 28. 8:17. SS 3:1-3. Ho 5:15. Mk +1:35.
seek thee. Ps 27:8. Dt 33:27. Mt 6:33.
my soul. Heb. *nephesh,* Ge +34:3. Ps 42:6. 43:5. 88:3. Jb +14:22.
thirsteth. Ps 42:1, 2. 68:9. 84:2. 107:4-6. 119:81. 143:6. Ex 15:23-25. 17:2-7. Nu 20:1-11. Jg 15:16-19. Jn 7:37. Re 7:16, 17.
flesh. Ps 102:3-5. SS 5:8.
dry and thirsty land, where no water is. Heb. weary land without water. Ex 17:3. Is 32:2. 35:7. 41:18. Mt 12:43.

2 **To see.** Ps 27:4. 78:61. 105:4. 145:11. Ex 33:18, 19. 1 S 4:21, 22. 1 Ch 16:11. 2 C 4:4-6.
thy glory. Ps 90:16, 17. Ex 33:13-18.
in the. Ps 68:24. 73:17, 18. 77:13, 14. 84:2-11. 96:6. 134:2. Is 60:13.

3 **Because.** Ps 4:6. 21:6. 30:5. Ph 1:23. 1 J 3:2.
lips. Ps 30:12. 51:15. 66:17. Ho 14:2. Ro 6:19. 12:1. 1 C 6:20. He 13:15. Ja 3:5-10.
shall praise thee. Ps 27:6. 30:12. 40:16. 54:6. 56:12. 61:8. 65:1. 69:34. 70:4. 86:12. 119:7. Is 12:1. Ac 16:25. Re 4:8-11. 5:11-14. 7:11, 12. 15:3, 4. 19:5.

4 **Thus.** Ps 104:33. 145:1-3. 146:1, 2.
I will lift. Ps +88:9.

5 **My soul.** Heb. *nephesh,* Ge +34:3. Ps 104:34. SS 1:4. Mt +5:6.
marrow. Heb. fatness. or, milk. Ps 17:10. 73:7.
and fatness. Ps 36:8. 65:11. Jg 9:9.
with joyful. Ps 4:7. 43:4. 71:23. 118:14, 15. 135:3. 149:1-3. Ezr 3:11-13. Re 19:5-7.

6 **I remember.** Ps 42:8. 77:4-6. 119:55, 147, 148. 139:17, 18. 149:5. SS 3:1, 2. 5:2. La 2:19.
my bed. Ps +4:4.
meditate. Jb 35:10.
the night watches. Ps 42:8. +119:55.

7 **Because.** Ps 54:3, 4.
therefore. Ps 5:11. 21:1. 1 S 17:37. 2 C 1:10.
wings. Ps +91:4.

8 **My soul,** etc. Heb. *nephesh,* Ge +34:3.
followeth. Ps 73:25. 143:6, 7. Ge 32:26-28. 2 Ch 31:21. SS 3:2. Is 26:9. Mt 11:12. Lk 13:24. 18:5-7.
thy. Ps 37:24. 94:18. Is 42:1. Ph 2:12, 13. Col 1:29.
right hand. Ps +18:35.

9 **seek.** Ps 35:4, 26. 38:12. 40:14. 70:2. 1 S 25:29.
to destroy. Ps 35:8. 33, 14 (desolation).
soul. Heb. *nephesh,* Ge +12:13.
go. Ps +9:17. 55:15, 23. 86:13. 88:6. 139:15. Nu 16:30-33. 1 S 28:19. Jb 40:13. Is 14:9, 15, 19. Ezk 32:18-32. Ac 1:25.

10 **They shall fall,** etc. Heb. They shall make him run out, like water, by the hands of the sword. Ps 77:2mg. 1 S 26:10. 31:1-6. 1 K +16:12mg. Jb 5:20mg. Je 18:21mg. Ezk 35:5mg.
a portion. SS 2:15. Ezk 39:4, 17-20. Re 19:17, 18.

11 **the king.** Ps +21:1. 1 S +24:20.
sweareth. Ge +21:23.
the mouth. Ps +107:42.

PSALM 64

1 A.M. 2943. B.C. 1061.
Hear. Ps +5:1. 27:7. 143:1-3. La 3:55, 56.
preserve. Ps 17:8, 9. 31:13-15. 34:4. 56:2-4. Ac 18:9, 10. 27:24.

2 **Hide me.** i.e. protect. Ps 17:8. 27:5. +31:20. 32:7. 61:3, 4. 83:3. +91:1. 143:9. Is 26:20. 32:2. Je 36:26.
secret. Ps 56:6. 109:2, 3. Ge 4:6. 1 S 23:22, 23. 2 S 17:2-4. Je 11:19. 18:23. Mt 26:3, 4. Ac 23:14, 15. 25:3.
insurrection. Ps 2:2. 3:1. Lk 23:18-23.

3 **whet.** Ps 57:4. Pr 12:18. 30:14. Is 54:17. Je 9:3. Ja 3:6-8.
bend. Ps 11:2. 58:7.
bitter words. Is 28:15.

4 **shoot.** Ps 10:8, 9. 11:2. Ne 4:11. Hab 3:14.
the perfect. Ps 59:3, 4. Jn 19:6. 1 P 2:22, 23.
suddenly. ver. 7. 1 S 18:11. 19:10. 2 S 15:14.

5 **encourage.** Ex 15:9. Nu 22:6. Pr 1:11-14. Is 28:15. 41:6. Re 11:10.
matter. *or,* speech. ver. 3. Ps 45:1. Pr +22:12mg. Ge 11:1.
commune. 1 S 23:19-23. Mt 23:15. 26:3, 4.
of laying snares. Heb. to hide snares. Ps +141:9.
Who. Ps +10:11. 59:7. 94:7.

6 **search.** Ps 35:11. 1 S 22:9-13. 24:9. 25:10. Da 6:4, 5. Mt 26:59-66. Jn 18:29, 30. 19:7.
they accomplish, etc. *or,* we are consumed by that which they have throughly searched.
a diligent search. Heb. a search searched. Ge +1:29.
both. Ps 5:9. Pr 20:5. Is 29:15. Je 17:9, 10. 1 C 4:5.

7 **shoot.** ver. 4.
arrow. Dt +32:23.
suddenly. ver. 4. Ps 73:19. Pr 6:15. 29:1. Is 30:13. Mt 24:40, 50, 51. 1 Th 5:2, 3.
shall they be wounded. Heb. their wound shall be. 1 K 22:34. 1 Ch 10:3-7.

8 **tongue.** Ps 59:12. 94:23. 140:9. Jb 15:6. Pr 12:13. 18:7. Mt 21:41. 27:25. Lk 19:22. 21:23, 24.
all that. Ps 31:11. 52:6. Nu 16:34. 1 S 31:3-7. Na 3:7. Re 18:4, 10.

9 **fear.** Ps 40:3. 53:5. 119:120. Je 50:28. 51:10. Re 11:13.

they. Ps 58:11. 107:42, 43. Is 5:12. Ezk 14:23. Ho 14:9. Ro +15:4. 1 C 10:11.

10 righteous. Ps 32:11. 33:1. 40:3. +58:10. Ph 4:4.

upright. Ps 97:11. 112:2. 1 C 1:30, 31. Ga 6:14.

PSALM 65

1 Praise. Ps 21:13. 115:1, 2.

waiteth. Heb. is silent. Ps +37:7mg. 62:1mg. Lk 2:25.

in Sion. S#6726h, elsewhere rendered Zion, 2 S +5:7. Ps 76:2. 78:68, 69. 1 Ch 11:7. 15:29. 16:41, 42. 25:1, etc. Re 14:1-3.

vow. Le +23:38.

2 thou. Ps 66:19. 1 K 18:29, 37. 2 Ch 33:13. Da 9:17-19. Lk 11:9, 10. +18:1. Ac 10:31. 1 J +5:14, 15.

unto thee. Ps 22:27. 66:4. 86:9. Is 49:6. 66:23. Jn 12:32. He 4:16. Re 11:15.

all flesh. Ps 2:8. 72:11. 86:9. Is 45:22, 23. 62:2. 66:23. Zp 3:8-10. Ml 1:11. Ro 14:11. Ph 2:10, 11. Re 5:13. 15:4.

3 Iniquities. Heb. Words. or Matters, of iniquities. Ps 35:20mg. +64:5mg. 105:27mg. 145:5mg.

prevail. Ps 38:4. 40:12. 2 S 12:7-13. Je 5:25. Mi 7:8, 9. Ro 7:23-25. Ga 5:17.

transgressions. Ps 51:2, 3, 7. 79:9. Is 1:18, 19. 6:7. Zc 13:1. Jn 1:29. He 9:14. 1 J 1:7-9. Re 1:5.

4 Blessed. Ps +1:1. Ep 1:3, 4.

choosest. Ps 4:3. 78:70, 71. 135:4. Dt +10:15. Jn 15:16. 1 P 2:4, 5.

causest. Ps 15:1. 23:6. 24:7. Jn 6:44, 65. 15:16. Re 3:12.

we shall be satisfied. Ps 84:4, 10, 11. 89:15, 16. 92:13. SS 2:3. Is 12:3. 48:17. 60:7. Mt +5:6. 18:20. Jn 3:20. Re 21:3, 4.

5 terrible. Ps 45:4. 76:3-9. +99:3. Dt 4:34. Is 37:36.

righteousness. Ps 145:17. Ro 2:5. 1 P 4:17, 18. Re 15:3, 4. 16:5. 19:1-3.

answer. Je 33:3.

O God. Ps +88:1.

the confidence. Is 45:22. Mt 28:19, 20. Ro 15:10-12.

all. Ps 22:27.

afar. Is 51:5. 60:5. 66:19. Zp 2:11. Zc 9:10. Ac 28:28. Ro 15:12. Ep 2:17, 18.

6 Which. Ps 24:2. 119:90. Mi 6:2. Hab 3:6.

girded. Ps 93:1. 1 S 2:4. Is 51:9.

7 Which stilleth. Ps 89:9. 107:29. Ge 8:1, 2. Jon 1:4, 15. Mt 8:26, 27. Mk 4:41.

of the seas. Ps 93:3, 4. Da 7:2. Hab 3:8. Re 13:1. 21:1.

noise of their. Ps 93:3, 4. 104:6-9. Jb 38:8-11.

tumult. Ps 2:1-4. 76:10. Is 17:12, 13. Jn 18:6.

8 in the. Ps 2:8.

afraid. Ps 48:5, 6. 66:3. 126:2. 135:9. Ex 15:14-16. Jsh 2:9-11. Hab 3:3, etc. Ac 5:38, 39. Re 11:13.

outgoings. Ps 19:5. 74:16. 104:20-23. 136:8. Ge 8:22. Dt 4:19. Jb 38:12.

the morning. Ge 1:5.

rejoice. or, sing. ver. 13. Ps 32:11. 81:1. 148:3. Jb 29:13.

9 visitest. Ps 104:13, 14. Dt 11:11, 12. Ru 1:6. Jb 37:6-13. Je 14:22. Ac 14:17.

and waterest it. or, after thou hadst made it to desire rain. Ps 63:1.

greatly. ver. 11. Ps 68:9, 10. 104:13-15. 147:8, 9. Jb 5:10, 11. Je 5:24. Jl 2:23-26.

the river. Ps 46:4. Dt 33:28. Re 22:1.

is full. Ps 104:16. Dt 33:28. Jn 7:37-39. Ac 2:16, 17. 14:17.

thou preparest. Ps 104:15. 107:37. Ge 26:12. 1 T 6:17, 18.

10 waterest. Ps 36:8mg. Pr 5:19mg. 7:18.

ridges. Jb 31:38. 39:10. Ho 10:4. 12:11.

settle the furrows thereof. or, causest rain to descend into the furrows thereof.

settlest. or, to go down. Jb 21:13. Jl 3:11.

furrows. Je 48:37.

makest it soft. Heb. dissolvest it. Ps 46:6. 75:3. Jb 30:22.

with showers. Ps 72:6. Dt 32:2. Je 3:3. 14:22. Mi 5:7.

blessest. Ps 85:12. 147:8. 1 C 3:6, 7. 2 C 9:10.

springing. Ge 19:24. Is 4:2.

11 crownest. Ps 5:12mg. 103:4. Pr 14:18. He 2:7-9.

with thy. Heb. of thy.

thy paths. Ps 25:10. 104:3. 147:8. Jl 2:14, 21-26. Hg 2:19. Ml 3:10.

fatness. Ps 36:8. Ro 11:17.

12 drop. Ps 104:10-13. Jb 38:26, 27.

rejoice. Heb. are girded with joy. ver. 6. Is 55:9-13. 61:10, 11.

13 pastures. Ps 104:24-28. Zc 9:17. Ac 14:17.

they shout. Ps 96:11-13. 98:7-9. Is 35:1, 2, 10. 52:9. 55:12. Je 48:33.

PSALM 66

1 A.M. 3469. B.C. 535.

Make. Ps 81:1. 95:1, 2. 98:4. 100:1. 1 Ch 15:28.

all ye lands. Heb. all the earth. Ps 96:1. 117:1, 2. 150:6. Ge 6:11. 1 Ch 16:23, 24. Is 24:16.

2 Sing forth. Ps 47:6, 7. 72:18. 96:3-10. 105:2, 3. 106:2. 107:15, 22. 1 Ch 29:10-13. Ne 9:5. Is 6:3. 12:4-6. 49:13. Re 4:8-11. 5:13.

his name. Ac 15:14, 17.

3 How terrible. ver. 5. Ps +99:3. Ex 15:1-16, 21. Jg 5:2-4, 20-22. Is 2:19. Je 10:10.

through. Ps 18:44. 22:28, 29. 68:30. 81:15.

submit themselves. *or*, yield feigned obedience. Heb. lie. Ps 17:1mg. 18:44mg. 78:35, 36. 81:15mg. Dt +33:29mg. 2 S 22:45mg. Je 3:10mg. 27:15mg. 29:9mg.

4 **All**. Ps +86:9. 96:1, 2. 117:1. Is +42:10-12. 49:22, 23. Da 7:14. Ml 1:11. Re 5:13. 7:9.

5 **Come**. ver. 16. Ps 46:8. 111:2, 3. 126:1-3. Nu 23:23.
terrible. ver. +3. Ezk 1:18.

6 **He turned**. Ex +14:21.
they. Jsh 3:14, 16.
there. Ps 106:11, 12. Ex 15:1, etc. Re 15:2, 3.

7 **ruleth**. Ps 62:11. Da 4:35. 6:26, 27. Mt 6:13. 28:18.
for ever. Heb. *olam*, Ex +12:24.
his eyes. Ps +11:4.
let. Ps 2:10-12. 52:1-5. 68:18. 73:3-12. 75:4, 5. Ex 18:11. Jb 9:4. Is 10:7-16. 37:28, 29. Da 5:20-28.
Selah. Ps +9:16.

8 **O bless**. Dt 32:43. Ro 15:10, 11.
make. ver. 2. Ps 47:1. Je 33:11. Re 5:11-14. 19:1, 5, 6.

9 **holdeth**. Heb. putteth. Ps 22:29. 104:3. 1 S 25:29. Ac 17:28. Col 3:3, 4.
soul. Heb. *nephesh*, Ge +12:13.
in life. Ps 7:5. 16:11. 17:14. 18:46. Col 3:3.
suffereth. Ps 37:23, 24. 62:2, 6. 94:18. 112:6. 121:3. 125:3. Nu 23:9. 1 S 2:9. Je 30:11.

10 **hast proved us**. Ps +17:3. Dt 4:20. 13:3.
tried. 1 P +1:7.
as silver. Is 1:25. Ezk 22:19. Zc 13:9.

11 **broughtest**. Jb 19:6. La 1:13. 3:2, etc. Ho 7:12. Mt 6:13.
upon. Dt 33:11.

12 **caused**. Ps 129:1-3. Is 51:23.
heads. Jg +5:30.
through fire. Da 3:27.
water. Ex 14:22, 29. Is 43:1, 2. Ac 14:22. 1 Th 3:3, 4.
but thou. Ps 33:19. 40:2, 3. Jb 36:16. Lk 16:25. Ja 5:11. Re 7:14, etc.
wealthy. Heb. moist. Ps 23:5. 107:35-37. Is 35:6, 7.

13 **go into**. Ps 51:18, 19. 100:4. 116:17. 118:19, 27. Dt 12:11, 12. He 13:15.
burnt offerings. Le +23:12.
vows. Ps 116:14. Le +23:38.

14 **uttered**. Heb. opened. S#6475h. Ps 22:13mg. 144:7 (rid), 10, 11. Jg 11:35, 36.
mouth. Nu 30:2, 8, 12.
when. Ge 28:20-22. 35:3. 1 S 1:11. 2 S 22:7.

15 **will offer**. Le +23:12.
fatlings. Heb. marrow. Is 5:17.
with the. Je 41:5.
I will offer. 2 S 6:13, 17-19. 1 Ch 16:1-3.
Selah. Ps +9:16.

16 **Come**. ver. 5. Ps 34:2, 11. 71:18. Ml 3:16. 1 T 1:15, 16. 1 J 1:3.

and I will declare. Ps 22:23, 24. 32:5, 6. 34:8. 40:9, 10. 71:20. 89:9. 107:29-31. 2 S 1:27. 2:1. Is 49:23. Da 2:23. 6:20, 23. Mk 7:36, 37. Jn 11:40. 1 C 15:8-10.
soul. Heb. *nephesh*, Ge +12:13.

17 **I cried**. Ps +3:4. 34:3, 4, 6.
he was. Ps 30:1. 145:1.

18 **If I regard iniquity**. Ps 5:5. 6:8. 7:14. 10:7mg. Ge 35:2, 3. Jg 10:15, 16. 1 S 7:4-6. Jb 11:13-15. 22:23. 27:8, 9. Pr 15:8, 29. 21:13. 28:9. Is 1:15-17. 55:6, 7. Jn +9:31. 2 T 2:19. Ja 4:3, 8-10.
my heart. Ps 4:7. 7:9, 10. 9:1. 10:6, 11. 1 S 16:7. 1 K 15:14. Re 2:23.
the Lord. Ps 2:4. 16:2. 22:30. 35:17.
not hear. Ps +4:3. 18:41. 38:13. 50:16, 17. Ge +16:11. Jb 27:9. 35:12, 13. Pr 1:28, 29. 15:8, 29. 21:13. 28:9. Is 1:11-15. 59:1, 2. Je 11:11. 14:10, 12. Ezk 8:18. 14:3. Mi 3:4. Zc 7:13. Mt 7:18. Lk 13:25. 18:14. Jn +9:31. He 11:6. Ja 1:6, 7. 4:3. 1 J 5:14.

19 **verily God hath**. Ps 6:9. 34:6. 116:1, 2. La 3:55, 56. He 5:7. 1 J 3:20-22.

20 **hath not turned**. Ps 22:24. 51:11. 86:12, 13. 2 S 7:14, 15.

PSALM 67

(Title.) A.M. cir. 3464. B.C. cir. 540.
Neginoth. Ps 4, 6, 76, titles.

1 **God**. Nu 6:24-27. Dt 21:8. 2 C 13:14.
bless us. Ps 28:9. 109:28. Ge 32:24-26. Dt 26:13-15. 1 Ch 4:10. Ep 1:3.
cause. Ps 4:6. 31:16. 80:1-3, 7, 19. 119:135. Ml 4:2. 2 C 4:6.
face to shine. Ps 34:5. Ex 34:29. Nu 6:25. 2 C 3:18.
upon us. Heb. with us.
Selah. Ps +9:16.

2 **That**. Ps 98:2, 3. Est 8:15-17. Zc 8:20-23. Ac 9:31.
thy way. Lk 3:3. Ac 13:10. 18:25. 22:4.
saving. Ps 43:5. 66:1-4. 117:2. Is 49:6. Mt 28:19. Mk 16:15. Lk 2:30, 31. 3:6. T 2:11.

3 **Let**. ver. 5. Ps 45:17. 66:4. 74:21. 119:175. 142:7. Is 38:18, 19.

4 **O let**. Ps 97:1. 138:4, 5. Dt 32:43. Is 24:14-16. 42:10-12. 54:1. Ro 15:10, 11. Ga 4:27.
for thou. Ps +7:8.
govern. Heb. lead. Ps 2:8. 82:6. Is 55:4. Re 11:15-17.
Selah. Ps +9:16.

5 **Let the people**. ver. 3. Mt 6:9, 10.

6 **Then**. Ps 85:9-12. Le 26:3, 4. Is 1:19. 30:23, 24. Ezk 34:26, 27. Ho 2:21, 22. 1 C 3:6-9.
our own. Ps 48:14. Ge 17:7. Ex 3:15. Je 31:1, 33. Ezk 34:24.

7 **God**. Ps 29:11. 72:17. Ge 12:2, 3. Ac 2:28. Ga 3:9, 14.
all the. Ps +89:6. 98:3. Is 45:22. 52:10. Mi

5:4. Zc 9:10. Ml 1:11. Ac 13:47.

fear. Ml 4:2. Ac 13:26.

PSALM 68

(*Title*.) A.M. 2962. B.C. 1042. This magnificent and truly sublime ode is supposed, with much probability, to have been composed by David, and sung at the removal of the ark from Kirjath-jearim. 2 S 6:12.

1 **God arise**. Ps +3:7. Is 42:13, 14.

be scattered. ver. 14, 30. Ps 59:11. 89:10. Is 33:3. 41:15, 16. Ezk 5:2. 12:14, 15. Da 2:35.

that hate. Ps 21:8. Ex 20:5. Dt 7:10. Jn 14:23, 24.

before him. Heb. from his face.

2 **As smoke**. Ps 37:20. Is 9:18. Ho 13:3.

as wax melteth. Ex +15:15. 2 P +3:10.

in the presence. Ps 76:7. 80:16. Na 1:5, 6. 2 Th 1:8, 9. Re 6:16, 17.

3 **But**. Ps +58:10.

rejoice. Ps 95:1, 2. 98:8, 9. Dt +12:7. Is 65:14. Jn 15:11. Re 5:11.

exceedingly rejoice. Heb. rejoice with gladness. Ps 21:1. 43:4. 1 P 1:8.

4 **Sing unto God**. Ps 34:1. 50:23. 66:4. 67:4. Is 12:4-6.

rideth. ver. 33. Dt +33:26.

his name. Ex +6:3.

JAH. S#3050h, Ex +15:2. Ps 115:17, 18. Is 12:2. JAH is an abbreviation of JEHOVAH, and signifies self-existence: He who derives his being from none, but gives being to all.

5 **A father**. Ex +22:22.

a judge. Ps 72:2, 4. Is +1:17. Ep 5:1.

in his. Ps 33:14. 2 Ch 6:2. 30:27mg. Is 57:15. 66:1. Ac 7:48, 49.

habitation. Dt +26:15. Zc 2:13mg. Jn 14:10. 2 C 5:19.

6 **God**. Ps 107:10, 41. 113:9. 1 S 2:5. Ga 4:27.

solitary. Ps 22:20mg. 25:16. 35:17mg.

families. Heb. a house. ver. 12 (home). 23:6. +113:9. Ge 6:14 (within). 7:1 (house). 12:1, 15, 17. 14:14. 15:2, 3. 17:12.

he bringeth. Ps +146:7.

the rebellious. ver. 18. Ps 66:7. 78:8. 107:34, 40. Dt 28:23, 24. Ho 2:3. Ml 1:3. Mt 23:37, 38. Ep 2:12.

dry. Ps 107:33, 34. Dt 8:14, 15.

7 **O God**. Ps 114:1, etc. Ex 13:21. Dt 4:34. Jg 4:14. Hab 3:3.

thou didst march. Dt +33:2. Jg 5:4. Is 16:1-5. 63:1-4. Mi 2:13. Hab 3:12.

the wilderness. Je +31:2.

8 **earth**. Ps 77:18. 114:7. Is 64:1, 3. Hab 3:13. He +12:26. Re 11:19.

the heavens. Jg 5:4, 5.

Sinai. Ex 19:16, 18. Dt 5:23-25.

the God. ver. 35. Ps 41:13. Is 45:3.

9 **didst**. Ps 65:9, etc. Ps 77:16, 17. 78:24-27. Dt 11:10-12, 14. Ezk 34:26.

send. Heb. shake out. Ex 20:25. 29:24mg. Le 23:11. 2 K 5:11mg. Pr 7:17. Is 10:15, 32. 11:15. 13:2.

plentiful rain. Ps 63:1. Ac 2:1-18.

confirm thine inheritance. Heb. confirm it. Ps 8:3 (ordain). 9:7 (prepared). 11:2 (made ready). 40:2 (established). 99:4. 119:90. 2 S 9:5-7.

10 **Thy congregation**. Ps 74:1, 2, 19. Ex 19:5, 6. Nu 16:3. 1 P 5:3.

thou. Dt 26:5, 9, 10. 32:8-14. 1 S 2:8. Jb 5:10, 11. Is 52:7. Mt 11:5. Lk 1:53.

11 **Lord**. Ps 40:3. Ex 14:15. 17:9, etc. Jg 4:6, etc. Ep 4:11.

great was. Is +66:19. Re 7:3, 4.

company. Heb. army. ver. 25. Ex 15:20, 21. Jg 5:1, etc. Is +27:6. Re 7:3, 9, 14. 19:13, 14.

that published. Is +27:6. 52:7. Mi 4:2. Na 1:15. Mt +24:14.

12 **Kings**. Ex 14:25. Nu 31:8, 9, 54. Jsh 10:16, 42. 12:7, 8. Jg 5:19. 11:34. 1 S 18:6. Re 6:2, 15, 16. 19:17-20.

did flee apace. Heb. did flee, did flee.

she. Nu 31:27. 1 S 30:24.

13 **Though ye have**. Ps 81:6. Ex 1:14. 1 C 6:9-11. 12:2. 15:49. Ep 2:1-3. T 3:3.

the wings. Ps 74:19. 105:37. 149:4. 1 K 4:20, 21. Ezk 16:6-14. Lk 15:16, 22. Ep 5:26, 27. Re 1:5, 6.

gold. Dt 7:6. 1 K 10:14, 27.

14 **When**. Nu 21:3, 21, etc. Jsh 10:10, etc. ch. 12. 24:31. Re 19:14-21.

Almighty. Ge +49:25.

in it, it was. or, for her, she was. Jg 2:7. Je 2:3.

as snow. Ps 51:7. Is 1:18.

15 **hill of God**. Ps 2:6. 78:68, 69. 87:1, 2. Is 2:2, 3. Zc 14:10.

of Bashan. Dt +32:14.

16 **Why**. Ps 114:4, 6. Is 2:2.

the hill. Ps 132:13, 14. Dt 12:5, 11. 1 K 9:3. He 12:22, 23. Re 21:2, 3.

for ever. Jb +4:20 (S#5331h).

17 **chariots**. Ps 18:10. 104:3. 2 K 2:11. 6:16, 17. 1 Ch 28:18. Is 19:1. Ezk 1:15, etc. Hab 3:8.

thousands. or, many thousands. Ne 7:71. Da 7:10. He 12:22. Re 5:11. 9:16.

of angels. Mt +13:41. 26:53. Re 5:11.

among them. Dt +7:21. Is +59:20. Zc 9:14. 12:8. Jn 1:14. +14:2, 3. 1 J 3:2.

as in Sinai. Ex 3:2-5. 19:22, 23. 24:15, 16. +33:2.

in the holy place. Ex 25:20-22. 40:34-38. Le 16:2. 1 Ch 28:18.

18 **Thou hast**. Ep 4:8.

ascended. Ps 24:3, 7-10. 47:5. 110:1. Mk

16:19. Lk 24:51. Ac 1:2-9. Ep 4:8-10. Col
2:15. He 4:14. 6:20. 8:1. 1 P 3:22.
led. Jg 5:12.
captivity. i.e. captives. Is 49:24. Je 29:14.
received. 2 S 6:12. 1 Ch 29:16. Lk 24:49. Jn
1:16. 3:34, 35. 14:16, 17. 16:7, 13-15. Ac 1:4.
2:4, 33-38. Ep 4:8.
for men. Heb. in the man. 1 C 15:45-47. Col
1:18, 19. 2:3, 9. He 1:3.
yea. Ps 145:9. Lk +6:35.
rebellious. Dt 9:7. Pr 1:22, 23. Is 55:7. Mt
9:13. Lk 24:47. Ac 2:23, 36, 38-41. 9:17. 1 C
6:9-11. 1 T 1:13-15. T 3:3-7.
that. Ps 78:60. 2 Ch 6:18. Ezk 48:35. Jn
14:17, 23. Re 1:20. 2:1.
dwell among. Ps 135:21. Ex +29:45.
19 **Blessed**. Ps 72:17-19. 103:1, etc. Ep 1:3.
daily. or, day by day. Ps 32:7. 61:8. 139:17,
18. Ex 16:5. Pr 8:30, 34. La 3:23. 1 T +4:8.
loadeth us. or, beareth our burdens. Ps 37:5.
55:22. 81:6. Nu 11:11, 12. Is 46:3, 4. 1 P 5:7.
with benefits. Ps 103:1, 2.
God. Ps +88:1.
Selah. Ps +9:16.
20 **our God**. Is 12:2. 45:17-22. Ho 1:7. 2:23. Jn
4:22.
unto. Ps 118:17, 18. Dt 32:39. 1 S 2:6. Jn
5:21, 23, 28, 29. 11:25, 26. He 2:14, 15. Re
1:18. 20:1.
issues. Pr 4:23.
21 **God**. Ps 110:6. Hab 3:13. Mk 12:4.
the hairy. Ps 55:23.
of such. ver. 18. Ps 7:12. Ex 34:7. Pr 1:24,
etc. Ezk 18:27-30. Lk 13:5. He 2:1-3. 12:25.
Re 2:14-16.
22 **Bashan**. Nu 21:33, 35. Is 11:11-16. 49:22.
the depths. Ex 14:22, 29. Is 51:10, 11. Je
23:5-8. Ezk 36:24. Ho 1:10, 11.
23 **That**. Ps 58:10.
dipped. Heb. red. Ex 14:30. Is 63:1-6.
the tongue. 1 K 21:19. 22:38. 2 K 9:33-37.
Re 19:17-21.
24 **even**. Ps 24:7-10. 47:5-7. 2 S 6:12-17. 1 Ch
13:8. 15:16-24.
sanctuary. Ps 63:2.
25 **the singers**. 1 Ch 15:16, 28. Re 19:1, 2.
the players. Ps 87:7. 150:3-5. 1 Ch 13:8. Re
14:2, 3. 15:2, 3.
among. Ps 148:12, 13. Ex +15:20.
damsels. or, virgins. Ge +24:43. Ex 2:8. Pr
30:19. SS 1:3. 6:8. Is 7:14. Je 31:11, 13.
timbrels. Na 2:7.
26 **Bless**. Ps 107:32. 111:1. 135:19-21. 1 Ch
16:7, 8, etc.
from the fountain. or, ye that are of the
fountain. Ps 36:9. Ge 35:11. Dt 33:28. Pr 5:16.
Is 48:1. Ac 13:26.
27 **There**. 1 Ch 13:5.
little. Ge 42:32. Jg 20:35, 48. 21:6, etc. 1 S
9:21. 1 Ch 12:16, 29. 15:3. 27:12.

princes. Ps 47:9. 60:7. Is 11:13. Ezk 37:19-27.
and their council. or, with their company.
28 **commanded**. Ps 42:8. 44:4. 71:3. Dt 28:8. Is
40:31. Mt 8:8. Jn 5:8, 9. Ac 3:6-8. 2 C 12:9,
10.
thy strength. Ps 18:1. 144:2.
strengthen. Ps 138:8. 1 Ch 29:12. Ep 3:17-
20. Ph 1:6. 2 Th 1:11.
hast wrought. Ps 31:19. Is 26:12. Ph 2:13.
29 **Because**. 1 Ch 17:4-12. 22:7-11. 28:10, etc.
29:3. 2 Ch 2:5, 6. 6:8, 9.
shall. Jg +3:15. Ezr 7:13-28. Ne 2:8. Is +49:7.
30 **Rebuke**. 2 S ch. 8, 10. 2 Ch ch. 14, 20. Is ch.
37.
company of spearmen. or, beasts of the
reeds. Je 51:32, 33.
multitude. Ps 22:12, 13. Is 34:7. Je 50:11.
every. Ps 2:12. 18:44. 2 S 8:2, 8-11.
scatter thou. or, he scattereth. ver. 14.
delight. Ps 120:7. Ro 7:22. Ja 4:1.
31 **Princes**. Ps 72:8-11. Is 19:18-25. 45:14. 60:6,
7. 66:19.
Ethiopia. Ge +2:13.
stretch. Ps +88:9. 2 Ch +30:8mg.
hands. ver. 29. Ps 22:27. 72:10. Is 49:7. 60:6,
9.
32 **ye kingdoms**. Ps 67:2-5. 100:1. 117:1, 2. Dt
32:43. Ro 15:10, 11. Re 15:4.
33 **rideth**. ver. +4. Ex 20:18.
heavens of heavens. Dt +10:14.
of old. Ps 44:1. 55:19. 74:2, 12. 77:5. 93:2.
102:25. Mi +5:2.
send out. Heb. give. ver. 11. Ps 14:7mg. 46:6.
53:6mg. 77:17.
his voice. Ezk +10:5.
34 **Ascribe**. Ps 29:1, 2. 96:6-8. 1 Ch 16:28, 29.
Re 19:6.
his excellency. Dt 33:26. 2 P 1:17.
clouds. or, heavens. Ps 18:11. 36:5. 57:10.
77:17. 108:4mg.
35 **terrible**. Ps 45:4, 5. +99:3. Ex 15:1. He 12:24-
29. Re 6:16, 17.
out of. Ps 110:2.
the God. Heb. *El*, Ex +15:2.
of Israel. Is +29:23.
giveth strength. ver. 28. Ps +18:1. 73:26. Dt
33:25. Zc 12:8. Ro 14:4.
Blessed. Ps 72:18, 19.

PSALM 69

(*Title*.) **Shoshannim**. Ps 45, 60, 80, titles.
A Psalm. It is uncertain when this Psalm was
composed; though it is probable that it was
written by David during the rebellion of
Absalom. It is an exceedingly fine composition; it evidently refers to the advent, passion,
and resurrection of our Lord, to the vocation
of the Gentiles, and the reprobation of the
Jews: see the Marginal References.

1 **the waters**. ver. 2, 14, 15. Ps +93:3. Is 28:17.
soul. Heb. *nephesh*, Ge +12:13.

2 **I sink**. Ps 40:2. Je 38:6, 22.
deep mire. Heb. the mire of depth. Ps 68:22.
deep waters. Heb. depth of waters. Ps 88:6,
7. Ezk 27:26-34.
the floods. Ps 32:6. Ge 7:17-23. Mt 7:25.
26:37, 38.

3 **I am**. Ps 6:6. 13:1-3.
crying. Ps +3:4. Mt 26:38.
my throat. ver. 21. Ps 22:15. Jn 19:28-30.
mine. Ps 119:82, 123. Dt 28:32, 65. Jb 11:20.
16:16. 17:5, 7. 31:16. Is 38:14. La 2:11. 4:17.
5:17.
I wait. Ps 25:21. +37:24. 39:7. 2 K 6:33. Jb
14:14. 29:21, 23. 30:26. 32:11, 16. Is +30:18.
42:4. Ezk 19:5. Mi 5:7. 7:7. 1 P 1:10, 11.

4 **hate me without**. Ps 109:2-5. Is 49:7. Jn
15:24, *25*. 1 P 2:22.
more than. Ps 40:12.
being. Ps 7:3-5. 35:12, 19. 38:19, 20. 109:3-5.
Mt 27:23.
then I. Le 5:15, 16. 6:4, 5. Is 53:4-7. Jn
+17:5. 2 C 5:21. 1 T +2:6. 1 P 2:24. 3:18.

5 **and my sins**. Heb. and my guiltiness. Ps
17:3. 19:12. 44:20, 21.
hid. Ps 38:9. Je 16:17.

6 **Let not**. Ps 7:7. 35:26, 27. Jl +2:26. Lk 24:19-
21. Jn 16:20. Ac 4:7-16. Ep 3:13.
wait. S#6960h, Ps 37:34. ver. 3.
O God of Israel. Is +29:23. Ac 13:17, 23.

7 **Because**. Ps 22:6-8. 44:22. Je 15:15. Jn
15:21-24.
shame. Is 50:6. 53:3. Mt 26:67, 68. 27:29, 30,
38-44. Lk 23:11, 35-37. He 12:2.

8 **stranger unto**. Ps 31:11. Jb 19:13-19. Is
63:3. Mt 26:48-50, 56, 70-74. Jn 1:11. 7:3, 5.
and an alien. Heb. *nokri*, S#5237h, Ge +31:15.
1 S 17:28. Mi 7:5, 6. Mt 10:21, 22, 35, 36. Mk
6:3. Jn 7:5.
mother's children. Mt +13:55. Mk 3:31.
+6:3. Ac 1:14.

9 **zeal**. Ps 119:139. 1 K 19:10. 1 Ch 15:27-29.
29:3. Is 56:7. Je 7:11. Mt 21:13. Mk 11:15-17.
Lk 19:46. Jn 2:14-17.
and the. Ps 89:50, 51. Ro *15:3*.

10 **I wept**. Ps 102:8, 9. 109:24, 25. Lk 7:33, 34.
chastened. Nu +29:7.
soul. Heb. *nephesh*, Ge +34:3.
with fasting. Mt +6:16.

11 **sackcloth**. Jb +16:15. 2 C 8:9.
I became. Ps 44:13, 14. Dt 28:37. 1 K 9:7. Je
24:9.

12 **They**. Dt 16:18. Mt 27:12, 13, 20, 41, 42, 62,
63. Lk 23:2. Ac 4:26, 27.
gate. Ge +14:7.
speak against. Ps 22:6, 7. Mt 27:12, 63. Jn
8:48.
I was. Ps 35:15, 16. Jb 30:8, 9. Mk 15:17-19.

drunkards. Heb. drinkers of strong drink. Da
5:2-4, 23.

13 **my prayer**. Ps 55:16, 17. 91:15. Da 9:21, 23.
Mt 26:36, etc. Lk 22:44. Jn 17:1, etc. He 5:7. 1
P 2:23.
acceptable time. Ps 30:5. 32:6. 62:12. 1 S
25:8. Est 5:2, 6. 7:2. Is 49:8. 55:6. 2 C +6:2.
in the. Ps 40:10, 11. 98:3. Ge 24:27. Mi 7:20.
Lk 1:72. Ac 13:32, 33. Ro 15:8, 9.

14 **Deliver**. Ps 40:1-3. Je 38:6-13. La 3:55. Jon
2:3-6. Jn 17:1. He 5:7.
let me. Ps 25:18, 19. 35:19. 109:3, 21. Lk
19:14, 27. Ac 5:30, 31.
out of. ver. 1, 2, 15. Ps 42:7. 124:4, 5. 144:7.
Mk 14:34, etc. 15:34.

15 **waterflood**. Is 43:1, 2. Jon 2:2-7. Mt 12:40.
Ac 2:23-27. Re 12:15, 16.
pit. Heb. *be-er*, Ge +16:14. Ge 37:24. Ps
+16:10. 88:4-6. Nu 16:33, 34. Ac 2:24, 31.

16 **for thy**. Ps 36:7. 63:3. 109:21.
turn. Ps +25:16. 26:11.
according. ver. 13. Ps +51:1. Is 63:7.

17 **hide**. Ps 22:24. Dt +31:17. Mt 27:46.
for I am. Mt 26:38.
hear me speedily. Heb. make haste to hear
me. Ps +40:17. Jb 7:21.

18 **Draw**. Ps 10:1. 22:1, 19. Je 14:8.
soul. Heb. *nephesh*, Ge +12:13.
redeem. Ps 31:5. 111:9. Jb 6:23.
because. Ps 27:11. Dt 32:27. Jsh 7:9.

19 **my reproach**. ver. 7-9. Ps 22:6, 7. Is 53:3. Jn
15:24. He 12:2. 1 P 2:23.
my shame. Ps 80:45. Ga 3:13. He 12:2.
dishonor. Jn 8:49.
mine. Ps 2:2-4. 38:9. Mt 27:39, 41. Lk 23:35-
37.

20 **Reproach**. Ps +31:11. 123:4.
broken my. Ps 147:3. Pr 25:15. Mt +26:67.
Jn 16:22.
I am. Ps 42:6. Mt 26:37, 38. Jn 12:27.
I looked. Is 63:5. Mt 26:40, 56. Mk 14:37,
50.
take pity. Heb. to lament with me. Jb 2:11.
42:11. La 1:12. Ro 12:15.
but there. Ps 142:4. Jn 16:32. 2 T 4:16, 17.
comforters. Jb +16:2. 19:21, 22. Mt 26:56.

21 **gall for my meat**. Dt +29:18. Mt 27:34, 48.
in my thirst. ver. 3. Ps 22:15. Jn 19:29, 30.
vinegar to drink. Mt 27:34. Mk 15:23, 36.
Lk 23:36. Jn 19:29, 30.

22 **Let their table**. Je +10:25. Ml 2:2. Ro *11:8-10*.
a trap. Is 8:14, 15. 1 P 2:8.

23 **Their eyes**. Is 6:9, 10. 29:9, 10. Mt 13:14, 15.
Jn 12:39, 40. Ac 28:26, 27. Ro 11:25. 2 C 3:14.
make their. Dt 28:65-67. Is 21:3, 4. Je 30:6.
Da 5:6. Ro 11:10.

24 **Pour**. Dt 28:15, etc. 29:18-28. 31:17. 32:20-
26. Is +66:14. Ezk +7:8. Mt 23:35-37. Lk
21:22. 1 Th 2:15, 16.

take. Ex 15:15. Is 13:8. Zc 1:6.

25 **Let their**. 1 K 9:8. Je 7:12-14. Mt 23:38. 24:1, 2. Ac *1:20*.

habitation. Heb. palace. Ge 25:16. Nu 31:10. Is 5:1. 6:11.

let none dwell. Heb. let there not be a dweller.

26 **For**. Ps 109:16. 2 Ch 28:9. Jb 19:21, 22. Zc 1:15. 1 Th 2:15.

whom. Is 53:4, 10. Zc 13:7.

they talk. Mk 15:28-32.

those, etc. Heb. thy wounded. Ps 88:5. 89:10. Ge 34:27.

27 **Add**. Ps 81:12. Ex 8:15, 32. 9:12. Le 26:39. Is 5:6. Mt 21:19. 23:31, 32. 27:4, 5. Ro 1:28. 9:18. 2 Th 2:11, 12. Re 22:10, 11.

iniquity. *or*, punishment of iniquity. Ps 109:17-19. 2 T 4:14.

let them. Ps 24:5. Is 26:10. Ro 9:31. 10:2, 3.

28 **blotted**. Is 65:15. Ho 1:9. Re +3:5.

book. Ex +32:32.

be written. Ph +4:3.

29 **I am poor**. Ps +40:17. Is 53:2, 3.

and sorrowful. Ps 13:2. 18:4-6. 2 S 22:6, 7. Da +10:16-19. Mt 26:37-39.

let thy. Ps 18:48. 22:27-31. 89:26, 27. 91:14-16. Ep 1:21, 22. Ph 2:9-11.

30 **I will**. Ps 28:7. 40:1-3. 118:21, 28, 29.

magnify. Ps 34:3.

31 **also shall**. Ps 50:13, 14, 23. Ho 14:2. Ep 5:19, 20. He 13:15. 1 P 2:5.

32 **The humble**. *or*, The meek. Ps 25:9. 34:2. Mt +5:5.

your heart. Ps 22:26, 29. Jn 16:22. 20:20.

live. 1 S +10:24mg.

that seek. Je +29:13.

33 **the Lord**. Ps 72:12-14. 102:17, 20. Is 66:2. Lk 4:18. 1 J +5:14.

his prisoners. Ps +146:7. Ep +3:1.

34 **Let**. Ps 96:11, 12. 98:7, 8. 148:1, etc. 150:6. Is 44:22, 23. 49:13. 55:12. Re 7:11-13.

moveth. Heb. creepeth. Ge 1:20mg.

35 **save Zion**. Ps 51:18. 147:12, 13. Is 14:32. +24:23. 44:26. 46:13. Zp 3:15.

build. Ps 48:11-13. +102:16. Ezk 36:35, 36.

dwell there. Am +9:15.

in possession. Ob 17.

36 **The seed**. Dt +29:11.

his servants. Ps 90:16, 17. 102:28. Is 44:3, 4. 61:9. Ac +2:39.

shall inherit. Mt +5:5. Ro +4:13. 8:17. Ep +1:11. 1 P +1:4.

love his name. Dt +6:5. 2 T 4:8. Re 21:27.

dwell therein. ver. 35. Ps 23:6. Mt 8:11.

PSALM 70

(**Title**.) A.M. 2983. B.C. 1021.

A Psalm. This Psalm is almost word for word the same as the last verses of Psalm 40; and it is written as a part of the succeeding Psalm in about 27 MSS. Both Psalms evidently appear to have been written by David during the rebellion of Absalom, and probably at the crisis when he heard of the sanguinary counsel which Ahithophel had given respecting him; or, as some suppose, when beyond Jordan. 2 S 17:1-21.

to bring. Ps 38, title.

1 **O God**. Ps +40:17. 69:18.

to help me. Heb. to my help. Ps 38:22mg.

2 **Let**. Ps +71:13.

my soul. Heb. *nephesh*, Ge +12:13.

be turned. Is 28:13. Jn 18:6.

3 **back**. Ps 40:15. Ac 1:18.

Aha, aha. Ps 35:21, 25. Pr 24:17, 18. Ezk 25:3. 26:2. 36:2.

4 **Let all**. Ps 5:11. +40:16. 97:12. Is 61:10. La 3:25. Jn 16:20.

rejoice. Ps +25:2.

5 **I am**. Ps +40:17.

make. 2 C 1:10.

O Lord. Ps 13:1, 2. He 10:37. Re 22:20.

PSALM 71

1 **do I**. Ps 22:5. 25:2, 3. 31:1-3. 125:1. 146:5. 2 K 18:5. 1 Ch 5:20. Ro 9:33. 1 P 2:6.

let me. Is 45:17. Je 17:18.

2 **Deliver**. Ps 31:1. 91:15.

in thy. Ps 17:2. 34:15. 43:1. 143:1, 11. Da 9:16. 2 Th 1:6.

cause. 1 C 10:13.

escape. Lk +21:36. Re 3:10.

incline. Ps +17:6.

thine ear. Ps +10:17.

3 **my strong habitation**. Heb. to me for a rock of habitation. Ps 31:2, 3. 91:1, 2. Pr 18:10. Is 32:2. 33:16.

continually resort. Mk 10:1. Jn 10:41.

thou hast. Ps 44:4. 68:28. 91:11, 12. Ezk 9:6. Re 7:2, 3.

my rock. Ps 18:2. 144:2.

fortress. Ps +31:3.

4 **Deliver**. ver. 2. Da 3:17.

out of the. Ps 17:8, 9, 13. 59:1, 2. 140:1-4. 2 S 16:21, 22. 17:1, 2, 12-14, 21.

5 **For thou**. Ps 13:5. +42:11. Ro 15:13.

my hope. Pr 13:12. Is 20:5. Ac 28:20. Ro 8:24. 1 T 1:1. T 2:13.

my trust. ver. 17. Ps 22:9, 10. 1 S 16:13. 17:33-37, 45-47. Ec 12:1. Lk 2:40. 2 T 3:15.

6 **By thee**. Ps 22:9, 10. Pr 8:17. Is 46:3, 4. 49:1, 2. Je 3:4.

thou art. Ps 139:15, 16. 145:1, 2. Is 49:1, 5. Je 1:5. Lk 1:31, 32. Ga 1:15.

my praise. ver. 14. Ps 34:1. Ep 5:20.

7 **as a wonder**. Is 8:18. Zc 3:8. Lk 2:34. Ac 4:13. 1 C 4:9. 2 C 4:8-12. 6:8-10.

thou art. Ps 62:7. 142:4, 5. Je 16:19.

8 **Let my mouth**. ver. 15, 24. Ps 34:1. 35:28. 51:14, 15. 107:2. 118:24. +141:2. 145:1, 2. 146:2.

thy honor. Ps 95:6. 1 Ch 16:29. Is 6:1-3. Da +4:34. Mt +6:9. 1 T +1:17. Ju 25. Re 4:8, 11.

9 **Cast**. ver. 18. Ps 92:13-15. Is 46:4. 2 T 1:12. 4:18.

old age. ver. 18. Pr 16:31. Is 46:4.

when. Ps 73:26. 90:10. 2 S 19:35. 21:15-17. Ec 12:1-7.

10 **and they**. Ps 10:9. 56:6. Pr 1:11.

lay wait for. Heb. watch or observe. Ps +5:8mg. +31:6. 37:32, 33. 1 S 19:11. Pr 1:11. Je 5:26. 20:10.

soul. Heb. nephesh, Ge +12:13.

take. Ps 2:2. 83:3. 2 S 17:1, etc. Mt 26:3, 4. 27:1. Mk 15:1.

11 **God**. Ps 3:2. 37:25, 28. 41:7, 8. 42:10. Mt 27:42, 43, 46, 49.

for there. Ps 7:2. 50:22. 2 Ch 32:13, 14. Da 3:15.

12 **O God**. Ps 22:11. 35:22. 46:1. 69:18.

make. Ps +40:17.

13 **Let them be**. ver. 24. Ps 6:10. 31:17, 18. 35:4, 8, 26. 40:14, 15. 70:2, 3. 83:16, 17. 109:6, 7, 9-20, 28, 29. 129:5. Is 41:11. Je +10:25. 20:11, 12. 1 C 16:22.

soul. Heb. nephesh, Ge +12:13.

covered. Ps 109:29. 132:18. 1 P 5:5.

14 **hope**. Ps +42:11. Jb 13:15. Ro +15:4. He 10:35.

praise. Ps 35:28. 51:15. 119:164. Is 12:1. +61:3. Lk 19:37. Ac 2:47. 16:25. He 13:15.

more and more. ver. 6. Ps 104:33. 145:1. Ph 1:9. 1 Th 4:10. 2 P +3:18. Re 4:8. 5:13.

15 **My mouth**. ver. 8, 24. Ps 22:22-25. 30:12. 37:30. 40:9, 10. 145:2, 5-14.

all the day. Ps 35:28. 89:16.

I know. Ps 40:5, 12. 139:17, 18.

16 **I will go**. Ps +18:1. 73:26. Dt 33:25. Jsh 1:9. 2 T 2:1.

I will make. Is 26:13. 63:7. Ro 1:16.

thy righteousness. ver. 2, 15, 19, 24. Ps 51:14. Mt 6:33. Ro 1:17. 3:21. 10:3. Ph 3:9. 2 Th 1:6.

17 **thou hast**. ver. 5. Ps 119:9, 102.

hitherto. Ps 66:16. 1 S 17:36, 37. 2 S 4:9. 22:1, etc. 1 Ch 16:4, etc.

18 **Now**. ver. 9. Ge 27:1. 1 S 4:15, 18. Is 46:4.

when I am old and greyheaded. Heb. unto old age and grey hairs.

until I. Ps 78:4-6. 145:4, 5. Ex 13:8, 14-17. 1 Ch 29:10, etc. Ac 13:36.

strength. Heb. arm. Ex +15:16.

19 **Thy righteousness**. Ps 36:5, 6. 57:10. 139:6. Pr 15:24. 24:7. Is 5:16. 55:9. Ro 3:26.

who hast. Ps 126:2, 3. Da +4:3.

who is like. Ps 8:5. Ex +8:10. Is +57:15.

20 **which**. Ps 40:1-3. 60:3. 66:10-12. 88:6, etc.

138:7. 2 S 12:11. Mk 14:33, 34. 15:34. 2 C 11:23-31. Re 7:14.

quicken. Ps 80:17, 18. 143:11. Is 26:19. Ho 6:1, 2. Ac 2:24, 32-34. +13:33. Ro 4:17. 8:29. Col 1:18. He 1:5, 6. 12:2. 1 P 3:18. Re 1:5.

shalt bring. Ps +16:10. 40:2. 86:13. Is 38:17. Ezk 37:12, 13. Jon 2:6. Jn 5:28, 29. Ac 17:31. Ep 4:9.

21 **increase**. Ps 72:11. 2 S 3:1. Is 9:7. 49:6. 53:10, 11. Re 11:15.

comfort. Ps 32:10. 2 C 1:4, 5. 2:14. 7:6, 13. 1 Th 3:9.

22 **psaltery**. Heb. instrument of psaltery. Ps 92:1-3. 150:3-5. Hab 3:18, 19.

even. Ps 25:10. 56:4. 89:1, 2. 98:3. 138:2. Mi 7:20. Ro 15:8.

O thou. Is +1:4. 57:15.

23 **my lips**. Ps 63:5. 104:33. Lk 1:46, 47.

my soul. Heb. nephesh, Ge +12:13. Ps +34:22.

24 **My tongue**. ver. 8, 15. Ps 37:30. Dt 11:19. Pr 10:20, 21. Mt 12:35. Ep 4:29.

for they. ver. 13. Ps 18:37-43. 92:11. 1 C +15:25. Ep 6:12.

PSALM 72

(*Title*.) A.M. 2989. B.C. 1015.

A Psalm. This Psalm seems to have been composed by David, in his last days, when he had set his beloved son on the throne. "Then," says Calmet, "transported with joy and gratitude, he addressed this Psalm to God, in which he prays Him to pour out His blessings on the young king, and upon the people. He then, wrapped up in a divine enthusiasm, ascends to a higher subject; and sings the glory of the Messiah, and the magnificence of his reign."

for. or, of. Ps 127, title.

1 **Give**. 1 K 1:39, etc. 1 Ch 22:12, 13. 29:19. 2 Ch 1:10. Is 11:2. Jn 3:34. He +1:8, 9.

thy judgments. 2 S 23:3. 1 K 3:9-12.

the king's. 1 K 1:47, 48. 2:1-4. Je 23:5, 6.

2 **He shall**. ver. 12-14. 1 K 3:5-10. Je +21:12.

thy poor. Ps 12:5. 82:3, 4. Jb 34:19.

3 **mountains**. ver. 16. Is 32:16, 17. 52:7. Ezk 34:13, 14. Jl 3:18.

bring peace. ver. 7. Is 2:4. 11:6-9. Jn 17:20-23. Ep 4:16.

little. Ps 65:12.

by righteousness. Ps 85:10, 11. 96:11-13. 98:8, 9. Is 32:17. Da 9:24. Ro 14:17. 2 C 5:19-21.

4 **He shall judge**. ver. 12-14. 109:31. Dt +32:36. Ezk 34:15, 16. Zc 11:7, 11. Mt 11:5.

the poor. Ja +2:5.

the needy. Mt +5:3. 11:5.

break. Ps 2:9. 94:5. Jb 19:2. 34:24. Pr 20:26. Je 51:20-23. Da 2:34, 35.

the oppressor. Is 9:4. 51:12, 13. Zc 9:8-10. Re 18:6-8, 20, 24. 19:2.

5 They shall. 1 S 12:18. 1 K 3:28.
as long. ver. 7, 17. Ps 89:29, 36, 37. Ge +8:22. Ec +1:4. Is 9:7. Je +31:35, 36. Da 2:44. 7:14, 27. Lk 1:32, 33. 1 C +15:24, 25. Ep 3:21. Re 11:15.
throughout all. Ps 89:4, 29, 36, 37. 102:28. 145:13. 146:10. Is 34:17. 51:8. 59:21. 60:15. 65:23. 66:22. Je 33:22. Ezk 37:25. Mt 5:5. Lk 1:32, 33.
generations. Ge +9:12.
6 like rain. Dt 32:2. 2 S 23:4. Pr 1:23. 16:15. 19:12. Is 5:6. 32:15. 44:3-5. Ezk 34:23-26. 39:29. Ho 6:3. 14:5-7. Jl 2:28, 29. Zc 12:10. 1 P 1:12.
mown grass. Is +26:19.
7 In his days. Ps +118:24. 132:15-18. Is 11:6-9. 32:3-8, 15-20. 35:1, etc. 54:11-17. 55:10-13. 60:1, 22. 61:3-6, 10, 11. Ml 4:2. Ac 4:32.
righteous flourish. Ps 92:12.
abundance. 1 K 4:25. 1 Ch 22:8, 9. Is 2:4. 9:6, 7. Da 2:44. Lk 1:33. 2:14. Ep 2:14-17. He 7:2.
as long as the moon endureth. Heb. till there be no moon. ver. +5, 17.
8 He shall. Ps 2:8. 80:11. 89:25, 36. 110:2. Ex 23:31. 1 K 4:21-24. Zc 9:10. 14:9. Re 11:15.
the river. Ps 80:11. Ge 15:18. 31:21. Ex 23:31. Nu 34:5. Dt 11:24. Jsh 13:3. 15:4, 47. 24:2. 1 K 4:21. 8:65. 1 Ch 18:3. 19:16mg. 2 Ch 9:26mg. Is 27:12. Ezk 48:28. Mi 7:12.
the ends. Ps 2:8. 22:27, 28. 59:13. 67:7. Is +43:6. Je +31:8.
9 They that. 1 K 9:18, 20, 21. Is 35:1, 2.
his enemies. Ps 2:9. 21:8, 9. 110:1, 6. Lk 19:27.
lick. Is 49:23. Mi 7:17.
10 The kings. 2 Ch 9:21. Is 43:6. +49:7.
Tarshish. Ge +10:4.
bring presents. Jg +3:15. Mt 2:11, 12.
offer gifts. Is 60:6. Mt 2:2, 11.
11 all kings. Is +49:7. Re 17:14. 21:24, 26.
all nations. Ps +86:9. Is 54:5. Ro 11:25. Re 20:1-6.
12 For. ver. 4. Je +21:12. Lk 4:18. 7:22. He 7:25. Re 3:17, 18.
the needy. Ps 9:18. 22:11.
crieth. Ps 10:17.
the poor. Ps 10:9-12. +40:17. 74:19-21.
him. Ec 4:1. Is 63:4, 5.
13 shall save. Ps +140:12. Ezk 34:16. Mt 5:3. 18:11. Ja 2:5, 6.
souls. Heb. *nephesh*, Ge +12:13.
14 he shall. Ps +34:22. +130:8. Lk 1:68-75.
soul. Heb. *nephesh*, Ge +12:13.
precious. Ps 116:15. Mt 23:30-36. 1 Th 2:15, 16. Re 2:10. 6:9-11. 17:6. 18:20-24. 19:2.
15 And he. Ps 21:4. Jn 11:25. 14:19. 16:23. Ro 8:34. 1 J 1:2. Re 1:18.
to him. 1 K 10:14. Mt 2:11.
shall be given. Heb. one shall give.

gold. Is 60:5-7.
prayer. ver. 19. Ps 45:4. Mt 6:10. 21:9. Jn 16:23, 24. 1 C 1:2, 3. 2 C 13:14. 1 Th 3:11. 2 T 4:22. He 10:19-22.
continually. 1 Ch +16:11.
daily. 2 Ch 2:11, 12. 9:1, 4-8, 23, 24. Jn 5:23. Ph 2:11. 2 P 3:18. Ju 25. Re 1:5, 6. 5:8-14. 7:9-12.
16 There. Jb 8:7. Is 30:23. 32:15, 20. Mt 13:31-33. Mk 16:15, 16. Jn 4:35. Ac 1:15. 2:41. 4:4. 1 C 3:6-9. Re 7:9.
upon. Is +2:2, 3.
the fruit. Ps 92:12-14. Is 29:17. 35:1, 2. Ho 14:5-7.
of the city. ver. 6. 1 K 4:20. Is 44:3-5. Je 33:22. Re 7:14. 21:10, 24.
17 His name. Ps 45:17. 89:36. Is 7:14. Mi 5:2. Mt 1:21, 23. Lk 1:31-33. Ph 2:10.
shall endure. Heb. shall be. Ps 104:31mg.
for ever. Heb. *olam*, Ex +12:24.
his name, etc. Heb. shall be as a son to continue his father's name for ever. Ep 3:14. Col 1:3. 1 P 1:3.
as long. ver. +5, 7.
men. Ge +12:3.
all nations. Je 4:2. Lk 1:48. Re 15:4.
18 Blessed. Is +29:23.
who only. Da +4:3.
19 blessed. Ne 9:5. Re 5:13.
for ever. Heb. *olam*, Ex +12:24.
and let. Is +40:5. Zc 14:9. Ml 1:11. Mt 6:10.
Amen. Mt +6:13.
20 The prayers. 2 S 23:1. Jb 31:40. Je 51:64. Lk 24:51.

PSALM 73

(*Title*.) of. *or*, for. Ps 50, 74-83, titles. 2 K +18:18.
1 Truly. *or*, Yet. Ps 2:6. 42:11.
God. ver. 18-28. Ps 84:11. Is 63:7-9. Lk 12:32.
to such. Jn 1:47. Ro 2:28, 29. 4:16. 9:6, 7.
of a clean heart. Heb. clean of heart. Ps 24:4. 51:10. Pr 20:9. Je 4:14. 32:39. Mt +5:8. T 3:5. Ja 4:8.
2 But. Ps 5:7. 17:15. 35:13. Jsh 24:15. 1 S 12:23. 1 Ch 22:7. Jb 21:4.
feet. Ps 116:8. 1 S 2:9. Ro 7:23, 24.
steps. Ps 17:5. 38:16. 94:18. Jb 12:5.
3 envious. Ps +37:1. Jb 21:7, 29, 30. Je 12:1-3.
I saw. Ps 17:14.
4 no. Ps 17:14. Jb 21:23, 24. 24:20. Ec 2:16. 7:15. Lk 16:22.
firm. Heb. fat. Ps 17:10. Ge 41:2, 4, 5, 7, 18, 20.
5 They are. ver. 12. Jb 21:6. Pr 3:11, 12. Je 12:1, 2. 1 C 11:32. He 12:8. Re 3:19.
in trouble as other. Heb. in the trouble of other.
like. Heb. with. 1 C 11:32.

6 Therefore. Dt 8:13, 14. 32:15. Est 3:1, 5, 6. 5:9-11. Jb 21:7-15. Ec 8:11. Je 48:11, 29. Ezk 28:2-5. Da 4:30.
as a chain. Jg 8:26. Pr 1:9. SS 4:9. Is 3:19. Ezk 16:11. Ja 4:6.
violence. Pr 3:31mg. 4:17. Mi 2:1, 2. 3:5. Ja +5:4-6.
covereth. Ps 61:2 (overwhelmed). 65:13. 102:t. 109:18, 29. 142:3. Jb 23:9 (hideth). 1 P 5:5.

7 eyes. Dt +31:20. Is 3:9. Ezk 16:49.
have, etc. Heb. pass the thoughts of the heart. ver. 12. Ps 17:14. 1 S 25:2, 36. Lk 12:16-21.

8 corrupt. Ps 53:1-4. Pr 30:13, 14.
speak wickedly. Ps +10:2, 10; 11. 12:4, 5. Ex 1:9, 10. 1 S 13:19. 1 K 21:7, etc. Je 7:9-11. Ho 7:16.
speak loftily. 2 P 2:10, 18. Ju 16.

9 set. Ex 5:2. 2 Ch 32:15. Jb 21:14. Da 3:15. 7:25. Re 13:6.
heavens. 2 Ch 32:20. Da 4:26. Mt 3:2. 21:25. Lk 15:18.
tongue. Ps 52:4. Lk 18:4. Ja 3:6.

10 Therefore. Je 2:19. Mt 24:12. 2 P 2:20.
waters. Ps 75:8. 144:13. Ge 23:9mg.

11 How. ver. 9. Ps 10:11. 94:7. Jb 22:13, 14. Ezk 8:12. Zp 1:12.
God. Heb. *El*, Ex +15:2.
is there. Ps 44:21. 139:1-6. Ho 7:2.

12 these. Ps 37:35. 52:7. Je 12:1, 2. Lk 16:19. Ja 5:1-3.
prosper. ver. 3.
world. Heb. *olam*, Le +25:32. Ec 3:11.
they. Ps 17:14. 62:10. Pr 11:4. Je 5:27, 28. Ho 12:7, 8.

13 Verily. Jb 9:27, 31. 21:15. 34:9. 35:3. Ml 3:14. Ac 24:16. 1 C 6:11. 1 J 3:3. 5:18.
in vain. Jb 21:15. 34:9. 35:3.
washed. Ps 24:4. 26:6. 51:10. Dt 21:6. He 10:19-22. Ja 4:8.

14 For all. Ps 34:19. 94:12, 13. Jb 7:3, 4, 18. 10:3, 17. Je 15:18. Am 3:2. He 12:5. 1 P 1:6.
chastened. Heb. my chastisement was. Ps 38:14.
morning. Jb 7:18.

15 offend. 1 S 2:24. Ml 2:8. Mt 18:6, 7. Ro 14:13, 15, 21. 1 C 8:11-13.
generation. Ps 22:30. 24:6. 1 P 2:9.

16 When. Ps 36:6. 97:2. Jb +11:7.
too painful for me. Heb. labor in mine eyes. Ps 39:6. Lk 18:32-34. Jn 16:18, 19.

17 Until. Ps 27:4. 63:2. 77:13. 119:24, 130.
the sanctuary. Ps 20:2. 68:35. 74:7. 78:69. 2 K 19:1. Is 37:14.
of God. Heb. *El*, Ex +15:2.
then. Ps 37:37, 38. Jb 27:8. Ps 119:130. Ec 8:12, 13. Je 5:31. Lk 12:20. 16:22, 23. 2 C 4:17, 18.

18 Surely. Ps 35:6. Dt 32:35. Je 23:12.

thou castedst. Ps 37:20, 24, 35-38. 55:23. 92:7. 94:23. 2 Th 1:9.

19 How. Ps 58:9. Jb 20:5. Is 30:13. Ac 12:23. 1 Th 5:3. Re 18:10.
they are. or, how are they. Ps 53:5. Nu 17:12, 13. 1 S 28:20. Jb 15:21. 18:11. 20:23-25. Pr 28:1. Is 21:3, 4. Da 5:6.

20 As a. Ps 90:5. Jb 20:8. Is 29:7, 8.
when. Ps 7:6. 78:65.
despise. or, tread down. Ps 44:5. Is 14:19. 63:18.
their image. Ps 39:6. Re +13:15.

21 my heart. ver. 3. Ps 37:1, 7.
in my. Jb 16:13. La 3:13.

22 So. Ps 49:10. 69:5. 92:6. Pr 12:1. 30:2. Ec 3:18.
ignorant. Heb. I knew not. Ps 35:8mg. 39:6. 92:6. 101:4.
as a. Ps 32:9. Is 1:3.
before thee. Heb. with thee.

23 Nevertheless. Ps 16:8. 23:4. 46:7. 139:1-12, 18. Ge 17:1. Mt 1:23. 28:20. He +13:5.
thou hast. Ps 37:17, 24. 63:8. Is 41:10, 13. 42:1.

24 Thou. Ps 16:7. +32:8. Ex 33:16. Is 48:17. 58:8, 11. Lk 11:13. Ja 1:5.
receive. Ps 49:15. 84:11. Lk 23:46. Jn 14:3. 17:5, 24. Ac 7:59. 2 C 5:1. 1 P 1:4, 5.

25 Whom. Ps 16:5, 11. 17:15. 37:4. 43:4. 63:3. 89:6. Mt +5:8. Ph 3:8. 1 J 3:2. Re 21:3, 22, 23.
none upon. Ps 9:2. 18:1. 42:1, 2. 104:34. 143:6-8. Is 26:8, 9. Hab 3:17, 18. Mt 10:37. Ph 3:8.
desire. Ps 45:11. SS 5:10, 16. Jn 6:68.

26 flesh. Ps 63:1. 84:2. 119:81, 82. Jb 13:15. 2 C 4:8-10, 16-18. Ph 1:21. 2 T 4:6-8. 2 P 1:14. Re 21:7.
but. Ps +18:1. 23:4. 138:3. 1 C +15:55.
strength. Heb. rock. Dt +32:31. Ps 18:2, 31, 46.
portion. Ps +16:5, 6. SS 2:16. Re 21:3, 4, 7.
for ever. Heb. *olam*, Ex +12:24.

27 lo. Ps 119:155. Jb 21:14, 15. Is 29:13. Je 12:2. Mt 15:7, 8. Ep 2:12, 13, 17.
that go. Ex +34:15. 1 J 2:15.

28 But. Ps 65:4. 84:10. 116:7. La 3:25, 26. 1 P 3:18.
for me. Jsh +24:15.
draw near. SS 1:4. Ho 11:4. Ja +4:8.
that I may. Ps 66:16. 71:17, 24. 107:22. 118:17.

PSALM 74

(Title.) A.M. 3416. B.C. 588.
Maschil of Asaph. *or*, A Psalm for Asaph to give instruction. Ps 78, title.

1 O God. Ps +9:10. 10:1. 42:9. +44:9.
for ever. Jb +4:20.
anger. Jg +2:14.
smoke. Ps 79:5. Le +26:30. Dt +4:24.

the sheep. Ps 79:13. 95:7. 100:3. Je 23:1. Ezk 34:8, 31. Lk 12:32. Jn 10:26-30.

2 **purchased**. Ex 15:16. Dt 9:29. Ac 20:28.
of old. Mi +5:2.
rod. *or*, tribe. Ps 2:9. 23:4. 45:6. 78:55.
thine. Ps 33:12. 106:40. 135:4. Dt 4:20. 32:9. Je 10:16.
redeemed. Is 43:3-5. 51:11. 62:12. 63:9-11. T 2:14. Re 5:9.
this mount. Ps 48:1, 2. 78:68, 69. 132:13, 14.

3 **Lift**. Ps 44:23, 26. Jsh 10:24. 2 S 22:39-43. Is 10:6. 25:10. 63:3-6. Mi 1:3.
feet. Ps 110:1. Is 60:13. 66:1.
the perpetual. Ps 102:13, 14. Ne 1:3. 2:3, 13. Jb +4:20. Is 64:10, 11. Da 9:17. Mi 3:12. Lk 21:24. Re 11:2.
all. Ps 79:1. Je 52:13. La 1:10. Da 8:11-14. 9:27. 11:31. Mk 11:17.

4 **Thine**. 2 Ch 36:17, 19. La 2:7. Lk 13:1. Re 13:6.
they set. Je 6:1-5. Da 6:27. Mt 24:15. Lk 21:20.

5 **was famous**. 1 K 5:5, 6. 2 Ch 2:14. Je 46:22, 23.

6 **the carved**. 1 K 6:18, 29, 32, 35.

7 **cast fire into thy sanctuary**. Heb. sent thy sanctuary into the fire. 2 K 25:9. Je +17:27. Mt 22:7.
defiled. Ps 89:39. Ezk 24:21.
dwelling. Ex 20:24. Dt 12:5. 1 K 8:20.

8 **said**. Ps 83:4. 137:7. Est 3:8, 9.
destroy. Heb. break. or, oppress. Ps 123:4. Je 25:38.
all the synagogues. or, meeting places. 2 K 2:3, 5. 4:23. 2 Ch 17:9. 23:5. Mt 4:23. Ac 15:21.

9 **We see**. Ex 12:13. 13:9, 10. 23:14. Jg 6:17. Ezk 20:12. He 2:4.
no more. 1 S 3:1. Ho 3:4. Am 8:11, 12. Mi 3:6, 7.
knoweth. 1 Ch +12:32. Lk 12:56.
how long. Da 9:2. Mt 24:36. Ac 1:6, 7.

10 **how long**. Ps +31:11. Is 63:6. 64:12. Da 9:17, 18. Re +6:10.
for ever. Jb +4:20.

11 **withdrawest**. Is 64:12. La 2:3.
right hand. Ps +18:35.
pluck it out. Ps 44:23. 78:65, 66.
bosom. Nu 11:12. Pr 19:24. 26:15. Is 40:11. Jn 1:18.

12 **God**. Ps 44:4. Ex 15:2. 19:5, 6. Nu 23:21, 22. Is 33:22.
of old. Mi +5:2.
working. Ps 106:43. Ex 15:2-15. Jg 4:23, 24. 1 S 19:5. Is 63:8. Hab 3:12-14.

13 **divide**. Heb. break. Ex +14:21. Is 11:15, 16.
brakest. Ps 89:10. 104:9. Ex 14:28. 15:4. Jb 7:12. 26:12, 13. 38:8, etc. Pr 8:29. Is 51:9, 10. Je 5:22. Ezk 29:3.

dragons. *or*, whales. Ps 91:13. 148:7. Ge 1:21. La 4:3mg. Ezk 32:2.

14 **leviathan**. Ps 104:25, 26. Jb 3:8mg. 41:1, etc. Is 27:1. Re 20:2.
meat. Ps 72:9. Ex 12:35, 36. 14:30. Nu 14:9.
to the people. Ps +83:3. Je 31:2. Ezk 20:35.
inhabiting the wilderness. Is +16:3, 4. Je +31:2. Ezk +20:35. Ho 2:14. Mt 24:16. Re +12:6, 14.

15 **cleave**. Ps 105:41. Ex 17:5, 6. Nu 20:11. Is 48:21.
fountain. Heb. *mayan*, Ge +7:11. Is 28:28. 33:12. 47:2.
flood. Jsh 3:13, etc. 2 K 2:8, 14. Is 11:16. 44:27. Hab 3:9mg. Re 16:12.
mighty rivers. Heb. rivers of strength. Ps 24:2. 46:4. 66:6.

16 **The day**. Ps 136:7-9. Ge 1:3-5.
prepared. Ps 8:3. 19:1-6. 136:7-9. Ge 1:14-18. Mt 5:45.
the light. Ge 1:3.

17 **set**. Ps 24:1, 2. Dt 32:8. Ac 17:26.
made summer. Heb. made them summer. Ge +8:22. Je +31:35, 36. Ac 14:17.

18 **Remember**. ver. 22. Ps 89:50, 51. 137:7. Is 62:6mg, 7. Re 16:19.
the foolish. ver. 22. Ps 14:1. 39:8. 94:2-8. Dt 32:27. Ezk 20:14.
blasphemed. Le +24:11.

19 **soul**. Heb. *nephesh*, Ge +12:13.
turtledove. Ps 68:13. SS 2:14. 4:1. 6:9. Is 60:8. Mt 10:16.
forget. Ps 68:10. 72:2. Zp 3:12. Ja 2:5, 6.
for ever. Jb +4:20.

20 **Have respect**. Ps 89:28, 34-36, 39. 105:8, 9. 106:45. Ge 17:7, 8. Ex 24:6-8. Le 26:40-45. Dt 9:27. 2 S +7:10-13, 15, 16. 23:5. Is +55:3. Je 31:33. +33:20-26. Zc 9:11. Ml 3:6. Lk 1:68-75. He 8:10.
the covenant. Ps 105:8-10. 106:45. Ge 30:1. 2 Ch +20:7. Mi +7:20.
the dark. Dt 12:31. Ro 1:29-31. Ep 4:17, 18.
habitations. Ps 5:8. Ge 49:5-7.

21 **O let not**. Ps 9:18. +12:5. 102:19-21. 109:22. Is 45:17.
poor. Ps 102:21. Ezr 3:11. Je 33:11.

22 **Arise**. Ps +3:7. 79:9, 10.
remember. ver. 18. Ps 75:4, 5. 89:50, 51. Is 52:5.

23 **Forget**. Ps +13:1.
tumult. ver. 4. Ps 2:1, 2. Is 37:29. La 2:16. Re 17:14.
increaseth. Heb. ascendeth. Ge 28:12. Jon 1:2.

PSALM 75

(Title.) A.M. 3294. B.C. 710.
Al-taschith. *or*, Destroy not. Ps 57, 58, titles.
A Psalm. Some consider this Psalm to have

been written by David on his accession to the throne over all Israel; others refer it to the time of the captivity, considering it as a continuation of the subject in the preceding; but Bp. Patrick and others are of opinion that it was composed by Asaph to commemorate the overthrow of Sennacherib's army, 2 K ch. 19.
of Asaph. *or*, for Asaph. 2 K +18:18.

1 **for that**. Ps 76:1. 138:2. Ex 23:21. 34:6, 7. Je 10:6.
  wondrous. Dt 4:7, 33, 34.
  works declare. Ps 9:16. 19:1, 2. Ac 14:17. Ro 1:20. 11:36. He 3:4.

2 **When**. Ps 78:70-72. 101:2. 2 S 2:4. 5:3. 8:15. 23:3, 4.
  receive the congregation. *or*, take a set time. Ec 3:17. Jn 7:6. Ac 1:7. 17:31.
  uprightly. Ps 17:2.

3 **earth**. Ps 60:1-3. 78:60-72. 1 S 31:1-7. Is 24:1-12. Ro 8:21, 22.
  I bear. 1 S 18:7. 25:28. 2 S 5:2. Is 49:8. He 1:3.
  pillars. 1 S 2:8.
  Selah. Ps +9:16.

4 **I said**. Ps 82:2, etc. 94:8. Pr 1:22. 8:5. 9:6.
  Lift. Ps 89:17. 148:14. Da 7:20, 21. Zc 1:21.

5 **speak**. 2 Ch +30:8. Ezk 2:4.
  stiff neck. 2 Ch +30:8.

6 **promotion cometh**. 1 S 16:7. Mt 7:21, 23.
  south. Heb. desert. Ps 29:8. 55:7. 63:1. 65:12.

7 **God**. Ps +7:8.
  he putteth. Ps 113:7, 8. 1 S 2:7, 8. 15:23, 28. 16:1. 2 S 3:17, 18. 5:2. 6:21. Je 27:4-8. Da 2:21, 22, 37. 5:18. Lk 1:52. Jn 15:16. Ro 11:15. Ga 1:15.

8 **For in**. Ps 11:6. 60:3. Jb 21:20. Is 51:17, 22. Je 25:15, 17, 27, 28. Hab 2:16. Re 14:9, 10. 16:19.
  it is full. Pr 23:30. Is 5:22.
  poureth. Heb. *nagar*, **S#5064h.** Ps 63:10mg. Ezk 35:5mg. Mi 1:4.
  but the dregs. Ps 73:10. Is 25:6. Je 48:11. Zp 1:12.

9 **But**. Ps 9:14. 34:1. 104:33. 145:1, 2.
  for ever. Heb. *olam*, Ex +12:24.

10 **All the horns**. Ps 101:8. Je 48:25. Zc 1:20, 21.
  but the horns. Ps +92:10.

PSALM 76

(Title.) **Neginoth**. Ps 4, 54, 61, 67, titles.
A Psalm. This Psalm is entitled in the Septuagint, which is followed by the Vulgate and Apollinarius, "An ode against the Assyrian;" and it is considered by many of the best commentators to have been composed by Asaph after the defeat of Sennacherib.
of Asaph. *or*, for Asaph. 2 K +18:18.

1 **In Judah**. Ps 48:1-3. 147:19, 20. Dt 4:7, 8,

34-36. Ac 17:23. Ro 2:17, etc. 3:1, 2.
  his. Ps 98:2, 3. 148:13, 14. 1 Ch 29:10-12. 2 Ch 2:5, 6. Da 3:29. 4:1, 2.

2 **Salem**. Ge 14:18. He 7:1, 2.
  dwelling. Ps 132:13, 14. 2 Ch 6:6. Is 12:6.

3 **There**. Ps 46:9. 2 K 19:35. 2 Ch 14:12, 13. 20:25. 32:21. Is 37:35, 36. Ezk 39:3, 4, 9, 10. Col 2:15.
  brake he. Ex 15:3.
  battle. Zc 14:3.
  Selah. Ps +9:16.

4 **mountains**. SS 4:8. Je 4:7. Ezk 19:1-4, 6. 38:12, 13. Da 7:4-8, 17, etc. Hab 3:6.

5 **stouthearted**. Jb 40:10-12. Is 46:12. Da 4:37. Lk 1:51, 52.
  they. Ps 13:3. Is 37:36. Je 51:39. Da 12:2. Na 3:18.
  and. Is 31:8. Ezk 30:21-25.

6 **At thy**. Ps 18:15. 80:16. 104:7. Ex 15:1, 21. Zc 14:3.
  both. Ex 14:27, 28. 15:4-6, 10. 2 S 10:18. Is 37:36. Ezk 39:20. Na 1:6. 2:13. 3:18. Zc 2:4.
  dead. 1 S 26:12. Je 51:39, 57.

7 **even thou**. Mt +10:28. Re 14:7.
  who. Ps 90:11. Na 1:6. 1 C 10:22. Re 6:16, 17.
  when. Ps 2:12.

8 **didst**. Ex 19:10. Jg 5:20. 2 Ch 32:20-22. Ezk 38:20-23.
  still. 2 Ch 20:29, 30. Hab +2:20.

9 **arose**. Ps +3:7.
  to judgment. Ps +7:8. 72:4. Je 5:28.
  to save. Ps 35:20. Mt +5:5.
  Selah. Ps +9:16.

10 **Surely**. Ge 37:18-20, 26-28. 50:20. Ex +9:16, 17. 15:9-11. 18:11. Da 3:19, 20, 28. Ac 2:36. 4:26-28. Ph +1:12. Re +11:18.
  remainder. Ps 46:6. 65:7. 104:9. Mt 2:13-16. 24:22. Ac 12:3, etc.

11 **Vow**. Le +23:38. Nu +30:2.
  let all. Ps 68:29. 89:7. Dt 16:16. 2 Ch 32:22, 23.
  bring presents. Le 7:16. +23:19. Dt 16:16. Pr 23:26. 2 C 8:5.
  unto him. Heb. to fear. Ge 31:42.
  be feared. Ps 9:20. Is 8:12. Je 32:21. Ml 1:6.

12 **cut off**. Ps 2:5, 10. 48:4-6. 68:12, 35. Jsh 5:1. 2 Ch 32:21. Da 5:6. Zp 3:6.
  spirit. Heb. *ruach*, Ge +41:8; +26:35.
  terrible. Is 13:6-8. 24:21. Re 6:15. 19:17-21.

PSALM 77

(Title.) A.M. cir. 3463. B.C. cir. 541.
Jeduthun. Ps 39, 62, titles. 1 Ch +9:16.
A Psalm. This Psalm is allowed by the best judges to have been written during the Babylonian captivity.
of Asaph. *or*, for Asaph. Ps 50, title. 2 K +18:18.

1   **I cried.** Ps +3:4.
     gave. Ps 116:1, 2.
2   **In the.** Ps 18:6. +50:15. 88:1-3. 102:1, 2.
     130:1, 2. Ge 32:7-12, 28. 2 K 19:3, 4, 15-20.
     Is 26:9, 16. Jon 2:1, 2. 2 C 12:7, 8. He 5:7. Ja
     5:13.
     my. Ps 6:2, 3. 38:3-8. 2 Ch 6:28. Is 1:5, 6. Ho
     5:13. 6:1.
     sore. Heb. hand. ver. 20. 78:42, 61. 80:17.
     89:21. Ex 9:29. 17:11, 12. 1 K +16:12mg.
     ran. or, spread out. Ps 63:10mg. 2 S 14:14
     (spilt). La 3:49 (trickleth down). 1 T +2:8.
     in the night. Ps 63:6. +119:55. Is 26:9.
     ceased not. Ps 38:8 (feeble). Hab 1:4
     (slacked). Ge 45:26 (fainted). Lk 18:1. 1 Th
     5:16. Ja 5:16.
     my soul. Heb. *nephesh,* Ge +34:3.
     refused. Ps 78:10.
     to be comforted. Ge 37:35. Est 4:1-4. Pr
     18:14. Je 31:15. Jn 11:31.
3   **I remembered.** Jb 6:4. 23:15, 16. 31:23. Je
     17:17.
     was troubled. Ps 42:5, 11. 46:3. 83:2. Jb
     23:15, 16.
     I complained. Ps 55:2. 88:3, etc. 102:3, etc.
     142:2. Nu +11:1. Ru +1:13. Jb 7:11. 10:1.
     23:2. Pr +19:3. Is 29:24. La 3:17, 39. Ezk
     +18:25. Ro +9:14. Ph +2:14. +4:11. He +13:5.
     spirit. Heb. *ruach,* Ps +106:33; Ge +26:35. Ps
     55:4, 5. 61:2. 142:2, 3. 143:4, 5.
     overwhelmed. or, feeble. **S#5848h.** Ps 61:2.
     65:13 (covered). 73:6. 77:3. 102:title. 107:5.
     142:3. 143:4. Ge 30:42 (feebler). Jb 23:9
     (hideth). Is 57:16 (fail). La 2:11 (swoon), 12
     (swooned), 19 (faint). Jon 2:7 (fainted).
     Selah. ver. 9, 15. Ps +9:16.
4   **holdest.** Ps 6:6. Est 6:1. Jb 7:13-15.
     I am. Jb 2:13. 6:3.
5   **have considered.** Ps 74:12-18. 143:5. Dt
     32:7. Jb 29:2-4. Is 51:9. 63:9-15. Mi 7:14, 15.
     of old. Mi +5:2 (**S#6924h**).
     of ancient times. Heb. *olam* plural, Ps +61:4.
6   **my song.** Ps 42:8. Jb 35:10. Hab 3:17, 18. Jon
     1:2. Ac 16:25. or, music. Ps 4:t (Neginoth).
     61:t (Neginah). 69:12. Jb 30:9. La 3:14. 5:14.
     Hab +3:19mg.
     night. ver. 2. 78:14. 88:1. 90:4. Is 50:10.
     commune. Ps 4:4. 63:6. 104:34. Ec 1:16.
     and. Ps 139:23, 24. Jb 10:2. La 3:40. 1 C
     11:28-32.
     spirit. Heb. *ruach,* Ps +106:33; Ge +26:35.
     search. Ge 31:35. 44:12. Je 29:13. La 3:40.
     Am 9:3. Zp 1:12. Jn +5:39. 1 C 11:31.
7   **the Lord.** Ps 37:24. +44:9. 71:9. 74:1. 89:30-
     34, 38, 46. +94:14. Je 23:24-26. La 3:31, 32.
     Ro +11:1, 2.
     for ever. Heb. *olam* plural, Ps +61:4.
     and will. Ps 79:5. 85:1, 5.
8   **Is his.** Ps 103:17, 18. Is 27:11. Lk 16:25, 26.
     for ever. Jb +4:20 (**S#5331h**).

     promise fail. Nu 14:34. 23:19. Je 15:18. Hab
     +3:9. Ml +3:6. Ro 9:6. +11:29. He 6:18.
     for evermore. Heb. to generation and gener-
     ation. Ps +33:11mg.
9   **God.** Ps +13:1. Is 40:27. 63:15. La 3:22, 23.
     Ho 11:8.
     gracious. Ex 34:6.
     anger. Ps 78:21, 31, 38, 49.
     shut up. Ps 107:42. Jb 5:16. Lk 13:25-28. Ro
     11:32mg. 1 J 3:17.
10   **This is**, etc. Ps 31:22. 73:22. 116:11. Jb 42:3.
     La 3:18-23. Mk 9:24.
     the years. ver. 5. Ex 15:6. Nu 23:21, 22. Dt
     4:34. Hab 3:2-13. or, changes. Ps 78:33. Ge
     1:14. 47:8, 9. Pr 3:2mg.
     right hand. Ps +18:35.
     most High. Ps +7:17.
11   **remember.** ver. 10. Ps 28:5. 44:1. Dt +7:18. 1
     Ch 16:12. Is 5:12.
     of old. Mi +5:2.
12   **meditate.** Ps 104:34. 143:5.
     talk. Ps 71:24. 105:2. 145:4, 11. Dt 6:7. Lk
     24:14-32.
13   **Thy way.** Ps 25:10. 27:4. 63:2. 68:25. 73:3,
     16, 17.
     who. Ps 89:6-8. Ex 15:11. Dt 32:31. Is 40:18,
     25. 46:5. Ro 11:33. Re 15:3, 4.
14   **the God.** Ps 105:5. Da +4:3.
     thou hast. Ex 13:14. 15:6. Jsh 9:9, 10. Is
     51:9. 52:10. Da 3:29. 6:27.
15   **with.** Ps 136:11, 12. Ex 6:6. Dt 9:26, 29. Is
     63:9.
     arm. Ex +15:16.
     the sons. Ge 48:3-20.
16   **The waters.** Ex +14:21. Hab 3:8-10, 15.
17   **clouds.** Ge 9:13.
     poured out water. Heb. were poured forth
     with water. Ps 68:8, 9. Heb. *zaram,* **S#2229h.** Ps
     77:17. 90:5.
     thine. Dt +32:23.
18   **voice.** Ezk +10:5.
     lightnings. Ps 97:4. Hab 3:4. Re 18:1.
     earth. Ex 19:18. 2 S 22:8, 14. Mt 27:51. 28:2.
     Re 20:11.
19   **way.** Ps 29:10. 97:2. Ne 9:11. Jb 26:14. Na
     1:3, 4. Hab 3:15.
     footsteps. Ps 89:51. Ex 14:28. Ro 11:33.
20   **Thou leddest.** Ex 13:21. 14:19. Is 63:11, 12.
     Ezk +31:34. Ho 12:13. Ac 7:35, 36.

PSALM 78

(*Title*.) A.M. 3074. B.C. 930.
Maschil. *or, A Psalm* for Asaph, to give
instruction. Ps 74, title.
1   **Give ear.** Ps 49:1-3. 51:4. Jg 5:3. Pr 8:4-6. Is
     51:4. 55:3. Mt 13:9.
     my people. ver. 20, 52, 62, 71. 2 K 4:13. Est
     7:3, 4.
     my law. ver. 5, 10.

incline. Ps 86:1. 88:2.
words. Ps 5:1. 19:14.

2 **I will open**. Jg +11:35. Mt 13:34, 35.
parable. Nu 23:7.
dark sayings. Ps 49:4. Nu +12:8. Jg 14:12. Pr 1:6. Da 8:23. Mt 13:11-13. Mk 4:34. 1 C 10:11.
of old. Mi +5:2.

3 **Which we**. Ps 44:1. 48:8. Ex 12:26, 27. 13:8, 14, 15.

4 **We will**. Ps 145:4-6. Dt 4:9. 6:7. Jl 1:3.
showing. Ps 71:17, 18. Dt 11:19. Jsh 4:6, 7, 21-24.
praises. Ps 9:14. 105:1-5. 145:5, 6. Is 63:7, etc.

5 **For he**. Ps 81:5. 119:152. 147:19. Dt 4:45. 6:7. 11:19. Is 8:20. Ro 3:2. 1 J 5:9-12.
testimony. Ex +16:34.
that they. ver. 3, 4. Ge +18:19. Dt +6:20. Is 38:19. Ml 4:6. Ep +6:4.

6 **That**. Note the cause/effect relationships expressed in this passage (ver. 5-8. See related note, Ps +9:10). Ps 48:13. 71:18. 102:18. 145:4. Est 9:28.
who. Ps 90:16. Dt 4:10. Jsh 22:24, 25. Jl 1:3.

7 **set their hope**. Ps 40:4. 62:5. 91:14. 130:6, 7. 146:5. Je 17:7, 8. Ac +26:6. Ro +15:4. 1 P 1:21.
not forget. Ps 77:10-12. 103:2. 105:5. Ex 12:24-27. Dt 4:9. 7:18, 19. 8:2, 11. Est 9:27, 28. 1 C 11:24.
God. Heb. *El*, Ex +15:2.
keep. Dt 5:29. Jn +13:17. 14:21-24. 1 J 3:22-24. 5:3. Re 14:12.

8 **as their fathers**. Ps 68:6. 106:7. 1 K 9:4. 22:52. 2 Ch 17:3. 22:3. 26:4. +30:8. Je 9:14. Ezk 2:3-8. 20:8, 18. Am 2:4. Mt 14:8. 23:31-33. 2 T 1:5.
stubborn. 1 S +15:23.
rebellious. Ps 68:6. Dt 31:27. 1 S +15:23.
set not. Heb. prepared not. ver. 37. 2 Ch +12:14mg. 30:19.
whose. ver. 37. Dt 4:4. Jsh 14:8, 9. Ac 11:23. Ph 1:27. 4:1.
spirit. Heb. *ruach*, Ge +41:8. Ezr 1:5. Da 5:12. 2 C +12:18.
stedfast. ver. 37. Ps 16:8. Nu +14:24. Jsh 24:15. 2 K 22:2. Jn 8:31. 1 C 15:58. 16:13. He 3:14. 4:14. 10:23.
God. Heb. *El*, Ex +15:2.

9 **The children**. ver. 21. Dt 1:41-44. Jsh 17:16-18. 1 S 4:10. 31:1.
carrying. Heb. throwing forth.
turned. Ps 30:11. 41:3mg. 66:6. 105:25. Jg 9:28, 38-40. Lk 22:33, 56-60.

10 **kept not**. Dt 31:16, 20. Jg 2:10-12. 2 K 17:14, 15. Ne 9:26-29. Je 31:32.

11 **forgat**. ver. 7. Ps 106:13, 21, 22. Dt 32:18. Je 2:32.

12 **Marvellous**. ver. 42-50. Ps 105:27-38. 135:9.

Ex ch 7-12. Dt 4:34. 6:22. Ne 9:10.
Zoan. ver. 43. Ge 32:3. Nu +13:22.

13 **He divided**. Ex +14:21. ch. 15. 1 C 10:2, 3.
made. Ps 33:7. Jsh 3:16. Hab 3:15.

14 **the daytime**. Ps 105:39. Ex +13:21.

15 **clave**. Ps 105:41. 114:8. Ex 17:6. Nu 20:11. Is 41:18. 43:20. Jn 7:37, 38. 1 C 10:4. Re 22:1, 17.

16 **brought streams**. Ps 105:41. Dt 8:15. 9:21. Is 43:19.

17 **they sinned**. ver. 32. Ps 95:8-10. 106:13-32. Dt 9:8, 12-22. He 3:16-19.
provoking. ver. 35, +40, 56. Is 63:10.
most High. ver. 35, 56. Ps +7:17. Is 14:14. Ro 9:5. 1 C 10:9. 1 Th 3:13.

18 **God**. Heb. *El*, Ex +15:2.
by asking meat. Ps 106:14, 15. Ex 16:2, 3. Nu 11:4. 1 C 10:6. Ja 4:2, 3.

19 **Yea**. Ex 16:8-10. Nu 21:5. 2 Ch 32:19. Jb 34:37. Ro 9:20. Re 13:6.
Can God. Heb. *El*, Ex +15:2. Nu 11:4, 13.
furnish. Heb. order. Ps 40:5. Jg 20:22. 1 S 17:8. Is 21:5 (prepare).
table. Ps +23:5.

20 **he smote**. Ex 17:6, 7. Nu 20:11.
can he give. ver. 41. Ge 18:12-14. Nu 11:21-23.

21 **the Lord**. ver. 31. Nu 11:10. 1 C 10:5, 11. Ju 5.
a fire. Nu 11:1-3. Dt 32:22. He 12:29.

22 **Because**. Ps 106:24. Is 7:9. He 3:12, 18, 19. 11:6. 1 J 5:10. Ju 5.

23 **Though**. Ps 33:9. Is 5:6.
opened. Dt 28:12. Ml 3:10.
the doors. Ge 7:11. 2 K 7:2, 19. Ml 3:10.

24 **had rained**. Ps 68:9. 105:40. Ex 16:4, 14. Dt 8:3. Ne 9:15, 20. Jn 6:31, 33, etc. 1 C 10:3.
the corn of heaven. Ex 16:22, 31.

25 **Man**, etc. *or*, Every one did eat the bread of the mighty. Ps 103:20. Jn 6:48-50.
he sent. Ex 16:8. Mt 14:20. 15:37.

26 **He caused**. Ps 135:7. Nu 11:31.
east wind. Ge +41:6.
blow. Heb. go.

27 **He rained**. Ex 16:12, 13. Nu 11:18, 19, 31, 32.
feathered fowls. Heb. fowl of wing. Ps 17:8.
as the sand. Ge +22:17.

28 **he let**. Ex 16:13.
fall. ver. 55.
camp. Ps 27:3. 106:16. SS 6:13.
habitations. or, tabernacles. ver. 60.

29 **for he gave**. Ps 106:15. Nu 11:19, 20.

30 **But**. Nu 11:33, 34. 22:20-22. Pr 1:32. Lk 16:19-23.

31 **fattest**. Dt +31:20.
smote down. Heb. made to bow.
chosen men. *or*, young men. ver. 63.

32 **they sinned**. Nu ch. 14, 16, 17. 21:1-6. ch. 25. 2 Ch 28:22. Ezk 20:13. Ho 13:2.
believed. ver. 22. Lk 16:31. Jn 12:37.

33 **days**. Ps 90:7-9. Nu 14:29, 35. 26:64, 65. Dt 2:14-16.
years. Ge 3:16-19. Jb 5:6, 7. 14:1. Ec 1:2, 13, 14. 12:8, 13, 14.

34 **When he slew**. Nu 21:7. Jg 3:8, 9, 12-15. 4:3. 10:7-10. Is 26:16. Je 22:23. Ho 5:15. 7:14.
returned. Dt 4:29-31. Jg 10:15, 16. La 3:39, 40. Ho 3:5. 12:6. 14:1, 2.
early. Mk +1:35.
God. Heb. *El*, Ex +15:2.

35 **remembered**. ver. 7, 11, 42. Ps 106:13, 21.
God was. Dt 32:4, 15, 30, 31.
the high. ver. +17, 56.
God. Heb. *El*, Ex +15:2.
their redeemer. Ex 6:6. 15:13. Dt 7:8. 15:15. Is +41:14. 63:8, 9. T 2:14.

36 **Nevertheless**. Ps 106:12, 13. Dt 5:28, 29. Is 29:13. Ezk 33:31. Ho 11:12.
lied. Ps 18:44mg.

37 **their heart**. Ps 119:80. Ho 7:14, 16. 10:2. Ac 8:21.
stedfast. ver. 8. Ps 44:17, 18. Dt 31:20. Ho 8:1.

38 **But he**. Ex +34:6-9. Nu 16:44-48. Is 44:21, 22.
full of. Jb 23:6. Mt 11:28-30. 28:18.
many. Is 48:9. Ezk 20:8, 9, 13, 14, 17, 21, 22.
did not. 2 K 21:29.

39 **remembered**. Ge +8:1.
flesh. Ps 103:14-16. Ge 6:3. Jn 3:6.
a wind. Ps 39:13. Jb 7:7, 16. Ja 4:14.

40 **How oft**. ver. 17. Ps 95:8-10. 106:14-33. Nu 14:11. Dt 9:21, 22.
provoke him. *or*, rebel against him. ver. +17. Jb 17:2. Is 3:8.
grieve. Ps 95:10. Is 7:13. +63:10. Ep 4:30. He 3:15-17.

41 **Yea**. Nu 14:4, 22. Dt 6:16. Ac 7:39. He 3:8-11. 2 P 2:21, 22.
God. Heb. *El*, Ex +15:2.
limited. ver. 19, 20. Ezk 9:4 (set). Mk 5:35, 36.

42 **remembered**. ver. 11, 21, 22. Ps 136:10-15. Ex 13:9. Is 11:11. Je 32:21.
the day. Ps 106:7-10. Ex 14:12, 30, 31.
delivered. Ps 31:5.
the enemy. *or*, affliction. ver. 61, 66.

43 **How**. Ps 105:27-38. 135:9. Ex 3:19, 20. Dt 4:34. 6:22. Ne 9:10.
wrought. Heb. set. ver. 5. Ps 19:4. 50:23. 54:3. 74:4. 81:5. 86:14. Ex +9:21mg. Jb 1:8mg. Zp 3:19mg.
wonders. ver. 12. Ps 71:7. 105:5, 27. 135:9.

44 **turned**. Ps 105:29. Ex 7:17-21. Re 16:3-6.

45 **sent**. Ps 105:31. Ex 8:21-24.
frogs. Ps 105:30. Ex 8:2-15. Re 16:13.

46 **the caterpillar**. 2 Ch 6:28. Is 33:4. Jl 1:4. 2:25.
labor. Dt +28:33.
locust. Ps 105:34, 35. Ex 10:4, 12-15, 19. 1 K

+8:37. Jl 1:4-7. 2:3, 25. Am 4:9. 7:1, 2. Re 9:2-11.

47 **destroyed**. *or*, killed. ver. 31.
with hail. Is +28:17.
sycamore. 1 K 10:27. 1 Ch 27:28.
frost. *or, great* hailstones.

48 **gave up**. Heb. shut up. ver. 62.
hot thunderbolts. *or*, lightnings. **S#7565h**. Ps 76:3h (arrows). Ex 9:28. Dt +32:24 **(S#7565h)**.

49 **cast**. Ps 11:6. Jb 20:23. Is 42:25. La 4:11. Zp 3:8. Ro 2:8, 9.
fierceness of. Ps 2:5. 58:9. 2 Ch +24:18. 30:8.
wrath. Ps 7:6. 85:3. 90:9, 11.
indignation. Ps 38:3. Is +66:14.
trouble. Ps 9:9. 10:1. 22:11.
by sending. Ex 12:13. 1 S 24:16. 1 K 22:21, 22. Jb 1:12. 2:6, 7. Zc 8:8.
evil angels. *or*, messengers. Pr 16:14. Is 14:32. 33:7. 37:9.

50 **made a way**. Heb. weighed a path. Ps 58:2. Pr 5:6. Is 26:7.
he spared. Jb 27:22. Ezk 5:11. 7:4, 9. 8:18. 9:10. Ro 8:32. 2 P 2:4, 5.
soul. Heb. *nephesh*, Ge +12:13.
life over to the pestilence. *or*, beasts to the murrain. Ex 9:3-6.

51 **smote**. Ps 105:36. 135:8. 136:10. Ex 12:12, 29, 30. 13:15. He 11:28.
the chief. Ge 49:3.
tabernacles. Ps 105:23. 106:22. Ge 9:22-25. 10:6.

52 **But**. Ps 105:37. Ne 9:12. Is 63:11-14.
like a. Is 40:11. Ezk +34:31. Lk 15:4-6.

53 **so that**. Ex 14:15, 19, 20. He 11:29.
but. Ps 136:15. Ex 14:27, 28. 15:10.
overwhelmed. Heb. covered. ver +55:5mg.

54 **And he**. Ex 15:13, 17. Da 9:16-20. 11:45.
his right. Ps +18:35.
purchased. Ep 1:14.

55 **cast**. Ps 44:2. 105:44, 45. 135:10-12. 136:18-22. Jsh ch. 6-21. Ne 9:22-25.
divided. Nu 33:54. Jsh 13:7. 19:51.
and made. Dt 6:10-12.

56 **they tempted**. ver. 40, 41. Dt 31:16-20. 32:15-21. Jg 2:11, 12. 2 K 17:7, etc. Ne 9:25, 26. Ezk 16:15-26.
most high. ver. +17, 35.

57 **But**. ver. 41. Jg 3:5-7, 12. Ezk 20:27, 28.
they were. ver. 8-10, 37. Ho 7:16.

58 **their high**. Dt 12:2, 4. 2 K +21:3.
moved. Ex +20:5. Jg 2:12, 20.
with. Ps 97:7. Ex +20:4. Jg 2:11, 17. 10:6. 1 K 11:7, 10. 12:31. 2 Ch +34:3. Je 8:19. Ho 13:2.

59 **God**. Ps 11:4. 14:2-5. Ge 18:20, 21.
greatly. Ps +106:40.

60 **tabernacle**. Ex +38:21.
Shiloh. Jg +21:19.

61 **his strength**. Ps 63:2. 132:8. Jg 18:30. 1 S
4:11. 5:1, 2. 1 Ch 16:11. 2 Ch 6:41.
glory. Ps 24:7. Ex 40:34. 1 S 4:21, 22.

62 **gave**. 1 S 4:2, 10, 11.
wroth. Ps 89:38. Is 64:9.

63 **fire**. ver. 21. Dt 32:22.
maidens. Ps 45:14. 148:12. Ge +24:16
(**S#1330h**). Is 4:1. Je 7:34. 16:9. 25:10.
given to marriage. Heb. praised. Ps 18:3.
48:1. 113:3. Ge 12:15. Pr 31:28, 31. SS 6:9. Je
7:34.

64 **priests**. 1 S 2:33, 34. 4:11, 17. 22:18, 19.
widows. Jb +27:15.

65 **Then**. Ps +3:7.
and like. Is 42:13, 14.
that shouteth. Is +42:13.

66 **And he**. 1 S 5:6-12. 6:4. Jb 40:12.
he put. Je 23:40.
perpetual. ver. 69. Ge +9:12.
reproach. Ps 15:3. 22:6. 31:11.

67 **he refused**. 1 S 6:21. 7:1, 2. 2 S 6:2, 17.

68 **chose**. Ge 49:8-10. Ru 4:17-22. 1 S 16:1. 2
Ch 6:6.
mount. 1 Ch +11:5.

69 **And he**. Ps 48:2, 3. 1 K 6:2. 9:8. 2 Ch 3:4.
high. 1 Ch 29:1, 19. 2 Ch 2:9. Ac 7:48, 49.
earth. Ps 102:25. 104:5. 119:90, 91. 1 S 2:8.
Jb 26:7. Is 48:13. 51:6. Col 1:16, 17. Re 20:11.
established. Heb. founded. Ps 8:2mg. 89:11.
Hab 1:12mg.
for ever. Heb. *olam*, Ex +12:24. Ps 89:36, 37.
104:5. 119:90, 91. Ec +1:4.

70 **chose**. Ps 89:19, 20. 1 S 16:11, 12. 2 S 3:18.
6:21. Is +55:3. Ac 13:22, 34.
and took. Ps 75:6, 7. Ex 3:1, 10. 1 S 17:15,
etc. 2 S 7:8. 1 K 19:19, 20. Pr 15:33. Am 7:14,
15. Mt 4:18-22. 1 C 1:26-29.

71 **From following**. Heb. From after. Je
+17:16mg.
ewes. Ge 33:13. Is 40:11.
great with young. or, suckling ones. **S#5763h**.
Ge 33:13. 1 S 6:7 (milch), 10. Is 40:11mg.
brought. Ps 75:6, 7. 113:7, 8. 1 S 2:7, 8. Je
27:5, 6.
feed. Is +40:11.

72 **according**. Ps 28:9. 75:2. 101:1-8. 2 S 8:15. 1
K 9:4. 15:5. Is 11:1-4. Ac 13:22, 36.
guided. Ps +32:8. 1 K 3:6-9, 28. Zc 11:15-17.
2 C 3:5, 6. 2 T 2:15. Ja 1:5.

PSALM 79

(*Title*.) A.M. 3416. B.C. 588.
A Psalm. This Psalm is supposed, with much
probability, to have been written on the
destruction of the city and temple of
Jerusalem by Nebuchadnezzar.
of Asaph. *or*, for Asaph. Ps 74, title, mg. 2 K
+18:18.

1 **the heathen**. Ps 74:3, 4. 80:12, 13. 2 K

21:12-16. 25:4-10. 2 Ch 36:3, 4, 6, 7, 17. Zc
14:2. Lk 21:24. Re 11:2.
into. Ps 74:2. 78:71. Ex 15:17. Is 47:6.
holy. Ps 74:7, 8. 2 K 24:13. La 1:10. Ezk 7:20,
21. 9:7.
have laid. Je +17:27. 26:18. Mi 3:12.

2 **dead bodies**. Je +7:33.

3 **Their**. ver. 10. Mt 23:35. Ro 8:36. Re 16:6.
17:6. 18:24.
and there, etc. ver. +2. Ps 141:7. Je 14:16.
15:3. Re 11:9.

4 **become**. Ps +31:11. 80:6. Dt 28:15, 37. Je
25:18. La 2:15, 16. Ezk 35:12. 36:3, 15.
scorn. 1 K 9:7. Ne 2:19. 4:1-4.
derision. Lk +16:14.

5 **How long**. Re +6:10.
wilt. Ps 85:5. 103:8-10. Is 64:9. Mi 7:18.
for ever. Jb +4:20 (**S#5331h**).
jealousy. Ex +20:5.
burn. Dt +32:22.

6 **Pour out**. Ezk +7:8. Jl 2:28, 29. Zc 12:10. Ac
2:17, 18, 33. Ro 5:5. T 3:6.
wrath. 1 S 28:18. Mi 7:9. Ro 2:5. 4:15. 13:4,
5. Ep 5:6.
upon. Is ch. 13, 21, 23. Je +10:25. 25:29. ch.
46-51.
not known. Ps 9:16, 17. Is 45:4, 5. Jn 16:3.
17:25. Ac 17:23. Ro 1:28. Ep 2:12.
2 Th 1:8.
not called. Ps 145:18. Je +10:25. Ro 10:12-
14. 1 C 1:2.

7 **For they**. Ps 80:13. Je +10:25. Zc 1:15.
Jacob. Dt +9:1.
laid. 2 Ch 36:21. Is 24:1-12. 64:10, 11.

8 **remember**. Ps 25:7. 130:3, 4. Ex 32:34. 1 K
17:18. Is 43:25. 64:9. Ho 8:13. 9:9. Re 18:5.
former iniquities. *or*, the iniquities of them
that were before us. Ge 15:16. Ezk 2:3. Da
9:16. Mt 23:32-36.
let thy. Ps 21:3. +51:1.
we are. Ps 106:43. 116:6. 142:6. Dt 28:43.

9 **for the glory**. Ps +119:158. 1 K 18:36, 37. 2
Ch 14:11. Is 37:20. Ml 2:2. Mt +6:13. 1 T
+1:17.
purge. Ps 25:11. 65:3. Da 9:9, 19.
for thy. Is +48:9.

10 **Wherefore**. Ps 42:3, 10. 115:2. Jl 2:17. Mi
7:10.
let him. Ps 9:16. 58:11. 83:17, 18. Ex 6:7.
7:5. Ezk 36:23. 39:21, 22.
by the. Je 51:35. Re 18:20.
revenging. Heb. vengeance. Ro 12:19.

11 **sighing**. Ps +12:5. 35:10. 69:33. 102:20. Ex
2:23, 24. Is 42:7.
prisoner. Ps 102:19, 20. Ac 12:5. Ep 6:18-20.
according. Ps 146:6, 7. Nu 14:17-19. Mt
6:13. Ep 3:20.
thy power. Heb. thine arm. Ex +15:16. Ezk
22:6mg.
preserve thou those that are appointed

to die. Heb. reserve the children of death. 1 S +20:31mg.

12 **render**. Ps 31:23. Ge 4:15. Le 26:21, 28. Is 65:5-7. Je 32:18. Lk 6:38.
wherewith. Ps +44:16. 74:18, 22. Zc 2:8.

13 **thy people**. Ps +74:1.
for ever. Heb. *olam*, Ex +12:24.
we will. Ps 45:17. 74:15, 22. 80:1. 145:4. Is 43:21.
all generations. Heb. generation and generation. Ps 12:7. 14:5. +33:11mg.

PSALM 80

(*Title*.) A.M. cir. 3463. B.C. cir. 541.
Shoshannim-Eduth. i.e. *lilies of testimony*, **s#7802h**. Ps 45, 60, 69, titles.
A Psalm. This Psalm is generally supposed to have been written during the Babylonian captivity; but some think it refers to the desolations made by Sennacherib.
of Asaph. *or*, for Asaph. Ps 79, title. 2 K +18:18.

1 **Give ear**. Ps +5:1.
O Shepherd. Ps 79:13. Jn +10:11.
leadest. Ps 77:20. 78:52. Is 49:9, 10. 63:11. Jn 10:3, 4.
Joseph. Ex +12:40. Am 5:15. 6:6.
dwellest. 1 S +4:4.
shine. ver. 3, 7, 19. Ps 50:2. 94:1. Dt 33:2. Jb 10:3. Is 60:1. Ezk 43:2. Da 9:17. Re 21:23.

2 **Before**. Nu 2:18-24. 10:22-24.
Ephraim. Ex +12:40. "Ephraim" includes the ten tribes, "Benjamin" includes Judah; and "Manasseh" includes the two-and-a-half tribes. Ps 78:9.
stir up. Ps +3:7. 78:38. Is 42:13, 14.
come and save us. Heb. come for salvation to us. Is 11:11. 25:9. 33:22. +59:20. Ro +11:26.

3 **Turn us**. ver. 7, 19. Ps 85:4. 1 K 18:37. Je 31:18, 19. La 5:19-21.
cause. ver. 1. Ps 4:6. 67:1. 119:135. Nu 6:25, 26.
be saved. Is 30:15. Je 4:14.

4 **how long**. Ps 85:5. Is 58:2, 3, 6-9. La 3:44. Ho 3:4, 5. 5:15. 6:1-3. Mi 5:3. Mt 15:22-28. Lk 18:1-8. Ac +3:19-21. Ja 4:3.
be angry. Heb. smoke. Ps 74:1. Dt +4:24. 29:20.

5 **feedest**. Ps 42:3. 102:9. Jb 6:7. Is 30:20. Ezk 4:16, 17.

6 **Thou**. Je 15:10.
our enemies. Jg 16:25. Is 36:8, 12-20. Lk +8:53. Re 11:10.

7 **Turn us**. ver. 3, 19. Ps 51:10. Lk 1:16, 17.
we shall. Is 30:15. 64:5. Je 4:14. Mk 4:12. 2 T +2:25, 26.

8 **a vine**. Is 5:1-7. 27:2, 3. Je 2:21. Ezk 15:6. 17:6. 19:10. Mt 21:33-41. Jn 15:1-8.

thou hast cast. Ps 44:2. 78:55. Je 18:9, 10.
planted. Je +11:17.

9 **preparedst**. Ps 105:44. Ex 23:28-30. Jsh 23:13-15. 24:12. Ne 9:22-25. Is 5:5, 6. Je 12:10. Na 2:2.
to take. Is 27:6. 37:31. Je 12:2.
and it. 1 K 4:20, 25. 1 Ch 21:5. 27:23, 24.

10 **goodly cedars**. Heb. cedars of God. Ps +36:6mg. 104:16.

11 **She sent**. Ps +72:8.
sea. Nu +34:6.
river. Ps +72:8.

12 **broken**. Ps 89:40, 41. Is 5:5. 18:5, 6. Na 2:2. Lk 20:16.

13 **The boar**. 2 K ch. 18, 19, 24, 25. 2 Ch ch. 32, 36. Je 4:7. 39:1-3. 51:34. 52:7, 12-14.

14 **Return**. Ps 7:7. 90:13. Is 63:15, 17. Jl 2:14. Ml 3:7. Ac 15:16.
look down. Ps 33:13. Is 63:15. La 3:50. Da 9:16-19.

15 **vineyard**. ver. 8. Is 5:1, 2. Je 2:21. Mk 12:1. Jn 15:1.
right hand. Ps +18:35.
the branch. Ps 89:21. Is +11:1. 49:5.

16 **burned**. Ps 79:5. Is 27:11. Ezk 20:47, 48. Jn 15:6.
cut down. Am +9:11. Lk 13:7, 9. Ac 15:16.
perish. Ps 39:11. 76:6, 7. 90:7. 2 Th 1:9.

17 **Let thy**. ver. 15. Ps 89:21. 110:1. 132:11. Is 53:5. Da +7:13, 14. Jn 5:21-29.
the man. 2 S 7:19. 1 Ch 17:17. Ac 2:30. 17:31. Ro 1:3. 1 T 2:5. 2 J +7.
right hand. Ps +110:1.
son of man. Ps +8:4. Mt +16:27.
madest strong. Ps +45:7. Is 41:10. 53:10. Mt 28:18. Ac 2:33.

18 **So will not**. Ps 79:13. Je +32:40. Jn 6:66-69. He 10:38, 39.
quicken. Ps 71:20. 85:6. 119:25, 37, 40, 50, 88, 107, 149, 154, 156, 159. 143:11. SS 1:4. Is 57:15. Ho 6:2. Mt 24:13. Jn 5:21. Ro 4:17. 8:11. Ph 2:12, 13. Ep 2:1-5. 1 P 3:18.
will call. Ps 3:4. 18:3, 6. 22:2. 27:7. Ge 4:26. Ac 15:17.
thy name. Ps +9:10. 105:1. Ac 2:21. Ro 10:13.

19 **Turn us**. ver. 3, 7. SS 1:4. Je 3:22, 23.
cause. ver. 1. Ps 27:4, 9. 31:16. 44:3.

PSALM 81

(*Title*.) A.M. 3489. B.C. 515.
Gittith. Ps 8, title.
A Psalm. Some suppose this Psalm to have been composed to be sung at the feast of Trumpets, before the time of David; and others think it was written at the removal of the ark to Mount Zion; but the most probable opinion is, that it was sung at the dedication of the second temple.

of Asaph. *or*, for Asaph. Ps 79, title. 2 K +18:18.

1 Sing. Ps 67:4. Je 31:7.
our strength. Ps 18:1, 2. 28:7. 52:7. Ph 4:13.
make. Ps 33:1-3. 46:1-7. 66:1. 95:1, 2. 100:1, 2.
the God. Ps 46:11. Ge 50:17. Mt 22:32.

2 a psalm. Mk 14:26. Ep 5:19. Col 3:16. Ja 5:13.
harp. Re +5:8.

3 Blow. Ps 98:6. Nu 10:1-9. 1 Ch 15:24. 16:6, 42. 2 Ch 5:12. 13:12, 14.
trumpet. Le 23:24.
new moon. Col +2:16.
solemn. Le +23:36.

4 statute. Ps 2:7. 50:16. 94:20.
a law. *or*, ordinance. Ps 1:5 (judgment). 7:6. Ge 18:19, 25 (right). Ex 15:25. Le 5:10mg. Nu 15:24mg.
God of Jacob. ver. 1.

5 in Joseph. Nu +1:10.
for a. Ps 78:6. Ex 13:8, 9, 14-16. Dt 4:45. Ezk 20:20.
through. *or*, against. Ex 12:12, 27, 29.
where. Ps 114:1. Ge 42:23. Dt 28:49. Is 28:11. Je 5:15. 1 C 14:21, 22.

6 I removed. Ex 1:14. 6:6. Is 9:4. 10:27. Mt 11:29.
were delivered. Heb. passed away. Ps 17:3. 37:36. 42:4. 57:1.
from the pots. Ps 68:13. Ex 1:14. 1 S 2:14. 2 K 10:7. 2 Ch 35:13. Jb 41:20. Je 24:2.

7 calledst. Ps 50:15. 91:14, 15. Ex 2:23. 14:10, 30, 31. 17:2-7.
secret. Ex 14:24. 19:16, 19. 20:18-21.
proved. Ex 17:6, 7. Nu 20:13, 24. Dt 33:8.
Meribah. *or*, strife. Ps 95:8. 106:32. Ge 13:8. Ex 17:7mg.
Selah. Ps +9:16.

8 Hear. Ps 50:7. Dt 32:46. Is 55:3, 4. Jn 3:11, 32, 33. Ac 20:21. 1 J 5:9.
if thou wilt. ver. 13. Dt 5:27. +15:5. Is 1:19.

9 There shall. Ex 20:3-5. 1 C 8:5, 6.
strange. Ps 18:44, 45. 137:4. 144:7, 11. Ex +12:43. Dt 6:14. 32:12. Is 43:12. Ml 2:11.

10 I am. Ex 20:2, 3, 5. Je 11:4. 31:31-33.
open. Ps 37:3, 4. Dt 15:10. Jn 7:37. 15:7. 16:23. Ep 3:19, 20. Re 21:6. 22:17.
fill it. Mt +5:6. Jn 10:10. 1 C 2:9. 1 T 6:17. Ja 1:5.

11 people. Ps 106:12, 13. Je 2:11-13. +7:26.
would none. Ex 32:1. Dt 32:15, 18. Pr 1:29, 30. He 10:29.

12 I gave. Ge 6:3. Ho 4:17. Ac 7:42. 14:16. Ro 1:24, 26, 27. 2 Th 2:9-11.
their own hearts' lust. *or*, the hardness of their hearts, *or* imaginations. Je +3:17mg.
they walked. Ex 11:9. Is 30:1. Je 7:24. 44:16, 17.
own counsels. Jsh 9:14. Je 7:24. 23:18, 22.

13 Oh that. Dt 5:29. 32:29. Is 48:18. Mt 23:37. Lk 19:41, 42.
had hearkened. Ex 19:5, 6. Le 26:3-12. Dt 4:5, 6, 40. 28:1-13.
had walked. Dt 10:12, 13.

14 I should. Nu 14:9, 45. Jsh 23:13. Jg 2:20-23.
turned. Am 1:8. Zc 13:7.
hand. Is +1:25.

15 The haters. Ps 18:45. 83:2, etc. Ex 20:5. Dt 7:10. Jn 15:22, 23. Ro 1:30. 8:7.
submitted themselves. *or*, yielded feigned obedience. Heb. lied. Ps +66:3mg.
time. Ps 102:28. Is 65:22. Jl 3:20.
for ever. Heb. *olam*, Ex +12:24.

16 fed. Ps 23:2. 36:8. 147:14. Dt 32:13, 14. Jl 2:24.
finest of the wheat. Heb. fat of the wheat. Ps 17:10. 63:5mg. 73:7. 147:14mg. Ge 30:14. Dt 32:14.
honey. Jg 14:8, 9, 18. 1 S 14:25, 26.
the rock. Ps 18:33. Ex 17:6. Dt 32:13. Jg 6:21. Jb 29:6. Ep 2:6.

PSALM 82

(*Title*.) A.M. 3108. B.C. 896.
A Psalm. Some refer this Psalm to the time of David, and others to that of Hezekiah; but it is more probable that it was composed when Jehoshaphat reformed the courts throughout his kingdom, 2 Ch 19:6, 7.
of Asaph. *or*, for Asaph. 2 K +18:18.

1 God, etc. Or, "God standeth in the assembly of God (*El*), he judgeth among the judges" (*elohim*). Ex +18:21. 2 Ch 19:6, 7. Ec 5:8.
the gods. ver. +6, 7. Ex +12:12.

2 How. Mt +17:17.
judge. Ps 58:1, 2. Mi 3:1-3, 9-12. Ja +2:1.
accept. Ro +2:11.
Selah. Ps +9:16.

3 Defend. Heb. Judge. Dt +32:36.
poor. Ps +12:5.
fatherless. Ex +22:22.
do. Je 7:5. Je +21:12. Ja 1:27.

4 Deliver. Je +22:16.
rid. Ps 140:12. Ne 5:1-13. Jb 5:15, 16.

5 They. That is, the judges know not.
know not. Ps 53:4. Jb 21:14, 15. Pr 1:29. Je 4:22. Mi 3:1. Ro 1:28.
walk. Pr 2:13. 4:19. Ec 2:14. Is 2:5. Jn 3:19. 12:35. 1 J 2:11.
all the, etc. Ps 11:3. 75:3. Ec 3:16. Is 5:7. 2 T 2:19.
out of course. Heb. moved. Ps 10:6. 13:4. 15:5. 16:8.

6 I have said. ver. 1. Ex 21:6. 22:8, 9, 28. Jn 10:34-36.
gods. Heb. *elohim*. Ps 8:5. Ex +12:12. Jn 1:1. +10:30, *34*, 35. Ro 9:5. T 2:13. 1 J 5:20.
children. 1 J +3:1.
most High. Ps +7:17.

7 **But**. Ps 49:12. Jb 21:32. Ezk 31:14.
like men. Or, "like Adam," *keadam*. Jg 16:7.
and fall, etc. Or, "and fall as one of them, O
ye princes." Ps 83:11. Ho 7:16.

8 **Arise**. Ps +3:7. 96:13. Mi 7:2, 7.
judge. Ps +7:8. Ac +24:10.
earth. Ge +6:11.
for thou. He 1:2.
inherit all nations. Ps 2:8. 69:36. +86:9.
96:10. +149:5-9. Mt +5:5. Jn 10:16. Ro 8:17,
32. Re +5:10.

PSALM 83

(*Title*.) A.M. 3416. B.C. 588.
A Song. Some refer this Psalm to the confederacy against Jehoshaphat, as William Kay
notes "Referred by Kimchi (with the highest
probability) to the time of Jehoshaphat's
prayer, 2 Ch 20:5-12, when Juda was threat-
ened by a confederacy of Moab, Ammon,
Edom, and others, acting in concert with
Syria, compare Am ch. 1" (*The Psalms with
Notes*, p. 272); and others to the destruction of
Jerusalem by Nebuchadnezzar.
of Asaph. *or*, for Asaph. Ps 79, title. 2 K
+18:18.

1 **Keep**. Ps 28:1. 35:22. 44:23. 50:3. 109:1, 2.
be not. Is 42:14.

2 **For, lo**. Ps 2:1, 2. 74:4, 23. 2 K 19:28. Is
37:29. Je 1:19. Mt 27:24. Ac 4:25-27. 16:22.
17:5. 19:28, etc. 21:30. 22:22. 23:10.
tumult. Ps 46:3. Is 17:12.
that hate. Ps 81:15. Ro 1:30.
lifted. Ps 75:4, 5, 93:3. Jg +8:28. Is 37:23. Da
5:20-23.
the head. Hab 3:13.

3 **crafty counsel**. Ps 10:9. 56:6. 64:2. 1 S
13:19. Is 7:6, 7. Lk 20:20-23.
against. Ps +122:6. Ge 12:3. Pr +21:30.
thy people. Dt +32:43.
thy hidden ones. Ps +64:2. 91:1. 1 K 17:3. Is
+16:3-5. 18:2. Ezk +20:35. Da +11:33. Hab
+3:4, 16. Zp +2:3. Zc +11:16mg. Ml +3:16. Lk
+21:36. Col 3:3, 4. 1 Th +1:10. 2 Th +1:7.

4 **Come**. Ex 1:10. Est 3:6-9. Pr 1:12. Je 11:19.
+31:36. Da 7:25. Mt 27:62-66. Ac 4:17. 9:1, 2.
23:14.
from being a nation. 2 Ch 20:11. Is 7:8. Zc
14:2.

5 **For**. Ps 2:2. Pr 21:30. Is 7:5-7. 8:9, 10. Jn
11:47-53. Ac 9:4. 23:12, 13. Re 17:13. 19:19.
consent. Heb. heart. Ps 4:7. 7:10.
they are. Jsh 10:3-5. 2 S 10:6-8. Is 7:2.

6 **The tabernacles**. Ps 15:1. 19:4. 27:5, 6.
Edom. 2 Ch 20:1, 10, 11.
Moab. Ezk +25:8.
Hagarenes. i.e. *fugitives*, **S#1905h**. Ge 25:12-
18. 1 Ch 5:10, 19, 20, Hagarites.

7 **Gebal**. i.e. *boundary*, **S#1380h**. Jsh 13:5. Ezk 27:9.

8 **Assur**. Ge 10:11mg, Asshur. 25:3.
Holpen. Heb. been an arm to. Is 33:2.
the children. Ge 19:37, 38. Dt 2:9.
Selah. Ps +9:16.

9 **as unto**. Nu 31:7, 8. Jg +7:22-25. Is 10:26.
Hab 3:7.
as to Sisera. Jg 4:15-24.
of Kison. i.e. *curved*, **S#7028h**, Jg +5:21, Kishon.

10 **Endor**. Taanach and Megiddo (Jg 5:19) were
near En-Dor (William Kay). Jsh 17:11. 1 S
28:7.
as dung. Je +16:4.

11 **Oreb**. Jg 7:25.
Zebah. Jg 8:12-21.

12 **Let us take**. ver. 4. Ps 74:7, 8. 2 Ch 20:11.
the houses. Heb. *neoth*. The lands of which
God has given the occupation to Israel
(William Kay). Ps +23:2. 74:20.

13 **O my**. Ps 22:1. 44:4. 74:11, 12.
like. Is 17:12-14.
as the. Ps 35:5. 68:1, 2. Mt 3:12. 1 C +3:12.

14 **As the fire**. Ps +97:3. 2 P +3:7.
the flame. Dt +32:22. Na 1:6, 10.

15 **persecute**. Ps 2:5. 11:6. 50:3. 58:9. Jb 9:17.
22:10. 27:20-23. Is +28:17. 29:6. 30:30. 31:8.
Je +23:19. Ezk 13:11-14. Am 1:14. Mt 7:27.
He 12:18.

16 **Fill**. Ps 6:10. 9:19, 20. 34:5.
thy name. 2 Ch 20:9.

17 **Let them**. Ps +71:13. Is 24:21, 22. 26:21.
+66:24. Da 2:44. Zc 14:12-14.
for ever. Ps +9:18.

18 **That men**. Ex 9:15, 16. Pr +16:4. Is 5:16. Je
16:21. Ezk +6:7. Jn +11:42. Ro 9:17, 22-24.
know. Is 64:1, 2. Ezk +6:10.
whose name. Ex +6:3. 2 Ch 20:9.
the most high. Ps +7:17. 87:5. 92:8. 2 Ch
20:6. Is 54:5. Mi 4:13. Zc 4:14. Mt 11:10. Ro
9:5. 1 C 10:9. 1 Th 3:13.
earth. Ps 97:5.

PSALM 84

(*Title*.) A.M. 3469. B.C. 535.
Gittith. Ps 8, 81, titles.
A Psalm. Some suppose this Psalm was composed by David when driven from Jerusalem
by Absalom's rebellion; but it is more probable that it was written at the foundation of
the second temple.
for. *or*, of.

1 **How**. Ps 26:8. 27:4. 48:1, 2. 87:2, 3. 122:1.
He 9:23, 24. Re 21:2, 3, 22, 23.
O Lord. Ps 103:20, 21. 1 K 22:19. Ne 9:6. Is
6:2, 3.

2 **soul**. Heb. *nephesh*, Ge +34:3. Ps 139:14. Is
26:9. Mt +11:29. Lk 1:46. 2:35. Ac 14:2, 22.
longeth. Ps 13:1, 2. 27:8. 42:1, 2. 63:1, 2.
73:26. 107:9. 119:20, 81. 143:6. SS 2:4, 5.
3:1-4. 5:8.

my heart. Ps +24:4. 1 S 13:14.
crieth. Jb 23:3. Is 26:9. 64:1. La 2:18. Ho 7:14.
the living God. Je +10:10.

3 **sparrow.** Ps 90:1. 91:1. 116:7. Mt 8:20. 23:37.
my King. Ps 5:2.

4 **Blessed.** Dt +28:3. Ps 23:6. 27:4. 65:4. 134:1-3.
they will. Ps 71:8, 15. 145:1, 2, 21. Is 12:4, 5. Re 4:8. 7:15.
Selah. Ps +9:16.

5 **Blessed.** Dt +28:3.
strength. Ps +18:1. 2 C 3:5.
in whose. Ps 40:8. 42:4. 55:14. Is 26:9. Je 31:33. 50:4, 5. Mi 4:2.

6 **Who.** Ps 66:10-12. Jn 16:33. Ac 14:22. Ro 5:3-5. 8:37. 2 C 1:5. 4:17. Re 7:14.
Baca, etc. i.e. *the weeper,* **S#1056h.** 2 S 5:22-24.
the rain. Ps 68:9. 2 K 3:9-20. **S#4175h:** Jl 2:23mg.
well. Heb. *mayan,* Ge +7:11 (**S#4599h**), a spring or fountain. Ps 74:15. 87:7. 104:10. Is 12:3.
filleth. Heb. covereth. Ps 71:13. 109:19, 29. Is 59:17.
pools. S#1293h, elsewhere generally translated *blessing,* Ge 12:2; 2 Ch 20:26mg; Ps 3:8; 21:3, 6. Ge 26:15. Jg 1:15.

7 **They.** Jb 17:9. Pr 4:18. Is 40:29, 31. Jn 1:16. 10:27, 28. 15:2. 2 C 3:18. Ph 3:13, 14. He 12:1. 2 P 3:18.
strength to strength. Heb. company to company. Ps 18:32, 39. 33:16. Ezk 41:7mg. Lk 2:44. Ro 1:17. 2 C 3:18.
in Zion. Ps 43:3. Dt 16:16. Is 46:13. Je 31:6. Zc 14:16. Jn 6:39, 40. 14:3. 1 Th 4:17.
appeareth. Ps 18:15. 42:2. 90:16. Is 47:3.

8 **Lord.** ver. 1, 2, 3, 11, 12, Jehovah.
God of hosts. Ps 59:5. 80:4, 7, 19.
prayer. Ps 4:1. 6:9. 35:13. 39:12.
give ear. Ps +5:1. 49:1.
God of Jacob. Ps +20:1. Ho 12:3-6.
Selah. Ps +9:16.

9 **our.** ver. 11. Ps 98:1. Ge 15:1. Dt 33:29.
the face. Ps 45:12mg. 80:3. 119:58mg. 132:10.
thine anointed. Ps 2:2, 6mg. 89:20. 132:17. 1 S 2:10. 16:6. 2 S 19:21. 23:1. 2 Ch 6:42. Ac 4:27.

10 **For.** ver. 1, 2. Ps 27:4. 43:3, 4. 63:2. Lk 2:46. Ro 8:5, 6. Ph 3:20.
thousand. Ex 18:21. Mi +5:2.
I had. Heb. I would choose rather to sit at the threshold. 2 K +12:9mg. Ja 2:3.
to dwell. Ps 17:14, 15. 26:8-10. 141:4, 5.

11 **a sun.** Ps 27:1. Le 16:12, 13. Hab 3:19. Ml +4:2. Jn 1:9, 10. Re 21:23.
shield. ver. 9. Ps 3:3. 28:7. 33:20. 47:9. 115:9-11. 119:114. Ge +15:1. Le 16:12, 13. Pr 2:7.

the Lord. Jn 1:16. Ro 8:16-18. 2 C 3:18. 4:17. Ph 1:6.
give grace. Je 30:9. 31:33. Mt +28:19. Lk 1:74, 75. Jn 17:17, 19. Ro 5:15, 17, 20. 1 C 6:11. 2 C 3:5, 18. +8:9. Ep 2:10. Ph 2:13. 4:13. Col 1:12, 21, 22. 1 Th 5:23. 2 Th 2:13. T 2:11, 14. He 10:29. Ja 4:6. 1 P 5:10.
glory. Ps 73:24. Ex 33:18. Ro 5:2. 8:30.
no good thing. Ps 3:8. 5:12. 16:6. 23:6. 34:9, 10. 58:11. 85:12. 106:15. Pr 3:32. 10:6, 24, 28. 11:18, 19, 28. 12:12. 13:9, 21. 21:21. Ec 8:12. Is 3:10. Je 5:25. +29:11. Mt 6:33. Ro 8:32. 1 C 3:21, 22. Ph 4:19. 1 T +4:8. Ja 4:3.
walk. Ps 15:2. Pr 2:7. 10:9. 28:6, 18. Mi 2:7. Ga 2:14.

12 **blessed.** Ps +1:1. 62:8. Is 30:18. 50:10. Je 17:5, 7, 8. Ro 15:13. 1 P 1:8.

PSALM 85

(*Title*.) A.M. 3468. B.C. 536.
for. or, of. Ps 42, title.

1 **Lord.** Le 26:42. Zc 1:16.
favorable unto. or, well pleased with. Ps 77:7.
thy land. Dt +32:43.
thou hast. Ps 126:1, 2. Ezr 1:11. 2:1. Je +23:3.

2 **forgiven.** Ps 32:1. 79:8, 9. Je 50:20. Mi 7:18. Ac 13:39. Col 2:13, 14.

3 **taken.** Is 6:7. 12:1. 54:7-10. Jn 1:29.
turned, etc. or, turned thine anger from waxing hot. Ex 32:11, +12, 22.

4 **Turn us.** Ps 80:3, 7, 19. 138:8. Je 31:18. La 5:21. Ml 4:6.
O God. Ps +88:1. Mi 7:7, 18-20. Jn 4:22.
cause. Ps 78:38. Is 10:25. Da 9:16.

5 **angry.** Ps 74:1. 77:9. 79:5. 80:4. 89:46. Is +41:9. 64:9-12. Mi 7:18. Zc +10:6.
for ever. Heb. *olam,* Ex +12:24.
draw. Lk 21:24. Re 18:21-23.

6 **Wilt thou.** Ps 80:14-16, +18. 122:6. SS 4:16. Is 62:6, 7. 64:1, 2. Je 14:20, 21. Da 9:17. Hab 3:2. Mt 6:10.
revive. Ps 80:18. 138:7. Ezr 9:8, 9. Is 57:15. Ho 6:1, 2. Hab 3:2.
people. Ps 53:6. Ezr 3:11-13. Je 33:11.

7 **thy mercy.** Ps 98:3. 106:45. Dt +32:43. Is 54:7, 8. Je 42:12. Mi 7:18, 20. Hab 3:2. Zc 10:6. Lk 1:50, 54, 55, 72, 78.
thy salvation. Ps 50:23. 91:16. Is 25:9. Lk 1:69. 2:30. He +9:28.

8 **hear.** Hab 2:1. He 12:25.
God. Heb. *El,* Ex +15:2.
speak peace. Ps 29:11. Je 29:11. Zc 9:10. Jn 20:19, 26. Ro +5:1.
to his. Ps 50:5. Ep 1:1, 2.
but. Ps 130:4. Jn 5:14. 8:11. Ac 3:26. Ga 4:9. 2 T 2:19. He 10:26-29. 2 P 2:20-22. Re 2:4, 5. 3:19.
folly. Ge +34:7. 1 S 25:25. Pr 26:11. 27:22.

9 **Surely.** Ps 24:4, 5. 50:23. 119:155. Is 46:13.

Mk 12:32-34. Jn 7:17. Ac 10:2-4. 11:13, 14.
13:26. Ro 10:8, 9. T 2:11-13.
that fear. Pr +3:7.
that glory. Ps +102:16. Ex 40:34, 35. 2 Ch
7:1, 3. Is 4:5. 46:13. Ezk 26:20. Hg 2:7-9. Zc
2:5, 8. Lk 2:32. Jn 1:14.

10 **Mercy**. Ps 61:7. 89:14. Ex +34:6, 7. Jn 1:17.
truth. ver. 11. Mi 7:20.
righteousness. Ps +46:10. 72:3. Is 32:16-18.
42:21. 45:24. Je 23:5, 6. Ho 2:19. Ro 3:25, 26,
31. 5:21. 14:17. 2 C 4:6. Ep 3:8-11. 1 T 1:11.
He 7:2. 1 P 1:12.
peace. Lk 2:14. Ro +5:1.
kissed. 2 S 15:5. 1 K 19:18. Pr 7:13.

11 **Truth**. Is 4:2. 45:8. 53:2. Jn 1:17. 14:6. 1 J
5:20, 21.
shall spring. Mk 16:6. Ga 4:4, 5.
righteousness. Dt 33:16. Is 32:17. 42:21.
45:24, 25. Je 23:5, 6. Mt 3:17. 17:5. Lk 2:14.
Ro 3:25, 26. 5:1, 2. 2 C 5:21. Ep 1:6.

12 **the Lord**. Ps 84:11. Mi 6:8. Mt 7:11. Lk
11:13. 1 C 1:30. Ep 1:3. Ja 1:17.
our land. Ps 67:6. 72:16. Is 30:23, 24. 32:15,
16. Mt 13:8, 23. Ac 2:41. 21:20. 1 C 3:6-9.

13 **Righteousness**. Ps 72:2, 3. 89:14. Is 58:8. Ps
119:35. Mt 20:27, 28. Jn 13:14-16, 34. 2 C
3:18. Ga 2:20. Ep 5:1, 2. Ph 2:5-8. 3:9, 16, 17.
He 12:1, 2. 1 P 2:18-24. 4:1. 1 J 2:1-3, 6.

PSALM 86

(*Title*.) **A Prayer of David**. *or*, a prayer,
being a Psalm of David. This Psalm is supposed to have been composed by David either
when persecuted by Saul, or driven from
Jerusalem by Absalom. Ps 102, 142, titles.

1 **Bow**. Ps 31:2. Is 37:17. Da 9:18.
for I am. Ps 10:14. +40:17. 119:22. 140:12. Is
66:2. Mt 5:3. Lk 4:18. Ja 1:9, 10. 2:5.

2 **Preserve**. Ps 4:3. 37:28. 119:94, 175. 145:19,
20. 1 S 2:9. Is 55:3. Jn 10:27-29. 17:11. 1 P
1:5. 5:3-5.
soul. Heb. *nephesh*, Ge +12:13.
holy. *or*, one whom thou favorest. Ps 18:19.
+43:1mg. 145:17mg. Dt 7:7, 8. Ro 9:18,
23, 24.
save. Ps 119:124, 125. 143:12. Jn 12:26.
trusteth. Ps 13:5. 16:1. 31:1. Is 26:3, 4. Ro
15:12, 13. Ep 1:12, 13.

3 **Be merciful**. Ps +4:1.
for I. Ps 55:17. Lk 2:37. 11:8-13. 18:7. Ep
6:18.
daily. *or*, all the day. Ps 25:5. 88:9. Is 58:2. Lk
+18:1. Ro 12:12.

4 **Rejoice**. Ps 51:12. Is 61:3. 65:18. 66:13, 14.
soul. Heb. *nephesh*, Ge +34:3.
do. Ps 25:1. 62:8. 143:8. 1 S 1:15.
soul. Heb. *nephesh*, Ge +34:3.

5 **thou**. ver. 15. Ps 25:8. 36:7. 52:1. 69:16.
119:68. Ex +34:6. 1 J 4:8, 9.

ready to forgive. Ps 32:5. Is 1:18. 43:25.
44:22. 55:6, 7. Ro 10:13.
plenteous. Ro 5:20, 21. Ep 1:6-8.
unto all. Ps 145:9, 18. Je 33:3. Ezk 36:33, 37.
Lk 11:9, 10. Jn 4:10. 6:37. Ac 2:21. Ro 10:12,
13. 1 J 4:8.

6 **Give ear**. Ps 5:1, 2. 17:1. 54:2. 55:1. 130:2.

7 **In the day**. Ps 18:6. 34:4-6. +50:15. 55:16-
18. 77:1, 2. 91:15. 142:1, 2. Is 26:16. La 3:55-
57. Jon 2:2. Lk 22:44. He 5:7.

8 **Among**. Ex +8:10. Da 3:29. 1 C 8:5, 6.
the gods. Heb. *elohim*. Ex +12:12.
neither. Ps 136:4. Dt 3:24. 4:34.

9 **All**. Ps 22:27-31. 65:5. 66:4. 67:2-4, 7. 72:8,
11, 19. 102:15, 18. Is 2:2-4. 11:9. 43:6, 7.
59:19. 66:18-20, 23. Zc 14:9. Ro 11:25. Re
11:15. 15:4. 20:3.
shall come. Is 66:18. Zc 14:16.
and shall. Re *15:4*.
glorify. Mt +9:8. Ro 15:9. Ep 1:12. 1 P 2:9.

10 **For**. ver. 8. Da +4:3. Ac 2:19-22. 4:30. Ro
15:18, 19.
God alone. Dt +6:3, 4. +32:39. Is 37:16, 20.
44:6-8. Mk 12:29. 1 C 8:4. Ep 4:6.

11 **Teach me**. Ps 5:8. 25:4, 12. +27:11. 32:8.
90:12. 119:12, 26, 33, 73, 108, 124. 143:8-10.
Jb 34:32. Lk 11:1. Jn 6:45, 46. Ep 4:21.
Ja 1:5.
I will. Ps 26:3. 119:30. Ml 2:6. 2 J 4. 3 J 3, 4.
unite. Je 32:38, 39. Ho 10:2. 14:8. Zp 1:5. Mt
6:22-24. Jn 17:20, 21. Ac 2:46. 1 C 6:17.
10:21. 2 C 11:3. Ga 5:17. Col 3:17, 22, 23.
to fear. Ps 33:8. 99:1. 1 K 8:40. 2 Ch 6:31.

12 **praise**. Ps 34:1. 103:1-3. 104:33. 145:1-5.
146:1, 2. 1 Ch 29:13, 20. Is 12:1. Re 5:9-13.
19:5, 6.
with all. Ps 9:1. Dt 6:5. Pr 3:5, 6. Ac 8:37. Ep
5:19.
glorify. Ro 15:6. 1 C 6:20. 10:31.
for evermore. Heb. *olam*, Ps +18:50.

13 **great**. Ps 57:10. 103:8-12. 108:4. Lk 1:58.
and thou. Ps +16:10. 56:13. 88:6. 116:8. 2 S
12:13. Jb 33:18, 22, 24, 28. Is 38:17. Jon 2:3-
6. 1 Th 1:10.
soul. Heb. *nephesh*, Ps +30:3.
lowest. Dt +32:22. Mt +10:15.
hell. *or*, the grave. Heb. *sheol*, Ps +30:3; Ge
+37:35. Ps 6:5. 9:17.

14 **O God**. Ps 36:11. 54:3. 119:51, 69, 85. 140:5.
2 S 15:1.
assemblies. 2 S 16:20-23. 17:1-4, 14. Mt
26:3, 4. 27:1, 2. Ac 4:27, 28.
violent. Heb. terrible. **S#6184h**. Ps 37:35 (great
power). 54:3 (oppressors). Jb 6:23 (mighty).
15:20 (oppressor). 27:13. Pr 11:16 (strong). Is
13:11. 25:3, 4, 5. 29:5, 20. Je 15:21. 20:11.
Ezk 28:7. 30:11. 31:12. 32:12.
soul. Heb. *nephesh*, Ge +12:13.
and have. Ps 10:4, 11, 13. 14:4. 36:1. Ezk
8:12. 9:9.

15 **But thou**. ver. 5. Ex +34:6, 7. Ro 5:20, 21. Ep 1:7. 2:4-7.
God. Heb. *El*, Ex +15:2.
full. Ps 103:8. 130:7.
mercy. Ps 85:10. 98:3. Jn 1:17. Ro 15:8, 9.
and truth. Ps 146:6. Dt +32:4. Ro 3:4. T +1:2. He 6:18.

16 **turn**. Ps +25:16. 90:13. 119:132.
give thy strength. Ps 27:14. 28:7, 8. 84:5. 119:28. 138:3. Jg 16:28. 1 Ch +16:11. Ne 6:9. Is 40:29-31. 45:24. Da 10:16-18. Zc 10:12. Ep 3:14-16. 6:10. Ph 4:13. Col 1:10, 11.
the son. Ps 116:16. 119:94. 2 T 1:5.
handmaid. Is +7:14. Mt 1:23. Lk 1:38.

17 **Show**. Ps 41:10, 11. 74:9. Is 38:22. 1 C 5:5.
that they. Ps 71:9-13. 109:29. Mi 7:8-10. Ph 2:7-10.
thou. Ps 40:1. 71:20, 21.

PSALM 87

(*Title*.) A.M. 3468. B.C. 536. **A Psalm**. It is highly probable that this Psalm was written by one of the descendants of Korah on the return from the Babylonian captivity. It seems to have been written in praise of Jerusalem; and, typically, of the Christian church.
for. *or*, of.

1 **His**. 2 Ch 3:1. Is 28:16. Mt 16:16, 18. 1 C 3:10, 11. Ep 2:20-22. He 12:22. 1 P 2:4-8.
the holy. Ps 48:1, 2. 68:16. 121:1. Is 2:2, 3. 56:7. Zc 8:3. 2 P 1:18.

2 **The Lord**. Ps 78:67-69. 132:13, 14. Dt 12:5. 2 Ch 6:6. Is 14:32. 56:7. Jl 2:32. 1 C 3:16. Ep 2:21.
gates. Ge +14:7.
dwellings. or, tabernacles. Ps 26:8. 43:3. 49:11.

3 **Glorious**. Ps 45:13. 48:2, 3, 11-13. 125:1, 2. Is 12:6. 19:14, etc. 46:13. 49:14-23. 54:2, 11, 12. 59:20, 21. 60:1, 2, 13, 15, 19. 61:3, etc. 62:1-3, etc. Je 3:14-17. 31:12, 13. Ezk 36:2, 11, etc. 37:27, 28. ch. 40-48. He 12:22, 23. Re 14:1. 21:10-27.

4 **Rahab**. Ps 89:10mg. Is 51:9.
Babylon. Ps 137:1, 8, 9. 2 K 20:17, 18. Is 13:1, etc. 14:4-6. Je 25:9. ch. 50, 51. Da 2:47, 48. 4:30. Re 17:5. 18:2.
Philistia. i.e. *watered*, **S#6429h**. Ps 60:8. 108:9.
Tyre. 1 K +7:13.
Ethiopia. Ge +2:13. Is 18:1, 7. Je 3:16.
this man. Ps 68:31. 1 S 17:8. 2 S 21:16-22. Is 19:11, 23-25. Ezk 28:2.
born. Ps +2:7.

5 **of Zion**. 1 Ch +11:5. Is 44:4, 5. 60:1-9. Zc 8:22. Jn 1:12-14. 3:3-5. Ga 3:26-28. He 11:32-40. 1 P 1:23, 24.
highest. Ezk 48:35. Mt 16:18. Ro 8:31.

6 **when**. Ps 22:30. Is 4:3. Ezk 9:4. 13:9. Lk 10:20. Ph 4:3. Re 13:8.

this man. Je 3:19. Ga 4:26-31. Re 20:15.
Selah. Ps +9:16.

7 **As well**. Ps 68:24, 25. 1 Ch 15:16, etc. 23:5. 25:1-6. Re 14:1-3. 15:3.
on instruments. Ps 150:4. Re 14:1-3.
all my. Ps 46:4. Dt 8:15. Is 12:3. Jn 1:16. 4:10, 14. 7:37-39. Ja 1:17. Re 21:6. 22:1, 17.
springs. Heb. *mayan*, Ge +7:11 (**S#4599h**).

PSALM 88

(*Title*.) A.M. cir. 2173. B.C. cir. 1531.
for. *or*, of. Ge +36:5.
Mahalath. Ps 53, title.
Maschil, etc. *or*, *A Psalm* of Heman the Ezrahite, giving instruction. Supposed to have been written by *Heman*, son of Zerah, and grandson of Judah, on the oppression of the Hebrews in Egypt.
Heman. 1 Ch +2:6.
Ezrahite. Ps 89, title. 1 K +4:31.

1 **Lord**. Ps 18:46. 24:5. 25:5. 27:1, 9. 51:14. 62:7. 65:5. 68:19, 20. 79:9. 85:4. 140:7. Ge 49:18. 1 Ch 16:35. Is 12:2. 17:10. Mi 7:7. Hab 3:18. Lk 1:47. 2:30. T 2:10, 13. 3:4-7.
cried. Ps +3:4. He 5:7.
day and night. Ps 22:2. 86:3. Ne 1:6. Is 62:6. La 2:18, 19. Lk 2:37. 18:7. 1 Th 3:10. 1 T 5:5. 2 T 1:3. Re 4:8.

2 **Let**. Ps 79:11. 141:1, 2. 1 K 8:31. La 3:8.

3 **soul**. Heb. *nephesh*, Ge +34:3. ver. 14, 15. Ps 22:11-21. 69:17-21. 77:2. 143:3, 4. Ge 25:8, 9, 17. 35:18. 1 K 17:22. Jb 6:2-4. +14:22. 33:18, 22. Is 53:3, 10, 11. La 3:15-19. Mt +10:28. 26:37-39. Mk 14:33, 34.
troubles. Ps +107:3.
life. Ps 107:18. Jb 33:22.
grave. Heb. *sheol*, Ge +37:35.

4 **counted**. Ps 15:4. 28:1. 30:9. 143:7. Jb 17:1. Is 38:17, 18. Ezk 26:20. Jon 2:6. Mt 27:42. 2 C 1:9.
down. Ps +146:4.
pit. Heb. *bor*, Ge +37:20.
as a man. Ps 31:12. 109:22-24. Ro 5:6. 2 C 13:4.

5 **Free among**. Jb 3:17. Is 14:9-12. 38:10-12. Ezk 32:18-32.
grave. Heb. *qeber*, Ge +23:4.
whom. Ps 136:23. Ge 8:1. 19:29. Jb 14:12.
cut off. ver. 16. Ps 31:22. Jb 6:9. 11:10. Is 53:8. Mt 27:46, 66.
from thy hand. *or*, by thy hand.

6 **lowest**. Ps 40:2. 86:13. Dt +32:22.
pit. Heb. *bor*, Ge +37:20.
darkness. Ps 143:3. Pr 4:19. La 3:2. Jn 12:46. Ju 6, 13.
deeps. Ps 69:15. 130:1.

7 **Thy wrath**. Ps 38:1-6. 90:7-11. 102:10. Jb 6:4. 10:16. Jn 3:36. Ro 2:5-9. Ga 3:13. 1 P 2:24. Re 6:16, 17.

with. Ps 42:7. Jon 2:3.
Selah. ver. 10. Ps +9:16.

8 **put**. ver. 18. Ps 31:11. 142:4. 1 S 23:18-20. Jb 19:13-19. Mt 26:21, 34, 56. Jn 11:57.
acquaintance. 2 K 10:11mg.
made. Is 49:7. 53:3. Zc 11:8. Mt 27:21-25. Jn 15:23, 24.
I am shut. Jb 12:14. 19:8. La 3:7-9.

9 **Mine**. Ps +6:7. +56:8.
called. ver. +1. Ps 55:17. 86:3.
stretched out. Ps 28:2. 44:20. 63:4. 68:31. 134:2. 141:2. 143:6. Ge 48:14, 15. Ex 9:29. 17:11. 1 K 8:22, 38, 54. 2 Ch 6:12, 13. Ezr 9:5, 6. Jb 11:13-15. Is 1:15. La 2:19. 3:41. Hab 3:10. 1 T 2:8.

10 **Wilt thou**. Ps 6:5. 30:9. 115:17. 118:17. Is 38:18, 19. Mk 5:35, 36. Jn 11:25.
shall. Jb 14:7-12. Is +26:19. Ezk 37:1-14. Lk 7:12-16. 1 C 15:52-57.

11 **declared in**. Ps +146:4.
grave. Heb. *qeber*, Ge +23:4 (**S#6913h**).
in destruction. Ps 55:23. 73:18. Jb 21:30. +26:6. Pr 15:11. Mt 7:13. Ro 9:22. 2 P 2:1.

12 **dark**. Ps 143:3. Jb 10:21, 22. Is 8:22. Mt 8:12. Ju 13.
in the land. ver. 5. Ps 31:12. Jb 24:20. Ec 2:16. 8:10. 9:5.

13 **and in**. Ps +119:147, 148. Mk +1:35.
prevent thee. Ps 21:3.

14 **Lord**. Ps +77:7. Mt 27:46.
soul. Heb. *nephesh*, Ge +12:13.
hidest. Dt +31:17.

15 **afflicted**. Ps 73:14. Jb 17:1, 11-16. Is 53:3.
die. Ge +49:33 (**S#1478h**).
while. Ps 22:14, 15. Jb 6:4. 7:11-16. Is 53:10. Zc 13:7. Lk 22:44.
thy terrors. Jn 12:27.

16 **fierce wrath**. Ps 38:1, 2. 89:46. 90:7, 11. 102:10. Is 53:4-6. Ro 8:32. Ga 3:13. Re 6:17.
cut me. Is 53:8. Da 9:26.

17 **They**. Ps 22:16. 42:7. 69:1, 2. 116:3. Jb 16:12, 13. 30:14, 15. La 3:5-7. Mt 27:39-44.
daily. *or*, all the day. ver. 9. Ps 25:5. 32:3. 35:28. 38:6.

18 **Lover**. ver. 8. Ps 31:11. 38:11. Jb 19:12-15.
mine acquaintance. 2 K 10:11mg.

PSALM 89

(*Title*.) A.M. cir. 3463. B.C. cir. 541.
Maschil, etc. *or*, *A Psalm* for Ethan the Ezrahite, *to give instruction*. This Psalm is generally supposed to have been written during the Babylonian captivity, when, the family of David being dethroned, and the royal family ruined, the Divine promises had apparently failed.
Ethan. 1 K 4:31. 1 Ch 2:6.

1 **I will**. Ps 86:12, 13. 101:1. 106:1. 136:1, etc.
mercies. Ro 12:1. 2 C 1:3.

for ever. Heb. *olam*, Ex +12:24.
with. Ps 40:9, 10. 71:8, 15-19.
thy faithfulness. ver. 5, 8, 33-49. Ps 36:5. 92:2. Is 25:1. La 3:23. Mi 7:20. T 1:2.
all generations. Heb. generation and generation. ver. 4. Ps +33:11mg.

2 **Mercy**. Ps 36:5. 103:17, 18. Ne 1:5. 9:17, 31. Lk 1:50. Ep 1:6, 7.
for ever. Heb. *olam*, Ex +12:24.
faithfulness. ver. 5, 37. Ps 119:89. 146:6. Nu 23:19. Mt 24:35. He 6:18.

3 **made**. ver. 28, 34, 39. 1 K 8:16. Is +55:3. Je 30:9. Ezk 34:23, 24. Ho 3:5. Lk +1:32, 33.
covenant. Ge +9:16.
my chosen. ver. 19. Ps 78:70. Is 42:1. Mt 3:17. 12:18-21. He 1:5.
sworn. ver. 35. Ps 132:11. 2 S 3:9. Ac +2:30, 31. He 7:21.
David. Ac +13:23.

4 **Thy seed**. ver. 1, 29, 36. Ps +45:6. 132:12. 1 K 9:5. 1 Ch 17:10-14. 22:10. Zc 12:8. Lk 20:41-44. Ac 13:32-37. Ro 1:3, 4. 15:12. Ph 2:9-11. Re 22:16.
for ever. Heb. *olam*, Ex +12:24. Ge +9:16.
throne. Ge +49:10.
generations. Ge +9:12.
Selah. ver. 37, 45, 48. Ps +9:16.

5 **heavens**. Ps 19:1. 50:6. 97:6. Is 44:23. Lk 2:10-15. Ep 3:10. 1 P 1:12. Re 5:11-14. 7:10-12.
in the congregation. ver. 7. Ps 111:1. Dt +33:2. Da 7:10, 22, 27. 2 Th 1:7. He 12:22, 23. Ju 14, 15. Re 19:1-6.

6 **For who**. ver. 8. Ps 40:5. 73:25. Ex +8:10.
the sons. Ps 29:1mg. 52:1. 103:20.

7 **God**. Heb. *El*, Ex +15:2.
is greatly. Le 10:3. Is 6:2-7. 66:2. Je +5:22. Mt +10:28. Ac 5:11.
feared. Ec +12:13.
in reverence. 1 Ch 13:7, 10. Hab +2:20.

8 **O Lord**. Ps 84:12. Jsh 22:22. Is 28:22.
a strong. ver. 13. Ps 24:8. 147:5. 1 S 15:29. Jb 9:19. Is 40:25, 26. Je 32:17. Mt 6:13.
like. ver. +6. Dt 32:31. 1 S 2:2.

9 **Thou rulest**. Ps 29:10. 65:7. 66:5, 6. 93:3, 4. 107:25-29. Jb 38:8-11. Na 1:4. Mt 8:24-27. 14:32. Mk 4:39, 41.

10 **Thou hast**. Ps 78:43, etc. 105:27, etc. Ex ch. 7-15.
Rahab. *or*, Egypt. Ps 87:4. Is 51:9.
scattered. Ps 59:11. 68:30. 144:6. Is 24:1.
thy strong arm. Heb. the arm of thy strength. Ex 3:19, 20. +15:16. Dt 4:34.

11 **The heavens**. Ps 24:1, 2. 50:12. 115:16. Ge 1:1. 2:1. 1 Ch 29:11. Jb 41:11. 1 C 10:26, 28.

12 **north**. Jb 26:7.
Tabor. Jg +4:6.
Hermon. Dt +3:8.
rejoice. Ps 65:12, 13. Is 35:1, 2. 49:13. 55:12, 13.

13 **a mighty arm**. Heb. an arm with might. ver. 10. Ps 62:11. Da 4:34, 35. Mt 6:13.

14 **Justice**. Ps +45:6, 7. 99:4. 145:17. Dt 32:4. Re 15:3.
habitation. *or*, establishment. Ps 33:14. 97:2mg. 104:5. Pr 16:12. Is 4:5.
throne. Ps +11:4.
mercy. ver. 2. Ps 85:13. Jn 1:17.

15 **Blessed**. Dt +28:3.
know. Ps 90:6. 98:4-6. 100:1. Le 25:9. Nu 10:10. 23:21. Is 52:7, 8. Na 1:15. Lk 2:10-14. Ro 10:15, 18.
joyful sound. or, trumpet sound. Le +23:24.
shall walk. *or*, walk habitually. Ps 55:14. 81:13. Lk +11:28.
in the light. Ps 4:6. 44:3. Nu 6:25, 26. Jb 29:3. Pr 16:15. Is 2:5. Jn 14:21-23. Ac 2:28. Re 21:23.

16 **name**. ver. 12, 24. Ps 33:21. 44:8. Lk 1:47. Ph 4:4. 1 P 1:8.
righteousness. Ps 40:10. 71:15, 16. Is 45:24, 25. 46:13. Je 23:6. Ro 1:17. 3:21-26. 2 C 5:21. Ph 3:8, 9.

17 **For thou**. Ps 28:7. 1 C 1:30, 31. Ph +4:13.
our horn. ver. 24. Ps +92:10.

18 **the Lord is**, etc. *or*, our Shield is of the Lord, and our King is of the Holy One of Israel. Ps 47:9. 62:1, 2, 6. 84:11. 91:1, 2. Ge 15:1. Dt 33:27-29. Pr 30:5.
Holy. Ps 30:4. Is +1:4.
king. Ps 44:4. Is 33:22.

19 **Then**. 1 S 16:1. 2 S 7:8-17. Lk 1:68-70. 2 P 1:21. 3:2.
to thy holy. Ps +16:10.
I have laid. Ge 49:24. 1 S 16:18. Jb 33:24. Is 9:6. Je 30:21.
mighty. Jsh 4:24. 1 S 16:18. Is 9:6. 63:1. Je 50:34. Am 5:12. Zp 3:17.
exalted. ver. 3. 1 K 11:34. Ph 2:6-11. He 2:9-17.

20 **I have found**. 1 S 16:1, 12, 13. Is 61:1-3. Mk 1:10. Jn 3:34. Ac 13:22.

21 **With**. Ps 18:32-39. 80:15-17. 2 S 7:8-16. Is 42:1. 49:8.
mine. ver. 13. Is 41:10. Ezk 30:24, 25. Zc 10:12.

22 **enemy**. Ps 129:2. 1 Ch 17:9. Mt 4:1-11.
son. Jn 17:12. 2 Th 2:3.

23 **I will**. Ps 2:9. 2 S 3:1. 7:1, 9. 22:40-44. Re 2:27.
plague. Ps 2:1-6. 21:8, 9. 109:3, etc. 110:1, 2. 132:18. Lk 19:14, 27. Jn 15:23.

24 **But my**. ver. 2-5, 28, 33. Ps 61:7. Jn 1:17. 2 C 1:20.
in my name. ver. 16. Dt +28:58.
horn. ver. 17. 1 S 2:1.

25 **I will**. Ps 2:8. 72:8-11. 80:11. 1 K 4:21. Re 11:15.
his hand. Dt +32:36. 1 Ch 18:1, 3.

26 **Thou**. 2 S 7:14. 1 Ch 22:10. Mt 26:39, 42. Lk

23:46. Jn 11:41. 20:17. He 1:5.
God. Heb. *El*, Ex +15:2. Ps 43:4. Mk 15:34.
rock. Ps 18:46. 62:2, 6, 7. 95:1. 2 S 22:47. Is 50:7-9.

27 **Also**. Ps 2:7. Ro 8:29. Col 1:15, 18.
him. ver. 20.
firstborn. Ge +48:14. 2 Ch +26:10. Je +31:9. Col +1:15.
higher. Ps 2:10-12. 72:11. Nu 24:7. 2 Ch 1:12. 9:23, 24. Is 49:7. Re 19:16. 21:24. or, Most High. Heb. *Elyon*. Ps +7:17. Ge +14:18. Re 1:5.

28 **mercy**. Is +55:3. Ac 13:32-34.
for evermore. Ps +18:50.
covenant. ver. +34. Ge +9:16.
stand fast. Jg +2:1.

29 **His seed**. ver. 4, 36. Ps 132:11. 1 Ch 17:11, 12. Is 59:21. Je 33:17-26.
for ever. Ps +9:18 (S#5703h).
throne. Ps +45:6. 1 Ch 22:10. Ezk 37:24, 25.
days of heaven. Ps 21:4. Dt +11:21. Mt 6:10. Ac +3:19, 21. He +11:13.

30 **If**. Ps 132:12. 2 S 7:14. 1 Ch +28:9. 2 Ch 7:17-22.
forsake. Ps 119:53. Pr 4:2. 28:4. Je 9:13-16.
walk. Ezk 18:9, 17. 20:19. Lk 1:6.

31 **If**. Ge +4:7.
break. Heb. profane. Ps 55:20mg.

32 **Then**. Ps +9:10. Ex 32:34. 2 S 7:14. 1 K 11:6, 14, 31, 39. Pr 3:11, 12. Am 3:2. 1 C 11:31, 32. He 12:6-11.

33 **Nevertheless**. 1 K 11:13, 32, 36. La 3:31, 32. 1 C 15:25. Re +2:6.
not utterly take. Heb. not make void. ver. 39. Ps 33:10. 94:14. 1 S 15:29. Is +55:3.
fail. Heb. lie. He 6:18.

34 **My covenant**. ver. 28. Le +26:42. Je +33:20, 21.
not break. Dt 31:16. Jg +2:1.
nor alter. Nu 23:19. Ml +3:6. Mt 24:35. Ro 11:29. Ja 1:17.

35 **Once**. Ps 14:3. 27:4. 34:20. 53:3. Jb +40:5.
have I sworn. Ps 110:4. 132:11. Am 4:2. 8:7. He 6:13, 17.
that I will not lie. Heb. If I lie. 2 T 2:13. T 1:2.
David. Ac +13:23.

36 **seed**. ver. 4, 29. Is 53:10. 59:21.
for ever. Heb. *olam*, Ex +12:24. Ec +1:4.
and. Ps +45:6. Je +33:20, 21. Jn 12:34.

37 **It shall**. Re +11:15.
faithful witness. Jb 16:19. Re 1:5. 3:14.
for ever. Heb. *olam*, Ex +12:24. Ps 72:7. 104:19. Ge 1:14-18. Je +31:35, 36.
and as. Ge 9:13-16. Is +54:9, 10.
Selah. Ps +9:16.

38 **But**. Ps +44:9, etc. Je 12:1.
and. Ps +106:40.
wroth. ver. 51. Ps 84:9. 2 S 1:21. 15:26. 2 Ch 12:1-12. La 4:20. Zc 13:7.

39 **void**. ver. 34-36. Ps 77:10. 116:11. Jn 13:7.
profaned. ver. 44. Ps 74:7. 143:3. Is 25:12.
43:28. La 5:16.

40 **broken**. Ps 80:12. Jb 1:10. Is 5:5, 6.
brought. 2 Ch 12:2-5. 15:5. La 2:2, 5. Re
13:1-7.

41 **All**. Ps 44:10-14. 80:13. Is 10:6. Je 50:17.
he is. Ps +31:11. Dt 28:37. Ne 5:9.

42 **set up**. Le 26:17, 25. Dt 28:25, 43. La 2:17.
Jn 16:20. Re 11:10.

43 **turned**. Ezk 30:21-25.
not made. Le 26:36, 37. Nu 14:42, 45. Jsh
7:4, 5, 8-12. 2 Ch 25:8.

44 **Thou**. 1 S 4:21; 22. 1 K 12:16-20. 14:25-28.
La 4:1, 2. 2 Th 2:3-10.
glory. Heb. brightness. Ex 24:10.
cast. ver. 39. Da 7:20-25.

45 **The days**. ver. 28, 29. 2 Ch 10:19. Is 63:18.
thou. Ps 44:15, 16. 109:29. Mi 7:10.

46 **How**. Ps 85:5. Re +6:10.
wilt. Dt +31:17. Is 45:15. Ho 5:15.
for ever. Jb +4:20 (**S#5331h**).
thy wrath. Ps 78:63. Dt +32:22.

47 **Remember**. Ps 39:5, 6. 119:84. Jb 7:7. 9:25,
26. 10:9.
how short. Ps 90:12. Jb 14:1, 5. 1 C 7:29-31.
Ep 5:16. Ja +4:14.
wherefore. Ps 144:4. Jb 14:1. Ja 4:14.

48 **What**. Ps 49:7-9. Jb 14:5. 30:23. Ec 3:19, 20.
8:8. 9:5. 12:7. He +9:27.
see death. Jn 8:51. He 11:5.
shall. Ps 49:15. Ac 2:27. 2 C 4:14.
soul. Heb. *nephesh*, Ps +30:3.
grave. Heb. *sheol*, Ps +30:3. Ge +37:35.
Selah. Ps +9:16.

49 **where**. Ps 77:9, 10. Is 63:7-15.
thou. ver. 3, 4, 35. Ps 54:5. 132:11, 12. 2 S
3:9. 7:15. Is +55:3. He 7:21.

50 **Remember**. Ps +31:11.

51 **they have**. Mt 5:10-12. Ac 5:41. 1 C 4:12,
13. He 10:33. 11:36.
footsteps. Ps 56:5, 6. 57:3. +77:19. 2 S 16:7,
8. Mt 12:24. 26:61. Jn 8:48. 1 P 2:20, 21.
3:16. 4:14-16. 2 P 3:3, 4.

52 **Blessed**. Ps 104:35. Ne 9:5. Jb 1:21. Hab
3:17-19. Ro 9:5. 1 T 1:17.
for evermore. Ps +18:50.
Amen. Mt +6:13.

PSALM 90

(Title.) A.M. 2514. B.C. 1490. **A Prayer**. *or*, A
prayer, being a Psalm of Moses. This Psalm is
supposed to have been composed by Moses,
when all the generation of the Israelites who
had offended God, were sentenced to fall in
the wilderness, at the age of seventy or eighty
years, except Moses, Caleb, and Joshua. Nu
ch. 13, 14.
the man. Ex 33:14-19. Dt +33:1.

1 **Lord**. Ps 71:3. 91:1, 9, 10. Dt 33:27. Is 8:13,
14. Ezk 11:16. Jn 6:56. 1 J 4:15, 16.
all generations. Heb. generation and generation. Ps +33:11mg.

2 **Before**. Jb 38:4-6, 28, 29. Pr 8:25, 26.
or ever. Ps 33:9. 146:6. Ge 1:1.
even from. Ps 102:24-27. 103:17. Pr 8:23. Is
44:6. Mi +5:2. Hab 1:12. He 1:10-12. 13:8. Re
1:8.
everlasting to. Heb. *olam* doubled, Ps
+41:13. 102:11, 12.
thou art. Dt 32:17. Is 44:6. 45:22. 57:15. Je
10:10mg. La 5:19, 20.
God. Heb. *El*, Ex 15:2.

3 **Thou**. Ps 104:29. +146:4. Ge 3:19. 6:6, 7.
Nu 14:35. Jb 12:10. 17:14. 34:14, 15.
Ec 12:7.
Return, ye children of men. Rather,
"Return, ye children of Adam;" i.e. to that
dust out of which ye were originally formed.
Ho 7:10.

4 **thousand years**. Ec 6:6. Is 65:17-25. 2 P 3:8.
Re 20:4-7.
is past. *or*, when he hath passed them.
and as. Mt 14:25. 24:43. Lk 12:38.

5 **Thou**. Jb 9:26. 22:16. 27:20, 21. Is 8:7, 8. Je
46:7, 8.
as a sleep. Ps 73:20. Is 29:7, 8.
morning. 1 P +1:24.
groweth up. *or*, is changed. Ps 102:26. Is
2:18mg.

6 **In the morning**. Ps 92:7. Jb 14:2. Mt 6:30.
groweth up. Jg 5:26 (stricken through). 1 S
10:3 (forward). Jb 9:26 (passed away). SS
2:11 (is over).

7 **For we**. ver. 9, 11. Ps 39:11. 59:13.
Nu 17:12, 13. Dt 2:14-16. He 3:10, 11, 17-19.
4:1, 2.
are we. Ex 14:24. Ro 2:8, 9.

8 **Thou**. Ps 10:11. 50:21. 139:1-4. Jb 34:21. Je
2:22. 9:13-16. 16:17. 23:24. Ezk 8:12. Re
20:12.
our. Ps 19:12. Pr 5:21. Ec 12:14. Lk 12:1, 2.
Ro 2:16. 1 C 4:5. He 4:12, 13. 1 J 3:20.
in the. Ps 80:16.

9 **For**. Ps 78:33. Is 57:16-18.
passed. Heb. turned. Ps 40:4 (respecteth).
102:17 (regard). Dt 16:7. 31:18. Ec 2:11
(looked), 12 (turned). Is 53:6.
We spend. Ep 5:16. Col 4:5.
a tale. Heb. a meditation. ver. 4. Ps 39:5.
49:3. Jb 37:2. Ezk 2:10.

10 **The days**, etc. Heb. As for the days of our
years, in them are seventy years. Ge +29:14.
47:9. Ex +23:26. Dt 34:7. Je +28:3mg.
strength. Ps 54:1. 65:6. 91:16. 1 K 3:14. Ep
6:2, 3. 1 P 3:10.
yet. 2 S 19:35. 1 K 1:1. Ec 12:2-7.
for. Ps 78:39. Jb 14:10mg. 24:24. Is 38:12. Lk
12:20. Ja 4:14.

11 Who knoweth. Ps 2:12. 7:11, 12. 76:7. Le 26:18, 21, 24, 28. Dt 28:59. 29:20, etc. 32:29. Jb +19:25. Is +33:14. Na 1:2, 3, 6. Lk 12:5. Jn 3:36. Ro 1:18. 1 C 10:22. 2 C 5:11. Ep 5:6. 1 Th 1:10. He 10:26, 27. Re 6:17. 19:15.

12 So teach. Ps 39:4. Dt 32:29. Ec 9:10. Lk 12:35-40. Jn 9:4. Ep 5:16, 17. Col 4:5.
to number. Ps 89:47. Ge 13:16. 1 Ch 21:1. Ec 9:10. Mt 24:44. Lk 12:35-37. 1 C 1:7, 8. 2 C 4:18. Ph 3:20. T 2:11-13. 1 P 4:7. 2 P 3:11.
that. Ps +49:11. 95:7-9. Jb 22:21. 28:28. 1 Ch +28:9. Pr 2:2-6. 3:13-18. 4:5, 7. 7:1-4. 8:32-36. 16:16. 18:1, 2. 22:17. 23:12, 23. 27:1. Ec 9:10. Mt +16:27. Lk +9:24. 2 C +6:2. He 2:1.
apply our hearts. Heb. cause our hearts to come. 1 S 9:27. Pr 1:7. 21:30.

13 Return. Ps 6:4. 80:14. Ex 32:12. Dt 32:36. Je 12:15. Jl 2:13, 14. Zc 1:16.
how. Re +6:10.
let it. Je +18:8.

14 satisfy. Ps 91:16. 145:15, 16. La 3:22, 23. Zc 9:17. Mt +5:6.
early. or, in the morning. Ps 97:11. Re +2:28.
that we. Ps 23:6. 85:6. 86:4. 149:2. Ph 4:4.

15 Make us glad. Ps 30:5. +118:24. 126:5, 6. Is 12:1. 40:1, 2. 61:3. 65:18, 19. Je 29:11. 31:12, 13. Mt +5:4. Jn 16:20. Re 7:14-17.
according to. Ge +18:25. Je 31:25, 28. 32:42. Mi 7:15. Zc 8:13. 10:6. Mt 5:11, 12. Mk 10:29, 30. Lk 6:20-23. Ro 8:18. 1 C 2:9. 2 C 4:17, 18. Ph 4:19. 1 J 3:2.
the days. Nu 14:34. Dt 32:7.
thou hast afflicted. Ps +119:75. Dt 8:2. Ru +1:13. Jb 1:12. Je 31:28. La 3:33. Am +3:2, 6. Ja 1:17. 1 P 5:10.
the years. Ps 31:10. Dt 2:14-16.
seen evil. Jb 2:10. Is +45:7.

16 Let. Ps 44:1. Nu 14:15-24. Hab 3:2.
and. Nu 14:22, 30, 31. Dt 1:39. Jsh 4:22-24. 23:14.

17 And let. Ps 27:4. 50:2. 80:3, 7. 110:3. Ezk 16:14. 2 C 3:18. 1 J 3:2.
establish. Ps 68:28. 118:25. Jb 22:28. Pr 16:3. Is 26:12. 1 C 3:7. Ph 2:12, 13. 2 Th 2:16, 17. 3:1.

PSALM 91

(*Title*.) This Psalm is supposed by some to have been composed by Moses on the same occasion as the preceding; but others think it was written by David, after his advice to his son Solomon, 1 Ch ch. 28.

1 dwelleth. Ps 2:4. 9:11. 17:12mg. 32:7. 52:8. 61:3, 4. 90:1. Is 8:14. Ezk 11:16. Ho 14:5, 6. 1 J 4:15, 16.
secret place. Ps 18:11. 27:5. 31:20. +64:2. SS 2:14. Col 3:3.
abide. Heb. lodge. Ps 25:13mg. +49:12. Ru 1:16. Jb 17:2mg. 39:28.

under. Ps 5:12. Ru 2:12.
shadow. Ps 17:8. 36:7. 57:1. 121:5. Jg 9:15. SS 2:3. Is 4:5, 6. 16:3. 25:4. 30:2. 32:2. 42:1. 49:2. 51:16. La 4:20. Ho 14:7.
Almighty. Ge +49:25.

2 I will. ver. 9. Ps +9:9. 71:3. Dt 32:30, 31.
fortress. Ps +31:3.
my God. Ps 43:4. 48:14. 67:6, 7. Ge 17:7. Dt 26:17-19. Je 31:1. Mt 1:23. Lk 20:38. Jn 1:36. He 11:16.
in him. Ps 62:5-8. 118:8, 9. Is 12:2. 26:3, 4.

3 snare. Ps +141:9. Pr 7:23. Ec 9:12. Ho 9:8. Am 3:5. 1 T 6:9. 2 T 2:26.
and from. ver. 6. Nu 14:37, 38. 16:46-48. 2 S 24:15. Jb 5:19-22.

4 wings. Ps 17:8. 36:7. 57:1. 61:4. 63:7. Dt 32:11, 12. Ru 2:12. Is 31:5. Ml 4:2. Mt 23:37. Lk 13:34.
his truth. Ps 89:23, 24. 138:2. 146:5, 6. Ge 15:1. Nu 23:19. Is 43:1, 2. Mk 13:31. T 1:2. He 6:17, 18.

5 Thou. Ps 3:6. 27:1-3. 46:2. 66:12. 112:7. 121:6. Jb 5:19, etc. Pr 28:1. Is 43:2. Mt 8:26. He +13:6.
terror. Ps 3:5. 55:4. 2 K 7:6. Jb 4:13-15. 18:11. 24:14-16. Pr 3:23-25. Is 21:4. Lk 12:20, 39. 1 C +15:55.
nor. Dt +32:23.

6 pestilence. Ps 121:5, 6. Ex 12:29, 30. 2 K 19:35.
destruction. Nu 16:48. 2 S 24:15. Mt 24:6, 7. 1 C 10:6-10.

7 A thousand. Ps 32:6. Ge 7:23. Ex 12:12, 13. Nu 14:37, 38. Jsh 14:10.

8 Only. Pr 3:25, 26. Ml 1:5.
and see. Is +66:24.
reward. Ge +6:13. Is 3:11. Ro 6:23. He 2:2.

9 Because. ver. 2. Ps 142:4, 5. 146:5, 6.
most high. ver. 1. Ps 71:3. 90:1.

10 no evil. Ps 31:23. 32:6, 7. 121:7. Jb 5:19. Pr 12:21. 15:19. Zp 3:15. Ro 8:28.
neither. Dt 7:15. Jb 5:24.

11 For. Ps 34:7. 71:3. 2 K 6:16, 17. Mt 4:6. 18:10. Lk *4:10, 11*. He 1:14.
in all. Pr 3:6. Is 31:1. Je 2:18.

12 They. Ex 19:4. Dt 1:31. Is 46:3. 63:9. Lk 4:11.
lest. Ps +37:24. Jb 5:23. Pr 3:23.

13 tread. Jg 14:5, 6. Jb 5:23. 1 S 17:37. Is +5:29. Ro 8:37.
adder. *or*, asp. Ps 58:4. Mk 16:18. Ac 28:3-6. Ro 3:13. 16:20.
the dragon. Is 27:1. Re 12:9. 20:1, 2.

14 set. ver. 9. Dt 28:1. Jg +5:31. 1 Ch 29:3. Jn 14:23. 16:27.
I will set. Ps 59:1mg. 89:16, 17. Is 33:15, 16. Ph 2:9-11.
known. Ps +9:10. Ga 4:9.
my name. Ex 23:13.

15 He shall. Ps +50:15. Je 33:3. Ro 10:12, 13. 1 J +5:14.

I will be. Ps 138:7. Ge 39:21, 23. Is +43:2. Jn 16:32.

deliver. Ps +34:4. 37:40. 2 C 1:9, 10.

honor. 1 S 2:30. Jn 5:23, 44. 12:26, 43. 1 P 1:21. 3:22. 5:4. Re 3:21.

16 **With long life**. Heb. With length of days. Ps 21:4. 23:6mg. 93:5mg. 102:24. Ge 15:15. +25:8. Dt +4:40. Pr 3:2mg, 16. Is 38:18, 19. La 5:20mg.

satisfy. Ps 90:14.

show. Ps +16:11. 50:23. Is 45:17. Lk 2:30. 3:6.

PSALM 92

(*Title*.) A.M. cir. 3464. B.C. cir. 540. **A Psalm**. Ps 3:1.

for. Is +58:13, 14. He 4:9mg. Re 4:8-11.

1 **thanks**. Ps +136:1.

sing. Ps 33:1. 50:23. 52:9. 54:6. 73:28. 107:1, 8, 15, 21, 22. 135:3. 147:1. Ep 5:19. He 13:15.

most. ver. 8. Ps +7:17. Is +57:15.

2 **show**. Ps 71:15. 89:1, 2. 145:2. Is 63:7. La 3:22, 23. Jn 1:17.

lovingkindness. Ge 24:12.

morning. Is 33:2. La 3:23.

faithfulness. Ge 24:27.

every night. Heb. in the nights. Ps 42:8. 77:2. Jb 35:10. Ac 16:25.

3 **instrument**. Ps 68:25. 2 Ch 23:5.

the harp, etc. *or*, the solemn sound with the harp. Re +5:8.

a solemn sound. Heb. *higgaion*. Ps 9:16mg.

4 **hast made**. Ps 9:2. 64:10. 104:31, 34. 106:47, 48. 126:3. 145:6, 7. Is +61:2-11. 65:13, 14. 66:10, 11. Je 31:7, 11-13. Zp 3:14-16. Lk 1:47. Jn 16:22. 2 C 2:14. Re 18:20.

thy work. Nu 23:23. Ph 2:12, 13. 1 Th 5:23, 24.

5 **O Lord**. Ps 66:3. Da +4:3.

thoughts. Ps +40:17. 139:17. Ge +50:20. Is 28:29. 55:8, 9. Je 23:20. Ro 11:33, 34.

deep. Ps 64:6. Ec 7:24. 1 C 2:10.

6 **A brutish**. Ps 32:9. 73:22. 94:8. Pr 30:2. Is 1:3. Je 10:14. 1 C 2:14.

a fool. Ps 14:1. 49:10. 75:4. Pr 1:22. 24:7. Lk 12:20.

7 **wicked**. 1 P +1:24.

workers. Ps 73:12, 18-20. Jb 12:6. 21:7-12. Je 12:1, 2. Ml 3:15. 4:1.

it is that. Ps 37:35, 36, 38. 73:18-20. 1 S 25:36-38. Pr 1:32. Mk +4:19. Lk 16:19-25.

destroyed. Dt 4:26. 7:23. 12:30.

for ever. Ps +9:18. Mt +25:41, 46.

8 **art most high**. Ps +7:17. 102:26, 27. Ex 18:11. Ec 5:8. Ac 12:1, 22-24.

for evermore. Heb. *olam*. Ps +18:50.

9 **For**. Ps 21:8, 9. 37:20. 68:1, 2. 73:27. 89:10. Jg 5:31. Lk 19:27. 2 Th 1:7-9.

scattered. Ps 1:4. 59:11. 68:30. Le 26:33. Nu

10:35. Dt 28:64. Is 17:13. Ezk 5:12. Mt 7:23. Lk 21:24.

10 **But**. Ps 18:2. 75:10. 89:17, 24. 112:9. 132:17. 148:14. 1 S 2:1, 10. 2 S 22:3. Lk 1:69.

an unicorn. Nu 23:22. 24:8.

I shall. Ps +45:7.

anointed. Ex +28:41. Lk +7:46.

11 **Mine eye**. Is +66:24. 2 Th 1:6.

12 **righteous**. ver. 7. Ps 52:8. 72:8. Is 55:13. 65:22. Ho 14:5, 6.

the palm tree. Ex 15:27. 1 K 6:29.

cedar. Nu +24:6.

13 **Those**. Is 60:21. Ro 6:5. 11:17. Ep 3:17. Col 1:23. 2:7.

planted. Ezk 18:26.

shall flourish. Is 61:3. 2 P 1:10, 11. 3:18.

in the. Ps 23:6. 100:4. 135:2. 2 Ch 4:9.

14 **fruit**. Ps 1:3. Mt 3:10. Jn 15:2-5. Ga 5:22, 23. Ph 1:11. Ju 12.

in old age. Ps 71:18. 1 Ch 29:1, etc. Jb 17:9. Pr 4:18. Is 40:31. 46:4. Je 17:8.

flourishing. Heb. green. Ezk 47:12.

15 **To show**. Jn 10:27-29. 15:1-3. 1 C 1:8, 9. 1 Th 5:23, 24. T 1:2. 1 P 1:4, 5.

my rock. Ps 18:2. 62:6. Dt 32:4.

and. Ps 5:4, 5. 145:17. Jb 34:10. Hab 1:13. Zp 3:5. Ro +9:14. 2 Th 1:6, 7. Ja 1:13.

PSALM 93

(*Title*.) It is highly probable that this Psalm was written on the same occasion as the preceding, as a part of which it is written in twelve MSS.

1 **Lord**. Ps 59:13. 96:10. 97:1. 99:1. 103:19. 1 Ch 16:31. 29:12. Is 52:7. Re 11:15-17. 19:6.

clothed. Ps 104:1, 2. Is 51:9. 59:17. 63:1.

majesty. 1 Ch +29:11.

he hath. Ps 18:32. 65:6. Is 11:5.

world. Ps 75:3. 96:10. Is 45:12, 18. 49:8. 51:16. He 1:2, 3.

2 **Thy**. Ps +45:6. Pr 8:22, 23. Da 4:34. Mi +5:2.

of old. Heb. from then.

thou. Ps 90:2. 102:24-27. He 1:10-12. 13:8. Re 1:8, 11, 17, 18. 2:8.

everlasting. Ge +17:7.

3 **The floods**. Ps 18:4. 42:7. 69:1, 2, 14-16. 124:4. 2 S 22:5. Is 43:2. 57:20. Je 12:5. +47:2. La 3:54. Jon 2:3. Mt 14:29, 30. Mk 4:39.

the floods. Ps 96:11. 98:8. Is 55:12.

lifted. Ge +22:13.

the floods lift. Ps 2:1-3. 107:25, 26. 124:3-5. Ac 4:25-27.

4 **mightier**. Ps 65:7. 89:6, 9. 114:3-5. Jb 38:11. Je 5:22. Mk 4:37-39.

5 **Thy**. Ps 19:7, 8. 119:111, 129, 138, 144. Is 8:20. Mt 24:35. He 6:17, 18. 1 J 5:9-13.

holiness. Ps 5:4-7. 99:5, 9. Le 10:3. 19:2. Is 52:11. Zc 14:20, 21. Jn 4:24. 1 C 3:16, 17. He 12:14. 1 P 1:16. Re 21:27. 22:14.

thine house. Ep 5:25-27. 1 T 3:15. He 3:6.
for ever. Heb. to length of days. Ps +91:16mg.

PSALM 94

(*Title*.) A.M. 3416. B.C. 588. Dr. Delaney supposes that this Psalm was written by David on occasion of his war with the Ammonites, in consequence of the indignities shown to his messengers; but it is more probable that it was written to bewail the destruction of Jerusalem and the temple.

1 **God**. Heb. *El*, Ex +15:2.
to whom vengeance belongeth. Heb. God of revenges. Ps 18:47.
O God. Heb. *El*, Ex +15:2.
to whom. Dt +32:35. Je +50:15. 2 Th 1:7, 8.
show thyself. Heb. shine forth. Ps 80:1.

2 **Lift**. Ps 7:6. 68:1. 74:22. Mi 5:9.
judge of the earth. Ps +7:8, 11. 9:4, 8, 13, 14, 16. 50:6. 75:7. 76:9. 96:10, 13. 97:1. Ge +18:25. Is 30:18, 19. Je +23:5-8. Mi +5:1, 2. Zc +14:9. Jn 5:22, 23. Ro 14:9-12. 2 C 5:10. 2 T +4:1. Re 20:11, 12.
render. Ps 31:23. Jb 40:11, 12. Pr 16:5. Is 2:11, 12, 17. 10:12. 37:23, 29, 36-38. Je 50:31, 32. Da 4:37. 5:22-24. 1 P 5:5. Re 18:6-8.

3 **Lord**. Ps 43:2. 73:8. Je 12:1, 2. Re +6:10.
the wicked. Est 5:11, 12. 6:6-10. 7:6, 10. Jb 20:5. Ac 12:22, 23.

4 **shall**. Ps 31:18. 59:7, 12. 64:3, 4. 73:8, 9. 140:3. Pr 30:14. Je 18:18. Mt 12:24, 34. Ju 14, 15.
boast. Ps 10:2-7. 52:1. Ex 15:9, 10. Jb 21:14, 15. Is 10:13-15. 37:24, 25. Da 7:8, 11, 25. 8:11. 11:36, 37. Re 13:5, 6.

5 **break**. Ps 7:2. 14:4. 44:22. 74:8, 19, 20. 79:2, 3, 7. 129:2, 3. Is 3:15. 52:5. Je 22:17. 51:20-23, 34. Mi 3:2, 3. Re 17:6.
afflict. Ex 2:23, 24. Je 50:11. Re 11:3.

6 **They slay**. Is 13:15-18.
widow. Is +1:17.
stranger. Ps 39:12. 119:19. 146:9. Ge +23:4. Ex 12:48mg.
fatherless. Ex +22:22.

7 **they say**. Ps 10:11-13. 44:21. 59:7. Jb 22:12, 13. Pr 15:3. Is 29:15. Ezk 8:12. 9:9. Zp 1:12. Lk 18:2, 4.

8 **brutish**. Ps 49:10. 73:22. 92:6. Pr 12:1. Is 27:11. Je 8:6-8. 10:8. Ro 3:11.
fools. Dt 32:29. Pr 1:22. 8:5. T 3:3.

9 **He that planted**. Ps 139:2, 4. Ex 4:11. 1 K +8:39. Pr 20:1, 12. Je 17:10.
hear. Ps 11:4. 17:3. 44:21. 139:1-12. Je 23:23, 24.

10 **chastiseth**. Ps 9:5. 10:16. 44:2. 135:8-12. 149:7. Is 10:12. 37:36. Je +10:25. Ezk 39:21.
he correct. Is 10:5, 6. Am 3:2. Hab 1:12. 3:12.

teacheth man. Ps 25:8, 9. 119:66. Ex 35:34. Jb 35:11. 36:22. Pr 2:6. Is 2:3. 28:26. 54:13. Jn 6:45.

11 **The Lord**. 1 C 3:20.
knoweth. Ps 49:10-13. Jb 11:11, 12. Ro 1:21, 22. 1 C 1:19, 21, 25. 3:18-20.
the thoughts. Ge 6:5. Is 55:8. Mi 4:12.

12 **Blessed**. Je +31:18.
teachest. Jb 33:16-25. Mi 6:9. Re 3:19.

13 **rest from**. Ps 27:5. 31:19, 20. 143:8, 9mg. Is 16:3-5. +26:20, 21. Hab +3:16. Zp +2:3. Lk +21:36. 2 C 4:17, 18. 2 Th 1:7, 8. He 4:9. Re +3:10. 14:13.
until the pit. Ps 9:15. 55:23. Is +24:22. Je 18:20, 22. 2 P 2:9. 3:3-7. Re 6:10, 11. 11:18.

14 **For**. Ps 37:28. 1 S 12:22. Is 49:14, 15. Je 32:39, 40. Jn 10:27-31. Ro 8:30, 38, 39. +11:1, 2. He +13:5.
not cast. Le +26:44. Is +41:9. +55:3. Ro +11:1.
forsake. 1 S +12:22. Is +60:10. Je +4:27. Ml +3:6. He +13:5.
his inheritance. ver. 5. Ps 2:8. 28:9. 33:12. Ex 15:17. Le 25:23. Dt 4:20. 9:26, 29. +32:9, 43. 1 S 10:1. 26:19. 2 S 20:19. 21:3. 1 K 8:51, 53. 2 K 21:14. Is 19:25. 63:17. 65:9. Je 10:16. Da +7:14. Zc 2:12. Lk +1:32, 33. Ro 8:17. Ep 1:18. Col +3:24. He 1:2. Re +11:15.

15 **But judgment**. ver. +2, 3. Ps +7:8, 9. 125:3. Dt 32:35, 36. Jb 35:14. Is +32:1. Da 7:22. Mi 7:9. Ml 3:18. 2 P 3:8-10. Re 15:3, 4. 20:4.
and all. Ps 37:5-7, 34. 125:4, 5. Jb 17:9. 23:11, 12. Ja 5:7-11. 1 J 2:19.
the upright. Pr 8:15, 16. Je 33:26. 1 C +6:2.
shall follow it. Heb. shall be after it.

16 **rise up**. Ex 32:26-29. Nu 25:6-13. Jg 5:23. 1 K 18:39, 40. 2 K 9:32. 10:15. Is 59:16. 63:5. Je 5:1. Ezk 22:30. Mt 12:30. 3 J 8.
stand up. Ne 5:7. Je 26:16-19. Jn 7:50, 51.

17 **Unless**. Ps 118:13. 124:1, 2. 125:1-3. 142:4, 5. Jn 16:32. 2 C 1:8-10. 2 T 4:16, 17.
soul. Heb. *nephesh*, Ps +30:3.
almost. *or*, quickly. Ps 2:12 (little). 37:10 (little while). 81:14 (soon).
dwelt. Ps 13:3. 31:17. 115:17.
silence. Heb. *dumah*, S#1745. Ps 115:17, only.

18 **My foot**. Ps 17:5. 37:23, 24. 38:16. 119:116, 117. 121:3. 1 S 2:9. Jb 12:5. Is 41:10. Lk 22:32. 1 P 1:5.
held me up. 2 P +1:10.

19 **In the multitude**. Ps 43:2-5. 61:2. 63:5, 6. 73:12-16. 77:2-10. Je 20:7-11. Hab 3:16-18. Ro 5:2-5. 2 C 1:4, 5. 1 P 1:7, 8.
soul. Heb. *nephesh*, Ge 34:3.

20 **throne**. Ps 52:1, 2. 82:1, 2. 1 S 22:17-19. Ec 3:16. +5:8. Am 6:3.
fellowship. 2 Ch 6:14-16. Is 1:11-20. Je 7:4-11. Jn 18:28. 2 C 6:14-16. Ep 5:11. 1 J 1:5, 6.
frameth. Ps 58:2. Ex 1:17. 1 K 12:32. Est 3:6-

12. Is 10:1. Da 3:4-7. 6:7-9. Mi 6:16. Jn 9:22. 11:57. Re 13:15-17.

21 **gather**. Ps 2:1-3. 22:16. 59:3. Pr 1:11, 16. Mt 27:1. Ac 4:5-7, 27, 28.
soul. Heb. *nephesh*, Ge +12:13.
condemn. Ex 23:7. 1 K 21:19. Pr 17:15. Je 26:15. Ezk 22:6, 12, 27. Mt 23:32-36. Ac 7:52, 58-60. Ja 5:6. Re 17:6.
blood. Dt +19:10. Pr 1:11. Ac 17:26.

22 **But**. ver. 10. Ps 27:1-3. 59:9, 16, 17. 62:2, 6.
the rock. Ps 18:2. Is 33:16.

23 **And he**. Ps 55:23. +57:6. 64:8. Pr 1:11, 18, 31.
cut them. Ps 12:3. 1 S 26:10, 11. Pr 2:22. 5:22. 14:32. Ezk 18:24. Da 9:26.

PSALM 95

1 **Come**. Ps 34:3. 66:8. 107:8, 15, 21. 117:1. 118:1. 136:1-3. 148:11-13. 150:6.
sing. Ps 47:6, 7. 66:1, 2. 81:1. 96:1, 2. 101:1. Ex 15:1, 21. 1 Ch 16:9. Ep 5:19. Col 3:16. Re 5:9. 14:3. 15:3.
let us make. Ps 66:1. 98:4-8. 100:1. Ezr 3:11-13. Is 12:4-6. Je 33:11. Mt 21:9. Re 19:6.
the rock. Ps 89:26. Dt 32:15. 2 S 22:47. Mt 16:16, 18. 1 C 10:4.

2 **Let us**. Ps 5:7. 100:2, 4. Je 31:12, 13.
come before his presence. Heb. prevent his face. Ps 17:13mg. 18:18. 21:3. Mi 6:6.
psalms. Ps 105:2. Ja 5:13.

3 **a great**. Ps 47:2. 48:2. Je 10:10, 11. 46:18. 48:15. Da +2:45. 4:37. Mt 5:35.
above. Is 44:8. Je 10:10-16. Mt 28:18. Ep 1:21. 1 P 3:22.
gods. Ex +12:12.

4 **In**. Ps 24:1. Jb 11:10.
his. Heb. whose.
deep. Ps 135:6.
the strength of the hills is his also. *or,* heights of the hills are his. Ps 65:6. 97:5. Jb 9:5. Mi 1:4. Na 1:5. Hab 3:6, 10.

5 **The sea is his**. Heb. Whose the sea is. Ps 33:7. Ge 1:9, 10. Jb 38:10, 11. Pr 8:29. Je 5:22.
he made. Jn 1:3.
hands. Nu +11:23. Pr 8:26.

6 **O come**. ver. 1. Ho 6:1. Mt 4:2. Re 22:17.
worship. Ps 72:9. Ex 20:5. Mt 4:9. Mk 14:35. Ac 10:25, 26. Re 22:8, +9.
let us. Ps 105:1-4. Ge 35:2, 3. Is 2:3. Jon 1:6. 3:6-9. Zc 8:21. He 4:16.
kneel. 1 K 8:54. 2 Ch 6:13. Ezr 9:5. Da +6:10. Lk 22:41. Ac 7:60. 20:36. 21:5. 1 C 6:20. Ep 3:14. Ph 2:10.
Lord. Ex +15:26.
our maker. Ps 100:3. Jb 35:10. Ec 12:1. Is 54:5. Jn 1:3. 1 P 4:19.

7 **For he**. Ps 48:14. 67:6. 115:3. Ex 15:2. 20:2. Je 31:33. He 11:16.

people. Ps 23:1. Ezk +34:31. I P 2:25.
pasture. Ps +74:1.
Today. He 3:7-11, +13, *15*. 4:7.
if ye. Pr 8:6. Is 55:3. Mt 3:2, 3. 17:5. Re 3:20.

8 **Harden**. Ex 8:15. 1 S 6:6. Da 5:20. Ac 19:9. Ro 2:5. He 3:8, +13. 12:25.
in the. Ex 17:2, 7. Nu +14:11, 22, 27. 20:13. Dt 1:34, 35. 6:16. He 3:8, 9, 15-19. Ju 5.
provocation. Heb. contention. S#4808h. Ps 81:7mg. 106:32. Ge 13:8. Ex 17:7mg. Nu 20:13mg, 24. 27:14, 14. Dt 32:51mg. 33:8. Ezk 47:19mg. 48:28mg. or, Meribah. i.e. *strife,* Ex +17:7.
temptation. S#4531h. Ex 17:7mg. Dt 4:34. 6:16. 7:19. 9:22. 29:3. 33:8. Jb 9:23. or, Massah. i.e. *trial,* Ex +17:7.
wilderness. Ps 29:8. 55:7. 65:12.

9 **When**. Ex +17:2.
saw. Nu 14:22. Mt 11:20-22. Jn 15:24.

10 **Forty**. Nu 32:13. Dt 1:3. 2:14-16. Jon +3:4. He 3:9, 10, 17.
grieved. Ge 6:6. Ep +4:30. He 3:10.
err. Ho +4:12.
and they. Pr 1:7, 22-29. Je 9:6. Jn 3:19-21. Ro 1:28.

11 **I sware**. Nu 14:23, 28-30. Dt 1:34, 35. He 3:11, 18. 4:3, 5.
that they should not enter. Heb. if they enter. Ge +4:7. Nu 14:23.
my rest. Ge 2:2, 3. Je 6:16. Mt 11:28, 29. Ro 5:1. He 4:4-11. Re 14:13.

PSALM 96

1 A.M. 2962. B.C. 1042.
O sing. Ps 33:3. 98:1. 149:1. 1 Ch 16:23-33. Is 42:10. Re 5:9. 14:3.
sing unto. Ps 67:3-5. 68:32. Ro 15:11.

2 **bless**. Ps 72:17, 18. 103:1, 2, 20-22. 104:1. 145:1, 10. 1 Ch 29:20. Ep 1:3. Re 5:13.
show. Ps 40:9, 10. 71:15. Is 40:9. 52:7, 8. Mk 16:15. Ac 13:26. Ro 10:14-18. 1 P 2:9.

3 **Declare**. Ps 22:27. 72:18, 19. ch. 117. Is 19:23-25. 49:6. Da 4:1-3. 6:26, 27. Mi 4:2. Zc 9:10. Mt 28:19. Mk 16:15. Lk 24:47. Re 14:6, 7.

4 **For the**. Ps 86:10. Ex 18:11. 1 S 4:8. Ne 9:5, 6. Da +2:45.
and greatly. Ps 18:3.
feared. Ps 66:3, 5. Je +5:22.
all gods. Ex +12:12.

5 **For**. Ps 115:3-8. 135:15-18. Is 44:8, etc. 46:1, 2. Je 10:3-5, 11, 12, 14, 15. Ezk +30:13. Ac 19:26. 1 C 8:4.
but. Ps 115:15. Ge 1:1. Is 42:5. Je 10:11.

6 **Honor**. Ps 8:1. 19:1. 63:2, 3.
majesty. 1 Ch +29:11.
strength. Ps 27:4. 29:1, 2, 9. 50:2.
sanctuary. 1 Ch 16:27.

7 **Give**. Ps 29:1, 2. 68:32-34. Lk 2:14. Ju 25.
O ye kindreds. Ps 22:27. 66:1, 2. 67:3, 4. Ro 15:9, 10. Re 5:9. 19:6.
glory. 1 Ch 29:11-13. Mt 6:13. Jn 5:23. 1 P 5:11. Ju 24, 25. Re 5:13. 7:12. 14:7. 19:1.
strength. Ps +8:2. 29:1.

8 **the glory**. Ps 108:3-5. 111:9. 148:13, 14. Ex +34:5-9. Re 15:4.
due unto. Heb. of.
his name. Ps +9:10. 68:4. 83:18. Mt 6:9. Jn 5:23. Ph 2:9, 10.
bring. Is 60:6, 7. Ml 1:11. Ro 12:1. 15:16. Ph 2:17. 4:18. He 13:13, 15, 16. 1 P 2:5. Re 8:3, 4.
come. Ps 100:4.

9 **in the beauty of holiness**. *or*, in the glorious sanctuary. Ps 29:2. 110:3. 2 Ch 20:21. Ezr 7:27. Ezk 7:20. Da 11:45. Lk 21:5, 6.
fear. Ps 33:8. 76:7, 11.

10 **say**. Ps 18:49. 46:6, 10. 126:2. Ml 1:11, 14. Ga 1:16.
the Lord. Ps 2:8-12. +93:1. Da 2:44. Mt 3:2.
the world. Is 49:8. Col 2:7. He 1:3.
judge. ver. 13. Ps +7:8. Ro 15:9.

11 **the heavens**. Ps 69:34. 148:1-4. Is 44:23. 49:13. Lk 2:10, 13, 14. 15:10. Re 12:12. 19:1-7.
the earth. Ro 8:21.
the sea. Ps 69:34-36. 98:7-9.

12 **Let**. Ps 65:12, 13. Is 42:10, 11. 55:12, 13. Ro 8:22.

13 **he cometh**. Dt +33:2. Is +35:4. 1 Th 4:16-18. 2 Th 1:10. 2 T 4:8. 2 P 3:8-10, 12-14. Re +11:18.
to judge. ver. +10. Ac 24:10.
the earth. Re +5:10.
with righteousness. Is 2:1-4. 11:3-9. Da +7:13, 14. 1 C 6:2, 3. Re 20:4-6.

PSALM 97

1 A.M. 3000. B.C. 1004.
Lord. Ps +93:1. Ob +21. Mt 3:3. 6:10, 13. Mk 11:10. Col 1:13.
the earth. Ps 2:11. 98:4-6. Is 49:13. Lk 2:10, 11.
let the multitude of isles. Heb. let the many, *or* great isles. Is +11:11.

2 **Clouds**. Ps 77:19. Ge +9:13. Ex 24:16-18. Na 1:3.
darkness. Ex +10:22.
righteousness. Ps 45:6, 7. 89:14. 99:4. Ge +18:25. He +1:8, 9.
judgment. Ro 11:33.
habitation. *or*, establishment. Ps 89:14mg. Pr 16:12.

3 **A fire**. Ps 18:8. 21:8, 9. 50:3. Nu 11:1. Dt 4:11, 24, 36. 5:4, 23, 24. +32:22. Is +24:6. 26:11. 29:6. 30:27, 30, 33. 33:11, 12, 14. 64:1, 2. Da 7:10. Na 1:5, 6. Hab 3:5. Ml +4:1. 2 Th

1:8. He 12:29. 2 P 3:7, 10-13. Re 11:5. 20:15.

4 **His**. Ps 77:18. 144:5, 6. Ex 19:16-18.
the earth. Ps 18:7. 104:32. 114:4, 7. Dt +32:22. Jb +26:11. Je +4:24. 10:10. Mt 27:50, 51. 28:2, 3. Re +6:12. 19:11.

5 **hills melted**. Jg 5:4, 5. Is 24:19, 20. Hab 3:6, 10. 2 P +3:10.
the Lord of. Ps 47:2. 83:18. Is 54:5. Mi 4:13. Zc 4:14. Mk 11:3. 1 C 1:2.

6 **The heavens**. Ps 19:1. 36:5, 6. 50:6. 89:2, 5. Is 1:2. Re 19:1, 2.
all the. Ps 67:4. 98:3. 2 S 22:47. Is +40:5. 45:6. Mt 6:9, 10.

7 **Confounded**. Ex +20:4. Is 2:20, 21. 37:18, 19. 41:29.
of idols. Ezk +30:13. Ho +14:8. Jn 5:43. 1 J 5:21.
worship. Ex 25:20. Dt 32:43. 2 Ch 3:13. He 1:6. 1 P 1:12. 3:22. Re 5:11-14.
gods. Ps +8:5. Ge 1:26. Ex +12:12. 2 Ch +35:22.

8 **Zion**. Ps 48:11. Is 51:3. 52:7-10. 62:11. Zp 3:14-17. Zc 9:9. Mt 21:4-9.
because. Ps 52:6. 58:10. Re 18:20. 19:1-7.

9 **Lord**. Ex +15:26.
high above. Heb. Most High. Ps +7:17. 18:13. Ep 1:21. Ph 2:9-11.
exalted. Is +12:4.
far. Ps 95:3. 96:4. 115:3-8. 135:5. Ex 18:11. Je 10:8, 10.
above all. Is 44:6. Jn 3:31. Ro 9:5.
gods. Ps +8:5. Ex +12:12.

10 **Ye that**. Jg +5:31.
hate evil. Pr +8:13. 2 T +2:19.
preserveth. Ps 31:23. 37:28, 39, 40. 145:20. Pr 2:8. Is 45:17. Jn 10:28-30. Ro 8:28-30. 2 T 4:17, 18. 1 P 1:5.
souls. Heb. *nephesh*, Ge +12:13.
delivereth. Ps 125:3. Je 15:21. Da 3:28. 6:22, 27. 2 Th 2:8-12. 3:2. 1 J 5:18. Re 13:8.

11 **Light**. Ps +112:4. Ge +1:3. Est 8:16. Is 60:1, 2. 62:1. Re 21:23. 22:5.
sown. Ps 126:5, 6. Pr 11:18. Jn 16:20. Ga 6:8. Ja 5:7-11.

12 **Rejoice**. Hab 3:17, +18. Zp 3:14-17.
give thanks. Ps 30:4. 60:6. Hab 1:12, 13. He 12:10.
at the remembrance. *or*, to the memorial. Ps 6:5. 9:6. 30:4mg.
holiness. Is 57:15. 1 Th 4:3. He 12:14.

PSALM 98

1 **Sing**. Ps 33:3. 96:1. 149:1. Is 12:5. 42:10. Re 5:9. 14:3.
for he. Ps 77:14. 86:10. 105:5. 136:4. 139:14. Ex 15:6, 11. Is 43:18-20. Je 31:22. Lk 1:49. 2:10-14. Ac 2:11. Re 15:3, 4.
hath done. Mk 7:37. Lk 13:17.
his right. Ps +18:35.

holy arm. Ex +15:16.
victory. Ps 2:5, 6. 45:3-5. 110:2-6. Ge 3:15.
Jn 16:33. Ac 2:32, 33. 19:20. Ro 8:37. Col
2:15. He 2:14, 15. Re 3:21. 6:2. 17:14. 19:11-
21.

2 **made**. Is 45:21-23. Mt 28:19. Lk +3:6. Ro
10:18. T 2:13.
righteousness. Ps 22:31. 24:5. Is 45:24, 25.
46:13. 62:2. Je 23:6. Jn 16:8-10. Ro 1:17.
3:21-26. 9:30. 10:3, 4. 2 C 5:21. Ph 3:9. 2 P
1:1.
openly showed. *or,* revealed. Le 20:11, 17,
18. Ro 1:17.

3 **remembered**. Ps 106:45. Le 26:42. Dt 4:31.
Mi 7:20. Lk 1:54, 55, 72. Ro 15:8, 9.
mercy. Ge +20:13.
all the ends. ver. 2. Ps 22:27. 67:7. Is 45:22.
49:6. 52:10. Lk 2:30, 31. 3:6. Ac 13:46, 47.
28:28. Ro 10:12, 18. Re 5:9.

4 **Make**. Ps 47:1-5. 66:1, 4. 67:4. 95:1. 100:1. Is
12:6. 42:11. 44:23. Je 33:11. Zp 3:14. Mt 21:9.
Re 19:1, 6.

5 **with the harp**. Re +5:8.

6 **trumpets**. Ps 47:5. 81:2-4. Le +23:24. Nu
10:1-10. 1 Ch 15:28. 2 Ch 5:12, 13. 29:27.
the King. Ps 47:6, 7. Mt 25:34. Re 19:16.

7 **Let**. Ps +96:11, etc. Ro 8:21, 22.
world. Ps 97:1. Is 49:13. 61:11.

8 **Let the floods clap**. Ps 47:1. 2 K 11:12. Is
55:12.
hills. Ps 65:12, 13. Is 55:12.

9 **for he cometh**. Ps +96:10, 13. Re 1:7.
with righteousness. Ps +7:8. 72:2. Is 5:16.
Ac 24:25. 2 P 3:13, 14. Re 20:4-6.
with equity. Ps 9:8. 17:2. 58:1.

PSALM 99

1 **Lord**. Ps 2:6. +93:1. Lk 19:12, 14.
people. Ps 2:11, 12. 21:8, 9. 97:4. Lk 19:27.
Ph 2:12.
he sitteth. 1 S +4:4.
earth. Ps 82:5mg. Je 4:24. 5:22. 49:21. 50:46.
Re 6:14. 20:11.
be moved. Heb. stagger. Is 19:14. 24:19, 20.

2 **great**. Ps 48:1-3. 50:2. 76:1, 2. Is 12:6. 14:32.
He 12:22-24. Re 14:1, etc.
high. Ps 66:7. 97:9. Is 6:1-7. Da 4:34, 35. He
12:18. Ja 4:6, 7.

3 **thy great**. Ps +47:2. 65:5. 66:3, 5. 68:35.
76:12. Ex 34:10. Dt 7:21. 10:17. +28:58. 1 Ch
17:21. Ne 1:5. 4:14. 9:32. Jb 37:22. Is 12:6.
64:3. Je 20:11. 44:26. Da +2:45. 9:4. Na 1:6,
7. He 12:21, 28. Re 6:16, 17.
for it. ver. 5, 9. Ps 111:9. 145:17. Ex 15:11.
Le 19:2. Jsh 24:19. 1 S 2:2. Jb 6:10. Is +1:4.
5:16. 6:3. 57:15. Lk 1:49. Jn 17:11. Re 3:7.
4:8. 15:4.

4 **strength**. Dt 32:3, 4. Jb 36:5-7. 37:23. Is
+11:4. He +1:8.

thou dost. Is 9:7. 42:4. 61:11.
executest. Dt 10:18. Ju 15.

5 **Exalt**. ver. 9. Is +12:4.
Lord. Ex +15:26.
footstool. Is +66:1.
he is holy. *or,* it is holy. ver. 3. Le 19:2. Is 6:3.

6 **Moses**. Ex 24:6-8. 29:11, etc. 40:23-29. Nu
16:47, 48.
his priests. He 7:24.
they called. Ex 14:15. 15:25. 32:11-14.
33:12-15. Nu 14:13-20. 16:21, 22. 1 S 7:9-12.
12:18-24. Je 15:1. He 7:25.
he answered. 1 K 18:36-38. 2 K 20:1-6, 10,
11. 1 Ch 4:10. 2 Ch 20:6-27. Ps +27:7. Da
9:20-23. Lk 1:13. Ac 10:4.

7 **He spake**. Ex 33:9.
in the cloudy. Ex +13:21.
kept. Ex 40:16. Nu 16:15. Dt 4:5. 33:9. 1 S
12:3-5. Pr 28:9. He 3:2. 1 J 3:21, 22.

8 **Lord**. Ex +15:26.
thou wast. Ps 89:31-33. Nu 14:20. Dt 9:19.
Je 46:28. Zp 3:7.
though. Ex 32:2, 34, 35. Nu 11:33, 34.
14:20-34. 16:47-49. 20:12, 24. Dt 3:26. 9:20.
Re 3:19.
their inventions. Ec 7:29. Ro 1:21.

9 **Exalt**. ver. +5.
his holy. Ps 2:6. 48:1, 2. 87:1-3.
for the. ver. 3, 5. Ps 107:8. 145:3. 148:13. 1 S
2:2. Is 5:16. 6:3. +57:15. Hab 1:12, 13. Lk
1:49. 1 P 1:15, 16. Re 3:7. 4:8.
Lord. Ex +15:26.

PSALM 100

(*Title.*) **A Psalm**. Ps 145, title.
praise. *or,* thanksgiving. ver. 4. Ps 26:7. 42:4.
50:14. 56:12.

1 **Make**. Ps 32:11. 47:1, 5. 66:1, 4. 95:1, 2.
98:4. Is 24:14-16. 42:10-12. Zp 3:14. Lk
19:37.
all ye lands. Heb. all the earth. Ps 67:4.
68:32. ch. 117. Dt 32:43. Zc +14:9. Ro 15:10.

2 **Serve**. Ps 9:2. 63:4, 5. 71:23. 107:21, 22. Le
25:9. Dt +12:7. 28:47. Lk 1:74. Col 3:23.
come. Ps 42:4. 95:2. 2 Ch 20:27, 28. 31:2. Ep
5:19.
presence. Ge +19:13.

3 **Know**. Ps 46:10. 95:3, 6, 7. Dt 4:35, 39. 7:9.
1 S 17:46, 47. 1 K 18:36-39. 2 K 19:19. Je
10:10. Jn 17:3. Ac 17:23, 24. 2 C 4:6. Ga 4:8,
9. 1 J 5:20.
it is he. Ps 95:6. 119:73. 139:13, etc. 149:2.
Jb 10:8-13. Ec 12:1. Ep 2:10. 1 P 4:19.
not we ourselves. *or,* his we *are.* Ps 12:4. 1 C
6:19, 20.
we are his. Ps +74:1, 2. Is 63:11, 19. Ezk
+34:31. 1 C 6:19, 20. 1 P 2:9, 25.

4 **Enter**. Ps 65:1. 66:13. 116:17-19. Is +35:10.
be thankful. Ps +136:1. Col +3:17.

bless his name. Ps 96:2. 103:1, 2, 20-22. 145:1, 2. 1 Ch 29:20. Jb 1:21. 1 P 2:9.

5 **is good**. Ps 52:1. 107:1, 8, 15, 22. +136:1.
his mercy. Ps 36:5. Ex +34:6.
everlasting. Ge +17:5.
and his truth. Ps 85:10. 89:1, 2. 119:90, 91. 146:6. Dt 7:9. Je +33:20, 21. Mi 7:20. Ro 15:8, 9. T +1:2. He 6:13-18.
all generations. Heb. generation and generation. Ps +33:11mg. 89:1mg.

PSALM 101

1 **I will sing**. Ps 89:1. 97:8. 103:6-8. 136:10-22. Re 15:3, 4. 19:1-3.
of mercy. Ps +100:5. Ro 9:15-18, 22, 23. +11:22.
unto thee. Ps 71:22, 23.

2 **behave**. ver. 6. Ps 75:1, 2. 119:106, 115. 143:8. 1 S 18:14, 15. 22:14. 2 S 8:15. 2 Ch 30:12. 31:20, 21. Je 23:5, 6.
O when. Ps +40:17. 143:7, 8.
walk within. Ge +18:19. Dt +6:7. Jsh +24:15. 2 S +6:20. Jb +1:5. Is 38:19. 1 T 3:4, 5. +4:12. T 1:6. 2:7.
my house. Jsh 24:15. Ec 4:9, 10. Is 41:13. Mt 6:33. Lk 16:13. 1 C 13:5. 2 C 3:5. Ep 4:32. Col 3:19. He 10:24. T 2:4. 1 P 3:7.
perfect heart. 1 K 9:4. 11:4. 2 K +20:3.

3 **set**. Ps 18:20-23. 26:4, 5. 39:1. 119:37, 113. Ex 20:17. 2 S 11:2-4. 1 K 21:2, etc. Jb 31:1. Pr +4:23. 6:25. 23:31-35. Ec 6:9. Is 33:15. Je 22:17. Ezk 23:14, 16, 20. Ho 7:6, 7. Mi 2:2. Mt 5:28. Mk 7:20-23. Ro 1:21-32. 13:13, 14. 1 C 3:16, 17. +6:9, 10. 2 C 10:5. 12:21. Ga 5:19-21. Ep 4:19-23. 5:3-5, 11, 12. 1 Th 5:22. 1 T 1:9, 10. 2 T 2:22. Ja 1:13-15. 1 P 2:11. 4:3-5. 2 P 2:14.
wicked thing. Heb. thing of Belial. 1 S +30:22.
I hate. Pr +8:13.
the work. Ps 26:5, 9. 119:104. Jb 21:16. T 1:16.
them. Ps 14:3. 36:3. 40:4. 78:41, 57. 125:5. Ex 32:8. Jsh 23:6. 1 S 12:20, 21. 15:11. Is 30:11. Zp 1:5, 6. Ga 4:9. He 10:39. 2 P 2:21. 1 J 2:19.
it shall not. Dt 13:17.

4 **A froward**. Pr 2:12-15. 3:32. 8:13. 11:20.
not know. Ps 6:8. 119:63, 115. Est +1:12. Pr 9:6. 22:24. Mt 7:23. 2 C 6:14-16. 15:33. 2 T 2:19.

5 **Whoso**. Ex +20:16. Le +19:16. Pr 6:16, 17. 20:19.
slandereth. Ps 74:18. 141:3. Le +19:16. Pr 4:24. +21:23. 24:28. +29:11. Ec +10:11. Ro 14:10. 1 C 5:11. 6:10. 15:33. Ep +4:31. 5:3, 4. 2 T 2:16. T 2:7, 8. Ja 1:21, 26. 1 P 3:9.
an high. Ps +119:21. 138:6. 1 S 2:3. Pr +6:17. Da 4:37. Ob 3, 4.
suffer. lit. I am not able (to bear). Is 1:13.

6 **Mine**. Ps 15:4. 34:15. 119:63. Pr 28:28. 29:2. Mt +24:45. Lk +12:42-44. Ro 13:1-4.
that they. Jn 12:26. 14:3. 17:24. Re 3:20, 21. 21:3.
in a perfect way. *or*, perfect in the way. Ps 119:1mg, 2, 3. Ge +17:1. Pr 11:20. 13:6. Ph 3:12-15.

7 **He that worketh**. 2 S 4:10-12. 2 K 5:26, 27. Pr 29:12. Ac 1:16-20, 25. 5:1-10.
tarry in my sight. Heb. be established. Ps 89:21, 27. 93:1. Ec 8:11. Ep 5:11.

8 **early**. lit. at morning. Je 21:12. Re +2:28.
destroy. Ps +58:10. Pr +2:22. 16:12. 20:8, 26. Is 11:4. 17:14. +24:6. 65:20. Mi 3:1-4, 9.
cut off. Ps +37:9. 75:10. Pr +2:22. Ho 9:3. Mi 2:8-10. Re 21:27. 22:14, 15.
the city. Ps 48:2, 8. 102:13, 16. Is 1:26. 26:1. 62:6, 7.

PSALM 102

(*Title*.) A.M. cir. 3464. B.C. cir. 540. **A Prayer**. This Psalm was evidently composed towards the close of the Babylonian captivity; and probably by the prophet Daniel.
of. *or*, for.
overwhelmed. Ps 12:5. 61:2. 69:1, 2. 142:2, 3. 143:4. La 3:18-20. Mk 14:33, 34. Lk 22:44. He 5:7.
poureth. Ps 42:4. 62:8. 77:3. 142:2. 1 S 1:15, 16.

1 **Hear**. Ps 5:2. 55:1-5. 57:1-3. 130:1, 2. 141:1, 2. 143:7. 145:19.
let my. Ps +3:4. 18:6. Jg 10:16. 1 S 9:16. 2 Ch 30:27. La 3:8, 44.

2 **Hide**. Dt +31:17. Is 43:2. 1 C 10:13.
incline. Ps 71:2. 88:2, etc.
in the day. Ps +40:17. Jb 7:21. Ac 12:5, etc.

3 **my days**. Ps 37:20. 119:83. Ja 4:14.
like smoke. *or*, (*as some read*) into smoke.
my bones. Ps 22:14, 15. 31:10. 38:3. Jb 30:30. La 1:13. 3:4.

4 **heart**. Ps 6:2, 3. 42:6. 55:4, 5. 69:20. 77:3. 143:3, 4. Jb 6:4. 10:1. La 3:13, 20. Mt 26:37, 38.
withered. ver. +11.
so that. ver. 9. 1 S 1:7, 8. Ezr 10:6. Ac 9:9.
bread. Ge +3:19.

5 **the voice**. Ps 6:6, 8. 32:3, 4. 38:8-10. Jb 19:20. Pr 17:22. La 4:8.
skin. *or*, flesh. Ps +16:9. Jb 12:10mg. Is 10:18mg. Ezk 10:12mg.

6 **like**. Jb 30:29, 30. Is 38:14. Mi 1:8.
a pelican. Is 34:11-15. Zp 2:14mg. Re 18:2.

7 **watch**. Ps 22:2. 77:4. 130:6. Dt 28:66, 67. Jb 7:13-16. Mk 14:33-37.
alone. Ps 38:11. La 3:28-30.

8 **Mine**. Ps +31:11. 55:3.
mad. Ps 2:1. Lk 6:11. Ac 7:54. 26:11.

are sworn. or, do curse by me. Dt 21:33. Je 29:22. Ac 23:12, etc.
against me. Ac 4:27.

9 **I have**. Ps 69:21. Is 44:20. La 3:15, 16. Mi 1:10. 7:17.
mingled. Jb +3:24. Lk +6:21.

10 **Because**. Ps 38:3, 18. 39:11. 90:7-9. Is +66:14. La 1:18. 3:39-42. 5:16. Da 9:8-14. Ro 3:19.
thou hast. Ps 30:6, 7. 73:18-20. 147:6. 1 S 2:7, 8. 2 Ch 25:8. Jn 12:32, 33. 2 C 4:9.

11 **My days**. Ps 103:15. Is 4:1. 9:4. Ho 9:9. Mt 2:1. Ac 5:36.
like a shadow. ver. 3. Ps 39:5, 6. 109:23. 144:4. Ec 6:12. Ja 4:14.
I am withered. ver. 4. Ps 39:11. 1 P +1:24.

12 **thou**. ver. 24-27. Ps 9:7. 90:1, 2. Dt 33:27. Is 44:6. 60:15. La 5:19. Ml 3:6. He 13:8. Re 1:17, 18.
for ever. Heb. *olam*, Ex +12:24. Re 5:14.
thy remembrance. Ps 135:13. Ex 3:15.
generations. Ge +9:12.

13 **Thou shalt arise**. Ps +3:7.
mercy upon. Ps 51:18. Is 14:32. 60:1, 10-14. Je 31:10-12, 23. Zp +3:8. Zc 1:12, 13. 2:10-12.
Zion. Is +24:23.
the set time. ver. +16. Ge +17:21. Ezr 1:1, etc. Is 40:2mg. Je 29:10, 12. Da 9:2, etc. 12:9, 12, 13. Ho 6:2. Mi +5:3. Zp +3:20. Ac 1:6, 7. +3:19. Ga 4:4. 2 P 3:8, 12. Re 11:15-18.

14 **thy servants**. Ps 79:1, 7-10. 137:5, 6. Ezr 1:5. 3:1-3. 7:27. Ne 1:3. 2:3, 17. 4:2, 6, 10. Da 9:16.
stones. Ne 4:2.

15 **heathen shall fear**. Ps 61:5. 68:31, 32. +86:9. 138:4. 1 K 8:43. Is 55:5. 60:3, etc. Je 25:12. Zc 8:20-23. Re 11:15. 21:24.
all the kings. Ps 138:4. 148:11.
thy glory. Is +40:5.

16 **When**. ver. +22. Is 2:2, 3. Ezk +34:27. 39:28. Ho 6:11. Zp 3:20.
shall build. Ps 51:18. 69:35. +147:2. Is 16:5. 44:26. 62:7. Je +1:10. 33:7, 10, 11. 42:10. Ezk 26:14. Am +9:11-15. Mi 3:12. 4:1-7. +5:3. 7:14, 15. Zc 1:17. Ac +3:19, 21. +15:16.
Zion. Ps 14:7. +50:2, 3. Is +24:23.
he shall appear. Ps +42:5mg. Je 31:3. Ezk +20:35-38. Zc 2:6-13. 9:14. 2 T +4:1.
his glory. Ps 85:9. 145:11, 13. Is +40:5. Mi 2:9. Zc 2:8. +6:13. 14:9. Mt 16:27. Mk 8:38. Col +3:4. 1 P +1:11.

17 **He will**. Ps 4:1. 6:9. 9:18. +34:6, 15. 72:12. Dt 4:29. 32:36. 1 S 2:8. Ne 1:6, 11. 2:1-8. Jb 34:28. 36:15. Is 30:19. Je 29:11-14. Da 9:3-21. Jl 2:18-20. Zc 10:6.
not despise. Ps 22:24. 69:33.

18 **written for**. Ps 71:18. 78:4-6. 119:105, 130. Ex 17:14. Dt 9:10. 31:19, etc. Jb 19:23, 24. Pr +8:9. +18:1. Is +8:20. Da 9:2. Jn 20:31. Ro 15:4. 1 C 10:11. 2 T 3:16, 17. 2 P 1:15, 18, 19.

the people. Ps 22:30, 31. 45:16, 17. Is 43:5-7, 21. 65:17-19. 2 C 5:17, 18. Ep 2:10. 1 P 2:9, 10.

19 **For he**. Ps 14:2. 33:13, 14. Dt 26:15. 1 K 8:39, 43. 2 Ch 16:9.
the height. Jb 22:12. He 8:1, 2. 9:23, 24.
from heaven. Mt +6:9.

20 **To hear**. Ps 79:11. Ex 2:23-25. 3:7. 2 K 13:4, 22, 23. Jb 24:12. Is 14:17. Je 51:34, 35.
to loose. Ps +146:7.
those that are appointed to. Heb. the children of. 1 S +20:31mg.

21 **To declare**. Ps 9:13, 14. 22:22. 51:14, 15. 79:13. Is 51:11. Ep 2:4-7. 3:21. 1 P 2:9.

22 **When**. ver. 16. Ps 72:8-11. Ge +49:10. Ezr 10:7. Est 2:8, 19. Ezk +34:27. Ro 15:19.
gathered. Is 66:18. Je +23:3. Ho 1:9-11. 2 Th +2:1.
the kingdoms. Ps 145:11-13. Ob +21. Mt +24:14. Re 11:15.
to serve. Ps 72:11. Is 49:22, 23. 60:3-5.

23 **He weakened**. Heb. He afflicted. Ps 89:38-47. 2 Th 2:3-12. 1 T 4:1-3. 2 T 3:1, etc. Re 11:2, etc. 12:13, etc.
shortened. Ps 110:3. Ex 12:5. Jb 21:21.

24 **I said**. Ps 39:13. Is 38:10, etc.
my God. Ps +24:10. Ho 1:7. He +1:8, 10-12.
in the midst. Ps 55:23. Jb 14:5, 14. 15:32. 21:21. 22:16. Pr 10:27. Ec +7:17. Is +38:10. Je 17:11. Lk 12:20.
thy years. ver. 12, 27. Ps 9:7. 90:1, 2. Jb +36:26. Hab 1:12. Re 1:4, 8.
generations. Ge +9:12.

25 **Of old**. Ge 1:1. 2:1. Ex 20:11. Jb 38:4-7. Pr 8:23, etc. Jn +1:3. He *1:10-12*.

26 **They shall perish**. Ec +1:4. Is 34:4. 51:6. 65:17. 66:22. Lk 21:33. Ro 8:20. 2 P 3:7-12. Re 20:11. 21:1.
endure. Heb. stand. ver. 12. Ex 3:14.

27 **thou art**. Ml +3:6. Jn 8:58. He 13:8. Ja 1:17. Re 1:8, 17, 18.
thy years. ver. 24. Ps 90:4. Jb 36:26.

28 **The children**. Ps 22:30, 31. 45:16, 17. 69:35, 36. 103:17. +145:13. Is +29:23. 53:10. 54:1. 59:20, 21. 65:22. 66:22. Ho 1:10. Jn 8:33-40. Ac 2:39. 2 P 3:13.
of thy servants. Ps 78:70. 89:3, 20. 105:6, 26, 42. Is 37:35. 41:8, 9. Je 33:21, 22, 26. Ezk 28:25. 34:23, 24. 37:24, 25. Mi 7:20. Zc 3:8. Ml 4:4. Ro 8:17, 19.
shall continue. Ps +72:5. Je +31:36. Jl 3:20. Mt 24:34. Lk +1:32, 33.
their seed. Ps 69:36. +72:5. 90:16, 17. 112:2.

PSALM 103

1 A.M. 2970. B.C. 1034.
Bless. ver. 22. Ps 30:4. 68:19. 104:1. 146:1, 2. Lk 1:46, 47.
my. Ps 104:1. 146:1. Is 42:1. Lk +1:46.

soul. Heb. *nephesh*, Ge +34:3; Nu +23:10; Ps +16:10.

all that. Ps 47:7. 57:7-11. 63:5. 86:12, 13. 111:1. 138:1. Mk 12:30-33. Jn 4:24. 1 C 14:15. Ph 1:9. Col 3:16.

holy name. Ps 99:3. Is 6:3. Re 4:8.

2 **soul**. Heb. *nephesh*, Ge +34:3.

forget not. Ps 105:5. 106:7, 21. 116:12. Dt 8:2-4, 10-14. 32:6, 18. 2 Ch 32:25. Is 63:1, 7. Je 2:31, 32. Lk 17:15-18. Ep 2:11-13.

3 **forgiveth**. Ps +32:5. 51:1-3. +130:8. Is 43:25. Je 33:8. Ezk 33:16. Mt 9:2-6. Mk 2:5, 10, 11. Ep 1:7.

healeth. Ps 30:2. 38:1-7. +41:3, 4, 8. 107:17-22. 147:3. Ex 15:26. +23:25. Nu 12:13. 21:7-9. Jsh 18:27, Irpeel. 2 K 20:5. Pr 3:7, 8. 4:22. Is 33:24. 53:5. Je 17:14. 33:6. Mt 8:16, 17. Ac 10:38. 2 T 4:20. Ja 5:14, 15. 3 J 2.

4 **redeemeth**. Ps 30:3. +34:22. 56:13. Jb 33:19-30. Ho 13:9.

crowneth. Ps 5:12mg. 8:5. 21:3. 65:11. Ja 1:12. 1 P 5:4.

5 **satisfieth**. Ps 23:5. 104:28. 145:15, 16. Mt +5:6. 1 T 6:17.

thy youth. Is 40:31. Ho 2:15. 2 C 4:16.

like the eagle's. Is +40:31.

6 **judgment**. Dt +32:36.

oppressed. Ps 9:9. 12:5. Dt 24:14, 15. Jb 27:13, etc. Pr 14:31. 22:22, 23. 23:10, 11. Is 14:4, etc., 17-19. 58:6, 7. Je 7:6, etc. Ezk 22:7, 12-14. Mi 2:1-3. 3:2-4. Ja 2:6. +5:1-6.

7 **He made**. Ps 77:20. 105:26, etc. Ex 19:8, 20. 20:21. 24:2-4. Nu 12:7, 8. Dt 29:29. 34:10. Ne 9:13, 14. Is 63:11, 12. Jn 5:45-47. Ac 7:35, etc.

his ways. Ex 33:13. +34:5, 6. Jn 5:20.

his acts. Ps 78:5. 147:19.

8 **merciful**. Ex +34:6, 7. Je 32:18. Ro 5:20, 21. Ep 1:7, 8.

slow. Jl 2:13. Jon 4:2. Na 1:3.

plenteous in mercy. Heb. great of mercy. Ps 18:16mg. +86:15.

9 **not always**. Ps 30:5. Jb +4:20. Is 27:4. Is +41:9. Je 3:5.

neither. Ps 30:5. Is 57:16. Je 3:5. Mi 7:18, 19.

for ever. Heb. *olam*, Ex +12:24.

10 **hath not dealt**. Ps 130:3. Ezr 9:13. Ne 9:31. Jb 11:6. Ec 8:11. 9:1, 2. La 3:22. Da 9:18, 19. Hab 3:2. Mt +6:5. Ro 4:7, 8.

rewarded. 1 S +1:22.

11 **as the**, etc. Heb. according to the height of heaven. Ps 36:5. 57:10. 89:2. Jb 22:12. Pr 25:3. Is 55:9. Ep 2:4-7. 3:18, 19.

his mercy. ver. 13, 17. Lk 1:50.

12 **as the east**. Ps 50:1. 113:3. Le +1:16. Is 45:6.

so far. Is 43:25. Je 31:34. 50:20. Mi 7:18. He 10:2-4. 1 J 1:7.

removed. Is 43:25. Je 33:8. Mi 7:19.

13 **Like**. Nu 11:12. Dt 8:5. Pr 3:12. Is 63:13, 15,

16. Je 31:9, 20. Mt 6:9, 32. Lk 11:11, 12. 15:21, 22. Jn 20:17. He 12:5-11.

them. ver. 11, 17. Pr +3:7. Ml 3:16, 17.

14 **he knoweth**. Ps +40:17. 78:38, 39. 89:47.

our frame. Ps +34:4. 38:10. 49:12. 1 S 20:3. Is 2:22. 64:6. Mk 8:3. Ro 7:15-25. 1 C 10:13.

remembereth. Ge +8:1.

dust. Ps 104:29. +146:4. Ge +3:19. Jb 7:5-7, 21. 10:9. 13:25. 14:2, 3. Ec 3:20. 12:7.

15 **his days**. 1 P +1:24.

a flower. Jb 14:1-3. Is 28:1, 4. Na 1:4.

16 **the wind**. Jb 27:20, 21. Is 40:7.

it is gone. Heb. it is not. Ge 5:24. 42:36. Jb 14:10.

and the. Jb 7:6-10. 8:18, 19. 20:9.

17 **the mercy**. ver. +8. Je 31:3. Ro 8:28-30. Ep 1:4-8. 2:4-7. 2 Th 2:13, 14. 2 T 1:9.

from everlasting to. Heb. *olam* doubled, Ps +41:13.

his righteousness. Ps 22:31. Is 46:13. 51:6. Da 9:24. Mi 6:5. Ro 1:17. 3:21-25. 2 P 1:1.

unto children's. Ps 25:13. 90:16. +102:28. Ex 20:6. Dt 10:15. Is 41:8. 59:20, 21. Je 33:24-26. Ac 13:32-34. Ro 15:8.

18 **To such**. Ps 25:10. 132:12. Ge 17:9, 10. Ex 19:5. 24:8. Dt 7:9. 2 Ch 34:31. He 8:6-13.

remember. Ps 119:9-11. Dt 4:23. 6:6-9. Pr 3:1. Mt 28:20. Lk 1:6. Ac 24:16. 1 Th 4:1, 2.

to do them. Lk +6:46.

19 **prepared**. Ps 9:7.

his throne. Ps +11:4. Re 1:4.

in the heavens. Mt +6:9.

his kingdom. Ps 47:2. 83:18. 2 Ch 20:6. Da 4:25, 34, 35. Mt +6:10, 13. Ep 1:21, 22. Ph 2:9, 10. 1 P 3:22.

over all. Ps 22:27. 59:13. 67:7. 1 C 15:24-28. Ep 1:10.

20 **Bless**. Ps 148:2. Lk 2:13, 14. Re 19:5, 6.

that excel in strength. Heb. mighty in strength. Ps 78:25. 2 K 19:35. Is 6:2. Jl 2:11. Mt 26:53.

do his. Mt 6:10. Lk 1:19. He 1:14.

21 **all ye his hosts**. Ps +24:10. 148:2, 3. Ge 32:2. Jsh 5:14. 1 K 22:19. 2 Ch 18:18. Ne 9:6. Lk 2:13.

ministers. Ps 68:17. 104:4. Da 7:9, 10. Mt 13:41. 24:30, 31. 2 Th 1:7, 8. He 1:6, 7, 14. Re 22:8, 9.

22 **all his works**. Ps 145:10. 148:3-12. 150:6. Is 42:10-12. 43:20. 44:23. 49:13. Re 5:12-14.

bless the Lord. ver. 1. Ps 104:1, 35. 146:1.

soul. Heb. *nephesh*, Ge +34:3.

PSALM 104

1 **Bless**. ver. 35. Ps 103:1, 2, 22.

my. Ps +103:1. Lk +12:19.

O my. Ps +42:5.

soul. Heb. *nephesh*, Ge +34:3.

O Lord. Ps 7:1-3. Da 9:4. Hab 1:12.

art very great. Je 23:24. Da +2:45. Re 1:13, etc.

clothed. Ps +93:1. Da 7:9.

honor. Ps 29:1-4.

and majesty. Ps 146:10. Ex 8:10, 11. 19:18. 20:18, 19. 1 Ch +29:11. Da 7:9, 10. Is +57:15.

2 **with light**. Da 7:9. Mt 17:2. 1 T 6:16. 1 J 1:5.

garment. Ps +93:1.

stretchest. Is +40:22.

3 **Who layeth**. Ps 18:10, 11. Am 9:6.

waters. Ge 1:7.

maketh. Mt 26:64. Re 1:7.

clouds. Ps 77:17. Ge +9:13. Ex +13:21. Mt +24:30. 26:64.

his chariot. Ps +68:17.

walketh. Ps 18:10. 139:9. 2 S 22:11. Na 1:3.

4 **Who maketh**. Ac 23:8. He 1:7, 14.

spirits. Heb. *ruach*. Thus, *ruach* is used of invisible spirit beings, here, angels. For Cherubim, see Ezk 1:12, 20, 21. 10:17. For neutral spirit beings, see Jb 4:15. Is 31:3. For evil spirit beings see Jg +9:23. For the other uses of *ruach*, see Ge 6:3.

ministers. 2 K 2:11. 6:17. Ezk 1:13, 14.

flaming fire. Is +24:6. Ho 7:6, 7. Zc 12:6. Mt 3:12. Mk 3:17. Lk 9:54. 12:49. 2 Th 1:8. Re 11:5. 16:8.

5 **Who laid the foundations of the earth**. Heb. He hath founded the earth upon her bases. Ps 24:2. 33:9. 136:6. Jb 26:7. 38:4-7.

should not. Ps 72:5, 17. 78:69. 89:36, 37. 93:1. 96:10. 119:90, 91. 1 Ch 16:30. Ec +1:4. Is 49:8. 51:16. 2 P 3:7, 10, 11. Re 6:14. 20:11.

for ever. lit. for ever and ever.

and ever. Ps +9:18 (**S#5703h**).

6 **coveredst**. Ge 1:2-10. 7:19, 20. 2 P 3:5, 6.

stood above. Ge 7:19.

7 **At thy**. Ge 1:9. 8:1. Pr 8:28, 29. Mk 4:39.

they fled. Ps 114:3-7.

8 **They go up**, etc. *or*, The mountains ascend, the valleys descend. Ge 8:5.

9 **hast set**. Ps 33:7. Ge 9:11-15. Jb 26:10. 38:10, 11. Is +54:9. Je 5:22.

10 **He sendeth**. Heb. Who sendeth. Ps 107:35. Dt 8:7. Is 35:7. 41:18.

springs. Heb. *mayan*, Ge +7:11.

run. Heb. walk. Ps 131:1mg. Pr 8:20mg. Ec 1:7. Hab 3:11mg.

11 **They give**. Ps 145:16.

the wild. Jb 39:5-8.

quench. Heb. break. Ps 105:16. Ex 12:46. Is 42:3.

12 **the fowls**. ver. 16, 17. Ps 50:11. 84:3. 148:10. Mt 6:26. *13:32*. Mk 4:32. Lk 13:19.

sing. Heb. give a voice. Ps 147:9.

13 **watereth**. Ps 147:8. Dt 11:11. Jb 38:25-28, 37. Je 10:13. 14:22. Mt +5:45. Ac 14:17.

his chambers. ver. 3. Ge 1:7. Am 9:6.

the earth. Ps 65:9-13.

14 **causeth**. Ps 145:15, 16. 147:8, 9. Ge 1:11, 12,

29, 30. 2:5. 1 K 18:5. Je 14:5, 6. Jl 2:22. Mt +5:45.

herb. Ge 1:29, 30. 2:9, 16. 3:18. 9:3.

that he. Ps 136:25. Ge 4:12. Jb 28:5. 1 C 3:7.

food. Heb. bread. Ge +3:19. Is 28:28.

15 **wine**. Ps 23:5. Le +23:13. Jg 9:13. Pr 31:6, 7. Ec 10:19. Je 31:12. Zc 9:15-17. Mk 14:23. Ep 5:18.

oil to make his, etc. Heb. to make his face shine with oil, *or* more than oil. Dt 28:40. Jg 9:9. Ec 8:1. SS 1:2-4. Lk +7:46. He 1:9. 1 J 2:20, 27.

bread. Ps 105:16. Le 26:26. Dt 8:3. Is 3:1. Ezk 4:16. 5:16. 14:13.

16 **trees**. Nu +24:6. Ezk 17:23.

are full. Ps 65:9. Dt 33:28.

17 **the birds**. ver. 12. Je 22:23. Ezk 31:6. Da 4:21. Ob 4. Mt 13:32.

as for. Le 11:19. Je 8:7.

the stork. Le 11:19. Dt 14:18. Jb 39:13mg. Je 8:7.

18 **the wild goats**. 1 S 24:2. Jb 39:1.

the conies. Dt 14:7. Pr 30:26.

19 **the moon**. Ps 8:3. 136:7-9. Ge 1:14-18. Dt 4:19. Jb 31:26-28. 38:12. Je 31:35.

seasons. Ge +17:21.

20 **makest**. Ps 74:16. 139:10-12. Ge 1:4, 5. +8:22. Is 14:7.

darkness. Ex +10:22.

of the forest do creep forth. Heb. thereof do trample on the forest. Ps 69:34mg. Ge 9:2. Le 20:25mg.

21 **The young**. Ps 34:10. Jb 38:39. Is 31:4. Ezk 19:2, etc. Am 3:4.

seek. Ps 147:9. Jb 38:41. Jl 1:18, 20. 2:22.

22 **The sun**. Jb 24:13-17. Na 3:17. Jn 3:20.

23 **goeth forth**. Ge 3:19. Jg 19:16. Ec 5:12. Ep 4:28. 2 Th 3:8-12.

24 **O Lord**. Ne +4:4.

how. Ps 8:3. Ne 9:6. Da +4:3.

in wisdom. Ps 136:5. Ge 1:31. Pr 3:19, 20. 8:22, etc. Je 10:12. Ro 11:33. Ep 1:8. 3:10.

the earth. Ps 24:1. 50:10-12. 65:11. Ge 1:11, 12, 24, 25. 1 T 6:17.

25 **this great**. Ps 95:4, 5. Ge 1:20-22, 28. Dt 33:14-16, 19.

beasts. Ge 3:1. Ac 28:5.

26 **There go**. Ps 107:23. Ge 49:13.

leviathan. Ps 74:14. Jb 3:8mg. 41:1, etc. Is 27:1.

made. Heb. formed. Ps 74:17. 94:9, 20. 95:5. Ge 2:7, 8. 19.

to play. Jb 41:5, 29.

27 **wait**. Ps 36:6. 136:25. 145:15, 16. 147:9. Jb 38:41. Lk 12:24-28.

meat in. Jb 36:31. Mt +24:45. Lk +12:42.

28 **gather**. Ex 16:4, 18, 22. Nu 11:8.

openest. Ps 38:13. 39:9. 49:4. 51:15. 145:16.

thine hand. Ps +37:24. Ru +1:13.

filled. ver. 13.

with good. Ps +145:9. 2 K +6:33. Je +29:11. Ja +1:17.

29 **hidest**. Ps 31:20. 64:2. Dt +31:17. Ro 8:20-22.
are troubled. Ps 6:10. 48:5. 83:17. 90:7.
thou takest. Ps +146:4. Jb 34:14, 15. Ec 12:7. Ac 17:25, 28.
breath. Heb. *ruach*, Ge +6:17. Jb 12:10. 27:3. 33:4. 34:14. +146:4. Ec 8:8. 12:7. Is 2:22. 42:5. Ezk 37:9mg. Ac 17:25.
die. Ge 6:17. 7:21. +25:8. 35:29. +49:33.
return. ver. 9. Ps 6:10. 7:12. 90:3. Ge +3:19.
dust. Ps 7:5. 18:42. 22:15. 30:9. Ec 3:20.

30 **sendest**. Ps 33:6. Jb 26:13. 33:4. Is 32:14, 15. Ezk 37:9. Jn 7:39. Ep 2:1, 4, 5. T 3:5.
spirit. Heb. *ruach*, Nu +16:22.
renewest. 2 K 2:11. 6:17. Is 11:6-9. 65:17, 25. 66:22. Ho 2:18. Mk 11:2. Ro 8:21. Re 21:5.
the face. Ge 1:2.

31 **The glory**. Ps 102:16. Ro 11:36. Ga 1:5. Ep 3:21. 2 T 4:18. He 13:21. 1 P 5:11. 2 P 3:18. Re 5:12, 13.
endure. Heb. be. Ps 72:17mg.
for ever. Heb. *olam*, Ex +12:24.
rejoice. Ge 1:31. Ex 31:17. Dt +30:9. Ezk 5:13.

32 **looketh**. Ps 77:16. +97:4. Is 64:2. Je 5:22. Am 8:8. Na 1:5, 6. Hab 3:5, 6, 10. Re 20:11.
he toucheth. Je 1:9. Am 9:5.
smoketh. Ps 50:3. Is 64:1, 2. Re +14:11.

33 **I will sing**. Ps 63:4. 145:1, 2.
as long. Ps 146:2. Dt +12:1.

34 **meditation**. Ps 1:2. +40:17. 63:5, 6. 77:12. 119:15, 16, 97, 103, 111, 127, 128, 167. 139:17, 18. Pr 24:14.
I will be. Hab 3:17, +18.

35 **sinners**. Ps 1:4. 37:38. 59:13. 68:1, 2. 73:27. +101:8. Jg 5:31. Pr 2:22. Ml +4:1, 3. Re 19:1, 2.
the wicked. Ps 37:9, 10.
Bless. ver. 1. Ps 89:52. 103:1, 2, 22. Ro 9:5.
soul. Heb. *nephesh*, Ge +34:3.

PSALM 105

(*Title*.) A.M. 2962. B.C. 1042.

1 **Give**. Ps +136:1-3. 1 Ch 16:7-22.
call. Is 12:4. Jl 2:32. Ac 9:14. Ro 10:13. 1 C 1:2.
make known. Ps 89:1. 96:3. 145:4-6, 11, 12. Nu 23:23. Is 12:4. 51:10. Da 3:29. 4:1-3. 6:26, 27.

2 **Sing unto**. Ps 47:6, 7. 96:1, 2. 98:1, 5. Jg 5:3. Is 12:5, 6. 42:10-12. Ep 5:19. Re 15:3, 4.
talk ye. Ps 77:12. 78:4-6. 119:27. Ex 13:8, 9, 14. Dt 6:6-9. Lk 24:14, etc.

3 **Glory**. Ps 34:2. Is 45:25. Je 9:23, 24. 1 C 1:29, 31. Ga 6:14.
let the heart. Ps +9:10. Pr 8:17. Is 45:19. 55:6, 7. La 3:25. Lk 11:9, 10.

4 **Seek**. Am 5:4-6. Zp +2:2, 3.
his strength. Ps 78:61. 132:8. 2 Ch 6:41.
seek his face. Ps 27:8. 63:1.

5 **Remember**. Ps 103:2. Dt +7:18, 19. 32:7. Lk 22:19. 1 C 11:24-26.
the judgments. Ps 119:13. Re 16:7. 19:2.

6 **ye seed**. Ex 3:6. Is 41:8, 14. 44:1, 2. Ro 9:4, etc.
his chosen. Dt 7:6-8. Jn 15:16. 1 P 2:9.

7 **the Lord**. Ps 95:7. 100:3. Ge 17:7. Ex 20:2. Dt 26:17, 18. 29:10-15. Jsh 24:15-24.
judgments. Ps 48:10, 11. Is 26:9. Re 15:4.

8 **He hath remembered**. ver. +42. 1 Ch 16:15.
for ever. Heb. *olam*, Ex +12:24. Ge +9:16.
a thousand. Dt 7:9.

9 **covenant**. Ge 17:2. 22:16, 17. 26:3. 28:13. 35:11. Ne 9:8. Ac 7:8. He 6:17.

10 **an everlasting**. Ge +9:16. +17:7, 8. 2 S 23:5. He 13:20.

11 **Unto thee**. Ge +13:15.
lot. Heb. cord. Ps 16:5, +6. 18:4, 5mg. 78:55. Jsh 17:5, 14.

12 **a few**. Ge 34:30. Dt 7:7. 26:5. Is 51:2. Ezk 33:24, etc.
and strangers. Ge 17:8. 23:4. Ac 7:5. He 11:9, 12.

13 **went from**. Ps 12:8. 39:6. Ge 13:17.
one nation to another. Ge 12:10. 15:13-16. 20:1. 46:3, 6. Nu 32:13.
from one kingdom. 1 Ch 16:20.

14 **He suffered**. Ge 12:14-17. 20:1-7. 26:14, etc. 31:24-29. 35:5. Ex 7:16, 17.

15 **Touch not**. Jb +1:11.
mine anointed. 1 K 19:16. 1 J 2:27.
and do. Ge 20:7. 27:39, 40. 48:19, 20. 49:8, etc.

16 **Moreover**. Am +3:6. 7:1-4. 8:11, 12. Hg 1:10, 11. 2:17. Mt 8:8, 9.
famine. 1 K +8:37.
brake. Ps 104:15. Ge 47:13, 19. Le +26:26.

17 **He sent**. Ge 45:5, 7, 8. 50:20.
Joseph. Ge 37:27, 28, 36. 39:1. 45:4. Ac 7:9.
was sold. Ge 39:1. Is 49:7. Ph 2:7.

18 **Whose**. Ge 40:15. 41:12. Ps 22:16. Mt 27:2. Pr +7:22. He +11:36.
he was laid in iron. Heb. his soul came into iron. Heb. *nephesh*, Ge +27:31. Ps 107:10.
iron. 2 K +6:5.

19 **his word**. Ps 44:4. Ge 41:11-16, 25, 39, 40. Pr 21:1. Da 2:30. Ac 7:10.
tried him. 1 P 1:6, 7. 4:19.

20 **The king**. Ge 41:14.
loosed. Ps +146:7. Ac 2:24.

21 **made**. Ge 41:40-44, 55. 45:8, 26. Ge 31:18.
substance. Heb. possession. Ps 104:24. Ge 31:18.

22 **To bind**. Ge 41:44. Nu 30:2. Jg 15:10, 12, 13.
princes. Ps 45:16. 68:27. 82:7. 119:23.
pleasure. Heb. *nephesh*, Ex +15:9.
teach. Ge 41:33, 38, 39. Is 19:11, 12.

senators. or, elders. Ps 107:32. 119:100. 148:12.

wisdom. Ps 119:98. Jb 35:11.

23 **Israel**. Ge 45:9-11. 46:2-7. Jsh 24:4. Ac 7:11-15.

Jacob. Ge 47:6-9, 28.

the land. ver. 27. Ps 78:51. 106:22. Ge 10:6.

24 **And he**. Ge 13:16. 46:3. Ex 1:7. Dt 26:5. Ac 7:17, 18. He 11:12.

made. Ge 26:16. Ex 1:8, 9. 12:37.

25 **He turned**. Ge 15:13. Ex 1:8-10. +4:21. 9:16. **to hate**. Ex 1:11-14, 16. 2:23. Ac 7:19.

26 **sent**. Ps 77:20. Ex 3:10. 4:12-14. 6:11, 26, 27. Jsh 24:5. Mi 6:4. Ac 7:34, 35.

his servant. Mt 12:18.

Aaron. Ex 4:14, 16. 7:1, 12. 28:1, 2, 12, 29-38. 29:5, etc. Le 8:7, etc. Nu 16:5-11, 40, 47, 48. 17:5. 1 S 12:6.

27 **They**. Ps 78:43-51. 135:8, 9. Ex ch. 7-11. Dt 4:34. Ne 9:10, 11. Is 63:11, 12. Je 32:20, 21.

his signs. Heb. words of his signs. Ps +65:3mg.

wonders. ver. 23. Ps 106:22.

28 **sent**. Ex +10:22.

rebelled. Ps 99:7. Ezk 2:4-8.

29 **turned**. Ps 78:44. Ex 7:20, 21. Is 50:2. Ezk 29:4, 5. Re 16:3.

30 **brought**. Ps 78:45. Ex 8:3-14. Re 16:13, 14.

31 **there**. Ps 78:45. Ex 8:21-24. Is 7:18.

and lice. Ex 8:16-18.

32 **He gave them hail for rain**. Heb. their rain hail. Is +28:17.

33 **He smote**. Re 9:4.

34 **the locusts**. Ps +78:46.

35 **eat up**. Ps 18:8. 21:9. 22:26. Ex 10:15.

the herbs. Ps 72:16. 92:7. 102:4, 11.

the fruit. Ps 1:3. 21:10. 58:11mg. 72:16.

36 **He smote**. Ps 78:51. 135:8. 136:10. Ex 4:23. 11:4, 5. 12:12, 29, 30. He 11:28.

chief. Ge 49:3.

37 **brought**. Ge 15:14. Ex 3:22. 12:35, 36. Ac 13:17.

and there. 2 Ch 28:15. Jb 4:4. Is 5:27.

38 **Egypt**. Ge +47:15.

glad. Ex 10:7. 12:33.

for. Ge 35:5. Jsh 2:9.

39 **spread**. Ps 78:14. Ex +13:21. 1 C 10:1, 2.

40 **asked**. Ps 78:18, 26-28. Ex 16:12, 13. Nu 11:4-6, 31-33.

satisfied. Ex 16:14-35. Nu 11:7-9. Dt 8:3. Jsh 5:12. Ne 9:20.

bread. Ps 78:23-25. Jn 6:31-33, 48-58.

41 **opened**. Ps 78:15, 16, 20. 114:8. Ex 17:6. Nu 20:11. Ne 9:15. Is 48:21. 1 C 10:4.

42 **For he**. ver. 8-11. Ge 12:7. 13:14-17. 15:14. Le +26:42.

remembered. Ge +8:1. Ml +3:6.

Abraham. Ex 32:13. Dt 9:5, 27. Mi 7:20.

43 **And he**. Ps 78:52, 53. 106:8-12. Ex 15:13. Dt 4:37, 38. Is 63:11-14. Ac 7:36. 13:17.

with joy. Is 35:10. 51:10, 11. 55:12. Je 31:11, 12.

gladness. Heb. singing. Ps 106:12. Ex 15:1, etc.

44 **gave**. Ps 44:2, 3. 78:55. 80:8. 135:10-12. 136:21, 22. Jsh 11:23. 21:43. 23:4. 24:8, 13. Ne 9:22-25.

inherited. Dt 6:10, 11. Jsh 5:11. 13:7, etc.

the labor. Dt +28:33.

45 **That**. Dt +4:1. 5:33. Ep 2:8-10. T 2:14. 1 J 2:3. 5:3.

Praise ye the Lord. Heb. Hallelujah. Ps 106:1. 150:1mg. Re 19:3, 4.

PSALM 106

1 **Praise ye the Lord**. Heb. Hallelujah. Ps 105:45.

O give. Ps +136:1. 1 Th 5:18.

is good. Ps +136:1. Lk 6:35.

his mercy. Ps 103:17. Ro 5:20, 21.

2 **utter**. Ps 40:5. 139:17, 18. 145:3-12. Jb 5:9. 26:14. Ro 11:33. Ep 1:19. 3:18-21.

all his praise. Ne 9:5.

3 **Blessed**. Ps +1:1-3. 119:1-3. Mk 3:35. Lk 6:47-49. +11:28. Jn +13:17. +14:21. 15:14. Ja 1:25. Re 7:15. 22:14.

keep. Ps 119:106, 112. Is 56:1, 2. Je 22:15, 16. Lk 11:42. Jn 14:21-23.

doeth. Ps 15:2. 119:44. Is 64:5. Ezk 18:21, 22. Lk 1:74, 75. Ac 24:16. Ro 2:7. Ga 6:9. Ja 1:25. 2:17, 23. Re 2:10. 22:14.

at all times. Ps 119:20, 112. Dt 5:29. 11:1.

4 **Remember**. Ps 25:7. 119:132. Ne +5:19. 13:14, 22, 31. Lk 23:42.

the favor. Ps 5:12.

visit. Ps +8:4. 65:9. 80:14. Ex +3:16. Jb 10:12. Lk 1:68, 69. Ac 15:14.

thy salvation. Ps 35:3. 119:123. Is 12:2. La 3:26. Mt 1:21. Ro 5:9. Ep 2:8. 2 C +6:2. He +9:28.

5 **thy chosen**. Ps 105:6, 43. Dt 7:6. +10:15. Jn 15:16. Ac 9:15. Ja +2:5.

rejoice. Ps +14:7. 16:11. 48:11. +118:24. Is 12:6. +35:10. 66:10. Jl 2:23. Zp 3:14. Zc 9:9. Jn 16:22. Ph 3:3.

glory. Is 45:25. Ep 1:17, 18. Col +3:4.

thine inheritance. Ps +94:14. Is 19:25. Col +3:24.

6 **have sinned**. Ps 78:8. Le 26:40, 42. Nu 32:14. 1 K 8:47. Ezr 9:6, 7. Ne 9:16, 32-34. Da 9:5-8. Mt 23:32. Ac 7:51, 52.

fathers. ver. 7. Ps 22:4. Ge +13:8.

7 **Our**. Dt 29:2-4. 32:28, 29. Pr 1:22. Is 44:18. Mk 4:12. 8:17-21. 2 Th 2:10-12.

they. Ps 78:42. Dt +7:18. 15:15.

multitude. ver. 45. Ps +5:7.

but. Ex 14:11, 12.

8 **Nevertheless**. Re +2:6.

he saved. Nu 14:13-16. Is +48:9.

that he. Ps 111:6. Ex 9:16. 15:6. Ro 9:17.

9 **He rebuked**. Ps 18:15. Ex +14:21. Is 11:14-16. Mk +4:39.
so he. Ps 77:19, 20.

10 **And he**. Ex 14:30. 15:9, 10. Dt 11:4. Ne 9:11.
redeemed. Ps +34:22. Ex 15:13. Jb 6:22, 23. Mi 6:4.

11 **the waters**. Ps 78:53. Ex 14:13, 27, 28. 15:5, 10, 19.

12 **believed**. Ex 14:31. 15:1, etc. 2 Ch 20:20. Lk +8:13. Jn 8:30, 31.
they sang. Ps +9:10. Ho +2:15.

13 **They soon forgat**. Heb. They made haste, they forgat. Ps 78:11. Is 15:17, 24. 16:2. 17:2, 7. Ezk 33:31.
waited not. 1 Ch 10:14. Pr 1:25, 30. Is 48:17, 18. Je 23:22. Ml 2:6.

14 **But**. Ps 78:18, 30. Nu 11:4, 33, 34. Dt 9:22. 1 C 10:6.
lusted exceedingly. Heb. lusted a lust. Ge +1:29mg. 1 C 10:6.
tempted. Ex +17:2.
God. Heb. *El*, Ex +15:2.

15 **he gave**. Ps 78:29-31. 84:11. Nu 11:31-34. 1 S 8:22. 12:13. Is 10:16. 24:16. 48:22. Ho 4:17. Ja 4:3.
but sent. Ge 19:20. Ex 32:31-35. Nu 11:18-20, 21-23, 30-33. 14:20-23. 16:44-49. 20:7-12. 21:6-9. Dt 3:23-27. Jg 20:23-25. 1 S 8:4-7. 2 S 24:10-15. 1 K 21:27-29. 2 K 22:18-20. 2 Ch 12:5-9. Is +66:4. Je +6:19. 15:1-4. 21:1-6. 37:3-10, 16, 17. Ezk 14:12-19.
soul. Heb. *nephesh*, Ge +12:13.

16 **envied**. Nu 16:1, 3, etc. Ps +37:1. Mk 15:10.
the saint. Ex 28:36. Nu +16:5, 7.

17 **The earth opened**. Nu 16:29-33. 26:10. Dt 11:6.

18 **a fire**. Nu 16:35-40, 46. He 12:29.

19 **made a calf**. Ex +32:4. 1 C 10:7.

20 **Thus**. Ps 89:17. Je 2:11. Ro 1:22, 23.
their glory. or, honor. Ps 3:3. +8:5. +16:9. 26:8. 30:12mg. Is +40:5.
into. Ex 20:4, 5. Is 40:18-25.

21 **forgat**. ver. 13. Ps 78:11, 12, 42-51. Dt 32:17, 18. Je 2:32.
God. Heb. *El*, Ex +15:2. Is 12:2. 45:21. 63:8. Ho 1:7. Lk 1:47. T 1:3. 2:10. 3:4-6.
which. Ps 74:13, 14. 135:9. Dt 4:34. 6:22. 7:18, 19. Ne 9:10, 11.

22 **Wondrous**. Ps 78:51. 105:23, 27-36.
terrible. Ex 14:25-28. 15:10.

23 **he said**. Ex 32:10, 11, 32. Dt 9:13, 14, 19, 25. 10:10. Ezk 20:13, 14.
his chosen. Ps 105:6, 26. Nu 16:5. Is 42:1. Zc 13:7. Mt 12:18. Jn 15:16, 19.
stood. Ex 32:14. Je 5:1. Ezk 13:5. 22:30. Ja 5:16.
lest. Ge +32:28.

24 **they despised**. Ge 25:34. Nu 13:32. 14:4, 31. Mt 22:5. He 12:16.

the pleasant land. Heb. a land of desire. Dt 8:7-9. 11:11, 12. Je +3:19mg.
they believed not. Nu 14:11. Dt 1:32. He 3:12-14, 18, 19. 4:2, 6, 14. Ju 5.

25 **murmured**. Ex +15:24. Ju +16.
hearkened. Ps 95:7-9. Nu 14:22. He 3:7, 8, 15.

26 **Therefore**. Ps 95:11. Nu 14:28-35. Dt 1:34, 35. He 3:11, 18.
lifted. Ge +14:22.

27 **overthrow**. Heb. make them fall.
to scatter. Je +9:16.

28 **joined**. Nu 25:1-3, 5. 31:16. Dt 4:3. 32:17. Jsh 22:17. Ho 9:10. Re 2:14.
of the dead. Ps 115:4-8. Je 10:8-10. 1 C 10:19, 20.

29 **with their**. ver. 39. Ps 99:8. Dt 32:16-21. Ec 7:29. Ro 1:21-24.
the plague. Nu 25:9. 1 C 10:8.

30 **Then stood**. Nu 25:6-8, 14, 15. Dt 13:9-11, 15-17. Jsh 7:12. 1 K 18:40, 41. Jon 1:12-15.

31 **was counted**. Nu 25:11-13. Dt 24:13. Mk 14:3-9.
generations. Ge +9:12.
for evermore. Heb. *olam*, Ps +18:50.

32 **angered**. Ps 78:40. 81:7. Nu 20:2-6, 13.
so that. Nu 20:12, 23, 24. 27:13, 14. Dt 1:37. 3:26. 4:21.
for their sakes. Is 53:5.

33 **Because**. Nu 20:10, 11.
provoked. ver. 7, 43. 78:17, 40. Jb 17:2. Is 3:8. Ep 4:26. Ja +1:20.
spirit. Heb. *ruach*, Ge +6:3. Here, "spirit" is used for the whole person. **S#7307h.** Ps 77:3, 6. Ezk 21:7. Da 2:1, 3. Ml 2:15, 16.
he spake. Ps 39:1. 141:3. Ge 30:1. 35:16-18. Jb 2:10. 38:2. 40:4, 5. 42:7, 8. Mt +12:36. Ep 5:11, 12. Ja 3:2. 5:16.

34 **did not**. Jsh 15:63. 16:10. 17:12-16. 23:12, 13. Jg 1:19, 21, 27-35. Mt 17:19-21.
concerning. Nu 33:52, 55, 56. Dt 7:2, 16, 23, 24. 20:16, 17. 1 S 15:3, 22, 23.

35 **But**. Jsh 15:63. Jg 1:27-36. 2:2, 3.
learned. Is 2:6. Je +10:2. 1 C 5:6. 15:33.

36 **And**. Ps 78:58. Ex 34:15, 16. Jg 2:12, 13, 17, 19. 3:5-7. 10:6. 2 K 17:8-11, 16, 17. 2 Ch 33:2-9. Ezk 16:15, etc. 20:28-32.
which. Ex +23:33.

37 **they sacrificed**. Dt +18:10.
devils. Le 17:7. Dt 32:17. 2 Ch 11:15. 1 C 10:20. Re 9:20.

38 **shed**. Dt +19:10. Je 2:34.
the land. Le +18:25. Is 1:15. 26:21. Ezk 7:23. 22:3.

39 **defiled**. Is 24:5, 6. 59:3. Ezk 20:18, 30, 31, 43.
went. Ex +34:15, 16.
their own. ver. 29. Is 1:4.

40 **the wrath**. Jg +2:14. Ne 9:27, etc.
abhorred. Ps 5:6. 10:3. 78:59. 89:38. Le

20:23. 26:11, 30, 44. Dt 32:19. Pr 22:14. Je 14:19, 21. La 2:7. Am 6:8. Zc 11:8.

his own. Ps 74:1, 2. Dt 9:29. La 2:7.

41 he gave. Dt 32:30. Jg +2:14. 4:1, 2. 6:1-6. Ne 9:27, etc.

and they. Dt 28:25, 29, 33, 48.

42 enemies. ver. 10. Ps 3:7. 6:10. 7:5. 8:2. 9:3.

oppressed. Ex 22:21. 23:9. Nu 22:25. Jg 4:3. 10:12.

into subjection. or, humbled. Le 26:41. Dt 28:25. Jg 3:30.

43 Many. Jg 2:16-18. 1 S 12:9-11. Ne 9:27, 28.

with their. ver. 29. Ps 1:1. 81:12.

brought low. or, impoverished, or weakened. Jg 5:8. 6:5, 6. 1 S 13:19-22.

44 Nevertheless. Re +2:6.

he regarded. Jg 2:18. 3:9. 4:3. 6:6-10. 10:10-16. 1 S 7:8-12. 2 K 14:26, 27. 2 Ch 33:12. Ne 9:27-31.

45 And he. Le +26:42. 2 K 13:22, 23.

remembered. Ge +8:1.

repented. Je +18:8.

the multitude. ver. +7.

46 He made. 1 K 8:50. Ezr 9:9. Je 15:11. 42:12. Da 1:9.

47 Save us. Ps 14:7. 126:1-4. 1 Ch 16:35, 36.

gather. Je +23:3.

to give thanks. Ps 107:1-3. Re 7:10-12.

triumph. Ps 92:4. 2 C 2:14.

48 Blessed. Is +29:23.

from everlasting to. Heb. olam doubled, Ps +41:13.

Amen. Mt +6:13.

Praise ye the Lord. Heb. Hallelujah. ver. 1. Ps 105:45mg.

PSALM 107

(Title.) A.M. 3468. B.C. 536. The author of this Psalm is unknown; but it was evidently written to commemorate the return of the Jews from the Babylonian captivity; and it may easily be perceived that it must have been sung in alternate parts, having a double burden, or two intercalary verses often recurring.

1 Give. Ps +136:1.

good. Ps +136:1.

for his mercy. Ex +34:6.

for ever. Heb. olam, Ex +12:24.

2 Let the redeemed. Ps +34:22. Dt 15:15. Is +43:1.

say so. Ps 32:3. 39:3. 126:2. Ex 12:14. Mk +5:19. 8:38. Ro 10:9, 10.

from. Ps 106:10. Dt 7:8. Je 15:21. 31:11. Mi 4:10. Lk 1:74.

hand. Ge +9:5.

3 gathered. Je +23:3. Re 5:9.

east. Is 43:5.

west. Is 11:11. 49:12. Je 31:10. Lk 13:29.

north. Je +1:14.

south. Heb. sea. ver. 23. Ps 8:8. 24:2. 106:7.

4 wandered. ver. 40. Ge 21:14-16. Nu 14:33. Dt 8:15. 32:10. Jb 12:24. Ezk 34:6, 10. He 11:38. Re 12:6.

solitary way. Mk 1:35.

they found. ver. 10, 17, 23.

5 Hungry. Jg 15:18, 19. 1 S 30:11, 12. Is 44:12. Je 14:18. Lk 2:19. Mk 8:2, 3.

soul. Heb. nephesh, Ge +34:3.

6 cried. Ps +3:4.

trouble. ver. 13, 17-19, 28. Ps 9:13. 31:7. 50:15. 88:3. 91:15. Jg 10:9, 10. 2 Ch 15:4. Ne 9:32. Is 41:17, 18. Je 29:12-14. Ho 5:15. He 4:15, 16.

he delivered. Ne +9:37. 2 C 1:8-10. 12:8-10. 2 T 3:11.

7 he led. Ps 77:20. 78:52. 136:16. Dt 32:11, 12. Ezr 8:21-23. Is 30:21. 35:8-10. 48:17. 49:8-11. 63:13, 14. Je 6:16. 31:9. 2 P 2:15, 21.

that they. ver. 4, 36. Ne 11:3. Je 31:24, 38-46. 33:10-13. He 4:9. 11:9, 10, 16. 12:22, 23. Re 21:2-4, 10-27.

8 Oh that men. ver. 15, 31. Ps 81:13-16. Dt 5:29. 32:39. Is 48:18.

praise. Ps 34:3. 92:1, 2. 147:1. Is 63:7.

goodness. Ps +136:1.

his wonderful. Ps 78:4. 111:4. Da +4:3.

9 he satisfieth. Ps +37:3. Mt +5:6.

soul. Heb. nephesh, Ge +34:3. Pr 6:30. Is 5:14. 29:8. Re +18:14.

and filleth. Ps 81:10. Mt 6:33. 1 P 2:2.

soul. Heb. nephesh, Ge +34:3.

10 Such. ver. +4.

darkness. Mt +4:16. 22:13.

shadow. Ps +23:4.

bound. Ps 105:18. Ex 2:23, 24. 2 Ch 33:11. Jb 36:8, 9. La 3:6, 7. Ro 6:20, 21. 2 P 2:19.

11 Because. Ps 68:6, 18. 106:43. Is 63:10, 11. La 3:39-42. 5:15-17.

God. Heb. El, Ex +15:2.

contemned. Ps 73:24. 113:7-9. 119:24. 2 Ch 25:15, 16. 33:10. Pr 1:25, 30, 31. Is 5:19. Je 23:22. 44:16. Lk 7:30. 16:14. Ac 20:27. Ro 1:28.

12 he brought. Ex 2:23. 5:18, 19. Jg 10:16-18. 16:21, 30. Ne 9:37. Is 51:19, 20, 23. 52:5. La 5:5, 6. Lk 15:14-17.

and there. Ps 18:40, 41. 22:11. 142:4. 2 K 6:26, 27, 33. Jb 9:13. Is 63:5.

13 they cried. ver. 6, 19, 28. Ps +3:4. Je 31:18-20.

14 brought. Ps 68:6. Jb 33:30. 42:10-12.

darkness. ver. 10. Jb 15:22, 30. 19:8. Mt +4:16. He 2:15.

shadow. Ps +23:4.

brake. Ps +146:7. Jb 36:8.

15 Oh that. ver. 8, 21, 31. Ps 116:17-19.

16 For he. Jg 16:3. Is 45:1, 2. Mi 2:13.

bars of iron. Ps 2:9. Jb 40:18. Is 45:2.

in sunder. Ac 12:6, 7.

17 **Fools**. ver. +4. Ps 14:1. 92:6. Pr 1:22. 7:7, 22. 26:3.
    because. Ps 38:1-8. Nu 11:33, 34. 12:10-13. 21:5-9. Is 57:17, 18. Je 2:19. La 1:8. 3:39.

18 **soul**. Heb. *nephesh*, Nu +11:6.
    abhorreth. Jb 33:19-22.
    meat. Ps 78:18, 30. 104:21, 27.Ge +3:19. Jb 6:7. Jn 4:8, 32, 34. 6:27. 21:5. He 12:16.
    and they. Ps 9:13. 88:3. Is 38:10.
    draw near. Jb 33:22. Is 38:1. Ph 2:27.
    the gates. Ge +14:7. Jb +38:17.
    of death. Pr +7:27.

19 **they cry**. ver. +6, 13, 28. Ps 78:34, 35. 2 S 22:5-7. Je 33:3. Ac 7:59, 60.

20 **He sent**. Ps 147:15, 19. 2 K 20:4, 5. Mt 8:8.
    healed. Ps +103:3, 4. Nu 21:8, 9. Jb 33:23-26. Mt 8:8.
    delivered. Ps 49:15. 56:13. Jb 33:28-30.

21 **Oh that**. ver. 8, 15, 31. Ps 66:5. 2 Ch 32:25. Lk 17:17, 18.

22 **sacrifice**. Le +7:12.
    declare. Ps 9:11. 73:28. 105:1, 2. 118:17. Is 12:4.
    rejoicing. Heb. singing. Ps +30:5mg. 42:4. 47:1.

23 **They**. ver. +4.
    go down. Ps 48:7. Ezk 27:26. Ac 27:9, etc. Re 18:17.

24 **his wonders**. Ps 95:5. 104:24-27. Jb 38:8-11.
    deep. Ge +1:2.

25 **he commandeth**. Ps 135:7. 148:8. Jon 1:4.
    raiseth. Heb. maketh to stand.
    lifteth. Ps 93:3, 4. Mt 8:24. Jn 6:18.

26 **mount up**. Ps 24:3. 104:8. 132:3. Ge +2:24. Dt 30:12. Ro *10:6*.
    go down. Ps 7:16. 18:9. 49:17. 55:15.
    their soul. Heb. *nephesh*, Ge +34:3.
    is melted. Ps 22:14. 119:28. 2 S 17:10. Is 13:7. Na 2:10.

27 **stagger**. Jb 12:25. Is 19:14. 29:9, 10.
    are at their wit's end. Heb. all their wisdom is swallowed up. Jb 37:20. Is 19:3mg. 28:7. Ac 27:15-20.

28 **they cry**. ver. +6, 13, 19. Jon 1:4-6, 13-15. Mt 8:23-26. 14:29-32. Mk 5:18. Ac 27:23-25, 33-37.

29 **He maketh**. Ps 65:7. 89:9. Jon 1:15. Mt 8:26. Mk 4:39-41. Lk 8:23-25.

30 **he bringeth**. Jn 6:21. Ac 27:44.

31 **Oh that men**. ver. 8, 15, 21. Ps 103:2. 105:1. Ho 2:8. Jon 1:16. 2:9. Mi 6:4, 5. Ro 1:20, 21. 2 T 3:2. He 13:15.
    his wonderful. Ps 71:17. 105:2. Da +4:3.

32 **exalt**. Ps 18:46. 46:10. 99:5, 9. Ex 15:2. Is 12:4. 25:1.
    in the congregation. Ps 22:22, 25. 40:9, 10. 66:16. 111:1. 119:46. Ac 4:8-12.

33 **turneth**. 1 K 17:1-7. Is 13:19-21. 19:5-10. 34:9, 10. 42:15. 44:27. 50:2. Ezk 30:12. Jl 1:20. Na 1:4. Zp 2:9, 13.
    watersprings. 1 K 18:5. Je 14:3. Am 4:7, 8.

34 **A fruitful**. Ge 13:10, 13. 19:25. Dt 29:23-28. Is 32:13-15.
    barrenness. Heb. saltness. Ge +14:3. Dt +29:23.
    the wickedness. Je 12:4.

35 **turneth**. Ps 114:8. Nu 21:16-18. 2 K 3:16-20. Is 35:6, 7. 41:17-19. 44:3-5. Ezk 47:6-12.
    and. Ge +8:22.

36 **And**. Ge +8:22.
    there he. Ps 146:7. Lk 1:53.
    a city. ver. 7. Ac 17:26.

37 **sow**. Is 37:30. Je 29:5. 31:5. Ezk 28:26. Am +9:13-15.
    which may. Ps 65:9-13. Ge 26:12. Jl 1:10-12. Hg 1:5, 6, 10, 11. 2:16-19. Zc 8:12. Ac 14:17. 1 C 3:7. 2 C 9:10.

38 **He blesseth**. Ps 128:1-6. Ge 1:28. 9:1. 12:2. 17:16, 20. Ex 1:7. Dt 28:4, 11. 30:9. Je 30:19. Ezk 37:26.
    suffereth. Ps 144:13, 14. Ge 30:43. 31:9. Ex 9:3-7. 12:38. Dt 7:14. Pr 10:22.

39 **they are**. Ps 30:6, 7. Ge 45:11. Ru 1:20, 21. 1 S 2:5-7. 2 K 4:8. 8:3. Jb 1:10-17.
    oppression. Ex 1:13, 14. 2:23, 24. Jg 6:3-6. 2 K 10:32. 13:7, 22. 14:26. 2 Ch 15:5, 6. Je 51:33, 34.

40 **poureth**. Jb 12:21, 24. Is 23:8, 9.
    contempt. Ps 78:66. Ex 8:3, 17, 24. Jsh 10:24-26. Jg 1:6, 7. 4:21. 1 S 5:9. 6:4. 1 K 21:19. 2 K 9:35-37. Da 4:33. 5:5, 6, 18-30. Ac 12:23. Re 19:18.
    causeth. ver. 4. Jb 12:24. Je 13:15-18.
    wilderness. or, void place. Ge 1:2. Dt 32:10.

41 **setteth**. Ps 113:7, 8. Ru 4:14-17. 1 S 2:8. Est 8:15-17. Jb 5:11. 8:7. 11:15-19. 42:10-12. Je 52:31-34. Ja 5:11.
    from. or, after.
    maketh. Ps 78:52. 128:6. Ge 33:5-7. 48:11. 1 S 2:21. Jb 21:11. 42:16. Pr 17:6. Is 49:20-22.

42 **righteous**. Ps +58:10, 11. Is 66:10, 11, 14.
    iniquity. Ps 31:18. 63:11. 112:10. Ex 11:7. Jsh 10:21. 1 S 2:9. Jb 5:15, 16. Pr 10:11. Mt 22:12. Ro 3:19. T 1:10, 11.

43 **is wise**. Ps 28:5. 64:9. Dt 32:29. Is 5:12. Je 9:12. Da 10:12. Ho 14:9. Lk 19:42.
    observe. Ps 47:7.
    they shall understand. Ps 25:14. 50:23. Je 9:24. Ep 3:18, 19.

PSALM 108

(*Title*.) A.M. 2964. B.C. 1040. This Psalm is composed of two Psalms; ver. 1-5 being the same as Ps 57:7-11; and ver. 6-13 the same as Ps 60:5-12; and it is probably to be referred to the same period as the latter. Ps 68, title.

1 **my heart**. Ps 57:7-11.
    I will. Ps 30:12. 34:1. 104:33. 138:1. 145:1, 2. 146:1, 2. Ex 15:1.

my glory. Ps +16:9. 30:12mg. 71:8, 15, 23, 24. 145:21.

2 **Awake**. Ps 33:2. 69:30. 81:2. 92:1-4. Jg 5:12.
I myself. Ps 57:8. 103:22.

3 **praise**. Ps 22:22, 27. 96:10. 117:1, 2. 138:4, 5. Zp 3:14, 20.

4 **thy mercy**. Ps 36:5. 85:10, 11. 89:2, 5. 103:11. Is 55:9. Mi 7:18-20. Ep 2:4-7.
clouds. *or*, skies. Ps 36:5. 68:34mg. 89:6, 37.

5 **Be thou**. Ps 8:1. Is +12:4.
thy glory. Ps 72:19. Is 6:3. Mt 6:9, 10, 13.

6 **That thy**. Ps 60:5-12. Dt 33:12. 2 S 12:25. Mt 3:17. 17:5. Ro 1:7. Ep 1:6. Col 3:12.
save. Ps 35:1-3. 54:1. 98:1, 2. 144:5-7. Ex 15:6. Is 51:2-11.
and answer me. 1 K 18:24, 26, 29, 36, 37. 2 Ch 32:20-22. Is +65:24. Je 33:3.

7 **spoken**. Ps 89:35, 36. Am 4:2.
I will rejoice. Ps 16:9-11. 2 S 7:20, etc. 1 P 1:3, 8. 2 P 1:3, 4.
Shechem. Ge +33:18.
the valley. Ge 33:17. Jg 8:5, 6.

8 **Gilead**. Ge +37:25.
Ephraim. Ge +41:52.
Judah. Ps +60:7. 122:5.

9 **Moab**. Ezk +25:8. Jn 13:8, 14.
I cast. Ru 4:7, 8.
over Philistia. 2 S 21:15-22. Is 14:29-32.

10 **who will lead**. Ps 20:6-8. 60, title. Is 63:1-6. Je +49:7-16. Ob 3, 4.

11 **who hast**. Ps +44:9. 1 S ch. 29, etc.
go forth. Nu 10:9. Dt 20:3, 4. 1 S 17:26, 36. 2 Ch 13:12. 14:11. 20:15.

12 **Give**. Ps 20:1, etc.
for vain. Ps +60:11. Jb 9:13. 16:2. Is 30:3-5.

13 **Through**. Ps 18:29-34. 118:6-13. 144:1. 2 Ch 20:12. Ro 8:37. 1 C 15:10. Ep 6:10-18.
valiantly. Je 9:3. 1 T 6:12.
tread. Ps 18:42. 60:12. Jg 15:8. Is 25:10. 63:3. Ro 16:20. 2 C 2:14.

PSALM 109

(*Title*.) A.M. 2942. B.C. 1062.

1 **Hold**. Ps 28:1. 35:22, 23. 83:1. Is 42:14.
O God. Ps 118:28. Ex 15:2. Dt 10:21. Je 17:14.

2 **the mouth**. Ps 31:13, 18. 64:3, 4. 140:3. 2 S 15:3-8. 17:1. Pr 15:28. Mt 26:59-62.
of the deceitful. Heb. of deceit. Ps 5:6. 10:7. 17:1. 24:4. 52:4.
are opened. Heb. have opened themselves. Ps 78:23. 105:41.
with. Ps 120:3. Pr 6:17. 12:19. Je 9:3, 5. Ac 6:13.

3 **compassed**. Ps 17:11. 22:12. 32:7. 88:17. 2 S 16:7, 8. Ho 11:12.
fought. Ps 35:7, 20. 59:3, 4. 69:4. 1 S 19:4, 5. 26:18. 2 S 15:12. Jn 15:24, 25.
without. Ps 59:4. Da 6:4. Jn 19:6.

4 **For my**. Ps 35:7, 12. 38:20. 2 S 13:39. Jn 10:32. 2 C 12:15.
but I. Ps 55:16, 17. 69:12, 13. 2 S 15:31, 32. Da 6:10. Lk 6:7, 11, 12. 23:34.
give myself unto. or, I (am) prayer. Ps 120:7.

5 **they**. Ps 35:7-12. 37:7. Ge 44:4. Pr 17:13.
hatred. Ps 55:12-15. 2 S 15:12, 31. Mk 14:44, 45. Lk 6:16. 22:47, 48. Jn 13:18.

6 **Set thou**. ver. 8, 20, 29. Ps +71:13. Mt 27:4.
and let. Zc 3:1. Jn 13:2, 27.
Satan. *or*, an adversary. ver. 4, 20, 29. Nu 22:22. 1 S 29:4. Zc 3:1mg. Mt 5:25.

7 **be condemned**. Heb. go out guilty, *or* wicked. Ro 3:19. Ga 3:10.
and let. 2 S 15:7, 8. Pr 15:8. 21:27. 28:9. Is 1:15. 66:3. Mt 23:14.
become sin. Pr 15:8. 28:9. Mt 23:14. Lk 20:46, 47.

8 **his days**. Ps 55:23. Mt 27:5.
let. Ac 1:20.
another. Ac 1:16-26.
office. *or*, charge. ver. 6. Nu 3:32. 4:16. 16:29. 1 Ch 24:3. Zc 3:7mg.

9 **his children**. Ex 22:24. Je 18:21. La 5:3.

10 **Let his**. Ps 37:25. Ge 4:12-14. 2 S 3:29. 2 K 5:27. Jb 24:8-12. 30:3-9. Is 16:2.

11 **extortioner**. Jb 5:5. 18:5, 9-19. 20:18-20.
strangers. Dt 28:29, 33, 34, 50, 51. Jg 6:3-6.

12 **none**. Is 27:11. Lk 6:38. Ja 2:13.
favor. Ps 137:8, 9. Is 13:18. Mt 27:25. Lk 11:50, 51.

13 **Let his**. Ps 37:28. 1 S 2:31-33. 3:13. 2 K 10:10, 11. Jb 18:19. Is 14:20-22. Je 22:30.
their name. Pr 10:7. Re +3:5.

14 **Let the**. Ex +20:5. Le 26:39. 2 S 3:29. 21:1, 8, 9. Mt 23:31-36.
let not. 2 K 8:27. 9:27. 10:13, 14. 11:1. 2 Ch 22:3, 4.
blotted. Ne 4:5. Is 43:25. Je 18:23.

15 **before**. Ps 51:9. 90:8. Dt 32:34. Je 2:22. Ho 7:2. Am 8:7.
cut off. ver. 13. Ps 34:16. Jb 18:17. Is 65:15.

16 **he remembered**. 2 S 17:1, 2. Mt 5:7. 18:33-35. Ja 2:13.
persecuted. Ps 10:2, 14. Ge 42:21. Jb 19:2, 3, 21, 22. Mt 27:35-46.
slay. Ps 34:18. 69:20-29. 2 S 16:11, 12. Mk 14:33-36.

17 **loved**. Pr 8:36. 13:24. 17:19.
cursing. Ps 52:4, 5. 59:12, 13. Pr 14:14. Ezk 35:6. Mt 7:2. 2 Th 2:10, 11. Re 16:6.

18 **As he**. Ps 73:6. Jb 29:14. Col 3:8, 12. 1 P 5:5.
so let. Nu 5:22, 27. Jb 20:12-16, 20-23. Mt 26:24. 27:3-5. Ac 1:18, 25.
into his bowels. Heb. within him. ver. 22. Ps 5:9. 36:1. 39:3.

19 **as the garment**. ver. 18, 29. Ps 35:26. 132:18.

20 **Let this**. Ps 2:5, 6, 12. 21:8-12. +71:13.

110:1, 5, 6. 2 S 17:23. 18:32. 1 K 2:44. Lk 19:27. 1 Th 2:15, 16.

them. Mt 11:19. 12:24. 26:66, 67. Mk 9:39. 1 C 12:3.

soul. Heb. *nephesh*, Ge +12:13.

21 **But do.** Ps +25:11. 69:29. Jn 17:1. Ph 2:8-11.
thy mercy. Ps 63:3. Ex +34:6.

22 **For I.** Ps 22:6. +40:17.
heart is wounded. ver. 16. Ps 88:15, 16. 102:4. 2 K 4:27. Jb 6:4. Is 53:3. Lk 22:44. Jn 12:27.

23 **gone.** Ps 102:11. 144:4. 1 Ch 29:15. Jb 14:2. Ec 6:12. 8:13. Ja 4:14.
I am tossed. Ps 102:10. Ex 10:13, 19.

24 **knees.** Ps 22:14. He 12:12.
are weak. Lk 23:26. Jn 19:17.
fasting. Mt +6:16.
my flesh. Ps 32:3, 4. 38:5-8. 102:4, 5. Jb 19:20.

25 **a reproach.** Ps +31:11. 35:15, 16. He 12:2.
when they. Je +18:16.

26 **Help.** Ps 40:12, 13. 119:86. He 5:7.
save me. Ps 57:1. 69:13, 16.

27 **they may know.** Ps 17:13, 14. 64:8, 9. 126:2. Ex 8:19. Nu 16:28-30. Jb 37:7. Is 53:10. Ezk +6:7, 10. Ac 2:32-36. 4:16.

28 **Let them.** ver. 17. Nu 22:12. 23:20, 23. 2 S 16:10-13.
but let. Is 65:13-16. Jn 16:22. He 12:2.

29 **be clothed.** ver. 17-19. Ps +71:13. 132:18. 140:9. Da 12:2. Mi 7:10.

30 **greatly.** Ps 7:17. 9:1. 22:22, 25. 71:22, 23. 108:1-3.
I will praise. Ps 22:22-25. 35:18. 107:32. 111:1. 116:12-18. 138:1, 4. He 2:12.

31 **For he.** Ps 16:8. 73:23. 110:5. 121:5.
poor. ver. 16. Ps 68:5. 72:4, 12, 13. 140:12.
to save. Ps 10:14. Ex 22:22-24. Pr 22:22, 23. Ec 5:8. Is 54:17. Ac 4:10-12. 5:30, 31.
those that condemn. Heb. the judges of.
soul. Heb. *nephesh*, Ge +12:13.

PSALM 110

(*Title.*) A.M. 2962. B.C. 1042. This Psalm was probably composed by David after Nathan's prophetic address; and, from the grandeur of the subject and the sublimity of the expressions, it is evident that it can only refer, as the ancient Jews fully acknowledged, to the royal dignity, priesthood, victories, and triumphs of the MESSIAH.

1 **The Lord.** Mt *22:44.* Mk *12:36.* Lk *20:42, 43.* Ac *2:34-36.* He *1:13.*
said. Ps 8:1. Mt 22:42-46. Mk 12:35-37. Lk 20:41-44.
Sit. He +1:3.
right hand. Ps 80:17. Mt 20:21, 23. 22:44. 26:64. Mk 10:37, 40. 12:36. 14:62. 16:19. Lk

20:42. 22:69. Ac 2:33, 34. 7:55, 56. Ro 8:34. Ep 1:20. Col 3:1. He 1:3, 13. 8:1. 10:12. 12:2. 1 P 3:22.

until. Ps 2:6-9. +45:6, 7. Is 7:14. 9:6. Mi 5:2. Ml 3:1. Mk 1:2. 1 C 15:25. He 1:3, 13. 10:12, 13.

footstool. Ps 8:6. 74:3. 1 C 15:25. Ep 1:22. He 1:13. 2:8.

2 **shall send.** Da +7:13, 14. Mt 26:29. Lk 1:32. 19:15. 22:29. Re +11:15. 22:3.
the rod. Ex 7:19. 8:5. Mi 7:14. Mt 28:18-20. Ac 2:34-37. Ro 1:16. 1 C 1:23, 24. 2 C 10:4, 5. 1 Th 2:13. 1 P 1:12.
out of Zion. Is +24:23. Je 3:17. Ezk 47:1. Zp 3:14, 15.
rule. Ps 2:8, 9. 18:43. 22:28, 29. 45:5, 6. 2 S 23:3. Je 23:5, 6.

3 **Thy.** Ps 22:27, 28. Jg 5:2. Je 24:7. Ac 2:41. Ro 11:2-6. 2 C 8:1-3, 5, 12, 16. Ph 2:13. He 13:21.
day. Ac 1:8. 2:33, 41. 4:30-35. 19:20. 2 C 13:4. Ga 1:15, 16.
beauties. Ps 96:9. Ezk 43:12. Ep 1:4. 1 Th 4:7. T 2:14.
from the womb, etc. *or*, more than the womb of the morning: thou shalt have, etc.
morning. Re +2:28.
thou hast. Ps 102:23, 24. Ex 12:5. Ac 4:4. 21:20. Re 7:9.
the dew. Dt +33:13. Is +26:19.

4 **Lord.** Ps 89:34-36. He 5:6. 6:13-18. 7:21, 28.
will not. Nu 23:19.
Thou. Ge 14:18-20. Zc +6:13. He *5:6, 10.* 6:20. 7:1-3, 11, *17, 21.* Re 1:6.
for ever. Heb. *olam*, Ex +12:24. He 7:15, 16, 24, 25.
the order. He 5:5, 6.

5 **at thy.** ver. 1. Ps 16:8. Mk 16:19. Ac 2:34-36. 7:55, 56.
strike. Ps 2:2-6, 9-12. 45:4, 5. 68:14, 30. 149:7-9. Is 29:8. Zc 9:9, 10, 13-15. Re 17:12-14. 19:11-21. 20:8, 9.
in the day. Ps 21:8, 9. Ezk 38:18, 19. Ro +2:5. Re 6:15-17. 11:18.

6 **judge.** Ps +7:8.
fill. Is 34:2-8. 43:2-4. 66:16, 17. Ezk 38:21, 22. 39:4, 11-20. Re 14:19, 20.
wound. Ps 68:21. Ge +3:15. Is 9:4, 5. Hab 3:13.
many. *or*, great.

7 **He shall.** Ps 102:9. Jg 7:5, 6. Jb 21:20. Is 53:12. Je 23:15. Mt 20:22. 26:42. Jn 18:11.
drink. 1 K 17:6.
brook. or, torrent. Ps 36:8. 74:15. Is 30:28. 66:12. Am 5:24.
in the way. Is 40:3. 43:19. Jl 2:7. Ml 3:1.
therefore. Is 53:11, 12. Lk 24:26. Ph 2:7-11. He 2:9, +10. 1 P 1:11.
lift. Ps 3:3. 27:6. Je 52:31.

PSALM 111

1 A.M. 3468. B.C. 536.
Praise ye the Lord. Heb. Hallelujah. Ps 106:1, 48.
I will. Ps 9:1. 103:1. 138:1.
assembly. Ps 22:25. 35:18. 40:9, 10. 89:5, 7. 107:32. 108:3. 109:30. 149:1. 1 Ch 29:10-20. 2 Ch 6:3, 4. 20:26-28.

2 **works**. Ps 139:14. Jb 26:12-14. ch. 38, 41. Is 40:12. Je 32:17-19. Da +4:3. Ep 1:19, 20. 2:7-10. Re 15:3.
sought. Ps 77:11, 12. 104:24, 34. 107:43. 143:5. Jb 37:7. Ec 3:11. 1 P 1:10-12.
that have. Ps 92:4. Pr 17:16. 18:1, 2. 24:14. Ro 1:28. 8:6.

3 **honorable**. Ps 19:1. 145:4, 5, 10-12, 17. Ex 15:6, 7, 11. Ep 1:6-8. 3:10. Re 5:12-14.
righteousness. Ps 103:17. 119:142, 144. Is 51:5, 6, 8. Da 9:24.
for ever. Ps +9:18.

4 **He hath**. Ps 78:4-8. Ex 12:26, 27. 13:14, 15. Dt 4:9. 31:19, etc. Jsh 4:6, 7, 21-24. 1 C 11:24-26.
gracious. Ex +34:6, 7. Ep 1:6-8. 1 T 1:14.
full. Ps 78:38. 112:4. 145:8.

5 **hath given**. Ps +37:3. Lk 12:30.
meat. Heb. prey. Ps 104:21. 124:6. Ge 49:9. Pr 31:15. Ml 3:10.
he will. Le +26:42. Is +55:3. Ml +3:6.
ever. Heb. *olam*, Ps +5:11.
covenant. ver. +9. Ge +9:16.

6 **showed**. Ps 78:12, etc. 105:27, etc. Dt 4:32-38. Jsh 3:14-17. 6:20. 10:13, 14.
that he. Ps 2:8. 44:2. 78:55. 80:8. 105:44.

7 **works**. Ps 85:10. 89:14. 98:3. Dt 32:4. 2 T 2:13. Re 15:3, 4.
all his. Ps 19:7. 105:8. 119:86, 151, 160.

8 **They**. Is 40:8. Mt 5:18. Ro 3:31.
stand fast. Heb. are established. Ps 112:8. Is 26:3.
for ever. Ps +9:18.
and ever. Heb. *olam*, Ps +21:4.
are done. Ps 19:9. 119:127, 128. Ro 7:12. Re 15:3.

9 **sent redemption**. Ps 130:7, 8. Dt 15:15. Is 44:6. +51:11. 63:9. Mt 1:21. Lk 1:68, 71, 72. Ga +3:13.
his covenant. ver. 5. 2 S 23:5. 1 Ch 16:15. Is +55:3. Je +33:20, 21. Ga 3:15-17. He 13:20.
for ever. Heb. *olam*, Ex +12:24.
holy. Ps 89:7. +99:3. Dt 28:58. Ml 1:11. 2:2.

10 **fear**. Dt +6:2.
a good understanding. *or*, good success. Ps 1:3. Dt 4:6. Jsh 1:7, 8. Pr 3:4. 2 T 3:15-17.
do his commandments. Heb. do them. Dt 4:6. Jn +13:17. Re 22:14.
his praise. Mt 25:21, 23. Jn 5:44. 12:43. Ro 2:7, 29. 1 C 4:5. 2 C 4:17. 1 P 1:7.
for ever. Ps +9:18.

PSALM 112

1 **Praise ye the Lord**. Heb. Hallelujah. Ps 111:1mg. 147:1mg. 148:11-14. 150:1mg.
Blessed. Ps 145:19. Pr +3:7.
delighteth. Ps 1:1, 2. 40:8. 119:16, 35, 47, 48, 70-72, 97, 143. Ro 7:22. 8:6.

2 **His seed**. Ge 22:17, 18. Dt +29:11. Ac 2:39.

3 **Wealth**. Pr 3:16. 15:6. Is 33:6. Mt 6:33. 2 C 6:10. Ph 4:18, 19. 1 T 6:6-8.
and riches. Jb 22:23, 24. Pr 10:4, 22. Mt 6:19, 20. Lk 6:20, 24. 12:21. Ja 5:1-3.
and his. ver. 9. Ps 111:3, 10. Is 32:17. 51:8. Da 9:24. Mt 24:22-24. Re 22:11.
for ever. Ps +9:18.

4 **there ariseth**. Ps 18:28. 37:6. 97:11. 118:27. Jb 11:17. 18:5, 6. 22:28. Pr 4:18. 13:9. Is 50:10. Mi 7:8, 9. Ml 4:2. Mt 13:43. Jn 8:12. 12:46.
he is gracious. Ps 106:1. Mi 6:8. Lk 6:36. 2 C 8:8, 9. Ep 4:32. 5:1, 2, 9, 15. Col 3:12, 13.
righteous. T 2:11, 12. 1 J 2:29. 3:7, 10.

5 **good**. Pr 2:20. 12:2. Lk 23:50. Ac 11:24. Ro 5:7.
showeth. Ps 37:25, 26. Dt 15:7-10. Jb 31:16-20. Lk +6:35.
lendeth. Pr 19:17. 22:7. Lk 14:12-14.
he will. Pr 17:18. 18:9. 22:26, 27. 24:27, 30-34. 27:23-27. Jn 6:12. Ro 12:11. Ep 5:15. Col 4:5.
guide his affairs. Pr +22:3. Lk 14:28.
discretion. Heb. judgment. Ps 1:5. 7:6. 9:4. 10:5. Ge +18:19. Mi +6:8. Ph 1:9.

6 **Surely**. Ps 15:5. 62:2, 6. 125:1. 2 P 1:5-11.
for ever. Heb. *olam*, Ex +12:24.
the righteous. Ne 13:22, 31. Pr 10:7. Mt 25:34-40. He 6:10.
everlasting. Heb. *olam*, Ge +17:7.

7 **shall not**. Ps 27:1-3. +34:4. 56:3, 4. Pr 1:33. 3:25, 26. Lk 21:9, 19, 26.
tidings. lit. hearing. Is 37:7. Je 49:14.
heart. Ps 57:7. 118:6. Is 26:3, 4. Da 3:16, 17. Ac 20:23, 24. 21:13.
fixed. 2 Ch +12:14mg.
trusting. Ps 62:8. 64:10. 118:8, 9. Jn 14:1. Ac 27:25.

8 **heart**. Ps 27:14. 31:24. He 13:9.
shall. Pr 3:33.
until he see. Ps 54:7. 59:10. 91:2, 8. 92:11. 118:7. Is +66:24.

9 **He**. 2 C 9:9.
dispersed. Dt 15:11. Pr 11:24, 25. 19:17. Ec 11:1, 2, 6. Is 32:8. 58:7, 10. Mk 14:7. Lk 11:41. 12:33. 18:22. Jn 13:29. Ac 4:35. 20:35. Ro 12:13. 2 C 8:9. 9:10-15. 1 T 6:18. He 13:16. Ja 2:15, 16. 1 J 3:16-18.
righteousness. ver. +3. Dt 24:13. Mt 6:4. Lk 14:12-14. 16:9. He 6:10.
for ever. Ps +9:18.
horn. Ps +92:10.

10 **wicked**. Est 6:11, 12. Is 65:13, 14.
gnash. Ps +37:12. Mt +25:30.

melt. Ex +15:15.
desire. Ps 36:12. Jb +8:13. Pr +10:28. 11:7. Is +38:18. Lk 16:23-26. He +9:27.

PSALM 113

(*Title*.) This and the following five Psalms form what is called by the Hebrews the great Hallel, or praise; which was sung on their most solemn festivals, and particularly after the celebration of the Passover (Mt 26:30. Mk 14:26). This and the following were probably composed after the return from the captivity.

1 **Praise ye the Lord**. Heb. Hallelujah. Ps 112:1.
Praise, O. Ps 33:1, 2. 103:20, 21. 134:1. 135:1-3, 20. 145:10. Ep 5:19, 20. Re 19:5.
the name. Is +30:27.

2 **Blessed**. Ps 41:13. 72:17-19. 106:48. 1 Ch 16:36. 29:10-13. Da 2:20. Ep 3:21. Re 5:13.
for evermore. Heb. *olam*, Ps +18:50.

3 **the rising**. Ps 72:11, 17-19. 86:9. Is 24:16. 42:10-12. 49:13. 59:19. Hab 2:14. Ml 1:11. Ro 15:9, 10. Re 11:15.

4 **high**. Ps 97:9. 99:2. Is 40:15, 17, 22.
his glory. Ps 8:1. 57:10, 11. 1 K 8:27. Is 66:1.

5 **like**. Ex +8:10.
dwelleth. Heb. exalteth himself to dwell. Is +12:4.

6 **humbleth**. Ps 11:4. Jb 4:18. 15:15. Is 6:2.
in heaven. Dt +10:14.
in the earth. Ps 138:6. Is 57:15. 66:2.

7 **raiseth**. Ps 75:6, 7. 107:41. Jb 5:11, 15, 16. Ezk 17:24. 21:26, 27. Lk 1:52, 53. 1 C 1:27. Ja 2:5.
out of. Ps 22:15. Is +26:19. Da +12:2, 3. Ac 2:31-33. Ep 1:20, 21. 1 P 3:21, 22.
needy. 1 S 2:7, 8. 24:14. 2 S 7:8, 9. Jb 2:8. 36:6, 7.

8 **may set**. Ps 68:13. Ge 41:41. Ph 2:8-11. Re +5:10.
the princes. Ps 47:9. Is +32:1.

9 **maketh**. Ps 68:6. Ge 21:5-7. 25:21. 30:22, 23. 1 S 2:5. Is +54:1. 56:4, 5. Lk 1:13-15. Ga 4:27.
barren. Ge +11:30. 29:31.
mother. Ps +127:3. Is +54:1.
keep house. Heb. dwell in an house. Ps 23:6. Is 60:7. Jn +14:2, 3.

PSALM 114

1 **Israel**. Ex 12:41, 42. 13:3. 20:2. Dt 16:1. 26:8. Is 11:16.
a people. Ps 81:5. Ge 42:23.

2 **Judah**. Ex 6:7. 19:5, 6. 25:8. 29:45, 46. Le 11:45. Dt 23:14. 27:9, 12. Ezk 37:26-28. 2 C 6:16, 17. Re 21:3.
dominion. Ex 19:6.

3 **sea**. Ex +14:21. 15:8.
Jordan. Ps 74:15. Jsh 3:13-16. Hab 3:9.

4 **mountains skipped**. Ps 29:6. 68:8, 16. Ex 19:18. 20:18. Jg 5:4, 5. Je 4:23, 24. Mi 1:3, 4. Na 1:5. Hab 3:6, 8. 2 P 3:7-11. Re 20:11.

5 **What ailed**. Je 47:6, 7. Hab 3:8.

6 **skipped**. ver. 4. Ps 29:6.

7 **Tremble**. Ps 77:18. +97:4. Jb 26:11. Is 64:1-3. Je 5:22. Mi 6:1, 2.

8 **Which turned**. Ps 78:15, 16. 105:41. 107:35. Ex 17:6. Nu 20:11. Dt 8:15. Ne 9:15. Is 14:23. 1 C 10:4.
the flint. Dt 8:15. 32:13. Jb 28:9mg. Is 50:7.
fountain. Heb. *mayan*, Ge +7:11. Jsh 15:9. 1 K 18:5. 2 K 3:19, 25.

PSALM 115

(*Title*.) A.M. 3108. B.C. 896. This seems to be an *epinikion*, or triumphal song, in which the victory is wholly ascribed to Jehovah; and to none can it be referred with more propriety than to that of Jehoshaphat over the confederated forces of his enemies, 2 Ch 20.

1 **Not unto us**. Ps 74:22. Jg 4:9. Is +48:9. Je 17:5. Re 4:10, 11.
thy name. Dt +28:58.
unto thy name. Mt 6:9.
for thy mercy. Ps 61:7. 89:1, 2. 2 Ch 32:25, 26. Mi 7:20. Jn 1:17. Ro 15:8, 9.

2 **Wherefore**. Ps 42:3, 10. 79:10. Ex 32:12. Nu 14:15, 16. Dt 32:26, 27. 2 K 19:10-19. Jl 2:17.

3 **But our**. Ps 47:2. 68:4. 83:18. 93:1. 123:1. 1 Ch 16:25. Mt +6:9, 13. Ac 17:24.
he hath. Ps 29:10. Ex +33:19. Dt +2:30. 1 Ch 29:12. Jb 9:12. +42:2. Is +14:27. Mt 20:15. Ro +9:18, 19.
whatsoever. Ps 135:6.

4 **Their idols**. Ex +20:4. Ho 8:6. Da 5:4. 1 C 10:19, 20.
silver. Ge +23:9.

5 **they speak not**. Je +10:5.
see not. Ps 135:16.

6 **They have ears**. Ps 135:17.
smell not. 1 C 10:19.

7 **hands**. ver. 4. Ps 8:6. 10:12. 17:14.
handle not. 1 S 5:4.
feet. Ps 8:6. 18:9. 22:16. 25:15.
walk. Ps 55:14. 81:13. 85:13. 86:11. 1 S 5:3. Is 46:7. Ac 17:29.
neither speak. Hab 2:18.

8 **make them**. Ps 135:18. 2 K 19:18. Is 44:9-20. Je 10:8. Ho 8:6. Jon +2:8. Hab 2:18, 19. Ac 17:29. Ro 1:23, 28. 2 C 4:4.
are like. Ps 135:18. 2 K 17:15. Je +2:5.

9 **Israel**. Ps 118:2-4. 135:19, 20. Ex 19:5.
trust. Ps 62:8. 125:1. 130:7. 146:5, 6. Je 17:7, 13. Ep 1:12.
their help. Ps 33:20, 21. 46:1.
their shield. Ps +84:11.

10 **house of Aaron**. Ex 28:1. Nu 16:5, 40. 18:7.
trust. Ph 4:6.

11 **Ye that.** Ps 33:18. 118:4. Pr +3:7. 30:5. Re
19:5.

12 **hath.** Ps 25:7. 136:23. Ge 8:1. Ex 2:24, 25. Jsh
17:14. 1 S 7:12. Is 44:21. 49:14-16. Ac 10:4.
the house of Israel. Ps 67:7. Ge 12:2, 3.
22:17, 18. Ac 3:26. Ga 3:14, 29. Ep 1:3.
will bless. Dt +28:4. Ep 1:3.

13 **He will bless.** Ps 29:11. Pr +3:7. Ml 3:16, 17.
Col 3:11.
both small. 2 K +23:2.
and. Heb. with. Ps 104:25. Dt 25:13.

14 **increase.** Ge 13:16. 2 S 22:36mg. 24:3. Is 2:2,
3. 27:6. 49:20, 21. 56:8. 60:4, etc. Je 30:19.
33:22. Ho 1:10. Zc 8:20-23. 10:8. Col 1:10.
2:19. Ja 4:6. Re 7:4, 9.
you. Ge 17:7. Je 32:38, 39. Ac 2:39. 3:25.

15 **blessed.** Ps 3:8. Ge 14:19. 32:26-29. Ep 1:3,
4. 1 P 3:9.
made. Ps 96:5. 146:5, 6. Ge 1:1.

16 **heaven.** Ps 89:11. 144:5. 148:4. Is 66:1. La
3:66. Jn 14:2, 3.
but the earth. Ps 50:12. Ge 1:28-30. 9:1-3.
Dt 32:8. Je 27:5, 6. Mt +5:5. 1 C 10:26.

17 **dead.** Ps 6:5. 30:9. 31:12. 88:10-12. 106:28.
118:17. Pr +21:16. Ec +9:5. Is 38:18, 19. Ro
12:1, 2. Re 20:5.
praise not. Ps +146:4.
go down. Ps 22:29. 28:1. 30:3. 31:17. 37:20.
49:14, 15, 19. 140:10, 13. 147:6. 1 S 2:9. Jb
27:13, 19. 40:12, 13. Pr 12:7. Is +24:22.
26:14. 42:7, 22. 43:17, 21.
silence. Heb. *dumah*, Ps 94:17, only.

18 **But we.** Ps 59:16. 102:18. Is 24:14, 16.
will bless. Ps 113:2. 118:17-19. 145:2, 21. Is
+51:11. Da 2:20. Re 5:13.
for evermore. Heb. *olam*, Ps +18:50.
Praise the Lord. Ps 105:45.

PSALM 116

(**Title.**) A.M. 3468. B.C. 536. From several
instances of the Chaldee dialect in this Psalm,
it appears to have been written after the
Babylonian captivity.

1 **love.** Ps 119:132. Dt +6:5. Jn 21:17.
because. Ps 18:6. 31:22, 23. 34:3, 4. 40:1, 2.
66:19, 20. 69:33, 34. Ge 35:2, 3. 1 S 1:26, 27.
Jn 16:24.

2 **therefore.** Ps 55:16, 17. 86:6, 7. 88:1, 2.
145:18, 19. Jb 27:10. Lk 18:1. Ph 4:6. Col 4:2.
as long as I live. Heb. in my days. 2 K 20:19.

3 **sorrows.** Ps 18:4-6. 88:6, 7. Jon 2:2, 3. Mk
14:33-36. Lk 22:44. He 5:7.
pains. Ps 118:5. La 1:3.
hell. Heb. *sheol*, Ge +37:35.
gat hold upon me. Heb. found me. 2 K
+9:21mg.
I found. Ps 32:3, 4. 38:6. Is 53:3, 4.

4 **called.** Ps +3:4. 118:5. 2 Ch 33:12, 13. Is
37:15-20. 38:1-3.

O Lord. Ps 6:4. 22:20. 25:17. 40:12, 13.
142:4-6. 143:6-9. Lk 18:13, 14. 23:42, 43.
deliver. Ps 56:1-3. Mt 24:19-21. Lk +21:36.
Ac 16:23-25. Ep 6:18-20. Ph 4:6. 2 Th 3:1, 2.
Ja 5:14, 15.
soul. Heb. *nephesh*, Ge +12:13.

5 **Gracious.** Ps 115:1. Ex +34:6, 7. Ep 1:6-8.
2:4. 1 T 1:14. T 3:4-7.
and righteous. Ps 119:137. 145:4-7, 17. Ezr
9:15. Ne 9:8, 33. Is 45:21. Da 9:7, 14. Ro 3:25,
26. 1 J 1:9.

6 **preserveth.** Ps 19:7. 25:21. Is 35:8. Mt 11:25.
Ro 16:19. 2 C 1:12. 11:3. Col 3:22.
simple. Pr +1:4.
I was. Ps 79:8. 106:43. 142:6.

7 **thy rest.** Ps 42:11. 95:11. Je 6:16. 30:10. Mt
11:28, 29. He 4:8-10.
soul. Heb. *nephesh*, Ge +34:3.
hath dealt. Ps 13:6. 119:17. Ho 2:7.
bountifully. 1 S +1:22.

8 **For thou.** Ps 56:13. 86:13.
soul. Heb. *nephesh*, Ge +12:13.
mine eyes. Lk +6:21.
and my feet. Ps 37:24. 56:13. 73:23. 94:18. 1
S 2:9. Lk 22:31, 32. Ju 24.

9 **walk.** Ps 61:7. Ge +17:1. 1 K 9:4.
in the land. Ps +27:13.

10 **I believed.** 2 C *4:13.* 5:7. He 11:1.
therefore. Nu 14:6-9. Pr 21:28. 2 P 1:16-21.
I was greatly. ver. 3.

11 **in my.** Ps 31:22. 1 S 27:1.
All. Ps 62:9. 2 K 4:16, 28. Je 9:4, 5. Ro 3:4.

12 **What shall.** Ps 51:12-14. 103:2, 3. Is 6:5-8.
Ro 12:1. 1 C 6:20. 2 C 5:14, 15.

13 **I will take.** ver. 17. Ps 36:8. Nu 15:2-5. Lk
22:17, 18, 20. 1 C 10:16, 21. 11:25-27.
call. ver. 2. Ps 105:1. Is 12:4.

14 **pay my vows.** ver. 18. Le +23:38. Mt 5:33.

15 **Precious.** Ps 37:32, 33. 49:7, 8. 72:14. 126:5,
6. 139:17. 1 S 25:29. Jb 5:26. Is 28:16. Ho
11:4. Lk 16:22. Re 1:18. 14:13.
the death. Ge 4:10. 1 C +15:55.

16 **truly.** Ps 86:16. 119:125. 143:12. Jn 12:26.
Ac 27:23. Ja 1:1.
the son. Ps 86:16.
handmaid. Ps 86:16. Mt 1:23.
thou hast. Ps +146:7. Ro 6:22.

17 **the sacrifice.** Le +7:12.
call. ver. 13. Ac 2:42.

18 **will pay.** ver. 14. Le +23:38.

19 **the courts.** Ps 96:8. 100:4. 118:19, 20. 122:3,
4. 135:2. 2 Ch 6:6.

PSALM 117

1 **O praise.** Ps 66:1, 4. 67:3. 86:9. Is 24:15, 16.
42:10-12. Ro *15:11.* Ep 3:5, 6. Re 15:4.
praise him. Ps 148:11-14. 150:6. Re 5:9. 7:9,
10.

2 **his merciful.** Ps 85:10. 89:1. 100:4, 5. Is

25:1. Mi 7:20. Lk 1:54, 55. Jn 14:6. Ro 15:8, 9. 1 J 5:6.

for ever. Heb. *olam*, Ex +12:24.

PSALM 118

1 **give thanks**. Ps +136:1.
  his mercy. Ex +34:6.
  for ever. Heb. *olam*, Ex +12:24.

2 **Let**. Ps 118:8, 9, 15, 16. 136:1, 2, 3.
  Israel now say. Ps 115:9-11. 135:19, 20. 145:10. 147:19, 20. Ga 6:16. He 13:15. 1 P 2:9, 10.
  his mercy. ver. 1.
  for ever. Heb. *olam*, Ex +12:24.

3 **the house of Aaron**. Ps 115:9-11. 134:1-3. 1 P 2:5. Re 1:6. 4:7-11. 5:8-10.
  mercy. ver. 1. Ep 2:4. 1 P 1:3.
  for ever. Heb. *olam*, Ex +12:24.

4 **Let them**. Ps 22:23. Re 19:5.
  his mercy. ver. +1.
  for ever. Heb. *olam*, Ex +12:24.

5 **called**. Ps 40:1-3. 77:2. 116:3, 4. 130:1, 2. Mk 14:34-36.
  in distress. Heb. out of distress. Ne +9:37.
  set me. Ps 18:19. 22:21. 31:8. He 5:7.

6 **The Lord**. Ps 27:1-3. 46:1, 11. 56:4, 9, 11. 146:5. Is 51:12. Je 20:11. Mi 7:8-10. Ro 8:31. He *13:6*.
  on my side. Heb. for me. Ps 56:9.
  not fear. Ps 3:6. 27:1-3. +34:4. 46:1, 2. 56:3, 4, 11. 146:5. Ge +15:1. 19:30. Dt 31:6, 8. Jsh 8:1. 1 K 18:8-16. 2 K 6:15, 16. Pr 29:25. Is 41:10, 13, 14. 43:1, 5. 44:2, 8. 51:7, 12. 54:4. Je 1:8. Ezk 2:6. Da 3:17, 18. 6:10. Mt +10:28-33. Mk 4:40. 16:6. Jn 14:27. Ac 4:13. 20:24. 27:24. He 13:6. 1 P 3:13, 14.

7 **taketh**. Ps 54:4. 55:18. 1 Ch 12:18.
  therefore. Ps +112:8.

8 **It is**. ver. +2.
  better to trust. Ps +9:10. 20:7. 23:4-6. 27:1. 49:6, 7. 56:4. 62:8, 9. 91:2. Pr 28:1, 26. Is +26:3, 4. Mi 7:5-7. Zc 4:6. Mk 10:24. Lk 12:19, 20. 2 C 1:9. Ga 6:7. 1 Th 5:2, 3. He 3:12, 14. 10:35, 36. 13:5. Ja 4:13-15.
  put confidence. 2 Ch 12:1. Is 30:2, 3.

9 **trust**. Ps 91:2. Is 26:4.
  than to put. Ps 146:3-5. Is 30:2, 3, 15-17. 31:1, 8. 36:6, 7. Ezk 29:7.

10 **All nations**. Ex +9:6. 2 S ch. 5, 8, 10. Zc 12:3. 14:1-3. Re 19:19-21. 20:8, 9.
  destroy them. Heb. cut them off. ver. 11, 12. Ps 58:7. 90:6. Jb 14:2.

11 **They compassed**. Ps 22:12-16. 88:17. 1 S 23:26. 1 Ch 19:10.

12 **like bees**. Dt 1:44.
  quenched. Ps 83:14, 15. Ec 7:6. Is 27:4. Na 1:10.
  in the name. Ps 8:9. 20:1, 5. 1 S 17:45. 2 S 23:6. 1 Ch 14:10, 11, 14-16. 2 Ch 14:9, 11,

12. 16:7-9. 20:17-22. 22:7, 8. 32:7, 8.
  destroy them. Heb. cut them down. ver. 10, 11.

13 **Thou hast**. Ps 18:17, 18. 56:1-3. 1 S 20:3. 25:29. 2 S 17:1-3. Mi 7:8. Mt 4:1-11. He 2:14.

14 **is my strength**. Ps +18:1. Mt 1:21-23.
  and song. Ge +43:11mg. Ex 15:2. Is 12:2.

15 **voice**. Ps 30:11, 12. 119:54, 111. Dt +12:7. Is 51:11. 65:13. Re 18:20. 19:1-5.
  the right hand. Ps +18:35.

16 **The right hand**. Ex 15:6. Ac 2:32-36.
  exalted. Is +12:4.

17 **not die**. Ps 6:5. Is 38:16-20. Hab 1:12. Jn 11:4. Ro 14:7-9.
  declare. Ps 40:5, 10. 71:17, 18. 73:28. 107:22. 119:13. 145:4. Je 51:10.

18 **chastened**. Ps 66:10-12. 2 S 12:10. ch. 13, 16. Jb 33:16-30. Je 10:24. 30:11. +31:18. Jon 2:6. 2 C 1:9-11. 6:9. He 12:10, 11.
  not given. Jb 2:6.

19 **Open**. Is 26:2. Re 22:14.
  I will go. Ps 9:13, 14. 66:13-15. 95:2. 100:4. 116:18, 19. Is 38:20, 22.

20 **This gate**. Ps 24:3, 4, 7, 9. Is 26:2. 35:8-10. Re 21:24-27. 22:14, 15.

21 **will praise**. Ps 22:23, 24. 69:33, 34. 116:1.
  and art. ver. 14. Ex 15:2. Is 12:2. 49:8.

22 **The stone**. Mt +*21:42*. Mk *12:10, 11*. Lk *20:17*. Ac *4:11*. 1 P 2:4-6, 7, 8.
  refused. Mt 21:42. Jn 7:48.
  the head. Zc 4:7.

23 **This**. Mt *21:42*. Mk *12:10-11*.
  the Lord 's doing. Heb. from the Lord. Ac 2:32-36. 3:14, 15. 5:31, 32. Ro 1:4. Ep 1:19-22.
  it is. Jb 5:9. Ac 4:13. 13:41.

24 **the day**. Ps 2:7. Dt 11:21. 33:12. Is +2:11. 24:21, 22. 25:9. 49:8. Ho +2:18. 6:2. Zc +3:9, 10. 14:7, 8. Mt 28:1-8. Jn 8:56. 20:19, 20. Ac +20:7. 1 C +5:5. 2 C +6:2. He 3:7, 13. Re +1:10.
  we will rejoice. Ps 84:10. 106:5. 1 K 8:66. 2 Ch 20:26-28. Ne 8:10. Is +58:13. Hab 3:17, 18.
  glad. Ps 97:11. Nu 10:10.

25 **Save now**. Ps 20:9. 22:21. 69:1, 13. Dt 28:67. Is 63:19. 64:1, 2. Ac 26:29. Ro 9:3.
  send now. Ps 90:17.

26 **Blessed**. Zc 4:7. Mt *21:9. 23:39*. Mk *11:9, 10*. Lk *13:35. 19:38*. Jn *12:13*.
  we have. Ps 134:3. Nu 6:23-26.

27 **God**. Heb. *El*, Ex +15:2. 1 K 18:21, 39.
  showed. Ps +112:4. Est 8:16. Is 9:2. 60:1. 1 P 2:9.
  bind. Ps 51:18, 19. 1 K 8:63, 64. +18:44mg. 1 Ch 29:21. Ro 12:1. He 13:15.
  sacrifice. lit. feast. Ex 23:18.
  the horns. Ex +27:2.

28 **my God**. Heb. *El*, Ex +15:2. Ps 22:1. 63:1. 89:26. 145:1. 146:2. Is 12:2. 25:1, 9.
exalt. Is +12:4.

29 **give thanks**. ver. +1. Is 63:7.
for ever. Heb. *olam*, Ex +12:24.

PSALM 119

ALEPH

1 One of several acrostic or alphabetical passages, the others being: Ps ch. 9, 10, 25, 34, 37. ch. 145. Pr 31:10-31. La ch. 1, 2, 3, 4.
Blessed. Ps +1:1-3. Mt +5:3-12. Lk +11:28. Jn +13:17. Ja 1:25. Re 22:14.
undefiled. *or*, perfect, *or* sincere, Ps +101:6mg. ver. +3, 165. Ps 147:11. Dt +33:9. Jsh +14:8, +14. 2 K +20:3. 2 Ch 31:20, 21. Jb +36:7. Is +60:21. Jn +1:12, +47. +17:6. Ac 24:16. Ro 13:8, 10. 2 C 1:12. Ep +5:25. T 2:11, 12. 1 J +1:8, 10. 3:3. Re 19:8.
walk. Ps 1:1-3. 25:10. Ezk 11:20. Ho 14:9. Lk 1:6. 1 Th 4:1, 2.

2 **Blessed**. Dt +28:3.
keep. ver. 22, 146. Ps 25:10. 105:45. Dt 6:17. 1 K 2:3. Pr 23:26. Ezk 33:31. 36:27. Jn +13:17. 14:23. 1 J 3:20.
seek. ver. 10. Ps +9:10. 27:8. Dt 4:29. 2 Ch 31:21. Je 3:10. 29:13. Ho 10:2. He 11:6.
whole heart. Dt 6:5. Jsh +14:8. Je 24:7. 29:13.

3 **do no iniquity**. Zp 3:13. Ro 6:14. 7:15. 13:10. 1 C +2:6. Ga 5:16, 17. Ph 3:12. 1 J +1:8. 2:15. 3:6, 9. 5:18.
they walk. Ps 44:18. +128:1. Jn 10:27. Col +1:10. 1 Th 4:1.

4 **commanded**. Dt 4:1, 9. 5:29-33. 6:17. 11:13, 22. 12:32. +26:16, 18. 28:1, etc. 30:16. Jsh 1:7. Je 7:23. Mt 7:21. 28:20. Lk 6:46. +11:28. Jn 14:15, +17, 21. Ph 4:8, 9. He 11:6. 1 J 2:3. 5:3.

5 **my ways**. ver. 32, 36, 44, 45, 131, 159, 173. Ps 51:10. Is 30:21. Je 31:33. Ro 7:22-24. 2 Th 3:5. He 13:21.

6 **shall I**. ver. 31, 80. Jb 22:23, 26. Da 12:2, 3. Ro 6:21. 1 J 2:28. 3:20, 21.
ashamed. Is 45:17. Ro 9:33.
I have. ver. 128. Mt 7:16-21. Jn 15:14. Ja 2:10, 17, +18. 1 J 2:3-6.

7 **I will**. ver. 171. Ps 9:1. 63:3. 86:12, 13. 1 Ch 29:13-17.
when. ver. 12, 18, 19, 27, 33, 34, 64, 73, 124. Ps 25:4, 5, 8-10. 143:10. Is 48:17. Jn 6:45.
thy righteous judgments. Heb. judgments of thy righteousness. ver. 138.

8 **I will**. ver. 16, 106, 115. Jsh +24:15.
O forsake. ver. 116, 117, 176. Ps 38:21, 22. 51:11. 2 Ch 32:30, 31. Is 54:7, 8. Ph 4:13. He +13:5.

BETH

9 **shall**. Ps 25:7. 34:11. Jb 1:5. 13:26. Pr 1:4, 10. 4:1, 10-17. 5:7, etc. 6:20, etc. 7:7. Ec 11:9, 10. 12:1. Lk 15:13. 2 T 2:22. T 2:4-6.
cleanse. Ps 19:9, 11, 12. Ex 30:18. Jn 15:3. 17:17. Ep 5:26, 27. He 10:22.
by taking. ver. 11, 97-105. Ps 1:1-3. 17:4. 19:7-11. 74:4-8. Dt 6:6-9. 17:18-20. Jsh 1:7. Pr 4:23. Lk 22:61, 62. Jn 15:3. 17:17, 19. 2 T 3:15-17. Ja 1:21-25.

10 **my whole heart**. ver. 2, 34, 58, 69. Ps 78:37. 1 S 7:3. 2 Ch 15:15. Is 26:9. Je 3:10. Ho 10:2. Zp 1:5, 6. Mt 6:24. Col 3:22. He 11:6. 1 J 2:15.
O let me not wander. ver. 17, 18, 21, 33-35, 118, 133, 176. Ps 23:3. 125:5. 143:8-10. 1 Ch 29:18, 19. Pr 2:13. 21:16. Is 35:8. Ezk 34:6. 2 P 2:15-22.

11 **Thy word**. ver. 97, 105. Ps 1:2. Je 15:16. Col 3:16. 1 J 2:14.
hid. Dt +6:6. Jsh 1:8. Lk 8:15.
that I. Ps 19:13. Ep 6:17, 18.

12 **Blessed**. 1 T 1:11. 6:15.
teach. ver. 26, 27, 33, 64, 66, 68, 71, 72, 108, 124, 125, 135. Ps 25:4, 5. 86:11. 143:10. Lk 24:45. Jn 14:26. 1 J 2:27.

13 **I declared**. ver. 46, 172. Ps 34:11. 37:30. 71:15-18. 118:17. Dt 11:18, 19. Mt 10:27. 12:34, 35. Ac 4:20.
all. Ac +20:20, 27.

14 **rejoiced**. ver. 47, 72, 77, 111, 127, 162. Ps 19:9, 10. 112:1. Jb 23:12. Is 35:8. Je 15:16. Mt 13:44. Jn +5:39. 14:6. Ac 2:41-47. 1 C 3:21, 22.

15 **meditate**. ver. 23, 48, 78, 97, 131, 148. Ps 1:2. Ja 1:25.
have respect. ver. 6, 117. Jb 23:11, 12.

16 **delight**. ver. 14, 24, 35, 47, 70, 77, 92. Ps 40:8. Ro 7:22. He 10:16, 17.
not forget. ver. 11, 83, 93, 109, 141, 176. Pr 3:1. Jn 14:26. He 2:1. Ja 1:23-25.

GIMEL

17 **Deal**. ver. 65, 124, 132. Ps 13:6. 116:7. Jn 1:16. 2 C 9:7-11. Ph 4:19.
bountifully. Ps 13:6. 116:7. 1 S +1:22 (S#1580h).
I may live. Ro 8:2-4. 2 C 5:14, 15. Ep 2:4, 5, 10. T 2:11, 12. 1 J 2:29. 5:3, 4.

18 **Open**. Heb. Reveal. Ps 146:8. Ge +3:7. Nu 22:31. 2 K 6:15-17, 20. Is 29:10-12, 18. 32:3. 35:5. 42:7, 16, 18. 43:8. Mt 9:30. 13:13. 16:17. 20:30-34. Lk +24:16, 31, 45. Jn 9:7, 32, 39. Ac 26:18. 2 C 2:11, 14. 3:14-18. 4:4-6. Ep 1:17, 18. Re 3:18.
that I. Mt 11:25. Jn 3:27. 6:45.
wondrous. ver. 96. Ho 8:12. 2 C 3:13. He 8:5. 10:1.

19 **a stranger**. Ps 39:12. 94:6. 146:9. Ge +23:4. 47:9. Ex 12:48mg. 1 K 8:41-43. 1 Ch 29:15.

Mi 2:10. Mt 8:20. 2 C 5:6. Ph 3:20. He 11:13-16. 13:14. 1 P 1:1-4. 2:11.

hide. ver. 10. Jb 39:17. Is 63:17. Lk 9:45. 24:45.

20 **soul.** Heb. *nephesh,* Ge +34:3.
breaketh. ver. 40, 131, 174. Ps 42:1. 63:1. 84:2. Pr 13:12. SS 5:8. Mt +5:6. Re 3:15, 16.
thy judgments. Is 26:8.
at all times. Ps 106:3. Jb 23:11, 12. 27:10. Pr 17:17.

21 **rebuked.** ver. 78.
the proud. ver. 51, 69. Pr +16:5. Ro +12:3. Ph +2:3.
cursed. ver. 10, 110, 118. Dt 30:19. Ne 9:16, 29. Is 42:24. Je 44:9-11, 16, 28, 29. Mt +25:41.
do err. Mk 12:24, 27.

22 **Remove.** ver. 39, 42. Ps 39:8. 42:10. 69:9-11, 19, 20. 123:3, 4. 1 S 25:10, 39. 2 S 16:7, 8. Jb 16:20.
reproach. Jb 19:2, 3. He 13:13. 1 P 2:20. 4:14.
contempt. Ps 123:3, 4.
for I have. Ps 37:3, 6. 1 P 2:20. 3:16, 17. 4:14-16.

23 **Princes.** Ps 2:1, 2. 1 S 20:31. 22:7-13. Lk 22:66. 23:1, 2, 10, 11.
thy servant. ver. 15. Da 6:9, 10.

24 **testimonies.** ver. 16, 77, 92, 143, 162. Jb 27:10. Je 6:10.
my counsellers. Heb. men of my counsel. ver. 97-100, 104, 105. Ps 19:11. 73:24. Dt 17:18-20. Jsh 1:8. Pr 6:20-23. Is 8:20. 40:13mg. 46:11mg. Col 3:16. 2 T 3:15-17.

DALETH

25 **soul.** Heb. *nephesh,* Ge +34:3. Ps 22:15. 44:25. Is 65:25. Mt 16:23. Ro 7:22-24. Ph 3:19. Col 3:2.
quicken. ver. 37, 40, 88, 93, 107, 149, 154, 156, 159. Ps 71:20. 80:18. 143:11. Is 40:31. Hab 3:2mg. Jn 10:10. Ro 8:2, 3.
according. ver. 28, 41, 76, 169. Dt 30:6. 2 S 7:27-29.

26 **declared.** ver. 106. Ps 27:11. 32:5. 38:18. 51:1, etc. 69:5. 143:8, 10. Jb 31:33. Pr +28:13.
thou heardest me. Ps +34:15, 17. 116:1, 2. Lk 15:18-22. Jn +9:31. He 4:13-16.
teach. ver. 12. Ps 25:4, 8, 9. 27:11. 86:11. 143:8-10. 1 K 8:36.

27 **understand.** ver. 34, 73, 125, 144, 169. 1 K 3:9. 1 Ch 22:11, 12. Da 9:13. Col 1:9. 2:2. 2 T 2:7.
so shall I talk. Ps 37:30. 71:17. 78:4. 105:2. 111:4. 145:5, 6. Ex 13:14, 15. Jsh 4:6, 7. Ml +3:16. Ac 2:11. Re 15:3.

28 **soul.** Heb. *nephesh,* Ge +34:3.
melteth. Heb. droppeth. Ps 22:14. 107:26-28. Jsh 2:11, 24. Jb 16:20. Ec 10:18.

strengthen. Ps 27:14. 29:11. 68:28. Dt 33:25. Is 40:29, 31. Zc 10:12. Ep 3:16. Ph 4:13.

29 **Remove.** ver. 37, 104, 128, 163. Ps 141:3, 4. Pr 30:7-9. Is 44:20. Je 16:19. Jon 2:8. Ep +4:25. 1 J 1:8. 2:4.
grant me. ver. 5. Je 31:33, 34. He 8:10, 11.

30 **chosen.** ver. 29, 11, 173. Jsh 24:15. Pr 1:29. Lk 10:42. Jn 3:19-21. 8:45. 1 P 2:2. 2 J 4.
thy judgments. ver. 24, 52. Dt 11:18-20.

31 **stuck.** ver. 48, 115. Dt +4:4. Pr 23:23. Jn 8:31. He 11:13. 2 P 2:21.
put me. ver. 6, 80. Ps 25:2, 20. Is 45:17. 49:23. Je 17:18. Jl 2:27. Ro 5:5. 1 J 2:28.

32 **run.** SS 1:41. Is 40:31. 1 C 9:24-26. He 12:1. 1 J 5:3.
enlarge. ver. 45. Ps 18:36. 1 K 4:29. Ne 8:10. Jb 36:15, 16. Is 60:5. 61:1. Lk 1:74, 75. Jn 8:32, 36. 2 C 3:17. 6:11. 1 P 2:16.

HE

33 **Teach.** ver. 12, 26, 27. Is 54:13. Jn 6:45.
I shall keep. ver. 8, 112. Je 32:40. Mt 10:22. 24:13. 1 C 1:7, 8. Ph 1:6. 1 J 2:19, 20, 27. Re 2:26.

34 **Give me.** ver. 73. Ps 111:10. Jb 28:28. Pr 2:5, 6. Jn 7:17. Ph 2:13. Ja 1:5. 3:13-18.
I shall. Dt 4:6. Mt 5:19. 7:24. Ja 1:25. 2:8-12. 4:11.
observe. ver. 10, 58, 69.

35 **Make me.** ver. 27, 36, 173. Ezk 36:26, 27. Ph 2:13. He 13:21.
the path. Ps 23:3. Pr 3:13, 17. 4:11, 18. 8:20. Is 2:3. 48:17.
therein. ver. 16. Is 58:13, 14. Ro 7:22. 1 J 5:3.

36 **Incline.** Ps 51:10. 141:4. 1 K 8:58. Je 32:29. Ezk 11:19, 20.
and not to. Ps 10:3. Ex +18:21. Ezk +33:31. Hab 2:9. Mt 6:24. Mk 7:21, 22. Lk 12:15. 16:14. 2 C 4:18. Ep 5:3, 5. Col 3:5. 1 T 6:9, 10, 17. He +13:5. 2 P 2:3, 14.

37 **Turn.** Heb. Make to pass. Nu 15:39. Jsh 7:21. 2 S 11:2. Jb 31:1. Pr 4:25. 23:5. Is 33:15. Mt 5:28. Ph 3:13, 14. 1 J 2:16.
quicken. ver. 25, 40.

38 **Stablish.** ver. 49. 2 S 7:25-29. 2 C 1:20.
who is devoted. Ps 103:11, 13, 17. 145:19. 147:11. Je 32:39-41.

39 **reproach.** ver. 22, 31. Ps +31:11. 57:2, 3. 2 S 12:14. Ne 4:4. Je 20:7-13. 1 T 3:7. 5:14. T 2:8.
for thy. ver. 20, 43, 75, 123, 131. Ps 19:9. Dt 4:8. Is 26:8. Ro 2:2. 7:12. Re 19:2.

40 **I have.** ver. 5, 20. Ps 37:4. Mt 26:41. Ro 7:22, 24. 2 C 7:1. Ga 5:17. Ph 3:13, 14.
quicken. ver. 25, 37, 88, 107, 149, 156, 159. Mk 9:24. Jn 5:21. 10:10. 1 C 15:45. Ep 2:5. 3 J 2.

VAU

41 Let. ver. 58, 76, 77, 132. Ps 35:3. 69:16.
106:4, 5. Lk 2:28-32. Ja 1:21.

42 So shall. Ps 3:2, 3. 42:10. 71:10, 11. 109:25.
Mt 27:40-43, 63.
have wherewith, etc. *or*, answer him that
reproacheth me in a thing. 2 S 16:7, 8. 19:18-
20. 1 P 3:15. 2 P 1:16, 19.
for I trust. ver. 49, 74, 81. Ps 56:4, 10, 11.
89:19, etc. 2 S 7:12-16. 1 Ch 28:3-6. Mi 7:8.
Ac 27:25.

43 take not. ver. 13. Ps 50:16. 51:14, 15. 71:17,
18. Is 59:21. Ep 1:13. Ja 1:18.
for I have. ver. 52, 120, 175. Ps 7:6-9. 9:4,
16. 43:1. 1 P 2:23.

44 keep. ver. 33, 34. Re 7:15. 22:11.
continually. Ps 119:109, 117. Is +58:11.
for ever. Heb. *olam*, Ps +21:4.
and ever. Ps +9:18.

45 And I will. ver. 133. Ps 12:8. 39:6. Is 26:12,
13. Lk 4:18. Jn 8:30-36. Ja 1:25. 2:12. 2 P
2:19.
at liberty. Heb. at large. ver. 32, 96. Ps 101:5
(proud). 104:25. 118:5. Ne 7:4mg. Pr 4:12. Is
22:18mg.
for I seek. ver. 19, 71, 94, 148, 162. Pr 2:4, 5.
18:1. Ec 1:13. Jn +5:39. Ep 5:17.

46 speak. Ps 138:1. Da 3:16-18. 4:1-3, 25-27. Mt
10:18, 19. Ac 26:1, 2, 24-29. 1 T 6:13.
will not. Mk 8:38. Ro 1:16. Ph 1:20. 2 T 1:8,
16. 1 P 4:14-16. 1 J 2:28.

47 I will delight. ver. 16, 24. Ps 112:1. Jn 4:34.
Ph 2:5. 1 P 2:21.
which. ver. 48, 97, 127, 140, 167, 174. Ps
19:7-10. Jb 23:11, 12. Ro 7:12, 16, 22.

48 hands. Ps 10:12. Ezk 44:12. Mi 5:9.
unto thy. Mt 7:21. Jn +13:17. 15:14. Ja 1:22-
25.
and I will. ver. 15. Ps 1:2.

ZAIN

49 Remember. Ge +8:1. Ps 105:2, 42. 106:4, 45.
Ge 8:1. 32:9-12. Jsh 23:14. 2 Ch 6:42. Ne 1:8,
9. Jb 7:7. Is 62:6mg.
upon which. ver. 43, 74, 81, 147. Ps +42:11.
2 S 5:2. 7:25. Ro 15:13. 1 P 1:13, 21.

50 This. Ps 27:13. 28:7. 42:8, 11. 94:19. Je
15:16. Ro 5:3-5. 8:28. 15:4. He 6:17-19.
12:11, 12.
thy word. ver. 11, 38, 41, 58, 67, 76, 82, 103,
116, 123, 133, 140, 148, 158, 162, 170, 172.
hath quickened. ver. +25, +40, 162. Ezk
37:10. Jn 6:63. Col 2:13. He 4:12. Ja 1:18. 1 P
1:23. 2:2.

51 proud. ver. +21. Ps +10:2.
derision. Lk +16:14, 15. 1 C 4:12, 13. 2 T
3:12. 1 P 2:23.
yet have. ver. 31, 157. Ps 44:18. Jb 23:11. Is
38:3. 42:4. Ac 20:23, 24. He 12:1-3.

52 remembered. Ps 42:6. 63:5, 6. 77:5, 11, 12.
78:34, 35. 105:5. 143:5. Ex 14:29, 30. Nu
16:3, etc. Dt 1:35, 36. 4:3, 4. Is 64:5. Jon 2:4.
2 P 2:4-9.
of old. Heb. *olam*, Ge +6:4.
comforted. Is 25:4. Ro 15:4.

53 Horror. ver. 136, 158. Ps 11:6. Ezr 9:3, 14.
10:6. Je 13:17. La 5:10mg. Da 4:19. Hab 3:16.
Lk 19:41, 42. Ac 17:16, 17. Ro 9:1-3. 2 C
12:21. Ph 3:18.
the wicked. 2 P 3:17.

54 Thy statutes. Ps 89:1. 101:1. Ge 47:9. He
11:13-16.

55 night. ver. 62, 148. Ps 22:2. 42:8. 63:5, 6.
72:2. 77:6. 139:18. Ge 20:3, 4. 26:24. 32:24-
28. Jb 35:9, 10. Is 26:9. La 2:19. Lk 6:12. Ac
16:25.
kept. ver. 17, 34. Jn 14:21. 15:10.

56 I kept. ver. 8, 22, 43, 47, 55, 58-60, 145, 146,
153, 165. Ps 18:18-22. 19:11. Dt 26:13-15. Is
32:17. Jn 14:23. 1 J 3:19-24.

CHETH

57 my portion. Ps +16:5.
I have. ver. 106, 115. Ps 66:14. Dt 26:17, 18.
Jsh 24:15, 18, 21, 24-27. Ne 10:29, etc.

58 I intreated. ver. 10. Ps 4:6. 51:1-3. 86:1-3.
Ge 32:26. Ho 7:14. He 10:22.
favor. Heb. face. Ps 27:8. 45:12mg. 102:12,
13. 106:4, 5. Jb +11:19mg. 33:26.
be merciful. ver. 41, 65, 76, 170. Ps 56:4, 10.
138:2. Mt 24:35.
according to. Ge 32:12. Ex 32:13. 2 S 7:25. 1
K 8:25.

59 thought. La 3:40. Ezk 18:28, 30. Hg 1:5, 7.
Lk 15:17-20. 2 C 13:5.
turned. ver. 112. Dt 4:30, 31. Je 8:4-6. 31:18,
19. La 3:40. Ezk 18:27, 28. 33:14-16, 19. Jl
2:13. Ac 17:28. 1 C 4:15. 2 C 12:21. Col 3:9,
10. 1 P 1:22.

60 made. Ps 95:7, 8. Ge +21:14. Ezr 10:6-8. Pr
27:1. Ec 9:10. Ac 24:25. Ga 1:16.

61 The bands. *or*, The companies. ver. 95. Ps
3:1. 1 S 30:3-6. Jb 1:17, 20, 21. Ho 6:9. He
10:34.
but I. ver. 176. 1 S 24:9-11. 26:9-11. Pr
24:29. Mt 6:20. Ro 12:17-21.

62 midnight. ver. 147, 164. Ps 42:8. 139:17, 18.
149:5. Mk 1:35. Ac 16:25.
thy. ver. 7, 75, 106, 137. Ps 19:9. Dt 4:8. Ro
7:12.

63 a companion. ver. 79, 115. Ps 15:4. 16:3.
45:7. 55:14. +101:4, 6, 7. 142:7. Jg 20:11. 1 S
23:16. 2 Ch 13:7. 19:2. Pr 2:20. 12:26. 13:20.
27:17. Ec 10:10. Ml 3:16-18. Lk 24:15, 32. Ro
1:12. +16:17. 1 C 12:13. +15:33. 2 C 6:14-17.
7:6, 7. Ep 5:3, 7, 11. Col 2:2. 2 T 2:19. He
+3:12, 13. 10:25. 1 P 3:8. 1 J 1:3. 3:14.
fear. ver. 120. Ps 55:19. 76:8. 103:11, 17.

112:1. 118:4. 128:4. 135:20. Ex +18:21. Pr 1:29. Ec 8:12. Ml 3:16.

keep. ver. 2, 4. Ps 103:18. Pr 1:10. Lk +11:28. 2 J 9-11.

precepts. ver. 56. Ps 111:10.

64 **earth**. Ps 33:5. 104:13. +145:9, 15, 16.

teach. ver. 12, 26. Ps 27:11. Is 2:3. 48:17, 18. Mt 11:29.

TETH

65 **dealt well**. ver. 17. Ps 13:6. 16:5, 6. 18:35. 23:5, 6. 30:11. 116:7. 1 Ch 29:14.

66 **Teach me**. ver 34. Ps 72:1, 2. 1 K 3:9, 28. Pr 2:1-9. 8:20. Is 11:2-4. Je 3:15. Mt 13:11. Ph 1:9, 10. 4:8, 9. Ja 3:13-18.

I have. ver. 128, 160, 172. Ne 9:13, 14.

67 **Before**. ver. 176. Ps 73:5, etc. Dt 32:15. 2 S 10:19. 11:2, etc. 2 Ch 33:9-13. Pr 1:32. Je 22:21.

but now. ver. 71, 75. Je 31:18, 19. La 3:27. Ho 2:6, 7. 5:15. 6:1. He 12:10, 11. Re 3:10.

68 **good**. Ps 5:4. 86:5. +136:1. Ex +34:6. Mt +5:45. Jn 3:14-17. Ro 5:8. 8:32. 1 T 2:3, 4. 2 P 3:9. 1 J 4:7-10.

teach. ver. 12, 26. Ps 25:8, 9.

69 **proud**. Ps 35:11. 109:2, 3. Jb 13:4. Je 43:2, 3. Mt 5:11, 12. 10:25. 26:59, etc. Ac 24:5, 13.

I will. ver. 51, 157.

with my whole. ver. 34, 58. Mt 6:24. He 11:6. Ja 1:8.

70 **as fat**. Dt +31:20. Ep 4:19. 1 T 4:2.

but I. ver. 16, 35. Ps +1:2. 40:8. Ro 7:22.

71 **good**. ver. 67. Is 27:9. Je +31:18. He 5:8. 12:10, 11. 1 P 1:6, 7.

72 **better**. ver. 14, 111, 127, 162. Ps 19:10. Pr 3:14, 15. 8:10, 11, 19. 16:16. Mt 13:44-46. Ep 3:8.

JOD

73 **Thy hands**. Ps 100:3. 138:8. 139:14-16. Jb 10:8-11.

give me. ver. 34, 125, 144, 169. Ps 111:10. 1 Ch 22:12. 2 Ch 2:12. Jb 32:8. Pr 2:3-6. 2 T 2:7. 1 J 5:20.

that I may. Ps 111:10. Ja 3:18. 1 J 2:3.

74 **fear thee**. ver. 79. Ps 34:2-6. 66:16. Ml +3:16.

glad when. Ro +15:7.

I have. ver. 42, 147. Ps 108:7. Ge 32:11, 12. Lk 21:33. Ro 15:4.

75 **I know**. ver. 7, 62, 128, 160. Le 10:3. Dt 32:4. Ezr 9:13. Jb 2:10. 34:23. Is 27:8. Je 12:1. La 3:39. Mi 7:18.

right. Heb. righteousness. ver. 137. Ps 145:17. Ge 18:25. Ex 9:27. Jg 1:7. 2 Ch 12:6. Je 10:24. Ro 3:4, 5. Ja +2:19.

thou in faithfulness. Ps 25:10. 39:9. 89:30-33. 94:11, 12. 107:43. Dt 8:16. 1 S 3:18.

16:10-12. 2 K 4:19, 20, 23, 26, 27. Jb 1:21. 13:15. Is 39:8. Je +29:11. 1 C 11:32. He 12:10, 11. Ja 5:11. 1 P 4:17, 19. Re 3:19.

afflicted me. ver. 67, 71. Ps 77:2, 7-10. 34:19. +90:15. 102:23mg. Ex 15:23-25. Ru +1:13. Ezr 9:13. Jb 11:6. 37:23. Is 27:9. 48:10. 64:12. La +3:33. Ho 2:6, 7, 14. Am 3:2. Na 1:12. Zc 13:9. Jn 15:2. 1 C 11:30, 31. He 12:6. Re 3:19.

76 **merciful**. Ps 86:5. 106:4, 5. 2 C 1:3-5.

for my comfort. Heb. to comfort me. Ge 37:35. 2 S 10:2. Is 66:13.

77 **thy tender**. ver. 41. Ex +34:6.

may live. Jn 10:10.

for thy. ver. 24, 47, 174. Ps 1:2. He 8:10-12.

78 **the proud**. ver. +21, 51, 85. Ps 35:26. 83:16-18.

dealt perversely. Ps 139:21. Mt 5:11, 12.

without. ver. 86. Ps 7:3-5. 25:3. 35:7. 69:4. 109:3. 1 S 24:10-12, 17. 26:18. Jn 15:24, 25. 1 P 2:20.

but I will. ver. 23. Ps 1:2.

79 **Let those**. ver. +63, 74. Ps 7:7. 133:1. 142:7. Est 10:3. Ac 2:46, 47. Ro 15:7. 1 C 11:1. 2 T 4:16. He 10:24. 3 J 11, 12.

turn. Ps 6:10. 7:12. 9:17. 18:37. Ga 6:2.

and those. ver. +63.

known. Ps 36:10. 37:18. 44:21.

80 **heart**. Ps 51:6. 95:10, 11.

sound. Ps 25:21. 32:2. Dt 26:16. 2 Ch 12:14. 15:17. 25:2. 31:20, 21. Pr +4:23. Ezk 11:19. Jn 1:47. 2 C 1:12. 1 T 4:16. 2 T 2:15. 4:3. Re 3:1, 2.

that I be. ver. 6. Ps 25:2, 3. 1 J 2:28.

CAPH

81 **soul**. Heb. *nephesh*, Ge +34:3.

fainteth. ver. 20, 40. Ps 42:1, 2. 73:26. 84:2. 106:4. 107:4-6. SS 5:8. Jon 2:7. Ph 1:23. Re 3:15, 16.

salvation. Ps 35:3. Ge 49:18. 2 S 23:5. Is 25:9. 1 Th 5:8.

but I hope in. ver. 42, 74, 77, 114, 147. Ro +15:4.

82 **Mine eyes**. ver. 123. Ps +69:3. Pr 13:12.

fail. La 2:11.

When wilt. Ps 86:17. 90:13-15. Is 8:17.

comfort. ver. 76. Ps 71:21. 86:17. 2 Th 2:16, 17.

83 **like a bottle in the smoke**. Ps 22:15. 102:3, 4. Jb 30:30.

yet do I. ver. 16, 61, 176.

84 **How**. Ps 39:4, 5. 89:47, 48. 90:12. Jb 7:6-8.

when. Ps 7:6. 2 Th 1:6. Re 6:10, 11.

85 **The proud**. ver. 78. Ps 7:15. +10:2. 35:7. Pr 16:27. Je 18:20.

which. Ps 58:1, 2.

86 **All thy**. ver. 128, 138, 142, 151. Ps 19:9. Ro 7:12.

faithful. Heb. faithfulness. ver. 30, 75, 90, 138mg.

they. ver. 78. Ps 7:1-5. 35:7, 19. 38:19. 59:3, 4. Je 18:20.

help. Ps 44:4-6. 70:5. 142:4-6. 143:9. 2 Ch 14:11, 12.

87 **almost**. 1 S 20:3. 23:26, 27. 2 S 17:16. Mt +10:28.

but I forsook not. ver. 51, 61. 1 S 24:6, 7. 26:9, 24.

88 **Quicken**. ver. 25, 40, 159. Col 3:3.

so shall I. ver. 2, 146. Ps 25:10. 78:5. 132:12. 2 C 3:5.

testimony. Jg 3:20. 1 S 3:9.

LAMED

89 **For ever**. Heb. *olam*, Ex +12:24. ver. 152, 160. Ps 89:2. Is 40:8. Je +33:20, 21, 25, 26. Ml 3:6. Mt 5:18. 24:34, 35. 1 P 1:25. 2 P 3:13.

thy word. Is 45:23. 1 P 1:25.

is settled. He 6:17-19.

in heaven. Ep 1:4.

90 **faithfulness**. Ps 89:1, 2. Dt 7:9. Mi 7:20.

unto all generations. Heb. to generation and generation. Ps +33:11mg.

thou hast. Ps 89:11. 93:1. 104:5. Jb 38:4-7. 2 P 3:5-7.

established. Ps 8:3. 9:7. 40:2.

abideth. Heb. standeth. Ps 10:1. 33:9. 38:11. 76:7. 78:69. 104:5. Ec +1:4. He 1:3.

91 **They continue this**. Ps 148:5, 6. Ge +8:22. Is 48:13. Je +33:25, 26.

according to. Ps 148:8. Jb 37:11, 12.

ordinances. Jb +38:33.

all are. Ge +50:20. Dt 4:19. Jsh 10:12, 13. Jg 5:20. Mt 5:45. 8:9.

92 **thy law**. ver. 24, 77, 143. Ro 15:4.

my delights. Jb 23:12. Je +15:16.

I should. Ps 27:13. 94:18, 19. Pr 6:22, 23.

93 **will never**. ver. 16, 50. Jn 8:31.

with them. Jn 6:63. 1 P 1:23.

thou hast. 1 C 3:7. Ph 2:13.

quickened. ver. +50. Jn 6:63. Ro 10:17. He 4:12. Ja +1:18.

94 **I am thine**. ver. 125. Ps 4:3. 74:2. 86:2. 143:12. Dt 32:9. Jsh 10:4-6. Is 41:8-10. 43:1, 10-12. 44:2, 5, 21, 22. 64:8-10. Zp 3:17. Ml 3:17. Lk 11:21, 22. Jn 6:37. 10:29. 17:6-11. Ac 20:28. 27:23, 24. Ro 6:16. 8:7-9. 1 C 3:23. 6:19, 20. Ep 2:10.

save me. ver. 146. Ps 3:7. 6:4. 7:1. 54:1. 69:1. 71:2. 80:2, 3. 86:2mg, 16. 106:47. 109:26. 118:25. 1 Ch 16:35. Je 17:14. Mt 8:25. 14:30.

for I have. ver. 27, 40, 173. Jn 10:27, 28.

sought. ver. 10, 45, 155. Ps +34:4. 109:10. Is 34:16. Jn +5:39. He 11:6.

95 **wicked**. ver. 61, 69, 85-87. Ps 10:8-10. 27:2. 37:32. 38:12. 1 S 23:20-23. 2 S 17:1-4. Zc 2:8. Mt 26:3-5. Lk 21:17-19. Ac 12:11. 23:21. 25:3.

but I. ver. 24, 31, 111, 125, 129, 167.

96 **I have seen**. Ps 39:5, 6. 1 S 9:2. 17:8, 49-51. 31:4, 5. 2 S 14:25. 16:23. 17:23. 18:14, 17. Ec 1:2, 3. 2:11. 7:20. 12:8. Mt 5:18. 24:35. Ph 3:6, 7. Ja 2:10.

but thy. Ps 19:7, 8. Pr 24:9. Mt 5:18, 28. 22:37-40. 24:35. Mk 12:29-34. Jn 6:28, 29. Ro 7:7, 9, 12, 14. Ga 3:13. He 4:12, 13. 1 J 3:23.

broad. ver. 45. Ge 34:21. Jb 11:9. Is 22:18mg. 33:21mg. 51:28. Ezk 23:32. Ro 3:22.

MEM

97 **O how**. ver. 48, 113, 127, 159, 165, 167. Ps 1:2. 138:2. Dt 6:6-9. 17:18, 19. Jsh 1:8. 1 K 22:8. Pr 2:10. 18:1.

meditation. ver. 99. Jb 15:4. 1 T 4:15.

98 **Thou**. Ps 25:12.

through. ver. 104. Dt 4:6, 8. 1 S 18:5, 14, 15, 30. Pr 2:6. Col 3:16.

wiser. Ps 105:22. Jb 35:11.

they are ever. Heb. it is ever. ver. 11, 30, 105. Ja 1:25.

ever. Heb. *olam*, Ps +5:11.

99 **understanding**. Jb 32:8.

than all. Dt 4:6, 8. 2 S 15:24-26. 1 Ch 15:11-13. 2 Ch 29:15, etc. 30:22. Je 2:8. 8:8, 9. Mt 11:25. 13:11. 15:6-9, 14. 23:24, etc. Lk 2:46, 47. He 5:12.

teachers. Ps 18:34. 94:10. 144:1.

for thy. ver. 24. 2 T 3:15-17.

100 **understand**. 1 S 3:19. 1 K 12:6-15. Jb 12:12. 15:9, 10. 32:4, 10.

the ancients. Ps +105:22. 107:32. 148:12. Jb 32:9. Ec 4:13.

because. Ps 111:10. Jb 28:28. Is 64:5. Je 8:8, 9. Mt 7:24. Jn 7:17. 14:21-23. Ja 3:13.

101 **refrained**. ver. 59, 60, 104, 128. Ps 18:23. 139:24. Pr 1:15. 10:23. 16:17. Is 53:6. 55:7. Je 2:36. Ro 12:9. 1 C 9:25. 2 C 7:1. Ga 5:23. 1 Th 5:22. T 2:11, 12. 1 P 2:1, 2. 3:10, 11. 2 P 1:6.

keep. Pr 7:2. Lk +11:28.

102 **departed**. Ps 18:21. 86:11. Dt 17:20. Jsh 23:6. 1 K 15:5. Pr 5:7. Je 17:5. 32:40.

for thou. Ps 27:11. 32:8. 86:11. 1 K 8:36. Is 30:20. 54:13. Je 31:33. Jn 6:45. Ep 4:20-24. 1 Th 2:13. 1 J 2:20, 27.

103 **sweet**. Ps 19:10. 56:10. 63:5. Jb 23:12. Pr 3:17. 8:11. 24:13, 14. SS 1:2-4. 5:1. Je 15:16.

taste. Heb. palate. Ps 137:6. Jb +31:30mg.

honey. Ps 19:10. 34:8. 81:16. Ge 43:11. Pr 24:13, 14. 27:7. 2 C 2:14.

104 **Through**. ver. 98, 100.

precepts. ver. 4, 15, 27, 35, 40, 45, 56.

get understanding. ver. 130. Ps 19:7. Pr 2:10, 11. 8:9. 16:21. Lk 24:32, 45. He 6:1. 2 P 3:18.

therefore. ver. 128. Pr +8:13. 13:5.

false way. ver. 29, 30, +128. Ps 49:13. Pr

14:12. Je 44:4. Mt 7:13. Ep 5:11, 12. 1 Th
5:22. 2 Th 2:10-12. 2 J 9-11.

NUN

105 **word**. Ps 19:8. 43:3. Pr 6:23. Ep 5:13. 2 P
1:19.
lamp. *or, candle*. Ps +18:28mg. Jb 29:3mg. Pr
6:23mg.
a light. ver. 130. Ps 4:6. 27:1. 36:9. 37:6.
38:10. Is 8:20. Mt 5:14. Jn 1:9. 1 J 1:5.
path. ver. 9. Ps 17:4. 142:3. Jg 5:6. Jb 19:8.
24:13.

106 **sworn**. Nu +30:2. 2 Ch 15:13, 14. Ne 10:29.
Je 50:5. Mt 5:33. 2 C 8:5.
that I will. ver. 115. 2 K 23:3.

107 **afflicted**. Ps 6:1-3. 22:14-18. 34:19. Ro 5:3-5.
2 C 4:17.
quicken. ver. 25, 88. Ps 71:20. 143:11. Hab
3:2. Jn 5:21. 6:63.

108 **Accept**. Ps 19:14. 50:14.
freewill offerings. Le +23:38.
of my mouth. Ps 69:30, 31. Ho 14:2. He
13:15.
teach. ver. 12, 26, 130, 169.

109 **My soul**. Heb. *nephesh*, Ge +12:13. Jg 12:3. 1
S 19:5. 20:3. Jb 13:14. Ro 8:36. 1 C 15:31. 2 C
1:9. 11:23.
yet do I not. ver. 61, 83, 93, 117, 141, 153,
176. Ja 1:22-25. 2 P 1:12.

110 **wicked**. ver. 85. Ps 10:8-18. +141:9. Pr 1:10-
15.
snare. ver. +128. Ex +23:33. Mt 24:4. 2 C
11:13-15.
yet I erred not. ver. 10, 21, 51, 87, 95. Da
6:10. Mk 12:24. Lk 20:19-26. Ep 4:14. Col
1:23. 2:7.

111 **Thy testimonies**. ver. 14, 127, 162. Ps 16:5,
6. Dt 33:4. Is 54:17. Ac 26:18. Col 1:12. He
9:15. 1 P 1:4.
heritage. Ps 61:5. Is 54:17.
for ever. Heb. *olam*, Ex +12:24. 1 P 1:25.
for they. ver. 77, 92, 174. Ps 19:8. Je 15:16. 1
P 1:8.

112 **inclined**. ver. 36. Ps 141:4. Jsh 24:23. 1 K
8:58. 2 Ch 19:3. Pr 4:23. Ph 2:12, 13.
perform. Heb. do. Dt 4:13. Jn +13:17.
alway. Heb. *olam*, Ge +6:3.
the end. ver. 33, 44. 1 P 1:13. Re 2:10.

SAMECH

113 **hate**. Ps 94:11. Pr 24:9. Is 55:7. Je 4:14. Mk
7:21. 2 C 10:5.
vain thoughts. 1 K 18:21mg. Je 23:26, 28.
Ja 1:8.
thy law. ver. 97, 103.

114 **my hiding place**. Ps +32:7.
my shield. Ps +84:11.
I hope. ver. 81. Ps 130:5, 6.

115 **Depart**. Ps +6:8. 26:5, 9. 1 C 15:33. 2 C 6:14,
17.
for I will. ver. 106. Jsh 24:15.

116 **Uphold**. Ps 37:17, 24. 41:12. 63:8. 94:18. Dt
33:25. Is 41:10. 42:1.
and let me. Ps 25:2. Is 45:17. Ro 5:5. 9:33.
10:11. 1 P 2:6.
ashamed. Ps +25:2.

117 **Hold**. Ps 17:5. 37:17. 51:12. 71:5, 6. 73:2, 23.
139:10. 145:14. SS 8:5. Is 41:10, 13. Jn 10:28,
29. Ro 14:4. 1 P 1:5. Ju 24.
and I will. ver. 6, 48, 111, 112.

118 **trodden**. Is 25:10. 63:3. Ml 4:3. Lk 21:24. Re
14:20.
err. ver. 10, 21. Ps 95:10. Dt 29:18-20. Mk
12:24, 27.
their deceit. ver. 29. Ps 78:36, 37, 57. Is
44:20. Ep 4:22. 5:6. 2 Th 2:9-11. 2 T 3:13. 1 J
2:21. Re 18:23.

119 **puttest away**. Heb. causest to cease. 1 S
15:23. Je 6:30. Ezk 22:18-22. Ml 3:2, 3. Mt
3:12. 7:23. 13:40-42, 49, 50.
like dross. Pr 25:4. 26:23. Is 1:22.
therefore. ver. 111, 126-128.

120 **My flesh**. ver. 53. Le 10:1-3. 1 S 6:20. 2 S
6:8, 9. 1 Ch 21:16, 17, 30. Da 10:8-11. He
12:21, 28, 29. 1 J 4:18. Re 1:17, 18.
trembleth. ver. 161. Is +66:2.
am afraid. Ps 37:32, 33. Ro 8:1, 33, 34. 2 C
1:12. 1 J 3:21.

AIN

121 **I have**. Ps 7:3-5. 18:18-25. 75:2. 1 S 24:11-15.
25:28. 2 S 8:15. Ac 24:16. 25:10, 11. 2 C 1:12.
leave me. Ps 37:33. 57:3, 4. Lk 18:7, 8. 2 P
2:9.

122 **surety**. Ge 43:9. Pr 22:26, 27. Is 38:14. Phm
18, 19. He 7:22.
let not. ver. +21. Ps +10:2.
oppress. Le +19:13. Dt 24:14, 15.

123 **Mine eyes fail**. ver. +82. Ps 22:1. +69:3.
130:6. 143:7.

124 **Deal**. ver. 76, +77, 132. 2 T 1:16-18.
teach. ver. 12, 26. Ps 143:10-12. Ne 9:20.

125 **I am thy**. ver. 94. Ps 86:16. 116:16. Ro 6:22.
give. ver. 34, 66. 2 Ch 1:7-10. 2 C 3:5, 6. 2 T
2:7. Ja 1:5. 3:13-17.
that I. ver. 11, 18, 19, 29. Pr 9:10. 14:8.

126 **time**. Ps 9:19. 102:13. Ge 6:3. 22:10, 11, 14.
Dt 32:36. Is 42:14. Ezk 9:4.
to work. Is 28:21. Je 18:23. Ml 3:17. Ro
+12:19. 1 P 4:17.
they. Je 8:8. Hab 1:4. Ml 2:8. Mt 15:6. Ro
3:31. 4:14.

127 **I love**. ver. 72. Ps 19:10. Pr 3:13-18. 8:11.
16:16. Mt 13:45, 46. Ep 3:8.

128 **Therefore**. ver. 104. Ps +9:10.
I esteem. ver. 6. Ps 19:7, 8. Dt 4:8. Jb 33:27.
Pr 30:5. Ro 7:12, 14, 16, 22.

all things. Lk 1:6. 2 C 7:1. Ph 1:9, 10. 2 T
3:16, 17. Ja 2:10.
right. Pr 3:6 (direct). 11:5. 15:21. Is 45:2,
13mg.
and I. ver. 104, 118.
false way. ver. +63, 101, 104. Ps 1:6. Pr
14:12. Je 10:2. Lk +6:46. 16:15. Jn 3:19. 5:23,
43. 1 C 6:9-11. 12:3. 2 C 6:14-18. Ga 5:16-21.
Ep 4:14. 5:3-7, 11, 12. He 10:25, 26. 1 J 1:10.
2:15-17. 2 J 9-11. Ju 3, 23.

PE

129 **testimonies**. ver. 18. Ps 139:6. Is 9:6. 25:1.
Ro 11:33. Re 19:10.
doth. ver. 2, 31, 146. Ps 25:10.
soul. Heb. *nephesh*, Ge +34:3.
130 **entrance**. ver. 105. Pr 6:23. Is 8:20. Lk 1:77-
79. Ac 26:18. 2 C 4:4, 6. Ep 5:13, 14. Ph 2:15,
16. 2 P 1:19.
it giveth understanding. Ps 19:7. Pr 1:4,
22, 23. 8:8, 9. 9:4-6. Ro 16:18, 19. 2 T 3:15-
17.
simple. Ps 19:7. 116:6. Pr +1:4. Mt 11:25.
131 **opened**. ver. 20. Ps 42:1. Is 26:8, 9. 1 P 2:2.
and panted. Is +42:14mg.
I longed. ver. 40, 162, 174. He 12:14.
132 **Look**. ver. 124. Ps 25:18. Ex 4:31. 1 S 1:11. 2
S 16:12. Is 63:7-9.
as thou usest to do unto those. Heb.
according to the custom toward those. Ps
22:4, 5. 71:4-6. 86:17. 106:4. Ge 19:19. Nu
14:19. 1 K 8:51-53. Da 9:15, 18. Jn 14:21, 23.
2 Th 1:6, 7.
133 **Order**. ver. 116. Ps 17:5. +32:8. 121:3. 1 S
2:9.
let not. Ps 19:13. Ro 6:12-14. 7:23, 24.
134 **Deliver**. ver. 121, 122. Ps 17:8, 9. 44:24, 25.
56:1, 2, 13. 105:43-45. Jg 4:3. 10:7-10. Is
19:19, 20. 38:14. Ezk 11:17-20. 36:24-27. Lk
1:74, 75. Jn 8:36. Ac 9:31.
oppression. Ex +2:23. 2 Ch +6:37. Is 19:20.
38:14. 1 T 2:2.
135 **Make**. Ps 4:6. 80:1, 3, 7, 19. Nu 6:25, 26. Jb
33:26. Re 22:4, 5.
and teach. ver. 12, 26. Jb 34:32. 35:11.
36:22. Lk 24:45. Jn 14:26. 2 C 4:6. He 8:10.
136 **Rivers**. ver. 53, 158. Ps 126:6. 1 S 15:11. Je
9:1, 17, 18. 13:17. 14:17. La 1:16. 2:11, 18,
19. 3:48, 49. Ezk 9:4. 21:6. Lk +6:21. 19:41.
Ro 9:2, 3. 1 C 5:2. 2 C 2:4. Ph 3:18.
because. Dt 9:18. Ezr 9:2, 3. Mk 3:5. 2 P 2:7.

TZADDI

137 **Righteous**. Ps 99:4. 103:6. 145:17. Dt 32:4.
Ezr 9:15. Ne 9:33. Is 45:21. Je 12:1. Da 9:7,
14. Ro 2:5. 3:5, 6. 9:14. Re 15:3, 4. 16:7. 19:2.
138 **testimonies**. ver. 86, 144. Ps 19:7-9. Dt 4:8,
45.

righteous. Heb. righteousness. ver. 75mg, 172.
faithful. Heb. faithfulness. ver. 75, 86mg.
139 **zeal**. Ps 69:9. 1 K 19:10, 14. Is 59:17. Jn 2:17.
Ro 12:11. T 2:14. Re 3:16, 19.
consumed me. *or*, cut me off. Ps 18:40. 54:5.
88:16. 101:5, 8. 143:12. La 3:53.
because. Ps 53:4. Mt 9:13. 12:3-5. 15:4-6.
21:13, 16, 42. 22:29. Ac 13:27. 28:23-27.
140 **Thy word**. ver. 9. He 12:14.
pure. Heb. tried, *or* refined. ver. +128. Ps
12:6. 18:30. 19:8. Pr +30:5. Ro 7:12, 16, 22. 1
P 2:2. 2 P 1:21.
141 **small**. Ps 22:6. +40:17. Pr 15:16. 16:8. 19:1.
Is 53:3. Lk 6:20. 9:58. 2 C 8:9. 10:10. Ep 3:8.
Ja 2:5.
yet do. ver. 109, 176. Pr 3:1.
142 **Thy righteousness**. Pr 24:21. Da 7:25. Ml
3:6. Mt 5:18. Jn 10:35.
an everlasting. Heb. *olam*, Ge +17:7.
righteousness. ver. 144. Ps 36:6. Is 51:6, 8.
Da 9:24. 2 Th 1:6-10.
and thy. ver. 151. Ps 19:9. Jn 17:17.
Ep 4:21.
143 **Trouble**. ver. 107. Ps 18:4, 5. 88:3, etc. 116:3.
130:1. Mk 14:33, 34.
taken hold on me. Heb. found me. Ps 116:3.
2 K +9:21mg.
yet thy. ver. 16, 47, 77. Jb 23:12. Jn 4:34.
16:33. Ro 15:4.
144 **righteousness**. ver. 138, 152. Mt 5:18. 1 P
1:23-25.
everlasting. Heb. *olam*, Ge +17:7.
give me. ver. 34, 66, 73, 169. 2 C 4:6. 1 J
5:20, 21.
understanding. Pr 10:21. Is 6:9, 10. 27:11.
Je 4:22. 9:23, 24. Da 12:10. Ho 4:6. Mt 13:19.
Jn 17:3. Ja 1:5.
shall live. 1 P 1:23.

KOPH

145 **cried**. ver. 10. Ps 61:1, 2. 62:8. 86:4. 102,
title. 141:1, 2. 142:1, 2. 1 S 1:10, 15. 1 S +7:8.
Je 29:13. Lk +18:1.
whole heart. ver. 58. Ps 5:1-3. 17:1, 6.
19:14. 20:9. 22:2, 19. 27:7, 8. 28:1, 2. 38:9.
39:12. 55:1, 2, 16, 17. 57:2. 61:2. 84:8. 88:1,
2, 9, 13. 102:1, 2. 130:1, 2. Ge 18:32. 32:26.
Ex 32:32. Dt 9:25. Jg 6:39. 16:28. 1 S 1:10.
Ezr 9:5. Ne 1:6. Is 62:1, 6, 7. 64:12. Je 29:13.
Da 9:3. Ho 12:3, 4. Jon 1:14. Mt 15:23. 20:31.
Lk 18:7. Ac 12:5. Ro 8:26. 2 C 12:8. Ja +5:17.
I will. ver. 44, 106, 115.
146 **and I shall keep**. *or*, that I may keep. ver.
134. Jg 10:15, 16. Mt 1:21. T 2:14. 3:4-8.
147 **I prevented**. Ps +5:3. 21:3. 42:8. 88:13.
130:6. 139:17, 18. Ge +22:3. Is 26:9. Mk
+1:35.
dawning. Ge 32:24. 1 S 30:17. 2 K 7:5. Jb
3:9.

and cried. Lk 6:12. Ju 20.
hoped. ver. +49, 74, 81. Ps 56:4.

148 **eyes**. ver. 62. Ps 63:1, 6. 139:17, 18. La 2:19.
Lk 6:12.
the night watches. Ps 63:6. 90:4. Ex 14:24.
Mk 6:48.

149 **Hear**. Ps 5:2, 3. 55:2. 64:1.
according unto. Ps 51:1, 69:16. 109:21. Is
63:7. Jn 10:10. Ro 8:32.
quicken me. ver. 25, 40, 154, 156. Is 30:18.

150 **draw nigh**. Ps 22:11-13, 16. 27:2. 1 S 23:26.
2 S 17:16. Mt 26:46, 47.
far from. Ps 50:17. Jb 21:14. Pr 1:7, 22. 28:9.
Ep 2:13, 14.

151 **near**. Ps 46:1. 75:1. 139:2. 145:18. Dt 4:7. Mt
1:23. Jn 16:32. Ep 2:13. Ph 4:5.
all. ver. 138, 142.

152 **thy testimonies**. ver. 144, 160. Ps 89:34-37.
111:7, 8. Ec 3:14. Lk 21:33.
of old. Mi +5:2.
founded. Ps 104:5.
for ever. Heb. *olam*, Ex +12:24.

RESH

153 **Consider**. ver. 159. Ps +9:13. Ex 3:7, 8.
affliction. Ps 25:16-18. 44:22-25. 106:43, 44.
107:17-19. Dt 26:6, 7. 1 S 26:24. 2 K 4:18-22.
2 Ch 33:11-13. Jb 1:20-22. 34:28. Mt 26:38,
39. 2 C 12:7, 8.
deliver. ver. 154. Ps 91:14, 15.
for I. ver. 16, 98, 109, 141, 176.

154 **Plead**. Ps 35:1. 43:1. 1 S 24:15. Jb 5:8. Pr
22:23. Je 11:20. 50:34. 51:36. Mi 7:9. 1 P
2:23. 1 J 2:1.
quicken. ver. 25, 40.

155 **Salvation**. Ps 73:27. 85:9. Jb 5:4. Is 46:12.
57:19. Lk 16:26. Ep 2:12, 13, 17, 18.
for they. Ps 10:4, 5. Jb 21:14, 15. Pr 1:7. Lk
16:24. Ro 3:11.

156 **Great**. Heb. Many. ver. 157, 162, 165.
are thy. Ex +34:6.
quicken. ver. 149.

157 **Many**. Ps 3:1, 2. 22:12, 16. 25:19. 56:2.
118:10-12. Mt 13:20, 21. 24:9. 26:47. Ac
4:27.
yet do I. ver. 51, 110. Ps 44:17. Jb 17:9.
23:11. Is 42:4. Ac 20:23, 24. 1 C 15:58.

158 **beheld**. ver. 53, 136. Ezk 9:4. Mk 3:5.
was grieved. ver. 136. Ps +79:9. Ezr 9:2-5.
10:6. Ezk 9:4. Ac 17:16. Ro 9:1-3. 2 P 2:7, 8.
kept not. 2 Ch 19:2. Is 8:20. Ep 5:6.

159 **Consider**. ver. 97, 153. 2 K 20:3. Ne 5:19.
13:22. Jb 1:8. Mt 5:6.
quicken. ver. 88.

160 **Thy word is true from the beginning**.
Heb. The beginning of thy word is true. ver.
86, 89, 90, 138. Pr +22:21. 30:5. Jn 17:17. 2 T
3:16.
and every one. ver. 75, 142, 144, 152. Ec

3:14. Mt 5:18.
for ever. Heb. *olam*, Ex +12:24.

SCHIN

161 **Princes**. ver. 23, 157. 1 S 21:23. 24:9-15.
26:18. Jn 15:25. 2 T 3:12. 1 P 3:17.
my heart. Ps 4:4. Ge 39:9. 42:18. 2 K 22:19.
Ne 5:15. Jb 31:23. Is +66:2. Je 36:23-25.

162 **rejoice**. ver. 72, 111. Je 15:16.
as one. 1 S 30:16. Pr 16:19. Is 9:3. Mt 13:45,
46.

163 **hate**. ver. 29, 113, 128. Ps 101:7. Pr +8:13.
26:25. 30:8. Ep +4:25.

164 **Seven times**. ver. 62. Ps 55:17. Jb 5:19. Pr
24:16. Da 6:10. Mt 18:21. Lk 17:4.
praise. Ps 34:1.
because. Ps 48:11. 97:8. Re 15:3. 19:2.

165 **Great peace**. Ps 29:11. 125:5. 147:14. Ge
+43:23. Le 26:6. Pr 3:1, 2, 13, 17. 16:7. Ga
6:15, 16. Ph +4:7.
nothing shall offend them. Heb. they shall
have no stumbling block. Is 8:13-15. 28:13.
57:14. Ezk 3:20. Mt 13:21. 24:24. 1 P 2:6-8.

166 **Lord**. ver. +49, 81, 174. Ge 49:18. 1 J 3:3.
and done. Ps 4:5. 24:3-5. 50:23. Jn 7:17. 1 J
2:3, 4.

167 **soul**. Heb. *nephesh*, Ge +34:3.
hath kept. ver. 5-8, 97, 111, 159. Jn 14:21-
24. 15:9, 10. He 10:17.
and I love. Ps 40:8. Ro 7:22.

168 **for all my**. Ps 44:20, 21. 90:8. 139:3. Jb
34:21. Pr 5:21. Je 23:24. He 4:13. Re 2:23.

TAU

169 **Let my cry**. ver. 145. Ps 18:6. 2 Ch 30:27.
give me. ver. 144. 1 Ch 22:12. 2 Ch 1:10. Pr
2:3-5, 7. Da 2:21. Ja 1:5.

170 **deliver me**. ver. 41. Ps 89:20-25. Ge 32:9-12.
2 S 7:25.

171 **My lips**. ver. 7. Ps 50:23. 71:17, 23, 24.

172 **tongue**. ver. 13, 46. Ps 37:30. 40:9, 10. 78:4.
Dt 6:7. Mt 12:34-36. Ep 4:29. Col 4:6.
speak. Jb +3:1.
for all thy. ver. 86, 138, 142, 144. Ro 7:12,
14.

173 **Let**. ver. 94, 117. Is 41:10-14. Mk 9:24. Jn
15:5. 2 C 12:9. Ep 6:10, etc. Ph 4:13.
hand. 1 Ch 4:10. Is 41:13.
I have chosen. ver. 30, 35, 40, 111. Dt 30:19.
Jsh 24:15, 22. 1 K 3:11, 12. Pr 1:29. Is +66:4.
Lk 10:42.

174 **longed**. ver. 81, 166. Ge 49:18. 2 S 23:5. Pr
13:12. SS 5:8. Mt +5:6. Ro 7:22-25. 8:23-25.
Ph 1:23.
and thy law. ver. 16, 24, 47, 77, 111, 162,
167. Ps 1:2.

175 **Let my**. Ps 9:13, 14. 30:9. 51:14, 15. 118:18,
19. Is 38:19.

soul. Heb. *nephesh*, Ge +12:13.
praise. 1 P 1:3.
and let thy. ver. 75. Is 26:8, 9. Ro 8:28. 1 C 11:31, 32. 2 C 4:17.

176 **gone astray**. Ps 51:7-12. Is +53:6. Je +14:7, 8, 9. 31:18, 19. Ezk 34:16. Ho 14:2-4. Mt 10:6. 15:24. Lk 22:61, 62. Jn 10:16. Ja 5:16. 1 P 2:25.
seek. SS 1:4. Je 31:18. Lk 19:10. Jn 10:27, 28. Ga 4:9. Ph 2:13. Ja 1:17.
for I do. ver. 61, 93. Ho 4:6.

PSALM 120

(*Title*.) **A Song of degrees**. Ps 121-134, titles.

1 **my distress**. Ps 30:7, 8. 50:15. 116:3, 4. Ne +9:37. Is 37:3, 4, 14, etc. 38:2-5. Lk 22:44. He 5:7.

2 **Deliver**. 2 T 4:18.
soul. Heb. *nephesh*, Ge +12:13. Nu +23:10. Mt +12:18.
from lying lips. Ps 5:6. 35:11. 52:2-4. 109:1, 2. 140:1-3. Mt 26:59-62. Re 21:8.

3 **What shall**, etc. *or*, What shall the deceitful tongue give unto thee? *or*, What shall it profit thee? Jb 27:8. Mt 16:26. Ro 6:21.
done. Heb. added. Ps 10:18 (more). 41:8. 61:6mg. 77:7. Pr 3:2.
false tongue. Ps 7:11-13. Ja 3:6.

4 **Sharp**, etc. *or*, It is as the sharp arrows of the mighty man, with coals of juniper. Ps 57:4. 59:7. Pr 11:9. 12:18. 16:27. 18:8, 21. Ja 3:5-8.
arrows. Ps 7:13. 52:5. 140:9-11. Dt 32:23, 24. Pr 12:22. 19:5, 9. Re 21:8.

5 **Woe**. Je 9:2, 3, 6. 15:10. Mi 7:1, 2. 2 P 2:7, 8. Re 2:13.
Mesech. i.e. *selection*, **S#4902h**. Ge +10:2, Meshech.
the tents. Ge +25:13. 1 S 25:1.

6 **soul**. Heb. *nephesh*, Ge +27:31.
dwelt. Ps 57:4. 1 S 20:30-33. Ezk 2:6. Mt 10:16, 36. Jn 15:18. T 3:3.

7 **am for**. or, am. Ps 109:4.
peace. *or*, a man of peace. Ps +34:14. 35:20. 55:20. 2 S 20:19. Ep 2:14-17.
when. 1 S 24:9-11. 26:2-4.

PSALM 121

(*Title*.) **A Song**. Ps 120, title.

1 **I will**, etc. *or*, Shall I lift up mine eyes to the *hills?* whence should my help come? Je 3:23. **lift up**. Ps 2:6. 68:15, 16. 78:68. 87:1. 123:1. Is 2:3. Ezk 18:6, 15.

2 **My help**. Ps 46:1. 124:8. 146:5, 6. Is 40:28, 29. 41:13. Je 20:11. Ho 13:9. He 13:6.

3 **will not suffer**. Ps 91:12. 1 S 2:9. Pr 2:8. 3:21, 23, 25, 26. 1 P 1:5.
thy foot. Ps 66:9.
slumber. Ps 76:5.

4 **he that**. Ps 27:1. 32:7, 8. 127:1. Is 27:3.
shall. Ps 127:2. 1 K 18:27. Ec 8:16. Re 7:15.
slumber. Is 5:27.

5 **The Lord is**. Nu 14:9. Pr 3:24.
thy shade. Ps +91:1. Ex 13:21. 33:23. Mt 23:37. Lk 1:35.
upon. Ps 16:8. 109:31.

6 **The sun**. Ps 91:5-10. Is 49:10. Re 7:16.

7 **preserve**. Ps 91:9, 10. 1 Ch 4:10. Jb 5:19, etc. Pr 12:21. Mt 6:13. Ro 8:28, 35-39. 2 T 4:18.
he shall. Ps 34:22. 41:2. 97:10. 145:20.
soul. Heb. *nephesh*, Ge +12:13.

8 **thy going out**. Nu +27:17. Dt 28:6, 19. 2 S 5:2. Ezr 8:21, 31. Pr 2:8. 3:6. Jn 10:9. Ja 4:13-16.
from this time. Ps 113:2. 115:18.
for evermore. Heb. *olam*, Ps +18:50.

PSALM 122

(*Title*.) **A Song of degrees**. Ps 120-134, titles.

1 **I was glad**. Ps 42:4. 55:14. 63:1-3. 84:1, 2, 10. 119:111.
Let us go. Is 2:3. Je 31:6. 50:4, 5. Mi 4:2. Zc 8:21-23. He 10:25.

2 **Our feet**. Ps 84:7. 87:1-3. 100:4. Ex 20:24. Dt 12:5, 14. 2 Ch 6:6.

3 **Jerusalem is builded**. 2 S 5:9. Ep 2:20, 21. 4:4-7. Re 21:10, etc.
as. Ge +25:31.
compact. Is 62:3. Je 31:38-40. Zc 14:10. Ac 4:32. Re 22:1, 2.

4 **Whither**. Ps 78:68. 132:13. Ex 23:17. 34:23, 24. Dt 12:5, 11. 16:16.
the testimony. Ex +16:34.
to give. Ps 66:13-16. 107:1-3. 116:17-19. 118:19.

5 **there**. Dt 17:8, 18. 2 S 15:2. 2 Ch 19:8.
are set. Heb. do sit. Ps 125:1. Jl 3:20.
the thrones. 2 S 8:18. 2 Ch 11:22. Is +2:3.

6 **Pray for**. Ps 51:18. 137:6, 7. Is 62:1, 6, 7. Je 51:50. Jn 17:20, 21.
the peace. ver. 7. Ro +5:1. Ep 4:3. 2 Th 3:16.
of Jerusalem. Ps 51:18. +147:2. Is +24:23. 52:9, 10. 65:18, 19. Da 9:16. Zc 1:12, 13.
they shall. Ge +12:3.
prosper. Ps +1:3.
that love. Jg +5:31. 1 J 3:14.

7 **Peace**. ver. +6. Ps 147:14. 1 Ch 12:18. Is 9:7. Ja 3:18.
within thy palaces. Ps 48:3.

8 **my brethren**. Ps 16:3. 42:4. +119:63. Ep 4:4-6. Ph 2:2-5. Ja 3:13-18.

9 **the house**. Ps 26:8. 69:9. 84:1, 2, 10. 1 Ch 29:3. Jn 2:17.
I will seek. Ps 102:13, 14. 137:5, 6. Ne 2:10. 13:14.

PSALM 123

(*Title.*) A.M. cir. 3463. B.C. cir. 541.
A Song of degrees. Ps 120-134, titles.

1 **lift I.** Ps 25:15. +121:1. 141:8. Ge +22:13. Lk 18:13.
   O thou. Ps 113:5, 6. Mt +6:9.

2 **as the eyes.** Jsh 9:23, 27. 10:6.
   look unto. Ps 27:8. 1 Ch 23:28. Mt 21:28. Lk 12:37.
   so our eyes wait. Ps +25:3. 32:8. 119:82, 123-125. Ge 32:26. 2 Ch 20:12. Lk 18:1. He 12:2.

3 **Have mercy.** Ps +4:1. 69:13-16. Lk 18:11-13.
   for we are. Ps 44:13-16. 89:50, 51. Ne 4:2-4. Is 53:3. Lk 16:14. 23:35.

4 **soul.** Heb. *nephesh,* Ge +34:3.
   with the scorning. Ps 73:5-9. 119:51. 1 S 17:42. Ne 4:2, 6. Jb 12:5. 16:4. Je 48:11, 27, 29. Ac 17:21, 32. 26:24. 1 C 4:13.
   at ease. Ezk +13:10. Am 6:1.
   contempt. Ps 80:6. 119:22. 1 S 17:28. Ne 2:19. 4:3. Mt 13:55. Jn 9:34.
   the proud. Ps +10:2.

PSALM 124

(*Title.*) **A Song.** Ps 120-134, titles.

1 **the Lord.** Ps 27:1. 46:7, 11. 54:4. 56:9, 118:6, 7. Ex 15:1. Is 8:9, 10. Ro 8:31. He 13:5, 6.
   now may. Ps 129:1.

2 **when men.** Ps 2:1, 2. 3:1. 22:12, 13, 16. 37:32. Nu 16:2, 3.

3 **Then they.** Ps 27:2. 74:8. 83:4. Est 3:6, 12, 13.
   swallowed. Ps +35:25. Jon 1:17.
   their wrath. Ps 76:10. 1 S 20:30-33. Da 3:19. Mt 2:16. Ac 9:2. 26:11.

4 **the waters.** Ps +93:3. Is 8:7, 8. 28:2. Da 9:26.
   soul. Heb. *nephesh,* Ge +12:13.

5 **the proud.** Ps 93:3, 4. Jb 38:11. Je 5:22.
   soul. Heb. *nephesh,* Ge +12:13.

6 **who hath not.** Ps 17:9-13. 118:13. 140:5, 6. Ex 15:9, 10. Jg 5:30, 31. 1 S 26:20. Is 10:14-19.

7 **Our soul.** Heb. *nephesh,* Ge +12:13.
   is escaped. 1 S 23:26, 27. 24:14, 15. 25:29. 2 S 17:2, 21, 22.
   as a bird. Ps 25:15. 91:3. Pr 6:5. Je 5:26. 18:22. 2 T 2:26.

8 **help.** Ps 121:2.
   made. Ps 115:15. 134:3. Jn +1:3. Ac 4:24.

PSALM 125

(*Title.*) A.M. 3468. B.C. 536. **A Song.** Ps 120-124, titles.

1 **that trust.** Ps 20:7. 21:7. 25:2, 3. 44:6. 62:2, 6. 147:11. 1 S 17:45. 1 Ch 5:20. Pr 3:5, 6. Is +26:3, 4. Ep 1:12, 13. 1 P 1:21. Re 3:12.
   be as mount. 1 Ch +11:5. Is 12:6. 14:32.

51:3, 11, 16. 52:1, 7, 8. Ob +21. Mi 4:2. Zc 1:14, 17.
   but abideth. Mt 16:16-18.

2 **As the mountains.** Is 54:10. La 4:12.
   round about. Ps 46:1-7. Pr 18:10. Is 43:2-6. 54:14, 17.
   the Lord. Ps 34:7. Dt 33:27. Is 4:5. Zc 2:5. Jn +10:28, 29.

3 **the rod.** Ps 103:9, 14. Pr 22:8. Is 9:4. 10:5. 14:5, 6. 27:8. 1 C 10:13. Re 2:10.
   the wicked. Heb. wickedness. Ps 5:4. 10:15. 45:7. 73:12-18. 89:22.
   rest. Ge 8:4. Ex 10:14. 20:11.
   lot. Ps +16:5. 22:18. 78:55. Le 16:8. Jsh +14:2.
   lest. Ps 103:14. Mt 24:22. 1 C 10:13. Ju 24.
   righteous. Ps 1:5. 5:12. 7:9. 11:3.
   put forth. Ps 18:14, 16. 20:2. 55:20. 57:3. 1 S 24:10. Ac 12:1.
   iniquity. Ps 37:1. 43:1mg. 89:22. 92:15. Ec 7:7.

4 **Do good.** Ps 41:1-3. 51:18. 73:1. Is 58:10, 11. Ep 6:18. He 6:10. 1 J 3:17-24.
   upright. Ps 32:2. 84:11, 12. 119:80. La 3:25. Jn 1:47. Re 14:5.

5 **As for such.** Ps 40:4. 101:3. 1 Ch 10:13, 14. Pr 14:14. Je 2:19. Zp 1:6. 1 C +15:2. He +10:38. 2 P 2:20, 21. 1 J 2:19.
   crooked. Jg 5:6mg. Pr 2:15. Is 59:8. Ph 2:15.
   lead them. Ps 106:9. Ex +9:16. 14:21. Dt +2:30. 1 S +18:10. Am +3:6. Ep +1:11.
   with the workers. Ps 5:5. 6:8. Mt 7:23. 24:48-51. He 10:26. 1 J 3:9. 5:18.
   peace. Je +29:7.

PSALM 126

(*Title.*) **A Song of degrees.** Ps 120-125, titles.

1 **turned again,** etc. Heb. returned the returning of Zion. Ps 53:6. 85:1. Ezr ch. 1. Jb 42:10. Je 31:8-10. Ho 6:11. Jl 3:1.
   we were like. Jb 9:16. Mk 16:11. Lk 24:11, 41. Ac 12:9, 14-16.

2 **Then was.** Ps 14:7. 53:6. 106:47, 48. 107:1, 2. 136:1. Ex 12:14. Ezr 3:11. Jb 8:21. Is 35:10. 49:9-13. Je 31:12, 13. 33:11. Re 11:15-17.
   laughter. Ge +21:6.
   then said. Nu 23:23. Jsh 2:9-11. 9:9, 10. Ne 6:16. Zc 8:22, 23. Ro 11:15.
   hath. Dt 16:13, 17. Zc 14:18.
   done great things for them. Heb. magnified to do with them. Ps 35:26. 38:16. 41:9mg. Je 48:26. Da +8:11. 11:36, 37. Jl 2:20mg. Zp 2:8, 10.

3 **great things.** Ps 18:50. 31:19. 66:5, 6. 68:7, 8, 22. Ezr 7:27, 28. Is 11:11-16. 12:4-6. 51:9-11. 52:9, 10. 66:14. Lk 1:46-49. Ep 1:18-22. Re 12:10. 19:1-7.

4 Turn again. ver. +1. Ps 85:4. Ho 1:11.
as the streams. Jsh 3:16. Is 41:18. 52:9, 10.

5 that sow. Ps 137:1. Jl 2:17, 23. Lk +6:21.
shall reap. Pr 11:18, 30. Is 66:8. Da 12:3. Mk 1:17. Lk 1:16. Jn 17:20. Ja 5:20.
joy. *or*, singing. Ps +30:5mg.

6 that goeth. Ps 30:5. Jb 11:13-17. Is 61:3. Je 50:4, 5. Ga 6:7, 8.
weepeth. Ps +119:136. Ac 20:31. 2 C 11:28. Ga 4:19. He +6:11. 13:17.
bearing. Ec 11:1.
precious seed. *or*, seed basket. **S#4901h**. Jb 28:18 (price). Am 9:13 (**S#4900h**).
shall doubtless. Is 9:2, 3. Lk 15:18-24. Ac 16:29-34. Re 7:15-17.
with rejoicing. 1 Th +2:19, 20. He +13:17.
bringing his sheaves. Pr +11:30. Da +11:33. +12:3.
with him. Mt 6:19, 20. Lk +16:9. Ph +4:17. He 10:34.

PSALM 127

(Title.) **A Song**. Ps 120-126, titles.
for Solomon. *or*, of Solomon. Ps 72, title.

1 Except the Lord. Ps 33:16-18. Pr 16:9. 21:30, 31. Ec 9:11. 1 C 3:6, 7.
build. 1 Ch 22:10, 11. 28:10, 20. 29:19. Ne 2:17. 1 C 3:9-15.
they labor. Ge 11:8, 9.
in vain. Ga +4:11.
that build it. Heb. that are builders of it in it. Ps 118:22. 147:2. 1 K 5:18.
except. Ps 121:3-5. Is 27:3. Zc 2:4, 5.
the watchman. SS 3:3. 5:7. Is 21:5-12. 56:10. 62:6. Je 51:12, 31. Ezk 33:2-9.

2 vain. Ps 39:5, 6. 121:4. Ec 1:14. 2:1-11, 20-23. 4:8.
rise up. Pr 31:15-18.
the bread. Ge 3:17-19. Ec 6:7.
so he. Ps 3:5. 4:8. Ge 32:24. Pr 10:22. Ec 5:12. Is 32:17, 18. Je 31:26. Ezk 34:25. Ac 12:5, 6.

3 children. Ps +113:9. 115:14. 128:3, 4. Ge 1:28. 4:1. 15:4, 5. 24:60. 30:1, 2. 33:5. 41:51, 52. 48:4. Dt 7:13. 28:4. 30:9. Jsh 24:3, 4. 1 S 1:19, 20, 27. 2:20, 21. 1 Ch 28:5. Jb 5:25. Is 8:18.
fruit. Ge +11:30. +29:31. Dt 7:14. Ru 4:13.

4 arrows. Je 50:9.
so are children. Pr 17:6. 31:28.

5 Happy. Ge 50:23. Jb 1:2. 42:12-16.
his quiver full of them. Heb. filled his quiver with them. Ps 107:9. Jb 29:23. Is 22:6. 49:2. Je 5:16. La 3:13.
they shall. Jb 5:4. Pr 27:11.
speak. *or*, subdue. Ps 18:47. *or*, destroy.
enemies. Ps 3:7. 6:10. 7:5. 8:2. 9:3. 13:2.
gate. Ps 9:13. 69:12. 87:2. Ge +14:7. +22:17.

PSALM 128

(Title.) **A Song of degrees**. Ps 120-127, titles.

1 every one. Pr +3:7.
walketh. Ps 1:1-3. 44:18. 81:13. 119:1, 3. Pr 8:32. Col +1:10.

2 thou shalt eat. Ps 58:11. Ge 3:19. Dt 28:4, 11, 39, 51. Jg 6:3-6. Ec +2:24. 5:18, 19. Is 62:8, 9. 65:13, 21-23.
labor. Dt +28:33. Pr 14:23. Lk 10:7.
happy. Ps 58:10. Dt 33:29. Pr 14:21. 16:20. 28:14. 29:18. Jn 13:17.
and it shall. Dt +4:40. Ps +1:3. Ec 8:12, 13. Je 22:15. 1 C 15:58. Ep +6:3.

3 a fruitful vine. Ge 49:22. Pr 5:15-18. Ezk 19:10.
olive plants. Ps 52:8. 144:12. Je 11:16. Ho 14:6, 7. Ro 11:24.
round about. Ps 127:5.

4 blessed. Ps 112:2. Jg 5:24.
feareth. Ps 111:10. Pr 1:7.

5 bless thee. Ps 20:2. 118:26. Ep 1:3.
out of Zion. Ps 20:2. 134:3. 135:21. Is +2:3. +24:23.
thou shalt see. Ps +122:6, 9. Is 33:20.

6 thou shalt see. Ps +102:28. Ge 50:23. Jb 42:16.
peace. Ps 125:5. Is 66:12. Ga 6:16.

PSALM 129

(Title.) A.M. 3470. B.C. 534. **A Song of degrees**. Ps 120-128, titles. This Psalm was most probably composed in consequence of the opposition of the Samaritans, Ezr ch. 4.

1 Many. *or*, Much. ver. 2. Ps 32:10. 34:19. 65:9.
have they. Ex 1:12-14, 22. 5:7-19. Jg 2:15. 10:8-12. 1 S 13:19. La 1:3.
from. Je 2:2. Ezk 23:3. Ho 2:15. 11:1.
may. Ps 124:1.

2 yet they have. Ps 34:19. 118:13. 125:1. Jb 5:19. Je 1:19. Mt 16:18. Jn 16:33. Ro 8:35-39. Re 12:8, 9.

3 The plowers. Ps 141:7. Is 51:23. Mi 3:12. Lk 22:63. Jn +19:1.

4 The Lord. Ezr 9:15. Ne 9:33. La 1:18. 3:22. Da 9:7. 2 Th 1:6, 7.
cut asunder. Ps 124:6, 7. 140:5-11. 2 P 2:9.

5 be confounded. Ps +71:13. 83:4-11. 122:6. Est 6:13. 9:5. Is 10:12. 37:22, 28, 29, 35. Zc 1:14-17. 12:3, 6. 1 C 16:22.

6 as the grass. Je 17:5, 6. Mt 13:6. 1 P +1:24.

7 he that bindeth. Ps 126:6. Is 17:10, 11. Ho 8:7. Ga 6:8.

8 The blessing. Ps 118:26. Ru 2:4.

PSALM 130

(Title.) A.M. cir. 3464. B.C. cir. 540. **A Song**. Ps 120-129, titles.

1 Out of. Ps 18:4-6, 16. 25:16-18. 40:1, 2. 42:7.

69:1, 2, 14, 15. 71:20. 88:6, 7. 116:3, 4. La 3:53-55. Jon 2:2-4. He 5:7.

2 **hear**. Ge +16:11.
let thine ears. Ps +5:1. +10:17. +17:6. 61:1, 2. 2 Ch 6:40. Ne 1:6, 11.

3 **shouldest mark**. Jb 10:14. Pr +20:9. Jn 8:7-9.

4 **forgiveness**. Ps 25:11. 32:1, 2. Ex +34:7. Is 1:18. 45:25. 55:7. Ro 8:1. 2 C 5:19. Ep 1:7. Col 1:14.
that thou mayest. Ps 2:11, 12. 1 K 8:39, 40. Je +5:22. Ac 9:31. 2 T 2:19. He 12:24-28.

5 **I wait**. Ps +25:3.
soul. Heb. *nephesh*, Ge +34:3.
and in his. Ps 119:42, 81. Ro +15:4.

6 **soul**. Heb. *nephesh*, Ge +34:3.
waiteth. Ps 63:1, 2, 5, 6. La 4:17. Ac 27:29. He +12:2.
I say more than they that watch for the morning. *or*, which watch unto the morning. Ps +119:147. 134:1. Is 21:8.

7 **Let Israel**. Ps 40:3. 71:5. 131:1, +3. Is 27:5. Zp 3:12.
for with. ver. 4. Ex +34:6. Ro 5:20, 21. 8:24. Ep 1:7, 8. 1 T 2:5, 6. He 10:35. 1 J 2:1, 2. Re 5:9.
plenteous. Ps +86:15.

8 **he shall redeem**. Ps 25:22. +34:22. Mt 1:21. Ro 6:14. 11:26. 1 J 3:5-8.
from all. Jb 5:24. Is +60:21. Je 31:31-34. 32:40. 50:20. Ezk 14:11. 36:27. Mi 7:19. Zp 3:13. Ro 11:26. 1 C 15:24-28. Re 21:3-7. 22:3.

PSALM 131

(*Title*.) A Song of degrees. Ps 122, 124, 133, titles.

1 **my heart**. Dt 17:20. 1 S 16:13, 18, 22. 17:15, 28, 29. 18:23. Mt +11:29. Ac 20:19. 1 Th 2:6, 7, 10.
neither. Ps 78:70-72. Je 17:16. 45:5. Am 7:14, 15. Ro 12:16.
exercise. Heb. walk. Ps +104:10mg.
high for me. Heb. wonderful for me. Ps 139:6. Jb 42:3. Ro 11:33.

2 **quieted**. Ps 42:5, 11. 43:5. 62:1mg. 1 S 24:10. 25:32, 33. 30:6. 2 S 15:25, 26. 16:11, 12. Is 30:15. La 3:26.
myself. Heb. my soul. *nephesh*, Ex +15:9. Lk 21:19. Jn 14:1, 2.
a child. Mt 18:3, 4. Mk 10:15. 1 C 14:20.
soul. Heb. *nephesh*, Ge +34:3.
weaned. 1 S +1:22.

3 **Let Israel**. Ps +42:11. 115:9-11.
from henceforth. Heb. from now. Ps 113:2. 115:18. Is 26:3, 4.
for ever. Heb. *olam*, Ex +12:24.

PSALM 132

(*Title*.) A.M. 2962. B.C. 1042. **A Song of degrees**. Ps 120-131, titles.

1 **remember**. Ps 25:6, 7. Ge 8:1. Ex 2:24. La 3:19. 5:1.
all his afflictions. 1 S ch. 18-30. 2 S ch. 15-20.

2 **he sware**. Ps 119:106. 2 S 7:1, 2. 2 Ch 15:12-15.
vowed. Le +23:38.
the mighty. ver. 5. Ge 49:24. Is +49:26. 60:16.

3 **I will not**. Ec 9:10. Hg 1:4. Mt 6:33.
go up. Ge 49:4. Ex 8:3. 2 K +1:16. Ec 10:20. Is 57:7.

4 **give sleep**. Ge 24:33. Ru 3:18. Pr 6:4.

5 **I find**. 2 S 6:17. 1 Ch 15:3, 12. Ac 7:46.
an habitation. Heb. habitations. 1 K 8:27. 2 Ch 2:6. Is 66:1. Ac 7:47-49. Ep 2:22.
for the mighty. ver. 2. Ps 46:11. 50:1. 146:5, 6.

6 **at Ephratah**. 1 Ch +2:50. Mi +5:2.
we found. 1 S 7:1. 1 Ch 13:5, 6. Jn 1:45.

7 **will go**. Ps 5:7. 66:13, 14. 118:19. 122:1. Is 2:3.
worship. Ps 95:6.
footstool. Is +66:1.

8 **Arise**. Ps +3:7.
the ark. Ps 62:7. 71:7. 78:61. 105:4.

9 **thy priests**. ver. 16. Ps 93:1. 104:1. Ex +28:2. Jb 29:14. Je 23:6. 1 C 1:30. 1 P 5:5.
let thy saints. Ps 35:26, 27. 68:3. 70:4. Jg 5:31.
shout. Ps 47:1. Ezr 3:11, 12. Is 65:14. Zp 3:14. Zc 9:9. 2 C 1:24.

10 **thy servant**. Ps 105:41, 42. Ex 32:13. Dt 9:27. 1 K 8:25. 11:12, 13, 34. 15:4, 5. 2 K 19:34. 2 Ch 6:16, 17, 42. Is 37:35. 42:1. Ho 3:5.
turn not. Ps 84:9. 89:38, 39. 2 Ch 6:42. Jn 11:42. 1 J 2:20.

11 **sworn**. Ps 110:4. 1 S 15:29. He 6:18.
unto David. Je 23:5. Ac 13:23. Ro 1:3.
not turn. Is +55:3. Ro 11:29.
Of the fruit. 2 S 7:12. 1 K 8:25. 2 Ch 6:16. Lk 1:69, 70. Ac 2:30.
body. Heb. belly. Dt 28:4, +11mg, 18. 30:9. Jb 19:17mg. Mi 6:7mg.
throne. 2 S 7:13.

12 **If**. Ge +4:7.
thy children. Ps 89:30-35.
teach them. Ps 25:12, 13.
their children. Ps 102:28. 115:14. Is 9:7. 59:21. Lk 1:32, 33.
thy throne. Re 3:21.
for evermore. Ps +9:18.

13 **the Lord**. Ps 76:1, 2. 78:68, 69. Is 14:32.
Zion. Ps 87:1, 2. Is +24:23. 56:7. 1 C 3:16. Ep 2:21.
he hath desired. Ps 48:1-3. 68:16. 87:2. 1 T 3:15.

14 **my rest**. ver. 8. Is 11:10. 66:1. Zp 3:16, 17.
for ever. Ps +9:18. Lk +1:32, 33.

here will. Ps 76:2. 135:21. Ex +29:45. Is 8:18. +24:23. Ezk 48:35. Re 21:23.
for I have. Ps 87:2.

15 **abundantly**. *or*, surely. Ge 2:17.
bless her provision. Ex 23:25. Le 26:4, 5. Dt 28:2-5. Pr 3:9, 10. Hg 1:6, 9. 2:16-19. Ml 2:2. Mt 14:19-21. 2 C 9:10, 11.
I will satisfy. Ps 22:26. +37:3. 149:4. Dt 14:29. Zc 11:7. Mt +5:6. Mk 8:6-9. Jn 6:57, 58.

16 **clothe**. ver. +9. Ps 149:4. 2 Ch 6:41.
with salvation. Ps 27:1. Lk 2:30.
her saints. Ho 11:12. Zc 9:9, 15-17. Jn 16:24.

17 **will I make**. Ps +92:10. Ezk 29:21.
I have ordained. 1 K 11:36. 15:4. 2 Ch 21:7. Lk 2:30-32.
lamp. *or*, candle. Ps +18:28mg. Ge 15:17. Lk 2:32.

18 **His enemies**. Ps 21:8, 9. 35:26. 109:29. Jb 8:22. Da 12:2. Lk 19:27.
but upon. Ps 72:8-11. Is 9:6, 7. 58:10-12. Mt 28:18. Lk 1:32, 33. Re +11:15. 17:14.

PSALM 133

(*Title*.) **A Song of degrees**. Ps 122, 124, 131, titles.

1 **how good**. Ps 122:6-8. Ge 45:24. 2 S 2:26, 27. Is 11:6-9, 13. Je 32:39. Jn 13:35. 17:21. Ro 12:9, 10. 13:8-10. 1 C 1:10. Ga 5:13, 14. Ep 5:1, 2. Ph 2:2-5. Col 2:2. 1 Th 3:12, 13. He +12:14. 13:1. 1 P 1:22. 3:8. 1 J 2:9-11. 3:10, 11, 14-19. 4:20, 21.
pleasant. Ps 45:8. SS 4:16.
together. Heb. even together.
unity. Mk 9:50.

2 **It is like**. Ps 141:5. Pr 27:9. SS 1:3. Jn 12:3.
ointment. Le 8:12, 30. 1 J 2:20.
that ran down. Ex +28:41.

3 **As the dew of Hermon**. Dt +3:8.
for there the Lord. Ps 42:8. Le 25:21. Dt 28:8.
even life. Ps 16:11. 21:4. Jn 4:14. 5:24, 29. 6:50, 51, 68. 11:25, 26. Ro 5:21. 6:23. 1 C 12:12, 13. Ga 5:22. 1 J 2:25. 5:11. Re 1:18.
for evermore. Heb. *olam*, Ps +18:50.

PSALM 134

(*Title*.) A.M. 3468. B.C. 536. **A Song of degrees**. Ps 120-133, titles.

1 **bless ye**. Ps 103:21. 135:1, 2, 19-21. 1 Ch 23:30-32. Re 19:5.
which by night. Ps 130:6. Le 8:35. 1 Ch 9:23, 33. Lk 2:37. Re 7:15.

2 **Lift up**. Ps +88:9.
in the sanctuary. *or*, *in* holiness. Ps 26:6. 1 T 2:8.

3 **Lord**. Ps 124:8. 146:5, 6.

bless thee. Ps 14:7. 20:2. 110:2. 128:5. 135:21. Nu 6:24. Ro 11:26.

PSALM 135

(*Title*.) A.M. 3000. B.C. 1004.

1 **Praise ye the Lord**. Ps 33:1, 2. 96:1-4. 106:1. 107:8, 15. 111:1. 112:1. 113:1. ch. 117. 150:6.
Praise ye the name. Ps 7:17. 102:21. 113:2, 3. 145:1, 2. 148:13. Ex +34:5-7. Ne 9:5.
O ye servants. Ps 113:1. 134:1. 149:1-3.

2 **that stand**. 1 Ch 16:37-42. 23:30. Ne 9:5. Lk 2:37.
the courts. Ps 92:13. 96:8. 116:19.

3 **Praise**. Ps 69:30, 31. 92:1, 2.
for the Lord. Ps 106:1. 107:1. 118:1. 119:68. 136:1. 145:7, 8. Is 63:7. Mt 19:17.
for it is. Ps 33:1. 63:5. 92:1, 2. 147:1.

4 **the Lord**. Dt +10:15. 1 S 12:22. Is 41:8. 43:20, 21. Zc 2:10-12.
Jacob. Ps 14:7.
Israel. Ge +9:27. Dt 33:28.
his peculiar. Ex +19:5, 6. Je 13:11.

5 **I know**. Ps 48:1. 89:6. Is 40:22, 25. Je 10:10, 11. Da +2:45. 3:29. 6:26, 27.
great. Ps 77:13. Is 12:6.
gods. Ex +12:12.

6 **Whatsoever**. Ps 33:9, 11. +115:3. Jb +42:2. Da 4:35. Am 4:13. 9:6. Mt 20:15. 28:18. Ro +9:18. Re 4:11.
in the seas. Ps 136:13-15. Mt 8:26, 27. 14:25.

7 **He causeth**. Ps 148:8. Ge 2:5, 6. 1 K 18:1, 41-45. Jb 5:10. Je 10:13. 14:22. 51:16. Zc 10:1.
he maketh lightnings. Jb 28:25, 26. 38:24-28, 35.
the rain. Je 14:22.
he bringeth. Ps 107:25. 148:8. Jb 38:22, 23. Jon 1:4. Jn 3:8.
treasuries. Dt +28:12.

8 **smote**. Ps 78:51. 105:36. 136:10. Ex 12:12, 29, 30. 13:15.
both of man and beast. Heb. from man unto beast.

9 **sent tokens**. Ps 78:43-50. 105:27-29. Ex ch. 7-15. Dt 4:34. Ne 9:10. Is 51:9, 10. Je 32:20, 21. Ac 7:36.
upon Pharaoh. Ps 136:15.

10 **smote**. Ps 44:2, 3. 136:17-22.

11 **Sihon**. Nu +21:21, 35.
and all the. Jsh ch. 10-12.

12 **gave their**. Ps 44:1-3. 78:55. 136:21, 22. Nu 33:54. Jsh 11:23. 12:7.

13 **Thy name**. Ps 8:1, 9. 72:17. 102:12, 21. Ex 3:15. 34:5-7. Ho 12:5. Mt 6:9, 13.
for ever. Heb. *olam*, Ex +12:24.
throughout all generations. Heb. to generation and generation. Ps +33:11mg.

14 **For**. He *10:30*.
the Lord. Ps +7:8.
he will repent. Dt +32:36. 1 Ch 21:15.
15 **idols**. Ex +20:4. Is 37:19.
16 **speak not**. Je +10:5.
eyes have they. Is 6:10. Mt 13:14-16.
17 **hear not**. Ps 115:6. 1 C 10:19.
neither. Ps 115:7. Je 10:14. 51:17. Hab 2:19.
breath. Heb. *ruach*, Ge +6:17.
18 **They that**. Ps 97:7. +115:8. 2 C 4:4.
are like. Ps 115:8. 2 K 17:15. Je +2:5.
19 **Bless**. Ps 115:9-11. 118:1-4. 145:10. 147:19,
20. 148:14. 2 C 1:3. Re 5:12. 19:5.
house of Aaron. Ps 115:10.
20 **Bless**. Ps 72:18. 2 C 1:3. Re 5:12.
ye that fear. Ps 22:23. 103:11, 13, 17.
115:11. 118:4. +119:63, 74. Pr 14:2.
21 **out of Zion**. Ps 76:2. 134:3. 2 Ch 6:6.
which dwelleth. Ps 48:1, 9. 132:13, 14. Is
12:6.
Praise. Jg +5:31. Ps 146:10.

PSALM 136

1 **Give thanks**. Ps 92:1. 100:4. 105:1. 106:1.
107:1. 118:1, 29. 1 Ch 16:34, 41. 25:3. 29:13.
Ezr 3:11. Col +3:17. 1 Th 5:18. He 13:15.
is good. Ps 25:8. 33:5. 34:8. 100:5. 106:1.
107:1, 8. 119:68. 126:1, 2. 145:7, +9. Is 63:7.
Je 33:11. Na 1:7. Mt 19:17. Ro 2:4. 11:22.
for his mercy. Ex +34:6. Ju 21.
for ever. Heb. *olam*, Ex +12:24.
2 **O give**. ver. +1.
God of gods. Ps 82:1. 97:7, 9. Ex 18:11. 2 Ch
2:5. Da +2:47.
3 **the Lord**. Dt +10:17.
4 **who alone**. Da +4:3.
5 **To him**. Ps 33:6. 104:24. Ge 1:1. Pr 3:19, 20.
8:22-29. Je 51:15.
6 **To him**. Ps 24:2. 104:2, 3. Ge 1:9. Jb 26:7.
37:18. Is 40:22. 44:24. Je 10:12. Zc 12:1. 2 P
3:5-7.
7 **great lights**. Ps 74:16, 17. 104:19. Ge 1:14-
19. Dt 4:19.
8 **The sun**. Ps 148:3. Je 31:35. Mt +5:45.
to rule. Heb. for the rulings. ver. 9. 103:22.
114:2.
by day. Ps 49:5. 50:15. 59:16.
9 **The moon and stars**. Ps 8:3. 89:36, 37. Jb
31:26.
10 **smote Egypt**. Ps 78:51. 105:36. 135:8. Ex
11:5, 6. 12:12, 29. He 11:28.
11 **brought out**. Ps 78:52. 105:37. Ex 12:51.
13:3, 17. 1 S 12:6-8.
12 **With a strong hand**. Ex 13:14. 15:6. Ac
7:36.
stretched. Ex +6:6.
arm. Ex +15:16.
13 **which divided**. Ex +14:21, 22, 29. He 11:29.
14 **pass through**. Ps 78:13. 106:9. Ex 14:22.

15 **But overthrew**. Heb. But shaked off. Ps
78:53. 135:9. Ex 14:27, 28. 15:4, 5, 10, 11. Ne
9:10, 11.
for his mercy. Ps 65:5. 79:6-9. 143:12. Ex
15:12, 13. Lk 1:71-74.
16 **which led**. Ps 77:20. Ex 13:18. 15:22. Nu
9:17-22. Dt 8:2, 15. Ne 9:12, 19. Is 49:10.
63:11-14.
17 **which smote**. Ps 135:10, 11. Jsh ch. 12.
great kings. ver. 18, 19, 20. Ps 48:2.
135:10.
18 **And slew**. Ps 10:8. 59:11. 78:31. 94:6.
famous kings. Ps 135:11.
19 **Sihon**. Nu +21:21, 23.
Amorites. Dt +20:17.
20 **Og**. Nu +21:33.
Bashan. Dt +32:14.
21 **gave their land**. Ps 44:2, 3. 78:55. 105:44.
135:12. Nu 32:33, etc. Dt 3:12-17. Jsh 12:1,
etc. ch. 13-21. Ne 9:22-24.
22 **an heritage**. Ps 47:4.
23 **remembered**. Ps 102:17. 106:42-45. Ge 8:1.
Dt 32:36. Is 63:9. Ezk 16:3-13. Lk 1:48, 52.
in our low estate. Ps 72:12-14. 113:7. 116:6.
142:6. 1 S 2:7, 8.
24 **hath redeemed**. Ex 15:13. Dt 15:15. Pr
23:10, 11. Is 63:9. Lk 1:68-74. T 2:14.
25 **Who giveth food**. Ps 104:27. +145:15.
147:9. Ge +3:19.
flesh. Ge +6:12.
26 **the God**. Heb. *El*, Ex +15:2.
of heaven. ver. 1-3. Ps 115:3. 123:1. Re
+11:13.
for ever. Heb. *olam*, Ex +12:24.

PSALM 137

(*Title*.) A.M. cir. 3463. B.C. cir. 541. The
author of this beautiful and affecting elegy is
unknown, but the occasion is evident; and it
was most probably composed during, or near
the close of, the captivity.
1 **the rivers**. Ge 2:10-14. Ezr 8:21, 31.
Ezk 1:1.
there sat. Ne 1:3, 4. 2:3. Jb 2:12, 13. Je
13:17, 18. 15:17. La 2:10. Ezk 3:15.
we wept. Ps 42:4. 102:9-14. Is 66:10. Je
51:50, 51. La 1:16. 2:11, 18. 3:48-51. Da 9:3.
10:2, 3. Lk 19:41. Re 11:3.
2 **We hanged**. Is 15:7. Am 8:10. Re +5:8.
3 **For there**. Ps 123:3, 4. La 2:15, 16.
a song. Heb. the words of a song. ver. 4. Ps
28:7. 33:3. 40:3. 42:8.
wasted us. Heb. laid us on heaps. Ps 79:1. Ne
4:2. Je 9:11. 26:18. La 1:7. Mi 3:12. Lk 21:6.
the songs of Zion. Ps 9:14. 65:1. 1 Ch 15:27,
28. 16:7. Is 35:10. 51:11. Je 31:12, 13. Re
14:1-3.
4 **How shall**. Ec 3:4. Is 22:12. La 5:14, 15. Ho
9:4. Am 8:3.

strange. Ps 18:44, 45. 81:9. 144:7, 11. Ex +12:43.

land. Heb. land of a stranger. Is 49:21.

5 **I forget**. Ps 84:1, 2, 10. 102:13, 14. +122:5-9. Ne 1:2-4. 2:2, 3. Is 62:1, 6, 7. Je 51:50. Da 6:10, 11.

let my right. Zc 11:17.

6 **let my tongue**. Ps 22:15. Is 41:17. La 4:4. Ezk 3:26.

if I prefer. Ps 84:10. Mt 6:33. Ac 20:24. Ph 1:20-25. 1 Th 3:7-9.

my chief joy. Heb. the head of my joy. Ps 21:6.

7 **Remember**. Ps 74:18. 79:8-12. Am +8:7. Zc 1:15.

the children. Je +49:7.

the day. Dt +4:32.

who said. Pr +17:5.

Rase it. Heb. Make bare. Is +3:17mg. Hab 3:13mg.

8 **daughter**. Nu +21:25. Is +47:1.

who art. Is ch. 13. 14:4-24. 21:1-10. 47:1. Je 25:12-14. ch. 50, 51. Re 14:8-11. ch. 17. 18:6.

destroyed. Heb. wasted. Ps 17:9mg.

happy. Ps +149:6-9. Is 13:3-5. 44:28. Re 17:5, 6, 14. 18:6, 20.

rewardeth, etc. Heb. recompenseth unto thee thy deed which thou didst unto us. Je 50:15-29. Re 18:6.

9 **Happy**. Pr 17:5.

taketh. Ps 48:6. 73:23. 77:4. 139:10.

and dasheth. Ps 2:9. 2 K 8:12. 15:16. Is 13:16. Je 13:14. Ho 10:14. 13:16. Am 1:13. Na 3:10. Zc 14:2.

little ones. Ps 8:2. 17:14. 1 S 15:3.

the stones. Heb. the rock. Ps 18:2. 31:3. 40:2. 42:9.

PSALM 138

(*Title*.) A.M. 3485. B.C. 519. **A Psalm of David**. Five MSS. omit *ledawid*; and the LXX. and Arabic prefix also the names of Haggai and Zechariah; and it is probable that it was composed to be sung at the dedication of the second temple.

1 **I will praise**. Ps +9:1. 86:12, 13. 111:1. 1 C 14:15. Ep 5:19.

before. Ps 119:46. Ac 23:5. He 1:14.

the gods. Or, God, *Elohim*. Ps +8:5. Ex +12:12. 2 S 19:21. Ro 13:1.

2 **toward**. Ps 99:5, 9. Da +6:10.

and praise. Ps 36:5, 6. 85:10. 86:15. 89:1, 2. 100:4, 5. 115:1. Is 63:7. La 3:23. Mi 7:18-20. Lk 1:68-72. Jn 1:17. Ro 15:8, 9.

for thou hast. Ps 56:4, 10. Is 42:21. Mt 5:18. 24:35. Jn 10:35.

magnified. Ps 35:26. 38:16. 41:9mg. 55:12. Is 42:21.

thy word. Ps 12:6. 17:6. 18:30. 56:4. 105:19. 119:11. Nu 11:23. Pr 13:13.

thy name. Ps 8:9. +9:10. Pr 18:10.

3 **In the day**. Ps 18:6. 2 K +20:4. Da 9:23. Lk 17:5.

cried. Ps +3:4.

strengthenedst. Ps +18:1. 63:8. Is 41:10. 1 P 5:10.

soul. Heb. *nephesh*, Ge +34:3.

4 **All the kings**. Ps 102:15, 22. Is +49:7. Re 21:24.

when they hear. Ps 22:22, 27. 51:13. 68:11. 69:30-32. 71:18. Is 11:9. 54:13. Ro 10:18.

5 **they shall**. Is 52:7-10. 65:14. 66:10-14. Je 31:11, 12. Zp 3:14, 15. Mt 21:5-9. Lk 19:37, 38.

for great. Ps 21:5. Ex 15:11. 33:18, 19. Is 6:1-3. Ml 1:11. Jn 13:31, 32. 17:1. 2 C 4:6. Ep 1:6, 12. Re 4:11. 5:12-14. 7:12. 19:1.

6 **Though**. Ps 51:17. 113:5, 6. 1 S 2:7, 8. Pr 3:34. Is +57:15. 66:2.

yet hath. Ps 34:18. Is 66:2.

but the proud. Pr +16:5.

afar off. Ps 139:2. Mt 25:41. 2 Th 1:9.

7 **Though I walk**. Ps 23:3, 4. 42:7, 8. 66:10-12. Jb 13:15. 19:25, 26. Is 57:16.

thou wilt. Ps 71:20, 21. 85:6. 119:49, 50.

thou shalt stretch. Ps 35:1-3. 56:1, 2, 9. 64:7, 8. 77:10. 144:1, 2. Ex +7:5. Mi 7:8-10.

and thy right. Ps 17:7. 18:35. 44:3, 5-7. 60:5. Is 41:10. Ac 2:33.

8 **perfect**. Ps 57:2. Is 26:12. 46:4. Je 32:39, 40. Jn 15:2. Ro 5:10. 8:28-30. Ph 1:6. 1 Th 5:24. 1 P 5:10. 2 P +1:10.

thy mercy. Ex +34:6.

for ever. Heb. *olam*, Ex +12:24.

forsake. Ps 71:6-9, 17, 18. Jb 10:3, 8. 14:15. Is 42:16. 43:21. He +13:5. 1 P 1:3-5. 4:19. Ju 1.

the works. Ps 100:3. Is 64:8.

PSALM 139

(*Title*.) A.M. 2956. B.C. 1048. **A Psalm**. Ps 3, title.

1 **thou hast**. ver. 23. Ps 11:4, 5. 17:3. 44:21. 1 K 8:39. Je 12:3. +17:10. Jn 21:17. 1 C 2:10.

and known. Jn 1:48.

2 **knowest**. Ps 56:8. Ge 16:13. 2 K 6:12. 19:27. Jb 31:4. Pr 15:3. Is 37:28. Zc 4:10.

understandest. Ps 94:11. Jn +2:25. 1 C 4:5.

afar off. Ezk 38:10, 11, 17.

3 **compassest**. or, winnowest. Jb 13:26, 27. 14:16, 17. 31:4. Mt 3:12.

my path. ver. 18. Ps 121:3-8. Ge 28:10-17. 2 S 8:14. 11:2-5, 27.

and art acquainted. 2 S 12:9-12. Pr 5:20, 21. Ec 12:14. Is 29:15. Je 23:24. Jn 1:48, 49. 6:70, 71. 13:2, 21. Ac 5:3, 4.

4 **there is not**. Ps 19:14. Jb 8:2. 38:2. 42:3, 6-8.

Zp 1:12. Ml 3:13-16. Mt 12:35-37. Ja 1:26. 3:2-10.

thou knowest. Ps 50:19-21. Je 29:23. He 4:12, 13.

5 **beset me.** Dt 33:27. Jb 23:8, 9.
before. Mi +5:2.
and laid. Ex 24:11. Re 1:17.

6 **knowledge.** Ps 40:5. 131:1. Jb +11:7. 42:3. Pr 30:2-4.
cannot. Lk 18:34.

7 **Whither.** 2 Ch 16:9. Je 23:23, 24. Jon 1:3, 10. Ac 5:9.
from thy. Ps 51:11. Ge 1:2. Jb 26:13. Is 11:1, 2. Ac 5:3, 4.
spirit. Heb. *ruach.* 2 S 23:2. Is 40:13. +48:16. Jn 4:24.
thy presence. Ps 51:11. Is 57:15. Je 23:23, 24. Mt +28:19. Jn 14:16, 17. 1 C 3:16. 6:19.

8 **ascend.** Ezk 28:12-17. Am 9:2-4. Ob 4. Mt 22:31, 32. Mk 12:26, 27.
in hell. Heb. *sheol,* Ge +37:35. Ps +16:10. 30:3. Jb 14:13. 26:6. 34:21, 22. Pr 15:11. Is 38:10. Am 9:2-4. Jon 2:2.

9 **the wings.** Ps 18:10. 19:6. Ml 4:2.
dwell. Ps 74:16, 17. Is 24:14-16.

10 **Even there.** Ps 143:9, 10.
right hand. Ps +18:35.
lead me. Ps +32:8.

11 **Surely.** Ps 10:11-13. 94:7. Jb 22:12-14. Is 29:15. Je 23:24.
even the night. Jb 12:22.

12 **the darkness.** Ex 14:20. 20:21. Jb 26:6. 34:22. Da 2:22. He 4:13.
hideth not. Heb. darkeneth not. Ps 105:28. Is 29:15. Je 13:16.
shineth. Ps 18:28. 67:1. 118:27.
the darkness, etc. Heb. as *is* the darkness, so *is* the light.

13 **For thou.** Jb 10:9-12.
covered me. Ps 22:9, 10. 71:6. Jb 31:15. Is 44:2. 46:3. Je 1:5.

14 **for I am fearfully.** lit. with fears and wonder. Ps 9:1. 26:7. 40:5. Ge 1:26, 27.
marvelous. Ps 92:4, 5. 104:24. 111:2. Jb 5:9. Re 15:3.
soul. Heb. *nephesh,* Ge +34:3. Ps +84:2. Mt +11:29.
right well. Heb. greatly. Ps 6:3. 21:1. 31:11. 38:6.

15 **substance.** or, strength, *or* body. Dt 8:17. Jb 30:21mg.
when I. ver. 13. Jb 10:8-11. Ec 11:5.
in the lowest. Ps 63:9. Ep 4:9.

16 **in thy book.** Ml 3:16. Re +3:5.
all my members. Heb. all of them.
written. Ps 69:28. 102:18. Ezr 8:34.
which in continuance were fashioned. or, what days they should be fashioned. Ps +90:12. Jb 17:7. 33:29.
when. Ac 13:48.

17 **precious.** Ps 40:5. 49:7, 8. 116:15. Jb 26:14. Pr 8:31. Is 28:16. 55:8, 9. Je 29:11. Ep 3:9, 10. 1 P 1:19. 2:7. 2 P 1:1, 4.
thy thoughts. Ge +50:20.
God. Heb. *El,* Ex +15:2.
how great. Ps 31:19. 36:7.

18 **they are more.** Ps 40:5, 12.
than the sand. Ge +22:17.
when I awake. ver. 3. Ps 3:5. 16:8-11. 17:15. 63:6, 7. Is +26:19. Da 12:2. 1 Th 5:10.

19 **Surely.** Ps 5:6. +9:17. 55:23. 64:7. 94:23. Is 11:4. Ju 14, 15.
depart from. Ps +6:8. 26:5. 101:4. 2 C 6:17. Re 18:4.
ye bloody. Ps 5:6. 26:9. 55:23. 59:2.

20 **For they speak.** Ps 73:8, 9. 74:18, 22, 23. Jb 21:14, 15. Is 37:23, 28, 29. Ju 15. Re 13:6.
thine. Ps 2:1-3. Ex +20:7.

21 **Do not I.** 2 Ch 19:2. Pr +8:13. 2 P 2:7, 8.
and am not. Ps 119:136, 158. Je 13:17. Mk 3:5. Lk 19:41. Ro 9:1-3.

22 **hate them.** Pr. +8:13. Lk 14:26.

23 **Search me.** ver. 1. Ps 26:2. 44:21. Pr 30:7, 8. Jn 3:20, 21.
God. Heb. *El,* Ex +15:2.
try me. Ps 26:2. 1 J 3:21.
know. Dt 8:2, 16. Jb 31:6. Pr 17:3. Zc 13:9. Ml 3:2, 3. 1 P 1:7.

24 **And see.** Ps 7:3, 4. 17:3. Pr 28:26. Je 17:9, 10. Jn 15:6.
wicked way. Heb. way of pain, *or* grief. 1 Ch 4:9, 10. Pr 28:10. Is 14:3. Je 36:3. He 12:15, 16.
and lead. Ps +32:8. 119:1, 32.
the way. Ps 1:6. 16:11. Mt 7:13, 14. Jn 14:6. Col 2:6.
everlasting. Heb. *olam,* Ge +17:7.

PSALM 140

1 A.M. 2942. B.C. 1062.
Deliver. Ps 43:1. 59:1-3. 71:4.
violent man. Heb. man of violences. ver. 4, 11. Ps 18:48mg. 25:19mg. Pr 3:31mg. Hab 1:2, 3.

2 **imagine.** Ps 2:1, 2. 21:11. 36:4. 38:12. 52:2. 62:3. 64:5, 6. Pr 6:14. 12:20. 16:27. Is 59:4. Ho 7:6, 15. Mi 2:1-3. Na 1:11.
continually. Ps 56:6. 120:7. 1 S 23:19-24. 24:11, 12. 26:1, etc.

3 **sharpened.** Ps 52:2, 3. 57:4. 59:7. 64:3, 4. Pr 12:18. Is 59:3-5, 13. Je 9:3, 5. Ja 3:6-8.
like a serpent. Ge 3:13. Pr 23:32. Mt 12:34. 2 C 11:3.
adders.' Ps 58:4. Ro 3:13, 14.
Selah. ver. 5, 8. Ps +9:16.

4 **Keep me.** Ps 17:8, 9. 36:11. 37:32, 33-40. 55:1-3. 71:4.
preserve. ver. 1.
overthrow. Ps 17:5. Pr 18:5.

5 **The proud**. Ps +10:2.
snare. Ps 10:4-12. 17:8-13. +57:6. +141:9. Lk 11:53, 54.

6 **I said unto**. Ps 16:2, 5, 6. 31:14. 91:2. 119:57. 142:5. La 3:24. Zc 13:9.
hear. Ps 27:7, 8. 28:1, 2. 55:1, 2. 64:1.

7 **the strength**. Ps 18:1, 2, 35. 27:1. 28:7, 8. 59:17. 62:2, 7. 89:26. 95:1. Dt 33:27-29. Is 12:2.
thou hast covered. Ps 144:10. Le 26:7, 8. Dt 32:30. 1 S 17:36, 37, 45-51. 2 S 8:6, 14. Zc 12:6, 8.

8 **Grant not**. Ps 27:12. 94:20, 21. 2 S 15:31. Jb 5:12, 13.
lest they exalt themselves. *or*, let them not be exalted. Dt 32:27.

9 **let the mischief**. Ps +57:6. 64:8. Pr 10:6, 11. 12:13. 18:7. Mt 27:25.

10 **burning coals**. Ps 11:6. 18:13, 14. 21:9. 120:4. Ge 19:24. Ex 9:23, 24. Re 16:8, 9.
let them. Da 3:20-25. Mt 13:42, 50.
into deep. Ps 55:23. Pr 28:10, 17. Re 20:15. 21:8.

11 **Let not**, etc. *or*, Let not an evil speaker, a wicked man of violence, be established in the earth: let him be hunted to his overthrow.
an evil speaker. Heb. a man of tongue. Ps +12:3, 4. Pr 6:17. 12:13. 17:20. 18:21. Ec +10:11.
evil. Ps 7:14-16. 9:16. 34:21. Pr 13:21. Is 3:11.

12 **maintain**. Ps 9:4, 18. 10:14, 17, 18. 22:24. 34:6. 35:10. 72:4, 12-14. 102:17. 109:31. +119:68. 146:9. 1 K 8:45, 49. Jb 5:15, 16. Pr 22:22, 23. 23:10, 11. Is 11:4. Je 22:16. Da 10:18. Mt 11:5. Ja +5:11.

13 **Surely**. Ps 32:11. 33:1. Is 3:10.
the upright. Ps 16:11. 23:6. 73:24. Jn +14:3. 17:24. 1 Th 4:17. Re 7:14-17. 21:24-27.
shall dwell. Jn +14:3.
thy presence. Ps +16:11. Ex 33:14. 2 Ch 15:2. Is +24:23. 41:10. Jl 2:27. Mt +5:8. Jn 14:23.

PSALM 141

1 A.M. 2946. B.C. 1058.
cry. Ps +3:4.
make haste. Ps +40:17. Jb 7:21.

2 **Let my prayer**. Pr 15:8.
set forth. Heb. directed. Ps 5:3.
as incense. Ex +30:1, 7-9, 34-38. 31:11. 37:29. Le 10:1, 2. 16:11-13. Nu 16:35, 46-48. Dt 33:10. 1 K 18:29. 2 Ch 13:11. Ml 1:11. Lk 1:9, 10. 2 C 2:15. Re 5:8mg. 8:3, 4.
the lifting. Ps +88:9.
the evening. Ex 29:39-42. 1 K 18:29, 36. Ezr 9:4, 5. Da 9:21. Mt 27:45, 46. Lk 23:44. Ac 3:1. 10:2, 3, 30.

3 **Set a watch**. Ps 17:3-5. 19:14. 39:1. 71:8.

+101:5. Pr 21:23. Mi 7:5. Ja 1:26, 27. 3:2.
keep. Ps +38:13. Mi 7:5.

4 **Incline not**. Ps 119:36. Dt +2:30. 29:4. 1 K 8:58. 22:22. Is 63:17. Mt 6:13. Ja 1:13.
to practice. 1 C 15:33. 2 C 6:17. Re 18:4.
with men. Ps 26:4. +119:63. 1 C 15:33.
and let me. Nu 25:2. Pr 23:1-3, 6-8. Da 1:5-8. Ac 10:13, 14. 1 C 10:27, 28, 31.

5 **the righteous**. 1 S 25:31-34. 2 S 12:7-13. 2 Ch 16:7-10. 25:16. Pr 6:23. 9:8, 9. 15:5, 22. 19:25. 25:12. 27:5, 6. Ga 2:11-14. 6:1. Re 3:19.
smite, etc. *or*, smite me kindly and reprove me; let not their precious oil break my head, etc.
reprove. Pr 13:18. 15:5. 17:10. 25:12.
for yet my. Ps 51:18. 125:4. Mt 5:44. 2 T 1:16-18. Ja 5:14-16.

6 **When their judges**. 1 S 31:1-8. 2 S 1:17, etc. 1 Ch 10:1-7.
they shall hear. 2 S 2:4. 5:1-3. 1 Ch 11:1-3. 12:38.
for they. Ps 45:2. 2 S 2:5, 6. 23:1. 1 Ch 13:2. Lk 4:22.

7 **bones**. Ps 44:22. 1 S 22:18, 19. Ro 8:36. 2 C 1:8, 9. He 11:37. Re 11:8, 9.
grave's. Heb. *sheol*, Ge +37:35.

8 **mine eyes**. Ps 25:15. 123:1, 2. 2 Ch 20:12, 14, 15.
leave not my soul destitute. Heb. make not my soul bare. Ps 25:16, 17. 102:17. +137:7mg. 143:3, 4. Is 41:17. Jn 14:18.
soul. Heb. *nephesh*, Ge +12:13.

9 **from the snares**. Ps 38:12. 64:5. 91:3. 119:110. 124:7. 140:5. 142:3. Pr 13:14. Je 18:22. Mt 22:15. Lk 20:20. 2 T 2:26.

10 **the wicked**. Ps +57:6. 64:7, 8. Pr 11:8.
escape. Heb. pass over. Ps 17:3 (transgress). 37:36. 42:4 (had gone). 57:1. 81:6mg. 90:4. 104:9. 148:6.

PSALM 142

(*Title*.) A.M. 2942. B.C. 1062. **Maschil of David**. *or*, A Psalm of David giving instruction. Ps 32, 54, 57, titles. 1 Ch 4:10.
when he was. 1 S 22:1, 2. 24:3. He 11:38.

1 **I cried**. Ps +3:4.
with my voice. Ps 28:2. 141:1.

2 **poured out**. Ps 42:4. 62:8. 102, title. 1 S 1:15, 16. Is 26:16. Ro 8:26.
I showed. Ps 18:4-6. Ph 4:6, 7. He 5:7.

3 **my spirit**. Heb. *ruach*, Ge +41:8. Ps 22:14. 61:2. 102:4. 143:4. Mk 14:33-36.
then thou. Ps 1:6. 17:3. 139:2-4. Jb 23:10.
In the way. Ps 31:4. 35:7, 8. 56:6. +141:9.

4 **I looked**, etc. *or*, Look on the right hand and see.
but there was. Ps 31:11. 69:20. 88:8, 18. Jb 19:13-19. La 1:12. Mt 26:38, 40, 47, 56. 2 T 4:16.

refuge. 1 S 23:11-13, 19, 20. 27:1.
failed me; no man cared for my soul. Heb.
perished from me; no man sought after my
soul.
  soul. Heb. *nephesh*, Ge +12:13.

5 **Thou art.** Ps +9:9. Jn 16:32. 2 T 4:17.
  my portion. Ps +16:5.
  in the land. Ps +27:13.

6 **for I am.** Ps 44:24-26. 79:8. 116:6. 136:23.
143:3, 7. Ge 41:14.
  for they. Ps 3:1. 38:19. 57:3, 4. 59:3. 1 S
24:14. Ro 8:33, 37.

7 **my soul.** Heb. *nephesh*, Ge +12:13. Ps 142,
title. Ps 9:13, 14. 31:8. 88:4-8. 143:11. 146:7.
Is 61:1. Ac 2:24.
  prison. Ps +146:7.
  the righteous. Ps 7:6, 7. 22:21-27. 34:2.
107:41, 42. 119:74.
  thou shalt. Ps 13:6. 116:7. 119:17. Ja 5:10,
11.

PSALM 143

1 **in thy faithfulness.** Ps 31:1. 71:2. 2 S 7:25.
La 3:22, 23. Da 9:16. 1 J 1:9.

2 **enter not.** Ps 130:3. Jb 14:3.
  in thy sight. Ex 34:7. Jb 4:17. Pr +20:9. Ro
3:20. Ga 2:16.
  no man. Mt 18:11. Ac 4:12. 13:38, 39. Ro
3:19, 20. 5:6. 9:31, 32. Ga 2:16, 20, 21. 3:10-
12, 18-24. Ph 3:4-7. He 9:23. Ja 2:10.

3 **the enemy.** Ps 7:1, 2. 17:9-13. 35:4. 54:3.
142:6.
  soul. Heb. *nephesh*, Ge +12:13.
  smitten. Ps 7:5. 2 S 2:22. 18:11.
  made me. Ps 31:12, 13. 88:4-6. Ezk 37:11.
  long. Heb. *olam*, Le +25:32. Ec 12:5.

4 **is my spirit.** Heb. *ruach*, Ge +41:8. Ps 55:5.
61:2. 77:3. 102, title. 124:4. 142:3. Jb 6:27.
  my heart. Ps 25:16. 102:3, 4. 119:81-83. Lk
22:44.

5 **remember.** Ps 42:6. 44:1. 77:5, 6, 10-12. Dt
+7:18. 1 S 17:34-37, 45-50.

6 **stretch forth.** Ps +88:9.
  my soul. Heb. *nephesh*, Ge +34:3. Ps 42:1, 2.
63:1. 84:2. Is 26:8, 9. 35:7. Jn 7:37.
  Selah. Ps +9:16.

7 **Hear me.** Ps 13:1-4. +40:17.
  my spirit. Heb. *ruach*, Ge +41:8. Ps 40:12.
69:3. Is 57:16. Lk 21:26.
  hide not. Ps 22:24. Dt +31:17.
  lest I be like, etc. or, for I am become like,
etc.
  like. Nu +21:27.
  unto them. *Ps 28:1.* 88:4-6, 10, 11. +146:4.
Is 38:18.
  pit. Heb. *bor*, Ge +37:20. Ps 7:15. 28:1. 30:3.
40:2. 88:4.

8 **to hear.** Ps 42:8. Ge 32:24-29. 2 Ch 20:20. Re
+2:28.

cause me. ver. 10. Ps +32:8. 119:27, 33, 34,
73. Is 48:17.
  for I lift up. Ps 25:1. 86:4. La 3:41.
  soul. Heb. *nephesh*, Ge +34:3.

9 **flee unto thee.** Heb. hide me with thee. Ps
31:2-4. 56:9. +64:2. 91:1, 4. 142:5. Pr 18:10.
He 6:18.

10 **Teach.** Ps +32:8. 119:5-7, 12, 35. Mi 4:2. Mt
28:20. Col 1:9, 10. 1 Th 4:1, 2. 1 J 2:27.
  to do. Ps 86:11. 119:5, 10, 35, 133.
  thy will. 1 Th +4:3.
  for thou art. Ps 22:1. 31:14. 63:1. 118:28.
140:6.
  thy spirit. Heb. *ruach*, Ge +41:38. Is +48:16.
  is good. Ne 9:20. Is 63:14. Mt +28:19. Mk
+10:18. Jn +10:11. 14:26. 16:13-15. Ro 5:5.
8:2, 14-16, 26. 15:13, 30. Ga 5:22, 23. Ep
4:30. 5:9. 2 T 1:7.
  the land. Ps 27:11, 13. Is 26:10.

11 **Quicken.** Ps 85:6. 119:25, 37, 40, 88, 107.
138:7. Hab 3:2. Ep 2:4, 5.
  name's sake. Is +48:9.
  for thy righteousness'. ver. 1. Ps 9:7, 8.
31:1. 71:2.
  bring. Ps 25:17. 34:19. 37:39, 40. 91:15, 16.
Re 7:14-17.
  soul. Heb. *nephesh*, Ge +34:3.

12 **of thy mercy.** Ps 54:5. 55:23. 136:15-20. 1 S
24:12-15. 25:29. 26:10.
  soul. Heb. *nephesh*, Ge +34:3.
  for I am thy. Ps 116:16. 119:94.

PSALM 144

1 **my strength.** Heb. my rock. Ps +18:1, 2, 31.
95:1.
  teacheth. Ps 18:34. 44:3, 4. 60:12. 2 S 22:35.
2 C 10:4. Ep 6:10, 11.
  to war. *or,* to the war, etc.

2 **My goodness.** *or,* mercy. Ps 52:1. 57:3.
59:10.
  my fortress. Ps +31:3. 2 S 22:2, 3, 40-48.
  who subdueth. Ps 18:47. 110:2, 3. 2 S 22:40.

3 **what is man.** Ps +8:4.
  or the son. Ps 146:3, 4.

4 **Man.** Ps 39:5, 6. 62:9. 89:47. Jb 4:19. 14:1-3.
Ec 1:2, 14. 12:8.
  his days. Ps 102:11. 103:15, 16. 109:23. 2 S
14:14. 1 Ch 29:15. Jb 8:9. Ec 8:13.

5 **Bow.** Ps 18:9. Is 64:1, 2.
  come down. Is 64:1-4. Re 22:17, 20.
  touch. Na 1:3-6. Hab 3:3-6. He 12:18.
  smoke. Re +14:11.

6 **Cast forth.** Ps 18:13, 14. 77:17, 18. 2 S
22:12-15.
  thine arrows. Dt +32:23.

7 **Send.** Ps 18:16. 2 S 22:17. Mt 27:43.
  hand. Heb. hands. Ps +31:5.
  deliver me. Ps 69:1, 2, 14, 15. 93:3, 4. Re
12:15, 16. 17:15.

the hand. ver. 11. Ps 54:3. Ne 9:2. Ml 2:11.
strange. ver. 11. Ps 18:44, 45. 81:9. 137:4. Ex +12:43. Is 56:3, 6.

8 **mouth.** Ps 10:7. 12:2. 41:6. 58:3. 62:4. 109:2, 3. Is 59:5-7.
their right hand. Is 44:20. Mt 5:30. Re 13:16, 17.

9 **sing a new.** Ps 33:2, 3. 40:3. 98:1. 149:1. Re 5:9, 10, 12, 13. 12:10. 14:3.
upon. Ps 81:1-3. 108:2, 3. 150:3-5. 1 Ch 25:1-6.

10 **that giveth.** Ps 18:50. 33:16-18. 2 S 5:19-25. 8:6, 14. 2 K 5:1.
salvation. *or*, victory. 2 S 19:2. Pr 21:31mg. Is 45:1-6. Je 27:6-8.
who delivereth. Ps 140:7. 1 S 17:45, 46. 2 S 21:16, 17.

11 **Rid.** Ps 35:1-5.
and deliver me. ver. 7, 8. 2 S 10:6, etc. 16:5, etc. 17:1, etc. La 1:3, 4.
strange. ver. +7.

12 **our sons.** 1 Ch 22:6, 11, 12. 29:19. Mt 19:13-15.
as plants. Ps 115:14, 15. 127:4, 5. 128:3. Is 44:3-5. La 4:2.
as corner stones. Jb 42:15. Pr 31:10-27. Is 3:16-24.
polished. Heb. cut. Zc 9:15.
the similitude. SS 8:8, 9. 1 P 3:3-6.

13 **our garners.** Ps 107:37, 38. Ge 28:20. Le 26:5, 10. Dt 28:8. 1 Ch 4:10. Jb 8:5-7, 22:23-28. Jl 2:19. Ml 3:10. Lk 12:16-20.
all manner of store. Heb. from kind to kind. 2 Ch 16:14.
our sheep. Ge 30:29-31. Dt 7:13, 14. 8:3. 28:4.

14 **strong to labor.** Heb. able to bear burdens, *or*, loaden with *flesh*.
no breaking in. Dt 28:7, 25. Jg 5:8. 6:3-6. 1 S 13:17-23. 31:7. Je 13:17-19. 14:18. La 1:4-6. Zc 8:3-5.
no complaining. Ps 102:11. 109:23. Jb 8:9. 14:2. Is 24:11. +29:24. Je 14:2. 46:12. Ju +16.
streets. Am +5:16.

15 **yea, happy.** Ps 33:12. 65:4. 89:15. 146:5. Dt 33:29. Ep 1:3.

PSALM 145

(Title.) A.M. 2989. B.C. 1015. **David's.** This incomparable song of praise, which is the last of the acrostic or alphabetical Psalms, each verse beginning with a consecutive letter of the Hebrew alphabet, is supposed to have been composed by David towards the close of his life.
Psalm of praise. Ps 100, title.

1 **extol thee.** Ps 30:1. 68:4. 71:14, etc. 103:1, 2. Da 4:37.
my God. Ps 44:4. 45:1, 6. 47:6-8. 48:2, 3.

95:3. 149:2. Is 33:22. Ml 1:14. Mt 25:34. Re 19:16.
I will bless. ver. 21. Ps 30:12. 52:9. 113:1, 2. 146:1, 2.

2 **Every day.** Ps 72:15. 119:164. Da 6:10. Re 7:15.

3 **Great.** Da +2:45.
and his greatness is unsearchable. Heb. and of his greatness there is no search. Jb +11:7-9.

4 **generation.** Ps 44:1, 2. 71:18. 78:3-7. Ex 12:26, 27. 13:14, 15. Dt 6:7. Jsh 4:21-24. Is 38:19.

5 **will speak.** Ps 40:9, 10. 66:3, 4. 71:17-19, 24. 96:3. 105:2. Is 12:4. Da 4:1-3, 37.
majesty. 1 Ch +29:11.
works. Heb. things, or words. Ps +65:3mg. 72:18.

6 **And men.** Ps 22:22, 23, 27, 31. 98:2, 3. 113:3. 126:2, 3. Jsh 2:9-11. 9:9, 10. Ezr 1:2. Je 50:28. Da 3:28, 29. 6:25-27. Hab 2:14.
I will declare thy greatness. Heb. thy greatness I will declare it. Ps 92:1, 2. 107:21, 22, 31, 32.

7 **abundantly.** Ps 36:5-8. Is 63:7. Mt 12:34, 35. 2 C 9:11, 12. 1 P 2:9, 10.
sing. Ps 36:10. 51:14. 71:15, 16, 19. 72:1-3. 89:16. Is 45:24, 25. Je 23:6. Ph 3:7-9. Re 15:3, 4. 19:1-3.

8 **Lord is gracious.** Ex +34:6, 7. Ep 1:6, 8. 2:4.
of great mercy. Heb. great in mercy. Ps 5:7. 6:4. 13:5. 17:7. 31:21.

9 **good to all.** ver. 7. Ps 8:3, 4. 36:6, 7. 52:1. 65:9-13. 68:18. 104:27, 28. 113:4-6. +136:1. Ge +18:25. Ex +34:6. Is 57:15. Je +29:11. Jon 4:11. Zc 9:17. Mt +5:45. Lk +6:35. Ac 14:17. 17:25. Ja +1:17.

10 **All thy.** Ps 19:1. 96:11-13. 98:3-9. 103:22. 104:24. 148:1-13. Is 43:20. 44:23. Ro 1:19, 20.
and thy saints. Ps 22:23. 30:4. 32:11. 97:12. 135:19-21. 148:14. Is 43:21. He 13:15. 1 P 2:5, 9. Re 7:9-12. 19:5, 6.

11 **the glory.** Ps +45:6, 7. 72:1, etc. 93:1, 2. 96:10-13. 97:1, etc. 99:1-4. +102:16. 1 Ch 29:11, 12. Is +24:23. 33:21, 22. Mt +6:10. Mk 11:9, 10. Lk 1:31-33. 1 Th 2:12. 2 T 2:10. Re 5:12, 13. 11:15-17.

12 **make known.** Ps 98:1. 105:5. 106:2. 110:2, 3. 135:6-12. 136:4, etc. Da 4:34, 35. Mt 28:18. Ac 2:8-11. Ep 1:19-21. 3:7, 8. Re 12:10. 19:15, 16.

13 **kingdom.** Ps +45:6. 146:10. 1 T +1:17.
everlasting kingdom. Heb. kingdom of all ages. Ps 100:5. 103:17. 1 C 15:21-28.
thy dominion. Ps +49:14. 72:8. Da 4:3, 34. Mi 4:8. Zc 9:10. 1 P 4:11. 5:11. Ju 25. Re 1:6.
all generations. Ps 45:17. +72:5.

14 **upholdeth.** Ps 37:24. 94:18. 119:117. Lk 22:31, 32.

raiseth up. Ps 146:8. Lk 13:11-13.
bowed down. Ps 35:14. 38:6. 42:5mg. 57:6.
15 **The eyes**. ver. 9. Ps 104:21, 27. 136:25.
147:8, 9. Ge 1:30. Jb 38:39-41. Jl 2:22. Mt
6:26. Lk 12:24. Ac 17:25.
wait upon thee. *or,* look unto thee. Ps
104:27. 119:166. Ru 1:13.
due season. Mt +24:45.
16 **openest**. Ps 104:21, 28. 107:9. 132:15. 147:9.
Jb 38:27, 41.
hand. Ps +104:28.
17 **righteous**. Ps 50:6. 89:14. 97:2. 99:3, 4.
103:6. Ge +18:25. Dt 32:4. 1 S 2:2, 3. Ne 9:33,
34. Is 45:21. Da 9:7. Zp 3:5. Zc 9:9. Ro 3:5, 6,
25, 26. Re 4:8. 15:3, 4. 16:5-7. 19:2, 11.
holy. *or,* merciful, *or* bountiful. Ps +43:1mg.
Mi 7:2mg.
18 **nigh unto**. Ps 34:18. 46:1, 5. Dt 4:7. 1 K
18:27, 28. Jn 14:23. Ac 10:34, 35. Ja +4:8.
call upon. Ps 17:1. 119:2. Ho 7:14. Mt 6:5-8.
23:14. 1 J +5:14, 15.
in truth. Dt 4:29. 1 S +16:7. Is 29:13, 14. Je
29:13. Mt 15:7, 8. Jn 4:24.
19 **fulfill the desire**. Ps 20:4, 5. 34:9. 37:4, 19.
140:8. Pr 10:24. Mt +5:6. Jn 15:7, 16. 16:24.
Ep 3:16-20. 1 J 5:15.
fear him. Dt +6:2. Ml +3:16.
will hear. Ps 10:17. 20:1. +34:15, 17. 37:39,
40. 91:15.
20 **preserveth**. Ps 37:28. Dt +6:5. Jn 10:27-29. 1
P 1:5-8.
all the wicked. Ps 1:6. +9:17. Mt 25:41.
21 **My mouth**. ver. 1, 2, 5. Ps 30:12. 51:15.
71:8, 15, 23, 24. 89:1.
let all flesh. Ps 65:2. 67:3, 4. 86:9. 103:22.
ch. 117. 150:6. Ge +6:12. Re 5:11-14.

PSALM 146

1 A.M. 3489. B.C. 515.
Praise ye the Lord. Heb. Hallelujah. Ps
105:45mg.
Praise the Lord. Ps 103:1, 22. 104:1, 35.
soul. Heb. *nephesh,* Ge +34:3. Ps +103:1. Lk
12:19.
2 **While I live**. Ps 63:4. 71:14, 15. 145:1, 2. Dt
+12:1. Re 7:9-17.
3 **Put**. Ps 62:9. Is 36:6.
in princes. Ps 107:40. Is 24:21.
son of man. Ps +8:4.
no help. *or,* salvation. Ps 33:17. 37:39. 40:10.
+60:11mg. Ac 4:12.
4 **His breath**. Heb. *ruach,* Ge +6:17. Ps +31:5.
104:29. Ge +2:7. 6:17. 7:15, 22. Jb 12:10.
14:10. 17:1. 27:3. Is 2:22. La 4:20. Da 5:23.
Mt +10:28. Ja 2:26.
goeth forth. Ps 17:2. 41:6. 44:9. Ec 8:8. Mt
27:50. Ac 7:59.
in that very day. Ps 37:9-13. +118:24. Is
2:12, 17. +24:21-23. Lk 23:43.

he returneth. Ps 9:15, 17. 90:3. +94:13.
103:14. 115:17. Ge +3:19. Ec 3:20. 12:7.
earth. Lk 12:16.
his thoughts. Heb. *eshtonoth,* only here.
William Kay notes that the Chaldi verb is
used in Da 6:4 of the labored artifices of
Daniel's enemies. Ps 6:5. +13:3. 28:1. 30:9.
33:10. 49:11. 88:4, 11. 94:11. +115:17. 143:7.
Jb 14:10, 21. 17:11. Pr 10:7. 11:7. 14:32. Ec
9:5, 10. Is 2:22. 38:18. 55:7. La 4:20. Jn 9:4.
12:35. 1 C 2:6. He +9:27. Ja 4:13, 14.
perish. Ps 9:6. 10:16. 41:5. 115:17, 119:92.
142:4. 1 S +2:9. Est 4:16. Jb 4:7. 11:20mg.
18:17. 30:2. Pr 11:7. Ec 5:14. 9:6. Is 26:14.
29:14. 57:1. Je 6:21. 7:28. 9:12. La 3:18. Jon
4:10. Mi 7:2. Ja 4:14.
5 **Happy**. Ps +1:1.
the God. Ps 46:7, 11. 84:8. Ge 32:24-29.
50:17. Ex 3:6.
whose hope. Ps +42:11. +94:13, 14. 115:18.
Ac +26:6. Ro +15:4. T +1:2. 1 P 1:21.
6 **made heaven**. Ps 136:5, 6. 148:5, 6. Ge 1:1.
2:1, 4. Jn +1:3. Ac 4:24. Re 14:7.
the sea. Ps 95:5. Ex 20:11. Jb 38:8-11. Pr
8:28, 29.
keepeth truth. Ps 89:2, 33. 98:3. 100:5. Dt
7:9. Is +55:3. Da 9:4. Mi 7:20. Ml +3:6. Jn
10:35. Ro +15:8. T +1:2. He 6:18.
for ever. Heb. *olam,* Ex +12:24.
7 **executeth judgment**. Dt +32:36. Ac 24:10.
oppressed. Ps +12:5. Is 9:4. Ml +3:5. Ro
12:17, 19.
which giveth food. Ps +37:3. 145:15, 16. Je
31:14. Mt 14:15-21. Lk 9:17.
looseth. Ps 68:6. 69:33. 102:20. 105:17-20.
107:10, 14-16. 116:16. 142:7. Dt 30:4. 2 Ch
33:11-13. Is 42:7, 22. 49:9, 25. 61:1. Je 15:11.
52:32-34. Zc 9:11, 12. Lk 4:18. 13:16. Ac
5:18, 19. 12:4-11. 16:26.
the prisoners. Ps 79:11. Jb 3:18. Is 42:22.
49:24mg. Ep +4:8.
8 **openeth**. Ps +119:18. Mt +11:5. 1 P 2:9.
raiseth. Ps 145:14. 147:6. Lk 13:11-13. 2 C
7:6.
loveth. Ps 11:7. Dt 33:3. Jn 14:21-23. 16:27.
1 J 4:16.
9 **preserveth**. Ezk 11:16.
strangers. Ps 39:12. 94:6. 119:19. Ge +23:4.
Ex 12:48mg. Is 14:1.
fatherless. Ex +22:22.
and widow. Is +1:17.
the way. Ps 1:6. 18:26. 83:13-17. 145:20.
147:6. 2 S 15:31. 17:23. Est 5:14. 7:10. 9:25.
Jb 5:12-14. Pr 4:19. 1 C 3:19.
he turneth. Is 24:18-20.
10 **reign**. Ps +102:15, 16. 145:13. Da 6:26. 1 C
15:24. Re +11:15.
for ever. Heb. *olam,* Ex +12:24.
thy God. Ps 147:12. Is 12:6. 40:9. 52:7. Jl
3:17.

O Zion. Ps +102:16. Is +24:23. +51:11. +59:20.

unto all. Ps +72:5. 115:14. Ge 17:5-8. Je 32:39, 40.

generations. Ge +9:12.

Praise ye. Ps 105:45mg.

PSALM 147

1 **for it is good**. Ps 63:3-5. 92:1. 135:3.

and praise. Ps 33:1. 42:4. 122:1-4. Re 5:9-14. 19:1-6.

2 **build**. Ps +102:16. Ne 3:1, etc. 7:4. Is 14:32. +24:23. 52:9, 10. Da 9:25. Mt 16:18.

he gathereth. Ge +49:10. Ezr 2:64, 65. 8:1, etc. Is +52:12mg. 56:8. Je +23:3. Ezk +20:34, 35. 38:8. Ep 2:12-19.

the outcasts. Is +27:13.

3 **healeth**. Ps +51:17. +103:3. Jb 5:18. Ho 6:1, 2. Ml 4:2. Mt 9:22. 12:20. Lk 4:18.

the broken. Ps 69:20.

bindeth up. Jb +5:18.

wounds. Heb. griefs. Ps 16:4. Jb 9:28. Pr 10:10. 15:13. Is 1:5, 6.

4 **He telleth**. Ps 8:3. 148:3. Ge +15:5. Is 40:26.

number. ver. 5. Ps 40:12. 104:25. 105:12.

stars. Ps 8:3. 136:9. 148:3. Ge 1:16.

5 **Great**. Ps 99:2. Da +2:45. Na 1:3. Re 15:3.

his understanding is infinite. Heb. of his understanding there is no number. Ps 40:5. 139:17, 18. Is 40:28. Ro 11:33.

6 **lifteth up**. Ps 145:14. 146:8, 9. 1 S 2:8. Jb 22:29. Ja 4:10. 1 P 5:6.

meek. Mt +5:5.

he casteth. Ps 55:23. 73:18, 19. 146:9. 2 P 2:4-9.

7 **Sing**. Ps 47:6, 7. 68:32. 95:1, 2. 107:21, 22. Ex 15:20, 21.

harp. Re +5:8-10.

8 **covereth**. Ps 135:7. Ge 9:14. 1 K 18:44, 45. Jb 26:8, 9. 36:27-33. 38:25-27. Is 5:6.

clouds. Ge +9:13.

prepareth. Ps 65:9-13. 104:13, 14. Jb 5:10. Je 14:22. Jl 2:23. Am 5:7, 8. Mt 5:45. Ac 14:17. Ja 5:17, 18.

9 **He giveth**. Ps 104:27, 28. 136:25. 145:15, 16. Jb 38:41. Mt 6:26. Lk 12:24.

10 **delighteth**. Ps 20:7. 33:16-18. Jb 39:19-25. Pr 21:31. Is 31:1. Ho 1:7.

he taketh. 1 S 16:7. 2 S 1:23. 2:18-23. Ec 9:11.

11 **taketh pleasure**. Ps 35:27. 149:4. Pr 11:20. 31:30. Is 62:4. Zp 3:17. Ml 3:16, 17. Col 1:10. He 11:5. 1 P 3:4.

that fear. Dt +6:2. Ml +3:16.

that hope. Ps +13:5. +42:11.

12 **praise thy God**. Ps 135:19-21. 146:10. 149:2. Is 12:6. 52:7. Jl 2:23.

13 **he hath**. Ps 48:11-14. 51:18. 125:2. Ne 3:1, etc. 6:1. 7:1. 12:30. La 2:8, 9. 4:12. Da 9:25.

blessed. Ps 115:14, 15. 128:3-6. 144:12. Is 44:3-5. Je 30:19, 20. Zc 8:3-5. Lk 19:42-44.

14 **He maketh peace**, etc. Heb. Who maketh thy border peace. Ps 29:11. 122:6. Le 26:6. 1 Ch 22:9. Is 9:6, 7. 60:17, 18. 66:12. Zc 9:8.

filleth. Ps 132:15. Ge 42:25. Dt 8:7, 8. Ezk 27:17.

finest of the wheat. Heb. fat of wheat. Ps 81:16mg. Dt 32:14.

15 **sendeth**. Ps 33:9. 107:20, 25. Jb 34:29. 37:12. Jon 1:4. Mt 8:8, 9, 13.

his word. Ps 68:11. 2 Th 3:1mg.

16 **giveth**. Ps 148:8. Jb 37:6. Is 55:10.

scattereth. Jb 37:9, 10. 38:29.

17 **casteth**. Ps 78:47, 48. Ex 9:23-25. Jsh 10:11. Jb 38:22, 23.

who can stand. Jb 38:29, 30.

18 **He sendeth**. ver. 15. Jb 6:16, 17. 37:10, 17.

19 **showeth**. Ps 76:1. 78:5. 103:7. Dt 33:2-4. Ml 4:4. Ro 3:2. 9:4. 2 T 3:15-17.

word. Heb. words. Ex 20:1, etc. Dt 4:12, 13mg. 5:22.

his statutes. Ex ch. 21-23. Dt +4:1.

20 **not dealt so**. Dt 4:32-34. Pr 29:18. Is 5:1-7. Mt 21:33-41. Ac 14:16. 26:17, 18. Ro 3:1, 2. Ep 2:12. 5:8. He 4:1, 2. 1 P 2:9, 10.

PSALM 148

1 **Praise ye the Lord**. Heb. Hallelujah. Ps 89:5. 146:1mg. Is 49:13. Mk *11:10*. Lk 2:13, 14. Re 5:13. 19:1-6.

2 **all his angels**. Ps 103:20, 21. Jb 38:7. Is 6:2-4. Ezk 3:12. Lk 2:14. Re 5:11-13.

all his hosts. Ps +103:21.

3 **sun**. Ps 8:1-3. 19:1-6. 89:36, 37. 136:7-9. Ge 1:14-16. 8:22. Dt 4:19. Je 33:20.

4 **heavens**. Ps 113:6. Dt +10:14.

waters. Ps 104:3. Ge 1:7. 7:11.

5 **for he**. Ps 33:6-9. 95:5. Ge 1:1, 2, 6. Je 10:11-13. Am 9:6. Re 4:11.

6 **He hath also**. Ps 89:37. 93:1. 102:26. 119:90, 91. Jb 38:10, 11, 33. Pr 8:27-29. Ec +1:4. Is 54:9. 65:17. Je +31:35, 36. 33:25. 2 P 3:10.

for ever. Ps +9:18.

and ever. Heb. *olam*, Ps +21:4.

7 **from the earth**. ver. 1.

ye dragons. Ps 74:13, 14. 104:25, 26. Ge 1:21. Jb 41:1, etc. Is 27:1. 43:20. 51:9, 10. Jl 2:22.

8 **Fire**. Ps 147:15-18. Ge 19:24. Ex 9:23-25. Le 10:2. Nu 16:35. Jb 37:2-6. Is 66:16. Jl 2:30. Am 7:4. Re 16:8, 9, 21.

hail. Is +28:17.

stormy. Ps 107:25-29. Ex 10:13, 19. 14:21. Am 4:13. Jon 1:4. Mt 8:24-27.

9 **Mountains**. Ps 65:12, 13. 96:11-13. 97:4, 5. 98:7-9. 114:3-7. Is 42:11. 44:23. 49:13. 55:12, 13. 64:1. Ezk 36:1, etc.

10 **Beasts**. Ps 50:10, 11. 103:22. 150:6. Ge 1:20-25.

flying fowl. Heb. birds of wing. Ge 7:14mg.
Ezk 17:23.

11 **Kings**. Ps 2:10-12. 22:27-29. 66:1-4. 68:31,
32. 72:10, 11. 86:9. 102:15. 138:4, 5. Pr 8:15,
16. Is 49:23. 60:3. Re 21:24.

12 **young men**. Ps 8:2. 68:25. 78:31, 63. Dt
32:35. Je 31:13. Zc 9:17. Mt 21:15, 16. Lk
19:37. T 2:4-6.
maidens. Ps 45:14. 78:63. Ge +24:16.
old men. Ps +105:22. 107:32. +119:100.
children. or, youths. Ps 37:25. 119:9. Ge
14:24. 2 K +2:23.

13 **for his name**. Ps 8:1, 9. 99:3, 4, 9. SS 5:9, 16.
Is 6:3. Zc 9:17. Ph 3:8.
excellent. Heb. exalted. Is +12:4. Mt 6:13.
glory. Ps 57:5. 72:19. 108:4. 113:4. Ep 4:10. 1
P 3:22.

14 **exalteth**. Ps +92:10. Lk 1:52.
the praise. Ps 145:10. 149:9. Lk 2:32. Re 5:8-
14.
a people. Ex +19:5, 6. Dt 4:7. 33:29. Jn 4:23.
Ep 1:4. 2:13, 17, 19. Ja 4:8.
Praise. Ps 105:45mg.

PSALM 149

1 **Praise ye the Lord**. Heb. Hallelujah. Ps
148:1.
Sing. Ps 33:3. 96:1. 98:1. 144:9. Is 42:10. Re
5:9. 7:10, 12.
in the congregation. Ps 22:22, 25. 68:26.
89:5. 111:1. 116:18. He 2:12.

2 **rejoice**. Ps 135:3, 4. Dt 7:6, 7. +12:7.
him that made. Ps 100:3. 1 S 12:22. Jb
35:10. Is 17:7. 27:11. 54:5. Ep 2:10.
children of Zion. Is 62:11, 12. Jl 2:23.
be joyful. Is +51:11. 52:7. Zc 9:9. Mt 21:5. Lk
19:37, 38. Ph 3:3. 4:4. Re 19:6.
their King. Ps 59:13. 114:2. Zp +3:15. Zc 9:9.
Mt 21:5. 25:34. Jn +1:49. 19:15, 19-22.

3 **in the dance**. or, with the pipe. Ex +15:20.
with the timbrel. 1 Ch 16:42. Ezr 3:10.
harp. Re +5:8.

4 **taketh pleasure**. Ps 22:8. 35:27. 44:3. 47:4.
117:11. 147:11. Pr 11:20. Is 62:4, 5. Je 32:41.
Zp 3:17. Col 1:10. He 11:5.
beautify. Ps 90:17. 132:16. Is 61:1-3, 10. 2
Th +1:10. He 12:10. 1 P 3:4. 5:5. Re 7:14.
the meek. Mt +5:5.
with salvation. Ps 9:13, 14. 14:7. 37:39, 40.
+42:5mg. 53:6. 98:2, 9. 102:16. 132:11-16. Is
+25:9. He +9:28.

5 **the saints**. Ps 23:1. 118:14, 15. 145:10. Ro
5:2. 1 P 1:8.
sing. Ps 42:8. 63:5, 6. 92:2. 119:55, 62. Jb
35:10.
upon their beds. Ps 4:4. 36:4. 41:3. Ge 49:4.
Re 7:15-17.

6 **the high**. Ps 96:4. Ne 9:5. Da 4:37. Lk 2:14.
Re 19:6.
God. Heb. El, Ex +15:2.
mouth. Heb. throat. Ps 5:9. 69:3. 115:7.
145:3-5. Is 58:1.
and a two-edged. Pr 5:4. Is 41:15mg. 2 C
10:4. Ep 6:17. He 4:12. Re 1:16. 2:12. 12:11.
in their hand. Ne 4:17. Lk +22:36. Jn 18:36.

7 **execute vengeance**. Ps 137:8, 9. Nu 31:2, 3.
Dt 32:41. Jg 5:23. 1 S 15:2, 3, 18-23. Ezk
28:26. Mi +5:8-15. Zc +9:13-16. 12:6. 14:17-
19. Ju 15. Re 19:11-21.
upon the heathen. Ezk +30:3. Mi 7:16, 17.

8 **To bind**. Jsh 10:23, 24. 12:7. Jg 1:6, 7.
their kings. Is 60:10.
fetters. 2 Ch +33:11.

9 **To execute**. Ps 137:8. Dt 7:1, 2. 32:42, 43. Jg
5:13, 31. Is 14:22, 23. Da +7:22. Ju 15. Re
2:26, +27. 17:14-16.
the judgment. Mt +3:11. Jn 20:22, 23.
written. Jb 13:26. Is 26:9.
this honor. Ps 148:14. Pr +22:29. 1 C 6:2, 3.
Re 3:21.
have all. 1 S 30:24. Pr 19:22. Da 7:18. Ho
+11:12. Zc +14:5. Jn +10:16. Ac +10:11. 1 C
12:11, 13. Ga 3:28. Ep +4:4. 1 Th 3:13. Ju 14.
Re 20:6.

PSALM 150

1 **Praise ye the Lord**. Heb. Hallelujah. Ps
105:45mg. 149:1.
God. Heb. El, Ex +15:2.
in his sanctuary. Ps 29:9. 66:13-16. 116:18,
19. 118:19, 20. 134:2.
in the firmament. Ge 1:6-8. Ezk 1:22-26.
10:1. Da 12:3.

2 **for his mighty**. Ps 145:5, 6. Re 15:3, 4.
according. Ps 96:4. 145:3. Dt 3:24. Je 32:17-19.

3 **with the sound**. Ps 81:2, 3. 98:5, 6. Nu
10:10. 1 Ch 15:24, 28. 16:42. Da 3:5.
trumpet. or, cornet. Ps 47:5. 81:3. 98:6. 2 Ch
+5:12.
the psaltery. 33:2. 57:8. 71:22. 81:2. 92:3.
108:2. 149:3. 1 S +10:5.
harp. Re +5:8.

4 **with the timbrel**. Ex +15:20.
with the timbrel. or, pipe. La 5:15.
stringed instruments. Ps 33:2. 45:8. 92:3.
144:9. Is 38:20. Hab 3:19.
organs. Jb 30:31.

5 **the loud cymbals**. 2 S 6:5. 1 Ch +13:8.
15:16, 19, 28. 16:5. 25:1, 6. Jb 41:7. Is 18:1.
sounding. Ps 18:44. Ge 29:13.

6 **Let everything**. Ps 103:22. 145:10. 148:7-
11. Ep 5:19, 20. Col 3:16. Re 5:13, 14.
breath. Heb. neshamah, Ge +2:7.
Praise ye. Ps 105:45mg.

PROVERBS

PROVERBS 1

1 **proverbs.** ver. 6. Pr 10:1. 25:1. 1 K +4:32. Ec 12:9. Jn 16:25.
Solomon. 2 S 12:24, 25. 1 K 2:12. 1 Ch 22:9. 28:5. 29:23.

2 **To know.** Pr 4:5-7. 7:4. 8:5. 16:16. 17:16. Dt 4:5, 6. 1 K 3:9-12. 2 T 3:15-17.
wisdom. Ep 4:14.
instruction. 2 P 1:6.
perceive. Is 6:10. Ph 1:10. He 5:14.

3 **receive.** Pr 2:1-9. 8:10, 11. Jb 22:22.
instruction. 2 P 1:6.
equity. Heb. equities. 1 K 3:28.

4 **subtilty.** ver. 22, 23. Pr 8:5. 9:4-6. Ps 19:7. 119:130. Is 35:8. Mt 10:16.
simple. ver. 22, 32. Pr 7:7. 8:5. 9:4, 13. 14:15, 18. 21:11. 22:3. Ps 19:7. 116:6. 119:130. Ezk 45:20. Ro 16:18, 19.
to the young. Pr 7:7-24. 8:17, 32. Ps 34:11. 119:9. Ec 11:9, 10. 12:1. 2 T 2:22. T 2:6.
discretion. or, advisement. Pr 2:11. 3:21. 5:2. 8:12. Ps 17:4. 1 Th 5:21.

5 **wise.** Pr 9:9. 12:1. Ps 119:98-100. 1 C 3:18. 10:15. Ph 3:12.
a man. 1 S 25:32, 33. 2 Ch 25:16.
unto wise counsels. Ps 119:18, 33, 34. Ac 8:34, 35. 18:24-26. 1 C 2:9, 10. He 13:9.

6 **a proverb.** Mt 13:10-17, 51, 52. Mk 4:11, 34. Ac 8:30, 31.
the interpretation. or, an eloquent speech. Hab 2:6.
the words. Ec 12:11.
dark. Ps +78:2. He 5:14. 2 P 3:16.

7 **fear.** Pr 15:33. Dt 17:18-20. Jb +28:28. Ps 5:7. 112:1. Lk 23:40. Ro 3:18.
beginning. or, principal part. Pr 3:9. 4:7. 8:22. 17:14.
but. ver. 22, 29, 30. Pr 5:12, 13. 15:5. 18:2. Ps 36:1. Je 8:9. Jn 3:18-21. Ro 1:28.

8 **My son.** ver. 10, 15. Pr 2:1. 3:1. 7:1. Mt 9:2, 22.
hear. Pr 4:1-4. 5:1, 2. 31:1. Ex +20:12. 1 S 2:25. 2 T 1:5. 3:14, 15. He 1:6.

9 **they.** Pr 3:22. 4:9. 6:20, 21. 1 T 2:9, 10. 1 P 3:3, 4.
an ornament. Heb. an adding. Ge 41:42. SS 1:10. 4:9. Is 3:19. Ezk 16:11. Da 5:7, 16, 29.

10 **if sinners.** Pr 7:21-23. 13:20. 20:19. Ge 3:6. 11:4. 39:7-13. Dt 13:6-8. Jg 16:16-21. 1 Ch 21:1. Ps 1:1. 50:18. +119:63, 101. Is 41:6. Ro 16:18. 1 C 15:33. 2 C 2:11. Ep 5:11. Ja 1:13-15.
consent thou not. Est +1:12. Ro 7:14-17, 20, 23.

11 **Come with.** ver. 14. Is 56:12.
let us lay. ver. 16. Pr 12:6. 30:14. Ps 56:6. 64:5, 6. 71:10. Je 5:26. Mi 7:2. Ac 23:15. 25:3.
blood. ver. 16, 18. Pr 6:17. 12:6. 28:17.
let us lurk. ver. 18. Ps 10:8-10. 17:12. 35:7. Je 11:19. 18:18-20. Mt 26:3, 4. Jn 15:25.

12 **swallow.** Ps +35:25. Mi 3:2, 3.
as the. Ps 5:9. Ro 3:13.
grave. Heb. sheol, Ge +37:35.
whole. Nu 16:30-33. 26:10. Ps 28:1. 143:7.
pit. Heb. bor, Ge +37:20.

13 **We shall find.** ver. 19. Jb 24:2, 3. Is 10:13, 14. Je 22:16, 17. Na 2:12. Hab 2:9. Lk 12:15. 1 T 6:9, 10. Re 18:9-16.

14 **lot.** Pr 16:33. 18:18. Le 16:8, 9.
among us. ver. 11. Ge 19:1.
purse. Pr 16:11. 23:31. Dt 25:13.

15 **walk not.** Pr 4:14, 15. 9:6. 13:20. 1 K 13:15-19. Ps 1:1. 26:4, 5. +119:63. 2 C 6:17.
refrain. Pr 4:27. 5:8. Ps 119:101. Je 14:10.

16 **For their.** Pr 4:16. 6:18. Is 59:7. Ro 3:15.
feet. Pr 6:18. Is 52:7. Ro 3:15.

17 **in vain.** Pr 7:23. Jb 35:11. Is 1:3. Je 8:7.
net. Ex 27:4, 5. 38:4. Ps +57:6.
sight of any bird. Heb. eyes of every thing that hath a wing. Pr 23:5.

18 **lay wait.** Pr 5:22, 23. 9:17, 18. 28:17. Est 7:10. Ps 7:14-16. 9:16. 55:23. Mt 27:4, 5.
lurk. 1 K 21:20. Ps 10:8.
lives. Heb. nephesh, Ge +44:30.

19 **every.** Pr 15:27. 23:3, 4. 2 S 18:11-13. 2 K 5:20-27. Je 22:17-19. Mi 2:1-3. 3:10-12. Hab 2:9. Ac 8:19, 20. 1 T 3:3. 6:9, 10. Ja 5:1-4. 2 P 2:3, 14-16.
greedy. Pr 15:27. 1 K 21:4. Mt 26:14-16. 27:3, 5. Lk 12:15.
taketh. Jb 31:39. Ps 7:15, 16. Ec 5:13.
life. Heb. nephesh, Ge +44:30.

20 **Wisdom.** Heb. Wisdoms, that is, excellent wisdom. Mt 13:34, 35. Lk 11:49. 1 C 1:24, 30. Col 2:3.

crieth. Pr 8:1-5. 9:3. Ps 40:9, 10. Jn 7:37. Re 3:20.

in the streets. lit. open places. Am +5:16. Jn 18:20. Ac 26:26. 2 P +1:16.

21　**She crieth**. Pr 9:3. Mt 10:27. 13:2. Lk 14:21, 23. Jn 18:20, 21. Ac 5:20. Ro 10:21.

gates. Ge +14:7.

22　**How**. Mt +17:17.

ye simple. ver. +4. Pr 7:7. 9:4-6, 16-18. Ps 94:8. Mt 9:13. 11:29, 30. 23:37. Lk 19:42. Re 22:17.

simplicity. 2 S 15:1. Ro 12:8. 2 C 1:12. 11:3.

the scorners. Pr 3:34. 14:6. 15:12. 19:29. 21:11. Jb 34:7. Ps 1:1. 2 P 3:3.

delight. or, have delighted. i.e. will delight. Ge +45:9.

fools hate knowledge. ver. 7, 29. Pr 5:12. Jb 21:14. 24:13. Mt 23:37. Lk 19:41, 42. Jn 3:20. Ro 1:20.

23　**Turn**. Is 1:18. Ezk 18:27-30. +33:11. Zc 9:12. 29:1. Ps 141:5. Re 3:19.

my reproof. ver. 25, 30. Pr 6:23. 10:17. 12:1. 29:1. Ps 141:5. Re 3:19.

behold. Is 32:15. 45:8. 59:21. Jl 2:28. Zc 12:10. Lk 11:13. Jn 4:10, 14. 7:36, 37. 14:16, 17. Ac 2:36-38. 1 C 2:12. Ga 3:14. 2 T 1:14. Re 3:16-18.

spirit. Heb. *ruach*, Ge +41:38; +26:35.

make known. Pr 28:5. Ps 25:12. 32:8. Jn 16:13. 1 J 2:27.

24　**I have called**. Is 50:2. 65:12. 66:4. 2 Ch 36:15, 16. Je 7:13. Zc 7:11, 12. Mt 22:3, 5, 6. 23:37, 38.

ye refused. Ps 58:4, 5. +119:68. +145:9. Jon +4:2. Mt 22:2-6. Lk 14:17-20. He +12:25, 26.

stretched. Pr 31:20. Is 49:22. 65:2. Ac 4:30. Ro 10:21.

25　**ye**. ver. 30. 2 Ch 36:16. Ps 107:11. Je 23:22. Lk 7:30.

set at nought. Ex 5:2. Dt 31:27. Ne 9:26. Ps 81:11. Is 1:2. 30:8, 9. 65:2, 3. Je 5:23. 25:4. Ezk 2:7, 8.

would. ver. 30. Pr 5:12. 12:1. Ps 81:11.

26　**will laugh**. Jg 10:14. Ps 2:4. 37:13. 59:8. Lk 14:24.

calamity. ver. 27. Pr 6:15. 17:5.

fear. ver. 27, 33. Pr 3:25. Ge +31:42.

27　**your fear**. Pr 3:25, 26. 10:24, 25. Ge +31:42. Ps 69:22-28. Lk 21:26, 34, 35. 1 Th 5:3. Re 6:15-17.

as a. Je +23:19.

distress. Lk 21:23-25. Ro 2:9.

28　**Then shall**. Ge 6:3. 1 S 8:18. 15:24-26. 28:5, 6. Ps 50:15. +66:18. Is 55:6. Je 15:1. Ezk 5:11. 7:25, 26. 14:13-20. 20:1-3. Ho 5:6, 7. Am 8:*11, 12*. Mt 7:22, 23. 25:10-12. Lk 13:25-28. 16:22-26. He 12:*15-17*. Re 6:15-17.

they shall seek. Pr 8:17. 1 Ch +28:9. Ps 78:34-36. Ho 5:15. 6:1-4.

not find. Lk 13:24, 25.

29　**hated knowledge**. ver. 22. Pr 5:12. 6:23. Jb 21:14, 15. Ps 50:16, 17. Is 27:11. 30:9-12. Jn 3:20. Ac 7:51-54.

did not choose. Ps 119:173. Is +66:4. Lk 10:42. He 11:25.

30　**would none**. ver. 25. Pr 15:32. Ps 81:11. 119:111, 173. Je 8:9. Lk 14:18-20.

31　**they eat**. Pr 14:14. Dt 28:63. Jb +4:8. Ga 6:7, 8. He 10:26, 27, 31.

32　**the turning**. *or*, ease. Ec 8:11. Je 48:11, 12. Mk +4:19.

the simple. ver. 4.

shall slay them. Pr 8:36. Jn 3:36. He 10:38, 39. 12:25.

prosperity. Dt 32:15, etc. Ps 69:22. 92:6, 7. Lk 12:16-21. 16:19-25. He 12:8. Ja 5:5.

fools. Pr +23:4. Mk +4:19. Lk 12:19-21.

33　**whoso**. Pr 8:32-35. 9:11. 12:15. Ps 25:12, 13. 81:13. Is 48:18. 55:3. Mt 17:5. Jn 10:27-29. 1 P 1:5.

dwell safely. Pr 3:23, 24. 18:10. Ge 7:13, 16. 9:2. Dt +12:10. 1 S 2:9. Jb 4:7. 5:21, 23. 11:18. Ps 16:8. 25:12, 13. 27:1. 34:20. 91:1, 2, 4, 10. 112:7. 121:1-8. 124:8. 125:2. Is 4:5, 6. 27:3. 33:16. 43:2, 3. Zc 2:5. 1 P 3:13.

and shall. Pr 3:21-26. 14:26. 31:21. Ps 112:7. Is 14:3. 26:3. Ml 4:1, 2. Lk 21:9, 19, 26, 28. Ro 8:35-39. 2 P 3:13.

fear. Ge +19:30.

PROVERBS 2

1　**if**. Pr 1:3. 4:1. 7:1. Jn 12:47, 48. 1 T 1:15.

hide. Pr 6:21. Dt +6:6. Mt 13:44.

2　**thou**. Pr 18:1. Ps 119:111, 112. Is 55:3. Mt 13:9.

incline. Zc 7:11, 12.

apply. Pr 22:17-21. 23:12. Ps 90:12. Ec 7:25. 8:9, 16. Lk 14:28. Ac 17:11.

3　**if**. Pr 3:6. 8:17. 1 K 3:9-12. 1 Ch 22:12. Ps 25:4, 5. 119:34, 73, 125, 169. Lk 11:13. Ep 1:17, 18. Ja 1:5.

liftest up thy voice. Heb. givest thy voice. Pr 1:20. 8:1. Ps 46:6.

4　**thou**. Pr 3:14, 15. 8:18, 19. 16:16. 23:23. Ps 19:10. 119:14, 72, 127. Mt 6:19-21. 13:44. 19:21, 22, 29.

searchest. Jb 28:12-20. Ec 4:8. Lk 16:8.

5　**shalt**. 2 Ch 1:10-12. Ho 6:3. Mt 7:7, 8. Lk 11:9-13.

the fear. Pr 9:10. Jb 28:28. Je 32:40, 41.

find. Je 9:24. 24:7. 31:34. Mt 11:27. Lk 10:22. Jn 17:3. 1 J 5:20.

knowledge. ver. 9. Pr 28:5. Is 2:3. 29:18, 24. 32:3. 35:8. 42:7. 52:6. Je 31:34. Ho 6:3. Mt 11:20. Lk 1:77-79. 4:18. Jn 8:12. 1 C 2:14, 15. 2 C 4:6. 1 J 5:20.

6　**the Lord**. Ex 31:3. 1 K 3:9, 12. 4:29. 1 Ch 22:12. Jb 32:8. Is 54:13. Da 1:17. 2:21, 23. Lk 21:15. Jn 6:45. Ep 1:17, 18. Ja 1:5, 17.

wisdom. Pr 8:9. Jb 28:20. Ps 16:7. 51:6. Ec 2:26. Ja 1:5.
out. Pr 6:23. 8:5-9. Ps 19:7. 119:98, 104. Is 8:20.

7 **layeth**. Pr 8:14. 14:8. Jb 28:28. 1 C 1:19, 24, 30. 2:6, 7. 3:18, 19. Col 1:5. 2:3. 2 T 3:15-17. Ja 3:15-17.
a buckler. Pr 28:18. 30:5. Ps 84:11. 144:2.

8 **keepeth**. Pr 8:20. Ps 1:6. 23:3, 4. 121:5-8. Is 35:9. 49:9, 10. Jn 10:28, 29.
and. Pr 3:21-24. Dt 33:3, 26-29. 1 S 2:9. Ps 37:23, 24, 28, 31. 66:9. 145:20. Je 32:40, 41. Lk 8:15. 1 P 1:5. Ju 24.

9 **Then shalt**. Pr 1:2-6. Ps 25:8, 9. 32:8. 119:99, 105. 143:8-10. Is 35:8. 48:17. Je 6:16. Mt 7:13, 14. Jn 14:6. T 2:11, 12.

10 **wisdom entereth**. Pr 14:33. 18:1, 2. 24:13, 14. Jb 23:12. Ps 19:10. 104:34. 119:97, 103, 111, 162. Je 15:16. Jn 14:23. Ro 6:17, 18. Col 3:16.
heart. Ge +3:7.
soul. Heb. *nephesh*, Ge +34:3; Ge +3:7.

11 **Discretion**. Pr 4:6. 6:22-24. Ps 25:21. 119:9-11. Ec 9:15-18. 10:10. Ep 5:15.

12 **deliver**. Pr 1:10-19. 4:14-17. 9:6. 13:20. Ps 17:4, 5. 26:4, 5. 141:4. 2 C 6:17.
from the man. Pr 3:32. 8:13. 16:28-30. Ps 101:4. Is 59:3-5. Ac 20:30. 1 C 15:33.

13 **leave**. Pr 21:16. Ps 14:3. 36:3. 125:5. Ezk 18:26. 33:12, 13. Zp 1:6. Mt 12:43-45. 2 T 4:10. He +3:13. 6:4-6. 2 P 2:20-22. 1 J 2:19.
walk. Pr 4:19. Jb 24:13-16. Jn 3:19, 20. 12:35. Ro 1:21. 1 Th 5:5-7. 1 J 1:6. 2:9-11.

14 **rejoice**. Pr 10:23. Je 11:15. Hab 1:15. Zp 3:11. 1 C 13:6.
and. Ho 7:3. Lk 22:4, 5. Ro 1:32.

15 **Whose ways**. Dt 32:5. Ps 125:5. Is 30:8-13. 59:8. Ph 2:15.

16 **deliver**. Pr 5:3-20. 6:24. 7:5-23. 22:14. 23:27. Ge 39:3-12. 1 K 11:1. Ne 13:26, 27. Ec 7:26.
flattereth. Pr 7:21. 29:5.

17 **the guide**. Pr 5:18. Je 3:4.
forgetteth. Ezk 16:8, 59, 60. Ml 2:14-16.

18 **her house**. Pr 5:4-14. 6:26-35. 7:22-27. 9:18. 1 C 6:9-11. Ga 5:19-21. Ep 5:5. Re 21:8. 22:15.

19 **None**. Ps 81:12. Ec 7:26. Je 13:23. Ho 4:14. Mt 19:24-26.
take. Pr 4:18. Ga 5:19, 21. Ep 5:5. He 6:18. Re 21:8.

20 **mayest walk**. Pr 13:20. Ps +119:63, 115. SS 1:7, 8. Je 6:16. He 6:12. 3 J 11.

21 **the upright**. Jb 1:1. 42:12. Ps 84:11. 112:4-6. Mt +5:5.

22 **the wicked**. Pr 5:22, 23. Jb 18:16-18. 21:30. Ps 37:20, 22, 28, 37, 38. 52:5. 101:8. 104:35. 145:20. 147:7-9. Is 3:10, 11. 11:4. +65:20.
rooted. or, plucked up. Pr +13:22. +28:8. Dt 7:22mg. 28:63. Mt 3:10. +13:30. 2 P 3:7.

PROVERBS 3

1 **forget not**. Pr 1:8. 4:5. 31:5. Dt 4:23. Ps 119:93, 153, 176. Ho 4:6.
let. Dt 4:9. +6:6. 8:1. 30:16-20. Ps 119:11, 16, 34, 47, 48. Ezk 11:19. 36:26, 27. Jn 14:21-24. Ro 7:22. Re 22:14, 20.

2 **length**. ver. 16. Pr 4:10. 9:11. Dt +5:16. Jb 5:26. Ps 34:11-14. 128:6. Ep 6:1-3. 1 T 4:8.
long life. Heb. years of life. ver. 16. Jb 12:12. Ps +91:16mg.
and peace. ver. 17. Ps 119:165. Is 48:17, 18. Ro +5:1.

3 **mercy**. Pr 16:6. 20:28. 2 S 15:20. Ps 25:10. 85:10. 89:14. 117:2. Ho 4:1. Mi 7:18-20. Ml 2:6. Mt 23:23. Ep 5:1, 2, 9. Col 3:12.
bind. Pr 6:21. 7:3. Ex 13:9, 16. Dt 6:8. 11:18-21. Ps 119:11.
write. Je 17:1. 2 C 3:3. He 10:16.
table of. Ex +25:21.

4 **find favor**. Ge 39:2-4, 21. 41:39, 40. 1 S 2:26. Ps 111:10. Da 1:9. Lk 2:52. Ac 2:47. Ro 14:17-19.
good under-standing. or, good success. Pr 12:8. 13:15. 16:22. 19:11mg. 23:9. Jsh 1:7mg, 8mg. Ps 111:10.

5 **Trust**. Pr 22:19. +25:19. Jb 13:15. Ps 4:5. +9:10. 37:3, 5, 7. 42:5. 62:8. 115:9-11. 125:1. 146:3-5. Is 12:2. 26:3, 4. 50:10. Je 17:7, 8. Ep 1:12. 1 P +1:21.
lean not. ver. 7. Pr 23:4. 28:26. Ge 3:5, 6. Ps 78:18-21. Is 47:10, 11. Je 1:6-8. 2:13. 9:23. 10:23. 17:5. Ro 12:16. 1 C 3:18-20. 8:1, 2. Ph 3:3.

6 **In**. Pr 16:3. 23:17. 1 S 23:4, 11, 12. 30:8. 1 Ch +28:9. Ezr 7:27. 8:22, 23. Ne 1:11. 2:4. 1 C 10:31. 2 C 8:16. Ph 4:6. Col 3:17, 23.
direct. Pr 11:5. 16:9. Ps +32:8. 37:23. Is 28:26. 42:16. 48:17. Je 10:23. Ja 1:5.

7 **Be**. ver. 5. Pr 26:12. Is 5:21. Ro 11:25. 12:16.
fear the Lord. Pr 8:13. 14:26, 27. 16:6. 19:23. Ne 5:9, 15. Jb 1:1. Ps 19:9. 25:12, 14. 31:19. 34:11-14. 85:9. 103:11. 111:10. 112:1. 115:13. 128:1. 147:11. Ec 7:18. 8:12. +12:13. Is 50:10. Ml 2:5. 4:2. Lk 1:50. Ac 9:31. 10:2, 22, 35. 13:16, 26.
depart. 2 T +2:19.

8 **shall**. Pr 4:22. 16:24. Ps 147:3. Is 1:6. Je 30:12, 13.
health. Heb. medicine. **S#7500h**, only here. Compare **S#7499h**: Je 30:13. 46:11. Ezk 30:21mg.
thy. Ezk 16:4, 5.
marrow. Heb. watering, *or* moistening. Jb 21:24. Ho 2:5mg.

9 **Honor**. Pr 14:31. Ge 14:18-21. 28:22. Ex 35:20-29. Nu 7:2, etc. 31:50, etc. 1 S 2:30. Hg 1:4-9. Ml 3:8, 9. 4:2. Mt 6:1. Mk 14:7, 8, 10, etc. Lk 14:13, 14. 1 C 16:2. 2 C 5:14, 15. 8:2, 3, 8, 9. Ph 4:17, 18. 1 J 3:17, 18.
with thy substance. Dt 14:29. Ml 3:10-12.

Ro 12:1. 1 C 6:20. 2 C 8:5. Ga 6:6-8. Ph 4:17-19. 1 T 5:17, 18.
firstfruits. Le +23:10.

10 So shall. Pr 11:24, 25. 19:17. 22:9. Le 26:2-5. Dt 28:8. Ne 8:10. Ec 11:1, 2. Hg 2:19. Ml 3:10, 11. Mt 10:42. Lk +6:38. 2 C 9:6-11. Ga 6:10. He 6:10.

11 My. Ps 139:23, 24. Je +31:18. La 3:40. He *12:5, 6*.
neither. Pr 24:10. Jb 4:5. Ps 77:2, 7-10. Is 40:30, 31. 2 C 4:1, 16, 17. 12:8-10. He 12:3, 7-12. Ja 5:11. 1 P 1:6, 7.
weary. S#6973h, Is +7:6.

12 whom the Lord. Dt 8:2, 15, 16. Ps 119:75. Je 29:11. 1 P 5:6. Re 3:19.
he correcteth. Pr 13:24. Jb 5:17. Ps 103:10. Is 48:10. Je 10:24. 30:11. La 3:31-33, 39. Zc 13:9. Ml 3:3. He *12:5, 6*.
as a father. Pr 29:17. Dt 8:5. Ps 103:13. 119:67, 71. He 12:10.

13 Happy. Pr 4:5-8. +8:10, 32-35. +16:22. 1 K 10:1-9, 23, 24. Ec 9:15-18.
getteth. Heb. draweth out. Pr 2:4. 8:35mg. 12:2. 18:1, 22. Ps 140:8.

14 the merchandise. Pr 2:4. 8:10, 11, 19. 16:16. 2 Ch 1:11, 12. Jb 28:13-19. Ps 19:10. 119:72, 111, 162. Mt 16:26. Ph 3:8, 9. Re 3:18.

15 more. Pr 8:11. 20:15. 31:10. Jb 28:15-18. Mt 13:44-46. Ph 3:7, 12, 14.
all. Ps 63:3. 73:25, 26. Ro 8:18.

16 Length. ver. +2. Ps 71:9. 1 T 4:8.
riches. Pr 4:6-9. 8:18-21. 15:6. Dt 11:14, 15. 28:11, 12. 30:9. 1 K 3:13. Jb 22:24, 25. Ps 19:11. 107:38. 112:3. Is 30:23. Mk 10:30. 1 C 3:21-23. 2 C 6:10.

17 ways of. Pr 2:10. 22:18. Ps 19:10, 11. 63:3-5. 112:1. 119:14, 47, 103, 174. Mt 11:28-30. He 11:26.
all. Ps 25:10. 37:11. 119:165. Is 26:3. 57:19. Lk 1:79. Jn 16:33. Ro 5:1. Ph 4:8, 9.

18 tree of life. Pr 10:11. 11:30. 13:12. 15:4. Ge 2:9. 3:22. Re 2:7. 22:2.
happy. Jn 15:11. 17:13. 2 C 6:10. 8:2. 1 P 1:6-8.

19 Lord. Pr 8:27-29. Ps 104:24. 136:5. Je 10:12. 51:15. Jn 1:3.
established. *or*, prepared. Ex 15:17. 2 S 7:13.

20 the depths. Ge 1:9. 7:11. Jb 38:8-11. Ps 104:8, 9.
the clouds. Ge 27:28, 37-39. Dt 33:28. Jb 36:27, 28. 38:26-28. Ps 65:9-12. Je 14:22. Jl 2:23.
dew. Dt +33:13. Is +26:19.

21 let. ver. 1-3. Dt 4:9. 6:6-9. Jsh 1:8. Jn 8:31. *15:6, 7. He 2:1-3*. 1 J 2:24, 27.
keep. Pr 2:7. Dt 32:46, 47. 2 P 1:12.

22 life. Pr 4:22. Ec 7:12. Is 38:16. Jn 8:12. 12:49, 50. 17:3.
soul. Heb. *nephesh*, Ge +34:3.
grace. Pr 1:9.

23 safely. Pr 2:8. 4:12. 10:9. Ps 37:23, 24, 31. 91:11, 12. 121:3, 8. Zc 10:12.

24 liest. Pr 6:22. Le 26:6. Ps 3:5. 4:8. 121:4-7. Jb 11:19. Is 26:9. Ezk 34:15.
afraid. Ge 19:30. Ezk 34:25-28.
and. Ps 127:2. Je 31:26. Ac 12:6. 1 Th 4:13, 14.

25 Be not. Pr 1:33. Jb 5:21, 22. 11:13-15. Ps 27:1, 2. +34:4. 46:1-3. 91:5. 112:7. Is 8:12, 13. 14:3. 41:10-14. Da 3:17, 18. Mt 8:24-26. 24:6. Mk 4:40. Lk 21:9. Jn 14:1. 2 T 1:7. 1 P 3:14.
fear. Ge +31:42.
neither. Pr 1:27. Ps 73:19. Is 57:20, 21. Mt 24:15. Lk 21:18-28.

26 Lord. Pr 14:26. Dt 33:27. Ps 91:1-3, 9, 10. Is 26:1, 20. Hab 3:17, 18. Lk 21:28, +36. Re 1:7.
shall keep. Pr 11:8. 1 S 2:9. Ps 25:15.

27 Withhold not. Pr 11:24, 26. 25:11. Ro 13:7. 2 C 9:7. Ga 6:10. T 2:14. Ja 2:15, 16. +5:4.
them to whom it is due. Heb. the owners thereof. Le +19:13.
in the power. Ge 31:29. Mi 2:1.

28 Go, and come again. Pr 27:1. Le +19:13. Dt +24:12-15. Ec 9:10. 11:6. 2 C 8:11. 9:3. 1 T 6:18.

29 Devise not evil. *or*, Practice no evil. Pr 6:14, 18. 16:29, 30. Dt 27:24. Ps 35:20. 55:20. 59:3. Je 18:18-20. Mi 2:1, 2.

30 Strive not. Ps 17:14. 18:6. 25:8, 9. 29:22. Mt 5:39-41. Ro 12:18-21. 1 C 6:6-8. Col 3:12-15. 2 T 2:24. He 12:14.

31 Envy. Ps +37:1.
the oppressor. Heb. a man of violence. Pr 16:29. 2 S 22:49. Ps 73:6. 140:1mg. Ec 5:8.
choose. Pr 1:15-18. 2:12-15. 12:12. 22:22-25.

32 the froward. Pr 6:16-19. 8:13. 11:20. 17:15. Ps 18:26. Lk 16:15.
his secret. Pr 14:10. Ge 18:17. Dt 29:29. Ps 25:14. Mt 11:25. 13:11. Jn 7:17. 14:21-24. 15:15. 1 C 2:12-15. Re 2:17.

33 curse. Pr 21:12. 26:2. Ge +6:13. Le 26:14, etc. Dt 7:26. 29:19, etc. Jsh 6:18. 7:13. Da 5:5, 6. Mt +25:41.
the house. Mi 6:10.
he blesseth. Dt 28:2, etc. 2 S 6:11. 1 K 21:20-22. 2 K 10:1-11. Jb 8:6, 7. Ps 1:3. 31:23. 91:10.

34 he scorneth. Pr 9:7, 8, 12. 19:29. 21:24. Ex 14:13. Ps 2:1-4. 138:6. Is 37:33, 34.
he giveth. Is 57:15. 66:2. Mt +5:3. 15:27, 28. Lk 18:13, 14. Ja *4:6*. 1 P *5:5*.

35 wise. Pr 4:8. 1 S 2:30. Ps 73:24.
but. Pr 13:18. Ps 132:18. Is 65:13-15. Da 12:2, 3. Ml 3:18. Mt 13:43.
shame. Pr 6:33. 9:7. 11:2. 12:16. Da 12:2. Ro 6:21.
shall be the promotion of fools. Heb. exalteth the fools. Pr 14:29.
fools. Pr 1:22. 8:5. 10:1. 12:23.

PROVERBS 4

1 **ye**. Pr 1:8. 6:20-23. Ps 34:11. 1 Th 2:11, 12.
attend. Pr 2:1-5. 5:1. 7:4. 8:32-36. 19:20.
22:17. He 2:1.

2 **good doctrine**. Pr 8:6-9. 22:20, 21. Dt 32:2.
Jb 33:3. Ps 49:1-3. Je 5:31. Jn 7:16, 17. 1 T
4:6, 16. T 1:9.
forsake. 1 Ch +28:9. 2 Ch 7:19. Ps 89:30-32.
Ga 1:6, 7.

3 **I was**. 2 S 12:24, 25. 1 K 1:13-17. 1 Ch 3:5.
22:5. 28:9. 29:1. Je 10:23. Ro 12:16.

4 **He**. Pr 22:6. Ge +18:19. 1 Ch 22:11-16.
+28:9. Ep 6:4. 2 T 1:5. 3:15.
Let. Pr +3:1. Dt 4:9. 6:6. Ps 119:11.
keep. Pr 7:2. Le 18:3-5. Is 55:3. Jn 12:50. He
5:9.

5 **Get wisdom**. Pr 1:22, 23. 2:2-4. 3:13-18. 8:5.
17:16. 18:1. 19:8. 23:23. 1 K 3:5, 6, 9, 11, 12.
Ja 1:5.
neither. 2 Ch 34:2. Jb 23:11. Ps 44:18.
119:51, 157.

6 **love**. ver. 21, 22. Pr 2:10-12. Ep 3:17. 2 Th
2:10.

7 **Wisdom is**. Ec 7:12. 9:16-18. Mt 5:6. 6:33.
13:44-46. Lk 10:42. Ph 3:8.
with. Pr 16:16. 21:6. Ps 49:16-20. Ec 2:4-9.
4:8. Mk 8:36, 37. Lk 12:20.
get understanding. Ps 119:104.

8 **promote thee**. Pr 3:35. 22:4. 1 S 2:30. 1 K
3:5-13. Da 12:3.

9 **give**. Pr 1:9. 3:22. 1 T 2:9, 10. 1 P 3:4.
a crown, etc. *or*, she shall compass thee with
a crown of glory. Pr 16:31. Is 28:5. He 2:7-9. 1
P 5:4. Re 3:21.

10 **my**. Pr 8:10. 19:20. Jb 22:22. Je 9:20. Jn 3:32,
33. 1 Th 2:13. 1 T 1:15.
the years. Dt +4:40. 1 T 4:8.

11 **taught**. ver. 4. Dt 4:5. 1 S 12:24. Jb 36:22. Ec
12:9.
led. Pr 8:6, 9, 20. Ps 23:3. 25:4, 5. 32:8. Ac
13:10.

12 **thou goest**. Pr 6:22. 2 S 22:37. Jb 18:7, 8. Ps
18:36.
thou shalt. ver. 19. Pr 3:23. Ps 91:11, 12.
119:165. Je 31:9. Jn 11:9, 10. Ro 9:32, 33. 1 P
2:8. 1 J 2:10, 11.

13 **Take**. Pr 3:18. 23:23. Is 48:17, 18. Ac 2:42.
11:23. 1 Th 5:21. He 2:1. Re 2:13. 12:11.
let. Ge 32:26. SS 3:4. Lk 24:27-29. Jn 4:39-
42. Ga 3:1. 2 T 3:14.
she. Pr 3:22. Dt 32:47. Ps 34:12-14. Ec 7:12.
Jn 6:68.

14 **not into the path**. Pr 1:10, 15. 2:11, 12. 9:6.
13:20. Ps 1:1. 17:4. 26:4, 5. +119:63, 114,
115. 1 C 15:33.

15 **Avoid it**. Pr 1:15. 5:8. 6:5. Ex 23:7. Jb 11:14.
22:23. Is 33:15. 2 C 6:17. Ep 5:11. Col 2:8. 1
Th 5:22.

16 **they sleep not**. Pr 1:16. Ps 36:4. Is 57:20. Mi
2:1. Lk 22:66. Jn 18:28. 2 P 2:14.

17 **they eat**. Pr 9:17. 20:17. Jb 24:5, 6. Ps 14:4.
Je 5:26-28. Ezk 22:25-29. Am 8:4-6. Mi 3:5.
6:12. Zp 3:3. Mt 23:14. Ja +5:4, 5.

18 **the path**. ver. 11. Pr 2:9. 2 S 23:4. Jb 11:17.
22:28. 23:10. 33:28. Ps 16:11. 23:3. 25:10.
119:14, 35, +105, 130. Is 2:3. 26:7. Ho 6:3. Zc
14:6, 7. Mt 5:14, 16, 45. Jn 8:12. Ac 20:30. 2
C 3:18. Ga 1:6, 7. Ep 4:14. Col 1:23. 2:3, 4, 6,
7. He 12:13. 2 P 1:19. 2:1, 2. 3:18. 1 J 2:3, 6.
Re 21:23. 22:5.
the just. Pr 3:32. 12:13. 20:7. Jb 36:7. Ps
34:15. 37:25. 92:12. Is 3:10. Mt 13:43.
shining light. Ps +112:4. 119:147. 130:6. Is
58:8, 10. Da 12:3. Ph 2:15.
more and more. 2 S 3:1. Ps 84:7. 97:11.
119:105. Da 12:4. Ml 4:2. Mt 5:14. 6:23.
13:12. 24:4. Mk 8:24, 25. Jn 1:46, 49-51.
16:13. 1 C 13:12. 2 C 3:18. 4:6. 11:13-15. Ep
3:17-19. Ph 3:12-15. 1 Th +4:1. 1 T 4:15, 16.
2 T 3:13. Ja 4:6. 2 P 1:19. Ju +3.
perfect day. Jb 11:17. 19:25. Is 60:20. Ho
+6:3 (prepared). Mt 13:43. 1 C 1:8. Col 3:4. 1
Th 5:8. 2 T 1:12. 2 P 3:10-14. 1 J 3:2, 3. Re
21:23.

19 **The way of the wicked**. Pr 2:13. Dt 28:29.
1 S 2:9. Jb 5:14. 12:25. 15:23. 18:5, 6, 18.
24:13. Ps 35:6. 82:5. Is +8:20. 59:9, 10. Je
13:16. 23:12. Zp 1:17. Mt 6:23. 7:23. +15:14.
Jn 3:19. 11:10. 12:35, 36. 1 J 1:6. 2:11.
as darkness. Is +9:2. Mi 3:6. Jn 1:5. Ro
13:12. Ep 5:8. 1 Th 5:4.
know not. Ps 73:18. Is 30:13. Je 13:16. Mt
7:26, 27. 23:13, 15. Mk 12:24, 27. Lk +11:52.
Jn 12:35, 36. 1 C 2:5. 10:12.
stumble. Mt 18:6. Ro 9:32, 33. 1 P 2:8.

20 **attend**. Pr 5:1. 6:20, 21. 7:1. Ps 78:1. 90:12.
Is 55:3. Mt 17:5.

21 **depart**. Pr 3:3, 21.
in the. Pr 2:1. Ps 40:8mg. Je 31:33.

22 **life**. ver. 4, 10.
health. Heb. medicine. Pr 6:15. 12:18. 13:17.
16:24. Ps +101:3.

23 **Keep thy heart**. Pr 16:9. 22:5. 23:19. 28:26.
Dt 4:9. 23:9. 2 S 15:6. 1 K 11:9. 2 K 10:31. Jb
15:12. 31:1. Ps 19:13. 25:20. 119:11, 37.
139:23, 24. 141:3, 4. Je +6:19. 17:9. Ho 4:11.
Mt +5:8. 6:22. 12:34, 35. Mk 14:38. Lk 6:45.
Ac 15:20, 29. Ro 6:17. Ep +4:14. Ph +4:7, 8.
Col 1:22, 23. 2:6, 7. 1 T +4:12. He 12:15. 13:9.
Ja 4:8. 1 P 1:22. 4:19.
with all diligence. Heb. above all keeping.
ver. 7. Pr 3:21. 11:16. 13:3. Ex +20:15.
+15:26. Ec 5:13. 1 C 10:12. Ph 2:12, 13. Col
1:10.
for. Pr 10:11. Mt 12:34, 35. 15:19. Mk 7:21-
23. Jn 4:14. Ph 4:8. 1 T 4:12. Ja 1:14, 15. 3:5,
6.

24 **Put away**. Jb 11:14. Ps 19:13. 141:3, 4. Ezk
18:31. Ep 4:25-31. Col 3:8. Ja 1:21, 26. 1 P
2:1.

a froward, etc. Heb. frowardness of mouth, and perverseness of lips. Pr 8:8, 13. 17:20. 1 T 6:5. T 2:9.

25 thine eyes. Pr 23:5, 33. Ex 2:12. Jb 31:1. Ps 119:37. Mt 6:22. Lk 9:62.
look straight. 1 K 13:18-22.

26 Ponder. Pr 5:6. Ps 119:59. 143:8-10. Ezk 18:28. Hg 1:5, 7. Ep 5:15, 17.
let all thy ways be established. or, all thy ways shall be ordered aright. Ps 37:23. 40:2. 1 Th 3:13. 2 Th 3:3. 1 P 5:10.

27 Turn. Nu 20:17. Jsh +1:7. Ga 2:11-13.
remove. 2 T +2:19. Ju 21, 24, 25.

PROVERBS 5

1 attend. Pr 2:1. 4:1, 20. Mt 13:9. Mk 4:23. Re 2:7, 11, 17, 29. 3:6, 13, 22.
bow. Pr 22:17. Ja 1:19.

2 thy lips. Pr 10:21. 15:2, 7. 16:23. 20:15. Ps 45:2. 71:15. 119:9, 11, 13, 59. SS 4:11. Ml 2:6, 7.

3 the lips. Pr +2:16. Re 17:2-6.
strange woman. 1 K 11:1, 2, 6-8.
mouth. Heb. palate. Jb +31:30mg.
smoother. Ps 55:21.

4 her. Pr 6:24-35. 7:22, 23. 9:18. 23:27, 28. Ec 7:26. He 12:15, 16.
wormwood. Dt +29:18.
sharp. Jg 16:4-6, 15-21. Ps 55:21. He 4:12.

5 down. Pr 1:12. 2:18, 19. 7:27. Ge 28:12.
death. Pr 2:18. 5:5. 7:27. 8:36. 10:2. 11:7. 14:12, 27, 32. Ps 9:13. 49:14, 17. 55:15. 78:50. 89:48. Ec 7:26. 8:8. 10:1mg. Is 25:8. 28:15, 18. 38:18. Ezk 33:11. Ro 6:23.
steps. Pr 4:12. 16:9. 30:29. 2 S 6:13.
take hold. Pr 4:4. 11:16. 28:17.
hell. Heb. sheol, Ge +37:35. Pr 7:27. 9:18. 15:11, 24. 23:14. 27:20. Dt +32:22. Jb 26:6. Is 5:14. 14:9, 15. 28:15. Jon 2:2.

6 ponder. Pr 4:26. Ps 119:59.
the path. Pr 11:19. Ps 16:11.
her. Pr 6:12, 13. 7:10-21. 2 Th 2:9, 10.

7 Hear. Pr 4:1. 8:32-36. 22:17-21. He 12:25.
and depart. Pr 3:21. 4:21.

8 thy way. Pr 4:15. 6:27, 28. Mt 6:13. Ep 5:11.

9 Lest thou give. Pr 6:29-35. Ge 38:23-26. Jg 16:19-21. Ne 13:26. Ho 4:13, 14.
years. Ps 90:12.

10 strangers. Pr 6:35. Ho 7:9. Lk 15:30.
wealth. Heb. strength. Pr 14:4. 20:29. 24:5, 10. +27:24mg. 31:3.
labors. Dt +28:33.

11 thou. Pr 7:23. Dt 32:29. Je 5:31. Ro 6:21. He 13:4. Re 21:8. 22:15.
when. Nu 5:27. 1 C 5:4, 5. 6:18.

12 How. Pr 1:7, 22, 29-30. 15:5. Ps 50:17. 73:22. Zc 7:11-14. Jn 3:19, 20.
and my. Pr 1:25. 6:23. 12:1. 13:18. Ge 19:9. Ex 2:13, 14. 2 Ch 24:20-22. 25:16. 33:10, 11.

36:16, 17. Je 44:4, 5. Zc 1:4-6.

13 not obeyed. Lk 15:18. 1 Th 4:8. 5:12, 13. He 13:7.

14 almost in all evil. Pr 13:20. Nu 25:1-6. Ho 4:11-14. 1 C 10:6-8. 2 P 2:10-18. Ju 7-13.

15 Drink waters. ver. 18, 19. Pr 9:5. 23:7. Ge 24:14. Jn 4:14. 7:37, 38. 1 C 7:2-5. He 13:4.
cistern. Heb. bor, Ge +37:20. Pr 1:12. 28:17. 2 K 10:14. 18:31. Ne 9:25. Ec 12:6.
running waters. Ps 78:16. SS 4:15. Je 2:13. Jn 4:10.
well. Heb. be-er, Ge +16:14.

16 thy. Dt 33:28. Ps 68:26. Is 48:1, 21.
fountains. Heb. mayan, Ge +7:11.
dispersed. Ge 24:60. Jg 12:9. Ps 127:3. 128:3.
abroad. Heb. chuts, Am 5:16 (S#2351h, highways).
streets. Heb. rechob, public square or broad street. Am 5:16 (S#7339h, streets).

17 strangers'. ver. 3, 10, 20. Ge 34:27. 1 K 11:1.

18 rejoice. Ec 9:9. Ml 2:14, 15.

19 as the. SS 2:9. 4:5. 7:3. 8:14.
satisfy thee. Heb. water thee. ver. 15. Ps 36:8mg. 65:10.
be thou ravished always with her love. Heb. err thou always in her love. 2 S 12:4.

20 with. Pr 2:16-19. 6:24. 7:5. 22:14. 23:27, 28, 33. 2 S 11:2, 3. 1 K 11:1.

21 the ways. Pr 15:3. 2 Ch 16:9. Jb 31:4. 34:21. Ps 11:4. 14:1-3. 17:3. 139:1-12. Je 16:17. 17:10. 23:24. 32:19. Ho 7:2. He 4:13. 13:4. Re 2:18, 23.

22 His. Pr 11:3, 5. Ge 29:25. 1 S 2:3. Jb +4:8. 31:4. Ec 12:14. Is 29:15. Ho 4:11-14. Ga 6:7, 8.
holden with. Pr 27:22. Ge 37:4. Ex 32:9. Jsh 24:19. Jb +21:15. Ec 7:26. 9:3. Is 48:4. Je 2:22. 3:5. 6:10. 13:23. 17:1, 9. Mt 7:18. 12:34. +13:38. 17:17. 23:33. Jn 6:44, 65. +17:14. Ro 8:7, 8.
sins. Heb. sin. 1 C 5:9, 10. Ga 5:19-21. Ep 5:5, 6. He 13:4.

23 shall die. Pr 10:21. 14:32. Jb 4:21. 36:12.
in the. Pr 14:14. Ps 81:12. 2 P 2:15-22.

PROVERBS 6

1 if thou be. Pr 11:15. 17:18. 20:16. 22:26. 27:13. Ge 43:9. 44:32, 33. Jb 17:3. Phm 18, 19. He 7:22.
hast stricken. Pr 17:18. 22:26. Jb 17:3.

2 snared. Pr 12:13. 18:7.

3 when. 2 S 24:14. 2 Ch 12:5. Ps 31:8.
go. Ex 10:3. 2 Ch 36:12. Ja 4:10.
and make sure thy friend. or, so shalt thou prevail with thy friend.

4 Give not sleep. ver. 10, 11. Ps 132:4. Ec 9:10. Mt 24:17, 18. Mk 13:35, 36.

5 Deliver thyself. Mt 5:25.

as a bird. Pr 1:17. Ps 11:1. 124:7.
fowler. Ps 91:3.

6 **the ant**. Pr 1:17. Jb 12:7, 8. 35:11. Is 1:3. Mt 6:26.
  thou sluggard. ver. 9. Pr 10:26. 13:4. 15:19. 18:9. 19:15, 24. 20:4. 21:25. 22:13. 24:30-34. 26:13-16. Mt 25:26. Ro 12:11. He 6:12.
  consider. Pr 4:26. Dt 4:39. 32:29. Jb 37:14. Ps +10:4. 28:5. 50:21, 22. 111:4. Ec 7:13, 14. Is 1:3. 5:12, 13. Ho 7:2. Hg 1:5.

7 **no guide**. Jb 38:39-41. 39:1-12, 26-30. 41:4, etc.

8 **her meat**. Pr 30:25. 1 T 6:19.

9 **How**. Pr 24:33, 34. Mt +17:17.
  when. Ps 13:3. 94:8. Jon 1:6. Ro 8:13. 13:11-14. Ep 5:14. 1 Th 5:2-7.
  arise. SS 2:10. Is 60:1. Mk 10:49. Lk 22:46. Jn 5:8. Ep 5:14.

10 **a little sleep**. ver. 6. Pr 19:15. #24:33, 34. +25:28. 1 Th 5:6.

11 **poverty come**. Pr 10:4. 13:4. 20:4.

12 **naughty**. Heb. "A man of Belial." Pr 16:27mg. 19:28mg.
  person. Pr 11:6. 17:4. 1 S 17:28. Je 24:2, 8-10. Ja 1:21.
  walketh. ver. 14. Pr 2:12. 4:24. 8:13. Ps 10:3, 7. 36:3. 52:2-4. 59:7. 73:8, 9. Mt 12:34. Ac 20:30. 1 T 5:13. T 1:10, 11. Ja 3:6.

13 **winketh**. Pr 5:6. 10:10. Jb 15:12. Ps 35:19.
  speaketh with. Is 3:16.

14 **Frowardness**. Pr 2:14. 16:28-30. 21:8. Mt 15:19.
  he deviseth. ver. 18. Ps 36:4. Is 32:7. 57:20. Ezk 11:2. Mi 2:1.
  soweth. Heb. casteth forth. ver. 19. Pr 16:28. 22:8. 26:17-22. Ho 8:7. Ro 2:8. 16:17. Ga 6:7, 8.

15 **shall his**. Pr 1:27. 29:1. Ps 73:18-20. Is 30:13. 1 Th 5:3.
  he be. 2 Ch 36:16. Ps 50:22. Je 19:11. Jn 3:7. T 3:3-5.

16 **six**. Pr 8:13. 30:18, 21, 24, 29. Am 1:3, 6, 9, 11. 2:1, 4, 6.
  yea, seven. Mt 11:9. Jn 16:32. Ac 26:27. 1 C 7:10. 15:10. Ga 1:6. 2:20. 4:9. 2 T 4:8. 1 J 2:2.
  an abomination. Pr 3:32. 11:1, 20. 15:8, 9. 17:15. 20:10, 23. Dt 18:10-12. 23:18. 24:4. 25:16. Re 21:27.
  unto him. Heb. of his soul. Ps 11:5. Heb. *nephesh*, Ex +15:9; Le +26:11.

17 **A proud look**. Heb. Haughty eyes. Pr +16:5. 21:4mg. 30:13. Ps 10:4. 73:6-8. 101:5. 131:1. Is 2:11, 17. 3:9, 16. 10:12. Lk 18:14. 1 P 5:5.
  lying. Pr 26:28. Ps 5:6. 120:2, 3. Ep +4:25.
  and hands. Pr 1:11. Ge 4:8. 9:6. Dt +19:10. 27:25. Mt 23:37, 38.

18 **heart**. Pr 24:8. Ge 6:5. 2 S 16:20, 21. Ps 36:4. Je 4:14. Mi 2:1. Zc 8:17.
  feet. Pr 1:16. Is 59:7. Zc 5:4. Ro 3:15. Ju 19.

19 **A false**. Pr 12:17. 21:28. 25:18. Ex 23:1. Dt

19:16-20. 1 K 21:10-15. Ps 27:12. 35:11. Ml +3:5. Mt 15:19. 26:59. Ac 6:13. Ep +4:25.
  that soweth. ver. 14. Pr 16:28. 22:10. 26:20. Ro 16:17, 18. 1 C 3:3, 4. 2 T 2:23. Ja 3:14-16, 18. 3 J 9, 10. Ju 19.

20 **keep thy**. Pr 7:1-4. Ex +20:12. Ep 6:1.
  forsake not. Pr 1:8.

21 **Bind them**. Pr 3:3. 4:6, 21. 7:3, 4. Ex 13:16. Dt 6:8. 2 C 3:3.
  continually. Is +58:11.

22 **When thou goest**. Pr 2:11. 3:23, 24. Dt 11:18-21. Ps 17:4. 43:3. 119:9, 11, 24, 54, 97, 148.
  sleepest. Pr 3:24. Le 26:6. Ps 3:5. 4:8. 121:4-7.

23 **the commandment**. Ps 19:8-11. 119:98-100, 105. Is 8:20. 2 T 3:16, 17. 2 P 1:19.
  lamp. *or*, candle. Pr 20:20mg, 27mg. 24:20mg. Ps +18:28mg. Re 2:5.
  and reproofs. Pr 5:12. 15:31, 32. 29:15. Le 19:17. Ps 141:5.
  the way. Pr 3:18. 4:4, 13. 15:24. Je 21:8.

24 **keep**. Pr +2:16. Ps 17:4, 5.
  flattery. Ps +12:3.
  of the tongue of a strange woman. *or*, of the strange tongue.

25 **Lust**. Ex 20:14, 17. Le 20:10. 2 S 11:2-5. Jb 31:1. Ps 119:37. Mt 5:28. Ja 1:14, 15.
  take. 2 K 9:30mg. SS 4:9. Is 3:16.

26 **by**. Pr 5:10. 29:3, 8. Lk 15:13-15, 30.
  a piece. 1 S 2:36.
  the adulteress. Heb. the woman of a man, *or*, a man's wife.
  hunt. Ge 39:14. Jb 2:4. Ezk 13:18.
  life. Heb. *nephesh*, soul, Ge +44:30.

27 **take fire**. Jb 31:9-12. Ho 7:4-7. Ja 3:5.

28 **go upon**. Is 43:2.
  hot coals. Pr 25:22. 26:21. Ps 140:10. SS 8:6.
  burned. Is 43:2.

29 **he that**. Ge 12:18, 19. Le 20:10. 2 S 11:3, 4. 12:9, 10. 16:21. Je 5:8, 9. Ezk 22:11. Ml +3:5.
  toucheth. Ge 20:4-7. 26:10, 11. 1 C 7:1.

30 **despise**. Pr 23:9, 22. 30:17.
  thief. Pr 29:24. Ex 22:2, 7. Dt 24:7.
  steal. Ge 31:19. 44:8. Ex 20:15.
  to satisfy. Jb 38:39. 1 C 6:10. 1 J 3:4.
  soul. Heb. *nephesh*, Nu +11:6. Ps 107:9. Is 5:14. 29:8. Re +18:14.
  hungry. Pr 19:15. Ge 41:55.

31 **restore**. Ex 22:1, 3, 4. 2 S 12:6. Jb 20:18. Lk 19:8.
  sevenfold. ver. 3. Ge 4:15, 24. Jb 20:18. Ps 79:12. Lk 19:8.
  he shall give. Mt 18:25.

32 **lacketh**. Pr 7:7. Ge 39:9, 10. 41:39. Ec 7:25, 26. Je 5:8, 21. Ro 1:22-24.
  understanding. Heb. heart. Pr 17:18mg. Ho 4:11, 12.
  destroyeth. Pr 2:18, 19. 5:22, 23. 7:22, 23.

8:36. 9:16-18. Ezk 18:31. Ho 13:9. He 13:4.
soul. Heb. *nephesh*, Ge +27:31.

33 **A wound**. Pr 5:9-11. Jg 16:19-21. Ps 38:1-8.
51:8.
and his. Ge 49:4. 1 K 15:5. Ne 13:26. Ps 51,
title. Mt 1:6.

34 **jealousy**. Pr 27:4mg. Nu 5:14. 25:11. Jg
19:29, 30. SS 8:6. 1 C 10:22.

35 **regard**. S#5375h. Heb. accept the face of. Pr
4:3. 7:13. 8:25. 18:5. 2 K 5:1mg. Is 2:9 (forgive). Ml 2:9mg.

PROVERBS 7

1 **My son**. Pr 1:8. 3:1.
keep. Lk 8:15. 11:28. Jn 14:23. 15:20. Re 1:3.
22:9.
lay. Pr 2:1-7. 10:14. Dt 11:18. Jb 22:22.

2 **Keep**. Pr 4:4, 13. Le 18:5. Is 55:3. Jn 12:49,
50. 14:21. 15:14. 1 J 2:3, 4. 5:1-3. Re 22:14.
as the. Dt 32:10. Ps 17:8. Zc 2:8.

3 **Bind them**. Pr 6:21. Dt +6:6, 8, 9. Ps 143:10.
Is 30:8. Je 17:1.
table of. Ex +25:21.

4 **Say**. Pr 2:2-4. 4:6-8.
Thou. Jb 17:14. SS 8:1. Mt 12:49, 50. Lk
11:27, 28.

5 **keep thee from**. Pr +2:16.
flattereth. Ps +12:3.

6 **at the**. Ge 26:8. 2 S 6:16.

7 **the simple**. Pr 1:4, 22, 32. 8:5. 14:15, 18.
19:25. 22:3. 27:12. Ps 19:7. 119:130. Ro
16:18, 19.
the youths. Heb. the sons.
void. Pr 6:32. 9:4, 16. 10:13. 12:11. 19:2.
24:30. Je 4:22. Mt 15:16.

8 **street**. Heb. *shuk*, properly, "an alley,"
S#7784h. Ec 12:4, 5. SS 3:2. Am 5:16.
near her corner. Pr 4:14, 15. 5:8. Jg 16:1. 2
S 11:2, 3. 1 C 6:18. 2 T 2:22. Ju 23.

9 **the twilight**. Ge 39:11. Jb 24:13-15. Ro
13:12-14. Ep 5:11, 12. 1 Th 5:7. 1 J 1:6.
evening. Heb. evening of the day. Ex
12:6mg.

10 **the attire**. Ge 38:14, 15. 2 K 9:22, 30. Is
3:16-24. 23:16. Je 4:30. 1 T 2:9. Re 17:3-5.
subtil. Ge 3:1. 2 C 11:2, 3.

11 **loud**. Pr 9:13. 25:24. 27:14, 15. 31:10-31.
her feet. Ge 18:9. 1 T 5:13, 14. T 2:4, 5.

12 **without**. Heb. *chuts*, Am 5:16 (S#2351h, highways). Outside, or narrow streets. Pr 9:14, 15.
23:28. Je 2:20, 33, 36. 3:2. Ezk 16:24, 25, 31.
Re 18:3, 23.
in the streets. Heb. *rechob*, Am 5:16 (S#7339h,
streets). *Public* square or broad streets. Pr
22:13.

13 **she**. Ge 39:7, 12. Nu 25:1, 6-8. 31:16. Ezk
16:33. Re 2:20.
with an impudent face said. Heb. she

strengthened her face and said. Is 50:7. Ezk
2:4, 6. 3:7-9.

14 **I have peace offerings with me**. Heb.
Peace offerings are upon me. Pr 15:8. 17:1.
21:27. Le +23:19.
this. 2 S 15:7-9. 1 K 21:9, 10. Jn 18:28.
vows. Le +23:38.

15 **came I forth**. 1 T 5:13-15. T 2:5.
meet. ver. 10.

16 **decked**. SS 1:16. 3:7-10. Re 2:22.
fine linen. Ex +26:1. Is 19:9.

17 **perfumed**. Ge 30:14, 15. SS 3:6. Is 57:7-9.
with myrrh. Mt +2:11.

18 **fill of love**. SS 1:2. 2:3. 4:10.
until morning. Pr 27:14. Ge 1:5. 19:27. Jg
19:25-27.
with loves. Pr 5:19. Ge 39:7, 12. Ho 8:9mg.

19 **the goodman**. Mt 20:11. 24:43. Lk 12:39.
he is gone. Mt 24:48. Mk 13:34-36. Lk
12:45, 46.

20 **bag**. Pr 26:8. Ge 42:25. 1 S 25:29.
money. Pr 2:4. 3:14. 8:10, 19. 10:20.
with him. Heb. in his hand.
the day appointed. *or*, the new moon. 2 Ch
+2:4.

21 **With her**. ver. 5. Pr 5:3. Jg 16:15-17. Ps 12:2.
forced. Mt 26:41. Ac +16:15.

22 **straightway**. Heb. suddenly. Pr 3:25. 6:15.
24:22.
as an ox. Pr 14:4. Ac 14:13.
slaughter. Pr 9:2mg. Ge 43:16mg. 1 S
25:11mg.
as a fool. ver. 6-9, 23. Pr 1:7. 10:8, 14, 21.
11:29. 12:15. He +13:4.
the correction. Jb 13:27. 33:11. Ps 105:18.
Je 20:2. 29:26. Ac 16:24.

23 **a dart**. Nu 25:8, 9.
as a bird. Pr 1:17. Ec 7:26. 9:12.
knoweth. Pr 9:18. Jg 16:6. Ho 4:11, 14. Ro
13:12, 13.
life. Heb. *nephesh*, Ge +44:30.

24 **O ye children**. Pr 4:1. 5:7. 8:32, 33. 1 C 4:14,
15. Ga 4:19. 1 J 2:1.

25 **thine**. Pr 4:14, 15. 5:8. 6:25. 23:31-33. Mt
5:28.
go not astray. Pr 5:23. Ps 119:176. Is 53:6.

26 **hath cast down**. Pr 6:33. Jg 16:21. 2 S 3:6-8,
27. 12:9-11. 1 K 11:1, 2. Ne 13:26. Ro 6:2, 3.
1 C 9:27. 10:8. 2 C 12:21. Ga 5:24. Col 3:1-5.
1 Th 4:3-5. 2 T 2:22. 1 P 2:11.

27 **Her house**. Pr 2:18, 19. 5:5. 9:18. Ec 7:26.
hell. Heb. *sheol*, Ge +37:35. 2 S 22:5, 6. Hab
2:5. Ro +6:23. 2 C +4:12. Re 6:8.
the chambers. Pr 18:8mg. 20:27. 26:22mg.
Dt 32:25mg. 1 K 20:30mg. 22:25mg. Is 14:18.
Lk 16:23, 26.
death. Pr 2:18. 5:5. 8:36. 14:12, 27. Jb
+18:13. +38:17. Ps 55:4. 107:18. Is 28:15, 18.
Hab 2:5. Re 21:8.

PROVERBS 8

1 **Doth not**. Pr 1:20, 21. 9:1-3. Is 49:1-6. 55:1-3. Mt 3:3. 4:17. 28:19, 20. Mk 13:10. 16:15, 16. Lk 24:47. Jn 7:37. Ac 1:8. 22:21. Ro 15:18-21.
wisdom. ver. 22-30. Mt 11:19. Lk 11:49. 1 C 1:24.

2 **standeth**. Ge 37:7. Ex 7:15. 15:8. Je +7:2. Re 3:20.
the top. ver. 23, 26. Pr 1:9, 21. 4:9.
high places. Pr 9:3, 14. Jg 5:18.
the way. ver. 13, 22, 32. Pr 1:15, 31.
paths. ver. 20. Pr 1:15. 3:17. 12:28.

3 **crieth**. Mt 22:9. Lk 14:21-23. Jn 18:20. Ac 5:20.

4 **Unto you**. Ps 49:1-3. 50:1. Mt 11:15. Mk 16:15. Jn 3:16. 7:37. 2 C 5:19, 20. Col 1:23, 28. 1 T 2:4-6. T 2:11, 12. Re 22:17.

5 **ye simple**. Pr +1:4, 22. 9:4. Ps 19:7. 94:8. Is 42:13. 55:1-3. Ac 26:18. 1 C 1:28. 6:9-11. Re 3:17, 18.

6 **for**. Pr 2:6, 7. 4:2, 20-22. 22:20, 21. Ps 19:7-11. 49:3. 1 C 2:6, 7. Col 1:26.
the opening. Jg +11:35. Mt 7:28, 29.

7 **my mouth**. Jb 36:4. Jn 1:17. 8:14, 45, 46. 14:6. 17:17. 18:37. Re 3:14.
an abomination to. Heb. the abomination of. Pr 12:22. 16:12. 29:27.

8 **All**. Ps 12:6. Is 45:23. 63:1.
there. ver. 13. Jn 7:46.
froward. Heb. wreathed. Jb 5:13.
perverse. Pr 2:15. 11:20. 17:20.

9 **all plain**. Pr 1:7. 2:6. 14:6. 15:14, 24. 17:24. 18:1, 2, 15. Dt 27:8. 30:11. Ps 19:7, 8. 25:12-14. 119:98-100, 104, 105, 130. Is 35:8. Am 3:10 (**S#5228h**). Mi 2:7. Mt 13:11, 12. Lk 10:21. Jn 6:45. 7:17. 1 C 2:14, 15. 2 T 2:7. Ja 1:5. 1 J 5:20.
that understandeth. Pr 14:6. 17:10, +24. 26:2, 7, 11. +28:5, 11. Da +11:33. Je 23:20.
right. Pr 2:7. 3:32. 11:3, 6, 11.
find knowledge. Pr 11:27. 18:15.

10 **Receive my**. Pr 2:4, 5. 3:13, 14. 10:20. 16:16. 23:23. Ps 119:72, 127, 162. Ec 7:11, 12. Lk 10:39. Ac 3:6. 2 C 6:10.
knowledge. Pr 4:7-9, 13. 22:17. 23:12. Jb +21:14. Lk +11:52.
rather than. Jb 28:15-28.

11 **wisdom**. Pr 3:13-18. 4:5-7. 16:16. 20:15. Jb 28:12-19, 28. Ps 19:10. +58:11. 119:127. Mt 16:26. Jn 6:29. 1 C 1:20. 3:18. Ph 3:8, 9. He +12:14.

12 **I wisdom**. Ps 104:24. Is 11:1, 2. 55:8, 9. Ro 11:33. Ep 1:8, 11. 3:10. Col 1:19. 2:3.
prudence. *or*, subtlety. ver. 5. Pr 1:4. Ex 21:14. Jsh 9:4. Mt 22:18-22. Jn 2:23, 24. Ep 1:7, 8.
knowledge. Ex 31:3-6. 35:30-35. 36:1-4. 1 K 7:14. 1 Ch 28:12, 19. 2 Ch 2:13, 14. Is 28:26.

13 **The fear**. Pr +3:7. Dt +6:2.
hate evil. Ex 18:21. Ps 5:4, 5. 15:4. 26:5. 31:6. 36:4. 45:7. 97:10. 101:3. 119:104, 113, 128, 163. 139:21, 22. Am 5:15. Mi 3:2. Zc 8:17. Ro 7:15. 12:9. 1 Th 5:22. 2 T 2:19. He 1:9. Ju 23. Re 2:2, 6, 15.
pride. Pr +16:5. Mt 20:28. Lk 22:27.
the froward. Pr 4:24. 6:12. 10:31.

14 **Counsel**. Is 9:6. 40:13, 14. Je 32:19. Jn 1:9. Ro 11:33, 34. 1 C 1:24, 30. Ep 1:11. Col 2:3. 1 J 2:1. Re 3:18. 19:16.
sound. Pr 2:6, 7. Ro 1:22.
understanding. Is 40:28, 29.
I have. Pr 24:5. Jb 9:4. Ps 89:19. Ec 7:19. 9:16-18. Is 26:4. Col 1:24.

15 **By**. 1 S 9:17. 16:1. 1 Ch 28:5. Je 27:5-7. Da 2:21. 4:25, 32. 5:18, etc. 7:13, 14. Mt 28:18. Ro 13:1-6. Re 19:16.
decree. 1 K 3:9, 28. 5:7. 10:9. Ps 72:1-4. 99:4. Is 1:26. 32:1, 2. Je 33:15. Re 19:11.

16 **princes**. Pr 19:10. 28:2. Ge 12:15.
rule. Pr 29:4. 2 Ch 1:10. Est 1:22. Is 32:1.
nobles. Pr 17:7, 26. 19:6. 25:7.
judges. Pr 29:14. Ge 18:25. Ex 2:14.

17 **I love**. 1 S 2:30. Ps 91:14. Jn 14:21, 23. 16:27. 1 J 4:19.
seek. Je +29:13.
early. Ps 63:1. Ec 12:1. Mk 10:14. Lk 13:24, 25. 2 C 6:2.
find. Mt 7:7. Ja 1:5.

18 **Riches**. Ro 2:4. 9:23. 10:12. 11:33. 2 C 8:9. Ep 1:7, 18. 2:4, 7. 3:8, 16. Ph 4:19. Col 1:27. 2:2, 3.
and honor. Pr 3:16. 4:7-9. Is 55:2. Ja 2:5.
durable. Ps 39:6. Ec 5:14-16. Mt 6:19, 20. Lk 10:42. 12:20, 21, 33. 16:11, 12. Ro 5:17. 2 C 6:10. Ep 3:8. Ph 4:19. 1 T 6:17-19. Ja 5:1-3. Re 3:18.
and righteousness. Pr 11:4. Mt 6:33. Ph 3:8, 9.

19 **My fruit**. ver. 10. Pr 3:14, 15. Ps 19:10. Ec 7:12.

20 **lead**. *or*, walk. Pr 3:6. 4:11, 12. 6:22. Ps 23:3. 25:4, 5. 32:8. +104:10mg. Is 2:3. 49:10. 55:4. Jn 10:3, 27, 28. Re 7:17.
in the midst. Pr 4:25-27. Dt 5:32.

21 **to inherit**. ver. 18. Pr 1:13. 6:31. Ge 15:14. 1 S 2:8. Mt 25:46. Jn 1:1, etc. Ro 8:17. He 10:34, 35. 1 P 1:4, 5.
fill. Ps 16:11. Ep 3:19, 20. Re 21:7.

22 **The Lord**. Pr 3:19. Jn 1:1, 2. Col 1:17.
possessed. Heb. acquired. **S#7069h**. Pr 1:5. 4:5, 7. Ge 4:1. 25:10. Ps 139:13. Je 32:15.
me. ver. 30. Mi +5:2. Lk 11:49. Jn 17:5. 1 C 1:24. He 13:8. Re 3:14.
beginning. Pr 1:7. 3:9. 4:7. 17:14.
before. Mi +5:2.

23 **set up**. or, anointed. Ge 1:26. Ps 2:6. Is 29:10. Mi +5:2. Jn 17:24. Ep 1:10, 11. 1 J 1:1, 2.

everlasting. Heb. *olam*, Ge +17:7.
from the beginning. Jn 1:1-3, 14, 18. 8:58.
+10:30. 17:5. Ph 2:6-11. 1 P 1:20. 1 J 1:1, 2.
Re 1:11.
or ever. ver. 25. 2 K 19:25. Mi +5:2. Jn 17:5.
24 **I was**. Ps 2:7. Jn 1:14. 3:16. 5:20. He 1:5, 6. 1
J 4:9.
fountains. Heb. *mayan*, Ge +7:11 **(S#4599h)**.
25 **Before the mountains**. Jb 15:7, 8. 38:4-11.
Ps 90:2. 102:25-28. Is 53:8. He 1:10.
26 **as yet**. Ge 1:1, etc.
fields. *or*, open places. Pr 1:20. 5:16. 7:12.
highest part. *or*, chief part. ver. 2, 23.
27 **When**. Ge 1:6.
he prepared. Ps 33:6. 103:19. 136:5. Je
10:12. Col 1:16. He 1:2.
compass. *or*, circle. Jb 22:14. Is 40:11, 12, 22.
28 **established**. or, strengthened. Pr 31:17. Dt
15:7.
clouds. Pr 3:20. Jb 35:5. 36:28.
strengthened. Jg 3:10. 6:2mg.
the fountains. Ge 7:11.
29 **he gave**. Ge 1:9, 10. Jb 38:8-11. Ps 33:7.
104:9. Je 5:22.
when he appointed. Jb 38:4-7.
30 **Then**. Col 1:16.
one. Jn 1:1-3, 18. 16:28-30.
I was daily. Is 42:1. Mt 3:17. 17:5. Jn 12:28.
Col 1:13.
31 **and my**. Ps 16:3. 40:6-8. Jn 4:34. 13:1. 2 C
8:9.
32 **for blessed**. Ps 1:1-4. 119:1, 2. 128:1, 2. Lk
+11:28.
33 **Hear**. Pr 1:2, 3, 8. 4:1. 5:1. +19:20. Dt 10:12,
13. Is 55:1-3. Lk +11:28. Ro 10:16, 17. Ja 1:25.
refuse. Pr 1:21-23. 1 S +25:17. Ps 81:11, 12.
Je 6:16. 44:16, 17. Lk 19:14. He +12:25.
34 **that heareth**. Is 55:3. Jn 5:24. Re 3:20.
watching. Pr 1:21-23. 2:3, 4. 3:13, 18. Ex
29:42. 33:11. 1 K 17:1. Ps 27:4. 84:10. 92:13.
Mt 7:24. 18:20. Lk 1:6. 2:37. 10:39. +11:28.
Jn 8:31, 32. Ac 2:42. 17:11, 12. Ja 1:22-25.
Re 3:2.
waiting. 1 Ch 6:33.
35 **whoso**. Pr 1:33. 3:13-18. Jn 1:4. 3:16, 36.
14:6. Ph 3:8, 9. Col 3:3. 1 J 5:11, 12.
obtain. Heb. bring forth. Pr 3:13mg.
favor. Pr 12:2. Ep 1:6.
36 **sinneth against**. Pr 1:31. 15:32. 20:2. Jn
3:19, 20. Ac 13:46. He 2:3. 10:29.
soul. Heb. *nephesh*, Ge +27:31.
all they. ver. 33. Pr 5:11, 12, 22, 23. Ezk
18:31. 33:11. Jn 15:23, 24. 1 C 16:22.
love. Ps +109:17.
death. Pr 21:6. 29:24.

PROVERBS 9

1 **Wisdom**. Pr 1:2, 7. 10:13, 23, 31.
builded. Mt 16:18. 1 C 3:9-15. Ep 2:20-22. 1

T 3:15. He 3:3-6. 1 P 2:5, 6.
pillars. 1 K 7:2, 3, 6, 21. Ga 2:9.
Re 3:12.
2 **killed**. Is 25:6. Mt 22:3, 4, etc. 1 C 5:7, 8.
beasts. Heb. killing. Pr 7:22. Ge +43:16mg.
mingled. ver. 5. Pr 23:30. Lk 14:17.
3 **sent**. Mt 22:3, 4, 9. Lk 11:49. 14:17, 21-23.
Ro 10:15. 2 C 5:20, 21.
maidens. Pr 27:27. 31:15. Ge +24:14
(S#5291h).
she crieth. ver. 14. Pr 1:20-23. 8:1-3. Jn
7:37. 18:20. Re 3:20.
4 **simple**. ver. 16. Pr 1:22. 6:32. 8:5. Ps 19:7.
119:130. Mt 11:25. Re 3:17, 18. 22:17.
5 **eat**. ver. 2, 17. Ps +22:26. SS 5:1. Je 31:12-14.
Mt 26:26-28.
6 **Forsake**. Pr 4:14, 15. 13:20. Ps 26:4-6. 45:10.
119:115. Ho 7:11. Ac 2:40. 2 C 6:17. Ja 4:4.
Re 18:4.
in. Pr 4:11. 10:17. Mt 7:13, 14. Lk 13:24.
7 **reproveth**. Pr 15:12. Ge 19:8, 9. 1 K 18:17.
21:20. 22:24, 27. 2 Ch 24:20-22. 25:15, 16.
36:16. Mt +7:6.
8 **Reprove not**. Pr 23:9. 29:1. Nu 14:6-10. 1 K
22:8. Mt +7:6. 15:14. He 6:4-8.
rebuke a wise man. Pr 13:18. 28:23. Ex
18:17-24. Le +19:17. 2 S 12:7-14. 1 K 1:23,
32-40. Ps 141:5. Ga 2:11-14. 2 P 3:15, 16.
9 **Give instruction**. Pr 1:5. 25:12. Ho 6:3. Mt
13:11, 12. 2 P 3:18. 1 J 2:20, 21. 5:13.
10 **The fear**. Pr 1:7. Jb +28:28.
the knowledge. Pr 2:5. 30:3. 1 Ch +28:9. Mt
11:27. Jn 17:3. 1 J 5:20.
11 **by me**. Dt +4:40.
12 **If thou**. Pr 16:26. Jb 22:2, 3, 21. 35:6, 7. Is
28:22. Ezk 18:20. 2 P 3:3, 4, 16.
thou alone. Nu +32:23. Ga 6:5, 7, 8.
13 **clamorous**. Pr 7:11. 21:9, 19. 1 T 6:4mg.
simple. Pr +1:4.
14 **she**. Pr 7:10-12.
in. ver. 3.
15 **To call**. Pr 7:13-15, 25-27. 23:27, 28.
16 **Whoso is**. ver. 4.
17 **Stolen**. Pr 20:17. 23:31, 32. Ge 3:6. Ro 7:8.
Ja 1:14, 15.
eaten in secret. Heb. of secrecies. Pr 7:18-
20. 30:20. 2 K 5:24-27. Ep 5:12.
18 **he**. Pr 1:7. Ps 82:5. 2 P 3:5.
the dead. Pr 2:18, 19. 5:5. 6:26. 7:27.
hell. Heb. *sheol*, +Ge 37:35.

PROVERBS 10

1 **proverbs**. Pr 1:1. 25:1. 1 K 4:32. Ec 12:9.
A wise. ver. 5. Pr 13:1, 24. 15:20. 17:21, 25.
19:13, 26. 20:20. 23:15, 16, 24, 25. 29:3, 15.
Ec 2:19.
glad father. Ge 45:28. 46:30.
heaviness of. Ge 26:34, 35. 1 S 2:24.
2 **Treasures**. Pr 11:4. 1 K 21:4-24. 2 K 5:22-27.

Ps 49:6-10. Is 10:2, 3. Zp 1:18. Lk 12:15-21.
16:22, 23. Ro 2:5. Ja 5:1-3.

profit nothing. ver. 4, 15, 22. Pr 11:4, 24,
28. 13:8, 11. 14:20. 18:11, 23. 19:1, 4, 7, 22.
20:21, 21:6, 20. 22:27. Ezk 7:19. Mt 27:3-5.
Ro 6:21.

but. Pr 12:28. Da 4:27. Ro 5:21. Ph 3:9.

3 **will.** Ps 10:14. Ps +37:3. He 13:5, 6.
not suffer. ver. 29. Pr 11:18, 21, 23, 25, 31.
12:2. 13:21, 22. 14:9, 11, 14. 15:6, 10, 25.
19:29. 20:30. 22:4.
soul. Heb. *nephesh*, Ge +12:15.
but. Mt 6:25, 26, 31.
1:18.
the substance of the wicked. *or, the
wicked for their wickedness.* Pr 14:32.

4 **becometh poor.** Pr 6:6-11. 11:24. 12:24.
19:15, 24. 20:4, 13. 24:30-34. Ec 10:18. Je
48:10. Mt 13:12. 25:29. Jn 6:27. He 6:11, 12.
2 P 1:5-10.
with a slack hand. *that is, slothfully and
negligently.* 13:4, 21:5. 1 C 15:58.
diligent. Pr 12:11, 24, 27. 13:4, 11. 14:23.
21:5. 22:29. 28:19, 20. Ro +12:11. Ep 6:5, 6.
Col 3:22, 23. 1 Th 4:11. 2 Th 3:10.
maketh rich. Thus "my responsibility," diligence; compare ver. 22. Ps 62:10. 1 T +6:9. 2
P 1:5-11.

5 **gathereth.** Pr 6:6-8. 30:25. Ge 41:46-56. Is
55:6, 7. Mt 20:30. Ga 6:10.
that sleepeth. Mt 25:5, 8-10.
in harvest. Je 8:20.
a son. Pr 12:4. 17:2. 19:26.

6 **Blessings.** Pr 11:26. 24:25. 28:20. Dt 28:1-6.
Jb 29:13. Mt +5:8. 2 T 1:16-18.
head. Jg +5:30mg.
but. ver. 11. Est 7:8. Ps 107:42. Ro 3:19.
violence covereth. ver. 9, 10, 11, 16, 21, 25,
27, 30. Pr 11:5, 6, 8, 19, 30. 12:5, 26. 16:27,
28, 29, 30. 17:4. 21:8, 12, 26, 29. 22:10.

7 **memory.** 1 K 11:36. 2 K 19:34. 2 Ch 24:16. Ps
+13:3. 112:6. +146:4. Ob 16. Mt 25:41. 26:13.
Mk 14:9. Lk 1:48. 2 T 1:5. Re 20:4, 5. 21:4.
the name. Jb 18:17. 27:23. Ps 9:5, 6. 109:13,
15. Ec 8:10. Je 17:13.

8 **wise in heart.** ver. 13, 14, 23. Pr 12:1, 8, 15,
23. 13:15, 16. 14:6, 7, 8, 15, 16, 18, 24, 33.
15:7, 14, 21. 17:10, 12, 24.
will receive. Pr 1:5. 9:9. 12:1. 14:8. Ps
119:34. 143:8-10. Ja 3:13.
but. ver. 10. Pr 12:13. 13:3. 14:23.
prating fool. Heb. a fool of lips. ver. 10 Jg
+7:22mg. Ec 10:12.
fall. *or, be beaten.* ver. 10mg. Pr 18:6,

9 **that walketh.** Pr 28:18. Ps 23:4. 25:21.
26:11, 12. 37:37. 84:11. Is 33:15, 16. 3:19-
29. Ga 2:13, 14. 1 J 3:18-22.
but. Pr 17:20. Lk 12:1, 2. Ac 5:1-10. 4:5.

10 **that.** Pr 6:13. Jb 15:12. Ps 35:19.
but. ver. 8. Pr 18:6, 7, 21.
prating. ver. 8mg. Jg +7:22mg.
fall. *or,* be beaten. ver. 8mg. Ho 4:14mg. 3 J
10.

11 **mouth of a.** ver. 20, 21, 32. Pr 13:14. 15:7.
16:22-24. 18:4. 20:15. Ps 37:30, 31. 45:2. Jn
4:14. 7:38. Ep 4:29.
but. ver. 6. Ps +107:42. Ec 10:12-14.
12:34-37. Ja 3:5-8.

12 **Hatred.** Pr 11:5, 6, 8, 17:9, 11,
13. 7. Pr 11:18. 16:27. 28:25. 29:22.
4:1.
love covereth. Pr 17:9. Ge 45:5, 8. Ps
106:33. Mt 8:21-3. 1 C 13:4. Ga 6:1. Col
3:13. Ja 5:20. 1 P 4:8.

13 **the lips.** ver. 1, 21. Pr 15:7. 16:
12:9-11. 1 K 3:12. Ec 10:12. Is 20:15. 2 S
but. 1 K 12:13, 14. Lk 4:22.
a rod. ver. 10. 22. 17:10. 26:3. 2
32:9. He 12:6, 7.
understanding. Heb. heart. Pr 6:32mg.

14 **lay up.** Pr 1:5. 9:9. 18:1, 15. 19:8. Mt 12:
13:44, 52. 2 C 4:6, 7.
the mouth. ver. 8. 10. Pr 13:3. 18:6, 7.
21:23. Ex 52. Ps 52:1, 4, 5. Lk 12:19, 20.

15 **rich.** Pr 18:11. Jb 31:24, 25. Ps 49:6. 52:7.
Ec 7:12. Je 9:23. Mk 10:24. Lk 12:19. 1 T
6:17.
the destruction. Pr 4:20. 19:7. 22:22, 23.
Mi 2:1, 2.
poor. Pr 14:20. 19:7. 2:7. Ec 9:16. Ja 2:5.

16 **labor.** Pr 11:30. Is 3:10. 11. Jn 6:27. Ro 8:13.
1 C 10:31. 15:58. Ga 6:9. Ph 2:12, 13. He
6:10.
the fruit. Mt 7:17, 18. 12:33, 34. 15:19. Ro
6:23. 2 T 2:17, 18. 3:13.

17 **the way.** Pr 3:1, +2, 18. 4:4, 13. 12:1. 22:17-
19. Mt 7:24-27. Lk +11:28. He 2:1. 2 P 1:5-11.
he that. Pr 1:25, 26, 30. 5:12. 15:10. 29:1. 2
C 25:15, 16. He 12:25.
refuseth reproof. Pr +8:33. 13:13, 14, 18.
16:3.
erreth. *or,* causeth to err. Ec 5:6. Ho +4:12.

18 **that hideth.** Pr 26:24-26. 1 S 18:21, 22, 29.
2 S 3:27. 11:8-15. 13:23-29. 20:9, 10. Ezr 4:1-
10. Ps 5:9. 12:2. 55:21. Lk 20:20, 21. Jn
13:34, 35.
that uttereth. Ep +4:31.
slander. Pr 19:5, 9, 28.

19 **the multitude.** Ec 5:3. 10:13, 14. Ja 3:2.
but. Pr 17:27, 28. Ps 39:1. Ja 1:19. 3:2.
refraineth. ver. 20, 31, 32. Pr 11:12, 13.
15:1, 2, 4, 23, 28. 16:21, 23, 24. 20:19.
+21:23. 22:11. Is +58:13.
is wise. Jb 13:5. Ps 141:3. Col 4:6. Ja 1:19.
3:2.

20 **tongue**. Pr 12:18. 15:2, 4. 16:13. 25:11, 12, 15. 31:26. Ps +5:9. Is 35:6. Mt 12:35.
the heart. Pr 23:7. Ge 6:5. 8:21. Je 17:9. Mt 12:34.

21 **The lips**. Pr 15:7. Ep 4:29. Col 3:16.
feed many. Pr 11:25. 12:18. 15:4. Jb 4:3, 4. 23:12. 29:21, 22. Ps 37:30. Ec 12:9, 10. Je foo 15:16. Da 12:3mg. Jn 6:11. 21:15-17. 1 Jn 3:19. Heb.
wisdom. Pr 15:16. Ex Mt 13:19.
The bssing. Pr 15:16. Ps 3:8. 37:5. Ec 2:26.

22 **The** 5:19, 20.
t maketh rich. Thus "God's sponsibility," compare ver. 4. Pr 28:0. Ge 4:2. 13:2. 14:23. 24:35. 2:12. t 8:17. 8. 1 S 2:7, 8. 2 Ch 25:24. 37:22. 07:38. 13:7, 8. 1 T +6:9. 20:21. 28:2. Jsh 6:8. 7:1, etc. 1 K . 2 K 5:26. 27. Jb 27. etc. Hab 2:6-12. 5:4. Ro 8:38. 39. 1 T 6. Ja 5:1-5.
s sport. Pr 14:9. 15:21. 26:18, 19. Ec 7:6. 11:9.
fool. Pr +14:13. Ec 7:4.

24 **fear**. Jb +3:25. 15:20, 21. Ps +34. Is 8:12. Je +10:5. He 10:27.
shall come. ver. 28. Pr 11:2, 30. 12:3, 7, 12, 20, 21, 28. 13:6, 9, 0. 14:19, 22, 0, 32. 16:20. 17:19, 20. 18. 19:16. 20:7. 21:5, 16, 17, 18, 21. 22:5.
the desire. Ps 21:. 37:4. 145:19. Mt +5:6. Jn 14:18. 16:24. 1 J 5:14, 15.

25 **the whirlwind**. e +23:19.
so. Jb 27:19-21. s 37:9, 10. 73:18-20.
everlasting. He. olam, Ge +17:7.
foundation. ve. 30. Ps 15:5. Mt 7:24, 25. 16:18. Ep 2:20. ol 1:23. 1 T 6:19. 2 T 2:19. 2 P 1:10. 1 J 2:17.

26 **vinegar**. Pr 25:13, 20.
as smoke. Is 6:5.
so. Mt 25:26. Ro 12:11. He 6:12.
the sluggard. Pr 12:11, 24, 27. 13:4. 4:4, 23. 15:19. 16:26. 18:9. 19:15, 24. 2:, 13. 21:25. 22:13. Ex 22:29. Ec 11:4. R 3:15, 16.

27 **fear**. Pr 3:2, 16. 9:11. 14:27. Ps 2:4. 34:11-13. 91:16.
prolongeth. Heb. addeth. Pr 3:2. Dt +4:40.
the years. Jb 36:14. Ps +102:24. Is 65:20.

28 **hope**. Ps 16:. 73:24-26. 97:11. 147:11. Is 12:3. 35:10. o 5:2. 12:12. 15:13. 2 Th 2:16. T 1:2. He 6:19.
but. Pr 11:7. 14:32. Jb +8:13. 11:20. +36:18. Ps 112:10. Mt 7:22, 23. Lk 16:23-26. He +9:27.

29 **way**. Ne 8:10. Jb 17:9. Ps 84:5, 7. Is 40:29 31. Zc 10:12. Ph 4:13.
but. Pr 21:15. Jb 31:3. Ps 1:6. 36:12. 37:20. 92:7. Mt 7:22, 23. Lk 13:26, 27. Ro 2:8, 9.

30 **never**. ver. 25. Ps 15:1, 2. 16:8. 37:22, 28, 29. 112:6. 125:1. Ro 8:35-39. 2 P 1:10, 11.
the wicked. Ps 37:9, 10, 22. 52:5. Ezk 33:24-26. Mi 2:9, 10. Mt 21:41.

31 **mouth**. ver. 11, 13, 20, 21. Jb 6:25. Ps 37:30. Ja 3:13.
63:11. 120:3, 4.
the froward. Ps 31:18. 4:27. T 2:8.

32 **know**. Ec 12:10. Da 4:27.
but. Pr 11:11. 12:6, 18. 15:2, 28. 18:6-8.
frowardness. Heb. frowardnesses. ver. 31. Pr 2:12, 14.

PROVERBS 11

1 **A false balance is**. Heb. Balances of deceit are. Pr 16:11. 20:10, 23. Le 19:35, 36. Dt 25:13-16. Ps 66:18. Ho 12:7. Am 8:5, 6. Mi 6:10, 11. Mt 7:12. Ph 4:8. 1 Th 4:6.
a just weight. Heb. a perfect stone. Pr 16:11. 1 Ch 23:29. Ezk 45:10-12.

2 **pride**. Pr 3:34, 35. +16:5.
cometh shame. Ge 3:5, 7. Nu 12:2, 9, 10.
but. Pr 15:33. Lk 14:10, 11.

3 **The integrity**. ver. 5. Pr 2:1, 2, 9. 5:2. 4:23, 25-27. 10:9. 12:22. 13:6. 14:30. 15:21. 16:11. 19:1. 20:7. 21:3. Ps 15:1-5. 24:3-5. 25:21. 26:1. Is 33:15, 16. Ezk 18:5, 7-9. Mi +6:8. Mt 6:22. Lk 3:13, 14. 6:31. 16:10. Jn 7:17. Ac +6:3. 24:16. Ro 13:1. 2 C 4:1, 2. Ep 6:14. Ph 4:8. Col 3:22, 23. 1 T 1:5. T 1:7-9. 1 P 2:11, 12. 3:13. 1 J 5:18.
the perverseness. Pr 21:7. 28:18. Ec 7:17. Is 1:28.

4 **Riches**. Pr 10:2. Jb 36:18, 19. Ps 49:6-8. Ezk 7:19. Zp +1:11, 18. Mt 16:26. Lk 12:20.
day of wrath. Jb +21:30. Ja +5:1.
but. Pr 12:28. Ge 7:1. 2 K 20:3-6. Ezk 14:20. 18:27. Ro 5:17. 1 T +4:8.

5 **direct**. Heb. rectify. Pr 3:6. 9:6. 15:21.
but. ver. 3. 2 S 17:23. Jb +4:8. Mt 27:4, 5.

6 **righteousness**. Ge 30:33. 31:37. 1 S 12:3, 4.
but. Nu 22:32. 2 S 15:6. 18:14. 1 K 2:32, 33, 44. Jb +4:8. Ec 10:8.

7 **expectation shall perish**. Pr +10:28. 13:12, 19. 14:32. Ex 15:9, 10. Jb 8:13, 14. 11:20. Ps +146:4. Ezk 28:9. Lk 12:19, 20.
the hope of unjust. Ps 49:17-19. Is 1:28. Zp 1:18.

8 **righteous is delivered**. Pr 21:18. Ex 14:21-23, 26. Est 5:14. 7:9, 10. Is 43:3, 4. Da 6:23, 24.
ut of trouble. 2 K 22:20. 23:29. 2 Ch 15:20-24. Is 57:1. Da 3:22. Lk +21:36.

9 **n hypocrite**. 2 S +15:6. 1 K 13:18-22. 22:6, 2-23. Jb +8:13. Ps 55:12, 20, 21. Mt 7:15. 15-14. Ac 20:30. 2 C 11:13-15. 2 Th 2:8-10. 1 4:1-3. 2 P 2:1-3.
thugh knowledge. Pr 2:10-16. 4:5, 6. 6:24. 1 S 14:24-45. 2 S 16:1-4. Mt 24:11, 24. k 12:24. 13:14, 22. 2 C 2:11. 11:3. Ep

4:13, 14. 2 P 3:16-18. 1 J 2:20, 21, 27.
be delivered. Pr 22:3. Ps 31:20. 37:19. Is 26:20. Hab 3:16.

10   **it goeth**. Pr 28:12, 28. Est 8:15, 16.
the righteous. ver. 11, 14, 26. Pr 14:34. 21:15.
when. Ex 15:21. Jb 27:23. Ps +58:10, 11.
shouting. Pr 29:2. Am 5:13.

11   **the blessing**. Pr 14:34. 29:8. Ge 41:38-42. 45:8. Jg 5:31. 2 Ch 32:20-23. Jb 22:30. Ec 9:15.
it. 2 S 20:1. Est 3:8-15. 9:1-16. Ja 3:6.

12   **that**. Jg 9:27-29, 38. Ne 4:2-4. Ps 123:3, 4. Mt 7:3-5. Lk 16:14. 18:9. Jn 7:48-52. 1 C 4:7.
void of wisdom. Heb. destitute of heart. Pr 6:32mg. 7:7. 9:4, 16.
a man. Pr 10:19. 1 S 10:27. 2 K 18:36. Ga 6:1. 1 P 2:23.

13   **A talebearer**. Heb. He that walketh being a talebearer. Le +19:16. 1 Th 4:11. 2 Th 3:10-12.
revealeth. Pr 25:9. 26:20-22. Ne 6:17-19.
he. Pr 14:5. Jsh 2:14, 20. Je 38:27.
spirit. Heb. *ruach*, Ge +41:8.

14   **no counsel is**. Pr 15:22. 16:22. 24:6. 1 K 12:1-19. Ec 10:10. Is 19:11-14. Ac 15:6.

15   **that is surety**. Pr 6:1-5. 17:18. 20:16. 22:26, 27.
smart. Heb. be sore broken. Pr 13:20. Is 1:27. 42:21. 53:10. Jn 10:15, 17, 18. Ga 3:13. Re 5:12.
suretiship. Heb. those that strike hands. Pr 3:24 (sweet). 6:1. 17:18. 20:16. 22:26. 27:13. Jb 17:3.

16   **gracious**. ver. 22. Pr 12:4. 18:22. 19:14. 21:9, 19. 31:30, 31. Ru 3:11. 1 S 25:32, 33. 2 S 20:16-22. Est 9:25. Mt 26:13. Lk 8:3. 10:42. 21:2-4. Ac 9:39. 16:14, 15. Ro 16:2-4, 6. 1 P 3:1-4. 2 J 1.
and strong. Ps +86:14 (**S#6184h**). Lk 11:21, 22.

17   **merciful**. Ps 41:1-4. 112:4-9. Is 32:7, 8. 57:1. 58:7-12. Da 4:27. Mt +5:7. 6:14, 15. 25:34-40. Lk 6:36. 2 C 9:6-14. Ph 4:17.
soul. Heb. *nephesh*, Ge +27:31.
but. Pr 15:27. Jb 20:19-23. Ec 4:8. Ja 2:13. 5:1-5.

18   **wicked**. Pr 1:18. 5:22. Ge 3:4, 5. Jb 27:13-23. Ec 10:8. Is 59:5-8. Ro 6:21. Ep 4:22.
but. Pr +3:27. 22:8. Ps 126:5, 6. Ho 10:12, 13. Ga 6:8, 9. Ja 3:18.
righteousness. Ps 112:9. 2 C 9:9.
reward. Mt +5:12.

19   **righteousness**. ver. 4. Pr 10:16. 12:28. 19:23. Ge 19:16. Is 3:10. Ac 10:35. 1 J 3:7, 10.
he that pursueth evil. Pr 1:16-19. 7:22, 23. 8:36. 1 Ch +28:9. Ro 2:8, 9.

20   **of a froward**. Pr 6:14, 16-19. 8:13. Ps 18:25, 26.
abomination. Pr 15:8, 9, 26, 29. Ps 11:5-7.

upright. Pr 2:7. 15:8. 16:17. 21:29. Ps 11:7. 51:6. 140:13.
his delight. Ps 147:11. Zp 3:17.

21   **hand**. Pr 16:5. Ge 11:1, 4, 6-8. Ex 23:2. Nu 16:1-33. Is 8:9. 41:7.
the seed. Pr 13:22. Ge 7:1. Nu 14:24. Dt +29:11. Ps 84:11. Is 27:4. Ac 2:39.

22   **a jewel**. Pr 31:30. Ezk 16:15, etc. Na 3:4-6. 1 P 3:3, 4. 2 P 2:22.
is without. Heb. departeth from. Pr 7:10. 9:13.

23   **desire**. Ps 10:17. 27:4. 37:4. 39:7, 8. 73:25. 119:5, 10. Is 26:8, 9. Je 17:16. Mt +5:6. Ro 7:15-17, 22.
expectation. ver. 7. Pr 10:28. Jn 3:36. Ro 2:8, 9. He 10:27.

24   **that scattereth**. ver. 18. Pr 19:17. 28:8. Dt 15:10. Ps 112:9. Ec 11:1, 2, 6. Lk 6:38. Ac 11:29, 30. 2 C 9:5-11.
yet increaseth. Is 15:9mg. Lk +6:38. 16:9.
withholdeth. Pr +3:27. 10:19. 13:24. 17:27. 21:13. 28:27. 2 Ch 29:7. Ps +10:3. Ec +5:13. Ezk +16:49. Mt 26:7, 8. Ac 5:1, 2. 1 J 3:17.
is meet. or, uprightness. Pr 2:13. 4:11. 14:2.
but. Hg 1:6, 9-11. 2:16-19.
poverty. Pr 6:11. 14:23. 21:5, 17.

25   **liberal soul**. Heb. soul of blessing. Heb. *nephesh*, Ge +12:5. Pr 28:27. Jb 29:13-18. 31:16-20. Is 32:8. 58:7-11. Mt +5:7. 25:34, 35. 2 C 9:6-11.
that watereth. Pr 10:21. 25:13, 25. Is 58:10. Da 12:3mg.
shall be. Ro 2:21.

26   **that withholdeth**. Pr 15:27. Je 48:10. Ezk 16:49. Am 8:4-6. Mt 25:26, 27. 1 J 3:17.
corn. Is 3:11.
shall curse. Pr 24:24. 28:27. Ex +22:22-24. Jg 9:57. Ja +5:4.
blessing. Pr 10:6. Jb 29:13. 2 C 9:11.
that selleth. Ge 41:53-57. 42:6. Is 55:1.

27   **diligently**. *Shochair*, properly, "rising early to seek" what is greatly desired. Jb +8:5 (**S#7836h**).
he that seeketh. Pr 17:11. Est 7:10. Ps 7:14-16. 9:15, 16. 10:2. 57:6.

28   **that trusteth**. Pr 10:15. Dt 8:12-14. Jb 31:24, 25, 28. Ps 52:7. 62:10. Is 26:4. Mk 10:24. Lk 12:19-21. 1 T 6:17.
but. Ps 1:3. 52:8. 92:12-14. Is 60:21. Je 17:7, 8.

29   **that troubleth**. Pr 15:27. 17:6. 18:19. 19:13. Ge 34:30. 49:7. Jsh 7:24, 25. 1 S 25:3, 17, 38. Je 29:28. Hab 2:9, 10.
inherit. Ec 5:16. Ho 8:7.
the wind. Heb. *ruach*. Ec 5:16.
servant to. Pr 14:19. 17:2. 22:7.
wise of heart. Pr 10:8. 16:21.

30   **fruit**. Pr 10:16. Da 12:2, 3. Lk 13:7. Jn 15:8, 16. 1 T 4:16. 2 T 2:12.

tree of life. Pr +3:18. 15:4. Is +61:3. Je 17:8. Ezk 33:8, 9. Da +12:3.

and. Da 12:3. Mt 4:19. Jn 4:36. 1 C 9:19-23. 1 Th 2:19. Ja 5:19, 20.

winneth. Heb. taketh. Pr 9:7. Ge 19:14. Ml 2:6. Mt 18:15. Lk 5:9, 10. Ja 5:19, 20.

souls. Heb. *nephesh*, Ge +12:5.

31 **the righteous.** 2 S 7:14, 15. 12:9-12. 1 K 13:24. Je 25:29. 1 C 11:30-32. 1 P *4:17, 18*.

in the earth. Mt +5:5.

PROVERBS 12

1 **loveth.** Pr 2:10, 11. 6:23. 8:17, 32. 10:17. 13:18. 15:5, 10, 31, 32. 18:1. 29:1. Ps 16:7. 119:27, 97-100. Ec 4:13. Je 31:18. 2 Th 2:10.

instruction. or, discipline. Pr 1:2, 3, 7, 8. 5:23. 6:23. 10:17.

he that. Pr 5:12, 13. 9:7, 8. 15:10. Ps 32:9. 92:6. Is 1:2, 3. Je 6:8.

2 **good.** Pr 8:35. Ps 4:6. 5:12. 63:3. 112:5. Is 58:8-11. Ac 11:24. Ro 5:7. 2 C 5:9, 10.

a man. Pr 1:31. 6:18. Ps 9:15. Is 32:5-7. 1 P 3:11, 12.

3 **be established.** Pr 10:25. Jb 5:3-5. 15:29. 20:5-9. 27:13-18.

the root. ver. 12. Ps 15:5. 62:2. 125:1, 2. 1 S 25:33. Is 54:17. Mi 7:8. Ro 8:31. Ep 3:17. Col 2:7.

4 **virtuous woman.** Pr 11:16. 14:1. 19:13, 14. 31:10-25, 28, 30, 31. Ac 9:36. 1 C 11:7, 11. T 2:5. 1 P 3:1.

she. Pr 21:9, 19. 27:15, 16. 1 K 21:25.

as. Pr 14:30. Hab 3:16.

5 **thoughts.** Pr 11:23. 24:9. Ps 119:15. 139:23. Is 55:7. Je 4:14. Ro 7:15-23.

counsels. Ps 12:2, 3. 36:2-4. 41:6, 7. 140:1-3. Mt 2:3-8, 16. 26:4. 1 C 4:5. 2 C 4:2.

6 **words.** Pr 1:11-19. Ge 37:18-20. 2 S 17:1-4. Ps 37:12, 22. Is 59:7. Je 5:26. Mi 7:1, 2. Mt 2:7, 8. Ac 23:12, 15. 25:3.

the mouth. Pr 14:3. Est 4:7-14. 7:4-6. Mt 22:46. Lk 21:14, 15.

7 **wicked.** Pr 11:21. 14:11. 15:25. Ge 6:5. Est 9:6-10, 14. Jb 5:3, 4. 11:20. 18:15-20. 27:18-23. Ps 37:10, 35-37. 73:18, 19. Je 17:9.

the house. Pr 3:33. 14:1, 11. 24:3, 4. 2 S 7:16, 26. 1 K 15:4. Jb 5:24. 8:6, 7. Ps 128:3-6. Mt 7:24-27. Re 3:12.

8 **commended.** Ge 41:39. 1 S 16:18. 18:30. Ec 8:1. Da 6:3. Lk 12:42-44. 16:8. 1 C 3:10-15. 4:5. 2 C 10:18.

he that. Pr 1:26. 3:35. 5:23. 1 S 13:13. +25:17. Ps 132:18. Da 12:2. Ml 2:8, 9. Mt 27:4, 5. Ac 12:23.

of a perverse heart. Heb. perverse of heart. 1 S 20:30. Est 1:16.

despised. Pr 18:3. Ge 38:23mg.

9 **He that is.** 2 Th 3:10. 1 T 5:8.

despised. Pr 13:7. Lk 14:11.

10 **righteous.** Ge 33:13, 14. Ex 9:19. Nu 22:28-32. Dt 25:4. Jon 4:11.

regardeth. Pr 14:21, 31. 17:5. 19:17. 21:10, 13. 22:9. or, knoweth. Pr 14:10. 17:27. 24:22. 28:2.

life. Heb. *nephesh*, soul, Ge +2:19. 9:4. Dt 12:23.

beast. Pr 30:30. Ge 1:24, 25, 26. 2:20.

but. Ge 37:26-28. Jg 1:7. 1 S 11:2. Jn 19:31, 32. Ja 2:13-16.

tender mercies. or, bowels. Ge 43:14, 30. Dt 13:17. 1 J 3:17.

cruel. Pr 5:9. 11:17. 17:11. Is 13:9.

11 **tilleth.** Pr 13:23. 14:4, 23. 27:27. 28:19. Ge 2:15. 3:19. Ps 128:2. Ep 4:28. 1 Th 4:11, 12. 2 Th 3:8, 10-12.

be satisfied. Ge 26:12. 31:40. 32:10.

he that followeth. Pr +1:10, etc. 4:14, 15. 9:6. 13:20. 24:21. Ex 23:2. Jg 9:4. 2 S 15:11. 2 Ch +13:7. Ps 26:4. +119:63. Jon 2:8. Ac 5:36, 37. 20:29, 30. T 1:10, 11.

void. Pr 6:32. 7:7. 9:13, 16.

12 **desireth.** Pr 1:17-19. 29:5, 6. Ps 9:15. 10:8-10. Je 5:26-28. Mi 7:2. Hab 1:15-17.

net. or, fortress. Pr 10:15. Ec 7:26. 9:14. Is 29:7.

the root. Ps 1:3. Is 27:6. 37:31. Je 17:7, 8. Lk 8:13-15. Jn 15:4, 5, 16. Ro 6:22.

13 **The wicked is snared by the transgression of his lips.** Heb. snare of the wicked is in the transgression of lips. Pr 6:2. 15:2. 18:6, 7. 2 S 1:2-16. 1 K 2:23. Ps 5:6. 64:8. Da 6:7, 8, 24. Mt 27:25.

but. Ge 48:16. 2 S 4:9. Ps +34:19. Ec 7:18. Ro 8:35-37.

14 **satisfied.** Pr 13:2. 18:20, 21. Ps 63:5. Ml 3:16, 17. Ja 3:2, 13.

and. Is 3:10, 11. Mt 10:41, 42. 16:27. Ga 6:7, 8. 2 Th 1:6, 7. He 2:2. 6:10. 11:26.

15 **way.** Pr 3:7. 14:12, 16. 16:2, 25. 21:2. 26:12, 16. 28:11. 30:12. Ps 32:9. Lk 18:11. Ga 6:3.

fool. Pr 14:8. 26:12. 28:26. 1 S 25:17, 25. Ps +5:9. Lk 11:39, 40. T 3:3.

is right. 1 K 12:13, 14.

but. Pr 1:5. 9:9. 19:20. 1 S +25:17. 1 K 12:6-15. 2 K 5:13, 14. Ec 4:13. Je 38:15, etc.

hearkeneth. Pr 1:33. 8:33.

is wise. Ja 1:5.

16 **fool's.** Pr 18:6. 20:3. 27:3. 29:11. 1 S 20:30-34. 1 K 19:1, 2. Ja +1:20.

wrath. **S#3708h.** Pr 17:25 (grief). 21:19. 27:3. Jb 6:2. 10:17 (indignation). 17:7 (sorrow). Ec 1:18 (grief). 2:23. 7:3mg, 9. 11:10mg.

presently. Heb. in that day. Ps 2:7. 18:18. 50:15.

but. Pr 10:12. 16:22. 17:9. 29:11. 1 S 10:27. Ro 12:18-21. Ja 1:19.

17 **that.** Pr 14:5, 25. 1 S 22:14, 15. Ps 119:163. 1 J 4:2.

truth. ver. 19, 22. Pr 13:5. 14:5, 25. 17:7.
but. Pr +6:19. 24:28. 1 P 3:16.

18 **that**. Pr 25:18. Ps 42:10. 52:2. 57:4, 59:7. 64:3. Ja 3:6-8.
like. Re 1:16.
but. Pr 10:20, 21. 13:17. 15:7. 16:24. Da 11:33. Col 4:6. Re 22:2.
health. Pr 4:22mg. 6:15. 13:17. 16:24.

19 **lip of truth**. ver. 22. Ps 15:1, 3. 34:12, 13. Zc 1:4-6. Mt 24:35. 1 P 3:10.
for ever. Ps +9:18.
but. Pr 19:9. 2 K 5:25-27. Jb 20:5. Ps 52:5. Ac 5:3-10.

20 **Deceit**. ver. 12. Pr 26:24-26. Ge 37:31, 32. Je 17:16. Mi 2:1. Mk 7:21, 22. 12:14-17. Ro 1:29.
but. Is 9:6, 7. Zc 6:13. Mt +5:9. He 12:14. 1 P 3:8-13.

21 **no evil**. Ge +24:44. Ps 34:19. +91:10. Ro 8:28. 1 C 3:22, 23. 2 C 4:17.
happen. S#579h. Ps 91:10 (befall). See also Ex 21:13 (deliver). 2 K 5:7 (seek). Young renders this clause, "No iniquity is desired by the righteous."
filled. Pr 1:31. 14:14. Ec 9:3. Je 13:12-14. Hab 2:16. Re 18:6.

22 **Lying**. Ps 5:6. Is 9:15. Ezk 13:19, 22. Jn 3:20, 21. Ep +4:25.
deal truly. Pr 20:14. Mt 7:12. Mk 10:19. Ep 4:1.
his delight. Pr 11:1, 20. 15:8. Je 9:24.

23 **A prudent**. Pr 10:19. 11:13. 13:16. Ec 3:7. Am 5:13. Mt 17:9. Lk 2:19.
but. Pr 15:2. Ec 10:3, 12-14.

24 **hand**. Pr 10:4. 13:4. 17:2. 22:29. 1 K 11:28. 12:20. Mt 25:21-23.
but. ver. 27. Pr 19:15. 21:25, 26. 22:13. 24:30-34. 26:13-16.
slothful. or, deceitful. ver. 27. Pr 10:4, +26. 19:15. Jb 13:4. 27:4. Je +38:10mg.

25 **Heaviness**. Pr 14:10. 15:13, 15, 23. 17:22. 18:14. Ge 37:34, 35. Jsh 7:6, 7, 10. Ne 2:1, 2. Ps 38:6. 42:5, 11. Je 18:11, 12. Mt 27:5. Mk 14:33, 34.
but. ver. 18. Pr 15:23. 16:24. 25:11. 27:9. Is 35:3, 4. 50:4. 61:1, 2. Zc 1:13. Mt 11:28. 2 C 1:4. 2:4-8.

26 **righteous**. ver. 13. Pr 17:27. Ps 16:3. Mt 5:16, 46-48. Lk 6:32-36. 1 P 2:18-21. 1 J 3:1.
excellent. or, abundant. Jg 1:23 (descry). Ec 1:13 (search). 2:3 (sought). 7:25 (search). Young renders this clause, "The righteous searcheth his companion." That is, he carefully selects his companions. Pr 13:20. 18:24. 22:24. Ex 23:2. 2 Ch 13:7. Ps +119:63. Je 10:2. 1 C 15:33. 2 C 6:14, 17.
but. Ps 81:12, 13. Is 44:20. Ja 1:13, 14. 2 P 2:18-22. 1 J 2:26. Re 12:9. 13:14.

27 **slothful**. Pr 13:4. 23:21. 26:15. Jsh 18:3. 2 J +8.

but. Pr 15:16. 16:8. Ps 37:16. Jn 15:8. Ph 1:11.

28 **In the way**. Pr 8:35. 9:11. 10:16. 11:19. Is 35:8. Ezk 18:9, 20-24. Mt 7:13, 14. Jn 14:6. Ro 5:21. 6:22, 23. T 2:11, 12. He 10:19-23. 1 J 2:29. 3:7. 3 J 11.
no death. Jn 5:24. 1 C +15:55.

PROVERBS 13

1 **wise**. Pr 4:1-14, 20-22. 10:1. 15:5, 20. He 5:8.
but. Pr 9:7, 8. 14:6. 1 S 2:25. Ps 1:1. Is 28:14, 15.
heareth not. Pr 1:7, 25. 15:12. 1 S +25:17. Je 5:3. Ezk +22:29. Am 5:10. Mt +7:6. Lk 3:19, 20. Jn 3:20. 7:7.
rebuke. ver. 8. Pr 17:10. 2 S 22:16. Is 1:4, 5. He 12:5.

2 **eat**. Pr 12:14. 18:20.
the fruit. Pr 1:31. 8:19. 11:30. 12:14. Mt 7:16-23.
the soul. Heb. nephesh, Ge +27:31.
violence. Pr 1:11-13, 18, 31. 4:17. 10:11. Ps 75:8. 140:11. Je 25:27-31. Hab 2:8, 17. Re 16:6.

3 **that keepeth**. Pr +21:23. Ps +38:13.
life. Heb. nephesh, soul, Ge +44:30.
openeth wide. Ezk 16:25.
shall have. 1 S 25:10, 11, 33.

4 **soul**. Heb. nephesh, Ge +34:3.
sluggard. Pr 6:6, 9. 10:26. 15:19.
desireth. Pr 10:4. 12:11, 24. 26:13. Nu 23:10.
soul. Heb. nephesh, Ge +34:3.
diligent. Pr 2:2-9. 8:34. 10:4. 12:24, 27. 21:5. Jn 6:27. He 6:11. 2 P 1:5-11.
shall be. Ho 6:3. Mt 11:12. 25:14-29.
made. Pr 11:25. 28:25. Ps 92:14. Is 58:11.

5 **righteous**. Pr 30:8. Ps 19:14. 51:15. Ep +4:25.
is. Ezk 6:9. 20:43. 36:31. Zc 11:8.
and. Pr 3:35. Da 12:2. Ac 12:21-23. Re 21:8.

6 **Righteousness**. Pr 11:3, 5, 6. Ge 7:1. 19:29. 39:9. Ps 5:8. 15:2. 25:21. 26:1. Is 33:15, 16.
wickedness. Pr 5:22. 21:12. 2 Ch 28:23. Ps 140:11.
the sinner. Heb. sin. Ge 4:7. Ex 29:14, 36. 30:10. 2 C 5:21.

7 **There is**. Pr 11:24, 25, 30. Is 55:1-3.
maketh himself rich. ver. 11. Pr 12:9. Lk 18:11-14. 1 C 4:8. 2 P 2:19. Re 3:17, 18.
that maketh himself poor. Ec 11:1, 2. 1 C 4:10, 11. 2 C 4:7. +6:10. Ph 3:7-9. Re 2:9.
yet. Lk +6:38.

8 **ransom**. Pr 6:35. Ex 21:30. Jb 2:4. Ps 49:6-10. Je 41:8. Mt 16:26. 1 P 1:18, 19.
life. Heb. nephesh, soul, Ge +44:30.
the poor. 2 K 24:14. 25:12. Je 39:10. Zp 3:12.
rebuke. ver. +1.

9 **light**. 1 K 11:36. Ps +112:4. Mt 5:14, 16.
lamp. or, candle. Ps +18:28mg. 49:17-19. Is 50:10, 11. Mt 22:13. 25:3, 8.

10 **Only.** Pr 21:24. Jg 12:1-6. 1 K 12:10, 11, 16. 2 K 14:10. Lk 22:24. 1 T 6:4. Ja 3:14-16. 4:1, 5, 6. 3 J 9, 10.
with. Pr 12:15, 16. 17:14. 19:20. 20:18. 25:8. Jg 8:1-3. Mt +5:5. Lk 14:28-32. Ac 6:1-5. Ph 2:3. Ja 3:17.
well advised. Pr 20:18. 1 K +12:7.

11 **Wealth.** Pr 10:2. 20:21. 28:8. Jb 15:28, 29. 20:15, 19-22. 27:16, 17. Ec 5:14. Je 17:11. Hab 2:6, 7. Hg 1:6. Ja 5:1-5.
he. ver. 22, 23. Pr 20:21. 27:23-27. Ps 128:2.
by labor. Heb. with the hand.

12 **Hope.** Ps +71:5.
deferred. Ge 15:2. Ps 42:1-3. 69:3. 119:81-83, 123. 143:7. SS 5:8. La 4:17.
when. ver. 19. Ge 21:6, 7. 46:30. 1 S 1:26-28. Ps 17:15. 40:2, 3. Hg 2:7. Lk 2:29, 30. 24:17, 21. Jn 16:22. He 10:37. Re 21:4. 22:7, 12, 20.
a tree. Pr 3:18. 11:30. Re 22:2.

13 **despiseth.** Pr 1:25, 30, 31. Ex 5:2. 14:28. 2 S 12:9, 10. 2 Ch 36:16. Je 36:23-32. 43:2. 44:16, 17. Ezk 20:13, 16, 24. Lk 16:31. He 2:2, 3. 10:28, 29. 12:25.
he. Ps 115:13. Is +66:2. Ml 3:16.
rewarded. Heb. in peace. Ps 19:11. 119:165. Mt 5:12. 2 J 8.

14 **law.** Pr 9:11. 10:11. 14:27. 16:22.
to depart. Pr 15:24. 16:6, 17. 2 S 22:6, 7. Ps 18:5. 116:3. 119:9, 11.

15 **Good understanding.** Pr 3:4. 14:35. 1 S 18:14-16. Ps 111:10. Lk 2:52. Ac 7:10.
way of transgressors. Pr 4:19. 15:10. Ge +6:13. Nu 22:22-31. +32:23. Ps 95:9-11. Is 57:20, 21. 59:8. Je 2:19. La 3:7. Ho 2:6. Ac 9:5. Ro 6:21, 23. Ga 6:7. Ja 4:6.

16 **prudent.** Pr 12:22, 23. 15:2. 21:24. Ezr 8:22. Ps 112:5. Is 52:13. Mt 10:16. Ac 16:37, 38. 22:25. Ro 16:19. 1 C 14:20. Ep 5:17.
with knowledge. Lk 14:28-32.
a fool. 1 S 25:10, 11, 17, 25. Ec 10:3.
layeth. Heb. spreadeth. Ex 9:29, 33. 37:9. Is 37:14.
folly. ver. 19, 20. Pr 1:22, 32. 3:25.

17 **wicked.** Pr 10:26. 26:6. 2 K 5:26, 27. Je 23:13-16, 28. Ezk 3:18. 33:7, 8. 2 C 2:17.
but. Pr 25:13, 23. 1 C 4:2. 2 C 5:20. 1 T 1:12. 2 T 2:2.
a faithful ambassador. Heb. an ambassador of faithfulness.
faithful. or, stedfast. lit. stedfastnesses. Pr 14:5. 17:2. 20:6. Dt 32:20. Is 26:2mg.
ambassador. Pr 25:13. 26:14. Ge 24:34, 37, 38, 51-56. Ac 20:27. 2 C 5:20.
health. Pr 4:22mg. 6:15. 12:18. 16:24.

18 **Poverty.** ver. 13. Pr 5:9-14. 12:1. 19:16. Je 5:3-9. Lk 15:12-16.
refuseth instruction. ver. +1, 8. 1 S +25:17. He +12:25.
regardeth reproof. Pr 9:9. 25:12. 2 K +5:13. Ps 141:5. 1 T +5:19. He 12:11.

19 **The desire.** ver. 12. 1 K 1:48. Ps 17:15. 21:1, 2. SS 3:4. 2 T 4:7, 8. Re 7:14-17.
soul. Heb. *nephesh*, Ge +34:3.
it is. Pr 29:27.
fools. Pr 27:22. Dt 32:5, 6.
depart. Pr 3:7. 16:6, 17. Jb 28:28. Ps 34:14. 37:27. 2 T 2:19.

20 **walketh with wise.** Pr 2:20. 12:26. 27:17. 1 K 10:8. Ps +119:63. SS 1:7, 8. Ml 3:16. Ac 2:42. He 10:24. 3 J +11.
but. Pr 1:11-19. 2:12-19. 7:22, 23, 27. 9:6. +12:11. 22:14. Ge 13:12, 13. 14:12. 1 K 12:8, 10. 22:4, 32. 2 Ch 13:7. 19:2. Ac 2:40. 1 C 15:33, 34. 2 C 6:14-18. Ep 5:11. Re 18:4.
destroyed. Heb. broken.

21 **pursueth.** Pr +17:13. Ge 4:7. Nu +32:23. 35:19. Jsh 7:20-26. Jg 9:24, etc. 1 K 21:19-23. 2 K 9:30-36. Est 7:7-10. 8:1. 9:10. Ps 140:11. Ac 28:4.
righteous. Jb 21:15. Ps +84:11. Mt 10:41, 42. Mk +10:29, 30. Lk +14:14. Ro 2:7-10. Ga 6:9. He 6:10.

22 **leaveth an inheritance.** Ge 17:7, 8. 2 Ch 21:7. Ps 25:12, 13. 102:28. 112:2. 128:6.
to his. Ge 48:15, 16, 20. Nu 14:24. Jsh 14:14.
the wealth. Pr +28:8. Ex 3:22. Est 8:1, 2. Jb 27:13, 16, 17. Ps 105:44. Ec 2:26. Is +60:5mg. Lk 19:24-26.
for the just. Ps +37:9. Zc +14:14. Mt +5:5. Ro +11:26.

23 **food.** Pr 12:11, 14. 27:18, 23-27. 28:19. Ec 5:9.
destroyed. Pr 6:6-11. 11:5, 6. Ps 112:5. Ec 8:5, 6. Je 8:7-10.
for want. Pr 17:15, 23, 26. 18:5, 17, 18. 21:28.

24 **spareth.** Pr 10:13. +19:18. 22:15. 23:13, 14. 26:3. 29:15, 17. Dt +27:16. He 12:9.
hateth. Pr 8:36. Ge 29:30, 31, 33. Dt 21:15. Ml 1:2, 3. Mt 6:24. Mt 10:37. Lk 14:26. 16:13. Jn 12:25. Ro 9:13.
he that. Pr 3:12. Ps 94:12. 103:13. Ep +6:4. He 12:6-8.
loveth. Ps +109:17.

25 **righteous.** Ps +37:3, 16, 18, 19. Jn 6:35, 55. 1 T 4:8. He 13:5.
soul. Heb. *nephesh*, Nu +11:6.
but. Pr 15:27. 16:11. 20:10, 14, 23.
belly. Pr 6:11. 24:34. Dt 28:48. 32:24. Is 65:13, 14. Ho 4:10. Mi 6:14. Lk 15:15-17. 2 Th 3:10.

PROVERBS 14

1 **wise.** Pr 16:22. 20:5, 18. 21:22. 24:3, 4. 31:10-31. Ru 4:11.
the foolish. Pr 9:13-15. 19:13. 21:9, 19. 1 K 16:31. 21:24, 25. 2 K 11:1.

2 **that walketh.** Pr 16:17. 28:6. 1 K 3:6. Jb 1:1.

28:28. Ps 25:21. 112:1. Ec 12:13. Ml 2:5, 6. Ac 9:31. 10:22, 35. 1 J 3:21.

feareth. ver. 27. Pr 21:3, 4, 27.

but. Pr 11:12. Jb 12:4. Ps 123:3, 4. Lk 10:16. 16:14. Ro 2:4, 5. 2 T 3:2, 3.

3 the mouth. Pr 18:6. 21:24. 22:8. 28:25. 1 S 2:3. Jb 5:21. Ps 10:5-14. 12:3, 4. 31:18. 52:1, 2. 57:4. Je 18:18. Da 7:20. Ja 3:5, 6. 2 P 2:18. Re 13:5, 6.

but. Pr 12:6. Ps 141:3. Ro 10:9, 10. Re 3:10. 12:11.

4 clean. Am 4:6. 1 C 3:9.

but. Pr 13:23. 1 C 9:9-11.

strength. Le 1:5.

5 faithful witness. ver. 25. Pr 12:17. Ex 23:1. 1 K 21:13. 22:12-14. Ps 51:6. Ep +4:25.

false witness. 2 C 11:13-15.

6 scorner. Pr 18:2. 26:12. Is 8:20. Je 8:9. Mt 6:22, 23. 11:25-27. Ro 1:21-28. 9:31, 32. 1 C 3:18, 19. 8:2. 2 P 3:3-5.

findeth it not. Ezk 14:3, 4. Jn 18:38.

knowledge. Pr 8:9. 15:14. 17:24. 24:7. Ps 119:18, 98-100. Mt 7:7, 8. 13:11, 12. Jn 7:17. Ac 8:27-39. Ja 1:5.

hath understanding. Pr +19:25.

7 Go from. Pr 9:6. 13:20. 19:27. Ps +119:63, 114, 115. Mt +7:6. 1 C 5:11. 15:33. Ep +4:14. 5:11. 1 T 4:7. 6:3-5. 2 P 2:1, 2. 2 J 10.

lips. Ge +11:1.

8 wisdom. Pr 2:9. 8:20. Ps 111:10. 119:5, 34, 35, 73. 143:8. Ec 8:5. 1 C 7:20. Ep 5:17. Col 1:9, 10. 1 Th 4:11. 2 T 3:15-17. Ja 3:13.

folly. Pr 11:18. 2 K 5:20-27. Je 42:20mg. Lk 12:19, 20. Ac 5:1-10. Ep 4:22. 2 T 3:13.

9 Fools. Pr 1:22. 10:23. 26:18, 19. 30:20. Jb 15:16. 34:7-9. Je 44:4, 5. Ju 18.

mock at sin. Ge 3:12, 13. 1 S 15:13-15. Ps +58:5. Je 7:9, 10. Ezk +33:20. Mt 25:44.

among. Pr 3:4. 8:35. 12:2. 13:15. Is 66:2-5. Ezk 9:4-6. Da 9:4-21. Mt 27:46. Ro 14:17, 18.

10 heart. ver. 13. Pr 15:13. 18:14. 1 S 1:10. 2 K 4:27. Jb 6:2-4. 7:11. 9:18. 10:1. Ezk 3:14. Mt 14:33, 34. Jn 12:27. 1 C 2:11.

his own. Heb. *nephesh*, Ex +15:9.

bitterness, etc. the bitterness of his soul. Ge 42:21. 2 K +4:27mg. Is 53:3. 63:9. Mk 14:34, 35.

and a. Ps 25:14. Jn 14:18, 23. Ph 4:7. 1 P 1:8. Re 2:17.

11 house. Pr +3:33. 12:7. 21:12. Jb 8:15. 15:34. 18:14, 15, 21. 20:26-28. 21:28. 27:13-23. Zc +5:4. Mt 7:24-27.

the tabernacle. Pr 11:28. 21:20. Jb 8:6. Ps 112:2, 3. 128:3. Is 40:29. 58:11, 12. He 11:9, 10.

12 is a way. Pr 12:15. 15:24. 16:12, 17, 25. 30:12. Is 53:6. Mt 7:13, 14. Lk 13:24. Ro 6:21. Ga 6:3. Ep 5:6. Ja 1:22.

seemeth right. Jg 17:13.

the end. ver. 13. Pr 5:4, 11. 16:25.

ways of death. Pr 16:25. Je 21:8. Ro 6:21.

13 in laughter. Pr 5:4. 21:17. Jb 21:11-14. Ec 2:1, 2, 10, 11. 7:2-5, 6. 11:9, 10. Lk 6:25. 16:25. 1 C 10:7. Ep +2:3. Ja 4:9. 1 P +4:7. 2 P 2:13. Re 18:7, 8.

the end. Pr 5:3, 4.

14 backslider. Pr 1:32. Je 2:19. 8:5. 17:5. Ho 4:16. Zp 1:6. He 3:12. 2 P 2:20-22.

filled. Pr 1:31. 12:14. Ezk 22:31.

a good. ver. 10. Jn 4:14. 2 C 1:12. Ga 6:4, 8.

15 simple. Pr 4:26. +22:3. 27:12. Ge 3:1-6. Ezk 14:10. Ro 16:18, 19. Ep +4:14. 5:17. 1 J 4:1.

believeth every. Jsh 9:14. 1 K 13:15-24. Ep +4:14. 2 T 3:6-8, 13. He 13:9. 2 P 2:2, 18-20.

the prudent. ver. +8. Pr +22:3. Am 5:13. Ac 13:7. Ro 14:12. 1 Th 5:21.

looketh well. Pr +15:14. 18:1, 17. Is +8:20. Mt 7:15. Ac +17:11. 20:28-30. 1 Th 5:21. 2 P 3:17. 1 J 4:1.

16 feareth. Pr 3:7. 16:6, 17. 22:3. Ge 39:9. 42:18. Ne 5:15. Jb 31:21-23. Ps 119:120. 1 Th 5:22.

the fool. Pr 7:22. 28:14. 29:9. 1 K 19:2. 20:10, 11, 18. Ec 10:13. Mk 6:17-19, 24, 25. Jn 9:40.

17 that. ver. 29. Ja +1:20.

a man. Pr 6:18. 12:2. Est 3:6. 7:5, 6. Is 32:7. Je 5:26-29.

18 simple. Pr +1:4.

inherit. Pr 3:35. 11:29. Je 16:19. 44:17. Mt 23:29-32. 1 P 1:18.

the prudent. Pr 4:7-9. 11:30. Da 12:3. 2 T 4:8. 1 P 5:4.

19 The evil bow. Ge 42:6. 43:28. Ex 8:8. 9:27, 28. 11:8. 2 K 3:12. Est 6:11. 7:7, 8. 8:1, 2. Ps 49:14. Is 60:14. Mi 7:9, 10, 16, 17. Ml 4:3. Ac 16:39. Re 3:9.

20 poor. Pr 10:15. 19:7. Jb 6:21-23. 19:13, 14. 30:10.

but. Pr 19:4, 6. Est 3:2. 5:10, 11.

the rich hath many friends. Heb. many are the lovers of the rich. Ru +3:10.

21 that despiseth. Pr 11:12. 17:5. 18:3. Jb 31:13-15. 36:5, 6. Ps 22:24. Lk 18:9. Ja 2:5, 6, 14-16.

he that hath. ver. 31. Pr 11:24, 25. 19:17. 28:27. Ps 41:1, 2. 112:5-9. Ec 11:1, 2. Is 58:7-12. Da 4:27. Mt 25:34. Lk 6:30-36. Ac 20:35. He 6:10, 12. 1 J 3:17-22.

22 err. ver. 17. Pr 12:2. Is 32:7, 8.

devise evil. Pr 6:18. Ge 11:4, 5. Ps 2:1, 4. Mt 27:5. Ja 1:15.

but. Ge 24:27. Ps 25:10. 61:7. Mt 5:7. Jn 1:17.

devise good. Pr 19:22. 1 K 8:17, 18. 2 Ch 6:8. Is 32:8.

23 all labor. Pr 12:24. +22:29. 28:19. Ge 3:19. 1 K 11:28mg. Ps 90:17. Ec 2:24. Mt 11:12. Lk 10:7. Jn 6:27. 1 C +15:58. Col 3:22-24. 2 Th 3:10, 12. He +6:10, 11.

but. Pr 10:10. Ec 5:3. Je 12:2. Lk +6:46. 2 Th 3:10-12. 1 T 5:13.

24 **crown**. ver. +18. 1 K 3:13. Ps 112:9. Ec 7:11, 12. Is 33:6. Lk 16:9.
foolishness. Pr 27:22. Ps 49:10-13. Lk 12:19, 20. 16:19-25.

25 **true witness**. ver. +5. Ac 20:21, 26, 27. 26:16-20. Ep 4:25. 1 T 4:16.
souls. Heb. *nephesh*, Ge +12:5.
speaketh lies. ver. 5. Je 5:31. 2 C 11:13-15. 2 T 4:1-3. 2 P 3:3.

26 **fear**. ver. 27. Pr +3:7, 8, 25, 26. Ge 31:42. Ps 130:4. Ml 3:16-18. He 12:28.
confidence. Pr 18:10. Hab 3:17-19. 1 J 4:18.
his children. Pr 18:10. Ge 22:12. Ps +83:3. Is 26:20, 21. Je 15:11. 32:39, 40.
refuge. Ps 94:13. Is +26:20. Je +31:2. Zp +2:3. Lk +21:36. He 6:18, 19.

27 **The fear**. Pr 10:27. Ps 103:17. Ml 4:2.
a fountain. Pr 13:14. Is 33:6. Jn 4:14. Re 21:6.
to. Pr 2:10-18. 22:5. Ps 18:5. Ec 7:26.

28 **the multitude**. Ex 1:12, 22. Dt 1:11. 1 K 4:20, 21. 20:27. 2 K 10:32, 33. 13:7. Re 7:9, 10.
king's honor. ver. 35. Pr 16:10, 12-15. 19:12. 20:2, 8, 9, 26, 28. 21:1.

29 **slow**. ver. +17. Mt +5:5. 1 C 13:4, 5. Ja +1:20. 1 P 2:21-23.
but. Da 3:19, etc. Jon 4:9. Mt 2:16.
hasty. Heb. short. Jb +21:4mg.
spirit. Heb. *ruach*, Ge +41:8.
exalteth. Pr 4:8. Ec 10:6. Mt 5:22. Ep 4:26, 27, 31.

30 **sound**. Pr 4:23. Ps 119:80. 2 T 1:7.
flesh. Ge +17:13.
envy. 1 S 18:9, 12, 29. 1 K 21:4. Ps +37:1. 112:10.
rottenness. Pr 3:8. 12:4. 17:22.

31 **that oppresseth**. Pr 17:5. Jb 31:13-16. Ps +12:5. Mt 25:40-46.
but. ver. +21. Pr 19:17. Le 25:35, 36. Dt 15:11. Mt 25:40. Jn 12:8. 2 C 8:7-9. 1 J 3:17-21. 4:21.
the poor. Mt 11:5. 26:11. Ja +2:5.

32 **wicked**. Pr +10:28.
driven. Jb 18:18. 27:20-22. Ps 1:4. 58:9. Is 8:21, 22. Da 5:26-30. Jn 8:21, 24. Ro 9:22. 1 Th 5:3.
the righteous. Ge 49:18. Jb 13:15. 19:25-27. Ps 23:4. 37:37. 39:7. Lk 2:29. 1 C 15:55-58. 2 C 1:9. +5:8. Ph 1:22, 23. 2 T 4:6-8, 18. Re 14:13.
death. 1 C +15:55.

33 **Wisdom**. Pr 2:10. Mt 22:15-46. Jn 14:23.
resteth. Pr 12:16, 23. 13:16. 15:2, +28. 29:11. Ec 10:3.
fools. Ec 5:3. 10:14.

34 **Righteousness**. Dt 4:6-8. 28:1-14. Jg 2:6-14. Is 58:13, 14. Je 2:2, etc. Ho 13:1.

but. Dt 28:15, etc. 29:18-28. Ne 13:15-18. Ps 107:34. Ezk ch. 16, 22, 23.
sin. or, sin offering. Pr 5:22. 10:16. 13:6. 20:9. Ge +4:7.
reproach. 2 S 12:14. Ps +31:11.
any people. Heb. nations. Ge 27:29. Is 17:12.

35 **king's**. Pr 16:12, 13, 15. 20:8, 26. 22:11. 25:5. 29:12. Ps 101:4-8. Da 6:1-3. Mt 24:45-51. Lk 12:42-48.
wise servant. Pr 17:2. 27:18. Mt 25:21. Lk 12:37. Ep 6:5-8. Col +3:22, 24.
him. Pr 10:5. 17:2. 19:26.

PROVERBS 15

1 **A soft answer**. Pr 25:11, 15. Jsh 22:30. Jg 8:1-3. 1 S 25:21-33. 2 S 2:5. 20:16-22. Ac 23:6. 2 C 6:3. 12:6. Ja 3:17, 18.
turneth away. Pr 16:7. 29:8. Je +2:24mg.
grievous. ver. 18. Pr 10:12. 28:25. 29:22. Jg 12:3-6. 1 S 25:10, 11, 21, 22. 2 S 19:43. 1 K 12:13-16. Ec 7:8, 9. Ac 15:39. Ja 3:5.

2 **tongue**. ver. 23, 28. Pr 12:23. 13:16. 16:23. 25:11, 12. Ps 45:1. Ec 10:12, 13. Is 11:2. 50:4. Mt 22:15-46. Mk 4:33. Jn 7:46. 1 C 3:2. 2 T 2:15.
fools. Pr 10:8. 18:7. Ps +101:5. Ec 5:3. 10:12-14.
poureth. Heb. belcheth, or, bubbleth. ver. 28. Pr 1:23. Jb 2:9, 10. Ps 19:2. 59:7. 145:7.

3 **eyes of**. ver. 11. Pr 5:21. Ps +11:4. Je 16:17. 32:19.
every place. 1 K 8:27. Ps 139:3-10. Is +57:15. Je 23:23, 24. Mt +18:20. +28:19. Ac 17:27. Ep 1:23.
beholding. 2 K 5:26. Ps 73:11. 139:23, 24. Is 29:15. Ho 7:2. Jn 1:48.

4 **A wholesome**. Heb. The healing of the. Pr 4:22mg. 12:18. 14:30. 16:24. Ec 10:4. Ml 4:2. Col 4:6. 1 T 6:3.
a tree. Pr 3:18. Ge 3:22-24. Re 2:7.
a breach. Pr 18:8, 14. 26:22. Ps 52:2-4. 109:22.
spirit. Heb. ruach, Ge +41:8.

5 **fool**. ver. 20. Pr 13:1, 18. 22:15. Ex +20:12. 1 S 2:23-25. 2 S 15:1-6. 1 Ch 22:11-13. 28:9, 20. La 3:27. Ep 6:1, 2.
instruction. ver. 31, 32. Pr 17:16. 18:15. 19:8, 18, 20, 27. 22:6, 15.
but. ver. 31, 32. Pr 1:23. 6:23. 19:20. 25:12. Ps 141:5. 1 T 1:13. 2:15.

6 **the house**. ver. 16. Pr 8:21. 13:22. 21:20. Ps 112:3. 1 C 2:9. 2 C 6:10. He 11:26.
treasure. lit. strength. Pr 27:24mg. Ro +11:25.
in the revenues. Pr 10:22. 16:8. Jb 20:19-23. Ps 37:16. Ec 4:6. 5:10-14. Ja 5:1-3.

7 **lips**. Ps 37:30. 45:2. 51:13-15. 71:15-18. 78:2-6. 119:13. Ec 12:9, 10. SS 4:11. Mt 10:27. 28:18-20. Mk 16:15. Ac 18:9, 10. Ro 10:14-17. 15:18-21. Ep 4:29. 2 T 2:2.

disperse. Jb 4:3, 4. Ps 40:9, 10. Mt 4:23. 2 C 9:6. 1 P 4:10.

the heart. Pr 10:20, 21. Mt 12:34. Jn 3:6.

8   **sacrifice of the wicked**. Pr 21:4, 27. 28:9. Ge 4:3-5. 1 S 15:22. Ec 5:1. Is 1:10-15. 29:13, 14. 61:8. 66:3. Je 6:20. 7:21-23. Am 5:21, 22. Mt 15:8, 9. Jn 4:24. Ac 8:22. T 1:15.

the prayer. ver. 29. 1 Ch 29:17. Ps 17:1. SS 2:14. Da 10:12. Ac 10:4.

the upright. Pr 21:21. Jn +17:6. Ph 3:12.

his delight. Ps 141:2. SS 2:14. 4:11. Da 9:23. 10:12. Jn 4:23, 24. Ro 8:26, 27. He 4:16. 10:19-22. Re 8:4.

9   **The way**. Pr 4:19. 21:4, 8. Ps 1:6. 146:8, 9. Is 29:13, 14. Mt 7:13.

an abomination. Je 44:4. Hab 1:13.

he loveth. Pr 21:21. Is 26:7. 51:1, 7. Da 9:23. Ho 6:3. 1 T 6:11. 2 T 2:22.

10   **Correction**. *or*, instruction. ver. 5, 32, 33. Pr 12:1. 23:12.

grievous. Pr 12:1. 13:1. 23:35. 1 K 18:17. 21:20. 22:8. 2 Ch 16:10. 36:16. Jn 3:20. 7:7.

and he. Pr 1:30. 5:12. 10:17. Is 1:5, 6. Ezk 24:13, 14.

11   **Hell**. Heb. *sheol*, Ge +37:35. Pr 27:20. Jb 26:6. Ps 139:7, 8. Re 1:18.

destruction. Jb 26:6.

the hearts. 2 Ch 6:30. Ps 7:9. 44:21. 139:23, 24. Je 17:9, 10. Jn +2:24, 25. 21:17. Ac 1:24. He 4:13. 1 J 3:20. Re 2:23.

12   **scorner**. ver. 10. Pr 9:7, 8. 1 K 22:8. Am 5:10. Jn 3:18-21. 7:7. 2 T 4:3.

neither. 2 Ch 18:7. Jb 21:14.

13   **merry**. ver. 15, 30. Pr 17:22. 1 S 1:17, 18. Ps 32:1, 2, 11. Ac 6:15. 2 C 1:12. Ph 4:4.

by. Pr 12:25. 18:14. Ne 2:2. Jn 14:1. 2 C 2:7-11. 7:10.

spirit. Heb. *ruach*, Ge +41:8.

14   **heart**. Pr +4:23.

hath understanding. Pr 1:5. 9:9.

seeketh knowledge. Pr 2:3-5. 4:7. +14:15. 18:1, 15, 17. 23:23. 1 K 3:6-12. 10:1. 2 Ch 1:10. Jb 28:12, 20. Ps 90:12. 119:33, 34, 66, 97, 100. Ec 1:13. 7:25. 8:16. 12:9, 10. Da 9:2. Mt 5:6. 12:42. Lk 10:39. Jn 3:1, 2. 5:39. Ac 8:28, 31. 10:33. 17:11. Ph 1:9. He 5:14. 6:1. 1 P 1:11. 2 P 3:18.

the mouth. ver. 21. Pr 12:23. 18:2. Is 30:10. 44:20. Ho 12:1. Ac 17:21.

15   **All**. Ge 37:35. 47:9. Ps 90:7-9, +15. Mk +10:30. 1 P 5:10.

but. *Pr 14:30*. 16:22. 17:22. Jb 1:21. 15:11. Hab 3:17, 18. Ac 16:25. Ro 5:2, 3, 11. 12:12. 2 C 1:5, 12. 6:10. He 10:34. 1 P 1:6-8. 4:13.

feast. Ps 4:6, 7. Ec 9:7. Jn 4:13, 14. 7:38, 39.

16   **little**. Pr 16:8. 28:6. Ps 37:16. Ph +4:11. 1 T 6:6.

great. Pr 10:22. Ec 2:10, 11. 18-23. 4:6. 5:10-12.

17   **a dinner**. Pr 17:1. 21:19. Ps ch. 133. Ph 2:1. 1 J 4:16.

18   **wrathful**. Pr 10:12. 19:19. 28:25. 2 S 19:43. 20:1. Ja 3:14-16.

stirreth up. Pr 28:25. 29:22.

strife. Pr 6:14. 16:28. 17:1, 14. 20:3.

slow to anger. ver. 1. Pr 25:15. Ge 13:8, 9. Jg 8:1-3. 1 S 25:24, etc. Ps 103:8. Ec 10:4. Mt +5:5, 9. Ac 6:1-5. Ja +1:20.

appeaseth. Jb 34:29. 37:17. Ec 10:4.

strife. Pr 17:1, 14. 18:6, 17. 20:3.

19   **way of the slothful**. Pr 22:5, 13. 26:13. Nu 14:1-3, 7-9. Mt 25:26, 27.

the way of the righteous. Pr 3:6. 8:9. Ps 5:8. 25:8, 9, 12. 27:11. Is 30:21. 35:8. Zc 4:7. Ph 4:13.

made plain. Heb. raised up as a causey. Is 57:14. Je 18:15.

20   **wise**. Pr 23:15, 16. 29:3. 1 K 1:48. 2:9. 5:7. Ph 2:22.

despiseth. Ex +20:12. 2 K 2:23. Jb 19:18. Mi 7:6.

21   **joy**. Pr 10:23. 14:9. 26:18, 19.

destitute of wisdom. Heb. void of heart. Pr 6:32mg. 11:12mg.

a man. Pr 14:16. Jb 28:28. Ps 111:10. Ep 5:15. Ja 3:13.

22   **Without counsel**. Pr 11:14. 20:18. Ec 8:6.

but in. Pr 24:6.

23   **joy**. Pr 12:14. 16:13. 24:26. 25:11, 12. Ep 4:29.

in due season. Heb. in his season. Ps 1:3. Ec 3:1. Is 50:4. 2 T 4:2.

how good. 1 S 25:32, 33. Mt 18:15.

24   **way**. Pr 6:23. Ps 16:11. 139:24. Je 21:8. Mt 7:14. Jn 14:6.

above. Mt 6:20. 2 C 4:18. Ph 3:20. Col 3:1, 2. He 11:16. 13:14.

that. Pr 2:18. 5:5. 7:27. 9:18. 23:14.

hell. Heb. *sheol*, Ge +37:35.

25   **destroy**. Pr 12:7. 14:11. Jb 40:11-13, Ps 52:1, 5. 138:6. Is 2:12. Da 5:20. Lk 1:51, 52. 1 P 5:5.

widow. Is +1:17.

26   **thoughts of the wicked**. Pr 6:16-19. 23:7. 24:9. Ps 94:11. Is 59:7. Je 4:14. Mt 15:19. He 4:13.

but. ver. 23. Pr 22:11. Ps 18:26. 19:14. 24:4. 37:30, 31. 45:1. Ml 3:16, 17. Mt +5:8. 12:34-37.

pleasant words. Heb. words of pleasantness. ver. 8. Pr 3:17. 15:1. +16:24. 1 T +4:12.

27   **greedy of gain**. Pr 1:13, 19. 11:19, 29. 20:21. 21:26. Ge 13:10, 11. Dt 7:26. Jsh 6:18. 7:1, 11, 12, 15, 21, 24, 25. 1 S 8:3-5. 15:19, 23. 1 K 15:19, 23. 2 K 5:20-27. Ps 10:3. Ec 5:10. Is 5:8-10. 56:11. Je 17:11. Am 2:7. Mi 3:11. Hab 2:9-11. Zc 5:3, 4. 9:3. Mt 26:15, 16. Jn 12:6. Ac 16:19. 24:26. 1 T 6:9, 10. Ja 5:3. 2 P 2:15.

but. Pr 28:16. 29:4. Ge 14:22, 23. Ex +18:21. 23:8. Dt 16:19. Is 33:15, 16.

28 **heart**. ver. 2. Pr 16:23. 1 K 3:23-28. Ne 2:4. Ec 5:2, 6. 10:2.

studieth. or, meditateth. Pr 8:7. 24:2. Jsh +1:8.

to answer. Ja 1:5. 1 P 3:15.

the mouth. Pr 10:19. 13:16. 29:11, 20. Ec 10:12-14. Mt 12:34-36. T 1:10, 11. Ja 3:6-8. 2 P 2:18.

29 **far from**. Jb 21:14. Ps 10:1. 34:16. +66:18. 73:27. 138:6. Is 46:12, 13. Je 18:17. 23:24. Am 9:4. Mt 25:46. Ac 13:38-46. 17:27, 28. Ep 2:12, 13. 2 Th 1:9.

wicked. ver. 8. 1 P 3:12.

he heareth. ver. 8. 1 S 1:13. Ps 6:8. 38:9. +66:18, 19. Is 38:14. La 3:56. Lk 18:1-7. Ro 8:26, 27. 1 J +5:14.

righteous. Jb 8:5, 6. Ps 4:4, 5. Is 58:8, 9. 64:5. Je 17:16. Jn +9:31. 17:6. Ja 5:16. 1 P 3:12. 1 J 2:1. 3:22.

30 **light**. Pr 13:9. Ezr 9:8. Ec 11:7. Re 21:23. 22:5.

a good. Pr 17:22. 25:25. Ps 89:15. Lk 2:10-19. 1 Th 3:6-9.

the bones. Pr 3:8. Is 58:11.

31 **ear**. ver. 5. Pr 1:23. 9:8, 9. 13:20. 19:20. 25:12. 2 S 12:13. Ps 141:5. Is 55:3. Mk 4:24. Lk 8:18. +11:28.

abideth. Pr 19:23. Ge 19:2. 24:23. Ps +49:12. Jn 15:3, 4. 1 J 2:19.

among. Pr 14:33.

32 **refuseth**. Pr 5:11, 12. 1 S +25:17. Ps 50:17. He +12:25.

instruction. or, correction. Pr +12:1. 29:1. Is 1:5. Ezk 24:13, 14.

soul. Heb. *nephesh*, Ge +27:31.

heareth. or, obeyeth. Pr 5:13. 25:12. Ge 22:18. 26:5. Dt 21:18, 20. Mt 7:24-27. Ja 1:22. Re 3:19.

reproof. Pr 1:30.

getteth understanding. Heb. possesseth an heart. ver. 14, 21mg. Pr 17:16. 18:15. 19:8mg.

33 **fear**. Pr 1:7. 8:13. Jb 28:28. Ps 34:11. 111:10.

and. Pr 18:12. 25:6, 7. 29:23. Lk 14:10, 11. Ph 2:5-11. Ja 4:10. 1 P 5:5, 6.

PROVERBS 16

1 **preparations**. or, disposings. ver. 9. Pr 19:21. 20:24. 21:1. 2 Ch 18:31. Ezr 7:27. Ne 1:11. Ps 10:17. 119:36. Je 10:23. 32:39, 40. Ezk 36:26, 27. 2 C 8:16. Ph 2:13. Ja 1:16-18.

heart. Ps 10:17. Je 10:23. 31:33. Da 1:8. Am 4:12. Jn 6:44, 45. Ac 16:14. 2 C 3:3, 5. 1 T 5:22.

and. Pr +15:28. Ex 4:11, 12, 15. Nu 22:18. Je 1:7-9. Mt 10:19, 20. Lk 12:11, 12. 21:14, 15.

from the Lord. ver. 2-7, 9, 33. Pr 17:3. 19:21. 20:12, 24, 27. 21:2, 30, 31. 22:12. Ph 2:13.

2 **the ways**. ver. 25. Pr 21:2. 1 S 15:13, 14. Ps

36:2. Je 2:22, 23. Lk 18:9-11. Ro 7:7-9.

clean. Pr 30:12. Is 5:20. Mt 6:23. Jn 16:2. 18:28. Ac 26:9.

but. Pr 5:21. 24:12. 1 S 2:3. 16:7. Is 26:7. Je 17:10. Da 5:27. Lk 16:15. Re 2:18, 23. 3:1.

spirits. Heb. *ruach*, Ge +41:8.

3 **Commit**. Heb. Roll. Ps 22:8mg. 37:5mg.

thy works. Ne 2:4-6. Jb 5:8. Ps 37:4, 5. 55:22. Mt 6:25, etc. Lk 12:22. Ph 4:6. 1 P 5:7.

thy thoughts. Pr 4:23. Jb 22:28. Ps 112:7. 127:2. Is 7:5-7. 26:3. Ph 4:8.

established. ver. 33.

4 **Lord**. Is 43:7, 21. Ro 11:36. Re 4:11.

for himself. Ps +46:10. +83:18. Is 42:8. 43:7, 21. 48:11. Ezk 20:9. 36:32. Jn +11:42. 1 C +15:28. Col 1:16. Re 4:11.

yea even. Ex 9:16. 14:17. Jb 21:30. Ezk 33:11. Mk 4:11, 12. Ro 9:17, 22, 23. 2 C 2:15. 13:5, 6. 1 P 2:8. 2 P 2:3, 9, 12. Re 19:3.

5 **proud**. ver. +18. Pr +6:17. 8:13. 15:26. Ge 3:5. Ex 5:2. 9:17. 10:3. 18:11. 1 S 2:3. 2 S 22:28. Jb 40:11, 12. Ps 2:1. +10:2. 12:3, 4. 18:27. 31:23. 119:21. 138:6. Is 2:12. 3:16-23. 5:15. 13:11. 26:5. 45:9. 65:5. Je +20:11. Ezk 28:2. Da 4:30-32, 37. Hab 2:4, 5. Mt 23:12, 29-31. Lk 1:51. 14:11. +16:15. 2 Th 2:4, 8. 1 T 3:6. 2 T 3:2. Ja 4:6, 16. 1 P 5:5.

though. Pr 11:21. Is 8:9, 10.

unpunished. Heb. held innocent. Pr 6:29. 11:21. 17:5mg. 19:5mg. Ex +20:7. Is 3:11. Ro 2:8, 9.

6 **mercy**. Pr 20:28. Ex 30:10. Le 4:20. Ps 85:10. 86:15. Da 4:27. Mi 7:18-20. Lk 11:41. Jn 1:17. 15:2. Ac 15:9. 1 P 1:22.

and truth. Pr 3:3. 12:19.

purged. Ps 65:3.

by the. Ex +1:17. Dt +6:2. Ec 7:18. 2 C 7:1. Ep 5:21.

7 **When**. Pr 10:12. +17:17. 18:24. +19:11. 25:15, 21, 22. 29:8. Mt 5:38-45. +10:16. +11:29. Lk 6:30, 35-37. Ro 12:14, 20, 21. Ga +6:1. Ep +4:32. 1 P 3:8, 13.

please. 2 Ch 14:3. Ps 69:31. Ro 8:31. Ph 4:18. Col 1:10. 3:20. He +12:14. 13:21. Ja +1:4. 1 J 3:22.

he maketh. Ge 27:41. 32:6, 7, 28. 33:4. 43:14. Jb 1:9, 10. Je 15:11mg. Da 1:9. 3:26-30. 6:24, 28. Ac 9:1, 2, 19, 20.

enemies. Dt 28:7. 2 K 6:16. 17:39. 2 Ch 14:11. Jb 8:22. Ps 17:7. 27:5, 6. 37:32, 33, 40. 76:10. 97:10. 112:8. 118:6, 7. 125:3. Is 25:5. 54:15, 17. Lk 1:71, 74, 75. 18:7, 8. Ac 18:10. He 13:6.

at peace. Ge 31:55. 33:1, 4. 39:21. 2 Ch 20:30. Jb 34:29. Ps 105:13-15. Ac 9:31. Ro 8:28, 31. 1 P 3:13.

8 **Better is**. Pr 15:16. Ps 37:16. 1 T 4:8. 6:6-9.

little. Pr 6:10. 10:20. 24:33. Ge 18:4. 1 K 17:10, 12.

with righteousness. Pr 11:1. 12:21. 15:27.

28:20. Dt 16:20. 25:15. Ps 15:5. Is 33:15, 16. 56:1, 2. Ezk 18:5, 7-9.

than great revenues. ver. 16, 19. Pr 13:11. 20:15. 21:6, 7. 22:1, 16. 28:8. 1 K 21:19. Je 17:11. Mi 6:10. Hab 2:6. Lk 19:8. 1 T 6:10. Ja 5:1-3.

without right. ver. 10 (judgment), 11 (just), 33 (disposing). Ge 18:19, 25. Ps 112:15mg. 140:12. Is 1:17 (judgment).

9 **heart deviseth**. ver. 1. Pr 19:21. 20:24. 21:30. Ps 37:23. Is 46:10.

directeth. Ge 45:5. Ps 33:11. 37:23. 107:7. Is 42:16. Je 10:23. La 3:37.

10 **A divine**. Heb. Divination. Dt +18:10. Je +27:9.

sentence. or, oath. ver. 12, 13. Ge 44:5, 15. Dt 17:18-20. 2 S 23:3, 4. Ps 45:6, 7. 72:1-4. 99:4. Is 32:1, 2. Je 23:5, 6.

transgresseth. Ho 10:4. Am 5:7. 6:12.

11 **just**. Pr 11:1. 20:10, 23. Le 19:35, 36. Dt 25:13-15. Ezk 45:10. Ho 12:7. Am 8:5. Mi 6:11.

weights. Heb. stones. Pr 11:1mg. 20:10mg. Le 19:36mg. Dt 25:13mg.

bag. S#3599h. Pr 1:14 (purse). 23:31 (cup). Dt 25:13. Is 46:6. Mi 6:11.

12 **an**. Pr 28:9. Dt 25:16. Lk +12:48.

for. Pr 20:18. 25:5. 29:14. 2 S 23:3, 4. 1 K 3:9. Ps 72:1. 99:4. Re 19:11.

13 **Righteous lips**. Pr 14:35. 22:11. 2 S 14:17. 45:7. 101:5-7. Is 11:2-4.

14 **wrath**. Pr 19:12. 20:2. Est 7:7. Ec 8:3, 4. Da 3:13, etc. Mt 22:13. Lk 12:4, 5. Re 6:16, 17.

messengers. Pr 17:11. 1 S 22:16. 1 K 2:25. 2 K 6:31-33. Da 2:12. Mk 6:27.

but. Ec 10:4. Ac 12:20. 2 C 5:20.

15 **the light**. Pr 19:12. Jb 29:23, 24. Ps 4:6. 21:6. Ac 2:28.

his favor. Pr 22:1. Est 5:2, 3. Jb 29:23. Ps 4:7. 30:5. 72:6. Ho 6:3. Zc 10:1. Col 1:20.

16 **better**. Pr 3:15-18. 4:7. 8:10, 11, 19. Jb 28:13, etc. Ps 119:27. Ec 7:12. Mt 16:26. Lk 12:21. Ph 3:7, 8. Col 2:3. Ja 1:5.

17 **highway**. Pr 4:24-27. Is 35:8. Ac 10:35. 24:16. T 2:10-14.

depart. Pr 14:16. Ps 18:23. Zc 7:10. 1 C 10:6. 1 Th 5:22. 2 T +2:19.

he. Pr 10:9. 19:16. Mt 24:13. He 10:39. Ju 21, 24. Re 3:10.

soul. Heb. *nephesh*, Ge +27:31.

18 **Pride goeth**. ver. +5. Pr 11:2. 17:19. 28:26. 29:23. Nu +32:23. Dt +17:20. Est 3:5, 6. 6:6. 7:9, 10. Is 37:10-13, 38. Je 50:31, 32. Da 4:30-37. 5:20-24. Ob 3, 4. Ml 4:1. Mt 26:33-35, 74. Ac 12:21-23. Ro 11:20.

haughty. Pr 18:12. 2 S 22:28.

spirit. Heb. *ruach*, Ge +41:8.

before a fall. 1 C 10:12. 2 C 12:9.

19 **to be**. Ps 34:18. 138:6. Is 57:15. Mt +5:3. Lk 1:51-53. 18:13, 14. Ph +2:3.

spirit. Heb. *ruach*, Ge +41:8.

than. Ex 15:9. Is 9:3. 10:6, 13-15. 53:12.

20 **handleth**. *or*, understandeth. Pr 8:35. 13:15. 17:2. 19:8. 24:3-5. Ge 41:38-40. Da 1:19-21. Mt 10:16.

whoso. Pr 22:19, 20. 1 Ch 5:20. Is +26:3, 4. 30:18. Da 3:28. 6:23. Ep 1:12, 13.

21 **wise**. ver. 23. Pr 10:8. 23:15. 1 K 3:12. Ho 14:9. Ro 16:19. Ja 3:17.

the sweetness. ver. 24. Pr 15:7. 27:9. Ps 45:2. Ec 12:10. Is 50:4. Lk 4:22. Jn 7:46.

22 **Understanding**. Pr 2:10-12. 3:13-18, 35. 4:5-9. Ec 7:12.

a wellspring. Pr 10:11. 13:14. 14:27. 18:4. Jn 4:14. 5:24. 6:63, 68. 7:38.

the instruction. Pr 15:2, 28. Mt +7:6. 15:14. 23:16-26. Lk 6:39, 40. Ro 1:22.

23 **heart**. Pr 15:28. 22:17, 18. Ps 37:30, 31. 45:1. Mt 12:34, 35. Col 3:16.

teacheth. Heb. maketh wise.

24 **Pleasant words**. Pr 12:6, 14, 18. 13:2. 15:4, 23, 26. 18:20, 21. 23:16. 25:11, 12. 27:9. Dt 32:2. SS 4:11. Ml 3:16, 17. Jn 20:19-21.

an honeycomb. Pr 24:13, 14. Ps 19:10. 119:103. Je 15:16. Lk 24:32.

soul. Heb. *nephesh*, Ge +34:3.

health. Pr 3:8mg. 4:22. 6:15. 12:18. 13:17. 29:1. 2 Ch 36:16mg. Je 8:15.

25 **a way**. Pr 12:26. 14:12. Ge 41:32. Is 28:15-19. Da 5:20. Jn 7:47-49. 9:40. 14:6. Ac 26:9. 1 C 10:12. 2 C 13:5. Re 3:11. 22:7.

seemeth right. Pr +30:12. Dt 11:16. Is 5:20. 44:20. Je 6:16. La +3:40. Mt 6:23. 7:22, 23. 24:4, 5. Lk 21:8. Jn 3:19. +5:43. 1 C 3:18. Ga 6:3, 7. Ep 4:18. 5:6. 2 Th 2:3, 11, 12. Re +3:17.

death. Ge +2:17. Is 5:1-7. 27:10, 11. 28:15-19. Ezk 15:2-5. +18:4. Ml 4:1. Mt 3:10. 25:41. Jn 15:6. 2 C 13:5. Ph 3:19. He 6:8. 12:17. Ja 1:15. Re 20:15.

26 **He**. Heb. The soul of him. Heb. *nephesh*, Ex +15:9.

laboreth for. Pr 9:12. 14:23. Ge 3:19. Ec 6:7. 1 Th 4:11, 12. 2 Th 3:8-12.

craveth it of him. Heb. boweth unto him.

27 **An ungodly man**. Heb. A man of Belial. 1 S +30:22mg. 2 S 20:1.

diggeth. Pr 2:4. Ps 7:14, 15. Is 5:18. Hab 2:13.

in. Ps 7:14. 52:2-4. 57:4. Ja 3:6-8.

28 **froward**. Pr 6:14, 19. 15:18. 18:8. 26:20-22. 29:22. 30:33. 1 T 6:3-5. Ja 3:14-16.

soweth. Heb. sendeth forth. Pr 6:14mg, 19. Ge 3:23. 8:7, 8, 12.

a whisperer. Pr 17:9. Ge 3:1, etc. 1 S 24:9. Ro +1:29.

29 **violent**. Pr 1:10-14. 2:12-15. 3:31. 1 S 19:11, 17. 22:7-9. 23:19-21. Ne 6:13. 2 P 3:17.

30 **shutteth**. Pr 6:12-14. 10:10. Is 6:10. Mt 13:15. Jn 3:20.

moving. ver. 27. Mi 7:3. Mt 14:7, 8. 27:23-26.

31 **hoary**. Pr 20:29. Le 19:32. Jb 32:6, 7. Ps 92:13, 14.
   if. Ge 47:7-10. 1 S 12:2-5. 1 Ch 29:10, etc. Ec 4:13. Lk 1:6. 2:29, etc., 37, 38. Phm 9.

32 **that is**. Ps 103:8. Ep 5:1. Ja +1:20.
   and he. ver. 19. Pr 25:28. 1 S 25:32, 33. Ro 12:19, 21. Ja 3:2. Re 2:7. 3:21.
   spirit. Heb. *ruach*, Ge +41:8.
   than he. Pr 25:28.

33 **the lot**. Jsh 7:14. +14:2. Mt 10:29, 30.
   whole disposing. Ep +1:11.

PROVERBS 17

1 **a dry morsel**. Pr 15:17. Ps 37:16. 1 T 6:6.
   an house. Pr 7:14.
   sacrifices. *or*, good cheer.
   with. Pr 21:9, 19.

2 **wise**. Pr 11:29. 14:35. Ge 24:4, etc. 30:27. Ec 4:13.
   that. Pr 10:5. 19:26. 29:15.
   have part. Ge 31:1.

3 **fining pot**. Pr 27:21. 1 P +1:7.
   but. Jb 23:10. Je +17:10. 1 C 3:13.

4 **wicked doer**. Pr 28:4. 1 S 22:7-11. 1 K 22:6, etc. Is 30:10. Je 5:30, 31. Mi 2:11. 2 T 4:3, 4. 1 J 4:5. Re 13:3-8.

5 **mocketh**. Pr 14:21, 31. Ps 69:9. 1 C 11:22. 1 J 3:17.
   glad at calamities. Pr 24:17, 18. Jb 31:29. Ps 35:15. 137:7. Je 17:16. 50:11. La 4:21, 22. Ezk 26:2, 3. 35:15. 36:5. Am 5:18. Ob 12. Mi 7:8. Ro 12:15, 20, 21.
   unpunished. Heb. held innocent. Pr +16:5mg.

6 **Children's**. Ge 48:11. 50:23. Jb 42:16, 17. Ps 127:3-5. 128:3-6.
   the crown. Pr 12:4. 16:31.
   and the glory. Ex 3:14, 15. 1 K 11:12. 15:4. Zc 10:7. Ml +4:6. Mt 3:9.

7 **Excellent speech**. Heb. A lip of excellency. Jg +7:22mg. Ep 4:29. Ph 1:27. Col 4:6.
   becometh not. Pr 26:7. Ps 50:16, 17. Mt 7:5.
   much. Pr 16:10-13. 29:12. 2 S 23:3. Jb 34:12. Ps 101:3-5.
   lying lips. Heb. a lip of lying. Pr 12:19.

8 **gift**. ver. 23. Pr 18:16. 19:6. 21:14. 29:4. Ex 23:8. Dt 16:19.
   precious stone. Heb. stone of grace. Pr 1:9. 3:4, 22, 34. 4:9.
   whithersoever. Ge 33:9-11. 43:11. 1 S 25:35. 2 S 16:1-4. Mi 7:3.
   prospereth. Dt +29:9.

9 **that covereth**. Pr 10:12. Ps 32:1. Ep 5:1, 2. 1 P 4:8.
   seeketh. *or*, procureth. ver. 19. Pr 21:6. 28:5. 29:26.

but. Pr 16:28.
repeateth. 1 T 5:13.

10 **A reproof**, etc. *or*, A reproof aweth more a wise man, than to strike a fool an hundred times. Pr 9:8, 9. 13:1. 15:5. 19:25. 27:22. 29:19. Ps 141:5. Ezk 36:26. Lk 22:61, 62. Re 3:19.
   than. 2 Ch 28:22. Je 5:3.

11 **An evil man**. ver. 13. Pr 19:19. 20:17. 21:7. 22:8, 16. 2 S 15:12. 16:5-9. 18:15, 16. 20:1, 22. 1 K 2:24, 25, 31, 46. Mt 21:41. 22:7. Lk 19:27.
   rebellion. Nu 17:10. Dt 21:18-23. 31:27. Or, "A rebel seeketh only evil." 1 S 15:23.
   messenger. Pr 16:14.

12 **a bear**. Pr 28:15. 2 S 17:8. 2 K 2:24. Ho 13:8.
   rather. Pr 27:3. 2 Ch 10:14-16. Mt 2:16.

13 **rewardeth evil**. Pr 20:22. 1 S 24:17. 25:21. 31:2, 3. 2 S 21:1, etc. Ps 35:12. 38:20. 55:12-15. 109:4-13. Je 18:20, 21. +37:18. Mt 5:39. 27:5, 25. John 10:32. Ro 12:17. 1 Th 5:15. 1 P 3:9.
   evil. 1 S 20:7. 25:17. 2 Ch 25:16. Est 7:7. Is 28:22. Da 9:24-27. 11:36. Lk 22:22.
   not depart. Pr 13:21. Ex +20:5. Nu +32:23. 2 S 12:10. 21:1, etc. Ps 32:10. Je 18:20-23. Am 7:9. Mt 27:5. Ga 6:7.
   his house. Mt 23:37, 38. +24:8. Lk 13:35.

14 **beginning**. ver. 19. Pr 26:21. 29:22. Jg 12:1-6. 2 S 2:14-17. 19:41-43. 20:1, etc. 2 Ch 10:14-16. 13:17. 25:17-24. 28:6.
   leave. Pr 13:10. 14:29. 16:32. 19:11. 20:3. 25:8. Jg 8:1-3. Ec 7:8, 9. Mt 5:39-41. Ac 6:1-5. 15:2, etc. 1 Th 4:11. 2 T 2:23, 24. He +12:14. Ja 3:14-18.

15 **that justifieth**. Pr 24:23, 24. Ge +9:5. Ex 23:7. 1 K 21:13. Is 5:23. 55:8, 9. Ezk 22:27-29. Am 5:7, 12. 6:12. Lk 23:18-25. Jn 18:40. Ro 4:5. Ja 5:6.
   condemneth the just. Lk +16:1. Jn +7:24, 51.
   abomination. Pr 6:16. 11:1. 15:8. 2 C 5:21.

16 **a price**. Pr 1:22, 23. 8:4, 5. 9:4-6. Is 55:1-3. Ac 13:46. 2 C 6:1.
   fool. Ps +10:4. Je 4:22.
   seeing. Pr 1:7, 25. 14:6. 18:15. 21:25, 26. Dt 5:29. Ps 81:11-13. Ho 4:11. Jn 3:20. Ac 28:26, 27.

17 **friend**. Pr +16:7. 18:24. 19:6. 27:9. 2 S 1:26.
   loveth. Pr 18:24. 19:7. Ru 1:16, 17. 1 S 18:3. 19:2. 20:17. 23:16. 2 S 1:26. 9:1, etc. Est 4:14. Jb 6:14. Jn 13:1. 15:13, 14. 1 C 13:4, 7, 8. He 2:11.
   a brother. Pr +18:19, 24. Ep 5:30. Ph 2:25.

18 **void**. Pr 7:7. 12:11. 18:2. 24:30. 28:16. Is 27:11. 44:19. Je 4:22. 5:21mg. +8:7. Mt 13:19. 2 C 4:4.
   understanding. Heb. heart. Pr +6:32mg. 10:13mg, 21mg. Je 5:21mg. Ho 7:11.
   striketh hands. Pr 6:1. 11:15mg. 22:26. Jb 17:3.

surety. Pr 6:1-5. 11:15. 20:16. 22:26, 27.
friend. Pr 3:28, 29. 6:1, 3, 29.

19 loveth. ver. 14. Pr 29:9, 22. Ps +109:17. 2 C 12:20. Ja 1:20. 3:14-16.
he that. Pr +16:5. 24:27. 1 S 25:36-38. 2 S 15:1. 1 K 1:5. Je 22:13-15. Mk 9:33, 34. Lk 22:24. 1 C 3:3, 4.

20 He that hath a froward heart. Heb. The froward of heart. Pr 3:32. 6:12-15. 8:13. Ps 18:26. La 3:27.
and he. Pr 10:10, 14, 31. 18:6, 7. Ec 10:12. Ja 3:6-8.

21 that. ver. 25. Pr 10:1. 15:20. 19:13. Ge 26:34, 35. 1 S 2:32-35. 8:3. 2 S 18:33. Ec 2:18, 19.
hath. Pr 23:15, 16. 2 C 2:3. Phm 19, 20. 3 J 4.

22 merry heart. Pr 12:25. 15:13, 15. 18:14. Ps 35:27. Ec 9:7-9. Ac 16:25. Ro 5:2-5.
like a medicine. Heb. to a medicine. Pr 4:22mg.
a broken. Ps 102:3-5. 2 C 2:7. 7:10.
spirit. Heb. *ruach*, Ge +41:8.
drieth. Jb 30:30. Ps 22:15. 32:3, 4.

23 taketh a gift. ver. 8. Pr 18:16. 28:21. 29:4. Ex 23:8. Dt 16:19. 1 S 8:3. 12:3. Is 1:23. 5:22, 23. 33:15, 16. Ezk 22:12. Mi 7:3. Mt 28:11-15. Mk 14:10, 11. Ac 8:18-20.
out of. Pr 21:14.

24 before. Pr 14:6. 15:14. Dt 30:11-14. Ec 2:14. 8:1. Jn 7:17.
understanding. Pr +8:9. 28:2, +5.
the eyes. Pr 12:11. 23:5. Ps 119:37. Ec 6:9. 1 J 2:16.
fool. Pr 16:3. Dt 29:29. Ps 37:5. Ec 8:17. 11:5. Lk +10:42. 13:23, 24. Jn 21:21, 22. Ac 17:21. 2 C 10:5. Ep 4:14. Col 2:18. 2 T 2:23.

25 foolish son. ver. 21. Pr 10:1. 15:20. 19:13. Ge 26:34, 35. 1 S 2:24, 25. 2 S 13:1, etc. 18:33. Ec 2:18, 19.

26 to punish. ver. 13, 15. Pr 18:5. Ge +18:25. 1 K 21:11, etc. Je +37:18. Mt 26:3, etc.
to strike. 1 S 24:5, 6. 2 S 3:23-25, 39. 16:7, 8. 19:7. Jb 34:18, 19. Ec 10:20. Mi 5:1. Jn 18:22, 23. 2 P 2:10.

27 spareth his words. Pr 15:28. 18:13. +21:23. Ps 39:1. Ec 9:17. Mt +7:6. Col 4:6. Ja 1:19.
an excellent spirit. *or*, a cool spirit. Heb. *ruach*, Ge +41:8. Pr 16:32. 25:25. Ec 9:17. Je 18:14. Ja 3:18.

28 Even a fool. Pr 10:19. 15:2. Jb 13:5. Ec 5:3. 10:3, 14.
understanding. Pr 1:5. 10:13. 14:6, 33.

PROVERBS 18

1 Through desire, etc. *or*, He that separateth himself seeketh, according to *his* desire, *and* intermeddleth in every business. Jb 23:12. Je 15:16. 1 P 2:2.
having separated. Ge 32:24. Ex 33:16. 1 S

9:27. Ps 55:7. Je 9:2. Zc 7:3. Mt 14:23. Mk +1:35. +6:31. Lk 5:16. 6:12. 9:10. Ro 1:1. 2 C 6:17. Ga 1:17. 1 Th 3:1. Ju 19.
seeketh. Pr 2:1-6. +14:15. +15:14. Is 34:16. Mt 13:11, 12, 44. Mk 4:11. Jn 5:39. Ac 17:11. Ep 5:15-17.
intermeddleth. Pr 8:8, 9. 14:10. 17:14. 20:3, 19. 24:21. 26:17. Ps 119:97-100, 104, 105. Is 26:8, 9. Je 15:17. Mk 1:35.
all wisdom. Pr 21:30. Is 8:20. Mk 12:24.

2 fool. Pr 1:7, 22. 15:14. 17:16. Jb +21:14. Ps 1:1, 2. 92:5, 6. Mt 8:34. 1 C 8:1.
but. Nu 24:15, 16. Ac 8:9, 19, 21. 1 C 14:12. Ph 1:15. 2 P 2:15-19.

3 wicked cometh. Pr 11:2. 22:10. 29:16. 1 S 20:30. Ne 4:4. Ps 69:9, 20. 123:3, 4. Mt 27:39-44. 1 P 4:4, 14.

4 words. Pr 10:11. 13:14. 16:22. 20:5. Mt 12:34. Jn 4:14. 7:38, 39. Col 3:16. 4:6.
the wellspring. Pr 5:18. 10:11. 13:14. 14:27. Ps 78:2. Mt 7:29. Lk 4:32. 24:32. Col 3:16.

5 not. Ro +2:11. Ja +2:1.
to overthrow. 1 K 21:9-14. Is 5:23. 59:14. Mi 7:3.

6 fool's. Pr 12:16. 13:10. 14:16. 16:27, 28. 17:14. 20:3. 27:3. Jg 8:6, 15, 16. 2 K 2:23, 24. Ps 52:1-5. Ec 10:12.
his. Pr 14:3. 19:19. 22:24, 25. 25:24. 29:9.

7 his destruction. Pr 10:8, 14. 12:13. 13:3. Ec 10:11-14.
his lips. Pr 6:2. Jg 11:35. 1 S 14:24, etc. Mk 6:23-28. Ac 23:14, etc.
soul. Heb. *nephesh*, Ge +12:13.

8 words. Pr 12:18. Le +19:16. Ps 52:2. 64:3, 4.
talebearer. *or*, whisperer. Ro +1:29.
as wounds. *or*, like as when men are wounded. Pr 12:18. 26:22. Col 3:12-14.
innermost parts. Heb. chambers. Pr 7:27. 20:27, 30.
belly. Jb +15:35.

9 that is slothful. Pr 6:6. 10:4, 26. 12:24, 27. 13:4. 15:19. 19:15, 24. 20:4. 21:25. 22:13. 23:20, 21. 24:30-34. 26:13-16. 31:27. Je 48:10mg. Mt 25:25, 26. Ro 12:11. 1 T 5:13. T 1:12. He 6:12.
is brother. Jb 30:29.
great waster. Pr 28:24. Lk 15:13, 14, 30. +16:1. 19:20.

10 name. Ge 17:1. Dt +28:58. Ps +9:10. Is 9:6. 57:15. Je 23:6. Mt 1:23. 2 C 1:3. 1 P 5:10. Re 1:8.
a strong tower. Dt 33:27-29. 2 S 22:3, 51. Ps 18:2. 27:1. 61:3, 4. 91:2. 144:2. Is 26:4.
the righteous. Ge 32:11, 28, 29. 1 S 30:6. 2 S 22:45-47. Ps 56:3, 4. Mi 7:18.
safe. Heb. set aloft. Ps 91:14. Hab 3:19.

11 The rich. Pr 10:15. 11:4. Dt 32:31. Jb 31:24, 25. Ps 49:6-9. 52:5-7. 62:10, 11. Ec 7:12. Mt 7:24-27. Lk 12:19-21.

12 **destruction**. Pr +16:5. Ezk 16:49, 50. Da 5:23, 24. Ac 12:21-23.
and. Pr 15:33. Jb 42:6, etc. Ps 113:7, 8. Is 6:5, etc. Da 9:20, 23. Mt +5:3. 1 C 4:7.

13 **that**. Dt 13:14. 2 S 16:4. 19:24-30. Est 3:10, etc. 8:5, etc. Jb 29:16. Da 6:9, 14. Jn 7:24.
answereth a matter. Heb. returneth a word. Pr 17:13. 24:26mg. 26:16. Jsh 22:16, 21. 1 S 17:30mg.
before. ver. 17. Pr 14:8. 15:22, +28. Le +19:15. Dt 19:15. Jb 32:4, 10, 11. Jn +7:51. 1 T +5:19.
folly. Pr 5:2, 3. 12:23. 13:16. 14:1.
shame. Jb 20:3. Ps 4:2. 35:26.

14 **spirit**. Heb. *ruach*, Ge +41:8; Ge +26:35. Jb 1:20, 21. 2:7-10. Ps 147:3. Ro 5:3-5. 8:35-37. 2 C 1:12. 12:9, 10. Ja 1:2. 1 P 1:6.
a wounded. Pr 17:22. Ge 4:13. 1 S 28:6, 15. 2 S 17:23. 1 K 16:18. Jb 6:4. 7:14, 15. 10:15-17. Ps 30:9, 10. 32:3, 4. 38:2-4. 42:10, 11. 55:3, 5. 77:2, 3. 88:14-16. 109:22. Mt 27:3-5. Mk 14:33, 34. Ro 8:35-37. 2 C 2:7. 1 Th 5:14. He 12:15.
spirit. Heb. *ruach*, Ge +41:8; Ge +26:35.

15 **getteth knowledge**. Pr 1:5. 4:5, 7. 9:9. 10:14. +15:14. 23:23. 1 K 3:9. Ps 119:97-104. Lk 8:8-10. 10:39. Ph 1:9. Col 1:10. 2 T 3:15-17. Ja 1:5. 2 P 3:18.

16 **gift**. Pr 17:8. Ge 24:30-33. Jg +3:15.
bringeth. Pr 22:29. 1 S 16:20. Jb 11:19. Ps 112:6. Mt 13:57. 23:12.

17 **He that is first**. ver. +13. Pr 12:15. 2 S 16:1-3. 19:24-27. Ac 17:11. 24:5, 6, 12, 13. Ep 4:14. 1 Th 5:21. 2 T 3:14. 1 P 3:15. 2 P 1:16.
but. Pr 14:15. Jn +7:24, 51. Ac +17:11. Ro 14:12. 1 Th 5:21.

18 **The lot**. Jsh +14:2.

19 **brother**. ver. +24. Pr 6:19. 17:17. Ge 4:5-8. 27:41-45. 32:6-11. 37:3-5, 11, 18-27. Nu 20:18. 2 S 13:22, 28. 19:43. 1 K 2:23-25. 12:16. 2 Ch 13:17. Ps 133:1. Lk 17:3-5. Ac 15:39.
than. Pr 10:15. 16:32.
bars. Ex 26:26-29. 35:11. Jg +16:3.
castle. 1 K 16:18. 2 K 15:25. 1 Ch +27:25.

20 **satisfied**. Pr 12:13, 14. 13:2. 22:18, 21. 25:11, 12.

21 **Death**. ver. 4-7. Pr 10:20, 21, 31. 11:30. +21:23. Ps 51:15. 141:3. Ac 16:30, 31. Ro 10:9, 10, 14, 15. 2 C 2:16. 11:15. Ep 4:29. Col 4:6. T 1:10, 11. 2 P 2:18.
and. Ec 10:12-14. Is 57:19.

22 **findeth a wife**. Pr 5:15, etc. 12:4. 19:14. 30:18, 19. 31:10, etc. Ge 2:18. +21:21. 24:57, 67. 28:8, 9. 29:20, 21, 28. Ex 2:21. Nu 12:1. 36:6. Dt 21:10-14. Jg 14:2, 3. 1 S 18:20-29. 2 S 3:12-16. Ec 9:9. SS 4:9. Ho 12:12. Mt 19:5. 1 C 7:2, 39. 14:35. 2 C 6:14. He 13:4.
and. Pr 3:4. 8:35.

23 **poor**. Ru 2:7. 1 S 2:36. 2 K 4:1, 2. Is 66:2. Mt +5:3. Ja 1:9-11.
rich. Ge 42:7, 30. Ex 5:2. 1 S 25:10-12, +17. Ja 2:3.

24 **that hath friends**. ver. 17. Pr 3:28, 29. 6:1. 12:26. 17:17. 22:24. 25:17. 27:9. 1 S 19:4, 5. 30:26, etc. 2 S 9:1, etc. 16:17. 17:27-29. 19:30-39. 21:7. 1 Ch 12:38-40. 2 Ch 13:7. Ps 38:11. Je 2:37. Mt 26:49, 50.
there. Pr 27:10. 2 S 1:26. Jn 14:3, 18. 15:14, 15. Ro +12:5. He 2:11, 14-18. 1 J 3:16.
brother. ver. +19. Pr 17:17. 27:10.

PROVERBS 19

1 **Better**. ver. 22. Pr 12:26. 15:16. 16:8. 28:6. Ps 37:26. Mt 16:26. 1 T 6:17-19. He 11:37, 38. Ja 2:5, 6.
perverse. 1 S +25:17, 25. Is 59:3. Mt 12:31-34.

2 **that the**. Pr 10:21. Ec 12:9. Is 27:11. Ho 4:6. Jn 16:3. Ro 10:2. Ph 1:9.
soul. Heb. *nephesh*, Ge +34:3.
and. Pr 1:16. 14:29. 21:5. 25:8. 28:22. Jb 31:5. Ec 7:9. Is 28:16.

3 **foolishness**. Ge 3:6-12. 4:5-14. Nu 16:19-41. 17:12, 13. 1 S 13:13. 15:23. 22:13, etc. 1 K 20:42, 43. 2 K 3:9, 10. +6:33. 2 Ch 16:9, 10. Jb 2:10. Ac 13:45, 46.
fretteth. Ru +1:13. Ps 37:1, 7. +77:3. Is 8:21, 22. 29:24. Ph +4:11. Ju +16. Re 16:9-11.
against. Is 45:9. Ezk +18:25. Ro +9:14, 20-24.

4 **Wealth maketh**. ver. 6, 7. Pr 14:20. Lk 15:13-15. 1 C 3:21-23.
the poor. Pr 10:15. Jb 6:15-23. 19:13-17. Ja 2:5.

5 **false**. ver. 9. Pr +6:19. Ps 120:3, 4. Da 6:24.
unpunished. Heb. held innocent. Pr +16:5mg. Dt 5:11. 1 K 2:9.
speaketh lies. ver. +9. Re 21:8.

6 **will**. ver. 12. Pr 16:15. 29:26. Ge 42:6. 2 S 19:19, etc. Jb 29:24, 25.
favor. Ex +32:11mg.
and. Pr 17:8. Ro 6:23.
him that giveth gifts. Heb. a man of gifts. Ge 34:12. Jg +3:15.

7 **the brethren**. ver. 4. Pr 14:20. 27:10. Ps 38:11. 88:8, 18. 113:7, 8. Ec 9:15, 16. Ja 2:6.
go far. Ps 38:11.
he pursueth. Pr 21:13. Lk 18:38-40.
yet. Pr 18:23. Ja 2:15, 16. 1 J 3:17, 18.

8 **that getteth**. Pr 1:5, 6. 3:13-18, 35. 4:6-9. 8:35. 9:12. 10:17. 11:29. 12:8. 13:15. 15:24. 16:20, 22. 21:20. 24:3-5, 13, 14. 28:26. Ps 107:43. Ec 7:12. 8:1. 10:10. Ho 14:9. Da 2:21. 12:3, 10.
wisdom. Heb. an heart. Pr 15:32mg. 17:16. Ezk 36:26.

loveth. Pr 8:35, 36. Jn 12:25. 1 P 3:10.
soul. Heb. *nephesh*, Ge +27:31.
he that keepeth. Pr 2:1-9. 3:18, 21. 4:4, 6, 21. 16:20. 22:18. Ps 19:11. Jn 14:21.

9 false witness. ver. 5.
and. Is 9:15-17. Je 23:25-32. 27:15-17. 28:15-17. 29:31, 32. Ezk 13:22. 2 Th 2:8-10. 1 T 4:1, 2. 2 P 2:1-3. Re 19:20. +21:8. 22:15.
lies. Pr 10:18. Ge +6:6. Ps 5:6. 59:12, 13. 62:3, 4. 63:11. Is 28:17. Ep +4:25.

10 Delight. Pr 30:21, 22. 1 S 25:36. Est 3:15. Ps 32:11. 33:1. Is 5:11, 12. 22:12-14. Ho 7:3-5. 9:1. Am 6:3-6. Lk 16:19, 23. Ja 4:9.
much. 2 S 3:24, 25, 39. Ec 10:5-7. Is 3:5.

11 discretion. Pr 2:11, 12. 3:21-23. 8:12. 11:22. 12:16. Jn 6:12. *or*, prudence. Pr 3:4mg. 12:8 (wisdom). 13:15 (understanding). 16:22. 23:9. 1 S +25:3 (**S#7922h**).
deferreth. Pr 12:16. 14:29. 15:18. 16:32. Ec 8:11. Mt +5:5. Ac +7:59. 1 C 13:4, 5, 7. Ga +6:1. Ep 4:1, 2, +32. Col 3:12, 13. He +12:14. Ja +1:4, 19. 1 P 2:18-23. 3:8, 9.
and. Pr 16:32. 20:3. 25:21, 22. Ge 45:4-15. 50:15-21. 1 S 24:7-19. Mt 5:44, 45. 18:21, 22. Ro 12:18-21. Ep 4:32. 5:1.
pass over. Le 19:18. Ps 38:12-14. Col 3:13. 1 P 3:9.

12 king's. Pr 16:14, 15. Est 7:8. Ec 8:4. Da 2:12, 13. 3:19-23. 5:19. Mt 2:16-18. Lk 12:4, 5.
roaring. Is +5:29.
as dew. Dt +33:13.

13 foolish. Pr 10:1. 15:20. 17:21, 25. Dt 21:18, etc. 2 S ch. 13-18. Ec 2:18, 19.
the contentions. Pr 21:9, 19. 25:24. 27:15, 16. Jb 14:19. 1 C 7:16. 14:34. Ep 5:22-24. Col 3:18. T 2:5. 1 P 3:1.

14 the inheritance. Pr 13:22. Dt 21:16. Jsh 11:23. 2 C 12:14.
prudent wife. Pr 3:6. 18:22. 31:10, etc. Ge 24:7. 28:1-4. Ja 1:17.

15 Slothfulness casteth. ver. 24. Pr 6:6, 9-11. 20:13. 23:21. 24:33, 34. Is 56:10. Ro 13:11, 12. Ep 5:14.
an idle. Pr 10:4, 5. 20:13. 23:21. 2 Th 3:10.
soul. Heb. *nephesh*, Ge +12:5.

16 keepeth the commandment. Pr 3:1. 29:18. Ps 103:17, 18. Ec 8:5. 12:13. Je 7:23. Lk 10:28. +11:28. Jn +13:17. 14:15, 21-23. 15:10-14. 1 C 7:19. 1 J 2:3, 4. 3:22. 5:3. Re 22:14.
keepeth his. Pr 16:17. 21:23. *22:5. Ps 19:11. 119:165. Ezk 33:5. Mt 16:26.*
soul. Heb. *nephesh*, Ge +27:31.
he that despiseth. Pr 13:13. 15:32. Le 26:21. Je 10:23. Hg 1:5, 7. Ga 6:7, 8. Ja 1:14, 15.

17 hath pity. Pr 14:21. 28:8, 27. Dt 15:7-11. 2 S 12:6. Ec 11:1. Mt 25:34-40. Lk 10:33-37. 14:12-14. 1 J 3:17.

lendeth. Pr 11:24, 25. 28:27. Dt 15:7-14. Is 58:7-11. Mt 10:41, 42. 25:40. 2 C 9:6-8. Ph 4:17. He 6:10.
that which he hath given. *or*, his deed. Pr 12:14. Jg 9:16. 2 Ch 32:25. 2 C 9:6-9.
pay him. Pr 6:31. 13:21. 20:22. Mt 10:42. Mk 10:30. Lk 6:38. Ro 11:35. 1 C 13:3.

18 Chasten. Pr +13:24. 22:6, 15. 23:13, 14. 29:15, 17. Ex +13:8. Ps 39:10. 89:30-32. Is 66:13. La 3:33. He 12:7-10. 1 P 5:6.
while. Pr 22:6. 29:1. 1 K 1:6. 2:24. Ps 103:13. Ec 1:15. 4:13. 8:11. 11:3. Col 3:21. 1 T 5:14. He 3:12, 13. 12:15. Re 22:11.
soul. Heb. *nephesh*, Ge +34:3.
spare. lit. lift not up thy soul. Pr 6:35 (regard), 9:12 (bear). 18:14 (bear). Ge 18:24, 26. Ps 25:1. 82:2 (accept). 86:4. Je 7:16. La 3:41.
for his crying. Ex 2:23, 24. Jg 10:16. *or*, to his destruction, *or*, to cause him to die. Pr 23:13. Dt 21:18-21.

19 man. 1 S 19:1-11. 20:30-33. 22:7, etc. 24:17, etc. 26:21, etc. 2 S 16:5, 6. Ja +1:20.
great wrath. Pr 6:34. Ge 4:5-8, 13.
deliver. Pr 10:2. 11:6. 12:6. Ps 138:8. Mt 11:29. Ro 7:22-25. 2 C 12:9.
do it again. Heb. add. ver. 4. Pr 1:5. 3:2. 9:9, 11. 10:22.

20 Hear. Pr 1:8. 4:1, 10. 5:7. 7:24. Mk 4:24. Lk 8:18. +11:28.
counsel. ver. 21. Pr 1:25, 30. 8:14. 12:15. 1 K 12:13. 2 Ch 25:16. Is 1:3.
receive instruction. Pr 1:8. 2:1-9. 4:7, 13. 8:17, +33, 34, 35. 1 S +25:17. 2 Ch 1:11, 12. Ho 6:3.
be wise. Nu 23:10. Dt 8:16. 32:29. Ps 90:12, 14.
thy latter end. Ps 37:37. Lk 16:19-23.

21 many. Pr 12:2. Ge 37:19, 20. Est 9:25. Ps 21:11. 33:10, 11. 83:4. Ec 7:29. Is 7:6, 7. Da 11:24, 25. Mt 26:4, 5. 27:63, 64.
nevertheless. Pr 16:1, 9. Ge 45:4-8. 50:20. Ps 2:6. 21:11. 94:11. Is +14:27. Ac 4:27, 28. He 6:17, 18. 1 P 2:8. Ju 4.

22 desire. 1 S 30:24. 1 Ch 29:2, 3, 17. 2 Ch 6:8. Ps +149:9. Mk 12:41-44. 14:6-8. Lk 21:4. 2 C 8:2, 3, 12.
and. ver. 1. Jb 6:15. 17:5. Ps 62:9. Ac 5:1-5. T 1:2.
poor. 2 C 8:9.
liar. ver. +9.

23 fear of the Lord. Pr +3:7. 10:27. Ps 33:18, 19. 145:18-20. Ml 3:16, 17. He 12:28. Re 15:4.
to life. Pr 3:2, 18, 22. 10:16.
shall abide. Ps 90:14. 91:16. Is 58:10, 11. Mt +5:6. Ph 4:11, 12. 1 T 4:8. 6:6-9. He +13:5, 6.
satisfied. Pr 27:7. Ge 25:8. 35:29.
he shall. Pr 12:21. Ro 8:28. 2 T 4:18.

24 slothful man. ver. 15. Pr 6:9, 10. 12:27. 15:19. 24:30-34. 26:13-16. Ps 74:11. Ec 4:5. Am 6:1. Ro 2:7. He 12:1, 2.

25 Smite. Pr 21:11. 23:13, 14. Ge 14:5, 7, 15. Dt 13:11. 21:21. Mt +5:39. Ac 13:9-11.
scorner. ver. 29. Pr 1:22. 3:34.
simple. Pr 1:4, 22, 32. 7:7. 8:5. 9:4.
beware. Heb. be cunning. or, act prudently. Pr 15:5. Ex 18:10, 11. Dt 19:20. 1 S 23:22. Ps 83:3. Re 11:13.
reprove. Pr 3:12. 9:8-10. 15:5. 17:10. 30:6. 1 S +25:17. Ps 141:5. Mt +7:6. Re 3:19.
hath understanding. Pr 1:5. +8:9. 10:13. +14:6, 33. +15:14.
knowledge. ver. 2, 27. Pr 1:4, 7, 22, 29.

26 wasteth. Ex +20:12. Lk 15:12-16, 30. Ro 1:30, 31.
a son. Pr 10:5. 17:2. 28:7.

27 Cease. Pr 14:7. Dt 4:2. 13:1-4. 1 K 22:22-28. 2 Ch 13:7. Ps +119:63. Is 30:10. Je 5:31. Mt 7:15. +15:14. 16:6, 12. Mk 4:24. 7:6-14. Jn 10:5. Ro 16:17. 2 C 10:5. 11:13-15. Ga 1:6, 7. 3:1-4. +5:4, 7, 8. Ep 4:14. 1 T 4:7. 6:3-5. 2 T 2:16, 17. 4:3. He 13:9. 2 P 2:1, 2. 1 J 4:1. 2 J 10. Re 2:2.
to err. Mk 12:24.

28 An ungodly witness. Heb. A witness of Belial. Pr +16:27mg. 1 S +30:22. Ac 6:11-13.
scorneth. Pr 14:9. Ps 10:5, 11. Is 28:14-18, 22. Lk 18:2-4.
the mouth. Pr 15:14. Jb 15:16. 20:12, 13. 34:7. Ho 4:8.

29 Judgments. Ex +7:4. Is 33:14. Je 31:18. Ezk 22:14. Ac 13:40, 41. He 10:31.
scorners. ver. 25. Pr 3:34. 9:12. Ps 1:1. Is 28:22. 29:20. 2 P 3:3-7.
and. Pr 7:22. 10:13. 17:10. 26:3. He 12:6.

PROVERBS 20

1 Wine. Pr 4:17. 9:2, 5. 21:17. Is 5:11, 13, 22. Ho 4:6-11. Hab 2:15.
a mocker. Pr 23:29-35. 31:4. Ge 9:21-23. 19:31-36. 1 S 25:36-38. 2 S 11:13. 13:28. 1 K 20:16-21. Is 28:7. Ho 4:11. 7:5. Hab 2:15, 16. 1 C 6:10. Ga 5:21. Ep 5:18.
strong drink. Pr 31:4, 6. Le 10:9.
raging. or, noisy. Pr 1:21. 7:11. 9:13. 1 K 1:41.
deceived. Pr 23:21, 29, 30, 34, 35. Ge 9:20, 21. Is 28:7, 8. 56:12. Je 25:27. Da 5:1, 4. Ho 4:11. 1 C 11:21. or, going astray. Ps 119:21, 118. Ezk 45:20.
not wise. 2 S 13:28. 1 K 16:9. Is 28:7. Lk 21:34. Ep 5:18.

2 fear. Pr 16:14, 15. Ec 10:4. Am +1:2.
sinneth. Pr 8:36. 1 K 2:23. Est 7:7. Ps 2:12.
soul. Heb. nephesh, Ge +27:31.

3 honor. Pr 3:16, 35. 8:18. 11:16.
to cease. Pr 14:29. 16:32. 17:14. 19:11. 25:8-

10. Ge 13:8. Ro 12:18, 21. Ep 1:6-8. 4:32. 5:1. Col 3:12-15.
but every fool. Pr 14:17. 18:6. 21:24. 2 K 14:9, 10. Ja 3:14-18. 4:1.
meddling. Pr 17:14. 18:1. 1 P 4:15.

4 sluggard. Pr 10:4, 19:15, 24. 26:13-16. Mt 25:26-30. Ro 13:11.
cold. or, winter. S#2779h. Ge 8:22. Jb 29:4 (youth). Ps 74:17. Je 36:22. Am 3:15. Zc 14:8.
therefore. Pr 6:10, 11. 19:15. 24:34. Mt 25:3-10, 24-28. 2 P 1:5-11.

5 Counsel. Pr 18:4. Ps 64:5, 6. Je 17:9. 1 C 2:11.
man of understanding. Pr +8:9. 14:6. +19:25. Ps 119:98.

6 proclaim. Pr 25:14. 27:2. 2 K 10:16, 31. Je 2:23, 35. Mt 6:2, 5, 16. Lk 16:15. 18:8, 11, 28. 22:33. Ro 2:17-23. 2 C 12:11.
goodness. or, bounty. ver. 28 (mercy). Pr 3:3. 11:17. 14:22.
but. Ps 12:1. Ec 7:28. Je 5:1. Mi 7:2. Lk 18:8. Jn 1:47.
faithful. Pr 13:17. 14:5. Dt 32:20. Ps 12:1. Is 26:2. Lk 18:8. Ph +2:12.

7 just. Pr 14:2. 19:1. Ge 17:1, 2. Ps 15:2. 26:1, 11. Is 33:15. Lk 1:6. 2 C 1:12. T 2:11, 12. 3 J 3, 4.
his children. Pr 13:22. Ge +18:19. Dt 4:40. 5:29. +29:11. Ps 147:13. Ac 2:39. 2 T 1:5.

8 A king. ver. 26. 16:12. 29:14. 1 S 23:3, 4. 2 S 8:15. 23:4. 1 K 10:9. Ps 72:4. 82:1. 89:14. 92:9. 99:4. 101:3-8. Is 32:1.
his eyes. Ps 5:5. Re 1:14.

9 Who. 1 K 8:46. 2 Ch 6:36. Jb 9:2. 14:4. 15:14-16. 25:4. Ps 14:3. 51:5, 10. 130:3. 143:2. Ec 7:20. Is 6:5. 53:6. 64:6. Mt 11:28. Lk +19:10. Jn 3:6. Ro 3:8-12. 7:18. 1 C 4:4. Ga 3:22. Ep 2:2, 3. 1 T 1:15. Ja 3:2, 8. 1 J 1:8-10.
can say. 1 C 12:3.
clean. Jb 8:6. Ps 24:4. 51:2, 7.

10 Divers weights, and divers measures. Heb. A stone and a stone, an ephah and an ephah. Dt 25:13.
both. ver. 23. Pr 11:1. 16:11. Le 19:35, 36. Dt 25:13-16. 32:4. Ps 5:6. 25:21. Am 8:4-7. Mi 6:10, 11.
abomination. Dt 7:25, 26. Re 21:8.

11 a child. Pr 21:8. 22:15. 1 S 2:26. 3:19, 20. Ps 51:5. 58:3. Mt 7:16. Lk 1:15, 66. 2:46, 47, 50-52. 6:43, 44. 2 T 3:14, 15.

12 hearing ear. Ex 4:11. Ps 94:9. 119:18. Mt 13:13-16. Mk +4:24. 8:25. Lk +8:18. Ac 26:18. Ep 1:17, 18.
seeing eye. Ge +3:7. Lk +24:31.
the Lord. Pr 2:6. Ex 4:11. Jn 16:14, 15. 1 C 4:7. 2 T 2:25.

13 Love not sleep. Pr 6:9-11. 10:4, 5. 12:11. 13:4. 19:15. 24:30-34. 1 K 19:5. Ps 127:2. Ro 12:11. 1 C 9:24, 25. 1 Th 5:6. 2 Th 3:10.
open. Jon 1:6. Ro 13:11. 1 C 15:34. Ep 5:14.

14 It is naught. ver. 14, 22, 30. Pr 1:16, 33. Le 19:18. 25:14. Ec 1:10. Is 5:20. Ho 12:7, 8. Mt 5:37. Ac 24:16. 1 Th 4:6.
boasteth. Ja 4:16.

15 There is gold. Mt 19:22. 1 T 6:9, 10.
but. Pr 3:15. 8:11. 10:20, 21. 15:7, 23. 16:16, 21, 24. 25:12. 1 K 3:9. Jb 28:12-19. Ec 12:9-11. Mt 13:45, 46. Ro 10:14, 15. Ep 4:29.

16 Take his. Pr 11:15. 22:26, 27. 27:13. Ex 22:26, 27.
a strange. Pr 2:16. 5:3. 7:5, 10. 23:27.

17 deceit. Heb. lying, *or* falsehood. Pr 4:17.
is sweet. Pr 9:17, 18. Ge 3:6, 7. 2 K 5:20, 26, 27. Jb 20:12-20. Ec 11:9. He 11:25.
afterwards. He 12:11.
his. La 3:15, 16.

18 purpose. Pr 15:22. 24:5, 6. 1 K 22:6. Is 9:6.
good advice. Pr 13:10. 1 K +12:7.
make war. Pr 25:8. Jg 1:1, 2. 9:29. 20:7, 18, 23, 26-28. 2 S 2:26, 27. 2 Ch 25:17-23. Ps 144:1. Lk 14:31. +22:36.

19 that goeth. Le +19:16.
meddle. Pr 24:21.
flattereth. *or*, enticeth. Pr 16:29. Ps +12:3.

20 curseth. Pr 30:11, 17. Ex +20:12. 21:15, 17-21. Le 20:9. Dt 27:16. Mt 15:4. Mk 7:10-13.
his. Pr 13:9. 24:20. Jb 18:5, 6, 18. Mt 22:13. 25:8. Ju 13.
lamp. *or*, candle. ver. 27mg. Ps +18:28mg.
put out. Pr 13:9. 24:20.
obscure. **S#380h**. Pr 7:2 (apple), 9 (black). Dt 32:10. Ps 17:8. Ju 13.
darkness. Pr 2:13. Ge 1:2, 4, 5, 18. Ex +10:22. Je 4:28. +8:15. La 3:2. Am 5:18, 20. Mi 7:8. Re 8:12. 9:2.

21 gotten. Pr 23:4. 28:20, 22. 2 S 15:10. 1 T 6:9.
but. Pr 13:22. 28:8. 2 S 18:9-17. 1 K 21:1-15. Jb 27:16, 17. Je 17:11. Hab 2:6. Zc 5:4. Ml 2:2.

22 I will recompense. Pr 17:13. 24:29. Ge 27:41. Dt 32:35. Ro 12:17-19, 21. 1 Th 5:15. He 10:30. 1 P 3:9.
wait. 2 S 16:12. Ps +25:3. Mt 5:38, 39. 1 P 2:23. 4:19. Re 6:10.

23 weights. ver. +10. Ezk 45:10.
a false balance. Heb. balances of deceit. Ho 12:7. Am 8:5. Mi 6:10, 11.

24 Man's. Ps 37:23. 119:32. Is 30:21. Je 10:23. Da 5:23. Ac 17:28.
how. Pr 14:8. 16:9. Ps 25:4, 12. 37:23. 73:24. Is 10:6, 7. Ro 1:10. Ph 2:13.

25 a snare. Pr 18:7. Le 5:15. 22:10-15. 27:30. Jsh 6:18. Ml 3:8-10.
after. Le 27:9, 10, 31. Nu +30:2. Mt 5:33.

26 wise. ver. 8. Pr 17:15. Ge +9:5. 2 S 4:9-12. 1 K 14:14. Ps 1:4. 101:5-8. Ml 3:2.
bringeth. 2 S 12:31. Is 28:27, 28.

27 spirit. Heb. *neshamah*, breath, Ge +2:7. Jb 32:8. Ro 1:19-21, 32. 2:14, 15. 1 C 2:11. 2 C 4:2-6. 1 J 3:19-21.

candle. *or*, lamp. ver. +20mg. Ps 119:105mg.
searching. ver. 30. Ac 24:16. He 4:12, 13. 1 J 3:20.
belly. Jb +15:35.

28 Mercy. Pr 16:6. Ps +61:7. 85:10. 89:14. 101:1.
his. Pr 16:12. 29:14. Ps 21:7. 26:1. Is 16:5. Mi 7:18.

29 glory. Is 40:29. Je 9:23, 24. 1 J 2:14.
the beauty. Pr +16:31. Le 19:32.

30 cleanseth away evil. Heb. is a purging medicine against evil. Pr 4:22mg. Ps 119:9, 11. Is 27:9.
stripes. Pr 19:25. 22:15. Ps 103:14. 119:75. Is 27:9. Je 10:24. He 12:10, 11.

PROVERBS 21

1 The king's. Pr 16:1, 9. 20:24. 28:2. Ge 20:6. Ezr 1:1. 7:27, 28. Ne 1:11. 2:4. Ps 76:10. 105:14, 25. 106:46. Je 52:3. Da 4:35. Ac 7:10. Re 17:17.
rivers. **S#6388h**. Pr 5:16. Jb 29:6. Ps 1:3. 46:4 (streams). 65:9. 119:136. Is 30:25. 32:2. La 3:48.
of water. Ps 1:3. 74:15. 93:4. 114:3, 5. Is 43:19. 44:27. Je 17:8. Re 16:4, 12.
turneth. Dt +11:10. Is 37:25. Ezk 32:2.
whithersoever. Pr 16:9, 33. Ezr 6:22. Ne 2:4. Est 4:11. 5:3. Je 10:23. Ep +1:11.

2 right. Pr +16:2, 25. Mt 19:20. Lk 18:11, 12. Ga 6:3. Ja 1:22.
the Lord. Pr 24:12. 1 S 16:7. Ps 139:23, 24. Je 17:9, 10. Lk 16:15. Jn +2:24, 25. Re 2:23.

3 do justice. Pr 15:8. 24:23. Le 19:15, 36. Dt 6:18. 16:20. 1 S 12:1-4. 15:22. Ps 50:8. 51:6. Is 1:11-17. 56:1. Je 7:21-23. Ho 6:6. Mi 6:6-8. Zc 7:9, 10. Mt 23:23. Mk 12:32-34. Lk 20:25. Jn +1:47. +8:50. Ac 10:35. Ro 12:1. 13:7, 8. 2 C +7:1. Ep 6:14. 1 Th 2:10. +4:6. 1 T 6:11. T 2:11, 12.

4 An high look. Heb. Haughtiness of eyes. Pr +6:17. 8:13. Je 48:29.
and the. ver. 27. Pr 15:8. Ro 14:23.
proud. Pr 28:25. Ge 34:21 (large). Ex 3:8.
plowing of the wicked. *or*, light of the wicked. Pr 20:27. Jb 4:8. Mt 6:23. Ro 2:4. 1 C 2:11.

5 thoughts. Pr 10:4. 13:4. 27:23-27. Ep 4:28. 1 Th 4:11, 12. He 6:11, 12. 12:1.
of every. Pr 14:29. 20:21. 28:22.

6 getting. Pr 10:2. 13:11. 20:14, 21. 22:8. 30:8. Je 17:11. 1 T 6:9, 10. T 1:11. 2 P 2:3.
seek. Pr 8:36. Ezk 18:31. Ro 6:23.

7 robbery. Pr 1:18, 19. 10:6. 22:22, 23. Ps 7:16. 9:16. Is 1:23, 24. Je 7:9-11, 15. Ezk 22:13, 14. Mi 3:9-12.
destroy them. Nu +32:23. Is 30:12, 13. Heb. saw them, *or*, dwell with them. Je 30:23mg. Zc 5:3, 4.
because. ver. 21. Ezk 18:18. Ep 5:6.

8 way. Ge 6:5, 6. Jb 15:14-16. Ps 14:2, 3. Ec 7:29. 9:3. 1 C 3:3. Ep 2:2, 3. T 3:3.
but. Pr 15:26. 30:12. Da 12:10. Mt +5:8. 12:33. Ac 15:9. T 1:15. 2:14. 3:5. 1 P 1:22, 23. 1 J 2:29. 3:3.

9 better. ver. 19. Pr 12:4. 19:13. 25:24. 27:15, 16.
brawling woman. Heb. woman of contentions. Pr 25:24.
in a wide house. Heb. in a house of society. Pr 15:17. 17:1. 25:24. Is +47:12. 1 P 3:3, 4.

10 soul. Heb. *nephesh*, Ge +34:3.
desireth. Pr 3:29. 12:12. Ps 36:4. 52:2, 3. Ec 8:11. Mk 7:21, 22. 1 C 10:6. Ja 4:1-5. 1 J 2:16.
findeth no favor. Heb. is not favored. ver. 13. 1 S 25:8-11. Ps 112:5, 9. Is 32:6-8. Mi 3:2, 3. Ja 2:13. 5:4-6.

11 the scorner. Pr +19:25, 29. Nu 16:34. Dt 13:11. 21:21. Ps 64:7-9. Ac 5:5, 11-14. 1 C 10:6-11. He 2:1-3. 10:28, 29. Re 11:13.
punished. Ex 21:22. Ec 8:11. Is 26:9.
simple. Pr +1:4.
when the wise. Pr 1:5. 8:33. 9:9. 15:14. 18:1, 15. 19:20. Ps 94:12. 119:71.
instructed. Ne 8:13mg.

12 wisely. Jb 5:3. 8:15. 18:14-21. 21:28-30. 27:13-23. Ps 37:35, 36. 52:5. 58:10, 11. 107:43. Ho 14:9. Hab 2:9-12.
overthroweth. Pr 11:3-5. 13:6. 14:32. Ge 19:29. Am 4:11. 1 C 10:5. 2 P 2:4-9. 3:6, 7.

13 stoppeth. Pr 24:11, 12. 31:8, 9. Le +25:35. Jb +27:13. Ps +12:5. 58:4. 82:34. Is 1:17. 16:3, 4. Je 21:12. Zc 7:11. Mt +5:7. Lk 6:38. Ac 7:57. 1 J 3:17.
at. Pr 28:27. Dt 15:7-11. Ne 5:1-5, 13. Is 58:6-9. Je 34:16, 17. Mt 6:14. 7:2. 18:30-35. 25:41-46. Ja 2:13-16.
cry himself. Lk 16:24.
but shall. Is 58:7, 9. Col 3:12.
not be heard. Ps +66:18. Is 58:7-11.

14 gift. Pr 17:8, 23. Ex 23:8. Dt 16:19. Jg +3:15. Ec 10:19.
in secret. Mt 6:3, 4.

15 joy. Pr 10:29. Jb 29:12-17. Ps 32:11. 40:8. 112:1. 119:16, 92. Ec 3:12. Is 32:17. 64:5. Mt 11:30. Jn 4:34. Ro 7:22.
destruction. ver. 12. Pr 5:20. 10:29. Mt 7:23. 13:41, 42. Lk 13:27, 28.

16 wandereth. Pr 13:20. 1 S +16:14. Ps 125:5. Je 14:10. Zp 1:6. Jn 3:19, 20. He 6:4-6. 10:26, 27, 38. 2 P 2:21, 22. 1 J 2:19.
remain. Pr 2:18, 19. 7:26, 27. 9:18. Je 22:17-19, 28-30. Ep 2:1. Ju 12. Re 20:5.
the dead. *or*, Rephaim. Pr 2:18. 9:18. Ge +14:5. Dt +2:20. Jsh +17:15mg. Jb 26:5. Ps 88:10. Is 14:9. 26:14, 19.

17 loveth. ver. 20. Pr 5:10, 11. 23:21. Ps +11:5. Lk 15:13-16. 16:24, 25. 1 T 5:6. 6:17. 2 T 3:4.
pleasure. Heb. sport. *or*, mirth. ver. 15. Pr

10:28. 12:20. 14:10, 13. 15:21, 23. 26:19. Ge 31:27. Jb 20:5. Ec 2:1, 2. 7:4. 8:15. Is 32:11. 47:8, 9. Lk 8:13. 12:19. 21:34. Ep 5:4. 2 P 2:13. Re 18:7.
wine. Pr 20:1. 23:20, 21, 29-35.
and oil. ver. 20. Pr 5:3. 27:9, 16. Ge 28:18.
rich. Pr 10:4, 22. 23:21. 1 S 17:25.

18 wicked. Pr 11:8. Jsh 7:25. Ps 49:7, 8. Is 43:3, 4. 53:4, 5. 55:8, 9. 1 P 3:18.

19 better. ver. +9. Ps 55:6, 7. 120:5, 6. Je 9:2. 1 C 7:15.
wilderness. Heb. land of the desert.

20 treasure. Pr 10:22. 15:6. Ge 41:48. Ps 112:3. Ec 5:19. 7:11. 10:19. Mt 6:19, 20. Lk 6:45.
oil. Ps 23:5. Je 41:8. Mt 25:4, 5.
desired. Ge 2:9. 3:6. Ps 19:10.
but. Mt 25:3, 4, 8. Lk 15:14. 16:1, 19-25.

21 that. Pr 15:9. Ps 63:8. Is 32:17. 33:15-17. 51:1. Ho 6:3. Mt 5:6. Ro 14:19. Ph 3:12-14. 1 Th 5:15. 1 T 6:11. 2 T 2:22. He 12:14.
findeth. Pr 22:4. Mt 10:41, 42. Jn 12:26. Ro 2:7-10. 1 C 15:58. 2 T 4:7, 8. He 6:10. 1 P 1:7.

22 wise. 2 S 20:16-22. Ec 7:19. 9:13-18. 2 C 10:4. Ep 6:10-12.

23 keepeth. Pr 10:19. 12:13. 13:3. 14:3. 17:27, 28. +18:21. Ps 34:12, 13. +101:5. Mt 12:36, 37. Ja 1:26. 3:2-13. 1 P 3:10.
soul. Heb. *nephesh*, Ge +27:31.

24 haughty. Pr 6:17. 16:18. 18:12. 19:29. Est 3:5, 6. Ec 7:8, 9. Is 2:12. Ml 4:1. Mt 2:16.
proud wrath. Heb. the wrath of pride. Jb 38:11mg. Is 66:2.

25 desire. Pr 6:6-11. 12:24, 27. 13:4. 15:19. 19:24. 20:4. 22:13. 24:30-34. 26:13, 16. Mt 25:26.
slothful. Ec +10:18.
refuse. Pr 19:15. 1 Th 4:11. 2 Th 3:10, 11. 1 T 5:13.

26 coveteth. Ex +20:17. Ac 20:33-35. Ph +2:21. Col +3:5. 1 Th 2:5-9.
greedily. Pr +15:27.
the righteous. Ps 37:26. 112:9. Lk 6:30-36. Ac 20:35. 2 C 8:7-9. 9:9-14.

27 sacrifice. Pr 15:8. 28:9. 1 S 13:12, 13. 15:21-23. Ps 50:8-13. Is 1:11-16. 66:3. Je 6:20. 7:11, 12. Am 5:21, 22. Ml 1:7, 8. Mt 15:7-9. Jn 14:6.
with a wicked mind. Heb. in wickedness. Mt 23:14. Jn 10:1.

28 false witness. Heb. witness of lies. Pr +6:19. Is 29:21.
the man. Pr 1:33. 8:34. 12:19. Ac 12:15. 2 C 1:17-20. 4:13. T 3:8. 1 J 1:1, 3.
constantly. Pr 12:19. Jb +4:20 (**S#5331h**). Jn 3:11. 2 P 1:16-18.

29 hardeneth. Pr 28:14. 29:1. 1 S +25:17. Je 3:2, 3. 5:3. 8:12. 36:25. 44:16, 17.
he directeth. *or*, he considereth. Pr 11:5. Ps 119:59. 2 K +5:13, 14. Ezk 18:28. Hg 1:5, 7. 2:15, 18, 19. Mt 6:22. Lk 15:17, 18. 1 Th 3:11.

30 **no wisdom**. Is +14:27. Je 9:23. +19:7. Jon 1:13. Ac 4:27, 28. 1 P 2:8.

nor understanding. Ro 11:33-36.

nor counsel. Pr +19:21. 2 S 16:23. 1 K 11:11, 40. 21:21. 22:30-34. 2 K 10:1-7. 11:2. Ezr 4:15. Jb 12:21, 22. Is +14:27.

against. Nu 23:23. Ge 11:8. Jb 42:2mg. Is 37:27. 40:23. 41:11. 45:16. Je 20:11. Lk 20:26. 2 C 13:8.

31 **horse**. Ps 20:7. 33:17, 18. 147:10. Ec 9:11. Is 31:1. Ho 14:3.

but. Ps 3:3, 8. 68:20.

safety. *or*, victory. Ps 144:10mg.

PROVERBS 22

1 **good name**. Pr 25:18. 1 K 1:47. Ps +101:5. Ec 7:1. Lk 10:20. Ph 4:3. He 11:39. Ju +8.

loving favor rather than. *or*, favor is better than, etc. Pr 16:15. Ac 7:10.

2 **rich**. Pr 29:13. 1 S 2:7. Ps 49:1, 2. Lk 16:19, 20. 1 C 12:21. Ja 2:2-5.

poor. Ex +23:3.

meet together. Jb 3:19. Is 53:6. 1 C 12:13. Ga 3:28. Re 20:12.

the Lord. Pr 14:31. Jb 31:15. 34:19. Ac 17:25, 26, 28.

3 **prudent**. Pr 12:16, 23. 13:16. 14:8, 15, 16, 18. 15:5. 16:21. 18:15. 27:12. Ex 9:20, 21. Ps 112:5. Is 26:20, 21. Je +8:7. Ho 14:9. Mt +7:6. 24:15-18. 1 Th 5:2-6. He 6:18. 11:7.

forseeth. Pr 6:8. 14:15. 24:27. 2 Ch 34:21. Ps +34:4. +112:5. Lk 12:33. 14:28. 22:36. Ro 11:20. 2 C 5:9-11. He 4:1, 11. 11:7.

the evil. Pr 14:16. Is 50:11. Mt 25:41.

hideth. Pr 18:10. 27:12. 28:12. Nu 35:11-13. 1 S 19:2, 12, 18. 20:5, 19. +21:10, 14. 23:19-21. 26:1. 27:1. 1 K +17:3. 18:4, 10. 19:3. Ps 55:12. Is 26:20. Je +36:19, 26. 37:12. Am 5:13. Mt +10:23. 24:15-18. Mk 3:6, 7. Lk +4:30. Jn 8:59. 10:39. 12:36. Ac 4:12. 9:23-25. 17:14. 23:12-24. He 6:18.

the simple. Pr 1:4, 22, 32. 7:7, 22, 23. 9:16-18. 14:15, 16. 29:1. Ps 116:6. Is 26:11.

punished. Pr 27:12. Ex 21:22. Mt 25:46.

4 **By**, etc. Heb. The reward of humility, etc. Pr 3:16. 21:21. Ps 34:9, 10. 112:1-3. Is 33:6. 57:15. Ml 3:14. Mt +5:3. 6:33. Lk 18:13, 14. 1 T 4:8. Ja 4:6, 10.

5 **Thorns**. Pr 13:15. 15:19. Jsh 23:13. Jb *18:8. Ps 11:6. 18:26, 27. Je 23:12*, 13.

he. Pr 13:3. 16:17. 19:16. Ps 91:1. 1 J 5:18. Ju 20, 21.

soul. Heb. *nephesh*, Ge +27:31.

6 **Train up**. Pr +19:18. Ex 10:2. +13:8. Dt 6:6-9. 11:18-21. 32:46. Jsh +1:8. Is 28:9. Ep 6:4. *or*, Catechize. **S#2596h**. Dt 20:5 (dedicated), 5 (dedicate). 1 K 8:63. 2 Ch 7:5.

a child. Ge +18:19. Dt 4:9. 6:7. 2 K +2:23. Ps 78:3-8. La 3:27. Ep 6:4. 2 T +3:15.

the way. Heb. his way. lit. mouth of the way. i.e. entrance on life.

when. 1 S 1:28. 2:26. 12:2, 3.

not depart. Pr 20:7. Ge 18:19. 1 K +8:36. Ps 37:26. 102:28. Ac +2:39. Ph +2:12. 2 T 1:5.

7 **rich**. ver. 16, 22. Pr 14:31. 18:23. Am 2:6. 4:1. 5:11, 12. 8:4, 6. Ja 2:6. 5:1, 4.

the borrower. Dt 15:6. 28:12. 2 K 4:1, 7. Ne 5:3-5. Ps 37:21. Is 24:2. Mt 18:24, 25. Lk 16:5, 6. Ro 13:8.

servant to. 2 K 4:1-7. 1 C 6:12.

lender. Heb. man that lendeth. Pr 19:17. 28:8. Dt 15:6. 24:6. +28:12. 2 K 4:1. Jb 24:3. Ps 37:26. 112:5. Is 24:2. Mt 5:42. Lk 6:34, 35.

8 **that**. Jb +4:8. Ho 8:7. 10:12, 13. Ga 6:7, 8.

the rod of his anger shall fail. *or*, with the rod of his anger he shall be consumed. Pr 14:3. Ps 125:3. Is 9:4. 10:5. 14:29. 30:31.

9 **He that hath a bountiful eye**. Heb. Good of eye. Pr 11:25. 19:17. 21:13. Dt 15:7-11. 28:56. Jb 31:16-20. Ps 41:1-3. 112:9. 145:16. Ec 11:1, 2. Is 32:8. 58:7-12. Mt 20:15. 25:34-40. Mk 7:22. Lk 6:35-38. 14:14. Ac 20:35. 2 C 8:1, 2. 9:6-11. 1 T 6:17-19. He 6:10. 13:16. 1 P 4:9.

10 **Cast out**. Pr 21:24. 26:20, 21. Ge 21:9, 10. Ne 4:1-3. 13:28. Ps 1:1. 101:5. Mt 18:17. 1 C 5:5, 6, 13.

11 **that**. Pr 16:13. Ps 101:6. Mt +5:8.

for the grace of his lips. *or*, and hath grace in his lips. Ps 45:2. Lk 4:22.

the king. Ge 41:39, etc. Ezr 7:6, etc. Ne 2:4-6. Est 10:3. Da 2:46-49. 3:30. 6:20-23.

12 **eyes**. 2 Ch 16:9. Ps 34:15. Is 59:19-21. Mt 16:16-18. Ac 5:39, 12:23, 24. Re 11:3-11. 12:14-17.

he. Jb 5:12, 13. Ac 8:9-12. 13:8-12. 2 Th 2:8. 2 T 3:8, 9.

words. *or*, matters. Jb 33:13. Ps +65:3mg. Ec 12:13. Je 7:22mg. 52:34mg. Ezk 9:11mg. Da 1:14.

13 **The slothful**. Pr 15:19. 26:13-16. Nu 13:32, 33.

without. Heb. *chutz*, Am +5:16 (**S#2351h**, high-ways), outside, or narrower streets.

the streets. Heb. *rechob*, Am +5:16 (**S#7339h**, streets), public square or broad streets.

14 **mouth**. Pr +2:16-19. Jg 16:20, 21.

a deep pit. Heb. *shuchah*, **S#7745h**. Pr 23:27 (ditch). Je 2:6 (pits). 18:20, 22.

abhorred. Ps 81:12. +106:40. Ro 1:28.

15 **Foolishness**. Jb 11:12. 14:4. Ps 51:5. Jn 3:6. Ep 2:3.

a child. Pr +19:18. Ex +13:8. 2 K 2:23, 24. **but**. Pr +13:24. +19:18. 23:13, 14. 29:13-17. He 12:7, 10, 11.

16 **oppresseth the poor**. ver. 22, 23. Pr 28:3. Ps +12:5. Je 22:13, 16. Mi 2:2, 3. Zc 7:9-14. Ja 2:13.

to increase. Lk +6:35. 1 T +6:9.

he that giveth. Lk 6:33-35. 14:12-14. 16:24.

17 **Bow**. Pr 2:2-5. 5:1, 2.
  and hear. Pr 1:3. 3:1. 4:4-8. 8:33, 34. Is 55:3.
  Mt 17:5.
  apply. Pr 23:12. Ps 90:12. Ec 7:25. 8:9, 16.

18 **it is**. Pr 2:10. 3:17. 24:13, 14. Ps 19:10.
  119:103, 111, 162. Je 15:16.
  keep them. Col 3:16.
  within thee. Heb. in thy belly. Jb 32:18mg,
  19. Jn 7:38.
  fitted. Pr 8:6. 10:13, 21. 15:7. 16:21. 25:11.
  Ps 119:13, 171. Ml 2:7. He 13:15.

19 **thy**. Pr 3:5. Ps 62:8. Is 12:2. 26:4. Je 17:7. 1 P
  1:21.
  even to thee. *or, trust* thou also.

20 **written**. Pr 8:6. Ps 12:6. Ho 8:12. 2 T 3:15-
  17. 2 P 1:19-21.

21 **I**. Lk 1:3, 4. Jn 20:31. 1 J 5:13.
  certainty. Pr 19:27. 21:30. **S#7189h,** Ps 60:4
  (truth). 119:160. Is 8:20. Lk 1:1-4. Jn 4:42.
  20:25-28. Ac 17:11. 1 C 2:5. 1 Th 1:5. 2 T
  1:12. 3:15. 2 P 1:15, 16.
  words of truth. Pr 8:8, 9. 30:5. Ps 119:160.
  Ec 12:10. Da 10:21. Jn 17:17. Ja 1:18.
  answer. Pr 8:6. 15:28. 1 P 3:15.
  them that send unto thee. *or,* those that
  send thee. Pr 10:26. 15:23. 25:13. 26:6. Ml
  2:7. 1 T 4:16. 2 T 2:2.

22 **Rob not**. Pr 21:7. 23:10, 11. 28:24. Ex
  +20:15. Le +19:13. Nu +32:23. Jb +27:13. Is
  61:8. Ezk 22:29-31. Mt +26:52. 1 Th +4:6. 1 T
  +1:10.
  oppress. ver. +16. Ex 23:6. 2 S 12:1-6. Jb
  29:12-16. 31:16, 21. Ezk 22:29. Zc 7:9, 10. Ml
  +3:5.
  in the gate. Ge +14:7. 2 S 19:8.

23 **the Lord**. 1 S 24:12, 15. 25:39. Ps +12:5.
  43:1. 68:5. +140:12. Je 50:34. 51:36. Mi 7:9.
  Ml +3:5.
  spoil. Is 33:1. Hab 2:8.
  soul. Heb. *nephesh,* Ge +12:5.

24 **Make no friendship**. Pr 21:24. Ps +119:63.
  2 C 6:14-17. 1 T 5:22.
  angry man. Pr 11:22 (snout). Ja +1:20.
  furious man. Pr 6:34.

25 **Lest thou learn**. Pr 13:20. Je +10:2. 1 C
  15:33.
  snare. Ex +23:33.
  soul. Heb. *nephesh,* Ge +34:3.

26 **strike hands**. Pr 6:1-5. 11:15. 17:18. 27:13.
  sureties. Pr 17:18. 20:16. Ne 5:3. Ezk 27:27.
  debts. Ex 22:26, 27. Dt 24:10, 12, 14.

27 **why should**. Pr 20:16. Ex 22:26, 27. 2 K 4:1.

28 **Remove not**. Pr +23:10. 1 K +12:7, 8, 13.
  ancient. Heb. *olam,* Jb +22:15.
  landmark. *or, bound.* Pr 15:25. 23:10mg. Ge
  10:19. 23:17. Dt 32:8. Jg 21:25. Jb 38:10, 11.
  2 T 3:7. 4:3, 4.

29 **Seest thou**. Pr 26:12. 29:20.
  a man diligent. Pr 10:4. 12:24. 13:4. 25:14.
  Ge 47:6. 1 K 11:28. Ezr 7:6. Ps 45:1. Ec 9:10.

Is +16:5. Mt 25:21, 23. Lk 19:13. Jn 12:26. Ro
12:8, 11. Ep 5:16. Col 4:5. 2 T 2:15. 4:2. He
6:11. 11:6. 2 P +1:10. 3:14.
he shall stand. That is, he shall have the
honor of serving kings; as the phrase denotes.
Pr 18:16. Ge 39:3-6. 41:40, 42. Dt +10:8. Ne
1:11. 2:1. Est 6:11. Jb 11:19mg. 29:7-12. Ps
+149:9. Da 2:48. 3:30. 5:29. 6:1-3, 28. Lk
10:7. +21:36. Re 7:15. 22:3, 4.
mean men. Heb. obscure men. **S#2823h,** only
here.

PROVERBS 23

1 **sittest**. Ge 43:32-34. Ju 12.

2 **put a knife**. Mt 18:8, 9. 1 C 9:27. Ph 3:19.
  appetite. Ec 6:7. Lk 21:34.

3 **not desirous**. ver. 6. Ps 141:4. Da 1:8. Lk
  21:34. Ro 13:14. 1 C 10:31. Ep 4:22. 2 P 1:5,
  6.

4 **Labor not**. Pr 28:20, 22. Jb 9:29. Is 5:8.
  40:28. Mt 6:20. Lk 12:15. Jn +6:27. Ph +4:11.
  1 T 6:8-10, 17. He 10:34. Ja 5:2, 3. 2 P 2:14-
  16. 1 J +5:4.
  cease. Pr 3:5. 26:12. Is 5:21. Ro 11:25. 12:16.
  1 C 1:30, 31.

5 **thou**. Ps 119:36, 37. Je 22:17. 1 J 2:16.
  set thine eyes upon. Heb. cause thine eyes
  to fly upon. Col 3:1-4.
  that which. Ge 42:36. Ec 1:2. 12:8. Is 55:2. 1
  C 7:29-31.
  riches. Pr 27:24. Jb 1:14-17. Ps 39:6. Ec 5:13,
  14. Mt 6:19. 1 T 6:17. Ja 5:1, 2.
  they fly away. Ec 1:2, 14. 2:4-11, 17-19.
  5:10, 11. Ge 31:9. Jb 1:14-17. Ja +4:14.

6 **an evil eye**. ver. 5, 26, 29, 31, 33. Pr 22:9. Dt
  15:9. 28:56. Mt 20:15. Mk 7:22. 1 C 5:11.
  desire. ver. 3. Ps 141:4. Da 1:8-10. Col 3:2.

7 **as**. Pr 19:22. Je +6:19. Mt 9:3, 4. Lk 7:39.
  heart. Heb. *nephesh,* soul, Ex +23:9. 1 K
  +8:18.
  Eat. Jg 16:15. 2 S 13:26-28. Ps 12:2. 55:21.
  Da 11:27. Lk 11:37, etc.

8 **morsel**. Pr 17:1. 28:21. Ge 18:5.
  vomit up. Le 18:25, 28. 20:22.
  lose. or, marr. Pr 9:8. Ge 38:9. Ex 21:26. Ec
  3:7.
  sweet. Pr 22:18. 24:4. 2 S +1:23mg.

9 **Speak**. Pr 9:7, 8. 26:4, 5. Is 36:21. Mt +7:6.
  Ac 13:45, 46. 28:25-28.
  he. Lk 16:14. Jn 8:52. 9:30-34, 40. 10:20. Ac
  17:18, 32. 1 C 1:21-24. 4:10-13.

10 **Remove**. Pr 22:28. Dt 19:14. 27:17. Jb 24:2.
  Ho 5:10.
  old. Heb. *olam,* Jb +22:15.
  landmark. *or, bound.* Pr +22:28mg.
  fatherless. Ex +22:22-24.

11 **their redeemer**. Dt 27:19. Ps +12:5. 103:6.
  136:1. Is +41:14. Je 51:36.

12 **Apply**. ver. 19. Pr 2:2-6. 5:1, 2. 15:28. 22:17.

Ps 119:18, 72. Is 28:13, 34:16. Ezk 33:31. Mt
13:52. Jn +5:39. 2 T 2:15. +3:15. Ja 1:21-25.

words of. Pr 2:5. 5:1. +22:21.

13 Withhold not correction. Pr +13:24.
+19:18. 29:15, 17. Ex +13:8. Le +19:17. 1 S
2:23-25. 3:13. 1 K 1:6. 2:24. La 3:33. Ep 6:4. 1
T 2:8. He 12:10.

from the child. Jb 11:12. Ps 58:3. Ec 11:10.

14 Thou shalt. Ex +13:8.
beat him. Pr 22:15. 1 C 5:5. 11:32.
rod. ver. 13. Pr 10:13. +13:24. 22:8. 29:15,
17.
deliver. 1 C 5:5. 11:32. He 12:10.
soul. Heb. *nephesh*, Ps +30:3.
hell. Heb. *sheol*, Ge +37:35. Pr +30:3.

15 My son. Pr 1:10. 2:1. 4:1. Mt 9:2. Lk 15:18-
20. Jn 21:5. 1 J 2:1.
if. ver. 24, 25. Pr 10:1. 15:20. 29:3. 1 Th 2:19,
20. 3:8, 9. 2 J 4. 3 J 3, 4.
even mine. *or*, even I will rejoice. Pr 29:3. Je
32:41. Zp 3:17. Lk 15:23, 24, 32. Jn 15:11. 2 T
1:2-5.

16 thy. Pr 8:6. Ep 4:29. 5:4. Col 4:4. Je 3:3.

17 not. Ps +37:1.
be thou. Pr 15:16. 28:14. Ps 111:10. 112:1.
Ec 5:7. +12:13, 14. Ac 9:31. 2 C 7:1. 1 P 1:17.

18 surely. Ps 37:37. Je 29:11. Lk 16:25. Ro 6:21,
22.
end. *or*, reward. Pr 24:14. Je +29:11. He
10:35. Ja 5:11. 1 P 1:9.
thine. Ps 9:18. Je +29:11. Ph 1:20.

19 Hear. Mt 13:9. Mk 4:24. Lk +8:18.
and guide. ver. 12, 26. Pr 4:10, 23.

20 not. ver. 29-35. Pr +20:1. 28:7. 31:6, 7. Is
5:11, 12, 22. 22:13. Mt 24:49. Lk 15:13, 14.
16:19. 21:34. Ro 13:13. Ep 5:18. 1 P 4:3, 4.
flesh. Heb. their flesh.

21 the drunkard. Pr 21:17. Dt 21:20. Is 28:1-3.
Jl 1:5. 1 C 5:11. 6:10. Ga 5:21. Ph 3:19.
drowsiness. Pr 6:9-11. 19:15. 24:30-34.

22 Hearken. Ex +20:12.
despise. Pr 30:11, 17. Le 19:3. Mt 15:4-6. Jn
19:26, 27.

23 Buy. Pr 2:2-4. 4:5-7. 10:1. 16:16. 17:16. Jb
28:12-19. Ps 119:72, 162. Is 55:1. Mt 13:44,
46. Ph 3:7, 8. Re 3:18.
sell. Mt 16:26. Ac 20:23, 24. He 11:26. Re
12:11.

24 father. ver. 15, 16, +22. 1 K 1:48. 2:1-3, 9. Ec
2:19.
shall have. Phm 19, 20.

25 and she. Pr 17:25. 1 Ch 4:9, 10. Lk 1:31-33,
40-47, 58. 11:27, 28.

26 My son. ver. 15.
give me. Pr 4:23. Dt 6:5. 1 Ch 29:14. Ps
76:11. Mt 10:37, 38. Lk 14:26. 20:25. Ro 12:1.
1 C 6:20. 2 C 5:14, 15. 8:5. Ep 3:17.
let. Pr 4:25-27. Ps 107:43. 119:2, 9-11, 105.
Ho 14:9. Ro 8:13. Ga 5:6. 2 P 1:19.

27 deep ditch. Pr +22:14 **(S#7745h).**

strange woman. Ec 7:26. Je 10:2.
pit Heb. *be-er*, Ge +16:14.

28 as for a prey. *or*, as a robber. Pr 2:16-19.
7:12, 22-27. 9:18. 22:14. Jg 16:4, etc. Ec 7:26.
Je 3:2.
increaseth. Nu 25:1. Ho 4:11. 1 C 10:8. Re
17:1, 2.

29 Who hath woe. ver. 21. Pr 20:1. 1 S 25:36,
37. 2 S 13:28.
Na 1:10. Ml K 20:16. Is 5:11, 22. 28:7, 8.
redness. Ge 49. 50. Lk 12:45, 46. Ep 5:18.

30 tarry long. 1 +20:1.
5:11. Am 6:6. 5:18. 9:21. Ps 127:2. Is
mixed. Pr 9:2. 75:8.

31 Look not. Pr 6:25. Ge 19:.
31:1. Ps 75:8. 119:37. Jl 1:5.
9:47. Ro 13:13. Ep 18. 1 P 4:3-2. Jb
color. lit. eye. Le +1:55. Mk

32 At the last. Pr 5:11. 28:3, 7, 8. Je
7:5, 6, 12. Lk 16:25, 26. Ro 6:21.
biteth. Ec 10:8. Je 8:7. Am 5:19. 93.
an adder. *or*, a cockatrice. Is 11:8mg.
59:5mg. Je 8:17.

33 eyes. Ge 19:32, etc.
and. Pr 31:5. Ps 69:12. Is 5:4. Ho 7:5. Ju
13.

34 thou. 1 S 25:33-38. 30:16, 17. 2 S 13:28. 1 K
16:9. 20:16, etc. Jl 1:5. Mt 2:38. Lk 17:27-
29. 21:34. 1 Th 5:2-7.
midst. Heb. heart. Pr 30:19mg. Ex 15:8. Je
51:1mg.

35 stricken. Pr 27:22. Je 5:3. 31:18.
I felt it not. Heb. I knew *it* not. Jb 20:20mg.
Ec 8:5mg. Ep 4:18, 19.
I will. Pr 26:11. Dt 29:19. Is 22:13. 56:12. 1 C
15:32-34. 2 P 2:22.

PROVERBS 24

1 not. ver. 19. Ps +37:1.
neither. Pr 1:11-15. 13:20. Ge 13:10-13.
19:1, etc. Ps 26:9. +119:63.

2 their heart. ver. 8. Pr 6:14. 1 S 23:9. Est 3:6,
7. Jb 15:35. Ps 7:14. 10:7. 28:3. 36:4. 64:2-6.
140:2. Is 59:4. Mi 7:3. Mt 26:3, 4. Lk 23:20,
21. Ac 13:10.

3 wisdom. Pr 9:1. 14:1. 1 C 3:9, 10.
house builded. Je 22:13-18.
it is. 2 S 7:26. Je 10:12. Col 2:7.

4 by knowledge. Pr 15:6. 20:15. 21:20. 27:23-
27. 1 K 4:22-28. 1 Ch 27:25, etc. 29:2, etc. 2
Ch 4:18-22. 26:4-11. Ne 10:39. 13:4-13. Mt
13:52.

5 A wise. Pr 8:14. 10:29. 21:22. Ec 7:19. 9:14-18.
strong. Heb. in strength.
increaseth strength. Heb. strengtheneth
might. Ps 84:7. Is 40:31. Col 1:11.

6 by. Pr 15:22. 20:18. Lk 14:31. 1 C 9:25-27. Ep
6:10, etc. 1 T 6:11, 12. 2 T 4:7.
and. Pr 11:14. 15:22.

Ps 10:5. 92:5, 6.

7 too. Pr 14:6. 15:24. 17:24.
Mt 11:25. 1 C 2:14.
openeth not. Ps +38:13.
in the gate. Pr 22:22. Ge +14:7. Je 29:7.
31:21. Ps 127:5. Is 29:21. Am 5:10, 12, 15.
18. 14:22.

8 that deviseth. ver. 2, 9. Pr 6:14-13. 32:7.
Ge 3:1. 1 K 2:44. Ps 21:11. Jb
Ezk 38:10, 11. Na 1:11. Ro 6:5. 8:21. Ps

9 thought. ver. 8. Pr 23:7. Ho 6:9 **(S#2154h,**
119:113. Is 55:7. Je 4. 15:9. Ac 8:22. 2 C
lewdness). Mt 5. Ps 1:1.
10:5. Pr 3:11, 12. x 15:1, 24. 16:3.
the s 14:4-6. 14:3. 33:27. 1 S 27:1. Jb

10 th 7:1-4. Ps 78. 20. 91:15. Is 40:28-
54:7. 61:3. Je 12. Jon 4:8. Mt 10:30.
14:30. 2 C 4:1. 12. Col 1:11. Ep 3:13. 2 T
1:15. 4:16. He 10:2-35. 12:1-5. +13:5. Ja 1:4.
Re 2:3, 13.
da of. Jb 5:17 Ps 50:15. Mt 13:20, 21. Lk
+13. He 12:5.
hall. Heb. narrow. Pr 23:27. Ge 12:10-13.
20:2. Ex 4:10-1. Nu 11:11. 22:26. Jsh 7:6-10.
1 S 27:1. 1 K 9:3, 4. Jb 41:15. Ps 31:1, 22.
116:11. Je 20:7-18. Jon 4:8, 9. Mt 26:35, 22.
56. 69-74.

11 forbear. 1S 26:8, 9. Is 58:6, 7. Je +21:12. Lk
10:31, 32 23:23-25. Ac 18:17. 21:31, 32.
23:10, 2, etc. 1 J 3:16, 17.

12 doth not he that. Pr 5:21. 21:2. 1 S 16:7. Ps
7:9. 17:3. 44:21. Ec 5:8. Je 17:10. Ro 2:16. 1 C
4:5. He 4:12, 13. Re 2:18, 23.
that keepeth. Pr 22:5. 1 S 2:6. 25:29. Ps
+6:6. 66:9. 121:3, 8. Da 5:23. Ac 17:28. Re
18.
soul. Heb. *nephesh*, Ge +12:15.
and shall. Mt +16:27. Ro 2:6.

13 eat. Pr 25:16, 27. SS 5:1. Is 7:15. Mt 3:4.
to thy taste. Heb. upon thy *palate*. Jb
+31:30mg.

14 shall the. Pr 22:18. Ps 19:10, 11. 119:103,
111. Je 15:16.
soul. Heb. *nephesh*, Ge +34:3.
when. Pr 2:1-5, 10. 3:13-18.
there. Pr 23:18. Mt 19:21, 29. Ph 4:7. Ja
1:25.

15 Lay. Pr 1:11. 1 S 19:11. 22:18, 19. 23:20-23.
Ps 10:8-10. 37:32. 56:6. 59:3. 140:5. Je 11:19.
Zc 2:8. Mt 26:4. Ac 9:24. 23:16. 25:3.
spoil. Ps 22:28. Is 32:18.

16 a just. Jb 5:19. Ps 34:19. 37:24. Mi 7:8-10. 2
C 1:8-10. 4:8-12. 11:23-27.
falleth. Pr 11:5, 14. 13:17. 17:20. 26:27.
28:10, 14, 18.
seven times. Ps 119:164. Mt 18:21.
Lk 17:4.
and riseth. Pr 31:28. Ge 37:7. 41:30. Ps
37:24, 39, 40. Ju 24.
but. Pr 13:17. 28:14-18. 1 S 26:10. 31:4. Est

7:10. Jb 15:30. Ps 7:16. 52:5. Am 5:2. 8:14. Ac
12:23. 1 Th 5:3. Re 18:20, 21.

17 Rejoice not. Pr 11:10. +17:5. Ex 15:1. Jg
16:25. 2 S 1:11, 12. 16:5-7, etc. Jb 22:19. Ps
58:10. Zc 1:15. Mt 5:44. Lk 19:41-44. 1

42:10.
1. Re 15:3, 4. 18:20. 19:1-6.
C 13:6,
Heb. be evil in his eyes. Nu

18 displease him. *Heb.*
+22:34mg.
and he. La 4:21, 22. Zc 1:15, 16.
turn away. Jg 16:25-30. Ps 137:7-9. Is 51:22,
23. Je 48:26, 27. La 1:21. Ezk 25:1-7. 26:2.
25. 36:5-7. Ob 10-14. Mi 7:10.
not company with the wicked.
Pr 12:26. 13:20. Nu 16:26. Ps 1:1. 26:4, 5.
37:1. +119:63, 115. 2 C 6:17. Ep 5:11. 2 T
3:2-5. Re 18:4.
neither. ver. 1. Ps +37:1.

20 there. Ps 9:17. 11:6. Is 3:11.
candle. *or,* lamp. Ps +18:28mg. Mt 8:12. 25:8.
Ja 2:26. Ju 13.

21 fear. Ex 14:31. 1 S 24:6. Ec 8:2-5. Mt 22:21.
Ro 13:1-7. 1 T 2:1, 2. T 3:1. 1 P 2:17.
3:16-18. Mt 17:24-27. Ac 4:18, 19. 5:27-29.
Ro 13:1-7. T 3:1. 1 P 2:13-17.
meddle. Ge 49:6. Nu 16:1-13. 1 S 8:5-7.
12:12-19. 2 S 15:10-13, etc. 1 K 12:16.
given to change. Heb. changers. Pr 17:9.
26:11. 31:5mg. 1 S 10:27. 1 K 16:8-22. Est
1:7. 3:8. Da 2:21. 7:25. Ro 13:2. Ep +4:14. 2 T
3:14. 2 P 2:10. Ju +3, 8.

22 their. Nu 16:31-35. 1 S 31:1-7. 2 S 15:13.
18:7-16. 2 Ch 13:16, 17. Ho 5:11. 13:10, 11.
who. Pr 16:14. 20:2. Ps 90:11. 2 S 18:7, 8. 20:1,
2, 22. 2 K 17:21, 23. Ec 8:2-5. Ac 5:36, 37.

23 things. Ps 107:43. Ec 8:1-5. Ho 14:9. Ja 3:17.
It. Pr 18:5. 28:21. Le 19:15. Dt 1:17. Ps 82:2-
4. Jn 7:24. Ro +2:11. 1 T 5:20, 21. Ja 2:4-6.

24 that. Pr 17:15. Ex 23:6, 7. Le 19:15. Dt 1:17.
16:19. Ps 82:2-4. Is 5:20, 23. Je 6:13, 14. 8:10,
11. Ezk 13:22.
him shall. Pr 11:26. 28:27. 30:10. Is 66:24.

25 them. Le 19:17. 1 S 3:13. 1 K 21:19, 20. Ne
5:7-9. 13:8-11, 17, 25, 28. Jb 29:16-18. Mt
14:4. 1 T 5:20. 2 T 4:2. T 1:13. 2:15.
a good blessing. Heb. a blessing of good. Pr
28:23.

26 shall kiss. Pr 15:23. 16:1. 25:11, 12. Ge
41:38, etc. Da 2:46-48. Mk 12-17, 28, 32-34.
giveth a right answer. Heb. answereth right
words. Pr 18:13mg. Jb 6:25.

27 Prepare. Pr +22:3. 1 K 5:17, 18. 6:7. Mt
18:17, 18. Lk 6:48. 14:28-30. 1 C 3:10-15. Ep
2:21, 22. 3:17. 4:11-16. Col 1:23. 2:7. 1 T
4:16. 2 T 2:2.

28 not. Pr 14:5. 19:5, 9. 21:28. Ex 20:16. 23:1. 1
S 22:9, 10. 1 K 21:9-13. Jb 2:3. Ps 35:7-11.
52, title. Mt 26:59, 60. 27:23. Jn 15:25.
deceive. Ps 52:4. 120:2-4. Ep 4:25. Col 3:9.
Re 21:8. 22:15.

so. ver. 22. Pr 16:28. 22:10. Ps 52:1-5. Ja 3:6.
talebearer. *or*, whisperer. ver. +22. Ro +1:29.
ceaseth. Heb. is silent. Ps 37:7mg. 107:30.
Jon 1:11mg, 12.

21 **As coals**. Pr 10:12. 15:18. 29:22. 30:33. 2 S
20:1. 1 K 12:2, 3, 20. Ps 120:4.

22 **words**. Le +19:16.
innermost parts. Heb. chambers. Pr +7:27.
belly. Jb +15:35.

23 **Burning lips**. ver. 24-26. Pr 10:18. 29:5. 2 S
20:9, 10. Ps 55:12-14. Ezk 33:31. Lk 22:47,
48.

24 **hateth**. Pr 11:15. 12:1. 13:24.
dissembleth. *or*, is known.
deceit. Pr 11:1. 12:5, 17, 20. 14:8.

25 **speaketh fair**. Heb. maketh his voice gracious. Ps 12:2. 28:3. Je 9:2-8. Mi 7:5.
believe. Je 12:6. Mt 24:23.
seven. Pr 6:16-19.

26 **Whose hatred is covered by deceit**. *or*,
Hatred is covered in secret. Ge 4:8. 1 S 18:17,
21. 2 S 3:27, etc. 13:22-28. Ps 55:21-23.
showed before. Lk 12:2.

27 **diggeth**. Pr 28:10. Jb +4:8. Ps 10:2. 57:6. Ec
10:8.
shall fall. Pr 27:18. Da 6:24.

28 **lying**. Je 14:14-16. Jn 8:40, 44-49. 10:32, 33.
15:22-24.
a flattering. Pr 27:1, 2. Ps +12:3. Lk 20:20,
21.

PROVERBS 27

1 **Boast not**. Ps 95:7. Is 56:12. Lk 12:19, 20.
17:29. 2 C 6:2. Ja 4:13-16.
tomorrow. Heb. tomorrow day. Pr 3:28. Jsh
+4:6mg.
thou. 1 S 28:19. Ps 37:5. Mt 24:48-51. 25:13.

2 **Let another**. Pr 25:27. Mt 5:16. 2 C 10:12,
18. 12:11. Ja 5:16.

3 **heavy**. Heb. heaviness. Ex 15:5. Is 21:15.
30:27mg. Na 3:3.
but. Pr 17:12. Ge 34:25, 26. 49:7. 1 S 22:18,
19. 25:32, 33. 2 S 13:22, 23. Est 3:5, 6. Da
3:19. Mt 2:16. Ep 4:26. 1 J 3:12.

4 **cruel, and anger is outrageous**. Heb. cru-
elty, and anger an overflowing. 1 S 25:13, 21.
Ja 1:19-21.
but. Pr 14:30. Ge 26:14. 37:11. Jb 5:2. Mt
27:18. Ac 5:17mg. 7:9. 17:5. Ro 1:29. Ja 3:14-
16. 4:5, 6. 1 J 3:12.
envy. *or*, jealousy. Pr 6:34. Ge 4:5-8. 1 S
18:6-9, 16, 17. Ps +37:1. SS 8:6. Da 6:3-5. Mk
7:21-23. 2 C 12:20.

5 **rebuke**. Pr 28:23. Le 19:17. Mt 18:15. Ga
2:14. 1 T 5:20.

6 **Faithful**. Le +19:17. Ps +141:5. Ga +2:11. 1 T
+5:19.
the wounds. 2 S 12:7, etc. Jb 5:17, 18. Ps
141:5. He 12:10. Re 3:19.

but. Ps 55:21. Lk 22:48.
the kisses. Pr 10:18. 26:23-26. Ge +27:27.
deceitful. *or*, earnest, *or*, frequent. Ezk 35:13
(multiplied).

7 **full**. Nu 11:4-9, 18-20. 21:5.
soul. Heb. *nephesh*, Ge +12:5.
loatheth. Heb. treadeth under foot. Ps 44:5.
60:12. 108:12.
honeycomb. Ex 16:31.
to. Jb 6:7. Lk 15:16, 17. Jn 6:9.
hungry. Pr 28:3, 6, 8, 11. 29:13.
soul. Heb. *nephesh*, Ge +12:5.
every. Ph 4:11. 1 T 6:6.

8 **a bird**. Jb 39:14-16. Is 16:2.
nest. Dt 22:6, 7.
man. Pr 21:16. Ge 4:16. 16:6-8. 1 S 22:5.
27:1, etc. 1 K 19:9. Ne 6:11-13. Jon 1:3, 10-
17. 1 C 7:20, 24. 1 T 6:6. Ju 13.
wandereth. Pr 26:17. Ge 34:1, 2. 1 T 5:13. T
2:5.
his place. Pr 14:8. Ne 10:39. SS 1:7, 8. Zc
11:7. Mk 9:38-40. Lk 16:2. Col 2:5. 1 Th 4:11.
5:21. 2 T 3:7. 4:3, 4. He 10:25.

9 **Ointment**. Pr 7:17. Jg 9:9. Ps 45:7, 8. 104:15.
133:2. SS 1:3. 3:6. 4:10. Jn 12:3, 7. Ro 12:15.
2 C 2:14-16.
so. Pr 15:23. 16:21, 23, 24. Ex 18:17-24. 1 S
23:16, 17. Ezr 10:2-4. Ps 55:14. Ac 28:15.
by hearty counsel. Heb. from the counsel of
the soul. Heb. *nephesh*, Ex +15:9.

10 **own**. 2 S 19:24, 28. 21:7. 1 K 12:6-8. 2 Ch
24:22. Is 41:8-10. Je 2:5.
father's friend. Ge 48:15, 16. 1 K 5:1-10. 1
Ch +28:9. Jn 15:15.
neither. Pr 17:17. 19:7. Jb 6:21-23. Ob 12-
14.
better. Pr 17:17. 18:24. 2 S 1:26. Lk 10:30-
37. Ac 23:12, 23, etc.
neighbor. Pr 25:17.
brother. Pr 17:17.
far off. Ge 39:4, 21. 41:39-45. 37:4-18. 1 S
17:28. ch. 20. Mt 13:57. Lk 4:24. 22:28. Jn
4:44. 7:3-5.

11 **be wise**. Pr 10:1. 15:20. 23:15, 16, 24, 25. Ec
2:18-21. Phm 7, 19, 20. 2 J 4. 3 J 4.
make. Pr 28:7, 24. 29:3.
that I. Ps 119:42. 127:4, 5.

12 **prudent**. Pr 18:10. +22:3. Ps 57:1-3. Mt 3:7.
2 P 3:7, 10-14.

13 **his garment**. Pr 6:1-4. 20:16. 22:26, 27. Ex
22:26.

14 **He that**. 2 S 15:2-7. 16:16-19. 17:7-13. 1 K
22:6, 13, 14. Je 28:2-4. Ac 12:22, 23.
loud voice. Jb 32:21. Is 36:13. Lk 11:27. Ac
16:16-18.
rising. Ge +21:14.

15 **A continual**. Pr 19:13. 21:9, 19. 25:24. Jb
14:19.

16 **the ointment**. Mt 26:73. Jn 12:3.

17 **Iron sharpeneth**. 1 S 13:20, 21.

so. ver. 9. Jsh 1:18. 2:24. 1 S 9:27. 11:9, 10. 23:16. 2 S 10:11, 12. Jb 4:3, 4. Ec 4:10. Is 35:3, 4. 41:6. Ml 3:16. 1 Th 3:3, 4. 2 T 1:8, 12. 2:3, 9-13. He +3:12, 13. 10:24. Ja 1:2. 1 P 4:12, 13.

18 **keepeth**. SS 8:12. 1 C 9:7, 13. 2 T 2:6.
so. Pr 17:2. 22:29. Ge 24:2, 3. 39:2-5, 22, 23. Ex 24:13. 2 K 3:11. 5:2, 3, 25, 27. Mk 10:43. Ac 10:7. Col 3:22.
waiteth. Ps +25:3.
shall be. 1 S 2:30. Ps 123:2. Mt 24:45, 46. 25:21, 22. Lk 12:37, 43, 44. Jn 12:26. 1 P 2:18, 21.

19 **in**. Ja 1:22-25.
so. Ge 6:5. Ps 33:15. Mk 7:21.

20 **Hell**. Heb. *sheol*, Ge +37:35. Pr 15:11. 30:15, 16. Jb 26:6. Is 5:14. Hab 2:5.
destruction. Jb +26:6.
never. Heb. not.
so. Pr 23:5. Ps 4:6. Ec 1:8. 2:10, 11. 5:10, 11. 6:7. Je 22:17. 1 J 2:16.

21 **the fining**. Pr 17:3. Ps 12:6. 66:10. Zc 13:9. Ml 3:3. 1 P 1:7. 4:12.
so. 1 S 18:7, 8, 15, 16, 30. 2 S 14:25. 15:6, etc. 1 C 4:7.

22 **Though thou**. Pr 23:35. Ex 12:30. 14:5. 15:9. 2 Ch 28:22, 23. Is 1:5. Je 5:3. 44:15, 16. Re 16:10, 11.
will not. Is +9:13. Je 13:23. Re 16:9-11, 21.

23 **diligent**. Ge 30:32-42. 31:38-40. 33:13. 1 S 16:11. 17:28. 1 Ch 27:29-31. 2 Ch 26:10. Ru 2:4, 5. 3:7. Ps 78:70, 71. Ezk 34:22-24, 31. Jn 21:15-17. Ro 12:11. Col 3:22-24. 1 P 5:2.
know the state. Pr 20:4. Ac 20:28. He +3:12, 13. +12:15. 13:20. 1 P 2:25. 5:2, 4.
look well. Heb. set thy heart. Pr 24:32mg. Ex 7:23. Dt 32:46. 1 S +4:20. Ps +48:13mg.

24 **For**. Pr 23:5. Zp 1:18. 1 T 6:17, 18.
riches. Heb. strength. Pr 5:10mg. 15:6. Ge +34:29. Is 10:14. 30:6. 33:6. 60:5mg. Je 20:5. Ezk 22:25. Ja 1:10.
for ever. Heb. *olam*, Ex +12:24.
doth. 2 S 7:16. Ps 89:36. Is 9:7.
every generation. Heb. generation and generation. Pr 30:11, 12, 13, 14. Ps +33:11mg. 72:5. 102:12. Je 50:39. La 5:19. Jl 3:20.

25 **hay**. Pr 10:5. Ps 104:14. 1 K 18:5. 2 K 19:26.

26 **lambs**. Jb 31:20.

27 **enough**. Pr 30:8, 9. Mt 6:33.
food. Pr 15:16. 23:28. Am 8:11. Mt +25:45. He 5:12-14. 1 P 2:2.
household. Ps 36:7. Ga 6:10. Ep 2:19. He 3:6.
maintenance. Heb. life. Dt 24:6. Is 57:10mg.
maidens. Pr 9:3. 31:15. Ge +24:14.

PROVERBS 28

1 **wicked**. Ge 3:9, 10. Le 26:17, 36. Dt 28:7, 25. 2 K 7:6, 7, 15. Ps 53:5. Is 7:2. Je 20:4.

the righteous. Ex 11:8. Ps 27:1, 2. 46:2, 3. 112:7. Is 26:3, 4. Da 3:16-18. 6:10, 11. Ac 4:13. 14:3. Ro 1:15, 16. 1 Th 2:2.

2 **For the**. Pr 21:1. Je 52:3. Ro 13:1-7.
the transgression. 1 K 15:25, 28. 16:8-29. 2 K 15:8-31. 2 Ch 36:1-12. Is 3:1-7. Ho 13:11.
land. Ge +6:11.
but. Ge 45:5-8. 2 Ch 32:20-26. Jb 22:28-30. Ec 9:15. Is 58:12. Da 4:27.
by a man, etc. *or*, by men of understanding *and* wisdom shall they likewise be prolonged. Pr 11:11.

3 **poor man**. Jb 20:10mg. Mt 18:28-30.
oppresseth. ver. 16.
which leaveth no food. Heb. without food.

4 **that**. 1 S 23:19-21. Ps 10:3. 49:18. Je 5:30, 31. Ml 3:15. Ac 12:22. 24:2-4. Ro 1:32. 1 J 4:5.
but. 1 S 15:14-24. 22:14, 15. 1 K 18:18, 21. 20:41, 42. 21:19, 20. 22:19-28. 2 K 3:13, 14. Ne 5:7, etc. 13:8-11, 17-20, 23-26, 28. Mt 3:7. 14:4. Ac 15:2. 19:9. Ga 2:3-6. Ep 5:11. 1 Th 2:2. Ju 3.
contend. Ne +13:11.

5 **Evil men**. Pr 15:24. 24:1. Jn 3:19.
understand not. Pr 14:6. 24:7. Ps 10:4. 25:14. 82:5. 92:6. Jb 21:14. Is 5:20. Je 4:22. Mt 13:12. 25:29. Mk 4:10-13. Jn 3:19. 7:17. 1 C 2:14, 15. Ep 4:18. 2 Th 2:10-12. Ja 1:5. 2 P 3:5. 1 J 2:20, 27.
but they. Ps 119:100.
that seek. Ps +9:10. 97:11. 105:4. 119:4, 5, 8, 10, 32, 173. Is 26:9. 55:6. Je 29:13. Mt 13:12. 25:29. Jn 6:37. Ph 2:12, 13. He 11:6.
understand all. Pr 1:23. +8:9. 14:6. Dt 29:29. Jb 32:7-9. Ps 25:9, 12, 14. 97:11. 119:98-100, 104, 130. Mt 11:25. Lk 7:35. 10:21. 2 C 4:6. 2 T 2:7. 3:15-17. 1 J 2:20.

6 **Better**. ver. 18. Pr 16:8. 19:1, 22. Dt 5:32. Lk 16:19-23. Ac 24:24-27.

7 **keepeth**. Pr 2:1, etc. 3:1, etc. Dt 4:6. Ps 119:9, 11.
but. ver. 24. Pr 19:26. 23:19-22. 29:3, 15. Ps +119:63, 115. Lk 15:13, 30. 1 P 4:3, 4.
is a companion of riotous men. *or*, feedeth gluttons. Pr 23:20, 21. Dt 21:20.
shameth. Pr 25:8. Ru 2:15mg. 1 S 20:34. Ps 44:9.

8 **that by usury**. Pr 13:22. Jb 27:16, 17. Ec 2:26. Is +24:2.
unjust gain. Heb. by increase. ver. 20, 22, 24. Pr 10:2. 11:24, 26. 13:7. 15:16, 17, 27. 16:8. 21:6, 7. 22:16. Je 17:11. +22:13. Ja 5:1-6.
increaseth. Lk 12:15.
gather it for. Pr 2:21, 22. 10:30. 11:31. 12:7. +13:22. 14:11, 19. 15:25.
pity. Pr 19:17. 2 S 12:6. Ps 140:12. Mt 5:3-7.

9 **turneth away**. Pr 21:13. Jb 21:14. 22:17. Is 58:7-11. Ezk 33:31, 32. Mt 15:8. 2 T 4:3, 4.
even. Ps +66:18. 109:7. Mt 25:41.

10 causeth. Nu 31:15, 16. 1 S 26:19. Mt 5:19. 18:6. Mk 9:42. Lk 17:1, 2. Ac 13:8-10. Ro 16:17, 18. 2 C 11:3, 4, 13-15. Ga 1:8, 9. 2:4. 3:1-4. 2 P 2:18-20. Re 2:14.
he shall. Jb +4:8. Ec 10:8.
but. Pr 10:3. 15:6. 21:20. Dt 7:12-14. Ps 37:11, 25, 26. Mt 6:33. Ro 8:39. 1 C 2:9. 1 P 1:4.

11 rich. Pr 18:11. 23:4. Is 10:13, 14. Ezk 28:3-5. Lk 16:13, 14. 1 C 3:18, 19. 1 T 6:17.
wise. 1 C 10:12.
his own conceit. Heb. his eyes. Pr 26:16. Is 5:21. Ro 11:25. 12:16.
the poor. Pr 18:17. 19:1. Jb 32:9. Ec 9:15-17.

12 righteous. ver. 28. Pr 11:10. 29:2. 1 Ch 15:25-28. 16:7, etc. 29:20-22. 2 Ch 7:10. 30:22-27. Est 8:15-17. Jb 29:11-20. Lk 19:37, 38.
but. 1 S 24:11. 1 K 17:3, etc. 18:4, 13. 19:3. Ec 10:6, 16. Je 36:26. He 11:37, 38.
hidden. Heb. sought for. Pr +22:3. Je 5:1.

13 covereth. Pr 10:12. 17:9. 30:20. Ge 3:7, 12, 13, 21. 4:9. 31:34, 35. 37:31-35. Ex 32:21-24. 1 S 15:13, 20, 21, 24. 2 S 11:15, 25. Jb 31:33. Ps 32:1, 3-5. 90:8. Is 5:20. Je 2:22, 23. Mt 23:25-28. 26:70. 27:24-26. Ac 5:1-8.
not prosper. Pr 13:15. Ge 3:9. +6:13. 4:10-12. 42:21. Nu +32:23. 1 S 15:21, 23. 2 K 5:27. Jb 34:21, 22. Ps 1:3, 4. 66:18. Ec 12:14. Is 30:1. Lk 12:2, 3. Jn 8:9. 1 C 4:5.
whoso confesseth. Le 26:40-42. Jsh 7:19, 20. 1 K 8:47-49. Jb 33:27. 40:4. 42:6. Ps 25:11. 51:1-5, 10. 119:26. Is 43:25, 26. Je 3:12, 13. Da 9:20-23. Ho 5:14, 15. Lk 15:18-24. +18:14. Ac +19:18. 2 C +7:10. Ja +5:16. 1 J 1:8-10.
and forsaketh. Ex 10:16, 17. 1 S 15:30. Jb 34:32. Ps 85:8. Je +33:15. Mt 27:4, 5.
shall have. Le 26:40-42. 2 Ch +7:14. Jb 33:27, 28. Ps +32:5. 85:2. Ho 5:15. Lk 23:43. 1 J 1:9.

14 Happy. Pr 23:17. Ps 2:11. 16:8. 112:1. Is 66:2. Je 32:40. Ro 11:20. He 4:1. 1 P 1:17.
that feareth. Mk 13:35-37. Lk 12:37, 38. 1 C 10:12. Re 16:15.
but. Pr 29:1. Ex 7:22, 23. 14:23, etc. Jb 9:4. Ro 2:4, 5.

15 a roaring. Is +5:29.
a ranging. Pr 17:12. 2 K 2:24. Ho 13:8.
so. Ex 1:14-16, 22. 1 S 22:17-19. 2 K 15:16. 21:16. Est 3:6-10. Mt 2:16.
wicked ruler. ver. 16. Pr 29:2, 4. 1 K 4:16. 2 Ch 33:9-11. Ps 12:8. 94:20, 21.

16 prince. 1 K 12:10, 11, 14. Ne 5:15. Ec 4:1. Is 3:12. Am 4:1.
oppressor. Ge +43:16.
hateth covetousness. Ex +18:21. +29:17. Ps +37:1. Is 33:15, 16. Je 22:15-17. Lk 12:15-21. Ga +5:14. Ep 5:3. Ph 2:4. Col 3:5. He 13:5.

17 doeth violence. Ge 9:6. Ex 21:14. Nu 35:14, etc. 1 K 2:28-34. 21:19, 23. 2 K 9:26. 2 Ch 24:21-25. Mt 27:4, 5. Ac 28:4. Ro 5:20.
person. Heb. *nephesh*, Jsh +10:28.
pit. Heb. *bor*, Ge +37:20.

18 walketh. Pr 10:9, 25. 11:3-6. Ge 17:1. Ps 11:7. 15:1, 2. 25:21. 26:11. 84:11. 97:11. 125:4. Ga 2:14.
but. ver. 6. Nu 22:32. Ps 73:18-20. 125:5. 1 Th 5:3. 2 P 2:1-3. Re 3:3.

19 that tilleth. Pr #12:11. 14:4. 27:23-27. Ec 9:10. Ro 12:11.
but. Pr 13:20. 23:20, 21. Jg 9:4. Lk 15:12-17.

20 faithful. Pr 10:4. 20:6. Ge 24:35. 1 S 22:14. 1 Ch 28:7. Ne 7:2. Ps 101:6. 112:4-9. Mt 25:21, 23. Lk +12:42. 16:1, 10-12. 17:10. 1 C 4:2-5. 15:58. Ja 1:6-8. Re 2:10, 13.
abound with blessings. Pr 10:22. 11:28, 31. Mt 25:21, 23. Mk +10:30. Lk 14:14. 16:10. Ph +4:17. Ja +2:5.
but. ver. 22. Pr 13:11. 20:21. 23:4. 2 K 5:20-27. 1 T 6:9, 10.
innocent. *or*, unpunished. Pr 6:29. 11:21. 16:5mg. 17:5mg. 19:5mg, 9. Ge 24:41. Je 25:29. 49:12.

21 respect. Ja +2:1.
persons. Ge +3:19.
for. Ezk +13:19.

22 that hasteth, etc. Heb. that hath an evil eye, hasteth to be rich. ver. 20. Pr 19:2. 23:5. Ge 13:2. Lk 12:15. 1 T 6:9, 10, 17.
an evil. Pr 23:6. Mt 20:15. Mk 7:22. 1 J 2:16.
and. Ge 13:10-13. 19:17. 1 K 21:2, 18, 19. Jb 20:18-22. 27:16, 17. Je 17:11. 22:13-19. Lk 12:19, 20.

23 that rebuketh. ver. 4. Pr 6:23. 13:18. 15:31, 32. +19:25. 24:24, 25. 25:12. 27:5, 6. Le +19:17. 2 S 12:7. 1 K 1:23, 32-40. Ps 141:5. Ezk 16:1. Mt 18:15. Lk 17:3. Ga 2:11. +6:1. Ep 5:11. Col 3:16. 1 Th 5:14. 2 P 3:15, 16.
afterwards. Pr 25:12. Ps 141:5. Mt +7:6. 1 P 2:12.

24 robbeth. Pr 19:26. Ge 31:19, 34, 35. Jg 17:2. Mt 15:4-6.
the same. ver. 7. Pr 13:20. 18:9.
a destroyer. Heb. a man destroying. Pr 6:32. 18:9. Ge 6:13.

25 that is. Pr 10:12. 13:10. 15:18. 21:24. 22:10. 29:22, 23.
heart. Heb. *nephesh*, soul, Ex +23:9.
he that putteth. Ps 37:5-7. Is +26:3. 1 T 6:6. 1 P 5:7.
made. Pr 11:25. 13:4. 15:30. Is 58:11.

26 that. Pr 3:5. Ge 3:6. 2 K 8:13. Je 17:9. Mt 26:33, 35, 41, 69, 70. Mk 7:21-23. 14:27-31. Ro 8:7.
but. Jb 28:28. Ep 5:16, 17. Col 1:10. 4:5, 6. 1 Th 4:1. 2 T 3:15. Ja 1:5. 3:13-18.

27 that giveth. Pr 19:17. 22:9. Dt 15:7, 10. Ps 41:1-3. 112:5-9. 2 C 9:6-11. He 13:16.

hideth. Is 1:15.
shall. Pr 11:26. 24:24. Mt 25:41-45. Ja 2:13.
28 **the wicked**. ver. 12. Pr 29:2. Is 51:12.
hide. Jb 24:4. Is 26:20. Am 5:13.
they perish. Est 8:17. Ac 12:23, 24.

PROVERBS 29

1 **He, that being often reproved**. Heb. A
man of reproofs. Pr 1:24-31. 1 S 2:25, 34. 1 K
17:1. 18:18. 20:42. 21:20-23. 22:20-23, 28,
34-37. 2 Ch 25:16. 33:10. 36:15-17. Is 48:8.
Je 25:3-5. 26:3-5. 31:18. 35:13-16. Zc 1:3-6.
Mt 26:21-25. Jn 6:70, 71. 13:10, 11, 18, 26.
Ac 1:18, 25.
hardeneth. Ex 9:34. 2 Ch +30:8. Is 48:4.
neck. Ex 32:9. Ac 7:51.
shall. Pr 6:15. 28:18. Is 30:13, 14. Zc 7:11-14.
Ro 11:32. 1 Th 5:3.
without remedy. 2 Ch 36:16. He 6:4-6.
2 **the righteous**. Pr 11:10. 28:12, 28. Est 8:15.
Ps 72:1-7. Is 32:1, 2. Je 23:5, 6. Re 11:15.
in authority. or, increased. ver. 16. Ge 7:17.
Ex 11:9. Ec 5:11.
when the wicked. Est 3:15. Ec 10:5. Mt 2:3,
16.
people mourn. Pr 11:10. Am 5:13.
3 **loveth**. Pr 10:1. 15:20. 23:15, 24, 25. 27:11.
Lk 1:13-17.
he. Pr 5:8-13. 6:26. 21:17, 20. 28:7, 19. Lk
15:13, 30.
4 **king**. ver. 14. Pr 16:12. 20:8. 1 S 13:13. 2 S
8:15. 1 K 2:12. 2 Ch 1:1. Ps 89:12, 14. 97:2.
99:4. Is 9:7. 32:1, 2. 49:8.
he that receiveth gifts. Heb. a man of oblations. 2 K 15:18-20. Je 22:13-17. Da 11:20.
Mi 7:3.
5 **flattereth**. 2 S 14:17. 15:1-14. 16:1-4. Ps
+12:3.
spreadeth. Pr 1:17. La 1:13. Ho 5:1. Lk
20:20, 21. Ro 16:18.
6 **the transgression**. Pr 5:22. 11:5, 6. 12:13. Jb
18:7-10. Ps 11:6. Is 8:14, 15. 2 T 2:26.
but. Ps 97:11. 118:15. 132:16. Is 35:10. Ac
16:25. Ro 5:2, 3. 1 C 15:55-57. Ja 1:2. 1 P 1:8.
1 J 1:4. Re 5:8-10.
7 **considereth**. lit. knoweth. Ge +39:6. Le
+19:15. Jb 29:11-16. 31:13, 21. Ps 31:7. 41:1.
Ga 6:1.
but. Pr 21:13. 1 S 25:9-11. Je 5:28. 22:15-17.
Ezk 22:7, 29-31. Mi 3:1-4.
8 **scornful**. Pr 11:11. Is 28:14-22. Mt 27:39-43.
Jn 9:40, 41. 11:47-50. 1 Th 2:15, 16.
bring a city into a snare. or, set a city on
fire. Ja 3:5, 6.
wise. Ex 32:10-14. Nu 16:48. 25:11. Dt 9:18-
20. 2 S 24:16, 17. Je 15:1. Ezk 22:30. Am 7:2-
6. Jon 3:5-10. Ja 5:15-18.
turn away. Pr 15:1. Ex 32:10-14. Nu 16:48.
Je +2:24mg. Ja 5:18.

9 **contendeth with**. Pr 26:4. Ec 10:13. Mt
+7:6. 11:17-19.
10 **The bloodthirsty**. Heb. Men of bloods. Ge
4:5-8, +10mg. 1 S 20:31-33. 22:11. 1 K 21:20.
22:8. 2 K +9:26mg. 2 Ch 18:7. Mt 5:12. Mk
6:18, 19, 24-27. Jn 7:7. 15:18, 19. Ac 7:52. Ga
4:29. 2 T 3:12. I J 3:12, 13. Re 17:6.
but. 1 S 15:11. Je 13:15-17. 18:20. 40:14-16.
Lk 23:34. Jn 5:34. Ac 7:60. Ro 10:1.
soul. Heb. nephesh, Ge +12:13.
11 **fool uttereth**. ver. 20. Pr 12:16, 23. 13:16.
14:16, 17, 33. 15:2. 18:7, +13. Jg 16:17. 1 S
16:1, 2. Ps +101:5. Am 5:13. Mi 7:5. Ep 5:4.
mind. Heb. ruach, spirit, Ge +26:35.
wise man. Pr 10:14. 16:32. 17:28. 30:32. Ps
141:3.
till afterwards. 1 S 25:36.
12 **ruler hearken**. Pr 20:8. 25:23. 1 S 22:8, etc.
23:19-23. 2 S 3:7-11. 4:5-12. 1 K +12:8. 16:2.
21:11-13. 2 K 10:6, 7. Ps 52:2-4. 101:5-7. Je
37:2. Zp 1:9. 1 T 5:19.
his servants. 2 K +5:13.
wicked. Ho +7:3.
13 **The poor**. Pr 10:4. 13:8, 23. 14:20. Ezk
18:25.
the deceitful man. or, the usurer. S#8501h,
only here. Is +24:2. Mt 9:9. 1 C 6:10.
meet. Pr 22:2.
Lord. Jb 25:3. Ps 13:3. 145:9. Mt +5:45. Ep
2:1.
14 **king**. ver. 4. Pr 16:12. 20:28. 25:5. 28:16. Dt
17:18-20. Jb 29:11-18. Ps 72:2-4, 12-14. 82:2,
3. 89:2. Is 1:17. 11:4. 28:6. Je 5:28. 22:16. Da
4:27.
his throne. Is 9:6, 7. Lk 1:32, 33. He 1:8, 9.
for ever. Ps +9:18.
15 **rod**. ver. 17, 21. Pr 10:13. 13:24. +19:18.
+22:6, 8, 15. 23:13, 14. Mi 6:9.
and reproof. Pr 10:17. 15:5, 10. 17:10.
25:12. 27:5. 29:1. Ex +13:8. Ps 141:5. Ec 7:5.
He 12:5.
give wisdom. 2 Ch 33:12. Ps 119:67, 71, 75.
He 12:9-11.
a child. Pr 10:1, 5. 17:21, 25. 22:6. 1 S 3:13.
1 K 1:6.
left to himself. Ex 4:24-26. 1 S +3:13. 1 K
1:6. Est 2:11. Is 16:2, 27:10. 2 C +12:14. 1 T
+5:8.
to shame. Pr 10:5. 12:4. 14:35. 17:2. 19:26.
16 **the wicked**. ver. 2mg. Ezk 16:49.
but. Ps 37:34, 36. 58:10. 63:10. 91:8. 92:9,
11. 112:8. Re 11:15. 15:4. 18:20.
17 **Correct thy son**. ver. 15. Pr 13:24. +19:18.
22:15. 23:13, 14. Ex +13:8.
soul. Heb. nephesh, Ge +34:3.
18 **there**. 1 S 3:1. 1 Ch 17:15. 2 Ch 15:3-5. Ps
74:9. La 2:9. Ho 4:6. Am 8:11, 12. 9:11, 12.
Ml 2:7. Mt 9:36. Ro 10:13-15.
perish. or, is made naked. Ex 32:25. 2 Ch
28:19.

but. Pr 19:16. Ps 19:11. 119:2. Lk +11:28. Jn +13:17. 14:21-23. Ro 2:13. Ja 1:25. Re 22:14.
happy. Ps +58:11. 119:1, 2. +128:2. Ro +7:12.

19 **servant**. Pr 26:3. 30:22. T 2:9.
though. Jb 19:16.

20 **Seest thou**. ver. 11. Ec 5:2. Ja 1:19.
words. *or*, matters. Pr 14:29. 21:5.
more. Pr 26:12.

21 **servant**. ver. 19. La 3:27. Ep 6:9. Col 4:1.
become. Pr 30:21, 22. Jn 15:15.
length. Pr 5:4, 11. 14:12, 13.

22 **angry**. Pr 10:12. 17:19. 30:33. Ep 4:26. Ja +1:20.
strife. 1 T 6:4. 2 T 2:23, 24. Ja 3:16.
a furious. Pr 17:19. Ja 3:16.

23 **man's**. 2 Ch 32:25, 26. 33:10-12, 23, 24. Jb 22:29. Ps 39:5. Ac 12:23.
pride. Pr +16:5.
honor. Pr 15:33. Ge 18:27. Dt 8:2, 3, 16. Jb 22:29. Is +57:15. 66:1, 2. Mt +5:3. 18:4. 23:12.
spirit. Heb. *ruach*, Ge +41:8.

24 **partner**. Pr 1:11-19. Ex 22:8. Ps 50:18-22. Is 1:23. Mk 11:17.
hateth. Pr 6:32. 8:36. 15:32. 20:2.
soul. Heb. *nephesh*, Ge +27:31.
he. Le 5:1. Nu 5:21. Jg 17:2. 1 K 22:16. Mt 26:63. Ep 5:11.

25 **fear**. Ge 12:11-13. 20:2, 11. 26:7. Ex 32:22-24. 1 S 15:24. 27:1, 11. 1 K 19:3. Is 57:11. Je 38:19. Mt +10:28. 15:12. 26:69-74. Jn 3:2. 9:22. 12:42, 43. 19:12, 13. Ga 2:11-13. 2 T 4:16, 17.
whoso. 2 K 6:31, 32. 1 Ch 5:20. Ec 7:18. Is +26:3. Da 3:28. 6:23. Ac 4:13, 19. 1 P 1:21.
safe. Heb. set on high. Ps 69:29. 91:14.

26 **seek**. Pr 19:6. Ps 20:9.
ruler's favor. Heb. face of a ruler. Pr 17:9, 19. 28:5.
but. Pr 16:7. 19:21. 21:1. Ge 43:14. Ezr 7:27, 28. Ne 1:11. Est 4:16. Ps 20:9. 62:12. Is 46:9-11. Da 4:35.

27 **unjust**. Pr 24:9. Ps 119:115. 139:21, 22. Zc 11:8. Jn 7:7. 1 J 3:13.
just. Mt 5:45.
and he. Jn 15:17-19, 23. Ro 8:7. 1 J 3:12, 13.

PROVERBS 30

1 **Agur**. i.e. *gatherer*, **S#94h**.
Jakeh. i.e. *obedient*, **S#3348h**.
even. Pr 31:1. 2 P 1:19-21.
Ithiel. i.e. *God has arrived; God is with me*, **S#384h**. ver. 1. Ne 11:7.
Ucal. i.e. *prevailing; devoured; I shall be completed, I shall be enabled*, **S#401h**.

2 **I am**. Jb 42:3-6. Ps 73:22. Is 6:5. Ro 11:25. 1 C 3:18. 8:2. Ja 1:5.
brutish. Pr 5:12. Ps 92:6. Je 10:14. 2 P 2:12-16.

3 **neither**. Je 10:7. Am 7:14, 15. Mt 16:17.
nor. Jb +11:7. Jn 17:3.
have. Heb. know. Pr 5:6. 10:32. 24:12.
the holy. Is 6:3. 30:11. 57:15. Re 3:7. 4:8.

4 **Who hath ascended**. Dt 30:12. Jn 3:13. Ro 10:6. Ep 4:9, 10.
who hath gathered. Jb 11:7-9. 38:4, etc. Ps 104:2, etc. Is 40:12, etc. 53:8.
what is his name. Ex 3:13-15. 6:3. 34:5-7. Dt 28:58.
and what. Ge 32:29. Jg 13:18. Ps 2:7. Is 7:14. 9:6. Je 23:6. Mt 1:21-23. 11:27. Lk 10:22.

5 **word**. Ps 12:6. 18:30. 19:8. 119:140. Ro 7:12. Ja 3:17.
pure. Heb. purified. 2 S 22:31. Ps 12:6. 18:30. 119:140mg.
shield. Ps +84:11. 144:2.

6 **Add**. Ge 3:3. Dt +4:2. Is +42:21. 2 P 3:15, 16.
and. Ge 3:3. Jb 13:7-9. 1 C 15:15.

7 **have**. 1 K 3:5-9. 2 K 2:9. Ps 27:4. Lk 10:42.
deny me them not. Heb. withhold not from me. Pr 3:27. 23:13. Ge 30:2. 2 S 13:13. Ps 21:2.

8 **vanity**. Pr 21:6. 22:8. Ps 62:9, 10. 119:37. Ec 1:2. Is 5:18. 59:4. Jon 2:8. Ac 14:15. 1 J 2:16.
and lies. Ps 119:29.
neither. Ge 28:20. Jb 1:21. Je 45:5. Ph 4:11, 12. 1 T 6:6-10.
poverty. Pr 6:11. +10:15. 11:24. 20:13. 21:17. 23:21. 24:34. 28:19. Le +25:35. Dt 15:11. Ps +12:5. +140:12. Is 3:7. Am 8:11. Mt +5:7. Lk +16:25. 2 C +6:10. Ja +2:5.
nor riches. Pr 23:4, 5. 1 K 3:13. Ec 5:10. Hab 2:5. Mt 13:22. Mk +4:19. Ph 4:11, 12. 1 T +6:5, 9, 10.
feed. Ge 28:20. 48:15, 16. Ex 16:15, 18, 21, 22, 35. Mt 6:11, 33. Lk 11:3. 1 T 6:6-8.
convenient for me. Heb. of my allowance. Ge +47:22. 1 K 4:27. 2 K 25:30. Je 37:21. 52:34. Mt 6:11.

9 **I be full**. Dt 6:10-12. 8:10-14, 17. 31:20. 32:15. Ne 9:25, 26. Jb 31:24-28. Je 2:31. Ezk 16:14, 15, 49, 50. Da 4:17, 30. Ho 13:6. Mk +4:19. Ac 12:22, 23. Ja 4:3.
deny thee. Heb. belie thee. Jsh 24:27. Jb 8:18. 21:13, 14. 22:17, 18. 31:28. Je 5:12.
Who. Ex 5:2. 2 Ch 32:15-17.
or. Pr 6:30, 31. Ps 125:3.
lest. Ps +9:10.
and steal. Ex +20:15. Dt 23:24. Ep 4:28. 1 P 4:15.
and take the name. Pr 29:24. Ex 20:7. Le 5:1. Mt 26:72, 74.

10 **Accuse not**. Heb. Hurt not with thy tongue. Pr 17:20. 24:23. Ge 21:25, 26. Le 19:16, 17. Dt 23:15. 1 S 22:9, 10. 24:9. 26:19. 30:15. 2 S 16:1-4. 19:26, 27. Ps +101:5. Ec 7:21. Da 3:8, etc. 6:13, 24. Mt 7:3-5, 12. 18:15. Ro 14:4. Ep 4:31, 32. Col 3:12, 13. T 3:2. Phm 8-10. Ja 2:13.

lest. Pr 11:26. 24:24. 26:2. 28:27. Dt 15:9. 1 S 26:19. 2 Ch 24:22-24. Ec 7:21.
and thou. Jn 8:3-9. Ro 2:1, 3, 21, 22.

11 **a generation**. ver. 12-14. Mt 3:7. 1 P 2:9.
that curseth. ver. 17. Pr +20:20. Dt 21:20, 21.
doth. 1 T 5:4, 8.

12 **that are pure**. Pr +16:25. 21:2. Jg 17:5, 13. 1 S 15:13, 14. Jb 33:9. Ps +10:4. 36:2. 51:10. Is 65:5. Je 2:22-24, 35. 17:9. Mt 19:20-22. Lk 11:39, 40. +16:15. 18:11. 2 T 3:5. T 1:15, 16. 1 J 1:8-10.
not. Ps 51:2, 7. Is 1:16. Je 4:14. Ezk 36:25. Zc 13:1. 1 C 6:11. T 3:5. 1 J 1:7. Re 1:5.

13 **how lofty**. Pr +6:17. Ezk 28:2-5, 9. Da 11:36, 37. Hab 2:4. Ph 2:5-8. 2 Th 2:3, 4.

14 **whose**. Pr 12:18. Jb 29:17. Ps 3:7. 52:2. 57:4. 58:6. Da 7:5-7. Re 9:8.
to devour. Pr 22:16. 28:3. Ps 10:8, 9. 12:5. 14:4. Ec 4:1. Is 32:7. Am 2:7. 4:1. 8:4. Mi 2:1, 2. 3:1-5. Hab 3:14. Zp 3:3. Mt 23:14. Ja 5:1-4.

15 **The horseleach**. Is 57:3, 4. Ezk 16:44-46. Mt 23:32. Jn 8:39, 44.
Give. Ezk +13:19. Ju 11, 12.
There. ver. 21, 24, 29. Pr 6:16. Am 1:3, 6, 9, 11, 13. 2:1, 4.
never satisfied. Pr 27:20. Ec 1:8. 4:8. 5:10. Ezk 16:28, 29. Am 4:8. Hab 2:5.
It is enough. Heb. Wealth. ver. 16. Ps 44:12.

16 **The grave**. Heb. *sheol*, Ge +37:35. Pr 27:20. Hab 2:5.

17 **eye that mocketh**. ver. +11. 2 S 18:9, 10, 14-17. 2 K 2:23. Jb 19:18.
father. Ex +20:12.
the ravens. 1 S 17:44, 46. 2 S 21:10.
valley. *or*, brook. Nu +13:23mg.

18 **too wonderful**. Jb 42:3. Ps 40:5. 131:1mg. 139:6. Ro 11:33.

19 **way of an eagle**. Jb 39:27. Is 40:31.
midst. Heb. heart. Pr 23:34mg. Ex +15:8.
and the. Pr 14:12, 13. Ex 22:16. 1 Th 5:22. 1 T 4:12. 5:2. 6:11. 2 T 2:22. He 3:13. 1 J 2:16.

20 **the way**. Pr 7:13-23. Nu 5:11-30.
no wickedness. He +3:13.

21 **For three**. Jb 40:5.
disquieted. Pr 29:9. Dt 2:25.
bear. Pr 18:5. Ge 4:13. 36:7.

22 **a servant**. Pr 19:10. 28:3. Ec 10:7. Is 3:4, 5. 1 C 14:40.
a fool. 1 S 25:3, 10, 11, 25, 36-38. 30:16.

23 **an odious**. Pr 19:13. 21:9, 19. 27:15.
an handmaid. Pr 29:21. Ge 16:4.

24 **little**. Jb 12:7.
exceeding wise. Heb. wise, made wise. Pr 1:5, 6. 3:7, 35. 9:8, 9.

25 **The ants**. Pr 6:6-8. Mt 6:20. Jn 6:27.

26 **The conies**. Le 11:5. Ps 104:18.
rocks. Ps 18:2. 91:1, 2. Je 48:28.

27 **The locusts**. Ps +78:46.
by bands. Heb. gathered together. Ezk 1:21-26.

28 **palaces**. Ps 144:12. Is 13:22. Da 1:4. Ep 2:6.

29 **three**. ver. 21. Jb +40:5.
go well. Ph 4:8.

30 **A lion**. Jg 14:18. Is +5:29.
among. Lk 1:42.

31 **greyhound**. *or*, horse. Heb. girt in the loins.
against. Pr 16:14. 20:2. Da 3:15-18.

32 **thou hast done**. Pr 26:12. Ec 8:3.
thought evil. Pr 16:3. Ec 10:20. Mt 5:28. 2 C 10:5. Ph 4:8.
lay. Pr 17:28. Jg +18:19. Jb 21:5. 40:4, 5. Ec 8:4. Mi 7:16, 17. Ro 3:19.

33 **so**. Pr 15:18. 16:28. 17:14. 26:21. 28:25. 29:22.

PROVERBS 31

1 **the prophecy**. Pr 30:1.
his. Pr 1:8. 6:20. 2 T 1:5. 3:15, 16.

2 **the son of my womb**. Is 49:15.
the son of my vows. 1 S 1:11, 28.

3 **strength**. Pr 5:9-11. 7:26, 27. Ho 4:11.
to that. Dt 17:17. Ne 13:26.

4 **not for kings**. Le 10:8-11. Nu 6:1-4. 1 K 20:12, 16-20. Est 3:15. Ec 10:17. Is 28:7, 8. Da 5:2-4. Ho 4:11, 12. 7:3-5. Hab 2:5. Mt +10:16. Mk 6:21-28.
Lemuel. i.e. *for whom is a mighty one; by God; unto God*, **S#3927h**. ver. 1.
drink. Da 5:2. Mt 11:18, 19. Lk 7:33, 34.

5 **drink**. Ec 10:17.
pervert. Heb. alter. 1 S 21:13. Est 2:9mg. Ps 89:34.
any of the afflicted. Heb. all the sons of affliction. Hab 2:5.

6 **strong**. Ps 104:15. 1 T 5:23.
of heavy hearts. Heb. bitter of soul. Heb. *nephesh*, Ex +23:9. 1 S +30:6mg.

7 **drink**. Ep 5:18.
remember his. Je 16:7.

8 **Open**. 1 S 19:4-7. 20:32. 22:14, 15. Est 4:13-16. Je +21:12. 26:16-19, 24. 38:7-10. Jn 7:51.
such, etc. Heb. the sons of destruction. or, change. 1 S +20:31mg. Jb 14:14.

9 **judge righteously**. Pr 16:12. 20:8. Le 19:15. Dt 1:16. 16:18-20. 2 S 8:15. Jb 29:12, 15, 16. Ps 58:1, 2. 72:1, 2, 12-14. Is 1:17, 23. 11:4. +21:7. 31:1, 2. Je 5:28. 22:3, 15, 16. 23:5. Da 4:27. Am 5:11, 12. Zc 7:9. 9:9. Jn 7:24. He 1:9. Re 19:11.

10 **can**. Pr 12:4. 18:22. 19:14. Ru 3:11. Ec 7:28. SS 6:8, 9. Ep 5:25-33.
her. Pr 3:15. 8:11. 20:15.
price. Ml 3:17.

11 **heart**. 2 K 4:9, 10, 22, 23. 1 P 3:1-7.
no need. SS 4:16.

12 **will do**. Ge 2:18. 1 S 25:18-22, 26, 27. Ro 7:18, 25. 1 C 7:34. Ep 5:31, 32.

13 **worketh**. Ge 18:6-8. 24:13, 14, 18-20. 29:9, 10. Ex 2:16. Ru 2:2, 3, 23. Is 3:16-24. 32:9-

11. Ac 9:39, 40. 1 Th 4:11. 2 Th 3:10-12. 1 T 5:10, 14. T 2:5.
willingly. Ro 6:19.

14 **is like**. ver. 24. 1 K 9:26-28. 2 Ch 9:10, 21. Ezk 27:3, etc.
from afar. Jn 6:33.

15 **riseth**. Jsh 3:1. 2 Ch 36:15. Ps 119:147, 148. Ec 9:10. Mk 1:35. Ro 12:11.
and giveth. Mt 24:45. Lk 12:42.
meat. lit. prey. Ps +111:5mg.
portion. Lk +12:42.
maidens. Pr 9:3. 27:27. Ge 24:14.

16 **considereth**. Jsh 15:18. SS 8:12. Mt 13:44.
buyeth. Heb. taketh. Pr 1:19. Nu 21:25. Ps 6:9. Is 55:1.

17 **girdeth**. Lk +12:35.
strengtheneth. Ge 49:24. Is 44:12. Ho 7:15.

18 **perceiveth**. Heb. tasteth. Is 14:24, 29, 43.
her candle. Ge 31:40. Ps 127:2. Mt 5:15, 16. Mk 25:3-10. 1 Th 2:9. 2 Th 3:7-9.

19 **She layeth**. Ex 35:25, 26.
her hands. Ep 4:28.

20 **She stretcheth**. Heb. She spreadeth. Pr 1:24.
to the poor. Mt 25:36.
she reacheth. Pr 19:17. 22:9. Jb 31:16-20. Ps 41:1. 112:9. Ec 11:1, 2. Mk 14:7. Ac 9:39-41. 20:34, 35. Ep 4:28. He 13:16.

21 **not afraid**. Pr 1:33. 25:20.
scarlet. or, double garments. Ge 38:28, 30. 45:22. Ex 25:4.

22 **coverings**. Pr 7:16.
clothing. Ge 41:42mg. Est 5:1. 8:15. Ps 45:13, 14. Ezk 16:10-13. 1 P 3:3, 4.
silk. Ex 39:27.

23 **husband**. Pr 12:4.
in the gates. Pr 24:7. Ge +14:7. Dt 16:18. 21:19. Ru 4:1, 2. Jb 29:7.

24 **She maketh**. ver. 13, 19. Ex +26:1.

25 **Strength**. Jb 29:14. 40:10. Ps 132:9, 16. Is 61:10. Ro 13:14. Ep 4:24. 1 T 2:8-10. 1 P 3:3, 4. 5:5, 6.
and she. Ps 97:11, 12. Is 65:13, 14. Mt 25:20, 21. Jn 16:20.

26 **openeth**. ver. 8, 9. Jg +11:35. 13:23. 1 S 25:24-31. 2 S 20:16-22. 2 K 22:15-20. Est 4:4. 5:8. 7:3-6. 8:3-6. Lk 1:38, 42-56. Ac 18:26. Ep 4:29. Col 4:5, 6. Ja 3:17.
in her. Pr 12:18. 16:24. 25:15. Ge 24:18-20. SS 2:14. 4:11. Ml 2:6. Ac 16:15. 1 P 3:1, 4, 5, 8, 9.

27 **looketh well**. Pr 14:1. Ph 2:12. 1 Th 4:11. 2 Th 3:6-12. 1 T 5:10, 13, 14. T 2:4, 5.

28 **children**. ver. 1. 1 K 2:19. Ps 116:16. 2 T 1:5. 3:15-17.
her husband. SS 7:1-9. Is 62:4mg, 5mg.
praiseth. 1 C 4:5.

29 **done virtuously**. or, gotten riches. ver. 3, 10. Pr 12:4. 13:22.
thou. SS 6:8, 9. Ep 5:27.

30 **Favor**. Pr 6:25. 11:22. 2 S 14:25. Est 1:11, 12. Ezk 16:15. Ja 1:11. 1 P 1:24.
a woman. Pr 1:7. 8:13. Ex 1:17-21. Ps 147:11. Lk 1:6, 46-50. 1 P 3:4, 5.
she. Ec 7:18. 12:13. Ro 2:29. 1 C 4:5. 1 P 1:7. 3:4.

31 **of the**. ver. 16. Pr 11:30. Ps 128:2. Mt 7:16, 20. Ro 6:21, 22. Ph 4:17.
and let. Mk 14:7-9. Ac 9:39. Ro 16:1-4, 6, 12. 1 T 5:10, 25. He 6:10. Re 14:13.

ECCLESIASTES

ECCLESIASTES 1

1 A.M. 3027. B.C. 977.
the Preacher. ver. 12. Ec 7:27. 12:8-10. Ne 6:7. Ps 40:9. Is 61:1. Jon 3:2. 2 P 2:5.
king. ver. 12. 1 K 11:42, 43. 2 Ch 9:30. 10:17-19.

2 **of vanities.** Ec 2:11, 15, 17, 19, 21, 23, 26. 3:19. 4:4, 8, 16. 5:10. 6:11. 11:8, 10. 12:8. Ps 39:5, 6, 11. 62:9, 10. 144:4. Ro 8:20, 21.

3 **profit.** Ec 2:22. 3:9. 5:15, 16. Pr 23:4, 5. Is 55:2. Hab 2:13, 18. Mt 16:26. Mk 8:36, 37. Jn 6:27.
under. Ec 2:11, 19. 4:3, 7. 5:18. 6:12. 7:11. 8:15-17. 9:3, 6, 13.

4 **One generation.** Ec 6:12. Ge 5:3-31. 10:1-32. 11:10-32. 36:9, etc. 47:9. Ex 1:6, 7. 6:16, etc. Ps 89:1, 2, 47, 48. 90:9, 10. Zc 1:5.
but. Ge +8:22. Ps 78:69. 89:36, 37. 102:24-28. 104:5. 119:90, 91. Mt 24:35. 2 P 3:10-13.
abideth. 1 Ch 16:30. Ps +102:25, 26.
for ever. Heb. *olam*, Ge +9:12. Ge +8:22. Ex +12:24. Ps 72:5, 7, 17. 78:69. 89:36, 37. 104:5. 148:6. Is +9:6, 7. Ezk +37:25.

5 **sun.** Ge 8:22. Ps 19:4-6. 89:36, 37. 104:19-23. Je 33:20.
hasteth. Heb. panteth. Jsh 10:13, 14. Ps 42:1. 119:131. Is +42:19mg. Am 2:7. Hab 3:11.

6 **The wind.** Jb 37:9, 17. Ps 107:25, 29. Jon 1:4. Mt 7:24-27. Jn 3:8. Ac 27:13-15.

7 **the rivers run.** Jb 38:10, 11. Ps 104:6-9.
return again. Heb. return to go.

8 **full.** Ec 2:11, 26. Ge 3:19. Mt 11:28-30. Ro 8:22, 23.
man. Ec 4:1-4. 7:24-26.
the eye. Ec 4:8. 5:10, 11. Ps 63:5. Pr 27:20. 30:15, 16. Is 55:2. Mt +5:6. Re 7:16, 17.

9 **that hath.** Ec 3:15. 7:10. 2 P 2:1.
and there. Is 43:19. Je 31:22. Re 21:1, 5.

10 **it hath.** Mt 5:12. 23:30-32. Lk 17:26-30. Ac 7:51, 52. 1 Th 2:14-16. 2 T 3:8.
of old time. Heb. *olam* plural, Ps +61:4.

11 **There is.** Ec 2:16. Ps 9:6. Is 41:22-26. 42:9.

12 *the Preacher.* ver. +1. 1 K 4:1, etc.

13 **I gave.** ver. 17. Ec 7:25. 8:9, 16, 17. Ps 111:2. Pr 2:2-4. 4:7. 18:1, 15. 23:26. 1 T 4:15.
by wisdom. 1 C 1:20.
this sore. Ec 3:10. 4:4. 12:12. Ge 3:19.
to be exercised. *or,* to afflict them.

14 **have seen.** ver. 17, 18. Ec 2:11, 17, 26. 1 K 4:30-32. Ps 39:5, 6.
spirit. Heb. *ruach,* Ge +41:8.

15 **crooked.** Ec 3:14. 7:12, 13. Est 5:11-13. Jb 11:6. 34:29. Pr +19:18. Is 40:4. La 3:37. Da 4:35. Mt 5:36. 6:27. Re +22:11.
cannot. Jb 12:14. Is 14:27. Da +10:12.
wanting. Heb. defect. 1 K 21:4. Jb 20:22.

16 **communed.** 2 K 5:20. Ps 4:4. 77:6. Is 10:7-14. Je 22:14. Ezk 38:10, 11. Da 4:30.
Lo. Ec 2:9. 1 K 3:12, 13. 4:29-31. 10:6, 7, 23, 24. 2 Ch 1:10-12. 2:12. 9:22, 23.
great experience of. Heb. seen much. He 5:14.

17 **I gave.** ver. +13. Ec 2:3, 12. 7:23-25. 1 Th 5:21.
I perceived. Ec 2:10, 11.
spirit. Heb. *ruach,* Ge +41:8.

18 **in much.** Ec 2:15. 7:16. 12:12, 13. Jb 28:28. Pr 3:13. 1 C 3:18-20. Ja 3:13-17.

ECCLESIASTES 2

1 **said.** ver. 15. Ec 1:16, 17. 3:17, 18. Ps 10:6. 14:1. 27:8. 30:6, 7. Lk 12:19.
Go to. Ge 11:3, 4, 7. 2 K 5:5. Is 5:5. Ja 4:13, 14. 5:1.
I will. Ec 8:15. 11:9. Is 50:5, 11. Lk 16:19, 23. Ja 5:5. T 3:3. Re 18:7, 8.
pleasure. ver. 10, 11. Pr +23:5.

2 **It is.** Ec 7:2-6. Pr 14:13. Is 22:12, 13. Am 6:3-6. 1 P 4:2-4.

3 **sought.** Ec 1:17. 1 S 25:36.
give myself unto wine. Heb. draw my flesh with wine.
yet. Pr +20:1. 31:4, 5. Ep 5:18.
and to lay. Ec 7:18. Pr 20:1. 23:29-35. Mt 6:24. 2 C 6:15-17.
till. Ec 6:12. 12:13.
all. Heb. the number of. Ge 47:9. Ex +23:26. Jb 14:14. Ps 90:9-12.

4 **made.** Ge 11:4. 2 S 18:18. Da 4:30.
I builded. Dt 8:12-14. 1 K 7:1, 2, 8-12. 9:1, 15-19. 10:19, 20. 2 Ch 8:1-6, 11. Ps 49:11.
I planted. 1 Ch 27:27. 2 Ch 26:10. SS 1:14. 7:12. 8:11, 12. Is 5:1.

5 **me.** SS 4:12-16. 5:1. 6:2. Je 39:4.
I planted. Ge 2:8, 9. Lk 17:27-29.

6 pools. Ne 2:14. SS 7:4.
to water. Ps 1:3. Je 17:8.
7 servants. 1 K 9:20-22. Ezr 2:58. Ne 7:57.
and had. Ge 17:12, 13.
servants born in my house. Heb. sons of
my house. Ge 15:3.
also. Ge 13:2. 2 K 3:4. 1 Ch 27:29-31. 2 Ch
26:10. 32:27-29. Jb 1:3. 42:12.
8 silver. 1 K 9:14, 28. 10:10, 14, 15, 21-28. 2
Ch 9:11, 15-21.
men singers. 2 S 19:35. Ezr 2:65.
musical instruments, etc. Heb. musical
instrument and instruments. 1 Ch 25:1, 6. Jb
21:11, 12. Ps 150:3-5. Da 3:5, 7, 15. Am 6:5.
9 I was great. Ec 1:16. 1 K 3:12. 10:7, 23. 1 Ch
29:25. 2 Ch 1:1. 9:22, 23.
10 whatsoever. Ec 3:22. 6:9. Ge 3:6. 6:2. Jg
14:2. Jb 31:1. Ps 119:37. Pr 23:5. 1 J 2:16.
kept not from. 1 K 11:1-3. Lk 15:13, 17, 18.
16:19, 22, 23. Mk +4:19. Ph +3:19. 1 T +2:9.
my heart rejoiced. ver. 22, 24. Ec +3:22.
11 I looked. Ec 1:14. Ge 1:31. Ex 39:43. 1 J
2:15-17.
behold. ver. 17-23. Ec 1:3, 14. 11:8. Hab
2:13. 1 T 6:6-11.
spirit. Heb. *ruach*, Ge +41:8.
12 I turned. Ec 1:17. 7:25.
even that which hath been already done.
or, in those things which have been already
done. ver. 25.
13 I saw. Ec 7:11, 12. 9:16. Pr 4:5-7. 16:16. Ml
3:18. 4:1, 2.
that wisdom excelleth folly. Heb. that
there is an excellency in wisdom more than
in folly, etc.
light. Ec 11:7. Ps 119:105, 130. Pr 4:18, 19.
Mt 6:23. Lk 11:34, 35. Ep 5:8.
14 wise. Ec 8:1. 10:2, 3. Pr 14:8. 17:24. Jn 13:7.
1 J 2:11.
walketh in darkness. 1 J 2:9.
one. Ec 9:1-3, 11, 16. Ps 19:10. 49:10.
15 even to me. Heb. to me, even to me.
and why. Ec 1:16, 18. 1 K 3:12.
Then I. ver. 1. Ec 1:2, 14.
16 there is. Ec 1:11. Ex 1:6, 8. Ps 88:12. 103:16.
Ml 3:16.
for ever. Heb. *olam*, Ex +12:24.
how. Ec 6:8. 2 S 3:33. Ps 49:10. Is 57:1, 2. Lk
16:22, 23. He +9:27.
17 I hated. Nu 11:14, 15. 1 K 19:4. Jb 3:20-22.
7:15, 16. 14:13. Je 20:14-18. Jon 4:3, 8. Ph
1:23-25.
work. Ec 1:14. 3:16. Ezk 3:14. Hab 1:3.
for. ver. 11, 22, 23. Ec 6:9. Ps 89:47.
spirit. Heb. *ruach*, Ge +41:8.
18 I hated. ver. 4-9. Ec 1:13. 4:3. 5:18. 9:9.
taken. Heb. labored.
I should. ver. 26. Ec 5:13, 14. 1 K 11:11-13.
Ps 17:14. 39:6. 49:10. Lk 12:20. 16:27, 28. Ac
20:29, 30. 1 C 3:10.

19 who knoweth. Ec 3:22. 1 K 12:14, etc.
14:25-28. 2 Ch 10:13-16. 12:9, 10. Jn 3:17. Ja
1:5.
labor. Dt +28:33.
wise under. Ec 9:13. Lk 16:8. Ja 1:17. 3:17.
20 to cause. Ge 43:14. Jb 17:11-15. Ps 39:6, 7. 1
C 15:19. 2 C 1:8-10. 1 Th 3:3, 4.
21 whose. ver. 17, 18. Ec 9:18. 2 Ch 31:20, 21.
33:2-9. 34:2. 35:18. 36:5, etc. Je 22:15, 17.
leave. Heb. give. Je 40:11.
22 hath man. Ec 1:3. 3:9. 5:10, 11, 17. 6:7, 8.
8:15. Pr 16:26. 1 T 6:8.
and of the. Ec 4:6, 8. Ps 127:2. Mt 6:11, 25,
34. 16:26. Lk 12:22, 29. Ph 4:6. 1 P 5:7.
23 all. Ec 1:18. Ge 47:9. Jb 5:7. 14:1. Ps 90:7-10,
+15. 127:2.
travail. Ec 1:13. 3:10.
his heart. Ec 5:12. Est 6:1. Jb 7:2, 3, 13, 14.
Ps 4:8. 6:6, 7. 32:4. 77:2-4. Je 31:26. Da 6:18.
Ac +14:22.
24 nothing. ver. 10. Ec +3:22. Dt +12:7. Ac
14:17. 1 T 6:8, 17.
make his soul. Heb. *nephesh*, Ge +34:3.
enjoy good. *or*, delight his senses. Ps +128:1,
2. Is 9:3. Jon 4:6.
his labor. Lk 10:7.
that it. Ec 3:13. 5:19. 6:2. Dt 8:18. Pr 10:22.
Ml 2:2. Lk 12:19, 20.
25 who can. ver. 1-12. 1 K 4:21-24.
26 in his sight. Heb. before him. Ge 7:1. Lk 1:6.
Ac 11:24, 25.
wisdom. 2 Ch 31:20, 21. Pr 3:13-18. Is 3:10,
11. Jn 16:24. Ro 14:17, 18. 1 C 1:30, 31. Ga
5:22, 23. Col 1:9-12. 3:16, 17. He 13:21. Ja
1:5. 3:17.
to the sinner. Jb 27:16, 17. Pr 13:22. 28:8.
may give. Jb 27:16, 17. Ps 39:6. Is 65:13, 14.
spirit. Heb. *ruach*, Ge +41:8.

ECCLESIASTES 3

1 every thing. ver. 17. Ec 7:14. 8:5, 6. 2 K
5:26. 2 Ch 33:12. Pr 15:23. Mt 16:3.
season. Ezr 10:14. Ne 2:6. Est 9:27, 31. Je
+8:7.
time. Jn +2:4.
under. Ec 1:13. 2:3, 17.
2 time to be born. Heb. time to bear. Ge
17:17, 21. 18:14. 21:1, 2. 1 S 2:5. 1 K 13:2. 2
K 4:16. Jb 7:1. Ps +113:9. Is 54:1. Lk 1:13, 20,
36. Jn 16:21. Ac 7:17, 20. Ga 4:4.
and a time to die. Ec +7:17. Ge 5:5. 47:29.
Ex 1:6. Nu 20:24-28. 27:12-14. Dt 3:23-26.
34:5. Jb 7:1. 14:5, 14. Ps 31:5, 15. Is 38:1, 5,
+10. Jn 7:30. He +9:27.
a time to plant. Je 1:10. +11:17. Am 9:15.
Mt 13:28, 29, 41. 15:13.
to pluck up. Ps 52:5. Je 18:7, 9.
3 time to kill. Ge 9:5, 6. Dt 32:29. 1 S 2:6, 25.
1 K 2:23, 24, 28, 29, 34, 36, 37, 46. Ps 78:31,

34. Je 12:3. Ho 6:1, 2. Ro 13:4.

a time to heal. Nu 21:6-9. Ps 107:20. 147:3. Is 38:5, 21. 57:18. Je 33:6. Lk 9:54-56. Ac 5:15, 16.

a time to break. Is 5:5, 6. 44:26. Je 31:28. 39:2, 8. 45:4. Ezk 13:14. 33:21. Da 9:25-27. Zc 1:12-17. Ml 1:4.

build up. Ne 2:17, 18, 20. Ps 102:13-16. Is 45:13. 58:12. 60:10. Da 9:25. Am 9:11.

4 **time to weep.** Ge 23:2. 43:30. 2 S 12:21. Ne 8:9-12. 9:1, etc. Ps 30:5. 126:1, 2, 5, 6. Is 22:12, 13. Je 22:10. Jl 2:17. Mt 9:15. 11:17. Lk 6:25. Jn 16:20-22. Ro 12:15. 2 C 7:10. Ja 4:9.

a time to laugh. Ec 2:1, 2. Ge 21:6. Ne 8:9. Ps 2:4. 37:13. Lk 1:13, 14, 58. 6:21-25.

to mourn. Ge 23:2. 1 S 16:1. Pr 29:2. Is 38:14. 61:2. Jl 1:9. Zc 12:10, 12. Mt +5:4. 9:15.

to dance. Ex +15:20.

5 **to cast.** Le 14:40, 45. Jg 20:16. Jsh 4:3-9. 10:27. 2 S 18:17, 18. 1 K 15:22. 3:25. Is 5:2. La 4:1.

gather stones. Ec 2:4. Ge 31:45, 46, 51, 52. Dt 27:4, 5. Jsh 4:3, 8, 20. 1 S 17:40. 1 K 18:31, 32. Ps 102:14. Is 54:11.

a time to embrace. Ec 2:3. Ge 29:13. 33:4. 48:10. Ex 19:15. 1 S 21:4, 5. 2 K 4:16. SS 2:6, 7. Jl 2:16. Zc 7:3. 1 C 7:5. He 13:4. 1 P 3:7.

refrain from. Heb. be far from. Ex 19:15. Pr 5:20. Jl 2:16. 1 C 7:5.

6 **time to get.** *or,* time to seek. or, to buy, or acquire. Ec 2:8. Ge 30:30, etc. 31:18. 42:2, 7, 10. Ex 12:35, 36. Dt 8:17, 18. Ru 4:5. 2 S 24:21. 2 K 5:26. 8:9. Pr 23:23. Is 55:1. Je 32:7. Ep 4:28.

and a time to lose. Ge 31:39. Is 47:9. Mt 10:39. 16:25, 26. 19:29. Mk 8:35-37. 10:28-30. Lk 9:24, 25.

to keep. 1 S 16:11. Pr 7:1. Lk 8:15. +11:28. Jn 2:10. 12:7. 2 T 1:14.

and a time to cast. Ec 11:1. Jg 15:17. 2 K 7:15. Ps 112:9. Is 2:20. 31:7. Ho 9:17. Jon 1:5. Ac 27:19, 38. Ph 3:7, 8. He 10:34, 35.

7 **time to rend.** Ge 37:29, 34. 1 S 15:27, 28. 2 S 1:11. 3:31. 1 K 11:11, 31. 13:3, 5. 14:8. 21:27. 2 K 5:7. 6:30. Je 36:24. Jl 2:13. Jn 19:24. Ac 9:39.

to sew. Ezr 4:12mg. Ezk 37:17, 22.

time to keep silence. Le 10:3. Dt +3:26. Jb 2:13. Ps 32:3. +38:13, 14. 50:16. Pr +12:23. 17:27, 28. 26:4, 5. Je 8:14. La 3:28. Am 8:3. Mi 7:5. Mt +7:6. Mk 1:25, 34. 3:12. Lk 1:19, 20, 22. 4:41. 1 T 2:11, 12. 1 P 2:15.

and a time to speak. Ge 44:18-34. Ex 7:2. Le +19:17. Nu 22:8. Jg +11:35. 1 S 19:4, 5. 25:24, etc. 2 S 7:17. Est 4:13, 14. 7:4. Jb 32:4, etc. Ps 2:5. 107:2. 145:6, 11, 21. Pr 24:11, 12. 25:11. 31:8, 9. Ezk 2:7. 3:18. Lk 19:37-40. Jn 16:13. Ac 4:20.

8 **time to love.** Je 2:2. Ezk 16:8. Da 1:9. Ga 5:13. Ep 3:19. 5:25, 28, 29. 2 Th 1:3. T 2:4.

a time to hate. 2 S 13:15. 2 Ch 19:2. Ps 105:25. 139:21. Pr 11:15. 15:27. 25:17. 28:16. Lk 14:26. Jn 12:25. Ju 23. Re 2:2.

a time of war. Ge 14:14-17. Ex 17:16. Nu 1:3, 20, 22. Dt 3:18. Jsh 8:1, etc. 11:23. Jg 3:2. 2 S 3:1. 10:6, etc. 1 K 5:4. 1 Ch +5:22. +20:1. 2 Ch 20:1, etc., 30. Jb 38:23. Je 6:4. Lk 14:31. Re 12:7. 19:11, 19.

of peace. Le 26:6. Jsh 11:23. 14:15. Jg 4:17. 1 S 7:14. Ps 72:3. 85:8. Pr +16:7. Is 9:7. Zc 9:10. Ro 5:1. Ep 4:3. He 12:14.

9 **What profit.** Ec 1:3. 2:11, 22, 23. 5:16. Pr 14:23. Mt 16:26.

10 **have seen.** Ec 1:13, 14. 2:26. Ge 3:19. 1 Th 2:9. 2 Th 3:8.

11 **hath made.** Ec 7:29. Ge 1:31. Dt 32:4. Ps 111:2. Mk 7:37.

also. Mt 13:22. Ro 1:19, 20, 28.

world. Heb. *olam,* Le +25:32. Ps 73:12.

so. Jb +11:7.

12 **but.** ver. +22. Dt 28:63. Ps 37:3. Is 64:5. Lk 11:41. Ac 20:35. 1 T 6:18.

13 **should eat.** Ec 2:24. 5:18-20. 6:2. 9:7. Dt 28:30, 31, 47, 48. Jg 6:3-6. Ps 128:2. Is 65:21-23.

14 **whatsoever.** Ps 33:11. 119:90, 91. Is 46:10. Da 4:34, 35. Ac 2:23. 4:28. Ro 11:36. Ep 3:11. T 1:2. Ja 1:17.

it shall be. Is +31:2. Ml +3:6. Ja +1:17.

for ever. Heb. *olam,* Ex +12:24.

nothing. Ps 76:10. Pr 19:21. 21:30. 30:6. Is 10:12-15. Da 8:8. 11:2-4. Jn 19:10, 11, 28-37. Ac 5:39.

God doeth it. Ps 64:9. Is 59:18, 19. Re 15:4.

15 **which hath.** Ec 1:9, 10. 1 C 10:13.

past. Heb. driven away.

16 **I saw.** Ec 4:1. 5:8. 1 K 21:9-21. Ps 58:1, 2. 82:2-5. 94:21, 22. Is 5:7. 59:14. Je 5:5. Mi 2:2. 7:3. Zp 3:3. Mt 26:59. Ac 23:3. Ja 2:6.

17 **said.** Ec 1:16. 2:1.

God. Ps +7:8. 2 Th 1:6-10.

for. ver. 1. Je 29:10, 11. Da 11:40. 12:4, 9, 11-13. Ac 1:7. 1 Th 5:1. 2 P 3:7, 8. Re 11:2, 3, 18. 17:12-17. 20:2, 7-9.

18 **concerning.** Ge 3:17-19. Jb 14:1-4. 15:16. Ps 49:14, 19, 20. 73:18, 19. 90:5-12. He +9:27. 1 P 1:24.

that God, etc. *or,* that they might clear God, and see, etc. Jb 40:8. Ps 51:4. Ro 3:4. 9:23.

and that. Ge 3:19. Jb 14:1. Ps 73:22. 2 P 2:12.

19 **that which.** Ec 2:16. Ps 49:12, 20. 92:6, 7.

one thing. Ps 27:4. Mk 10:21. Lk 10:42. Jn 9:25. Ph 3:13. 2 P 3:8.

as the. 2 S 14:14. Jb 14:10-12. Ps 104:29. Is 2:22.

breath. Heb. *ruach,* Ge +6:17. Ec +12:7. Ge

7:22. Nu 27:16. Jb 27:3, 4. Ps 104:29. +146:4. Re 16:3.

no preeminence. Ge 5:22, +24. 15:15. +25:8. 35:29. 37:35. Nu 20:24. 27:13. Mt +10:28. 22:32. Lk 16:26. Jn 5:24. 8:51. 11:25. 12:25. 1 Th 5:23. 2 T 1:10. He 11:16, 26. Ju 14, 15.

for. Ec 2:20-23. Ps 39:5, 6. 89:47, 48.

20 **go**. ver. 21. Ec 6:6. 9:10. Ge 25:8, 17. Nu 27:13. Jb 7:9. 17:13. 30:24. Ps 49:14.

all are. Ge 3:19. Jb 10:9, 10. 34:15. Ps 104:29. +146:4. Da 12:2.

21 **Who knoweth**. Ec 12:7. Lk 16:22, 23. Jn 14:3. Ac 1:25. 2 C 5:1, 8. Ph 1:23.

spirit. Heb. *ruach*, Nu +16:22. Ec 12:7. Jb +14:22. 32:8. Da 7:15. Mt 22:32. Mk 2:8. Lk 16:22, 23. 23:43, 46. Ac 7:59. 1 C 2:11. 2 C 5:8. Ph 1:23. 2 T +1:10. He 12:23. Re 6:9. 16:3.

of man. Heb. of the sons of man. ver. 18, 19.

goeth upward. Heb. is ascending. Ec 12:7.

spirit. Heb. *ruach*, Nu +16:22.

22 **nothing**. ver. 12. Ec 2:10, 11, 24. 5:18-20. 8:15. 9:7-9. 11:9. Dt +12:7. 26:10, 11. 28:47. Ro 12:11, 12.

who. Ec 6:12. 8:7. 9:12. 10:14. Jb 14:21. Da 12:9, 10, 13. Mt 6:34.

ECCLESIASTES 4

1 **I returned**. Jb 6:29. Ml 3:18.

and considered. Ec 3:16. +5:8. 7:7. Ex 1:13, 14, 16, 22. 2:23, 24. 5:6-19. Dt 28:33, 48. Jg 4:3. 10:7, 8. Ne 5:1-5. Jb 24:7-12. Ps 10:9, 10. Pr 28:3, 15, 16. Is 5:7. 51:23. 59:7, 13-15. Ml +3:5.

the tears. Ps 42:3, 9. 80:5. 102:8, 9. Ml 2:13. Ja +5:4.

they had. Jb 16:4. 19:21, 22. Ps 69:20. 142:4. Pr 19:7. La 1:2, 9. Mt 26:56. 2 T 4:16, 17.

side. Heb. hand. Ex 2:5.

2 **I praised**. Ec 2:17. 9:4-6. Jb 3:17-21. Ph 1:23. Re 14:13.

3 **better**. Ec 6:3-5. Jb 3:10-16. 10:18, 19. Je 20:17, 18. Mt 24:19. Lk 23:29. Ro 8:28. 2 C 4:17.

who. Ec 1:14. 2:17. Ps 55:6-11. Je 9:2, 3.

4 **every**, etc. Heb. all the rightness of work, that this *is* the envy of a man from his neighbor. Ge 4:4-8. 1 S 18:8, 9, 14-16, 29, 30. Ps +37:1. 1 J 3:12.

This is. ver. 16. Ec 1:14. 2:21, 26. 6:9, 11. Ge 37:4, 11.

spirit. Heb. *ruach*, Ge +41:8.

5 **fool**. Pr 6:9-11. 12:27. 13:4. 20:4. 24:33, 34.

eateth. Jb 13:14. Pr 11:17. Is 9:20.

6 **an handful**. Ps 37:16. Pr 15:16, 17. 16:8. 17:1.

spirit. Heb. *ruach*, Ge +41:8.

7 **I returned**. ver. 1. Ps 78:33. Zc 1:6.

8 **one**. ver. 9-12. Ge 2:18. Is 56:3-5.

he hath. Ge 15:2, 3.

no. Is 5:8.

eye satisfied. Ec 1:8. 5:10. Pr 27:20. Hab 2:5-9. 1 J 2:16.

For. Ps 39:5, 6. Is 44:19, 20. Lk 12:20.

soul. Heb. *nephesh*, Ge +27:31.

it is. Ec 1:13. 2:23. Is 55:2. Mt 11:28.

9 **Two**. 1 K 22:4.

are. Ge 2:18. Ex 4:14-16. Nu 11:14. Pr 27:17. Hg 1:14. Mk 6:7. Ac 13:2. 15:39, 40. 1 C 12:18-21.

a good. Ru 2:12. Jn 4:36. 2 J 8.

10 **if**. Ex 32:2-4, 21. Dt 9:19, 20. 1 S 23:16. 2 S 11:27. 12:7, etc. Jb 4:3, 4. Is 35:3, 4. Lk 22:31, 32. Ga 2:11-14. 6:1. 1 Th 4:18. 5:11.

but. Ge 4:8. 2 S 14:6.

11 **if two**. 1 K 1:1, 2.

12 **and a**. 2 S 23:9, 16, 18, 19, 23. Da 3:16, 17. Mt 18:20. Ep 4:3.

13 **is a poor**. Ec 9:15, 16. Ge 37:2. Pr 19:1. 28:6, 15, 16.

will no more be. Heb. knoweth not to be. 1 S +25:17. 1 K 22:8. 2 Ch 16:9, 10. 24:20-22. 25:16.

14 **For out**. Ge 41:14, 33-44. 2 S 7:8. Jb 5:11. Ps 113:7, 8.

also. 1 K 11:43. 12:13-20. 14:26, 27. 2 K 23:31-34. 24:1, 2, 6, 12. 25:7, 27-30. La 4:20. Da 4:31.

15 **child**. 2 S 15:6.

16 **no end**. 2 S 15:12, 13. 1 K 1:5-7, 40. 12:10-16.

they also. Jg 9:19, 20. 2 S 18:7, 8. 19:9.

this. Ec 1:14. 2:11, 17, 26.

spirit. Heb. *ruach*, Ge +41:8.

ECCLESIASTES 5

1 **thy foot**. Ge 28:16, 17. Ex 3:5. Le 10:3. Jsh 5:15. 2 Ch 26:16. Ps 89:7. Is 1:12. 1 C 11:22. He 12:28, 29.

thou goest. Ep 2:18. He 4:16. 7:25. 10:22. 11:6.

ready. Ac 10:33. 17:11. Ja 1:19. 1 P 2:1, 2.

give. Ge 4:3-5. 1 S 13:12, 13. 15:21, 22. Ps 50:8-18. Pr 15:8. 21:27. Is 1:10-15. 66:3. Je 7:21-23. Ho 6:6, 7. Ml 1:10, 11. He 10:26.

for. Am 5:21-23.

2 **not rash**. Ge 18:27, 30, 32. 28:20-22. Nu 30:2-5. Jg 11:30-36. 1 S 14:24-45. 25:10, +17. Ps 77:7-10. Pr 20:25. Mt 20:21, 22. Mk 6:23.

to utter. Jb 37:20.

thing. *or*, word.

for. Is 55:9. Mt +6:9.

let thy. ver. 3, 7. 1 S +23:4. Jb +6:24. Ps +25:5. Pr 10:19. 17:27. Is +58:13. Ml 3:5. Mt 6:7. 23:14. Mk 12:40. Lk +6:12. 18:1. Ja 3:2.

3 **dream**. ver. 7. Ge 20:3, 6. 31:10. Jb 20:8. 33:15. Je 23:25.

multitude. ver. 7. Ec 1:18. 11:1.
business. ver. 14. Ec 1:13. 2:13, 16.
a fool's. Ec 10:12-14. Pr 10:19. 15:2. 18:2.
by. Pr 17:28.

4 **vowest**. Ge 35:1, 3. Nu +30:2. Mt 5:33.
vow. Le +23:38.
for. Ps 147:10, 11. Ml 1:10. He 10:6.

5 **Better**. Dt 23:22. Pr 20:25. Ac 5:4.
vow. Le +23:38.

6 **thy mouth**. ver. 1, 2. Ja 1:26. 3:2.
before. Le 5:4, 5. Ge 48:16. Nu 22:34. Ps
+35:6. Ho 12:4, 5. Ml 2:7. 3:1. Ac 7:30-35. 1
C 11:10. 1 T 5:21. He 1:14.
it was. Le 5:4-6. 27:9, 10.
destroy. Hg 1:9-11. 2:14-17. Mt 10:28. 1 C
3:13-15. 2 J 8.
but fear. Ec +12:13.

7 **in the**. ver. 3. Mt 12:36.
but fear. ver. +6.

8 **thou seest**. Pr 29:12, 24. Ep +5:11.
oppression of the poor. Ec 3:16. 4:1. Le
+19:13. Ps +12:5. Ezk +16:49. Am 2:7. +5:12.
Mt 23:14.
violent. Ps 55:9. 58:2. Ezk 8:17. Hab 1:2, 3,
13.
perverting of judgment. Ec 3:16. Le
+19:15. Dt 24:17. Ps 82:2. Pr 29:27. 31:4, 5.
Mi +6:8. Hab +1:4. Lk +16:10.
and justice. Dt +16:20. Lk +16:10. Ph 4:8.
marvel. Zc 8:6. 1 J 3:13. Re 17:6, 7.
matter. Heb. will, *or* purpose. Is 10:5-7, 12.
46:10, 11. Hab 1:12. Ac 4:27, 28. Ro 11:33.
for. Is 57:15. Lk 1:32, 35, 76.
regardeth. 1 K 21:19, 20. Jb 27:8-23. Ps
+12:5. 58:10, 11. 82:1. 83:18. 140:11, 12. Is
5:7. 59:13-16. Je 22:17-19. Ezk 22:6-14. Am
5:12. 6:2-6, 12. Mi 2:1-3, 9. 3:1-4, 9-12. 6:10-
13. Zc 7:9-13. Ml +3:5. Ja 2:13.
higher than they. 1 Ch 21:15, 16. Ps 95:3.
Pr 8:15, 16. Is 37:36. Mt 13:41, 42. Ac 12:7-
10, 23.

9 **the profit**. Ge 1:29, 30. 3:17-19. Ps 104:14,
15. 115:16. Pr 13:23. 27:23-27. 28:19. Je
40:10-12.
the king. 1 S 8:12-17. 1 K 4:7-23. 1 Ch
27:26-31.

10 **He that**. Ec 4:8. 6:7. Ps 52:1, 7. 62:10. Pr
30:15, 16. Hab 2:5-7. Mt 6:19, 24. Lk 12:15. 1
T 6:9, 10. Ja 5:1-3.
this. Ec 1:17. 2:11, 17, 18, 26. 3:19. 4:4, 8,
16.

11 **they**. Ge 12:16. 13:2, 5-7. 1 K 4:22, 23. 5:13-
16. Ne 5:17, 18. Ps 119:36, 37.
what. Ec 6:9. 11:9. Jsh 7:21-25. Pr 23:5. Je
17:11. *Hab 2:13. 1 J 2:16.*

12 **sleep**. Ps 4:8. 127:2. Pr 3:24. Je 31:26.
abundance. Ps 62:10. Mk +4:19.

13 **a sore**. Ec 4:8. 6:1, 2.
riches kept. Ec 8:9. Ge 13:5-11. 14:16.
19:14, 26, 31, etc. Pr 1:11-13, 19, 32. 11:4,

24, 25. 21:13. 28:27. Is 2:20. 32:6-8. Zp 1:18.
Lk 12:16-21. 16:1-13, 19, 22, 23. 18:22, 23.
19:8. Jn 12:5. Ac +5:2. 1 T +6:9, 10. Ja 2:5-7.
5:1-4.

14 **those**. Ec 2:26. Jb 5:5. 20:15-29. 27:16, 17. Ps
39:6. Pr 23:5. Hg 1:9. 2:16, 17. Mt 6:19, 20.
and he. 1 S 2:6-8, 36. 1 K 14:26. Ps 109:9-12.

15 **came forth**. Jb 1:21. Ps 49:16, 17. Lk 12:20.
1 T 6:7.

16 **a sore**. ver. 13. Ec 2:22, 23.
what. 1 S 12:21. Je 2:8. Mk 8:36.
for. Ec 1:3. Pr 11:29. Is 26:18. Ho 8:7. Jn 6:27.

17 **he eateth**. Ge 3:17. 1 K 17:12. Jb 21:25. Ps
78:33. 102:9. 127:2. Ezk 4:16, 17.
much. 2 K 1:2, 6. 5:27. 2 Ch 16:10-12. 24:24,
25. Ps 90:7-11. Pr 1:27-29. Ac 12:23. 1 C
11:30-32.

18 **it is good and comely**. Heb. there is a good
which is comely, etc. Ec +3:22. 1 T 6:17-19.
the days. Heb. the number of the days. Ec
2:3mg.
it is his. Ec 3:22. Je 52:34.

19 **to whom**. Ec 2:24. 3:13. 6:1, 2. Dt 8:18. 1 K
3:13.
this is. Ec 2:24-26.

20 **For he shall not much remember**. *or,*
Though he give not much, yet he remembereth, etc. Ps 37:16.
because. Dt 28:8-12, 47. Ps 4:6, 7. Is 64:5.
65:13, 14, 21-24. Ro 5:1-5, 11.

ECCLESIASTES 6

1 **an evil**. Ec 5:13.

2 **man**. Ec 5:19. 1 K 3:13. 1 Ch 29:25, 28. 2 Ch
1:11. Da 5:18.
so. Ec 2:4-10. Dt 8:7-10. Jg 18:10. Jb 21:9-15,
17. Ps 17:14. 73:7. Lk 12:19, 20.
soul. Heb. *nephesh*, Ge +27:31.
but. Ec 4:8. Dt 28:33, 43. Ps 39:6. La 5:2. Ho
7:9.
vanity. Ec 4:4, 8. 5:16.

3 **a man**. Ge 33:5. 1 S 2:20, 21. 2 K 10:1. 1 Ch
28:5. 2 Ch 11:21. Est 5:11. Ps 127:4, 5. Pr
17:6.
so. Ec 5:17-19. Ge 47:9.
soul. Heb. *nephesh*, Ge +34:3.
not filled. ver. 6.
and also. 2 K 9:35. Est 7:10. 9:14, 15. Is
14:19, 20. Je 22:19. 36:30.
burial. Heb. *qeburah*, Ge +35:20.
that an. Ec 4:3. Jb 3:16. Ps 58:8. Mt 26:24.

4 **his name**. Ps 109:13.

5 **this**. Jb 3:10-13. 14:1. Ps 58:8. 90:7-9.

6 **though**. Ge 5:5, 23, 24, 27. Is 65:22.
yet. ver. 3. Jb 7:7. Ps 4:6, 7. 34:12. Is +65:20.
Je 17:6.
do. Ec 3:20. 12:7. Jb 1:21. 30:23. He +9:27.

7 **the labor**. Ge 3:17-19. Pr 16:26. Mt 6:25. Jn
6:27. 1 T 6:6-8.

appetite. Heb. soul. *nephesh*, Nu +11:6. ver. 3. Ec 5:10. Is 56:11mg. Lk 12:19.

8 **what hath the wise**. Ec 2:14-16. 5:11. 1 T 6:6, 7.

the poor. Ge 17:1. Ps 101:2. 116:9. Pr 19:1. Lk 1:6. 1 T 6:17.

living. 1 S +10:24.

9 **Better**. Ec 2:24. 3:12, 13. 5:18.

wandering of the desire. Heb. walking of the soul. Heb. *nephesh*, Ex +15:9. Jb 31:7. Pr 30:15, 16. Je 2:20.

this. ver. 2. Ec 1:2, 14. 2:11, 22, 23. 4:4.

spirit. Heb. *ruach*, Ge +41:8.

10 **which**. Ec 1:9-11. 3:15.

and it. Ge 3:9, 17-19. Jb 14:1-4. Ps 39:6. 82:6, 7. 103:15.

neither. Jb 9:3, 4, 32. 33:10, 11, 13. 40:2. Is 45:9, 10. Je 49:19. Ezk 22:14. Ro 9:19, 20. 1 C 10:22.

11 **many things**. Ec 1:6-9, 17, 18. 2:3-11. 3:19. 4:1-4, 8, 16. 5:7. Ps 73:6. Ho 12:1.

12 **who knoweth**. Ec 2:3. 12:13. Ps 4:6. 16:5. 17:15. 47:4. La 3:24-27.

good for. Mi 6:8.

the days of his vain life. Heb. the number of the days of the life of his vanity. Ec 8:13. 9:6. 1 Ch 29:15. Jb 8:9. 14:2. Ps 39:5, 6. 89:47. 90:10-12. 102:11. 109:23. 144:4. Ja 4:14.

for who can. Ec 2:18, 19. 3:22. 8:7. Jb 14:21.

ECCLESIASTES 7

1 **good**. Pr 22:1. SS 2:13.

name. Pr 15:30. 22:1. Is 56:5. Lk 10:20. He 11:2, 39.

precious. Ec 10:1. Ps 133:2. Pr 27:9. SS 1:3. 4:10. Jn 12:3.

the day. Ec 4:2. Jb 3:17. 5:7. Is 57:1, 2. Lk 16:22, 23. 2 C 5:1, 8. Ph 1:21-23. Re 14:13.

2 **better**. Ge 48:1, etc. 49:2, etc. 50:15-17. Jb 1:4, 5. Is 5:11, 12. 22:12-14. Am 6:3-6. Mt +5:4. 14:6, etc. 1 P 4:3, 4.

that. Nu 23:10. Dt 32:29. Ro 6:21, 22. Ph 3:19. He +9:27.

living. Dt 32:46. Is 47:7. Hg 1:5mg. Ml 2:2.

3 **Sorrow**. *or*, Anger. ver. 9. Ec 1:18. 2:23. 2 C 7:10.

better. Ne 8:10. Ps 119:67, 71. Da 9:3. 10:2, 3, 19. Mt +5:4. Ph 4:4.

by. Ro 5:3, 4. 2 C 4:16, 17. He 12:10, 11. Ja 1:2-4.

4 **heart**. Ne 2:2-5. Is 53:3, 4. Mt 8:14-16. Mk 5:38, etc. Lk 7:12, 13. Jn 11:31-35.

the heart. 1 S 25:36. 30:16. 2 S 13:28. 1 K 20:16. Is 21:4. Je 51:39, 57. Da 5:1-4, 30. Ho 7:5. Na 1:10. Mk 6:21, etc.

5 **better**. Ps 141:5. Pr 9:8. 13:18. 15:31, 32. 17:10. 27:6. Re 3:19.

the song. Ps 69:12.

6 **as**. Ec 2:2. Ps 58:9. 118:12. Is 65:13-15. Am 8:10. Lk 6:25. 16:25. 2 P 2:13-17. Ju 12, 13.

crackling. Heb. sound. Ec 5:3, 6. 10:20. 12:4.

the laughter. Pr 29:9.

7 **oppression**. Dt 28:33, 34, 65. Am 3:10. 2 P +3:5.

a gift. Ex 23:8. Dt 16:19. 1 S 8:3. 12:3. Pr 17:23. Is 1:23. 33:15.

8 **Better**. Ps 126:5, 6. Is 10:24, 25, 28-34. Lk 16:25. He 12:11. Ja 5:11. 1 P 1:13.

the patient. Mt +5:5. Lk 21:19. Ro 2:7, 8. He 10:36. Ja 5:8, 10, 11. 1 P 2:20, 21. 5:5, 6.

in spirit. Heb. *ruach*, Ge +41:8. Mt 5:3.

the proud. Ps 31:23. +119:21. Pr 13:10. 28:25. Ro 12:3, 16. Ph +2:3.

in spirit. Heb. *ruach*, Ge +41:8.

9 **hasty**. 1 S 25:21, 22. 2 S 19:43. Est 3:5, 6. Jon 4:9. Ep 4:26, 27. Ja +1:20.

spirit. Heb. *ruach*, Ge +41:8; Ge +26:35.

anger. Ge 4:5, 6, 8. 34:7, 8, 25, 26, 30, 31. 2 S 13:22, 28, 32. Pr 26:23-26. Mk 6:19, 24.

10 **What**. Jg 6:13. Je 44:17-19. Mt 24:38, 39. Ac 17:30. 2 T 3:13.

wisely. Heb. out of wisdom. Ge 6:11, 12. Ps 14:2, 3. Is 50:1. Ro 1:22-32. 3:9-19.

11 **good with an inheritance**. *or*, as good as an inheritance, yea, better too. Ec 9:15-18. 1 K 3:6-9. Lk 16:8, 9. 1 T 6:17-19.

them. Ec 11:7.

12 **wisdom**. Jb 1:10. 22:21-25. Pr 2:7, 11. 8:11. 14:20. 16:16. 18:10, 11. Is 33:6.

a defence. Heb. a shadow. Jg 9:15. Ps 57:1. Is 30:2. 32:2.

money is. Jb 22:25.

the excellency. Dt 30:19, 20. 32:47. Pr 3:18. 8:35. 9:11. 11:4. Jn 12:50. 17:3. Ph 3:8. 2 T 3:15.

13 **Consider**. Dt 8:2, 5. Jb 37:14. Ps 8:3. 107:43. Is 5:12. Ro 8:28.

who. Ec 1:15. Jb 9:12. 11:10. 12:14. 34:29. Is 14:27. 43:13. 46:10, 11. Da 4:35. Ro 9:15, 19. Ep +1:11.

14 **the day**. Ec 3:4. Dt 28:47, 48. Ps 30:11, 12. 40:3. 73:25. Mt 9:13. Jn 16:22, 23, 33. Ja 5:13.

but. Dt 8:3. 1 K 8:47. 17:17, 18. 2 Ch 33:12, 13. Jb 10:1, 2. Ps 94:12, 13. 119:71. Is 22:12-14. 26:11. 42:25. Je 23:20. Mi 6:9. Hg 1:5-7. Lk 15:17, 18. Ac 14:22.

set. Heb. made. 2 Ch 2:18.

to the. Ec 12:8, 13. Ho 2:6, 7.

15 **have I**. Ec 2:23. 5:16, 17. 6:12. Ge 47:9. Ps 39:6. Jn 13:7.

there is a just. Ec 3:16. 8:14. 9:1, 2. 1 S 22:18, 19. 1 K 21:13. 2 Ch 24:21, 22. Jb 9:22, 23. Is 57:1. Mt 23:34, 35. Lk 16:25. Jn 16:2. Ac 7:52, 59.

there is a wicked. Ec 8:12, 13. Jb 21:7-15. Ps 73:3-13. 92:7. Is 65:20. Je 12:1, 2.

16 **Be not**. Pr 25:16. Mt +5:48. 6:1-7. 9:14. 15:2.

23:5, 23, 24, 29. Lk 18:12. Ro 10:2. Ph 3:6,
12. 1 T 4:3.

neither. Ec 12:12. Ge 3:6. Jb 11:12. 28:28. Pr
23:4. Ro 11:25. 12:3. 1 C 3:18, 20. Col 2:18,
23. Ja 3:13-17.

destroy thyself. Heb. be desolate. Mt 23:38.
Re 18:19.

17 **not**. Je 2:33, 34. Ezk 8:17. 16:20. Ja 1:21.
why. Ge 38:7-10. 1 S 25:38. Ac 5:5, 10.
12:23.
before thy time. Heb. not in thy time.
Ps +102:24. Mt 8:29. Jn 7:8, 30. 1 C 11:30,
32.

18 **good**. Ec 11:6. Pr 4:25-27. 8:20. Lk 11:42.
for. Pr +3:7. Je 32:40.

19 **strengtheneth the wise**. Ec 9:15-18. 2 S
20:16-22. Pr 21:22. 24:5. Col 1:9-11.

20 **there**. Pr +20:9. Ro 3:23.
doeth. Is 64:6.

21 **take no heed**. Heb. give not thine heart. 2 S
19:19. Pr 19:11. 20:3.
unto. 2 S 16:10. Is 29:21. 1 C 13:5-7.

22 **also**. 1 K 2:44. Mt 15:19. 18:32-35. Jn 8:7-9.
Ja 3:9.

23 **I said**. Ge 3:5. 1 K 3:11, 12. 11:1-8. Ro 1:22.
1 C 1:20.

24 **which is far off**. Dt 30:11-14. Jb +11:7.
28:12-23, 28. Ps 36:6. Is 55:8, 9. 1 T 6:16.
deep. Dt 29:29.

25 **I applied mine heart**. Heb. I and my heart
compassed. Ec 1:13-17. 2:1-3, 12, 20.
the reason. ver. 27mg. Ec 2:15. 3:16, 17. 9:1,
2. Je 12:1, 2. 2 P 2:3-9. 3:3-9.
know. Ec 9:3. 10:13. Ge 34:7. Jsh 7:13. 2 S
13:12. Pr 17:12. 26:11.

26 **I find**. Jg 16:18-21. Pr 2:18, 19. 5:3-5. 7:21-
27. 9:18. 22:14. 23:27, 28.
whoso pleaseth God. Heb. he that is good
before God. Ec 2:26.

27 **saith**. Ec 1:1, 2. 12:8-10.
**counting one by one, to find out the
account**. or, weighing one thing after
another, to find out the reason. ver. 25.

28 **yet**. ver. 23, 24. Is 26:9.
one. Jb 33:23. Ps 12:1.
soul. Heb. nephesh, Ge +34:3.
one man. 1 K 19:14, 18.
but. 1 K 11:1-3.

29 **God**. Ge +1:26, 27. 3:6. 5:1.
they. Ge 3:6, 7. 6:5, 6, 11, 12. 11:4-6. Ps
99:8. 106:29, 39. Je 2:12, 13. 4:22. Ezk 22:6-
13. Mk 7:8, 9. Ac 7:40-43. Ro 1:21-32. 3:9-
19. Ep 2:2, 3. T 3:3.

ECCLESIASTES 8

1 **as the**. Ec 2:13, 14. 1 C 2:13-16.
who knoweth. Ge 40:8. 41:15, 16, 38, 39.
Jb 33:23. Pr 1:6. Is +8:20. Da 2:28-30, 47.
4:18, 19. Mk +12:24. Jn +5:39. Ac 8:30, 31.

17:11. 1 T 4:16. 2 T 2:15. 2 P +1:20. 1 J 2:20,
27.

a man's. Ex 34:29, 30. Pr 4:8, 9. 17:24. 24:5.
Mt 17:2. Ac 6:15. Ja 3:17.

face. Nu +6:26.

and the. Dt 28:50. Ac 4:13, 29. Ep 6:19.

boldness. Heb. strength. 2 T 4:17.

2 **I counsel**. Ec 12:13. Pr 24:21. Ro 13:1-4. T
3:1. 1 P 2:13-17.
in regard. 1 K 2:43. 1 Ch 29:24. Ezk 17:13-
20. Ro 13:5.

3 **not hasty**. Ec 10:4. Pr 14:29.
stand. 1 K 1:50-52. 2:21-24. Ps 68:21. Is
48:4. Je 44:16, 17. Ac 5:8, 9.
for. Pr 16:14, 15. 30:31. Da 4:35. 5:19.

4 **Where**. Ge 1:3. Mk +4:39. Jn 2:5. 1 C 4:20.
the word. 1 K 2:25, 29-34, 46. Pr 19:12.
20:2. 30:31. Da 3:15. Lk 12:4, 5. Ro 13:1-4. 1
T +2:1, 2.
What. Jb 33:12, 13. 34:18, 19. Da 4:35. Ro
9:20.

5 **keepeth**. ver. 2. Ex 1:17, 20, 21. Ps 119:6. Ho
5:11. Lk 20:25. Ac 4:19. 5:29. Ro 13:5-7. 1 P
3:13, 14.
feel. Heb. know. Jb 20:20mg. Pr 23:35mg.
a wise. Ec 2:14. 10:2. 1 Ch +12:32. Pr 17:24.
Lk 12:56, 57. 1 C 2:14, 15. 2 C 6:2. Ep 5:15-
17. Ph 1:9, 10. Col 1:9. He 5:14.

6 **to every**. Ec 3:1, 11, 17. 7:13, 14.
therefore. Ec 11:9, 10. 12:1. Is 3:11-14.
22:12-14. Lk 13:25. 17:26-30. 19:41-44. He
3:7-11.

7 **he knoweth**. Ec 6:12. 9:12. 10:14. Pr 24:21,
22. 29:1. Mt 24:44, 50. 25:6-13. 1 Th 5:1-3.
when. or, how.

8 **is no**. Ec 3:21. 2 S 14:14. Jb 14:5. 34:14. Ps
49:6-9. 89:48. He +9:27.
power. 1 C 15:43. 2 C 13:4.
spirit. Heb. ruach, Nu +16:22. Ec 11:5. Pr
30:4.
to retain. Ps 31:15. Lk 12:20.
the spirit. Heb. ruach, Nu +16:22.
neither hath. Ec 3:19. 9:2.
discharge. or, casting off weapons. Dt 20:1-8.
2 K 7:15.
neither. Ps 9:17. 52:5-7. 73:18, etc. Pr 14:32.
Is 28:15, 18.

9 **this**. Ec 1:14. 3:10, 16. 4:7, 8. 7:25.
there is. Ec 5:8, 13. Ex 14:5-9, 28. Dt 2:30. 2
K 14:10-12. 25:7.

10 **so**. 2 K 9:34, 35. Jb 21:18, 32, 33. Lk 16:22.
the place. Ps 122:1-5. Ac 6:13.
they were. Ec 2:16. 9:5. Ps 31:12. Pr 10:7. Je
17:13. He 10:38.

11 **Because**. Ps +9:10.
sentence. Ex 8:15, 32. Jb 21:11-15. Ps 10:6.
50:21, 22. Is 5:18, 19. 26:10. 57:11. Je 48:11.
Mt 24:49, 50. Ro 2:4, 5. 2 P 3:3-10.
fully. Je 42:15.

12 **a sinner**. Ec 5:16. 7:15. 1 K 2:5-9. 21:25.

22:34, 35. Pr 13:21. Is 65:20. Ro 2:5. 9:22. 2 P 2:9.

surely. Ps 37:11, 18-20. Pr 1:32, 33. +3:7. Is 3:10, 11. 65:13, 14, 20-24. Mt +10:28. 25:33, 34, 41-46.

fear before. Ec 3:14. 1 Ch 16:30. Ps 96:9.

13 **it shall**. Jb 18:5. 20:5. 21:30. Ps 11:5. Is 57:21. Ml 3:15, 17, 18. Mt 13:49, 50. Jn 5:29.

neither. Ps 55:23. Is 30:13. 2 P 2:3.

as a. Ec 6:12. Jb 7:6, 7. 14:2. Ps 39:5. 144:4. Ja 4:14.

14 **a vanity**. Ec 4:4, 8. 9:3. 10:5.

there be just. Ec 2:14. 7:15. 9:1-3. Jb 9:22-24. 21:17, etc. 24:21-25. Ps 73:13, 14. Ml 3:15. Ro 8:28. 1 C 15:19.

15 **Then I**. Ec +3:22. 1 T 4:3-5. 6:17.

16 **When I**. ver. 9. Ec 7:25.

there is that. Ec 2:23. 4:8. 5:12. Ge 31:40. Ps 127:2.

17 **that a man**. Jb +11:7.

ECCLESIASTES 9

1 **considered in my heart**. Heb. gave, *or* set to my heart. Ec 1:17. 7:25. 8:16. 12:9, 10.

to declare. Mt +5:45. Lk +6:35. 13:2, 3. Jn 9:3.

that the. Ec 8:14. Dt 33:3. 1 S 2:9. 2 S 15:25, 26. Jb 5:8. Ps 10:14. 31:5. 37:5, 6. Pr 16:3. Is 26:12. 49:1-4. Je 1:18, 19. 9:23, 24. Jn 10:27-30. 1 C 3:5-15. 2 T 1:12. 1 P 1:5.

no man. Ec 7:15. Ps 73:3, 11-13. Ml 3:15-18.

2 **alike**. Ec 2:14-16. Jb 9:22. 21:7-9, 12-15, 17, 18. Ps 73:2, 3, 12, 13. Ezk 21:3. Ml 3:14, 15. Mt +5:45. He 13:15, 16.

as is. Ec 2:26. 7:18. 8:12-14.

feareth. Ge 24:3, 8, 9. Jsh 2:17-20. 1 S 14:26. Ezk 17:18, 19. Zc 5:3, 4. Ml +3:5, 18.

3 **also**. Ec 8:11. Ge 6:5. 8:21. 1 K +8:18. Jb 15:16. Ps 51:5. Pr 20:9. Je 17:9. Mt 15:19, 20. Mk 7:21-23. Jn 3:19. Ro 1:29-31. 6:21. 8:7, 8. 1 C 2:14. Ep 4:17-19. 5:8. T 1:15. 3:3.

and madness. Ec 1:17. 7:25. Lk 6:11. 15:17. Ac 26:11, 24. 2 P 2:16.

after. Ec 12:7. Pr 14:32. Ac 12:23.

4 **to him**. Jb 14:7-12. 27:8. Is 38:18. La 3:21, 22. Lk 16:26-29.

hope. Ec 8:8.

living dog. Is 38:19. Mt 15:27. Ph 3:2.

dead lion. 2 Ch 35:24. Pr 30:30.

5 **the living**. Ec 7:2. Ge 3:19. 47:30. Jb 30:23. Ro 5:12. He +9:27.

the dead. Jb 14:21. Ps 6:5. 88:10, 11. Is 63:16.

know not. ver. +10. Dt +18:10, 11. 1 S 20:39. 28:7-20. 2 S 15:11. Jb 14:21. Ps 31:17. 115:17. 139:7, 8. +146:4. Pr 15:11. Is 14:10, 16. 38:18. 63:16. Mt 8:6. Lk 16:19-31. Jn 11:11. He 11:36, 37. 1 J +4:18.

reward. Ec 2:26. 3:21. 12:7. Jb +14:22. Ps

6:5. +13:3. 62:12. 91:8. Mt 16:27. 25:41.

for the. Ec 2:16. 8:10. Jb 7:8-10. Ps 31:12. 88:5, 12. 109:15. Is 26:14.

forgotten. Ec 6:4. 8:10. Dt 32:26. Jb 18:17. Ps +9:5. 34:16. 109:15.

6 **their love**. Ex 1:8. Jb 3:17, 18. Ps 146:3, +4. Pr 10:28. Mt 2:20.

neither have they. Ec 2:18-23. 6:12. 8:8.

portion. ver. 9. Ec 2:10, 21. 3:22. Ps 17:14. Lk 16:25. 1 P 1:3, 4.

for ever. Heb. *olam*, Ex +12:24.

7 **Go**. Ge 12:19. Mk 7:29. Jn 4:50.

eat. Ec +3:22. 10:19. Dt +12:7. 1 Ch 16:1-3. 29:21-23.

for. Ge 4:4, 5. Ex 24:8-11. Lk 11:41. Ac 10:35. Ro 5:1, 2. 1 T 6:17. 1 P 2:5.

8 **thy garments**. 2 S 19:24. Est 8:15. Re 3:4, 5. 7:9, 13, 14. 16:15. 19:8, 14.

let thy head. Lk +7:46.

9 **Live joyfully**. Heb. See, or Enjoy life. Ec 1:10. 2:1. 7:13.

with the wife. Pr 5:18, 19. 18:22. 19:14. Ml 2:15.

all the days of the life. Ec 6:12. Ps 39:5. 144:4.

given thee. Mt 19:6. Ep 6:4.

for. Ec 2:10, 24. 3:13, 22. 5:18.

10 **thy hand findeth**. Nu 13:30. Jg 9:33mg. 1 Ch 22:19. 28:20. 29:2, 3. 2 Ch 31:20, 21. Ezr 6:14, 15. Ne 2:12-20. 3:1, etc. 4:2, 6, 9-13, 17-23. 13:8-31. Ps 71:15-18. Pr 10:29. +22:29. Is 40:29-31. Je 29:13. Mt 6:33. Jn 4:34. Ac 9:6. Ro 12:11. 15:18-20. 1 C 9:24, 26. 15:10. 16:10. Ep 5:16. Col 3:23. 2 P 1:12-15.

do it with. Ec 11:6. 2 Ch 31:21. Ph 2:12. Col 3:23. 1 Th +4:11.

for. ver. 5, 6. Ec +11:3. Jb 14:7-12. Ps 6:5. 88:10-12. Is 38:18, 19. Ho 13:9. Jn 9:4. Ac 20:25-31.

no work. Ps +146:4. Jn 9:4.

nor knowledge. Ec 1:16, 18. 2:21, 26. Is 38:18.

nor wisdom. ver. 13, 15, 16, 18. Ec 1:13. Ps +146:4.

grave. Heb. *sheol*, Ge +37:35. 42:38. 44:29. Nu 16:33. 1 K 2:6. Jb 30:23. Is 5:14. 14:10, 16. Lk 16:31.

whither. Jb 30:23. Ps 115:17.

11 **returned**. Ec 2:12. 4:1, 4. Ml 3:18.

that the race. 1 S 17:50. 2 S 2:18-23. 17:14, 23. Ps 33:16, 17. 75:6, 7. 147:10, 11. Je 9:23. 46:6. Am 2:14-16. Ro 9:16.

bread. Ge +3:19.

but. Ec 2:14, 15. 3:14, 17. 7:13. 1 S 2:3-10. Jb 5:11-14. 34:29. Pr 21:30, 31. La 3:37, 38. Da 4:35. Ep +1:11.

chance. 1 K 5:4 (occurrent). 22:34. Est 6:1-11. Lk 10:31.

happeneth. Ec 2:14, 15. Nu 11:23.

12 man. Ec 8:5-7, 11. Lk 19:42-44. 2 C 6:2. 1 P 2:12.
as the fishes. Pr 7:22, 23. Hab 1:14-17. 2 T 2:26.
as birds. Mt 10:29, 30.
the sons. Ps +4:2.
snared. Jb 18:8-10. Pr 29:6. Lk +21:35.
it falleth suddenly. 1 S 20:3. Ps 102:23, 24. Pr 6:15. Is 30:13. Mt +25:13. Lk 12:20, 39. 17:26-31.
13 This wisdom. ver. 11. Ec 6:1. 7:15. 8:16.
14 There was. 2 S 20:15-22. 2 K 6:24-33. 7:1, etc.
15 delivered. Pr 11:11.
yet. Ge 40:23. Est 6:2, 3.
16 Wisdom. ver. 18. Ec 7:19. Pr 21:22. 24:5. 1 C 12:31.
the poor. Pr 10:15. Mk 6:2, 3. Jn 7:47-49. 9:24-34. 1 C 1:26-29. Ja 2:2-6.
not heard. 1 C 2:8.
17 of wise. Ge 41:33-40. 1 S 7:3-6. Pr 28:23. Is 42:2, 4. Ja 1:20. 3:17, 18.
18 better. ver. 16.
sinner. Jsh 7:1, 5, 11, 12. 22:20. 1 S 14:28, 29, 36-46. 2 S 20:1, 2. 1 C 5:6. Ga 5:9. 2 Th 2:8-12. 2 T 2:16-18. 3:8. 4:3, 4. T 1:10, 11. He 12:15, 16. 3 J 10.

ECCLESIASTES 10

1 Dead flies. Heb. Flies of death.
the ointment. Ex 30:34, 35.
a little. 2 Ch 19:2. Ne 6:13. 13:26. Mt 5:13-16. Ga 2:12-14.
2 wise. Ec +9:10. Pr 14:8. Lk 14:28-32.
right hand. Ge +48:13.
but. ver. 10, 14. Pr 17:16. Lk 12:18-20.
left. Ge +48:13. Jg +20:16.
3 wisdom. Heb. heart. Jb +12:3.
and he. Ec 5:3. Pr 13:16. 17:28. 18:2, 6. 1 P 4:4.
4 spirit. Heb. *ruach*, Ge +41:8.
leave. Ec 8:3.
for. 1 S 25:23, 24, 32, 33. Pr 25:15.
5 an evil. Ec 4:7. 5:13. 6:1. 9:3.
as an. Ec 3:16. 4:1.
from. Heb. from before.
6 Folly. Jg 9:14-20. 1 K 12:13, 14. Est 3:1. Ps 12:8. Pr 28:12, 28.
dignity. Heb. heights. Jg 5:18. 2 S 22:17.
the rich. Ja 2:3-5.
7 have seen. Pr 19:10. 30:22.
8 that. Jg 9:5, 53-57. 2 S 17:23. 18:15. Est 7:10. Ps 7:15, 16. 9:15, 16. Pr 26:27. 28:10.
a serpent. Am 5:19. 9:3.
9 stones. Ec 3:5. Ge 2:12. 11:3.
hurt. Ge 45:5. 1 S 20:3. Ne 8:10, 11.
cleaveth. Ps 141:7. Is 63:12.
10 wisdom. ver. 15. Ec 9:15-17. Ge 41:33-39. Ex +18:19-23. 1 K 3:9. 1 Ch +12:32. 2 Ch

23:4-11. Mt 10:16. Ac 6:1-9. 15:2, etc. Ro 16:19. 1 C 14:20. Ep 5:15-17. Col 4:5. Ja 1:5.
11 the serpent. Ps 58:4, 5. Je 8:17.
a babbler. Heb. the master of a tongue. Ps 34:13. 52:2. 64:3. 101:5. 140:11mg. Pr 18:21. Ja 3:6-8.
12 words. Jb 4:3, 4. 16:5. Ps 37:30. 40:9, 10. 71:15-18. Pr 10:13, 20, 21, 31, 32. 12:13, 14, 18. 15:2, 23. 16:21-24. 22:17, 18. 25:11, 12. 31:26. Mt 12:35, 36. Lk 4:22. Ep 4:29. Col 4:6.
wise man's. Pr +1:5.
gracious. Heb. grace. Ec 9:11. Ge 6:8. 18:3. 1 S +25:17. 2 K +5:13. Ep +6:9.
but. 2 S 1:16. 1 K 20:40-42. Ps 64:8. 140:9. Pr 10:8, 10, 14. 18:6-8. 19:5. 26:9. Lk 19:22.
13 beginning. Jg 14:15. 1 S 20:26-33. 22:7, 8, 16-18. 25:10, 11. 2 S 19:41-43. 20:1. 2 K 6:27, 31. Pr 29:9. Mt 2:7, 8, 16. Lk 6:2, 11. 11:38, 53, 54. Jn 12:10. Ac 5:28-33. 6:9-11. 7:54-59. 19:24-28.
talk. Heb. mouth. Dt +21:5mg.
mischievous madness. ver. 5. Ec 1:13. 2:17, 21.
14 fool. Ec 5:3. Pr 10:19. 15:2.
is full of words. Heb. multiplieth words. Jb 34:37. 35:16. Ezk 35:13.
a man. Ec 3:22. 6:12. 8:7. Ja 4:13, 14.
15 labor. ver. 3, 10. Is 44:12-17. 47:12, 13. 55:2. 57:1. Hab 2:6, 13. Mt 11:28-30.
because. Ps 107:4, 7. Is 35:8-10. Je 50:4, 5.
16 when. 2 Ch 13:7. 33:1, etc. 36:2, 5, 9, 11. Is 3:4, 5, 12.
and. Pr 20:1, 2. Is 5:11, 12. 28:7, 8. Ho 7:5-7.
in the. Je 21:12.
17 Blessed. Dt +28:3.
when. ver. 6, 7. Pr 28:2, 3. Je 30:21.
and thy. Pr 31:4, 5.
due season. Mt +24:45. Lk 12:42, 45.
drunkenness. Lk 12:45.
18 slothfulness. Pr 12:24. 14:1. 18:9. 19:15. 20:4. 21:25. 22:13, +29. 23:21. 24:30, 31. 26:13. Mt 25:26. Ro 12:11. 2 Th 3:11. He 6:11, 12. 2 P 1:5-10.
19 feast. Ec 2:1, 2. 7:2-6. Ge +19:3. 43:34. Da 5:1, etc. 1 P 4:3.
and wine. Ec 9:7. 1 S 25:36. 2 S 13:28. Ps 104:15. Is 24:11. Lk 12:19. Ep 5:18, 19.
maketh merry. Heb. maketh glad the life.
but. Ec 7:11, 12. 1 Ch 21:24. 29:2, etc. 2 Ch 24:11-14. Ezr 1:6. 7:15-18. Ne 5:8. Ps 112:9. Is 23:18. Mt 17:27. 19:21. Lk 8:3. 16:9. Ac 2:45. 11:29. Ph 4:15-19. 1 T 6:17-19.
20 Curse. Ex 22:28. Is 8:21. Ac 23:5. 1 P 2:13. 2 P 2:10.
thought. *or*, conscience. Ec 7:21, 22. Lk 19:40. Ro 13:5.
curse not. Pr 11:24-26.
in thy bedchamber. Ex 3:8. 2 S 4:7. 2 K 1:16. 6:11, 12. 11:2. 2 Ch 22:11. Est 2:21-23. Hab 2:11. Lk 10:40. 12:2, 3.

hath wings. Ps 15:3. Pr 1:17mg. Ezk 11:5. 33:20. Lk 12:2, 3. 19:40.

ECCLESIASTES 11

1 **thy bread.** Dt 15:7-11. Pr 11:24, 25. 22:9. Is 32:8.
waters. Heb. face of the waters. Is 32:20.
for. ver. 6. Dt 15:10. Ps 41:1, 2. 126:5, 6. Pr 3:9, 10. 11:18. 19:17. Is 32:8. Mt 10:13, 42. 25:40. Mk 4:8. Lk 6:35. 14:14. +16:9. 2 C 9:6, 8, 9. Ga 6:8-10. He 6:10. Ja 5:7.

2 **a portion.** Ne 8:10. Est 9:19, 22. Ps 112:9. Lk 6:30-35. 1 T 6:18, 19.
seven. Jb 5:19. Ps 119:164. Pr 6:16. Mi 5:5. Mt 18:22. Lk 17:4.
for. Da 4:27. Ac 11:28-30. Ga 6:1. Ep 5:16. He 13:3.

3 **the clouds.** Ge +9:13. 1 K 18:45. Ps 65:9-13. Is 55:10, 11. 1 J 3:17.
if the tree. Ec 7:13. Pr +19:18. 20:4. Mt 3:10. 7:19, 20. Lk 13:7. 16:22-26. Ja 2:15-17. Re 22:11.

4 **that observeth.** Pr 3:27, 28. 20:4. 22:13.
wind. Ge +9:14.
clouds. Ge +9:13.

5 **thou knowest not what.** Jn 3:8.
spirit. Heb. *ruach*, Nu +16:22. Ec 1:6.
nor. Ps 139:14, 15.
even. Jb +11:7. 38:4, etc. ch. 39-41.

6 **morning.** Jb +7:18.
sow. Ec +9:10. Is 55:10. Ho 10:12. Mk 4:26-29. Jn 4:36-38. 2 C 9:6. Ga 6:9. 2 T 4:2.
thou knowest. Ec 9:1. Hg 1:6-11. 2:17-19. Zc 8:11, 12. Ac 11:20, 21. 1 C 3:5-7. 2 C 9:10, 11.
prosper. Heb. be right. **S#3787h.** Ec 10:10 (direct). Est 8:5 (right).

7 **the light.** Jb 33:28, 30. Ps 56:13. Pr 15:30. 29:13.
a pleasant. Ec 7:11. Ps 84:11. Mt +5:45.

8 **if a man.** Ec 6:6. 8:12.
rejoice. Ec 3:12, 13. 5:18-20. 8:15.
yet. Ec 7:14. 12:1-5. Dt 32:29. Jb 10:22. 14:10. 15:23. 18:18. Je 13:16. Jl 2:2. Mt 22:13. Jn 12:35. Ju 18.
All that. Ec 2:1-11, 15, 17, 19, 21-23, 26. 4:8, 16. 5:15, 16. 6:11.

9 **Rejoice.** 1 K 18:27. +22:15. Lk 15:12, 13.
in thy youth. Ec 12:1. 1 K 18:12. La 3:27.
walk. Nu 15:39. 22:32. Dt 29:19, 20. Jb 31:7. Ps 81:12. Je 7:24. 23:17. 44:16, 17. Ac 14:16. Ep 2:2, 3. 1 P 4:3, 4.
in the sight. Ec 2:10. Ge 3:6. 6:2. Nu 15:39, 40. Jsh 7:21. 2 S 11:2-4. Mt 5:28. 1 J 2:15, 16.
know. Ps +7:8. Ac 24:25. 2 P 3:7.

10 **remove.** Ec 12:1. Jb 13:26. Ps 25:7. 2 P 3:11-14.
sorrow. *or*, anger. Ps 90:7-11.

and put. Jb 20:11. 2 C 7:1. 2 T 2:22.
for. Ec 1:2, 14. Ps 39:5. Pr 22:15.

ECCLESIASTES 12

1 **Remember.** Ec 11:10. Ge 39:2, 8, 9, 23. Dt 8:18. 1 S 1:28. 2:18, 26. 3:19-21. 16:7, 12, 13. 17:36, 37. 1 K 3:6-12. 14:13. 18:12. 2 Ch 34:2, 3. Ne 4:14. Ps 22:9, 10. 34:11. 63:6. 71:17, 18. 78:35. 119:55. Pr 8:17. +22:6. Is 26:8. Je 51:50. La 3:27. Da 1:8, 9, 17. Lk 1:15. 2:40-52. 18:16. Ep 6:4. 2 T 3:15.
youth. Je 3:4.
while. Ec 11:8. Jb 17:1. 30:2. Ps 90:10. Ho 7:9.
when. 2 S 19:34, 35.

2 **the sun.** Ec 11:7, 8. Ge 27:1. 48:10. 1 S 3:2. 4:15, 18.
nor. Ps 42:7. 71:20. 77:16-20.
clouds. Ge +9:13.

3 **strong.** 2 S 21:15-17. Ps 90:9, 10. 102:23. Zc 8:4. He 12:12.
and those. ver. 2. Ge 48:10.

4 **all.** 2 S 19:35.

5 **the almond.** Ge 42:38. 44:29, 31. Le 19:32. Jb 15:10. Ps 71:18. Pr 16:31. 20:29. Is 46:4. Je 1:11.
because. Ec +9:10. Jb 17:13. 30:23. Ps 49:10-14. He +9:27.
long. Heb. *olam*, Le +25:32. Ps 143:3.
the mourners. Ge 50:3-10. Mt +9:23.

6 **Or ever.** ver. 1, 2.
silver cord. 2 S 8:2. 17:13. 22:6.
golden bowl. Ec 2:8. Ge 2:11, 12. 13:2, etc. SS 5:11.
broken. Is 42:4.
pitcher. Ge 24:14-18, 20, 43.
fountain. Jb 21:24. Is 35:7. 49:10.
wheel. Ps 83:13. Is 5:28.
cistern. Heb. *bor*, Ge +37:20. 40:15. 41:14.

7 **Then shall.** 1 S 20:3. Ezk 33:11. He +9:27.
dust. Ec +3:20. Ge +2:7. +3:19. 15:15. 18:27. Jb 4:19, 20. 7:21. 20:11. 34:14, 15. Ps 90:3. 104:29. +146:4. Is 25:8. Da 12:2. Jn 6:40. Ro 8:23. Ph 3:21.
the spirit. Heb. *ruach*, Nu +16:22. Ec +3:19, +21. +9:5. Ge +2:7. Nu +27:16. 1 K 17:17, 21, 22. Jb 14:22. 27:3, 4. 33:4. +34:14. Ps 104:29. Pr 20:27. Da 7:15. Zc +12:1. Mk 2:8. Lk 23:46. Ac 7:59. Ro +8:10. 1 C 2:11. 5:3, 5. 6:20. 2 C 4:16. 1 Th 5:23. Ja 2:26. Re 11:11.
return unto God. Ge +2:7. Nu 16:22. 27:16. Jb 20:8. Is 57:16. Je 38:16. Ezk +18:4. Zc 12:1. Lk 16:22-25. 20:37, 38. 23:43. 1 C 8:4. 2 C 5:6-8. T 2:13.
who gave. Ge +2:7. Jb 27:3mg. Is 42:5. Zc 12:1. He +12:9, 23.

8 **of vanities.** Ec 1:2, 14. 2:17, 26. 4:4. 6:12. 8:8. Ps 62:9.

9 **moreover, because the Preacher was
wise**. *or*, the more wise the Preacher was, etc.
he still. 1 K 8:12, etc. 10:8.
he gave. 1 K 4:32. Pr 1:1. 10:1. 25:1.

10 **Preacher**. Ec 1:1, 12.
sought. Pr 16:21.
acceptable words. Heb. words of delight. Pr
15:23, 26. 16:21-24. 25:11, 12. Is 50:4. Lk
4:22. Jn 7:46. 1 C 2:4. 1 T 1:15.
written. Pr 1:1-6. 8:6-10. 22:17-21. Lk 1:1-4.
Jn 3:11. Col 1:5.
words of truth. Pr +22:21. Da 10:21.
Ja 1:18.

11 **as goads**. Je 23:29. Mt 3:7. Ac 2:37. 2 C 10:4.
He 4:12. 1 P 1:10, 11. 2 P 3:1, 2.
nails. Ex +27:19.
by. or, are the words.
masters. Jn 3:10.
which. or, both of these.
given. Ge 49:24. Ps 23:1. 80:1. Is 40:11. Ezk
34:23. Jn 10:14. He 13:20. 1 P 5:4.

12 **by these**. Lk 16:29-31. Jn 5:39. 20:31. 21:25.
2 P 1:19-21.
study. *or*, reading. **S#3854h**, only here.
weariness. Ec 1:18.

13 **Let us hear the conclusion of the whole
matter**. *or*, The end of the matter, even all
that hath been heard is. Pr +22:12mg.
Fear God. Ec 5:7. Dt +6:2. 2 K 17:35, 36. Ps
33:8. Pr 1:7. +3:7. Is 8:13. Je +5:22. Mt +10:28.
Lk +10:42. He 12:28. 1 P 1:17. 2:17. Re 19:5.
keep. Dt 13:4. Ps 95:6-8. 96:9. 99:5. Mt
+4:10. +5:48. Ac +4:32. Ro 12:1. Col 3:23, 24.
He +10:25. 1 J +2:3. Ju +21.
for. Ec 2:3. 6:12. Dt 10:12, 13.
whole duty. Mi +6:8.

14 **God shall**. Ps +7:8. Lk 12:1, 2. Jn 5:29.
every work. Ec 11:9. Ne +9:6. Ps +62:12.
+102:24. Mt 12:36. Lk 12:2, 3. Ro 2:16. 1 C
3:13. 4:5. 2 T 4:1.
every secret. 1 C 4:5.
whether good. 2 C 5:10.

SONG OF SOLOMON

SONG OF SOLOMON 1

1 **song.** Ps 14, title. Is 5:1.
of songs. Ps 33:1-3. 34:1-3. 51:15. 92:1-3. 104:34. 147:7. Ep 5:19. Col 3:16. Re 5:9. 15:2-4.
Solomon's. 2 S 12:24. 1 K 4:32. 1 Ch 22:7-10. Ne 13:26. Is 9:6, 7. Da 7:13, 14. Mt 3:17. Lk 1:31-33. 11:31. 24:31. Jn 21:7. Re 19:16.
2 **him.** SS 5:16. 8:1. Ge 27:26, 27. 29:11. 45:15. Ps 2:12. Lk 15:20. Ac 21:7. Ep 5:29. 1 P 5:14.
his mouth. 1 S 3:9. Jb 23:12. Ps 119:103. Je 15:16. Mt 4:4. 11:28-30. Mk 10:14. Lk 4:22. Jn 7:37, 46. 8:11. 20:15. 1 P 2:22.
thy love. Heb. thy loves. ver. 4. SS 2:4. 4:10. 7:6, 9, 12. 8:2. Ps 36:7. 63:3-5. Is 25:6. 55:1, 2. Je 31:3. Mt 26:29. Jn 13:1. 15:9. Ro 8:38, 39. 1 J 4:8, 16, 18, 19.
3 **the savor.** SS 3:6. 4:10. 5:5, 13. Ex 30:23-38. Ps 45:7, 8. 133:2. Pr 27:9. Ec 7:1. Is 61:3. Jn 12:3. Ac 4:13. 2 C 2:14-16. Ep 5:2. Ph 4:18. Col 2:9. 1 P 2:7.
thy name. Dt +28:58. 1 S 18:30mg. Ps 8:1. +9:10. 45:17. 89:15, 16. Is 7:14. 9:6, 7. Je 23:5, 6. Mt 1:21-23. Jn 16:23.
ointment. ver. 12. 1 Ch 9:30.
the virgins. ver. 4. SS 6:8. Ge +24:43. Ex 2:8. Ps 45:14. Mt 25:1. 2 C 11:2. Re 14:1-5.
4 **Draw me.** Ps 73:28. Je 30:21. 31:3. Ho 11:4. Jn 6:37, 44. 12:32. 2 C 5:14. Ph 2:12, 13. 1 J 4:19.
we will. Ps 45:14, 15. 119:32, 60. Ph 3:12-14. He 12:1.
the king. SS 2:3-5. 3:4. Ps 45:14, 15. Mt 25:10. Jn 14:2, 3. Ep 2:6. He 6:20.
his chambers. Ps 27:4, 5. 65:4. Re 22:4, 5.
we will be glad. Ps 4:6, 7. 45:15. 98:4-9. 149:2. Is 25:8, 9. 45:25. 61:3, 10. Mi 4:2. Hab 3:17, 18. Zp 3:14-17. Zc 9:9. Lk 2:10. Ph 3:3. 4:4. 1 P 1:8.
remember. ver. 2. Ps 42:4. 48:9. 63:5, 6. 103:1, 2. 104:34. 111:4. Is 63:7. Lk 22:19. 1 C 11:23-26. Re 1:5.
thy love. SS 2:4. 8:6. Ps 63:3. Jn 15:9. Ro 5:5. 1 J 4:9.
the upright love thee. or, they love thee uprightly. ver. 3. SS 8:7. Ps 84:11. Jn 21:15-17. Ro 12:9. Ep 6:24. Ju 21.

5 **black.** ver. 6. Ge 8:21. Le 13:45. Jb 40:4. 42:6. Ps 51:5. Is 1:5, 6. 6:5. 53:2. Je 17:9. Ezk 16:6. Mt 10:25. Lk 5:8. Ro 3:10. 7:14, 18, 21, 23, 24. 1 C 4:10-13. 1 J 3:1. or, dark. SS 5:11. Le 13:31, 37. Zc 6:2, 6.
but comely. ver. 8-10. SS 2:10, 14. 4:1, 7. 6:4-10. Nu +23:21. 2 S 12:13. Ps 51:7. 90:17. 149:4. Is 6:7. 61:10. Ezk 16:14. Mt 9:2. 22:11. Lk 15:22. Ro 7:22. 13:14. 2 C 5:21. 6:9, 10. 12:10. Ep 1:6. 5:26, 27. Ph 3:9. Col 1:28. 2:10. Ja 2:5. Re 7:14. 19:7, 8.
O ye daughters. SS 2:7. 3:5, 10, 11. 5:8, 16. 8:4. Ps 45:9. +48:11. Lk 23:28. Ga 4:26.
as the tents. Ps 120:5.
6 **Look.** Ru 1:19-21. Ob 12, 13. Mt 18:10.
because I. Jb 30:30. Je 8:21. La 4:8. 5:10. Mk 4:6, 17. Ac 14:22.
my mother's. Ps +69:8. Je 12:6. Mi 7:6. Mt 10:22, 25, 35, 36. Lk 12:51-53. Ga 4:29.
were angry. 2 T 3:12.
keeper. SS 8:11, 12. Lk +10:42. 12:35, 36, 38. 2 T 4:2. 2 P 3:14.
not kept. Pr 24:30, 31. 1 C 9:27. 11:28, 31. He 12:15.
7 **O thou.** SS 2:3. 3:1-4. 5:8-10, 16. Ps 18:1. 116:1. Is 5:1. 26:9. Mt 10:37. Jn 21:17. 1 P 1:8. 2:7.
where. Jb 23:3, 4, 8-12. Ps 25:4, 5. 27:11. 43:3. 119:105.
thou feedest. Ge 37:16. Ps 23:1, 2. 80:1. Is +40:11.
rest. Ps 23:2, 3. 73:24, 25. 119:176.
for. 1 S 12:20, 21. Ps 28:1. Jn 6:67-69. 1 J 2:19, 20.
turneth aside. or, is veiled. Ge 38:15. 2 C 3:14-18.
8 **know not.** Ps 25:8, 9. 32:8. Pr 8:17-21. Is 30:21. Jn +5:39. 14:6. 16:13. He 13:22. Ja 1:5. 1 P 3:12.
O thou. ver. 15. SS 2:10. 4:1, 7, 10. 5:9. 6:1, 4-10. 7:1, etc. Ps 16:3. 45:11, 13. Ep 5:27. Re 19:7, 8.
go thy way. Pr 6:22, 23. Lk 1:78, 79. Ep 5:1. 1 P 2:21, 25. 2 P 1:19.
forth by. Pr 8:34. Je 6:16. 1 C 11:1. He 6:12. 11:4, etc. 13:7. Ja 2:21, 25. 5:10. 1 P 3:6.
feed. Jn 21:15. 1 P 5:2.

the shepherd's. Zc 13:7. He 13:20, 21. 1 P 5:4.

9 **O my**. SS 2:2, 10, 13. 4:1, 7. 5:2. 6:4. Jn 15:14, 15.
   to a. 1 K 10:28. 2 Ch 1:14-17. Jb 39:21-25. Is 31:1. Zc 10:3.

10 **thy cheeks**. Ge 24:22, 47. Is 3:18-21. Ezk 16:11-13. 2 P 1:3, 4.
   thy neck. SS 4:9. Ge 41:42. Nu 31:50. Pr 1:9. 1 P 3:4.

11 **We will**. SS 8:9. Ge 1:26. Ps 45:9, 13, 14. 149:4. Is 61:10. Je 2:32. Ep 5:25-27. Ph 3:21.

12 **the king**. SS 7:5. Ps 45:1. Mt 22:11. 25:34. Jn 18:37. Re 19:16.
   sitteth. SS 4:16. Mt 18:20. 22:4. 26:26-28. Lk 12:37. 24:30-32. 1 C 10:16. Re 3:20.
   my. SS 4:13-16. Jn 12:1-3. Ph 4:18. Re 8:3, 4.
   spikenard. 1 Ch 9:30.
   sendeth. Mk 7:24. Jn 12:3.
   smell. ver. 3. SS 4:10. Ex +30:1. Mt 26:7. Jn 12:3.

13 **bundle**. Mt +2:11.
   he shall. SS 2:7. 3:5. 8:3, 4. Ep 3:17.

14 **beloved**. ver. 13. SS 2:3. Mt 12:18. 17:5. 1 P 2:7.
   camphire. or, cypress. SS 4:13, 14.
   En-gedi. Jsh +15:62.

15 **thou art fair**. ver. 8. SS 4:1, 7, 10. 5:12. 7:6. Nu 23:21. Jb 40:4. Ps 45:11. Je 6:2. Ep 1:4, 5. 5:27. Ju 24.
   my love. or, my companion. Ml 2:14.
   thou hast. SS 4:1. 5:12. 2 C 11:2, 3. Ep 1:17, 18.

16 **thou art**. SS 2:3. 5:10-16. Ps 45:2. 90:17. Zc 9:17. 1 C 1:30. Ph 3:8, 9. Re 5:11-13.
   also. SS 3:7. Ps 110:3.

17 **beams**. SS 8:9. 2 Ch 2:8, 9. Ps 92:12. 1 T 3:15, 16. He 11:10. 1 P 2:4, 5.
   our house. Ps 23:6. 92:13. Jn 14:20. 17:21. 1 C 3:9. Ep 2:19, 20, 22. He 3:6. 1 P 2:4-7. Re 21:22.
   cedar. SS 5:15. 8:9. Le 14:4, 49. 1 K 5:8. 6:15-18.
   rafters. or, galleries. SS 7:5. Ezk 41:16. 42:3.

SONG OF SOLOMON 2

1 **the rose**. Ps 85:11. Is 35:1, +2.
   lily. ver. 16. SS 6:3. Is 57:15. Mt 6:28, 29.
   valley. 2 C 8:9. Ep 4:2. Ph 2:7. Ja 1:9-11. 2:5.

2 **lily**. Is 55:13. Ho 14:5. Mt 6:28, 29. 10:16. Ph 2:15, 16. 1 P 2:12.
   among thorns. Nu 33:55. Mt 10:16. 13:3, 7, 24-28. Ph 2:15.
   daughters. Is 32:9, 11.

3 **the apple tree**. SS 8:5. Is 4:2. Ezk 17:23, 24. Jn 15:1-8.
   my beloved. SS 5:9, 10, 16. Ps 45:2. 89:6. Jn 1:14-18. 3:29-31. He 1:1-6. 3:1-6. 7:23-26. 12:2.

among the sons. SS 5:10. Jg 9:8-15. Jn 7:46. Ph 2:11.
   I sat, etc. Heb. I delighted and sat down, etc. Dt 33:3. Jg 9:15, 19, 20. Lk 10:39. 1 P 1:8. 1 J 1:3, 4.
   his shadow. Ps +91:1.
   his fruit. ver. 5. Ge 3:22-24. Ps 63:1. Ezk 47:12. Jn 1:16. 6:55, 57. Re 22:1, 2.
   taste. Heb. palate. Jb +31:30mg. Ps 34:8. Je 15:16.

4 **brought**. SS 1:4. 5:1. Ps 23:5. 40:2. 63:2-5. 65:4. 84:10. Is 25:6. 55:1, 2. Lk 14:17. Jn 14:21-23. Re 3:20. 22:17.
   banqueting house. Heb. house of wine. SS 1:1, 4. 1 Ch 9:33. Est 7:7. Ps 16:11. 36:8. Re 19:9.
   his banner. SS 6:4. Ex 17:15. Jb 1:10. Ps 60:4. Is 11:10. Jn 15:9-15. Ro 5:8-10. 8:28-39. 1 C 15:57.

5 **Stay**. SS 2:3. Ps 4:6, 7. 42:1, 2. 63:1-3, 8. 104:15. Is 26:8, 9. Lk 22:20. 24:32. Jn 6:55, 57. Ph 1:23.
   flagons. 2 S 6:19. Ho 3:1.
   comfort me. Heb. straw me. Ps 55:6. 73:25. Is 40:1. He 4:9. Re 22:3, 4.
   for. SS 5:8. 2 S 13:1, 2. Ps 84:1, 2. 119:130, 131. Is 6:11. Ga 2:20. Re 22:20.

6 **left hand**. SS 8:3-5. Ge 13:9. Is 54:5-10. 62:4, 5. Je 32:41. Zp 3:17. Jn 3:29. Ep 5:25-29.
   under. Dt 33:27. Ps 37:24. 55:22. Is 26:3. 40:11. 41:10. Mt 14:30, 31. 1 P 5:7.
   right hand. Dt 33:12. Ps 31:5. Is 40:29. Jn 10:28-30.

7 **charge you**. Heb. adjure you. Mt 26:63.
   O ye. SS 1:5.
   by the roes. SS 3:5. Pr 5:19.
   ye stir. SS 8:4. Ep 5:22-33.
   till he please. Mt 6:9, 10. 2 Th 3:5. 1 T 6:14-17. Ja 1:4. 5:8. Re 13:10.

8 **voice**. SS 5:2. Jn 3:29. 10:4, 5, 27. Re 3:20.
   behold. Nu 23:9. Is 33:17. Ju 14. Re 1:7.
   he cometh. Mt 25:6. Jn 11:28, 29. 1 Th 5:1, 2. T 2:13. Re 16:15.
   leaping. 2 S 6:16. Is 35:6. Je 48:27. Lk 6:23. Ac 3:8. 14:10.
   the mountains. Is 40:3, 4. 44:23. 49:11-13. 55:12, 13. Lk 3:4-6.

9 **like**. ver. 17. SS 8:14. Ps 70:5.
   behold. Re 22:7, 20.
   he standeth. 1 C 13:12. 2 C 3:13-18. Ep 2:14, 15. Col 2:17. He 9:8, 9. 10:1, 19, 20.
   showing. Heb. flourishing. Lk 24:35. Jn 5:39, 46. 12:41. 1 P 1:10-12. Re 19:10.

10 **spake**. ver. 8. 2 S 23:3. Ps 85:8. Je 31:3.
   Rise. ver. 13. SS 4:7, 8. 5:2. Ge 12:1-3. Ps 45:10, 11. Pr 6:9. Is 52:1, 2. 60:1-5. Mi 2:10. Ml 4:2. Mt 4:19-22. 9:9. Mk 10:49. Lk 22:46. Jn 5:8. 2 C 6:17, 18. 11:2. Ep 5:14. Re 19:7-9. 22:17.

come away. Ex 33:15. Je 29:11. Jn 14:2, 3. He 13:14.

11 **the winter**. Ec 3:4, 11. Is 12:1, 2. 40:2. 54:6-8. 60:1, 2. Mt +5:4. Ep 5:8. Re 11:14, 15.
is past. Is 44:22. Je 50:20. 2 C 5:17. Ep 2:1. 5:8.
rain. Ge 8:13. 9:15. Ps 126:5. Re 7:17. 21:3, 4.

12 **flowers**. SS 6:2, 11. Is 35:1, 2. Ho 14:5-7.
appear. Ps 90:17. 92:12, 13.
time. Ps 40:1-3. 89:15. 148:7-13. Is 42:10-12. 55:12. Je +8:7. Mt 16:3. Ep 5:18-20. Col 3:16.
of the turtle. Ro 15:9-13. Ep 1:13, 14.

13 **fig tree**. SS 6:11. 7:8, 11-13. Is 18:5. 55:10, 11. 61:11. Ho 14:6, 8. Hg 2:19. Mt 24:32, 33. Lk 13:6, 7.
vines with. or, the vines (are) blossoms.
smell. SS 4:13, 14. 7:12, 13. Ex 30:8, 34. Ho 14:6, 7. Ph 4:18.
Arise. ver. 10. Pr 8:17. Mt 18:10. 19:14. Lk 19:42. 2 C 5:20. 6:1, 2.
and come. 1 Th 4:17. He 6:10.

14 **my dove**. SS 5:2. 6:9. Ps 68:13. 74:19. Is 60:8. Ezk 7:16. Mt 3:16. 10:16.
that art. Ex 3:6. 4:11-13. Ezr 9:5, 6. Jb 9:16. Is 6:5. Da 9:7. Lk 8:47, 48.
clefts. Ex 33:22, 23. Ps 71:3. Is 2:21. 33:16. Je 49:16. Ob 3.
secret. Dt 13:6. 27:15, 24. Ps 27:5. 91:1. Is 26:20.
stairs. Ezk 38:20.
let me hear. Ec 8:13. Ps 50:14, 15. Pr 15:8. He 4:16. 10:22.
for sweet. Ps 22:3. 50:23. Is 51:3. Re 4:8-10. 5:8. 7:9, 10.
voice. SS 8:13. Ps 29:3. Jn 10:3.
thy countenance. SS 1:5, 8. 6:10. Ps 17:15. 45:11. 110:3. Ep 5:27. Col 1:22. 1 P 3:4. Ju 24.

15 **the foxes**. Ps 80:13. Ezk 13:4-16. Lk 13:32. 2 P 2:1-3. Re 2:2.
the little. Ps 19:12. Pr 4:23. Mt 16:6, 12. 1 C 5:6-8. Ga 5:7. Re 2:4, 7.
that spoil. Pr 17:14. 1 T 6:10, 11. 2 T 2:21-23. He 12:1, 15. 1 J 2:15, 16.
tender. ver. 13. SS 7:12. Mt 12:20. Lk 8:14. Re 3:2, 8.

16 **beloved**. SS 6:3. 7:10, 13. Ps 48:14. 63:1. Pr 8:31. Je 31:33. Jn 4:32, 34. 1 C 3:21-23. 6:20. Ga 2:20. Re 21:2, 3.
I am his. SS 7:10. Nu 18:20. Ps 73:25, 26. Is 9:6. 43:6. 55:4. Ezk 34:23. Ml 4:2. Jn 3:16. 6:37. Ro 14:7, 8. He 10:22.
he. ver. 1. SS 1:7. 6:3. Mt 18:20.

17 **Until**. Ps 42:8. 1 Th 5:2, 4-6. 2 Th 2:3.
the day. SS 4:6. Lk 1:78. Ro 13:12. 2 P 1:19. Re 22:20.
the shadows. 1 C 13:10, 12. Col 2:16, 17. He 8:5. 10:1.
beloved. ver. 9. SS 8:14.

Bether. *or*, division. **S#1335h**. Ge 15:10 (piece). Je 34:18, 19 (parts).

SONG OF SOLOMON 3

1 **night**. Ps +4:4. 6:6. 22:2. 63:6-8. 77:2-4. Is 26:9. Am 6:1. Ro 13:11. Ep 5:14.
him whom. SS 1:7. 5:8. Jn 21:17. 1 P 1:8.
soul. Heb. *nephesh*, Ge +34:3.
I sought. SS 5:6. Jb 23:8, 9. Ps 30:7. 130:1, 2. Is 55:6. Lk 12:37. 13:24. Ro 12:11. 1 P 1:13. 2 P 3:13, 14.

2 **will rise**. SS 5:5. Is 64:7. Jon 1:6. Mt 26:40, 41. Ro 13:11. 1 C 15:34. Ep 5:14.
and go. SS 1:8. Lk 15:18-20.
the streets. Heb. *shuk*, Am 5:16 (alleys). Pr 1:20, 21. +7:8 (**S#7784h**). 8:2, 3, 34. Mk 6:56. Lk 14:21-23.
broad ways. Heb. *rechob*, Am 5:16 (**S#7339h**, streets), public square or broad streets.
seek him. Jb 23:8, 9. Ps 22:2. Is 26:9. Je 29:13. Jn 5:39.
soul. Heb. *nephesh*, Ge +34:3.
loveth. SS 1:4. Jn 21:15-17. Ep 6:24.
I sought. Ps 22:1, 2. 42:7-9. 43:2-5. 77:7-10. Jn 6:68, 69.

3 **watchmen**. SS 5:7. Is 21:6-8, 11, 12. 56:10. 62:6. Je 6:17. Ezk 3:17. 33:2-9. Ml 2:7. He 13:17.
Saw. Jn 12:20-22. 20:15.
soul. Heb. *nephesh*, Ge +34:3.

4 **but**. SS 6:12. Pr 8:17. Is 45:19. 55:6, 7. Je 29:13. La 3:25. Mt 7:7.
found him. Ge 24:27. Ps 145:18. Pr 8:17. Is 45:19. 55:6, 7. Mt 7:7. Jn 20:11-16. Ga 6:9.
soul. Heb. *nephesh*, Ge +34:3.
I held. SS 7:5. Ge 32:26. Pr 4:13. Ho 6:1-3. 12:3, 4. Mt 28:9. Jn 20:16, 17. Re 3:11, 12.
I had. Is 49:14-18. 54:1-3. Ga 4:26.
conceived me. Jn 1:12, 13. 3:5-8. Ja 1:18. 1 P 1:23. 1 J 5:1, 4-7.

5 **charge**. SS +1:5. Mi 4:8.
till he. 2 C 13:14. 1 J 1:3.

6 **this**. SS 8:5. Dt 8:2. Is 43:19. Je 2:2, 3. 31:2. Re 12:6, 14.
that cometh. Ge 24:63. Nu 23:21. Dt 32:12.
like. Ex 13:21, 22. Nu 10:35. Jl 2:29-31. Ac 2:18-21. Col 3:1, 2.
perfumed. Ex 30:1-9, 34-38. 2 C 2:14-16. Ph 4:18. Re 5:8.
myrrh. Mt +2:11.

7 **his bed**. ver. 9mg. SS 1:16.
threescore. 1 S 8:16. 14:52. 28:2. 1 K 9:22. 14:27, 28. 2 K 6:17. He 1:14.
the valiant. 1 K 4:26, 27. 10:26-29. Ps 68:17, 18.

8 **all**. Ps 45:3. 149:5-9. Is 27:3. 2 C 10:4. Ep 6:12, 16-18. 1 P 5:8. 1 J 3:8. Re 19:14.
because. Ne 4:21, 22. Ps +34:4. 1 Th 5:6-8.

9 **a chariot**. *or*, a bed. ver. 7. 2 S 23:5. Re 14:6.
Lebanon. 1 K 5:13-16.
10 **the pillars**. 1 K 7:21. Ps 87:3. 1 T 3:15, 16.
Re 3:12.
the midst. Ro 5:8. Ep 3:18, 19. Re 1:5.
for. Re 21:9-11, 21.
11 **Go**. SS 7:11. He 13:13.
O ye. SS 1:5. 2:7. Ps 9:14. 45:14, 15. 48:11.
daughters. Mt +21:5.
of Zion. Ps 2:6. 76:1, 2. Is 62:1-5.
behold. Is 9:6. Mt 12:42. Ph 2:9-11. He 2:9.
Ju 24. Re 1:7. 19:12, 16.
his mother. SS 8:5. Col 1:18. Re 5:9, 10.
in the day of his. Is 62:5. Je 2:2. Ho 2:19,
20. Jn 3:29. Re 19:7. 22:9, 10.
in the day of the. Is 53:11. Je 32:41. Zp
3:17. Lk 15:6, 7, 23, 24, 32. Jn 15:11. 1 C 2:9.
Re 22:5.

SONG OF SOLOMON 4

1 **thou art fair**. ver. 9, 10. SS 1:15. 2:10, 14. Ps
45:11. Ezk 16:14. 2 C 3:18.
thou hast. SS 5:12. Mt 11:29. Ph 2:3-5.
dove's. SS 1:15. 2:14. 5:2, 12. Mt 5:5. 6:22.
10:16. 11:29. Ph 2:15.
within. ver. 3. SS 6:7.
thy hair. SS 5:11. 6:5, 7. 7:5.
flock. Lk 12:32. Jn 10:16. 1 P 5:2.
appear from. or, eat of, etc.
mount. Ge 31:25. Nu 32:1, 40. Dt 3:12.
2 **teeth**. SS 6:6. Je 15:16. Jn 15:7. Col 1:4-6. 1
Th 2:13. 2 P 1:5-8.
flock. Ps 78:52. 79:13. 95:7.
came up. SS 6:6. Ge 19:15, 28.
washing. SS 6:6. Is 1:18. Zc 13:1. Jn 15:3. 1
C 6:11. T 3:5. He +10:22. Re +1:5. 7:14. Heb.
rachtsah, **S#7367h**: SS 6:6.
bear twins. SS 7:3. Ge 25:24. 38:27.
and none. Ex 23:26. Dt 7:13, 14.
barren. SS 6:6. 2 S 17:8. Ps +113:9. +127:3.
Pr 17:12. Je 18:21. Ho 13:8.
3 **lips**. ver. 11. SS 5:13, 16. 7:9. Ps 37:30. 45:2.
119:13. Pr 10:13, 20, 21. 16:21-24. Mt 12:35.
Lk 4:22. 1 C 1:23. 2 C 5:18-21. Ep 4:29. Col
3:16, 17. 4:6.
scarlet. Le 14:4, 6, 49-52. Nu 4:8. 19:6. Jsh
2:18. Pr 31:26. He 9:19. Re 5:9, 12.
thy temples. SS 6:7. Ge 32:10. Ezr 9:6. Ezk
16:63.
4 **neck**. SS 1:10. 7:4. 2 S 22:51. Ep 4:15, 16.
Col 2:19. 1 P 1:5.
tower. SS 5:13. 7:4. 8:10. Ge 11:4.
Ps 144:12.
an armoury. Ne 3:19.
there hang. Ezk 27:10, 11. Is 22:23, 24.
a thousand. 2 Ch 9:15, 16. 12:9-11.
shields. 2 S 8:7-11. 2 K 11:10. 2 Ch 23:9.
mighty men. 2 S 23:8-39. 2 Ch 11:10, etc.
ch. 12. Lk 11:21, 22. Ro 8:37. Ep 6:10. 1 J 5:4.

5 **two breasts**. SS 1:13. 7:3, 7. 8:1, 10. Pr 5:19.
Is 66:10-12. 1 P 2:2.
feed. SS 2:16. 6:3. Ps 133:1, 2. Ro 12:9, 10. 1
C 1:10. 10:16, 17. Ep 4:3.
6 **Until**. Mt 28:20. He +13:5.
day. SS 2:17. Ml 4:2. Lk 1:78. 2 P 1:19. 1 J
2:8. Re 22:16.
break. Heb. breathe. SS 2:17. Ezk 21:31.
the mountain. Ex 20:24. 30:8, 23-26. 37:29.
Dt 12:5, 6. Ps 66:15. Is 2:2. Ml 1:11. Lk 1:9,
10. Re 5:8.
of myrrh. ver. 14.
7 **all fair**. ver. 1. SS 5:16. 6:10. Nu 24:5. Jb
40:4. Ps 45:11, 13. 90:17. Ep 5:25-27. Col
1:22. 2 P 3:14. Ju 24. Re 21:2.
no spot. Ep 5:27.
8 **with me**. SS 2:13. 7:11. Ps 45:10. Pr 9:6. Lk
9:57. Jn 12:26. Col 3:1, 2. Re 14:4.
from Lebanon. Dt +1:7.
look from. Ge 19:17. Mt 4:8, 9. Lk 22:31. 1 P
5:8.
Amana. i.e. *support, confirmation, faithfulness;
constancy, a settled provision*, **S#549h**. SS 4:8. 2 K
5:12.
Shenir. Dt +3:9. Jsh 12:1. 1 Ch +5:23.
Hermon. Dt +3:8.
from the lion's. Ge 49:9. Nu 23:24. Ps 76:1,
4.
leopards. Is 11:6. Je 5:6.
9 **ravished**. *or*, taken away, etc. Ro 8:35. Ep
3:19.
my sister. ver. 10, 12. SS 5:1, 2. Ge 20:12.
Mt 12:50. 1 C 9:5. He 2:11-14.
my spouse. SS 3:11. Ps 45:9. Is 54:5. 62:5.
Ezk 16:8. Ho 2:19, 20. Jn 3:29. 2 C 11:2. Re
19:7, 8. 21:2, 9, 10.
thou hast. SS 6:12. 7:5, 6, 10. Pr 5:19, 20. Zp
3:17.
with one of. SS 1:15. 6:5.
one chain. SS 1:10.
10 **love**. Heb. loves. SS 1:2mg. Mt 11:19. Ep 2:4-
7. 5:25, 32.
how much. SS 1:2, 4.
the smell. SS 1:3, 12. 3:6. 5:5. Mt 26:6-12.
Lk 7:36-50. 2 C 1:21, 22. Ga 5:22, 23. Ph
4:18. Re 5:8.
ointments. SS +1:3. 1 Ch +9:30.
11 **lips**. ver. 3. SS 5:13. 7:9. Ps 71:14, 15, 23, 24.
Pr 16:24. Ho 14:2. He 13:15.
drop. Dt 32:2. 1 P 3:15, 16.
honey. SS 5:1. Pr 24:13, 14. Is 7:15.
the smell. ver. 10. Ge 27:27. Ps 45:8. Ho
14:7.
thy garments. Ex 22:9, 26. Dt 24:13. 29:5.
Ps 45:13, 14. Is 61:10. Ezk 16:14. Mt 22:11.
Lk 15:22. Ph 3:8, 9. Col 1:12. Ju 24, 25. Re
19:7, 8.
12 **garden**. ver. 15, 16. SS 5:1. 6:2, 11. Ge 2:8-
10. Ps 1:3. 80:8-16. 92:12, 13. 125:2. Pr 5:15-
18. Is 58:11. 61:10, 11. Je 31:12. Ho 6:3. 14:5.

Zc 2:5. Jn 15:19. 17:9. 1 C 6:13, 19, 20. 7:34. Ph 2:15. 1 J 5:19. Re 21:27.

inclosed. Heb. barred. Jg 3:23, 24. 2 S 13:17, 18. Ps 91:1.

fountain. Heb. *mayan*, Ge +7:11 (S#4599h). ver. 15. Ge 8:2. Pr 5:15. Is 27:3.

sealed. Dt 32:34. Ne 9:38. 2 C 1:22. Ep +1:13. 4:30. Re 7:3.

13 are an orchard. SS 6:11. 7:12. 8:2. Ps 92:14. Ec 2:5. Is 60:21. 61:11. Jn 15:1-3. Ph 1:11.

pleasant. ver. 16. SS 2:13. 6:2. 7:13. Ex 30:8, 34. Dt 33:13-16.

fruits. ver. 16. SS 2:3. 8:11, 12. Je 17:7, 8. Mt 7:16, 17. Jn 15:2, 8. Ro 6:22. Ga 6:7, 8. Ep 5:9. Ja 5:7.

camphire. *or*, cypress. ver. 14. SS 1:14mg.

spikenard. SS 1:12. Mk 14:3. Jn 12:3.

14 calamus. Ex 30:23. Ezk 27:19.

cinnamon. Ex 30:23. Pr 7:17. Re 18:13.

trees. 1 K 4:33.

of frankincense. ver. 6. Mt +2:11.

myrrh. ver. 6. Mt +2:11.

aloes. Nu 24:6. Ps 45:8. Pr 7:17.

the chief. 1 C 12:4-6. 15:41.

spices. SS 6:2. Ge 43:11. 1 K 10:10. 2 Ch 9:9. Ps 141:5. Mk 16:1.

15 fountain. Heb. *mayan*, Ge +7:11 (S#4599h). ver. 12. Ps 42:1. 63:1. Ec 2:6. Is 12:3. Re 21:6.

of gardens. ver. 12, 16. SS 5:1. 6:2.

a well. Heb. *be-er*, Ge +16:14. Ge 14:10. 21:19. Ps 36:8, 9. 46:4. Jn 4:10, 14. Re 22:1.

living waters. Ge 26:19. Le 14:5, 6, 51, 52. 15:13. Nu 19:17. Pr 5:15, 16. Is 58:11. Je 2:13. 17:13. Zc 14:8. Jn 4:14. 7:37, 38.

streams. Ge 2:10. Ex 15:8. Ps 78:16. Is 32:2. Je 18:13, 14. Ezk 47:1-10. Jl 3:18. Ja 1:17. Re 22:1.

16 Awake. SS 1:4. Jg 5:12. Ps 7:6. Ec 1:6. Is 51:9-11. 64:1. Ezk 37:9. Jn 3:8. Ac 2:1, 2. 4:31.

north wind. Pr 25:23.

south. Ex 26:18, 35. 27:9. 36:23.

blow. Ge 1:2. Ezk 37:9. Zc 4:6. Jn 3:8. 6:63. 14:26. Ac 9:31. 1 C 12:11.

garden. ver. 12, 15. SS 5:1. 6:2.

the spices. ver. 13, 14. SS 7:12, 13. Ps 45:8. 133:1, 2. 2 C 9:10-15. Ph 1:9-11. Col 1:9-12. 1 Th 2:12, 13. He 13:20, 21. 2 P 3:18.

may flow. Nu 24:7. Dt 32:2.

Let. SS 5:1. 8:12. Mt 25:14-30. 26:10, 12. Jn 15:8. Ro 15:16, 28. 1 P 2:5, 9, 10.

his garden. Lk 13:6-9.

pleasant fruits. ver. 13. SS 7:13. Dt 33:13-16. Ps 23:3. 119:67. Pr 31:11. Is 42:3. Lk 4:18. 2 C 7:11. Ga 5:22, 23. He 12:11.

SONG OF SOLOMON 5

1 come. SS 4:16. 6:2, 11. 8:13. Is 5:1. 33:17. 45:19. 51:3. 58:11. 61:11. 66:14. Hg 2:7. Jn 10:10. 14:21-23. Re 3:11.

my sister. SS 4:9-12. 8:1. Mt 15:28. He 2:12-14.

I have gathered. SS 4:13, 14. Ps 80:12. 147:11. Is 53:11.

myrrh. ver. 5, 13. Mt +2:11.

honey. SS 4:11. Ge 43:11. Ex 3:8. 1 S 14:27.

wine. Pr 9:5.

eat. Dt 16:13-17. 26:10-14. 2 Ch 31:6-10. Ps 16:3. Is 23:18. 55:1, 2. 62:8, 9. 65:13. 66:14. Mt 25:40. Jn 6:53-57. Ac 11:29. 2 C 9:11-15. Ep 5:18. 1 Th 3:8, 9.

O friends. Jg 14:20. Ps 23:5. Lk 12:4. 15:6, 7, 9, 10. Mt 9:15. Jn 3:29. 15:14, 15. Re 19:9.

drink. Mt 5:6. Jn 1:16.

yea, drink abundantly, O beloved. *or*, and be drunken with loves. Pr 7:18. Zc 9:15-17. Ro 14:17. Ph 4:19. 2 P 1:11. Re 22:17.

2 sleep. SS 3:1. 7:9. Da 8:18. Zc 4:1. Mt 25:4, 5. 26:40, 41. Lk 9:32. Ro 13:11. Ep 5:14. 1 Th 5:6. He 6:12. 1 P 1:13.

but. Ro 7:21-23. Ga 5:17. He 12:1.

the voice. SS 2:8, 10. Ps 119:50. Jn 5:28, 29. +10:4, 27.

knocketh. Re 3:20.

Open. Ps 24:7-10. 81:10. Pr 23:26.

my dove. SS 2:14. 6:9. Ps 119:1. Re 3:4. 14:4.

my head. SS 8:7. Ge 29:20. 31:40, 41. Is 50:6. 52:14. 53:3-5. Mt 8:17. 25:35-45. Mk 1:35. Lk 6:12. 22:44. 2 C 5:14, 15. Ga 2:20.

3 have put. Pr 3:28. 13:4. 22:13. Mt 25:5. 26:38-43. Lk 11:7. Ro 7:22, 23.

I have washed. Ge +18:4. Ex +29:4, 17. 30:19, 21. 40:31.

how shall. Ps 123:4. Is 32:9. Is 47:8. 64:7. Am 6:1. Zp 1:12. Mt 22:5. Mt 24:12. Lk 9:59. 14:18-20.

4 put. SS 1:4. Ps 38:2. 44:21. 110:3. Ac 16:14. 2 C 8:1, 2, 16. Ph 2:13.

hole. *or*, network. 1 S 14:11. 2 K 12:9. Ezk 8:7.

my bowels. Ge 15:4. 25:23. Is 26:8, 9. +63:15. Lk 22:61, 62.

were moved. Ps 46:6. Je 51:55. Zc 9:15.

for him. *or*, (as some read,) in me.

5 rose. ver. 2. Ps 119:59. Lk 12:36. Ep 3:17. Ph 1:6. 2:13. Re 3:20.

open. Dt 15:8, 11. Ne 8:5.

my hands. ver. 13. SS 3:6. 4:13, 14. 2 C 7:7, 9-11.

sweet smelling. Heb. passing, *or* running about.

myrrh. Ps 45:8.

6 but my. Ps 30:7. Is 8:17. 12:1. 50:2. 54:6-8. Ho 5:6, 15. Mt 15:22-28. Re 3:19.

withdrawn. Jb 29:2, 3.

my soul. Heb. *nephesh*, Ge +34:3. ver. 2, 4. Ge 42:28. 2 S 16:10. Ps 69:3. 77:3. Is 57:16. Mt 26:75. Mk 14:72. Lk 22:61, 62.

I sought. SS 3:1, 2. 1 S 28:6. Jb 23:3-9. Ps 22:1, 2. 28:1. 80:4. 88:9-14. Is 26:9. 58:2-4, 7-9. La 3:8. Zc 7:13.

not find. Je 2:17.
I called. Ps 143:7.
no answer. Jb 30:20. La 3:8, 44.

7 **watchmen**. SS 3:3. Is 56:10, 11. 62:6. Ezk 3:17. Ho 9:7, 8. Ac 20:29, 30. 2 C 11:13. He 10:25.
they smote. Ps 141:5. Pr 9:8. Ho 6:5. Jn 16:2. Ac 26:9, 10. 2 C 7:10. Ga 2:11. Ph 3:6. 1 T 5:20, 21. T 1:13. 2:15. Ja 5:16. 1 P 1:6, 7. Re 3:19. 17:5, 6.
the keepers. SS 8:11. Is 62:6. Mt 21:33-41. 23:2, 29-36. He 13:17.
took away. Lk 6:22. Ac 5:40, 41. 1 C 4:10-13. He 11:36, 37. 12:2. 1 P 4:14-16. or, lifted up. Ge 13:6 (bear). 18:26 (spare). 19:21 (accepted). Ex 6:8mg. Ezr 9:2. Ps 123:1. Is 5:26.
veil. Is 3:23.

8 **charge**. SS +2:7. 3:5. 8:4. Ro 15:30.
daughters of Jerusalem. ver. 16. SS +1:5.
if ye. Ge 32:36. Ro 15:30. Ga 6:1, 2. Ja 5:16.
that ye. Heb. what ye.
I am. Ps 42:1-3. 63:1-3. 77:1-3. 119:81-83. Pr 13:12.

9 **What is**. Is 53:2. Mt 16:13-17. 21:10. Jn 1:14, 46. 7:41-43. 2 C 4:3-6.
O thou. SS 1:8, 15. 6:1, 9, 10. Ps 45:13. 87:3.

10 **beloved**. SS 2:1. Dt 32:31. Ps 45:17. Is 66:19. He 7:26.
white. or, clear. Is 18:4. 32:4. Je 4:11. La 4:7. Da 7:9. Mt 17:2. Re 1:14.
ruddy. Ge 25:30. Nu 19:2. 1 S +16:12. 17:42.
the chiefest. Heb. a standard bearer. SS 6:4, 10. Ps 45:2, 7. 73:25. 89:6. Is 10:18. 59:19. Mt 13:46. Mk 10:44. Jn 6:68. Ro 8:29. 9:5. Ph 2:9-11. Col 1:15-18. T 2:13. He 1:2. +2:10. 4:14. 7:26. 13:20. 1 P 2:6. 5:4. Re 1:5, 8.
ten thousand. Ge 24:60. Le 26:8. 2 S 18:3. Ec 7:28.

11 **head**. Da 2:37, 38. 1 C 11:3. Ep 1:21, 22. Col 1:18.
his locks. SS 7:5. Da 7:9. Re 1:14.
bushy. or, curled.

12 **His eyes**. SS 1:15. 4:1. 2 Ch 16:9. Ps 32:8. Pr 15:3. He 4:13.
fitly set. Heb. sitting in fulness, *that is*, fitly placed, and set as a precious stone in the foil of a ring.

13 **cheeks**. SS 1:10. Is 50:6.
as a. Ps 4:6, 7. 27:4. 89:15. Re 21:23.
sweet flowers. or, towers of perfumes. SS 3:6.
his lips. SS 4:11. Ps 45:2. 85:8. 89:15. Pr 8:6-10. Is 50:4. Lk 4:22. Jn 6:63.
dropping. ver. 5.

14 **hands**. Ex 15:6. Jb 10:8. Ps 31:5. 45:4-7. 99:4. 104:24. 139:9, 10. 145:15, 16. Is 9:7. 49:16. 52:13. Mt 14:31. 2 T 1:12. 1 P 4:19.
his belly. SS 7:2. Ex 24:10. Is 54:11. Ezk 1:26-28.

15 **legs**. Re 1:15.
pillars. Dt 32:4. Ps 75:3. 80:17. Pr 8:22, 23.
sockets. Ex 26:19.
his countenance. SS 2:14. Nu 6:25, 26. Jg 13:6. Ps 4:6. 31:16. 44:3. Mt 17:2. 28:3. Ac 2:28. Re 1:16.
as Lebanon. SS 4:11. Ps 92:12. Ho 14:7. Zc 9:17. 1 T 3:16.

16 **mouth**. Heb. palate. SS 1:2. Jb +31:30mg. Ps 19:10. Je 15:16. Jn 7:46.
most. SS 1:16. 2:1, 3. Ps 45:2. 89:6. 148:13. Is 9:6, 7. Ph 3:8. 1 P 2:6, 7.
altogether lovely. Ge 39:6. Ps 8:9. 24:10. 34:2. Col 2:9.
my beloved. SS 2:16. 6:3. Ps 73:25. Jn 6:68. Ga 2:20.
friend. Pr 17:17. 18:24. Je 3:20mg. Ho 3:1. Jn 15:14, 15. He 2:11. Ja 2:23. 4:4.

SONG OF SOLOMON 6

1 **O thou**. ver. 4, 9, 10. SS 1:8. 2:2. 5:9.
that. SS 1:4. Ru 1:16, 17. 2:12. Is 2:5. Je 14:8. Zc 8:21-23. Jn 6:24. Ac 5:11-14.
seek him. Pr 8:17. La 3:25. Mt 7:7, 8. Jn 20:15, 16. Ro 10:6, 8. He 11:6.

2 **gone**. ver. 11. SS 4:12-16. 5:1. Ec 2:5. Is 58:11. 61:11. Mt 18:20. 28:20.
the beds. SS 5:13.
feed. SS 1:7, 8. Is 40:11. Ezk 34:23. Zp 3:17. Jn 4:34, 35. Re 7:17.
and to gather. SS 2:2. Is 57:1. Mk 4:29. Jn 14:3. 17:24. Ph 1:21-23. 1 Th 4:13, 14. Re 14:15.

3 **my beloved's**. SS 2:16. 7:10. Ps 23:1. 63:1. La 3:24. Lk 1:46, 47. Jn 20:28. He 8:10. Re 21:2-4.
he feedeth. SS 2:2, 16.

4 **beautiful**. ver. 10. SS 2:14. 4:7. 5:2. Ezk 16:13, 14. Ep 5:27.
as Tirzah. Nu +26:33.
comely. Ps 48:2, 13. La 2:15. Re 21:2.
as Jerusalem. Ps 50:2. 122:3. 125:2. He 12:22.
terrible. ver. 10. SS 4:4. Nu 24:5-9. Ps 144:4-8. Zc 12:3. 2 C 10:4. Re 19:14-16.

5 **away**. SS 4:9. Ge 32:26-28. Ex 32:10. Ps 25:15. 123:2. Je 15:1. Mt 15:27, 28.
overcome me. or, puffed me up. Ge 32:28. Ps 138:3. Pr 8:31. Ho 12:4. Lk 24:29. Ja 5:16.
thy. SS 4:1-3.

6 **teeth**. SS +4:2. Mt 21:19. 25:30. Lk 12:32.

7 **a piece**. SS 4:3.

8 **are**. Ge +4:19.
threescore. SS 3:7. Ge 5:15, 18, 20. 1 K 11:1. 2 Ch 11:21. Ps 45:14. Re 7:9.
queens. ver. 9. 1 K 10:1, 4, 10.
fourscore. Ge 5:25, 26, 28. 16:16.
concubines. ver. 9. 1 Ch +2:48.

virgins. SS 1:3. Ge +24:43. Ex 2:8.
without number. Ge 34:30.

9 **My dove**. SS 2:14. 5:2.
but one. Ge 2:23. Mt 19:4-6. Jn 10:16. 17:22.
1 C 15:48. Ep 4:4. 1 T 3:2.
only one. Nu 23:9. Ps 45:9. Ga 4:26. Ep 4:3-6.
the choice. Pr 31:29.
The daughters. Dt 4:6, 7. 33:29. Ps 45:12-15. 126:2. Pr 31:28, 29. 2 Th 1:10. Re 21:9, 10.
praised her. Pr 31:10-31. Re 21:26.

10 **Who**. SS 3:6. 8:5. Is 63:1. Re 21:10, 11.
looketh. 2 S 23:4. Jb 11:17. Pr 4:18. Is 58:8. Ho 6:5. 2 C 3:18. Ph 2:16. Re 22:16.
morning. 2 S 23:4. Jn 17:22.
fair. Jb 31:26. Ep 5:27.
moon. Ge 1:16.
clear. Ps 14:5. Pr 4:18. Ml 4:2. Mt 13:43. 17:2. Re 10:1. 12:1. 21:23. 22:5.
the sun. 2 P 1:19. Re 12:1.
terrible. ver. 4. Ro 8:37.

11 **the garden**. ver. 2. SS 4:12-16. 5:1. Ge 2:9. Ps 1:3. 92:12-15. Jn 15:16.
to see the. SS 7:12. Is 5:2-4. Mk 11:13. Lk 13:7. Ac 15:36.
fruits. Mk 4:28, 29. Jn 15:5. 1 P 3:4.

12 **Or ever I was aware**. Heb. I knew not.
my soul. Heb. *nephesh*, Ge +34:3; Le +26:11. Je 31:18-20. Ho 11:8, 9. Lk 15:20.
made me like the chariots of Amminadib. *or*, set me on the chariots of my willing people. Ge 41:43. 46:29. Ps 110:3. Is 6:8. Ho 2:1. Ac 9:6.

13 **return**. SS 2:14. Je 3:12-14, 22. Ho 14:1-4.
Shulamite. i.e. *complete, having peace; the perfect, the peaceful; that recompenses*, **S#7759h**.
What. SS 1:6. Lk 7:44. 15:10. 2 Th 1:10.
see in. Ac 4:13.
Shulamite. Ge 49:10. Ps 76:2. Is 8:6. Jn 9:7. He 7:2.
As. Jn 10:16. Ro 3:29. Ep 2:14-17.
two armies. *or*, Mahanaim. Ge +32:2. Ps 34:7. Ro 7:23. Ga 5:17. Ep 6:10-19.

SONG OF SOLOMON 7

1 **thy feet**. Ep +6:15. Ph 1:27.
with shoes. Dt 33:25.
O prince's. 1 S 2:8. Ps 45:13. Lk 8:48. Ro 8:17. 2 C 6:17, 18. 1 J 3:1. Re 21:7.
the joints. Da 2:32. Ep 4:15, 16. Col 2:19.
the work. Ex 28:15. 35:35.

2 **navel**. Pr 3:8.
goblet. Ex 24:6. Ps 23:5. Is 22:24.
wanteth not. Dt 33:23. Ps 23:5. 34:9, 10.
liquor. Heb. mixture.
thy belly. SS 5:14. Ps 45:16. Is 46:3. Je 1:5. Ro 7:4.
wheat. Ps 147:14. Mt 3:12. 13:30.

3 **Thy two**. SS 4:5. 6:6.
4 **neck**. SS 1:10. 4:4.
ivory. SS 5:14. 1 K 10:18, 22. 22:39. Ps 45:8. 144:12.
thine eyes. That is, "Thine eyes are dark, deep, clear, and serene, as the fishpools in Heshbon." SS 4:1, 9. 6:5. Ep 1:17, 18. 3:18, 19.
Heshbon. Nu +21:25.
gate. Ge +14:7. 19:1. 22:17. 23:10.
Bath-rabbim. i.e. *daughter of many* (a village dependent on a city, Nu +21:25mg), **S#1337h**.
thy nose. That is, "Thy nose is as finely formed as the tower of Lebanon." Ph 1:9, 10. He 5:14.
the tower. SS 4:8. 5:15. 1 K 7:2. 9:19. 2 Ch 8:6.
Damascus. Ge +14:15.

5 **head**. Is 35:2. Ep 1:22. 4:15, 16. Col 1:18. 2:19.
Carmel. *or*, crimson. Jsh +19:26.
the hair. SS 4:1. 5:11. Re 1:14.
the king. Ge 32:26. Ps 68:24. 87:2. Mt 18:20. 28:20.
held. Heb. bound. Ge 32:26. Ex 32:10, 11, 14. Re 21:3.
galleries. SS 1:17mg. Ge 30:38, 41. Ex 2:16.

6 **fair**. ver. 10. SS 1:15, 16. 2:14. 4:7, 10. Ge 12:11, 14. 24:16. 29:17. Dt 21:11. 2 S 13:1. 14:27. 1 K 1:3, 4. Est 2:7. Jb 42:15. Ps 45:11. Is 62:4, 5. Am 8:13. Zp 3:17.
pleasant. Ge 49:15. 2 S 1:26.
O love. Ac 20:28. Ep 5:32. Re 21:9.
delights. Ps 104:31. Pr 19:10. Ec 2:8. Mi 1:16. 2:9. Zp 3:17.

7 **thy stature**. Ps 92:12. Je 10:5. Ep 4:13. He 6:1.
thy breasts. ver. 3, 8. SS 1:13. 4:5. 8:8. Is 66:10, 11. Ep 3:17-19.
clusters. Re 7:9.

8 **I will go**. SS 4:16. 5:1. Je 32:41. Jn 14:21-23.
the vine. Jn 15:1-5.
the smell. SS 1:3. 2:3. 2 C 2:14.

9 **the roof**. SS 2:3mg, 14. 5:16mg. Jb 6:30mg. Pr 16:24. Ep 4:29. Col 3:16, 17. 4:6. He 13:15.
thy mouth. Nu 12:6. 24:2-4. Jb 33:14-17. Je 23:28, 29. 2 C 12:1-4.
the best wine. Is 62:8, 9. Zc 9:15-17. Jn 2:10. Ac 2:11-13, 46, 47. 4:31, 32. 16:30-34. Ep 5:18, 19. 2 P 1:21.
that goeth. Ge 2:4. 13:5. 15:2. Pr 23:31.
sweetly. Heb. straightly. SS 1:4mg. 1 Ch 29:17. Pr 23:31.
those that are asleep. *or*, the ancient. SS 5:2. 1 S 26:7, 12. 1 K 3:20. Ro 13:11. 1 Th 4:13, 14. Re 14:13.

10 **my**. SS 2:16. 6:3. Ps 116:16. 119:94, 125. Ac 27:23. 1 C 6:19, 20. Ga 2:20. 2 T 1:12.
his desire. ver. 5, 6. Jb 14:15. Ps 45:11. 147:11. Is 26:8. Lk 22:15. Jn 15:9. 17:24. Ro 8:38, 39. Ep 2:4. 1 J 4:16-19.

11   **let us go**. SS 1:4. 2:10-13. 4:8.

12   **get**. Pr 8:17. Ec 9:10. Mk +1:35. 6:31.

     let us see. SS 6:11. Pr 24:30, 31. Ac 15:36. 2 C 13:5. 1 Th 3:5, 6. He 12:15.

     the tender. SS 2:13, 15. Is 18:5.

     appear. Heb. open. Jb 12:18. 30:11. 39:5. Mk 4:28. 2 P 1:8.

     there will I give thee. ver. 6. SS 4:16. Ex 25:22. Ps 43:4. 63:3-8. 73:25. 122:5. Pr 8:17. Ezk 20:40, 41. Mk 10:13, 14, 16. Ro 5:11. 2 C 5:14, 15. Ep 6:24. He 4:16.

13   **mandrakes**. Ge 30:14-16. Je 24:1.

     at our. SS 4:16. 5:1. Jn 15:8. Ga 5:22, 23. Ep 5:9. Ph 1:11.

     new. Mt 13:52.

     I have. 1 Ch 28:12. Ps 16:11. 36:8. Is 23:18. 60:6, 7. Mt 6:20. 25:40. Ro 15:25-27. 1 C 2:9, 10. 16:2. 2 C 8:8, 9. Col 3:17. 1 P 4:11. Re 22:14.

SONG OF SOLOMON 8

1   **that thou**. Is 7:14. 9:6. Hg 2:7. Zc 9:9. Ml 3:1. Mt 13:16, 17. Lk 2:26-32, 38. 10:23, 24. 1 T 3:16. He 2:11, 12.

     my brother. Pr 17:17. 18:24. Jn 1:14. He 2:17. 4:15, 16.

     sucked. Is 66:11, 12. Ga 4:26.

     find thee. Ps 63:1-5. Jn 1:14. 3:13. 8:42. 13:3. 16:28. He 2:9-14. 9:26-28.

     I would. SS 1:2. Ps 2:12. 45:10, 11. Lk 7:45-48. 9:26. 12:8. Jn 7:46-52. 9:25-38. Ga 6:14. Ph 3:3, 7, 8.

     yea. Ps 51:17. 102:16, 17. Mk 12:42-44. 14:6-9.

     I should not be despised. Heb. they should not despise me. Is 60:14. Lk 10:16. 18:9. 1 C 1:28.

2   **bring**. SS 3:4. Ga 4:26.

     who. Lk 16:29-31. Jn 5:39, 46, 47. Ac 17:11, 12. 2 T 3:15. 1 P 1:10-12. 2 P 1:19. Re 19:10.

     instruct. Mt 10:20. Lk 12:12. Jn 14:26. 16:13. Ac 6:5, 6.

     I would cause. SS 4:10-16. 5:1. 7:9, 12.

     spiced. Pr 9:2.

3   **left hand**. SS 2:6. Ge 13:9. Dt 33:27. Is 62:4, 5. 2 C 12:9.

     under. Dt 33:27. Ps 145:14.

     right hand. Ps 63:7, 8.

     embrace. SS 2:6. Ge 29:13. 33:4. Ps 55:22.

4   **charge**. SS 2:7. 3:5. 5:8, 9.

     daughters of Jerusalem. SS +1:5.

     that ye stir not up. SS 2:7. 3:5. Pr 10:12.

     nor awake. Heb. why should ye stir up, *or, why awake, etc*. SS 2:7. 3:5. Dt 32:11.

     love. ver. 6, 7. SS 2:4, 5, 7. 3:5.

     he please. or, she please. SS 2:7. 3:5. Dt 25:7.

5   **Who is this**. SS 3:6. 6:10. Ge 24:65.

     cometh up. Dt 33:2. Ps 50:5. Zc 14:5. 1 C 15:52. 1 Th 3:13. 2 Th 1:10. Ju 14. Re 21:9.

     from the wilderness. SS 3:6. 4:8. Ge 14:6. 16:7. Ps 45:10, 11. 107:2-8. Is 40:3. 43:19. Je 2:2. Ho 2:14. Ac 7:38. Re 12:6.

     leaning. 2 Ch 32:8mg. Ps 63:8. Is 26:3, 4. 36:6. Mi 3:11. Jn 13:23. Ac 27:23-25. 2 C 12:9, 10. Ep 1:12, 13. 1 P 1:21.

     I raised. SS 2:3. Ho 12:4. Jn 1:48-51.

     there she. ver. 1. SS 3:4, 11. Is 49:20-23. Ro 7:4. Ga 4:19.

6   **as a seal**. Ex 28:9-12, 21, 29, 30. Is 49:16. Je 22:24. Hg 2:23. Zc 3:9. 2 C 1:22. Ep +1:13. +4:30. 2 T 2:19.

     upon thine heart. Ex 28:30. Pr 23:26.

     love. SS 5:8. Ps 42:1, 2. 63:1. 84:2. Jn 21:15-19. Ac 20:24. 21:13. 2 C 5:14, 15. Ph 1:20-23. Re 12:11.

     is strong. Ro 8:35, 38, 39.

     jealousy. Ex 20:5. 34:14. Nu 5:14. 25:11. Dt 32:21. Pr 6:34. Na 1:2. 2 C 11:2.

     cruel. Heb. hard. Pr 27:4mg.

     grave. Heb. *sheol*, Ge +37:35.

     coals. Dt 32:24. Jb 5:7. Ps 120:4. Pr 25:22. Ro 12:20.

     of fire. Ge 15:17. 19:24. 22:6, 7.

     flame. Le 6:13.

7   **Many waters**. Ps 93:4. Is 43:2. Mt 7:24, 25. Ro 8:28-39.

     quench. Ezk 32:7mg.

     love. ver. 4, 6. SS 2:4, 5, 7. 3:10. Je 31:3. Jn 3:16. Ro 5:7, 8. 1 C ch. 13. Ep 2:4. 1 J 4:9, 10.

     floods. Ge 2:10, 13, 14. 15:18.

     drown. Jb 14:19. Ps 69:15mg.

     if a man. Pr 6:31, 35. Ro 13:8-10.

     substance. Ps 44:12. 112:3. 119:14.

     be contemned. or, tread. ver. 1. Pr 6:30. 23:9, 22.

8   **a little**. Ezk 16:46, 55, 56, 61. 23:33. Lk 8:14. Jn 10:16. Ac 15:14-17. Ro 15:9-12. 1 C 3:1, 2. 11:30. He 5:12-14.

     she hath. ver. 10. SS 4:5. 7:3. Ps 147:19, 20. Ac 7:38. Ro 3:1, 2. Ep 2:12.

     what. Ps 2:8. 72:17-19. Is 49:6. 60:1-5, 10, 11. Ac ch. 10. 11:1-18. 16:9. 18:26. 22:21. 26:17, 18. Ro 10:12-15. 14:1. 15:1. Ep 2:13-15, 19-22. 1 Th 2:7.

     in the day. Lk 19:44. 1 P 2:12.

9   **a wall**. SS 2:9. Re 21:12-19.

     we will. Is 58:12. 60:17. 61:4. Zc 6:12-15. Mt 16:18. Ac 15:16. 1 C 3:10-12. Ep 2:20-22.

     build upon. Ph 1:6. Ep 2:19-22. He 6:1. 1 P 2:5. Ju 20.

     a door. Ac 14:27.

10   **a wall**. ver. 9. Ne 12:27-43. Re 21:10-21.

     my. SS 4:5. 7:3, 4, 7, 8. Ezk 16:7. Col 2:7.

     then. Ge 6:8. Dt 7:7, 8. Pr 3:4. Is 60:10. Lk 1:30. Ep 1:6-8. 1 T 1:16.

     in his eyes. Mt 5:48. Lk 6:40. Jn +17:6. 1 C 11:1. 2 C 13:9. Ph 3:14-17.

     favor. Heb. peace. or, grace. Ge 15:15. 26:29, 31. Ro 5:1-10. 8:33. 1 C 15:10. 1 J 3:21.

11 vineyard. ver. 12. SS 1:6, 14. 2:15. 4:13, 16. 7:12. Ec 2:4, 5. Is 5:1-7. 27:2, 3. Mt 21:33-43. Mk 12:1-9. Lk 20:9-16. 1 C 9:7.

Baal-hamon. i.e. *lord of the multitude; place of the sun,* **S#1174h.**

he let. Ps 80:8. Mt 21:33. Lk 20:9, etc.

keepers. ver. 12. SS 1:6. Na 1:2.

fruit. ver. 12. SS 2:3. 4:3, 16. Mk 13:34. Lk 19:13.

a thousand. Ge 20:16. Is 7:23.

silver. ver. 9. SS 1:11. 3:10.

12 vineyard. SS 1:6. Pr 4:23. Ac 20:28. 1 T 4:15, 16.

thou. Ps 72:17-19. Ro 14:7-9. 1 C 6:20. 2 C 5:15.

those. 1 Th 2:19, 20. 1 T 5:17, 18.

13 dwellest. SS 2:13. 4:16. 6:2, 11. 7:11, 12. Mt 18:20. 28:20. Jn 14:21-23.

the companions. SS 1:7. 3:7-11. 5:9-16. Jg 11:38. 14:11. Ps 45:14.

voice. SS 2:14. 1 S 3:9. Ps 29:3. Is 40:2. Ho 2:14. Jn +10:3, 27.

cause. SS 2:14. Ps 50:15. Jn 14:13, 14. 15:7. 16:24.

to hear. Is 30:21. Hab 2:1. Mt 13:9. Re 2:29.

14 Make haste. Heb. Flee away. SS 2:17. Ge 16:6, 8. Ps +40:17. Lk 19:12. Ph 1:23. 3:20, 21. 2 P 3:9. Re 22:17, 20.

be thou like. SS 2:9, 17.

young. SS 2:9, 17. 4:5. 7:3.

hart. SS 2:9, 17. Dt 12:15, 22.

spices. SS 4:10, 14, 16. Ex 25:6.

ISAIAH

ISAIAH 1

1 A.M. 3244. B.C. 760.
vision. Is 21:2. Nu 12:6. 24:4, 16. 2 Ch 26:22.
32:32. Ps 89:19. Je 23:16. Ezk 1:1. Na 1:1.
Hab 2:2. Mt 17:9. Ac 10:17. 26:19. 2 C 12:1.
Isaiah. i.e. *safety of Jahu* or *a safety (is) Jahu;*
salvation of the Lord; the salvation of Jehovah,
S#3470h. 2 K 19:2, 5, 6, 20. 20:1, 4, 7-9, 11, 14,
16, 19. 2 Ch 26:22. 32:20, 32. Is 1:1. 2:1. 7:3.
13:1. 20:2, 3. 37:2, 5, 6, 21. 38:1, 4, 21. 39:3,
5, 8. See for the same Hebrew name belonging to other persons, rendered "Jesaiah," 1 Ch
+3:21; "Jeshaiah," 1 Ch +25:3.
Amoz. 2 K +19:2.
saw. Is 2:1. 13:1. 2 P 1:21.
the days. Is 6:1. 2 Ch ch. 26-32.
Uzziah. 2 Ch +26:1.
Jotham. Jg +9:5.
Ahaz. 1 Ch +8:35.
Hezekiah. 2 K +16:20.
2 **Hear**. Dt 4:26. 30:19. 32:1. Ps 50:4. Je 2:12.
6:19. 22:29. Ezk 36:4. Mi 1:2. 6:1, 2.
O heavens. Dt +32:1.
for the Lord. Je 13:15. Am 3:1. Mi 3:8. Ac
4:20. Ro 3:1, 2. 9:4. He 1:1.
I have. Is 5:1, 2. 46:3, 4. Dt 1:31. 4:7, 8. 7:6.
Ps 147:20. Je 31:9. Ezk 16:6-14. 20:5, etc. Ro
3:1, 2. 9:4, 5. He 12:7.
they have. Is 63:9, 10. Dt 9:22-24. 32:5, 6,
15. Je 2:5-13. Ml 1:6.
3 **ox**. Pr 6:6. Je +8:7. Ho 11:4.
but Israel. Is 5:12. 27:11. 44:18. Dt 29:2, 4.
32:28, 29. Ps 94:8. Je 4:22. 9:3-6. 10:8, 14. Mt
13:13-15, 19. Ro 1:28. 2 P 3:5.
know. Jb +19:25.
4 **sinful**. ver. 23. Is 10:6. 30:9. Ge 13:13. Mt
11:28. Ac 7:51, 52. Re 18:5.
laden with iniquity. Heb. of heaviness.
a seed. Is 57:3, 4. Nu 32:14. Ps 78:8. Je 7:26.
16:11, 12. Mt 3:7. 23:33.
children. Je 2:33. Ezk 16:33.
corrupters. *Dt 32:5.*
forsaken. ver. 28. Is 6:12. 7:16. 10:3 (leave),
14 (left). 17:2, 9. 18:6 (left). 27:10. 32:14.
41:17. 49:14. 54:6. 55:7. 58:2. 60:15. 62:4, 12.
Dt 29:25. Je +1:16.
provoked. Is 3:8. 65:3. Nu 14:11, 23. 16:30.

Dt 31:20. 32:19. Ps 78:40. Je 7:19. 1 C 10:22.
the Holy one of Israel. Is 5:19, 24. 10:20.
12:6. 17:7. 29:19. 30:11, 12, 15. 31:1. 37:23.
41:14, 16, 20. 43:3, 14, 15. 45:11. 47:4. 48:17.
49:7. 54:5. 55:5. 60:9, 14. 2 K 19:22. Jb 6:10.
Ps +16:10. 71:22. 78:41. 89:18. Je 50:29. 51:5.
Ezk 39:7. Ho 11:9. Hab 1:12, 13. 3:3.
gone away backward. Heb. alienated, *or*
separated. Ps 58:3. Je 2:5, 31. Ro 8:7. 10:21.
Col 1:24.
5 **Why should**. Je 6:28-30. +31:18. Ezk 24:13.
ye will. 2 Ch 28:22. Je 9:3. Re 16:8-11.
revolt more and more. Heb. increase revolt.
Je +28:16mg.
the whole. ver. 23. Ne 9:34. Je 5:5, 31. Da
9:8-11. Zp 3:1-4.
head. Is 7:20. 30:28.
6 **the sole**. Dt 28:35. 2 S 14:25. Jb 2:7, 8. Lk
16:20, 21.
no soundness. Ps 38:7, 8.
bruises. 2 Ch 6:28, 29. Ps 77:2. Je 6:14mg.
30:12. Na 3:19.
sores. Lk 16:20.
they have. Jb 5:18. Ps 38:3-5. Je 6:14. 8:21,
22. 33:6. Ho 5:12, 13. Ml 4:2. Mt 9:12, 13. Lk
10:34.
ointment. *or*, oil. Is 5:1mg. 10:27 (anointing). 25:6 (fat). 28:1, 4. 39:2. 41:19 (oil tree).
59:9. 61:3. Dt +33:24.
7 **country**. Is 5:5, 6, 9. 6:11. 24:10-12. Le
26:34. Dt 28:51, 52. 2 Ch 28:5, 16-21. Ps
107:34, 39. Je 6:8.
desolate. Is 6:11. 17:9. 33:8. 49:8, 19. 54:1,
3. 61:4. 62:4. Je +18:16.
burned. Is 9:5. 34:9. Je 2:15.
strangers. Is 5:17. Dt 28:33, 43, 48-52. La
5:2. Ezk 30:12. Ho 7:9. 8:7.
overthrown by strangers. Heb. the overthrow of strangers.
8 **daughter**. Nu +21:25. Mt +21:5.
cottage. Jb 27:18. La 2:6.
besieged. Is 8:8. 10:32. Je 4:17. Lk 19:43, 44.
9 **of hosts**. Ps +24:10.
left. La 3:22. Hab 3:2. Ro *9:29*.
a very. Is 6:13. 17:6. 24:13. 1 K 19:18. Zc
13:8, 9. Mt 7:14.
remnant. Is 37:4, 31, 32. 46:3. Le +23:22. Jb

1:12. Mi +5:3. Zc 13:9. Jn +6:12. Re 6:16, 17. 12:12-17. 13:7.
we should. Ge 18:26, 32. +19:24.
Sodom. Ge 19:1-29.

10 **Hear**. Je +7:2.
Sodom. Ge 13:13. +18:20 Je 9:26. Am 9:7. Re 11:8.
the law. Is 2:3. 5:24. 8:16, 20. 24:5. 30:9. 42:4, 21, 24. 51:4, 7.

11 **To what purpose**. Is 66:3. 1 S 15:22. Ps 50:8, 9. 51:16, 17. Pr 15:8. 21:27. Je 6:20. 7:21. Am 5:21, 22. Mi 6:7. Mt 9:13.
saith the Lord. ver. 11, 18. Is 33:10. 40:1, 25. 41:21, 21. 66:9. Ps 12:5.
burnt offerings. Le +23:12.
and the. Is 3:16-23. 58:6, 7. Ps 15:2-5. Mi 6:8. Ro 1:29-31. 1 T 4:1-3. 2 T 3:1-7. 1 P 4:3.
fat. Ex +29:13.
he goats. Heb. great he goats. Is 14:9mg.

12 **When**. Is 58:1, 2. Ex 23:17. 34:23. Dt 16:16. Ec 5:1. Mt 23:5.
to appear. Heb. be seen. Ex 23:15. 34:20.
required. Ps 40:6. Mi 6:6-8.
tread. Ezk 26:11. 34:18. Da 8:7, 10.

13 **Bring no more**. Ps +50:16.
vain. Ezk 20:39. Ml 1:10. Mt 15:9. Lk 11:42.
oblations. ver. +11.
incense. Is 66:3. Pr 21:27.
new moons. Col +2:16.
assemblies. or, convocations. **S#4744h**. Is 4:5. Ex 12:16, 16. Le 23:2-4, 7, 8, 21, 24, 27, 35, 36, 37. Nu 10:2. 28:18, 25, 26. 29:1, 7, 12. Ne 8:8.
cannot. Ge +32:28.
away with. i.e. I am not able to endure. Je 44:22.
it is. 1 C 11:17. Ph 1:15.
iniquity. or, grief. Ps 78:40. Ep 4:30.
solemn. Le +23:36.

14 **new moons**. Col +2:16.
appointed feasts. Ge +17:21. Le 23:2.
my soul. Heb. nephesh, Ge +34:3; Le +26:11. Is 61:8. Am 5:21.
hateth. Ex +15:7.
I am weary. Is 43:24. Ps 50:8, 9. Am 2:13. Zc 11:8. Ml 2:17.

15 **when**. Ps +88:9.
your hands. Dt +32:36.
I will hide. Is 58:7. Dt +31:17. Ps 55:1. 77:7-9.
make many prayers. Heb. multiply prayer. Mt 6:7. 23:14.
not hear. Ps +66:18.
your hands. Is 10:13. Ge 6:11. 2 K 19:11. Ezk +22:29. Ezk 33:25, 26. Mt 23:14. Lk 13:25-27. Ro +3:15.
full of. Is 59:2, 3. Je 7:8-10. Ezk 7:23-26. Mi 3:9-11.
blood. Heb. bloods. 2 K +9:26mg.

16 **Wash**. Ge 18:4. 19:2. 2 S 11:8. 2 K +5:13. Jb 11:13, 14. Ps 26:6. Je 4:14. 2 C 7:1. Ja 4:8.

put away. Is 55:6, 7. Je +33:15. Ep 4:22-24. T 2:11-14. 1 P 2:1.
mine eyes. Ps +11:4.
cease. Jg 2:19. Ps 34:14. 37:27. Am 5:15. Ro 12:9. Ep 4:25-29. 1 P 3:11.

17 **seek judgment**. or, justice. Is 58:6. Pr 31:9. Da 4:27. Mi 6:8. Zp 2:3. Zc 8:16. Lk 3:8.
relieve. or, righten. Je +22:3, 16.
judge. Je +21:12.
fatherless. ver. 23. Ex +22:22.
plead. Ps 35:1.
widow. ver. 23. Is 10:2. Ex 22:22. Dt 10:18. 14:29. 16:11, 14. 24:17, 19-21. 26:12. 27:19. Jb 22:9. 24:3, 21. 29:13. 31:16. Ps 68:5. 94:6. 146:9. Pr 15:25. Je 7:6. 22:3. 49:11. Ezk 22:7. Mi 2:9. Ml 3:5. Mt 23:14. Lk 2:37. 4:26. 7:12. 18:3, 5. 21:2, 3. Ac 6:1. 9:39, 41. 1 C 7:8. 1 T 5:3-5, 9, 11, 16. Ja 1:27. Re 18:7.

18 **Come now**. Ps +119:68. Pr 1:20-23. Je 22:29. Ezk 33:11. Mi 6:1-3. Mt +14:14. Ja +5:11.
and let us reason. lit. clear up. Is 41:21. 43:24-26. Jsh 20:4. 1 S 12:7. Ec 3:11. Je 2:5. Mi 6:2, 3. Ac +17:2. 18:4. 24:25.
though your. Is 44:22. Ps 51:7. Mi 7:18, 19. Ro 5:20. Ep 1:6-8. Re 7:14.
sins. ver. 16, 17. Pr 20:9. Ro 3:23. 6:23. Ja 4:17. 1 J 1:9. 5:17.
as scarlet. Is 24:2. 32:2. 66:12.
they shall be. Ps 51:7.
snow. 2 K +5:27.

19 **If**. Ge 4:7.
willing. Is 3:10. 55:1-3, 6, 7. Je 3:12-14. 31:18-20. Ho 14:1-4. Jl 2:26. Mt 21:28-32.
obedient. Lk 6:46. Jn 3:36. +13:17. He 5:9.

20 **if**. Ge +4:7.
ye refuse. Is 3:11. 1 S 12:25. 2 Ch 36:14-16. He 2:1-3.
sword. Ex +5:3.
for the mouth. Is +21:17. 40:5. 58:14. Le 26:33. Nu 23:19. 1 S 15:29. T 1:2.

21 **the faithful**. Is 48:2. Ne 11:1, 18. Ps 46:4. 48:1, 8. Ho 11:12. Zc 8:3. He 12:22.
become. Ps 73:23. Je 2:20, 21. 3:1. La 1:8, 9. Ezk ch. 16, 22, 23. Lk 13:34. Re 11:2, 8.
harlot. Is +32:9.
it was full. Is 5:7. 2 S 8:15. 1 K 3:28. 2 Ch 19:9. Ezk 22:3-7. Mi 3:2, 3. Zp 3:1-3.
lodged. Ps +49:12.
but now. Is 59:9. 65:13, 14. La 1:1. Lk 2:14. Ro 5:18, 19. 6:7, 8. 8:5, 13. 15:12. 2 C 4:17, 18. 6:8-10. Ph 3:7. 2 P 2:19.
murderers. Ac 7:52.

22 **silver**. Je 6:28-30. La 4:1, 2. Ezk 22:18-22. Ho 6:4.
wine. Pr 6:17. Ho 4:18. 2 C 2:17. Re 14:10.

23 **Thy princes**. Is 3:14. 2 K 17:9-11. 2 Ch 24:17-21. 28:22. 36:14. Je 5:5. Ezk 22:6-12. Da 9:5, 6. Ho 7:3-5. 9:15. Mi 3:1-3, 11. Ac 4:5-11.
companions. Pr 29:24. Mt 21:13. Mk 11:17. Lk 19:46.

every. Is 33:15. Ex 23:8. Dt 16:19. Pr 17:23. Je 22:17. Ezk 22:12. Ho 4:18. Mi 7:3.
they judge not. Is 10:1, 2. Je 5:29. Ml +3:5.
fatherless. Ex +22:22.
widow. ver. +17.

24 **the mighty One of Israel**. Is 30:29. 49:26. 60:16. Ge 49:24. Je 50:34. Re 18:8.
Ah. Dt 28:63. 32:43. 2 K 15:37. Pr 1:25, 26. Ezk 5:13. 16:42. 21:17. He 10:13.
avenge. Ex +15:7. Dt +32:35, 41. Jg 16:28. Ro +12:19.

25 **And I**. Zc 13:7-9. Re 3:19.
turn. Ps 81:14. Am 1:8.
hand. Ps 81:14. Am 1:8. Zc 13:7.
purely. Heb. according to pureness. 2 S 22:21, 25. Jb 9:30. 22:30. Ps 18:20, 24.
purge. ver. 22. Is 4:4. 6:11-13. Je 6:29. 9:7. Ezk 20:38. Zp 3:11. Ml 3:3. Mt 3:12.
thy dross. Nu 31:22, 23. Ps 66:10. Ezk 22:18-22. Zc 13:9. 1 C 3:13, 15.

26 **And I will**. Is 32:1, 2. 60:17, 18. Nu 12:3. 16:15. 1 S 12:2-5. Je 33:7, 15-17. Ezk 34:23, 24. 37:24, 25. 45:8.
judges. Ex +21:6. Dt 21:2.
afterward. Is 59:20, 21. Ezk +38:8, 16. Da +9:24. Zc 12:10. 13:1.
thou shalt. ver. 21. Is +60:21. 62:1. Je 31:23. Zp 3:9, 13. Zc 8:3, 8. Re 21:27.
righteousness. Da +9:24.

27 **Zion**. Is +59:20.
redeemed. Is 45:21-25. Ro 3:24-26. 11:26, 27. 2 C 5:21. Ep 1:7, 8. T 2:14. 1 P 1:18, 19.
with judgment. Is 5:16. Mt +3:11. Re 3:19.
her converts. or, they that return of her. Is 10:21. 1 C 1:30.

28 **the destruction**. Heb. the breaking. Is +51:19mg. Jb 31:3. Ps 1:6. 5:6. 37:38. 73:27. 92:9. 104:35. 125:5. Pr 29:1. Lk 12:45, 46. 1 Th 5:3. 2 Th 1:8, 9. 2 P 3:7. Re 21:8.
they that. Is 30:13, 14. 50:11. 1 S 12:25. 1 K 9:6-9. Je +1:16. Zp 1:4-6. Lk 3:9.

29 **ashamed**. Is 30:22. 31:7. 45:16. Dt 16:21. Ezk 16:63. 36:31. Ho 14:3, 8. Ro 6:21.
the oaks. Is +57:5mg. 65:3. 66:17. Ezk 6:13. Ho 4:13.
the gardens. Is 65:3. 66:17. Je 2:20. 3:6.
chosen. Is 7:15, 16. 14:1. 40:20. 41:8, 9, 24. 43:10. 44:1, 2. 48:10. 49:7. 56:4. 58:5, 6. 65:12. 66:3, 4.

30 **ye shall be**. Is 5:6. Je 17:5, 6. Ezk 17:9, 10, 24. Mt 21:19, 20.
an oak. Is 6:13. Ezk 6:13.
garden. Is 58:11. Je 31:12. Ezk 31:4, etc.

31 **the strong**. Ezk 32:21.
as tow. Is 27:4. 43:17. 50:11. Jg 15:14. Ps 68:1, 2. He 12:29. Re 6:14-17.
the maker of it. or, his work.
and they. Is 9:18. 34:9, 10. 2 S 23:6, 7. Ps

37:20. Ezk 20:47, 48. Ml 4:1. Mt +25:41. Lk 12:5.
quench. Mt +3:12.

ISAIAH 2

1 **saw**. Is 1:1. 13:1. Am 1:1. Mi 1:1. 6:9. Hab 1:1.

2 **And it shall**. Mi 4:1-3.
in the last days. Ge +49:1. Jb 19:25. Je 33:15, 16. Am 9:13-15.
the mountain. Is 24:23. 25:6, 7. 27:13. 30:29. 56:7. 65:11. Ps 68:15, 16. 72:16. Ezk 20:40. Da 2:35, 45. Mi 4:1, 2. Zc 8:3. He 12:22. Re 20:4. 21:10, etc.
the Lord's house. Is +60:13. Ezk +37:26. 40:2. Jl 2:1. Mi 4:1, 2. Zc 1:16. 6:12, 13.
established. or, prepared. Is 16:5. 45:18. 54:14. Ge 41:32mg. Ps 48:8. 57:8mg.
the hills. Ps 68:15. Zc 14:10.
and all. Ex +9:6. i.e. many from all nations. ver. 3. Is +11:10. 27:13. Ps 2:8. +86:9.

3 **Come ye**. Je 31:6. 50:4, 5. Zc 8:20-23. Lk 24:47. Jn 4:22. Ep 2:13.
he will teach. Dt 6:1. Ps 25:8, 9. Mt 7:24. Lk +11:28. Jn 7:17. Ac 10:33. Ja 1:25.
paths. Is 3:12. 26:7, 8. 30:11. 33:8 (highways). Is 40:14. 41:3.
out of Zion. Is +24:23. Lk 24:47. Ac 1:8. 13:46-48. Ro 10:18.
the law. Is +1:10.

4 **And**. Ge +8:22.
he shall judge. Ps +7:8. Jn 16:8-11.
rebuke. Is 11:4. 37:4. Ge 21:25.
and they shall. Is 9:7. 11:6-9. Ps 46:9. Ho 2:18. Jl 3:10. Mi 4:3. Zc 9:10.
swords. Is 1:20. 3:25. 13:15.
plowshares. Ge +49:10. 1 S 13:20, 21. Jl 3:10. Mi 4:3.
pruning hooks. or, scythes. Is 18:5. Jl 3:10mg. Mi 4:3mg.
neither. Is 60:17, 18. Ps 72:3-7.

5 **house of Jacob**. ver. 6. Is 8:17. 10:20. 14:1. 29:22. 46:3. 48:1. 58:1.
come ye. ver. 3. Is 50:10, 11. 60:1, 19. Ps 89:15. Lk 1:79. Jn 12:35, 36. Ro 13:12-14. Ep 5:8. 1 Th 5:5, 6. 1 J 1:7. Re 21:23, 24.
walk. Is 50:11. Ps 82:5. 1 Th 1:3. 1 J 1:7.

6 **Therefore**. Dt 31:16, 17. 2 Ch 15:2. 24:20. 28:16-19. La 5:20. Ro +11:1, 2, 20.
from the east. or, more than the east. Ge +29:1. 1 K +4:30.
and are. Is 8:19. 47:12, 13. Ex 22:18. Le 19:31. 20:6. Dt +18:10-14. 1 Ch 10:13.
soothsayers. 2 K +21:6.
and they. Ex 34:16. Nu 25:1, 2. Dt 21:11-13. 1 K 11:1, 2. Ne 13:23. Je +10:2.
please themselves in. or, abound with, etc. Pr 29:21. or, strike hands. Pr 6:1. Ezk 17:18.

7 **land**. Dt 17:16, 17. 1 K 10:21-27. 2 Ch 9:20-

25. 27:5, 6. Je 5:27, 28. Ja 5:1-3. Re 18:3, 11-17.

their land is. Is 30:16. 31:1. Dt 17:16. 1 K 4:26. 10:26. Ps 20:7. Ho 14:3.

horses. Is 31:1. Mi 5:10.

8 **is full**. Is 57:5. 2 Ch 27:2. 28:1-4, 23-25. 33:3-7. Je 2:28. 11:13. Ezk 16:23-25. Ho 12:11. Ac 17:16.

idols. lit. empty, vain things; nothings. Le 26:1. Dt 27:14, 15.

worship. Is 37:19. 44:15-20. Dt 4:28. Ps 115:4-8. Ho 8:6. 13:2. 14:3. Hab 1:16. Re 9:20.

9 **the mean**. Is 5:15. Ps 49:2. Je 5:4, 5. Ro 3:23. Re 6:15-17.

humbleth. Is 57:9. Col 2:18, 23.

therefore. Is 27:11. Jsh 24:19. Je 18:23. Mk 3:29.

10 **Enter**. ver. 19-21. Is 10:3. 42:22. Jg 6:1, 2. Jb 30:5, 6. Ho 10:8. Lk 23:30. Re 6:15, 16.

hide. Ge +3:22.

for fear. Is 6:3-5. Jb 31:23. Ps 33:8. 90:11. Je 10:7, 10. Lk 12:5. Re 15:3, 4.

majesty. 1 Ch +29:11.

11 **lofty**. ver. +17. Is 5:15, 16. Je 50:31, 32. Ml 4:1.

and the Lord. Je 9:24. 1 C 1:29-31. 2 C 10:17.

exalted. Is +12:4.

in that day. ver. 17. Is 4:1. 10:20. 11:10, 11. 12:1, 4. 14:3. 17:7. 24:21. 25:9. 26:1. 27:1, 2, 12, 13. 28:5. 29:18. 30:23. 52:6. Jb +21:30. Ps 118:24. Je 30:7, 8. Ezk 29:21. 38:14, 19. 39:11, 22. Da 12:1. Ho 2:16, 18, 21. Jl 3:18. Am 9:11. Ob 8, 15. Mi 4:6. 5:10. 7:11, 12. Zp 3:11, 16. Zc 2:11. 3:9, 10. 9:16. 12:3, 4, 6, 8, 9, 11. 13:1, 2, 4. 14:4, 6, 8, 9, 13, 20, 21. Ml 3:17. Mt 7:22. Lk 10:12. Ac 15:16. 17:31. 1 C 3:13. 1 Th 5:4. 2 Th 1:10. 2 T 1:12, 18. 4:8. Re 1:10.

12 **the day of the Lord**. Ps 92:6-9. La 2:22. Ezk +30:3. 1 C +3:13. 5:5. 2 Th +1:10.

be upon. Is 23:9. Pr +16:5.

13 **upon all**. Is 10:33, 34. 14:8. 37:24. Ezk 31:3-12. Am 2:5.

oaks. Ezk 27:6. Zc 11:2.

14 **high mountains**. Is 30:25. 40:4. Ps 68:16. 110:5, 6. 2 C 10:5.

15 **high tower**. lit. great place. Zp 1:16.

fenced wall. Is 25:2. 27:10. 36:1.

16 **the ships of Tarshish**. Ge +10:4. Re 18:17-19.

pleasant pictures. Heb. pictures of desire. Nu 33:52. Is +32:12mg. Re 18:11, 12.

17 **the loftiness**. ver. 11. Is 13:11. 24:21. Ps 9:19, 20. 37:13, 35, 36. Pr +6:17. 8:13. 16:18, 19. Je 9:24. 48:29, 30. Ezk 28:2-7. Zc 11:2. 1 C 1:29-31.

exalted. ver. +11.

18 **the idols**. Is 10:10, 11. 27:9. Ezk 36:25. 37:23. Ho 14:8. Zp 1:3. Zc 13:2.

he shall utterly abolish. or, shall utterly pass away. Mi 1:7.

19 **they shall go**. ver. 10, 21. 1 S 13:6. 14:11. Je 16:16. Ho 10:8. Mi +7:17. Lk 23:30. Re 6:15. 9:6.

holes. or, caverns. Is 32:14.

caves. lit. pierced places. S#4247h, only here. Ge +19:30.

earth. Heb. dust. ver. 10. Is 25:12. 26:5, 19. Ge 2:7. 3:14, 19.

for fear. ver. 10. 2 Th 1:9.

when he ariseth. Nu +10:35.

to shake. Is 30:32. Ps 7:6. 18:6-15. 76:7-9. 114:5-7. Mi 1:3, 4. Hab 3:3-14. He +12:26. 2 P 3:10-13. Re 20:11.

20 **cast**. Is 30:22. 31:7, 27. 46:1, 2. Le 1:16. 14:40. Nu 19:6. Ho 14:8. Ph 3:7, 8.

his idols of silver. Heb. the idols of his silver, etc. Is 31:7. 46:6.

each one for himself to. or, for him to.

worship. lit. bow themselves to. Ge 37:10. Le 26:1. Jg 2:19.

bats. Le 11:19. Dt 14:18.

21 **go into**. ver. 10, 19. Ex 33:22. Jb 30:6. SS 2:14.

clefts. Ex 33:22.

tops. lit. boughs. Is 17:6. 27:10. 57:5.

for fear. Ps 9:19, 20. 33:8. 90:11. Mt +10:28.

when he ariseth. Ps +3:7. Ml 4:5. 1 Th 5:2, 3. 2 P 3:10-13. Re 6:15, 16. 20:11.

shake terribly. or, terrify. Ps 10:18. Ho 10:8. Mt 7:26, 27. Lk 23:30. He +12:26.

22 **Cease**. Is 1:16. Ex 14:12. Ps +60:11. 62:9.

whose. Is +1:2. Ge 7:22. Jb 27:3.

breath. Heb. *neshamah*, Ge +2:7. Is 30:33. 42:5. 57:16 (soul). Ps +146:4.

for wherein. Is 40:17. Jb 7:15-21. Ps 8:4. 144:3, 4. Je 17:5.

ISAIAH 3

1 **behold**. Is 2:22.

the Lord. Is 1:24. 36:12. 51:22.

the stay. Le +26:26. Je 37:21. 38:9.

bread. Ge +3:19.

2 **mighty**. Is 2:13-15. 2 K 24:14-16. Ps 74:9. La 5:12-14. Am 2:3.

prophet. Ps +74:9.

prudent. 1 Ch 12:32. Pr 16:10.

the ancient. Is 9:15. Ezk 8:12. 9:5, 6.

3 **captain**. Ex +18:21. Dt 1:15. 1 S 8:12. 2 K 1:9, 14.

the honorable man. Heb. a man eminent in countenance. Jg 8:18. 2 K +5:1mg.

cunning artificer. Is 5:21. 19:11. 1 S 13:19, 20. 2 K 24:14.

eloquent orator. or, skilful of speech. Ex 4:10, 14-16. Heb. the skilful of charm. Is +26:16. Pr 16:10. Ec 10:11. Je 8:17. Ho 3:4.

4 **children**. 1 K 3:7-9. 2 Ch 26:1. 33:1. 34:1. 36:2, 5, 9, 11. Ec 10:16.

5 the people. Is 9:19-21. 11:13. Je 9:3-8. 22:17. Ezk 22:6, 7, 12. Am 4:1. Mi 3:1-3, 11. Zc 7:9-11. Ml +3:5. Ja 2:6. +5:4.
child. Is 1:4. Le 19:32. 2 K 2:23. Jb 19:18. 30:1-12. Pr 30:17.
base. 2 S 16:5-9. Ec 10:5-7. Mt 26:67, 68. 27:28-30, 44. Mk 14:65. Lk 22:64.

6 a man. Is 4:1. Jg 11:6-8. Jn 6:15.
clothing. ver. 7.
ruler. Is 1:10. Jsh 10:24.
ruin. Zp 1:3.

7 swear. Heb. lift up the hand. Ge +14:22.
healer. Heb. binder up. Is 58:12. Je 14:19. La 2:13. Ho 5:13. 6:1.
neither bread. 2 S 19:31-40. 1 K 4:22, 23. Ne 5:17, 18. Je 41:17, 18.

8 Jerusalem. 2 Ch 28:5-7, 18, 19. 33:11. 36:17-19. Je 26:6, 18. La 5:16, 17. Mi 3:12.
because. Is 5:18, 19. 57:4. Ps 73:8, 9. Ezk 8:12. 9:9. Ho 7:16. Ml 3:13-15. Mt 12:36, 37. Ju 15.
to provoke. Is 65:3-5. Dt 31:16-18. 2 Ch 33:6, 7. Jb 17:2. Ps 78:17. Ezk 8:4-6, 17, 18. Hab 1:13. 1 C 10:22.
the eyes. 1 K 9:3. Hab 1:13.

9 The show. ver. +16. 1 S 15:32. 2 K 9:30. Je 3:3. 6:15. Da 7:20.
and they declare. Ge 13:13. 18:20, 21. 19:5-9. Jb 36:14mg. Je 44:16, 17. Ezk 23:16.
Woe. La 5:16. Ho 13:9.
soul. Heb. *nephesh*, Ge +12:3.
unto. Jb +36:14mg. Ro 1:27.

10 Say ye. Is 26:20, 21. Ec 8:12. Je 15:11. Ezk 9:4. 18:9-19. Zp 2:3. Ml 3:18. Ro 2:5-11.
they shall eat. Ps +1:3. 18:23, 24. Ga 6:7, 8. He 6:10.

11 Woe. Is 48:22. 57:20, 21. 65:13-15, 20. Ps 1:3-5. 11:5, 6. Ec 8:13.
for the reward. Ps 28:4. Pr 1:31. Mt +16:27. Ja 2:13.
given him. Heb. done to him. Ps 120:3, 4. Ro 2:6-9.

12 children. ver. +4. 2 K 15:8-25. Ec 10:16. Ho 7:3-7.
women rule over them. Jg 4:4. 1 K 10:1-13. 2 K 11:1-16. 2 Ch 9:1-9, 12. 22:2, 3, 10-12. 23:1-15. Ne 2:6. Na 3:13. Zc 5:7, 8. Mt 13:33. Ac 8:27. 1 T 2:12. Re ch. 17. 19:2.
lead thee. *or*, which call thee blessed. Nu 6:23-27. Mt +15:14.
err. Ho +4:12.
destroy. Heb. swallow up. Is 9:16mg. 25:7mg, 8. 28:4mg. Ps 35:25. La 2:5, 16. Mt 23:14.
paths. Is 2:3.

13 standeth up. Ps 12:5. Pr 22:22, 23. 23:10, 11. Ho 4:1, 2. Mi 6:2.

14 enter. Jb 22:4. 34:23. Ps 143:2.
the ancients. ver. +2, 3.
ye have eaten. *or*, ye have burnt. Is 5:5, 7.

Jb 24:2-7. Je 5:27. Am 4:1. Mi 2:2. 6:10. Mt 21:33-41.
the spoil. Ja 5:2-5.

15 What mean. Ezk 18:2. Jon 1:6.
ye beat. Is 58:4. Ex 5:14. Am 2:6, 7. 8:4-6. Mi 3:2, 3.
grind. Ex 32:20. Nu 11:8. Jb 31:10.
poor. Is 11:4. 26:6. 29:19.

16 the daughters. Is 1:8. 4:4. SS 3:11. Mt 21:5. Lk 23:28.
are haughty. Is 24:4. 32:9-11. Pr +6:17. Ec 7:8. Ezk 16:49, 50. Zp 3:11. Ml 3:15. 1 P 3:3, 4.
walk with. Lk 18:11, 13. 1 P 3:3.
wanton eyes. Heb. deceiving with their eyes. Pr 7:10, 11. 29:3. Lk 15:30. Ja 5:5. 2 P 2:14, 18. Or, as *mesakkaroth ainayim* is rendered in the Targum, "painting their eyes with stibium." Ezk 23:40.
mincing. *or*, tripping nicely.
tinkling. ver. 18.

17 smite. Le 13:29, 30, 43, 44. Dt 28:27. Re 16:2.
daughters. Is +32:9.
and. Ge +8:22.
discover. Heb. make naked. ver. 24. Is 20:4. 47:2, 3. Ge 24:20. 2 Ch 24:11. Ps +137:7mg. 141:8. Je 13:22. La 1:8. Ezk 16:36, 37, 39. 23:9, 10, 25-29. Ho 2:3, 9, 10. Mi 1:11. Na 3:5. Zc 14:2.

18 tinkling ornaments. ver. 16.
and. Ge +8:22.
cauls. *or*, networks.
round tires. Jg 8:21mg.

19 chains. *or*, sweet-balls. Jg 8:26.
and. Ge +8:22.
the bracelets. Ge 24:22, 30, 53. 38:18, 25. Ex 35:22. Nu 31:50. Ezk 16:11.
mufflers. *or*, spangled ornaments.

20 bonnets. Is 61:3, 10. Ex 39:28. Ezk 24:17, 23.
and. Ge +8:22.
ornaments. lit. "steppings." **S#6807h**. 2 S 5:24 (a going). 1 Ch 14:15.
tablets. Heb. houses of the soul. Heb. *nephesh*, Nu +23:10. Probably perfume boxes, as rendered by Bp. Lowth.
the earrings. Ge 35:4. Ex 32:2. Ezk 16:12. Ho 2:13.

21 rings. Ge 41:42. Est 8:2. SS 5:14. Lk 15:22. Ja 2:2.
and. Ge +8:22.
nose jewels. Ge 24:47. 1 T 2:9, 10. 1 P 3:3, 4.

22 The changeable suits. Zc 3:4. 1 T 2:8-10. 1 P 3:3, 4. 5:5.
and. Ge +8:22.
mantles. Ru 3:15.
crisping pins. or, purses. 2 K 4:23.

23 glasses. Ex 38:8.
and. Ge +8:22.

fine linen. Ge 41:42. 1 Ch 15:27. Ezk 16:10. Lk 16:19. Re 19:8, 14.

vails. Ge 24:65. Ru 3:15. SS 5:7.

24 **And**. Ge +8:22.

instead. Is 57:9. Pr 7:17.

baldness. ver. 17. Is 15:2. 22:12. Le 13:40. 21:5. Dt 14:1. 2 K 2:23. Ezr 9:3. Jb 1:20. Je 7:29. 16:6. 47:5. 48:37. Ezk 7:18. 27:31. 29:18. Am 8:10. Mi 1:16.

a girding. Jb +16:15.

burning. Is 4:4. Le 26:16. Dt 28:22. 32:24. Re 16:9. 18:9.

25 **Thy men**. 2 Ch 29:9. Je 11:22. 14:18. 18:21. 19:7. 21:9. 39:1-10. La 2:21. Am 9:10. Zc 14:2-5, 14. Re 19:11-21.

and. Ge +8:22.

mighty. Heb. might. Is 11:2. 28:6. 30:15. Jg 5:31. Je 41:2, 3.

26 **And**. Ge +8:22.

her gates. Is 24:12. Je 14:1, 2. La 1:4.

mourn. Is 19:8. 24:4, 7. 33:9. 57:18. 60:20. 61:2, 3. 66:10. Jb 1:20. 2:13.

desolate. or, emptied. Heb. cleansed. **S#5352h**. Ge 24:8 (clear). Ex 21:19 (be quit). Nu 5:28 (be free), 31 (guiltless). Jg 15:3 (blameless). Ps 19:13 (innocent). Je 2:35. Zc 5:3mg.

shall sit. Is 47:1. Jb 2:8, 13. Ps 137:1. La 2:10. 3:28. Je 6:26. Ezk 26:16. Mi 1:10. Lk 19:44.

ISAIAH 4

1 **And**. Ge +8:22.

in that day. Is +2:11. Ps +102:11. Lk 21:22, 23.

seven. Is 3:25, 26. 13:12. Jb 5:19.

women. Is 24:6. Je 15:8.

one man. Is 3:25, 26. +24:6.

We will eat. 2 Th 3:12.

let us be called by thy name. Heb. let thy name be called upon us. Nu 6:27. Dt 28:10.

to take away. or, take thou away.

reproach. Ps 78:63. Lk +1:25.

2 **that day**. Is 2:12.

the branch. Is +11:1. 53:2. 60:21. Ps 80:15, 17. Ezk 17:22, 23. 34:29. Lk 1:78. 23:31. Ro 15:12. Re 5:5. 22:16.

beautiful and glorious. Heb. beauty and glory. Ex 28:2. Zc 9:17. Jn 1:14. 2 C 4:6. 2 P 1:16, 17. Re 22:16.

the fruit. Is 27:6. 30:23. 45:8. Le +23:10. Ps 67:6. 85:9-13. Ezk 34:29. Ho 2:22, 23. Jl 2:23-25. 3:18. Am 9:11-15. Zc 9:17.

them that are escaped. Heb. the escaping. Is 10:20-22. 27:12, 13. 37:31, 32. Ezr 9:14. Ezk 9:4. Ob +17mg. Mt 24:22. Lk +21:36. Ro 11:4, 5. Re 7:9-14. 14:1-5.

3 **Zion**. Ps 87:5, 6.

Jerusalem. Ga 4:26. He 12:22.

shall be. Is 1:27. 52:1. 60:21. Ezk 36:24-28.

43:12. Zc 14:20, 21. 1 C 1:2. Ep 1:4. Col 3:12. He 12:14. 1 P 2:9.

written. Ex +31:18. Re +3:5.

among the living. or, to life. Ps 69:28. 87:5, 6. Ml 3:16. Ac 13:48.

4 **When**. Is 52:1. Re 21:27.

washed away. Ps +51:2. Is 3:16, etc. La 1:9. Ezk 16:6-9. 22:15. 36:25-27, 29. Jl 3:21. Zp 3:1. Zc 3:3, 4. 13:1, 9. Ml 3:2, 3. or, bathed. Ex 29:4, 17. 30:19, 21.

filth. lit. "outgoing." Is 28:8. 36:12. 2 K 18:27. Pr 30:12.

have purged. Is 26:20, 21. Ex 40:38. 2 Ch 4:6. Ezk 24:7-14. Mt 23:37.

blood. lit. bloods. Is 1:11, 15. 9:5. Ge +4:10mg. 2 K +9:26mg.

spirit. Heb. ruach, Ex +15:8.

of judgment. Is 9:5. Ezk 22:18-22. Mt +3:11, 12. Jn 16:8-11.

spirit. Heb. ruach, Ex +15:8.

of burning. Is 5:5. 40:16. 44:15. 2 Ch 4:20. 13:11. Ne 10:34. Mt +3:11.

5 **upon every**. Is 32:18. 33:20. Ps 87:2, 3. 89:7. 111:1. Mt 18:20. 28:20.

assemblies. Is +1:13. Le 23:2.

a cloud. Ex +13:21.

upon. or, above.

all the glory. Is +40:5. 46:13. Ps 85:9. 87:3.

a defence. Heb. a covering. Is 31:4, 5. 37:35. 62:4. Ex 26:1, 7. Ps 19:5. Jl 2:16.

6 **tabernacle**. Is 8:14. Ps 27:5. +91:1. Pr 18:10. Ezk 11:16. He 6:18. Re 7:16. or, covering. lit. "booth." Is 1:8. Ge 33:17. Le 23:34.

place. Ps +32:7.

for a covert. Is 32:2, 18, 19. Mt 7:24-27. He 11:7. Re 21:2-4.

rain. Is 5:6. 30:23. Ex 9:33.

ISAIAH 5

1 **Now**. Dt 31:19-22. Jg 5:1, etc. Ps 45:1. 101:1.

wellbeloved. SS 2:16. 5:2, 16. 6:3. Mk 1:11.

touching his. Is 27:2, 3. Ps 80:8. SS 8:11, 12. Je 2:21. Mt 21:33. Mk 12:1. Lk 20:9. Jn 15:1.

a very fruitful hill. Heb. the horn of the son of oil. Is 21:10mg. Dt 8:7-9. Zc 4:14mg.

2 **fenced it**. or, made a wall about it. Ex 33:16. Nu 23:9. Dt 32:8, 9. Ps 44:1-3. 105:44, 45. Ro 9:4.

gathereth out. Is 62:10. 2 S 16:6, 13.

planted. Je +11:17.

the choicest vine. or, Sorek. Is 27:2-6. Jg +16:4. Ps 44:1, 2. 80:8. SS 8:12. Je 2:21. 12:10. Ho 10:1. 14:5-7. Jn 15:1.

and built. Is 1:8. Mi 4:8.

made. Heb. hewed. Is 22:16. Dt 6:11. Pr 9:1. Ho 6:5.

a winepress. Is 63:2, 3. Ne 13:15. Re 14:18-20.

he looked. ver. 7. Is 1:2-4, 21-23. Dt 32:6.
Mt 21:33, 34. Mk 11:13. 12:2. Lk 13:7. 20:10,
etc. 1 C 9:7.
wild grapes. Dt 32:32, 33. Ho 10:1.

3 **And now**. Je 23:23. Ml 1:6. Lk 11:19. Ac
4:19. 1 C 4:21. 10:15. 11:13, 14. Ga 3:1, 2, 5.
4:21.
judge. Ps 50:4-6. 51:4. Je 2:4, 5. Mi 6:2, 3.
Mt 21:40, 41. Mk 12:9-12. Lk 20:15, 16. Ro
2:5. 3:4.

4 **What could**. Is 1:5. 2 Ch 36:14-16. Je 2:30,
31. 6:29, 30. Ezk 24:13. Mt 23:37. Ac 7:51,
etc. Ro 1:24, 28. 2 Th 2:7.

5 **go to**. Ge 11:4, 7.
my vineyard. Ps 80:9. Je 12:10. Na 2:2.
I will take. Is 27:10, 11. Le 26:31-35. Dt
28:49-52. 2 Ch 36:4-10. Ne 2:3. Jb 1:5, 10. Ps
74:1-10. 80:12-16. La 1:2-9. 4:12. Lk 13:7.
trodden down. Heb. for a treading. Is 10:6.
25:10. 28:3, 18. La 1:15. Da 8:13. Mt 23:38.
Lk 21:24. Re 11:2.

6 **I will lay**. ver. 9, 10. Is 6:11, 12. 24:1-3, 12.
27:3. 32:13, 14. Le 26:33-35. Dt 29:23. 2 Ch
36:19-21. Je 25:11. 45:4. Lk 21:24.
it shall. Is 7:23-25. Ho 3:4.
I will also. Is 30:23. Le 26:19. Dt 28:23, 24.
Am 4:7. Zc 14:16, 17. He 6:6-8. Re 11:6.
clouds. Ge +9:13.

7 **the vineyard**. Ps 80:8-11, 15. Je 12:10.
the Lord of hosts. Is 1:9. 1 S 1:3.
house of Israel. Is 14:2. 46:3. 63:7.
his pleasant plant. Heb. plant of his pleasures. Is 62:5. Ps 147:11. 149:4. SS 7:6. Zp
3:17.
judgment. or, justice. ver. 2. Is 58:6-8. Ex
22:22-27. Mi +6:8. Zc 7:9-14. Mt 3:8-10.
23:23. Jn 15:2. 1 C 6:8-11. 1 J 3:7, 8.
oppression. Heb. a scab. Is 1:6. 3:14, 15, 17.
Ps +12:5.
a cry. Ex +22:23, 27. Ne 5:1-5.

8 **Woe unto them**. Ps 10:3. Je 22:13-17. Ezk
33:31. Mi 2:2. Hab 2:9-12. Mt 23:14. Lk
12:15-24. Ep 5:3. He 13:5. 2 P 2:14.
field. 1 K 21:16, 20.
no place. Is 34:12. 40:17. 41:12, 29. 45:6, 14.
46:9. 47:8, 10. 52:4. 54:15.
they. Heb. ye.
placed. Ezk 11:15. 33:24.

9 **In mine ears, said**. or, This is in mine ears,
saith, etc. Is 22:14. Am 3:7.
Of a truth, etc. Heb. If not many houses desolate, etc.
desolate. ver. 6. Is 27:10. 2 Ch 36:21. Am
5:11. 6:11. Mt 22:7. 23:38.

10 *one bath*. Le 27:16. Ezk 45:10, 11. Jl 1:17.
Hg 1:9-11. 2:16.

11 **rise**. ver. 22. Is 28:1. Pr 23:29, 30. Ec 10:16,
17. Ho 4:11. 7:5, 6. Hab 2:15. Lk 21:34. Ro
13:13. 1 C 6:10. Ga 5:21. Ep 5:18, 19. 1 Th
5:6, 7.

inflame. or, pursue. Is 28:7, 8. Pr +20:1.
23:32.

12 **the harp**. Is 22:13. Da 5:1-4, 23. Am 6:4-6.
Lk 16:19. Col 3:16. Ja 5:13. Ju 12. Re +5:8.
are in. or, are. Ge +49:9.
they regard. ver. 19. Jb 34:27. Ps 28:5. 92:5,
6. Ho 4:10, 11.

13 **my people**. Is 1:7. 42:22-25. 2 K 17:6. 2 Ch
28:5-8.
because. Is 1:3. 27:11. Je +8:7. Ho 4:6. Mt
23:16-27. Lk 19:44. Jn 3:19, 20. Ro 1:28. 2 P
3:5.
honorable men are famished. Heb. glory
are men of famine. Is 3:8. 4:2, 5. 6:3. Je
14:18. La 4:4, 5, 9.
multitude. Je 14:3. Am 8:13.

14 **hell**. Heb. *sheol*. Ge +37:35. Is 14:9-15. 30:33.
Ps 49:14. Pr 27:20. Ezk 32:18-30. Hab 2:5. Mt
7:13. Re 6:8. 20:13-15.
enlarged. Ge +4:10.
herself. Heb. *nephesh*. Ex +15:9. Re +18:14.
opened. Nu 16:30-34. Pr 1:12.
he that rejoiceth. Is 21:4. 1 S 25:36-38. 2 S
13:28, 29. Ps 55:15. Da 5:3-6, 30. Na 1:10. Lk
12:19, 20. 16:20-23. 17:27. 21:34. Ac 12:21-
23.
shall descend. Ge +3:19. Ec +3:18-20.

15 **the mean**. Is 9:14-17. 24:2-4. Ps 62:9. Je 5:4,
5, 9. Ja 1:9-11. Re 6:15, 16.
the eyes. Is 37:23, 29. Pr +16:5.

16 **the Lord**. Ps +24:10.
exalted. Is +12:4.
in judgment. Ps 9:16. Ezk 28:22. 38:22, 23.
Ro 2:5. Re 19:1-5.
God that is holy. or, the holy God. Heb. the
God the holy. Heb. *El*, Ex +15:2. Ps +99:3.
sanctified. Is +8:13. 1 P 2:15. Re 19:11.

17 **shall the lambs**. Is 7:21, 22, 25. 17:2. 32:14.
40:11. 65:10. Zp 2:6, 14.
the waste. Dt +31:20. Am 4:1-3.
strangers. Is 1:7. Le 26:43. Dt 28:33. 2 Ch
36:21. Ne 9:37. La 5:2. Ho 8:7. Lk 21:24.

18 **draw**. Is 28:15. Jg 17:5, 13. 2 S 16:20-23. Ps
10:11. 14:1. 36:2. 94:5-11. Je 5:31. 8:5-9.
23:10, 14, 24. 28:15, 16. 44:15-19. Ezk 13:10,
11, 22. Zp 1:12. Jn 16:2. Ac 26:9.

19 **Let him**. Is 66:5. Je 5:12, 13. 17:15. 36:20-
26. Ezk 12:22, 27. Am 5:18, 19. 2 P 3:3, 4, 9.
let the. Is 30:11. Je 23:18, 36.

20 **them**. Pr 17:15. Ml 2:17. 3:15. Mt 6:23. 15:3-
6. 23:16-23. Lk 11:35. 16:15. 2 T 3:1-5. 2 P
2:1, 18, 19.
call evil good. Heb. say concerning evil, *It is*
good, etc. Nu 11:5, 6. Pr 24:24. Je 44:16-18.
Jn 16:2. Ro 3:8.
put darkness. Jb 10:22. Pr 16:25. Mt +6:23.
15:12-14. Jn 3:19, 20.

21 **wise**. Is 47:10. Jb 11:12. 37:24. Pr 3:7. 26:12,
16. Lk 16:15. Jn 9:41. Ro 1:22. 11:25. 12:16.
1 C 3:18-20.

in their own sight. Heb. before their face. Ge 19:21mg. 23:4, 8. Dt 4:37. 2 S 7:9mg.

22 **mighty**. ver. 11. Is 28:1-3, 7. Pr 23:19, 20. Hab 2:15.

23 **justify**. Ex 23:6-9. Pr 17:15. 24:24. 31:4, 5.
for reward. Is 1:23. Dt 16:19. 2 Ch 19:7. Pr 17:23. Mi 3:11. 7:3.
take. Is 10:2. 1 K 21:13. Ps 94:21. Mt 23:35. 27:24, 25. Ja 5:6.

24 **fire**. Heb. tongue of fire. Jn 15:6.
devoureth. 1 C +3:12, 13.
the flame. Mt +3:12. Lk +3:17.
their root. Is 9:14-17. Jb 18:16. Ho 9:16. Am 2:9.
cast away. 1 S 15:22, 23, 26. 2 K 17:14, 15. Ne 9:26. Ps 50:17. Je 6:19. 8:9. Lk 7:30. Jn 12:48. He 10:28, 29.
the law. Is +1:10.
despised. Is 30:12, 14. 2 S 12:9, 10. Lk 10:16. Ac 13:41. 1 Th 4:8.

25 **the anger**. Jg +2:14. 2 K 13:3. 22:13-17. Je 17:4, 27. La 2:1-3. 5:22. 1 Th 2:16.
stretched forth. Ex +7:5.
the hills. Ps 18:7. 68:8. 77:18. 114:7. Je 4:23-26. La 3:2. Ezk 32:7, 8. Jl 2:10. Mi 1:4. Na 1:5. Hab 3:10. Mt 24:7. Re 20:11.
torn. *or*, as dung. 1 K 16:4. Je 15:3. +16:4.
For all this. Is +9:12.
anger. Le 26:14, 18, 21, 23, 24, 28. Ps 78:38. Da 9:16. Ho 14:4. Re 9:12.
stretched out still. Ex +6:6.

26 **he will**. Is 11:12. 18:3. Je 51:27.
ensign. Ex +17:15.
from afar. Is 39:3. Dt 28:49. Je 5:15, 16.
hiss unto. 2 Ch +29:8.
end. Is 39:3. Dt 28:49. Ps 72:8. Je 5:15. Ml 1:11.
they shall come. Is 30:16. Je 4:13. La 4:19. Jl 2:7. Hab 1:6-10.

27 **shall be**. Jl 2:7, 8.
neither. Is 45:1, 5. 1 K 2:5. Ps 93:1. Da 5:6. Lk +12:35.
nor the latchet. Dt 32:25.

28 **arrows**. Ps 45:5. 120:4. Je 5:16. Ezk 21:9-11.
their horses. Jg 5:22. Je 47:3. Mi 4:13. Na 2:3, 4. 3:2.
whirlwind. Je +23:19.

29 **roaring**. Is 38:13. Ge 49:9. Nu 23:24. 24:9. Dt 33:20, 22. Jb 4:11. 10:16. 38:39, 40. Ps +7:2. Pr +19:12. 30:30. Je +2:15. Ezk 19:2. Da 6:24. 7:4. Ho 5:14. 13:7. Am +1:2. Mi 5:8. Na 2:11, 12. Zp 3:3. Zc 11:3. 2 T 4:17. 1 P 5:8. Re 5:5.
lion. Da 7:2-4, 7. Mt ch. 24. Jn 11:48.
lay hold. Is 42:22. 49:24, 25.
none shall. Ps 50:22. Je 32:5, 28. 37:8-10.

30 **like**. Ps 93:3, 4. Je 6:23. 50:42. Lk +21:25.
if one look. La 3:2. Re 6:12.
darkness. Ex +10:22.

sorrow. *or*, distress. Is 25:4. 26:16.
and the light, etc. *or*, when it is light, it shall be dark in the destructions thereof. Jl 3:15. Zc 14:6.

ISAIAH 6

1 A.M. 3245. B.C. 759.
the year. 2 K 15:7, Azariah. 2 Ch 26:22, 23.
I saw also. Ex 24:10, 11. Ex 33:20. Nu 12:8. Ezk 1:1, 25-28. Jn 1:18. 12:41, 45. 1 T 6:16.
sitting. Ezk 10:1. Da 7:9.
throne. Ps +11:4.
high. Is 12:4. 57:15. Ps 46:10. 108:5. 113:5. Ezk 1:26. Ep 1:20, 21.
his train. *or*, the skirts thereof. Ex 28:33, 34. 39:24-26. Je 13:22, 26. La 1:9. Na 3:5.
filled. 1 K 8:10, 11. Re 15:8.

2 **stood**. 1 K 22:19. Jb 1:6. Da 7:10. Zc 3:4. Lk 1:19. Re 7:11.
seraphims. Ps 104:4. Ezk 1:4. He 1:7.
wings. Ex 25:20. 37:9. 1 K 6:24, 27. 8:7. Ezk 1:6, 9, 24. 10:21. Re 4:8.
covered his face. Ge 17:3. Ex 3:6. 1 K 19:13. Ps 89:7.
his feet. Jb 4:18. 15:15. Ezk 1:11.
did fly. ver. 6. Ps 18:10. 103:20. Ezk 10:16. Da 9:21. Re 8:13. 14:6.

3 **one cried unto another**. Heb. this cried to this. Ex 15:20, 21. Ezr 3:11. Ps 24:7-10.
Holy. Ps +99:3. Mt 6:9.
the Lord. Is 40:10, 11. Ps +24:10.
the whole earth, etc. Heb. his glory *is* the fulness of the whole earth. Is 24:16. Ps 19:1-3. 57:11. Zc 14:9. Ep 1:18-23.
his glory. Is +40:5. Jn 12:41.

4 **posts**. Ezk 1:24. 10:5. Am 9:1.
door. Heb. thresholds. 2 K +12:9mg.
the house. Ex +13:21. Ezk 1:28.
filled. Ps 18:8. Re 11:19. 15:8.

5 **said I**. Jb 42:5, 6. Da 10:6-8. Hab 3:16. Lk 5:8, 9. Re 1:16, 17.
Woe. Is 5:8, 11, 18, 20.
undone. Heb. cut off. Is 15:1mg. Ps 31:17mg, 22.
a man. Ex 4:10. 6:12, 30. Jb 42:5, 6. Je 1:6. Zc 3:1-7. Mt 12:34-37. Lk 5:8. Ja 3:1, 2.
I dwell. Is 29:13. Je 9:3-8. Ezk 2:6-8. 33:31. Ja 3:6-10.
mine eyes. Is 33:17. Ge +32:30. Jn 12:41. Re 1:5-7, 17.
the King. Is 44:6.
the Lord of hosts. Ps +24:10. Jn 12:37-41. Ac 5:3, 4. 28:25, 26.

6 **flew**. ver. 2. Da 9:21-23. He 1:7, 14.
having, etc. Heb. and in his hand a live coal. Ezk 10:2. Mt 3:11. Ac 2:3, 4. Re 8:3-5.
which. Le 16:12. He 9:22-26. 13:10. Re 8:3-5.
tongs. Ex 25:38. 37:23 (snuffers).
the altar. Le 6:9. 1 K 18:38.

7 **he laid it upon**. Heb. caused it to touch. Je 1:9. Da 10:16.

thine iniquity. Is 43:25. 53:5, 10. Mt 9:2. Ro 8:1. He 1:3. 9:13, 14. 1 J 1:7. 2:1, 2.

thy sin. Is 38:17. 43:25. Lk 1:77. 24:47. Ro 5:11, 18, 19. 2 C 5:21. He +9:22.

8 **I heard**. Ge 3:8-10. Dt 4:33-36. Ezk 1:24. 10:5. Ac 28:25-28.

the voice of the Lord. Ex 16:7 w He 3:7-9. Ac 5:3, 4. 28:25-27.

Whom. 2 S 23:15. Ro 7:24.

send. Ex 4:10-13. 1 K 22:20. Ac 22:21. 26:16, 17.

who will go. Ezk 22:30.

us. Ge +1:26. 3:22. 11:7. Da 4:17. Mi +5:2. Mt +9:4. +18:20. +28:19. Jn +5:18. 1 C +1:24. 2 C 13:14. Ep 2:18. Col +1:16. +2:10. He +9:14. +13:8. 1 P 1:2. 1 J 5:7.

Then. Mt 4:20-22. Ac 20:24. Ep 3:8.

Here am I. Heb. Behold me. Is 65:1. Ge 22:1mg. Jb 38:35mg.

send me. Ezk 22:30. Ac 9:6.

9 **Go**. Is 23:16. 47:1.

and tell. Is 29:13. 30:8-11. Ex 32:7-10. Je 15:1, 2. Ho 1:9.

Hear ye. Is 43:8. 44:18-20. Mt *13:14, 15*. Mk *4:12*. Lk *8:10*. Jn 12:40. Ac *28:26, 27*. Ro *11:8*.

indeed. *or*, without ceasing. Heb. in hearing. Ge +2:16.

indeed. Heb. in seeing.

perceive not. Jn 8:43. Ac 7:51. 2 Th 2:11, 12.

10 **Make**. Ge +2:17. +31:7. Ps +16:9. Je 1:10. Ezk 43:3. Am +3:6. Mt *13:15*. Lk +8:10. Jn *12:40*. Ac 10:15. *28:27*.

the heart. Is 29:10. 63:17. Ex 7:3. 10:27. 11:10. 14:17. Dt 2:30. Ezk 3:6-11. Jn *12:40*. 2 C 2:16.

fat. Dt +31:20.

ears heavy. Je 6:10. Zc 7:11. Ac 7:51.

eyes. Ps 69:23.

lest. Jn 3:19, 20. He 3:8-11.

convert. Ac +3:19.

healed. Is 19:22.

11 **Lord**. Re +6:10.

how long. Ezk 11:13. Ro 11:25. Re 11:1, 2.

Until the. Is 1:7. 3:26. 24:1-12. 27:10. 32:13, 14. 2 Ch 36:21. Je 26:6, 9, 18. Mi 3:12. Lk 21:24.

utterly desolate. Heb. desolate with desolation. Je +18:16.

12 **the Lord**. Is 26:15. 2 K 25:11, 21. Je 15:4. 52:28-30.

a great. Je 4:29. 12:7. La 5:20. Ro +11:1, 2, 15.

13 **But yet**. Is 4:3. Ezk 11:16. Mi +4:7. Mt 24:22. Mk 13:20.

and it shall return, etc. *or*, when *it* is returned, and hath been broused.

teil tree. Is 1:29, 30.

an oak. Jb 14:7.

substance. *or*, stock, *or* stem. Jb 14:7-9.

so the holy. Is 11:1. 27:6. 65:8, 9. Ge 22:18. +49:10. Ezr 9:2. Ml 2:15. Mt 1:23. Lk +1:35. Jn 5:26. 15:1-3. Ac 4:27. Ro 9:5. 11:5, 24. Ga 3:16-19, 28, 29. Re 22:16.

ISAIAH 7

1 **the days**. 2 K 16:1-6. 2 Ch 28:1-6.

Rezin. Is 8:6. 2 K 15:27, 37. 16:5. Ps 83:3-5.

but could. ver. 4-9. Is 8:9, 10. Ps 27:1, 2. 112:7, 8. Pr 28:1.

2 **the house**. ver. 13. Is 6:13. 37:35. 2 S 7:16. 1 K 11:32. 12:16-20. 13:2. Je 21:12.

is confederate with. Heb. resteth on. ver. 17. Is 11:13. 2 Ch 25:10. 28:12. Ezk 37:16-19. Ho 12:1.

Ephraim. Ge +41:52.

And his heart. Is 8:12. 37:27. Le 26:36, 37. Nu 14:1-3. Dt 28:65, 66. 2 K 7:6, 7. Ps 11:1. 27:1, 2. 112:7, 8. Pr 28:1. Mt 2:3.

3 **Then said**. Is 65:24. Ja 5:11.

Go forth. Ex 7:15. Je 19:2, 3. 22:1.

Shear-jashub. *that is*, The remnant shall return. **S#7610h**. Is 6:13. 10:21, 22. 55:7. Ro 9:27.

the end. Is 36:2. 2 K 18:17. 20:20.

conduit. lit. a "thing causing to go up." Is 36:2. 2 K 20:20.

upper. Is 22:9, 11. 2 K 18:17. 20:20. Ne 2:14. 3:16.

pool. lit. "blessing," because of the value of water.

highway. *or*, causeway. Is 11:16. 19:23. 33:8. 35:8. 36:2. 40:3. 49:11. 57:14. 59:7. 62:10.

fuller's. or, washerman. Is 36:2. 2 K 18:17.

4 **Take heed**. Is 28:16. 30:7, 15. Ex 14:13, 14. 2 Ch 20:17. La 3:26.

fear not. Is 8:11-14. 35:4. 41:14. 51:12, 13. Mt +10:28. 24:6.

neither be fainthearted. Heb. let not thy heart be tender. Dt 20:3. 1 S 17:32. 2 S 3:39mg.

the two tails. ver. 8. Is 8:4. 2 K 15:29, 30. Am 4:11.

5 **Syria**. Ps 2:2. 83:3, 4. Na 1:11. Zc 1:15.

Ephraim. ver. 2.

the son. Is 8:6.

6 **go up**. Is 2:3. 5:24. 14:8, 13.

vex. *or*, waken. lit. "disgust." **S#6973h**. Ge 27:46 (weary). Ex 1:12 (grieved). Le 20:23 (abhorred). Nu 21:5 (loatheth). 22:3 (distressed). 1 K 11:25 (abhorred). Pr 3:11 (weary). Is 7:16 (abhorrest).

Tabeal. i.e. *goodness of God; good is God; good for nothing*, **S#2870h**. Is 7:6. Ezr 4:7.

7 **It shall not**. Is 10:6-12. 37:29. 46:10, 11. Ps 2:4-6. 76:10. Je +19:7. Da 4:35. Ac 4:25-28.

8 **For the head**. 2 S 8:6.

Syria. i.e. *sublime, deceiving; exalted*, S#758h.
ver. 1, 2, 4, 5, 8. Is 17:3. Jg 10:6. 2 S 8:6, 12.
15:8. 1 K 10:29. 11:25. 15:18. 19:15. 20:1, 20,
22, 23. 22:1, 3, 31. 2 K 5:1, 5. 6:8, 11, 23, 24.
7:5. 8:7, 9, 13, 28, 29. 9:14, 15. 12:17, 18.
13:3, 4, 7, 17, 19, 22, 24. 15:37. 16:5-7. 2 Ch
1:17. 16:2, 7. 18:10, 30. 20:2. 22:5, 6. 24:23.
28:5, 23. Ezk 16:57. 27:16. Ho 12:12. Am 1:5.
within. Is 8:4. 17:1-3. 2 K 17:1-6, etc. 19:17.
Ezr 4:2.
Ephraim. Ge +41:52.
that it be not a people. Heb. from a people.
Ho 1:6-10.

9 **the head**. 1 K +16:24.
Ephraim. ver. 8.
If ye, etc. *or*, ye not believe? *it is* because ye
are not stable. 2 Ch +20:20. Ac 27:11, 25. Ro
11:20. He 11:6. Ja 1:8. 1 J 5:10.

10 **Moreover**, etc. Heb. and the Lord added to
speak. Is 1:5, 13. 8:5. 10:20. Ho 13:2mg.

11 **Ask**. Is 45:11. Dt 4:32. 32:7. Ml 3:10. Mt 7:7.
sign. or, "token." ver. 14. Is 8:18. 19:20. 20:3.
37:30. 38:7, 8, 22. 44:25. 55:13. 66:19. Ge
1:14. 15:7, 8. 24:14. Ex 4:1, 8, 9. 12:13. Jg
6:36-40. 2 K 20:8-11. Ps 86:17. Je 19:1, 10.
51:63, 64. Mt 12:38-40. 16:1-4. Lk 21:7. Jn
2:18. 6:30, 31. Ac 4:29, 30.
ask it either in the depth. *or*, make *thy*
petition deep.
the height. Ezk 21:26.

12 **I will not ask**. 2 K 16:7, 8, 15. 2 Ch 28:22.
neither. Ezk 33:31.
tempt. Ex +17:2.

13 **O house**. ver. 2. 2 Ch 21:7. Je 21:12. Lk 1:69.
Is it a small. Ge 30:15. Nu 16:9, 13. Ezk
16:20, 47. 34:18.
to weary. 2 Ch 36:15, 16. Je 6:11.
will ye. Is 1:14, 24. 43:24. 63:10. 65:3-5. 2
Ch 28:5, 6. Ps 78:40. Am 2:13. Ml 2:17. Ac
7:51. He 3:10, 11.

14 **sign**. ver. 11. Is 38:7.
Behold. Ge +3:15. Ps 22:10. 69:8. 86:16.
116:16. Je 31:22. Mi 5:3. Mt +1:23. Lk +1:35.
a virgin. or, the virgin. S#5959h. Ge +24:43.
Ex 2:8. Ps 68:25. Pr 30:19. SS 1:3. 6:8. Mt
1:18, 20, 21, 23, 25. Lk 1:27 (S#3933g), 34, 38.
2:7. Ga 4:4. For related words, see S#1330h, Ge
+24:16; S#1331h, Le +21:13; S#3207h, Ge +34:4;
S#5291h, Ge +24:14; S#5291h with S#1330h, Dt
+22:23; S#3933g, Mt +1:23.
shall. Is 37:22. Ge 38:24.
conceive. S#2030h. Ge 16:11. 38:24, 25. Ex
21:22. Jg 13:5, 7. 1 S +4:19. 2 S 11:5. 2 K 8:12.
15:16. Is 7:14. 26:17. Je 20:17. 31:8. Am 1:13.
a son. Is +9:6.
shall call. *or*, thou, *O virgin*, shalt call. Ge 4:1,
2, 25. 16:11. 29:32. 30:6, 8. 1 S 1:20. 4:21.
Immanuel. i.e. *with us (he is) God; God with us*,
S#6005h. Is 8:8, 10. 9:6. 44:6. Mt 1:22, 23. Jn
1:1, 2, 14. Ro 9:5. 1 T 3:16.

15 **Butter**. ver. 22. Mt 3:4.
know. Ps 51:5. Am 5:15. Lk +1:35. 2:1-5, 40,
52. Ro 12:9. Ph 1:9, 10.

16 **before**. Dt 1:39. Jon 4:11.
the land. Is 8:4. 9:11, 12. 17:1-3. 2 K 15:29,
30. 16:9.

17 **bring upon**. Is 8:7, 8. 10:5, 6. ch. 36, 37. 2 K
ch. 18, 19. 2 Ch 28:19-21. ch. 32. 33:11. 36:6-
20. Ne 9:32.
the day. 1 K 12:16-19. 2 Ch 10:16-19.

18 **hiss**. 2 Ch +29:8.
fly. Is 30:1, 2. 31:1. Ex 8:21, 24. Dt 1:44.
7:20. Jsh 24:12. Ps 118:12.
rivers of Egypt. Ex 7:19. 8:5. 2 K 19:24. Jb
28:10. Ps 78:44.
bee. ver. 17. Dt 1:44. Jg 14:8. 2 K 23:29, 33,
34. Ps 118:12.

19 **desolate valleys**. Le 26:31-33.
in the holes. Is 2:19, 21. 2 Ch 33:11. Je
16:16. Mi 7:17.
bushes. *or*, commendable trees.

20 **shave**. Is 10:6. 2 K 15:19. 16:7, 8, 17, 18.
17:3. 2 Ch 28:20, 21. Je 27:6, 7. Ezk 5:1-4.
29:18, 20.
the head. Is 1:5, 6. 9:14-17. 24:2.

21 **a man**. ver. 25. Is 5:17. 17:2. 37:30. Je 39:10.

22 **butter and honey**. ver. 15. 2 S 17:29. Mt
3:4.
land. Heb. midst of the land.

23 **a thousand vines**. SS 8:11, 12. Mt 21:33.
be for briers. Is 5:6. 32:12-14. Je 4:26. He
6:8.

24 **arrows**. Is 5:28. 37:33. 49:2. Ge 27:3. Jg 5:6,
11.

25 **but it**. ver. 21, 22. Is 13:20-22. 17:2. Le
26:34, 35. Zp 2:6.

ISAIAH 8

1 **Take thee**. Je 32:11. 36:2, 28, 32.
write. Is 30:8. Jb 19:23, 24. Hab 2:2, 3.
a man's pen. Re 13:18. 21:17.
Maher-shalal-hash-baz. Heb. in making
speed to the spoil, he hasteneth to the prey.
Or, Make speed, etc. hasten, etc. i.e. *hasting
the prey*, S#4122h.

2 **I took**. Ru 4:2, 10, 11. 2 C 13:1.
Uriah. 2 S +11:3. 2 K 16:10, 11. 18:2.
Zechariah. 2 K 18:2. Zc +1:1.
Jeberechiah. i.e. *Jah blesses; he will be blessed
of the Lord*, S#3000h.

3 **went**. Heb. approached. Ge 27:41. 37:18.
the prophetess. Ex +15:20.
she conceived. Ho 1:3-9.
Call his name. Is 7:13, 14.
Maher-shalal-hash-baz. ver. 1.

4 **before**. Is 7:15, 16. Dt 1:39. Jon 4:11. Ro
9:11.
the riches of Damascus, etc. *or*, he that is
before the king of Assyria shall take away the

riches, etc. Is 10:6-14. 17:3. 2 K 15:29. 16:9.
17:3, 5, 6.

5 A.M. 3263. B.C. 741.
spake. Is 7:10.

6 refuseth. 1 K 7:16. 2 Ch 13:8-18.
the waters of. Ne 3:15. Jn 9:7, Siloam.
Shiloah. i.e. *thing sent; sent forth*, **S#7975h**. Is
8:6. Ne 3:15.
that go softly. 2 S 18:5. 1 K 21:27. Jb 15:11.
Je 2:13, 18. 18:14.
rejoice. Is 7:1, 2, 6. Jg 9:16-20.

7 the Lord bringeth. Is 59:19. Ge 6:17. Dt
28:49-52. Je +47:2. Lk 6:48.
strong. Ezr 4:10. Ps 72:8.
the king. Is 7:1-6, 17. 10:8-14. Ezk 31:3, etc.
he shall come. 2 K 17:3-6, 23, 24. 18:9-16.
banks. Nu 34:12.

8 he shall pass. Is 10:28-32. 22:1-7. 28:14-22.
29:1-9. ch. 36, 37.
reach. Is 30:28.
the stretching, etc. Heb. the fulness of the
breadth of thy land shall be the stretchings
out of his wings. Ezk 17:3.
O Immanuel. Is 7:14. Mt 1:23, Emmanuel.
28:20.

9 Associate. Is 7:1, 2. 54:15. Je 46:9-11. Ezk
38:9-23. Jl 3:9-14. Mi 4:11-13. Zc 14:1-3. Re
17:12-14. 20:8, 9.
and ye. *or*, yet ye. Is 14:5, 6. 28:13. Ps 37:14,
15. Pr 11:21.
gird yourselves. Is 45:5. 50:11.
be broken. Is 37:36. 1 K 20:11.

10 Take counsel. Ps 2:1, 2. 46:1, 7. 83:3, etc. Je
+19:7. Na 1:9-12. Ac 5:38, 39.
for God. Heb. *El*, Ex +15:2.
with us. Is 7:14. 9:6. +43:2. 2 Ch 13:12. Pr
11:21. Ac 5:39. 1 J 4:4.

11 with a strong hand. Heb. in strength of
hand. Je 20:7, 9. 1 K +18:46. Ac 4:20.
instructed. Ps +32:8. Pr 1:15. Je 15:19. Ezk
2:6-8.

12 Say ye not. Is 7:2-6. 51:12, 13. 2 K 16:5-7.
A confederacy. 2 K +11:14.
neither fear ye. Is 7:4. 51:12, 13. +36:18.
57:9-11. Jb +3:25. Ps 53:5. Je 1:17-19. Mt
28:2-5. Lk 12:4, 5. 21:9. 1 P *3:14, 15*.

13 Sanctify. Is 5:16. 26:3, 4. 29:23. Le 10:3.
22:32. Nu 20:12, 13. 27:14. Dt 32:51. Je
+12:3. Ezk 20:41. 28:22, 25. 36:23. +37:28.
38:16, 23. 39:27. Mt 6:9. Ro 4:20. 1 C 7:14. 1
P 2:5-8. 3:15.
and let him. Ge 31:53. Mt +10:28. 1 P *3:13-15*.
fear. Ec +12:13.

14 he shall be. Is 26:20. Ps 46:1, 2. Pr 18:10.
Ezk 11:16.
a stone. Is 28:16. Zc 3:9. Lk 2:34. Ro 9:32, *33*.
11:9-11, 35. Ep 2:20, 21. 1 P 2:8.
a snare. Ps 11:6. 69:22. Mt 13:57. Lk 21:35.

15 stumble. Da +2:44. Mt 11:6. 15:14. Jn 6:66.
Ro 11:25. 1 C 1:23. 1 P 2:7, 8.

16 Bind up. Is 29:11. Da 12:4.
the testimony. ver. 20. Ex +34:16. Dt 4:45.
2 K 11:12. Jn 3:32, 33. He 3:5. 1 J 5:9-12. Re
+19:10.
seal. Da 9:24. Re 5:1, 5. 10:4.
law. Is +1:10.
among. Is 54:13. Ps 25:14. Pr +8:8, 9. Da
12:9, 10. Mt 13:11. Mk 4:10, 11, 34. 10:10. 1
C 2:14. 2 C 3:14-16. Re 2:17.
disciples. lit. taught ones. **S#3928h**. Is 50:4
(learned; lit. disciples). 54:13. Je 2:24mg.
13:23mg.

17 I will. Is 64:4. Ps +25:3. 1 Th 1:10. 2 Th 3:5.
He 9:28. 10:36-39.
hideth. Is 54:8. Dt +31:17.
I will look. Is 50:10. Lk 2:38. He *2:13a*. 9:28.

18 I and the. ver. 3. Is 7:3, 16. 53:10. Ps 22:30.
He 2:*13b*, 14.
for signs. Is 20:3. Ex 7:3. Dt 4:34. 6:22. 7:19.
13:1, 2. 26:8. 28:46. 29:3. 34:11. Ps 71:7. Ezk
14:8. Zc 3:8. Lk 2:34. 1 C 4:9-13. He 10:33.
which. Is 12:6. 14:32. 24:23. 1 Ch 23:25. Ps
9:11. Zc 8:3. He 12:22.

19 Seek. Is 2:6. 1 S 28:8.
familiar spirits. lit. "bottles." Dt +18:11. Jb
32:19 (like bottles).
wizards. 2 K +21:6.
that peep. Is 10:14. 29:4.
should not. 1 S 28:16. 2 K 1:3. 2 P 2:1.
for the living. Ps 106:28. Je 10:10. 1 Th 1:9.

20 To the law. ver. +16. Jsh 1:8. Ezr 10:3. Ps
119:1. Mt 4:7. Lk 10:26. 16:29-31. Jn 5:39,
46, 47. Ac 17:11. Ro 4:3. Ga 3:8, etc. 4:21, 22.
2 T 3:15-17. 2 P 1:19.
testimony. ver. 16. Ru 4:7.
if they speak not. Ps +119:63. Pr +19:27. Mt
24:4. Mk +4:24. Lk +8:18. Ac 20:28-32. 2 C
4:2. Ga 1:6, 7. 3:1. Ep 4:14. 2 T +3:5. 2 P 2:1.
3:16. 2 J 9, 10.
according. Dt 30:11. Ps 8:2. +102:18. Pr
+8:9. Is 29:11-13. Ezk 14:10. Mt 7:21-23.
11:25. 15:3-6, 9. Mk 7:7-9. 12:24, 27. Jn
5:24-47. 12:48. Ac 17:11. Ro 2:16, 18. 14:12.
1 C 1:2. 2 C 10:12. 11:4. Ga 1:8. Ep 1:1. Ph
1:1. Col 1:2.
to this word. Dt +4:2. Pr 30:5, 6. Je 23:28,
29. Mk 12:24. Jn 8:31, 32.
it is. Is 30:8-11. Ps 19:7, 8. 119:130. Je 8:9.
Mi 3:6. Mt 6:23. 22:29. Mk 7:7-9. Ro 1:22. 2
P 1:19.
light. Heb. morning. lit. "darkness," either of
morning or of evening (Young). Is +17:14. Ge
32:25, 27. Jsh 6:15. 1 S 9:26. Jb 24:16. 38:12.
Ps 119:105, 130. 139:9. Pr +4:18, 19. 20:20.
Mt 6:23. 8:12. Jn 1:9. 3:19. 8:12. 2 C 4:3, 4. 2
P 1:19. 1 J 1:5, 7. 2:11. Ju 13. Re +2:28.

21 through. ver. 7, 8.
hardly bestead. or, sore distressed. Is 9:20.
Dt 28:33, 34, 53-57. 2 K 25:2, 3. Je 14:18.
52:6. La 4:4, 5, 9, 10.

hungry. Mt 4:4. 5:6. 2 P 2:2.
they shall fret. Pr 19:3. Re 16:11, 21.
curse. Ex 22:28. 2 K 6:33. Jb 1:11. 2:5, 9. Re 9:20, 21. 16:9-11.
look upward. 2 S +22:42.

22 **look**. Is 9:1. 2 Ch 15:5, 6. Je 30:6, 7. Am 5:18-20. Mt 8:12.
and darkness. Ex +10:22.
dimness. Pr 20:20.
driven to darkness. Is 3:11. Jb 18:18. Pr 14:32. Je 23:12. Mi 3:6. Mt 22:13.

ISAIAH 9

1 A.M. 3264. B.C. 740.
the dimness. Is 8:22.
when. 1 K 15:19, 20. 2 K 15:29. 2 Ch 16:4.
afterward. Le 26:23, 24, 28. 2 K 17:5, 6. 1 Ch 5:26.
by the way. Mt 4:15.
Galilee of the nations. *or*, Galilee the populous. Mt 4:12-16, 23.

2 **walked**. Is 50:10. Ec 2:14. Mi 7:8, 9. Mt *4:14-16*. Jn 1:4, 5, 9. 12:35, 36, 46. 1 J 1:5-7. Re 21:23, 24. 22:5.
darkness. Is 42:16. 50:10. Mt +4:16. 6:22, +23. Lk 1:79. Jn 1:5. 3:19, 21. 8:12. 11:9, 10. 12:35. Ac 26:18. Ro 1:21. 13:12, 13. 1 C 4:5. 2 C 4:6. 6:14. Ep 5:8, 11, 14. 1 Th 5:4, 5. 1 P 2:9. 1 J 1:5-7. 2:8-11.
shadow of death. Ps +23:4.
the light shined. Jb 22:28. Mt 4:12-16.

3 **hast multiplied**. Is 26:15. 49:20-22. Ne 9:23. Ps 107:38. Ho 4:7. Zc 2:11. 8:23. 10:8.
not increased the joy. *or*, to him increased the joy.
they joy. Is 12:1. 25:9. 35:2, 10. 54:1. 55:12. 61:7, 10. 65:18. 66:10. Ps 4:7. 126:5, 6. Je 31:7, 12-14. Ac 8:8. Ph 4:4. 1 P 1:8.
according. Is 16:9, 10.
and as men. Jg 5:30. 1 S 30:16. 2 Ch 20:25-28. Ps 119:162. Lk 11:22.

4 **For thou hast broken**. *or*, When thou brakest. Is 14:25. 47:6. Ge 27:40. Le 26:13. Je 30:8. Na 1:13.
the staff. Is 10:5, 27. 14:3-5. 30:31, 32.
the rod. Ps +125:3.
as in the day. Is 10:26. Ge +25:2. Ps 83:9-11. Ps +102:11.

5 **For every battle**, etc. *or*, When the whole battle of the warrior was, etc.
confused noise. Is 13:4. 1 S 14:19. Je 47:3. Jl 2:5. Na 3:2.
garments. Is 63:1-3. Re 19:13.
but this shall be. or, and it was, etc.
burning. Is 37:36. Ps 46:9. Ezk 39:8-10. Hab 3:5. Mt +3:11. 2 Th 1:8.
fuel. Heb. meat. ver. 19. Le 3:11, 16.

6 **For unto**. Is 7:14. Lk 1:35. *2:11*.
us. Lk 2:4. 3:23. Jn 4:22. Ro 9:5.

a child. Is 2:6. 8:18. 29:23.
is born. Is +7:14. 44:6. Mt 1:23. Lk 1:35. 2:11.
a son. lit. a "builder up." Is 1:1, 2.
is given. Jn 1:14. 3:16, 17. +8:35. 16:30. Ro 8:32. He 1:2. 1 J 4:10-14.
and. Is 6:12. Lk 4:18, 21.
the government. Is 22:21, 22. Ge 41:40. +49:10. Ps 2:6-12. 8:6. 110:1-4. Je 23:5, 6. Zc 6:12, 13. 9:9, 10. Mt 11:27. Lk 22:29. 1 C 15:25. Ep 1:22, 23. Re 1:6. +2:27. 19:16.
upon his shoulder. Is 22:22.
his name. Is +7:14. Jg 13:18. Ps +9:10. +20:1. Je 31:22. Mt +1:23. 1 T 3:16.
Wonderful. Is 28:29. Jg 13:18mg. Mt 21:15. Ac 2:22.
Counsellor. Is 11:2. 28:29. Pr 8:14. Je 32:19. Zc 6:13. Mt 7:28, 29. 12:42. Lk 21:15. Jn 1:16. 1 C 1:30. Ep +1:11. Col 2:3. 1 J 2:1. Re 3:18.
The mighty. Is 1:24. +10:21 (**S#1368h**). 44:6, 8. +49:26. Ps 45:3. 89:19. +99:3. Re 1:8.
God. Heb. *El*, Ex +15:2. Is 45:24, 25. Ps 45:3, 6. 50:1. Je 23:5, 6. Zc 13:7. Mt 1:23. Lk 1:47, 76. Jn 1:1, 2. +8:24, 58. +20:28. Ac 20:28. Ro 9:5. Col 2:9. 1 T 6:14-16. T 2:13. He 1:2, 3, +8. 1 J 5:20.
The everlasting. Is 40:28. 63:16. Ps +9:18 (**S#5703h**). Pr 8:27. Jn +1:1-3. +8:58. Col +1:17.
Father. Is 8:18. 53:10. 64:8. Pr +8:23. Jn +10:30. 1 C 15:22. He 2:13, 14. 9:12. Re 1:18.
The Prince of Peace. Is 11:6-9. 53:5. Ps 72:3, 7. 85:10. Da 9:24, 25. Mi 5:4, 5. Lk 2:14. Jn 14:27. Ac 10:36. Ro 5:1-10. 2 C 5:19. Ep 2:14-18. Col 1:20, 21. 2 Th 3:16. He 7:2, 3. 13:20.

7 **the increase**. 2 S 7:16. Ps 2:8. 72:8-11. 89:35-37. 145:13. Je 33:15-21. Da 2:35, 44. 4:3. 7:14, 18, 27. Lk *1:32, 33*. 1 C +15:24-28.
no end. Ge +9:12, +16. Ps 89:4. Da 2:44. +7:14. Lk 1:32, 33.
throne of David. Ps +132:11. Lk 1:32. Ac +2:30. +13:23. Re 3:7.
to establish it. Is 32:1, 2. Ps 45:4-6. 72:1-3, 7. He 1:8.
judgment. Ps +7:8.
for ever. Heb. *olam*, Ex +12:24. Ge +9:12, +16. 1 P 4:11. Re +11:15.
The zeal. Is 37:32. 59:17. 63:4-6, 15. 2 K 19:31. Ps +69:9. Ezk 36:21-23.

8 **sent a word**. Is 7:7, 8. 8:4-8. Mi 1:1-9. Zc 1:6. 5:1-4. Mt 24:35.

9 **And all**. Is 26:11. 1 K 22:25. Jb 21:19, 20. Je 30:24. 44:28, 29. Ezk 7:9, 27. 30:19. 33:33.
even Ephraim. Is 7:9. 10:9-11.
in the pride. Is 46:12. 48:4. Pr 16:18. Ml 3:13. 4:1. 1 P 5:5.

10 **bricks**. 1 K 7:9-12. 10:27. Ml 1:4.
but we. Le 26:18. Pr 16:18. Ezk 7:9. Ml 1:4. 1 P 5:5.

11 set up. Is 8:4-7. 10:9-11. 17:1-5. 2 K 15:29. 16:9.
join. Heb. mingle. Is 19:2mg.

12 Syrians. 2 K 16:6. 2 Ch 28:18. Je 35:11.
devour Israel. Dt 31:17. Ps 79:7. 129:3-6. Je 10:25.
open mouth. Heb. whole mouth.
For all this. ver. 17, 21. Is 5:25. 10:4. Je 4:8.
stretched. Ex +7:5.
still. Je 44:28. Mt 24:35.

13 the people. Is 26:11. Jb 36:13. Je +31:18. Ezk 24:13. Ho 5:15. 7:10, 16.
turneth not. Dt 4:29, 30. Jb 10:15-18. 16:12. Pr +27:22. La 1:12, 13. 3:10-12. Am 4:6, 7-11. Ju +16.
neither. Is 31:1. Dt 4:29. Je +29:11. 50:4, 5. Ho 3:4, 5.

14 will cut. Is 3:2, 3. 19:15. 2 K 17:6-20. Ho 1:4, 6, 9. 4:5. 5:12-14. 8:8. 9:11-17. 13:3. Am 2:14-16. 3:12. 5:2, 3. 6:11. 7:8, 9, 17. 9:1-9. Mi 1:6-8.
rush. Is 19:15. 58:5. Jb 41:2, 20.
in one day. Is 10:17. 30:13. Ho 10:15. Re 18:8, 10, 17.

15 ancient. Is 3:5. 5:13. 1 S 9:6.
head. Dt 28:13, 44.
the prophet. Is 28:17. 29:10. 1 K 13:18. 22:22-24. Je 5:31. 14:14, 15. 23:9, 14, 15, 25-27. 27:9, 10, 14, 15. 28:15, 16. 29:21, 31, 32. Ezk 13:1-16, 19, 22. Ho 9:8. Ml 2:9. Mt 7:15, 16. 24:24. 2 C 11:13-15. Ga 1:8, 9. 2 Th 2:9-12. 2 T 4:2, 3. 2 P 2:1-3. 1 J 4:1. Re 19:20.
tail. Dt 28:13, 44.

16 the leaders, etc. or, they that call them blessed. Is 3:12mg.
cause them to err. Ho +4:12. Mt +15:14. 18:6. 23:2, 3, 15, 16. Mk 9:42. +12:24, 27. Lk 17:1, 2. 1 T 4:2. 6:3, 4. 2 T 4:3. T 1:11. 2 P 2:1.
led of them. or, called blessed of them. Nu 6:23-26. 1 K 8:55, 56. 2 Ch 30:27. He 7:7.
destroyed. Heb. swallowed up. Is +3:12mg.

17 have no joy. Is 10:2. 13:18. 27:11. 62:5. 65:19. Ps 147:10, 11. Je 18:21. Zc 9:17.
for every. Jb +8:13. Je 5:1, 2. Mi 7:2. Mt +6:2.
every mouth. Is 32:6, 7. Mt 12:34.
folly. or, villany. S#5039h. Is 32:6. Ge 34:7. Dt 22:21. Jsh 7:15mg. Jg 19:23, 24mg. 20:6, 10. 1 S 25:25. 2 S 13:12. Jb 42:8. Je 29:23.
For all. ver. +12. Ezk 20:33.
stretched. Ex +7:5.

18 wickedness. Is 33:12. 66:16, 17. Nu 11:1-3. Dt +32:22. Jb 31:11, 12. Am 7:4. Na 1:6, 10. Ml 4:1. Mt +25:41.
it shall. Is 10:16-18. 27:4. He 6:8.
thorns. 2 S 23:6. Mi 7:4.
shall kindle. Mt +3:12.
mount. Is 5:24. Ps 37:20. Ho 13:3. Jl 2:30. Re 14:11.

19 is the land. Is 5:30. 8:22. 24:11, 12. 60:2. Je

13:16. Jl 2:2. Am 5:18. Mt 27:45. Ac 2:20.
fuel. Heb. meat. ver. 5.
no man. Is 13:18. Ezk 9:5. Mi 7:2, 6. 2 P 2:4.

20 And he. Is 49:26. Le 26:26-29. Je 19:9. La 4:10.
snatch. Heb. cut. 2 K 6:4. Jb 22:28 (decree). Hab 3:17.
right hand. Ge +48:13. Ec 10:2.
shall eat. Le +26:26.
left hand. Ge +48:13. Jg +20:16.
not be satisfied. Is 1:11. 66:11. Dt 6:11.
they shall. Is 49:26. Ec 4:5.

21 Ephraim. Jg 7:22. 1 S 14:20. 2 K 15:30, 37. 2 Ch 28:6-8. Mt 24:10. Ga 5:15.
For all this. ver. +12.
stretched. Ex +7:5.

ISAIAH 10

1 A.M. 3291. B.C. 713.
Woe. Is 3:11. 5:8, 11, 18, 20-22. Je 22:13. Hab 2:6, 9, 12, 15, 19. Mt 11:21. 23:13-16, 23, 27, 29, 33. 26:24. Lk 11:42-44, 46, 47, 52. Ju 11.
them. 1 K 21:13. Est 3:10-13. Ps 58:2. 94:20, 21. Da 6:8, 9. Mi 3:1-4, 9-11. 6:16. Jn 9:22. 19:6.
that write grievousness. or, to the writers that write grievousness.

2 turn aside. Is 29:21. La 3:35, 36. Am 2:7. 5:11, 12. Ml +3:5.
judgment. Is 5:7.
poor. Is 3:14.
that widows. Is +1:17.

3 And what. Is 20:6. 33:14. Jb 31:14. Je 5:31. Ezk 24:13, 14. Re 6:15-17.
the day. Is 26:21. Je +8:12. 1 P 2:12.
in the desolation. Is 5:26. 30:27, 28. 39:3, 6, 7. Dt 28:49.
to whom. Is 30:1-3, 16. 31:1-3. Ho 5:13.
where. Is 2:20, 21. 5:14. Ge 31:1. 2 K 7:6-8, 15. Ps 49:16, 17. Pr 11:4. Zp 1:18.

4 Without me. Le 26:17, 18, 36, 37. Dt 31:15-18. 32:29, 30. Je 37:10. Ho 9:12.
For all this. Ps +118:1. Is +9:12.
stretched. Ex +7:5.

5 O Assyrian. or, Woe to the Assyrian. Heb. O Asshur. Ge 10:11.
the rod. ver. 15. Is 5:26. 7:18. 8:4. 13:5. 14:5, 6. 41:15. Dt 28:49, 50. Jg 3:12. 1 K 11:14. Ps 17:13, 14. 125:3. Je 5:15. 6:22. 27:8. 51:20-24. Ezk 23:24. 29:19, 20. Da 2:37. Lk 19:43.
and. or, though.
indignation. ver. 25. Is +66:14.

6 against. Is 19:17. 29:13. 30:9-11. Jb +8:13. Je 3:10. 4:14. Mt +6:2.
will I give. ver. 13, 14. Is 37:26, 27. 41:25. 45:1-5. Je 25:9. 34:22. 47:6, 7.
tread them. Heb. lay them a treading. Is 22:5. 63:3, 6. 2 S 22:43. Mi 7:10. Zc 10:5.

7 **he meaneth**. Ge 50:20. Mi 4:11, 12. Ac 2:23. 13:27-30.
but. 2 K 18:13-37. 19:1-37.
in his heart. Is 36:18-20. 37:11-13.

8 **Are not**. Is 36:8, 9. 2 K 18:24. 19:10. Ezk 26:7. Da 2:37.

9 **Calno**. i.e. *his perfection; fortified dwelling,* **S#3641h**. Ge 10:10. Am 6:1, 2, Calneh.
Carchemish. i.e. *fortress of refuge; fortress of Chemosh* (i.e. *as if departing, as if feeling; the swift,* i.e. *the sun,* Nu +21:29), *the head* (or *lamb*) *as if departed,* **S#3751h**. 2 Ch 35:20. Je 46:2.
Hamath. Nu +13:21.
Samaria. Is 7:8, 9. 17:3. 2 K 16:9, 10. 17:5, 6. 18:9, 10.

10 **my hand**. Is 46:10, 11. Ps 76:10. Mt 23:37. 1 P 4:17.
the kingdoms. ver. 14. 2 K 18:33-35. 19:12, 13, 17-19. 2 Ch 32:12-16, 19.

11 **as I have**. Is 36:19, 20. 37:10-13.

12 **when the Lord**. ver. 5, 6. Is 14:24-27. 27:9. 46:10, 11. Ps 76:10. 1 P 4:17.
I will. ver. 16-19, 25-34. Is 17:12-14. 29:7, 8. 30:30-33. 31:5-9. 37:36-38. 50:15. Je 50:18.
punish. Heb. visit upon. Is 24:21mg. Je +9:25mg.
the fruit of the stout heart. Heb. visit upon the fruit of the greatness of the heart. Is 9:9. 2 K 19:36, 37. Ps 21:10. 62:9. Pr 18:12. Je 50:18. Mt 12:33. 15:19.
king of Assyria. Da 11:40. Mi +5:5, 6. Hab 3:16.
the glory. Ezk 31:10, 14. Da 4:37.
high looks. Pr +6:17. Da 11:36, 37.

13 **For he saith**. ver. 8. Is 37:23, 24. Dt 8:17. 2 K 19:20-24. Ezk 25:3. 26:2. 28:2-9. 29:3. Da 4:30. Am 6:13. Hab 1:16.
I have removed. 2 K 15:29. 17:6, 24. 18:11, 32. 1 Ch 5:26. Am 5:27. 6:1, 2.
bounds. Dt 32:8.
robbed. 2 K 16:8. 18:15. Ho 13:15, 16.
a valiant man. *or*, many people.

14 **And my**. Is 5:8. Jb 31:25. Pr 18:12. 21:6, 7. Ho 12:7, 8. Na 2:9-13. 3:1. Hab 2:5-11.
riches. Ge +34:29.

15 **the axe**. ver. +5. Ps 17:13, 14. Je 51:20-23. Ezk 28:9. Jn 19:11. Ro 9:20, 21.
boast itself. Is 44:23. Ex 8:9.
against him. Pr 3:27. 25:11.
the rod should shake itself against them. *or*, a rod should shake them.
itself, as if it were no wood. *or, that which is* not wood.

16 **the Lord of hosts**. Is 14:24-27. 29:5-8. 37:6, 7, 29, 36. 2 Ch 32:21.
fat ones. Dt +31:20.
leanness. Ps 106:15. Ac 12:23.
and under. Is 9:5. 30:30-33. 33:10-14.

17 **the light**. Is 60:19. Ps 27:1. 84:11. Re 21:23. 22:5.

fire. Is 9:19. Mt +3:11.
for a flame. Is 64:1, 2. 66:15, 16, 24. Nu 11:1-3. Ps 18:8. 50:3. 83:14, 15. Mt +3:12. 2 Th 1:7-9.
devour. Is 27:4. 37:36. Ps 97:3. Na 1:5, 6, 10.
in one day. Is 9:14. 2 K 19:35.

18 **consume**. ver. 33, 34. Is 9:18. 2 K 19:23, 28. Je 21:14. Ezk 20:47, 48.
both soul and body. Heb. from the soul and even to the flesh. Heb. *nephesh*, Ge +12:13. Jb +14:22. Da 7:15. Mt +10:28.
fainteth. Ps 27:1, 2.

19 **few**. Heb. number. Is 37:36. Nu 9:20. Dt 33:6. 1 S 27:7mg. 2 S 2:11mg. 1 Ch 16:19mg. Jb 16:22mg. Ezk 12:16mg.

20 **that day**. ver. 27. Is +2:11. 19:18, 19.
the remnant. Is 4:2, 3. Ezk 7:16. Mi +5:3.
no more. 2 K 16:7. 2 Ch 28:20. Ezk 23:12. Ho 5:13. 14:3.
but shall stay. Is 17:7, 8. +26:3, 4. 2 Ch 14:11. Je 21:2. Ho 3:5. 6:1. Mi 3:11. 7:7.
Holy One. Is +1:4. 57:15. Le 11:44. 19:2.
in truth. Is 16:5. 38:3. 48:1. 61:8.

21 **remnant**. ver. +20. Jl 3:1, 2.
return. Is 1:27mg. 7:3. 9:13. 19:22. 55:7. 65:8, 9. 2 Ch 30:1-13. Ho 6:1. 7:10, 16. 14:1-3. Ac 26:20. 2 C 3:14-16.
the mighty. **S#1368h**. Ge 6:4. 1 Ch +9:13mg, 26 (chief). Ps 19:5 (strong man). 24:8. 45:3. 89:19. Is +9:6. +10:21. Je 32:18. Zp 3:17.
God. Is +9:6. 45:22. 49:26. 60:16. Ex 3:6. Dt 7:21. 10:17. Ps 24:8. 45:3. Je 32:18. Zp 3:17. Mt 11:21. Lk 9:43. Ep 1:21. Re 7:10, 12.

22 **though thy**. Ro 9:27, 28. 11:5, 6.
as the sand. Ge +22:17.
yet a remnant. Is 6:13.
of. Heb. in, *or*, among.
the consumption. Is 6:11. 8:8. 27:10, 11. 28:15-22. Dt 28:65. Da 9:27. Ro 9:28.
with. *or*, in. Ge +18:25. Ac 17:31. Ro 2:5. 3:5, 6.

23 **consumption**. Is 28:22.
determined. Is 14:26, 27. 24:1, etc. Da 4:35. 8:19. Ro 9:28.
midst. Ge +45:6.

24 **O my people**. Is +30:19.
be not afraid. Is 8:12, 13. 33:14-16. 35:4. 37:6, 22, 33-35.
smite thee. ver. 5. Is 9:4. 14:29. 27:7.
and shall lift his staff against thee. *or*, but he shall lift up his staff for thee.
after the manner. Ex 1:10-16. 14:9, 21-31. 15:6-10.

25 **For yet**. ver. 33, 34. Is 12:1, 2. 14:24, 25. 17:12-14. 30:30-33. 31:4-9. 37:36-38. 54:7. 2 K 19:35. Ps 37:10. Da 11:36. He 10:37. 2 P 3:8.
the indignation. ver. +5. Da +8:19.

26 **stir up**. ver. +16-19. 2 K 19:35. Ps 35:23.
according. Is 9:4. Jg 7:25. Ps 83:11.

his rod. ver. +24. Is 11:16. 51:9, 10. Ex 14:25-27. Ne 9:10, 11. Ps 106:10, 11. Hab 3:7-15. Re 11:18. 19:15.

27 **his burden**. Is 9:4. 14:25. 2 K 18:13, 14. Na 1:9-13.
be taken away. Heb. remove.
because. Is 37:35. 2 S 1:21. Ps 2:1-3, 6mg. 20:6. +45:7. 84:9. 89:20-22, etc. 105:14, 15. 132:10, 17, 18. Da 9:24-26. Lk 4:18. Jn 1:41mg. Ac 4:27. 1 J 2:20, 27.
anointing. Is 30:23. 55:2. Ex +28:41.

28 **He is come**. 2 K 17:5.
Aiath. i.e. *a heap of ruins*, s#5857h. Jsh 7:2, Ai. Ne 11:31, Aija.
Migron. 1 S 14:2.
Michmash. 1 S 13:2, 5. 14:5, 31.

29 **the passage**. 1 S 13:23. 14:4.
Geba. 1 S +13:3.
Ramah. Je +31:15.
Gibeah. Jg +19:12.

30 **Lift up thy voice**. Heb. Cry shrill with thy voice.
Gallim. 1 S 25:44.
Laish. Jg 18:7, 29.
Anathoth. 1 Ch +7:8.

31 **Madmenah**. i.e. *dunghill*, s#4088h, only here. Is 25:10mg. Jsh 15:31, Madmannah. Je 48:2.
Gebim. i.e. *trenches, pits; beams, locusts*, s#1374h. See s#1356h, Je +14:3.

32 **Nob**. 1 S 21:1. 22:19. Ne 11:32.
shake. ver. 24. Is 11:15. 13:2. 19:16. Zc 2:9.
hand. Is +19:16.
the mount. Is 2:2. 37:22.
daughter. Nu +21:25.

33 **lop**. ver. 16-19. Is 37:24-36, 38. 2 K 19:21-37. 2 Ch 32:21.
the high ones. Am 2:9.
and the haughty. Is 2:11-17. Jb 40:11, 12. Da 4:23, 37. Lk 14:11.

34 **cut down**. ver. 18. Is 37:24. Je 22:7. 46:22, 23. 48:2. Na 1:12.
Lebanon. Zc 11:1, 2.
by a mighty one. *or*, mightily. Is 31:8. 37:36. Ps 89:6. 103:20. Da 4:13, 14, 23. 2 Th 1:7. He 1:13. 2 P 2:11. Re 10:1. 18:21.

ISAIAH 11

1 **shall come**. Is 53:2. Zc 6:12. Re 5:5. 22:16.
of Jesse. ver. 10. 1 Ch +2:12. Mt +1:6-16. Lk 2:23-32. 3:23-32.
a Branch. Is +4:2. Je 23:5, 6. 33:15. Zc 3:8. 6:12, 13.
his roots. Jn *1:1, 14. Ro 15:12*. Col 1:17.

2 **the Spirit**. Heb. *ruach*, Ge +41:38. Is 42:1. 57:15. 59:21. 61:1. Ge 1:2. Nu 11:25, 26. Jb 26:13. Ps 51:11. 139:7. Mt 3:16. Lk 4:16-21. Jn 1:32, 33. 3:34. Ac 6:10. 10:38. 1 C 2:10. 12:8. Ep 1:17. Col 1:9. 2:3. Ja 3:17.

rest upon. Is 61:1. Ps +45:7. Mt 3:16. Jn 3:34. Ac 10:38.
the spirit. Heb. *ruach*, Ge +41:38.
of wisdom. Ex 31:2, 3. Dt 34:9. Mt +28:19. Jn 14:17. 15:26. 16:13. 1 C 1:30. Ep 1:17, 18. Col 1:8, 9. 2:2, 3. 2 T +1:7. Ja 3:17, 18.

3 **shall make him**. Is 33:6. Pr 2:5, 9. Lk 2:46, 47, 52.
understanding. Heb. scent, *or*, smell. Ge 42:23. Jb 12:11. 34:3. Ph 1:9, 10. He 5:14.
and he shall not judge. 1 S 16:7. 2 S 14:17. 1 K 3:9, 28. Jn 5:22, 23, 27, 30. 7:24. 8:15, 16, 28, 38. 1 C 2:13-15. 4:3-5.

4 **But with righteousness**. 2 S 23:2-4. Ps 9:4mg. +45:6, 7. 96:13. 98:9. 99:4. Je +21:12. Mt 11:5. Jn 7:24. Re 19:11.
reprove. *or*, argue. Is 1:17. Pr 31:8, 9. Je 5:28.
for the meek. Mt +5:5.
he shall smite. Jb 4:9. Ps 2:9. 110:2. Ml 4:6. Ep 6:17. 2 Th 2:8. Re 1:16. 2:16. 19:15.
mouth. Nu +12:8.
with the breath. Heb. *ruach*, Ex +15:8. Is 30:33. Ps 18:8. Ac 9:1. 2 Th +2:8.
slay the wicked. Ps 101:8. Pr +2:22.

5 **righteousness**. Is +59:17. Ps 93:1. Ro 14:17. 1 P 4:1. Re 1:13. 15:3.
and faithfulness. Is 25:1. Ho 2:20. He 2:17. 1 J 1:9. Re 3:14. 19:11, 13.

6 **The wolf**. Is 55:13. 65:17, +25. Jb 5:23. Ps 8:6-8. Ezk 34:25. Ho +2:18. Jl 2:22. Mt 19:28. Ac +3:21. 9:13-20. Ro 8:19-21. 14:17. 1 C +6:9-11. 2 C 5:14-21. Ga 3:26, 27. Ep 4:22-32. Col 3:3-8. T 3:3-5. Phm 9-16. He 2:8. Re 5:9, 10.

7 **cow**. Ge 32:15. 41:2-4, 18-20.
feed. Is 27:10. 30:23. 40:11.
young ones. lit. "children." Is 2:6.
the lion. Is 35:9.
ox. Jb 40:15. Ho 2:18.

8 **weaned child**. 1 S +1:22. Mt 18:3. 1 C 14:20.
cockatrice'. *or*, adder's. Is 59:5mg. Ps 91:13. 140:3. Pr 23:32mg. Mk 16:18.

9 **not hurt**. ver. 13. Is 2:4. 35:9. 60:18. Jb 5:23. Ho 2:18. Mi 4:2-4. Mt +5:44, 45. Ac 2:41-47. 4:29-35. Ro 12:17-21. Ga 5:22-24. Ph 2:14, 15. 1 Th 5:15. Re 21:27.
in all. Zc 14:9. Ac 4:32.
holy mountain. Is +2:2. 27:13. 56:7. 57:13. 65:11, 25. 66:20. Ezk 20:40. Da 11:45. Jl 3:17. Ob 16. Zc 8:3.
for the earth. Is 30:26. +40:5. 49:6. Ps 22:27-31. 98:2, 3. Ec +1:4. Zc +14:9. Mt +5:5. Ro 11:25, 26. Re 20:2-6.
be full. Je 31:34. He 8:11.
the knowledge. Is 1:3. 6:3. Ps +9:10. Jn 17:3. 1 C 13:8, 12.

10 **in that day**. ver. 1. Is +2:11. Ro *15:12*. Re 22:16.

root. Ro 15:12. Re 5:5. 22:16.

Jesse. ver. +1.

which shall. Is 59:19. Ge +49:10. Jn 3:14, 15. 12:32.

ensign. Ex +17:15.

to it shall the Gentiles. Is 2:2-5. Ge 49:10, 22. Ps 22:27. Je 3:17. Mi 4:1, 2. Zc 2:11. 8:20-23. Ml 3:12. Mt 2:1, 2. 8:11. +12:18, 21. Jn 3:14, 15. 10:16. 12:20, 21, 32. Ac 10:45, 47.

his rest. Is 32:17, 18. 66:10-12. Ps 91:1, 4. 116:7. Je 6:16. Zp 3:17. Hg 2:9. Mt 11:28-30. 2 Th 1:7-12. He 4:1, 3, 6, 8, 9, etc. 1 P 1:7-9. 5:10.

glorious. Heb. glory. Is +40:5. Ps 149:5. Mt 25:31. Ro 8:18, 21. 1 C 2:9, 10. 2 C 3:10. 4:17. Ph 4:19. T 2:13. 1 P 5:1, 10.

11 set his hand. Nu +11:23. Is 26:19-21. ch. 60-66. Le 26:40-42. Dt 4:27-31. 30:3-6. Ps 68:22. Je 23:7, 8. 30:8-11. 31:36-40. 33:24-26. Ezk 11:16-20. 34:23-28. 36:24, etc. ch. 37-48. Ho 1:11. 3:4, 5. Jl ch. 3. Am 9:9, 14, 15. Mi 7:14, 15. Zc 10:8-12. ch. 12-14. Ro 11:15, 25, 26. 2 C 3:16.

the second time. Israel's full restoration was not accomplished with the return from the Babylonian captivity but is still future (Dt 30:4). The second regathering (the Bible does not predict a third) precedes the restoration. The regathering brings Israel back to the land in unbelief (Zp 2:1, 2) before the Day of the Lord (Zp +2:3) and the great tribulation (Je +30:7. Da +12:1). The initial regathering of Israel to the land (Is 54:7. Ezk +34:13. +37:25) sets the stage for the further working out of God's prophetic purposes. Christ in the Olivet discourse assumes Israel is in the land (Mt 24:15) before the tribulation. The purpose of the regathering and final restoration is to make possible the fulfillment of the Abrahamic and Davidic covenants (Is +55:3. Ac +7:5). This regathering (Mt 24:31) must be distinguished carefully from the final restoration. The following predictions were not fulfilled by the return from Babylon, and therefore relate to the initial regathering in unbelief, the future glorious restoration and final regathering. The regathered and/or restored nation will (1) speak Hebrew (Ne 13:24. Je 31:23. Zp 3:9). (2) return the second time (Is 11:11). (3) no more be removed (Is 60:21. Ezk 37:23-27. Am +9:15). Since Israel was removed in A.D. 70, long after the return from Babylon, these predictions cannot refer to the return from Babylon, but must refer to a future return. (4) The return of Christ at the second advent takes place with the resurrection of the righteous dead and the translation (He 11:5) of living believers (1 Th +4:16, 17). (5) The restoration of Israel is contingent upon their final repentance and spiritual

awakening (Ezk 39:22. Ho 5:15. Ml 3:7) brought about at the height of the great tribulation when Jerusalem is taken and all hope of survival is gone (Zc 14:2). (6) God responds to the cry of an apparently very small believing remnant (Is +17:6. 24:13, 14. 30:19. Ps 80:2mg. Zc 13:9). (7) This believing remnant, probably accounting for one third or less of the Jews at that time (Zc 13:8. 14:2) may have been prepared spiritually by careful students of the Bible among them who taught others (Da +11:33), and some of these may be the Jewish evangelists to the world during the tribulation (Is +27:6). This spiritual response may also be directly related to the appearance of Elijah (Ml 4:5). (8) The repentance of this remnant determines the timing of the Second Advent (Ho 6:1. Ac +3:19-21). (9) In the final moments of tribulation crisis the question is asked, "Where is their God?" (Jl 2:17). (10) Israel shall cry, "My God, we know thee" (Ho 8:2. Zc 13:9). (11) When Israel's cry ascends, God will hear (Is 30:19). In answer to this prayer the Lord will (12) be jealous for his land and pity his people (Jl 2:18). (13) God will remove the northern army (Jl 2:20). (14) God will put Israel's enemies to flight (Is 59:19). All this is contingent upon Israel's final repentance (Ho 5:15. Ml 3:7, 16, 17. 4:2). (15) When Israel turns from transgression, the Messiah will come to deliver her (Is +59:19, 20. Lk 21:28. Ac +3:19-21. Ro +11:26). (16) God awaits (Is +30:18) and will plead with them in the wilderness (Ezk 20:35, 36. Ho 2:14) till they acknowledge their guilt and call upon Him (Is +59:20. Ho 5:15. Jl 2:12, 17, 18). A portion of the Jews will be in Jerusalem (Ezk 22:19, 20. Zc 14:2) and the land of Israel; another portion will be in the wilderness (Ezk 20:35, 36. Ho 2:14. Re +12:6, 14) at this time. A third portion will be scattered throughout the nations of the earth. (17) The words of the prayer (Ps 60:1. Ho 14:2). (18) The swift answer to the prayer (Is +65:24). (19) God will immediately answer (Is 30:19. Je 33:3). (20) God will defend Judah and Jerusalem against the armies of Antichrist (Zc +12:8), delivering the tents of Judah first (Zc 12:7). (21) The Lord will be literally seen over them, protecting and defending them, and defeating their enemies (Zc 9:14). (22) They shall know from then on that the Lord is their God (Ezk 39:22. Jl 2:27). Upon this repentance God will (23) take away Israel's judgments, cast out the enemy, be the king of Israel, the Lord in the midst of them, and Israel shall not see evil any more (Zp 3:15). (24) The Messiah will return to the earth before the open manifestation of the Second Advent (Re 11:17. 16:5) to the region of Sinai (Dt +33:2. Ps +68:7, 8. Is +16:1-5) to organize his kingdom; proceed with judgment upon the enemies of Israel, to Bozrah (Is 34:1-10), for the Jews have sought refuge and have been hidden there (Is +16:1-5), perhaps at Petra (2 K 14:7. Is 16:1mg. Je 49:16. Ezk 35:9. Ob +3); Christ proceeds to destroy His enemies (Is 63:1-3), and to march victoriously (Dt 33:2) to Jerusalem, where he will ascend the mount of Olives (Zc 14:4) and come to Zion (Is +51:11). Israel returns from the wilderness at the start of the Millennium (Ho 2:14-23), led by God at this time. (25) All the saints will return with God and Christ at the visible final stage of the Second Advent (Ps +149:9. Ho +11:12. Jl 3:11. Ob +21). (26) This will be a time of great singing and rejoicing (Is 24:14-16. Ho +2:15. Jl 2:23. Zc +2:10). (27) As a result of the earthquake at the Second Advent of Christ, the physical features of the land and mount Zion experience topographical changes which will raise Jerusalem to a more eminent position, making it "beautiful for situation" (Ps 48:2), leveling the present surrounding towering mountains like a plain (or, the Arabah, a hollow depression), providing the space needed for the millennial temple (Ezk 42:16. Zc 14:4, 10). (28) Israel will at last possess the full geographical extent of the land covenanted to Abraham (1 K 4:21. Is +26:15. Je +7:7. +33:21. Ac +7:5. He +11:13, 39). (29) The captivity will be ended, the commencement of the final and complete regathering begins, and Israel will be a name and a praise among all the nations of the earth (Zp 3:20). (30) Israel will experience a supernatural return, apparently after the tribulation just prior to the millennium (Is 27:12. Ezk 34:12. Am 9:9), to be distinguished from the initial regathering in unbelief. (31) This will be a complete return (Ezk 39:28). (32) Unlike the return from Babylon, this is a worldwide return (Is 43:6. Je 31:8. Ezk 38:8). (33) It is a return in joy without sorrow (Is 65:19). (34) It includes the return of the resurrected (Ezk 37:12). (35) The land will be crowded (Is 49:19. Zc 2:4. 8:4, 5. 10:9, 10). (36) The millennium is preceded by the universal cleansing of the earth by fire to rid the world of the wicked (Ps 97:3. Is 24:1-6. +66:24. Jl 2:30. Zp 2:3. Ml 4:1. Mt 3:11, 12. +13:40-42. 2 Th 1:8. He 10:27. 2 P 3:7, 10-13). (37) In the land of Israel preparatory cleansing of the land will take place so the millennial temple can be built (Zc 13:1). (38) The millennial temple will be built by the Messiah (Zc 6:12, 13). (39) Christ in victory will judge the nations to determine which nations will be permitted to enter the millennium (Mt +10:15. 25:31-46). (40) Jewish evangelists will travel throughout the world to preach the gospel among the unconverted Gentile nations at the beginning of the millennium (Is +66:19). (41) Thereafter knowledge of the Lord will be universal (Is 54:13. Hab 2:14. Jn +6:45. He +8:11). (42) Israel will be the spiritual center of the world (Mi 4:1, 2. Zc 8:3, 22, 23. 14:16). (43) Israel will never suffer God's wrath or fury again (Is 51:22). (44) Israel will dwell in supernatural righteousness (Is +60:21). (45) Israel will be as though God had never cast them off (Jl +2:25. Zc +10:6. Ml 3:4). (46) Through Messiah Israel will be "head of the heathen," with Messiah as king over all the earth, ruling from Jerusalem (Ps 18:43. 110:2. Is 24:23. Je 3:17. Mi 4:7. Zp 3:15. Zc 14:9). (47) Israel will "eat the riches of the Gentiles" (Is 61:6). (48) This is what marks the "fullness of the Gentiles" (Ro 11:25). (49) Israel will be a praise among all people of the earth (Is 60:15. 61:9, 11. Zp 3:20. Zc 8:13. Ml 1:11. 3:12). (50) Israel will no more be a reproach among the heathen (Jl 2:19. Zc 8:13). (51) Israel shall never be invaded by foreign powers again (Jl +3:17. Ml 4:1-3), pertaining of course to the restoration, not necessarily the initial regathering. (52) Israel will "take them captives whose captives they were" (Is 14:2. 60:14. 61:5). (53) Israel will not depart from the Lord (Is 59:21. Je 32:40). The restoration of Israel (54) inaugurates universal peace and righteousness on earth (Is 2:4. Mi 4:3-5. Zc 9:10); (55) results in the restoration of all nature and the removal of the curse (Is 11:6-9. 24:6. 65:25. Ezk 34:25. Ml 4:6. Ac +3:19. Ro 8:19-23. Re 22:3); and (56) is accompanied by the universal removal of all false religion (Is 45:22. Ho 2:17. Mi 4:5. 5:8, 12, 13. Zc 13:2. Ml 1:11). Ex 15:16, 17. Je +23:8. 29:14. +31:36. Am +9:14, 15. Zc 8:7, 8. Ml 3:4, 6, 12, 18. Ro +11:1.

remnant. Mi +4:7.

from Assyria. ver. 16. Is 27:12, 13. Mi 7:12. Zc 10:10.

Egypt. Is 19:23. Je 44:1.

Pathros. i.e. *extension of ruin; a morsel moistened,* S#6624h. Ge +10:14, Pathrusim. Je 44:1, 15. Ezk 29:14. 30:14.

Cush. Ge +2:13.

Elam. Ge +10:22.

Shinar. Ge +10:10.

Hamath. Nu +13:21.

the islands. Is 20:6. 23:2, 6. 24:15. 40:15. 41:1, 5. 42:4, 10, 12, 15. 49:1. 51:5. 59:18. 60:9. 66:19. Ge 10:5. Est 10:1. Ps 72:10. 97:1. Je 2:10. 31:10. Ezk 27:3, 6. 39:6. Da 11:18. Zp 2:11.

12 set up. ver. 10. Is 18:3. 59:19. 62:10. Re 5:9.
shall assemble. Is 49:11, 12. 56:8. Dt 32:26.

Ps 68:22. Zp 3:10. Jn 7:35. Ja 1:1.
outcasts of Israel. Is +27:13.
gather together. Je +23:3.
corners. Heb. wings. Is +24:16mg. Jb
37:3mg.

13 **the envy**. Is 7:1-6. 52:7, 8. 60:14. Je 3:18.
Ezk 37:16-24. Ho 1:11. Jn 11:52. 13:34, 35.
the adversaries. Nu 24:17.

14 **the Philistines**. Je +47:4.
toward. Is 59:19. 66:19, 20. Mt +8:11.
spoil. Is 33:1. Je 49:28. Ezk ch. 38, 39.
them of the east. Heb. the children of the
east. Is 2:6. Ge +29:1.
they shall lay, etc. Heb. Edom and Moab
shall be the laying on of their hand; the children of Ammon their obedience. Is 60:14. Da
11:41. Ob 18. Re 15:3, 4.
Edom. Je +49:7.
Moab. Ezk +25:8.

15 **the Lord shall**. Is 27:12. Re 16:12.
utterly. Is 50:2. 51:9, 10. Zc 10:11. Re 21:1.
with his mighty. Ex 14:16, 21, 29.
he shake. Is 19:16.
shall smite. Is 19:5-10. Ex 7:19-21. Ps 74:13-
15. Ezk 29:10. 30:12. Zc 10:11. Re 16:12.
go over. or, tread it. Jg 20:43. Jb 28:8. Pr
4:11.
dryshod. Heb. in shoes. **S#5275h**. Is 5:27. 20:2.
Ge 14:23. Ex 3:5. 12:11. Dt 25:9, 10. 29:5. Jsh
5:15. 9:5, 13. Ru 4:7, 8. 1 K 2:5. Ps 60:8.
108:9. SS 7:1. Ezk 24:17, 23. Am 2:6. 8:6.

16 **And there shall**. ver. 11. Is 19:23. 27:13.
35:8-10. 40:3, 4. 49:12. 57:14.
like as it was. Is 42:15, 16. 48:20, 21. 51:10.
63:12, 13. Ex 14:22, 26-29.
in the day. Ge 2:4, 17. 1 K 2:37. Ezk 36:33.

ISAIAH 12

1 **And in that**. Is +2:11. 35:10.
O Lord. Is 25:1, 9. 49:13. 60:18, 19. Ps 34:1,
etc. 67:1-4. 69:34-36. 72:15-19. 149:6-9. Ro
11:15. Re 15:3, 4. 19:1-7.
though. Is 10:4, 25. 40:1, 2. 51:3. 54:8.
57:15-18. 66:13. Dt 30:1-3. Ps 30:5. 85:1-3. Je
31:18-20. Ezk 39:24-29. Ho 6:1. 11:8. 14:4-9.
thou comfortedst. Is 49:13.

2 **God**. Heb. *El*, Ex +15:2. Is 7:14. +9:6, 7. Ps
27:1. Je 23:6. Mt 1:21-23. Lk 2:30-32. Ro
1:16. 1 T 3:16. Re +7:10.
I will trust. Is 8:17. 2 S 22:3. Ps 56:3. He
2:13.
not be afraid. Is 42:3. Jb 11:15. Ps +34:4. 2 T
1:7. 1 J 4:18.
the Lord. Ps 118:14. Ho 1:7.
Jehovah. Is 26:4. Ex 3:13, 14. 6:3. Ps 83:18.
my strength. Is 35:3, 4. Nu 23:22. Jb 9:19.
Ps +18:1. 31:24. 89:8, 13. Jl 3:16. Zc 12:8.
my salvation. Is 52:9, 10. Je 3:23. Mt 1:21.
Ac 4:12.

3 **with joy**. Is 49:10. 55:1-3. Dt +12:7. Ps 36:9.
51:12. SS 2:3. Je 2:13. Jn 1:16. 4:10-14. 7:37-
39. Re 7:17. 21:6. 22:1, 17.
wells. Heb. *mayan*, Ge +7:11.
salvation. Ge 49:18. Ex 14:13. 15:2. Dt
32:15.

4 **in that day**. ver. 1. Ps 65:1. 106:47, 48.
113:1-3. ch. 117.
call upon his name. *or*, proclaim his name.
Ex 33:19. 34:5-7. 1 Ch 16:8. Ps 105:1.
declare. Is 66:19. Ps 9:11. 22:31. 40:5. 71:16-
18. 73:28. 96:3. 107:22. 145:4-6. Je 50:2.
51:9, 10. Jn 17:26. 2 Th 1:10.
his name. Ps +9:10.
exalted. Is 2:11, 17. 5:16. 25:1. 30:18. 33:5,
10. Ex 15:2. 2 S 22:47. 1 Ch 29:11. Ne 9:5. Ps
18:46. 21:13. 34:3. 46:10. 47:9. 57:5, 11. 97:9.
99:5, 9. 108:5. 113:5mg. 118:16, 28.
148:13mg. Ho 11:7. Ph 2:9-11.

5 **Sing**. Ex 15:1, 21. Ps 68:32-35. 98:1. 105:2.
Re 15:3. 19:1-3.
excellent things. Mk 7:37. Lk 13:17.
this is known. Is 40:9. Ps 72:19. Hab 2:14.
Re 11:15-17.

6 **Cry out**. Is 40:9. 52:7-10. 54:1. Zp 3:14. Zc
9:9. Lk 19:37-40.
thou. Is +30:19. 33:24.
inhabitant. Heb. inhabitress. Je 10:17mg.
for great. Is 8:18. 25:9. Ps 68:16. Je 23:5, 6.
Ezk 48:35. Zp 2:5. 3:15-17. Zc 2:5, 10, 11.
Holy One. Is +1:4.
in the midst. Ps +16:11. Ex +29:45. Jl 2:27.
Zp 3:14, 15, 17. 12:10. Jn 12:35, 36. Re 21:23.

ISAIAH 13

1 A.M. 3292. B.C. 712.
burden. Is 14:28. 15:1. 17:1. 19:1. 21:1, 11,
13. +22:1, 25. 23:1. Nu 24:3. Je 23:33-38. Ezk
12:10. Na 1:1. Hab 1:1. Zc 9:1. 12:1. Ml 1:1.
of Babylon. Is 14:4, etc. 21:1-10. 43:14. 44:1,
2. 47:1, etc. Ge 10:10. Je 25:12-26. ch. 50, 51.
Da 5:28-31, etc. Re 16:19. ch. 17, 18.
which Isaiah. Is 1:1.

2 **Lift ye up**. Is 5:26. 11:12. 18:3. Je 50:2.
51:27, 28.
upon the high. Je 51:25.
shake. Is 10:32. 11:15.
hand. Is +19:16.
go into. Is 45:1-3. Je 51:58.

3 **commanded**. Is 23:11. 44:27, 28. 45:1, 4, 5.
Ezr 1:1-4. Ps 149:5-7, +9. Je 50:21, etc. Re
19:14-16.
mighty ones. Je 51:20-24. Jl +3:11. Mt
13:41. Re 17:12-18. 18:1, 2, etc.
them that. Ezr ch. 1, 6. 7:12-26. Ps 149:2, 5-
9. Re 18:4-8, 20-24. 19:1-7.

4 **noise**. Is 22:1-9. Je 50:2, 3, 21, etc. 51:11, 27,
28. Ezk 38:3-23. Jl 3:14. Zc 14:1-3, 13, 14. Re
19:11-21.

like as. Heb. the likeness of. Jl 2:4-11. Re 9:7-10, 14-19.

the Lord. Is 10:5, 6. 45:1, 2. Je 50:14, 15. 51:6-25. Jl 2:1-11, 25. Re 18:8.

mustereth. 1 S +11:8.

5 **from a far country.** ver. 17. Je 50:3, 9. 51:11, 27, 28. Mt 24:31.

end of heaven. Dt 4:32. 30:4. 2 S +22:8. Ne 1:9. Mt 24:31.

and the weapons. Je 51:20, etc.

his indignation. Is +66:14.

the whole land. Ge +41:57.

6 **Howl ye.** Is 14:31. 15:2, 3, 8. 16:7. 23:1, 6. 52:5. 65:14. Je 4:8. 25:34. 47:2. 48:20, 31, 39. 49:3. 51:8. Ezk 21:12. 30:2. Jl 1:5, 11, 13. Am 8:3. Mi 1:8. Zp 1:10, 11, 14. Zc 11:3. Ja 5:1. Re 18:10.

day of the Lord. ver. 9. Dt +4:32. Ezk +30:3. 1 C +3:13.

as a. Jb 31:23. Jl 1:15.

Almighty. Ge +49:25.

7 **shall all.** Is 10:3, 4. 37:27. 51:20. Je 50:43. Ezk 7:17. 21:7. Na 1:6.

be faint. or, fall down. Zp 3:16mg.

every. Ex +15:15.

8 **pangs.** Je +4:31. 51:30, 31. Da 5:5, 6, 30, 31. **be amazed one at another.** Heb. wonder every man at his neighbor. Ge 43:33.

flames. Heb. faces of the flames. Jb +41:21. Jl 2:6. Na 2:10. 3:3mg.

9 **the day.** ver. 6. Is +34:8.

cruel. ver. 15-18. Is 47:10-15. Je 6:22, 23. 50:40-42. 51:35-58. Na 1:2, 6. Ml +4:1. Re 17:16, 17. 18:8. 19:17-21.

the land. Re 16:2.

destroy the sinners out. Is +24:6. Ps 37:9, 10, 20. 104:35. Pr 2:22. 2 P +3:7.

10 **the stars.** Is 14:13. 47:13. Ge 1:16.

constellations. Jb 9:9. Am 5:8.

give their light. Is 38:18 (celebrate). 41:16. 45:25 (glory). 62:9. 64:11 (praise). 2 S 22:29. Ps 18:28. 19:1-3. 145:10. Jl 2:30, 31. Zc 14:6. Re 6:12.

darkened. Is 34:4. Ex +10:22. Jb 18:6. Jl 3:15. Mt 24:29.

going forth. Is 37:28. Ge 8:7.

to shine. 2 S 22:29. Ps 18:28.

11 **I will punish.** Is 14:21. 24:4-6. Je 51:34-38. Re 12:9, 10. 18:2, 3.

the world. ver. 1. Is 14:17. Lk 2:1.

and I will cause. Is 2:17. 5:15. 14:12-16. 47:1. Ps 110:5. Je 50:29-32. Da 5:22, 23.

12 **a man.** ver. 15-18. Is 4:1. 10:19. 24:6. Ps 137:9.

more precious. or, rare. Is 24:6. Pr 8:12, 14-16, 18, 19. Ezk 22:18.

Ophir. 1 K +9:28.

13 **I will.** He +12:26.

the earth. Mt 24:35. 2 P 3:10. Re 20:11.

in the wrath. Ps 110:5, 6. La 1:12. Na 1:4-6. Re 19:17-19, 21.

fierce anger. Je 51:1-4, 6. He 12:28, 29.

14 **as the.** Is 17:13. 1 K 22:17, 36.

they shall. Is 47:15. Je 50:16. 51:9. Re 18:9, 10.

15 **that is found.** Is 14:19-22. 47:9-14. Je 50:27, 35-42. 51:3.

thrust. Je +37:10.

16 **children.** ver. 18. Ps +137:9.

and their. La 5:11. Zc 14:2.

17 **I will.** ver. 3-5. Is 21:2. 41:25. Je 50:9. 51:11, 27, 28. Da 5:28-31.

shall not regard. Pr 6:34, 35.

18 **shall dash.** ver. +16. Na 2:1.

their eye. Ge +31:35mg. 2 Ch 36:17. Ezk 9:5, 6, 10.

19 **Babylon.** Is 14:4-6, 12-15. Je 51:41. Da 2:37, 38. 4:30. Re 14:8. 18:10, 21.

when God overthrew. Heb. the overthrowing of. Ge +19:24, 25.

20 **never.** Jb +4:30 (S#5331h).

be inhabited. Is 14:23. 15:6, 7. 21:9. 34:11. 46:1. 47:1-11. Je 25:12-14. 50:3, 13, 21, 39, 45. 51:25, 29, 43, 62-64. Zp 3:6. Re 18:21-23.

21 **But.** Is 34:11-15. Re 18:2.

wild beasts. Heb. Ziim.

doleful creatures. Heb. Ochim.

owls. or, ostriches. Heb. daughters of the owl. Is +34:13mg.

satyrs. Le +17:7.

22 **the wild beasts.** Heb. Iim.

desolate houses. or, palaces. Ezk 19:7.

dragons. Is 35:7.

her time. Dt 32:35. Je 51:33. Ezk 7:7-10. Hab 2:3. 2 P 2:3. 3:9, 10.

ISAIAH 14

1 **the Lord.** Is 40:1, 2. 44:21, 22. 54:7, 8. Le 26:40-45. Dt 4:29-31. Ne 1:8, 9. Ps 98:3. 102:13. 136:10-24. 143:12. Je 50:4-6, 17-20, 33, 34. 51:4-6, 34-37. Lk 1:54, 72-74.

choose. Is 27:6. Zc 1:17. 2:12.

set. Dt 30:3-5. Je 24:5-7. 29:14. 30:18-22. 31:8-12. 32:37-41. Ezk 36:24-28. 39:25-29.

the strangers. Ge +23:4. Ex 12:48mg. Ps 146:9. Je 7:6.

be joined. Is 19:24, 25. 49:16-23. 56:6-8. 60:3-5, 10. 66:20. Ru 1:14-18. Est 8:17. Je 12:15, 16. Zc 2:11. 8:22, 23. Ml 1:11. Lk 2:32. Ac 15:14-17. Ep 2:12-19.

2 **and the house.** Is 18:7. 60:9-12. 61:5. Ezr 2:65. Ro 15:27. 2 C 8:4, 5. Ga 5:13.

for servants. Is 49:22, 23.

and they. Ps 68:18. 2 C 10:5. Ep 4:8.

whose captives they were. Heb. that had taken them captives.

they shall rule over. Is 60:14. Je 30:16. Da

7:18, 25-27. Zc 14:2, 3. Re 3:9. 11:11-18. 18:20-24.

3   **in the day**. Is +2:11.
     rest. Is 12:1. 32:18. Dt 28:48, 65-68. Ezr 9:8, 9. Je 30:10. 46:27, 28. 50:34. Ezk 28:24. Zc 8:2, 3, 8. Mt 11:28. Re 18:20. 19:1-3.
     thy fear. Ps +34:4. Pr 1:33. 3:25.

4   **take up**. Nu 23:7, 18. 24:3, 15, 20, 21, 23. Jb 27:1. 29:1. Mi 2:4. Hab 2:6.
     proverb. *or*, taunting speech. Je 24:9. Ezk 5:15. Hab 2:6.
     Babylon. Ge +10:10.
     How. ver. 6, 17. Is 47:5. 49:26. 51:23. Je 25:9-14. 27:6, 7. 37:6, 7. 50:22, 23. 51:20-24, 34, 35. Da 7:19-25. Hab 1:2-10. 2:6-12, 17. Re 13:15-17. 16:5, 6. 17:6. 18:5-8, 20.
     golden city. *or*, exactress of gold. Is 13:19. 45:2, 3. 2 Ch 36:18. La 4:1. Da 2:38. Re 18:16.

5   **broken the staff**. ver. 29. Is 9:4. 10:5. Ps 125:3. 129:4. Je 48:15-17.

6   **who smote**. Is 33:1. 47:6. 2 Ch 36:17. Je 25:9. Da 7:19-21. Ja 2:13.
     continual stroke. Heb. a stroke without removing. lit. "turning aside." Is 1:5. 31:6.
     is persecuted. Is 13:14-18. 21:1-10. 47:1, etc. Je 25:26. 50:2, 31. 51:25. Re 17:16, 17. 18:8-10.
     and none. Is 46:10, 11. Jb 9:13. Pr +21:30. Da 4:35. Ja 2:13.

7   **they**. Is 49:13. Ps 96:11-13. 98:7-9. 126:1-3. Pr 11:10. Je 51:48. Re 18:20. 19:1-6.
     break forth. Is 44:23. 49:13. 52:9. 54:1. 55:12.

8   **fir trees**. Is 37:24. 41:19. 55:13. 60:13. Ezk 17:2, 3, 11, 12.
     rejoice. Is 55:12, 13. Ezk 31:16. Zc 11:2.

9   **Hell**. *or*, The grave. Heb. *sheol*, Ge +37:35. Jb 13:14. Ps 16:8-11. Pr 15:24.
     from beneath. Is 30:33. Pr 15:24. Ezk 32:21. Mt +12:40. Ju 6.
     is moved. Ezk 32:18-32. Mk 9:43-50. Lk 16:27-31.
     the dead. Heb. *rephaim*, **S#7496h**, Pr +21:16. Dt +2:20. Jsh +17:15.
     chief ones. Heb. leaders, *or*, great goats. Is 1:11mg. Je 50:8.

10   **Art thou also**. Jb 30:23. Ps 49:6-14, 20. 82:6, 7. Ec 2:16. Lk 16:20-23.
     become like. Nu +21:27.

11   **pomp**. Is 21:4, 5. 22:2. Jb 21:11-15. Ezk 26:13. 32:19, 20. Da 5:1-4, 25-30. Am 6:3-7. Re 18:11-19.
     grave. Heb. *sheol*, Ge +37:35.
     viols. Is 5:12.
     the worm. Is 66:24. Ge +3:19. Jb 17:13, 14. 19:26. 21:26. 24:19, 20. Mk 9:43-48.
     spread. Est 4:3. Ps 139:8.
     worms. Is 41:14. 66:4. Dt 28:39.
     cover. Is 23:18. Le 9:19. Jb 21:26.

12   **How art thou fallen**. Is 13:10. 34:4. La 2:1. Ezk 28:13-17. Lk 10:18. 2 P 2:4. Re 8:10. 12:7-10.
     Lucifer. *or*, day star. i.e. *morning star*, **S#1966h**, only here. 2 P 1:19. Re 2:28. 22:16.
     son of the morning. Dt 25:2. Jb 38:32. Jon 4:10. Jn 17:12.
     weaken. ver. 4-6. Je 50:23. 51:20-24.

13   **thou**. Is 47:7-10. Ezk 27:3. 28:2. 29:3. Da 4:30, 31. Zp 2:15. Re 18:7, 8.
     I will ascend. Jb 20:6. Je 51:53. Ezk 28:9, 12-16. Da 3:1, 13-15. 8:10-12. Am 9:2.
     I will exalt. Da 8:10. Ob 4. Ezk 28:2. 2 Th 2:4.
     of God. Heb. *El*, Ex +15:2.
     the mount. Is 2:2. Ps 75:2. +82:1. Ezk 28:14.
     sides. lit. "thighs." ver. 15. Is 37:24. 1 S 24:3. Ezk 32:23.
     of the north. Jb 26:7. Ps 48:2. 75:6.

14   **ascend**. Is 37:23, 24.
     clouds. Ge +9:13.
     I will be. Is 47:8. Ge 3:5. 2 Th 2:4.

15   **thou**. ver. 3-11. Ezk 28:8, 9. Mt 11:23. Ac 12:22, 23. Re 19:20.
     hell. Heb. *sheol*, Ge +37:35.
     to the sides. ver. 13. Ezk 32:23.
     pit. Heb. *bor*, Ge +37:20 **(S#953h)**.

16   **shall narrowly**. Ps 58:10, 11. 64:9.
     Is this. ver. 4, 5. Ps 52:7. Je 50:23. 51:20-23. Da 4:30, 31, 33. Ac 12:23.

17   **made**. Is 13:19-22. 64:10. Ezk 6:14. Jl 2:3. Zp 2:13, 14.
     world. Is +13:11.
     opened not the house of his prisoners. *or*, did not let his prisoners loose homewards. Is 45:13. 58:6. 2 Ch 28:8-15. Ezr 1:2-4. Ep 4:8.

18   **all of**. Is 22:16. 2 Ch 24:16, 25. Ec 6:3. Ezk 32:18, etc.
     house. Jb 30:23. Pr 7:27. Ec 12:5.

19   **cast out**. 1 K 21:19, 24. Je +7:33.
     grave. Heb. *qeber*, Ge +23:4.
     thrust. Je +37:10.
     go down. Je 41:7, 9. Ezk 32:23, 24.
     pit. Heb. *bor*, Ge +37:20 **(S#953h)**. ver. 15. A rock-hewn buryingplace. Ps 28:1. 30:3. 88:6. The Hebrew term *bor* is rendered (1) *cistern*, 2 K 18:31. Pr 5:15. Ec 12:6. Is 36:16; (2) *dungeon*, Ge 40:15. 41:14. Ex 12:29. Je 37:16. 38:6, 6, 7, 9, 10, 11, 13. La 3:53, 55; (3) *fountain*, Je 6:7; (4) *well*, Pr 6:11. 1 S 19:22. 2 S 3:26. 23:15, 16. 1 Ch 11:17, 18. 2 Ch 26:10. Ne 9:25; (5) *pit*, Ge 37:20, 22, 24, 28, 29. Ex 21:33, 34. Le 11:36. 2 S 23:20. 2 K 10:14. 1 Ch 11:22. Ps 7:15. 28:1. 30:3. 40:2. 88:4, 6. 143:7. Pr 1:12. 28:17. Is 14:15, 19. 24:22. 38:18. 51:1. Je 41:7, 9. Ezk 26:20. 31:14, 16, 18, 23, 24, 25. 32:29, 30. Zc 9:11.

20   **not be joined**. Ec 6:3.
     burial. Heb. *qeburah*, Ge +35:20 **(S#6900h)**.

the seed. Is 13:15-19. Jb 18:16, 19. Ps 21:10. 37:28. 109:13. 137:8, 9. Da 5:18, 20, 22, 23, 30, 31.

21 **slaughter**. Ex 20:5. Le 26:39. Mt 23:35.
iniquity of their fathers. Ex +20:5.
do not. Is 27:6. Ps 140:8, 10. Hab 2:8-12.
face. Ge +1:2. +11:8.

22 **I will**. Is 13:5, 6. 21:9. 43:14. 47:9-14. Je 50:26, 27, 29-35. 51:3, 4, 56, 57.
Babylon. Is 13:17-22. 45:1-3. ch. 47. Je 50:23-40. 51:30-44. Ezk 26:7-11. 29:18-20. Da 2:31-35. 7:24, 25. ch. 7-12. Na ch. 2, 3. Zp 2:13-15. Mt 24:1, 2, 15, 16, 21. Lk 19:43, 44. 2 Th 2:3, 4.
the name. Jb 18:5, 6, 16-19. Ps 21:10. 37:28. 109:13. Pr 10:7. Je 51:62-64.
remnant. 1 K 14:10.

23 **make**. Pr 13:21, 22. 34:11-15. Je 50:39, 40. 51:42, 43, 61, 62. Zp 2:14. Re 14:8. 18:2, 21-23.
I will sweep. 1 K 14:10. 2 K 21:13. Je 51:25, 26.

24 **hath sworn**. Is 45:23. 54:9. 62:8. Ex 17:16. Dt 1:8. 2:14. 4:31. Ps 110:4. Je 44:26. Am 8:7. He 4:3. 6:16-18.
Surely. Is 46:10, 11. Jb 23:13. Ps 33:10. 92:5. Pr 19:21. 21:30. Je 23:30. 29:11. La 3:37. Mt 11:25, 26. Ac 4:28. Ep 1:9, +11.
purposed. ver. +27.

25 **I will**. Is 9:4. 10:16-19, 32-34. 17:12-14. 30:30-33. 31:8, 9. 37:36-38. 2 K 19:35-37. Ezk 39:4.
break. Ge 27:40.
then. ver. 5. Is 10:24-27. Na 1:13.

26 **the purpose**. Is 5:19, 25. 8:10. 11:2. Jb +14:5. Zp 3:6-8.
hand. Ac 4:28.

27 **Lord of hosts**. Ps +24:10.
purposed. ver. 24, 26. Is 23:9. 44:13. 46:9-11. 55:11. Jb 23:13. 40:8. Ps +115:3. Je 4:28. 50:45. 51:29. Ac 5:39. Ro 8:28, 31. Ep +1:11. 3:11.
his hand. Is 9:12.
stretched. Ex +7:5.
who shall. Is 43:13. 46:10. 2 Ch 20:6. Jb 9:12. 23:13. Ps 33:11. Pr 19:21. +21:30. Da 4:31-35. Mt 24:35. Ep +1:11.

28 **A.M. 3278. B.C. 726.**
In the year. Is 6:1.
Ahaz. 2 K 16:20. 2 Ch 28:27.

29 **Rejoice**. Pr 24:17. Ezk 26:2. 35:15. Ho 9:1. Ob 12. Mi 7:8. Zp 3:11.
whole. Jsh 13:3. 1 S 6:17, 18.
because. 2 Ch 26:6. 28:18.
for. 2 K 18:8.
cockatrice. or, adder. Is 11:8mg.
a fiery. Is 30:6.

30 **the firstborn**. i.e. the poorest of the poor. Jb +18:13.
the poor. Is 5:17. 7:21, 22. 30:23, 24. 33:16. 37:30. 65:13, 14.

and I. Je ch. 47. Ezk 25:15-17. Jl 3:4-8. Am 1:6-8. Zp 2:4-7. Zc 9:5-7.

31 **Howl**. Is +13:6.
O city. 1 S +22:19.
for. Is 20:1. Je 1:14. 25:16, 20.
none shall be alone. or, he shall not be alone.
appointed times. or, assemblies. S#4151h, only here; compare S#4150h, Ge +17:21; Ex +27:21. Is 5:27. 40:29-31. Ge 18:14.

32 **shall one**. Is 39:1. 2 S 8:10. 2 K 20:12, etc.
the Lord. Is 12:6. 37:32. Ps 87:1, 5. 102:16, 28. 132:13-15. Mt 16:18.
and the poor. Is 11:4. 25:4. Zp 3:12. Zc 11:7, 11. Ja 2:5.
trust in it. or, betake themselves unto it. Pr 18:10. Mt 24:15, 16. He 12:22.

ISAIAH 15

1 **burden**. Is 13:1. 14:28.
Moab. Ezk +25:8.
in the night. Ex 12:29, 30. 1 Th 5:1-3.
Ar. Nu 21:28. Dt 2:9, 18.
brought to silence. or, cut off. Is 6:5mg. Je 47:5. 48:2mg.
Kir. Is 16:7, Kir-hareseth. ver. 11, Kir-haresh. 2 K 3:25, Kir-haraseth. Je 48:31, 36, Kir-heres.

2 **is gone**. Is 16:12. Jsh 13:17. Je 48:18, 22, 23.
Bajith. i.e. the house, S#1006h.
high places. 2 K +21:3.
Moab. ver. +1.
howl. Is +13:6.
Nebo. Nu +32:3.
Medeba. Nu 21:30. Jsh 13:16.
all. Is +3:24.
beard. Le +19:27.

3 **sackcloth**. Jb +16:15.
on the. Dt +22:8.
weeping abundantly. Heb. descending into weeping; or, coming down with weeping. ver. 5.

4 **Heshbon**. Nu +21:25.
Jahaz. Nu +21:23.
his. Ge 27:46. Nu 11:15. 1 K 19:4. Jb 3:20-22. 7:15, 16. Je 8:3. 20:18. Jon 4:3, 8. Re 9:6.
life. Heb. nephesh, soul, Ge +44:30.

5 **My heart**. Is 16:9-11. Je 8:18, 19. 9:10, 18, 19. 13:17. 17:16. 48:31-36. Lk 19:41-44. Ro 9:1-3.
his fugitives, etc. or, to the borders thereof, even as an heifer.
Zoar. Ge +13:10.
three. Is 16:14. Je 48:34.
the mounting. Je 48:5, 34.
Luhith. i.e. tables made of boards; tabular; pertaining to the table, S#3872h. Is 15:5. Je 48:5.
with. 2 S 15:23, 30.
Horonaim. i.e. two caverns, S#2773h. Is 15:5. Je 48:3, 5, 34.

destruction. Heb. breaking. Is 22:5. +51:19mg. Je 4:20.

6 **waters**. ver. 9. Is 1:22, 30. 3:1.
Nimrim. i.e. *rebellious ones; leopards*, **S#5249h**. Nu 32:3, 36, Nimrah, Beth-nimrah. Jsh 13:27, Beth-nimrah. Je 48:34.
desolate. Heb. desolations. Je 48:34mg. 51:62mg.
the grass. Is 16:9, 10. Jl 1:10-12. Ps 129:6-8. Hab 3:17, 18. Re 8:7.

7 **the abundance**. Is 5:29. 10:6, 14. Na 2:12, 13.
to the. Ps 137:1, 2.
brook of the willows. *or*, valley of the Arabians. Jg +16:4mg.

8 **the cry**. ver. 2-5. Je 48:20-24, 31-34.
Eglaim. i.e. *two pools; double reservoir*, **S#97h**. Ezk 47:10, En-eglaim.
Beer-elim. i.e. *well of heroes, strong ones, princes*, or *oaks; well of the gods* or *mighty ones*, **S#879h**.

9 **Dimon**. i.e. *silence; undisturbed silence, secure rest*, **S#1775h**.
more. Heb. additions. Le 26:18, 21, 24, 28. Je 48:43-45.
lions. Le 26:22. 2 K 17:25. Je 15:3. Am 5:19.
him. Is 4:2. Jg 3:28-30. 2 K 17:25. Je 49:19.

ISAIAH 16

1 **Send**. Is +59:20. Ac 3:20.
the lamb. 2 S 8:2. 2 K 3:4, 5. Ezr 7:17.
from. 2 K 14:7.
Sela. *or*, Petra. Heb. a rock. i.e. *fortress*, **S#5554h**. 2 K +14:7.
to the wilderness. Ps +68:7. Je +31:2.
the mount. Is 10:32. 59:20. Mi 4:8.
daughter. Nu +21:25.

2 **as**. Is 13:14. Pr 27:8.
cast out of the nest. *or*, a nest forsaken.
the fords. Nu +21:13.

3 **Take**. Heb. Bring.
execute. Je +21:12. Da 4:27.
make. Is +9:6. Ps +91:1. Jon 4:5-8.
hide. Is +26:20. Zp +2:3. Mt 25:35. Lk +21:36. He 13:2.
the outcasts. Is +27:13. Ob 12-14.
bewray. i.e. expose, reveal, make known.
that wandereth. Mt 24:16-21. Re 12:6, 14.

4 **mine**. Dt 23:15, 16. 24:14. Je 21:12.
Moab. Da 11:41.
spoiler. Is 14:4. 21:2, 3. 33:1. 51:13. Je 48:8, 18. Zc 9:8.
extortioner. Heb. wringer. **S#4160h**, only here.
oppressors. Heb. treaders down. Is 15:6. 25:10. Mi 5:5, 6. Zc 10:5. Ml 4:3. Lk 21:24. Ro 16:20mg. Re 11:2.

5 **in mercy**. Ps 61:6, 7. 85:10. 89:1, 2, 14. 2 S 23:3. Ps 89:14. Pr 20:28. 29:14. Mt 25:31, 32, 34-37, 40. Lk 1:69-75.
throne. Ps +45:6.

established. *or*, prepared. Is 30:33.
in the tabernacle. Is +9:6, 7. 2 S 5:9. 7:16. Je 23:5, 6. Da 7:14, 27. Am 9:11. Mi 4:7. Lk 1:31-33. Ac 15:16, 17.
of David. Is +55:3. Ac 13:34.
judging. 2 S 23:3. 2 Ch 31:20, 21. Ps +7:8. 99:4. Je +21:12. Am 9:11. Zc 9:9. Ac +24:10. 1 C +6:2. He +1:8, 9.
hasting. 2 P 3:11, 12.

6 **have**. Is 2:11. Ob 3, 4. 1 P 5:5.
Moab. Ezk +25:8.
very proud. Jb 40:11, 12. Ps 12:3. 31:23. Pr 6:16, 17. 16:5.
but. Is 28:15, 18. 44:25. Je 50:36.

7 **Moab howl**. Is +13:6.
Kir-hareseth. i.e. *an earthen wall; city* or *wall of brick*, **S#7025h**. ver. 11. Is 15:1. 2 K 3:25.
mourn. *or*, mutter. Is 8:19. 33:18 (meditate). 38:14. 59:3.
stricken. 2 K 3:24-27. Ps 119:21.

8 **the fields**. Is 15:4. 24:7, 8. 2 S 1:21.
languish. Is 19:8.
the vine. ver. 9.
Sibmah. i.e. *river of water; sweet smell; why hoary?* **S#7643h**. ver. 9. Nu 32:3, Shebam, 38, Shibmah. Jsh 13:19. Je 48:32.
the lords. Is 10:7. Je 27:6, 7.
Jazer. Nu +32:1.
stretched out. *or*, plucked up. Is 33:23. Jg 15:9. Am 5:2.

9 **I will bewail**. Is +15:5. Je 48:32-34.
O Heshbon. Is 15:4.
for. Is 9:3. Jg 9:27. Je 40:10, 12.
the shouting for. *or*, the alarm is fallen upon, etc. ver. 10. Je 25:30. 48:33.
summer. Is 28:4. 2 S 16:1. Je 40:10, 12. 48:32. Am 8:1, 2. Mi 7:1.

10 **gladness**. Is 24:8, 9. 32:10. Je 48:33. Am 5:11, 17. Hab 3:17, 18. Zp 1:13.

11 **my**. Is 15:5. +63:15. 2 K 8:11. Je 4:19. 13:17. 48:36. Lk 19:41.
Kir-haresh. i.e. *the wall is earthen*, **S#7025h**. ver. 7, Kir-hareseth. Je 48:31, 36.

12 **when**. Is 15:2. 26:16. Nu 21:29. 22:39, 41. 23:1-3, 14, 28. 24:17. Jg 11:24. Pr 1:28. Je 48:7, 13, 35.
high place. 2 K +21:3.
he shall. Is 37:38. 1 K 11:7. 2 K 3:27. Je 48:7, 13, 46.
sanctuary. Is 16:12. Le 26:31. Ezk 21:2. Am 7:9.
but. Is 47:13. 2 K 19:12, 16-19. Ps 115:3-8. Je 10:5.

13 **since**. Is 44:8. Nu 24:15-17.

14 **But now**. Ac 1:6, 7.
three. Is 7:16. 15:5. 21:16. Dt 15:18.
the glory. Is 17:4. 23:9. Ge 31:1. Est 5:11. Je 9:23. Na 2:9, 10.
and the remnant. Je 48:46, 47.
feeble. *or*, not many.

ISAIAH 17

1 A.M. cir. 3263. B.C. cir. 741.
   burden. Is 15:1. 19:1.
   Damascus. Ge +14:15.
   Damascus is. Is 8:4. 10:9. 2 K 16:9.
   a ruinous. Is 25:2. 37:26. Je 49:2. Mi 1:6.
   3:12.
2 **Aroer**. Nu +32:34.
   they shall. Is 5:17. 7:23-25. 1 K 22:3. Zp
   +2:6.
   none. Je 7:33.
3 **fortress**. Is 7:8, 16. 8:4. 10:9. 2 K 16:9. 17:6.
   Ho 1:4, 6. 3:4. 5:13, 14. 8:8. 9:16, 17. 10:14.
   13:7, 8, 15, 16. Am 2:6-9. 3:9-15. 5:25-27.
   6:7-11. 8:14. 9:1-10. Mi 1:4-9.
   Damascus. 1 K 15:18, 19. 20:34.
   they shall. Is 16:14. 28:1-4. Ho 9:11.
4 **the glory**. Is 9:8, 21. 10:4. Ho 9:11. 12:2. Mi
   1:5.
   the fatness. Is 10:16-19. 24:13, 16. 28:1. Dt
   32:15-27. Ezk 34:20. Zp 2:11mg.
5 **as when**. Ps 129:6, 7. Je 9:22. 51:33. Ho
   6:11. 10:12-14. Jl 3:13. Mt 13:30, 39-42. Re
   14:15-20.
   corn. lit. harvest. Dt +24:19.
   the valley. Dt +2:20.
6 **gleaning grapes**. Is 1:9. 10:22. 24:13. Dt
   4:27. 24:20. Jg 8:2. 1 K 19:18. Ezk 36:8-15.
   37:19-25. 39:29. Ob 5. Mi 7:1. Ro 9:27. 11:4-
   6, 26.
   Lord God. Is 29:23. Ex 32:27. Jsh 9:18, 19.
   10:40, 42.
   of Israel. Is +29:23.
7 **At that day**. Is +2:11.
   shall a man look. Is +26:9.
   to his Maker. Is 10:20, 21. 19:22. 22:11.
   24:14, 15. 29:18, 19, 24. Jg 10:15, 16. 2 Ch
   30:10, 11, 18-20. 31:1. 35:17, 18. Je 3:12-14,
   18-23. 31:4-10. Ho 3:5. 6:1. 14:1-3. Mi 7:7.
   have respect. Zc 9:1.
8 **he shall**. Is 1:29. 2:18-21. 27:9. 30:22. 2 K
   16:10, 11. 23:11, 12. 2 Ch 34:4, 6, 7, 33. Ezk
   36:25. Ho 14:8. Zp 1:3. Zc 13:2.
   the work. Is 2:8. 31:6, 7. 44:15, 19, 20. Ho
   8:4-6. 10:1, 2. 13:1, 2. Mi 5:13, 14.
   the groves. 2 K +17:10.
   images. or, sun images. Le +26:30mg.
9 **In that day**. ver. 4, 5. Is 6:11-13. 7:16-20.
   9:9-12. 24:1-12. 27:10. 28:1-4. Ezr 9:7. Ho
   10:14. 13:15, 16. Am 3:11-15. 7:9. Mi 5:11.
   6:16. 7:13.
10 **thou hast forgotten**. Is 51:13. Dt 6:12. 8:11,
   14, 19. Ps 9:17. 106:13, 21. Je 2:32. 17:13. Ho
   2:13, 14. 4:6. 8:14. 13:6, 7.
   the God. Ps +88:1.
   the rock. Is 26:4. Dt 32:4, 15, 18, 30, 31. Ps
   18:2. 31:2, 3. 1 C 10:4.
   shalt thou. Is 65:21, 22. Le 26:16, 20. Dt
   28:30, 38-42. Je 12:13. Am 5:11. Zp 1:13.
11 **the harvest**. Is 18:5, 6. Jb 4:8. Je 5:31. Ho

8:7. 9:1-4, 16. 10:12-15. Jl 1:5-12. Ga 6:7, 8.
   **a heap in the day of grief and of desper-
   ate sorrow**. or, removed in the day of inheritance, and there shall be deadly sorrow. Is
   65:13, 14. Mt 8:11, 12. Ro 2:5, 8, 9. 2 C 7:10.
12 **multitude**. or, noise. Is 9:5.
   make a noise. Is 5:26-30. 2 K 15:29. 17:3. Ps
   18:4. 46:1-3. 65:6, 7. Je 6:23. +47:2. Ezk 43:2.
   Lk 21:25.
   mighty. or, many. Ps 29:3.
13 **shall rush**. Je 6:23.
   but. Is 10:15, 16, 33, 34. 14:25. 25:4, 5. 27:1.
   30:30-33. 31:8, 9. 33:1-3, 9-12. 37:29-38. Ps
   9:5. 46:5-11.
   rebuke. Jb 38:11. Mk 4:39-41.
   shall be. Lk +3:17.
   a rolling thing. or, thistle-down. Ps 83:13
   (wheel).
   whirlwind. Je +23:19.
14 **at eveningtide**. Is 10:28-32. 2 K 19:3, 35. Ps
   37:36.
   before the morning. Is 8:20mg. 37:29, 33-
   36. Ps 9:5. 78:65, 66. Re +2:28.
   he is not. Is +24:22. Ps +37:9, 10. +101:8. Pr
   13:9.
   the portion. Is 33:1. Jg 5:31. Jb 20:29. Pr
   22:23. Je 2:3. 13:25. Ezk 39:10. Hab 2:16, 17.
   Zp 2:9, 10. Zc 14:2, 3, 12-15.
   that spoil us. Zc 14:1, 2.

ISAIAH 18

1 A.M. cir. 3290. B.C. cir. 714.
   Woe. Is 1:4, 24. 5:8, 11.
   the land. Is 20:3-6. 30:2, 3. 31:1.
   shadowing. Ru 2:12. Ps 17:8. 36:7. 57:1.
   61:4. 63:7. 91:4. Mt 23:37.
   which. 2 K 19:9. Ezk 30:4, 5. Zp 2:12. 3:10.
   Ethiopia. 2 Ch 14:9. 16:8.
2 **sendeth**. Is 30:2-4. Ezk 30:9.
   vessels. Ex 2:3.
   bulrushes. Is 35:7. Ex 2:3. Jb 8:11. Ps 83:3.
   to a nation. ver. 7.
   scattered and peeled. or, outspread and
   polished. ver. 7. 1 K 7:45. Ezk 21:10, 11.
   to a people. Ge 10:8, 9. 2 Ch 12:2-4. 14:9.
   16:8.
   meted out and trodden down. or, that
   meteth out and treadeth down. Heb. of line
   and line and treading under foot.
   have spoiled. or, despise. Is 19:5-7.
3 **All ye**. Is 1:2. Ps 49:1, 2. 50:1. Je 22:29. Mi
   6:2.
   see ye. Is 5:26. 7:18. 13:2, 4. 26:11. Mi 6:9.
   trumpet. Le +23:24. Ho +8:1. Re 8:2, 13.
   hear ye. Mt 11:15. 13:9, 16.
4 **I will take**. Is 26:21. Ps 132:13, 14. Ho 5:15.
   consider my dwelling place. or, regard my
   set dwelling. ver. 7. Is 12:6. 14:32. 31:9.
   46:13. Nu 24:8, 9. 2 K 19:6-14. Jl 3:17.

like a clear. 2 S 23:4. Ps 72:6.
upon herbs. *or*, after rain. 2 K 4:39.
5 **afore harvest**. Is +17:11. SS 2:13, 15. Ezk 17:6-10.
6 **shall be left**. Is 14:19. 34:1-7. Le 26:43. Jb 18:4. Je 7:33. 15:3. Ezk 32:4-6. 39:17-20. Re 19:17, 18.
fowls. Lk +17:37.
7 **shall the present**. Is 16:1. 23:17, 18. 45:14. Jg +3:15. Ps 68:29-31. 72:9-15. 87:4. Je 3:16. Ezk 39:10. Zp 3:10. Ml 1:11. Ac 8:27, 28. Ro +11:25.
scattered and peeled. *or*, outspread and polished. ver. 2.
to the place. ver. +4. Is 60:6-9. Ps 132:13, 14. Mi 4:13. Zc 14:16, 17.

ISAIAH 19

1 **Egypt**. Je 25:19. 43:8-13. 44:29, 30. ch. 46. Ezk ch. 29-32. Jl 3:19. Zc 10:11. 14:18, 19.
rideth. Dt +33:26.
swift cloud. 2 Ch +5:13. Ps +104:3. Mt +24:30. 26:64, 65. Re 1:7.
the idols. Is 21:9. 46:1, 2. Ex +12:12. 1 S 5:2-4. Je 50:2. 51:44.
the heart. ver. 16. Ex +15:15. Je 46:5, 15, 16.
2 **I will**. ver. 13, 14. Is 9:21. Jg +7:22. 9:23. Mt 12:25. Re 17:12-17.
set. Heb. mingle. Is 9:11mg.
3 **the spirit**. Heb. *ruach*, Ge +41:8. ver. 1, 11-13. Is 57:16. 1 S 25:37. Ps 76:12. Je 46:15. Ezk 21:7. 22:14.
fail. Heb. be emptied. Is 24:1, 3. Jsh 2:11. Da 5:7-9. Na 2:2.
and I. Is 14:27. 2 Ch 25:16-20. Je +19:7.
destroy. Heb. swallow up. Ps 107:27mg.
and they. Is 15:2. 47:12. Da 2:2. 4:6, 7. 5:7.
familiar spirits. Dt +18:11.
wizards. 2 K +21:6.
4 **give over**. *or*, shut up. 1 S 23:7. Ps 31:8.
a cruel lord. ver. 2. Is 20:4. Je 46:26. Ezk 29:19. Da 11:5-45.
5 **the waters**. Is 11:15. Je 51:36. Ezk 30:12. Zc 10:11. 14:18.
fail. Is 41:17. Je 51:30.
6 **and the**. Is 37:25. 2 K 19:24.
the reeds. Is 18:2. Ex 2:3. Jb 8:11.
7 **everything sown**. Is 32:20. Dt 11:10. Je 14:4. Ezk 19:13. Jl 1:17, 18.
be no more. Heb. shall not be.
8 **fishers**. Je 7:21. Nu 11:5. Ezk 30:10-12. 47:10. Hab 1:15.
angle. Jb 41:1.
shall languish. Is 16:8.
9 **work**. Ex +26:1.
weave. Is 38:12. 59:5. Ex 28:32. 35:35. 39:22.
net works. *or*, white works.

10 **purposes**. Heb. foundations. Ps 11:3.
make. Ex 7:19. 8:5. Dt 11:10.
for fish. *or*, of living things. Heb. *nephesh*, Ge +2:19. Nu 11:5.
11 **the princes**. ver. +3, 13. Is 29:14. Ezk 7:26.
Zoan. Nu +13:22.
brutish. Ps 73:22. 92:6. Pr 30:2. Je 10:14, 21.
I am. Ge 41:38, 39. 1 K 4:30. Ac 7:22.
the son. Ps 72:1.
ancient. Heb. *kedem*, Mi +5:2.
12 **where are thy**. Is 5:21. 47:10-13. Jg 9:38. Je 2:28. 1 C 1:20.
let them. Is 40:13, 14. 41:22, 23. 44:7. Jb 11:6, 7. Ro 11:33, 34.
13 **princes of Zoan**. ver. +11. Ro 1:22.
Noph. i.e. *presentability*, S#5297h. Je 2:16. 44:1. 46:14, 19. Ezk 30:13, 16.
stay. *or*, governors. Heb. corners. Is 28:16. Ex 27:2. Nu 24:17. Jg 20:2. 1 S 14:38mg. Zc 10:4. 1 P 2:7.
14 **hath mingled**. ver. +2. Is 29:10, 14. 47:10, 11. 1 K 22:20-23. Jb 12:16. Ezk 14:7-9. 2 Th 2:11, 12.
perverse spirit. Heb. spirit of perverseness *or*, perversities. S#5773h, only here; the root is S#5753h, which occurs at Is 24:1mg. 1 S 20:30. 2 S 19:19. Pr 12:8.
as a drunken. Is 28:7, 8. 29:9. Jb 12:25. Je 25:15, 16, 17, 19, 27. 48:26.
15 **Neither shall**. Is 9:14, 15. Ps 128:2. Pr 14:23. Hab 3:17. Hg 1:11. 1 Th 4:11, 12.
head or tail. Is 9:15.
16 **like**. Is 30:17. Ps 48:6. Je 30:5-7. 50:37. 51:30. Na 3:13.
the shaking. Is 10:32. 11:15. 30:30-32. Zc 2:9.
hand. Is 10:32. 11:15. 13:2.
17 **the land**. Is 31:1-5. 36:1. Je 25:19, 27-31. 43:8-13. 44:28-30. Ezk 29:6, 7.
because. Is 14:24, 26, 27. 20:2-5. 46:10, 11. Da 4:35.
18 **that day**. ver. 19, 21. Is 2:11. Zc 2:11.
shall five. Is 11:11. 27:13. Ge +43:34. 2 K +7:13. Ps 68:31.
speak. Zp 3:9.
language. Heb. lip. Ge 11:1mg. Jg +7:22mg.
and swear. Ge +21:23. Ne 10:29.
destruction. Heb. Heres, *or*, the sun. Je 43:13mg. Ezk 30:17mg.
19 **an altar**. Is 66:23. Ge 12:7, 8. 13:4. 26:25. 28:18. Ex 24:4. Jsh 22:10, 26, 27. 1 K 18:35, 36. Zc 6:15. He 13:10.
pillar. S#4676h, Ex +34:13. ver. 21. Ge 28:18. 35:14. Le 26:1mg. Dt 12:5. 16:22mg.
20 **for a**. Is 55:13. Jsh 4:20, 21. 22:27, 28, 34. 24:26, 27.
they shall. ver. 4. Is 20:4. 52:5. Ex 2:23. 3:7. 2 K 13:4, 5. Ps 50:15. Ja +5:4.
he shall send. Is 37:36. 45:21, 22. Ne +9:27. Lk 2:11. T 2:13.

21 **the Lord shall**. Is 11:9. 37:20. 55:5. 1 S
18:46. 1 K 8:43. Ps 67:2. 98:2, 3. Je 16:19-21.
Hab 2:14. Jn 17:3. Ga 4:8, 9.
and shall. Zp 3:10. Ml 1:11. Jn 4:21-24. Ro
15:27, 28. 1 P 2:5, 9.
shall vow. Is 44:5. Le +23:38.
22 **he shall smite**. ver. 1, etc. Dt +32:39. Jb
5:17, 18. Ho 5:15. 6:1, 2. He 12:11.
they shall. Is 6:10. 55:7. Ho 14:1. Am 4:6-12.
Ac 26:17-20. 28:26, 27.
23 **a highway**. Is 11:16. 35:8-10. 40:3-5. Ep
2:18-22. 3:6-8.
24 **shall**. Is 6:13. 49:6, 22. 65:8, 22. 66:12, 19-
21. Dt 32:43. Ps ch. 117. Zc 2:10, 11. 8:20-23.
Lk 2:32. Ro 10:11-13. 15:9-12, 27.
a blessing. Is 65:8. Ge +12:2. Ezk 34:26. Zc
8:13. Ga 3:14.
25 **the Lord**. Is 61:9. 65:23. Nu 6:24, 27. 24:1.
Ps 67:6, 7. 115:15. Ro 11:12. Ep 1:3. 2:14.
Blessed. Is 29:23. Ps 100:3. 138:8. Ho 2:23. Ro
3:29. 9:24, 25. Ph 1:6. Col 3:10, 11. 1 P 2:10.
my people. Ho 2:23.
the work. Ro 10:12. Ga 6:15. Ep 2:10.
and Israel. Dt +32:9.
mine inheritance. Dt +32:43. Ps +94:14. Zc
+2:12.

ISAIAH 20

1 **Tartan**. 2 K 18:17.
Ashdod. Jsh +11:22.
Sargon. i.e. *the legitimate king; stubborn rebel;
prince of the sun*, **S#5623h**.
and took. Je 25:29, 30.
2 **Isaiah**. Heb. by the hand of Isaiah. 1 K
+16:12mg.
Go. Je 13:1-11. 19:1, etc. Ezk 4:5, 6. Mt
16:24.
sackcloth. 2 K 1:8. Jb +16:15. Zc 13:4. Mt
3:4.
put. Ex 3:5. Jsh 5:15. Ezk 24:17, 23.
naked. ver. 3, 4. Is 47:3. 58:7. Ge 2:25. 3:7,
10, 11. Ex 32:25. 1 S 19:24. 2 S 6:20. 2 Ch
28:15, 19. Jb 1:20, 21. 22:6. 24:7, 10. 26:6. Ec
5:15. La 1:8. 4:21. Ezk 18:7. Ho 2:3. Am 2:16.
Mi 1:8, 11. Na 3:5. Mab 2:15. Mt 25:36, 38,
43. Mk 14:51, 52. Jn 21:7. Ac 19:16. Ro 8:35.
1 C 4:1, 2, 9-13. 2 C 5:3. Ja 2:15. Re 3:17, 18.
16:15.
3 **naked**. ver. +2.
barefoot. 2 S 15:30. Je 2:25.
three years. Is 16:14. 37:30. Nu 14:34. 1 K
2:11. Ezk 4:5, 6. Re 11:2, 3.
a sign. Is +7:11. 8:18. Ex 7:3. Dt 4:34. 1 C
4:9.
upon Egypt. Is 18:1, etc.
4 **shall**. Is 19:4. Je 9:25, 26. 46:26. Ezk 30:18.
Egyptians. Heb. captivity of Egypt.
with their. Is 3:17. 2 S 10:4. Je 13:22, 26. Mi
1:11.

uncovered. ver. 2, 3. Is 30:14 (take). 47:2
(make bare). 52:10. 58:7. Ps 29:9 (discovereth). Je 13:26. 49:10. Ezk 4:7. Jl 1:7. Hg
2:16 (draw out).
shame. Heb. nakedness. Is +3:17. Ge 9:22,
23. 42:9, 12. Ex 20:26. 28:42. Le 18:6-19.
20:11, 17-21. Dt 23:14mg. 24:1mg. 1 S 20:30.
Ezk 22:10. Re 3:18.
5 **afraid**. Is 30:3, 5, 7. 36:6. 2 K 18:19-21. Ezk
29:6, 7.
their expectation. Je 37:7, 8. 42:13-22.
43:7. 46:26. La 5:6. Ezk 17:15.
their glory. Is 2:22. Je 9:23, 24. 17:5. 1 C 3:21.
6 **isle**. *or*, country. Jb 22:30. Je 47:4.
whither. Is 28:17. 30:1-7, 15, 16. 31:1-3. Jb
6:20.
and how. Mt 23:33. 1 Th 5:3. He 2:3.

ISAIAH 21

1 **The burden**. Is 13:1. 14:4, 23. 17:1. Je 50:1,
etc. 51:1, etc.
the desert. Is 13:20-22. 14:23. Je 51:42.
As whirlwinds. Jb 37:9. Da 11:40. Zc 9:14.
from. Is 13:4, 5, 17, 18. Ezk 30:11. 31:12.
2 **grievous**. Heb. hard. Is 48:4mg. Ps 60:3. Pr
13:15.
the treacherous. Is 24:16. 33:1. 1 S 24:13. Je
51:44, 48, 49, 53. Jn 8:44. Re 13:10.
Go up. Is 13:2-4, 17, 18. Je 50:14, 34. 49:34.
51:11, 27, 28. Da 5:28. 8:20.
all the sighing. Is 14:1-3. 35:10. 47:6. 51:11.
Ps 12:5. 79:11. 137:1-3. Je 31:11, 12, 20, 25.
45:3. 51:3, 4. La 1:22. Mi 7:8-10. Zc 1:15, 16.
3 **are**. Is 15:5. 16:9, 11. Hab 3:16.
pangs have. Je +4:31. Mi 4:9, 10.
I was bowed. Dt 28:67. Ps 38:6. Da 5:5, 6.
4 **heart panted**. *or*, mind wandered. Is 16:8
(wandered). 53:6 (gone astray). Ps 119:110
(erred), 176.
the night. Is 5:11-14. 1 S 25:36-38. 2 S
13:28, 29. Est 5:12. 7:6-10. Jb 21:11-13. Je
51:30, 39, 57. Da 5:1, 5, 30. Na 1:10. Lk
21:34-36.
turned. Heb. put.
5 **eat**. Is 22:13, 14. Da 5:1-5. 1 C 15:32.
arise. Is 13:2, 17, 18. 45:1-3. Je 51:11, 27, 28.
6 **Go**. Is 62:6. 2 K 9:17-20. Ps 127:1. Je 51:12,
13. Ezk 3:17. 33:2-7. Hab 2:1, 2.
7 **And he saw**. ver. 9. Is 37:24.
he hearkened. Je 51:31. He 2:1.
diligently. 1 K 18:29.
8 **cried, A lion**. *or*, cried as a lion. Is 5:29. Je
4:7. 25:38. 49:19. 50:44. Da 7:2-4. 1 P 5:8.
I stand. Is 56:10. 62:6. Ps 63:6. 127:1. Hab
2:1, 2.
whole nights. *or*, every night.
9 **behold**. Je 50:3, 9, 29, 42. 51:27.
Babylon. Is 13:19. 14:4. Je 50:2. 51:8, 64. Re
14:8. 18:2, 21.

all. Is 46:1, 2. Je 50:2, 38. 51:44, 47, 52.
graven images of. Dt 7:25. 12:3.

10 **my threshing**. Is 28:27. 41:15, 16. 2 K 13:7.
Je 51:33. Jl 3:14mg. Am 1:3. 9:9. Mi 4:13.
Hab 3:12. Re 14:14, 15.
corn. Heb. son. Is 5:1mg.
floor. or, threshingfloor. Ge +50:10.
that which. 1 K 22:14. Ezk 3:17-19. Ac
20:26, 27.

11 **burden**. Is 13:1.
Dumah. Ge +25:14. 1 Ch 1:30.
to me out of Seir. Ge +14:6. Je +49:7-22.
Watchman. Ezk 3:17. 33:1-9. Mt 13:35-37.
what. ver. 6. Je 37:17.

12 **The morning**. Is 17:14. Je 50:27. Ezk 7:5-7,
10, 12.
if. Is 55:7. Je 42:19-22. Ezk 14:1-6. 18:30-32.
Ac 2:37, 38. 17:19, 20, 30-32.
enquire. Is 63:1. Je 49:7-22. Ezk 35:1-15. Ob
1-21.
return. 2 S 23:4. 1 Th 5:1, 2, 5, 6. Re 22:16.
come. SS 2:17. Re 22:17, 20.

13 **Arabia**. 2 Ch +9:14. Je 49:28-33.
O ye. Is 13:20.
Dedanim. i.e. *leading forward; inhabitants of*
Dedan, **S#1720h**, only here. Ge +10:7.

14 **Tema**. Ge +25:15.
brought. *or*, bring ye. Is 16:3, 4. Jg 8:4-8. Pr
25:21. Je 12:9mg. Ro 12:20. 1 P 4:9.

15 **from the swords**. *or*, for fear of the swords.
Heb. from the face of. Jb 6:19, 20.

16 **according**. Is 16:14. Jb 7:1.
Kedar. Ge +25:13.

17 **archers**. Heb. bows. Is 22:3mg.
the mighty. Is 10:18, 19. 17:4, 5. Ps 107:39.
for. Is 1:20. Nu 23:19. Je 44:29. Zc 1:6. Mt
24:35.
hath spoken. Is +1:20. 22:25. 24:3. 25:8.

ISAIAH 22

1 A.M. cir. 3292. B.C. cir. 712.
burden. Is 13:1. 23:1. Na 1:1. Hab 1:1. Ml
1:1.
the valley. Ps 125:2. Je 21:13.
of vision. 1 S 3:1. Ps 147:19, 20. Pr 29:18. Mi
3:6. Ro 3:2. 9:4, 5.
What. Ge 21:17. Jg 18:23. 1 S 11:5. 2 S 14:5.
2 K 6:28. Ps 114:5.
that thou. Dt +22:8.

2 **that art**. ver. 12, 13. Is 23:7. 32:13.
Am 6:3-6.
thy slain. Is 37:33, 36. Je 14:18. 38:2. 52:6.
La 2:10. 4:9, 10.

3 **thy rulers**. Is 3:1-8. 2 K 25:2-7, 18-21. Je
39:4-7. 52:24-27.
by the archers. Heb. of the bow.
Is 21:17mg.

4 **Look**. Ru 1:20, 21. Ezr 9:3. Je 4:19. 9:1.
13:17. Lk 1:2.

weep bitterly. Heb. be bitter in weeping. Is
33:7. Je 6:26. Mi 1:8. Mt 26:75.
labor. Ps 77:2. Je 8:18. 31:15. Mt 2:18.

5 **a day**. Is 37:3. 2 K 19:3. Je 30:7. Ezk 7:7. Am
5:18-20. Zp 1:15.
treading. Is 5:5. 10:6. 25:10.
perplexity. Est 3:15. Mi 7:4.
breaking. 2 K 25:8-10. La 1:5. 2:2.
crying. Ho 10:8. Mt 24:16. Lk 23:30. Re 6:16,
17.

6 **Elam**. Ge +10:22.
quiver. Is 49:2.
Kir. Is 15:1. 2 K 16:9. Am 1:5. 9:7.
uncovered. Heb. made naked. Is +3:17mg.
21:5. Hab 3:9. Zp 2:14mg.

7 **thy choicest valleys**. Heb. the choice of thy
valleys. Is 37:24. Ge 23:6. Ex 15:4.
full. Is 8:7, 8. 10:28-32. 37:34. 2 K 24:10. Je
39:1-3.
at. *or*, toward.

8 **he discovered**. Is 36:1-3.
the armor. 1 K 7:2. 10:17. 14:27, 28. 2 Ch
12:10. SS 4:4.

9 **have seen**. 2 K 20:20. 2 Ch 32:1-6, 30.
breaches. or, clefts. Am 6:11.
gathered. Is 11:12. 40:11. 43:5.
lower. Is 7:3. A reference to the pool of
Siloam, the "old pool." Is 7:3. 8:6. 36:2. 2 S
5:8. 2 K 20:20. 2 Ch 32:3-5, 30. Ne 2:14. Ps
46:4.
pool. lit. blessing. ver. 11. Is 7:3. 36:2.

10 **numbered**. Le 15:13, 28. 23:15.
broken. Ex 34:13. Dt 7:5.

11 **a ditch**. or, reservoir. Ne 3:16.
old pool. ver. 9. Is 7:3. Ne 2:13-15. 7:1-4. ye
have. Is 8:17. 17:7. 31:1. 37:26. 2 Ch 6:6.
16:7-9. Je 33:2, 3. Mi 7:7.

12 **call**. 2 Ch 35:25. Ne 8:9-12. 9:9. Ec 3:4, 11. Je
36:22-24. Jl 1:13. 2:17, 18. Ja 4:8-10. 5:1.
mourning. Jl +2:12.
to baldness. Is +3:24.
sackcloth. Jb +16:15.

13 **behold**. Is 5:12. 21:4, 5. 56:12. Am 6:3-7. Lk
17:26-30.
let. Is 56:12. 1 C 15:32. Ja 5:5.

14 **it was**. Is 5:9. 1 S 9:15. Am 3:7.
Surely. Nu 15:25-31. 1 S 3:14. 2 K 24:4. Ezk
24:13. Mt 12:31, 32. Jn 8:21-24. He 10:26,
27. 1 J 5:16. Re 22:11, 12.
iniquity shall not be purged. Is 6:7. 27:9.
Ex 30:10. Le 4:20.

15 **treasurer**. 1 Ch 27:25. Ac 8:27.
Shebna. Is 36:3. 37:2. 2 K 18:18, 37. 19:2.
which. 1 K 4:6. 2 K 10:5.

16 **What hast**. Is 52:5. Mi 2:10.
hewed. Is 14:18. 2 S 18:18. 2 Ch 16:14. Jb
3:14. Mt 27:60.
sepulchre. Heb. *qeber*, Ge +23:4.
as he. *or*, O he.
sepulchre. Heb. *qeber*, Ge +23:4.

17 **will carry**, etc. *or*, who covered thee with an excellent covering, and clothed thee gorgeously, shall surely violently turn, etc. ver. 18.
a mighty captivity. Heb. the captivity of a man.
cover. Est +6:12.

18 **surely.** Is 17:13. Am 7:17.
a large country. Heb. a land large of spaces. Is 33:21mg. Ps 119:45mg.

19 **I will drive.** Jb 40:11, 12. Ps 75:6, 7. Ezk 17:24. Lk 1:52.

20 **Eliakim.** Is 36:3, 11, 22. 37:2. 2 K +18:18.

21 **clothe.** Ge 41:42, 43. 1 S 18:4. Est 8:2, 15. Jn 1:14. Ph 2:7, 8. 1 T 3:16. He 2:8-14, 16.
thy girdle. Is 11:5. Ex 28:4, 39, 40. 29:9, +39. 39:29. Le 8:7, 13. 16:4. Lk 17:8.
a father. Is +9:6, 7. Ge 45:8.

22 **And the key.** Jg 3:25. 1 Ch 9:27. Mt 16:18, 19. Lk +11:52. Re 1:18.
so he. Jb 12:14. Mt 18:18, 19. 28:18. Re 3:7.
open. Jb +12:14.

23 **I will.** Jn 10:18. Ro 1:4.
a nail. ver. 25. Ex +27:19.
a glorious. Ge 45:9-13. 1 S 2:8. Est 4:14. 10:3. Jb 36:7. Lk 1:31-33. 22:29, 30. Ac 2:29-31. Re 3:21.

24 **hang.** Ge 41:44, 55. 47:11-25. Da 6:1-3. Mt 28:18. Jn 5:22-27. 20:21-23. Re 5:12, 13. 19:12.
offspring. Is 34:1. 42:5. 44:3. 48:19. 61:9. 65:23. Jb 5:25. 21:8. 27:14. 31:8.
and the issue. Ezk 4:15.
vessels of small. Ezk 15:3. Ro 9:22, 23. 2 T 2:20, 21.
vessels of cups. Ex 24:6.
vessels of flagons. *or*, instruments of viols. Je 48:12. La 4:2.

25 **the nail.** ver. 15, 16, 23.
cut down. Is 53:8. Jn 19:11. Ac 2:23. 3:17, 18. 8:33. 1 C 1:23. 2 C 13:4.
and fall. Lk 24:21, 25-27. Jn 19:30. Ph 2:8.
the burden. Est 9:5-14, 24, 25. Ps 52:5-7. 146:3, 4. Je 17:5, 6.
for the. Is 46:11. 48:15. Je 4:28. Ezk 5:13, 15, 17. Mi 4:4.

ISAIAH 23

1 A.M. 3289. B.C. 715.
burden. Is +22:1. 1 K +7:13. Je 25:15, 22. 47:4. Ezk ch. 26-28. Jl 3:4-8. Am 1:9, 10. Zc 9:2, 4.
Howl. Is +13:6. Re 18:17-19.
ye ships. Is 2:16. 60:9. 1 K 22:48. 2 Ch 9:21. Ps 48:7. Ezk 27:25.
Tarshish. Ge +10:4.
for it is. Is 15:1. Je 25:10, 11. Re 18:22, 23.
the land. ver. 12. Nu 24:24. Je 2:10. Ezk 27:6. Da 11:30.

2 **still.** Heb. silent. Is 41:1. 47:5. Ps 46:10. Je 47:6. Hab 2:20.
the isle. Ezk 27:3, 4. 28:2.
the merchants. Ezk 27:8, etc.

3 **great waters.** Ps 29:3mg. 32:6.
Sihor. 1 Ch 13:5. Je 2:18.
the harvest. Is 32:20. Dt 11:10.
river. Is 7:18. Ex 7:19. 8:5.
she is. ver. 8. Ezk 27:33. 28:4, 5. Jl 3:5, 6. Re 18:11-13.
mart. ver. 18. Is 45:14. Pr 3:14. 31:18.

4 **I travail.** Je 47:3, 4. Ezk 26:3-6. Ho 9:11-14. Re 18:23.

5 **at the.** Is 19:16. Ex 15:14-16. Jsh 2:9-11.
so shall. Ezk 26:15-21. 27:29-36. 28:19. Re 18:17-19.

6 **Pass.** ver. 10, 12. Is 21:15. Jon 1:3.
Tarshish. Ge +10:4.
howl. ver. +1, 14.

7 **your.** Is 13:3. 22:2. 24:8. 32:13.
whose. Jsh 19:29.
antiquity. S#6927h. Is 23:7. Ps 129:6 (afore). Ezk 16:55, 55 (former). 36:11 (former estate).
ancient. Heb. *kedem*, Mi 5:2. Is 19:11.
her own. Is 47:1, 2. Ec 10:7.
carry. Ps 60:9. 68:29. 76:11.
afar off. Heb. from afar off. Is 5:26.

8 **Who hath.** Dt 29:24-28. Je 50:44, 45. Re 18:8.
the crowning. Ezk 28:2-6, 12-18. Zc 9:3.
merchants. Is 10:8. 36:9.

9 **Lord.** Is 10:33. 14:24, 27. 46:10, 11. Je 47:6, 7. 51:62. Ac 4:28. Ep +1:11. 3:11.
to stain. Heb. to pollute. Is 2:11, 12, 17. 5:15, 16. 13:11. Jb 40:11, 12. Da 4:37. Ml 4:1. Ja 4:6.
bring. Jb 12:21. Ps 107:40. 1 C 1:26-29.

10 **O daughter.** ver. 12.
Tarshish. Ge +10:4.
no more. ver. 14. 1 S 28:20. Jb 12:21. La 1:6. Hg 2:22. Ro 5:6.
strength. Heb. girdle. Ps 18:32. 109:19.

11 **stretched.** Is 2:19. 14:16, 17. Ex 15:8-10. Ps 46:6. Ezk 26:10, 15-19. 27:34, 35. 31:16. Hg 2:7.
the Lord. Is 10:6. Ps 71:3. Je 47:7. Na 1:14.
against the merchant city. *or*, concerning a merchantman. ver. 3. Ho 12:7, 8.
the merchant city. Heb. Canaan. Ge 9:25. 10:15-19. Zc 14:21. Mk 11:17. Jn 2:16.
strong holds. *or*, strengths. Zc 9:3, 4.

12 **Thou shalt.** ver. 1, 7. Ezk 26:13, 14. Re 18:22.
thou oppressed. Je +18:13.
daughter. Nu +21:25.
Zidon. ver. 2. Ge +49:13.
pass. ver. 1. Nu 24:24. Ezk 27:6.
there also. Dt 28:64-67. La 1:3. 4:15.

13 **land.** Is 13:19. Ge 11:28, 31. Jb 1:17. Hab 1:6. Ac 7:4.

the Assyrian. Ge 2:14. 10:10, 11. 11:9. 2 K 17:24. 20:12. 2 Ch 33:11. Ezr 4:9, 10. Da 4:30.
for them. Ps 72:9.
and he. Ezk 26:7, etc. 29:18.

14 **Howl**. ver. 1, 6. Ezk 27:25-30. Re 18:11-19.
ships. ver. 1.
Tarshish. Ge +10:4.

15 **Tyre shall**. Je 25:9-11, 22. 27:3-7. 29:10. Ezk 29:11.
one. Heb. *echad*, Dt +6:4. A compound unity; here, a dynasty, the Babylonian dynasty.
king. Da 7:14. 8:21. Re 17:10.
seventy years. Je 25:9-11. 27:2-7. 29:10.
shall Tyre sing as an harlot. Heb. it shall be unto Tyre as the song of an harlot. Is +32:9. Ezk 27:25. Ho 2:15.

16 **harp**. Re +5:8.
go about. Pr 7:10-12. Je 30:14.
thou harlot. Is +6:9.

17 **visit**. Je 29:10. Zp 2:7. Ac 15:14.
and she shall. Dt 23:18. Ezk 16:31. 22:13. 27:6, etc. Ho 12:7, 8. Mi 1:7. 3:11. 1 T 3:3, 8. 1 P 5:2.
shall commit. Na 3:4. Re 17:2-5. 18:9-14. 19:2.
the face. Ge +1:2.

18 **her merchandise**. Is 60:6, 7. 2 Ch 2:7-9, 11-16. Ps 45:12. 72:10. 87:4. Zc 14:20, 21. Mt 21:31. Mk 3:8. Lk 7:47. Ac 21:3-5.
it shall. Mt 6:19-21. Lk 12:18-20, 33. 16:9-13.
for them. Dt 12:18, 19. 26:12-14. Pr 3:9, 10. 13:22. 28:8. Ec 2:26. Ml 3:10. Mt 6:19. 25:35-40. Lk 8:3. Ac 9:39. Ro 15:25-27. Ga 6:6. Ph 4:17, 18.
durable. Heb. old. Pr 8:18.

ISAIAH 24

1 A.M. 3292. B.C. 712.
maketh the. Is 1:7-9. 5:6. 6:11, 12. 7:17-25. 27:10. 32:13, 14. 42:15. Je 4:7, 23, 26. Ezk 5:14. 6:6. 12:20. 24:11. 35:14. Na 2:10. Lk 21:24.
turneth it upside down. Heb. perverteth the face thereof. Is 29:16. 2 K 21:13. Ps 146:9. Ac 17:6.
scattereth. Dt 4:27. 28:64. 32:26. Ne 1:8. Je 9:16. 40:15. 50:17. Ezk 5:2. Zc 13:7-9. Ja 1:1.

2 **with the people**. Is 2:9. 3:2-8. 5:15. 9:14-17. 2 Ch 36:14-17, 20. Je 5:3-6. 23:11-13. 41:2. 42:18. 44:11-13. 52:24-30. La 4:13. 5:12-14. Ezk 7:12, 13. 14:8-10. Da 9:5-8. Ho 4:9, 10. Ro 2:11. 1 C 7:29-31. Ep 6:8, 9.
priest. *or*, prince. Ge 41:45mg, 50mg. Ex 2:16mg. 2 S 8:18mg. 20:26mg.
servant. Ex 21:2. Mt 6:24. Col 3:22. 4:1.
master. Col +4:1.
maid. Ge 16:1. 2 S 6:22. 14:6.

the buyer. Pr 20:14. Ezk 7:12. Ho 12:7.
lender. Ex 22:25, 27. Dt 15:2. 24:10, 11. 28:12. Pr 22:7.
taker of usury. Ex +22:25. Le 25:36, 37. Dt 15:3. 23:19, 20. Ne 5:2-5, 7, 11. Ps 15:5. Pr 28:8. 29:13mg. Je 15:10. Ezk 18:8, 13, 17. 22:12. Mt 5:42. 25:27. Lk 6:34, 35. 14:28. 16:8-10. 19:22, 23.

3 **shall**. ver. 1. Is 6:11. Le 26:30-35. Dt 4:27. 29:23, 28. 2 Ch 36:21. Ezk 36:4. Lk 21:24. Ja 1:1.
emptied. Ezk 36:4. Ro 2:7. Ga 5:19-21. 5:22, 23.
the Lord. Is +21:17. 22:25. Nu 23:19. Je 13:15. Mi 4:4.

4 **mourneth**. Is 3:26. 28:1. 33:9. 64:6. Je 4:28. 12:4. Ho 4:3.
haughty people. Heb. height of the people. Is +2:11, 12.

5 **defiled**. Ge 3:17, 18. 6:11-13. Le 18:24-28. 20:22. Nu 35:33, 34. 2 Ch 33:9. Ps 106:36-39. Je 3:1, 2. Ezk 7:20-24. 22:24-31. Mi 2:10. Ro 8:20-22.
because. Is 1:2-5. 50:1. 59:1-3, 12-15. Dt 32:15, 20. 2 K 17:7-23. 22:13-17. 23:26, 27. Ezr 9:6, 7. Ezk 20:13, 24. Da 9:5, 10.
changed. Jsh 24:25. Da 7:25. Mk 7:7-9. Lk 1:6. He 9:1.
broken. Is 59:13-15. Ge 17:13, 14. Ps 14:2, 3. Je 50:5. Jl 3:13. Am 8:11. Mt 24:24. Lk 18:8. Ro 3:9, 10, 23. 2 Th 2:3, 4, 7. 2 T 3:1-5. 2 P 2:1, 2. 3:3, 4. Ju 17-19. Re 3:10. 11:3, 7, 10. 12:12. 13:3, 4. 16:13, 14.
everlasting. Heb. *olam*, Ge +17:7. Is +55:3. Ge +9:16.

6 **hath**. Is 42:24, 25. Dt 28:15-20. 29:22-28. 30:18, 19. Jsh 23:15, 16. Zc +5:3, 4. Ml 2:2. 3:9. 4:1, 6. Mt 27:25.
the curse. Ge 3:17. Mt +25:41.
that dwell. Re +3:10.
are desolate. or, found guilty. Ps 5:10mg.
are burned. Is 1:31. 4:4. 31:9. 42:25. 66:15, 16, 24. Ps +97:3. +104:4. Zp 1:18. 3:8. Ml +4:1. 2 P +3:7. Re 16:9. 19:20.
and few. ver. 13. Is 4:1. 13:12. 45:20. 66:16. Le 26:22. Dt 4:27. 28:62. 29:20. Ps 92:7-9. Ezk 5:3. 36:36. Zc 13:8-14:5. Mt +7:14. Lk 18:8. Ro 9:27. 1 Th 4:15. 2 P 3:10. Re 6:4, 8. 8:9, 11. 9:15, 18. 11:13. 13:15. 14:15, 16, 20. 16:3, 18, 21. 18:8. 19:15, 18, 21.

7 **new wine**. Is 16:8, 10. 32:9-13. Ho 9:1, 2. Jl 1:10-12.
the vine. Jl 1:7.

8 **mirth**. Is 23:15, 16. Je 7:34. 16:9. 25:10. Ezk 26:13. Ho 2:11. Re 18:22.

9 **drink wine**. Is 5:11, 12. Ps 69:12. Ec 9:7. Am 6:5-7. 8:3, 10. Zc 9:15. Ep 5:18, 19.

10 **city**. ver. 12. Is 25:2. 27:10. 32:14. 34:13-15. 2 K 25:4, 9, 10. Je 39:4, 8. 52:7, 13, 14. Mi 2:13. 3:12. Lk 19:43, 44. 21:24.

of confusion. Heb. *tohu*, Ge 1:2. 29:21 (naught). 34:11. 40:17, 23. 41:29. 44:9 (vanity). 45:18, 19 (in vain). 49:4 (naught). 59:4 (vanity). Ge 11:9mg. Je 9:25, 26. Mt 23:34, 35. Re 11:7, 8. 17:5, 6. 18:2.

11 **a crying**. Pr 31:6. Ho 7:14. Jl 1:5.
　all joy. ver. 7-9. Is 8:22. 9:19. Je 48:33. La 5:14, 15. Am 5:16-20. Mt 22:11-13. Lk 16:25.

12 **the city**. Is 32:14. Je +18:16. La 2:9. 5:18. Mi 1:9, 12. Mt 22:7.
　the gate. Is 3:26. 14:31. 45:2. Ge +14:7. 2 K 25:10. Lk 21:24.

13 **there**. Is 6:13. 17:5, 6. Le 19:9, 10. Je 44:28. Ezk 7:16. 9:4-6. 11:16-20. 14:22, 23. +34:4. Mi +5:3. Mt 24:22. Re 3:4. 11:2, 3.

14 **shall lift**. Is 25:1. 26:1. 27:2. 40:9. 42:10-12. 52:7-9. 54:1. Je 30:19. 33:11. Zc +2:10.
　majesty. 1 Ch +29:11.

15 **glorify**. ver. 23. Jb 35:9, 10. Da 3:16-18. Hab 3:17, 18. Zc 13:8, 9. Ac 16:25. 1 P 1:7. 3:15. 4:12-14. Re 15:2-4.
　fires. *or*, valleys. Is 44:16mg. 59:19. Ps +49:14. +59:16.
　God of Israel. Is +29:23. Ge 33:20. Ex 24:10. Nu 16:9.
　isles. Is +11:11. Zc 10:9-12. Ml 1:11.

16 **From the**. Is 26:15. 45:22-25. 52:10. 66:19, 20. Ps 2:8. 22:27-31. 67:7. 72:8-11. 98:3. ch. 117. Mi 5:4. Mk 13:27. Ac 13:47.
　uttermost part. Heb. wing. Is 11:12mg. Ge 7:14mg. 1 K 6:24. Jb 37:3mg. Ezk 5:3mg. 39:4mg.
　heard songs. Zc +2:10.
　glory. ver. 23. Ex 15:11. Ps 58:10, 11. Re 15:3. 16:5-7. 19:1-6.
　the righteous. ver. 15. Is 26:2. Ac 3:14. 7:52. 22:14.
　But. Is 10:16. 17:4. Ps 106:15.
　My leanness. Heb. Leanness to me. *or*, My secret to me. Is 26:3. 29:1. 41:27. 65:1.
　the treacherous. Ho 10:1. 2 C 10:12. Ga 5:7. Ep 1:3.
　have dealt. Is 21:2. 33:1. 48:8. 63:5. Je 3:20. 5:11. 12:1, 6. La 1:2. Ho 5:7. 6:7. Hab 1:3.

17 **and the pit**. Le 26:21, 22. 1 K 19:17. Je 8:3. Ezk 14:21.
　snare. ver. +18.

18 **he who fleeth**. Dt 32:23-26. Jsh 10:10, 11. 1 K 20:29, 30. Jb 18:8-16. 20:24. Am 5:19.
　for the. Ge 7:11. 19:24. 2 K 7:2.
　snare. Lk +21:35.
　the windows. Ge 7:11. 2 P 3:5-7, 10.
　the foundations. Is 40:21. Dt 32:22. Ps 18:7, 15. 46:2, 3. He +12:26.

19 **utterly broken**. ver. 1-5. Is 34:4-10. Je 4:23-28. Na 1:5. Hab 3:6. Mt 24:3. Re 20:11.
　dissolved. 2 P 3:11.

20 **reel**. Is 19:14. 29:9. Ps 18:7. 107:27.
　removed. Is 1:8. 38:12.
　the transgression. Is 5:7-30. Ps 38:4. La

1:14. Ho 4:1-5. Mt 23:35, 36.
　shall fall. Je 8:4. 25:27. Da 11:19. Am 8:14. Zc 5:5-8. Re 18:21.

21 **in that day**. Is +2:11. Re 12:7, 8, 12, 13. 20:1-3.
　the Lord. Is 10:25-27. 14:1, 2. 25:10-12. 34:2, 4, 5, etc. Ps 76:12. 149:6-9. Ezk ch. 38, 39. Jl 3:9-17, 19. Hg 2:21, 22. Zc 14:12-19. Re 6:14-17. 17:14. 18:9. 19:17-21. 20:1-3.
　punish. Heb. visit upon. Heb. *pakad*, lit. looking again after what has been long neglected. Is 10:12mg. 23:17. Je +9:25mg. 27:22. Re 20:7.
　high ones. Ep 2:2. 6:12. Re 12:7-9. 20:1-3.
　the kings. Ps 2:2. 76:12. Zc 14:2. 2 Th 2:8. Re 19:11-21.

22 **they shall**. ver. 17. Is 2:19. Jsh 10:16, 17, 22-26.
　be gathered. Is +17:14. Ps +37:9. 101:8. Mi 4:11-13. Zp 3:8. Mt 13:28, 30, 40-42.
　as prisoners are gathered. Heb. with the gathering of prisoners.
　pit. *or*, dungeon. Heb. *bor*, Ge +37:20. 14:15, 19. 36:16. 38:18. 51:1. Ps 94:13.
　shut up in the prison. Is 42:7. Ps 142:7. Re 20:1-7.
　after many days. Ezk 37:25, 26, 28. 38:8. Ho 6:2. Re 20:2-7.
　shall they. Je 38:6-13. Zc 9:11, 12.
　visited. *or*, found wanting. Is 10:3. 23:17. 26:14, 16. 29:6. Ps +6:10. 109:28. Je 27:22. Ezk +38:8. Re 20:7-10.

23 **the moon**. lit. the pale. Is 4:5. 30:26. 60:19. Hab 3:11. Mt +24:29. Mk 13:24-26. Re 20:11. 21:23.
　confounded. Ps 71:24.
　ashamed. Is 19:9. 20:5. 37:27.
　shall reign. Is 52:7. Ex 15:21. Ps 18:43. 97:1. Je +23:5. Mi +4:7. Zc +9:9. +14:9. Mt 6:10, 13. Lk 1:32, 33. Re +11:15. 19:4, 6.
　in mount Zion. Is +2:3. 4:3, 4. 12:6. +30:19. +51:3, 11. 52:8. +59:20. 60:14, 15. 62:1-4. Ps 2:6, 8. 69:35, 36. +102:13, 16. 110:2. 122:6. 132:13, 14. Je 3:17. Jl 2:32. 3:17, 20, 21. Ob 17. Mi 4:2, 7. Zc 2:10-13. 8:2, 3, 15. He 12:22. Re 14:1.
　in Jerusalem. Is 2:3. 62:7, 12. 65:17-19. 66:13. Ps 51:18. 122:5, 6. +147:2. Je +3:17. Zc 2:12. 8:15, 22. 12:6. 14:17-21. Lk +19:11.
　before his ancients gloriously. *or*, *there shall be* glory before his ancients. ver. 16. Ps +102:16. 145:10, 11. Col +3:4. 1 P +1:11.
　before. Lk +21:36.
　his ancients. Is 35:10. Jb 38:4-7. Ps 140:13. Da 7:9, 10, 18, 22, 27. Jl 3:11. Zc +14:5. Mt 8:11. +13:43. Re 4:4. +5:10. 20:4-6. 22:4, 5.

ISAIAH 25

1 **thou art**. Is 26:13. 61:10. Ps 145:1. SS 6:3. 2 T 1:12. Re 5:9-14. 7:12.

my God. Heb. *Elohim,* Ge +1:1. ver. 9.
exalt. Is +12:4. Ps 46:10. 96:1-13. 98:1-9.
146:2. Re 15:3.
thou hast. Ps 78:4. 98:1. 111:4. Da +4:3.
thy counsels. Is 28:29. 46:10. Nu 23:19. Ps
33:10, 11. Je 32:17-24. Ezk 38:17-23. Ro
11:25-29. Ep +1:11. He 6:17, 18. Re 19:11.
2 For. ver. 12. Is 14:23. 17:1. 21:9. 23:13. Dt
13:16. Je 51:26, 37, 64. Na 3:12-15.
palace. Is 13:22. Re 18:1-3, 19, 21-24.
never be built. Is 13:20. 14:22, 23. Je 50:3,
39. 51:26, 29, 37, 62. Re 14:8. 16:19-21.
17:15-18. 18:2, 19, 21. 19:1-3.
3 shall the strong. Is 49:23-26. 60:10-14.
66:18-20. Ps 46:10, 11. 66:3. 72:8-11. Ezk
38:23. 39:21, 22. Zc 14:9, 16. Re 11:13, 15-
17.
4 strength. Is 33:2. Ps +18:1.
to the poor. Is 11:4. 14:32. 29:19. 66:2. Jb
5:15, 16. Ps +12:5. 35:10. 72:4, 13. 107:41.
119:31. Zp 3:12. Ja 2:5.
a refuge. Is 4:5, 6. 32:2.
when. Is +28:17. 37:3, 4, 36. Mt 7:25-27.
shadow. Is 26:20. Ps +91:1. Da 3:24, 25.
6:19-22.
blast. Heb. *ruach,* Ge +26:35. Is 37:7. Ex 15:8.
2 K 19:7.
5 shalt bring. Is 10:8-15, 32-34. 13:11. 14:10-
16. 17:12-14. 30:30-33. 49:25, 26. 54:15-17.
64:1, 2. Ps 74:3-23. 79:10-12. Je 50:11-15.
51:38-43, 53-57. Ezk 32:18-32. 38:9-23. 39:1-
10. Da 5:30. 7:23-27. 11:36-45. Re ch. 16-19.
20:8, 9.
as the heat. Is 18:4. 49:10. Ps 105:39. Jon
4:5, 6.
branch. Is 14:19, 20. Jb 8:16-19.
6 in this mountain. ver. 10. Is +2:2, 3.
make. Pr 9:1-5. SS 2:3-5. 5:1. Je 31:12, 13.
Zc 9:16, 17. Mt +5:6. 22:1-10. Lk 14:16-23.
22:29, 30. Re 19:9.
all people. Is 49:6-10. Da 7:14. Mt +8:11.
Mk 16:15, 16.
of wines. SS 1:2, 4. Je 48:11. Mt 26:29. Lk
5:39.
7 he will. Is 60:1-3. Mt 27:51. Lk 2:30-32. Ac
17:30. 2 C 3:13-18. Ep 3:5, 6. 4:18. 5:8. He
9:8, 24. 10:19-21.
destroy. Heb. swallow up. ver. 8. Is 3:12mg.
Ex +15:7. Ps 35:25. La 2:2, 5, 16.
cast. Heb. covered. **S#3874h**. 1 S 21:9
(wrapped). 1 K 19:13.
the vail. 2 C 3:15. 4:3, 4. Ep 4:18. Re 20:1-3.
8 He will. Da +12:2. Ho 13:14. Jn 19:30. 1 C
15:26, 54, +55. 2 T 1:10. He 2:14, 15. Re
20:14. 21:4.
swallow up. An example of double reference
in prophecy (Ho +11:1. Mt +16:23), applied
by Paul in 1 C 15:54 to the rapture (1 C
15:51, 52), but applied by Isaiah to the
Second Advent of Christ. ver. 7 (destroy). Nu

16:30. Ps 69:15. 106:17. Jon 1:17.
victory. Heb. *nezach,* Jb +4:20. Is 13:20.
28:28. 33:20. 34:10. 57:16. 1 S 15:29mg. 1 Ch
29:11. 1 C *15:54*.
wipe away tears. Is +65:19. Ezk +16:49, 55,
60.
rebuke of his people. Is 30:26. 37:3. +54:4-
10. 60:15. 61:7. 66:5. Dt +32:43. Ps 69:9.
89:50, 51. Jl 2:19. Am 9:9. Zp +3:20. Mt 5:11,
12. Ro 11:25, 26, 29, 32-36. 1 P 4:14.
take away. Is 65:17. Jl +2:25. Zp +3:15. Zc
8:13-15. 10:6. Ml 3:4.
off. Ml 3:17, 18.
9 it shall. Is 12:1. Zp 3:14-20. Re 1:7. 19:1-7.
in that day. Is +2:11.
Lo. Is 8:17. 26:8, 9. 30:18, 19. Ge 49:18. Ps
27:14. 37:5-7. 62:1, 2, 5-7. Mi 7:7. Zp 3:17.
Lk 2:25, 28-30. Ro 8:23-25. T 2:13. 2 P 3:12,
13. Re 22:20.
our God. ver. 1. Is 52:7. Jb +19:26. Ps +45:6,
7. Jn 1:1. +20:28. Ro 9:5. 2 C 5:19. Col 2:8, 9.
1 T 3:16. T 2:13. He +1:8. 2 P 1:1. Ju 4. Re
21:7.
we have waited. Is +35:4. Nu 24:17. Jb
+19:26. Ps +25:3. 92:2. Mt 24:27. Ac 1:9-11. 1
Th 4:16, 17.
we will. Is 12:2-6. 66:10-14. Ps 9:14. 20:5.
21:1. 95:1. 100:1. +118:24. Zc 9:9. Ro 5:2, 3.
Ph 3:1, 3. 1 P 1:6, 8, 9.
his salvation. Is 12:2. 26:1. 33:16-22. 35:4.
45:17. 49:8-11, 26. 59:16-21. 60:18. 61:10.
62:1. 63:5. Ps 9:14. 14:7. +37:9, 39. 42:5mg.
53:6. 74:12, 20. 85:7, 9. 98:2, 9. 118:14.
132:11, 16. 149:4. Je 23:6. 30:7. Ezk 37:23.
Mi 7:7. Lk 2:25, 30. Ro 13:11. 1 Th 5:9. 2 T
2:10. He +9:28.
10 in this. ver. 6. Is 11:10. 12:6. 18:4. Ps 132:13,
14. Ezk 48:35. Zp 3:15-17. Zc 9:9-11.
Moab. Ezk +25:8.
trodden down. *or,* threshed. Is 41:15, 16. Mi
4:13.
even. Is 5:25. 10:6. 14:19. 26:6. Ps 83:10. La
1:15.
for the dunghill. *or,* in Madmenah. Is
+10:31.
11 he shall spread. Is 5:25. 14:26. 65:2. Col
2:15.
he shall bring. ver. 5. Is 2:11. 10:33. 13:11.
14:12. 16:6. 53:12. Ps 2:5, 8-12. ch. 110. Je
48:29, 42. 50:31, 32. 51:44. Da 4:37. Ja 4:6.
Re 18:6-8. 19:18-20.
12 the fortress. Is 26:5. Je 51:58, 64. 2 C 10:4,
5. He 11:30. Re 18:21.
to the dust. Is 13:19-22. 14:23.

ISAIAH 26

1 that day. Is +2:11.
this song. Is 5:1. 27:1, 2. Ex 15:2-21. Nu
21:17, 18. Jg ch. 5. 2 S 22:1, etc. Je 33:11. Ep

5:19, 20. Re 5:9-14. 7:9-17. 11:15-18. 14:3.
15:3, 4. 19:1-7.

in the land. Ezr 3:11. Ps 137:3, 4.

strong city. Ps 48:11-13.

salvation. Is 60:18. 62:11. Ps 31:21. 48:12,
13. 125:1, 2. Ezk 48:35. Zc 2:4, 5. Mt 16:18.
Re 21:12-22.

2 Open. Is 60:11. 62:10. Ps 118:19, 20. Ezk
48:31-34. Zc 8:20-23. Ac 2:47. Re 21:13, 24-27.

righteous. Is +60:21. Ex 19:6. Dt 4:6-8. Ps
106:5. Ph 3:8, 9. 1 P 2:9. 2 P 3:13. Re 5:9.
19:8. 21:27. 22:14, 15.

truth. Heb. truths. Dt 32:20. Pr 13:17. Ju 3.

3 wilt keep. Is +9:6, 7. Dt 32:10. Ps 12:7. Mi
5:5. Ro +5:1.

in perfect peace. Heb. peace, peace. Is
24:16.

mind. or, thought, or, imagination. Is 29:16.
Ge 6:5. 8:21. 2 C 10:5.

stayed. Is 31:1. 48:2. 50:10. 2 Ch +20:20.
29:18. Ps 111:8mg. 112:8.

because. 1 Ch 5:20. 2 Ch 13:18. 16:8. Ps
+9:10. 84:11, 12. 146:3-6. Je 17:7, 8. Ro 4:18-
21.

he trusteth. Is 57:13. 2 S 22:31. Ps 2:12.
17:7. 28:7. 31:19, 20, 24. 32:10. 34:8, 22.
37:3. 38:15. 40:4. 84:12. 112:6-8. 118:8, 9.
125:1. 146:5. Pr 16:20. 18:10. 28:25. 29:25.
30:5. Je 17:7, 8.

4 Trust. Is 12:2. 50:10. 2 Ch 13:18. +20:20.
32:8. Ps 46:1. 55:22. 62:8. 91:2. 115:9-11.
118:8, 9. Pr 3:5, 6. Ro 4:20, 21.

for ever. Heb. olam plural, Ps +61:4; Ps +9:18
(**S#5703h**, ad).

in the Lord Jehovah. Is 12:2. 45:17, 24. 63:1.
Ex 3:13, 14. 6:3. Jb 9:19. Ps 46:1. 62:11. 66:7.
83:18. 93:1. 125:1. Mt 6:13. 28:18. Ph 4:13.

everlasting strength. Heb. the Rock of ages.
Is 17:10. 30:29. 32:2. 44:8. Dt 32:4, 15, 18,
30, 31. 1 S 2:2. 2 S 23:3. Ps 18:2, 46. 62:1, 2.
144:1mg. Hab 1:12. Mt 6:13. 16:18. 1 C 10:4.
Ph 4:13. He 13:8.

5 bringeth. Is 14:13-15. 25:11. Pr +16:5. 2 C
10:5.

the lofty. Is 25:12. 32:19. 47:1. Je 50:31, 32.
51:25, 26, 37, 64. Re 18:2.

6 foot. Is 25:10. 37:25. 60:14. Jsh 10:24, 25. Je
50:45. Da 7:27. Zp 3:11, 12. Ml 4:3. Lk 1:51-
53. 10:19, 20. Ro 16:20. 1 C 1:26, 27. Ja 2:5.
Re 2:26, 27. 3:9.

7 way. Is 35:8. 1 Ch 29:17. Jb 27:5, 6. Ps 18:23-
26. 37:23. Pr 20:7. 2 C 1:12. Ep 2:10. 1 J 3:7,
10, 22.

uprightness. 1 Ch 29:17. Ps 143:10.

most. 1 S 2:2-4. Jb 31:6mg. Ps 1:6. 11:4, 7.
Zp 3:5. 1 C 4:5.

dost weigh. 1 S 2:3. Jb 1:8. 31:6.

8 in. Is 64:4, 5. Nu 36:13. Jb 23:10-12. Ps
18:23. 44:17, 18. 65:6. 106:3. 119:102. Ml
4:4. Lk 1:6. 1 C 4:5. 2 C 1:12.

waited. Ps +25:3. 63:1. Ac 1:4, 14. 2:1. 2 Th
3:5. Ja 5:7-11.

desire. 2 S 23:5. Ps 13:2. 42:1, 2. 63:1-3.
73:25. 77:10-12. 84:2. 143:5, 6. SS 1:2-4. 2:3-
5. 5:8. 7:10.

soul. Heb. nephesh, Ge +34:3.

remembrance. Ex 3:15. Ps 102:12. 135:13.
Ho 12:5.

9 With my. 2 S 23:5. Ps 42:1, 2.

soul. Heb. nephesh, Ge +34:3. Ps +84:2. Mt
+11:29.

have I desired. Ps 63:6, 7. 73:25. 77:2, 3.
119:62. 130:6. SS 3:1-4. 5:2-8. Mk 1:35. Lk
6:12.

the night. Ps 63:6. +119:55. Pr +3:24. SS 3:1.

spirit. Heb. ruach, Ge +41:8. Ps +51:10. Mk
+2:8.

seek thee. Ps 63:1. Pr 8:17. Ho 5:15. Mt 6:33.
He 11:6.

early. Ge +19:27. Mk +1:35.

for when. Is 27:9. Ex +7:4. Nu 14:21-23. Ps
58:11. 64:9, 10. 83:18. 105:7. 119:155. Ho
5:15. 1 T +2:6. Re 7:14-17. 11:13. 15:4.

will learn. Ps 119:67, 71. Re 15:4.

10 favor. Is 63:9, 10. Ex 8:15, 31, 32. 9:34. Dt
32:15. 1 S 15:17-23. Ps 106:43. Pr 1:32. Ec
3:16. 8:11. Ho 13:6. Ro 2:4, 5. Re 2:21.

in the. Is 3:10. 24:5. 27:13. Ps 78:54-58.
143:10. Je 2:7. 31:23. Ezk 22:2, etc. Ho 9:3.
Mi 2:10. 3:10-12. Mt 4:5. 23:37. 24:15.

and will not. Is 2:10. 5:12. 22:11. Ps 28:4, 5.
Ho 11:7. Jn 5:37, 38.

11 when. Ex +9:3.

will not see. Is 18:3. Ex 7:23. 1 S 6:9. Jb
34:27. Je 5:3. 44:17-23. Mi 6:9. Ac 28:27. Re
9:20.

they shall see. Ex 9:14. 11:6, 7. 14:25. 1 S
5:6-11. 1 K 22:25. Ps 37:32-34. Je 44:28. Mi
6:9. Zc 1:6. Lk 16:23.

be ashamed. Is 11:13. 60:14. 66:5. Ps 76:17.
1 P 3:16. Re 3:9.

at the. or, towards thy.

fire. Is 64:2. +66:24. Ps +97:3. Mt +3:11.
+25:41.

12 ordain. ver. +3. Ps 37:37. Pr +16:7. Mi 5:5. Jn
20:19, 21.

for. Dt 30:6. Ps 51:10. Je 31:33. 32:39, 40.
Ezk 36:25-27. Jn 3:21. Ep 2:10. He 13:20, 21.

hast wrought. Ps 68:28. Ph 2:13.

in us. or, for us. Ps 57:2. Ezk 20:9, 14, 22. 1 C
15:10. Ph 2:13.

13 other. Is 51:22, 23. 2 Ch 12:8. Ne 9:28, 36,
37. Je 50:17. La 5:8. Mt 6:24. Jn 8:32-36. Ro
6:20, 22. Ep 2:1-3. 1 T 1:12-15. T 3:3-7.

by thee. Is 12:4. 48:1. Ex 23:13. Jsh 23:7. Am
6:10. 1 C 4:7. 15:10. 2 T 2:19. He 13:15.

14 dead. ver. 19. Is 8:19. 51:12, 13. Ex 14:30. Ps
106:28. Hab 2:18-20. Mt 2:20. Jn 5:28, 29. Re
18:2, 3. 19:19-21. 20:5.

deceased. Heb. rephaim. ver. 19. Is 14:9.

17:5. Jb 26:5. Ps 88:10. Pr 2:18. 9:18. +21:16.

shall not rise. 1 P 3:19. 2 P 2:4. Ju 6.

visited. or, inspected. ver. 16. Is 13:11. 34:16.

destroyed. Is 13:9. Nu 33:52. Jb 19:10. Ps 37:1, 2, 9, 10, 20, 35, 36, 38.

and made. Is 14:19-22. 33:14. Ps 9:6. 109:13. +146:4. Pr 10:7. Ec +9:5. Mt +10:28.

15 **increased.** Is 9:3. 10:22. Ge 12:2. 13:16. Nu 23:10. Dt 10:22. Ne 9:23. Je 30:19.

thou art glorified. Is 44:23. 49:18-21. 60:7-10, +21. Ps 86:9, 10. Jn +13:31. Re 11:15-18.

thou hadst. Is 6:12. Dt 4:27, 28. 28:25, 64. 32:26, 27. 1 K 8:46, 47. 2 K 17:6, 23. 23:27. Je 32:37. Ezk 5:12. 36:24. Lk 21:24. Ro 11:12.

removed it far. Is 60:21. Ge 15:18. Ex 23:31. Dt 11:24. Jsh 21:43. 1 K 4:21. Je +7:7. 33:21. Ac +7:5. He +11:13, 39.

16 **in trouble.** Dt 4:29-31. Jg 10:9, 10. 2 Ch 6:37, 38. 33:12, 13. Ps 50:15. 77:1, 2. 91:15. Je 22:23. Ho 5:15. 7:14. Re 3:19.

they poured. 1 S 1:15. Ps 42:4. 142:2. La 2:19. Da 6:10.

prayer. Heb. secret speech. S#3908h. Ec 10:11 (enchantment). Is 3:3 (orator; mg, skilful of speech), 20 (earrings). Je 8:17 (charmed).

17 **as a woman.** Is 37:3. 42:14. 66:7, 9. Ge +3:16. 30:6. Je +4:31. Mt +24:8.

18 **we have been in.** Is 37:3. 2 K 19:3. Ho 13:13.

brought forth wind. Ec 2:11, 17.

we have not. Ex 5:22, 23. Jsh 7:7-9. 1 S 11:13. 14:45.

the inhabitants. Ps 17:14. Jn 7:7. 1 J 5:19.

19 **dead men.** Is 25:8. 1 S +2:6. Jb 14:14. Ezk 37:1-14. Da 12:2. Ho 6:2. 13:14. Jn 5:28, +29. Ac 24:15. Ro 11:15. 1 C 15:22, 23. 1 Th 4:14, 15. Re 20:5, 6, 12.

my dead body. Jb +19:25, 26. Ezk 37:11-14. Ho 13:14. Mt 12:38-40. +27:52, 58. Mk 8:31-33. 9:9, 10. 10:32-34. Jn +2:19, +21. 10:18. 11:25, 26. 12:31-34. 20:6-10. 1 C 15:20, 23. Ph 3:10, 21.

shall they arise. Ezk 37:1-8. Da 12:1-4. Mt +11:5. Mk 12:18-27. Lk 7:22. Jn 5:28, 29.

Awake. Is 51:17. 52:1, 2. 60:1, 2. Ps 17:15. 22:15. +71:20. 139:18. Da 12:2. Ep 5:14. Re 11:8-11.

thy dew. Is 66:14. Ge 2:5, 6. Dt 32:2. 33:13, 28. 2 S 17:12. Jb 29:19. Ps 72:6. 110:3. Pr 3:20. Ho 14:5. Zc 8:12.

the earth. Re 20:13.

cast out. Ho 13:14. Zc 9:12. Ac 24:15.

the dead. Heb. rephaim. ver. +14 (deceased). Is 17:5. Lk 14:5. 15:20.

20 **my.** Is 51:4, 16. Je 7:23. 31:14.

enter. Is 32:18, 19. Ge 7:1, 16. Ex 12:22, 23. Ps 32:6, 7. 91:4. Pr 14:26. 18:10. +27:12. Ezk 11:16. Zc 9:12. Mt 23:37. Re 14:13.

shut. Mt 6:6.

hide. Is 16:1-5. 42:11-13. 63:1-5. Ps 60:6-12.

+64:2. 94:12, 13. 108:8-13. Pr +22:3. Ezk 20:33-44. Da 11:36-45. Ho 2:14-23. Ml 3:16-18. Mt 24:15-22. Lk +21:36. Col 3:3, 4. Re 12:6, 14.

for a little. Is 54:7, 8. Ps 30:5. 57:1. 2 C 4:17.

moment. S#7281h. Is 27:3. 47:9. 54:7, 8. Ex 33:5. Nu 16:21, 45. Ezr 9:8mg. Jb 7:18. 20:5. 21:13. 34:20. Ps 6:10 (suddenly). 30:5. 73:19. Je 4:20. 18:7 (instant), 9. La 4:6. Ezk 26:16. 32:10.

until the indignation. Is +66:14. Da 9:27. Mt 24:15-22. 1 Th 4:13, 14.

be overpast. Jb 14:13. Ps 57:1. Hab 3:16. Zp 2:2, 3. Lk +21:36. 1 Th 5:9. 2 P 2:9. Re 3:10.

21 **Lord cometh.** Is 18:4. +35:4. Ps 9:12. +102:16. Ezk 8:6. 9:3-6. 10:3-5, 18, 19. Ho 5:14, 15. Zc 8:3. 2 Th 1:7-10.

his place. 1 K +8:39.

punish. Is +24:21.

also. Ge 4:10, 11. Nu 35:32, 33. Jb 16:18. Ps 79:10. Ezk 24:7, 8. Lk 11:50, 51. Re 6:9-11. 16:6, 7. 18:24.

blood. Heb. bloods. 2 K +9:26mg.

ISAIAH 27

1 **that day.** Is +2:11.

with his. Is 34:5, 6. 66:16. Dt 32:41, 42. Jb 40:19. Ps 45:3. Je 47:6. Ep 6:17. He 4:12, 13. Re 1:16. 2:16. 19:13, 15, 21.

sword. Dt +32:41.

leviathan. Jb 12:1, etc. Jb 41:1, 33, 34. Ps 74:14. 104:26.

piercing. or, crossing like a bar. S#1281h. Is 43:14mg. Jb 26:13 (crooked).

crooked. Is 65:25. Jb 26:13.

serpent. Ge 3:1, 14, 15.

the dragon. Is 51:9. Ps 74:13, 14. Je 51:34. Ezk 29:3. 32:2-5. Re 12:3-17. 13:1, 2, 4, 11. 16:13. 20:2.

in the sea. Je 51:13. Re 13:1. 17:1, 15.

2 **sing.** Is 5:1-7. Nu 21:17.

A vineyard. Ps 80:8, 14, 15. Je 2:21. Mt 21:33, etc. Lk 20:9, etc.

red wine. Ge 49:11, 12.

3 **I the Lord.** Is 46:4, 9. 60:16. Ge 6:17. 9:9. Ezk 34:11, 24. 37:14, 28.

do keep. Dt 33:26-29. 1 S 2:9. Ps 46:5, 11. 121:3-5. Jn 10:27-30. 15:1, 2.

water. Is 5:6. 35:6, 7. 41:13-19. 55:10, 11. 58:11.

every moment. Jb 7:18.

will keep. Is 42:6. Dt 11:12. Ps 34:15. 121:4, 5. Pr 15:3. SS 4:12-16. Zc 4:10. 2 T 1:12. 1 P 3:12.

4 **Fury.** Is 12:1. 26:20, 21. 54:6-10. Ex 34:6, 7. Ps 85:3. 103:9. Ezk 16:63. Na 1:3-7. 2 P 2:9.

not in me. Ezk 18:23. Lk +6:35. 2 P 3:9.

who would. Is 5:6. 9:18. 10:17. 2 S 23:6. Ml 4:3. Mt 3:12. Lk 6:44. 14:31, 32. He 6:8.

briars and thorns. Is 5:6. He 6:8.
go through. *or*, march against.
burn them. Is 9:18.

5 **let him**. Is 25:4. 26:3, 4. 45:24. 56:2. 64:7. Ge
32:24-28. Jsh 9:24, 25. 10:6. Jb 22:21. Lk
13:34. 14:32. 19:42. Ep 2:8. He 6:18.
and he. Le 3:2, 3, 5. Ezk 34:25, 26. Ho 2:18-
20. Lk 19:42. Ro +5:1.

6 **cause them**. Is 6:13. 37:31. 49:20-23. 54:1-3.
60:22. Ge 49:22. Ps 92:13-15. Je 30:19. Ho
2:23. 14:5, 6. Zc 2:11. 6:12. 10:8, 9. Ro 11:12,
16-26. Ga 3:29. Ph 3:3. Re 11:15.
Israel shall. Ezk 39:25.
take root. Is 4:2. 11:10. 37:31. 2 K 19:30. Ps
80:9. Ho 14:5.
blossom and bud. Is 35:1, 2. Ge 40:10.
and fill. Ge 49:10. Ps 68:11. Na 1:15. Hab
2:14. Mt +24:14. Ac 5:28. 1 T +2:6. Re 11:15.
face. Ge +1:2.
the world. Is 42:12. 48:20. 49:6. 61:6.
+66:19. Ge +12:3. Mt +24:14. 28:19, 20. Mk
16:15. Ac +1:8. 17:6.
with fruit. Is 37:31. 52:7. 2 K 19:30. Ps
68:11. 72:16. Pr +11:30. Ezk 17:23. 36:8. Da
+11:33. +12:3. Ho 14:5, 6, 8, 9. Na 1:15. Jn
15:5, 16. Col 1:6. Re 7:3, 9, 14.

7 **Hath he smitten**. Is 10:20-25. 14:22, 23.
17:3, 14. Je 30:11-16. 50:33, 34, 40. 51:24.
Da 2:31-35. Na 1:14. 3:19.
as he smote. Heb. according to the stroke of.

8 **measure**. Is 57:16. 2 S 24:14. Jb 23:6. Ps 6:1.
38:1. 78:38. 103:9, 10, 14. Je 4:27. 10:24.
30:11. 46:28. Ml 3:17. Jn 3:34. 1 C 10:13. 1 P
1:6.
it shooteth forth. or, thou sendest it forth.
thou wilt. Is 1:5, 18-20. 5:3, 4. Jg 10:10-16.
Je 2:17-37. Ho 4:1. 6:1, 2. 11:7-9. Mi 6:2-5.
debate. or, strive. Is 1:17. 3:13. 49:25. 50:8.
51:22. Je 2:9, 29. 12:1. 50:34. Mi 7:9.
he stayeth, etc. or, when he removeth it. Pr
25:4, 5.
his rough. Is 10:5, 6, 12. Ps 76:10. 78:38. Je
4:11, 27.
east wind. Ge +41:6.

9 **this therefore**. Is 1:24, 25. 4:4. 48:10. Ps
119:67, 71. Pr 20:30mg. Ezk 20:38. 24:13. Da
11:35. Ml 3:2, 3. 1 C 11:32. He 12:6, 9-11.
be purged. Is +60:21. Nu 35:33. Dt 32:43. Ps
+130:8. Da +9:24. Jl 3:21. Zc 13:1.
this is. He 12:11.
take away his sin. Is +60:21. Ro *11:*27.
when. Is 64:10, 11. 2 K 25:8, 9, 13-17. 2 Ch
36:19. Ezr 3:2, 3. Ezk 11:18. 24:11-14.
the groves. Is 1:29. 2:12-21. 2 K +17:10. Ho
14:8. Zc 13:2.
images. or, sun images. Le +26:30.
shall not stand. Le 26:30. Ho 14:8.

10 **the defenced**. Is 5:9, 10. 6:11, 12. 17:9. 25:2.
64:10. Le 26:31-35. Je 26:6, 18. La 1:4. 2:5-9.
5:18. Ezk 36:4. Mi 3:12. Lk 19:43, 44. 21:20-24.

there shall. Is 7:21, 22, 25. 17:2. 32:13, 14.
Je 39:10.
the branches. Is 17:6.

11 **the boughs**. Ps 80:15, 16. Ezk 15:2-8. 20:47.
Mt 3:10. Jn 15:6.
withered. Jn 15:6.
broken off. Ro 11:17, 18, 20.
on fire. Jn 15:6.
for it is. Is 1:3. 44:18-20. Dt 4:6. 32:28, 29. Je
4:22. 5:4, 5, 21, 22. +8:7. Ho 4:6. Mt 13:15,
19. Ro 1:28, 31.
no understanding. Ps +49:20.
therefore. Is 43:1, 7. 44:20, 21, 24. +54:7. Ge
6:6, 7. Dt 32:18-25. 2 Ch 36:16, 17. Ps 106:40.
Ezk 9:5, 10. 1 Th 2:16. 2 Th 1:8, 9. Ja 2:13.
no favor. Ge +6:6. Ex 34:6, 7. Jb +27:8. Ezk
7:9. Da +12:2. Na 1:3.

12 **beat off**. Is 11:11-16. 24:13-16. 56:8. Ge
15:18. Dt 24:20. Jg 6:11. Ps 68:22. 72:8.
the channel. Jg 12:6.
the river. Is 7:20. 8:7. 11:15. Ps +72:8.
stream of Egypt. Ge 15:18. Nu 34:5. Jsh
13:3. 15:4, 47. 1 K 8:65. 2 K 24:7. 2 Ch 7:8.
Ps +72:8. Ezk 47:19. 48:28.
ye shall be. Dt 30:3, 4. Ne 1:9. Je 3:14. 43:7.
Am 9:9. Mt 18:12-14. Lk 15:4. Jn 6:37. 10:16.
gathered. or, gleaned. Is 17:6. Le +23:22.

13 **And it**. Is +2:11.
the great trumpet. Is 18:3. Le +23:24. 25:9,
52. Nu 10:2-4. 1 Ch 15:24. Ps 47:5. 81:3.
89:15. Zc 9:13-16. Mt 24:31. Lk 4:18. Ro
10:18. 1 Th 4:16, 17. Re 8:2, 6-13. 9:1, 14.
10:7. 11:15-18. 14:6.
and they. Is 11:16. 19:23-25. 2 K 17:6. Ho
9:3. 11:11. Zc 10:8-12.
Assyria. 2 K 17:6.
the outcasts. Is 11:12. 16:3, 4. 56:8. Ps
147:2. Je 30:17.
Egypt. Je 43:7. 44:28. Ho 8:13.
and shall. Is +2:2, 3. Zc 14:16. Ml 1:11. Jn
4:21-24.
holy mount. Is +11:9.
at. Is 24:23.

ISAIAH 28

1 A.M. 3279. B.C. 725.
the crown. ver. 3. Ho 5:5. 6:10.
drunkards. ver. 7. Is 5:11, 22. Pr +23:29. Ho
4:11. 7:5. Am 2:8, 12. 6:6.
whose. ver. 4. Is 7:8, 9. 8:4. 2 K 14:25-27.
15:29. 18:10-12. 2 Ch 28:6. 30:6, 7. Ho 13:1.
Am 6:1.
overcome. Heb. broken. Pr 23:35
(beaten).

2 **the Lord**. Is 9:9-12. 27:1. Ezk 30:10, 11.
as a tempest. ver. 15-19. Is 8:7, 8. 25:4. 2 K
15:29. 17:5, 6. Ps +83:15. Na 1:8.
Re 18:8.

3 **The crown**. ver. 1.

shall. Is 25:10. 26:6. 2 K 9:33. La 1:15. Da 8:13. He 10:29. Re 11:2.

under feet. Heb. with feet.

4 **shall be**. ver. 1. Is 1:30. Ps 73:19, 20. Ho 6:4. 9:10, 11, 16. 13:1, 15. Mt 21:19, 20. Ja 1:10, 11.

the hasty. Mi 7:1. Na 3:12. Re 6:13.

summer. Is +16:9.

eateth. Heb. swalloweth. Is 3:12mg. 9:16mg.

5 **In that day**. Is +2:11.

shall the. Is 41:16. 45:25. 60:1-3, 19. 62:3. Je 9:23, 24. Zc 6:13-15. Lk 2:32. 1 C 1:30, 31. 2 C 4:17. 1 P 5:4.

crown of glory. Is 62:3. 2 Th 1:10.

for a diadem. Jb 29:14. Ps 90:16, 17. 149:4.

residue. Is 11:16. Mi +5:3.

6 **for a spirit**. Heb. *ruach*, Ex +15:8. Is 11:2-4. 32:15, 16. Ge 41:38, 39. Nu 11:16, 17. 27:16-18. 1 K 3:28. 2 K 18:1-7. Ps 72:1-4. Pr 20:8. Jn 3:34. 5:30. 1 C 12:8.

and for strength. Dt 20:4. Jsh 1:9. Ps 18:32-34. 46:1, 11. 144:1, 2, 10.

7 **priest and the prophet**. Ml 2:7.

erred through wine. Is 19:14. 56:10-12. Le 10:9, 10. 2 K 17:18, 19. Pr +20:1. 31:4, 5. Ec 10:17. Ezk 44:21. Ho 4:11. Mi 2:11. Mt 24:29. Lk 21:34. Ep +5:18.

are swallowed. Is 19:3mg. Ps 107:27mg.

err in vision. Is 9:16. Je 14:14. 23:13, 16. La 2:14. Ezk 13:7. Ho +4:12.

8 **all tables**. Pr 26:11. Je 48:26. Hab 2:15, 16.

9 **shall he teach**. Is 30:10-12. Ps 25:9. 50:17. Pr 1:29, 30. Je 5:31. 6:10. Jn 3:19. 12:38, 47, 48.

weaned. 1 S +1:22. Mt 11:25. 21:15, 16. Mk 10:15. 2 T 3:15. 1 P 2:2.

to understand. Is +29:24.

doctrine. Heb. the hearing. ver. 19mg. Is 53:1mg.

10 **For precept**. ver. 13. Is 5:4. Dt 6:1-6. 2 Ch 36:15, 16. Ne 9:29, 30. Je 11:7. 25:3-7. Mt 21:34-41. Ph 3:1. 2 T 3:7. He 5:12. 6:1.

must be. *or*, hath been.

upon precept. Ge +6:17.

line. ver. 13. Ge +6:17.

little. Ge +6:17. Dt 6:7mg. Pr 22:6. Col 3:21. He 5:12.

11 **with**. Dt 28:49. Je 5:15. 1 C *14:21*.

stammering lips. Heb. stammerings of lips. S#3934h. Ps 35:16 (mockers). For the related root, S#3932h, see Is +33:19mg.

will he speak. *or*, he hath spoken.

12 **This**. Is 30:15. 2 Ch 14:11. 16:8, 9. Je 6:16. Mt 11:28, 29.

yet. Ps 81:11-13. Je 6:10. 44:16. Zc 7:11-14. Jn 3:19. He 12:25.

13 **the word**. 2 Ch 36:15, 16. Ne 9:30.

precept upon precept. ver. 10. Je 23:36-38. Ho 6:5. 8:12. Ph 3:1. 2 T 3:7.

that. Is 6:9, 10. 8:14, 15. Ps 69:22. Mt 13:14.

14 **ye**. ver. 22. Is 1:10. 5:9. 29:20. 30:10. Pr 1:22. 3:34. 29:8. Ho 7:5. Ac 13:41.

15 **We have**. Is 5:18, 19. Jb 5:23. 15:25-27. Ec 8:8. Je 36:21-24. 37:9, 10. 44:17. Ezk 8:12. Ho 2:18. Zp 1:12.

made a covenant. Is 24:5. 33:8. 54:10. 55:3. 56:4, 6. 59:21. 61:8.

hell. Heb. *sheol*, Ge +37:35.

when. Is 8:7, 8. Da 11:22.

we have made. Is 30:10. Je 5:31. 14:13, 14. 16:19. 28:15-17. Ezk 13:16, 22. Am 2:4. Jon 2:8. 2 Th 2:9-12.

16 **Behold**. Is 8:14. Ge +49:10, 42. Mt +21:42. Ro *9:33. 10:11*. 1 C 3:11. 1 P *2:6-8*.

foundation. Ep 2:19-22. Col 1:17.

a stone. Is 26:4mg. Ge 49:24. Ps 62:1, 2.

precious. Ps 49:7, 8. 116:15. 139:17. 1 P 1:19. 2:7. 2 P 1:1, 4.

corner stone. 1 P 2:6, 7.

foundation. Is +8:14.

he that. Is 30:18. Ps 22:4, 5. 112:7, 8. Hab 2:3, 4. Ja 5:7, 8. 1 P 3:6.

make haste. LXX reads, "be ashamed." Is 35:4mg. Ps +25:2.

17 **Judgment**. Is 10:22. 2 K 21:13. Ps 94:15. Je 7:4-8, 14, 20. Am 7:7-9. Ro 2:2, 5, 6, 25. 9:28. Re 19:2.

and the hail. ver. 2, 15. Is 25:4. 30:30. 32:2, 18, 19. Ex 9:18, 19, 22-26. Jsh 10:11. Jb 38:22. Ps 18:12, 13. 78:47, 48. 105:32. 148:8. Je +23:19. Ezk 13:10-16. 38:22. Hg 2:17. Re 8:7. 11:19. 16:21.

and the waters. Is 30:28. Jb 22:16. Je +47:2. Mt 7:27. 2 P 3:6, 7.

18 **your covenant**. Is 7:7. 8:10. Je 44:28. Ezk 17:15. Zc 1:6.

your agreement. Je 19:7. Da +9:27.

hell. Heb. *sheol*, Ge +37:35. Is 57:9. Ezk 31:16, 17. 32:21, 27.

when. ver. 2, 15. Is 8:8. +10:5, 6. Je 47:2. Da 8:9-13. 9:26, 27. 11:40. Re 12:15, 16. 17:15.

trodden down by it. Heb. a treading down to it. ver. 3. Ml 4:1-3.

19 **the time**. Is 10:5, 6. 2 K 17:6. 18:13. Ezk 21:19-23.

morning by. 2 S 13:4mg.

and it. Is 33:7. 36:22. 37:3. 1 S 3:11. 2 K 21:12. Je 19:3. Da 7:28. 8:27. Hab 3:16. Lk 21:25, 26.

to understand the report. *or*, when he shall make *you* to understand doctrine. lit. hearing. ver. 9mg. Is 29:24. 53:1mg.

20 **the bed**. Is 57:12, 13. 59:5, 6. 64:6. 66:3-6. Je 7:8-10. Mt 5:20. Ro 9:30-32. 1 C 1:18-31. Ph 3:8, 9.

21 **in mount Perazim**. i.e. *breaches; defeats*, S#6556h, as a name only here; compare S#1188h, 2 S +5:20. 2 S 5:20. 1 Ch 14:11.

the valley. Jsh 10:10, 12. 2 S 5:25, Geba. 1 Ch 14:16. Ps 18:13-15.

his strange work. ver. 19. Is 29:13, 14. Dt 29:21-24. Ps 119:126. Je 30:14. La 2:15. 3:33. Ezk 33:21. Hab 3:11. Lk 19:41-44. Ac 13:41.

22 be ye. ver. 15. Je 15:17. Lk +22:63. Ac 13:40, 41. 2 P 3:3-12.

lest. 2 Ch 33:11. Ps 107:16. Je 39:7. La 1:14. Re 22:18, 19.

a consumption. Is 10:22, 23. 24:1, 3, 4, etc. 32:12-14. Je 25:11. Da 9:26, 27. Lk 21:24.

23 Give ye ear. Is 1:2. Dt 32:1. Je 22:29. Mt 11:15. 13:3-43. Re 2:7, 11, 14, 17, 29.

24 plow. 1 C 3:9. 9:9, 10.

break. Je 4:3. Ho 10:11, 12.

25 made plain. or, level, or, equal. Is 38:13. Mt 3:12.

cast abroad. or, scatter. Is 24:1. Ge 11:9.

scatter. or, sprinkle. Ex 9:10. 24:8. Le 7:2.

in the principal, etc. *or*, the wheat in the principal *place*, and the barley in the appointed *place*.

rye. *or*, spelt. Ex 9:31, 32. Ezk 4:9.

place. Heb. border. Dt 32:8. Ps 74:17.

26 For his God, etc. *or*, And he bindeth it in such a sort as his God doth teach him. Ex 28:3. 31:3-6. 36:2. Jb 35:11. 39:17. Ps 144:1. Da 1:17. Ja 1:17.

doth instruct. Is 8:11. 30:21. 42:16. Ps 5:8. 25:5, 9. 27:11. 32:8. 48:14. 73:24. 119:102. 139:9, 10. 143:10. Pr 1:23. Jn 7:16, 17. Ja 1:5.

27 threshed. Is +21:10.

threshing instrument. Is 41:15.

the fitches. Is 27:7, 8. Je 10:24. 46:28.

28 Bread. ver. 27. Is 21:10. Jb 28:5. Ps 104:14. Am 9:9. Mt 3:12. 13:37-43. Lk 22:31, 32. Jn 12:24. 1 C 3:9. 9:9, 10.

bruised. Is 53:5. Ex +27:20. Nu 11:8. He +2:10.

ever. Jb +4:20 (**S#5331h**).

the wheel. ver. 27.

29 cometh. ver. 21, 22. Is +9:6. Jb 37:23. Je 32:19. Da +4:3.

wonderful in. Is +9:6. Mt 21:15. Ac 2:22.

excellent. Jb 37:23. 1 C 15:35-38, 42-44, 51-54.

ISAIAH 29

1 A.M. 3292. B.C. 712.

Woe, etc. *or*, O Ariel, *that is*, the lion of God. **S#740h**: Is 29:1, 2, 7. Ezr 8:16. ver. 15. Is 31:9. Ge 49:9. Ezk 43:15mg, 16.

Ariel. Ge +10:10.

the city. *or*, of the city. 2 S 5:7-9.

add. Is 1:11-15. Ps 50:8-17. Je 7:21. Ho 5:6. 8:13. 9:4. Am 4:4, 5. Mi 6:6-9. He 10:1.

kill. Heb. cut off the heads. 66:3. Mi 6:6, 7.

sacrifices. lit. feasts. Ex +23:18.

2 I will. Is 5:25-30. 10:5, 6, 32. 17:14. 24:1-12.

33:7-9. 36:22. 37:3. Je 32:28-32. 39:4, 5.

heaviness. Is 10:32. 37:3. Je 7:14. Ezk 9:6.

and it shall. Is 34:6. Ezk 22:31. 24:3-13. 39:17. 43:15. Zp 1:7, 8. Re 19:17, 18.

3 camp against. 2 K 18:17. 19:32. 24:11, 12. 25:1-4. Ezk 21:22. Mt 22:7. Lk 19:43, 44.

4 thou shalt. Is 2:11-21. 3:8. 51:23. 2 K 18:26, 36, 37. Ps 44:25. La 1:9.

whisper. Heb. peep, *or* chirp. Is +8:19.

out of the dust. 1 S 13:6. 14:11. Je 41:9.

5 the multitude. Is 10:16-19. 25:5. 31:3, 8. 37:36.

as chaff. Lk +3:17.

at an. Is 30:13. Nu 6:9. Ps 46:5, 6. 76:5, 6. 1 Th 5:3.

6 visited. Is 5:26-30. 1 S 2:10. 12:17, 18. 2 S 22:14.

with earthquake. Mt +24:7. Re +6:12.

storm and tempest. Ps +83:15.

devouring fire. Ps +97:3. Mt +3:11.

7 the multitude. Is 37:36. 41:11, 12. Je 25:31-33. 51:42-44. Na 1:3-12. Zc 12:3-5. 14:1-3, 12-15. Re 20:8, 9.

that distress. ver. +2.

shall be. Is 54:17. Jl 3:11.

as a dream. Jb 20:8. Ps 73:20.

8 as when. Is 10:7-16. 2 Ch 32:21.

dreameth. Is 37:36. Jb 20:8. Ps 73:20.

he awaketh. 2 S 4:31. Ps 3:5. 73:20. 139:18.

soul. Heb. *nephesh*, Nu +11:6. Ps 107:9. Pr 6:30. Is 5:14. Re +18:14.

behold. Is 44:12.

soul. Heb. *nephesh*, Nu +11:6.

hath appetite. Is 33:4. Ps 107:9. Pr 28:15.

so shall. Ezk 38:3-23. 39:8-29. 2 P 2:9. Re 20:9.

9 and wonder. Is 1:2. 33:13, 14. Je 2:12. Hab 1:5. Ac 13:40, 41. Re 17:6.

cry ye out, and cry. *or*, take your pleasure and riot. Is 22:12, 13. Mt 26:45. Mk 14:41.

they are. ver. 10. Is 19:14. 28:7, 8. 49:26. 51:21, 22. Je 23:9. 25:27. 51:7. La 4:21.

10 the Lord. ver. 14. Is 6:9, 10. Dt +2:30. 1 S 26:12. Ps 69:23. Mi 3:6. Ac 28:26, 27. Ro *11:8*.

poured out. Is 40:19. 44:10.

spirit. Heb. *ruach*, Ge +41:8; +26:35.

deep sleep. Ge 2:21. 15:12. Jb 4:13.

hath closed. Is 44:18. Ge +19:11. Ezk 14:9. 2 C 4:4. 2 Th 2:9-12.

rulers. Heb. heads. Is 3:2, 3. Mi 3:1.

the seers. Is 30:10. 1 S 9:9. Je 26:8-11. Am 7:12, 13.

he covered. Je 26:8.

11 book. or, letter. 2 S 11:14.

that is sealed. Is 8:16.

I cannot. Da 12:4, 9. Mt 11:25. 13:11. 16:17. Re 5:1-9. 6:1.

12 I am not. ver. 18. Is 28:12, 13. Je 5:4. Ho 4:6. Lk 14:18. Jn 5:40. 7:15, 16.

13 Forasmuch. Is 10:6. 48:1, 2. 58:2, 3. Ps 17:1.

Je 3:10. 5:2. 12:2. 42:2-4, 20. Ezk 33:31-33. Mt 15:7-9. Mk 7:6.

their fear. 2 Ch ch. 29-31. Pr 30:6. Mt 15:2-6. Mk 7:2-13. Col 2:22.

taught by. Is +8:20.

14 I will. ver. 9. Is 28:21. Hab 1:5. Jn 9:29-34.

proceed. Heb. add. Is 38:5. Dt 5:25mg.

for the wisdom. ver. 10. Je +19:7. Lk +8:10. Jn 9:39-41. Ro 1:21, 22, 28. 1 C 1:19-24.

15 Woe. Is 30:1, 2.

seek. Is 5:18, 19. 28:15, 17. 30:1. Jb 22:13, 14. Ps 10:11-13. 64:5, 6. 139:1-8. Je 23:24. Ezk 8:12. 9:9. Zp 1:12. Re 2:23.

to hide. Jb 34:22. Ps 94:7, 9.

and their works. Jb 24:13-17. 34:22. Lk 12:1-3. Jn 3:19. 1 C 4:5. 2 C 4:2, 5.

in the dark. Ep +5:11.

Who seeth. Is 47:10. Ps 59:7. 73:11. 94:7-9. Ml 2:17.

16 your turning. Is 24:1. Ac 17:6.

as the potter's. Is 45:9, 10. Je 18:1-10. Ro 9:19-21.

or shall. Is 45:11. Ps 94:8, 9.

17 yet a very. Is 63:18. Hab 2:3. Hg 2:6. He 10:37.

Lebanon. Is 32:15. 35:1, 2. 41:19. 49:5, 6. 55:13. 65:12-16. Ho 1:9, 10. Mt 19:30. 21:43. Ro 11:11-17.

the fruitful. Is 5:6. Ezk 20:46, 47. Ho 3:4. Mi 3:12. Zc 11:1, 2. Mt 21:18, 19. Ro 11:19-27.

18 in that day. Is +2:11.

the deaf. ver. 10-12, 24. Is 35:5. 42:18. 43:8. Ex 4:11. Dt 29:4. Je 31:33, 34. Ezk 12:2. Mt 11:5. 13:14-16. 16:17. Mk 7:37. Lk 7:22. Jn 6:45. 8:43. 2 C 3:14-18. 4:2-6.

words of the book. ver. 11. Ne 8:8. Ps 119:18. Jn +5:39. Ac 17:11.

shall see. Is 42:16. Pr 20:12. Lk 4:18. Ac 26:18. Ep 1:17-19. 5:14. 1 P 2:9. Re 3:18.

19 meek. Mt +5:5. Ph 2:1-3. Ja 2:5. 1 P 2:1-3.

increase. Heb. add. Is 15:9mg. 26:15.

the poor. Is 41:17, 18. 57:15. 66:2. Ps 9:18. 12:5. Zp 3:12-18. Mt +5:3. 11:5. 1 C 1:26-29. Ja 1:9. 2:5.

rejoice. Is 41:16. 61:10. Hab 3:18. Ph 3:1-3. 4:4.

20 the terrible. ver. 5. Is 10:24-26. 13:3. 14:12. 25:4, 5. 49:25. 51:13. Jb 1:6-12. 2:1-7. +8:13. Ps 109:6. Da 7:7, 19-25. Hab 1:6, 7. Zc 3:1, 2. Lk 22:31. Ro 16:20.

is brought. Lk 10:18. 1 Th 2:18. Re 12:10.

the scorner. Is 28:14-22. Lk 16:14. 23:11, 35.

and all. Mi 2:1. Mk 2:6, 7. 3:2-6. Lk 6:7. 13:14-17. 20:20-23. Re 12:10.

21 make. Jg 12:6. Mt 22:15. Lk 11:53, 54.

and lay. Je 18:18. 20:7-10. 26:2-8. Am 5:10-12. 7:10-17. Mi 2:6, 7.

reproveth. Je 17:19, 20. 19:2. Am 5:10.

gate. Ge +14:7.

and turn. Is 30:10. Pr 28:21. Ezk 13:19. Am 5:11, 12. Ml +3:5. Mt 22:15. 26:15. Ac 3:14. Ja 5:6.

nought. Is 59:4. Mt 26:14, 15. Lk 6:7.

22 the Lord. Jn 8:56.

who redeemed. Is 41:8, 9, 14. 44:21-23. 51:2, 11. 54:4. Ge 48:16. Jsh 24:2-5. Ne 9:7, 8. Lk 1:68. 1 P 1:18, 19. Re 5:9.

Jacob shall. Is 44:21-26. 45:17, 25. 46:3, 4. 49:7, etc. 60:1-9. 61:7-11. Je 30:5-7, 10. 31:10-12. 33:24-26. Ezk 37:24-28. 39:24-29. ch. 40-48. Jl +2:26, 27. Ro 11:11, etc.

pale. Je +30:6.

23 But when. Ezk 36:25. +39:28.

seeth his children. Is +26:19. Mt +8:11. +19:28. Ac +2:39.

the work. Is 19:25. 43:21. 45:11. 60:21. Ps 100:3. Ep 2:10.

sanctify my name. Is +8:13. Ps +9:10. Mt +6:9. 2 C 5:5. Re 11:15-17.

shall fear. Ho 3:5. Ac 2:36-39. 8:14, 15. 10:44, 45. 11:18. Re 15:4. 19:5.

the God of Israel. Is 17:6. 21:10, 17. 41:17. 45:3, 15. 48:1, 2. 52:12. Ge 33:20. Ex 24:10. Nu 16:9. Jsh 22:16. 1 S 1:17. 5:7, 8, 10, 11. 6:3, 5. 2 S 23:3. 1 K 8:26. 1 Ch 4:10. 5:26. 17:24. 29:10. 2 Ch 29:7. Ezr 3:2. 7:15. 8:35. 9:4. Ps 41:13. 68:35. 69:6. 72:18. 106:48. Ezk 8:4. 9:3. 10:19, 20. 11:22. 43:2. Mt 15:31.

24 They also. ver. 10, 11. Is 28:7. Ps 95:10. Pr 12:8. Ho 3:5. Zc 12:10. Mt 21:28-32. Lk 7:47. 15:17-19. Ac 2:37. 6:7. 9:19, 20. Ro 11:26. 1 C 6:11. 1 T 1:13-15. He 5:2. Re 20:2, 3.

that erred. Ge 37:15. Ex 23:4. Jb 6:24. Ps 95:10. Pr 21:16. Mk +12:24. 1 T 5:13-15. 2 T 3:6-8. He 3:12, 13. 2 P 3:16, 17.

in spirit. Heb. *ruach*, Ge +41:8. Ps +51:10.

shall come. Notice the implicit cause/effect relationships which point to the Biblical medicine (Pr 4:22mg) to cure a wrong spirit and murmurings (Ps +9:10). Ps 18:28. +119:130. Pr 29:13. Ac 26:18. 2 C 4:6. Ep 1:18. 1 P 2:9.

to understanding. Heb. know understanding. Is 32:4. 41:20. Ps +9:10. 94:10. 111:10. +119:97-105. Pr 1:1-6. 4:7. Jn 17:3. 1 C 2:14. Col +1:10. 2 T 2:15. +3:15-17. He +8:11.

they that murmured. Ru +1:13. Ps +77:3. Je +29:11. Ezk +18:25. Ro +9:14. Ph +4:11. Ju +16.

shall learn. Is 28:9. 42:16. Ps +25:9. Pr 16:21, 23. Je 42:3. Mt 13:23. Lk 10:39. Ac 2:41. 17:11. 1 Th 2:13.

doctrine. Is 28:9. Jb 11:4. Pr 4:2. Ac 2:42. 1 T +4:16. 2 T +3:16.

ISAIAH 30

1 A.M. cir. 3291. B.C. cir. 713.

Woe. Is 31:1.

the rebellious. ver. 9. Is 1:2. 63:10. 65:2. Dt

9:7, 24. 29:19. 1 S 15:22, 23. Je 4:17. 5:23.
Ezk 2:3. 3:9, 26, 27. 12:2, 3. Ho 7:13. Ac 7:51,
52.

that take. Is 8:19. 29:15. Jsh 9:14. I Ch
10:13, 14. Ho 4:10-12.

cover. Is 4:5mg. 28:15, 20. 32:2. Ps 61:4.
91:1-4. Ezk 28:14.

spirit. Heb. *ruach*, Ge +41:38.

add. Is 1:5. 5:18. Nu 32:14. Ho 13:2. Ro 2:5.
2 T 3:13.

2 walk. Is 20:5, 6. 31:1-3. 36:6. Dt 28:68. 2 K
17:4. Je 37:5-7. 43:7. Ezk 29:6, 7.

and have. Nu 27:21. Jsh 9:14. 1 K 22:7. Je
21:2. 42:2, 20.

strengthen themselves. 2 Ch 12:1.

to trust. Ps 60:11, 12. 118:8, 9.

the shadow. Is 18:1. Ps +91:1.

3 the strength. ver. 5-7. Is 20:5. Je 37:5-10.

the trust. Je 42:1-3, 13-16, 20.

your confusion. Is 45:16, 17. Je 17:5, 6. Ro
5:5. 10:11.

4 his princes. Is 57:9. 2 K 17:4. Ho 7:11, 12, 16.

Zoan. Nu +13:22.

Hanes. i.e. *grace has fled; ensign of grace*,
S#2609h, only here. Je +43:7, Tahpanhes.

5 ashamed. ver. 16. Is 20:5, 6. 31:1-3. Je 2:36.

6 burden. Is 46:1, 2. 57:9. Ho 8:9, 10. 12:1.

beasts. 1 K 10:2. Mt 12:42.

the south. Ge +12:9.

into the land. Is 19:4. Ex 1:14. 5:10-21. Dt
4:20. 8:15. 17:16. Je 11:4.

the viper. Is 59:5. Nu 21:6, 7. Dt 8:15. Je 2:6.

riches. Ge +34:29. 2 Ch 9:1. 16:2. 28:20-23.

7 the Egyptians. Is 31:1-5. Je 37:7.

in vain. Ps +60:11.

concerning this. *or*, to her. Their. ver. 15. Is 2:22. 28:12. 41:10. Ps 76:8,
9. 118:8, 9. Ho 5:13.

strength. Ge +34:29.

sit still. Is 7:3, 4. 46:10. Ex 14:13, 14. La
3:26. Mt 8:25, 26.

8 write. Is 8:1. Dt 31:19, 22. Jb 19:23, 24. Je
36:2, 28-32. 51:60. Hab 2:2.

note. Ex 17:14. 24:4. 34:27, 28. Nu 33:2. Dt
31:9, 24.

the time to come. Heb. the latter day. Is 2:2.
Nu 24:14. Dt 4:30. 31:29. Jb 19:25. Je 23:20.
48:47. Ezk 38:16. Ho 3:5. 1 T 4:1. 2 P 3:3. Ju
18.

for ever. Ps +9:18.

and ever. Heb. *olam*, Ps +21:4. Mt 24:35. 1 P
1:23-25.

9 this is. ver. 1. Is 1:4. Dt 31:27-29. 32:20. Je
44:2-17. Zp 3:2. Mt 23:31-33. Ac 7:51.

lying. Is 59:3. 63:8. Je 9:3-5. Ho 4:2. Re
+21:8. 22:15.

will not. 2 Ch 33:10. 36:15, 16. Ne 9:29, 30.
Pr 28:9. Je 7:13. Zc 1:4-6. 7:11, 12. Ro 2:21-
23.

the law. Is 1:10.

10 say. 1 K 21:20. 2 Ch 16:9, 10. 18:7-27. 24:19-
21. 25:16. Je 5:31. 11:21. 26:11, 20-23. 29:27.
38:4. Am 2:12. 7:13. Mi 2:6. Ac 4:17, 18.
5:28, 40. Ro 8:7. 1 Th 2:15, 16. Re 11:7.

speak. 1 K 22:8-13, 27. Je 6:13, 14. 8:10, 11,
23:17, 26-29. Ezk 13:7-10, 18-22. Mi 2:11. Jn
7:7. 8:45. Ro 16:18. Ga 4:16.

11 Get you out. Is 29:21. Am 7:13.

cause. Jn 15:23, 24. Ro 1:28, 30. 8:7. Ep
4:18.

12 Because. ver. 1, 7, 15-17. Is 5:24. 31:1-3. 2 S
12:9, 10. Am 2:4. Lk 10:16. 1 Th 4:8.

and trust. Is 28:15. 47:10. Ps 52:7. 62:10. Je
13:25.

oppression. *or*, fraud. **S#6233h**. Is 54:14.
59:13. Le 6:4 (thing). Ps 62:10. 73:8. 119:134.
Ec 5:8. 7:7. Je 6:6. 22:17. Ezk 18:18. 22:7mg,
12 (extortion), 29.

perverseness. **S#3868h**. Pr 2:15. 3:32. 14:2.

13 as a breach. 1 K 20:30. Ps 62:3. Ezk 13:10-
15. Mt 7:26, 27. Lk 6:49.

cometh. Is 29:5. Jb 36:18. Ps 73:19, 20. Pr
6:15. 29:1. 1 Th 5:1-3.

14 he shall break. Da +2:44.

potter's vessel. Heb. bottle of potters.

he shall not. Is 27:11. Dt 29:20. Jb 27:22. Je
13:14. Ezk 5:11. 7:4, 9. 8:18. 9:10. 24:14. Zc
7:13. Ro 8:32. 11:21. 2 P 2:4, 5.

so that. Is 47:14. Ps 31:12. Je 48:38. La 4:2.
Ezk 15:3-8.

15 the Holy One. ver. 11. Is +1:4. Je 23:36.

In returning. ver. 7. Is 7:4. 26:3, 4. 32:17. 1
Ch 5:20. 2 Ch 16:8, 9. 32:8. Ps 125:1, 2. Je
3:22, 23. Ho 14:1-3.

and rest. Ex 14:13. Mt 8:25, 26.

in quietness. Jb 34:29.

and ye. Ps 80:11-13. 81:13, 14. Je 6:16.
44:16, 17. Mt 22:3. 23:37. Lk 13:34. Jn 5:40.
He 12:25.

16 for we will. Is 5:26-30. 10:28-32. 31:1. Dt
28:25. 2 K 25:5. Ps 33:17. 147:10. Je 52:7.
Am 2:14-16. 9:1. Mi 1:13.

horses. Dt 17:16.

therefore. Dt 28:49. Je 4:13. 39:4, 5. La 4:19.
Hab 1:8.

17 thousand. Le 26:8, 36. Dt 28:25. 32:30. Jsh
23:10. Pr 28:1. Je 37:10.

till ye. Is 1:7, 8. 37:3, 4. Ne 1:2, 3. Zp 3:12. Zc
13:8, 9. Mt 24:21, 22.

a beacon. *or*, a tree bereft of branches, *or*,
boughs, *or*, a mast. Is 6:13. 27:11. Jn 15:2-6.
Ro 11:17-19.

18 therefore. Is 32:2. 55:8, 9. Ex 34:6, 7. Ho
2:14. Ro 5:20. 9:15-18.

wait. Is 18:4. 57:17, 18. Jb 32:4. Ps +25:3.
69:3. 106:13. Da 12:12. Ho 5:15. 6:1, 2, 9. Mt
+23:39. Lk +21:31. Ac +3:19-21.

be gracious. Ex +34:6. Is 31:18-20. Jon 3:4-
10. Zp 3:15. Zc 10:6. Mt 15:22-28. Lk 6:35.
15:20. Ro 9:22, 23. 2 P 3:9, 15.

be exalted. Is +12:4. Ps 76:5-10. Lk 24:26, 27. Ac 2:33-39. 5:31. Ep 1:6, 20-23.

have mercy. Is 60:10. Ex +34:6, 7. Jb 11:6. Ps 85:10. 98:3. 147:10, 11. Je 31:20. Ho 2:23. 11:8, 9. Zc 10:6. Ja 2:13. 2 P 3:9, 15.

God of judgment. Is 33:5. 45:21. 55:8. Dt +32:4. 1 S 2:3. Jb 35:14. Ps +7:8. 92:15. 99:4. 103:6. Je +10:24, 25. Mi 7:18-20. Zp 3:5. Ml 2:17. Jn 5:30. Ep 1:8.

blessed. Is +26:3. 32:20. 56:2. Dt +28:3.

wait for him. Ps +25:3. Ac 1:4. Ja 5:7, 11.

19 **dwell**. Is 10:24. 12:6. +24:23. 46:13. 65:9. Je 31:6, 12. 50:4, 5, 28. 51:10. Ezk 20:40. 37:25-28. Zp 3:14-20. Zc 1:16, 17. 2:4-7. 8:3-8. Ro 11:26.

thou shalt weep. Is 12:3-6. 40:1, 2. 54:6-14. 60:20. 61:1-3. 65:18, 19. Je 30:12-19. Mi 4:9, 10. Lk +6:21. Re 5:4-6.

gracious unto thee. Zc 12:10.

voice of thy cry. Ps 60:1. Ho +5:15. 8:2. +14:2. Zc 13:9.

he will answer. Ps 38:15mg. Je 33:3. Ezk 36:37. Mt 7:7-11. Ep 3:20. 1 J +5:14, 15.

20 **the bread**. Dt 16:3. 1 K 22:27. 2 Ch 18:26. Ps 30:5. 80:5. 102:9. 127:2. Ezk 4:13-17. 24:22, 23. Jn 16:33. Ac 14:22.

affliction. *or*, oppression. Ex 3:9. Jg 2:18.

yet shall. Ps 74:9. Am 8:11, 12. Mt 9:38. Ep 4:11.

thy teachers. 2 Ch +15:3. 35:3. Je 3:15. 23:3, 4. Ezk 34:23. Da +11:33.

21 **thine ears**. Is 35:8, 9. 42:16. 48:17. 58:11. Ps +32:8. Jn 14:26. 15:26, 27. 16:13, 14. 1 J 2:20, 27.

shall hear. Jn +10:4.

This is. Je 3:15. 42:3.

when ye turn to the right. Jsh +1:7.

22 **defile**. Is 2:20, 21. 17:7, 8. 27:9. 31:7. 2 K 23:4-20. 2 Ch 31:1. 34:3-7. Ezk 36:31. Mi 5:10-14. Zc 13:2. Re 19:20.

covering. Ex 38:17, 19. Nu 16:38, 39.

thy graven images of silver. Heb. the graven images of thy silver. Is 31:7mg. 46:6. Ex 32:2-4. Jg 17:3, 4.

ornament. Ex 28:8 (ephod). 39:5.

cast. Heb. scatter. Is 41:16. Ex 32:20. Nu 16:37. Je 15:7. Ezk 5:2.

as a. La 1:17. Ezk 18:6.

Get. Ho 14:8. 1 J 5:21.

23 **shall he**. Is 5:6. 32:20. 44:2-4. 55:10, 11. 58:11. Ps 65:9-13. 104:13, 14. 107:35-38. Je 14:22. Ezk 36:25, 26. Ho 2:21-23. Jl 2:21-26. Am 4:7, 8. Zc 8:11, 12. 10:1. Ml 3:10. Mt 6:33. 1 T 4:8.

it shall. Is 4:2. Le 26:9, 10. Dt 28:3-12. Ps 36:8.

in that day. Is +2:11.

thy cattle. Ge 41:18, 26, 47. Ps 144:12-14. Ho 4:16. Ml 4:2.

24 **oxen**. Dt 25:4. 1 C 9:9, 10.

ear the ground. Ge 45:6. Ex 34:21. Dt 21:4. 1 S 8:12.

clean. *or*, savory. Heb. leavened. **S#2548h**, only here.

25 **upon every high**. Is 2:14, 15. 35:6, 7. 41:18, 19. 43:19, 20. 44:3, 4. Ezk 17:22. 34:13, 26. Jn 7:38. Re 22:1.

high. Heb. lifted up. Is 2:14.

streams. Is 44:4. Ezk 47:1-12.

in the day. Is 34:2-10. 37:36. 63:1-6. Ezk 39:17-20. Re ch. 16-19.

when. Is 32:14. Na 3:12. 2 C 10:4.

towers. lit. "great places." Is 2:15. 5:2. 33:18.

26 **the light of the moon**. Is 11:9. 24:23. 60:19, 20. Zc 12:8. 14:7. Re 21:23. 22:5.

bindeth. Is 1:6. Dt 32:39. Jb 5:18. Je 33:5, 6. La 2:13. Ho 6:1, 2. Am 9:11. Re 21:4.

healeth. Re 22:2.

27 **the name**. Dt +28:58.

cometh. Is 63:1. Re 19:11-13.

burning. Is 34:9. Dt 33:2. Ps 79:5. +97:3. La 1:12, 13. Mt +3:11.

the burden thereof. *or*, the grievousness of flame. Is 13:8mg.

heavy. Heb. heaviness. Pr +27:3mg.

lips. Nu +12:8.

indignation. Is +66:14.

28 **his breath**. Heb. *ruach*, Ex +15:8. Jb +4:9. Lk 22:31. 2 Th 2:8. He 4:12. Re 1:16. 2:16.

an overflowing. Is 8:8. 28:17, 18. 29:6. Hab 3:12-15.

to sift. Is 19:12-14. 33:10-12. Ho 13:3. Am 9:9. Mt 3:12.

a bridle. Is 37:29. 2 K 19:28. Ps 32:9. Pr 26:3.

causing. Is 19:3, 13, 14. 2 S 17:14. 1 K 22:20-22. Jb 39:17. Ezk 14:7-9. 2 Th 2:11.

29 **Ye shall**. Is 12:1. 26:1. Ex 15:1, etc. 2 Ch 20:27, 28. Ps 32:7. Je 33:11. Re 15:3, 4. 19:1-7.

in the night. Le 23:32. Dt 16:6, 14. Ps 42:4. 81:1-4. Mt 26:30.

holy solemnity. Le 23:2.

with a pipe. 1 Ch 13:7, 8. Ps 42:4. 95:1, 2. 150:3-5.

the mountain. Is +2:2, 3.

mighty One. Heb. Rock. Is 26:4mg. Dt 32:4, 15, 18, 30, 31. Ps 18:31.

30 **the Lord**. Is 29:6. Ps 2:5. 18:13, 14. 46:6.

his glorious voice. Heb. the glory of his voice. Ps 46:6. Ezk +10:5. Re 1:15.

arm. Ex +15:16.

indignation. Na 1:6.

the flame. 1 S 7:10. Ps 76:5-8. +97:3. Mi 1:4. Mt 24:7. Re 6:12-17. 14:16-20.

devouring fire. Mt +3:11. 2 Th 1:8.

the tempest. Je +23:19.

hailstones. Is +28:17.

31 **the voice**. ver. 30. Is 37:32-38.

the Assyrian. Is 10:12. 31:8.

which smote. Is 9:4. 10:5, 15, 24. Ps 17:13, 14. 125:5. Mi 5:5, 6.

32 **every place**, etc. Heb. every passing of the rod founded.
grounded staff. Is 9:4. 10:5, 15, 24, 26. 14:5.
lay. Heb. cause to rest.
it shall be. ver. 29. Is 24:8. Ge 31:27. 1 S 10:5. Jb 21:11, 12. Ps 81:1, 2. Re 14:2, 3. 19:5, 6.
shaking. Is 2:19. 11:15. 19:16. Jb 16:12. He 12:26.
with it. *or*, against them.
33 **Tophet**. Jsh +15:8. Je +7:31. Mt 4:22. 18:8, 9.
ordained. Mt 25:41. 1 P 1:8. Ju 4.
of old. Heb. from yesterday. 1 S 14:21. 2 S +3:17mg. He 13:8.
for the king. "The king" is a title of the antichrist (Da 11:36). Is 14:9-20. 37:38. Ezk 32:22, 23. Re 19:18-20.
fire. Lk +16:24.
the breath. Heb. *neshamah*, Ge +2:7. ver. 27, 28. Jb +4:9. Ps 40:5, 6. 2 Th 2:8.
brimstone. Re +9:17.
doth kindle. Is 1:31. Dt +32:22. Mt +25:41. Ja 3:6.

ISAIAH 31

1 **Woe**. Is 30:1.
to them. Is 30:1-7. 36:6. 57:9. Ezk 17:15. Ho 11:5.
go down. Is 30:2. Jg 4:8. 1 S 17:39. Ho 1:7. Zc 4:6. 2 C 10:4.
stay on horses. Is 2:7. 30:16. 36:9. Dt 17:16. Ps 20:7. 33:16, 17. Mi 5:10.
they look. Is 5:12. 17:7, 8. 22:11. 2 Ch 16:7. Je 2:13. 17:5. Ho 14:3.
neither seek. Is 9:13. 30:2. 64:7. Dt 17:16. Da 9:13. Ho 7:7, 13-16. Am 5:4-8.
2 **he also**. 1 S 2:3. Jb 5:13. Je 10:7, 12. 1 C 1:21-29. Ju 25.
will bring. Is 19:11, 12. 30:13, 14. 45:7. Jsh 23:15. Am +3:6.
will not. Nu 23:19. Jb 23:13. Ps 33:11. Pr 19:21. Ec 3:14. 7:13. Je 36:32. 44:29. Zc 1:6. Ml +3:6. Mt 24:35. He 6:17, 18. Ja +1:17.
call back. Heb. remove. Is 18:5. 36:7. 2 K 17:23. 18:4.
arise. Is 28:21. 63:4-6. Nu 10:35. Ps 12:5, 6. 68:1, 2. 78:65, 66. Zp 3:8.
against the help. ver. 3. Is 20:4-6. 30:3. Je 44:29, 30. Ezk 29:6, 7.
3 **the Egyptians**. Is 20:5. 36:6. Dt 32:30, 31. Ps 9:20. 146:3-5. Ezk 28:9. Ac 12:22, 23. 2 Th 2:4-8.
God. Heb. *El*, Ex +15:2.
their horses. Ps 33:17.
not spirit. Heb. *ruach*, Ps +104:4.
stretch. Ex +7:5. Jsh 23:15.
both. Je 37:7-10.
4 **Like as**. Is +5:29. Am +1:2.

shepherds. Lk 2:8.
noise. *or*, multitude. Is 29:5, 7, 8. 63:15mg. Je +10:13mg.
so shall. Is 10:16. 12:6. 37:35, 36. 42:13. 2 Ch 20:15. Ps 46:5, 8, 9. 125:1, 2. Zc 2:5. 9:8, 15. +12:8. +14:3.
5 **as birds flying**. Is 10:14. Ex 19:4. Dt 32:11. Ps 46:5. 91:4. Zc 9:14.
defend. Is 37:35. 38:6. 2 K 19:34. 20:6. Zc 9:15. 12:8.
defending. 2 K 19:34. 20:6. Ps 37:40.
passing. Ex 12:13, 23, 27.
6 **Turn**. Je 31:18-20. Zc +1:3.
deeply. Is 1:4. 29:15. 48:8. 2 Ch 33:9-16. 36:14. Je 5:23. Ho 9:9.
7 **in that**. Is 2:20. 30:22. Dt 7:25. Ezk 36:25. Ho 14:3, 8.
his idols of gold. Heb. the idols of his gold. Is 30:22mg.
for a sin. 1 K 12:28-30. Ho 8:11.
8 **shall the**. Is 10:16. 19:33, 34. 14:25. 29:5, 8. 30:27-33. 37:35, 36. 2 K 19:34-37. 2 Ch 20:15. 32:21. Ps 37:40. Ho 1:7.
Assyrian. Is 30:31.
he shall flee. Is 37:37, 38.
from the sword. *or*, for fear of the sword. Is 1:20. 2:4. 3:25. Je +12:12.
discomfited. *or*, tributary. Heb. for melting, *or* tribute. Is 10:18. 13:7.Ge 49:15. Pr 12:24.
9 **he shall pass over to his strong hold for fear**. Heb. his rock shall pass away for fear.
his strong hold. *or*, his strength.
the ensign. Is 11:10. 18:3.
whose fire. Is 4:4. 10:17. 29:6. Le 6:13. 10:2. Ps 50:2, 3. Ezk 22:18-22. Zc 2:5. Ml +4:1.
in Zion. Ps +50:2, 3.
his furnace. Ps 21:9. La 5:10.

ISAIAH 32

1 **king**. Is +9:6, 7. +11:4. 40:1-5. Dt 17:14, 15. 2 S 23:3. 2 Ch 31:20, 21. Ps 99:4. Je +21:12. Ho 3:5. Zc 9:9. Ro 5:21. He 1:8, 9.
princes. Is 28:6. Je 33:26. Re +5:10. 17:14.
2 **a man**. Is +7:14. 8:10-14. +9:6. Ps 146:3-5. Mi 5:4, 5. Zc 13:7. 1 T 2:5. 3:16.
an hiding. ver. 18, 19. Is 28:17. 30:18. 44:3. Ps +64:2. Mt 7:24-27.
rivers of water. Is 35:6, 7. 41:18. 43:20. Ex 17:6. Pr +21:1. Jn 7:37. 19:34. Re 22:1.
the shadow. Ps +91:1.
great. Heb. heavy. Is 36:2. 2 K 6:14mg.
rock. Ps 31:2, 3. Ex 33:22.
weary. Ps 63:1mg.
3 **the eyes**. Is 30:26. 54:13. 60:1, 2. Ps +119:18. Je 31:34. Mt 13:11. Mk 7:37. 8:22-25. 1 J 2:20, 21.
the ears. Mt 13:9.
4 **heart**. Is 29:24. Ne 8:8-12. Mt 11:25. 16:17. Ac 6:7. 26:9-11. Ga 1:23.

rash. Heb. hasty. Is 35:4mg. Jb 5:13. Hab 1:6.
the tongue. Ex 4:11. SS 7:9. Lk 21:14, 15. Ac 2:4-12. 4:13.
plainly. or, elegantly. **S#6703h**. Is 18:4 (clear). SS 5:10 (white). Je 4:11 (dry).

5 vile. Is 5:20. Ps 15:4. Ml 3:18. Re 20:12. 22:11, 12.
nor. 1 S 25:3-8. Pr 23:6-8.

6 the vile. Is 29:20. 1 S 24:13. 25:10, 11. Je 13:23. Mt 12:34-36. 15:19. Ja 3:5, 6.
will speak. Is 5:20. Lk 6:45. Re +22:11.
and his heart. Ps 58:1, 2. Ho 7:6, 7. Mi 2:1, 2. Ac 5:3, 4. 8:21, 22. Ja 1:14, 15.
practice hypocrisy. Jb +8:13.
empty. Jb 22:5-9. 24:2-16. Pr 11:24-26. Am 2:6, 7. 8:6. Mi 3:1-3. Mt 23:14. Ja 1:27.
soul. Heb. nephesh, Ge +34:3.

7 instruments. Is 1:23. 5:23. Je 5:26-28. Mi 2:11. 7:3. Mt 26:14-16, 59, 60.
the churl. 1 S 25:10, 11.
deviseth. Ps 10:7-10. 64:4-6. 82:2-5. Je 18:18. Mi 7:2. Mt 26:4.
to destroy. Mt 23:14.
lying. Is 59:3, 4. 1 K 21:10-14. Mt 12:34, 35. Ac 6:11-13.
the needy speaketh right. or, he speaketh against the poor in judgment. Ml +3:5. Ja +5:4.

8 the liberal. 2 S 9:1, etc. Jb 31:16-21. Ps 112:9. Pr 11:24, 25. Lk +6:33-35. Ac 9:39. 11:29, 30. 2 C 8:2. 9:6-11.
stand. or, be established. Is 14:24. 40:8. Dt 19:15. Pr 15:22. 19:21.

9 ye women. ver. 11. Is 1:21. 3:16. 23:15-17. 47:7, 8. 57:3. Dt 28:56. 31:16. Jg 2:17. SS 2:2. Je 3:1-3. 4:30. 6:2-6. 48:11, 12. La 4:5. Ezk 16:13. 23:2. Am 6:1-6. Mi 7:8-10. Na 3:4.
give ear. Is 28:23. Dt 4:33, 36. Jg 9:7. Ps 49:1, 2. Mt 13:9.

10 Many days and years. Heb. Days above a year. Is 3:17-26. 24:7-12. Je 25:10, 11. Ho 3:4, 5. Mi 7:15. Mt +25:19.
for. Is 7:23. 16:10. Dt 8:8. Je 8:13. Ho 2:12. Jl 1:7, 12. Hab 3:17. Zp 1:13.

11 ye women. ver. 9. Is 3:16, 17, 24.
be troubled. Is 2:19, 21. 22:4, 5. 33:14. Lk 23:27-30. Ja 5:5.
strip. Is 20:4. 47:1-3. Dt 28:48. Ho 2:3. Mi 1:8-11.
gird. Jb +16:15.

12 lament. Dt 28:48. Ps 137:1. La 2:11. 4:3, 4. Lk 23:28.
pleasant fields. Heb. fields of desire. Is 2:16mg. 44:9mg. 54:12mg. Ge 27:15mg. Dt 8:7, 8. 11:11, 12. 1 K 20:6mg. 2 Ch 32:27mg. Jb 33:20mg. Je +3:19mg. +25:34mg. La 1:7mg, 10mg. 2:4mg. Ezk 24:16. +26:12mg. Da 9:23mg. 10:3mg, 11mg, 19mg. 11:37, 38mg. Ho 9:6mg, 16mg. Jl 3:5mg. Am 5:11mg.

13 come. Is 6:11. 7:23. 34:13. Ps 107:33, 34. Ho 9:6. 10:8.
yea, upon. or, burning upon, etc. Je 39:8. Re 18:7, 8.
in the. Is 22:2, 12, 13.

14 the palaces. Is 5:9. 24:1-3, 10, 12. 25:2. 27:10. 2 K 25:9. Ps 106:40-42. Lk 21:20, 24.
forts and towers. or, clifts and watchtowers. 2 K +5:24mg. Ne 2:11-15.
for. Is 13:19-22. 34:11-17. Re 18:2, 3.
for ever. Heb. olam, Ex +12:24.

15 Until. Is 62:1, 2. Ezk 36:24-26, 31. Jl 2:28. Zp 3:8-10.
the spirit. Heb. ruach, Ge +41:38. Is 11:2, 3. 44:3, 4. 45:8. 59:19-21. 63:11. Ps 104:30. 107:33. Pr 1:23. Ezk 37:9. 39:29. Jl 2:28, 29. Zc 12:10. Lk 24:49. Jn 7:39. Ac 2:17, 18, 33. 2 C 3:8. T 3:5, 6.
poured. Is 3:17. 22:6. 53:12.
wilderness. Is 29:17. 35:2, 7. 54:1-3. 55:11-13. 60:1, etc. 61:3-5. Ho 1:10, 11. Ro 11:18-26.

16 judgment. Is 35:8. 42:1, 4. 56:6-8. +60:21. Ps 94:14, 15. Ho 3:5. 1 C 6:9-11. T 2:11, 12. 1 P 2:9-12. 4:1-4.

17 the work. Is 26:3. 48:18. 66:12. Ps 72:2, 3. 119:165. Ro +5:1.
quietness. Is 2:3, 4. 9:7. 11:6-9, 13. Ps 112:6-9. Pr 14:26. Ezk 37:21, 22, 25. 39:29. Mi 4:3, 4. 2 C 1:12. He 6:11. 2 P 1:10, 11. 1 J 3:18-24. 4:17.
for ever. Heb. olam, Ex +12:24.

18 my people. Is 33:20-22. 35:9, 10. 60:17, 18. Je 23:5, 6. 33:16. Ezk 34:25, 26. Ho 2:18-23. Zc 2:5, 8. He 4:9. 1 J 4:16.
sure dwellings. Am +9:14, 15. Ob +17.
resting places. Dt 33:12. Je 50:6. Mt 9:36mg.

19 it shall. Is 26:20, 21. +28:17. 37:24. Mt 7:25.
on the. Zc 11:2.
the city shall be low. or, the city shall be utterly abased. Is 14:22, 23. 26:5. Na 1:1, 8. 2:10-13. Re 18:21.

20 Blessed. Is 19:5-7. 30:18, 23. 55:10, 11. 56:2. Dt 28:8. Ps 3:8. Pr +10:22. Ec 11:1. Ac 2:41. 4:4. 5:14. 1 C 3:6. 9:11. Ga 6:7-10. Ja 3:18.
that sow. Is 49:4. Dt 10:9. 33:11. Ps 132:16. Je 1:7, 8, 19. 15:19-21. 20:11. 31:14. Ezk 3:8, 9. Da 12:3. Mt 10:19, 20. 28:20. Lk +12:42-44. 21:15. Jn 4:36. 1 T 4:16. 1 P 5:1-4. Re 2:1.
the ox. Is 30:24. 1 C 9:9-11.

ISAIAH 33

1 thee that. Is 10:5, 6. 17:14. 24:16. 2 K 16:17, 18. 18:13-17. 2 Ch 28:16-21. Hab 2:5-8.
when thou shalt cease. Is 10:12. 21:2. 37:36-38. Jg 1:7. 2 K 19:6, 7. Je 25:12-14. 27:7. Ob 10-16. Zc 14:1-3. Mt 7:2. Re 13:10. 16:6. 17:12-14, 17.

2 be gracious. Is 30:18, 19. Ho 14:2.

waited. Ps +25:3.
be thou. Is 25:4. Ex 14:27. Ps 25:3.
83:8mg.
morning. Is 17:14. 37:36. Jb +7:18. Ps 143:8.
La 3:23.
our salvation. Is 26:16. Ps 37:39. 46:1, 5.
50:15. 60:11. 90:15. 91:15. Je 2:27, 28. 14:8.
2 C 1:3, 4.

3　the noise. Is 10:13, 14, 32-34. 17:12-14.
37:11-18, 29-36. Ps 46:6.

4　your spoil. ver. 23. 2 K 7:15, 16. 2 Ch 14:13.
20:25.
the running. Jl 2:9, 25.

5　The Lord. ver. 10. Is +12:4. 37:20. Ex 9:16,
17. 15:1, 6. 18:11. Jb 40:9-14. Ps 115:1, 2. Da
4:37. Ro 3:26. Re 19:1-6.
he dwelleth. Is 57:15. 66:1. Ps 113:5, 6.
123:1. Ep 1:20, 21.
he hath. Is 1:26, 27. 4:2-4. 32:1, 15-18. 52:1.
54:11-14. 60:21. 61:3, 11. 62:1, 2. 2 Ch 31:20,
21. Ro 11:26.

6　wisdom. Is 11:2-5. 38:5, 6. 2 Ch 32:27-29. Ps
45:4. Pr 14:27. 24:3-7. 28:2, 15, 16. 29:4. Ec
7:12, 19. 9:14-18. Je 22:15-17.
strength. Ps 27:1, 2. 28:8. 140:7.
salvation. Heb. salvations. Is 26:18. Ps
28:8mg.
fear. 2 Ch 32:20, 21. Ps 112:1-3. Pr 15:16.
19:23. Mt 6:33. 2 C 6:10. 1 T 4:8. 6:6.
treasure. Dt +28:12.

7　valiant ones. or, messengers. Is 29:1 (Ariel).
the ambassadors. Is 36:3, 22. Ge +10:1. 2 K
18:18, 37. 19:1-4.

8　highways. Is 10:29-31. Jg 5:6. La 1:4.
he hath broken. 2 K 18:14-17.
he hath despised. Is 10:9-11. 36:1. 2 K
18:13.
he regardeth. Is 10:13, 14. 1 S 17:10, 26. 2
K 18:20, 21. Ps 10:5. Lk 18:2-4.

9　earth. Is 1:7, 8. 24:1, 4-6, 19, 20. Je 4:20-26.
languisheth. Is 16:8.
Lebanon. Is 14:8. 37:24. Zc 11:1-3.
hewn down. or, withered away. Is 19:6.
Sharon. Is +35:2.
Bashan. Dt +32:14.
Carmel. Jsh +19:26.
shake off. ver. 15. Is 52:2.

10　Now will I rise. Is 10:16, 33. 42:13, 14.
59:16, 17. Dt 32:36-43. Ps +3:7.
now will I be exalted. ver. +5. Ex 14:18.
15:9-12. Am 6:1.
will I lift. Dt 32:36. 2 K 19:7, 8. Ps 7:6. 12:5.
46:9. 102:13.

11　conceive. Is 8:9, 10. 10:7-14. 29:5-8. Ps 2:1.
83:5-18. Ja +1:15.
chaff. *Is 17:13.*
stubble. 1 C +3:12.
your breath. Heb. *ruach*, Ge +41:8. Jb 19:17.
shall devour. Is 31:8, 9. 37:23-29. Ps +97:3.

12　the people. 2 K 19:32-35.

the burnings. i.e. as fuel for lime-kilns. Am
2:1.
thorns. Is 9:18. 27:4. 37:36. 2 S 23:6, 7.

13　Hear. Is 18:3. 37:20. 49:1. 57:19. Ex 15:14,
15. Jsh 2:9-11. 9:9, 10. 1 S 17:46. Ps 46:6-11.
48:10. 98:1, 2. Da 3:27-30. 4:1-3. 6:25-27. Ac
2:5-11. Ep 2:11-18.
ye that are near. Ps 97:8. 99:2, 3. 147:12-14.
148:14.
acknowledge. Da 4:37.

14　sinners. Is 7:2. 28:14, 15, 17-22. 29:13. 30:8-
11. Nu 17:12, 13. Jb 15:21, 22. 18:11. Ps 53:5.
Pr 28:1. Re 6:15-17.
fearfulness. Jb 4:14. Ps 2:11. 48:6.
the hypocrites. Jb +8:13. Mt 22:12.
Who among us shall dwell with the. Is
5:24. 29:6. 30:27-33. Dt 4:24. 5:24, 25. 9:3. Ps
11:6. +97:3.
fire. Lk +16:24.
everlasting. Heb. *olam*, Ge +17:7. 2 Th 1:9.
burnings. Is 26:11. 34:9, 10. Mt +25:41, 46.

15　that walketh. Is 56:1, 2. Ps 1:1-3. 15:1, 2.
24:4, 5. 26:1, 2, 11. 106:3. Ezk 18:15-17. Ml
2:6. Lk 1:6. Ro 2:7. T 2:11, 12. 1 J 3:7.
righteously. Heb. in righteousnesses. Is
45:24mg. Jg +5:11mg. 1 K 3:6.
uprightly. Heb. in uprightnesses. lit. upright
things. Is 26:7. 45:19. 1 Ch 29:17.
despiseth. Ex +18:21. Ne 5:7-19. Jb 31:13-
25. Lk 3:12-14. 19:8. Ja +5:4.
oppressions. or, deceits. Pr 28:16.
shaketh. Ex 23:6-9. Nu 16:15. Dt 10:17.
16:19. 27:25. 1 S 12:3. Je 5:26-28. Mi 7:3, 4.
Mt 26:15. Ac 8:18-23. 2 P 2:14-16.
stoppeth. 1 S 24:4-7. 26:8-11. Jb 31:29-31.
Ps 26:4-6, 9-11. Je 40:15, 16. Ep 5:11-13.
blood. Heb. bloods. Is 1:15mg. 26:21mg. Ge
+4:10mg. 2 K +9:26mg. Pr 1:11.
shutteth. Ps 119:37.

16　shall dwell. Is 32:18. Ps 15:1. 90:1. 91:1-10,
14. 107:41. Pr 1:33. 18:10. Hab 3:19.
high. Heb. heights, or high places. ver. 5. Is
22:16. Dt 28:1. Jg 5:18. Ps +91:14. 102:19.
148:1. Pr 8:2. 9:3. Hab 3:19. Re 3:10.
his place. Is 26:1-5. Ps 18:33.
bread. Ge +3:19. Ps +37:3. Mt 6:11. Lk
12:29-31.
waters. 2 Ch 32:30.

17　eyes. Is 32:1, 2. 37:1. 2 Ch 32:23. Ps 45:2. SS
5:10. Zc 9:17. Mt 17:2. Jn 1:14. 14:21. 17:24.
1 J 3:2.
shall see. Jb +19:27. Ps 17:15.
beauty. S#3308h. Is 3:24. Est 1:11. Ps 45:11.
50:2. Pr 6:25. 31:30. La 2:15. Ezk 16:14, 15,
25. 27:3, 4, 11. 28:7, 12, 17. 31:8. Zc 9:17.
that is very far off. Heb. of far distances. Is
39:3. Ps 31:8. Je 8:19. 2 C 4:18. He 11:13-15.

18　heart. Is 38:9, etc. 1 S 22:33-36. 30:6. 2 K
19:14. 2 Ch 32:17-21. Ps 31:7, 8, 22. 71:20. 2
C 1:8-10. 2 T 3:11.

Where is the scribe. 1 C 1:20.
receiver. Heb. weigher. Ge 23:16. 2 K 15:19, 20. 18:14, 15, 31.
where is he. Is 10:16-19. Ps 48:12, 13.

19 **shall not**. Ex 14:13. Dt 28:49, 50. 2 K 19:32.
fierce. Dt 28:49, 50.
deeper. Is 28:11. Je 5:15. Ezk 3:5, 6. 1 C 14:21.
speech. Ge +11:1.
stammering. *or*, ridiculous. Is 28:11mg. 37:22 (scorn). Jb 21:3. Ps 2:4 (derision). Pr 1:26 (mock). Je 20:7.

20 **Look**. Is 26:1-3. Ps 48:12, 13.
the city. Dt 12:5. Ps 78:68, 69.
solemnities. Is 1:14. 14:13. Ge +17:21. Ex +27:21. Le 23:2.
thine eyes. Ps 46:5. 125:1, 2. 128:5, 6.
quiet habitation. Is 32:17, 18.
a tabernacle. Is 16:5. Am +9:11. Ac 15:16. Re 21:3.
not be taken down. Am +9:15.
not one. Is 37:33. 54:2. Ezk 48:35. Mt 16:18. He 12:28. Re 3:12.
stakes. Ex +27:19.
be removed. Am +9:15.
ever. Jb 4:20 (S#5331h).

21 **the glorious**. Ps 29:3. Ac 7:2. 2 C 4:4-6.
a place. Ps 46:4, 5.
broad rivers and streams. Heb. broad of spaces, *or* hands. Is 22:18mg. Ne 7:4. Ezk 47:1-5. Re 22:1.

22 **the Lord is our judge**. Ps +7:8.
lawgiver. Heb. statute-maker. Dt 33:2. Ne 10:14. Ps 147:19, 20. Ja 4:12.
the Lord is our king. Ps 44:4. 74:12. 89:18. Je 23:5, 6. Zc 9:9. Mt 21:5. 25:31-34, 46. Re 19:16.
he will. Is 12:2. +25:9. Zp 3:15-17. Mt 1:21-23. Lk 2:11. Ac 5:31. T 3:4-6. He 5:9.

23 **Thy tacklings are loosed**. *or*, They have forsaken thy tacklings. ver. 21. Ezk 27:26-34. Ac 27:19, 30-32, 40, 41.
then. ver. 1-4. 2 Ch 20:25. Re 19:17, 18.
prey. 2 K 7:16.
the lame. 1 S 30:10, 22-24. 2 K 7:8. 19:35. Ps 68:12. 1 C 1:27.

24 **the inhabitant**. Is 58:8. Dt 7:15. 28:27. 2 Ch 30:20. Ps +103:3. Ezk 47:6, 7, 12. Re 21:4. 22:2.
shall be forgiven. Ex 23:21. +34:7. Je +31:34.

ISAIAH 34

1 **Come**. Is 18:3. 33:13. 41:1. 43:9. 49:1. Jg 5:3, 31. Ps 49:1, 2. 50:1. 96:10. Mk 16:15, 16. Re 2:7.
let the. Is 1:2. Dt 4:26. 32:1. Je 22:29. Mi 6:1, 2.
all that is therein. Heb. the fulness thereof. Ps 24:1. 1 C 10:26, 28.

2 **the indignation**. Is 24:1, etc. +66:14. Je 25:15-29. Jl 3:9-14. Am ch. 1. 2:1-6. Zp 3:8. Zc 14:3, 12-16. Ro 1:18. Re 6:12-17. 14:15-20. 19:15-21. 20:9, 15.
and his. Is 30:27-30. Na 1:2-6.
destroyed. or, devoted. ver. 5. Is 3:4. 8:18. 11:15. 22:22. Le 27:29. Nu 21:2. Jsh 6:17mg. Jg 21:11. Ezr 10:8mg.
hath delivered. Je 27:2-6. Re 16:14.

3 **slain**. Is 66:24. Je +7:33.
and the mountains. ver. 7. Ezk 32:5, 6. Re 14:20. 16:3, 4.

4 **all the host**. Is 14:12. Ps 102:25, 26. Mt +24:29. 2 P 3:7-12. Re 20:11.
leaf falleth. Is 24:6, 13. 1 Th 4:15, 17. He +12:26.

5 **my sword**. Ps 17:13. Je +12:12.
bathed. Heb. *ravah*, S#7301h. ver. 7mg. Is 16:9. Ps 36:8. 65:10. Pr 5:19mg. Je 46:10.
upon Idumea. i.e. *earthy*, S#123h. ver. 6. Ezk 25:12-14. 35:15. 36:5. or, Edom. Je +49:7-22.
the people. Dt 27:15. 29:18-21. Mt 25:41. 1 C 16:22. Ga 3:10. 2 P 2:14.
my curse. ver. 2. Is 43:28. Le 27:29. Zc 14:11. Ml 4:6.

6 **sword**. Dt +32:41.
filled. Is 63:3. Je 49:13. Ezk 21:4, 5, 10.
the fat. Dt 32:14.
the Lord hath. ver. 5. Is 63:1. Ps 37:20. Je 50:27. 51:40. Ezk 39:17-20. Zp 1:7. Re 19:17, 18.
Bozrah. Is 63:1-3.
great slaughter. Jl 3:13, 14. Re 14:19, 20.
Idumea. ver. +5.

7 **unicorns**. *or*, rhinoceroses. Nu 23:22. 24:8. Dt 33:17. Jb 39:9, 10. Ps 92:10.
the bullocks. Ps 68:30. Je 46:21. 50:11, 27.
soaked. *or*, drunken. ver. 3, 5. Is +43:24mg.
with blood. Ezk 32:5, 6.
fatness. S#2459h. ver. 6. Is 1:11. 43:24. Ge 4:4. 45:18. Ex 23:18. Le 3:3, 4, 9, 17, etc. Nu 18:12. Dt 32:14, 38. Jg 3:22. 1 S 15:22. Jb 15:27. Ps 17:10. 63:5. 73:7. 81:16mg. 119:70. 147:14mg. Ezk 34:3. 39:19. 44:7, 15.

8 **the day**. Is 26:21. 35:4. 49:26. 59:17, 18. 61:2. 63:4. Dt 32:35, 41-43. Ps 94:1. Je +46:10. Ezk +30:3. Mi 6:1. Lk 18:7. Ro 2:5, 8, 9. 1 Th +5:2. 2 Th 1:6-10. Re 6:10, 11. 9:15. 18:20. 19:2.
vengeance. Is +61:2. +63:4. Dt +32:35. Ezk +30:3.
year of recompences. Is 63:4. Ho +9:7.
Zion. Ps 102:13, 16.

9 **the streams**. Is 11:15. 27:12. 30:28.
pitch. S#2203h. Ex 2:3.
brimstone. Re +9:17.

10 **shall not**. Mt +3:12.
the smoke. Re 14:10, +11.
from. Is 13:20. Ezk 29:11. Ml 1:3, 4.

for ever. Heb. *olam*, Ex +12:24.
and ever. Jb +4:20 (**S#5331h**, doubled here).

11 **cormorant**. *or*, pelican. Is 13:20-22. 14:23.
Zp 2:14. Re 18:2, 21-23.
stretch. 2 S 8:2. 2 K 21:13. La 2:8. Ml 1:3, 4.
the line. Zc 1:16.
confusion. Heb. *tohu*. Ge 1:2.
emptiness. Heb. *bohu*. Ge 1:2. Je 4:23.

12 **call**. Is 3:6-8. Ec 10:16, 17.
nothing. Is 41:24. 1 C +8:4. 13:2. 2 C 12:11.

13 **thorns**. Is 32:13, 14. Jb +30:7.
an habitation. Is +13:21, 22. 35:7. Je 9:11.
10:22. 49:33. 50:39, 40. 51:37. Ml 1:3. Re
18:2, 20-24.
owls. *or*, ostriches. Heb. daughters of the owl.
Is 13:21mg. 43:20mg. Jb +30:29.

14 **The wild beasts of the desert**. Heb. *Ziim*. Is
13:21mg.
the wild beasts of the island. Heb. *Ijim*. Is
13:22mg.
satyr. *or*, goat. lit. "hairy one." **S#8163h**. Is
13:21. Ge 27:11, 23. 37:31 (kid). Le 4:23, 24
(goat). 2 Ch 11:15 (devils).
screech owl. *or*, night-monster.

15 **nest**. Ps 104:17. Je 48:28. Ezk 31:6.
lay. lit. "letteth escape." Is 46:4.
hatch. lit. "cleave." Ne 9:11.
gather under. Je 17:11.
the vultures. Dt 14:13.

16 **Seek**. Is 1:17. 8:19, +20. 28:13. 55:16. Dt
31:21. Jsh 1:8. Pr 23:12. Da 10:21. Am 3:7.
Ml 3:16. Mt 4:10. Mk +12:24. Jn +5:39.
10:35. Ac 17:3, 11. 2 T 3:15. 2 P 1:19.
book. roll or scroll. ver. 4. Is 19:11. 30:8. Ex
+17:14. Da 9:2. 2 T +3:16.
read. lit. "call." Is 8:3 (call). 12:4mg. 29:11,
12. 40:2 (cry), 6. 55:6. 58:1. Dt 17:19. Ac
8:28. Re 1:3.
no one. Is 55:11. Mt 5:18. Lk 21:33.
shall fail. Is 40:26.
want her mate. 1 S 20:6. 25:15.
my mouth. Is 46:10. Ge 6:17. Nu 23:19. Ps
33:6, 9.
spirit. Heb. *ruach*, Ex 15:8.

17 **he hath cast**. Jsh +14:2. 18:8.
divided. Dt 32:8, 9. Ps 78:55. Ac 13:19.
17:26.
they shall. ver. 10. Is 13:20-22. Ps +72:5.
for ever. Heb. *olam*, Ex +12:24.

ISAIAH 35

1 **wilderness**. Is 29:17. 32:15, 16. 40:3. 51:3.
52:9, 10. Ezk 36:35.
be glad. Dt 28:63. 30:9. Ps 48:11. 97:8. Je
32:41. Re 19:1-7.
desert. Is 4:2. 27:6. 55:12, 13. 61:10, 11.
66:10-14. Ho 14:5, 6.

2 **blossom abundantly**. Is 25:6. 41:18. 60:5-7,
13. Ps 72:16. Jl 2:21-26. 3:18. Ac +3:21.

and rejoice. Is 42:10-12. 49:13. 55:12, 13. 1
Ch 16:33. Ps 65:12, 13. 89:12. 96:11-13. 98:7-
9. 148:9-13. Zc 10:7. Ro 10:15. 15:10. Re
14:2, 3.
the glory. Is 33:9. 41:19. 60:13, 21. 61:3.
65:8-10. Ps 72:16. Ho 14:6, 7.
the excellency. Is 60:13. Ezk 34:25, 26. Am
9:13-15. Mi 7:14, 15. Zp 3:19, 20. Zc 14:20,
21. Ac 4:32, 33.
Sharon. i.e. *a great plain*, **S#8289h**. Is 33:9.
65:10. Jsh 12:18. 1 Ch 5:16. 27:29. SS 2:1.
they shall. Is +40:5. 66:18, 19. Ps 50:2. Jn
17:24.

3 **Strengthen**. Is 40:1, 2. 52:1, 2. 57:14-16. Jg
7:11. Jb 4:3, 4. 16:5. Lk 22:32, 43. Ac 18:23.
He 12:12.

4 **fearful**. Heb. hasty. Is 28:16. 32:4mg. Ps
116:11. Hab 2:3.
Be strong. Jsh +1:6.
fear not. Is 44:2. Ge +15:1. Jn *12:15*. Re 2:10.
behold. Is 25:9. 26:20, 21. 40:9, 10. 52:7-10.
61:2. 64:1, 2. 66:15. Dt 32:35-43. Ps 50:3.
96:13. Da 7:13, 14, 18, 22, 27. Ho 1:7. Mi 1:3.
Hab 2:3. Hg 2:7. Zc 2:8-10. 14:5. Ml 3:1. Mt
1:21-23. Mt +11:3. Lk 21:28. T 2:13. He 9:28.
10:37, 38. Ja 5:7-9. Ju 14, 15. Re 1:7. 22:20.
with vengeance. Dt +32:35.

5 **the eyes**. Ps +119:18. Mt +11:5. Jn 11:47. Ac
9:17, 18. Ep 5:14.
the ears. Is +29:18. 48:8. Jb 33:16. Pr 20:12.
Je 6:10. Mk 9:25, 26.

6 **shall the lame**. Mt +11:5. Jn 5:8, 9.
the tongue. Is 32:4. Ps 51:15. Mt +9:33. Lk
1:64. Col 3:16.
for. Is 41:17, 18. 43:19, 20. 48:21. 49:10, 11.
Ex 17:6. Nu 20:11. Ne 9:15. Ps 46:4. 78:15,
16. Ezk 47:1-11. Zc 14:8. Jn 7:37-39. Re 22:1,
17.

7 **the parched**. Is 29:17. 44:3, 4. Mt 21:43. Lk
13:29. Jn 4:14. 7:38. 1 C +6:9-11.
springs. Is 41:18. 43:20. 44:3, 4. 49:10. Je
31:12. Jn 7:38, 39. Re 22:17.
in the habitation. Is 34:13. Ho 1:10, 11. Ac
26:18. 1 J 5:19, 20. Re 12:9-12. 18:2. 20:2, 3.
grass with reeds. *or*, a court for reeds, etc. Is
19:6.

8 **an highway**. Is 11:16. 19:23. 40:3, 4. 42:16.
49:11, 12. 57:14. 62:10. Je 31:21. Jn 14:6. He
10:20-23.
The way. Is 7:3. 59:8. Ep 2:10. 1 Th 4:7. 2 T
1:9. T 2:11-14. He 10:19-22. 12:14. 1 P 1:14,
15. 2:9, 10.
the unclean. Is 52:1, 11. 60:21. Ezk 43:12.
44:9. Jl 3:17. Zc 14:20, 21. Jn 14:6. 2 P 3:13.
Re 21:27.
but it shall be for those. *or*, for he *shall be*
with them. Is 49:10. Ps 23:4. Mt 1:23. Re
7:15-17.
the wayfaring. Is 30:21. Ps 19:7. 25:8, 9.
119:130. Pr +4:18. 8:8, 9, 20. Je 32:39, 40.

50:4, 5. Jn 7:17. 1 J 2:20, 27.

not err. Nu 35:32. Dt +27:8. Pr +8:8, 9. Je 31:21. Hab 2:2. Lk 10:21. Ja 2:5.

9 **No lion**. Is 11:6-9. 65:25. Le +26:6. 1 P 5:8. Re 20:1-3.

but. Is +43:1.

10 **the ransomed**. Is 51:10, 11. Jb 33:24. Ho 13:14. Mt 20:28. 1 T 2:5, 6.

and come. Ps 84:7. Je 31:11-14. 33:11. Jn 16:22. Ju 21. Re 14:1-4. 15:2-4. 18:20. 19:1-7.

with songs. Zc +2:10.

everlasting. Heb. *olam*, Ge +17:7.

joy. Is 25:8. 52:9. 65:18, 19. Zp 3:14-17.

heads. Jg +5:30.

and gladness. Ps 51:8.

and sorrow. Is +65:19.

ISAIAH 36

1 **it came**. 2 K 18:13, 17. 2 Ch 32:1.

that Sennacherib. Is 1:7, 8. 7:17. 8:7, 8. 10:28-32. 33:7, 8. This account is parallel to 2 K 18:13-20:19 and 2 Ch 32:1-33.

2 A.M. 3294. B.C. 710.

sent. 2 K 18:17, etc. 2 Ch 32:9, etc. Is 7:3. 22:9-11.

great. 2 K 6:14mg.

upper pool. or, blessing. Is 7:3. 2 K 18:17.

fuller's. or, washerman. Is 7:3. 2 K 18:17.

3 **Eliakim**. Is 22:15-21.

house. Ge +7:1.

Shebna. 2 S 8:16, 17. 20:24, 25.

scribe. *or*, secretary. 2 S 8:17mg. 2 K 18:18mg. 22:3. Je 52:25.

Joah. i.e. *whose helper is Jehovah*, **S#3098h**. 2 K 18:18, 26, 37. 1 Ch 6:21. 26:4. 2 Ch 29:12. 34:8. Is 36:3, 11, 22.

recorder. or, remembrancer. ver. 22. 2 S +8:16mg.

4 **Thus saith**. Is 10:8-14. 37:11-15. Pr 16:18. Ezk 31:3, etc. Da 4:30. Ac 12:22, 23. Ju 16.

the great king. Ps 47:2.

Assyria. Ge +2:14.

What. 2 K 18:5, 19, etc. 19:10. 2 Ch 32:7-10, 14-16. Ps 42:3, 10. 71:10, 11.

trustest. Ps 121:3. 125:1, 2. 127:1. 130:5-8.

5 **vain words**. Heb. a word of lips. Jg +7:22mg. Pr 14:23.

I have counsel and strength for war. *or, but* counsel and strength are for the war. Pr +21:30, 31. 24:5, 6.

that. 2 K 18:7, 19, 20. 24:1. Ne 2:19, 20. Je 52:3. Ezk 17:15.

6 **thou trustest**. Is 20:5, 6. 30:1-7. 31:3. 2 K 17:4. 18:21. Je 37:5-8. Ezk 29:6, 7.

7 **We trust**. 2 K 18:5, 22. 1 Ch 5:20. 2 Ch 16:7-9. 32:7, 8. Ps 18:1, 2, 50. 22:4, 5. 42:5, 10, 11.

is it not. 2 K +21:3. 2 Ch 30:14. 1 C 2:15.

8 **pledges**. *or*, hostages. 2 K 14:14.

and I. Is 10:13, 14. 1 S 17:40-43. 1 K 20:10, 18. 2 K 18:23. Ne 4:2-5. Ps 20:7, 8. 123:3, 4.

9 **face**. Ge +3:19.

the least. Is 10:8. 2 K 18:24.

and put. ver. 6. Is 30:16, 17. 31:1, 3. Dt 17:16. Ps 20:7, 8. Pr 21:31. Je 2:36.

10 **am I now**. Is 10:5-7. 37:28. 1 K 13:18. 2 K 18:25. 2 Ch 35:21. Ps 94:20. 115:2-4. Da 3:15, 17. Am +3:6. Jn 19:11.

11 **in the Syrian**. 2 K 18:26, 27. Dt 28:49. Ezr 4:7. Je 5:15. Da 2:4.

in the Jews' language. Is 19:18.

12 **that sit upon**. 2 K 18:27.

that they may. Is 9:20. Le 26:29. Dt 28:53-57. 2 K 6:25-29. 31:18. Je 19:9. La 4:9, 10. Ezk 4:16.

13 **cried**. 1 S 17:8-11. 2 K 18:28-32. 2 Ch 32:18. Ps 17:10-13. 73:8, 9. 82:6, 7.

Hear. ver. 4. Is 8:7. 10:8-13. Ezk 31:3-10. Da 4:37.

14 **Let not**. Is 37:10-13. 2 K 19:10-13, 22. 2 Ch 32:11, 13-19. Da 3:15-17. 6:20. 7:25. 2 Th 2:4. Re 13:5, 6.

15 **make you trust**. ver. 7. Is 37:23, 24. Ps 4:2. 22:7, 8. 71:9-11. Da 3:14, 15. Mt 27:43.

16 **Make an agreement with me by a present**. *or*, Seek my favor *by* a present. Heb. Make with me a blessing. Jg +3:15.

come out. 1 S 11:3. 2 K 24:12-16.

eat ye. 1 K 4:20, 25. Mi 4:4. Zc 3:10.

cistern. Heb. *bor*, Ge +37:20.

17 **I come**. 2 K 17:6, etc. 18:9-12. 24:11. Pr 12:10.

a land of corn. Ge +27:28. Ex 3:8. Dt 8:7-9. 11:12. Jb 20:17. The other copy in 2 K 18:32, adds here, "a land of oil olive, and of honey; that ye may live, and not die: and hearken not unto Hezekiah when he seduceth you."

wine. Ge +27:28.

and vineyards. Ge +18:27.

18 **lest**. ver. 7, 10, 15. Is 37:10. Ps 12:4. 92:5-7. **Hath**. Is 37:12, 13, 17, 18. 2 K 18:33-35. 19:12, 13, 17, 18. 2 Ch 32:13-17. Ps 115:2-8. 135:5, 6, 15-18. Je 10:3-5, 10-12. Da 3:15. Hab 2:19, 20.

gods of the nations. Jg 11:24. 1 K 20:23.

19 **Hamath**. Nu +13:21.

Arphad. i.e. *firmly laid; resting place*, **S#774h**. 2 K 18:34. 19:13. Is 10:9, Arpad. 36:19, 37:13. Je 49:23, Arpad. Ezk +27:8, Arvad.

Sepharvaim. 2 K 17:24.

and have. Is 10:10, 11. 2 K 17:5-7. 18:10-12.

20 **that the Lord**. Is 37:18, 19, 23-29. 45:16, 17. Ex 5:2. 2 K 19:22, etc. 2 Ch 32:15, 19. Jb 15:25, 26. 40:9-12. Ps 50:21. 73:9. Da 3:15.

21 **they held**. Ps +38:13-15. Pr 9:7. 26:4. Mt +7:6.

22 **Then came**. 2 K 18:37.

Eliakim. ver. 3, 11.

recorder. ver. 3mg. 2 S +8:16mg.
with their. Is 29:2. 2 K +18:37.

ISAIAH 37

1 **it came**. 2 K 19:1, etc.
he rent. 2 K +18:37.
sackcloth. Jb +16:15.
and went. Ezr 9:5. Jb 1:20, 21. Ps 26:8.
73:16, 17. 122:1, 9. 134:1, 2. Da 6:10.
the house. 1 K 8:26-30. 9:3.

2 **sent Eliakim**. ver. 14. 2 K +18:18. 22:12-14.
2 Ch +20:20. Ps 50:15. 91:15. Ja 5:16-18. Jl
1:13.
elders of the priests. 2 K 19:2. Je 19:1.

3 **This day**. Is 25:8. 33:2. 2 K 19:3. 2 Ch 15:4.
Ps 50:15. 91:15. 116:3, 4. Je 30:7. Ho 5:15.
6:1. Re 3:19.
blasphemy. *or*, provocation. Ps 95:8mg.
120:2, 3. 123:3, 4.
for the. Is 26:17, 18. 66:9. Ho 13:13.

4 **It may**. Jsh 14:12. 1 S 14:6. 2 S 16:12. Am
5:15.
to reproach. ver. +23, 24. Is 36:20. 1 S
17:26, 36. 2 Ch 32:15-19.
living. Je +10:10.
and will. ver. 23. Ps 50:21.
lift up. 1 S 7:8. 12:19, 23. 2 Ch 32:20. Ps
106:23. 120:1. 123:1-3. 130:1, 2. Jl 2:17. Ja
5:16.
for the. Is 8:7, 8. 2 K 17:18. 18:9-16. 2 Ch
28:19. Je 33:3. Ezk 36:37. Mi +5:3.
left. Heb. found. Est +1:5mg.

6 **Thus shall**. 2 K 19:5-7. 22:15-20.
Be not. Is 7:4. 10:24, 25. 35:4. 41:10-14.
43:1, 2. 51:12, 13. Ex 14:13, 14. Le 26:8. Jsh
11:6. 2 Ch 20:15-20. Mk 4:40. 5:36.

7 **I will**. Is 10:16-18, 33, 34. 17:13, 14. 29:5-8.
30:28-33. 31:8, 9. 33:10-12. Jb 4:9. Ps 58:9.
Je +49:14.
send a blast upon him. *or*, put a spirit into
him. Heb. *ruach*, Ex +15:8.
I will cause. ver. 36-38. 2 Ch 32:21.

8 **Rabshakeh**. 2 K 19:8, 9. Nu 33:20, 21.
Libnah. Nu +33:20.
Lachish. Jsh +10:3.

9 **he heard**. 1 S 23:27, 28.
Ethiopia. Ge +2:13. 2 K 17:30.

10 **Let not**. Is 36:4, 15, 20. 2 K 18:5. 19:10-13. 2
Ch 32:7, 8, 15-19. Ps 22:8. Mt 27:43.

11 **thou hast heard**. ver. 18, 19. Is 10:7-14.
14:17. 36:18-20. 2 K 17:4-6. 18:33-35.

12 **the gods**. Is 36:18, 20. 46:5-7.
Gozan. 2 K +17:6.
Haran. Ge +11:26.
Eden. Am +1:5.
Telassar. i.e. *hill of Assur; Assyrian hill; weari-*
ness of the prince, **S#8515h**. 2 K 19:12. Ge 14:1. 2
K 19:12, Thelasar.

13 **Hamath**. Nu +13:21.

Hena. i.e. *shaken*, **S#2012h**. 2 K 18:34. 19:13.
Ivah. 2 K 17:24, 30, 31, Ava, Avites. +18:34.
19:13.

14 **received**. 2 K 19:14.
and Hezekiah went. ver. 1. 1 K 8:28-30, 38,
44, 45. 9:3. 2 Ch 6:20, etc. Ps 27:5. 62:1-3.
74:10, 11. 76:1-3. 123:1-4. 143:6. Jl 2:17-20.
and spread. 1 S 23:4.

15 **prayed**. 1 S 7:8, 9. 2 S 7:18-29. 2 K 19:15-19.
2 Ch 14:11. 20:5-12, 22. Da 9:3, 4. Ph 4:6,
7. Ja 5:13.

16 **Lord**. Ps +24:10.
dwellest. 1 S +4:4. He 4:16.
thou art. ver. 20. Is 43:10, 11. 44:6. 45:22.
54:5. 1 K 18:39. 2 K 5:15. Ps 86:10. Re 11:15-
17.
hast made. Ps 121:1, 2. 123:1. 124:8. 134:3.
Jn +1:3.

17 **Incline**. Jb 36:7. Ps +17:6.
hear. ver. 4. 2 S 16:12. Ps 10:14, 15. 74:10,
22. 79:12. 83:1-4, 17, 18. 89:50, 51. 93:3, 4.
open. Zc +12:4.

18 **the kings**. 2 K 15:29. 16:9. 17:5, 6, 24. 1 Ch
5:26. Na 2:11, 12.
laid waste. 2 K 19:17. Je 51:36.
nations. Heb. lands.

19 **And have**. Is 10:9-11. 36:18-20. 46:1, 2. Ps
86:8. 89:6. 96:5, 6. Je 10:15, 16.
cast. Heb. given. Is 36:8. 61:3.
fire. Dt +7:5.
no gods. Is 40:19-21. 41:7. 44:9, 10, 17. Ps
115:4-8. Je 10:2-6, 11. Ho 8:6. 1 C +8:4.

20 **that all**. Is 42:8. Ex 9:15, 16. Jsh 7:8, 9. 1 S
17:45-47. 1 K 8:43. 18:36, 37. Ps 46:10.
59:13. 67:1, 2. 83:17, 18. Ezk 36:23. Ml 1:11.
even. ver. 16.
thou only. Is 43:11. Dt +6:4. +32:39. Ps
83:18. 86:10. Mk 12:29. Jn 20:17. 1 C 8:6. Ep
1:17. 4:5, 6. 1 T 2:5.

21 **Whereas**. Is 38:3-6. 58:9. 65:24. Ge 32:28. 2
S 15:31. 17:23. 2 K 19:20, 21. Jb 22:27. Ps
91:15. Da 9:20-23. Ac 4:31. 1 Th 5:17. Ja
5:16. 1 J 5:14, 15.

22 **The virgin**. Ge +24:16. Je +18:13. Ezk 16:35.
the daughter. Nu +21:25. Mt +21:5.
hath despised. Is 8:9, 10. 1 S 17:36, 44-47.
Ps 2:2-4. 27:1-3. 31:18. 46:1-7. Jl 3:9-12.
shaken. Ps 105:14, 15. Je +18:16.

23 **Whom hast**. ver. 4, 10-13. Ex 5:2. Le +24:11.
Ps +31:11. 73:9. Re 13:1-6.
against whom. Is 10:13-15. 14:13, 14. Ex
9:17. Pr 30:13. Ezk 28:2, 9. Da 5:20-23. 7:25.
2 Th 2:4.
the Holy One. Is +1:4. Ex 15:11.

24 **By thy**. Heb. By the hand of thy. 1 K
+16:12mg. 2 K 14:25. 19:23mg.
servants. ver. 4. Is 36:15-20. 2 K 19:22, 23.
By the. Is 10:13, 14. 36:9. Ex 15:9. Ps 20:7.
Da 4:30.
Lebanon. Is 14:8.

tall cedars thereof, and the choice fir trees thereof. Heb. tallness of the cedars thereof *and* the choice of the trees thereof. Is 10:18. 14:8. Ezk 31:3, etc. Da 4:8-14, 20-22. Zc 11:1, 2.

of his Carmel. *or, and* his fruitful field. Is 29:17. Jsh +19:26.

25 **digged**. 2 K 19:24.

with the sole. Is 36:12. 1 K 20:10. 2 K 19:23, 24.

my feet. Dt +11:10. Pr 21:1.

dried up. Is 19:5. 44:12. 51:17. Ex 17:6.

rivers. arms, or canals. Is 19:6. Mi 7:12.

besieged. *or*, fenced and closed. Is +27:12. 2 K 19:24mg. 2 Ch 32:10mg. Ps 31:21mg. 60:9mg. Je 10:17. Mi 7:12. Zc 9:3.

26 **long ago**, etc. *or, how* I have made it long ago, *and* formed it of ancient times? Should I now bring it to be laid waste, *and* defenced cities *to be* ruinous heaps?

how I. Is +10:5, 6, 15. 45:7. 46:10, 11. Ge 50:20. Ps 17:13. 76:10. Am +3:6. Ac 2:23. 4:27, 28. 15:18. 1 P 2:8. Ju 4.

ancient. Mi +5:2.

formed. or, purposed. Is 10:5, 15. 30:32.

lay waste. Is 54:16. 2 K 19:25.

defenced cities. Is 25:2.

ruinous heaps. Is 10:30. 25:2. 37:26. 48:18.

27 **their inhabitants**. Is 19:16. Nu 14:9. 2 K 19:26. Ps 127:1, 2. Je 5:10. 37:10.

of small power. Heb. short of hand. Jb 14:1. Pr 14:17, 29.

as the grass of. 1 P +1:24.

28 **I know**. Ps 139:2-11. Pr 5:21. 15:3. Je 23:23, 24. Jn +2:24, 25. Ac 1:24. He 4:12, 13. Re 2:13.

abode. *or*, sitting. Is 40:22. 44:13.

going out. Nu +27:17. Is 13:10. Ge 8:7. 12:4.

coming in. Is 2:21. 13:22. 14:9.

29 **rage**. ver. 10. Is 36:4, 10. 2 K 19:27, 28. Jb 15:25, 26. Ps 2:1-3. 46:6. 93:3, 4. Na 1:9-11. Jn 15:22, 23. Ac 9:4.

tumult. Ps 74:4, 28. 83:2. Am 6:1. Mt 27:24. Ac 22:22.

will I. Is 30:28. Jb 41:2. Ps 32:9. 92:5-8. Ezk 29:4. 38:4. Am 4:2.

turn thee back. Ps 129:4, 5.

30 **this shall**. Is +7:14. 38:7. Ex 3:12. 1 K 13:3-5. 2 K 19:29. 20:9.

Ye shall. Is 7:21-25. Le 25:4, 5, 20-22. Ps 126:5, 6. 128:2.

groweth of itself. Le 25:5, 11. 2 K 19:29. Jb 14:19.

third year. Is 20:3.

31 **remnant that is escaped of the house of Judah**. Heb. escaping of the house of Judah that remaineth. Is 6:13. Je 44:28. Mi +5:3.

shall. 2 K 19:30-34. Ps 121:2-8. 124:1-3, 6. 125:2. 126:2, 3. 127:1.

take root. Is 11:1, 10. 27:6. 65:9. 2 K 19:30,

31. Ps 80:9. Je 30:19. Ga 3:29. Re 22:16.

upward. Zc 3:8. 6:12. Jn 15:5.

32 **a remnant**. Ro 11:5.

they that escape. Heb. the escaping.

the zeal. ver. 20. Is +9:7. Ex 20:5. Nu 25:11. Jl 2:18. Zc 1:14.

33 **He**. Is 8:7-10. 10:32-34. 17:12, 14. 33:20. 2 K 19:32-35. Da 4:34, 35.

shields. Heb. shield. 2 K 19:32.

cast. Ezk 21:22. Lk 19:43, 44.

34 **the way**. ver. 29. Pr +21:30.

35 **I will**. Is 31:5. 38:6. 2 K 20:6.

for mine. Is +48:9.

and for. 1 K 11:12, 13, 36. 15:4. Je 23:5, 6. 30:9. 33:15, 16. Ezk 37:24, 25.

my servant. Is 41:8. 42:1.

David's sake. Is +9:7. 2 S 23:1, 5. Ps 132:1, 10. Je +33:20, 21. Lk 1:31-33.

36 **the angel**. Is 10:12, 16-19, 33, 34. 17:13, 14. 29:7, 8. 30:30-33. 31:8. 33:10-12. Ex 12:23. 2 S 24:16. 2 K 19:35. 1 Ch 21:12, 16. 2 Ch 32:21, 22. Jb 4:9. Ps 35:5, 6. 73:18, 19. 90:5, 6. 92:1. 98:1. Ac 12:23.

and when. Ex 12:30. Jb 20:5-7. 24:24. Ps 46:6-11. 76:5-7. 1 Th 5:2, 3.

37 **Sennacherib**. ver. 7, 29. Is 31:9.

Nineveh. Ge +10:11.

38 **his god**. ver. 10. Is 14:9, 12. 36:15, 18. 2 K 19:36, 37. 2 Ch 32:14, 19, 21.

smote him. Is 14:12. Ps 94:20-23.

Armenia. Heb. Ararat. Ge 8:4. Je 51:27.

Esar-haddon. Ezr 4:2.

ISAIAH 38

1 A.M. 3291. B.C. 713.

was Hezekiah. 2 K 20:1-11. 2 Ch 32:24.

sick unto death. 2 K 13:14. Ps 107:18. Jn 11:1-5. Ac 9:37. Ph 2:27-30. 2 T +4:20.

And Isaiah. Is 37:21. 39:3, 4.

Set thine house in order. Heb. Give charge concerning thy house. 2 S 17:23mg. 2 K 20:1mg. Ec +9:10. Lk 9:61.

for thou. Je 18:7-10. Jon 3:4, 10.

2 **turned**. 1 K 8:30. Ps 50:15. 91:15, 16. Mt 6:6.

and prayed. Is 37:4, 14. 39:2.

3 **Remember**. Ne 5:19. 13:14, 22, 31. Ps 18:20-27. 20:1-3. He 6:10.

I have. Ge +17:1. 2 Ch 31:20, 21. Jb 23:11, 12. Ps 16:8. 18:23, 24. 32:2. Jn 1:47. 2 C 1:12. 1 J 3:21, 22.

in truth. 2 J 4. 3 J 3, 4.

a perfect heart. 2 K +20:3. Ps 101:2. 119:80. 2 C 13:9.

have done. 2 Ch 31:20, 21.

good. Ne 13:14.

wept. Ps +56:8.

sore. Heb. with great weeping. 2 K +20:3mg.

5 **and say**. 2 S 7:3-5. 1 Ch 17:2-4.

God. Is 7:13, 14. 1 K 8:25. 9:4, 5. 11:12, 13.

15:4. 2 Ch 34:3. Ps 89:3, 4. Mt 22:32.

of David. Is +55:3. 2 S +7:15. Ps +89:28, 33, 37. +132:11. Ac +13:34. Ro +11:1, 2, 29.

I have heard. Is 65:24. 2 K 19:20. 20:5. Ps 34:5, 6. 55:1. Da 9:21, 22. Mt 7:7, 8. Lk 1:13. 1 J 5:14, 15.

I have seen. Ps +56:8. 147:3.

I will. Jb 14:5. Ps 116:15. Ac 27:24.

6   **I will deliver**. Is 10:12. 12:6. 14:25. 31:4. 37:35. 2 Ch 32:22. 2 T 4:17.

I will defend. Is 31:5. Lk 18:7, 8.

7   **this shall be a sign**. ver. 22. Is 7:10-14. 37:30. Ge 9:13. Jg 6:17-22, 37-39. 2 K 20:8, etc.

8   **I will bring**. Jsh 10:12-14. 2 K 20:11. 2 Ch 32:24, 31. Mt 16:1.

the sun dial. Heb. the degrees by, *or*, with the sun.

9   **writing**. Is 12:1, etc. Ex 15:1, etc. Jg 5:1, etc. 1 S 2:1-10. Ps 18, title. 30:11, 12. 107:17-22. 116:1-4. 118:18, 19. Jon 2:1-9.

he had. Dt 32:39. 1 S 2:6. Jb 5:18. Ho 6:1, 2.

10   **in the cutting off of my days**. ver. 1. Jb 6:11. 7:7. 17:11-16. Ps 31:22. 88:1-7. 130:1. 2 C 1:9.

the gates. Ge +14:7; Ge +15:15. Jb +38:17.

grave. Heb. *sheol*, Ge 37:35. Jb +14:13. Ps +16:10. 30:3. 139:8.

deprived. Jb 17:11, 15. 2 C 1:9.

residue. Is 40:24. 65:15, 20. 1 S 25:38. Ps 37:22, 28. 90:10, 12. +102:24. Ec 3:2. Mt 8:29. Jn 7:8, 30. 1 C 11:30, 32.

11   **I shall not**. Jb 35:14, 15. Ps 6:4, 5. 31:22. Ec +9:5, 6.

see. or, appear before. Is 1:12. Ex 23:15. 34:20.

the land of the living. Jb 28:15. Ps +27:13.

behold man. Ps 88:8, 9, 18.

12   **departed**. Ja 4:14.

is removed. Jb 4:19. 7:7. Ps 89:45-47. 102:11, 23, 24. 2 C 5:1.

as a. Is 1:8. 13:20.

I have Jb 7:6. 9:25, 26. 14:2. Ja 4:14.

cut off. or, rolled up. Is 34:4. 2 T 4:7. He 1:12.

he will cut. Jb 6:9. 7:3-5. 17:1. Ps 31:22. 32:4. 109:23.

with pining sickness. *or*, from the thrum. i.e. the ends of the threads by which the web is fastened to the beam. or, loom.

from day. Jb 4:20. Ps 73:14.

13   **as a lion**. Is +5:29. 1 K 13:24-26. 20:36. Jb 16:12-14. Ps 39:10. 50:22. 51:8. 1 C 11:30-32.

break. Jb 9:17. 30:17. Ps +2:9. 10:10mg. 51:8. La 3:4.

from day. ver. 12. Jb 4:20. Ps 88:13. 130:6.

an end. Is 27:4, 5. Ps 55:4, 6.

14   **a crane**. Jb 30:29. Ps 102:4-7.

I did mourn. Mt +5:4.

dove. Is 59:11. Le 1:14. Na 2:7. Mt 10:16.

mine eyes. Ps +69:3. 123:1-4. Jn 17:1.

O Lord. Mt 6:9.

I am. Ps 119:122. 143:7.

undertake for me. *or*, ease me. Is 40:29. Jb 17:3. Ps 6:2-4. 61:1, 2. 2 C 12:9, 10.

15   **What**. Jsh 7:8. Ezr 9:10. Ps 39:9, 10. Jn 12:27.

spoken. Mi 6:8. Mt 11:28-30.

himself hath done. Ps 39:9. Ezk 14:23. Mk 7:37. Jn 13:7.

I shall. Ph 4:6, 7. 1 P 5:6, 7.

go softly. 1 K 21:27.

in the bitterness. 1 S +1:10mg. 2 K 4:27. Jb 7:11. 10:1. 21:25.

soul. Heb. *nephesh*, Ge +34:3.

16   **by these**. Is 64:5. Dt 8:3. Jb 33:19-28. Ps 71:20. Mt 4:4. 1 C 11:32. 2 C 4:17. He 12:10, 11.

life of. Ps 119:25, 37, 40, 88, 107, 149, 156, 159. Mt +10:28. 1 C 5:5. He +12:23. Ja 1:18, 21. 2:26. 5:20.

spirit. Heb. *ruach*, Ge +41:8.

so wilt. Is 53:10. Jb 23:10. Ps 119:75. Mt 10:24, 25. 2 C 4:17. He 2:10. 1 P 5:10.

17   **for peace I had great bitterness**. *or*, on my peace *came* great bitterness. Jb 3:25, 26. 29:18. Ps 30:6, 7.

in love to my soul delivered it from the pit. Heb. loved my soul from the pit. Heb. *nephesh*, Ps +30:3. 40:2. 86:13. 88:4-6. Jon 2:6.

delivered. Ge 37:24. Jb 33:24, 28. Ps 40:2. 103:3-5. 118:17, 18. 1 C +15:55-57. Ph 2:27.

pit. Heb. *shachath*, Jb +9:31. 33:18.

thou hast cast. Is 43:25. Ex 34:6, 7. Ps 10:2. 32:1, 2. 51:9. 85:2. Je 31:34. Ezk 18:31. Mi 7:18, 19. Mk 2:5, 6. Ac 5:31. 13:38. Ep 1:7. Col 1:14. Ja 5:15. Re 7:14.

all my sins. Ps 130:4, 7, 8. Je +50:20. 1 J 1:7-9.

behind. Contrast unforgiven sins said to be "before His face." Ps 90:8. 109:14, 15. Je 16:17. Ho 7:2.

18   **the grave**. Heb. *sheol*, Ge +37:35.

cannot praise. Ps 6:5. 30:9. 88:10-12. 115:17, 18. +146:4. Ec +9:5, 6, 10.

they that. Nu 16:33. Pr 14:32. Mt 8:12. 25:46. Lk 16:26-31.

pit. Heb. *bor*, Ge 37:20.

cannot hope. Jb +8:13. 11:20. 27:8. +36:18. Ps 36:12. 112:10. Pr +10:28. 11:7. 14:32. Ezk 16:49, +55, +60. Lk 16:26. Ac 3:21. 2 C 5:11. He +9:27. Ju 7. Re 22:11.

19   **the living**. Ps 103:1, 2. 146:2. Ec +9:10. Jn 9:4.

the father. Ge +18:19. Ex 12:26, 27. +13:8, 14, 15. Dt 4:9, 10. +6:6, 7, 20. Jsh 4:21, 22. Ps 78:3-8. +127:3. 128:3. 145:4. Jl 1:3.

20   **ready to save**. Ps 21:4. 116:9. Jn 11:25.

therefore. Ps 9:13, 14. 27:5, 6. 30:11, 12. 51:15. 66:13-15. 145:2.

we will sing. Is 26:19. Ps 16:11. 33:1. 89:1. 95:1, 2. 101:1. 105:1.

my songs. By Hezekiah: Ps 120, 121, 123, 125, 126, 128, 129, 130, 132; David, Ps 122, 124, 131, 133; Solomon, Ps 127.

to the stringed instruments. ver. 9. Jb 30:9. Ps 4, 61, 67, titles. 69:12. 76, title. 77:6. 150:4. Hab 3:19, 21.

in the house. Ps 122:1, 9. 134:1, 2.

21 **For Isaiah**. 2 K 20:7. Mk 7:33. Jn 9:6.

lump of figs. 1 S 25:18.

22 **What**. 2 K 20:8. Ps 42:1, 2. 84:1, 2, 10-12. 118:18, 19. 122:1. Jn 5:14.

ISAIAH 39

1 A.M. cir. 3292. B.C. cir. 712.

Merodach-baladan. i.e. *baal worshipper; baal is lord; thy rebellion, Merodach is not a lord; death and slaughter, Mars is a worshipper of Baal,* **S#4757h**, only here. 2 K 20:12, etc., Berodach-baladan.

king. Is 13:1, 19. 14:4. 23:13.

sent letters. 2 S 8:10. 10:2. 2 Ch 32:23.

2 **was glad**. 2 Ch 32:25, 31. Jb 31:25. Ps 146:3, 4. Pr 4:23. Je 17:9.

showed. Is 10:13. 14:13. 47:10. 2 K 5:11. 20:13. Ex 5:2. 2 Ch 26:16. 32:25, 27, 31. Est 2:20. 3:5. Pr 11:2. 15:33. 16:18. 18:12. 25:6mg. Da 4:30. 5:23. Ob 3. Lk 12:15-21.

precious things. *or,* spicery. 1 K 10:2, 10, 15, 25. 2 Ch 9:1, 9.

the silver. Dt 17:17.

armor. *or,* jewels. Heb. vessels, *or* instruments. 2 K 19:35. 20:15mg. 2 Ch 32:22, 23, 27.

and all. Is 33:1, 23. 2 K 18:15, 16.

there was. Ec 7:20. 2 C 12:7. 1 J 1:8.

nor in all. Ge +7:19. 1 K 18:10. Mt 5:29.

dominion. 2 K 20:13. 2 Ch 8:6.

3 **came Isaiah**. Is 38:1, 5. 2 S 12:1. 2 K 20:14, 15. 2 Ch 16:7. 19:2. 25:15, 16. Je 22:1, 2.

They are. Dt 28:49. Jsh 9:6, 9. Je 5:15.

4 **All that**. Jsh 7:19. Jb 31:33. Pr 23:5. 28:13. 1 J 1:9.

5 **Hear**. 1 S 13:13, 14. 15:16.

the Lord of hosts. 1 S 1:3.

6 **that all**. Is 46:11. Dt 28:49-51. 2 K 20:17-19. 24:12, 13. 25:13-15. 2 Ch 36:10, 18. Je 20:5. 27:21, 22. 52:17-19. Da 1:2.

7 **of thy sons**. 2 K 24:12. 25:6, 7. 2 Ch 33:11. 36:10, 20. Je 39:7. Ezk 17:12-20.

they shall be. Fulfilled Da 1:2-7.

eunuchs. 2 K +8:6mg.

8 **Good**. Le 10:3. Jg +10:15. La 3:22, 39. Ja 5:10, 11. 1 P 5:6.

For. 2 Ch 32:26. 34:28. Zc 8:16, 19.

ISAIAH 40

1 **comfort**. Is 3:10. 35:3, 4. 41:10-14, 27. 50:10. 57:15-19. 60:1, etc. 62:11, 12. 65:13, 14. Ne 8:10. Ps 85:8. 94:19. Zc +1:17. 9:9. Jn 14:26. 2 C +1:3, 4. 1 Th 4:18. He 6:17, 18.

2 **Speak ye**. Is 49:13. 61:2. 65:16-19. 66:10-13. Re 21:4, 5.

comfortably. Heb. to the heart. Ge +34:3mg.

warfare. *or,* appointed time. 1 Ch +20:1. Ps 102:13, etc. SS 2:11-13. Je 29:11. Da 9:2, 24-27. 11:35. +12:4, 9. Hab 2:3. Ac 1:7. Ga 4:4. Re 6:10, 11. 11:15-18.

that her iniquity. Is 12:1. 43:25. 61:7. Ps +32:5. Je 33:8, 9. 1 C +6:9-11.

double. Ge +43:12. Jb 42:10-12. Da 9:12. Zc 1:15. Ro 5:15, 20. 1 C 2:9. 2 C 4:17, 18. Ga 6:7-9. Ep 3:20.

3 **The voice**. Mt *3:1-3*. Mk *1:2-5*. Lk 3:2-6. Jn *1:23*.

of him. Ml 4:5, 6. Mt 11:10-12.

wilderness. Je +31:2.

Prepare. Is 35:8. 54:17. 62:10, 11. Ml 3:1. 4:5, 6. Mk 1:2-4. Lk 1:16, +17, 76, 77. Jn 1:19-25.

the Lord. Heb. Jehovah. Ne +9:6. Ps 24:7, 10. Jn 5:23. 8:24. 1 C 12:3. 1 P +2:3.

make. Is 43:19. 49:11. Ps 68:4.

desert. Heb. *arabah,* Dt +11:30. Am +6:14.

highway. Is +11:16.

our God. Ps +47:2. Hab +3:3.

4 **valley**. Is 42:11, 15, 16. 1 S 2:8. Ps 113:7, 8. Ezk 17:24. 21:26. Lk 1:52, 53. 3:5. 18:14.

every mountain. Is 2:12-15. Jb 40:11-13.

and the. Is 42:16. 45:2. Pr 2:15. Ac 9:1-22.

straight. *or,* a straight place.

plain. *or,* a plain place.

5 **the glory**. Is 4:5. 6:3. 11:9, 10. 35:2. 58:8. 59:19. 60:1-3, 19. 66:18. Ex +24:16. 33:18. Nu 14:21. 16:19, 42. 1 K 8:11. Ps 72:19, 96:6. 97:6. 102:15, 16. 106:20. Je 2:11. Ezk 39:21. 43:2, 5. 44:4. Hab 2:14. 3:3, 4. Hg 2:3, 7, 9. Lk 2:10-14, 32. Jn 1:14. 2:11. 12:41. 2 C 3:18. 4:6. He +1:3. 1 P 4:14. Re 21:11, 23.

all flesh. Lk 2:32. +3:6. Jn 1:9.

for the mouth. Is 1:20. 58:14. Nu 23:19. Je 9:12. Mi 4:4.

6 **Cry**. ver. 3. Is 12:6. 61:1, 2. Je +2:2. Ezk 33:2-9.

All flesh. 1 P *1:24, 25*.

7 **withereth**. ver. 8. Is 15:6. 19:5.

the flower. 1 P 1:23, 24.

fadeth. ver. 8. Is 24:4. Ps 39:11. Pr 30:32.

spirit. Heb. *ruach,* Ex +15:8.

bloweth upon. Ps 103:16.

8 **the word**. Is 25:1. 46:10, 11. 55:10, 11. Ps 19:9. 93:5. 119:89-91, 142. Zc 1:5, 6. Mt 5:18. 24:35. Mk 13:31. Jn +10:35. 12:34. Ro 3:1-3. 1 P 1:25.

for ever. Heb. *olam,* Ex +12:24.

9 **O Zion, that bringest good tidings**. *or,* O

thou that tellest good tidings to Zion. Is 41:27.
52:7. Ezr 1:1, 2. Lk 24:47. Ro 10:18.
get. Jg 9:7. 1 S 26:13, 14. 2 Ch 13:4.
O Jerusalem, that bringest good tidings.
or, O thou that tellest good tidings to
Jerusalem. Ps +122:6. 128:5.
lift up. Is 52:8. 58:4. Ge +22:13. Je 22:20. Ac
2:14.
be not. Is 35:3, 4. 51:7, 12. Ac 4:13, 29. 5:41,
42. Ep 6:18, 19. Ph 1:28, 29. 1 P 3:14.
Behold. Is +9:6. 12:2. +25:9. Ps +45:6. 47:7,
8. Zc 9:9. 13:7. Jn 1:1, 14. +20:28. 1 C 15:24,
25. Ph 2:5, 6. 1 T 3:16. He +1:6, 8. 1 J 5:20,
21. Re 11:15. 19:16.

10　**the Lord God.** Is +9:6, 7. 59:15-21. 60:1, etc.
Jn 12:13, 15.
will come. Is +35:4. Jn 1:18.
with strong hand. *or,* against the strong. Is
49:24, 25. 53:12. Mt 12:29. He 2:14. 1 J 3:8.
his arm. Ex +15:16. Ps 2:8, 9. 66:3. 110:1, 2,
6. Mt 28:18. Ep 1:20-22. Ph 2:10, 11. Re 2:26,
27. 17:14. 19:11-16. 20:11.
his reward. Is 62:11. Mt +16:27. Lk +14:14.
Re +11:18. 22:12.
with him. Mt 25:10, 31-46. Lk +14:14. Ju
14, 15. Re +11:18.
his work. *or,* recompence for his work. Is
+62:11mg. Ro 2:5, 6. 14:10. 2 C 5:10.

11　**feed.** Is 49:9, 10. 2 S 5:2. 7:7. 1 Ch 11:2. Ps
28:9. 78:71, 72. SS 1:7. Je 3:15. 23:4. Ezk
34:2, 13, 14, 23, 29. Mi 5:4. 7:14. Zc 11:4. Mt
2:6mg. Jn +10:11. 21:15-17. Ac 20:28. 1 P
5:2. Re 7:17.
his flock. Is 63:11. Ezk +34:31. Lk +12:32.
like a shepherd. Zc 13:7. Mt 26:31. Jn
10:11.
he shall gather. Is 42:3. Ge 33:13. Ezk
34:16. Jn 21:15-17. 1 C 3:1, 2.
and carry. Is 46:4. 63:9.
his bosom. Ps 74:11.
gently. Is 42:3. Ge 33:13. Ps 103:14. Mt
11:28. 12:15, 20. He 4:15.
lead. Is 11:1-9. 42:1-4. Mt 12:15, 20. Jn
+10:4, 11-18. He 4:15.
are with young. *or,* give suck. Ps +78:71.

12　**Who hath.** Ps 33:8, 9. 93:1, 2.
measured. Is 48:13. Jb 11:7-9. 38:4-11. Ps
102:25, 26. 104:2, 3. Pr 8:26-28. 30:4. He
1:10-12. Re 20:11.
span. Ex +31:18.
measure. Heb. *tierce.* i.e. *a third.* Jb 28:25. Ps
80:5.
weighed. Jb 28:25.

13　**hath directed.** Jb 21:22. 36:22, 23. Lk 10:22.
Jn 1:13. 3:8. Ro *11:34. 1 C 2:9-11, 16.* Ep
+1:11.
Spirit. Heb. *ruach,* Is +48:16. God the Holy
Spirit is unequaled (Je +10:6. Mt +8:27.
+28:19). Is 11:2. 42:1.
being. or, who as.

his counsellor. Heb. man of his counsel. lit.
"and a man, his counsellor." Compare for similar grammatical construction the renderings of
the following passages (Ge 13:8mg. Ex 2:14mg.
Le 22:12mg. Jsh 2:1. Jg 6:8mg. 11:1mg. 15:15.
16:1. 19:1mg. 21:12mg. 1 K 1:2mg. 2 K 9:4. Je
3:3. 20:15mg. Lk 2:15mg). Is +9:6. 41:28. Jb
15:8. 29:4. Ps 119:24mg. Je 23:18.

14　**With.** Jb 38:4.
counsel. Is +9:6. Ro 11:33-36. Ep +1:11.
instructed him. Heb. made him understand.
Jb 40:2. 42:1-3.
understanding. Heb. understandings. 1 C
12:4-6. Col 2:3. Ja 1:17.

15　**the nations.** ver. 22. Jb 34:14, 15. Je 10:10.
are as. 1 S 14:16.
small dust. Ps 103:14.
the isles. Is +11:11.

16　**not sufficient.** Ne 10:39.
nor. Ps 40:6. 50:10-12. Mi 6:6, 7. He 10:5-10.

17　**as nothing.** Is +5:8. 1 S 14:16. Jb 25:6. Ps
62:9. Da 4:34, 35. 2 C 12:11.
vanity. ver. 23. Is 24:10. Ge 1:2.

18　**To whom.** ver. 25. Ex +8:10. +20:4. 1 S 2:2.
Jb 40:9. Ps 8:5. Col +1:15. He +1:3.

19　**workman.** Is 37:18, 19. 41:6, 7. Ex +20:4.
+34:17. Ho 8:6.

20　**is so impoverished that he hath no oblation.** Heb. is poor of oblation.
chooseth. Is 2:8, 9. 44:13-19. Je 10:3, 4. Da
5:23.
shall not. Is 41:7. 46:7. 1 S 5:3, 4.

21　**not known.** Is 27:11. 44:20. 46:8. Ps 19:1-5.
115:8. Je 10:8-12. Ac 14:17. Ro 1:19-21, 28.
3:1, 2.

22　**It is he that sitteth.** *or,* Him that sitteth, etc.
Is 19:1. 66:1. Ps 2:4. 29:10. 68:33.
the circle. Jb 22:14 (circuit). 26:7. Ps 8:27
(compass).
the inhabitants. ver. 15, 17. Nu 13:33. Ps
33:13, 14.
stretcheth. Is 42:5. 44:24. 45:12. 51:13. Jb
9:8. 37:18. 38:4-9. Ps 102:25, 26. 104:2. Je
10:12. 51:15. Zc 12:1. He 1:10-12.
as a curtain. Ps 104:2.

23　**bringeth.** Is 19:13, 14. 23:9. 24:21, 22. Jb
12:21. 34:19, 20. Ps 76:12. 107:40. Je 25:18-
27. Lk 1:51, 52. Re 19:18-20.

24　**they shall not be planted.** Is 14:21, 22.
17:11. 1 K 21:21, 22. 2 K 10:11. Jb 15:30-33.
18:16-19. Je 22:30. Na 1:14.
he shall also. ver. 7. Is 11:4. 30:33. 37:7. 2 S
22:16. Jb 4:9. Hg 1:9.
and the. Je +23:19.
as stubble. 1 C +3:12.

25　**To whom.** ver. +18. Is 55:9. Dt 4:15-18, 33.
5:8. Ps 147:5.
liken me. Ge 1:26. 3:5, 22. 5:1.

26　**Lift.** Is 51:6. Dt 4:19. Jb 31:26-28. Ps 8:3, 4.
19:1.

who hath. Is 45:7. 48:13. Ge 1:1. 2:1, 2. Ps 148:3-6. Jn +1:3.
bringeth. Ps 147:4, 5.
by the greatness. Ps 89:11-13. Je 32:17-19.
faileth. Is 34:16. 1 S 30:19. 2 S 17:22.

27 **sayest**. Is 49:14, 15. 54:6-8. 60:15. 1 S 12:22. Jb 3:23. Ps 31:22. 77:7-10. Je 33:24. Ezk 37:11. Ro +11:1, 2.
my judgment. Is 49:4. Jb 27:2. 34:5. Ml 2:17. Lk 18:7, 8.

28 **Hast thou not known**. Je 4:22. Mk 8:17, 18. 9:19. +12:24. 16:14. Lk 24:25. Jn 14:9. 1 C 6:3-5, 9, 16, 19.
the everlasting. Heb. *olam*, Ge +17:7. Is 57:15. Ge 21:33. Dt 33:27. Je 10:10. Ro 16:26. 1 T 1:17. He 9:14.
the Lord. Ne +9:6. Jn 1:3.
the ends. Is 45:22. 49:6. 1 S 2:10. Ac 13:47.
fainteth. Is 59:1. 66:9. Ps 138:8. Jn 5:17. Ph 1:6.
no searching. Is 55:8, 9. Jb +11:7. Ps 147:5.

29 **giveth power**. Is 38:14. 41:10. Ge 18:14. 49:24. Dt 33:25. Jb 26:2. Ps +18:1. 119:28. He 11:34.
to the faint. Is 50:4. Je 31:25.
no might. ver. 26. Ho 12:3.
increaseth strength. ver. 31. Is 41:10. 1 S 2:4. 2 S 22:33, 40. Ps 18:32, 39. 28:8. 46:1. 73:26. 81:1. 86:16. 89:21. 138:3. Zc 12:8. Ro 14:4.

30 **youths shall**. Is 9:17. 13:18. Ps 33:16. 34:10. 39:5. Ec 9:11. Am 2:14.
faint. Dt 20:8. Ml 1:13. Ro 2:7. 1 C 15:58. Ga 6:9. 2 Th 3:13.

31 **they that wait**. Ps +25:3. 84:7. 92:1, 13. 1 Th 1:10.
renew. Heb. change. Jg 16:28. Jb 17:9. 33:24-26. Ps 103:5. 138:3. 2 C 1:8-10. 4:8-10, 16. 12:9, 10.
strength. Ps +18:1.
mount up. Ex 19:4. Ps 84:7. SS 8:5. 2 C 11:5. 12:11. Re 4:7.
as eagles. Ex 19:4. Dt 32:11, 12. Ps 103:5. Mt +24:28. Lk +17:37.
run. Ep 3:8.
walk. Je 9:1. La 4:1, 2. Ezk 22:18. Da 2:38, 39. Am 9:2, 3. Ph 2:6-8.
not faint. Ps 27:13. Lk 18:1. 2 C 4:1, 16. Ga 6:9. He 12:1. Re 2:3.

ISAIAH 41

1 **Keep silence**. Hab +2:20.
islands. Is +11:11. 49:1.
let the people. ver. 6, 7, 21, 22. Is 8:9, 10. Jb 38:3. 40:7. Jl 3:10, 11.
strength. Jb 26:2. Ro 5:6.
let us. Is 1:18. Jb 23:3-7. 31:35, 36. 40:8-10. Mi 6:1-3.

2 **Who raised**. ver. 25. Is 45:13. 46:11. Ge

11:31. 12:1-3. 17:1. Ps 47:7-9. 105:5, 6. He 11:8-10.
the righteous man. Heb. righteousness. ver. 10.
his foot. Jg 5:15mg.
kings. Ge 14:1, 8, 9.
gave. ver. 45. Is 45:1. Ge 14:14, 15. Ezr 1:2. Ga 3:18. He 7:1.
as the dust. ver. 15, 16. 2 S 22:43. 2 K 13:7.
as driven. Is 40:24.

3 **pursued**. Is 5:11. Ge 14:14, 15.
safely. Heb. in peace. Is 57:2. Jb 5:24.

4 **hath**. ver. 26. Is 40:12, 26. 42:24. 46:11.
calling. Is 44:7. 46:10. 48:3-7. Dt 32:7, 8. Ac 15:18. 17:26.
I the Lord. Is 43:10. 44:6. 48:12. Re 1:11, 17. 2:8. 22:13.
the first. Is 44:6. 48:12.
with the. Is 46:3, 4. Mt 1:23. 28:20.
I am. Is 43:10, 13. 46:4. 48:12. 52:6. Dt 32:39. 1 Ch 21:17. Jn +8:58.

5 **isles**. Is +11:11. Ezk 26:15, 16.
the ends. Ex 15:14, 15. Jsh 2:10, 11. 5:1. Ps 65:8. 66:3, 4. 67:7.

6 **helped**. Is 40:19. 44:12. 1 S 4:6-9. 5:3-5. Da 3:1-7. Ac 19:24-28.
said to. 1 Th 4:18.
of good courage. Heb. strong. Is 35:4. Jl 3:9-11.

7 **the carpenter**. Is 40:19. 44:12-15. 46:6, 7. Je 10:3-5, 9. Da 3:1, etc.
goldsmith. *or*, founder. Jg 17:4.
him that smote the anvil. *or*, the smiting.
saying, it is ready for the sodering. *or*, saying of the solder, It *is* good.
that it. Is 40:20. 46:7. Jg 18:17, 18, 24.

8 **thou**. Is 44:1, 2, 21. 48:12. 49:3. Ex +19:5, 6. Le 25:42. Dt 10:15. Ps 33:12. 105:6, 42-45. Je 33:24.
the seed. Mt 3:9. Lk 1:54, 55. Jn 8:33-44. Ro 4:12, 13. 9:4-8. Ga 3:16, 19. 4:22-31. He 2:16.
my friend. Ge 18:17. 2 Ch 20:7. Mt 17:5. Jn 15:14, 15. Ja 2:23.

9 **whom**. ver. 2. Jsh 24:2-4. Ne 9:7, etc. Ps 107:2, 3. Lk 13:29. Re 5:9.
called. Dt 7:7. 1 C 1:26-29. Ja 2:5.
I have chosen. Ge 12:1. Dt 7:6. 10:15. 14:2. Jsh 24:2-4. Ne 9:7. Ac 7:2-7. Ro +11:29.
not cast. ver. 17. Is 42:3, 16. 54:9, 10. +55:3. Le +26:44. 1 S 12:22. 1 K 11:39. 2 K 13:23. Ps +94:14. Je 31:37. 33:20, 21, 25, 26. Zc 10:6. Ro +11:1, 2.

10 **Fear thou not**. ver. 13, 14. Is 12:2. Ge +15:1. Dt 20:1. 2 Ch 20:17. Ps +118:6. Ro 8:31. 2 T +1:7.
with thee. Is +43:2.
for I am thy God. Is 52:7. 60:19. Ge +17:7. Ps 147:12. Ho 1:9. Jn 8:54, 55.

I will strengthen. Dt 33:27-29. Ps +18:1.
will help. Is 30:7. 2 Ch 32:8. Ps 60:11. Ro 8:31.
I will uphold. Ps 37:17, 23, 24. 41:12. 63:8. 119:117. 145:14.
the right. Ps +18:35. 99:4. 144:8, 11.

11 **all they**. Is 45:24. 49:26. 54:17. 60:12-14. Ex 11:8. 23:22. Zc 12:3. Ac 13:8-11. 16:39. Re 3:9.
ashamed. Je +20:11.
as nothing. ver. 24, 29. Is 40:17. Da 4:35.
they that strive with thee. Heb. the men of thy strife. Jb 31:35.
shall perish. Is 60:12. Ps 37:1, 2, 7.

12 **shalt seek**. Jb 20:7-9. Ps 37:35, 36.
them that contend with thee. Heb. the men of thy contention.
they that war against thee. Heb. the men of thy war.

13 **will hold**. Is 43:6. 45:1. 51:18. Dt 33:26-29. Ps 63:8. 73:23. 109:31. 2 T 4:17.
Fear not. ver. +10. Ps 32:8. 91:15. Mt 11:28. 28:20. Ph 4:6, 7. He +13:5.
help thee. Is 50:9. Ps 119:173.

14 **thou worm**. Jb 25:6. Ps 22:6.
Jacob. Is 43:1. 44:1, 2.
men. *or*, few men. Dt 7:7. Mt 7:14. Lk 12:32. Ro 9:27.
help thee. Is 50:9.
thy redeemer. Is 44:6, 24. 47:4. 48:17. 49:7, 26. 54:5, 8. 59:20. 60:16. 63:16. Ge 48:16. Ex 6:6. 15:13. Jb +19:25. Ps 19:14. 78:35. Pr 23:11. Je 50:34. Ga 3:13. T 2:14. Re 5:9.
Holy One. Is +1:4.

15 **I will make**. Is +21:10.
teeth. Heb. mouths. Ps +149:6 (twoedged).
thou shalt. Ps 18:42. Zc 4:7. 2 C 10:4, 5.
chaff. Lk +3:17.

16 **shalt fan**. Mt +3:12.
whirlwind. Je +23:19.
thou shalt rejoice. Is 12:6. 25:1-3. 45:24, 25. Je 9:23, 24. Hab +3:18. 1 C 1:30, 31. 2 C 10:17. Ph 3:3.

17 **the poor**. Is 61:1. 66:2. Ex 22:25-27. Dt +24:14, 15. Ps +40:17. 68:9, 10. Mt +5:3.
needy. Ps 40:17. +72:12.
seek water. Is 55:1. Ge 21:15, 16. Ex 17:3, 4, 6. Ps 42:2. 63:1, 2. Am 8:11-13. Mt +5:6. Lk 16:22-24. Jn 4:10-15. 7:37-39. Re 21:6. 22:17.
their tongue. Ps 22:15. La 4:4. Lk 16:24.
I the Lord. Is 30:19. Jg 15:18, 19. Ps 34:6. 50:15. 102:17. 107:5, 6. 2 C 12:9.
not forsake. ver. +9. Is 42:16. Ge 28:15. 1 S +12:22. Ps +94:14. He +13:5, 6.

18 **open**. *Is 45:8. 53:7.* Ge 8:6.
rivers. Is 12:3. 30:25. 32:2. 35:6, 7. 43:19, 20. 48:21. 58:11. Ps 46:4. 78:15, 16. 105:41. 107:35. Ezk 47:1-8. Jl 3:18. Zc 14:8. Mt +5:6. Re 22:1.

fountains. Heb. *mayan*, Ge +7:11.
I will make. Ex 17:6. 2 K 3:16. Ps 114:8.

19 **plant**. Is 27:6. 32:15. 37:31, 32. 51:3. 55:11, 13. 60:21. 61:3, 11. Ps 92:12-14. Ezk 17:22-24. 47:12.

20 **may see**. Is 43:7-13, 21. 44:23. 45:6-8. 66:18. Ex 9:16. Nu 23:23. Jb 12:9. Ps 109:27. Ep 2:6-10. 4:24. Col 3:10. 2 Th 1:10. Re 4:11.

21 **Produce**. Heb. Cause to come near. Is 1:18. Jsh 20:4. Jb 23:3, 4. 31:37. 38:3. 40:7-9. Mi 6:1, 2.

22 **and show**. Is 42:9. 43:9-12. 45:21. 48:14. Jn 13:19. 16:14.
happen. Nu 11:23. Ru 2:3mg.
consider them. Heb. set our heart upon them.

23 **that we may know**. Is 42:9. 44:7, 8. 45:3. 46:9, 10. Ps +82:1, 6, 7. Ezk 33:33. Jn 13:19. 14:29. Ac 15:18.
do good. Is +45:7. 46:7. Je 10:5.

24 **ye are**. ver. 29. Ex +20:4. 1 C 8:4.
of nothing. *or, worse* than nothing.
of nought. *or, worse* than of a viper. Is 30:6. 59:5.
an abomination. Is 66:24. Dt 7:26. 27:15. Re 17:5.

25 **raised**. Is 21:2. 44:28. 45:1-6, 13. 46:10, 11. Je 51:27-29.
north. Je +1:14.
he shall come. Ml 4:2, 3.
the rising of the sun. Jg 5:31.
shall he call. Is 45:3, 4. 2 Ch 36:22, 23. Ezr 1:2, 3.
come upon. ver. 2. Is 10:6. 2 S 22:43. Mi 7:10. Zc 10:5.
princes. Ezr 9:2 (rulers). Ne 2:16, 16. 4:14, 19. 5:7, 17. 7:5. 12:40. 13:11. Je 51:23, 28, 57. Ezk 23:6, 12, 23.
as the potter. Je 18:1-6.

26 **declared**. ver. 22. Is 43:9. 44:7. 45:21. Hab 2:18-20.
righteous. ver. 23.

27 **first**. ver. 4. Is 43:10. 44:6. 48:12. Re 2:8.
I will give. Is 40:9. 44:28. 52:7. Ezr 1:1, 2. Na 1:15. Ml 3:1. Lk 1:76-80. 2:10, 11. Ro 10:15.

28 **I beheld**. Is 45:21. 63:5. Da 2:10, 11. 4:7, 8. 5:8.
answer. Heb. return. Ex 19:8.

29 **they are all**. ver. +24. Ex +20:4.
vanity. Is 58:9. Dt +32:21. Ps 10:7.
molten images. Ex +34:17.
wind. Je 5:13.

ISAIAH 42

1 **my servant**. Is 43:10. 49:3-6. 52:13. 53:11. Ex +28:39 (girdle). Ps 106:23. Mt *12:18-21.* Lk 23:35. Ph 2:6-8.
whom I. Is 49:7, 8. 50:4-9. Jn 16:32.
mine elect. Ps 89:19, 20. Jn 6:27. 1 P 2:4, 6.

my soul. Heb. *nephesh*, Ge +34:3; Le +26:11. Je 9:9. Am 6:8. Mt 3:17. 17:5. Mk 1:11. Lk 3:22. Ep 1:4, 6. Col 1:13mg. He 10:38.
I have. Is 11:2-5. 59:21. 61:1. Mt 3:16. Mk 1:10. Lk 3:22. Jn 1:32-34. 3:34. Ac 10:38.
my spirit. Heb. *ruach*, Ge +6:3; +41:38. Is +48:16. Ac +5:4. The Trinity is seen here, for we have the Father as the speaker; the Son as the Servant, the Messiah; and the Holy Spirit. All three persons of the Trinity are also mentioned together in Mt 3:16, +17; +28:19; Lk 1:35; Jn 14:16, 26; 15:26; Ro 15:30; 1 C 12:4-6; 2 C 13:14; Ep 2:18; 4:4-6; 2 Th 3:5; He 9:14; 1 P 1:2; 1 J 5:7; Ju 20, 21; Re 1:4, 5.
he shall. Is 32:16. Ps 94:15.
to the Gentiles. Mt +12:18, 21. Jn 10:16. Ac 10:45, 47.

2   **not cry**. Mt +11:29. 12:15-20. Lk 17:20. 2 T 2:24.

3   **bruised**. Is 35:3, 4. 40:11, 29-31. 50:4, 10. 57:15-18. +58:6mg. 61:1-3. 66:2. Ps 103:3, 10, 13, 14. 147:3. Je 30:11-17. 31:18-20, 25. Ezk 34:16. Mt 11:28. 18:11-14. Mk 1:40, 41. Lk 22:31, 32, 60-62. Jn 8:10, 11. 20:19-21, 27. Ro 5:6, 8, 9. He 2:17, 18.
not break. Is +40:11. Mt 12:15, 20. He 4:15.
smoking. *or*, dimly burning. 1 S 3:2.
flax. Is 43:17.
quench. Heb. quench it. 2 S 21:17. 2 Ch 29:7.
he shall. Is 11:3, 4. Ps 72:2-4. 96:13. 98:9. Mi 7:9. Jn 5:30. 18:37, 38. 1 T 6:13. Re 19:11.

4   **shall not**. Is +9:7. +49:5-10. 52:13-15. 53:2-12. Jn 17:4, 5. He 12:2-4. 1 P 2:22-24.
discouraged. Heb. broken. Is 58:6mg. Ec 12:6.
judgment. Ps +7:8.
and the isles. ver. 12. Is 2:2-4. +11:11. 55:5. Ge +49:10. Ps 22:27. 72:8-11. 98:2, 3. Mi 4:1-3. Zc 2:11. Mt 12:21. Ro 16:26. 1 C 9:21. He 12:2. Ju 24, 25.

5   **he that created**. Is 40:12, 22, 28. 44:24. 45:12, 18. 48:13. Ge +1:1. Jb 26:13, 14. Ne 9:6. Ps 33:6, 9. 102:25, 26. 104:2, etc. Je 10:12. 32:17. Am 4:13. 9:6. Zc 12:1. Jn +1:1, 3, 14. Ep 3:9. Col 1:16. He 1:2, 10-12. 3:4. Re 4:11.
and stretched. lit. they that stretched. Is +40:22. Ge +1:26.
he that spread. Ge 1:10-12, 24, 25. Ps 24:1, 2. 136:6.
he that giveth. Ge +2:7. Jb 12:10. 27:3. 33:4. 34:14. Jb 14:10. Ps 33:6. Ezk 37:5, 6. Da 5:23. Ac 17:25.
breath. Heb. *neshamah*, Ge +2:7.
spirit. Heb. *ruach*, Nu +16:22. Jb 32:8. Ec +12:7. He +12:9.

6   **called**. Is 32:1. 43:1. 45:13. 49:1-3. Ps +45:3, 6, 7. Je 23:5, 6. 33:15, 16. Ro 3:25, 26. He +1:8, 9. 7:2, 26.
and will hold. ver. 1. Is 41:13.

will keep. Is 27:3.
and give. Is 49:8. Mt +26:28. Lk 1:69-72. Ro +15:8, 9. 2 C 1:20. Ga 3:15-17. He 8:6. 9:15. 12:24. 13:20.
for a covenant. Is 49:8. Ge +3:15. Ho +6:7. Ml 3:1. Mt 26:28. Ro 8:3. 1 C +15:45. Ga 3:21. He 10:5-10. +13:20.
a light. Is 51:4, 5. Lk *2:32*. Jn 8:12. 1 P 2:9.
Gentiles. ver. +1.

7   **open**. ver. 16. Ps +119:18. Mt +11:5.
to bring. ver. 22. Is 9:2. Ps +146:7. Ep 5:8. Col 1:13. 2 T 2:26. He 2:14, 15. 1 P 2:9.
sit. Mt 4:16. Lk 1:79. Ac 18:11.

8   **I am**. Is 48:11. Ex 3:15. Ne +9:6. Jn 8:24.
my name. Ex 4:5. +6:3. Ps 29:1, 2. 1 C +12:3.
my glory. Is 48:11. Ex 20:3-5. 34:14. Jn 5:23. 17:5. 1 C +2:8. Ja +2:1. Re 5:12, 13.
not give. Ex 20:5.
praise. Heb. *halal*. Is 13:10. 38:18.

9   **the former**. Ge 15:12-16. Jsh 21:45. 23:14, 15. 1 K 8:15-20. 11:36.
new things. Is 41:22, 23. 43:19. 44:7, 8. 45:11. 46:9, 10. 48:5, 6. Je 1:5. Da 2:28, 29. Jn 13:19. Ac +2:23. 15:18. 1 P 1:10-12. 2 P 1:19-21.
I tell. Dt +29:29.

10   **Sing**. Is 24:14-16. 44:23. 49:13. 65:14. Ps 33:3. 40:3. 96:1-3. 98:1-4. ch. 117. 149:1. Ro 15:9-11. Re 5:9. 14:3.
ye that go. Ps 107:23-32. 148:1-14. 150:6.
all that is therein. Heb. the fulness thereof.
the isles. ver. +4.

11   **Let the wilderness**. Is 32:16. 35:1, 2, 6. 40:3. 41:18, 19. 43:19. Ps 72:8-10.
Kedar. Ge +25:13.
let the inhabitants. Je 21:13. 48:28. 49:16. Ob 3.

12   **give glory**. Is 24:15, 16. 60:12. 66:18, 19. Ps 2:10-12. 22:27. 29:1. 68:31-34. 96:3-10. ch. 117. Re 7:9-12. +11:13.

13   **go forth**. Is 41:15, 16. Re 6:2. 19:11.
as a mighty. Is 59:16-19. 63:1-4. Ex 15:1-3. Ps 78:65, 66. 110:5, 6. Je 25:30.
stir up. Pr 10:12. SS 2:7.
jealousy. Ex +20:5.
shall cry. ver. 14. Ps 78:65.
roar. Am +1:2.
prevail. *or*, behave himself mightily. Jb 15:25. 36:9. Ps 118:16. Re 1:7. 19:11.

14   **long time**. Heb. *olam*, Le +25:32. Jb 32:18, 20. Ps 50:21. 83:1, 2. Ec 8:11, 12. Je 15:6. 44:22. Lk 18:7. 2 P 3:9, 10, 15.
refrained. Is 63:15. 64:12. Ge +45:1. 1 S 13:12. Est 5:10.
cry. ver. +13.
like a travailing. Je +4:31. Mt +24:8.
devour. Heb. swallow, *or* sup up. Ob 16mg. Lk 12:49. **S#7602h**. Jb 5:5. 7:2mg. 36:20. Ps 56:1, 2. 57:3. 119:131. Ec 1:5mg. Je 2:24. 14:6. Ezk 36:3. Am 2:7. 8:4.

15 **will make**. Is 2:12-16. 11:15, 16. 44:27. 49:11. 50:2. Ps 18:7. 107:33, 34. 114:3-7. Je 4:24. Na 1:4-6. Hab 3:6-10. Hg 2:6. Zc 10:11. Re 6:12-17. 8:7-12. 11:13. 16:12, 18. 20:11.

16 **I will bring**. Is 30:21. 48:17. 54:13. 60:1, 2, 19, 20. Je 31:8-10. Ho 2:14. Mt +11:5. Lk 1:78, 79. Ep 5:8.
lead. Is 40:10, 11. 41:3. 48:17. 55:4. 57:18. 58:11. 61:8. Jsh 3:4. Ps +23:3. 25:12. 32:8. Pr +8:9. Ho 2:6. Jn 9:25. 2 C 4:3.
darkness. Is 9:2.
crooked. Is 40:4. 45:2. Ec 1:15. 7:13. Lk 3:5.
straight. Heb. into straightness. Is 40:4.
These things. Dt 31:6.
not forsake. Is +41:9. Ro 5:8-10. 8:29-31. 2 Th 2:13, 14. 1 P 1:3-5.

17 **greatly ashamed**. Is 1:29. 44:9, 11. 45:16, 17. Ps 97:7. Je 2:26, 27. 17:13. Hab 2:18-20. Re 22:15.
say to. Is 44:17.
molten. Ex +34:17.

18 **ye deaf**. Is 29:18. 43:8. Ex 4:11. Pr 20:12. Ezk 12:2. Mk 7:34-37. Lk 7:22. Jn 8:43. 9:39. 2 C 3:15. Re 3:17, 18.

19 **Who is blind**. Is 6:9. 29:9-14. Je 4:22. 5:21. Ezk 12:2. Mt 13:14, 15. +15:14-16. Mk 8:17, 18. Jn 7:47-49. 9:39, 41. 12:40. Ro 2:17-23. 11:7-10, 25. 2 C 3:14, 15. 4:4.
my messenger. Ml 3:1. Lk 7:23.
perfect. i.e. an intimate friend or trusted one. Heb. *meshullam*, to be at peace with. Nu 23:21. 2 S 20:19. Jb 22:21. Ps 7:4.

20 **Seeing**. Is 1:3. 48:6-8. Nu 14:22. Dt 4:9. 29:1-4. Ne 9:10-17. Ps 106:7-13. 107:43. Jn 9:37-40. 11:47-50.
but thou. Ro 2:21.
opening. Is 58:2. Je 42:2-5. Ezk 33:31. Mk 6:19, 20. Ac 28:22-27.
heareth not. Je 5:21. 6:10. Ezk 12:2. Mt 13:14. Jn 12:40.

21 **well**. Is 1:24-27. 46:12, 13. Ps 71:16, 19. 85:9-12. Da 9:24-27. Mt 3:17. 5:17. 17:5. Jn 8:29. 15:10. Ro 3:25, 26. 2 C 5:19-21. Ph 3:9.
he will magnify. Is 66:2. Ps 40:8. 138:2. Pr +30:6. Mt +3:15. +5:18. Ro 3:31. 7:12. 8:3, 4. 10:4. Ga 3:13, 21. 5:22, 23. He 8:10. 1 J 3:4, 5.
it. Heb. *or*, him. Jn 13:31, 32. 17:4, 5.

22 **a people**. Is 1:7. 18:2. 36:1. 52:4, 5. 56:9. 2 K 24:11-13. 25:9. Je 50:17. 51:34, 35. 52:4, etc. Lk 19:41-44. 21:20-24.
they are all of them snared. *or*, in snaring all the young men of them.
are hid. ver. +7. Is 14:17. 45:13. *Ps 102:20. Je 52:31.*
a spoil. Heb. a treading. Is 51:23. Dt 28:29-33. Ps 50:22.

23 **will give**. Is 1:18-20. 48:18. Le 26:40-42. Dt 4:29-31. 32:29. Pr 1:22, 23. Je 3:4-7, 13. Mi

6:9. Mt 13:9. 21:28-31. Ac 3:19, 22, 23. 1 P 4:2, 3.
time to come. Heb. after-time. Pr 29:11.

24 **gave Jacob**. Is 10:5, 6. 45:7. 47:6. 50:1, 2. 59:1, 2. 63:10. Dt 28:49. 29:24-28. 32:30. Jg 2:14. 3:8. 10:7. 2 Ch 15:6. 36:17. Ne 9:26, 27. Ps 106:40-42. Je 5:15. 25:8, 9. La 1:14, 18. Am +3:6. Mt 22:7.
Israel. Ge 32:28. 43:6. 45:26, 28.

25 **he hath poured**. Dt 32:22. Ezk +7:8.
and it hath. 2 K 25:9.
he knew. Is 9:13. Je 5:3. Ho 7:9. Re 9:18-21. 16:9.
yet he laid. Is 57:11. Ml 2:2.

ISAIAH 43

1 **created**. ver. 7, 15, 21. Is 44:2, 21, 24. Ps 100:3. 102:18. Je 31:3. 33:24, 26. Ep 2:10.
O Jacob. Ge 32:27, 28.
Fear. ver. +5.
redeemed. ver. 14. Is 35:9, 10. +41:14. 48:17. +51:11. 62:12. Ge 48:16. Ex 15:13, 16. Ps 107:2. Lk +24:21. Ga +3:13. T 2:14. Re 5:9.
I have called. Is 42:6. 44:5. 45:4. 49:1. Ex 33:17. Ac 27:20, 25.
thou art mine. Ex +19:5, 6. Ezk 16:8. Zc 13:9. Ml 3:17. 2 T 2:19. He 8:8-10.

2 **When**. Mt 14:29, 30.
passest. Is 8:7-10. 11:15, 16. Ex 14:29. Dt 31:6, 8. Jsh 3:15-17. Ps 66:10, 12. 91:3, 5-7. Am 9:8, 9. Mt 7:25-27. He 11:29.
I will be with. Is 8:10. 41:10, 14. Ge +28:15. Nu 14:9. 23:21. Dt 20:1. 31:6-8. Jsh 1:5, 9. Jg 6:12, 13. 1 S 18:14, 28. 2 K 6:16. 18:7. 2 Ch 13:12. 32:7, 8. Ps 23:4. 46:4-7, 11. 91:15. Da 3:25. Mt 1:23. +28:20. Lk 1:28. Ac 18:9, 10. Ro 8:31. 2 C 12:9, 10. Ph 4:9. 2 T 4:17, 22. 1 J 4:4.
not overflow. Jb 28:11. Ps 93:3, 4.
when thou walkest. Ps 23:4. Da 3:25-27. Zc 13:9. Ml 3:2, 3. 4:1. Lk 21:12-18. 1 C 3:13-15. He 11:33-38. 1 P 4:12, 13.

3 **the Lord**. Ex +6:2, 3.
the Holy One. Is +1:4. 6:3. 45:15, 21. 49:26. 60:16. Le 19:2. Ps 22:3. 145:17. Ho 13:4. T 2:10-14. 3:4-6. Ju 25.
thy Savior. Is +63:16. T 3:5.
I gave. Ex 10:7. 2 Ch 14:9-14. Pr 11:8. 21:18.
Egypt. Ge +13:1. Ps 68:31.
Ethiopia. Ge +2:13.
Seba. Ge +10:7. Ps 72:10.
for thee. Pr 11:8. 21:18.

4 **precious**. Ex 19:5, 6. Dt 7:6-8. 14:2. 26:18. 32:9-14. Jb 28:10. Ps 135:4. Ml 3:17. T 2:14. 1 P 2:9.
thou hast been. Ge 12:2. Ps 112:9. Jn 5:44. 1 P 1:7.
I have. Je 31:3. Ho 11:1. Ml 1:2. Jn 16:27. 17:23, 26. Ro 8:32. Re 3:9.

life. *or*, person. Heb. *nephesh*, soul, Ge +44:30.

5　Fear not. ver. 2. Ge +15:1.
I will. 49:12. 60:1-11. 66:19, 20. 1 K 8:46-51. Ps 22:27-31. 50:5. Je +23:3. Zc 8:7. Lk 13:29. Jn 10:16.
gather thee. Mt 24:31. Mk 13:27.

6　to the north. Je +23:8. Ezk +38:6, 15.
bring my sons. Is 11:11. 18:7. Je 3:14, 18, 19. Ho 1:10, 11. Ro 9:7, 8, 25, 26. 2 C 6:17, 18. Ga 3:26-29.
ends of the earth. Ps 72:8. Je +31:8. Ezk 38:8.

7　every one. Ho 1:10. Ac 11:26. Ep 3:14, 15. 2 T 2:19.
called. Is 62:2-5. 63:19. Je 33:16. Ac 11:26. Ja 2:7. Re 3:12.
for I. ver. 1. Is 29:23. Ps 95:6, 7. 100:3. Jn 3:3-7. 2 C 5:17. Ga 6:15. Ep 2:10. Ph 1:6. T 3:5-7. He 13:20, 21.
for my. ver. 21. Is 48:11. Ps 50:23. Jn 15:8. Ro 9:23. Ep 1:5, 6, 12. 2:4-7. 1 P 2:9. 4:11, 14. Re 4:11.

8　Bring forth. Is 6:9. 42:18-20. 44:18-20. 2 C 4:4-6.
the blind people. Is 6:10. 42:19, 20. Lk +8:10.
the deaf. Mt 13:43.

9　all the. Is 45:20, 21. 48:14. Ps 49:1, 2. 50:1, 4. Jl 3:11.
who among. Is 41:21-26. 44:7-9. 46:10. 48:5, 6.
that they may. ver. 26. Jsh 24:15-24. 1 K 18:21-24, 36-39. Ro 3:4.
truth. Jn 18:37, 38.

10　my witnesses. ver. 12. Is 44:8. Jn 1:7, 8. 15:27. Ac +1:8. 5:32. 10:41. Ro 3:1, 2. 1 C 15:15. He 12:1.
saith the Lord. Ne +9:6. 1 C +12:3.
and my servant. Is 42:1. 55:4. Ph 2:7. Col 1:7. Re 1:2, 5. 3:14.
ye may know. Is 40:21, 22. 41:20. 45:6. 46:8, 9. Jn 8:12. 10:9, 14. 17:3. 20:31.
I am he. Is 41:4. 44:6-8. Mk 13:6. Jn 4:26. 8:19, 20, +24, 45, +58. 13:19.
before me. Ps 90:2. 93:2. Pr 8:22, 23. Mi +5:2. Jn +8:58. Col 1:17.
no God formed. *or*, nothing formed of God. Heb. *El*, Ex +15:2.
no God. Dt 32:39. Mk +12:32. Jn +1:1.
formed. Ph +2:6, 11. Re +3:14.

11　I, even I. ver. 25. Ne +9:6. 1 C 12:13.
am the Lord. ver. 3. Dt 6:4. Ho 1:7. 13:4. Lk 1:47. 2:11. Jn 10:28-30. T 2:10, 13. 2 P 3:18. 1 J 4:14. 5:20, 21. Ju 25. Re 1:11, 17, 18. +7:10.
beside me. Dt 32:39. Ps 49:7. Pr 8:22-31.
no savior. Is +63:16. 1 S 14:45. 2 K 13:5. Ne 9:27. Ho 13:4. Ob 21. Lk 1:46, 47. 2:11. Ac 4:12. 1 T 1:1. 2:3. 4:10. 2 T 1:10. T 1:3. 2:10. 3:4. 2 P 2:20. 1 J 4:14. Ju 25.

12　declared. Is 37:7, 35, 36. 46:10. 48:4-7.
no strange. Dt 32:12, 16. Ps 81:8-10.
my witnesses. ver. 10. Is 37:20. 44:8. 46:9.

13　before. Is 57:15. Ps 90:2. 93:2. Pr 8:23. Mi +5:2. Hab 1:12. Jn +1:1, 2. 8:58. 1 T 1:17. He 13:8. Re +1:8.
none that can. Dt 28:31. 32:39. Ps 50:22. Ho 2:10. 5:14. Jn 10:27, 28.
I will work. Jb 34:14, 15, 29. 42:2. Ro 9:18, 19. Ph 2:13.
let it. Heb. turn it back. Is 1:25, 26. +14:27. Je +2:24mg. Am 1:3, 6, 9, 11, 13. 2:1, 4, 6.

14　the Lord. ver. 1. Is +41:14.
For. ver. 3, 4. Is 44:24-28. 45:1-5. Je 50:2-11, 17, 18, 27-34. 51:1-11, 24, 34-37. Re 18:20, 21.
nobles. Heb. bars. Is +27:1mg. 45:2. Je 50:36mg.
whose cry. Ezk 27:29-36. Re 18:11-19.

15　the Lord. ver. 3. Is +1:4. 40:25. Re 3:7.
your Holy One. 2 Ch 12:8. Ps 44:4. Ac 27:23.
the creator. ver. 1, 7, 21. Is 33:22. 40:21-24. 44:2, 21, 28. 45:11-13, 18. 51:13. 54:5. Je 27:5. 31:35, etc. 33:25, etc. Mt 25:34.
your King. Is 33:17, 22. Ps 74:12. 98:6. Jn 18:36, 37. Re 19:12, 16.

16　maketh. ver. 2. Is 11:15, 16. Ex +14:21, 22, 29. Re 16:12.

17　bringeth. Ex 14:4-9, 23-28. 15:4. Ps 46:8, 9. 76:5, 6. Ezk 38:8-18.
they shall. Is 14:20-22. Re 19:17-24. 20:8, 9.
they are. Is 1:31.
tow. lit. flax. Is +42:3.

18　Remember ye not. Is 65:17. Dt +7:18. 1 Ch 16:12. Je 16:14, 15. 23:7, 8. 2 C 3:10.

19　I will do. Is 42:9. 48:6. Je 31:22. Re 21:5.
I will even. Is 35:6-10. 40:3, 4. 48:21. Lk 3:4, 5.
rivers. Is 41:18, 19. 48:21, 22. Ex 17:6. Nu 20:11. Dt 8:15. Ps 78:15-20. 105:41. Ezk 47:7, 8. Jl 3:18. Jn 4:10. 7:37-39.

20　beast. Is 11:6-10. Ps 104:21. 148:10. Lk 10:17, 19.
owls. *or*, ostriches. Heb. daughters of the owl. Is +34:13mg.
I give waters. Ex 17:6. Nu 20:11.
to give drink. ver. 19. Is 41:17. 48:21. 49:10. 55:1, 2. Ge 24:19. Je 31:9. Jl 3:18. Jn 4:10, 14. 7:37-39. Re 21:6. 22:17.
my chosen. Is 42:1. 65:15. 1 Ch 16:13. Ps 33:12. Mk 13:20. 1 P 2:9. Re 17:14.

21　This people. ver. 1, 7. Is 50:7. 60:21. 61:3. Ps 4:3. 102:18. Pr 16:4. Lk 1:74, 75. 1 C 6:19, 20. 10:31. Ep 1:5-12. 3:21. Col 1:16. T 2:14. He 13:15. 1 P 2:9.

22　not called. Je +10:25. Ho 14:1, 2. Ja 4:2, 3.
thou hast been. Jb 21:14, 15. 27:9, 10. Je 2:5, 11-13, 31, 32. Mi 6:3. Ml 1:12-14. 3:14. Jn 6:66-69.

23 hast not. Am 5:25. Ml 1:7, 8, 13, 14. 3:8.
small cattle. Heb. lambs, *or*, kids. Is 66:3. Ex 12:3mg.
honored. Is 1:11-15. 25:3. 66:3. Pr 15:8. 21:27. Am 5:21, 22. Zc 7:5, 6. Mt 11:30.
thy sacrifices. Is 56:7. 1 K 18:33-36. Ps 20:1-4. Jon 1:16.
nor wearied. Is 1:14. Mi 6:3. Mt 11:30.

24 no sweet. Ex 30:7, 23, 24, 34. Je 6:20.
neither. Ex +29:13. Ps 50:9-13.
filled me. Heb. made me drunk, *or*, abundantly moistened. Is 34:5 (bathed), 7mg. 55:10 (watereth). Je 31:25 (satiated). La 3:15.
thou hast made. Is 1:14, 24. 63:10. Ps 95:10. Ezk 6:9. 16:43. Am 2:13. Ml 1:17. 2:13-17.
wearied me. Is 7:13. Ml 2:17.

25 even I. ver. 11. Ne +9:6. Je +50:20. Da 9:9. Mi 7:18, 19. Mk +2:7. Ro 5:20.
blotteth out. Ps +51:1. Hab 1:13.
thy transgressions. Ps 103:12. Je 33:8.
for mine. Is +48:9.
will not remember. Is 55:7. Ps 32:5. 79:8. Je +31:34. He 9:14. 1 J 1:7, 9. Re 1:5, 6.

26 Put. Is 1:18. Ge 32:12. Jb 16:21. 23:3-6. 40:4, 5. Ps 141:2. Je 2:21-35. Ezk 36:37. Ro 11:35.
declare. ver. 9. Jb 40:7, 8. Ps 32:5, 6. Mt 7:7, 8. Lk 10:29. 11:2, 4. 16:15. 18:9-14. Ro 3:24-26. 5:1. 8:33. 10:3.

27 first father. Nu 32:14. Dt 26:5. Ps 78:8. 106:6, 7. Je 3:25. Ezk 16:3, 45. Zc 1:4-6. Ml 3:7. Ac 7:51. Ro 5:12.
and thy. Is 3:12. 28:7. 56:10-12. Je 5:31. 23:11-15. La 4:13, 14. Ezk 22:25-28. Ho 4:6. Mi 3:11. Ml 2:4-8. Mt 15:14. 27:1, 41. Jn 11:49-53. Ac 5:17, 18. Ro 3:19.
teachers. Heb. interpreters. **S#3887h**. Ge 42:23. 2 Ch 32:31mg. Jb 16:20 (scorn). 33:23.

28 I have. Is 47:6. 2 S 1:21. Ps 89:39. La 2:2, 6, 7. 4:20.
princes. *or*, holy princes. Ps +82:6, 7. Ge 12:15. Ex 1:11 (taskmasters). 2:14. 18:21, 25 (rulers).
and have. Is 42:24, 25. Dt 28:15-20. 29:21-28. Lk 21:21-24. 1 Th 2:16.
to the curse. Je +26:6.
reproaches. Ps 79:4.

ISAIAH 44

1 now. Is 42:23. 48:16-18. 55:3. Ps 81:11-13. Je 4:1. Lk 13:34. He 3:7, 8.
O Jacob. Is 41:8. 43:1. Ge 17:7. Dt 7:6-8. Ps 105:6, 42, 43. Je 30:10. 46:27, 28. Ro 11:5, 6.

2 that made. ver. 21. Is +43:1, 7, 21.
formed. ver. 24. Is 46:3, 4. 49:1. Ps 46:5. 71:6. Je 1:5. Ezk 16:4-8. 20:5-12. He 4:16.
Fear. Ge +15:1. Ro 8:30. Ep 1:4. 1 Th 1:4.
Jesurun. i.e. *upright; the righteous one, a little righteous*, **S#3484h**. Dt 32:15. 33:5, Jeshurun, 26.

3 pour. 2 K 3:11. Ezk 36:25. Ac +1:5. Re 19:13.
water. Is 41:17, 18. 59:21. Je +2:13. Ezk 34:26. Jl 3:18. Re 21:6. 22:17.
thirsty. Ps 42:2. Mt +5:6.
floods. Is 32:2. 35:6, 7. 43:19, 20. 48:21. Ps 78:15, 16. 107:35.
dry ground. Ps 63:1. Mt 12:43.
I will. Ps +7:13.
pour my. Is 32:15. 59:21. Pr 1:23. Ezk 36:25-30. 39:29. Jl 2:28, 29. Zc 12:10. Ac 2:16-18, 33, 39. 10:45. 28:25, 26. T 3:5, 6.
spirit. Heb. *ruach*, Ge +41:38.

4 spring up. Is 58:11. 61:11. Ge 39:3, 23. Dt 29:9. Jsh +1:8. Ps +1:3. 92:13-15. Je 17:7, 8. Ac 2:41-47. 4:4. 5:14. Col 1:6.
willows. Nu 24:6. Ps 137:1, 2. Ezk 17:5.
water courses. Is 30:25.

5 shall say. Mt 10:32, 33. Ro 10:9, 10.
I am. Dt 26:17-19. Ps 22:27. 116:16. Je 50:5. Mi 4:2. Zc 8:20-23. 13:9.
subscribe. Ne 9:38. 10:1-29. 2 C 8:5.
the name. Ga 6:16. 1 P 2:9.

6 the Lord. Ex 3:14. Dt +32:39.
the King. Is 33:22. 43:15. Ml 1:14. Jn +1:49.
his redeemer. ver. 24. Is +41:14. Ge 48:16. Ex 6:6. 15:13.
the Lord of hosts. Ex +15:26. Ps +24:10.
the first. Is 41:4. 48:12. Re +1:8, 11, 17, 18. 2:8. 22:13.
beside me. ver. 8. Is 37:16, 20. 42:8. +43:10, 11. 45:6, 21, 22. Dt 4:35, 39. +6:4. +32:39. Ps 86:10. Mk +12:32. 1 T 3:16.

7 who. Is +41:22, 26. 43:9, 12. 45:21. 46:9, 10. 48:3-8.
since. Is 41:4. Ge 17:7, 8. Dt 32:8. Ac 17:26. 2 Th 2:13.
ancient. Heb. *olam*, Jb +22:15. lit. the everlasting nation. Ge +17:7. Ps 111:5, 7, 8. Ro +11:1, 2.

8 neither. ver. +2. Pr 3:25, 26. Je 10:7. Jn 6:10.
have declared. Is 42:9. 48:5. Ge 15:13-21. 28:13-15. 46:3. 48:19. 49:1-28. Le ch. 26. Dt 4:25-31. ch. 28.
ye are. Is +43:10, 12. Ezr 1:2. 8:22. Da 2:28, 47. 3:16-28. 4:25. 5:23-30. 6:22. Lk 24:48. Ac +1:8. 14:15. 17:23-31. He 12:1. 1 J 1:2.
Is there. ver. +6. Is 45:5, 6. 46:9, 10. Dt 4:35, 39. +32:39. 1 S 2:2. 2 S 22:32. Je 10:6. Jn +1:1. 10:30.
beside me. ver. +6. Dt 4:35, 39. +32:39. Mk +12:32.
no God. Heb. no rock. Is +26:4. Dt 32:4, 31. Ps 18:31. 1 C 10:4.

9 make. Ex +20:4.
vanity. Heb. *tohu*, Ge 1:2. Is +24:10. Dt +32:21.
and their. Is 2:20, 21. 37:18-20. 46:1, 2, 6, 7. Jg 10:14. 1 K 18:26-40. Je 2:11, 27, 28. 14:22.

16:19, 20. Da 5:23. Ho 8:4-6. Hab 2:18-20. 1 C +8:4.

delectable. Heb. desirable. Is +32:12mg. Da 11:38mg.

their own. ver. 18, 20. Is 42:18. 43:8, 9. 45:20. Ps +115:8. Ep 4:18. 5:8.

10 **formed a god**. 1 K 12:28. Je 10:5. Da 3:1, 14. 1 C +8:4.

molten. Ex +34:17.

11 **all his**. Is +42:17. 1 S 5:3-7. 6:4, 5. Je 10:14. 51:17.

let them all. Is +41:5-7. Jg 6:29-31. 16:23-30. 1 K 18:19-29, 40. Da 3:1, etc. 5:1-6. Ac 19:24-34. Re 19:19-21.

12 **The smith**. Is 40:19. 41:6, 7. 46:6, 7. Ex 32:4, 8. Je 10:3, etc. Ac 19:24, 25.

the tongs. or, an ax. Je 10:3.

with hammers. 1 K 6:7.

yea, he is. Hab 2:13.

13 **he marketh**. Ex 20:4, 5. Dt 4:16-18, 28. Ac 17:29. Ro 1:23.

that it may. Ge 31:19, 30, 32. 35:2. Dt 27:15. Jg 17:4, 5. 18:24. Ezk 8:12.

14 **heweth**. Is 40:20. Je 10:3-8. Ho 4:12. Hab 2:19.

strengtheneth. or, taketh courage.

nourish. Ho 9:12.

15 **he maketh a god**. ver. +10. Is 45:20. Jg 2:19. 2 Ch 25:14. Re 9:20.

16 **part thereof**. or, half of it. ver. 19. Ex 24:6. Je 10:3-5.

seen the fire. lit. seen light. Is 24:15mg.

17 **Deliver me**. Is 36:19, 20. 37:38. 1 K 18:26. Da 3:17, 29. 6:16, 20-22, 27.

18 **have not**. ver. 9, 20. Is 45:20. 46:7, 8. Je 10:8, 14. Ro 1:21-23.

for he hath. Is 29:10. Ge +19:11. Dt +2:30. Ps 81:12. Lk +8:10. Ac 14:16. Ro 1:28. 2 C 4:3, 4. 2 Th 2:9-12.

shut. Heb. daubed. Le 14:42. Ezk 13:10, 12, 14. 22:28.

cannot understand. Is 56:11. Ps 92:6. Pr 2:5-9. 28:5. Da 12:10. Ho 14:9. Mt 12:34. Jn 5:44. 8:43. 12:39, 40. 2 P 2:14.

19 **considereth in his heart**. Heb. setteth to his heart. Is 46:8. Ex 7:23. Dt 32:46. Pr 24:32mg. Je +31:21. Ezk 40:4. Hg 1:5mg. Ho 7:2.

an abomination. Dt 27:15. 1 K 11:5, 7. 2 K 23:13.

the stock of a tree. Heb. that which comes of a tree.

20 **feedeth**. Jb 15:2. Ps 102:9. Pr 15:14. Ho 12:1. Lk 15:16.

a deceived. 1 K 22:20-23. Jb 15:31. Ps 14:1-3. 97:7. Ho 4:12. Ro 1:20-22, 28. 2 Th 2:11. 2 T 3:13. 1 J 5:21. Re 12:9. 13:14. 14:9-11. 18:23. 20:3.

turned him. Is 42:17. 45:16.

soul. Heb. nephesh, Ge +12:13.

Is there. Is 28:15-17. Je 16:19. Hab 2:18. 2 Th 2:9-11. 1 T 4:2.

21 **Remember**. Is 42:23. 46:8, 9. Dt 4:9, 23. 31:19-21. 32:18. Ezk 23:19. Ho 4:6. Jon 2:7, 8. 2 T 2:8. He 11:15.

thou art. ver. 1, 2. Is 41:8, 9. 43:1, 7, 15.

O Israel. Ge 32:26.

thou shalt. Is +41:9. 49:14-16. Ro 11:28, 29. He +13:5.

22 **blotted out**. Ps +51:1. 103:12. Je +31:34.

as a thick. Jb 37:11. La 3:42-44.

return. Ezk +33:11. Lk 22:61, 62. 24:47.

have redeemed. Is 1:27. 38:17. +51:11. 59:20, 21. Je 50:20. Lk +1:68, 73, 74. 1 C 6:20. Ga +3:13.

23 **Sing**. Is 42:10-12. 49:13. 55:12, 13. Ps 69:34. 96:11, 12. 98:7, 8. Je 51:48. Lk 2:10-14. Ro 8:19. Re 5:8-14. 12:12. 18:20. 19:1-6.

glorified. Is 26:15. 49:3. 60:21. Ezk 36:1, 8. 39:13. Ep 1:6, 7. 3:21. 2 Th 1:10-12. 1 P 4:11.

24 **thy redeemer**. ver. +6.

and he. ver. 2. Is 43:1, 7. 46:3, 4. 49:1. Jb 31:15. Ps 71:6. 139:13-16. Ga 1:15.

I am. Is 40:22. 42:5. 45:12. 48:13. 51:13. Jb 9:8. 26:7. Ps 104:2. Je 51:15.

maketh all. Col 1:16, 17. He 1:2.

by myself. Jn +1:3.

25 **frustrateth**. Is 47:12-14. 1 K 22:11, 12, 22-25, 37. 2 Ch 18:11, 34. Je 27:9, 10. 28:9-17. 50:36.

maketh. Ex 9:11. Da 1:20. 2:10-12. 4:7. 5:6-8.

diviners. Nu 24:1. Dt +18:10. 1 S 6:2. 28:8. Ezk 22:28.

turneth. Je +19:7. 51:57. Da 5:8.

26 **confirmeth**. Is 42:9. Ex 11:4-6. 12:29, 30. 1 K 13:3-5. 18:36-38. Ezk 38:17. Da 4:14, 28, 29. Zc 1:6. Mt 26:56. Lk +24:44. Ac 2:25-28. 2 P 1:19-21.

that saith. Is 54:3, 11, 12. 60:10. Ezr 2:70. Ps +102:16. Da 9:25. Zc 2:4. 12:6. 14:10, 11.

and I will. Is 58:12. Ne 1:3. 2:3. 3:1, etc. Am 9:14.

decayed places. Heb. wastes. Is 61:4. Ezk 36:10.

27 **Be dry**. Is 11:15, 16. 42:15. 43:16. 51:15. Ps 74:15. Je 50:38. 51:31, 32, 36. Re 16:12.

28 **Cyrus**. Is 41:25. 45:1, 3. 46:11. 48:14, 15. Da 10:1.

my shepherd. Is 63:11. Ps 78:71, 72.

shall perform all. Ac 13:22.

saying. Is 45:13. 2 Ch 36:22, 23. Ezr 1:1-3. 6:3, etc.

foundation. Ezr 3:11.

ISAIAH 45

1 **to his**. Is 13:3. 44:28. 1 K 19:15. Je 27:6.

Cyrus. i.e. supreme power; the sun; spiritual sense, **S#3566h**. Is 44:28. 45:1. 2 Ch 36:22, 23.

Ezr 1:1, 2, 7, 8. 3:7. 4:3, 5. Da 1:21. 10:1.
whose. Is 41:13. 42:6. Ps 73:23.
holden. *or*, strengthened. Ezk 16:49. 30:21-24.

to subdue. Is 41:2, 25. Ezr 1:1. Je 50:3, 35-37. 51:11, 12, 20-24. Da 5:6, 28-30. 7:5. 8:3.
to loose the loins. Jb 12:18, 21mg. Is 22:21. Da 5:6, 30, 31.
to open. Na 2:6.
shut. Is 60:11. Nu 12:14, 15.

2 **go before**. Is 13:4-17.
make. Is 40:4. 42:16. Ec 1:15. Lk 3:5.
straight. Ps +5:8.
break. Ps +2:9. Ps 107:16.

3 **I will give**. Ezr 1:7, 8. Je 27:5-7. 50:37. 51:53. Ezk 29:19, 20. Da 6:28.
that thou. Is 41:23. Ezr 1:2.
which call. Is 43:1. 48:15. 49:1. Ex 33:12, 17.
by thy name. Ge 17:19. 1 K 13:2. 1 Ch 22:9.

4 **Jacob**. Is 41:8, 9. 42:1. 43:3, 4, 14. 44:1. Ex 19:5, 6. Je 50:17-20. Mt 24:22. Mk 13:20. Ro 9:6. 11:7.
mine elect. Is 65:9, 22. Mt 24:21-31. Mk 13:22, 27. Lk 18:7, 8. 1 P 1:2. 2 J +1.
I have even. ver. 1. Is 44:28.
though. Ac 17:23. Ga 4:8, 9. Ep 2:12. 1 Th 4:5.

5 **the Lord**. ver. 14-18, 21, 22. Is 44:8.
none else. ver. 18, 22. Is 46:9. Dt 4:35, 39. +32:39. 1 K 8:60. Ho 13:4. Jl 2:27. Jn +1:1. He +1:8, 9.
no God. Dt +6:4.
I girded thee. Is 22:21. Ezr 1:2. Jb 12:18, 21mg. Ps 18:32, 39.

6 **they may know**. Is 37:20. Ps 46:10. 102:15, 16. Ezk +6:7, 10. Ml 1:11.
none else. Dt 4:35, 39. +32:39.

7 **form**. Ge 1:3-5, 17, 18. Ps 8:3. 104:20-23. Je 31:35. 2 C 4:6. Ja 1:17.
light. Ge +1:3.
create darkness. Ex 10:22. 14:20.
I make peace. Is 10:5, 6. Jb 2:10. 34:29. Ps 29:11. 75:7. Ec 7:13, 14. Je 18:7-10. 51:20. Ezk 14:15-21. Am 5:6. Ac 4:28.
create. Heb. *bara*, Poel Participle, which with "evil" requires the rendering "bring about" (CB).
evil or, calamity. Is 31:2. +47:11. Nu 11:1mg. Ps 5:4. Pr 1:16, 33. Am +3:6.
do all. Dt +2:30. Ep +1:11.

8 **Drop down**. Is 32:15. 44:3. Ps 72:3, 6. 85:9-12. Ezk 34:26. Ho 10:12. 14:5-8. Jl 2:28, 29. 3:18. Ac 2:33. T 3:3-6.
let the earth. Is 4:2. 11:1. 53:2. 61:3, 11. 1 C 3:6-9.
open. Nu 16:32. 26:10. Ps 106:17.
I the Lord. Is 65:17, 18. 66:22. Je 31:22. 2 C 5:21. Ep 2:10. 4:24.

9 **unto him**. Is 64:8. Ex 9:16, 17. Jb 15:24-26.

40:8, 9. Ps 2:2-9. Pr +21:30. Je 50:24. 1 C 10:22.
Shall the clay. Is 10:15. 29:16. Je 18:6. Ro 9:20, 21.

10 **that saith**. Dt +27:16. Ml 1:6. He 12:9.

11 **the Holy One**. Is +1:4.
Ask me. Ge 32:26. Est 8:8. Je 33:3. Ezk 36:37. Da 2:18. 9:2, 3, 24-27. Mt 7:7, 9-11. Mk 11:24. Lk 8:9, 10. 12:41. 13:23, 24. 18:26-30. 20:1-8, 27-35. 21:7-9. Jn 3:4-9. 9:36-38. 10:24, 25. 15:7.
things to come. Da 8:13-15. 9:20-23. Mt 24:3. Ac 1:6, 7. Re 1:3.
concerning my sons. Je 3:19. 31:1, 9. Ho 1:10. Ro 9:4-8. 2 C 6:18. Ga 3:26-29.
concerning the work. Is 29:23. 43:7. 60:21. Ep 2:10.
command. Is 5:6. 10:6. +62:7. Ge 2:16. 32:26. Jg 16:23. Jsh 10:12. Jb 22:28. Ho 12:4.

12 **made the earth**. ver. 18. Ge +1:1, 26, 27. Jn +1:3.
my hands. Is +40:22. Je 27:5. 32:17. Zc 12:1.
all their host. Dt +4:19. Je 31:35.

13 **raised him**. ver. 1-6. Is 41:2, 25. 46:11. 48:14, 15.
in righteousness. Is 42:6. Ps 65:5.
direct. *or*, make straight. ver. 2. Ps +5:8.
he shall build. Is 44:28. 49:23. 52:2, 3. 60:10, 16. 2 Ch 36:22, 23. Ezr 1:1-3. Ro 3:24-26. 1 P 1:18, 19.
price. Is 13:17.

14 **The labor**. Is 18:7. 19:23-25. 23:18. 49:23. 60:5, 6. 61:5, 6. 66:19, 20. Dt +28:33. Ps 68:30, 31. 72:10-15. 138:4. Zc 8:22, 23.
the Sabeans. i.e. *drunkards*, S#5436h. Is 45:13. Ezk 23:42. Jb 1:15. Ezk 23:42. Jl 3:8.
men of stature. Is 10:33. Nu 13:32. 2 S 21:20. Ezk 31:3.
come after. Mt +8:11.
in chains. Is 14:2. 49:23. Ps 149:6, 8.
they shall fall. Is 60:14. 61:5, 9. Ex 11:8. Est 8:17. Ac 10:25, 26. 1 C 14:24, 25. Re 3:9.
Surely. ver. 24. Je 16:19. Zc 8:20-23. 1 C 8:4-6. 14:25. 1 Th 1:9.
and there. ver. 5, 6. Is 44:8.

15 **a God**. Is 8:17. 57:17. Ex 20:21. Ps 44:24. 77:19. 97:2. Jn 12:35, 36. 13:7. Ro 11:33, 34.
O God. ver. 17. Is 46:13. 60:16. Ps 68:26. Mt 1:22, 23. Ac 5:31. 13:23. 2 P 3:18. Re +7:10.

16 **be ashamed**. ver. 20. Is 41:29. +42:17. Je 10:14, 15. 1 J 5:21. Re 14:9, 10.

17 **Israel**. ver. 25. Is 26:4. Ho 1:7. Ro 2:28, 29. 8:1. 11:26. 1 C 1:30, 31. 2 C 5:17-21. Ph 3:8, 9. 1 J 4:15. 5:11, 12.
in the Lord. Jn 14:20.
an everlasting. Heb. *olam* plural, Ps +61:4. Is 51:6, 8. 54:8. 60:19. Ps 103:17. Je 31:3. Jn 5:24. 6:40. 10:28. 2 Th 2:13, 14, 16. He 5:9. 1 J 5:11-13.

ye shall not. Jl +2:26, 27. Ro 8:1. 1 P 2:6.
without end. lit. unto the ages of perpetuity.
Ps +9:18 (**S#5703h**).

18 **that created**. Heb. *bara*. Is 42:5. Je 10:12.
51:15.
  God himself that. Pr 8:22, 23, 30, 31. Jn
  1:1-3.
  he created. ver. 12. Ge 1:1, 28. 9:1. Ps
  115:16. Ezk 36:10-12.
  in vain. Heb. *tohu*. Ge 1:2. Ps 107:40mg. Je
  4:23.
  I am. ver. 5, 6.

19 **spoken**. Is 43:9, 10. 48:16. Dt 29:29. 30:11-
  14. Pr 1:21. 8:1-4. Am 3:7. Jn 7:26, 28, 37-39.
  18:20. Ac 2:4-8.
  Seek. Is 1:15. Le 26:40-45. Dt 30:1, 2, 11. 1 K
  8:47-50. 1 Ch 28:8, 9. 2 Ch 6:37-39. Ps 24:6.
  116:1, 2. Pr 15:8. Je +29:13. Ml 3:13, 14. Mt
  15:8, 9. Ja 4:3.
  speak righteousness. Is 63:1. Nu 23:19, 20.
  Dt 32:4. Ps +9:10. 12:6. 19:7-10. 111:7, 8.
  119:137, 138. Pr 8:6, 8, 9. +30:5.

20 **yourselves**. Is 41:5, 6, 21. 43:9.
  and come. Mt 11:28. Ro 3:29.
  escaped. Is 4:2. Je 25:15-29. 50:28. 51:6-9.
  Ep 2:12, 16. Re 18:3-18.
  they. Is 42:17, 18. 44:17-20. 46:7. 48:7. 1 K
  18:26-29. Ps 115:8. 135:15-18. Je 2:27, 28.
  10:8, 14. 51:17, 18. Hab 2:18-20. Ro 1:21-23.
  god. Heb. *El*, Ex +15:2.

21 **Tell ye**. Ps 26:7. 71:17, 18. 96:10. Je 50:2. Jl
  3:9-12.
  and bring. Is 41:1-4.
  who hath declared. Is 41:22, 23. 43:9. 44:7,
  8. 46:9, 10. 48:3, 14.
  ancient. Heb. *kedem*, Mi +5:2. Is 19:11. 23:7.
  37:26. 46:10. 51:9.
  and there is. ver. 5, 14, 18. Is 44:8.
  a just. ver. 25. Is 43:3, 11. 63:1. Ge +18:25.
  Ps 116:5. Je 23:5, 6. Zp 3:5, 17. Zc 9:9. Ro
  3:25, 26. 4:5. T 2:13, 14. 1 J 1:9.
  God. Heb. *El*, Ex +15:2.
  none beside. Dt 4:35. 6:4. Mk 12:32.

22 **Look**. Nu 21:8, 9. 2 Ch 20:12. Mi 7:7. Zc
  12:10. Lk 23:42, 43. Jn 1:29. 3:13-16. 6:40.
  12:32. 19:37. He 12:2.
  for. ver. 21. Jn 10:28-30. T 2:13. 2 P 1:1.
  ends of the earth. Ps 22:27. 65:5.
  God. Heb. *El*, Ex +15:2.
  none else. ver. +5.

23 **sworn**. Ge 22:15-18. Je 22:5. 49:13. Am 6:8.
  He 6:13-18.
  the word. ver. 19. Is 55:11. Nu 23:19.
  That unto. Is +43:10. 48:11. Ne +9:6. Ro
  11:4. 14:10-12. Ph 2:10.
  bow. Ro 14:11. Ph 2:10.
  every tongue. Is 44:3-5. Ge +21:23. 2 Ch
  15:14, 15. Ne 10:29. Ps 132:2.

24 **Surely**, etc. *or*, Surely he shall say of me, In
  the Lord *is* all righteousness and strength.

in the Lord. ver. 25. Is 54:17. 61:10. Je 23:5,
  6. 1 C 1:30. 2 C 5:21. 2 P 1:1mg.
righteousness. Heb. righteousnesses. Is
  33:15mg. Jg +5:11mg. 1 S 12:7mg. Da 9:18.
strength. Dt 31:23. Ps +18:1, 2. Jl 3:10.
even. Is 55:5. 60:9. Ge +49:10. Mt 11:27, 28.
  Jn 7:37. 12:32. Ro 11:26. Ep 6:10. Re 22:17.
and all. Is 41:11. Ps 2:1-12. 21:8, 9. 72:9.
  110:2. Lk 13:17. 19:27. Re 11:18.

25 **the Lord**. ver. 17, 24. Ac 13:39. Ro 3:24, 25.
  5:1, 18, 19. 8:1, 30, 33, 34. 1 C 6:11. 2 C 5:21.
  the seed. ver. 19. Is 61:9. 65:9, 23. 1 Ch
  16:13. Ps 22:23. Ro 4:16. 9:6-8. Ga 3:27-29.
  be justified. Is 53:11. +60:21. Nu 23:21. Ezk
  36:25. Ac 13:39. Ro 3:24. 5:1, 9, 18, 19. 8:1,
  33, 34. 2 C 5:21. T 3:7. 1 J +2:12.
  glory. Is 41:16. Ps 64:10. Je 9:23, 24. 1 C
  1:31. 2 C 10:17. Ga 6:14. Ph 3:3.

ISAIAH 46

1 **Bel**. i.e. *lord, master*, **S#1078h**. Is 46:1. Je 50:2.
  51:44.
  boweth down. Is 21:9. 41:6, 7. Ex 12:12. 1 S
  5:3, 4. Je 48:1, etc. 50:2. 51:44, 47, 52.
  Nebo. i.e. *a prophet*, the Mercury of the
  Babylonians, "Anubis, Hermes, Mercury." Nu
  +32:3. Ac 14:12.
  their idols. lit. grievous things. Is 10:11.
  21:9. Da 3:1.
  your carriages. Am 5:26.
  a burden. Is 2:20. Je 10:5.

2 **they could**. Is 36:18, 19. 37:12, 19. 44:17.
  45:20.
  but. Jg 18:17, 18, 24. 2 S 5:21. Je 43:12, 13.
  48:7.
  themselves are. Heb. their soul is. Heb.
  nephesh, Ge +27:31.

3 **Hearken**. Is +44:1, 21. 48:1, 17, 18. 51:1, 7.
  Ps 81:8-13.
  the remnant. Is +1:9.
  borne. Is 44:1, 2. 49:1, 2. 63:9. Ex 19:4. Dt
  1:31. 32:11, 12. Ps 22:9, 10. 71:6. Ezk 16:6-
  16.

4 **even to your**. Is 41:4. 43:13, 25. Ps 92:14.
  102:26, 27. Ml 2:16. 3:6. Ro 11:29. He 1:12.
  13:8. Ja 1:17.
  even to hoar. Ps 48:14. 71:18.
  hairs. Ru +4:15.
  will I carry. Is 40:11. 63:9. Dt 33:27.

5 **To whom**. ver. +9. Is +40:18. Ph 2:6.
  compare. Nu +21:27.

6 **lavish**. Is 40:19, 20. 41:6, 7. 44:12-19. 45:20.
  Ex 32:2-4. Jg 17:3, 4. 1 K 12:28. Je 10:3, 4, 9,
  14. Ho 8:4-6. Hab 2:18-20. Ac 17:29.
  maketh it a god. Ps 115:4-8.
  they fall. Is 2:8. 44:17. Da 3:5-15.

7 **they carry him**. 1 S 5:3. Je 10:5. Da 3:1.
  one shall cry. Is 37:38. 45:20. Jg 10:12-14. 1
  K 18:26, 40. Je 2:28. Jon 1:5, 14-16.

8 Remember. Is 44:18-21. Dt 32:7, 29. Ps 115:8. 135:18. Je 10:8. Ac 7:51. 1 C 14:20.
bring. Is 47:7. Ezk 18:28. Hg 1:5, 7. Lk 15:17. Ep 5:14.

9 the former. Is 42:9. 65:17. Dt 32:7. Ne 9:7, etc. Ps ch. 78, 105, 106. 111:4. Je 23:7, 8. Da 9:6-15.
of old. Heb. *olam*, Ge +6:4.
I am God. Is +45:5, 6, 14, 18, 21, 22.
and there is none like. ver. +5. Ex +8:10.

10 the end. Is 41:21-23. 44:7. 45:21. Ge +3:15. 12:2, 3. +49:10, 22-26. Nu 24:17-24. Dt 4:25-31. 28:15, etc. Ac 15:18.
ancient. Mi +5:2.
My counsel. ver. 11. Is +14:27. Ps 135:6. Ac 3:23. 4:27, 28. Ro 11:33, 34. He 6:17.
will do my. Is +14:27. Ex +33:19. Dt +2:30. Mt 20:15.

11 Calling. Is 13:2-4. 21:7-9. 41:2, 25. 45:1-6. Je 50:29. 51:20-29.
a ravenous bird. Ezk 39:4.
the man. Is 44:28. 45:13. 48:14, 15. Ezr 1:2. Ps 76:10. Da 7:2-4. Ac 4:28.
that executeth my counsel. Heb. of my counsel. Ps 119:24mg.
I have spoken. Is 38:15. Nu 23:19.
purposed. Is +14:27.

12 Hearken. ver. 3. Is 28:23. 45:20. Ps 49:1. Pr 1:22, 23. 8:1-5. Je 50:45. Ep 5:14. Re 3:17, 18.
ye stouthearted. Is 48:4. Ps 76:5. Zc 7:11, 12. Ml 3:13-15. Ac 7:51.
that. Ps 119:150, 155. Je 2:5. Ep 2:13.

13 bring. Is 51:5. 61:11. Ro 1:17. 3:21-26. 10:3-15.
shall not tarry. Ps 14:7. 46:1, 5. Hab 2:3. He 10:37.
salvation. Is 12:2, 6. 28:16. 61:3. 62:11. Jl 3:17. Lk 2:11. 1 P 2:6.
Israel. Is 43:7. 44:23. 60:21. 61:3. Je 33:9. Hg 1:8. Jn 17:10. Ep 1:6. 2 Th 1:10, 12.

ISAIAH 47

1 Come. Is +6:9.
down. Is 3:26. 26:5. 52:2. Jb 2:8, 13. Ps 18:27. Je 13:18. 48:18. La 2:10, 21. Ezk 26:16. 28:17. Ob 3, 4. Jon 3:6.
O virgin. Je +18:13.
daughter. Is 13:1. Nu +21:25. Ps 137:8. Je 50:42. 51:33. Zc 2:7.
there is. Is 14:13, 14. Ps 89:44. Hg 2:22.
thou shalt. ver. 7-9. Is 32:9-11. Dt 28:56, 57. La 4:5. Re 16:19. 17:1-6. 18:7.

2 the millstones. Ex 11:5. Jg 16:21. Jb 31:10. Je 27:7. La 5:13. Mt 24:41. Lk 17:35.
grind meal. Ex 11:5. Mt 24:41.
make bare. Is +3:17.
uncover. Is 20:2.

3 Thy. Is +20:2.

I will take. Is 13:6. 59:17, 18. Dt +32:35, 41-43. Ps 137:8, 9. Je 13:22, 26. 51:4, 11, 20-24. 34-36, 56. Na 3:5. Re 16:19. 17:14, 16, 17.

4 our redeemer. Is +41:14. 62:11. 63:1. Je 31:11. Mt 1:21. Lk 2:11. Jn 1:29. 4:42. Ac 5:31. Ro 11:26.
Lord of hosts. Ps +24:10.
his name. Ex 3:15. 15:3.

5 silent. Is 13:20. 14:23. 1 S 2:9. Ps 31:17. 46:10. Je 25:10. La 1:1. Hab 2:20. Zc 2:13. Mt 22:12, 13. Ju 13. Re 18:21-24.
for. ver. 7. Is 13:19. 14:4. Da 2:37, 38. Re 17:3-5, 18. 18:7, 16-19.

6 wroth. Is 10:6. 42:24, 25. 2 S 24:14. 2 Ch 28:9. Ps 69:26. Zc 1:15.
I have polluted. Is 43:28. La 2:2. Ezk 24:21. 28:16.
thou didst. Is 13:16-18. 14:17. Ps 137:1-3. Ob 10, 16. Mt 7:2. Ja 2:13.
no mercy. 2 K 25:5, 6, 26. Je 50:17. 51:34.
upon. Dt 28:50.
the ancient. La 4:16.

7 thou saidst. ver. 5. Ezk 28:2, 12-14. 29:3. Da 4:29, 30. 5:18-23. Re 18:7.
for ever. Heb. *olam*, Ex +12:24.
so that. Is 46:8, 9. Dt 32:29. Je 5:31. Ezk 7:3-9.

8 given. Is 21:4, 5. 22:12, 13. 32:9. Jg 18:7, 27. Je 50:11. Da 5:1-4, 30. Zp 2:15. Re 18:3-8.
I am. ver. 10. Je 50:31, 32. 51:53. Da 4:22, 30. 5:23. 11:36. Hab 2:5-8. 2 Th 2:4.
none else. Is 45:6, 14. 46:9.
I shall not. Ps 10:5, 6. Na 1:10. Lk 12:18-20. 17:27-29. Re 18:7.

9 these two. Is 51:18, 19. Ru 1:5, 20. Lk 7:12, 13.
in a moment. Is 13:19. Ps 73:19. Da 5:30. 1 Th 5:3. Re 18:8-10.
they shall come. Is 13:20-22. 14:22, 23. Je 51:29, 62-64. Re 14:8. 18:21-23.
for the multitude. ver. 12, 13. Da 2:2. 4:7. 5:7. 2 Th 2:9, 10. Re +9:21.

10 thou hast trusted. Is 28:15. 59:4. Ps 52:7. 62:10.
thou hast said. Is 29:15. Jb 22:13, 14. Ps 10:11. 64:5. 94:7-9. Ec +8:8. Je 23:24. Ezk 8:12. 9:9.
Thy wisdom. Is 5:21. Ezk 28:2-6. Ro 1:22. 1 C 1:19-21. 3:19.
perverted thee. or, caused thee to turn away. Je 50:6.
I am. ver. 8.

11 evil. S#7451h, Is +45:7. Ge 19:19. 44:4. Jb 20:12. Ps 97:10.
thou shalt not know. Is 37:36. Ex 12:29, 30. Ne 4:11. Re 3:3.
from whence it riseth. Heb. the morning thereof. Is +8:20. 14:12. 17:14.
thou shalt not be. Ps 50:22. Je 51:39-42. Da 5:25-30. 1 Th 5:3. Re 18:9, 10.

put it off. Heb. expiate. Nu 35:33. Mt 18:34. Lk 12:59.

desolation. Is 10:3. Jb 30:3, 14. Ps 35:8.

suddenly. Pr 6:15. 24:22. 29:1. Ec 9:12. Is 29:5. 30:13. Je 15:8. 1 Th 5:3. Re 18:21.

not know. Pr 5:6.

12 **Stand now**. ver. 9, 10. Is 8:19. 19:3. 44:25. Ex 7:11. 8:7, 18, 19. 9:11. Je 2:28. Ezk 21:21-23. Da 5:7-9. Na 3:4. Ac 13:8-12. 2 Th 2:9-12. Re 17:4-6.

enchantments. ver. 9. Dt +18:11. Ps 58:5. Pr 21:9mg.

sorceries. ver. +9. 2 Ch +33:6. Je +27:9.

13 **wearied**. Is 57:10. Ezk 24:12. Hab 2:13.

Let now. Is 44:25. Da 2:2, 10. 5:7, 8, 15, 16, 30.

astrologers, the stargazers. Heb. viewers of the heavens.

stargazers. Is 29:10. 30:10. 1 Ch 29:29. 2 Ch 19:2. 29:25, 30. 33:18, 19. Mi 3:7.

the monthly prognosticators. Heb. that gave knowledge concerning the months.

monthly. Ge 7:11. 8:4. 29:14.

prognosticators. Je 16:21. Da 8:19.

14 **as stubble**. 1 C +3:12.

the fire. Zp 3:8. Mt 3:12. 2 Th 1:8. He 10:27. 2 P 3:7. Re 19:3.

themselves. Heb. their souls. Heb. *nephesh*, Nu +23:10. Mt +10:28. 16:26.

there shall. Is 30:14. Je 51:25, 26. Re 18:21.

15 **thy merchants**. Is 56:11. Ezk 27:12-25. Re 18:11-19.

they shall. Je 50:37. 51:6-9. Re 18:15-17.

ISAIAH 48

1 **Hear**. Mt 13:9.

house of Jacob. Is +2:5.

which are. Ge 32:28. 35:10. 2 K 17:34. Jn 1:47. Ro 2:17, 28, 29. 9:6, 8. Re 2:9. 3:9.

come. Nu 24:7. Dt 33:28. Ps 68:26. Pr 5:16.

which swear. Is 44:5. Dt 5:28.

make mention. Is 26:13. 62:6. Ex 23:13.

not in truth. Is 1:10-14. Le 19:12. Ps 50:16-20. 66:3mg. Je 4:2. 5:2, 3. 7:9, 10. Ml +3:5. Mt 15:7-9. 23:14. Jn 4:24. 1 T 4:2. 2 T 3:2-5.

2 **they call**. Is 52:1. 64:10, 11. Ne 11:1, 18. Ps 48:1. 87:3. Da 9:24. Mt 4:5. 27:53. Re 11:2. 21:2. 22:19.

and stay. Is 10:20. Jg 17:13. 1 S 4:3-5. Je 7:4-11. 21:2. Mi 3:11. Jn 8:33, 40, 41. Ro 2:17.

The Lord. Ps +24:10.

3 **declared**. Is 41:22. 42:9. 43:9. 44:7, 8. 45:21. 46:9, 10.

and I. Is 10:12-19, 33, 34. 37:7, 29, 36-38. Nu 23:19. Jsh 21:45. 23:14, 15. Ps 89:2. 119:89, 90.

4 **I knew**. Is 46:12. Ps 78:8. Zc 7:11, 12.

obstinate. Heb. hard. Is 14:3. 19:4. 21:2mg.

27:1, 8. 2 S 3:39. Je 5:3. Ezk 3:4-7. Da 5:20. Ro 2:5. He +3:13.

and thy neck. 2 Ch +30:8. Ps 75:5. Pr 29:1. Zc 7:12.

thy brow. Je 3:3. Ezk 3:7-9.

5 **even**. ver. 3. Is 44:7. 46:10. Lk 1:70. Ac 15:18.

before. Ge +1:28.

Mine idol. Is 42:8, 9. Ex 32:4. Je 44:17, 18.

6 **hast heard**. Ps 107:43. Je 2:31. Mi 6:9.

and will. Is 21:10. 43:8-10. Ps 40:9, 10. 71:15-18. 78:3-6. 119:13. 145:4, 5. Je 50:2. Mt 10:27. Ac +1:8.

showed. Is 42:9. Da 12:8-13. Am +3:6. Jn 15:15. Ro 16:25, 26. 1 C 2:9. 1 P 1:10-12. Re 1:19. 4:1. 5:1, 2. 6:1, etc.

new things. Is 65:17. Ro 16:25.

hidden things. Is 42:9. 49:6. 1 P 1:10-12.

not know. Dt 1:31, 32. 4:9.

7 **created**. or, produced. lit. prepared. Ex 34:10. Ps 148:5. Ezk 21:30.

now. Is 65:17, 18.

not from. Is 45:21.

I knew. Is 43:10. 46:10. Ex 6:7. Ezk 39:6. Jl 3:17.

8 **thou heardest**. Is 6:9, 10. 26:11. 29:10, 11. 42:19, 20. Je 5:21. Mt 13:13-15. Jn 12:39, 40.

thine ear. Is 50:5. Ps 40:6. 139:1-4. Je 6:10.

I knew. ver. 4. Is 21:2. Je 3:7-11, 20. 5:11. Ho 5:7. 6:7. Ml 2:11.

a transgressor. Ex 32:8. Dt 9:7, 24. Ps 51:5. 58:3. Ezk 16:3-5. Ep 2:3.

9 **my name's**. ver. 11. Is 37:35. 43:25. Dt 32:27. Jsh 7:9. 1 S +12:22. Ps 25:11. 79:9. 106:8. 115:1. 143:11. Je 14:7. Ezk 20:9, 14, 22, 44. 36:22, 32. Da 9:17-19. Ep 1:6.

defer. Nu 14:17-21. Ne 9:30, 31. Ps 78:38. 103:8-10. Pr 19:11.

10 **I have refined**. Is 1:25, 26. Ezk 20:38. 22:18-22. He 12:10, 11. 1 P 1:7. Re 3:19.

with silver. *or*, for silver.

I have chosen. Dt 4:20.

affliction. Ps 118:18. 119:67. 2 C 4:17, 18. He 12:6.

11 **mine own**. ver. 9.

for how. Is 52:5. Nu 14:15, 16. Dt 32:26, 27. Ezk 20:9, 39. Ro 2:24.

I will not give. ver. 5. Is 42:8. 45:23. Ex 20:5. Ne +9:6. Ps 115:1. Je 23:5. Jn 5:23. +17:5.

12 **Hearken**. Is 34:1. 46:3. 49:1. 51:1, 4, 7. 55:3. Pr 7:24. 8:32.

my called. Dt 7:6. Mt 20:16. Ro 1:6. 8:28. 1 C 1:24. 1 P 2:9. Re 17:14.

I am he. Is 41:4. 44:6. Dt +32:39. Jn +8:24. Re +1:8, 11, 17, 18. 2:8. 22:13.

the first. Is 41:4. 44:6. Re 22:13, 14.

13 **hand**. Is 42:5. 45:18. Ge 1:1. Ex 20:11. Ps 102:25. Jn 1:3. He 1:10-12.

and. Is 40:12.

my right hand hath spanned. *or*, the palm of my right hand hath spread out. Is 40:22. Jb 37:18. Ps +18:35.
spanned. Ex +31:18.
when. Is 40:26. Ps 119:89-91. 147:4. 148:5-8.

14 **assemble**. Is 41:22. 43:9. 44:7. 45:20, 21.
The Lord. Is 45:1-3. Mk 10:21.
he will do. Is 13:4, 5, 17, 18. 44:28. 46:11. Je 50:21-29. 51:20-24.

15 **prosperous**. Ps +1:3. 45:4. Ezk 1:2.

16 **Come ye near**. Ja +4:8.
I have not. ver. +3-6. Is 45:19. Dt 30:11. Jn 18:20.
there am I. Ex 3:14. Jn +1:1. 1 P 1:10, 11.
the Lord God. Is 11:1-5. +42:1. 61:1-3. Zc 2:8-11. Lk 4:18. Jn 3:34. 20:21, 22.
and his. Ge +1:26.
Spirit. Heb. *ruach*, **S#7307h**. Is 40:13. 59:19, 21. 61:1. 63:10, 11-14. Ge 6:3. 2 S 23:2. 1 K 18:12. 22:24. 2 K 2:16. 2 Ch 18:23. Ne 9:20, 30. Jb 26:13. 33:4. Ezk 3:12, 14a. 8:3. 11:1, 24. 37:1, 14. 43:5. Ho 9:7mg. Mi 2:7. 3:8. Zc 4:6. 6:8. 7:12. Ml 2:15. For the other uses of *ruach*, see Ge +6:3.

17 **the Lord**. ver. 20. Is +1:4. 43:14. 44:6-24. 54:5.
which teacheth. Is 2:3. 30:20. 54:13. Dt 8:17, 18. 1 K 8:36. Jb 22:21, 22. 36:22. Ps 25:8, 9, 12. 71:17. 73:24. Je 31:33, 34. Mi 4:2. Jn 6:45. Ep 4:21.
which leadeth. Ps +23:3. Je 6:16.

18 **O that**. Dt +5:29.
thou hadst. Dt 5:29. 32:29. Ps 81:13-16. Mt 23:37. Lk 19:41, 42.
hearkened to. Jn +13:17.
then had. Is 32:15-18. 66:12. Ps 36:8. 119:165. Am 5:24. Mt 11:21, 23. Ro 14:17.

19 **seed**. Ge +22:17.
his name. ver. 9. Is 9:14. 14:22. Jsh 7:9. Ru 4:10. 1 K 9:7. Ps 9:5. 109:13. Zp 1:4.

20 **ye forth**. Re 18:4.
with a voice. Is 12:1. 26:1. 45:22, 23. 49:13. 52:9. Ex 15:1, etc. 19:4-6. Ps 126:1, 2. Je 31:12, 13. 51:48. Re 18:20. 19:1-6.
utter it even. ver. 6. Je 31:10. 50:2.
redeemed. 2 S 7:23. Is +51:11.

21 **they thirsted**. Is 30:25. 35:6, 7. 41:17, 18. 43:19, 20. 49:10. Je 31:9.
he led them. Dt 8:2.
he caused. Ex 17:6. Nu 20:11. Ne 9:15. Ps 78:15, 20. 105:41.

22 **no peace**. Is 57:20, 21. Jb 15:20-24. Je 6:14. 8:11. Ezk 13:10, 16. Mt 12:43. Lk 19:42. Ro 3:16, 17. Re 14:11.

ISAIAH 49

1 **Listen**. Is +11:11. 45:22.
and hearken. Is 55:3. 57:19. Ep 2:17. He 12:25.

The Lord. ver. 5. Ps 71:5, 6. Je 1:5. Mt 1:20, 21. Lk 1:15, 31-35. 2:10, 11. Jn 10:36. Ga 1:15. 1 P 1:20.
mother. Is +7:14. Mt 1:23.

2 **he hath made**. Is 11:4. 50:4. 51:16. Ps 45:2-5. Je 1:6-10. Ho 6:5. Jn 6:63. He 4:12. Re 1:16. 2:12, 16. 19:11, 13, 15.
in the shadow. Ps +91:1. Lk 23:46.
made me. Is 50:4. 61:1-3. Ps 45:5. Je 1:18. 15:19, 20. 2 C 10:5.

3 **my servant**. Is 42:1. 43:21. 44:23. 52:13. 53:10, 11. Zc 3:8. Mt 17:5. Jn +13:31, 32. Ep 1:6. Ph 2:6-11. 1 P 2:9.
glorified. Ga 1:24.

4 **I have labored**. Is 65:2. Ezk 3:19. Mt 17:17. 23:37. Jn 1:11. 7:5. Ro 10:21. Ga +4:11.
spent. Le 26:20. 2 C 12:15.
yet. Is 53:10-12. Ps 22:22-31. Mt 11:25-27. Lk 24:26. Jn +17:4, 5. 2 C 2:15. Ph 2:9, 10. He 12:2.
work. *or*, reward. Is +62:11mg.

5 **that formed**. ver. 1. Ph 2:6, 7.
to bring. Is 56:8. Mt 15:24. Ac 10:36. Ro 15:8.
Though, etc. *or*, That Israel may be gathered to him, and I may, etc. Is 9:3. Ge +49:10. Mt 23:37. Jn 6:37. 17:1, 2, 12. Ep 1:5, 6.
Israel. Mt 21:37-41. 23:37. Lk 19:42. 1 Th 2:15, 16.
yet. Ps 110:1-3. Mt 3:17. 11:27. 17:5. 28:18. Jn 3:35. 5:20-27. Ep 1:20-22. 1 P 3:22.

6 **It is a light thing that**. *or*, *Art thou* lighter, than that, etc. 2 K 3:18. 20:10.
restore. Is 62:1, 2. Ezk 34:11-14. Ac +1:6. +3:19, 21. +15:26.
preserved. *or*, desolations. Is 1:8. 48:6. +65:4 (monuments).
I will also. Ml +4:2. Mt +4:16. Ro 15:10.
that thou mayest. Is +11:10. 24:14-16. 46:13. Lk +3:6. 24:46, 47.
the end. Ge 41:57.

7 **the Redeemer**. Is +48:17. Re 3:7.
whom man despiseth. *or*, to him that is despised in soul.
man. Heb. *nephesh*, Ex +15:9. Ps 42:5, 6. Zc 11:8. Mt 26:67. Lk +22:63. Jn 15:25. 18:40. 19:6, 15. 1 C 2:14.
the nation abhorreth. Mt 27:17-22. Lk 4:27-30.
to a. Mt 20:28. Lk 22:27.
servant of rulers. Ge 39:1. Ps 2:2. Mt 27:41. Ph 2:7.
Kings. ver. 23. Is 52:15. 60:3, 10, 16. Ps 2:10-12. 68:29, 31. 72:10, 11. 138:4. Re 11:15.
princes shall worship. Ps 72:10, 11. Mt 2:1, 2, 11.
and he. Is 42:1. Lk 23:35. 1 P 2:4.

8 **In an**. Ps 69:13. Lk 2:14. Jn 11:41, 42. 2 C 6:2. Ep 1:6. He 5:7. 7:25.
day of salvation. Ps 102:13. +118:24. Ho 6:3.

have I helped. Is 42:1. 50:7-9. Ac 2:24-32.
give thee. Is 42:6. Mt 26:28. He 8:6. 12:24.
for a covenant. Ge 17:10. Ex +8:23. 12:11.
Lk 22:20. 1 C 10:16.
to establish. *or*, raise up. Is 51:16. 1 Ch
16:30. Ps 75:3.
to cause. ver. 19. Is 51:3. 54:3. 58:12. 61:4.
Ps 2:8. Ep 2:12-19.
9 **to the**. Ps +146:7. Col 1:13. 1 P 2:9.
go forth. Jn 5:25. 11:25.
to them. Is +9:2.
They shall feed. Is 5:17. +40:11. Ps +22:26.
23:1, 2. Jl 3:18. Jn 10:9.
high. Dt 32:13.
10 **shall not hunger**. Mt +5:6. Jn 6:35.
nor thirst. Jn 4:14.
neither. Is 4:6. 25:4. 32:2. Ps 121:5, 6.
he that. Is 54:10. Ps 23:2-4. Je 31:9. Ezk
34:23.
shall lead. Jn +10:3, 4.
even by. Jn 7:38, 39.
guide. Is 58:11. Ps 25:9, 10. 34:5, 11. Lk
10:21. Jn 14:26. 1 J 2:27.
11 **I will make**. Is 11:16. 35:8-10. 40:3, 4.
43:19. 57:14. 62:10. Ps 107:4, 7. Lk 3:4, 5. Jn
14:6.
highways. Is +7:3.
12 **these shall**. Is +11:10. Ps 72:10, 11, 17. Lk
+13:29. Re 7:9. 11:15.
Sinim. i.e. *thorns*, **S#5515h**, only here.
Understood by some to be a possible reference
to China. Others refer the name to "Sin,"
mentioned in Ezk 30:15; to Syene, Ezk 30:6;
or "Sin" in Sinai, Ex 16:1. Compare "Sinite,"
Ge 10:17; 1 Ch 1:15.
13 **O heavens**. Is 42:10, 11. 44:23. 52:9. 55:12.
Ps 96:11-13. 98:4-9. Lk 2:13, 14. 15:10. Re
5:8-13. 7:9-12. 14:3.
break forth. Is +14:7.
the Lord. Is 12:1. Zc +1:17. 2 C 7:6. 2 Th
2:16, 17.
have mercy. Is +54:8.
14 **Zion said**. Mt 3:9. Ro 3:3. 4:2. 6:1, 2. 7:7.
9:14, 15. 9:19. 11:20, 21. 1 C 14:35. 15:35, 36.
The Lord. Is 40:27. Ps 22:1. 31:22. 77:6-10.
89:38-46. Ro +11:1-5.
forsaken. Is +1:4. +54:7. Zc 2:10-12.
my Lord. Ps +13:1.
15 **a woman**. 1 K 3:26, 27. Ps 103:13. Ml 3:17.
Mt 7:11.
forget. Je 2:32.
suckling. Is 65:20.
that she should not have compassion.
Heb. from having compassion. Is +22:4.
they may. Le +26:29. 2 K 11:1, 2. Ps 27:10.
Ro 1:31.
yet. Is 44:21. Je 31:20. Ho 11:1. Ro +11:28,
29.
not forget. Is +41:9. Ps +13:1. 77:9. +94:14.
Ro 8:38, 39. He +13:5.

16 **I have**. Ex 13:9. 28:9-30. SS 8:6. Je 22:24. Hg
2:23. Re 13:16.
palms. Ge +3:7. 1 S 5:4.
thy walls. Is 26:1. 54:12. 60:18. Re 21:10-21.
17 **children**. Is 51:18-20. 62:5. Ezr 1:5. Ne 2:4-9,
17. Ezk 28:24.
haste. Is 51:14.
thy destroyers. ver. 19. Is 51:13, 22, 23.
60:10, 18.
18 **Lift up**. Is 60:4. Ge 13:14. +22:13. Mt 13:41,
42. Re 22:15.
all these. ver. 12, 22. Is 43:5, 6. 54:1-3. 60:5-
11. 66:12, 13, 20. Je 31:8. Ga 3:28, 29.
As I live. Is 54:9. Ge 22:16. Dt +32:40.
thou shalt. Is 61:10. Pr 17:6.
as a bride. Je 2:32. Re 21:2.
19 **thy waste**. ver. 8. Is 51:3. 54:1, 2. Je 30:18,
19. 33:10, 11. Ezk 36:9-15. Ho 1:10, 11. Zc
2:4, 11. 10:10. Ro 11:11, 12.
they that. ver. 17, 25, 26. Ps +35:25. Je
30:16.
20 **children**. Is 60:4. Ho 1:10. Mt 3:9. Ga 4:26-
28.
The place. Is 51:3. 54:1, 2. Jsh 17:14-16. 2 K
6:1.
21 **Who hath**. 1 S 17:7.
seeing. Je 31:15-17. Mt 3:9. Ro 11:11-17, 24.
Ga 3:29. 4:26-29.
am desolate. Is 3:26. 51:17-20. 52:2. 54:3-8.
60:15. 62:4. 64:10. La 1:1-3. Mt 24:29, 30. Lk
21:24. Ro 11:26-31. Ep 2:13.
22 **Behold**. ver. 12. Is 2:2, 3. 11:10, 11. 42:1-4.
60:3-11. 66:7-12, 18-20. Ps 22:27. 67:4-7.
72:8, 17. 86:9. Ml 1:11. Lk +13:29. Ro 11:15.
lift up. Pr +1:24.
set up. Is 62:10.
shall bring. Is 14:2. 60:9. Ps 126:2. Jn 3:14,
15. 12:32.
arms. Heb. bosom. Ne 5:13. Ps 129:7.
daughters. Is 60:4.
carried upon. Is 66:12.
23 **kings**. ver. +7. Is 62:2. Ezr 1:2-4. 6:7-12.
7:11-28. Ne 2:6-10. Est ch. 8-10. Ps 2:10-12.
68:31. 72:10, 11. 138:4. Re 21:24-26.
nursing fathers. Heb. nourishers. lit. "stedfast ones" or "supporters." Nu 11:12. 2 K
10:15. 1 Th 2:7.
queens. Heb. princesses. or, king's daughters.
1 K 11:3. Est 1:18. La 1:1.
bow. Is 45:14. 60:14. Ge 43:26. Ps 72:9. Re
3:9.
lick up. Nu 22:4. Ps 72:9. Mi 7:17.
shalt know. Ex 6:7.
for they. Is 25:9. 50:7. 64:4. Ps 34:22. 69:6. Jl
+2:26. 1 P 2:6.
wait. Is 40:31. Ge 48:18. Ps 27:14. 37:9. 62:5.
24 **Shall**. Ezk 37:3, 11.
prey. Is 42:22. 53:12. Nu 31:11, 12, 26, 27,
32. Ps 22:15. 124:6, 7. 126:1-3. Zp +3:8. Mt
12:29. Lk 11:21, 22.

lawful captive. Heb. captivity of the just. Ezr 9:9, 13. Ne 9:33, 37. Ps 68:18. 69:33. 79:11. +102:13, 16, 20. 116:8, 9. Je 25:6-9, 11-14. 29:14.

25 **Even**. Is 10:27. 52:2-5. Je 29:10. 50:17-19, 33, 34. Zc 9:11. He 2:14, 15. 1 J 3:8.
captives. Heb. captivity. Is 61:1. Nu 31:12, 19, 26mg. 2 Ch 28:17mg. Ps 68:18. Je 48:46mg. Da 11:8. Am 4:10mg.
I will contend. Is 41:11, 12. 54:15-17. Ge 12:3. Nu 23:8, 9. Je 50:34. 51:35, 36. Zc 9:13-16. 12:3-6. 14:3, 12. Ro 8:31-39. Re 18:20.
I will save. Is +24:13. 25:9. 33:22. 41:1, 2, 9, 10, 11. 54:13. Ps 50:2-5. Je +30:7. Ga 4:26.

26 **I will feed**. Is 9:20. Ex 4:22, 23. 14:8, 27, 30, 31. 15:1. Jg 7:22.
drunken. Re 14:19, 20. 16:6. 17:6.
sweet wine. *or*, new wine. SS 8:2. Jl 1:5.
and all. Is 41:14-20. 45:6. 60:16. Ps 9:16. 58:10, 11. 83:18. Ezk 39:7. Da 7:21-27. Re 15:3, 4.
thy Savior. Is 12:2. 25:9. 26:1. 35:4. 63:1. Je 23:6. 30:7. Da 4:37. Mt 12:29. Lk 11:21, 22. He 2:14, 15. 9:28.
the mighty. Is +9:6. +10:21. 60:16. Ge 49:24. Dt 10:17. Ps 50:1. Je 32:18. Hab 1:12. Mt 11:21. Lk 9:43. Ep 1:21. Re 7:10, 12.
One of Jacob. Ps +132:2.

ISAIAH 50

1 **the bill**. Dt 24:1-4. Je 3:1, 8. Ho 2:2-4. Mk 10:4-12.
divorcement. Dt 24:1, 3. Je 3:8.
sold. Le +25:39.
for your iniquities. Is 59:1, 2. Je 3:8. 4:18. 31:31, 32.
your mother. 2 S +20:19. Ga 4:26.

2 **when I came**. Is 59:16. 63:3, 5. Pr +1:24. Je 5:1. 8:6. 35:15. Ho 11:2, 7. Jn 1:11. 3:19.
no man. Je 5:1. Jn 1:11. Ac 13:46. 18:6. 28:28.
Is my. Is 59:1. Ge 18:14. Nu 11:23.
have I. Is 36:20. 2 Ch 32:15. Da 3:15, 29. 6:20, 27.
at my. Ps 114:3, 5, 7. Mk +4:39.
I dry. Is 42:15. Ex +14:21.
their fish. Ex 7:18, 21.
rivers. Is 44:27. Jsh 4:7, 18. Ps 107:33.

3 **I clothe**. Ex 10:21. Ps 18:11, 12. Mt 27:45. Re 6:12.
sackcloth. Jb +16:15.

4 **God**. Is 49:2. Ex 4:11, 12. Ps 32:3, 8. 45:2. Je 1:9. Mt 10:19. 22:46. Mk 13:11. Lk 2:46, 47, 52. 4:22. 21:15. Jn 7:46. 1 C 1:30. Col 2:3. 3:16.
learned. Is +8:16.
that I should know. Jb 4:3, 4. Jn 7:16. 8:28, 38, 46, 47. 12:49. 14:10, 24. 17:8. 2 C 1:4.

a word. Is 57:15-19. Pr 15:23. 25:11. Mt 11:28. 13:54.
weary. Jn 4:6, 7.
morning by. Is 28:19. 2 S 13:4mg.
waketh mine ear. 1 S 9:15, 17. 15:22. Ps +10:17. 78:1. Ezk 3:10. Hab 2:1.
learned. Is +8:16. Jn 7:15-17.

5 **opened mine ear**. Is 48:8. Ex 21:2-6. Ps 40:6-8. Mt 26:39. Jn 8:29. 14:31. 15:10. Ph 2:8. He 5:8. 10:5-9.
not rebellious. Mt 26:39. Jn 4:34. 14:31. He 5:8. 10:5.

6 **gave**. Le +1:3. Jn 10:18. He 12:2.
my back. Mt +27:30. Jn 19:1. He 12:2.
the smiters. Zc 13:7. Mt 26:31.
my cheeks. 2 S 10:4. 2 S 20:9.
that plucked. Ne 13:25.
I hid not. Is 53:5. He 12:2.
spitting. Mt +26:67. 27:30. Mk 14:65.

7 **the Lord**. ver. 9. Is 42:1. 49:8. Ps 89:21-27. 110:1. Lk 22:43. Jn 16:33. He 13:6.
I set. Je 1:18. Ezk 3:8, 9. Mt 23:13-36. 26:53, 54. Lk 9:51. 11:39-54. Ro 1:16. 1 P 4:1, 16.
ashamed. Is 49:23.

8 **near that**. Is 53:6. Ro 8:32-34. 1 T 3:16.
let us. Is 41:1, 21. Ex 22:9. Dt 19:17. Jb 23:3-7. Mt 5:25.
mine adversary. Heb. the master of my cause. Ge +3:14, 15. Zc 3:1, etc. Mt 4:10, 11. Jn 12:31. Re 12:10.

9 **help me**. Is 41:13, 14. 42:1. 1 P 2:21-23.
who is. Ro 8:33, 34.
they all. Is 51:6-8. Jb 13:28. Ps 39:11. 102:26. Mt 24:35. He 1:11, 12.

10 **is among**. Pr +3:7. Ml 3:16.
obeyeth. Is 42:1. 49:3. 53:11. He +5:9.
that walketh in darkness. Is 9:2. 59:9. Jb 29:3. Ps 23:4. La 3:2.
hath no light. Ps +112:4.
let him trust. Is 26:3, 4. 1 S 30:6. 1 Ch 5:20. 2 Ch 13:18. 20:12, +20. Jb 13:15. 23:8-10. Ps 4:5. +9:10. 10:14. 22:4, 5. 25:20. 27:13, 14. 28:7. 31:1. 37:5, 6. 40:1-4. 42:11. 46:1. 57:1. 62:8. 71:5. 73:28. 112:7, 8. 118:8, 9. 141:8. 145:21. La 3:25, 26. Mi 7:7-9. Hab 3:17, 18. 2 C 1:8-10. He 10:35. 1 P 5:7.
the name. Ps +9:10.
and stay. 2 Ch 13:18.

11 **all ye**. Is 28:15-20. 30:15, 16. 55:2. Ps 20:7, 8. Je 17:5-7. Jon 2:8. Mt 15:6-8. Ro 1:21, 22. 10:3.
that kindle. Is 64:2. Dt 32:22. Je 15:14. 17:4.
compass. or, gird. Is +8:9.
walk. Is 2:5. Ec 11:9, 10. Ezk 20:39. Am 4:4, 5. 1 Th 1:3. 1 J 1:7.
This shall. Jn 9:39.
ye shall. Is 8:22. 65:13-16. Ps 16:4. 32:10. Mt 8:12. 22:13. Lk 16:22, 23. Jn 8:24. 1 C +6:9. 2 Th 1:8, 9. Re 19:20. 20:15.

ISAIAH 51

1 Hearken. ver. 4, 7. Is 46:3, 4. 48:12. 55:2, 3.
ye that follow. ver. 7. Ps 94:15. Pr 15:9.
21:21. Mt +5:6. 6:33. Ro 9:30-32. 14:19. Ph
3:13. 1 T 6:11. 2 T 2:22. He 12:14.
ye that seek. Is 45:19. 55:6. Ps 24:6. 105:3,
4. Am 5:4, 6. Zp +2:3.
look. Ge 17:15-17. Jsh 24:2. Ep 2:11, 12.
pit. Heb. *bor,* Ge +37:20. Jb 33:30. Ps 40:2.
2 Abraham your father. Ge 15:1, 2. 17:17.
18:11-13. Jsh 24:3. Ro 4:1-5, 16-24.
for. Ge 12:1-3. 13:14-17. 15:4, 5. 22:17. 24:1,
35, 36. Ne 9:7, 8. Ezk 33:24. Ga 3:9-14. He
11:8-12.
alone. Ge 12:4. Ex 12:38. Ne 13:3. Ezk 33:24.
Ml 2:15. Mt 10:37.
3 shall comfort. ver. 12. Is 12:1. Ps 85:8. Zc
+1:17. 2 C 1:3, 4.
Zion. Ps +102:13.
all. Is 44:26. 49:8. 52:9. 61:4. Ps 102:13, 14.
Je 33:12, 13.
waste places. Is 40:1. 49:13.
make. Is 35:1, 2, 7-10. 41:18, 19. Am +9:13.
like the garden. Ge 2:8, 9. 13:10. Ezk 31:8-
10. 36:35. Jl 2:3. Re 10:7. 22:3.
joy. Je 33:11. 1 P 1:8. Re 19:1-7.
melody. Ps 98:5.
4 Hearken. Ps 50:7. 78:1.
O my. Is 26:2. Ex 19:6. 33:13. Ps 33:12.
106:5. 147:20. 1 P 2:9.
a law. Is 2:3. Mi +4:2. Ro 8:2-4. 1 C 9:21.
I will make. Is 42:1-4, 6. 49:6. Ps 119:105.
Pr 6:23. Mt 12:18-20. Lk 2:32. Jn 1:9. 16:8-
11.
5 righteousness. Is 46:13. 56:1. Dt 30:14. Ps
85:9, 10. Mt 3:2. Ro 1:16, 17. 10:6-10.
my salvation. Is 2:2, 3. Ezk 47:1-5. Mt
28:18, 19. Mk 16:15. Lk 24:47. Ro 10:17, 18.
mine. Ps +7:8.
the isles. Is +11:11. Ro 1:16. 15:9-12.
6 Lift up. Is 40:26. Ge +22:13. Dt 4:19. Ps 8:3,
4.
the heavens. Is 34:4. 50:9. Ps 102:26, 27. Mt
24:35. He 1:11, 12. 2 P 3:10-12. Re 6:12-14.
20:11.
my salvation. ver. 8. Is 45:17. Ps 103:17. Da
9:24. Jn 3:15, 16. 5:24. 10:27-29. 2 Th 2:16.
He 5:9. 9:12, 15.
for ever. Heb. *olam,* Ex +12:24.
7 Hearken. ver. +1.
ye that. Ph 3:8-10. T 2:11, 12.
in whose. Dt +6:6. He 10:16.
fear. Ge +15:1. Je 1:17. Ezk 2:6. Mt 5:10, 11.
Lk 6:22. 12:4, 5. Ac 5:41. 1 P 4:4, 14.
8 For. Je +20:11.
the moth. Is 50:9. 66:24. Jb 4:19. 13:28. Ho
5:12.
my righteousness. ver. +6. Is 45:17. 46:13.
Lk 1:50.
for ever. Heb. *olam,* Ex +12:24.

generation. Ge +9:12.
9 Awake. ver. +17. Is 27:1. Ps +3:7.
put on. Is 52:1. Ps 21:13. 74:13, 14. +93:1.
Re 6:10. 11:17.
O arm. ver. 5. Ex +15:16.
as in. Jg 6:13. Ne 9:7-15. Ps 44:1.
ancient. Mi +5:2.
of old. Heb. *olam* plural, Ps +61:4.
Art thou. Jb 26:12mg. Ps 87:4. 89:10.
Rahab. Is 30:6. Jb 9:13.
the dragon. Is 27:1. Ps 74:13, 14. Ezk 29:3.
Hab 3:13. Re 12:7-9.
10 dried. Is 42:15. 50:2. Ex +14:21, 22, 29.
15:13.
deep. Ge +1:2.
11 the redeemed. Is +43:1. 44:22, 23. 48:20. Ps
111:9. Je 30:18, 19. 31:11, 12. 33:11. Ac 2:41-
47. Ep +1:14. Re 5:9-13. 7:9, 10. 14:1-4. 19:1-
7.
shall return. Is +52:12mg. +54:7.
and come. Ho 2:15.
with singing. Ps +30:5mg. Zc +2:10.
unto Zion. Is +24:23. +59:20. 66:5-8. Ps
51:18.
everlasting. Heb. *olam,* Ge +17:7. Is 60:19.
61:7. 2 C 4:17, 18. 2 Th 2:16. Ju 24.
and sorrow. Is +65:19. 2 C 4:17. Re 22:3.
12 I, even I. Ge +6:17.
that comforteth. ver. 3. Is 43:25. 53:3.
57:15-18. 61:1. 66:13. Dt 33:27. Jb 20:14. Je
8:18. La 3:22, 33. Jn 13:7. 14:16-18, 26, 27.
Ac 9:31. 2 C 1:3-5. 7:5, 6. Ja 5:11.
afraid of. ver. 7, 8. Is 2:22. 1 S 15:24. Ps
+118:6. Lk 12:4, 5.
son of man. Ps +8:4.
made as grass. 1 P +1:24.
13 forgettest. Is +17:10. Dt 6:12. 32:18. Ps
+9:17. Je 2:32.
that hath stretched. Is +40:22. Ge 1:1.
feared. Is 8:12, 13. 57:11. He 2:15.
were ready. *or,* made *himself* ready. Is 10:29-
32. Ex 14:10-13. 15:9, 10. Est 5:14. Da 3:15,
19. Re 20:9.
where is. Is 10:33, 34. 14:16, 17. 16:4. +25:8.
33:18, 19. 37:36-38. Ex 14:13. Est 7:10. Jb
20:5-9. Ps 9:6, 7. 37:35, 36. 76:10. Da 4:32,
33. Mt 2:16-20. Jn 14:27. Ac 12:23. 1 C 1:20.
+15:55. 2 C 1:3, 4. Re 19:20.
14 captive. Is 48:20. 52:2. Ezr 1:5. Ac 12:7, 8.
Ro 7:24. 8:19. 2 C +5:2.
die. Je 37:16. 38:6-13. La 3:53, 54. Zc 9:11.
15 that divided. ver. +10. Am 9:5, 6.
The Lord. Ps +24:10.
16 I have put. Is 50:4. 59:21. Dt 18:18. Jn 3:34.
8:38-40. 17:8. Re 1:1.
my words. Je 23:28.
I have covered. Dt 33:27.
shadow. Ps +91:1.
plant. Is 45:18. 60:21. 61:3. 65:17. 66:22. Ps
92:13. 2 P 3:13.

the heavens. Hg +2:6.
and lay. Is 48:13. 49:8. Ps 75:3.
Thou art. Is 60:14, 15. Je 31:33. 32:38. Zc 8:8. 13:9. He 8:10.

17 **awake**. ver. +9. Jg 5:12. 1 C 15:34. Ep 5:14.
which hast. Dt 28:28, 34. Jb 21:20. Ps 11:6. 60:3. 75:8, 22. Je 25:15-17, 27. Ezk 23:31-34. Zc 12:2. Re 14:10. 18:6.

18 **none**. Is 3:4-8. 49:21. Ps 88:18. 142:4. Je 5:30, 31. La 2:9. Zc 1:5. Mt 9:36. 15:14.
that taketh. Is 41:13. 45:1. Jb 8:20mg. Je 31:32. Mk 8:23. Ac 9:8. 13:11. He 8:9.

19 **two things**. Is 47:9. Ezk 14:21.
are come. Heb. happened. Ge +24:44. Jg 14:5mg. 2 S 1:6mg. Ps 59:4mg.
who shall. Jb 2:11. Ps 69:20. Je 9:17-21. La 1:9, 12, 17. Am 7:2.
destruction. Heb. breaking. Is 1:28mg. 15:5mg. 59:7mg. 65:14mg. Jg +7:15mg. Je 4:6mg. 6:14mg. Am 6:6mg.
by whom. Is 22:4. 61:2. Jb 42:11. Ec 4:1. La 1:16. Am 7:2. 2 C 7:6, 7, 13. 2 Th 2:16, 17.

20 **sons**. Is 40:30. Je 14:18. La 1:15, 19. 2:11, 12. 4:2. 5:13. Am 7:2.
a wild. Is 8:21. Ezk 12:13. 17:20. Re 16:9-11.
full. ver. 17, 21. Is 9:19-21. Ps 88:15, 16. La 3:15, 16. Re 14:10.
the rebuke. Ps 39:10, 11.

21 **hear**. ver. 1.
thou afflicted. Is 3:14, 15. 10:2. 54:11.
drunken. Is 29:9. Re 17:6.
but. Is 29:9. 49:26. Ezk 39:19.

22 **pleadeth**. Is 41:13. 1 S 25:39. Ps 35:1. Pr 22:23. Je 50:34. 51:36. Jl 3:2. Mi 7:9.
I have. ver. 17. Is +54:7-10. 62:8. Ezk 39:29. Zc 12:2.
no more drink it again. Is 11:11. 52:1. +54:7. Je 31:40. Ho +2:19. Am +9:15. Zc +9:8. Lk 1:71.

23 **I will**. Is 49:25, 26. Pr 11:8. 21:18. Je 25:17-29. Zc 12:2. Re 17:6-8, 18.
soul. Heb. *nephesh*, Ge +27:31.
Bow. Jsh 10:24. Ps 66:11, 12. Re 11:2. 13:16, 17.

ISAIAH 52

1 **awake**. Ps +3:7. Da 10:9, 16-19. Hg 2:4. Ep 6:10.
put on thy beautiful. Is +61:3, 10. SS 6:4, 10. Ezk 16:14. Lk 15:22. Ro 3:22. 13:14. Ep 4:24. Re 19:7, 8, 14.
the holy. Is 1:21, 26. 48:2. Ne 11:1. Je 31:23. Zc 14:20, 21. Mt 4:5. Re 21:2, 27.
henceforth. Is +60:21. Jb +5:24. Ps +130:8.
there shall. Is 1:26. 26:2. 35:8. 60:21. 2 Ch 23:19. Ezk 44:9. Na 1:15. Zp 3:13. Zc 14:9. Re 20:9. 21:27.
unclean. Is 35:8-10.

2 **Shake**. Is 3:26. 51:23. Je 51:6, 45, 50. Zc 2:6, 7. Re 18:4.
arise. Re 18:7.
loose. Is 45:13. 49:21. 51:14. 61:1, 3. Lk 4:18. 21:24.

3 **have sold**. Is 45:13. Dt +32:30.

4 **My people**. Ge 46:6. Ac 7:14, 15.
the Assyrian. Is 14:25. ch. 36, 37. Ex 1:8. Je 50:17. Ac 7:18.
without. Jb 2:3. Ps 25:3. 69:4. Jn 15:25.

5 **what**. Is 22:16. Jg 18:3.
people. ver. 3. Ps 44:12.
make. Is 47:6. 51:20, 23. Ex 1:13-16. 2:23, 24. 3:7. Ps 137:1, 2. Je 50:17. La 1:21. 2:3. 5:13-15. Zp 1:10.
my name. Ezk 20:9, 14. 36:20-23. Ro 2:24.
blasphemed. Le +24:11.

6 **my people**. Ex 33:19. 34:5-7. Ps 48:10. Ezk 20:44. 37:13, 14. 39:27-29. Zc 10:9-12. He 8:10, 11.
know my name. Ex 3:14, 15. Ps +9:10.
in that day. Is +2:11.
I am he. Is 42:9. Nu 23:19. He 6:14-18.

7 **How beautiful**. Na *1:15*. Lk 2:10. Ro 10:12-*15*. Ep +6:15.
feet. Pr +1:16.
that bringeth. Jn 1:41, 45. 4:29.
good tidings. Is 40:9. 61:1-3. 2 S 18:26. 2 K 7:9. Re 22:17.
publisheth. Ps 68:11. SS 2:8. Mk 13:10. 16:15. Lk 24:47. Ac 10:36-38. Re 14:6.
Thy God. Is 24:23. 25:9. 33:22. Jb +19:26. Ps +45:6. +93:1. Mi +4:7. Zc 9:9. Mt 25:34. 28:18. Jn +1:1. +20:28. Ac +20:28. Ro 9:5. 2 C 5:19. Col 2:8, 9. 1 T 3:16. T 2:13. He +1:8. 2 P 1:1. Ju 4. Re 11:15. 21:7.

8 **Thy**. Is 56:10. 62:6, 7. SS 3:3. 5:7. Je 6:17. 31:6, 7. Ezk 3:17. 33:7. He 13:17.
lift. Is 24:14. 40:9. 58:1.
with. Is 12:4-6. 26:1. 27:2. 35:10. 48:20. Je 33:11. Ac 2:46, 47. Re 5:8-10. 18:20. 19:4.
sing. Is +51:11.
see. Is 30:26. Je 32:39. Zp 3:9. Zc 12:8. Ac 2:1. 4:32. 1 C 1:10. 13:12. Ep 1:17, 18.
eye to eye. lit. face to face. Zc 9:14. 12:10. Jn 1:51.
shall bring again. or, returneth to. Is +59:20. Ps +102:16. Ho +5:15. +6:3. Mi +2:13. +5:3, 4. Mt +23:39. Ac +3:19-21.
Zion. Is +59:20.

9 **Break**. Is 14:7. 42:10, 11. 44:23. 48:20. 49:13. 54:1-3. 55:12. 65:18, 19. 66:10-13. Ps 96:11, 12. Zp 3:14, 15. Ga 4:27.
ye waste. Is 44:26. 51:3. 61:4.

10 **made**. Is 66:18, 19. Ac 2:5-11. Re 11:15-17. 15:4.
arm. Ex +15:16.
eyes. Is 40:5. 49:26.

all. Is 49:6. Ps 22:27. Lk 3:6. Ac 13:47. Re 11:15. 14:6. 19:1-3.

11 depart ye. 2 C 6:17. Re +18:4.
touch. Le 5:2, 3. 11:26, 27, 45, 47. 15:5, etc. Ezk 44:23. Hg 2:13, 14. Ac 10:14, 28. Ro 14:14. Ep +5:11. 1 P 1:14-16. 2:5, 11.
be ye clean. Le 10:3. 11:45. 22:2, 3. Ezr 1:7-11. 8:25-30.
that bear. 1 P 2:5, 9. Re 5:9, 10.

12 ye shall. Is 28:16. 51:14. Ex 12:33, 39. 14:8. Dt 16:3.
for. Is 45:2. Ex 13:21, 22. 14:19, 20. Dt 20:4. Jg 4:14. 1 Ch 14:15. Ezr 1:1-11. Mi 2:13. Jn +10:4.
the God of Israel. Is +29:23.
be your rereward. Heb. gather you up. Is 14:1-3. 24:13, 14, 23. 25:6. 26:1, 2, 9, 13, 15. 30:19. 33:20. +35:10. 44:23. 46:13. 49:6, 12, 19. 58:8mg. 60:4. Ex 14:19. Nu 10:25. Dt +30:3. Jsh 6:9, 13. Ps 27:10mg. Je 3:17. +23:3. 30:3, 10. 31:8, 10. 32:37-40. 33:7, 26. 46:27. 50:19. Ob 17. Mi 5:7. Zc 2:12. 9:16.

13 my servant. Is 11:2, 3. +37:35. 42:1. 49:3, 6. 53:11. Ezk 34:23. Zc 3:8. Ph 2:7, 8.
deal prudently. or, prosper. Is 53:10. Jsh +1:7mg, 8mg. 1 S 18:14mg. Je 23:5. Mt 22:34-40.
he shall. Is +9:6, 7. 49:6. Ps 2:6-9. 110:1, 2. Mt 28:18. Jn 3:31. 5:22, 23. Ep 1:20-23. Ph 2:5, 9-11. Col 1:19. 2:3, 9. He +1:3. 2:7, 8. Re 5:6-13.
exalted. Is 53:12.

14 many. Ps 71:7. Mt 7:28. 22:22, 33. 27:14. Mk 5:42. 6:51. 7:37. 10:26, 32. Lk 2:47. 4:36. 5:26.
astonied. Archaic for "astonished," as in Jb 17:8. Ps 22:17. Lk 23:35.
marred. Is 50:6. 53:2-5. Ps 22:6, 7, 15, 17. 102:3-5. Zc 13:6. Mt 26:67. 27:29, 30. Lk 22:64. Jn 19:5. 1 T 3:16.

15 sprinkle. Heb. nazah, Nu +19:21. Le +1:5. 2 K 9:33. Jl 2:28. Mt 28:19. Ac +1:5. 2:17, 33. 8:36. T 3:5, 6.
kings. Is +49:7. Jb 21:5. 29:9, 10. 40:4. Mi 7:16, 17. Zc 2:13.
for. Is 51:5. 55:5. Ro 15:20, 21. 16:25, 26. 1 C 2:9. Ep 3:5-9.

ISAIAH 53

1 Who hath believed. lit. remained stedfast. Ge +15:6. 45:26. Ex 4:8. Jn 1:7, 12. 7:5. 12:38. Ro 10:16, 17. 1 C 1:18, 24. 2 C 4:3, 4.
report. or, doctrine. Heb. hearing. Is 28:9mg, 19mg. 37:7. 1 S 2:24.
the arm. Ex +15:16. Mt 11:25. 13:11. 16:17. Ro 1:16. 1 C 1:18, 24. Ep 1:18, 19.
revealed. Is 40:5. Mt 11:25. 16:17. Ro 1:17, 18.

2 he shall grow. Is +11:1. Mk 6:3. Lk 2:7, 39, 40, 51, 52. 9:58. Ro 8:3. Ph 2:6, 7. 1 T 3:16.

dry ground. Mt 6:3. Lk 9:58.
he hath no form. Is 52:14. Mk +14:44. Lk +4:30. Jn +8:59. 18:4-8.
no beauty that. Mk 9:12. Jn 1:10-14. 7:24. 9:28, 29. 18:40. 19:5, 14, 15. 1 P 2:4.

3 despised. Zc 11:8, 12, 13. Mt +26:67. Mk 3:21, 30. 6:3. 9:12. Lk 4:22, 24. +8:53. 9:22, 58. +16:14. +22:63. 23:18, etc. Jn 8:48. 9:16, 24.
and rejected. Ge 6:5. Mt 27:25. Lk 17:25. 19:14. 20:13-15. Jn 1:10, 11. 7:41, 52. 8:48. 10:20. Ac 7:51, 52. 13:46.
a man of sorrows. ver. 4, 10. Ge 49:23. 1 Ch 4:9. Ps 69:29. Mt 26:37, 38. Mk 14:34. Lk 19:41. Jn 11:35. He 2:15-18. 4:15. 5:7.
we hid as it were our faces from him. or, he hid as it were, his face from us. Heb. as a hiding of faces from him, or from us. lit. "making secret," as if he were ashamed; as in Is 8:17. Is 50:6. Ps 22:6, 7. Mk 3:20, 21. Jn 8:48. 18:40.
we esteemed. Dt 32:15. Ps 69:8. 118:22. Zc 11:13. Mt 21:42, 43. 26:15. 27:9, 10. Jn 1:10, 11. 7:5, 48. 18:40. Ac 3:13-15.

4 he hath. ver. 5, 6, 11, 12. He 8:17. Lk 4:2. Jn 11:35. Ga 3:13. He 2:17, 18. +4:15. 9:28. 1 P 2:24. 3:18. 1 J 2:2.
borne. Ex 28:38, 43. Ezk +4:4.
our griefs. Da 9:26. Mt 20:28.
yet. Mt 26:37. Jn 19:7.
smitten. Is +50:6. Mi 5:1. Mt 26:67, 68. 27:30. Jn 19:3.

5 But he was. ver. 6-8, 11, 12. Da 9:24. Zc 13:7. Mt 20:28. Ro 3:24-26. 4:25. 5:6-10, 15-21. 1 C +15:3. 2 C 5:21. Ga 3:13. Ep 5:2. He 9:12-15, 28. 10:10, 14. 1 P 3:18.
wounded. or, tormented. Is 51:9. Ps 109:22.
for our. Ps 106:32.
transgressions. Le +5:6.
bruised. ver. 10. Ge +3:15. Ex +27:20. Le 2:1. +23:13. Mt 27:26-29. He +2:10.
iniquities. 1 J 3:5.
the chastisement. 1 P 2:24.
peace. Le 7:29, 30. +23:19. Ro 5:1. Ep 2:14.
with his. 1 P 2:24.
stripes. Heb. bruise. Is 1:6. Ge 4:23. Ex 21:25.
healed. Le 13:18, 37. 14:3. Nu 21:9. Ps +103:3. Mt 8:17. Jn 3:14, 15.

6 All. Pr +20:9.
we like sheep. Ps 23:1, 3. 119:176. Mt 18:12-14. Lk 15:3-7. Ro 3:10-19. 1 P 2:25.
turned. That is, turned the face. Is 8:21. 56:11.
his own. Is 55:7. 56:11. Pr 14:12. Ezk 3:18. Ro 4:25. Ja 5:20. 1 P 3:18.
the Lord hath. ver. 10. Jn 3:16. Ro 3:25. Ga 4:4, 5. 1 J 4:9, 10.
laid on him the iniquity of us all. Heb. made the iniquities of us all to meet on him.

Is 50:8. Le +23:19. Ps 69:4.

the iniquity. Je 23:6. Da 9:24. Jn 3:17. 6:51, 55. 10:9. Ro 1:16, 17. 3:21, 22. 5:10, 11, 15-21. 10:3, 4. 2 C 5:14, 15. Ep 5:2. Ph 3:9. 1 J 2:2. 3:5. 4:9, 10. Re 5:9.

7 **yet**. Mt +11:29. 26:63. 27:12-14. Mk 14:61. Lk 23:9. Jn 19:9.

opened not. Ps +38:13.

he is brought. Ge 3:24. Le 17:5. Jn 18:13. Ac 8:32, 33.

as a lamb. Ex 12:5, 13. Ac 8:32-35. Re 13:8.

sheep. Le 1:10.

is dumb. Mt 27:12-14. 1 P 2:23.

8 **from prison and from judgment**:

and. or, by distress and judgment: but, etc. Ps 22:12-21. 69:12. Mt 26:65, 66. 27:23, 24. Jn 19:4, 7. Ac 8:33.

who shall declare. Mt 1:1. 12:50. Jn 7:27. Ac 8:33. Ro 1:4. 2 C 5:16.

his generation. Da +9:26. Jn 16:32.

cut off. Ps 102:23, 24. Da +9:24-26. Mk 14:41. Lk 3:1, 2, 23. Jn 8:20. 11:49-52. 13:1. 18:13, 14.

land. Ps +27:13.

for the transgression. Jn 11:51, 52.

was he stricken. Heb. was the stroke upon him. 1 P 3:18.

9 **And he made**. or, appointed. lit. gave. Is 7:14. 55:4. Ge 15:18. Ps 72:15. Ec 2:21mg. Je 1:4. Mt 27:57-60. Mk 15:43-46. Lk 23:50-53. Jn 19:38-42. 1 C 15:4.

grave. Heb. qeber, Ge +23:4. Is 14:19. 22:16. 65:4.

wicked. or, "wrong ones." Is 3:11. Lk 23:32.

with the rich. Mt 27:57-60. Mk 15:43, 46. Lk 23:53. Jn 19:40-42.

death. Heb. deaths. i.e. most bitter death. Mk 15:42-47. Jn 19:38, 39.

done no violence. Jn 19:4.

neither. Jn 8:46. 1 P 2:22, 23.

deceit. Ex 12:5. Le 1:3, 10. 2 C 5:21. He +4:15. 7:26. 9:14. 1 P 2:22. 1 J 3:5.

in his mouth. Ja 3:2.

10 **pleased**. Is 42:1. Mt 3:17. 17:5.

bruise. ver. +5. Le +23:13.

he hath. Ps 69:26. Zc 13:7. Mt 27:46. Lk 22:44. Jn 12:27. 18:11. Ro 8:32. Ga 3:13. 1 J 4:9, 10.

when thou shalt make his soul. Heb. nephesh, Ge +12:13. or, when his soul shall make. Da 9:24. Lk +9:24. Ro 8:3. 2 C 5:21. Ep 5:2. 1 T 2:6. He 7:27. 9:14, 25, 26. 10:6-12. 13:10-12. 1 P 2:24.

an offering. Heb. asham, the trespass offering. Le +5:6. 14:12, 21. +23:19.

he shall see. Ps 22:30. 45:16, 17. 110:3. Jn 12:24. He 2:13.

he shall prolong. Is +9:7. Ps 16:9-11. 21:4. 72:17. 89:29, 36. Ezk 37:25. Da 7:13, 14. Lk 1:33. 23:42, 43. Ac 2:24-28. Ro 6:9. Re 1:18.

the pleasure. Is 55:11-13. 62:3-5. Ps 72:7. 85:10-12. 147:11. 149:4. Je 32:41. Ezk 33:11. Mi 7:18. Zp 3:17. Lk 15:5-7, 23, 24. Jn 6:37-40. 10:17, 18. Ep 1:5, 9. 2 Th 1:11.

shall prosper. Ge 39:3. Ps 22:30. 110:3. Mt 12:20. Lk 1:33. Jn 6:40. 12:23, 24. Ro 6:9. Ep 1:5. He 2:13. Re 1:18. 14:3, 4.

11 **see**. Lk 22:44. Jn 12:24, 27-32. 16:21. Ga 4:19. He 12:2. Re 5:9, 10. 7:9-17.

travail. Ga 41:51. Ga 4:19.

soul. Heb. nephesh, Ge +12:13.

satisfied. Ps 17:15. Jn 19:30.

by his knowledge. Mt 7:11. Mk 5:29. Lk 1:77. Jn 4:39-42. 17:3. 1 C 4:19. 2 C 1:9. 4:6. Ph 3:8-10. 2 P 1:2, 3. 3:18.

my righteous. Is 42:1. 49:3. 1 J 2:1. 2 J 1, 3.

justify. Is 45:25. 61:10. Le +23:12. Ps 85:10. Lk +19:10. Ro 3:22-24. 4:24, 25. 5:1, 9, 18, 19. 1 C 6:11. Ph 3:9. T 3:6, 7.

bear. ver. 4-6, 8, 12. Mt 20:28. He 9:28. 1 P 2:24. 3:18.

12 **will I**. Is 49:24, 25. 52:15. Ge +3:15. Ps 2:8. 24:7-10. Da 2:45. Mt 12:28, 29. Ac 26:18. Ep 4:8-10. Ph 2:8-11. Col 1:13, 14. 2:15. He 2:14, 15.

a portion. Is 52:15 with 53:12. Ps 110:2-5. Re 19:11-16.

spoil. Mk 3:27. Ro 16:20. 1 J 3:8.

the great. Ac 2:33, 36. 2 C 13:4. Ph 2:9. Re 17:14. 19:12.

poured. Is 32:15. Le 4:30. +23:19. Ps 22:14. Ph 2:17mg. He 12:2.

soul. Heb. nephesh, Ge +12:13.

unto death. Mt 27:50.

numbered with. Mk 15:28. Lk 22:37. 23:25, 32, 33.

he bare. ver. +11. Le 10:17. Nu 9:13. 18:32. 1 T 2:5, 6. T 2:14. He 9:26, 28.

of many. Many is sometimes put for all. Da 12:2. Mt 20:28. +26:28. Jn 6:50. Ro 5:15, 19. 8:29. He 2:10. 9:28.

made intercession. Ps 109:4. Lk 23:34. Ro 8:34. He 7:25. 9:24. 1 J 2:1, 12.

for the transgressors. Lk 23:43. Jn 17:20. Ro 5:8.

ISAIAH 54

1 **Sing**. Is 44:23. 49:13.

O barren. Is 62:4. Ge +11:30. 2 S 2:1, 5. SS 8:8. Je 3:20. Ezk 16:15, 20, 21, 36, etc. Ho 2:4. 4:6. 5:7. 9:14-17. 10:1. Ga 4:27. He 11:11, 12.

thou. lit. she.

break. Is +14:7. 42:10, 11. 44:23. 49:13. 52:9. 55:12, 13. Ps 67:3-5. 98:3-9. Zp 3:14. Zc 9:9. Re 7:9, 10.

into singing. Is 12:6. 49:13. Zp 3:14. Zc +2:10.

for more. Is 27:6. 49:17, 18, 20. Ge +22:16-

18. 1 S 2:5. Ps +113:9. Je 31:27, 28. 33:22. Ezk 36:10, 11, 37, 38. Ho 1:10. Zc 2:3-5. He 11:11, 12. 12:22, 23. Re 21:2.

are the children. Ps +102:28. Ho 1:10.

of the desolate. Is 62:4.

than the children. Mt +7:14. Lk 20:35, 36. Ro 8:23.

married wife. 2 C 11:2. Ep 5:27. Re 19:7-9.

2   **Enlarge.** Is 33:20. 49:19, 20. Je 10:20.

stakes. Ex +27:19.

3   **thou shalt.** Is 2:2-4. 11:9-12, 14. 35:1, 2. 42:1-12. 43:5, 6. 49:12. 60:3-11. Ge +49:10. Ps 72:8-11. Am +9:11, 12. Ob 18-20. Ro 9:25, 26. 10:18. 11:12. Col 1:23.

and thy. Is 49:18. 55:5. 60:10-13. 61:5-9.

make. Is 49:8, 19. 52:9. Ezk 36:35, 36.

4   **Fear not.** Ge +15:1.

ashamed. Is 61:7. Le 26:6. Jl +2:26. 1 P 2:6.

thou shalt forget. Je 31:19. Ezk 16:22, 43, 60-63. Ho 3:1-5.

shame of thy youth. Je 3:24, 25.

the reproach. Is 50:1. Je 3:14.

5   **thy Maker.** Ps 45:10-17. Je 3:14. 31:32. Ezk 16:8. Ho 2:19, 20. Jn 3:29. 2 C 11:2, 3. Ep 5:25-27, 32.

the Lord of hosts. Ps +24:10. Lk 1:32.

is his name. Ex +6:3.

thy Redeemer. or, kinsman-Redeemer. Ge 48:16. Ex 6:6. 15:13.

the Holy One of Israel. Is +1:4.

The God. Is +42:1. Jsh 3:11, 13. Zc 6:5. 14:9. Ro 3:29, 30. 11:12. Re 11:15.

6   **a woman.** Is 49:14. 62:4. Ho 2:1, 2, 14, 15. Mt 11:28. 2 C 7:6, 9, 10.

forsaken. Is 1:4.

grieved. 1 S +1:10.

spirit. Heb. *ruach,* Ge +41:8.

a wife. Pr 5:18. Ec 9:9. Ml 2:14.

7   **a small.** Is 26:20. 60:10. Ps 30:5. 2 C 4:17. 2 P 3:8, 9.

forsaken thee. Is +41:9. 60:15. Dt 31:17. 2 K 13:23. 21:14. 1 Ch +28:9. 2 Ch 12:5. 15:2. 24:20. Ps 78:60, 61. Is 27:11. Je 6:30. 12:7. 23:33, 39. La 5:20, 22. Ho 1:6, 9. 9:12, 15, 17. Am 5:2. Mt 21:43. Re 11:2.

with. Is 11:11. 14:1. 40:11. 49:18. 60:4. 66:18. Ex +34:6. Je 29:10. Mt 23:37. Ep 1:10.

gather thee. Is +52:12mg. +56:8. 1 Ch 16:35. Ne 1:9. Je 16:15. +23:3. 24:6. 50:19. Ezk 20:34, 41. 28:25.

8   **a little.** Is 47:6. 57:16, 17. 60:10. Ps 30:5. Zc 1:15.

I hid. Is 8:17. 45:15. 53:3. Dt +31:17.

but. Is +55:3. Ps 103:17, 18. Je 31:3. 2 Th 2:16. 1 T 1:16.

everlasting. Heb. *olam,* Ge +17:7. Ge +9:16.

have mercy. Is 49:13-17. Ho 2:14, 16mg, 19. **the Lord.** ver. 5. Is 48:17. 49:26. He 9:12.

9   **For this.** Je +33:25, 26. Ro +11:1, 2.

the waters of Noah. Is 12:1. 55:11. Ge

+8:21, 22. 9:11-16. 1 Ch 1:4. Ps 104:9. Je +5:22. +31:35, 36. +33:20-26. Ezk 14:14, 20. 39:29. He 6:16-18. Re 4:3.

no more. Ge +8:21, 22. +9:16.

so have. Ge +22:16-18. Je 31:35-37. Lk 1:73. He 6:13, 14.

sworn that. Is 55:11. Ps 119:89, 90. Mi 7:20. He 6:18.

10   **the mountains.** Is 51:6, 7. Ps 46:2. 125:2. Mt 5:18. 16:18. 24:35. Ro 11:29. 2 P 3:10-13.

not depart. Is +41:9, 17. Ge +8:22. Ezk 16:60.

the covenant. Is +55:3. Ge +9:16. Ps 89:33, 34. Ml 2:5. He 8:6-13.

that hath. Is 49:10. Ep 2:4, 5. T 3:5.

11   **thou afflicted.** ver. 6. Is 49:14. 50:10. 51:17-19, 23. 52:1-5. 60:15. Ex 2:23. 3:2, 7. Dt 31:17. Ps 34:19. 129:1-3. Je 30:17. Jn 16:20-22, 33. Ac 14:22. Re 7:13, 14. 11:3-10. 12:13-17.

tossed. Mt 8:24. Ac 27:18-20.

not comforted. La 1:1, 2, 16, 17, 21.

I will lay. 1 K 5:17. 1 Ch 29:2. Ezk ch. 40-42. 1 C 3:12, 13. Ep 2:20. 1 P 2:4-6. Re 21:18-21.

sapphires. Ex 24:10. 28:17-20. 39:10-14. SS 5:14. Ezk 1:26. 10:1.

12   **windows.** or, pinnacles. Is 14:31. 22:7. 24:12.

agates. Ezk 27:16. Re 21:21.

pleasant stones. or, stones of delight. lit. "desire, pleasure." Is +32:12mg. 44:28. 46:10. 48:14.

13   **all.** Is 2:3. 11:9. Ps 25:8-12. 71:17. Je 31:34. Mt 11:25-29. 16:17. Lk 10:21, 22. 24:45. Jn 6:45. 14:26. 1 C 2:10. Ep 4:21. 1 Th 4:9. He +8:10, 11. 1 J 2:20, 27.

taught. Is +8:16. 48:17, 18. Mi 4:2. 1 J 2:27.

great. Is 26:3. Ps 119:165. Je 33:6. Ezk 34:25, 28. 37:26. Ho 2:18. Ro +5:1.

of thy children. Dt +29:11. 2 T +3:15.

14   **righteousness.** Is 1:26, 27. 45:24. 52:1. +60:21. 61:10, 11. 62:1. Je 23:6. 31:23. Ezk 36:27, 28. 37:23-26. Jl 3:17-21. Zc 8:3. 2 P 3:13.

thou shalt be. Is 51:13. Ex 22:26, 27. Ps 12:5. 35:10. 72:4, 14. 109:31. 146:7. Ec 5:8. Zc 9:8.

for thou. Is 2:4. 60:18. Pr 3:25, 26. Je 23:3, 4. 30:10. Mi 4:3, 4. Zp 3:13-16. Zc 2:4, 5.

15   **they shall.** Ps 56:7. 59:4. Ezk 38:8-23. Jl 3:9-14. Re 16:14. 19:19-21. 20:8, 9.

shall fall. Is 43:3, 4, 14. Ps 37:12, 13. Pr 15:25. Zc 2:8. 12:3, 9. 14:2, 3.

16   **I have.** Is 10:5, 6, 15. 37:26. +45:7, 8. 46:11. Ex +9:16. Pr +16:4. Da 4:34, 35. Jn 19:11.

17   **no weapon.** ver. 15. Ps 2:1-6. Pr +21:30. Ezk 38:9, 10. Mt 16:18. Jn 10:28-30. Ro 8:1, 28-39.

every. Is 50:8, 9. Jb 1:11. 2:5. 22:5, etc. 42:7, 8. Ps 32:6. Je +20:11. Zc 3:1-4. Re 12:10.

the heritage. Is 58:14. Jb 20:29. Ps 16:6. 61:5. 119:111. Da 3:26-28. 6:20-22. Mt +5:5. Ro 6:22, 23.

and their. Is 45:24, 25. 61:10. Ps 24:5. 71:16, 19. Je 23:6. Ro 3:22. 10:4. 1 C 1:30. 2 C 5:21. Ph 3:9. 2 P 1:1.

ISAIAH 55

1 Ho. Ru 4:1. Pr 1:21-23. 8:4. Zc 2:6.

every. Is 41:17, 18. Ps 42:1, 2. 63:1. 143:6. Jn 4:10-14. 7:37, 38. Re 21:6. 22:1, 17.

waters. Je +2:13.

buy, and. Ps 31:16. Mt 13:44-46. Ph 3:7. Re 3:18.

buy wine. Ps 104:15. SS 1:2, 4. 5:1. Zc 9:15. 10:7. Mt 26:29. Jn 2:3-10.

milk. Jl 3:18. 1 C 3:2. 1 P 2:2.

without money. Is 52:3. Ge 47:25. Ro 3:24. 11:6. Ep 2:4-8.

2 do ye. Is 44:20. Je 2:13. Ho 8:7. 12:1. Hab 2:13. Mt 15:9. Lk 15:15, 16. Ro 9:31. 10:2, 3. Ph 3:4-7. He 13:9.

spend. Heb. weigh. Is 46:6. Ge 23:16. Je 32:9.

hearken. Is 51:1, 4, 7. Dt +15:5. Ps 34:11. Pr 1:33. 7:24. 8:32. Mk 7:14. Ro 10:17.

eat. Ps +22:26. Mt +5:6.

soul. Heb. *nephesh*, Ge +34:3.

delight. Is 58:14. Jb 22:26. 27:10.

fatness. S#1880h: Jg 9:9. Jb 36:16. Ps 65:11. See also S#1880h: Le 1:16 (ashes). 4:12, 12. 6:10, 11. 1 K 13:3, 5. Je 31:40.

3 Incline. Ps 78:1. 119:112. Pr 4:20.

come. Mt 11:28. Jn 6:37, 44, 45. 7:37.

hear. Mt 13:16. 17:5. Jn 5:24, 25. 8:47. 10:27.

soul. Heb. *nephesh*, Ge +12:13.

and I will. Is 54:8. 61:8. Ge 17:7. Je 31:33, 34. 32:40. 50:5. He 13:20.

everlasting. Heb. *olam*, Ge +17:7. Ge +9:16.

covenant. Jg 2:1. 2 S 7:10-16. Ps +74:20. 89:34.

the sure mercies. Is +41:9. +54:8-10. +59:21. 2 S +7:10, 15. 23:5. Ps +89:3, 28, 33, 35-37. +132:11. Je +33:20, 21, 25, 26. Ezk 37:24, 25. Ac +13:34.

of David. Is 38:5. Ac +13:23.

4 I have. Jn 3:16. 18:37. 1 T 6:13. Re +1:5. +3:14.

a leader. Is 49:8-10. 63:12, 13. Jsh 5:14. Ps 2:6. 67:4mg. 77:20. Je 30:9. Ezk 34:23, 24. Da 9:25. Ho 3:5. Mi +5:2-4. Mt 2:6. 28:18-20. Jn 10:3, 27. 12:26. 13:13. Ac 5:31. 2 Th 1:8. Ep 5:24. He +2:10. 5:9. Re 19:16.

5 thou shalt. Is 11:10, 11. 52:15. 56:8. Ge +49:10. Ps 18:43. Ro 15:20, 21. Ep 2:11, 12. 3:5, 6.

nations. Is 49:5, 6. 60:5. Ho 1:10. Zc 2:11. 8:20-23. Ep 2:13.

Holy One of Israel. Is +1:4.

hath glorified. Is 60:9. Ps 110:1-3. Lk 24:26. Jn 12:28. 13:31, 32. 17:1. Ac 3:13. 5:31. He 5:5. 1 P 1:11.

6 Seek. 2 Ch 19:3. Ps 14:2. 27:8. 32:6. 95:7. Je +29:13.

while he may. Ps 32:6. Mt 5:25. 25:11, 12. Lk 13:24, 25. Jn 7:33, 34. 8:21. 12:35, 36. 2 C 6:1, 2. He 2:3. +3:13.

while he is near. Is 12:6. 46:13. Ge +6:3. Dt 4:7. Ps 75:1. 145:18. 148:14. Pr 1:28. Ezk 8:6. Ho 5:6. 9:12. 2 C +6:2. Ep 2:13, 17.

7 the wicked. Is 1:16-18. 2 Ch +7:14. Je 3:3. 8:4-6. Ezk 3:18, 19. Jon 3:10. Mt 9:13. Lk 15:10, 24. Ac +3:19. 1 C +6:9-11. Ja 4:8-10.

forsake. 2 Ch +7:14. Jb 34:31, 32. Ps 37:11. Pr 28:13. Jon 3:7, 8.

unrighteous man. Heb. man of iniquity.

his thoughts. Ge 6:5. Jb 17:11. Ps 66:18. +146:4. Je 4:14. Zc 8:17. Mt 15:18, 19. Mk 7:21, 23. Lk 11:39, 40. Ac 8:21, 22. Ja 1:15.

return. Je +33:15.

have mercy. Ex +34:6. Jn +3:36.

for. Is 43:25. 44:22. Je 3:12, 13. Lk 7:47. Ro 5:16-21. Ep 1:6-8. 1 T 1:15, 16.

abundantly. Heb. multiply to. Is 1:15mg. Ge 3:16. Ps 18:35mg. Lk 15:20. Ro 5:20.

pardon. Mi 7:18, 19.

8 my thoughts. Ge +50:20. 2 S 7:19. Ps 25:10. 40:5. 92:5. 94:11. Pr 21:8. 25:3. Je 3:1, 4. Ezk 18:29. Da 4:37. Ho 14:9. Mi 4:12.

9 the heavens. Ps 36:5-7. 77:19. 89:2. 103:11, 12. Mt 11:25, 26. Ro 11:31-36.

ways higher. Is 57:15. 64:4. Ps +8:5. Ec 3:11. 8:17. 1 C 2:9.

your ways. 2 S 7:19. 1 J 4:10.

my thoughts. ver. 8. Ps 40:5, +17.

10 as the rain. Is 5:6. 30:23. 61:11. Dt 32:2. 1 S 23:4. Ps 65:9-13. 72:6, 7. Ezk 34:26. Ho 10:12. Mt +5:45. Re 11:6.

returneth not. Ps 135:7. Je 10:13. 51:16.

that it. 2 C *9:10*.

give seed. Ge 47:23. 2 C 9:9-11.

eater. Jg 14:14.

11 shall my word. Is +54:9. Nu 23:19. Dt 8:3. 32:2. Ps 119:89. 138:2. Ezk 12:25. Mt 24:35. Lk 8:11-16. Jn 6:63. Ro 10:17. 1 C 1:18. 3:6-9. Ep 6:17. 1 Th 2:13. He 6:7. Ja 1:18. 1 P 1:23.

my mouth. Nu +12:8.

not return. 1 S 3:19.

it shall accomplish. Is 44:26-28. 45:23. 46:10. Ep 1:9-11.

please. Ps +115:3.

12 ye shall. Is 49:9, 10.

with joy. Is 35:10. 51:11. 65:13, 14. Ps 105:43. Je 30:19. Ro 5:11. Col 1:11-13.

peace. Je 33:6, 11. Ro +5:1.

the mountains. Is 14:8. 35:1, 2. +49:13. Ps 65:13. 148:4-13. Re 19:1-6.

singing. Is +48:20. Zc 2:7-10.
the trees. Is 41:19, 20. 61:3. Ps 92:12.
104:16.
clap. 1 Ch 16:32, 33. Ps 47:1.

13 **Instead**. Is 11:6, 7. 65:25. Ac +3:21.
of the thorn. Is 11:6-9. 41:19. 60:13, 21.
61:3. Mi 7:4. Ro 6:19. 1 C +6:9-11. 2 C 5:17.
for a. Is 43:21. Je 13:11. 33:9. Lk 2:14. Jn
15:8. Ep 3:20, 21. 1 P 2:9, 10. 4:11.
an everlasting. Heb. *olam*, Ge +17:7. Is
54:10. Je 50:5.

ISAIAH 56

1 **Keep**. Is 1:16-19. 26:7, 8. 55:7. Ps 24:4-6.
50:23. Je 7:3-11. Ml 4:4. Mt 3:2. Jn +7:17.
judgment. *or*, equity. Is 1:17. 26:9. 59:8mg.
for. Is 46:13. 51:5. Ps 50:23. 85:9. Mt 3:2.
4:17. Mk 1:15. Lk 3:3-9. Ro 1:16. 10:6-10.
13:11-14.
my righteousness. Ro 1:17. 3:21, 22.
2 **Blessed**. Ps +1:1-3. 15:1-5. 119:1-5.
layeth hold. ver. 4. Pr 4:13. Ec 7:18.
keepeth the sabbath. Is 58:13. Ex +20:8-11.
keepeth his. Ps 34:14. 37:27. 119:101. Pr
4:27. 14:16. 16:6, 17. Ro 12:9.
3 **the son**. Nu 18:4, 7. Dt 23:1-3. Zc 8:20-23.
Mt +8:10, 11. Ac 8:27. 10:1, 2, 34. 13:47, 48.
17:4. 18:7. Ro 2:10, 11. 15:9-12, 16. Ep 2:12-
22. 1 P 1:1.
stranger. ver. 6. Is 60:10. 61:5. 62:8. Ex
+12:43. Ps 144:7, 11.
joined. Je 50:5. Zp 2:11. 1 C +6:17.
The Lord hath. Mt 15:26, 27. Lk 7:6-8. Ro
2:10, 11. Ep 2:19.
neither. ver. 4, 5. Is 39:7. Ge +37:36mg. Dt
23:1. Je 38:7-13. 39:16, 17. Da 1:3, etc. Mt
19:12, etc. Ac 8:26-40.
dry tree. Le 21:20. Ezk 17:24. Mt 19:12.
4 **choose**. Is +66:4. Jsh 24:15, 22. Ps 119:63,
111, 173. Lk 10:42.
take hold. Is 27:5. +55:3. 2 S 23:5. Je 50:5.
He 6:17, 18.
5 **will I**. Mt 16:18. Ep 2:22. 1 T 3:15. He 3:6.
give. Is 27:5. Mt 15:26, 27.
mine house. Ezk 43:7. Zc 6:12, 13. Mt 21:13.
a place. Ex 33:21. Dt +16:16. Jsh 20:4. Zc
3:7. Jn 14:2, 3. *or*, station. lit. "hand." Is 1:12.
1 S 15:12. 2 S 18:18.
and a name. Is 62:12. 65:15. Lk 10:20. Jn
1:12. Ro 8:15-17. 1 J 3:1. Re 2:17. 3:12. 21:7.
better. 1 S 1:8.
everlasting. Heb. *olam*, Ge +17:7.
name. Ex 32:32.
that shall. Is 48:19. 55:13. 65:23. 66:22. Je
33:18. 35:19. Re 3:5.
6 **stranger**. ver. +3. Is 60:10. Ac 10:34, 35.
17:4. Re 7:9.
join. ver. +3. Is 44:5. Je 50:5. Ac 2:41. 11:23.
2 C 8:5. 1 Th 1:9, 10. He 12:23. 1 P 1:1, 2.

to love the name. Ps +9:10. Dt +6:5. 1 C
16:22. Ga 5:6. Ep 6:24.
every. ver. 2. Is 58:13. Re 1:10.
7 **them will**. Is +2:2, 3. Ps 2:6. Ml 1:11. Jn
12:20, etc. Ep 2:11-13. 1 P 1:1, 2.
holy mountain. Is +11:9.
house of prayer. Zc 8:22. Mk 11:17.
their burnt offerings. Le +23:12. Lk 22:15-
18, 30.
sacrifices. Ps 50:14, 23. Je 33:18. Ro 12:1. He
13:15. 1 P 2:5.
for mine house. Ps 132:13. Ml 1:11. Mt
21:13. 23:38. Mk *11:17*. Lk *19:46*. Jn 4:21-23. 1
T 2:8.
for all. 1 T +2:2.
8 **which gathereth**. Je +23:3.
outcasts. Is +27:13.
Yet. Is 43:6. 49:12, 22. 60:3-11. 66:18-21. Ge
+49:10. Jn +10:16. 11:51, 52. Ep 1:10. 2:14-
16.
beside those that are gathered. Heb. to his
gathered. ver. 3. Is 66:21. Jn +10:16.
9 **ye beasts**. 1 K +14:11. Da 7:2-28. Re 13:1-
18.
10 **watchmen**. Is 52:8. Ezk 3:17, 18.
are blind. Is 29:10. Je 14:13, 14. Ho 4:6. 9:7,
8. Mt +15:14.
they are all dumb dogs. Is 58:1. Je 6:13, 14.
23:13, 14. Ezk 3:15-18, 26, 27. 13:16. 33:6.
Ph 3:2.
sleeping. *or*, dreaming, *or*, talking in their
sleep.
loving. Pr 6:4-10. 24:30-34. Jon 1:2-6. Na
3:18. Mk 13:34-37.
11 **Yea, they are**. Ex +18:21. Ezk +13:19. 34:2,
3. Ac 20:29, 33, 34. Ph 3:2, 19. 1 T 3:2, 3, 8. T
1:7, 11. Ju 11, 16. Re 22:15.
greedy. Heb. strong of appetite. Heb. *nephesh*,
Nu +11:6. Ec 6:7mg. Ph +3:19.
can never have enough. Heb. know not to
be satisfied. Ec 5:10. Ph 4:11.
are shepherds. Mi 3:6. Zc 11:15-17. Mt
13:14, 15. Jn 8:43. 2 C 4:4.
all look. Ex 23:3. Je 22:17. 2 P 2:15, 16.
his gain. Ex +18:21. Ps 10:3. Lk 16:13, 14. 1
C +6:10. Ep 5:5. Col +3:5. 1 T +6:5, 17-19. 2 T
3:1, 2.
12 **I will**. Is 5:22. 28:7, 8. Pr 23:29-32. 31:4, 5.
Ho 4:11. Am 6:3-6. Mt 24:49-51. Lk 12:45, 46.
21:34. 1 C 6:10. Ep +5:18. 1 Th 5:6-8. T 1:7.
tomorrow. Is 22:13, 14. Ps 10:6. Pr 23:35.
27:1. Je 18:18. Lk 12:19, 20. 1 C 15:32. Ja
4:13, 14.

ISAIAH 57

1 **righteous**. 2 Ch 32:33. 35:24. Ec 7:15.
no man. ver. 11. Is 42:25. 47:7. Ml 2:2.
merciful men. Heb. men of kindness, *or* god-
liness. Ps 12:1. Mi 7:2.

the righteous. 1 K 14:13. 2 K 22:20. 2 Ch 34:28. Lk 19:43, 44.

taken away. 2 K 22:20. 23:29. Ps 7:7. Jl 2:32. Zp +2:3. Mt 24:40. Lk +21:36. Ro 5:9. 1 Th 1:10. 4:17. 5:9, 10. Re +3:10.

the evil to come. *or*, that which is evil. Is +45:7. Je 22:20. 1 Th 1:10. 2 T 3:1. 1 J 2:18. Re 8:13.

2 He shall. Jb 3:17. Ec 12:7. Mt 25:21. Lk 16:22. 1 C 15:18. 2 C 5:1, 8. Ph 1:23. Re +14:13.

enter into. *or*, go in. Lk 2:29. 7:50.

rest. Is 14:18. 2 Ch 16:14. Ezk 32:25.

in his uprightness. *or*, before him. Ge 17:1. Am +3:10 (**S#5228h**). Lk 1:6.

3 draw. Is 45:20. Jl 3:9-11.

sons. Ho 1:2. Mt +3:7. 16:4. Ja 4:4. Re 17:1-5.

sorceress. Is +32:9. 2 K +21:6.

4 Against. Is 10:15. 37:23, 29. Ex 9:17. 16:7, 8. Nu 16:11. Lk 10:16. Ac 9:4.

sport. Jg 16:25-27. Ps 69:12. Mt 27:29, 39-44. 2 P 2:13.

make. Ps 35:21.

draw. Jsh 10:21. Jb 16:9, 10. Ps 22:7, 13, 17. La 2:15, 16.

are ye. Is 1:4. 30:1, 9. Ezk 2:4. Ho 10:9. Mt 13:38. Ep 2:2, 3. 5:6. Col 3:6.

5 Inflaming. Ex 32:6. Nu 25:1, 2, 6. Je 50:38. 51:7. Ho 4:11-13. 7:4-7. Am 2:7, 8. Re 17:1-5. 18:3.

with idols. *or*, among the oaks. Is 1:29. Ge 12:6. 13:18. 14:13. 18:1. 21:33. 35:4. Jsh 24:26. Jg 6:11, 19. 9:6, 37. 1 S 10:3. 22:6. 31:13. Ho 4:13.

under every green tree. Is +1:29. Dt 12:2. 1 K 14:23. 2 K 16:3, 4. 17:10. 2 Ch 28:4. Je 2:20. 3:6, 13. 17:2. Ezk 6:13. Ho 4:13.

slaying the children. Dt +18:10. 1 K 11:7. Ho 13:1.

valleys. or, brooks. Is 15:7mg. Jg +16:4mg.

6 the smooth. Je 3:9. Hab 2:19.

to them. Is 65:11. Dt 32:37, 38. Je 7:18. 19:13. 32:29. 44:17-25.

drink offering. Le +23:13.

meat offering. Le +23:13.

Should. Is 66:3. 1 K 12:32, 33. Ezk 20:39.

comfort. Ezk 5:13.

7 a lofty. Je 2:20. 3:2. Ezk 16:16, 25. 20:28, 29. 23:17, 41.

8 the doors. Ezk 8:8-12. 23:14, 41.

also and the posts. i.e. door posts.

for. Ezk 16:32.

made thee a covenant with them. *or*, hewed *it* for thyself *larger* than theirs.

thou lovedst. Ezk 16:25-28. 23:2-20.

where thou sawest it. *or*, thou providedst room. or, station. lit. "hand." Is +56:5.

9 thou wentest to the king. *or*, thou respectedst the king. Is 30:1-6. 31:1-3. 2 K 16:7-11. 2

Ch 28:22, 23. Ezk 16:33. 23:16. Ho 7:11, 12. 12:1. or, the idol. Is 30:33. 1 K 11:7.

perfumes. Pr 7:17.

and didst debase. Is 2:9. Col 2:18.

unto hell. Heb. *sheol*, Ge +37:35. Is 5:14.

10 wearied. Is 47:13. Je 2:36. 9:5. Ezk 24:12. Hab 2:13.

There is. 2 Ch 28:22, 23. Je 2:25. 44:17, 18. Ro 7:9.

life. *or*, living. Pr 27:27mg.

therefore. Je 3:3. 5:3.

11 of whom. Is 51:12, 13. Pr 29:25. Mt 26:69-75. Ga 2:12, 13.

that thou. Is 30:9. 59:3, 4. Je 9:3-5. 42:20. Ezk 13:22. Ho 11:12. Ac 5:3. 2 Th 2:9. 1 T 4:2. Re +21:8. 22:15.

and hast. Je +2:32. 3:21.

nor. ver. +1.

have not. Is 26:10. Ps 50:21. Ec 8:11.

of old. Heb. *olam*, Ge +6:4.

12 I will declare. Is 1:11-15. 58:2-6. 59:6-8. 64:5. 66:3, 4. Je 7:4-11. Mi 3:2-4. Mt 23:5, 14. Ro 3:10-20. 10:2, 3.

thy righteousness. Is 64:6. T 3:5.

not profit. Mk 8:36.

13 let. ver. 9, 10. Jg 10:14. 2 K 3:13. Je 22:22. Zc 7:13.

but the wind. Is 40:24. 41:16. Jb 21:17, 18. Ps 1:4. 37:9. 58:9. 115:8. Ho 13:3.

vanity. i.e. vain men. Ps 144:4. Ja 4:14.

but he. Is 26:3, 4. Ps +9:10. +37:3, 9. 84:12. 118:8, 9. 125:1. Pr 28:25. Je 17:7, 8.

my holy. Is +11:9.

14 Cast. Is 35:8. 40:3, 9. 62:10. Lk 3:3-6.

take. 1 C +8:9, 13. 2 C 6:3. He 12:13.

15 the high. Is 6:1. Ps +8:5. 83:18. 97:9. 138:6. 139:7. Da 4:17, 24, 25, 34. Ho 11:9.

that inhabiteth. Is 40:28. Ge 21:33. Dt 33:27. Ps 90:2. Pr 8:23. Je 10:10. Ro 1:20. He 9:14.

eternity. Heb. *ad*, Ps +9:18.

whose. Ps +99:3. Ac 3:14.

I dwell. Ex +29:45. Ps 68:4, 5. 113:4-6. 138:6, 8. 139:7. Zc 2:13. Mt +6:9. Jn 1:38.

with. 2 Ch 33:12, 13. 34:27. Ps +51:17. 138:6. Ezk 16:63. Ja 4:6. 1 P 5:5.

contrite. Ps 51:10, 11, 17. Jl 2:13. 2 C +7:10.

humble. 2 Ch +7:14. Pr 16:19. Mt +5:3. Ja 4:6.

spirit. Heb. *ruach*, Ge +41:8.

to revive. Is 61:1-3. 2 K 5:7. Ezk 13:22mg. Mt +5:4. Lk 4:18. 15:20-24. 2 C 1:4. 2:7. 7:6.

the spirit. Heb. *ruach*, Ge +41:8.

contrite ones. Dt +33:9. Ps 34:18. Lk 15:7, 21, 22.

16 I will not. Ps 78:38, 39. 85:5. 103:9-16. Je 10:24. Mi 7:18.

for ever. Heb. *olam*, Ex +12:24.

neither. Is 54:7, 8. Ps 30:5.

always. Heb. *nezach*, Jb +4:20 (**S#5331h**).
the spirit. Heb. *ruach*, Ge +41:8.
should fail. 2 C 2:7. Col 3:21.
the souls. lit. breathing things. Heb. *neshamah*, Ge +2:7. Is 2:22. 30:33. 42:5. Ge 6:3. Nu 16:22. Jb 34:14, 15. Ec +12:7. Je 38:16. Zc 12:1. He +12:9.

17 the iniquity. Is 5:8, 9. 56:11. Je 6:13. 8:10. 22:17. Ezk 33:31. Mi 2:2, 3. 3:10, 11. Lk 12:15. Ep 5:3-5. Col 3:5. 1 T 6:9, 10. 2 P 2:3, 14, 15.
I hid. Is 8:17. 45:15.
and he. Je +31:18. Lk 15:14-16.
frowardly. Heb. turning away. **S#7726h**. Je 3:14 (backsliding), 22. 50:6 (turned them away).
in the. Ec 6:9.

18 have. Is 1:18. 43:24, 25. 48:8-11. Je 31:18-20. Ezk 16:60-63. 36:22, etc. Lk 15:20. Ro 5:20.
will heal. Je 3:22. 31:3. 33:6. Ho 14:4-8.
will lead. Is 49:10. Ps 23:2. Re 7:17.
restore. ver. 15. Is 12:1. 61:2, 3. 66:10-13. Ps 51:12. Ro 15:5. 2 C 1:4. 7:6. Re 7:17.
to his. Je 13:17. Ec 9:4.

19 I create the fruit. Ex 4:11, 12. Ho 14:2. Lk 21:15. Ep 5:18, 19. 6:19. Col 4:3, 4. He 13:15.
Peace. Ge +43:23. Mk 16:15. Ac 2:39. Ro +5:1.
near. Ps 148:14.
will heal. Is 1:5, 6. Ex +15:26. Ps +103:3. 147:3.

20 like. Is 3:11. Jb 15:20-24. 18:5-14. 20:11, etc. Ps 78:18-20. Pr 4:16, 17. Ju 12, 13.

21 no peace. Is 3:11. +48:22. 2 K 9:22.

ISAIAH 58

1 aloud. Heb. with the throat. Ps 149:6.
spare. Is 56:10. Ps 40:9, 10. Je 1:7-10, 17-19. 7:8-11. 15:19, 20. Ezk 2:3-8. 3:5-9, 17-21. 20:4. 22:2. Mi 3:8-12. Mt 3:7-9. Ac 7:51, 52. 20:26, 27. T 2:15. Re 14:9, 10.
lift up. Is +40:9, 10.
like. Is 27:13. Ho +8:1. Re 1:10. 4:1.
trumpet. Le +23:24.
and show. Mt 23:1-3, 33. Lk 20:45-47. Ac 7:51. 20:26, 27. 2 C 13:2.

2 they seek. Is 1:11-15. 29:13. 48:1, 2. Dt 5:28, 29. 1 S 15:21-25. Pr 15:8. Ezk 33:30-33. Mt 15:7-9. Mk 4:16, 17. 6:20. Jn 5:35. T 1:16. He 6:4-6. Ja 1:22.
they ask. Je 42:2, 3, 20. Mk 12:14, 15. Ja 1:21, 22. 1 P 2:1, 2.

3 have we fasted. Nu 23:4. Mi 3:9-11. Zc 7:5-7. Ml 3:14. Mt 20:11, 12. Lk 15:29. 18:9-12.
afflicted. Nu +29:7.
soul. Heb. *nephesh*, Ge +27:31.
in the day. Da 10:2, 3. Jon 3:6-8.

exact. Ne 5:7. Pr 28:9. Je 34:9-17. Mt 18:28-35.
labors. *or*, things wherewith ye grieve others. Heb. griefs. **S#6092h**, only here. Is 47:6. Ex 2:23, 24.

4 ye fast. Jg +20:26. 1 K 21:9-13. 2 Ch +7:14. Pr 21:27. Mt +6:16. 23:14. Lk 20:47. Jn 18:28.
and to smite. Ac 23:1, 2. Ph 1:15, 16.
shall not fast as ye do this day. *or*, fast not as this day. Pr 21:27. Lk 18:9-14.
to make. Jl 2:13, 14. Jon 3:7. Mt 6:16-18.

5 Is it such. Mt +6:16.
a day for a man to afflict his soul. *or*, to afflict his soul *for* a day. Heb. *nephesh*, Ge +27:31. ver. 3. Le 16:29.
to spread. Jb +16:15.
ashes. Est +4:1.
an acceptable. Is 49:8. 61:2. Ps 69:13. Lk 4:19. Ro 12:2. 1 P 2:5.

6 Is not this. Mi +6:8.
the fast. Mt 6:17, 18. 1 P 2:5.
to loose. Ne 5:10-12. Je 34:8-11. Mi 3:2-4.
bands. or, pangs. Ps 73:4.
heavy burdens. Heb. bundles of the yoke.
to let. Lk *4:18*.
oppressed. Heb. broken. Jg +10:8.
go free. Ex 21:2. Le 25:39, 50. Dt 15:12. Je 34:9.
ye break. 1 T 6:1.

7 to deal. lit. divide or break. Dt 26:14. Jb 42:11. Je 16:7mg. La 4:4. Ezk 18:7. 24:17. Ho 9:4. Mt 14:19. 15:36. 26:26. Mk 8:6, 19. 14:22. Lk 22:19. 24:30, 35. Ac 2:42, 46. 20:7, 11. 27:35. 1 C 10:16. 11:24.
bread. Ge +3:19.
to the hungry. ver. 10. Jb 22:7. 31:18-21. Ps 112:9. Pr 22:9. 25:21. 28:27. Ec 11:1, 2. Ezk 18:7, 16. Da 4:27. Mt 25:35-40. Lk 11:41. 19:8. Ro +12:20, 21. 2 C 9:6-10. 1 T 5:10. Phm 7. Ja 2:15, 16. 1 J 3:17, 18.
bring. Is 16:3, 4. Ge 18:2-5. 19:2. Jg 19:20, 21. Ac 16:15, 34. Ro 12:13. He 13:2, 3.
the poor. Ps 41:1.
cast out. *or*, afflicted. **S#4788h**. La 1:7 (miseries). 3:19 (misery).
to thy house. Ps 68:6mg.
the naked. Is +20:2. 2 Ch 28:15. Jb 31:19, 20. Mt 25:35-45. Lk 3:11.
hide not thyself. Ps 55:1. Dt 22:1, 3, 4. Jb 6:16. Mt 15:5. Mk 7:11-13.
thine own. Ge 29:14. 37:27. Jg 9:2. 2 S 19:12, 13. Ne 5:5. Mt 22:39. Lk 10:26-36. Ro 11:14. Ga 6:10. Ep 5:29. 1 T 4:10. +5:8. 1 J 3:17.
flesh. that is, kindred. 1 T 5:8mg.

8 thy light. ver. 10, 11. Jb 11:17. Ps 37:6. 97:11. 112:4. Pr +4:18. Ho 6:3. Ml 4:2.
and thine health. Heb. thy healing. Is 57:18. Je +8:22. 33:6. 38:17. Ho 6:2. 14:4. Mt 13:15.
and thy. Ps 85:13. Ac 10:4, 31, 35.

the glory. Is 52:12. Ex 14:19.
be thy rereward. Heb. gather thee up. Is 40:11. +52:12mg. Ge 42:17mg. Ex 14:19, 20. Ps 27:10mg.

9   **shalt thou**. Is 30:19. Ps 34:15-17. 37:4. +66:18, 19. 118:5. 1 J +5:14.
Here. Ge 27:18. 1 S 3:4-8.
the yoke. ver. 6.
the putting. Is 57:4. Pr 6:13.
speaking vanity. Is 59:3, 4. Ps 12:2. 36:3. 1 S 25:10, 11. Pr 18:23. Ezk 13:8. Zc 10:2. Mt 12:34. Ep 4:31.

10   **draw out**. ver. 7. Dt 15:7-10. Ps 41:1, 2. 112:5-9. Pr 11:24, 25. 14:31. 28:27. Lk 18:22.
thy soul. Heb. *nephesh*, Ge +34:3. 1 C 16:2. 2 C 8:3, 11. 9:7.
satisfy. ver. 11. Dt 15:7, 8.
soul. Heb. *nephesh*, Ge +34:3.
light rise. ver. 8. Is 60:1. Ex 22:3. Dt 33:2.
in obscurity. Is 29:18. 59:9. Ge +1:2 (darkness).
thy darkness. Is 9:2. 42:7, 16. 49:9. 60:2. Ps 107:10. Mi 7:8.
noon day. Is 16:3. 59:10. Ge 43:16. Jb 11:17. Ps 37:6.

11   **guide thee**. Is 49:10. 62:20. Ge 24:27. Ex 13:17. Ps 25:9. +32:8. 48:14. 73:24. Jn 16:13. 1 Th 3:11mg.
continually. S#8548h. Is 21:8. 49:16. 51:13. 52:5. 58:11. 60:11. Ps 35:27. 40:11, 16. 70:4. 71:3, 6, 14. 72:15. 73:23. 119:44, 109, 117. Pr 6:21.
and satisfy. Is 33:16. Jb 5:20. Ps 33:18, 19. 34:9, 10. 37:19. Je 17:8. Ho 13:5.
soul. Heb. *nephesh*, Ge +34:3.
drought. Heb. droughts. Ps 68:6.
make fat. Ps 92:14. Pr 3:8. +11:25. 13:4. 28:25.
be like. Is 61:11. SS 4:15. Je 31:12. Ezk 36:35.
a spring. Is 41:18.
whose waters. Jn 4:14.
fail. Heb. lie, *or* deceive. Is 57:11. Jb 6:15-20.

12   **build**. Is 51:3. 61:4. Ne 2:5, 17. 4:1-6. Je 31:38. Ezk 36:4, 8-11, 33. Am +9:14, 15.
old. Heb. *olam*, Jb +22:15.
waste. Is 51:3. 52:9.
The repairer. Ne 4:7. 6:1. Da 9:25. Am 9:11.

13   **turn**. Ex +20:8-11.
from doing thy pleasure. Ge 4:3. 29:27. Mt 23:23. Lk +13:14. Ro 14:5. 1 J 2:15, 16.
call. Ps 27:4. 37:4. 42:4. 84:2, 10. 92, title, 1, 2. 122:1. Re 1:10.
honor him. Is 8:13. 25:1. Ps 29:2. 34:3. 57:5. 71:8. 107:32. 145:5. Pr 3:9. 14:31. Ml 1:6. Mt *15*:8. Mk 7:6. 11:8. Lk 4:15. 19:35. Jn +5:23, 44. 8:49, 54. 12:13. Re 5:13. 19:7.
own ways. Is 55:8. 66:3. Am 8:5. Ep 5:8.
nor speaking. Is 59:3, 13.
words. Is 29:24. Pr 10:19. Ec 5:1, 2. Hab

+2:20. Mt 6:7. 12:36. 1 C 14:34. Ep 5:4. 1 T 2:11, 12. Ju +16.

14   **delight**. Jb 22:26. 27:10. 34:9. Ps 36:8. 37:4, 11. Hab 3:18. Ph 4:4. 1 P 1:8.
cause thee to ride. Is 33:16. Dt 32:13. 33:29. Ps 45:4. Hab 3:19. Re 6:2.
and feed. Is 1:19. Ge 28:14. Ps 105:9-11. 135:12. 136:21, 22. Je 3:19.
the mouth. Is 1:20. 40:5. 55:10, 11. Mi 4:4. Mt 24:35.

ISAIAH 59

1   **the Lord's**. Is 50:2. Ge 18:14. Nu 11:23. Je 32:17.
that it cannot save. Is 63:1. 1 S 17:37. 2 C 1:10. 2 T 4:17. He 7:25. 2 P 2:9.
his ear. Is 6:10. 65:24. Da 9:21. Mt 13:15.

2   **your iniquities**. Is +50:1. Dt 32:19. Jsh 7:11, 12. Pr 15:29. Je 5:25.
have separated. Ge 4:16. Je 44:4. Lk 16:26.
your sins. Ho 14:4. 1 J 1:9.
hid. *or*, made *him* hide. Is 57:17. Dt +31:17. Mt 6:22, +23. 2 P +3:5.
not hear. 1 S 14:36-38. Ps +66:18.

3   **your hands**. Is 1:15, 21. Je 2:30, 34. 22:17. Ezk 7:23. 9:9. 22:2-6. 35:6. Ho 4:2. Mi 3:10-12. 7:2. Mt 27:4, 25.
your lips. Je 7:8. 9:3-6. 42:20. 44:16. Ezk 13:8. Ho 7:3, 13. Mi 6:12. 1 T 4:2.

4   **calleth**. ver. 16. Je 5:1, 4, 5. Ezk 22:29-31. Mi 7:2-5.
trust. Is 30:12. Jb 15:31. Ps 62:10. Je 7:4, 8.
and speak. ver. 3. Ps 62:4.
they conceive. ver. 13. Pr 4:16. Mi 2:1. Mt 23:27, 28. Ja +1:15.

5   **cockatrice'**. *or*, adder's. Is 11:8mg. 14:29mg. Pr 23:32mg.
crushed breaketh out into a viper. *or*, sprinkled *is as if* there brake out a viper. Mt +3:7.

6   **webs**. Is 28:18-20. 30:12-14. Jb 8:14, 15.
garments. Is 61:10.
neither. Is 30:1. 57:12. 64:6. Ro 3:20-22. 4:6-8. Re 3:17, 18.
their works. Is 5:7. Ge 6:11. Ps 58:2. Je 6:7. Ezk 7:11, 23. Am 3:10. 6:3. Mi 2:1-3, 8. 3:1-11. 6:12. Hab 1:2-4. Zp 1:9. 3:3, 4.

7   **feet**. Pr 1:16. 6:17, 18. Ro *3:15-17*.
and they. ver. 3. Je 22:17. La 4:13. Ezk 9:9. 22:6. Mt 23:31-37. Re 17:6.
innocent blood. Dt +19:10. 27:25.
their thoughts. Pr 15:26. 24:9. Mt 15:18, 19. Mk 7:21, 22. Ac 8:20-22.
wasting. Is 60:18. Ro *3:16*.
destruction. Heb. breaking. Is +51:19mg.
paths. Is +7:3.

8   **way**. Is 57:21. Ps 120:7. Pr 3:17. Lk 1:79. Ro *3:17*.

no. ver. 14, 15. Is 5:7. Je 5:1. Ho 4:1, 2. Am 6:1-6. Mt 23:23.

judgment. *or*, right. Is 56:1mg. Ps 58:1, 2.

crooked. Ps 125:5. Pr 2:15. 28:18.

whosoever. Is 48:22. 57:20, 21.

9 **is judgment**. La 5:16, 17. Hab 1:13.

we wait. Is 5:30. Jb 30:26. Je 8:15. 14:19. Am 5:18-20. Mi 1:12. 1 Th 5:3.

but. Is +1:21.

we walk. Pr +4:19. Je 13:16.

10 **grope**. Dt +28:29. Jb 5:14. Pr +4:19. Je 13:16. La 4:14. Am 8:9. Jn 11:9, 10. 12:35, 40. 1 J 2:11.

the blind. 1 S 3:1. 28:6. Mt +15:14. 2 P 1:9.

night. Is 5:11. 21:4. Jb 24:15. Pr 7:9. 2 K 7:5, 7. Je 13:16.

in desolate. La 3:6.

11 **roar**. Is 51:20. Ps +22:1.

mourn. Mt +5:4.

like doves. Le 1:14. Mt 10:16.

for salvation. Ps 85:9. 119:155.

12 **our transgressions**. Is 1:4. Le 16:21. Ezr 9:6. Je 3:2. 5:3-9, 25-29. 7:8-10. Ezk 5:6. 7:23. 8:8-16. 16:51, 52. 22:2-12, 24-30. 23:2, etc. 24:6-14. Ho 4:2. Mt 23:32, 33. 1 Th 2:15, 16.

our sins. Le 16:21. Je 14:7. Ho 5:5. 7:10. Ro 3:19, 20.

iniquities. Le 16:21.

we know. Ezr 9:13. Ne 9:33. Da 9:5-8.

13 **lying**. Is 32:6. 48:8. 57:11. Ps 78:36. Je 3:10. 42:20. Ezk 18:25. Ho 6:7. 7:13. 11:12. Ac 5:3, 4.

departing. Is 31:6. Je 3:20. 32:40. Ezk 6:9. He +3:12.

speaking. Je 5:23. 9:2-5. Mt 12:34-36. Mk 7:21, 22. Ro 3:10-18. Ja 1:15. 3:6.

14 **judgment**. ver. 4. Is 5:23. 10:1, 2. Ps 82:2-5. Ec 3:16. Je 5:27, 28, 31. Am 5:7, 11, 12. Mi 3:9-11. 7:3-5. Hab 1:4. Zp 3:1-3.

15 **truth**. Is 48:1. Ps 5:9. 12:1, 2. Je 5:1, 2. 7:28. Ho 4:1, 2. Mi 7:2. Mt +23:13, 14.

faileth. Is 34:16.

he that. Hab 1:13, 14. Ac 9:1, 23. Ro 8:36. He 11:36-38. 1 J 3:11, 12.

maketh himself a prey. *or*, is accounted mad. 1 S 21:14mg. 2 K 9:11. Mk 3:21. Jn 8:52. 10:20. 2 T +1:7.

displeased him. Heb. was evil in his eyes. Nu +22:34mg.

16 **he saw**. Is 50:2. 64:7. Ge 18:23-32. Ps 106:23. Je 5:1. Ezk 22:30. Mk 6:6.

no man. Is 63:3.

wondered. Ps 143:4. Mk 6:6.

intercessor. Is 53:12. Je 15:11.

therefore. Jb 40:14.

his arm. Ex +15:16.

17 **he put on righteousness**. Is 11:5. 51:9. Jb 29:14. Ro 13:12-14. 2 C 6:7. Ep 6:14, 17. 1 Th 5:8. Re 19:11.

breastplate. Ex +39:8. Ps +35:2.

garments of vengeance. Ps +93:1. Je +50:15.

and clad. Ep 6:13.

with zeal. Is +9:7. Zc 1:14.

18 **According**. Is 63:6. Jb 34:11. Ps 18:24-26. 62:12. Je 17:10. 50:29. Mt 16:27. Ro 2:6. Re 20:12, 13.

deeds. Heb. recompences. 2 S 19:36. Je 51:56.

fury. Is 1:24. 49:25, 26. 63:3, 4, 6. 66:15, 16. Le +26:28. Ps 21:8, 9. La 4:11. Ezk 5:13, 15. 6:12. 8:18. 14:19-21. 16:42. 21:17. 24:13. 36:6. 38:18. Na 1:2, 6. Lk 19:27. 21:22. Re 16:19. 19:15.

19 **fear the name**. Is 11:9-16. 24:14-16. 49:12. 66:18-20. Ps 22:27. 102:15. 113:3. Da 7:27. Zp 3:8, 9. Ml 1:11. Re 11:15.

his glory. Is +40:5. Ezk 39:21.

the rising. Is +24:15. Ps 113:3. Ml 1:11.

When. Ezk +39:28.

the enemy. Is 29:19, 20. Re 12:10, 15-17. 17:14, 15.

like a flood. Je +47:2. Ezk +38:15, 16. Jl 3:2, 11, 14. Zc 14:2-4. Mt +24:8.

the Spirit. Heb. *ruach*, Is +48:16. Is 11:10. Ge +41:38. Ps 51:12. Jl 2:28-32. 3:1, 7-17. Zc 4:6. 2 Th 2:8. Re 20:1-3.

lift up a standard against him. *or*, put him to flight. ver. 17. Is 10:18. 11:4. 27:1. 41:11, 12, 15, 16. 49:22, 24-26. 60:14. 62:10. Ex +17:15. Ps 92:7. 110:2, 5, 6. Ezk 38:4. 39:2-4. Jl 2:20. Re 20:9.

20 **the Redeemer**. Is 25:9. Ob 17-21. Ro *11:26, 27*.

shall come. Is +16:1. 52:8. Ps 85:9. +102:16. Jl 2:12, 17-21. Zc 12:8. +14:3, 4. Ac +3:20.

to Zion. Is 1:27. +24:23. Ps 14:7. Ho 2:14, 15. Jl 3:16, 17. Zc 1:16, 17. Ro *11:26*.

turn from. Is 44:21-23. 62:1. Dt 30:1-10. Je 31:2, 3. Ezk 18:30, 31. Da 9:13. Ho 5:15. 14:2. Jl 2:17, 18. Zc +13:9. Ac 2:36-39. +3:19, 26. 26:20. T 2:11-14. He 9:28. 12:14. 2 P 3:14.

21 **As for me**. Ps 55:16.

this. Is 49:8. +55:3. Je 31:31-34. 32:38-41. Ezk 36:25-27. 37:25-27. 39:25-29. He 8:6-13. 10:16.

My spirit. Heb. *ruach*, Is +48:16. Is 11:1-3. 32:15. 44:3. 61:1-3. Ezk 37:14. 39:29. Pr 1:23. Jn 1:33. 3:34. 4:14. 7:39. Ac 2:38. Ro 8:9. 1 C 12:13. 2 C 3:8, 17, 18.

my words. Is 51:16. Jn 7:16, 17. 8:38. 17:8. 1 C +15:3. 1 P 1:25.

shall not depart. Is +41:9. +55:3. Je 3:19. 32:40. Ezk 16:63. Am +9:15.

for ever. Heb. *olam*, Ex +12:24. Ge +9:12.

ISAIAH 60

1 **Arise**. Ps +3:7. Mt 5:16. Jn 5:8. Ep +5:14. Ph 2:15.

shine; for thy light is come. *or*, be enlightened, for thy light cometh. ver. 19, 20. Ml +4:2. Jn +1:9. Ep 5:8. 1 J 1:5. Re 1:16. +2:28. 21:23. 22:5.

is come. Ge 6:13. Mt 12:28. He 12:22.

the glory. Is +40:5.

2 **the darkness**. Ps 74:20. Mt +15:14. Jn 3:19. Ac 26:18. Ro 1:21-32. Ep 4:17-20.

gross darkness. Je 13:16. Mt 6:23. Lk 18:8. Jn +21:3. Ep 5:8. Col 1:13. 1 P 2:9.

his glory. Is +40:5. Le 9:23. Ps 80:1. Ezk 10:4. Ml 4:2.

3 **the Gentiles**. Ps 67:1-4. Mt 2:1-11. +12:18. 28:19. Lk 24:47.

kings. ver. 10, 16. Is +49:7. Re 21:24.

4 **Lift**. Is 49:18. Ge +22:13. Jn 4:35. Ac 13:44.

they gather. Ge +49:10.

they come. Is 42:6. 49:20-22. 66:11, 12. Mt +8:11. Ga 3:28, 29.

thy sons. Je 31:10. Ezk 34:11-15.

nursed. Is 49:22mg.

5 **thou shalt see**. Is +11:10. 61:6. Je 33:9. Ho 1:10, 11. 3:5. Ac 10:45. 11:17.

fear. Ho 3:5 (praise).

be enlarged. Is 54:2. 1 S 2:1. Re 21:26.

abundance of the sea shall be converted unto thee. *or*, noise of the sea shall be turned towards thee. Is 24:14, 15. Ps 98:7-9. Je 51:16mg.

forces. *or*, wealth. ver. 11. Is 10:3. 23:18. 61:6. Ge +31:1. +34:29. Jb 36:19. Pr 13:22. Mi 4:13. Zc 14:14. Ac 24:17. Ro *11:25*. 15:26.

6 **multitude**. Is 30:6. Jg 6:5. 7:12. 1 K 10:2. 2 K 8:9.

Midian. Ge +25:2.

all. Is 45:14. 1 K +10:1.

they shall bring. Is 61:6. Ps 72:10. Ml 1:11. Mt 2:2, +11.

they shall show. Ro 15:9. Ph 2:17. 1 P 2:5, 9. Re 5:9, 10. 7:9-12.

7 **of Kedar**. Ge +25:13.

Nebaioth. i.e. *high places; heights; prophecies; increasings; fruitfulnesses*, **S#5032h**. Is 60:7. 1 Ch 1:29. See also Ge +25:13. 28:9. 36:3 (Nebajoth).

they shall. Is 56:7. Jb 42:8. Ro 12:1. 15:16. He 13:10, 15, 16.

I will. Hg 2:7-9.

8 **fly**. ver. 4. Is 2:3, 5. Zc 8:21. Lk +13:29.

a cloud. He 12:1.

as the. Ge 8:8-11.

9 **the isles**. Is +11:11. Ge 9:27.

the ships. 1 K +22:48.

thy sons. ver. +4. Ps 68:30, 31. Zc 14:14. 2 C 8:4, 5. Ga 3:26. 4:26.

unto. Ex 33:19. 34:5-7. Jsh 9:9. 1 K 8:41. 10:1. Pr 18:10. Je 3:17. Jn 17:26. Ac 9:15.

because. Is 14:1, 2. 43:4. 52:1-6. 55:5. 57:17. Je 30:19. Lk 2:32. Jn 17:4.

10 **the sons**. Is 61:5. Zc 6:15.

of strangers. Is 56:3, 6. 61:5. Ex +12:43. Le 22:25.

their kings. ver. +3. Is 49:23. Ezr 6:3-12. 7:12-28. Re 21:24, 26.

in my wrath. Is 12:1. 54:7, 8. 1 S +12:22. Ps 30:5. Zc 1:15.

in my favor. Is 14:1. 49:8. Ps 69:13. 77:7. 85:1. +102:13. 106:4.

had mercy. Is +55:3. Ps 106:46. Je 12:15. 31:20. +33:25, 26. 42:12. La 3:32. Ezk 39:25. Ho 1:7. 2:23. Mi 7:19. Zc 1:16. 10:6.

11 **thy gates**. Ne 13:19. Re 21:25.

forces. *or*, wealth. ver. +5mg.

12 **the nation**. Is 41:11. 54:15. Ps 2:12. Da +2:44. Zc 14:12-19. Lk 19:27.

13 **The glory**. Is 35:2. 41:19, 20. 55:13. Ho 14:6, 7.

to beautify. Is 41:19. 51:3. Ezr 7:27. Re 3:12.

my sanctuary. Ezk +37:26. 43:7. Zc 1:16. 6:12, 13.

the place. Is 35:2. 66:1. 1 Ch 28:2. Ps 96:6. 99:5. 132:7.

my feet. Ps +74:3. Ezk 43:7. Zc 14:4.

14 **sons**. Is 14:1, 2. 45:14. 49:23. Je 16:19. Re 3:9.

afflicted. or, oppressed. Is 1:7, 8. 6:12. 7:16.

shall come bending. Ml 1:11. Mt +8:11. Re 3:9.

The city. Is 62:12. Ps 87:3. He 12:22. Re 3:12. 14:1.

Zion. Is +24:23.

15 **thou**. Is 49:14-23. 54:6-14. Je 30:17. La 1:1, 2. Re 11:2, 15-17.

forsaken. Is +1:4, 7-9. 6:11-13. +54:7. 62:4. Je 30:17. Zc 10:6. Ro 11:15.

and hated. Is 66:5. Dt 21:15. Ps 9:13. 25:19. 35:19. 38:19. 69:4. 109:3. 119:78, 86. Mt 10:22.

eternal. Heb. *olam*, Le +25:32.

excellency. Ps 47:4.

a joy. Is 35:10. 61:7. Je 33:11. Re 21:2.

16 **suck the milk**. Is 49:23. 61:6. 66:11, 12.

thou shalt know. Is +43:3, 4. 66:14. Ezk 34:30.

thy Redeemer. Is +41:14.

the mighty. Is +49:26.

One of Jacob. Ps +132:2.

17 **brass**. Is 30:26. 1 K 10:21-27. Zc 12:8. He 11:40. 2 P 3:13.

make. Is 1:26. 32:1, 2.

thine exactors. Is 3:12. Lk 3:13.

18 **Violence**. Is 2:4. 11:9. Ps 72:3-7. Mi 4:3. Zc 9:8.

but. Is +26:1. Re 19:1-6.

thy walls. Re 21:18.

Salvation. Re 19:1.

Praise. Is 61:11. Ps 89:16.

19 **sun**. Ps 36:9. Re 21:23. 22:5.

everlasting. Heb. *olam*, Ge +17:7.

thy God. Ps 3:3. 4:2. 62:7. Zc 2:5. Lk 2:32.

20 **sun**. Ps 27:1. 84:11. Am 8:9. Ml 4:2.

the Lord shall. Is 58:11.
everlasting. Heb. *olam*, Ge +17:7.
the days. Is +65:19.

21 **people**. Is 4:3, 4. 52:1. 62:4. Zc 14:20, 21. 2 P 3:13. Re 21:27.
all righteous. Is +27:9. 61:3. 62:2. Dt +30:6. Ps +130:8. Ezk 37:23, 24. Da +9:24. Na 1:15. Zp +3:13. Re 21:27.
inherit. Mt +5:5. Re 21:7.
the land. 2 Ch +20:7. Zc 3:9. Ac +7:5.
for ever. Heb. *olam*, Ex +12:24. Is 11:11. +41:9. +55:3. Ge 17:8. 2 Ch 20:7. Am +9:15. He +11:39.
the branch. Is +4:2. 29:23. 43:7. 45:11. 61:3. Ps 92:13. Mt 15:13. Jn 15:2.
the work. Is 29:23. 43:21. Hab 3:2. Ep 2:10.
that I. Is +49:3. Ep 1:6, 12. 2:7. 2 Th 1:10.

22 **little**. Is 66:8. Da 2:35, 44. Mt 13:31, 32. Mk 4:28, 29. Ac 2:41. 5:14. Re 7:9.
I the Lord. Is 5:19. Hab 2:3. Lk 18:7, 8. He 10:36, 37. 2 P 3:8, +9.

ISAIAH 61

1 **Spirit**. Heb. *ruach*, Is +48:16. Is 11:2-5. 42:1. 59:21. Mt 3:16. Lk *4:18, 19*. Jn 1:32, 33. 3:34.
anointed. Ex +28:41. Jn +1:41. Ac 10:38.
to preach. Is 52:9. Mt +5:3-5. 11:5. Lk 4:16-21, 43. 7:22.
meek. Mt +5:5.
to bind. Jb +5:18. Ps +51:17. Ho 6:1. 2 C 7:6.
to proclaim. Ex 9:13. Le 25:11, 52. Je 34:8. Lk 4:16-22. Jn 8:32-36. Ac 26:18. Ro 6:16-22. 7:23-25. 2 C 3:17. 2 T 2:25, 26. He 2:8-10.
opening. Is +14:17. Ps 79:11. +146:7. La 3:34.

2 **the acceptable year**. Is 49:8. 63:4. Ge 2:4. Le 25:9-13. Ps 90:4. Je 11:23. 48:44. Lk *4:19*. 2 C 6:2. 2 P 3:7, 8. There is an unannounced time gap between this clause and the next. Other time gaps between adjacent statements can be seen at: Ps 118:22. Is 9:6. 53:10, 11. La 4:21, 22. Da 2:39-45; 7:3-28; 8:3-25; 9:26, 27; 11:20, 21; 11:35, 36; 12:2. Ho 2:13, 14. 3:4, 5. 5:15—6:1. Am 9:10, 11. Ob 21. Mi 2:12, 13. 5:2, 3. Hab 2:13, 14. Zp 3:7, 8. Zc 8:2, 3. 9:9, 10. Ml 3:1-3. Mt 10:23. 12:20. Lk 1:31, 32. 21:24, 26. Jn 1:5, 6. 5:28, 29. 1 P 1:11. Re 1:19; 4:1. 12:5, 6.
day of vengeance. Is 66:14. Ps 110:5, 6. Je +50:15. Ml 4:1-3. 1 Th 1:10. 2:16.
to comfort. Is 40:1. Je 31:13. 2 Th 2:16, 17.
mourn. Is +3:26. Mt +5:4.

3 **mourn**. Ezk 26:15, 16. Mt +5:4.
beauty. Is 12:1. Est 4:1-3. 8:15. 9:22. Ps 30:11. Ezk 16:8-13.
for ashes. Est +4:1.
the oil. Ps 23:5. +45:7. 104:15. Ec 9:8. Jn 16:20. He 1:9.
the garment of praise. ver. 10. Zc 3:5. Lk 15:22. Re 7:9-14.

the spirit. Heb. *ruach*, Ge +41:8.
of heaviness. S#3544h: Is 42:3 (smoking; mg, dimly burning). Le 13:6 (somewhat dark), 21, 26, 28, 39 (darkish), 56. 1 S 3:2 (wax dim). Compare S#3543h, 1 S +3:13 (restrained). 2 T +1:7. 1 P 4:14.
be called. Is 60:21. Ps 92:12-15. Je 17:7, 8. Mt 7:17-19.
trees of righteousness. Is 41:19, 20. 57:5. +60:21. Ps +1:3. Pr +11:30. Je +31:2. Da +12:3.
the planting. Nu 24:6. Ps +1:3. 92:12, 13. Je +11:17. Ezk 19:10. Mt 7:19. 15:13. Jn 15:1, 2. Ro 6:5. 1 C 3:9.
that he. Is 26:15. 44:23. 49:3. +60:21. Ex 14:18. Le 10:3. Ezk 28:22. 39:13. Hg 1:8. Mt +9:8. 1 C 6:20. 1 P 2:9.

4 **shall build**. Is 49:6-8. 58:12. Ezk 36:23-26, 33-36. Am 9:14, 15.
old. Heb. *olam*, Jb +22:15.
raise up. Am 9:11, 12. Ac +15:16.
desolations. Is +1:7. Ps 74:3.

5 **strangers**. Is 14:1, 2. 56:3, 6. 60:10-14. 62:8. Ex 12:43. Jsh 9:21. Ep 2:12-20.

6 **named**. Is 60:17. Ex +19:6. 1 P 2:5, 9.
call. Ezk 14:11. 1 C 3:5. 4:1. 2 C 6:4. 11:23. Ep 4:11, 12.
Ministers. Ex 28:35. Nu 16:9. Dt 10:8. 17:12. 1 C 4:1.
ye shall eat. Is 23:18. 60:5-7, 10, 11, 16. 66:12. Ac 11:28-30. Ro 15:26, 27.
riches of the Gentiles. Is +60:5. Mi 4:13. Zc 14:14. Ro +11:25.

7 **your shame**. Is 40:2. Dt 21:17. 2 K 2:9. Jb 42:10. Zc 9:12. Ro 5:20, 21. 2 C 4:17.
ye shall have. Jl +2:25. Zc 10:6.
double. or, double (honor). Ge +43:12.
everlasting. Heb. *olam*, Ge +17:7. Is 35:10. +51:11. +60:19, 20. Ps +16:11. Mt +25:46. 2 Th 2:16.

8 **I the Lord**. Ps 11:7. 33:5. 37:28. +45:7. 99:4. Je +9:24. Zc 8:16, 17.
I hate. Is 1:11-13. 1 S 15:21-24. Je 7:8-11. Am 5:21-24. Mt 23:14.
I will direct. Ps 25:8-12. +32:8. Pr +3:6. 8:20. 2 Th 3:5.
I will make. Is +55:3. Ps 50:5.
everlasting. Heb. *olam*, Ge +17:7.
covenant. Ge +9:16.

9 **their seed**. Is 44:3. Ge 22:18. Zc 8:13. Ac +2:39. 3:25. Ro 9:3, 4.
they are. Is 65:23. Ps 115:14. Zc 8:13. Ac 3:26. Ro 11:16-24.

10 **will greatly**. Is 35:10. 51:11. Ps 28:7. Hab +3:18. 1 P 1:8. Re 19:7, 8.
rejoice. Zp 3:17.
soul. Heb. *nephesh*, Ge +34:3. Ge 23:8. Le 26:43. 1 S 18:1. Ps 119:28.
clothed me. ver. 3. Is 52:1. Ex +28:2. 2 Ch 6:41. Jb 29:14. Ezk 26:15, 16. Lk 15:22. Ro 14:17. Ph 3:9. Re 4:4. 7:9-14. 21:2.

covered me. Is 59:6. Re 19:7, 8.
as a bridegroom. Is 49:18. Ps 45:8, 9, 13, 14.
Je 2:32. Ezk 16:8-16. Re 19:7, 8. 21:2, 9.
decketh himself. Heb. decketh as a priest.
Ex 28:2, 40.
with her. Ge 24:53.

11 **as the earth**. Is 55:10, 11. 58:11. SS 4:16.
5:1. Mt 13:3, 8, 23. Mk 4:26-32.
so. Is 45:8. 62:1. Ps 72:3, 16. 85:11. 97:11. 2
C 1:20.
righteousness. Is 4:3, 4. 45:8. +60:21. Ps
72:5. 85:10, 11, 13. Re 19:8.
praise. Is 60:18. 62:7. 1 P 2:9.

ISAIAH 62

1 **Zion's**. ver. 6, 7. Ps 51:18. 137:6. Is +24:23.
Mt 24:27. Lk 10:2. 21:24. 2 Th 3:1. He 7:25.
the righteousness. Is 1:26, 27. 32:15-17.
51:5, 6, 9. 61:10, 11. Ps 98:1-3. Pr +4:18. Mi
4:2. Mt 5:16. Lk 2:30-32. Ph 2:15, 16. 1 P 2:9.
lamp. Zc 4:2. Re 21:23, 24.

2 **the Gentiles**. Is 52:10. 61:9. Mi 5:8. Mt
+12:18. 24:27. Col 1:23.
thy righteousness. Is +60:21.
all kings. Is 49:23. 60:11, 16. Ps 72:10, 11.
138:4, 5.
thou shalt. ver. 4, 12. Is 65:15. Ge 17:5, 15.
32:28. Je 11:16. 33:16. Ezk 48:35. Ac 11:26.
Ga 4:26. He 12:22. Re 2:17. 21:2, 9, 10.

3 **crown**. Ps 132:18. Pr 12:4. SS 3:11. Re
19:12.
of glory. Is 28:5. Zc 9:16. Lk 2:14. 1 Th 2:19.

4 **shalt no more**. ver. 12. Is 32:14, 15. 49:14.
50:1. 54:1, 6, 7. Je 3:8. Ho 1:9, 10. 2:2. Ro
9:25-27. He +13:5. 1 P 2:10.
Hephzibah. *that is*, My delight *is* in her.
S#2657h. ver. 5. Ps 16:3. 149:4. 2 K 21:1. Je
32:41. Zp 3:17.
Beulah. *that is*, Married. Is 54:5. 61:10. Ps
48:2. SS 4:7. Je 3:14. Ezk 16:8, 14. Ho 2:19,
20. Mt 23:39. Jn 3:29. 2 C 11:2. Ep 5:25-27.
Re 21:2, 9, 10. **S#1166h**: Is 54:1. 62:4. Ge
20:3mg. Dt 22:22. Pr 30:23.

5 **shall thy sons**. Is 49:18-22. Ps 45:11-16.
the bridegroom rejoiceth. Heb. with the
joy of the bridegroom. ver. 4. Ps 45:11. SS
3:11. Jn 3:29. 2 C 11:2. He 12:2. 1 P 1:8. Re
21:2.
rejoice. Dt +30:9.

6 **set watchmen**. Is 21:11, 12. 52:8. 56:10. 2
Ch 8:14. SS 3:3. 5:7. Je 6:17. Ezk 3:17-21.
33:2-9. 1 C 12:28. Ep 4:11, 12. He 13:17.
which. ver. 1. Ps 134:1, 2. Re 4:6-8.
make mention of the Lord. *or, are the
Lord's remembrancers.* Is 26:13. 43:26. Ge
32:12. Nu 14:17-19. 2 S +8:16mg. Ps 74:2, 18.
137:5, 6. Ac 10:4, 31.
keep. Ps 83:1. Mt 15:22-27. Lk +18:1-8, 39.
Re 6:10.

7 **give him**. Is +45:11. Mt 6:9, 10. Lk +18:1-8.
1 Th +5:17.
no rest. Heb. silence. ver. 6. Ps 83:1.
till he make. ver. 1-3. Is 61:11. 64:9-12. Ps
+102:13, 16. +122:6. Je 33:9. Zp 3:19, 20. Mt
6:9, 10, 13. Re +11:15.
Jerusalem. Is +24:23. Zc +2:12.
a praise. Zp 3:20. Zc 12:2.

8 **sworn**. Dt 32:40. Ezk 20:5.
arm. Ex +15:16.
Surely I will no more give. Heb. if I give,
etc. Is 65:21-23. Le 26:16. Dt 28:30, 31, 33. Jg
6:3-6. Je 5:17.
stranger. Is 56:3, 6. 60:10. 61:5. Ex +12:43.
Je 5:19.

9 **gathered it**. Dt 20:6. 28:30. Je 31:5.
shall eat. Dt 12:7, 12. 14:23-29. 16:11, 14.
and praise. Dt 14:23, 26. 16:11, 14.
brought it together. Dt 12:12.

10 **go through**. Is 18:3. 40:3. 48:20. 52:11.
57:14. Ex 17:15. Mt 22:9. He 12:13.
high-way. Is +7:3.
gather out. Jn 11:39.
lift up. Is 11:12. 49:22.

11 **the Lord**. Ps 98:1-3. 102:18, 21, 22. Je 33:9.
Zp 3:20. Mk 16:15. Ro 10:11-18.
Say. Mt +21:5.
his reward. Is +40:10. 49:4. Re 22:12.
work. *or*, recompence. Is 40:10mg. 49:4mg.
61:8. Le +19:13.

12 **The holy**. Is +60:21. Dt 7:6. 26:19. 28:9. 1 P
2:9.
The redeemed. Is 35:9. 43:1. Ps 107:2. 1 P
1:18, 19. Re 5:9.
Sought out. Is 65:1. Ezk 34:11-16. Zc 8:23.
14:16. Mt 18:11-13. Lk 15:4, 5. +19:10. Jn
4:23. +10:16.
not forsaken. ver. +4. Is +41:9. 49:14-16. 1 S
+12:22. Ps 87:3. +94:14. Mt 16:18. 28:20. He
+13:5.

ISAIAH 63

1 **Who is this**. Ps 24:7-10. SS 3:6. 6:10. 8:5. Mt
21:10.
from Edom. Is 34:5, 6. Ps 137:7. Ob 1, 8, 9,
21.
dyed. ver. 2, 3. Is 9:5. Re 19:13.
Bozrah. Am 1:11, 12.
glorious. Heb. decked.
travelling. Ps 45:3, 4. Re 11:17, 18.
speak. Is 45:19, 23. Nu 23:19.
mighty. Jsh 4:24. Ps 89:19. Am 5:12. Zp
3:17. Lk 1:49. Jn 10:28-30. He 7:25. 1 P 1:5.
Ju 24, 25.

2 **Wherefore art thou**. Re 19:13.
red. Ge 25:30. Nu 19:2.
treadeth. Ps 68:23. La 1:15. Re 14:19, 20.
19:15.
winefat. Jg 6:11. Ne 13:15. Jl 3:12-14.

3 **trodden**. Is 25:10. La 1:15. Ml 4:3. Re 14:19, 20. 19:13-15.
alone. Ps +69:8. Jn 1:11. 7:3, 5. He 9:7.
none with me. Is 59:16.
tread. Is 22:5. 28:3. Ps 60:12.
and trample. ver. 6. Is 34:2-5. 2 K 9:33. Ezk 38:18-22. Mi 7:10. Zc 10:5.
fury. Is +59:18.
sprinkled. Le +1:5. 2 K 9:33. Re 19:13.

4 **day of vengeance**. Is +24:6. Dt +32:35. Ps +58:10. Je +50:15. Zp +3:8. 2 Th 1:8. 2 P 3:7. Re 11:13.
the year of. Is 34:8. +61:2. Ps 97:8. 98:9. +102:13. Ro 11:25-29.

5 **looked**. ver. 3. Is 41:28. 50:2. Jn 16:32. Ac 4:12. He 7:25.
mine own. Ex +15:16. Ps 44:3. Ho 1:7. 1 C 1:24. He 2:14, 15.
my fury. Is 59:16-18.

6 **in mine anger**. Ps 76:7-9. 99:1.
make. ver. 2, 3. Is 49:26. 51:21-23. Jb 21:20. Ps 60:3. 75:8. Je 25:16, 17, 26, 27. La 3:15. Re 14:10. 16:6, 19. 18:3-6.
I will bring. Is 25:10-12. 26:5, 6. Re 18:21.

7 **mention**. Is 41:8, 9. 51:2. Ne 9:7-15, 19-21, 27, 31. Ps 63:3. 78:11, etc. 105:5, etc. 107:8, 15, 21, 31. 136:1. 147:19, 20. Je 2:2. Ezk 16:6-14. Ho 2:19.
the great goodness. 1 K 8:66. 2 Ch 7:10. Ne 9:25, 35. Zc 9:17. Ro 2:4.
according to his. Ex +34:6, 7. Ep 1:6, 7. 2:4. 1 T 1:14. T 3:4-7.

8 **Surely**. Is 41:8. Ge 17:7. Ex 3:7. 4:22, 23. 6:7. 19:5, 6. Ro +11:1, 2, 28.
children. Is 57:11. Ex 24:7. Ps 78:36, 37. Zp 3:7. Jn 1:47. Ep +4:25.
so he. Is 12:2. 19:20. 43:3, 11. 45:21, 22. Dt 33:29. Ps 106:21. Je 14:8. Ho 13:4. 1 J 4:14. Ju 25.

9 **all their**. Ex 3:7-9. Jg 10:16. La 3:33. Zc 2:8. Mt 25:40, 45. Ac 9:4. He 2:18. +4:15.
the angel. Ex 32:34. 33:2, 14. Ho 1:7. Zc +12:8. Ac 12:11. 1 C 10:9.
in his love. Dt 7:7, 8. Ps 78:38. 106:7-10. Jn 16:27. T 2:14. 1 J 4:9, 10. Re +1:5. 5:9.
redeemed them. Ex 15:13.
bare them. Ex 19:4. Dt 1:31. 4:37. 32:11. Ac 13:18.
carried. Is 40:11. 46:3, 4. Ex 19:4. Dt 1:31. 32:11, 12. Lk 15:5.
of old. Heb. *olam*, Ge +6:4.

10 **they rebelled**. Is 1:2. 65:2. Ex 15:24. 16:8. 32:8. Nu 14:9, 11, 34. 16:1, etc. Dt 9:7, 22-24. Ne 9:16, 17, 26, 29. La 1:18, 20. Ezk 2:3, 7. 20:8, 13, 21.
vexed. Is 7:13. 43:24. Ge 6:3, 6. Ex 23:21, 22. Jg 10:16. Ps 78:8, 40, 49, 56. 95:9-11. Ezk 6:9. 16:43. Mk 3:5. Ac 7:51. Ep +4:30.
his holy. Ne 9:20. Hg 2:4, 5.
Spirit. Heb. *ruach*, Is +48:16.

he was. Ex 23:21. Le 26:17, etc. Dt 28:15, etc. 32:19-25. Je 21:5. 30:14. La 2:4, 5. Mt 22:7.

11 **he remembered**. Le 26:40-45. Dt 4:30, 31. Ps 25:6. 77:5-11. 89:47-50. 143:5. Lk 1:54, 55.
of old. Heb. *olam*, Ge +6:4.
Where is he that brought. ver. 15. Is 51:9, 10. Ex 14:30. 32:11, 12. Nu 14:13, 14, etc. Je 2:6.
shepherd. *or*, shepherds. Ex 3:1. Ps 79:13. Jn +10:11.
where is he that put. Nu 11:17, 25, 29. Ne 9:20. Da 4:8. Hg 2:5. Zc 4:6. Jn 3:34.
Spirit. Heb. *ruach*, Is +48:16.

12 **That led**. Is 55:4. Nu 24:8. Ps 77:20.
with. Ex 15:6, 13, 16. Ps 80:1.
dividing. Ex +14:21.
to make. Is 55:13. Ex 14:16, 17. 2 S 7:23. Ro 9:17.
everlasting. Heb. *olam*, Ge +17:7.

13 **led them**. Ps 106:9. Hab 3:15.
deep. Ge +1:2.

14 **the Spirit**. Heb. *ruach*, Is +48:16. Jsh 22:4. 23:1. He 4:8-11.
to make. ver. 12. Nu 14:21. 2 S 7:23. 1 Ch 29:13. Ne 9:5. Lk 2:14. Ep 1:6, 12, 14.

15 **Look down**. Dt 26:15. Nu 14:17-20. Ps 33:14. 80:14. 102:19, 20. La 3:50.
the habitation. Is +57:15. 66:1. 1 K 8:27. 2 Ch 30:27. Ps 113:5, 6. 123:1. 138:6.
where. Is +9:7. 51:9, 10. Ps 89:49.
sounding. *or*, multitude. Is 31:4mg. Ps 51:1.
thy bowels. ver. 9. Is 16:11. 49:15. Ge 43:30. 1 K 3:26. Ps 25:6mg. 51:1. Je 31:20. Ho 11:8. Mt +9:36. 14:14. 15:32. Lk 1:78mg. Ph 1:8. 2:1. Col 3:12. Phm 7, 12, 20. 1 J 3:17.
Are. Ps 77:7-9.

16 **thou art**. Is 64:8. Ex 4:22. Dt 32:6. 1 Ch 29:10. Je 3:19. 31:9. Ml 1:6. 2:10. Mt 3:9. 6:9.
our father. Dt 32:6. Ml 1:6. 2 C 1:21.
though Abraham. Mt +8:11. Ga 3:16, 26-29.
be ignorant of us. 2 K 2:9. Jb +14:21. Ec +9:5. Mt 22:32. Mk 12:26, 27. Lk +16:23.
Israel. 1 C 3:6. 7:16.
redeemer; thy name is from everlasting. *or*, Redeemer from everlasting is thy name. ver. 12. Is +41:14. He +13:8. 1 P 1:18-21. Re 1:8. 4:8. 11:17. 16:5.
everlasting. Heb. *olam*, Ge +17:7.

17 **why hast**. Ps 119:10, 36. 141:4. Ezk 14:7-9. 2 Th 2:11, 12.
made us to err. Is +45:7. 2 K 21:9. La 3:9. Am +3:6.
and hardened. Ex +4:21.
Return. Nu 10:36. Ps 74:1, 2. 80:14. 90:13. Zc 1:12.

18 **people**. Is 62:12. Ex 19:4-6. Dt 7:6. 26:19. Da 8:24. 1 P 2:9.

our. Is 64:11, 12. Ps 74:3-7. 79:1. La 1:10. 4:1. Mt 23:38. 24:2. Lk 21:24. Re 11:2.

19 are thine. Ps 79:6. 135:4. Je 10:25. Ac 14:16. Ro 9:4. 11:28. Ep 2:12.
they were not called by thy name. *or,* thy name was not called upon them. Dt 28:10. Je +14:9mg.

ISAIAH 64

1 Oh that. Ps 18:7-15. 144:5, 6. Mk 1:10mg.
rend. Ml 3:10.
that thou wouldest come. Is +35:4. 63:15. Ex 3:8. 19:11, 18, 19. Ps 144:5. Da 7:13. Mi 1:3, 4. Hab 3:1-13. Mt 26:64. Ac 1:9-11. 3:20, 21. Re 1:7. 22:17, 20.
that the. Jg 5:4, 5. Ps 68:8. 114:4-7. 2 P +3:10-12. Re 20:11.

2 melting fire. Heb. fire of meltings. 2 P +3:10.
to make. Is 37:20. 63:12. Ps 46:10. 67:1, 2. 79:10. 98:1, 2. 102:15, 16. 106:8. Ezk +38:16, 22, 23. 39:27, 28. Hab 3:2.
that the nations. Ps 48:4-6. 99:1. Je 5:22. Mi +7:17. Re 11:11-13.

3 thou didst. Dt 4:34. Jg 5:4, 5. 2 S 7:23. Ps 68:8. +99:3. 105:27-36. 106:22.
the mountains. ver. 1. Ex 19:18. Na 1:5, 6. Hab 3:3, 6.

4 beginning of the world. Heb. *olam,* Le +25:32.
have not. Ps 31:19. 1 C 2:9, 10. Ep 3:5-10, 17-21. Col 1:26, 27. 1 T 3:16. 1 J 3:1, 2. 4:10. Re 21:1-4, 22-24. 22:1-5.
seen, etc. *or,* seen a God besides thee, *which* doeth so for, etc.
prepared. Ps 31:19. Mt 25:34. Jn 14:2, 3. He 11:16.
waiteth. Ps +25:3. 1 C 1:7. 1 Th 1:10. Ja 5:7.

5 meetest. Ge 32:1. Ex 20:24. 25:22. 29:42, 43. 30:6. He 4:16.
rejoiceth. Ps 25:10. 37:4. 112:1. Ac 10:2-4, 35. Ph 3:13-15.
worketh righteousness. Zp +2:3.
those that. Is 26:8, 9. 56:1-7.
remember thee. Ml +3:16, 17.
thou art wroth. Is 63:10. Ps 90:7-9.
in those. Ps 103:17, 18. Je 31:18-20. Ho 6:3. 11:8, 9. Ml 3:6.
continuance. Heb. *olam,* Le +25:32. Is 63:9, 11, 16, 19. Jn 6:54. Ep 1:21. 3:21.
we shall be saved. Ro 8:38, 39. +11:26.

6 are all. Jb 40:4. 42:5, 6. Pr +20:9. T 3:3.
unclean thing. Le 5:2. Ezk 36:17.
all our righteousnesses. Is 57:12. Dt 6:12. Je 23:6. Ezk +33:13. Zc 3:3, 4. Ph 3:8, 9. Re 3:17, 18. 7:13, 14.
filthy. S#5708h, only here. Le 12:2. 15:20.
rags. S#899h. Is 51:6, 8 (garment). 59:6. Ge 24:53 (raiment). 27:15, 27. 38:14, 19. Ex +28:2. Zc 3:5.

we all. Is 40:6-8. Ps 90:5, 6. Ja 1:10, 11. 1 P 1:24, 25.
our iniquities. Is 57:13. Ps 1:4. Je 4:11, 12. Ho 4:19. Zc 5:8-11.

7 none. Is 50:2. 59:16. Je +10:25. Ezk 22:30. Da 9:13.
to take hold. Is 27:5. 56:4. +62:7. 2 Ch +7:14. Ezk 22:30.
hast hid. Is 45:15. 53:3. 54:8. 57:17. Dt +31:17. Ho 5:15.
consumed. Heb. melted. Ps 46:6. 90:7-9. Je 9:7. Ezk 22:18-22. 24:11. Am 9:5.
because. Heb. by the hand, as Jb 8:4mg.

8 thou art. Is 63:16. Ex 4:22. Dt 32:6. Ga 3:26, 29.
are the clay. Is 29:16. 45:9. Je 18:2-6. Jn 9:6. Ro 9:20-24.
all are. Is 43:7. 44:21, 24. Jb 10:8, 9. 26:13. Ps 100:3. 119:73. 138:8. Jn 1:3. Ac 17:24, 26. 2 C 6:1. Ep 2:10.

9 wroth. Ps 6:1. 38:1. 74:1, 2. 79:5-9. Je 10:24. Hab 3:2.
remember. Je 3:12. La 5:20. Mi 7:18-20. Ml 1:4. 2 P 2:17. Re 20:10.
for ever. Heb. ad, Ps +9:18 (S#5703h).
we are. Is 63:19. Ps 79:13. 119:94.

10 holy cities. Is 1:7. 2 K 25:9. 2 Ch 36:19-21. Ps 79:1-7. La 1:1-4. 2:4-8. 5:18. Da 9:26, 27. 12:7. Mi 3:12. Lk 21:21, 24. Re 11:1, 2.
desolation. Mt 23:38. 24:2.

11 holy. Je +17:27. La 2:7. Ezk 7:20, 21. 24:21, 25. Mt 24:2.
house. 2 Ch 6:19, 20. 7:12. Ps 74:2-8. 79:1-7.
where. 1 K 8:14, 56. 2 Ch 6:4. 7:3, 6. 29:25-30.
all our. La 1:7, 10, 11.
pleasant things. 2 Ch 36:19.

12 refrain thyself. Is 42:14. 63:15. Ge 43:31. 45:1. Ps 10:1. 74:10, 11, 18, 19. 79:5. 80:3, 4. 83:1. 89:46-51. Zc 1:12. Re 6:10.

ISAIAH 65

1 I am sought. Is 2:2, 3. 11:10. 55:5. Ps 22:27, 28. Mt 8:10. 15:21-28. Jn 16:5. Ro 9:24-26, 30. *10:20, 21.* Ep 2:12, 13.
Behold. Is 40:9. 41:27. 45:22. Jn 1:29.
unto. Is 43:1. 63:19. Ho 1:10. Zc 2:11. 8:22, 23. 1 P 2:10.
a nation. Dt 32:21.

2 I have. Ro *10:21.*
spread. Pr +1:24. Mt 23:37. Lk 13:34. 19:41, 42.
a rebellious. Is 1:2. 63:10. Dt 9:7. 31:27. Je 5:23. Ezk 2:3-7. Ac 7:51, 52. 1 Th 2:15, 16.
which. Is 59:7, 8. Ps 36:4. Pr 16:29.
after. Is 55:7. Ge 6:5. Nu 15:39. Dt 29:19. Ps 81:11, 12. Je 3:17. 4:14. 7:24. Mt 12:33, 34. 15:19. Ro 2:5. Ja 1:14, 15.

3 **A people**. Is 3:8. Dt 32:16-19, 21. 2 K 17:14-17. 22:17. Ps 78:40, 58. Je 32:30-35. Ezk 8:17, 18. Mt 23:32-36.
to my face. Jb 1:11. 2:5.
that sacrificeth. Is 1:29. 57:5. 66:17. Le 17:5. Je 2:20. 3:6. Ezk 20:28.
altars. Heb. bricks. Is 9:10. Ex 20:24, 25. 30:1-10. 2 K 23:12.

4 **remain**. Nu 19:11, 16-20. Dt 18:11. 2 Ch 34:5. Mt 8:28. Mk 5:2-5. Lk 8:27.
graves. Heb. qeber, Ge +23:4.
monuments. Is 48:6 (hidden things).
which eat. Is 66:3, 17. Le 11:7. Dt 14:8.
broth. or, pieces. Ex 23:19. 34:26. Dt 14:3, 21. Jg 6:19, 20. Ezk 4:14.
abominable things. Le 7:18. 19:7. Ezk 4:14.

5 **Stand**. Mt 9:11. Lk 5:30. 7:39. 15:2, 28-30. 18:9-12. Ac 22:21, 22. Ro 2:17, etc. Ju 19.
come not. Ml 3:16. Lk 9:49, 50. 11:52. Ac 10:28. Ro 15:7. 3 J 9, 10. Ju 19.
I am holier than thou. Dt 9:4. Jb 9:20. 35:2. Pr 12:15. 20:6. 30:12. Mt 6:5. Lk 18:9. Ac 11:2, 3. Ro 12:3. 2 C 10:12. Ph 2:3. Ja 1:27.
These. Pr 10:26. +16:5.
nose. or, anger.
a fire. Dt 29:20. 32:20-22.

6 **it is written**. Is 30:8. Ex 17:14. Dt 32:34. Ml 3:16. Re +3:5.
I will. Is 42:14. 64:12. Ps 50:3, 21.
but. Ps 79:12. Je 16:18. Ezk 11:21. 22:31. Jl 3:4.
recompense. Dt 32:35. 1 Th 2:16.

7 **Your iniquities**. Ex 20:5. Le 26:39. Nu 32:14. Ps 106:6, 7. Da 9:8. Mt 23:31-36.
burned. Is 57:7. 1 K 22:43. 2 K 12:3. 14:4. 15:35. 16:4. Ezk 18:6.
blasphemed. Ezk 20:27, 28.
therefore. ver. +6. Je 5:9, 29. 7:19, 20. 13:25. Mt 23:32. 1 Th 2:16.

8 **a blessing is**. Jb 14:7. Jl 2:14. Lk 13:6-9.
not destroy. Is 6:13. 10:21, 22. Je 30:11. +31:37. 46:28. Am 9:8, 9. Mt 24:22. Mk 13:20. Ro 9:27-29. +11:1, 5, 6, 24-26.

9 **I will**. Is 10:20-22. 11:11-16. 27:6. Je 31:36-40. 33:17-26. Ezk 36:8-15, 24. 37:21-28. 39:25-29. Am 9:11-15. Ob 17-21. Zp 3:20. Zc 10:6-12.
a seed. Is 26:2. 66:7, 8. Mt 21:43.
mine elect. ver. 15, 22. Mt 24:22. Ro 11:5-7, 28.

10 **Sharon**. Is +35:2. Ezk 34:13, 14. 35:2.
fold of flocks. Ps 23:1. SS 1:7. Jn 10:11.
valley of Achor. Jsh 7:24-26. Ho 2:15.
for my people. Is 6:13. Ga 3:29.

11 **they that forsake**. Dt 29:25. Je +1:16. Jn 1:11. 1 C 10:21.
my holy. ver. +25. Is +2:2. Ps 132:13, 14. Re 21:2, 3.
prepare. Is 57:5-10. Dt 32:17. Je 2:28. Ezk 23:41, 42. 1 C 10:20, 21.

troop. or, Gad. or, Fortune. Ge +30:11. Jsh 11:17. 12:7. 13:5. 15:37. Ezr 2:12. Ps 37:16, 21. 1 T 6:5. Ja 4:13.
drink offering. Is 5:22. Le +23:13. Pr 23:30.
number. or, Meni. or, fill up mingled wine unto Destiny. i.e. Fate. Ge 50:20. Da 5:25, 26. Ja 4:14.

12 **will I**. Is +3:25. 10:4. 31:8. 34:5, 6. 66:16. Je +12:12. Mt 22:7.
because. Pr +1:24. Mt 21:34-43. Jn 1:11.
did evil. ver. 3. Is 1:16. Je 16:17.
and did. Is 66:3, +4.

13 **Behold**. Is +2:7.
my servants shall eat. Ps +22:26. +37:3. Ml 3:18. Lk 14:23, 24. 16:24, 25.
but ye. Is +1:21.
be hungry. Lk 6:25.
my servants shall rejoice. Is 26:2. 61:7. 66:5, 14. Da +12:2. Mt 21:43.

14 **my servants**. Is 24:14. 52:8, 9. Jb 29:13. Ps 66:4. Je 31:7. Ja 5:13. Re 14:3.
but ye shall. Is +1:21. Mt +25:30. Lk 16:22, 23. Ja 5:1.
vexation. Heb. breaking. Is +51:19mg. Pr 15:4.
spirit. Heb. ruach, Ge +41:8.

15 **name**. Pr 10:7.
curse. Je +26:6.
my chosen. ver. 9, 22.
the Lord. ver. 12. Is 66:15, 16. Mt 21:41. 22:7. 1 Th 2:16.
shall slay thee. Is +38:10.
his servants. Is 42:1. 62:2. Ac 11:26. Ro 9:26. 1 P 2:9, 10.
another name. Is 60:18. 62:2, 4, 12. Ge +17:5. Dt +7:24. Jb 34:24. Je 23:6. 33:16. Ezk 48:35. Re 2:17.

16 **he who blesseth**. Ge 22:18. 26:4. Ps 72:17. Je 4:2.
in the God. Dt 32:4. Ps 31:5. 86:15. Je 10:10. Jn 1:14, 17. 14:6. He 6:17, 18. 1 J 5:20. Re 3:14.
of truth. or, faithfulness. 2 C 1:20.
sweareth. Ge +21:23.
because. ver. 19. Is 11:16. 12:1. 35:10. 54:4. Je 31:12. Ezk 36:25-27. Da 12:1, 11, 12. Zp 3:14-20. Re 20:4.
are hid. Is 64:4. 1 C 2:9.
mine eyes. Ps +11:4.

17 **I create**. Is 51:16. 66:22. Ps 102:25, 26. 2 P 3:13. Re 21:1-5.
the former. Je 3:16.
not be remembered. Is 25:8.
into mind. Heb. upon the heart. Je +3:16mg.

18 **be ye glad**. Is 12:4-6. 42:10-12. 44:23. 49:13. 51:11. 52:7-10. 66:10-14. Ps 67:3-5. 96:10-13. ch. 98. Zp 3:14. Zc 9:9. 1 Th 5:16. Re 11:15-18. 19:1-6.
for ever. Heb. ad, Ps +9:18.

19 **I will**. Dt +30:9. SS 3:11.
my people. Is 51:16. 66:22.
the voice of weeping. Is 25:8. 35:10. 51:3, 11. 60:20. Je 31:12, 15-17. Re 7:17. 21:4.

20 **There shall**. Ps 91:16.
an infant of days. Dt +4:40. Jn 3:36. 10:10, 28. 17:3. Ro 6:23.
filled. Ge 21:19. 24:16. 25:8. Dt 4:40. Jb 5:26. Ps 34:12.
the child. Je 31:17.
but the sinner. Is 3:11. 11:2-4. 22:14. Pr +10:27. Ec +7:17. 8:12, 13. Je 31:30. Zp 3:13. Ro 2:5-9.
accursed. or, cut off, or, lightly esteemed. Ne +13:25. Jb 24:18. Ps 101:8. Pr 2:22. Is 11:4. Mt +25:41. Ro 2:5. 6:23.

21 **they shall build**. Is 62:8, 9. Le 26:16. Dt 28:30-33, 41. Jg 6:1-6. Je 31:4, 5. Am +9:14.
inhabit. Ezk 36:10.
shall plant. Is 30:23. 37:30. 62:8, 9. Je 31:5.

22 **for as the days**. ver. 9, 15. Ge 5:5, 8, 11, 27. Le 26:16. Re 20:3-5.
of a tree. Ps 92:12-14.
elect. S#972h. ver. 9, 15 (chosen). Is 42:1. 43:20. 45:4. 2 S 21:6. 1 Ch 16:13. Ps 89:3. 105:6, 43. 106:5, 23.
long enjoy. Heb. make them continue long, or, shall wear out. Ge 18:12. Jb 13:28. 21:13. 36:11.
the work. Ps 90:17.

23 **not labor in vain**. Is 55:2. 61:9. Le 26:3-10, 20, 22, 29. Dt 28:3-12, 38-42. Ho 9:11-14. Hg 1:6, 9. 2:19. Ml 3:10, 11. Ga +4:11. 1 C 15:58. Re 22:3.
bring forth. Dt 28:41.
for trouble. Ps 78:33.
for they. Is 61:9. Ge 12:2. Dt +29:11. Ps 115:14, 15. Zc 10:8, 9. Ac 3:25, 26. Ro 4:16. 9:7, 8. Ga 3:29.

24 **before they call**. Ge +24:15, 45. 2 K +20:4. Ps 32:5. 138:3. Da 9:20-23. 10:12. Ho +5:15. 8:2. Mt 6:8. Mk 11:24. Lk 15:18-20. Ac 4:31. 10:30-32. 12:5-16.
I will answer. Ge +17:20. Ps +27:7. 38:15mg. +99:6. Je 33:3. Ac +3:20.
I will hear. Ps 38:15. 1 J +5:14, 15.

25 **wolf**. Is 11:6-9. 35:9. Ezk 34:25. Ho +2:18. Jl 2:22. Ac 9:1, 19-21. Ro 8:19-21. 1 C +6:9-11. T 3:3-7.
shall feed. Is 11:6, 7. 55:13. Ac +3:21.
together. i.e. "as one," one of others. Heb. echad, Dt +6:4 (one). Is 4:1. 5:10. 6:2, 6. 9:14. 10:17. 19:18. 23:15. 27:12. 30:17, 17. 34:16. 36:9. 47:9. 51:2. 65:25. 66:8, 17.
dust. Ge 3:14, 15. Ps 72:9. Pr 20:17. Ro 16:20. He 2:14. Re 12:7-9. 20:2, 3.
the serpent's meat. Ge 3:14. Re 20:1-3.
shall not. Is 2:4. 11:9. Mi 4:3.
my holy mountain. ver. 11. Is +11:9. Ezk 43:11, 12. Zc 14:20, 21. Re 14:1.

ISAIAH 66

1 **The heaven**. Dt +10:14. Ps 99:9. Mt +6:9. Ac 7:49, 50. 17:24. Ep 1:20. He 9:24.
my throne. Ps +11:4.
footstool. 1 Ch 28:2. Ps +74:3. 99:5. 132:7. La 2:1. Mt 5:35. Ac 7:49.
where is. 2 S 7:5-7. Je 7:4-11. Ml 1:11. Mt 24:2. Jn 4:20, 21. Ac 7:48-50. Re 21:22.
the house. Is 2:2. 60:13. Ezk +37:26. 40:2. Jl 2:1. Mi 4:1, 2. Hg 2:7. Zc 1:16. 6:12, 13.

2 **For all those**. Jn +1:3. Ac 7:50.
to this. 2 Ch 34:27, 28.
will I look. Jn 4:23, 24.
poor. Mt +5:3. Ja 2:5.
contrite. Ps +51:17. 138:6. Je 31:19, 20.
spirit. Heb. ruach, Ge +41:8.
trembleth. ver. 5. Ezr 9:4. 10:3. 2 Ch 34:21, 27. Ps 119:120, 136, 161. Pr 13:13. 28:14. Je 36:16, 23, 24. Ezk 9:4, 6. Hab +3:16. Ml 3:16. Ac 9:6. 16:29, 30. Ph 2:12.

3 **killeth**. Is 1:11-15. Pr 15:8. 21:27. Am 5:21, 22.
lamb. or, kid. Is 43:23mg. Ex 12:3mg.
cut off. Ex 13:13. Dt 23:18.
as if he offered. ver. 17. Is 65:3, 4. Le 11:7. Dt 14:8.
burneth. Heb. maketh a memorial of. Is 62:6mg. Le 2:2. 2 S +8:16mg.
they have. Is 65:12. Jg 5:8. 10:14.
own ways. Is 58:13.
soul. Heb. nephesh, Ge +34:3.

4 **I will choose**. 2 S 22:27. 1 K 22:19-23. Ps 81:12. Pr 1:31, 32. Ezk 14:9. Mt 24:24. 2 Th +2:10-12. Re 17:17.
delusions. or, devices. Is 3:4 (babes). Je +6:19.
will bring. Pr 10:24.
fears. Ps +34:4.
when I called. Pr +1:24.
not hear. Je +7:26.
they did evil. Is 65:3. 2 K 21:2, 6.
and chose. Is +56:4. 58:10, 13. 65:12. Ge 19:20. Dt +30:19. 1 K 3:11, 12. +18:21. Jb 36:21. Ps +50:23. 106:15. Pr 1:29. Je 9:6. 21:8. Da 1:8. 3:16-18. 6:10. Ml 3:16. Mt 16:24. 27:25. Lk 19:14. Jn 3:18. 18:40. Ro 1:28. +12:1, 2. 14:19. 1 C +6:9, 10. 2 C +6:17. 2 Th 2:10-12. He 11:25. Ja 4:4. 1 J 2:15-17. Re 3:20.
delighted not. Is +58:13, 14. Jb 34:9. Ps +37:4. Pr 11:1, 20. 12:22. 15:8. 18:2. Je 9:24.

5 **ye that**. ver. 2.
Your. Ps 38:20. SS 1:6. Ml 3:16-18. Mt 5:10-12. 10:22. Lk 6:22, 23. Jn 9:34. 15:18-20. 16:2. Ac 26:9, 10. 1 Th 2:15, 16. 1 J 3:13.
Let. Is 5:19.
but. Ac 2:33-47. 2 Th 1:6-10. T 2:13. He +9:28. 1 P 4:12-14.

6 **voice of noise**. Is 5:14. 13:4. 42:14. Je 51:55. Zc 12:3-6. 14:3.

voice from. Re 19:1-3.
a voice of the Lord. Is 34:8. 59:18. 65:5-7. Jl 3:7-16. Am 1:2, etc.

7 **travailed**. Is 54:1. Mt +24:8. Jn +16:21. Ga 4:26. Re 12:1-4.
delivered. ver. 8. Da 12:1.
man child. Re +12:5.

8 **hath heard**. Is 64:4. 1 C 2:9.
the earth. Zc 12:10-13. 13:9. Mt 24:15-22. Ro 11:25-29.
shall a nation. Is 26:2. 49:20-22. Mt 21:43. Ac 2:41. 4:4. 21:20. Ro 15:18-21.
travailed. ver. 7. Da 12:1. Mi +5:3. Zc 12:10—13:1. Mt +24:8, 15-22. Re 12:1-6, 14.
brought forth. Ro 8:14. Ga 3:26. 4:26. 1 J 3:1.

9 **bring to**. Is 37:3. Ge 18:14.
cause to bring forth. *or*, beget. Ge 11:27.
saith. Is +1:11.
shut. Ge 16:2.
the womb. Ge 20:18.

10 **Rejoice ye**. Is 44:23. 65:18. Dt 32:43. Ro 15:9-12.
all ye that love. Ps 26:8. 84:1-4. +122:6. 137:5, 6. Re 20:9.
that mourn. Mt +5:4. 23:37. Re 11:3-15.

11 **ye may suck**. Is 49:23. 60:5, 16. Nu 11:12. Ps 36:8. Je 3:15. Jl 3:18. 1 P 2:2.
and be satisfied. Is 49:23. Mt +5:3, 6. Lk 18:13, 14.
breasts of. Ge 49:25.
abundance. *or*, brightness. Is 25:6.
her glory. Is 60:1, 2. 62:2. Lk 2:32.

12 **I will**. Is +9:7. 48:18. 60:4, 5. Ps 72:3-7.
the glory. ver. 19, 20. Is 45:14. 49:19-23. 54:3. 60:4-14.
then. ver. 11. Is 49:22. 60:16.
ye shall. Is 60:4.

13 **one**. Is 40:1, 2. 51:3. 1 Th 2:7.
comfort you. Is 51:12. Ps 103:13. 2 C +1:4.
ye shall. ver. 10. Is 65:18, 19. Ps 137:6. Mt +5:4.
in Jerusalem. Is +24:23. Zc 2:12.

14 **your heart**. Zc 10:7. Jn 16:22.
your bones. Is +26:19. 58:11. Pr 3:8. 17:22. Ezk 37:1-14. Ho 14:4-8. Ro 11:15.
like an herb. Is +26:19. Dt 32:2.
the hand. ver. 5. Is 65:12-16. Ru +1:13. Ezr 7:9. 8:18, 22, 31. Ps 37:24. Ml 3:18. He 10:27.
toward. Is 54:7-9. Ps +102:13. Zc 8:15.
his servants. Is 54:17.
indignation. Is 10:5. 13:5. 26:20. 30:27, 30. 34:2. Ps 69:24. 78:49. 102:10. Je 10:10. Da +8:19. 11:36. Mi 7:9. Na 1:6. Hab 3:12. Zp 1:18. 3:8. Ro 2:8. He 10:27. Re 14:10.

15 **the Lord**. Is +35:4. Ezk 20:38. 38:16-23. Mt 24:29-31. 25:31.
with fire. Is +24:6. Ps 11:6. +97:3. Ezk 38:22. Am 7:4. Mt +3:11. 22:7. 2 Th 1:6-10. 2 P 3:10-12.

with his chariots. Is 5:28. Dt 33:2. 2 K 6:16, 17. Ps +68:17. Je 4:13. Da 7:10. 11:40. Hab 3:8. He 12:22. Re 9:16.
like a whirlwind. Ps 50:3. Je +23:19.
with fury. Is +59:18.
with flames. Nu 16:35. 2 Th 1:8. 2 P +3:7.

16 **by fire**. Is 30:30. Jb 36:18. Ezk 38:22. Zc 13:9.
by his sword. Is 27:1. Je +12:12. Ezk 38:21, 22. 39:2, etc. Jl 3:13. Re 19:11-21.
plead with. Is 59:4.
flesh. Ge +6:12.
the slain. ver. +24. Is 22:2. Zc 13:8, 9. 14:2, 3.
be many. Jl 3:14. Re 19:21.

17 **in the gardens**. Is 1:29. 65:3, 4.
behind one tree in the midst. *or*, one after another.
tree. or, Asherah. Dt 16:21, grove, or Asherah. Ex 34:13. Dt 23:17mg. Jg 6:25, 28. 1 K 16:33. 18:19-40. 2 K 17:10. 21:3. 23:6, 7. Ezk 16:17.
eating. Is 65:4. Le 11:2-8. Dt 14:3-8.
abomination. Heb. *shakaz*. Le 7:21. 11:10-13, 20, 23, 41-43. 20:25. Dt 7:26. Ezk 8:10.
the mouse. Le 11:29. 1 S 6:4, 5, 11, 18.
consumed together. Is 1:28, 31. Est 9:28. Ps 37:20, 38.

18 **I know**. Is 37:28. Dt 31:21. Am 5:12. Re 2:2, 9, 13.
their thoughts. Is 59:7. 65:2. Ezk 38:10. Jn +2:25. 1 C 3:20.
that I. Is 2:2. Ps 67:2. 72:11, 17. 82:8. 86:9. Jl 3:2. Ro 15:8-12. 16:26. Re 11:15.
will gather. Is 45:22-25. Je 3:17. Jl 3:2. Zp 2:11. 3:8.
shall come. Ps 86:9. Zc 14:16-19.
see my glory. ver. 19. Is +40:5. Lk +9:32. Jn 17:24.

19 **I will set**. Is 11:10-12. 18:3, 7. 30:17. 31:9. 49:22. 59:19. 62:10. Lk 2:34.
sign. Is +7:11.
I will send. ver. 12, 20. Is 49:7, 8, 9, 18. 52:7-10. 55:5. 56:6-8. 60:3-5, 14, 15. 61:4, 6, 9. 62:2. Zc 13:9. Mk 16:15. Ro 11:1-6, 15. Ep 3:8. Re 21:24-26. 22:2.
Tarshish. Ge +10:4.
Lud. Ge +10:22.
that draw the bow. Ezk 38:2.
Tubal. Ge +10:2.
the isles. Is +11:11. 43:6.
that have. Is 29:24. 52:15. 55:5. 65:1. Ml 1:11. Mt +8:11, 12. 28:19. Ro 15:21. Re 1:7.
they shall declare. Is 12:4. 42:12. 43:10-12, 21. 44:22, 23. 52:7. 53:1. 1 Ch 16:24. Ps 9:11. ch. 47, 97. 98:1-3. 118:17. 138:1-5. Ml 1:11. He 2:4.
my glory. ver. +18. Hg 2:9. Re 15:4.
among the Gentiles. Is +11:10. 25:6-9. +27:6. 48:20. 62:1-4. Dt 32:43. Ps ch. 67. 96:3. 102:15, 21, 22. Ezk 36:36. 37:28. 38:16, 23. 39:7, 21-23. Mt +24:14.

20   **shall bring**. Is 14:2.
     all your brethren. Is 43:6. 49:12, 22. 54:3.
     60:3-14.
     an offering. Reference to the "meat offer-
     ing," or meal offering, or gift offering. Le
     +23:13. Ro 12:1, 2. 15:16. Ph 2:17. 1 P 2:5.
     upon horses. Is 60:9.
     litters. _or_, coaches. Nu 7:3. SS 3:9.
     mules. 2 S 13:29. 18:9.
     swift beasts. Ge 31:34.
     my holy mountain. Is 2:2, 3. +11:9.
     bring an offering. Le +23:13.
     clean vessel. Is 52:11.

21   **I will also take**. Is +56:8. Ex +19:6. Je
     13:18-22.
     for Levites. Dt 17:9. Jsh 3:3. 8:33. 2 Ch
     30:27. Ne 11:20. Je 33:21. Ezk 43:19. 44:10,
     13, 15. Ho 2:23. Mi 5:3. Mt 21:43. Jn 1:11.
     10:16. Ro 9:23-26.

22   **the new heavens**. Is 65:17. He 12:27, 28. 2
     P _3:13_. Re 21:1.
     shall remain. or, are standing. Is 3:13. 6:2.
     11:10. Ec +1:4.
     your seed. Is 53:10. 61:8, 9. 65:22, 23. Mt
     28:20. Jn 10:27-29. 1 P 1:4, 5.
     your name. Is 56:5.

remain. Ps +72:5, 17. Mt 28:20. Lk 1:33. Re
11:15.

23   **one new**, etc. Heb. new moon to his new
     moon, and from sabbath to his sabbath. Col
     +2:16.
     shall all. ver. +18. Ps +86:9. Zc 8:20-23. 14:14,
     16, 17. Ml 1:11. Jn 4:23. He 4:9. Re 15:4.
     flesh. Ge +6:12.
     worship before me. Is 19:21, 23. 27:13.
     49:7.

24   **and look**. Ge 19:28. Ex 14:30. Jb 22:19.
     34:26. Ps 37:34. 52:6. 58:10, 11. +112:8. Je
     11:20. 20:12. 51:24. Ezk 28:17. 39:9-16. Zc
     14:12, 18, 19. Lk +13:28. 16:23. Re 14:10.
     19:17-21.
     carcasses. ver. 16. Je +7:33. Zc 14:12. Mt
     +24:28.
     transgressed. Is 1:28. 24:20-22.
     their worm. S#8438h. Is 14:11b. 41:14. Ex
     16:20. Dt 28:39. Jb 25:6b. Ps 22:6. Jon 4:7.
     Mk _9:44-49_.
     not die. Is 14:9, 10. Jb 36:18. Ezk 32:21. Da
     +12:2.
     their fire. Mt +3:12. +25:41, 46.
     and they. Is 34:3. 65:15. Da 12:2. 1 Th 2:15,
     16.

JEREMIAH

JEREMIAH 1

1 A.M. 3375. B.C. 629.

words. 2 Ch 36:21. Is 1:1. 2:1. Am 1:1. 7:10.

Jeremiah. i.e. *Jah is the exalted one; high one of Jah*, **S#3414h**. Je 1:1, 11. 7:1. 11:1. 14:1. 18:1, 18. 19:14. 20:1-3. 21:1, 3. 24:3. 25:1, 2, 13. 26:7-9, 12, 20, 24. 28:12. 29:27, 29, 30. 30:1. 32:1, 2, 6, 26. 33:1, 19, 23. 34:1, 6, 8, 12. 35:1, 3, 12, 18. 36:1, 4, 5, 8, 10, 19, 26, 27, 32. 37:2, 3, 4, 6, 12-18, 21. 38:1, 6, 7, 9-17, 19, 20, 24, 27, 28. 39:11, 14, 15. 40:1, 2, 6. 42:2, 4, 5, 7. 43:1, 2, 6, 8. 44:1, 15, 20, 24. 45:1. 46:1, 13. 47:1. 49:34. 50:1. 51:59-61, 64. 52:1. 2 K 23:31. 24:18. 1 Ch 12:13. 2 Ch 35:25. 36:12, 21, 22. Also **S#3414h**: Je 27:1. 28:5, 6, 10-12, 15. 29:1. 1 Ch 5:24. 12:4, 10. Ezr 1:1. Ne 10:2. 12:1, 12, 34. Da 9:2.

Hilkiah. 2 K +18:18.

of the priests. Ezk 1:3.

in Anathoth. 1 Ch +7:8.

2 **the word**. ver. 4, 11. 1 K 13:20. Ho 1:1. Jon 1:1. Mi 1:1.

in the days. 2 K 21:25, 26. ch. 22, 23. 2 Ch ch. 34, 35.

3 **It came also**. Je 25:1-3. ch. 26, 35, 36. 2 K 24:1-9. 2 Ch 36:5-8.

unto the end. Je ch. 21, 22, 28, 29, 34, 37-39, 52. 2 K 24:17-20. ch. 25. 2 Ch 36:11-21.

in the fifth. Is 52:12, 15. 2 K 25:8. Zc 7:5. 8:19.

4 **the word**. ver. +2. Ezk 1:3. 3:16.

5 **Before I**. Ps 71:5, 6. Is 49:1, 5. Lk 1:76. Ga 1:15, 16.

I knew. Ge +39:6. Ex 33:12, 17. Jn 10:14. Ro 8:29. 2 T 2:19-21.

and before. Lk 1:15, 41. Ro 1:1.

and I ordained. Heb. and I gave. Jn 15:16. 20:21-23. Ac 1:8. Ep 1:22. 4:11, 12.

6 **Ah, Lord**. Is 4:10. 14:13. 32:17.

I cannot speak. Ex 4:1, 10-16. 6:12, 30. 1 S 16:2. 1 K 3:7. 18:14. Is 6:5. Ep +6:19.

for I am. 1 K 3:7-9. Mk 10:15. Lk 10:21. 2 C 3:5.

7 **for thou shalt**. ver. 17, 18. Ex 4:12. 7:1, 2. Nu 22:20, 38. Dt 4:2. 1 K 22:14. 2 Ch 18:13. Is 55:11. Ezk 2:3-5. 3:17-21, 27. Mt 10:19, 20. 28:20. Mk 16:15, 16. Ac 20:27. T 2:15.

8 **not afraid**. ver. 17. Ps +118:6. Ezk 3:8, 9. Lk 12:4, 5. Ac 4:13, 29. Ep 6:20.

for I am. Je 15:20, 21. 20:11. Ex 3:12. Dt 31:6, 8. Jsh 1:5, 9. Is 43:2. Mt 28:20. Ac 7:9, 10. 18:10. 26:17. 2 C 1:8-10. 2 T 4:17, 18. He +13:5, 6.

9 **and touched**. Ex 4:11, 12. Ps +104:32. Is 6:6, 7. 49:2. 50:4. Lk 21:15.

Behold. Je 5:14. Ex 4:15, 16. Is 51:16. Ezk 3:10. Mt 10:19. Lk 12:12.

10 **I have**. Je 25:15-27. 27:2-7. ch. 46-51. 1 K 17:1. Is +6:10. Re 11:3-6.

to root out. Je 18:7-9. Ge +2:17. 1 K 19:17. Ezk 32:18. 43:3. Am 3:7. Zc 1:6. Mt 18:18. 2 C 10:4, 5. Re 19:19-21.

to build. Je 18:9. 24:6. 30:18. 31:4, 5, 28, 38. Ps +102:16. Is 44:26-28. Ezk 36:36. Am 9:11.

11 **what seest thou**. Am 7:8. 8:2. Zc 4:2. 5:2.

I see a rod. Nu 17:8. Ezk 7:10, 11.

12 **Thou hast**. Dt 5:28. 18:17. Lk 10:28. 20:39.

I will hasten. Je ch. 39, 52. Dt 32:35. 2 K 24:2. Ezk 12:22, 23, 25, 28. Am 8:2. Re 22:10.

13 **the second time**. Ge +22:15. +41:32. 2 C 13:1, 2.

I see. Ezk 11:2, 3, 7. 24:3-14.

seething. Jb 41:20. Ezk 22:21.

pot. Je 52:18, 19. Ex 16:3. 27:3. Ezk 24:3.

toward the north. Heb. from the face of the north. ver. +14, 15.

14 **Out of the north**. Je 3:12, 18. 4:6. 6:1, 22. 10:22. 13:20. +23:8. 25:9. 31:8. 46:6, 10, 20. 47:2. 50:3, 9, 41. Ps +48:2. 75:6. 107:3. Is 41:25. 43:6. Ezk 1:4. 32:30. +38:6, 15. 39:2. Da 11:44. Jl +2:20. Zp 2:13. Zc 2:6.

break forth. Heb. be opened. Ne 7:3. Jb 12:14.

15 **I will call**. Je 5:15. 6:22. 10:22, 25. 25:9, 28, 31, 32.

of the north. ver. +14.

and they. Je 39:3. 43:10. Is 22:7.

and against. Je 4:16. 9:11. 33:10. 34:22. 44:6. 52:4, 5. Dt 28:49-53. La 5:11. Mt 23:37-39.

16 **And I**. Je 4:12, 28. 5:9, 29. Ezk 24:14. Jl 2:11. Mt 23:35, 36.

forsaken me. Je 2:13, 17, 19. 5:7, 19. 15:6. 16:11. 17:13. 19:4. Dt 28:20. 31:16, 17. 32:15. Jsh 24:20. Jg 2:12, +13. 10:6, 10, 13. 1 S

12:10. 2 K 22:17. 1 Ch 28:9. 2 Ch 7:19, 22.
12:1. 15:2. 24:20. 34:25. Ezr 8:22. Is 1:4, 28.
65:11. Lk 8:13. 1 C 15:2. He 10:38, 39.
and have. Je 7:9. 11:12, 17. 44:17. Is 65:3.
Ezk 8:9-11. Ho 11:2.
worshipped. Je 10:8, 9, 15. 51:17. Is 2:8.
37:19. 44:15-17. Ho 8:6. Ac 7:41. Ja 4:4. Re
2:20-23.
17 **gird up**. Ps +18:32. Lk +12:35.
and speak. ver. 7. Je 23:28. Ex 7:2. Ezk 3:10,
11. Jon 3:2. Ac 20:20, 27.
be not. ver. +8. Je 17:18. Ex 3:12. Ezk 2:6, 7.
Mt +10:28. 1 Th 2:2.
confound thee. *or,* break thee to pieces. Ezk
3:14-18. 33:6-8. 1 C 9:16.
18 **I have**. Je 6:27. 15:20. Is 50:7. Ezk 3:8, 9. Mi
3:8, 9. Jn 1:42.
against. Je 21:4-14. ch. 22. 26:12-15. 34:3,
20-22. 36:27-32. 37:7-10. 38:2, 18-23. 42:22.
19 **And they**. Je 11:19. 15:10-21. 20:1-6. 26:11-
24. 29:25-32. 37:11-21. 38:6-13.
not prevail. Ps 129:2. Ac 5:39. 2 T 4:17, 18.
for I am. ver. +8. Je 15:20, 21. Jsh 1:9.

JEREMIAH 2

1 **the word**. Je 1:11. 7:1. 23:28. Ezk 7:1. He
1:1. 2 P 1:21.
2 **cry**. Je 3:12. 7:2. 11:6. 19:2. 31:6. Pr 1:20.
8:1-4. Is 40:6. 58:1. Ho 5:8. 8:1. Jon 1:2. Mt
11:15. Lk 12:3.
I remember. ver. 3. Nu 23:19-21. Ne 5:19.
6:14. 13:14, 22, 29, 31. Ps 79:8. 98:3. 106:45.
132:1. 137:7. Ho 2:19, 20. 11:1. Am 2:10.
5:25, 26. Ac 7:39-43. Re 2:2-4.
thee. *or,* for thy sake.
the kindness. Ex 14:31. 15:1-20. Is 63:7. SS
6:3. Ezk 16:8, 22, 60. 23:3, 8, 19. Ho 2:15, 19,
20.
thine espousals. Ex 24:3-8. SS 3:11. Ezk
16:8.
when. ver. 6. Dt 2:7. 8:2, 15, 16. Ne 9:12-21.
Is 63:7-14.
3 **holiness**. Ex 19:5, 6. Dt 7:6-8. 14:2. 26:19. Zc
14:20, 21. Ep 1:4. 1 P 2:9.
the firstfruits. Le +23:10.
all that. Je 12:14. 50:7. Ex 4:22, 23. Ps 81:14,
15. 105:14, 15, 25-36. Is 41:10, 11. 47:6. Jl
1:3, 7, 8. Zc 1:15. 2:8. 12:2-4. Ac 9:4, 5.
offend. Le 4:13, 22, 27. 5:2, 3, 4, 5, 17, 19.
6:4. Nu 5:6, 7.
evil. Is +45:7.
4 **Hear ye**. Je 5:21. +7:2. 13:15. Is 51:1-4.
house of Jacob. Je 5:20. Am 3:13.
all the families. Je 31:1. 33:24.
house of Israel. ver. 26. Je 3:18, 20. 5:11, 15.
9:26. 10:1. 11:10, 17. 13:11. 18:6. 23:8. 31:27,
31, 33. 33:14, 17. 48:13. Is +5:7. Ezk 18:31.
5 **What**. ver. 31. Dt 32:4. Is 5:3, 4. 43:22, 23.
Mi 6:2, 3.

fathers. ver. 7. Jg 2:10.
are gone. Je 12:2. Is 29:13. Ezk 11:15. Mt
15:8.
walked. Dt +32:21. 1 C 8:4.
vanity. Je 8:19. 14:22.
are become vain. Ps +115:8. Ho 9:10. 2 C
3:18.
6 **Where**. ver. 8. Je 5:24. Jg 6:13. 2 K 2:14. Jb
35:10. Ps 77:5. Is 64:7.
brought us up. Ex ch. 14, 15. Nu 13:27.
14:7, 8. Dt 6:10, 11, 18. Is 63:9, 11-13. Ho
12:13. 13:4.
led us. ver. +2. Dt 8:14-16. 32:10.
deserts. Je 5:6. 17:6. 50:12. Mt 12:43.
pits. Je 18:20, 22. Pr +22:14 (**S#7745h**). 23:27.
drought. Is 35:1.
the shadow. Ps +23:4.
7 **brought**. Nu 13:27. 14:7, 8. Dt 6:10, 11, 18.
8:7-9. 11:11, 12. Ne 9:25. Ezk 20:6. 1 C 2:9,
10.
a plentiful country. *or,* the land of Carmel.
Je 4:26. 48:33. Jsh +15:55.
ye defiled. Je 3:1, 9. Le +18:25-28. Ps 78:58,
59.
my land. Dt +32:43.
8 **priests**. ver. 6. Je 5:31. 8:10, 11. 23:9-15. 1 S
2:12. Is 9:16. 28:7. 29:10-12. 56:9-12. Ho 4:6.
Mt +15:14.
and they that. Je 8:8, 9. Le 10:11. Dt 17:11.
33:10. Ml 2:6-9. Lk 11:46, 52. Ro 2:17-24. 2 C
4:2.
handle the law. 2 K 14:6. 22:8.
knew me not. Je 4:22. Mk 12:24. Jn 8:55.
16:3.
the pastors. Je 10:21. 12:10. 23:1, 2.
prophets. Je 23:13. 1 K 18:19, 22, 40.
do not. ver. 11. Je 7:8. 1 S 12:21. Is 30:5. Hab
2:18. Mt 16:26.
9 **I will**. ver. 29, 35. Is 3:13. 43:26. Ezk 20:35,
36. Ho 2:2. Mi 6:2.
with your. Ex 20:5. 34:6, 7. Le 20:5.
10 **over**. *or,* over to.
the isles. Is +11:11.
Chittim. Ge +10:4.
Kedar. Ge +25:13.
and see. Je 18:13, 14. Jg 19:30. 1 C 5:1.
11 **a nation**. ver. 5. Mi 4:5. 1 P 1:18.
no gods. Je 16:20. Ps 115:4. Is 37:19. 1 C
+8:4. Ga 4:8.
changed their glory. ver. 8. Dt 33:29. Ps 3:3.
Is +40:5. Ro 1:23.
not profit. ver. 8.
12 **Be astonished**. Je 6:19. 22:29. Dt 32:1. Is
1:2. Mi 6:2. Mt 27:45, 50-53.
ye heavens. Is 1:2.
13 **For my**. ver. 31, 32. Je 4:22. 5:26, 31. Ps
81:11-13. Is 1:3. 5:13. 63:8. Mi 2:8. 6:3.
forsaken me. ver. 17, 19. Je +1:16. Jn 18:40.
the fountain. Je 17:13. 18:14. Ps 36:9. Is
55:1, 2. Jn 4:14. 7:37-39. Re 21:6. 22:1, 17.

waters. Je 17:13. Ps 36:8, 9. Is 44:3. 55:1.
Ezk 36:25. Jl 2:28, 29. Zc 12:10. 14:8. Jn 4:10,
14. 7:38. Ac 2:17, 18, 33. T 3:5, 6.
broken cisterns. ver. 11, 26, 27. Ps 115:4-8.
146:3, 4. Ec 1:2, 14. 2:11, 21, 26. 4:4. 12:8. Is
44:9-12. 46:6, 7. 55:2. 2 P 2:17.

14 **Israel**. Ex 4:22, 23. Is 50:1.
he a homeborn. Ge 14:14. 15:3. Ec 2:7.
spoiled. Heb. *become* a spoil.

15 **young lions**. Je 4:7. 5:6. 25:30. 49:19. 50:17,
44. 51:38. Jg 14:5. Is +5:29. La 3:10.
yelled. Heb. gave out their voice. Je 4:16.
they made. Is +1:7. 24:1. Ezk 5:14.
his cities. Je +18:16. 33:10. 34:22. 44:22. Is
5:9. Zp 1:18. 2:5. 3:6.

16 **Also the**. 2 K +18:21. 23:33.
Noph. Is +19:13.
Tahapanes. i.e. *beginning of the age or world;
thou wilt fill hands with pity*, **S#8471h**, only here.
Je +43:7, Tahpanhes.
have broken the crown. *or*, feed on thy
crown. Dt 33:20. Is 1:6, 7. 8:8.

17 **Hast thou**. ver. 19. Je 4:18. Le 26:15, 17, etc.
Nu +32:23. Dt 28:15, etc. Jb +4:8. Is 1:4. Ho
13:9. Ga 6:7, 8.
in that. ver. +13.
when he. Dt 32:10, 12, 19. Ps 77:20. 78:53,
54. 107:7. 136:16. Is 63:11-14.

18 **what hast**. ver. 36. Je 37:5-10. Is 8:6, 7.
30:1-7. 31:1-3. La 4:17. Ezk 17:15. Ho 7:11.
the way of Egypt. Dt 17:16.
Sihor. i.e. the Nile. Jsh 13:3.
or what hast. 2 K 16:7-9. 2 Ch 28:20, 21. Ho
5:13.

19 **Thine**. ver. 17. Jb +4:8. Is 3:9. 5:5. 50:1. Ho
5:5.
and thy. Je 3:6-8, 11-14. 5:6. 8:5. Ho 4:16.
11:7. 14:1. Zc 7:11.
bitter. Je 4:18. Jb 20:11-16. Am 8:10.
forsaken. Je +1:16.
and that my. Je 5:22. 36:23, 24. Ps 36:1. Ro
3:18.
Lord God of Hosts. Je +6:6. 46:10. 49:5.
50:25, 31.

20 **For of**. Je 30:8. Ex 3:8. Le 26:13. Dt 4:20, 34.
15:15. Is 9:4. 10:27. 14:25. Na 1:13.
old time. Heb. *olam*, Jsh +24:2.
and thou saidst. Ex 19:8. 24:3. Dt 5:27.
26:17. Jsh 10:16. 24:16-24. 1 S 12:10.
transgress. *or*, serve. Je 5:19. 16:11. 22:9, 13.
Ge 25:23. 29:18. Ex 3:12. 20:9. 34:21. Jg 2:7,
11, 17.
when upon. 1 K 12:32. Ps 78:58. Ezk 16:24,
25, 31.
high hill. 2 K +17:10.
green tree. Is +57:5.
playing. Je 3:1, 6-8. Ex 34:14-16. Dt 12:2. Is
1:21. Ezk 16:15, 16, 28, 41. 23:5. Ho 2:5. 3:3.

21 **Yet I**. Je +11:17. Mt 21:33. Mk 12:1. Lk 20:9.
Jn 15:1.

noble vine. Ge 49:11. Is 5:2.
wholly. Ge +18:19. 26:3-5. 32:28. Dt 4:37.
Jsh 24:31. Ps 105:6. Is 41:8.
into the degenerate. Dt 32:32. Is 1:21. 5:4.
La 4:1.

22 **For though**. Jb 9:30, 31. Ps 51:1, 2. Ml 3:2.
yet thine iniquity. Je 16:17. 17:1. Dt 32:34.
Jb 14:17. Ps 90:8. 130:3. Ho 13:12. Am 8:7.

23 **How canst**. ver. 34, 35. Ge 3:12, 13. 1 S
15:13, 14. Ps 36:2. Pr 28:13. 30:12, 20. Ml
3:7, 8, 13. Lk 10:29. Ro 3:19. 1 J 1:8-10. Re
3:17, 18.
see. Je 3:2. Ps 50:21. Ezk ch. 16, 23.
valley. Je 7:31. Is 57:5, 6.
thou art a swift. *or*, O swift. Est 8:16.

24 **A wild ass**. *or*, O wild ass, etc. Je 14:6. Jb
11:12. 39:5-8.
used. Heb. taught. Je 13:23mg. Is +8:16.
her pleasure. Heb. the desire of her heart.
or, her soul. Heb. *nephesh*, Ge +2:19.
turn her away. *or*, reverse it. Je 15:19.
23:22. 32:44. Pr 15:1. 29:8. Is 43:13mg. La
3:21mg. Ezk 16:34.
in her month. ver. 27. Ho 5:15.

25 **Withhold**. Je 13:22. Dt 28:48. Is 20:2-4. La
4:4. Ho 2:3. Lk 15:22. 16:24.
There is no hope. *or*, Is the case desperate?
Je 18:12. Is 57:10.
for I have. Je 3:13. Is 2:6.
after. Je 44:17. Dt 29:19, 20. 32:16. 2 Ch
28:22. Lk 15:21-24. Ro 2:3-5. 8:24.

26 **the thief**. ver. 36. Je 3:24, 25. Ezr 9:6. Pr
6:30, 31. Is 1:29. Ro 2:21. 6:21.
their kings. Je 32:32. Ezr 9:7. Ne 9:32-34.
Da 9:6-8.

27 **to a stock**. Je 10:8. Ps 115:4-8. Is 44:9-20.
46:6-8. Hab 2:18-20.
stone. Je 3:9.
brought me forth. *or*, begotten me. Je 14:5.
15:10. 17:11. 20:14. 22:26. Ge 4:18. Is 66:7, 8.
for they. Ezk 8:16. 23:35.
their back. Heb. the hinder part of the neck.
Je 7:26. 17:23.
but in the time. ver. 24. Je 22:23. Jg 10:8-
16. Ps 78:34-37. Is 26:16. Ho 5:15, 7:14.

28 **But where**. Dt 32:37, 38. Jg 10:14. 2 K 3:13.
Is 45:20. 46:2, 7.
trouble. Heb. evil. ver. 3. Je 1:14. Is +45:7.
57:1.
to the number. ver. 32. Je 11:13. 44:28. 2 K
17:30, 31. Ho 10:1.

29 **will ye plead**. ver. +23, 25. Je 3:2.
ye all have. Je 5:1. 6:13. 9:2-6. Da 9:11. Ro
3:19. 1 J 2:1.

30 **In vain**. Je 6:29, 30. 7:28. +31:18. 2 Ch
28:22. Ezk 24:13. Re 9:20, 21. 16:9.
your own sword. Je 26:20-24. 1 K 18:4, 13.
19:10, 14. 2 K 21:16. 2 Ch 24:21. 36:16. Ne
9:26. Mt 21:35, 36. 23:29, 34-37. Mk 12:2-8.
Lk 11:47-51. 13:33, 34. Ac 7:52. 1 Th 2:15.

31 **O generation**. Dt 32:5. Ps 22:30. 24:6. 78:8. 112:2. Is 53:8. Je 7:29. Mt 3:7. 11:16. 12:34, 39, 41-45. 16:4. 17:17.
see ye. Am 1:1. Mi 6:9.
Have I been. ver. +5, 6. 2 S 12:7-9. 2 Ch 31:10. Ne 9:21-25. Ho 2:7, 8. Ml 3:9-11.
We are lords. Heb. We have dominion. Dt 8:12-14. 31:20. 32:15. Ps 10:4. 12:4. Pr 30:9. Ho 13:6. 1 C 4:8. Re 3:15-17.

32 **a maid**. ver. 11. Je 14:17. 18:13. 31:4. Ge +24:16, 22, 30, 53. 2 S 1:24. Ps 45:13, 14. Is 61:10. Ezk 16:10-13. 1 P 3:3-5. Re 21:2.
forget. Is 49:15.
yet my people. Je 3:21. 13:10, 25. 18:15. Ps 9:17. 106:21. Is 17:10. Ezk 22:12. Ho 8:14.

33 **Why**. ver. 23, 36. Je 3:1, 2. 7:3. Is 57:7-10. Ho 2:5-7, 13.
love. Je 12:7. Ho 9:10.
hast. 2 Ch 33:9. Ezk 16:27, 47, 51, 52. Ro 1:32.

34 **Also**. Je 7:31. 19:4. 2 K 21:16. 24:4. Ps 106:37, 38. Is 57:5. 59:7. Ezk 16:20, 21. 20:31. Lk 11:49, 50. Re 17:6, 7.
blood of. Ge 9:5. Ezk 22:27.
souls. Heb. *nephesh*, Jsh +10:28.
I have. Je 6:15. 8:12. Ezk 24:7.
secret search. Heb. digging. Ex 22:2. Mt 24:43.

35 **Because**. ver. +23, 29. Jb 33:9. Pr 28:13. Is 58:3. Ro 7:9.
I will. ver. +9. 1 J 1:8-10. Re 3:16-18.

36 **gaddest**. ver. 18, 23, 33. Je 31:22. Ho 5:13. 7:11. 12:1.
thou also shalt. Je 37:7. Is 20:5. 30:1-7. 31:1-3. La 4:17. 5:6. Ezk 29:7.
as thou wast. 2 Ch 28:16, 20, 21. Ho 5:13. 10:6. 14:3.

37 **thine hands**. Je 14:3, 4. 2 S 13:19.
for the Lord. ver. 36. Je 17:5. 37:7-10. 1 S 15:22, 23. Is 10:4. Ezk 17:15-20.
and thou. Je 32:5. Nu 14:41. 2 Ch 13:12.

JEREMIAH 3

1 **They say**. Heb. Saying. Jg 16:2.
If a man. Dt 24:1-4.
put away. Ml 2:16.
return unto her. 1 Ch 8:9. Ho 2:7.
shall not that. ver. 9. Je +2:7. Le 18:24-28. Is 24:5. Mi 2:10.
but thou hast. Je 2:7, 20, 23. Dt 22:21. Jg 19:2. Ezk 16:26, 28, 29. 23:4, etc. Ho 1:2. 2:5-7.
harlot. Is +32:9.
yet return. ver. 12-14, 22. Je 8:4-6. +33:15. Dt 4:29-31. Ml 3:7. Lk 15:16-24.

2 **Lift**. Je 2:23. *Ezk 8:4-6. Lk 16:23*.
unto. Je 2:20. Dt 12:2. 1 K 11:3. 2 K 23:13. Ezk 16:16, 24, 25. 20:28.
In the. Ge 38:14. Pr 7:11, 12. 23:28. Ezk 16:24, 25.

thou hast. ver. +1, 9. Je 2:7.
whoredoms. Ex +34:16.

3 **the showers**. Je 9:12. 14:4, 22. Le 26:19. Dt 11:17. 28:23, 24. Is 5:6. Jl 1:16-20. Am 4:7. Hg 1:11.
withholden. Je 5:24, 25. Am 4:7. Zc 14:17. Ml 3:10.
latter rain. Je 5:24. Zc 10:1.
a whore's. Je 5:3. 6:15. 8:12. 44:16, 17. Ezk 3:7. 16:30-34. Zp 3:5.
thou refusedst. Je 5:3. Ne 9:17. Zc 7:11, 12. He 12:25.

4 **Wilt thou**. ver. 19. Je 31:9, 18-20. Ho 14:1-3.
My father. Je +2:27. Ro 8:15. Ga 4:6.
the guide. Je 2:2. Ge 48:15. Ps 48:14. 71:5, 17. 119:9. Pr 1:4. 2:16, 17. Ho 2:15. Ml 2:14.
youth. Je +2:2. Ps 129:1. Ezk 16:22. 23:3. Ho 11:1.

5 **Will he**. Ps 30:5. 103:9.
reserve. ver. 12. Ps 77:7-9. 85:5. 103:8, 9. Is 57:16. 64:9.
for ever. Heb. *olam*, Ex +12:24.
the end. Heb. *netsach*, Jb +4:20.
thou hast spoken. Ezk 22:6. Mi 2:1. 7:3. Zp 3:1-5.

6 A.M. 3292. B.C. 612.
backsliding. ver. 8, 11-14. Je +2:19. 7:24. 2 K 17:7-17. Ezk 23:11.
she is. 2 K +17:10. Ezk 16:24, 25, 31.
green tree. Is +57:5.
played. ver. +1.

7 **Turn thou**. ver. 12. 2 K 17:13, 14. 2 Ch 30:6-12. Ho 6:1-4.
her treacherous. ver. 8-11. Ezk 16:46. 23:2-4. 37:16, 17.

8 **when for**. ver. 1. 2 K 17:6-18. 18:9-11. Ezk 23:9. Ho 2:2, 3. 3:4. 4:15-17. 9:15-17.
and given her. Dt 24:1. Is 50:1.
feared not. 2 K 17:19. Ezk 23:11-21. Ho 4:15.

9 **lightness**. or, fame. Ge 18:21. Ezk 23:10.
she defiled. ver. 2. Je 2:7.
committed. Je 2:27. 10:8. Is 57:6. Ezk 16:17. Ho 4:12. Hab 2:19.

10 **Judah**. 2 Ch 34:33. 35:1-18. Ps 78:36, 37. Is 10:6. Ho 7:14.
feignedly. Heb. in falsehood. Ps +66:3mg.

11 **The backsliding**. ver. 8, 22. Ho 4:16. 11:7.
justified. Ezk 16:47, 51, 52. 23:11.
herself. Heb. *nephesh*, Ge +27:31.

12 **toward the north**. ver. 18. Je +1:14. 2 K 15:29. 17:6, 23. 18:11.
Return. ver. 1, 7, 22. Je +33:15. Is 44:21-23. Ho 6:1.
backsliding. Ho 4:16.
for I am. Je 30:11. 31:20. 33:26. Dt 4:29-31. 2 Ch 30:9. Ps 86:5, 15. 103:8, 17. 145:8. Ezk 16:60. 39:25. Ho 11:8, 9. Mi 7:18-20. Ro 5:20, 21.

will not keep. ver. 5. Ps 79:5.
for ever. Heb. *olam*, Ex +12:24.

13 **acknowledge**. ver. 25. Je 31:18-20. Le
26:40-42. Dt 30:1-3. 2 S 12:13. Jb 33:27, 28.
Pr 28:13. Lk 15:18-21. 1 J 1:8-10.
and hast scattered. ver. 2, 6. Je 2:20, 25.
Ezk 16:15, 24, 25.
green tree. Is +57:5. +66:17.

14 **Turn**. ver. 22. Ho 10:12. Re 2:4, 5. 3:1, 2, 3.
O backsliding. ver. 22. Je +2:19. Is
+57:17mg.
for I am married. ver. 1, 8. Je 2:2. 31:32. Is
54:5. Ho 2:19, 20.
one of a city. Je 23:3. 31:8-10. Is 1:9. 6:13.
10:22. 11:11, 12. 17:6. 24:13-15. 27:13. Ezk
34:11-14. Zc 13:7-9. Ro 9:27. 11:4-6.

15 **will give**. Je 23:4. 31:12, 14. 1 S 13:14. Ps
23:2. Is 30:20, 21. 41:18. 49:9, 10. 52:7, 8.
56:7. 62:6. Ezk 34:15, 23. 37:24. Mi 5:4, 5. Jn
10:1-5. 21:15-17. Ep 4:11, 12. 1 P 5:1-4.
pastors. Lk 1:2. Ac 15:6, 23. 20:28. Ep 4:11,
12. Ph 1:1. 1 T 2:7. 3:1. 2 T 1:11. 1 P 5:1-3.
which shall. Pr 10:21. Is 30:20, 21. +40:11.
Lk 1:31, 32. +12:42. Ac 2:34-36. 1 C 2:6, 12,
13. 3:1, 2. He 5:12-14. 1 P 2:2.

16 **when**. Je 30:19. 31:8, 27. Is 60:22. 61:4. Ezk
36:8-12. 37:26. Ho 1:10, 11. Am 9:9, 14, 15.
Zc 8:4, 5. 10:7-9.
say. Je 7:4. Zp 3:11. Mt 3:9.
The ark. Ex 25:22. 2 Ch 35:3. Ps 87:4. Ezr
1:7. Is 18:7. 65:17. 66:1, 2. Ml 1:11. Jn 4:20-
24. He 9:9-12. 10:8, 9, 19-21.
to mind. Heb. upon the heart. Je 7:31mg.
19:5. 32:35. 2 K 12:4mg. Is 65:17mg. Ezk
38:10.
visit. or, inspect. Je 5:9. 9:9. 29:10. 2 K 25:9,
13-15.
neither shall. Ezr 1:7.
that be done. *or, it* be magnified. **S#6213h**. Je
5:13. Ge 20:9. 29:26. 34:7. Ex 12:16. 31:15.
Le 23:3. Ezk 12:11, 25, 28. 15:5mg. 2 C 3:7, 8,
11. He 9:3, 4, 11, 12.

17 **call Jerusalem**. Ps 87:2-7. Is 60:1. 65:18.
66:7-13, 20.
the throne. Je 31:23. 1 S 2:8. Ps +11:4. 87:3.
Is +24:23. 46:13. Ezk 37:24-28. Zp 3:8, 14-17.
Ga 4:26.
and all the nations. Is +11:10.
to the name. Is 26:8. 56:6. 59:19. 60:9.
walk. Je 7:24. 9:14. 11:8. 16:12. 18:12. Ge
8:21. Nu 15:39. Ro 1:21. 6:14. 2 C 10:4, 5. Ep
4:17-19.
imagination. *or*, stubbornness. Je 7:24mg.
9:14mg. 11:8mg. 13:10mg. 16:12mg. 18:12.
23:17mg. Dt 29:19mg. Jg 2:19. Ps 78:8.
81:12mg.

18 **In**. Je +23:3. 50:4, 20.
house of Judah. Je 5:11. 11:10, 17. 12:14.
13:11. 22:6. 31:27, 31. 33:14. 36:3.
with. *or*, to.

land of the north. ver. +12.
to the land. Je +7:7. Am +9:15. Zc 3:9.
given, etc. *or*, caused your fathers to possess.
Zc 8:12.

19 **How**. Je 5:7. Ho 11:8.
put thee. ver. 4. Je 31:9, 20. 1 J +3:1-3.
pleasant land. Heb. land of desire. Je
12:10mg. Ps 106:24mg. Is +32:12mg. Ezk
20:6, 15. Da 8:9. 11:16mg, 41mg, 45mg. Zc
7:14mg.
goodly heritage. Heb. heritage of glory, *or*
beauty. Pr 3:35. Ac +20:32.
Thou shalt. ver. +4. Is 63:16. 64:8. Mt 6:8, 9.
Ro 8:15-17. Ga 4:5.
shalt not. Je +32:39, 40. He 10:39.
from me. Heb. from after me. Je +17:16mg.

20 **husband**. Heb. friend. SS 5:16. Ho 3:1.
so have. ver. 1, 2, 8-10. Je 5:11. Is 48:8. Ezk
16:15, etc. Ho 5:7. 6:7. Ml 2:11.

21 **A voice**. Je 30:15-17. 31:9, 18-20. 50:4, 5. Is
15:2. Ezk 7:16. Zc 12:10-14. 2 C 7:10.
for they have. Nu 22:32. Jb 33:27. Pr 10:9.
19:3. Mi 3:9.
and they have. Je +2:32. Is 17:10. Ezk
23:35. Ho 8:14. 13:6.

22 **Return**. ver. +12, 14. Ho 6:1.
backsliding. Je 50:6. Is +57:17mg.
will heal. Jn +12:40. Ac +3:19-21.
Behold. Je 31:18. Ps 27:8. SS 1:4. Ho +3:5. Zc
13:9.

23 **in vain**. ver. 6. Je 10:14-16. Ps 121:1, 2. Is
44:9. 45:20. 46:7, 8. Ezk 20:28, 29.
Jon 2:8, 9.
mountains. Ezk 18:6, 11, 15. Mi 1:4.
in the Lord. Je 14:8. Ps 121:1, 2. Is 63:1, 16.
Ho 1:7. Re +7:10.

24 **shame**. ver. +25. Je 11:13. Ho 2:8. 9:10. 10:6.
labor. Dt +28:33.

25 **lie down**. Je 2:26. 6:26. Ezr +9:6-15. Ps
109:29. Is 50:11. La 5:16. Ezk 7:18. Da +12:2.
Ro 6:17, 18, 20, 21.
for we have sinned. Je 2:17, 19. Dt 31:17,
18. Ezr 9:6. Ezk 36:32.
we and our. Je 2:2. Ezr 9:7. Ne 9:32-34. Ps
106:7. Is 48:8. La 5:7. Da 9:6-9.
and have not. Je 22:21. Jg 2:2. Pr 5:13. Da
9:10.

JEREMIAH 4

1 **wilt return**. ver. 4, 14.
return. Je +33:15. Is 31:6. Ho 7:16.
put away. Ge 35:2. Dt 27:15. Jsh 24:14. Jg
10:16. 1 S 7:3. 2 K 23:13, 24. 2 Ch 15:8. Ezk
11:18. 18:13. 20:7, 8. 43:9. Ho 2:2. Ep 4:22-
31.
then shalt. Je 15:4. 22:3-5. 24:9. 25:5. 36:3.
2 Ch 33:8.

2 **shalt swear**. Je 5:2. Ge +21:23.
liveth. 1 K +17:1.

in truth. Je 9:24. 1 K 3:6. Ps 99:4. Ho 2:19. Zc 8:8.

in judgment. Je 23:5.

in righteousness. Three words used, but one thing meant, just and righteous truth. Da 3:7. Mt 6:13. Jn 14:6.

and the nations. Ge +22:18. Ps 72:17. Is 65:16. Ga 3:8.

and in him. Je 9:24. Is 45:25. 1 C 1:29-31. 2 C 10:17. Ph 3:3.

3 **Break**. Ge 3:17, 18. Ho 10:12. Mt 13:7, 22. Ga 6:7, 8.

4 **take**. ver. +1. Dt +30:6.

lest my fury. Le +26:28. Is 51:17.

like fire. Dt +32:22.

quench. Mt +3:12.

evil. Is +45:7.

5 **Declare ye**. Je 5:20. 9:12. 11:2.

Blow. Ho +8:1-4.

Assemble. Je 8:14. 35:11. Jsh 10:20.

6 **the standard**. ver. 21. Je 50:2. 51:12, 27. Is 62:10.

retire. or, strengthen. **S#5756h**. Je 6:1 (gather). Ex 9:19. Is 10:31.

for I will. Je +1:14.

and a great. Je 50:22. 51:54.

destruction. Heb. breaking. Is +51:19mg. Zp 1:10.

7 **lion**. 2 K 24:1. 25:1. Is +5:29.

destroyer. Je 25:9. 27:8. Ezk 21:19-21. 26:7-10. 30:10, 11. Da 5:19.

to. Je +18:16. Is 1:7. 5:9.

8 **gird**. Jb +16:15.

howl. Is +13:6.

the. Is +9:12. 12:1.

9 **that the heart**. Je 39:4-7. 52:7. 1 S 25:37, 38. 2 K 25:4-7. Ps 102:4. Is 19:3, 12, 16. 21:3, 4. 22:3-5.

and the priests. Je 5:31. 6:13, 14. 37:19. Is 29:9, 10. Ezk 13:9-16. Ac 13:40, 41.

10 **Ah**. Je 1:6. 14:13. 32:17. Ezk 11:13.

surely. Je 14:13, 14. 1 K 22:20-23. Is 63:17. Ezk 14:9, 10. Ro 1:24, 26, 28. 2 Th 2:9-12.

deceived. Am +3:6.

Ye shall have. Je 5:12. Is 30:10. 37:35. Ezk +13:10.

the sword. ver. 18. Ex 9:14. La 2:21.

soul. Heb. nephesh, Ge +12:13. Ps 69:1.

11 **A dry wind**. Je +23:19. 51:1. Ge +41:6. Is 64:6.

daughter. Je 6:26. 8:19, 21, 22. 9:1, 7. 14:17. Is 22:4. La 2:11. 3:48. 4:3, 6, 10.

not to fan. Mt +3:12.

12 **a full wind from those**. or, a fuller wind than those.

give sentence. Heb. utter judgments. Je 1:16. 39:5mg. 2 K 25:6mg. Ezk 5:8. 6:11-13. 7:8, 9.

13 **Behold**. Is 13:5. 19:1. Na 1:3. Mt 24:30. Re 1:7.

clouds. Ge +9:13.

his chariots. Ps +68:17.

whirlwind. Je +23:19.

his horses. Dt 28:49. La 4:19. Da 7:4. Ho 8:1. Hab 1:8.

Woe. ver. +31. Je 9:19. 10:19.

14 **wash**. ver. +1. Je 13:27. Mt 12:33. 15:19, 20. 23:26, 27, 37-39. Lk 11:39. Ja 4:8.

How long. Mt +17:17.

vain thoughts. Je +6:19. Ps 66:18. 119:113. Ac +8:22. Ro 1:21. 1 C 3:20.

15 **a voice**. Je 6:1. Ge +14:14.

mount Ephraim. Jsh +17:15.

16 **ye**. Je 6:18. 31:10. 50:2. Is 34:1.

watchers. ver. 17. Je 5:6. 16:16. 39:1.

from. Je 5:15. Dt 28:49-52. Is 39:3, 4.

give out. Je 2:15. Ezk 21:21, 22.

17 **keepers**. Je 6:2, 3. 2 K 25:1-4. Is 1:8. Lk 19:41, 43, 44. 21:20-24.

because. Je 5:23. Ne 9:26, 30. Is 1:20-23. 30:9. La 1:8, 18. Ezk 2:3-7. Da 9:7, etc.

18 **Thy way**. Je 2:17, 19. 5:19. 6:19. 26:19. Jb 20:5-16. Ps 107:17. Pr 1:31. 5:22. Is 50:1.

it reacheth. ver. +10.

19 **My bowels**. Je 9:1, 10. 13:17. 14:17, 18. 23:9. 48:31, 32. Ps 119:53, 136. Is 15:5. 16:11. 21:3. 22:4. La 1:16. 2:11. 3:48-51. Da 7:15, 28. 8:27. Hab 3:16. Lk 19:41, 42. Ro 9:2, 3. 10:1. Ga 4:19.

my very. Heb. the walls of my.

O my. Ge 49:6. Jg 5:21. Ps 16:2. 42:5, 6. 103:1. 116:7. 146:1.

soul. Heb. nephesh, Ge +27:31.

sound. ver. +5, 21.

20 **upon destruction**. ver. +6. Je 17:18. Le 26:18, 21, 24, 28. Ps 42:7. Is 13:6. La 3:47. Ezk 7:25, 26. 14:21. Jl 1:15. Mt +10:28. 2 Th 1:9.

suddenly. Je 10:19, 20. Is 33:20. 54:2. La 2:6-9. Hab 3:7.

curtains. 2 S +7:2.

a moment. Ex 33:5. Nu 16:21, 45. Ps 73:19. Is 47:9. 2 Th 5:2-5.

21 **How long**. ver. +14.

shall I. ver. 5, 6, 19. Je 6:1. 2 Ch 35:25. 36:3, 6, 7, 10, 17.

22 **For my**. Je 5:4, 21. 8:7-9. Dt 32:6, 28. Ps 14:1-4. Is 1:3. 6:9, 10. 27:11. 29:10-12. 42:19, 20. Ho 4:1, 6. Mt 23:16-26. Ro 1:22. 3:11. 1 C 1:18.

they have. Ho 5:4. Jn 16:3. Ro 1:28. 1 C 1:20, 21.

known me. Je 9:24. Ho 4:1.

they are wise. 2 S 13:3. 16:21-23. Mi 2:1. Lk 16:8. Ro 16:19. 1 C 14:20.

23 **the earth**. Je 9:10. Ge 1:2. Dt 32:10. Is 24:19-23. Re 20:11.

void. Ge +1:2. Is 34:11. 45:18.

the heavens. Is 5:30. Mt +24:29.

24 **mountains**. Je 8:16. Jg 5:4, 5. 1 K 19:11. Ps +97:4. Is 5:25. Mi 1:4. He +12:26.

25 **there was no man.** Ho 4:3. Zp 1:2, 3.

26 **the fruitful.** Je 12:4. 14:2-6. Dt 29:23-28. Ps 76:7. 107:34. Is 5:9, 10. 7:20-25. 24:18-20. Mi 3:12. Mt 24:29, 30. Ac 2:16-21. Re 21:23-25.

27 **The.** ver. +7. Je +18:16. Is 24:1, 3-12.
yet. Je 5:10, 18. Le +26:44. Is 24:12, 13. Ezk 11:13. Mi 7:18. Zc 10:6. Ro 9:27-29. +11:1-7.

28 **the earth.** ver. 23-26. Je 12:4. 23:10. Is 24:4. 33:8, 9. Ho 4:3. Jl 1:10.
the heavens. Is 50:3. Mt +24:29.
black. Ex +10:22.
because. Je 7:16. 14:11, 12. 15:1-9. Nu 23:19. 1 S 15:29. Is +14:27. Ezk 24:14. Ho +13:14. He 7:21.

29 **city.** 1 S +22:19.
shall flee. Je 39:4-6. 52:7. 2 K 25:4-7. Is 30:17. Am 9:1.
they shall go. 1 S 13:6. 2 Ch 33:11. Is 2:19-21. Lk 23:30. Re 6:15-17.
every. ver. 27.

30 **And when.** Je 5:31. 13:21. Is 10:3. 20:6. 33:14. He +2:3.
Though. Ezk 23:40, 41. 28:9, 13. Re 17:4.
face. Heb. eyes. 2 K 9:30mg. Ezk 23:40.
in vain. Je 22:20-22. La 1:2, 19. 4:17. Ezk 16:36-41. 23:9, 10, 22-24, 28, 29. Re 17:2, 13, 16-18.
lovers. Ezk 23:5.
will despise. Je 30:14. La 1:2, 19.
life. Heb. nephesh, Ge +44:30.

31 **I have heard.** Je 6:24. 13:21. 22:23. 30:6, 7. 48:41. 49:22, 24. 50:43. Ps 48:6. Is 13:8. 21:3. 26:17. Ho 13:13. Mt +24:8mg. 1 Th 5:3.
the voice. Je 6:2, 23. Mt 21:5.
daughter. Nu +21:25.
spreadeth. Is 1:15. La 1:17.
Woe. Je 10:19. 15:18. 45:3. Ps 120:5. Is 6:5. Mi 7:1. 1 C 9:16.
for my. Ge 27:46. Jb 10:1.
soul. Heb. nephesh, Ge +34:3.
because. Je 14:18. 18:21. La 1:20. 2:21. Ezk 9:5, 6. 23:46, 47. Re 17:3-6.

JEREMIAH 5

1 **Run ye.** 2 Ch 16:9. Da 12:4. Jl 2:9. Am 8:12. Zc 2:4.
streets. Heb. chuts, Am 5:16. Je 6:11.
broad places. Heb. rechob, Am +5:16. Je 9:21. 48:38. Pr 8:3. SS 3:2. Lk 7:32. 14:21.
if ye can find. Ge 18:26. 1 K 19:10. Pr 20:6. Ezk 22:30. Mt +7:14. Lk 18:8.
if there. Ge 18:23-32. Ps 12:1. 14:3. 53:2-4. Ezk 22:30. Mi 7:1, 2. Ro 3:10.
that seeketh. Pr 2:4-6. 23:23. Is 59:4, 14, 15. 2 Th 2:10.
will pardon. Ge 18:24-32.

2 **though.** Je +4:2.
falsely. Je 7:9. Le 19:12. Is 48:1. Ho 4:1, 2,

15. 10:4. Zc 5:3, 4. Ml +3:5. 1 T 1:10. 2 T 3:5. T 1:15, 16.

3 **are not thine.** Je 32:19. 2 Ch 16:9. Ps 11:4-7. 51:6. Pr 22:12. Ro 2:2.
thou hast stricken. Je +31:18. Pr 23:35. 27:22. Is 42:25. Ezk 24:13. Ml 3:13, 14.
not grieved. Mt 11:16, 17.
refused. 1 S +25:17. He +12:25.
they have made. Pr 21:29. Is 48:4. Ezk 3:7-9. Zc 7:11, 12. Ro 2:4, 5. He 12:9.

4 **Surely.** Je 4:22. 7:8. 8:7. Is 27:11. 28:9-13. Ho 4:6. Mt 11:5. Jn 7:48, 49.

5 **get me.** Am 4:1. Mi 3:1. Ml 2:7.
but these. Je 6:13. Ps 2:2, 3. Ezk 22:6-8, 25-29. Mi 3:1-4, 11. 7:3, 4. Zp 3:3-5. Mt 19:23-26. Lk 18:24. 19:14. Ac 4:26, 27. Ja 2:5-7.

6 **a lion.** Is +5:29. Ezk 14:16-21. Am 5:18, 19.
and a wolf. Ps 104:20. Ezk 22:27. Hab 1:8.
evenings. or, deserts. Je 50:12. Jsh 18:18mg. Ezk 47:8mg.
a leopard. Da 7:6. Ho 13:7. Re 13:2.
because. Je +2:17, 19. 9:12-14. 14:7. 16:10-12. 30:24. Nu 32:14. Ezr 9:6. 10:10. Is 59:12. La 1:5. Ezk 16:25. 23:19.
increased. Heb. strong. Je 15:8. 30:14, 15. Is 31:1.

7 **How shall.** Je 3:19. Ho 11:8. Mt 23:37, 38.
forsaken me. Je +1:16.
sworn by. Je 12:16. Jsh 23:7. Ho 4:15. Am 8:14. Zp 1:5.
no gods. Je +2:11. Dt 32:21. 1 C +8:4. Ga 4:8.
I had fed. Je +2:31. Dt 32:15. Ezk 16:49, 50. Ho 13:6. Ja 5:1-5.
they then. Je 9:2. 13:27. 23:10. 29:22, 23. Ex 20:14. Le 20:10. Dt 5:18. Ps 50:18. Ezk 22:11. Ho 4:2, 13, 14. 7:4. Ml +3:5. 1 C +6:9. He +13:4. Ja +4:4.
committed adultery. Je 7:30, 31. 19:4, 5. 32:34, 35. Is +66:17. Ezk 16:17. Ho 4:12-14. Am 2:7-9.
by troops. Nu 25:1-3.

8 **every one.** Je 13:27. Ge 39:9. Ex 20:14, 17. Dt 5:18, 21. 2 S 11:2-4. Jb 31:9. Mt 5:27, 28.

9 **I not visit.** ver. 29. Je +11:22. La 4:22. Ho 8:13.
and shall. Je 44:22. Le 26:25. Dt +32:35, 39-41, 43. Ezk 5:13-15. 7:9.
soul. Heb. nephesh, Ge +34:3; Le +26:11.

10 **Go ye up.** Je 6:4-6. 25:9. 39:8. 51:20-23. 2 K 24:2-4. 2 Ch 36:17. Is 10:5-7. 13:1-5. Ezk 9:5-7. 14:17. Mt 22:7.
but make. ver. 18. Je +4:27. 30:11. 46:28. Ezk 12:15, 16. Am 9:8, 9.
they are not. Je 7:4-12. Ps 78:61, 62. Ho 1:9.

11 **the house.** Je 3:6-11, 20. Is 48:8. Ho 5:7. 6:7.

12 **have belied.** ver. 31. Je 4:10. 14:13, 14. 23:14-17. 28:15-17. 43:2, 3. Dt 29:19. 1 S 6:9. 2 Ch 36:16. Is 28:14, 15. Ezk 12:22-28. 13:6. Mi 2:11. 3:11. Hab 1:5, 6. 1 J 5:10.
neither. Je 23:17. 28:4. Ps 10:6. 1 Th 5:2, 3.

13 **the prophets**. Je 14:13-15. 18:18. 20:8-11. 28:3. Jb 6:26. 8:2. Ho 9:7. 1 C 2:14-16.

14 **the Lord God of hosts**. Je 15:16. 35:17. 49:5.
  I will make. Je 1:9. 23:29. 28:15-17. 2 K 1:10-15. Ho 6:5. Zc 1:6. Re 11:3, 5, 6.
  fire. Je 20:9. 23:29.

15 **I will**. Je +1:15. 4:16. 6:22. 25:9. Dt 28:49. Is 5:26. 39:3, 6.
  O house. ver. 11. Je +2:4, 26. Mt 3:9, 10.
  a mighty. Da 2:37, 38. 7:7. Hab 1:5-10.
  ancient. Heb. *olam*, Jb +22:15. Ge 10:10.
  a nation. Is 28:11. 33:19. 1 C 14:21-25.
  language. The Chaldee, which, though a dialect of the Hebrew, is so very different in its words and construction, that in hearing it spoken they could not possibly understand it.

16 **quiver**. Ps 5:9. Is 5:28. Ro 3:13.
  sepulchre. Heb. *qeber*, Ge +23:4.

17 **And they**. Le 26:16. Dt 28:30, 31, 33. Jg 6:3, 4. Is 62:9. 65:22. Hab 3:17, 18.
  they shall impoverish. Je +2:15. 4:7, 26. La 2:2. Ezk 36:4. Zp 3:6. Ml 1:4.

18 **I will not make**. ver. +10. Je 4:27. Ezk 9:8. 11:13. Ro +11:1-5.

19 **Wherefore**. Je +2:35. 13:22. 16:10. 22:8, 9. Dt 29:24-28. 1 K 9:8, 9. 2 Ch 7:21, 22.
  Like as. Je +1:16. Dt 4:25-28. 28:47, 48. La 5:8.
  strange. Je 8:19. Ex 12:43. Is 62:8.

21 **O foolish**. ver. +4. Je 4:22. 8:7. 10:8. Dt 32:6. Ps 94:8. Is 27:11. Lk +8:10.
  understanding. Heb. heart. Pr 17:16. Ho 7:11.
  which have eyes. Mk *8:18.*

22 **Fear ye not**. Je 10:7. 33:9. Dt +6:2. Jb 37:24. Ps 76:7. 89:7. 96:4. 130:4. Ho +3:5. Mt +10:28. Lk 12:5. Re 15:4.
  tremble. Ps 99:1. Is +66:2. Da 6:26.
  placed. Jb 26:10. 38:10, 11. Ps 33:7. 93:3, 4. 104:9. Pr 8:29. Is 50:2. +54:8-10. Am 9:6. Na 1:4. Mk 4:39.
  perpetual. Ge +9:12.
  toss. Je 46:7.
  roar. Je 51:55. Ps 46:3.

23 **a revolting**. ver. +5. Je 6:28. 17:9. Ps 95:10. Is 1:5. 31:6. Ho 4:8. 11:7. He +3:12.

24 **Let us now**. ver. +22. Je 50:5. Is 64:7. Ho 3:5. 6:1.
  that giveth rain. Je 3:3. 14:22. Dt 11:13, 14. 28:12. 1 K 17:1. Jb 5:10. 36:27, 28. 38:37. Ps 147:8. Jl 2:23. Am 4:7. Zc 10:1. Ml 3:10. Mt +5:45. Ac 14:17. Ja 5:7, 17, 18. Re 11:6.
  former. Dt +11:14.
  the appointed. Ge +8:22.

25 **iniquities**. Je 2:17-19. 3:3. Dt 28:23, 24. Ps 107:17, 34. Is 59:2. La 3:39. 4:22.
  withholden good. Ps 84:11.

26 **For**. Je 4:22. Is 58:1. Ezk 22:2-12.
  lay wait. *or*, pry as fowlers lie in wait. Je

18:22. 1 S 19:10, 11. Ps 10:9, 10. 64:5. 71:10. Pr 1:11, 17, 18. Hab 1:14, 15.
  catch. Lk 5:10.

27 **cage**. *or*, coop. Re 18:2-4.
  so are. Pr 1:11-13. Ho 12:7, 8. Am 8:4-6. Mi 1:12. 6:10, 11. Hab 2:9-11.

28 **waxen**. Dt +31:20. Am 4:1. Ja 5:4, 5.
  overpass. Je 2:33. Ezk 5:6, 7. 16:47-52. 1 C 5:1.
  judge. Je +22:16.
  fatherless. Ex +22:22.
  yet. Je 12:1. Jb 12:6. Ps 73:12.

29 **not visit**. ver. +9. Ml +3:5. Ja +5:4.
  soul. Heb. *nephesh*, Ge +34:3; Le +26:11.

30 **A wonderful and horrible thing**. *or*, Astonishment and filthiness. Je 2:12. 23:14. Is 1:2. Ho 6:10.

31 **prophets**. Je 14:14. 23:25, 26. La 2:14. Ezk 13:6. Mi 3:11. Mt 7:15-17. 2 C 11:13-15. 2 P 2:1, 2.
  bear rule. *or*, take into their hands. Ne 9:28. Ps 49:14. 72:8. La 1:13.
  my people. Is 30:10, 11. Mi 2:6, 11. Jn 3:19-21. 2 Th 2:9-12. 2 T 4:2-4.
  and what. Je 4:30, 31. 22:22, 23. Dt 32:29. Is 10:3. 20:6. 33:14. La 1:9. Ezk 22:14. Zp 2:2, 3.

JEREMIAH 6

1 **O ye**. Jsh 15:63. 18:21-28. Jg 1:21.
  Benjamin. "Benjamin" is put for all Judah, on account of their close connection with the Gibeathites (Jg 19:16. Ho 9:9. 10:9).
  gather. Je 4:29. 10:17, 18.
  blow. Ho +8:1.
  Tekoa. 1 Ch +2:24.
  Beth-haccerem. i.e. *the vineyard house,* **S#1021h.** Ne 3:14.
  evil. ver. +22. Je 1:14, 15. 4:6. 10:22. 25:9. Ezk 26:7, etc.
  north. The *north* is put for Media and Persia, with respect to Babylon. For other examples of this use see Je 50:3, 41.

2 **daughter**. Nu +21:25. Is 3:16, 17.
  comely and delicate woman. *or, a woman* dwelling at home. Dt 28:56. 2 K 4:13.

3 **shepherds**. Na 3:18.
  they shall. Je 4:16, 17. 39:1-3. 2 K 24:2, 10-12. 25:1-4. Lk 19:41-44.

4 **Prepare**. Je 5:10. 51:27, 28. Is 5:26-30. 13:2-5. Jl 3:9.
  at noon. Je 15:8. 2 S 4:5. SS 1:7. Is 32:2. Zp 2:4.
  for the. Je 8:20.
  shadows. SS 2:16, 17.

5 **let us destroy**. Je 9:21. 17:27. 52:13. 2 Ch 36:19. Ps 48:3. Is 32:14. Ho 8:14. Am 2:5. 3:10, 11. Zc 11:1.

6 **Lord of hosts**. ver. 9. Je 8:3. 9:7, 17. 10:16. 11:17, 20, 22. 19:11. 20:12. 23:15, 16, 36.

32:10. Dt +28:32mg. 1 S 2:25. Ezk 14:3, 14-
20. 1 J 5:16.
I will. 1 S 8:18. Is 1:15. Mi 3:4.

17 Seest thou not. Je +6:27. Ezk 8:6-18. 14:23.

18 children. Je +44:17-19, 25. 1 C 10:22.
queen of heaven. *or,* frame, *or* workmanship
of heaven. Je 44:17, 18, 19, 25. Dt 4:19. 1 K
11:5. 1 Ch 11:44. Jb 31:26-28.
drink offerings. Le +23:13.
that they. Je 25:7. Is 3:8. 65:3.

19 they provoke. Je 2:17, 19. Dt 32:16, 21, 22.
Is 1:20, 24. Ezk 8:17, 18. 1 C 10:22.
the confusion. Je 20:11. Ezr 9:7. Is 45:16.
Da 9:7, 8.

20 Behold. Je 12:4. 14:16.
anger. Je 4:23-26. La 2:3-5.
fury. Le +26:28.
shall burn. Je +17:27. Ezk 22:22.
shall not. Mt +3:12.

21 Put. Le +23:12. Ho 8:13.

22 nor. Ex 15:26. 19:5. Mi 6:6-8. Mt 9:13. 12:7.
23:23. Mk 12:33.
burnt offerings. Heb. the matter of burnt
offerings. Le +23:12.

23 Obey. Je 11:4, 7. 26:13. Ex 15:26. 19:5, 6.
23:21, 22. Le 26:3-12. Dt 5:29, 33. 6:3. 11:27.
13:4. 28:1. 30:2, 8, 20. 1 S 15:22. Zc 6:15. Mt
28:20. Jn +13:17. Ro 16:26. 2 C 10:5. He 5:9.
and I. Je +31:33.
that it. Je 42:6. Dt 4:10. 5:16, 33.

24 they. ver. +26. Ex 32:7, 8.
walked. Je 23:17. Dt 29:19.
counsels. Je 23:18, 22.
imagination. *or,* stubbornness. Je +3:17mg.
went. Heb. were.
backward. ver. 26. Je 2:27. 8:5. 32:33. Ne
9:29. Ho 4:16.

25 the day. Je 32:30, 31. Ex ch. 12-15. Dt 9:7,
21-24. 1 S 8:7, 8. Ezr 9:7. Ne 9:16-18, 26. Ps
106:13-22. Ezk 2:3. 20:5, etc. 23:2, 3.
sent. ver. 13. 2 Ch +24:19.
my. Je +26:5.

26 hearkened not. ver. 13, 24. Je 6:17, 19.
11:8, 10. 17:23. +25:3, 4, 7. 26:5. 29:19.
32:33. 34:14. 35:14-17. 44:4, 5, 16. Dt
+28:15. 2 K 17:14. 21:9. 2 Ch 33:10. Ne 9:16,
17, 29, 30. Ps 81:11. 106:25. Is 48:18. Ezk
20:8. Da 9:6. Zc 1:4. 7:7, 11-13.
but. 2 Ch +30:8. Pr +29:1. Ro 2:5.
they did. Je 16:12. Mt 21:36-39. 23:32, 33.

27 thou shalt speak. Je 1:7. 26:2. Ezk 2:4-7.
3:17, 18. Ac 20:27.
hearken. Je 1:19. Is 6:9, 10. Ezk 3:4-11.
also. Is 50:2. 65:12. Zc 7:13.

28 nor. Je 6:29, 30. +31:18.
correction. *or,* instruction. Je +6:8.
truth. Je 5:1. 9:3-8. Is 59:14, 15. Ho 4:1. Mi
7:2-5.

29 Cut. Is +3:24.

and take. Je 9:17-21. Ezk 19:1. 28:12.
for. Je 6:30. 2 K 17:20. Zc 11:8, 9.
generation. Dt 32:5. Mt 3:7. 12:39. 16:4.
23:36. Ac 2:40.

30 they. Je 23:11. 32:34. 2 K 21:4, 7. 23:4-6, 12.
2 Ch 33:4, 5, 7, 15. Ezk 7:20. 8:5-17. 43:7, 8.
Da 9:27.

31 the high. 2 K +21:3. 2 Ch 33:6.
of Tophet. i.e. *contempt; a spitting (as an object
of contempt); place of burning, burial, or of drums,*
S#8612h. Je 7:31, 32. 19:6, 11, 12, 13. 2 K
23:10. Is +30:33.
the valley. Jsh +15:8.
to burn. Dt +18:10.
which I. Le 18:21. 20:1-5. Dt 17:3. 18:10. Pr
30:6.
came it into. Heb. came it upon. lit. ascend
upon. Je +3:16mg.

32 the days. Je 19:6. Le 26:30. Ezk 6:5-7.
Tophet. ver. +31. Is +30:33.
the valley. ver. +31. Je 19:5.
slaughter. Je 12:3. 19:6. Zc 11:4, 7.
for. Je 19:11, 13. 2 K 23:10.

33 the carcasses. Je 8:1, 2. 9:22. 12:9. +16:4.
19:7. 22:19. 25:33. 34:20. 36:30. Le 26:30. Dt
28:26. 1 S 17:44, 46. 2 K 9:36, 37. Ps 79:1-3.
Is 5:25. 14:19. 34:3. 66:24. Ezk 6:4, 5. 39:4,
18-20. 43:7, 9. Mt 24:28. Re 19:17, 18.
none shall. Je 9:22. 14:16. Is 17:2.

34 to cease. Je 16:9. 25:10. 33:10, 11. Is 24:7, 8.
Ezk 26:13. Ho 2:11. Re 18:23.
for. Je +18:16. Is 3:26.

JEREMIAH 8

1 At that time. Je 7:32-34. 1 K 13:2. 2 K
23:16, 20. 2 Ch 34:4, 5. Ezk 6:4, 5. 37:1, 3.
Am 2:1.
bring out the bones. 2 Ch 34:5.
graves. Heb. *qeber,* Ge +23:4.

2 and all. Je 7:18. Dt +4:19. Ezk +8:16.
they shall be. Je +7:33. Ec 6:3.
face. Ge 1:2.

3 death shall be chosen. Je 20:14-18. 1 K
19:4. Jb 3:20-22. 7:15, 16. Jon 4:3. 2 C 5:4.
Ph 1:23-25. Re 6:16. 9:6.
evil family. Am 3:1. Mi 2:3.
in all. Je 23:3, 8. 29:14, 28. 32:36, 37. 40:12.
Dt 30:1, 4. Da 9:7.

4 Shall they. Pr 24:16. Ho 14:1. Am 5:2. Mi
7:8. Ro 11:11.
shall he. Ml 3:7.
turn. Je 3:1, 22. 4:1. 23:14. 36:3. 1 K 8:38. Is
44:22. 55:7. Ezk 18:23. Ho 6:1, 2. 7:10. Lk
15:32.

5 slidden. Je 2:32. 3:11-14. 7:24-26. Ho 4:16.
11:7.
they hold. Je 9:6. Pr 4:13. Is 30:10. 44:20. 1
Th 5:21. 2 Th 2:9-12. Re 2:25.

they refuse. Je 5:3. Is 1:20. Zc 7:11. Jn 5:40. He 12:25.

6 **hearkened**. Jb 33:27, 28. Ps 14:2. Is 30:18. Ml 3:16. 2 P 3:9.

no man. Je 5:1. Is 59:16. Ezk 22:30. Mi 7:2.

saying. Jb 10:2. Ezk 18:28. Hg 1:5, 7. Lk 15:17-19.

as. Je 2:24, 25. Jb 39:19-25.

7 **stork**. Jb 39:13mg. Pr 6:6-8. Is 1:3.

appointed times. Ge +17:21. Le 23:2. Nu 28:2. Ec 3:1. Mt +24:44, 45.

turtle. SS 2:12.

people. Je 5:4, 5. Is 1:3. 5:12.

know not. Je 5:4, 5. 1 Ch +12:32. Is 27:11. Da 12:4, 9, 10. Lk +11:52.

8 **We**. Jb 5:12, 13. 11:12. 12:20. Jn 9:41. Ro 1:22. 2:17, etc. 1 C 3:18-20.

the law. Ps 147:19, 20. Ho 8:12.

Lo. Mt 15:6.

in vain, etc. or, the false pen of the scribes worketh for falsehood. Pr 17:16. Is 10:1, 2. Lk +11:52. 2 C 2:17mg. 4:2. 11:13. 2 T 2:15. 2 P 3:16.

pen. Je 17:1. Jb 19:24. Ps 45:1.

scribes. 1 Ch 2:55. 2 Ch +15:3. 17:7-9. 34:13. Ezr 7:6, 12. Ne 13:13. Mt 2:4.

9 **The wise men are**. or, Have they been, etc. Je 6:15. 49:7. Jb 5:12, 13. Is 19:11, 12. Ezk 7:26. 1 C 1:26-29.

lo. Dt 4:6. Ps 19:7. 119:98-100. Is +8:20. 1 C 1:18-29. 2 T 3:15.

rejected. Je 6:10. 20:8. 36:23. 2 Ch 36:16. Ps 50:17. Is 5:24. 30:12. Zc 7:12. Mk +7:9, 13. Ac 13:46.

what wisdom. Heb. the wisdom of what thing, etc. Pr 1:7. +21:30. 1 C 1:20.

10 **will I**. Je 6:12. Dt 28:30-32. Am 5:11. Zp 1:13.

for. Je +6:13. Ex +18:21. Ac +8:10. 20:33, 34. 2 C 12:14. T 1:7, 11.

from the prophet. Je +5:31. 23:11-17, 25, 26. 32:32. Is 28:7. La 4:13. Ezk 22:27, 28.

11 **they**. Je 14:14, 15. 27:9, 10. 28:3-9. 1 K 22:6, 13. Is +48:22. La 2:14. Mi 2:11.

12 **ashamed when**. Je 3:3. 6:15. Ps 52:1, 7. Is 3:9. Zp 3:5. Ph 3:18, 19.

therefore. Is 9:13-17. 24:2. Ezk 22:25-31. Ho 4:5, 6.

in the time. Je 10:15. 11:23. 23:12. 46:21. 48:44. 50:27. 51:18. Dt 32:35. Is 10:3. Ho 5:9. 9:7. Mi 7:4. Lk 19:44.

13 **I will surely consume**. or, In gathering I will consume. Is 24:21, 22. Ezk 22:19-21. 24:3-11. Zp 1:2, 3.

there. Le 26:20. Dt 28:39-42. Is 5:4-6, 10. Ho 2:8, 9. Jl 1:7, 10-12. Hab 3:17. Hg 1:11. 2:17. Mt 21:19. Lk 13:6-9.

the leaf. Je 17:8. Ps +1:3, 4. Ja 1:11.

14 **do**. 2 K 7:3, 4.

enter. Je 4:5, 6. 35:11. 2 S 20:6.

be silent. Je 48:2. 49:26. 50:30. 51:6. Le 10:3. 1 S 2:9. Ps 39:2. La 3:27, 28. Am 6:10. Hab +2:20.

water. Je 9:15. 23:13. 22:15, 17. Nu 5:18-24. Mt 27:34.

gall. or, poison. Dt +29:18.

15 **We looked**. Je 4:10. 14:19. Jb 30:26. Mi 1:12. 1 Th 5:3.

health. Je 14:19. 33:6. 2 Ch +21:18.

trouble. or, terror. **S#1205h**, only here and Je 14:19. Jb 3:26. 19:8. 23:17. 30:26. Pr +20:20. Ec 6:4. Is 59:9. La 3:2.

16 **was heard**. Ge +14:14.

the whole. Je 4:24. Hab 3:10.

trembled. Je 49:21. Jg 5:4. Ps 68:8. Ezk 38:20. Jl 2:10. 3:16. Na 1:5.

at the. Je 6:23. 47:3. Jg 5:22. Na 1:4, 5. 3:2.

all that was in it. Heb. the fulness thereof. Je 47:2mg. Dt 33:16. Ps 24:1. 1 C 10:26, 28.

17 **I will**. Dt 32:24. Is 14:29. Am 5:19. 9:3. Re 9:19. 12:9.

which. Ps 58:4, 5. Ec 10:11.

18 **comfort**. Is 51:12.

my. Je 6:24. 10:19-22. Jb 7:13, 14. Is 22:4. La 1:16, 17. Da 10:16, 17. Hab 3:16.

in. Heb. upon.

19 **the voice**. Je 4:16, 17, 30, 31. Is 13:5. 39:3.

them, etc. Heb. the country of them that are afar off.

the Lord. Je 14:19. 31:6. Ps 135:21. Is 12:6. 52:1. Jl 2:32. 3:21. Ob 17. Zc 14:3, 4. Re 2:1.

her king. Ps 146:10. 149:2. Is 33:22. Lk 1:32, 33.

Why. ver. 5, 6. Dt 32:16-21. Is 1:4.

provoke. Je 7:19. Dt 32:21. 1 K 15:30. 21:20.

graven images. Ex +20:4.

strange. Je 5:19. Ex 12:43. Ezk 44:7, 9.

vanities. Dt +32:21. 1 C 8:4.

20 **harvest is past**. Le +23:22. Pr 10:5. Mt 13:30. 25:1-13. Lk 10:2. 13:25. 19:43, 44. Jn 4:35. 1 Th 4:16, 17. He +3:7-15. Re 14:15.

21 **the hurt**. Je 4:19. 9:1. 14:17. 17:16. Ne 2:3. Ps 137:3-6. Lk 19:41. Ro 9:1-3.

I am black. Je 4:28. 14:2. SS 1:5, 6. Jl 2:6, 10. 3:15. Mi 3:6. Na 2:10.

22 **no balm**. Ge +37:25.

Gilead. Ge +37:25.

no physician. Jb +13:4.

why. Je 30:12-17.

health. lit. prolongation. **S#724h**. Je 30:17. 33:6. 2 Ch 24:13mg. Ne 4:7 (made up; lit., healing went up to the walls). Is 58:8.

daughter. Je +4:11.

recovered. Heb. gone up. Is 1:5, 6.

JEREMIAH 9

1 **Oh that**. Heb. Who will give, etc. Je 4:19. Ps +119:136. Is 16:9.

waters. ver. 18.

weep. Ps 42:3.
the daughter. Je +4:11.

2 **that I had**. Ps 55:6-8. 120:5-7. Mi 7:1-7.
for they. Ps +50:16.
all adulterers. Je 5:7, 8. 23:10. Ge 19:5. Le 18:22-25. 1 S 2:22. Ezk 22:9-11. Ho 4:2. 7:4. Mt 12:39. Jn 8:7, 9. Ga 5:19. Ja 4:4. 1 P 4:3, 4.
an assembly. Je 12:1, 6. Ho 5:7. 6:7. Mi 7:2-5. Zp 3:4. Ml 2:11.

3 **they bend**. ver 5, 8. Ps 52:2-4. 64:2-4. 120:2-4. Is 59:3-5, 13-15. Mi 7:3-5. Ro 3:13.
valiant. Mt 10:31-33. Mk 8:38. Ro 1:16. Ph 1:28, 29. Ju +3. Re 12:11.
for they. Je 7:26. 2 T 3:13.
they know. Je 4:22. 22:16. +31:34. Jg 2:10. 5:23. 1 S 2:12. Ho 4:1-3. Jn 8:54, 55. 17:3. Ro 1:28. 2 C 4:4-6.

4 **ye heed**. Je 12:6. Ps 12:2, 3. 55:11, 12. Pr 26:24, 25. Mi 7:5, 6. Mt 10:17, 21, 34, 35. Lk 21:16.
neighbor. *or*, friend. Ge 38:12.
every brother. Ge 25:26. 27:35, 36. 32:28. 1 Th 4:6.
walk. Le +19:16. Pr 25:18. Ep +4:31.

5 **they will**. ver. +8. Is 59:13-15. Mi 6:12. Ep 4:25.
deceive. *or*, mock. Ge 31:7. Jg 16:10. Jb 11:3.
taught. ver. 3. Jb 15:5. Ps 50:19. 64:3. 140:3. 1 T 4:1-3.
weary. Ge 19:11. Ps 7:14. Pr 4:16. Is 5:18. 41:6, 7. 44:12-14. 57:10. Ezk 24:12. Mi 6:3. Hab 2:13.

6 **habitation**. Je 11:19. 18:18. 20:10. Ps 120:2-6.
refuse. Je 13:10. Jb 21:14, 15. Pr 1:24, 29. Ho 4:6. Jn 3:19, 20. Ro 1:28. 1 C 15:34. 2 Th +2:10.

7 **I will**. Je 6:29, 30. Pr 1:23-27. Is 1:25. Ezk 22:18-22. 24:11, 12. 1 P +1:7.
shall. Je 31:20. 2 Ch 36:15. Ho 6:4, 5. 11:8, 9. Zc 1:14-16.

8 **tongue**. ver. 3, 5. Ps 12:2. 57:4. 64:3, 4, 8. 120:3. Ro 3:13.
one. 2 S 3:27. +4:6. 20:9, 10. Ps 28:3. 55:21. Pr 26:24-26. Mt 26:48, 49.
in heart. Heb. in the midst of him. Ge 41:21mg.
his wait. *or*, wait for him.

9 **visit them**. ver. +25.
soul. Heb. *nephesh*, Ge +34:3. Le +26:11.
avenged. Ex +15:7.

10 **the mountains**. Je 4:19-26. 7:29. 8:18. 13:16, 17. La 1:16. 2:11.
habitations. *or*, pastures. lit. comely places. Je 23:10. 25:37. Ps 23:3.
because. Je 12:4, 10. 14:6. 23:10. Jl 1:10-12.
burned up. *or*, desolate. ver. 12. Je 2:15. 10:22. 46:19.
so. Je 2:6. Is 34:19. Ezk 14:15. 29:11. 33:28.

both, etc. Heb. from the fowl even to, etc. Je 4:25. Ho 4:3.

11 **Jerusalem**. Je 26:18. 51:37. Ne 4:2. Ps 79:1. Is 25:2. Mi 1:6. 3:12. Mt 24:1, 2. Mk 13:1, 2. Lk 21:6.
a den. Je 10:22. Is 13:22. 34:13. Re 18:2.
the cities. Je 34:22. Is 44:26. La 2:2, 7, 8.
desolate. Heb. desolation. Je +18:16. La 3:47. Mi 6:16.

12 **the wise**. Dt 32:20, 29-31. Ps 107:43. Ho 14:9. Mt 24:15. Re 1:3.
for. Je 5:19, 20. 16:10-13. 22:8, 9. Dt 29:22-28. 1 K 9:8, 9. Ps 107:34. Ezk 14:23. 22:25-31. Ho 13:9.

13 **Because**. Je 22:9. Dt 31:16, 17. 32:15, 21. 2 Ch 7:19. Ezr 9:10. Ps 89:30. 119:53. Pr 28:4. Zp 3:1-6.
my law. Ex ch. 20.

14 **walked**. Je 3:17. 7:24. Ge 6:5. Ro 1:21-24. Ep 2:3. 4:17-19.
imagination. *or*, stubbornness. Je +3:17mg.
which. Je 44:17. Zc 1:4, 5. Ga 1:14. 1 P 1:18.

15 **the Lord of hosts**. Je +7:3.
I will. Je 25:15. Ps 60:3. 75:8. 80:5. Is 2:17, 22.
wormwood. Dt +29:18.
water of gall. Dt +29:18.

16 **scatter**. Je 13:24. 15:4. 18:17. Le 26:33. Dt 4:27. 28:25, 36, 64. 30:3. 32:26. Ne 1:8. Est 3:8. Ps 44:11. 106:27. Ezk 5:2, 12. 6:8. 11:16, 17. 12:15. 17:21. 20:23. 22:15. 36:19. Zc 7:14. Jn 11:52. Ja 1:1. 1 P 1:1.
and I. Je +12:12.

17 **Lord of hosts**. ver. 7. Je 2:19. +6:6.
call for. Je 22:18. 34:5. 1 S 1:24.
the mourning women. Mt +9:23.

18 **take**. ver. 10, 20.
our eyes. ver. +1. Je 6:26. La 1:2.

19 **a voice**. Je 4:31. Ezk 7:16-18. Mi 1:8, 9.
we are. Je 2:14. 4:13, 20, 30. Dt 28:28, 29. La 5:2. Mi 2:4.
our. Le 18:25, 28. 20:22. Jb 8:18. La 4:15. Ezk 19:12. Da 8:11. Mi 2:10.

20 **hear**. Is 3:16, 18-24. 32:9-13. Lk 23:27-30.
receive. Jb 22:22.
and teach. ver. +17, 18.

21 **death is come**. Je 6:11. 15:7. 2 Ch 36:17. Ezk 9:5, 6. 21:14, 15. Am 6:10, 11.
windows. lit. pierced places. Je 22:14. Ge 8:6. 26:8. Jl 2:9.
from without. Heb. *chuts*, Am 5:16 (**S#2351h**, highways), outside or narrow streets.
streets. Heb. *rechob*, Am 5:16 (**S#7339h**, streets), public square or broad streets.

22 **fall**. Je +7:33. +16:4.

23 **Let not**. Pr +21:30.
wise. Jb 5:12-14. Ps 49:10-13, 16-18. Ec 2:13-16, 19. 9:11. Is 5:21. 10:12, 13. Ezk 28:2-9. Ro 1:22. 1 C 1:19-21, 27-29. 3:18-20. Ja 3:14-16.

neither. Dt 8:17. 1 S 17:4-10, 42. 1 K 20:10, 11. Ps 33:16, 17. Is 10:8. 36:8, 9. Ezk 29:9. Da 3:15. 4:30, 31, 37. 5:18-23. Am 2:14-16. Ac 12:22, 23.

rich. Jb 31:24, 25. Ps 49:6-9. 52:6, 7. 62:10. Pr 11:4. Ezk 7:19. Zp 1:18. Mk 10:24. Lk 12:19, 20. 1 T 6:10.

24 **let him**. Je 4:2. Ps 44:8. Is 41:16. 45:25. Ro 5:11. 1 C *1:31*. 2 C *10:17*. Ga 6:14. Ph 3:3.
knoweth me. Je 4:22. 31:33, 34. Ps 91:14. Pr 2:5. Ho 4:1. Mt 11:27. Lk 10:22. Jn 17:3. 2 C 4:6. 1 J 5:20.
lovingkindness. Ex 34:5-7. Ps 36:5-7. 51:1. 107:43. 145:7, 8. 146:7-9. Ro 3:25, 26.
for. 1 S 15:22. Ps 99:4. Is 61:8. Mi +6:8. 7:18.
I delight. Is +66:4.

25 **that**. Ezk 28:10. 32:19-32. Am 3:2. Ro 2:8, 9, 25, 26. Ga 5:2-6.
punish. Heb. visit upon. Je +11:22mg. 21:14mg. 23:34mg. 30:20. 36:31mg. 44:13. 51:47mg. Is 10:12mg. 24:21mg. Ho 4:9mg. 12:2mg. Zp 1:8mg. Zc 10:3mg.
circumcised. Le +26:41, 42. Dt 10:16. 30:6.
with the. Ro 2:25-29.

26 **Egypt**. Je 25:9-26. 27:3-7. ch. 46-52. Is ch. 13-24. Ezk ch. 24-32. Am ch. 1, 2. Zp ch. 1, 2.
Judah. Is 19:24, 25.
in the utmost corners. Heb. cut off into corners; *or*, having the corners *of their hair* polled. Le 21:5. Je 25:23. 49:32. Le +19:27.
nations. Dt 32:8, 9.
uncircumcised in. Le +26:41.

JEREMIAH 10

1 A.M. 3397. B.C. 607.
Hear. Je +7:2. 13:15-17. Ps 50:7. 1 Th 2:13.

2 **Learn not**. Le 18:3, 27. 20:23. Ex 23:2, +13, 24. Dt 12:30, 31. 18:14. +20:18. 22:5. Jg 6:10. 1 S 8:5, 19, 20. 2 K 5:18. 17:15. Ps 16:4. 106:35. Pr 22:25. Is 2:6. Ezk 20:32. Jon 2:8. Mt 6:7, 8. 23:2, 3. 1 C 11:1. Ph 4:8.
be not dismayed. ver. +5. Dt 18:10, 14. Is +8:12. 47:12-14. Jl 2:30, 31. Mt 24:7. Lk 21:11, 25-28.

3 **customs**. Heb. statutes, *or* ordinances, are vanity. ver. +2, 8. Je +2:5. 13:23. Le 18:30. Dt +32:21. Jg 11:39mg. 1 K 18:26-28. Pr +5:22. Mt 6:7. Mk +7:9. Ro 7:19-24. 1 P 1:18. 1 J +1:8.
vain. or, a breath. Pr 21:6. Is 49:4. 57:13. Mt 6:7. Ro 1:21.
one cutteth a tree. Is 40:19, etc. 44:9-20. 45:20. +66:17. Ho 8:4-6. Hab 2:18, 19.
work of the hands. 1 P 1:18, 19.

4 **deck**. Ps 115:4. 135:15. Is 40:19, 20.
fasten. Is 41:6, 7. 44:12. 46:7.

5 **speak not**. Ps 115:5-8. 135:16-18. Is 46:7. Hab 2:19. 1 C 12:2. Re 13:14, 15.
be borne. Is 46:1, 7.

not afraid. ver. +2. Jb +3:25. Ps 53:5. Is +8:12.
do evil. Is 41:23, 24. 44:9, 10. 45:20. 1 C +8:4.

6 **none like**. Ex +8:10. Is 40:13, 14, 18, 25. 55:8, 9. Mt +8:27. +28:19.
thou. Ps 77:13, 14. Is 12:6. Da +2:45. 4:3, 34, 35.
might. Jb 36:22, 23.

7 **would**. Re +15:4.
O King. Ps 22:28. 72:11. 86:9. 89:6. Is 2:4. Zc 2:11. Re 11:15. *15:3*.
to thee. *or*, it liketh thee. Ps 76:7.
among. ver. +6. Ps 89:6. 1 C 1:19-21.

8 **altogether**. Heb. in one, *or* at once. Nu 10:4. Dt +6:4. Jb 33:14. Pr 28:18. Is +65:25.
brutish. ver. 14. Dt +32:21. Ps 14:2. 92:6. 94:8. +115:8. Pr 30:2.
the stock. Je 2:27. Is 44:19. Ho 4:12.

9 **Silver**. ver. +4.
Tarshish. Ge +10:4.
Uphaz. i.e. *island of gold*; *desire of fine gold*; *pure gold*, **S#210h**. Je 10:9. Da 10:5. Compare Ophir, 1 K +9:28. 2 Ch +8:18.
are all. Ps 115:4.

10 **the Lord**. 1 K 18:39. 2 Ch 15:3. Jn 17:3. 1 Th 1:9. 1 J 5:20.
true God. Heb. God of truth. Dt 32:4. Ps 31:5. 100:5. 146:6. 1 J 5:20.
the living. Je 23:36. 44:26. Dt 5:26. 1 S 17:26, 36. Ps 42:2. 84:2. Is 37:4, 17. Da 6:26. Mt +16:16. 26:63. Ac 14:15. 1 Th 1:9. 1 T 6:17. He 10:31.
everlasting king. Heb. king of eternity. Heb. *olam*, Ge +17:7. Ps 2:6-9. 93:1, 2. 99:1. Is 57:15. Da 4:3, 34. 1 T +1:17.
wrath. Is +66:14. Jn +3:36. 1 Th +5:9. Re 14:10.
tremble. Ps 68:11. +97:4. Re 20:11.
the nations. Ps 76:7. 90:11. Jl 2:11. Na 1:6. Ml 3:2.
his indignation. Is +66:14.

11 **Thus**. "In the Chaldean language."
The gods. Ps 96:5.
they. ver. 15. Je 51:18. Is 2:18. Zp 2:11. Zc 13:2. Re 20:2, 3.
under. La 3:66.

12 **hath made**. Je 51:15-19. Jb 38:4-7. Ps 136:5, 6. 148:4, 5. Jn +1:3.
established. Ps 24:2. 78:69. 93:1. 119:90. Pr 3:19. 30:4. Is 45:18. 49:8.
by his wisdom. Ps 19:1, 2. 104:24. Pr 3:19, 20. Ro +11:33.
stretched. Jb 26:7. Is +40:22. 48:13.

13 **uttereth**. Jb 37:2-5. 38:34, 35. Ps 18:13. 29:3-10. 68:33.
multitude. *or*, noise. Je 3:23. 47:3 (rumbling). 51:16mg. Is 31:4mg. Ezk 7:11mg. 39:11mg.
he causeth. 1 K 18:41, 45, 46. Jb 36:27-33. Ps 135:7. 147:8.

maketh. Ex 9:23. 1 S 12:17, 18. Jb 38:25-27, 34, 35. Zc 10:1mg.
with. *or,* for.
bringeth. Jb 38:22. Ps 135:7.
treasures. Dt +28:12.

14 **man**. ver. +8.
brutish in his knowledge. *or,* more brutish than to know. ver. 21. Je 51:17mg. Is 19:11.
founder. Ps 97:7. Is 45:16.
molten. Ex +34:17.
falsehood. Hab 2:18. Ro 1:25.
and. Ps +135:17.
breath. Heb. *ruach,* Ge +6:17.

15 **vanity**. ver. 8. Dt +32:21.
time of their visitation. ver. 11. Je +8:12. Is 2:17-21. Zp 1:3, 4. Zc 13:2.

16 **portion**. Ps +16:5, 6.
former. ver. +12. Pr +16:4. Is +45:7.
Israel. Ex +19:5. Ps 74:2. Is 47:6.
The Lord of hosts. Je +6:6. 31:35. 32:18. 46:18. 50:33, 34. 51:19. Ps +24:10.
is his name. Ex +6:3.

17 A.M. 3404. B.C. 600.
thy wares. Je 6:1. Ezk 12:3-12. Mi 2:10. Mt 24:15-18. Re 18:4.
inhabitant. Heb. inhabitress. Je 21:13mg. 48:19mg. 51:35mg. Is 12:6mg. Mi 1:11mg.

18 **I will**. Je 15:1, 2. 16:13. Dt 28:63, 64. 1 S 25:29.
that. Je 23:20. Ezk 6:10. Zc 1:6.

19 **Woe**. Je +4:19, 31. 8:21. 9:1. 17:13. La 1:2, 12, etc. 2:11, etc. 3:48.
Truly. Ps 39:9. 77:10. Is 8:17. La 3:18-21, 39, 40. Mi 7:9. Ja 1:2.

20 **tabernacle**. Je 4:20. Is 54:2. La 2:4-6.
my children. Je 31:15. Jb 7:8. Pr 12:7. Is 49:20-22.
there. Je 4:20. Is 51:16.

21 **the pastors**. ver. +8, 14. Je 2:8. 5:31. 8:9. 12:10. 22:22. 23:9, etc. 25:34. 50:6. Is 9:16. 56:10-12. Ezk 22:25-30. 34:2-10. Zc 10:3. Mt +15:14. Jn 10:12, 13.
brutish. ver. 8, 14. Je 5:31. 51:17. Ps 94:8. Is 19:11. 44:18.
not sought. ver. +25. Je 2:5. 8:2. 1 Ch +28:9. 2 Ch +7:14.
not prosper. Je 20:11. 22:30. Ps 1:3.
their. Je 9:16. 23:1. 49:32. 50:17. Ezk 34:5, 6, 12. Zc 13:7.

22 **the noise**. Je 1:15. 4:6. 5:15. 6:1, 22. Hab 1:6-9.
bruit. *Archaic* for *report, rumor.* Na 3:19.
north country. Je +1:14. 5:15.
a den. Je +9:11. Ml 1:3.

23 **I know**. Ps 17:4, 5. 37:23, 24. 119:116, 117. Pr +16:1. 20:24.
the way. Pr 14:12. 16:25. Mt 7:22, 23.
direct his steps. Pr 16:9.

24 **correct me**. Je 30:11. Ps +6:1. 38:1. Pr +19:18. 29:17. Hab 3:2.

lest. Je 30:11. Jb 6:18. Is 40:23. 41:11, 12.
bring me to nothing. Heb. diminish me. Ex 30:15mg. Le 25:16. Ezk 5:11.

25 **Pour out**. Je 6:6. Jg 6:20. Ps +79:6, 7. Jn +17:9. 2 Th 1:6-8. For other instances of imprecatory prayer see: Je 11:20. 12:3. 15:15. 17:18. 18:21-23. Nu 16:15. Dt 33:11. Jsh 8:33, 34. Jg 16:28. 1 S 26:19. 2 Ch 24:22. Ne 4:4, 5. 5:13. 6:14. Jb 27:7. Ps 5:10. 9:20. 10:2, 15. 28:4. 54:5. 55:9, 15. 56:7. 58:7. 59:5, 11, 13, 15. 68:1, 2. 69:22-24, 27, 28. +71:13. 79:10, 12. 94:2. 119:78, 84. 140:9, 10. 143:12. 144:6. La 1:22. 3:64-66. 1 C 16:22. Ga 1:8, 9. 2 T 4:14. Re 6:10.
that know thee not. Jb 18:21. Jn 17:25. Ac 17:23. 1 C 15:34. 1 Th 4:5. 2 Th 1:8.
call not. ver. 21. Ge +6:6. Jsh +9:14. Jb 15:4. 21:15. +27:10. Ps 10:4. 14:4. 53:4. 79:6. Is 43:22. 64:7. 65:1. 66:4. Da 9:13. Ho 7:7, 10, 14. Jon 1:6. Zp 1:6. Ja 4:2.
thy name. Ge +4:26. Dt +28:58.
eaten. Je 8:16. 12:9. 50:7, 17. 51:34, 35. Ps 14:4. 27:2. 53:4. 79:7. Is 9:12. 56:9. La 2:22. Ezk 25:6-8. 35:5-10. Am 8:4. Ob 10-16. Mi 3:2, 3. Zc 1:15. Mt 23:14. Mk 12:40. Lk 20:47. 2 C 11:20. Ga 5:15. Ja 5:3. Re 17:16.
desolate. Je +18:16.

JEREMIAH 11

2 A.M. 3406. B.C. 598.
the words. ver. 6. Je 34:13-16. Ex 19:5. 2 K 11:17. 23:2, 3. 2 Ch 23:16. 29:10. 34:31.

3 **the Lord God of Israel**. Je 13:12. 21:4. 23:2. 24:5. 25:15. 30:2. 32:36. 33:4. 34:2, 13. 37:7. 42:9. 45:2.
Cursed be. Je +10:25. Dt 27:26. 28:15, etc. 29:19, 20. Jsh 24:19-22. Ga 3:10-13.

4 **I commanded**. Je 31:32. Ex 24:3-8. Dt 5:2, 3. 29:10-15. Ezk 20:6-12. He 8:8-10.
in the day. Ge +2:17.
iron. Dt 4:20. 1 K 8:51. Is 48:10.
Obey. Je +7:23.
ye be. Ge +17:7.
I will be. Le 26:3-12.

5 **perform**. Ge 22:16-18. 26:3-5. Ps 105:9-11. Ac +7:2-5.
the oath. Dt 7:12.
a land. Je 32:22. Dt 7:12, 13.
honey. Ex +3:8.
So be it. Heb. Amen. lit. stedfast. **S#543h**. Je 28:6. Nu 5:22. Dt 27:15-26. 1 K 1:36. 1 Ch 16:36. Ne 5:13. 8:6. Ps 41:13. 72:19. 89:52. 106:48. Is 65:16, 16 (truth). Mt +6:13. Lk 10:21.

6 **Proclaim**. Je +2:2. Zc 7:7.
Hear. ver. +2-4. Ps 15:5. Jn +13:17. Ro 2:13. Ja 1:22.

7 **I earnestly**. 1 S 8:9. Ep +4:17. 2 Th 3:12.
in the day. Ex 15:26. 23:21, 22. Dt 4:6. 5:29.

6:2. 8:6. 10:12, 13. 11:26-28. 12:32. 28:1, etc. 30:20.

rising. Je +25:3.

8 **obeyed not.** Je 3:17. 44:17. Ne 9:16, 17, 26, 29. Ezk 20:8, 9, 18-21.

nor. Je 6:17. 7:24, 26. 35:15. Zc 7:11, 12.

walked. Je 6:16. 9:13, 14.

imagination. *or,* stubbornness. Je +3:17mg.

therefore. Je 17:18. 19:7, 15. 35:17. 36:31. Le 26:14, 16, 21. Dt 28:15, etc. 29:21-24. 30:17-19. 31:17, 18, 20, 21. 32:20-26. Jsh 23:13-16. Ezk 20:37, 38. Mi 3:12.

9 **A conspiracy.** Je 5:31. 6:13. 8:10. 2 K +11:14. Ezk 22:25-31. Ho 6:9. Mi 3:11. 7:2, 3. Zp 3:1-4. Mt 21:38, 39. 26:3, 4, 15. Jn 11:53. Ac 23:12-15.

10 **turned.** Je 3:10. 1 S 15:11. 2 Ch 34:30-33. Ho 6:4. 7:16. Zp 1:6.

iniquities. Jg 2:17, 19. Ps 78:8-10, 57, 58. Ezk 20:18-21. Zc 1:4. Ac 7:51, 52.

the house of Israel. Je +3:6-11. 31:32. Le 26:15. Dt 31:16. 2 K 17:7-20. Ezk 16:59. 44:7. Ho 6:7. 8:1. He 8:9.

11 **I will bring.** ver. 17. 2 K 22:16. 2 Ch +34:24. Ezk 7:4, 5.

which. Je 15:2, 3. Pr 29:1. Is 24:17. Am 2:14, 15. 5:19. 9:1-4. 1 Th 5:3. He 1:3. Re 6:16, 17.

escape. Heb. go forth of. Je 29:2. 38:17, 21. Ge 8:7mg. 1 S 14:41. Ezk 26:18. Mt 24:40, 41. Lk +21:36.

cry. Ps +66:18.

12 **go.** Je +2:28. 44:17-27. Dt 32:37, 38. Jg 10:14. 2 Ch 28:22, 23. Is 45:20.

trouble. Heb. evil. ver. 8, 11, 14. Is +45:7.

13 **For according.** Je 2:28. 3:1, 2. Dt 32:16, 17. 2 K 23:4, 5, 13. Is 2:8. Ho 12:11.

set up altars. Je 19:5. 32:35. 2 K 21:4, 5.

shameful thing. Heb. shame. Je 2:26. 3:24. 48:13. Nu 25:1-3. Jg +6:32. Is 66:17. Ho 9:10.

14 **pray not.** Je +7:16. 14:11. 15:1. Ex 32:10. Pr 26:24, 25. 1 J +5:16.

for. ver. +11. Ps +66:18. Ho 5:6.

trouble. Heb. evil. ver. 11. Is +45:7.

15 **What,** etc. Heb. What is to my beloved in my house? Lk 8:28.

my beloved. Je 2:2. 3:14. 12:7. Ho 3:1. Mt 22:11, 12. Ro 11:28.

to do. Je 3:8. 7:8-11. 15:1. Ps 50:16. Pr 15:8. 21:27. 28:9. Is 1:11-15. 50:1.

seeing. Je 3:1, 2. Ezk +16:25, etc. 23:2, etc.

the holy flesh. Je 7:21. Hg 2:12-14. T 1:15.

thou doest evil. *or,* thy evil *is.* Pr 2:14. 10:23. 26:18, 19. Ro 1:32. 1 C 13:6. Ja 4:16.

16 **A green.** Ps 52:8. Ro 11:17-26.

with. Ps 80:16. Is 1:30, 31. 27:11. Ezk 15:4-7. 20:47, 48. Mt 3:10. Jn +15:6.

17 **the Lord of hosts.** Je +6:6.

that planted. Je +2:21. 12:2. 18:9. 24:6. 31:28. 32:41. 42:10. 45:4. Ex 15:17. 2 S

+7:10. 1 Ch 17:9. Ps 44:2. 80:8, 15. Ec 3:2. Is 5:1, 2, 4. 60:21. 61:3. Ezk 17:5. Am 9:15.

pronounced. ver. +11. Je 16:10, 11. 18:8. 19:15. 26:13, 19. 35:17. 36:7. 40:2.

to provoke. Je 7:18.

18 **the Lord.** ver. 19. 1 S 23:11, 12. 2 K 6:9, 10, 14-20. Ezk 8:6, etc. Mt 2:13. Ac 27:23, 24. Ro 3:7.

hath given me knowledge. Is 11:2. Jn +2:25.

19 **I was.** Pr 7:22. Is 53:7, 8.

and I. Je 18:18. 20:10. Ps 31:13. 35:15. 37:32, 33. Is 32:7. Mt 26:3, 4.

saying. Je 50:5.

destroy. Je 6:5. 13:9.

tree with the fruit. Heb. stalk with his bread. or, dish in his food. i.e. the food in his dish.

let us cut. Ps 83:4. Is 53:8, 10. Da 9:26. Lk 20:10-15.

from. Ps +27:13.

that his name. Ps 109:13. 112:6. Pr 10:7. Is 38:11. Na 1:14.

no more remembered. Jb 24:20. Ezk 21:32.

20 **judgest righteously.** Je 12:1. Ge +18:25. Ps 98:9. Ac 17:31.

triest. Je +17:10. Is 53:11.

let. Je +10:25. Re 18:20.

see. Dt +32:43. Is +66:24.

revealed. 1 S 24:9, 15. Jb 5:8. Ps 10:14, 15. 35:1. 43:1. 57:1. Ph 4:6. 1 P 2:23.

21 **that seek.** Je 12:5, 6. 20:10. +34:20. Mi 7:6. Mt 10:21, 34-36. 13:57. Lk 4:24.

life. Heb. *nephesh,* soul, Ge +44:30.

Prophesy not. Is 30:9, 10. Am 2:12. 7:13-16. Mi 2:6, 11.

thou. Je 20:1, 2. 38:1-6. Mt 21:35. 22:6. 23:34-37. Lk 13:33, 34. Ac 7:51, 52.

22 **punish.** Heb. visit upon. **S#6485h.** Je 5:9, 29. 9:9, +25mg. 13:21mg. 23:2. 25:12mg. 29:32. 44:29. 46:25. 50:18. Ex +20:5. +32:34. 34:7. Nu 14:18. 16:29. Dt 5:9. Ho 2:13. 8:13. Am 3:2mg.

young. Je +18:21. La 2:21. 1 Th 2:15, 16.

23 **no.** ver. 19. Je 44:27. Is 14:20-22.

the year. Is +61:2. Je 5:9, 29. +8:12.

JEREMIAH 12

1 **Righteous.** Hab 1:13. Ro 2:17-20. 1 C 4:8. 2 C 10:1. 12:16. Ga 4:15. Ja 2:19.

art thou. Je 11:20. Ge +18:25. Dt 32:4. Ezr 9:15. Ps 51:4. 119:75, 137. 145:17. La 1:18. Da 9:7. Hab 1:13-17. Zp 3:5. Ro 3:5, 6.

talk. *or,* reason the case. Je 39:5mg. Jb 13:3. Ps 127:5mg. Is 41:21.

Wherefore doth. Je 5:28. Jb 12:6. 21:7-15. Ps 37:1, 35. 73:3-5, 7. 92:7. 94:3, 4. Pr 1:32. Hab 1:4. Ml 3:15.

deal. ver. 6. Je 5:11. Is 48:8. Ho 6:7.

2 **hast**. Je +11:17. Ezk 19:10-13.
grow. Heb. go on.
near. Is 29:13. Ezk 33:31. Mt 15:8. Mk 7:6. T 1:16.

3 **knowest**. Je 11:20. 2 K +20:3. 1 Ch 29:17. Jb 23:10. Ps 17:3. 26:1. 44:21. 139:1, 23. Jn 21:17. 1 J 3:20, 21.
toward. *or*, with.
pull. Je +10:25. 20:12. 48:15. 50:27. 51:4.
prepare. or, sanctify. Je 6:4. Is +8:13.
the day. Je 11:19. Ps 44:22. Ja 5:5.

4 **long**. Re +6:10.
mourn. Je 9:10. 14:2. 23:10.
the herbs. Ps 107:33, 34. Jl 1:10-17.
beasts. Je 4:25. 7:20. Ho 4:3. Hab 3:17. Ro 8:22.
He. Je 5:13, 31. Ps 50:21. Ezk 7:2-13.

5 **if**. He 12:1.
thou hast. Pr 3:11. 24:10. He 12:3, 4. 1 P 4:12-14.
canst. Je 26:8. 36:26. 38:4-6.
then how wilt. Mt 7:14-23. 25:14-30, 34-40. Lk 16:10. Ro 8:18. 1 C 2:9. 3:13-15. 9:24-27. He 6:11, 12, 18. 2 P 3:14.
swelling. Je 49:19. 50:44. Jsh 3:15. 1 Ch 12:15. Jb 41:34. Ps 42:7. 69:1, 2. Zc 11:3.

6 **thy brethren**. Je 9:4. 11:19, 21. 20:10. Ge 37:4-11. Jb 6:15. Ps +69:8, 9. Ezk 33:30, 31. Mi 7:5, 6. Mt 10:21. Mk 13:12. Jn 7:5.
yea. Is 31:4. Ac 16:22. 18:12. 19:24-29. 21:28-30.
have called, etc. *or*, cried after thee fully.
believe them not. Ro 3:13.
though. Ps 12:2. Pr 26:25. Mt 22:16-18.
fair words. Heb. good things. 2 K 25:28mg.

7 **have forsaken**. Je 11:15. 51:5. Is 2:6. +54:7. Jl 2:17. 3:2.
I have given. Je 7:14. La 2:1, etc. Ezk 7:20, 21. 24:21. Lk 21:24.
dearly beloved. Heb. love. Je +2:33.
soul. Heb. *nephesh*, Ge +34:3.

8 **crieth out**. *or*, yelleth. Heb. giveth out his voice. Je 2:15. 51:38.
therefore. Ho 9:15. Am 6:8. Zc 11:8.

9 **speckled bird**. *or*, a bird having talons.
the birds. Je 2:15. 2 K 24:2. Ezk 16:36, 37. 23:22-25. Re 17:16, 17.
come ye. Je +7:33. Is 56:9.
come. *or*, cause them to come. Is 21:14mg.

10 **pastors**. Je +6:3. 25:9. 39:3.
my vineyard. Ps 80:8-16. Is 5:1-7. Na 2:2. Lk 20:9-16.
trodden. Is 43:28. 63:18. La 1:10, 11. Lk 21:14. Re 11:1, 2.
pleasant portion. Heb. portion of desire. Je +3:19mg.

11 **made it**. Je +18:16.
it mourneth. ver. 4-8. Je 14:2. 23:10. La ch. 1-5. Zc 7:5.
layeth. Ec 7:2. Is 42:25. 57:1. Ml 2:2.

12 **spoilers**. Je 4:11-15. 9:19-21.
high places. 2 K +21:3.
the sword. Je 14:12. 21:7, 9. +24:10. 25:16, 27, 29. 29:17. 32:24. 42:16, 22. 43:11. 44:12, 13, 27. 46:10, 14. 47:6. 48:2. 49:37. 50:35. 1 Ch 21:12. Is +65:12. La 1:20. Ezk 12:14. 21:3. 38:21. Ho 11:6. Am 9:4. Na 2:13. Zp 2:12. Ep 6:17. Re +1:16.
no. Is 57:21. Mt 24:21, 22. Re 6:4.

13 **sown**. Le 26:16. Dt 28:38. Mi 6:15. Hg 1:6. 2:16, 17.
shall reap. Nu +32:23.
put. Je 3:23-25. Is 30:1-6. 31:1-3. 55:2. Hab 2:13. Ro 6:21.
they. *or*, ye.

14 A.M. 3401. B.C. 603.
against. Je 48:26, 27. 50:9-17. 51:33-35. Ezk 25:3-15. Am 1:2-15. Zp 2:8-10.
that touch. Je 2:3. 49:1, 7. Jb +1:11. Ob 10-16. Zc 1:15. 12:2-4.
to inherit. Je 3:18. Ex 32:13.
I will. Je ch. 48-51. Ezk ch. 25-32, 35.
and pluck. Je 3:18. 32:37. Dt 30:3. Ps 106:47. Is 11:11-16. Ezk 28:25. 34:12, 13. 36:24. 37:21. 39:27, 28. Ho 1:11. Am 9:14, 15. Zp 3:19, 20. Zc 10:6-12. 2 C 3:15, 16.

15 **after**. Dt +30:3. Is 23:17, 18. Mi 7:19.
heritage. Nu 32:18. Dt 3:20.

16 **if**. Je +7:5.
my name. Ge +21:23. SS 1:8.
as they. Jsh 23:7. Ps 106:35, 36.
built. Is 19:23-25. 56:5, 6. Zc 2:11. Ro 11:17. 1 C +3:9. 1 P 2:4-6.

17 **if**. Je +7:5. Ps 2:8-12. Is 60:12. Zc 14:16-19. Lk 19:27. 2 Th 1:8. 1 P 2:6-8.
pluck. ver. 14, 15. Je 18:7. 31:28. 45:4. Ezk 19:12. Da 7:4-8. 11:4.

JEREMIAH 13

1 A.M. 3405. B.C. 599.
Go. ver. 11. Je 19:1. 27:2. Ezk 4:1, etc. 5:1, etc. He 1:1, 2.

2 **according**. Pr 3:5. Is 20:2. Ezk 2:8. Ho 1:2, 3. Jn 13:6, 7. +15:14.

3 **the word**. ver. 3, 8.
second time. Ge +41:32.

4 **go**. Je 51:63, 64. Ps 137:1. Mi 4:10.

5 **as**. Ex 39:42, 43. 40:16. Mt 21:2-6. Jn 2:5-8. Ac 26:19, 20. 2 T 2:3. He 11:8, 17-19.

6 **Arise**. ver. 2-5.

7 **it was**. ver. 10. Je 24:1-8. Is 64:6. Ezk 15:3-5. Zc 3:3, 4. Lk 14:34, 35. Ro 3:12. Phm 11.

9 **After**. Je 18:4-6. La 5:5-8.
the pride. ver. 15-17. Le 26:19. Jb 40:10-12. Pr 16:18. Is 2:10-17. 23:9. Ezk 16:50, 56. Na 2:2mg. Zp 3:11. Lk 18:14. Ja 4:6. 1 P 5:5.
the great. Je 48:29. Is 16:6.

10 **evil**. Je 5:23. 8:5. 11:7, 18. 15:1. +25:4. Nu 14:11. 2 Ch 36:15, 16.

walk. Je 7:24. 9:14. 11:8. 16:12. Ec 11:9. Ep 4:17-19.

imagination. *or*, stubbornness. Je +3:17mg. Ac 7:51.

shall. ver. 7. Je 15:1-4. 16:4. Is 3:24.

11 I caused. Ex 19:5, 6. Dt 4:7. 26:18. 32:10-15. Ps 135:4. 147:20.

for a name. Je 33:9. Is 43:21. 55:13. +62:12. 1 P 2:9.

but. ver. 10. Je 6:17. Ps 81:11. Jn 5:37-40.

12 Every bottle. or, jar. **S#5035h**. Je 48:12. 1 S 1:24. 10:3. 25:18. Jsh 9:4. 2 S 16:1. Jb 38:37. Is 30:14mg. La 4:2 (pitchers).

shall be filled. Je 25:15. Ge 6:11.

and they shall. Ezk 11:2, 3. 24:19.

13 I will. Je 25:15-18, 27. 51:7. Ps 60:3. 75:8. Is 29:9. 49:26. 51:17, 21. 63:6. Hab 2:16.

with drunkenness. Ezk 23:33. 39:19.

14 I will dash. Je 19:9-11. 48:12. Jg 7:20-22. 1 S 14:16. 2 Ch 20:23. Ps +2:9. Is 9:20, 21.

one against another. Heb. a man against his brother. 1 S 10:11mg.

even. Je +6:21. 47:3. Ezk 5:10. Mt 10:21. Mk 13:12.

I will not. Je 21:7. Dt 29:20. Is 27:11. Ezk 5:11. 7:4, 9. 8:18. 9:5, 10. 24:14.

but destroy. Heb. from destroying. Je 15:3. 51:11.

15 and. Is 42:23. Jl 1:2. Re 2:29.

be. Is 28:14-22. Ja 4:10.

for. Je 26:15. Am 7:15. Ac 4:19, 20.

16 Give. Ps 96:7, 8. 1 T +1:17. Re +11:13.

before. Je 4:23. Ec 11:8. 12:1, 2. Is 59:9. Jn 12:35.

cause. Am +3:6. 5:8.

darkness. Ex +10:22.

your. Pr +4:19. 1 P 2:7, 8. 1 J 2:8-11.

while. Je 8:15. 14:19. Is 59:9. La 4:17.

the shadow. Ps +23:4.

gross darkness. Ex 10:21. Is +60:2. Mt +8:12.

17 if. Je 22:5. Ml 2:2.

my soul. Heb. *nephesh*, Ge +34:3. Je 17:16. Ps +119:136.

pride. ver. 15. Jb 33:17. Ps +119:21.

mine eye. Je 9:1.

run down. Mt 26:38. Lk 19:41. 22:41, 44, 45.

because. ver. 19, 20. Is 63:11. Ezk +34:31.

18 unto. Je 22:26. 2 K 24:12, 15. Ezk 19:2, etc. Jon 3:6.

Humble. Ex 10:3. 2 Ch 33:12, 19, 23. Mt 18:4. Ja 4:10. 1 P 5:6.

sit. Is 3:26. 47:1. La 2:10.

principalities. *or*, head tires. lit. "first estates." **S#4761h**, only here. Compare **S#7218h**, Jsh 11:10. 19:51. 22:21, 30. 2 S 23:8, 13, 18. 1 K 21:9mg. 2 K 9:30. Ezk 24:23.

19 cities. Je 17:26. 33:13. Dt 28:52. Jsh 18:5. Ezk 20:46, 47.

south. Ge +12:9. Is +30:6. Da 11:5.

shut. Dt 28:52. Jb 12:14.

Judah. Je 39:9. 52:27. Le 26:31-33. Dt 28:15, 64-68. 2 K 25:21.

20 Lift. Ge +22:13.

and. Hab 1:6.

north. Je +1:14.

where. ver. +17. Is 56:9-12. Ezk 34:7-10. Zc 11:16, 17.

21 wilt. Je 5:31. 22:23. Is 10:3. Ezk 28:9.

punish. Heb. visit upon. Je +11:22mg.

for. 2 K 16:7. Is 39:2-4.

shall not. Je +4:31.

22 if. Dt +7:17. Lk 5:21, 22.

Wherefore. Je +5:19. 16:10, 11.

the greatness. Je 2:17-19. 9:2-9. Ho 12:8.

skirts. ver. 26. Is +3:17. Re 3:18.

heels. Ge 3:15. Ro 16:20.

made bare. *or*, shall be violently taken away. La 2:6. Mt 11:12.

23 Ethiopian. Nu +12:1.

change his skin. Je 2:22, 30. 5:3. 6:29, 30. 17:9. Pr 27:22. Is 1:5. Mt 19:24-28.

then may. Jb 14:4. Mt 7:16-18. 12:33. Jn 6:44, 65. Ro 11:35, 36. 1 C 2:14. 4:7. 2 C 3:5.

accustomed. Heb. taught. Je 2:24mg. 9:5. Is +8:16.

24 will. Je +9:16. Lk 21:24.

stubble. 1 C +3:12.

wind. Je 4:11, 12. Ps 1:4. 83:13-15. Is 17:13. 41:16. Ho 13:3, 15. Zp 2:2.

25 thy lot. Le 16:8-10. Nu 26:55. Jb 20:29. Ps 11:6. Is 17:4. Mt 24:51.

because. Je 2:13, 32. Dt 32:16-18. Ps +9:17. 106:21, 22.

trusted. Je 7:4-8. 10:14. Dt 32:37, 38. Is 28:15. Mi 3:11. Hab 2:18, 19.

26 I discover. ver. +22.

27 thine adulteries. Je 2:20-24. 3:1, 2. 5:7, 8. Ezk 16:15, etc. 23:2, etc. Ho 1:2. 4:2. 2 C 12:21. Ja 4:4.

neighings. Je 5:8. 8:16.

lewdness. Je 11:15.

hills. 2 K +17:10.

Woe. Je 4:13. Ezk 2:10. 24:6. Zp 3:1. Mt 11:21. Re 8:13.

wilt. Je 4:14. Ps 94:4, 8. Ezk 24:13. 36:25, 37. Lk 11:9-13. 2 C 7:1.

when, etc. Heb. after when yet? Je +17:16mg.

shall. Pr 1:22. Ho 8:5.

JEREMIAH 14

1 A.M. 3399. **B.C.** 605.

The word. Je 1:2, 4.

the dearth. Heb. the words of the dearths, *or* restraints. Je 17:8mg.

2 mourneth. Je +4:28. 12:4. Is 3:26. Ho 4:3. Jl 1:10, 12.

the gates. Is 24:4, 7. 33:9. Ge +14:7.
they. Je 8:21. La 2:9. 4:8, 9. 5:10. Jl 2:6.
are black. or, sit in black. Je 8:21. 13:18. Jb
2:8, 13. Ps 35:14. Is 3:26. 15:3.
the cry. Je 11:11. 18:22. 46:12. Ex +2:24. 1 S
5:12. 9:16. Jb 34:28. Ps 144:14. Is 5:7. 15:5.
Zc 7:13.

3 **their nobles**. 1 K 18:5, 6.
pits. Je 2:13. 1 K 17:7. 2 K 18:31. Ps 63:1. Jl
1:20. Am 4:8.
they were. Je 2:26, 27. 20:11. Ps 40:14.
109:29. Is 45:16, 17.
covered. ver. +4.

4 **the ground**. Le 26:19, 20. Dt 28:23, 24.
29:23. Jl 1:19, 20.
the plowmen. Jl 1:11, 17.
ashamed. Jb 29:23.
they covered. Est +6:12.

5 **the hind**. Jb 39:1-5. Ps 29:9.

6 **the wild**. Je 2:24. Jb 39:5, 6.
their. 1 S 14:29. La 4:17. 5:17. Jl 1:18.

7 **though**. Is 59:12. Ho 5:5. 7:10.
do. ver. 20, 21. Is +48:9.
for our backslidings. Je +2:19. Ezr 9:6, 7,
15. Ne 9:33, 34. Ps 51:7, 12. +119:176. Da
9:5-16.

8 **the hope**. Ps +42:11. Ac 28:20. 1 T 1:1.
savior. Is 43:3, 11. 45:15, 21.
in time. Ps 9:9. 37:39, 40. 46:1. 50:15. 91:15.
138:7. 2 C 1:4, 5.
why. Ps 10:1.
stranger. Je 7:6. 22:3. Ge +23:4.
a wayfaring. Jg 19:17.
tarry. Lk 24:28, 29.

9 **cannot**. Nu 11:23. 14:15, 16. Ps 44:23-26. Is
50:1, 2. 51:9. 59:1.
in the midst. Ex 29:45, 46. Le 26:11, 12. Dt
23:14. Ps 46:5. 84:1. Is 12:6. Zc 2:5. 2 C 6:16.
Re 21:3.
we are called by thy name. Heb. thy name
is called upon us. Je 7:10mg, 11. 15:16mg.
25:29mg. 2 S 12:28mg. 1 K 8:43mg. 2 Ch
6:33mg. Is 63:19mg. 65:1. Da 9:18mg, 19. Am
9:12mg. Ac 15:17. Ja 2:7.
leave. 1 S +12:22. Ps 27:9. 119:121. He
+13:5.

10 **have they**. Je 2:23-25, 36. 3:1, 2. 8:5. Ho
11:7, 9.
wander. ver. +11. Je 50:6. Jg 9:9, 11, 13. Ps
119:176. Pr 21:16. 27:8. Is 53:6. La 4:14. Ezk
34:6. 1 T 1:6. 1 P 2:25. 2 P 2:15. Ju 13.
refrained. Je 2:25. Ps 119:101.
the Lord. Je 6:20. Is 1:13, 14. Am 5:21, 22.
Ml 1:8-13.
he will. Je 31:34. 44:21, 22. 1 S 15:2. 1 K
17:18. Ps 109:14, 15. Ho 8:13. 9:9. He 8:12.

11 **Pray not**. Je +7:16. 11:14. 15:1. Ex 32:10,
31-34.

12 **they fast**. Is 58:3.
not hear. Je +7:16. 11:14. Am 5:23.

and when. Je 6:20. 7:21, 22. Pr 21:27.
burnt offering. Le +23:12.
not accept. Ps +66:18.
sword. Je +12:12. Ex +5:3.

13 **Ah**. Je +1:6. 4:10.
behold. Je 5:31. 28:2-5. Ezk +13:10-16, 22.
Mi 3:11. 2 P 2:1-3.
sword. Ex +5:3.
assured peace. Heb. peace of truth. Je 4:10.
23:17.

14 **The prophets**. Je +23:25, 26, 30. 27:10, 14.
28:13. 29:21. 37:19. Dt 18:20-22. Pr +4:18. Is
9:15. Zc 13:3. 1 T 4:1-3. Re 13:13-15.
I sent. Je 23:14-16, 21-32. 27:14, 15. 28:15.
29:8, 9, 31. Is 30:10, 11. 2 Th 2:9-11.
false vision. Je 23:16, 26. 27:9, 10. Ezk
12:24. 14:10. 2 C 11:3, 4, 13, 14. Ga 1:8.
divination. Je +27:9. Dt +18:10.
and the. Je 23:26. Is 30:10. La 2:14.
their heart. Nu +16:28.

15 **Sword**. Ex +5:3.
and famine shall not. Je 5:12, 13. 20:6.
23:14, 15. 28:15-17. 29:20, 21, 31, 32. 1 K
22:25. Ezk 14:9, +10. Am 7:17. 2 P 2:1-3, 14-
17.

16 **the people**. Je 5:31. Is 9:16. Mt +15:14.
be cast. Je +7:33. 9:22. 15:2, 3. 16:4. 18:21.
19:6, 7. Ps 79:2, 3.
sword. Ex +5:3.
for. Je 2:17-19. 4:18. 13:22-25. Pr 1:31. Re
16:1.
wickedness. Ge +19:15.

17 **Let mine**. Ps +119:136.
for. Je +18:13.
daughter. Je +4:11.
with a very. Je 30:14, 15. Ps 39:10. Mi 6:13.

18 **sword**. Je +12:12.
famine. 1 K +8:37.
yea. Je 6:13. 8:10. 23:21. Dt 28:36, 64. Is
28:7. La 4:13-16.
go about, etc. or, make merchandise against
a land, and men acknowledge it not. Je 2:8.
5:31. Ge 34:10. Mi 3:11. 2 P 2:3.
into a land. Je 9:16. +16:13.

19 **utterly**. Ps +44:9.
hath. Je 12:8. Zc 11:8, 9.
soul. Heb. nephesh, Ge +34:3; Le +26:11.
no healing. Je +8:22. 15:18. 2 Ch 36:16. La
2:13.
we. Je +8:15. Jb 30:26. La 4:17. 1 Th 5:3.

20 **We acknowledge**. Je 3:13, 25. Le 26:40-42.
Ezr 9:6, 7. Ne 9:2. Ps 32:5. 51:3. 106:6, etc. Da
9:5-8. 1 J 1:7-9.
for. 2 S 12:13. 24:10. Jb 33:27. Ps 51:4. Lk
15:18-21.

21 **not abhor**. ver. 19. Ps 51:11. +106:40.
for. ver. +7. Ezk 39:25. Ep 2:4-7.
disgrace. Ps 74:3-7, 20. La 1:10. 2:6, 7, 20.
Ezk 7:20-22. 24:21. Da 8:11-13. Lk 21:24. Re
11:2.

throne. Ps +11:4.

remember. Ex 32:13. Le +26:42. Ps 74:2, 18-20. 89:39, 40. Is 64:9-12. Zc 11:10, 11. He 8:6-13.

22 **Are**. Je 10:15. 16:19. Dt 32:21. Is 41:29. 44:12-20.

vanities. Dt +32:21. 1 K 17:1. 18:1, 41, 44, 45. Ps 74:1, 2. 1 C +8:4.

Art. Je 5:24. 10:13. 51:16. Dt 28:12. 1 K 8:36. 17:14. 18:39-45. Jb 5:10. 38:26-28. Ps 147:8. Is 30:23. Jl 2:23. Am 4:7. Mt +5:45.

wait upon. Ps +25:3. 135:7. Hab 3:17-19.

JEREMIAH 15

1 **Then said**. Je 7:16. 1 J 5:16.

Though. Je 7:16. 11:14. 14:11. Ezk 14:14-21.

Moses. Ex 17:11. 32:11-14. Nu 14:13-20. 1 S 7:9. 8:6. 12:23. Ps 99:6. Ezk 14:14. He 7:25.

stood. Je 18:20. Ge 19:27. Ps 106:23. Zc 3:3. He 9:24.

my mind. Heb. *nephesh*, soul, Ge +23:8; Le +26:11. Jg 5:9. Pr 14:35.

not be toward. Je 21:1-7. 37:3-10. Ex 32:30-35. Nu 16:44-46. Dt 3:23-26. Jg 10:10-14. 1 S 15:10, 11. 16:1. Ezk 14:1-3. 14:13-21. Mt 20:20-23. Mk 5:18, 19. Lk 9:59-62. 12:13-15. 13:23, 24, 25-27. 16:24, 25, 27-30. Ac 1:6, 7. 2 C 12:7-9.

cast. Ps +44:9.

2 **for death**. Je +12:12. 2 S 8:2. 12:31. Is 24:18. Da 9:12. Am 5:19. Zc 11:9. Re 6:3-8. 13:10.

to death. Ge +2:17. Nu 15:30. 16:26-32. 1 S 2:25. Pr +16:25. Da 12:2, 3. Mt 12:31, 32. Mk 3:28-30. Ro 6:21-23. 2 T 4:14. He 6:4-6. 10:26-31. 2 P 2:20-22. Ja 5:20. 1 J +5:16. Re 2:11. 20:6, 14. +21:8.

3 **I will**. Je 7:33. Dt 28:26. 1 K 21:23, 24. 2 K 9:35-37. Is 18:6. 56:9, 10. Ezk +5:17. Re 19:17, 18.

kinds. Heb. families. Je 1:15. 2:4.

4 **cause them to be removed**. Heb. give them for a removing. Je +9:16. 24:9mg. 29:18. 34:17mg. La 1:8mg. Ezk 23:46mg.

because. 2 K 21:3, 11-13. 23:26, 27. 24:3, 4.

5 **For who**. Je 16:5. 21:7. Jb 19:21. Ps 69:20. Is 51:19. La 1:12-16. 2:15, 16. Na 3:7. Mt 23:37-39.

how thou doest. Heb. of thy peace. Jg +18:15mg.

6 **forsaken**. Je +1:16.

thou art. Je 7:24. 8:5. Is 1:4. 28:13. Ho 4:16. 11:7. Zc 7:11.

stretch. Ex +7:5.

weary. Je 6:11. 20:9. Ps 78:38-40. 106:43-45. Ezk 12:26-28.

repenting. Je +18:8.

7 **I will fan**. Ps 1:4. Mt +3:12.

gates. Ge +14:7.

bereave. Je 9:21. 18:21. Dt 28:18, 32, 41, 53-56. Ho 9:12-17.

children. *or*, whatsoever is dear. Ge 42:36. Ezk 24:21, 25.

since. Je 5:3. 8:4, 5. Is 9:13. Am 4:10-12. Zc 1:4.

8 **widows**. Je 7:6. 18:21. 22:3. Is 3:25, 26. +4:1.

sand. Ge +22:17.

the mother, etc. *or*, the mother *city* a young man spoiling, etc. *or*, the mother *and* the young men. Je 6:11.

a spoiler. Je 4:16. 5:6. 6:4, 5, 26. Lk 21:35.

at noon day. Je 6:4.

suddenly. Is 47:11. 1 Th 5:3.

terrors. Le 26:16. Ps 78:33. Is 65:23.

9 **She that hath**. 1 S 2:5. Is 47:9. La 1:1. 4:10.

seven. Ru 4:15. 1 S 2:5. Jb 1:2.

languisheth. Je 14:2. 1 S 2:5.

given up. Jb 11:20.

ghost. Heb. *nephesh*, soul, Nu +23:10.

her sun. Am 8:9, 10.

and the. ver. 2, 3. Je 44:27. Ezk 5:12.

10 **my**. Je 20:14-18. Jb 3:1-3, etc.

a man. ver. 20. Je 1:18, 19. 20:7, 8. 1 K 18:17, 18. 21:20. 22:8. Ps 120:5-7. Ezk 2:6, 7. 3:7-9. Mt 10:21-23. 24:9. Lk 2:34, 35. 21:17. Ac 16:20-22. 17:6-8. 19:8, 9, 25-28. 28:22. 1 C 4:9-13.

neither. Dt +19:5.

lent on usury. Is +24:2.

curse. Ps 109:28. Pr 26:2. Mt 5:44. Lk 6:22.

11 **The Lord said**. Je 46:25. Lk 11:39. 12:42. 18:6. 22:31.

Verily it. Ps 37:3-11. Ec 8:12.

verily I. Je 29:11-14. 39:11, 12. 40:2-6. Ps 106:46.

cause the enemy to entreat thee. *or*, entreat the enemy for thee. Pr +16:7. 21:1.

12 **Shall iron**. Je 1:18, 19. 21:4, 5. Jb 40:9. Is 45:9. Hab 1:5-10.

13 **substance**. ver. 8. Je 17:3. 20:5.

without. Dt +32:30.

14 **pass**. ver. 4. Je +16:13. Le 26:38, 39. Dt 28:25, 36, 64. Am 5:27.

a fire. Je +17:27.

15 **thou**. Je 12:3. 17:16. Jb 10:7. Ps 7:3-5. 17:3. Jn 21:15-17. 2 C 5:11.

remember. Je 20:12. Ne 5:19. 6:14. 13:22, 31. Ps 106:4. 109:26-29. 119:84, 132-134. Lk 18:7, 8. Ro 12:19. Re 18:20.

visit. Ps 59:5. 80:14, 15. 106:4.

revenge me. Je +10:25.

take. Ps 39:13. 102:24. Is 38:3.

know. ver. 10. Je 11:21. 20:8. Ps 69:7-9. Mt 5:10-12. 10:22. 19:29. Lk 6:22, 23. 21:17. Ro 8:35. 1 P 4:14-16.

16 **Thy words**. Jsh 1:8. Ps 119:16, 24, 35, 127, 162. Is 8:20. Mk 12:24.

found. 2 K +22:8. 2 Ch +34:14, 15.

I did. Ezk 3:1-3. 1 C 12:13. Re 10:9.

eat them. Jb +23:12. Ps 119:92, 103. Jn 6:51, 53, 63. He 5:12-14. 1 P 2:2. Re 10:10.

thy word. Je 6:10. Jb 23:12. Ps 19:10. 119:72, 97, 101-103, 111. Mi 2:7.

rejoicing. Ps 119:111, 162.

heart. Dt +6:6.

I am called by thy name. Heb. thy name is called upon me. Je +14:9mg. 2 Ch +7:14. Jn 17:14.

O Lord God of hosts. Je +5:14.

17 **sat not**. Ps +26:4.

mockers. He +11:36.

sat alone. Je 13:17. La 3:28. Ezk 3:24, 25. Da 7:28.

for. Je 1:10. 6:11. 20:8, 9.

indignation. Da +8:19.

18 **my pain**. Je 14:19. Ps 6:3. 13:1-3. La 3:1-18.

perpetual. Jb +4:20 (S#5331h).

my wound. Je 30:12, 15. Jb 34:6. Mi 1:9.

as a. Je 1:18, 19. 20:7. Ezk 5:22, 23.

and as. Je 14:3. Jb 6:15-20. Is 58:11.

fail. Heb. be not sure. Ps 78:8, 37. 93:5. Pr 11:13. Is 7:9mg. 22:23. Mi 1:14mg.

19 **If**. Je +7:5.

return. ver. 10-18. Je 20:9. Ex 6:29, 30. Jon 3:2.

stand. ver. 1. Dt +10:8. Lk +21:36.

take. Ge +18:25. Le 10:10. Is 32:5, 6. Ezk 22:26. 44:23. He 5:14.

as my. Ex 4:12, 15, 16. Lk 10:16. 12:12. 21:15.

let them. Je 38:20, 21. Ezk 2:7. 3:10, 11. Ac 20:27. 2 C 5:16. Ga 1:10. 2:5.

20 **I will**. Je 1:18, 19. 6:27. Ezk 3:9. Ac 4:8-13, 29-31. 5:29-32.

fight. 2 T 3:12. 1 P 5:10.

but. Je 20:11, 12. Ps 124:1-3. 129:1, 2. Ro 8:31-39.

for. Je 20:11, 12. Ps 46:7, 11. Is +7:14. 8:9, 10. 41:10. Ac 18:9, 10. 2 T 4:16, 17, 22.

21 **deliver**. Ge 48:16. Ps 27:2. 37:40. Is 49:24, 25. 54:17. Mt 6:13. Lk +21:36. Ro 16:20. 2 C 1:10.

redeem. Ex 6:6. 13:13.

the terrible. Is 13:11. 25:3-5. 29:5, 6, 20.

JEREMIAH 16

1 **The word**. Je +1:2, 4. 2:1.

2 **not take**. Ge 19:14. Mt 24:19. Lk 21:23. 23:29. 1 C 7:26, 27.

3 **thus saith**. ver. 5, 9.

their fathers. Je 6:21.

that begat. Is 66:9.

4 **die**. Je 14:16. 15:2, 3. Ps 78:64.

not. ver. 5-7. Je 22:18. 25:33. Am 6:9, 10.

neither. Je 7:33. 22:19. 36:30. Ps 79:1-3.

as dung. Je 8:2. 9:22. 25:33. 1 K 14:10, 11. 21:23, 24. 2 K 9:10, 36, 37. Jb 20:7. Ps 83:10. Is 5:25mg. Zp 1:17. Ml 2:3.

consumed. Je +12:12. 14:15.

meat. Je 34:20. Ps 79:2. Is 18:6. Ezk 39:17-20. Re 19:17, 18.

5 **Enter**. ver. 6, 7. Ezk 24:16-23.

mourning. or, mourning feast. Am 6:7.

neither go to lament. Mt 8:22. Lk 9:60.

I have. Je 15:1-4. Dt 31:17. 2 Ch 15:5, 6. Is 27:11. Zc 8:10. Re 6:4.

taken away. Heb. asaph. Ps 26:9. 27:10.

6 **the great**. Je 13:13. Is 9:14-17. 24:2. Ezk 9:5, 6. Am 6:11. Re 6:15. 20:12.

they. ver. +4. Je 22:18, 19.

nor cut. Le +19:28.

bald. Is +3:24.

7 **tear themselves**. or, break bread. Is +58:7. Mt 25:35.

cup. Pr 31:6, 7.

8 **the house**. Je 15:17. Ps 26:4. Ec 7:2-4. Is 22:12-14. Am 6:4-6. Mt 24:38. Lk 17:27-29. 1 C 5:11. Ep +5:11.

to sit. Am 6:1.

9 **the Lord of hosts, the God of**. Je +7:3.

I will. Je 7:34. 25:10. Is 24:7-12. Ezk 26:13. Ho 2:11. Re 18:22, 23.

the bride. Je 7:34. 25:10. 33:11.

10 **Wherefore**. Je +2:35. 5:19. 13:22. 22:8, 9. Dt 29:24, 25. 1 K 9:7-9. Ho 12:8.

evil. Is +45:7.

11 **Because**. Je +1:16. 2:8. Ne 9:26-29. Ps 106:35-41. Da 9:10-12.

walked. Je 8:2. 9:14. Ezk 11:21. 1 P 4:3.

my law. Ex ch. 20.

12 **worse**. Je +7:26. 13:10. Jg 2:19. Mt 23:32. 2 T 3:13.

imagination. or, stubbornness. Je +3:17mg. Dt 9:27. 1 S 15:23.

evil. Je 17:9. Ge 6:5. 8:21. Ec 8:12. 9:3. Mk 7:21-23. He +3:12-14.

13 **will I**. Je 6:15. Le 18:26-28. Dt 4:26-28. 28:36, 63-65. 29:28, 29. 30:17, 18. Jsh 23:15, 16. 2 Ch 7:20.

into a land. Je 14:18. 15:4, 14. 17:4. 22:28. 52:27.

and. Dt 4:26-28. 28:36. Ps 81:12.

14 **behold**. Je 23:7, 8. Is 43:18, 19. Ho 3:4, 5.

that brought. Ex +20:2. Dt 15:15. Mi 6:4.

15 **that brought**. Je 3:18. 24:6. 30:3, 10. 31:8. 32:37. 50:19. Dt 30:3-5. Ps 106:47. Is 11:11-16. 14:1. 27:12, 13. 43:5, 6. Ezk 34:12-14. 36:24, 27, 28. 37:21-24. 39:28, 29. Am 9:14, 15. Lk 21:20-24.

the land of the north. Je 3:12, 18. 6:22. 10:22. 23:8. 31:8. Is 41:25.

bring them again. Je 30:3. Ezk 38:14.

I gave. Dt +30:3.

16 **I will send**. Je 25:9. Ezk 12:13. Am 4:2. Hab 1:14, 15. Mk 1:17.

fish them. Jb 19:6. Ezk 32:3. Ho 7:12. Mt +13:47.

hunters. Ge 10:9. 1 S 24:11. 26:20. Mi 7:2.

every mountain. Is 24:17, 18. Am 5:19. 9:1-3. Lk 17:34-37. Re 6:15-17.

holes of the rocks. Je 13:4. Ge +19:30. Is 7:19.

17 mine eyes. Ps +11:4. 90:8. 139:3, 4. Pr 5:21. Is 29:15. Ezk 8:12. 9:9. Mt 12:36. Lk 12:1-3. 1 C 4:5.

18 double. Ge +43:12.

they have defiled. Je 3:1, 2, 9. Le +18:25, 27, 28. Zp 3:1-5.

my land. Dt +32:43.

the carcases. Le 18:21. 26:30. Ezk 11:18, 21. 43:7-9.

19 my strength. Je 17:17. Ps +18:1. 27:5. 144:1, 2. Is 25:4.

fortress. Ps +31:3. Pr 18:10. Na 1:7.

refuge. Ps +9:9. Ezk 11:16.

Gentiles. Ps 67:2-7. 68:31. 72:7-12. 86:9. Mt +12:18. Lk 1:31-33. Re 7:9-11. 11:15. 21:23, 24.

Surely. Je +3:23. Hab 2:18, 19. 1 P 1:18.

vanity. Dt +32:21.

wherein. Je +2:11. 10:5. Is 44:10.

20 make gods. Ps 115:4-8. 135:14-18. Is 36:19. 37:19. Ho 8:4-6. Ac 19:26. Ga 1:8. 4:8-11.

21 I will this. Ex 9:14-18. 14:4. Ps 9:16. Ezk 6:7. 24:24, 27. 25:14.

and they. Je 33:2. Ex +15:3. Ps 83:18. Is 43:3. Am 5:8.

my name. Ex 3:15. +6:3. 15:3.

The Lord. *or*, JEHOVAH. Ps 83:18.

JEREMIAH 17

1 written with. Jb 19:23, 24. Ps 45:1.

point. Heb. nail.

graven. Pr 3:3. 7:3. 2 C 3:3.

table of. Ex +25:21.

and upon. Le 4:7, 18, 25. Ho 12:11.

2 their children. Je 7:18. Ho 4:13, 14.

their altars. 2 Ch 33:3, 19. Ps 78:58. Is 1:29. 17:7, 8.

groves. 2 K +17:10. Is 66:17.

green trees. Is +57:5.

high hills. 2 K +17:10.

3 my. Je 26:18. Is 2:2, 3. La 5:17, 18. Mi 3:12. 4:1, 2.

I will. Je 15:13. 52:15-20. 2 K 24:13. 25:13-16. Is 39:4-6. La 1:10. Ezk 7:20-22.

and thy. 2 K +21:3. Is 27:9.

4 thyself. Heb. in thyself.

shalt. Je 16:13. 25:9-11. Le 26:31-34. Dt 4:26, 27. 28:25. Jsh 23:15, 16. 1 K 9:7. 2 K 25:21.

and I. Je 5:29. 27:12, 13. Dt 28:47, 48. Ne 9:28. Is 14:3.

for. ver. 27. Dt 29:26-28. 32:22-25. Is 5:25. La 1:12. Ezk 21:31, 32. Na 1:5, 6. Mt +25:41.

for ever. Heb. *olam*, Ex +12:24.

5 Cursed. La +3:65.

that trusteth. Jg 4:9. Ps +60:11. 62:9. Is 30:1, etc. 31:1, etc. 36:6. Ezk 29:6, 7.

flesh. Ge +6:3.

his arm. 2 Ch 32:8.

whose. 2 Ch 12:1. Ezk 6:9. He +3:12.

6 like. Je 48:6. Jb 8:11-13. 15:30-34. Ps +1:4. 92:7. 129:6-8. Is 1:30.

and shall. 2 K 7:2, 19, 20. Jb 20:17.

a salt. Dt +29:23.

7 Blessed is. Ps +1:1. Is +26:3, 4. +30:18. Ep 1:12.

hope. Ps +42:11.

8 he shall. Jb 8:16. Ps +1:3. 92:10-15. Pr 11:28. Is 58:11. Ezk 31:4-10. 47:12. Re 22:2.

the waters. *or*, rivulet. Je 15:18. Is 58:11. Jn 4:13, 14.

drought. *or*, restraint. Je 14:1mg.

9 The heart. Je 16:12. Ge 6:5. 8:21. Jb 14:4. 15:14-16. Ps 51:5. 53:1-3. Pr 28:26. Ec 9:3. Mt 12:34, 35. 15:19. Mk 7:21, 22. Jn 3:19. Ro 8:7, 8. 1 C 2:14. Ep 4:17-19. 5:8. T 1:15. He +3:12. Ja 1:14, 15.

10 the Lord. Ne +9:6.

search the heart. Je 11:20. 1 S 16:7. 1 Ch +28:9. 29:17. 2 Ch 6:30. Jb 13:9. Ps 7:9. 26:2. 139:1, 2, 23, 24. Pr 17:3. Jn +2:25. Ro *8*:27. He 4:12, 13. Re *2*:23.

try. Ps +11:5.

even. Mt +16:27.

fruit. Je 6:19. 21:14. Mi 7:13. Ro 6:21. Ga 6:7, 8.

11 sitteth, etc. *or*, gathereth *young* which she hath not brought forth.

he that. Je 5:27, 28. 22:13, 17. Pr 1:18, 19. 13:11. 15:27. 21:6. 28:8, 16, 20, 22. Is 1:23, 24. Ezk 22:12, 13. Ho 12:7, 8. Am 3:10. 8:4-6. Mi 2:1, 2, 9. 6:10-12. 7:3. Hab 2:6-12. Zp 1:9. Zc 5:4. 7:9-13. Ml +3:5. Mt 23:14. 1 T 6:8, 9. T 1:11. Ja +5:3-5. 2 P 2:3, 14.

shall leave. Pr 23:5. Ec 5:13-16.

in the midst. Ps +102:24.

a fool. Lk 12:20.

12 glorious high. 2 Ch 2:5, 6. Ps +11:4. 96:6. He 4:14, 16.

13 the hope. ver. +7, 17. Ps 22:4, 5. Ac 28:20. 1 T 1:1.

all that. Is +42:17. 65:11-14. 66:5. Ezk 16:63. 36:32. Da 12:2.

they that. ver. 5. Ps 73:27. Pr 14:14. Is 1:28.

written. Pr 10:7. Lk 10:20. Jn 8:6-8. Re 20:15.

forsaken. Je +1:16. Ps 36:8, 9. Jn 4:10, 14. 7:37, 38. Re 7:17. 21:6. 22:1, 17.

waters. Je +2:13.

14 Heal. Je 15:18. 31:18. Ge 20:17. Dt +32:39. 1 K 13:6. 2 K 20:1-3. 2 Ch 16:12. Ps 6:2, 4. 12:4. 60:1, 2. +103:3. Is 6:10. 57:18, 19. Mt 8:2, 3, 5-7. 14:35, 36. 15:22. 17:14-18. Mk 1:40, 41. 7:32-35. Lk 4:18. 5:12, 13. 17:12-18.

save. Je 15:20. Ps 60:5. 106:47. Mt 8:25. 14:30.

thou. Dt 10:21. Ps 109:1. 148:14.

15 Where is the word. Je 20:7, 8. Is 5:19. Ezk 12:22, 27, 28. Am 5:18. 2 P 3:3, 4.

16 I have. Je 1:4-10. 20:9. Ezk 3:14-19. 33:7-9. Am 7:14, 15. Ja 1:19. 3:1.

to follow thee. Heb. after thee. Je 3:19mg. 13:27mg. 32:40mg. 48:2mg. 2 S 7:8mg. Ps 78:71mg. Ezk 13:3mg. Am 7:15mg.

neither. Je 4:19, 20. 9:1. 13:17. 14:17-21. 18:20. Ro 9:1-3.

desired. Jb 36:20. Am 5:18.

woeful. ver 9 (desperately wicked). Jb +34:6 (S#605h).

day. ver. +18.

that. Ac 20:20, 27. 2 C 1:12. 2:17. 4:3, 4.

17 a terror. Jb 31:23. Ps 77:2-9. 88:15, 16.

thou. ver. 7, 13. Je 16:19. Ps 41:1. 59:16. Na 1:7. Ep 6:13.

18 Let them. Je +10:25.

confounded. Je 20:11. Ps 35:4, 26, 27. 40:14. 70:2. 83:17, 18.

but let not me be confounded. Ps 25:2, 3. 71:1.

bring. Je +11:8.

the day of evil. ver. 16, 17. Je 18:19-23. Is +45:7.

destroy them with double destruction. Heb. break them with a double breach. Je 11:20. 14:17. Jb 16:14. Ezk 21:6.

double. Ge +43:12.

19 A.M. cir. 3393. B.C. cir. 611.

Go and stand. Je +7:2.

gate. Ge +14:7.

20 Hear. Je +7:2. 13:18. Ps 49:1, 2. Ezk 2:7. 3:17.

21 Take. Dt 4:9, 15, 23. 11:16. Jsh 23:11. Pr 4:23. Is 65:5. Mk +4:24. Lk +8:18. Ac 20:28. He 2:1-3. 12:15, 16.

yourselves. Heb. *nephesh*, Ge +27:31.

bear. ver. 22-27. Ex +20:8. 23:12. Nu 15:32-36. Jn 5:9-12. Ga 4:9-11. Col 2:16, 17.

22 neither do. Ex +20:8-10. 23:12. Lk 6:5, 9-11. Re 1:10.

23 they obeyed. Ezk 20:13, 16, 21.

made. Pr +29:1. Zc 7:11, 12.

not hear. Je +7:26.

nor. Je +6:8. Pr 1:3, 5. 5:12. 8:10. Jn 3:19-21.

24 if. Je +7:5. Ezk 43:11.

diligently hearken. Dt +15:5. +26:16. Ezr +7:10. Is 21:7. Zc 6:15. Lk +11:28. He 11:6. 2 P 1:5-10.

to bring. ver. 21, 22. Ne 13:15, 19. Jn 5:10.

sabbath day. Is 56:2, 6, 7.

but hallow. Is +58:13, 14.

25 shall there. Je 22:4.

sitting. Je 13:13. 22:30. 33:15, 17, 21. 2 S 7:16. 1 K 9:4, 5. Ps 89:27, 29-37. 132:11, 12. Is +9:6, 7. Lk 1:32, 33. Ac 2:34-36.

riding. Dt 17:16. 1 S 8:11. 2 S 8:4.

and this. Ex 12:14. Ps 132:13, 14. Am 9:11, 15. He 12:22.

for ever. Heb. *olam*, Ex +12:24.

26 from the cities. Je 32:44. 33:13. Jsh 15:21, etc.

the plain. Jsh 15:33. Zc 7:7.

the south. Ge +12:9.

bringing. Le ch. 1-7. Ezr 3:3-6, 11.

burnt offerings. Le +23:12.

sacrifices. Ge 46:1. Ex 18:12. Jg 2:5. 1 S 1:21. 6:15. 11:15. 2 S 6:13. 1 Ch 21:28. 29:21. 2 Ch 5:6. Jon 1:16.

meat offerings. Le +23:13.

incense. Je 6:20. 41:5. Ex +39:38. Le 2:1. 5:11. 6:15. 24:7. Nu 5:15. 1 Ch 9:29. Ne 13:5. Is 43:23. 60:6. 66:3.

sacrifices of praise. Le +7:12. Ps 65:1. 119:108. Re 1:5, 6.

27 if. Je +7:5.

ye will not hearken. ver. 24. Je 6:17. 26:4-6. 44:16. Is 1:20. Zc 7:11-14. He 12:25.

hallow the sabbath. ver. +21, 22. Is +58:13, 14. Ezk 22:8.

then. ver. +4. Je 15:14. 21:10, 12, 14. 32:29. 34:2, 22. 37:8, 10. 38:3, 18, 21-23. 39:8. 49:27. 50:32. 52:13. Dt +32:22. 2 K 25:9. 2 Ch 36:19. Ps 74:6-8. 79:5. Is 9:18, 19. 64:11. La 4:11. Ezk 16:41. 24:9. Ho 8:14. Am 1:4, 7, 10, 12, 14. 2:2, 4, 5.

shall devour. Je 39:8. 52:13. 2 K 25:9. 2 Ch 36:19. Am 2:5.

shall not. Mt +3:12.

JEREMIAH 18

2 A.M. 3396. B.C. 608.

and go. Je 13:1. 19:1, 2. Is 20:2. Ezk 4:1, etc. 5:1. Am 7:7, 8. He 1:1.

cause. Je 23:22. Ac 9:6.

3 I went. Jon 1:3. Jn 15:14. Ac 26:19.

wheels. *or*, frames, *or*, seats. Ex 1:16.

4 made of clay was marred in. *or*, made was marred, as clay in.

made it again. Heb. returned and made. Nu 11:4mg.

as. ver. 6. Is 45:9. Ro 9:20-23.

6 cannot I do. ver. 4. Is 64:8. Da 4:34, 35. Mt 20:15. Ro 11:32-36.

7 to pluck. Je +1:10. 12:14-17. 25:9, etc. 45:4. Am 9:8. Jon 3:4.

8 If. Je +7:5.

that nation. Je 7:3-7. 36:3. Jg 10:15, 16. 1 K 8:33, 34. 2 Ch 12:6, 7. Is 1:16-19. Ezk 18:21. 33:11, 13. Jon 2:5-10. Lk 13:3-5.

I will repent. Je 15:6. 26:3, 13, 19. 42:10. Ge +6:6. Ex 32:12, 14. Dt 32:36. Jg 2:18. 2 S 24:16. Ps 90:13. 106:45. 135:14. Ho 11:8. 13:14. Jl 2:13, 14. Am 7:3-6. Jon 3:9, +10. 4:2.

9 to build. Je +1:10. Am 9:11-15.

plant. Je +11:17.

10 If. Je +7:5.

do evil. Je 7:23-28. Ps 125:5. Ezk 3:20. 18:24. 33:18. Zp 1:6.

then. Nu 14:22, 23, 34. 1 S 2:30. 13:13, 14. 15:11, 35.

repent. Ge +6:6. Jon +3:10.

11 go to. Ge 11:3, 4, 7. 2 K 5:5. Is 5:5. Ja 4:13. 5:1.

and devise. ver. 18. Je 4:23. 11:19. 51:11. Mi 2:3.

return. Je +35:15. 2 K 17:13. 27:13. La 3:39-41. Ezk 13:22.

12 There. Je +2:25. 2 K 6:33. Is 57:10. Ezk 37:11.

we will walk. Je 3:17. 7:24. 11:8. 16:12. 23:17. 44:17. Ge 6:5. 8:21. Dt 29:19. Mk 7:21, 22. Lk 1:51.

imagination. Je 3:17.

13 Ask. Je 2:10-13.

who. 1 S 4:7. Is 66:8. 1 C 5:1.

virgin. Je 2:13. 14:17. 31:4. 46:11. Nu +21:25. 2 K 19:21. Is 23:12. 37:22. 47:1. La 1:15. 2:13. Am 5:2.

a very. Je 5:30. 23:14. Ho 6:10.

14 Will. Jn 6:68.

the snow, etc. *or*, my fields for a rock, *or for* the snow of Lebanon? shall the running waters be forsaken for the strange cold *waters*? Je 2:13. Jb 9:30.

15 my people. Je 2:13, 19, 32. 3:21. 13:25. 17:13.

burned. Je 10:15. 16:19. 44:15-19, 25. Is 41:29. 65:7. Ho 2:13. 11:2.

caused. Is 3:12. 9:16. Ezk 14:10. Ml 2:8. Mt 15:6-9. 23:13, 15. Mk +12:24. Ro 14:21.

the ancient. Heb. *olam*, Jb +22:15.

paths. Je +6:16.

to walk. Je 19:5. Is 57:14.

a way. Pr 15:19. Is 57:14. 62:10.

16 desolate. Je 2:15. 4:7, 27. 6:8. 7:34. 9:11. 10:22, 25. 12:11. 19:8. 25:9, 11, 18, 38. 26:9. 33:10. 34:22. 44:2, 22. 49:13. 50:13. Le 26:31-34, 43. Dt 29:23. 2 Ch 36:21. Is +1:7. 6:11. 24:12. 64:10. La 1:4. 5:18. Ezk 6:14. 12:19. 33:28, 29. Mi 3:12. 7:13. Mt 23:38.

a perpetual. Heb. *olam*, Ge +9:12. 2 Ch +29:8.

shall be. Dt 28:59.

wag. 2 K 19:21. Jb 16:4. Ps 22:7. 44:14. 109:25. Is 37:22. La 2:15. Mt 27:39. Mk 15:29.

17 scatter. Je +9:16.

east wind. Ge +41:6.

show. Je 2:27. 32:33. Dt +31:17. Jg 10:13, 14.

the day. Je 46:21. Dt 32:35. Pr 7:25, 26.

18 come. ver. 11. Je 11:19. Ps 21:11. Is 32:7. Mi 2:1-3.

for the law. Je 13:13, 14. 14:14-16. 29:25-29. Le 10:11. 1 K 22:24. Ml 2:7. Lk 11:45. Jn 7:47-49. 9:40.

counsel. 2 S 15:31. 17:14. Jb 5:13.

Come and let us smite. Je 26:11. Ps 52:2. 57:4. 64:2, 3. Pr 18:21.

with. *or*, for.

tongue. Ps +5:9.

and let us not. Je 5:12, 13. 43:2. 44:17.

19 Give. Je 20:12. Ps 55:16, 17. 56:1-4. 64:1-4. 109:4, 28. Mi 7:8. Lk 6:11, 12.

hearken. 2 K 19:16. Ne 4:4, 5. 6:9.

20 evil. 1 S 24:17-19. Ps 35:12. 38:20. 109:4, 5. Pr 17:13. Jn 10:32. 15:25.

digged. ver. 22. Jb 6:27. Ps 7:15. 35:7. 57:6. 119:95. Pr 26:27. Ec 10:8.

pit. Heb. *shuchah*, Pr +22:14 (**S#7745h**).

soul. Heb. *nephesh*, Ps +30:3.

Remember. Je 7:16. 11:14. 14:7-11, 20-22. 15:1. Ge 18:22-32. Ps 106:23. Ezk 22:30, 31. Zc 3:1, 2.

21 deliver. Je +10:25. 20:1-6, 11, 12. Ps 109:9-20.

pour out their blood. Heb. pour them out. Ps 63:10mg. Ezk 35:5.

let their wives. Je 15:2, 3, 8. 16:3, 4. Ex 22:24. Dt 32:25. La 5:3.

let their young. Je 9:21. 11:22. 2 Ch 36:17. Am 4:10.

22 a cry. Je 4:19, 20, 31. 6:26. 9:20, 21. 25:34-36. 47:2, 3. 48:3-5. Is 10:30. 22:1-4. Zp 1:10, 11, 16.

for. ver. 20.

pit. Heb. *shuchah*, Pr +22:14.

and hid. Je 20:10. Ps 56:5-7. 64:4, 5. +141:9.

23 thou. ver. 18. Je 11:18-20. 15:15. Ps 37:32, 33.

their counsel. Jn 11:53.

to slay me. Heb. for death. Je 15:2.

forgive not. Ps 35:4. 59:5. Is 2:9. Mt 18:18. Lk 23:34. Jn 20:23.

neither blot. Ps +51:1.

in the time. Je 8:12. 11:23. Is 10:3. Lk 21:22. Ro 2:5.

JEREMIAH 19

1 A.M. 3397. B.C. 607.

Go. ver. 10, 11. Je 18:2-4. 32:14. Is 30:14mg. La 4:2. 2 C 4:7.

bottle. **S#1228h**. ver. 10. 1 K 14:3mg. Compare Je +13:12.

the ancients of the people. Je 26:17. Ex 3:16. 12:21. 18:12, +21. Nu 11:16, 17. Jsh +20:4. 1 Ch 24:4-6. Ezk 9:6. Mt 26:3. 27:1, 41, 42.

ancients of the priests. Dt 21:2. 2 K 19:2. Is 37:2. Ac 5:21.

2 the valley. Jsh +15:8. Ne 2:13.

east gate. Heb. sun gate. Ne 3:29. or, the gate of potsherds. i.e. the pottery gate. Is 30:14.

and proclaim. Je 1:7. +2:2. +7:2. Ezk 3:10, 11. Jon 3:2. Mt 10:27. Ac 20:27.

3 Hear. Je +7:2. 13:18. Ps 2:10-12. 102:15. 110:5. Mt 10:18.

Lord of. ver. 15. Je +7:3.

I will bring. Je +6:19. Am +3:6.
evil. Is +45:7.
his ears. 1 S *3:11*. 4:16-18. 2 K *21:12*, 13. Is 28:19.

4 **forsaken**. Je +1:16. Da 9:5-15.
estranged. 2 K 21:4, 5, 7. 23:11, 12. 2 Ch 33:4-7.
burned. Je 7:9. 11:13. 18:15. 32:29-35. Dt 13:6, 13. 28:36, 64. 32:17.
whom neither. Dt 32:17.
filled. Je 2:30, 34. 7:31, 32. 22:17. 26:15, 23. 2 K 21:6, 16. 24:4. Is 59:7. La 4:13. Mt 23:34, 35. Lk 11:50. Re 16:6.

5 **the high**. 2 K +21:3.
to burn. Dt +18:10.
which. Je +3:16mg. Le 18:21.
neither. Ezk 38:10. Da 2:29.
mind. Ge +6:6.

6 **this**. ver. +2, 11, 12. Je 7:32, 33. Jsh 15:8. Is +30:33.

7 **I will make void**. Je 8:9. 49:7. 2 S 15:31. 17:14, 23. Ne 4:15. Jb 5:12, 13. 12:16, 17. Ps 33:10, 11. Pr +21:30. Is 7:7. 8:10. 19:3, 11-14. 28:17, 18. 29:14. 30:1-3. 44:25. La 3:37. Ob 8. Ro 3:31. 4:14. 1 C 1:19, 20. 3:19, 20. Ja 4:13-15.
the counsel. Is +28:18. Da +9:27.
I will cause. Je 9:21. 15:2, 9. 18:21. 22:25. 46:26. Le 26:17. Dt 28:25.
lives. Heb. *nephesh*, Ge +44:30.
and their. Je +7:33.

8 **desolate**. Je +18:16.
hissing. 2 Ch +29:8.

9 **eat the**. Le +26:29. Is 9:20.
lives. Heb. *nephesh*, Ge +44:30.

10 **break the bottle**. Je 48:12. 51:63, 64.

11 **Lord of hosts**. Je +6:6.
Even. Je 13:14. La 4:2. Da +2:44.
made whole. Heb. healed. Je 15:18.
bury. ver. 6. Je +7:31, 32.

12 **make**. lit. give. Je 10:13. 11:5.
as Tophet. Je +7:31.

13 **defiled**. 2 K 23:10, 12, 14. Ps 74:7. 79:1. Ezk 7:21, 22.
upon. Dt +22:8.
have poured. Je 7:18.
drink offerings. Le +23:13.

14 **from**. ver. 2, 3.
he stood. Je +7:2. Lk 21:37, 38.

15 **bring**. Je +11:8.
because. Je 35:15-17. 2 Ch +30:8. Zc 7:11-14.
hardened. Dt 10:16. 2 Ch 30:8mg.
that they. Je +7:26. Ps 58:2-5.

JEREMIAH 20

1 **Pashur**. i.e. *prosperity round about; freedom*, s#6583h. Je 20:1-3, 6. 21:1. 38:1. 1 Ch 9:12. Ezr 2:38. 10:22. Ne 7:41. 10:3. 11:12.

son of. 1 Ch 7:15, 17.
Immer. 1 Ch +9:12.
chief. 2 K 25:18. 2 Ch 35:8. Ac 4:1. 5:24.

2 **smote**. Je 1:19. 19:14, 15. 26:8. 36:26. 37:15, 16. 38:6. 2 Ch 24:21. Am 7:10-13. Mt 5:10-12. 21:35. 23:34-37. Ac 7:52. He +11:36, 37. Re 17:6.
the stocks. Pr +7:22.
in the high gate. Je 37:13. 38:7. Zc 14:10.

3 **Pashur**. Ac 4:5-7. 16:30, 35-39.
hath. Je 7:32. 19:2, 6. Ge 17:5, 15. 32:28. Is 8:3. Ho 1:4-9.
Magor-missabib. *that is*, Fear round about. i.e. *terror on every side*, s#4036h, only here. ver. 10. Je 6:25. 46:5. 49:29. Ps 31:13. La 2:22.

4 **I will make**. Dt 28:65-67. Jb 18:11-21. 20:23-26. Ps 73:18, 19. Ezk 26:17-21. Mt 27:4, 5.
thine. Je 29:21. 39:6, 7. Dt 28:32-34. 1 S 2:33. 2 K 25:7.
I will give. Je 19:15. 21:4-10. 25:9. 32:27-31.

5 **I will deliver**. Je 3:24. 4:20. 12:12. 15:13. 24:8-10. 32:3-5. 39:2, 8. Is +39:6. La 1:7, 10. 4:12. Ezk 22:25.
strength. Is 60:5mg.
labors. Dt +28:33.

6 **thou, Pashur**. Je 28:15-17. 29:21, 22, 32. Ac 13:8-11.
thy friends. ver. 4. Je 5:31. 6:13-15. 8:10, 11. 14:14, 15. 23:14-17, 25, 26, 32. Is 9:15. La 2:14. Ezk 13:4-16, 22, 23. 22:28. Mi 2:11. Zc 13:3. 2 P 2:1-3.
thou hast. Le 26:17. Dt 28:25.

7 **deceived**. *or*, enticed. Je 1:6-8, 18, 19. 4:10. 15:18. 17:16. Ex 5:22, 23. 22:16. Nu 11:11-15. 1 K 22:20mg. Ps 19:7. Ezk 14:9. Ho 2:14.
thou art. ver. 9. Ezk 3:14. Mi 3:8. 1 C 9:16.
I am. Je 15:10. 29:26. Ho 9:7. Lk +16:14. 1 C 4:9-13. He +11:36.

8 **I cried**. Je 4:19, etc. 5:1, 6, 15-17. 6:6, 7. 7:9. 13:13, 14. 15:1-4, 13, 14. 17:27. 18:16, 17. 19:7-11. 28:8.
the word. ver. +7. 2 Ch 36:16.
reproach. Ps +31:11.
derision. Lk +16:14.

9 **I will not**. Ex 4:13. 1 K 19:3, 4. Jon 1:2, 3. 4:2, 3. Lk 9:62. Ac 15:37, 38.
was in. Je 6:11. Jb 32:18-20. Ps 39:3. 119:11. Ezk 3:14. Ac 4:20. 17:16. 18:5. 1 C 9:16, 17. 2 C 5:13-15.
fire. Je 5:14. 23:29.
could not. Ac 4:20.

10 **I heard**. Ps 31:13. 57:4. 64:2-4. Mt 26:59, 60.
defaming. Ge 39:16. Ps 37:12.
fear. ver. +3.
Report. Je 18:18. Ne 6:6-13. Pr 10:18. Is 29:21. Ezk 22:9. Lk 20:20. Ac 6:11-15. 24:1-9, 13.
All my familiars. Heb. Every man of my

peace. Je 38:22mg. Jb 19:19mg. Ps 41:9mg. 55:13, 14. Lk 11:53, 54. 12:52, 53.
we shall. 1 K 19:2. 21:20. 22:8, 27. Mk 6:19-28. Ac 5:33. 7:54. 23:12-15.

11 the Lord. Je +1:8, 19. 15:20. Is 41:10, 14. Ro 8:31. 2 T 4:17.
a mighty. Ps +99:3.
my. Je 17:18. Dt 32:35, 36. Ps 27:1, 2. Jn 18:4-6.
not prevail. Je 1:19. 15:20. +17:18. Ps +37:9, 12-15. 47:3. Pr +16:5. Is 41:11. 51:7, 8. 54:17. 60:14. +66:5. Da +12:2. Mi 7:9, 10. Ml 4:2, 3. Lk +16:25. Ro 16:20. 2 Th 1:4-8. Re 3:9. 18:20. 19:3.
everlasting. Heb. *olam*, Ge +17:7. Je 23:40. Ps 6:10. 35:26. 40:14. Is 45:16. Da +12:2, 3.

12 Lord of hosts. Je +6:6.
that. Je +17:10. Ps 11:5. 17:3.
let. Je +10:25.
me see. Is +66:24.
thy vengeance. Ps 109:6-20. Re 18:20. 19:2, 3.
for. 1 S 1:15. Ps 62:8. 86:4. Is 37:14. 38:14. 1 P 2:21-23. 4:19.

13 for. Ps 34:6. 35:9-11. 69:33. 72:4. 109:30, 31. Is 25:4. Ja 2:5, 6.
soul. Heb. *nephesh*, Ge +12:13.

14 Cursed be the day. Je +15:10. Jb 3:3-16.

15 A man child. lit. a son, a male. Je 1:5. Ge 21:5, 6. Is 40:13mg. Lk 1:14. Re 12:5.

16 as. Ge +19:24, 25. Ho 11:8.
repented not. Je 18:8. 26:13. Jon 3:4, 9, 10. 4:2.
let him. Je 4:19. 18:22. 48:3, 4. Ex 32:17, 18. Ezk 21:22. Ho 10:14. Am 1:14. 2:2. Zp 1:16.

17 he slew. Jb 3:10, 11, 16. 10:18, 19. Ec 6:3. He 10:36, 37.
grave. Heb. *qeber*, Ge +23:4.
always. Heb. *olam*, Ge +6:3.

18 Wherefore. Ge 27:46. Jb 3:20. 6:11. 7:6. 10:1. Ec 2:17. 4:1, 2. Jon 4:8.
came. Jb 3:20. 14:1, 13. La 3:1.
to see. Je 8:18. Ge 3:16-19. Ps 90:10. La 1:12. Jn 16:20. He 10:36.
with. Ps 69:19. Is 50:6. 51:7. Ac 5:41. 1 C 4:9-13. 2 T 1:12. He 10:36, 37. 11:36. 12:2. 13:13. 1 P 4:14-16.

JEREMIAH 21

1 A.M. cir. 3415. B.C. cir. 589.
The word. Je ch. 21, 34, 32, 33, 38, 39.
when. Je 32:1-3. 37:1. 52:1-3. 2 K 24:17-20. 25:1, 2. 1 Ch 3:15. 2 Ch 36:9-13.
Pashur. *Je +20:1.*
Melchiah. i.e. *the Lord is king,* **S#4441h.** Je +38:1, Malchiah. 1 Ch +9:12, Malchijah.
Zephaniah. Zp +1:1.
Maaseiah. i.e. *work of Jehovah; whose refuge is Jehovah,* **S#4641h.** Je 29:21, 25. 37:3. Ezr 10:18,

21, 22, 30. Ne 3:23. 8:4, 7. 10:25. 11:5, 7. 12:41, 42. Also **S#4641h:** Je 35:4. 1 Ch 15:18, 20. 2 Ch 23:1. 26:11. 28:7. 34:8.

2 Inquire. Je 37:3, 7. 38:14-27. 42:4-6. Jg 20:27. 1 S 10:22. 28:6, 15. 1 K 14:2, 3. 22:3-8. 2 K 1:3. 3:11-14. 22:13, 14. Ezk 14:3-7. 20:1-3.
for. Je 32:24. 39:1, 2. 52:3-6. 2 K 25:1, 2.
Nebuchadrezzar. i.e. *Nebo, the fire of brightness; may Nebo protect the crown,* **S#5019h.** ver. 7. Je 22:25. 24:1. 25:1, 9. 29:21. 32:1, 28. 35:11. 37:1. 39:1, 22. 43:10. 44:30. 46:2, 13, 26. 49:28, 30. 50:17. 51:34. 52:4, 12, 28, 29, 30. Ezk 26:7. 29:18, 19. 30:10.
according. Ex ch. 14, 15. Jsh ch. 10, 11. Jg ch. 4, 5. 1 S 7:10-12. 14:6-14. 17:45-50. 2 Ch 14:9-13. 20:1-30. 32:21. Ps 44:1-4. 46:8-11. 48:4-8. 105:5, etc. 136:1, etc. Is 59:1, 2.

4 Behold. Je 32:5. 33:5. 37:8-10. 38:2, 3, 17, 18. 52:18. Is 10:4. Ho 9:12.
and I. Je 39:3. Is 5:5. 13:4, 14. La 2:5, 7. Ezk 16:37-41. Zc 14:2. Mt 22:7.

5 I myself. Is 63:10. La 2:4, 5.
with an. Je 32:17. Ex +7:5.
strong arm. Je 20:5, 7.
anger. Is 5:25. Na 1:5, 6.

6 I will. Je 7:20. 12:3, 4. 33:12. 36:29. Ge 6:7. Is 6:11. 24:1-6. Ezk 14:13, 17, 19, 21. 33:27-29. Ho 4:3. Mi 3:12. Zp 1:3. Lk 21:24.
they. Je 32:24. 34:17. 42:22. Ezk 5:12, 13. 7:15. 12:16.

7 I will. Je 24:8-10. 32:4. 34:3, 19-22. 37:17. 38:18, 21-23. 39:4-7. 52:8-11, 24-27. 2 K 25:5-7, 18-21. 2 Ch 36:17-20. La 4:20. Ezk 12:12-16. 17:11, 16, 20, 21. 21:25, 26.
life. Heb. *nephesh*, Ge +44:30.
he shall. Je 13:14. Dt 28:50. 2 Ch 36:17. Is 13:17, 18. 27:11. 47:6. Ezk 7:9. 8:18. 9:5, 6, 10. Hab 1:6-10.

8 I set. Dt 11:26. 30:15, 19. Is 1:19, 20. Re +3:20.
life. Dt 32:47.
death. Pr 11:19. 14:12. Jn 3:18, 36. Ro 6:23.

9 that abideth. ver. +7. Je 27:13. 38:2, 17-23.
life. Heb. *nephesh*, Ge +44:30.
a prey. Je 38:2. 39:18. 45:5.

10 I have. Ezk +15:7. Am 9:4.
face. Ge +19:13.
it shall. Je +17:27. 26:6. Zc 1:6.

11 the house. Je 13:18. 17:20. Mi 3:1.

12 house. Is 7:2, 13. Lk 1:69.
Execute. Heb. Judge. Je 5:28. 22:2, 3, 15-17. 23:5, 6. 33:15. 2 S 8:15. 1 K 10:9. 1 Ch 18:14. Jb 29:12-14. Ps 72:1-4, 12-14. 82:2-4. Is 1:17. +11:4. 16:3-5. 32:1, 2. Ezk 45:9-12. Mi 6:8. Zc 7:9-11. Re 19:11.
morning. Ex 18:13. Ps 101:8. Ec 10:16, 17. Zp 3:5.
deliver. Jb 29:12-17. Ps 72:12-14. 82:4. Pr 24:11, 12. 31:8, 9. Is 1:17. Lk 18:3-5. Ro 13:4.

lest. ver. 5, +14. Je 5:14. Le +26:28. Dt 22:18-22, 31. 24:8-14. +32:22. Zp 1:18.

none. Mt +3:12.

13 **I am**. ver. 5. Je 23:30-32. Ex 13:8, 20. Ezk +15:7.

inhabitant. Heb. inhabitress. Je +10:17mg.

of the valley. Jsh 15:8. Ps 125:2. Is 22:1.

Who. Je 7:4. 49:4, 5, 16. 2 S 5:6, 7. La 4:12. Ob 3, 4. Mi 3:11.

14 **punish**. Heb. visit upon. Je +9:25mg.

according. Je 6:19. 17:10. 32:19. Pr 1:31. Is 3:10, 11. Ga 6:7, 8.

kindle a fire. ver. +10. Is +30:33.

in the. Je 22:7. Is 10:18, 19. 27:10, 11. 37:24. Ezk 20:46-48. Zc 11:1.

forest. Je 22:7.

shall. Je 52:13. 2 Ch 36:19.

JEREMIAH 22

1 A.M. cir. 3406. B.C. cir. 598.

Go. Je 21:11. 34:2. 1 S 15:16-23. 2 S 12:1. 24:11, 12. 1 K 21:18-20. 2 Ch 19:2, 3. 25:15, 16. 33:10. Ho 5:1. Am 7:13. Mk 6:18. Lk 3:19, 20.

2 **Hear**. ver. 29. Je +7:2. 13:18.

that sittest. ver. 4, 30. Je 17:25. 29:16, 17. 36:30. Is +9:7. Lk 1:32, 33.

enter. Je 7:2. 17:20.

3 **Execute**. Je 9:24. Je +21:12. Ex 23:6-9. Le +19:15. Dt 16:18-20. 25:1. 2 S 23:3. Mi 3:11. +6:8.

judgment and. ver. 15. Ge +1:26. Ezk 18:5mg. Jn +7:24.

do no wrong. ver. +17.

do no violence. Ml +3:5. Lk 3:14.

stranger. Je 7:6. 14:8. Ezk +47:22.

fatherless. Ex +22:22.

widow. Is +1:17.

neither. ver. 17. Je 7:6. 26:16. Dt 19:10-13. 2 K 24:4. Ps 94:21. Pr 6:17. Is 1:15-20. Jl 3:19.

4 **if**. Je +7:5.

then. Je +17:25.

upon the throne of David. Heb. for David upon his throne.

5 **if**. Je +7:5. 17:27. 2 Ch 7:19, 22. Is 1:20.

I swear. Ge 22:16. Nu 14:28-30. Dt 32:40-42. Ps 95:11. Am 6:8. 8:7, 8. He 3:18. 6:13, 17.

that. Je +7:13, 14. 26:6-9. 39:8. Mi 3:12.

6 **unto**. ver. 24. Je 21:11. Ge 37:25. Dt 3:25. SS 5:15.

house of Judah. Je +3:18.

Thou. Ge 31:21. SS 4:1.

Lebanon. ver. 23. 1 K 7:2. Is 33:9.

surely. Je 4:20. 7:34. 9:11. 19:7, 8. 21:14. 25:9, 10. 26:6-9, 18. Ps 107:34. Is 6:11. 24:1-6. 27:10. Ezk 33:27, 28.

7 **I will**. Je 4:6, 7. 5:15. 6:4. 50:20-23. 51:27, 28. Is 10:3-7. 13:3-5. 54:16, 17. Ezk 9:1-7. Mt 22:7.

cut. Je 21:14. Is 10:33, 34. 27:10, 11. 37:24. Zc 11:1.

cedars. Je 21:14.

8 **many nations**. Dt 29:23-25. 1 K 9:7-9. 2 Ch 7:20-22. La 2:15-17. 4:12. Da 9:7.

9 **they shall answer**. Je 2:17-19. 40:2, 3. 50:7. Dt 29:25-28. 1 K 9:9. 2 K 22:17. 2 Ch 34:25. Da 9:7.

10 **Weep ye not**. 2 K 22:20. 23:30. 2 Ch 35:23-25. Ec 4:2. Is 57:1. La 4:9. Lk 23:28.

sore. 2 K +20:3.

for him. ver. 11. 2 K 23:30-34. Ezk 19:3, 4.

11 **Shallum**. 2 K +15:10. 2 Ch 36:1-4, Jehoahaz.

12 **he shall die**. ver. 18. 2 K 23:34.

13 **unto**. ver. 18. 2 K 23:35-37. 2 Ch 36:4.

buildeth. Le +19:13. +Dt 24:14, 15. Jb 24:10, 11. Mi 3:10. Hab 2:9-11. Ml +3:5. 1 T +5:18. Ja +5:4.

work. lit. wages. Le +19:13. Lk 10:7.

14 **I will**. Pr 17:19. 24:27. Is 5:8, 9. 9:9, 10. Da 4:30. Ml 1:4. Lk 14:28, 29.

large. Heb. through aired.

windows. or, my windows. lit. "holes." Je 9:21. Ex 8:6.

ceiled with cedar. 2 S 7:2. 2 Ch 3:5. SS 1:17. Hg 1:4.

vermilion. Ezk 23:14. Na 2:3.

15 **thy**. ver. 18. 2 K 23:25. 1 Ch 3:15.

eat. 1 K 4:20-23. 2 Ch 35:7, 8, 12-18. Ec 2:24. 9:7-10. 10:16, 17. Is 33:16. Lk 11:41. Ac 2:46. 1 C 10:31.

and do. ver. +3. Je +21:12. 2 K 22:2. 23:25. 2 Ch 34:2. Pr 20:28. 21:3. 25:5. 29:4. 31:9. Is +9:7.

judgment and justice. ver. 3.

then. Je 42:6. Dt +4:40. Ps 128:1, 2. Ec 8:12. Is 3:10.

16 **judged**. Je 5:28. Ge +1:29. Jb 29:12-17. Ps 72:1-4, 12, 13. 82:3, 4. 109:31. Pr 21:13. 22:22, 23. 24:11, 12. Is 1:17.

know me. Je 9:3, 16, 24. 31:33, 34. 1 S 2:12. 1 Ch +28:9. Ps +9:10. Jn 8:19, 54, 55. 16:3. 17:3, 6. T 1:16. Ja 1:27. 1 J 2:3, 4.

17 **thine eyes**. Jsh 7:20, 21. Jb 31:7. Ps 119:36, 37. Ezk 19:6. 33:31. Mk 7:21, 22. Ja 1:14, 15. 2 P 2:13, 14. 1 J 2:15, 16.

covetousness. Ex +18:21. Ps 10:3. Lk 12:15-21. 16:13, 14. Ro 1:29. 1 C +6:9, 10. Ep +5:3-5. Col 3:5. 1 T +6:9, 10. 2 P 2:3, 14.

shed. ver. 3. Je 6:11. 26:22-24. 1 K 21:19. 2 K 24:4. 2 Ch 36:8. Ezk 19:6. Zp 3:3.

violence. or, incursion. Je 8:6. 23:10mg. 2 S 18:27. 1 C 6:10.

18 **They**. ver. 10. Je 16:4, 6. 2 K 23:34-37. 2 Ch 21:19, 20. 35:25.

Ah my brother. 2 S 1:26. 3:33-38. 1 K 13:29, 30.

19 **buried**. Je 36:30. Jb +22:6. 2 Ch 36:6.

burial. Heb. qeburah, Ge +35:20.

of an ass. Je +7:33. 15:3. 36:6, 30. 1 K 14:10, 11. 21:23, 24. 2 K 24:6. 2 Ch 36:6. Ec 6:3.

20   **Go**. Ge +3:22.

    lift. Ge +22:13.

    and cry. Je 2:36, 37. 30:13-15. 2 K 24:7. Is 20:5, 6. 30:1-7. 31:1-3.

    Bashan. Dt +32:14.

    passages. Nu 27:12. 33:47, 48. Dt 32:49.

    for. ver. 22. Je 4:30. 25:9, 17-27. La 1:2, 19. Ezk 23:9, 22.

21   **I spake**. Je 2:31. 6:16, 17. 35:15. 36:21-26. 2 Ch 33:10, 11. 36:16, 17. Pr 30:9.

    prosperity. Heb. prosperities. Ps 119:67. 122:7. Mk +4:19.

    will not hear. Pr 1:24-30.

    This. Je 3:25. 7:22-28. 32:30. Dt 9:7, 24. 31:27. 32:15-20. Jg 2:11-19. Ne 9:16, etc. Ps 106:6, etc. Is 48:8. Ezk 20:8, 13, 21, 28. 23:3-39.

22   **wind**. Je 4:11-13. 30:23, 24. Is 64:6. Ho 4:19. 13:15.

    thy pastors. Je 2:8. 3:15. 5:30, 31. 10:21. 12:10. 23:1, 2. Ezk 34:2-10. Zc 11:8, 17. Ac 7:51, 52.

    thy lovers. ver. +20.

    surely. Je +2:26, 27, 37. 20:11.

    wickedness. Is +45:7.

23   **inhabitant**. Heb. inhabitress. Je 10:17mg. Is 12:6mg.

    Lebanon. ver. 6. Zc 11:1, 2.

    makest. Je 21:13, 14. 48:28. 49:16. Nu 24:21. Am 9:2, 3. Ob 4. Hab 2:9.

    how gracious. Je 3:21. 50:4, 5. Ho 5:15. 6:1. 7:14.

    when. Je +4:31.

24   **As I live**. Dt +32:40.

    Coniah. i.e. *made ready of Jah; established of the Lord; Jehovah has established*, **S#3659h**. Je 22:24, 28. 37:1. 2 K +24:6, Jehoiachin. Je +24:1, Jeconiah. Mt 1:11, 12, Jechonias.

    the signet. ver. 6. SS 8:6. Hg 2:23.

25   **I will give**. ver. 28. Je +34:20. 2 K 24:15, 16.

    life. Heb. *nephesh*, Ge +44:30.

    whose. Pr 10:24.

26   **I will cast**. Je 15:2-4. 2 K 24:15. 2 Ch 36:9, 10. Is 22:17. Ezk 19:9-14.

27   **to the**. ver. 11. Je 44:14. 52:31-34. 2 K 25:27-30.

    desire. Heb. lift up their mind. Heb. *nephesh*, Ex +15:9. Je 44:14mg. Ps 86:4. Ezk 24:25mg.

28   **Coniah**. ver. +24.

    a despised. Je 48:38. 1 S 5:3-5. 2 S 5:21. Ps 31:12. Ho 8:8. 13:15. Ro 9:21-23. 2 T 2:20, 21.

    his seed. ver. 30. 1 Ch 3:17-24. Mt 1:12-16.

    which. Je +16:13.

29   **O earth**. Je 6:19. Dt 4:26. 31:19. +32:1. Is 1:1, 2. 34:1. Mi 1:2. 6:1, 2.

30   **Write**. 1 Ch 3:16, 17. Mt 1:12-16.

    childless. 1 Ch 3:16, 17. Mt 1:12.

sitting. Je +36:30. Ps 94:20. 1 Ch 22:8-10. 28:5. Mt 1:1, 11, 12, 16. Lk 1:27, 32, 33. 3:23, 31.

JEREMIAH 23

1   **Woe**. Je 2:8, 26. Ezk 13:3. 34:2. Zc 11:17. Mt 23:13-29. Lk 11:42-52.

    pastors. ver. 2, 11-15. Je 2:8. 10:21. 12:10. 22:22. 25:34-36. 50:6. Is 56:9-12. Ezk 22:25-29. 34:2-10, 21. Mi 3:11, 12. Zp 3:3, 4. Zc 11:5-7, 15-17. Mt 9:36. +15:14. Jn 10:10, 12-15.

2   **not visited**. 1 S 12:23. Jl 2:17. Mt 25:36, 42, 43-45. Ac 20:31. Ro 1:9. 2 C 11:2. 12:14, 15. Ga 4:19, 20. Ph 1:3-5, 8. Col 1:9-11, 28. 4:12, 13. 1 Th 2:6-12. 3:7-10. Ja 1:27.

    visit upon. ver. 34mg. Je +8:12. +11:22mg.

3   **I will gather**. ver. 8. Je 29:10, 14. 30:3, 18. 31:8, 10, 23. 32:37, 44. 33:7, 11, 26. Dt +30:3-5. Ps 14:7. 53:6. 85:1. 102:22. 106:47. 107:3. 147:2. Is 11:11-16. 27:12, 13. 43:5, 6. 52:12mg. 54:7. 56:8. Ezk 11:17. 28:25. 34:12-16, 23-31. 36:24, 33, 37. 37:21, 25. 38:8. 39:25, 27, 28. Ho 1:11. 6:11. Jl 3:1. Am 9:9, 14, 15. Mi 2:12. 4:6, 12. 7:12. Zp 3:18-20.

4   **set up shepherds**. Je 33:26. Is 11:11. 30:20, 21. Ho 3:3-5.

    feed. Is +40:11.

    neither. Nu 31:49. Jn 6:39, 40. 10:27-30. 17:12. 18:9. 1 P 1:5.

5   **the days**. ver. 7. Je 29:10. 30:3. 31:27, 31-34, 38. +33:14. Ge 22:18. +49:10. Am 9:11, 13. Lk 17:22. He 8:8.

    the Lord. Ne +9:6.

    I will raise. Je 33:15. Ps 72:1, 2. Is 32:1, 2. 40:10, 11. Da 9:24. Am 9:11. Zc 9:9. Re 19:11.

    righteous. Zc 13:7. 1 C 1:30.

    Branch. Is +11:1. 40:9, 11. Jn 1:45.

    King. Ps +47:2.

    shall reign. Ps 47:8. 96:10. 146:10. Is +9:7. +24:23. 32:1. 52:7. Mi +4:7. Zc +14:9. Lk +1:32, 33. 1 C +15:25. 2 T 2:12. Re 11:15, 17. 19:6. +20:4.

    and prosper. Je 22:30. Ps 45:4. Is 52:13mg. 53:10.

    and shall. Je +21:12. Is 40:10, 11.

    judgment and justice. Ge +1:26. Ps +7:8. Da 9:24. Am 9:11. Zc 9:9. Re 19:11.

    in the earth. Is 26:9. Re +5:10.

6   **Judah**. Dt 33:28, 29. Ps 130:7, 8. Is 12:1, 2. 33:22. 45:17. Ezk 37:24-28. Ho 1:7. Ob 17, 21. Zc 10:6. Mt 1:21. Lk 1:71-74. 19:9, 10. Ro 11:26, 27.

    dwell. Je 30:10. Dt +12:10. Is 2:4. 35:9. Zp +3:13. Zc 2:4, 5. 3:10. 14:9-11.

    and this. Is +7:14. +9:6. Mt +1:21-23.

    THE LORD OUR RIGHTEOUSNESS. Heb. *JEHOVAH-tsidkenu*. Je 33:15, 16. Ex +15:26. Dt 6:25. Is 45:24, 25. 54:17. 64:6. Da 9:24. Ro

3:22. 5:19. 10:2-4. 1 C 1:30. 2 C 5:21. Ph 3:9. 2 P 1:1.

7 the days come. ver. 3. Je +16:14, 15. 31:31-34. Is 43:18, 19.
which brought. Ex ch. 12-15.

8 which brought. ver. +3. Is 14:1. 65:8-10.
the house of Israel. Je +2:4.
the north country. Is 43:6. Ezk +38:6, 15. Da 11:44.
they shall dwell. Is 65:9, 10. Ezk 37:25. Am +9:14, 15. Zc 8:7, 8.
own land. Dt +32:43. Is +60:21.

9 A.M. 3399. B.C. 605.
heart. Je 9:1. 14:17, 18. 2 K 22:19, 20. Ezk 9:4, 6. Da 8:27. Hab 3:16.
because. Je +5:31.
like a drunken. Je 25:15-18. Ps 60:3. Is 6:5. 28:1. 29:9. 51:21. La 3:15. Ro 7:9.

10 full. Je 5:7, 8. 7:9. 9:2. Ezk 22:9-11. 23:9-12. Ho 4:2, 3. Ml +3:5. Mt 5:27, 28. 1 C +6:9, 10. Ga +5:19-21. He +13:4. Ja 4:4.
because. Zc 5:3, 4. 1 T 1:10.
swearing. Heb. cursing. Je 29:18mg. Ge 24:41 (oath). Le 5:1. Pr 29:24. Is 24:6.
the land. Je 12:3, 4. 14:2. La 1:2-4. Jl 1:10.
the pleasant. Je 9:10. Ps 107:34. Is 24:6.
course. or, violence. Je 8:6. 22:17. 2 S 18:27.

11 both. ver. 15. Je 5:31. 6:13. 8:10. Ezk 22:25, 26. Zp 3:4.
in. Je 7:10, 11, 30. 11:15. 32:34. 2 Ch 33:5, 7. 36:14. Ezk 7:20. 8:5, 6, 11, 16. 23:39. Mt 21:12, 13.

12 as. Je 13:16. Ps 35:6. 73:18. Pr +4:19.
in the. Jb 18:18. Is 8:22. Jn 12:35. 1 J 2:11. Ju 13.
the year. Je +8:12. Ex 32:34.

13 folly. or, an absurd thing. Heb. unsavory. Jb 1:22. 24:12. La 2:14.
prophets. Ho 9:7, 8.
prophesied. Je 2:8. 1 K 18:18-21, 25-28, 40.
and caused. 2 Ch 33:9. Is 9:16.
to err. ver. 32. Je 42:20.

14 in the. Je 5:30, 31. 14:14. 26:32. Ezk 13:2-4, 16. 22:25. Is 41:6, 7. Mi 3:11. Zp 3:4. 2 P 2:1, 2.
an horrible thing. or, filthiness. Je 5:30. 18:13.
they commit. Je 29:23. 2 P 2:14-19.
walk. ver. 17, 25, 26, 32. Je 14:14. Ezk 22:25. 2 Th 2:9-11. 1 T 4:2. Re 19:20. +21:8. 22:15.
strengthen. Ezk +13:22, 23.
Sodom. Ge 13:13, +18:20. 19:24. Ml 1:1. 2 P 2:6. Ju 7.

15 Lord of hosts. Je +6:6.
will. Dt +29:18.
profaneness. or, hypocrisy. **S#2613h**, only here. Is 32:6.

16 Hearken. Je 27:9, 10, 14-17. 29:8. Pr 19:27. Mt 7:15, 16. 2 C 11:13-15. Ga 1:8, 9. 1 J 4:1.
they make. Je +2:5. 2 K 17:15. Ro 1:21.

a vision. ver. 21, 26. Je 14:14. Ezk 13:3, 6, 16, 23. 22:28. Mi 2:11.
own heart. ver. 26. Nu +16:28.

17 that despise. Nu 11:20. 1 S 2:30. 2 S 12:10. Ml 1:6. Lk 10:16. Jn 5:23. 1 Th 4:7, 8.
Ye. Is 3:10, 11. La 2:14. Ezk +13:10, 15, 16, 22. Mi 3:5, 11. Zc 10:2.
imagination. or, stubbornness. Je +3:17mg.
No. Je 18:18. Am 9:10. Mi 3:11. Zp 1:12.

18 who. ver. 22. Nu 9:8. 1 K 22:24. Jb 15:8-10. 2 Ch 18:23. Is 40:13, 14. 1 C 2:16.
counsel. or, secret. Je 7:24. Ps 25:14. 81:12. Am 3:7. Jn 15:15.

19 a whirlwind. Je 4:11, 13. 25:32. 30:23. Jb 21:18. 37:9. 38:1. 40:6. Ps 58:9. Pr 1:24-27. 10:25. Is 5:25-28. 17:13. 21:1. 30:30. 40:24. 41:16. 66:15, 16. Ezk 1:4. Da 11:40. Ho 13:3, 15. Am 1:14. Na 1:3-6. Hab 3:14. Zc 7:14. 9:14.

20 until. Je 30:24. Is 14:24. Zc 1:6. 8:14, 15.
in the latter days. Ge +49:1.
ye shall consider. or, understand. 1 K 8:47. Pr 5:11-14. +21:30. Da 11:33, 35. 12:9, 10. Mt 24:15.

21 not sent. ver. 32. Je +14:14. Is 6:8. Jn 20:21. Ac 13:4. Ro 10:15.

22 if. ver. +18. Ezk 2:7. 3:17. Ac 20:27.
my counsel. ver. 18. Je 7:24. Ps 81:12. 106:13. 107:11. Pr 1:25.
had caused. ver. 28.
then. Je 25:5. 35:15. 36:3. Ezk 13:22. 18:30. Zc 1:4. Ac 26:18-20. 1 Th 1:9, 10. 5:6.
turned them. Ml 2:6.

23 a God at hand. 1 K +20:23, 28. Ps 113:5, 6. 139:1-10. Ezk 20:32-35. Jon 1:3, 4.

24 hide. Je 49:10. Ge 16:13. Jb 22:13, 14. 24:13-16. Ps 10:11. +11:4. 90:8. 139:7, 11-16. Is 29:15. Ezk 8:12. 9:9.
Do not I fill. Ps 148:13. Pr +15:3. Is 57:15. Da 4:35. Mt +28:19. Ep 1:22, 23.
heaven. Dt +10:14.

25 heard. Je 8:6. 13:27. 16:17. 29:23. Ps 139:2, 4. Lk 12:3. 1 C 4:5. He 4:13. Re 2:23.
dreamed. ver. 28, 32. Je 29:8. Ge 37:5, 9. Nu 12:6. Jl 2:28. Mt 1:20.

26 How. Je 4:14. 13:27. Ps 4:2. Ho 8:5. Ac 13:10.
shall this be. Je 31:6, 16, 17. Pr 8:21. 18:24. Lk 7:25.
prophets of. Je +14:14. 17:9. Is 30:9, 10. 2 Th 2:9-11. 1 T 4:1, 2. 2 T 4:3. 2 P 2:13-16.
own heart. ver. 16. Nu +16:28.

27 think. Dt 13:1-5. Ac 13:8. 2 T 2:17, 18. 3:6-8.
as. Jg +2:11. +6:25.

28 that hath. Heb. with whom is.
a dream. ver. 32. Is +8:20. Ezk 13:7.
speak my word. Pr 14:5. 30:6. Mt +24:45. Lk +12:42. Jn 16:8-14. 1 C 4:2. 2 C 2:17. 1 T 1:12. 2 T 3:15-17. 1 P 2:2. 2 P 1:21.

faithfully. Da +11:33. 1 T +4:16. 2 T +2:15. 4:2.

What. Lk +3:17. 1 C 3:11-13.

29 **my word**. Je +15:16.

like as. Je 5:14. 20:9. Lk 24:32. Jn 6:63. Ac 2:3, 37. 2 C 2:16. 10:4, 5. He 4:12. Re 11:5.

30 **I am against**. Je +14:14, 15. 44:11, 29. Le 20:3. 26:17. Dt 18:20. 29:20. Ps 34:16. Ezk 13:2, 3, 8, 9, 20, 22. 15:7. 1 P 3:12.

that steal. Lk 8:12.

31 **use**. *or*, smooth. Is 30:10. Mi 2:11.

He saith. ver. +17. Ge 22:16. Nu 14:28. 24:3, 4, 15, 16. 2 Ch 18:5, 10-12, 19-21.

32 **false dreams**. ver. +28.

to err. ver. +16. Je 27:14, etc. 28:15-17. 29:21-23, 31. Dt 13:1, etc. 18:20. Is 3:12. Ezk 13:7-18. Ho +4:12. Zc 13:2, 3. Mk +12:24. Re 19:20.

and by. Zp 3:4. 2 C 1:17.

therefore. ver. +22. Je 7:8. La 2:14. Mt +15:14.

33 **What**. ver. 35, 36.

the burden. Je 17:15. 20:7, 8. Is 13:1. 14:28. Na 1:1. Hab 1:1. Ml 1:1.

forsake you. ver. +39, 40. Je 32:19, 20. Is +54:7.

34 **punish**. Heb. visit upon. ver. +2. Je +9:25mg.

35 **every one**. Je 31:34. He +8:11.

What. ver. 33.

36 **for every**. Ps 12:3. 64:8. 120:3. 140:9. Pr 17:20. Is 3:8. Mt 12:36. Lk 19:22. 2 P 2:17-19. Ju 15, 16.

for ye. Is 28:13, 14, 22. Ga 1:7-9. 6:5. 2 P 3:16.

living God. Je +10:10.

37 **What hath**. ver. 35. Je 33:3. 42:4.

38 **ye say**. 2 C +11:13, 14.

the burden. ver. +30. Is +8:20.

ye shall not say. Ps +50:16. Mk +3:12.

39 **I, even I**. Ge +6:17.

forget. Ps +13:1.

forsake you. ver. +33. Je 32:28-35. 35:17. 36:31. Dt 31:17. Pr 13:13. Is +41:9. +54:7. Ezk 8:18. 9:6. Ho 4:6.

cast. Ps +44:9. Mt +25:41. 2 Th 1:8, 9.

40 **everlasting**. Heb. *olam*, Ge +17:7.

reproach. Je +20:11. 24:9. 42:18. 44:8-12. Dt 28:37. Ezk 5:14, 15. Da 9:16. +12:2. Ho 4:7.

perpetual. Ge +9:12.

JEREMIAH 24

1 A.M. 3406. B.C. 598.

Lord. Am 3:7. 7:1, 4, 7. 8:1, 2. Zc 1:20. 3:1.

two. Dt 26:2-4.

after. Je 22:24-28. 29:2. 2 K 24:12-16. 2 Ch 36:10. Ezk 19:9.

Jeconiah. i.e. *he will be established of the Lord; Jehovah will establish*, S#3204h. Je 27:20. 28:4. 29:2. 1 Ch 3:16, 17. Est 2:6. Mt 1:11. Variant

of the name Jehoiachin, 2 K +24:8, and Coniah, Je +22:24.

carpenters. Je 10:3, 9. 29:2. Ex 28:11.

smiths. Je 29:2. 1 S 13:19, 20. 2 K 24:14.

2 **One basket**. ver. 5-7.

first ripe. Ex 22:29. Nu 18:13. Is 28:4. Ho 9:10. Mi 7:1.

naughty. ver. 8-10. Is 5:4, 7. Ezk 15:2-5. Ml 1:12-14. Mt 5:13.

they were so bad. Heb. for badness.

3 **What**. Je 1:11-14. 1 S 9:9. Am 7:8. 8:2. Zc 4:2. 5:2, 5-11. Mt 7:17, 19. 25:32, 33.

5 **God of Israel**. Je +11:3.

I acknowledge. lit. know. Ge +39:6. Na 1:7. Zc 13:9. Mt 25:12. Jn 10:27. 1 C 8:3. Ga 4:9. 2 T 2:19.

them that are carried away captive. Heb. the captivity. Je 28:4mg.

for. Dt 8:16. Ps 94:12-14. 119:67, 71. Ro 8:28. He 12:5-10. Re 3:19.

6 **For I will**. Je 21:10. Ne 5:19. Jb 33:27, 28. Ps +11:4.

and I will bring. Je +23:3.

I will build. Je +1:10. Ps +102:16.

plant. Je +11:17.

7 **I will give**. Je 31:33, 34. 32:39. Dt 30:6. Ezk 11:19, 20. 36:24-28.

and they. Ge +17:7. Dt 26:17-19.

for they. Je 3:10. 29:12-14. Dt 4:29-31. 30:2-5. 1 S 7:3. 1 K 8:46-50. 2 Ch 6:38. Is 55:6, 7. Ho 14:1-3. Ro 6:17. 2 C 3:16, 17.

8 **as**. ver. +2, 5. Je 29:16-18.

So will. Je +21:7.

and them. Je ch 43, 44.

9 **to be removed**. Heb. for removing, *or* vexation. Je +15:4mg. Ezk 5:1, 2, 12, 13.

to be a. Je 19:8.

reproach. Ps +31:11.

proverb. Dt +28:37.

a taunt. Dt 28:37 (byword). La 2:15-17. Ezk 25:3. 26:2. 36:2, 3.

a curse. Je +26:6. Ps 109:18, 19.

10 **I will send**. Je 5:12. 9:16. 14:15, 16. 15:2. 16:4. 19:7. 34:17. Le 26:6, 25, 26, 33, 36. Dt 28:21-24. 32:25, 41, 42. Is 51:19. Ezk 5:2, 12-17. 6:11-14. 7:15. 14:17, 21. 33:27.

JEREMIAH 25

1 A.M. 3398. B.C. 606.

in the. Je 36:1. 46:2. 2 K 24:1, 2. Da 1:1, 2.

2 **spake unto**. Je 18:11. 19:14, 15. 26:2. 35:13. 38:1, 2. Ps 49:1, 2. Mk 7:14-16.

3 **thirteenth**. Je 1:2. 1 K 22:3. 2 Ch 34:3, 8.

rising early. ver. 4. Je 7:13, 25. 11:7. 26:5. 29:19. 32:33. 35:14, 15. 44:4. Ge +21:14. Ex 8:20. 2 Ch 36:15. Is 55:2. Mk +1:35. Jn 8:2, 47. 2 T 4:2.

not hearkened. Ps 81:13. Jn 8:47.

4　rising early. That is, "sending them diligently." ver. +3. 2 Ch +24:19.

not hearkened. ver. 3, 7. Je +7:26. 11:8-10. 13:10, 11, 17. 16:12. 17:23. 18:12, 18. 19:15. 22:21. 34:14, 15. 36:31. Zc 1:4. 7:11, 12. Mt 21:32-40. Jn 1:11, 12. Ac 7:51, 52. He 12:25.

5　Turn. Je +35:15. 2 K 17:13, 14. Jon 3:8-10. Lk 13:3-5. Ja 4:8-10.

dwell. Je +7:7. Ge 17:8. Ps 37:27. 105:10, 11.

ever and for. Heb. *olam* doubled, Da +2:20.

6　go not after. Je 7:6, 9. +10:2. 35:15. Ex +20:3, 23. Dt 6:14. 8:19. 13:2. 28:14. Jsh 24:20. 1 K 11:4-10. 14:22. 2 K 17:35.

7　that ye. Je +7:18, 19. 32:30-33. Dt 32:21. 2 K 17:17. 21:15. Ne 9:26. Pr 8:36.

8　the Lord of hosts. Je +6:6.

9　I will. Je 5:15, 16. 8:16. Le 26:25, etc. Dt 28:45-50. Pr +21:1. Is 5:26-30. 10:5. 39:7. Hab 1:6-10.

north. Je +1:14.

Nebuchadrezzar. Je 27:6. 40:2. 43:10. Is 13:3. 44:28. 45:1. Ezk 29:18-20.

my servant. Je 27:6. 43:10. Is +10:5. 44:24, 28.

against. ver. 17-26. Je 27:3-8. Ezk 26:7. 29:19. 30:10, 11.

an astonishment. Je 24:9. 2 Ch +29:8.

perpetual. Ge +9:12.

desolations. Je +18:16.

10　take from. Heb. cause to perish from. Est 3:13. 7:4. 8:11.

voice of mirth. Je 7:34. 16:9. 33:10, 11. Is 24:7-12. Ezk 26:13. Ho 2:11. Re *18:22, 23*.

the sound. Ec 12:2-4.

11　seventy years. Beginning B.C. 606, 2 K 14:1; ending B.C. 536, Ezr 1:1; Da 9:2. ver. 12. 2 Ch 36:21, 22. Is 23:15-17. Da 9:2. Zc 7:5.

12　it shall come. Is 44:26-28.

when. Je 29:10. 2 K 24:1. Ezr 1:1, 2. Da 9:2.

that I. ver. 14. Je ch. 50, 51. Dt 32:35-42. Is ch. 13, 14, 21, 46, 47. Da ch. 5. Hab ch. 2. Re ch. 18.

punish. Heb. visit upon. Je +11:22mg.

perpetual. Je 50:3, 13, 23, 39, 40, 45. 51:25, 26, 62-64. Ge +9:12. Is 13:19. 14:23. 15:6. 20:1, etc. 47:1. Ezk 35:9.

13　hath. Je +1:5, 10. Da 5:28, 31. Re 10:11.

14　many. Je 27:7. 50:9, 41. 51:6, 27, 28. Is 14:2. 45:1-3. Da 5:28. Hab 2:8-16.

I will recompense. Je 50:29-34. 51:6, 20-27, 35-41. Ps 137:8. Is 66:6. Re 18:20-24.

15　Lord God of Israel. Je +11:3.

Take. Je 13:12-14. Jb 21:20. Ps 11:6. 75:8. Is 51:17, 22. Zc 12:2. Re 14:9, 10, 19, 20.

all. ver. 27-33.

16　shall drink. ver. 27. Je 51:7, 39. La 3:15. 4:21. Ezk 23:32-34. Na 3:11. Re 14:8, 10. 16:9-11. 18:3.

because of. Je +12:12.

17　and made. ver. 28. Je 1:10. 27:3. ch. 46-51. Ezk 43:3.

18　Jerusalem. Je 1:10. 19:3-9. 21:6-10. Ps 60:3. Is 51:17, 22. Ezk 9:5-8. Da 8:12. 9:12. Am 2:5. 3:2. 1 P 4:17.

to make. ver. +9, 11.

curse. Je +26:6. Jsh 6:18.

as it. Je 44:22. 1 K +8:24.

19　Pharaoh. Je 43:9-13. 46:2, 13-26. Ezk ch. 29-32. Na 3:8-10.

20　the mingled. ver. 24. Je 49:28-33. 50:37. Ex 12:38. Ezr 9:2. Ps 106:35. Ezk 30:5. Da 2:43.

Uz. Ge +10:23.

Philistines. Je +47:4.

Ashkelon. Jg +14:19.

remnant. Ne 13:23-27. Is 20:1. Am 1:8.

21　Edom. Je 27:3. +49:7.

Moab. Ezk +25:8.

Ammon. Ge +19:38.

22　Tyrus. i.e. *rock, strength; to distress*, **S#6865h**. Je 27:3. 47:4. 1 K +7:13, Tyre. Ezk 26:2-4, 7, 15. 27:2, 3, 8, 32. 28:2, 12, 18. 29:18. Ho 9:13. Am 1:9, 10. Zc 9:2, 3.

Zidon. Ge +49:13.

isles which are beyond the sea. *or*, region by the seaside. Je 49:23-27. Am 1:3-5. Zc 9:1.

23　Dedan. Ge +10:7.

Tema. Ge +25:15.

Buz. Ge 22:21.

in the utmost corners. Heb. cut off into corners, *or* having the corners *of the hair* polled. Je +9:26. 49:32.

24　Arabia. 2 Ch +9:14.

the mingled. ver. +20. Ge 25:2-4, 12-16. 37:25-28.

25　Zimri. Ge 25:2, Zimran.

Elam. Ge +10:22.

Medes. Is +13:17.

26　all the kings. ver. 9. Je 50:9. Ezk +32:27, 30.

and the. Je 51:41.

Sheshach. i.e. *thy fine linen; confusion; gates of iron; house of the prince*, **S#8347h**. Je 25:26. 51:41.

drink. ver. 12. Je ch. 50, 51. Is ch. 13, 14, 47. Da ch. 5. Hab 2:16. Re ch. 18.

27　Lord of hosts, the God of Israel. Je +7:3.

Drink. Is 51:21. 63:6. La 4:21. Hab 2:16.

because. ver. 16. Je +12:12. Ezk 21:4, 5. 24:21-25.

28　if. Jb 34:33.

Ye. Je 4:28. 51:29. Is 14:24-27. 46:10, 11. Da 4:35. Ac 4:28. Ep +1:11.

29　I begin. Je 49:12. Pr 11:31. Ezk 9:6. 38:21. Ob 16. Lk 23:31. 1 P 4:17.

which is called by my name. Heb. upon which my name is called. Je +14:9mg.

Ye shall. Je 30:11. 46:28. 49:12. Pr 11:21. 17:5.

unpunished. Ex 20:7. 34:7. Nu 14:18.

I will. Je +12:12. Zc 13:7.

30 roar. Am +1:2.
his holy. Je 17:12. Dt 26:15. 1 K 9:3. 2 Ch 30:27. Ps 11:4. 68:5. 132:14. Zc 2:13.
give. Je 48:33. Ps 78:65. Is 16:9. 63:1-3. Re 14:18-20. 19:15.
31 A noise. Je 45:5. Is 34:8. Ho 4:1. 12:2. Mi 6:2.
plead. Is +66:16. Ezk 20:35, 36. 38:22. Jl 3:2.
32 evil. 2 Ch 15:6. Is 34:2. +45:7. 66:18. Lk 21:10, 25, 26.
and a. Je +23:19. Zp 3:8.
33 the slain. ver. 18-26. Je 13:12-14. Is 34:2-8. 66:16. Zp 2:12. Re 14:19, 20. 19:17-21.
they shall not. Je +7:33. Re 11:9.
they shall be. Je +16:4.
34 Howl. ver. 23, 36. Is +13:6.
ye shepherds. Ezk 34:10, 16.
wallow. Je 6:26. 48:26. Ezk 27:30, 31.
ye principal. Ezk 34:17, 20.
the days of your. Heb. your days for. ver. 12. Je 27:7. 51:20-26. Is 10:12. 33:1. La 4:21, 22.
ye shall. Je 19:10-12. 22:28. Ps +2:9. Is 30:14.
pleasant vessel. Heb. vessel of desire. 2 Ch 32:27mg. 36:10mg. Ezr 8:9mg. Is +32:12mg. Da 11:8mg. Ho 13:15mg. Na 2:9mg.
35 the shepherds, etc. Heb. flight shall perish from the shepherds, and escaping from, etc. Je 32:4. 34:3. 38:18, 23. Jb 11:20. Is 2:12-22. 24:21-23. Ezk 17:15, 18. Da 5:30. Am 2:14. 9:1. Re 6:14-17. 19:19-21.
nor. Je 48:44. 52:8-11, 24-27. Am 9:1-3.
36 cry of. ver. +34. Je 4:8. Zc 11:3.
37 peaceable habitations. Is 27:10, 11. 32:14.
38 hath. Is +5:29. Am 8:8.
desolate. Heb. a desolation. ver. 12. Je 44:6, 22.

JEREMIAH 26

1 A.M. 3394. B.C. 610.
the beginning. 2 K 23:34-36. 1 Ch +3:15.
2 Stand. Je +7:2. 23:28. Lk 19:47, 48. 20:1. 21:37, 38. Jn 8:2. 18:20.
cities. 1 S +22:19.
all the words. Je 1:17. 42:4. Is 58:1, 2. Ezk 3:10, 17-21. Mt 28:20. Ac 20:20, 27.
diminish. Dt +4:2.
3 If. Je +7:5.
so. Je 18:7-10. 36:3. Is 1:16-19. Ezk 18:27-30. Jon 3:8-10. 4:2.
hearken. Dt +15:5.
that I. ver. 13. Je +18:7-10. 1 K 21:27, 29.
repent. Je +18:8.
4 If. Je +7:5.
will not hearken. Le 26:14, etc. Dt 28:15, etc. 29:18-28. 31:16-18, 20. 32:15-25. Jsh 23:15, 16. 1 K 9:6, 7. 2 Ch 7:19, 20. Ne 9:26-30. Is 1:20. 42:23-25.

my law. Ex ch. 20.
which. Je 44:10. Dt 4:8, 44. 11:32. He 6:18.
5 my servants the. Je 7:13, 25. 11:7. 25:4. 2 K 9:7. 17:13, 23. 21:10. 24:2. 29:19. 35:15. 44:4. Ezr 9:11. Ezk 38:17. Da 9:6-10. Am 3:7. Zc 1:6. Re 10:7. 11:18.
whom. Je +25:3, 4. Mk 12:2.
6 will I. Je +7:12-14.
a curse. Je 24:9. 25:18. 29:18, 22. 42:18. 44:8, 12, 22. Dt 29:20, 21, 27. 2 K 22:19. Is 43:28. 65:15. La +3:65. Da 9:11. Zc +5:3. 8:13. 12:2, 3. Ml 4:6.
7 the priests. Je 5:31. 23:11-15. Ezk 22:25, 26. Mi 3:11. Zp 3:4. Mt 21:15. Ac 4:1-6. 5:17.
8 the priests. Je 2:30. 11:19-21. 12:5, 6. 18:18. 20:1, 2, 8-11. 2 Ch 36:16. La 4:13, 14. Mt 21:35-39. 22:6. 23:31-35. 26:3, 4, 59-66. Ac 5:33. 7:52. Re 18:24.
Thou shalt. Dt 18:20.
surely die. Ge +2:16, 17.
9 Why. 2 Ch 25:16. Is 29:21. 30:9-11. Am 5:10. 7:10-13. Mi 2:6. Mt 21:23. Ac 4:17-19. 5:28. 6:14.
desolate. Je +18:16.
And all. Ex +9:6. Mt 27:20. Mk 15:11. Ac 13:50. 16:19-22. 17:5-8. 19:24-32. 21:30. 22:22.
in the. Jn 8:20, 59.
10 the princes. ver. 16, 17, 24. Je 34:19. 36:12-19, 25. 37:14-16. 38:4-6. Ezk 22:6, 27.
in the entry. or, at the door.
the new gate. Je 36:10. 2 K 15:35.
11 saying. Dt 18:20. Mt 26:65, 66. Lk 23:1-5. Jn 18:30. 19:7. Ac 22:22. 24:4-9. 25:2-13.
This man is worthy to die. Heb. The judgment of death is for this man. ver. 16. Ex +6:6. Dt 19:6. 21:22. 22:26. Ac 23:29. 25:11, 25. 26:31.
for he. Je 38:4. Ac 6:11-14.
12 The Lord. ver. 2, 15. Je 1:17, 18. 19:1-3. Am 7:15-17. Ac +4:19, 20. +5:29.
13 amend. Je +35:15.
obey. Je +7:23. 38:20. Is 1:19.
repent. ver. 3, 19. Je +18:8.
evil. Is +45:7.
14 As for. Je 38:5. Jsh 9:25. Da 3:16.
as seemeth good and meet unto you. Heb. as it is good and right in your eyes. 2 S 15:26.
15 ye shall. Je 2:30, 34. 7:6. 22:3, 17. Ge 4:10. 42:22. Nu 35:33. Dt 19:10, 13. 2 K 24:4. Pr 6:17. Mt 23:30-36. 26:4, 25. 27:4, 25. Ac 7:60. 1 Th 2:14-16. Re 16:6.
for of. ver. +12.
16 Then said. Je 36:19, 25. 38:7-13. Est 4:14. Pr +16:7. Mt 27:23, 24, 54. Lk 23:13-15, 41, 47. Jn 10:21. Ac 5:34-39. 23:9, 29. 25:25. 26:31, 32.
17 Then rose. Mi 1:1. Ac 5:34.
elders of. Ge 50:7. Jsh +20:4.
18 Micah. S#4320h. Mi 1:1.

Morasthite. i.e. *native of Moresheth (i.e. possession)*, **S#4183h**. Je 26:18. Mi 1:1.
Lord of hosts. Je +6:6.
Zion. Mi *3:12*.
Jerusalem. Je +9:11. 51:37. 2 K 19:25. Ne 4:2. Ps 79:1.
the mountain. Je 17:3. Is 2:2, 3. Mi 4:1. Zc 8:3.

19 **did he**. 2 Ch 29:6-11. 32:20, 25, 26. 34:21. Is 37:1, 4, 15-20.
fear the Lord. Ac 5:39. 23:9.
besought the Lord. Heb. besought the face of the Lord. Ex +32:11mg. 2 K 13:4.
and the Lord. ver. +3. Ex 32:14. 2 S 24:16.
repented. ver. 3, 13.
Thus. ver. 15. Nu 16:38. 35:33, 34. Is 26:21. La 4:13, 14. Mt 23:35. 27:24, 25. Lk 3:19, 20. Ac 5:39. Re 6:9, 10. 16:6. 18:20-24.
souls. Heb. *nephesh*, Ge +12:13.

20 **Urijah**. i.e. *light of the Lord; my light is Jehovah*, **S#223h**. ver. 20, 21, 23. 2 K 16:10, 11, 15, 16. Ne 3:4, 21. 8:4.
Kirjath-jearim. Jsh +9:17.

21 **the king sought**. Je 32:3. 36:26. Ex 10:28. Nu 24:11. 1 K 13:4. 22:27. 2 K 5:12. 2 Ch 16:10. 24:21. 26:19. Ps 119:109. Mt 14:3, 5. Mk 6:19.
he was. 1 K 19:1-3. Pr +22:3. 29:25. Mt 10:23, 28, 39. 16:25, 26.

22 **men**. Ps 12:8. Pr 29:12.
Achbor. Ge +36:38.

23 **who**. ver. +15. Je 2:30. Ezk 19:6. Mt 14:10. 23:34, 35. Ac 12:1-3. 1 Th 2:15. Re 11:7.
and cast. Je 22:19. 36:30.
graves. Heb. *qeber*, Ge +23:4.
common people. Heb. sons of the people. Ezk 23:42mg.

24 **Ahikam**. 2 K +22:12.
the son of. Je 29:3. 36:10.
that. Je 1:18, 19. 15:19-21. 1 K 18:4. Is 37:32, 33. Ac 23:10, 20-35. 25:3, 4. 27:43. Re 12:16.

JEREMIAH 27

1 A.M. 3409. B.C. 595.
the beginning. ver. 3, 12, 19, 20. Je 26:1. 27:1. 28:1. Ge 1:1.

2 **saith the Lord**. *or*, hath the Lord said. Am 7:1, 4.
Make. ver. 12. Je 28:10-14.
put. Je 13:1-11. 18:2-10. 19:1-11. 28:10. 1 K 11:30, 31. Is 20:2-4. Ezk ch. 4, 5, 12. 24:3-12.

3 **Edom**. Je +25:19-26. ch. 47-49. Ezk ch. 25-28. 29:18. Am 1:9-15. 2:1-3.
the messengers. 2 Ch 36:13. Ezk 17:15-21.

4 **to say unto their masters**.
Thus. *or*, concerning their masters, saying, Thus.
the Lord. ver. 21. Je +7:3. 10:10, 16. 51:19. Ex 5:1.

5 **made**. Je 10:11, 12. 32:17. 51:15. Ge +1:1. 9:6. Ex 20:11. Jb 26:5-14. 38:4, etc. Ps 102:25. 136:5-9. 146:5, 6. 148:2-5. Is 40:21-26. 45:12. 48:13. 51:13. Jn +1:1-3. Ac 14:15. Col +1:16. He 1:2, 10, 11. Re 4:11.
great power and. Ex +6:6.
and have. Ge 1:29, 30. 9:2, 3. Nu +33:53. Dt 2:7, 9, 19. 5:16. Jsh 1:2, 3. Ezr 1:2. Da 2:21.

6 **have I given all**. Je 28:14. Da 2:37, 38. 5:18, 19.
my servant. Je 24:1. 25:9. 43:10. 51:20-23. Is 44:28. Ezk 29:18-20.
the beasts. Je 28:14. Ps +50:10-12. Da 2:38.

7 **all**. Je 25:11-14. 50:9, 10. 52:31. 2 Ch 36:20, 21.
until. Je 25:12. 50:27. Ps 37:13. 137:8, 9. Is 13:1, 8, etc. 14:22, 23. 21:9. 47:1-5. Da 5:25-31. Hab 2:7. Zc 2:8, 9. Re 13:5-10. 14:8, 15-20. 16:19. 17:16, 17. 18:2-8.
many. Je 25:14. ch. 50, 51. Is 14:4-6.
great kings. Da 2:39.

8 **that nation**. Je 25:28, 29. 38:17-19. 40:9. 42:10-18. 52:3-6. Ezk 17:19-21.
with the sword. Je 24:10. Le 26:25, 26. Dt 28:21-24. Ezk 14:21.

9 **hearken not**. ver. 14-16. Je 23:16, 25, 32. Ml +3:5. Re+9:21.
diviners. Je 29:8. Dt +18:10. Jsh 13:22mg. Ezk 12:24. Mi 3:6, 7, 11. Zc 10:2.
dreamers. Heb. dreams. Je 23:27, 28. +29:8. Is 47:12-14.
enchanters. 2 K 21:6 (**S#6049h**, observed times).
sorcerers. **S#3786h**, only here. Compare **S#3784h**, Ml +3:5; **S#3785h**, Is 47:12.

10 **they**. ver. +14. Je 28:16. Ezk 14:9-11.
to. Je 32:31. La 2:14.
I. ver. +15.

11 **bring**. ver. 2, 8, 12.
those. Je 21:9. 38:2. 40:9-12. 42:10, 11.

12 **Zedekiah**. ver. 3. 1 K +22:11. Pr +1:33. Ezk 17:11-21.
Bring. ver. 2, 8.

13 **Why**. Je 38:20. Pr 8:36. Ezk 18:24, 31. 33:11. Jn 5:40.
by the sword. ver. 8. Je 24:9. 38:2. Ezk 14:21.

14 **hearken not**. ver. +9. Is 28:10-13. 2 C 11:13-15. Ph 3:2.
they. ver. 10. Je +14:14. 1 K 22:22, 23. Ezk 13:6-15, 22, 23. Mi 2:11. Mt 7:15. 2 P 2:1-3. 1 J 4:1.

15 **a lie**. Heb. in a lie, *or* lyingly. Ps +66:3.
that I. ver. 10. 2 Ch 18:17-22. 25:16. Ezk 14:3-10. Mt 24:24. 2 Th 2:9-12. 2 T 2:17-19. 4:3, 4. Re 13:7, 8, 12-14.
ye. Je 6:13-15. 8:10-12. 14:15, 16. 20:6. 23:15. 28:16, 17. 29:22, 23, 31, 32. Mi 3:5-7. Mt +15:14. Re 19:20.

16 **Behold**. Je 28:3. 2 Ch +4:19.
for. ver. 10, 14. Is 9:15. 44:24, 25.

17 serve. ver. 11, 12.
 wherefore. ver. 13. Je 38:17, 23.
18 they. 1 K 18:24, 26.
 let them. Je 7:16. 15:1. 18:20. 42:2. Ge
 18:24-33. 20:17. 1 S 7:8. 12:19, 23. 2 Ch
 32:20. Jb 42:8, 9. Ezk 14:14, 18-20. 22:30. Ml
 1:9. Ja 5:16-18.
 the Lord of hosts. Je +10:16.
19 the pillars. Je 52:17-23. 1 K 7:15, etc. 2 K
 25:13, 17. 2 Ch 4:2-16.
20 when. Je +24:1. 2 Ch 36:10, 18.
21 the vessels. Je 20:5.
22 carried. Je 29:10. 34:5. 2 Ch +4:19.
 until. Je 25:11, 12. 29:10. 32:5. 2 Ch 36:21-
 23. Ezr 1:1-5. Pr +21:30. Is +24:22. Da 9:2.
 then. Ezr 1:7, 11. 5:13-15. 7:9, 19.

JEREMIAH 28

1 the same. Je 27:1.
 Hananiah. ver. 11. Je 36:12. 37:13.
 Azur. i.e. *helpful*, **S#5809h**. Je 28:1. Ne 10:17,
 Azzur. Ezk 11:1.
 the prophet. Je 23:28. Is 9:15. Zc 13:2-4.
2 the Lord of. ver. 14. Je +7:3.
 I have. Je 27:2-12. Ezk 13:5-16. Mi 3:11.
3 two full years. Heb. two years of days. Ge
 47:8, 28mg. Ps 90:10mg. Am 4:4mg.
 all the vessels. 2 Ch +4:19.
4 Jeconiah. Je +24:1.
 captives. Heb. captivity. Je 24:5mg. 29:22.
 Ezk 1:1mg.
 I will break. ver. 2, 10. Je 2:20. 30:8. Ge
 27:40. Is 9:4. Na 1:13.
5 unto the prophet. ver. 1. Ezk 21:4. Mt 8:12.
 9:13. Lk 2:48. 1 C 1:21, 25. 5:11. 2 C 4:4. Ga
 1:6. T 1:12. Ja 2:14, 17, 20, 24, 26.
 the house. ver. 1. Je 7:2. 19:14. 26:2.
6 Amen. Mt +6:13.
 the Lord perform. ver. 3. Je 11:5. 17:16.
 18:20.
7 Nevertheless hear. 1 K 22:28.
8 of old. Heb. *olam*, Ge +6:4.
 prophesied. Le 26:14, etc. Dt 4:26, 27. 1 S
 2:27-32. 1 K 14:7-15. 21:18-24. 22:8. Is 5:5.
 6:11. ch. 24. Jl 1:2, etc. Mi 3:8-12. Na ch. 1-3.
 Am 1:2.
9 which. Ezk +13:10.
 then. Dt 18:21, 22. Ezk 13:10-16.
10 took. ver. 2, 4. Je 27:2. 36:23, 24. 1 K 22:11,
 24, 25. Ml 3:13.
11 Thus. Je 29:9. 1 K +13:18. 2 Ch 18:5, 10, 22,
 23. Pr 14:7.
 Even. ver. +2-4.
12 the word. Je 1:2. 29:30. 2 K 20:4. 1 Ch 17:3.
 Da 9:2.
13 Thou hast. Je 27:15. Ps 149:8. La 2:14.
14 I have put. Je 27:7. Dt 28:48. Is 14:4-6.
 that they. Je 25:9-26. Re 17:12, 13.
 and I. Je +27:6.

15 The Lord hath not sent thee. ver. 11. Je
 +14:14. 1 K 22:23. Ezk +22:28.
16 face. Ge +1:2.
 this year. ver. 3. Je 20:6. Nu 14:37. 16:28-35.
 Dt 13:5-11.
 die. Dt 18:20.
 because. Ezk 13:10-15. Ac 13:8-11.
 rebellion. Heb. revolt. Je 29:32mg. Dt
 13:5mg. 2 K 24:17. 2 Ch 36:13. Ezk 17:15, 18.
17 Hananiah. Is 44:24-26. Zc 1:6.

JEREMIAH 29

1 Cir. A.M. 3407. B.C. 597.
 Now. This transaction is supposed to have
 taken place in the first or second year of
 Zedekiah.
 words. Je 25:1. 26:1. 27:1. 30:1.
 of the letter. ver. 25-29. 2 Ch 30:1-6. Est
 9:20. Ac 15:23. 2 C 7:8. Ga 6:11. He 13:22. Re
 ch. 2, 3.
 the elders. Je 24:1-7. 28:4. Jsh +20:4.
 the prophets. Ezk 1:1. Da 1:6.
2 Jeconiah. Je +24:1.
 the queen. Je 13:18. 22:26. 2 K 24:12, 15.
 eunuchs. *or*, chamberlains. Je 34:19. 38:7.
 41:16. 52:25. 2 K +8:6mg.
 carpenters. Je 10:3, 9. 24:1. Ex 28:11.
 the smiths. 2 K 24:14.
3 Shaphan. 2 K +22:3.
 Gemariah. Je 36:25. 2 K 22:12. 2 Ch 34:20.
4 Lord of. ver. 8, 21, 25. Je +7:3.
 whom I have caused. Je 24:5. Is 5:5. 10:5,
 6. +45:7. 59:1, 2. Am +3:6.
5 Build ye houses. ver. 10, 28. Ezk 28:26.
6 Take ye. Je 16:2-4. Ge 1:27, 28. 9:7.
 1 T 5:14.
 take wives. Ge 29:19. Nu +12:1.
 Jg 1:12-14.
 that ye. Je +30:19. Ge 1:28. 15:5. 22:17.
7 seek. Da 4:27. 6:4, 5. Ro 13:1, 5. 1 P 2:13-17.
 peace. Ge +43:23. Is 26:12. Da 4:1. 6:25. Mt
 10:13. Lk 10:5, 6. Ro 1:7. +5:1. 1 C 1:3. 2 C
 1:2. Ga 1:3. 6:16. Ep 1:2. 6:23. Ph 1:2. Col
 1:2. 1 Th 1:1. 2 Th 1:2. 3:16. 1 T 1:2. 2 T 1:2.
 T 1:4. Phm 3. 1 P 1:1, 2. 5:14. 2 P 1:2. 2 J 3. 3
 J 14. Ju 2. Re 1:4.
 pray. 1 T 2:1, +2.
8 Let not. Je +14:14. Ezk +14:10. Zc 13:4. Mt
 24:4, 5, 11, 24. Mk 13:5, 6, 9, 22, 23, 33. Lk
 21:8. Ro 16:18. 2 C +11:13-15. Ep +4:14. 5:6.
 2 Th 2:3, 9-11. 2 T 3:13. 1 J 2:18, 26. 4:1. 2 J
 +7-9. Re 13:13, 14. 19:20.
 diviners. Je +27:9.
 deceive you. Mt 24:4.
 neither hearken. Je +23:28. +27:9. Jb 20:8.
 Ps 73:20. Ec 5:3. Is 29:7, 8. Zc 10:2.
 your dreams. Je 5:31. +23:28. Mi 2:11. Lk
 6:26. 2 P 2:2, 3.
9 falsely. Heb. in a lie. ver. 23, 31. Ps +66:3.

10 **after**. Je 25:12. 27:7, 22. 2 Ch 36:20-23. Ezr 1:1, 2. Da +9:2. Zc 7:5.
I will. Je +24:6, 7. 32:42-44. Zp 2:7.

11 **I know**. Jb 23:13. Ps 33:11. 40:5. Is +46:10, 11. 58:8-12. Mi 4:12. Zc 1:6. 8:14, 15.
thoughts. Je 3:12-19. 23:5, 6. 30:9, 10, 18-22. ch. 31-33. Ge +50:20. Ps 40:5, +17. Is ch. 40-46. Ezk 11:5. 34:11-31. ch. 36, 37, 39. Ho 2:14-23. 3:5. 14:2-9. Jl 2:28-32. Am 9:8-15. Mi 5:4-7. 7:14-20. Zp 3:14-20. Zc 9:9-17. 12:5-10. 14:20, 21. Re 14:8-14.
of peace. Ps +85:8.
not of evil. Ge 50:20. Ex +34:6. Ru +1:13. Ps +9:10. 55:22. 66:9-12. +84:11. 89:33. 97:10. +104:28. 121:3, 7. +145:9. Pr 10:3. Is +45:7. Mt 6:25-34. 25:24. Lk +6:35. Ro 8:28. +9:14. 2 C 9:8. 2 T 3:11. Ja 1:13, 17. 5:11.
expected end. Heb. end and expectation. Pr 3:5, 6. La 3:26. 1 C 2:9. 1 J 3:2.
expectation. **S#8615h**. Jsh 2:18, 21 (line). Ru 1:12 (hope). Jb 6:8mg. 11:18, 20. 27:8. Ps 9:18. 62:5. 71:5. Pr 10:28. 11:7. +19:18. 23:18. 24:14. Je +31:17. Ho +2:15. or, hope in your latter end.
hope. Ro +15:4.
latter. Ps +118:24. Am 9:11-15. Zc 9:12. 10:6. Ja +5:11.
end. Pr +23:18. Mt 5:12. Lk 14:14. 1 C 2:9. 15:58. Ep 3:20. Re 11:18.

12 **Then shall**. Je 31:9. 33:3. Ne 2:4, etc. Ps 102:16, 17. Ezk 36:37. Da 9:3, etc. 2 C 3:14-16. 1 J +5:14.

13 **seek me**. Dt 4:29-31. 1 Ch 28:9. 2 Ch 15:2. Ezr 8:22. Jb 8:5, 6. Ps +9:10. 69:32. Pr 8:17. Is 8:19, 20. 45:19. 55:6, 7. 58:1-3. La 3:25. Ho 5:15. 6:1-3. 10:12. Am 5:4-6. Zp 2:1-3. Mt 6:33. Lk 11:9, 10. He 11:6. Ja 4:8.
with. Je 3:10. 24:7. 2 Ch 22:9. Ps 119:2, 10, 58, 69, 145. Jl 2:12. Mt +22:37. Ac 8:37. 17:27.

14 **I will be**. Dt 4:7. 1 Ch +28:9. 2 Ch 15:12-15. Ps 32:6. 46:1. Is 45:19. 55:6. Ro 10:20.
and I will turn. Je 16:14, 15. 23:3-8. 24:5-7. 30:3, 10. 31:8, etc. 32:37, etc. 33:7, etc. 46:27, 28. 50:4, 5, 19, 20, 33, 34. 51:10. Ps 126:1, 4. Ezk 11:16-20. ch. 34, 36-39. Am 9:14. Mi 4:12. Zp 3:20.
your captivity. Dt 4:27-29. Ezr 8:21-23. Ps 68:18. Is 49:24. Ezk 3:15, 16. Da 9:17, 18. 10:12.
will gather. Je 23:3. 32:37. Ps 107:3.
whither. ver. 18. Je 8:3. 23:3, 7, 8. Is 11:11, 12. 43:5, 6.
bring you again. ver. 10. Je 3:14. 12:15. 16:15. +23:3. 24:6.

15 **The Lord hath**. ver. 8, 9. Je 28:1, etc. Ezk 1:1, 3.

16 **of the king**. ver. 3. Je 24:2. 38:2, 3, 17-23. Ezk ch. 6-9. 17:12-21. 21:9-27. 22:31. 24:1-14.

17 **the Lord of hosts**. Je +10:16.
Behold. ver. 18. Je 15:2, 3. 24:8-10. 34:17-22. 43:11. 52:6. Ezk 5:12-17. 14:12-21. Lk 21:11, 23, 25-27.
the sword. Je +12:12.
them like. Je 24:1-3, 8.

18 **will deliver**. Je +15:4. Le 26:33. 2 Ch 29:8. Ps 44:11. Ezk 6:8. 12:15. 22:15. 36:19. Am 9:9. Zc 7:14. Lk +21:24.
to be a curse. Heb. for a curse. ver. 22. Je +26:6.
astonishment. 2 Ch +29:8.

19 **not hearkened**. Je +7:26. Lk +8:18. He 12:25.
rising up early. Je +25:3.
would not hear. Je +25:4. Jb +21:14. Lk 19:14. Ac 7:39. Ro 1:28. 2 P 3:5.

20 **Hear**. Je +7:2.
all ye. Ezk 3:11, 15.
whom. Je +24:5. Mi 4:10.

21 **which**. ver. 8, 9. Je 14:14, 15. La 2:14.

22 **shall be**. Ge 48:20. Ru 4:11. Is 65:15. 1 C 16:22.
roasted. Da 3:6, 21.

23 **villany**. Is +9:17.
and have. Je 7:9, 10. 23:14, 21. Ps +50:16-18. Zp 3:4. 2 P 2:10-19. Ju 8-11.
lying. ver. 8, 9, 21. La 2:14.
even I. Je 13:27. 16:17. 23:23, 24. Pr 5:21. Ml 2:14. +3:5. He 4:13. Re 1:5. +3:14.

24 **Shemaiah**. ver. 31, 32.
Nehelamite. *or*, dreamer. **S#5161h**. ver. +8, 31, 32.

25 **Because**. 1 K 21:8-13. 2 K 10:1-7. 19:9, 14. 2 Ch 32:17. Ezr 4:7-16. Ne 6:5, 17, 19. Ac 9:2.
Zephaniah. ver. 29. Zp +1:1.

26 **officers**. Je 20:1, 2. 2 K 11:15, 18. Ac 4:1. 5:24.
for every. 2 K 9:11. Mk 3:21. Jn 7:20. 10:20, 39. 2 T +1:7.
and maketh. ver. 27. Dt 13:1-5. Zc 13:3-6. Mt 21:11, 23. Lk 7:39. Jn +5:18. 8:53. +10:33.
prison. He +11:36.
stocks. Pr +7:22.

27 **therefore**. Nu 16:7. 2 Ch 25:16. Am 7:12, 13. Jn 11:47-53. Ac 4:17-21. 5:28, 40.
which. ver. 26. Je 43:2, 3. Nu 16:3. Mt 27:63. 2 T 3:8.

28 **This captivity is long**. ver. 1-10.

29 **Zephaniah the priest**. ver. 25.

31 **Send**. ver. 20.
Because. ver. +8, 9, 23. Ezk 13:8-16, 22, 23. 2 P 2:1.

32 **punish**. Je +11:22mg. 20:6. Nu 16:27-33. Jsh 7:24, 25. 2 K 5:27. Ps 109:8-15. Is 14:20-22. Am 7:17.
he shall. Je 22:30. 35:19. 1 S 2:30-34.
behold. ver. 10-14. Je 17:6. 2 K 7:2, 19, 20.
rebellion. Heb. revolt. Je 28:16mg. Dt 13:5mg.

JEREMIAH 30

1 Cir. A.M. 3417. B.C. 587.
The word. Je 1:1, 2. 26:15.

2 **Write.** Je 36:2-4, 32. 51:60-64. Ex 17:14. Dt 31:19, 22-27. Jb 19:23, 24. Is 8:1. 30:8. Da 12:4. Hab 2:2, 3. Ro +15:4. 1 C 10:11. 2 P 1:21. Re 1:11, 18, 19.

3 **the days.** Je +23:5. Lk 19:43. 21:6.
that I. ver. 10, 18. Je +23:3. 27:22. Ob 19, 20.
and I. Je 16:15. 23:8. 27:11. Ezr 3:1, 8, 12. Ezk 20:42. 28:25, 26. 36:24. 37:21-25. 39:27, 28. 47:14.

4 **concerning Israel and.** Je 31:6. Is 11:13. Ho 1:11. Ezk 20:40.

5 **a voice.** Je 4:15-20, 31. 6:23, 24. 8:19. 9:19. 25:36. 31:15, 16. Is 5:30. 59:11. Am 5:16-18. 8:10. Zp 1:10, 11. Lk 19:41-44. 21:25-27. 23:28-30.
of fear, and not of peace. *or, there is* fear, and not peace. Je 46:5.

6 **a man.** Heb. a male. Ge 1:27. Ezk 16:17mg.
every. Je +4:31. Ps 48:6. Is 13:6-9. 42:14. +66:7, 8. Da 5:6. Mi 4:9, 10. 5:3. Zc 12:9-13:1. 14:1-15. Mt +24:8. Jn 16:21, 22. Ro 11:25-29. Re 12:2.
paleness. Is 29:22. Dt 28:22. Jl 2:6. Na 2:10.

7 **Alas.** Jg +6:22.
that day is great. Is 2:12-22. Ezk 7:6-12. Ho 1:11. Jl 2:11, 18, 31. Am 5:18-20. Zp 1:14-18. Zc 14:1-4. Ml 4:1. Ac 2:20. Re 6:17.
none is like it. La 1:12. 2:13. 4:6. Da 9:12. 12:1. Jl 2:1, 2. Mt +24:21, 22. Mk 13:19, 20.
even the time. Ge 32:7, 24-30. 43:6. 45:26, 28. Ezk +30:3. Da +12:1. Ho 12:2-4.
Jacob's trouble. Is 22:5. Ezk 20:33. Da 9:27. 11:40-45. 12:1-7. Ho 12:2-4. Zp 1:4, 12, 14, 15. Mt 24:15-31. Re 12:1—20:6.
but he. ver. +10. Je 50:18-20, 33, 34. Ps 25:22. 34:19. Is 14:1, 2. 49:25. Ro 11:26.
out of. Lk +21:36. Ro 11:26.

8 **come to pass.** Dt 30:1-6.
in that day. Is +2:11.
Lord of hosts. Je +6:6.
I will break. Je 27:2. 28:4, 10, 11, 13, 14. Is 9:4. 10:27. 14:25. Ezk 34:27. Na 1:13.
serve. Je 25:14. 27:7.

9 **David their king.** Is +55:3-5. Ezk 34:23-25. 37:24, 25. Ho 3:4, 5. Lk 1:69. Ac 2:30, 34. 13:34.

10 **fear.** Ge +15:1.
I will save. ver. +3. Je 3:18. 23:3, 8. 29:14. 46:27. Is 46:11, 13. 49:25. 60:4, etc. Ezk 16:53.
and shall. Je 23:6. 33:16. Is 35:9. Ezk 34:25-28. 38:11. Ho 2:18. Mi 4:3, 4. Zp 3:15. Zc 2:4, 5. 3:10. 8:4-8.

11 **I am.** Je 1:8, 19. 15:20. 46:28. Is 8:10. 43:25. Ezk 11:16, 17. Mt 1:23. 28:20. Ac 18:10. 2 T 4:17, 18, 22.

though. Je 5:10, 18. 46:27, 28. Ezk 11:13. Ro 9:27-29. 11:5-7.
not make. Je 31:10. Le +26:44. Is +41:9. Ro +11:1, 11, 12.
but I. Je +10:24. Ps 6:1. Is 27:7, 8.
unpunished. or, guiltless. Ex 20:7. 34:7. Nu 14:18.

12 **Thy bruise.** ver. +15. Je 14:17. 15:18. 2 Ch 36:16. Is 1:5, 6. Ezk 37:11.

13 **none.** Ps 106:23. 142:4. Is 59:16. Ezk 22:30. 1 T 2:5, 6. 1 J 2:1.
that, etc. Heb. for binding up, or pressing. Lk 10:30-34.
no healing medicines. ver. 17. Je +8:22. 17:14. 33:6. Ex +15:26. Dt 32:29. Jb 5:18. 34:29. Is 1:6. Ho 6:1. 14:4. Na 3:19. 1 P 2:24.

14 **lovers.** Je 2:36. 4:30. 22:20, 22. 38:22. La 1:2, 19. Ezk 23:9, 22. Ho 2:5, 6, 10-16. Re 17:12-18.
I have wounded. Jb 13:24-28. 16:9. 19:11. 30:21. La 2:5. Ho 5:14.
because. ver. +15. Je 5:6. Ps 90:7, 8. Ezk 9:8-10.

15 **Why.** Je 15:18. Jsh 7:10, 11. La 3:39. Mi 7:9.
thy sorrow. ver. 12, 17. Je 46:11. Jb 34:6, 29. Is 30:13, 14. Ho 5:12, 13. Mi 1:9. Ml 4:1, 2.
for the multitude. ver. 14. Je 2:19, 28-30. 5:6-9, 25-31. 6:6, 7, 13. 7:8-11. 9:1-9. 11:13. 32:30-35. 2 Ch 36:14-17. Ezr 9:6, 7, 13. Ne 9:26-36. Is 1:4, 5, 21-24. 5:2. 59:1-4, 12-15. La 1:5. 4:13, 14. 5:16, 17. Ezk ch. 16, 20, 22, 23. Zp 3:1-5.

16 **all they.** Je 10:25. 12:14. 25:12, 26-29. 50:7-11, 17, 18, 28, 33-40. 51:34-37. Ex 23:22. Ps 129:5. 137:8, 9. Is 14:2. 33:1. 41:11, 12. 47:5, 6, 11. 54:15, 17. La 1:21. 4:21, 22. Ezk 25:3, etc. 26:2, etc. 29:6, 7. 35:5, etc. Mi 4:11-13. 7:10-17. Na 1:8-14. Hab 2:16, 17. Zp 2:8-10. Zc 1:14, 15. 2:8, 9. 12:2-4. 14:2, 3. Re 13:10.
shall be. Ge +12:3.

17 **restore health.** ver. +13. Je 3:22. +8:22. 31:20. 33:6. Ex +15:26. Ps 23:3. +103:3. 107:20. Is 30:26. 33:24. 35:5, 6. 42:3. Ezk 34:16. Ho 6:1. Ml 4:2. 1 P 2:24. Re 22:2.
they. Ne 4:1-4. Ps +12:5. 44:13-16. 79:9-11. Is 11:12. La 2:15-17. Ezk 35:12, 13. 36:2, 3, 20.

18 **Behold.** ver. 3. Je +23:3. 46:27. 49:6, 39.
the city. Je 31:40. Ne ch. 3. 7:4. Is 44:24, 26. Zc 12:6. 14:10, 11.
heap. *or,* little hill. Je 21:10. 31:38, 39. 34:2. 37:10. Ezk 48:30-35.
the palace. 1 Ch 29:1, 19. Ezr 6:3-15. Ps 78:69. Is 44:28. Ezk 7:20-22. Hg 2:7-9. Zc 1:16, 17.

19 **out.** Je 31:4, 12, 13. 33:10, 11. Ezr 3:10-13. 6:22. Ne 8:12, 17. 12:43-46. Ps 53:6. 126:1, 2. Is 12:1. 35:10. 51:11. 52:9. Zp 3:14-20. Zc 8:19.
and I. Je 31:27. 33:22. Is 27:6. 60:22. Ezk 36:10-15, 37. 37:26. Zc 2:4, 5. 8:4, 5. 10:8.

I will. Je 33:9. Is 60:19. 62:2, 3. Zp 3:19, 20.
Zc 9:13-17. 12:8. Jn 17:22. 1 P 1:7.

20 **children**. Je 32:39. Ge 17:5-9. Ps 90:16, 17.
102:18, 28. Is 1:26, 27.
aforetime. Heb. *kedem*, Mi +5:2. Je 33:7.
and I. ver. +16. Je 2:3. 50:33, 34. Is 49:25,
26. 51:22, 23.
punish. Je +9:25mg.
all that. Ge +12:3.

21 **nobles**. Ge +49:10. Ezr 2:2. 7:25, 26. Ne 2:9,
10. 7:2.
governor. Je +23:5, 6. 33:15. Dt +18:18.
33:5. 2 S +7:13. Ps 89:29. 110:1-4. Is +9:6, 7.
Ezk 34:23, 24. 37:24. Mi +5:2-4. Zc 9:9, 10.
Mt 2:2. 21:5-11. 27:37. Mk 11:9, 10. Lk 1:32,
33. Jn 18:36, 37. 19:19-22. Ac 2:34-36. 5:31.
Re 19:16.
the midst. Ge +49:10. Dt +17:15.
and I. Nu 16:5, 40. 17:12, 13. Ps 110:4. Am
+9:11, 14, 15. Zc 6:12, 13. Mt 3:17. Lk 24:26.
Ro 8:34. He +1:3. 4:14-16. 7:21-26. 9:15-24.
1 J 2:2. Re 5:9, 10.
draw near. Ps 73:28. SS 1:4. Ho 11:4.
for. Je 49:19. 50:44. Is 63:1. Mt 21:10.
engaged. Ge 18:27, 30, 32. Jb 23:3-5. 42:3-6.
He 7:26. 9:24.

22 **ye shall**. Ge +17:7. Dt 26:17-19. SS 2:16. Ho
2:23.

23 **the whirlwind**. Je +23:19.
continuing. Heb. cutting. Pr 21:7mg.
fall. *or*, remain. 2 S 3:29mg. Ho 11:6.

24 **fierce**. Je 4:28. 1 S 3:12. Jb 23:13, 14. Is
14:24, 26, 27. 46:11. Ezk 20:47, 48. 21:5-7.
in the latter days. Je +23:20. Ge +49:1.

JEREMIAH 31

1 **same time**. Je +30:24.
will I. ver. 33. Ge +17:7. Ps 48:14. 144:15.
of all. Je 3:18. 23:6. 30:3, 10. 33:7, 14, 24-26.
50:4. Is 11:12, 13. Ezk 37:16-27. Ho 1:11. Zc
10:6, 7. Ro 11:26-29.
they shall. Je 30:22. 32:38. Le 26:12.

2 **The people**. Ex 1:16, 22. 2:23. 5:21. 12:37.
14:8-12. 15:9, 10. 17:8-13.
were left. Je 3:14. Is +24:6, 13. Zc 13:8. Mt
24:13. Lk 13:23. 18:8. Ro 11:5.
found grace. Je 2:2. Dt 1:30, 33. 2:7. 8:2, 3,
16. Ne 9:12-15. Ps 78:14-16, 23-29, 52.
105:37-43. 136:16-24. Is 32:16. 63:7-14. Ezk
20:14-17.
in the wilderness. Dt +33:2, 3. Jg 5:4, 5. Ps
68:7. +74:14. Is +16:1. 32:15, 16. 35:1, 6.
40:3. 41:19, 20. 61:3. Ezk 20:35, 36. Ho 2:14.
Mt 24:16. Re +12:6, 14.
when. Nu 10:33. Dt 1:33. 12:9. Ps 23:2.
95:11. Is 63:14. Ezk 34:15. Mt 11:28, 29. He
4:8, 9.
rest. Ps +94:13. Hab +3:16. 2 Th 1:7.

3 **appeared**. Ge +35:9.
of old. Heb. from afar.
I have. Dt +33:3, 26-29. Ps 139:16. Jn 3:16.
Ep 1:4.
an. Ps 103:17. Is 45:17. 54:8, 9. Ro 11:28, 29.
2 Th 2:13-16. 2 T 1:9.
everlasting. Heb. *olam*, Ge +17:7.
with lovingkindness have I drawn. *or*,
have I extended lovingkindness unto. SS 1:4.
Ezk +20:35, 36. Ho +2:14. 11:4. Jn 6:44, 45.
Ro 8:30. Ep 1:3-5. 2:4, 5. T 3:3-6. Ja 1:18. 1 P
1:3, 4.

4 **build**. Je +1:10. Ps +102:16. Ac 15:16. Ep
2:20-22. Re 21:10, etc.
O virgin. ver. 21. Je +18:13. Ge +24:16. Nu
+21:25.
again. ver. 13. Ex +15:20. Re 19:1-8.
tabrets. *or*, timbrels. Ex +15:20.

5 **yet**. Dt 28:30. Is 62:8, 9. 65:21, 22. Am 9:14,
15. Mi 4:4. Zc 3:10.
mountains. Ezk 36:8. Ob 19. Ac 8:5.
eat. Heb. profane. Le 19:23-25. Dt 20:6.
28:30. 1 S 21:5.

6 **a day**. Je 6:17. Is 40:9. 52:7, 8. 62:6. Ezk
3:17. 33:2. Ho 9:8.
upon. Je 50:19. 2 Ch 13:4. 30:5-11. Ac 8:5-8.
Arise. Je 50:4, 5. Ezr 1:5. 8:15-20. Is 2:2-4.
11:11-13. Ho 1:11. Mi 4:1-3. Zc 8:20-23.

7 **Sing**. Dt 32:43. Ps ch. 67. 96:1-3. 98:1-4. ch.
117. 138:4, 5. Is 42:10-12. Zc +2:10.
O Lord. Ps 14:7. 28:9. 69:35. 106:47. 118:25.
Ho 1:7.
remnant. Mi +5:3.

8 **I will**. Je 3:12. +23:3. Zc 2:6.
from the north country. Je +1:14.
gather them. Is +52:12mg. Ezk 20:34, 41.
+34:13. +37:25.
coasts of the earth. Ps 65:5. 72:8. 98:3. Is
43:6. 45:22. 49:6. 52:10.
the blind and. Is 40:11. 42:16. Ezk 34:16. Mi
4:6. Zp 3:19. Mt 12:20. Jn 21:15. 1 C 8:10. 1
Th 5:14. He 4:15. 12:12, 13.

9 **come**. Je 3:4. Da 9:17, 18. Mt +5:4.
Ro 8:26.
supplications. *or*, favors. Je 3:21, 22. 2 Ch
6:21. Zc 12:10.
I will. Ps 23:2. Is 35:6-8. 41:17-19. 43:16, 19.
49:9-11. Re 7:17.
in a. Is 40:3, 4. 57:14. 63:13. Mt 3:3. Lk 3:4-
6. He 12:13.
for I. ver. 20. Dt 32:6. 1 Ch 29:10. Is 63:16.
64:8. Mt 6:9. He 12:23. 1 J +3:1.
Ephraim. Ex 4:22. Ezk 34:12-14.
my firstborn. 1 Ch +5:1. +26:10. Ps 89:20.
27. Col +1:15.

10 **declare**. Is +11:11. 48:20.
scattered. Je +9:16. 50:17-20.
gather. Je +23:3. Is 40:11. Ezk 20:34, 41.
and keep. Je +30:11. Is 40:11. Ezk 34:12.

37:24. Mi 5:4, 5. Zc 9:16. Lk 12:32. Jn 10:26-29. Ac 20:28, 29.

11 **redeemed**. Je 15:21. 50:33, 34. Is 49:24-26. +51:11. Mt 20:28. Ga +3:13. He 2:14, 15.
stronger. Ps 142:6. Mt 12:29. 22:29. Lk 11:21, 22.

12 **Therefore**. ver. +4. Je 33:9-11. Is ch. 12. 35:10. 51:11.
the height. Is 2:2-5. Ezk 17:23. 20:40. Mi 4:1, 2.
and shall. Je 33:9. Ps 130:4. Ho 3:5. Ro 2:4.
wheat. Ho 2:20-23. Jl 3:18. Zc 9:15-17.
and their. Is 1:30. 58:11.
soul. Heb. *nephesh*, Ge +34:3.
watered garden. Is 58:11.
and they. Is +65:19. Jn 16:22.

13 **shall**. ver. +4. Ne 12:27, 43. Ps 30:11. 149:3. Zc 8:4, 5, 19.
for. Ezr 6:22. Est 9:22. Is 35:10. 51:3, 11. 60:20. 61:3. 65:18, 19. Jn 16:22.

14 **satiate**. Dt 33:8-11. 2 Ch 6:41. Ne 10:39. Ps 132:9, 16. Is 61:6. Jn 6:35. 1 P 2:9. Re 5:9, 10.
soul. Heb. *nephesh*, Ge +34:3.
my people. ver. 25. Je 33:9. Zc 9:15-17. Mt +5:6. Ep 1:3.

15 **A voice**. Ge 35:19. Ezk 2:10. Mt 2:16-18.
Ramah. i.e. *high place*, S#7414h. Je 40:1. Jsh 18:25. 19:8 (Ramath), 29, 36. Jg 4:5. 19:13. 1 S 1:1, Ramathaim-zophim, 19. 2:11. 7:17. 8:4. 15:34. 16:13. 19:18, 19, 22, 23. 20:1. 22:6. 25:1. 28:3. 1 K 15:17, 21, 22. 2 K 8:29. 2 Ch 16:1, 5, 6. 22:6. Ezr 2:26. Ne 7:30. 11:33. Is 10:29. Ho 5:8. Mt *2:18*, Rama. 27:57, Arimathea.
bitter weeping. Je 6:26. Ho 12:14.
Rahel. i.e. *ewe*, S#7354h. Ge +29:28, Rachel.
refused. Ge 37:35. Ps 77:2. Is 22:4.
her children. 2 S 12:23.
because. Ge 42:13, 36. Jb 7:21. Ps 37:36. La 5:7. Mt 2:16-18.

16 **Refrain**. Ge 43:31. 45:1. Ps 30:5. Mk 5:38, 39. Jn 20:13-15. 1 Th 4:13, 14.
from weeping. Is +25:8. Re +21:4.
for thy work. Je 2:2. Ru 2:12. 2 Ch 15:7. Ec 9:7. 1 C 15:58. He 6:10. 11:6.
they. ver. 4, 5. Je +23:3. 29:14. 30:3, 18. 33:7, 11. Ezr 1:5-11. Ezk 11:17, 18. 20:41, 42. Ho 1:11. 2:15.
the enemy. 1 C +15:26.

17 **there is hope**. Je 29:11-16. 46:27, 28. Ps +102:13, 14. Pr +14:32. Is 6:13. 11:11, etc. +26:19. La 3:18, 21, 26, 27. Ezk 37:11-14, 25. 39:28. Ho 2:15. 3:5. Am 9:8, 9. Mt 24:22. Ro 11:23-26. 2 C 3:14-16.
thy children. 2 S 12:23. Is 65:20. Ac +2:39.
come again. Dt +32:39-43. 1 S 2:6. Ps +27:13. 79:11. 102:13-22. Is +26:19.

18 **surely**. Jb 33:27, 28. Ps 102:19, 20. Is 57:15-18. Ho 5:15. 6:1, 2. Lk 15:18-20.

Ephraim. ver. 6, 9. Je 3:21, 22. 50:4, 5. Ho 11:8, 9. 14:4-8.
Thou hast. Je 2:30. 5:3. 7:28. 2 Ch 28:22. Jb 5:17. Ps 39:8, 9. 94:12. 118:18. 119:67, 71, 75. Pr 3:11. Is 1:5. 9:13. 57:17. Ho 5:12, 13. Zp 3:2. 1 C 11:32. He 12:5. Re 3:19.
as a. Ps 32:9. Pr 26:3. 29:1. Is 51:20. 53:7. La 3:27-30. Ho 10:11.
the yoke. Mt 11:29.
turn. Je 17:14. Ps 80:3, 7, 19. 85:4. La 5:21. Ml 4:6. Lk 1:17. Ac 3:26. Ph 2:13. Ja 1:16-18.
for. Je +3:22, 25. Is 63:16.

19 **Surely after**. Dt 30:2, 6-8. Ezk 36:26, 31. Zc 12:10. Lk 15:17-19. Jn 6:44, 45. Ep 2:3-5. 2 T 2:25. T 3:3-7.
I smote. Ezk 21:12. Lk 18:13. 2 C 7:10, 11.
I was ashamed. Je Le 26:41, 42. Ezr +9:6. Ezk 6:9. 20:43, 44. 36:31, 32.
I did. Je 3:25. 22:21. 32:30. Jb 13:26. 20:11. Ps 25:7. Is 54:4, 7. Ezk 23:3. Lk 15:30.

20 **Is Ephraim**. ver. 9. Je 3:19. Ps 103:13. Pr 3:12. Lk 15:20, 24, 32.
for. Dt 32:36. Jg 10:16. Is 57:16-18. La 3:31, 32.
my bowels. SS 5:4. Is +63:15, 16.
are troubled. Heb. sound. Je 48:36. Is 16:11. 63:15.
I will. Is 55:7. 57:18. Ho 14:4. Mi 7:18, 19.
have mercy. Je 30:17. Ezk 34:16. Lk +19:10.

21 **Set thee**. Is 57:14. 62:10.
waymarks. Nu 35:32. Dt +27:8. Jsh +20:7. 2 K 23:17. Is 35:8. Ezk +39:15. Hab 2:2.
set thine. Je 50:5. Dt 32:46. 1 Ch 29:3. 2 Ch 11:16. 20:3. Ps 62:10. 84:5. Pr 24:32mg. Is 44:19mg. 57:14. Ezk 40:4. Hg 1:5mg.
even. Je 6:16.
turn. Je 51:6, 50. Is 48:20. 52:11, 12. Zc 2:6, 7. 10:9.
O virgin. ver. +4. Je 3:14.

22 **How**. Je 2:18, 23, 36. 4:14. 13:27. Ho 8:5.
go about. SS 5:6.
backsliding. Je 3:6, 8, 11, 12, 14, 22. 7:24. 8:4-6. 14:7. 49:4. Ho 4:16. 11:7. 14:4. Zc 7:11.
created. Nu 16:30.
new thing. Je 30:14. Dt 24:4. Is +7:14. Ho 2:19. Mt 1:23.
A woman. ver. 21. S#5347h. Ge 1:27. 5:2. 6:19. 7:3, 9, 16. Le 3:1, 6. 4:28, 32. 5:6. 12:5, 7. 15:33. 27:4, 5, 6, 7. Nu 5:3. 31:15. Dt 4:16.
shall. Ge +3:15. Is +7:14. Mt +1:21. Lk 1:34, 35. Ga 4:4.
compass. Ps 7:7. 26:6. Jon 2:5.
a man. Ps 10:15-18. La 3:1. Zc 13:7.

23 **As yet**. Je 23:5-8. 33:15-26. Is 1:26. +60:21. Zc 8:3.
The Lord. Je +7:3. Ru 2:4. Ps 28:9. +122:5-8. 128:5. 129:8. 134:3.
when. Je +23:3.
O habitation. Je 50:7. Is 1:21.

and mountain. Ps 48:1, 2. 87:1-3. Ob 17. Mi 4:1. Zc 8:3.

24 **in Judah**. Je 33:11-13. Ezk 36:10, 11. Zc 2:4. 8:4-8.

25 **satiated**. ver. +14. Is 32:2. 50:4. Mt 11:28. 2 C 7:6.
  soul. Heb. *nephesh*, Ge +34:3.

26 **I awaked**. Ps 127:2. Zc 4:1, 2.

27 **the days**. ver. +31.
  that I. Je 30:19. Ezk 36:9. Ho 2:23. Zc 10:9, 10.

28 **And**. Ge +8:22.
  that like. Je 44:27. Da 9:14.
  to pluck. Je +1:10.
  so. Je 32:41, 42. Ps +102:16. Da 9:25. Ac 15:16.
  plant. Je +11:17.

29 **The fathers**. ver. 30. La 5:7. Ezk 18:2-4.
  sour grape. ver. 30. Is 18:5.
  children's. Ex +20:5. 34:7. Dt 5:9. He 7:10. 12:9.
  on edge. Ec 10:10.

30 **every one**. Ex +20:5. Dt 24:16. Is 3:10, 11. Ezk 3:18, 19, 24. 18:4, 20. 33:8, 13, 18. Ga 6:5, 7, 8. Ja 1:15.
  his own. 2 K +14:6.

31 **Behold**. He *8:8-12. 10:16, 17*.
  the days. ver. 27. Je +23:5.
  new covenant. Ge +9:16. Mt +26:28. He 10:16, 17.
  with. Je 50:4, 5. Ga 6:16. Ph 3:3.

32 **Not according**. ver. +1. Je 34:14. Ex 19:5, 6. 24:6-8. Dt 5:3, 4. 29:1, 10. Jsh 24:22. 1 K 8:9. Ezk 16:8, 60-62. He 9:18-22.
  that I made. Ex 24:3-8.
  in the day. Ge +2:17. Dt 1:31. 32:11, 12. Ps 73:23. SS 8:5. Is 41:13. 51:18. 63:12-14. Ho 11:1, 3, 4. Mk 8:23.
  which. Je 11:7-10. 22:9. Le 26:15. Dt 29:21, 25. 31:16, 20. Is 24:5. Ezk 16:59. 20:37. He *8:9*.
  although I was. *or*, should I have continued? Je 2:2. 3:14. Is 54:5. Ezk 16:8. 23:4. Ho 2:2. 3:1. Jn 3:29. 2 C 11:2.

33 **But this shall be**. Je 32:40.
  covenant. Ge +9:16.
  I will. Dt +6:6. 30:6. Ezk 11:19, 20. 36:25-27. Ro 7:22. 8:2-8. Ga 5:22, 23. He 8:10. 10:16.
  in their. Ex +25:21.
  write. Ex +31:18.
  and will. ver. +1.

34 **teach no more**. 1 Th 4:9. He 5:12. 8:12. 1 J 2:27.
  Know the Lord. 1 S +2:12. 1 Ch +28:9. Jn 17:3.
  for they. Je 24:7. Is 11:9. 30:26. 54:13. 60:19-21. Hab 2:14. Mt 11:27. Jn 6:45. +17:6. 1 C 2:10. 2 C 4:6. 1 J 2:20. 5:20.
  know. Jb +19:25. Ezk 34:27. He 8:11.
  from the least. Ac +8:10.

for I. Je 33:8. 50:20. Ps 32:1. Is 33:24. 43:25. 44:22. Am 8:7. Mi 7:18, 19. Ac 10:43. 13:38, 39. Ro 11:26, 27. Ep 1:7. He 8:12, *10:17*.
  remember. Ge +8:1.
  no more. Ge +9:16. Zc +10:6.

35 **which giveth**. Ge 1:14-18. 8:22. Dt 4:19. Jb 38:33. Ps 19:1-6. 72:5, 17. 74:16. 89:2, 36, 37. 119:89. 136:7-9. Mt +5:45. Ro 1:20. He 11:3.
  ordinances. Ge 8:22. Jb +38:33.
  which divideth. Ex +14:21.
  when. Je 5:22. Jb 38:10, 11. Ps 93:3, 4. 107:25-29. Is 51:15. Mt 8:25, 26.
  The Lord of hosts. Ps +24:10.
  is his name. Je +10:16. Ex +6:3.

36 **If**. Ge 8:22. 13:15.
  those. Je 33:20-26. Ps 72:5, 17. 89:36, 37. 102:28. 119:89. 148:6. Is +54:9, 10.
  then. Le +26:44. Ps 72:5, 7, 18. 102:28. Is 11:11. Ro +11:1.
  cease. Is 46:28. Dt 32:26. Am 9:8, 9.
  for ever. Heb. *olam*, Ge +9:12.

37 **If**. Je 33:22. Jb 11:7-9. Ps +89:2, 28, 34. Pr 30:4. Is 40:12.
  I will cast. Le +26:44.

38 **the days**. ver. 27. Je +23:5.
  that. ver. +28. Ne 2:17-20. 12:30-40. Ezk 48:30-35.
  the tower. Ne 3:1. 12:39. Zc 14:10.
  the gate of. 2 K 14:13. 2 Ch 26:9.

39 **measuring line**. 1 K 7:23. Ezk 40:3, 8. Zc 1:16. 2:1, 2. Re 11:1.
  Gareb. i.e. *scabby, leprous; reviler*, **S#1619h**, 2 S +23:38. 1 Ch 11:40.
  Goath. i.e. *lowing; fatigue*, **S#1601h**, only here.

40 **the whole**. Je 7:32. 19:11-13. 32:36. Ezk 37:2.
  the brook. 2 S +15:23.
  unto. 2 K 11:16. 2 Ch 23:15. Ne 3:28.
  shall be holy. Ezk 45:1-6. 48:35. Jl 3:17. Zc 14:20, 21.
  not be plucked up. Je +18:7. Is 51:22. Ezk 37:25. 39:28, 29. Am +9:15. Zc +9:8.
  for ever. Heb. *olam*, Ex +12:24.

JEREMIAH 32

1 A.M. 3415. B.C. 589.
  in the. Je 39:1, 2. 52:4, 5. 2 K 25:1, 2. 2 Ch 36:11.
  the eighteenth. Je +25:1.

2 **then**. 2 K +25:18.
  Jeremiah. ver. 3, 8. Mt 5:12. He +11:36.
  in the. Ne 3:25.

3 **Zedekiah**. Je 2:30. 5:3. 2 K 6:31, 32. 2 Ch 28:22.
  Wherefore. Je 26:8, 9. 38:4. Ex 5:4. Am 7:13. Lk 20:2. Ac 6:12-14.
  Behold. ver. 28, 29, 36. Je +21:4-7. 27:8. 34:2, 3. 37:6-10. 38:3.

4 **shall not escape**. Je +21:7.
delivered into. Je 34:3.
shall speak. Je 34:3mg.
5 **until**. Je 27:22. 34:4, 5.
though. Je 2:37. 21:4, 5. 33:5. 37:10. Nu
14:41. 2 Ch 13:12. 24:20. Pr +21:30. Ezk 17:9,
10, 15.
7 **Behold**. 1 K 14:5. Mk 11:2-6. 14:13-16.
Hanameel. i.e. *gift of God; place of God's favor;*
God is a rock or safety, **S#2601h**. ver. 8, 9, 12.
my field. Nu 35:5.
Anathoth. 1 Ch +7:8.
for. Le 25:23-25, 32-34, 49. Nu 35:2. Ru 4:4-
9. Re 5:1-5.
8 **court**. ver. 2. Je 33:1.
Anathoth. ver. +7.
Then I. 1 S 9:16, 17. 10:3-7. 1 K 22:25. Zc
11:11. Jn 4:53. Ac 10:17-28.
9 **weighed**. Ge 23:15, 16. 1 K 20:39mg. Est
3:9mg. Is 55:2mg.
seventeen shekels of silver. *or,* seven
shekels, and ten *pieces* of silver. Ge 37:28. Ho
3:2. Zc 11:12, 13.
10 **I**. ver. 12, 44. Is 44:5.
subscribed the evidence. Heb. wrote in the
book. Jsh 18:9. Is 30:8.
and sealed. Dt 32:34. Jb 14:17. SS 8:6. Da
8:26. Jn 3:33. 6:27. 2 C 1:22. Ep 1:13. 4:30.
Re 7:2. 9:4.
and took. ver. 12, 25, 44. Ru 4:9-11. Is 8:1, 2.
11 **according**. Lk 2:27. Ac 26:3. 1 C 11:16.
12 **Baruch**. i.e. *bent of knee* or *blessed,* **S#1263h**. Je
32:12, 13, 16. 36:4, 5, 8, 10, 13-19, 26, 27,
32. 43:3, 6. 45:1, 2. Ne 3:20. 10:6. 11:5.
Neriah. i.e. *light of Jah; lamp of the Lord; my*
lamp is Jehovah, **S#5374h**. Je 32:12, 16. 36:4, 8.
43:3. 45:1. 51:59. Also Je 36:14, 32. 43:6.
and in. 2 C 8:21.
14 **Lord of hosts, the God of**. Je +7:3.
Take. ver. 10-12.
sealed. Jb 14:17.
earthen vessel. Je +19:1. Le 6:28.
15 **Houses**. ver. 37, 43, 44. Je +30:18. 31:5, 12,
24. 33:12, 13. Am 9:14, 15. Zc 3:10.
16 **I prayed**. Je 12:1. Ge 32:9-12. 2 S 7:18-25.
Ezk 36:35-37. Ph 4:6, 7.
17 **Ah**. Je 1:6. 4:10. 14:13. Jg +6:22. Ezk 9:8.
11:13.
thou. Je 27:5. 51:15, 19. Ge +1:1. Ex 20:11. 2
K 19:15. Ne +9:6. Ps +115:3. 136:5-9. Is
48:12, 13. Da 4:35. Zc 12:1. Jn +1:3. Ac 7:49,
50. 14:15. 17:24.
there. ver. 27. Jb +42:2.
too hard for thee. *or,* hid from thee. Is 46:9,
10. Da 2:22. Ac 15:18. Ep 3:9-11.
18 **showest**. Ex 20:5, 6. 34:7. Nu 14:18. Dt 5:9,
10. 7:9, 10.
recompensest. Jsh 7:24-26. 2 S 21:1-9. 1 K
14:9, 10. 16:1-3. 21:21-24. 2 K 9:26. Mt
23:31-36. 27:25.

the Great. Ne 1:5. Is 57:15. Da +2:45.
Mighty. Is +49:26.
God. Heb. *El,* Ex +15:2. Je 51:56.
the Lord of hosts. Ps +24:10.
is his name. Je +10:16.
19 **Great**. Pr 8:14. Is +9:6. 28:29. 40:13. 46:10,
11. Ro 11:33, 34. Ep +1:11. Col 2:3. 1 J 2:1.
Re 3:18.
work. Heb. doing. Ex 15:11. Da 4:35.
for. Ps +11:4. Pr 5:21.
to give. 1 K 8:32. Ec 12:14. Mt +16:27. Jn
5:29.
20 **hast set**. Ex 7:3. 10:2. Dt 4:34. 6:22. 7:19.
13:1, 2. 26:8. 28:46. 29:3. 34:11. Ne 9:10. Ps
78:43-51. 105:27-36. 135:8, 9. Ac 7:36.
and hast. Ex 9:16. 2 S 7:23. 1 Ch 17:21. Ne
9:10. Is 63:11, 12. Da 9:15.
21 **brought**. Ex 6:6. 13:14, 15. Ps 105:37, 43.
106:8-11.
with a strong. Ex +6:6. 13:9. Ps 89:8-10.
22 **which**. Ge +13:15. Ex 13:5. Nu 14:16, 30. Ac
+7:5.
honey. Ex +3:8.
23 **possessed**. Ne 9:15, 22-25. Ps 44:2, 3. 78:54,
55. 105:44, 45.
but. Je +7:23, 24. 11:7, 8. Jg 2:11-13. 10:6.
Ezr 9:7. Ne 9:26-30. Ezk 20:8, 18, 21. Da 9:4-
6, 10-14. Zc 1:2-4.
they have. Lk 17:10. Jn +15:14. Ga 3:10. Ja
2:10.
therefore. Le 26:14, etc. Dt 28:15, etc. Jsh
23:16. Ezr 9:7. La 1:8, 18. 5:16, 17. Da 9:11,
12.
evil. Is +45:7.
come. 2 S +1:6.
24 **mounts**. *or,* engines of shot. Je 6:6. 33:4. 2 S
20:15. Ezk 21:21, 22.
the city is. ver. 3, 25, 36. Je 21:4-7. 37:6-10.
because. Je +12:12. 52:6. La 2:21, 22. 4:3-10.
what. Dt 4:26. 31:16, 17. 32:24, 25. Jsh
23:15, 16. Zc 1:6. Mt 24:35.
25 **thou**. ver. 8-15.
for. *or,* though. ver. 24. Ps 77:19. 97:2. Jn
13:7. Ro 11:33, 34.
27 **God**. Nu +16:22. 27:16.
flesh. Is 64:8. Lk +3:6. Ro 3:29, 30.
is there anything. ver. 17. Je 33:3. Mt
19:26. Mk 9:23. 11:22. Lk 18:27.
28 **Behold**. ver. 3, 24, 36. Je 19:7-12. 20:5.
29 **and set**. Je +17:27. Mt 22:7.
upon. Je 7:18. 44:17-19, 25. Dt +22:8.
to provoke. Dt 4:25. 9:18. 31:29. 32:21.
30 **children**. Je 2:7. 3:25. 7:22-26. Dt 9:7-12,
22-24. 2 K 17:9-20. Ne 9:16, etc. Ps 106:6, 7.
Is 63:10. Ezk 16:15, etc. 20:8, 28. 23:43, 44.
Ac 7:51-53.
from. Je 22:21. Ge 8:21. Ezk 23:3.
31 **this city**. Je 5:9-11. 6:6, 7. 23:14, 15. 1 K
11:7, 8. 2 K 21:4-7, 16. 22:16, 17. 23:13, 15.
Ezk 22:2-22. Mt 23:37. Lk 13:33, 34.

a provocation of mine anger. Heb. for my anger. ver. 37. Je 2:35. 4:8.
that I. Je 27:10. 2 K 23:27. 24:3, 4. La 1:8.

32 **they**. Je 2:26. Ezr 9:7. Ne 9:32-34. Is 1:4-6, 23. 9:14, 15. Ezk 22:6, 25-29. Da 9:6, 8. Mi 3:1-5, 9-12. Zp 3:1-4.

33 **turned**. Je 2:27. 7:24. 18:17. Ezk 8:16. Ho 11:2, 7. Zc 7:11, 12.
back. Heb. neck.
rising. Je +25:3, 4.

34 **set their abominations**. Je +7:30.
which is called. Je 7:10mg.

35 **they built**. Dt +18:10.
the valley. Jsh +15:8.
Molech. Le +18:21.
which. Je +7:31. Le 18:21. 20:2-5. Dt +18:10-12. 1 K 11:33.
neither came. Je +3:16.
to cause. Ex 32:21. Dt 24:4. 1 K 14:16. 15:26, 30. 16:19. 21:22. 2 K 3:3. 21:11. 23:15. 2 Ch 33:9.

36 **now**. Je 16:12-15. Is 43:24, 25. 57:17, 18. Ezk 36:31, 32. Ho 2:14. Ro 5:20. Ep 2:3-5.
the Lord, the God of. Je +11:3.
It shall. ver. +3, 24, 28.

37 **I will gather**. Je +23:3. Ho 1:11. 3:5. Ob 17-21.
I will cause. Le 23:43. Dt +12:10. Ezk 36:11, 33. Ho 11:11. Jl 3:20. Zc 2:4, 5. 3:10. 10:6. 14:11.

38 **they shall**. Ge +17:7. Dt 26:17-19. Ps 144:15. 1 J 3:1, 2.

39 **I will**. 2 Ch 30:12. Is 52:8. Ezk 11:19, 20. 36:26. 37:22. Jn 17:21. Ac 4:32. 2 C 13:11. Ph 2:1, 2.
one way. Je 6:16. Is 35:8. Jn 14:6. He 10:20.
they may fear. ver. 40. Dt +6:2. Ps 112:1. Pr 14:26, 27. 23:17. Ac 9:31.
for ever. Heb. all days. Je 33:18. 35:19. Ge +9:12. Lk 1:75.
for the. Ge 17:7. 18:19. Dt 5:29. 11:18-21. Ps 115:13-15. 128:6. Ezk 37:25. Ac +2:39. 3:39. 13:33. Ro 11:16. 1 C 7:14.

40 **I will make**. Is +55:3. Ezk 16:60. Lk 1:72-75. Ga 3:14-17. He 6:13-18. 12:24.
everlasting. Heb. olam, Ge +17:7.
covenant. Ge +9:16.
that I. Ezk 39:29. Jn 10:27-30. Ro 8:28-39.
will not. Je +31:36. +33:25, 26. Ps 94:14. Is +41:9. 51:22. 54:7. Ro +11:1. 15:8. He +13:5.
from them. Heb. from after them. Je +17:16mg. 2 K 10:29.
but I. Je 31:33. Ezk 36:26. Ro 15:8. 2 C 3:14. He 4:1. Ja 1:17. 1 P 1:5.
not depart. Je 3:19. Ps 80:18. +130:8. Is +11:11. +41:9. +55:3. +59:21. Ezk 16:63.

41 **Yea, I**. Dt +30:9.
rejoice. Ps +104:31.
do them good. Ezk 36:11. Zc 10:6.
and I. Je +11:17. Am 9:15.

assuredly. Heb. in truth, or stability. Je 2:21. 26:15. 28:9. Ho 2:19, 20.
whole. Mt +22:37.
heart. Ge +6:6.
soul. Heb. nephesh, Ge +34:3; Le +26:11.

42 **Like**. Je 31:28. Jsh 23:14, 15. Zc 8:14, 15. Mt 24:35.
so. Je +31:28. 33:10, 11.
promised. Je 29:10. 33:17, 20, 21, 22, 25, 26. Is +55:3. Ro 11:29. +15:8.

43 **ye say**. ver. 36. Je 33:10. Ezk +12:19. 37:11-14.

44 **buy**. ver. 6-15.
in the land. Je 17:26.
for I. ver. +37. Ps 126:1-4.

JEREMIAH 33

1 A.M. 3416. B.C. 588.
he. He +11:36.

2 **the maker**. Ps 87:5. 102:16. Is 14:32. 37:26. 43:1, 21. 62:7. He 11:10, 16. Re 21:2, 10.
the Lord. or, Jehovah. Je +32:18. Ex 3:14, 15. 6:3. 15:3. Am 5:8. 9:6.

3 **Call**. Je 29:12. Ps 6:9. 86:5, 7. Is 55:6, 7. +65:24. Jl 2:32. Lk 11:9, 10. Ro 10:12, 13. He 4:14-16. Ja 4:8. 1 J +5:14.
will answer. Is +65:24.
show. Je 32:27. Jb 28:11. Ps +51:6. Mi 7:15. Ep 3:20.
great and. 2 K 4:1-7. 2 Ch 17:3-5. Jb 42:10-13. Is 41:17, 18. +55:1-3. 64:4. Lk 8:24, 25. 12:31. 2 C 12:7-11. Ep 3:20, 21. Ja 5:17, 18. Re 3:20, 21.
mighty. Heb. hidden. Zc 11:2mg. Re 2:17.
things. Mt 21:22. Ro +8:32.
which thou. Ps 25:14. Is 45:3. 48:6. Am 3:7. Mt 13:35. 1 C 2:7-11.

4 **the Lord, the God of**. Je +11:3.
thrown. Je 32:24. Ezk 4:2. 21:22. 26:8. Hab 1:10.

5 **come**. Je 21:4-7. 32:5. 37:9, 10.
I have hid. Dt +31:17.

6 **I will bring**. Je +8:22. Ps +103:3. Is 58:8. Ho 6:1. 7:1. Mt 14:36.
and will. Ex 34:6. Ps 37:11. 72:7. Is 26:2-4. 55:7. 66:12. Mi 4:3. Jn 10:10, 11. T 3:5, 6.

7 **will cause**. ver. 11, 26. Je +23:3.
will build. Ps +102:16. Is 1:26. Ho 2:15. Zc 1:17.

8 **will cleanse**. Je +31:34. Ps 85:2, 3. Is 40:2. 56:7. Ezk 36:25, 33. Jl 3:21. Zc 13:1. He 9:11-14. 1 J 1:7-9. Re 1:5, 6.
will pardon. Ps 103:12. Is 43:25. Mi 7:19.

9 **a name**. Je 13:11. 31:4. Dt +30:9. Ps 126:3, 4. Is 62:2, 3, 7, 12. Zc 8:20-23. 12:2, 3.
before. Je 26:6. 29:1. 44:8.
fear. Ho +3:5.

10 **which ye**. Je +32:36, 43. Ezk 37:11.

11 **voice of joy**. Je 7:34. 16:9. 25:10. Jn 3:29. Re 18:23.

the voice of them. Je 31:12-14. Is 12:1-6. 51:11. Zp 3:14, 15.
Praise the. Ex +34:6.
Lord of hosts. Je +6:6.
for ever. Heb. *olam*, Ex +12:24.
sacrifice. Le +7:12. Ezk 43:27mg. 45:17mg. Am 4:5.
of praise. Je +17:26.
For I. ver. +7, 26.

12 **without**. Je 32:43. 36:29. 51:62.
in all. Je +17:26. 31:24. 32:44. 50:19, 20. Is 65:10. Ezk 34:12-14. 36:8-11. Ob 19, 20. Zp 2:6, 7. Jn 10:2, 3.

13 **shall**. Le 27:32. Lk 15:4-7. Jn 10:3, 4, 14.

14 **the days come**. ver. +17. Je +23:5. Is 32:1, 2. Ezk 34:23-25. Da 2:44. 7:13, 14. 9:25. Mi +5:2. Zp 3:15-17. Zc 9:9, 10. Ml +3:1. Lk 10:24. Ac 13:32, 33. 2 C 1:20. He 11:40. 1 P 1:10-12. Re 19:10.

15 **the Branch**. Is +11:1. 61:11.
unto David. 2 S 7:12.
and he. Is +9:7. +11:4. 42:21. Jn 5:22-29. He 7:1, 2.

16 **In those days**. Zc 12:8.
shall Judah. Je +23:6. Is 45:17, 22. Ro 11:26.
dwell safely. Dt +12:10. Ps 102:13, 14, 16. Is 4:5, 6. 27:2, 3. 33:20-22. 51:3. 54:14, 15, 17. 65:18, 19. 66:10-12. Da 7:27.
The Lord our righteousness. *JEHOVAH-tsidkenu*. Je 23:6. Ex +15:26. Is 45:24, 25. Ro 3:22. 5:19. 10:4. 1 C 1:30. 2 C 5:21. Ph 3:8, 9. 2 P 1:1.

17 **David shall never want**. Heb. There shall not be cut off from David. Je 35:19. 2 S 3:29. 7:14-16. 1 K 2:4. 8:25mg. 1 Ch 17:11-14, 27. Ps 89:29-37. Is +9:7. Lk 1:32, 33, 69, 70.

18 **Neither shall**. Is 56:7. 61:6. Ezk 43:19-27. 44:9-11. 45:4, 5. Ml 3:3. Ro 12:1, 2. 15:16. 1 C 2:2. Ep 1:6, 7. He 13:15, 16. 1 P 2:5, 9. Re 1:6. 5:9, 10.
the priests the Levites. Nu 25:10-13. Dt 17:9. Is 66:21. Ezk 43:18, 19. 44:10, 14, 15. Ml 2:5.
burnt. Le +23:12.
sacrifice. Is +56:7.
continually. He 13:15, 16.

20 **If ye can break**. ver. 25, 26. Je +31:35, 36. Ge +8:22. Jb 38:12. Ps 89:30-37. 104:19-23. Is +54:9, 10. Ro +11:1.
covenant. Ge +9:16.

21 **may**. 2 Ch 7:18. 21:7. Is +55:3. Mt 24:35. Lk 1:69, 70.
covenant. Ge +9:16.
with David. Is +55:3. He 6:17, 18.
that he. ver. 20, 25, 26. Je +7:7. 31:35-37. Jsh 21:43. 1 K 4:21. Is +9:6, 7. +26:15. 60:21. Da 7:14. Mt 8:11. Lk 1:32, 33. Ac 7:5. He 11:13, 39.
and with. ver. +18. Re 5:10.

22 **the host**. Je 31:37. Ge +15:5. 28:14. Re 7:4, 9, 10.
sand of the sea. Ge +22:17.
so. Ps 22:30. 89:3, 4, 29. Is 53:10-12. Ezk 37:24-27. Zc 12:8.
multiply. Ac 9:31. He 2:10.
the Levites. Is +66:21, 22. Ezk 44:15.

24 **The two**. ver. 21, 22. Ps +44:9. +94:14. Ro +11:1-6.
thus. Ne 4:2-4. Est 3:6-8. Ps 44:13, 14. 71:11. 83:4. 123:3, 4. La 2:15, 16. 4:15. Ezk 25:3. 26:2. 35:10-15. 36:2.

25 **If my**. ver. +20. Ge +8:22. 9:9-17.
and if. Je +31:35, 36. Ps 74:16, 17. 104:19.
ordinances of heaven. Jb +38:33.

26 **Then**. Je 31:36. Dt 4:31. Jg 2:1. Is +54:9, 10. Ro +11:1.
will I. Je +31:37. Ge +49:10.
cast away. Je 23:39. Is +41:9. +54:7.
I will cause. ver. 7-11. Ezr 2:1, 70.
Abraham. Ge 50:24. Ex 2:24. 3:6. 6:3, 4. Ps 105:9, 10. Mt +8:11. +22:32. Mk +12:26, 27. Lk 1:72, 73.
for I. Je +23:3. 31:36, 37. Ro +11:1.
and have. Je 31:20. Is 14:1. +41:9. 54:8. Ezk 39:24, 25. Ho 1:7. 2:23. Zc 10:6. Ro 11:32.

JEREMIAH 34

1 A.M. 3415. B.C. 589.
when. ver. 7. Je 32:2. 39:1-3. 52:4, etc. 2 K 25:1-9. 2 Ch 36:11-17.
all the kingdoms. Je 1:15. 27:5-7. Da 2:37, 38. 4:1, 22. 5:19.
of his dominion. Heb. the dominion of his hand.

2 **Go**. Je 22:1, 2. 37:1-4. 2 Ch 36:11, 12.
Behold. ver. 22. Je +17:27.

3 **And thou**. ver. 21. Je +21:7.
and thine. Je 39:6, 7. 52:10, 11. 2 K 25:6, 7. Ezk 12:13. 17:18-20. 21:25.
he shall speak with thee mouth to mouth. Heb. his mouth shall speak to thy mouth.

4 **Yet hear**. Je +7:2. 38:17, 20.

5 **But thou**. 2 K 22:20. 2 Ch 34:28. Ezk 17:16.
and with. 2 Ch 16:13, 14. 21:19.
so. Da 2:46.
and they. Je +22:18. 2 Ch 21:20. La 4:20.

6 **spake**. 1 S 3:18. 15:16-24. 2 S 12:7-12. 1 K 21:19. 22:14. Ezk 2:7. Mt 14:4. Ac 20:27.

7 **fought against**. ver. +1. Je 4:5. 8:14. 11:12. Dt 28:52.
Lachish. Jsh +10:3.
for. 2 Ch 11:5-10. 27:4.

8 **had**. 2 K 11:17. 23:2, 3. 2 Ch 15:12-15. 23:16. 29:10. 34:30-33. Ne 9:38. 10:1, etc.
to proclaim. ver. +14, 17. Ex 21:2-4. 23:10, 11. Le 25:10, 39-46. Dt 15:12. Ne 5:1-13. Is 9:4. 10:27. 14:25. 61:1, 2. Ezk 46:17. 1 C 7:21.

9 **Hebrew**. Ge 14:13. 40:15. Ex 2:6. 3:18. Dt 15:12. 1 S 4:6, 9. 14:11. 2 C 11:22. Ph 3:5.
Hebrewess. i.e. *a Hebrew woman*, **S#5680h**, with this rendering only here. For **S#5680h**, Hebrew, see Ge +14:13.
serve. ver. 10. Je 25:14. 27:7. 30:8. 1 C 6:6-8.

10 **when**. Je 26:10, 16. 36:12, 24, 25. 38:4.
then. Je 3:10, 11. Is 29:13. Mk 6:20.

11 **afterward**. ver. 21. Je 37:5. Ex 8:8, 15. 9:28, 34, 35. 10:17-20. 14:3-9. 1 S 19:6-11. 24:19. 26:21. Ps 36:3. 78:34-36. 125:5. Pr 26:11. Ec 8:11. Ho 6:4. 7:16. Zp 1:6. Mt 12:43-45. Ro 2:4, 5. 2 P 2:20-22.

12 **from the Lord**. Ge +19:24.

13 **I made**. Je 31:32. Ex 24:3, 7, 8. Dt 5:2, 3, 27. 29:1. He +8:10, 11.
in the day. Je +7:22. 11:4, 7. Ge +2:17. Dt 7:8. 15:15. 16:12. 24:18. Jsh 24:17. Jg 6:8.
out of. Ex 13:3, 14. Dt 5:6. 6:12. 8:14. 13:10. Jsh 24:17. Jg 6:8.

14 **At the**. ver. 8, 9. Ex 21:1-4. 23:10, 11. Dt 15:12. 1 K 9:22. 2 Ch 28:10. Is 58:6. Am 8:6.
been sold. *or*, sold himself. Le +25:39.
but. Je +7:26. 1 S 8:7, 8. 2 Ch 36:16, 21.

15 **ye**. 1 K 21:27-29. 2 K 10:30, 31. 12:2. 14:3. Is 58:2. Mt 15:8.
now. Heb. today.
in proclaiming. ver. +10, 11.
ye had. ver. +8. 2 K 23:3. Ne 10:29. Ps 76:11. 119:106.
which is called by my name. Heb. whereupon my name is called. Je +7:10mg, 11.

16 **ye turned**. ver. +11. 1 S 15:11. Ezk 3:20. 18:24. 33:12, 13. Lk +8:13-15.
polluted. Ex 20:7. Le 19:12. Ezk 17:16-19. 20:39. 39:7. Ml 1:7, 12.
pleasure. Heb. *nephesh*, Ex +15:9; Ge +23:8.
and brought. Mt 18:28-34.

17 **behold**. Le 26:34, 35. Dt 19:19. Jg 1:6, 7. Est 7:10. Da 6:24. Mt 7:1, 2. Lk 6:37, 38. Ga 6:7. Ja 2:13. Re 16:6.
liberty. Le 25:42, 55.
to the sword. Je +12:12.
I will. Je 24:9, 10. 29:18.
to be removed. Heb. for a removing. Je +15:4mg.

18 **have transgressed**. Dt 17:2. Jsh 7:11. 23:16. Ho 6:7. 8:1.
when. Ge +15:10, 17, 18. Dt 29:12mg. Jsh 9:7. Ps 50:5.

19 **princes**. ver. 10. Ezk 22:27, etc. Da 9:6, 8, 12. Mi 7:1-5. Zp 3:3, 4.
the eunuchs. Je +29:2.

20 **and into**. ver. 21. Je 4:30. 11:21. 21:7. 22:25. 38:16. 44:30. 49:37.
life. Heb. *nephesh*, Ge +44:30.
and their. Je +7:33. 1 K +14:11.

21 **Zedekiah**. ver. +3-5. Je +21:7.
life. Heb. *nephesh*, Ge +44:30.
which are. Je 37:5, 11.

22 **I will command**. 2 S 16:11. 2 K 24:2, 3. 2 Ch 36:17. Is 10:5-7. 13:3. 37:26. 45:1-3. Am +3:6. Mt 22:7.
cause. Je +37:8-10.
shall fight. ver. +2.
and I will. Je +18:16. Is 24:12. 64:10, 11. La 1:1. Zc 1:12. 7:14.

JEREMIAH 35

1 A.M. 3397. B.C. 607.
in the. Je 1:3. 1 Ch +3:15.

2 **the house**. ver. 8. 2 K 10:15, 16. 1 Ch 2:55.
Rechabites. i.e. *descendants of Rechab* (i.e. *horseman*, 2 S +4:2), **S#7397h**, Je 35:2, 3, 5, 18. Nu 10:29. Jg 1:16. 4:11-17. 5:24. 1 S 15:6.
into one. ver. 4. Je 36:10. 1 K 6:5, 6, 10. 1 Ch 9:26, 27. 23:28. 2 Ch 3:9. 31:11. Ezr 8:29. Ne 13:5, 8, 9. Ezk 40:7-13, 16. 41:5-11. 42:4-13.

3 **Habaziniah**. i.e. *God's light; the hiding of God's thorn; whom the Lord makes a buckler or shield*, **S#2262h**.

4 **into the chamber**. Je 36:10-12.
Igdaliah. i.e. *Great is Jah; Jehovah will wax great*, **S#3012h**.
a man. Dt +33:1. 1 T +6:11.
the princes. Je 26:10.
the keeper. Je 52:24. 2 K 12:9. 25:18. 1 Ch 9:18, 19, 27. 2 Ch 8:14. 31:14. Ps 84:10.
door. Heb. threshold, *or* vessel. 2 K +12:9mg. Ezk 43:8.

5 **Drink**. ver. 2. Ec 9:7. Am 2:12. 2 C 2:9.

6 **Jonadab**. i.e. *the Lord gave freely; Jehovah is a willing giver; whom Jehovah impels*, **S#3122h**. Je 35:6, 10, 19. 2 S 13:3, 32, 35. 2 K +10:15. 1 Ch 2:55.
Ye shall. Le 10:9. Nu 6:2-5. Jg 13:7, 14. Lk 1:15. 1 C 7:26-31.
for ever. Heb. *olam*, Ex +12:24.

7 **all**. ver. 10. Ge 25:27. Le 23:42, 43. Ne 8:14-16. Ep +5:18. He 11:9-13. 1 P 2:11.
live many. Dt +4:40.
land where. Ge 36:7. 1 Ch 16:19. Ps 105:12.

8 **we obeyed**. Ex 20:12. Pr 1:8, 9. 4:1, 2, 10. 6:20. 13:1. Col 3:20.
Jonadab. **S#3082h**, 2 K +10:15. ver. 14, 16, 18.

9 **neither have**. ver. 7. Nu 16:14. 2 K 5:26. Ps 37:16. 1 T 6:6, 9.

10 **we have**. ver. 8.

11 **when**. 2 K 24:2. Da 1:1, 2.
Come. Je 4:5-7. 8:14. Mk 13:14. Lk 21:20, 21.
Syrians. Is 9:12.

13 **Will**. Je 5:3. 6:8-10. 9:12. 32:33. Ps 32:8, 9. Pr 8:10. 19:20. Is 28:9-12. 42:23. He 12:25.

14 **words**. ver. +6-10.
rising. Je +25:3, 4. Pr 1:20-33.
but ye. Je +7:26. Is +30:9. 50:2.

15 sent. 2 Ch +24:19. Lk 10:16. 1 Th 4:8.
Return. Je 3:12, 14, 22. 4:1, 4, 14. 7:3-5.
17:20-23. 18:11. 23:14. 24:7. 25:5. 26:13.
31:19, 20. 36:3. 44:4, 5. Pr 28:13. Is 1:16-19.
55:6, 7. Ezk 18:21-23, 30-32. 33:11. Ho 14:1-
4. Jl 2:12, 13. Zc +1:3, 4. Mt 3:8. Ac +3:19.
26:18-20.
ye shall dwell. Je +7:7.
ye have. Lk 13:34, 35.
16 the sons. ver. 14. Is 1:3. Ml 1:6. Mt 11:28-30.
Lk 15:11-13, 28-30.
17 Lord God of. Je 38:17. 44:7.
Behold. Je +11:8. 15:3, 4. 21:4-10. Ge 6:17.
Dt 29:19-28. 31:20, 21. 32:16-42.
evil. Is +45:7.
because. Je +7:13, 26, 27. 26:5. +29:19.
32:33. Pr 1:24-31. 13:13. 16:2. Is 50:2. 65:12.
66:4. Lk 13:34, 35. Ro 10:21.
18 Because. Ex +20:12. Dt 5:16. Ep 6:1-3.
19 Jonadab, etc. Heb. There shall not a man be
cut off from Jonadab the son of Rechab to
stand, etc. Je +33:17mg. 1 Ch 2:55.
stand. Je 33:17, 18. Lk +21:36.

JEREMIAH 36

1 fourth year. Je +25:1. 35:1. 2 K 24:1, 2.
2 a roll. ver. 6, 23, 29. Je 30:2. 45:1. 51:60. Ex
17:14. Dt 31:24. Ezr 6:2. Jb 31:35. Ps 40:7. Is
8:1. 30:8, 9. Ezk 2:9. 3:1-3. Hab 2:2, 3. Zc 5:1-
4. Re 5:1-9.
write. Je +30:2. Ho 8:12.
against Israel. Je 2:4. 3:3-10. 23:13, 14.
32:30-35. 2 K 17:18-20.
against all. Je 1:5, 10. 25:9-29. ch. 47-51.
from the days. Je +1:2, 3. 25:3.
3 may be. ver. 7. Je 18:8. 26:3. Dt 5:29. Ezk
12:3. Zp 2:3. Lk 20:13. 2 T 2:25, 26. 2 P 3:9.
hear. Ezk 18:27, 28. 33:7-9, 14-16. Mt 3:7-9.
Lk 3:7-9.
they may. Je +35:15. Dt 30:2, 8. 1 S 7:3. 1 K
8:48-50. 2 Ch 6:38, 39. Ne 1:9. Jon 3:8-10.
that I. Is 6:10. Mt 13:15. Mk 4:12. Ac 3:19.
26:18. 28:27.
4 Baruch. ver. 26. Je 32:12. 43:3, 6. 45:1-5.
wrote. ver. 17, 18, 32. Je 45:1, 2. Ro 16:22.
upon. ver. 21, 23, 28, 32. Is 8:1. Ezk 2:9. Zc
5:1.
5 I am shut. Je 40:4. He +11:36.
6 and read. ver. 8. Ezk 2:3-7.
the words. Je +7:2. 18:11. 19:14. 22:2. 26:2.
upon. ver. +9. Le 16:29-31. 23:27-32. Ac
27:9.
fasting day. 2 K 24:1. 2 Ch 36:6.
7 It may. ver. +3. Je 26:3. 1 K 8:33-36. 2 Ch
33:12, 13. Ezk 12:3. Da 9:13. Ho 5:15. 6:1.
14:1-3. Am 5:15. Zp +2:3.
they will present their supplication. Heb.
their supplication shall fall. Je 37:20mg.
38:26. 42:2mg, 9.

and will. Je +1:3. 25:5. Jon 3:8. Zc 1:4.
for. Je 16:10. 19:15. Dt 28:15, etc.
29:18-28.
anger. Je 21:5. 2 K 22:13, 17. 2 Ch 34:21.
fury. Le +26:28.
8 did. ver. 4. Je 1:17. Mt 16:24. 1 C 16:10. Ph
2:19-22.
in the. Ne 8:3. Lk 4:16, etc.
9 A.M. 3398. B.C. 606.
in the fifth year. ver. +1.
they proclaimed. Le 23:27. Mt +6:16.
came. ver. 6.
10 Then. ver. 6, 8.
in the chamber. Je +35:4.
Gemariah. i.e. *perfected of the Lord; complete-*
ness of Jah, **S#1587h**. ver. 11, 12, 25. Je 29:3.
Shaphan. ver. +11.
the scribe. 2 S +8:17.
entry. *or*, door. Je 26:10. 2 K 15:35.
gate. Ge +14:7.
11 Shaphan. ver. 10. 2 K +22:3.
12 Elishama. ver. 20, 21. Je 41:1.
Delaiah. i.e. *drawn up of the Lord; Jah has*
delivered, **S#1806h**. ver. 25. 1 Ch +3:24, Daliah.
24:18. Ezr 2:60. Ne 6:10. 7:62.
Elnathan. ver. 25. 2 K +24:8.
Gemariah. ver. +10.
Hananiah. Je 28:1, etc. 1 Ch +25:23.
13 declared. 2 K 22:10, 19. 2 Ch 34:16-18, 24.
Jon 3:6.
14 Jehudi. i.e. *a Jew; praise of the Lord*, **S#3065h**.
ver. 21, 23.
Nethaniah. Je 40:8. 41:1, 2, 16, 18. 2 K
25:23.
Cushi. Zp 1:1.
took. ver. +2. Ezk 2:6, 7. Mt 10:16, 28.
15 and read. ver. +21.
16 they were. ver. 24. Ac 24:25, 26.
We. Je 13:18. 38:1-4. Am 7:10, 11.
17 Tell. Jn 9:10, 11, 15, 26, 27.
18 He pronounced. ver. 2, 4. Je 43:2, 3. Pr
+26:4, 5.
with ink. 2 C 3:3. 2 J 12. 3 J 13.
19 Go, hide. ver. 26. Je 26:20-24. 2 Ch 25:15. Pr
+22:3. Am 7:12. Lk 13:31. Ac 5:40.
20 laid up. ver. 12, 21.
21 Jehudi. ver. 14.
And Jehudi. ver. 15. Je +23:28. 26:2. 2 K
22:10. 2 Ch 34:18-20. Ezk 2:4, 5, 7.
22 the winterhouse. Je 22:14-16. Jg 3:20. Am
3:15.
23 he cut. ver. 29-31. Dt 29:19-21. 1 K 22:8, 27,
28. Ps 50:17. Pr 1:30. 5:12. 13:13. 19:21.
+21:30. 29:1. Is 5:18, 19. 28:14, 15, 17-22. Re
22:19.
24 they were not afraid. ver. 16. Jb 15:4. Ps
36:1. 64:5. Is 26:11. Ro 3:18.
nor rent. Je 5:3. 2 K +18:37. Jon 3:6. Mt
12:41.
25 Elnathan. ver. +12.

made. Je 13:15-17. Ge 37:22, 26-28. Mt 27:4, 24, 25. Ac 5:34-39.
but. 1 S +25:17. Pr 21:29.

26 **Hammelech**. *or*, the king. *i.e. the king; counselor*, **S#4429h**. Je 38:6mg. 1 K 22:26. 2 K 10:2. Zp 1:8.
Abdeel. *i.e. servant of God*, **S#5655h**.
to take. Je 2:30. 26:21-23. 1 K 19:1-3, 10, 14. Mt 23:34-37. 26:47-50. Jn 7:32. 8:20. 11:57.
but. ver. 5, 19. Je 1:19. 15:20, 21. 2 K 6:18-20. Ps +64:2. +91:1. 121:8. Pr +22:3. Zp 2:3. Ac 12:11.

27 **after that**. ver. +23. 2 T 2:9.
and the words. ver. 4, 18.

28 **another roll**. Je 28:13, 14. 44:28. Jb 23:13. Zc 1:5, 6. Mt 24:35. 2 T 2:13.

29 **Thou hast**. Dt 29:19. Jb 15:24-27. 40:8-10. Is 45:9. Ac 5:39. 1 C 10:22.
Why. Je 26:9. 32:3. Is 29:21. 30:10. Ac 5:28.
The king. Je 21:4-7, 10. 28:8. 32:28-30. 34:21, 22.

30 **He shall**. Je 22:30. Dt 29:19, 20. 2 K 24:12-15.
and his dead body. Je +22:18, 19.
in the day. Ge 31:40.

31 **punish**. Heb. visit upon. Je +9:25mg.
will bring. Je +11:8. 29:17-19. 44:4-14. Pr 29:1.
but. Je +25:4. Mt 23:37-39.

32 **took**. ver. +28-30.
who wrote. ver. 4, 18. Ex 4:15, 16. Ro 16:22.
were added. Le 26:18, 21, 24, 28. Da 3:19. Re +22:18, 19.
like words. Heb. words as they.

JEREMIAH 37

1 A.M. 3406-3416. B.C. 598-588.
Zedekiah. 1 K +22:11.
Coniah. Je +22:24.
made king. Ezk 17:12-21.

2 **neither**. 2 K 24:19, 20. 2 Ch 36:12-16. Pr 29:12. Ezk 21:25. 1 Th 4:8.
by the prophet. Heb. by the hand of the prophet. 1 K +16:12mg.

3 **Jehucal**. *i.e. potent; he will be made strong; Jehovah will prevail*, **S#3081h**.
Zephaniah. Zp +1:1.
Pray now. Je 2:27. 21:1, 2. 42:2-4, 20. Ge 27:38. Ex 8:8, 28. 9:27, 28. 10:16, 17. Nu 12:10-13. 21:6, 7. 1 S 7:8. 12:19. 1 K 13:6. 2 K 2:9. 4:27. 19:3, 4. Jb 42:8, 9. Ml 1:9. Lk 23:42. Ac 8:24. Ro 15:30-32. 2 C 1:11. Ep 6:18-20. Col 4:3, 4. 1 Th 5:25. 2 Th 3:1, 2. He 13:18, 19. Ja 5:14, 15.

4 **for**. ver. 15. Je 32:2, 3.

5 **Pharaoh's**. ver. 7. 2 K 24:7. Ezk 17:15.

they. ver. 11. Je 34:21.

7 **Thus**. ver. 3. Je 21:2. 2 K 22:18.
the Lord, the God of. Je +11:3.
Pharaoh's. Je 17:5, 6. Pr +21:30. Is 30:1-6. 31:1-3. La 4:17. Ezk 17:17. 29:6, 7, 16.

8 **fight against**. Je +17:27.

9 **Thus saith**. Ezk 24:14.
Deceive not. Ob 3. Mt 24:4, 5. Ga 6:3, 7. Ep 5:6. 2 Th 2:3. Ja +1:22.
yourselves. Heb. your souls. Heb. *nephesh*, Ex +15:9. Est 9:31mg.

10 **though**. Je 21:4-7. 49:20. 50:45. Le 26:36-38. Is 10:4. 30:17.
wounded men. Heb. men thrust through. Is 14:19. lit. pierced. **S#1856h**. Je 51:4. Nu 25:8. Jg 9:54. 1 S 31:4. 1 Ch 10:4. Is 13:15. La 4:9. Zc 12:10. 13:3.
yet. Jl 2:11.
burn. Je +17:27.

11 **that**. ver. +5.
broken. Heb. made to ascend. Je 34:21. Ex 40:36.

12 **Then**. Lk 21:20, 21.
went. 1 K 19:3, 9. Pr +22:3. Ne 6:11. Mt 10:23. 1 Th 5:22.
the land. Je 1:1. Jsh 21:17, 18. 1 Ch 6:60.
separate himself thence. *or*, slip away from thence. or, receive a portion thence. Je 32:9. 1 S 30:24. Pr +22:3.
in the midst. Lk +4:30.

13 **in the gate**. Je 38:7. 2 K 14:13. Ne 8:16. Zc 14:10.
Irijah. *i.e. fear of Jah; protection of the Lord; he will see the Lord*, **S#3376h**. ver. 14.
Hananiah. Je 28:1, 10-17. 36:12.
Thou. Je 18:18. 20:10. 21:9. 27:6, 12, 13. 28:14. 38:4, 17. Am 7:10. Lk 23:2. Ac 6:11. 24:5-9, 12, 13. 2 C 6:8-10.

14 **said**. Je 40:4-6. Ne 6:8. Ps 27:12. 35:11. 52:1, 2. Mt 5:11, 12. Lk 6:22, 23, 26. 1 P 3:16. 4:14-16.
false. Heb. falsehood, *or*, a lie. Je 3:10mg, 23 (in vain). 5:2, 31. 8:8mg. 10:14.
princes. Je 26:16. 38:1.

15 **the princes**. Je 20:1-3. 26:16. Mt 21:35. 23:34. 26:67, 68. Lk 20:10, 11. 22:64. Jn 18:22. Ac 5:28, 40. 23:2, 3.
put. He +11:36.
in the. ver. 20. Je 38:6, 26.

16 A.M. 3415. B.C. 589.
into the dungeon. Heb. *bor*, Ge +37:20. lit. house of the pit. Je 6:7. 38:6, 10-13. Ge 21:19. 40:15. Is 14:19. La 3:53, 55.
cabins. *or*, cells.
remained. ver. 21. Je 38:13, 28.

17 **asked**. Je 38:5, 14-16, 24-27. 1 K 14:1-4.
secretly. Je 38:16. 40:15. Dt 13:6.
Is there. ver. 3. Je 21:1, 2. 1 K 22:16. 2 K 3:11-13. Pr 8:21. 18:24. Mk 6:20. Lk 7:25.
thou shalt. Je +21:7. 29:16-18.

18 **What have I offended**. Je 26:19. Ge 31:36. 1 S 24:9-15. 26:18-21. Pr 17:13, 26. Da 6:22. Jn 10:32. Ac 23:1. 24:16. 25:8, 11, 25. 26:31. Ga 4:16.

19 **Where**. Je 2:28. Dt 32:36, 37. 2 K 3:13.
your prophets. Je 6:14. 8:11. 14:13-15. 23:17. 27:14-18. 28:1-5, 10-17. 29:31. La 2:14. Ezk 13:10-16.

20 **be accepted before**. Heb. fall before. Je 36:7mg. 42:2mg. Da 9:18mg.
lest. Je 26:15. 38:6-9, 26. Ac 23:16-22. 25:10, 11. 28:18, 19.

21 **into the**. Je 32:2, 8. 38:13, 28.
and that. 1 K 17:4-6. Jb 5:20. Ps 33:18, 19. 34:9, 10. 37:3, 19. Pr +16:7. 21:1. Is 33:16. Mt 6:33.
daily. Mt +6:11.
piece. lit. cake. Je 52:6. Ex 29:23. Jg 8:5. Lk 11:5.
until. Je 38:9. 52:6. Dt 28:52-57. 2 K 25:3. La 2:11, 12, 19, 20. 4:4, 5, 9, 10. 5:10.
were spent. or, till the consumption. Je 1:3. 24:10. 27:8.
Thus. Ac 12:5. 28:16, 30. He +11:36.

JEREMIAH 38

1 **Shephatiah**. 2 S +3:4.
Jucal. i.e. *mighty; he will be made able*, **S#3116h**. Je 37:3, Jehucal.
Pashur. Je +20:1.
Malchiah. i.e. *Jehovah's king*, **S#4441h**. Je 21:1. 1 Ch 6:40. +9:12, Malchijah. Ezr 10:25, 31. Ne 3:14, 31. 8:4. 11:12.
heard. Ac 4:1, 2, 6-10. 5:28.

2 **He that**. ver. 17-23. Je 21:8, 9. 24:8, 9. 27:13. 29:18. 34:17. 42:17, 22. 44:13. Ezk 5:12-17. 6:11, 12. 7:15. 14:21. Mt 24:7, 8. Re 6:4-8.
shall have. Je 21:9. 39:18. 45:5.
life. Heb. *nephesh*, Ge +44:30.

3 **This city**. Je +21:10. 32:3-5.

4 **the princes**. Je 26:11, 21-23. 36:12-16. 2 Ch 24:21. Ezk 22:27. Mi 3:1-3. Zp 3:1-3.
thus. Ex 5:4. 1 K 18:17, 18. 21:20. Ezr 4:12. Ne 6:9. Am 7:10. Lk 23:2. Jn 11:46-50. Ac 16:20. 17:6. 24:5. 28:22.
weakeneth. Ezr 4:4.
welfare. Heb. peace. Je +29:7. 33:9. Jg +18:4mg. Ps 69:22.
hurt. Is +45:7.

5 **for**. 1 S 15:24. 29:9. 2 S 3:39. 19:22. Pr 29:25. Jn 19:12-16.

6 **took**. Je 37:21. Ps 109:5. Lk 3:19, 20.
into. Je +37:16. La 3:55. Ac 16:23, 24. 2 C 4:8, 9. He 10:36, 37.
dungeon. Heb. *bor*, Ge +37:20. Je 37:16.
Hammelech. or, the king. Je +36:26mg.
and they. ver. 11, 12.

And in. ver. 22, 26. Je 37:20. Ge 37:24. Ps 40:2. 69:2, 14, 15. La 3:52-55. Zc 9:11.
dungeon. Heb. *bor*, Ge +37:20.

7 **Ebed-melech**. i.e. *servant of the king*, **S#5663h**. ver. 8, 10-12. Je 39:16-18.
Ethiopian. Nu +12:1. Mt 8:11, 12. 20:16. Lk 10:30-37. 13:29, 30. 23:26. Ac 8:27-39.
eunuchs. Je +29:2mg.
dungeon. Heb. *bor*, Ge +37:20.
the king. Je 37:13. Dt 21:19. Jb 29:7-17. Am 5:10.

9 **these**. ver. 1-6. Est 7:4-6. Jb 31:34. Pr 24:11, 12. 31:8, 9.
dungeon. Heb. *bor*, Ge +37:20.
is like to die. Heb. will die.
for there. Je 37:21. 52:6.

10 **the king**. Est 5:2. 8:7. Ps 75:10. Pr 21:1.
with thee. Heb. in thine hand. Je 39:11mg. 43:9. 2 S 18:2.

11 **let them**. ver. 6.

12 **Ebed-melech**. Je 39:16-18. Mt 10:40-42. 25:34-40.
the Ethiopian. ver. 7.
Put. Ro 12:10, 13, 15. Ep 4:32.

13 **So**. ver. 6.
Jeremiah. ver. 28. Ac 23:35. 28:16, 30.
dungeon. Heb. *bor*, Ge +37:20.
remained. Je 37:16. He +11:36.

14 **sent**. Je 21:1, 2. 37:17.
third. or, principal. 1 K 10:5. 2 K 16:18.
I will. Je 42:2-5, 20. 1 S 3:16-18. 1 K 22:16. 2 Ch 18:15.

15 **wilt thou not surely**. Ge +2:16. Lk 22:67, 68.

16 **sware secretly**. Je 37:17. Jn 3:2.
that made. Nu 16:22. 27:16. Ec +12:7. Is 57:16. Zc 12:1. He +12:9.
soul. Heb. *nephesh*, Ge +12:5.
of these. ver. +1-6. Je +34:20.
life. Heb. *nephesh*, soul, Ge +44:30.

17 **the God of hosts**. Je +35:17. Ps 80:7, 14. Am 5:27.
the God of Israel. 1 Ch 17:24. Ezr 9:4.
If thou. ver. 2. Je 7:6, 7. 21:8-10. 27:12, 17. 39:3. Jb 23:13.
soul. Heb. *nephesh*, Ge +12:13.

18 **if thou**. 2 K 24:12. 25:27-30.
then. ver. 3, 23. Je +21:7.

19 **I**. ver. 5. 1 S 15:24. Jb 31:34. Pr 29:25. Is 51:12, 13. 57:11. Jn 12:42. 19:12, 13.
mock. ver. 22. Jg 9:54. 16:25. 1 S 31:4mg. Is 45:9, 10.

20 **Obey**. Je 26:13. 2 Ch +20:20. Da 4:27. Ac 26:29. 2 C 5:11, 20. +6:1. Phm 8-10. Ja 1:22.
and thy. Is +55:3.
soul. Heb. *nephesh*, Ge +12:13.

21 **if thou refuse**. Je 5:3. Ex 10:3, 4. 16:28. Jb 34:33. Pr 1:24-31. Is 1:19, 20. He 12:25.
to go. ver. 2, 17. Je 27:12. 2 K 24:12.

this is. Je 15:19-21. 26:15. Nu 23:19, 20. 24:13. Jb 23:13. Ezk 2:4, 5, 7. 3:17-19. Ac 18:6. 20:26, 27.

22 **all**. Je 41:10. 43:6. La 5:11.
Thy friends. Heb. The men of thy peace. ver. 4-6. Je 20:10mg. Ps 41:9mg. Ob 7mg.
have set. ver. 19. La 1:2. Mi 7:5.
thy feet. ver. +6. Ps 69:2, 14.
they are. Je 46:5, 21. Is 42:17. La 1:13.

23 **they shall**. ver. 18. Je 39:6. 41:10. 52:8-13. 2 K 25:7, 9, 10. 2 Ch 36:20, 21.
shalt cause, etc. Heb. shalt burn, etc. Je +17:27. 27:12, 13. Ezk 14:9. 43:3.

24 **Let no man know**. Je 37:17. 1 S 16:2. Mt 10:32, 33. Lk 16:8. 1 C 12:3.

25 **if the princes hear**. ver. +4-6, 27.

26 **I presented**. Je 37:15, 20. 42:2. Est 4:8.

27 **and he told**. 1 S 10:15, 16. 15:16. 16:2-5. 2 K 6:19. Mt 2:8, 12, 16. Ac 23:6.
according. ver. 24.
left off speaking with him. Heb. were silent from him. 1 S 7:8mg.

28 **abode**. ver. +13. Je 15:20, 21. 37:21. 39:14. Ps 23:4. 2 T 3:11. 4:17, 18.

JEREMIAH 39

1 A.M. 3414. B.C. 590.
the ninth. Je 52:4-7. 2 K 25:1, 2, etc. Ezk 24:1, 2. Zc 8:19.
the tenth. This was the month *Tebeth* (Est 2:16), which began with the first moon of January; and it was on the 10th of this month that Nebuchadnezzar invested the city.

2 A.M. 3416. B.C. 588.
the fourth. This was the month *Tammuz*, which commences with the first moon of July: the siege had lasted just eighteen months. 2 K 25:3.
was. Je 5:10. 52:6, 7. 2 K 25:4. Ezk 33:21. Mi 2:12, 13. Zp 1:10.

3 **all the**. Je 1:15. 21:4. 38:17.
Nergalsharezer. i.e. *fire prince; the splendor of brightness*, S#5371h. ver. 13. 2 K 17:29, 30.
Samgar-nebo. i.e. *warrior; sword of Nebo*, S#5562h.
Sarsechim. i.e. *prince of the coverts*, S#8310h.
Rab-saris. i.e. *chief eunuch*, S#7249h. 2 K 18:17.
Rab-mag. i.e. *chief soothsayer; much melting*, S#7248h.

4 **when**. Je +21:7. Le 26:17, 36. Dt 28:25. 32:24-30. Is 30:15, 16. Am 2:14.
betwixt. Je 52:7, etc. 2 Ch 32:5.

5 **Chaldeans'**. Je +21:7. 2 Ch 33:11. La 1:3.
in the plains. Jsh +4:13.
Riblah. Je 52:9, 26, 27. 2 K 23:33. 25:5, 6.
Hamath. Nu +13:21.
gave judgment upon him. Heb. spake with

him judgments. Je 4:12mg. 2 Ch 36:10, 13. Ezk 17:15-21.

6 **slew the**. Je 52:10. 2 K 25:7.
before. Ge 21:16. 44:34. Dt 28:34. 2 K 22:20. 2 Ch 34:28. Est 8:6. Is 13:16.
slew all. Je +21:7.

7 **he put**. Je 32:4, 5. 52:11. 2 K 25:7. Ezk 12:13.
chains. Heb. two brasen chains, *or* fetters. 2 Ch +33:11.
to carry him. Je 52:11. 2 K 25:7. 2 Ch 36:6.

8 **burned**. Je 7:20. 9:10-12. +17:27. Is 5:9. La 1:10. 2:2, 7. Am 2:5. Mi 3:12.
and brake. Je 52:14. 2 K 25:10. 2 Ch 36:19. Ne 1:3.

9 **Nebuzar-adan**. ver. 13. Je 40:1. 52:12-16, 26. 2 K 25:11, 20.
captain of the guard. *or*, chief marshal. Heb. chief of the executioners, *or* slaughter-men; *and so* ver. 10, 11, etc. Ge 37:36mg. 39:1. 2 K 25:8mg.
carried. Je 10:18. 16:13. 20:4-6. 52:28-30. Le 26:33. Dt 4:27. 2 K 20:18. Is 5:13.

10 **left of**. Je 40:7. 2 K 25:12. Ezk 33:24.
at the same time. Heb. in that day.

11 **gave**. Je 15:11, 21. Jb 5:19. Ac 24:23.
to. Heb. by the hand of. Je 37:2mg.

12 **look well to him**. Heb. set thine eyes upon him. Je 24:6. 40:4mg. Pr 23:5. Am 9:4. 1 P 3:12.
do him. Ps 105:14, 15. Pr +16:7. 21:1. Ac 7:9, 10. 1 P 3:13.

13 **Nebuzar-adan**. ver. 3, 9.
Nebushashban. i.e. *deliverance of Nebo*, S#5021h.

14 **took**. ver. 15. Je 37:21. 38:13, 28. 40:1-4. Ps 105:19.
committed. Je 40:5-16. 41:1-3. 2 K 25:22-25.
Ahikam. 2 K +22:12.

15 **while**. ver. 14. He +11:36.

16 **Ebed-melech**. Je 38:7-13.
the Lord of hosts, the God of Israel. Je +7:3.
Behold. Je 5:14. 19:11, 12. 21:7-10. 24:8-10. 26:15, 18, 20. 32:28, 29. 34:2, 3, 22. 35:17. 36:31. 44:28, 29. Jsh 23:14, 15. 2 Ch 36:20, 21. Da 9:12. Zc 1:6. Mt 24:35.
evil. Is +45:7.
before thee. Ps 91:8, 9. 92:11.

17 **I will**. Je 1:19. Jb 5:19-21. Ps 41:1, 2. 50:15. 91:14-16. Da 6:16. Mt 10:40-42. 25:40. 2 T 1:16-18.
of whom. Je 38:1, 9. Ge 15:1. 2 S 24:14.

18 **but**. Je 21:9. 38:2. 45:4, 5.
life. Heb. *nephesh*, Ge +44:30.
a prey. or, spoil. Je 21:9. 38:2. 45:5.
because. Je 17:7, 8. Ru 2:12. 1 Ch 5:20. Ps

2:12. 25:2. 33:18. 34:22. 37:3, 39, 40. 84:12. 146:3-6. 147:11. Is 26:3, 4. Ep 1:12, 13. 1 P 1:21.

JEREMIAH 40

1 **after**. Je 39:11-14.
Ramah. Je +31:15.
bound. Ps 68:6. 107:16. Ac +21:33.
chains. *or*, manacles. ver. 4. 2 Ch +33:11.
that were. Je 28:4.
2 **of the guard**. Je +39:9mg.
The Lord. Je 22:8, 9. Dt 29:24-28. 1 K 9:8, 9. 2 Ch 7:20-22. La 2:15-17.
evil. Is +45:7.
3 **because**. Je 50:7. Dt 29:24, 25. Ne 9:28, 33. Da 9:11, 12. Ro 2:5. 3:19.
4 **were upon thine hand**. *or, are* upon thine hand. ver. 1mg.
look well unto thee. Heb. set mine eye upon thee. Je 39:11, 12mg.
all the. Ge 13:9. 20:15. 47:6.
5 **Go back**. Je 39:14. 41:2. 2 K 25:22-24.
Ahikam. ver. 6, 9, 14. 2 K +22:12.
or go. ver. 4. Je 15:11. Ezr 7:6, 27. Ne 1:11. 2:4-8. Pr +16:7. 21:1.
gave him. Je 52:31-34. 2 K 8:7-9. Jb 22:29. Ac 27:3, 43. 28:10. He 13:6.
victuals and a reward. 2 K 25:30.
6 **Then**. Je 39:14.
Mizpah. Je 41:5-9. Ge +31:49.
7 **all the**. Je 39:4. 2 K 25:4, 22, 23, etc.
governor. Ezk 17:15-19.
the poor. Je 39:10. Ge +34:29. Ezk 33:24-29. 52:16.
8 **came**. ver. 6, 11, 12.
even. ver. 14. Je 41:1-16. 2 K 25:23, 25.
Johanan. 2 K +25:23.
Jonathan. Je 37:15, 20. 38:26.
Kareah. i.e. *bald*, S#7143h. ver. 13, 15, 16. Je 41:11, 13, 14, 16. 42:1, 8. 43:2, 4, 5.
Ephai. i.e. *languid; wearying of the Lord; great languishing*, S#5778h.
Netophathite. 2 S +23:28.
Jezaniah. i.e. *the Lord hears*, S#3153h. Je 42:1.
Maachathite. Dt 3:14. Jsh 12:5. 2 S 10:6, 8. 23:34. 1 Ch 2:48.
9 **sware**. 1 S 20:16, 17. 2 K 25:24.
Fear. Je 27:11. 38:17-20. Ge 49:15. Ps 37:3. 128:2.
10 **serve**. Heb. stand before. Lk +21:36.
gather. Je 39:10.
summer. ver. 12. Is +16:9.
11 **all the Jews**. Je 24:9. Is 16:4. Ezk 5:3, 12. 25:2, 6, 8, 12. 35:5, 15. Ob 11-14.
12 **returned**. Je 43:5.
driven. Je 43:5. 49:5.
unto Mizpah. Je 41:1.
summer fruits. ver. +10. Je 8:20.
13 **Johanan**. ver. 6-8.

14 **Baalis**. i.e. *son of exultation; lord of the banner*, S#1185h.
Ammonites. Ge +19:38. 1 S +11:11.
Ishmael. ver. 8. Je 41:2, 10. Pr 26:23-26. Is 26:10. Mi 7:5.
slay thee? Heb. strike thee in soul? Heb. *nephesh*, Jsh +10:28; Ge +9:5. ver. 15. Ge 37:21. Dt 19:6mg.
believed. 1 C 13:5-7.
15 **Let**. 1 S 24:4. 26:8. Jb 31:31.
wherefore. Je 12:3, 4. 2 S 18:3. 21:17. Ezk 33:24-29. Jn 11:50.
slay thee. Heb. *nephesh*, Jsh +10:28. ver. +14.
16 **Thou shalt**. Je 41:2. Mt 10:16, 17. Ro 3:8.
falsely. Je 3:10, 23. 5:2, 31. 37:14. 2 K 9:12.

JEREMIAH 41

1 **the seventh month**. Je 39:2. 52:6. 2 K 25:3, 8, 25. Zc 7:5. 8:19.
Ishmael. Je +40:6, 8.
Elishama. Je 36:12, 20.
of the. Pr 13:10. 27:4. Ja 4:1-3.
seed royal. 2 K 11:1. 2 Ch 22:10. Ezk 17:13.
they did. Je 40:14-16. 2 S 3:27. 20:9, 10. Ps 41:9. 109:5. Pr 26:23-26. Da 11:26, 27. Lk 22:47, 48. Jn 13:18.
2 **and smote**. 2 K 22:25.
whom. Je 40:7.
3 **slew all**. ver. 11, 12. 2 K 25:25. Ec 9:18. La 1:2.
4 **after**. 1 S 27:11. Ps 52:1, 2.
5 **came**. 2 K 10:13, 14.
Shechem. Ge +33:18.
Shiloh. Jg +21:19.
Samaria. 1 K +16:24.
their beards. Le +19:27. 2 S 10:4.
cut. Le +19:28.
offerings. Le 2:1. Le +23:13.
incense. Je +17:26.
to bring. Le 23:23, 34. Nu 29:12. Dt 16:13.
to the house. 1 S 1:7. 2 K 25:9. Ps 102:14.
6 **weeping**, etc. Heb. in going and weeping. Je 50:4. 2 S 1:2, etc. 3:16. Pr 26:23-26.
7 **slew**. 1 K 15:28, 29. 16:10-12. 2 K 11:1, 2. 15:25. Ps 55:23. Pr 1:16. Is 59:7. Ezk 22:27. 33:24-26. Ro 3:15.
cast them. Ps 74:7. 89:39. 118:5.
pit. Heb. *bor*, Ge +37:20. ver. 9.
8 **Slay**. Jb 2:4. Ps 49:6-8. Pr 13:8. Mt 6:25. 16:26. Mk 8:36, 37. Ph 3:7-9.
treasures. Jg 6:11.
9 **the pit**. Heb. *bor*, Ge +37:20. Je 37:16. 1 K 15:22. 2 K 10:14. 2 Ch 16:6.
because of Gedaliah. *or*, near Gedaliah. Heb. by the hand, *or* by the side of Gedaliah. Je 38:10mg. 46:6.
was it. Jsh 10:16-18. Jg 6:2. 1 S 13:6. 14:11, 22. 24:3. 2 S 17:9. He 11:38.
for fear. 1 K 15:17-22. 2 Ch 16:1-10.

10 **all the**. Je 40:11, 12.
  king's daughters. Je 22:30. 38:23. 39:6. 43:5-7. 44:12-14.
  whom. Je 40:7.
  to the. Je 40:14. Ne 2:10, 19. 4:7, 8. 6:17, 18. 13:4-8.

11 **Johanan**. ver. 2, 3, 7. 2 K +25:23.

12 **to fight**. Ge 14:14-16. 1 S 30:1-8, 18-20.
  the great waters. 2 S 2:13.

13 **and all**. ver. 13, 16. Je 40:13.
  were glad. Pr 29:2.

14 **So all**. ver. 10, 16.
  cast about. or, turn round. Je 52:21. Ge 37:7.

15 **escaped**. 1 S 30:17. 1 K 20:20. Jb 21:30. Pr 28:17. Ec 8:11, 12. Ac 28:4.
  eight men. ver. 2. 2 K 25:25.

16 **even**. ver. 10. Je 42:8. 43:4-7.
  children. Nu +16:27.

17 **habitation**. or, inn. 2 S 19:31-40. Lk 2:7.
  Chimham. 2 S 19:37, 38.
  to go. Je 42:14, 19. 43:7. Is 30:1-3.

18 **for they**. Je 42:11, 16. 43:2, 3. Ge +19:30. 2 K 25:25. Ps +34:4. Is 30:16, 17. 51:12, 13. 57:11. Lk 12:4, 5.
  because. ver. 2.
  whom. Je 40:5.

JEREMIAH 42

1 **all the**. ver. +8.
  Jezaniah. Je +40:8. 2 K +25:23, Jaazaniah.
  from. ver. 8. Je 5:4, 5. Ac +8:10.
  came. ver. 20. Is 29:13. 48:1. 58:1, 2. Ezk 14:3, 4. 20:1-3. 33:31. Mt 15:8.

2 **be accepted before thee**. Heb. fall before thee. Je 36:7mg. 37:20mg.
  and pray. Je 17:15, 16. 21:2. 37:3. Ex 8:28. 9:28. 1 S 7:8. 12:19, 23. 1 K 13:6. Is 1:15. 37:4. Ac 8:24. Ja +5:16.
  remnant. Mi +5:3.
  left. Le 26:22. Dt 4:27. +28:62. Is 1:9. La 1:1. Ezk 5:3, 4. 12:16. Zc 13:8, 9. Mt 24:22.

3 **may show us**. Dt 5:26, 27, 29. 1 K 8:36. Ezr 8:21. Ps +32:8. 86:11. Is 2:3. Mi 4:2. Mk 12:13, 14.

4 **I will pray**. Ex 8:29. 1 S 12:23. Ro 10:1.
  whatsoever. Je +23:28. 1 K 22:14-16. 2 Ch 18:13-15. Ezk 2:7.
  I will keep. Ac +20:20, 27.

5 **The Lord be**. Je 5:2. Ge +31:49, 50. Ex 20:7. Jg 11:10. 1 S 12:5. 20:42. Mi 1:2. Ml 2:14. +3:5. Ro 1:9. Re 1:5. 3:14.
  if we. Ex 20:19. Dt 5:27-29.

6 **it be good**. Ro 7:7, 13. 8:7.
  evil. Is +45:7.
  that it. Je +7:23. Dt 5:29, 33. 6:2, 3. Ps 81:13-16. 128:2. Is 3:10, 11. Ro 8:7, 8. 1 J 3:2, 3, 22, 23.

7 **after ten days**. Ps 27:14. Is 28:16. Hab 2:3.

8 **Johanan**. ver. +1. Je 40:8, 13. 41:11-16. 43:2-5.

9 **the Lord, the God of Israel**. Je +11:3.
  unto. ver. +2. 2 K 19:4, 6, 20, etc. 22:15-20.

10 **abide**. Ge 26:2, 3. Ps 37:3.
  then. Ps +102:16. Ezk 36:36. Ac 15:16.
  build. Je 1:10.
  plant. Je +11:17.
  for I repent. Je +18:8.

11 **afraid**. Je 27:12, 17. 41:18. 2 K 25:26. Mt +10:28.
  for I. Je 1:19. 15:20. Dt 20:4. Jsh 1:5, 9. 2 Ch 32:7, 8. Ps 46:7, 11. Is 8:8-10. 41:10. 43:2, 5. Mt 28:20. Ac 18:9, 10. Ro 8:31. 2 T 4:17, 18.

12 **that he**. Ne 1:11. Ps 106:45, 46. Pr +16:7.

13 **But if ye**. ver. 10. Je 44:16. Ex 5:2.

14 **we will go**. Je 41:17. 43:7. Dt 29:19. Is 30:15, 16. 31:1.
  nor hear. Je 4:19, 21. Ex 16:3. 17:3. Nu 11:5. 16:13.

15 **hear**. Je +7:2.
  Lord of hosts, the God of Israel. ver. 18. Je +7:3.
  If. ver. 17. Je 44:12-14. Ge 31:21. Dt 17:16. Da 11:17. Lk 9:51.

16 **that the sword**. ver. 13. Je +12:12. Pr 13:21. Ezk 11:8. Zc 1:6. Jn 11:48.
  follow close. Heb. cleave after you. 2 K 5:27.
  there ye. Je 44:11, 12, 27.

17 **it be with all the men**. Heb. all the men be.
  they shall. ver. 22. Je 24:10. 44:14.
  none. Je 44:28.

18 **As mine**. Je 6:11. 7:20. 39:1-9. 52:4, etc. 2 K 25:4, etc. 2 Ch 34:25. 36:16-19. La 2:4. 4:11. Ezk 22:22. Da 9:11, 27. Na 1:6. Re 14:9, 10. 16:2, etc.
  ye shall be. 2 Ch +29:8.
  curse. Je +26:6.
  and ye shall see. Je 22:10-12, 27.

19 **Go**. Dt 17:16. Is 30:1-7. 31:1-3. Ezk 17:15.
  know. Je 38:21. Ezk 3:21. Ac 20:26, 27.
  admonished you. Heb. testified against you. Dt 8:19. 31:21. 2 K 17:13. 2 Ch +24:19. Ne 9:26, 29, 30, 34. 13:15. Ps 50:7. Mi 6:3. Lk +16:28. Ep +4:17. 1 Th +4:6.
  this day. Dt +4:26. Lk 23:43. Ac 20:26.

20 **For ye**. Je 3:10. 17:10. 41:17. Ps 139:2. Ezk 14:3, 4. 33:31. Mt 22:15-18, 35. Jn 1:48. +2:24, 25. Ga 6:7.
  dissembled in your hearts. Heb. have used deceit against your souls. Heb. *nephesh*, Ex +23:9. Nu 16:38. Ps 18:44mg. 65:3mg. Pr 14:8. Ja 1:22.
  Pray. ver. +2.

21 **I have**. Dt 11:26, 27. Ezk 2:7. 3:17. Ac 20:20, 26, 27.
  this day. ver. 19. Dt +4:26. Lk 23:43. Ac 20:26.
  but. Je 7:24-27. Dt 29:19. Zc 7:11, 12.

22 **know**. ver. +17. Je 43:11. Ezk 5:3, 4. 6:11.
by the sword. Je +12:12.
in the. Ho 9:6.
to go and sojourn. *or,* to go to sojourn. ver.
15. Je 44:12, 14.

JEREMIAH 43

1 **had made**. Je 26:8. 42:22. 51:63.
all the words. Je 1:7, 17. 26:2. 42:3-5. Ex
24:3. 1 S 8:10. Mt 28:20. Ac 5:20. 20:27.
2 **Azariah**. Je 40:8. 42:1, Jezaniah.
Johanan. 2 K +25:23.
all the. Je 13:15. Ps +10:2. Pr 30:9. Is 9:9, 10.
Thou speakest. Je 5:12, 13. 2 Ch 36:13. Is
7:9.
3 **Baruch**. ver. 6. Je 32:12. 36:4, 10, 26. 45:1-3.
to deliver. Je 38:4. Ps 109:4. Mt +5:11, 12.
Lk 6:22, 23, 26.
4 **obeyed not**. Je 42:5, 6. 44:5. 2 Ch 25:16. Ec
9:16.
to dwell. Je 42:10-13. Ps 37:3.
5 **took**. Je 40:11, 12. 41:15, 16. 1 S 26:19.
6 **the king's**. Je 41:10. 52:10.
every. Je 39:10. 40:7.
person. Heb. *nephesh*, soul, Ge +12:5.
Jeremiah. Ec 9:1, 2. La 3:1. Jn 21:18.
7 **So**. 2 Ch 25:16.
Tahpanhes. i.e. *beginning of the age* or *world;
thou wilt fill hands with pity; temptation,* **S#8471h**.
ver. 8, 9. Je 2:16, Tahapanhes. 44:1. 46:14. Is
30:4, Hanes. Ezk 30:18, Tehaphnehes.
8 **Then came**. Ps 139:7. 2 T 2:9.
9 **great**. Je 13:1, etc. 18:2, etc. 19:1, etc. 51:63,
64. 1 K 11:29-31. Is 20:1-4. Ezk 4:1, etc. 5:1,
etc. 12:3, etc. Ho 12:10. Ac 21:11. Re 18:21.
in the brickkiln. or, brick pavement. Ex
1:14. 2 S 12:31. Na 3:14.
10 **Lord of hosts, the God of Israel**. Je +7:3.
I will send. Je 1:15. 25:6-26. 27:6-8. Ezk
29:18-20. Da 2:20, 21. 5:18, 19.
my servant. Je +25:9. 27:6. 46:27, 28. Is
+10:5. 44:27, 28, 45:1. Mt 22:7.
his royal. 1 K 20:12, 16. Ps 18:11. 27:5.
31:20.
11 **he shall smite**. Je 25:19. 46:1-26. Is ch. 19.
Ezk 29:19, 20. ch. 30-32.
such as are for death. Je +12:12. 2 S 12:31.
Jb 20:29. Zc 11:9. Mt 25:31-46.
12 **in the**. Je 48:7. 50:2. 51:44. Ex +12:12. 2 S
5:21. Is 21:9. 46:1.
array. Est 6:9. Jb 40:10.
putteth. Ps 109:18, 19. 132:16, 18. Is 49:18.
52:1. 59:17. 61:5, 10. Ro 13:12. Ep 4:24. 6:11.
Col 3:12, 14.
13 **images**. Heb. statues, *or* standing images. 2 K
+17:10mg. Is +66:17.
Beth-shemesh. *or,* the house of the sun. or,
temple of the sun. Is 19:18mg. Ezk 30:17mg.
S#1053h: Jsh 15:10. 19:22, 38. 21:16. Jg 1:33. 1

S 6:9, 12, 13, 15, 19, 20. 1 K 4:9. 2 K 14:11,
13. 1 Ch 6:59. 2 Ch 25:21, 23. 28:18.
that is in. To distinguish it from the Beth-
shemesh of Jsh 15:10. Jg 1:33. 1 S 6:9, 19.
and the. ver. 12.

JEREMIAH 44

1 Cir. A.M. 3433. B.C. 571.
concerning. Je 42:15-18. 43:5-7.
Migdol. Ex +14:2.
Tahpanhes. Je +43:7.
Noph. Is +19:13.
Pathros. Is +11:11.
2 **Lord of hosts, the God**. Je +7:3.
Ye have. Je +39:1-8. Ex 19:4. Dt 29:2. Jsh
23:3. Zc 1:6.
a desolation. ver. 22. Je +18:16. 2 K 21:13.
Is 24:12. La 1:1, 16. 5:18. Mi 3:12.
3 **of their**. Je 2:17-19. 4:17, 18. 5:19, 29. 9:12-
14. 11:17. 16:11, 12. 19:3, 4. 22:9. Ezr 9:6-11.
Ne 9:33. La 1:8. 4:13. Ezk 8:17, 18. 9:9.
22:25-31. Da 9:5-8. Zc 7:12, 13.
gods. Dt 13:6. 29:26. 32:17.
4 **I sent**. 2 Ch +24:19.
this abominable. Je 16:18. Ezk 8:10.
16:36, 47. Ep 5:5. Col 3:5, 6. 1 P 4:3.
Re 17:4, 5.
5 **they**. Je +7:26. 2 Ch 36:16. Re 2:21, 22.
burn. ver. 17-21. Je +19:13.
6 **my fury**. Le +26:28. Is 51:17, 20.
wasted. ver. +2, 3. Is 6:11.
7 **the Lord, the God of hosts**. Je +35:17.
against. Je 7:19. 25:7. 42:20mg. Nu 16:38. Pr
1:18. 5:22. 8:36. 15:32. Ezk 33:11. Hab 2:10.
souls. Heb. *nephesh*, Ge +12:13.
to cut. ver. 8, 11. Je 9:21. 51:22. Jsh 6:21. Jg
21:11.
child. Dt 32:25. 1 S 15:3. 22:19. La 2:11.
Judah. Heb. the midst of Judah. Je 50:8.
51:6.
to leave. ver. 12, 14, 27, 28.
8 **ye provoke**. Je +25:6, 7. Dt 32:16, 17. 2 K
17:15-17. Is 3:8. 1 C 10:21, 22. He 3:16.
that ye might cut. ver. +7. Ezk 18:31, 32.
a curse. ver. 12. Je +26:6. 2 Ch +29:8.
9 **ye forgotten**. Jsh 22:17-20. Ezr 9:7-15. Da
9:5-8.
wickedness. Heb. wickednesses, *or* punish-
ments, etc. Is +45:7.
the wickedness of your. ver. 15-19. Je
7:17, 18.
10 **are not**. Je 8:12. Ex 9:17. 10:3. 1 K 21:29. 2
Ch 12:6-12. 32:26. 33:12, 19. 34:27, Da 5:20-
22. Ja 4:6-10. 1 P 5:6.
humbled. Heb. contrite. 2 K 22:19. Ps 34:18.
+51:17. Is 57:15. 66:2. Ezk +9:4.
neither. Je 10:7. 36:24. Ex 9:30. Pr 8:13.
14:16. 16:6. 28:14. Ec 8:12, 13. Ml 4:2. Mt
27:54. Lk 23:40. Ro 11:19, 20. Re 15:4.

11 **I will**. Ezk +15:7. Am 9:4.
for evil. Is +45:7.

12 **I will take**. Je +42:15-18, 22.
from the. Ho 4:6.
by the sword. Je +12:12. 46:19.
an execration. Je 42:18. 46:19.
astonishment. 2 Ch +29:8.
a curse. ver. +8.

13 **I will punish**. ver. 27, 28. Je +9:25mg. 21:9.
24:10. 42:18. 43:11.
by the sword. Je +12:12. 46:19.

14 **So**. ver. 28.
which are. Is 30:1-3.
shall escape. ver. 27. Je +42:17. Mt 23:33.
Lk +21:36. Ro 2:3. He 2:3.
which they. Je 22:26, 27. 42:22.
have a desire. Heb. lift up their soul. Heb.
nephesh, Ex +15:9. Je 22:27mg.
for none. ver. 28. Is 4:2. Mi +4:7.

15 **all the**. Je 5:1-5. Ge 19:4. Ne 13:26. Pr 11:21.
Is 1:5. Mt 7:13. 2 P 2:1, 2.

16 **the word**. Ps 19:7, 8. Ho 8:12. 1 C 15:1-4.
we will not hearken. Je +7:26. 8:6, 12.
38:4. Ex 5:2. Jb 15:25-27. 21:14, 15. Ps 2:3.
73:8, 9. Is 3:9. Da 3:15. 7:25. Mt 15:6. Lk
19:14, 27.

17 **we will**. Ex +22:30. 32:1. Dt 31:16, 20.
certainly do. Da 11:36. Mk 7:5-13. Ro 1:16,
25. Ga 1:8. 2 Th 2:4, 9-12.
whatsoever. ver. 25. Nu 30:2, 12. Dt 23:23.
Jg 11:36. Ps 12:4. Mk 6:26.
queen of heaven. *or*, frame of heaven. Je
7:18mg. 2 K 17:16.
drink offerings. Le +23:13.
as we. Je 19:13. 32:29-32. 2 K 22:17. Ne
9:34. Da 9:6-8.
our fathers. Ne 9:34. Ps 106:6. Ezk 20:8. Da
9:5, 6, 8. 1 P 1:18.
in the cities. ver. +9, 21.
then. Ex 16:3. Is 48:5. Ho 2:5-9. Ph 3:19.
victuals. Heb. bread. 1 K 11:18.

18 **we have**. Je +40:12. Nu 11:5, 6. Jb +21:14,
15. Ps 73:9-15. Ml 3:13-15.

19 **we burned**. ver. +15. Je 7:18.
without. Ge 3:6, 11, 12, 16, 17.
Dt 7:3, 4. 1 K 21:25. 2 Ch 21:6. Pr 11:21.
Mk 6:19-27.
men. *or*, husbands. ver. 15. Nu 30:6.

20 **the men**. Je 43:6.

21 **and in**. ver. 9, 17. Je 11:13. Ezk 16:24.
did. Je 14:10. 1 S 15:3. 1 K 17:18. Ps 79:8. Is
64:9. Ezk 21:23, 24. Ho 7:2. Am 8:7. Re
16:19. 18:5.

22 **So that**. Je 5:9, 29.
could. Je 15:6. Ge 6:3, 5-7. Ps 95:10, 11.
101:5. Is 1:24. 7:13. 43:24. Ezk 5:13-15. Am
2:13. Ml 2:17. Ro 2:4, 5. 9:22. 2 P 3:7-9.
your land. ver. +2, 6, 12.
astonishment. 2 Ch +29:8.
curse. Je +26:6.

without an inhabitant. Je 4:7. 9:11. 26:9.
34:22. Is 6:11.
as at this day. Je 25:18. 1 K +8:24.

23 **ye have burned**. ver. +8, 18, 21. Je 32:31-
33. 2 Ch 36:16. La 1:8. 1 C 10:20. 2 C 6:16-
18.
nor walked. Ps 119:150.
nor in his statutes. Ps 119:155.
nor in his testimonies. Ps 78:56.
therefore. 1 K 9:9. Ne 13:18. Da 9:11, 12.
is happened. 2 S +1:6.
as at. ver. +22.

24 **Hear**. ver. 16. Je +7:2.
all Judah. ver. 15, 26. Je 43:7. Ezk 20:32, 33.

25 **Ye and**. ver. +15-19. Is +28:15. Ju 13.
We will. Mt 14:9. Ac 23:12-15.
vows. Le +23:38.
ye will. Jb 34:22. Ja 1:14, 15.

26 **I have sworn**. Je 46:18. Ge 22:16. Nu 14:21-
23, 28. Dt 32:40-42. Ps 89:34. Is 62:8. Am 6:8.
8:7. He 3:18. 6:13, 18.
great name. Ps +99:3.
that my name. Ps 50:16. Ezk 20:39. Am
6:10.
The Lord God. Je 4:2. 5:2. 7:9. Is 48:1, 2. Zp
1:4, 5.

27 **will watch**. Je 1:10. +21:10. 31:28. Ezk 7:5,
6.
shall be. ver. +12, 18. 2 K 21:14.

28 **a small**. ver. 14. Is 27:12, 13.
shall know. ver. 16, 17, 25, 26, 29. Nu
14:28, 29, 41. Ps 33:11. Is 14:24-27. 28:16-18.
46:10, 11. La 3:37, 38. Zc 1:5, 6. Mt 24:35.
mine, or theirs. Heb. from me or them.

29 **a sign**. ver. 30. Nu +26:10. Mt 24:15, 16, 32-
34. Mk 13:14-16. Lk 21:20, 21, 29-33.
punish. Je +11:22mg.
my words. Pr 19:21. Is 40:8.

30 **I will**. Je 43:9-13. 46:13-26. Ezk ch. 29, 30.
31:18. ch. 32.
Pharaoh-hophra. i.e. *Pharaoh, priest of the
sun; his nakedness, covering evil,* **S#6548h.**
as I. Je 34:21. 39:5-7. 52:8-11. 2 K 25:4-7.
life. Heb. *nephesh*, Ge +44:30.

JEREMIAH 45

1 A.M. 3397. B.C. 607.
Baruch. Je 32:12, 16. 43:3-6. 51:59. 2 Ch
34:8.
when. Je 36:1, 4, 8, 14-18, 26, 32.
the fourth year. Je 25:1-3. 26:1. 36:1, 9.
46:2. Da 1:1.

2 **the Lord, the God of Israel**. Je +11:3.
unto. Is 63:9. Mk 16:7. 2 C 1:4. 7:6. He 2:18.
4:15.

3 **Woe**. Je 9:1. 15:10, etc. 20:7, etc. Ps 120:5.
added. Ge 37:34, 35. 42:36-38. Nu 11:11-15.
Jsh 7:7-9. Jb 16:11-13. 23:2. Ps 42:7. La 3:1-
19, 32.

I fainted. Je 8:18. Ps 27:13. 77:3, 4. Pr 24:10. La 1:13, 22. 2 C 4:1, 16. Ga 6:9. 2 Th 3:13. He 12:3-5.

4 that which. Je +1:10. Ge 6:6, 7.
planted. Je +11:17.

5 seekest. 2 K 5:26. Ps 131:1. Lk 6:26. Ro 12:16. 1 C 7:26-32. 1 T 6:6-9. He +13:5.
seek them not. 1 K 3:11. Hab 2:6. Mt 6:25-33. Mk 9:33-37. 10:35-45. 12:38, 39. Jn 5:44. 1 J 2:16. 3 J 9, 10.
I will bring. Je 25:26. Zp 3:8.
evil. Is +45:7.
flesh. Lk +3:6.
thy life. Heb. *nephesh*, Ge +44:30; Ge +9:5. Je 21:9. 38:2. 39:18.

JEREMIAH 46

1 The word. Je 7:1. 11:1.
against. Je 1:10. 4:7. 25:15-29. Ge 10:5. Nu 23:9. Zc 2:8. Ro 3:29.

2 Against Egypt. ver. 14. Je 25:9, 19. Ezk ch. 29-32.
Pharaoh-necho. i.e. *Pharaoh the lame*, **S#6549h**. 2 K 23:29, 33, 34, 35, Pharaoh-nechoh. 2 Ch 35:20, 29, Necho.
Carchemish. Is 10:8, 9.
in the fourth year. Je 25:1. 36:1. +45:1.

3 Order ye. Je 51:11, 12. Is 8:9, 10. 21:5. Jl 3:9. Na 2:1. 3:14.

4 furbish. Ezk 21:9-11, 28.
brigandines. or, coats of mail. Je 51:3. 1 S 17:5, 38. 2 Ch 26:14. Ne 4:16.

5 and their. Re 6:15.
beaten down. Heb. broken in pieces. Jb 4:20mg.
fled apace. Heb. fled a flight. ver. 15. Ge 19:17. 2 K 7:6, 7. Na 2:8.
fear. Je +6:25. 20:3, 4mg, 10. 49:29. Is 19:16. Ezk 32:10. Re 6:15-17.

6 not. Jg 4:15-21. Ps 33:16, 17. 147:10, 11. Ec 9:11. Is 30:16, 17. Am 2:14, 15. 9:1-3.
stumble. ver. 12. Je 20:11. 50:32. Jg 5:26, 27. Ps 27:2. Is 8:15. Da 11:19, 22.
toward. ver. 10, 20. Je +1:14.

7 Who. SS 3:6. 8:5. Is 63:1.
as a flood. Je +47:2.

8 riseth. Ezk 29:3. 32:2.
I will go. Ex 15:9, 10. Is 10:13-16. 37:24-26.

9 rage. Na 2:3, 4.
Ethiopians. Heb. Cush. Ge +2:13.
Libyans. Heb. Put. i.e. *afflicted*, **S#6316h**, so rendered only here. Ge +10:6, Phut. Ac 2:10.
Lydians. i.e. *a magnet; to firebrand, travailing*, **S#3866h**. Ge 10:13. 1 Ch 1:11, Ludim. Is 66:19. Ezk 27:10, Lud. 30:5. Na 3:9, Lubim.

10 the day. Je +50:15. Ezk +30:3. 1 Th 5:1-5. 2 P 3:10.
adversaries. Je 30:16. 48:5.

the sword. Je +12:12. Ezk 39:17-21. Zp 1:7, 8. Re 19:17-21.
drunk. Dt 32:42.
hath a sacrifice. Is +34:6.
the north. ver. 2, +6. 2 K 24:7.

11 Gilead. Ge +37:25.
O virgin. Je +18:13. Nu +21:25.
in vain. Is 30:12-15. Ezk 30:21-25. Mi 1:9. Na 3:19. Mk 5:25-28. Lk 8:43, 44.
thou shalt not be cured. Heb. no cure *shall be* unto thee.

12 heard. Ezk 32:9-12. Na 3:8-10.
thy cry. Je 14:2. 48:34. 49:21. 51:54. 1 S 5:12. Is 15:5-8. Zp 1:10.
stumbled. ver. +6. Is 10:4. 19:2.

13 Cir. A.M. 3398. B.C. 606.
Nebuchadrezzar. Je 43:10-13. 44:30. Is ch. 19. Ezk ch. 29-32.

14 Migdol. Ex +14:2.
Noph. Is +19:13.
Tahpanhes. Je +43:7.
Stand. ver. 3, 4. Je 6:1-5. Jl 3:9-12.
the sword. ver. +10. Je 2:30. 2 S 2:26. Is 1:19, 20.

15 thy. ver. 5, 21. Jg 5:20, 21. Is 66:15, 16.
the Lord. Ex 6:1. Dt 11:23. Ps 18:14, 39. 44:2. 68:2. 114:2-7.

16 made many to fall. Heb. multiplied the faller. Ps 78:38.
one. Le 26:36, 37.
they said. ver. 21. Je 51:9.

17 Pharaoh. Ex 15:9. 1 K 20:10, 18. Is 19:11-16. 31:3. 37:27-29. Ezk 29:3. 31:18.
hath passed. Je 37:7. 2 S 20:5.
time appointed. Ge +17:21.

18 saith. Je 10:10. 44:26. 48:15. 51:57. Is 47:4. 48:2. Ml 1:14. Mt 5:35. 1 T 1:17.
the Lord of hosts. Je +10:16.
Tabor. Jg +4:6.
Carmel. Jsh +19:26.

19 thou. Je 48:18.
dwelling. or, inhabitress of. Je 48:18. Ezk 12:2.
furnish thyself to go into captivity. Heb. make thee instruments of captivity. Is 20:4, 5. Ezk 12:3mg, 4-12.
Noph. Is +19:13.
waste. Je 26:9. 34:22. 51:29, 37. Zp 2:5.

20 a very. Je 50:11. Ho 10:11.
heifer. ver. 15.
it cometh. ver. +6, 10.

21 her hired. ver. 9, 16. 2 S 10:6. 2 K 7:6. Ezk 27:10, 11. 30:4-6.
like. Dt +31:20.
fatted bullocks. Heb. bullocks of the stall. Pr 15:17. Am 6:4.
they did. ver. 5, 15, 16.
the day. Je 18:17. Dt 32:35. Ps 37:13. Is 10:3. Ezk 35:5. Ho 9:7. Ob 13. Mi 7:4.
time of. Je +8:12.

22 voice. Is 29:4. Mi 1:8. 7:16, 17.
and come. Je 51:20-23. Is 10:15, 33, 34.
14:8. 37:24. Zc 11:2.
23 cut. Is 10:18, 19. Ezk 20:46, 47.
because. 2 K +8:37.
24 daughter. ver. 11, 19. Ps 137:8, 9.
she shall. ver. 20. Je 1:15. Ezk ch. 29-32.
25 Lord of hosts, the God of. Je +7:3.
punish. Je +11:22mg.
multitude. *or*, nourisher. Pr 8:30. Heb.
Amon. Na 3:8mg.
No. Ezk 30:14-16. Na 3:8-10.
with their. Ex +12:12.
and their. Ezk 32:9-12. Na 3:9.
and all. Je 17:5, 6. 42:14-16. Is 20:5, 6. 30:2,
3. 31:1-3. Ezk 39:6, 7.
26 I will. Je +44:30. Ezk 32:11.
lives. Heb. *nephesh*, souls, Ge +44:30.
and afterward. Je 48:47. 49:39. Ezk 29:8-14.
old. Heb. *kedem*, Mi +5:2.
27 fear. Ge +15:1.
I will save. Je 23:3, 4. 29:14. 31:8-11. 32:37.
Is 11:11, etc. Ezk 34:10-14. 36:24. 37:21, 22.
39:25. Am 9:14, 15. Mi 7:11-16.
and be. Je +23:6. 33:16. 50:19. Ezk 34:25,
26. 39:25.
28 Fear thou not. Ge +15:1.
for I am. Je 1:19. 15:20. 30:11. Jsh 1:5, 9. Ps
46:7, 11. Is 8:9, 10. 41:10. 43:2. Mt +1:23.
28:20. Ac 18:10. 2 T 4:17, 22.
make. Je 25:9. Is 45:23. Da 2:35.
but I will not. Je 5:10, 18. 10:24. 32:42-44.
Le +26:44. Is +41:9. +60:10.
correct. Je +10:24. Hab 3:2. 1 C 11:32.
will I. Is 27:7, 9. He 12:5-10. Re 3:19.
not leave thee wholly unpunished.
or, not utterly cut thee off. Ex 20:7. 34:7.
Nu 14:18.

JEREMIAH 47

1 Cir. A.M. 3387. B.C. 617.
against. Je 48:1. 49:1, 7, 23. Ezk 25:15-17.
Am 1:6-8. Zp 2:4-7. Zc 9:5-7.
Gaza. Heb. Azzah. Ge +10:19mg.
2 waters. Je 46:7, 8. 51:42. Ps +93:3. Is 8:7, 8.
17:12, 13. 28:17. 59:19. Ezk 26:19. 27:26. Da
9:26. 11:10, 22. Am 8:8. 9:5, 6. Na 1:8. Re
12:15, 16. 17:1, 15.
north. Je +1:14.
all that is therein. Heb. the fulness thereof.
Je 8:16mg. Ps 24:1. 50:12. 96:11. 98:7. Am
6:8mg. 1 C 10:26, 28.
then the. Je 46:12. Is 22:1, 4, 5.
shall howl. Is +13:6.
3 the noise. Je 8:16. 46:9. Jg 5:22. Jb 39:19-25.
Ezk 26:10, 11. Na 2:4. 3:2, 3.
rumbling. Je +10:13mg.
the fathers. Dt 28:54, 55. La 4:3, 4.
4 the day. Je +46:10. Ps 37:13. Is 10:3. Ezk

7:5-7, 12. 21:25, 29. Ho 9:7. Lk 21:22.
Philistines. i.e. *wanderers; wallowing; watered*,
S#6430h. ver. 1. Je 25:20. Ge 21:32, 34. 26:1, 8,
14, 15, 18. Ex 13:17. 23:31. Jsh 13:2, 3. Jg
3:3, 31. 10:6, 7, 11. 13:1, 5. 14:1, 4. 15:5, 11,
14. 16:5, 23, 30. 1 S 4:1, 2. 5:2, 8. 6:4, 16, 18.
13:5, 19-23. 29:2, 7. 2 S 1:20. 3:14, 18. 5:17,
etc. 23:9-14. 1 K 4:21. 15:27. 2 K 8:2, 3. 18:8.
1 Ch 1:12. 10:1, etc. 2 Ch 9:26. 17:11. 21:16.
26:6, 7. 28:18. Ps 83:7. Is 2:6. 9:12. 11:14. Ezk
16:27, 57. 25:15, 16. Am 1:8. 6:2. 9:7. Ob 19.
Zp 2:5. Zc 9:6.
Tyrus. Je +25:22.
every. Jb 9:13. Is 20:6. 31:3. Ezk 30:8.
the remnant. Ezk 25:16. Am 1:8. 9:7.
country. Heb. isle. Jb 22:30. Is 20:6.
Caphtor. i.e. *crown; hollow goblet*, **S#3731h**. Ge
+10:14, Caphtorim. Dt 2:23. Am 9:7.
5 Baldness. Is +3:24.
Gaza. ver. +1.
the remnant. ver. 4. Je 25:20. Ezk 25:16.
how. Le +19:28.
6 thou sword. Je +12:12. 51:20-23. Ps 17:13.
Is 10:5, 15.
how long. Mt +17:17.
put up thyself. Heb. gather thyself. Je 4:5.
Ge 49:1.
into. 1 Ch 21:27. Ezk 21:30. Jn 18:11.
7 can it. Heb. canst thou.
the Lord. 1 S 15:3. Is 10:6. 13:3. 37:26. 45:1-
3. 46:10, 11. Ezk 14:17. Am +3:6.
the sea. Ezk 25:16. Zp 2:6, 7.
hath he. Mi 6:9.

JEREMIAH 48

1 A.M. cir. 3420. B.C. cir. 584.
Moab. Je 27:3. Jg 3:12, 28. 1 S 14:47. 2 K
1:1. 3:4-27. 13:20. 2 Ch 20:10-12. Is 27:3. Ezk
+25:8-11.
the Lord of hosts, the God of Israel. Je
+7:3.
Nebo. ver. 22. Nu +32:3.
Kiriathaim. i.e. *double city*, **S#7156h**. Je 48:1,
23. Ezk 25:9. See also **S#7156h**, Nu 32:37,
Kirjathaim. Compare **S#7741h**, Ge 14:5, Shaveh
Kiriathaim.
Misgab. *or*, The high place. i.e. *height, safety*,
S#4870h.
2 no more. ver. 17. Is 16:14.
Heshbon. ver. 34, 45. Nu +21:25.
come. ver. +42. Je 31:36. 33:24. 46:28.
thou shalt. Je 25:15, 17.
cut down. *or*, brought to silence. Je 8:14. Ps
31:17mg. Is 15:1mg.
Madmen. i.e. *dunghill*, **S#4086h**, only here. Is
25:10mg, Madmenah.
sword. Je +12:12.
pursue thee. Heb. go after thee. Je
+17:16mg.

3 **voice**. Je 4:20, 21. 47:2. Is 15:2, 8. 16:7-11. 22:4.
Horonaim. ver. 5, 34. Is 15:5.
4 **Moab**. Nu 21:27-30.
her. Est 8:11. Ps 137:9.
5 **Luhith**. ver. 34. Is 15:5.
continual weeping. Heb. weeping with weeping. 2 S 13:36.
6 **Flee**. Je 51:6. Ge 19:17. Ps 11:1. Pr 6:4, 5. Mt 24:15-18. Lk 3:7. 17:30-33. He +6:18.
lives. Heb. *nephesh*, Ge +44:30.
be like. Je 17:6. Jb 30:3-7.
the heath. *or*, a naked tree. Je 17:6.
7 **because**. Je 9:23. 13:25. Ps 40:4. 49:6, 7. 52:7. 62:8-10. Is 59:4-6. Ezk 28:2-5. Ho 10:13. 1 T 6:17. Re 18:7.
Chemosh. ver. 13, 46. Je 43:12. Nu +21:29. Is 46:1, 2.
his priests. Je 49:3.
8 **the spoiler**. ver. 18. Je 6:26. 15:8. 25:9. 51:56.
and no. ver. 20-25. Ezk 25:9.
city. 1 S +22:19.
9 **wings**. ver. 28. Ps 11:1. 55:6. Is 16:2. Re 12:14.
the cities. Je 46:19. Zp 2:9.
10 **Cursed**. La +3:65.
that doeth. Nu 31:14-18. Jg 5:23. 1 S 15:3, 9, 13, etc. 1 K 20:42. 2 K 13:19.
work of the Lord. Je 50:25. 1 C 15:58. He 6:10.
deceitfully. *or*, negligently. Ge +27:12. Ex +15:26. 2 Ch 24:5. Ne 3:5. Jb 13:7. Ps 32:2. 78:57. Pr +10:4. 12:24mg. Ezk 33:31. Mi 6:12. Mt 25:26. Lk 16:10. Ro 12:11, 17. 1 Th 5:22. He +6:12.
11 **hath been**. Ps 55:19. 73:4-8. 123:4. Pr 1:32mg. Zc 1:15.
he hath. Is 25:6. Zp 1:12.
emptied. Je 51:34. Is 24:3. Na 2:2, 10.
therefore. ver. 29. Is 16:6. Ezk 16:49, 50.
remained. Heb. stood.
12 **wanderers**. ver. 8, 15. Je 25:9. Is 16:2. Ezk 25:9, 10.
empty. ver. 11, 38. Je 14:3. 19:10. 25:34. Ps 2:9. Is 30:14. Na 2:2.
13 **ashamed**. ver. 7, 39, 46. Jg 11:24. 1 S 5:3-7. 1 K 11:7. 18:26-29, 40. Is 2:20. 16:12. 45:16, 20. 46:1, 2.
as the. 1 K 12:28, 29. Ho 8:5, 6. 10:5, 6, 14, 15. Am 5:5, 6.
house of Israel. Je +2:4.
14 **How**. Je 8:8. Ps 11:1. Is 36:4, 5.
We. Je 9:23. 49:16. Ps 33:16. Ec 9:11. Is 10:13, 16. 16:6. Ezk 30:6. Zp 2:10.
15 *spoiled*. *ver. 8, 9, 18, 25.*
his chosen. Heb. the choice of his, etc. Is 40:30, 31.
gone. ver. 4. Je 50:27. 51:40. Is 34:2-8.
saith. Je 46:18. 51:57. Ps 24:8-10. 47:2. Da 4:37. Zc 14:9. Ml 1:14. Re 19:16.

whose name is. Je +10:16. Ex +6:3. Ps +68:4. +83:18.
Lord of hosts. Je +6:6. Ja +5:4.
16 **near**. Je 1:12. Dt 32:35. Is 13:22. 16:13, 14. Ezk 12:23, 28. 2 P 2:3.
17 **bemoan**. ver. 31-33. Je 9:17-20. Is 16:8. Re 18:14-20.
How. ver. 39. Is 9:4. 10:5. 14:4, 5. Ezk 19:11-14. Zc 11:10-14.
18 **daughter**. Je 46:18, 19. Is 47:1.
Dibon. ver. 22. Nu +21:30.
and sit. Ge 21:16. Ex 17:3. Jg 15:18. Is 5:13. Ezk 19:13.
the spoiler. ver. 8.
19 **inhabitant**. Heb. inhabitress. Je +10:17mg.
Aroer. Nu +32:34.
ask. 1 S 4:13, 14, 16. 2 S 1:3, 4. 18:24-32.
20 **confounded**. ver. 1-5. Is 15:1-5, 8. 16:7-11.
Arnon. Nu +21:13.
21 **the plain**. ver. 8. Ezk 25:9. Zp 2:9.
Jahazah. Jsh +13:18, Jahaza.
22 **Dibon**. ver. +18.
Beth-diblathaim. i.e. *house of two fig cakes*, **S#1015h**, only here. Nu 33:46, Almon-diblath-aim. Ezk 6:14, Diblath.
23 **Kiriathaim**. ver. +1. Ge 14:5, Shaveh Kiriathaim. Jsh 13:19, Kirjathaim.
Beth-gamul. i.e. *house of the weaned; house of recompense; house of the rewarded*, **S#1014h**, only here.
Beth-meon. i.e. *house of habitation*, **S#1010h**. Nu 32:38, Baal-meon. Jsh 13:17, Beth-baal-meon.
24 **Kerioth**. ver. 41. Am 2:2.
Bozrah. Dt 4:43, Bezer. Jsh 21:36, Bezor. Zp 2:8-10.
25 **horn**. Ps 75:10. La 2:3. Da 7:8. 8:7-9, 21. Zc 1:19-21.
and his. Nu 32:37. Jb 22:9. Ps 10:15. 37:17. Ezk 30:21-25.
26 **ye him**. Je 13:13, 14. 25:15-17, 27-29. 51:7, 39, 57. Ps 60:3. 75:8. Is 29:9. 51:17. 63:6. La 3:15. 4:21. Ezk 23:31-34. Na 3:11. Re 16:19.
for he. ver. 42. Ex 5:2. 9:17. Jb 9:4. Is 10:15. Ezk 35:12, 13. Da 5:23. 8:11, 12. 11:36. Zp 2:8-10. 2 Th 2:4.
wallow. Is 19:14. 29:9. Hab 2:16.
and he also. ver. 39. Ps 2:4. 59:8. La 1:21. Ezk 23:32.
27 **was not**. Pr 24:17, 18. La 2:15-17. Ezk 25:8. 26:2, 3. 35:15. Ob 12, 13. Mi 7:8-10. Zp 2:8, 10. Mt 7:2. Lk +16:14.
was he found. Je 2:26. Mt 26:55. 27:38.
skippedst. *or*, movedst thyself. Je 31:18. Is 24:20.
28 **leave**. ver. 9. Jg 6:2. 1 S 13:6. Is 2:19. Ob 3, 4.
dwell in. Pr 30:26.
like. Je 49:16. Ps 55:6, 7. SS 2:14.
29 **heard**. Pr 8:13. Is 16:6. Zp 2:8-10, etc.

his loftiness. Jb 40:10-12. Ps 138:6. Pr 18:12. 30:13. Is 2:11, 12. Da 4:37. Lk 14:11. Ja 4:6.

30 **know**. Is 16:6. 37:28, 29.
his lies shall not so effect it. *or*, those on whom he stayeth (Heb. his bars) do not right. Je 50:36. Jb 9:12, 13. Ps 33:10. Pr +21:30.

31 **will I howl**. Is +13:6. 15:5.
Kir-heres. i.e. *city or wall of brick; the wall is earthen*, **S#7025h**. ver. 36. 2 K 3:25, Kar-haraseth. Is 16:7, Kir-hareseth, 11, Kir-haresh.

32 **vine**. Nu 32:37, 38, Shibmah. Jsh 13:19. Is 16:8, 9.
Jazer. Nu +32:1.
the spoiler. ver. 8, 15, 18. Je 40:10.

33 **joy**. Je 25:9, 10. Is 9:3. 16:9. 24:7-12. 32:9-14. Jl 1:12, 16. Re 18:22, 23.
caused. Is 5:10. 7:23. 16:10. Jl 1:5, 12, 13. Hg 2:16.

34 **the cry**. ver. 2. Is 15:4-6.
Elealeh. Nu 32:37.
Jahaz. ver. +21, Jahazah.
Zoar. ver. 3, 5. Ge +13:10.
Nimrim. Nu 32:3, Nimrah, 36, Beth-nimrah. Is 15:6.
desolate. Heb. desolations. Is 15:6mg.

35 **him that offereth**. ver. 7. Nu 22:40, 41. 28:14, 28-30. Is 15:2. 16:12.
high places. 2 K +21:3.

36 **mine heart**. Je 4:19. Is 15:5. 16:11. 63:15.
like pipes. Mt 9:23.
Kir-heres. ver. 31.
the riches. Je 17:11. Pr 11:4. 13:22. 18:11. Ec 5:13, 14. Is 15:7. Lk 12:20, 21. Ja 5:2, 3.

37 **every head**. Is +3:24.
clipped. Heb. diminished.
cuttings. Le +19:28.
upon the loins. Jb +16:15.

38 **upon**. Dt +22:8.
broken. Je 22:28. 25:34. Ps 2:9. Is 30:14. Ho 8:8. Ro 9:21, 22. 2 T 2:20, 21. Re 2:26, 27.

39 **How is it**. ver. 17. La 1:1. 2:1. 4:1. Re 18:9, 10, 15, 16.
back. Heb. neck. Je 46:5.
a derision. ver. 26, 27. Is 20:4-6. Ezk 26:16-18.
dismaying. Je 49:37. Ezk 32:23mg.

40 **he shall**. Je 4:13. Dt 28:49. La 4:19. Ezk 17:3. Da 7:4. Ho 8:1. Hab 1:8.
as an eagle. Dt 28:49.
spread. Je 49:22. Is 8:8.

41 **Kerioth**. *or*, The cities. ver. 24.
as the heart. Je +4:31. 51:30. Mi 4:9, 10.

42 **Moab**. Je 46:28.
from. ver. 2. Je 30:11. Est 3:8-13. Ps 83:4-8. Is 7:8. Mt 7:2.
magnified. ver. 26-30. Pr 16:18. Is 37:23. Da 11:36. 2 Th 2:3, 4. Re 13:5, 6.

43 **Fear**. Dt 32:23-25.
snare. Lk +21:35.

44 **that fleeth**. Je 16:16. 1 K 19:17. 20:30. Is 37:36-38. Am 2:14, 15. 5:19. 9:1-4.
and he that. Is 24:17, 18.
the year. Je +8:12. Is +61:2.

45 **a fire**. Nu 21:28. Am 2:2.
devour. Nu 24:17. Zc 10:4. Mt 21:42.
tumultuous ones. Heb. children of noise.

46 **Woe**. Nu 21:29. Ezk +34:2.
the people. ver. 7, 13. Jg 11:24. 1 K 11:7. 2 K 23:13.
of Chemosh. Nu +21:29.
captives. Heb. in captivity. Is 49:25mg.

47 **Yet will I bring**. The Moabites are one of several nations promised to be regathered in the latter days: Elam, Je 49:39; Ammon, Je 49:6; Israel, Je 46:27, 28. Moab and Ammon were the children of Lot. Je 46:26. 49:6, 39. Is 18:7. 19:18-23. 23:18. Ezk +16:49, 53-55, 60.
in the latter. Ge +49:1. Jb +19:25. Ezk 38:8.

JEREMIAH 49

1 A.M. 3421. B.C. 583.
Concerning. *or*, Against. ver. 7, 23, 28. Je 48:1.
Ammonites. Ge +19:38. 2 Ch 20:1, 23.
their king. *or*, Melcom. Jg 10:7, 8. 11:13-15. 1 S 11:1-3. 2 K 10:33. +23:13. 24:2. Ne 2:19. 4:7. 13:1, 2.
cities. Ps 9:6.

2 **that I will**. Je 4:19. Ezk 25:4-6. Am 1:14.
Rabbah. Jsh +13:25.
her daughters. Nu +21:25mg. Ps +48:11.
shall Israel. ver. 1. Is 14:1-3. Ob 19.

3 **Howl**. Is +13:6.
gird. Jb +16:15.
run. Jb 30:3-7. Is 15:2.
their king. *or*, Melcom. ver. 1. 1 K 11:5, 33. 2 K 23:13, Milcom. Zp 1:5, Malcham.
shall go. Je 46:25. 48:7. Am 1:15.

4 **gloriest**. Je +9:23. Is 28:1-4. 47:7, 8. Re 18:7, 8.
thy flowing valley. *or*, thy valley floweth away.
O backsliding. Je 3:14. 7:24. Ho 4:16.
trusted. Je 48:7. Ps 49:6. 52:7. 62:10. Pr 10:15. Ezk 28:4-7. 1 T 6:17.
Who. ver. 16. Je 21:13. Ob 4, 5.

5 **I will**. ver. 29. Je 15:8. 20:4. 48:41-44. Jsh 2:9. 2 K 7:6, 7. 19:7. Jb 15:21. Pr 28:1.
Lord God of hosts. Je +2:19.
ye shall. Je 46:5. Am 4:3.
none. Is 16:3. Ob 12-14.

6 **afterward**. ver. 39. Je 46:26. 48:47. Is 19:18-23. 23:18. Ezk 16:53.

7 **Edom**. Je 25:9, 21. 27:3. Ge +25:30. 27:41. +36:21. Nu 20:14-21, 23. +24:17, 18. Dt 23:7. 2 S 8:14. 2 K 8:20. 1 Ch 18:12, 13. Ps 60:8, 9. 83:4-10. 108:9, 10. 137:7. Is 11:14. 34:5, 6. 63:1-6. La 4:21, 22. Ezk 25:12-14. 32:29. ch.

35. Da 11:41. Jl 3:19. Am 1:6, 9, 11, 12. 9:12. Ob 1, 8, 10-14. Ml 1:3, 4.

Lord of hosts. Je +6:6.

Is wisdom. Je 18:18. +19:7. Ro 1:22, 23.

Teman. ver. 20. Ge +36:11.

8 **Flee**. ver. 30. Je 6:1. 48:6. Mt 24:15-18. Re 6:15.

turn back. *or*, they are turned back. Ezk 9:2mg.

dwell deep. Je 48:28. Jg 6:2. 1 S 13:6. Is 2:21. Am 9:1-3. Ob 3, 4.

Dedan. Ge +10:7.

for. ver. 32. Je 46:21. 48:44. La 4:21, 22.

9 **grapegatherers**. Is 17:6. Ob 5, 6.

till they have enough. Heb. their sufficiency. Ex 36:7.

10 **I have made**. Ml +1:2-4. Ro +9:12, 13.

his secret. Je 23:24. Is 45:3. Am 9:3.

his seed. Ps 37:28. Is 14:20-22. Ob 9.

he is not. Ps 37:35, 36. Is 17:14.

11 **the fatherless**. Ex +22:22. Jon 4:11. Ml +3:5.

let thy. 1 T 5:5.

12 **they whose**. Je 25:28, 29. 30:11. 46:27. Pr 17:5. La 4:21, 22. Ob 16. 1 P 4:17, 18.

cup. Ezk 23:32. Lk 22:17, 20. 1 C 10:16, 21. 11:25, 26, 27, 28.

not go unpunished. Ex 34:7.

13 **I have**. Je +44:26. Ge 22:16. Is 45:23. Ezk 35:11. Am 6:8.

Bozrah. ver. 22. Ge +36:33.

a desolation. ver. 17, 18. Is 34:9-15. Ezk 25:13, 14. 35:2-15. Jl 3:19. Ob 18, 19. Ml 1:3, 4.

perpetual. Ge +9:12.

14 **heard**. Je 51:46. 2 K 7:6. 19:7. Is 37:7. Ezk 7:25, 26. Ob 1. Mi +7:17. Mt 24:6. Mk 13:7.

an ambassador. Is 18:2, 3. 30:4.

Gather. Je 50:9-16. 51:11, 27, 28. Is 13:2, 3.

15 **I will make**. 1 S 2:7, 8, 30. Ps 53:5. Ob 2. Mi 7:10. Lk 1:51.

16 **terribleness**. Or, monstrous thing; i.e. an Edomite Asherah. Je 48:29. Pr 16:18. 18:12. 29:23. Is 25:4, 5. 49:25. 66:17. Ob 3.

dwellest. SS 2:14. Is 2:21.

the rock. Probably *Sela*, or Petra. 2 K 14:7.

though. Je 48:28. Jb 39:27, 28. Is 14:13-15. Ezk 28:11-19. Am 9:2. Ob 4.

17 **Edom**. ver. 13. Is 34:9-15. Ezk 25:13, 14. 35:7, 15.

astonished. 2 Ch +29:8.

shall hiss. 2 Ch +29:8.

18 **in the overthrow**. Ge +19:24, 25. Re 11:8.

no man. ver. 33. Jb 18:15-18. Is 34:10. Re *18:21-23*.

19 **he shall come**. Is +5:29.

the swelling. Je +12:5. Jsh 3:15. 1 Ch 12:15.

who is like. Ex 15:11. Ps 89:6, 8. 113:5, 6. Is 40:25.

appoint me the time. *or*, convent me in

judgment. Jb 9:19-21. 23:3-7. 40:2-8. 42:3-5. Ps 143:2.

that shepherd. Je +30:21. Jb 41:10. Ps 76:7. Na 1:6. Re 6:17.

20 **the counsel**. Je 50:45. Ps 33:11. Pr 19:21. Is 14:24-27. 46:10, 11. Ac 4:28. Ep +1:11.

Teman. ver. +7. Jb 6:19, 20.

Surely. Je 37:10. 50:45. Zc 4:6. 1 C 1:27-29.

make. ver. 13, 17, 18. Ml 1:3, 4.

21 **earth**. Je 50:46. Is 14:4-15. Ezk 26:15, 18. 31:16. 32:10. Re 18:10.

Red sea. Heb. Weedy sea. 1 K 9:26.

22 **he shall**. Je 4:13. 48:40, 41. Dt 28:49. Da 7:4. Ho 8:1.

Bozrah. ver. 13.

the heart of the. ver. 24. Je +4:31. Ps 18:5.

23 **Damascus**. Ge +14:15. 2 C 11:32.

Hamath. Nu +13:21.

evil. Is +45:7.

fainthearted. Heb. melted. Ex +15:15.

sorrow. Is 57:20.

on the sea. *or*, as on the sea. Ps 107:26, 27. Lk 8:23, 24. 21:25, 26. Ac 27:20. Re 15:2.

24 **anguish**. ver. +22.

25 **How**. Je 33:9. 48:2, 39. 51:41. Ps 37:35, 36. Is 1:26. 14:4-6. Da 4:30. Re 18:10, 16-19.

not left. Dt 32:36. 1 K 14:10. Ps 49:10. Ml 4:1.

26 **young men**. Je 9:21. 11:22. 50:30. 51:3, 4. La 2:21. Ezk 27:27. Am 4:10.

27 **I will**. Am 1:3-5.

Ben-hadad. 1 K +15:18. 2 K 13:5.

28 **Kedar**. Ge +25:13.

Hazor. ver. 30, 33. Jsh +15:23.

Arise. ver. 14, 31. Je 50:14-16. Is 13:2-5.

spoil. Is 11:14.

east. Ge +29:1.

29 **tents**. Ps 120:5. Is 13:20. 60:7.

curtains. Je 4:20. 10:20. Hab 3:7.

camels. Ge 37:25. Jg 6:5. 7:12. 8:21, 26. 1 Ch 5:20, 21. Jb 1:3.

Fear. ver. 24. Je 6:25. 20:3mg, 4, 10. 46:5. Ps 31:13. La 2:22. 2 C 4:8-10. 7:5.

30 **get you far off**. Heb. flit greatly. Je 50:8. Ps 11:1.

dwell. ver. 8.

for. Je 25:9, 24, 25. 27:6. Is 10:7.

31 **wealthy nation**. *or*, nation that is at ease. Je 48:11. Jb 16:12. Ps 123:4. Is 32:9, 11. Ezk 23:42.

that. Jg 18:7-10, 27. Is 47:8. Ezk 30:9. 38:11. 39:6. Na 1:12. Zp 2:15.

which dwell. Nu 23:9. Dt 33:28. Jg 18:28. Ezk 38:11, 12. Mi 7:14.

32 **their camels**. ver. +29.

I will scatter. ver. 36. Dt 28:64. Ezk 5:10, 12. 12:14, 15.

in the utmost corners. Heb. cut off into corners, *or*, that have the corners *of their hair* polled. Je 9:26mg. 25:23mg.

33 Hazor. ver. 28.
a dwelling. ver. 17, 18. Je 9:11. 10:22. 50:39, 40. 51:37. Is 13:20-22. 14:23. 34:9-17. Zp 2:9, 13-15. Ml 1:3. Re 18:2, 21, 22.
for ever. Heb. *olam*, Ex +12:24.

34 Cir. A.M. 3406. B.C. 598.
Elam. Ge +10:22.

35 break. Je 50:14, 29. 51:56. Ps 46:9. Is 22:6.

36 the four winds. Da 7:2, 3. 8:8, 22. 11:4. Re 7:1.
scatter. ver. 32. Dt 28:25, 64. Ezk 5:10, 12. Am 9:9.
the outcasts. Je 30:17. Ps 147:2. Is 11:12. 16:3, 4. 27:13. 56:8.

37 to be. ver. 5, 22, 24, 29. Je 43:39. 48:39. 50:36. Ps 48:4-6. Ezk 32:23mg.
their enemies. Je +34:20, 21.
life. Heb. *nephesh*, Ge +44:30.
I will send the sword. Je +12:12.

38 will set my throne. Je 43:10. Da 7:9-14.

39 latter days. Ge +49:1.
I will. ver. +6. Jb 42:10. Ezk 16:53-55. 29:14. 39:25. Am 9:14.

JEREMIAH 50

1 A.M. 3409. B.C. 595.
against Babylon. Je 25:26, 27. 27:7. 51:1, etc. Ps 137:8, 9. Is 13:1-3. 14:4. 21:1-10. ch. 47. Hab 2:5-20. Re ch. 18.
the land. Ge 11:31. Jb 1:17. Is 23:13. Ac 7:4.
Jeremiah. Heb. the hand of Jeremiah. 2 S 23:2. 1 K +16:12mg. 2 P 1:21.

2 Declare. Je 6:18. 31:10. 46:14. Ps 64:9. 96:3. Is 12:4. 48:6. 66:18, 19. Re 14:6-8.
set up. Heb. lift up. Je 4:5, 6. 46:14. Is 13:2.
Babylon is taken. Je 51:8. Is 21:9. Re 14:8. 18:2, 6, 10, 21.
Bel. Je 51:44. Is 46:1.
Merodach. i.e. *death and slaughter; warlike*, **S#4781h**, only here. Je 52:31. Is 39:1.
her idols. Je +43:12, 13. 51:47. Is 37:19. Zp 2:11.
images. Le 26:30. Ezr 1:7. Is 21:9. 46:1. Je 50:2. 51:44, 47, 52. Da 1:2.

3 out of the north. ver. 9, 41. Je +6:1. 51:11, 27, 48. Is 13:5, 17, 18, 20.
which. ver. 12, 13, 35-40. Je 51:8, 9, 25, 26, 37-44, 62. Is 13:6-10, 19-22. 14:22-24. Re 18:21-23.
both. Je 7:20. 21:6. Ge 6:7. Ex 12:12. Ezk 14:13-31. Zp 1:3.

4 those. ver. 20. Je 3:16-18. 33:15. 51:47, 48. Is 63:4.
the children of Israel. ver. 19, 20, 33, 34. Je 3:18. 23:6-8. 30:10, 11. 31:6, 7, 31. 33:7. Is 11:12, 13. 14:1. Ezk 37:16-22. 39:25. Ho 1:11.
going. Ezr 3:12, 13. Jl 2:12. Zc 12:10-14. Lk +6:21. Re 1:7.

seek the. Je 29:12-14. Ps 105:4. Is 45:19. 55:6. Ho 3:5. Zc 8:21-23.

5 ask. Je 6:16. Ps 25:8, 9. 84:7. Is 35:8. Jn 7:17.
Come. Is 2:3-5. Mi 4:1, 2. Ac 11:23. 2 C 8:5.
join. Is +56:3. 1 C +6:17.
in a. Is +55:3. 56:6, 7.
perpetual. Heb. *olam*, Ge +9:12. Je 3:18-4:2. 11:1-6. 31:31.
that shall. 1 K 19:10, 14. He 8:6-10.

6 people. ver. 17. Nu +27:17. Ps 119:176. Is 53:6. Mt 18:11-13. Lk 15:4-7. Ro 11:26.
their shepherds. Je 10:21. 23:11-15. Is 56:10-12. Ezk 34:4-12. Zc 11:4-9.
turned. Je 3:14, 22. Is +57:17mg.
on the. Je 2:20. 3:6, 23. Ezk 34:6.
have forgotten. Je 2:32. Ps 32:7. 90:1. 91:1. 116:7. Is 30:15. 32:2.
resting place. Heb. place to lie down in. Ps 23:2. SS 1:7, 8. Is 32:18. Ezk 34:14, 25-28. Mt 9:36mg.

7 have devoured. ver. 17, 33. Je +10:25.
We offend. ver. 15, 23, 29. Je 2:3. 25:14, 15. 40:2, 3. 51:11, 24, 56. Is 10:5-7, 12. 47:6. 54:15-17. Da 9:6, 16. Zc 1:14-16. 11:5.
the habitation. Je 31:23. Ps 90:1. 91:1.
the hope. Ps 22:4, 5. +42:11. 1 T 1:1.

8 out of the midst. 2 Th 2:7, 8. Re +18:4.
he goats. Pr 30:31.

9 I will raise. ver. 3, 21, 26, 41, 42. Je 15:14. 51:1-4, 11, 27, 28. Ezr 1:1, 2. Is 13:2-5, 17. 21:2. 41:25. 45:1-4.
north. ver. +3.
they shall. ver. 14, 29.
expert man. or, destroyer. or, successful. Je 10:21. 23:5. 1 S 18:14.
none. 2 S 1:22. Is 13:18.

10 Chaldea. i.e. *occultism, astrologer; clod breakers; land of the Chaldeans*, **S#3778h**. Je 25:12. 27:7. 51:24, 35. Ezk 11:24. 16:29. 23:15, 16.
all that. Is 33:4, 23. 45:3. Re 17:16.

11 ye were. Pr +17:5. La 1:21. 2:15, 16. Ezk 25:3-8, 15-17.
ye destroyers. ver. 17. Je 51:34, 35. Ps 74:2-8. 79:1-4. 83:1-5. Is 10:6, 7. 47:6. Zc 2:8, 9. 14:1-3, 12.
ye are. ver. 27. Ps 22:12. Ho 10:11. Am 4:1.
fat. Heb. big, or corpulent. Dt +31:20.
bellow as bulls. or, neigh as steeds. Je 5:8.

12 mother. Je 49:2. Ga 4:26. Re 17:5.
the hindermost. ver. 17. Je 25:26. Is 23:13.
a wilderness. ver. 35-40. Je 25:12. 51:25, 26, 43, 62-64. Is 13:20-22. 14:22. Re 18:21-23.
desert. Je 5:6mg.

13 Because. Zc 1:15.
not be inhabited. ver. +39. 1 P 5:13.
every. Je 25:12. Is 14:4-17. Hab 2:6, etc.
hiss. 2 Ch +29:8.

14 in array. ver. 9. Je 51:2, 11, 12, 27. 1 S 17:20. 2 S 10:9. Is 13:4, 17, 18.
bend. ver. 29, 42. Je 46:9. 49:35. Is 5:28.

for she. ver. 7, 11, 29. Ps 51:4. Hab 2:8, 17. Re 17:5.

15 **Shout**. Je 51:14. Jsh 6:5, 20. Ezk 21:22.
she hath. 1 Ch +29:24mg.
hand. 1 Ch +29:24.
her foundations. Je 51:25, 44, 58, 64.
for it. ver. 14, 28. Je 46:10. 51:6, 11, 36. Dt +32:35. Ps 94:1. 149:7. Is 59:17. 61:2. 63:4. Na 1:2. Lk 21:22. Ro 3:5. 12:19. 2 Th 1:8.
as she. ver. 29. Jg 1:6, 7. 1 S 15:33. Ps 137:8, 9. Mt 7:2. Ja 2:13. Re 16:6. 18:6. 19:2.

16 **the sower**. Je 51:23. Jl 1:11. Am 5:16.
sickle. *or*, scythe. Jl 3:13.
they shall turn every one. Je 46:16. 51:9. Is 13:14.

17 **a scattered**. ver. +6. Jl 3:2. Lk 15:4-6.
the lions. Is +5:29.
first. 2 K 15:29. 17:6, etc. 18:9-13. 2 Ch 28:20. 32:1, etc. 33:11. Is 7:17-20. 8:7, 8. 10:5-7. ch. 36, 37.
this. Je ch. 39. 51:34, 35. 52:1. 2 K ch. 24, 25. 2 Ch ch. 36. Is 47:6. Da 6:24.

18 **Lord of hosts, the God of Israel**. Je +7:3.
will punish. Je +11:22mg.
as I. Is 37:36-38. Ezk 31:3-17. Na ch. 1-3. Zp 2:13-15.

19 **bring**. ver. 4, 5. Je 3:18. +23:3. Is 65:9, 10.
he shall. Is 33:9. 35:2. Mi 7:14, 18.
his soul. Heb. *nephesh*. Ge +34:3. Je 31:14, 25.
mount. Jsh +17:15.
Gilead. Ge +37:25.

20 **In those**. ver. +4. Je 33:15.
the iniquity. Je +31:34. Nu +23:21. Is 11:1, 2. Ac 3:19, 26. Ro 8:33, 34.
and there. Ps +130:8. Ro 5:16. 2 P 3:15.
I will pardon. Je 44:14. Ps +32:5. Is 1:9. Ro 5:16. 6:13. 11:6, 26, 27.

21 **up**. ver. 3, 9, 15.
Merathaim. *or*, the rebels. i.e. *double rebellion; double bitterness*, S#4850h, only here.
Pekod. *or*, visitation. Ezk 23:23.
and do. Je 34:22. 48:10. Nu 31:14-18. 1 S 15:3, 11-24. 2 S 16:11. 2 K 18:25. 2 Ch 36:23. Is 10:6. 44:28. 48:14.

22 **A sound**. Je 4:19-21. 51:54-56. Is 21:2-4.

23 **How is**. Je 51:20-24. Is 14:4-6, 12-17. Da 2:40. Re 18:16-19, 21.

24 **snare**. Ec 9:12.
and thou wast. Je 51:8, 31-39, 57. Is 21:3-5. Da 5:30, 31. Re 18:7, 8.
because. Ex 10:3. Jb 9:4. 40:2, 9. Is 13:11. 45:9. 2 Th 2:4.

25 **opened**. ver. 35-38. Je 51:11, 20. Ps 45:3, 5. Is 13:2-5, 17, 18. 21:7-9.
armory. *Dt +28:12*.
weapons. Ps +35:2.
indignation. Da +8:19.
this. ver. +15. Je 51:12, 25, 55. Is 14:22-24. 46:10, 11. 48:14, 15. Am +3:6. Re 18:8.
Lord God of hosts. Je +2:19.

26 **against**. ver. 41. Je 51:27, 28. Is 5:26.
the utmost. Heb. the end. Je 51:31.
open. ver. 10. Je 51:44. Is 45:3.
cast her up. *or*, tread her. Ps 119:118. Is 10:6. 25:10. 63:3, 4. La 1:15. Mi 7:10. Re 14:19, 20. 19:15.
destroy. ver. 13, 15, 23. Je 51:25, 26, 64. Is 14:23. Re 18:21-24.

27 **bullocks**. ver. 11. Je 46:21. Ps 22:12. Is 34:7. Ezk 39:17-20. Re 19:17, 18.
their day. ver. 31. Je 27:7. +48:44. Ps 37:13. La 1:21. Ezk 7:5-7. Re 16:17-19. 18:10.
time of. Je +8:12.

28 **voice**. Je 51:50, 51. Is 48:20.
to declare. ver. 15. Je 51:10, 11. Ps +149:6-9. Da 5:3-5, 23, 26, 27. Zc 12:2, 3.
vengeance of his. ver. +15. La 1:10. 2:6, 7. Da 5:3.

29 **the archers**. ver. 9, 14, 26.
recompense. ver. +15. Je 51:56.
for she hath. ver. 24, 32. Ex 10:3. Is 14:13, 14. 37:23. 47:10. Da 4:37. 5:23. 11:36. 2 Th 2:4. Re 13:5, 6.

30 **her young**. Je 9:21. 18:21. 48:15. 49:26. 51:3, 4. Is 13:15-18.
all her. ver. 36. Je 51:56, 57. Re 6:15-17. 19:18.

31 **I am**. Ezk +15:7.
O thou. ver. 29, +32. Je 48:29. 49:16.
most proud. Heb. pride. ver. 32mg.
for. ver. +27.

32 **the most proud**. Heb. pride. ver. 31mg. Pr +16:5. Is 14:13-15.
none. Je 51:26, 64. Re 18:8, 21.
kindle. Je +17:27.

33 **and all**. ver. 7, 17, 18. Je 51:34-36. Is 14:17. 47:6. 49:24-26. 51:23. 52:4-6. Zc 1:15, 16.
they refused. Je 34:15-18. Ex 5:2. 8:2. 9:2, 3, 17, 18. Is 14:17. 58:6.

34 **Redeemer**. Ex 6:6. Pr 23:11. Is +41:14. Mi 4:10.
strong. Ps 89:19. Re 18:8.
Lord of hosts. Ps +24:10.
is his name. Ex +6:3.
plead. Je 51:36. Ps 35:1. 43:1. Pr +22:23. Is 51:22. Am 5:12. Mi 7:9. Ja +5:4.
that he. Is 14:3-7. 2 Th 1:6, 7. Re 19:1-3.

35 **sword**. Je +12:12. Zc 11:17.
upon her princes. ver. 27, 30. Je 51:39, 57. Is 41:25. Da 5:1, 2, 30.
her wise men. Je 8:9. 10:7. Is 19:11-13. 29:14. 44:25. 47:13, 14. Da 5:7, 8. 1 C 1:25.

36 **A sword**. Dt +28:4.
upon the liars. *or*, upon the chief stays. Heb. bars. Je 48:30. Is 43:14mg. 44:24, 25. 2 Th 2:9-11. 1 T 4:2. 1 J 2:22. Re 19:20. +21:8. 22:15.
dote. 2 S 15:31. 17:14. 2 Ch 25:16. Is 47:10-15. 1 T 6:4.
her mighty. ver. +30. Je 49:22. 51:23, 30, 32. Na 2:8. 3:7, 13, 17, 18.

37 **their horses**. Je 51:21. Ps 20:7, 8. 46:9. 76:6. Ezk 39:20. Na 2:2-4, 13. Hg 2:22.
all the. Je +25:20.
as women. Je +48:41. Is 19:16. Na 3:13.
her treasures. ver. 26. Is 45:3.

38 **A drought**. ver. 12. Je 51:32-36. Is 44:27. Re 16:12. 17:15, 16.
the land. ver. 2. Je 51:44, 47, 52. Is 46:1-7. Da ch. 3. 5:4. Hab 2:18, 19. Re 17:5.
mad. Je +51:7. Is 44:25. Ac 17:16.

39 **wild beasts**. ver. 12, 13. Je 25:12. 51:26, 37, 38, 43, 62-64. Is 13:20-22. 14:23. 34:11-17. Re 16:17-21. 18:2, 21-24.
no more inhabited. ver. 3, 13. Je 25:12. 51:29, 43, 62. Is 13:20.
for ever. Jb +4:20 (S#5331h).

40 **overthrew Sodom**. Je 51:26. Ge +19:24, 25. Ho 11:8, 9. Re 11:8. 18:8, 9.

41 **a people shall**. ver. 2, 3, 9. Je 6:22, 23. 25:14. 51:1, 2, 11, 27, 28. Is 13:2-5, 17, 18. Re 17:16.
north. Je +6:1.

42 **hold**. Je +6:22, 23.
they are cruel. Ps 74:20. 137:8, 9. Is 13:17, 18. 14:6. 47:6. Hab 1:6-8. Ja 2:13. Re 16:6.
their voice. Ps 46:2, 3, 6. Is 5:30.
shall ride. Je 8:16. 47:3. Is 5:28. Hab 1:8. Re 19:14-18.
daughter. Is +47:1.

43 **king**. Je 51:31. Is 13:6-8. 21:3, 4. Da 5:5, 6.
pangs. Je +4:31.

44 **like a lion**. Is +5:29.
the swelling. Je +12:5.
who is a. Jb 41:10, 11. Is 41:25. 46:11.
for who. Ex +15:11. Ps 89:6, 8. Is 40:18, 25. 43:10.
appoint me the time. *or*, convent me to plead. Je 49:19mg. Jb 9:19.
who is that. Je +49:19. Jb 41:10.

45 **hear**. Je 51:10, 11. Is +14:27. Ac 4:28. Re 17:16, 17.
the least. Je 37:10. 49:20.
surely he. Is 13:9.

46 **the noise**. Je 49:21. Is +14:9, 10. Ezk 26:18. 31:16. 32:10. Re 18:9-19.

JEREMIAH 51

1 **I will**. Je 50:9, 14-16, 21. Is 13:3-5. Am +3:6.
midst. Heb. heart. Pr 23:34mg.
rise. Je 50:24, 29, 33. Zc 2:8. Ac 9:4.
a destroying wind. Je +4:11, 12. 49:36. 2 K 19:7. Ezk 19:12. Ho 13:15.

2 **fanners**. Mt +3:12.
fan. Ge +1:29.
in the day. ver. 27, 28. Je 50:14, 15, 29, 32.

3 **let the**. Je 50:14, 41, 42.
brigandine. Je 46:4.

spare. Je 9:21. 50:27, 30. Dt 32:25. Ps 137:9. Is 13:10-18. Ja 2:13.
destroy. Je 50:21.

4 **thrust**. Je +37:10. 49:26. 50:30, 37.

5 **Israel**. Je 50:4, 5, 20. Le +26:44. 1 K 6:13. Ezr 9:9. Is 44:21. 49:14, 15. +54:3-11. 62:12. Ho 1:10. Am 9:8, 9. Ro +11:1, 2.
nor. Zc 2:12. 12:6, 8.
Lord of hosts. Je +6:6.
though. Je 16:18. 19:4. 23:15. 31:37. 2 K 21:16. Ezr 9:13. Ne 9:17, 31. Ezk 8:17. 9:9. 22:24-31. Ho 4:1, 2. Mi 7:18, 20. Zp 3:1-4. Jn 6:37. Ro 5:8.
Holy One. Is +1:4.

6 **Flee**. ver. 9, 45, 50. Re +18:4.
soul. Heb. *nephesh*, Ge +12:13.
be not. Pr 13:20. 1 T 5:22.
for this. ver. 11. Je 27:7. +50:15. Re 16:19. 18:5, 6.
he will render. Je 25:14, 16.

7 **a golden**. Is 14:4. Da 2:32, 38. Re 17:4, 5.
the nations. Je 25:9, 14-27. Da 3:1-7. Hab 2:15, 16. Re 14:8. 17:2. 18:3, 23. 19:2.
are mad. Je 25:16. 50:38.

8 **suddenly fallen**. ver. 41. Je 50:2. Is 21:9. 47:9, 11. Re 14:8. 18:2, 8, 10, 17, 19.
howl. Is +13:6. Ezk 27:30-32. Da 5:24, 31.
take balm. Je 30:12-15. Ge +37:25. Na 3:19.

9 **would have**. Je 23:22. 1 S 13:13, 14. Ps 81:13, 14. Is +30:15. Mt 26:53, 54. Lk 13:34.
forsake. Je 8:20. 46:16, 21. 50:16. Is 13:14. 47:15. Mt 25:10-13.
her judgment. 2 Ch 28:9. Ezr 9:6. Da 4:20-22. Re 18:5.

10 **brought**. Ps 37:6. Is 54:17. Mi 7:9, 10. 2 C 5:21.
let us. Je 31:6-9. 50:28. Ps 9:14. 102:19-21. 116:18, 19. 126:1-3. Is 40:2. 51:11. 52:9, 10. Re 14:1-3. 19:1-6.

11 **Make**. Je 46:4, 9. 50:9, 14, 25, 28, 29. Is 21:5.
bright. Heb. pure. or, cleanse. Je 4:11.
the Lord hath. ver. 27, 28. 1 K 11:14, 23. 1 Ch 5:26. 2 Ch 36:22. Ezr 1:1. Is 10:26. 13:17, 18. 21:2. 41:25. 45:1, 5. 46:11. Re 17:16, 17.
the spirit. Heb. *ruach*, Ge +41:8; Ge +26:35.
his device. ver. 12, 29. Je 50:45.
the vengeance. ver. 24, 35. Je 50:15, 28. Ps 74:3-11. 83:3-9. Hab 2:17-20. Zc 12:2, 3. 14:2, 3, 12.

12 **the standard**. Je 46:3-5. Pr +21:30. Is 8:9, 10. 13:2. Jl 3:2, 9-14. Na 2:1. 3:14, 15.
make the watch. Is 21:5, 6.
ambushes. Heb. liers in wait. Jsh 8:4, 13mg, 14.
the Lord hath both. ver. 11, 29. La 2:17.

13 **dwellest**. ver. 36. Re 17:1, 15.
upon many waters. ver. 36, 42. Je 50:38. Nu 24:7. Jn +3:23. Re 17:1, 15.
abundant. Je 50:37. Is 45:3. Hab 2:5-10. Re 18:11-17.

thine. Je 17:11. 50:27, 31. Ge 6:13. La 4:18. Ezk 7:2-12. Da 5:26. Am 8:2. 1 P 4:7.
and the. Hab 2:9-11. Lk 12:19-21. 2 P 2:3, 14, 15. Ju 11-13. Re 18:19.

14 sworn. Je +49:13. Am 6:8. He 6:13.
himself. Heb. his soul. Heb. *nephesh*, Ge +27:31; Le +26:11.
as with. Je 46:23. Jg 6:5. Jl 1:4-7. 2:3, 4, 25. Na 3:15-17.
lift up. Heb. utter. Je +50:15. Ex 32:18.

15 hath made. Je 10:12-16. 32:17. Ge 1:1-6. Ps 107:25. 146:5, 6. 148:1-5. Is 40:26. Ac 14:15. 17:24. Ro 1:20. Col +1:16, 17. He +1:2, 3. Re 4:11.
by his wisdom. Ps 104:24. 136:5. Pr 3:19. Ro 11:33.
and hath. Is +40:22. 48:13.

16 he uttereth. Je +10:12, 13. Jb 37:2-11. 40:9. Ps 18:13. 29:3-10. 46:6. 68:33. 104:7. Ezk 10:5.
there is. Jb 36:26-33. 37:13. 38:34-38. Ps 135:7. Am 9:6.
multitude. *or*, noise. Je +10:13mg. Is 60:5mg. Ezk 7:11mg. Am 5:23.
and he causeth. Ps 135:7.
bringeth. Ge 8:1. Ex 10:13, 19. 14:21. Jb 38:22. Ps 78:26. 135:7. 147:18. Jon 1:4. 4:8. Mt 8:26, 27.
treasures. Dt +28:12.

17 Every. Je +10:8, 14. Ps 53:1, 2. 1 C 1:19-21.
brutish by his knowledge. *or*, more brutish than to know. Je 10:14mg.
no breath. Heb. *ruach*, Ge +6:17. Ps +135:17.

18 vanity. Dt +32:21.
time of. Je +8:12. 43:12, 13. 46:25. 48:7. 50:2. Ex 12:12. Is 19:1. 46:1. Zp 2:11. 1 P 2:12.

19 portion. Ps +16:5. 115:3.
the former. ver. +15.
the rod. Je 12:7-10. 50:11. Ex 19:5, 6. Dt 32:8, 9. Ps 33:12. 74:2. 135:4. 1 P 2:9.
the Lord of hosts. Ps +24:10.
is his name. Ex +6:3.

20 art. Je 50:23. Is 10:5, 15. 13:5. 14:5, 6. 37:26. 41:15, 16. Mi 4:13. Zc 9:13, 14. Mt 22:7.
weapons. Ps +35:2.
with thee. *or*, in thee, *or*, by thee.
break. Je 25:9, 11. 27:5-7.

21 the horse and. Je 50:37. Ex 15:1, 21. Ps 46:9. 76:6. Ezk 39:20. Mi 5:10. Na 2:13. Hg 2:22. Zc 10:5. 12:4. Re 19:18.

22 man and. Je 6:11. Dt 32:25. 1 S 15:3. 2 Ch 36:17. Is 20:4. La 2:11. Ezk 9:5, 6.

24 I will render. ver. 11, 35, 49. Je 50:15, 17, 18, 28, 29, 33, 34. Ps 137:8, 9. Is 47:6-9. 51:22, 23. 61:2. 63:1-4. 66:6. 1 Th 2:15, 16. Re 6:10. 18:20, 24. 19:2-4.
in your sight. Is +66:24.

25 I am. Ezk +15:7.
O destroying. ver. 53, 58. Ge 11:4. Is 13:2. Da 4:30. Zc 4:7.

which destroyest. ver. 7, 20-23. Je 25:9, 18-27. Re 8:8. 17:1-6.
and will. 2 P 3:10. Re 8:8. 18:9, 19.

26 shall not. ver. +37, 43. Je 50:12, 13. Is 13:19-22. 14:23.
desolate for ever. Heb. everlasting desolations. Je 50:40, 41. Is 34:8-17. Re 18:20-24.
for ever. Heb. *olam*, Ex +12:24.

27 Set ye up. ver. 12. Je 50:2, 41. Is 13:2-5. Zc 14:2-4.
blow. Ho +8:1.
prepare. Je 25:14.
Ararat. Ge 8:4.
Minni. i.e. *division; from me; part*, **S#4508h**.
Ashchenaz. i.e. *fire that spreads*, **S#813h**. Ge 10:3, Ashkenaz. 1 Ch 1:6.
cause. ver. +14. Je 46:23. 50:41, 42. Jg 6:5. Jl 2:2, 3. Na 3:15-17. Re 9:7-11.

28 the kings. ver. 11. Je 25:25. Ge 10:2. 1 Ch 1:5, Madia. Est 1:3. 10:2. Is 13:17. 21:2. Da 5:28-30. 6:8. 8:3, 4, 20. 9:1, 2.

29 the land. Je +8:16. 10:10. 50:36, 43. Is 13:13, 14. 14:16. Jl 2:10. Am 8:8.
every purpose. Pr +21:30. Ep +1:11.
without an inhabitant. ver. 8, 26. ver. 11, 12, 43, 62-64. Je 50:13, 39, 40, 45. Is 13:19, 20. 14:23, 24. 46:10, 11. ch. 47. Re 18:2, 21-24.

30 The mighty. ver. 32, 57. Je 48:41. 50:36, 37. Ps 76:5. Is 13:7, 8. 19:16. Na 3:13. Re 18:10.
her bars. Je 50:36mg. Ps 107:16. 147:13. Is 45:1, 2. La 2:9. Am 1:5. Na 3:13.

31 post. Je 4:20. 50:24. 1 S 4:12-18. 2 S 18:19-31. 2 Ch 30:6. Est 3:13-15. 8:10, 14. Jb 9:25.
to show. Je 50:43. Is 21:3-9. 47:11-13. Da 5:2-5, 30.
one. or, each.

32 the passages. Je 50:38. Is 44:27.
the men. ver. +30. Je 50:37.

33 Lord of hosts, the God of Israel. Je +7:3.
daughter. Is +47:1.
is like. Is +21:10.
threshingfloor. Ge +50:10.
it is time to thresh her. *or*, in the time that he thresheth her. Is 21:10.
the time. Is 17:5. 18:5. Ho 6:11. Jl 3:13. Mt 13:30, 37-39. Re 14:15-20.

34 the king. ver. +49. Je 39:1-8. 50:7, 17. La 1:1, 14, 15.
he hath made. Je 48:11, 12. Is 24:1-3. 34:11. Na 2:2, 9, 10.
swallowed. ver. 44. Ps +35:25. Mt 23:14.

35 The violence. Heb. My violence. Je 50:29. Jg 9:20, 24, 56, 57. Ps 9:12. 12:5. 137:8, 9. Is 26:20, 21. Zc 1:15. Mt 7:2. Ja 2:13. Re 6:10. 16:6. 18:6, 20.
flesh. *or*, remainder. Le 18:6mg.
inhabitant. Heb. inhabitress. Je +10:17mg.

36 I will plead. Je +50:33, 34. Ps 140:12. Pr

22:23. 23:11. Is 43:14. 47:6-9. 49:25, 26. Mi 7:8-10. Hab 2:8-17.
take. ver. +6. He 10:30, 31. Re 19:1-3.
and I will. Je +50:38. Ps 107:33, 34. Is 44:27. Re 16:12.

37 **become**. ver. 25, 26, +29. Je 25:9, 12, 18. Is 34:8-17. Re 18:2, 21-23.
an hissing. 2 Ch +29:8.
without an inhabitant. ver. 29. 1 P 5:13.

38 **roar**. Is +5:29. 35:9.
yell. *or*, shake themselves. Jg 16:20.

39 **their heat**. Je 25:27. Is 21:4, 5. 22:12-14. Da 5:1-4, 30. Na 1:10. 3:11.
and sleep. ver. 57. Ps 13:3. 76:5, 6.
perpetual. Heb. *olam*, Ge +9:12.

40 **like lambs**. Je 50:27. Ps 37:20. 44:22. Is 34:6. Ezk 39:18.

41 **Sheshach**. Je 25:26. Da 5:1-3.
the praise. Je 49:25. 50:23. Is 13:19. 14:4. Da 2:38. 4:22, 30. 5:4, 5. Re 18:9-19.
an astonishment. ver. 37. Je 50:46. Dt 28:37. 2 Ch 7:21. Ezk 27:35.

42 **The sea**. Ps 18:4, 16. 42:7. 65:7. Je +47:2. Lk 21:25.

43 **cities**. ver. +29, 37. Je 50:39, 40.
a land. Je 2:6. Is 13:20. Ezk 29:10, 11.

44 **I will punish**. ver. 18, 47. Je 50:2. Is 46:1, 2.
I will bring. ver. +34. 2 Ch 36:7. Ezr 1:7. Da 1:2. 5:2-4, 26.
the nations. Is 2:2. 60:5. Da 3:2, 3, 29. 4:1, 22. 5:19, 31. Re 18:9-19.
the wall. ver. 53, 58.

45 **go**. ver. 6, 10, 50. Re 14:8-11. +18:4.
deliver. Ac 2:40.
soul. Heb. *nephesh*, Ge +12:13.

46 **lest**. *or*, let not. Je +49:14. Lk 21:9-19, 28.
a rumor shall. Is 13:3-5. 21:2, 3.
ruler against. Jg +7:22.

47 **I will**. ver. 52. Je +50:2. Is 21:9. 46:1, 2.
do judgment upon. Heb. visit upon. ver. 18. Je +9:25mg.
her whole. ver. 24, 43. Je 50:12-16, 35-40.

48 **the heaven**. ver. 10. Ps +58:10, 11. Is 44:23. 48:20. 49:13. Re 15:1-4. 16:4-7.
sing. Je 31:12. Ge +4:10.
the spoilers. ver. +11. Je 50:3, 9, 41.

49 **As Babylon**, etc. *or*, Both Babylon *is* to fall, O ye slain of Israel, and with Babylon shall fall the slain of all the country.
hath. ver. 10, 11, 24, 35. Je 50:11, 17, 18, 29, 33, 34. Jg 1:7. Ps 137:8, 9. Mt 7:2. Ja 2:13. Re 18:5, 6.
of all. Is 14:16, 17.
the earth. *or*, the country.

50 **escaped**. ver. 6, 45. Je 31:21. 44:28. Is 51:11. Re +18:4.
remember. Je 29:12-14. Dt 4:29-31. 30:1-4. Ezr 1:3-5. Ne 1:2-4. 2:3-5. Ps 102:13, 14. 137:5, 6. Da 9:2, 3, 16-19.
Jerusalem. Ps +122:6.

51 **are confounded**. Je 3:22-25. 31:19. Ps 74:18-21. 79:4, 12. 123:3, 4. 137:1-3. La 2:15-17. 5:1. Ezk 36:30.
shame. Je 3:25. 14:3. Ps 44:13-16. 69:7-13. 71:13. 109:29. Ezk 7:18. Mi 7:10.
for strangers. Je 52:13. Ps 74:3-7. 79:1. La 1:10. 2:20. Ezk 7:21, 22. 9:7. 24:21. Da 8:11-14. 9:26, 27. 11:31. Re 11:1, 2.

52 **that I**. ver. +47. Je 50:38.
the wounded. Is 13:15, 16. Ezk 30:24. Da 5:30, 31.

53 **mount**. ver. 25, 58. Je 49:16. Ge 11:4, 9. Ps 139:8-10. Is 14:12-15. 47:5, 7. Ezk 31:9-11. Da 4:30. Am 9:2, 4. Ob 3, 4.
from. ver. 1-4, 11, 48. Je 50:9, 10, 21, 25, 31-34, 45. Is 10:6, 7. 13:2-5, 17. 41:25. 45:1-5.

54 **A sound**. Je 48:3-5. 50:22, 27, 43, 46. Is 13:6-9. 15:5. Zp 1:10. Re 18:17-19.

55 **destroyed**. ver. 38, 39. Je 25:10. 50:10-15. Is 15:1. 24:8-11. 47:5. Re 18:21-23.
her waves. Ps 65:7. 93:3, 4. Is 17:13. Ezk 26:3. Lk 21:25. Re 17:15.

56 **the spoiler**. ver. 48. Je 50:10. Is 21:2. Hab 2:8. Re 17:16.
her mighty. ver. +30. Je 50:36.
every. Je 49:35. Ge 49:24. 1 S 2:4. Ps 37:15. 46:9. 76:3. Ezk 39:3, 9.
the Lord. ver. +6, 24. Je 50:28, 29. Dt 32:35. Ps 94:1, 2. 137:8. Is 34:8. 35:4. 59:18. 2 Th 1:6. Re 18:5, 6, 20. 19:2.
God. Heb. *El*, Ex +15:2.

57 **I will**. ver. +39. Je 25:27. Is 21:4, 5. Da 5:1-4, 30, 31. Na 1:10. Hab 2:15-17. Re 18:6, 7, 9.
sleep a. Ps 76:5, 6. Is 37:36.
perpetual. Heb. *olam*, Ge +9:12.
the king. Je +46:18. 48:15. Ml 1:14.

58 **The broad walls of Babylon**. *or*, The walls of broad Babylon. ver. 44. Je 50:15.
utterly. lit. being broken shall be broken. Ge +2:16.
broken. *or*, made naked. **S#6209h**. Is 23:13. 32:11.
high gates. ver. 30. Is 45:1, 2.
the people. ver. 9, 64. 2 Th +2:1.

59 **Neriah**. Je +32:12. 36:4. 45:1.
with. *or*, on the behalf of.
quiet prince. *or*, prince of Menucha, *or*, chief chamberlain. lit. prince of rest. Je 45:3, 5. Ps 23:2. Is 32:18.

60 **wrote in a book**. Je 30:2, 3. 36:2-4, 32. Is 8:1-4. 30:8. Da 12:4. Hab 2:2, 3. Re 1:11, 19.
evil. Is +45:7.

61 **and shalt see**. Mt 24:1, 2. Mk 13:1, 2.
read. Je 29:1, 2. Col 4:16. 1 Th 4:18. 5:27. Re 1:3.

62 **to cut**. ver. +25, 26, 29, 37. Je 50:3, 13, 39, 40. Is 13:19-22. 14:22, 23. Re 18:20-23.
desolate. Heb. desolations. ver. 26. Je 25:9, 12. 48:34mg. Is 15:6mg. Ezk 35:9.
for ever. Heb. *olam*, Ex +12:24.

63 **thou shalt bind**. Je 19:10, 11. Re 18:21.
Euphrates. Ge +2:14.
64 **Thus shall**. ver. 42. Je 25:27. Na 1:8, 9. Re
14:8. 18:2, 21.
not rise. Is 13:20.
evil. Is +45:7.
they shall. ver. 58. Ps 76:12. Hab 2:13.
Thus far. Jb 31:40. Ps 72:20.

JEREMIAH 52

1 A.M. 3406-3416. B.C. 598-588.
one and twenty. 2 K 24:18. 2 Ch 36:11.
began to reign. Heb. reigned.
Libnah. Nu +33:20.
2 **he did**. 1 K 14:22. 2 K 24:19, 20. 2 Ch 36:12,
13. Ezk 17:16-20. 21:25.
according. Je 26:21-23. 36:21-23, 29-31.
3 **through**. 2 S 24:1. 1 K 10:9. Pr +21:1. 28:2.
Ec 10:16. Is 3:4, 5. 19:4.
cast. Ps +51:11.
Zedekiah. 2 Ch 36:13. Ezk 17:15-21.
4 A.M. 3414. B.C. 590.
the ninth year. Je 39:1. 2 K 25:1. Ezk 24:1,
2.
in the tenth month. Zc 8:19.
pitched. ver. 7. Je 6:3-6. 32:24. Le 26:25. Dt
28:52-57. Is 29:3. 42:24, 25. Ezk 4:1-7. 21:22.
Lk 19:43. 21:20.
6 A.M. 3416. B.C. 588.
the fourth month. Je 39:2. 2 K 25:3. Zc 8:19.
the famine. Je 15:2. 19:9. 21:9. 25:10. Ge
+12:10. Le +26:26.
bread. Je 37:21.
7 **the city**. Je 34:2, 3. 2 K 25:4.
all the men. Je +39:4-7. 49:26. 51:32. Le
26:17, 36. Dt 28:25. 32:30. Jsh 7:8-12.
8 **overtook Zedekiah**. Je +21:7. Is 30:16, 17.
Am 2:14, 15. 9:1-4.
9 **they took**. Je 32:4, 5. 2 Ch 33:11. Ezk 21:25-
27.
Riblah. Je 39:5. 2 K 23:31-33. 25:4-6.
Hamath. Nu +13:21.
10 **slew**. Je 22:30. 39:6, 7. Ge 21:16. 44:34. Dt
28:34. 2 K 25:7.
he slew. ver. 24-27. 2 K 25:18-21. Ezk 9:6.
11:7-11.
11 **put out the eyes of Zedekiah**. Heb. blinded
Zedekiah. Je 32:4. 34:3-5. 2 K 25:6, 7mg. Ezk
12:13.
chains. or, fetters. 2 Ch +33:11.
prison. Heb. house of the wards.
12 **fifth month**. 2 K 25:8. Zc 7:3-5. 8:19.
the nineteenth. ver. 29. 2 K 24:12. 25:8.
captain of the guard. or, chief slaughter-
men, and so ver. 14. Je 39:9mg. Ge 37:36mg.
served. Heb. stood before. Je 40:10.
13 **burned**. Je 7:14. +17:27. Ps 79:1. La 2:7. Ezk
7:20-22. 24:21. Mi 3:12. Zc 11:1. Mt 24:2. Ac
6:13, 14.

the king's. Je 22:14. Ezk 24:1-14. Am 3:10,
11. 6:11.
14 **brake**. Je +39:8.
15 **carried**. Je 15:1, 2. Zc 14:2.
the poor. 2 K 25:11, 12. Pr 10:15. 14:31.
19:4, 17. 22:9, 16, 22. 28:3, 8, 11, 15. 29:7,
14.
16 **certain**. Je 39:9, 10. 40:5-7. 2 K 25:12. Ezk
33:24.
the poor. Mt 11:5. Ja 2:5.
17 **pillars**. ver. 21-23. 1 K 7:15-22, 27, 50. 2 Ch
4:12, 13. Is +39:6. La 1:10. Da 1:2.
the bases. 1 K 7:23-26. 2 Ch 4:14, 15.
18 **caldrons**. Ex 27:3. 38:3. 2 K 25:14-16. Ezk
46:20-24.
the shovels. or, instruments to remove the
ashes. Nu 4:14. 1 K 7:40, 45. 2 Ch 4:11, 16.
the snuffers. Ex 37:23. 2 Ch 4:22.
bowls. or, basons. Ex 25:29. 37:16. 1 K
+7:40, 50. Ezr 1:10.
the spoons. Nu 7:13, 14, 19, 20, 26, 32, 38,
44, 50, 56, 62, 84, 86. 2 Ch 24:14.
19 **basons**. Ex 12:22.
firepans. or, censers. Le 26:12. Nu 16:46. 2 K
25:15. Re 8:3-5.
bowls. 1 K +7:40.
and the candlesticks. Ex +25:31.
20 **two**. ver. 17.
the brass. Heb. their brass.
without. 1 K 7:47. 2 K 25:16. 1 Ch 22:14. 2
Ch 4:18.
21 **concerning**. 1 K 7:15-21. 2 K 25:17. 2 Ch
3:15-17.
fillet. Heb. thread.
22 **with network**. Ex 28:14-22, 25. 39:15-18. 1
K 7:17. 2 Ch 3:15. 4:12, 13.
23 **all the**. 1 K 7:20.
24 **the captain**. ver. +12, 15. 2 K 25:18.
Seraiah. 2 S +8:17.
Zephaniah. Je 21:1. 29:25, 29. 37:3. 2 K
25:18.
door. Heb. threshold. 2 K +12:9mg.
25 **an eunuch**. Je +29:2.
seven. 2 K 25:19.
were near the king's person. Heb. saw the
face of the king. 2 K 25:19mg. Est 1:14. Mt
18:10.
principal scribe of the host. or, scribe of
the captain of the host. 2 S +8:17.
27 **the king**. Je 6:13-15. 2 K 25:20, 21. Ezk
8:11-18. 11:1-11.
Riblah. ver. +9. Nu 34:8-11. 2 S 8:9.
Thus. Je 24:9, 10. 25:9-11. 39:10. Le 26:33-
35. Dt 4:26. 28:36, 64. 2 K 17:20, 23. 23:27.
25:21. Is 6:11, 12. 24:3. 27:10. 32:13, 14. Ezk
33:28. Mi 4:10.
28 A.M. 3404. B.C. 600.
in the seventh year. 2 K 24:2, 3, 12-16. Da
1:1-3.
29 A.M. 3415. B.C. 589.

the eighteenth year. ver. 12. Je 39:9. 2 K 25:11. 2 Ch 36:20.

persons. Heb. souls. Heb. *nephesh*, Ge +12:5. 14:21. 36:6. Ex 1:5.

30 **carried**. ver. 15. Je 6:9. 41:18.

persons. Heb. *nephesh*, souls, Ge +12:5.

31 A.M. 3442. B.C. 562.

it came. 2 K 25:27-30.

Jehoiachin. 2 K +24:8.

in the twelfth. Nearly answering to our 25th of April, A.M. 3442. 2 K 25:27.

king of Babylon. Pr +21:1.

lifted up. Ge 40:13, 20. Jb 22:29. Ps 3:3. 27:6.

32 **kindly unto him**. Heb. good things with him. Pr 12:25.

set. Je 27:6-11. 2 K 25:28. Da 2:37. 5:18, 19.

33 **changed**. Ge 41:14, 42. 2 K 25:29. Ps 30:11. Is 61:1-3. Zc 3:4.

he did. 2 S 9:7, 13. 1 K 2:7.

continually. Is +58:11.

bread. Ge +3:19.

34 **there was**. 2 S 9:10. Mt 6:11.

continual. 1 K 8:59. 2 K 25:30. Is +58:11. Da 1:5.

every day a portion. Heb. the matter of the day in his day. Ex +5:13mg. Lk 11:3.

LAMENTATIONS

LAMENTATIONS 1

1 How doth. La 2:1. 4:1. Is 14:12. Je 50:23. Zp 2:15. Re 18:16, 17.
sit. La 2:10. 3:28. Is 3:26. 47:1, 5. 52:2, 27. Je 9:11. Ezk 26:16.
full. Ps 122:4. Is 22:2. Zc 8:4, 5.
as a. Is 47:7-9. 54:4. Re 18:7.
great. 1 K 4:21. 2 Ch 9:26. Ezr 4:20.
how is. La 5:16. 2 K 23:33, 35. Ne 5:4. 9:37.

2 weepeth. ver. +16. Jb 7:2, 3. Ps 6:6. 77:2-6.
lovers. ver. 19. Je 2:17, 27, 36, 37. 4:30. 22:20-22. 30:14. Ezk 16:37. 23:22-25. 29:6, 7, 16. Ho 2:7. Re 17:13, 16.
none. ver. 9, 16, 17, 21. Is 51:18, 19.
all her friends. Jb 6:15. 19:13, 14. Ps 31:11. Pr 19:7. Mi 7:5.
enemies. Je 12:14.

3 gone. 2 K 24:14, 15. 25:11, 21. 2 Ch 36:20, 21. Je 39:9. 52:15, 27-30.
because of great servitude. Heb. for the greatness of servitude.
she. La 2:9. Le 26:36-39. Dt 28:64-67. Je 24:9. Ezk 5:12.
all. La 4:18, 19. Je 16:16. 52:8. Am 9:1-4.
between the straits. Ps 116:3. 118:5.

4 ways. Je 2:6, 7. 5:13. Is 24:4-6. Je 14:2. Mi 3:12.
solemn feasts. La 2:6. Ge +17:21h. Le 23:2. Ps 74:8.
all her gates. La 2:9. Je 9:11. 10:22. 33:10-12.
her priests. ver. 11, 12, 18-20. La 2:10, 11, 19-21. Is 32:9-14. Jl 1:8-13.
bitterness. Je 7:34. 16:9. 25:10. 31:13. 33:11.

5 adversaries. La 2:17. 3:46. Le 26:17. Dt 28:13, 43, 44. Ps 80:6. 89:42. Is 63:18. Je 12:7. Mi 7:8-10.
for. ver. 18. La 3:39-43. Le 26:15, etc. Dt 4:25-27. 28:15, etc. 29:18-28. 31:16-18, 29. 32:15-27. 2 Ch 36:14-16. Ne 9:33, 34. Ps 90:7, 8. Je 5:3-9, 29. 23:14. 30:14, 15. 44:21, 22. Ezk 8:17, 18. 9:9. 22:24-31. Da 9:7-16. Mi 3:9-12. Zp 3:1-8.
her children. La 2:11, 19, 20. 4:4. Je 39:9. 52:27-30.

6 from. 2 K 19:21. Ps 48:2, 3. Is 1:21. 4:5. 12:6. Zp 3:14-17.

daughter. Nu +21:25.
all. La 2:1-7. 2 S 4:21, 22. Ps 50:2. 96:9. 132:12, 13. Je 52:8, 11, 13. Ezk 7:20-22. 11:22, 23. 24:21, 25.
her princes. Le 26:36, 37. Dt 28:25. 32:30. Jsh 7:12, 13. Ps 44:9-11. Je 29:4. 48:41. 51:30-32. 52:7.
harts. Je 14:5, 6. 47:3.

7 remembered. Jb 29:2, etc. 30:1. Ps 42:4. 77:3, 5-9. Ho 2:7. Lk 15:17. 16:25.
all her. Dt 4:7, 8, 34-37. 8:7-9. Ps 147:19, 20. Is 5:1-4.
pleasant. or, desirable. ver. 10mg. Is +32:12mg.
old. Heb. kedem, Mi +5:2.
the adversaries. La 2:15, 16. Ps 79:4. 137:3, 4. Mi 4:11.
sabbaths. Is +58:13. Je 17:21-23, 27. Ezk 22:8, 26. 23:38.

8 hath. ver. 5, 20. 1 K 8:46, 47. 9:7, 9. Is 59:2-13. Je 6:28. Ezk 14:13-21. 22:2-15.
grievously sinned. lit. sinned a sin.
removed. Heb. become a removing, or, wandering. Je +15:4mg.
all. La 4:15, 16. 5:12-16. 1 S 2:30.
they. La 4:21. Is +3:17. Re 3:18.
she sigheth. ver. 4, 11, 21, 22. La 2:10. Je 4:31.

9 filthiness. ver. 17. Je 2:34. 13:27. Ezk 24:12, 13.
she remembereth. Dt 32:29. Is 47:7. Je 5:31. 1 P 4:17.
came. ver. 1. La 4:1. Is 3:8, 9. Je 13:17, 18.
she had. ver. 2, 17, 21. La 2:13. Ec 4:1. Is 40:2. 54:11. Ho 2:14. Jn 11:19.
behold. Ex 3:7, 17. 4:31. Dt 26:7. 1 S 1:11. 2 S 16:12. 2 K 14:26. Ne 9:32. Ps 25:18. 119:153. Da 9:17-19.
for. Dt 32:27. Ps 74:8, 9, 22, 23. 140:8. Is 37:4, 17, 23, 29. Je 48:26. 50:29. Zp 2:10. 2 Th 2:4-8.

10 spread. ver. 7. Is 5:13, 14. Je 15:13. 20:5. 52:17-20.
pleasant. or, desirable. ver. 7mg. Ps 74:4-8. 79:1-7. Is 63:18. 64:10, 11. Je 51:51. 52:13. Ezk 7:22. 9:7.
whom. Dt 23:3. Ne 13:1. Ezk 44:7. Mk 13:14.

11 **seek**. ver. 19. La 2:12. 4:4-10. Dt 28:52-57. 2 K 6:25. Je 19:9. 38:9. 52:6. Ezk 4:15-17. 5:16, 17.
relieve the soul. Heb. make the soul to come again. Heb. *nephesh*, Ge +12:13; Ge +2:7n. 1 S 30:11, 12.
see. ver. 9, 20. La 2:20. Jb 40:4. Ps 25:15-19.
for I. La 3:45. Je 30:17.

12 **Is it nothing**. *or, It is* nothing. Am 6:6.
pass by. Heb. pass by the way. La 2:15mg.
if. La 2:13. 4:6-11. Da 9:12. Mt 24:21. Lk 21:22, 23. 23:28-31.
be. *or*, exists. Heb. *yesh*. Ge 18:24. Pr 8:21 (substance; i.e. what exists). 18:24 (there is; i.e. there exists).
my sorrow. Ps +45:7. He 12:2, 3.

13 **above**. La 2:3, 4. Dt 32:21-25. Jb 30:30. Ps 22:14. 31:10. 102:3-5. Na 1:6. Hab +3:16. 2 Th 1:8. He 12:29.
he hath spread. La 4:17-20. Jb 18:8. 19:6. Ps 66:11. Ezk 12:13. 17:20. 32:3. Ho 7:12.
he hath turned. Ps 35:4. 70:2, 3. 129:5. Is 42:17.
desolate. ver. 22. La 5:17. Dt 28:65. Je 4:19-29.

14 **yoke**. Dt 28:47, 48. Pr 5:22. Is 14:25. 47:6. Je 27:8-12. 28:14.
delivered. Je 25:9. 34:20, 21. 37:17. 39:1-9. Ezk 11:9. 21:31. 23:28. 25:4, 7. Ho 5:14.

15 **trodden**. 2 K 9:33. 24:14-16. 25:4, etc. Ps 119:118. Is 5:5. 28:18. Je 50:26mg. Da 8:13. Mi 7:10. Ml 4:3. Lk 21:24. He 10:29.
crush. Jg +10:8mg.
the virgin, etc. *or*, the winepress of the virgin, etc. Je +18:13.
as in. Is 63:3. Re 14:19, 20. 19:15.

16 **I weep**. ver. 2, 9. Ps +119:136.
relieve. Heb. bring back. ver. +11, 19. Ho 9:12.
soul. Heb. *nephesh*, Ge +12:13.
my children. ver. 5, 6. La 2:20-22. 4:2-10. Je 9:21.

17 **spreadeth**. 1 K 8:22, 38. Is 1:15. Je 4:31.
none. ver. 2, 9, 16, 19, 21.
commanded. La 2:1-8, 17-22. 2 K 24:2-4. 25:1. Je 6:3. 16:6. 21:4, 5. 34:22. Ezk 7:23, 24. Ho 8:8. Lk 19:43, 44.
Jerusalem. ver. 9. La 4:15. Le 15:19-27. Ezk 36:17.

18 **Lord**. Ex 9:27. Dt 32:4. Jg 1:7. Ezr 9:13. Ne 9:33, 34. Ps 119:75. 145:17. Je 12:1. Da 9:7, 14. Zp 3:5. Ro 2:5. 3:19. Re 15:3, 4. 16:5-7.
for I. La 3:42. 1 S 12:14, 15. 15:23. Ne 1:6-8. 9:26. Ps 107:11. Da 9:9-16.
commandment. Heb. mouth. Dt +21:5mg.
hear. ver. 12. Dt 29:22-28. 1 K 9:8, 9. Je 22:8, 9. 25:28, 29. 49:12. Ezk 14:22, 23.
my virgins. ver. 5, 6. Dt 28:32-41.

19 **for**. ver. 2. La 4:17. Jb 19:13-19. Je 2:28. 30:14. 37:7-9.

my priests. ver. 11. La 2:20. 4:7-9. 5:12. Je 14:15-18. 23:11-15. 27:13-15.
ghost. Heb. *gava*, Ge +49:33 (**S#1478h**).
while. ver. 11.
souls. Heb. *nephesh*, Ge +12:13.

20 **Behold**. ver. 9, 11. Is 38:14.
my bowels. La 2:11. Jb 30:27. Ps 22:14. Is 16:11. Je 4:19. 31:20. 48:36. Ho 11:8. Hab 3:16.
for. ver. 18. Le 26:40-42. 1 K 8:47-50. Jb 33:27. Ps 51:3, 4. Pr 28:13. Je 2:35. 3:13. Lk 15:18, 19. 18:13, 14.
abroad. La 4:9, 10. Dt 32:25. Je 9:21, 22. 14:18. Ezk 7:15.

21 **have heard that**. ver. 2, 8, 11, 12, 16, 22.
they are. La 2:15. 4:21, 22. Ps 35:15. 38:16. 137:7. Je 48:27. 50:11. Ezk 25:3, 6, 8, 15. 26:2. Ob 12, 13.
thou wilt. Is ch. 13, 14, 47. Je 25:17-29. ch. 46-51. Ezk ch. 25-32. Am ch. 1.
the day. Ps 37:13. Je 25:17-26. Jl 3:14.
called. *or*, proclaimed. ver. 15, 19. Je 3:12. 12:6mg. 36:6 (read), 9, 14. 51:61 (read).
they shall. La 4:22. Dt 32:41-43. Ps 137:8, 9. Is 51:22, 23. Je 50:15, 29, 31. 51:24, 49. Mi 7:9, 10. Hab 2:15-17. Re 18:6.

22 **Let**. Je +10:25.
all their. Ps 109:14, 15. 137:7-9. Je +10:25. 51:35. Lk 23:31.
my heart. ver. 13. La 5:17. Is 13:7. Je 8:18. Ep 3:13.

LAMENTATIONS 2

1 **How**. La 1:1. 4:1.
covered. La 3:43, 44. Ezk 30:18. 32:7, 8. Jl 2:2.
daughter. Nu +21:25.
and cast. Is 14:12-15. Ezk 28:14-16. Mt 11:23. Lk 10:15, 18. Re 12:7-9.
the beauty. 1 S 4:21. 2 S 1:19. Is 64:11. Ezk 7:20-22. 24:21.
his footstool. Is 60:13. +66:1.

2 **swallowed**. ver. 17, 21. La 3:43. Jb 2:3mg. Ps 21:9. Is 27:11. Je 13:14. 21:7. Ezk 5:11. 7:4, 9. 8:18. 9:10. Zc 11:5, 6. Mt 18:33.
he hath thrown. ver. 5, 17. Je 5:10. Mi 5:11, 12. Ml 1:4. 2 C 10:4.
brought them down to. Heb. made to touch. Ps 89:39. Is 25:12. 26:5.
polluted. Ps +89:39, 40. Is 23:9mg. 43:28. 47:6.

3 **the horn**. Jb 16:15. Ps 75:5, 10. 89:24. 132:17. Je 48:25. Lk 1:69.
he hath. Ps 74:11.
he burned. Dt +32:22. Ps 79:5. 89:46. Is 1:31. 42:25. Lk 3:17.

4 **bent**. ver. 5. Jb 16:12-14. Is +63:10. Je 21:5. 30:14.
bow. Dt +32:23.

like an enemy. Ru +1:13, 21. Jb +13:24.
that were pleasant to the eye. Heb. the desirable of the eye. Is +32:12mg. Ezk 24:25.
he poured. Is 51:17-20. 63:6. Ezk +7:8.

5 **was**. ver. 4. Je 15:1. 30:14.
he hath swallowed up Israel. ver. 2. 2 K 25:9. 2 Ch 36:16, 17. Je 52:13.
mourning. Ezk 2:10.

6 **he hath violently**. Ps 80:12. 89:40. Is 5:5. 63:18. 64:11.
tabernacle. *or*, hedge. Jb 27:18. Is 1:8.
as if. Is 1:8.
solemn feasts. Ge +17:21. Le +23:36.
sabbaths. Is 1:13.
the king. La 4:16, 20. 5:12. Is 43:28. Je 52:11-27. Ezk 12:12, 13. 17:18. Ml 2:9.

7 **cast off**. ver. 1. Le 26:31, 44. Ps 78:59-61. Is 64:10, 11. Je 7:12-14. 26:6, 18. 52:13. Ezk 7:20-22. 24:21. Mi 3:12. Mt 24:2. Ac 6:13, 14.
abhorred. Ps +106:40.
given up. Heb. shut up. ver. 5. 2 Ch 36:19. Je 32:29. 33:3, 4. 39:8. Ezk 7:24. Am 2:5.
they have. Ps 72:4, etc. 74:3-8. Ezk 7:21, 22.
solemn feast. Ge +17:21. Le 23:2.

8 **purposed**. ver. 17. Is 5:5. Je 5:10.
stretched. 2 S 8:2. 2 K 21:13. Is 28:17. 34:11. Am 7:7, 8.
he hath not. Jb 13:21. Ezk 20:22.
destroying. Heb. swallowing up. ver. 2, 5.
he made. Is 3:26. Je 14:2.

9 **gates**. Ne 1:3. Je 39:2, 8. 51:30. 52:14.
her king. La 1:3. 4:15, 20. Dt 28:36. 2 K 24:12-16. 25:7. Je 52:8, 9. Ezk 12:13. 17:20.
the law. 2 Ch +15:3. Ezk 7:26. Ho 3:4.
her prophets. Ps +74:9. Am 8:11, 12. Mi 3:6, 7.

10 **elders**. La 4:5, 16. 5:12, 14. Jb 2:13. Is 3:26. 47:1, 5.
sit. La 1:1. Jb 2:13. Is 3:26.
and keep. La 3:28. Je 8:14. Am 5:13. 8:3.
cast up. Jsh +7:6.
sackcloth. Jb +16:15.
the virgins. La 1:4. Am 8:13.

11 **eyes**. La 1:16. 3:48-51. 1 S 30:4. Ps +6:7. +69:3.
tears. ver. 19. Zc 8:5.
my bowels. La 1:20. Je 4:19.
my liver. Jb 16:13. Ps 22:14.
for. Je +4:11.
because. ver. 19, 20. La 4:3, 4, 9, 10. Lk 23:29.
swoon. *or*, faint. Is 57:16.

12 **Where is**. La 1:11.
as the wounded. Ezk 30:24.
soul. Heb. *nephesh*, Ge +12:13. Is 53:12.

13 **shall I take**. La 1:12. Da 9:12.
daughter. Nu +21:25.
for thy breach. 2 S 5:20. Ps 60:2. Je 14:17. Ezk 26:3, 4.

who can. Is 51:19. Je 8:22. 30:12-15. 51:8, 9.

14 **prophets**. Is 9:15, 16. Je 2:8. 5:31. 6:13, 14. 8:10, 11. 14:13-15. 23:11-17. 27:14-16. 28:15. 29:8, 9. 37:19. Ezk 13:1-16. Mi 2:11. 3:5-7. 2 P 2:1-3.
they have. Is 58:1. Je 23:22. Ezk 13:22.
false. Je 23:14-17, 31, 32. 27:9, 10. Ezk 22:25, 28. Mi 3:5. Zp 3:4.

15 **that pass**. Dt 29:22-28. 1 K 9:7-9. 2 Ch 7:21. Je 18:16.
by. Heb. by the way. La 1:12mg.
clap. La 1:8. Jb 27:22, 23. Ezk 25:6. Na 3:19.
hiss. ver. 16. 2 Ch +29:8.
wag. Je +18:16.
Is this. ver. 6. Ps 48:2. 50:2. Is 64:11.

16 **thine**. La 3:46. Jb 16:9, 10. Ps 22:13. 35:21. 109:2.
gnash. Ps +37:12.
We have swallowed. Ps +35:25. Je 50:7, 17. Ezk 25:3, 6, 15. Zp 2:8-10.
we have seen. Ps 35:21. 41:8. Ob 12-16.

17 **done**. ver. 8. Le 26:14, 16, 17. Dt 28:15, etc. 29:18-23. 31:16, 17. 32:15-27. Je 18:11. Mi 2:3.
old. Heb. *kedem*, Mi +5:2.
he hath thrown. ver. 1, 2. Ezk 5:11. 7:8, 9. 8:18. 9:10.
he hath caused. La 1:5. Dt 28:43, 44. Ps 38:16. 89:42.

18 **heart**. Ps 119:145. Is 26:16, 17. Ho 7:14.
O wall. ver. 8. Hab 2:11.
let tears. Ps +119:136. Je 4:31.
the apple. Ps 17:8.

19 **cry out**. Ps 42:8. 62:8. +119:55, 147, 148. 130:6. Is 26:9. Mk +1:35. Lk 6:12.
watches. Jg 7:19. Mt 14:25. Mk 13:35.
pour. 1 S 1:15. 7:6. Jb 3:24. Ps 62:8. 142:2.
like water. ver. 11. Zc 8:5.
lift up. Ps +88:9.
life. Heb. *nephesh*, Ge +44:30.
that faint. ver. 11, 12. La 4:1-9. Is 51:20. Ezk 5:10, 16. Na 3:10.

20 **consider**. Ex 32:11. Dt 9:26. Is 63:16-19. 64:8-12. Je 14:20, 21.
Shall the women. Le +26:29.
of a span long. *or*, swaddled with their hands. ver. 22.
shall the priest. La 1:19. 4:13, 16. Ps 78:64. Is 9:14-17. Je 5:31. 14:15-18. 23:11-15. Ezk 9:5, 6.

21 **young**. Dt 28:50. Jsh 6:21. 1 S 15:3. 2 Ch 36:17. Est 3:13. Je 51:22. Ezk 9:6.
my virgins. La 1:15, 18. Ge +24:16. Ps 78:63. Je 9:21. 11:22. 18:21. Am 4:10.
by the sword. Jb 27:14.
thou hast killed. ver. 2, 17. La 3:43. Is 27:11. Je 13:14. 21:7. Ezk 5:11. 7:4, 9. 8:18. 9:5, 10. Zc 11:6.

22 **solemn day**. ver. +6. Ge +17:21.

my terrors. Ps 31:13. Is 24:17, 18. Je 6:25. 20:3, 10. 46:5. 49:29. Am 9:1-4.
those. Dt 28:18. Je 16:2-4. Ho 9:12-16. Lk 23:29, 30.

LAMENTATIONS 3

1 **the man**. Da 2:31.
hath. lit. he hath.
seen affliction. La 1:12-14. Jb 19:21. Ps 71:20. 88:7, 15, 16. Is 53:3. Je 15:17, 18. 20:14-18. 38:6.
his wrath. Jb 9:34. 21:9. Ps 2:9. 88:7. 89:32. Is +10:5.

2 **brought**. ver. 53-55. La 2:1. Dt 28:29. Jb 18:18. 30:26. Is 59:9. Je 13:16. Am 5:18-20. Ju 6, 13.
darkness. Pr +20:20.

3 **against me**. La 2:4-7. Dt 29:20. Ru +1:13. Jb 31:21. Is 1:25. 63:10.
hand. Ex +9:3.

4 **My flesh**. Jb 16:8, 9. Ps 31:9, 10. 32:3. 38:2-8. 102:3-5.
he hath. Ps 22:14. 51:8. Is 38:13. Je 50:17.

5 **builded**. ver. 7-9. Jb 19:8.
compassed. Ps 32:7, 10.
gall. ver. 19. Dt +29:18.

6 **in dark**. Ps 88:5, 6. 143:3, 7.
of old. Heb. *olam*, Ge +6:4.

7 **hedged**. ver. 9. Jb 3:23. 19:8. Ps 88:8. Pr +13:15. Je 38:6. Ho 2:6.
made. La 1:14. 5:5. Da 9:12.
chain. lit. brass. Jg 16:21. 2 K 25:7. 2 Ch 33:11. 36:6. Je 39:7.

8 **when I cry**. ver. 44. Jb 19:7. 30:20. Ps 22:2. 80:4. Hab 1:2. Mt 27:46.

9 **enclosed**. Je 36:5.
made. ver. 11. Is 30:28. 63:17. Je 36:5.

10 **unto**. Is +5:29. Ho 6:1. Am 5:18-20.
in secret. Ps 10:9. 17:12.

11 **pulled**. Jb 16:12, 13. Ps 50:22. Je 5:6. 51:20-22. Da 2:40-44. 7:23. Mi 5:8. Ho 6:1.
he hath made. La 1:13. Jb 16:7. Is 3:26. Je 6:8. 9:10, 11. 19:8. 32:43. Mt 23:38. Re 18:19.

12 **bent**. Jb 16:12, 13.
bow. Dt +32:23.

13 **arrows**. Heb. sons. Dt +32:23.

14 **a derision**. ver. 63. Ne 4:2-4. Ps 69:11, 12. 123:3, 4. 137:3. 1 C 4:9-13.
song. ver. 63. Ps 69:12.

15 **filled**. ver. 19. Ru 1:20. Jb 9:18. Ps 60:3. Is 51:17-22. Je 25:15-18, 27.
bitterness. Heb. bitternesses. Ex 12:8. Nu 9:11. 1 S +1:10.
wormwood. Dt +29:18.

16 **broken**. Jb 4:10. Ps 3:7. 58:6.
gravel. Pr 20:17. Mt 7:9. Lk 11:11.
hath. Ps 102:9.
covered me with ashes. *or*, rolled me in the ashes. Jb 2:8. Je 6:26. Jon 3:6.

17 **thou**. La 1:16. Ps 119:155. Is 38:17. 54:10. 59:11. Je 8:15. 14:19. 16:5. Zc 8:10.
soul. Heb. *nephesh*, Ge +34:3.
I forgat. Ge 41:30. Jb 7:7. Je 20:14-18.
prosperity. Heb. good. Ge 1:4. Jb 2:10. Ec 7:14, 18, 20, 26. Je 18:20.

18 **I said**. 1 S 27:1. Jb 6:11. 17:15. Ps 31:22. 116:11. Is 40:27. Ezk 37:11.
strength. 1 S 15:29. Jb +4:20. Is 63:3.

19 **Remembering**. *or*, Remember. Ne 9:32. Jb 7:7. Ps 89:47, 50. 132:1.
the. ver. +5, 15.

20 **soul**. Heb. *nephesh*, Ge +34:3; Le +26:11.
hath. Jb 21:6.
humbled. Heb. bowed. Ps 42:5, 6, 11. 43:5. 146:8.

21 **recall to my mind**. Heb. make to return to my heart. Ps 77:7-11. Je 2:24mg.
therefore. ver. 24-29. Ps +42:11. Hab 2:3.

22 **of**. Ezr 9:8, 9, 13-15. Ne 9:31. Ps 78:38. 106:45. Ezk 20:8, 9, 13, 14, 21, 22. Ml 3:6.
mercies. Ex +34:6.
because. Ps 77:8.

23 **new**. Ps 30:5. Is 33:2. Zp 3:5.
morning. Jb +7:18. Ps 92:2. Is 33:2.
great. Ex 34:6, 7. Ps 36:5. 89:1, 2, 33. 146:6. T 1:2. He 6:18. 10:23.
faithfulness. Ps 143:1.

24 **my portion**. Ps +16:5.
soul. Heb. *nephesh*, Ge +34:3.
therefore. ver. 21. 1 S 30:6. 1 Ch 5:20. Jb 13:15, 16. Ps +42:11. 62:8. 84:12. Ro 15:12, 13. 1 P 1:21.

25 **good**. Ex +34:6. Ps 25:8-10. 86:5. Je +29:11. Na 1:7. Mt +5:45. Lk +6:35.
that wait for. ver. 26. Ge 49:18. Ps +25:3. 39:7. Is 49:23. 1 Th 1:10. Ja 5:7.
soul. Heb. *nephesh*, Ge +12:5.
that seeketh. 2 Ch 19:3. 30:19. 31:21. Ps 22:26. 27:8. 105:3, 4. 119:2. Is 26:9. Je +29:13.

26 **good**. Ps 52:9. 54:6. 73:28. 92:1. Ga 4:18.
hope. Ro 8:25. He +3:14. 10:35. 1 P 1:13.
quietly. Ex 14:13. 2 Ch 20:17. Ps +25:3. 119:166, 174. Is 30:7, 15.

27 **bear**. Ps 90:12. 94:12. 119:71. Ec 12:1. Mt 11:29, 30. He 12:5-12.

28 **sitteth alone**. La 2:10. Ps 39:9. 102:7. Je 15:17.

29 **putteth**. 2 Ch 33:12. Jb 40:4. 42:5, 6. Ezk 16:63. Ro 3:19.
if. Jl 2:14. Jon 3:9. Zp +2:3. Lk 15:18, 19. 18:13.

30 **his cheek**. Mt 26:67. +27:30.
filled. La 1:12. Ps +31:11. 123:3.

31 **not cast off**. Ps +77:7. 103:8-10. Le +26:44. Is 57:16. Je +32:40. 33:24. Mi 7:18, 19. Ro +11:1-6. He +13:5.
for ever. Heb. *olam*, Ex +12:24.

32 **though he cause**. ver. +22. Ex 2:23-25. 3:7. Jg 10:16. 2 K 13:23. Ps 30:5. 78:38. 103:11-

13. 106:43-45. Je 31:20. Ho 11:8, 9. Mi 7:19. Lk 15:20.

33 afflict. Jb 37:23. Ps +90:15. +119:75. Is 28:21. 63:9. Ezk 18:32. 33:11. Jn 16:27. He 12:9, 10.

willingly. Heb. from his heart. Nu 16:28. Je 14:14. 23:16. 31:20. Ezk 13:17. Jn 5:30. 6:38.

nor grieve. Ru +1:13. Is 55:7. Mt 23:37. Lk +6:35. 1 C 10:13. Ja 1:13, 17.

34 crush. Jg +10:8. Je 50:17, 33, 34.

all. Ps 79:11. +146:7. Is 14:17.

35 turn aside. Dt 16:19. 24:17. 27:19. Ps +12:5. 140:12. Pr 17:15. Zc 1:15, 16.

the most High. or, a superior. Dt 26:19.

36 the Lord. 2 S 11:27. Is 59:15. Hab 1:13.

approveth. Heb. seeth. Ps 54:7.

37 saith. Pr 16:9. 19:21. Is 46:10, 11. Je +19:7. Da 4:35. Ro 9:15, 16. Ep +1:11.

38 most High. Ps +7:17.

proceedeth not evil and good. Jb 2:10. Ps 75:7. Pr 29:26. Is +45:7. Am +3:6. Mt +5:45.

39 doth. ver. 22. Nu 11:11. Pr 19:3. Is 38:17-19.

complain. or, murmur. Ju +16.

a man. Ge 4:5-7, 13, 14. Le 26:41, 43. Nu 16:41. 17:12, 13. Jsh 7:6-13. 2 S 6:7, 8. 2 K 3:13. 6:32, 33. Ezr 9:13. Jb 11:6. Is 51:20. Jon 2:3, 4. 4:8, 9. Mi 7:9. He 12:5-12. Re 16:9.

40 Let us search. 1 Ch 15:12, 13. Jb 11:13-15. 34:31, 32. Ps 4:4. 119:59. 139:23, 24. Pr +16:25. Je 29:13, 14. Ezk 18:28. Hg 1:5-9. 1 C +5:8. 11:28, 31. 2 C 13:5. Ga 6:4.

turn. Zc +1:3, 4. Ac +3:19-21. +9:35.

41 lift. Ps 25:1. 86:4. 116:4. 119:48. 143:6-8.

with. Ps +88:9.

God. Heb. El, Ex +15:2.

42 transgressed. La 1:18. 5:16. Ne 9:26. Jb 33:27, 28. Je 3:13. Da 9:5-14. Lk 15:18, 19.

thou. 2 K 24:4. Je 5:7, 9, 29. Ezk 24:13, 14. Zc 1:5, 6.

43 covered. La 2:1. Ps 44:19.

persecuted. ver. 66. Ps 83:15.

thou hast slain. La 2:2, 17, 21. 2 Ch 36:16, 17. Ezk 7:9. 8:18. 9:10.

44 covered. Ps 97:2.

that. ver. +8. Ps 80:4. Je 14:11, 12. 15:1. Zc 7:13.

45 as. ver. 14. La 2:15. 4:14, 15. Dt 28:13, 37, 44. 1 C 4:11-13.

46 have. La 2:16. Ex 11:7. Jb 30:9-11. Ps 22:6-8. 44:13, 14. 79:4, 10. Mt 27:38-45.

47 snare. Lk +21:35.

desolation. La +1:4, 13. 2:1-9. Is 51:19.

48 Mine eye runneth. Ps +119:136. Je 4:19.

49 and. La +1:16. Ps 77:2. Je 14:17.

50 Till the Lord look down. La 2:20. 5:1. Ps 80:14-16. 102:19, 20. Is 62:6, 7. 63:15. 64:1. Da 9:16-19.

51 eye. Ge 44:34. 1 S 30:3, 4. Je 4:19-21. 14:18. Lk 19:41-44.

mine heart. Heb. my soul. Heb. nephesh, Ex +23:9.

because of all. or, more than all.

the daughters. La 1:18. 2:21. 5:11. Je 11:22. 14:16. 19:9.

52 chased. Je 37:15, 16. 38:4-6.

without. 1 S 24:10-15. 25:28, 29. 26:18-20. Ps 35:7, 19. 69:4. 109:3. 119:161. Je 37:18. Jn 15:25.

53 cut. Ps 88:6. Je 37:20. 38:6, 9, 10.

in the. Je 37:16. 38:6, 9, 10.

dungeon. Heb. bor, Ge +37:20.

and. Da 6:17. Mt 27:60, 66.

54 Waters. Ps +93:3.

I said. ver. +18. Is 38:10-13. Ezk 37:11. 2 C 1:8-10.

55 called upon. 2 Ch 33:11, 12. Ps 18:5, 6. 40:1, 2. 69:13-18. 116:3, 4. 130:1, 2. 142:3-7. Je 38:6. Jon 2:2-4. Ac 16:24-28.

thy name. Ps +9:10. 20:1.

dungeon. Heb. bor, Ge +37:20.

56 hast. 2 Ch 33:13, 19. Jb 34:28. Ps 3:4. 6:8, 9. 34:6. 66:19. 116:1, 2. Is 38:5.

hide. Ps 55:1. 88:13, 14. Ro 8:26.

at my breathing. Ml 3:16.

57 drewest. Ps 69:18. Is 58:9. Ja +4:8.

thou saidest. Is 41:10, 14. 43:1, 2. Je 1:17. Ac 18:9, 10. 27:24. Re 1:17. 2:10.

58 thou hast pleaded. 1 S 25:39. Ps 35:1. Je 51:36.

soul. Heb. nephesh, Ge +12:13.

thou hast redeemed. Ps +34:22.

59 thou hast. Je 11:19-21. 15:10. 18:18-23. 20:7-10. ch. 37, 38.

judge. Ge +1:29. 31:42. Ps 9:4. 26:1. 35:1, 23. 43:1. 1 P 2:23.

60 hast seen. ver. 59. Ps 10:14. 56:6. Je 11:19, 20.

61 hast heard. ver. +30. Zp 2:8.

62 lips. Ps 59:7, 12. 140:3. Ezk 36:3.

and. Je 18:18.

63 their sitting. Ps 139:2.

I am. ver. 14. Jb 30:9.

64 Render. Ps 28:4. Je +10:25. 50:29. Re 18:6.

65 sorrow. or, obstinacy. Dt +2:30. Is 6:10.

thy curse. Ps 109:17, 18. Ml 1:14. 2:2. 3:9. Mt +25:41.

66 Persecute. ver. 43. Ps 35:6. 83:15.

under. Dt 7:24. 25:19. 29:20. 2 K 14:27. Je 10:11.

heavens. Ps 8:3. 115:16. Is 66:1.

LAMENTATIONS 4

1 How is the gold. 2 K 25:9, 10. Is 1:21, 22. 14:12. Ezk 7:19-22.

the stones. La 2:19. Je 52:13. Mt 24:2. Mk 13:2. Lk 21:5, 6.

2 sons. Is 51:18. Zc 9:13.

how. La 2:21. 5:12. Is 30:14. Je 19:11. 22:28. Ro 9:21-23. 2 C 4:7. 2 T 2:20.

earthen. Je 18:1-6. 19:1-10.
pitchers. Is 22:24. Je 48:12.
3 **sea monsters**. *or*, sea calves. Ps 74:13mg. Je 9:11.
the daughter. ver. 10. Le +26:29. Je +4:11.
like. Jb 39:13-16. Ro 1:31.
4 **tongue**. Ps 22:15. 137:6.
the young. La 1:11. 2:11, 12. Dt 32:24. Mt 7:9-11.
breaketh. Is +58:7.
5 **that did**. Dt 28:54-56. Is 3:16-26. 24:6-12. 32:9-14. Je 6:2, 3. Am 6:3-7. Lk 7:25. 1 T 5:6mg. Re 18:7-9.
brought. 2 S 1:24. Pr 31:21. Lk 16:19.
embrace. Jb 24:8. Je 9:21, 22. Lk 15:16.
6 **punishment of the iniquity of the daughter**, *or*, iniquity of the daughter, etc. Is 1:9, 10. Ezk 16:48-50. Mt 11:23, 24. Lk 10:12. 12:47.
greater than. Mt +10:15.
the punishment. ver. 9. Ge 19:25. Da 9:12. Mt 24:21.
7 **Nazarites**. Nu 6:2, etc. Jg 13:5, 7. 16:17. Am 2:11, 12. Lk 1:15.
purer. 1 S 16:12. Ps 51:7. 144:12. SS 5:10. Da 1:15.
their polishing. Ex 24:10. Jb 28:16.
8 **visage**. La 5:10. Jb 30:17-19, 30. Jl 2:6. Na 2:10.
blacker than a coal. Heb. darker than blackness. La 5:10. Jb 30:30.
they. ver. 1, 2. Ru 1:19, 20. Jb 2:12. Is 52:14.
their skin. Jb 19:20. 33:21. Ps 32:4. 38:3. 102:3-5, 11. 119:83.
9 **for**. Le 26:39. Ezk 24:23. 33:10.
pine away. Heb. flow out. Ps 78:20.
10 **hands**. ver. +3.
pitiful. Is 49:15.
in. La 3:48.
11 **Lord**. ver. 22. La 2:8, 17. Je 6:11, 12. 9:9-11. 13:14. 14:15, 16. 15:1-4. 19:3-11. 23:19, 20. 24:8-10. Ezk +7:8. 20:47, 48. Zc 1:6. Lk 21:22.
kindled. Je +17:27.
12 **kings of**. Dt 29:24-28. 1 K 9:8, 9. Ps 48:4-6. 79:1.
13 **the sins**. La 2:14. Je 5:31. 6:13. 14:14. 23:11-21. Ezk 22:26-28. Mi 3:11, 12. Zp 3:3, 4.
that. Je 2:30. 26:8, 9. Mt 23:31, 33-37. Lk 11:47-51. Ac 7:52. 1 Th 2:15, 16.
14 **have wandered**. Dt 28:28, 29. Is 29:10-12. 56:10. 59:9-11. Mi 3:6, 7. Mt +15:14. Ep 4:18.
they have polluted. Nu 35:33. Is 1:15. Je 2:34.
with blood. Nu 19:11, 16. 2 K 21:16.
so that men could not touch. *or*, in that they could not *but* touch. Nu 19:16. Ho 4:2.
15 **Depart ye**. Nu 16:26. 19:16. Ps 6:8. 139:19. Mi 2:10. 2 C +6:17.
it is unclean. *or*, ye polluted. Le 13:45.
16 **anger**. *or*, face. Jb 23:15.

hath divided. Ge 49:7. Le 26:33-39. Dt 28:25, 64, 65. 32:26. Je 15:4. 24:9.
he will. Ps 106:44. He 8:9.
they respected. La 5:12. 2 K 25:18-21. 2 Ch 36:17. Is 9:14-16.
17 **our eyes**. La 1:19. 2 K 24:7. Is 20:5, 6. 30:1-7. 31:1-3. Je 2:18, 36. 8:20. 37:7-10. Ezk 29:6, 7, 16.
watched for. Ps 130:6.
18 **hunt**. La 3:52. 1 S 24:14. 2 K 25:4, 5. Jb 10:16. Ps 140:11. Je 16:16. 39:4, 5. 52:7-9.
our end is near. Je 1:12. 51:33. Ezk 7:2-12. 12:22, 23, 27. Am 8:2.
19 **persecutors**. Dt 28:49. Is 5:26-28. 30:16, 17. Je 4:13. Ho 8:1. Hab 1:8. Mt 24:27, 28.
the eagles. Dt 28:49. Je 48:40. 49:16, 22.
they pursued. Am 2:14. 9:1-3.
20 **breath**. Heb. *ruach*, Ge +6:17. La 2:9. Ge 2:7. 44:30. 2 S 18:3. Ps +146:4.
the anointed. 1 S 12:3, 5. 16:6. 24:6, 10. 26:9, 11, 16, 23. 2 S 1:14, 16, 21. 19:21. Ps 89:20, 21.
was taken. Je +21:7. Ezk 19:4, 8.
pits. Ps 107:20. Je 2:6. 18:20, 22.
we shall live among. Note the unannounced time gap between this verse and the next (Is +61:2).
21 **Rejoice**. Ps 35:19. Pr +17:5.
be glad. Ps 83:3-12. Ec 11:9. Ezk 25:6, 8.
the land. Ge +10:23.
the cup. Je 25:15-29. +49:7, 12, 13. Ezk 35:3-9.
and shalt. Is +20:2.
22 **The punishment of thine iniquity**. *or*, Thine iniquity. ver. 6mg. Is 40:1, 2. Je 46:27, 28. 50:20.
no more carry. Is 52:1. 60:18. Je +32:40. Ezk 37:28.
he will visit. ver. 21. Ps 137:7, 8.
discover thy sins. *or*, carry *thee* captive for thy sins. Na 2:7mg.

LAMENTATIONS 5

1 **Remember**. La 1:20. 2:20. 3:19. Ne 1:8. Jb 7:7. 10:9. Je 15:15. Hab 3:2. Lk 23:42.
behold. La 2:15. Ne 1:3. 4:4. Ps +31:11. 123:3, 4.
2 **inheritance**. Dt 28:30, etc. Ps 79:1, 2. Is 1:7. 5:17. 63:18. Je 6:12. Ezk 7:21, 24. Zp 1:13.
3 **orphans**. Ex 22:24. Je 18:21. Ho 14:3.
fatherless. Dt +10:18.
4 **have**. Dt 28:47, 48. Is 3:1. Ezk 4:9-17.
for money. lit. silver. Ge 13:2.
is sold. Heb. cometh for price.
5 **Our necks are under persecution**. Heb. On our necks are we persecuted. La 1:14. 4:19. Dt 28:48, 65, 66. Je 27:2, 8, 11, 12. 28:14. Mt 11:29. Ac 15:10.
labor. Ne 9:36, 37.

6 **given**. 1 Ch +29:24mg.
to the Egyptians. Is 30:1-6. 31:1-3. 57:9. Je 2:18, 36. 44:12-14. Ho 5:13. 7:11. 9:3. 12:1.

7 **fathers**. Ex +20:5. Je 16:12. 31:29. Ezk 18:2. Mt 23:32-36.
and are. Ge 42:13, 36. Jb 7:8, 21. Je 31:15. Zc 1:5.
borne. Is 53:4, 11. Mt 27:25.

8 **Servants**. Ge 9:25. Dt 28:43. Ne 2:19. 5:15. Pr 30:22.
there. Jb 5:4. 10:7. Ps 7:2. 50:22. Is 43:13. Ho 2:10. Zc 11:6.

9 **gat our bread**. Jg 6:11. 2 S 23:17. Je 40:9-12. 41:1-10, 18. 43:14, 16. Ezk 4:16, 17. 12:18, 19.
lives. Heb. *nephesh*, souls, Ge +44:30; Ge +9:5.
sword. Ezk 21:3, 4.

10 **skin**. La 3:4. 4:8. Jb 30:30. Ps 119:83. Re 6:5, 6.
black. or, burning. Ge 43:30. 1 K 3:26. Ho 11:8.
terrible famine. *or*, terrors, *or* storms, of famine. Ps 11:6mg. 1 K +8:37.

11 **ravished**. Dt 28:30. Is 13:16. Zc 14:2.
women. Ge 2:22, 23. Ps 58:8.
maids. Ge +24:16.

12 **Princes**. La 2:10, 20. 4:16. Is 47:6. Je 39:6, 7. 52:10, 11, 25-27.
hanged up. Ge 40:19. Dt 21:22, 23. Est 2:23. 7:9mg, 10.
faces. Ge +3:19.
elders. ver. 14. La 4:16.
not honored. La 2:6. 4:16. Le +19:32.

13 **the young men**. Ex 11:5. Jg 16:21. Jb 31:10. Is 47:2.
grind. Ec 12:3, 4. Mt 24:41.
fell. Ex 1:11. 2:11. 23:5. Jsh 9:27. Ne 5:1-5. Is 58:6. Mt 23:4.

14 **elders**. La 1:4, 19. 2:10. Dt 16:18. Jb 29:7-17. 30:1. Is 3:2, 3.

the gate. Jsh 20:4.
the young. Jb 30:31. Is 24:7-11. Je 7:34. 16:9. 25:10. Ezk 26:13. Re 18:22.

15 **our dance**. Ex +15:20. Am 6:4-7. 8:10. Ja 4:9, 10.

16 **The crown**. La 1:1. Jb 19:9. Ps 89:39. Je 13:18. Ezk 21:26. Re 2:10. 3:11.
is fallen from our head. Heb. of our head is fallen.
woe. La 1:8, 18. 2:1. 4:13. Pr 14:34. Is 3:9-11. Je 2:17, 19. 4:18. Ezk 7:17-22. 22:12-16. 2 P 2:4-6.

17 **our heart**. La 1:13, 22. Le 26:36. Is 1:5. Je 8:18. 46:5. Ezk 21:7, 15. Mi 6:13.
our eyes. Ps +6:7. +69:3.

18 **of the**. La 2:8, 9. 1 K 9:7, 8. Ps 74:2, 3. Je 17:3, 26:9. 52:13. Mi 3:12.
the foxes. Ps 63:10. Is 32:13, 14. Je 9:11.

19 **remainest**. Dt 33:27. Ps 9:7. 10:16. 29:10. 90:2. 102:12, 25-27. Hab 1:12. 1 T 1:17. 6:15, 16. He 1:10-12. +13:8. Re 1:4, +8, 17, 18.
for ever. Heb. *olam*, Ex +12:24.
thy throne. Ps +45:6. 145:13. 146:10. Da 2:44. 7:14, 27. He +1:8, 9.

20 **dost**. Ps +13:1, 2. 74:1. 79:5. 85:5. 89:46. 94:3, 4. +102:13, 16. Is 64:9-12. Je 14:19-21. Ac +1:6.
for ever. Jb +4:20 (**S#5331h**).
forsake us. Is +54:7.
so long time. Heb. for length of days. Ps +91:16mg. Mt +25:19.

21 **Turn**. 1 K 18:37. Jb 23:3, 4. Ps 42:1, 2. 51:11, 12. 63:1, 2, 4-6. 80:3, 7, 19. 85:4. Je 31:18. +32:39, 40. Ezk 11:19, 20. 36:25-27, 37. Hab 3:2. Ep 3:16-19. Re 3:20.
renew. Ps 51:10. Is 60:20-22. Je 31:4, 23-25. 33:10, 13. Zc 8:3-6. Ml 3:4.
old. Mi +5:2.

22 **But thou hast utterly rejected us**. *or*, For wilt thou utterly reject us? Ps +44:9. Is +41:9. +54:7. Je +4:27. Ezk 37:11. Zc 10:6.

EZEKIEL

EZEKIEL 1

1 A.M. 3409. B.C. 595.
in the thirtieth year. Nu 4:3. Lk 3:23.
as I. 2 K 24:14. Ec 9:1, 2. Je 24:5-7.
captives. Heb. captivity. Je 28:4mg.
by the river. ver. 3. Ezk 3:15, 23. 10:15, 20,
22. 43:3. Ps 137:1.
Chebar. i.e. *abundant, vehement,* S#3529h. ver.
1, 3. Ezk 3:15, 23. 10:15, 20, 22. 43:3. 2 K
17:6. 1 Ch 5:26.
the heavens. Mt 3:16. Lk 3:21. Jn 1:51. Ac
7:56. 10:11. Re 4:1. 19:11.
I saw. Ezk 8:3. 11:24. Ge 15:1. 46:2. Nu 12:6.
Is 1:1. Da 8:1, 2. Ho 12:10. Jl 2:28. Mt 17:9.
Ac 9:10-12. 10:3. 2 C 12:1.
2 **the fifth year.** Ezk 8:1. 20:1. 29:1, 17. 31:1.
40:1. 2 K 24:12-15.
3 **word.** Je 1:2, 4. Ho 1:1. Jl 1:1. 1 T 4:1.
Ezekiel. Heb. Jehezkel. i.e. *God will strengthen,*
S#3168h. ver. 3. Ezk 24:24. 1 Ch 24:16.
Buzi. i.e. *sprung from Buz (i.e. contempt), to dis-*
respect, S#941h, only here.
and the hand. 1 K +18:46.
4 **a whirlwind.** Je +23:19.
north. Je +1:14. Hab 1:8, 9. Ac 2:2. Re 4:5.
a great. Ezk 10:2-4. Ex +13:21.
infolding itself. Heb. catching itself.
color. lit. eye. ver. 27. Ezk 8:2. 10:8, 9. Re
1:15.
midst of the fire. 2 Ch 5:13, 14. Is 4:5.
5 **the likeness.** Re 4:6. 6:6.
6 **And every one had four faces.** ver. 10, 15.
Ezk 10:10, 14, 21, 22. Re 4:7, 8.
every one had four wings. ver. 8-11. Ex
25:20. 1 K 6:24-27. Is 6:2.
7 **straight feet.** Heb. a straight foot.
like the sole. Le 11:3, 47.
the color. ver. 13. Ps 104:4. Da 10:6. Re 1:15.
8 **the hands.** Ezk 8:3. 10:2, 7, 8, 18, 21. Is 6:6.
9 **joined.** ver. 11. 2 Ch 3:11, 12. 1 C 1:10.
they turned. ver. 12. Ezk 10:11, 22. Pr 4:25-
27. Lk 9:51, 62.
10 **for the.** Ezk 10:14. Re 4:7.
the face of a man. Nu 2:10. Is 46:8. Lk
15:10. 1 C 14:20.
the face of a lion. Nu 2:3. Jg 14:18. 1 Ch
12:8. Re 5:5.

the face of an ox. Ezk 10:14, Cherub. Nu
2:18. Pr 14:4. 1 C 9:9, 10.
the face of an eagle. Nu 2:25. Dt 28:49. Jb
39:27. Is 40:31. Da 7:4.
11 **and their.** Ezk 10:16, 19.
stretched upward. *or,* divided above.
and two. ver. 23. Ge 3:24. Ex 26:1. 1 K 6:23-
29. Is 6:2. Re 4:6-8. 5:8-10.
12 **they went every.** ver. 9, 17. Ezk 10:22.
whither. ver. 20, 21. Jn 17:22. Ro 8:14. 1 C
3:16. 6:17, 19. 12:6. 2 C 6:16. He 1:14.
spirit. Heb. *ruach,* Ps +104:4.
13 **their appearance.** ver. 7. Ge 15:17. Ps 104:4.
Is 6:2. Da 10:5, 6. Mt 28:3. Ac 2:3. Re 4:5.
10:1. 18:1.
14 **ran and.** Ps 147:15. Da 9:21. Zc 2:3, 4. 4:10.
Mt 24:27, 31. Mk 13:27.
15 **one.** ver. 19-21. Ezk 10:9, 13-17. Da 7:9.
with. ver. 6. Re 4:7.
16 **the color.** ver. 10. Ex 39:13. Da 10:6.
a wheel. Ezk 10:10. Jb 9:10. Ps 36:6. 40:5. Ro
11:33. 1 C 2:9, 10, 16. Ep 3:10.
17 **and.** ver. 9, 12. Ezk 10:11. Is 55:11.
18 **they were so.** Jb 37:22-24. Ps 77:16-19.
97:2-5. Is 55:9.
rings. *or,* strakes. 1 K 7:33.
full. Ezk 10:12. 2 Ch 16:9. Ps 34:15. Pr 15:3.
Zc 4:10. Re 4:6, 8.
19 **And when.** Ezk 10:16, 17. Ps 103:20.
20 **Whithersoever.** Jn 6:63. Ro 8:1, 2, 5, 9, 11,
16, 26, 27. Ep +1:11.
the spirit. Heb. *ruach,* Ps +104:4. ver. 12. 1 C
14:32.
spirit. Heb. *ruach,* Ps +104:4.
for the. Ezk 10:17. Zc 6:1-8.
spirit. Heb. *ruach,* Ps +104:4.
of the living creature. *or,* of life.
21 **When.** ver. 21-26. Pr 30:27. Lk 2:27. Mt 4:1.
Ac 2:4. 8:29. 10:19. 16:7.
those went. ver. 19, 20. Ezk 10:17.
spirit. Heb. *ruach,* Ps +104:4.
of the living creature. *or,* of life. Ro 8:2.
22 **the likeness.** ver. 26. Ezk 10:1. Ge 1:6. Ex
24:10. Jb 37:22. Re 4:3, 6. 21:11.
crystal. Ge 31:40.
23 **their wings.** ver. 12, 24.
which. ver. 11. Jb 4:18. Ps 89:7. Lk 17:10.

24 like. Ezk 43:2. Re 1:15. 19:6.
as the voice. Ezk +10:5. Re 1:10. 16:17, 18.
Almighty. Ge +49:25.
as the noise. 2 K 7:6. Da 10:6.
25 and had. ver. 24.
26 And above. ver. 22. Ezk 10:1.
over. Mt 28:18. Ep 1:21, 22. Ph 2:9, 10. 1 P 3:22.
the likeness of a throne. Ps +11:4. +45:6. Da 7:9, 10, 14. Zc 6:13. Ac 7:56. He +1:8.
as the. Ex 24:10. Is 54:11.
the appearance of a man. Ge 32:24-30. Jsh 5:13-15. 6:1, 2. Is +9:6, 7. Je +23:5, 6. Da 10:18. Jn 6:62. Ro 8:3. Ph 2:7, 8. Col 2:9. 1 T 2:5. 3:16. He 2:14. Re 1:13. 3:21. 5:6. 14:14.
27 as the color. ver. 4. Ezk 8:2.
the appearance of fire. Dt 4:24. Ps 50:3. 97:2, 3. Is 6:1. Da 7:9. 10:6. 2 Th 1:8. He 12:29. Re 1:14-16.
brightness. Ps 80:1. 99:1. Mt 17:2. Ph 3:21. 1 T 6:16. He 1:2, 3. 1 J 1:5.
28 the appearance of the bow. Ge 9:13-16. Ex 24:10. Is +54:8-10. Re 4:3. 10:1.
This. Ex +24:16. 33:18-23. Nu 12:6-9. 1 C 13:12.
the glory. Ezk 3:12, 23. 8:4. 9:3. 10:4, 18, 19. 11:22, 23. 43:2, 4, 5. 44:4. Jn +17:5. 1 T 3:16.
I fell. Ezk 3:23. 9:8. 43:3. 44:4. Ge +17:3.

EZEKIEL 2

1 Son of man. ver. 3, 6, 8. Ezk 3:1, 4, 10, 17. 4:1. 5:1. 6:2. 7:2. 8:6, 12, 15. 12:3. 13:2. 14:3, 13. 15:2. 16:2. 17:2. 20:3. 37:3. Ps +8:4. Mt +8:20. 16:13-16. Jn 3:13, 16. Ac 7:56. He 2:6. Re 14:14.
stand. Ezk 1:28. Da 10:11, 19. Mt 17:7. Ac 9:6. 26:16. Re 1:17.
I will speak. Ex 25:17-22. Nu 7:89.
2 the spirit. Heb. *ruach*, Ge +41:38.
entered. Ezk 3:12, 14, 24. 36:27. Nu 11:25, 26. Jg 13:25. 1 S 16:13. Ne 9:30. Jl 2:28, 29. Re 11:11.
and set. Ezk 3:24. Da 10:11.
3 I send. Ezk 3:4-8. 2 Ch 36:15, 16. Is 6:8-10. Je 1:7. 7:2. 25:3-7. 26:2-6. 36:2. Mk 12:2-5. Lk 24:47, 48. Jn 20:21, 22. Ro 10:15.
a rebellious nation. Heb. rebellious nations. Ezk ch. 16, 20, 23.
rebelled. Ezk 17:15. 20:18-30, 38. Nu 20:10. 32:13, 14. Dt 9:24, 27. 1 S 8:7, 8. 2 K 17:17-20. Ezr 9:7. Ne 9:16-18, 26, 33-35. Ps 106:16-21, 28, 32-40. Je 3:25. 16:11, 12. 44:21, 22. Da 9:5-13. Ac 7:51.
4 they. Ezk 3:7. Dt 10:16. 31:27. 2 Ch 30:8. 36:13. Ps 95:8. Is 48:4. Je 3:3. 5:3. 6:15. 8:12. Mt 10:16.
impudent. Heb. hard of face. Pr 21:29.

stiffhearted. Ex 32:9. 33:3, 5. 34:9. Dt 9:6, 13. 10:16. 31:27. Jg 2:19. Is 48:4. Ac 7:51.
Thus. 1 K 22:14. Je 26:2, 3. Ac 20:26, 27.
5 whether. ver. 7. Ezk 3:10, 11, 26, 27. Mt 10:12-15. Mk 6:11. Ac 13:46. Ro 3:3. 2 C 2:15-17. 2 T 4:2, 3.
rebellious. Nu 17:10. Dt 31:27. 1 S 15:23. Ne 9:17. Jb 23:2. Pr 17:11. Is 30:9.
yet. Ezk 3:19. 33:9, 33. Lk 10:10-12. Jn 15:22.
6 be not. Ezk 3:8, 9. 2 K 1:15. Ps +118:6. Mi 3:8. Lk 12:4. Ac 4:13, 19, 29. Ep 6:19. Ph 1:28. 2 T +1:7.
briers. *or*, rebels. 2 S 23:6, 7. Is 9:18. Je 6:28. Mi 7:4.
scorpions. Lk 10:19. Re 9:3-6.
though they. Ezk 3:9, 26, 27. Pr 30:13, 14. Is 51:7. Je 18:18. Am 7:10-17. He 11:27. 1 P 3:14.
7 thou. Ezk 3:10, 17. Ge 3:2, 3. Je 1:7, 17. +23:28. 26:2. Jon 3:2. Mt 28:20.
whether. ver. 5. 2 T 4:2.
most rebellious. Heb. rebellion. ver. 5. Ps 107:11. Is 30:9.
8 hear. Jb +37:2. Lk +8:18. Re 2:7, 11, 17, 29.
Be. Le 10:3. Nu 20:10-13, 24. 1 K 13:21, 22. Is 50:5. 1 P 5:3.
open. Ezk 3:1-3, 10. Ps 119:130, 131. Je 1:7, 9. 15:16. 1 T 4:14-16. Re 10:9.
9 an hand. Ezk 8:3. Je 1:9. Da 5:5. 10:10, 16-18.
a roll. Ezk 3:1. Ps 40:7. Je 36:2. He 10:7. Re 5:1-5. 10:8-11.
10 spread. Is 30:8-11. Hab 2:2.
was written within and without. Re 5:1.
lamentations. Is 3:11. Je 36:29-32. Re 8:13. 9:12. 11:14.

EZEKIEL 3

1 eat. ver. 10. Ezk 2:8, 9. Je +15:16. 1 T 4:15. Re 10:9, 10.
go. ver. 11, 15, 17-21. Ezk 2:3. Je 24:1-7.
house. Ge +7:1.
2 opened my mouth. Je 25:17. Ac 26:19.
3 and fill. Ezk 2:10. Jb 32:18, 19. Je 6:11. 20:9. Jn 7:38. Col 3:16.
Then. Ps 119:11. Je 15:16. Jn 6:53, 63.
it was. Jb 23:12. Ps 19:10. 119:97, 103. Pr 16:24. 1 Re 10:9, 10.
4 go. ver. 11. Ezk 2:3, 7. Mt 10:5, 6. 15:24. Jn 20:21. Ac 1:8.
speak with. Mt 12:34, 35. Jn 3:34. 7:16. 1 C 11:23.
5 thou. Jon 1:2. 3:2-4. Ac 26:17, 18.
of a strange speech and of an hard language. Heb. deep of lip and heavy of tongue: and so ver. 6. Jg +7:22mg. Ps 81:5. Is 33:19.
6 of a strange speech and of an hard language. Heb. deep of lip, and heavy of language. ver. +5mg.

Surely, etc. *or*, If I had sent thee to them, would they not have hearkened? etc. Jon 3:5-10. Mt +11:20-24. 12:41, 42. Lk 11:30-32. Ac 28:28. Ro 9:30-33.

7 **Israel will not**. 1 S 8:7. Je 25:3, 4. 44:4, 5, 16. Mt 23:37. Lk 10:16. 13:34. 19:14. Jn 1:11. 5:40-47. 10:20. 15:20-24.
  all the. Ezk 2:4. 24:7. Is 3:9. Je 3:3. 5:3.
  impudent and hardhearted. Heb. stiff of forehead and hard of heart. Ezk 2:4mg. Ex 32:9. Dt 9:6, 13.

8 **I have made**. Ex 4:15, 16. 11:4-8. 1 K 21:20. Ps +58:11. Is 50:7. Je 1:18, 19. 15:19-21. Mi 3:8. Mt 28:20. Lk 6:22, 23. 21:15. Ac 7:51-56. 2 T 4:7, 8. He 11:27, 32-37.

9 **adamant**. Zc 7:12.
  fear. Ge +15:1. Is 50:7. Je 17:18. Mi 3:8. 1 T 2:3. 2 T 2:6.

10 **all my words**. Is 50:4.
  receive. ver. 1-3. Ezk 2:8. Jb 22:22. Ps 119:11. Pr 8:10. 19:20. Lk 8:15. 1 Th 2:13. 4:1. 1 T 4:15.
  and hear. Lk +8:18.

11 **get**. ver. 15. Ezk 11:24, 25. Da 6:13.
  the children. Ezk 33:2, 12, 17, 30. 37:18. Ex 32:7. Dt 9:12. Da 12:1.
  speak. ver. 27. Ezk 2:5, 7. Ac 20:26, 27.
  whether. Jn 3:11. 2 T 4:2.

12 **spirit**. Heb. *ruach*, Is +48:16. ver. +14. Ezk 2:2.
  a voice. Ac 2:2. Re 1:10, 15.
  Blessed. Ps 72:18, 19. 103:20, 21. 148:2. Is 6:3. Re 5:11-14. 19:6.
  glory. Ezk +1:28. Ex +24:16. 1 S 4:21, 22.

13 **the noise**. Ezk 1:24. 10:5. 2 S 5:24. Jn 3:8. Ac 2:2-4. 4:31.
  touched. Heb. kissed. Ge 33:4.
  and the noise. Ezk 10:16, 17.

14 **the spirit**. Heb. *ruach*, Is +48:16. ver. 12.
  lifted. Ezk +8:3.
  took me away. Jb 20:9.
  and I went. Ex 4:13.
  in bitterness, in the heat of my spirit. Heb. bitter in hot anger. Heb. *ruach*, Ge +41:8. Nu 11:11-19. Ps 32:3. 51:14. Je 6:11. 20:14-18. Jon 4:1, 3, 9.
  but. 1 K +18:46. 2 K 2:16. Je 20:7-9. 1 C 9:16.

15 **Telabib**. i.e. *corn hill, heap of green ears,* **S#8512h**, only here.
  that dwelt. ver. 23. Ezk 1:1, 3. 10:15. 43:3.
  sat. Ge 50:10. Jb 2:13. Ps 137:1. Je 23:9. Hab 3:16.

16 **And it came to pass**. Je 42:7.

17 **I have**. Ezk 33:2-9. 1 C 12:28. Ep 4:11.
  a watchman. Ezk 33:2, 6, 7. SS 3:3. 5:7. Is 21:6, 8, 11, 12. 52:8. 56:10. 62:6. Je 6:17. 31:6. Ac 20:28-31. He 13:17.
  hear. Ezk 33:6-8. 2 Ch 19:10. Is 58:1. Je 6:10. Hab 2:1. Mt 3:7. 1 C 4:14. 2 C 5:11, 20. Col 1:28. 1 Th 5:14.

give them warning. ver. 18-21. Ezk 33:3-9. Je 6:1 (sign of fire).

18 **I say**. Ezk 18:4, 13, 20. 33:6, 8. Ge 2:17. 3:3, 4. Nu 26:65. 2 K 1:4. Is 3:11. Lk 13:3, 5. Ep 5:5, 6.
  surely. Ge +2:16.
  to save. Ezk 18:30-32. Ac 2:40. +3:19. 1 T 4:16. Ja 5:19, 20.
  the same. Ezk 33:6, 9, 10. Pr 14:32. Jn 8:21, 24.
  but. Ezk 34:10. Lk +11:50, 51. Ac +18:6.

19 **if thou**. 2 K 17:13, etc. 2 Ch 36:15, 16. Pr 29:1. Je 42:19-22. 44:4, 5. Lk 10:10, 11. Ac 18:5, 6. 20:31. 1 Th 4:6. He 2:1-3. 12:25.
  he shall. ver. 18. Jn +8:21, 24. 2 Th 1:8, 9. He +10:26, 27.
  but thou. ver. 21. Ezk 14:14, 20. 33:5, 9. Is 49:4, 5. Ac 13:45, 46. 18:6. 20:26. 2 C 2:15-17. 1 T 4:16.
  soul. Heb. *nephesh*, Ge +12:13.

20 **When**. Ezk 18:24, 26. 33:12, 13. 2 Ch 24:2, 17-22. Ps 36:3. 125:5. Zp 1:6. Mt 13:20, 21. 2 T 2:15. He 10:38. 2 P 2:18-22. 1 J 2:19.
  righteousness. Heb. righteousnesses. Is 64:6. Da 9:18.
  and I lay. Dt 13:3. Lk 2:34. 1 C +8:9. +11:19. 2 Th 2:9-12.
  because. ver. 18. Le 19:17. 2 S 12:7-13. 2 Ch 19:2-4. 25:15, 16. Pr 25:12. Mt 18:15.
  and his. Ezk 18:24, 26. 33:12, 13. Mt 12:43-45. Lk 8:15. Ro 2:7, 8. He 10:38. 2 P 2:21.
  but his. ver. 18. Ezk 33:6. He 13:17.

21 **if thou**. Mt 24:24, 25. Ac 20:31. 1 C 4:14. 10:12. Ga 1:6-10. 5:2-7. Ep 4:17-21. +5:5, 6. Col 1:28. 3:5-8. 1 Th 4:6-8. 5:14. 2 T 4:1, 2. T 2:15. 1 J 3:6-9. Re 3:19.
  he shall. ver. 20. Ps 19:11. Pr 9:9. 17:10. Ga 2:11-13. Ja +5:20.
  also. ver. 19. Ps 51:14. 1 T 4:6, 16.
  soul. Heb. *nephesh*, Ge +12:13.

22 **the hand**. ver. 14. Ezk 1:3. 37:1.
  Arise. Ezk 8:4. Ac 9:6.
  talk. Ex +33:9.

23 **the glory**. Ezk +1:28. Ex +24:16. Jn 1:14. Ac 7:55.
  as the. Ezk 1:24.
  river. Ezk 1:1-3.
  and I fell. Ezk +1:28.

24 **the spirit**. Heb. *ruach*, Ge +41:38. Ezk 2:2. 37:10. Da 10:8-10, 19.
  Go. Ezk 4:1-4.

25 **they shall**. Ezk 4:8. Mk 3:21. Jn 21:18. Ac 9:16. 20:23. 21:11-13.

26 **I will**. Ps 137:6. Je 1:17. Lk 1:20-22.
  and shalt. La 2:9. Ho 4:17. Am 5:10. 8:11, 12. Mi 3:6, 7.
  a reprover. Heb. a man reproving. Is 29:21.
  for. Ezk 2:3-8. Is 1:2.

27 **I will**. Ezk 11:25. +24:27. Ex 4:11, 12.

Thus. ver. 11. Mt 11:15. 13:9. Re +22:10, 11.
for they. ver. 9, 26. Ezk 12:2, 3.

EZEKIEL 4

1 **take**. Ezk 5:1, etc. 12:3, etc. 1 S 15:27, 28. 1
K 11:30, 31. Is 20:2-4. Je 13:1-14. 18:2, etc.
19:1, etc. 25:15, etc. 27:2, etc. Ho 1:2, etc. ch.
3. 12:10.
even. Je 6:6. 32:31. Am 3:2.
2 **lay**. Je 39:1, 2. 52:4. Lk 19:42-44.
battering rams. or, chief leaders. Ezk 21:22.
3 **an iron pan**. *or*, a flat plate, *or*, slice. Le 2:5.
set thy face. Le 17:10. 20:3, 5, 6. 26:17. Je
21:10. 44:11.
besieged. 2 K 25:1-10. Je 21:3-10. 37:8.
This. Ezk 12:6, 11. 24:24-27. Is 8:18. 20:3. Lk
2:34. 1 C 4:9. He 2:4.
4 **upon**. ver. 5, 8.
and lay. 2 K 17:21-23.
according to the number. Nu 14:34.
thou shalt bear. Ezk 16:54. 18:19, 20. 23:49.
32:24, 25, 30. 44:10, 12. Ex 28:38, 43. Le
10:17. 16:22. 17:16. Nu 5:31. 14:34. 18:1.
30:15. Is 53:11, 12. La 5:7. Mt 8:17. He 9:28.
1 P 2:24.
5 **I have**. Is 53:6.
three. This number of years will take us back
from the year in which Judea was finally desolated by Nebuzar-adan, B.C. 975, to the
establishment of idolatry in Israel by
Jeroboam, B.C. 584. "*Beginning from* 1 K
12:33. *Ending* Je 52:30."
6 **forty days**. "*Beginning from* 2 K 23:3, 23.
Ending Je 52:30." Jon +3:4.
each day for a year. Nu 14:34. Da 9:24-26.
12:11, 12. Re 9:15. 11:2, 3. 12:14. 13:5.
7 **set**. ver. 3. Ezk 6:2.
and thine. Is 52:10.
8 **I will**. Ezk 3:25. Ac 9:16. 2 C 11:23-27.
from one side to another. Heb. from thy
side to thy side.
9 **wheat**. ver. 13, 16.
fitches. *or*, spelt. Ex 9:32. Is 28:25.
three. ver. 5.
10 **by weight**. ver. 16. Le +26:26. Dt 28:51, etc.
11 **shalt drink**. ver. 16. Is 5:13. Jn 3:34.
by measure. Le 19:35.
hin. Ezk 45:24. 46:5, 7, 11, 14.
12 **cake**. lit. a "round" thing. Ge 18:6.
dung. or, filth. lit. "outgoing." Dt 23:13.
in their sight. Ezk 12:3.
13 **Even thus**. Is 30:20. Da 1:8. Ho 9:3, 4.
14 **Ah**. Ezk 9:8. 20:49. Je 1:6.
my soul. Heb. *nephesh*, Ge +27:31. Ac 10:14.
from my youth. Mt 19:20. Mk 10:20. Lk
18:21. Ac 10:14. 26:4.
have I eaten. Ex 22:31. Le 11:39, 40. 17:15.
which dieth. Le 11:1-47. 21:1, etc. 22:1, etc.
Dt 14:3.

abominable. Le 7:18. 19:7. Dt 14:3. Is 65:4.
66:17.
15 **cow's dung**. Am 7:6.
16 **I will break**. ver. +10.
eat. ver. 10, 11. Ps 60:3. La 1:11. 4:9, 10.
+5:9.
17 **and consume**. Ezk 24:23. 33:10. Le 26:39.

EZEKIEL 5

1 **take**. Ezk 44:20. Le 21:5. 2 S 14:26. Is 7:20.
then. Da 5:27.
2 **shalt burn**. ver. 12. Je 9:21, 22. 15:2. 24:10.
38:2. Jg 9:15, 19, 20. Zc 13:8, 9. Lk 12:49.
the city. Ezk 4:1-8.
I will draw. ver. 12. Je +12:12. Am 9:2, 3.
3 **a few**. 2 K 25:12. Je 39:10. 40:6. 52:16. Mt
7:14. Lk 13:23, 24. 1 P 4:18.
skirts. Heb. wings. Is +24:16mg.
4 **take**. 2 K 25:25. Je ch. 41-44. 52:30.
shall a fire. Je 4:4. 48:45.
5 **This**. Ezk 4:1. Ps 48:2. Je 6:6. Lk 22:19, 20. 1
C 10:4.
I have. Ezk 16:14. Dt 4:6. Mi 5:7. Mt 5:14.
6 **she hath**. Ezk 16:47. Dt 32:15-21. 2 K 17:8-
20. Ps 106:20. Ro 1:23-25. 1 C 5:1. Ju 4.
changed. or, rejected or rebelled against. Ezk
20:8, 13, 21. Nu 20:24. 27:14. Dt 32:6. Is 1:2.
for they. Ne 9:16, 17. Ps 78:10. Je 8:5. 9:6.
He +12:25.
7 **neither have done**. ver. 11. Ezk 16:47, 48,
54. 2 K 21:9-11. 2 Ch 33:9. Is 5:2, 4. Je 2:10,
11.
8 **I, even I**. Ge +6:17.
against. Ezk +15:7. Dt 29:20. Is 5:5-7. La 2:5.
3:3. 4:6. Am 3:2. Zc 14:2, 3. Mt 22:7.
in the. Ezk 25:2-6. 26:2. 29:6, 7. 35:10-15. Dt
29:23-28. 1 K 9:8, 9. Je 22:8, 9. 24:9. 50:7. La
2:15-17.
9 **that which**. La 4:6, 9. Da 9:12. Am 3:2. Mt
24:21.
10 **the fathers**. Le +26:29. Is 9:20. 49:26.
the whole. ver. 2, 12. Ezk 6:8. 12:14. 20:23.
22:15. 36:19. Le 26:33. Dt 4:27. 28:64. 32:26.
Ne 1:8. Ps 44:11. Je 9:16. 44:12. 50:17. Am
9:9. Zc 2:6. 7:14. Lk 21:24.
11 **as I live**. Dt +32:40. Ps 95:11. Am 8:7.
thou hast. Ezk 8:5, 6, 16. 23:38. 44:7. 2 K
21:4, 5, 7. 23:12. 2 Ch 33:4, 7. 36:14. Je 7:9-
11. 32:34.
detestable. Ezk 7:20. 11:18, 21. Dt 7:25, 26.
Je 16:18. 44:4.
will I. Ezk 16:27. 29:15. Ps 107:39. Je
10:24mg. Ro 11:12.
neither shall. Ezk 7:4, 9. 8:18. 9:5, 10.
24:14. Dt 13:8. 29:20. La 2:21. Zc 11:6. Ml
3:17. Ro 8:32. 11:21. 2 P 2:4, 5.
eye. Dt +11:12.
12 **third part of**. ver. 2. Ezk 6:12. Je 15:2. 21:9.
44:14. Zc 13:7-9.

and I will scatter. ver. 2, 10. Je +9:16.
and I will draw. ver. +2.

13 **shall mine.** Ezk +7:8. 13:15. 20:8, 21. Pr 1:26. Je 25:12. Da 9:2. 11:36.
I will cause. Ezk 16:42, 63. 21:17. 23:25. 24:13. Is +59:18.
I will be comforted. Dt 32:36. Is 1:24. +57:6. Zc 6:8.
spoken. Ezk 6:10. 36:5, 6. 38:18, 19. Is +9:7. 59:17.

14 **I will.** Dt +28:37. Ne 2:17. Ps +31:11. Je +18:16.
the nations. ver. 8.

15 **reproach.** Dt 28:37.
an instruction. Dt 29:22-28. 1 K 9:7-9. Ps 79:4. Is 26:9. Je 22:8, 9. 1 C 10:11.
when. Ezk 25:17. Is 66:15, 16. Na 1:2.

16 **the evil.** Dt +32:23, 24.
and will. Le +26:26. 2 K 6:25.

17 **and evil.** Ezk 14:15, 21. 33:27. 34:25-28. 39:4. Ex 23:29. Le 26:6, 22. Dt 32:23, 24. 1 K 20:36. 2 K 2:24. 17:25. Je 15:3. Re 6:7, 8.
and pestilence. ver. 12. Ezk +38:22.
and I. Ezk 11:8. 23:47. 29:8. Je +12:12.
I the Lord. ver. 13, 15. Ezk 17:21, 24. 21:32. 22:14. 24:14. 26:14. 30:12. 37:14. Is 14:27. Je 1:12. 44:28. Mt 24:35.

EZEKIEL 6

1 **And the word.** ver. 3. Ezk 7:1.

2 **set.** Ezk 4:7. 13:17. 20:46. 21:2. 25:2. 38:2, 3.
the mountains. Ezk 19:9. 33:28. 34:14. 35:12. 37:22. Dt 11:11. Jsh 11:21. Ps 87:1. 125:2. Mi 6:1, 2.

3 **Ye.** Ezk 36:1-4, 8. Je 22:29. Mi 6:2.
to the mountains. Je 2:20. 3:6, 23.
rivers. Ezk 36:4, 6. 2 S 22:16.
bring a sword. Je +12:12.
and I will. Le 26:30. Is 27:9.
high places. 2 K +21:3.

4 **images.** *or,* sun images: and so ver. 6. Le +26:30mg. Je 43:13mg.
and I. ver. 5, 13. Le 26:30. 1 K 13:2. 2 K 23:14, 16-20. 2 Ch 34:5. Je 8:1, 2.

5 **lay.** Heb. give. ver. 13, 14. Ezk 5:14. 7:3.
carcases. lit. "faint ones." Ezk 43:7, 9.
I will scatter. 2 K 23:14.
the bones. Ps 53:5. 2 Ch 34:5. Je 7:32.

6 **all your.** Is 6:11. Je 9:19. Zp 3:7.
the cities. Ezk 5:14. Is 24:1-12. 32:13, 14. 64:10. Je 2:15. 9:11. 10:22. 34:22. Mi 3:12. Zp 1:2-6, 18. 3:6.
laid waste. Le 26:31.
and the. 2 K +21:3.
your altars. Ezk 30:13. Is 2:18, 20. 27:9. Ho 10:2. Mi 1:7. 5:13. Zp 1:3, 4. Zc 13:2.
images. ver. 4mg.
your works. Ps +115:8. Is 1:31. Hab 2:18.

7 **slain.** Ezk 9:7. Je 14:18. 18:21. 25:33. La 2:20, 21. 4:9.
and ye shall know. ver. +10, 13, 14. Ezk 7:4, 9, 27. 11:10, 12. 12:15, 16, 20. 13:9, 14, 21, 23. 14:8. +15:7. +23:49. +32:15. Ex 7:5. 10:2. 14:4, 18. 1 K 20:13, 28. 2 K 19:19. Ps 9:16. 83:17, 18. Is 64:2. Je 24:7. Da 4:1-3, 34-37. 6:26, 27. Jl 2:27. 3:16, 17.

8 **leave a remnant.** Ezk +12:16. Is 27:7, 8. Je 46:28. Mi +5:3.
scattered. Je +9:16.

9 **remember.** Le 26:40, 41. Dt 4:29-31. 30:1-3. Ps 137:1. Je 51:50. Da 9:2, 3. Zc 10:9.
I am. Ezk 5:13. 16:43. Ps 78:40. Is 7:13. 43:24. 63:10. Je 3:6, 13. Am 2:13.
their eyes. Ezk 14:4-7. 20:7, 24, 28. 23:14-16. Nu 15:39. 2 K 16:10. 2 P 2:14.
they shall. Ezk 7:16. 12:16. 16:63. 20:43. 36:31, 32. Le 26:39. Jb 42:6. Is 64:6. Je 30:18, 19. 2 C 7:11.

10 **they shall know.** ver. +7, 14. Ezk 12:15. 14:22, 23. 20:26. 30:8. 32:15. Le 23:43. 1 S 17:46, 47. 1 K 8:41-43. 18:37. 2 Ch 6:33. Ps 59:13. 109:27. Is 19:12. 41:20. 45:6. Je 5:12-14. 31:34. 44:28. Da 9:12. Zc 1:6.
not said in vain. Nu 23:19.
evil. Is +45:7.

11 **Smite.** Ezk 21:14-17. Nu 24:10. Is 58:1. Je 9:1, 10.
Alas. Ezk +9:4. Je +30:7. Jl 1:15. Am 5:16. Re 18:10, 16-19.
fall. Je +12:12.
sword. lit. mouth of the sword. Ge +34:26.

12 **far off.** Da 9:7.
thus. Le 26:14-39. Dt 28:15-68. Is 40:2. +59:18.

13 **when.** ver. 4-7. Is 37:20, 36-38.
upon. Ezk 20:28. Is 65:3, 4. 66:17.
green tree. Is +57:5.
oak. Is +1:29.

14 **will I stretch.** Ex +7:5. Is 26:11.
more desolate than the wilderness. *or,* desolate from the wilderness. Je +18:16.
Diblath. i.e. *fertile; place of the fig-cakes,* **S#1689h**, only here. Nu 33:46, Almon-diblath-aim. Je 48:22, Beth-diblathaim.
shall know. ver. +7. Ps 83:16-18. Am 3:2.

EZEKIEL 7

2 **unto.** Ezk 12:22. 21:2. 40:2. 2 Ch 34:7.
An end. ver. 3, 5, 6. Ezk 11:13. Ge 6:13. Dt 32:20. Je 5:31. 51:13. La 1:9. 4:18. Am 8:2, 10. Mt 24:6, 13, 14. 1 P 4:7.

3 **and I.** ver. 8, 9. Ezk 5:13. 6:3-7, 12, 13.
will judge. ver. 8, 27. Ezk 11:10, 11. 16:38. 18:30. 33:20. 34:20-22. 36:19. Re 20:12, 13.
recompense. Heb. give. ver. 4, 8, 20, 21.

4 **mine eye.** ver. 9. Ezk 5:11. 8:18. 9:10. 24:14. Dt +11:12. Je 13:14. Zc 11:6.

but. Ezk 11:21. 16:43. 22:31. 23:49. Je 16:18. 25:14. Ho 9:7. 12:2. He 10:30.
and ye. ver. 9, 27. Ezk +6:7.

5 **An evil**. Ezk 5:9. 2 K 21:12, 13. Da 9:12. Am 3:2. Na 1:9. Mt 24:21.

6 **An end**. ver. 3. Je 44:27.
watcheth for thee. Heb. awaketh against thee. 2 K +4:31. Zc 13:7.
behold. ver. 10. Ezk 21:25. 39:8. 2 P 2:5.

7 **morning**. Ge 19:15, 24. Is 17:14. Am 4:13.
the time. ver. 12. Ezk 12:23-25, 28. Is 13:22. Zp 1:14-16. 1 P 4:17.
the day of trouble. Is 22:5. Je +30:7.
sounding again. or, echo. Is 16:9. 22:5. Je 25:30.

8 **pour**. Ezk 9:8. 14:19. 20:8, 13, 21, 33, 34. 21:31. 22:31. 30:15. 36:18. Le +26:28. 2 Ch 34:21, 25. Ps 69:24. +79:6. Is 42:25. Je 7:20. La 2:4. 4:1, 11. Da 9:11, 27. Ho 5:10. Na 1:6. Re 14:10. 16:1.
accomplish. Ezk 6:12.
thy ways. Ezk +22:31.
and I. ver. 3, 4.

9 **recompense**. Je 51:56.
thee. Heb. upon thee.
and ye. ver. 4.
that I am. Ex 15:26.
the Lord. Is 9:13. Mi 6:9. Ga 6:7. Re 20:13.
that smiteth. Ho 6:1.

10 **behold, it**. ver. 6. 1 Th 5:3.
the morning. ver. 7.
the rod. Ezk 19:14. 21:10, 13. Nu 17:8. Is 10:5.
pride. Le 26:18, 19. Pr 14:3. 16:18. Is 28:1. Da 4:37. Ja 4:6.

11 **Violence**. ver. 23. Is 5:7. 9:4. 14:29. 59:6-8. Je 6:7. Am 3:10. 6:3. Mi 2:2. 3:3. 6:12. Ja 2:13.
none. ver. 2, 16. Ezk 5:4, 11. 6:11. Ps 50:16-22. Zp 1:18.
multitude. or, tumult.
theirs. or, their tumultuous persons. Je +10:13mg.
neither. Ezk 24:16-24. Ps 78:64. Je 16:5, 6. 22:18. 25:33.

12 **time**. ver. 5-7, 10. 1 C 7:29-31. Ja 5:8, 9.
let. Is 24:1, 2. Je 32:7, 8, 24, 25.
for. ver. 13, 14. Ezk 6:11, 12. Is 5:13, 14.

13 **the seller**. Le 25:24-28, 31. Ec 8:8.
they were yet alive. Heb. their life were yet among the living.
neither. Ezk 13:22. 33:26, 27. Jb 15:25. Ps 52:7.
in, etc. or, whose life is in his iniquity.
the iniquity of his life. Heb. his iniquity.

14 **have**. Ho +8:1.
for. ver. 11, 12. Is 24:1-7. Je 6:11. 7:20. 12:12.

15 **The sword**. i.e., war, or destruction. Je +12:12. 14:18. 34:1.

16 **they**. Ezk 6:8. Ezr 9:15. Is 1:9. 37:31. Je 44:14, 28.
like. Ezk 6:9. Is 38:14. 59:11.
mourning. Ezk 36:31. Pr 5:11-14. Zc 12:10-14. Lk +6:21.

17 **hands**. Ezk 21:7. Is 13:7, 8. Je 6:24. He 12:12.
be weak as water. Heb. go into water. Ezk 21:7mg.

18 **shall also**. Jb +16:15.
and horror. Ge 15:12. Jb 21:6. Ps 35:26. 55:4, 5. Je 3:25. Re 6:15-17.
and baldness. Is +3:24.

19 **shall cast**. 2 K 7:7, 8, 15. Pr 11:4. Is 2:20. 30:22. Zp 1:18. Mt 16:26.
removed. Heb. for a separating, or, uncleanness.
deliver. Pr +11:4. Zp +1:11, 18.
day of the wrath. Jb 20:28. +21:30. Pr +11:4. Zp +1:18. Ro +2:5. Ja +5:1.
they shall not. Jb 20:12-23. Ps 78:30, 31. Ec 5:10. Is 55:2. Lk 12:19, 20.
souls. Heb. nephesh, Ge +34:3.
it is the stumblingblock of their iniquity. or, their iniquity is their stumblingblock. 1 C +8:9.

20 **the beauty**. Ezk 24:21. 1 Ch 29:1, 2. 2 Ch 2:9. ch. 3. Ezr 3:12. Ps 48:2. 50:2. 87:2, 3. Is 64:11. Hg 2:3.
but. Ezk 5:11. 8:7-10, 15, 16. 2 K 21:4, 7. 23:11, 12. 2 Ch 33:4-7. 36:14. Je 7:30.
set it far from them. or, made it unto them an unclean thing. ver. 22. Ezk 9:7. 24:21. Je 7:14. La 1:10. 2:1, 7.

21 **I will give it**. 2 K 24:13-15. 25:9, 13-16. 2 Ch 36:18, 19. Ps 74:2-8. 79:1. Je 52:13.

22 **face**. Ps 10:11. 35:22. 74:10, 11, 18-23. Je 18:17.
my secret place. He 9:3.
robbers. or, burglers. Ezk 18:10. Ps 17:4. Je 7:11. Da 11:14.

23 **a chain**. Ezk 19:3-6. Je 27:2. 40:1. La 3:7. Na 3:10.
for. Ezk 9:9. 11:6. 22:3-6, 9, 13, 27. 2 K 21:16. 24:4. Is 1:15. 59:3, 7. Je 2:34. 7:6. 22:17. Ho 4:2. Mi 2:2. 7:2. Zp 3:3, 4.

24 **I will bring**. Ezk 21:31. 28:7. Ps 106:41. Je 4:7. 12:12. Hab 1:6-10.
they shall. Je 6:12. La 5:2.
I will also. Ezk 33:28. Is 5:14.
their holy places shall be defiled. or, they shall inherit their holy places. Ezk 21:2. 22:16. Jsh 14:1. 2 K 24:20. 25:8, 9. 2 Ch 7:19. Ps 83:12.

25 **Destruction**. Heb. Cutting off. Is 38:12.
and they. Is 57:21. 59:8-12. Je 8:15, 16. La 4:17, 18. Mi 1:12.

26 **Mischief**. or, Accident. Is 47:11.
shall come. Le 26:18, 21, 24, 28. Dt 32:23. Je 4:20.
rumor. lit. hearing. Is 53:1mg. Je +49:14.

then. Ezk 14:1. 20:1-3. 33:31. Je 21:2. 37:17. 38:14, etc.

but the law. Dt 17:8-13. 33:10. Ps +74:9. La 2:9. Am 8:11, 12. Mi 3:6.

ancients. Ezk 8:1. 14:1. 20:1. Je 18:18.

27 **king**. Ezk 12:10-22. 17:15-21. 21:25. Je 52:8-11.

desolation. 2 K +18:37.

I will. ver. 4-8. Ezk 18:30. Is 3:11. Ro 2:5-10.

according to their deserts. Heb. with their judgments. Mt 7:2. Ja 2:13.

and they. ver. +4. Ps 9:16.

EZEKIEL 8

1 **in the sixth year**. Ezk 1:2. 20:1. 24:1. 26:1. 29:1, 17. 31:1. 32:17. 40:1.

and the. Ezk 14:1, 4. 20:1. 33:31. Jsh +20:4. Ml 2:7. Ac 10:33.

that the hand. 1 K +18:46.

2 **I beheld**. Ezk 1:4, 26, 27. Da 7:9, 10. Re 1:14, 15.

brightness. Da 10:6. Mt 17:1, 2. Ac 26:13. 1 T 6:16. He 1:2, 3. 1 J 1:5. Re 1:15.

3 **he put**. Ezk 2:9. Da 5:5. 10:10, 18.

the spirit. Heb. *ruach*, Is +48:16.

lifted me up. Ezk 3:14. 11:1, 24. 37:1. 40:2, 3. 43:5. 1 K 18:12. 2 K 2:16. Mt 4:1. Lk 4:1. Ac 8:39. 2 C 12:2-4. Re 1:10. 4:2. 17:3. 21:10.

to the door. ver. 5. 2 K 16:14.

the image. Ezk 5:11. 7:20. 2 K 21:7. Je 7:30. 23:11. 32:34.

of jealousy. Dt 4:16. 2 Ch 33:7, 15.

provoketh. Ex +20:5. Dt 5:9.

4 **the glory**. Ezk 1:26-28. 3:22, 23. 9:3. 10:1-4. 11:22, 23. 43:2-4. Ex 25:22. 40:34, 35. 2 C 3:18. 4:4-6. He 1:3.

5 **lift**. Je 3:2. Zc 5:5-11.

at the. ver. 3. Ps 48:2.

this image. 2 K 21:7. Is +66:17.

6 **seest**. ver. 12, 17. Je 3:6. 7:17.

even. ver. 9, 17. Ezk 5:11. 7:20-22. 23:38, 39. 2 K 23:4-7. Pr 5:14. Je 7:30. 23:11. 32:34. 44:17.

that I. Ezk 10:19. 11:22, 23. Dt 31:16-18. 2 Ch 36:14-17. Ps 78:60. Je 26:6. La 2:6, 7.

greater. ver. 11, 14, 16.

7 **the door**. 1 K 7:12. 2 K 21:5.

8 **dig now**. Jb 34:22. Is 29:15. Je 2:34mg. 23:24. Am 9:2, 3.

9 **that they**. Ezk 20:8.

10 **every**. Ex +20:4. Le 7:21. 11:10-12, 29-31, 42-44. 20:25. Dt 7:26. 14:3, 7, 8. Is 57:6-10. +66:17. Je 2:26, 27. 3:9. 16:18.

11 **seventy**. Ge +46:27. 2 Ch 19:8. Je 5:5. 19:1. 26:17. Da 9:8.

Jaazaniah. 2 K +25:23.

Shaphan. 2 K +22:3.

every. Nu 16:17, 35. 2 Ch 26:16, 19. Je 7:9.

12 **hast**. ver. 6, 15, 17.

ancients. ver. 11. Jsh +20:4. Ep 5:12.

in the dark. ver. 7, 8. Jb 24:13-17. Jn 3:19, 20. Ep +5:11, 13.

The Lord seeth. Ezk 9:9. Jb 22:12, 13. Ps 73:11. 94:7-11. Is 29:15.

13 **greater**. ver. 6, 15. Je 9:3. Ro 1:24, 25. Ep 5:12. 2 T 3:13.

14 **toward**. Ezk 44:4. 46:9.

Tammuz. i.e. *sprout of life; hidden; giver of the vine; dissolution; shrivelled up*, S#8542h, only here. Ps 106:28. Is 17:10. Je 22:18. Am 8:10. Zc 12:10.

15 **Hast**. ver. 6, 12. 2 T 3:13.

greater. ver. 9, 13.

16 **the inner**. Ezk 10:3. 40:28. 43:5. 45:19.

at the door. 2 K 16:14. 2 Ch 7:7. Jl 2:17.

about. Ezk 11:1.

with their. Ezk 23:35. 1 K 8:29. 2 Ch 29:6. Je 2:27. 32:33.

their faces. Dt 4:19. 17:3. 2 K 23:5, 11. 2 Ch 14:5. Jb 31:26-28. Je 8:1-3. 44:17. Ac 7:42, 43.

17 **Is it a light**, etc. or, Is there any thing lighter than to commit, etc.

for. Ezk 7:23. 9:9. 11:6. Ge 6:13. 2 K 21:16. 24:4. Je 6:7. 19:4. 20:8. Am 3:10. 6:3. Mi 2:2. 6:12. Zp 1:9.

to provoke. Je 7:19.

the branch. Is 66:17.

18 **will I also**. Ezk 7:4-9. 9:5, 10. Is +59:18.

mine eye. Ezk 5:11. 7:4, 9. 9:5. Dt 13:8. Je 21:7.

and though. Jg 10:13, 14. Ps +66:18.

mine ears. Ps +10:17.

EZEKIEL 9

1 **cried**. Ezk 43:6, 7. Is 6:8. Am 3:7, 8. Re 1:10, 11. 14:7.

Cause. Ex 12:23. 2 K 10:24. 1 Ch 21:15, 16. Is 10:6, 7. He 1:7, 14.

2 **six**. Je 1:15, 16. 5:15-17. 8:16, 17. 25:9.

the higher. 2 K 15:35. 2 Ch 27:3. Je 26:10.

lieth. Heb. is turned. Je 49:8mg.

slaughter weapon. Heb. weapon of his breaking in pieces.

and one. Ezk 10:2, 6, 7. Le 16:4. Re 15:6.

inkhorn. Je 36:18. 2 C 3:3. 2 J 12. 3 J 13.

by his side. Heb. upon his loins.

beside. Ex 27:1-7. 40:29. 2 Ch 4:1.

3 **the glory**. Ezk 3:23. 8:4. 10:4, 18. 11:22, 23. 43:2-4.

from the cherub. Ge +3:24.

clothed with linen. Da 10:5, 6. Re 1:13.

4 **set a mark**. Heb. mark a mark. Ex 12:7, 13. Jsh 2:12, 18. 1 S 21:13mg. Jb 31:35mg. Ps 78:41. Ml 3:16. Jn 6:27. 2 C 1:22. Ep +4:30. 2 T 2:19. Re 7:2, 3. 9:4. 13:16, 17. 14:1. 20:4.

that sigh. Ezk 6:11. Ps +12:5. +51:17. 119:53, 136. 2 C 12:21. 2 P 2:8, 9.

5 **hearing**. Heb. ears. 1 S 9:15. Is 5:9. 22:14.
  Go. ver. 10. Ezk 5:11. 7:4, 9. 8:18. 24:14. Ex
  32:27. Nu 25:7, 8. Dt 32:39-42. 1 K 18:40.
6 **Slay**. Ge 19:22.
  utterly. Heb. to destruction. Ezk 23:47. 26:8,
  11, 15.
  old. Nu 31:15-17. Dt 2:34. 3:6. Jsh 6:17-21. 1
  S 15:3. 2 Ch 36:17.
  young. Ezk 23:6.
  maids. Ezk 44:22.
  children. Nu +16:27.
  but. Ex 12:23. Jsh 2:18, 19. 6:22-25. 2 T 2:19.
  He 11:28. Re 7:3. 9:4. 14:4.
  and begin. Ezk 8:5-16. 2 K 10:23. Is 10:12.
  Je 25:29. 49:12. Am 3:2. 9:9. Ml +3:5. Lk
  +12:47. 1 P *4:17, 18.*
  at the. Ezk 8:11, 12, 16. 11:1, 13.
7 **Defile the house**. Ezk 7:20-22. 2 Ch 36:17.
  Ps 79:1-3. La 2:4-7. Lk 13:1.
8 **that I**. Ge +17:3. Ezr 9:5. Ga 3:19.
  Ah. Ezk 4:14. 11:13. Ge +18:23. Je 4:10.
  14:13, 19. Am 7:2-5.
  pouring out. Ezk +7:8.
9 **The iniquity**. Ezk 7:23. 22:2-12, 25-31. Dt
  31:29. 32:5, 15-22. 2 K 17:7, etc. 2 Ch 36:14-
  16. Is 1:4. 59:2-8, 12-15. Je 5:1-9. 7:8, 9. Mi
  3:9-12. Zp 3:1-4.
  and the land. Ezk 8:17. 2 K 21:16. 24:4. Je
  2:34. 22:17. La 4:13, 14. Mt 23:35-37. Lk
  11:50.
  full of. Heb. filled with. 2 K 15:35.
  perverseness. *or*, wresting of *judgment*. Ezk
  22:27-29. Mi 3:1-3. 7:3, 4. Hab +1:4mg.
  The Lord hath. Ezk 8:12. Jb 22:13. Ps 10:11.
  94:7. Is 29:15.
10 **mine**. ver. 5. Ezk 5:11. 7:4. 8:18. 21:31, 32. 2
  K 24:4.
  but. Ezk 7:8, 9. 11:21. 22:31. Dt 32:41. 2 Ch
  6:23. Is 65:6. Ho 9:7. Jl 3:4. He 10:30.
11 **reported the matter**. Heb. returned the
  word. Pr +22:12mg.
  I have. Ps 103:20. Is 46:10, 11. Zc 1:10, 11.
  6:7, 8. Re 16:2, 17.

EZEKIEL 10

1 **I looked**. Is 21:8, 9. Hab 2:1.
  in the. Ezk 1:22-26. Ex 24:10. Ep 1:22. Re
  4:2, 3.
  above. ver. 20. Ezk 11:22. Ps 18:10. 68:17,
  18. Ep 1:20. 1 P 3:22.
  as the. Ezk 1:22, 26. Ge 18:2, 17, 22, 31.
  32:24, 30. Jsh 5:13-15. 6:2. Jg 13:6, 8, 18-22.
  Jn 1:18. Re 1:13-18.
  throne. Ex 24:*10.* He +1:8. Re 3:21. 4:1-10.
2 **unto**. ver. 7. Ezk 9:2, 3, 11.
  Go. ver. 8-13, 16. Ezk 1:15-20.
  thine hand. Heb. the hollow of thine hand.
  coals. Ezk 1:13. Ex 9:8-10. Ps 18:12, 13.
  140:10. Is 6:6, 7. Re 8:5.

scatter. Ezk 20:47, 48. 24:9-14. 2 K 25:9. Is
  30:30. Je 24:8-10.
3 **and the cloud**. ver. 8. Ezk 9:3. 43:4. Ex
  +13:21.
4 **the glory**. ver. 18. Ezk +1:28. Is +40:5.
  went up. Heb. was lifted up.
  and the house. Ezk 43:5. Ex +13:21. Hg 2:9.
  Re 15:8.
5 **the sound**. Ezk 1:24.
  outer. Ezk 46:21. 1 K 7:9. 2 Ch 4:9.
  the voice. Ezk 1:24. Ex 19:16, 19. 20:18, 19.
  Dt 4:12, 13. Jb 37:2-5. 40:9. Ps 18:13. 29:3-9.
  68:33. 77:17, 18. Is 30:30. Jn 12:28, 29. He
  12:18, 19. Re 10:3, 4. 11:12, 15, 19.
  Almighty God. Ge +17:1.
6 **that when**. ver. 2. Ps 80:1. 99:1.
7 **stretched forth**. Heb. sent forth.
  unto the. ver. 6. Ezk 1:13.
  and went. Ezk 41:23-28. Is 6:6. Mt 13:41,
  42, 49, 50. 24:34, 35. Re 8:5.
8 **the form**. ver. 21. Ezk 1:8. Is 6:6.
9 **behold**. Ezk 1:15-17.
  as the. Da 10:6. Re 21:20.
  a beryl. or, a stone of Tarshish.
10 **as if**. Ezk 1:16. Jb 23:13. Ps 36:6. 97:2.
  104:24. Ro 11:33.
11 **they went upon**. ver. 22. Ezk 1:17.
  whither. Ezk 1:20. Mt 8:8-10.
12 **body**. Heb. flesh. Ps 102:5mg.
  were. Ezk 1:18. Col 1:12. Re 4:6, 8.
13 **it was cried**, etc. *or*, they were called in my
  hearing, Wheel, *or*, Galgal. ver. 2. Ezk 23:24.
  26:10. Ps 77:18. 83:13. Ec 12:6. Is 5:28. 17:13.
  Je 47:3. Da 7:9.
14 **every**. ver. 21. Ezk 1:6-10. 1 K 7:29, 36. Re
  4:7.
  the face of a cherub. Ezk 1:10.
15 **lifted**. ver. 18, 19. Ezk 8:6. 11:22. Ho 9:12.
  This. ver. 20. Ezk 1:5, 13, 14. 43:3.
16 **And when**. Ezk 1:19-21.
17 **When**. Ep +1:11.
  for. Ezk 1:12, 20, 21.
  spirit. Heb. *ruach*, Ps +104:4.
  of the living creature. *or*, of life. Ge 2:7. Ro
  8:2. Re 11:11.
18 **the glory**. ver. 4. Ezk 7:20-22. Ps 78:60, 61.
  80:1. Je 6:8. 7:12-14. Ho 9:12. Mt 23:37-39.
  and stood. ver. 3, 4. Ge 3:24. 2 K 2:11. Ps
  18:10. 68:17, 18.
19 **the cherubims**. Ezk 1:17-21. Ge +3:24.
  of the east. Ezk 8:16. 43:4.
  and the glory. ver. 1. Ezk 1:26-28.
20 **the living**. ver. 15. Ezk 1:22-28. 3:23.
  the river. Ezk 1:1.
  and I. 1 K 6:29-35. 7:36.
21 **had four**. ver. 14. Ezk 1:8-10. 41:18, 19. Re
  4:7.
  and the. ver. 8.
22 **the likeness**. Ezk 1:10. Ex 25:18-20, 40.
  they went. ver. 11. Ezk 1:12. Ho 14:9.

EZEKIEL 11

1 **the spirit**. Heb. *ruach*, Is +48:16. ver. 24. Ezk +8:3. 41:1.
the east gate. Ezk 10:19. 43:4.
eastward. S#6921h. Ezk 17:10. 40:6, 10, 19, 22, 23, 32, 44. 41:14. 42:9, 10, 12, 15, 16. 43:1, 2, 4, 17. 44:1. 45:7. 46:1, 12. 47:1, 2, 3, 18. 48:1-8, 10, 16-18, 21, 23, 24, 25, 26, 27, 32. Ge +41:6.
behold. Ezk 8:16.
gate. Ge +14:7.
five and. Is 43:28. Je 38:4.
Jaazaniah. 2 K +25:23.
Pelatiah. ver. 13. Ezk 22:27. Is 1:10, 23. Ho 5:10.
2 **these are**. Est 8:3. Ps 2:1, 2. 36:4. 52:2. Is 30:1. 59:4. Je 5:5. 18:18. Mi 2:1, 2.
3 **Which say**. Je 28:1-17.
It is not, etc. *or, It is* not *for us* to build houses near. Ezk 7:7. 12:22, 27. Is 5:19. Je 1:11, 12. Am 6:3, 5. 2 P 3:4.
this city. ver. 7-11. Ezk 24:3-14. Je 1:13.
4 **prophesy against**. Ezk 13:2, etc., 17, etc. 20:46, 47. 21:2. 25:2. Is 58:1. Ho 6:5. 8:1.
5 **the Spirit**. Heb. *ruach*, Ge +41:38. Ezk 2:2. 3:24, 27. 8:1. Nu 11:25, 26. 1 S 10:6, 10. Ac 10:44. 11:15.
Speak. Ezk 1:3. 2:4, 5, 7. 3:11. Is 58:1. 2 P 1:21.
Thus have. Ezk 28:2. 29:3. 38:11. Ps 50:21. Is 28:15. Ml 3:13, 14. Mk 3:22-30. Ja 3:6.
for I know. Ezk 38:10. Je 16:17. 17:10. 29:11. Jn +2:25.
mind. Heb. *ruach*, spirit, Ge +26:35.
6 **have multiplied**. Ezk 7:23. 9:9. 22:2-6, 9, 12, 27. 24:6-9. 2 K 21:16. Is 1:15. Je 2:30, 34. 7:6, 9. La 4:13. Ho 4:2, 3. Mi 3:2, 3, 10. 7:2. Zp 3:3. Mt 23:35.
7 **Your**. Ezk 24:3-13. Mi 3:2, 3.
but. ver. 3, 9-11. 2 K 25:18-22. Je 52:24-27.
8 **have feared**. Jb 3:25. 20:24. Pr 10:24. Is 24:17, 18. 30:16, 17. 66:4. Je 38:19-23. 42:14-16. 44:12, 13. Am 9:1-4. Jn 11:48. 1 Th 2:15, 16.
9 **and deliver**. Ezk 21:31. Dt 28:36, 49, 50. 2 K 24:4. Ne 9:36, 37. Ps 106:41. Je 5:15-17. 39:6.
and will. Ezk 5:8, 10, 15. 16:38, 41. 30:19. Ps 106:30. Ec 8:11. Jn 5:27. Ro 13:4. Ju 15.
10 **fall**. 2 K 25:19-21. Je 39:6. 52:9, 10, 24-27.
in the border. Nu 34:8, 9. Jsh 13:5. 1 K 8:65. 2 K 14:25. 25:18-21. Je 52:24-27.
and ye. Ezk +6:7. Ps 9:16. Je 9:24.
11 **This city**. ver. 3, 7-10.
the border. ver. 10. Je 39:5-7. 52:9, 10.
12 **shall know**. Ps 9:16.
for ye have not walked. *or,* which have not walked. ver. 21. Ezk 20:16, 21, 24. Le 26:40. 1 K 11:33. 2 K 21:22. Ezr 9:7. Ne 9:34. Ps 78:10. Je 6:16. Da 9:10.
but. Ezk 8:10, 14, 16. 16:44-47. Le 18:3, 24-

28. Dt 12:30, 31. 2 K 16:3, 10, 11. 17:11, etc. 18:12. 21:2. 2 Ch 13:9. 28:3. 33:2-9. 36:14. Ps 106:35-39. Je +10:2.
13 **when**. ver. 1. Ezk 37:7. Nu 14:35-37. Dt 7:4. 1 K 13:4. Pr 6:15. Je 28:15-17. Ho 6:5. Ac 5:5, 10. 13:11.
Then. Dt 9:18, 19. Jsh 7:6-9. 1 Ch 21:16, 17. Ps 106:23. 119:120.
Ah. Ezk 9:8. Am 7:2, 5.
full end. Je +4:27. 5:10, 18. Ro 11:4, 5.
15 **thy brethren**. Je 24:1-5.
Get. 1 S 26:19. Is 65:5. 66:5. Jn 16:2.
unto. Ezk 33:24.
16 **Thus saith**. Le 26:44. Dt 30:3, 4. 2 K 24:12-16. Ps 44:11. 84:11. Je 24:5, 6. 30:11. 31:10.
as a. Ps 31:20. 61:3. 90:1. 91:1, 9, etc. Pr 18:10. Is 4:5. 8:14. Je 29:7, 11. 42:11.
17 **gather you**. Ezk 28:25. Is +52:12mg. Je 3:12, 18. +23:3. 24:5. Mk 13:27. 2 Th 2:1.
the land of Israel. Ezk +21:2. +37:25.
18 **shall take away**. ver. 21. Ezk 5:11. 7:20. 37:23. 43:7, 8. Is 1:25-27. 30:22. Je 16:18. Ho 14:8. Mi 5:10-14. Col 3:5-8. T 2:12.
19 **I will give**. Dt +30:6. 2 Ch 30:12. Je 24:7. Zp 3:9. Jn 17:21-23. Ac 4:32. 1 C 1:10. Ep 4:3-6. Ph 2:1-5.
I will put. Ezk 18:31. 2 K 22:19. Ps 51:10. Lk 11:13. Jn 14:26. Ro +12:2. 2 C 5:17. Ga 6:15. Ep 4:23.
spirit. Heb. *ruach*, Ge +41:38; Ps +51:10.
I will take. Ezk 36:26, 27. Is 48:4. Zc 7:12. Ro 2:4, 5.
heart of flesh. 2 C 3:3.
20 **they may**. ver. 12. Dt +4:1. 12:30, 31. Ro 16:26. 1 C 11:2. T 2:11, 12.
and they. Ge +17:7. Ho 2:23.
21 **whose**. Ec 11:9. Je 17:9. Mk 7:21-23. He +3:12, 13. 10:38. Ja 1:14, 15. Ju 19.
their detestable. ver. 18. Je 1:16. 2:20.
I will. Ezk 9:10. 20:31, 38. 22:31. Ex 34:7. Is 63:10. Je 29:16-19. Ga 6:7.
22 **the cherubims**. Ezk 1:19, 20. Ge +3:24.
23 **the glory**. Ezk +1:28. Ho 9:12. Zc 14:4. Mt 23:37-39. 24:1, 2.
went up. Lk 24:50. Ac 1:9.
which. Ezk 43:2. Zc 14:4.
24 **the spirit**. Heb. *ruach*, Is +48:16. ver. +1.
into. Ezk 1:3. 3:12, 15. Ps 137:1.
So. Ge 17:22. 35:13. Ac 10:16.
25 **I spake**. Ezk 2:7. 3:4, 17, 27.

EZEKIEL 12

2 **thou**. Ezk 2:3, 6-8. 3:9, 26, 27. 17:12. 24:3. 44:6. Dt 9:7, 24. 31:27. Ps 78:40. Is 1:23. 30:1, 9. 65:2. Je 4:17. 5:23. 9:1-6. Da 9:5-9. Ac 7:51, 52.
which have. Pr 18:1. Is 29:9-12. 42:19, 20. Mk 8:17, 18. Lk +8:10. Jn 9:39-41. 2 C 3:14.

4:3, 4. 8:12. 2 Th 2:10, 11. He 5:14. 6:1. 2 P +3:18.
for. Ezk 2:5.

3 **prepare**. ver. 10-12. Ezk 4:1, etc. Je 13:1, etc. 18:2, etc. 19:1, etc. 27:2.
stuff. *or*, instruments. Je 46:19mg.
it may. Ezk 33:11. Dt 5:29. 32:29. Ps 81:13. Je 18:11. 25:4-7. 26:3. 36:3, 7. Lk 13:8, 9, 34. 20:13. 2 T 2:25.

4 **at even**. ver. 12. 2 K 25:4. Je 39:4. 52:7.
they that go forth into. Heb. the goings forth of.

5 **Dig thou**. Heb. Dig for thee. 2 K 25:4. Je 39:2-4.

6 **cover**. Ge +27:16. 1 S 28:8. 2 S 15:30. Jb 24:17.
for I. ver. 11. Ezk 2:8. 4:3. 24:24. Is 8:18. 20:2-4.

7 **I did so**. Ezk 2:8. 24:18. 37:7, 10. Je 32:8-12. Mt 21:6, 7. Mk 14:16. Jn 2:5-8. +15:14. Ac 26:19.
I brought. ver. 3-6.
digged. Heb. digged for me.
in their sight. Ps 71:7.

9 **the rebellious**. ver. 1-3. Ezk 2:5-8.
What. Ezk 17:12. 20:49. 24:19. Re 3:15, 16.

10 **This**. 2 K 9:25. Is 13:1. 14:28. Ml 1:1.
prince. That is, Zedekiah king of Judah. Ezk 7:27. 17:13-21. 21:25-27. Je 21:7. 24:8. 38:18.

11 **I am**. ver. 6.
remove and go. Heb. by removing go. Je 15:2. 52:15, 28-30.

12 **the prince**. ver. 6. 2 K 25:4. Je 39:4. 52:7.

13 **My net**. Ezk 19:8, 9. 32:3. Jb 19:6. Ps 9:16. 11:6. Is 24:17, 18. Je 50:24. La 1:13. 3:47. Ho 7:12. Lk 21:35.
and I. Je +21:7.
bring him. 2 K +5:19.

14 **I will scatter**. Ezk 5:10-12. 17:21. 2 K 25:4, 5.
I will draw. Je +12:12.

15 **they shall know**. ver. 16, 20. Ezk 5:13. +6:7. 33:33. Ps 9:16.
scatter. Je +9:16.

16 **I will leave**. 2 K 24:14. 25:12. Is 24:13. Je 4:27. 30:11. +42:2. Am 9:8, 9. Mi +4:7. Mt 7:14. 24:22.
a few men. Heb. men of number. Ge 13:16. 34:30. Is 10:19, +20mg. Ro 9:27.
that they. Ezk 14:22, 23. 36:31. Le 26:40, 41. Je 3:24, 25. Da 9:5-12.
and they. Dt 29:24-28. 1 K 9:6-9. Je 22:8, 9.

18 **eat thy bread with**. Ezk 4:16, 17. 23:33. Le 26:26, 36. Dt 28:48, 65. Jb 3:24. Ps 60:2, 3. 80:5. 102:4-9.

19 **with carefulness**. 1 K 17:10-12.
that her. Ezk 36:3. Je +18:16. 32:43. Zc 7:14.
all that is therein. Heb. the fulness thereof. Ps 24:1. 1 C 10:26, 28.

because. Ezk 7:23. Ge 6:11-13. Ps 107:34. Je 6:7. Mi 3:10-12.

20 **the cities**. Ezk 15:6-8. Le 26:31. Is 3:26. 7:23, 24. 24:3, 12. 64:10, 11. Je 4:7, 23-29. 12:10-12. 16:9. 19:11. 24:8-10. 25:9. 34:22. La 5:18. Da 9:17.

22 **what**. Ezk 18:2, 3. Je 23:33-40.
The days. ver. 27. Ezk 11:3. Is 5:19. Je 5:12, 13. Am 6:3. 2 P 3:3, 4.

23 **I will**. Ezk 18:3. Is 28:22.
proverb. Dt +28:37.
The days. ver. 25. Ezk 7:2, 5-7, 10-12. Jl 2:1. Zp 1:14. Ml 4:1. Mt 24:34. Ja 5:8, 9.

24 **no more**. Ezk 13:23. 1 K 22:11-13, 17. Je 14:13-16. 23:14-29. La 2:14. Zc 13:2-4. 2 P 2:2, 3.
flattering. Ps +12:3.

25 **I will**. ver. 28. Ezk 6:10. Nu 14:28-34. Is 14:24. 55:11. La 2:17. Da 9:12. Zc 1:6. Mt 24:35. Lk 21:13, 33.
in your. Je 16:9. Hab 1:5. Mk 13:30, 31.
O rebellious. ver. 1, 2.

27 **for**. ver. 22. Is 28:14, 15. Da 10:14. 2 P 3:4.

28 **There shall**. ver. 23-25. Nu 23:19. Je 4:7. 44:28. Mt 24:48-51. Mk 13:32-37. Lk 21:34-36. 1 Th 5:2, 3. Re 3:3.

EZEKIEL 13

2 **prophesy against**. Ezk 14:9, 10. 22:25, 28. 2 Ch 18:18-24. Is 9:15. 56:9-12. Je 5:30, 31. 6:13, 14. 8:10. 14:13-15. 23:2, 11-22, 25, 26. 27:14, 18. 28:12-17. 29:8, 9, 22, 23. 37:19. La 4:13. Mi 3:6, 11. Zp 3:4. 2 P 2:1-3.
prophesy out of. Heb. are prophets out of. ver. 3, 17. Nu +16:28. Je 14:14. 23:16, 26.
Hear. Je +7:2. 28:15.

3 **Woe**. ver. 18. Ezk 34:2. Je 23:1. Mt 23:13-29. Lk 11:42-47, 52. 1 C 9:16.
foolish. Pr 15:2, 14. La 2:14. Ho 9:7. Zc 11:15. Mt 23:16-26. Lk 11:40. 1 T 6:4. 2 T 3:9.
follow. Heb. walk after. Je +17:16mg.
spirit. Heb. *ruach*, Ge +41:8; Ge +26:10. Mk +2:8.
have seen nothing. *or*, *things which* they have not seen. ver. 6, 7. Je 23:28-32.

4 **like**. SS 2:15. Mi 2:11. 3:5. Mt 7:15. Ro 16:18. 2 C 11:13-15. Ga 2:4. Ep 4:14. 2 Th 2:9, 10. 1 T 4:1, 2. T 1:10-12. Re 13:11-14. 19:20.

5 **have not**. Ezk 22:30. Ex 17:9-13. 32:11, 12. Nu 16:21, 22, 47, 48. 1 S 12:23, 30. Ps 106:23, 30. Je 15:1. 23:22. 27:18. Ml 1:9.
gaps. *or*, breaches. Is 58:12. La 2:13, 14. Am 4:3.
made up the hedge. Heb. hedged the hedge. Ge +1:29. Nu 22:24. Ps 80:12. Is 5:5. Ho 2:6mg.
to stand. Jb 40:9. Ps 76:7. Is 27:4. Ep 6:13, 14. Re 16:14. 20:8, 9.
the day. Ezk 7:7. +30:3. Zp 2:2, 3.

6 **have seen**. ver. 23. Ezk 12:23, 24. 22:28. La 2:14. 2 P 2:18.
lying. Dt +18:10. Je +27:9.
saying. ver. 7. Je 23:31, 32. 28:2, 15.
made. ver. 22. 1 K 22:6, 27, 37. Pr 14:15. Je 29:31. 37:19. Mk 13:6, 22, 23. 2 Th 2:11.

7 **The Lord**. ver. 2, 3, 6. Ezk 2:5-7. Je 23:21. Mt 24:23, 24.

8 **behold**. Ezk +15:7. Ps 5:6. 1 T 4:1, 8.

9 **mine**. Ezk 11:13. 14:9, 10. Ps 101:7. Je 20:3-6. 28:15-17. 29:21, 22, 31, 32. Re 19:20.
assembly. or, secret, or council. Je 23:18mg.
neither shall they be. Ezr 2:59, 62, 63. Ne 7:62, 64. Ps 87:6. Ho 9:3. Re +3:5.
neither shall they enter. Ezk 20:38.
and ye. ver. 14. Ezk +6:7. 1 K 22:24, 25. Je 23:20.

10 **seduced**. 2 K 21:9. Pr 12:26. Je 23:13-15. 1 T 4:1. 2 T 3:13. 1 J 2:26. Re 2:20.
Peace. ver. 16. Ezk 23:42. 1 K +13:9, 18. Ps 123:4. Is 57:21. Je 4:10. 6:14. 8:11, 15. 14:13. 23:17. 28:9. Am 6:1. Ml 3:15.
a wall. or, a slight wall.
others. ver. 11, 14, 15. Ezk 22:28. Le 14:42. 2 Ch 18:12. Is 30:10. 44:18mg. Je 5:31. Mi 2:11. Mt 23:27. Ac 23:3.

11 **there shall**. Ezk 38:22. Jb 27:21. Ps 11:6. 18:13, 14. 32:6. Is 25:4. 28:2, 15-18. 29:6. 32:19. Na 1:3, 7, 8. Mt 7:25, 27. Lk 6:48, 49.
hailstones. ver. +13.

12 **Where**. Dt 32:37. Jg 9:38. 10:14. 2 K 3:13. Je 2:28. 29:31, 32. 37:19. La 2:14, 15.

13 **a stormy**. Le 26:28. Ps +83:15. 107:25. 148:8. Jon 1:4.
and great hailstones. ver. 11. Is +28:17.

14 **the foundation**. Ps 11:3. Mi 1:6. Hab 3:13. Mt 7:26, 27. Lk 6:49. 1 C 3:11-15.
ye shall be. Je 6:15. 8:12. 14:15. 23:15.
and ye shall know. ver. 9, 21, 23. Ezk +6:7.

15 **The wall**. Ne 4:3. Ps 62:3. Is 30:13.

16 **visions of peace**. ver. +10. Je 5:31. 29:31. 1 Th 5:3.
no peace. Is +48:22.

17 **set thy**. Ezk 4:3. 14:8. 20:46. 21:2. 29:2. 38:2.
the daughters. Is 3:16, etc. 4:4.
prophesy. Ex +15:20. 2 P 2:1.
out of. ver. +2. Nu +16:28. Re 2:20.

18 **Woe**. ver. 3.
that sew. ver. 10, 16. 2 K 23:7. Is 26:11. 52:10. Je 4:10. 6:14. 2 T 4:3.
armholes. or, elbows.
hunt souls. Heb. nephesh, Ge +12:5. Ezk 22:25. Pr 6:26. Ep 4:14. 2 P 2:14.
will ye save. ver. 22.
souls. Heb. nephesh, Ge +12:13.

19 **pollute**. Ezk 20:39. 22:26.
for handfuls. 1 S 2:16, 17, 29. Pr 28:21. 30:15. Is 56:11. Ho 4:8, 18. Mi 3:5, 11. 7:3. Ml 1:10. Ro 16:18. 1 P 5:2, 3. 2 P 2:3, 13-15.

to slay. ver. 22. Pr +19:27. Mt 23:15. Ro 14:15. 1 C 8:11.
souls. Heb. nephesh, Ge +12:13.
to save. Je 23:14, 17.
souls. Heb. nephesh, Jsh +10:28.
by your lying. Pr 21:6.

20 **I am against**. ver. 8, 9, 15, 16. Pr 6:16-19. Am 6:1.
to make them fly. or, into gardens. Ezk +8:14. Nu 17:8. SS 6:11. 7:12. Is +66:17.
and will. 2 T 3:8, 9.

21 **and ye shall**. ver. +9.

22 **with lies**. Ezk 9:4. Ge 3:4. Dt 29:19. Ps +14:1. Pr 12:19, 22. Je 4:10. 14:13-17. 23:9, 14. La 2:11-14. Jn 8:44. He +3:12. 2 P 3:5. Re +21:8.
and strengthened. Je 23:14. 27:14-17. 28:16. 29:32.
by promising him life. or, that I should save his life. Heb. by quickening him. ver. 16. Ge 3:4, 5. Je 6:14. 8:11. 23:17. Mt +6:23. +23:15. 2 P 2:18, 19.

23 **ye shall see**. ver. 6, etc. Ezk 12:24. Dt 18:20. Mi 3:6, 7. Zc 13:3, 4. 2 T 3:9.
for I. ver. 21. Ezk 34:10. Mt 24:24. Mk 13:22. 1 C 11:19. Ju 24. Re 12:9, 11. 13:5, 8. 15:2.
and ye. ver. +9, 21.

EZEKIEL 14

1 **certain**. Jsh +20:1.
and sat. Ezk 33:31. Jg 20:26. Is 29:13. Lk 10:39. Ac 22:3.

2 **the word**. 1 K 14:4, 5. Am +3:7.

3 **these men**. ver. 4, 7. Ezk 6:9. 11:21. 20:16. 36:25. Je 17:1, 2, 9. Ep 5:5.
idols in their heart. Ezk 8:17, 18. 20:31. Is 16:12. Je 11:11-14. Ho 5:6, 7. Mk 7:21-23. Ep 5:5. Ph +3:19. Col 3:5. 1 T +6:9-11, 17-19. 1 J 5:21.
and put. Je 44:16-18. 1 C +8:9.
should. Ezk 20:3. 1 S 28:6. 2 K 3:13. Ps +66:18. 101:3. Pr 21:27. Is 33:15. Je 7:8-11, +16. 42:20, 21. Lk 20:8.

4 **speak**. Ezk 2:7. 3:4, 17-21.
I the Lord. ver. 7. 1 K 21:20-25. 22:19-22. 2 K 1:16. Is 3:11. 66:4.

5 **I may**. ver. 9, 10. Ho 10:2. Zc 7:11-14. 2 Th 2:9-11.
estranged. Dt 32:15, 16. Is 1:4mg. Je 2:5, 11-13, 31, 32. Zc 11:8. Ro 1:21-23, 28, 30. 8:7. Ga 6:7. Ep 4:18. Col 1:21. He +3:12.
through. Col 3:5, 6. 2 Th 2:11, 12.

6 **Repent**. 1 S 7:3. 1 K 8:47-49. Ne 1:8, 9. Is 55:6, 7. Je 8:5, 6. 31:18-20. 50:4, 5. La 3:39-41. Ho 14:1-3, 8. Jon 3:7-9. Lk +13:3.
yourselves. or, others.
turn. ver. 4. Ezk 8:16. 16:63. 36:31, 32. 2 Ch 29:6. Is 2:20. 30:22. Je 13:27. Zp 3:11. Ro 6:21.

7 **of the stranger**. Ezk +47:22. Le 20:2. 24:22. Nu 15:15, 16, 29. Je 22:3.

separateth. Ho 4:14. 9:10. Ju 19.
and setteth. ver. 3, 4.
and cometh. Ezk 33:30-32. 2 K 8:8, etc. Is
58:1, 2. Je 21:1, 2. 37:1-3, 9, 10, 17. 38:14-
23.
by. ver. 4, 7, 8.

8 I will set. Ezk +15:7.
a sign. Ezk 5:15. Nu +26:10. Is 65:15.
proverb. Dt +28:37.
I will cut. Ge 17:14. Ex 12:15, 19. 30:33, 38.
Le 7:20, 21, 25, 27. 17:4, 9. 19:8. 20:3. 22:3.
23:29. Nu 9:13. 19:20. Ps 37:22. Ro 11:22. 1 C
10:11.
and ye. Ezk +6:7.

9 if the. Ezk 20:25. 2 S 12:11, 12. 1 K 22:20-
23. Jb 12:16. Ps 81:11, 12. Is 63:17. 66:4. Je
4:10. 2 Th 2:9-12.
I the Lord have deceived. Ge +31:7. Is
+45:7. Je 20:7. Am +3:6. 2 Th 2:11.
and I will. Ex +7:5.

10 they shall bear. Ezk 17:18-20. 23:49. Ge
4:13. Ex 28:38. Le 5:1, 17. Nu 5:31. 14:34.
31:8. Mi 7:9. Ga 6:5.
the punishment. ver. 4:7, 8. Dt 13:1-10.
17:2-7. Je 6:14, 15. 8:11, 12. +14:15. Re
19:19-21.
punishment of him that seeketh. Pr
+19:27. Is +8:20. Je +18:15. Mt 10:41.
+15:14. Mk +4:24. Ro 14:12. 1 C 11:19. 1 T
4:16. 2 P 3:17.

11 the house. Ezk 34:10. 44:10, 15. 48:11. Dt
13:11. 19:20. Ps 119:67. +130:8. Is 9:16. Je
23:15. 50:6. 2 P 2:15, 22.
neither be. Ezk 11:18-20. 36:25-29. 37:23.
that they. Ge +17:7.

13 when. Ezk 9:9. Ezr 9:6. Is 24:20. La 1:8, 20.
Da 9:5, 10-12.
land. Ge +6:11.
trespassing. Le 5:15. 6:2. 26:40. Nu 5:6, 12,
27.
break. Le +26:26.
and will cut. ver. 17, 19, 21. Ezk 25:13. Ge
6:7. Je 7:20. 32:43. 36:29.

14 these. ver. 16, 18, 20.
Noah. Ge +5:29.
Daniel. Ezk 28:3. Da 9:21. 10:11. Mt 24:15.
Job. Jb 1:5, 8. 42:8, 9. Je +7:16. 11:14. 14:11,
12. 15:1.
deliver. ver. +20. Pr 10:2. 11:4. 2 P 2:9.
souls. Heb. *nephesh*, Ge +12:13.

15 noisome. Ezk 5:17.
spoil. *or*, bereave. Ezk 36:12. Le 26:22.

16 these. ver. 14, 18. Mt 18:19, 20. Ja 5:16.
in it. Heb. in the midst of it. ver. 9, 14, 18, 20.
as I live. ver. 20. Dt +32:40.
they shall. Ge 18:23-33. 19:29. Jb 22:30. Ac
27:24. He 11:7.

17 I bring. Ezk 29:8. 32:11. Jb 27:14. Je +12:12.
25:9. Re 6:3, 4.
a sword. Ex +5:3.

so that. ver. 13. Ezk 25:13. Je 33:12. Ho 4:3.
Zp 1:3.

18 Though. ver. +14.

19 if I. Ezk 5:12, 17. 38:22. Nu 14:12. 16:46-50.
Dt 28:21, 22, 59-61. 2 S 24:13, 15. 1 K 8:37. 2
Ch 6:28. 7:13. 20:9. Ps 91:3, 6. Is 37:36. Je
14:12. 21:6, 9. 24:10. Am 4:10. Mt 24:7.
and pour. Ezk +7:8.

20 Noah. ver. 14, 16.
Daniel. ver. 14.
souls. Heb. *nephesh*, Ge +12:13.
by. Ezk +18:20, 22. Jb 5:19-24. Ps 33:18, 19.
Ho 10:12. Zp 2:3. Ac 10:35. 1 J 2:29. 3:7, 10.

21 How much more when. *or*, Also when.
my four. ver. 13, 15, 17, 19. 1 K +8:37. Pr
10:2. Je +12:12.

22 behold, therein. Le +26:44. 2 Ch 36:20. Is
17:4-6. 24:13. 40:1, 2. 65:8, 9. Je 5:19. 52:27-
30. Mi +5:3. Mk 13:20. He 12:6-11.
ye shall see. Ezk 6:9, 10. 16:63. 20:43. 36:31.
Je 31:17-21.
ye shall be. Je 3:21-25.

23 shall comfort. Is 40:1, 2.
that I have not. Ezk 8:6-18. 9:8, 9. Ge
18:22-33. Dt 8:2. Ne 9:33. Pr 26:2. Je 7:17-28.
22:8, 9. Da 9:7, 14. Ro 2:5. Re 15:4. 16:6.
have done. Ps 39:9. Is 38:15. Mk 7:37. Jn 13:7.

EZEKIEL 15

2 What. Dt 32:32, 33. Ps 80:8-16. SS 2:13, 15.
6:11. 7:12. 8:11, 12. Is 5:1-7. Je 2:21. Ho 10:1.
Mt 21:33-41. Mk 12:1-9. Lk 20:9-16. Jn 15:1-
6.
among. Is 44:23. Mi 3:12. Zc 11:2.

3 wood. Je 24:8. Mt 5:13. Mk 9:50.
men take. Jn 15:5, 6.
pin. Ex +27:19.

4 it is cast. Ps 80:8, 14-16. Is 27:11. Jn 15:6. He
6:8.
the fire. Is 1:31. Am 4:11. Ml 4:1. Mt 3:12.
He 12:28, 29.
Is it meet. Heb. Will it prosper.

5 meet. Heb. made fit. Je +3:16mg.

6 As the vine. ver. 2. Ezk 17:3-10. 20:47, 48. Is
5:1-6, 24, 25. Je 4:7. 7:20. 21:7. 24:8-10.
25:9-11, 18. 44:21-27. Zc 1:6.
so will I give. 2 K 25:9.

7 I will set. Ezk 5:8. 13:8. 14:8. 21:3. 26:3.
28:22. 29:3, 10. 35:3. 38:3. 39:1. Le 17:10.
20:3-6. 26:17. Ps 34:16. Je 21:10, 13. 44:11.
50:31. 51:25. Na 2:13. 3:5. 1 P 3:12.
they shall. 1 K 19:17. Is 24:18. Je 48:43, 44.
Am 5:19. 9:1-4.
and ye shall. Ezk +6:7. 16:62. 17:21, 24.
20:12, 20, 38, 42, 44. 21:5. 22:16, 22. +23:49.

8 I will. Ezk 6:14. 14:13-21. 33:29. Is 6:11.
24:3-12. Je 25:10, 11. Zp 1:18.
committed a trespass. Heb. trespassed a
trespass. Ezk 14:13. 2 Ch 36:14-16.

EZEKIEL 16

2 **cause**. Ezk 20:4. 22:2. 23:36. 33:7-9. Is 58:1.
Ho 8:1.
abominations. Ezk 8:9-17.

3 **Thy birth**. Heb. Thy cutting out, *or* habitation. ver. 45. Ezk 21:30. 29:14. Ge 11:25, 29.
Jsh 24:14. Ne 9:7. Is 1:10. 51:1, 2. Mt 3:7.
11:24. Lk 3:7. Jn 8:44. Ep 2:3. 1 J 3:10.
the land. Ge 15:18-21.
Amorite. Ge +10:16.
Hittite. Dt +20:17.

4 **for**. Ezk 20:8, 13. Ge 15:13. Ex 1:11-14. 2:23,
24. 5:16-21. Dt 5:6. 15:15. Jsh 24:2. Ne 9:7-9.
Ho 2:3. Ac 7:6, 7.
to supple thee. *or*, when I looked *upon
thee*.
nor swaddled. La 2:20mg, 22. Lk 2:7, 12.

5 **eye**. Ex 2:6. Is 49:15. La 2:11, 12, 19. 4:3, 4,
10.
but thou. Ge 21:10. Ex 1:22. Nu 19:16. Je
9:21, 22. 22:19.
person. Heb. *nephesh*, soul, Ge +12:5.

6 **and saw**. Ex 2:24, 25. 3:7, 8. Ex 20:2. Ho
11:1. Ac 7:34.
polluted. *or*, trodden under foot. Is 14:19.
51:23. Mi 7:10. Mt 5:13. He 10:29. Re 14:20.
Live. Ezk 20:5-10. Ex 19:4-6. Dt 9:4, 5. Ps
105:10-15, 26-37. Jn 5:25. Ro 9:15. Ep 2:4, 5.
T 3:3-7.

7 **caused**, etc. Heb. made thee a million. Ge
22:17. Ex 1:7. 12:37. Ac 7:17.
excellent ornaments. Heb. ornament of
ornaments. ver. 10-13, 16. Ex 3:22. Dt 1:10.
4:8. 32:10-14. 33:26-29. Ne 9:18-25. Ps 135:4.
147:20. 148:14. 149:2-4. Is 61:10. 62:3.
hair. Is 7:20.
whereas. ver. 22. Jb 1:21. SS 4:5. Ho 2:3, 9,
10. Re 3:17, 18.

8 **thy time**. ver. 6. Dt 7:6-8. Ru 3:9. 1 S
+12:22. Is +41:8, 9. 43:4. 63:7-9. Je 2:2, 3.
31:3. Ho 11:1. Ml 1:2, 3. Ro 5:8. 9:10-13.
and I. Dt 22:30. Ru 3:9.
I sware. Ezk 20:5, 6. Ex 19:4-8. 24:1-8.
32:13. Dt 4:31. Je 2:2, 3. 31:32. Ho 2:18-20.
Ml 2:14.

9 **washed**. ver. 4. Ezk 36:25. Ru 3:3. Ps 51:7. Is
4:4. Jn 13:8-10. 1 C 6:11. 10:2. He 9:10-14. 1
J 5:8. Re 1:5, 6.
blood. Heb. bloods. ver. 6. 2 K +9:26mg.
anointed. Ps 23:5. 2 C 1:21. 1 J 2:20, 27.

10 **clothed**. ver. 7. Ps 45:13, 14. Is 61:3, 10. Lk
15:22. Re 21:2.
broidered. ver. 13, 18. Ex 28:5. 1 P 3:3, 4.
badgers' skin. Ex 25:5. 26:14. Nu 4:6.
I girded. Ex 39:27, 28. Re 7:9-14. 19:8.
covered. Ge 41:42mg. Ex +26:1.

11 **I put**. Ge 24:22, 47, 53.
a chain. Ge 41:42. Pr 1:9. 4:9. SS 1:10. 4:9. Is
3:19. Da 5:7, 16, 29.

12 **forehead**. Heb. nose. Ge 24:22mg. Is 3:21.

earrings. Ge 35:4. Ex 32:2. 35:22. Nu 31:50.
Jg 8:24. Jb 42:11. Pr 25:12. Ho 2:13.
and a. Le 8:9. Est 2:17. Is 28:5. La 5:16. Re
2:10. 4:4, 10.
crown. Jn 19:2.

13 **wast thou**. Is +32:9.
thou didst. ver. 19. Dt 8:8. 32:13, 14. 1 S
12:13. Ps 45:13, 14. 81:16. 147:14. Ho 2:5.
honey. Ex +3:8.
and thou wast. ver. 14, 15. Ps 48:2. 50:2. Is
64:11. Je 13:20.
and thou didst. Ge 17:6. 1 S 12:12. 2 S 8:15.
1 K 4:21. Ezr 4:20. 5:11. Ps 50:2. La 2:15.

14 **thy renown**. Dt 4:6-8, 32-38. Jsh 2:9-11.
9:6-9. 1 K 10:1, etc., 24. 2 Ch 2:11, 12. 9:23.
La 2:15.
beauty. Ps 48:2, 12, 13. 90:17. SS 6:4.
perfect. Ep 1:6.
through. 1 C 4:7.
put upon. Is 52:1.

15 **thou didst**. Ezk 33:13. Dt 32:15. Is 48:1, 2.
Je 7:4. Mi 3:11. Zp 3:11. Mt 3:9.
and playedst. Ezk 20:8. 23:3, 8, 11, 12, etc.
Ex 32:6, etc. Nu 25:1, 2. Jg 2:12, 13. 3:6. 10:6.
1 K 11:5-8. 12:28. 2 K 17:7. 21:3-11. Ps
106:35-39. Is 1:21. 57:8. Je 2:20, 23-28. 3:1,
2, 6, 20. 7:4. Ho 1:2. 4:10-14. Re 17:5.
and pouredst. ver. 25, 36, 37.

16 **of thy garments**. ver. 17, 18. Ezk 7:20. 2 K
23:7. 2 Ch 28:24. Ho 2:8.
high places. 2 K +21:3.
and playedst. Is 1:21.

17 **hast also**. Ezk 7:19. 23:14, etc. Ex 32:1-4. Ho
2:13. 10:1.
men. Heb. a male. Is 57:8. 66:17. Je 30:6mg.
Da 3:1.
and didst. Is 44:19, 20. 57:7, 8. Je 2:27, 28.
3:9. +5:7.

18 **And tookest**. ver. 10. Ho 2:8.

19 **meat**. ver. +13. Dt 32:14-17. Ho 2:8-13.
honey. Ex +3:8.
a sweet savor. Heb. a savor of rest. Ezk 6:13.
Ge +8:21mg.

20 **thy sons**. ver. 21. Ezk 23:4. Ge 17:7. Ex 13:2,
12. Dt 29:11, 12.
and these. Ezk 20:26, 31. 23:37, 39. Jsh
15:8. 2 K 16:3. 2 Ch 33:6. Ps 106:37, 38. Is
57:5. Je 7:31. 32:35. Ho +13:2mg. Mi 6:7.
be devoured. Heb. devour.
Is this. Ezk 8:17. Nu 16:9. Je 2:34, 35.

21 **my children**. Ps 106:37.
to pass. Dt +18:10.

22 **not remembered**. ver. 3-7, 43, 60-63. Je
2:2. Ho 2:3. 11:1.

23 **woe**. Ezk 2:10. 13:3, 18. 24:6. Je 13:27. Zp
3:1. Mt 11:21. 23:13-29. Re 8:13. 12:12.
woe. Ps +42:2. Ro 9:3.

24 **thou hast**. ver. 31, 39. Ezk 20:28, 29. 2 K
21:3-7. 23:5-7, 11, 12. 2 Ch 33:3-7.
eminent place. *or*, brothel house.

and hast. Le 26:30. Ps 78:58. Is 57:5, 7. Je 2:20. 3:2. 17:3.

25 **high place**. 2 K +21:3.
at every. ver. 31. Ge 38:14, 21. Pr 9:14, 15. Is 3:9. Je 2:23, 24. 3:2. 6:15. 11:13.
hast made thy beauty to be abhorred. Ezk 23:9, 10, 32. Re 17:1-5, 12, 13, 16.
opened thy feet. Ge 38:14. Dt 28:57. Jg +3:24. Pr 9:14. 23:28.

26 **with the**. Ezk 8:10, 14. 20:7, 8. 23:3, 8, 19-21. Ex 32:4. Dt 29:16, 17. Jsh 24:14. Is 30:21. Je 2:33.
neighbors. lit. settlers down. Ex 3:22.
great of flesh. or, appetite. ver. +17. Ezk 23:20. Le 15:2, 3.

27 **I have**. Ezk 14:9. Is 5:25. 9:12, 17.
stretched. Ex +7:5.
and have. Dt 28:48-57. Is 3:1. Ho 2:9-12.
thine ordinary. Ge +47:22.
delivered. ver. 37. Ezk 23:22, 25, 28, 29, 46, 47. Ps 106:41. Je 34:21. Re 17:16.
will. Heb. *nephesh*, Ex +15:9.
daughters. *or*, cities. Nu +21:25mg. 2 K 24:2. 2 Ch 28:18, 19. Is 9:12.
which. ver. 47, 57. Ezk 5:6, 7.

28 **hast played**. Ezk 23:5-9, 12, etc. Jg 10:6. 2 K 16:7, 10-18. 21:11. 2 Ch 28:23. Je 2:18, 36. Ho 10:6.

29 **in the land**. Ezk 13:14-23. Jg 2:12-19. 2 K 21:9.
unto. Ezk 23:14, etc.

30 **weak**. Pr 9:13. Is 1:3. Je 2:12, 13. 4:22.
the work. Jg 16:15, 16. Pr 7:11-13, 21. Is 3:9. Je 3:3. Re 17:1-6.

31 **In that thou buildest thine**. *or*, In thy daughters *is* thine, etc. ver. +24, 39.
makest. ver. 25. Ho 12:11.
in that thou scornest. ver. +33, 34. Is 52:3.

32 **as a wife**. ver. 8. Ezk 23:37, 45. Je 2:25, 28. 3:1, 8, 9, 20. Ho 2:2. 3:1. 2 C 11:2, 3.

33 **give**. Ge 38:16-18. Dt 23:17, 18. Ho 2:12. Jl 3:3. Mi 1:7. Lk 15:30.
but thou. Is 30:3, 6, 7. 57:9. Ho 8:9, 10.
hirest. Heb. bribest.

34 **thou givest**. Ho 8:9.
reward. ver. 31, 33, 41. Dt 23:18. Is 23:17, 18. Ho 9:1. Mi 1:7.
no reward. ver. 36.

35 **O harlot**. Is 1:21. 23:15, 16. Je 3:1, 6-8. Ho 2:5. Na 3:4. Jn 4:10, 18. Re 17:5.
hear. Ezk 13:2. 20:47. 34:7. 1 K 22:19. Is 1:10. 28:14. Ho 4:1. Am 7:16.

36 **Because**. ver. 15, etc. Ezk 22:15. 23:8. 24:13. 36:25. La 1:9. Zp 3:1.
filthiness. *Heb.* brass. Ezk 24:11.
and thy. Ezk 23:10, 18, 29. Ge 3:7, 10, 11. Ps 139:11, 12. Je 13:22-26. Re 3:18.
idols. lit. "rolled or dungy ones." Ezk 6:4, 5, 6, 9, 13. 2 K +23:24 (**S#1544h**).
and by. ver. +20, 21. Je 2:34.

37 **I will gather**. Is +3:17. Je 4:30. 22:20. Ho 8:10. Re 17:16.

38 **as women**. Heb. with judgments of women, etc. ver. 40. Ezk 23:45-47. Ge 38:11, 24. Le 20:10. Dt 22:22-24. Mt 1:18, 19. Jn 8:3-5.
shed. ver. 20, 21, 36. Ge 9:6. Ex 21:12. Nu 35:31. 2 K 24:3, 4. Ps 79:3-5. Je 18:21. Na 1:2. Zp 1:17. Re 16:6.

39 **they shall throw**. ver. 24, 25, 31. Ezk 7:22-24. Is 27:9.
shall strip. ver. 10-20. Ezk 23:26, 29. 2 K 25:13-15. Is 3:16-24. Ho 2:3, 9-13.
thy fair jewels. Heb. instruments of thine ornament. ver. 17.

40 **shall also**. Hab 1:6-10. Jn 8:5-7.
and thrust. Ezk 23:10, 47. 24:21. Je 25:9.

41 **burn**. Dt 13:16. Je +17:27. Mi 3:12.
and execute. Ezk 5:8. 23:10, 48. Dt 13:11. 22:21, 24. Jb 34:26.
and I. Ezk 23:27. 37:23. Is 1:25, 26. 2:18. 27:9. Ho 2:6-17. Mi 5:10-14. Zc 13:2. 1 T 5:20.

42 **will I**. 2 S 21:14. Is +59:18. Zc 6:8.
my jealousy. Ex 34:14.
and will. Ezk 39:29. Is 40:1, 2. +54:9, 10.

43 **thou hast**. ver. 22. Ps 78:42. 106:13. Je 2:32.
but hast. Ezk 6:9. Dt 32:21. Ps 78:40, 58, 59. 95:10. Is +63:10. Am 2:13. Ac 7:51. Ep 4:30.
thy way. Ezk +22:31.
thou shalt not. Le 19:29.

44 **proverb**. Dt +28:37.
As is. ver. 3, 45. 1 K 21:26. 2 K 17:11, 15. 21:9. Ezr 9:1. Ps 106:35-38.

45 **that lotheth**. ver. 8, 15, 20, 21. Ezk 23:37-39. Dt 5:9. 12:31. Is 1:4mg. Zc 11:8. Ro 1:30, 31.
your mother. ver. 3.
Amorite. Ge +10:16.

46 **elder**. ver. 51. Ezk 23:4, 11, 31-33. Je 3:8-11. Mi 1:5.
thy younger sister. Heb. thy sister lesser than thou. ver. 48, 49, 53-56, 61. Ge 13:11-13. +18:20, etc. 19:24, 25. Dt 29:23. La 4:6mg. Lk 17:28-30. 2 P 2:6. Ju +7.
her daughters. ver. +27mg. Ezk 26:6. Ge 14:8. 19:29. Ho 11:8.

47 **as if that were a very little thing**. *or*, that was lothed as a small *thing*. Ezk 8:17. 1 K 16:31. Pr 5:14 (almost). The word denotes "quickly, shortly, in a little time."
thou wast. ver. 48, 51. Ezk 5:6, 7. 2 K 21:9, 16. Jn 15:21, 22. 1 C 5:1.

48 **Sodom thy sister**. Mt +10:15. +11:23, 24. Mk 6:11. Lk 10:12. Ac 7:52.

49 **Sodom**. Is 3:9. Mt +10:15.
pride. Ezk 29:3. Ge 19:9. Ps +10:2. Is 16:6.
fulness. Ge 13:10. 18:20. Dt 32:15. Pr 30:9. Is 22:13, 14. Je 5:28. 50:11mg. Am 6:3-6. Mk +4:19. Lk 6:25. 12:16-20. 16:19. 17:28. 21:34. Re 3:17.

abundance of idleness. or, prosperous ease. Dt 6:11, 12. 11:21. Pr 1:32. 10:4. 19:15. +22:29. Is 56:10. Je +48:10mg. Mt 12:36. 20:6, 7. 25:18, 26-30. Lk 12:19. 13:6, 7. 19:20-24. Ac 17:21. Ro +12:11. 2 Th 3:10, 11. 1 T +5:13. He +6:12.

neither. Ezk 34:4. Jb 24:4. Ps +12:5. +62:10. 109:16. Pr 30:14. Is 32:7. Am 2:6. 5:11, 12. Mi 3:2-4. Hab 3:14. Zc 7:10. 11:16. Mt +5:7. 25:43. Lk 16:20, 21. Ja +4:17.

50 and committed. Ge 13:10, 13. 18:20. 19:5. Le 18:22. Dt 23:17. 2 K 23:7. Pr 16:18. 18:12. Ro 1:26, 27. Ju +7.

therefore. Ge +19:24. Re 18:9.

51 Samaria. Lk +12:47, 48. Ro 3:9-20.

justified. Ezk 23:11. Je 3:8-11. Mt 12:41, 42. Re 2:20-22.

52 which hast. ver. 56. Mt 7:1-5. Lk 6:37. Ro 2:1, 10, 26, 27.

bear thine. ver. 54, 63. Ezk 36:6, 7, 15, 31, 32. 39:26. 44:13. Je 23:40. 31:19. 51:51. Ho 10:6. Ro 1:32. 6:21.

they are more. Ge 38:26. 1 S 24:17. 1 K 2:32.

53 bring. ver. 60, 61. Ezk 29:14. 39:25. Dt 30:3. Jb 42:10. Ps 14:7. 85:1. 126:1. Is 1:9. Je 20:16. 31:9, 10, 23. 48:47. 49:6, 39. Jl 3:1.

captivity of Sodom. Ezk 47:8. Zc 14:8.

in the midst. Is 19:24, 25. Je 12:16. Ro 11:23-31.

54 thou mayest. ver. 52, 63. Ezk 36:31, 32. Je 2:26. La 4:6.

in that. Ezk 14:22, 23.

55 Sodom. Is 1:9, 10. 3:9. Je 23:14. Zp 2:9. Re 11:8.

her daughters. Mi 4:8. Zp 3:10, 14. Zc 9:9.

former estate. ver. 53. Ezk 37:1-14. Is 25:7, 8. Je 48:47. Ho 13:14. Ju 7.

then. ver. 53. Ezk 36:11. Is 1:9. Ml 3:4.

56 was not. Is 65:5. Zp 3:11. Lk 15:28-30. 18:11.

mentioned. Heb. for a report, or a hearing. Ezk 7:26. Heb. prides, or excellencies.

57 thy wickedness. ver. 36, 37. Ezk 21:24. 23:18, 19. Ps 50:21. La 4:22. Ho 2:10. 7:1. 1 C 4:5.

reproach. 2 K 16:5-7. 2 Ch 28:5, 6, 18-23. Is 7:1. 14:28.

Syria. Heb. Aram. Ge 10:22, 23. Nu 23:7.

the daughters. ver. 27mg.

despise. or, spoil. Je 33:24.

58 hast. Ezk 23:49. Ge 4:13. La 5:7.

borne. Heb. borne them. Ezk 3:14. 32:8.

59 I will. Ezk 7:4, 8, 9. 14:4. Is 3:11. Je 2:19. Mt 7:1, 2. Ro 2:8, 9.

which. Ezk 17:13-16, 19. Ex 24:1-8. Dt 29:10-15, 25. 2 Ch 34:31, 32. Is 24:5. Je 22:9. 31:32.

60 I will remember. ver. 8. Le +26:42. Je 2:2. Ho 2:15.

I will establish. Is +55:3. Ho 2:19, 20. He 8:10. 12:24.

everlasting. Heb. olam, Ge +17:7.

covenant. Ge +9:16. Is 44:7.

61 remember. ver. 63. Ezk 20:43. 36:31, 32. Ps 119:59. Je 50:4, 5.

be ashamed. Le 26:40, 41. Ezr +9:6.

when. ver. 53-55. SS 8:8, 9. Is 2:2-5. 11:9, 10. Ho 1:9-11. Ro 11:11. 15:8, 9, 16. Ga 4:26, 27. Ep 2:12-14. 3:6.

I will. Is 49:18-23. 54:1, 2. 60:4. 66:7-12. Ga 4:26, etc.

but not. Je 31:31, etc. Jn 15:16. He 8:13.

62 I will. ver. 60. Je 31:31, 32. 50:5. Da 9:27. Ho 2:18-23. He 8:8.

and thou. Ezk +6:7.

63 remember. ver. 61. Ezk 36:31, 32. Ezr +9:6. Da 9:7, 8.

and never. Jb 40:4, 5. Ps 39:9. Is +59:21. Je 3:19. 31:34. 32:40. La 3:39. Zc +10:6. Ro 2:1. 3:19, 27. 9:19, 20.

open thy mouth. Ezk +24:27. 29:21.

when. Ps +102:13, 16. Ho 5:15. Ac +3:19-21.

pacified. Pr 16:14. Zc 10:6. Ro 5:1, 2. 1 C 4:7. Ep 2:3-5. T 3:3-7.

EZEKIEL 17

2 put forth. Ezk 20:49. Jg 9:8-15. 14:12-19. 2 S 12:1-4. Ho 12:10. Mt 13:13, 14, 35. Mk 4:33, 34. 1 C 13:12mg.

riddle. Nu +12:8.

parable. Nu +21:27. +23:7.

3 A great. ver. 7, 12, etc. Dt 28:49. Je 4:13. 48:40. 49:16, 22. La 4:19. Ho 8:1. Mt 24:28.

great wings. Da 2:38. 4:22. 7:4.

divers colors. Heb. embroidering. 1 Ch 29:2.

came. ver. 12. 2 K 24:10-16. 2 Ch 36:9, 10. Je 22:23-28. 24:1.

the highest. ver. 12. Je 22:23, 24.

branch. or, foliage. lit. "pruned" thing. Ezk 8:17. Nu 13:23.

the cedar. Ezk 31:3, 10.

4 into. Is 43:14. 47:15. Je 51:13. Re 18:3, 11-19.

a city. 2 K 24:12.

5 the seed. Zedekiah, brother to Jeconiah. ver. 13. 2 K 24:17. Je 37:1.

planted it in a fruitful field. Heb. put it in a field of seed. Dt 8:7-9.

he placed. Ezk 19:11, 12. Is 15:7. 44:4.

6 it grew. ver. 14. Pr 16:18, 19. Je 52:10.

7 another. ver. 15. 2 K 24:20. 2 Ch 36:13. Je 37:5-7.

8 soil. Heb. field. ver. 5, 6.

9 Shall it. ver. 10, 15-17. Nu 14:41. 2 Ch 13:12. 20:20. Is 8:9, 10. 30:1-7. 31:1-3. Je 32:5.

shall he. 2 K 25:4-7. Je 21:4-7. 24:8-10. 39:4-7. 52:7-11.

the fruit. Je 52:10.

even. Je 37:10.

10 **shall it**. Is 20:5. Mt 21:19. Mk 11:20. Jn 15:6. Ju 12.
east wind. Ge +41:6.
toucheth. Ge +26:29.

12 **to the**. Ezk 2:5, 8. 3:9. 12:9. Is 1:2.
Know. Ezk 24:19. Ex 12:26. Dt 6:20. Jsh 4:6, 21. Mt 13:51. 15:16, 17. 16:11. Mk 4:13. Lk 9:45. Ac 8:30.
Behold. ver. 3. Ezk 1:2. 2 K 24:10-16. 2 Ch 36:9, 10. Je 22:24-28.
and led. Is 39:7. Je 52:31-34.

13 **hath taken**. ver. 5. 2 K 24:17. Je 37:1.
taken an oath of him. Heb. brought him to an oath. Ezk 16:59. 2 Ch 36:13. Je 5:2.
he hath also. 2 K 24:15, 16. Je 24:1. 29:2.

14 **the kingdom**. ver. 6. Ezk 29:14. Dt 28:43. 1 S 2:7, 30. Ne 9:36, 37. La 5:16. Mt 22:17-21.
base. Or, *low*; a tributary kingdom, dependent on the king of Babylon.
but that by keeping of his covenant it might stand. Heb. to keep his covenant, to stand to it. Je 27:12-17. 38:17-21.

15 **he rebelled**. ver. 7. 2 K 24:20. 2 Ch 36:13. Je 52:3.
in. Dt 17:16. Is 30:1-4. 31:1-3. 36:6-9. Je 37:5-7.
Shall he prosper. ver. +9. Dt 29:12-15. Je 22:29, 30.
shall he escape. ver. 18. Ezk 21:25. Pr 19:5. Je 32:4. 34:3. 38:18, 23. Mt 23:33. He 2:3.
or shall. Ps 55:23.

16 **whose oath**. ver. +18, 19. Ezk 16:59. Ex +20:7. Nu 30:2. Jsh 9:20. 2 S 21:2. Ps 15:4. Ec 8:2. Ho 10:4. Zc 5:3, 4. Ml +3:5. Ro 1:31. 1 T 1:10. 2 T 3:3.
even. ver. 10. Je +21:7.

17 **shall**. Ezk 29:6, 7. 2 K 24:7. Is 36:6, 9. Je 37:7. La 4:17.
by. Ezk 4:2. Je 33:5. 52:4.
persons. Heb. *nephesh*, souls, Jsh +10:28.

18 **Seeing**. Nu 30:2. Jsh 9:19, 20.
given his hand. 1 Ch +29:24mg.
he shall. ver. +15.

19 **surely**. Ezk 21:23-27. Dt 5:11. Je 5:2, 9. 7:9-15.
hath broken. Ps 33:10. 89:33mg.

20 **I will spread**. Ezk 12:13. 32:3. Jsh 10:16-18. 2 S 18:9. 2 K 25:5, 7. 2 Ch 33:11. Jb 10:16. Ec 9:12. Je 39:5-7. La 1:13. 4:20. Ho 7:12. Lk 21:35.
plead. Ezk 20:35, 36. 38:22. Je 2:9, 35. 50:44. Ho 2:2. Mi 6:2.
trespass. Ezk +15:8.

21 **all his fugitives**. Ezk 5:12. 12:14. 2 K 25:5, 11. Je 48:44. 52:8. Am 9:1, 9, 10.
shall know. Ezk +6:7. Is 26:11.

22 **highest branch**. Is +4:2. Mt 1:11, 12, 16.
a tender. Is +53:2.
upon. Ezk 20:40. 40:2. Ps 2:6. 72:16. Is 2:2, 3. Da 2:35, 44, 45. Mi 4:1.

23 **and it**. Ps 92:12, 13. Is 27:6. Jn 12:24. 15:5-8.
cedar. Is +4:2.
under. Ezk 31:6. Ge +49:10. Ps 22:27-30. 72:8-11. Is 2:2. 11:6-10. 49:18-23. 60:4-12. Da 4:10-14, 21-23. Ho 14:7. Mt 13:32, 47, 48. Lk 14:21-23. Jn 12:32. Ac 10:11, 12. Ga 3:28. Ep 1:10. Col 3:11. 2 Th +2:1. Re 11:15.

24 **all the trees**. Ps 96:11, 12. Is 55:12, 13. Da 2:44, 45. ch. 4.
have brought. 1 S 2:7, 8. Jb 5:11. 40:12. Ps 75:6, 7. 89:38-45. Is 2:13, 14. +9:6, 7. 11:1, etc. 26:5. Am 9:11. Lk 1:33, 52, 53. 1 C 1:27, 28.
dry tree. Is 56:3.
I the Lord have spoken. Ezk 12:25. 22:14. 24:14. Mt 24:35. Lk 23:31.

EZEKIEL 18

2 **mean**. Ezk 17:12. Is 3:15. Ro 9:20.
proverb. Dt +28:37.
the land. Ezk 6:2, 3. 7:2. 25:3. 36:1-6. 37:11, 19, 25.
The fathers. Je 15:4. 31:29, 30. La 5:7. Mt 23:36.
the children's. Ex +20:5. 34:7. Dt 5:9. 24:16. La 5:7.

3 **ye shall not**. ver. 19, 20, 30. Ezk 33:11-20. 36:31, 32. Je 31:31, 32. Ro 3:19.
proverb. Dt +28:27.

4 **all souls**. Heb. *nephesh*, Ge +12:5. Nu 16:22. 27:16. Zc 12:1. He +12:9.
are mine. Ro +14:8.
as the soul of. Heb. *nephesh*, Ge +12:5.
the soul. Heb. *nephesh*, Ge +12:5. 17:14.
that sinneth. ver. 20. Ro 6:23. Ga 3:10-13, 22.
it shall die. Nu 23:10. Dt +24:16. Jsh +11:11. Ps 78:50. Ec 3:19. 12:7. Is 53:12. Je 31:30. Mt +10:28. 22:32. 25:46. Mk 12:26. 14:34. Lk 6:9. 9:60. 12:48. 16:24. Ac 3:23. Ro 6:23. 14:12. Ga 6:5, 7. Ep 2:1. 1 T 5:6. Re 19:20. 20:10.

5 **if**. Ps 15:2-5. 24:4-6. Mt 7:21-27. Ro 2:7-10. Ja 1:22-25. 2:14-26. 1 J 2:3, 4, 29. 3:7, 8, 24. 5:2-5. Re 22:14.
that, etc. Heb. judgment and justice. Ezk +33:14mg. Ge +18:19. Pr 21:3. Je 22:3, 15. 23:5.

6 **not**. ver. +11, 15. Ezk 6:13. 20:28. 22:9. Ex 34:15. Nu 25:2, 3. Dt 12:2. 1 C 10:20, 21, 28.
mountains. Je +3:23.
neither hath lifted. ver. 12, 15. Ezk 20:7, 8, 24. 33:25, 26. Ge +22:13. Dt 4:19. Ps 121:1. 123:1, 2.
neither hath defiled. Ezk 22:10, 11. Le 18:19, 20. 20:10, 18. Dt 22:22, etc. Je 5:8, 9. Mt 5:28. 1 C +6:9-11. Ga 5:19-21. He 13:4.
come near. Le 18:19. 20:18.
menstrous. La 1:17.

7 **hath not oppressed**. ver. 12, 16, 18. Ezk 22:12, 13, 27-29. Ex +22:21-24. 23:9. Le +19:13, 15. 25:14. Dt 23:16. 1 S 12:3, 4. Jb 31:13-22. Pr 3:31. 14:31. 22:22, 23. Is 1:17. 5:7. 33:15. 58:6. Je 7:6, 7. Am 2:6, 7. 8:4-6. Mi 2:1, 2. 3:2-4. Zc 7:9-11. Ml +3:5. Ja +5:1-6.
hath restored. Ezk 33:15. Ex 22:26. Dt 24:6, 10, 12, 13, 17. Jb 22:6. 24:3, 9, 10. Am 2:8.
hath spoiled. Ezk 7:23. Ge 6:11, 12. Is 59:6, 7. Je 22:3, 16, 17. Am 3:10. 5:11, 12. 6:3. Zp 1:9.
hath given. ver. 16. Dt 15:7-11. Jb 31:16-20. Ps 41:1. 112:4, 9. Pr 11:24, 25. 28:8, 27. Is 58:7-11. Mt 25:34-46. Lk 3:11. 2 C 8:7-9. 9:6-14. Ja 2:13-17. 1 J 3:16-19.
bread. Is +58:7.
to the hungry. Jb 31:17. Pr 25:21. Ec 11:1. Is 58:7, 10. Mt 25:35. Lk 3:11. Ja 2:15, 16.
covered the naked. Jb 31:19. Is +20:2. Lk 3:11.

8 **hath not**. ver. 13, 17. Is +24:2.
hath withdrawn. 2 S 22:24. Ne 5:15. Is 33:15. Ep +5:11. 1 Th 5:22.
hath executed. Le 19:15, 35. Dt 1:16, 17. 16:18-20. Jb 29:7-17. Pr 31:8, 9. Is 1:17. Je 22:15, 16. Zc 7:9, 10. 8:16. Mt 7:2. Jn 7:24.

9 **walked**. ver. 17. Ezk 33:15. Dt +4:1. 10:12, 13. Ne 9:13, 14. Ac 24:16. Ja 1:22-25.
is just. Ps 24:4-6. Mi 6:8. Hab 2:4. Ro 1:17. Ja 2:18-26. 1 J 2:29. 3:7.
he shall. Le +18:5. Am 5:4, 14, 24.

10 **that is**. Ex 22:2. Le +19:13. Ml 3:8, 9. Jn 18:40.
a robber. *or*, a breaker up of an house. Ezk 7:22. Ex 22:2. Da +11:14mg.
a shedder. Ge +9:5, 6. Ex 21:12. Nu 35:31. Ro 13:3, 4. 1 J 3:12-15.
the like to any one of these things. *or*, to his brother besides any of these.

11 **that**. ver. 7-9. Mt 7:21-27. Lk +11:28. Jn +13:17. 15:14. Ph 4:9. Ja 2:17. 1 J 3:22. Re 22:14.
eaten. ver. 6, 15. Ezk 6:3. 22:9. Ex 34:15. Nu 25:2. Dt 12:2. 1 K 13:8, 22. Is 65:7. Je 3:6. Ho 4:13. 1 C 10:20.
mountains. Je +3:23.

12 **oppressed**. ver. 7, 16. Ezk +16:49. 22:29. Ho 12:7. Am 4:1. Zc 7:10. Ja 2:6.
hath committed abomination. ver. 6. Ezk 8:6, 17. Le 18:22, 26-30. 2 K 21:11. 23:13.

13 **given**. ver. 8, 17.
shall he. ver. 24, 28, 32.
surely. Ge +2:16.
blood. Heb. bloods. 2 K +9:26mg. Ac +18:6.

14 **if he**. ver. 10. Pr 17:21. 23:24.
that seeth. Ezk 20:18. 2 Ch 29:3-11. 34:21. Je 9:14. 44:17. Mt 23:32. 1 P 1:18.
considereth. ver. 28. Ps 119:59, 60. Is 44:19. Je 8:6. Ho 7:2. Hg 1:5, 7. 2:18. Lk 15:17-19.

15 **not eaten**. ver. +6, 7, 11-13.
mountains. Je +3:23.
lifted. Ps +121:1.

16 **withholden the pledge**. Heb. pledged the pledge, *or* taken to pledge. ver. 7, 12. Jb 22:6.
but hath. ver. 7. Jb 22:7. 31:19. Pr 22:9. 25:21. 31:20. Ec 11:1, 2. Is 58:7-10. Mt 25:34-46. Lk 11:41. 14:13. Ja 2:15, 16. 1 J 3:17.

17 **hath taken**. ver. 8. Jb 9:33. 29:16. Pr 14:31. 29:7, 14. Je 22:16. Da 4:27. Mt 18:27-35. Lk 19:8.
that hath not. ver. +8, 9, 13. Le 18:4, 26, 30.
he shall not. ver. 19, 20. Ezk 20:18, 30. Dt 24:16. Je 16:11-13, 19. Ml 3:7. Mt 23:29-33.
he shall surely. ver. 9, 19, 21, 28. Ezk 3:21. 33:13, 15, 16. Is 3:10.

18 **cruelly oppressed**. Ec 5:8.
even he shall die. ver. 4, 20, 24, 26. Ezk 3:18. Is 3:11. Jn +8:21, 24.

19 **Why**. Ex +20:5. Dt 5:9. 2 K 23:26. 24:3, 4. Je 15:4. La 5:7.
When. Ezk 20:18-20, 24, 30. Zc 1:3-6.

20 **the soul**. Heb. *nephesh*, Ge +12:5.
that sinneth. ver. +4, 13. Dt 24:16. 1 K 14:13. 2 K 14:6. 22:18-20. 2 Ch 25:4. Je 31:29, 30.
not bear. Ezk 4:4. Le 5:1, 17. 10:17. 16:22. 19:8. Nu 18:1. Ps 49:7. Is 53:11. Ga +6:5. He 9:28. 1 P 2:24.
righteousness. ver. 30. Ezk 14:14. 33:10. 1 K 8:32. 2 Ch 6:23, 30. Is 3:10, 11. Mt 16:27. Ro 2:6-9. 2 C 5:10. Re 2:23. 20:12. 22:12-15.

21 **if the**. ver. 27, 28, 30. 2 Ch 33:12, 13. Je +35:15. Lk 24:47. Ac +3:19. 1 T 1:13-16. Ja 4:8-10.
and keep. ver. 9. Ezk 36:27. Ge 26:5. Ps 119:80, 112. Lk 1:6. Ja 2:14, 26.
and do. ver. 5, 19, 27. Ps 119:1. Ga 5:22-24. T 2:11-14.
he shall surely. ver. 17, 28. Ezk 3:21. Ro 8:13.
not die. Lk 3:7. Re 2:11.

22 **his transgressions**. ver. 24. Ezk 33:16. 1 K 17:18. Ps 25:7. 32:1, 2. 51:1. 103:12. Is 43:25. Je 31:34. 50:20. Mi 7:19. Ro 8:1. He 8:12. 10:3, 4.
not be mentioned. Is 43:25. Jn 5:24. +17:6. Ro 4:3-5, 20-25. 5:1. 8:1. 2 C 5:21. Col 1:22. 1 J 1:9. Ju 24.
in his. 2 Ch 6:23. Ps 18:20-24. 19:11. Ro 2:6, 7, 10. Ga 6:7, 8. Ja 2:21-26. 2 P 1:5-11. 1 J 3:7.

23 **any pleasure**. ver. 32. Ezk 33:11. La 3:33. Ho 11:8. 1 T 2:4. 2 P 3:9.
not that. Ex 34:6, 7. Jb 33:27, 28. Ps 147:11. Je 31:20. Mi 7:18. Lk 15:4-7, 10, 22-24, 32. Ja 2:13.

24 **But when**. ver. 26. Ezk 3:20, 21. 33:12, 13, 18. 1 S 15:11. 1 Ch +28:9. 2 Ch 24:2, 17-22.

Ps 36:3, 4. 125:5. Zp 1:6. Mt 13:20, 21. Lk +8:13. Jn 6:66-70. 1 C +15:2. Ga 5:7. Col +1:23. He +10:26, 29, 38, 39. 2 P +1:10. 2:18-22. 1 J 2:19. 5:16-18. Ju 12.

and doeth. ver. 10-13. Mt 12:43-45. Ro 1:28-31. 2 C 12:20, 21. 2 T 3:1-5. He 10:26.

All his. ver. 22. Mk 13:13. Ga 3:4. He 6:4-6. 10:26-31. 2 J +8. Re 2:10. 3:11.

in his. ver. 18. Pr 14:32. 21:16. Mt 7:22, 23. Jn +8:21, 24.

25 **way.** ver. 29. Ezk 33:17, 20. Jb 32:2. 34:5-10. 35:2. 40:8. 42:4-6. Ml 2:17. 3:13-15. Mt 20:11-15. Ro 3:5, 20. 9:20. 10:3.

not equal. Ru +1:13. 2 K +6:33. Jb 12:6. 21:7. Ps 73:14. +77:3. Pr +19:3. Ec 7:15. 9:2. Is +29:24. Je 12:1. Hab 1:2. Mt 20:12. 25:24. Ro +9:14. Ph +4:11. He +13:5.

my way equal. Ge +18:25. Dt 32:3, 4. Ps 50:6. 145:17. Is 55:8, 9. Je 12:1. Zp 3:5. Lk +6:35. Ro 2:5, 6.

are not. ver. 29. Ezk 33:17.

your ways unequal. Ps 50:21. Je 2:17-23, 29-37. 16:10-13.

26 **When.** ver. 24.

turneth away. Ho 6:3. 1 C 11:28-32. 1 J 5:17.

27 **when.** ver. 21. Is 1:18. 55:7. Mt 9:13. 21:28-32. Ac +3:19. 20:21. 26:20.

he shall. Ezk 33:5. Ac 2:40. 1 T +4:16.

soul. Heb. *nephesh*, Ge +12:13.

28 **he considereth.** ver. 14. Ezk 12:3. Dt 32:29. Ps 119:1, 6, 59. Je 31:18-20. Lk 15:17, 18.

turneth. ver. 21, 31. Ezk 33:12. 1 S 7:3, 4. Col 3:5-9. T 2:14. Ja 2:10-12.

29 **The way.** ver. 2, +25. Pr +19:3.

your ways. ver. +25.

30 **I will.** Ezk 7:3, 8, 9, 27. Ps +7:8.

every. Ml 3:18. Mt +16:27. 25:32. Ga 6:4, 5.

Repent. ver. 21. Da 9:13. Ho 12:6. Lk +13:3.

yourselves. *or, others.* ver. 32mg. Da 12:3. 1 T +4:16.

so. ver. 21. Lk 13:3, 5. Ro 2:5. Ja 1:15. Re 2:21-23.

ruin. Ezk 21:15. Is 3:6.

31 **Cast away.** Ezk 20:7. Ps 34:14. Is 1:16, 17. 30:22. 38:17. 55:7. Ro 8:13. Ep 4:22-32. Col 3:5-9. Ja 1:21. 1 P 1:14. 2:1. 4:2-4.

make. Ezk 11:19. 36:26. Ps 51:10. Je 32:39. Mt 12:33, 34. 23:26. Ac +3:19. Ro 8:13. 12:2. 2 C 5:17. Ja 4:8. 1 P 1:22.

spirit. Heb. *ruach*, Ge +41:8; Ps +51:10. Lk 1:46, 47. Jn 4:24. 6:63.

for why. Ezk 33:11. Dt 30:15, 19. Pr 8:36. Je 21:8. 27:15. Ac 13:46.

32 **I have.** ver. 23. La 3:33. Mt 18:14. 1 T +2:4. 2 P +3:9.

yourselves. *or, others.* ver. 30mg. Da 12:3. 1 T +4:16.

EZEKIEL 19

1 **take.** ver. 14. Ezk 2:10. 26:17. 27:2. 32:16, 18. Je 9:1, 10, 17, 18. 13:17, 18.

the princes. 2 K 23:29, 30, 34. 24:6, 12. 25:5-7. 2 Ch 35:25. 36:3, 6, 10. Je 22:10-12, 18, 19, 28, 30. 24:1, 8. 52:10, 11, 25-27. La 4:20. 5:12.

2 **A lioness.** Is +5:29.

whelps. Ge 49:9. Re 5:5.

young lions. Is 11:6-9.

3 **it became.** ver. 6. 2 K 23:31, 32. 2 Ch 36:1, 2.

4 **He was.** 2 K 23:31, 33, 34. 2 Ch 36:4, 6. Je 22:11, 12, 18.

5 **another.** ver. 3. 2 K 23:34-37. 2 Ch 36:4.

a young lion. ver. 2.

6 **he went.** 2 K 23:35, 37. 24:1-7. 2 Ch 36:5. Je 22:13-17. ch. 26, 36.

he became. ver. 3.

7 **knew.** Ge +4:1. 2 Ch 36:8.

desolate palaces. *or,* widows. Is 13:22mg.

and the land. Ezk 22:25. Pr 19:12. 28:3, 15, 16.

the fulness. Ezk 12:19mg. 30:12mg. Am 6:8mg. Mi 1:2mg.

8 **the nations.** 2 K 24:1-6. 2 Ch 36:6.

and spread. ver. 4. Ezk 12:13. 17:20. La 4:20.

9 **chains.** *or,* hooks. ver. 4. Ezk 29:4. 38:4. Ex 35:22 (bracelets). 2 K 19:28. Is 37:29.

and brought. 2 Ch 36:6. Je 22:10-12, 18, 19. 36:30, 31.

that his. ver. 7. Ezk 6:2. 36:1.

10 **mother.** ver. 2. Ho 2:2, 5.

like. Ezk 15:2-8. 17:6. Is 5:1-4. Mt 21:33-41.

blood. *or,* quietness, *or,* likeness. Ezk 16:6, 22.

she was. Nu 24:6, 7. Dt 8:7, 9. Ps 80:8-11. 89:25-29.

11 **she had.** ver. 12, 14. Ezk 21:10, 13. Ge +49:10. Nu 24:7-9, 17. Ezr 4:20. 5:11. Ps 2:8, 9. 80:15, 17. 110:2. Is 11:1.

her stature. Ezk 31:3. Da 4:11, 20, 21.

12 **she was.** Ezk 15:6-8. Ps 52:5. 80:12, 13, 16. 89:40-45. Is 5:5, 6. Je 31:28.

the east. Ge +41:6. Je 4:11, 12.

strong. ver. 11. 2 K 23:29, 34. 24:6, 14-16. 25:6, 7. Je 22:10, 11, 18, 19, 25-27, 30.

the fire. Ezk 15:4. Dt +32:22. Is 27:11. Mt 3:10. Jn +15:6.

13 **now.** Ezk 1:3. 2 K 24:12-16.

she is. ver. 10. Dt 28:47, 48. Je 52:27-31.

in a dry. Ps 63:1. 68:6. Ho 2:3.

14 **fire.** Ezk 17:18-20. Jg 9:15. 2 K 24:20. 2 Ch 36:13. Is 9:18, 19. Je 38:23. 52:3.

she hath. ver. 11. Ezk 21:25-27. Ge +49:10. Ne 9:37. Ps 79:7. 80:15, 16. Je 22:28-30. Ho 3:4. 10:3. Am 9:11. Jn 19:15.

This is. ver. 1. La 4:20. Lk 19:41. Ro 9:2-4.

EZEKIEL 20

1 A.M. 3411. B.C. 593.
in the seventh. Ezk 1:2. 8:1. 24:1. 26:1. 29:1, 17. 30:20. 31:1. 32:1. 40:1.
that certain. Ezk 14:1-3. 33:30-33. 1 K 14:2-6. 22:15. 2 K 3:13. Is 29:13. 58:2. Je 37:17. Mt 22:16.
and sat. Ezk 8:1. Jg +20:26. Lk 2:46. 8:35. 10:39. Ac 22:3.

3 **Are.** Is 1:12. Mt 3:7. Lk 3:7.
As I. ver. 31. Ezk 14:3, 4, 7, 8. 1 S 28:6. Ps 50:15-21. Pr 1:24-31. 15:8. 21:27. 28:9. Is 1:15. Mi 3:7. Mt 15:8, 9. Jn 4:24.

4 **judge them.** *or*, plead for them. Ezk 14:14, 20. 22:2. 23:36, 45. Is 5:3. Je 7:16. 11:14. 14:11-14. 15:1. 22:21. 1 C +6:2, 3.
cause. Ezk 16:2, 3. Mt 23:29-37. Lk 11:47-51. 13:33-35. Ac 7:51, 52.

5 **In the day.** Ge +2:17. Ex 6:6, 7. 19:4-6. 20:2. Dt 4:37. 7:6. 14:2. Ps 33:12. Is 41:8, 9. 43:10. 44:1, 2. Je 33:24. Mk 13:20.
lifted up mine hand. *or*, sware. ver. 6, 15, 23, 28, 42. Ge +14:22.
and made. Ezk 35:11. Ex 3:8. 4:31. 6:3. Dt 4:34. 11:2-7. Ps 103:7.
I am. Ex 3:6, 16. 20:2, 3.

6 **In the day.** Ge +2:17.
lifted. ver. +5.
to bring. Ge 15:13, 14. Ex 3:8, 17. ch. 14, 15.
into. Dt 8:7-9. 11:11, 12. 32:8.
flowing. ver. 15.
honey. Ex +3:8.
which is. ver. 15. Ps 48:2. Da 8:9. 11:16, 41. Zc 7:14.

7 **Cast.** ver. 8. Ezk 18:6, 15, 31. Is 2:20, 21. 31:7.
the abominations. Ezk 6:9. 14:6. 2 Ch 15:8.
of. ver. 24.
defile. Ezk 23:3, 8. Le 17:7. 18:3. Dt 29:16-18. Jsh 24:14.
I am. ver. 19. Ex 16:12. Le 11:44. 20:7.

8 **they rebelled.** Dt 9:7. Ne 9:26. Is 63:10.
they did not. ver. 7. Ezk 32:4-6. Ex 32:3, 4.
then I. ver. 13, 21, 33. Ezk +7:8.
accomplish. Ge +3:9.

9 **I wrought.** ver. 14, 22, 44. Ezk 39:7. Ex 32:12. Nu 14:13, etc. Dt 9:28. Is +48:9.
in whose. Jsh 2:10. 9:9, 10. 1 S 4:8.

10 **I caused.** Ex 13:17, 18. 14:17-22. 15:22. 20:2.

11 **I gave.** Ne 9:13, 14. Ro 3:2.
showed them. Heb. made them to know. Ezk 16:2.
judgments. Dt +4:1.
which. ver. 13, 21. Le +18:5. Dt 30:15, 16.

12 **I gave.** Ex +20:8-11. 35:2. Le 23:3, 24, 32, 39. 25:4. Col 2:16.
to be. ver. 20.
know. Ezk +6:10.

I am. Ezk 37:28. Ex 19:5, 6. Le 20:8. 21:8, 15, 23. Jn 17:17-19. 1 Th 5:23. Ju 1.
Lord. Ex +15:26.

13 **rebelled.** ver. 8. Ex 16:28. 32:8. Nu 14:22. Dt 9:12-24. 31:27. 1 S 8:8. Ne 9:16-18. Ps 78:40, 41. 95:8-11. 106:13-33. Is 63:10.
and they. ver. 16, 24. Le 26:15, 43. 2 S 12:9. Pr 1:25. 13:13. Am 2:4. 1 Th 4:8. He 10:28, 29.
which. ver. 11.
and my. ver. 21. Ex 16:27, 28. Nu 15:31-36. Is 56:6.
I said. ver. +8. Ex 32:10. Nu 14:11, 12, 29. 16:20, 21, 45. 26:65. Dt 9:8. Ps 106:23.
pour out. Ps +79:6.

14 **I wrought.** ver. +9.

15 **I lifted.** ver. +5. Ex +9:3. Nu 26:64, 65. Dt 1:34, 35. Ps 95:11. He 3:11, 18. 4:3.
flowing. ver. 6.

16 **they.** ver. 13, 14.
for their. ver. 8. Ezk 14:3, 4. 23:8. Ex 32:1-8, 23. Nu 15:39. 25:2. Am 5:25, 26. Ac 7:39-43. 1 C 10:5, 6.

17 **mine.** Ezk 8:18. 9:10. Dt 4:31, 32. 1 S 24:10. Ne 9:19. Ps 78:37, 38.
eye. Dt +11:12.
neither. Ezk 7:2. 11:13. Je +4:27. 5:18. Na 1:8, 9.

18 **I said.** Nu 14:32, 33. 32:13-15. Dt 4:3-6. Ps 78:6-8.
the statutes. Mi 6:16. Zc 1:2-4. Lk 11:47, 48. Ac 7:51. 1 P 1:18.
defile. ver. 7. Je 2:7. 3:9.

19 **the Lord.** Ex +20:2, 3. Dt 5:6, 7. 7:4-6. Ps 81:9, 10. Je 3:22, 23.
walk. Dt +4:1. Ne 9:13, 14. T 2:11-14.

20 **hallow my sabbaths.** ver. +12. Ex +20:11. Ps 118:24. Col 2:16. Re 1:10, 11.

21 **the children.** Nu 21:5. 25:1-8. Dt 9:23, 24. 31:27. Ps 106:29-33. Ac 13:18.
if a man. ver. 11, 13.
I would. ver. +8.
pour out. Ps +79:6.
accomplish. Ezk 13:15. Da 11:36.

22 **I withdrew my hand.** ver. 17. Jb 13:21. La 2:8.
wrought. ver. +9.

23 **lifted.** ver. +5.
that I. Je +9:16.

24 **they had.** ver. 13, 16.
their eyes. Ezk 6:9. 18:6, 12, 15. Dt 4:19. Jb 31:26, 27. Am 2:4.

25 **I gave.** ver. 26, 39. Ezk 14:9-11. Ge +2:17. +31:7. Ex 4:21. 5:22. Dt 4:27, 28. 28:36. Jg 15:1. 1 S 24:7. 2 S 21:10. Ps 16:10. 81:12. Is 66:4. Je 4:10. Mt 6:13. 11:25. 13:11. Ro 1:21-28. 9:18. 2 Th 2:9-11.

26 **polluted.** ver. 31. Ps 106:15. Is 63:17. Ro 11:7-10. 2 Th 2:11.

in that. Ex 13:12. Dt +18:10. Ho +13:2mg.
all that. Ex 13:12. Lk 2:23.
to the end. Ezk +6:7.
27 **speak**. Ezk 2:7. 3:4, 11, 27.
Yet. Ro 2:24. Re 13:5.
committed. Heb. trespassed. Ezk 14:13.
15:8.
28 **when I**. Jsh 23:3, 4, 14. Ne 9:22-26. Ps
78:55-58.
the which. ver. 6, 15. Ge 15:18-21. 26:3, 4.
Ps 105:8-11.
they saw. Ezk 6:13. Ps 78:58. Is 57:5-7. Je
2:7. 3:6.
sweet savor. Ge +8:21.
drink offerings. Le +23:13.
29 **I said**, etc. *or*, I told them what the high place
was, or, Bamah. 2 K +21:3.
And the. Ezk 16:24, 25, 31.
30 **Are ye**. Nu 32:14. Jg 2:19. Je 7:26. 9:14.
16:12. Mt 23:32. Ac 7:51.
31 **ye offer**. ver. +26.
and shall. ver. 3. Ezk 14:3, 4. 1 S 28:5, 6. 2 K
3:13, 14. Jb 27:8, 10. Ps 66:18. Pr 1:27, 28.
28:9. Is 1:15. Je 14:12. Zc 7:13. Mt 25:11, 12.
Ja 4:1-3.
32 **that which**. Ezk 11:5. 38:10. Ps 139:2. Pr
19:21. +21:30. La 3:37.
mind. Heb. *ruach*, Ge +26:35.
We will. Je +10:2. 44:16, 17, 29. Ro 12:2.
to serve. Dt 4:28. 28:36, 64. 29:17. Is 37:19.
Da 5:4. Re 9:20.
33 **surely**. Dt 4:34.
stretched. Ex +7:5.
with fury. Le +26:28.
poured out. Ps +79:6.
34 **I will bring**. ver. 38. Ezk 11:17. 28:25.
+34:16. Is 27:9-13. Am 9:9, 10. Mi 2:12, 13.
Zp 3:15.
will gather. Ezk 22:20. Ps +147:2. Zc 10:8. 2
C 6:17.
fury. Ezk +7:8.
35 **I will**. ver. 36. Ezk 19:13. +38:8. Ho 2:14. Mi
4:10. 7:13-15. Re 12:14.
into the wilderness. Ps 74:14. Is +26:20, 21.
Je +31:2. Zp +2:3. Re +12:6, 14.
of the people. Ps +74:14. +83:3. Is +16:3, 4.
and there. Ezk 17:20. 38:22. Je 2:2, 3, 9, 35.
25:31. Ho 4:1. Mi 6:1, 2.
plead with. Je 2:9. Ho 2:14.
face to face. Dt +5:4. Zc 12:10. Mk +1:2.
36 **Like as**. Dt +33:2. Mi +7:15.
I pleaded. ver. 13, 21. Ex 32:7, etc. Nu ch.
11. 14:21-23, 28, 29. ch. 16, 25. Ps 106:15,
etc. 1 C 10:5-10.
37 **pass**. Ezk 34:17. Le 27:32. Je 33:13. Am 9:9.
Mt 25:32, 33.
I will. Ezk 16:59, 60. Le 26:25. Ps 89:30-32.
Je +11:8. Am 3:2.
the bond. *or*, a delivering.
38 **I will purge**. Ezk 11:21. 34:17, 20-22. Nu

14:28-30. Am 9:9, 10. Zc 13:8, 9. Ml 3:3. 4:1-
3. Mt 3:9, 10, 12. 25:32, 33. Ro 9:27-29.
they shall. Ezk 13:9. Nu 14:30. Ps 15:1.
95:11. Je 44:14. 1 C 10:5. He 3:19. 4:6. Ju 5.
and ye. Ezk +6:7. Ps 9:16.
39 **Go ye**. Ge +3:22. ver. 25, 26. Jg 10:14. 2 K
3:13. Ps 81:12. Ho 4:17. Am 4:4, 5. Ro 1:24-
28. 2 Th 2:11.
but. Ezk 23:37-39. Pr 21:27. Is 1:13-15. 61:8.
66:3. Je 7:9-11. Zp 1:4, 5. Mt 6:24. Re 3:15, 16.
40 **in mine**. Ezk 17:23. Ps 2:6. Is +2:2, 3. +11:9.
54:1-7. 62:1-9. Je 31:12. Re 21:10.
there shall. Ezk 37:22-28. Is 56:7. 60:7.
66:23. Zc 8:20-23. Ml 1:11. 3:4. Ro 12:1. He
13:15. 1 P 2:5.
offerings. i.e. heave offerings. Le +7:14.
firstfruits. *or*, chief. Le +23:10.
41 **sweet savor**. Heb. savor of rest. ver. 28. Ezk
6:13. Ge +8:21mg. Ml 3:4.
I bring. Ezk 11:17. 34:19. 36:24. 37:25. 38:8.
Is 11:11-16. 27:12, 13. Je 23:3. 30:3, 18.
32:37. Am 9:14, 15. Ob 17-21. Mi 7:12-16.
gather. ver. +34.
and I will. Is +8:13. Lk 2:14. Ro 12:1.
42 **ye shall**. ver. 38, 44. Ezk +6:7. Je 31:34. Jn
17:3. 1 J 5:20.
when I. Ezk 11:17-20. 34:13. 36:24. 37:21, 25.
for the which. ver. 15. Le 26:44, 45. Dt 30:4,
5.
43 **shall ye**. Ezk 6:9. Le 26:39-41. Ezr 9:5, 6, 15.
Ne 1:8-10. ch. 9. Ho 5:15.
and ye shall. Ezk 16:61-63. 36:31. Jb 42:6.
Je 31:18. Zc 12:10-14. Lk 18:13. 2 C 7:11.
44 **And ye shall**. ver. +38.
when I. ver. +9. 1 T 1:16.
45 **Moreover**. This is the beginning of another
prophecy, and properly belongs to the following chapter.
46 **set**. Ezk 4:7. 6:2.
south. Heb. Negeb. Ge +12:9.
and drop. Ezk 21:2. Dt 32:2. Jb 29:22. Is
55:10. Am 7:16. Mi 2:6mg.
the forest. Je 13:19. 22:7. Zc 11:1, 2.
47 **south**. Ge +12:9.
I will kindle. Ezk 15:6, 7. 19:14. 22:20, 21.
Dt +32:22. Is 9:18, 19. 30:33. Je 21:14.
green. Ezk 17:24. Lk 23:31.
the flaming. Mt +3:12. He 12:29.
from the south. Ezk 21:3, 4. Is 24:1-6.
48 **all flesh**. Dt 29:24-28. 2 Ch 7:20-22. Is 26:11.
Je 40:2, 3. La 2:16, 17.
49 **Doth he not speak**. Mt 13:11, 13-15. Jn
16:25. Ac 17:18.
parables. Nu +21:27. 23:7.

EZEKIEL 21

2 **set**. Ezk 4:3, 7. 20:46. 25:2. 28:21. 29:2. 38:2.
Ep 6:19.
and drop. Dt 32:2. Am 7:16. Mi 2:6mg, 11.

holy places. Le 26:31. Is 16:12. Am 7:9.
against. Ezk 4:7. 6:2. 20:46. 36:1. Je 26:11, 12. Ac 6:13, 14.
the land. Ezk 11:17. 12:19, 22. 13:9. 18:2. 20:38, 42. 25:3, 6. 33:24. 36:6. 37:12. 38:18, 19.

3 **to the land**. ver. +2. Ezk 7:2. +27:17.
Behold. Ezk +15:7.
will draw. ver. 9-11, 19. Ex 15:9. Ps 17:13. Is 10:5. Je +12:12. 51:20. Zc 13:7.
the righteous. Ezk 9:5, 6. Jb 9:22, 23. Ec 9:2. Je 15:2-4.

4 **against**. Ezk 6:11-14. 7:2. 20:47. Ps 16:4.
5 **all**. Ezk 20:48. Nu 14:21-23. Dt 29:24-28. 1 K 9:7-9.
it shall. ver. 30. 1 S 3:12. Is 45:23. 55:11. Je 23:20. Na 1:9.

6 **Sigh**. ver. 12. Ezk 6:11. 9:4. Is 22:4. Je 4:19. 9:17-24. Jn 11:33-35.
with the. Is 16:11. 21:3. Je 30:6. Da 5:6. 8:27. Na 2:10. Hab 3:16.
before. Ezk 4:12. 12:3-5. 37:20. Je 19:10.

7 **Wherefore**. Ezk 12:9-11. 20:49. 24:19.
For the. Ezk 7:26. 2 K 21:12. Is 7:2. 28:19. Je 6:22-24. 49:23.
and every. Ex +15:15.
all hands. Jb 4:3, 4. Is 35:3. Je 50:43. Lk 21:26. He 12:12.
spirit. Heb. *ruach*, Ps +106:33.
faint. Je 8:18. La 5:17.
weak as water. Heb. go into water. Ezk 7:17mg.
it cometh. Ezk 7:2-12. 12:22-28. 1 P 4:7.

9 **A sword**. ver. +3, 15, 28. Jb 20:25.
sharpened. Ps 7:11-13. Is 27:1. 34:5, 6. He 4:12. Re 19:15.

10 **it is furbished**. Je 46:4. Na 3:3. Hab 3:11.
should. Est 3:15. Ec 3:4. Is 5:12-14. 22:12-14. Am 6:3-7. Na 1:10. Lk 21:34, 35.
it contemneth the rod of my son, as every tree. *or, it is* the rod of my son, it despiseth every tree. ver. 25-27. Ezk 19:11-14. 20:47. 2 S 7:14. Ps 2:7-9. 89:26-32, 38-45. 110:5, 6. Re 2:27.

11 **to give**. ver. 19. Je 25:9, 33. 51:20-23.
12 **howl**. ver. 6. Ezk 9:8. Is +13:6.
terrors by reasons of the sword shall be upon my. *or,* they are thrust down to the sword with my.
smite. ver. 14. Ezk 6:11. Je 31:12.

13 **Because**, etc. *or,* When the trial hath been, what then? shall they not also belong to the despising rod? Je 12:5. 1 C 4:21.
a trial. Jb 9:23. 2 C 8:2.
contemn. ver. 10, 25.
it shall. ver. 27. Is 1:5.

14 **smite**. ver. 17. Ezk 6:11. Nu 24:10.
hands together. Heb. hand to hand. ver. 17.
let the. Le 26:21, 24. 2 K 24:1, 10-16. 25:1, etc. Da 3:19.

entereth. Ezk 8:12. 1 K 20:30. 22:25. Am 9:2.
15 **point**. *or,* glittering, *or* fear.
against. ver. 22. Ezk 15:7. Je 17:27. 32:3.
that their. ver. 7. Ezk 20:47.
ruins. lit. stumblingblocks. Ezk 3:20. 7:19. Je 18:23.
it is made. ver. 10, 28.
wrapped up. *or,* sharpened. ver. 9-11.

16 **Go**. ver. 4, 20. Ezk 14:17. 16:46.
either. Ge 13:9.
or on the left. Heb. set thyself, take the left hand.

17 **smite**. ver. 14. Ezk 22:13. Nu 24:10.
and I. Dt 28:63. Is +59:18. Zc 6:8.

19 **appoint thee two**. Ezk 4:1-3. 5:1, etc. Je 1:10.
the sword. Ps 17:13. Is +10:5.
a place. lit. Heb. hand. i.e. a signpost. Nu 35:32. Dt 23:12mg.

20 **Rabbath**. Dt +3:11.
the defenced. 2 S 5:9. 2 Ch 26:9. 32:5. 33:14. Ps 48:12, 13. 125:1, 2. Is 22:10. La 4:12.

21 **the king**. Pr 16:33. +21:1.
parting. Heb. mother. Mt 22:9.
at the head of. Ezk 16:24, 25. Ge 38:14. Pr 9:14. Je 3:2.
to use divination. Dt +18:10.
he made his. Ge 48:13. Jsh 14:2. Jg 20:16. Pr 16:33.
arrows. *or,* knives.
images. Heb. teraphim. Ge +31:19mg. Ho 4:12.
the liver. Only here.

22 **captains**. *or, battering* rams. Heb. rams. Ezk 4:2.
to lift. Ex 32:17, 18. Jsh 6:10, 20. 1 S 17:20. Jb 39:25. Je 51:14.
to appoint. Ezk 4:2. Je 32:24. 33:4. 52:4.

23 **as a**. Ezk 11:3. 12:22. Is 28:14, 15.
to them that have sworn oaths. *or,* for the oaths made unto them. Ezk 17:13-19. 2 Ch 36:13.
but. 2 K 24:20. 25:1-7. Je 52:3-11.
call. ver. 24. Ezk 29:16. Nu 5:15. 1 K 17:18. Re 16:19.
remembrance. 2 S +8:16mg. Ps 90:8. He 4:13.

24 **your transgressions**. Ezk 16:16, etc. 22:3-12, 24-31. 23:5, etc. 24:7. Is 3:9. Je 2:34. 3:2. 5:27, 28. 6:15. 8:12. 9:2-7. Ho 4:2. Mi 3:10-12.
ye shall. 2 K 25:1-4. 2 Ch 36:17. Is 22:17, 18. Je 15:2. Am 9:1-3.

25 **profane**. Ezk 17:18, 19. 2 Ch 36:13. Je 24:8. 52:2. or, wounded. lit. "pierced through." ver. 14, 29. i.e. deadly wounded one. Zedekiah a type of the future Antichrist (CB). Re 13:3.
whose. ver. 29. Ezk 7:6. 30:3. 35:5. Ps 7:9. 9:5, 6. Je 51:13.

26 **Remove**. Ezk 12:12, 13. 16:12. 2 K 25:5-7, 27, 28. Je 13:18. 39:6, 7. 52:9-11, 31-34. La 5:16.
exalt. Ezk 17:24. 1 S 2:7, 8. Ps 75:7. 113:7, 8. Lk 1:52.

27 **I will overturn, overturn, overturn, it.** Heb. Perverted, perverted, perverted, will I make it. Hg 2:21, 22. He 12:26, 27.
until he come. ver. 13. Ezk 17:22, 23. 34:23. 37:24, 25. Ge +49:10. Nu 24:19. 2 S 3:17, 18. 5:1, 2. Ps 2:6. 72:7-10. Is +9:6, 7. 42:1. Je +23:5, 6. 30:21. 33:15-17, 21, 26. Da 2:44. 9:25. Ho 3:5. Am 9:11, 12. Mi +5:2. Hg 2:7. Zc 6:12, 13. 9:9. 14:9. Ml 3:1. 4:2. Mt 28:18. Lk 1:32, 69. 2:11. Jn 1:49. Ac 15:14-17. Ep 1:20-22. Ph 2:9, 10. 1 P 3:22. 4:13. Re 6:2. 11:15. 19:11-16. 20:1-10.

28 **concerning the**. ver. 20. Ge +19:38.
The sword. ver. 9, 10.

29 **they see**. Ezk 22:28. Je +27:9.
to bring. Ezk 13:10-16. La 2:14.
whose. ver. 25. Jb 18:20. Ps 37:13.
day. Dt +4:32.

30 **Shall I cause it to return**. or, Cause it to return. ver. 4, 5. Je 47:6, 7.
I will. Ezk 16:38. 28:13, 15. Ge 15:14.
in the. Ezk 16:3, 4.

31 **pour**. Ezk +7:8. Is +66:14.
I will blow. Ezk 22:20, 21. Ps 18:15. Is +30:33. 37:7. 40:7. Hg 1:9.
brutish. or, burning.
and skilful. Is 14:4-6. Je 4:7. 6:22, 23. 51:20, 21. Hab 1:6-10.

32 **for fuel**. Ezk 20:47, 48. Ml 4:1. Mt 3:10, 12.
thy blood. ver. 30. Is 34:3-7.
thou shalt be no. Ezk 25:9, 10. Zp 2:9.
for I. Nu 23:19. Mt 24:35. 1 P 1:23.

EZEKIEL 22

2 **wilt thou**. Is +6:10.
judge. or, plead for. Ezk 20:4mg. 23:36mg.
bloody city. Heb. city of bloods. Ezk 23:45. 24:6, 9. 2 K +9:26mg. 21:16. 24:3, 4. Je 2:30, 34. Mt 23:35. 27:25. Lk 11:50. Ac 7:52.
thou shalt. Ezk 16:2. Is 58:1. 1 T 5:20.
show her. Heb. make her know. ver. 26. Ezk 20:11mg.
her abominations. Ezk 8:9-17. ch. 16, 23.

3 **sheddeth**. ver. 27. Ezk 24:6-9. Zp 3:3.
that her. ver. 4. Ezk 7:2-12. 12:25. Ro 2:5. 2 P 2:3.
and maketh. 2 K 21:2-9. Je ch. 2, 3.

4 **that thou**. ver. 2. 2 K 21:16.
and thou hast. Nu 32:14. Mt 23:32, 33. 1 Th 2:16.
days. Dt +4:32.
have I. Ezk +5:14, 15. 16:57. 21:28. Ps +31:11.

5 **infamous and much vexed**. Heb. polluted of name, much in vexation. Je 15:2, 3.

6 **the princes**. ver. 27. Ne 9:34. Is 1:23. Je 2:26, 27. 5:5. 32:32. Da 9:8. Mi 3:1-3, 9-11. Zp 3:3.
power. Heb. arm. Ps 79:11mg. Mi 2:1.

7 **set**. Pr +20:20.
dealt. ver. 29. Ps +12:5. Ml +3:5.
oppression. or, deceit. ver. 29mg. Le 6:4. Is 30:12mg.
stranger. ver. 29. Ezk +47:22.
fatherless. Ex +22:22.
widow. Is +1:17.

8 **despised**. ver. 26.
profaned my sabbaths. Ex +20:8. Am 8:4-6. Ml 1:6-8, 12.

9 **men that carry tales**. Heb. men of slanders. Ex +20:16. Le +19:16. 1 K 21:10-13. Ps +101:5. Pr 10:18. Je 37:13-15. 38:4-6. Mt 26:59. Ac 6:11-13. 24:5, 13. Re 12:9, 10.
they eat. Ezk 18:6, +11, 15. Ps 106:28. 1 C 10:18-21.
they commit lewdness. Ezk 16:43. 24:13. Jg 20:6. Pr +5:3. Je +9:2. Ho 4:2, 10, 14. 6:9. 7:4. Ac +15:20. He +13:4.

10 **discovered**. Ge 35:22. 49:4. Le 18:7, 8, 9. 20:11. Dt 27:20, 23. 2 S 16:21, 22. 1 Ch +5:1. Am 2:7. 1 C 5:1.
humbled. Ezk 18:6. 36:17. Le 18:19. 20:18.

11 **one**. or, every one. ver. 6.
committed. Ezk 18:11. Ex +20:14. Le 18:19, 20. 20:10. Dt 22:22. Jb 31:9-11. Je 5:7, 8. +9:2. 29:23. Ml +3:5. Mt 5:27, 28. 1 C +6:9. Ga 5:19. He +13:4.
another. or, every one. ver. 6.
hath lewdly. or, hath by lewdness. ver. +9. Le 18:15. 20:12, 17.
his sister. Le 18:9. 20:17. Dt 27:22. 2 S 13:1, 14, 28, 29.

12 **taken gifts**. Ex 23:7, 8. Dt +16:19. 27:25. Is 1:23. Mi 7:2, 3. Zp 3:3, 4.
to shed blood. ver. 3.
thou hast taken usury. Is +24:2.
greedily gained. Pr 1:19. Is 56:11. Mt 23:14, 25. Lk 3:13. 18:11. 19:8. 1 C 5:11. +6:10. 1 T 3:3. 6:9, 10. Ja +5:1-4. Ju 11.
extortion. Ezk 18:12. Je 22:17. Mi 2:2.
and hast forgotten me. Ezk 23:35. Dt 32:18. Ps 50:21, 22. 106:21. Je 2:32. 3:21.

13 **I have**. Ezk 21:14, 17. Nu 24:10.
hand. Ezk +21:17.
thy dishonest gain. ver. 27. Pr 28:8. Is 33:15. Je 5:26, 27. 7:9-11. Am 2:6-8. 3:10. 8:4-6. Mi 2:1-3. 6:10, 11. Ep 5:5, 6. Col 3:5, 6. 1 Th +4:6.
and at. ver. 2-4.

14 **thine heart**. Ezk 21:7. 28:9. Jb 40:9. Is 31:3. 45:9. Je 13:21. 1 C 10:26. He 10:31.
I the. Ezk 5:13. 17:24. 24:14. Nu 23:19. 1 S 15:29. Mk 13:31.

15 **scatter**. Ezk 34:6. Je +9:16.
consume. ver. 18-22. Ezk 20:38. 23:47, 48.

24:6-14. Is 1:25. Zc 13:9. Ml 3:3. 4:1. Mt 3:12. 1 P 4:12.

16 take thine inheritance in thyself. *or,* be profaned in thyself. Ezk 7:24. 25:3. Is 43:28. 47:6.
thou shalt know. Ezk +6:7. Ex 8:22. Ps 9:16. Is 37:20. Da 4:25, 32-35. Am 3:2.

18 the house. Ps 119:119. Is 1:22. Je 6:28-30.
dross. Is 1:25. 13:12.
brass. ver. 20. Is 48:4. La 4:1, 2.
in the midst. Pr 17:3. Is 31:9. 48:10.
dross. Heb. drosses. ver. 19.

19 dross. Ps 66:10. Is 1:25. Zc 13:9. Ml 3:2, 3.
I will. Ezk 11:7. 24:3-6. Mi 4:12. Mt 12:30, 40-42.

20 As they gather. Heb. *According* to the gathering.
to blow. ver. 21. Ezk 21:31, 32. Is 54:16.
will I gather. Ezk +20:34. Zc 10:8.
in mine. Ezk 24:13. Je 4:11, 12, 20.

21 and blow. Ezk 15:6, 7. 20:47, 48. 22:20-22. Dt 4:24. 29:20. 32:22. 2 K 25:9. Ps 21:9. 50:3. Is +30:33. Je 21:12. Na 1:6. Zp 1:18. 1 C 3:13. He 12:29.
and ye. Ps 68:2. 112:10. Is 64:2mg, 7mg. Je 9:7.

22 ye shall know. ver. +16.
poured out. ver. +31.

24 Thou art. 2 Ch 28:22. 36:14-16. Is 1:5. 9:13. Je 2:30. 5:3. 6:29. 44:16-19. Zp 3:2.

25 a conspiracy. Ezk 13:10-16. 1 K 22:11-13, 23. 2 K +11:14. Je 5:30, 31. 6:13. La 2:14. 4:13. 2 P 2:1-3.
like. ver. 27-29. Is 56:11. Ho 6:9. Mi +3:5-7. Re 13:11, 15.
ravening. ver. 27. Jb 18:4. Ps 22:13. Na 2:12. Mt 7:15. Lk 11:39.
they have devoured. Ezk 13:19. Je 2:30, 34. Mt 23:14. Mk 12:40. Lk 20:47. Re 17:6. 18:13.
souls. Heb. *nephesh,* Jsh +10:28.

26 priests. 1 S 2:12-17, 22. Je 2:8, 26, 27. La 4:13. Mi 3:11, 12. Zp 3:3, 4. Ml 1:6-8. 2:1-3, 7, 8.
violated. Heb. offered violence to. Zp 3:4.
profaned. Le 22:2, etc. 1 S 2:15, 29.
put no difference. Ezk 44:23. Le 10:1-3, 10. 11:47. 20:25. 22:22. Ps +119:63. Je 15:19. Hg 2:11-13. Ac 10:14. 15:29. 2 C +6:14-17. He 5:14.
hid their. ver. +8. Ezk 20:12, 13.
I am profaned. Ezk 36:20-23. Ro 2:24.

27 princes. ver. 6. Ezk 19:3-6. 45:9. Is 1:23. Ho 7:1-7. Mi 3:2, 3, 9-11. 7:8. Zp 3:3. Ja 2:6, 7.
souls. Heb. *nephesh,* Jsh +10:28.
to get. ver. 13. Mt 21:13. Ja +5:1-4.

28 prophets. ver. 25. Ezk 13:10-16. Is 30:10. Je 8:10, 11.
seeing. Ezk 13:22, 23. 21:29. Je 23:25-32. La 2:14. Zp 3:4.

Thus saith the Lord. Ezk 13:6, 7. Je 23:21. 28:2, 15. 29:8, 9, 23. 37:19.

29 people. ver. 7. Ezk 18:12. Is 5:7. 10:2. 59:3-7. Je 5:26-28, 31. 6:13. Am 3:10. Mi 2:2. 3:3. Ja +5:4.
oppression. *or,* deceit. ver. +7mg. Ezk +27:13. Ex 5:15-19. Pr +13:19. Mi 3:2, 3. Na 3:1. 1 T +1:10.
oppressed. ver. 7. Ex 22:21. 23:9. Le 19:33, 34. Ps 94:6. Mt 25:43.
stranger. ver. +7. Ezk 47:22.
wrongfully. Heb. without right. Je +22:13.

30 I sought. Is 41:28. 59:16. 63:5. Je 5:1.
make. Ezk 13:5. Ge 18:23-32. Ex 32:10-14. Ps 106:23, 30. Je 15:1.
found none. Ps 14:3. Mt +7:14. Lk 18:8.

31 Therefore. Pr 1:24, 31. Mt 23:37, 38.
have I poured. ver. 21, 22. Ezk +7:8.
own way. Ezk 7:3, 4, 8, 9. 9:10. 11:21. 16:43. Ro 2:8, 9.

EZEKIEL 23

2 two women. Ezk 16:44, 46. Is +32:9. Je 3:7-10.
mother. 2 S +20:19.

3 in Egypt. Ezk 20:8. Le 17:7. Dt 29:16, 17. Jsh 24:14.
in their. ver. 8, 19, 21. Ezk 16:22. Ho 2:15.

4 the elder. Ezk 16:40. 1 K 12:20.
they were. Ezk 16:8, 20. Ex 19:5, 6. Ps 45:11-16. Je 2:2, 3. Ro 7:4.
Samaria. Is 7:9.
Aholah. *that is,* His tent, *or* tabernacle. i.e. *her own tent,* **S#170h.** ver. 4, 5, 36, 44. 1 K 12:26-33. Jn 4:22.
Jerusalem. 1 Ch 11:4, 7.
Aholibah. *that is,* My tabernacle in her. **S#172h.** ver. 4, 11, 22, 36, 44. 1 K 8:29. Ps 76:2. 132:13, 14.

5 Aholah. 1 K 14:9, 16. 15:26, 30. 16:31, 32. 21:26. 2 K 17:7-18.
doted. ver. 7, 9, 12, 16, 20. Ezk 16:37. Je 50:38.
on the. Ezk 16:28. 2 K 15:19. 16:7. 17:3. Ho 5:13. 8:9, 10. 10:6. 12:1.

6 all of. ver. 12-15.

7 committed her whoredoms with them. Heb. bestowed her whoredoms upon them. Ezk 16:15.
the chosen men of Assyria. Heb. the choice of the children of Asshur. Ge 10:22.
with all their. ver. 30. Ezk 20:7. 22:3, 4. Ps 106:39. Ho 5:3. 6:10.

8 whoredoms. ver. 3, 19, 21. Ex 32:4. 1 K 12:28. 2 K 10:29. 17:16.

9 I have delivered. 2 K 15:29. 17:3-6, 23. 18:9-12. 1 Ch 5:26. Ho 11:5. Re 17:12, 13, 16.

10 discovered. ver. 29. Is +3:17.

they took. ver. 47.
famous. Heb. a name. ver. 48. Je 22:8, 9.

11 **her sister**. ver. 4. Je 3:8.
was more corrupt in her inordinate love than she. Heb. she corrupted her inordinate love more than she.
her sister in whoredoms. Heb. the whoredoms of her sister. Ezk 16:47-51. Je 3:8-11.

12 **upon**. ver. 5. Ezk 16:28. 2 K 16:7-15. 2 Ch 28:16-23.
captains. ver. 6, 23.

13 **that they**. ver. 31. 2 K 17:18, 19. Ho 12:1, 2.

14 **portrayed**. Ezk 8:9, 10. +16:17. Is 46:1. Je 50:2.
vermilion. Je 22:14. Na 2:3.

15 **with girdles**. 1 S 18:4. Is 22:21.
all of. Jg 8:18. 2 S 14:25.

16 **as soon as she saw them with her eyes**. Heb. at the sight of her eyes. Ezk 16:29. Ge +3:6. 6:2. 39:7. 2 S 11:2. 2 K 20:12-19. Jb +31:1. Ps +101:3. 119:37. Pr 6:25. 23:33. Mt 5:28. 1 J 2:16. 2 P 2:14.
she doted. ver. 20.
and sent. ver. 40, 41. Ezk 16:17, 29.

17 **Babylonians**. Heb. children of Babel. Ge 10:10. 11:9.
and her. ver. 22, 28. Ezk 16:37. 2 S 13:15.
mind. Heb. *nephesh*, Ge +23:8. ver. 22, 28. Ezk 20:32. Ge +2:7.
alienated. Heb. loosed, *or* disjointed. Je 6:8mg.

18 **discovered**. Ezk 16:36. 21:24. Is 3:9. Je 8:12. Ho 7:1.
then. Dt 32:19. Ps 78:59. 106:40. Je 6:8. 12:8. 15:1. La 2:7. Ho 2:2. Am 6:8. Zc 11:8.
my mind. Heb. *nephesh*, Ge +23:8; Le +26:11.
alienated. Ge +32:28.

19 **multiplied**. ver. 14. Ezk 16:25, 29, 51. Am 4:4.
in calling. ver. 3, 8, 21. Ezk 16:22. 20:7.
remembrance. Is +44:21.

20 **she doted**. ver. 16.
paramours. Ezk 16:20, 26.
whose flesh. Je 2:23, 24. 5:8. 13:27.
as the flesh. Ezk +16:26.
issue. Ge 38:9. Le 15:16-18, 32. 18:20. 19:20. 22:4. Nu 5:2. Dt 23:10. 2 S 3:29. Mt 9:20.
horses. Ezk 17:15. Je 5:8.

22 **I will raise**. ver. 9, 28. Ezk 16:37. Is 10:5, 6. 39:3, 4. Hab 1:6-10. Re 17:16.
from. ver. 17.
mind. Heb. *nephesh*, Ge +23:8. ver. 17, 28.
and I. Je 6:22, 23. 12:9-12.

23 **Babylonians**. Ezk 21:19, etc. 2 K 20:14-17. 25:1-3.
the Chaldeans. 2 K 24:2. Jb 1:17. Is 23:13. Ac 7:4.
Pekod. i.e. *punishment*, **S#6489h**. Je 50:21.
Shoa. i.e. *opulent, noble, free; cry; fruitful*, **S#7772h**, only here.

Koa. i.e. *alienation; curtailment; a prince*, **S#6970h**, only here.
the Assyrians. Ge 2:14. 25:18. Ezr 6:22.
desirable. ver. 6, 12.

24 **with chariots**. Ezk 26:10. Je 47:3. Na 2:3, 4. 3:2, 3.
I will set. ver. 45. Ezk 16:38. 21:23. Dt 28:49, 50. 2 S 24:14. Je 39:5, 6.

25 **I will set**. Ezk 5:13. ch. 8. 16:38-42. Ex 34:14. Dt 29:20. 32:21, 22. Pr 6:34. SS 8:6. Zp 1:18.
fall by the sword. 2 Ch 36:17.
they shall take thy. ver. 47. Ho 2:4, 5.
thy residue. Ezk 15:6, 7. 20:47, 48. 22:18-22. Re 18:8.

26 **strip**. ver. 29. Is +3:17. Re 17:16. 18:14-17.
fair jewels. Heb. instruments of thy decking. Is 3:17-24. 1 P 3:3, 4.

27 **will I**. Ezk 16:41. 22:15. Is 27:9. Mi 5:10-14. Zc 13:2.
and thy. ver. 3, 19.
so that. Mi 5:13. Zc 13:2.
from the land. Is 31:1.

28 **whom thou**. ver. 17, 22. Ezk 16:37. Je 21:7-10. 24:8. 34:20.
mind. Heb. *nephesh*, Ge +23:8. ver. 22.

29 **deal**. ver. 25, 26, 45-47. Ezk 16:39. Dt 28:47-51. 2 S 13:15.
labor. Dt +28:33.
the nakedness. ver. +10, 18.

30 **thou hast**. ver. 12-21. Ezk 6:9. Ps 16:4. 106:35-38. Je 2:18-20. 16:11, 12. 22:8, 9.
because thou art. ver. 7, 17.

31 **walked**. ver. 13. Ezk 16:47-51. Je 3:8-11.
her. 2 K 21:13. Je 7:14, 15. Da 9:12.
cup. Is 51:17. Re 14:9, 10.

32 **drink**. Ps 60:3. Is 51:17. Je 25:15-28. 48:26. Mt 20:22, 23. Re 16:19. 18:6.
cup. Je +49:12.
thou shalt be. Ezk 22:4, 5. 25:6. 26:2. 35:15. 36:3. Dt 28:37. 1 K 9:7. Ps 79:3. Je 25:9. La 2:15, 16. Mi 7:8.

33 **filled**. Je 25:27. Hab 2:16.
with the cup of astonishment. Is 51:17, 22.

34 **drink**. Ps 75:8. Is 51:17.
and pluck. ver. 3, 8. Mt 5:29, 30. Re 18:7.

35 **Because**. Ezk 22:12. Is 17:10. Je 2:32. 3:21. 13:25. 23:27. 32:33. Ho 8:14. 13:6. Ro 1:28. He 10:29.
and cast. 1 K 14:9. Ne 9:26.
therefore. ver. 45-49. Ezk 7:4. 44:10. Le 24:15. Nu 14:34. 18:22.

36 **wilt**. Ezk 20:4. 22:2. Je 1:10. 1 C 6:2, 3.
judge. *or*, plead for. Ezk 22:2mg. Je 11:14. 14:11.
Aholah. ver. 4.
declare. Ezk 16:2. Is 58:1. Ho 2:2. Mi 3:8-11. Mt 23:13-35. Lk 11:39-52. Ac 7:51-53.

37 they have. ver. 5. Ezk 16:32. Ho 1:2. 3:1.
   and blood. ver. 39, 45. Ezk 16:36, 38. 22:2-
   4. 24:6-9. 2 K 24:4. Ps 106:37, 38. Is 1:15. Je
   7:6, 9. Ho 4:2. Mi 3:10. Lk 13:34.
   have also. ver. 4. Dt +18:10.
38 they have. Ezk 7:20. 8:5-16. 2 K 21:4, 7.
   23:11, 12.
   defiled. Jn 2:13-16.
   and have. Ex +20:8.
39 they came. Ezk 33:31. Is 3:9. 66:3. Je 7:8-11.
   11:15. Mi 3:11. Jn 18:28.
   thus. ver. 38. Ezk 44:7. 2 K 21:4. 2 Ch 33:4-
   7. Je 23:11.
40 ye have. ver. 16. Is 57:9.
   to come. Heb. coming. 2 K 20:13-15.
   thou didst. Ru 3:3. Est 2:12.
   paintedst. 2 K 9:30mg. Is 3:16. Je 4:30mg. 1
   P 3:3.
   and deckedst. Ezk 16:13-16. Pr 7:10. Is
   3:18-23.
41 stately. Heb. honorable. Est 1:6. Pr 7:16, 17.
   Is 57:7-9. Am 2:8. 6:4. He +13:4.
   a table. Ezk 44:16. Is 65:11. Ml 1:7.
   whereupon. Ezk 16:18, 19. Pr 7:17. Je
   44:17. Ho 2:8, 9.
42 a voice. Ezk 32:6, 18, 19. Ho 13:6. Am 6:1-6.
   common sort. Heb. multitude of men. Je
   26:23mg.
   were brought. Ge 10:7, 28. 25:3. 1 K 10:1.
   Sabeans. *or*, drunkards. S#5433h, only here.
   Compare S#5436h, Is 45:14; S#7614h, Jb 1:15;
   S#7615h, Jl 3:8. Jb 1:15. Jl 3:8.
   bracelets. Ezk 16:11, 12. Re 12:3.
43 old. *or*, worn out. lit. "faded" one. Jsh 9:4, 5.
   Ezr 9:7. Ps 106:6. Je 13:23. Da 9:16.
   whoredoms with her. Heb. her whoredoms. Ezk 16:15, 19.
44 so went. ver. 3, 9-13. Ps 106:39.
45 the righteous. ver. 36. Je 5:14. Ho 6:5. Zc
   1:6. Jn 8:3-7.
   after the manner of adulteresses. ver. 37-
   39. Ezk 16:38-43. Le 20:10. 21:9. Dt 22:21-
   24. Jn 8:7. Re 16:5, 6. 19:2, 3.
   because. ver. 37.
46 I will. ver. 22-26. Ezk 16:40. Je 25:9.
   to be removed and spoiled. Heb. for a
   removing and spoil. Je +15:4mg.
47 the company. ver. 25, 29. Ezk 9:6. 16:41. Dt
   22:24. Je 33:4, 5.
   dispatch them. *or*, single them out. Ezk
   24:6.
   shall slay. Ezk 24:21. 2 Ch 36:17-19.
   and burn. Dt 13:16. Je 39:8. 52:13.
48 I cause. ver. 27. Ezk 6:6. 22:15. 36:25. Mi
   5:11-14. Zp 1:3.
   that. Ezk 5:15. 16:41. Dt 13:11. Is 26:9.
   +66:24. Ro 15:4. 1 C 10:6-11. 2 P 2:6.
49 they shall. Ezk 7:4, 9. 9:10. 11:21. 16:43.
   22:31. Is 59:18.
   ye shall bear. ver. 35. Ps 106:43.

and ye shall know. Ezk +6:7. 24:24, 27.
   25:5, 7, 11, 17. 26:6. 28:22, 23, 24, 26. 29:6,
   9, 16, 21. 30:8, 19, 25, 26. +32:15.

EZEKIEL 24

1 A.M. 3414. B.C. 590.
   the ninth year. This was the ninth year of
   Zedekiah, about Thursday, January 30, A.M.
   3414, the very day in which Nebuchadnezzar
   began the siege of Jerusalem. Ezk 1:2. 8:1.
   20:1. 26:1. 29:1, 17. 31:1. 32:1, 17. 33:21.
   40:1. 2 K 24:12.
2 write. Is 8:1. 30:8, 9. Hab 2:2, 3.
   of this. 2 K 25:1. Je 39:1. 52:4.
3 utter. Ezk 19:2, etc. Mk 12:12. Lk 8:10.
   parable. Nu +23:7.
   the rebellious. Ezk 2:3, 6, 8. 3:9. 12:2, 25.
   17:12. Is 1:2. 30:1, 9. 63:10. Ac 7:51.
   Set. ver. 6. Ezk 11:3. 17:12. Je 1:13, 14.
4 the pieces. Ezk 22:18-22. Mi 3:2, 3.
   Mt 7:2.
5 the choice. Ezk 20:47. 34:16, 17, 20. Je 39:6.
   52:10, 11, 24-27. Re 19:20.
   burn. *or*, heap. ver. 9, 10.
6 Woe. ver. 9. Ezk 11:6, 7. 22:2, 3, 6-9, 12, 27.
   23:37-45. 2 K 21:16. 24:4. Mi 7:2. Na 3:1. Mt
   23:35. Re 11:7, 8. 17:6. 18:24.
   to the pot. ver. 11-13. Je 6:29.
   bring. Ezk 9:5, 6. 11:7-9, 11. Jsh 10:22.
   let no. Jsh 7:16-18. 1 S 14:40-42. 2 S 8:2. Jl
   3:3. Ob 11. Jon 1:7. Na 3:10.
   let no lot. Jsh 14:2.
7 her blood. 1 K 21:19. Is 3:9. Je 2:34. 6:15.
   she poured. Le 17:13. Dt 12:16, 24. Jb
   16:18. Is 26:21.
8 it might. Ezk 5:13. 8:17, 18. 22:30, 31. Dt
   32:21, 22. 2 K 22:17. 2 Ch 34:25. 36:16, 17.
   Je 7:18-20. 15:1-4.
   I have set. Ezk 16:37, 38. 23:45. Dt 29:22-28.
   Je 22:8, 9. Mt 7:2. 1 C 4:5. Re 17:1-6. 18:5-
   10, 16-20.
9 Woe. ver. +6. Na 3:1. Hab 2:12. Lk 13:34, 35.
   Re 14:20. 16:6, 19.
   I will. Ezk 22:19-22, 31. Is +30:33. 31:9. 2 Th
   1:8. 2 P 3:7-12. Ju +7. Re +21:8.
10 Heap on wood. Is +30:33.
   spice it well. Ezk 43:24. Le 2:13. Jb 6:6. Mt
   5:13. Mk +9:50. Lk 14:34, 35. Ep 4:29. Col
   4:6. He +3:12, 13.
   and let. 2 Ch +34:5. Je 17:3. 20:5. La 1:10.
   2:16.
11 set it. Je 21:10. 32:29. 37:10. 38:18. 39:8.
   52:13.
   that the filthiness. Ezk 20:38. 22:15, etc.
   23:26, 27, 47, 48. 36:25. Is 1:25. 4:4. 27:9. Mi
   5:11-14. Zc 13:1, 2, 8, 9. Ml 4:1. Mt 3:12. 1 C
   3:12, 13.
12 wearied. Is 47:13. 57:9, 10. Je 2:13. 9:5.
   10:14, 15. 51:58. Ho 12:1. Hab 2:13, 18, 19.

her great. ver. 6, 13. Ge 6:5-7. 8:21. Is 1:5. Je 5:3. 44:16, 17. Da 9:13, 14.

her scum. 2 Ch +34:5. 1 P 4:12, 17. 2 P 3:10-14.

13 **thy filthiness**. ver. 11. Ezk 23:36-48. 2 C 7:1.

because. Ezk 22:24. 2 Ch 36:14-16. Is 5:4-6. 9:13-17. Je 6:28-30. 25:3-7. 31:18. Ho 7:1, 9-16. Am 4:6-12. Zp 3:2, 7. Mt 23:37, 38. Lk 13:7-9. Re +22:11.

have purged. Ex +8:18.

till I. Is +59:18. Ro 2:8, 9.

14 **the Lord**. Nu 23:19. 1 S 15:29. Ps 33:9. Is 55:11. Je 23:20. Mt 24:35.

neither will I spare. Ezk 5:11. 7:4, 9. 8:18. 9:10. Je 13:14.

according to thy ways. Ezk 16:43. 18:30. 22:31. 23:24, 29, 49. Is 3:11. Je 4:18. Mt 16:27. Ro 2:5, 6.

16 **the desire**. ver. 18, 21, 25. Ps 45:11. Pr 5:19. SS 7:10. Is +32:12mg.

with a. Jb 36:18. Ps 39:10.

stroke. S#4046h. Ex 9:14 (plagues). Nu 14:37 (plague). 16:48, 49, 50. 25:8, 9, 18. 26:1. 31:16. 1 S 4:17. 6:4. 2 S 17:9 (slaughter). 18:7. 24:21, 25. 1 Ch 21:17, 22. 2 Ch 21:14mg. Ps 106:29, 30. Ezk +38:22. Zc 14:12, 15, 15, 18.

yet. ver. 21-24. Le 10:2, 3. Je 22:10, 18. 1 Th 4:13.

thy tears. Mt +9:23.

run. Heb. go.

17 **Forbear to cry**. Heb. Be silent. Ps 37:7mg. 39:9. 46:10. Am 8:3. Hab 2:20mg.

make. Je 16:4-7.

bind. ver. 23. Le 10:6. 13:45. 21:10.

put. ver. 23. 2 S 15:30. Is 20:2.

cover. ver. 22. Le 13:45. Mi 3:7.

lips. Heb. upper lip, and so ver. 22. Le 13:45. 2 S 19:24.

eat. Ho 9:4.

the bread of men. Is +58:7.

18 **and at**. Mt 19:29. 1 C 7:29, 30.

19 **Wilt thou**. Ezk 12:9. 17:12. 20:49. 21:7. 37:18. Ml 3:7, 8, 13.

21 **I will**. Ezk 7:20-22. 9:7. Ps 74:7. 79:1. Is 64:10, 11. Je 7:14. La 1:10. 2:6, 7. Da 11:31. Ac 6:13, 14.

the excellency. Ps 96:6. 105:4. 132:8.

the desire. ver. 16. Ps 27:4. 84:1.

that which your soul pitieth. Heb. the pity of your soul. Heb. *nephesh*, Ge +34:3. Jb 31:30.

your sons. Ezk 23:25, 47. Je 6:11. 9:21. 16:3, 4.

22 **ye shall do**. ver. 16, 17. Jb 27:15. Ps 78:64. Je 16:4-7. 47:3. Am 6:9, 10.

23 **tires**. Je 13:18mg.

shall not. Je 16:4-7.

But. Ezk 4:17. 33:10. Le 26:39.

and mourn. Is 59:11.

24 **Ezekiel**. Ezk 4:3. 12:6, 11. Is 8:18. 20:3. Ho 1:2, etc. 3:1-4. Lk 11:29, 30. 1 C 4:9.

when. 1 S 10:2-7. Je 17:15. Lk 21:13. Jn 13:19. 14:29. 16:4.

ye shall know. Ezk +6:7.

25 **take from**. Ps 78:64.

their strength. ver. 21. Ps 48:2. 50:2. 122:1-9. Je 7:4.

that whereupon they set their minds. Heb. the lifting up of their soul. Heb. *nephesh*, Ge +23:8. Je 22:27mg.

their sons. Dt 28:32. Je 11:22. 52:10.

26 **he that escapeth**. Ezk 33:21, 22. 1 S 4:12-18. Jb 1:15-19.

27 **thy mouth**. Ezk 3:26, 27. 29:21. 33:22. Ex 4:11, 12. Lk 1:64. 21:15. 2 C 6:11. Ep 6:19. Col 4:3, 4.

be opened. Jg +11:35.

no more dumb. Ezk 33:22. Lk 1:20, 62-65.

shalt be. ver. 24.

they shall know. Ezk +6:10.

EZEKIEL 25

2 **thy face**. Ezk 6:2. 20:46. 21:2. 35:2.

the Ammonites. Ge +19:38.

3 **Ammonites**. ver. +2.

thou saidst. ver. 6, 8. Ezk 35:10-15. 36:2. Ps 40:15. 70:2, 3. Pr +17:5. La 1:21, 22.

the land. Ezk +11:17.

4 **men**. Heb. children. Jg 6:3, 33. 7:12. 8:10. 1 K 4:30.

of the east. Ezk 21:19, 20. Ge +29:1. Is 41:2. Je 25:21.

they shall eat. Le 26:16. Dt 28:33, 51. Jg 6:3-6. Is 1:7. 62:8, 9. 65:22.

5 **Rabbah**. Jsh +13:25.

a stable. Is 17:2. 32:14. Zp 2:14, 15.

and ye. ver. 7, 11, 17. Ezk +6:7. Is 37:20.

6 **thou hast**. Jb 27:23. 34:37. Je 48:27. La 2:15. Na 3:19. Zp 2:15.

hands. Heb. hand.

stamped. Ezk 6:11.

feet. Heb. foot.

rejoiced. ver. 15. Ezk 35:15. 36:5. Ne 4:3, 4mg. Pr 24:17. Ob 12. Zp 2:8, 10.

heart. Heb. soul. Heb. *nephesh*, Ex +23:9.

against. Je 40:14. 41:10.

7 **I will stretch**. ver. 13, 16. Ex +7:5.

and will. Je 49:2. Am 1:14.

a spoil. *or*, meat.

thou shalt know. ver. +5. Jn +11:42.

8 **Moab**. Ge +19:37. Nu 21:26, 29. 24:17, 18. Dt 34:5, 6. 2 S 8:2. 1 Ch 18:2. Ps 60:8. 83:4-8. 108:9. Is 11:14. 15:1, 2, 5. 16:4, 6, 7. 25:10. Je 9:26. 25:21. ch. 48:1-5, 20, 26, 28-31, 36, 39, 42, 45-47. Am 2:1-3. Mi 6:5. Zp 2:8-11.

Seir. ver. 12-14. Ge +14:6. Je +49:7.

the house. Is 10:9-11. 36:18-20.

9 **side**. *or*, shoulder. Ezk 3:16. 33:2, etc. Jsh 18:12.
Beth-jeshimoth. Nu +33:49.
Baal-meon. Nu +32:38.
Kiriathaim. Je +48:1, 23.

10 **the men**. ver. 4.
with the Ammonites. *or*, against the children of Ammon. ver. 2-7.
may. Ezk 21:32. Ps 83:3-6. Is 23:16.

11 **I will**. ver. 17. Ezk 5:8, 10, 15. 11:9. 16:41. 39:21. Ex +7:4. Ps 9:16. 149:7. Ju 15.
upon. Je 9:25, 26. 25:21. ch. 48.
and they. ver. 5. Ezk +6:10. 35:15.

12 **Because**. ver. 8. Ezk ch. 35. Ge 36:8. 2 Ch 28:17, 18. Je +49:7, etc.
taking vengeance. Heb. revenging revengement. Ge 27:41, 42. Am 1:11, 12. Ob 10-16.

13 **I will also**. ver. 7, 16. Je +49:7.
and will. Ezk 14:8, 13, 17, 19-21. 29:8. Ge 6:7. Je 7:20.
Teman. Ge +36:11.
of Dedan shall fall by the sword. *or*, shall fall by the sword unto Dedan. Ge +10:7.

14 **by the hand**. Ge 27:29. Nu 24:17-19. Is 11:14. 63:1, etc. Je 49:2.
and they shall know. Dt 32:35, 36. Ps 58:10, 11. Na 1:2-4. He 10:30, 31. Re 6:16, 17.

15 **Because**. ver. 6, 12. Is 14:29-31. Je +47:4. Jl 3:4, etc.
dealt. Is 9:12.
heart. Heb. *nephesh*, Ex +23:9.
to destroy. Jg ch. 14-16. 1 S ch. 4-6, 13, 14, 17, 31. 2 S 8. 1 Ch 7:21.
for the old hatred. *or*, with perpetual hatred. Heb. *olam*, Jb +22:15. Ezk 35:5mg.

16 **I will stretch**. ver. 7, 13. Ps 60:8, 9. 108:9, 10. Is 11:14. Je 47:1-7. Am 1:6-8.
Cherethims. i.e. *exterminators, executioners*, S#3774h. 2 S +8:18, Cherethites.
and destroy. Je 47:4.
sea coasts. *or*, haven of the sea. Ge 49:13. Je 47:7.

17 **I will**. ver. 11. Ezk 5:15.
vengeance. Heb. vengeances. Ps 94:1.
they shall. ver. 5, 11, 14. Ezk 6:7, +10. Ps 9:16.

EZEKIEL 26

1 **the eleventh year**. Ezk 1:2. 8:1. 20:1. Je 39:2.

2 **Tyrus**. Je +25:22.
Aha. Ezk 25:2, 3, 6. 36:2. Ps 35:21-23. 40:15. 70:3. 83:2-4. Pr +17:5.
the gates. Ge +14:7. La 1:1. Ac 2:5-10.
she is. Ezk 35:10. Je 49:1.

3 **Behold**. Ps 45:12. 72:10. Is 23:15-18. Zc 9:1-7.
I am against. Ezk +15:7.
many. Mi 4:11. Zc 14:2.

as the sea. Ezk 27:26, 32-34. Ps 107:25. Is 5:30. Je 6:23. +47:2. Lk 21:25.

4 **destroy**. ver. 9. Is 23:11. Je 5:10. Am 1:10. Zc 9:3, 4.
scrape her dust. ver. 12. Le 14:41-45.
make her like. Ezk 24:7, 8.

5 **the spreading of nets**. ver. 14, 19. Ezk 27:32. 47:10.
and it. Ezk 25:7. 29:19.

6 **her daughters**. ver. 8. Nu +21:25mg.
and they. Ezk +6:7.

7 **I will**. ver. 3. Ezk 28:7. 29:18-20. 30:10, 11. 32:11, 12. Je 25:9-11, 22. 27:3-6.
Nebuchadrezzar. Ezk 29:18, 19. 30:10.
a king of kings. Ezk 17:14-16. Ezr 7:12. Is 10:8. Je 52:32. Da 2:37, 38, 47. Ho 8:10.
with horses. ver. 10, 11. Ezk 23:23, 24. Je 4:13. 6:23. Na 2:3, 4. 3:2, 3.

8 **he shall make**. Ezk 21:22. 2 S 20:15. Je 52:4.
cast a mount. *or*, pour out the engine of shot. Je 6:6mg. 32:24mg. 33:4. Lk 19:43.

9 **engines**. 2 Ch 26:15.
he shall. Zc 9:3, 4.

10 **By reason**. Ezk 29:18-20.
the abundance. ver. 7. Je 47:3.
shake. ver. 15. Ezk 27:28. Na 2:3, 4.
enter. Jsh 6:5, 20.
as men enter into a city wherein is made a breach. Heb. according to the enterings of a city broken up.

11 **hoofs**. Is 5:28. Je 51:27. Hab 1:8.
and thy. Is 26:5.
garrisons. Heb. pillars, 2 K +17:10mg.

12 **make a spoil**. ver. 5. Mt 6:19, 20.
thy merchandise. Ezk 27:3-36. Is 23:8, 11, 17, 18. Zc 9:3, 4. Re 18:11-13.
destroy. Am 1:9, 10.
thy pleasant houses. Heb. houses of thy desire. Is +32:12mg.

13 **the noise**. Ezk 28:13. Is 14:11. 22:2. 23:7, 16. 24:8, 9. Je 7:34. 16:9. 25:10. Ho 2:11. Am 6:4-7. Ja +5:1-5. Re 18:22, 23.
to cease. Je 47:4.

14 **like**. ver. 4, 5, 12.
be built no more. Dt 13:16. Jb 12:14. Ps +102:16. Ml 1:4.
for I. Ezk 5:13, 15, 17. 17:21-24. 21:32. 22:14. 30:12. Nu 23:19. Jb 40:8. Is 14:27. Mt 24:35.

15 **shake**. ver. 18. Ezk 27:28, 35. 31:16. 32:10. Is 2:19. Je 49:21. He 12:26, 27.
when. Is 61:3, 10.

16 **all the princes**. Ezk 27:29-36. 32:21-32. Is 14:9-13. 23:1-8. Re 18:11-19.
come. Ex 33:4, 5. Jb 2:12. Jon 3:6.
clothe. Ezk 7:8. Jb 8:22. Ps 35:26. 109:18, 29. 132:18. 1 P 5:5.
trembling. Heb. tremblings.
sit. Jb 2:13. Is 3:26. 47:1. 52:2. La 2:10.

tremble. Ezk 32:10. Ex 15:15. Da 5:6. Ho 11:10, 11. Re 18:15.
be astonished. Ezk 27:35.

17 take. Ezk 19:1, 14. 27:2, 32. 28:12, etc. 32:2, 16. Je 6:26. 7:29. 9:20. Mi 2:4.
How art. 2 S 1:19, 25-27. Is 14:12. La 1:1. Jl 1:18. Ob 5. Zp 2:15. Re 18:9, 10, 16-19.
seafaring men. Heb. the seas.
strong. Ezk 27:3, etc. 28:2, etc. Jsh 19:29. Is 23:4, 8.

18 the isles tremble. ver. 15. Ezk 27:28-30.
at thy. Is 23:5-7, 10-12. Zc 9:5.

19 bring. ver. +3.

20 I shall bring. Ezk 32:18-32, 34. Nu 16:30, 33. Ps 28:1. Is 14:11-19. Lk 10:15.
pit. Heb. *bor*, Ge +37:20.
of old time. Heb. *olam*, Jsh +24:2.
in places. Jb 30:3-6. Ps 88:3-6. Is 59:10. La 3:6.
of old. Heb. *olam*, Ge +6:4.
pit. Heb. *bor*, Ge +37:20.
and I shall set. Ezk 28:25, 26. 39:7, 25-29. Is 4:5. Zc 2:8.
in the land of the living. Ps +27:13.

21 a terror. Heb. terrors. ver. 15, 16. Ezk 27:36. 28:19.
though. ver. 14. Ps 37:36. Je 51:64. Re 18:21.
yet shalt. ver. 19. Da 7:24-26. Mt 11:21, 22. 2 Th 2:8. Re 18:2. 19:19, 20. 20:7-9.

EZEKIEL 27

2 take up. ver. 32. Ezk 19:1. 26:17. 28:12. 32:2. Je 7:20. 9:10, 17-20. Am 5:1, 16.

3 O thou. ver. 4, 25. Ezk 26:17. 28:2, 3. Is 23:2.
a merchant. ver. 12, etc. Is 23:3, 8, 11. Re 18:3, 11-15.
for many isles. Is +11:11.
I am. ver. 4, 10, 11. Ezk 28:12-17. Ps 50:2. Is 23:9.
of perfect beauty. Heb. perfect beauty. La 2:15. Ezk 28:12.

4 midst. Heb. heart. Ezk 26:5. Ex +15:8. Ps 46:2mg.
builders. Is 62:5.
perfected thy. Jsh 19:29. Ho 9:13.

5 made. Heb. built.
of Senir. Dt 3:9. SS 4:8, Shenir.
cedars. 1 K 5:1, 6. 2 S 5:11. Ps 29:5. 92:12. 104:16. Is 14:8.

6 the oaks. Is 2:13. Zc 11:2.
Bashan. Dt +32:14.
the company, etc. *or,* they have made thy hatches of ivory well trodden.
company. Heb. daughters.
the isles. Is +11:11.
of Chittim. Ge +10:4.

7 linen. Ex +26:1. Is 19:9.
blue and purple. *or,* purple and scarlet. Ex 25:4. Je 10:9.
Elishah. Ge 10:4. 1 Ch 1:7.

8 Zidon. Ge +49:13.
Arvad. i.e. *place of fugitives,* **S#719h.** ver. 11. Ge 10:18. 2 K 18:34. Is 10:9. Je 49:23, Arpad.
wise. ver. 28. 1 K 5:6. 9:27. 2 Ch 2:13, 14.

9 Gebal. Jsh 13:5. 1 K 5:18mg. Ps 83:7.
calkers. *or,* stoppers of chinks. Heb. strengtheners. ver. 27. 2 K 12:5.
mariners. lit. "salt" men. ver. 27, 29. Jon 1:5.

10 Persia. Ezk 38:5. Da 5:28.
of Lud. Ge +10:22. Na 3:9.
Phut. Ge +10:6.
they hanged. ver. 11. SS 4:4.

11 of Arvad. ver. 8.
Gammadims. i.e. *dwarfs; courageous; deserters; cutters,* **S#1575h,** only here.
they hanged. ver. +10.
thy walls. 2 S 24:7.
they have. ver. 3, 4.

12 Tarshish. Ge +10:4.
fairs. ver. 14, 16, 19, 22, 27, 33 (wares).

13 Javan. Ge +10:2.
Tubal. Ge +10:2.
traded the persons. Heb. *nephesh,* souls, Ge +12:5. Ezk +22:29. Pr +22:22. Jl 3:3-8. 2 P 2:3. Re 18:2, 11-13.
brass. 1 K 7:14.
market. *or,* merchandise. ver. 9, 17, 19.

14 Togarmah. Ezk 38:6. Ge 10:3. 1 Ch 1:6.
with horses and. 1 K 10:29.

15 Dedan. ver. 20. Ge +10:7.
of ivory. 1 K 10:22. Re 18:12.

16 Syria. Ge 10:22, Aram. 28:5. 2 S 8:5. 10:6. 15:8. Is 7:2.
the wares of thy making. Heb. thy works. ver. 18. Ne 13:16. Ac 12:20.
occupied. *or,* traded. ver. +21, 27. Lk 19:13.
agate. *or,* chrysoprase. Is 54:12.

17 land of Israel. Ezk 11:17. +21:2, 3. 40:2. 47:18.
traded. ver. 16. 1 K 5:8-11, 18. 9:11-13.
wheat. Dt 8:8. 32:14. 1 K 5:9, 11. 2 Ch 2:10, 15. Ezr 3:7. Ac 12:20.
Minnith. Jg 11:33.
Pannag. i.e. *preparing of affliction; pastry,* **S#6436h.**
oil. Ezr 3:7.
balm. *or,* rosin. Ge +37:25.

18 Damascus. Ge +14:15.
Helbon. i.e. *the fat one; very fat,* **S#2463h,** only here.

19 Dan. Jg 18:28, 29.
going to and fro. *or,* Meuzal. Ge 10:27.
cassia. Ex 30:23, 24. Ps 45:8. SS 4:13, 14.

20 Dedan. ver. +15.
precious clothes. Heb. clothes of freedom.

21 Arabia. 2 Ch +9:14.
Kedar. Ge +25:13.
occupied with thee. Heb. *were* the merchants of thy hand. ver. 15. 1 Ch +29:24mg. Lk 19:13.

in lambs. 2 Ch 17:11. Is 60:7.

22 **Sheba**. 1 K +10:1.
and gold. Ge 2:11, 12.

23 **Haran**. Ge +11:26.
Canneh. i.e. *surname; flattering title*, S#3656h, only here. Ge 10:10, 22, Calneh. Is 10:9, Calno. Am 6:2, Calneh.
Eden. Ge 2:8. Am +1:5.
Sheba. ver. +22.
Asshur. Ge +10:22. Is 7:18, 20.
Chilmad. i.e. *complete clothing; defense; seven; complete measure; enclosure, fortress*, S#3638h, only here.

24 **all sorts of things**. *or*, excellent things.
clothes. Heb. foldings. 2 K 2:8.

25 **ships of Tarshish**. ver. +12. 1 K +22:48.
glorious. ver. 4.

26 **rowers**. Is 33:23.
great. Je +47:2.
the east wind. ver. 34. Ge +41:6. Ac 27:14, 41.
midst. Heb. heart. ver. 4mg.

27 **Thy riches**. ver. 7-9, 12, 18, 19, 22, 24, 34. Ezk 26:12. Pr 11:4. Re 18:11, etc.
occupiers. or, traders. ver. 15, 21mg. Mt 25:16. Lk 19:13.
and in all. *or*, even with all.
shall fall. Ezk 26:14, 21.
midst. Heb. heart. ver. 26mg.

28 **suburbs**. *or*, waves. Is 57:20.
shake. ver. 35. Ezk 26:10, 15-18. 31:16. Ex 15:14. Na 2:3.

29 **all that handle**. Re 18:17, etc.
shall come. Ezk 26:16. 32:10.

30 **shall cause**. ver. 31, 32. Ezk 26:17. Is 23:1-6. Re 18:9-19.
cast. Jsh +7:6.
shall wallow. Est +4:1-4.

31 **they shall make**. Is +3:24.
sackcloth. Jb +16:15.
they shall weep. Is 16:9. 22:4. Mi 1:8.
bitterness. 1 S 1:10mg.
heart. Heb. *nephesh*, Ex +23:9.

32 **take up**. ver. 2. Ezk 26:17.
What city. La 1:12. 2:13. Re 18:9-18.
the destroyed. ver. 26. Ezk 26:4, 5.

33 **thy wares**. ver. 3, 12, etc. Is 23:3-8. Re 18:3, 12-15, 19.
with the. ver. 27. Ezk 28:16.

34 **be broken**. ver. 26, 27. Ezk 26:12-15, 19-21. Zc 9:3, 4.

35 **the inhabitants**. Ezk 26:15-18. Is 23:5-11.
their kings. Ezk 28:17-19. 32:10. Re 18:9, 10.

36 **hiss**. Ezk 26:2. 2 Ch +29:8.
thou shalt. Ezk 26:14, 21.
a terror. Heb. terrors.
never shalt be any more. Heb. *shalt* not *be* for ever. Heb. *olam*, Le +25:32. Ps 37:10, 36.

EZEKIEL 28

2 **Because**. ver. 5, 17. Ezk 31:10. Dt +17:20. Pr 18:12.
I am a god. ver. 6, 9. Ge 3:5. Ac 12:22, 23. Re 17:3.
I sit. ver. 12-14. Is 14:13, 14. Da 4:30, 31. 2 Th 2:4.
in the midst. Heb. in the heart. Ezk 27:3, +4mg, 26mg, 27mg.
yet. ver. 9. Ps 9:20. +82:6, 7. Is 31:3.
thou set. ver. 6. 2 Th 2:3, 4.

3 **thou art wiser**. Da 1:17, 20. 2:48. 5:11, 12. Zc 9:2, 3.
Daniel. Ezk 14:14.
no secret. 1 K 4:29-32. 10:3. Jb 15:8. Ps 25:14. Ec 10:20. Da 2:22, 27, 28, 47. 5:12.

4 **With thy wisdom**. Ezk 29:3. Dt 8:17, 18. Pr 18:11. 23:4, 5. Ec 9:11. Hab 1:16. Zc 9:2-4.
riches. lit. strength. ver. 5.

5 **thy great wisdom**. Heb. the greatness of thy wisdom. Pr 26:12. Is 5:21. Ro 12:16.
and by. Ezk 27:12, etc. Ps 62:10. Is 23:3, 8. Ho 12:7, 8. Zc 9:3. Ja 4:13, 14.
and thine. ver. 2. Ezk +16:49. Dt 6:11, 12. 8:13, 14. 2 Ch 25:19. 32:23-25. Jb 31:24, 25. Ps 52:7. 62:10. Pr 11:28. 30:9. Is 10:8-14. Da 4:30, 37. Ho 13:6. Lk 12:16-21. 1 T 6:17.
because of. Mk +4:19.
riches. lit. strength. ver. 4.

6 **Because**. ver. 2. Ge 3:4, 5. Ex 9:17. Jb 9:4. 40:9-12. 1 C 10:22. 2 Th 2:4. Ja 1:11.

7 **I will**. Ezk 26:7-14. Is 23:8, 9. Je 27:2-7. Am +3:6.
the terrible. Ezk 30:11. 31:12. 32:12. Dt 28:49, 50. Is 25:3, 4. Da 7:7. Hab 1:6-8.
defile. ver. 15-17.

8 **shall bring**. Ezk 32:18-30. Jb 17:16. 33:18, 28. Ps 28:1. 30:9. 55:15. 88:4, 5. Pr 1:12. 28:17. Is 14:12. 38:17.
are slain. Ezk 27:26, 27, 34.

9 **yet say**. ver. 2. Is 45:9. Da 4:31, 32. 5:23-30. Ac 12:22, 23. 2 Th 2:4.
I am God. ver. +2. Ps +8:5. 82:6.
thou shalt. Ps 82:7. Is 31:3.
slayeth. *or*, woundeth.

10 **the deaths**. Ezk 31:18. 32:19, 21, 24-30. 44:7, 9. Le 26:41. Jg 8:21. 9:54. 1 S +14:6. Je 6:10. 9:25, 26. Jn +8:24. Ac 7:51. Ph 3:3.
by the. ver. 7. Ezk 11:9. Je 25:9.

12 **take up**. ver. 2. Ezk 19:1, 14. 26:17. 27:2, 32. 32:2, 16. 2 Ch 35:25. Is 14:4. Je 9:17-20.
Thou sealest. ver. 2-5. Ezk 27:3, 4. Ro 15:28. 2 C 1:22.
full. Jb 38:3, 4, 7. Pr +21:30. Is 10:13. Je 9:23. Lk 2:40. Ac 6:3. 1 C 1:19, 20. 3:19. Col 1:9. 2:3. Ja 3:13-18.
beauty. Is +33:17.

13 **in Eden**. Ezk 31:8, 9. 36:35. Ge 2:8. 3:23, 24. 13:10. Is 51:3. Jl 2:3. Re 2:7.

the garden. lit. "covered, protected" place. Ezk 31:8, 9.

every. Ezk 27:16, 22. Ge 2:11, 12. Ex 28:17-20. 39:10-21. Is 54:11, 12. Re 17:4. 21:19, 20.

sardius. *or*, ruby. Ex 28:17. 39:10. Re 4:3.

topaz. Jb 28:19. Re 21:20.

diamond. Ex 28:18. 39:11.

beryl. *or*, chrysolite. Ezk 1:16. 10:9. Ex 28:20. 39:13. SS 5:14. Da 10:6.

onyx. Ge +2:12.

jasper. Ex 39:13. Re 4:3. 21:19.

sapphire. Ezk 1:26. 10:1. Re 21:19.

emerald. *or*, chrysoprase. Ezk 27:16mg. Re 4:3. 21:19.

carbuncle. Ex 28:17. 39:10.

gold. Ge 2:12.

the workmanship. Ezk 26:13. Is 14:11. 23:16. 30:32.

tabrets. Ps 150:4. Is 5:12. 24:8. 30:32. Je 31:4.

pipes. lit. things "pierced" with holes.

thou wast. ver. 15. Ezk 21:30.

14 the anointed. ver. 16. Ex 25:17-20. 30:26. 40:9.

cherub. Ge +3:24.

that covereth. ver. 16. Ex 25:20. 37:9. 1 Ch 28:18. Is 30:1. Na 2:5mg.

and I. Ex 9:16. Ps 75:5-7. Is 10:6, 15. 37:26, 27. Da 2:37, 38. 4:35. 5:18-23. Jn 11:51. Ro 9:17.

upon. ver. 2, 16. Ezk 20:40. Is 14:12-15. 2 Th 2:4.

the stones. ver. 13, 17. Ex 24:9, 10. Re 18:16.

15 Thou wast. ver. 3.

perfect. ver. 3-6, 12. Ezk 16:14. 27:3, 4.

till iniquity. ver. 17, 18. Ge 1:26, 27, 31. 6:5, 6. Pr 14:34. Ec 7:29. Is 14:12. La 5:16. Ro 7:9. 2 P 2:4.

16 the multitude. Ezk 27:12, etc. Is 23:17, 18. Ho 12:7. Lk 19:45, 46. Jn 2:16. 1 T 6:9, 10.

filled. Ezk 8:17. Ge 6:11. Am 3:9. Mi 2:2. 6:12. Hab 2:8, 17. Zp 1:9.

thou hast sinned. Ro 6:23.

therefore. Ge 3:24. Le 18:24-28. Is 22:19. 23:9. Mi 2:10. 2 P 2:4-6. Ju 6. Re 12:9.

O covering. ver. 14.

17 heart. ver. +2, 5. Ezk 16:14, 15. Pr 11:2. Lk 14:11.

beauty. Is +33:17.

thou hast. Is 19:11-13. Je 8:9. Ro 1:22-25. 1 C 1:19-21.

I will cast. Jb 40:11, 12. Ps 73:18. 147:6.

I will lay. Ezk 16:41. 23:48. 32:10. Is 14:9-11.

may behold. Is +66:24.

18 defiled. ver. 2, 13, 14, 16.

by the iniquity. Mk 8:36.

therefore. Ezk 5:4. Jg 9:15, 20. Am 1:9, 10, 14. 2:2, 5. Re 6:15-17. 18:8.

I will bring. Ml 4:3. 2 P 2:6.

19 they. Ezk 27:35, 36. Ps 76:12. Is 14:16-19. Re 18:9, 10, 15-19.

thou shalt. Ezk 26:14, 21. 27:36. Je 51:63, 64. Re 18:21.

a terror. Heb. terrors. Ezk 27:36mg.

any more. Heb. *olam*, Le +25:32. Ps 37:10.

21 set. Ezk 6:2. 25:2. 29:2.

Zidon. Ge +49:13.

22 I am against. Ezk +15:7. Na 1:6.

I will. ver. 25. Ezk 39:13. Ex 9:16. 14:4, 17. 15:21. Le 10:3. 1 S 17:45-47. Ps 9:16. 21:12, 13. 83:17, 18. Is 5:15, 16. 37:20. Re 19:1, 2.

shall be. Is +8:13.

23 I will send. Ezk +38:22. Je 15:2.

and they shall. Ezk +6:7.

24 a pricking. Ex +23:33. 2 S 23:6, 7. Is 35:9. 55:13. Je 12:14. Mi 7:4. Zc 14:21. 2 C 12:7. Re 21:4.

and they. ver. 23, 26. Ezk +6:7.

25 When. Le 26:44, 45. Dt +30:3, 4. Jl 3:7.

be sanctified. ver. +22.

then shall. Ezk 36:28. 37:25. Je 23:8. 27:11.

to my. Ge 28:13, 14.

26 and they shall dwell. Dt +12:10. Zc 2:4, 5.

safely. *or*, with confidence. Pr 14:26.

build. Is 65:21, 22. Je 29:5, 6, 28. 31:4, 5. 32:15. Am 9:13, 14.

when I. ver. 24. Ezk ch. 25-32, 35. Is ch. 13-21. Je ch. 46-51. Zc 1:15.

despise. *or*, spoil. Ezk 39:10. Is 17:14. 33:1. Je 30:16. La 1:8. Hab 2:8. Zp 2:8, 9.

and they. ver. 22, 24. Ezk +6:7. Ex 29:46.

EZEKIEL 29

1 A.M. 3415. B.C. 589.

tenth year. ver. 17. Ezk 1:2. 8:1. 20:1. 26:1. 40:1.

2 set. Ezk 6:2. 20:46. 21:2. 25:2. 28:21, 22.

Pharaoh. Je 44:30.

against all. Ezk ch. 30-32. Is ch. 18. 19:1-17. ch. 20. Je 9:25, 26. 25:18, 19. 43:8-13. 46:2-26. Jl 3:19. Zc 14:18, 19.

3 I am. ver. 10. Ezk +15:7. Ps 76:7. Je 44:30. Na 1:6.

the great. Ezk 32:2. Ps 74:13, 14. Is 27:1. 51:9. Re 12:3, 4, 16, 17. 13:2, 4, 11. 16:13. 20:2.

My river. ver. 9. Ezk 28:2. Dt 8:17. Is 10:13, 14. Da 4:30, 31.

4 I will put hooks. Ezk 38:4. 2 K 19:28. Jb 41:1, 2. Is 37:29. Am 4:2.

the fish. Hab 1:14, 15.

5 I will leave. Ezk 31:18. 32:4-6. 39:4-6, 11-20. Ps 110:5, 6. Je 8:2. 16:4. 25:33.

open fields. Heb. face of the field. Je 9:22.

I have. 1 K +14:11. Ps 74:14.

6 **know**. Ezk +6:7. Ex 9:14.
a staff. 2 K 18:21. Is 20:5, 6. 30:2-7. 31:1-3.
36:6. Je 2:36. 37:7. La 4:17.

7 **they took**. Ezk 17:15-17. Je 37:5-11.
thou didst. Ps 118:8, 9. 146:3, 4. Pr 25:19. Je
17:5, 6.

8 **I will**. ver. 19, 20. Ezk 6:3. 11:8. 30:4, 5, 10,
11. Je +12:12.
cut. Ezk 25:13. 32:10-13. Ge 6:7. Ex 12:12. Je
7:20. 32:43.

9 **the land**. ver. 10-12. Ezk 30:7, 13-17. Je
43:10-13.
because. ver. 3. Jb 41:1, 34. Pr 16:18. 18:12.
29:23.

10 **I will**. ver. 11. Ezk 30:12. Hab 3:8.
utterly waste. Heb. wastes of waste.
desolate. Jl 3:19.
from the tower of. *or*, from Migdol to
Syene. Ex +14:2.
Syene. Heb. Seveneh. i.e. *opening, key; seven*,
S#5482h. Ezk 30:6.

11 **foot of man**. Ezk 30:10-13. 31:12. 32:13.
33:28. 36:28. Je 43:11, 12.
forty. 2 Ch 36:21. Is 23:15, 17. Je 25:11, 12.
29:10. Da 9:2. Jon +3:4.

12 **desolate in**. Ezk 30:7. Je 25:15-19. 27:6-11.
Na 3:8, 9.
and I will scatter. Ezk 30:23, 26. Je 46:19.

13 **At the**. Is 19:22, 23. Je 46:26.

14 **Pathros**. Is +11:11.
habitation. *or*, birth. Ezk 16:3mg.
base. Heb. low. ver. 15. Ezk 17:6, 14. Zc
10:11.

15 **the basest**. Ezk 17:6, 14. 30:13. Is 19:23. Zc
10:11.
rule. Ezk 31:2. 32:2. Da 11:42, 43. Na 3:8, 9.

16 **the confidence**. ver. 6, 7. Ezk 17:15-17. Is
20:5. 30:1-6. 31:1-3. 36:4-6. Je 2:18, 19, 36,
37. 37:5-7. La 4:17. Ho 5:13. 7:11. 12:1. 14:3.
bringeth. Ezk 21:23. Nu 5:15. 1 K 17:18. Ps
25:7. 79:8. Is 64:9. Je 14:10. Ho 8:13. 9:9. He
10:3, 17. Re 16:19.
remembrance. 2 S +8:16mg.
but. ver. 6, 9, 21. Ezk +6:7.

17 A.M. 3432. B.C. 572.
the seven and twentieth year. ver. 1. Ezk
1:2.

18 **Nebuchadrezzar**. Ezk 26:7-12. Je 25:9. 27:6.
bald. Is +3:24.

19 **I will**. ver. 8-10. Ezk 30:10-12. Je 43:10-13.
take her spoil , and take her prey. Heb.
spoil her spoil, and prey her prey. Ezk
38:12mg.

20 **labor**. *or*, hire.
served. 2 K 10:30. Is 10:6, 7. 45:1-3. Je 25:9.
Da 4:32.

21 **In that day**. Is +2:11.
I cause. Ezk 28:25, 26. Ps +92:10. Is +4:2.
27:6.

the opening. Ezk +24:27. Am 3:7, 8.
they shall know. ver. +6, 9, 16.

EZEKIEL 30

2 **Howl**. Is +13:6.

3 **the day is**. Ezk 7:7, 12. Ps 37:13. Jl 2:1. Ob
15. Zp 1:7, 14. Mt 24:33. Ph 4:5. Ja 5:9. Re
6:17.
the day of the Lord. Ezk 7:7. 13:5. Is 2:12.
13:6. +34:8. Je 46:10. Jl 1:15. 2:1, 2, 11, 31.
3:14. Am 5:18, 20. Ob 15. Zp 1:7, 8, 14, 15,
18. 2:2, 3. Zc 14:1. Ml 4:1, 5. 1 Th +5:2. 2 Th
2:2. 2 P 3:10. Re 1:10. 3:3, 11. 6:17. 16:14, 15.
a cloudy. ver. 18. Ezk 32:7. 34:12. Ge +9:13.
Ex 14:20, 24. Is 19:1. Jl 2:1, 2. Am 5:16-20.
the time of the heathen. Ezk 29:12. Ps
110:6. +149:7-9. Is 24:21-23. 34:2, etc. Je
25:15-29. +30:7. Da 9:27. 12:7. Jl 3:11-14. Ob
15. Zp 3:6, 7. Zc 14:3-19. Lk +21:24. Ro
+11:25. Re 19:13-21.

4 **the sword**. Ezk 29:8. Is 19:2. Je 50:35-37.
pain. *or*, fear. ver. 9. Ex 15:14-16. Ps 48:6, 7.
Is 19:16, 17. Re 18:9, 10.
in Ethiopia. ver. 9. Je 46:9.
and they. ver. 10. Ezk 29:12, 19.
and her. Is 16:7. Je 50:15.

5 **Ethiopia**. Ge +2:13.
Libya. Heb. Phut. i.e. *heart of the sea; afflicted*,
S#6316h. Ge +10:6.
Lydia. Heb. Lud. i.e. *birth; travail*, S#3865h. Ge
+10:22. Na 3:9.
all the. Je +25:20.
Chub. i.e. *Christ's thorn; bearing fruit; clustered;
a horde*, S#3552h, only here.
men. Heb. children.
that is. Je 44:27.
by the sword. Je 12:12.

6 **They also**. Jb 9:13. Is 20:3-6. 31:3. Na 3:9.
from the tower of Syene. *or*, from Migdol
to Syene. Ezk 29:10mg.
by the sword. Jg 7:18. Ps 7:11-13.

7 **they shall**. Ezk 29:12. 32:18-32. Je 25:18-26.
ch. 46-51.

8 **shall know**. Ezk +6:7. Ps 58:11.
when I. ver. 14, 16. Ezk 22:31. Dt +32:22.
Am 1:4, 7, 10, 12, 14. 2:2, 5.
destroyed. Heb. broken. ver. 6.

9 **messengers**. ver. 5, 6. Is 18:1, 2. 20:3-5. Zp
2:12.
careless. Ezk 38:11. 39:6. Jg 18:7. Is 32:9-11.
47:8. Je 49:31. Zp 2:15. 1 Th 5:2, 3.
great. ver. 4. Ezk 26:16. 27:35. 32:9, 10. Is
19:17. 23:5. Je 49:21. Zc 11:2, 3.
lo. Ezk 33:33. Am 4:2.

10 **I will**. Ezk 29:4, 5, 19. 32:11-16.
by the. ver. 24, 25.

11 **the terrible**. Ezk 28:7. 31:12. 32:12. Dt
28:50. Is 14:4-6. Je 51:20-23. Hab 1:6-9.

and fill. Ezk 35:8. 39:4, 11-20. Is 34:3-7. Zp 1:17, 18. Re 14:20. 19:18.

12 **I will make**. Ezk 29:3. Is 19:4-10. 44:27. Je 50:38. 51:36. Na 1:4. Re 16:12.
dry. Heb. drought. Ge 7:22. Ex 14:21.
sell. Jg 2:14. Is 19:4.
all that is therein. Heb. the fulness thereof. Ezk +19:7. 1 C 10:26.
by the hand. Ezk 28:10. 31:12.

13 **I will also**. Ex +12:12. Zc 13:2.
idols. 2 K +23:24.
images. S#457h. Le 19:4 (idols). 26:1. 1 Ch 16:26. Jb 13:4 (no value). Ps 96:5. 97:7. Is 2:8, 18, 20. 10:10, 11. 19:1, 3. 31:7. Je 14:14 (thing of nought). Hab 2:18. Zc 11:17.
Noph. Is +19:13. Ho 9:6, Memphis. Heb. Moph.
there shall. Ezk 29:14, 15. Zc 10:11.
put. Is 19:16. Je 46:5.

14 **Pathros**. Is +11:11.
Zoan. or, Tanis. Nu +13:22.
will execute. Je +46:25.

15 **I will pour**. Ps 11:6. Ezk +7:8.
Sin. i.e. thorn; clay, mire, S#5512h. or, Pelusium. ver. 16. Ex 16:1. 17:1. Nu 33:11, 12.
the multitude of No. Je +46:25.

16 **set fire**. ver. 8, 9. Ezk 28:18.

17 **Aven**. i.e. vanity; perverseness; nothingness, S#206h. or, Heliopolis. Ge 41:45, On. Ho 10:5, 8, Beth-aven. Am 1:5.
Pibeseth. i.e. mouth of loathing, S#6364h, only here. or, Pubastum.
by the sword. Is 66:16.

18 **Tehaphnehes**. S#8471h. Je +43:7.
the day. Ex 10:15, 22, 23. Is 5:30. 9:19. 13:10. Jl +3:15. Mt +24:29.
darkened. or, restrained.
I shall break. Ezk 29:15. Is 9:4. 10:27. 14:25.
the pomp. Ezk 31:18. Is +14:11. Je 46:20-26.
a cloud. ver. 3. Is 19:1.

19 **execute judgments**. ver. 14. Ezk 5:8, 15. 25:11, 17. 39:21. Ex +7:4. Nu 33:4. Ps 9:16. 149:7. Ro 2:5, 6. Re 17:1.
shall know. Ezk +6:7.

20 A.M. 3416. B.C. 588.
eleventh year. Ezk 1:2. 26:1. 29:1, 17.

21 **I have**. ver. 24. Ps 10:15. 37:17. Je 48:25.
it shall not. Is 1:6. Je 30:13. 46:11. 51:8, 9. Na 3:19. Re 18:21.

22 **I am**. Ezk 29:3. Je 46:25.
will break. Ps 37:17.
the strong. Ezk 34:16.
and that. 2 K 24:7. Je 37:7. 46:1-12. I will. Je 46:21-25.

23 **scatter the Egyptians**. ver. 17, 18, 26. Ezk 29:12, 13. Da 4:35.

24 **I will**. ver. 25. Ne 6:9. Ps 18:32, 39. 37:17. 144:1. Is 45:1, 5. Je 27:6-8. Zc 10:11, 12.

and put. Dt 32:41, 42. Ps 17:13. Is 10:5, 6, 15. Zp 2:12.
he shall. Ezk 26:15. Jb 24:12. Je 51:52.

25 **I will strengthen**. Ps 75:7. Da 4:32, 37.
they shall know. ver. 19, 26. Ezk +6:7. Ps 9:16.
put my sword. Ps 17:13, 14. Da 4:17.

26 **I will**. ver. 17, 18, 23. Ezk 6:13. 29:12. Da 11:42.
they shall. ver. +8.

EZEKIEL 31

1 **in the eleventh**. On Sunday, June 19, A.M. 3416, according to Usher; and about a month before the capture of Jerusalem. Ezk 1:2. 30:20. Je 52:5, 6.

2 **speak**. Je 1:5, 17. Pr 27:19. Re 10:11.
to his. Ezk 29:19. 30:10. Na 3:8-10.
Whom. ver. 18. Is 14:13, 14.

3 **the Assyrian**. Na 3:1, etc. Zp 2:13.
a cedar. Ezk 17:3, 4, 22. Is 10:33, 34. 37:24. Da 4:10, 20-23. 5:20. Zc 11:2.
with fair branches. Heb. fair of branches. Ezk 33:32mg.
of an high. ver. 6. Jg 9:15. Da 4:12.

4 **waters**. Ezk 17:5, 8. Pr 14:28. Je 51:36. Re 17:1, 15.
made him great. or, nourished him.
set. or, brought.
little rivers. or, conduits.

5 **his height**. Ps 37:35, 36. Is 10:8-14. 36:4, 18, 19. 37:11-13. Da 4:11.
multitude of waters. ver. 7. Dt +11:10.
he shot forth. or, it sent them forth.

6 **the fowls**. Ezk 17:23. Da 4:12, 21. Mt 13:32.

7 **his branches**. ver. 9, 12. Ezk 17:6. Da 4:14.
great waters. lit. many waters. Ezk 29:3. Jn +3:23.

8 **cedars**. Ezk 28:13. Ge 2:8. 13:10. Ps 80:10. Is 51:3.
nor any. Ps 37:35. Is 10:7-14. 36:4-18. 37:11-13.
garden of God. Ezk 28:13. Ge 2:8. +6:2. 13:10.

9 **made**. Ezk 16:14. Ex 9:16. Ps 75:6, 7. Je 46:20. Da 2:21, 37, 38. 4:22-25. 5:20-23.
all the trees. Ezk 17:22-24. Jg 9:8-20. Ps 96:12, 18. Is 55:12, 13. Zc 11:2.
of Eden. Ge 2:8.
garden of God. Ge +6:2.
envied. Ge 26:14. 37:11. 1 S 18:15. Ps 73:3. Pr 27:4. Ec 4:4. Ja 4:5, 6.

10 **Because**. Mt 23:12.
and his. ver. 14. Dt +17:20. Jb 11:11, 12. Pr 8:13. 11:2. 18:12. Is 14:13-15. Da 4:30. Ob 3.

11 **delivered**. Ezk 11:9. 21:31. 23:28. Jg 16:23. Je 43:8-10. 44:30. 46:22-24. 1 T 1:20.
the mighty. Ezk 32:11, 12. Je 25:9. Da 5:18, 19.

he shall surely deal with him. Heb. in doing he shall do unto him. Jg 1:7. Ps 39:11. Mt 7:1, 2. Ja 2:13.
I have driven. Le 18:24-28. 20:22, 23. Dt 18:12. La 1:21. Na 3:18.

12　**strangers**. Ezk 28:7. 30:11. Is 19:4. Hab 1:6, 11.
upon. Ezk 32:4, 5. 35:5, 8. 39:4. Is 34:5-7.
rivers. or, torrents. S#650h. Ezk 6:3. 32:6. 34:13. 35:8. 36:4, 6. 2 S 22:16. Jb 6:15. Ps 18:15. 42:1. 126:4. SS 5:12. Is 8:7. Jl 1:20. 3:18.
gone. Da 4:12-14. Na 3:17, 18. Re 17:16.

13　**his ruins**. Ezk 29:5. 32:4. Is 18:6. Re 19:17, 18.

14　**the end**. Dt 13:11. 21:21. Ne 13:18. Da 4:32. 5:22, 23. 1 C 10:11. 2 P 2:6.
stand up in their height. or, stand upon themselves for their height.
delivered. Ps 82:7. Ec +12:7, 8. He +9:27.
the nether. or, lowest. Dt +32:22 (S#8482h). Ezk 32:18-32. Ps 63:9, 10.
pit. Heb. bor, Ge 37:20.

15　**grave**. Heb. sheol, Ge +37:35. Ezk 32:27.
I caused a. Na 2:8-10. Re 18:9-11, 18, 19.
mourn. Heb. be black. Ml 3:4.

16　**made**. Ezk 26:10, 15. 27:28. Na 2:3. Hg 2:7. He 12:26, 27. Re 11:13. 18:9, etc.
when I. Ezk 32:18, etc. Is 14:15.
hell. Heb. sheol, Ge +37:35. Ezk 32:27.
pit. Heb. bor, Ge +37:20 (S#953h). Is 14:19.
and all. ver. 9, 18. Is 14:8. Hab 2:17.
of Lebanon. Is 10:12, 13, 17-19, 33, 34.
shall be comforted. ver. 14. Ezk 32:31. Is 14:15.
nether. ver. 14. Dt +32:22 (S#8482h).

17　**went**. Ezk 32:20-30. Ps 9:17. Is 14:9-15.
into. ver. 15, 16. Ezk 32:21.
hell. Heb. sheol, Ge +37:35. Ezk 32:27.
that were. Ezk 30:6-8, 21-25. Na 3:17, 18.
dwelt. ver. 3, 6. Ezk 32:31. La 4:20. Da 4:11, 12. Mk 4:32.

18　**art thou**. ver. 2. Ezk 32:19.
among the trees. Ps 37:35, 36. Is 14:18-20. Je 46:24, 26.
with the. ver. 9, 16.
thou shalt. Ezk +28:10. 32:10, 19, 21, 24, etc. 1 S 17:26, 36. 2 S 1:20. Je 9:25, 26.
This is. 2 Ch 28:22. Ps 52:7. Mt 13:19. 26:26-28. 1 C 10:4.

EZEKIEL 32

1　A.M. 3417. B.C. 587.
in the twelfth. ver. 17. Ezk 1:2. 29:1, 17. 30:20.

2　**take up**. ver. 16, 18. Ezk 19:1. 27:2, 32. 28:12. Je 9:18.
Thou art like. Ezk 19:2-6. 38:13. Ge 49:9. Nu 24:9. Pr 28:15. Je 4:7. Na 2:11-13.

and thou art as. Ezk 29:3. Ps 74:13, 14. Is 27:1. 51:9.
whale. or, dragon. lit. long "extended" object. Ezk 29:3. Jb 30:29.
and troubledst. Ezk 34:18.
with thy feet. Dt 11:10. Pr +21:1.
fouledst. Ezk 34:18, 19. Nu 19:17mg. Ro 6:4.
rivers. lit. "flowings." ver. 14. S#5104h. Ezk 1:1, 3. 31:4, 15. Ge 2:10. 15:18. Jg 3:8mg. Jb 20:17mg. Zc 9:10.

3　**I will**. Ezk 12:13. 17:20. Ec 9:12. Je 16:16. La 1:13. Ho 7:12. Hab 1:14-17. Mt +13:47.

4　**leave thee upon**. Ezk 31:12, 13. 39:4, 5, 17-20. 1 K +14:11. Ps 63:10. 74:14. 79:2, 3. 83:9, 10. 110:5, 6. Is 14:19. 18:6. 34:2-7. +66:24. Jl 3:19.

6　**water**. Ex 7:17. Is 34:3, 7. Re 14:19, 20. 16:6.
wherein thou swimmest. or, of thy swimming.
rivers. 2 S +22:16.

7　**put thee out**. or, extinguish thee. 2 S 14:7 (quench). 21:17. 2 Ch 29:7. Jb 18:5, 6. Pr 13:9. SS 8:7 (quench). Is 42:3. +66:24.
I will cover the heaven. Ezk 30:3, 18. Ex 10:21-23. Is 13:9-11. 34:4. Je 13:16. Jl 2:2, 31.
make the stars. Mt +24:29. Mk 13:24. 2 P 3:10, 12.
dark. Pr +20:20.
the moon. Re 8:12.

8　**All**. Ge +2:24.
bright lights of heaven. Heb. lights of the light in heaven. Ge 1:14.
dark. Heb. them dark. Ex +10:22.
set darkness upon. Jl 2:10.

9　**vex**. Heb. provoke to anger, or grief. Re 11:18. 18:10-15.
when. Ezk 29:12. 30:23, 26. Je 25:15-25.

10　**amazed**. Ezk 27:35. Dt 29:24. 1 K 9:8.
my sword. Dt 32:41.
horribly afraid. Jsh 2:11.
and they. Ezk 26:16. 30:9. Ex 15:14-16. Je 51:9. Zc 11:2. Re 18:10.
life. Heb. nephesh, Ge +44:30.
in the day. Ezk 27:27.

11　**The sword**. Ezk 26:7. 30:4, 22-25. Je 27:6. 43:10. 46:13, 24-26.

12　**the mighty**. Ezk 31:11.
the terrible. Ezk 28:7. 30:11. 31:12. Dt 28:49, 50. Hab 1:6, 7.
they shall. Ezk 29:19. Is 25:2, 3.

13　**destroy**. Ezk 29:8. 30:12.
neither. ver. 2. Ezk 29:11. 34:18.

14　**and cause**. Ezk 34:18. Jb 41:1.

15　**destitute of that whereof**. Heb. desolate from the fulness thereof. Ezk 29:12, 19, 20. Ps 24:1. 107:34.
then. Ezk +6:7. 33:29. 34:27, 30. 35:4, 9, 12, 15. 36:11, 23, 36, 38. 37:6, 13, 14, 28. 38:16, 23. 39:6, 7, 22, 23, 28.

16 **the lamentation**. ver. 2. Ezk 26:17. 2 S 1:17.
3:33, 34. 2 Ch 35:25. Je 9:17, 18.
the daughters. Jg 11:40.
17 **in the twelfth year**. ver. 1. Ezk 1:2.
the fifteenth. That is, of the twelfth month,
just a fortnight (for fourteen nights, or two
weeks) after the preceding prophecy.
18 **wail**. ver. 2, 16. Ezk 21:6, 7. Is 16:9. Mi 1:8.
Lk 19:41. Ro 12:15.
cast them down. Ezk 20:25. 43:3. Je 1:10.
Ho 6:5.
the daughters. Nu +21:25mg.
unto the. ver. 21, 24, etc. Ezk 26:20. +31:14.
Ps 30:9. 63:9. Is 14:15.
nether. Dt +32:22 (S#8482h).
with them. Ge 6:5.
pit. Heb. *bor*, Ge +37:20.
19 **Whom dost**. Ezk 27:3, 4. 28:12-17. 31:2, 18.
go down. Is 14:9-15.
with the uncircumcised. ver. 21, 24, 29,
30. Ezk +28:10.
20 **fall**. ver. 23-26, 29, 30. Ezk 29:8-12.
she is delivered to the sword. *or*, the
sword is laid.
draw her. Ps 28:3. Pr 24:11. Je 22:19.
21 **The strong**. ver. +27. 1 S 28:12.
shall speak. Ezk 31:15, 16. Is 14:10, 16. Lk
16:24.
out of. Is 1:31. 14:9, 10. +30:33. +66:24. Lk
16:23, 24.
hell. Heb. *sheol*, Ge +37:35.
gone down. ver. +19, 24, 25. Nu +16:30-34.
Ps +9:17. +55:15. Pr +14:32.
22 **Asshur is there**. ver. 24, 26, 29, 30. Ge
+10:22. 2 K 19:35. Is +30:33. 37:36-38. Na
1:7-12. 3:1, etc. Re 19:20. 20:10.
graves. Heb. *qeber*, Ge +23:4.
23 **graves**. Heb. *qeber*, Ge +23:4. Ezk 26:20. Is
14:15.
pit. Heb. *bor*, Ge +37:20.
grave. Heb. *qeburah*, Ge +35:20.
which caused. ver. 24-27, 32. Ezk 26:17, 20.
Is 14:16. 51:12, 13.
terror. *or*, dismaying. or, downfall. ver. 24,
25, 26, 27, 30, 32. Ezk 26:17. Je 48:39. 49:37.
the land of the living. ver. 26. Ps +27:13.
24 **Elam**. Ge +10:22.
grave. Heb. *qeburah*, Ge +35:20.
which are. ver. 18, 21. Ezk 26:20.
which caused. ver. 23.
borne their shame. ver. 25, 30. Ezk +16:52,
54. 34:29. 36:6, 7, 15. 39:26. 44:13. Je 3:24,
25. Hab 2:16.
pit. Heb. *bor*, Ge +37:20.
25 **set her**. Ps 139:8. Re 2:22.
a bed. 2 S 4:7. 2 K 6:12. Jb 7:13.
all of them uncircumcised. ver. +19, 21.
Ezk +28:10. 44:7, 9. 2 S 1:20. 1 Ch 10:4. Ac
7:51.
though their terror. Mt +10:28. Lk 12:4, 5.

land of. Ezk +26:20.
pit. Heb. *bor*, Ge +37:20.
26 **Meshech**. Ge +10:2. Je 51:27, Minni.
Tubal. Ge +10:2.
graves. Heb. *qeber*, Ge +23:4.
all of them uncircumcised. ver. 19, 20, 24.
caused their terror. ver. 23, 27, 32.
27 **shall not lie with**. ver. 21. Jb 3:13-15. Is
14:18, 19.
to hell. Heb. *sheol*, Ge +37:35. ver. 19, 21.
Ezk 18:4, 20. Dt 29:29. Mt 25:46. Mk 9:43-46.
Lk 16:24. Ac 7:22. 2 T 1:10.
with. Ps 16:10. Am 9:2.
their weapons of war. Heb. weapons of
their war. Is 54:17. 2 C 10:4.
but their iniquities. Ezk +18:20. Jb 20:11.
Ps 49:14. 92:7, 9. 109:18. Pr +14:32.
Jn +8:24.
28 **thou shalt be broken**. Je 25:15, 16, 18-26.
Da 2:34, 35.
29 **Edom**. Ezk ch. 25, 35. Je +49:7-22.
laid. Heb. given, or put. ver. 23. Ezk 31:14.
35:12.
pit. Heb. *bor*, Ge +37:20.
30 **the princes**. Ezk 38:6, 15. 39:2. Je +1:14.
4:6.
the Zidonians. Ezk 28:21-23. Ge 10:15. 1 K
5:6. Je 25:22.
and bear. ver. 24, 25.
pit. Heb. *bor*, Ge +37:20.
31 **Pharaoh shall**. Ezk +28:9.
shall be comforted. Ezk 14:22. 31:16. La
2:13. Lk 16:24.
32 **I have caused**. ver. +27. Ge 35:5. Jb 31:23.
Je 25:15, 29-33. Zp 3:6-8. 2 C 5:11. He 10:31.
Re 6:15-17.

EZEKIEL 33

2 **speak**. ver. 17, 30. Ezk 3:11, 27.
When I bring the sword upon a land. Heb.
A land when I bring a sword upon her. Ezk
6:3. 11:8. Je +12:12. 25:31. Zc 13:7.
set. ver. 7. 2 S 18:24-27. 2 K 9:17-20. Is 21:6-
9. 56:9, 10. 62:6. Je 51:12. Ho 9:8.
3 **blow the trumpet**. ver. 8, 9. Ne 4:18, 20. Ho
+8:1. 1 C 14:8.
4 **whosoever heareth**. Heb. he that hearing
heareth. 2 Ch 25:16. Pr 29:1. Je 6:17, +19.
42:20-22. Zc 1:2-4. Ja 1:22.
his blood. ver. 5, 9. Ac +18:6.
head. Jg +5:30.
5 **heard**. Ps 95:7. He 2:1-3.
trumpet. Am +3:6.
his blood. Is 51:2. Jn 8:39.
But. Ex 9:19-21. 2 K 6:10. Ac 2:37-41. Col
1:28. 1 T 4:6, 16. He 11:7.
soul. Heb. *nephesh*, Ge +12:13.
6 **and blow**. Is 56:10, 11. Am +3:6. 1 C 14:8.
person. Heb. *nephesh*, Jsh +10:28.

he is. ver. 8, 9. Ezk +18:20, 24. Pr +14:32. Jn +8:21-24.

his blood. Ezk 34:10. Lk +11:50.

7 **I have**. Ezk 3:17-21. SS 3:3. 5:7. Is 62:6. Je 6:27. 31:6. Mi 7:4. Ep 4:11. He 13:17.

thou shalt. Ezk 2:7, 8. 1 K 22:14, 16-28. 2 Ch 19:10. Je 1:17. +23:28. 26:2. Ac +20:20, 26, 27. 1 C 11:23. 1 Th 4:1, 2.

8 **O wicked**. ver. 14. Ezk 18:4, 10-13, 18, 20. Ge +2:17. 3:4. Pr 11:21. Ec 8:13. Is 3:11. Je 8:13.

surely. Ge +2:16.

if thou. Ezk 13:9, 10. Je 8:11, 12. 14:13-16.

that wicked. ver. 6. Nu 27:3. Ac 20:26, 27.

9 **if thou**. Ezk 3:19, 21. Ps 40:9, 10. Mt +24:4, 25. Ac 13:40. 18:5, 6. 28:23-28. Ga 5:19-23. 6:7, 8. Ep 5:3-6. Ph +3:18, 19. 1 Th 4:3-8. 5:14. Re +1:5.

if he. Pr 15:10. 29:1. Lk +12:47. Jn +8:24. Ac 13:46. He 2:3. 12:25.

thou hast. Ac 20:26. 2 C 2:15-17.

soul. Heb. *nephesh*, Ge +12:13.

10 **If our**. Ezk 24:23. Le 26:39.

pine away. Ezk 4:17. Le 26:39.

how. Ezk 37:11. Ps 130:7. Is 49:14. 51:20. Je 2:25.

11 **As I live**. Dt +32:40.

I have. Ezk 18:23, 32. 2 S 14:14. La 3:33. Ho 11:8. Lk 15:20-32. 1 T +2:4. 2 P +3:9.

no pleasure. Je 27:13. Jn 5:40.

but that. Lk 15:7.

turn ye. Ezk 14:6. Le 26:39-42. Dt 30:10. 2 Ch 30:6. Pr 1:23. 8:36. Zc +1:3. Ac +3:19.

12 **say**. ver. 2.

The righteousness. ver. 18. Ezk 3:20, 21. 18:24-26. 2 S 24:10-15.

as for. ver. 19. Ezk 18:21, 27-32. 1 K 8:48-50. 2 Ch +7:14. Mt 21:28-31. Ro 3:25.

neither. 1 J 2:1.

13 **if**. Ge +4:7. Je +7:5. 2 P +1:10.

he trust. Ezk 3:20. 18:24. Lk 18:9-14. Ro 10:3. Ph 3:9. He +10:38. 2 P 2:20-22. 1 J 2:19.

to his own righteousness. Is 64:6. Ro 10:3. He 6:4-6. 10:26, 29. 2 P 1:9.

he shall die. Ezk 18:4, 24. Ro 6:23.

14 **Thou shalt**. ver. 8. Ezk 3:18, 19. 18:27. Is 3:11. Je 18:7, 8. Lk 13:3-5.

surely. Ge +2:16.

if. Je +7:5. 1 C +15:2.

he turn. Pr 28:13. Is 55:7. Je 4:1. Ho 14:1. Ac +3:19.

and do. Mt 7:21. Jn +13:17. He +5:9.

that which is lawful and right. Heb. judgment and justice. Ezk 18:5mg, 21, 27. Ps +15:1-5. Je +22:3. Mi +6:8. Ml +3:5. Mt 9:13. 1 C +6:9-11. Ga 5:19-23. He 6:9-12. Ja 1:26, 27. 3:17. 4:17. 2 P 1:5-11. 1 J 2:3, 29. 5:17.

15 **restore**. Ezk 18:7, 12, 16. Ex 22:26, 27. Le 6:2, 4, 5. Dt 24:6, 10-13, 17. Jb 22:6. 24:3, 9. Am 2:8.

give again. Ex 22:1-4. Le 6:2-5. Nu 5:6-8. Lk 19:8, 9. Ep 4:28.

walk. Ezk 20:11, 13, 21. Le 18:5. Ps 119:93. Lk 1:6. Col +1:10.

statutes of life. Le 18:5. Ro 3:20. 7:10, 12, 16, 22. Ga 2:16, 21. 3:24.

he shall. Ezk 18:27, 28. Le 18:5. Ro 2:7. Re 22:12-14.

16 **None of his sins**. Ezk +18:22. Ps 79:8. Is 1:18. 43:25. 44:22. Mi 7:18, 19. Ro 4:7. 5:16, 21. He 8:12. 1 J 2:1-3.

17 **the children**. ver. 20. Ezk +18:4, 20, 25, 29. Jb 35:2. 40:8. Mt 25:24-26. Lk 19:21, 22.

The way. Ezr 9:13. Ps 50:21.

their way. Is 55:8, 9.

not equal. Ezk +18:25.

18 **righteous turneth from**. ver. 12, 13. Ezk 18:26, 27. 2 Ch 24:2, 17, 18, 24, 25. He +10:38, 39. 2 P 2:20-22.

19 **But if**. ver. +14. Je +7:5.

turn from. Ezk 18:27, 28. 2 Ch +7:14. 33:1, 2, 12, 13.

20 **Yet**. ver. 17. Ezk 18:25, 29. Ge +18:25. Pr +14:9. 19:3. Mt 25:24, 25. Lk +19:14. Ro 3:7, 8. 9:9-19, +20, 21.

I will judge. Dt 32:4, 5. Ps +7:8. Zp 3:5. Mt +16:27. Jn 5:29.

21 **in the twelfth**. Ezk 1:2.

one that. Ezk 24:26, 27.

The city. Ezk 24:26. 2 K 24:4, etc. 25:2, 4. 2 Ch 36:17, etc. Je 39:2-8. 52:4-14.

22 **the hand**. 1 K +18:46.

and my. Ezk +24:27.

24 **they that**. ver. 27. Ezk 5:3, 4. 34:2. Je 39:10. 40:7-10. 52:6.

wastes. ver. 27. Ezk 36:4.

the land of Israel. Ezk 11:17.

Abraham was one. Heb. *echad*, Dt +6:4. Is 51:2.

he inherited the land. Ac +7:5.

but we. Mi 3:11. Mt 3:9. Lk 3:8. Jn 8:33, 39. Ro 4:12. 9:7. 1 Th 5:3.

is given us. Nu ch. 34. Dt 34:3, 4. Jsh ch. 13-16, 18, 19.

25 **Ye eat**. Le +3:17.

lift up. Ezk 18:6, 12, 15. Dt 4:19. Ps 24:4. Je 44:15-19.

idols. Ezk +30:13.

and shed. Ezk 9:9. 22:6, 9, 27.

shall ye. Je 7:9, 10.

26 **Ye stand**. Ge 18:8, 22. 27:40. Mi 2:1, 2. Zp 3:3.

work abomination. Ezk 18:12. Le 18:26-30. 20:13. 1 K 11:5-7. 1 P 4:3. Re +21:8, 27.

ye defile. Ezk 18:6, 11, 15. 22:9-11. Ex +20:14. Je 5:8, 9. 23:10. Ja 4:4.

shall ye possess. Le 18:25, 28. 20:22. Dt 4:25, 26. 29:18-23. Jsh 23:15, 16. 1 S 2:30. Ps 50:16-20. 94:20, 21. Is 1:19, 20. Mt +5:5.

27 **surely**. ver. +2, 24.

will I give. Ezk +5:17.
to be devoured. Heb. to devour him.
forts. Jg +6:2.
in the caves. Ge +19:30. 1 S 23:14. Je 41:9.

28 **I will lay**. Ezk 15:8. 36:34, 35. Je 16:16.
+18:16. 25:11. Zc 7:13, 14.
most desolate. Heb. desolation and desolation. ver. 29. Ezk 6:14. 35:3mg, 7mg.
and the pomp. Ezk 7:24. 24:21. 30:6, 7.
and the mountains. Ezk 6:2-6. 36:4.

29 **shall**. Ezk +6:7. Ps 9:16.
because. Ezk 6:11. 8:6-15. 22:2-15, 25-31.
36:17, 18. 2 K 17:9-18. 2 Ch 36:14-17. Je 5:1-
9, 25-31. Mi 6:9-12. Zp 3:1-4.

30 **the children**. Je 11:18, 19. 18:18.
against thee. *or*, of thee. 2 K 6:12. Ec
+10:20. Lk 12:3.
Come. Is 29:13. 58:2. Je 23:35. 42:1-6, 20.
Mt 15:8. 22:16, 17.

31 **as the people cometh**. Heb. according to
the coming of the people. Ezk 8:1. 14:1. 20:1,
etc. Lk +10:39. Ac 10:33.
they sit before thee as my people. *or*, my
people sit before thee. Mt 15:7, 8. 23:27, 28.
and they hear. Je 6:16, 17, +19. 43:1-7.
44:16. Pr 23:12. Mt 7:24-27. Lk +6:48, 49.
8:21. +11:28. Ja 1:22-24. 1 J 3:17, 18.
will not do. Lk +6:46. Ja +1:22.
with their mouth. Ps 78:36, 37. Is 29:13. Ja
2:14-16. 1 J 3:17, 18.
show much love. Heb. make loves, *or* jests.
Is 28:13. Je 23:33-38. Mt +12:36. Lk +16:14.
Ep 5:4. 1 J 3:18.
their heart. 2 S +24:45mg. Hab +2:9. Mt
6:24. 13:22. 19:22. Lk 12:15-21. Ep +5:5. Col
3:5. 1 T 6:9, 10.
their covetousness. Ezk +16:49. Ps +10:3. Pr
+11:24. Ac 5:2. 1 T +6:5.

32 **of one**. Mk 4:16, 17. 6:20. Jn 5:35.
a pleasant voice. Heb. a song of loves. Ezk
31:3mg.
play well. 1 S 16:17. Ps 33:3. Is 23:16.
they hear. Is +6:9. Jb +37:2. Je +29:19. Lk
+8:18. +11:28.
do them not. 2 S +24:45mg. Mt 7:21, 26, 27.
Lk +6:46.

33 **when**. 1 S 3:19, 20. Je 28:9. Jn 8:28.
it will come. Mt 24:35.
shall. Ezk 2:5. 2 K 5:8. Is 41:23. Lk 10:11. Jn
14:29.

EZEKIEL 34

2 **the shepherds**. Ezk 33:24. Je 2:8. 3:15.
10:21. 12:10. *Jn 10:1, 2, 12.*
Woe. ver. 8-10. Ezk 13:19. Dt 28:16. Ru 1:16.
1 S 3:17. Ps 109:6-19. Is 3:11. Je 23:1. 48:46.
Mi 3:1-3, 11, 12. Zp 3:3, 4. Zc 11:17. Mt
11:21. +24:45-51. Lk +12:42-46. 20:46, 47.
Ro 16:18. 2 T +4:14. 2 P 2:3.

feed themselves. Is 56:11. Zc 11:5, 16, 17.
feed the flocks. Is +40:11.

3 **eat**. Le 3:14-17. 7:23, 25. Dt 32:14. 1 S 2:15-
17. Ne 8:10. Is 56:11, 12. Zc 11:5, 16.
ye kill. Ezk 19:3, 6. 22:25-28. 33:25, 26. 1 K
21:13-16. 2 K 21:16. Is 1:10, 15. Je 2:30.
22:17. La 4:13. Mi 3:1-3. Zp 3:3.

4 **diseased**. ver. 16. Is 56:10. Je +8:22. Zc
11:15, 16. Mt 9:36. He 12:12.
neither. Lk 18:29. Jn 1:13. Ro 8:35. 1 C 3:21,
22. 2 Th 2:2.
sought. Mt 10:6. 18:12, 13. Lk 15:4-6.
but with. Ex 1:13, 14. Le 25:46, 53. Je 22:13.
Mt 21:35. 24:49. 2 C 1:24. Ja +5:1-6. 1 P 5:2,
3. Re 13:14-17. 17:5, 6.

5 **they were**. ver. 6. Ezk 33:21, 28. Nu +27:17.
because there is no shepherd. *or*, without
a shepherd, and so ver. 8. Nu 27:15-17. Zc
10:2, 3.
and they became. ver. 8. Is 56:9. Je 12:9-12.
Jn 10:12. Ac 20:29-31.

6 **wandered**. Ezk 7:16. Je 13:16. 40:11, 12. Mt
18:12. He 11:37, 38. 1 P 2:25.
my flock. Jn 10:16.
scattered. Mt 26:31.
face. Ge +1:2.
and none. Ps 142:1. Je 5:1.

7 **ye shepherds**. ver. 9. Ps 82:1-7. Je +7:2.
13:13, 18. Ml 2:1. Mt 23:13-36. Lk 11:39.

8 **prey**. ver. 5, 6, 31.
the shepherds. ver. 2, 3, 10, 18. Ac 20:33. 1
C 9:15. 2 P 2:13. Ju 12.

9 **O ye shepherds**. ver. 7.

10 **I am**. Ezk 5:8. 13:8. 21:3. 35:3. Je 21:13.
23:1, 2. 50:31. Na 2:13. Zc 10:3. 1 P 3:12.
and I will. Ezk 3:18, 20. 33:6-8. Je 13:18-20.
Ro 14:10. 2 C 5:10. He 13:17.
and cause. 1 S 2:29-36. Je 39:6. 52:9-11, 24-
27.
neither shall. ver. 2, 8.
for I will. ver. 22. Ps 23:5. 72:12-14. 102:19,
20.

11 **I, even I**. Ge +6:17. Is 45:12.
search. Ps 119:176. Is 56:8. Je 23:3, 4. 31:8,
10. Mt 13:11, 12. Lk +19:10. Jn +10:11.

12 **As a shepherd seeketh out**. Heb. According
to the shepherd's seeking of, etc. 1 S 17:34,
35. Lk 15:4-6. Jn 10:11, 12.
all places. Ezk 28:25. 36:24. 37:21, 22. Dt
+30:3. Je 23:3, 4.
in the cloudy. Ezk +30:3. Ge +9:13. Ex
+10:22. Is 50:10. Am 5:18-20. Ac 2:19-21.

13 **I will bring**. ver. 23-29. Ezk 20:40-42. 28:25,
26. 38:8. Is 65:9, 10. 66:19, 20. Je +23:3. Ho
3:4, 5. Lk 21:24.
and feed. ver. +2. Ezk 36:18-25.
rivers. 2 S +22:16.

14 **feed them**. ver. 27. Ps 23:1, 2. 34:8-10. Is 25:6.
30:23, 24. +40:11. Je 31:12-14, 25. Jn 10:9.
there shall. Je 33:12, 13.

15 feed. Ps 23:2. Je 23:4.
I will cause. Ps 23:2. SS 1:7, 8. Is 11:6, 7. 27:10. 65:9, 10. Je 3:15. 31:2. Ho 2:18. Zp 3:13. Jn 21:15.

16 seek that. ver. 4, 11. Is 40:11. 61:1-3. Mi 4:6, 7. Mt 11:28. 15:24. Lk +19:10. 22:31, 32.
and bring. Jn +10:16.
but I. Ezk 39:18. Dt +31:20. Am 4:1-3.
I will feed. Is 49:26. Je 9:15. 10:24. 23:15. Mi 7:14.

17 I judge. ver. 20-22. Ezk 20:37, 38. Zc 10:3. Mt 25:31-33.
cattle and cattle. Heb. small cattle of lambs and kids. Ex 12:3mg.
he goats. Heb. great he goats. Ezk 39:18mg. Is 1:11mg.

18 a small. Ezk 16:20, 47. Ge 30:15. Nu 16:9, 13. 2 S 7:19. Is 7:13.
to have. ver. 2, 3. Mi 2:2. 3 J 9, 10.
tread. Ezk 32:2. Mt 15:6-9. 23:13. Lk 11:52.
deep waters. Ezk 32:14.
foul. Ezk 32:2. Nu 19:17. Ro 6:4.
with. Is 1:12.

20 Behold. ver. 10, 17. Ps 22:12-16. Mt 25:31-46.
fat cattle. Is 10:16. Am 4:1.

21 ye have. ver. 3-5. Da 8:3-10. Zc 11:5, 16, 17.
pushed. Lk 13:14-16.

22 will I. ver. 10. Ps 72:12-14. Je 23:2, 3. Zc 11:7-9.
and I. ver. 17.

23 I will. Ec 12:11. Jn +10:11.
shall feed. Is 30:20, 21. +40:11.
my servant David. ver. 24. Ezk 37:24, 25. 1 K 11:32, 34. 14:8. Is 11:1. +55:3, 4. Je 30:9. Ho 3:5. Lk 1:32, 33. Re 22:16.

24 I the Lord will. ver. 30, 31. Ge +17:7. Is 43:2, 3.
a prince. Ezk 37:22. Jsh 5:13-15. Ps 2:6. Is +9:6, 7. 55:4. Je 23:5, 6. 33:15-17. Mi +5:2. Mt 28:18. Lk 1:31-33. Ac 5:31. 1 C 15:25. Ep 1:21, 22. Ph 2:9-11. He +2:9, 10. Re 19:13-16.

25 I will make. Ezk 37:26. Is +55:3. Je 31:31-33. Zc 6:13. He 13:20.
and will. Le 26:6. Jb 5:22. Is 35:9.
and they. ver. 28. Dt +12:10.
wilderness. Ps 65:12.

26 make them. Ge +12:2. 22:18. Is 19:24. 49:6. 53:11. Zc 8:13, 23. Ep 2:13-15.
my hill. Ezk 20:40. Ps 2:6. 68:16. 132:14-16. 133:3. Is 2:2-4. 56:7. Mi 4:1, 2.
I will cause. Le 26:4.
showers. Dt 28:12. Ps 68:9. Is 32:15, 20. 44:3. Zc 10:1. Ml 3:10.

27 the tree. Ezk 47:12. Le 26:4. Ps 85:12. 92:12-14. Is 4:2. 35:1, 2. 61:3. Je 31:12. Jn 15:5-8.
the earth. Ezk 35:14. 36:30. Le +26:4. Ps 67:6. 85:12. Ro +8:18-23.
safe in their land. Ezk 28:26. 38:8, 11. Is +11:11. Je +23:6. Am 9:14, 15.

know that. Ezk +6:7. He +8:10, 11.
when I. ver. 10. Le 26:13. Is 9:4. 10:27. 14:2, 3. 52:2, 3. Je 2:20. 30:8. Ro +11:25.
the bands of. Is 58:6.
served. Je 25:14. 27:7.

28 they shall. ver. 8. Ezk 36:4, 15. Is +11:11. Am 9:11-15.
neither. ver. 25, 29. Je 30:10. 46:27.
dwell safely. ver. +25.
none shall. Zp 3:13.

29 I will. Is +4:2.
of renown. or, for renown. Ps 72:17. Is +9:6.
consumed. Heb. taken away. ver. +23, 26, 27. Ezk 36:29.
neither. Ezk 36:3-6, 15. Re 21:3, 4.

30 they know. ver. 24. Ezk 16:62. 37:27. Ps 46:7, 11. Is 8:9, 10. Mt 1:23. 28:20.

31 ye my flock. Ezk 36:38. Ps 77:20. 78:52. 80:1. SS 1:7, 8. Is 40:11. Je 13:17, 20. 23:2-4. Mi 7:14. Lk +12:32. Jn 10:11, 16, 26-30. 21:15-17. Ac +20:28. 1 P 5:2, 3.
my pasture. Ps +74:1.
I am your God. ver. +24. Ex 29:46. Jn +20:28.

EZEKIEL 35

1 word of the Lord came. Ezk 21:1. 22:1. 34:1. 2 P +1:21.

2 set. Ezk 6:2. 20:46. 21:2. 25:2. Is 50:7. Ep 6:19.
mount. Ge +14:6.
and prophesy. Je 9:25, 26. +49:7-22.

3 I am. Ezk +15:7.
and I will stretch. Ex +7:5. Je 51:25.
most desolate. Heb. desolation and desolation. ver. 7mg. Ezk 5:15. 33:28mg.

4 lay. ver. 9. Ezk 6:6. Je +49:7, 8.
thou shalt know. ver. 9, 12, 15. Ezk +6:7. Ex 9:14.

5 thou hast had. ver. 12. Ge 25:22, 23. 27:26, 28, 29, 41, 42. Je +49:7.
perpetual hatred. or, hatred of old. Heb. olam, Ge +9:12. Ezk 25:15.
shed the blood of. Heb. poured out. Je 18:21mg.
force. Heb. hands. Je 18:21.
in the. Ezk 21:25, 29. Da 9:24.

6 I will. Ps 109:16. Is 63:2-6. Ob 15. Mt 7:2. Re 16:5-7. 18:6, 24. 19:2, 3.
since. Ps 109:17.

7 most desolate. Heb. desolation and desolation. ver. 3mg, 9. Ezk 33:28mg.
passeth. Ezk 29:11. Jg 5:6, 7. 2 Ch 15:5, 6.

8 fill his mountains. Ezk 31:12. 32:4, 5. 39:4, 5. Is 34:2-7.

9 I will make. 2 K 14:7. Je 49:16.
perpetual. Heb. olam, Ge +9:12. ver. 4. Ezk 25:13. Je 49:17, 18. Zp 2:9. Ml 1:3, 4.
and ye. Ezk +6:7.

10 **thou hast**. Ezk 36:5. Le 25:23. Nu 35:34. Ps 83:4-12. Je 49:1. Ob 13.

whereas. *or*, though. Ezk 36:2, 5. 48:35. Ps 48:1-3. 76:1. 132:13, 14. Is 12:6. 31:9. Zp 3:15-17. Zc 2:5.

11 **I will even**. Ps 137:7. Am 1:11. Mt 7:2. Ja 2:13.

and I. Ps 9:16. 83:17, 18.

12 **And thou**. ver. 9. Ezk +6:7.

I have heard. Ps 94:9, 10.

they are given. Ezk 36:2. Ps 83:12.

consume. Heb. devour. ver. 10. Ezk 39:4mg.

13 **with**. 1 S 2:3. 2 Ch 32:15, 19. Is 10:13-19. 36:20. 37:10, 23, 29. Da 11:36. Ml 3:13. 2 P 2:18. Ju 15, 16. Re 13:5, 6.

boasted. Heb. magnified. Je 48:26, 42.

have multiplied. Jb 34:37. 35:16. Ps 73:8, 9. Ec 10:14mg.

I have. ver. 12. Ex 16:12. Nu 14:27. 2 K 19:28. Je 29:23.

14 **whole earth rejoiceth**. Ezk +34:27. Is 14:7, 8. 35:1, 2, 6, 7. 65:20-25. Ro 8:20-22.

I will. Is 65:13-15. Je 48:47. Ml 1:3, 4.

15 **didst rejoice at**. Pr +17:5.

shalt. ver. 3, 4.

Idumea. Ezk 36:5. Is 34:5, 6. Mk 3:8.

and they. ver. +4. Ps 9:16. La 4:21, 22.

EZEKIEL 36

1 **the mountains**. Ezk 6:2, 3. 33:28. 34:14. 37:22. Ps 125:2.

hear. ver. 4, 8. Ezk 20:47. 37:4. Je 22:29.

2 **Because**. ver. 5. Ezk 25:3. 26:2. Ps 40:15.

hath said. Ex +15:9.

even. Dt 32:13. Ps 78:69. Is 58:14. Hab 3:19.

ancient. Heb. *olam*, Jb +22:15.

high places. Ge 49:26. Dt 33:15. 2 K +21:3.

our's. Ezk 35:10. Je 49:1.

3 **Because**. Heb. Because for because. Ezk 13:10. Le 26:43.

they have made. Je ch. 39, 41, 52. La ch. 1-5.

swallowed. Ps +35:25. Ec 10:12.

and ye. Dt 28:37. 1 K 9:7, 8. Ps 44:13, 14. 79:10. Je 18:16. 24:9. 33:24. La 2:15. Da 9:16.

taken up in the lips of talkers. *or*, made to come upon the lip of the tongue.

and are. Jb 30:1-10. Ps 35:15, 16. 69:12. Mt 27:39-44. 1 C 4:13.

4 **to the mountains**. ver. 1, 6. Dt 11:11. Mi 6:2.

rivers. *or*, bottoms, *or*, dales. Ezk +31:12. 2 S 22:16.

desolate. ver. 33-35. Ezk 6:14. 33:24, 27. 2 Ch 36:17-21. Is 6:11. 24:1-12.

a prey. Ezk 34:28. Ps 79:4. Is 64:10, 11. Je 25:9-13. 29:10.

5 **Surely**. Dt +4:24. Zc 1:15.

against the. ver. 3. Je 25:9, 15-29. Zp 2:8-10.

against all. Ezk 25:8-14. ch. 35. Ps 137:7. Is 34:5. 63:1-6. Je 49:7-22. La 4:21. Am 1:11, 12. Ob 1, etc. Ml 1:2-4.

appointed. Ezk 35:10-12. Ps 83:4-12. Je 49:1.

with the. Pr +17:5.

with despiteful. Ezk 25:12, 15. Am 1:11.

minds. Heb. *nephesh*, Ge +23:8.

6 **the land of Israel**. Ezk +11:17.

the mountains. ver. 4, 5, 15. Ezk 34:29. Ps 74:10, 18, 23. 123:3, 4.

7 **I have lifted**. Ge +14:22.

the heathen. Ezk ch. 25-35. Je 25:9, 15-29. ch. 47-51. La 4:22. Am ch. 1. Zp ch. 2.

8 **ye shall**. Ezk 34:26-29. Ps 67:6. 85:12. Is 4:2. 27:6. 30:23. Ho 2:21-23. Am 9:13-15.

at hand. Ezk 12:25. Ph 4:5. He 10:37. Ja 5:8, 9.

9 **I am for you**. Le 26:42. Dt 11:11. Ps 46:11. Ro 8:31.

I will turn. Ps 99:8. Ho 2:21-23. Jl 3:18. Am 9:14. Hg 2:19. Zc 8:12. Ml 3:10, 11.

10 **I will**. ver. 37. Is 27:6. 47:17-23. Je 30:19. 31:27, 28. 33:12. Zc 8:3-6.

the wastes. ver. 33. Is 51:3. 52:9. 58:12. 61:4. Je 31:10-14. Am 9:14, 15.

11 **I will multiply**. Je 31:27. 33:12.

and I will settle. Je 30:18. 31:38-40. Ho 2:22, 23. Ob 19-21. Mi 7:14, 15.

will do better. ver. 35. Is 30:26. +54:7-10. +65:17. Je 23:5-8. 31:17. Jl 3:18-21. Am 9:15. Hg 2:6-9. Zc 8:11-15. 10:6. He +8:8-13. 11:40.

and ye. Ezk +6:7. Is 52:4-6. Ho 2:20. 1 J 5:20.

12 **they shall**. Je 32:15, 44. Ob 17-21.

no more. ver. 13. Ezk 5:17. 14:15. Ge 42:36. Nu 13:32. Je 15:7.

13 **thou land devourest**. Nu 13:32. 2 K 17:25, 26.

14 **no more**. Ezk 37:25-28. Is 35:9. 60:21. Am 9:15.

bereave. *or*, cause to fall.

15 **men**. ver. 6. Ezk 34:29. Is 54:4. 60:14. Mi 7:8-10. Zp 3:19, 20.

thou bear. Ps +31:11.

17 **they defiled**. Le 15:19. +18:25-28, 30.

as the. Ezk 22:10. Le 15:19. 18:19. Is 64:6.

18 **I poured**. Ezk +7:8.

for the. Ezk 16:36-38. 23:37. Nu 35:33. 2 K 24:3, 4.

idols. ver. 25. 2 K +23:24.

19 **I scattered**. Je +9:16. Am 9:9.

according to their way. Ezk 7:3, 8. 18:30. 22:31. 39:24. Ro 2:6. Re 20:12-15.

20 **they profaned**. ver. 23. Is 52:5. Le 18:21. 19:12. Am 2:7. Ro 2:24.

These. Ex 32:11-13. Nu 14:15, 16. Dt 28:63. Jsh 7:9. 2 K 18:30, 35. 19:10-12. Je 33:24. Da 3:15.

21 **I had pity**. Ezk 20:9, 14, 22. Dt 32:26, 27. Ps 74:18. Is 37:35. 48:9.

profaned among. Ro 2:24.

22 **not for your sakes**. ver. 32. Dt 7:7, 8. 9:5-7. Is +48:9. T 3:5.

23 **sanctify**. Dt 28:58. Ps 46:10. Is +8:13. 48:11. +52:5. Ro 2:24.
and the heathen. Ezk 39:28. Ex 15:4-16. Ps 102:13-16. 126:1-3. Da 2:47. 3:28, 29. 4:2, 3, 34-37. 6:26, 27.
when I shall. Ezk 20:41. 28:22. 37:28. 38:23. 1 P 2:9.
in you. ver. 22-29, 32. Jn 14:3. 16:12-15. Ga 4:9. 1 Th 5:1, 3. 2 T 3:14, 15. Re 8:7-12.
their. *or*, your. Ezk 28:25. 38:16.

24 **take you from**. Le 25:23. Je +23:3. 50:17-20. Ro +11:25, 26.

25 **Then**. Ezk +34:27, "then." Ex 17:8. Jl +2:28, "afterward." Ml 3:4, 16. Mt 25:1. 1 Th 4:17.
will I sprinkle. Le +1:5. Ps 51:7. Is 44:3. 52:15. Jn +3:5. Ac +1:5. T 3:5, 6. He 9:13, 14, 19. +10:22. 1 J 5:6.
water. Je +2:13.
filthiness. ver. 17, 29. Ezk 37:23. Ps 51:2. Pr 30:12. Is 4:4. Je 33:8. Zc 13:1. Ac +22:16. 1 C 6:11. 2 C 7:1. Ep 5:26, 27. T 2:14. He 9:14. 1 J 1:7. Re +1:5. 7:14.
from all your idols. Is 2:18-20. 17:7, 8. Je 3:22, 23. Ho 14:3, 8. Zc 13:2.
cleanse. Ps +51:2.

26 **new heart**. Dt +30:6. Ps 51:10. 110:3. Je 24:7. 50:4, 5. Jn 3:3-5. 2 C 3:18. 5:17. Ga 6:15. Ep 2:10. 2 T 1:9. T 3:5. Re 21:5.
the spirit. Heb. *ruach*, Ge +41:38.
stony. Ezk 11:19, 20. Zc 7:12. Mt 13:5, 20, 21. Mk 4:16, 17. 2 C 3:3.

27 **I will**. Ezk 37:14. 39:29. Pr 1:23. Is 44:3, 4. 59:21. Jl 2:28, 29. Zc 12:10. Lk 11:13. Ro 8:9, 14-16. 1 C 3:16. 6:19. Ga 5:5, 22, 23. Ep +1:13, 14. 2 Th 2:13. T 3:3-6. 1 P 1:2, 22. 1 J 3:24.
spirit. Heb. *ruach*, Ge +41:38.
and cause you. Ezk 37:24. Je +31:33. Ga 5:16. Col 2:6. Ph 2:12, 13. T 2:11-14. He 13:21. 1 J 1:6, 7. 2 J 6.
my statutes. Ex 12:24, 43. 30:21. Dt +4:1. He 9:1.
my judgments. Dt +4:1.

28 **dwell in the land**. ver. 10. Ezk 28:25. 37:25. 39:28. Ge 13:14-17. Am 9:15.
be my people. Ge +17:7. SS 6:3. Ho 1:10. 2 C 7:1.

29 **save**. ver. +25. Je 33:8. Ho 14:2, 4, 8. Jl 3:21. Mi 7:19. Zc 13:1. Mt +1:21. Ro 6:14. 11:26. T 2:14. 1 J 1:7-9.
call for. ver. 8, 9. Ezk +34:27, 28. Ps 105:6. Ho 2:21-23. Mt 6:33.
lay no famine. Ezk 34:29.

30 **I will**. Ezk +34:27. Hg 2:19.
reproach. Dt 29:23-28. Jl 2:17, 26.

31 **shall ye**. Ezk 6:9. 16:61-63. 20:43. Le 26:39. Ezr 9:6, etc. Ne 9:1-3, 26-35. Je 31:18-20. Da 9:4-20.
evil. Is +45:7.

shall lothe yourselves. Jb 42:6. Is 6:5. +64:6. Zc 12:10, 11. Lk 18:13. Ro 6:21. 2 C 7:10, 11.

32 **not for your**. ver. +22. Dt 9:5. Mt +8:8. Ac +20:24. 1 C +4:7. 2 T 1:9. T 3:3-6.
be ashamed. Ezk 16:63. Ezr 9:6. Ro 6:21. 1 P 4:2, 3.

33 **In the day**. Ge +2:17.
cleansed you. Dt 9:4, 6. Mi 7:18.
cause you to dwell. Zc 8:7, 8.
wastes. ver. 10. Is 58:12. Je 32:43. 33:10. 50:19, 20. Am 9:14, 15.

34 **shall be tilled**. La 3:31, 32.
whereas it lay desolate. Ezk 6:14. Dt 29:23-28. 2 Ch 36:21. Je 25:9-11.

35 **they shall**. Ps 58:11. 64:9. 126:2. Je 33:9.
like the garden of Eden. Ezk 28:13. 37:13. Ge 2:8, 9. 13:10. Is 51:3. Jl 2:3.

36 **the heathen**. Ne 4:6-9.
shall know. Ezk +6:7. Mi 7:15-17.
I the Lord have. Ezk 22:14. 24:14. 37:14. Nu 23:19. Ho 14:4-9. Mt 24:35. 2 C 1:20.

37 **I will yet**. Ezk 14:3. 20:3, 31. Ps 102:17. Is 55:6, 7. Je 50:4, 5. Zc 10:6, 7. 13:9. Ph 4:6. He 4:16. 10:21, 22. Ja 4:2, 3. 1 J +5:14, 15.
I will increase. ver. 10. Ps 81:10.

38 **holy flock**. Heb. flock of holy things. Is 66:20. Ro 12:1. 15:16. Ph 2:17.
as the flock. 2 Ch 7:8. 30:21-27. 35:7, etc. Ps 23:1, 2. Ezk +34:31. Zc 8:19-23. Jn 10:14. Ac 2:5-11.
solemn feasts. Ge +17:21. Le 23:2.
the waste. ver. 33-35. Ezk 34:31. Je 30:19. 31:27, 28. Jn 10:16. Re 7:4-9.
flocks of men. Ex 23:17. 34:23. Dt 16:16.

EZEKIEL 37

1 **The hand**. 1 K +18:46. 2 P 1:21.
carried. Ezk +8:3. Lk 4:1.
in the spirit. Heb. *ruach*, Is +48:16. 2 Th 2:2. 1 J 4:1-3. Re 1:10. 4:2. 17:3. 21:10.
the valley. ver. 2. Ezk 3:22, 23 (plain). 17:22-24. Am 1:5. Zc 12:11. 14:4, 5.
full of bones. ver. 11. Ps 141:7. Da +12:2. 1 C 15:22. Ep 2:1.

2 **pass by them**. Ne 2:12-16. Ps 48:12-14. Lk 19:41-44.
valley. *or*, champaign. Dt 11:30.
they were. ver. 11. Ps 32:4. 141:7. Ep 2:1.

3 **can**. Je 30:10-17. Jn 6:5, 6. Ro 11:15.
O Lord God. Dt 32:39. 1 S 2:6. Je 32:17, 27. Jn 5:21. 11:25, 26. Ac 26:8. Ro 4:17. 2 C 1:9, 10. He 11:19.

4 **Prophesy**. ver. 11, 15, 16. Nu 20:8. 1 K +13:2. +17:20-22. Mt 21:21. Lk 7:14. Jn 2:5. 11:43.
O ye. Ezk 36:1. Is +26:19. 42:18. Je 22:29. Mi 6:2. Jn 5:25, 28, 29. Ac 17:30.
hear. Ps 119:25, 50. Jn 5:24. He 4:12.

5   **I will**. ver. 9, 10, 14. Ge +2:7. Ps 104:29, 30. Jn 20:22. Ro 8:2. Ep 2:5.
breath. Heb. *ruach*, Ge +6:17. ver. 6, 8, 9, 10, 14. Ge 7:15. Jn 6:63.

6   **I will**. ver. 8-10.
sinews. 2 K 5:14. Je 30:17. 1 C 15:35, 38.
put. Ge +2:7.
breath. Heb. *ruach*, Ge +6:17.
ye shall know. ver. 14, 28. Ezk +6:7. Dt 29:6. Is 49:23.

7   **I prophesied as**. Je 13:5-7. 26:8. Ac 4:19. 5:20-29.
there. 1 K 19:11-13. Ac 2:2, 37. 16:26-29.
bones came together. Ezr 2:1. Je 50:4.

8   **the sinews and**. Is 66:14.
skin covered. Ne 10:29.
breath. Heb. *ruach*, Ge +6:17. Ge +2:7. Mt 23:13-28.

9   **Prophesy unto**. Jn 5:25, 28, 29.
wind. *or*, breath. Heb. *ruach*, Nu +16:22. Am 4:13mg.
Come. ver. 5, 14. SS 4:16. Jn 3:8. Ac 2:2.
four winds. Da 7:2. 11:4. Re 7:1.
breath. Heb. *ruach*, Ge +6:17.

10   **the breath**. Heb. *ruach*, Ge +6:17. Ps 104:30. Pr 1:23. Re 11:11. 20:4, 5.
and stood. Is 51:17. 52:1, 2. Lk 7:14, 15. Jn 11:43, 44. Re 11:11.
great army. Ps +149:6-9. Is 60:8, 9.

11   **whole house**. ver. 16, 19. Ezk 36:10. 39:25. 1 K 18:31, 32. Is 11:12, 13. Je 31:1. 33:24-26. Ho 1:11. Ro 11:26. 2 C 5:14. Ep 2:1.
Our bones. ver. 1-8. Nu 17:6, 12, 13. Ps 77:7-9. 102:3. 141:7. Is 40:27. Je 2:25. La 2:21, 22. 3:4.
hope is lost. Ezk 33:10. Is 49:14. Ro +11:1, 2.
cut off. 2 Ch 36:14-21. La 3:54. Ho 1:6, 9.

12   **Therefore**. Jb 35:14, 15.
I will open. ver. 21. Dt 32:39. Ps 17:15. 49:14, 15. Is 25:6, 9. +26:19. 66:14. Da +12:2. Ho 6:2. 13:14. Ro 11:15. 1 Th 4:16. Re 20:13.
graves. Heb. *qeber*, Ge +23:4.
come up out. Ps 71:20. Is 26:19. 66:10-14. Ho 6:1-3. 13:14. Lk 15:24. Jn 5:24-29. Ro 8:10, 11. 11:15. 1 C +15:45. Ep 2:4, 5. Re 11:11. 20:4-6, 11-15.
and bring. ver. 25. Ezk 28:25. +34:13. 36:24. Ezr 1:2. Am 9:14, 15.
land of Israel. Ezk +11:17.

13   **ye shall know**. ver. 6. Ezk 16:62. Ps 126:2, 3.
when. Ezk +36:25. Ro 1:4. 8:11. 2 C 4:14. Re 11:11.

14   **shall put**. ver. 9. Ezk 11:19. 18:31. 36:27. 39:29. Is 32:15. Jl 2:28, 29. Zc 12:10. Ac 2:16, 17. Ro 8:2, 11. 1 C +15:45. T 3:5, 6.
spirit. Heb. *ruach*, Is +48:16.
I the Lord. ver. 6. Ezk 5:13, 17. 17:24. 22:14. 36:36, 38.

16   **take thee**. Nu 17:2, 3.
stick. lit. wood. Ge +40:19.

For Judah. Ge 49:8-12. 1 Ch 5:2. 2 Ch 10:17. 11:11-17. 15:9. 30:11-18. Zc 10:6.
For Joseph. Ge 49:22-26. 1 K 11:26. 12:16-20. 1 Ch 5:1. 2 Ch 10:19. Is 11:13. Je 31:6. Ho 5:3, 5.

17   **join them**. ver. 22-24. Is 11:13. Je 50:4. Ho 1:11. Zp 3:9.

18   **Wilt**. Ezk 12:9. 17:12. 20:49. 24:19. Mt 24:3.

19   **Behold**. ver. 16, 17. 1 Ch 9:1-3. Am +5:6. Ep 2:13, 14. Col 3:11.
be one. ver. +22.

20   **in thine**. Ezk 12:3. Nu 17:6-9. Ho 12:10.

21   **I will take**. Is 49:12. Je 16:15. +23:3. 29:14. 50:19. Ob 17-21. Mi 7:11, 12.

22   **I will make**. Is 11:12, 13. Je 3:18. 32:39. 50:4. Ho 1:11. Zc 10:6. Ep 2:19-22.
the mountains. Ezk 6:2. 17:22. 20:40. 34:13. 36:1, 36. 40:2. 43:12.
and one king. ver. 24. Ezk 34:23, 24. Ge +49:10. Ps 72:1, 8. Je 30:1, 21. 33:14-17, 26. Lk 1:32, 33. Jn +1:49. 10:16. Re 11:15.
no more two. Ezk 35:10.

23   **Neither shall they defile**. Ezk 14:11. 20:43. 36:25, 29, 31. 39:7. 43:7, 8. Is 2:18. Je 3:17. Ho 14:8. Zc 13:1, 2. 14:21.
idols. 2 K +23:24.
detestable things. Ezk +16:17mg. Is +66:17.
transgressions. Ezk 14:11. 18:22, 28, 30, 31. 21:24. 33:10, 12. 39:24. Is 53:5, 8.
but. Ezk 20:41. 28:25. 36:24, 29. Le 20:7, 8. Mi 7:14, 18-20.
will cleanse. Ezk 36:25. Je 50:20. Ep 5:26, 27. He 9:13, 14. 1 J 1:7, 9.
so shall. ver. 27. Ge +17:7. Ps 68:20, 35. Ho 1:10.

24   **David**. ver. 22, 25. Is +55:3, 4. Je 23:5. 30:9. Ho 3:5. Lk +1:32, 33.
my servant. Ezk 34:23, 24. 1 K 11:32. 14:8.
one shepherd. ver. 22. Ec 12:11. Jn +10:11. Ep 4:4-6.
they shall. Ezk 36:27. Dt 30:6. Je 31:33. 32:39. 1 C 11:2. Ep 2:10. Ph 2:12, 13. T 2:11-13. 3:3-8. 1 J 2:6.
judgments. Ezk +33:14mg.
and do. Ezk +33:31.

25   **they shall dwell in**. ver. 21. Ezk 16:60, 61. 20:34, 35, 37, 38, 40. 28:25. 37:26. Je +23:3. 32:41. 50:4, 5, 19, 20. Ho 2:14, 15, 19. 3:4, 5. Ob 17, 21. Mi 5:3, 4, 7, 13. 7:14, 17. Zp 3:9. Zc 2:10, 12. 12:6, 10. Lk 21:24. Ro +11:2, 12, 15, 23-33. 2 C 3:15, 16.
even they. Is +60:21. 66:22. Jl 3:20. Am 9:15. Zp 3:14, 15. Zc 14:11.
children's children. Ac +2:39.
for ever. Heb. *olam*, Ex +12:24. Ps +72:5.
my servant. 2 S 3:18.
David. ver. 22, +24. Is +9:6, 7. Da 2:44, 45. 7:13, 14, 18. Ho 3:5. Zc 6:12, 13. Jn 12:34. He 7:2, 21.
for ever. Heb. *olam*, Ex +12:24.

26 **I will make**. Ezk 34:25. Ge 17:7. Ps 89:3, 4. Is +55:3. Ho 2:18-23. Jn 14:27.

everlasting. Heb. *olam*, Ge +9:16. +17:7. Is 44:7.

covenant. Ge +9:16 +17:7. Dt +30:1. Is +55:3. Je 32:40. He 12:24. 13:20.

multiply. Ezk 36:10, 37. Is 27:6. 49:21. Je 30:19. 31:27. Ho 1:10, 11. Zc 8:4, 5. He 6:14.

set my sanctuary. ver. 28. Ezk 11:16. 40:2. 43:7. 45:1, etc. 48:8, 10, 21. Le 26:11, 12. 1 K 8:20, 21. Ps 68:18. Is 2:2. 60:13. Jl 2:1. Mi 4:1, 2. Hg 2:7. Zc 1:16. 2:5. 6:12, 13. Jn 1:14. 2 C 6:16. Re 21:3.

in the midst. Ho 11:9. Jl 2:27. Re 21:3.

for evermore. Heb. *olam*, Ps +18:50.

27 **tabernacle**. Le 26:11. Is 60:13. Am 9:11. Zc 6:12, 13. Jn 1:14. Col 2:9, 10. Re 21:3, 22.

I will. ver. +23. Ho 2:23. 2 C 6:16.

28 **the heathen**. Ezk +6:7. Ps 46:10, 11. 79:10. 102:15. 126:2. Zc 14:9. Ro 11:15.

sanctify. Ezk 20:12. Ex 31:13. Le 20:8. 21:8. Jn 17:17-19. 1 C 1:30. Ep 5:26. 1 Th 5:23.

when. Ezk +34:27. 36:25.

my sanctuary. ver. +26. Is 60:13. Zc 6:12, 13. Re 21:3.

in the midst. ver. +26. Ezk 43:9. Zp 3:5, 15, 17.

for evermore. Heb. *olam*, Ps +18:50.

EZEKIEL 38

1 **the word**. Ezk 37:15.

2 **Son**. ver. 14. Ezk 2:1. 39:1, 17.

set. Ezk 6:2. 20:46. 25:2. 35:2, 3.

Gog. i.e. *mountain*, in reference to the Caucasus mountains, chief seat of the Scythian people. Rather, "Gog (the prince) of the land of Magog, the prince of Rosh, Meshech, and Tubal." Dt 3:1-13. 1 Ch +5:4. Re 20:8, 9.

Magog. Ge 10:2. 1 Ch 1:5. Compare "Agag," Nu 24:7.

the chief prince of. *or*, prince of the chief of. Rather, prince of Rosh. ver. 2, 3. Ezk 39:1. Ge +46:21.

Meshech. Ge +10:2.

Tubal. Ge +10:2.

3 **I am against**. Ezk +15:7.

4 **I will**. 2 S 24:1. 1 Ch 21:1.

turn thee. Ezk 29:4. 39:2. 2 K 19:28. Is 37:29. +59:19mg.

back. or, lead thee away enticingly. Is 47:10 (perverted). Je 50:6.

put hooks. Ezk 29:4. Is 30:28. 37:29.

bring thee forth. Zc 12:1-8. Mt 24:14-30. Re 16:14. 17:14. 19:17-21.

all thine army. ver. 15. Da 11:40. Re 9:16.

horses. ver. 15. Ps 20:7. Pr 21:31. Da 11:40. Ro 16:20.

all of them clothed. Ezk 23:12.

company. or, gathered host. Ezk 16:40.

bucklers. Ezk 23:24.

handling. 1 Ch 12:8. 2 Ch 25:5. Je 46:9.

5 **Persia**. Now Iran. Ezk 27:10. Da 2:32, 39. 5:28-31. 8:20.

Ethiopia. Ge +2:13. Da 11:43. Zp 2:12.

Libya. *or*, Phut. Ge +10:6. Da 11:43.

6 **Gomer**. Ge 10:2. 1 Ch 1:5.

his bands. ver. 9, 22. Ezk 12:14. 39:4.

Togarmah. Descendants of Gomer, the son of Japheth, supposed to have settled in the northern part of Armenia (Ezk 32:26. Minni, Je 51:27). Ezk 27:14. Ge 10:3. 1 Ch 1:6. Da 11:40.

of the north. Contrast Re 20:8, where Gog comes from the four quarters of the earth, thus a worldwide gathering of enemies against Jerusalem, whereas here Gog is from the north, showing these are two different events (see ver. 4, 16). ver. 15. Je +1:14.

7 **Be thou prepared**. 2 Ch 25:8. Ps 2:1-4. Pr +21:30. Is 8:9, 10. 37:22. 54:17. Je 46:3-5, 14-16. 51:12. Jl 3:9-12. Am 4:12. Zc 14:2, 3.

and prepare. Je 46:14.

8 **After many days**. ver. 16. Is 24:22. Ho 3:3-5. Hab 2:3. Mt +25:12. ver. 12. Ho 3:5. Zp 2:1.

thou shalt be visited. Ex +20:5. Is 24:22. 29:6. Je +11:22mg. 32:5. La 4:22.

in the latter years. ver 14, 16, 18. Ezk 39:8, 11. Ge +49:1.

into the land. ver. 12. Ezk +34:13. 36:24, etc. 37:21, +25, etc. 39:27-29. Is 11:11, 12, etc. 66:8. Je 30:3, 7, 18. 32:37. Am 9:14, 15.

the sword. Is 1:20. Ho 11:6.

gathered. ver. 12. Ezk 20:34. 28:25. Je +23:3.

out of many people. ver. 12. Is 11:11. 43:6. Je 31:8. Mt 24:31. Lk 21:24.

the mountains. Ezk +34:13. 36:1-8. 37:22.

always waste. Ezk 5:14. Is 61:4. Je 2:15. 22:5.

it is brought. 1 P 2:9.

and they shall. ver. 11. Da 9:27.

safely. or, confidently. lit. "leaningly." ver. 11, 14. Dt 12:10.

9 **shalt ascend**. Ezk 13:11. Is 21:1, 2. 25:4. 28:2. Da 11:40.

and come. Is 10:3.

like. ver. 16. Je 4:6-13. Jl 2:2.

storm. ver. 22. Ezk 13:11. Is 4:6. 25:4. 28:2. 30:30. 32:19.

cloud. Ezk 30:3. 34:12. Is 4:5. 25:4, 5. Je 4:13.

all thy. Is 8:9, 10.

10 **that at**. Ps 83:3, 4. 139:2. Pr 19:21. Is 10:7. Mk 7:21. Jn 13:2. Ac 5:3, 9. 8:22. 1 C 4:5.

come into. 2 K +12:4.

think an evil thought. *or*, conceive a mischievous purpose. Ps 36:4. Pr 6:14, 18. 12:2. Je +6:19. Da 11:44, 45. Mi 2:1. Re 17:13.

11 go up. Ex 15:9. Ps 10:9. Pr 1:11-16. Is 37:24, 25. Je 49:31. Ro 3:15. Re 20:7-9.
unwalled villages. Dt 3:5. Est 9:19. Zc 2:4.
go to. Jg 18:7, 27. Je 49:31, 32. Zc 2:4, 5.
safely. *or,* confidently. ver. +8. Ps 16:9mg. Pr 3:29, 30.
without walls. Is 26:1. Je 49:31.

12 take a spoil, and to take a prey. Heb. spoil the spoil, and to prey the prey. Ezk 29:19mg. Ge +1:29. Ps 83:4. Pr 1:13. Is 10:6. 17:12-14. Je 30:16.
to turn. Is 1:24, 25. Am 1:8. Zc 13:7.
the desolate. ver. 8. Ezk 36:33-35. Je 32:43, 44. 33:12, 13. Zc 1:12, 17.
and upon. ver. 8. Zc 10:8-10.
the people. Ezk 39:13.
gathered out. ver. 8.
which have gotten. Is 60:5-9. 61:6. Je 49:31.
cattle and goods. ver. 13. Ge 31:18.
midst. Heb. navel. Ezk 5:5. Dt 32:8. Jg 9:37mg. Is 2:2. Zc 2:8.

13 Sheba. Ezk 27:12, 15, 20, 22, 23, 25. 1 K +10:1. Jb 1:15.
Dedan. A country in the Arabian peninsula, not far from the Edomites. Ge +10:7.
the merchants. Ezk 27:12, 25.
of Tarshish. Ge +10:4.
with all. Ezk 19:3-6. 32:2. Nu 23:24. Ps 57:4. Is 11:6. Je 50:17. 51:38. Mi 5:8. Na 2:11-13. Zc 11:3.
Art thou come. 1 P 5:8.

14 in that day. ver. 19. Is +2:11.
my people. Dt +32:43. Compare verse 16, "my land."
dwelleth. ver. 8, 11. Je 23:6. Zc 2:5, 8.
shalt. Ezk 37:28.

15 thou shalt come. Ezk 39:2. Da +9:26. 11:40, 44. Hab +3:16.
thy place. ver. 6. Ezk 39:2. Is 14:31. Je 1:14. 6:22. 46:20, 24. Da 11:40, 44.
north parts. ver. 6. Ezk 39:2. Da 11:44.
riding upon horses. ver. 4. Ezk 23:6. 26:7, 10. Is 31:1, 3. Ho 1:7. Jl 1:6. Hab 1:8.
and many. ver. 4, 6. Jl 3:2. Zp 3:8. Zc 12:2-4. 14:2, 3. Re 16:14, 16. 20:8.
a mighty army. Jl 2:1-20. Re 6:4.

16 shalt come up against. Mi 5:6.
as a cloud. ver. 9.
it shall be. ver. 8. Dt 31:29. Is 2:2. +11:11. Da 2:28. 10:14. Ho 3:5. Mi 4:1. 1 T 4:1. 2 T 3:1.
the latter days. ver. +8. Je 49:39. Da 2:28.
I will bring thee. Ex +9:16. Dt +2:30. 1 S +18:10. Is +45:7. Am +3:6. Ep +1:11.
my land. Dt +32:43. Compare "my people," ver. 14, and "my mountains," ver. 21.
heathen may know. ver. 23. Ezk +6:7. 35:11. Da 3:24-29. Mi 7:15-17. Hab 3:2. Mt 6:9, 10.

when I. ver. 23. Ge +12:3. Ps +122:6. Is +8:13.

17 Art thou he. Je 6:22, 23. 2 Th 2:3, 7.
whom. ver. 10, 11, 16. Nu 24:17-24. Ps 2:1-3. 110:5, 6. Is 10:20-27. 11:4. 14:24-27. 27:1. 29:1-8. 34:1-6. 63:1-6. 66:15, 16. Je 30:1-11. Da 2:44, 45. 11:40-45. Jl 2:20. 3:9-17, 19. Mi 5:3-15. Zp 1:14. 3:8. Zc 12:2-9. 14:1-3.
by. Heb. by the hands of. 1 K +16:12mg.
years. Is 63:4.

18 same time. Ge +2:17.
land of Israel. Ezk 11:17.
that my fury. Dt +32:22. Ps 89:46. Is +59:18. Da 8:25. He 12:29.
my face. Is 11:4. 2 Th 2:8. Re 2:16. 19:15, 21.

19 in my. Ex +20:5.
fire of my wrath. Is +24:6.
Surely. Is 30:32. He +12:26.

20 the fishes. Je 4:23-26. Ho 4:3. Na 1:4-6. Zc 14:4, 5. Re 6:12, 13.
the fowls. Ho 4:3.
face. Ge +1:2.
shall shake. Ps 18:7-15. Is 5:25. He +12:26.
at my presence. Ps 68:2, 8. +97:4, 5.
the mountains. Ps 68:8. Is 5:25.
steep places. *or,* towers, *or* stairs. SS 2:14. Is 30:25. Na 1:6. 2 C 10:4.

21 I will. Ezk 14:17. Ps 105:16.
a sword. Je +12:12.
my mountains. Is 14:25. 49:11. 65:9.
every. Jg +7:22.

22 I will plead. Ezk 17:20. Is 66:16. Je 25:31. Zc 14:12-15.
with pestilence. Ezk 6:11, 12. 7:15. 12:16. +14:19, 21. 24:16. 28:23. 33:27. Ex 5:3. Le 26:25. 1 Ch 21:12, 14. Je 27:8, 13. 28:8. 29:17, 18. 32:24, 36. 34:17. 38:2. 42:17, 22. 44:13. Hab 3:5. Zc 14:12. Lk 21:11. Re 6:8.
and with blood. Ezk 5:17. 14:19. 28:23. 32:6. Nu 23:24. 2 S 1:22. Is 34:3, 7. 49:26. Je 25:27. Re 8:7. 14:20. 16:6.
an overflowing rain. Ge 19:24. Ps 11:6. 77:16-18. Is 29:6. Mt 7:27.
great hailstones. Is +28:17.
fire. Ezk 39:6. Is 29:6. 30:30. 2 P +3:7. Re 8:7, 8.
brimstone. Re +9:17.

23 magnify. Ezk 36:23.
sanctify myself. ver. 16. Is +8:13.
and I. ver. +16. Ezk +6:7. Ex 7:5, 17. 8:10, 22. 9:14-16. Da 11:40-45. 12:1. Zp 1:7mg. Ro 9:17, 22. Re 15:3, 4. 19:1-6.
they shall know. Ezk 6:10. Ps 9:16.

EZEKIEL 39

1 son. Ezk 38:2, 3.
Behold. Ezk +15:7.
the chief prince of Meshech and Tubal.

Or, "prince of Rosh, Meshech, and Tubal." Ezk +38:2.

2 **I will**. Ezk 38:4. Ps 40:14. 68:2. Is 37:29.
turn thee back. Is +59:19mg. Jl 2:20.
leave but the sixth part of thee. *or*, strike thee with six plagues; *or*, draw thee back with a hook of six teeth, as Ezk 38:4. 45:13.
and will cause. Ezk 38:15. Da 11:40.
to come up. Ezk 38:15. Hab +3:16.
north parts. Heb. sides of the north. Ezk +38:6.
the mountains. ver. 4, 17. Ezk 6:2. 38:8, 21.

3 **I will smite**. Ezk 30:21-24. Ps 11:2. 37:14. 46:9. 58:7. 76:3-5. Je 21:4, 5. Ho 1:5. 2:18.

4 **fall**. ver. 17-20. Ezk 38:21. Ps 9:3-10. Is 14:25-27. 34:4.
all thy bands. Ezk 38:6.
I will. Ezk 29:5. 32:4, 5. Is 34:2-8. Re 19:17-21.
ravenous birds. Is 46:11.
sort. Heb. wing. Ezk 5:3mg. Ge 7:14. Is +24:16mg.
beasts. ver. 17. Ezk +5:17.
to be devoured. Heb. to devour. Ezk 35:12mg.

5 **open field**. Heb. face of the field. Ezk 29:5mg. 32:4. Je 8:2. 22:19.
for I have spoken. Ezk 17:24. Nu 23:19. Is 55:11.

6 **I will send a fire**. Ezk 28:18. 30:8, 16. 38:19-22. 1 K 18:24, 38. 2 K 1:10. Ps 11:6. Is 66:14-16. Am 1:4, 7, 10. Na 1:6. Zc 14:12. He 12:28, 29. Re 20:9.
Magog. Ezk 38:2.
carelessly. *or*, confidently. Ezk +38:8, 11mg. Jg 18:7.
in the isles. Ezk 26:15, 18. 38:6, 13. Is +11:11. Je 25:22.
they shall know. Ezk +6:7.

7 **will I**. ver. 22. Ezk 38:16, 23. Is 52:6.
and I will. Ezk 20:9, 14, 39. 36:20, 21, 36. Ex +20:7. Le 18:21.
the heathen. Ezk +6:7.
the Holy One. Is +1:4.

8 **it is come**. Ezk 7:2-10. 21:7. Is 33:10-12. Re 16:17. 21:6.
it is done. Re +10:7.
this. Ezk +38:17. Jl 2:11, 31. Zp 1:14. 2 P 3:8. Ju 6. Re 6:17. 10:7.

9 **shall go**. Ps 111:2, 3. Is +66:24. Ml 1:5.
and shall. ver. 10. Jsh 11:6. Ps 46:9. Zc 9:10.
handstaves. *or*, javelins.
burn them with fire. *or*, make a fire of them. Is 44:15.
the weapons. ver. 10. Ps 140:7.
the shields. Ezk 23:24.

10 **shall spoil**. Ex 3:22. 12:36. Jg 6:1, 6. 7:19-25. 2 Ch 14:9-15. ch. 20. Is 9:4. 10:24-34. 14:2. 33:1. Mi 5:8. Hab 2:8. Zp 2:9, 10. Mt 7:2. Ro +11:25. Re 13:10. 18:6.

11 **in that day**. Is +2:11.
graves. Heb. *qeber*, Ge 23:4. Ps 49:14. Is 34:1-3.
on the east. Ezk 47:18. Nu 34:11. Jl 2:20. Zc 14:8. Lk 5:1. Jn 6:1.
noses. *or*, *mouths*.
Hamon-gog. *that is*, The multitude of Gog. Nu 11:34mg. Je +10:13mg.

12 **cleanse**. ver. 14, 16. Nu 19:16. Dt 21:23.

13 **shall bury**. Ps 53:5. Is +66:24.
a renown. Ezk 34:29. Dt 26:19. Ps 149:6-9. Je 33:9. Zp 3:19, 20. 1 P 1:7.
the day. ver. 21, 22. Ezk 28:22. Ps 126:2, 3.

14 **they shall**. Nu 19:11-19.
continual employment. Heb. continuance. Is +58:11.
to cleanse. ver. 12.
seven months. ver. 12.

15 **bone**. Nu 19:11.
set. Heb. build. Ezk 4:2. Lk 11:44.
a sign. S#6725h. 2 K 23:17h (title). Je +31:21h (waymarks).
in the valley. ver. 11.
Hamon-gog. i.e. *the multitude of Gog*, S#1996h. ver. 11.

16 **Hamonah**. *that is*, The multitude. S#1997h.
cleanse. ver. 12. Nu 35:33.

17 **Speak**. Ge 31:54. 1 S 9:13. 16:3. Is 56:9. Je 12:9. Zp 1:7. Re 19:17, 18.
every feathered fowl. Heb. the fowl of every wing. ver. 4. Is 18:6.
Assemble. Je 12:9.
to my. ver. 4. 1 S 17:46. Is 11:4. 18:6. 34:6. Je 46:10. Zp 1:7. 2 Th 1:7-9.
sacrifice. *or*, slaughter.
may eat. Ezk 44:15. Le 3:11-17.

18 **eat**. Ezk 29:5. 34:8. Re 19:17, 18, 21.
goats. Heb. great goats. Ezk 34:17mg.
of bullocks. Ps 68:30. Is 34:7. Je 50:11, 27. 51:40.
fatlings. Dt 32:14. Ps 22:12. Am 4:1.
of Bashan. Ge 49:16, 17. Dt +32:14.

19 **eat fat till ye be full**. Is 23:18.

20 **be filled**. Ezk 38:4. Ps 76:5, 6. Hg 2:22. Re 19:18.

21 **I will set**. Ezk 36:23. 38:16, 23. Ex 9:16. 14:4. Is 26:11. 37:20. Ml 1:11.
my glory. ver. 13. Is +40:5.
my judgment. Ezk 28:25, 26. Ps 9:16. Is 26:9. 42:1-4. Mi 5:15.
and my hand. Ex +9:3. Ps 10:16. Mi 4:11-13.

22 **know**. ver. 7, 28. Ezk +6:7. Ps 9:16. ch 46. 59:13. Is 12:4-6. Je 31:34. Ho +8:2. 13:4. Jn 17:3. 1 J 5:20.
that day. Is +2:11.
and forward. Ezk 43:27. 1 S 18:9. Is 18:2, 7.

23 **the heathen**. Ezk 36:18-23, 36. 2 Ch 7:21, 22. Je 22:8, 9. 40:2, 3. La 1:8. 2:15-17.
into captivity. Dt 28:15-68.

for their iniquity. Ge +6:13. Ex +22:20. +35:2. Le 26:14-39. +32:23. Dt 4:25-27. 28:15-25, 33, 37-48, 58-63, 66, 67. 2 Ch 24:20-24. Ne 9:25-30. Jb +27:13. Ps +12:5. +34:16. +37:9. +58:11. Je 25:8-14. 44:6-11. Zc +10:11.

hid I. ver. 29. Ezk 22:26. Dt +31:17. Is 28:15. 53:3. +54:8. 57:17.

gave them. Le 26:25. Dt 32:30. Jg 2:14. 3:8. Ps 106:41. Is 42:24.

24 **According**. Ezk 36:19. Le 26:24. 2 K 17:7, etc. Ezr 9:7. Ps 78:55-64. Is 1:20. 3:11. 59:2, 17, 18. Je 2:17, 19. 4:18. 5:25. Da 9:5-10.

25 **Now**. Ezk 38:2.
will I. Is 56:8. Je 3:18. +23:3. Ro 11:26-31.
bring again. Ezk 16:53. 20:34. Dt 30:3. Jb 42:10. Ps 14:7. Je 32:44. Jl 3:1-8.
the whole. Ezk 20:40. 37:21, 22. Je 30:3. 31:1. Ho 1:11. Ro 11:26, 27.
and will. Ex +20:5.

26 **they have borne**. Ezk 16:52, 57, 58, 63. 32:24, 25, 30. Ps 99:8. Je 3:24, 25. 30:11. Da 9:16.
when they. Dt +12:10. 28:47, 48. 32:14, 15.
none made. Ezk 34:28. Le 26:6. Is 17:2. Je 7:33.

27 **I have**. ver. 25. Ezk 28:25, 26. Is 27:6, 7.
and am. ver. 13. Is +8:13.

28 **shall they**. ver. +22. Ho 2:20.
which caused them. Heb. by my causing of them, etc. ver. 23.
but I have. Note the time element signaled by "but" here, in contrast with "when" in the following references: Ezk 28:25. 32:7. 34:27. 35:11. 36:23. 37:13, 28. Compare "then" at Ezk 36:25. Is 59:19.
have left none. Ne 1:8-10. Je +23:3. Am 9:9. Mt 24:31. Ro 9:6-8. +11:1-7.

29 **hide**. ver. 23-25. Ezk 37:26, 27. Is 45:17. +54:8-10.
for. Ezk 36:25-27. 37:14. Is 32:15. 44:3-5. 59:20, 21. Jl 2:28. Zc 12:10. Ac 2:17, 18, 33. 1 J 3:24.
spirit. Heb. *ruach*, Ge +41:38.

EZEKIEL 40

1 **In the five**. On Tuesday, April 20, A.M. 3430. B.C. 574. Ezk 1:2. 8:1. 29:17. 32:1, 17.
after. Ezk 33:21. 2 K ch. 25. Je ch. 39, 52.
selfsame. Dt +32:48.
hand. 1 K +18:46. Re 1:10.

2 **the visions**. Ezk 1:1. 8:3. Is 60:13. Da 7:1, 7. Zc 6:12, 13. Ac 2:17. 16:9. 2 C 12:1-7.
land of Israel. Ezk +27:17.
a very. Ezk 17:22, 23. Is 2:2, 3. Da 2:34, 35. Mi 4:1. Re 21:10.
by. *or*, upon.
as the. Ezk 48:30-35. Ga 4:26. Re 21:2, 10-23.

frame. 1 Ch 28:12, 19.
on the south. Ps 48:2. Is 14:13.

3 **whose**. Ezk 1:7, 27. Da 10:5, 6. Re 1:15.
with. Ezk 47:3. Is 8:20. 28:17. Zc 2:1, 2. Re 11:1. 21:15.

4 **behold**. Ezk 2:7, 8. 3:17. 43:10, 11. 44:5. Mt 10:27. 13:9, 51, 52.
shall show thee. Re 1:1, 19.
declare all. Is 21:10. Je 26:2. Ac 4:20. 20:27. 22:14, 15. 1 C 11:23. 1 J 1:1, 3.

5 **a wall**. Ezk 42:20. Ps 125:2. Is 26:1. 60:18. Zc 2:5. Re 21:12.
by the cubit. Ezk 43:13. Dt 3:11.
hand breadth. ver. 43. Ex 25:25. 37:12.
so he. Ezk 42:20. Re 21:16.

6 **unto**. ver. 20. Ezk 8:16. 11:1. 43:1. 44:1. 46:1, 12. 1 Ch 9:18, 24. Ne 3:29. Je 19:2.
which looketh. Heb. whose face was the way. Ezk 43:1. Re 7:2.
stairs. ver. 26. 1 K 6:8.
threshold. Ezk 10:18. 43:8. 46:2. 47:1. Ps 84:10mg.
one reed. ver. 5, 7.

7 **little chamber**. Ezk 42:5. 1 K 6:5-10. 1 Ch 9:26. 23:28. 2 Ch 3:9. 31:11. Ezr 8:29. Je 35:4.

9 **the posts**. Ezk 45:19.

10 **the little**. ver. 7.
they three. 1 K 6:5, 6.

12 **space**. Heb. limit, *or*, bound.
six cubits. ver. 5, 7. 1 K 6:10.

13 **the gate**. The whole arch of the east gate, measured from the southern extremity of the opposite room, was 25 cubits; including the dimensions of the two rooms, or twelve cubits, ver. 7; the spaces before the rooms or two cubits, ver. 12; and the breadth of the entrance, ten cubits, ver. 11; making in all 24 cubits, leaving one cubit for the thickness of the walls.

14 **the court**. Ezk 8:7. 42:1. Ex 27:9. 35:17. Le 6:16. 1 Ch 28:6. Ps 100:4. Is 62:9.

15 **the face of the gate**. ver. 6, 7, 17. Ezk 41:21, 25.

16 **narrow**. Heb. closed. Ezk 41:16, 26. 1 K 6:4. Ps 58:4. Pr 17:28. 1 C 13:12.
the little. ver. 7, 12.
arches. *or*, galleries, *or* porches. ver. 21, 22, 25, 30. Ezk 41:15. 42:3. Jn 5:2.
inward. *or*, within. 1 K 6:30. 2 Ch 29:16.
palm trees. Ezk 41:18. 1 K 6:29, 32, 35. 2 Ch 3:5. Ps 92:12. Re 7:9.

17 **the outward**. Ezk 10:5. 42:1. 46:21. Re 11:2.
they were. 1 K 6:5. 1 Ch 9:26. 23:28. 2 Ch 31:11.
thirty. Ezk 42:4. 45:5.
pavement. 2 S 12:31. Je 43:9-11. Mt 25:32.

18 **pavement**. Je 43:9. Jn 19:13.

19 **he measured**. 1 Ch 28:11, 12.

unto the. ver. 23, 27. Ezk 46:1, 2.
without. *or*, from without.
20 **the gate**. ver. 6.
that looked. Heb. whose face was. ver. 6mg.
21 **the little**. ver. 7, 10-16, 29, 30, 36, 37.
arches. *or*, galleries, *or* porches. ver. 16, 26, 30-34.
after. ver. 8, 10, 13, 15, 25, 29.
22 **palm trees**. ver. 16, 31, 37. 1 K 6:29, 32, 35. 7:36. 2 Ch 3:5. Re 7:9.
and they. ver. 6, 26, 31, 34, 37, 49. He 6:1.
seven steps. 1 K 6:8.
23 **the gate of**. ver. 19, 27, 28, 44.
and he. Ex 27:9-18. 38:9-12.
24 **and behold**. ver. 6, 20, 35. Ezk 46:9.
and he. ver. 21, 28, 29, 33, 35, 36.
25 **windows**. ver. 16, 22, 29. Jn 12:46. 1 C 13:12. 2 P 1:19.
the length. ver. 21, 33.
26 **seven**. ver. 6, 22. 2 P 3:18.
palm trees. ver. 16, 22. Ps 92:12, 13. SS 7:7, 8.
27 **in the**. ver. 23, 32.
and he. ver. 19, 23, 47.
28 **according**. ver. 32, 35.
29 **the little**. ver. 7, 10, 12. 1 Ch 28:11, 12. 2 Ch 31:11. Ne 13:5, 9. Je 35:2-4. 36:10.
and there. ver. 16, 22, 25.
30 **five and**. ver. 21, 25, 29, 29, 33, 36.
five cubits. Instead of five cubits, it seems evident, from the parallel places, that we should read twenty-five: the word *esrim* appears to have been lost out of the text.
broad. Heb. breadth.
31 **and palm**. ver. 26, 34.
eight. ver. 22, 26, 34, 37.
32 **into the**. ver. 28-31, 35.
33 **it was**. ver. 21, 25, 36.
34 **palm trees**. ver. 31.
eight steps. ver. 6, 22, 26, 31, 34, 37, 49.
35 **to the**. ver. 27, 32. Ezk 44:4. 47:2.
36 **little**. ver. 21, 29, 36.
37 **the posts**. ver. 31, 34.
the utter court. That is, "the *outer* court."
38 **the chambers**. ver. 12. Ezk 41:10, 11. 1 K 6:8.
where. Le 1:9. 8:21. 2 Ch 4:6. He +10:22.
burnt offering. Le +23:12.
39 **tables on that**. Ex +25:23. Lk 22:30.
the burnt offering. Le +23:12.
the sin offering. Le +23:19.
the trespass offering. Le +5:6.
40 **at the side**. ver. 38, 39. Ezk 41:22.
as one goeth up. *or*, at the step. ver. 35.
north gate. Le 1:11.
42 **of hewn stone**. Ex 20:25. La 3:9. Am 5:11.
instruments. Ex 38:3.
43 **hooks**. *or*, end-irons. *or*, the two hearth-stones.
upon. Le 1:6, 8, 12. 8:20.

44 **the inner**. ver. 23, 27.
chambers. ver. 7, 10, 29. 1 Ch 6:31, 32. 16:41-43. 25:1, etc. Ep 5:19. Col 3:16.
45 **whose**. Ezk 8:5.
the keepers. Le 8:35. Nu 3:27, 28, 32, 38. 18:5. 1 Ch 6:49. 9:23. 2 Ch 13:11. Ps 134:1. Ml 2:4-7. 1 T 6:20. Re 1:6.
charge. *or*, ward, *or*, ordinance, and so ver. 46. Ezk 44:8mg. 1 Ch 9:23. Ml +3:14mg.
46 **the keepers**. Ezk 44:15. Le 6:12, 13. Nu 18:5.
these. Ezk 43:19. 44:15, 16. 48:11. 1 K 2:35. 1 Ch 29:22.
which come. Le 10:3. Nu 16:5, 40. Ep 2:13.
47 **measured**. Ezk 43:13-16.
an hundred cubits long. ver. 19, 23, 27.
foursquare. Ezk 48:20. Re 21:16.
48 **the porch**. 1 K 6:3. 2 Ch 3:4.
49 **the steps**. ver. 31, 34, 37.
pillars. 1 K 7:15-21. 2 Ch 3:15, 17. Je 52:17-23. Re 3:12.

EZEKIEL 41

1 **he brought**. Ezk +40:2, 3, 17.
to the temple. 1 K 6:2. Zc 6:12, 13. Ep 2:20-22. 1 P 2:5. Re 3:12. 11:1, 2. 21:3, 15.
and measured. Ex 26:15, etc.
2 **the door**. *or*, the entrance. Ex 26:36. 36:37. 1 K 6:31-35. 2 Ch 3:7. 29:7. Jn 10:7, 9.
the length. 1 K 6:2, 17. 2 Ch 3:3.
the breadth. 1 K 6:3.
3 **two cubits**. ver. 2, 4.
4 **twenty cubits**. 1 K 6:20. 2 Ch 3:8. Re 21:16.
This. Ex 26:33, 34. He 9:3-8.
most holy. The Holy of Holies. ver. 21, 23. Ezk 44:13. 45:3. 1 K 6:16.
5 **side chamber**. ver. 6, 7. Ezk 42:3-14. 1 K 6:5, 6.
6 **one over another**. Heb. side chamber over side chamber.
thirty in order. *or*, three and thirty times, *or* feet.
and they. 1 K 6:6, 10.
have hold. Heb. be holden. 1 P 1:5.
but. Ne 13:4, 5.
7 **there was**, etc. Heb. *it was* made broader, and went round. 1 K 6:8. Mt 13:32. He 6:1.
increased. Ps 84:7.
8 **a full**. Ezk 40:5. 2 Ch 3:3. Re 21:16.
9 **was five**. ver. 5.
that which. ver. 11. Ezk 42:1, 4.
11 **and the breadth**. ver. 9. Ezk 42:4.
12 **separate**. ver. 13-15. Ezk 42:1, 10, 13. Re 21:27. 22:14, 15.
13 **he measured**. ver. 14, 15.
15 **galleries**. *or*, several walks, *or*, walks with pillars. ver. 16. Ezk 42:3, 5. SS 1:17. 7:5. Zc 3:7.
an hundred. Ezk 40:47.
with the inner. ver. 17. Ezk 42:15.

16 **door posts**. *or*, thresholds. Ezk 40:6, 7.
narrow. ver. 26. Ezk 40:16, 25. 1 K 6:4. 1 C
13:12.
cieled with wood. Heb. cieling of wood. 1 K
6:15. 2 Ch 3:5. Hg 1:4.
from the ground up to the windows. *or*,
the ground unto the windows.
covered. 1 K 6:18.
17 **measure**. Heb. measures. Ezk 42:15.
18 **with cherubims**. ver. +20.
palm trees. Ezk 40:16, 22. Re 7:9.
and every. Ezk 1:10. 10:14, 21. Re 4:7-9.
19 **the face**. Ezk 1:6, 10. 10:14.
20 **cherubims**. ver. 18. Ge +3:24. 2 Ch 3:7.
21 **posts**. Heb. post. Ezk 40:14. 1 S 1:9. 1 K
6:33mg.
22 **altar**. Lk +1:11.
This is. Ezk 23:41. Ex +25:23. Pr 9:2. SS 1:12.
Re 3:20.
before. Ex 30:8.
23 **the temple**. 1 K 6:31-35. 2 Ch 4:22.
24 **the doors**. 1 K 6:31-35.
two leaves. Ezk 40:48.
25 **cherubims**. ver. 16-20.
26 **narrow windows**. ver. +16. Ezk 40:16.

EZEKIEL 42

1 **he brought**. Ezk 40:2, 3, 24. 41:1.
the utter court. Ezk 40:20. Re 11:2.
chamber. ver. 4. Ezk 41:9, 12-15.
3 **the twenty**. Ezk 41:10.
the pavement. Ezk 40:17, 18. 2 Ch 7:3.
gallery against. Ezk 41:15, 16. SS 1:17. 7:5.
4 **before**. 1 K 6:5, 6.
a walk. ver. 11.
a way. Mt 7:14. Lk 13:24.
5 **were higher than these**. *or*, did eat of these.
Ezk 41:7.
than the lower, and than the middle-
most of the building. *or, and* the building
consisted of the lower and middlemost. ver. 6.
6 **three stories**. Ezk 41:6. 1 K 6:8.
8 **the length**. Ezk 41:15.
before. ver. 11, 12.
9 **from under**. *or*, from the place of. Ezk 46:19.
the entry. *or*, he that brought me. Ezk 44:5.
46:19.
as one goeth. *or*, as he came. 1 K 6:8-10.
10 **the thickness**. Ezk 41:12.
over against. ver. 1, 13. Ezk 41:13-15.
11 **the way**. ver. 2-8.
12 **was a door**. ver. 9.
13 **they be holy**. Ex +29:31.
approach. Ezk 40:46. Le 10:3. Nu 16:5, 40.
18:7. Dt 21:5.
the most holy. Le +2:3. Ne 13:5.
meat offering. Le +23:13.
sin offering. Le +23:19.
trespass offering. Le +5:6.

14 **they not go**. Ezk 44:19. Ex 28:40-43. 29:4-9.
Le 8:7, 13, 33-35. Lk 9:62.
and shall put. Le 16:3, 4, 23. Is 61:10. Zc
3:4, 5. Ro 3:22. 13:14. Ga 3:27. 1 P 5:5.
15 **measuring**. Ezk 41:2-5, 15.
gate. Ezk 40:6, etc.
16 **side**. Heb. wind. ver. 17-20. Ezk 37:5.
the measuring reed. Ezk 40:3. Ps 48:2. Is
35:7. Zc 2:1. 14:4, 10. Re 11:1, 2.
20 **it had**. Ezk 40:5. SS 2:9. Is 25:1. 26:1. 60:18.
Mi 7:11. Zc 2:5.
five hundred. Ezk 45:2. 48:20. Re 21:12-17.
a separation. Ezk 22:26. 44:23. 48:15. Le
10:10. Lk 16:26. 2 C 6:17. Re 21:10-27.

EZEKIEL 43

1 **the gate that**. Ezk 40:6. 42:15. 44:1. 46:1.
2 **the glory**. Ezk +1:28. Is +40:5.
came. Ezk 11:23.
and his voice. Ezk 1:24. Re 1:15. 14:2. 19:1,
6.
the earth. Ezk 10:4. Is +40:5. Re 18:1.
3 **according to the appearance**. Ezk 1:4-28.
8:4. 9:3. 10:1-22. 11:22, 23.
I came. Is +6:10.
to destroy the city. *or*, to *prophesy* that the
city should be destroyed. Ezk 9:1, 5. 32:18. Je
1:10. Re 11:3-6.
the river. Ezk 1:3. 3:23.
fell. Ezk +1:28.
4 **the glory**. Hg 2:5-9.
came. Ezk 10:18, 19. 40:6. 42:15. 44:1, 2.
46:1.
5 **the spirit**. Heb. *ruach*, Is +48:16.
took. Ezk +8:3.
and brought. SS 1:4. 2 C 12:2-4.
inner court. Ezk 8:16.
the glory. Ex +24:16. Is +40:5.
6 **I heard**. Ezk 1:26-28. Le 1:1. Is 66:6. Re 16:1.
the man. Ezk 40:3.
7 **the place of my throne**. Ezk 10:1. Ps +11:4.
99:1.
and the place. 1 Ch 28:2. Ps 99:5. Is 60:13.
66:1. Mt 5:34, 35.
where I will dwell. ver. 9. Ezk 37:26-28.
48:35. Ex +29:45. Mt 28:20. Jn 1:14. 14:23.
in the midst. Ps 46:5.
for ever. Heb. *olam*, Ex +12:24. Ge +9:12. Lk
+1:32, 33.
no more defile. Ezk 20:39. 23:38, 39. 39:7.
Ho 14:8. Zc 13:2. 14:20, 21.
whoredom. ver. 9. Ezk 16:15-17, 25, 26. Je
3:1-5. Ho 4:13, 14. 9:1. Ja 4:4.
by the carcasses. ver. 9. Le 26:30. 2 Ch 34:5.
Je 16:18.
high places. 2 K +21:3.
8 **setting**. Ezk 5:11. 8:3-16. 23:39. 44:7. 2 K
16:10, 14, 15. 21:4-7. 23:11, 12. 2 Ch 33:4, 7.
by my thresholds. Is 6:4.

their post. Is +66:17.
my posts. Ezk 41:21. 46:2.
and the wall between me and them. *or*,
for *there was but* a wall between me and them.
Is 59:2.
defiled my holy name. Ezk 23:39.
abominations. Ezk 23:26. Le 26:30. 1 K
12:28. Ml 2:11.

9 **Now let**. Ezk +18:30, 31. Ho 2:2. Col 3:5-9.
the carcasses. ver. +7. Ezk 37:23.
and I. ver. 7. Ezk 37:26-28. 2 C 6:16-18.
for ever. Heb. *olam*, Ex +12:24.

10 **show**. Ezk 40:4. Ex +25:40.
that they. ver. 11. Ezk 16:61, 63. 31:31, 32.
Ro 6:21.
pattern. *or*, sum, *or* number.

11 **And if**. Je +7:5. 17:24, 25.
ashamed. ver. 10.
show them. Ezk ch. 40-42. 44:5, 6. He 8:5.
all the ordinances. 1 C 11:2.
and do. Ezk 11:20. 36:27. Mt 28:20. Jn
+13:17.

12 **Upon**. Ezk 40:2. 42:20. Ps 93:5. Is 2:2, 3. Jl
3:17. Mi 4:1, 2. Zc 14:20, 21. Re 21:27.

13 **the measures**. Ex 27:1-8. 2 Ch 4:1.
The cubit. Ezk 40:5. 41:8.
bottom. Heb. bosom. ver. 14, 17.
edge. Heb. lip. Ezk 3:5, 6. 36:3. +47:7mg. Ex
26:4. Jg +7:22mg.

14 **the lower settle**. or, ledge.

15 **the altar**. Heb. Harel, *that is*, the mountain of
God.
the altar. Heb. Ariel, *that is*, the lion of God.
Is 29:1mg, 2, 7.
four horns. Ex +27:2.

16 **twelve cubits**. Ex 20:26. 27:1, 2. 2 Ch 4:1.
Ezr 3:3.
square. Ex 38:1, 2.

17 **and the border**. Ex 25:25. 30:3. 1 K 18:32.
his stairs. Rather, "its ascents." Ex 20:26.
look toward. Ex 8:16. 40:6. 1 K 6:8.
Ne 9:4.

18 **to offer**. Le +23:12. He 9:21-23. 10:4-12.
12:24.
to sprinkle. Ezk 10:2. Le +1:5. 2 Ch 34:4. Jb
2:12. Is 28:5. Ho 7:9.

19 **the priests the Levites**. Ezk 40:46. 44:15.
48:11. Dt 17:9. Jsh 3:3. 8:33. 1 S 2:35, 36. 1 K
2:27, 35. 2 Ch 30:27. Ne 11:20. Is 61:6. 66:21,
22. Je 33:18-22. 1 P 2:5, 9.
which approach. Nu 16:5, 40. 18:5.
a young. Ezk 45:18, 19. Ex 29:10, 11. Le 4:3,
etc. 8:14, 15. 2 C 5:21. He 7:27.
sin offering. Le +23:19.

20 **take**. ver. 15. Ex +29:12, 36.
and on the four. ver. 16, 17.
thus shalt. ver. 22, 26. Ezk 45:18, 19. Le
16:19. He 9:21-23.

21 **burn**. Ex 29:14. Le 4:12, 21. 8:17. He 13:11,
12.

22 **a kid**. ver. 25. Ex 29:15-18. Le 4:27, 28, 30.
8:18-21. Is 53:6, 10. 1 P 1:19.
and they. ver. 20, 26.

24 **offer them**. Le 1:3-6.
cast salt. Le +2:13.
burnt offering. Le +23:12.

25 **Seven days**. Ex 29:35-37. Le 8:33.
sin offering. Le +23:19.

26 **Seven days**. Ex 29:35, 36.
they shall. Le 8:33, 34.
consecrate themselves. Heb. fill their
hands. Ex +28:41mg.

27 **that upon**. Le 9:1-6, 23, 24.
make. Ro 15:16. Ph 2:17. He 13:15.
burnt offerings. Le +23:12.
peace offerings. *or*, thank offerings. Le
+23:19. Je +33:11.
I will accept. Ezk 20:40, 41. Le 22:27. Dt
33:11. Jb 42:8. Ho 8:13. Ro 12:1. Ep 1:6. Col
1:20, 21. 1 P 2:5.

EZEKIEL 44

1 **the outward**. Ezk 40:6, 17. 42:14. 2 Ch 4:9.
20:5. 33:5. Ac 21:28-30.
looketh. Ezk 43:1, 4. 46:1.

2 **because**. Ezk 43:2-4. Ex 24:10. Is 6:1-5.

3 **for**. Ezk 34:23, 24. 37:24, 25. 46:2, 8. 2 Ch
23:13. 34:31.
the prince. Ezk 34:24. 37:25. 45:8, 22.
46:18. Zc 6:12, 13.
to eat. Ge 31:54. Ex 24:9-11. Dt 12:7, 17, 18.
Is 23:18. 62:9. 1 C 10:18, etc. Re 3:20.
he shall enter. Ezk 40:9. 46:2, 8-10.

4 **the way**. Ezk 40:20, 40.
the glory. Ezk +1:28. Is +40:5. Ml 3:1.
and I fell. Ezk +1:28. Ps 89:7.

5 **mark well**. Heb. set thine heart. Ezk 40:4. Ex
9:21mg. Dt 32:46. 1 Ch 22:19. 2 Ch 11:16. Pr
24:32mg. Da 10:12. He 8:5.
concerning. Ezk 43:10, 11. Dt 12:32. Mt
28:20.
and mark well. Ps 119:4.
the entering. Ps 96:8, 9. Ac 8:37.

6 **thou shalt say**. Ezk 2:5-8. 3:9, 26, 27. Is 6:1,
9. Jn 12:41. Ro 10:21.
rebellious. Heb. rebellion, put for rebellious
people.
let it suffice. Ezk 45:9. 1 P 4:3.

7 **ye have brought**. ver. 9. Ezk 7:20. 22:26.
43:7, 8. Le 22:25. Ac 21:28.
strangers. Heb. children of a stranger. ver. 9.
Ex +12:43 (**S#5236h**). Ps 18:44mg. Is 56:6, 7. Je
8:19. Da 11:39. Ml 2:11.
uncircumcised in heart. Le +26:41.
when. Le 3:16. 21:6, 8, 17, 21. 22:25. Ml 1:7,
12-14. Jn 6:52-58.
the fat. Ex +29:13.
broken. Ge 17:14. Le 26:15. Dt 31:16, 20. Is
24:5. Je 11:10. 31:32. He 8:9.

8 ye have not. Le 22:2, etc. Nu 18:3-5. Ne 13:4-9. Ac 7:53. 1 T 6:13, 14. 2 T 4:1.
set keepers. 1 K 12:31. 13:33, 34. 2 K 17:32.
charge. *or*, ward, *or* ordinance, and so ver. 14, 16. 1 Ch 23:32. Ezr 8:24-30. Ml +3:14mg.

9 Thus saith. Ezk 31:10, 15. 43:18. 45:9, 18. 46:1, 16. 47:13.
No stranger. ver. 7. Nu 16:9, 39, 40. Ps 50:16. 93:5. Da 11:39. Jl 3:17. Zc 14:21. Mk 16:16. Jn 3:3-5. T 1:5-9.

10 the Levites. ver. 15. Ezk 22:26. 48:11. 2 K 23:8, 9. 2 Ch 29:4, 5. 36:14. Ne 9:34. Je 23:11. Zp 3:4. 1 T 5:22.
idols. 2 K +23:24.
bear. Ge 4:13. Le 19:8. Nu 5:31. Ps 38:4. Is 53:11.

11 having charge. ver. 14. Ezk 40:45. 1 Ch 26:1, etc.
ministering to the house. 2 Ch 29:4, 5.
shall slay. 2 Ch 29:34. 30:17. 35:10, 11.
and they. ver. 15. Nu 16:9. 18:6. Dt +10:8.

12 they ministered. 1 S 2:29, 30. 2 K 16:10-16. Is 9:16. Ho 4:6. 5:1. Ml 2:8, 9.
caused the house of Israel to fall into iniquity. Heb. were for a stumblingblock of iniquity unto, etc. 1 C +8:9.
therefore. Ezk 20:6, 15, 23, 28. Dt 32:40-42. Ps 106:26. Am 8:7. Re 10:5, 6.
and they shall. ver. 10, 13.

13 they shall not. ver. 15. Nu 18:3. 2 K 23:9. 1 C 3:12-15.
bear. Ezk 32:30. 36:7.

14 keepers. Nu 18:4. 1 Ch 23:28-32. 2 Ch 29:34.

15 the sons. Ezk 40:46. 43:19. 48:11. 1 S 2:35. 1 K 2:35. 1 Ch 29:22. 1 T 3:3-10. 2 T 2:2. Re 2:1, 8, 12, 18. 3:1, 7, 14, 22.
when. ver. 10.
come near. ver. 13. 1 C 3:12-15.
they shall stand. Dt +10:8. Zc 3:1-7.
the fat. ver. +7.
the blood. Le 17:5, 6.

16 They shall enter. He 10:19. Re 1:6.
to my table. Ex +25:23.
keep. Nu 18:1, 5, 7, 8. Dt 10:8. 33:8-10. 1 Ch 23:28, 32.

17 they shall. Ex 28:29, 40, 42, 43. 39:27-29. Le 16:4. Re 4:4. 19:8.

18 bonnets. Ezk 24:17. Ex 28:40, 41. 39:28. Is 61:10. 1 C 11:4-10.
linen breeches. Ex 28:42, 43. 1 C 14:40.
with anything that causeth sweat. *or*, in sweating *places*. Heb. in, *or* with sweat.

19 they shall put. Ezk 42:13, 14. Le 6:10, 11.
sanctify. Ezk 46:20. Ex 29:37. 30:29. Le 6:27. Mt 23:17-19. 1 C 3:5, 6.

20 shave. Le +19:27.
nor suffer. Nu 6:5. 1 C 11:14.

21 drink wine. Le 10:9. Lk 1:15. 1 T 3:8. 5:23. T 1:7, 8.

22 a widow. Le 21:7, 13, 14. Dt 25:5. 1 T 3:2, 4, 5, 11, 12. T 1:6.
put away. Heb. thrust forth. Dt 24:1-4.
that had a priest before. Heb. from a priest.

23 shall teach. Ezk 22:26. Le 10:10, 11. Dt 33:10. Ho 4:6. Mi 3:9-11. Zp 3:4. Hg 2:11-13. Ml 2:6-9. Ga 6:6. 1 T 4:11, 12. 2 T 2:24, 25. T 1:9-11.

24 in controversy. Dt 17:8-13. 1 Ch 23:4. 2 Ch 19:8-10. Ezr 2:63.
they shall keep. 1 T 3:15.
in all. Le ch. 23. Nu ch. 28, 29. Ne ch. 8.
hallow my sabbaths. Ex +20:8.

25 come at no dead person. Le 21:1-6. 22:4. Mt 8:21, 22. Lk 9:59, 60. 2 C 5:16. 1 Th 4:13-15.

26 And after. Nu 6:10, etc. 19:11-13. He 9:13, 14.

27 unto the inner. ver. 17.
he shall offer. Le 4:3, etc. 8:14, etc. Nu 6:9-11. He 7:26-28.
sin offering. Le +23:19.

28 for an inheritance. Col 3:24.
I am their inheritance. Ezk 45:4. 48:9-11. Nu 18:20. Dt 10:9. 18:1, 2. Jsh 13:14, 33. Ro 8:17. Ep 1:11. 1 P 1:4. 5:2-4.
no possession. Ac 4:32. 1 C 7:30. 2 C 6:10.
possession. SS 2:16.

29 eat. Le +7:7.
meat offering. Le +23:13.
sin offering. Le +23:19.
trespass offering. Le +5:6.
dedicated. *or*, devoted. Le 27:21, 28 with Nu 18:14. 1 C 3:21-23.

30 first. *or*, chief. Ezk 20:40. 48:14. Ex 13:2, 12, 13. 22:29, 30. Nu 3:13. 18:12, 13.
all the firstfruits. Ex 13:2, 12. Le +23:10. Nu 3:13.
oblation. or, heave offering. Ezk 20:40. 45:6, 7, 13, 16. 48:8-10, 12, 18, 20, 21. Le +7:14.
first of your dough. Nu 15:20.
that he may. Dt 26:10-15. Pr 3:9, 10. Ml 3:10, 11.

31 priest shall not. Ex 22:31. Le 17:15. 22:8. Dt 14:21. Ro 14:20, 21. 1 C 8:13.

EZEKIEL 45

1 shall divide by lot. Heb. cause the land to fall by lot. Jsh +14:2.
ye shall offer. ver. 2-7. Ezk +44:30. 48:8-23. Ex 29:27. Le 25:23. Ezr +8:25. Pr 3:9, 10.
an holy portion. Heb. holiness. Zc 14:20, 21.
the length. ver. 2. Ezk 42:16-19.
five and twenty thousand. Ezk 48:8.

2 five hundred in length. Ezk 42:16-20.
suburbs. *or*, void places.

3 and in it. Ezk 48:8, 10.

4 holy portion. ver. 1. Ezk 44:28. 48:11.
which. Ezk 40:45. 43:19. 44:13, 14. Nu 16:5.

a place for their houses. 2 K 23:11. 1 Ch 26:12, 13.
holy place for. Ezk 48:10.

5 **the five**. Ezk 48:10, 13, 20.
the ministers. 1 C 9:13, 14.
for a possession. Ezk 40:17. 1 Ch 9:26-33. Ne 10:38, 39.

6 **the city**. Ezk 48:15-18, 30-35.
whole house. Ezk 48:19.

7 **for the prince**. Ezk 34:24. 37:24. 46:16-18. 48:21. Ps 2:8, 9. Is +9:5, 6. Lk +1:32, 33.

8 **and my princes**. Ezk 19:3-7. 22:27. 46:18. 2 K 15:19, 20. Pr 28:16. Is 11:3-5. 32:1, 2. 60:17, 18. Je 22:17. 23:5. Mi 3:1-4. Zp 3:13. Ja 2:6. +5:1-6. Re 19:11-16.
according. Jsh 11:23.

9 **Thus saith**. Ezk +44:9.
Let it. Ezk 44:6. 1 P 4:3.
princes of. Dt 17:14-20.
remove. Ne 5:10. Zc 8:16. Lk 3:14.
execute. Ezk 43:14-16.
take away. Ne 5:1-13. 1 C 6:7, 8.
exactions. Heb. expulsions. Jb 20:19. 22:9. 24:2-12. Mi 2:1, 2, 9.

10 **just balances**. Le 19:35, 36. Pr 11:1. 16:11. 20:10. 21:3. Am 8:4-6. Mi 6:10, 11.
just ephah. Dt 25:13-15. Pr 20:10.

11 **ephah**. Le +27:16. Is 5:10.
the measure. Ex +5:8.

12 **the shekel**. Ex +30:13.

13 **the oblation**. Ezk +44:30.
give the sixth. Ezk 39:2.

14 **ordinance of oil**. ver. 25. Nu 28:5.
the tenth. ver. 11.
the cor. 1 K +4:22mg.

15 **lamb**. or, kid. Ezk 34:17mg. Ex 12:3mg.
out of the fat pastures. or, well-watered land. Ge 13:10. Pr 3:9, 10. Ml 1:8, 14.
meat offering. Le +23:13.
burnt offering. Le +23:12.
peace offerings. or, thank offerings. ver. 17.
to make. He +2:17. 9:22, 23.

16 **the people**. Ex 30:14, 15. 2 Ch 29:31.
shall give this. Heb. shall be for.
for. or, with. Is 16:1.

17 **the prince's**. Ezk 40:38. 44:16. 46:4-12. 2 S 6:19. 1 K 8:63, 64. 1 Ch 16:2, 3. 29:3-9. 2 Ch 5:6. 7:4, 5. 8:12, 13. 30:24. 31:3. 35:7, 8. Je 33:18. Ezr 1:5. 6:8, 9. Ps 68:18. Jn 1:16. Ro 11:35, 36. Ep 5:2.
burnt offerings. Le +23:12.
meat offerings. Le +23:13.
drink offerings. Le +23:13.
in the feasts. Ge +17:21. Le 23:2. Nu ch. 28, 29. Is 66:23.
new moons. ver. 18. Col +2:16.
the sabbaths. Is +58:13, 14.
he shall prepare. ver. 22-24. Le 14:19. Nu 6:16, 17. Ps 22:15-26, 29. Jn 6:51-57. 1 C 5:7, 8. He 13:10. 1 P 2:24. +3:18.

sin offering. Le +23:19.
meat offering. Le +23:13.
burnt offering. Le +23:12.
peace offerings. or, thank offerings. Le +23:19. Je +33:11. Col 3:17.
make reconciliation. 2 Ch 29:20-24.

18 **In the first month**. Ex 12:2. Nu 28:11-15. Mt 6:33.
bullock. Ex 29:1-14.
without blemish. Le +1:3.
and cleanse. Ezk 43:22, 26. Le 8:1-13. 16:16, 33. He 9:22-25. 10:3, 4, 19-22.

19 **and upon the four corners**. Ezk 43:14, 20. Le 16:18-20.
the settle. Ezk 43:14.

20 **every one**. Le 4:27-30. Ps 19:12. Ro 16:18, 19. He 5:2.
that is simple. Ps 19:7. Pr +1:4. 19:25.
so shall. ver. 15, 17. Le 16:20.

21 **ye shall**. Ex ch. 12. Le 23:5-8. Nu 9:2-14. 28:16-25. Dt 16:1-8. 1 C 5:7, 8.
passover. Ex 12:18. Le +23:5.
unleavened bread. Le +23:6.

22 **the prince**. Mt 20:28. 26:26-28.
bullock. Le 4:14. 2 C 5:21.

23 **seven days**. Le 23:8.
a burnt. Le +23:12.
seven bullocks. Nu +23:1. He 10:8-12.

24 **he shall prepare**. Ezk 46:5-7. Nu 28:12-15, 20, 21.

25 **In the seventh**. Le +23:34.
sin offering. Le +23:19.
burnt offering. Le +23:12.
meat offering. Le +23:13.
according to the oil. ver. +14. Le 5:11. Nu 18:12. Dt 12:17.

EZEKIEL 46

1 **shall be shut**. Ezk 44:1, 2.
six working. Ge 3:19. Ex +20:9. Lk 13:14.
on the sabbath. Ezk 45:17. Le 23:3. 2 Ch 23:31. Is +58:13, 14. 66:23. He 4:9, 10.
new moon. Col +2:16.

2 **the porch**. Jn 10:1-3.
by the post. ver. 8. Ezk 44:3. 2 Ch 23:13. 34:31.
the priests. Col 1:28.
his. Ezk 45:16, 17, 20, 22.
burnt offering. Le +23:12.
peace offerings. Le +23:19.
he shall worship. 1 K 8:22, 23. 1 Ch 17:16. 29:10-12. 2 Ch 6:13. 29:29. Mt 26:39. He 5:7, 8.
but the gate. ver. 12.

3 **people of the land**. Ezk 45:16. Is 66:23. Lk 1:10. Jn 10:9. He +10:19-22.

4 **the burnt**. Le +23:12.

5 **the meat**. ver. 7, 11, 12. Le +23:13.
as he shall be able to give. Heb. the gift of

his hand. Le 14:21. Nu 6:21. 9:10. Dt 16:17.
and. Nu 28:9.

8 **he shall go**. ver. 2. Ezk 44:1-3. Col 1:18.

9 **when the people**. 1 C 14:40.
come before. Ex 23:14-17. 34:23. Dt 16:16.
Ps 84:7. Ml 4:4.
solemn feasts. Ge +17:21. Le 23:2.
he that entereth. Ezk 1:12, 17. Ph 3:13, 14.
He 10:38. 2 P 2:20, 21.

10 **the prince in the midst**. 2 S 6:14-19. 1 Ch
29:20, 22. 2 Ch 6:2-4. 7:4, 5. 20:27, 28. 29:28,
29. 34:30, 31. Ne 8:8, 9. Ps 42:4. 122:1-4. Mt
18:20. 28:20. He 3:6. 4:14-16. Re 2:1.
when they go in. Ex 23:14-17. Dt 16:16.
go forth. 2 S 5:24. Jn +10:4.

11 **in the feasts**. Le ch. 23. Nu ch. 15, 28, 29. Dt
ch. 16.
the meat. ver. 5, 7.

12 **a voluntary**. Le +23:38. 1 K 3:4. 1 Ch 29:21.
2 Ch 5:6. 7:5-7. 29:31. Ezr 6:17. Ps 40:7, 8. Ro
12:1. Ep 5:2.
burnt offering. Le +23:12.
peace offerings. Le +23:19.
open him. ver. 1, 2, 8. Ezk 44:3.
as he did. Ezk 45:17.

13 **Thou shalt daily**. Ex 29:38-42. Nu 28:3-8,
10. Da 8:11-13. Jn 1:29. 1 P 1:19, 20. Re 13:8.
of the first year. Heb. a son of his year. Ex
12:5. Le 12:6mg.
every morning. Heb. morning by morning. 2
S +13:4mg. Ps 92:2. Is 50:4.

14 **every morning**. ver. +13.
the sixth. Nu 28:5.
perpetual. Heb. *olam*, Ge +9:12.

15 **every morning**. ver. +13.
a continual. Ex +29:38. He 9:26. 10:1-10.

16 **If the prince**. Ge 25:5, 6. Nu 27:1-11. 36:7. 2
Ch 21:3. Ps 37:18. Mt 25:34. Lk 10:42. Jn
8:35, 36. Ro 8:15-17, 29-32. Ga 4:7.

17 **to the year**. Le +25:10. Mt 25:14-29. Lk
19:25, 26. Ga 4:30, 31.

18 **the prince**. Ezk 45:8. 1 K 21:4-7, 16. Ps 72:2-
4. 78:72. Is 11:3, 4. 32:1, 2. Je 23:5, 6.
thrust. Ezk 22:27. 1 K 21:19. Mi 1:1, 2. 3:1-
3.
inheritance out. Ps 68:18. Jn 10:28. Ep 4:8.
my people. Ezk 34:3-6, 21.

19 **the entry**. Ezk 40:44-46. 42:9. 44:4, 5.

20 **boil the trespass offering**. Le +5:6. 1 S
2:13-15. 2 Ch 35:13.
sin offering. Le +23:19.
bake the meat offering. Le +23:13.
to sanctify. Ezk +44:19.

21 **in every corner of the court there was a
court**. Heb. *a court in a corner of a court; and
a court in a corner of a court*.

22 **joined**. *or*, made with chimneys.
corners. Heb. cornered.

24 **where the ministers**. ver. 20. 1 Ch 23:27-
29. Mt +24:45. Jn 21:15-17. 1 P 5:2.

EZEKIEL 47

1 **the door**. Ezk 41:2, 23-26. Ps 46:4. Is 30:25.
55:1. Je 2:13. Jl 3:18. Zc 13:1. 14:8. Jn 7:37-
39. Re 22:1, 17.
came down. or, were coming down. Is 12:3.
44:3. Jl 3:18. Zc 14:8. Re 22:1.
from under. ver. 12. 2 K +18:17. 20:20. 2 Ch
32:3-5. Ne 2:14. Is 2:3. Is 22:11.

2 **northward**. Ezk 44:2, 4.
there ran. Lk 24:47. Jn 4:22.

3 **the man**. Ezk 40:3. Zc 2:1. Re 11:1. 21:15.
waters were to the ancles. Heb. waters of
the ancles. Lk 24:49. Ac 2:4, 33. 10:45, 46.
11:16-18.

4 **the waters were to the knees**. Ac 8:4.
19:10-20. Ro 15:19. Col 1:6.

5 **waters to swim in**. Heb. waters of swimming. Is 11:9. Da 2:34, 35. Hab 2:14. Mt 13:31,
32. Jn 7:37-39. Re 7:9. 11:15. 20:2-4. 22:1.

6 **hast thou**. Ezk 8:17. 40:4. 44:5. Je 1:11-13.
Zc 4:2. 5:2. Mt 13:51.

7 **at the**. Is 44:18, 19. 43:19. Jl 3:18.
bank. Heb. lip. Jg +7:22mg.
many. ver. 12. Ge 2:9, 10. Nu 24:6. Ps 1:3. Je
17:8. Re 22:2.

8 **east country**. Jsh 22:11.
and go down. Is 35:1, 7. 41:17-19. 43:20.
44:3-5. 49:9, 10. Je 31:9.
desert. *or*, plain. Heb. Arabah. Dt 3:17. 4:49.
Jsh 3:16. Je 5:6mg.
the sea. Jsh 3:16.
the waters. 2 K 2:19-22. Is 11:6-9. Ml 1:11.
Mt 13:15.

9 **that every**. Jn 3:16. 11:26.
thing. Heb. *nephesh*, soul, Ge +2:19. Le 11:10.
which moveth. Ge 1:20.
rivers. Heb. two rivers. Ps 78:16.
shall live. Is 12:3. Jn 4:10, 14. 5:25. 6:63.
11:25. 14:6, 19. Ro 8:2. 1 C 15:45. Ep 2:1-5.
a very great. Is 49:12. 60:3-10. Zc 2:11. 8:21-
23. Ac 2:41, 47. 4:4. 5:14. 6:7. 21:20.
for they. Ex +15:26. Ps +103:3. Is 30:26.

10 **fishers**. Mt 4:19. 13:47-50. Mk 1:17. Lk 5:4-
10. Jn 21:3-11.
En-gedi. Jsh +15:62.
Eneglaim. i.e. *spring of two heifers*, S#5882h,
only here.
the great sea. ver. 15. Nu +34:6.
exceeding. Is 49:12, 20.

11 **shall not be healed, they shall be**. *or*, and
that which shall not be healed, shall be, etc. He
+6:4-8. +10:26-31. 2 P 2:19-22. Re +21:8.
22:11, 15.
given. Dt +29:23.

12 **by the river**. ver. 7. Ps 92:12. Is 60:21. 61:3.
grow. Heb. come up. Is 53:2.
trees for meat. Ge 2:9. Re 2:7.
whose. Jb 8:16. Ps +1:3. Je +17:8.
new. *or*, principal.
their waters. SS 4:12. 7:12, 13.

medicine. *or*, bruises and sores. Is 1:6. Je +8:22. Re 22:2, 14.

13 **This shall**. Nu 34:2-12.
Joseph. Ezk 48:4-6. Ge 48:5, 21, 22. 49:26. 1 Ch +5:1. Je 3:18. 31:1.

14 **lifted up mine hand**. *or*, swore. Ezk 20:42. 36:7, +25. Ge +14:22. 22:16, 17. He 6:13.
to give. Ezk 20:42. Ge 12:7. +13:15. 15:7. 17:8. 26:3. +28:13. 50:24. Nu 14:16, 30.
fall. Ezk 48:29. Pr 16:33.

15 **And this**. ver. 17-20.
Hethlon. i.e. *hiding place*, S#2855h. Ezk 48:1.
Zedad. Nu 34:8, 9.

16 **Hamath**. Nu +13:21.
Berothah. i.e. *place of wells; cypress-like*, S#1268h. 2 S 8:8, Berothai.
Sibraim. i.e. *double hope*, S#5453h, only here.
Damascus. Ge 14:15. 1 Ch 18:5. Ac 9:2.
Hazar-hatticon. *or*, the middle village. S#2694h.
Hauran. i.e. *cavernous; very white*, S#2362h. ver. 18.

17 **Hazar-enan**. Ezk 48:1. Nu 34:9.

18 **east side**. Nu 34:10-12.
from. Heb. from between. 2 K 16:14.
from Gilead. Ge 31:23, 47, Galead. +37:25.
land of Israel. Ezk +27:17.
Jordan. Ge 13:10. Jb 40:23.

19 **south side**. Nu 34:3-5.
Tamar. Ezk 48:28.
strife. *or*, Meribah. Nu 20:13. Dt 32:51. 33:8. Ps 81:7.
river. *or*, valley. Nu 34:5. Jsh 12:3.
southward. *or*, toward Teman. Jsh 12:3mg.

20 **west side**. Nu 34:6.
Hamath. 1 Ch 13:5.

21 **divide this land**. Nu 34:13-15.

22 **ye shall divide**. ver. 13, 14. Jsh +14:2.
and to the. Is 56:3-8. Jn +10:16. Ac 2:5-10. 11:18. Ep 2:12, 13, 19-22. 3:6. Re 7:9, 10.
strangers. ver. 23. Ezk 14:7. 22:7, 29. Dt +26:11. Zc 7:10. Ml 3:5.
born in. Ex 12:19, 48, 49. Le 16:29.
they shall have. Ac 15:9. Ro 10:12. Ga 3:28, 29. Col 3:11.

23 **the stranger**. ver. +22.

EZEKIEL 48

1 **the names**. Ex 1:1-5. Nu 1:5-15. 13:4-15. Re 7:4-8.
From. Ezk 47:15-17. Nu 34:7-9.
a portion. Heb. one portion.
Dan. Ge +14:14. 1 Ch 7:12. Mt 20:15, 16.

2 **Asher**. Ge +30:13. Nu +1:13. Dt +33:24.

3 **Naphtali**. Ge 30:7, 8. Jsh 19:32-39.

4 **Manasseh**. Ge +41:51. Nu +1:10.

5 **Ephraim**. Jsh ch. 16. 17:8-10, 14-18.

6 **Reuben**. Ge +29:32. Nu +1:5.

7 **Judah**. Ge 29:35. Jsh ch. 15. 19:9.

8 **the offering**. Ezk +44:30. 45:1-6. Ex 29:27.
the sanctuary. ver. 35. Is 12:6. 33:20-22. Zc 2:11, 12. 2 C 6:16. Ep 2:20-22. Col 2:9. Re 21:3, 22. 22:3.

9 **the oblation**. ver. +8, 10, 21. Ezk +44:30.

10 **for the priests**. Ezk 44:15, 28. 45:4. Nu 35:1-9. Jsh ch. 21. Mt 10:10. 1 C 9:13, 14.
toward the east. Nu 3:38.
and the sanctuary. ver. 8.

11 **It shall be for the priests that are sancti-fied**. *or*, The sanctified *portion shall be* for the priests.
the sons. Ezk 40:46. 43:19. 44:15, 16.
charge. *or*, ward, *or* ordinance. Ml +3:14mg. Mt +24:45, 46. 2 T 4:7, 8. 1 P 5:4. Re 2:10.
as the Levites. Ezk 44:10.

12 **a thing**. Ezk 45:4. Le 27:21.

13 **Levites**. Nu 1:53. Jsh 21:1.
five and twenty thousand in. Ezk 45:3, 5. Dt 12:19. Lk 10:7.

14 **not sell**. Ex 22:29. Le 25:32-34. 27:10, 28, 33. Nu 18:12-14.
firstfruits. Le +23:10.
for. ver. 12. Le 23:20. 27:9, 32. Ml 3:8-10.

15 **a profane**. Ezk 22:26. 42:20. 44:23. 45:6.
for the city. 1 T 3:15. Re 21:16.

18 **that serve**. Jsh 9:27. Ezr 2:43-58. Ne 7:46-62.

19 **shall serve**. Ezk 45:6. 1 K 4:7-23. Ne ch. 11.

20 **foursquare**. Ezk 40:47. He 12:27. Re 21:16.

21 **the residue**. ver. 22. Ezk +45:7, 8. Ho 1:11.
and westward. ver. 8-10.

23 **Benjamin**. ver. 1-7. Ge +35:18. Jsh 18:21-28.
a portion. Heb. one *portion*. ver. 1.

24 **Simeon**. Ge +29:33. 49:5-7. Jsh 19:1-9.

25 **Issachar**. Ge +30:18. Jsh 19:17-23.

26 **Zebulun**. Ge +30:20. Jsh 19:10-16.

27 **Gad**. Ge +30:11. Nu 32:33-36. Jsh 13:24-28.

28 **from Tamar**. Ezk 47:19. 2 Ch 20:2.
strife in Kadesh. Heb. Meribah-kadesh. Nu 20:1, 13. Ps 106:32.
the river. or, brook (of Egypt). Ps +72:8.
the great sea. Nu +34:6.

29 **the land**. Ezk 47:13-22. Nu 34:2, 13. Jsh ch. 13-21.
divide by lot. Jsh +14:2.

30 **the goings**. ver. 16, 32-35. Re 21:16.
four. ver. 15. Ezk 42:16. Is 37:36.

31 **the gates**. Is 26:1, 2. 54:12. 60:11. Re 21:12, 13, 21, 25.

35 **and the name**. Ge 22:14. Je 33:16. Zc 14:21.
The Lord. Heb. *Jehovah shammah*. i.e. *The Lord is there*. Signifying the personal presence of Messiah who will reign visibly in Israel (Is +9:6, 7. 24:23. Lk +1:32, 33. Re 11:15. 20:4-10). Ex +15:26. 17:15. Jg 6:24. Ps 46:5. 48:3, 14. 68:18. 77:13. 132:14. Is 12:6. 14:32. Je 3:17. Jl 3:21. Zc 2:10. Re 21:3. 22:3.

DANIEL

DANIEL 1

1 **the third year of**. 2 K 24:1, 2, 13. 2 Ch 36:5-7.
Babylon. 2 K +17:24.

2 Cir. A.M. 3398. B.C. 606.
the Lord gave. Da 2:37, 38. 5:18. Dt 28:49-52. 32:30. Jg 2:14. 3:8. 4:2. 2 K 24:3. Ps 106:41, 42. Is 42:24.
with part. Da 2:42. 2 Ch +4:19.
Shinar. Ge +10:10.
and he. Da 5:2, 3. Jg 16:23, 24. 1 S 5:2. 31:9, 10. Ezr 1:7. Je 51:44. Hab 1:16.

3 **Ashpenaz**. i.e. *nose of a horse*, **S#828h**.
the master. 2 K 18:17. Je 39:3.
eunuchs. ver. 18. 2 K +8:6mg.
certain of the children. Foretold 2 K 20:17, 18. Is 39:7. Je 41:1.
the princes. Est 1:3. 6:9.

4 **Children**. ver. 10, 13, 15, 17. Ge 21:8, 14-16. 1 S 1:2. 1 K 12:8. 2 K 2:23, 24. Is 9:6. La 4:10.
in whom. Le 21:18-21. 24:19, 20. Jg 8:18. 2 S 14:25. Ac 7:20. Ep 5:27.
and skilful. Da 2:20, 21. 5:11. Ec 7:19. Mt 2:1. Ac 7:22.
ability. ver. 17-20. Pr 22:29.
the tongue. Dt 28:49.
Chaldeans. Da 2:2, 4. 9:1. Je 22:25. Ezk 23:23.

5 **a daily**. 1 K 4:22, 23. 2 K 25:30. Mt 6:11. Lk 11:3.
provision. Ex +5:13mg.
which he drank. Heb. of his drink.
stand. ver. 19. Dt +10:8. Lk +21:36.

6 **Daniel**. Da 2:17. Ezk 14:14, 20. 28:3. Mt 24:15. Mk 13:14.

7 **the prince**. ver. 3, 10, 11.
gave names. Da 4:8. 5:12. Ge 41:45. 2 K 23:34. 24:17.
Belteshazzar. i.e. *Bel's prince* or *superior; lord of the straitened's treasure*, **S#1095h**. Da 10:1. Also **S#1096h**. Da 2:26. 4:8, 9, 18, 19, 19, 19. 5:12.
Hananiah. Da 2:49. 3:12-30.
Shadrach. i.e. *rejoicing in the way; little friend of the king*, **S#7714h**. Also **S#7715h**. Da 2:49. 3:12-14, 16, 19, 20, 22, 23, 26, 28-30.
Meshach. i.e. *agile, expeditious; waters of quiet*,

S#4335h. Also **S#4336h**. Da 2:49. 3:12-14, 16, 19, 20, 23, 26, 28-30.
Abednego. i.e. *servant of light* or *the sun*, **S#5664h**. Also **S#5665h**. Da 2:49. 3:12-14, 16, 19, 20, 22, 23, 26, 28-30.

8 **Daniel**. i.e. *judge of God, my God is judge; divine judgment*, **S#1840h**. ver. 6-11, 17, 19, 21. Da 2:19. 8:1, 15, 27. 9:2, 22. 10:1, 2, 7, 11, 12. 12:4, 5, 9. 1 Ch 3:1. Ezr 8:2. Ne 10:6. Ezk 14:14, 20. 28:3.
purposed. Ru 1:17, 18. 1 K 5:5. Ps 119:106, 115. Pr 23:7. Ac 11:23. 1 C 7:37. 2 C 9:7.
heart. Pr 16:1.
defile. Ex 34:15. Le 3:17. 7:26. 11:45-47. 17:10-14. 19:26. Dt 32:38. Ps 106:28. 141:4. Ezk 4:13, 14. Ho 9:3, 4. Ac 10:14-16. 15:29. Ro 14:15-17. 1 C 8:7-10. 10:18-21, 28-31. 1 T 5:22.
king's meat. Ezk 4:13. Ho 9:3.
wine. Jg 13:4.

9 **God had brought**. Ge 32:28. 39:21. Ex 3:21. 1 K 8:50. Ezr 7:27, 28. Ne 1:11. 2:4. Ps 4:3. 75:6, 7. 106:46. Pr +16:7. Ac 7:9, 10.

10 **I fear**. Pr 29:25. Jn 12:42, 43.
worse liking. Heb. sadder. Ge 40:6. Mt 6:16-18. Lk 24:17.
sort. or, term, or continuance.
endanger. Da 5:19.

11 **Melzar**. or, the steward. i.e. *chief butler*, **S#4453h**. ver. 16.

12 **Prove**. Re 2:10.
pulse to eat. Heb. of pulse that we may eat, etc. ver. 16. Ge 1:29, 30. Dt 8:3. Ro 14:2.

13 **our countenances**. La 4:7.

15 **their**. Ex 23:25. Dt 28:1-14. 2 K 4:42-44. Ps 37:16. Pr 10:22. Hg 1:6, 9. Ml 2:2. Mt 4:4. Mk 6:41, 42.
appeared. 1 S 16:12. Ps 45:2.

16 **Melzar**. ver. 11mg.
took away. Le 11:4-23. Ezk 4:14. Ac 10:14.

17 **God**. Da 2:21, 23. 1 K 3:12, 28. 4:29-31. 2 Ch 1:10, 12. Jb 32:8. Ps +119:98-100. Pr 2:6. Ec 2:26. Is 28:26. Lk 21:15. Ac 6:10. 7:10. Col 1:9. Ja +1:5, 17.
knowledge. Ac 7:22.
Daniel had understanding. or, he made Daniel understand. Da 4:9, 10. 5:11, 12, 14.

10:1. Ge 41:8-15. Nu 12:6. 2 Ch 26:5. Ezk 28:3. 1 C 12:7-11.

18 eunuchs. ver. 3. 2 K +8:6mg.

19 A.M. 3401. B.C. 603.
communed. 1 K 10:2.
therefore. ver. +5. Da 2:49.

20 in all. 1 S 18:30. 1 K 4:29-34. 10:1-3, 23, 24. Ps +119:99. Lk 21:15.
wisdom and understanding. Heb. wisdom of understanding.
ten. Ge 31:7. Nu 14:22. Ne 4:12. Jb 19:3.
the magicians. Da 2:2-11, 21-23. 4:7, 8, etc. 5:7, 8, 11, 12, 17. Ge +41:8. 2 T 3:8, 9.

21 Daniel continued. Da 6:28. 10:1. Ex 25:30. 27:20. 28:29, 30, 38. 29:38, 42. 30:8. Ezk 39:14. "He lived to see that glorious time of the return of his people from the Babylonian captivity, though he did not die then. So *till* is used Ps 110:1. 112:8."

DANIEL 2

1 in. Da 1:1-5. 2 Ch 36:5-7.
the second. 2 K 23:36. 24:12. Je +25:1.
Nebuchadnezzar. ver. 3. Da 4:5. Ge 40:5-8. 41:1, etc. Jb 33:15-17.
his spirit. Heb. *ruach*, Ps +106:33; Ge +26:35. ver. 3.
and his. Da 6:18. Est 6:1.

2 commanded. Da +1:20. 4:6. 5:7. Ge 41:8. Ex 7:11. 22:18. Dt +18:10-12. Is 8:19. 19:3. 47:12, 13. Ml +3:5.
magicians. S#2748h. Da 1:20. 2:2. Ge 41:8, 24. Ex 8:11, 22. 8:7, 18, 19. 9:11. For S#2749h, see ver. 10.
astrologers. Da 1:20. 2:10, 27. 4:7. 5:7, 11, 15. Is 47:13.
sorcerers. Is +47:12. Ml +3:5.
the Chaldeans. ver. 4, 5, 10. Da 1:4.

3 I have dreamed. ver. 1. Ge 40:8. 41:15.
spirit. Heb. *ruach*, Ps +106:33; Ge +26:35. Da 4:5. Ge 41:8.

4 in. Ge 31:47. Ezr 4:7. Is 36:11. Je 10:11.
Syriack. S#762h. 2 K 18:26. Ezr 4:7, 7. Is 36:11.
O king. 1 S +10:24. Ne +2:3.
live. 2 S 16:16mg.
for ever. Chal. *alam*, Ex +12:24.
tell. Da 4:7. 5:8. Ge 41:8. Is 44:25.

5 ye shall. Da 3:29. 1 S 15:33. Ps 50:22. 58:7.
cut in pieces. Chal. made pieces.
made. Dt 13:16. Jsh 6:26. 2 K 10:27. Ezr 6:11.

6 ye shall. ver. 48. Da 5:7, 16, 29. Nu 22:7, 17, 37. 24:11.
rewards. *or*, fee. Da 5:17mg.

7 Let. ver. 4, 9. Ec 10:4.

8 gain. Chal. buy. ver. 9. Est 3:7. Ep 5:16. Col 4:5.

9 there is. Da 3:15. Est 4:11.

for. 1 K 22:6, 22. Pr 12:19. Is 44:25. Ezk 13:6, 17, 19. 2 C 2:17.
lying. Zc 10:2.
the time. ver. 21. Da 5:28, 31. 7:25.
I shall know. Is 41:22-24, 28, 29.

10 magician. S#2749h. ver. 10, 27. 4:7, 9. Da 5:11.
Chaldean. i.e. *inhabitant of Chaldea*, S#3779h. See Da 5:30. Also see ver. 5, 10. Da 3:8. 4:7. 5:7, 11.

11 and there. ver. 27, 28. Da 5:11. Ge 41:39. Ex 8:19. Mt 19:26.
except. Is 44:24, 25.
whose. Ex 29:45. Nu 35:34. 1 K 8:27. 2 Ch 6:18. Ps 68:18. 113:5, 6. 132:14. Is 8:18. +57:15. 66:1, 2. Jl 3:21. Jn +1:1-3, 14. 14:17, 23. 2 C 6:16. Re 21:3.

12 For this cause. Da 3:13. 5:19. Jb 5:2. Ps 76:10. Pr 16:14. 19:12. 20:2. 27:3, 4. 29:22. Mt 2:16. 5:22.

13 the decree. Da 6:9-15. Est 3:12-15. Ps 94:20. Pr 28:15-17. Is 10:1.
and they. Da 1:19, 20. 6:12. Je 36:26.

14 answered. Chal. returned. Da 3:16.
with. 2 S 20:16-22. Ec 9:13-18.
Arioch. Ge 14:1.
captain of the king's guard. *or*, chief marshal. Chal. chief of the executioners, *or* slaughtermen. Ge 37:36mg. 39:1. 40:3. 2 K 25:8. Je 39:9mg. 52:12mg, 14.

15 hasty. Hab 1:6.
made. ver. 9.

16 and desired. ver. 9-11. Da 1:18, 19. He 11:1.

17 Hananiah. Da 1:7, 11. 3:12.

18 they would. Da 3:17. 1 S 17:37. Est 4:15-17. Ps 50:15. 91:15. Pr 3:5, 6. Is 37:4. Je 33:3. Mt 18:12, 19. Ac 4:24-31. 12:4, 5. Ro 15:30, 31. 2 T 4:17, 18.
mercies. Ex 34:5, 6. Pr 18:10. Ph 4:6, 7.
of the God of heaven. Chal. from before God.
concerning this secret. ver. 18, 19, 27, 28, 29, 30, 47. 4:9. Am 3:7.
Daniel and his fellows should not perish. *or*, they should not destroy Daniel, etc. Ge 18:28. Ml 3:18. 2 P 2:9.

19 was. ver. 22, 27-29. Da 4:9. 2 K 6:8-12. Ps 25:14. Am 3:7. 1 C 2:9, 10.
in. Da 7:7. Nu 12:6. Jb 4:13. 33:15, 16. Mt 2:12, 13.

20 answered and said. Dt 1:41.
Blessed. Ge 14:20. 1 K 8:56. 1 Ch 29:10, 20. 2 Ch 20:21. Ps 41:13. 50:23. 72:18, 19. 103:1, 2. 113:2. 115:18. 145:1, 2.
ever and ever. Chal. *alam* doubled, Ps +41:13. Da 7:18. 1 Ch 16:36. 29:10. Ne 9:5. Je 7:7. 25:5.
for wisdom. ver. 21-23. 1 Ch 29:11, 12. Jb 12:13, 16-22. Ps 62:11. 147:5. Pr 8:14. Je 32:18, 19. Mt 6:13. Ju 24, 25. Re 5:12, 13.

21 he changeth. ver. 9. Da 7:25. 11:6. 1 Ch

29:30. Est 1:13. Jb 34:24-29. Ps 31:14, 15. Ec 3:1-8. Je 27:5-7.

he removeth. Da 4:17, 32. 1 S 2:7, 8. Jb 12:18. Ps 75:6, 7. 113:7, 8. Pr 8:15, 16. Lk 1:51, 52. Ac 13:21, 22. Re 19:16.

he giveth. Ex 31:3, 6. 1 K 3:8-12, 28. 4:29. 10:24. 1 Ch 22:12. 2 Ch 1:10-12. Pr 2:6, 7. Lk 21:15. 1 C 1:30. Ja +1:5, 17. 3:15-17.

22 **revealeth**. ver. 11, 28, 29. Ge 37:5-9. 41:16, 25-28. Jb 12:22. Ps 25:14. Is 41:22, 24, 26. 42:9. Am 4:13. Mt 11:25. 13:13. Ro 16:25, 26. 1 C 2:9-11. Ep 3:5. Col 1:25-27.

he knoweth. Jb 26:6. Ps 139:11, 12. Je 23:24. Lk 12:2, 3. Jn 21:17. 1 C 4:5. He 4:13.

the darkness. Jb 38:19.

and the. Da 5:11, 14. Ps 36:9. 104:2. Jn 1:9. 8:12. 12:45, 46. 1 T 6:16. Ja 1:17. 1 J 1:5.

23 **thank**. 1 Ch 29:13. Ps 50:14. 103:1-4. Is 12:1. Mt 11:25. Lk 10:21. Jn 11:41.

O thou. Ge 32:9-11. Ex 3:15. 1 K 8:57. 18:36. 1 Ch 29:10. 2 Ch 20:6.

who hast. ver. +20, 21. Pr 8:14. 21:22. 24:5. Ec 7:19. 9:16, 18.

and hast. ver. 18, 29, 30. Ge 18:17. Ps 25:14. Je 29:11, 12. Am +3:7. Jn 15:15. Re 1:1. 5:5.

24 **Arioch**. ver. 15.

Destroy. ver. 12, 13. Ac 27:24.

25 **brought**. Pr 24:11, 12. Ec 9:10.

I have. Chal. That I have.

captives of Judah. Chal. children of the captivity of Judah. Da 1:6. 6:13. Ne 7:6. Je 29:1. 1 C 1:27, 28.

26 **Daniel**. Da 1:7. 4:8, 19. 5:12.

Art. ver. 3-7. Da 4:18. 5:16. Ge 41:15. 1 S 17:33.

27 **cannot**. ver. 2, 10, 11. Da 5:7, 8. Jb 5:12, 13. Is 19:3. 44:25. 47:12-14.

28 **a God**. Ps 115:3. Mt 6:9. Ja 1:17.

that revealeth. ver. 18, 47. Ge 40:8. 41:16. Is 41:22, 23. Am 4:13.

maketh known. Chal. hath made known.

latter days. Da 10:14. Ge +49:1.

29 **came into thy mind**. Chal. came up. Je 3:16mg. Ezk 38:10.

he that. ver. 22, 28, 47. Am 4:13.

30 **this secret**. Ge 41:16. Ac 3:12. 1 C 15:8-12.

but. ver. 17, 18, 49. Is 43:3, 4. 45:4. Mt +24:22. Mk 13:20. Ro 8:28. 1 C 3:21-23. 2 C 4:15.

their sakes that shall make known the interpretation to the king. or, the intent that the interpretation may be made known to the king.

and. ver. 47.

31 **sawest**. Chal. wast seeing.

a great image. Jb 4:13-16.

and the form. Da 7:3-17. Mt 4:8. Lk 4:5.

terrible. Is 13:11. 25:3-5. Ezk 28:7. Hab 1:7.

32 **head**. ver. 37, 38. Da 4:22, 30. 7:4. Is 14:4. Je 51:7. Re 17:4.

breast. ver. 39. Da 7:5. 8:3, 4. 11:2.

belly. ver. 39. Da 7:6. 8:5-8. 11:3, etc.

thighs. or, sides.

33 **legs of iron**. ver. 40-43. Da 7:7, 8, 19-26.

34 **a stone**. ver. 44, 45. Da 7:13, 14, 27. Ps 118:22. Is 28:16. Zc 12:3. Mt 16:18. Mt 21:42, 44. Ac 4:11. 1 P 2:4, 6-8. Re 11:15.

was cut. Da 8:25. Jb 34:20. La 4:6. Zc 4:6. Jn 1:13. 2 C 5:1. He 9:24.

without hands. or, which was not in hands. ver. 45mg. Da 8:25. Jb 34:20. La 4:6. Ac 7:48. 17:24, 25. 19:26. 2 C 5:1. Ep 2:11. Col 2:11. He 9:11, 24.

which smote. Ps 2:8-12. 110:5, 6. +149:6-9. Is 60:12. Zc 12:3. Re 17:14. 19:11-21.

and brake. Da 8:25. Ps 2:9. Is 8:9, 14, 15. 30:14. Re 2:27.

35 **like the chaff**. Mi 4:13. Lk +3:17.

no place. Jb 6:17. Ps 37:10, 36. 103:16. Re 12:8. 20:11.

became. Is +2:2, 3. Ps 89:25, 27.

and filled. Ps 2:8. 22:27. 46:9. 66:4. 67:1, 2. 72:8, 16-19. 80:9, 10. 86:9. Is 11:9. Zc 9:10. 14:8, 9. 1 C 15:25. Re 11:15. 20:2, 3.

36 **we will tell**. ver. 23, 24.

37 **a king of kings**. Ge +9:25. 1 K 4:24. Ezr 7:12. Is 10:8. 47:5. Je 27:6, 7. Ezk 26:7. Ho 8:10. Re +1:5. 17:14.

the God of heaven. Da 4:25, 32. 5:18. Pr 8:15. Je 28:14. Re +11:13. 19:16.

power. Da 4:3, 34. 1 Ch 29:11, 12. Ps 62:11. Mt 6:13. Jn 19:11. Re 4:11. 5:12, 13.

and glory. Is 13:19.

38 **the beasts**. Da 4:21, 22. Ps 50:10, 11. Je 27:5-7. 28:14. Ezk 26:7.

Thou art. ver. +32. Da 4:20-22. 7:4.

39 **another kingdom**. ver. 32. Da 5:25-31. 7:5. 8:3, 4, 20. 11:2. 2 Ch 36:20, 22, 23. Ezr 1:2. Is 13:17. 21:2. 44:28. 45:1-5. Je 51:11.

another third. ver. 32. Da 7:6, 7, 23. 8:5, etc., 21, 22. 10:20. 11:1-4, etc. Jl 3:6. Zc 6:3-6. 9:13. Re 13:1, 2. 17:3, 16, 17.

40 **the fourth**. ver. 33. Da 7:7, 19-26. 8:24, 25. +9:26, 27. 11:36-45. Lk 2:1. 3:1. Mt 17:24-27. 22:17-21. Jn 11:48. 19:12. Ac 16:37, 38. 22:25-28. 25:9-11.

forasmuch. Da 7:7. Je 15:12. Am 1:3.

41 **the feet**. ver. 33-35. Da 7:7, 8, 20-24. Lk 21:24. Re 12:3. 13:1-18. 17:12-17.

42 **the toes**. Da 7:24. Re 13:1.

broken. or, brittle.

43 **mingle**. Je +25:20.

one to another. Chal. this with this.

even. Da 7:7, 8, 23, 24. Re 13:1, etc. 17:12-17.

44 **in the days**. Chal. in their days. ver. 41, +43.

these kings. The days of the ten yet future kings. Re 17:12-18.

God of heaven. ver. 28, +37.

set up a kingdom. Da 4:3, 34. Ge +49:10. Is

11:2-9. 24:23. Mt +6:10. 28:18. Jn 18:36, 37.
1 C +15:24-28. Ep 1:20-22. 2 Th 1:7-10. Ju
14, 15. Re +11:15. 20:1-10.

which shall never. Da 4:3, 34. 6:26. 7:13,
14, 27. Ps +45:6. Ezk 37:25. Mi 4:7. Lk +1:32,
33. Jn 12:34. He 12:28.

be destroyed. Zc 14:3. Re 19:11-19.

kingdom. Chal. kingdom thereof.

not be left. Da 7:18. Jl 3:17. Am +9:15. Mi
4:1-3, 7. Ac +1:6. 3:19-21. 15:16, 17.

break in pieces. ver. 34, 35. Da 8:25. Ps 2:9.
21:8, 9. Is 8:15. 30:14. 60:12. Je 19:10, 11. Mi
4:13. Zc 12:3. Mt 21:44. Lk 20:18. 1 C 15:24,
25. Re 2:27. 19:15-20.

and consume. Lk 20:18.

for ever. Chal. *alam*, Ex +12:24. 1 C 15:24,
25. Re 20:3.

45 **thou sawest**. ver. 34, 35. Is 28:16. Zc 12:3.
Mt 21:24.

without hands. *or*, which *was* not in hands.
ver. 34mg. Lk 17:20. 2 C 10:4, 5.

the great God. Da +4:3. Ex 15:16. Dt +3:24.
10:17. 2 S 7:22. 1 Ch 16:25. 2 Ch 2:5. Ezr 5:8.
Jb 36:26. Ps 47:2. 48:1. 95:3. 96:4. +99:3.
104:1. 135:5. 147:5. Je 10:6. 32:18, 19. Ml
1:11, 14. Re 19:17.

made known. Ge 41:28, 32. Mt 24:35. Re
1:19. 4:1.

hereafter. Chal. after this.

sure. Nu 23:19.

46 **fell**. 2 S 14:22. Mt +8:2. Lk 17:16. Ac +10:25.
14:11-18. 28:6. Re 11:16. +19:10. +22:8, 9.

and commanded. Ac 14:13.

and sweet. Le 26:31. Ezr 6:10.

47 **a God of gods**. Da 11:36. Dt 10:17. Jsh
22:22. Ps 136:2.

a Lord. ver. 37. Da 4:17, 32, 34, 35. Jb 12:19.
Ps 2:10, 11. 72:11. 82:1. Pr 8:15, 16. 1 T 6:15.
Re +1:5. 17:14. 19:16.

a revealer. ver. 19, 28. Da 4:8, 9. Ge 41:39.
Am +3:7.

48 **a great**. ver. 6. 5:16. Ge 41:39-43. Nu 22:16,
17. 24:11. 1 S 17:25. 25:2. 2 S 19:32. 2 K 5:1.
Jb 1:3. Je 5:5.

ruler. Da 5:29. 6:1, 2.

and chief. Da 4:9. 5:11.

governors. Da 3:2, 3, 27. 6:7.

49 **he set**. ver. 17. Da 1:17. 3:12-30. Pr 28:12.

sat. Est 2:19, 21. 3:2. Je 39:3. Am 5:15.

DANIEL 3

1 A.M. 3424. B.C. 580.

made. Da 2:31, 32. 5:23. Ex 20:23. 32:2-4,
31. Nu 33:52. Dt 7:25. Jg 8:26, 27. 1 K 12:28.
2 K 19:17, 18. Ps 115:4-8. 135:15-18. Is 2:20.
30:22. 40:19, etc. 46:6. Je 10:9. 16:20. Ezk
7:20. +16:17. 23:14. Ho 8:4. Hab 2:19. Ac
17:29. 19:26. Re 9:20.

threescore. Is +58:13, 14.

in the plain. Ge 11:2.

Dura. i.e. *circle* or *dwelling*, **S#1757h**, only here.

in the province. ver. 30. Da 2:48. Est 1:1.

2 **sent**. Ex 32:4-6. Nu 25:2. Jg 16:23. 1 K 12:32.
Pr 29:12. Re 17:2.

rulers of. Est 1:1.

3 **the princes**. Est 3:12. Ps ch. 82. Ac 19:34,
35. Ro 1:21-28. 3:11. 1 C 1:24-26. Re 13:13-
16. 17:13, 17.

the governors. ver. 3, 27. Da 2:48. 6:7.

captains. Ne 5:14, 18. Est 3:13. Hg 1:14.

the treasurers. Ezr 7:21.

4 **aloud**. Chal. with might. Da 4:14. Pr 9:13-15.
Is 40:9. 58:1. Re 18:2.

it is commanded. Chal. they command. Ho
5:11. Mi 6:16.

O people. Da 4:1. 6:25. Est 8:9.

5 **the cornet**. *Karna*, the *horn*. ver. +10, 15.

flute. ver. 10, 15.

dulcimer. *or*, singing. Chal. symphony. ver.
10, 15. Lk 15:25.

worship. Ex 34:14.

6 **falleth**. ver. 11, 15. Ex +20:5. Is 44:17. Mt
+4:9. Re 13:15-17.

the same. Da 2:5, 12, 13. Mk 6:27.

hour. or, moment. ver. 15. Da 4:19, 33. 5:5.

a burning. Ge 19:28. Je 29:22. Ezk 22:18-22.
Mt 13:42, 50. Re 9:2. 14:11.

7 **when**. ver. 10.

all the people. Je +4:2. 51:7. Ac 14:16. 1 J
5:19. Re 12:9. 13:3, 8, 14. 17:8, 19:20.

worshipped. Ex 34:17. Is 2:8, 9.

8 **and accused**. Da 6:12, 13. Ezr 4:12-16. Est
3:6, 8, 9. Ac 16:20-22. 17:6-8. 28:22. 1 P 4:3,
4.

9 **king**. ver. 4, 5.

O king. Ne +2:3. Ro 13:7.

for ever. Chal. *alam*, Ex +12:24.

10 **hast made**. ver. 4-7. Da 6:12. Ex 1:16, 22.
Est 3:12-14. Ps 94:20. Ec 3:16. Is 10:1. Jn
11:57. Re 13:16, 17.

the cornet. Ex 15:20, 21. 32:18, 19. 1 Ch
15:16, 28. 16:5, 6. 25:1-6. 2 Ch 29:25. Ps
81:1-3. 92:1-3. 149:3, 4. 150:3-6. Am 6:5.

12 **certain**. Da 2:49. 6:13. 1 S 18:7-11. Est 3:8.
Pr 27:4. Ec 4:4.

not regarded thee. Chal. set no regard upon
thee. Da 6:13. Ac 5:28. 17:7.

13 **in his**. ver. 19. Da 2:12. Ge 4:5. 1 S 20:30-33.
Est 3:5, 6. Pr 17:12. 27:3. 29:22. Lk 6:11.

Then. Mt 10:18. Mk 13:9. Lk 21:12. Ac 5:25-
27. 24:24.

14 **true**. *or*, of purpose. Ex 21:13, 14.

my gods. ver. 1. Da 4:8. Is 46:1. Je 50:2.

15 **ye hear**. ver. 10.

harp. 1 Ch 13:8.

ye fall. Lk 4:7, 8.

have made. Ex +32:32.

well. ver. 17. Ge 30:27. Ex 32:32. Lk 13:9.

and who. ver. 28, 29. Da 6:16, 20. Ex +5:2. 2

K 18:35. 2 Ch 32:15-17. Is 36:20. 37:23. Mt 27:43.

16 **answered and said**. Dt 1:41.
we are. Mt 10:19. Mk 13:11. Lk 12:11. 21:14, 15. Ac 4:8-12, 19. 5:29. 6:15. 24:10-13. Ph 4:6, 7. 1 P 5:7.

17 **our God**. Da 4:35. 6:20-22, 27. Ge 17:1. 18:14. 1 S 17:37, 46. Jb 5:19. 34:29. Ps 27:1, 2. 62:1-6. 73:20. 115:3. 121:5-7. Pr 18:10, 11. Is 12:2. 26:3, 4. 54:14. Lk 1:37. Ac 20:24. 21:13. 27:20-25. Ro 8:31. He 7:25. 11:1.
will deliver. Is +57:1. 2 T 4:17.

18 **But if not**. Ge 28:20. Est 4:16. Jb 13:15. Is 45:11. Mt 6:10. 26:39, 42. Lk 11:2. 22:42. Ac 21:14. 1 J 5:14.
be it. Jb 13:15. Pr 28:1. Is 51:12, 13. Je 26:12-15. Mt 10:28, 32, 33, 39. 16:25. Lk 12:3-9. Ac 4:10-13, 19. 5:29-32. 7:51-60. He 11:33, 34. Re 2:10, 11. 12:11.
will not serve. Ex +20:3-5. Le 19:4. Jsh 24:15. 1 K 19:14, 18. 1 C +12:3. +15:58.

19 **was Nebuchadnezzar**. ver. +13. Pr 16:14. 19:12. 21:24. Is 51:33. Lk 12:4, 5. Ac 5:33. 7:54.
full. Chal. filled.
the form. Da 5:6. Ge 4:5, 6. 31:2.
he spake. Ex 15:9, 10. 1 K 20:10, 11. 2 K 19:27, 28. Ps 76:10. Pr 16:14. 27:3, 4.
one seven times. Da 6:24. Le 26:18, 21, 24, 28.
than. 1 K 18:33-35. Mt 27:63-66.

20 **most mighty men**. Chal. mighty of strength.
to bind. ver. +15. Ac 12:4-7. 16:23, 25.

21 **coats**. or, mantles.
hats. or, turbans.

22 **commandment**. Chal. word.
urgent. Ex 12:33.
flame. or, spark.
slew. Da 6:24. Ps 9:15. 10:14. Pr 11:8. 21:18. Zc 12:2, 3. Mt 27:5. Ac 12:19.

23 **fell**. Da 6:16, 17. Ps 34:19. 66:11, 12. 124:1-5. Je 38:6. La 3:52-54. 2 C 1:8-10. 4:17. 1 P 4:12, 13.

24 **astonied**. Da 5:6. Ac 5:23-25. 9:6. 12:13.
counsellors. or, governors. ver. 2, 3.
O king. ver. 9, 10, 17. Da 4:22, 27. 5:18. 6:7, 22. 1 S 17:55. Ac 26:13, 27.

25 **walking**. Is +43:2.
the midst. Zp 3:15. Mt 18:20.
the fire. Zc 2:5.
they have no hurt. Chal. there is no hurt in them. Ps 91:3-9. Mk 16:18. Ac 28:5, 6. 1 P 3:13.
the fourth. Ac 12:6, 7.
the Son of God. ver. 18, +28. Jb +1:6. 38:7. Ps 34:7. Pr 30:4. Mt 27:54. Lk +1:35. Jn 1:34. 19:7, 8. Ro 1:4.

26 **mouth**. Chal. door.
ye servants. ver. 17. Da 2:47. 6:20. Ezr 5:11. Ac 16:17. 27:23. Ga 1:10. Re 19:5.

the most. Ps +7:17.
come forth. Jsh 3:17. 4:10, 16-18. Is 28:16. 52:12. Ac 16:37.

27 **the princes**. ver. 2, 3. 1 S 17:46, 47. 2 K 19:19. Ps 83:18. 96:7-9. Is 26:11. Ac 2:6-12. 26:26.
upon. Is 43:2. He 11:34.
nor was. Mt 10:30. Lk 21:17, 18. Ac 27:34.

28 **Blessed**. Da +2:47. 4:34. 6:26. Ge 9:26. Ezr 1:3. 7:23-28. Ps 76:10. 138:7.
hath sent. ver. 25. Da 6:22, 23. Ge 19:15, 16. Nu 20:16. 2 Ch 32:21. Ps 34:7, 8. 103:20. Is 37:36. Mt 18:10. Ac 5:19. 12:7-11. He 1:14.
his angel. ver. 25. Ge +12:7. +16:13. +17:1. 18:10, 13, 17, 20, etc. +19:24. 21:17. Ex 23:23. 33:2. Pr 8:31. Zc +12:8. Jn 8:56, 58. Ac 12:6, 7.
delivered. ver. 17. Ps 91:1-3.
that trusted. Da 6:23. 1 Ch 5:20. 2 Ch +20:20. Ps 22:4, 5. 33:18, 21. 34:8, 22. 62:8. 84:11, 12. 118:8, 9. 146:5, 6. 147:11. Is 26:3, 4. Je 17:7, 8. 2 C 1:9, 10. Ep 1:12, 13. 1 P 1:21.
and have. Ezr 6:11. Ac 4:19.
yielded. Ro 12:1. 14:7, 8. Ph 1:20. He 11:37. Re 12:11.
serve. ver. 16-18. Ex +20:5. Mt 4:10.

29 **Therefore**. Da 6:26, 27.
I make a decree. Chal. a decree is made by me.
amiss. Chal. error. 2 S 6:7mg.
the God. ver. 15, 17, 28.
cut in pieces. Chal. made pieces. Da +2:5mg.
because. Da 6:27. Dt 32:31. Ps 3:8. 76:10. 89:8. 113:5.

30 **the king**. Da 5:19. 1 S 2:30. Ps +91:14. Jn 12:26. Ro 8:31.
promoted. Chal. made to prosper. Ps +1:3.

DANIEL 4

1 **unto all**. Da 3:4, 29. 7:14. Est 3:12. 8:9. Zc 8:23. Ac 2:6.
Peace. Je +29:7.

2 **I thought it good**. Chal. It was seemly before me. Jsh 7:19. Ps 51:14. 71:18. 77:13, 14. 78:12-16, 43-55. 89:1, 2. 92:1, 2. 105:1, 2. 106:2. 107:8. 111:2.
that. Da 3:26. Ps 66:16. Ac 22:3-16. 26:9-16.

3 **great**. ver. 34. Da +2:45. 6:27. 7:18. Ex 15:11. Dt 4:32-34. Jb +11:7. 36:26. 37:5. Ps 40:5. 71:19. 72:18. 77:11-14, 19. 86:10. 92:5. 104:24. 105:27. 107:8, 31. 111:2. 136:4. 145:3, 6. Is 25:1. 28:29. He 2:4. Re 15:3.
his kingdom. ver. 17, 34, 35. Da 6:26. +7:14, 27. Ps 66:7. Is +9:7. Je +10:10. Lk +1:32, 33. Re 11:15.
everlasting. Chal. *alam*, Ge +17:7. Ps 90:1, 2. 103:19. Mi 4:7. Lk +1:32, 33.
his dominion. Ps +145:13.
is from. Jb 25:2. 1 P 4:11.

4 was. Ps 30:6, 7. Is 47:7, 8. 56:12. Je 48:11. Ezk 28:2-5, 17. 29:3. Zp 1:12. Lk 12:19, 20. 1 Th 5:2, 3.

5 a dream. Da +2:1. 5:5, 6, 10. 7:28. Ge +31:24.

and the thoughts. Da 2:28, 29.

6 to bring. Da +2:2. Ge 41:7, 8. Is 8:19. 47:12-14.

7 Then came. Da 2:1, 2. 1 S 6:2. Ezk +21:21.

but. Da 2:7. Ge 41:8. Is 44:25. Je 27:9, 10. 2 T 3:8, 9.

8 Belteshazzar. Da 1:7. 5:12. Is 46:1. Je 50:2.

according to. Is 46:1. Je 50:2. 51:44.

and in. ver. 9, 18. Da 2:11. 5:11, 14. Nu 11:17, etc. Is 63:11.

spirit. Ge +41:38.

9 master. Da 1:20. 2:48. 5:11.

the spirit. ver. 8. Ge +41:38. 1 S 4:8. Is 63:11. 2 P 1:21.

no secret. ver. 5. Da 2:3. Ge 11:6-8. Is 33:18. 54:14. Ezk 28:3.

tell. ver. 18. Da 2:4, 5. Ge 40:9-19. 41:15, etc. Jg 7:13-15.

10 saw. Chal. was seeing.

a tree. ver. 20-26. Ps 37:35, 36. Is 10:33, 34. Je 12:2. Ezk 31:3-18.

11 reached. ver. 21, 22. Ge 11:4. Dt 9:1. Mt 11:23.

12 the beasts. Je 27:6, 7. Ezk 17:23. 31:6.

shadow. La 4:20.

the fowls. Mt 13:32. Lk 13:19.

13 in the visions. ver. 5, 10. Da 7:1.

a watcher. ver. 17, 23. Ps 103:20.

an holy. Da 8:13. Dt 33:2. Ps 89:7. Zc 14:5. Mt 25:31. Mk 1:24. Lk 4:34. Ju 14. Re 14:10.

14 aloud. Chal. with might. Da 3:4. Re 10:3. 18:2.

Hew. ver. 23. Da 5:20. Mt 3:10. 7:19. Lk 3:9. 13:7-9.

let. ver. 12. Je 51:6, 9. Ezk 31:12, 13.

15 leave. ver. 25-27. Jb 14:7-9. Is 14:4, 12-17. Ezk 29:14, 15.

16 be changed. ver. 32, 33. Is 6:10. Hab 1:11. Mk 5:4, 5. Lk 8:27-29.

seven times. ver. 23, 25, 31. Da 7:25. 11:13. 12:7. Re 12:14.

17 by the decree. ver. 13, 24, 1 K 22:19, 20. 1 T 5:21.

the demand. Ge 24:47. Jg 4:20. 1 P 3:21.

the holy. ver. 8, 9, 13. Jb 1:6. Is 6:3, 8. Re 4:8.

that the living. Ps 9:16. 83:17, 18. Ezk 25:17.

the most High. ver. 25, 32-35. Da 2:21. 5:18-21. Je 27:5-7.

giveth. 1 K 19:15. 2 K 8:12. Ps 75:6, 7. Ezk 20:24-26. Ho 13:11. Jn 19:11.

the basest. ver. 25. Da 11:21. Ex 9:16. 1 S 2:8. 1 K 21:25. 2 K 21:6, etc. 2 Ch 28:22. Ps 12:8. 113:7, 8. Ezk 7:24. 1 C 1:28.

18 forasmuch. ver. 7. Da 2:7. 5:8, 15. Ge 41:8, 15. Is 19:3. 47:12-14.

but. ver. 8, 9. Da 2:26-28. 1 K 14:2, 3. Am +3:7.

spirit. Ge +41:38.

19 Daniel. ver. 8. Da 1:7. 2:26. 5:12.

was astonied. ver. 9. Da 7:28. 8:27. 10:16, 17. Je 4:19. Hab 3:10.

for one hour. 2 C 7:8. Ga 2:5.

let not. ver. 4, 5. 1 S 3:17.

My lord. ver. 24. Da 10:16. Ge 31:35. 32:4, 5, 18. Ex 32:32. 1 S 1:15. 24:8. 26:15. 2 S 18:31. 1 K 18:7.

the dream. 1 S 25:26. 2 S +18:32. 1 T +2:2.

20 The tree. ver. 10-12. Ezk 31:3, 16.

21 Whose leaves. ver. 12.

under which. Da 2:38.

the fowls. ver. 12. Ezk 17:23. 31:6. Mt 13:32.

22 thou. Da 2:37, 38. 2 S 12:7. Mt 14:4.

thy greatness. Da 5:18-23. Ge 11:4. 28:12. 2 Ch 28:9. Ps 36:5. 108:4. Je 27:4, 6-8. Re 18:5.

23 saw. ver. 13-17.

and let his. ver. 15. Da 5:21.

24 the decree. ver. 17. Jb 20:29mg. Ps 2:7. 148:6. Is 14:24-27. 23:9. 46:10, 11.

come. Jb 1:12-19. 40:11, 12. Ps 107:40.

25 drive. ver. 32, 33. Da 5:21, etc. Jb 30:3-8. Mk 5:3, 4.

to eat. Ps 106:20.

till. ver. 17, 32, 34, 35. Da 2:21. 5:21. Ps +7:17. 75:7. Je 27:5. Jn 19:11.

26 to leave. ver. 15. Jb 14:7-9.

the heavens. Ps +73:9. Mt 5:34. 21:25. Lk 15:18, 21.

27 let. Ge 41:33-37. Ps 119:46. Ac 24:25. 2 C 5:11.

break off. Ge 27:40. Ex 32:2, 3, 24. Jb 34:31, 32. Ps 136:24. Pr 16:6. 28:13. Is 55:6, 7. Ezk 18:21, 27-32. Mt 3:8. Ac 8:22. 26:20. Ja 4:8-10. 1 P 4:8.

by showing mercy. Le 18:9, 10. 25:35. Dt 15:10, 11. Jb +6:14. Ps 41:1-3. Pr +21:13. Is 58:5-7, 10-12. Ezk 18:7. Mt 25:35. Lk 3:11. 11:41. 16:9. Ac 10:2-4. Ga 5:6, 13, 22. Ep 4:28. Ja 1:27. 2:1-9. 1 J 3:17.

the poor. Ezk +16:49.

if it. Da 7:12. 1 K 21:29. Jl 2:14. Jon 3:9. Zp 2:2, 3.

lengthening of thy tranquillity. or, healing of thine error.

28 All this came. Da 5:21-23. Nu 23:19. Pr 10:24. Zc 1:6. Mt 24:35.

29 end. Ge 6:3. Ec 8:11. 1 P 3:20. 2 P 3:9, 10, 15. Re 2:21.

in. or, upon.

30 Is not. Ps 73:8. 75:4, 5. Pr +16:5. Hab 1:15, 16. Lk 12:19, 20.

great. Ge 10:10. 11:2-9. Re 16:19. 17:5. 18:10, 21.

that. 1 Ch 29:12-14. 2 Ch 2:5, 6. Is 10:8-15. 37:24, 25. Ezk 28:2-5. 29:3.

and for. Da 5:18, 19. Est 1:4. Ps 49:20. 104:1. 145:5-12. 1 C 10:31. Re 21:24-26.

31 **the word**. Da 5:4, 5. Ex 15:9, 10. Jb 20:23. Lk 12:20. Ac 12:22, 23. 1 Th 5:3.

fell. ver. 24, 34. Mt 3:17. Jn 12:28. Ac 9:3-5. Re 16:7.

The kingdom. Da 5:28. 1 S 13:14. 15:23. Ezk 31:10, 11.

32 **they shall drive**. ver. 14-16, 25, 26. Da 5:21. Jb 30:5-7.

until. ver. 17, 25. Ex 8:10. 9:14, 29. Jsh 4:24. Jb 12:18-21. Ps 9:16. Pr 8:15, 16. Is 37:20. 45:3. Je 27:5.

33 **same**. Da 5:5. Jb 20:5. Is 30:13, 14. 1 Th 5:2.

fulfilled. Nu 23:19.

and he was. ver. 25, 32.

34 A.M. 3441. B.C. 563.

at the end. ver. 16, 26, 32.

lifted. Ps 121:1. 123:1. 130:1, 2. Jon 2:2-4. Lk 15:18. 18:13.

understanding returned. Lk 15:17. 2 T +1:7.

I blessed. 1 Ch 29:10, 11. Jb 1:21. Ps 50:14. 103:1-4. 107:8, 15, 22, 31. Is 24:15. La 3:19-23.

the most High. ver. 17, 32. Ps +7:17.

praised. Ps 71:8. Je 33:11. He +13:15.

honored. Ps 71:8. 96:6. 104:1. 145:5. Jn 5:23. 1 T +1:17.

him. Da 12:7. Ps 90:2. 102:24. 146:10. Je 10:10. Jn 5:26. 1 T 1:17. 6:16. Re 4:10. 10:6.

for ever. Chal. *alam*, Ex +12:24.

whose dominion. ver. 3. Da 2:44. +7:14. Ps 10:16. 145:13. Is +9:6, 7. Je 10:10. Mi 4:7. Lk +1:33. Re 11:15.

everlasting. Chal. *alam*, Ge +17:7.

is from. Ps 90:1. +102:28.

35 **all**. Jb 34:14, 15, 19-24. Is 40:15-17, 22-24.

and he. 1 S 3:18. Jb 34:29. Ps 135:6. Is +14:27. Mt 11:25, 26. Ac 4:28. Ph 2:10, 11.

the inhabitants. Ps 33:8, 14. 49:1. Is 26:9.

none. Jb 9:4, 13. 34:29. 40:9-12. 42:2. Ac 9:5. 11:17. 1 C 10:22.

What. Jb 9:12. 33:12, 13. 40:2. Is 45:9-11. Ro 9:19, 20. 11:33-36. 1 C 2:16.

36 **my reason**. ver. 34.

mine. ver. 15, 16, 32. 2 Ch 33:12, 13.

added. 1 S 2:30. Jb 13:12. 42:12. Ps 103:2-5, 8-10. Pr 22:4. Mt 6:33. 2 C 4:17.

37 **I Nebuchadnezzar**. ver. 3, 34. Da 5:4, 23. 1 P 2:9, 10.

the King. Da 5:23. Mt 11:25. Ac 17:24.

all. Dt 32:4. Ps 33:4, 5. 99:4. 119:75. 145:17, 18. Is 5:16. Re 4:11. 15:3. 16:7. 19:1, 2.

those that walk. ver. +30, 31. 2 Ch 33:11, 12, 19. Ezk 16:56, 63.

DANIEL 5

1 **Belshazzar**. i.e. *the splendor of brightness; lord of whose treasure*, S#1113h. ver. 1, 2, 9, 22, 29, 30. Da 7:1.

made. Ge 40:20. Est 1:2, 3, 7, 8. Is 21:4, 5. 22:12-14. Je 51:39, 57. Na 1:10. Mk 6:21, 22.

feast. Ge +3:19.

lords. Da 4:36.

2 **Belshazzar**. ver. 29. Je 27:7.

tasted the wine. Pr +20:1. 23:29-32. 31:4. Hab 2:5.

the golden. 2 Ch +4:19.

father. *or*, grandfather. ver. 11, 13, 18. 1 K +15:10mg. Ro 9:10.

taken out. Chal. brought forth. Ezr 1:7.

wives. Ge +4:19.

concubines. 1 Ch +2:48.

might. ver. 4, 23.

3 **golden vessels**. Da 1:2. 2 K 25:15. 2 Ch 36:10. Je 52:19.

4 **praised**. ver. 23. Da +4:37. Jg 16:23, 24. Is 42:8. Ho 2:8-13. Re 9:20, 21.

of gold. Da 3:1-7, 8, etc. Ps 115:4-8. 135:15-18. Is 40:19, 20. 42:17. 46:6, 7. Je 10:4-9. Hab 2:19. Ac 17:29. 19:24-28. Re 9:20.

5 **the same hour**. Da 3:6. 4:19, 31, 33. Jb 20:5. Ps 78:30, 31. Pr 29:1. Lk 12:19, 20. 1 Th 5:2, 3.

wrote. ver. 8, 15, 24-28. Col 2:14. Re 20:12-15.

6 **the king's**. ver. +9. Da 2:1. 3:19. Jb 15:20-27. 20:19-27. Ps 73:18-20. Is 21:2-4.

countenance. Chal. brightnesses. ver. 9.

was changed. Chal. changed it.

and his thoughts. ver. 10. Da +4:5, 19. 7:28.

so that. Ps 69:23. Is 13:7, 8. 21:3, 4.

joints. *or*, girdles. Is 5:27. 45:1. Chal. bindings, *or* knots.

and his knees. Is 35:3. Ezk 7:17. 21:7. Na 2:10. He 12:12.

7 **aloud**. Chal. with might. Da 4:14mg.

to bring. Da +2:2. 4:6. Ge 41:8. Is 44:25, 26. +47:13.

be clothed. ver. 16, 29. Da 2:6. Ge 41:42-44. Nu 22:7, 17. 24:11. 1 S 17:25.

scarlet. *or*, purple.

a chain. Pr 1:9. SS 1:10. Ezk 16:11.

the third. Da 2:48. 6:2, 3. Est 3:1. 10:2, 3.

8 **but**. Because, probably, it was written in the ancient Hebrew or Samaritan character. Da +2:27. 4:7. Ge 41:8. Is 47:9, 12-15.

9 **greatly**. ver. 6. Da 2:1. Jb 18:11-14. Ps 18:14. Ac 22:6, 9. Re 6:15.

countenance. Chal. brightnesses. ver. 6mg. Da 10:8.

changed. Ps 48:6. Is 13:6-8. 21:2-4. Je 6:24. 30:6. Mt 2:3.

10 **O king**. Ne +2:3.

live. 1 S +10:24mg.

for ever. Chal. *alam*, Ex +12:24.

let not. Ge 35:17, 18. 1 S 4:20-22. Jb 13:4. 21:34.

11 **a man**. Da +2:47. 4:8, 9, 18. Ge 41:11-15.

spirit. Chal. *ruach*, Ge +41:38.

father. *or*, grandfather. ver. +2.
light. Da 2:11. 2 S 14:17. Ac 12:22. 14:11. Re 3:9.
Nebuchadnezzar. 1 K +15:10.
father. *or*, grandfather.
king. ver. 2mg.
master. Da +2:48. 4:8, 9. Ac 16:16.

12 **an excellent**. ver. 14. Da 6:3. Ps 16:3. Pr 12:26. 17:27. Col 1:29.
spirit. Chal. *ruach,* Ge +41:38; Nu +11:17. Ps 78:8. 2 C +12:18.
interpreting of. *or*, of an interpreter of, etc.
dissolving. *or*, of a dissolver.
doubts. Chal. knots. ver. 16. 1 K 10:1-3. 2 Ch 9:1, 2.
whom . Da 1:7. 4:8, 19.

13 **Art thou**. ver. 11. Da 1:21. 2:48. 8:1, 27.
the children. Da 1:6. 2:25. 6:13. 2 K 24:11-15. Ezr 4:1. 6:16, 19, 20. 10:7, 16.
father. *or*, grandfather. ver. +2, 11, 18.
Jewry. i.e. *land of Judea,* **S#3061h**, so rendered only here. Lk 23:5. Jn 7:1, 3, Judea.

14 **that the spirit**. Chal. *ruach,* Ge +41:38. ver. 11, 12.

15 **And now**. ver. 7, 8. Da +2:3-11. Is 29:10-12. 47:12, 13.

16 **make**. Chal. interpret. Ge 40:8.
thou shalt. ver. +7. Ac 8:18.

17 **Let**. ver. 29. Ge 14:23. Ex 23:8. 2 K 3:13. 5:16, 26. Ac 8:20.
rewards. *or*, fee. Da 2:6mg.
I will read. Ps 119:46.

18 **O thou**. Da 3:17, 18. 4:22. 6:22. Ac 26:13, 19.
the most high God. Da 2:37, 38. 4:17, 22-25, 32. Ps +7:17.
father. ver. 2.

19 **that he**. Da 3:4. 4:17, 22. Je 25:9, etc. 27:5-7. Hab 2:5. Ro 13:1.
whom he would he slew. Da 2:12, 13. 3:6, 20, 21, 29. Pr 16:14. Jn 19:11.

20 **when**. Da 4:30-33, 37. Ex 9:17. 18:11. 2 S 22:28. Jb 15:25-27. 40:11, 12. Pr 16:5, 18. Is 14:12-17. Lk 1:51, 52. 18:14.
mind. Chal. *ruach,* Ge +26:35.
hardened. Ex +4:21. 2 K 17:14. Je 19:15. He +3:13.
in pride. *or*, to deal proudly.
deposed. Chal. made to come down. Is 47:1. Je 13:18. 48:18. Ezk 30:6.

21 **he was driven**. Da +4:25, 32, 33. Jb 30:3-7.
his heart was made like. *or*, he made his heart equal, etc.
till. Da +4:17, 25, 32, 35, 37. Ex 9:14-16. Ps +7:17. Ezk 17:24.

22 **thou**. ver. 18. Ps 119:46. Mt 14:4. Ac 4:8-13.
his son. ver. 2mg. 1 K +15:10.
hast. Ex 10:3. 1 S 6:6. 2 Ch 33:22, 23. 36:12. Is 26:10, 11. Mt 21:32. Ac 5:29-33. 1 P 5:5, 6.

though. Pr 29:1. Lk +12:47. Jn +13:17. Ja 4:6, 17.

23 **lifted**. ver. 3, 4. Dt +17:20. Ps 14:1. Pr 18:12. 28:14. Is 10:33. 33:10. 37:23. Je 50:29. Re 13:5, 6.
the Lord. Da +4:37. Ge 14:19. Ps 115:16.
and they. ver. 2-4. 1 S 5:1-9.
hast praised. Jg 16:23.
which. Ps 115:4-8. 135:15-17. Is 37:19. 46:6, 7. Hab 2:18, 19. 1 C +8:4.
in whose. Ge 2:7. Jb 12:10. 34:14, 15. Ps 104:29. +146:4. Is 42:5. Ac 17:25, 28, 29.
breath. Chal. *nishma,* same as Heb. *neshamah,* Ge +2:7.
and whose. Jb 31:4. Ps 139:3. Pr 20:24. Je 10:23. He 4:13.
hast thou. Ro 1:21-23. Ro 3:23.

24 **Then was**. ver. 5.

25 **MENE**. i.e. *who is numbered,* **S#4484h**. ver. 26. Ezr 7:25 (set). Compare **S#4483h**: Da 2:24 (ordained), 49 (set). 3:12. Had these words been written in the Chaldean character, every one who knew the alphabet of the language could at least have read them: they are pure Chaldee, and literally denote "He is numbered, he is numbered; he is weighed; they are divided."
TEKEL. i.e. *be weighed,* **S#8625h**. ver. 27.
UPHARSIN. i.e. *divided,* **S#6537h**. ver. 28.

26 **God**. Da 9:2. Jb +14:14. Is ch. 13, 14. 21:1-10. ch. 47. Je 25:11, 12. 27:7. ch. 50, 51. Ac 15:17.

27 **Thou art weighed**. 1 S 2:3. Jb 31:6. Ps 62:9. Je 6:30. Ezk 22:18-20.
art found wanting. Mt 22:11, 12. Ro 3:23. 1 C 3:13.

28 **PERES**. *Peres,* he was divided, **S#6537h**. ver. 25. Pronounced *paras,* denotes Persians, who seem evidently referred to.
Thy. ver. 31. Da 6:28. 7:5. 8:3, 4, 20. 9:1. Ezr 1:2. Is 13:17. 21:2. 45:1, 2.
Medes. Is 21:2.
Persians. **S#6540h**. ver. 28. 6:8, 12, 15. Ezr 4:24. 6:14.

29 **they clothed**. ver. 7, 16.

30 **In that night**. ver. 1, 2. Ps 76:5. Is 21:4-9. 47:9. Je 51:11, 28-32, 39-42, 56, 57.

31 **Darius**. Da 6:1. 9:1.
Median. i.e. *one from Media,* **S#4077h**.
took. Da 7:18. Ps 75:7.
being. Chal. *he as* the son of, etc.
about. *or*, now.

DANIEL 6

1 **Darius**. Da 5:31. 8:3, 4. 1 P 2:14.
an. Ex +18:21, 22. Est 1:1.

2 **of**. Da 2:48, 49. 5:16, 29. 1 S 2:30. Pr 3:16.
that. Mt 18:23. Lk 16:2.

and the. Ezr 4:22. Est 7:4. Pr 26:6. Lk 19:13, etc. 1 C 4:2.

3 **was preferred**. Da 2:46-48. 4:18. 5:11, 12. Pr 22:29.

an. Da 5:12, 14. 9:23. Ge 41:38-41. Ne 7:2. Pr 3:3, 4. 17:27. Ec 2:13.

spirit. Heb. *ruach*, Ge +41:8; Nu +11:17.

4 Cir. A.M. 3467. B.C. 537.

sought. Da 3:8. Ge 43:18. Jg 14:4. Ps 37:12, 13, 32, 33. 109:3. Pr 29:27. Ec 4:4. Je 18:18, 23. 20:10. Mt 26:4. 27:18. Lk 20:20. 22:2. 1 P 2:20.

but. 1 S 18:14. 19:4, 5. 22:14. Lk 23:14, 15. Jn 19:4. 2 C 11:12. Ph 2:15. 1 T 5:14. T 2:8. 1 P 2:12. 3:16. 4:14-16.

find none. Ne 5:9. Jb 1:1. Ps 59:4. Ezk 14:14. Jn 19:6. T 2:8.

faithful. Lk +16:10, 12. 1 C 4:2. He 3:5.

5 **We shall**. 1 S 24:17. Est 3:8. Is +54:17. Jn 19:6, 7. Ac 24:13-16, 20, 21.

6 **assembled together**. or, came tumultuously. ver. 11. Ps 56:6. 62:3. 64:2-6. Mt 27:23-25. Lk 23:23-25. Ac 22:22, 23.

King. ver. 21. Ne +2:3. Pr 26:28. Ac 24:2, 3.

live. 2 S 16:16mg.

for ever. Chal. *alam*, Ex +12:24.

7 **All**. ver. 2, 3. Da 3:2, 27.

captains. Da 3:2, 27. Ezr 5:3. Ne 2:7. Est 3:12. Hg 1:1, 14. 2:2, 21. Ml 1:8.

have consulted. Ps 2:2. 59:3. 62:4. 83:1-3. 94:20, 21. Mi 6:5. Mt 12:14. 26:4. Mk 15:1. Jn 12:10. Ac 4:5-7, 26-28.

decree. or, interdict.

save of thee. Ps 12:2, 3. 62:3, 4. Pr 26:23-26, 28.

he shall. Da 3:6, 11. Ps 10:9. Na 2:12.

8 **establish**. Est 3:12. 8:10. Is 10:1.

according. ver. 12, 15. Est 1:19. 8:8.

altereth not. Chal. passeth not. Mt 24:35.

9 **signed**. Ps 62:9, 10. 118:9. 146:3. Pr 6:2. 7:21-23. Ec 9:12. Is 2:22.

10 **when Daniel knew**. Ex 1:17, 19-21. Mt 2:13, 14. Lk +14:26. Ac 4:17-19. +5:29.

his windows. 1 K 8:30, 38, 44, 47-50. 2 Ch 6:38. He +4:16.

his chamber. Ac 9:39, 40.

toward Jerusalem. Ps 5:7. 28:2. +122:6. 138:2. Jon 2:4.

he kneeled. 1 K 8:54. 19:18. 2 K 1:13. 2 Ch 6:13. Ezr 9:5. Ps +95:6. Mt 17:14, 15. Mk 1:40. 10:17. Lk 5:8. 22:41. Ac 7:60. 9:40. 20:36, 37. 21:4, 5. Ep 3:14.

three times. ver. 13. Ps +55:17. 86:3mg. 119:164. Lk 18:7. 21:36. Ac 1:14. 2:1, 2, 15. *3:1. 6:4. 10:2, 4, 9, 31. 12:5*, 16, 17. Ro +12:11, 12. Ep 6:18. Ph 4:6. Col 4:2. 1 Th 5:17. 2 T 1:3.

gave thanks. Ps 34:1. Col +3:17.

as he did aforetime. Ne 6:11. Ps 11:1, 2. Mt +10:28-33. Lk 12:4-9. Ac 4:18, 19, 29. 5:20,

29, 40-42. 20:24. Ph 1:14, 20. Re 2:10, 13. +12:11.

11 **assembled**. ver. +6. Ps 10:9. 37:32, 33.

12 **they**. Da 3:8-12. Ac 16:19, 24. 24:2-9.

The thing. ver. 8. Est 1:19.

13 **That Daniel**. Da 1:6. 2:25. 5:13.

regardeth not. Da 3:12. Est 3:8. Ac +5:29. 17:7.

14 **was sore**. Da 3:13. Mt 27:17-24. Mk 6:26. Lk 23:13-21. Jn 19:7-12.

and he. 2 S 3:28, 29.

15 **Know**. ver. 8, 12. Est 8:8. Ps 94:20, 21.

16 **the king**. 2 S 3:39. Pr 29:25. Je 26:14. 38:5. Mt 14:8-10. 27:23-26. Mk 6:25-28. 15:14, 15. Jn 19:12-16. Ac 24:27. 25:9, 11. Ro 13:3.

Thy God. ver. 20. Da 3:15, 17, 28. Dt 32:31. Jb 5:19. Ps 37:39, 40. 91:14-16. 118:8, 9. Is 43:2. Ac 27:23, 24.

17 **a stone**. La 3:53. Mt 27:60-66. Ac 12:4. 16:23, 24.

18 **and passed**. 2 S 12:16, 17. 19:24. 1 K 21:27. Jon 3:3-9.

instruments. or, table. Jb 21:12. Ps 137:2. Pr 18:14. Ec 2:8. Is 24:8, 9. Am 6:4-6. Re 18:22.

and. Da 2:1. Est 6:1. Ps 77:4.

19 **arose very early**. Mt 28:1. Mk +1:35. 16:2. 2 C 2:13. 1 Th 3:5.

20 **is**. ver. 16, 27. Da 3:15, 17, 28, 29.

servest. 1 Ch 16:11. Ps 71:14-18. 73:23. 119:112. 146:2. Pr 23:17, 18. Ho 12:6. Lk 18:1. Ac 6:4. Ro 2:7. Col 4:2. 1 Th 5:17, 18. Ja 1:25.

able. Da 3:17. Ge 18:14. Nu 11:23. 14:15, 16. Je +32:17. Mk 4:40. Lk 1:37. 2 C 1:10. 2 T 1:12. 4:16-18. He 7:25. Ju 24.

21 **O king**. ver. +6.

live. 2 S 16:16mg.

for ever. Chal. *alam*, Ex +12:24.

22 **My God**. ver. 20. 2 S 22:7. Ps 31:14. 38:21. 46:1. 118:28. Mi 7:7. Mt 27:46. Jn 20:17, 28.

hath sent. Da +3:28. Nu 20:16. 2 Ch 32:21. Ps 34:7. Is 63:9. Ac 12:11. 27:23. He 1:14.

hath shut. 1 S 17:37. Ps 91:11-13. 2 T 4:17. He 11:33.

not hurt. Is 43:2.

forasmuch. ver. 23. Ps 18:19-24. 26:6. 84:11. Is 3:10. Ac 24:16. 2 C 1:12. 1 P 4:19. 1 J 3:19-21.

and also. Ge 40:15. 1 S 24:9-11. 26:18. Ps 7:1-4. Ac 25:8-11.

23 **was**. ver. 14, 18. Ex 18:9. 1 K 5:7. 2 Ch 2:11, 12.

because. Da 3:25, 27, 28. 1 Ch 5:20. 2 Ch +20:20. Ps +9:10. 37:40. 118:8, 9. 146:3-6. Pr 18:10. Is 26:3. Mt 9:28-30. 17:20. Mk 9:23. Lk 7:50. 17:5, 6. Jn 11:40. He 11:33.

24 **and they brought**. Dt 19:18-20. Jg 1:7. Est 7:10. 9:25. Ps 7:15-17. Pr 11:8.

them. Dt +24:16. Jsh 7:24, 25. 2 K 14:6. Est 9:10. Ps 9:16. 10:15. Pr 26:27. Ro 12:19.

the lions. Da 3:22. Ps 54:5. Is +5:29.

25 **king**. Da 4:1. Ezr 1:1, 2. Est 3:12. 8:9.
   Peace. Je +29:7.
26 **make**. Da 3:29. Ezr 6:8-12. 7:12, 13.
   tremble. Ps 2:11. 99:1-3. 119:120. Is 66:2. Je
   10:10. Lk 12:5. He 12:29.
   the living. Da 4:34. Ru 1:16. Ezr 1:3. Je
   +10:10. Ac 17:25. Re 5:14.
   and stedfast. Ps 93:1, 2. 146:10. Ml +3:6. He
   6:17, 18. Ja 1:17.
   for ever. Chal. *alam*, Ex +12:24.
   and his kingdom. Da +2:44. 4:3, 34. 7:14,
   27. Ps 10:16. 29:10. 145:12, 13. Is +9:7. Mt
   6:13. Lk +1:33. Re 11:15.
   not be destroyed. Ps 10:16.
27 **delivereth**. Jb 36:15. Ps 18:48, 50. 32:7.
   35:17. 97:10. Lk 1:74, 75. 2 C 1:8-10. 2 T
   4:17, 18.
   and he. Da 4:2, 3, 34. Je 32:19, 20. Mk
   16:17, 18. Ac 4:30. He 2:4.
   power. Chal. hand.
28 **and in**. Da 1:21. 2 Ch 36:22, 23. Ezr 1:1, 2. Is
   44:28. 45:1.
   Persian. i.e. *inhabitant of Persia*, **S#6543h**, only
   here.

DANIEL 7

1 Cir. A.M. 3449. B.C. 555.
   Belshazzar. Da 5:1, 22, 30. 8:1. Je 27:7.
   Daniel. Da 2:1, 28, 29. 4:5. Nu 12:5, 6. Jb
   33:14-17. Je 23:28. Jl 2:28. Am +3:7. Ac 2:17,
   18.
   had. Chal. saw.
   a dream. Ge +31:24.
   visions. ver. 7, 13, 15. Ge 15:1. 46:2. Jb 4:13.
   Ezk 1:1. 2 C 12:1.
   he wrote. Is 8:1. 30:8. Hab 2:2. Ro +15:4. Re
   +1:19. 10:4.
   matters. *or*, words.
2 **the four winds**. Da 8:8. 11:4. Ezk 37:9. Zc
   2:6. Re 7:1.
   the great sea. ver. 17. Nu 34:6. Ps 65:7. 93:3,
   4. Hab 3:8. Is 17:12, 13. 27:1. 57:20. Re 13:1.
   17:15. 21:1.
3 **four**. ver. 17. Da 2:32, 33, 37-40. Zc 6:1-8.
   beasts. ver. 4-8, 17. Ps 74:13, 14. 76:4. Is
   27:1. 51:9. Ezk 19:3-8. 29:3. 32:2. Re 13:1, 2.
4 **The first**. Da 2:37, 38.
   like a lion. 2 S 1:23. Is +5:29.
   eagle's wings. Dt 28:49, 50. Je 4:13. 48:40.
   49:22. La 4:19. Ezk 17:3. Hab 1:6-8.
   Mt 24:28.
   the wings. Da 4:31-33. Je 50:30-32.
   and it. *or*, where with it, etc.
   lifted. Da 4:30. 5:18-23. Is 14:13-17. Je 25:9-
   26. Hab 2:5-10.
   and a. Da 4:32, 36, 37. Jb 25:6. Ps 9:20. Ezk
   28:2, 9.
5 **another**. Da 2:39. 8:3. 2 K 2:24. Pr 17:12. Ho
   13:8.

a bear. 1 S 17:34-36. 2 S 17:8. Pr 28:15. Is
13:17, 18. Ho 13:8. Am 5:19.
itself on one side. *or*, one dominion. Da
5:28, 31. 8:3, 4, 20. 11:2. Ezr 1:2.
Arise. 2 Ch 36:20. Is 13:17, 18. 21:2. 56:9. Je
50:21-32. Ezk 39:17-20.
6 **and lo**. Da 2:39. 8:5-7, 20, 21. 10:20. 11:3,
etc. Ho 13:7. Re 13:2.
like a leopard. SS 4:8. Je 5:6. 13:23. Ho
13:7. Hab 1:8.
which had. Da 8:5.
four wings. ver. 4. Ezk 17:3.
four heads. Da 8:8, 22. 11:3, 4, etc.
dominion was given. Da 2:39.
7 **I saw**. ver. 2, 13.
a fourth. ver. 19, 23. Da 2:40. 8:10. 2 S
22:43. Re 13:1-10.
and stamped. Re 6:16, 17. 14:19. 16:1.
19:15-21.
and it had ten. ver. 24. Da 2:41, 42, 44. Re
12:3. 13:1. 17:7, 12.
8 **another**. ver. 20-25. Da 8:9-12. Re 13:5-8,
11-13.
eyes like. Da 8:23-25. Zc 11:17. Re 9:7.
a mouth speaking great. ver. 25. Da 8:11.
11:36. 1 S 2:3. Ps 12:3. 2 Th 2:4. 2 T 3:2. 2 P
2:18. Ju 16. Re 13:1, 5-8.
9 **till**. Da 2:34, 35, 44, 45. 1 K 22:19. 1 C
+15:24, 25. Re 4:2, 3. 19:18-21. 20:1-4.
were cast down. rather, were set in place. 2
S 12:30, 31. Ps 9:7. Je +43:11. Mt 25:31-33.
Re 4:2.
the Ancient. ver. 13, 22. Ps 90:2. 102:24, 25.
Is +9:6. Mi +5:2. Hab 1:12.
of days. Mi 5:2mg. He 13:8. 2 P 3:18.
did sit. Ps 9:5. 29:10. Is 28:6.
whose garment. Ps 45:8. 104:2. Mt 17:2. Mk
9:3. Ph 3:9. 1 T 6:16. 1 J 1:5. Re 1:13, 14.
was white. Is 1:18. Mt 28:3. Re 3:5. 4:4.
19:8, 11.
his throne. Is 6:1-3. Ac 2:30, 33. 2 Th 1:7, 8.
2 P 3:7-10.
and his wheels. Ps 104:3, 4. Ezk 1:13-21.
10:2-7, 9-13.
burning fire. Ex 3:2. 19:18. Dt 4:24. 9:3. Ps
18:8. 50:3. Ezk 1:4. He 12:29. Re 4:5.
10 **fiery**. Ps +97:3. Is 66:15, 16. 2 P +3:7.
thousand thousands. Dt 33:2. 1 K 22:19. Jb
25:3. Ps 68:17. Zc 14:5. Mt 16:27. 25:31. He
12:22. Ju 14. Re 5:11.
stood before. Da +1:5. Zc 3:4. Lk +21:36.
the judgment. ver. 22, 26. Ps 9:4, 7. 96:11-
13. Ml 3:16-18. Re 11:18. 20:11-15.
the books. Is 65:6. Re +3:5.
11 **the voice**. ver. 8, 25. 2 P 2:18. Ju 16. Re
13:5, 6. 20:4, 12.
even. ver. 26. Da 8:25. 11:45. Ps 7:6. 2 Th
2:8. Re 18:8. 19:20. 20:10.
his body. Mt +24:28. Lk +17:37.
the burning flame. Ps 11:6. 50:3. 97:3. Is

+30:33. 2 Th 1:7-10. 2:8. 2 P +3:7, 10, 12. Re 20:7-9.

12 **the rest**. ver. 4-6. Da 8:7. Jn 12:20. Ac 2:9.
taken away. Da 2:34, 35.
their lives were prolonged. Chal. a prolonging in life was given them. Da 2:44, 45.
a season and time. Da +2:21.

13 **one like**. Ps +8:4, 5. Is +9:6, 7. Ezk 1:26. Mt 13:41. 24:30. 25:31. 26:64. Mk 13:26. 14:61, 62. Lk 21:27, 36. Jn 3:13. 5:27. 12:34. Ac 7:56. Ph 2:6-8. He 2:14. Re 1:7, 13, 18. 14:14.
Son of man. Ps +8:4, 5. 80:17. Mt 8:20. 9:6. 10:23. 11:19. 16:13, +27, 28. 19:28. 24:30. 25:31. 26:64. Jn 1:51. +3:13. 5:25, 27. Ac 7:56. 2 T 4:1. He 2:7. Re 1:13. 14:14.
came. Is +35:4.
the clouds of heaven. Ge +9:13. Mt 24:30. 26:64. Mk 13:26. Ac 1:9-11. Re 1:7.
the Ancient. ver. 9, 22.
and they. Ps 47:5. 68:17, 18. Je 49:19. Ep 1:20, 21. 1 T 6:16. He 9:24.

14 **given**. ver. 27. Ps 2:6-8. 8:6. 110:1, 2. Mt 11:27. 28:18. Lk 10:22. 19:11, 12, 15. Jn 3:35. 5:22-27. 1 C 15:27. Ep 1:20-22. Ph 2:9-11. He 1:3, 4. 1 P 3:22. Re 3:21.
that all. Da 3:4, 7, 29. Ps 72:17. Is 60:12. Ph 2:9, 11. Re 11:15. 17:14.
an everlasting. Chal. alam, Ge +17:7. Ge +9:12. Is +9:7. Lk +1:32, 33. Re +11:15.
dominion. ver. 18, 27. Da 2:35, 44. 6:26. Ps +45:6. Ob +21. Jn 12:34. 1 C +15:24-28. He +12:28. Re 20:1-6.
his kingdom. Da 2:44, 45. Ps 2:6. Is +9:6, 7. 11:3-5. Mi 4:1-7. 5:2-5. Zc 14:9, 16, 17. Lk +1:32, 33. 2 T 4:1.

15 **was grieved**. ver. 28. Da 8:27. 10:8, 16. Je 15:17, 18. 17:16. Hab 3:16. Lk 19:41-44. Ro 9:2, 3. Re 10:9-11.
in my spirit. Jb +14:22. Pr 20:27. Ec +12:7. Mt +10:28. Mk 2:8. 1 C 2:11. 2 C 5:8. Ph 1:21-24. He 12:23. Ja 2:26. 1 P 3:4. Re 6:9-11.
body. Chal. sheath. Ge +2:7. 1 Ch 21:27. Jb +14:22. Is +10:18mg. 2 P 1:14.
the visions. Da 2:1, 3. 4:5. Ge 40:7, 8. 41:8.

16 **one**. ver. 10. Da 8:13-16. 10:5, 6, 11, 12. 12:5, 6. Ge 40:8. Zc 1:8-11. 2:3. 3:7. Re 5:5. 7:13, 14.

17 **great**. ver. 3, 4. Da 2:37-40. 8:4, 19-22. Nu 34:6.
arise out. ver. 3. Ps 17:14. Jn 18:36. Re 13:1, 11.

18 **the saints**. ver. 22, 27. Da 4:13, 23. Ps +149:9. Is 60:12-14. Zc 13:8, 9. 1 Th 3:13. Re +5:10.
most High. Chal. high ones, that is, things, or places. ver. 22, 25, 27. Ps +7:17. Jn +14:2. Ro 9:5. 1 C 10:9. Ep 1:3. 2:4-7. 6:12.
shall take. or, receive. ver. 22, 27. Da 2:6. 5:31. Ps +149:6-9. Mt 11:12. 25:34. 2 T 4:8. Re 20:4.

possess the kingdom. Is 11:11, 12. 26:9. Mt 4:8, 9. +5:5. 25:34. Lk 12:32. 13:28, 29. 14:15. 17:20, 21. 21:31. 22:16, 18, 29, 30. 2 C 4:4. Ep 2:2. 2 T 2:11, 12. He 12:28, 29. 1 P 5:8. Re 2:26, 27. 5:10. 12:9. 20:2, 3.
for. Chal. ad, Ps +9:18.
ever and ever. Chal. alam doubled, Da +2:20. Ps +41:13. Je 7:7. 25:5.

19 **the fourth**. ver. 7. Da 2:40-43.
the others. Chal. those.

20 **the ten horns**. ver. 8, 11, 23. Da 8:9-11. Re 17:12.
mouth. ver. 8. Da 11:37. Re 13:5, 6.
whose look. ver. 25. Da 11:36, 37.

21 **the same horn**. ver. 25. Da 8:12, 24. 9:26, 27. 11:31-35. 12:7. Re 11:7-9. 12:3, 4, 13-17. 13:5-7, etc. 17:6, 14. 19:19.
prevailed against. Da 8:10, 24. Zc 13:8, 9. 14:1, 2. Re 13:7-10, 16, 17. 14:12.

22 **the Ancient**. ver. 9-11. Da 8:25. 2 Th 2:8. Re 11:11-18. 14:8-20. 19:11-21. 20:9-15.
came. ver. 9, 13, 14. Dt 30:3. Zc 14:5. Mt 24:29-31. Ep +1:10. T 2:13.
judgment. ver. 10, 18, 26. Ps +149:9. Is 63:4. Re +5:10. 11:2. 19:20.
saints possessed. ver. +18. Da +2:44, 45. Ge 9:12. Ps 49:14. Is +9:7. Re 1:5, 6. +5:10. 11:15. 22:4, 5.

23 **the fourth**. ver. 7, 17. Da 2:40. Lk 2:1. Jn 11:48.

24 **the ten horns**. ver. 20. Re 12:3. 13:1, 2. 17:3, 12, 13, 16-18.
another shall rise. ver. 8, 20. Da 8:9-12. 11:36. Mi 5:5. 2 Th 2:3-10. 1 T 4:1-3.

25 **he shall speak**. ver. 8, 20. Da 8:11, 24, 25. 11:28, 30, 31, 36, 37, 40, 41. Is 37:23. 2 Th 2:3, 4. Re 13:5, 6, 11.
great words. ver. 8, 11.
the most High. Da 4:17.
shall wear out. Dt 8:4. Jsh 9:4, 5. Je 30:4-7. Mt 24:15-22. Re +6:9, 10. 11:7-10. 12:6, 14. 13:7-10. 14:12. 16:6. 17:6. 18:24.
the saints. ver. 18, 22.
and think. Da 2:21. 11:31, 36-38. 12:11. 2 Th 2:4. 1 T 4:1-3. Re 13:15-17.
change times and laws. Ge 1:14. 17:21. 18:14.
until. Re 17:14.
a time. Da 4:25, 32. 8:14. 9:26, 27. 12:7, 11, 12. Nu 14:34. Ps 90:4. Ezk 4:5. 2 P 3:8. Re 11:2, 3. 12:6, 14. 13:5, 7.

26 **the judgment shall sit**. ver. 10, 11, +22. 2 Th 2:8. Re 11:13. 20:10, 11.
his dominion. ver. 24, 25.
to consume and. Da 2:44. Is 60:12. Re 11:15. 19:20.
unto the end. Da 8:17-19. 9:26. 11:40. 12:4, 9, 13. Mt 24:14.

27 **the kingdom and**. ver. 14, 18, 22. Ps +149:5-9. Is 49:23-26. 54:3. 60:11-16. Zp 3:19, 20. Zc 14:9. Re 20:4.

whose kingdom. Da 4:34. Ps +45:6. Jn 12:34. Ac 2:34-36. Ph 2:9.

shall be given. ver. +18. Re 2:26, 27. 3:21.

and all. Ps 2:6-12. +86:9. Is 60:12. Ob 21. Re 11:15.

dominions. *or*, rulers. Re 17:14. 19:16.

serve and obey. 2 T 2:12. Re 5:10. 20:6.

him. or, them. Dt 28:1-14. Is 65:17-25. Zc 14:2-4. Re 19:11-21.

28 **the end**. Da 8:17, 19. 11:27. 12:9, 13.

my cogitations. ver. 15. Da 8:27. 10:8, 16.

but. Ge 37:10. Mk 9:10. Lk 2:19, 51. 9:44.

DANIEL 8

1 Cir. A.M. 3451. B.C. 553.

the third. Da +7:1.

me Daniel. ver. 15. Da 7:15, 28. 9:2. 10:2, 7. 11:4.

2 **I saw in**. ver. 3. Da +7:2, 15. Nu 12:6. He 1:1.

Shushan. i.e. *lily; joyfulness*, S#7800h. Ne 1:1. Est 1:2, 5. 2:3, 5, 8. 3:15. 4:8, 16. 8:14, 15. 9:6, 11-15, 18.

the palace. 1 Ch 29:1.

province. Ge +10:22.

I saw. Ezk 8:3.

the river. ver. 3, 6. Je 17:8.

Ulai. i.e. *muddy water; senseless; my leader*, S#195h. ver. 16.

3 **I lifted**. Da 10:5. Ge +22:13. Nu 24:2. Jsh 5:13. 1 Ch 21:16. Zc 1:18. 2:1. 5:1, 5, 9. 6:1.

a ram. ver. 20. Da 2:39. 7:5. 2 Ch 36:20.

one. Da 5:31. 6:28. Ezr 1:2. 4:5. Est 1:3. Is 13:17. 21:2. 44:28. Je 51:11.

the other. Heb. the second. Ge 4:19.

4 **pushing**. Da 2:39. 5:30, 31. 7:5. 11:2. Is 45:1-5. Je ch. 50, 51. Ezk 34:21.

neither. ver. 7. Jb 10:7. Ps 7:2. 50:22. Mi 5:8.

but. Da 5:19. 11:3, 16, 36. Is 10:13, 14.

5 **an he goat**. ver. 21. Da 2:32, 39. 7:6.

the face. Ge 1:2.

touched not the ground. *or*, none touched *him* in the earth.

a notable horn. Heb. an horn of sight. ver. 8, 21. Da 11:3.

6 **to the**. ver. +3.

7 **moved**. Da 11:11.

and there was no. Le 26:37. Jsh 8:20.

but. Da +7:7.

there was none. ver. +4.

8 **waxed**. Dt 31:20. Est 9:4. Je 5:27. Ezk 16:7.

when. Da 4:31. 5:20. 2 Ch 26:16. Ps 82:6, 7. Ezk 28:9.

the great. ver. 22. Da 7:6. 11:4.

toward. Da 2:39. 7:2. Mt 24:31. Mk 13:27. Re 7:1.

9 **came**. ver. 23, 24. Da 7:8, 20-26. 11:21, 25, etc.

the pleasant. Ps 48:2. Je +3:19mg.

10 **to the host**. *or*, against the host. ver. 24, 25.

Da 11:28, 30, 33-36. 12:3. Ge 15:5. 22:17. Ex 12:41. Is 14:13. Je 33:22. Mt 24:29. Re 1:20. 12:4.

and stamped. ver. 7. Da 7:7, 21, 25.

11 **he magnified**. ver. 25. Da 5:23. 7:25. 11:36. 2 K 19:22, 23. 2 Ch 32:15-22. Is 14:13, 14. 37:23, 29. Je 48:26, 42. Jl 2:20mg. Zp 2:8, 10. 2 Th 2:4. Re 13:5-7.

to. *or*, against. Ps 2:1-3.

the prince. ver. 25. Da 11:36. Jsh 5:14, 15. He 2:10. Re 17:14. 19:13-16.

by him. *or*, from him.

the daily. ver. 12, 13. Da 9:27. 11:31. 12:11. Ex +29:42. 2 Ch 29:7. Is +58:11. Ezk 46:14.

and the place. Da +9:26, 27. Ex 15:17. 1 K 8:13, 39, 43. Lk 21:5, 6, 24.

12 **an host was given him against the daily sacrifice**. *or*, the host was given over for the transgression against the daily *sacrifice*. Da 11:31-35. 12:11. Re 13:7.

and it cast. Ps 119:43, 142. Is 59:14. 2 Th 2:10-12.

and it practiced. ver. 4. Da 11:28, 36. 1 S 23:9. Jb 12:6. Je 12:1, 2. Re 13:11-17.

13 **one saint**. Da 4:13. +7:16. 12:5, 6. Dt 33:2. Jb 5:1. 15:15. Ps 89:5, 7. Zc 1:9-12, 19. 2:3, 4. 14:5. 1 Th 3:13. 1 P 1:12. Ju 14.

that certain saint. *or*, the numberer of secrets, *or*, the wonderful numberer. Heb. *Palmoni*. Jg 13:18mg. Ru 4:1. Ps 12:6. 87:6. 138:2. 139:6. 147:4. Is +9:6. 40:12, 26. Mt 10:29, 30. 11:27. Lk 10:22. Jn 1:18.

How. Re +6:10.

the vision. ver. +11, 12.

daily. ver. 11.

and the. Da 9:27. 11:31. 12:11. Mt 24:15. Mk 13:14. Lk 21:20.

of desolation. *or*, making desolate. Da 9:27. 11:31. 12:11. Mt 24:15.

the host. Nu 4:23, 30, 35, 39, 43. 8:24, 25.

to be trodden. ver. 10. Da 7:23. Is 63:18. Lk +21:24. He 10:29. Re 11:2.

14 **Unto**. Da 7:25. 9:27. 12:7, 11. Re 11:2, 3. 12:14. 13:5.

two thousand and three hundred. ver. 17. Da 9:27. Nu 14:34. Ps 90:4. Ezk 4:5. 2 P 3:8.

days. Heb. evening, morning. ver. +26. Ge 1:5.

then. Is 1:27. Ro 11:26, 27. 1 P 1:12. Re 11:15.

sanctuary. Ex 15:17. Ps 78:54. Ezk 37:27, 28. 39:12-15.

cleansed. Heb. justified. Da 9:24. Le 8:10. 16:20. Is 45:25. Ezk 39:12-15. Ga 3:8. He 9:23. 10:10-13.

15 **I Daniel**. Da +7:28.

sought. Da 7:16-19. 12:8. Mt 13:36. 24:15. Mk 4:12. 13:14. 1 P 1:10, 11. Re 13:18.

as. Da 10:5, 16. Jsh 5:14. Is +9:6. Ezk 1:26-28. Mt 24:30. Re 1:13.

16 **I heard**. Da 10:11, 12. Ac 9:7. 10:13. Re 1:12.
between. ver. 2. Da 12:5-7.
Gabriel. i.e. *man of God*, **S#1403h**. Da 9:21, 22.
Lk 1:19, 26.
make. Da 9:22, 23. 10:14, 21. 12:7, 8. Zc 1:9.
2:4. He 1:14. 1 P 1:10, 11. Re 22:16.

17 **I was**. Da 10:7, 8, 16. Ge +17:3. Mt 17:8.
Understand. ver. 15. Da 9:23. 10:11.
O son of man. Da +7:13. Ps +8:4. Ezk +2:1.
at the time of the end. ver. 19. Da 7:26.
+9:26, 27. 11:35, 36, 40. 12:4, 9, 13. Je +30:7.
Hab 2:3. Mt 24:14.

18 **I was**. ver. 17, 27. Da 10:8, 9. Ge 2:21. 15:12.
1 S 26:12. Jb 4:13. 33:15. Pr 19:15. Is 29:10.
Lk 9:32. 22:45. Ac 20:9.
on my face. Ezk 1:28. 2:1, 2.
he touched. Da 10:10, 16, 18. Ge 15:12. Jb
4:13. Ezk 2:2. Zc 4:1. Ac 26:6. Re 1:17.
set me upright. Heb. made me stand upon
my standing.

19 **I will**. ver. +15-17. Re 1:1.
what shall be. Mt 24:3-44.
the last end. ver. +17, 23, 24. Da +9:26, 27.
11:27, 35, 36. 12:4, 7, 8. Hab 2:3. Re 10:7.
11:18. 15:1. 17:17.
indignation. Is +66:14. Je +30:7. Mi 7:9. Re
14:10. **S#2195h**: ver. 19. Da 11:36. Ps 38:3
(anger). 69:24. 78:49 (indignation). 102:10. Is
10:5, 25. 13:5. 26:20. 30:27. Je 10:10. 15:17.
50:25. La 2:6. Ezk 21:31. 22:24, 31. Ho 7:16
(rage). Na 1:6. Hab 3:12. Zp 3:8.
time appointed. Ge +17:21.
the end shall be. Mt 24:6, 13, 14, 15. Lk
21:24.

20 **The ram**. ver. +3. Da 11:1, 2.
Media and. Da 5:28, 31. Ezr 1:2.

21 **the rough**. ver. +5-7. Da 10:20. 11:2.
Grecia. i.e. *supple; clay; unstable; effervescing*,
S#3120h. Da 10:20. 11:2. Ge +10:2, Javan.
the great. ver. +8. Da 11:3.

22 **being broken**. ver. 8.
whereas. ver. 3. Da 11:4.

23 **in the latter time**. Da 10:14. Nu 24:24. Ezk
+38:8, 16. 1 T 4:1. 2 T 3:1. 1 J 2:18. 4:3.
when. Ge 15:16. Mt 23:32. 1 Th 2:16.
come. Heb. accomplished. Da 9:24.
to the full. Re 14:15, 18. 18:5.
a king. ver. +9-12. Da 7:8, 11, 20, 25.
fierce countenance. Dt 28:50. Re 17:13, 17.
19:19.
and understanding. ver. 25. Da 11:21, 24. 2
Th 2:9-11. Re 13:11-14. 17:13. 19:20.
dark sentences. Ps +78:2.
shall stand. ver. 6.

24 *not by his own power*. ver. 22. 2 Th 2:9,
10. Re 13:2-9. 17:12, 13, 17.
shall prosper. ver. +12. Da 11:36.
shall destroy. ver. 10, 12. Da 7:8, 23, 25.
11:31-36. Zc 13:8, 9. 14:1, 2. Re 13:10. 16:6.
17:6. 19:2.

holy people. Heb. people of the holy ones.
Da 7:18, 22, +25. Is 63:18. Re 14:12.

25 **through his policy**. ver. +23, 24. Da 7:8.
11:21-25, 32, 33. Pr 29:12.
craft. 2 Th 2:9, 10. Re 13:12-14. 16:13, 14.
magnify. ver. 11. Da 7:8, 25. 11:36, 37. Je
48:26. 2 Th 2:4. Re 13:5, 6.
peace. or, prosperity. Da 11:21. Ps 122:7. Zc
7:7. 1 Th 5:3.
stand up. ver. +11. Da 11:36. Re 17:14.
19:16.
against the Prince. 1 T 6:15. Re 1:5. 17:14.
19:16, 19.
but he. Da 2:34, 35, 44, 45. 7:26. 11:45. Ps
92:7. Is 10:12. 14:25. 31:8. Mi 5:5-7. Na 1:11.
Zp 2:13. Zc 10:11. Ac 12:23. 2 Th 1:7-9. Re
19:19-21.
broken. Da +2:44.
without hand. Da 2:34, 45. Jb 34:20. La 4:6.
Is 11:4. 2 Th 2:8.

26 **the vision of**. ver. +11-15. Da 10:1.
wherefore shut. Da 12:4, 9. Is +8:16. Ezk
12:27. 2 Th 2:6-10. Re 10:4. 22:10.
for it. Da 10:1, 14. Is 24:22. Ho 3:3, 4.
days. ver. 14. Da 12:11, 12. Ezk 12:27. Re
9:15. 11:3. 12:6.

27 **fainted**. ver. +7. Da 7:28. 10:8, 16. Hab +3:16.
and did. ver. 2. Da 2:48, 49. 5:14. 6:2, 3. 1 S
3:15.
but. ver. +15-17.

DANIEL 9

1 A.M. 3466. B.C. 538.
Darius. Da 1:21. 5:31. 6:1, 28. 11:1.
which. or, in which he, etc.

2 **understood by books**. Da 8:15, 16. Ps
119:24, 99, 100. +126:5. Je 29:1. Mt 24:15.
Mk +12:24. 13:14. Jn +5:39. Ac 8:34. 18:9-
11. Ro 10:17. 1 T 4:13. 2 T 2:15. 3:15-17. 1 P
1:10-12. 2 P 1:19-21. Re 1:3.
to Jeremiah. 2 Ch 36:21. Je 25:11, 12. 27:7.
29:10. Zc 7:5.
desolations of. Ps 74:3-7. 79:1, 2. Is 6:11,
12. 24:10-12. 64:10. Je 7:34. 25:18. 26:6, 18.
La 1:1. Mi 3:12.

3 **I set**. Da +6:10. Ne 1:4, etc. Ps 102:13-17. Je
29:10-13. 33:3. Ezk 36:37. Ja 5:16-18.
by prayer and. Ph 4:6.
with fasting. Da 10:2, 3. Ezr 9:5. 10:6. Mt
+6:16. Ja 4:8-10.
and sackcloth. Jb +16:15.
and ashes. Est +4:1.

4 **made**. ver. 5-12. Le 26:40-42. 1 K 8:47-49. 2
Ch +7:14. Ne 9:2, 3. Ps 32:5. Pr 28:13. Je
3:13. 1 J 1:8-10.
the great. Ex +20:6. 34:6, 7. Nu 14:18, 19. Dt
5:10. 7:9. 1 K 8:23. Ps +99:3. Je 32:17-19. Mi
7:18-20. Lk 1:72. Ro 8:28. Ja 1:12. 2:5. 1 J
5:2, 3.

the covenant. Dt +7:9. Ps 74:20.
and mercy. Ex +20:6. 34:6, 7.

5 **We**. 1 J 1:8.
have sinned. ver. 15. 1 K 8:47-50. 2 Ch 6:37-39. Ezr 9:6. Ne 1:6-8. 9:33, 34. Ps 106:6. Is 64:5-7. Je 3:25. 14:7.
departing. Ps 18:21. 119:102. Is 59:13. Ezk 6:9. Ho 1:2. Ml 3:7. He +3:12.

6 **have we**. ver. 10. 2 Ch 36:15, 16. Is 30:10, 11. Je +7:26. Mt 23:37. Lk 20:10-12. Ac 13:27. 1 Th 2:15, 16.
servants. 2 K 17:13. Je +26:5.
which spake. Ex 4:16. 7:1. Dt 33:1. He 1:1.
our kings. Ezr 9:7. Ne 9:32, 34.

7 **righteousness**. ver. 8, 14. Dt 32:4. Ezr 9:13. Ne 9:33, 34. Ps 19:9. 51:4, 14. 119:137. 145:17. Je 12:1. Lk 23:40, 41.
belongeth unto thee. or, thou hast, etc.
unto us. Ezr +9:6, 7. Ezk 36:31.
all Israel. ver. 11. 1 K 12:17. Ezr 2:70. 7:13. 10:5.
near. Dt 4:27. 2 K 17:6, 7. Is 11:11. Je 24:9. Am 9:9. Ac 2:5-11.
whither. Le 26:33, 34.

8 **to us**. ver. 6, 7.
because. Je 14:20. La 1:7, 8, 18. 3:42. 5:16.

9 **To the Lord**. ver. 7. Ex +34:7. Ep 1:6-8. 2:4-7.
though. ver. 5. Ne 9:18, 19, 26-28. Ps 106:43-45. Je 14:7. Ezk 20:8, 9, 13, 14.

10 **which**. ver. 6. 2 K 17:13. 18:12. Ezr 9:10, 11. Ne 9:13-17. He 1:1.

11 **all**. ver. 7. 2 K 17:18-23. Is 1:4-6. Je 8:5-10. 9:26. Ezk 22:26-31.
the curse. Le 26:14, etc. Dt 27:15-26. 28:15, etc. 30:17-19. 31:17, 18. 32:19-42. Je +26:6. Zc +5:3.
Moses the servant. 1 Ch 6:49. 2 Ch 24:9. Ne 10:29.

12 **confirmed**. 2 K 17:13. Is 44:26. La 2:17. Ezk 13:6. Zc 1:6. Mt +5:18. Ro 15:8.
our judges. 1 K 3:9. Jb 12:17. Ps 2:10. 148:11. Pr 8:16.
bringing upon. Am +3:6.
evil. Is +45:7.
for under. La 1:12. 2:13. 4:6. Ezk 5:9. Jl 2:2. Am 3:2. Mt 24:21. Mk 13:19. Lk 21:22.

13 **As it is written**. ver. 11. Le 26:14, etc. Dt 28:15, etc. Is +42:9. La 2:15-17. Jn +10:35. 13:19. +14:29. 16:4.
law of Moses. Ex +24:4.
yet. Je 36:24.
made we not our prayer before. Heb. intreated we not the face of, etc. Ex +32:11. Jb 36:13. Is 9:13. Je 2:30. 5:3. +10:25.
that. Ps +9:10.
we might turn. Dt 29:4. Ps 85:4. 119:18, 27, 73. Is 64:7. Je 44:27. Lk 24:45. Jn 6:45. 8:32. Ac +3:19.
and understand. Ps +119:27. Ep 1:17, 18. Ja +1:5.

14 **watched**. Je 31:28. 44:27.
the Lord. ver. 7. Ne 9:33. Ps 51:14.
for. ver. 10.

15 **hast brought**. Ex 6:1, 6. 12:41. 14:18. ch. 15. 32:11. 1 K 8:51. Ne 1:10. Ps +119:132. Je 32:20-23. 2 C 1:10.
hast gotten. Ex 9:16. 14:18. Ne 9:10. Ps 106:8. Is 55:13. Je 32:10.
gotten thee renown. Heb. made thee a name. Ex 14:18. 1 Ch 17:21. Ne 9:10. Is 63:12, 14. Je 32:20.
we have sinned. ver. 5. Lk 15:18, 19, 21. 18:13.

16 **according to**. 1 S 12:7. Ne 9:8. Ps 31:1. 44:4. 71:2. 143:1, 11. Mi 6:4, 5. 2 Th 1:6. 1 J 1:9.
be turned. Ps 85:4, 5. Jon 3:8, 9. Hab 3:2.
thy holy. ver. 20. Ps 87:1-3. Jl 3:17. Zc 8:3.
for the. Ex +20:5. Le 26:39, 40. Ps 106:6, etc. Ezk 18:4, 20. Mt 23:31, 32. Lk 11:47-51.
Jerusalem. 1 K 9:7-9. Ps 44:13, 14. 79:4. Is 64:9-11. Je 24:9. 29:18. La 1:8, 9. 2:15, 16.
a reproach. Ps +31:11.

17 **cause**. Nu 6:23-26. Ps 4:6. 67:1. 80:1, 3, 7, 19. 119:135. +122:6-9. 137:5, 6. Re 21:23.
face. Ge +19:13.
thy sanctuary. La 5:18.
for. ver. 19. Jn 16:24. 2 C 1:20.

18 **incline**. Ps +17:6. Is 63:15-19. 64:12. Zc +12:4.
behold. Ex 3:7. Ps 80:14-19.
which is called by thy name. Heb. whereupon thy name is called. Je +14:9mg. 1 C 1:2.
for we. ver. 5. Da 2:17, 18. Mt 18:19, 20.
present. Heb. cause to fall. Je 36:7mg. 37:20mg.
for our righteousnesses. Is 64:6. Je 14:7. Ezk 36:32.
great mercies. ver. +9.

19 **O Lord, forgive**. Le 26:40-42. Nu 14:19. Dt 30:1-3. 1 K 8:30-39. 2 Ch 6:21, 25-30, 39. Am 7:2. Lk 11:8.
defer. Ps 44:23-26. 74:9-11. 79:5. 85:5, 6. 102:13, 14. Is 64:9-12.
thine. Ps 102:15, 16. Is +48:9. Ezk 39:25. Ep 3:10.
for thy. ver. 18. Ps 79:6, 9, 10. Je +14:9mg.

20 **whiles**. Da +10:12. Ps 32:5. 65:2, 3. 86:5-7. 145:18. Is 58:9. +65:24. Ac 4:31. 10:30, 31.
confessing my. ver. 4. Ec +7:20. Is 6:5. Ro 3:23. Ja 3:2. 1 J 1:8-10.
for. ver. 16. Ps 137:5, 6. Is 56:7. 62:6, 7. Zc 8:3. Re 21:2, 10.

21 **speaking**. Ps 69:13. 91:15. 145:18, 19. Is +65:24.
the man Gabriel. Da 8:16. 10:16. Lk 1:19, 26.
to fly. Ps 103:20. 104:4. Is 6:2. Ezk 1:11, 14. He 1:7.

swiftly. Heb. with weariness, *or* flight.

touched. Da 8:18. 10:10, 16, 18. Is 6:6, 7. Ac 12:7. He 1:14.

about the time. 2 S 24:15. 1 K 18:29, 36-39. Ezr 9:5. Mt 27:46. Ac 3:1. 10:3, 9.

evening. Ezr 9:5. Mt +14:23.

oblation. Le +23:13.

22 he informed. ver. 24-27. Da 8:16. 10:11, 12, 19, 21. Zc 1:9, 14. 6:4, 5. Re 4:1.

give thee skill and understanding. Heb. make thee skilful of understanding.

23 at the beginning. Da 10:12. Ps 69:13. Ezk 14:14.

commandment. Heb. word.

for. Da 10:11, 19. Lk 1:28.

greatly beloved. Heb. *a man of* desires. SS 7:10. Is +32:12mg.

understand. Mt 24:15.

24 Seventy weeks. Le 25:8. Nu 14:34. Ezk 4:6. Ac +1:6, 7. Ro +11:25.

holy city. Is 48:2. Zc 8:3.

finish. *or*, restrain. Ge 8:2. 23:6. Ex 36:6. Is 66:7-14. Ezk 36:24-30. Ro 11:25-29.

the transgression. Is +60:21. Mt 1:21. 1 J 3:8.

and to. La 4:22. Col 2:14. He 9:26. 10:14.

make and end of. *or*, seal up. 1 K 21:8. Jb 14:17. Ezk 28:12.

to make. He +2:17.

reconciliation. Ps +130:8. Zc 13:1.

to bring in. Is 51:6, 8. 53:10, 11. 56:1. Je 23:5, 6. Ro 3:21, 22, 25. 1 C 1:30. 2 C 5:21. Ph 3:9. He 9:12-14. 2 P 1:1. Re 14:6.

everlasting. Heb. *olam* plural, Ps +61:4.

righteousness. Is 1:26.

to seal up. Is 11:9. Je +31:31-40. Mt 11:13. Lk 21:22. +24:25-27, 44, 45. Jn 19:28-30. Ro 11:25-29.

prophecy. Heb. prophet. Ac 3:22. 1 C 13:8-10.

and to anoint. Da +8:14. Ex +28:41. Le 8:10. Ps 2:6. +45:7. Is +56:7. 60:13. +61:1-3. Je 33:18. Ezk 20:40, 41. +37:26-28. 40:2, 38. 43:7, 12, 26, 27. Zc 6:12, 13. 14:16, 17. Lk +4:18-21. Jn 1:41. 2:13-22. 3:34. Ac 10:38. He +1:8, 9. 9:11.

the most holy. or, saint of saints. Le +2:3. Ps +16:10. He +4:15.

25 and understand. ver. 23. Mt 13:23. 24:15. Mk 13:14. Ac 8:30.

from the going forth. Ezr 4:24. 6:1-15. 7:1, 8, 11-26. Ne 2:1-8. 3:1.

restore and to build Jerusalem. *or*, build again Jerusalem: as 2 S 15:25. Ps 71:10.

unto the Messiah. *i.e. the anointed*. Ge +49:10. Ps 2:2, 3, 6. 110:4. Zc 6:13. Mt 2:1, 2. Mk +1:15. Lk 2:25, 26. 3:15. Jn 1:41. 4:25, 26.

the Prince. Da 8:11, 25. 1 S +9:16 (**S#5057h**). 2 S 7:25-29. 1 Ch +5:2mg. Ps 89:3, 4. Is

+55:3, 4. Lk 2:4. Jn +1:49. Ac 3:14, 15. 5:30, 31. Re +1:5. 19:16.

be built again. Heb. return and be builded.

wall. *or*, breach, *or*, ditch.

even in. Ne 4:8, 16-18. Ep 5:16.

troublous times. Heb. strait of times. Ne 4:8, 16-18. 6:15. 9:36, 37.

26 And after. Lk +2:10. Jn +5:39. Ro +1:4.

Messiah. Ps 22:15. 89:44, 45. Is 53:8. Mk 9:12. Lk 24:25-27, 45-47. Jn 11:51, 52. 12:32-34. 2 C 5:21. Ga 3:13. 1 P 2:21, 24. 3:18.

cut off. Ge 9:11. Ex 12:15. 30:33, 38. Le 7:20. 18:29. 20:17. Dt 20:20. Ps 37:9, 34. Pr 2:22. Is 44:14. Je 10:3. 11:19. Ac 2:22, 23.

but not. *or*, and shall have nothing. Da 11:17. Ge 5:24. 42:36. Ps 22:6, 7. Is 53:4-6, 8, 12. Je 31:15. Zc 13:7. Mt 20:28. 26:56. Mk 14:50. Jn 1:11. +14:30.

for himself. Is 50:6. 53:4-6, 12. Mt 20:28. Jn 10:11, 18. 1 C +15:3. 1 P 2:24. Re +1:5, 6.

and the people, etc. *or*, and the Jews they shall be no more his *people*. Da 11:17. Is 60:21. Ho 1:9. Mi 5:3.

and the people. *or*, and the prince's (Messiah's, ver. 25) future people.

the prince that shall come. Da 7:8, 20, 21, 24-26. 8:9-12, 23-25. 11:36-45. Mi 5:5, 6. Hab +3:16.

shall destroy the city and. Mt 21:41. 22:2, 7. 23:38. +24:2, 3. Mk 13:2. Lk 19:41-44. 21:6, 12-24. Ac 6:13, 14.

and the end. Mt 24:6-14. Mk 13:7. Lk 21:12-24.

with a flood. Je +47:2.

the war. Mt 24:6, 7, 14. Lk 21:20, 24.

desolations are determined. *or*, it shall be cut off by desolations.

desolations. Mt 23:38.

are determined. ver. 25 (wall, or ditch). 11:36. Jb 14:5. Is 10:22. Note the unannounced time gap between ver. 26 and ver. 27 (Is +61:2).

27 And he. ver. 26. Da 7:8, 23, 24. 8:23-25. 11:36-45. 1 J 2:18.

shall confirm. Is 42:6. 53:11. +55:3. Je +31:31-34. +32:40-42. Ezk 16:60-63. Mt 26:28. Ro 5:15, 19. 15:8, 9. Ga 3:13-17. He 6:13-18. 8:8-13. 9:15-20, 28. 10:16-18. 13:20, 21.

the covenant. *or*, a covenant. Da 11:21-24. Is 28:18. Je 19:7.

for one week. Ge 29:27. Re 11:7.

cause the sacrifice. Da 7:25. 8:11, 12, 13. 11:31. 12:11. Mt 24:15. 27:51. 2 Th 2:4. He 10:4-22. Re 11:3. 12:6, 14. 13:1, 5, 6.

for the overspreading of abominations he shall make it desolate. *or*, with the abominable armies. *or*, upon the battlements shall be the idols of the desolator. Da 8:13. 12:11. Is 8:8. Mt *24:15*. Mk 13:14. Lk 21:20.

abominations. Da 11:31. 12:11. 2 K 23:13. Is 10:22, 23. 28:22. 44:19. 66:3. +66:17. Lk 21:24. Ro 11:26. Re 13:14, 15. 14:9-11. 19:20. 20:4.

make it. That is, the Jewish temple. Da 8:9-14. 11:45. 12:1, 7, 11. Mt 24:15. 2 Th 2:4. Re 11:1, 2. 13:6, 14, 15.

until the consumation. Is 10:22, 23. +28:22. Je 4:27. 5:10, 18. 30:11. 46:28. Ezk 11:13. Jl 3:1, 2, 9-16. Na 1:8, 9. Zc 14:1-3. Mt 24:29-31. 25:31-46. Ro 11:25-29. Re 16:19.

that determined. Da 11:36. Le 26:14, etc. Dt 4:26-28. 28:15, etc. 29:18, etc. 30:17, 18. 31:28, 29. 32:19, etc. Jb 14:5. Ps 69:22-28. Pr 16:4, 5. Is 10:22, 23. 28:18-22. 66:5, 6. Lk 2:34. Ro 11:26. 1 Th 2:15, 16. 2 Th 2:3-12.

shall be poured. Ezk +7:8. Re 16:1-4, 8, 10, 12, 17.

upon the desolate. *or*, upon the desolator. Da 7:11, 25, 26. 8:25. 11:45. Is 11:4. 2 Th 1:7-10. 2:3-12. Ju 14, 15. Re 19:20. 20:10.

DANIEL 10

1 A.M. 3470. B.C. 534.
Cyrus. Da 1:21. 6:28. 2 Ch 36:22, 23. Ezr 1:1, 2, 7, 8. 3:7. 4:3, 5. 5:13-17. 6:3, 14. Is 49:28. 45:1.
whose. Da 1:7. 4:8. 5:12.
and the. Da 8:26. 11:2. Ge 41:32. Lk 1:20. Re 19:9. 21:5. 22:6.
but. ver. 14. Da 12:4, 9.
time appointed. Heb. *tzaba*. Generally rendered "host" or "army." Here, "warfare" or "conflict." Da 8:10, 11, 12. Jb 10:17. Is 40:2.
long. Heb. great.
and he. Da 1:17. 2:21. 5:17. 8:16. 9:22, 23. Ep 1:18. 3:17-19.

2 **I Daniel**. Ezr 9:4, 5. Ne 1:4. Ps 42:9. 43:2. 137:1-5. Is 66:10. Je 9:1. Mt 9:15. Ro 9:2, 3. Ja 4:9, 10. Re 11:5.
three full weeks. Heb. weeks of days. Da +9:24-27.

3 **I ate**. Da 6:18. Is 24:6-11. 1 C 9:27.
pleasant bread. Heb. bread of desires. ver. 11mg. Is +32:12mg.
neither did. 2 S 12:20. 19:24. Pr 27:9. Lk +7:46.

4 **as**. Da 8:2. Ezk 1:3.
Hiddekel. Ge 2:14.

5 **and behold**. Da 12:6, 7. Jsh 5:13. Zc 1:8. Re 1:13-15.
a certain man. Heb. one man.
clothed. Da 12:6, 7. Ezk 9:2.
loins. Is 11:5. Ep 6:14. Re 1:13-15. 15:6, 7. **Uphaz**. Je 10:9.

6 **like the beryl**. Ex 28:20. Ezk 1:16. 10:9. Re 21:20.
his face. Ezk 1:14. Mt 17:2. Lk 9:29. Re 1:13-17. 19:12.

his arms. Ezk 1:7. Re 1:15. 10:1.
like the voice. Ezk 1:24. Re 10:3, 4.

7 **alone**. 2 K +6:17. Ac 9:7. 22:9.
but. Ezk 12:18. He 12:21.
so. Ge 3:10. Is 2:10. Je 23:24.

8 **I was**. Ge 32:24. Ex 3:3. Jn 16:32. 2 C 12:2, 3.
and there. Da +7:28. 8:27. Hab 3:16. Mt 17:6. Mk 9:6. Re 1:17.
comeliness. *or*, vigor. Jb 42:5, 6. Is 6:5.
turned. Ge 32:25, 31. 2 C 12:7.

9 **deep sleep**. Da +8:18. Ge 2:21. 15:12. Jb 4:13. 33:15. SS 5:2. Lk 9:32. 22:45. Re 1:17.
on my face. Ezk 3:23, 24.

10 **an hand**. ver. 16, 18. Da 8:18. 9:21. Je 1:9. Re 1:17.
set. Heb. moved. Am 9:9mg.

11 **a man**. Da +9:23. Ezk 14:14, 20. Jn 13:23. 21:20.
greatly beloved. Heb. of desires. ver. +3mg. Ps 45:11. SS 7:10.
understand. Da +8:16, 17. 9:22, 23.
upright. Heb. upon thy standing. Ac +26:16.
I stood. Jb 4:14-16. 37:1. Mk 16:8. Ac 9:6.

12 **Fear not**. ver. 19. Ge +15:1. Lk 24:38. 2 T +1:7.
from. ver. 2, 3. Da 9:3, 4, 20-23. Ps +13:1. Is 58:9. +65:24. Ac 10:4, 30, 31. Ep +6:12.
chasten. Da 9:3, 4, 20-23. Nu +29:7.
thy words were heard. Da 9:21-23. 1 S 12:18. 1 K 18:37, 38. Ps +3:4. +4:3. 84:11. +126:5. Je 15:1. 33:3. Mt +5:14. Lk 18:7, 8. Ac 12:5, 7. 1 T +2:1-3, 8. Ja 4:3, 8. 1 P 3:12. 1 J +5:14. Re 8:3, 4.
and I. ver. 11. Da 9:20-22. Ac 10:3-5, 30, 31. 1 T +2:1, 2.

13 **the prince**. ver. 20. Ezr 4:4-6, 24. Is 24:21. Je 46:25. Zc 3:1, 2. Mt 4:8. 1 C 8:5. 10:20. 2 C 4:4. Ep 6:12. 1 Th 2:18.
Michael. ver. 21. Da 12:1. Ju 9. Re 12:7.
one. *or*, the first. Col 2:10. 1 P 3:22.

14 **in the latter days**. Da 2:28. Ge +49:1. Ju 18. **the vision**. ver. 1. Da 8:26. 12:4, 9. Hab 2:3. He 2:3.

15 **I set**. ver. +9. Da 8:18. Ezk 24:27. 33:22. Lk 1:20.
became dumb. Ps 39:2, 9.

16 **like**. ver. 5, 6, 18. Da 8:15. 9:21. Ezk 1:26. Ph 2:7, 8. Re 1:13.
touched. ver. 10. Is 6:7. Je 1:9. Ezk 3:27. 33:22. Lk 1:64.
opened. Jg +11:35.
my lord. ver. 17. Da 12:8. Ex 4:10, 13. Jsh 5:14. Jg 6:13, 15. 13:8. Jn +20:28.
my sorrows. ver. 8, 9. Da 7:15, 28. 8:17, 27. 2 S 22:5-8. Ps +69:29. Ec 1:18.

17 **the servant of this my lord**. *or*, this servant of my lord. Mt 22:43, 44. Mk 12:36.
talk. Ge 32:30. Ex 24:10, 11. 33:20. Jg 6:22. 13:21-23. Is 6:1-5. Jn 1:18.

straightway. ver. +8.

breath. Heb. *neshamah*, Ge +2:7.

18 **again**. ver. +10, 16. Da 8:18.

he touched. Is 6:6-8.

he strengthened. 1 S 23:15. Jb 16:5. 23:6. Ps 27:14. Is 35:3, 4. Lk 22:32, 43. Ac 18:23. 2 C 12:9, 10. Ep 3:16. Ph 4:13. Col 1:11.

19 **O man**. ver. 11. Da 9:23. Jn 11:3, 5, 36. 15:9-14. 19:26. 21:20.

beloved. ver. 11.

fear not. ver. +12. Jg 6:23. Lk 24:36-38. Jn 16:33.

be strong. Jsh +1:6.

Let. 1 S 3:9, 10.

thou hast. ver. +18. Ps 138:3. 2 C 12:9.

20 **knowest thou wherefore**. Nu 24:12, 14. Jsh 5:13-15.

to fight. ver. +13. Is 37:36. Ac 12:23. Ep +6:12.

the prince of Grecia. Da 7:6. 8:5-8, 21. 11:2-4.

21 **I will**. Da 8:26. ch. 11, 12. Is 41:22, 23. 43:8, 9. Am +3:7. Ac 15:15-18.

show thee. 1 S 9:27. +23:16. Ml 2:7. Lk 24:27. Jn +5:39. 2 T +3:15.

scripture of truth. Pr +22:21. Ec 12:10. Jn 17:17. Ja 1:18.

holdeth. Heb. strengtheneth himself. ver. 19. 1 Ch +11:10mg.

Michael. ver. 13. Da +9:25. +12:1. Ju 9. Re 12:7.

DANIEL 11

1 **in the**. Da +5:31. 9:1.

Mede. i.e. *measure*, S#4075h, only here.

to confirm. Da 10:18, 19. Ac +14:22.

2 **will I**. Da 8:26. 10:1, 21. Pr 22:21. Am +3:7. Jn 10:35. 18:37, 38. Re 21:5.

three. Ezr 4:5, 6.

far richer. Ps 73:6, 7.

stir. ver. 25. Da 2:32, 39. 7:5. 8:4.

through his riches. Ezr 4:4-7, 23, 24.

3 **a mighty**. Da 7:6. 8:5-9, 21.

rule. Ge +1:29.

do. ver. 16, 36. Da 4:35. 5:19. 8:4, etc. Ep +1:11. He 2:4. Ja 1:18.

4 **he shall stand**. Jb 20:5-7. Ps 37:35, 36. 49:6-12. 73:17-20. Lk 12:20.

and shall be. Da 7:6. 8:8, 22. Ps 39:6. Ec 2:18, 19. 4:8. Mt 12:25.

be plucked. Da 7:8. Je 12:15, 17. 18:7. 31:40. 45:4.

5 **the king**. ver. 8, 9, 11, 14, 25, 40. Is 19:1, etc.

south. ver. +40. Je 13:19.

and one. ver. 3, 4.

6 **the end of years**. ver. 13mg. 2 Ch 18:2mg. Ezk +38:8, 9, 16.

join themselves. Heb. associate themselves. ver. 23. 2 Ch 20:35.

king. ver. 7, 13, 15, 40.

an agreement. Heb. rights. Ps 17:2.

retain. Jb 38:15. Ps 10:5. Ezk 30:21. Zc 11:16, 17.

he that begat her. *or*, whom she brought forth.

7 **out of**. Jb 14:7. Is 9:14. 11:1. Je 12:2. Ml 4:1.

one stand. ver. 20. Ps 49:10-13. 109:8. Lk 12:20.

in his estate. *or*, in his place, *or*, office. ver. 20, 21, 38. Pr 28:2.

and shall prevail. Ps 55:23. Ezk 17:18.

8 **carry captives**. lit. shall bring into captivity. Is 49:25mg.

their gods. Ge 31:30. Ex 12:12. Nu 33:4. Dt 12:3. Jg 18:24. Is 37:19. 46:1, 2. Je 43:12, 13. 46:25. Ho 8:6. 10:5, 6.

their precious vessels. Heb. vessels of their desire. Da 1:2, 3. Je +25:34mg.

10 **be stirred up**. *or*, war.

overflow. ver. 22, 40. Je +47:2.

then shall he return, and be stirred up. *or*, then shall he be stirred up again. Da 9:25.

to his. ver. 7, 39. Is 25:12.

11 **king of the south**. ver. 5, 9.

moved. ver. 44. Da 8:7. Ps 76:10.

the multitude. ver. 10. Da 2:38. 1 K 20:13, 28. Ps 33:16, 17. Ec 9:11, 12. Je 27:6.

12 **his heart**. Da 5:19, 20, 23. 8:25. Dt 8:14. 2 K 14:10. 2 Ch 25:19. 26:16. 32:25. Pr 16:18. Is 10:7-12. Ezk 28:2, 5, 17. Hab 2:4-6. Ac 12:22, 23. 1 T 3:6. 1 P 5:5.

not be. 1 P 5:5.

13 **the king**. ver. +6, 7.

certainly. Ge +2:16.

after certain years. Heb. at the end of times, *even* years. ver. 6. Da 4:16. 12:7.

14 **robbers of thy people**. Heb. children of robbers. or, destroyers. lit. "breakers forth." 1 K 12:15. Ps 17:4. Ezk 18:10mg.

exalt themselves. Ac 4:25-28. Re 17:17.

to establish. Ac 13:27.

but they shall fall. Ge 27:8. Is 41:4, 22, 23. 26. 43:9, 13. 44:7. 45:21. 46:10. 48:14.

15 **cast up**. Je 5:10. 6:6. 33:4. 52:4. Ezk 17:17.

most fenced cities. Heb. city of munitions.

shall not. ver. +6. Da 8:7. Jsh +1:5. Pr +21:30, 31.

his chosen people. Heb. the people of his choices. Ex 15:4.

16 **shall do**. ver. +3, 36. Da 8:4, 7.

glorious land. *or*, goodly land. Heb. land of ornament. ver. 41mg, 45mg. Is 8:8. Je +3:19mg.

17 **set his face**. ver. 19. 2 K 12:17. 2 Ch 20:3. Pr +19:21. Ezk 4:3, 7. 25:2. Lk 9:51.

upright ones. *or*, much uprightness, *or*, equal conditions. Nu 23:10. Jb 1:1, 18. Ps 11:7. Pr 16:13.

corrupting her. Heb. to corrupt. 1 S 18:21.

not stand. Est +1:12.
neither. Da +9:26. Ps 56:9. Ezk 17:17. Mt 12:30. Lk 11:23. Ro 8:31.

18 **the isles**. Is +11:11.
for his own behalf. Heb. for him.
the reproach. Heb. his reproach.
he shall cause. Nu +32:23. Jg 1:7. Est 7:10. Pr 26:27. Ho 12:14. Mt 7:2.

19 **not be found**. Jb 20:8. Ps 27:2. 37:36. Je 46:6. Ezk 26:21.

20 **estate**. *or*, place. ver. 7, 21mg.
a raiser of taxes in the. Heb. one that causeth an exactor to pass over the, etc. Dt 15:2, 3. 2 K 23:35.
glory of the kingdom. ver. 16, 41.
anger. Heb. angers. Pr 30:33.

21 **estate**. *or*, place. ver. 7, 20.
shall stand. Da 7:8. 8:9, 23, 25.
a vile person. 1 S 3:13. Ps 12:8. 15:4. Is 32:5, 6. Na 1:14.
peaceably. Da 8:25. Ezk 16:49.
by flatteries. ver. 32, 34. Jg 9:1-20. 2 S 15:2-6. Ps +12:3. 55:21.

22 **with**. ver. +10.
also. Da 8:10, 11, 25.

23 **work deceitfully**. Da 8:25. Ge +34:13. Ps 52:2. Pr 11:18. Ezk 17:13-19. Ro 1:29. 2 C 11:13. 2 Th 2:9, 10. Re 13:12-14.

24 **peaceably**. ver. 21. Da 8:25.
even upon the fattest. *or*, into the peaceable and fat, etc. Ge 27:28, 39.
he shall scatter. Jg 9:4. Pr 17:8. 19:6. 22:16.
forecast his devices. Heb. think his thoughts. Da 7:25. Pr 23:7. Ezk 38:10. Mt 9:4.

25 **stir up**. ver. 2, 10. Pr 15:18. 28:25.
courage. lit. heart.
the south with. ver. 5.

26 **that feed**. 2 S 4:2-12. 2 K 8:14, 15. 10:6-9. Ps 41:9. Mi 7:5, 6. Mt 26:23. Mk 14:20. Jn 13:18, 26.
the portion. Da 1:5, 8.
overflow. ver. 10, 22.

27 **hearts**. Heb. their hearts.
shall be to do mischief. 2 S 13:26-28. Ps 12:2. 52:1, 2. 58:2. 64:6. Pr 12:20. 23:6-8. 26:23-26.
speak lies. Ps 62:9. Je 9:3-5. 41:1-3.
but. Pr +19:21. Ezk 17:9, 10, 15.
for yet. ver. 29, 35, 40. Da 8:19. 10:1. 12:9. Hab 2:3. Ac 1:7. 17:31. 1 Th 5:1.
time appointed. ver. 29, 35. Ge +17:21.

28 **the holy covenant**. ver. +22, 30-32. Da 8:24. Ac 3:25.

29 **time appointed**. ver. 27, 35. Da +8:19. 10:1. Ge +17:21. Is 14:31. Ac 17:26. Ga 4:2.
as the former. ver. 23, 25.

30 **the ships of Chittim**. Ge +10:4.
and have indignation. ver. +28. Da 7:25. Re 12:12, 13, 17.

against the holy covenant. ver. 28. Da +9:27.
have intelligence. Ne 6:12-14. Mt 24:10.
forsake the holy covenant. ver. 28. 1 C +12:3. He +10:26, 29.

31 **arms**. Da 8:24, 25. Re 17:12-14.
they shall pollute. Da +8:11. 12:11. La 1:10. 2:7. Is 66:17. Ezk 7:20, 21. 9:7. 24:21, 22.
shall take. Da +8:12, 13, 26. +9:27. Ho 3:4.
daily sacrifice. Da +8:11. +9:27. 12:11.
place the abomination. Da 8:13. +9:27. 12:11. Mt 24:15. Mk 13:14. Lk 21:20.
maketh desolate. *or*, astonisheth. Da 8:13. Ac 13:40, 41.

32 **shall he**. Pr 19:5. 26:28.
corrupt. *or*, cause to dissemble. 1 C +12:3. 2 Th 2:9-12. Re 13:12-15.
by flatteries. Ps +12:3. Ep 6:10-18. Re 13:8. 14:12.
the people. 1 Ch +28:9. Ps +9:10. 46:1. Je 31:34. Jn 17:3. 2 C 4:3-6. 1 J +2:3, 4. 5:20.
shall be strong. Mi 5:7-9. 7:15-17. Zc 9:13-16. 10:3-6, 12. 12:3-7. 14:1-4. Ml 4:2, 3. 2 T +2:1-3. He 10:32, 33. 1 P 1:5. 1 J 5:4. Re 6:11. 7:9, 10. 12:7-11.

33 **understand among the people**. Da 12:3, 4, 10. 2 Ch +15:3. 35:3. Ps +102:18. Pr +8:9. 18:1. Is +8:16, 20. 30:20. 32:3, 4. Je +23:28. Zc 8:20-23. Ml +2:7. Mt +13:11, 51, 52. +24:45, 46. 28:20. Lk +24:44-47. Jn +6:14. Ac 4:2-4. 11:26. 14:21. +18:2, 26. Ro 15:7. 16:3, +5. 1 C 16:19. He 5:12-14. 1 P 4:10. 2 P 1:20. 2 J +10.
shall instruct. Da 12:3. 1 T +4:16. 2 T 2:24, 25.
shall fall. Mi 7:8. Zc 12:8mg. Mt 10:21. 20:23. +24:9. Jn 16:2. Ac 12:2, 3. 1 C 4:9. 2 T 1:12. 3:12. 4:6. He 11:34-37. Re 1:9. 2:10, 13. 6:9. 7:14. 12:11. 13:7-10. 17:6.

34 **shall fall**. ver. 14, 19, +33. Pr 24:17.
they shall be. Re 12:2-6, 13-17. 13:1-4.
but many. Da 7:21. Mt 24:11, 12. Re 13:7.
cleave. Je +23:28. Ezk +33:32. Mt 7:15. Ac 20:29, 30. Ro 16:18. 2 C 11:13-15. Ga 2:4. Ep 4:14. 1 T 4:1, 2. 2 T 3:1-7. 4:3. T 1:11. 2 P 2:1-3, 18, 19. 1 J 2:18, 19. 4:1, 5. 2 J 7-10. Ju +3, 4. Re 2:20. 13:11-14.

35 **some**. ver. +33. Da 8:10. 12:10. Mt 16:17, 23. 26:56, 69-75. Lk 22:31. Jn 20:25. Ac 13:13. 15:37-39.
shall fall. 2 P +3:17.
to try. Da 12:10. Dt 8:2, 3, 16. 2 Ch 32:31. Pr 17:3. Zc 13:9. Ml 3:2-4. 4:1-3. Ja 1:2, 3. 1 P 1:6, 7. 4:12. Re 2:10.
them. *or*, by them.
make them white. 2 P 3:14. Ju 24. Re 7:9, 13, 14.
even. ver. 29, 40. Da +8:17, 19. +9:27. 10:1. 12:4, 11. Hab 2:3. Mt 24:13. Re 13:10. 14:15. 17:17.

time appointed. ver. 27, 29. Da 9:26, 27. Ge +17:21. Is 61:2 (time gap).

36 the king. ver. 27. Da 7:8, 24. +8:23. +9:26.
do according to his will. ver. +3, 16. Da 7:25. 8:4. Is 13:13, 14. Jn 5:30. 6:38. Re 13:7. 17:13.
exalt. Da +7:8, 20, 25. 8:11, 25. Is 14:13. 2 Th *2:3, 4*. Re 13:5, 6. 17:3.
speak. Da +8:11, 24, 25. Re 13:6.
the God of gods. Da +2:47.
till the indignation. Da 7:20-25. +8:19. 12:7, 11-13. Ps 92:7. Is +26:20. +66:14. Re 11:2, 3. 12:14. 13:5. 14:10.
for that determined. Da 4:35. +9:26, 27. Nu 23:19. Jb 23:13, 14. Ps 33:10, 11. Pr +19:21. Is 46:10, 11. Ac 4:28. Re 10:7. 17:17.

37 Neither shall. Jn 5:43.
the desire of women. Ge 3:16. Dt 5:21. 21:11. 1 S 9:20. 2 S 1:26. SS 7:10. Is +32:12mg. Je 7:18. 44:17. Ezk 8:14. 24:16. 1 T 4:3.
nor regard any god. Ge 3:5. Is +14:13. 2 Th 2:4.

38 But in his estate. *or*, But in his stead. Heb. But as for the almighty God, in his seat he shall honor, yea, he shall honor a god whom, etc. 1 T 4:1, 2.
forces. *or*, munitions. Heb. *Mauzzim, or*, gods protectors. ver. 7, 10, 19, 31, 39. Is +60:5.
a god. Re 13:12-17. 17:1-5. 18:12.
honor with. Re 9:20, 21.
pleasant things. Heb. things desired. ver. +8mg. Is +32:12mg.

39 most strong holds. Heb. fortresses of munitions.
strange. Ex 12:43 (S#5236h). Ezk 44:7, 9. Ml 2:11.
rule over. Re 13:15.
gain. Heb. a price. Dt 23:18. 2 S 24:24. Pr 1:13, 14. La 5:4mg. Re 18:9-13.

40 at the time of the end. ver. +35. Da +8:17, 19. +9:27. 12:4, 9.
the king of the south. i.e. Egypt. ver. +5, 6, 9, 11, 14, 25. Ezk 38:14-18.
the king of the north. i.e. Syria. ver. 6, 7, 13, 15. Mi +5:5.
shall come. Da 9:26. Hab +3:16.
like a whirlwind. Je +23:19.
with horsemen. Ezk 38:3-6, 15. Re 9:16. 16:12.
overflow. ver. +10, 22.

41 enter. ver. +45. Ezk 38:8-13.
glorious land. *or*, goodly land. Heb. land of delight, *or* ornament. ver. +16mg.
escape. Da 12:1.
Edom. Is 11:13-15. Je 9:26.
Moab. Is 16:4. Je 48:47.
Ammon. Je 49:6.

42 stretch forth. Heb. send forth. Ex 9:15.
land of Egypt. Ezk 29:14, 15. Zc 10:10, 11. 14:17, 18. Re 11:8.

43 the Libyans. Je +46:9. Ezk 38:5, 6.
at his steps. Jg 4:10. Ezk 11:8mg.

44 tidings. Je 51:31.
east. ver. 11, 30. Ezk 38:9-12. Re 9:16. 16:12. 17:13. 19:19-21.
north. Je +1:14.
make away many. Re 13:7.

45 he shall. Zc 13:8, 9. 14:2.
between. Jl 2:20. Zc 14:8.
in the. ver. 16, 41. Da 8:9. Ps 48:2. Is 2:2. 14:13. Mi 4:2. 2 Th 2:4.
glorious holy mountain. *or*, goodly. Heb. mountain of delight of holiness. ver. 41mg. Is +11:9.
he shall come. Da 2:35. 7:26. 8:25. Ezk 38:22, 23. 39:2. Jl 3:2, 12. 2 Th 2:8. Re 13:10. 14:14-20. 16:14. 19:19-21. 20:2, 9.
none shall help him. Is 11:4. 24:21, 22. Zc 12:1-9. 14:1-3, 12, 13. 2 Th 2:8. Re 19:20.

DANIEL 12

1 at that time. Da +11:35. Is +2:11.
Michael. i.e. *who is like unto God?*, S#4317h. Da 10:13, 21. 12:1. Ju +9. Re 12:7-9.
stand up. He 10:12. Ju +9.
the great prince. Da +9:25. 10:21. Is +9:7. Ezk 34:24. 37:24. Ep 1:21. Re +1:5. 17:14. 19:11-16.
time of trouble. Da 8:24, 25. +9:12, 26. Is 22:5. +26:20, 21. Je +30:7. Zp 1:4, 12, 15. Mt 24:21. Mk 13:19. Lk 21:23, 24. Re 16:17-21.
never was. Je 30:7. Jl 2:1, 2.
thy people. Is 11:11, etc. 27:12, 13. Je +30:7. Ezk 37:21-28. 39:25-29. Ho 3:4, 5. Jl 3:16-21. Am 9:11-15. Ob 17-21. Zc 12:3-10. Ro 11:5, 6, 15, 26.
written. Ex +31:18. Re +3:5.
book. Ex +32:32.

2 many. Jb +19:25-27. Is +26:19. +53:12. Ezk +37:1-4, 12. Ho +13:14. Mt 22:29-32. Lk *2:34*. Jn 11:23-26. 1 C +15:20-22, 51-54. 1 Th 4:14, +16. Re 20:4-6, 12.
that sleep. 2 K +24:6. Jb 7:21. +14:21. Ps 6:5. +13:3. Ec +9:5. Mt 9:24. +27:52. Jn 11:11. Ac 7:60. 13:36. 1 C +11:30. 15:6, 18, 20, 35, 51. 1 Th 4:13-18. 5:10. Ja 2:26. He +12:23. 2 P 3:4.
the dust. Ge +2:7. +3:19. Jb 7:21. Ps 22:15. +146:4. Ec +3:19-21.
shall awake. Jb +19:25, 26. Is +26:19. +43:10. Mt +27:52. Jn +2:19, 21. +5:28, 29. Re +14:13.
some to everlasting life. Heb. *olam*, Ge +17:7. Ps 49:14, 15. Ezk 37:11-14. Mt 25:46. Jn 5:28, 29. Ac 24:15. 26:8. 1 C 15:20, 23, 51, 52. 1 Th 4:16. He 11:35.
and some. Is +26:19, 21. 27:6. 1 C 15:23. Re 20:5.
shame. Je 23:40. Ju 13.

everlasting. Heb. *olam,* Ge +17:7.
contempt. Jb 22:15, 16, 19. Ps 2:4, 5. 52:1, 5, 6. 59:7, 8. Pr 1:26, 27. 3:34. Is +66:24. Je +20:11. Lk +13:28. Ro 9:21. 2 Th 1:7-10.

3 they that be. Da +11:33, 35. Pr +11:30. Mt +24:45. 1 C 3:10. 2 T 3:15-17. 2 P 3:15. Re 20:4-6.
wise. *or,* teachers. 2 Ch 30:22. Pr 16:23. Ac 13:1. Ep 4:11. 1 T +4:16. He +5:12.
shine. Pr 4:18. Mt 13:43. 19:28. 1 C 15:40-42. 1 Th 2:19, 20. Re 1:20.
turn many. Pr 10:21. 11:25, 30. Je 23:22. Ml 2:6. Lk 1:16, 17. Jn 4:36. Ro 1:16, 17. Ph 2:16, 17. Ja 5:19, 20. Ju 22, 23.
as the stars. Nu 24:17.
for ever. Heb. *olam,* Ps +21:4 **(S#5769h).**
and ever. Heb. *ad,* Ps +9:18.

4 shut. Da 8:26. Re 10:4. 22:10.
to the. ver. 9. Da 8:17. 10:1. 11:40. Re 5:1-5.
many. Da 11:33. Is 11:9. 29:18, 19. 30:26. 32:3. Zc 14:6-10. Mt 24:14. Ro 10:18. Re 14:6, 7.
to and fro. 2 Ch 16:9. Je 5:1. Ezk 22:30. Am 8:12. or, apostatize (Gesenius, p. 962a). Ps 40:5. 2 Th 2:3, 7. 1 T 4:1. 2 T 3:1-5.
knowledge. or, wickedness. ver. 10. 1 Ch +12:32. Pr +4:18. Is 11:9. 25:6, 7. 29:18, 24. 35:6-8. 41:18, 19. 52:7, 8. 54:13. Je +8:7. Mt +24:45. 2 Th 2:7, 8. 2 P 3:18.

5 other two. Da 10:5, 6, 10, 16.
bank. Heb. lip. Jg +7:22mg.
of the river. Da 10:4.

6 one said. Da 8:16. Zc 1:12, 13. Ep 3:10. 1 P 1:12.
man. Da +10:5, 6. Ezk 9:2. Re 15:6. 19:14.
upon. *or,* from above. Re 10:2-5.
How long. Re +6:10.

7 he held. Ge +14:22.
liveth. Da 4:34. Jb 27:2. Je 4:2.
for ever. Heb. *olam,* Ex +12:24.
that it. ver. 11, 12. Da +7:25. 8:14. 11:13. Re 11:2, 3, 15. 12:6, 14. 13:5.
a time. Da +8:19. Ge +17:21.
and half. or, a part.
and when. Lk 21:14. Re 10:7. 11:7-15.
the holy. Da +8:24. Dt 7:6. 26:19. Is 62:12. 1 P 2:9.
be finished. Lk 21:24.

8 but. Lk 18:34. Jn 12:16. Ac 1:7. 1 P 1:11.
what. ver. +6. Da 10:14.

9 Go. ver. 13.
closed. ver. 4. Da 8:26. Is +8:16. 29:11. Re 10:4.

10 shall be. Da 11:35. Ps 51:7. Is 1:18. Ezk 36:25. Zc 13:9. 1 C 6:11. 2 C 7:1. T 2:14. He 12:10. 1 P 1:7, 22. Re 3:18. 7:13, 14. 19:8, 14.
but the wicked. 1 S 24:13. Ec +1:15. Is 32:6, 7. Ezk 47:11. Ho +14:9. Ro 11:8-10. 2 Th 2:10-12. Re 9:20, 21. 16:11. 22:11.
but the wise. ver. 3. Da +11:33, 35. Ps 107:43. Pr 1:5. 2:1-5. Mk 4:11. Lk +24:45. Jn +7:17. 8:47. 18:37. 1 C 2:10-16. 1 Jn 5:20.
shall understand. 1 Ch +12:32. Je +8:7. 23:20. Mt 24:15. Mk 12:24. 1 J 2:18-22.

11 the time. Da 8:11, 12, 26. 11:31.
the abomination. Heb. to set up the abomination, etc. Mt 25:31-46.
daily sacrifice. Da +8:11, 13. +9:27. +11:31.
abomination. Da +9:27. +11:31. Mt 24:15. Mk 13:14. Re 11:2.
maketh desolate. *or,* astonisheth. Da 7:25. 2 Th 2:4.
a thousand. Da 1:12. 7:25. 8:14. Re 11:2. 12:6. 13:5.

12 Blessed. Ps +1:1. Mt 10:22. Ro 11:15. Re 20:4.
waiteth. Ps 37:9. 130:5-8. Is 30:18. Mt 24:13. Mk 13:13. 1 C +15:58. He 10:36. Re 2:26.
thousand three hundred and. ver. 11. Da +7:18, 22. Ge 15:18. Ps +149:9. Is 2:2-4. +26:9, 15. 27:12. 43:6. Je +7:7. 31:8. +33:21. Ezk 34:12. 39:28. Am 9:9. Mt 19:28. 25:34. Lk 22:29, 30. Ac +7:5. Ro 11:15. 1 C 6:2, 3. He 11:13, 39. Re 5:10. 11:15. 20:4.

13 go. ver. 9.
for thou. *or,* and thou, etc.
shalt rest. ver. 3. Is 57:1, 2. Zc 3:7. Mt 19:28. Lk 22:29, 30. 2 C 5:1. 2 Th 1:7. 2 T 4:7, 8. Re 14:13.
stand. ver. 2. Jb 19:25. Ps +1:5. 16:11. 17:15. Is +26:19. Lk +21:36. Ac +24:15. Ju 14, 15.
in thy lot. Jg 1:3. Ps +16:5, 6. 105:11. 125:3. Jn 14:2. Col 1:12. 1 P 1:4.
at the end. 2 T 1:12. He +11:13.

HOSEA

HOSEA 1

1 **word**. Je 1:2, 4. Ezk 1:3. Jl 1:1. Jon 1:1. Zc 1:1. Jn 10:35. 2 P 1:21.
Hosea. i.e. *deliverer*, **S#1954h**. Ho 1:1, 2, 2. 2 K +15:30. Ro 9:25, Osee.
in the days. Is 1:1. Mi 1:1.
Uzziah. 2 K 14:16-20. 15:1, 2, 32. ch. 16, 18. 2 Ch ch. 26-32.
2 **beginning**. Mk 1:1.
by. Nu 12:6, 8. Hab 2:1. Zc 1:9.
Go. Ho 3:1. Is +20:2, 3. Je 13:1-11. Ezk ch. 4, 5.
a wife of whoredoms. Ho 4:2, 12. 5:3, 4. 6:10. 7:4.
children. Ho 2:4. 2 P 2:14mg.
for the land. lit. earth. Ho 4:1. Jl 1:2.
whoredom. Ex +34:15. Je 2:13.
departing. Ho 4:10. 7:8. 8:11, 14. 10:1. 12:14. 13:9.
3 **he went**. Is 8:1-3.
Diblaim. i.e. *double fig cake*, **S#1691h**.
4 **Call**. ver. 6, 9. Is +7:14. +9:6. Mt +1:21. Lk 1:13, 31, 63. Jn 1:42.
Jezreel. 1 Ch +4:3.
little while. Ho 10:14.
and I. 2 K 9:24, 25. 10:7, 8, 10, 11, 17, 29-31. 15:8, 10-12.
avenge. Heb. visit. Ho 2:13. 9:7. Je +9:25mg. 23:2.
blood. Dt +19:12.
will cause. 2 K 15:29. 17:6, etc. 18:9-12. 1 Ch 5:25, 26. Je 3:8. Ezk 23:10, 31.
5 **at that day**. 2 K 17:6. 18:11.
I will. Ho 2:18. Ps 37:15. 46:9. Je 49:34, 35. 51:56.
in the valley. Jsh 17:16. Jg 6:33.
6 **Lo-ruhamah**. *that is*, Not having obtained mercy. i.e. *the uncompassionate*, **S#3819h**. ver. 6, 8. Ho 2:23. Ro 9:25. 1 P 2:10.
for. 2 K 17:6, 23, etc. Is 27:11.
no more have. Heb. not add any more to have.
but I will utterly take them away. *or*, that I should altogether pardon them. Ho +9:15-17. Ge 18:24. Ex 23:21. Is 2:9.
7 **I will**. Ho 11:12. 2 K 19:35. Is 7:5-8. ch. 36. 37:35, 36.

will save. Is +7:14. +12:2. 49:6. Je +23:5, 6. Zc 2:6-11. 4:6. 9:9, 10. Mt +1:21-23. T 3:4-6.
by the Lord. 2 K 19:35. Is 11:4. Da +3:25, +28. 2 Th 2:8.
their God. Ne +9:6. Ps 102:24. Ec 12:14. Je 23:5. Zc 13:7. T 2:13.
not save. 1 S 17:39. Is 31:1. Zc 4:6. 2 C 10:4.
by bow. Ps 33:16. 44:3-6.
8 **weaned**. 1 S +1:22.
9 **Call**. Ho 3:4. Ro +11:1, 25.
Lo-ammi. *that is*, Not my people. ver. 10. Ho 2:23. Ps +44:9. +54:7. Ezk 11:19, 20. Da +9:26. 1 P 2:10.
10 **the number**. Ge 12:7. 26:4. Ex 6:4. 32:13. Nu 23:10. Is 27:6. 60:22. 65:23. Ezk 37:26.
the sand. Ge +22:17.
cannot be measured. Nu 23:10.
and it. Ro *9:25, 26*.
in the. *or*, instead of that.
it was said. Ho 2:23. Is 43:6. 49:17-22. 54:1-3. 60:4, etc. 65:1. 66:20. 1 P *2:9, 10*.
Ye are the sons. Is 63:16. 64:8. 1 J +3:1.
living God. Je +10:10.
11 **the children of Judah**. Ho 3:5. Je 3:18, 19. +23:3. 50:4, 5, 19. Ezk 16:60-63. 34:23, 24. Ro 11:25, 26.
one. Heb. *echad*, Dt +6:4.
head. Ho 3:5. Is 26:13. Je 23:5, 6. 30:9, 21. Ezk 34:23. 37:24. Ep 1:22, 23. 5:23.
for. Ho 2:22, 23. Ps 22:27-30. 110:3. Is +54:7. Je 24:6. 31:28. 32:41. Am 9:15. Zc 10:6. Ro 11:15.
day. Dt +4:32.

HOSEA 2

1 **unto**. Ho 1:9-11.
Ammi. *that is*, My people. **S#5971h**. Ex 19:5, 6. Je 31:33. 32:38. Ezk 11:20. 36:28. 37:27. Zc 13:9.
Ruhamah. *that is*, Having obtained mercy. **S#7355h**. ver. 23. Ro 11:30, 31. 2 C 4:1. 1 T 1:13. 1 P 2:10.
2 **Plead with**. Is 58:1. Je 2:2. 19:3. Ezk 20:4. 23:45. Mt 23:37-39. Ac 7:51-53. 2 C 5:16.
mother. 2 S +20:19.
she is not. Is +32:9. Is 50:1. Je 3:6-8.

let her. Ho 1:2. Je 3:1, 9, 13. Ezk 16:20, 25. 23:43.
whoredoms. Ex +34:15.
3 **I strip**. ver. 10. Is +3:17. Re 17:16.
was born. Ezk 16:4-8, 22.
as. Is 32:13, 14. 33:9. 64:10. Je 2:31. 4:26. 12:10. 22:6. Ezk 19:13. 20:35, 36.
a dry. Je 2:6. 17:6. 51:43.
and slay. Ex 17:3. Jg 15:18. Am 8:11-13.
4 **I will not**. Ho 1:6. Is 27:11. Je 13:14. 16:5. Ezk 5:11. 8:18. 9:10. Zc 1:12. Ro 9:18. 11:22. Ja 2:13.
children of. Ho 1:2. 2 K 9:22. Is 57:3. Jn 8:41.
5 **their mother**. ver. 2. Ho 3:1. 4:5, 12-15. Is 1:21. 50:1. Je 2:20, 25. 3:1, 6-9. Ezk 16:15, 16, 28, etc. 23:5-11. Re 2:20-23. 17:1-5.
hath done. Ho 9:10. Ezr 9:6, 7. Je 2:26, 27. 11:13. Da 9:5-8.
I will. ver. 13. Ho 8:9. Is 57:7, 8. Je 3:1-3. Ezk 23:16, 17, 40-44.
lovers. or, my Baals, or lords. Je 44:17, 18. Ezk 23:5.
give. ver. 8, 12. Jg 16:23. Je 44:17, 18.
drink. Heb. drinks.
6 **I will**. Ge +6:13. Jb 3:23. 19:8. Pr 13:15. La 3:7-9. Lk 15:14-16. 19:43.
make a wall. Heb. wall a wall. Ge +1:29. Ezk 13:5mg.
7 **she shall follow**. Ho 5:13. 2 Ch 28:20-22. Is 30:2, 3, 16. 31:1-3. Je 2:28, 36, 37. 30:12-15. Ezk 20:32. 23:22.
I will go. Ho 5:15. 6:1, 2. 14:1. Ps 116:7. Je 3:22-25. 31:9, 18. 50:4, 5. La 3:40-42. Lk 15:17-20.
first. 1 Ch 8:9. Je 2:2. 3:1. 31:32. Ezk 16:8. 23:4.
for. Ho 13:6. Dt 6:10-12. 8:17, 18. 32:13-15. Ne 9:25, 26. Je 14:22. Da 4:17, 25, 32. 5:21.
8 **she**. Is 1:3. Hab 1:16. Ac 17:23-25. Ro 1:28.
her corn. ver. 5. Ho 10:1. Jg 9:27. Je 7:18. 44:17, 18. Ezk 16:16-19. Da 5:3, 4, 23. Lk 15:13. 16:1, 2.
wine. Heb. new wine. Ho 4:11. Is 24:7-9.
which they prepared for Baal. or, wherewith they made Baal. Ho 8:4. 13:2. Ex 32:2-4. Jg 17:1-5. Is 46:6.
9 **will I**. Da 11:13. Jl 2:14. Ml 1:4. 3:18.
take. ver. 3. Is +3:17-26. 17:10, 11. Zp 1:13. Hg 1:6-11. 2:16, 17.
season. Ge +17:21.
recover. or, take away. or, rescue. Ge 31:16.
10 **now**. ver. 3. Is 3:17. Je 13:22, 26. Ezk 16:36, 37. 23:29. Lk 12:2, 3. 1 C 4:5.
lewdness. Heb. folly, or, villany. **S#5040h**, only here. Hebrew root word is **S#5036h**, rendered "fool" at Ps 14:1, "vile person" at Is 32:5, 6.
and none shall. Ho 5:13, 14. 13:7, 8. Ps 50:22. Pr 11:21. Mi 5:8.
11 **cause**. Ho 9:1-5. Is 24:7-11. Je 7:34. 16:9. 25:10. Ezk 26:13. Na 1:10. Re 18:22, 23.

her feast. 1 K 12:32. Is 1:13, 14. Am 5:21. 8:3, 5, 9, 10.
new moons. Col +2:16.
sabbaths. Is +58:13.
solemn feasts. Ge +17:21. Le 23:2.
12 **destroy**. Heb. make desolate. Je 22:6. **S#8074h**. Le 26:31, 32. Jb 16:7. Ps 79:7 (laid waste). Je 10:25. Ezk 14:8 (make him; lit. make him desolate). 30:12 (waste), 14. 32:10 (amazed).
These. ver. 5. Ho 9:1.
rewards. or, my hire, or fee. Dt 23:18.
I will. Ps 80:12, 13. Is 5:5, 6. 7:23. 29:17. 32:13-15. Je 26:18. Mi 3:12.
13 **I will visit**. Ho 9:7, 9. Je +11:22.
the days. Ho 9:10. 13:1. Jg 2:11-13. 3:7. 10:6. 1 K 16:31, 32. 18:18, etc. 2 K 1:2. 10:28. 21:3.
she burned. Ho 11:2. Je 7:9. 11:13. 18:15.
she decked. Ezk 23:40-42.
earrings. or, ring. i.e. a nose ring. Ge 24:22. 35:4.
jewels. lit. "smooth thing." Pr 25:12.
she went. ver. 5, 7. Je 2:23-25.
forgat. Dt 6:12. 8:11-14. 32:18. Jg 3:7. 1 S 12:9. Jb 8:13. Ps 78:11. 106:13, 21. Is 17:10. Je 2:32. Ezk 22:12. 23:35. Note time gap between ver. 13 and 14 (Is +61:2).
14 **Therefore**. Is 30:18. Je 16:14.
I will. SS 1:4. Jn 6:44. 12:32.
and bring. ver. 3. Is 11:16. Je 2:2. Ezk 20:10, 35, 36. Re 12:6, 14.
into the wilderness. Ho 9:10. 11:1. 12:10, 14. 13:4. Ps +74:14. Is 4:5. 9:16. 32:16. 43:16. 48:21. 50:2. 51:10. Je 2:6. 7:22, etc. 9:3, etc. 14:14. 23:7. +31:2. 34:13. Ezk 20:5, etc. Am 2:10. 3:1. Mi 6:4. 7:15. Hg 2:6.
and speak. Is 35:3, 4. 40:1, 2. 49:13, etc. 51:3, etc. Je 3:12-24. 30:18-22. 31:1-37. 32:36-41. 33:6-26. Ezk +20:35, 36. 34:22-31. 36:8, etc. 37:11-28. 39:25-29. Am 9:11-15. Mi 7:14-20. Zp 3:9-20. Zc 1:12-17. 8:19-23. Ro 11:26, 27.
comfortably. or, friendly. Heb. to her heart. Ge +34:3mg. Jg 19:3mg. Is 40:2mg.
15 **I will**. ver. 12. Le 26:40-45. Dt 30:3-5. Ne 1:8, 9. Is 65:21. Je 32:15. Ezk 28:26. Am 9:14.
from thence. Nu 16:13, 14. Is +51:11.
the valley. Ex +17:14. Jsh 7:26. Is 65:10.
for a door. La 3:21. Ezk 37:11-14. Zc 9:12. Jn 10:9. Ac 14:27.
of hope. An allusion to the contrasting meaning of Achor (trouble).
she shall sing. Ex 15:1-21. Nu 21:17. Ps 30:5mg. 106:12. Zc +2:10.
as in the days. Ho 11:1. Je 2:2. Ezk 16:8, 22, 60.
and as in the day. Ezk 20:36. Mi +7:15.
when she came up. Ex 1:10. 4:22. 12:38. 13:18.

16 **Ishi**. *that is,* My husband. **S#376h**. ver. 7. Is 54:5. Je 3:14. Jn 3:29. 2 C 11:2. Ep 5:25-27. Re 19:7.
Baali. *that is,* My lord. **S#1180h**.

17 **I will**. Ex +23:13. Is 2:18. Ezk 6:6. 36:25, 26. 37:23.
and they. Je 10:11. Zc 13:2.

18 **in that day**. Is +2:11.
will I. Le +26:6. Ps 91:1-13. Is +65:25. Jl 2:22. Ro 8:19-21.
I will break. Ps 46:9. Is 2:4. Ezk 39:9, 10. Mi 4:3. Zc 9:10.
and will. Dt +12:10. Ps 23:2. Je 30:10. Zc 3:10.

19 **And I will**. Ps 36:5-7. Is 54:5. 62:3-5. Je 3:14, 15. Jn 3:29. Ro 7:4. 2 C 11:2. Ep 5:25-27. Re 19:7-9. 21:2, 9, 10.
betroth. Ex 22:16. Dt 20:7. 22:23, 25, 27, 28. 28:30. 2 S 3:14.
for ever. Heb. *olam,* Ex +12:24. Is 51:22. +54:8-10. Je +31:31-37. +32:38-41. Ezk +37:25-28. 39:29. Jl 3:20.
in righteousness. Ps 85:10. +130:8. Is 45:23-25. 54:14. +60:21. Je 4:2. Ro 3:25, 26. Ep 1:7, 8. 5:23-27.
in mercies. Is +55:3.

20 **thou shalt know the Lord**. Ex 6:7. Is 1:3. 11:9. 54:13. Je 9:24. 24:7. +31:33, 34. Ezk 38:23. Mt 11:27. Lk 10:22. 19:42, 44. Jn 6:45. +8:55. 17:3. 2 C 4:6. Ph 3:8. Col +1:10. 2 T 1:12. He +8:11. 1 J 4:6. 5:20.

21 **in that day**. Is +2:11.
I will hear, saith. Is +65:24. Zc 8:12. 13:9. Mt 6:33. Ro 8:32. 1 C 3:21-23.

22 **the earth**. Jl 1:3, 4. Jn 1:1, 2. 1:4, 5. Ro 5:3, 4, 5. 8:29, 30. 10:14, 15. Ja 1:3, 4. 1:14, 15. 2 P 1:5-7.
shall hear. Ps 67:6. Zc 8:12.
and they. Ho 1:4, 11.

23 **I will sow**. Ps 72:16. Is 61:9. Je 31:27. Zc 10:9. Ac 8:1-4. Ja 1:1. 1 P 1:1, 2.
and I will have mercy. ver. 1mg. Ho 1:6, 7. Ps 68:20. Is +55:3. 65:1. Mi 7:19. Zc 1:16. 10:6. Ro 9:25. 11:30-32. 1 P 2:9, 10.
not obtained mercy. Ho 1:6, +9.
and I will say. Ho 1:10. Zc 2:11. 13:9. Ro 9:25, 26.
they shall say. Ho 1:11. Zc 13:9. Ro 9:26. 1 P 2:10.
Thou art my God. Ho 8:2. Dt 26:17-19. Ps 22:27. 68:31. 118:28. SS 2:16. Is 44:5. Je 16:19. 32:38. Zc 8:22, 23. 13:9. 14:9, 16. Ml 1:11. Jn +20:20. Ro 3:29. 15:9-11. 1 Th 1:9, 10. Re 21:3, 4.

HOSEA 3

1 **Go yet**. Ho 1:2, 3.
friend. Je 3:1, 20mg. Mt 26:50.
according. Ho 11:8. Dt 7:6, 7. Jg 10:16. 2 K

13:23. Ne 9:18, 19, 31. Ps 106:43-46. Je 3:1-4, 12-14. 31:20. Mi 7:18-20. Zc 1:16. Lk 1:54, 55.
look to other gods. Dt 31:18, 20. Ps 123:2. Is 17:7, 8. 45:22. Mi 7:7.
love flagons. Ho 4:11. 7:5. 9:1, 2. Ex 32:6. Jg 9:27. Am 2:8. 6:6. 1 C 10:7, 21. 1 P 4:3.
wine. Heb. grapes. Ge 40:10. 49:11.

2 **I bought**. Ge 31:41. 34:12. Ex 22:17. 1 S 18:25.
fifteen shekels. Ex 21:7, 32. Le 27:4.
an homer. Le 27:16. Is 5:10. Ezk 45:11.
half homer. Heb. *lethech.*

3 **Thou shalt abide**. ver. +4. Dt 21:13. Je 30:22-24. 31:1-9.
not play. Je 2:20. Ja 4:4.
be for thee. Ex 6:7.

4 **many days**. ver. 3. Dt 28:59. Mi +3:6. Mt +25:19. Ac +1:6. Ro 11:25.
a king. Ho 10:3. Ge +49:10. Je 15:4, 5. Mi 4:9. Jn 19:15.
prince. Ho 8:4.
without a sacrifice. 2 Ch 15:2. Da +8:11-13. +9:27. +12:11. Mt +24:1, 2. Lk 21:24. Ac 6:13, 14. He 10:26.
an image. Heb. a standing, *or* statue, *or* pillar. 2 K +17:10. Is 19:19, 20.
ephod. Ex +28:4. Ezr 2:63. Ne 7:65.
without teraphim. Ge +31:19mg. Ezk 20:32. Mi 5:11-14. Zc 13:2.

5 **Afterward**. ver. 4. Ho 6:2. Is 24:22. Ezk +38:8, 16. Hab 2:3.
return. Ho 2:7. 5:4, 15. 6:1. 7:10. 11:5. 12:6. 13:4. 14:1-3, 8. Je +3:22. 31:6-10. Ezk +34:16.
seek the Lord. Ho 5:6, 15. 2 Ch +7:14. Is 27:12, 13. Je 50:4, 5.
and David their king. 1 K 12:16. Is +55:3, 4. Je +30:9. +33:17. Ezk 34:23, 24. +37:22-25. Am 9:11. Mi 2:13. Mt 8:11. Ac 15:16-18.
shall fear. Ex 15:14-16. 2 Ch 20:29. Ne 6:16. Is 60:5, 6. Je +5:22. Ezk 16:63. Mi 7:16 +17. Zc 12:2. Lk +1:65.
his goodness. Ho 14:2 (graciously). Ex 18:9. 33:19. Nu 10:32. 2 S 7:28. 1 K 8:66. 1 Ch 17:26. 2 Ch 7:10. Ne 9:25, 35. Is 63:7. Je 31:12. 33:9. Zc 9:17. Ro 2:4.
in the latter days. Ge +49:1. Ro +11:25.

HOSEA 4

1 Cir. A.M. 3224. B.C. 780.
Hear. Is 34:1. Je +7:2. 9:20.
for. Ho 12:2. Is 1:18. 3:13, 14. 5:3. 34:8. Je 25:31. Mi 6:2.
controversy. Ho 12:2. Is 1:18. 3:13, 14. Je 25:31. 30:31. Mi 6:2.
land. Ho +1:2.
no truth. Is 59:13-15. Je 6:13. 7:3-6. Mi 7:2-5.

nor mercy. Ho 6:6. Mi +6:8.

nor knowledge. ver 6. Ho 2:20. 5:4. Je 4:22, 28. 5:4. 9:24. 22:16. Mk 12:24. Jn +8:55. Ro 1:21, 28. 1 C 15:34. 1 J 2:3, 4. 4:7, 8.

2   **swearing**. Is 24:5. 48:1. 59:2-8, 12-15. Je 5:1, 2, 7-9, 26, 27. 6:7. 7:6-10. 9:2-8. 23:10-14. Ezk 22:2-13, 25-30. Mi 2:1-3. 3:2, 9-12. 6:10-12. 7:2-4. Zp 3:1-5. Zc +5:3, 4. 7:9-11.

blood. Heb. bloods. 2 K +9:26mg.

toucheth. Ho 5:2. 6:9. La 4:13-15. Mt 23:35-37. Ac 7:52. 1 Th 2:15. Re 17:6.

3   **the land**. Is 24:4-12. Je 4:27, 28. 12:4. Jl 1:10-13. Am 1:2. 5:16. 8:8-10. Na 1:4.

with the beasts. Je 4:25. 12:4. Ezk 38:20. Zp 1:3.

4   **let**. ver. 17. Am 5:13. 6:10. Mt 7:3-6.

as. Nu 16:1, etc. Dt 17:12. Je 18:18. Ro 2:8. 10:21.

5   **in the day**. Je 6:4, 5. 15:8.

and the prophet. Ho 9:7, 8. Is 9:13-17. Je 6:4, 5, 12-15. 8:10-12. 14:15, 16. 15:8. 23:9. Ezk 13:9-16. 14:8-10. Mi 3:5-7. Zc 11:8. 13:2.

destroy. Heb. cut off.

thy. Ho 2:2. Is 50:1. Je 15:8. 50:12. Ezk 16:44, 45. Ga 4:26.

6   **My people**. ver. 12. Is 1:3. 3:12. 5:13. Je 4:22. 8:7.

destroyed. Heb. cut off.

for lack of. ver. 1. Ho 6:6. 2 Ch 15:3. Jb 36:12. Pr 19:2. 29:18. Is 5:13. 27:11. 45:20. Je 5:3, 4, 21. Mt +15:14. 2 C 4:3-6.

because. 1 S 2:12. Pr 1:30-32. Is 28:7. 56:10-12. Je 2:8. 8:8, 9. Ml 2:7, 8. Mt 23:16-26.

rejected. Ho 8:12. Je 6:10, 19.

I will also reject. Zc 11:8, 9, 15-17. Ml 2:1-3, 9. Mt 21:41-45. Mk 12:8, 9. Lk 20:16-18.

seeing. Ho 8:14. 13:6. 2 K 17:16-20. Ps 119:61, 139. Is 17:10. Mt 15:3-6.

forgotten. Is +44:21.

I will also. Ho 1:6. 1 S 2:28-36. 3:12-15.

forget. Ps +13:1.

7   **they were**. ver. 10. Ho 5:1. 6:9. 13:6, 14. Dt 32:15. Ezr 9:7.

therefore. 1 S 2:30. Je 2:26, 27. Ml 2:9. Ph 3:19.

8   **eat**. Le 6:26, 30. 7:6, 7. Nu 18:9.

sin. or, sin offering. Ge +4:7. Le +23:19.

set their heart on their iniquity. Heb. lift up their soul to their iniquity.

heart. Heb. *nephesh*, soul, Ex +23:9. Ps 24:4. 25:1. Ezk +13:19. 14:3, 7. T 1:11.

9   **like people**. Is 9:14-16. 24:2. Je 5:31. 8:10-12. 23:11, 12. Ezk 14:10. 22:26-31. Mt +15:14.

punish. Heb. visit upon. Ho 1:4mg. Je +9:25mg.

reward them. Heb. cause to return. Ps 109:17, 18. Pr 5:22. 17:13. Is 3:10, 11. Zc 1:6.

10   **they shall eat**. Le +26:26. Pr 13:25. Is 65:13-16. Ml 2:1-3.

they shall commit. ver. 14. Ho 9:11-17.

left off. 1 Ch +28:9. 2 Ch 24:17, 18. Ps 36:3. 125:5. Je 34:15, 16. Ezk 18:24, 26. Zp 1:6. Lk +8:13. 1 C +15:2. 2 P 2:20-22.

to take heed. Lk +8:18. +10:28. +11:28. He 2:1. 2 P +1:5-11, 19.

11   **take**. ver. 12. Pr 6:32. +20:1. 23:27-35. Ec 7:7. Is 5:12. 28:7. Lk 21:34. Ro 13:11-14.

heart. Is 5:12. 28:7.

12   **ask**. Nu 27:21. Jg 18:5. Je 2:27. 10:8. Ezk 21:21. Hab 2:19.

stocks. i.e. wooden idols. Is 45:20. Je 2:27.

their staff. i.e. wooden divining rods. Ezk 21:21.

for. Ho 5:4. Is 44:18-20. Mi 2:11. 2 Th 2:9-11.

spirit. Heb. *ruach*, Ge +41:8.

caused. Ps +9:10.

to err. or, go astray, wander. Ge 20:13. 2 Ch 33:9. Ps 95:10. Pr +10:17. 14:22. +19:27. Is 3:12. 9:16. 19:14. 21:4mg. 28:7. 30:28. 35:8. 53:6. 63:17. Je 23:13, 32. 42:20mg. 50:6. Am 2:4. Mi 3:5. Mt 22:29. Mk +12:24, 27. He 3:10. Ja 1:16. +5:19.

gone. Ho 9:1. Ex +34:15. Je 5:7.

from under. Nu 5:19, 29. Ezk 23:5.

13   **sacrifice**. Ezk 16:16, 25. 20:28, 29.

oaks. Is +57:5.

therefore. 2 S 12:10-12. Jb 31:9, 10. Am 7:17. Ro 1:23-28.

14   **I will not**. *or*, Shall I not, etc.

punish. ver. 17. Is 1:5. He 12:8.

for. 1 C 6:16.

are separated. Ju 19.

and they. 1 K 14:23, 24. 15:12. 2 K 23:7.

harlots. Ge 38:21, 22. Dt 23:17.

therefore. ver. 1, 5, 6. Ho 14:9. Pr +28:5. Is 44:18-20. 56:11. Da 12:10. Jn 8:43. Ro 3:11. Ep 4:18.

fall. *or*, be punished. Pr 10:10mg.

15   **play the harlot**. ver. 12. Je 3:6-10. Ezk 23:4-8.

yet. Ho 11:12. 2 K 17:18, 19. Je 3:10, 11. Lk +12:47, 48. Ep +5:11.

Gilgal. Jsh +4:19.

Beth-aven. Ho 5:8. 10:5, 8. Jsh +7:2. 1 K 12:28, 29. 13:1. 2 K 10:29. 17:6-23. Je 48:13. Am 3:14. 7:13.

nor. Is 48:1. Je 5:2. Ezk 20:39. Am 6:10. 8:14. Zp 1:5, 6.

16   **slideth**. Ho 11:7. 1 S 15:11. Je 3:6, 8, 11, 12. 5:6. 7:24. 8:5. 14:7. Ps 125:5. Zc 7:11mg. He +3:12.

as a lamb. Le 26:33. Is 7:21-25. 22:18.

17   **Ephraim**. Ho 11:2. 12:1. 13:2.

let. ver. 4. Ps 81:12. Mt +15:14. Re +22:11.

18   **drink**. Dt 32:32, 33. Is 1:21, 22. Je 2:21.

sour. Heb. gone. Ml 3:7.

committed. ver. 2, 10. 2 K 17:7-17.

her. Ex 23:8. Dt 16:19. 1 S 8:3. 12:3, 4. Ezk +13:19. Am 5:12.

rulers. Heb. shields. Ps 47:9.
Give ye. Ho 8:13.

19 **wind**. Ho 13:15. Is 57:13. Je 4:11, 12. 51:1. Zc 5:9-11.
and. Ho 10:6. Is 1:29. 42:17. Je 2:26, 27, 36, 37. 3:24, 25. 17:13.

HOSEA 5

1 **O priests**. Ho 4:1, 6, 7. 6:9. Ml 1:6. 2:1.
O house. Ho 7:3-5. 1 K 14:7-16. 21:18-22. 2 Ch 21:12-15. Je 13:18. 22:1, etc. Am 7:9. Mi 3:1, 9.
for. Ho 9:11-17. 10:15. 13:8.
ye have. Ho 9:8. Mi 7:2. Hab 1:15-17.
Tabor. Jg +4:6.

2 **the revolters**. Ho 6:9. 9:15. Je 6:28.
profound. Ps 64:3-6. 140:1-5. Is 29:15. Je 11:18, 19. 18:18. Lk 22:2-5. Ac 23:12-15.
though. *or*, and, etc.
a rebuker. lit. a correction. Ho 6:5. Is 1:5. Je 5:3. 25:3-7. Am 4:6-12. Zp 3:1, 2. Re 3:19.

3 **know**. Ge +39:6. Am 3:2. He 4:13. Re 3:15.
Ephraim. ver. 9, 11, 13. Ge +41:52.
thou. Ho 4:17, 18. 1 K 12:26-33. 14:14-16. Ezk 23:5.

4 **They will not frame their doings**. lit. They will not give. *Or,* Their doings will not suffer them. Ps 36:1-4. 78:8. Jn 3:19, 20. 2 Th 2:11, 12.
for. Ho 4:12. Je 50:38.
and. Ho 4:1. 1 S 2:12. Ps +9:10. Je 9:6, 24. 22:15, 16. 24:7. Jn +8:55. 16:3. 1 J 2:3, 4.

5 **the pride**. Ho 7:10. Pr 30:13. Is 3:9. 9:9, 10. 28:1-3. Am 8:7.
testify. Is 44:9. 59:12. Je 14:7. Mt 23:31. Lk 19:22.
fall in. Ho 4:5. 14:1. Pr 11:5, 21. 14:32. 24:16. Je 3:3. Am 5:2.
Judah. ver. 14. Ho 8:14. 2 K 17:19, 20. Ezk 23:31-35. Am 2:4, 5.

6 **go**. Ex 10:9, 24-26. Pr 15:8. 21:27. Je 7:4. Mi 6:6, 7.
to seek. Dt 4:29.
not find. Pr 1:28. Is 1:11-15. 66:3. Je 11:11. La 3:44. Ezk 8:18. Am 5:21-23. Mi 3:4. Jn 7:34.
he. SS 5:6. Lk 5:16.
withdrawn. Ho 9:12. Ge +6:3.

7 **dealt**. Ho 6:7. Is 48:8. 59:13. Je 3:20. 5:11. Ml 2:11.
begotten. Ne 13:23, 24. Ps 144:7, 11. Ml 2:11-15.
a month. 2 K 15:13. Ezk 12:28. Zc 11:8.

8 **Blow**. *Ho +8:1.*
Gibeah. Jg +19:12.
Ramah. Je +31:15.
Beth-aven. Ho 4:15. Jsh +7:2. 1 K 12:29.
after. Jg 5:14. 20:40.

9 **Ephraim**. ver. 12, 14. Ho 8:8. 9:11-17. 11:5,

6. 13:1-3, 15, 16. Jb 12:14. Is 28:1-4. Am 3:14, 15. 7:9, 17.
have. Is 46:10. 48:3, 5. Am +3:7. Zc 1:6. Jn 16:4.

10 **princes**. ver. 5.
remove. 1 K 15:16-22. 2 K 16:7-9. 2 Ch 28:16-22. Pr +23:10. Is 5:8. Mi 2:2.
pour. Ezk +7:8.
like. Ps 32:6. 88:17. 93:3, 4. Pr 17:14. Mt 7:27. Lk 6:49.

11 **oppressed**. Dt 28:33. 2 K 15:16-20, 29. Am 5:11, 12.
he willingly. *or,* willfully. 1 K 12:26-33. 2 K 10:29-31. Ps +119:63. Mi 6:16. Ac 5:29. Ro 6:13. He +10:26.

12 **as a moth**. Jb 13:28. Is 50:9. 51:8.
rottenness. *or,* a worm. Pr 12:4. Jon 4:7. Hab +3:16. Mk 9:44-48.

13 **his wound**. Je 30:12, 14. Mi 1:9.
went. Ho 7:11. 10:6. 12:1. 2 K 15:19, 29. 16:7. 2 Ch 28:16-18.
to king Jareb. i.e. *contender,* S#3377h. Ho 5:13. 10:6. *or,* to the king of Jareb; *or,* to the king *that* should plead.
yet. 2 Ch 28:20, 21. Is 1:6. Je 30:12, 15.

14 **as a lion**. Is +5:29.
will tear. Ps 50:22.
none. Dt 28:31. Jb 10:7. Am 2:14.

15 **return**. ver. 6. Ex 25:21, 22. 1 K 8:10-13. Ps 132:14. Is 26:21. Ezk 8:6. 10:4. 11:23. Mi 1:3.
my place. Is 18:4.
till. Ho 8:2. 14:1-3. Le +26:40-42. Dt 4:29-31. 30:1-3. 1 K 8:47, 48. 2 Ch 6:36, 37. +7:14. Ne 1:8, 9. Jb 33:27. Is 64:5-9. Je 3:13. 29:12-14. 31:18-20. Ezk 6:9. 20:43. 36:31. Da 9:4-12. Ac 3:19-21.
acknowledge their offense. lit. be guilty. Ho 4:15. 6:1. 14:1-3. Ezk 39:23-29. Hab 1:11. Zc 12:10, 11.
seek my face. Ho 3:5. Je +29:13. Zc 8:21, 22.
in their affliction. Dt +4:30. Jg 4:3. 6:6, 7. 10:10-16. 2 Ch 33:12, 13. Jb 27:8-10. Ps 50:15. 78:34. 83:16. 119:67. Pr 1:27, 28. Is 26:9, 16. 64:9-12. Je 2:27. Ezk 20:44. Zp 2:1-3. Lk 13:25.
seek me early. ver. 6. Jb 8:5. 24:5. Ps 63:1. 78:34. Pr 1:28. 7:15. 11:27. 13:24. Is 65:24. Zc 12:9, 10. 13:9. Re +2:28.

HOSEA 6

1 **let us return**. Ho 5:15. 1 S 14:36. 1 Ch +28:9. 2 Ch 15:2. Jb 33:27, 28. Is 2:3-5. 58:2. Je 3:22. 50:4, 5. Zp +2:1-3. Zc +1:3. Ml 2:7. Jn 14:6. Ac +3:19-21. Ep 3:12. Ja +4:8.
he hath torn. Ho 5:12-14. 13:7-9. Dt 32:39. 1 S 2:6. Jb 5:18. 34:29. Ps 30:7-11. Is 29:13. 30:22. Je 30:12-17. 33:5, 6. La 3:32, 33. Ezk 7:9.
will heal. Ex +15:26. Je 30:17.
will bind. Jb +5:18. Ep 2:13-18.

2 **after two days**. Ps 30:4, 5. +102:13, 16. 1 C +15:4, 20.

revive us. Ho +13:14. Ezr 9:8. Ps 71:20. +80:18. 85:6. Is +26:19, 20. Hab 3:2.

the third day. 2 K 20:5. Ps 90:4. +118:24. Is 24:22. Lk 13:32. 2 P 3:8. Re 11:11.

raise us up. Ezk 37:11-13. Da +12:2. Am 9:11, 14, 15. Lk 2:25. Ac +1:6. +3:19-21.

we shall live. Ge 17:18. Ps 61:7. Jn 14:19. Ro 14:8.

in his sight. Ho 7:2. Jb 19:26. Is 24:23. Mt 19:28. 23:39. Lk 21:36. Jn 1:51. 1 J 3:2.

3 **we know**. Ho 2:20. Is 54:13. Je 24:7. +31:34. Mi 4:2. Jn 17:3.

if. Pr 2:1-5, 9. Mt 13:11, 12. Jn 7:17. 8:12, 31, 32. Ac +3:19-21. 17:11, 12. Ph 3:13-15. He 3:14.

follow on. Pr 23:12. Da +11:33. Mt 24:13. Lk 8:11-15. 22:31, 32. Jn 8:31. 15:9, 10. Ac 11:23. 14:22. Ro 2:7-9. Ga 4:11. 5:7. 6:9. Col +1:10. 1 Th 3:5. 2 P 3:18.

his going forth. Ps 19:4-10. Mi +5:2. Ml +4:2. Jn 16:28.

prepared. or, sure, or fixed. Ge 41:32mg. Dt 13:14 (certain). 2 S 7:16, 26 (established). 2 Ch +12:14mg. Ps 51:10mg. 93:2. Pr 4:18 (perfect). Is 2:2. Mi 4:1.

as the morning. Ho +14:5. Ge +8:22. Je +31:35, 36. +33:25, 26. Re +2:28.

unto us. Ps 72:6. Zc 9:9. Mi +5:2.

as the rain. Ho 10:12. 14:5. Dt 32:2. Jb 29:23. Ps 65:9. 72:6. Is 5:6. 32:15. 44:3. Ezk 36:25. Jl 2:23, 24. Mi 5:7. Zc 10:1.

former rain. or, as the latter rain *sprinkling* the earth. Dt 11:14. 1 Ch 10:3 (archers). 2 Ch 35:23. Pr 26:18 (casteth). Je 5:24.

4 **what**. Da 11:8. Is 5:3, 4. Je 3:19. 5:7, 9, 23. 9:7. Mt 23:37, 38. Lk 13:7-9. 19:41, 42.

what shall. Ho 11:8. Mt 21:25, 26. Lk 16:3.

for. Jg 2:18, 19. Ps 78:34-37. 106:12, 13. Je 3:10. 34:15, 16. Mt 13:21. 2 P 2:20-23.

goodness. or, mercy, or, kindness.

as a. Ho 13:3.

it goeth away. Mk +4:17. Lk +8:13.

5 **have I**. 1 S 13:13. 15:22, 23. 1 K 14:6-12. 17:1. 18:17, 18. 2 K 1:16. 2 Ch 21:12-17. Is 58:1. Je 1:10, 18. 5:14. 13:13, 14. 23:29. Ezk 3:9, 10. 43:3. Ac 7:31-44.

I have. 1 K 19:17. Is 11:4. Je 23:29. 2 C 10:5, 6. He 4:12. Re 1:16. 2:16. 19:15, 21.

and thy judgments are as. or, that thy judgments might be as, etc. Ho 14:9. Ge +18:25. Dt 33:2. Jb 34:10, 11. Ps 37:6. 119:120. Zp 3:5. Ro 2:5. Ep 6:17. 1 P 2:7.

6 **I desired mercy**. 1 S 15:22. Ps 50:8, 9. Pr 21:3. Ec 5:1. Is 1:11-17. 58:6-10. Je 7:22, 23. Da 4:27. Am 5:21-24. Mi +6:6-8. Mt +5:7. *9:13. 12:7.* +23:23. Mk 12:33.

not sacrifice. Ps 50:8, 9. Pr 21:3. Is 1:11.

the knowledge of God. Ho 4:1. 1 Ch +28:9.

Jb 22:21. Je 9:23, 24. 22:16. Col +1:10. 1 J +2:3. 3:6.

burnt offerings. Le +23:12.

7 **men**. or, Adam. Ge 3:6, 11. Jb 31:33. Ps 49:12. 82:7.

transgressed. Ho 8:1. 2 K 17:15. 18:12. Is 24:5. Je 31:32. Ezk 16:59-61. 20:37. He 8:9.

the covenant. Ge 2:16, 17. Jsh 24:1, 25. Is +42:6. Ro 5:12, 19. 1 C 15:22, +45, 47. Ga 3:10. 1 Th 5:9.

they dealt. Ho 5:7. Is 24:16. 48:8. Je 3:7-11, 20. 5:11. 9:6.

8 **Gilead**. Ge +37:25.

polluted with blood. or, cunning for blood. Ho 5:1, 2. 2 S 3:27. 20:8-10. 1 K 2:5. Ps 10:8, 9. 59:2, 3. Is 59:6, 7. Je 11:19. Mi 7:2. Mt 26:15, 16. Ac 23:12-15. 25:3.

9 **as troops**. Ho 7:1. Ezr 8:31. Jb 1:15-17. 12:6. 24:2-17. Pr 1:11-19.

so. Ho 5:1, 2. Je 11:9. Ezk 22:25, 27. Mi 3:9-11. Zp 3:3, 4. Mk 14:1. Lk 22:2-6. Jn 11:47-53. Ac 4:24-28.

company. Is +47:12 (**S#2267h**).

by consent. Heb. with *one* shoulder, *or* to Shechem. 1 K 12:25. Zp 3:9mg.

lewdness. *or*, enormity. **S#2154h**. Le 18:17 (wickedness). 19:29. 20:14, 14. Jg 20:6. Jb 17:11 (purposes). 31:11 (heinous crime). Ps 26:10 (mischief). 119:150. Pr 10:23. 21:27mg. 24:9 (thought). Is 32:7. Je 13:27. Ezk 16:27, 43, 58. +22:9, 11. 23:21, 27, 29, 35, 44, 48, 49. 24:13.

10 **I have seen**. Je 2:12, 13. 5:30, 31. 18:13. 23:14.

there. Ho +4:11, 17. 5:3, 4. 1 K 12:28-30. 15:30. 2 K 17:7-23. Je 3:6-11. Ezk 23:5-11.

11 **harvest for thee**. Ho 8:7. 10:12, 13. Pr 22:8. Is 17:5-8. Je 51:33. Jl 3:12, 13. Mi 4:12. Mt +13:30, 39. Lk 3:17. Ga 6:7, 8. Re 14:14-20.

when. Ps +102:16, 22.

I returned the captivity. Jb 42:10. Ps 126:1, 4. Je +23:3. Ezk 20:34, 41. Zp 2:7. Ac +1:6.

HOSEA 7

1 **I would**. Je 51:9. Mt 23:37. Lk 13:34. 19:42.

the iniquity. Ho 4:17. 6:8-10. 8:9. 11:12. 12:14. 13:1, 2, 16. Is 28:1-3. Mi 6:16.

wickedness. Heb. evils. Ho 8:5. 10:5. Ezk 16:46, 51. 23:4. Am 8:14.

they commit. Ho 5:1. 6:10. 11:12. 12:1, 7. Is 59:12-15. Je 9:2-6. Mi 7:3-7.

the troop. Ho +6:9.

spoileth. Heb. strippeth. Is 32:11.

2 **consider not in**. Heb. say not to. Dt 32:29. Ps 50:22. Is 1:3. 5:12. 44:19. 57:1.

I remember. Ho 9:9. Ps 25:7. 90:8. Je 14:10. 17:1. Am 8:7. Lk 12:2, 3. 1 C 4:5. Re 20:12, 13.

their own. Nu +32:23. Jb 20:11-29. Ps 9:16. Pr 5:22. Is 26:16. Je 2:19. 4:18.
have beset. He 12:1.
are before. Jb 34:21. Ps 90:8. Pr 5:21. Je 16:17. 32:19. He 4:13.

3 They make. Ho 5:11. 1 K 22:6, 13. Pr 17:4. 20:26. 28:4. 29:12. Je 5:31. 9:2. 28:1-4. 37:19. Am 7:10-13. Mi 6:16. 7:3. Ro 1:32. 1 J 4:5.

4 are all. Ex +9:6.
adulterers. Ho +4:2, 12. Je 5:7, 8. 9:2. Ja 4:4.
as an oven. ver. 6, 7.
who ceaseth, etc. or, the raiser will cease.
raising. or, waking. Ps 73:20.

5 the day. Ge 40:20. Da 5:1-4. Mt 14:6. Mk 6:21, 22.
made. Pr +20:1. Is 5:11, 12, 22, 23. 28:1, 7, 8. Hab 2:15, 16. Ep +5:18. 1 P 4:3, 4.
bottles of wine. or, heat through wine. **S#2534h**. Ezk 3:14.
he stretched. 1 K 13:4.
with scorners. Ps +1:1. 69:12. Pr 13:20. 23:29-35. Da 5:4, 23.

6 they. ver. 4, 7. 1 S 19:11-15. 2 S 13:28, 29. Ps 10:8, 9. Pr 4:16. Mi 2:1.
made ready. or, applied. Is 41:21mg. Ezk 9:1.

7 devoured. Ho 8:4. 1 K 15:28. 16:9-11, 18, 22. 2 K 9:24, 33. 10:7, 14. 15:10, 14, 25, 30.
there. ver. 10, 14. Ho 5:15. Jb 36:13. Is 9:13. Je +10:25. Ezk 22:30. Da 9:13.

8 he hath. Ho 5:7, 13. 9:3. Ezr 9:1, 2, 12. Ne 13:23-25. Ps 106:34, 35. Je +10:2. Ezk 23:4-11. Ml 2:11.
a cake. Ho 8:2-4. 1 K 18:21. Zp 1:5. Mt 6:24. Re 3:15, 16.

9 Strangers. Ps +7:13.
devoured. Ho 8:7. 2 K 13:3-7, 22. 15:19, 29. Pr 23:35. Is 42:22-25. 57:1, 11.
here and there. Heb. sprinkled. Ezk 36:25.
knoweth it not. Jg 16:20.

10 the pride. Ho +5:5. Je 3:3.
and they. ver. 7. Ho 6:1. Dt 4:29. Pr 27:22. Is 9:13. Je 8:5, 6. 25:5-7. 35:15-17. Am 4:6-13. Zc 1:4.
nor. Ps 10:4. 14:2. 53:2. Je 3:10. Ro 3:11.

11 a silly. Ho 11:11.
without. Ho 4:11. Pr 6:32mg. 15:32mg. 17:16.
they call. Ho 5:13. 8:8, 9. 9:3. 12:1. 14:3. 2 K 15:19. 17:3, 4. Is 30:1-6. 31:1-3. Je 2:18, 36. Ezk 23:4-8.

12 I will spread. Jb 19:6. Je 16:16. Ezk 12:13. 17:20. 32:3. Mt +13:47.
I will bring. Ec 9:12.
as their. Le 26:14, etc., 28. Dt 27:14-26. 28:15, etc. 29:22-28. 31:16-29. 32:15-43. 2 K 17:13-18. Je 44:4. Re 3:19.
congregation. Ex +12:3.

13 Woe. Ho 9:12. Is 31:1. La 5:16. Ezk 16:23. Mt 23:13-29. Re 8:13.

have fled. Ho 11:2. Ge 3:8. Jb 11:12. 21:14, 15. 22:17. Ps 139:7-9. Je 2:5, 13. Jon 1:3, 10.
destruction. Heb. a spoil. Ho 9:6mg. Ezk 45:9. Am 3:10mg. Hab 1:3.
transgressed. Ho 14:9.
though. Dt 7:8. 9:26. 15:15. 21:8. 24:18. Ne 1:10. Ps 106:10. 107:2, 3. Is 41:14. 43:1-3. 63:8-10. Mi 6:4. 1 P 1:18, 19.
spoken. ver. 3. Ho 11:12. Is 59:13. Je 18:11, 12. 42:20. 44:17, 18. Ezk 18:2, 25. Ml 3:13-15. 1 J 1:10.

14 they have not. Jb 35:9, 10. Ps 78:34-37. Is +29:13. Je 3:10. Zc 7:5.
when. Is 52:5. 65:14. Am 8:3. Ja 5:1.
assemble. Ho 3:1. Ex 32:6. Jg 9:27. Is 58:5. Am 2:8. Mi 2:11. Ro 16:18. Ph +3:19. Ja 4:3.
rebel against. or, apostatized from. Ps 101:4. Pr 5:7. +22:6. Je 17:5. 32:40. Da 9:5, 11.

15 I have. 2 K 13:5, 23. 14:25-27. Ps 18:34. 106:43-45. 144:1.
bound. or, chastened. ver. 12. Jb 5:17. Ps 94:12, 13. Pr 3:11, 12. He 12:5-11. Re 3:19.
imagine. Ps 2:1. 62:3. Pr +21:30. Je +17:9. Na 1:9, 11. Ac 4:25. Ro 1:21. 2 C 10:5.

16 return. Ho 6:4. 8:14. 11:7. Ps 78:37. Je 3:10. Lk +8:13. 11:24-26.
most High. Ho 11:7.
like. Ps 78:57.
the rage. ver. 13. Ps 12:4. 52:2. 57:4. 73:9. Is 3:8. Je 18:18. Mt +12:36, 37. Ja 3:5-8. 2 P 2:8. Re 13:5, 6.
this. Ho 8:13. 9:3, 6. Ezk 23:32. 36:20.
land of Egypt. Ho 9:3, 6. Is 30:3, 5.

HOSEA 8

1 the trumpet. Ho 5:8. Is 18:3. 58:1. Je 4:5, 19. 6:1. 51:27. Ezk 7:14. 33:3-6. Jl 2:1, 15. Am +3:6. Zp 1:16. Zc 9:14. 1 C 15:52.
thy mouth. Heb. the roof of thy mouth. Jb +31:30mg.
He shall come. Dt 28:49.
as. Dt 28:49. Je 4:13. 48:40. Hab 1:8. Mt 24:28.
the house. Ho 9:15. 2 K 18:17. Am 8:3. 9:1. Zc 11:1. Ep 2:19-22. He 3:6. 1 P 2:5. 4:17.
transgressed. Ho 6:7. Is 24:5. Je 31:32. Ezk 16:59. He 8:8-13.
my covenant. Dt 4:13.

2 shall cry. Ho +5:15. 7:13, 14. Dt 4:29-31. 2 K 10:16, 29. 2 Ch 15:10-15. 20:21, 22. Jb 8:5-7. 22:23-30. Ps +50:15. 78:34-37. Is 48:1, 2. +65:24. Je 7:4. 36:7. Jl 2:15-19, 32. Mi 3:11. Zc 12:10. 13:9. Mt +7:21-23. 25:11, 12. Lk 13:25-27. T 1:16. 1 J 2:4.
we know thee. Is 29:13. Ezk 39:22. Jl 2:17, 27. Zc 13:9. Mt 7:22. 15:8. Jn +8:54, 55.

3 cast. Ps 36:3. 81:10, 11. Am 1:11. 1 T 5:12.
good. Ho 3:5. 14:2.
the enemy. Le 26:36. Dt 28:25. La 3:66. 4:19.

4 **set**. Ho 7:7. 1 K 12:16-20. 2 K 15:10-30, Shallum, Menahem, Pekahiah.
I knew it not. Ps 1:6. Mt 7:23. 25:12. Mk +13:32. Lk 13:25, 27. Jn 10:14. 1 C 8:3. Ga 4:9.
of. Ho 2:8. 13:2. 1 K 12:28. 16:31.
that they. Ho 13:9. 1 K 13:34. Je 44:7, 8. Ezk 18:31.

5 **calf**. ver. 6. Ex +32:4. Is 14:20. 45:20.
mine. Dt 32:22. 2 K 17:16-18, 21-23.
how. Je 13:27. Mt +17:17.

6 **from**. Ps 106:19, 20.
the workman. Ps +115:8. Ac 17:29. 19:26.
the calf. Ho 10:2, 5, 6. Je 43:12, 13. 50:2.
shall. 2 K 23:15, 19. 2 Ch 31:1. 34:6, 7.

7 **sown**. Ho 10:12, 13. Nu +32:23. Jb 4:8. Pr 22:8. Ec 5:16. Ga 6:7, 8.
it hath. Is 17:11. Je 12:13.
stalk. or, standing corn. Ex 22:6.
the strangers. Ho 7:9. Dt 28:33. Jg 6:3-6. 2 K 13:3-7. 15:19, 29.

8 **swallowed**. 2 K 17:1-6. 18:11. Ps +35:25. Je 50:17.
among. Le 26:33. Dt 28:25, 64.
a vessel. Is 30:14. Je 22:28. 48:38. 51:34. Ro 9:22. 2 T 2:20, 21.

9 **they**. Ho 5:13. 7:11. 2 K 15:19. Ezk 23:5-9.
a wild. Jb 39:5-8. Is 1:3. Je 2:24.
hath. Ho 2:5-7, 10-13. 12:1. 2 Ch 28:20, 21. Is 30:6. Ezk 16:33, 34.
lovers. Heb. loves. Pr 7:18.

10 **now**. Ho 10:10. Ezk 16:37. 23:9, 10, 22-26, 46, 47.
sorrow a little. or, begin to sorrow in a little while, as Hg 2:6.
for. 2 K 14:26. 15:19, 20. 17:3. 1 Ch 5:26.
the king. Is 10:8. 36:13. Ezk 26:7. Da 2:37.

11 **Ephraim**. Ho 4:17. Ps 106:15.
many. Ho 10:1, 2, 8. 12:11. Is 10:10, 11.
altars. Dt 4:28. Je 16:13.

12 **written**. Ex 17:14. 24:4, 7. 34:27. Nu 33:1, 2. Dt 4:6-8. Ne 9:13, 14. Ps 119:18. 147:19, 20. Pr 22:20, 21. Ezk 20:11, 12. Ro 3:1, 2. 7:12.
but. Ho 4:6. 2 K 17:15, 16. Ne 9:26. Ps 50:17. Is 30:9. Je 6:16, 17, +19. 8:8, 9. 44:16. Mk +7:9.

13 **They sacrifice**, etc. or, In the sacrifices of mine offerings, they sacrifice flesh and eat it. Je 7:21-23. Zc 7:6.
but. Ho 5:6. 9:4. 12:11. 1 S 15:22, 23. Pr 21:27. Is 1:11, 15. 66:3. Je 14:10-12. Am 5:22. 1 C 11:20, 29.
now will. Ho 9:9. Je +11:22. Am 8:7. Re 16:19.
they shall. Ho 2:15. 7:16. 9:3, 6. 11:5. Dt 28:68.

14 **forgotten**. Ho 13:6. Dt 32:18. Ps 106:21. Is 17:10. Je 2:32. 3:21. 23:27.
Maker. Ps 100:3. Is 29:23. 43:21. 64:8. Ep 2:10.

and buildeth. 1 K 12:31, 32. 16:31, 32. 2 Ch 23:17. 24:7.
and Judah. 2 Ch 26:10. 27:4. Is 22:8-11.
I will send. 2 K 18:13. Is 42:13, 25. Je +17:27.
his cities. 2 K 18:13.

HOSEA 9

1 **Rejoice**. Ho 10:5. Is 17:11. 22:12. La 4:21. Ezk 21:10. Am 6:6, 7, 13. 8:10. Ja 4:16. 5:1.
as. Ezk 16:47, 48. 20:32. Am 3:2.
gone. Ho +4:12. 5:4, 7.
thou hast loved. Ho 2:12. Je 44:17.
reward. Dt 23:18.
upon. or, in, etc.

2 **floor**. Ho 2:9, 12. Ge +50:10. Jl 1:3-7, 9-13. Am 4:6-9. 5:11. Mi 6:13-16. Hg 1:9. 2:16, 17.
winepress. or, winefat.
fail. lit. lie. Ge 18:15. Le 6:2.

3 **shall not dwell**. Dt 28:63. Mi +2:10. Zc 7:14.
the Lord's land. Dt +32:43. Zc 2:12. Ml 3:12.
but. ver. 6. Ho 8:13. 11:5. Dt 28:68. Is 11:15, 16.
and. Ezk 4:13. Da +1:8. Ac 10:14.
in Assyria. Ho 11:11. 2 K 17:6.

4 **shall not**. Ho 3:4. Jl 1:13. 2:14.
neither. Ho 8:13. Is 1:11-15. 57:6. 66:3. Je 6:20. Am 4:4, 5. 5:22. Ml 1:9, 10.
pleasing. Ho 8:13. Je 6:20.
bread. Ge +3:19.
of mourners. Nu 19:11, 14. Ne 8:9-12. Is +58:7. Ml 2:13.
their bread. Ex 40:23. Le +17:11. 21:6, 8, 17, 21. Nu 4:7. 28:2. Am 8:11, 12. Jn 6:51.
soul. Heb. nephesh, Ge +12:13.

5 **What**. Is 10:3. Je 5:31.
in. Ho 2:11. Jl 1:13.
solemn. Ge +17:21.

6 **they**. Dt 28:63, 64. 1 S 13:6. 2 K 13:7.
destruction. Heb. spoil. Ho 7:13mg.
Egypt. ver. 3. Ho 7:16. 8:13. 11:11. Is 11:11. 27:12. Zc 10:10, 11.
shall gather them up. Je 8:2. Ezk 29:5.
Memphis. i.e. gate of the blessed, **S#4644h**, only here.
the pleasant places for their silver, nettles. or, their silver shall be desired, the nettle shall, etc. Heb. the desire of. ver. 16mg. Is +32:12mg.
nettles. Ho 10:8. Jb +30:7. Ps 107:34. Is 5:6. 7:23. 32:13.
tabernacles. Ex +27:21.

7 **days of visitation**. Ex 32:34. Is 34:8. Je +8:12. Ezk 7:2-7. 12:22-28. Am 8:2. Zp 1:14-18. Lk 21:22. Re 16:19.
days of recompence. **S#7966h**. Is 34:8. Mi 7:3 (reward).
Israel. Is 26:11. Ezk 25:17. 38:23.
the prophet. ver. 8. Je 6:14. 8:11. 23:16, 17.

La 2:14. Ezk 13:3, 10. Mi 2:11. Zp 3:4. Zc 11:15-17.

spiritual man. Heb. man of the spirit. Heb. *ruach*, Is +48:16.

mad. 2 K 9:11. Mk 3:21. 2 T +1:7.

the multitude. Ezk 14:9, 10. 2 Th 2:10-12.

8 **watchman**. SS 3:3. Is 21:6-11. 62:6. Je 6:17. 31:6. Ezk +3:17, 18. 33:7. Mi 7:4. He 13:17.

with. 1 K 17:1. 18:1, 36-39. 22:28. 2 K 2:14, 21. 3:15-20. 4:1-7, 33-37, 41, 43. 5:14, 27. 6:17, 18. 7:2, 19. 13:21.

but. Ho 5:1. 1 K 18:19. 22:6, 11, 22, 23. Je 6:14. 14:13. La 2:14. 4:13, 14.

in the. *or*, against the. Jn 15:24. Ro 8:7.

9 **deeply**. Is 24:5. 31:6.

days. Ps +102:11.

Gibeah. Ex +24:4. Jg +19:12, 22-30. ch. 20, 21. 2 K 14:6. 22:8.

therefore. Ho 8:13.

10 **found**. Ho 11:1. Ex 19:4-6. Dt 32:10. Je 2:2, 3. 31:2.

grapes. Ho 2:15. Nu 13:23, 24. Is 28:4. Mi 7:1.

fig tree. Mt 21:19.

but. Nu 25:3. Dt 4:3. Ps 106:28.

Baal-peor. Nu 25:3. Dt 4:3. Ps 106:28.

separated. Ho 4:14. Jg 6:32. 1 K 16:31. Je 11:13. Ro 6:21.

that shame. Is +66:17. Je 3:24. 11:13.

and their. Nu 15:39. Dt 32:17. Ps 81:12. Je 5:31. Ezk 20:8. Am 4:5.

were according. *or*, became abominable like that which they loved. Je +2:5. 2 C 3:18.

as they loved. *or*, to their love.

11 **their**. Ge 41:52. 48:16-20. 49:22. Dt 33:17. Jb 18:5, 18, 19.

from the birth. Ps 58:8. 71:6. Ec 6:3. Am 1:13.

from the womb. ver. 14. Dt 28:18, 57. Ps 139:14-16. Lk 23:29.

conception. Ge 3:16. Ru 4:13. Je 1:5.

12 **yet**. ver. 13, 16. Le 26:22. Dt 28:32, 41, 62. 32:25. Jb 27:14. Je 15:7. 16:3, 4. La 2:20.

not. Nu 26:65. Jg 4:16.

woe. Ho 5:6. 7:13. Dt 31:17. 1 S 16:14. 28:15, 16. 2 K 17:18, 23.

depart. Ho 5:6. Ge +6:3.

13 **as**. Ezk ch. 26-28.

shall. ver. 16. Ho 10:14. 13:8, 16. 2 K 15:16. Je 9:21. Am 7:17.

14 **what**. ver. 13, 16. Mt 24:19. Mk 13:17. Lk 21:23. 23:29. 1 C 7:26.

wilt. Jn 6:62. Ac 23:9.

give them. Ro 3:4.

a miscarrying womb. Heb. a womb that casteth the fruit. Jb 21:10. Je 50:9.

15 **is in**. Jsh +4:19.

I hated. Le 26:30. Ezk 23:18. Zc 11:8.

I will drive. ver. 3, 17. Ho 1:6, 9. 3:4. 1 K 9:7-9. 2 K 17:17-20. Ps 78:60. Je 3:8. 11:15. 33:24-26. Am 5:27.

all. Ho 5:1, 2. Is 1:23. Je 5:5. Ezk 22:27. Mi 3:11. Zp 3:3. Ac 4:5-7, 27. 5:21.

revolters. *or*, apostates. lit. "turners aside." Ho 4:16. Dt 21:18 (stubborn), 20. Ps 78:8. Is 1:23. Zc 7:11. 1 T 4:1.

16 **their root**. ver. 11-13. Jb 18:16. Is 5:24. 40:24. Ml 4:1.

the beloved fruit. Heb. the desires. ver. 6mg. Ps +113:9. +127:3. Is +32:12mg. Ezk 24:21.

17 **My God**. 2 Ch 18:13. Ne 5:19. Ps 31:14. Is 7:13. Mi 7:7. Jn +20:17, 28. Ph 4:19.

cast them away. Is +54:7.

because. Ho 7:13. 1 K 14:15, 16. 2 K 17:14-20. 2 Ch 36:16. Ps 81:11-13. Pr 29:1. Is 48:18. Je 25:3, 4. 26:4-6. 35:15-17. Zc 1:4. 7:11-14. Ac 3:23.

not hearken. Je +29:19.

wanderers. Dt 28:64, 65. 32:36. 2 K 17:6, 18-20, 23. Am 8:2. 9:9. Jn 7:35. Ja 1:1.

HOSEA 10

1 Cir. A.M. 3264. B.C. 740.

Israel is. Is 5:1-7. Ezk 15:1-5. Na 2:2. Jn 15:1-6.

an empty vine. *or*, a vine emptying the fruit which it giveth. Jg 9:8-13. 2 K 4:39.

fruit. Ho 13:15. Jb +21:15. Is 1:5. Col 3:5. 1 J 5:17.

unto himself. Pr 13:7. Zc 7:5, 6. Lk 12:21. Ro 14:7, 8. 2 C 5:16. Ph 2:21.

to the multitude. Ho 2:8. 8:4, 11. 12:8, 11. 13:2, 6. 13:2, 6. Je 2:28.

images. Heb. statues, *or* standing images. 2 K +17:10mg. Is +66:17.

2 **Their heart is divided**. *or*, He hath divided their heart. Ho 7:8. 1 K 18:21. 2 K 17:32, 33, 41. Is 44:18. Zp 1:5. Mt 6:24. Lk 16:13. 2 Th 2:11, 12. Ja 1:8. 4:4. 1 J 2:15. Re 3:15, 16.

found faulty. *or*, held guilty. Ho 9:17.

he shall. Ex 23:24. 34:13. Dt 7:5. 12:3.

break down. Heb. behead. ver. 5-8. Ho 8:5, 6. 1 S 5:4. Je 43:13. Mi 5:13. Zc 13:2.

3 **We have**. ver. 7, 15. Ho 3:4. 11:5. 13:11. Ge +49:10. Mi 4:9. Jn 19:15.

4 **swearing**. Ho 6:7. 2 K 17:3, 4. Ezk 17:13-19. Ro 1:31. 2 T 3:3.

thus. Dt +29:18. Is 5:7. 59:13-15. He +12:15.

5 **Samaria**. ver. +7.

the calves. Ex +32:4.

Beth-aven. Jsh +7:2.

for the people. Jg 18:24. Re 18:11-19.

the priests. *or*, Chemarim. 2 K 23:5mg. Zp +1:4.

rejoiced. lit. leaped, or exulted. 1 K 18:26.

for the glory. Ho 9:11. 1 S 4:21, 22. Ac 19:27.

6 **carried**. Ho 8:6. Is 46:1, 2. Je 43:12, 13. Da 11:8.

present. Ho 5:13. 2 K 17:3.

receive. Ho 4:19. Is 1:29. 44:9-11. 45:16. Je 2:26, 27, 36, 37. 3:24, 25. 48:13. Ezk 36:31, 32.

ashamed. Ho 11:6. Jb 18:7. Is 30:3. Je 7:24. Mi 6:16.

7 **Samaria**. 1 K +16:24.

king. ver. 3, 15. 2 K 15:30. 17:4.

the water. Heb. the face of the waters. Ge +1:2. 7:18. Jb 24:18. Ju 13.

8 **high places**. ver. 5. Ho 4:15. 5:8. 2 K +21:3.

the sin. Dt 9:21. 1 K 12:28-30. 13:34. 14:16. Am 8:14. Mi 1:5, 13.

the thorn. Ho 9:6. Ge 3:18. Ex 22:6. Is 32:13. 34:13.

their altars. 1 K 13:2. 2 K 23:15. 2 Ch 31:1. 34:5-7.

they shall. Is 2:19. Lk *23:30*. Re *6:16*. 9:6.

mountains. Ge 49:22, 26. Jg 4:5.

9 **from**. Jg +19:12, 22-30.

the battle. Jg 20:17-48.

did not. Ge 6:5. 8:21. Zp 3:6, 7. Mt 23:31, 32.

10 **in my desire**. Dt 28:63. Is 1:24. Je 15:6. Ezk 5:13. 16:42.

and the. Ho 8:1, 10. Je 16:16. 21:4. Ezk 16:37. 23:9, 10, 46, 47. Mi 4:10-13. Zc 14:2, 3. Mt 22:7.

they, etc. *or*, I shall bind them for their two transgressions, *or*, in their two habitations.

two. Ho 3:5. 1 K 12:26-33. Is 5:20. Je 2:13.

furrows. **S#5869h**, Ge +24:13. Ho 2:10 (sight).

11 **an heifer**. Ho 4:16. Je 50:11. Mi 4:13.

and loveth. Ho 2:5. 3:1. 9:1. Dt 25:4. Ro 16:18.

but. Ho 11:4.

her fair neck. Heb. the beauty of her neck.

Judah. 2 Ch 28:5-8. Is 28:24.

12 **Sow**. Ho 8:7. Ps +126:5, 6. Pr 11:18. 18:21. Ec 11:6. Is 32:20. Ja 3:18.

reap. Ga 6:7-9.

break. Je 4:3, 4.

time. Dt 4:29. Ps 105:4. Is 31:1. 55:6. Je 29:12-14. 50:4, 5. Am 5:4, 6, 8, 14, 15. Zp 2:1-3. Lk 13:24, 25. 2 C 6:2. He 3:7.

rain. Ho 6:3. Dt 32:2. Ps 72:6. Is 5:6. 30:23. 44:3. 45:8. Ezk 34:26. Ac 2:18. 1 C 3:6, 7.

13 **plowed**. Ho 8:7. Jg 14:18. Jb 4:8. Pr 22:8. Ga 6:7, 8.

eaten. Pr 1:31. 12:19. 18:20, 21. 19:5.

didst. Ps 52:7. 62:10.

in the. Ps 33:16. Ec 9:11.

14 **shall a**. Ho 13:16. Is 22:1-4. 33:14. Am 3:8, 9. 9:5.

and all. 2 K 17:6. 18:9, 10. Is 17:3. Je 48:41. Mi +5:11. Na 3:12. Hab 1:10.

as. 2 K 18:33, 34. 19:11-13.

Shalman. i.e. *peaceable; he spoiled them; their peace offering*, **S#8020h**.

Beth-arbel. i.e. *house of the ambush of God*, **S#1009h**.

the mother. Ge 32:11. Ps +137:9.

15 **shall Bethel**. ver. 5. Am 7:9-17.

your great wickedness. Heb. the evil of your evil. Ro 7:13.

in a morning. ver. 3, 7. Is 16:14.

the king. 2 K 17:4, 23.

HOSEA 11

1 **Israel**. Ho 2:15. Dt 7:7, 8. +33:3. Je 2:2. Ezk 16:6, 22.

called. Ex 4:22, 23. Mt *2:15*. An illustration of the "law of double reference." See 2 S 7:12-16; Dt 18:15 with Ac 3:22, 23. Is 25:8. Je ch. 50, 51 w Re 18:9-21; Ge 3:15. Mt +16:23 ("law of double reference").

out of Egypt. Mt +2:14, 15.

2 **they called**. ver. 7. Dt 29:2-4. 1 S 8:7-9. 2 K 17:13-15. 2 Ch 36:15, 16. Ne 9:30. Is 30:9-11. Je 35:13. 44:16, 17. Zc 1:4-6. 7:11, 12. Lk 13:34. Jn 3:19-21. Ac 7:51, 52. 2 C 2:15, 16.

they sacrificed. Ho 2:13. 13:1, 2. Jg +2:11, 13. +6:25. 2 K 17:16.

burned. 1 K 12:33. Is 65:7. Je 18:15. 44:15.

3 **taught**. Ex 19:4. Nu 11:11, 12. Dt 1:31. 8:2. 32:10-12. Is 46:3. +63:9. Ac 13:18.

I healed. Ho 2:8. 7:1. 14:4. Ex 15:26. +23:25. Is 1:2. 30:26. Je +8:22. 30:17.

4 **drew**. Ps 73:28. 116:15. SS 1:4. Is +63:9. Je 30:21. 31:32. Mt 11:29. Jn +6:44. 12:32. 2 C 5:14.

of a man. 2 S 7:14.

I was. Le 26:13.

take off. Heb. lift up. Ge 14:22. Is 30:28.

and I laid. Ho 2:8. Ps 78:23-25. 105:40. Jn 6:32-58.

5 **shall not**. Ho 7:16. 8:13. 9:3, 6.

but. Ho 5:13. 10:6. 2 K 15:19, 29. 17:3-6. 18:11. Is 8:6-8. Am 5:27. "They became tributaries to Salmanasser."

because. Ho 6:1. 2 K 17:13, 14. 18:12. Je 8:4-6. Am 4:6, 8-10. Zc 1:4-6.

6 **the sword**. Ho 10:14. 13:16. Je +12:12. Mi 5:11.

consume. Ps 80:11-16. Is 9:14. 18:5. 27:10, 11. Ezk 15:2-7. 20:47. Ml 4:1.

because. Ho 10:6. Ps 106:39, 43. Is 30:1.

7 **are bent**. Ho 4:16. 14:4. Ps 78:57, 58. Pr 14:14. Je 3:6, 8, 11. 8:5. 14:7.

they called. ver. 2. Ho 7:16. Ex 2:23. 3:7. Jg 10:16. 2 K 13:23. 2 Ch 30:1-11. Ps 30:5. 78:38. 81:11. 103:11. 106:43-45. Je 31:20. La 3:22. Am 5:4-6, 14, 15. Mi 7:18, 19. Lk 15:20.

none at all would exalt him. Heb. together they exalted not. Is +12:4.

8 **How shall I give**. Ho 6:4. Je 9:7. La 3:33. Mt 23:37. Lk 19:41, 42.

Admah. Ge 14:2, 8. +19:24, 25. Re 11:8. 18:18.

Zeboim. Dt 29:23.

Mine. Jg 10:16. 2 K 13:23. Is +63:15. Je 3:12. +18:8.

heart. La 1:20.

within. Is +63:15.

repentings. Je +18:8.

9 **not execute**. Ho 14:4. Ex 32:10-14. Dt 32:26, 27. Ps 78:38. Is 27:4-8. 48:9. Je 30:11. 31:1-3. Ezk 20:8, 9, 13, 14, 21-23.

return. 1 S 26:8. 2 S 20:10.

for. Nu 23:19. Is 55:8, 9. Mi 7:18-20. Ml +3:6. Ro +11:28, 29.

not man. Is +57:15.

the Holy One. Is +1:4. Ezk 37:27, 28. Zp 3:15-17.

in the midst. Ex 33:5.

10 **walk**. Is 2:5. 49:10. Je 2:2. 7:6, 9. 31:9. Mi 4:5. Zc 10:12. Jn 8:12. Ro 8:1. 2 P 2:10.

he shall roar like. Am +1:2.

shall tremble. Jb 37:1. Ps 2:11. 119:120. Is 64:2. Je 5:22. 33:9. Hab +3:16. Ac 24:25.

west. Is 11:11. Zc 8:7.

11 **out**. Ho 3:5. 9:3-6. Is 11:11. Zc 10:10.

as a dove. Ho 7:11. Is 60:8.

and I. Je 31:12. 32:37. Ezk 28:25, 26. 36:33, 34. 37:21, 25. Am 9:14, 15. Ob 17.

12 **compasseth**. Ho 7:16. 12:1, 7. Ps 78:36. Is 29:13. 39:8. 44:20. 59:3, 4. Mi 6:12.

with deceit. Is 29:13. Ezk +33:31. Mt 15:8, 9. Mk 7:6, 7.

Judah. Ho 4:15. 2 K 18:4-7. 2 Ch 13:10-12. ch. 29-32.

ruleth. Ge 32:28. 1 C 6:2. Re 1:6. 3:21. 5:10.

saints. *or*, most holy. Jsh 24:19. Ps +149:9. Pr 30:3.

HOSEA 12

1 **feedeth**. Ho 8:7. Jb 15:2. Je 22:22.

east wind. Ge +41:6.

he daily. Ho 11:12.

and they. Ho 5:13. 7:11. 2 K 15:19. 17:4-6. Is 30:6, 7.

oil is carried. Ho 5:13. 2 K 17:4. Is 30:2-7. 57:9.

2 **a controversy**. Ho 4:1. Je 25:31. Mi 6:2.

and will. 2 K 17:19, 20. Is 8:7, 8. 10:6. Je 3:8-11. Ezk 23:11, etc., 31, 32.

punish. Heb. visit upon. Ho 2:13. 8:13. 9:9. Je +9:25mg.

according to his doings. Is 3:11. 59:18. Mt 16:27. Ro 2:6. Ga 6:7.

3 **took**. Ge 25:22, 26. *Ro 9:11-13*.

had, etc. Heb. was a prince, *or*, behaved himself princely. Ge 32:24-28. Ja 5:16-18.

4 **power**. Ge 32:28.

angel. ver. 5. Ge 32:29, 30. Zc +12:8.

made. Ge 32:9-12. He 5:7.

found. Ge 28:11-19. +35:9.

spake. Ps 66:6. 1 Th 4:17. He 6:13-18.

5 **Even**. Ge 28:16. 32:30. 35:7.

of hosts. Ps +24:10.

is his memorial. Ex 3:14, 15.

6 **turn**. Pr 1:23. Zc +1:3. Ac +2:38.

keep. Ho 4:1. Pr 21:3. Is 1:16, 17. 58:6-11. Je 22:15, 16. Am 5:24. Mi +6:8. Zc 7:9, 10. 8:16, 17. Ja 1:27. 2:13.

wait. Ps +25:3. Mk 15:43. Lk 23:51.

continually. 1 K 10:8. 1 Ch +16:11.

7 **a merchant**. *or*, Canaan. Ezk 16:3. Zc 14:21. Jn 2:16.

the balances. Le 19:35, 36. Pr 11:1. 16:11. Am 8:4-6. Mi 6:10, 11. 1 T 6:9, 10.

he loveth. Le 6:2. 19:13. Is 3:5. Ezk 22:29. Am 2:7. 3:9, 10. 4:1. 5:11, 12. Mi 2:1, 2. 3:1-3. 7:2, 3. Ml +3:5. Mt 23:14. Ja +5:4.

oppress. *or*, deceive. 1 S 12:3.

8 **Yet**. Jb 31:24, 25. Ps 49:6. 52:7. 62:10. Zc 11:5. Lk 12:19, 20. 16:13, 14. 1 T 6:5, 17. Re 3:17.

I have. Dt 8:17. Is 10:13, 14. Hab 1:16. 2:5, 6.

in all, etc. *or*, all my labors suffice me not; *he shall have* punishment of iniquity in whom *is* sin.

they. Pr 30:12, 20. Je 2:23, 35. Ml 2:17. 3:13. Lk 10:29. 16:15.

that. Heb. which.

9 **I that**. Ho 13:4. Ex 20:2. Le 19:36. 26:13. Nu 15:41. Ps 81:10. Mi 6:4.

yet. Ge 25:27. 2 S 7:2. 11:11. Je 35:7. He 11:9-13.

as in. Le +23:40-43.

tabernacles. Le +23:34, 39, 42. Lk 9:27, 33.

solemn feast. Ge +17:21. Le 23:2.

10 **have also**. 1 K 13:1, etc. 14:7-16. 17:1, etc. 18:21-40. 19:10. 2 K 17:13. Ne 9:30. Je 25:4. Am 7:14, 15. He 1:1. 2 P 1:21.

multiplied. Nu 12:6. Jl 2:28. Ac 2:17, 18. 2 C 12:1, 7.

used. Ho 1:2-5. 3:1. Is 5:1-7. 20:2-5. Je 13:1-14. 19:1, 10, 11. Ezk ch. 4, 5, 15. 20:49. 23:2, etc.

ministry. Heb. hand. 1 K +16:12mg.

11 **iniquity**. Ho 6:8. 1 K 17:1.

surely. Je 10:8, 15. Jon +2:8.

they sacrifice. Jsh +4:19.

their altars. Ho 8:11. 10:1. 2 K 17:9-11. Je 2:20, 28.

12 **Jacob**. Ge 27:43. 28:5. 29:1. Dt 26:5.

Israel. Ge 32:27, 28.

served. Ge 29:18-28. 31:41.

kept sheep. Ge 30:31.

13 **by a prophet**. Ho 13:4, 5. Ex 12:50, 51. 13:3. Nu 12:6-8. Dt 18:15. 1 S 12:8. Ps 77:20. Is 63:11, 12. Am 2:11, 12. Mi 6:4. Ac 3:22, 23. 7:35-37.

and by. Jn 6:32.

14 **provoked**. 1 K 12:25-13:5. 2 K 17:7-18. Ezk 23:2-10.

most bitterly. Heb. with bitternesses. Je 6:26.

therefore. 2 S 1:16. 1 K 2:33, 34. Ezk 18:13. 24:7, 8. 33:5.

blood. Heb. bloods. 2 K +9:26mg.

and his. Ho 7:16. Dt 28:37. 1 S 2:30. Da 11:18.

HOSEA 13

1 **Ephraim**. 1 S 15:17. Pr 18:12. Is 66:2. Lk 14:11.

spake. Jsh 4:14. Jb 29:21-25.

trembling. Je 49:24.

exalted. Nu 2:18-21. 10:22. 13:8, 16. 27:16-23. Jsh 3:7. 1 K 12:25. Lk 14:11.

offended. Ho 11:2. 1 K 16:29-33. 18:18, 19. 2 K 17:16-18.

died. Ge 2:17. Ro 5:12. 2 C 5:14.

2 **now**. Nu 32:14. 2 Ch 28:13. 33:23. Is 1:5. 30:1. Ro 2:5. 2 T 3:13.

sin more and more. Heb. add to sin. Jg 10:6. Is 7:10mg.

have made. Ho 2:8. 8:4. 10:1. Ps 115:4-8. Je 10:4.

molten images. Ex +34:17. 1 K 12:28.

according. Ho 10:6. 11:6. Ps 135:17, 18. Is 44:17-20. 45:20. 46:8. Je 10:8. Ro 1:22-25, 31. 1 C 2:14. 2 C 4:3, 4. Ep 4:17, 18.

the men that sacrifice. *or*, the sacrifices of men. Dt +18:10. Jsh 15:8. 1 K 12:26-33. Mi 6:7.

kiss. Ps +2:12. Ro 11:4.

calves. Ex +32:4.

3 **as the morning cloud**. Ho 6:4.

as the chaff. Ps 68:2. Je +13:24. Lk +3:17.

whirlwind. Je +23:19.

4 **I am**. Ho +12:9. Is 43:3, 10, 11. 44:6-8. 45:21. Ju 21.

for. Ac 4:12. Re +7:10.

5 **know**. Ex 2:25. Ps 1:6. 31:7. 142:3. Am 3:2. Na 1:7. 1 C 8:3. Ga 4:9.

in the wilderness. Dt 2:7. 8:15. 32:10. Je 2:2, 6.

great drought. Heb. droughts. Ps 63:1.

6 **According to**. Ho 10:1. Dt 8:12-14. 32:13-15. Ne 9:25, 26, 35. Je 2:31.

therefore. Ho 8:4. Dt 6:10-12. 8:12-14. 32:15, 18. Ps 10:4. Is 17:10. Je 2:32.

7 **I will be**. Is +5:29. Am +1:2.

8 **as a bear**. 2 S 17:8. Pr 17:12. Am 9:1-3.

wild beast. Heb. beast of the field. Ho 2:12, 18. Le 26:22. Ps 80:13. Is 5:29. 56:9. Je 12:9.

9 **thou**. Ho 14:1. Dt 32:5. 2 K 17:7-17. Ps 103:4. Pr 6:32. 8:36. Is 3:9, 11. Je 2:17, 19. 4:18. 5:25. Ml 1:9.

but. ver. 4. Dt 33:26. Ps 33:20. 46:1. 121:1, 2. 146:5. Ep 1:3-5. T 3:3-7.

is thine help. Heb. in thy help.

10 **I will be their king**. *or*, Where is thy king?

"King Hosea being then in prison, 2 K 17:4." Ps 10:16. 44:4. 47:6, 7. 74:12. 89:18. 149:2. Is 33:22. 43:15. Je 8:19. Zc 14:9. Jn 1:49.

where. ver. 4. Ho 10:3. Dt 32:37-39. Je 2:28.

thy judges. Ho 8:4. Jg 2:16-18. 1 S 8:5, 6, 19, 20. 12:11, 12. 1 K 12:20.

11 **I gave thee a king**. Ho 10:3. 1 S 8:7-9. 10:19. 12:13. 15:22, 23. 16:1. 31:1-7. 1 K 12:15, 16, 26-32. 14:7-16. 2 K 17:1-4. Pr 28:2.

12 **iniquity of Ephraim**. Dt 32:34, 35. Jb 14:17. 21:19. Ps 32:3, 5. Ro 2:5.

bound up. Dt 32:32, 35.

13 **sorrows**. Je +4:31. Mi 4:9, 10. Mt +24:8.

an unwise son. Pr +22:3. Ac 24:25.

for he. 2 K 19:3. Is 26:17, 18. 37:3. 66:8, 9. Ac 16:29-34. 2 C 6:2. He 3:7, 8.

stay. 2 K 4:6.

long. Heb. a time.

the breaking forth. 2 K 19:3.

14 **I will ransom**. Ho 6:2. Jb 19:25-27. 33:24. Ps +16:10. 30:3. 31:5. 49:7, 8, 15. 71:20. 86:13. 130:7, +8. Is 25:8. 29:22. Ezk 37:11-14. Ro 11:15.

them from. Ezk +16:49, 55, 60. Ac 3:21. Ju 7.

power. Heb. hand.

of the grave. Heb. *sheol*, Ge +37:35. Ezk 37:12. Ac 2:31, 32. Re 1:18.

redeem. S#1350h. Ex 6:6. Nu 5:8. Ru 2:20mg. 3:9mg, 13 (kinsman). 4:4, 6, 14mg. 1 K 16:11. Jb 19:25. Is +43:1. 51:10. 52:3. 63:4. Je 31:11. 32:7, 8. He 2:14, 15.

O death. Is +26:19. 1 C 15:21, 22, +55. 2 C 5:4. Ph 3:21. 1 Th 4:14-17. Re 20:13, 14. 21:4.

O grave. Heb. *sheol*, Ge 37:35. Dt +32:1.

repentance shall be hid. Nu 23:19. 1 S 15:29. Je 15:6. Ml +3:6. Ro 11:29. Ja 1:17.

mine eyes. Ps +11:4.

15 **Though**. Ho 10:1.

he be fruitful. Ge 41:52. 48:19. 49:22. Dt 33:17.

an east wind. Ho 4:19. Ge +41:6. Ps 1:4. Je +23:19.

his spring. Ho 9:11-16. Dt 33:28. Jb 18:16-19. Ps 109:13. Pr 5:18. Is 14:21, 22.

fountain. Heb. *mayan*, Ge +7:11. Pr 5:16.

pleasant vessels. Heb. vessels of desire. Je +25:34mg.

16 **Samaria**. "Fulfilled 2 K 17:6, 18." 2 K 8:12. 15:16. Is 17:3. Am 9:1-4. Mi 6:16.

rebelled. or, been bitter. S#4784h. Nu 20:24. 27:14. Dt 21:18, +21. 1 S 12:15. 1 K 13:21, 26. Ps 5:10. 105:28. Is 1:20. 50:5. 63:10. Je 4:17. La 1:18, 20. 3:42.

their infants. Ps +137:9.

ripped up. 2 K +8:12.

HOSEA 14

1 **return**. Ho 5:15. 8:2. Zc +1:3.

thou. Ho 13:9. Je 2:19. La 5:16. Ezk 28:14-16.

2 **Take with you words**. Ho 8:2. Le 26:40. 1 K 8:33. Jb 34:31, 32. Pr 28:13. Jl 2:17. Mt 6:9-13. Lk 18:13. 1 J 1:9.
say. Ps 60:1. Is 30:19.
Take away. 2 S +12:13. Is 44:22. Ezk 36:25, 26. Mi 7:19. Zc 3:4. +13:9. Jn 1:29. Ro 11:27. T 2:14. 1 J 1:7. 3:5.
receive, etc. *or*, give good. Mt 7:11. Lk 11:13. 15:21-24. Ep 1:6, 7. 2:7, 8. 2 T 1:9.
graciously. *or*, O Gracious One. Ho 3:5. 8:3.
render. Ps 66:13, 14. 116:14, 18. Jon 2:9.
the calves. Ps 51:17. He 13:15.
lips. Dt +17:6. Ps 69:30, 31. 116:17. 141:2. Ro 10:9, 10. He *13:15*. 1 P 2:5, 9.

3 **Asshur**. Ho 5:13. 7:11. 8:9. 12:1. 2 Ch 16:7. Ps 146:3. Je 31:18, etc.
we will not. Dt 17:16. Ps 20:7, 8. 33:17. Is 30:2, 16. 31:3. 36:8.
neither. ver. 8. Ho 2:17. Is 1:29. 2:20. 27:9. Ezk 36:25. 37:23. 43:7-9. Mi 5:10-14. Zc 13:2.
for. Ex +22:22-24. Jn 14:18mg.

4 **heal their backsliding**. Ho 11:7. Ex +15:26. Is 43:25. 48:9, 11. 57:18. 59:2. Je 3:12, 22. 5:6. 8:22. 14:7. 17:14. 33:6. Mt 9:12, 13. 1 J 1:9.
I will love. Dt 7:7, 8. Zp 3:17. Ro 3:24. Ep 1:6, 7. 2:4-9. 2 T 1:9. T 3:4-7.
for. Nu 25:4, 11. Ps 78:38. Is 12:1. 2 C 5:19-21.

5 **as the dew**. Ho 6:4. 13:3. Dt +33:13. Ps 133:3. Is +26:19. 44:3.
he shall. Ho 6:3. SS 2:1, 2, 16. 4:5. Mt 6:28, 29. Lk 12:27.
grow. *or*, blossom. Ps 72:16. 92:12. Is 27:6. 35:2.
cast. Heb. strike. 2 K 19:30.
roots. Jb 29:19. Ep 3:17.

6 **branches**. Ps 80:9-11. Ezk 17:5-8. 31:3-10.

Da 4:10-15. Mt 13:31, 32. Jn 15:1, etc. Ro 11:16-24.
spread. Heb. go. 2 Ch 26:8mg.
and his beauty. Ps 52:8. 128:3.
his smell. Ge 27:27. SS 4:11-15. 2 C 2:14, 15. Ph 4:18.

7 **that dwell**. Ps +91:1.
revive. Ho 6:2. Ps 85:6. 138:7. Is 61:11. Jn 11:25. 12:24. 1 C 15:36-38.
grow. *or*, blossom. ver. 5mg. SS 6:11. Zc 8:12.
scent. *or*, memorial. Ho 12:5.
wine. SS 1:2, 3.

8 **What have**. ver. 2, 3. Jg +11:12. Jb 34:32. Ac 19:18-20. 2 C 6:16. 1 Th 1:9. 1 P 1:14-16. 4:3, 4.
with idols. Ps 96:5. 97:7. Is 2:6, 8, 18, 20, 22. 17:7, 8. Zc 10:2. Jn 5:43. Re 9:20.
I have heard. Jb 33:27. Je 31:18-20. Lk 10:39. 15:20.
observed. Jn 1:47, 48. 2 C 3:18.
I am. Is 41:19. 55:13. 60:13.
From me. Is 45:24. Jn 1:16. 15:1-8. Ga 5:22, 23. Ep 5:9. Ph 1:11. 2:13. 4:13. Ja 1:17.

9 **wise**. Ps 107:43. Pr 1:5, 6. 4:18. Je 9:12. Da +11:33. +12:10. Mt 13:11, 12. Lk 1:17. Jn 8:47. 18:37.
prudent. Pr +22:3.
for the ways. Ps 25:10.
are right. Ho 6:5. Ge +18:25. Dt 32:4. Jb 26:14. 34:10-12, 18, 19. 36:23. Ps 18:30. 19:7, 8. 77:19. 119:75, 128. 145:17. Pr 10:29. Ezk 18:25. 33:17-20. Da 4:37. Zp 3:5. Ro 7:12.
the just shall walk. Jb 17:9. Ps 84:5, 7. Pr 10:29. Is 8:13-15. Mt 11:19. Lk 1:17.
but. Ex 14:20. 1 S 5:11. Ps 119:165. Pr +4:19. 10:29. 11:5. 15:9. Da +12:10. Mi 2:7. Na 3:3. Mt 21:44. Lk 2:34. 4:28, 29. 5:8. 7:23. Jn 3:19, 20. 8:9. 9:39. 15:24. Ro 9:32, 33. 1 C 1:23, 24. 2 C 2:15, 16. 7:10. 2 Th 2:9-12. 1 P 2:6-8.

JOEL

JOEL 1

1 A.M. 3204. B.C. 800.
word. Je 1:2. Ezk 1:3. Ho 1:1. Ac 1:16.
2 P 1:21.
to. Ac 2:16.
Pethuel. i.e. *man of God*, S#6602h, only
here.

2 **Hear**. Dt 32:1. Ps 49:1. Is 34:1. Je 5:21. Ho
5:1. Am 3:1. 4:1. 5:1. Mi 1:2. 3:1, 9. Mt 13:9.
Re 2:7.
ye old. Jb 8:8. 12:12. 15:10. 21:7.
land. lit. earth. Ho +1:2.
Hath. Jl 2:2. Dt 4:32-35. Is 7:17. Je 30:7. Da
+12:1. Mt 24:21.

3 **Tell ye your children**. Ex 10:1, 2. 13:14. Dt
4:9. 6:6, 7. 11:19. Jsh 4:6, 7, 21, 22. Ps 44:1.
71:18. 78:3-8. 145:4. Is 38:19.

4 **That which the palmer worm hath left**.
Heb. The residue of the palmer-worm. Jl 2:25.
Ex 10:4. Am 4:9.
the locust eaten. Ps +78:46.
the canker-worm eaten. Na 3:15-17.
the caterpillar. 1 K +8:37.

5 **Awake**. Is 24:7-11. Am 6:3-7. Lk 21:34-37.
Ro 13:11-14.
howl. ver. 11, 13. Is +13:6.
for. Is 32:10-12. Lk 16:19, 23-25.

6 **nation**. Jl 2:2-11, 20, 25. Pr 30:25-27.
my land. Dt +32:43. Ps 107:34. Is 8:8. 32:13.
Ho 9:3.
whose. Pr 30:14. Re 9:7-10.

7 **laid my vine**. ver. 12. Ex 10:15. Ps 80:8, 13,
14. 105:33. Is 5:1-6. 24:7. 27:2. Je 8:13. Ho
2:12. 10:1. Hab 3:17.
barked my fig tree. Heb. *laid* my fig tree for
a barking. Ho 9:10. Mt 21:19. Lk 13:6, 7.

8 **Lament**. ver. +13-15. Jl 2:12-14. Is 24:7-12.
62:5. Je 9:17-19. Ja 4:8, 9. 5:1.
the husband. Pr 2:17. Je 3:4. Ml 2:15.

9 **meat offering**. ver. 13, 16. Le +23:13.
drink offering. Le +23:13. Ho 9:4.
the priests. Jl 2:17. La 1:4, 16.
the Lord's. Ex 28:1. 2 Ch 13:10. Is 61:6.
ministers. Nu 3:6.

10 **field**. ver. 17-20. Le 26:20. Is 24:3, 4. Je 12:4,
11. 14:2-6. Ho 4:3.

the new wine. ver. 5, 12. Jl 2:19, 24. Is 24:7,
11. Je 48:33. Ho 9:2. Hg 1:11.
dried up. *or*, ashamed. ver. 11. Je 2:26.
languisheth. Is 16:8.

11 **ashamed**. ver. 10mg. Je 14:3, 4. Ro 5:5.
because. Is 17:11. Je 9:12.

12 **The vine**. ver. 10. Hab 3:17, 18.
the pomegranate. Nu 13:23. Ps 92:12. SS
2:3. 4:13. 7:7-9.
joy. ver. 16. Ps 4:7. Is 9:3. 16:10. 24:11. Je
48:33. Ho 9:1, 2.

13 **Gird**. ver. 8, 9. Jl 2:17. Je 4:8. 9:10. Ezk 7:18.
ye ministers. Ex 30:20. 1 C 9:13. He 7:13,
14.
lie. 2 S 12:16. 1 K 21:27. Jon 3:5-8.
sackcloth. Jb +16:15.
ye ministers. Is 61:6. 1 C 4:1. 2 C 3:6. 6:4.
11:23.
for. ver. 9. Le 2:8-10. Nu 29:6.
meat offering. Le +23:13.
drink offering. Le +23:13.

14 **Sanctify**. Jl 2:15, 16. Mt +6:16.
solemn assembly. *or*, day of restraint. Jl
2:15. Le +23:36.
the elders. Dt 29:10, 11. Jsh +20:4. 2 Ch
20:13. Ne 9:2, 3.
cry. Jon 3:8.

15 **Alas**. Jg +6:22.
for the day. Jl 2:2. Dt +4:32. Je +30:7. Am
5:16-18.
the day of the Lord. Jl 2:1. Ps 37:13. Ezk
7:2-12. 12:22-28. +30:3. Lk 19:41-44. Ja 5:9.

16 **the meat**. ver. 5-9, 13. Am 4:6, 7.
joy. Dt 12:6, 7, 11, 12. 16:10-15. Ps 43:4.
105:3. Is 62:8, 9.

17 **seed**. Heb. grains.

18 **the beasts groan**. ver. 20. 1 K 18:5. Je 12:4.
14:5, 6. Ho 4:3. Ro 8:22.

19 **to thee**. Ps +50:15. 91:15. Mi 7:7. Hab 3:17,
18. Lk 18:1, 7. Ph 4:6, 7.
the fire. Jl 2:3. Je 9:10. Am 7:4.
pastures. *or*, habitations. Jl 2:22. Ps 65:12.

20 **cry**. Jb 38:41. Ps 104:21, +27. 145:15. 147:9.
the rivers. Jl 3:18. 2 S 22:16. 1 K 17:7. 18:5.
Ezk +31:12.
dried up. Is 5:13. Am 4:8.

JOEL 2

1 **Blow**. ver. 15. Nu 10:3, 8, 9.
trumpet. *or*, cornet. Le +23:24. 1 Ch 15:28. Ho +8:1.
and sound. Nu 10:5-7, 9.
in my. Jl 3:17. Ps 87:1. Da 9:16, 20. Zp 3:11. Zc 8:3.
holy mountain. or, mountain of my sanctuary. Is 60:13. Ezk +37:26. 40:2. Zc 1:16. 6:12, 13.
let. Ezr 9:3, 4. Ps 119:120. Is 66:2, 5. Je 5:22. 10:7, 10. Da 6:26. Ph 2:12.
for the day of the Lord. ver. 11, 31. Jl 1:15. Ezk 7:5-7, 10, 12. 12:23. +30:3. Am 8:2. 1 C +3:13. Ja 5:9. 1 P 4:7.

2 **A day of darkness**. ver. 10, 31. Jl 3:14, 15. Ex +10:22. Am 5:18-20.
clouds. Ge +9:13. Ezk +30:3. 34:12.
as the morning. Am 4:13.
a great. ver. 5, 11, 25. Jl 1:6.
there hath not been. Jl 1:2, 3. Ex 10:6, 14. Je 30:7. Da +12:1. Mt 24:21. Mk 13:19.
ever. Heb. *olam*, Ps +5:11.
many generations. Heb. generation and generation. Ps +33:11mg.

3 **fire**. Jl 1:19, 20. Ps 50:3. Am 7:4.
devoureth before. Is 24:6, 10. Re 9:16.
the land. Ge 2:8. 13:10. Is 51:3. Ezk 28:13. 31:8, 9. 36:35.
and behind. Jl 1:4-7. Ex 10:5, 15. Je 5:17. Zc 7:14.
desolate wilderness. Jl 3:19. Ps 107:34mg.

4 **as the appearance**. Hab 1:8. Re 9:7.

5 **the noise**. Na 2:3, 4. 3:2, 3. Re 9:9.
like the noise of a. Is 5:24. 30:30. Mt 3:12.
a strong people. ver. 2.

6 **all**. Ps 119:83. Is 13:8. Je 8:21. +30:6. La 4:8.
blackness. Heb. pot.

7 **They shall run**. 2 S 1:23. 2:18, 19. Ps 19:5. Is 5:26-29.
climb. ver. 9. 2 S 5:8. Je 5:10.
they shall march. Pr 30:27.

8 **sword**. or, dart. 2 Ch 23:10. 32:5mg. Ne 4:17, 23. Jb 33:18. 36:12. SS 4:13.

9 **enter**. Ex 10:6. Je 9:21. Jn 10:1.
windows. Is 24:10. Je 9:21.
like a thief. Mt 24:43, 44. Lk 12:39. 1 Th 5:2. 2 P 3:10.

10 **earth**. Ps +97:4. He +12:26. Re 20:11.
the heavens. Is +34:4.
the sun. ver. 2, 31. Jl 3:15. Mt +24:29.
dark. Ex +10:22.

11 **utter**. 2 S 22:14, 15. Ps 46:6. Is 7:18. Am +1:2.
his army. *ver. 25*.
he is. Je 50:34. Re 18:8.
the day of the Lord. ver. +1, 31. Je +30:7. Ezk +30:3.
who. Nu 24:23. Je 10:10. Na 1:6. Zp 1:14. Ml 3:2. Re 6:17.

12 **now**. Ac 17:30. 2 C 6:2.
turn. 2 Ch 7:13, +14. Je 29:12, 13. Ho 5:15. Zc +1:3.
with all your heart. Dt +6:5. 2 K +20:3. 1 Ch 12:38. Ps 95:7, 8.
with fasting. ver. 15. Mt +6:16.
weeping. Lk +6:21.
with mourning. Is 22:12. Da 10:12. Mt +5:4.

13 **rend**. 2 K 22:19. Ps 34:18. 51:17. 147:3. Is 57:15. 66:2. Ezk 9:4. Mt +5:3, 4.
not your garments. 2 K +18:37. Is 58:5. Mt 6:16-18. 1 T 4:8.
he is gracious. Ex +34:6, 7. Ro 2:4.
and merciful. Jon 4:2.
slow. Ne 9:17. Ps 103:8. Na 1:3. Ja 1:19, 20. 2 P +3:9.
and repenteth. Je +18:8. 2 C 12:10.

14 **Who**. Ex 32:30. Jsh 14:12. 1 S 6:5. 2 K 19:4. Jon +3:9. Zp 2:3. 2 T 2:25.
and leave. Is 65:8. Hg 2:19. 2 C 9:5-11mg.
even. Jl 1:9, 13, 16.
meat offering. Le +23:13.
drink offering. Le +23:13.

15 **Blow**. ver. +1.
sanctify a fast. ver. +12. Jl 1:14. 1 K 21:9, 12. Je 36:9.
solemn. Le +23:36.

16 **sanctify**. Ex 19:10, 14, 15, 22. Jsh 7:13. 1 S 16:5. 2 Ch 29:5, 23, 24. 30:17, 19. 35:6. Jb 1:5.
assemble. Jl 1:14. Dt 29:10, 11. 2 Ch 20:13. Jon 3:7, 8.
gather the children. Dt +29:11.
let. Zc 12:11-14. Mt 9:15. 1 C 7:5.
closet. Ps 19:5. Is 4:5.

17 **the priests**. Jl 1:9, 13.
between. 1 K 6:3. 2 Ch 8:12. Ezk 8:16. Mt 23:35.
and let. Ho 14:2.
Spare. Ex 32:11-13. 34:9. Dt 9:16-29. Ne 13:22. Ps 118:25. Is 37:20. 64:9-12. Da 9:18, 19. Am 7:2, 5. Ml 1:9.
and give. Ps 44:10-14. 74:10, 18-23. 79:4. 89:41, 51. Ezk 36:4-7.
thine heritage. Dt 32:9.
that. Ne 9:36, 37. Is 63:17-19.
rule over them. *or*, use a by-word against them. Dt +28:37.
wherefore. Nu 14:14-16. Dt 9:26-29. 32:27. Ps 42:10. 79:10. 115:2. Ezk 20:9. 39:22. Mi 7:10. Mt 27:43.

18 **Then**. ver. 12, 17, 28. Ezk 36:25. 39:28. Ho 5:15.
be jealous. Ex +20:5.
his land. Dt +32:43.
and pity. Dt 32:16, 36, 43. Jg 10:16. Ps 103:13, 17. Is 60:10. 63:9, 15. Je 31:20. La 3:22. Ezk 36:21. Ho 11:8, 9. Lk 15:20. Ja 5:11.
his people. Dt +32:43.

19 **will answer**. Is +65:24.

I will send. ver. 24. Jl 1:10. Is 62:8, 9. 65:21-24. Ezk 36:29. Ho 2:15, 22. Am 9:13, 14. Hg 2:16-19. Zc 9:17. Ml 3:10-12.

be satisfied. ver. 26. Ps 81:13, 16. Mt 6:33.

and I. Ezk 34:29. 36:15. 39:29. Zp 3:19, 20.

20 remove. ver. 2-11. Jl 1:4-6. Ex 10:19. Is +59:19. Ezk 39:2-4.

the northern army. Je +1:14, 15. Da +11:40-45. Ezk 38:6, 15. 39:2. Re 9:3-11, 13-19.

will drive him. Is 59:19.

the east sea. Ge 14:13. Nu 34:3, 12. Dt 3:17. 4:49. Jsh 3:16. 12:3. 15:25. 18:19. 2 K 14:25. Ezk 47:7, 8, 18. Zc 14:8.

the utmost sea. or, western. Dt 11:24. 34:2. Zc 14:8.

his stink. Is +66:24. Ezk 39:12-16.

because. 2 K 8:13.

he. Da ch 7, 8.

done. Heb. magnified to do. Ps +126:2mg, 3. Je 48:26. Da +8:11, 25. +11:36. 2 Th 2:4. Re 13:5-7.

21 Fear not. Ge 15:1. Is 41:10. 54:4. Je 30:9, 10. Zp 3:16, 17. Zc 8:15.

be glad. Ps 65:12, 13. 96:11, 12. 98:8. Is 35:1, 2. 44:23. 55:12, 13. Ho +2:15, 21, 22.

for the Lord. ver. 20. Dt 4:32. 1 S 12:16, 24. Ps 71:19. +126:1-3. Je 33:3.

22 Be not afraid. Jl 1:18-20. Ps 36:6. 104:11-14, 27-29. 145:15, 16. 147:8, 9. Is 11:6-9. 30:23, 24. 65:25. Ezk 34:25. Ho +2:18. Jon 4:11. Ro 8:19-21.

for the pastures. Jl 1:19. Ps 65:12. Is 51:3.

for the tree. Le 26:4, 5. Ps 67:6. 107:35-38. Ezk 34:26, 27. 36:8, 30, 35. Ho 14:5-7. Am 9:14, 15. Hg 2:16-20. Zc 8:12. Ml 3:10-12.

yield. Ge 4:12. Ro 8:19-23. 1 C 3:7. Re 22:3.

strength. Ge +34:29.

23 Be glad. Is 65:18.

ye children of Zion. Ps 149:2. La 4:2. Zc 9:13. Ga 4:26, 27.

rejoice. Dt +12:7. Ps 28:7. 33:1. 95:1-3. 104:34. Is 41:16. 61:10. Zc +2:10. 9:9. 10:7. Lk 1:46, 47.

the former rain. or, a teacher of righteousness. ver. 28, 29. Dt 32:2. Jb 33:23. Ps 72:6, 7. Is 30:21, 23. Da +11:33. Ho 10:12. Ep 4:8-11.

moderately. Heb. according to righteousness. or, in due measure. Le 26:4. Dt 11:14. 28:12.

he will. Le 26:4. Dt +11:14. 28:12. Pr 16:15. Je 3:3. 5:24. Ho +6:3. Zc 10:1. Ja 5:7, 8.

in the first. Ge 8:13. Nu 9:5. Ezk 29:17. 45:18, 21. Am 4:7. or, as at the first. Is 1:26. Ho +2:15. Ml 3:4.

24 the floors. Jl 3:13, 18. Ge +50:10. Le 26:10. Dt +16:13mg. Pr 3:9, 10. Am 9:13. Ml 3:10.

the fats. Jl 3:13. Is 5:2.

25 I will restore. Jb 42:10mg. Pr 22:4. Is 54:4. 61:7. Ezk 18:22. Zc 10:6. Mt +19:28. Ac +3:19, 21. Ro 8:19-23.

the years. Jb 42:10. Ps 31:15. +90:12. +91:16. Is +38:10. 61:7.

that the locusts. Ps +78:46.

my great army. ver. 2-11, 20.

26 ye shall eat. Le 26:5, 26. Dt 6:11, 12. 8:10. Ne 9:25. Ps 22:26. 103:5. Pr 13:25. SS 5:1. Is 55:2. 62:8, 9. Mi 6:14. Zc 9:15, 17. 1 T 6:17.

and praise. Le 19:24. Dt 12:7, 12, 18. 16:11. 26:10, 11. 1 T 4:3-5.

that he. ver. 20, 21. Ge 33:11. Ps 13:6. 72:18. 116:7. 126:2, 3. Is 25:1.

my people. Dt +32:43.

never be ashamed. Ps 25:2, 3, 20. 31:17. 37:19. 69:6. Is 29:22, 23. 45:17. 49:23. 54:4. Zp 3:11. Ro 5:5. 9:33. 10:11-13. Ph 1:20. 1 J 2:28.

27 ye shall know. ver. 17. Jl 3:17. Le 26:11-13. Dt 23:14. Ps 9:16. Ezk +39:22. Ho 8:2.

in the midst. Jl 3:17. Le 26:11, 12. Dt 23:14. Ps 46:5. 68:18. Is +12:6. Ezk 37:26-28. Zp 3:5, 15, 17. Zc 2:5. 2 C 6:16. Re 21:3.

that I am the Lord. Is +45:5. 52:6. 53:6. Ezk +39:22, 28.

my people. Dt +32:43.

shall never be ashamed. ver. 26. 1 P 2:6.

28 And it shall. Zc 13:4. Ac 2:17-21.

afterward. ver. +18. Ge 12:3. Is +32:15. +55:3. Ezk 36:25. Mi 4:1, 2. Zc 8:3, 22, 23. Ac +3:19, 21.

that I. Pr 1:23. Is 32:15. 44:3. Ezk 39:29. Jn 7:39. Ac 2:16-18. 1 C 12:8. Ep 4:8, 11.

pour out. Ps +79:6. Je +2:13. Zc 12:10.

spirit. Heb. ruach, Ge +41:38.

all flesh. Is 49:6. Lk +3:6. Ac 2:2-4, 33, 39. 10:44-47. 11:15-18. 15:7, 8.

your daughters. Is 54:13. Hab 2:14. Ac 21:9. Ga 3:28. He +8:11. 1 J 2:20.

shall prophesy. Ex +15:20. Nu 11:16, 17, 29. Ac 21:9. 1 C 11:5, 13.

dream. Ge 37:5-10. Nu 12:6. Je 23:28.

29 upon the servants and. 1 C 7:21. 12:13. Ga 3:28. Col 3:11.

pour out. Ps +79:6. Je +2:13.

spirit. Heb. ruach, Ge +41:38.

30 show wonders in the heavens. Mt +24:29.

pillars of smoke. Re +14:11.

31 The sun shall. ver. 10. Jl 3:1, 15. Mt 24:29. 27:45. Mk 13:24, 25.

the moon into. Re 6:12.

before. Ml 4:5.

the great and terrible. ver. 11. Zp +1:14. Ml 4:1, 5.

day of the Lord. ver. +1, +11.

32 whosoever shall call. Ps +50:15. Is 55:6, 7. Je 33:3. Zc 13:9. Ac 2:21. Ro 10:11-14. 1 C 1:2.

delivered. Is 57:1. Lk +21:36. Ro 10:13. 1 Th 4:17.

for in mount Zion. Is +24:23. 46:13. Ob 17, 21. Zc 14:1-5. Jn 4:22. Ro 11:26.

shall be deliverance. Na 1:2. Lk +21:36. 1 Th +1:9, 10. 5:9.

and in the remnant. Mi +5:3. Jn +10:16. Ac 2:39. 15:17. Ro 8:28-30.

shall call. 2 T +1:9.

JOEL 3

1 in those days. Jl 2:29. Da +12:1. Zp 3:19, 20.

when. Jl +2:25. 2 Ch 6:37, 38. Jb 42:10. Ps 126:1, 4. Je +23:3. Ezk 16:53. 38:14-18.

2 also gather. Zp 3:8. Zc +12:2. 14:2-4. Re 16:14, 16. 19:19-21. 20:8.

the valley of Jehoshaphat. ver. 12. 2 Ch 20:21-26. Ezk 39:11. Zc 14:4.

will plead. Is 66:16. Je 25:31. Ezk 38:22. Am 1:11. Ob 10-16. Zc 12:3, 4. Re 11:18. 16:6. 18:20, 21.

My people. Dt +32:43. Ho 2:23. Mt 25:31-46.

My heritage. Dt 32:9.

Israel. Ezk 37:22.

and parted my land. Je 12:14. 49:1. Ezk 25:8. 35:10. Zp 2:8-10.

3 They have. Ob 16. Na 3:11.

cast lots. Jsh +14:2. 2 Ch 28:8, 9. Am 2:6. Ob 11. Na 3:10. Re 18:13.

4 and what. Jg +11:12. 2 Ch 21:16. 28:17, 18. Ac 9:4.

O Tyre. Am 1:6-10, 12-14. Zc 9:2-8.

Palestine. i.e. land of wanderers, S#6429h. Ex 15:14. Ps 60:8. 83:7. 87:4. 108:9. Is 14:29, 31.

will ye. Ezk 25:12-17.

swiftly. Dt 32:35. Is 34:8. 59:18. Je 51:6. Lk 18:7. 2 Th 1:6. He 10:30.

5 ye. 2 K 12:18. 16:8. 18:15, 16. 24:13. 25:13-17. Je 50:28. 51:11. Da 5:2, 3.

into. 1 S 5:2-5.

pleasant. Heb. desirable. Is +32:12mg.

6 children of. Ge +11:5.

sold. ver. 3, 8. Le +25:39. Ezk +27:13.

Grecians. Heb. sons of the Grecians.

7 I will raise. Is 49:12. Je +23:3, 8. 30:10, 11, 16.

and will. ver. 4. Ge +6:13. Jg 1:7. 1 S 15:33. Est 7:10. Mt 7:2. Ro +12:19. 2 Th +1:6, 7. Ja 2:13. Re 13:10. 16:6, 7. 19:2.

8 I will. ver. +6.

your sons and. Is 14:1, 2. 60:14.

Sabeans. i.e. they who come; go about; busybodies, S#7615h, only here. Ge 10:7. Jb 1:15. Ezk 23:42.

far off. Je 6:20.

9 Proclaim. Ps 96:10. Is 34:1. Je 31:10. 50:2.

Prepare. Heb. Sanctify. Ezk 21:21, 22. Re 16:14.

wake. Is 8:9, 10. Je 46:3, 4. Ezk 38:7.

10 your plowshares. Is 2:4. Ho 2:18. Mi 4:3. Lk +22:36.

pruning hooks. or, scythes.

let. 2 Ch 25:8. Is 45:24. Zc 12:8. 2 C 12:9.

11 Assemble. ver. 2. Ezk 38:9-18. Mi 4:12. Zp +3:8. Zc 14:2, 3. Re 16:14-16. 19:19, 20. 20:8, 9.

cause, etc. or, the Lord shall bring down thy mighty ones. Ps 103:20. Is 10:34. 13:3. 37:36. Mt 13:41. 2 Th 1:7. Re 19:14.

to come down. Ps +149:9. Ho +11:12. Zc +14:5. Ju 14, 15. Re 17:14.

12 valley. ver. 2, 14. 2 Ch 20:26. Ezk 39:11. Zc 14:4, 5.

and come up. Ps 2:8, 9. 7:6. Is 3:13. Ezk +30:3.

Jehoshaphat. ver. 2. Re 16:16.

there will I sit. ver. 2. 2 S 12:30, 31. Je +43:11. Mt 25:31-46.

to judge. Ps +7:8.

13 the sickle. Dt 16:9. Je 50:16. Mk 4:29. Re 14:15, 16, 18.

the harvest. Dt +24:19. Je 51:33. Ho 6:11. Mt 13:39.

for the press. Jl 2:24. Is 63:3. La 1:15. Re 14:17-20.

for their. Ge 13:13. 15:16. 18:20. Da 8:23. Mt 23:32.

14 multitudes. ver. 2. Is 34:2-8. 63:1-7. Ezk 38:8-23. 39:8-20. Re 16:14-16. 19:17-21.

decision. or, concision. Ph 3:2. or, threshing. Is +21:10.

for the day of the Lord. Jl +2:1. Ps 37:13. Ezk +30:3. 2 P 3:7.

15 The sun. Jl +2:10, 31. Is 5:30. Mt +24:29.

16 roar. Ezk 38:18-22. Am +1:2.

shall shake. Is 2:19, 21. He +12:26, 27.

hope. Heb. place of repair, or, harbor. Ps 18:2. +42:11. ch. 46. 61:3. 91:1, 2. Pr 18:10. Is 33:16, 21. 51:5, 6, 16. Je 36:26. Hab 3:16. Zp 2:3.

and the strength. 1 S 15:29. Ps 29:11. Zc 10:6, 12. 12:5-8.

17 shall ye know. ver. 21. Jl 2:27. Ps 9:11. 76:2. Ezk +6:7. 48:35. Zp 3:14-16.

dwelling in Zion. Is +24:23.

my holy mountain. Is +11:9.

Jerusalem. Is 4:3.

holy. Heb. holiness. Je 31:23. Ezk 43:12. Ob 17. Zc 14:20.

there. Is 35:8. 52:1. Na 1:15. Zc 14:21. Re 21:27.

18 in that day. Ps +118:24. Is +2:11.

the mountains. Jb 29:6. Is 55:12, 13. Am 9:13, 14.

and all. Is 30:25. 35:6. 41:17, 18.

rivers. Jl 1:20. 2 S 22:16. Is 41:18, 19. 43:19. Ezk +31:12.

flow. Heb. go. Zc 14:8.

and a fountain. Heb. mayan, Ge +7:11. Ps 46:4. Ezk 47:1-12. Zc 14:8. Re 22:1, 2, 17.

of the house. Ezk 47:1.

the valley. Nu 25:1. Mi 6:5.

Shittim. Nu 25:1. 33:49. Jsh 2:1. Mi 6:5.

19 **Egypt**. Is 11:15. 19:1, etc. Zc 10:10, 11. 14:18, 19.

Edom. Je +49:7. 17.

for the violence. Je 51:35. Ob 10-16. Hab 2:8. 2 Th 1:6.

innocent blood. Dt +19:10. 27:25.

20 **Judah**. Is 33:20. Ezk +37:25. Am 9:15.

dwell. *or*, abide. or, remain, be established.

S#3427h. ver. 12 (sit). Ps 9:7 (endure). 29:10 (sitteth). Is 13:20 (inhabited). Je 50:13, 39, 40. La 5:19 (remainest). Ho 3:3, 4.

for ever. Heb. *olam*, Ex +12:24.

21 **will cleanse**. Nu 35:23. Is 4:4. Ezk 36:25, 29. Mt 27:25.

cleansed. or, cleared. or, avenged. Ex 34:7. Nu 14:18. Dt 32:42, 43. 2 K 9:7. Re 6:10, 11.

for the Lord. *or*, even I the Lord that. ver. 17. Ps 87:3. Ex +29:45. Ezk 48:35. Re 21:3.

AMOS

AMOS 1

1 **The words**. Je 1:1. 7:27.
Amos. i.e. *to lade, to burden*, **S#5986h**. Am 7:8, 10, 11, 12, 14. 8:2.
who. Am 7:14. Ex 3:1. 1 K 19:19. Ps 78:70-72. Mt 4:18, 19. 1 C 1:27.
Tekoa. 1 Ch +2:24.
he saw. Is 1:1. Mi 1:1.
in the. 2 Ch +26:1. Ho +1:1.
and in. Am 7:9-11. 2 K 14:23-29.
the earthquake. Zc 14:5.

2 **roar**. Am 3:4, 7, 8, 12. Pr 20:2. Is +5:29. 31:4. 42:13. Je 25:30. Ho 11:10. 13:8. Jl 2:11. 3:16. Re 10:3.
the habitations. Am 4:7, 8. Is 33:9. Je 12:4. 14:2. Jl 1:9-13, 16-18.
Carmel. Jsh +19:26.

3 **For three**. ver. 6, 9, 11, 13. Am 2:1, 4, 6. Jb 5:19. 19:3. 33:29mg. Pr 6:16. 30:15, 18, 21, 29. Ec 11:2.
Damascus. Is +17:1.
and four. *or*, yea, for four.
turn away the punishment thereof. *or*, convert it, *or*, let it be quiet, *and so* ver. 6, 9, etc.
because. 1 K 19:17. 2 K 8:12. 10:32, 33.
threshed Gilead. Is +21:10.

4 **I will**. Jg 9:19, 20, 57. Je +17:27. Ezk 30:8. 39:6.
Hazael. 2 K +8:8.
palaces. or, fortresses. ver. 7, 10, 12, 14. Am 2:2, 5. 3:9-11. 6:8.
Ben-hadad. 1 K +15:18.

5 **break**. Dt 3:5. 1 K 4:13. Is 43:14mg. Je 50:36mg. 51:30. La 2:9. Na 3:13.
the plain of Aven. *or*, Bikath-aven. Ho 4:15. 5:8. 10:5, 8.
the house of Eden. *or*, Beth-eden. 2 K 19:12. Is 37:12. Ezk 27:23.
the people. Am 9:7. 2 K 16:9. Is 22:6.

6 **three**. ver. 3, 9, 11.
Gaza. Ge +10:19. 2 Ch 28:18. Is 14:28-31. Je 47:4, 5. Ezk 25:15, 16.
carried, etc. *or*, carried them away with an entire captivity. 2 Ch 21:16, 17. 28:17mg. Je 13:19. 47:1. Jl 3:6.

7 **I will**. Dt 32:35, 41-43. Ps 75:7, 8. 94:1-5. Zp 2:4. Ro 12:19.
a fire. ver. 4. 2 K 18:8. 2 Ch 26:6. Je 25:18-20. 47:1. Zc 9:5-7.
wall. ver. 10, 14.

8 **I will cut**. Is 20:1. Je 47:5. Ezk 25:16.
from Ashkelon. Jg +14:19.
turn. Ps 81:14. Is +1:25. Zc 13:7.
and the. Is 14:29-31. Je 47:4, 5. Ezk 25:16. Zp 2:4-7.

9 **Tyrus**. Is ch. 23. Je +25:22. Ezk ch. 26-28.
because. ver. 6, 11.
brotherly covenant. Heb. covenant of brethren. 2 S 5:11. 1 K 5:1-11. 9:11-14. 2 Ch 2:8-16.

10 **send a fire**. ver. +4. Ezk 26:12. Zc 9:4.
wall. ver. 7.

11 **Edom**. Is 21:11, 12. Je +49:7-22.
because. Ge 27:40, 41. Nu 20:14-21. Dt 2:4-8. 2 Ch 28:17.
his brother. Ge 25:24-26.
did cast off all pity. Heb. corrupted his compassions.
tear. 2 Ch 28:17.
perpetually. Heb. *ad*, Ps +9:18.
kept his wrath. Ps 85:5. 137:7. Ec 7:9. Is 57:16. Mi 7:18. Ep 4:26, 27. 5:1.
for ever. Heb. *netsach*, Jb +4:20.

12 **Teman**. Ge +36:11.
Bozrah. Ge +36:33.

13 **the children**. Ge +19:38.
and for. 1 S 11:1, 2. 2 S 10:1-8. 2 K 24:2. 2 Ch 20:1, 10. Ne 2:19. 4:7, etc.
because. 2 K +8:12. Ho 10:14.
ripped up the women with child. *or*, divided the mountains.
enlarge. Is 5:8. Je 49:1. Ezk 35:10. Hab 2:5, 6.

14 **kindle**. Je +17:27.
wall. ver. 7.
Rabbah. Jsh +13:25.
with shouting. Am 2:2. Jb 39:25. Is 9:5.
tempest. Ps +83:15.
whirlwind. Je +23:19.

15 **their king**. Je 49:3.

AMOS 2

1 **For three**. ver. 4, 6. Am 1:3, 6, 9, 11, 13. Nu ch. 20-25. Dt 23:4, 5. Ps 83:4-7. Mi 6:5.
of Moab. Ezk +25:8.
because. 2 K 3:9, 26, 27. Pr 15:3.

2 **Kirioth**. i.e. *cities*, **S#7152h**. Jsh 15:25. Je 48:24, 41.
with tumult. Am 1:14. Is 9:5. Je 48:34.

3 **cut off**. Nu +24:17, 18. Je 48:7, 25.

4 **For**. Dt 31:16-18. 32:15-27.
Judah. Am 3:2. 2 K 17:19. Je 9:25, 26. Ho 5:12, 13. 6:11. 12:2.
because. Le 26:14, 15, 43. Jg 2:17-20. 2 S 12:9, 10. 2 K 22:11-17. 2 Ch 36:14-17. Ne 1:7. 9:26, 29, 30. Is 5:24, 25. Je 8:9. Ezk ch. 16. 20:13, 16, 24. 22:8. 23:11, etc. Da 9:5-12. Ac 7:51. 13:40, 41. 1 Th 4:8.
and their lies. 2 K 17:15. Ps 40:4. Is 9:15, 16. 28:15. 44:20. Je 16:19, 20. 23:13-15, 25-32. 28:15, 16. Ezk 13:6-16, 22. 22:28. Hab 2:18. Ro 1:25.
after. Jg 2:11-17. 10:6. 2 Ch 30:7. Je 8:2. 9:14. Ezk 20:13, 16, 18, 24, 30. 1 P 1:18.

5 **I will**. Je +17:27.

6 **For three**. Am 6:3-7. 2 K 17:7-18. 18:12. Ezk 23:5-9. Ho 4:1, 2, 11-14. 7:7-10. 8:4-6. 13:2, 3. Mi 6:10-16.
because they sold. Am 5:11, 12. 8:4-6. Le +25:39. Is 5:22, 23. 29:21. Mi 3:2, 3.
and the poor. Ex 23:6-8. Ezk +16:49.
a pair of shoes. Ru 4:7.

7 **pant**. Am 4:1. 1 K 21:4. Pr 28:21. Mi 2:2, 9. 7:2, 3. Hab 2:6. Zp 3:3. Ja 2:6.
turn aside. Am +5:12. Is 10:2.
way of the meek. Mt +5:5. Ja +2:5. +5:4, 6.
man and his father. Le 18:8, 15. Ezk 22:11. 1 C 5:1.
go in. Ge +29:30. 38:2, 9, 16.
maid. *or*, young woman. Ge +24:14 (**S#5291h**).
to profane. Le 18:21. +19:8. 20:3. 2 S 12:14. Is 48:11. Ezk 20:9, 14. 36:20-23. Ml 1:12. Ro 2:24. 1 C 5:1.

8 **laid**. Ex +22:26, 27. Dt 24:12-17. Ezk 18:7, 12.
by every altar. Am 6:4. Is 57:7. Ezk 23:41. 1 C 8:10. 10:7, 21.
they drink. Am 6:6. Jg 9:27. Ho 4:8.
the condemned. *or*, such as have fined, *or* mulcted.

9 **yet destroyed I**. Ge +10:16.
whose height. Nu +13:33. Dt +2:20.
I destroyed. Jsh 11:21, 22. 2 S 23:16-22. Jb 18:16. Is 5:24. Ml 4:1.

10 **I brought**. Ex 12:51. Dt 4:47. Ne 9:8-12. Ps 105:42, 43. 136:10, 11. Je 32:20, 21. Ezk 20:10. Mi 6:4.
and led. Nu 14:34. Dt 2:7. 8:2-4. Ne 9:21. Ps 95:10. Ac 7:42. 13:18.
to possess. Nu 14:31-35. Dt 1:20, 21, 39.

11 **I raised**. 1 S 3:20. 19:20. 1 K 17:1. 18:4. 19:16. 20:13, 35, 41. 22:8. 2 K 2:2-5. 6:1. 17:13. 2 Ch 36:15. Je +7:25. 2 P 1:20, 21.
Nazarites. Nu 6:2. Jg 13:4-7. La 4:7. Lk 1:3-17.
Is it not. Is 5:3, 4. Je 2:5, 31. Mi 6:3, 4.

12 **ye gave**. Ex 32:21-23.
wine. Nu 6:3.
and commanded. Am 7:12, 13. Is 30:10, 11. Je 11:21. 26:11. Mi 2:6. Mt 21:34-38. Ac 4:18. 5:28. 7:51. 1 Th 2:15, 16.

13 **Behold**. Ps 78:40. Is 1:14. 7:13. 43:24. Ezk 6:9. 16:43. Ml 2:17.
I am pressed, etc. *or*, I will press your place, as a cart full of sheaves presseth.

14 **the flight**. Am 9:1-3. Jb 11:20mg. Ec 9:11. Is 30:16, 17. Je 9:23. 46:6.
the strong. Ps 33:16.
himself. Heb. his soul, or life. Heb. *nephesh*, Nu +23:10.

15 **neither**. Ps 33:16, 17.
himself. Heb. his soul, *or* life. Heb. *nephesh*, Nu +23:10.

16 **courageous**. Heb. strong of his heart. Je 48:41.
shall flee. Jg 4:17. 2 K 7:8, etc. Mk 14:52.

AMOS 3

1 **Hear**. 2 Ch 20:15. Is 46:3. 48:12. Je +7:2.
against the whole family. Je 8:3. 31:1. 33:24-29. Ezk 37:16, etc. Mi 2:3.
which. Am 2:10. Ex 12:51.

2 **only**. Ex 19:5, 6. Dt 7:6. 10:15. 26:18. 32:9. Ps 147:19, 20. Is 63:19.
known. Ge +39:6.
all. Ge 10:32. Je 1:15. 10:25. Na 3:4. Zc 14:17, 18. Ac 17:26.
therefore. Ezk 9:6. 20:36-38. Da 9:12. Mt +11:20-24. Lk +12:47, 48. Ro 2:9. 1 P +4:17.
punish. Heb. visit upon. Je +11:22mg.

3 **Can two walk**. Ge +5:22. Le 23:17. Ps +119:63. 2 C +6:14-16.

4 **a lion**. ver. +8. Ps 104:21. Is +5:29.
cry. Heb. give forth his voice.
den. Ps 104:22.

5 **a bird fall**. Ec 9:12. Je 31:28. Ezk 12:13. Da 9:14.

6 **a trumpet**. Ho +8:1.
and the people. Je 5:22. 10:7. 2 C 5:11.
be afraid. *or*, run together.
shall there. Ge 50:20. Is 14:24-27. +45:7. Ac 2:23. 4:28.
be evil. Am 5:13. 2 S 17:14. Jb +2:10. +9:22. Ps 5:4. 141:5. Is +45:7. Ja 1:13.
the Lord hath not done it? *or*, and shall not the Lord do *somewhat*? 1 K 11:14. Ps 94:7, 9, 10. Is 9:13. Mi 6:9. Mt 18:7. 1 C 2:8. 1 T 1:13, 16.

done it. Ex +4:21. Le 14:34. Nu 16:41. Jsh 6:21. 10:40. Jg 9:23. 14:4. 21:15. Ru +1:13. 1 S +18:10. 2 S 12:11. 24:1. 1 K 12:15. 2 K +6:33. Je 4:10. +29:11. Ezk 14:9. 20:25. +38:16. Ep +1:11. Re +17:17.

7 Surely. Jb 31:18. Mi 6:4.
will do. Ex 12:12. Nu 5:30. 33:4. Dt 10:18. 33:21.
but he revealeth. Ge 6:13. 18:17. 20:7. Ex 33:13. Nu 12:7, 8. Dt +29:29. 1 K 22:19-23. 2 K 3:17-20. 6:12. 22:13, 20. Ps 25:14mg. 103:7. Da 2:10, 11, +19. 8:15, 16. +9:22-27. +10:21. 11:2. Mt 13:11. Lk 2:26, 29, 36, 37. Jn 15:15. Re 1:1, 19. 4:1. ch. 6-20.
his servants. Je +26:5.

8 lion. ver. 4. Am +1:2. Re 5:5.
who can. Am 2:12. 7:12-17. Jb 32:18, 19. Je 20:9. Ac 4:20. +5:20, 29. 1 C 9:16.

9 Publish. 2 S 1:20. Je 2:10, 11. 31:7-9. 46:14. 50:2.
Ashdod. Jsh +11:22.
the mountains. Am 4:1. 6:1. Je 31:5. Ezk 36:8. 37:22.
and behold. Dt 29:24-28. Je 22:8, 9.
oppressed. or, oppressions. Am 4:1. 8:6. Le +19:13. Dt +24:14. Jb 35:9. Ec 4:1.

10 know not to do. Am 5:7. Ps 14:4. Je 4:22. 5:4. 2 P 3:5.
right. S#5228h. 2 S 15:3. Pr +8:9. 24:26. Is 26:10. 30:10. 59:14.
who store. Hab 2:8-11. Zp 1:9. Zc 5:3, 4. Ja +5:3, 4.
robbery. or, spoil. Ho 7:13mg.

11 An adversary. Am 6:14. 2 K 15:19, 29. 17:3-6. 18:9-11. Is 7:17, etc. 8:7, 8. 10:5, 6, 9-11. Ho 11:5, 6.
there shall be. or, shall come.
and thy. ver. 10, 15. Am 2:5. 6:8. 2 Ch 36:19.

12 As the. 1 S 17:34-37. Is 31:4.
taketh. Heb. delivereth.
so shall. Am 9:2, 3. 1 K 20:30. 22:25. Is 8:4. 17:1-6. Ro +11:4, 5. 1 P +4:17, 18.
in Damascus in a couch. or, on the bed's feet. or, in the corner of a couch. 1 K 20:34. 2 K 16:9.

13 and testify. Dt 8:19. 30:18, 19. 2 K 17:13, 15. 2 Ch 24:19. Ac 2:40. 18:5, 6. 20:21. Ep 4:17. 1 Th 4:6.
the Lord God. Am 5:27. Jsh 22:22. Is 1:24. Re 15:3.
the God of hosts. Ja +5:4.

14 in the. Ex 32:34.
visit the transgressions of Israel upon him. or, punish Israel for his transgressions. ver. +2mg.
I will. Am 9:1. 1 K 13:2-5. 2 K 23:15. 2 Ch 31:1. 34:6, 7. Je 48:13. Ho 10:5-8, 14, 15. Mi 1:6, 7.

15 the winter house. Je 36:22.
the summer house. Jg 3:20.

the houses. 1 K 22:39. Ps 45:8.
the great. ver. 11. Am 6:11. Is 5:9.

AMOS 4

1 ye kine. Dt +32:14. Je 50:11, 27.
the mountain. Am 6:1. 1 K +16:24.
which oppress. Am 2:6, 7. 3:9, 10. 5:11. Le +19:13. Dt +15:9-11. 1 S 12:3, 4. Ps +12:5. 140:12. Is 1:17-24. 5:8. 58:6. Je 5:26-29. 6:6. 7:6. Ezk 22:7, 12, 27, 29. Mi 2:1-3. 3:1-3. Zc 7:10, 11. Ml +3:5.
crush. Dt 28:33. Jb 20:19mg. Je 51:34.
Bring. Am 2:8. Is 56:11, 12. Jl 3:3.

2 hath sworn. Am 6:8. Ge 22:16. Ps +89:35. He 6:13.
with hooks. 2 Ch 33:11. Jb 40:24. 41:2. Is 37:29. Je 16:16. Ezk 29:4, 5. Hab 1:15, 16.
posterity. or, remnant of you. Ezk 23:25.

3 ye shall go. 2 K 25:4. Ezk 12:5, 12.
before her. Jsh 6:5, 20.
them into the palace. or, away the things of the palace. 2 K 7:7, 8, 15. Is 2:20. 31:7. Zp 1:18. Mt 16:26.

4 Come. Am 3:14. 5:5. Ec 11:9. Ezk 20:39. Ho 4:15. 9:15. 12:11. Jl 3:9-12. Mt 23:32. 26:45. Mk 14:41.
Bethel. 1 K 12:29.
at Gilgal. Jsh +4:19.
and bring. Nu 28:3, 4. Le 7:13.
sacrifices. Le +23:12. Ho 6:6.
every morning. Nu 28:4.
and your tithes. Dt 14:28, 29. 26:12.
three years. Heb. three years of days. Ge +24:55. Nu 28:3. Dt 14:28. Je +28:3mg.

5 offer a sacrifice. Heb. offer by burning. Le 7:12, 13. +23:17. Ps 56:12. Je 17:26. +33:11. He 13:15.
with leaven. Ex 12:15. 13:3, 7. 23:18. +24:4. 34:25. Le 2:11, 12. 6:17. 7:13. 23:17. Dt 16:3. Ho 9:9.
proclaim. Le 22:18-21. Dt 12:6, 7. Mt 6:2.
free offerings. Le +23:38.
for. Ps 81:12. Mt 15:9, 13, 14. 23:23. Ro 1:28. 2 Th 2:10-12.
this liketh you. Heb. so ye love. Ho 9:1, 10.

6 cleanness of teeth. Is 3:1. Je 14:18.
and want. Le +26:26. Ezk 16:27.
yet. ver. +8, 9. 2 Ch 28:22. Is 1:5. 9:13. 26:11. Je 5:3. 8:5-7. Ho 5:15. 6:1. 7:14-16. Jl 2:12-14. Hg 2:17. Zc 1:3-6. Re 2:21. 9:20, 21. 16:10, 11.

7 I have. Le 26:18-21, 23, 24, 27, 28. Dt 28:23, 24. 1 K 8:35, 36. 2 Ch +7:13, 14. Is 5:6. Je 3:3. 5:24, 25. 14:4, 22. Ezk 22:23, 24. Hg 1:10, 11. Zc 10:1. 14:17. Ml +3:10. Ja 5:17. Re 11:6.
when. Jl 2:23. Jn 4:35.
and I. Ex 8:22. 9:4, 26. 10:23. Jg 6:37-40. 1 C 4:7.
and the. Jl 1:10-18.

8 two. 1 K 18:5. Is 41:17, 18. Je 14:3.
but. Ezk 4:16. Mi 6:14. Hg 1:6.
yet. ver. +6, 9-11. Je 23:14. Ho 7:10.

9 with. Dt +28:22.
when, etc. *or*, the multitude of your gardens, etc., did the palmer worm, etc.
the palmer-worm. Ps +78:46.
yet. ver. +6, 8. Jb 36:8-13. Is 42:24, 25.

10 pestilence. Ex 9:3-6. 12:29, 30. +15:26. Dt 7:15. Ps 78:49, 50. Ezk +38:22.
after the manner. *or*, in the way. Ex 9:3, 6. 12:29. Dt 28:27. Ps 78:50. Is 10:24, 26.
your young. Le 26:25. 2 K 8:12. 10:32. Je 6:11. 11:22. 18:21. 48:15.
and have taken away your horses. Heb. with the captivity of your horses. Nu 31:26mg. 2 K 13:3-7. Is 49:25mg.
the stink. Am 8:3. Dt 28:26. Je 8:1, 2. 9:22. 15:3. 16:4. Jl 2:20.
yet. ver. +6. Ex 8:19. 9:12, 17, 34, 35. 10:3, 27. 14:4.

11 as God. Ge +19:24, 25. Ho 11:8.
as a firebrand. Zc 3:2. 1 C +3:15. Ju +23.
yet. ver. 6. Je 6:28-30. Ezk 22:17-22. 24:13. Re 9:20.

12 thus. ver. +2, 3. Am 2:14, 15. 9:1-4. Ps 10:17.
prepare. Am 5:4-15. 2 K 20:1. Ps 98:9. Pr 16:1. Is 47:3. Ezk 13:5. 22:30. Ho 10:8. 13:8. Zc +14:5. Mt 5:25. 24:44-51. 25:1-13. Mk 13:32-37. Lk 12:35, 36, 47. 14:31, 32. +21:34-36. 1 Th 5:2-4. Ja 4:1-10. Ju 14. Re 3:3. 19:7.

13 he that. Jb 38:4-11. Ps 65:6. Is 40:12. 42:5. Zc 12:1.
and createth. Heb. *bara*, Ge 1:1. Ps 51:10. 89:12, 47. 102:18. 104:30. 135:7. 147:18. 148:5. Ec 12:1. Is +45:18 (**S#1254h**). Je 10:13. 51:16.
wind. *or*, spirit. Pr 30:4. Ec 3:21. Ezk 37:9mg. Jn 3:8.
and declareth. Da 2:28. Lk 7:39, 40. Jn +2:25.
unto men. LXX adds, "his Christ."
that maketh. Ex 14:20.
darkness. Ex +10:22.
and treadeth. Dt 32:13. 33:29. Mi 1:3. Hab 3:19.
The Lord. Am 3:13. 5:8. 6:8. 9:5, 6. Is 47:4. 48:2. Je 10:16. 51:19.
The God of hosts. LXX renders, "The Lord God Almighty." 2 S 7:26, 27; Je 31:35; 50:34; Ho 12:5; Zc 2:8, 9, 11; 3:7, 10, 11; 13:7; Ml 3:1 all have "Lord (or Lord God) Almighty" where the Hebrew reads "Lord of Hosts" (Ps +24:10). Re *1:8*.
is his name. Ex +6:3. 15:3. Ps +68:4. +83:18.

AMOS 5

1 Hear. Am 3:1. 4:1.
I take. ver. 16. Je 7:29. 9:10, 17, 20. Ezk

19:1, 14. 26:17. 27:2, 27-32. 28:12. 32:2, 16. Mi 2:4.

2 virgin. Ge +24:16. Nu +21:25. Je +18:13.
is fallen. 2 K 15:29. 17:6. Is 3:8. Ho 14:1.
she shall. Is 14:21. 24:20. 43:17. Je 51:64.
she is. Is +54:7. Je 4:20.
none. Am 7:2-5. 9:11. Is 51:17, 18. Je 2:27, 28. 30:12-14. La 1:16-19. Ezk 16:36, 37. Ho 6:2.

3 The city. Dt 4:27. 28:62. Is 1:9. 10:22. 30:17. Ezk 12:16. Ro 9:27.
by a thousand. Dt 32:30.

4 Seek ye me. ver. 6. Dt 12:5. 30:1-8. 2 Ch 20:3. 34:3. Ps +9:10. 14:2. 27:8. Is 9:13. Je 10:21. +29:13. Zp 1:6. 2:3.
and. Ps 22:26. 69:32. 105:3, 4. Is +55:3.
shall live. Le 18:5. Dt 30:19. Ne 9:29. Is +26:19. 38:16. +55:3. Ezk 3:21. 18:19. 20:11. 33:11, 19. 37:3, 5, 6, 14. Ho 6:2. Hab 2:4. Lk 10:28. Ro 1:17. 10:5. Ga 3:12. He 10:38.

5 seek not. Am 4:4. Ho 4:15. 9:15. 10:14, 15. 12:11.
Beer-sheba. Am 8:14. Ge +21:31.
Gilgal. Jsh +4:19.
and Bethel. Am 7:17. Le 26:30-32. Dt 28:41. Ho 4:15. 10:8, 15.
come. Jb 8:22. Ps 33:10. Is 8:10. 29:20. 1 C 1:28. 2:6. Re 18:17.

6 Seek. ver. 4.
lest. Ex 22:6.
the house. Am 6:6. Ge 48:8-20. Jsh 18:5. Jg 1:22, 23. 2 S 19:20. 1 K 11:28. 1 Ch 7:29. Ezk 37:19. Ob 18. Zc 10:6. Re 7:8.
there. Mt +3:12.

7 turn. ver. 11, 12. Is 1:23. 5:7. 10:1. 59:13, 14. Hab 1:12-14.
wormwood. Dt +29:18.
leave. Ps 36:3. 125:5. Ezk 3:20. 18:24. 33:12, 13, 18. Zp 1:6.

8 the seven stars. Jb 9:9. 38:31, 32. Is 13:10.
shadow of death. Ps +23:4.
into the morning. Jb 38:12, 13.
maketh. Ex +10:22. 14:24-28. Is 59:10.
that calleth. Am 9:6. Ge 7:11-20. 1 K 18:44, 45. Jb 37:13. 38:34. Is 48:13. 2 P 3:5, 6.
face. Ge +11:8.
The Lord. Am 4:13.

9 strengtheneth. 2 K 13:17, 25. Je 37:10. Mt 11:12. Lk +1:52. He 11:34.
against the strong. Am 2:14. Jb 5:3. Is 29:5.
spoiled. Heb. spoil. Am 3:10mg. Ho 7:13mg.
come against. Mi +5:8-11.

10 hate. Am 7:10-17. 1 K 18:17. 21:20. 22:8. 2 Ch 24:20-22. 25:16. 36:16. Pr 9:7, 8. Is 29:21. Je 20:7-10. Jn 7:7. 15:19, 22-24. Re 11:10.
in the gate. ver. 12. Ge +14:7.
abhor. Je 17:16, 17. Jn 3:20. 8:45-47.

11 treading. Am 4:1. Is 5:7, 8. 59:13, 14. Mi 2:2. 3:1-3. Ja 2:6. Re 11:8-10.
ye have built. Dt 28:30, 38, 39. Is 65:21, 22. Mi 6:15. Zp 1:13. Hg 1:6.

pleasant vineyards. Heb. vineyards of desire. Is +32:12mg.

12 I know. Dt 31:21. Is 66:18. Je 29:23. He 4:12, 13.

manifold. 2 K 17:7-17. Ne 9:27. Is 47:9.

mighty. Ps 89:19. Is 63:1. Je 50:34. Re 18:5.

they afflict. Am 2:6, 7, 26. Ac 3:13, 14. 7:52. Ja +5:4, 6.

take. 1 S 8:3. Ps 26:9, 10. Is 1:23. 33:15. Mi 3:11. 7:3.

bribe. *or*, ransom. Ex 30:12. Nu 35:31, 32. Pr 6:35. 13:8. 21:18. Is 43:3.

and they turn aside. Am 2:7. Ex 23:6. Dt 16:19. 24:17. Is 10:2. 29:21. La 3:34, 35. Ezk +16:49. Ml +3:5.

the poor. Ezk +16:49.

in the gate. ver. 10. Ge +14:7. Dt 16:18. Ru 4:1. Jb 29:7, etc. 31:21. Pr 22:22.

13 the prudent. Pr +22:3.

keep silence. Am 6:10. Jb 24:4. Ps +38:13. Pr 11:10. 28:12, 28. 29:2. Je 8:14. Ho 4:4. Mi 7:5-7.

an evil. Ec 9:12. Is 37:3. Mi 2:3. Hab +3:16. Zp +2:2, 3. Ep 5:15, 16. 6:13. 2 T 3:1.

14 Seek. Ps 34:12-16. Pr 11:27. Is 1:16, 17. 55:2. Mi +6:8. Mt 6:33. Ro 2:7-9.

and so. Am 3:3. Ge 39:2, 3, 23. Ex 3:12. Le 26:12. Jsh 1:9. 1 K 6:13. 1 Ch 28:20. 2 Ch 15:2. Ps 46:11. Is 8:10. Mt 1:23. 28:20. Ph 4:8, 9. 2 T 4:22.

as. Nu 16:3. Is 48:1, 2. Je 7:3, 4. Mi 3:11.

15 Hate the evil. Ps 37:27. Pr +8:13. Is 1:16, 17. Ro 8:7. 1 Th 5:21, 22. 3 J 11.

love the good. Mi +6:8. Ph 4:8.

establish. ver. 10, 24. Am 6:12. 2 Ch 19:6-11. Ps 82:2-4. Je 7:5-7.

in the gate. Ge +14:7.

it may. Ex 32:30. 2 S 16:12. 1 K 20:31. 2 K 19:4. Jl 2:14. Jon 3:9. Zp +2:3.

the remnant. ver. 6. 2 K 13:7. 14:26, 27. 15:29. Mi +5:3.

Joseph. ver. 6. Ex 12:40. Ob 18. Zc 10:6.

16 the Lord. ver. 27. Am 3:13.

Wailing. Am 8:10. Is 15:2-5, 8. 22:12. Je 4:31. 9:10, 18-20. Jl 1:8, 11, 14. Mi 1:8. 2:4. Re 18:10, 15, 16, 19.

streets. lit. open places. Heb. *rechob*, **S#7339h**, courtyard or public square, broad streets. Ge 19:2. Dt 13:16. Jg 19:15, 17, 20. 2 S 21:12. 2 Ch 29:4. 32:6. Ezr 10:9. Ne 8:1, 3, 16. Est 4:6. 6:9, 11. Jb 29:7. Ps 55:11. 144:14. Pr 1:20. 5:16. 7:12. 22:13. 26:13. SS 3:2 (broad ways). Is 15:3. 59:14. Je 5:1 (broad places). 9:21. 48:38. 49:26. 50:30. La 2:11, 12. 4:18. Ezk 16:24, 31. Da 9:25. Na 2:4 (broad ways). Zc 8:4, 5.

highways. Heb. *chuts*, **S#2351h**, out of doors or narrow streets. Jb 5:10mg. 18:17. Pr 5:16. 7:12. 22:13. Je 5:1. 9:21. Na 2:4. Mt 7:13, 14. 22:9. Lk 14:23.

such. Mt +9:23.

17 in. Is 16:10. 32:10-12. Je 48:33. Ho 9:1, 2.

I will. Ex 12:12, 23. Jl 3:17. Na 1:12, 15. Zc 9:8.

pass through. Ex +12:12.

18 that desire the day. Is 5:19. 28:15-22. Jb 36:20. Je 17:16. Ezk 12:22, 27. Ml 3:1, 2. 2 P 3:4.

the day of the Lord is. Is 9:19. 24:11, 12. Je +30:7. Ezk +30:3. Da +12:1.

19 As if. Am 9:1, 2. 1 K 20:29, 30. Jb 20:24, 25. Is 24:17, 18. Je 15:2, 3. 48:43, 44. Ac 28:4.

a bear. 2 K 2:24. La 3:10. Da 7:5.

20 darkness. Ex +10:22. Jb 3:4-6. 10:21, 22.

not light. Ge +40:23. 2 S 22:13.

21 hate. Pr 15:8. 21:27. 28:9. Is 1:11-16. 66:3. Je 6:20. 7:21-23. Ho 8:13. Mt 23:14.

feast days. Le 23:2. Dt 16:16.

I will not. Ge +8:21. Le 26:31. 1 S 15:22.

smell in your solemn assemblies. *or*, smell your holy days. Le +23:36.

22 offer. Ps 50:8-13. Is 66:3. Mi 6:6, 7.

burnt offerings. Le +23:12.

meat offerings. Le +23:13.

I will not accept. Le 1:4. Ml 1:7.

peace offerings. *or*, thank offerings. Am 4:4, 5. Le +23:19. Je +33:11.

23 the noise. Am 6:5. 8:3, 10. 1 Ch 25:1, 7. Is 5:12.

viols. or, lutes. Am 6:5. 1 S 10:5 (psaltery). 1 Ch 13:8.

24 let. ver. 7, 14, 15. Jb 29:12-17. Pr 21:3. Is 1:17. Je 22:3. Ezk 45:9. Ho 6:6. Mi +6:8. Mk 12:32-34.

25 Have ye offered. Le 17:7. Dt 32:17-19. Jsh 5:5-7. 24:14. Ne 9:18, 21. Is 43:23, 24. Je 7:22, 23. Ezk 20:8, 16, 23, 24. Ho 9:9, 10. Zc 7:5. Ac 7:42, 43.

unto me. Le 17:7. Dt 32:17. Ps 106:37. 1 C 10:7.

26 the tabernacle of your Moloch. *or*, Siccuth your king. Le +18:21. 2 K +23:13, Milcom. **Moloch**. i.e. *a king; rule*, **S#4432h**. Le +18:21, Molech.

Chiun. i.e. *image, pillar; Raiphan* or Saturn. Ac 7:43.

27 beyond. Am 3:12. 2 K 15:29. 16:9. 17:6. Is 8:4. Ac 7:43.

whose. Am 4:13.

AMOS 6

1 to them. Jg 18:7. Is 32:9-11. 33:14. Je 48:11. 49:31. Lk 6:24, 25. 12:17-20. Ja 5:5. 1 P 5:7.

at ease. *or*, secure. Is 22:12, 13. Je 7:4. +48:10. Zp 1:12. Re 3:17.

and trust. Am 4:1. 8:14. 1 K +16:24.

named. Ex 19:5, 6. Nu 1:17. La 1:1.

chief. *or*, firstfruits. Ex 19:5. Le +23:10. Dt 28:13.

2 Pass. Je 2:10, 11. Na 3:8.
Calneh. Ge 10:10. Is 10:9, Calno. Ezk 27:23,
Canneh.
Hamath. Ge 10:18. Nu +13:21.
Gath. Jsh +11:22.
better. Is 10:9-11. 36:18, 19. 37:12, 13. Ezk
31:2, 3. Na 3:8.
3 put far away. Am 5:18. 9:10. Ec 8:11. Is
47:7. 56:12. Ezk 12:22, 27. Mt 24:48. 1 Th
5:3. 2 P 3:4. Re 18:7.
the evil day. Am +3:6. 5:13. 9:10.
and cause. ver. 12. Am 5:12. Ps 94:20.
seat. *or*, habitation.
4 lie. Is 5:11, 12. 22:13. Lk 16:19. Ro 13:13, 14.
Ja 5:5.
stretch themselves upon their couches.
or, abound with superfluities. 1 S 25:36-38. Ps
73:7. Lk 12:19, 20.
5 chant. *or*, quaver.
to the. Ge 31:27. Jb 21:11, 12. Ec 2:8. Is 5:12.
1 P 4:3. Re 18:22.
like. Am 5:23. 8:3. 1 Ch 23:5.
6 wine in bowls. *or*, in bowls of wine. 1 K
+7:40. Ho 3:1. 1 T 5:23.
chief. Mt 26:7-9. Jn 12:3.
but. Ge 37:25-28. 42:21, 22. Est 3:15. Ro
12:15. 1 C 12:26.
not grieved. La 1:12.
affliction. *or*, breach. 2 K 15:29. 17:3-6. Is
30:26. +51:19mg. Je +30:7.
Joseph. Am 5:6, 15. Ex +12:40.
7 shall they. Am 5:5, 27. 7:11. Dt 28:41. Lk
21:24.
and the. 1 K 20:16-20. Est 5:8, 12-14. 7:1, 2,
8-10. Is 21:4. Da 5:4-6. Na 1:10.
8 sworn. Am 4:2. 8:7. Ge 22:16. Je 51:14. He
6:13-17.
himself. Heb. *nephesh*, Ge +27:31; Le +26:11.
Is 42:1. Je 9:9. He 10:38.
I abhor. Ps +106:40.
the excellency. Am 8:7. Ps 47:4.
Ezk 24:21.
and hate. Am 3:11. La 2:5.
therefore. Mi 1:6-9.
all that is therein. Heb. the fulness thereof.
Ps 24:1. 50:12.
9 if. Am 5:3. 1 S 2:33. Est 5:11. 9:10. Jb 1:2, 19.
20:28. Ps 109:13. Is 14:21.
10 that burneth. Am 8:3. Jsh 7:25. 1 S 31:12. 2
K 23:16. 2 Ch 16:14. 21:19. Je 16:6.
34:5.
bring out the bones. Jb 7:15mg. 19:20. 2 Ch
34:5.
Hold. Am 5:13. Nu 17:12, 13. 2 K 6:33. Ezk
24:21-23.
for. Je 44:26. Ezk 20:39.
we may not make. *or*, they will not make,
or, have not made. That is, call upon, or
invoke. Is 26:13. 49:1. 62:6.
11 the Lord. Am 3:6, 7. 9:1, 9. Ps 105:16, 31,

34. Is 10:5, 6. 13:3. 46:10, 11. 55:11. Ezk
29:18-20. Na 1:14.
he will. ver. 8. Am 3:15. 2 K 25:9. Ho 13:16.
Zc 14:2. Lk 19:44.
breaches. *or*, droppings. Ec 10:18.
12 horses. Is 48:4. Je 5:3. 6:29, 30. Zc 7:11, 12.
for. Am 5:7, 11, 12. 1 K 21:7-13. Ps 94:20,
21. Is 59:13, 14. Ho 10:4, 13. Mi 7:3. Hab 1:3,
4. Ac 7:51, 52.
hemlock. Dt +29:18.
13 which. Ex 32:18, 19. Jg 9:19, 20, 27. 16:23-
25. 1 S 4:5. Jb 31:25, 29. Ec 11:9. Is 8:6. Je
9:23. 50:11. Jon 4:6. Hab 1:15, 16. Zp 3:11.
Lk 12:19, 20. Jn 16:20. Ja 4:16.
Re 11:10.
Have. 2 K 13:25. 14:12-14, 25. 2 Ch 28:6-8.
Is 7:1, 4. 17:3, 4. 28:14, 15. Da 4:30.
14 I will. Dt 28:49. 2 K 15:29. 17:6. Is 7:20. 8:4-
8. 10:5, 6. Je 5:15-17. Ho 10:5, 6.
from the entering. Nu +13:21.
Hemath. Ezk 48:1.
unto. 2 K 14:25.
river. *or*, valley. Am +5:24. Ge 26:17. Jsh
13:3. 15:47.
the wilderness. or, Arabah. Dt +11:30. Jb
24:5. 39:6. Is 33:9. 35:1, 6. 40:3. 41:19. 51:3.
Je 2:6. 5:6. 17:6. 50:12. 51:43.

AMOS 7

1 showed. ver. 4, 7. Je 1:11-16. +24:1. Ezk
11:25.
he. Ps +78:46. Na 3:15-17.
grasshoppers. *or*, green worms.
mowings. Dt 18:4.
the king's mowings. 1 K 4:7. 18:5.
2 when. Ex 10:15. Re 9:4.
O Lord. ver. 5. Ex 32:11, 12. 34:9. Nu 14:17-
19. Je 14:7, 20, 21. Da 9:19. Ja 5:15, 16.
by whom shall Jacob arise. *or*, who *of* (or,
for) Jacob shall stand? ver. 5. Is 51:19. Ezk
9:8. 11:13.
for. Ps 12:1. 44:22-26. Is 37:4. Je 42:2. Zc
4:10.
3 repented. ver. 3, 6. 1 Ch 21:15. Je +18:8. Ja
5:16.
4 showed. ver. 1, 7. Re 4:1.
called. Am 1:4, 7. 4:11. 5:6. Ex 9:23, 24. Le
10:2. Nu 16:35. Is 27:4. 66:15, 16. Je 4:4.
21:12. Jl 2:30. Mi 1:4. Na 1:6. He 1:7.
a part. Mi 2:4.
5 cease. ver. 2. Ps 85:4. Is 10:25.
for. ver. 2, 3. Is 1:9. Je 30:19.
6 repented. Jg 10:16. Je +18:8.
7 a wall. 2 S 8:2. 2 K 21:13. Is 28:17. 34:11. La
2:8. Ezk 40:3. Zc 2:1, 2. Re 11:1. 21:15.
8 Amos. Je 1:11-13. Zc 5:2.
A plumbline. 2 K 21:12, 13. Is 28:17. 34:11.
La 2:8. Da 5:27.
I will set. La 2:8.

I **will not**. Am 8:2. Je 15:6. Ezk 7:2-9. Mi 7:18. Na 1:8, 9.

9 **the high places**. Am 3:14. 5:5. Ge 26:23-25, Beer-sheba. 46:1. Le 26:30, 31. 2 K +21:3.
Isaac. Ge +9:27. Ps 105:9, 10. Je 33:26.
sanctuaries. Le 26:31. Is 16:12. Ezk 21:2.
Israel. Ge +9:27.
I will. "Fulfilled, 2 K 15:8-10."

10 **the priest**. 1 K 12:31, 32. 13:33. 2 K 14:23, 24. 2 Ch 13:8, 9. Je 20:1-3. 29:26, 27. Mt 21:23.
of Bethel. Am 3:14. 4:4. 5:5, 6.
hath conspired. 1 K 18:17. Je 26:8-11. 37:13-15. 38:4. Lk 23:2. Ac 5:28. 24:5.
against thee. 1 K 12:26-33.
in the midst. or, openly. ver. 8. Da 6:10. Ep +5:11.
not able. Ge 37:8. Je 18:18. Ac 7:54.

11 **thus**. Je 26:9. 28:10, 11. Ac 6:14.
Jeroboam shall die. ver. 9. Ps 56:5. Mt 26:61. Ac 17:6, 7. 24:5.
sword. lit. mouth of the sword. Ge +34:26.
and Israel. Am 6:7, 8. 2 K 17:6.

12 **O thou**. 1 S 9:9. 2 Ch 16:10. Is 30:10.
go. Am 2:12. Mt 8:34. Lk 8:37, 38. 13:31. Ac 16:39.
eat. 1 S 2:36. Is 56:11. Ezk 13:19. Ml 1:10. Ro 16:18. 1 C 2:14. 1 P 5:2.

13 **prophesy**. Am 2:12. Ac 4:17, 18. 5:28, 40.
for. 1 K 12:29, 32. 13:1.
chapel. or, sanctuary. ver. 9.
king's court. Heb. house of the kingdom. Da 4:30.

14 **neither**. 1 K 20:35. 2 K 2:3, 5, 7. 4:38. 6:1. 2 Ch 16:7. 19:2. 20:34.
an herdman. Am 1:1. Zc 13:5. 1 C 1:27.
sycamore fruit. or, wild figs. 1 K 10:27. 1 Ch 27:28. 2 Ch 1:15. 9:27. Ps 78:47. Is 9:10.

15 **the Lord took me**. Ex 3:1-10. Jg 6:11. 1 S 2:18, 35, 36. 9:16. 2 S 7:8. 1 K 11:28mg. 19:19. Ne 1:11. Ps 78:70-72. Da 1:19. Mt 4:18, 19. 9:9. Ac 9:3. Ro +12:11. Ph 3:5, 6. 1 T 1:13.
as I followed. Heb. from behind. Ge +24:27. Je +17:16mg.
Go. Je 1:7. Ezk 2:3, 4. Lk 24:46-48. Ac +1:8. 4:20. 5:20, 29-32.

16 **hear**. 1 S 15:16. Je +7:2. 28:15-17.
Prophesy not. ver. 13. Is 30:10. Mi 2:6.
Israel. ver. 9. Ge +9:27.
and drop. Dt 32:2. Ezk 20:46. 21:2. Mi 2:6mg.
Isaac. Ge +9:27.

17 **Thy wife**. Is 13:16. Je 20:6. 28:12, 16. 29:21, 25, 31, 32. La 5:11. Ho 4:13, 14. Zc 14:2.
thy land. Ps 78:55.
die. 2 K 17:6. Ezk 4:13. Ho 9:3.
divided by line. Jsh +17:14. 2 S 8:2. Ps 60:6. Mi 2:5. Zc 2:1.
and Israel. ver. 11. Le 26:33-39. 2 K 15:29. 17:6, 23. Je 36:27-32.

AMOS 8

1 **showed unto me**. Am 7:1, 4, 7.
summer fruit. ver. 2. Is +16:9.

2 **Amos**. Am 7:8. Je 1:11-14. Ezk 8:6, 12, 17. Zc 1:18-21. 5:2, 5, 6.
A basket. ver. 1. Dt 26:1-4. Je 24:1-3.
The end. Je 1:12. 5:31. La 4:18. Ezk 7:2, 3, 7, 10. 12:23. 29:8. Re 14:15, 18.
I will not. Am 7:8.
pass by. Am 7:8.

3 **the songs**. ver. 10. Am 5:23. Ho 10:5, 6. Jl 1:5, 11, 13. Zc 11:1-3.
shall be howlings. Heb. shall howl. Is +13:6.
many. Am 4:10. Is 37:36. Je 9:21, 22. Na 3:3.
they shall. Am 6:9, 10. Je 22:18, 19.
with silence. Heb. be silent. Am 6:10. Le 10:3. Ps 37:7mg. 39:9.

4 **Hear**. Am 7:16. 1 K 22:19. Is 1:10. 28:14. Je 5:21. 28:15.
swallow. Am 2:6, 7. 5:11, 12. Ps +12:5. 14:4. +35:25. 140:12. Pr 30:14. Is 32:6, 7. 42:14. Mt 23:14. Ja 5:6.
the needy. Pr 14:31.
the poor. Ex 22:25. Pr 14:21. Ezk +16:49.

5 **new moon**. or, month. Col +2:16.
be gone. Ml 1:13.
and the sabbath. Ex +20:8-10. Ne 13:15-21. Is +58:13, 14. Je 17:27. Mt 15:8. Ro 8:6, 7.
set forth. Heb. open. Ge 44:11.
making. Le 19:36. Dt 25:13-16. 1 Ch 23:29. Pr 11:1. 16:11. 20:10, 23. Is 1:22. Ezk 45:10-12. Mi 6:10-12.
falsifying the balances by deceit. Heb. perverting the balances of deceit. Ho 12:7. Hab +2:9mg.

6 **buy the poor**. ver. 4. Am +2:6. Ex 21:2. Le 25:39-42. Ne 5:1-5, 8. Jl 3:3, 6.
pair of shoes. Am 2:6. Ru 4:7.
and sell. Pr 20:14. Je 22:13. Ezk 22:29. Ho 12:7. Mi 6:10, 11. Mk 10:19.

7 **sworn**. Am 6:8. Dt 33:26-29. Ps 47:4. 68:34. Lk 2:32.
the excellency of Jacob. Am 4:2. 6:8. Ex 15:7. 1 S 15:29. Ho 5:5. 7:10.
I will. Ex 17:14, 16. 1 S 15:2, 3. Ps 10:11. 137:7. Je 17:1. +31:34. Ho 7:2. 8:13. 9:9.
never. Jb +4:20.
forget. Ps +13:1.

8 **the land**. Ps 18:7. 60:2, 3. 114:3-7. Is 5:25. 24:19, 20. Je 4:24-26. Mi 1:3-5. Na 1:5, 6. Hab 3:5-8. Hg 2:6, 7.
every one mourn. ver. 10. Am 9:5. Je 4:28. 12:4. Ho 4:3. 10:5. Mt 24:30.
rise. Je +47:2.

9 **I will cause**. Jb 5:14. Is 29:9, 10. 59:9, 10. Je 15:9. Mi 3:6.
and I. Ex +10:22. Mt 27:45.

10 **I will turn**. ver. 3. Am 5:23. 6:4-7. Dt 16:14. 1 S 25:36-38. 2 S 13:28-31. Jb 20:23. Is 21:3, 4. 22:12-14. Da 5:4-6. Ho 2:11. Na 1:10.

your feasts. Ex 12:14. 23:15, 16. Le +23:2.
sackcloth. Jb +16:15.
and baldness. Is +3:24.
as the mourning. Je 6:26. Zc 12:10. Lk 7:12, 13.
a bitter. Jb 3:5mg.

11 **but**. Ge 41:56. 1 S 3:1. 28:6, 15. 2 Ch 15:3. Ps +74:9. Pr 29:18. Is 5:6. 30:20, 21. La 2:9. Ezk 7:26. Mi 3:6. Mt 9:36. Lk 15:14. Jn 6:35. Ep 2:12. 1 T 6:5. Re 3:17.

12 **shall run**. Pr 14:6. Da +12:4. Mt 11:25-27. 12:30. 24:23-26. Jn 7:34. Ro 9:31-33. 11:7-10. 2 T 3:6, 7.

13 **the fair**. Dt 32:25. Ps 63:1. 144:12-15. Is 40:30. 41:17-20. Je 48:18. La 1:18. 2:10, 21. Ho 2:3. Zc 9:17.
virgins. Ge +24:16.

14 **swear**. Ho 4:15. Zp 1:5.
sin. Dt 9:21. 1 K 12:28, 29, 32. 14:16. +16:24. 2 K 10:16, 29.
Thy god. Ex 32:4, 5.
manner. Heb. way. Ac 9:2. 18:25, 26. 19:9, 23. 24:14.
Beer-sheba. Am 5:5.
shall fall. Dt 33:11. 2 Ch 36:16. Ps 36:12. 140:10. Pr 29:1. Is 43:17. Je 25:27. 51:64.

AMOS 9

1 **I saw**. 2 Ch 18:18. Is 6:1. Ezk 1:28. Jn 1:18, 32. Ac 26:13. Re 1:17.
upon. Am 3:14. Ezk 9:2. 10:4.
the altar. Am 7:13. 1 K 13:1. The altar of burnt offerings (Ex +40:6), called: the brasen altar (Ex 38:30); the altar that is by the door of the tabernacle (Le +1:5); the altar of the Lord (Le +17:6). For New Testament allusions to the altar of burnt offerings see Mt +5:23.
Smite. Is 6:3, 4. Ezk 9:5. Zc 11:1, 2.
lintel. or, chapiter, or knop.
posts. 1 K 6:33, 35.
cut them. or, wound them. Jg 16:29, 30. Jb 6:9. Is 38:12. Jl 2:8.
in the head. Ps 68:21. Is 9:14. Hab 3:13.
shall not flee. Am 2:14, 15. Is 24:17, 18. 30:16. Je 48:44.
not be delivered. Am 6:1. Pr 11:4.

2 **they dig**. Jb 26:6. Ps 139:7-10. Is 2:19. Je 23:24. Ezk 8:8. 12:5, 7.
into. Ge 42:38. 44:29, 31. Nu 16:30, 33. Ps 9:17. Ezk +32:27. Mt 5:29, 30. +10:28. Lk 12:5.
hell. Heb. sheol, Ge +37:35. Ge 37:35. Dt 32:22. 2 S 12:23. Ps +16:8-11. 49:14. 86:13. 141:7. Pr 9:18.
climb. Jb 20:6, 7. Is 14:13-16. Je 49:16. 51:53. Ezk 28:13-16. Ob 4. Lk 10:18.

3 **hide**. Jb 34:22. Je 23:23, 24.
hid. Ps 139:9-11. Je 16:16.

my sight. Ps +11:4.
the serpent. Is 27:1.

4 **go**. Le 26:33, 36-39. Dt 28:64, 65. Ezk 5:2, 12. Zc 13:8, 9.
command the sword. Je +12:12.
set. Le 17:10. 20:5. Dt 28:62, 63. 2 Ch 16:9. Ps 34:15, 16. Je 24:6. 39:12. 44:11.
for evil. Am +3:6. Is +45:7. Je 21:10.
not for good. Je 44:11, 27.

5 **toucheth**. Ps 144:5. Hab 3:10. Re 20:11.
melt. 2 P +3:10.
and all. Am 8:8. Je 12:4. Ho 4:3.
shall rise. Ps 32:6. Je +47:2. Mt 7:27.

6 **buildeth**. Ps 104:3, 13.
stories. or, spheres. Heb. ascensions. 2 K 9:13 (stairs). 20:9 (degrees), 10, 11 (degrees, dial). Ps 120:t. 121:t. 122:t. 123:t. 124:t. 125:t. 127:t. 128:t. 131:t. 132:t. 133:t. 134:t. Is 38:8.
in the heaven. Is 48:13.
troop. or, bundle. Ge 2:1.
calleth. Am 5:8. Ge 7:11-19. Je 5:22.
face. Ge +1:2.
The Lord. Am 4:13. Ex 3:14, 15.
is his name. Ex +6:3. +15:3.

7 **ye not as**. Je 9:25, 26. 13:23.
Have not. Am 2:10. Ex 12:51. Is 43:3. Ho 12:13.
brought up Israel. Ex 13:3, 9, 14, 16. 33:1. Dt 5:15. 6:21.
the Philistines. Dt 2:23. Je +47:4.
the Syrians. Am 1:5. 2 K 16:9.
Caphtor. or, Crete. Dt 2:23.
Kir. i.e. a wall, fortress, S#7024h. Am 1:5. 2 K 16:9. Is 15:1. 22:6.

8 **the eyes**. ver. 4. Ps 11:4-6. Pr 5:21. 15:3. Je 44:27.
and I. Ge 6:7. 7:4. Dt 6:15. 1 K 13:34. Ho 1:6. 9:11-17. 13:15, 16.
saving. Dt 4:31. Is 10:21, 22. 27:7, 8. Je 5:10. 30:11. +31:35, 36. +33:24-26. Jl 2:32. Ob 16, 17. Ro +11:1-7, 28, 29.
not utterly destroy. 1 S +12:22. Is +41:9. +60:10. Je +4:27. Zc 10:6. Ro +11:1, 2.

9 **and I**. Le 26:33. Dt 28:64.
sift. Heb. cause to move. Lk 22:31, 32.
among all. Le 26:33. Ja 1:1.
like as. Is 27:8.
yet shall not. Ge 19:22. 2 K 10:23. Ezk +9:6. 39:28. Zc 10:9. 13:8, 9. Ml 3:6. Lk 22:31. Re 7:3.
grain. Heb. stone.

10 **the sinners**. Is 33:14. Ezk 20:38. 34:16, 17. Zp 3:11-13. Zc 13:8, 9. Ml 3:2-5. 4:1. Mt 3:10-12. 13:41, 42, 49, 50.
The evil. Am 6:1, 3. Ps 10:11. Ec 8:11. Is 5:19. 28:14, 15. 56:12. Je 18:13. Ml 3:15. Mt 24:50.

11 **that day**. Is +2:11. Ac 15:15-17. 2 Th +1:10.
raise. 2 S 7:13. 1 K 11:38, 39. Ps +102:13. Is +9:6, 7. 11:1-10. Je +23:5, 6. 30:9. 33:14-16,

20-26. Ezk 17:24. 34:23, 24. 37:24, 25. Ho
3:5. Mi +5:2. Lk +1:31-33, 69, 70.
Ac 2:30-36.
the tabernacle. 2 S 7:13. Is 16:5. Ezk 21:25-
27. 37:27. La 2:6. Ac +15:16.
of David. Ac +13:23. +15:16.
is fallen. Ps 80:16. Mt 23:38. Lk 13:35.
close. Heb. hedge, *or* wall. Jb 1:10. Ps 80:12.
89:40. Is 5:5.
build. Ps +102:16.
as in. Ps 143:5. Is 63:11. Je 46:26. La 5:21.
Ezk 36:11. Mi 7:14.
of old. Heb. *olam*, Ge +6:4.

12 **possess**. Is 11:14. 14:1, 2. Jl 3:8. Ob 18-21.
Edom. Ge +25:23.
which are called by my name. Heb. upon
whom my name is called. Dt 28:10. Is 43:7. Je
+14:9mg. Ac *15:17*.

13 **plowman**. Le 26:5. Ezk 36:35. Ho 2:21-23.
Jn 4:35.
shall overtake. Is 29:17. 35:1-9. +51:3.
55:12, 13. 60:13-17. 65:25. Je 31:5, 6. Ezk
34:26, 27. 36:8, 29, 30, 35. Ho 2:21. Jl 3:18.
the reaper. Ps 144:13-15. Jn 4:36.
soweth. Heb. draweth forth.

the mountains. Is 35:1, 2. 55:13. Jl 3:18, 20.
sweet wine. *or*, new wine.
the hills. ver. +5. Jg 5:5.

14 **I will bring**. Am 5:11. Je +23:3. Ezk 16:53.
+28:25. Zp 2:7. Zc 8:7, 8. Ro +11:1.
build. Ps +102:16. Is 61:4. +65:21, 22. Ezk
+36:10, 33-36. 37:25-28.
and inhabit. Ho 11:11.
plant. Am 5:11. Is 62:8, 9. Ezk 28:26. Ho
2:21-23. Jl 2:23. 3:18. Zp 1:13. Zc 8:12.
and drink. Zc 9:17.

15 **I will plant**. Le 25:18, 19. 26:5. Je +11:17. Zc
8:8.
their land. Ge 13:15. 17:8. Dt +32:43. 1 K
+4:21. Is +60:21. Je +7:7. 24:6. 32:41. Ezk
28:25. +34:28. 36:24, 28. 37:12, 21, 25. 38:8.
Jl 3:20, 21. Mi 4:4. Zc 3:9.
no more be pulled up. Is +11:11. 32:18.
33:20. 51:22. 60:21. Je 7:7. +23:8. 24:6.
31:40. 32:41mg. Ezk 34:28. 36:11. 37:23-27.
Ho +2:19. Jl 3:20. Mi 4:4. Zp 3:15. Zc +9:8.
+14:11.
which I have given them. Nu 32:7, 9. Dt
3:18. 26:15. 28:52. Jsh 2:9, 14. 18:3. 23:13,
15. 2 Ch +20:7. Je 25:5. Ezk 28:25.

OBADIAH

OBADIAH 1

1 A.M. 3417. B.C. 587.

Obadiah. i.e. *servant of Jehovah*, **S#5662h**. 1 Ch 3:21. 7:3. 8:38. 9:16, 44. 12:9. 2 Ch 17:7. Ezr 8:9. Ne 10:5. 12:25. Ob 1. Also **S#5662h**: 1 K 18:3, 3, 4, 5, 6, 7, 16. 1 Ch 27:19. 2 Ch 34:12.

concerning. Is 21:11, 12. Je 9:25, 26. +49:7-22.

We. Je +49:14.

rumor. lit. hearing. Le +13:55.

from the Lord. Am +3:6.

and an. Is 18:2, 3. 30:4.

Arise. Je 6:4, 5. 50:9-15. 51:27, 28. Mi 2:13.

2 **made thee small**. Nu 24:18. 1 S 2:7, 8. 2 K 14:7. Jb 34:25-29. Ps 107:39, 40. Is 23:9. Je *49:15*. Ezk 29:15. Mi 7:10. Ml 1:3. Lk 1:51, 52.

3 **pride**. Jb 20:5-7. Pr +16:5. Is 10:14-16. 14:13. 16:6. Je 48:29, 30. 49:16. Ezk +16:49. Ml 1:4.

clefts. Heb. *chagavim*, chasms. **S#2288h**. SS 2:14. Je 49:16.

rock. Heb. *sela*, a cliff or abrupt and elevated rock. Here without the Hebrew article, as Is 16:1. With the article, applied as a proper name to *Petra*, 2 K 14:7. 2 Ch 25:12. Possibly Jg 1:36. Certain descriptive terms are used exclusively in connection with *Sela*: (1) *Chagavim*, in this verse, "clefts." (2) *Seiph*, a cleft. **S#5553h**. Jg 15:8, 11. Is 2:21. 57:5. (3) *Tsechiach*, a bald spot, as the summit of a rock exposed to the drying sun. **S#6706h**. Ne 4:13. Ezk 24:7, 8. 26:4, 14. (4) *Nekik*, a cranny or fissure. **S#5357h**. Is 7:19. Je 13:4. 16:16. (5) *Shen*, a tooth or sharp edge or end of a crag. **S#8127h**. 1 S 14:4, 5. Jb 39:28. Used as a proper name, 1 S 7:12 (Shen).

whose habitation. Ps 60:9. Hab 2:9.

saith in his heart. Is 14:13-15. 47:7, 8. Je 49:4. Re 18:7, 8.

4 **exalt**. Jb 20:6, 7. 39:27, 28. Je 49:16. Hab 2:9.

set thy nest. Nu 24:21. Hab 2:9.

among. Ps 139:8. Is 14:12-15. Je 51:53. Am 9:2.

5 **if robbers**. Je *49:9*.

how. 2 S 1:19. Is 14:12. Je 50:23. La 1:1. Zp 2:15. Re 18:10.

if the grape gatherers. Dt 24:21. Is +17:6. 24:13. Je 6:9. *49:9*. Mi 7:1.

some grapes. or, gleanings. Jg 8:2. Is 17:6.

6 **are the**. Ps 139:1. Is 10:13, 14. 45:3. Je 49:10. 50:37. Mt 6:19, 20.

how are his. Da 2:22.

7 **the men of**. Ps 55:12, 13. 83:5-8. Je 4:30. 30:14. La 1:19. Ezk 23:22-25. Re 17:12-17.

men that were at peace with thee. Heb. men of thy peace. Ps 41:9mg. Je 20:10mg. 38:22mg.

they that eat thy bread. Heb. the men of thy bread. Ps 41:9. Jn 13:18.

there is. ver. 8. Is 19:11-14. 27:11. Je 49:7. Ho 13:13.

in him. or, of it.

8 **in that day**. ver. 15, 16. Is +2:11. 63:1-6. Je 49:13.

even. Je +19:7.

9 **thy**. Ps 76:5, 6. Is 19:16, 17. Je 49:22. 50:36, 37. Am 2:16. Na 3:13.

O Teman. Ge +36:11.

every. Is 34:5-8. 63:1-3.

mount. ver. 21. Dt 2:5.

10 **violence**. Ge 32:6-8. Am 1:11.

shame. Ps 69:7. 89:45. 109:29. 132:18. Je 3:25. 51:51. Ezk 7:18. Mi 7:10.

and. Je +49:7.

for ever. Heb. *olam*, Ex +12:24.

11 **in the day that the**. 2 K 24:10-16. 25:11. Je 52:28-30.

captive his forces. or, his substance. ver. 13mg. Ge +34:29. Is 60:5mg. Ro 11:25.

cast. Jl 3:3. Na 3:10.

even. Ps 50:18. 137:7. Je 39:4, 5.

12 **thou**, etc. or, do not behold, etc.

looked. Ps 22:17. 37:13. 54:7. 59:10. 92:11. Mi 4:11. 7:8-10. Mt 27:40-43.

the day. Dt +4:32.

rejoiced. Pr +17:5. Ezk 25:6, 7. Mt 5:44. Lk 19:41.

thou have. 1 S 2:3. Ps 31:18.

spoken proudly. Heb. magnified thy mouth. Dt +21:5mg. Ps 35:21. Is 37:24. 57:4. Ezk 35:13. Ja 3:5. 2 P 2:18. Ju 16. Re 13:5.

13 **looked**. 2 S 16:12. Ps 22:17. Zc 1:15.

substance. or, forces. ver. 11mg.

14 **neither shouldest**. Am 1:6, 9.
    delivered up. *or*, shut up. Ps 31:8.
    in the day. ver. 12. Ge 35:3. Is 37:3. Je
    +30:7.

15 **the day of the Lord**. Ps 37:12, 13. 110:5, 6.
    Is +2:11, 17. 10:25. Je 9:25, 26. 25:15-29.
    49:12. La 4:21, 22. Ezk +30:3. Jl 3:11-14. Mi
    5:15. Zc 14:14-18. 1 P 4:17.
    all the heathen. Ezk +30:3. Mi 5:15. Zc 14:2.
    Re +13:3, 7, 8, 16, 17.
    as thou hast done. Ge +12:3. Jg 1:7. Ps
    137:8. Ezk 35:15. Jl 3:7, 8. Hab 2:8. Mt 7:2.
    25:31-46. Ja 2:13.

16 **as ye**. Ps 75:8, 9. Is 49:25, 26. 51:22, 23. Je
    25:15, 16, 27-29. 49:12. 1 P 4:17.
    mountain. Is +11:9.
    so shall. Je 30:16. Ezk 25:12-14. Mt 7:2. Ja
    2:13.
    swallow down. *or*, sup up. Jb 6:3. Is
    +42:14mg. Hab 1:9.
    and they shall be. Is 8:9, 10. 26:14. 29:7, 8.
    La 4:21, 22. Ezk 35:14, 15.

17 **upon**. Is +24:23. 46:13. Jl +2:32.
    shall be. Je 46:28. Jl 2:32. 3:16. Am 9:8. Ro
    +11:26.
    deliverance. *or*, they that escape. Ps 71:2.
    83:3. +94:13. Is 16:1-5. +26:20. 57:1. Je 44:14,
    28. Ezk 7:16. Jl 2:32. Zp +2:3. Lk +21:36.
    there shall be holiness. *or*, it shall be holy.
    Is 1:26, 27. 4:3, 4. +60:21. Jl 3:17. Zc 8:3.
    14:20, 21. Re 21:27.
    shall possess. Nu 24:18, 19. Ps 69:35. Is
    14:1, 2. +26:15. Jl 3:19-21. Am 9:11-15. Mi
    4:11-13. Ac +7:5.

18 **shall be a fire**. Dt 4:24. Jb 31:3. Is 10:17, 18.
    31:9. Mi 5:8. Zc 12:6. He 12:29.
    the house of Joseph. Am +5:6.
    for stubble. 1 C +3:12.
    there shall not be. ver. 9, 10, 16.
    any remaining. ver. 14. Nu 24:19. Is 63:1-6.
    Je 49:7-22.

19 **the south**. Nu 24:18, 19. Jsh 15:21. Ps 60:6-
    12. Is +30:6. Je 32:44. Am 9:12. Mi 7:8-10.
    Ml 1:4, 5.
    the plain. Jsh 13:2, 3. 15:33, 45, 46. Jg 1:18,
    19. Is 11:13, 14. Ezk 25:16. Am 1:8. Zp 2:4-7.
    Zc 9:5-7.
    Philistines. Ge +10:14.
    the fields of Ephraim. 2 K 17:24. Ezr 4:2, 7-
    10, 17. Ps 69:35. Je 31:4-6. Ezk 36:6-12, 28.
    +37:21-25. 47:13-21. 48:1-9.
    Benjamin. Jsh 13:25, 31. 18:21-28. 1 Ch
    5:26. Je 49:1. Am 1:13. Mi 7:14.

20 **the captivity of this**. Je 3:18. +23:3.
    Zarephath. 1 K 17:9, 10. Lk 4:26, Sarepta.
    Sepharad. i.e. *drawn apart; end of wandering;*
    end of spreading out; boundary, limit, **S#5614h**.
    which is in Sepharad, shall possess. *or*,
    shall possess that which is in Sepharad, they
    shall possess. Je 13:19. 32:44. 33:13.

21 **saviors**. Ne +9:27. Da +12:3. Ho +11:12. Jl
    +2:32. +3:11. Mi 5:4-9. Zc 9:11-17. 10:5-12. 1
    T +4:16. Ja +5:20.
    shall come. Is 63:1. Mi 4:7.
    to judge. Ps +149:5-9. Da 7:27. Lk 22:30. 1 C
    +6:2, 3. Re 19:11-13. +20:4.
    and the kingdom. Ps 102:15. Mt +6:10, 13.
    Lk 1:32, 33. 1 C +15:24, 25, 28.

JONAH

JONAH 1

1 A.M. 3142. B.C. 862.

the word of the Lord. Jon 2:10. 3:1, 3. 4:4, 9, 10. Dt 18:18, 19. Jn 7:16. 8:28, 46, 47. 12:49. 14:10, 24. 17:8. 2 P +1:21.

Jonah. i.e. *a dove*, **S#3124h**. ver. 1, 3, 5, 7, 15, 17. 2:1, 10. Jon 3:1, 3. 4. 4:1, 5, 6, 8, 9. 2 K 14:25. Mt 12:39-41. 16:4. Lk 11:29, 30, 32, Jonas.

2 **Nineveh**. Ge +10:11.

cry. Jon 3:2, 4. Jg 7:3, 20. Is 58:1. Je 1:7-10. Ezk 2:7, 8. 3:5-9. Jl 3:9. Am 4:5. Mi 3:8. Mt 10:18.

for. Ge 18:20, 21. Ezr 9:6. Ja +5:4. Re 18:5.

3 **to flee**. Jon 4:2. Ex 4:13, 14. 1 K 19:3, 9. Je 20:7-9. Ezk 3:14. Lk 9:62. Ac 15:38. 26:19. 1 C 9:16.

Tarshish. Ge +10:4.

from the presence. Ge 3:8. 4:16. Nu 35:34. Jb 1:12. 2:7. Ps 139:7-12. Pr 27:8. 2 Th 1:9.

Joppa. Jsh 19:46. 2 Ch 2:16. Ezr 3:7. Ac 9:36.

going. lit. coming. Mk 16:2. Jn 6:17. 11:29. Ac 28:14. Re 6:1, 3, 5, 7.

Tarshish. 1 K 10:22. 2 Ch +9:21. 20:36, 37. Is 2:16. 23:1, 6, 10. 60:9. Je 10:9. Ezk 27:12, 25.

4 **the Lord**. Ex 10:13, 19. 14:21. 15:10. Nu 11:31. Ps 48:7. 107:24-31. 135:7. Am 4:13. Mt 8:24-27. Ac 27:13-20.

send out. Heb. cast forth.

like. Heb. thought.

5 **mariners**. lit. "salt-men." Ezk 27:9, 27, 29.

cried. ver. 6, 14, 16. Ex 2:23. 1 K 18:26. Is 44:17-20. 45:20. Je 2:28. Ho 7:14.

every man. Mi 4:5.

and cast. Jb 2:4. Ac 27:18, 19, 38. Ph 3:7, 8.

wares. or, tackling. lit. "vessels, instruments." Ge 24:53.

the sides. lit. "thighs." Ge 49:13. 1 S 24:3. Ezk 32:23. Am 6:10.

ship. The deck, or covered part. Hebrew root *saphan*, to cover. Dt 33:21mg. 1 K 6:9. 7:3, 7. Je 22:14. Hg 1:4.

and was. Jg 16:19. Mt 25:5. 26:40, 41, 43, 45. Lk 22:45, 46.

6 **shipmaster**. lit. chief of the rope. Heb. *rab hachobel. rab*, captain or head. 2 K 25:8. Est 1:8. Da 1:3. *chobel*. Ezk 27:8, 27, 28, 29 (pilot).

What. Is 3:15. Ezk 18:2. Ac 21:13. Ro 13:11. Ep 5:14.

O sleeper. Ps 13:3. Lk 22:46. 1 Th 5:6.

arise. Ps 78:34. 107:6, 12, 13, 18-20, 28, 29. Je 2:27, 28. Mk 4:37-41.

if. Jon 3:9. 2 S 12:22. Est 4:16. Jl 2:14. Am 5:15.

call upon. ver. 13-15. Ps 107:23-30. Mk 4:37-39.

7 **every**. Jg 7:13, 14. Is 41:6, 7.

and let. Jsh +14:2.

for. Jsh 7:10-13. 22:16-20. 1 S 14:38, 39. Jb 10:2.

evil. Is +45:7. Am +3:6.

and the. Nu +32:23. Jsh 7:18. 1 C 4:5.

8 **Tell**. Jsh 7:19. 1 S 14:43. Ja +5:16.

What is thine. Ge 47:3. 1 S 30:13.

9 **I am**. Ge 14:13. 39:14. 40:15. Ex 3:18. Ph 3:5.

and I. 2 K 17:25, 28, 32-35. Jb 1:9. Ps 146:5, 6. Ho 3:5. Ac 27:23. Re 15:4.

the Lord. or, Jehovah.

the God of heaven. Re +11:13. 16:11.

which. Ge 1:1, 10. Ne 9:6. Ps 95:5, 6. 146:5, 6. Ac 14:15. 17:23-25.

10 **were**. Jsh 2:11. 1 S 15:22, 23. 1 K 13:20-22. Jn 19:8.

exceedingly afraid. Heb. afraid, with great fear. Ge +1:29. Da 5:6-9.

Why. Jsh 7:25. 2 S 24:3.

he fled. ver. 3. Jb 27:22.

11 **What**. 1 S 6:2, 3. 2 S 21:1-6. 24:11-13. Mi 6:6, 7.

calm unto us. Heb. silent from us. ver. 12. Ps +37:7mg. Pr 26:20mg.

wrought, and was tempestuous. or, grew more and more tempestuous. Heb. went and was, etc.

12 **Take**. 2 S 24:17. Jn 11:50.

for I know. Jsh 7:12, 20, 21. 1 Ch 21:17. Ec 9:18. Ac 27:24.

for my sake. Ps 32:5. 51:3, 4. Je 3:13. 14:20.

13 **rowed**. Heb. digged. Am 9:2.

but. Jb 34:29. Pr +21:30.

14 **they cried**. ver. 5, 16. Ps 107:28. Is 26:16.

let us not. ver. 4-6. Ge 4:13-15. 20:3, 7. 21:14-16. 32:9-12. Is 38:1-5. Mt 8:23-25. 14:28-30. 26:39. 1 J 5:16, 17.

life. Heb. *nephesh*, soul, Ge +44:30.
lay not. Ge 9:6. Dt 21:8. Ac 28:4.
for thou hast done. Ps 115:3. 135:6. Da 4:34, 35. Mt 11:26. Ep 1:9, +11.

15 **they**. Jsh 7:24-26. 2 S 21:8, 9. Ps 39:9.
took up. Ge 47:30. Ex 28:12, 29.
and the. Ps 89:9. 93:3, 4. 107:29. Mt 8:26. Lk 8:24.
ceased. Heb. stood. Ge 19:17.

16 **feared**. ver. 10. Is 26:9. Da 4:34-37. 6:26. Mk 4:41. Ac 5:11.
offered, etc. Heb. sacrificed a sacrifice unto the Lord, and vowed vows. Ge 8:20. Jg 13:16. 2 K 5:17. Ps 76:11. 107:22. Is 60:5-7.
made vows. Le +23:38.

17 **the Lord**. Jon 4:6. Ge 1:21. Ps 104:25, 26. Hab 3:2.
prepared. or, appointed, or assigned. Jon 4:6, 7, 8. Jb 7:3. Da 1:5, 10, 11. 5:25, 26.
great fish. Mt 12:40, Greek, *ketos*, any large marine monster; whence *cetaceae*, the mammalian order of fish.
in. Mt 12:39, 40. 16:4. Lk 11:30.
belly. Heb. bowels. Jon 2:1.
for three days and. Jsh 5:11. 1 S 30:12. 1 K 16:8.

JONAH 2

1 **prayed**. 2 Ch 33:11-13. Ps +50:15. 91:15. Is 26:16. Ho 5:15. 6:1-3. Ja 5:13.
out. Jb 13:15. Ps 130:1, 2. La 3:53-56. Ac 16:24, 25.

2 **I cried**. Jon 1:2, 6, 14. Ge 32:7-12. 24-28. 1 S 30:6. Ps +3:4. 4:1. 22:24. 65:2. 120:1. 130:1. Lk 22:44. He 5:7.
by reason of mine. *or*, out of mine. 1 S 1:16.
he heard. Ps 65:2. Is 45:19.
out. Ps 18:5, 6. 61:2. 86:13. 88:1-7. 116:3. Mt 12:38-41.
hell. *or*, the grave. Heb. *sheol*, Ge +37:35. Dt +32:22. Jb 26:6. Ps +9:17. +16:10. 139:7, 8. Is +14:9, 11. Ezk +32:27. Am +9:2. Hab 2:5. Mt 12:40. Ac 2:27, 31.
and thou heardest. Ps 34:6. 65:2.

3 **thou**. Jon 1:12-16. Ps 69:1, 2, 14, 15. 88:5-8. La 3:54.
deep. or, shady place. Jb 41:31. Ps 68:22. 69:2, 15. 107:24.
midst. Heb. heart. Pr 23:34.
the floods. or, tides. lit. "river." Ge 2:10, 13. 2 K 5:12. Ezk +32:2.
all thy billows. lit. "heaps." Ge 31:46, 47, 48, 51, 52. Jsh 7:26. 8:29. Ps 42:7.

4 **I said**. Ps 31:22. 77:1-7. Is 38:10-14, 17. 49:14. Ezk 37:11.
out. 1 K 9:7. Je 7:15. 15:1.
yet will. Ps 42:5, 11. 43:5.
toward. Da +6:10.

5 **waters compassed**. Ge 7:18. Ps 40:2. 69:1, 2. La 3:54.
soul. Heb. *nephesh*, Ge +12:13.
the depth. **S#8415h**. Ge 1:2 (deep). 7:11. 8:2. 49:25. Ex 15:5, 8. Dt 8:7. 33:13. Jb 28:14. 38:16, 30. 41:32. Ps 33:7. 36:6. 42:7. 71:20. 77:16. 78:15. 104:6. 106:9. 107:26. 135:6. 148:7. Pr 3:20. 8:24, 27, 28. Is 51:10. 63:13. Ezk 26:19. 31:4, 15. Am 7:4. Hab 3:10.

6 **bottoms**. Heb. cuttings off. **S#7095h**. 1 K 6:25 (cut down). 7:37 (size).
mountains. Dt 32:22. Ps 65:6. 104:6, 8. Is 40:12. Hab 3:6, 10.
the earth. Jb 38:4-11. Pr 8:25-29.
yet. Ps +16:10. Is 38:17. Ac 13:33-37.
her bars. Je 51:30. La 2:9. Am 1:5. Na 3:13.
for ever. Heb. *olam*, Ex +12:24.
corruption. *or*, the pit. Jb +9:31 (**S#7845h**). 33:24, 28. Ps 9:15. 30:3, 9. 55:23. 143:7. Is 38:17.

7 **my soul**. Heb. *nephesh*, Ge +34:3; +9:5. Ps 22:14. 27:13. 107:5. 119:81-83. He 12:3.
fainted. Jon 4:8. Ps 27:13. 77:3. 84:2. 107:4-6. 142:3 (overwhelmed). Je 14:2. La 2:12 (swooned).
I remembered. 1 S 30:6. Ps 20:7. 42:5, 11. 43:5. 77:10, 11. 143:5. Is +44:21. 50:10. La 3:21-26. 2 C 1:9, 10.
my prayer. 2 Ch 30:27. Ps 18:6. 66:19. Is +65:24. Re 5:8. 8:3, 4.
holy. ver. 4. Ps 5:7. 11:4. 65:4. Mi 1:2. Hab 2:20.

8 **observe**. Dt +32:21. Je 2:13. +10:2. Hab 2:18-20.
lying vanities. or, vanities of emptiness. 1 C 8:4.
forsake. Je 17:13.
mercy. Jon 4:2. Ps 103:8.

9 **I will sacrifice**. Ge 35:3. Le +7:12. +23:19. Je +33:11. Ro 12:1.
I will pay. Le +23:38.
Salvation. Ac 4:12. Re +7:10.

10 **spake**. Jon 1:17. Ge 1:3, 7, 9, 11, 14. Ps 8:6-9. 33:9. 105:31, 34. Is 50:2. Mt 8:8, 9, 26, 27.

JONAH 3

1 **the word**. Jon 1:1. Lk 10:30.
the second time. Ge +22:15. 41:32. Jn 21:15-17.

2 **Nineveh**. ver. 3. Jon 1:2. Ge +10:11. 1 S 15:22, 23. Na 2:6, 10. 3:1, 18.
preach. Je 1:17. 15:19-21. Ezk 2:7. 3:17. Mt 3:8. Jn 5:14.

3 **arose**. Ge 22:3. Mt 21:28, 29. 2 T 4:11.
Nineveh was. Na 2:8, 9.
an exceeding great city. Heb. a city great of God. Ps +36:6mg.

4 Yet. ver. 10. Dt 18:22. 2 K 20:1, 6. Is 38:1. Je 18:7-10.

forty. Ge 7:4. 18:28, 29. 50:3. Ex +16:35. 24:18. Nu 13:25. 14:34. Dt 9:9, 18, 25. 25:3. 29:5. Jsh 5:6. 14:7. Jg 3:11. 5:31. 8:28. 13:1. 1 S 4:18. 17:16. 2 S 5:4. 15:7. 1 K 2:11. 11:42. 19:8. 2 K 12:1. Ps 95:10. Ezk 4:6. 29:11-13. Mt 4:2. Ac 1:3. 7:30, 36, 42. 13:18, 21. He 3:9, 17.

5 believed. Ex 9:18-21. Ob +21. Mt 12:41. Lk 11:32. Ac 27:25. He 11:1, 7.

and proclaimed. Mt +6:16.

from. Ac +8:10.

6 word. Je 13:18.

and he arose. Ps 2:10-12. Ja 1:9, 10. 4:6-10.

and covered. Est +4:1-4.

7 proclaimed. ver. 5. 2 Ch 20:3. Ezr 8:21. Jl 2:15, 16.

published. Heb. said.

nobles. Heb. great men. 2 K 10:11.

herd. Jl 1:18. Ro +8:20-22.

8 and beast. ver. 7. Jon 4:11.

sackcloth. Jb +16:15.

cry mightily. Jon 1:6, 14. Ps 130:1, 2.

let. Is 1:16-19. 55:6, 7. 58:6. Ezk 18:21-24, 27, 30-32. 33:11. Da 4:27. Mt 3:8. Ac +3:19. 26:20.

the violence. Is 59:6.

9 Who can tell. Jon 1:6. 2 S 12:22. Je +18:8. Ezk 18:21-23. Am 5:15. Lk 15:18-20.

if. 2 Ch 34:19-21. Ps 90:11. Ec 2:19. 3:21. 6:12. 8:1. Is 39:5, 8. Jl 2:14.

turn. Ex +32:12.

10 God saw. 1 K 21:27-29. Jb 33:27, 28. Je 31:18-20. Lk 11:32. 15:20.

and God repented. Je +18:8. Ezk 33:14, 15.

JONAH 4

1 it displeased Jonah. ver. 4, 9. 2 K 14:25-27. Je 20:7, 8. Mt 20:15. Lk 7:39. 15:28. Ac 13:46. Ja 4:5, 6.

he was very angry. ver. 8-11. Ja 1:19, 20.

2 he prayed. 1 K 19:4. Je 20:7.

I fled. Jon 1:3. Lk 10:29.

Tarshish. Ge +10:4.

thou art. Ps 78:38. Ho 11:8, 9.

God. Heb. *El*, Ex +15:2.

and merciful. Ex +34:6, 7. Dt +33:9. Jb +36:7. Ps 119:64. 138:8. Jn 6:37. Ep 2:4-7.

slow to anger. Jn 3:36.

and of. Je +18:8.

and repentest. Is 55:9. Ezk 18:25, 27.

3 take. Nu 11:15. 20:3. 1 K 19:4. Jb 3:20, 21. 6:8, 9. Je 20:14-18. Ph 1:21-25.

life. Heb. *nephesh*, soul, Ge +44:30.

for. ver. 8. Jb 7:15, 16. Ec 7:1. 1 C 9:15.

4 Doest thou well to be angry? *or*, Art thou greatly angry? ver. 9. Nu 20:11, 12, 24. Ps 37:8. 106:32, 33. Ec 7:8, 9. Mi 6:3. Mt 20:15. Ep 4:26. T 1:7. Ja 1:19, 20.

5 Jonah. Jon 1:5. 1 K 19:9, 13. Is 57:17. Je 20:9.

till. Ge 19:27, 28. Je 17:15, 16. Lk 19:41-44.

6 the Lord. Jon 1:17. Ps 103:10-14.

gourd. *or*, palmerist.

So Jonah. Est 5:9. Pr 23:5. Is 39:2. Am 6:13. Lk 10:20. 1 C 7:30.

was exceeding glad. Heb. rejoiced with great joy.

7 God prepared. Jb 1:21. Ps 30:6, 7. 102:10. He 12:5-7.

a worm. Dt 28:39.

it withered. Ps 90:5, 6. Is 40:6-8. Jl 1:12.

8 that God prepared. ver. 6, 7. Jon 1:4, 17. Ezk 19:12. He 12:9, 10. Re 3:19.

vehement. *or*, silent. *or*, cutting. **S#2759h**, only here. From Hebrew root **S#2790h**: 2 S 19:10mg. Jb 1:14 (plowing). Zp 3:17mg.

east wind. Ge +41:6. Ex 10:13, 19.

and the sun. Ps 121:6. SS 1:6. Is 49:10. Re 7:16.

and wished. ver. 3. Le 10:3. 1 S 3:18. 2 S 15:25, 26. Jb 2:10. Ps 39:9.

in himself. Heb. *nephesh*, Ex +15:9.

9 Doest thou well to be angry. *or*, Art thou greatly angry. ver. 4.

I do well to be angry. *or*, I am greatly angry. Ge 4:5-14. Jb 18:4. 40:4, 5. Ja 3:8-10.

even. Jg 16:16. Jb 5:2. Mt 26:38. 2 C 7:10. Re 9:6.

10 had pity on. *or*, spared. lit. hast hastened upon. ver. 11. Ge 45:20mg. Ps 72:13. Ezk 16:5.

neither madest it grow. or, nourished it. lit. make great. Ge 12:2.

came up in a night. Heb. was the son of the night. 1 S +20:31. Ge 17:12mg.

11 should. ver. 1. Is 1:18. Mt 18:33. Lk 15:28-32.

Nineveh. Ge +10:11.

that great city. Jon 1:2. 3:2, 3. Ps 48:2. Ezk 48:35. Zc 8:3. Mt 7:6. 9:35-38. 10:11-14, 23. 11:1. 23:37. Lk 13:6-10. Jn 4:4, 5. Ac +1:8. 13:1-3. 14:3, 28. 18:1. 19:1, 8-10, 20, 21. 20:2, 3, 31. 28:11, 14. He 12:22.

are. Heb. *yesh*, Pr 8:21.

that cannot. Dt 1:39.

discern. Is 7:16.

and also. Ps 36:6. 104:14, 27, 28. 145:8, 9, 15, 16.

much cattle. Jon 3:2, 7.

MICAH

MICAH 1

1 A.M. 3254. B.C. 750.
Micah. i.e. *who is like Jehovah?* ver. 14, 15.
S#4318h. Jg 17:5, 8-10, 12, 13. 18:2-4, 13, 15, 18, 22, 23, 26, 27, 31. 1 Ch 5:5. 8:34, 35. 9:40, 41. 23:20. 24:24, 25. 2 Ch 18:14. 34:20. Je 26:18.
Morasthite. ver. 14. Je 26:18. Micah is one of several prophets who did come out of Galilee (Jn 7:52).
Jotham. Jg +9:5. 2 Ch ch. 27-32.
which. Is 1:1. Am 1:1. Ob 1. Na 1:1. Hab 1:1.
concerning. ver. 5. Ho 4:15. 5:5-14. 6:10, 11. 8:14. 12:1, 2. Am 2:4-8. 3:1, 2. 6:1.

2 **all ye people**. Heb. ye people all of them.
hearken. Dt 32:1. 1 K 22:28. Ps 49:1, 2. 50:1, 4. Is 1:2. Je +7:2. 22:29. Mk 7:14-16.
all that therein is. Heb. the fulness thereof. Ps 24:1. 50:12. Je 47:2mg. Am 6:8mg.
let. Ge 31:50, 51. Ps 50:7. Je 29:23. Ml 2:14. +3:5.
the Lord from. Ps 11:4. 28:2. Jon 2:7. Hab 2:20.

3 **cometh**. Is +35:4.
his place. 1 K +8:39. Ps 115:3. Ezk 3:12. Ho 5:14, 15.
and tread. Dt 33:29. Jb 40:12. Is 2:10-19. 25:10. 63:3, 4. Am 4:13.
the high. Dt 32:13. 33:29. Is 58:14. Hab 3:19.

4 **the mountains**. Dt 32:22. Jg 5:4, 5. 2 K ch. 17, 25. 1 Ch 12:15. Je +3:23. Hab 3:6, 10. 2 P +3:10-12. Re 20:11.
the valleys. Zc 14:4.
as wax. Ps 68:2.
a steep place. Heb. a descent. Jsh 7:5.

5 **the transgression of Jacob**. 2 K 17:7-23. 2 Ch 36:14-16. Is 50:1, 2. 59:1-15. Je 2:17, 19. 4:18. 5:25. 6:19. La 5:16. 1 Th 2:15, 16.
is it. 1 K +16:24.
high places. 2 K +21:3.
they. 2 K 16:3, 4, 10-12. 2 Ch 28:2-4, 23-25.

6 **I will make**. Mi 3:12. 2 K 19:25. Is 25:2, 12. Je 9:11. 51:37. Ho 13:16.
and I will pour. Je 51:25. La 4:1. Ezk 13:14. Hab 3:13. Mt 24:2.

7 **all the graven images**. Ex +20:4. +23:24. +32:4. Le +26:30. Is 2:18.
the hires. Dt 23:18. Je 44:17, 18. Ho 2:5, 8, 12. 8:9, 10. 9:1.
for. Dt 23:18. Jl 3:3. Re 18:3, 9, 12, 13.

8 **I will wail**. Is 16:9. 21:3. 22:4. Je 4:19. 9:1, 10, 19. 48:36-39.
howl. Is +13:6.
I will go. Is 20:2-4.
naked. Is 32:11.
a wailing. Jb 30:29. Ps 102:6.
owls. Heb. daughters of the owl. Jb +30:29. Is 13:21mg.

9 **her wound is incurable**. *or, she* is grievously sick of her wounds. Is 1:5, 6. Je 10:19. 15:18. 30:11-15.
it. 2 K 18:9-13. Is 8:7, 8.
he. ver. 12. 2 Ch 32:1, etc. Is 10:28-32. 37:22-36.
the gate. Ge +22:17. Ob 11, 13.

10 **Declare**. 2 S 1:20. Am 5:13. 6:10.
Gath. Jsh +11:22.
Aphrah. i.e. *dust*. **S#1036h**. Jsh 18:23, Ophrah.
roll. Jsh +7:6. Jb 2:8. Je 6:26. La 3:29.

11 **Pass**. Is 16:2. Je 48:6, 9.
thou inhabitant. Heb. inhabitress. Je +10:17mg.
Saphir. i.e. *fair; beautiful*, **S#8208h**. *or*, thou that dwellest fairly.
having. ver. 8. Is +3:17.
Zaanan. *or*, the country of flocks. **S#6630h**.
Beth-ezel. *or*, a place near. **S#1018h**.

12 **Maroth**. i.e. *bitterness, bitter fountains*, **S#4796h**. Ru 1:20.
waited carefully. *or*, was grieved. 1 S 4:13. Jb 30:25. Is 59:9-11. Je 8:15. 14:19.
but. ver. 9. Is +45:7. Am +3:6.

13 **Lachish**. Jsh +10:3.
bind. Ge 19:17. 2 K +9:21mg. Is 10:31. Je 4:29.
she. Ex 32:21. 1 K 13:33, 34. 14:16. 16:31. Re 2:14, 20. 18:1-5.
for. 2 K 8:18. 16:3, 4. Je 3:8. Ezk 23:11.

14 **give**. 2 S 8:2. 2 K 16:8. 18:14-16. 2 Ch 16:1-3. Is 30:6.
to. *or*, for.
Moresheth-gath. i.e. *possession of Gath*, **S#4182h**. ver. 1.
houses. Ps 62:9. 118:8, 9. 146:3, 4.

Achzib. *that is,* a lie. Jsh 15:44. 19:29. Jg 1:31.

15 **will.** Is 7:17, etc. 10:5, 6. Je 49:1.
Mareshah. Jsh +15:44.
he, etc. *or,* the glory of Israel shall come to, etc. Is 5:13. 10:3.
Adullam. Jsh +12:15.

16 **Make thee bald.** Is +3:24.
thy delicate. Dt 28:56, 57. Is 3:16, etc. La 4:5-8.
for. Dt 28:41. 2 K 17:6. Is 39:6, 7.

MICAH 2

1 Cir. A.M. 3274. B.C. 730.
devise iniquity. Est 3:8, 9. 5:14. 9:25. Ps 7:14-16. 140:1-8. Pr 6:12-19. 12:2. Is 32:7. 59:3-8. Je 18:18. Ezk 11:2. Na 1:11. Lk 20:19, 20. 22:2-6. Ac 23:12. Ro 1:30.
work evil. Ps 36:4. Pr 4:16.
upon their beds. Ps 4:4.
when. Ho 7:6, 7. Mt 27:1, 2. Mk 15:1. Ac 23:15.
because. Ge 31:29. Dt 28:32. Ne 5:5. Pr 3:27. Ec 4:1. Jn 19:11.
is. Heb. *yesh,* Pr 8:21.

2 **they covet fields.** Ex 20:17. Le 6:4. Dt 5:21. 1 K 21:2-19. Jb 31:38, 39. Is 5:8. Je 22:17. Am 8:4-6. Hab 2:5-9. 1 T 6:10.
so they. Mi 3:9. Ex +22:21-24. 2 K 9:26. Ne 5:1-5, 11. Jb 24:2-12. Ezk 18:12, 13. 22:12, 27, 29. Am 8:4-6. Ml +3:5.
oppress. *or,* defraud. Le +19:13. 1 S 12:3, 4. Ml +3:5. Mk 10:19. 1 Th +4:6.

3 **this family.** Je 8:3. Am 3:1, 2.
do. ver. 1. Je 18:11. 34:17. La 2:17. Ja 2:13.
devise an evil. Is +45:7. Am +3:6.
from which. Am 2:14-16. 9:1-4. Zp 1:17, 18.
necks. Je 27:12. La 1:14. 5:5. Ro 16:4.
go haughtily. Is 2:11, 12. 3:16. 5:19. 28:14-18. Je 13:15-17. 36:23. 43:2. Da 4:37. 5:20-23.
for. Am 5:13. Ep +5:16. 6:13.

4 **shall.** Nu +23:7, 18. Is 14:4. Ezk 16:44.
and lament. 2 S 1:17. 2 Ch 35:25. Je 9:10, 17-21. 14:17, 18. Jl 1:8, 13. Am 5:1, 17.
a doleful lamentation. Heb. a lamentation of lamentations. Ge +1:29. La ch. 1-5. Ezk 2:10.
We be. Dt 28:29. Is 6:11. 24:3. Je 9:19. 25:9-11. Zp 1:2.
he hath changed. ver. 10. Mi 1:15. 2 K 17:23, 24. 2 Ch 36:20, 21. Ps 15:4. Is 63:17, 18.
how hath. Ps +2:4.
turning away he. *or,* instead of restoring, he, etc.

5 **cast.** Nu 26:55, 56. Dt 32:8, 9. Jsh +14:2. 18:4-6, 10. Ps +16:6. Ho 9:3.
cord. Jsh +17:14.
the congregation. Dt 23:2, 3, 8. Ne 7:61-65.

6 **Prophesy ye,** etc. *or,* Prophesy not *as they* prophesy. Heb. Drop, etc. Is 30:10. Je 5:31. 11:21. 26:8, 9, 20-23. Ezk 20:46. 21:2. Am 2:12. 7:13-16. Ac 4:17-19. 5:28, 29, 40-42. 7:51, 52. 1 Th 2:15, 16.
they shall not prophesy. Ps 74:9. Ezk 3:26. Am 8:11-13.
that they. Je 6:14, 15. 8:11, 12.

7 **named.** Mi 3:9. Is 48:1, 2. 58:1. Je 2:4. Mt 3:8-10. Jn 8:39, 40. Ro 2:28, 29. 9:6-13. 2 T 3:5.
is. Nu 11:23. Is 50:2. 59:1, 2. Zc 4:6. 2 C 6:12.
spirit. Heb. *ruach,* Is +48:16.
straitened. *or,* shortened. Jb +21:4mg.
do not my words. Jb 23:12. Ps 19:7-11. 119:70, 71, 92, 93, 99-103. Pr +8:8, 9. Is 34:16. Je +15:16. Jn +5:39. Ro 7:13. 2 T +3:15, 16.
walketh. Ps +1:1. 15:2. 84:11. Pr 2:7. 10:9, 29. 14:2. 28:18. Ho 14:9. Col +1:10. 1 Th 4:1.
uprightly. Heb. upright. Pr 21:27. T 1:15.

8 **of late.** Heb. yesterday. Ps 90:4.
risen. 2 Ch 28:5-8. Is 9:21.
with the garment. Heb. over against a garment. Lk 10:30.
that pass by. Lk 10:30-37.
securely. 2 S 20:19. 2 Ch 28:8. Ps 55:20, 21. 120:6, 7. Pr 3:29, 30.

9 **women.** *or,* wives. Ge 4:19.
cast. ver. 2. Mt 23:14. Mk 12:40. Lk 20:47.
from their children. 1 S 26:19. Jl 3:6.
my glory. Ps 72:19. Ezk 39:21. Hab 2:14. Zc 2:5. 2 C 3:18. 4:6.
for ever. Heb. *olam,* Ex +12:24.

10 **and depart.** Dt 4:26. 30:18. Jsh 23:15, 16. 1 K 9:7. 2 K 15:29. 17:6. 2 Ch 7:20. 36:20, 21.
for this. Dt 12:9. Ps 95:11. He 4:1-9.
because. Le +18:25-28. 20:22-26.
it shall destroy. Le 18:28. 20:22. 26:38. Je 9:19. 10:18. Ezk 36:12-14.

11 **a man.** 1 K 13:18. 22:21-23. 2 Ch 18:19-22. Is 9:15. Je 14:14. 23:14, 25, 32. 27:14, 15. 28:2, 3, 15. 29:21-23. Ezk 13:3-14, 22. 22:28. 2 C 11:13-15. 2 Th 2:8-10. 2 P 2:1-3. 1 J 4:1. Re 16:13, 14.
walking in the spirit and falsehood do lie. *or,* walk with the wind and lie falsely.
spirit. Heb. *ruach,* Ge +41:8.
and. Ge +1:26. By Hendiadys, a false and lying spirit.
saying. Ex +15:9.
I will. Mi 3:5, 11. 1 K 22:6. Je 6:13, 14. 8:10, 11. 23:17. Ro 16:18. Ph 3:19. 2 P 2:13-19.
he shall. Is 30:10, 11. Je 5:31. 2 Th 2:11.

12 **surely assemble.** Is 14:1. Je 3:18. Ro 11:26.
gather. Je +23:3.
remnant. Mi +4:7.
I will put. Mi 7:14. Je 31:10. Ezk 34:11, 12, 22, 31.
Bozrah. Ge +36:33.

they. Je 31:7-9. Ezk 36:37. Zc 8:22, 23. 9:14, 15. 10:6-8.

13 **breaker**. Ex 19:22, 24. 2 S 5:20. 1 Ch 14:11. 15:13. Is 42:7, 13-16. 45:1, 2. 49:9, 24, 25. 51:9, 10. 55:4. 57:14. 59:16-19. 62:10. Je 51:20-24. Da 2:34, 35, 44. Ho 13:14. Zc 12:8. 1 C 15:21-26. He 2:14, 15.
they have. Zc 10:5-7, 12. 12:3-8.
their king. Is 49:10. 51:12. 52:8, 12. Je 23:5, 6. Ezk 20:33-44. 34:23, 24. Ho 1:11. +3:5. Zp +3:15. Zc 2:10-13. 9:14, 15. 14:3-5. Mt +23:39. Jn 10:27-30. He +2:9, 10. 6:20. Re 7:17. 17:14. 19:13-17.
and the Lord. Mi 4:7. Is 52:12. Ho 3:5.

MICAH 3

1 Cir. A.M. 3294. B.C. 710.
Hear. ver. 9, 10. Je +7:2. 13:15-18. Am 4:1.
Is it. Dt 1:13-17. 16:18. +17:18-20. 2 Ch 19:5-10. Ps 14:4. 82:1-5. Je 5:4, 5. 1 C 6:5.

2 **hate**. 1 K 21:20. 22:6-8. Am 5:10-14. Lk 19:14. Jn 7:7. 15:18, 19, 23, 24. Ac 7:51, 52. Ro 12:9. 2 T 3:3.
love. 2 Ch 19:2. Ps 15:4. 139:21, 22. Pr 28:4. Jn 18:40. Ro 1:32.
pluck. Ps 53:4. Is 3:15. Ezk 22:27. 34:3. Am 8:4-6. Zp 3:3. Zc 11:4, 5.

3 **eat**. Je +10:25.
and chop. Ezk 11:3, 6, 7.

4 **Then**. Mi 2:3, 4. Je 5:31.
cry. Ps +66:18. Je 2:27, 28. Mt 7:22, 23. Ja 2:13. 1 P 3:12.
not hear. Ps +66:18.
he will even. Dt +31:17. Is 59:1-15.
as. Is 3:11. Am 8:4-6, 11, 12. Zc 7:9-13. Ro 2:8, 9.

5 **concerning**. ver. 11. Je 14:14, 15. 23:9-17, 27, 32. 28:15-17. 29:21-23. Ezk 13:10-16. 22:25-29.
make my people err. Is +8:16, 20. Ezk 13:19, 22. Ho 4:9, +12. Mt +15:14. Mk 12:24, 27. Ac 20:29, 30. Ep 4:14. 1 T +4:16.
that bite. Mi 2:11. Je 8:11. Ezk 13:10, 18, +19. Zc 9:7. Mt 7:15.

6 **night**. Ps 74:9. Is +8:20-22. Je 13:16. Ezk 13:22, 23. Zc 13:2-4.
that ye shall not have a vision. Heb. from a vision. Am +8:11.
that ye shall not divine. Heb. from divining. Je +27:9.
the sun. Is 29:10. 59:10. Je 15:9. Ho +3:4. Am 8:9, 10.

7 **the seers**. Ex 8:18, 19. 9:11. 1 S 9:9. Is 44:24, 25. 47:12-14. Da 2:9-11. Zc 13:4. 2 T 3:8, 9.
cover. Le 13:45. Ezk 24:17, 22.
lips. Heb. upper lip. Le 13:45. Ezk 24:17mg, 22.
no answer. 1 S 14:37. 28:6, 15. Ps +74:9. Am +8:11.

8 **I am**. Jb 32:18. Is 11:2, 3. 58:1. Je 1:18. 6:11. 15:19-21. 20:9. Ezk 3:14. Mt 7:29. Mk 3:17. Ac 4:8-12, 19, 20. 7:54-57. 13:9-12. 18:5, 6, 9-11. 1 C 2:4, 12, 13.
power. Lk 24:49. 2 T +1:7.
spirit. Heb. *ruach*, Is +48:16.
to declare. Is 58:1. Ezk 16:2. 20:4. 22:2. 43:10. Mt 3:7-12. Ac 7:51, 52.

9 **I pray**. ver. 1. Ex 3:16. Ho 5:1.
that. Le 26:15. Dt 27:19. Ps 58:1, 2. Pr 17:15. Is 1:23. Je 5:28.

10 **build up Zion**. Je +22:13-17. Ezk 22:25-28. Hab 2:9-12. Zp 3:3. Mt 27:25. Mk 12:40. Jn 11:50.
blood. Heb. bloods. 2 K +9:26mg.

11 **heads**. Nu 16:15. 1 S 8:3. 12:3, 4. Is 1:23. Ezk 22:12, 27. Zp 3:3.
judge for reward. Dt 27:25. Ja +2:1.
and the priests. Je 6:13. 8:10. 1 T 3:3. T 1:11.
and the prophets. ver. 5. Ezk +13:19. Ac 8:18-20. 2 P 2:1-3, 14, 15. Ju 11.
yet. 1 S 4:3-6. Is 48:2. Je 7:4, 8-12. Ezk +33:31. Mt 3:9. Ro 2:17, etc.
and say. Heb. saying. Ge 1:22. Ex +15:9.
none evil can come. Je 23:17. Ezk 12:27. Am 6:3. 9:10. 2 P 3:3, 4.

12 **Therefore**. Je +11:8.
Zion. Mi 1:6. Ps 79:1. 107:34. Je 26:18. Mt 24:2. Ac 6:13, 14.
heaps. Mi 1:6.
the mountain. Mi 4:1, 2. Is 2:2, 3.

MICAH 4

1 **in the last days**. Ge +49:1. Mt 24:6, 14. Jn 6:39, 40. 1 P 1:5, 20. 1 J 2:18. Ju 18.
the mountain. Mi 3:12. Ps 24:3. Is +2:2-4. 11:9. Ezk 17:22-24. 28:16. 40:2. Da 7:14, 18, 22, 27. Re 11:15. +20:4. 21:1, etc.
house of the Lord. 2 S 7:13, 16. Is +2:2. 60:13. Ezk 40:2. Am +9:11. Acts 15:16.
top of the mountains. Is 2:2. 25:6, 7. 41:15. Ezk 17:23.
and people. Ps 68:29-32. 72:7-11, 16-19. 86:9. I10:3. Is +11:10. 27:13. 43:6. 54:2. Je 16:19. Zp 3:9, 10. Zc 14:16-21. Acts 15:17. Ro +11:25, 26. Re 15:4.

2 **shall come**. SS 1:4.
and say. Is 2:3. Je 31:6. 50:4, 5. Zc 8:20-23.
and he. Dt 6:1. Ps 25:8, 9, 12. Is 54:13. Mt 11:25-30. Jn 6:45. 7:17. Ac 10:32, 33. 13:42. Ja 1:19-25.
for the law. Ps 110:2. Is 26:9. 42:1-4. 51:4, 5. Ho +6:3. Zc +14:8, 9. Mt 28:19, 20. Mk 16:15, 16, 20. Lk 24:47. Ac +1:8. 13:46, 47. Ro 10:12-18. 15:19.
the word. Ge 15:1-4. 1 S 3:1-21. 2 S 7:4. 1 K 17:8-24. Ps 33:6. Is 40:8. Je 25:3. Jn 1:1-14. +3:34. Lk 1:2. He 4:12. 11:3. 1 P 1:23. 2 P 3:5. Re 19:13.

3 **he shall judge**. Ps 2:5, 9. +7:8. 72:8, 11, 17. Jn 16:8-11.

and rebuke. Mi 5:15. Ps 2:5-12. 68:30, 31. Is 25:3. Da +2:44. Zc 12:3-6. 14:3, +12-19. Re 20:8, 9.

they shall. Ps 46:9. Is 2:4. 11:6-9. Ho 2:18. Jl 3:10. Zc 9:10.

pruninghooks. *or*, scythes. Is 2:4mg. Jl 3:10mg.

neither. Ps 72:7. Is +9:7. 60:17, 18. +65:25. He 7:2.

4 **they**. Is 36:16. Zc 3:10.

none shall. Le 26:6. Dt +12:10. Is 54:14. Je 30:10.

for. 2 S +1:3. Ps +24:10. Is 1:20. 40:5. 44:6. 58:14. Je +6:6.

5 **all**. 2 K 17:29, 34. Je 2:10, 11.

name of. Jon 1:5, 6.

and we. Ge +17:1. Ps 71:16. Is 2:5. Zc 10:12. Col +2:6. 3:17.

the name. Ex +3:14, 15. Ps 20:7. 48:14. 145:1, 2. Is 26:13.

for ever. Heb. *olam*, Ps +21:4.

and ever. Heb. *ad*, Ps +9:18.

6 **In that day**. ver. 1. Is +2:11. Je 33:14.

will I assemble. Mi 2:12. Ps 38:17. Is 35:3-6. Je 31:8. Ezk 34:13-17. Zp 3:19. He 12:12, 13.

will gather. Is 56:8. Je 3:18. +23:3. Lk 19:10. Jn 10:16.

7 **I will**. Mi +5:3. Ezr 9:8, 14. 2 K 19:4, 30, 31. Is 6:13. 49:21-23. 60:22. 66:8. Je 42:2. 44:14, 28. Ho 1:10. Zc 8:6, 12. 9:13-17. 10:5-12.

cast far off. Is +41:9. Zc 10:6.

the Lord shall reign. Is +24:23. Je +23:5. Re +11:15.

in mount Zion. Mi 3:12. Is +24:23. 65:19.

for ever. Heb. *olam*, Ex +12:24.

8 **O tower**. 2 K +5:24mg. Ps 48:12, 13. Is 5:2. Mt 21:33. Mk 12:1.

the flock. *or*, Edar. Ge 35:21.

the strong. 2 S 5:7. Is 10:32. Zc 9:12.

the daughter. Mt +21:5.

the first. Nu 24:19. Ps 18:43. Je 3:17. Da 2:44. 7:18. Ob +21. Zp 3:20. Zc 9:10. 12:6-9. Lk 24:47. Ep 1:21. Re 22:5.

9 **why**. Je 4:21. 8:19. +30:6, 7.

is there. Is 3:1-7. La 4:20. Ho +3:4. 10:3. 13:10, 11.

for pangs. Ge +3:16. Je +4:31. Mt +24:8.

10 **and labor**. Is 66:7-9. Ho 13:13. Jn 16:20-22.

go forth out. 2 K 20:18. 25:4. 2 Ch 33:11. 36:20. Ho 1:10. 2:14. Zc 14:2. Re +12:14.

Babylon. Am 5:25-27. Ac 7:42, 43.

there shalt. Mi 7:8-13. Ezr 1:1, 2. Is 45:13. 48:20. 52:9-12. Zc 2:7-9.

redeem. Ps 106:10. Je 15:21.

11 **many**. Is 5:25-30. 8:7, 8. 33:3. Ps 21:11. Je 52:4. La 2:15, 16. Jl 3:2, etc. Zc 12:3.

gathered against. Zp +3:8. Re +16:16.

Let her. Nu 35:33. Ezk 25:3. 26:2. 36:2. Ob 12.

let our. Mi 7:10. Ob 12.

12 **they know not**. Ps 94:11. Is 55:8. Je 29:11. Ro 11:33, 34.

he shall gather. Is 17:5-8. 21:10. Jl 3:12, 13. Zp +3:8. Zc 14:1-3. Mt +13:30, 39. Lk 3:17. 17:34-37. Re 14:14-20. +16:16.

floor. Ge +50:10.

13 **and thresh**. Is +21:10. Ho 10:11.

daughter. Mt +21:5.

thine horn. Am 6:13.

hoofs. Dt 25:4. 33:25. Is 5:28.

thou shalt beat. Mi 5:8-15. Je 51:19, 20. Da +2:44. Zc 9:13-15. 10:3-5. 12:6. Ml +4:3. Jn +18:36.

I will consecrate. Le 27:28. Jsh 6:19, 24. 2 S 8:10, 11. Ps 68:29. 72:10. Is 18:7. 23:18. 60:5-9. +61:6. Zc 14:14. Ro +11:25. 15:25-28. 1 C 16:2. Re 21:24-26.

their substance. Ob +11mg. Zc 14:20, 21.

the Lord of. Ps 97:5. Zc 4:14. 6:5.

MICAH 5

1 **gather**. Dt 28:49. 2 K 24:2. Is 8:9, 10. 10:6. Je 4:7. 25:9. Jl 3:9-11. Hab 1:6-10. +3:16.

he hath. Dt 28:51-57. 2 K 25:1-3, 21. Ezk 21:21, 22. 24:2. Lk 19:43, 44.

they. Jb 16:10. La 3:30. Mt 5:39. 26:67. 27:30. Jn 18:22. 19:3. Ac 23:2. 2 C 11:20.

judge. 1 S 8:5, 6. 1 K 22:24. Ps 7:8, 11. 9:4, 13. +50:6. 94:2. 96:13. Is 33:22. La 3:30. 4:20. 5:8, 12. Am 2:3.

rod. Mi 7:14. Mt 27:30.

upon the cheek. Mt 26:67. +27:30.

2 **But thou**. Mt 2:6. Jn 7:42.

Bethlehem. Mt 2:1, 6. Lk 2:4-6. Jn 7:42. He 7:14.

Ephrath. Ge +48:7, Ephrath. Jsh 12:9. Ru +1:2. 1 Ch +2:50.

little. 1 C 1:27-29.

among. 1 S 10:19. 23:23.

thousands. Ex +18:21, 25. Jsh +22:21.

of Judah. 1 Ch +5:2. Ps +60:7. Mt 2:6. He 7:14. Re 5:5.

yet. Is 11:1. 53:2. Ezk 17:22-24. Am 9:11. Lk 2:4-7. 1 C 1:27, 28.

come forth. Zc 9:9. 1 Th 4:16.

that is. Ge +49:10. 1 Ch 5:2. Is +9:6, 7. Je +23:5, 6. Ezk 34:23, 24. 37:22-25. Zc 9:9. Mt 28:18. Lk 1:31-33. 23:2, 38. Jn 19:14-22. Re 19:16.

ruler. Je 30:9. Ac 7:35.

whose. Ps 90:2. 102:25-27. Pr 8:22, 23. Jn +1:1-3. 8:58. Col 1:17. He +13:8. 1 J 1:1, 2. Re 1:11-18. 2:8. 21:6.

of old. Heb. *kedem*, **S#6924h**. Always used of the past; rendered (1) *ever*, Pr 8:23. (2) *eternal*, Dt 33:27. (3) *everlasting*, Hab 1:12. (4) *old*, Ne 12:46. Ps 44:1. 55:19. 68:33. 74:2. 77:5, 11.

78:2. 119:152. 143:5. Je 46:26. La 1:7. 2:17. Mi 7:20. (5) *ancient*, Dt 33:15. 2 K 19:25. Is 19:11. 23:7. 37:26. 45:21. 46:10. 51:9. (6) *past*, Jb 29:2. (7) *aforetime*, Je 30:20. (8) *before*, Ps 139:5. Pr 8:22.

from. Ps 72:17. Pr 8:22-24. Jn +1:1, 2. +8:35, 58. 17:5. 1 J 1:1, 2. Re +1:8, 17.

everlasting. *or*, the days of eternity. Heb. *olam*, Ge +17:7. Mi 7:14. Ps 90:2. 93:2. Pr 8:22, 23. Da +7:9. Jn 1:1, 2.

3 Therefore. Mi 7:13. Ho 2:9, 14.

give them up. Mi 6:14. 1 K 14:16. 2 Ch 30:7. Is 49:1-23. Ho 11:8. Zc 13:7-9. Mt 21:43.

until the time. Ps +102:13, 16. Ho 3:4, 5. +5:15. 6:2. Mt 19:28. +23:39. Lk 21:24. Ac +3:19. Ro +11:25.

she which travaileth. Mi 4:10. Ge +3:15. Is +7:14. +66:7, 8. Mt 1:21, 23. +24:8. Jn 16:21, 22. Re 12:1, 2.

brought forth. Mt 19:28.

then the remnant. ver. 7, 8. Mi 2:12. +4:7. 7:18. Is +1:9. 10:5, 6, 20-22. 11:11. 37:4, 31. Je 23:3. 31:1, 7-9. Ezk 6:8. +14:22. Jl 2:32. Am 5:15. Zp 2:7, 9. 3:13. Ro 9:27, 28. 11:4-6.

his brethren. Mt 12:50. 25:40. Ro 8:29. He 2:11, 12.

4 stand. Mi 7:14. Is 49:9, 10. Jn +10:11.

feed. *or*, rule. Ps 2:8. Is +40:11.

in the majesty. Ex 23:21. 1 Ch +29:11, 12. Ps 72:19. Mt 25:31. Jn 5:22-29. 10:38. 14:9-11. Re 1:13-18.

name. Dt +28:58.

the Lord. Jn 20:17. Ep 1:3.

shall abide. Mi 4:4 (sit). Ezk 34:25, 28 (dwell). 38:8. Jl +3:20mg. Am 9:14 (inhabit). Mt 16:18. 1 P 1:5. Ju 1.

shall he be great. Ps 22:27. 72:8, 17. 98:3. Is 49:5, 7. 52:10, 13. Zc 9:10. Lk 1:32. Re 11:15.

5 this. Ps 72:7. Is +9:6, 7. 14:3-5, 25. Zc 9:10. Lk 2:14. Jn 14:27. 16:33. Ep 2:14-17. Col 1:20, 21.

when the Assyrian. Is +7:14, 20. 8:7-10. 10:12, 24. 14:25. 30:31. 31:8, 9. 37:31-36. 65:8, 9. Je 33:15-26. Da 11:40.

tread in our palaces. Da +9:27. 11:40-45. Mt +24:15. 2 Th 2:3, 4. Re 11:1, 2.

then shall we. Is 44:28. 59:19. Zc 1:18-21. 9:13-16. 10:3-6. 12:6-9. Re 17:14. 19:14, 15.

seven. Ge +21:28, 31. Jb 5:19. Pr 6:16. 30:18, 29. Ec 11:2. Am 1:3, 6.

shepherds. Da +11:33. 1 P 5:1-4.

eight. Ec 11:2.

principal men. Heb. princes of men. Jsh 13:21. Ps 83:12. Ezk 32:30.

6 they. Is 10:12. 14:2. 30:31. 31:8, 9. 33:1. Na 2:11-13. 3:1-3.

waste. Heb. eat up. lit. feed on. Nu 14:9. Je 6:3. Ac 10:13.

the land of Nimrod. Ge 10:8-11mg. 1 Ch 1:10.

in the entrances thereof. *or*, with her own naked swords. or, passes. Na 3:13.

thus shall he deliver. Is 14:25. Ezk 39:2. Mt 24:30, 31. Lk 1:71, 74. Ro +11:26.

the Assyrian. 2 K 15:29. 17:3-5. 18:9-15. 19:32-35. 2 Ch 33:11. Is 10:5-12.

when he cometh. Ezk 39:16.

7 the remnant. ver. +3, 8.

as a dew. Dt 32:2. +33:13. Jg 6:36-40. Ps 133:3. Is 32:13-17. 44:3-5. 66:19. Ezk 47:1-12. Ho +6:3. Zc 14:8. Mt 28:19. Ac 9:15. 11:15-18. 13:46-48. Ro 11:12-15. 15:19, 20. 1 C 3:6.

as the showers. Dt 32:2. Ps 65:10. Zc 10:1.

tarrieth not. Is 55:10, 11. Je 14:22. Ac 16:9, 10. Ro 9:30. 10:20.

8 among the Gentiles. Mi +4:7. 7:16. Zp 3:15, 20.

as a lion. Mi 4:13. Ps 2:8-12. 110:5, 6. Is +5:29. 41:15, 16. Ob 18, 19. Zc 9:15. 10:5. 12:3-6. Mt 10:14, 15. Ac 18:6. 2 C 2:15-17.

sheep. *or*, goats. Ex 12:21.

treadeth down. Mi 4:13. Ml +4:3.

and none. Ps 50:22. Ho 5:14. He 2:3. 12:25.

9 hand. Ex +9:3. Is 1:25. 11:14. 14:2-4. 33:10. 37:36. Lk +19:27. 1 C 15:25. Re +19:13-21. 20:8, 9.

10 in that day. Mi 4:1, 6. Is +2:11.

that I. Ps 20:7, 8. 33:16, 17. 147:10, 11. Je 3:23. Ho 1:7. 14:3. Hg 2:22. Zc 4:6. 9:10.

will cut. ver. 9. Dt 17:16. Is 2:7. 31:1. Zc 9:10.

11 I will cut. ver. 14. Dt 29:23. Is 1:7. 6:11.

and throw. Is 2:12-17. La 2:2. Ezk 38:11. Ho 10:14. Am 5:9. Zc 2:4, 5. 4:6.

12 cut off. Is 2:6-8, 18, 20. +8:19, 20. 27:9. Zc 13:2-4. Re 19:20. 22:15.

witchcrafts. or, sorceries. Ex 22:18. Le 19:26. 2 Ch +33:6. Re +9:21.

soothsayers. 2 K +21:6.

13 graven images. Ex +20:4. +23:24. Is 17:7, 8. Ho +2:17. 14:3, 8.

cut off. Zc 13:2.

standing images. *or*, statues. ver. 14. 2 K +17:10mg.

no more worship. Is 2:8, 18. Ezk 6:9. 23:27. Zc 13:2.

the work. Ps 115:4. 135:15. Is 2:8.

14 groves. 2 K +17:10. Is +66:17.

cities. *or*, enemies. ver. 11.

15 execute vengeance. ver. 8. Ps +58:10. +149:7-9. Is 65:12. Jl 3:12. 2 Th 1:8.

MICAH 6

1 ye. 1 S 15:16. Je +7:2. 13:15. He 3:7, 8.

contend. Dt 4:26. 32:1. Ps 50:1, 4. Is 1:2. Je 22:29. Ezk 36:1, 8. Lk 19:40.

before. *or*, with. Mi 1:4. Is 2:12-14.

let. Ezk 37:4.

2 Hear ye. Dt 32:1.
foundations. Dt 32:22. 2 S 22:8, 16. Ps 104:5. Pr 8:29. Je 31:37.
a controversy. Is 1:18. 5:3, 4. 43:26. Je 2:9, 29-35. 25:31. Ezk 20:35, 36. Ho 4:1. 12:2.

3 O my. ver. 5. Ps 50:7. 81:8, 13.
what. Je 2:5, 31.
wherein. Is 43:22, 23.
testify. Ps 51:4. Je +42:19. Ro 3:4, 5, 19.

4 I brought. Ex 12:51. 14:30, 31. 20:2. Dt 4:20, 34. 5:6. 9:26. Ne 9:9-11. Ps 77:20. 78:51-53. 106:7-10. 136:10, 11. Is 63:9-12. Je 32:21. Ezk 20:5-9. Am 2:10. Ac 7:36.
and redeemed. Ex 6:6. 13:13-16. Dt 7:8. 15:15. 24:18. 2 S 7:23.
house of servants. Ex 13:3mg, 14. 20:2. Dt 5:6. 6:12. 7:8.
Moses. Ex +2:10.
Miriam. Ex +15:20.

5 remember now. Nu 22:5. 23:7. 24:10, 11. 25:1. 31:16. Dt +7:18. 9:7. 16:3. 23:4, 5. Ps 103:1, 2.
Balak. Nu ch. 22-25. 31:16. Dt 23:4, 5. Jsh 24:9, 10. Jg 11:25. Re 2:14.
Balaam. Nu +31:8.
Shittim. Nu 22:41. 23:13, 14, 27, 28. 25:1. 33:49. Jsh 4:19. 5:9, 10. 10:42, 43.
know the righteousness. Jg 5:11mg. Ps 36:10. 71:15, 16, 19. 143:11. Ro 3:25, 26. 1 J 1:9.

6 Wherewith. 2 S 21:3. Mt 19:16. Lk 10:25. Jn 6:28. Ac 2:37. 16:30. Ro 10:2, 3.
bow. Ps 22:29. 95:6. Ep 3:14.
the high. Ge 14:18-22. Da 3:26. 4:9. 5:18, 21. Mk 5:7. Ac 16:17.
with. Le 1:3, etc. Nu 23:1-4, 14, 15, 29, 30. He 10:4-10.
burnt offerings. Le +23:12.
of a year old. Heb. sons of a year. Ex 12:5mg. Le 9:3. 23:12.

7 pleased. 1 S 15:22. Ps 50:8-13. 51:16. Is 1:11-15. 40:16. Je 7:21, 22. Ho 6:6. Am 5:22.
ten thousands. Ge +2:24.
rivers. Jb 29:6.
shall I give. Le +18:21. Dt +18:10. Jsh 15:8. Jg 11:31, 39. 2 K 3:27. 16:3. +21:6. 23:10. Je +7:31. 19:5. Ezk 16:20, 21. 23:37. Ho +13:2mg.
body. Heb. belly. Ps 132:11mg. Phm 12.
for the sin. Ps 49:7, 8.
soul. Heb. nephesh, Ge +27:31.

8 O man. Ro 9:20. 1 C 7:16. Ja 2:20.
what is good. 1 S 12:23, 24. Ne 9:13. Ps 73:28. Ec 6:12. La 3:26, 27. Am 5:15. Lk +6:35. 10:42. Ro 7:16. 2 Th 2:16, 17.
require of thee. Dt 10:12, 13. Ps 15:2-5. Is 33:15-17. 58:6, 7. Je 9:24. 22:3. Ezk 18:5-9. Zc 8:16. Mt 19:17. Jn 3:7. Ro 3:23, 24. 6:23. Ep 2:8-10. T 3:5-8. 1 J +2:3, 4. 3:23, 24. 5:11-13.
to do justly. Ge +18:19. Le +19:15. 1 S

15:22. Ps 82:3. 112:5mg. 119:121. Pr 21:3. Ec 12:13. Is 1:16-19. 56:1. 58:6-11. Je 7:3-6. 22:15, 16. 23:5. Ezk 45:9. 12:6. Am 5:24. Zp 2:3. 3:5. Zc 7:9, 10. Mt 3:8-10. Mk 12:30-34. Lk 11:42. +16:10. Ro 13:7. Col +4:1. T 2:11, 12. Ja 1:27. 2 P 1:5-8.
love mercy. Ps 37:26. 112:4, 9. Pr 3:3. 11:17. Is 57:1, 2. Ho 6:6. Zc 7:9. Mt +5:7. 18:32-35. Lk +6:36. Ep 4:32. Col 3:12, 13. 1 P 3:8, 9.
walk humbly. Heb. humble thyself to walk. Ge +5:22. Le 26:41. 2 Ch +7:14. 30:11. 32:26. 33:12, 13, 19, 23. 34:27. Is +57:15. 66:2. Ezk 16:63. Da 4:37. Mt +5:3. Lk 14:10. 18:13-17. 22:26. Ro 10:1-3. 12:3. Ph +2:3. Ja 4:6-10. 1 P 5:5, 6.

9 Lord's. Mi 3:12. Is 24:10-12. 27:10. 32:13, 14. 40:6-8. 66:6. Je 19:11-13. 26:6, 18, 20. 37:8-10. Ho 13:16. Am 2:5. 3:8-15. 6:1. Jon 3:4. Zp 3:2.
city. 1 S +22:19.
and. 2 K 22:11-20. Ps 107:43. Pr 22:3. Is 26:11. Ho 14:9.
the man of wisdom shall see thy name. or, thy name shall see that which is wisdom. Ex 34:5-7. Ps +9:10, 16. 48:10. 83:18. Is 30:27.
hear. 2 S 21:1. Jb 5:6-8, 17. 10:2. Is 9:13. 10:5, 6. Je 14:18-22. La 3:39-42. Jl 2:11-18. Am 4:6-12. Jon 3:5-10. Hg 1:5-7. He 12:5. Re 3:19.

10 Are, etc. or, Is there yet unto every man an house of the wicked, etc.
the treasures. Jsh 7:1. 2 K 5:23, 24. Pr 10:2. 21:6. Je 5:26, 27. Am 3:10. Hab 2:5-11. Zp 1:9. Zc +5:3, 4. Ja +5:1-4.
the house. Pr 3:33.
and. Le 19:35, 36. Dt 25:13-16. Pr 11:1. 20:10, 23. Ezk 45:9-12. Ho 12:7, 8. Am 8:5, 6. Lk 6:38.
scant measure. Heb. measure of leanness.
abominable. Nu 23:7, 8. Pr 22:14.

11 count them pure. or, be pure. Pr +17:15. 24:24.
the wicked balances. Dt 25:13-16. Ho 12:7.
the bag. Pr 16:11.

12 the rich. Mi 2:1, 2. 3:1-3, 9-11. 7:2-6. Is 1:23. 5:7. Je 5:5, 6, 26-29. 6:6, 7. Ezk 22:6-13, 25-29. Ho 4:1, 2. Am 5:11, 12. 6:1-3. Zp 3:3.
spoken. Is 32:7. 59:3-15. Je 9:2-6, 8. Ho 7:1, 13. Ro 3:13. 1 C 6:8.
deceitful. Je 9:5. 17:9. Ho 12:7. Ac 5:2. Ro 3:13.

13 I make. Le 26:16. Dt 28:21, 22. Jb 33:19-22. Ps 107:17, 18. Is 1:5, 6. Je 14:18. Ac 12:23. 1 C +11:30.
sick. 1 K +22:34mg.
in making. La 1:13. 3:11. Ho 5:9. 13:16.

14 eat. Le +26:26. Is 9:20. 65:13. Hg 2:16.
and thou. Dt 32:22-25. Is 3:6-8. 24:17-20. Je 48:44. Ezk 5:12. Am 2:14-16. 9:1-4.

15 **shalt sow**. Le 26:20. Dt 28:38-40. Is 62:8, 9. 65:21, 22. Je 12:13. Jl 1:10-12. Am 5:11. Zp 1:13. Hg 1:6.

16 **the statutes**. Le 20:8. 2 K 17:34. Je 10:3.
of Omri are kept. *or*, he doth much keep the, etc. 1 K 16:25-32. Ho 5:4, 11.
the works. 1 K 16:30-33. 18:4. 21:25, 26. 2 K 16:3. 21:3. Is 9:16. Re 2:20.
the house of Ahab. 1 K 16:30, etc. 21:25, 26. 2 K 21:3.
ye walk. Ps +1:1. Je 7:24.
that. 2 Ch 34:25. Je 24:8, 9. Ezk 8:17, 18.
desolation. *or*, astonishment. Dt 28:37.
hissing. 2 Ch +29:8.
therefore. Ps 44:13, 14. Is 25:8. Je 51:51. La 5:1. Ezk 39:26. Da 9:16.

MICAH 7

1 **Woe**. Ps 120:5. Is 6:5. 24:16. Je 4:31. 15:10. 45:3.
when they have gathered the summer fruits. Heb. the gatherings of summer. Is +16:9.
as the grapegleanings. Jg 8:2. Is 17:6. 24:13.
my soul. Heb. *nephesh*, Nu +11:6.
desired. Is 28:4. Ho 9:10. Mk 11:13.

2 **good**. *or*, godly, *or*, merciful. Mi 6:8. Ps +43:1mg. 86:2mg. 145:17mg. Is 57:1.
is perished. Ps 12:1. 14:1-3. Is 57:1. Je 5:1. Mt +7:14. Ro 3:10-18.
they all. Pr 1:11. 12:6. Is 59:7. Je 5:16. 16:16. La 4:18. Hab 1:15-17.

3 **do evil**. Pr 4:16, 17. Je 3:5. Ezk 22:6. Ep 4:19.
the prince. Is 1:23. Je 8:10. Ezk +13:19. 22:27. Am 5:12. Mt 26:15.
the judge. Mi 3:11.
asketh. or, judgeth. 1 S +13:8.
the great. 1 K 21:9-14.
for a reward. Dt 16:19.
his mischievous desire. Heb. the mischief of his soul. Heb. *nephesh*, Ex +15:9.
wrap. Is 26:21. Lk 12:1, 2. 1 C 4:5.

4 **as a brier**. 2 S 23:6, 7. Is 9:18. 55:13. Ezk 2:6. He 6:8.
the day. Dt +4:32. Is 22:5. Ezk 12:23, 24. Ho 9:7, 8. Am 8:2.
thy visitation. Je +8:12.
now. Is 22:5. Na 1:10. Lk 21:25.

5 **Trust ye not in**. Jb 6:14, 15. Ps 118:8, 9. Je 9:4, 5. Mt 10:16.
keep the doors. Jg 16:5-20. Ps 141:3. Ec 10:20. Mt 10:36.

6 **son**. Ge 9:22-24. 49:4. 2 S 15:10-12. 16:11, 21-23. Pr +15:20. 30:11, 17. Ezk 22:7. Ml +4:6. Mt 10:21, 35, *36*. Lk *12:53*. 21:16. 2 T 3:2, 3.
dishonoreth. Ex 20:12. Dt 5:16.

a man's. Ps 41:9. 55:12-14. Je 12:6. 20:10. Ob 7. Mt *10:36*. 26:23, 49, 50. Jn 13:18.

7 **I will look**. Ps 5:3. 34:5, 6. 55:16, 17. 109:4. 142:4, 5. Hab 3:17-19. Lk 6:11, 12. He +12:2.
wait. Ps +25:3. Hab 2:1.
God of. Ps +88:1.
my salvation. Is +25:9. He +9:28.
my God. Ps +4:3. 17:6. 20:1. 38:15. 1 J +5:14, 15.

8 **Rejoice**. Ps 13:4-6. 35:15, 16, 19, 24-26. 38:16. Pr +17:5. Ezk 25:6. Jn 16:20. Re 11:10-12.
when I fall. Ps 37:24. 41:10-12. Pr 24:16. Da 11:33. Zc 12:8mg. Ro 11:11. 14:4. Ju 24.
I shall arise. Jb 13:15. Ps 112:4.
when I sit. Ps +112:4. Is 49:9. Mt +4:16.
darkness. Pr +20:20. Lk 22:53. Jn 12:27. Col 1:12, 13.
the Lord. Ps 27:1. 84:11. +112:4. Is 2:5. 60:1-3, 19, 20. Ac 26:18. 2 C 4:6. Re 21:23. 22:5.

9 **I will bear**. Le 26:41. 1 S 3:18. 2 S 16:11, 12. 24:17. Jb 34:31, 32. Je 10:19. La 1:18. 3:39-42. Lk 15:18, 19. He 12:6, 7.
indignation. Is +66:14.
until. 1 S 24:15. 25:39. 26:10. Ps 7:6. 35:1. 43:1. Je 50:17-20, 33, 34. 51:35, 36. Hab 3:2. Re 6:10, 11. 18:20.
and execute judgment. Ps 7:8. 37:6. Is 50:7-9.
he will. Jb 23:10. Ps 17:15. 37:6. Ml 3:18. 1 C 4:5. 2 Th 1:5-10. 2 T 4:8.

10 **Then**, etc. *or*, And thou wilt see her that is mine enemy, and cover her with shame.
she that. Ps 137:8, 9. Is 47:5-9. Je 50:33, 34. 51:8-10, 24. Na ch. 2, 3. Re 17:1-7.
shame. Ps 35:26. 109:29. Je 51:51. Ezk 7:18. Ob 10.
her. Is +32:9.
Where. Ps 42:3, 10. 79:10. 115:2. Is 37:10, 11. Da 3:15. Jl 2:17. Mt 27:43.
mine eyes. Mi 4:11. Ps 58:10. Ml 1:5. Re 18:20.
now shall. 2 S 22:43. 2 K 9:33-37. Ps 18:42. Is 25:10-12. 26:5, 6. 41:15, 16. 51:22, 23. 63:2, 3. Zc 10:5. Ml 4:3.
trodden down. Heb. for a treading down.

11 **the day**. Ne 2:17. 3:1, etc. 4:3, 6. Ps +102:13, 14, 16. Da +9:25. Am 9:11-15. Ac 15:16.
shall the decree. Heb. *chok*, prescribed limit or boundary. Ezr 4:12-24. Ne 2:8. Jb 26:10. 38:10. Pr 8:29. Is 24:5. Je 5:22.
far removed. Is 9:4.

12 **In that day**. Is +2:11.
also. Mi +5:5. Is 19:23-25. 49:12. 60:4-9. 66:19, 20. Je 3:18. +23:3. Ho 11:11. Zc 10:10.
and from. *or*, even to.
the fortified cities. Is 19:6. +37:25mg.
the river. Ps +72:8.

13 **Notwithstanding the land shall be**. *or*, After that the land hath been. Le 26:33-39. Is 6:11-13. 24:3-8. Je 25:11. Da +9:26, 27. Lk 21:20-24.

for the fruit. Mi 3:12. Jb 4:8. Pr 1:31. 5:22. 31:31. Is 3:10, 11. Je 17:10. 21:14. 32:19. Ga 6:7, 8.

14 Feed. *or*, Rule. Ps 23:1-4. +45:6. Is +40:11. Je 50:19. Ezk +34:31.
with thy rod. Ps +23:4. 110:2.
which dwell. Ex 33:16. Nu 23:9. Dt 33:28. Je 49:31. Jn 17:16.
in the midst. Jsh +19:26. Is 65:10. Ezk +34:13, 14. Zp 3:13.
Bashan. Dt +32:14.
as in. Ps 77:5-11. 143:5. La 1:7. 5:21. Am 9:11. Ml 3:4.
of old. Heb. *olam*, Ge +6:4.

15 according to the days. Mi +6:4. Ex 12:51. Ps 68:22. 78:12, etc. Is 11:16. 51:9. 63:11-15. Je 23:7, 8. Ezk 20:36. Ho 2:15. Re +12:6, 14.
I will show. Mi 2:12, 13. Ex 34:10. Is 11:15, 16. 19:20. 27:12. Zc 14:4. Jn +1:51. 14:12.

16 nations. Mi +5:8. Ps 126:2. +149:5-9. Is 26:11. 60:6-10. 66:18. Ezk 38:23. 39:17-21. Zc 8:20-23. 9:13-16. 12:9. Re 11:18.
their might. Mi 4:8. Zc 12:6. 14:12-21.
lay their hand. Jg +18:19. Jb 21:5. 29:9, 10. 40:4. Is 52:15. Ro 3:19.

17 lick the dust. Ge +3:14, 15. Ps 72:9. Is 49:23. 60:14. +65:25. La 3:29. Re 3:9.
move. 1 S 14:11. Ps 18:45. Je 16:16.
worms. *or*, creeping things. Dt 32:24.
they shall be afraid. Ge +35:5. Nu 22:3. Dt 2:25. 11:25. Jsh 9:24. Ps 9:20. Is 2:10, 11, 19-21. 26:11. 64:2. Je 33:9. Zc 14:5. Re 6:15-17. 18:9, 10.
shall fear. Je +5:22.

18 a God. Heb. *El*, Ex +15:2.
like. Ex +8:10.
that pardoneth. Ex +34:7. Ps 65:3. Is 1:18. 55:7. Je +31:34. Lk 24:47.
passeth. Nu 23:21. Ezk 33:11. Am 7:8. 8:2.
the remnant. ver. 14. Mi +5:3. He 8:9-12.
he retaineth. Ps 77:6-10. 85:4, 5. 103:9. Is 57:10, 16. Je 3:5, 12. La 3:31, 32. Zp 3:17.
for ever. Heb. *ad*, Ps +9:18.
he delighteth. Is 62:5. 65:19. Je 32:41. Ezk 33:11. Zp 3:17. Lk 15:5-7, 9, 10, 23, 24, 32. Ep 2:4, 5. Ja 2:13.
in mercy. Ex +34:6. Ezk 33:11. Zc 10:6.

19 turn. Dt 30:3, 6. 32:36. Ezr 9:8, 9. Ps +25:16. 80:14. 90:13, 14. Is 63:15-17. Je 31:20. La 3:32. Ho 14:4. Zc 1:3. Ac +3:19-21.
have compassion. Je 12:15. 31:20. La 3:32. Ezk 36:25-27.
subdue. Dt 30:6. 1 Ch 17:10. Ps +130:8. Is 38:17. Ezk 11:19, 20. Ro 6:14, 17-22. 7:23-25. 8:2, 3, 13. T 2:14. Ja 4:5, 6. 1 J 3:8.
cast. Ps 32:1. 103:12. Is 38:17. 43:25. Je 31:34. 33:8. 50:20. Da +9:24.

20 wilt perform. Ge 12:2, 3. 17:7, 8. 22:16-18. 26:3, 4. 28:13, 14. Ps 105:8-10. Je +33:25, 26. Ml 3:6. Lk 1:54, 55, *72-74*. Ac 3:25, 26. +7:5. Ro 11:26-31. He 6:13-18.
mercy to Abraham. 2 Ch +20:7. Mt 8:11. Lk 13:28, 29. Ac +7:5. Ro +4:13. Ga 3:9, 14-18, 29.
sworn unto. Ge 50:24. Ps 105:9, 10, 42. Is +55:3. Ac +7:5. Ro +15:8. He 6:16-18.
from the days. Je 46:26.
of old. Heb. *kedem*, Mi +5:2.

NAHUM

NAHUM 1

1 Cir. A.M. 3291. B.C. 713.
burden. Is 13:1. 14:28. 15:1. 21:1. +22:1. 23:1. Je 23:33-37. Zc 9:1.
Nineveh. Ge +10:11.
Nahum. i.e. *comforted*, **S#5151h**.
Elkoshite. i.e. *God my bow*, i.e. *defense; of the gathered of God*, **S#512h**. A dweller in Elkosh. Jn +7:52.

2 **God is jealous, and the Lord revengeth**. *or*, The Lord *is* a jealous God, and a revenger. Ex +20:5.
revengeth. Ex +15:7. Is 65:6, 7. Je +50:15.
is furious. Heb. that hath fury. lit. lord of wrath. Jb 20:23. Is 51:17, 20. +59:18. Je 25:15. Mi 5:15. Zc 8:2. Jn +3:36.
reserveth. Dt 32:34, 35, 41-43. Je 3:5. Mi +7:18. Ro 2:5, 6. 2 P 2:9. Ju 13.
wrath. Je +2:14.
for his enemies. 1 Th +5:9.

3 **slow**. Ex 34:6, 7. Ne 9:17. Ps 103:8. 145:8. Pr 14:17. Jl 2:13. Jon 4:2. Ja 1:19.
great. Jb 9:4. Ps 62:11. 66:3. 147:5. Ep 1:19, 20.
and will not. Ex 34:7. Nu 14:18. Jb 10:14, 15.
his way. Ex +13:21. Dt 5:22-24. 1 K 19:11-13. Jb 38:1. Is 66:15. Da 7:13. Hab 3:5-15. Zc 9:14. Mt 26:64. Re 1:7.
the clouds. Ge +9:13.

4 **rebuketh**. Ex 14:21, 22, 27-29. Jb 38:11. Ps 18:15. 104:7. 114:3, 5. Is 51:10. Am 5:8. Mk +4:39.
and drieth. Jsh 3:13-15. 4:23. Ps 74:15. Is 19:5-10. 44:27. Ezk 30:12.
Bashan. Dt +32:14.
Carmel. Mi 7:14.
flower. Le +19:23.

5 **mountains quake**. 2 S 22:8. Ps 29:5, 6. 68:8. +97:4, 5. Is 2:12-14. Mi 1:3, 4. Mt 28:2. Re 20:11.
hills melt. Jg 5:5. 2 P +3:10.
the earth. 2 P 3:7-12.

6 **can stand**. Jb 9:4. Ps 2:12. 76:7. 90:11. Is 27:4. Je 10:10. Ml 3:2. Re 6:17.
indignation. Is +66:14.
abide. Heb. stand up. Je 10:10. 51:64. Ml 3:2.

his fury. ver. 2. Dt 32:22, 23. Is 10:16, 17. Ezk +7:8. Re 16:1, 8, 9.

7 **Lord is good**. Ex +34:6. Dt 4:31. Ps +136:1. Je +29:11. La 3:25. 1 J 4:8-10.
strong hold. *or*, strength. Jg 6:26mg. Ps +9:9. 27:5. 71:3. 84:11. 144:1, 2. Is 26:1-4.
in the day. Ps 20:1. +50:15. 59:16. 77:2. 86:7. 91:15. Is 37:3, 4. Je +30:7. Hab +3:16.
and he knoweth. Mt 7:23. Jn +2:25. Ga 4:9.
that trust. 1 Ch 5:20. 2 Ch 16:8, 9. 32:8, 11, 21. Ps +9:10. Is +26:3. Da 3:28. 6:23. Mt 27:43. 2 T 1:12mg.

8 **with**. Je +47:2. Ezk 13:13. Mt 7:27. 2 P 3:6, 7.
utter end. Ps 1:6.
the place. ver. 1. Na 2:8. Zp 2:13-15.
darkness. Ex +10:22. Jb 30:15. Pr 4:19. Mt 8:12.

9 **imagine against**. ver. 11. Ps 2:1-4. 21:11. 33:10. +140:2. Pr +21:30. Is 8:9, 10. Ezk 38:10, 11. Ho +7:15. Ac 4:25-28. 2 C 10:5.
he will make. 1 S 3:12. 26:8. 2 S 20:10. Ezk 20:17. Zp 2:13-15.
affliction. ver. 7.
not rise up. ver. 6mg. Is 10:25. Je 51:64. Zp 3:15.
second time. Is +11:11.

10 **while they be**. 2 S 23:6, 7. Mi 7:4. 1 Th 5:2, 3.
thorns. Is 10:17. 27:4.
drunken. Na 3:11. 1 S 25:36-38. 2 S 13:28. Je 51:39, 57.
they shall. Ps 68:2. Is 9:18. 10:17-19. 27:4. Ml 4:1.

11 **one**. ver. 9. 2 K 18:13, 14, 30. 19:22-25. 2 Ch 32:15-19. Is 10:7-15. Da 7:8, 21. 8:9, 23-25.
wicked counsellor. Heb. counsellor of Belial. 1 S +30:22mg. 2 S 20:1. 2 K +18:13, +17, 26-28. 2 Ch 13:7. Ps 120:2. 123:3.

12 **Though**, etc. *or*, If *they would have been* at peace, so *should they have been* many, and so should they have been shorn, and he should have passed away.
yet. 2 K 19:35, 37. Is 10:32-34. 14:24-27. 17:14. 30:28-33. 31:8, 9. 37:36.
cut down. Heb. shorn. Is 7:20.
pass. ver. 15. Ex 12:12. Is 8:8. Da 11:10.

I will. Ps 30:5. 103:9. 125:3. Is 30:19. 51:22. 54:8, 11. 60:18-20. Jl 2:19. Re 7:16.

13 **will I**. Ge 27:40. Is 9:4. 10:5, 12, 27. 14:25. Je 2:20. Mi 5:5, 6.
will burst. Ps 107:14. Je 5:5. 30:8.

14 **given**. Ps 71:3. Is 14:24. 33:13.
that. Ps 109:13. Pr 10:7. Is 14:20-22.
out. Ex 12:12. Le 26:30. 2 K 19:37. Is 19:1. 46:1, 2. Je 50:2.
cut off. Ezk 31:3.
graven image. Ex +20:4.
molten image. Ex +34:17.
I will make. Na 3:4-6. 2 K 19:37. 2 Ch 32:21.
grave. Heb. *qeber*, Ge +23:4.
for. 1 S 3:13. Is 37:37, 38. Da 11:21.

15 **upon**. Is 18:3. 40:9, 10. +52:7.
feet. Ep +6:15.
bringeth good tidings. Is 41:27.
that publisheth. Ps +68:11. Is +27:6. Lk 2:10, 14. Ac 10:36.
keep. Heb. feast. Ge +1:29. Dt 16:16. 23:21.
solemn. Le +23:36.
perform. Ps 107:8, 15, 21, 22. 116:12-14, 17, 18. Is 19:21.
vows. Le +23:38.
the wicked. Heb. Belial. ver. 11mg, 12. 1 S +30:22.
no more. Is 37:36-38. 52:1. Jl 3:17. Zc 14:21.
he is. ver. 14. Is 29:7, 8.

NAHUM 2

1 **He that dasheth in pieces**. *or*, The disperser, *or*, hammer. Ps 68:2. Pr 25:18. Is 14:6. Je 23:29. 25:9. 50:23. 51:20-23. Ezk 9:2mg. Mi 2:13.
keep. Na 3:14, 15. 2 Ch 25:8. Je 46:3-10. 51:11, 12. Jl 3:9-11.
make thy. Jb 40:7. Je 1:17.
fortify. Pr 24:5.

2 **hath turned away**. Ps 80:9. Is 5:5, 6. 10:5-12. Je 12:10. 25:29.
excellency of Jacob, as the excellency. *or*, the pride of Jacob as the pride. Je 13:9. Zp 3:11.
for. Ge 49:22, 23. Ps 80:12-15. Je 49:9. Ho 10:1.

3 **mighty men**. 2 S 23:8. 1 K 1:8, 10.
made red. Is 63:1-3. Zc 1:8. 6:2. Re 6:4. 12:3.
valiant men. Jg 3:29. +6:12. 1 S 18:17. 31:12. 2 S 11:16.
in scarlet. *or*, dyed scarlet. Je 22:14. Ezk 23:14.
flaming. *or*, fiery.
preparation. Je 46:14. Ezk 7:14. 38:7.
the fir trees. Is 14:8. Ho 14:8. Zc 11:2.

4 **chariots**. Na 3:2, 3. Is 37:24. 66:15. Je 4:13. Ezk 26:10. Da 11:40.
rage. 2 K 9:20. Je 46:9.

streets. Heb. *chuts*, Am 5:16 (**S#2351h**, highways), outside, or narrow streets.
justle. Is 33:4. Jl 2:9.
broad ways. Heb. *rechob*, Am 5:16 (**S#7339h**, streets), public square or broad streets.
they shall seem. Heb. their show.
like torches. lit. with the fire of steels. Jsh 17:16.

5 **He**. Na +3:18. Mi +5:5, 6.
recount. Is 21:5. Je 50:29. 51:27, 28.
worthies. *or*, gallants. Na 3:18. Jg 5:13. 2 Ch 23:20.
they shall stumble. Na 3:3. Is 5:26, 27. Je 46:12.
make haste. Hab 1:6-10.
defence. *or*, covering, *or* coverer.

6 **gates**. Is 45:1, 2.
dissolved. *or*, molten. Jsh 2:9. 2 P 3:10, 11.

7 **Huzzab**. *or*, that which was established; *or*, there was a stand made. i.e. *established; beautifully beaming*, **S#5324h**.
led away captive. *or*, discovered. La 4:22mg.
doves. Is 38:14. 59:11. Lk 23:27, 48.
tabering. *Taber* means to beat as a taber or tabret. Ex +15:20. 1 S 10:5.

8 **Nineveh**. Ge +10:11.
of old. *or*, from the days *that* she *hath been*.
like. Je 51:13. Re 17:1, 15.
Stand. Na 3:17. Is 13:14. 47:13. 48:20. Je 50:16. 51:30.
look back. *or*, cause *them* to turn.

9 **ye**. Is 33:1, 4. Je 51:56.
for there is none end of the store. *or*, and *their* infinite store, etc. ver. 12, 13.
pleasant furniture. Heb. vessels of desire. Je +25:34mg.

10 **empty**. Na 3:7. Ge 1:2. Is 13:19-22. 14:23. 24:1. 34:10-15. Je 4:23-26. 51:62. Zp 2:13-15. 3:6. Re 18:21-23.
the heart. Ex +15:15.
the knees. Da 5:6.
and much. Is 21:3. Je 30:6.
and the faces. Jl 2:6.

11 **Where is**. 2 K 18:34. Ps 37:10, 35, 36.
the dwelling. Na 3:1. Is +5:29.
none. Ge 49:9. Is 31:4.

12 **The lion**. Jb 4:10, 11. Je 4:7. Da 7:4.
and filled. Ps 17:12. Is 10:6-14. Je 51:34.

13 **I am**. Ezk +15:7.
I will burn. Jsh 11:9. 2 K 19:23. Ps 46:9. Is +30:31-33.
and the sword. Is 37:36-38. Je +12:12.
I will cut. Na 3:1, 12. Is 33:1-4. 49:24, 25.
the voice. 2 K 18:17, 19, 27-35. 19:9, 23. 2 Ch 32:9-16, 19.

NAHUM 3

1 **Woe to**. Is 24:2. Ezk 22:2, 3. 24:6-9. Jon 1:2. Hab 2:12. Zp 3:1-3.

bloody city. Heb. city of bloods. 2 K +9:26mg. Ezk 24:6, 9.
full. Na 2:12. Is 17:14. 42:24. Ho 4:2.

2 **noise**. Na 2:3, 4. Jg 5:22. Jb 39:22-25. Is 9:5. Je 27:4-8. 47:3. Hab 1:6-10.

3 **bright sword and the glittering spear**. Heb. flame of the sword, and lightning of the spear. Na 2:4. Ge 3:24. Jb +41:21. Is 13:8mg. Hab 3:11.
and there. Is 37:36. Je 33:5. Ezk 31:3-13. 39:4.

4 **Because**. Pr 14:34. Ezk 23:7, 11, 12.
harlot. Is +32:9. Re 17:2.
the mistress. Dt +18:10. Is 23:15-17. Re +9:21. 17:1-5. 18:2, 3, 9, 23.
witchcrafts. 2 Ch +33:6.
that selleth nations. Dt 32:30. Jg 2:14. 3:8. 2 K 16:10.
families. Je 25:9. Ezk 20:32.

5 **I am**. Nu +32:23. Ezk +15:7. 23:25.
I will discover. Na 2:13. Is +3:17mg. Hab 2:16.
skirts. Ex 28:33, 34. 39:24.
I will show. Je 13:26.
thy shame. Je 13:26.

6 **I will cast**. Jb 9:31. 30:19. Ps 38:5-7. La 3:16. Ml 2:3. 1 C 4:13.
make. Na 1:14. Jb 30:8. Ml 2:9.
will set. 1 K 9:7, 8. Is 14:16-19. Je 51:37. Zp 2:15. 1 C 4:9. He 10:33. Ju 7.

7 **that all**. Nu 16:34. Je 51:9. Re 18:10.
Nineveh. Na 2:9, 10. Je 51:41-43. Re 18:16-19.
who. Is 51:19. Je 15:5. La 2:13.

8 **thou**. Ezk 31:2, 3. Am 6:2.
populous No. or, nourishing No. Heb. No-amon. i.e. temple, portion, **S#4996h**. Je 46:25mg, 26. Ezk 30:14-16.
the rivers. Ex 7:19. 8:5.
that had. Is 19:5-10.
the sea. Jb 41:31. Is 18:2. 19:5.

9 **Ethiopia**. Ge +2:13.
infinite. lit. "and there is no end." ver. 3. Na 2:9. Is 2:7.
Put. i.e. extension; afflicted, **S#6316h**. Ge +10:6, Phut.
Lubim. i.e. dwellers in a thirsty land, **S#3864h**. 2 Ch 12:3. 16:8. Da 11:43.
thy helpers. Heb. in thy help.

10 **she carried**. Ps 33:16, 17. Is 19:4. 20:4.
went into captivity. Dt 28:41. Is 20:4.

her young. Ps +137:9.
at. La 2:19. 4:1.
cast lots. Jsh +14:2. Jl 3:3. Ob 11.

11 **shalt be drunken**. Na 1:10. Ps 11:6. 75:8. Is 29:9. 49:26. 63:6. Je 25:15-17, 27. 51:57. Re 14:10.
thou shalt be hid. Na 1:8. 2:12. 1 S 13:6. 14:11. Is 2:10, 19. Ho 10:8. Am 9:3. Ob 16. Mi 7:17. Lk 23:30. Re 6:15-17.
thou also. Na 2:1. Je 4:5. 8:14.
seek strength. Ep 6:10, 11.

12 **thy strong holds**. Hab 1:10. Re 6:13.

13 **thy people**. Is 19:16. Je 50:37. 51:30.
the gates. Na 2:6. Ps 107:16. Is 45:1, 2.
thy bars. Ps 147:13. Je 51:30.

14 **Draw**. 2 Ch 32:3, 4, 11. Is 22:9-11. 37:25.
fortify. Na 2:1. Is 8:9, 10. Je 46:3, 4, 9. Jl 3:9-11.
brick-kiln. or, the brickwork. Heb. malben, fortifications or walls built with bricks. 2 S +12:31. Je 43:9.

15 **shall the**. ver. 13. Na 2:13. Zp 2:13.
it. Jl 1:4. 2:25.
make thyself many as the locusts. Ex 10:13-15.

16 **above**. Ge +15:5.
spoileth. or, spreadeth himself. Ho 7:1.

17 **Thy crowned**. Re 9:7.
thy captains. Je 51:27.
great grasshoppers. Am 7:1.
not known. Ps 37:10, 35, 36. 92:7. Ob 16.

18 **Thy shepherds**. Na +2:6. Ex 15:16. Ps 76:5, 6. Is 56:9, 10. Je 51:39, 57.
O king. Je 50:18. Ezk 31:3, etc. 32:22, 23. Mi 5:5, 6.
nobles. or, valiant ones. Is 47:1. Je 14:3. Re 6:15.
shall dwell. Ge 3:19.
thy people. 1 K 22:17. Is 13:14.
no man gathereth. Dt 30:4.

19 **There is no**. Je 30:13-15. 46:11. 50:18. Ezk 30:21, 22. Mi 1:9. Zp 2:13-15.
healing. Heb. wrinkling. Le 13:6.
thy bruise. Ps 60:2. La 2:11.
thy wound. Ps 64:7. Mi 1:9.
is grievous. Je 10:19. 14:17. 30:12.
the bruit. i.e. noise or rumor. Je 10:22.
shall clap. Jb 27:23. Ps 47:1. Is 14:8, etc. 55:12. La 2:15. Ezk 25:6. 31:3. Re 18:20.
upon. Na 2:11, 12. Is 10:6-14. 37:18. Re 13:7. 17:2. 18:2, 3.

HABAKKUK

HABAKKUK 1

1 A.M. 3404. B.C. 600.
burden. Is +22:1. Na 1:1.
Habakkuk. i.e. *embracing continually*, **S#2265h**.
Hab 3:1.
2 how. Re +6:10.
cry. Dt +24:15. Jb 19:7. Ps 18:6, 41. 22:24. Je
20:8.
and thou wilt not save. Ps 22:1, 2. Je 14:9.
La 3:8.
3 show me iniquity. Ps 12:1, 2. 55:9-11. 73:3-
9. 120:5, 6. Ec 4:1. 5:8. Je 9:2-6. Ezk 2:6. Mi
7:1-4. Mt 10:16. 2 P 2:8.
for spoiling. Hab 2:17. Ho 7:13.
violence. Mi 6:12.
strife and. 1 K 19:10. Je 15:10. 20:14.
4 the law. Ps 11:3. 119:126. Pr 28:4. Ec 8:11.
Mk 7:9. Ro 3:31.
slacked. **S#6313h**. Ge 45:26 (fainted). Ps 38:8
(feeble). 77:2 (ceased). See also **S#6314h**. La
2:18 (rest).
never. Jb +4:20 (**S#5331h**).
for the wicked. 1 K 21:13. Jb 21:7. Ps 22:12,
16. 58:1, 2. 59:2, 4. 82:1-5. 94:3, 20, 21. Pr
17:4. 29:12. Is 1:21-23. 59:2-8, 13-15. Je
5:27-29. 12:1, 6. 26:8, 21-23. 37:14-16. 38:4-
6. Ezk 22:25-30. Ho 10:4. Am 5:7, 12. Mi 2:1,
2. 3:1-3. 7:2-4. Mt 23:34-36. 26:59-66. 27:1,
2, 25, 26. Ac 7:52, 59. 23:12-14. Ja 2:6, 7.
wrong. *or*, wrested. Ex +23:2, 6. Dt 16:19. Jb
19:7. Ec +5:8. Is 29:21. Ezk 9:9mg. Mi 3:9.
judgment. Le +19:15, 35. Pr 17:15. 28:5. Mi
+6:8. Mt +23:23. Jn +7:24. Ja +5:4, 6.
5 Behold. Ac *13:41*.
ye among. Dt 4:27. Je 9:25, 26. 25:14-29.
and regard. Is 29:14. La 4:12. Da 9:12. Ac
13:40, 41.
for. Is 28:21, 22. Je 5:12, 13. 18:18. Ezk
12:22-28. Zp 1:12. Ac 6:13, 14.
6 I raise. Dt 28:49-52. 2 K 24:2. 2 Ch 36:6, 17.
Is 5:26, 27. 23:13. 39:6, 7. Je 1:15, 16. 4:6, 7.
5:15. 6:22, 23. 21:4. 25:9.
breadth. Heb. breadths.
7 their judgment, etc. *or*, from them shall
proceed the judgment of these and the captivity of these. Je 39:5-9. 52:9-11, 25-27. Da
5:19, 27.

8 horses. Dt 28:49. Is 5:26-28.
fierce. Heb. sharp. Pr 27:17.
evening. Je 5:6. Zp 3:3.
they. Dt 28:49, 50. Je 4:13. La 4:19. Ezk 17:3,
12. Ho 8:1. Mt 24:28. Lk 17:37.
9 for. ver. 6. Hab 2:5-13. Dt 28:51, 52. Je 4:7.
5:15-17. 25:9.
their faces shall sup up as the east. *or*, the
supping up of their faces, as, etc. *or*, their
faces shall look toward the east. Heb. the
opposition of their faces shall be toward the
east. Ge +41:6. Jb 39:24. Je 4:11, 12.
they shall gather. Hab 2:5.
as the sand. Ge +22:17.
10 scoff. 2 K 24:12. 25:6, 7. 2 Ch 36:6, 10.
they shall deride. Is 14:16. Je 32:24. 33:4.
52:4-7.
11 shall his. Da 4:30-34.
mind. Heb. *ruach*, Ge +26:35.
change. Da +9:27.
imputing. Da 5:3, 4, 20. 11:36, 38.
12 thou not. Dt 33:27. Ps 90:2. 93:2. 102:27. Is
40:28. +57:15. La 5:19. Mi +5:2. 1 T 1:17.
6:16. He 1:10-12. +13:8. Re +1:8, 11.
mine. Is +1:4. Ac 3:14.
we. Hab 3:2. Ps 102:28. 118:17. Is 27:6-9. Je
4:27. 5:18. 30:11. +33:24-26. 46:28. Ezk
37:11-14. Am +9:8, 9. Mt +22:32.
shall not die. 1 C 15:53, 54. 1 T 6:16.
thou hast ordained. 2 K 19:25. Ps 17:13. Is
10:5-7. 37:26. Je 25:9, etc. Ezk 30:25.
mighty God. Heb. Rock. Dt 32:4, 15, 18, 30,
31. 1 S 2:2. 2 S 23:3. Ps 18:1, 2, 31, 46.
19:14.
established. Heb. founded. Ps 8:2mg.
for. Is 27:9, 10. Je 30:11. 31:18-20. 46:28. He
12:5, 6.
13 Thou art. Je +12:1.
of purer eyes than. Jb 15:15. Ps 5:4, 5. 11:4-
7. 34:15, 16. Ja 1:13. 1 P 1:15, 16.
evil. Is +45:7.
canst not. Ps 5:4. Is 43:25. Ro 3:26.
iniquity. *or*, grievance. ver. 3. Is 10:1.
wherefore lookest. Ps 10:1, 2, 15. 73:3, Je
12:1, 2. 2 P 3:9.
deal. Is 21:2. 33:1.
holdest. Est 4:14. Ps 35:22. 50:3, 21. 83:1. Pr

31:8, 9. Is 64:12. 1 C 2:8. Ep 5:11-13. 1 T
1:13, 16. Ja 4:17. 2 P 3:9.

the wicked. ver. 3, 4. 2 S 4:11. 1 K 2:32. Ps
37:12-15, 32, 33. 56:1, 2. Ac 2:23. 3:13-15. 2
Th 2:8.

14 **creeping**. *or*, moving. Ge 9:3.
no ruler. Pr 6:7.

15 **take**. Je 16:16. Ezk 29:4, 5. Am 4:2. Mt
17:27.
they catch. Ps 10:9. Lk 5:5-10. Jn 21:6-11.
drag. *or*, flue-net. ver. 16. Is 19:8. Mt 13:47.
therefore. Je 50:11. La 2:15, 16. Ezk 25:6.
26:2. 35:15. Re 11:10.

16 **they**. ver. 11. Dt 8:17, 18. Is 2:8. 10:13-15.
37:24, 25. Ezk 28:3-5. 29:3. Da 4:30. 5:23.
plenteous. *or*, dainty. Heb. fat. Ge 41:2, 4, 5, 7.

17 **and**. ver. 9, 10. Hab 2:5-8, 17. Is 14:16, 17. Je
25:9-26. ch. 46-49, 52. Ezk ch. 25-30.

HABAKKUK 2

1 **stand**. Ps 73:16, 17. Is 21:6, 8, 11, 12.
tower. Heb. fenced place. 2 S 18:24. 2 K
9:17. 17:9. Is 21:5. 62:6.
and will watch. Hab 1:12-17. Nu 9:8. Jb
+37:2. Ps 5:3. 85:8. Mi 7:7.
unto me. *or*, in me. 2 C 13:3. Ga 1:16.
what I shall answer. Is 50:4.
when I am reproved. *or*, when I am argued
with. Heb. upon my reproof, *or*, arguing. Jb
23:5-7. 31:35, 37. Je 12:1.

2 **Write**. Dt 27:8. 31:19, 22. Is 8:1. 30:8. Je
36:2-4, 27-32. Da +12:4. Re 1:18, 19. +14:13.
19:9. 21:5-8.
make it plain. Nu 35:32. Dt +27:8. Pr +8:9.
Is 35:8. Je 31:21. Jn 16:28, 29. 1 C 14:19. 2 C
3:12.
upon tables. Lk 1:63.
may run. Jb 9:25. Ps 18:10. Je 23:21. 51:31.
Hg 1:9. Zc 2:4.

3 **the vision**. Je 27:7. Da 8:19. +9:24-27.
+10:1, 14. 11:27, 35. 12:9. Ac 1:7. 17:26. Ga
4:2. 2 Th 2:6-8. Re 22:10.
is. or, is deferred.
appointed time. Ge +17:21. Mi +5:3.
but. Ex 12:41. Ps 102:13. Je 25:12, etc. He
10:36, 37.
wait. 2 K 6:33. Ps +25:3. Ja 5:7, 8.
it will surely. Is 55:11. Lk 18:7, 8. 2 P 2:3. 3:9.
not tarry. He 10:37.

4 **his**. Pr +16:5. 2 Th +2:4.
soul. Heb. *nephesh*, Ge +34:3.
lifted. Dt +17:20.
but the just. Is 30:15. Jn 3:36. Ro *1:17*. Ga
2:16. *3:11, 12*. He *10:38*. 1 J 5:10-13.
by his faith. 2 K 12:15 (faithfully).

5 **Yea also**. *or*, How much more. Dt 31:27. 1 S
14:30. 23:3. 2 S 4:11. 16:11. Jb 15:16. Pr
15:11. 19:7. 21:27. Ezk 14:21.
he transgresseth. Pr +20:1. 23:29-33. 31:4,

5. Is 5:11, 12, 22, 23. 21:5. Je 51:39. Da 5:1-4,
23. Na 1:9, 10. Re 17:6.
by wine. Heb. *yayin*, **s#3196h**. Ge 9:21. 14:18.
1 S 25:36, 37. Is 28:1. Je 23:9.
a proud man. ver. +4. Pr 30:13, 14. Is 14:13-
16. 16:6. Je 50:29. Ezk 28:17. Da 8:25. 11:36,
37. 2 Th 2:4.
keepeth. 2 K 14:10. 1 Th 4:11.
who enlargeth. Is 5:8. 10:7-13.
desire. Heb. *nephesh*, Ex +15:9.
as hell. Heb. *sheol*, Ge +37:35. Pr 27:20.
30:15, 16. Ec 5:10. Is 5:14.
gathereth. ver. 8-10. Is 14:16, 17. Je 25:9,
17-29. Re 20:8.

6 **take**. Is 14:4-19. Je 29:22. 50:13. Ezk 32:21.
parable. Nu +23:7.
proverb. Nu +12:8. Ps 78:2.
Woe to him. *or*, Ho, he. ver. 9, 12, 15, 19.
that increaseth. Hab 1:9, 10, 15. Jb 20:15-
29. 22:6-10. Pr 22:16. Je 17:11. +48:10.
51:34, 35. Ezk +16:49. 28:4, 5, 8. Am +8:5. Ja
+5:1-4.
how. Ps 94:3. Lk 12:20. 1 C 7:29-31. 1 P 4:7.
ladeth. ver. 13. Is 44:20. 55:2.
thick clay. or, pledges. Dt 15:6. Am 2:8.

7 **they**. Pr 29:1. Is 13:1-5, 16-18. 21:2-9. 41:25.
45:1-3. 46:11. 47:11. 48:14, 15. Je 50:21-32.
51:11, 27, 28, 57. Da 5:25-31. Na 1:9, 10. 1
Th 5:3. Re 18:10, 17.
bite. Ec 10:8. Je 8:17.

8 **thou**. ver. 10, 17. Is 33:1, 4. Je 25:12, 14.
27:7. 30:16. 50:10, 37. 51:13, 44, 48, 55, 56.
Zc 2:8, 9. Re 13:10.
blood. Heb. bloods. ver. 12, 17. 2 K +9:26mg.
the violence. Ps 137:8. Is 47:6. Je 50:11, 17,
18, 28, 33, 34. 51:8, 11, 24, 34, 35. Jl 3:19. Mi
4:11-13. Zc 1:15. 2:8. 12:2-4. 14:12. Re 6:10.
18:20-24.

9 **that coveteth an evil covetousness**. *or*,
that gaineth an evil gain. Ge 13:10-13. 19:26-
38. Dt 7:25, 26. Jsh 7:21-26. 1 K 21:2-4, 19-
24. 2 K 5:20-27. Jb 20:19-28. Pr 1:19. 15:27.
Je 6:13. 8:10. +22:13-19. Ezk 14:3. 22:27.
+33:31. Am +8:5. Mi 2:2. Zc 5:1-4. Lk 12:15.
Ac 1:17-25. Ju 11.
set his nest. Nu 24:21. Jb 39:27. Ps 10:3-6.
49:11. 52:7. Pr 18:11, 12. Is 28:15. 47:7-9. Je
49:16. Ob 4. Lk 12:19.
on high. Ge 11:4. Is 14:13.
delivered from. Pr 11:28. +21:30. Is 14:24-
27. 28:15. 47:8. Je 5:12. 21:13. 49:4. Am
+9:1-4, 10. Ob 3. Ro 2:3. 1 Th 5:3. He 2:3. 2 P
2:18-20. Re 6:15-17. 18:7.
power of evil. Heb. palm of the hand. Is
+45:7. 49:16.

10 **consulted**. 2 K 9:26. 10:7, 8. Is 14:20-22. Je
22:30. 36:31. Na 1:14. Mt 27:25.
sinned. Nu 16:38. 1 K 2:23. Pr 1:18. 8:36. Is
33:11.
soul. Heb. *nephesh*, Ge +12:13.

11 cry out. Ex +22:23. Jsh 24:27. Jb 31:38-40.
Je +10:25. Lk 19:40. He 12:24. Re 6:10.
beam. *or*, piece, *or*, fastening.
answer it. *or*, witness against it.

12 Woe to him. Ge 4:11-17. Jsh 6:26. 1 K
16:34. Je +22:13-17. Ezk 24:9. Da 4:27-31. Mi
3:10. Na 3:1. Jn 11:47-50. Re 17:6.
blood. Heb. bloods. ver. 8. 2 K +9:26mg.

13 is it not. Ge 11:6-9. 2 S 15:31. Jb 5:13, 14. Ps
39:6. 127:1, 2. Pr +21:30. Is 41:5-8. 50:11.
55:2. Je 51:58, 64. Ml 1:4.
Lord of hosts. Ex 15:26. 1 S +1:3. Ps +24:10.
people. Heb, *am*, S#5971h. ver. 5, 8, 10. Hab
3:13, 16. Ge 33:15. Ex 33:13. Ps 18:43.
people. Heb. *leom*, S#3816h. Ge 25:23 (people,
meaning races). 27:29 (nations). Ps 2:1. 47:3.
Pr 14:34. 24:24. Je *51:58* (folk).
weary themselves. Is 47:13.
for very vanity. *or*, in vain. Is 65:23. Je
51:58.

14 the earth. Ps 22:27. 67:1, 2. 86:9. 98:1-3. Is
11:9. +40:5. Zc +14:8, 9. Re 11:15. 15:4.
shall be filled. Is +27:6. +66:19.
with the knowledge of the glory. *or*, by
knowing the glory. Is +40:5. Ezk 28:22. He
8:11.

15 unto him. Ge 4:9-11. 19:32-35. Ex 21:28-30.
Dt 32:33-35. 2 S 11:13. 13:26-28. 2 K 21:9-
12. Je 25:15. 51:7. Ml +2:10. Jn 3:19. Re 17:2,
6. 18:3.
that puttest. Ho 7:5.
bottle. Ge 21:14, 15, 19.
makest him drunken. Ge 9:22. Pr +20:1. Is
5:11, 13.
that thou. Ge 9:22. Ezk 22:10. 23:14, 16, 18,
20.
nakedness. Is +20:2.

16 with shame for glory. *or*, more with shame
than with glory. Pr 3:35. Is 47:3. Ho 4:7. Ph
3:19.
drink. Ps 75:8. Is 49:26. 51:21-23. Je 25:26,
27. 51:57. Re 18:6.
and let. Is 20:4. 47:3. Na 3:5, 6. Re 17:16.
the cup. Je 25:27-29.
shameful spewing. Is 28:7, 8. Ho 7:5.

17 the violence. Zc 11:1.
because. ver. 8. Ps 55:23. 137:8. Pr 28:17. Re
10:20-24.
blood. ver. 8mg. 2 K +9:26mg.
of the city. Je 50:28, 33, 34. 51:24, 34-37.

18 profiteth. Is 37:38. +42:17. 46:1, 2, 6-8. Je
10:3-5. 50:2. Ro 6:21.
molten. Ex +34:17.
a teacher of lies. Is 28:15. Je 10:8, 14, 15.
Jon +2:8. Zc 10:2. Mt +15:14. +23:13, 15. Ro
1:23-25. Ep 4:14. 2 Th 2:9-11. 1 T 4:1, 2. 2 T
3:13. 2 J +9-11. Ju +3. Re 13:11-15. 19:20.
that the. Ps +115:8. Is 1:31.
maker of his work. Heb. fashioner of his
fashion.

dumb. Je +2:5. 14:14. Ezk +30:13. 1 C 12:2.

19 that. 1 K 18:26-29. Ps 97:7. Is 44:17. Je
51:47. Da 3:7, 18, 29. 5:23. Jon 1:5.
dumb. Je +10:5.
it is. Ps 115:4-8. Is 40:19. 46:6. Je 10:4, 9. Da
3:1. Ac 17:29. Re 17:4.
no breath. Heb. *ruach*, spirit, Ge +6:17. Ps
+135:17. Re 13:15.

20 the Lord. Ps 11:4. 115:3. 132:13, 14. Is 6:1.
66:1, 6. Jon 2:4, 7. Ep 2:21, 22.
holy temple. Mi 1:2.
let all the earth keep silence before him.
Jg 3:19. 1 Ch 13:7, 10. Ne 8:11. Jb 37:14.
40:4. Ps 4:4. +37:7mg. 46:10. 76:8, 9. 89:7. Is
41:1. +58:13. Je 8:14. Zp 1:7. Zc 2:13. Re 8:1.

HABAKKUK 3

1 prayer. Ps 86, 90, titles.
upon Shigionoth. *or*, according to variable
songs, *or* tunes, *called in Hebrew*, Shigionoth.
i.e. *wanderings*, S#7692h. Ps 7, title.

2 I have. ver. 16. Hab 1:5-10. Ex 9:20, 21. 2 Ch
34:27, 28. Jb 4:12-21. Ps 119:120. Is 66:2. Je
36:21-24. Da 8:17. He 11:7. 12:21. Re 15:4.
speech. Heb. report, *or* hearing. Is 53:1. Ro
10:16, 17.
afraid. Ex 14:31. Am 3:8.
O Lord. Ezr 9:8. Ps 85:6. 90:13-17. 138:7, 8.
Is 51:9-11. 63:15-19. 64:1-4. Ho 6:2, 3. Jn
10:10. Ph 1:6.
revive. *or*, preserve alive. Ps 85:5-7. +119:25
(quicken). Is 63:15, 17. Ho 5:6. 6:2.
thy work. Is +60:21.
in the midst. Je 25:11, 12. 52:31-34. Da 9:2,
+27.
make known. Is 64:1, 2. Ezk +38:16. +39:7.
in wrath. Ex 32:10-12. Nu 14:10-23. 16:46,
47. 2 S 24:10-17. Ps 6:1, 2. 38:1. 78:38. Is
54:8. +61:2. Je 10:24. 29:10. La 3:32. Na 1:2.
Zp 1:15. Zc 1:12. 1 Th +1:10.
remember mercy. Dt +32:43. Ps 85:1, 5, +7.
Is +26:20. 54:7, 8, 10. Mi 7:18, 20. Zp +2:3. Zc
10:6. Lk 1:72, 78. +21:36.

3 God came. Dt +33:2. Jg 5:4, 5. Ps 68:7, 8. Is
63:1-5. 64:3.
from. Ge +36:11.
Teman. *or*, the south. Jsh 12:3mg.
Holy One. Is +1:4.
Paran. Ge +21:21. Dt 33:2.
Selah. ver. 9, 13. Ps +9:16.
His glory. Ex 19:16-20. 20:18. 24:15-17. Dt
5:24. Ps 68:17. 114:3-7. Is +40:5. Mt +24:30.
and the earth. Is 6:3. 2 C 3:7-11. Re 5:13,
14.
his praise. Zc +2:10.

4 brightness. Ex 13:21. 14:20. Ne 9:12. Ps
18:12. 104:2. Is 60:19, 20. Mt 17:2. 2 Th +2:8.
1 T 6:16. Re 1:13, 17. 21:23, 24. 22:5.
horns coming out of his hand. *or*, bright

beams out of his side. Ge 19:11. Ps 31:8.
37:24. Is 62:3. 66:14. Da 12:3.

the hiding. Jb 26:14. Ps +83:3. Pr 18:10. Is
49:2.

his power. Ps +149:9.

5 **went.** Ex 12:29, 30. Ex 23:27. Ps 68:1, 2.
78:50, 51. Je 25:30-33. Ezk +38:22. Na 1:2, 3.
Re 19:19-21.

and. Ps 18:7-13.

burning coals. or, burning diseases. Dt 32:24.
Ps +11:6mg. 18:8. 76:3. 78:48. 140:10. Zc
14:5, 12, 15, 18.

6 **and measured.** Ex 15:17. 23:31. Nu ch. 34.
Dt +32:8. Jb 42:2. Is 40:12. Ac +17:26.

and drove. Jsh 10:42. 11:18-23. Ne 9:22-24.
Ps 135:8-12. Re 19:17, 18.

the everlasting. Heb. ad, Ps +9:18 (**S#5703h**).

mountains. ver. +10. Ge 49:26. Dt 33:15. Zc
+14:4, 5, 10.

perpetual. Heb. olam, Ge +9:12.

his ways. Ps 90:2. 103:17. Is 51:6, 8. Mi +5:2.
Mt 24:35. Lk 1:50. He +13:8.

everlasting. Heb. olam, Ge +17:7.

7 **saw the.** Ex 15:14-16. Nu 22:3, 4. Jsh 2:10.
9:24.

Cushan. or, Ethiopia. i.e. blackness, **S#3572h**,
only here. Ge +10:6, 7.

in affliction. or, under affliction, or vanity.
S#205h. Hab 1:3 (iniquity). Nu 23:21. Dt 26:14
(mourning). Jb 4:8. 15:35mg. Ps 5:5. 10:7.
36:4mg. 66:18. Pr 11:7 (unjust). 12:21 (evil).
17:4 (false). 22:8. Is 1:13mg. 10:1 (unrighteous). 55:7mg. 58:9. 59:7. 66:3 (an idol). Je
4:14 (vain), 15. Ezk 11:2 (mischief). +30:17
(Aven). Ho 9:4 (mourners). Am 5:5 (nought).
Mi 2:1. Zc 10:2.

curtains. 2 S +7:2.

Midian. Ge +25:2. Ps 83:5-10.

8 **Was the Lord.** Ex 14:21, 22. Is 50:2. Na 1:4.
Mk 4:39. Re 16:12.

the rivers. Is 8:7, 8. Je 46:7, 8. 47:2.

against the sea. Ps 65:7. 89:9. 93:3, 4. Is
5:30. 51:42. Da 7:2. Na 1:4. Re 13:1. 21:1.

ride. ver. 15. Dt +33:26, 27. Ps 45:4. Re 6:2.
19:11, 14.

thy chariots. Ps +68:17.

of salvation. or, were salvation.

9 **bow.** Dt 32:23. Ps 7:12, 13. 35:1-3. 45:4, 5. Is
51:9, 10. 52:10. La 2:4.

according. Ge +15:18-21. +17:7, 8. +22:16-
18. 26:3, 4. 28:13, 14. Ps 77:8. 105:8-11. Is
41:2-4. Zc 9:11-17. Lk 1:72-75. Ac +26:6, 7.
He 6:13-18.

Selah. ver. 3, 13. Ps +9:16.

Thou. Ex 17:6. Nu 20:11. Ps 78:15, 16.
105:41. 1 C 10:4.

the earth with rivers. or, the rivers of the
earth. Ps 74:15. 78:15, 16. 105:41.

10 **mountains.** ver. 6. Ex 19:16-18. Ps 68:7, 8,
16. 77:18. +97:4. Je +4:24. Re 20:11.

trembled. Ps 60:2. He +12:26.

the overflowing. Ex 14:22-28. Jsh 3:15, 16.
4:18, 23, 24. Ne 9:11. Ps 18:15. 66:6. 74:13-
15. 77:16-19. 114:3-8. 136:13-15. Is 11:15,
16. 63:11-13. He 11:29. Re 16:12.

the deep. Ge +1:2. Ex 14:22. Ps 42:7. 65:13.
93:2-5. 96:11-13. 98:7, 8. Is 43:20. 55:12.

lifted. Ps +88:9.

11 **sun.** Is 24:23. Jl 3:15. Mt 24:29.

stood still. Jsh 10:12, 13. Is 28:21. 38:8.

habitation. Ps 19:4.

at the light of thine arrows they went. or,
thine arrows walked in the light. Dt +32:23.
Jsh 10:11.

spear. Dt 32:41.

12 **didst march.** Dt +33:2. Nu 21:23-25. Jsh ch.
6-12. Jg 5:4. Ne 9:22-24. Ps 44:1-3. 68:7.
78:55. Is 63:1-6. Ac 13:19. 2 Th 1:7-10. Re
19:11-16.

indignation. Is +66:14.

thresh. Ps 18:42. Is +21:10. 41:2.

13 **wentest.** Ex 14:13, 14. 15:1, 2. Ps 68:7, 19-
23.

for the salvation. Is 35:4, 10.

salvation with. Ps 77:20. 89:19-21. 99:6.
105:15, 26. Is 63:11, 12. He +9:28. Re 12:10.

thine anointed. Ps 105:15. +149:6-9. Ro
+8:19. Re 2:26, 27.

thou woundedst. Ex 12:29, 30. Jsh 10:11,
24, 42. 11:8, 12. Ps 18:37-45. 68:21. 74:13,
14. 110:6. Re 19:19-21.

the head. Ps 83:2.

discovering. Heb. making naked. Ps
+137:7mg.

the foundation. Ml 4:1.

unto the neck. 2 Th +2:8.

Selah. Ps +9:16.

14 **the head.** Ex 11:4-7. 12:12, 13, 29, 30.
14:17, 18. Ps 78:50, 51. 83:9-11.

they. Ex 14:5-9. 15:9, 10. Ps 83:2-8. 118:10-
12. Ac 4:27, 28.

came out. Heb. were tempestuous. Jon 1:11,
13.

whirlwind. Je +23:19.

their. Ex 1:10-16, 22. Ps 10:8. 64:2-7.

15 **walk through.** ver. 8. Ps 68:17. 77:19.
89:23-25.

heap. or, mud. Ge 11:3 (morter). Ex 8:14
(heaps). Nu +11:32. Jb 4:19 (clay). 30:19
(mire).

16 **I heard.** ver. 2. Hab 1:5-11.

my belly. Ps 119:120. Je 4:19. 23:9. Ezk 3:14.
Da 8:27. 10:8.

rottenness. Jb 13:28. Pr 12:4. 14:30. Ho 5:12.

I trembled. Is +66:2.

that I might rest. Ps 91:15. 94:12, 13. Is
+26:20, 21. 57:1. Je 15:10, 11. 31:2. 45:3-5.
Ezk 9:4-6. Zp +2:3. Lk +21:36. 1 Th +5:9. 2 Th
1:6-10. Re +11:18.

the day of trouble. Je +30:7. Da +12:1.

when he cometh. Is 10:12. Ezk 38:15. 39:2. Da +9:26. +11:40, 44. Mi 5:5, 6. Zc 14:3, 13. 2 Th 1:8. 2:9.

up unto. Jg 20:23. 2 S 5:19.

the people. Is 26:11. 44:7.

he will. Hab 1:6. Dt 28:49-52. 2 K 24:1, 2. Je 25:9-11.

invade them. *or*, cut them in pieces. Ge 49:19. Zc 12:9.

with his troops. Is 59:19. Da 11:25. Zc 12:8.

17 **the fig tree**. Dt 28:15-18, 30-41. Je 14:2-8. Jl 1:10-13, 16-18. Am 4:6-10. Hg 2:16, 17.

shall not. Lk 21:25, 26.

fail. Heb. lie. Le 6:2, 3.

18 **Yet**. Hab 2:4. Jb +13:15. Lk 13:2-5. Jn 9:2, 3.

Ro 8:35-39. 2 C 5:7. He 10:34. 11:1. 12:4.

I will rejoice. Dt +12:7. Jb 13:15. Ps 4:7. 33:1. 46:1-5. 85:6. 97:12. 104:34. 118:15. 149:2. Is 41:16. 61:10. Zp 3:14. Zc 10:7. Lk 1:46, 47. Ro 5:2, 3. Ph 4:4. Ja 1:2, 9, 10. 1 P 1:8. 4:12, 13.

the God. Ex 15:2. Ps +88:1. 118:14. He +9:28.

19 **my strength**. Ps +18:1. 46:1. 84:11.

like. 2 S 1:23. 22:34. 1 Ch 12:8. Ps 18:33.

to walk. Dt 32:13. 33:29. Is 58:14. Am 4:13. Mi 1:3.

high places. Is 33:16mg.

stringed instruments. Heb. *Neginoth*, Ps ch. 4, 6, 54, 55, 67, 76, titles. Ps 150:4.

ZEPHANIAH

ZEPHANIAH 1

1 A.M. 3374. B.C. 630.

word of the Lord. Ezk 1:3. Ho 1:1. 2 T 3:16. 2 P 1:19.

Zephaniah. i.e. *protected; Jehovah hides; treasured up of Jehovah*, **S#6846h**. 2 K 25:18. 1 Ch 6:36. Je 21:1. 29:25, 29. 37:3. 52:24. Zc 6:10, 14.

Cushi. i.e. *blackness; the Ethiopian*, **S#3569h**. 2 S 18:21-23, 31, 32. Je 36:14.

Gedaliah. 1 Ch +25:3.

Amariah. Ezr +7:3.

Hizkiah. i.e. *strength of God; my strength is Jehovah*, **S#2396h**.

in the days. 2 K ch. 22, 23. 2 Ch ch. 34, 35. Je 1:2. 25:3.

2 **I will**, etc. Heb. By taking away I will make an end.

utterly. 2 K 22:16, 17. 2 Ch 36:21. Is 6:11. Je 6:8, 9. 24:8-10. 34:22. 36:29. Ezk 33:27-29. Mi 7:13.

all. Jb 42:2. Ps 8:6. Is 44:24.

land. Heb. face of the land. Ge 4:14. 6:1. 7:23. Ex 33:16. Nu 12:3. Dt 7:6. 14:2. 2 S 14:7mg. Is 23:17. Je 25:26. 28:16. Ezk 38:20. Am 9:8.

3 **consume man**. Je 4:23-26. 12:4. Ho 4:3.

stumbling blocks. *or*, idols. Is 3:6. 27:9. Ho 14:3, 8. Mi 5:11-14. Zc 13:2. Mt 13:41. 1 C +8:9.

cut off man. Ezk 14:13-21. 15:6-8.

4 **stretch**. Ex +7:5. 2 K 21:13. 23:8.

I will cut off. Mi 5:13.

the remnant of Baal. "Fulfilled, 2 K 23:4, 5. 2 Ch 34:4."

the Chemarims. i.e. *mourning; changed ones; blackness, sadness; one who goes about in black, in mourning, an ascetic, a priest*, **S#3649h**. 2 K 23:5mg. Ho 10:5mg.

5 **worship the host of heaven**. Dt +4:19.

upon. Dt +22:8.

and them. 1 K 18:21. 2 K 17:33, 41. Mt +6:24.

and that swear. Ge +21:23. Je 5:2. Ho 4:15.

by the Lord. *or*, to the Lord. Is 44:5.

swear by. Jsh 23:7.

Malcham. 1 K 11:33, Milcom. Am 5:26, Moloch.

6 **turned**. 1 S 15:11. Ps 36:3. 125:5. Is 1:4. Je 2:13, 17. 3:10. 15:6. Ezk 3:20. Ho 4:15, 16. 11:7. He 10:38, 39. 2 P 2:18-22.

from the Lord. Ho 1:2.

and those. Je +10:25. Ro 3:11. He 2:3.

not sought. Dt 4:29. 1 Ch +28:9. He 11:6.

7 **Hold thy peace**. 1 S 2:9, 10. Is 6:5. Am 6:10. Hab +2:20. Ro 3:19. 9:20.

for the day of the Lord. ver. 14. Ezk +30:3. Ph 4:5.

for the Lord. Is 34:6. Je 46:10. Ezk 39:17-20. Re 19:17, 18.

he hath. Pr 9:1-6. Ezk 39:17-21. Mt 22:4. 24:27, 28. Lk 14:16, 17. 17:34-37. Re 19:17, 18, 21.

bid. Heb. sanctified, *or* prepared. 1 S 16:5. 20:26. Lk 14:17. Col 1:12.

8 **the day**. Is +2:12. 13:6.

sacrifice. ver. +7.

punish. Heb. visit upon. Je +9:25mg.

the princes. 2 K 23:30-34. 24:12, 13. 25:6, 7, 19-21. Is 39:7. Je 22:11-19, 24-30. 39:6, 7.

king's children. 1 K 22:26. 2 K 11:2. Je 36:26. 39:6.

strange. Dt 22:5. 2 K 10:22. Is 3:18-24. Mt 22:11.

9 **leap**. 1 S 5:5. 2 S 22:30. 1 K 18:26. Ps 18:29. SS 2:8. Is 35:6.

which fill. 1 S 2:15, 16. 2 K 5:20-27. Ne 5:15. Pr 29:12. Ac 16:19.

10 **in that day**. ver. 7, 15. Je 39:2.

the noise. Is 22:4, 5. 59:11. 66:6. Je 4:19-21, 31. Am 8:3.

the fish gate. 2 Ch 33:14. Ne 3:3.

the second. 2 K 22:14mg. 2 Ch 34:22mg. Ne 11:9.

from the hills. 2 S 5:7, 9. 2 Ch 3:1.

11 **Howl**. Is +13:6.

Maktesh. i.e. *a mortar, hollow place*, **S#4389h**.

all the merchant. Ne 3:31, 32. Ho 12:7, 8. Jn 2:16. Re 18:11-18.

that bear silver. Pr +11:4. Ezk 7:19. Ja 5:1. Re 18:11.

12 **that I**. Je 16:16, 17. Am 9:1-3. Ob 6. Lk 15:8. 19:10.

search. Ps 7:9. 26:2. Je 11:20. 17:10. 20:12. Re 2:23.

with candles. Ps 119:104. Pr 6:23. 20:27. Lk 15:8. Ph 2:15. 2 P 1:19.

the men. Je 48:11. Am +6:1. Re 2:23.

settled. Heb. curded, or thickened. Ex 15:8. Jb 10:10. Zc 14:6mg.

on their lees. Ps 55:19. Je 48:11.

The Lord will not do. Jb 21:15. 22:12-14. Ps 10:4, 5, 11-13. 14:1. 94:7. Is 5:19. 41:23. Je 10:5. Ezk +8:12. 9:9. Ml 2:17. 3:14, 15. 2 P 3:4.

13 **their goods**. ver. 9. Is 6:11. 24:1-3. Je 4:7, 20. 5:17. 9:11, 19. 12:10-13. Ezk 7:19, 21. 22:31. Mi 3:12.

build. Dt 28:30, 39, 51. Is 5:8, 9. 65:21, 22. Am 5:11. +9:14. Mi 6:15.

wine. Hab 2:5.

14 **the great day of the Lord**. ver. 7. Je +30:7. Ezk +30:3. Ac 2:20. 1 C +3:13.

it is near. Ezk 7:6, 7, 12. 12:23. Am 8:2. Ro 13:12. Ph 4:5. He 10:37. Ja 5:9. 2 P 2:3.

hasteth greatly. He 10:37. Re 22:30.

even the voice. ver. 10. Is 22:4, 5. 66:6. Je 25:36. Jl 2:11. 3:16. 1 Th 4:16. He 12:26.

the mighty man. Is 15:4. 33:7. Je 48:41. Re 6:15-17.

15 **day of wrath**. ver. +18. Zp +2:2, 3. Jb +21:30. Ps 110:5. Pr 11:4. Je +30:7. Ezk 7:19. 38:18, 19. Am 5:18-20. Na 1:2. Ml 4:1. Lk 21:22, 23. Ro 2:5. 1 Th +1:10. 2 P 3:7. Re 6:17.

trouble and distress. Jb 15:24. Is 22:5. Je +30:7. Da +12:1. Jl 2:11. Ml 3:2. Lk 21:25, 26.

wasteness and desolation. Jb 30:3. 38:27.

a day of darkness. Jb 3:4-8. Mt +8:12.

clouds. Ge +9:13.

thick darkness. Ex +10:22.

16 **day of the trumpet**. Is 59:10. Je 8:16. Ho +8:1. Am 2:2. Hab 1:6-10. 3:6. 1 Th +4:16. Re +11:18, 19.

and against. Ps 48:12, 13. Is 2:12-15, 32:14.

high towers. Heb. corners. 2 Ch 26:15.

17 **distress**. Dt 28:52, 53.

they shall walk. Dt 28:28, 29. Ps 79:3. Is 29:10. 59:9, 10. La 4:14. Mt +15:14. Jn 9:40, 41. Ro 11:7, 25. 2 C +4:4. 2 P 1:9. 1 J 2:11. Re 3:17.

because. Is 24:5, 6. 50:1. 59:12-15. Je 2:17, 19. 4:18. La 1:8, 14, 18. 4:13-15. 5:16, 17. Ezk 22:25-31. Da 9:5, etc. Mi 3:9-12. 7:13.

and their blood. Ps 79:2, 3. Je 15:3. 18:21. La 2:21. 4:14. Am 4:10.

as dust. Ge +13:16.

dung. Je +16:4.

18 **their silver**. ver. +11. Ps 49:6-9. 52:5-7. Pr +11:4. 18:11. Is 2:20, 21. Je 9:23, 24. Ezk +7:19. Mt 16:26. Lk 12:19-21. 16:22, 23.

in the day. ver. +15. Jb +21:30. Is +66:14.

but. Zp 3:8. Le 26:33-35. Dt 29:20-28. 31:17. Je 4:26-29. 9:11.

the fire. Zp 3:8. Dt 9:3. +32:22. Ps 11:6. 21:8,

+9. 50:3. 68:2. 79:5. +97:3, 5. Is 9:5, 18, 19. 10:16, 17. 24:1-12. 26:11. 27:4. 30:30. 33:14. 64:2. 66:15, 16, 24. Je 7:20, 34. Ezk 20:47, 48. 30:8. 38:22. Mi 1:4. Na 1:5, 6. Hab 3:5. Ml 4:1. Mt 3:10, 12. 13:30. 2 Th 1:8. He 10:27. 2 P 3:7, 10. Re 16:8, 9.

jealousy. Ex +20:5. Ezk 16:38.

he shall. ver. 2, 3. Is 1:24.

ZEPHANIAH 2

1 **Gather**. Ex 5:7, 12. Nu 15:32, 33. 1 K 17:10, 12.

gather together. 2 Ch 20:4. Ne 8:1. 9:1. Est 4:16. Jl 1:14. 2:12-18. Mt 18:20.

O nation. Is 1:4-6, 10-15. Je 12:7-9. Zc 11:8.

desired. *or*, desirous. or, longing. Ge 31:30. Dt 9:24. Jb 14:15. Ps 84:3. Is 26:8, 9. Ac +3:19-21.

2 **Before the decree**. Zp 3:8. 2 K 22:16, 17. 23:26, 27. Ezk 12:25. Mt +24:35. 2 P 3:4-10.

as the chaff. Lk +3:17.

before the fierce. Zp +1:18. 2 K 23:26. 2 Ch 36:16, 17. Ps 2:12. 50:22. Je 23:20. La 4:11. Na 1:6. Ml 4:1, 2. Lk 13:24-28.

before the day of. Zp +1:15. Ps 95:7, 8.

3 **Seek ye**. Ps 45:4. 105:4. Je 3:13, 14. 4:1, 2. +29:13. Ho 7:10. Am 5:4-6, 14, 15.

all ye meek. 2 Ch 34:27, 28. Je 22:15, 16. Zc 8:19. Mt +5:5.

judgment. or, ordinances. Is 58:2. Je 8:7.

seek righteousness. Ph 3:13, 14. 1 Th 4:1, 10. 1 P 1:22. 2 P +3:18.

seek meekness. 2 Ch +7:14. Ps 25:9. 1 T +2:8.

it may. Ge +18:25, 32. 2 S 12:22. Je 5:1-3. Jl 2:13, 14. Am +5:15. Jon 3:9. Mt +7:14.

hid. i.e. escape (the Lord's) judgment (Gesenius, p. 711b). Ge 7:15, 16. Ex 12:27. Ps 27:5. 31:20. 32:6, 7. 57:1. +83:3. 91:1. +94:13. Pr 14:26. 18:10mg. 22:3. Is +26:20, 21. 51:16. Je 36:26. 39:18. 45:5. Jl 3:16mg. Hab +3:16. Ml 3:16-18. Lk +21:36. Col 3:2-4. 1 Th +1:10. Re +3:10.

in the day. Zp 1:14, 15, 18.

4 **Gaza**. Ge +10:19. Ezk 25:15-17.

Ashkelon. Je 47:5.

Ashdod. Jsh +11:22.

at the noon day. Ps 91:6. Je 6:4. 15:8.

5 **Cherethites**. 2 S +8:18.

the word. Am 3:1. 5:1. Zc 1:6. Mk 12:12.

O Canaan. Jsh 13:3. Jg 3:3. Zc 14:21.

6 **the sea**. ver. 14, 15. Is 17:2. Je 47:7. Ezk 25:5.

7 **the coast**. Is 14:29-32. Ob 19. Zc 9:6, 7. Ac 8:26, 40.

the remnant. ver. 9. Mi +5:3. Hg 1:12. 2:2.

Ashkelon. Zc 9:6.

for. *or*, when, etc.

shall visit. Ge 50:24. Ex 3:16. 4:31. Lk 1:68. 7:16.

turn. Zp 3:20. Ps 85:1. 126:1-4. Is 14:1. Je 3:18. 23:3. 29:14. 30:3, 18, 19. 33:7. Ezk 39:25. Am 9:14, 15. Mi 4:10.

8 heard. Ezk +25:8.
the revilings. Ge +19:38. Ezk 36:2.
magnified. Da +8:11.

9 as I. Dt +32:40.
Surely. Je 49:1-7. Ezk +25:8. Am 1:13-15.
as Gomorrah. ver. 14. Ge +19:24, 25.
nettles. Jb +30:7.
saltpits. Dt +29:23.
perpetual. Heb. olam, Ge +9:12. Je 25:12.
the residue. ver. +7. Jl 3:19, 20.

10 for. ver. 8. Pr 11:2. 16:18. 18:12. Is 16:6. Je 48:29. Da 4:37. 5:20-23. Ob 3. 1 P 5:5.
and magnified. Ex 9:17. 10:3. Is 10:12-15. 37:22-29. Ezk 38:14-18. Da +8:11.

11 for. Dt 32:38. Ho 2:17. Zc 13:2.
famish. Heb. make lean. Is 17:4.
the gods. Ex +12:12.
and men. Ps 2:8-12. 22:27-30. 72:8-11, 17. 86:9. 97:6-8. ch. 117. 138:4. Is 2:2-4. 11:9, 10. Mi 4:1-3. Zc 2:11. 8:20-23. 14:9-21. Ml 1:11. Jn 4:21-23. 1 T 2:8. Re 11:15.
isles of the heathen. Is +11:11.

12 Ethiopians. Ge +2:13.
my. Ps 17:13. Is 10:5. 13:5. Je +12:12. 51:20-23.

13 he will. Ps 83:8, 9. Is 10:12, 16. 11:11. Ezk 31:3, etc.
stretch. Ex +7:5.
north. Je +1:14.
will make. Na 1:1. 2:10, 11. 3:7, 15, 18, 19. Zc 10:10, 11.

14 flocks. ver. 6. Is 13:19-22. 34:11-17. Re 18:2.
cormorant. or, pelican. Ps 102:6.
upper lintels. or, knops, or chapiters. Am 9:1.
for he shall uncover. or, when he hath uncovered. Is 22:6mg.
the cedar. Je 22:14.

15 the rejoicing. Is 10:12-14. 22:2. 47:7. Re 18:7-10.
I am. Is 47:8. Ezk 28:2, 9. 29:3. Re 18:7.
how is. Is 14:4, 5. La 1:1. 2:1. Re 18:10-19.
every. Ps 52:6, 7. Na 3:19. Mt 27:39.
hiss. 2 Ch +29:8.

ZEPHANIAH 3

1 her that is filthy. or, gluttonous. Heb. craw. Le 1:16. Ezk +16:49.
polluted. Je 2:23.
the oppressing city. Dt +24:14. Is 1:21. 5:7. 30:12. 59:13. Je 6:6. 22:17. Ezk +16:49. 22:7, 29. Am 3:9. 4:1. Mi 2:2. Zc 7:10. Ml +3:5.

2 obeyed not. Dt +28:15, etc. Ne 9:26. Je 7:23-28. 22:21. Zc 7:11-14.
she received not. 1 S +25:17. Je +31:18. Ezk 24:13.

correction. or, instruction. Ps 50:17. Pr 1:7. 3:11. 5:12. Je 32:33. 35:13, 17. Jn 3:18, 19. 2 T 3:16.
trusted not. Ps +9:10. 78:22. Is 30:1-3. 31:1. Je 17:5, 6.
drew not near. Ps 10:4. Is 29:13. 43:22. He +10:22. Ja +4:8.

3 princes. Jb 4:8-11. Ps 10:8-10. Pr 28:15. Is 1:23. Je 22:17. Ezk 22:6, 25-27. Mi 3:1-4, 9-11.
judges. Ex +21:6.
evening. Je 5:6. Hab 1:8.

4 light. Is 9:15. 56:10-12. Je 5:31. 6:13, 14. 8:10. 14:13-15. 23:9-17, 25-27, 32. 27:14, 15. La 2:14. Ezk 13:3-16. Ho 9:7. Mi 2:11. 3:5, 6. Mt 7:15. 2 C 11:13-15. Ep 4:14. 2 P 2:1-3. 1 J 4:1. Re 19:20.
her priests. 1 S 2:12-17, 22. Ezk 22:26. 44:7, 8. Ho 4:6-8. Ml 2:8.
polluted. Le 19:8. 21:23. 22:15. Nu 18:32.
done violence. Je 2:8. Ezk 22:26mg.

5 just. Dt 32:4. Ps 99:3, 4. 145:17. Ec 3:16, 17. Is 45:21. Hab 1:13. Zc 9:9. Ro 3:26. 1 P 1:17.
in the midst. ver. 15, 17. Nu 5:3. Dt 7:21. 23:14. Is 12:6. Ezk 48:35. Mi 3:11. Zc 2:5.
he will. Ge +18:25. Jb 8:3. 34:10, 17-19. Ro 1:18. Ja 1:13.
every morning. Heb. morning by morning. 2 S +13:4mg. Is 28:19. 33:2. 50:4. Je 21:12. La 3:23. Re +2:28.
bring. Ps 37:6. Is 42:3, 4. Mi 7:9. Lk 12:2. Ro +2:5. 1 C 4:5.
but. Je 3:3. 6:15. 8:12.

6 cut. Is ch. 10, 15, 16, 19. 37:11-13, 24-26, 36. Je 25:9-11, 18-26. Na ch. 2, 3. 1 C 10:6, 11.
towers. or, corners. Zp 1:16. 2 K 14:13. 2 Ch 26:9, 15. Je 31:38.

7 Surely. ver. 2. Is 5:4. 63:8. Je 8:6. 36:3. Lk 19:42-44. 2 P 3:9.
so their dwelling. Je 5:1. 7:7. 17:25-27. 25:5. 38:17.
howsoever. 2 Ch 28:6-8. 32:1, 2. 33:11. 36:3-10.
they rose early. Mi 2:1, 2.
corrupted. Ge 6:12. Dt 4:16. Ho 9:9.

8 Therefore wait. Ps +25:3. Ja 5:7, 8.
until the day. Ml +4:5.
rise up. Jb 19:25 (stand). Ps +3:7. Is 42:13, 14. 59:16-18.
to the prey. Zp +2:2. Ge 49:27. Is 33:23. 49:24, 25. 60:5mg. 61:6. Ezk 39:10, 21. Mi 4:12, 13. Zc 14:14. Mt 24:28. Lk 17:37. Ro +11:25. Ja 5:3.
gather the nations. Ezk 38:14-23. Jl 3:2, 9-16. Mi 4:11-13. Zc 12:3. 14:2, 3. Mt +25:32. Re +16:14, 16. 19:17-19.
to pour. Je +10:25.
indignation. Is +66:14.
for all the earth. SS 8:6. 2 P 3:10.
the fire. Is +24:6.
my jealousy. Ex +20:5.

9 will I turn. Ne 13:24. Is 19:18. Je 31:23. Mt +12:35. Ep 4:29. Col 4:6.

pure. 2 S 22:27. Jb 33:3 (clearly). Da 12:10 (purified).

language. Heb. lip. Ge +11:1mg. Jg +7:22mg. Is 6:5. 19:18mg.

  that. 1 K 8:41-43. Ps 22:27. 86:9, 10. 113:3. Je 16:19. Hab 2:14. Zc 2:11. 8:20-23. +14:9. Ac 2:4, etc. Ro 15:6-11. Re 11:15.

  to serve. Re 7:14, 15.

  with one. Je 31:34. 32:39.

  consent. Heb. shoulder. Ho 6:9mg.

10 beyond. Ps 68:31. 72:8-11. Is 11:11. 18:1, 7, etc. 27:12, 13. 49:20-23. 60:4-12. 66:18-21. Ml 1:11. Ac 8:27. 24:17. Ro 11:11, 12. 15:16. 1 P 1:1.

11 In that day. Is +2:11.

  shalt thou. ver. 19, 20. Ps 49:5. Is 61:7. 65:13, 14. Je 31:19. Jl +2:26, 27. Ro 6:21. 1 P 2:6.

  that rejoice. Nu 16:3. Is 13:3. 48:1, 2. Je 7:4, 9-12. Ezk 7:20-24. 24:21. Mi 3:11. Ml 4:1. Mt 3:9. Ro 2:17.

  because of my holy. or, in my holy. Ps 48:2, 3. 87:1, 2. Is 11:9. Da 9:16, 20.

12 leave. Is 14:32. 61:1-3. Zc 11:11. 13:8, 9. Mt +5:3. 11:5. 1 C 1:27, 28. Ja 2:5.

  they shall trust. Ps 37:40. Is 50:10. Na 1:7. Mt 12:21. Ro 15:12. Ep 1:12, 13. 1 P 1:21.

  in the name. Ps +9:10. 20:1.

13 remnant. Zp 2:7. Is 6:13. Mi +5:3.

  not do iniquity. Ps +130:8. Is 11:6-9. 35:8. 65:20. Je 31:33. 32:40. Jl 3:17, 21. Zc 14:20, 21. Mt 13:41. 1 J 3:2, 9, 10. 5:18.

  nor speak lies. Is 63:8. Jn 1:47. Col 3:9. Re 14:5. +21:8, 27.

  they shall feed. Le 26:5, 6. Ps 23:2. Is 65:10. Je 23:4. Ezk 34:13-15, 23-28. Mi 4:4. 5:4, 5. 7:14. Re 7:15-17.

  and none. Le 26:6. Ps +118:6. Is 17:2. 54:14. Ezk 34:28. 39:26. Mi 4:4. 2 T +1:7.

14 Sing. Dt +32:43. Zc +2:10. Lk +23:41.

  daughter. Mt +21:5.

  shout. Ezr 3:11-13. Ne 12:43. Ps 14:7. 47:5-7. 81:1-3. 95:1, 2. 100:1, 2. 126:2, 3. Is 12:6. 24:14-16. 35:2. 40:9. 42:10-12. 51:11. 54:1. 65:13, 14, 18, 19. Je 30:19. 31:13. 33:11. Zc 2:10, 11. 9:9, 10, 15-17. Mt 21:9. Lk 2:10-14. Re 19:1-6.

  O daughter of Jerusalem. Mi 4:8.

15 hath taken. Ge 30:23. Ps 85:3. Is 25:8. 40:1, 2. 51:22. Mi 7:18-20. Zc 1:14-16. 8:13-15. 10:6, 7.

  he hath. Is ch. 13, 14. Je ch. 50, 51. Mi 4:6,

7. 7:10, 16, 17. Hab 2:8, 17. Zc 2:8, 9. 12:3. Ro 8:33, 34. Re 12:10.

  the king. Is 33:22. Jn +1:49. Re 19:16.

  in the midst. ver. 5, 17. Dt 7:21. Is 12:6. Ezk 37:26-28. 48:35. Da 3:25. Jl 3:20, 21. Zc 2:5, 10. Re 7:15. 21:3, 4.

  thou. Ps 91:10. Is 35:10. 51:22. 60:18. 65:19. Je 31:40. Ezk 39:29. Jl 3:17. Am 9:15. Zc 14:11.

16 In that day. Is +2:11.

  be said. Ge +15:1. Hg 2:4, 5. He 12:12.

  Fear thou not. Dt 7:21.

  slack. or, faint. Is 13:7. 2 C 4:1. Ga 6:9. Ep 3:13. He 12:3-5. Re 2:3.

17 in the midst. ver. 5, 15. Ps +102:13, 16. Zc 14:3, 5.

  is mighty. Ge 17:1. 18:14. Dt 10:17. Jsh 4:24. Ps 24:8-10. 89:19. Is +9:6. 12:2, 6. 63:1, 12. He 7:25.

  will rejoice. Nu 14:8. Dt +30:9. Ps 149:4. Is 61:10.

  with joy. Ps 147:11.

  he will. Ge 1:31. 2:2. Is 18:4. Jn 13:1.

  rest. Heb. be silent. Ps 37:7mg.

  joy over. Ps 149:4. Pr 11:20.

  with singing. Is +51:11.

18 gather. ver. 20. Dt 30:3, 4. Je 23:3. 31:8, 9. Ezk +34:13. 36:24. +37:25. Ho 1:11. Ro +11:25, 26.

  sorrowful. Ps 42:2-4, 10. 43:3. 63:1, 2. 84:1, 2. 137:3-6. La 1:4, 7. 2:6, 7. Ho 9:5.

  solemn assembly. Ge +17:21. Ex 27:21. Le +23:36.

  the reproach of it was a burden. Heb. the burden upon it was reproach.

19 I will undo. ver. 15. Is 25:9-12. 26:11. 41:11-16. 43:14-17. 49:25, 26. 51:22, 23. 66:14-16. Je 30:16. 46:28. 51:35, 36. Ezk 39:17-22. Jl 3:2-9. Mi 7:10. Na 1:11-14. Zc 2:8, 9. 12:3, 4. 14:2, 3. Re 19:17-21. 20:9.

  and I will save. Je 31:8. Ezk 34:16. Mi 4:6, 7. He 12:13.

  and I will. Dt 26:19. Is 60:14. 61:7. 62:7. Je 33:9. Ezk 39:26.

  get them praise. Heb. set them for a praise. Ps 78:43mg.

  where they have been put to shame. Heb. of their shame.

20 bring you. Ezk +34:13. +37:25.

  in the time. Ps +102:13, 16.

  gather. Is 56:8. Je +23:3. Ezk 28:25, 26.

  for I will. ver. 19. Dt 26:19. Is 25:8. 60:15, 18. 61:9. 62:7, 12. Mi 4:8. Ml 3:12. Re 5:13.

  I turn. Zp 2:7. Ps 35:6. Je +23:3. Ezk 16:53.

HAGGAI

HAGGAI 1

1 second. Hg 2:1, 10, 20. Ezr 4:5, 24. 5:1, 2. Zc 1:1, 7.

the king. Da 11:2.

the sixth. *Elul*, the sixth month of the ecclesiastical year, answering to a part of *September*.

first day of the month. 2 Ch +2:4.

by. Heb. by the hand of. ver. 6, 8. Hg 2:5, 11, 12, 13, 17. Ex 4:13. 9:35. 35:29. Le 10:11. 26:46. Nu 4:37, 45. 9:23. 10:13. 15:23. 16:40. 27:23. 36:13. Jsh 14:2. 20:2. 21:2, 8. 22:9. Jg 3:4. 1 K 8:53, 56. 12:15. +16:12mg. 17:16. 2 Ch 34:14mg. Ezr 6:14. Ne 8:14mg. 9:14. 10:29mg. Est 1:12mg. Is 20:2mg. Je +37:2mg. 50:1mg. Ezk 38:17mg. Ho 12:10mg. Zc 7:12mg.

Haggai. i.e. *festive, feast*, or *festival; exaltation* or *festival of the Lord*, **S#2292h**. ver. 1, 3, 12, 13. Hg 2:1, 10, 13, 14, 20. Ezr 5:1, 2. 6:14.

unto Zerubbabel. i.e. *sown in Babylon*, **S#2216h**. ver. 12, 14. Hg 2:2, 4, 21, 23. 1 Ch 3:19. Ezr 2:2. 3:2, 8. 4:2, 3. 5:2. Ne 7:7. 12:1, 47. Zc 4:6, 7, 9, 10. Mt 1:12, 13, Zorobabel. Lk 3:27.

son of. or, grandson of. 1 K 15:10. 1 Ch 3:19. 6:20. 7:6. Ezr 5:1. 7:1.

Shealtiel. i.e. *asked for from God*, **S#7597h**. Hg ver. 1. 2:23. 1 Ch 3:17, Salathiel. Ezr 3:2, 8. Ne 12:1. Also Hg 1:12, 14. 2:2. Mt 1:12, Salathiel. Lk 3:27.

governor. *or*, captain. Ezr 1:8. 2:63. Ne 5:14. 8:9.

Joshua. Hg 1:12, 14. 2:2, 4. Ezr 2:2. 3:8. 5:2. Ne 12:1, 10. Zc 3:1, 3, 8, 9. 6:11.

Josedech. i.e. *Jehovah is righteous*. **S#3087h**. Hg ver. 1, 12, 14. 2:2, 4. 1 Ch 6:14, 15, Jehozadak. Zc 6:11.

2 the Lord of hosts. Ex +15:26. Ps +24:10.

This. Nu 13:31. Ezr 4:4, 5, 23, 24. 5:1, 2. Ne 4:10. Pr 22:13. 26:13-16. 29:25. Ec 9:10. 11:4. SS 5:2, 3.

The time. Ps 1:3.

be built. Ezr 3:2.

3 by Haggai. Ezr 5:1. Zc 1:1.

4 Is it time. Je 33:10, 12.

to dwell. 2 S 7:2. Ezr 2:70. Ps 132:3-5. Mt 6:33. Ph 2:21.

cieled. or, paneled. 1 K 6:9. 7:3, 7. Je 22:14.

and this house. Ps 74:7. 102:14. Je 26:6, 18. 52:13. La 2:7. 4:1. Ezk 24:21. Da +9:17, 18, 26, 27. Mi 3:12. Mt +24:1, 2.

5 thus. ver. 7. Hg 2:15-18. La 3:40. Ezk 18:28. Lk 15:17. 2 C 13:5. Ga 6:4.

Consider your ways. Heb. Set your heart on your ways. ver. 7. Hg 2:15, 18. Ex 7:23. 9:21mg. Jb 1:8. 2:3. Ps 48:13mg. Pr +6:6. 24:32mg. Is 41:22. 44:19mg. Ezk 40:4. Da 6:14. 10:12. 1 C 11:31.

6 have sown. ver. 9. Hg 2:16. Le 26:20. Dt 28:38-40. 2 S 21:1. Ps 107:34. Is 5:10. Je 14:4. Ho 4:10. 8:7. Jl 1:10-13. Am 4:6-9. Mi 6:14, 15. Zc 8:10. Ml 2:2. 3:9-11.

eat. Le +26:26. 1 K 17:12. Jb 20:22. Je 44:18.

earneth wages. or, is hiring himself out. lit. "making himself sweet." Zc 8:10.

with holes. Heb. pierced through. Jb 20:28. Zc 5:4. 1 T +6:17.

7 Consider. ver. +5. 1 S 2:30. Ps 119:59, 60. Pr +6:6. +14:12, 13. Is 28:10. Da 10:12. 2 C 13:5. Ph 3:1.

8 to. 2 Ch 2:8-10. Ezr 3:7. 6:4. Zc 11:1, 2.

and build. ver. +2-4. Jon 3:1, 2. Mt 3:8, 9.

and I will take pleasure. Hg 2:7, 9. 1 K 8:29. 9:3. 2 Ch 7:16. Ps 87:2, 3. 133:13, 14. Zp 3:17.

I will be glorified. Hg 2:7. Ex 29:43. Le 10:3. Ps 132:13, 14. Is 60:7, 13. 66:11. Jn 13:31, 32.

9 Ye looked. ver. +6. Hg 2:16, 17. Is 17:10, 11. Ml 3:8-11.

blow upon it. *or*, blow it away. 2 S 22:16. 2 K 19:7. Is 40:7. Ml 2:2.

Why. Jb 10:2. Ps 77:5-10.

Because. ver. +4. Jsh 7:10-15. 2 S 21:1. Mt 10:37, 38. 1 C +11:30-32. Re 2:4. 3:19.

unto his own. Ph 2:21.

10 the heaven. Le 26:19. Dt 28:23, 24. 1 K 8:35. 17:1. Je 14:1-6. Ho 2:9. Jl 1:18-20.

11 And. Ge +8:22.

I called. Dt 28:22mg. 1 K 17:1. 2 K 8:1. Jb 34:29. Je 14:3, 4. La 1:21. Am 5:8. 7:4. 9:6.

new wine. Heb. tirosh, Ge +27:28.

upon all. Hg 2:17.

12 Zerubbabel. ver. 14. Ezr 5:2. Is 55:10, 11. Col 1:6. 1 Th 1:5, 6. 2:13, 14.

sent him. Je 43:1.

fear. Ge 22:12. Ps 112:1. Pr 1:7. Ec 12:13. Is 50:10. Ac 9:31. He 12:28.

13 **the Lord's**. Jg 2:1mg. Is 42:19. 44:26. Ezk 3:17. Ml 2:7. 3:1, 2 C 5:20.

I am with you. Hg 2:4. 2 Ch 15:2. 20:17. 32:8. Ps 46:7, 11. Is 8:8-10. 41:10. 43:2. Je 15:20. 20:11. 30:11. Mt 1:23. 18:20. 28:20. Ac 18:9, 10. Ro 8:31. 2 C 12:9. 2 T 4:17, 22.

14 **stirred up**. 1 Ch 5:26. 2 Ch 36:22. Ezr 1:1, 5. 7:27, 28. Ps 110:3. 1 C 12:4-11. 2 C 8:16. He 13:21.

the spirit. Heb. *ruach*, Ge +41:8; +26:35. 1 Ch 5:26. 2 Ch 21:16. 36:22. Ezr 1:1. Je 51:11.

governor of. ver. 1. Hg 2:21.

and they. Hg 2:4. Ezr 5:2, 8. Ne 4:6. 1 C 15:58. Ph 2:12, 13.

15 **the four and**. ver. 1. Hg 2:1, 10, 18, 20.

HAGGAI 2

1 **the seventh**. ver. 10, 20. Hg 1:15.

the prophet. Heb. the hand of the prophet, etc. Hg +1:1mg. 2 P 1:21.

2 **Zerubbabel**. Hg +1:1.

governor. Hg 1:14. Ezr 1:8. 2:63. Ne 8:9.

Josedech. 1 Ch 6:15.

3 **is left**. Ezr 3:12. Zc 4:9, 10.

this house. ver. 7.

first. 1 K 5:15-17. 6:7, 15, 18, 20-22, 30, 35. 7:48-51. 1 Ch 22:5.

glory. Is +40:5. Ezk 7:20. Lk 21:5, 6.

4 **now**. Jsh +1:6. Jg 6:14.

saith the Lord. Is 43:1.

and work. Zc 6:15. 8:9, 13.

with you. Hg 1:13. Ex 3:12. Jsh 1:7, 8. Jg 2:18. 1 S 16:18. 2 S 5:10. Mk 16:20. Ac 7:9. 2 T 4:17.

5 **According to**. Ex 29:45, 46. 33:12-14. 34:8, 10.

the word. Dt 28:1-42. Ps 105:8.

I covenanted. Ps 89:34. 111:5. Ml +3:6.

when ye came. Ex 12:51.

so. Nu 11:25-29. Ne 9:20, 30. Ps 51:11, 12. Is 63:11-14. Zc 4:6. Jn 14:16, 17.

spirit. Heb. *ruach*, Ge +41:38. Ne 9:20. Is 63:10, 11. Zc 4:6.

fear. Jsh 8:1. 2 Ch 20:17. Is 41:10, 13. Zc 8:13, 15. Mt 28:5. Lk 12:32. Ac 27:24. Re 1:17.

6 **Yet**. ver. 21, 22. He 12:26-28.

once. or, first. Heb. *echad*, one of several. Hg 1:1. 2:1. Dt +6:4. He *12:26, 27*.

a little while. Ps 37:10. Is 10:25. 29:17. Je 51:33. He 10:37.

and I will shake. ver. 7, 21, 22. Ps 46:3. 77:18. Ac 2:19, 20. He +12:26.

the heavens. ver. 21, 22. Is 13:10-13. 14:12-15. 34:4, 5. 51:16. Je 4:23-25. Ezk 32:7. Jl 2:10.

and the earth. Ge 6:11. Re 12:16.

7 **I will shake**. Ezk 21:27. Da 2:44, 45. 7:20-

25. Jl 3:9-16. Lk 21:10, 11. He +12:26. Re 6:12-17.

all nations. Ex +9:6. Is 24:21, 22. Da 12:1.

and the desire. Ge +3:15. 22:18. +49:10. 1 S 9:20. 2 Ch 21:20. Zc 9:9, 10. Lk 2:10, 11, 27, 29, 30, 46. Ro 15:9-15. Ga 3:8.

all nations. Ex +9:6.

shall come. Ge +49:10. Is +35:4. Da 7:14, 18, 27. Ml 3:1.

I will fill. Ex 40:34, 35. 1 K 8:11. 2 Ch +5:13, 14. Ps 80:1. Lk 19:47. 20:1. 21:38. Jn 1:14. 2:13-17. 7:37-39. 10:23-38. Col 2:9.

this house. Is 60:13. Ezk +37:26. 40:2. Jl 2:1. Zc 1:16. 6:12, 13. Ml 3:1. Mt 21:12. 24:15. Lk 2:27, 32.

glory. ver. 9. Ps 24:7-10. Is 9:6. +40:5.

8 **The silver**. 1 K 6:20-35. 1 Ch 29:12-16. Ps 24:1. 50:10-12. Is 2:7. 60:13, 17. 61:6.

9 **glory**. ver. +7. Ps 24:7-10. Is +40:5. Lk 2:14. 2 C 3:9, 10. 1 T 3:16. 1 Th 2:19, 20. He 12:28. Ja 2:1.

latter house. Ezk 43:2, 4, 5. 44:4. Ml 3:1. Mt 21:12. Lk 2:27, 32.

give. Ps 85:8, 9. Is +9:6, 7. 54:4, 10, 13. 57:18-21. Mi 5:5. Lk 2:14. Jn 14:27. Ac 10:36. Ep 2:14-17. Ph 4:7. Col 1:19-21.

peace. Is +9:6. Mi +5:5. Zc 9:9, 10.

10 **the four and**. ver. 1, 20. Hg 1:1, 15.

by. Hg +1:1mg.

11 **Ask now**. Le 10:10, 11. Dt 17:11. 21:5. 33:10. Is +8:20. Ezk 44:10-12, 23, 24. Ml 2:7. Mt 8:4. T 1:9.

12 **If one bear**. Ex 29:37. Le 6:27, 29. 7:6. Ezk 44:19. Mt 23:19.

holy flesh. Je 11:15.

skirt. lit. wing. Ru 3:9.

wine. Heb. *yayin*, Hab 2:5.

No. Le 6:27.

13 **If one**. Le 7:19. Nu 5:2, 3. 9:6-10. 19:11-22. Ezk 44:25.

body. Heb. *nephesh*, soul, Le +19:28.

unclean. Le 22:4, 6.

14 **So is this people**. Hg 1:4-11. Pr 15:8. 21:4, 27. 28:9. Is 1:11-15. T 1:15. Ju 23.

and that. Ezr 3:2, 3.

unclean. Is 6:5. 64:6. Ro 14:20. T 1:15.

15 **consider**. ver. 18. Hg 1:5, 7. Ps 107:43. Is 5:12. Ho 14:9. Ml 3:8-11. Ro 6:21. 1 C 11:31.

from before. Ezr 3:10. 4:24.

stone was laid. Is 28:16. Mk 4:19. 1 P 2:6, 7.

16 **when one came to an**. Hg 1:6, 9-11. Pr 3:9, 10. Is 9:20. Zc 8:10-12. Ml 2:2. Mk 4:20.

press. Is 63:3.

17 **with blasting**. Hg 1:9. Ge 41:6, 23, 27. Dt +28:22. Is 37:27.

with hail. Is +28:17.

in all. Hg 1:11. Ps 78:46. Is 62:8. Je 3:24.

yet. 2 Ch 28:22. Jb 36:13. Je +5:3. 6:16, 17. 8:4-7. Ho 7:9, 10. Am 4:8-11. Zc 1:2-4. 7:9-13. Re 2:21. 9:20, 21.

18 Consider. ver. 15. Dt 32:29. Lk 15:17-20.
even. Hg 1:14, 15. Ezr 5:1, 2. Zc 8:9, 12. He
11:10.
19 as yet. Hab 3:17, 18.
from this day. Ge 26:12. Le 26:3, etc. Dt
15:10. 28:2-15. Ps 84:10-12. 128:1-5. 133:3.
Pr 3:9, 10. Zc 8:11-15. Ml 3:10. Mt 6:33. 1 C
6:14-18.
I will bless. Ge 22:17, 18. Is 1:19. Ro 11:26.
1 T 4:8.
20 in the four. ver. 10.
21 Zerubbabel. Hg 1:1.
I will shake. ver. 6, 7. Ps 46:6. Ezk 26:15. He
+12:26, 27. 2 P 3:10, 12. Re 16:17-19.
the heavens and the earth. ver. 6. Ge 1:1.
Ex 20:11. 31:17. Dt 4:26. 30:19. 31:28. 2 K
19:15. 2 Ch 2:12. Is 37:16. Je 23:24. 32:17.
22 overthrow. Is 60:12. Ezk 21:27. +38:8, 9, 21.

Da 2:34, 35, 44, 45. 7:25-27. 8:25. +11:40.
12:1. Mi +5:8, 15. Zp 3:8. Zc 10:11. 12:2-5.
14:3. Mt +24:7. Re 11:15. 17:14.
and I will overthrow the chariots. Ex
14:17, 28. 15:4, 19. Ps 46:9. 76:6. Ezk 39:20.
Mi 5:10. Zc 4:6. 9:10.
every. Jg +7:22. Is 43:16, 17.
23 O Zerubbabel. Ezk 34:23.
my servant. 2 S 7:12, 16. Ps ch. 63. Is 42:1.
Zc 4:7-10.
and will. Ge 41:42. Est 3:10. SS 8:6. Je
22:24. Zc 4:7-10. 6:13. Jn 6:27. 2 T 2:19.
signet. Je 22:24.
for. Is 42:1. +43:10. 49:1-3. Zc 4:6-14. Mt
12:17, 18. Lk 3:23, 27. 23:35. Jn 7:42. 1 P
2:4-6. Re 19:16.
chosen thee. Dt +10:15. 1 K 8:16. 11:34. Is
+9:6, 7. Ro +8:28-30, 33.

ZECHARIAH

ZECHARIAH 1

1 A.M. 3484. B.C. 520.
the eighth. ver. 7. Zc 7:1. Ezr 4:24. 6:15. Hg 1:1, 15. 2:1, 10, 20.
Zechariah. i.e. *remembered of Jehovah*, **S#2148h.** ver. 1, 7. Zc 7:1, 8. Ezr 5:1. 6:14. Also 2 K 14:29. 15:11. 18:2. 1 Ch 9:21, 37. 15:20. 16:5. 2 Ch 17:7. 24:20. 34:12. Ezr 8:3, 11, 16. 10:26. Ne 8:4. 11:4, 5, 12. 12:16, 35, 41. Also 2 K 15:8. 1 Ch 5:7. 15:18, 24. 24:25. 26:2, 11, 14. 27:21. 2 Ch 20:14. 21:2. 26:5. 29:1, 13. 35:8. Is 8:2. Mt 23:35. Lk 11:51.
Iddo. Ezr +5:1.

2 **Lord.** 2 K 22:16, 17, 19. 23:26. 2 Ch 36:13-20. Ezr 9:6, 7, 13. Ne 9:26, 27. Ps 60:1. 79:5, 6. Je 44:6. La 1:12-15. 2:3-5. 3:42-45. 5:7. Ezk 5:11-13. 22:18, 31. Da 9:11, 12. Zp 2:1-3. Mt 23:30-32. Ac 7:52.
sore displeased. Heb. with displeasure. ver. 14, 15. Zc 8:2.

3 **Turn.** Dt 30:2, 10. 1 S 7:3. 1 K 8:47, 48. 2 Ch 6:38. 15:4. 30:6-9. Ne 1:9. 9:28. Je 3:12, 14, 22. 4:1. +35:15. Ho 6:1. Ml 3:7. Lk 15:18-20. Ac +9:35.
and. Je 12:15. 29:12-14. 31:18-20. La 5:21. Ho 14:4. Mi +7:19, 20. Lk 15:21, 22. Ac +3:19-21.

4 **as.** 2 Ch 29:6-10. 30:7. 34:21. Ezr 9:7. Ne 9:16. Ps 78:8. 106:6, 7. Ezk 18:14-17. 1 P 1:18.
unto. Zc 7:11-13. 2 Ch 24:19-22. 36:15, 16. Ne 9:26, 30. Is 30:9-11. Je 6:16, 17. 7:25. 13:16-18. 17:19-23. 25:3-7. 35:15. 36:2, 3, etc. 44:4, 5. Ezk 3:7-9. Mi 2:6. Ac 7:51, 52. 1 Th 2:15, 16.
Turn. ver. +3. Am 5:13-15, 24.
but. Je +7:26. 36:23, 24.

5 **Your fathers.** Mt 7:21-23. 12:31, 32. 15:18-20. Mk 7:20-23. Jn 21:15-17. Col 2:14, 15.
where are they. Jb 14:10-12. Ps 90:10. Ec 1:4. 9:1-3. 12:5, +7. Is 64:6. La 5:7. Ac 13:36. He 7:23, 24. +9:27. 2 P 3:2-4.
for ever. Heb. *olam*, Ex +12:24.

6 **my words.** Is 55:1.
did. Nu 23:19. +32:23. 2 Ch 36:17-21. Is 44:26. Je 26:15. 44:28. La 2:17. Ezk 12:25-28. Da 9:7, 11, 12. Am 4:6. Mt 24:35.

take hold of. *or*, overtake. Dt +28:15, 45. Je 42:16. Am 9:10. 1 Th 5:4.
they returned. Jb 6:29. Ml 3:18.
Like. La 1:18. 2:17. 4:11, 12. Ezk 37:11.
thought. Nu 33:56. Je 23:20.
according to our ways. Dt 28:20. Is 3:8-11. Je 4:4. 18:8-11. Ezk 20:43. Ho 9:15. Ro 2:6-11.

7 A.M. 3485. B.C. 519.
the eleventh. ver. 1.
Sebat. i.e. *smite thou; tribe*, **S#7627h**, only here. *Sebat* is the Chaldee name of the eleventh month of the ecclesiastical year, but the fifth of the civil year, answering to part of January and February.
Berechiah. i.e. *blessed of Jehovah*, **S#1296h.** ver. 1. 1 Ch 3:20. 9:16. 15:23. Ne 3:4, 30. 6:18.

8 **by night.** Ge 20:3. 1 K 3:5. Jb 4:13. Da 2:19. 7:2, 13.
behold. Zc 13:7. Jsh 5:13. Ps 45:3, 4. Is 63:1-4.
riding. Zc 6:2-7. Re 6:2, 4, 5, 8. 19:11, 14, 19-21.
among. SS 2:16. 6:2. Is 41:19. 55:13. +57:15. Re 2:1.
speckled. *or*, bay. Zc 6:6, 7.

9 **what.** ver. 19. Zc 4:4, 11. 6:4. Da 7:16. 8:15. Re 7:13, 14.
the angel. ver. 11, 12, 13, 14, 19. Zc 2:3. 4:1, 5. 5:5, 10. 6:4, 5. Ge 31:11. Da 8:16. 9:22, 23. 10:11-14. Re 17:1, 7. 19:9, 10. 22:8-16.

10 **the man.** ver. 8, 11. Zc 13:7. Ge 32:24-31. Ho 12:3-5.
These. ver. 11. Zc 4:10. 6:5-8. Jb 1:6, 7. 2:1, 2. Ps 34:7. 68:17. 103:20, 21. Ezk 1:5-14. He 1:14. 1 P 5:8. Re 12:7-12.

11 **they answered.** ver. 8, 10. Ps 68:17. 103:20, 21. Mt 6:10. 13:41, 49. 24:30, 31. 25:31. 2 Th 1:7. Re 1:1.
We. Zc 6:7. Da 10:20. Re 16:13, 14.
is. ver. 15. 1 Th 5:3.

12 **the angel.** ver. 8, 10, 11. Zc +12:8. He 7:25.
how long. Zc 7:9. Ps +102:13. Is 14:1. 49:13. 64:9-12. Re +6:10.
thou hast. Zc 7:5. 2 Ch 36:21. Je 25:11, 12. 29:10. Da 9:2.

13 **with good.** ver. 14-16. Zc 2:4-12. 8:2-8, 19.

Is 40:1, 2. Je 29:10. 30:10-22. 31:3, etc. Am 9:11-15. Zp 3:14-20.

comfortable words. ver. 17. Ps +102:13. Is 40:1, 2.

14 **the angel**. ver. 9, 13. Zc 2:3, 4. 4:1.
Cry. ver. 17. Is 40:1, 6.
I am. Is +9:7. Ho 11:8.
jealous. Ex +20:5.
for Zion. Is 37:32.

15 **sore displeased**. ver. 2, 11. Is 47:7-9. Je 48:11-13. Re 18:7, 8.
at ease. Is 32:9, 11. Am 6:1.
for. Is 54:8. He 12:6, 7.
and. Ps 69:26. 83:2-5. 137:7. Is 10:5-7. 47:6. Je 51:24, 34, 35. Ezk 25:3-7, 12-17. 26:2, 3. 29:6, 7. 35:3-9. 36:4, 5. Am 1:3-6, 9-13. Ob 10-16.
the affliction. Is +45:7. 47:11. Je 44:11.

16 **I am**. Zc 2:10, 11. 8:3. Is 12:1. 54:8-10. Je 31:22-25. 33:10-12. Ezk 37:24-28. 39:25-29. 48:35. Ho +5:15.
my house. Zc 4:9. 6:12, 13. Ezr 6:14, 15. Is 44:26-28. 60:13. Ezk 40:2. Hg 1:14.
and. Zc 2:1, 2. Ne 6:15, 16. Jb 38:5. Is 34:11. Je 31:39, 40. Ezk 40:1-3. 47:3. Da +9:25.

17 **My cities**. Ne 11:3, 20. Ps 69:35. Is 44:26. 61:4-6. Je 31:23, 24. 32:43, 44. 33:13. Ezk 36:10, 11, 33. Am 9:14. Ob 20.
prosperity. Heb. good.
the Lord shall. Is 40:1, 2. 49:13. 51:3, 12. 52:9. 54:8. 61:2. 66:13. Je 31:13, 14. Zp 3:15-17. Mt 23:37.
choose. Zc 2:12. 3:2. 2 Ch 6:6. Ps 132:13, 14. Is 14:1. +41:8, 9. Ro 11:28, 29. Ep 1:4.

18 **lifted**. Zc 2:1. 5:1, 5, 9. Ge +22:13. Jsh 5:13. Da 8:3.
four horns. ver. 21. 2 K 15:29. 17:1-6. 18:9-12. 22:11. ch. 24, 25. Ps 75:4, 5. Da 2:37-43. 7:3-8. 8:3-14. 11:28-35.

19 **What**. ver. 9, 21. Zc 2:2. 4:11-14. Re 7:13, 14.
scattered. ver. 21. Zc 8:14. 2 K 24:2, 10. 25:8-10. Ezr 4:1, 4, 7. 5:3. Je 50:17, 18. Da 12:7. Hab 3:14.

20 **four**. Zc 9:12-16. 10:3-5. 12:2-6. Dt 33:25. Jg 2:16, 18. 1 S 12:11. Ne 9:27. Is 54:15-17. Ob +21. Mi +5:5, 6, 8, 9.

21 **These are the**. ver. 19. Da 12:7.
fray. That is, to *terrify*, or *affright*, from the French *effrayer*. Zp 3:13.
which. Ps 75:4, 5. Is 43:14. Je 50:8, 9. La 2:17. Ezk 25:1, etc.

ZECHARIAH 2

1 **lifted**. Zc 1:18. Ge +22:13.
a man. Zc 1:16. Ezk 40:3, 5. 47:4. Re 11:1. 21:15, 16.

2 **Whither**. Zc 5:10. Jn 16:5.
To. Je 31:39. Ezk 45:6. 48:15-17, 30-35. Re 11:1. 21:15-17.

3 **the angel**. Zc 1:9, 13, 14, 19. 4:1, 5. 5:5.
and another. Zc 1:8, 10, 11. He 1:14.

4 **young**. Je 1:6. Da 1:17. 1 T 4:12.
Jerusalem. Zc 1:17. 8:4, 5. 12:6. 14:10, 11. Is 33:20. 44:26. 54:2. Je 30:18, 19. 31:24, 27, 38-40. 33:10-13. Ezk 36:10, 11. 38:11. Mi 7:11, 12.

5 **a wall**. Zc 9:8. Ex 14:19-24. Ps 46:7-11. 48:3, 12-14. Is 4:5. 12:6. 26:1, 2. 33:21. 60:18, 19. Da 3:25. Zp 3:15.
the glory. Zc +6:13. Ex +13:21, 22. Ps 3:3. 68:18. Is 40:5. 60:19. Ezk 43:1-7. Hg 2:7-9. Mt +24:30. +25:31. Lk 2:32. 2 P +1:17. Re 21:10, 11, 23. 22:3-5.
in the midst. Ps 46:5. Ezk 48:35. Jl 3:21.

6 **ho**. Ru 4:1. Is 55:1.
and flee. ver. 7. Je 1:14. 3:18. 31:8. Re +18:4.
land of the north. Je +1:14. Ezk +38:6.
spread. Dt 4:37. 28:64. Ps 68:14. Je 15:4. 31:10. Ezk 5:12. 11:16. 12:14, 15. 17:21. Am 9:9.

7 **Deliver**. Ac 2:40. Re +18:4.
that. Is 52:2. Mi 4:10.
daughter. Is +47:1.

8 **of hosts**. ver. 9, 11. Ps +24:10.
After. ver. 4, 5. Zc 1:15, 16. Is 11:10. 60:15. Jl 2:28. Mt 24:29, 30.
the glory. ver. 5. Zc +6:13. Ps +102:16. Is 11:10. 60:7-14. 61:1-3. Mt +24:30. Jn 17:4. 2 Th +1:7-10. 1 P +1:11.
sent. ver. 9, 11. Is 48:15, 16. Ml 3:1. Jn 14:23, 24, 26. 15:21-23. 17:18. 1 J 4:9, 10, 14.
the nations. 2 K 24:2. Is 52:10. Je 50:17, 18. 51:34, 35. Ezk 25:6, 7, 12, 15. 26:2. 35:5. Jl 3:2-8. Am 1:3-5, 9, 11, 13. Ob 10-16. Mi 4:11. 5:6. 7:10. Hab 2:8, 17. Zp 2:8.
which spoiled. Is 17:12-14. Ezk +38:12. 2 Th 1:6.
for. Ge 20:6. Ps 105:13-15. Ac 9:4. 2 Th 1:6.
toucheth. Ge +26:29.
the apple. Dt 32:10. Ps 17:8. Mt 25:40, 45.
his eye. 2 S +16:22.

9 **I will**. Is 10:32. 11:15. 13:2. 19:16.
and they. Is 14:2. 33:1, 23. Je 27:7. Ezk 39:10. Hab 2:8, 17. Zp 2:9.
and ye. ver. 8. Zc 4:9. 6:15. Je 28:7-9. Ezk 33:33. Jn +13:19. 16:4.

10 **Sing**. Ps +47:2. Is 12:5, 6. 24:14, 16. +35:10. 44:23. +51:11. Je 31:7, 12. Ho +2:15. Jl 2:23. Hab 3:3. Zp 3:14, 17.
and rejoice. Zc 9:9. Ps 47:1-9. 98:1-3. Is 12:6. 35:10. 40:9. 42:10. 51:11. 52:9, 10. 54:1. 61:10. 65:18, 19. 66:14. Je 30:19. 31:12. 33:11. Zp 3:14, 15. Ph 4:4.
daughter. Mt +21:5.
lo. Ps 40:7.
I come. Is +35:4.
I will dwell. Ex +29:45. Ezk 37:27. Zp 3:17. Mt 28:20. Jn 1:14. Re 2:1.

11 **many nations**. Zc 8:20-23. Ex 12:49. Nu

9:14. Ps 68:29-31. 72:8-11, 17. 102:21, 22. Is +11:10. 19:24, 25. 45:14. 52:10. 54:2, 3. Je 16:19. Lk 2:32. Ac 28:28. 1 P 2:9, 10. Re 11:15.

in that day. Zc 3:10. Is +2:11.

my people. Ex 12:49.

thou. ver. 9. Ezk 33:33. Jn 17:21, 23, 25.

12 **inherit**. Ex 19:5, 6. 34:9. Dt 9:29. 32:9. Ps +82:8. +94:14. 135:4. Is 19:25. Je 10:16. 51:19.

holy land. Zc 7:14. Da 11:41. Ho 9:3. Ml 3:12.

choose Jerusalem again. Zc 1:16, 17. Ps 101:8. Is +11:11. +24:23. +41:9. 52:9, 10. 62:6, 7. 66:13. Am +9:11. Ac 15:16.

13 **Be silent**. Hab +2:20. Ro 3:19. 9:20.

flesh. Lk +3:6.

for he. Ps 78:65. Is +26:20, 21. 42:13-15. 51:9. Zp 3:8.

his holy habitation. Heb. the habitation of his holiness. Dt 26:15. 2 Ch 30:27mg. Ps 11:4. 68:5. Is +57:15. 63:15. Je 25:30.

ZECHARIAH 3

1 **he**. Zc 1:9, 13, 19. 2:3.

Joshua. ver. 8. Zc 6:11. Ezr 5:2. Hg 1:1, 12. 2:4.

standing. Dt +10:8. 1 S 6:20.

the angel. Zc +12:8.

Satan. *that is*, an adversary. Nu 22:22, 23. 1 Ch 21:1. Jb 1:6-12. 2:1-8. Ps 109:6mg. Lk 22:31. Ep 6:11, 12. 1 P 5:8. Re 12:9, 10.

at his right hand. Jb 30:12. Ps 109:6.

resist him. Heb. be his adversary. Ge +3:15. Nu 22:32mg. 1 S 29:4. 2 S 19:22. 1 K 5:4. 11:14, 23, 25.

2 **the Lord said**. Ps 109:31. Lk 22:32. Ro 16:20. 1 J 3:8.

The Lord rebuke. Da 12:1. Mk +4:39. Re 12:9, 10.

chosen. Zc 1:17. 2:12. 2 Ch 6:6. Jn 13:18. Ro 8:33. Re 17:14.

a brand. Am 4:11. Ro 11:4, 5. Ju 23.

3 **was clothed**. 2 Ch 30:18-20. Ezr 9:15. Pr 30:12. Is 4:4. 64:6. Da 9:18. Mt 22:11-13. Re 3:17. 7:13, 14. 19:8.

4 **those**. ver. 1, 7. Is 6:2, 3. Lk +21:36. Re 5:11.

Take. Is 43:25. Ezk 36:25. Ga 3:27, 28. Ph 3:7-9. Re 7:14.

I have. 2 S 12:13. Ps 32:1, 2. 51:9. Is 6:5-7. Jn 1:29. Ro 6:23. He 8:12.

from thee. 2 S 12:13. 24:10. Jn 7:21.

and I will. Ex +28:2. Lk 15:22. 1 C 6:11. 2 C 5:21. Ph 3:9. Col 3:10, 11.

5 **Let them set**. Ex 29:5, 6.

fair. Zc 6:11. Ex 28:2-4. 29:6. Le 8:6-9. He 2:8, 9. 4:14-16. 5:1-6. Re 4:4, 10. 5:8-14.

mitre. or, turban. Ex 28:37.

6 **the angel of**. ver. 1. Ge 22:15, 16. 28:13-17.

48:15, 16. Ex 23:20, 21. Is 63:9. Ho 12:4. Ac 7:35-38.

protested. Ge 43:3. Dt 8:19. Je 11:7.

7 **of hosts**. Ps +24:10.

If. Je +7:5. Jn 15:7, 14.

wilt walk. Col +1:10. 1 Th 4:1. 1 J +2:3, 6.

if thou wilt keep. Ge 26:5. Le 8:35. 10:3. 1 K 2:3. 1 Ch 23:32. Ezk 44:8, 15, 16. 48:11. Ml 2:7. 1 T 6:13, 14. 2 T 4:1, 2.

charge. *or*, ordinance. Ps 109:8mg. Ml +3:14mg.

judge. Dt 17:8-13. 1 S 2:28-30. Je 15:19-21. Ml 2:5-7. Mt +19:28. Lk +22:30. 1 C +6:2, 3. Re 3:21.

I will. Zc 1:8-11. 4:14. 6:5. Ex 33:21. Jsh 20:4. Is 56:5. Lk 20:35, 36. Jn +14:2. He 12:22, 23. Re 5:9-14.

places. Heb. walks. Ep 1:3. Re 3:4, 5.

these that. Lk 22:19. Ps 103:21. Mt 18:10. Lk +21:36. 1 T 5:21.

8 **for**. Ps 71:7. Is 8:18. 20:3. 1 C 4:9-13.

wondered at. Heb. of wonder, *or* sign, as Ezk 12:11. 24:24. Is 8:18. 20:3. 1 C 4:9.

my. Is 42:1. 49:3, 5. 52:13. 53:11. Ezk 34:23, 24. 37:24. Mt 12:18. Ph 2:6-8.

the Branch. Is +11:1. Lk 1:78mg.

9 **the stone**. Zc 4:7. Is +8:14, 15. Da 2:34, 44. Mt 16:18. +21:42.

I have laid. Hg 2:23.

upon. or, fixed upon. Dt 11:12. 1 K 9:3. Ezr 5:5.

seven. Zc 4:10. Ge +21:28, 31. Re 5:6.

eyes. 2 Ch 16:9. Mk 6:20. Lk 20:20. Re 5:6.

I will engrave. Ex 28:11, 21, 36. Jn 6:27. 2 C 1:22. 3:3. 2 T 2:19.

remove. Zc 13:1. Is 53:4, etc. +60:21. Je +31:34. 50:20. Ezk 37:23. Da +9:24-27. Mi +7:18, 19. Jn 1:29. Ep 2:16, 17. Col 1:20, 21. 1 T 2:5, 6. He 7:27. 9:25, 26. 10:10-18. 1 J 2:2.

that land. Dt +32:43. Is 60:21. Je 3:18. +7:7. Am +9:15.

in one day. Zc 12:10, 11. Ge 27:45. 1 S 2:34. 1 K 20:29. 2 Ch 28:6. Is 9:14. 10:17. 47:9. 66:5-9. He 7:27. 9:12, 26, 28. 10:10, 12, 14.

10 **In that day**. Is +2:11.

shall. Zc 2:11. 1 K 4:25. Is 2:4. 36:16. Ho 2:18. Mi 4:4. Hg 2:9. Jn 1:45-48.

ZECHARIAH 4

1 **the angel**. Zc 1:9, 13, 19. 2:3. 3:6, 7.

waked. 1 K 19:5-7. Je 31:26. Da 8:18. 10:8-10. Lk 9:32. 22:45, 46.

2 **What**. Zc 5:2. Je 1:11-13.

a candlestick. Ex +25:31. Is 62:1, 2.

a bowl. Heb. her bowl. 1 K 7:50.

seven. Re +1:12.

seven pipes to the seven lamps. *or*, seven several pipes to the lamps, etc. ver. 12. Re 11:3-12.

3 **olive trees**. ver. 11, 12, 14. Ex 27:20, 21. Jg
9:9. Ro 11:17, 24. Re 11:4.
4 **What**. ver. 12-14. Zc 1:9, 19. 5:6. 6:4. Da
7:16-19. 12:8. Mt 13:36. Re 7:13, 14.
5 **Knowest**. ver. 13. Mk 4:13.
No. Ge 41:16. Ps 139:6. Da 2:30. 1 C 2:12-15.
6 **Not**. Zc 9:13-15. Nu 27:16. 2 Ch 14:11. Is 11:2-
4. 30:1. 32:15. 63:10-14. Ezk 37:11-14. Ho 1:7.
Hg 2:2-5. 1 C 2:4, 5. 2 C 10:4, 5. 1 P 1:12.
Not by. 1 S 17:39. Is 31:1. Ho 1:7. 2 C 10:4.
might. *or*, army. Ge 34:29. 47:6. Ex 14:4, 9.
Dt 33:11. Ru 3:11. 1 S 2:4. 17:20. 2 Ch 32:7,
8. Jb 20:21. Ps 20:6-8. 33:16, 20, 21. 44:3-7.
84:7. Pr 12:4. Ec 10:10.
power. Dt 8:18. Jg 16:5. Is 37:3. 44:12.
but by. Mi 3:8. Lk 4:14. Ac +1:8. 4:33. 1 C
2:4. Ep 3:16. 1 Th 1:5. 2 T +1:7.
spirit. Heb. *ruach*, Is +48:16. Ge 6:3. Ps 51:11,
12.
7 **O great**. Zc 14:4, 5. Ps 114:4, 6. Is 40:3, 4.
41:15. 64:1-3. Je 51:25. Da 2:34, 35. Mi 1:4.
4:1. Na 1:5, 6. Hab 3:6. Hg 2:6-9, 21-23. Mt
17:20. 21:21. Mk 11:23. Lk 3:5. Re 16:20.
become a plain. Is 40:4. 42:16.
headstone. ver. 9. Ps 24:7-10. 118:22. Is
28:16. Mt 21:42. Mk 12:10. Lk 20:17. Jn
19:30. 20:17. Ac 4:11. Ep 2:20. 4:8. 1 P 2:7.
shoutings. Ezr 3:11-13. 6:15-17. Jb 38:6, 7.
Re 5:9-13. 19:1-6.
Grace. Je 33:11. Ro 11:6. Ep 1:6, 7. 2:4-8.
9 **have**. Ezr 3:8-13. 5:2, 16.
his hands. Zc 6:12, 13. Ezr 6:14, 15. Mt
16:18. He 12:2.
and. Zc 2:8, 9, 11. 6:15. Is 48:16. Je 28:7-9.
Jn 3:17. 5:36, 37. 8:16-18. 17:21.
10 **despised**. Ezr 3:12, 13. Ne 4:2-4. Jb 8:7. Pr
+4:18. Da 2:34, 35. Ho +6:3. Hg 2:3. Mt
13:31-33. 1 C 1:28, 29.
for they, etc. *or*, since the seven eyes of the
Lord shall rejoice. Is 66:11, 14. Lk 15:5-10, 32.
and shall. Am 7:7, 8.
plummet. Heb. stone of tin. Ex +7:19.
those. Zc 3:9. Re 8:2.
they are. Zc 1:10, 11. Ps +11:4. Ezk 1:15-20.
Re 5:6.
11 **What**. ver. 3. Ne +8:15. Re 11:4.
12 **What be**. Mt 20:23. Re 11:4.
through. Heb. by the hand of. Hg +1:1mg.
empty, etc. *or*, empty out of themselves *oil
into* the gold.
the golden. Heb. the gold.
13 **Knowest**. ver. 5. He 5:11, 12.
14 **These**. Zc 6:13. Ex 29:7. 40:15. Le 8:12. 1 S
10:1. 16:1, 12, 13. Ps 2:6mg. 89:20. 110:4. Is
61:1-3. Da +9:24-26. Hg 1:1, 12. He +1:8, 9.
7:1, 2. Re 11:3, 4.
anointed ones. Heb. sons of oil. Is 5:1mg.
21:10mg.
that. Zc 3:1-7. 6:5. Dt +10:8. Je 49:19. Re
11:3-13.

the Lord. Zc 6:5. 14:9. Jsh 3:11, 13. Ps 8:1, 6,
9. 97:5. Is 54:5. Mi 4:13.

ZECHARIAH 5

1 **lifted**. Ge +22:13.
roll. ver. 2. Is 8:1. Je 36:1-6, 20-24, 27-32.
Ezk 2:9, 10. Re 5:1, etc. 10:2, 8-11.
2 **What**. Zc 4:2. Je 1:11-14. Am 7:8.
flying. Zp 1:14. 2 P 2:3.
the length. Ge 6:11-13. Re 18:5.
3 **the curse**. Le 26:14. Nu 22:6. Dt 11:28, 29.
29:19-28. Pr 26:2. Mt +25:41. Re +21:8. 22:3,
15.
the face. Ml 4:6. Lk 21:35.
every one, etc. *or*, every one of this *people*
that stealeth, holdeth *himself* guiltless, as it
doth.
stealeth. Ex +20:15. Dt +19:5. Pr 29:24. 30:9.
Je 7:9. Ho 4:2. Ml 3:8-10. 1 C +6:7-10. Ep
4:28. Ja +5:4.
sweareth. ver. 4. Zc 8:17. Le 19:12. Ec 9:2. Is
48:1. Je 5:2. 23:10. Ezk 17:13-16. Ml +3:5. Mt
5:33-37. 23:16-22. 1 T 1:9, 10. Ja 5:12.
shall be cut off. or, hath been let off, or
declared innocent, or goeth unpunished. Nu
5:31. Ps 19:12, 13. Je 2:35. 49:12.
4 **the house**. Pr +3:33.
the thief. Ex 21:16. 22:1-4, 10, 12. Le 6:2-5.
Dt 24:7. Pr 6:30, 31. Ezk 18:10, 13. Mt 27:38,
44. 1 C +6:10. Ep 4:28. T 2:10. 1 P 4:15.
him that. ver. 3. Zc 8:17. Le 19:12. Ml +3:5.
and it shall remain. Ex +20:5. Le 14:34-45.
Dt 7:26. Jb 18:15. 20:26. Pr +3:33. Hab 2:9-
11. Ja 5:2, 3.
shall consume it. Le 14:45.
5 **the angel**. Zc 1:9, 14, 19. 2:3. 4:5.
Lift. ver. 1.
6 **This is an ephah**. Ezk 45:10, 11. Am 8:5.
7 **talent**. *or*, weighty piece. Is 13:1. 15:1. 22:11.
is a woman. Je 3:1, 2. Ezk ch. 16, 23. Ho ch.
1-3. Mt 13:33. Re 2:20. 17:1, 5, etc., 18.
8 **This is wickedness**. Ge 15:16. Mt 12:43-45.
23:32. 1 Th 2:16. 2 Th 2:7-12.
the weight. ver. 7. Ps 38:4. Pr 5:22. La 1:14.
Am 9:1-4. Re 17:15, 16. 18:21.
9 **lifted**. ver. 1.
for. Dt 28:49. Da +9:26, 27. Ho 8:1. Mt 24:28.
wings of a stork. Le 11:19. Dt 14:18.
10 **Whither**. Je 7:11. Ezk 39:12. Jn 2:16.
11 **To**. Dt 28:59. Je 29:28. Ho 3:4. Lk 21:24.
the land of Shinar. Ge +10:10. 1 T 4:1-5. 1 J
4:1-6. Re 3:14-22. 9:1-21. 16:13-16, 19. 18:1-
5, 21-24.

ZECHARIAH 6

1 **I turned**. Zc 5:1.
lifted. Ge +22:13.
four. Zc 1:18, 19. Da 2:38-40. 7:3-7. 8:22.

and the. 1 S 2:8. Jb 34:29. Ps 33:11. 36:6. Pr +21:30. Is 14:26, 27. 43:13. 46:10, 11. Da 4:15, 35. Ac 4:28. Ep +1:11. 3:11.
brass. Dt 8:9.

2   **red**. Zc 1:8. Re 6:2-5. 12:3. 17:3.
black. ver. 6. Re 6:5, 6.

3   **white**. Re 6:2. 19:11. 20:11.
grisled. ver. 6, 7. Zc 1:8. Ge 31:10, 12. Da 2:33, 40, 41. Re 6:8.
bay. *or,* strong.

4   **unto**. Zc 1:9, 19-21. 5:5, 6, 10. He 1:14.

5   **These**. Zc 1:10, 11. 2 K 6:15-17. Ps 68:17. 104:3, 4. Ezk 1:5, etc. 10:9-19. 11:22. Da 7:10. He 1:7, 14. Re 7:1-3. 9:14, 15. 14:6, etc.
spirits. *or,* winds. 1 K 19:11. Ps 148:8. Da 7:2. 10:13, 20, 21.
go. Zc 4:10. 1 K 22:19-22. 2 Ch 18:18; 19. Jb 1:6. 2:1, 2. Da 7:10. Mt 18:10. Lk 1:19. 1 P 5:8. Re 9:2, 3, 9.
the Lord. Zc 4:14. Is 54:5.

6   **the north**. Je 1:14, 15. 4:6. 6:1. 25:9. 46:10. 51:48. Ezk 1:4.
go forth after. Da 7:5, 6. 11:3, 4.
toward. Da 11:5, 6, 9, 40.

7   **the bay**. Zc 1:10. Ge 13:17. 2 Ch 16:9. Jb 1:6, 7. 2:1, 2. Da 7:7, 19, 24.

8   **cried he upon**. or, called to, or appealed to. Jg 4:10, 13. Jon 3:7.
quieted. Zc 1:15. Jg 8:3. 15:7. Jb 15:13. 34:29. Ec 10:4. Is 1:24. 18:3, 4. 32:17. 42:13-15. 48:14. 51:22, 23. Je 51:48, 49. Ezk 5:13. 16:42, 63. Re 18:21, 22.
spirit. Heb. *ruach,* Is +48:16.

9   **the word**. Zc 1:1. 7:1. 8:1.

10   **captivity**. 2 K 24:15, 16. Ezr 1:11. 2:1. Ne 7:6. Est 2:6. Je 28:6. Ezk 1:1.
which. Ezr 7:14-16. 8:26-30. Is 66:20. Ac 24:17. Ro 15:25, 26.
the son. ver. 14.

11   **make**. Zc 3:5. Ex 28:36-38. 29:6. 39:30. Le 8:9. Ps 21:3. SS 3:11. He 2:9. Re 19:12.
Joshua. Zc 3:1. Hg 1:1, 14. 2:4.

12   **Behold**. Zc 13:7. Is 32:1, 2. Mi 5:5. Mk 15:39. Jn 19:5. Ac 13:38. 17:31. He 7:4, 24. 8:3. 10:12.
whose. Is +11:1. Lk 1:31-35, 78mg. Jn 1:45. Ac 13:22, 23. Re 22:16.
grow up out of his place. *or,* branch up from under him.
he shall build. Zc 1:16. 4:6-9. 8:9. Ps 127:1. Is 2:2. 28:16. Mt 16:18. 26:61. Mk 14:58. 15:29. Jn +2:19-21. 1 C 3:9-11, 16, 17. 6:19. 2 C 6:16. Ep 2:20-22. He 3:3, 4. 1 P 2:4, 5.
the temple. Zc 1:16. Is 56:7. 60:13. Ezk +37:26. 40:2. Jl 2:1. Hg 2:7.

13   **and**. Ge +8:22.
bear the glory. Zc +2:5, 8. Ps 21:5. 45:3, 4. 72:17-19. Is +9:6. 11:10. 22:24. 49:5, 6. Je +23:6. Da +7:13, 14. Hg 2:7-9. Mt 16:27. 24:30. 25:31. Lk 24:26. Jn 13:31, 32. 17:1-5.

Ep 1:20-23. Ph 2:5-11. He 1:3. 2:7-9. 3:3. 1 P 1:11. 3:22. Re 3:21. 5:9-13. 19:11-16.
sit. He +1:3.
a priest. ver. 11. Ge 14:18. Ps 110:4. He 3:1. 4:14-16. 6:20. 7:1, 24, 25, etc. 10:12, 13.
counsel of peace. Zc 4:14. Is 54:10. Da +9:25-27. Mi +5:4, 5. Ro +5:1. Col 2:18-20. He 7:1-3.

14   **Helem**. i.e. *hammer; strength, smiter,* **S#2494h**. ver. 10. See **S#1987h**, 1 Ch 7:35, Helem. 27:15, Heldai.
Hen. i.e. *gracious gift,* **S#2581h**.
a memorial. Ex +12:14. 1 S 2:30.

15   **And they**. Is 2:2, 3. 60:5-7. Mi 4:1, 2.
far off. Ac +2:39.
come and build. Is 56:6-8. 57:19. 60:10. 1 C 3:10-15. Ep 2:13-22. 1 P 2:4, 5.
and ye. ver. 12. Zc 2:8-11. 4:8, 9. Jn 17:20, 21.
And this. Zc 3:7. Is 3:10. 58:10-14. Ro 16:26. 2 P 1:5-10.
if. Ge +4:7. Je +7:5. 26:3.
diligently obey. Is +58:10-14. Je +7:23. Mt 3:1, 2. 4:17. 7:21-23. Lk +6:46. +11:28. Ac 2:38. +3:19. He +11:6. 1 J +2:3. 3:21, 24. Re 22:14.

ZECHARIAH 7

1   **the fourth**. Zc 1:1. Ezr 6:14, 15. Hg 2:10, 20.
Chisleu. i.e. *confidence,* **S#3691h**. Answering to part of *November* and part of *December*. Ne 1:1.

2   **they**. Zc 6:10. Ezr 6:10. 7:15-23. 8:28, etc. Is 60:7.
Sherezer. i.e. *prince of fire, he beheld treasure; Asur protect the king,* **S#8272h**. 2 K 19:37. Is 37:38. Zc 7:2.
Regemmelech. i.e. *royal friend; stoning of the king,* **S#7278h**.
pray before the Lord. Heb. intreat the face of the Lord. Zc 8:21. Ex +32:11mg. 1 K 8:28-30.

3   **speak**. Dt 17:9-11. 33:10. Ezk 44:23, 24. Ho 4:6. Hg 2:11. Ml 2:7.
Should. ver. 5. Ne 8:9-11. 9:1-3. Ec 3:4. Is 22:12, 13. Jl 2:17. Mt 9:15. Ja 4:8-10.
fifth. Zc 8:19. 2 K 25:8, 9. Je 52:12-14.
should I. Is 58:3. Ml 3:14.
separating. Zc 12:12-14. 1 C 7:5.

5   **When**. Is 58:5.
seventh. Zc 8:19. 2 K 25:23, 25. Je 40:8. 41:1-4, 15-18.
seventy. ver. +3. Zc 1:12. Je 25:11.
did. ver. 6. Is 1:11, 12. 58:4-6. Ho 7:14. Mt 5:16-18. 6:2, 5, 16. 23:5. Ro 14:6-9, 17, 18. 1 C 10:31. 2 C 5:15. Col 3:23.

6   **did not ye eat for**. *or, be* not ye they that did eat for, etc. Dt 12:7. 14:26. 1 S +16:7. 1 Ch 29:22. Je +17:9, 10. Ho 8:13. 9:4. 1 C 10:31. 11:20, 21, 26-29. Col 3:17.

7 Should ye not hear the words. *or, Are* not *these* the words, etc. Is +55:3, 6, 7.
cried. Zc 1:3-6. Is 1:16-20. Je 7:5, 23. 36:2, 3. Ezk 18:30-32. Da 9:6-14. Ho 14:1-3. Am 5:14, 15. Mi +6:6-8. Zp 2:1-3.
former. Heb. the hand of the former. ver. +12mg.
the south. Heb. *Negeb*. Dt 34:3. Is +30:6. Je 17:26. 32:44. 33:13.
the plain. Je 17:26. Ob 19.

9 saying. ver. +7. Zc 8:16, 17. Le +19:15, 35-37. Dt 10:18, 19. +15:7-14. 16:18-20. Pr 21:3. Is 58:6-10. Je 7:5-7, 23. Ho 10:12, 13. Am 5:24. Mi +6:8. Mt 23:23. Lk 11:42. Ja 2:13-17.
Execute true judgment. Heb. Judge judgment of truth. Ge +1:29. Je +21:12mg. Jn +7:24, 51.
show mercy. Mi +6:8. Mt 23:23. Ja 1:27.

10 oppress not. Ex 22:21-24. 23:9. Dt +24:14-18. Ps 72:4. Pr 22:22, 23. Is 1:16, 17, 23. Je 22:15-17. Ezk 22:7, 12, 29. Am 4:1. 5:11, 12. Mi 2:1-3. 3:1-4. Zp 3:1-3. Ml +3:5. Mt 23:14. 1 C +6:10. Ja +5:4.
the widow. Is +1:17.
fatherless. Ex +22:22.
stranger. Ezk +47:22, 23.
poor. Dt +24:14. Ps +12:5. Ezk +16:49.
imagine evil. Zc 8:17. Ps 21:11. 36:4. 140:2. Pr 3:29. 6:18. 23:7. Je 11:19, 20. 18:18. Mi 2:1. Mk +7:21-23. Ja 1:14, 15. 1 J 3:15.

11 refused to hearken. Zc 1:4. Ex 10:3. 1 S +25:17. Pr 1:5, 24-32. 2:2. Is 1:19, 20. Je +7:26. +25:4. Ezk 3:7. Ho 4:16. Zp 3:2.
pulled away the shoulder. Heb. gave a backsliding shoulder. Dt 10:16. Ne 9:29. Je 8:5. Ho 4:16. +9:15. He +10:38, 39.
stopped. Heb. made heavy. Ps 58:4, 5. Is 6:10. Ac 7:57.

12 their hearts. Ne 9:29. Jb 9:4. Is 48:4. Je 5:3. 7:23-26. Ezk 2:4. 3:7-9. 11:19. 36:26.
lest. Ne 9:29, 30. Ps 50:17. Is 6:10. Mt 13:15. Mk 4:12. Lk 8:12. Jn 3:19, 20. Ac 28:27. 2 Th 2:10-12.
Lord of hosts. Je +6:6.
sent. Ne 9:30. Ac 7:51, 52. 1 P 1:11, 12. 2 P 1:21.
spirit. Heb. *ruach*, Is +48:16.
by the former. Heb. by the hand of the former. ver. 7mg. Ezr +9:11. Hg +1:1mg.
therefore. 2 Ch 36:16. Je 26:19. Da +9:11, 12. 1 Th 2:15, 16.

13 as he cried. Ps 81:8-12. Is 50:2. Je 6:16, 17. Lk 19:42-44.
so. Ezk 20:3. Mt 25:11, 12.
I would not hear. Ps +66:18.

14 scattered. Zc 2:6. Je +9:16.
whirlwind. Je +23:19.
whom. Dt 28:33, 49. Je 5:15.
the land. Le 26:22. 2 Ch 36:21. Je 52:30. Da 9:16-18. Zp 3:6.

the pleasant land. Heb. the land of desire. Zc 2:12. Ps 48:2. Je +3:19mg. Ho 9:3. Ml 3:12.

ZECHARIAH 8

2 I was jealous. Ex +20:5. Is 59:17. 63:4-6, 15. La 4:11, 12.

3 I am. Zc 1:16. Je 30:10, 11.
dwell. Ex +29:45. La 4:22. Ezk 48:35. Jl 2:17. Jn 1:14. Col 2:9.
a city. Zc 14:20, 21. Is 1:21, 26. 60:14. Je 31:23. 33:16. Ezk 48:35.
the mountain. Is +2:2, 3.
the holy. Is +11:9. Re 21:10, 27.

4 There. 1 S 2:31. Jb 5:26. 42:17. Is 65:20-22. La 2:20, 21, etc. 5:11-15. He 12:22.
streets. broad or open places. Am +5:16.
very age. Heb. multitude of days. Jb 32:7. Ec 11:1.

5 playing. Zc 2:4. Ps 128:3, 4. 144:12-15. Je 30:19, 20. 31:27. 33:11. La 2:11, 19. Mt 11:16, 17.

6 marvellous. *or*, hard, *or* difficult. 2 S 13:2.
should. Ge +18:14. 2 K 7:2. Ps 90:4. Is 55:8-11. Ro 4:20, 21. 6:19-21.

7 I will save. Is 49:12. 59:19. 66:19, 20. Je +23:3. Ml 1:11. Ro 11:25-27.
east country. Ps 50:1. 113:3. Is 43:5. 59:19. Ml 1:11.
west country. Heb. country of the going down of the sun. Dt 11:30. Ps 50:1. 113:3. Ml 1:11.

8 and they shall dwell. Je 3:17, 18. +23:3, 8. 32:41. Jl 3:20.
they shall be my. Ge +17:7. Je 4:2. Ho 2:19-23.
in truth. Je 4:2.

9 Let. ver. 13, 18. Jsh +1:6.
the prophets. Ezr 5:1, 2. Hg 1:1, 12. 2:21.
foundation. Hg 2:18.

10 before. Hg 1:6-11. 2:16-18.
there was no hire for man. *or*, the hire of man became nothing, etc.
neither. Jg 5:6, 7, 11. 2 Ch 15:5-7. Je 16:16.
for. Is 19:2. Am +3:6. 9:4. Mt 10:34-36.

11 But now. ver. 8, 9. Ps 103:9. Is 11:13. 12:1. Hg 2:19. Ml 3:9-11.
former days. 1 K 4:20.

12 the seed. Ge 26:12. Le 26:4, 5. Dt 28:3-12. Ps 67:6, 7. Pr 3:9, 10. Is 30:23. Ezk 34:26, 27. 36:30. Ho 2:21-23. Jl 2:22. Am 9:13-15. Hg 2:19.
prosperous. Heb. of peace. Ps 72:3. Ja 3:18.
ground shall give. Le 26:4, 20. Dt 11:17. Ps 78:46. 85:12.
the heavens. Ge +27:28. Pr 19:12. Hg 1:10.
the remnant. ver. 6. Mi +4:7. 1 C 3:21.
to possess. Is 61:7. Ezk 36:12. Ob 17-20. Mt 6:33.

13 a curse. Dt +28:37. 29:23-28. Je +26:6.

O house. Zc 1:19. 9:13. 10:6. 2 K 17:18-20. Is 9:20, 21. Je 32:30-32. 33:24. Ezk 37:11, 16-19.
ye shall. ver. 20-23. Zc 10:6-9. Ge 12:2, 3. 26:4. Ru 4:11, 12. Ps 72:17. Is 19:24, 25. Mi 5:7. Zp 3:20. Hg 2:19. Ga 3:14, 28, 29.
fear not. ver. 9, 15. Ge +15:1. 1 C 16:13.
be strong. ver. +9.

14 **As.** Zc 1:6. Ps 33:11. Is 14:24. Je 31:28.
I repented not. 2 Ch 36:16. Je 4:28. 15:1-6. 20:16. Ezk 24:14. Ja 1:17.

15 **have.** Nu 23:19. Je 29:11-14. 32:42. Ezk 39:25-29. Mi 4:10-13. 7:18-20.
fear. ver. +13.

16 **are.** Dt 10:12, 13. 11:7, 8. Is 1:16, 17. Mi +6:8. Lk 3:8-14. Ep 4:17. 1 P 1:13-16.
Speak. ver. 19. Zc 7:9. Mi 6:12. Ep +4:25. 1 Th 4:6.
execute the judgment of truth and peace. Heb. judge truth and the judgment of peace. Zc 7:9mg. Is +9:7. 11:3-9. 32:17. Am 5:15, 24. Mt +5:9. Jn +7:24.
gates. Ge +14:7.

17 **let.** Zc 7:10. Pr 3:29. 6:14. Je 4:14. Mi 2:1-3. Mt 5:28. 12:35. 15:19. Ep 4:25.
evil. Is +45:7.
love no false oath. Zc +5:3, 4. Le 6:3. 19:12. Je 4:2. Ml +3:5.
things. Ps 5:5, 6. 10:3. Pr 6:16-19. 8:13. Je 44:4. Hab 1:13.

19 **the fourth.** 2 K 25:3, 4. Je 39:2. 52:6, 7.
the fifth. Zc 7:3. Je 52:12-15.
the seventh. Zc 7:5. Le 16:29. 23:27, 29, 32. 2 K 25:25. Ps 35:13. 69:10. Je 41:1-3.
the tenth. Le 16:29. 23:27, 29, 32. Je 52:4. Ezk 24:1, 2.
joy. Est 8:17. 9:22. Ps 30:11. Is 12:1. 35:10. 51:11. Je 31:12, 13.
feasts. Heb. solemn, or, set times. Ge +17:21. Le 23:2. 2 K 4:16mg.
therefore. ver. 16. Lk 1:74, 75. T 2:11, 12. Re 22:15.

20 **there.** Zc 2:11. 14:16, 17. 1 K 8:41, 43. 2 Ch 6:32, 33. Ps 67:1-4. 72:17. 89:9. ch. 117. 138:4, 5. Is +11:10. Je 16:19. Ho 1:10. 2:23. Am 9:12. Ac 8:27. 15:14-18. Re 11:15.

21 **Let.** Ps ch. 122.
speedily. or, continually. Heb. going. Ho 6:3. Is 2:3. Jon 1:11mg. Mi 4:2.
pray before the Lord. Heb. intreat the face of the Lord. Zc 7:2mg.
I will. Ps 103:22. 146:1, 2.

22 **many people.** Is 25:7. 55:5. 56:7. 60:3, etc. 66:23. Je 4:2. Mi 4:3. Hg 2:7. Ga 3:8. Re 15:4. 21:24.
to pray. Mk 11:17.

23 **ten men.** Ge 31:7, 41. Nu 14:22. Jb 19:3. Ec 11:2. Mi +5:5. Mt 18:21, 22.
out. Is 66:18. Ac 2:9-11. Re 7:9, 10. 14:6, 7.
take. 1 S 15:27, 28. Is 3:6. 4:1. Lk 8:44. Ac 19:12.

We will. Nu 10:29-32. Ru 1:16, 17. 2 S 15:19-22. 2 K 2:6. 1 Ch 12:18. Is 55:5. 60:3. Ac +13:47, 48.
we have. Ge 30:27. Nu 14:14-16. Dt 4:6, 7. Jsh 2:9-13. 1 K 8:42, 43. 1 C 14:25.

ZECHARIAH 9

1 Cir. A.M. 3494. B.C. 510.
burden. Is 13:1. Je 23:33-38. Ml 1:1.
Hadrach. i.e. spherical, round, **S#2317h.**
Damascus. Ge +14:15.
the rest. Zc 5:4. Is 9:8, etc.
when. Zc 8:20-23. 2 Ch 20:12. Ps 25:15. 123:1, 2. 145:15. Is 17:7, 8. 45:20-22. 52:10. Je 16:19. 32:19, 20. Mt +24:30. Re +1:7.

2 **Hamath.** Nu +13:21.
Tyrus. Je +25:22.
Zidon. Ge +49:13. Ob 20.
it be very wise. Ezk 28:3-5, 12.

3 **build.** Jsh 19:29. 2 S 24:7.
heaped. 1 K 10:27. Jb 22:24. 27:16. Is 23:8. Ezk 27:33. 28:4, 5.
as the dust. Ge +13:16.
fine gold. Pr 3:14.

4 **the Lord.** Pr 10:2. 11:4. Is 23:1-7. Ezk 28:16. Jl 3:8.
he will. Ezk 26:17. 27:26-36. 28:2, 8.
shall. Ezk 28:18. Am 1:10.

5 **Ashkelon.** Jg +14:19. Is 14:29-31. Ezk 25:15-17.
Gaza. Ge +10:19.
and be. Je 51:8, 9. Ezk 26:15-21. Re 18:9-11, 15-17.
for. Is 20:5, 6. Ro 5:5. Ph 1:20.

6 **a bastard.** Dt 23:2. Ec 2:18-21. 6:2. Is 2:12-17. 23:9. 28:1. Da 4:37. Am 1:8. Zp 2:10. He 12:8. 1 P 5:5.
Ashdod. Jsh +11:22.
Philistines. Je +47:4.

7 **I will.** 1 S 17:34-36. Ps 3:7. 58:6. Am 3:12.
blood. Heb. bloods. 2 K +9:26mg.
out of his mouth. Ps 16:4. Ezk 33:25.
abominations. 2 K 23:24. 1 Ch 15:8mg. Is 66:3. Je 4:1. 7:30. Da +9:27. 11:31. 12:11. Ho 9:10.
from between his teeth. Ps 58:6. Am 3:12.
he that remaineth. Zc 8:23. Jg 1:21. Is 11:12-14. 19:23-25. Je 48:47. 49:6, 39. Ezk 12:57-61. 16:53, 55.
a governor. Zc 12:5, 6. Is 49:22, 23. 60:14-16. Je 13:21. Mi +5:2. Ga 3:28.
a Jebusite. Ge +10:16. 1 Ch 22:1. Is 11:14.

8 **I will.** Zc 2:5. 12:8. Ge 32:1, 2. Ps 34:7. 46:1-5. 125:1, 2. Is 4:5. 26:1. 31:5. 33:20-22. 52:12. Jl +3:16, 17. Re 20:9.
mine house. Je 12:7. Ho 8:1. 9:15.
because of him that passeth by. 2 K 23:29. 24:1. Je 46:2, 13. Da 11:6, 7, 10-16, 27-29, 40-45.

no oppressor. Zc 14:11. Ps 72:4. Is 52:1. 54:14. 60:18. Je 31:12. Ezk 28:24, 25. 39:29. Am 9:15. Re 20:1-3.

for now. Zc 4:10. Ex 3:7, 9. 2 S 16:12. 2 Ch 16:9. Ac 7:34.

9 Rejoice. Zc 2:10. Ps 97:6-8. Is 12:6. 40:9. 52:9, 10. 62:11. Zp 3:14, 15.

daughter. Mt +21:5.

behold. Ps 45:1. Is 32:1, 2. Je 30:9. Mk 11:9, 10. Jn +1:49.

thy King. Mt 21:1-5.

cometh unto. Mi +5:2. Mt *21:5*. Jn *12:15*. 1 Th 5:2, 3. 2 Th 2:8.

he is just. 2 S 23:3. Ps +45:6, 7. 85:9-12. Is 45:21. Je 23:5. Mt 1:21. Ac +3:14. Ro 3:24-26. 1 J 2:1, 29.

having salvation. *or*, saving himself. i.e. showing himself a Savior. Ps 33:16. Is 63:5.

lowly. Ps 22:24. Mt +11:29. Mk 11:7. Lk 19:30-35. Jn 12:14-16.

riding upon. Jg 5:10. 10:4. 12:14. 2 S 13:29. 16:2. 17:23. 18:9. 19:26. 1 K 1:33, 38, 44. 10:25-29. 13:13, 23, 27. Ec 10:7. Je 17:25. 22:19. Jn 12:12-16.

the foal. Mt 21:1, 2. Note the unannounced time gap between ver. 9 and 10 (Is +61:2).

10 I will. Ho 1:7. +2:18. Mi 5:10, 11. Hg 2:22. 2 C 10:4, 5.

cut off. Zc 14:12-15. Is 63:1-6. Jl 2:2-11, 20. 3:2, 9-16. Re 19:11-21.

the battle. Zc 10:4, 5.

he shall speak peace. Ps 46:9. 47:3. 72:3, 7, 17. 85:8. Is +9:6, 7. 11:10. 49:6. 57:18, 19. Mi 4:2-4. +5:5. Ac 10:36. Ro 15:9-13. 2 C 5:18, 20. Ep 2:13-17. Col 1:20, 21.

unto the heathen. Zc 14:16-21. Is 2:2-4. 11:4-12. 35:1-8. 65:20-25. Lk 1:32, 33. Re 20:1-10.

his dominion. Ps 2:8-12. *72:8-11*. 98:1-3. Is +9:6, 7. 60:12. Mi 5:4. Re 11:15.

from the river. Ge 15:18. Ex 23:31. Dt 11:24. 1 K 4:21. Is +27:12.

11 As for thee. Dt 5:31. 2 S 13:13. 2 Ch 7:17. Da 2:29.

by the blood of thy covenant. *or*, whose covenant *is* by blood. Ex 24:5-8. Mt 26:28. Mk 14:24. Lk 22:20. 1 C 11:25. He 9:10-26. 10:29. 13:20.

I have. Ps +147:6. Is 51:14. 53:12. Ac 26:17, 18. Col 1:13, 14.

out of. Ge 37:24. Jb 33:24. Ps 30:3. 40:2. Is 38:17. 51:14. Je 38:6. Lk 16:24. Re 20:3.

pit. Heb. *bor*, Ge +37:20.

12 Turn you. Is +26:20, 21. 52:2. Je 31:6. 50:4, 5, 28. 51:10. Jl 3:16. Mi 4:8. Na 1:7. He 6:18.

strong hold. Heb. *bizzaron*, only here. A safe because inaccessible place. 2 K 14:7. Je 49:16. Ezk 35:9. Ob +3.

prisoners of hope. Ps 119:49. Is 42:7. 49:9. 61:1.

even. Is 38:18. 49:9. Je 31:17. La 3:21, 22. Ezk 37:11. Ho +2:15.

I will render double. Ge +43:12. Pr 1:23.

13 When. Zc 12:8.

bent Judah. Zc 1:21. 10:3-7. 12:2-8. Mi +5:4-9. Re 17:14.

and raised up. Ps +149:2-9. La 4:2. Am 2:11. Ob +21.

against thy. Da +8:21-25. +11:32-24. Jl 3:6-8. Mi 4:2, 3. Mk 16:15-20. Ro 15:16-20. 1 C 1:21-28. 2 C 10:3-5. 2 T 4:7.

O Greece. i.e. *hot and active*, **S#3120h**. Ge +10:2 (Javan).

made thee. Zc 12:8. Ps 18:32-35. 45:3. 144:1. 149:6. Is 41:15, 16. 49:2. Ep 6:17. He +4:12. Re 1:16. 2:12. 19:15, 21.

14 seen over them. Zc 2:5. 12:8. 14:1-5. Ex 14:24, 25. Jsh 10:11-14, 42. Is 31:5. 63:1-6. Jl 2:11. Mt 28:20. Ac 4:10, 11. Ro 15:19. 2 Th 1:7-10. He 2:4. Ju 14, 15. Re 11:15. 19:11-21.

his arrow. Dt +32:23. Is 30:30. Re 6:2.

as the lightning. Mt +24:27.

blow the trumpet. Jsh 6:4, 5. Is 27:13. Ho +8:1. Mt +24:31. 2 C 10:4, 5. 1 Th 4:16. Re 10:7. 11:15.

whirlwinds. Is +66:15. Je +23:19.

15 defend them. Zc 12:8. Is 31:5. 37:35.

they shall devour. Zc 10:5. 12:6. 14:14. Mi 5:8. Re 19:13-21.

subdue. 1 S 17:45-51. 1 C 1:18, 25.

with sling stones. *or*, with the stones of the sling. Jb 41:28, 29. 1 S 17:49. +25:29.

shall drink. ver. 17. Zc 10:7. Ps 78:65. SS 1:4. 5:1. 7:9. Is 55:1. Ac 2:13-18. Ep +5:18.

wine. Heb. *yayin*, Hab 2:5.

filled like bowls. *or*, fill both the bowls, etc. 1 K +7:40.

the corners. Ex 27:2. Le 1:5, 11. 4:7, 18, 25.

the altar. Dt 12:27. Am +9:1.

16 in that day. Is +2:11.

as the flock. Ps 100:3. Is 40:10, 11. Je 23:3, 4. Ezk 34:22-26, 31. Mi 5:4, 5. 7:14. Lk 12:32. Jn 10:11, 27-30. 1 P 5:2-4.

as the stones. Is 62:3. Hg 2:23. Ml 3:17.

lifted. Zc 8:23. Is 10:18. 11:10-12. 60:3, 14. Zp 3:20.

his land. Dt +32:43.

17 how great is his goodness. Ps 23:6. 31:19. 33:5. 36:7-9. 86:5, 15. 145:7, 8. Is 63:7, 15. Jn 3:16. Ro 5:8, 20, 21. Ep 1:7, 8. 2:4, 5. 3:18, 19. T 3:4-7. 1 J 4:8-11.

how great is his beauty. Ex 15:11. Ps 45:2. 50:2. 90:17. SS 2:3, 4. 5:10-16. Is 33:17. Jn 1:14. 2 C 4:4-6. Re 5:12-14.

corn. Is 62:8, 9. 65:13, 14. Ezk 36:29. Ho 2:21, 22. Jl 2:26. 3:18. Am 8:11-14. 9:13, 14. Ep 5:18, 19.

cheerful. *or*, grow, *or* speak. SS 7:9.

new wine. Heb. *tirosh*, Ge +27:28.

maids. Ge +24:16.

ZECHARIAH 10

1 Ask ye. Ezk 36:37. Mt 7:7, 8. Jn 16:23, 24. Ja 5:16-18.

rain in. Dt 11:13. 28:23, 24. 1 K 17:1. 18:41-45. Is 5:6. 30:23. Je 14:22. Ezk 34:26. Am 4:7. Ml 3:10.

the time. Dt 11:14. Jb 29:23. Pr 16:15. Ho +6:3. Jl +2:23, 24. Ja 5:7.

latter rain. Je 3:3. 5:24, 25.

bright clouds. *or*, lightnings. Jb 36:27-31. 37:1-6. Je 10:13. 51:16.

and give. Ps 65:9-13. 72:6. 104:13, 14. Is 44:3-5. Ezk 34:26. Ho 10:12. Mi 5:7. 1 C 3:6, 7.

2 the idols. Heb. the *teraphims*. Ge +31:19mg. Is 44:9, 10. 46:5-7. Je 10:8-14. 14:22. Hab 2:18.

vanity. Dt +32:21.

the diviners. Je +27:9. La 2:14.

false dreams. Je +23:25-28. 29:8, 21, 22.

they comfort. Jb 13:4. 21:34. Je 6:14. 8:11. 14:13, 14. 23:17. 28:4-6, 15. 37:19.

therefore. Je 13:17-20. 50:17. 51:23. Mi 2:12.

a flock. Is 14:9. Je 51:40.

troubled, because there. *or*, answered that *there*. Nu +27:17.

3 anger. Zc 11:5-8, 17. Is 56:9-12. Je 10:21. 23:1, 2. 50:6. Ezk 34:2, 7, 10, etc.

and I. Ezk 34:16, 17, 20, 21. Mt 25:31-33, 41.

punished. Heb. visited upon. Je +9:25mg.

visited. Ex 4:31. Ru 1:6. Zp 2:7. Lk 1:68, 78. 1 P 2:12.

as. Pr 21:31. SS 1:9.

4 of him came forth. Zc 1:20, 21. 9:13-16. 12:6-8. Nu 24:17. Is 41:14-16. 49:2. 54:16. Je 1:18, 19. 30:21. Mi +5:5-8. Mt 9:38. 2 C 10:4, 5. Ep 4:8-11. 6:10-17. 2 T 2:4, 5. He 7:14. Re 17:14. 19:13-15.

the corner. 1 S 14:38mg. Is 19:13mg. 28:16. Mt 21:42. Ep 2:20.

the nail. Ex +27:19.

the battle bow. Zc 9:8, 10. Ge 49:24. Ps +44:6. Re 6:2.

5 as mighty. Zc 9:13. 12:8. 1 S 16:18. 2 S 23:8. Ps 45:3. 76:1-4. Lk 24:19. Ac 7:22. 18:24. 2 C 10:4.

tread. Ps 18:42. Is 10:6. 25:10. 63:6. Mi 7:10. Mt 4:3.

streets. Am +5:16.

because. Zc 14:3, 13, 14. Dt 20:1. Jsh 10:14, 42. Is 8:9, 10. 41:12, 13. 42:13. Jl 3:12-17. Mt 28:20. Ro 8:31-37. 2 T 4:7, 17. Re 19:13-15.

and the riders on horses shall be confounded. *or*, they shall make the riders on horses ashamed. Zc 12:4. Ps 20:7, 8. 33:16, 17. Ezk 38:15. 39:18-20. Hg 2:22. Re 19:17, 18.

6 I will strengthen. ver. 12. Ps 89:21, 22. Is 41:10. Ezk 37:16. Ob +18-21. Mi 4:6, 7. 18. 5:8, 9. 7:16, 17. Zp 3:19, 20.

I will save. Zc 8:7, 8. Je 3:18. +23:6-8. 31:1,

31. 33:24-26. 46:27, 28. 50:4, 5. Ezk 39:25. Ho 1:11. Am +5:6. Ro 11:25, 26.

bring them. Ezk 37:19-22.

for I have mercy. Is 14:1. Je 31:20. +33:26. Ho 1:7. 2:23. 14:4-8. Mi +7:18-20. Na 1:7. Ro 11:32.

as though. Zc 8:11. Is 30:26. 49:17-21. +54:7-10. 60:14-17. 61:7. Je 30:18-20. Ezk +36:11. Jl +2:25. Zp 3:15. Ro 11:15.

for I am. Zc 13:9. Is 41:17-20. 65:23, 24. Je 33:2, 3. Ezk 36:37.

7 and their. Zc 9:15, 17. Ge 43:34. Ps 104:15. Pr 31:6, 7. Ac 2:13-18. Ep +5:18, 19.

yea. Ge +18:19. Ps 90:16. 102:28. Is 38:19. Je 32:39. Ac 2:39. 13:33.

their heart. Ps 13:5. 28:7. Hab 3:18. Jn 16:22. Ac 2:26. 1 P 1:8.

as through. Ps 104:15.

wine. Heb. *yayin*, Hab 2:5.

8 hiss. 2 Ch +29:8.

gather. Is 11:11, 12. 27:12, 13. +55:1-3. Ezk +20:34. 22:20. Mt 11:28. Re 22:17.

for. Zc 9:11. Ex 15:13. Ps 106:10. 107:1-3. Is 44:22. 47:4. 51:11. 52:1-3. Je 31:10, 11. 1 T 2:4-6. Re 14:3, 4.

and they. Ex 1:7. 1 K 4:20. Is 49:19-22. Je 30:19, 20. 33:22. Ezk 36:10, 11, 37, 38. Ho 1:10.

9 sow. Est 8:17. Je 31:27. Da ch. 3-6. Ho +2:23. Am +9:9. Mi 5:7. Ac 8:1, 4. 11:19-21. ch. 13, 14, etc. Ro 11:11-15.

remember. Dt 30:1-4. 1 K 8:47, 48. Ne 1:9. Je 51:50. Ezk 6:9.

live. Is 65:9, 23. Ac 2:38, 39. 3:25, 26. 13:32, 33. Ro 11:16, 17, 24.

10 bring them again. Dt +30:3, 5.

out of the. Is 19:23-25.

into. Je 22:6. Ezk 47:18-21. Ob 20. Mi 7:14.

place. Is 49:19-21. 54:2, 3. 60:22.

11 he shall. Ps 66:10-12. Is 11:14-16. 42:15, 16. 43:2.

with affliction. Zc 12:2, 3, 6, 9. 13:8, 9. 14:1-3, 12-16, 20. Ge +6:13. Ps 124:1-5. Je 30:7, 11. Ezk 20:33-37. 38:8-12, 16, 21, 22. +39:23. Jl 3:1, 2, 12, 17. Mi 4:11-13.

smite. Ex 14:21, 22, 27, 28. Jsh 3:15-17. 2 K 2:8, 14. Ps 77:16-20. 114:3, 5. Is 11:15, 16. Re 16:12.

deeps of the river. Na +3:8.

the pride. Ezr 6:22. Is 10:24-27. 14:25. 30:31. Mi +5:5, 6.

the scepter. Ezk 29:14-16. 30:13, 20, 21. 31:1, etc. 32:1, etc.

12 I will. ver. 6. Zc 12:5. Ps +18:1. 2 T 2:1.

walk. Ge 5:24. 6:9. 17:1. 24:40. Is 2:5. Mi 4:5. +6:8. Col 2:6. 3:17. 1 Th 2:12. 4:1. 1 J 1:6, 7.

ZECHARIAH 11

1 O Lebanon. Zc 10:10. Je 22:6, 7, 23. Hab 2:8, 17. Hg 1:8.

that. Zc 14:1, 2. Dt 32:22. Mt 24:1, 2. Lk 19:41-44. 21:23, 24.

2 Howl. Is 2:12-17. 10:33, 34. 14:8. Ezk 17:3, 22-24. 31:2, 3, 17, 18. Am 6:1, 2. Na 3:8, etc. Lk 23:31.

    fir tree. Dt +32:1.

    mighty. *or,* gallants.

    oaks. Is +2:13.

    for. Is 32:15-19. Ezk 20:46-48.

    forest of the vintage. *or,* defenced forest. Je +33:3mg.

3 a voice. ver. 8, 15-17. Is +13:6. Mt +15:14. 23:13-33.

    for their. 1 S 4:21, 22. Is 65:15. Je 7:4, 11-14. 26:6. Ezk 24:21-25. Ho 1:9, 10. 10:5. Zp 3:11. Mt 3:7-10. 21:43-45. Ac 6:11-14. 22:21, 22. Ro 11:7-12.

    a voice. Ps 22:21. Je 2:30. Ezk 19:3-6. Zp 3:3. Mt 23:31-38. Ac 7:52.

    for the pride. Je +12:5. 49:19. 50:44.

4 Lord. Zc 14:5. Is 49:4, 5. Jn 20:17. Ep 1:3.

    Feed. ver. 7. Is +40:11. Mt 15:24. 23:37. Lk 19:41-44. Ro 8:36. 15:8. 1 C 15:31, 32.

5 possessors. Je 23:1, 2. Ezk 22:25-27. 34:2, 3, 10. Mi 3:1-3, 9-12. Mt 23:14. Jn 16:2.

    hold. Je 2:3. 50:7.

    sell. Ge 37:26-28. 2 K 4:1. Ne 5:8. Mt 21:12, 13. 2 P 2:3. Re 18:13.

    Blessed. Dt 29:19-21. Ho 12:8. 1 T +6:5-10.

    I am rich. Ps +62:10. 1 T +6:9. Re 3:17.

    and their. Ezk 34:4, 6, 18, 19, 21. Jn 10:1, 12, 13.

6 no more pity. ver. 5. Is 27:11. +54:7. Ezk 8:18. 9:10. Ho 1:6. Mt 18:33-35. 22:7. 23:35-38. Lk 19:43, 44. 21:22-24. 1 Th 2:16. He 10:26-31. Ja 2:13.

    deliver. Heb. make to be found. ver. 9, 14. Zc 8:10. Is 3:5. 9:19-21. Je 13:14. Mi 7:2-7. Hg 2:22. Mt 10:21, 34-36. 24:10. Lk 12:52, 53. 21:16, 17.

    into the hand. Da +9:26, 27. Mt 22:7. Jn 19:15.

    they shall. Ml 4:6.

    and out. Ps 50:22. Is 2:19. Ezk 9:5. Ho 2:10. Mi 5:8. 6:14. He 2:3. 10:26, 27.

7 I will. ver. 4, 11. Zc 13:8, 9.

    even you, O poor. *or, verily* the poor. Is 11:4. 61:1. Je 5:4, 5. Zp 3:12. Mt 11:5. Mk 12:37. 1 C 1:26. Ja 2:5.

    staves. ver. 10, 14. Le 27:32. 1 S 17:40, 43. Ps 23:4.

    one. Ps ch. 133. Ezk 37:16-23. Jn 17:21-23.

    Bands. *or,* Binders. Jn 10:16. Ep 2:13-16.

    I fed. Ps 23:1. Is 40:11. Jn 10:11. 14:16. He 13:20. 1 P 5:4.

8 in. Ho 5:7. Mt 23:34-36. 24:50, 51.

    and my. Ps 5:5. +106:40. Je 12:8. Ho 9:15. He 10:38.

    soul. Heb. *nephesh,* Ge +34:3.

    lothed them. Heb. was straitened for them.

Is 49:7. Lk 12:50. 19:14. Jn 7:7. 15:18, 23-25.

    soul. Heb. *nephesh,* Ge +34:3.

9 I will. Je 23:33, 39. Mt 13:10, 11. 21:43. 23:38, 39. Jn 8:21, 24. 12:35. Ac 13:46, 47. 28:26-28.

    that that dieth. Ps 69:22-28. Je 15:2, 3. 43:11. Mt +15:14. 21:19. Re +22:11.

    and let. Dt 28:53-56. Is 9:19-21. Je 19:9. Ezk 5:10.

    another. Heb. his fellow, *or,* neighbor.

10 Beauty. ver. 7. Ps 50:2. 90:17. Ezk 7:20-22. 24:21. Da +9:26. Lk 21:5, 6, 32. Ac 6:13, 14. Ro 9:3-5.

    that. Nu 14:34. 1 S 2:30. Ps 89:39. Je 14:21. 31:31, 32. Ezk 16:59-61. Ho 1:9. Ga 3:16-18. He 7:17-22. 8:8-13.

11 broken. Is 53:5, 10.

    so, etc. *or,* the poor of the flock, etc., certainly knew.

    poor. ver. 7. Ps 69:33. 72:12-14. Is 14:32. Zp 3:12. Lk 7:22. 19:48. Ja 2:5, 6.

    that waited upon. or, were watching me. 1 S 1:12. 19:11. Ps 59:t. Is 8:17. 26:8, 9. 40:31. La 3:25, 26. Mi 7:7. Lk 2:25, 38. 23:48, 51. Ac 1:21, 22.

    knew. ver. 6. Le 26:38, etc. Dt 28:49, etc. 31:21, 29. 32:21-42. Lk 24:49-53. Jn 6:68, 69. Ro 11:7, etc. Ja 5:1-6.

12 ye think good. Heb. *it be* good in your eyes. Jsh +22:30mg.

    give. Mt 26:15. Jn 13:2, 27-30.

    So. Ge 37:28. Ex 21:32. Mt 26:15. Mk 14:10, 11. Lk 22:3-6.

    thirty pieces. Mt 26:14, 15.

13 Cast it. Ge 21:15. 2 Ch 24:10. Is 54:7-10. Mt 27:3-10, 12. Ac 1:18, 19.

    the potter. Je 18:2. Mt 27:7.

    a goodly price. Is 53:2, 3. Ac 4:11.

14 I cut. ver. 9. Ge +49:10. Is 9:21. 11:13. Ezk 37:16-20. Mt 24:10. Jn 11:49, 51, 52. Ac 23:7-10. Ga 5:15. Ja 3:14, 16. 4:1-3.

    Bands. or, Binders. ver. 7.

15 foolish shepherd. Ps 14:1. Is 56:10-12. Je 2:26, 27. La 2:14. Ezk 13:3. Da +7:24-26. +9:27. Mt +15:14. 23:17. 24:15. Lk 11:40. Jn 5:43. 2 Th 2:4-8, 10-12. Re 13:1-10.

16 which. Je 23:2, 22. Ezk 34:2-6, 16. Mt 7:15, 16. 23:2-4, 13-29. Lk 12:45, 46. Jn 10:12, 13.

    cut off. *or,* hidden. ver. 8, 9. Ps +83:3, 4. Da 11:41. Zp +2:3. Re +12:6, 14.

    neither. Ge 33:13. 1 S 17:34, 35. Is 40:11.

    feed. *or,* bear. Am 7:10. Ac 20:28-30.

    but. Ge 31:38. Is 56:11. Ezk 34:10, 21. Jn 10:1.

17 Woe. 1 K 13:30. Is 1:4. 17:12. 28:1. Je 22:18. 23:1. Ezk 13:3. 34:2. Am 5:18. Hab 2:6. Mt 23:13, 16. Lk 11:42-52. 2 Th 2:8-10. Re 19:20. 20:10.

    idol shepherd. Jb 13:4. Is 9:15. 44:10. Je 23:32. Ezk +30:13. 1 C 8:4. 10:19, 20.

that leaveth. Jn 10:12, 13.
the sword. Is 6:9, 10. 29:10. 42:19, 20. Je 50:35-37. Ho 4:5-7. Am 8:9, 10. Mi 3:6, 7. Jn 9:39. 12:40. Ro 11:7. Re 13:10-12.
his arm. 1 S 2:31. 1 K 13:4. Ezk 30:22-24.
utterly darkened. Ge 27:1. Dt 34:7. Jb 17:7.

ZECHARIAH 12

1   Cir. A.M. 3594. B.C. 500.
burden. Zc 9:1. Is 14:28. 15:1. 17:1. La 2:14. Ezk 12:10. Na 1:1. Ml 1:1.
for Israel. Is 51:22, 23. Je 30:10, 16. 50:34. Ezk 36:5-7. Jl 3:19-21. Ob 16, 17.
which stretcheth. Jb 26:7. Ps 136:5, 6. Is +40:22. 48:13.
and layeth. Ps 24:2. 102:25. 104:2-5. Am 4:8, 13.
formeth. Ge +2:7. Nu 16:22. 27:16. Jb 12:10. +14:22. 27:3. +34:14. Ps 51:10. +146:4. Ec +12:7. Is 42:5. 43:7. 44:24. 57:16. Je 38:16. Ezk +18:4, +20. Da 5:23. Am 4:13mg. Ac 17:25, 28. 1 C 2:11. He +12:9, 23.
spirit. Heb. *ruach*, Nu +16:22.

2   **a cup**. Ps 75:8. Is 51:17, 22, 23. Je 25:15, 17. 49:12. 51:7. La 4:21. Hab 2:16. Re 14:10. 16:19. 18:6, 20, 24.
trembling. *or*, slumber. Je 51:57. *or*, poison. Je 8:14mg.
when they, etc. *or*, and also against Judah *shall he be*, which shall be in siege against Jerusalem. Zc 14:2, 3, 14. Jl 3:2. Mi 5:5, 6. Hab +3:16.

3   **in that day**. ver. 4, 6, 8, 9, 11. Zc 2:8, 9. 10:3-5. 13:1. 14:2, 3, +4. Is +2:11. 60:12. 66:14-16. Ezk ch. 38, 39. Jl 3:8-16. Ob 18. Mi 5:8, 15. 7:15-17. Hab 2:17. +3:16. Zp 3:19. Hg 2:22.
will I make. Is 49:16.
a burdensome stone. Je +26:6. Da +2:44.
shall be cut. Ge +12:3.
though all. Zc 14:2, 3. Mi 4:11-13. Re 16:14. 17:12-14. 19:19-21. 20:8, 9.
be gathered. Zp +3:8. Re +16:16.

4   **that day**. ver. +3. Is 24:21.
I will smite. Zc 10:5. 14:15. Dt 28:28. 2 K 6:14, 18. Ps 76:5-7. Ezk +38:3, 4. 39:20.
I will open. Zc 9:8. 1 K 8:29. 2 K 19:16. 2 Ch 6:20, 40. 7:15. Ne 1:6. Ps +11:4. Is 37:17. Da 9:18. Ho +5:15. Lk 22:61. Ac 17:30.

5   **the governors**. ver. 6. Jg 5:9. Is 1:10, 23, 26. 29:10. 32:1. 60:17. Je 30:21. 33:26. Ezk 45:8, 9.
The inhabitants, etc. *or*, *There is* strength to me, *and to* the inhabitants, etc. Zc 10:6, 12. Ps 3:6. 18:32, 39. 20:6, 7. 27:3. 46:1, 5. 68:34, 35. 118:10-14. 144:1. Is 28:6. 41:10-16. Jl +3:16. 2 C 12:9, 10.

6   **like an hearth**. Is 10:16, 17. Je 5:14. Ob 18. Re 20:9.

like a torch. Ps 11:6. 97:3.
they shall devour. Zc 9:15. Ps 46:6, 7. +149:6-9. Is 41:15, 16. Da 2:34, 35, 44, 45. Mi +4:13. +5:5-8. Re 19:19, 20.
on the right. Is 9:20. 54:3. 2 C 6:7.
Jerusalem shall. Zc 1:16. 2:4, 12. 8:3-5. 14:10, 11. Ne ch. 11. Je 30:18. 31:38-40. Ezk 48:30-35.

7   **save the tents of Judah**. Zc 4:6. 11:11. Is 2:11-17. 23:9. Je 9:23, 24. Mt 11:25, 26. Lk 1:51-53. 10:21. Jn 7:47-49. Ro 3:27. 1 C 1:26-31. 2 C 4:7-12. Ja 2:5. 4:6.
do not magnify. Jb 19:5. Ps 35:26. 38:16. 55:12.

8   **In that day**. ver. 3. Is +2:11.
defend. Zc +2:5. +9:8, 15, 16. 14:3. Is 63:1-6. Jl 2:11. +3:16, 17. 2 Th 1:7-10. Ju 14, 15. Re 11:19-21.
he that is. Zc 9:13. Is +30:19, 26. Je +30:19-22. Ezk +34:23, 24. Jl 3:9, 10. Mi 5:8. 7:16. He 11:34.
feeble. *or*, abject. Heb. fallen. Is 49:7. 53:3. Je 27:10. Da 11:33, 34. Mi +7:8.
shall be as David. 1 S 17:32-51. Is +40:29.
the house of David. Ps 2:6, 7. +45:6, 7. 110:1, 2. Is +7:13, 14. +9:6, 7. Je +23:5, 6. 33:15, 16. Ezk +37:24-26. Ho 1:7. +3:5. Mi +5:2-4. Mt 1:23. Jn 17:21-23. Ro 1:3, 4. 9:5. 1 T 3:16. Re 22:13, 16.
as the angel. Zc 1:12. 3:1. Ge 16:7. 18:1. 22:11, 15-17. 31:11. 48:16. Ex +3:2. 14:19. 23:20. Jsh 5:13, 14. Jg 2:1. 6:11, 12. 13:3, 21. 2 S 14:17-20. 2 K 19:35. Ps 34:7. 35:5, 6. Is +63:9. Da +3:25, 28. Ho 12:4. Ml 3:1. Ac 7:30, 38. 12:23.

9   **in that day**. ver. 3. Is +2:11.
I will seek. ver. 2-6. Zc 9:13. Is 54:17. Ezk 39:2-5. Jl 3:2, 14, 16. Hg 2:22.
all the nations. Zc 14:2.
come against. Ge 34:27. Pr 28:22.

10   **I will pour**. Ps +79:6. Pr 1:23. Is 32:15. 44:3, 4. 59:19-21. Je +2:13. Ezk 39:29. Jl 2:28, 29. Ac 2:17, 33. 10:45. 11:15. T 3:5, 6.
the house. ver. 7.
the spirit. Heb. *ruach*, Ge +41:38. Ps 51:12.
of grace. Is +30:18, 19. He +10:29.
of supplications. Zc 13:9. Ps 10:17. +122:6. Is +30:19. +65:24. Je 3:21. 31:9. 50:4. Ho +5:15. 8:2. Ro 8:15, 26, 27. 2 C 7:10. Ga 4:6. Ep +6:18. Ju 20.
and they shall. Ps 22:16, 17. Jn 19:34-37. He +12:2. Re +1:7.
look upon me. *or*, look unto me. Zc 2:10. 14:9. Ge 15:5. 19:17, 26. Ex 33:8. Is +45:22. Ezk 20:35. Ho 5:15. Mt 23:39. *24:30*. Lk 23:35. Jn 3:14, 15. *19:37*. 2 C 3:16. 5:21.
whom they have. Zc 13:7. Jn 19:34-37. Re +1:7.
pierced. Zc 13:3. Ps 22:16. Is 53:5. Je +37:10mg (**S#1856h**). Jn 19:34, 37. Re 1:7.

they shall mourn. Ge 45:3. Ex 11:6. 12:29, 30. Je 6:26. Jl +2:12. Am 5:17. 8:10. Mt +24:30. 26:75. Ac 2:37. 2 C 7:9-11.

11 as the mourning. 2 K 23:29, 30. 2 Ch 35:20-25.

Hadadrimmon. i.e. *sound of the pomegranate,* **S#1910h.**

valley of Megiddon. Jsh +12:21.

12 the land. Je 3:21. 4:28. 31:18. Mt +24:30. Re +1:7.

every family apart. Heb. families, families. Ex 12:30. Ezk 24:23.

the family of the house of David apart. Je 13:18. Jon 3:5, 6.

and their wives apart. Zc 7:3. Jl 2:16. 1 C 7:5.

Nathan. 2 Ch +9:29.

13 Levi. Nu +1:49.

apart. Mt 26:3, 4. Jn 18:35.

Shimei. *or,* Simeon, as LXX. Heb. **S#8097h,** Nu +3:21, Shimites. Compare **S#8096h,** 2 S +16:5.

14 and their wives apart. ver. 12. Pr 9:12. Mt +5:4.

ZECHARIAH 13

1 In that day. ver. 2, 4. Zc 12:3, 8, 11. Is +2:11.

a fountain. Zc 14:8. Jb 9:30, 31. Ps 51:2, 7. Is 1:16-18. Ezk +36:25. Jn 1:29. 19:34, 35. 1 C 6:11. Ep 5:25-27. T 3:5-7. He 9:13, 14. 10:10, 14. 1 J 1:7. 5:6. 1 P 1:18, 19. Re +1:5, 6. 7:13, 14.

the house of David. Zc 12:7, 10.

and to. Lk 24:47. Ac +1:8. Ro +1:16.

uncleanness. Heb. separation for uncleanness. Le 15:2, etc. Nu 19:9-22. Ezk 36:17, 29. 37:23.

2 I will cut off. Ex +23:13. Ezk 30:13. Ho +2:17. Zp +1:3, 4. 2:11.

the names. Ex +23:13.

cause. 1 K 22:22. Je 8:10-12. 23:14, 15. 29:23. Ezk 13:12-16, 23. 14:9. Mi 2:11. Mt 7:15. 24:24. 2 C 11:13-15. 2 P 2:1-3, 15-19. 1 J 4:1, 2. Re 19:20.

unclean. Mt 12:43. Lk 11:20. Re 16:13, 14. 18:2. 20:1-3.

spirit. Heb. *ruach,* Jg +9:23.

3 and his father and. Ex 32:27, 28. Dt 13:6-11. 18:20. 33:9. Mt 10:37. Lk 14:26. 2 C 5:16.

thrust. Zc 12:10. Je +37:10 **(S#1856h).**

4 come to pass. Jl 2:28.

the prophets. Je 2:26. Mi 3:6, 7.

wear. 2 K 1:8. Is 20:2. Mt 3:4. 11:8, 9. Mk 1:6. Re 11:3.

rough garment. Heb. *garment of hair.* Ge 27:16. 2 K 1:8.

to deceive. Heb. to lie. Is 59:13.

5 I am no. Am 7:14. Ac 19:17-20.

6 What. 1 K 18:28. 20:35-41. Re 13:16, 17. 14:11.

I was. Ps 22:16. Pr 27:5, 6. Jn 18:35. 19:14-16.

my friends. Mk 3:21. Jn 1:11.

7 O sword. Dt +32:41, 42. Is 27:1. Je 47:6. Ezk 21:4, 5, 9, 10, 28.

my shepherd. Zc 11:4, 7. Ps 106:23. Jn +10:11.

the man. Is +9:6. Je +23:5, 6. Ho 12:3-5. Mt 1:23. 11:27. Jn +1:1, 2. +5:17, 18, 23. +8:58. +10:30, 38. 14:1, 9-11, 23. 16:15. 17:21-23. 1 C 15:47. Ph +2:6. Col +1:15-19. 1 T +2:5. He +1:6-12. Re +1:8, 11, 17. 2:23. 21:6. 22:13-16.

my fellow. or, my equal. Is 6:1-3. Jn +5:18. Ph 2:6. or, neighbor. Le 6:2. 18:20. 19:15, 17. 25:14, 15, 17.

the Lord. Ho 1:7.

of hosts. Ps +24:10.

smite. Is +53:4-10. Da +9:24-26. Mt 26:31. Mk *14:27.* Jn 1:29. 3:14-17. 10:11, 14-18. Ac 2:23. 4:26-28. Ro 3:24-26. 4:25. 5:6-10. 8:32. 2 C 5:21. Ga 3:13. Col 1:19, 20. He 10:5-10. 1 P 1:18-20. 2:24, 25. 3:18. 1 J 2:2. 4:9, 10. Re 13:8.

the sheep. Mt 26:31, 56. Mk 14:27, 50. Jn 16:32.

I will turn. Zc 11:7, 11. Ps 81:15. Is 1:25. Ezk 38:12. Am 1:9. Mt 10:17, 18, 42. 18:10, 11, 14, 34, 35. 24:9. Lk 12:32. 17:2. Jn 15:18, 20. 18:8, 9.

hand. Is +1:25.

little ones. Je 49:20. Lk 12:32.

8 two. Zc 11:6-9. Dt 28:49-68. Is 65:12-15. 66:4-6, 24. Ezk 5:2-4, 12. Da +9:27. Ml 3:1, 2, +5. 4:1-3. Mt 3:10-12. 21:43, 44. 22:7. 23:35-37. 24:21. Lk 19:41-44. 20:16-18. 21:20-24. 23:28-30. 1 Th 2:15, 16. Re 8:7-12. 16:19.

die. Ge +49:33.

but the third. Zc 14:1, 2. Is 6:13. 10:20-22. Je 30:11. Jl 2:31, 32. Am +9:8, 9. Mt 24:22. Mk 13:20. Ro 9:27-29. +11:1-5.

9 bring the third. Ps 66:10-12. Is 10:20-22. 43:2. Da +11:35. 1 C 3:11-13. 1 P 4:12.

fire. 1 P 4:12.

refine. 1 P +1:7.

try them. Ps +17:3. Is 1:25. Ezk 22:19-22. Da +12:10. Mt +26:41.

they shall call. Zc +12:10. Ho +5:15. 6:1-3. 8:2. 14:2. Jl 2:32. Ac 2:21. Ro 10:12-14.

I will hear. Zc 10:6. Is +65:24. Ho 2:21-23. 1 J +5:14.

It is my people. Ge +17:7. Dt 26:17-19. Ps 144:15. Is 44:1-6. Ho +2:23.

they shall say. Ezk 37:27, 28.

ZECHARIAH 14

1 the day of the Lord. Je +30:7, 8. Ezk +30:3. Ac 2:20.

2 gather all nations. Dt 28:9, etc. Ps 79:1. Is 5:26. +59:19. Je 30:7, 8. 34:1. Ezk +38:14-17.

Da 2:40-43. 8:13. Jl 3:2, 11. Ob 15. Mt 22:7. Lk 2:1. 2 Th 2:8. Re 11:7. 13:7. 16:12-14. 17:14.

against. Ps 83:4. Is 29:3-7.

the city. Mt 23:37, 38. 24:15, 16. Mk 13:14, 19. Lk 19:43, 44. 21:20-24.

the houses. Is 13:16. La 1:10. 5:11, 12. Am 7:17. Mt 24:19-21.

women ravished. La 5:11.

go forth into. Mi 4:10.

the residue. Lk 21:24.

shall not. Zc 13:8, 9. Is 65:6-9, 18. Mt 24:22. Ro 9:27-29. Ga 4:26, 27.

3 and fight. ver. 12, 13. Zc 2:8, 9. 10:4, 5. 12:2-6, +8, 9. Ps 46:5, 8, 9. 83:9-17. Is 10:24, 25. 14:25. 29:7, 8. 30:26-32. 31:4-9. 34:1-4. 63:1-6. 66:15, 16. Da 2:34, 35, 44, 45. Jl 3:2, 9-17. Zp 3:19. Hg 2:21, 22. Re 6:4-17. 8:7-13.

as when. Ex 15:1-6. Jsh 10:42. 2 Ch 20:15.

fought. Jsh 10:14.

battle. 2 S 17:11.

4 his feet. ver. 7. Is 52:7. Ezk 11:23. 43:2. Ac 1:11, 12.

in that day. ver. 6, 8, 9, 13, 20, 21. Zc +12:3. Is +2:11.

cleave. Zc 4:7. Ps 46:2, 3. Is 64:1, 2. Ezk 38:19, 20. +42:16. 45:1. 47:1. Mi 1:3, 4. Na 1:5, 6. Hab 3:6. Mk 11:23.

a very. ver. 10. Jl 3:12-14.

half of the. Ezk 47:1-12.

5 the mountains. or, my mountains.

for the, etc. or, when he shall touch the valley of the mountains to the place he separated.

ye shall flee. Nu 16:34. Am 2:14-16. Re 11:13. 16:18-21.

ye fled. Is 29:6. Am 1:1.

the Lord. Mt 16:27. 24:3, 27-31. 25:31. Mk 13:26, 27. Lk 21:27. 2 Th 2:8. Ja 5:8. Re 6:16, 17. 20:4, 11.

Azal. i.e. proximity, he has reserved, **S#682h**, only here.

the Lord. Ex 15:26.

God shall come. Is +35:4.

and all. Dt +33:2. Ps +149:9. Is 24:23. Ho +11:12. Jl 3:11. Ro 8:19. 1 Th 3:13. 2 Th 1:7-10. Ju 14.

the saints. Jb 5:1. Ps 89:5, 7. Is 13:3. Da 4:13. 8:13. Mt 16:27. +24:30, 31. +25:31. Ju 14.

6 that the. Is 5:30. Mt +24:29.

not. Ps 97:10, 11. 112:4. Pr +4:18, 19. Is 50:10. 60:1-3. Ho 6:3. Lk 1:78, 79. Jn 1:5. 12:46. Ep 5:8-14. Col 1:12. 2 P 1:19. Re 11:3, 15.

clear. Heb. precious. Ps +37:20mg.

dark. Heb. thickness. Zp 1:12.

7 it shall be one day. or, the day shall be one. Ps 118:24. Re 21:23. 22:5.

which. Ps 37:18. Mt +24:36. Mk +13:32. Ac +1:7. 15:18. 17:26, 31. 1 Th 5:2.

at evening. Is +9:7. 11:9. 30:26. 60:19, 20.

Da +12:4. Ho 3:5. 1 C 2:9. Re 11:15. 14:6. 20:2-4. 21:23. 22:5.

8 in that day. Jl 3:18.

living waters. Je +2:13. Ezk 47:1-12. Jl 3:18. Lk 24:47. Jn 4:10, 14. 7:38. Re 22:1, 2, 17.

the former. or, eastern. Jl 2:20.

hinder sea. Jl +2:20.

in summer. Is 35:7. 41:17, 18. 49:10. 58:11. Re 7:16, 17.

9 the Lord. Zc 8:20-23. Ge +49:10. 1 S 2:10. Ps 2:6-8. 47:2-9. +86:9. Is 24:23. 45:22-25. 49:6, 7. 52:10. 54:5. 60:12-14. Ezk 48:35. Am 9:12. Mi 4:1-3. 5:4. Zp 3:9. Ml 1:11.

shall be king. Zc 2:10. 12:10. Ps 18:43. 45:6. +47:2, 7. 59:13. 102:16. Is 12:6. Je 23:5, 6. Ob +21. Zp 3:14, 15.

all the earth. Zc 4:14. 6:5. Ps 72:8. Re +11:15.

in that day. Is +2:11.

one Lord. Zc 13:7. Mk +12:32. 1 C 2:8. 15:47. Ep 4:5, 6. Ja 2:1.

and his name one. Dt +6:4. Je 23:6. Mt 1:23. +28:19. Ep 3:14, 15.

10 the land shall be. ver. 4. Zc 4:6, 7. Ps 46:2, 3. Is 29:17. 40:3-5. Ezk +42:16. 45:1. 47:1. Hab 3:6. Lk 3:4-6.

turned. or, compassed. Ge 19:4.

plain. Heb. arabah. Dt +11:30.

from Geba. 1 S +13:3.

Rimmon. Jsh +15:32.

lifted up. Ps 48:2. 68:15. Is 2:2.

inhabited. or, shall abide. Zc 2:4. 12:6. Je 30:18.

from Benjamin's. 2 Ch 25:23. Ne 3:1. 8:16. 12:39. Je 20:2. 31:38-40. 37:13. 38:7.

corner gate. 2 Ch 26:9.

the tower. Je 31:38.

Hananeel. i.e. graciously given of God, **S#2606h**. Ne 3:1. 12:39. Je 31:38.

11 no more utter destruction. or, curse. Nu 21:3. Is 11:6-9, 11, 12. 60:18. Je +31:40. Ezk +37:26. Jl 3:17, 20. Am +9:15. Ml 4:6. Ro 8:18-25. Re 21:4. 22:3.

shall be safely inhabited. or, shall abide. Zc 2:4. 8:4, 8. +12:6. Le 26:5. Is 26:1, 2. 66:22. Je +23:5, 6. 30:10. 33:15, 16. Ezk 28:26. +34:22-29.

12 the plague wherewith. ver. 3. Zc 12:9. Ps 110:5, 6. Is ch. 34. 66:15, 16, 24. Ezk 38:18-22. 39:4-6, 17-20. Jl 3:1, 2, 9-16. Mi 4:3, 11-13. 5:8, 9. 7:16, 17. Re ch. 16. 19:17-21.

Their flesh. Le 26:18, 21, 24, 28. Dt 28:59. 2 Ch 21:15, 18, 19. Ps 90:11. Ac 12:23. Re 9:5, 6. 16:10, 11, 21. 17:16. 18:6-8.

their tongue. Lk 16:24.

consume. Dt 4:24. 9:3. He 12:29.

13 a great. Zc 12:4. Re 17:12-17.

his hand. Jg +7:22.

14 Judah also shall. or, thou also, O Judah, shalt, etc. Zc 10:4, 5. 12:5-7.

at. *or*, against. Not *against*, but *at* or *in*. For same idiom, see Ex 17:8, "at Rephidim;" Jg 5:19, "fought...in Taanach;" 2 Ch 35:22, "in the valley of Megiddo." ver. 3. Jg 9:45. 1 S 23:1. 2 S 12:27.

and the. 2 K 7:6-18. 2 Ch 14:13-15. 20:25-27. Is 23:18. Ezk 39:9, 10, 17, etc.

wealth. Is +60:5. +61:6. Mi 4:13.

15   so shall. ver. 12. Jsh 7:24, 25. Ro 8:20-22.

16   that every. Zc 8:20-23. 9:7. Is 60:6-9. 66:18-21, 23. Jl 2:32. Ac 15:17. Ro 9:23, 24. 11:5, 16, 26. Re 11:13, 15-17.

go up. Ps 86:9. Is 66:18.

the King. ver. 17. Ps 24:7-10. Is 6:5. Je 46:18. 48:15. 51:57. Ml 1:14. Lk 19:38. Jn 1:49. Ph 2:9-11. Re 19:16.

the Lord of hosts. Je +6:6.

keep the feast. ver. 18, 19. Le +23:34-36, 43. Mt +17:4.

17   that. Ps 2:8-12. 110:5, 6. Is 45:23. 60:12. Je 10:25. Ro 14:10, 11.

all. Ge 10:32. +12:3. 28:14. Am 3:2. Ac 17:26, 27.

even. Dt 11:17. 28:23, 24. 1 K 8:35. 17:1. 2 Ch 6:26. 7:13. Is 5:6. Je 14:4, 22. Am 4:7, 8. Ja 5:17. Re 11:6.

18   And if. Dt 16:13, 17. Ps 126:1-3.

that have no. Heb. upon whom *there is* not. Dt 11:10, 11.

feast of. Le +23:34.

tabernacles. Le +23:42.

19   punishment. *or*, sin. Ezk 18:20. Jn 3:19.

20   shall there. Pr 21:3, 4. Is 23:18. Jl 3:17. Ob 17. Zp 2:11. Ml 1:11. Lk 11:41. Ac 10:15, 28. 11:9. 15:9. Ro 14:17, 18. Col 3:17, 22-24. T 1:15, 16. 1 P 4:11.

bells. *or*, bridles. Ex 28:33-35.

HOLINESS. Ex 28:36. 39:30. Le 8:9. Ps 110:3. Is 4:3. 35:8. Je 31:40. 1 C 3:16, 17. 1 P 2:5, 9. Re 1:6. 5:10. 20:6. 21:27.

and the. Le 6:28. 1 S 2:14. Ezk 46:20-24.

the bowls. Ex 25:29. 37:16. 1 K +7:40.

21   every. Zc 7:6. Dt 12:7, 12. Ne 8:10. Ro 14:6, 7. 1 C 10:31. 1 T 4:3-5.

in that day. ver. 4. Is +2:11.

no more. Is 4:3. 35:8. Ezk 44:9. Ho 12:7mg. Jl 3:17. Mt 21:12, 13. Mk 11:15-17. Jn 2:15, 16. 1 C +6:9-11. Re 18:11-15. 21:27. 22:15.

Canaanite. Zc 11:7, 11. Zp 1:11. Mt 21:12.

in the house. Ep 2:19-22. 1 T 3:15. He 3:6. 1 P 4:17.

MALACHI

MALACHI 1

1 Cir. A.M. 3684. B.C. 420.

burden. Is 13:1. +22:1. Hab 1:1. Zc 9:1. 12:1.

by. Heb. by the hand of. Hg +1:1mg. 2:1mg.

Malachi. i.e. *my messenger or worker, messenger of the Lord,* **S#4401h.**

2 **I have.** Dt 32:8-14. +33:3. Is 41:8, 9. 43:4. Ro 11:28, 29.

Wherein. ver. 6, 7. Ml 2:17. 3:7, 8, 13, 14. Je 2:5, 31. Lk 10:29.

yet I. Ge 25:23. 27:27-30, 33. 28:3, 4, 10-17. 32:28-30. 48:4. Ro 9:10-*13.*

Jacob. Ge +9:27.

3 **Esau.** Ge +9:27. Ezk +35:5, 9.

hated. Ge 29:30, 31. Dt 21:15, 16. Mt 10:37. Lk 14:26.

laid. Je +49:7.

the dragons. Is 13:21, 22. 34:13, 14. 35:7. Je 9:11. 10:22. 49:33. 51:37.

4 **but.** Is 9:9, 10. Ja 4:13-16.

Lord of hosts. Je +6:6.

They shall build. Jb 9:4. 12:14. 34:29. Ps 127:1. Pr +21:30. Is 10:4, 15, 16. La 3:37. Ezk 35:2-4, 7, 9, 14, 15. Ob 1, 10, 16-18. Mt 12:30.

The border. Je 31:17. Ezk 11:10. Am 6:2.

The people. ver. 3. Ps 137:7. Is 11:14. 34:5, 10. 63:1-6. La 4:21, 22. Ezk 25:14. 35:9.

indignation. Is +66:14.

for ever. Heb. *olam,* Ex +12:24.

5 **your.** Dt 4:3. 11:7. Jsh 24:7. 1 S 12:16. 2 Ch 29:8. Lk 10:23, 24.

The Lord. Ps 35:26, 27. 58:10, 11. 83:17, 18. Ezk 38:16, 23. 39:21, 22.

from. *or,* upon. Heb. from upon.

6 **son.** Ex +20:12. Ho 11:1.

a servant. Ps 123:2. Is 41:8. 1 T 6:1, 2. T 2:9, 10. 1 P 2:17-19.

if then. Ex 4:22, 23. Is 1:2. 64:8. Je 31:9. Mt 6:9, 14, 15. Lk 6:36, 46. 1 P 1:17.

a father. Ml 2:10. Dt 32:6. Is 63:16.

and if. Mt +7:21. Lk +6:46. Jn +13:13-17.

unto you. Is +5:3.

O priests. Ml 2:8. 1 S 2:28-30. Je 5:30, 31. 23:11. Ezk 22:26. Ho 4:6. 5:1.

And ye. Ml 2:14-17. 3:7, 8, 13, 14. Je 2:21, 22. Ho 12:8. Lk 10:29.

7 **Ye offer,** etc. *or,* Bring unto my, etc.

polluted. Le 2:11. 21:6. Dt 15:21.

bread. Ge +3:19.

The table. ver. 12. Ex +25:23. 1 S 2:15-17. 1 C 11:20-22, 27-32.

8 **if ye offer the blind.** ver. 14. Le 22:19-25. Dt 15:21.

for sacrifice. Heb. to sacrifice.

or accept. ver. 10, 13. Jb 42:8. Ps 20:3. Je 14:10. Ho 8:13.

thy governor. Ne 5:14, 15.

9 **beseech.** 2 Ch 30:27. Jb 42:8. Je 27:18. Ho 13:9. Jl 1:13, 14. 2:17. Zc 3:1-5. Jn +9:31. He 7:26, 27.

God. Heb. the face of God. Heb. *El,* Ex +15:2. Ex +32:11mg. La 2:19.

be gracious. Jb 33:24. Zc +12:10.

by your means. Heb. from your hand. 1 K +10:29mg.

will he. Ac 19:15, 16. Ro 2:11. 1 P 1:17.

10 **even.** 1 S 2:36. Jb 1:9-11. Je 6:13. 8:10. Ezk +13:19. Jn 10:12. Ph 2:21.

neither. 1 C 9:13.

I have. Is 1:11-15. Je 6:20. Am 5:21-24. He +10:38.

an offering. Heb. *minchah,* meal offering, Le +23:13.

11 **from.** Ps 50:1. 113:3. Is 45:6. 59:19. +60:3, 5. Zc 8:7.

my name. ver. 14. Ps 67:2. 72:11-17. 98:1-3. Is +11:10. 45:22, 23. 54:1-3, 5. Am 9:12. Mi 5:4. Zp 3:9. Mt 6:9, 10. 28:19. Ac 15:7-9, 17, 18. Ep 3:1-3, 5-8. Re 11:15. 15:4.

great among. Zc +14:9.

and in every. Is 24:14-16. 42:10-12. Zp 2:11. Jn 4:21-23. Ac 10:30-35. Ro 15:9-11, 16. 1 T 2:8. Re 8:3.

incense. Ps +141:2. Is 60:6. Ro 12:1. Ph 4:18. He 13:15, 16.

pure offering. Jn 4:21, 23.

for my name. Is +66:19, 20.

12 **ye have.** ver. 6-8. Ml 2:8. 2 S 12:14. Ezk 36:21-23. Am 2:7. Ro 2:24.

The table. ver. 7, 13. Nu 11:4-8. Da 5:3, 4.

13 **Behold.** 1 S 2:29. Is 43:22. Am 8:5. Mi 6:3. Mk 14:4, 5, 37, 38.

weariness. Dt 20:8. Is 40:30, 31. Ro 2:7. 1 C

15:58. Ga 6:9. 2 Th 3:13. He 6:12.

and ye have snuffed at it. *or,* whereas ye might have blown it away.

torn. ver. 7, 8. Le 22:8, 19-23. Dt 15:21. Ezk 4:14. 44:31.

should I accept. Ml 2:13. Le 22:20. Is 1:12. 57:6. Je 7:9-11, 21-24. Am 5:21-23. Zc 7:5, 6. Mt 6:1, 2, 5, 16.

14 **cursed**. Ml +3:9. Ge 27:12. Jsh 7:11, 12. Pr +3:33. Je 48:10. Mt +24:51. Lk 12:1, 2, 46. Ac 5:1-10. Re +21:8.

which hath in his flock. *or,* in whose flock is. Ec 5:4, 5. Mk 12:41-44. 14:8. 2 C 8:12.

for I. ver. 8, 11. Dt 28:58. Ps +47:2. Is +57:15. Je 10:10. Da 4:37. 1 T 6:15.

great. Da +2:45.

my name. Ps 68:35. 76:12. Da 9:4. He 12:29. Re 15:4.

MALACHI 2

1 **O ye priests**. Ml 1:6. Je 13:13. La 4:13. Ho 5:1.

2 **If**. Ge +4:7. Je +7:5. 2 P +1:10.

ye will not hear. Le 26:14, etc. Dt +28:15, etc. 30:17, 18. Ps 81:11, 12. Is 30:8-13. Je 6:16-20. 13:17. 25:4-9. +29:19. 34:17. Ezk 3:7. Zc 1:3-6. 7:11-14.

if ye will not lay. Is 42:25. 47:7. 57:11.

to give. Ro +1:21, 24, 27. Re +11:13.

my name. Ps +9:10.

Lord of hosts. Je +6:6.

send a curse. Ge 3:17-19. Dt 28:20. Ho 6:1.

curse your blessings. Dt 28:2, 16-18, 53-57. Ps 69:22. 109:7-15. Da +9:11. Ho 4:7-10. 9:11-14. Hg 1:6, 9. 2:16, 17. Lk 23:28-30.

I have cursed. Ml +3:9. Dt +28:20. Is +45:7. Am +3:6. Hg 1:11. Ac 12:23. Ro 1:27.

3 **I will**. Jl 1:17.

corrupt. *or,* reprove. Ml 3:11. Ezr 10:18. Ps 106:9. Is 17:13. Je 29:27.

spread. Heb. scatter. ver. 9. 1 S 2:29, 30. Je +16:4. Na 3:6. Lk 14:35. 1 C 4:13.

feasts. Ex +23:18mg.

one shall take you away with it. *or,* it shall take you away to it.

4 **ye**. 1 K 22:25. Is 26:11. Je 28:9. Ezk 33:33. 38:23. Lk 10:11.

that my covenant. Is 1:24-28. 27:9. Ezk 20:38-41. 44:9-16. Mt 3:12. Jn 15:2. He 8:6.

5 **covenant**. Nu 3:45. 8:15. 16:9, 10. 18:8-24. 25:10-13. Dt 33:8-10. Ps 106:30, 31. Ezk 34:25. 37:26. 44:15, 16.

life and peace. Ro 8:6.

I gave. Ex 32:26-29. Dt 33:8-11.

the fear. He 12:28.

6 **law of truth**. Ps 37:30. 106:13. 119:142. Je 23:22. Ezk 44:23, 24. Da +10:21. Ho 4:6. Mt 22:16. Mk 12:14. Lk 20:21. Ep 4:15. 2 T 2:15, 16. T 1:7-9. Re 14:5.

iniquity. 1 P 2:1.

he walked. Ge +5:22.

with me. 1 J 1:3.

turn many. Je 23:22. Da +12:3. Lk 1:16, 17. Ac 26:17, 18. 1 Th 1:9, 10. Ja +5:19, 20.

7 **the priest's**. Le 10:11. Dt 17:8-11. 21:5. 24:8. 33:10. 2 Ch +15:3. 17:8, 9. 30:22. 35:3. Ezr +7:10. Ne 8:2-8. Je 15:19. 18:18. Da +11:33. Hg 2:11-13. 2 T 2:24, 25.

knowledge. Mk +12:24. Ro 15:14. 1 T +4:16. T 2:1.

the messenger. Ml 3:1. Is 42:19. 44:26. Hg 1:13. Jn 13:20. 20:21. Ac 16:17. 2 C 5:20. Ga 4:14. 1 Th 4:8.

Lord of hosts. Je +6:6.

8 **ye are**. Ps 18:21. 119:102. Is 30:11. 59:13. Je 17:5, 13. Ezk 44:10. Da 9:5, 6. He 3:12.

ye have caused. ver. 9. 1 S 2:17, 24, 30. Is 9:16. Je 18:15. 23:11-15. Mt 15:2-5. Lk 11:45, 46. Ro 2:19-24. 14:21.

stumble at. *or,* fall in. Mt +15:14. 18:6, 7.

ye have corrupted. ver. 5, 10. Le 21:15. Ne 13:29. Ezk 22:26. 44:10. Zp 3:4.

9 **made**. ver. 3. 1 S 2:17, 30. Pr 10:7. Da +12:2, 3. Mi +3:6, 7.

before. 1 K 22:28. Je 28:15, 16. 29:20-22, 31, 32. Ezk 13:12-16, 21. Mk 7:13, 14. Lk 20:45-57.

but. ver. 8. Mt 5:21, 22, 27, 28, 33-37, 43, 44. 19:17, 18. 23:16-24. Mk 7:8-13. Lk 10:29. 11:42. Ro 7:7-10.

have been partial in. *or,* lifted up the face against. Heb. accepted faces. Dt 1:17mg. Mi 3:11. Ja +2:1, 4. 2 P 3:16.

10 **all**. Ml 1:6. Jsh 24:3. Is 51:2. 63:16. 64:8. Ezk 33:24. Mt 3:9. Lk 1:73. 3:8. Jn 8:33, 39, 41, 53, 56. Ac 7:2. Ro 4:1. 9:10. 1 C 8:6. Ep 4:6. He +12:9.

father. Dt 32:6. Ps 103:13. Is 63:16. 64:8. Je 3:4, 19. 31:9.

hath not. Jb 31:15. Ps 100:3. Is 43:1, 7, 15. 44:2. Jn 8:41. Ac 17:25-29.

one. Dt 6:4. Ps 83:18. Mk 10:18. +12:32. Jn 4:24. Ac 17:26. Ro 3:29,30. 1 C +8:6. Ep 4:6.

God. Heb. *El,* Ex +15:2.

created. Heb. *bara,* **S#1254h**. Ge 1:1, 27. 2:3. 5:2. 6:7. Dt 4:32. Ps 89:12, 47. Is 4:5. 41:20. 43:7. 45:8, 12, 18. 54:16, 16. Je 31:22.

why. ver. 11, 14, 15. Je 9:4, 5. Mi 7:2-6. Mt 7:12. 10:21. 22:16, 37-40. Ac 7:26. 1 C 6:6-8. Ga 5:14. Ep 4:25. 1 Th 4:6.

by profaning. ver. 8, 11. Ex 34:10-16. Jsh 23:12-16. Ezr 9:11-14. 10:2, 3. Ne 13:29.

11 **Judah hath**. Je 3:7, 8, 20. 5:11.

and an. Le 18:24-30. Je 7:10. Ezk 18:13. 22:11. Re +21:8.

profaned. Ex 19:5, 6. Le 20:26. Da 7:3-6. 14:2. 33:26-29. Ps 106:28, 34-39. Je 2:3, 7, 8, 21, 22.

loved. *or,* ought to love.

and hath. Jg +3:6. Ezr 10:2. Ho 6:7.
the daughter. Ex 34:16.
strange. Ex 12:43 (S#5236h). Da 11:39.
god. Heb. *El*, Ex +15:2.

12　cut off. Le 18:29. 20:3. Nu 15:30, 31. Jsh
23:12, 13. 1 S 2:31-34. Ho 4:9. 1 C +11:30. He
13:17.
the master and the scholar. *or*, him that
waketh, and him that answereth. 1 Ch 25:8.
Ezr 10:18, 19. Ne 13:28, 29. Ps 134:1. Is 9:14-
16. 24:1, 2. Ezk 14:10. Ho 4:4, 5. Mt +15:14.
2 T 3:13. Re 19:20.
out of. Nu 24:5. Zc 12:7.
and him. ver. 10. Ge 4:3-5. 1 S 3:14. 15:22,
23. Is 61:8. 66:3. Am 5:22.
an offering. Heb. *minchah*, a meal offering,
Le +23:13.

13　covering. Dt 15:9. 1 S 1:9, 10. 2 S 13:19, 20.
Ps 78:34-37. Ec 4:1.
tears. Ps 39:12. Je 11:11.
crying out. Dt +24:15.
insomuch. Dt 26:14. Ezr 10:9-14. Ne 8:9-12.
Pr 15:8. 21:27. Is 1:11-15. Je 6:20.

14　Wherefore. Ml 1:6, 7. 3:8. Pr 30:20. Is 58:3.
Je 8:12.
the Lord. Ml +3:5. Ge 31:50. Jg 11:10. 1 S
12:5. Je 42:5. Mi 1:2.
the wife. ver. 15. Pr 5:18, 19. Ec 9:9. Is 54:6.
1 C 7:10, 11.
thy companion. Ge 2:18. Pr 2:17. SS
1:15mg. Ezk 16:8.

15　did. Ge +1:27. +2:20-24. Mt 19:4-6. Mk 10:6-
8. 1 C 7:2.
make one. Ge 2:24. Dt +6:4.
residue. *or*, excellency.
the spirit. Heb. *ruach*, Is +48:16. Ge +2:7. Jb
+27:3. Ec +12:7. Jn 20:22.
wherefore one. Is 51:2. Ezk 33:24.
That he. Ge 24:3-7, 44. 26:34, 35. 27:46.
28:2-4. Dt 7:4. Ezr 9:2. Ne 13:24. Je 2:21. 1 C
7:14. Ep 6:4. 1 T 3:4, 5, 11, 12. T 1:6.
godly seed. Heb. seed of God. Ge 6:2. Ps
25:13. Pr 11:21. 20:7. Ho 1:10. Ac 3:25. 1 C
7:14. 2 C 6:18.
take heed. ver. 14. Pr +4:23. 6:25. 7:25. Mt
5:28, 29. 15:19. 1 C 7:2-5. Ep 5:28, 33. He
12:15. Ja 1:14, 15. 1 P 3:7.
spirit. Heb. *ruach*, Ps +106:33.
treacherously. *or*, unfaithfully. Ge 2:24. Pr
5:18. Ec 9:9. Mk 10:7. 1 C 7:11. Ep 5:25. 1 P
3:7.
the wife. Ge +4:19.

16　the Lord. Dt 24:1-4. Is 50:1. Mt 5:31, 32.
19:3-9. Mk 10:2-12. Lk 16:18.
that he hateth putting away. *or*, if he hate
her, put *her* away. Heb. to put away. Dt 24:1.
Mt 5:31. Mt 19:6. 1 C 7:27.
covereth. Le 13:47-58. Ps 73:6. 109:18, 29.
Pr 28:13. Is 28:20. 30:1. 59:6. Mi 7:2, 3. Re
7:14.

17　wearied the Lord. Ps 95:9, 10. Is 1:14. 7:13.
43:24. Je 15:6. Ezk 16:43. Am 2:13. Ep +4:30.
Wherein. ver. 14. Ml 1:6, 7. 3:8.
When ye say. Ps +50:16, 17.
Every one. Ml 3:13-15. Jb 34:5-9, 17, 36.
36:17. Ps 73:3-15. Mt 11:18, 19.
Where. Ex 17:7. Dt 32:4. 1 S 2:3. Ps 10:11-
13. Ec 8:11. Is 5:18, 19. +30:18. Ezk 8:12. 9:9.
Zp 1:12. 2 P 3:3, 4.

MALACHI 3

1　Behold. Mt *11:10*.
I will. Ml 2:7. 4:5. Mt 11:10, 11. Mk 1:2, 3.
Lk *1:76. 7:26-28*. Jn 1:6, 7.
send my messenger. Ml 4:5, 6. Mt +11:14.
17:9-13. Mk 9:13. Lk 1:15-17, 76, 77. 7:37.
and he. Is 40:3-5. 62:10. Mt 3:1-3. 17:10-13.
Lk 1:16, 17. 3:3-6. Jn 1:15-23, 33, 34. 3:28-
30. Ac 13:24, 25. 19:4.
and. Ps 110:1. Is +7:14. +9:6. Hg 2:7-9. Lk
2:11, 21-32, 38, 46. 7:19, 20. 19:47. Jn 2:14-
16.
the Lord. Ex 23:20. 33:14, 16. Ne +9:6. Ps
110:1. Zc 13:7. Mt 22:41-45. Ac 2:34-36.
suddenly come. Ge +49:10. Lk 2:1, 2, 7.
to his temple. Hg 2:7, 9. Mt 21:12. Lk 2:27,
32.
even the messenger. Zc +12:8. He 8:6. 9:15.
12:24.
of the covenant. Is +42:6. 49:8. 1 C +15:45.
T 1:2. He +13:20. 1 P 1:20.
he shall come. Hg 2:7. Lk 10:1.
the Lord of hosts. Ps +24:10. Note time gap
between ver. 1, 2 (Is +61:2).

2　who may abide. Ml 4:1. Jl 2:11. Am 5:18-
20. Mt 3:7-12. 21:31-44. 23:13-35. 25:10. Lk
2:34. 3:9, 17. 7:23. 11:37-47, 52-54. +21:36.
Jn 6:42-44. 8:41-48, 55. 9:39-41. 15:22-24.
Ac 7:52-54. Ro 9:31-33. 11:5-10. He 10:28,
29. 12:25. 1 P 2:7, 8. 2 P 3:10. Re 1:6, 7. 6:17.
his coming. Is +35:4.
who shall stand. Ps +1:5.
for. Zc +13:9. Mt +3:11. Re 2:23.
like fullers. Ps 2:7. Is 1:18. Je 2:22. Mk 9:3.
Re +1:5. 7:14. 19:8.
soap. Jb 9:30. Je 2:22. Mk 9:3.

3　sit. Ps 2:4. Pr 25:4. Is 1:25. Je 6:28-30. Ezk
22:18-22. Da 12:10. Lk 3:16. Ep 5:26, 27. T
2:14. He 12:10. 1 P 1:7. Re 3:18.
a refiner. Jb 23:10.
purify. Ps +17:3. Is 1:25mg. Ezk 22:19.
the sons. Ml 1:6-10. 2:1-8. Is 61:6. 66:19-21.
Je 33:18, 22. Ezk 44:15, 16. Re 1:6. 5:10.
purge. Ps 51:7. Is 4:4. Mt 3:12. 2 T 2:20, 21.
as gold and. 2 T 2:20, 21. 1 P 1:7.
that they. Le 6:28. Pr 25:4. 2 C 4:10, 11.
an offering. Ml 1:11. Le +23:13. Ps 4:5.
50:14, 23. 69:30, 31. 107:21, 22. 116:17.
141:1, 2. Ho 14:2. Jn 4:23, 24. Ro 12:1. 15:16.

1 C 2:2. Ep 1:6, 7. Ph 2:17. 4:18. 2 T 4:6. He 13:15, 16. 1 P 2:5, 9.

4 the offering. Ps 51:19. Is 1:26, 27. 56:7. Je 30:18-20. 31:23, 24. Ezk 20:40, 41. 43:26, 27. Zc 8:3. 14:20, 21. Jn 4:24.
as in. 1 Ch 15:26. 16:1-3. 21:26. 29:20-22. 2 Ch 1:6. 7:1-3, 10-12. 8:12-14. 29:31-36. 30:21-27. 31:20, 21. Je 2:2, 3.
of old. Heb. *olam*, Ge +6:4.
former. *or*, ancient. 1 S +24:13 (**S#6931h**).

5 I will come near. Ml 2:17. Ex +32:34. Ps 50:3-6. +96:13. 98:9. Ezk 34:20-22. Lk 18:7, 8. He 10:30, 31. Ja 5:8, 9. Ju 14, 15. Re 2:14, 20-23. 18:21, 23, 24.
a swift. Ml 2:14. Ps 50:7. 81:8. Je 29:23. Mi 1:2. Mt 23:14-35.
the sorcerers. 2 Ch 33:6. Je 7:9, 10. Ezk 22:6-12. Da 2:2. 1 C +6:9, 10. Re +9:21.
adulterers. Ex +20:14. Le 20:10. Dt +5:18, 21. Je 7:9. Ezk 22:11. He +13:4.
false swearers. Le 6:3-5. 19:12. Dt +5:11, 20. Je 7:9. Zc +5:3, 4. 8:17. Re +21:8.
against those. Ex 22:21-24. Le +19:13. Dt +24:14, 15, 17. 27:19. Ps 12:5. Pr 22:22, 23. 23:10, 11. Je 22:13-17. Ezk +16:49. 22:7. Mi 2:2. Ja +5:4, 12.
oppress. *or*, defraud. Ex 22:21. Dt +24:14. Mk 10:19. 1 Th +4:6.
the widow. Is +1:17.
fatherless. Ex +22:22.
stranger. Dt +26:11. Mt +25:35.
fear not. Ge 20:11. 42:18. Ex 1:17. 18:21. Ne 5:15. Jb +21:14, 15. Ps 36:1. Pr 8:13. 16:6. Is 1:2. Je +10:25. 22:13, 16. Lk 18:4. 23:40. Ro 3:18.

6 I am. Ge 15:7, 18. 22:16. Ex 3:14, 15. Ne 9:7, 8. Is 41:13. 42:5-8. 43:11, 12. 44:6. 45:5-8. Je 32:27. Ho 11:9.
I change not. Nu 23:19. 1 S 15:29. Ps 33:11. 102:26. Is +31:2. 59:1. Ho 13:14. Mt 12:32. +28:19. Ro +11:29. He 1:12. 6:17, 18. +13:8. Ja 1:17. Re +1:8. 22:13.
therefore. Ps 78:38, 57. 103:17. 105:7-10. Is 40:28-31. La 3:22, 23. Ro 5:10. 8:28-32. 11:28, 29. Ph 1:6. 2 Th 2:13, 14.
not consumed. Le +26:42. Is +41:8, 9. +54:7-10. +55:3. La 3:22. Zc 10:6.

7 from the. Ex 32:9-14. Dt 9:7-21. 31:20, 27-29. Ne 9:16, 17, 26, 28-30. Ps 78:8-10. Ezk 20:8, 13, 21, 28. Lk 11:48-51. Ac 7:51, 52.
Return unto me. Le 26:40-42. Ezk 18:30-32. Zc +1:3.
Wherein. ver. 13. Ml 1:6. Is 65:2. Mt 23:27. Lk 15:16. Ro 7:9. 10:3, 21.

8 Will a man. Ps 29:2. Pr 3:9, 10. Mt 22:21. Mk 12:17. Lk 20:25. Ro 13:7.
rob. ver. 9. Pr 22:22.
In tithes. Ml 1:8, 13. Ge +14:20. Le 5:15, 16. 27:2-34. Nu 18:21-32. Dt 12:17, etc. 14:22-

29. Jsh 7:11. Ne 10:37-40. 13:4-14. Ps 119:126. Mt +23:23. Ro 2:22.
and offerings. Ex 29:27. Dt 18:3. Ezr +8:25. Ezk 44:30. 1 C 9:13.

9 cursed with a curse. Ml 2:2. Dt 28:15-19. Jsh 7:12, 13. 22:20. Pr +3:33. +26:2. Is 43:28. Da +9:11. Hg 1:6-11. 2:14-17. Zc +5:3. Ga 3:13.

10 all the tithes. Ge 14:20. 2 Ch 31:4-10. Ne 10:33-39. Pr 3:9, 10. Mt 6:2. 23:23. Lk 11:41, 42. 2 C 8:12.
into the storehouse. 1 Ch 26:20. 2 Ch 31:11-19. Ne 10:38. 12:44, 47. 13:5, 10-13.
meat. lit. prey. Ps +111:5mg.
and prove. 1 K 17:13-16. Ps 37:3. Hg 2:19. Mt 6:33. 2 C 9:6-8.
open. Ge 7:11. 8:2. 41:56. Dt 28:12. 2 K 7:2, 19. Ps 78:23. Je 3:3. 5:24, 25. Am 4:7. Zc 10:1. Lk +6:38.
of heaven. Is 64:1.
pour you out. Heb. empty out. Ec 11:3.
a blessing. 1 K 10:13. Ps 37:4. Hg 2:18, 19. Ep 3:20.
that there. Ex 36:6. Le 26:10. 2 Ch +31:10. Lk 5:6, 7. 12:16, 17. Jn 21:6-11. Ep 3:20.

11 rebuke. Jl 2:20. Am 4:9. 7:1-3. Hg 2:17.
the devourer. Jl 1:4. Am 4:9.
destroy. Heb. corrupt. Je 11:19. Ezk 16:47. Da 8:24, 25. 9:26.
neither. Dt 11:14. Is 65:18, 19, 21. Je 8:13. Jl 1:7, 12. 2:22. Mi 4:4. Hab 3:17. Zc 3:10. 8:12.

12 all. Dt 4:6, 7. 2 Ch 32:23. Ps 72:17. Is 61:9. Je 33:9. Zp 3:19, 20. Zc 8:23. Lk 1:48.
a delightsome. Dt 8:7-10. 11:12. Is 62:4. Ezk 20:15. Da 8:9. 11:41. Ho 9:3. Zc 2:12. 7:14mg.

13 Your. Ml 2:17. Ex 5:2. 2 Ch 32:14-19. Jb 34:7, 8. Ps 10:11. Is 5:19. 28:14, 15. 37:23. 2 Th 2:4.
What. ver. 8. Ml 1:6-8. 2:14, 17. Jb 40:8. Je 8:12. Ro 9:20.

14 It is. Jb +21:14, 15. 22:17. 34:9. 35:3. Ps 73:8-13. Is 58:3. Zp 1:12.
ordinance. Heb. observation. Le 18:30. 22:9. 2 K 11:5, 6, 7 (watch). Ezk 40:45mg. 44:8mg. 48:11mg. Hab 2:1 (watch). Zc 3:7mg.
and that. Is 58:3. Jl 2:12. Zc 7:3-6. Ja 4:9.
mournfully. Heb. in black. Is 50:3.

15 we call. Ml 4:1. Est 5:10-14. Ps 10:3, 4. 49:18, 19. 73:3, 12-17. Da 4:30, 31. 37. 5:20-28. Ac 12:21-23. 1 P 5:5.
yea. Ml 2:17. Jb 12:6. 21:7-15, 30. Pr 12:12. Ec 9:1, 2. Je 12:1, 2. Hab 1:13-17.
set. Heb. built. Jb 22:23. Je 12:16.
they that tempt. Ex +17:2.

16 that feared. ver. 5. Ex +18:21. Ps 66:16. 119:74. Pr +3:7. Je 8:6. Re 15:4.
spake often. Dt 6:6-8. 1 S 9:27. 23:16-18. Est 4:5-17. Ps 16:3. 66:16. 73:15-17. 119:27, +63. Pr 13:20. 18:24. Ezk 9:4. Da 2:17, 18. +11:33. Lk 2:38. 24:14-31. Jn 1:40-47. 12:20-

22. Ac 1:13. 2:1. 4:23-30. Ro +15:7. Ep 5:19. 1 Th 5:11, 14. He +3:12, 13. 10:24, 25. 12:15.

one to another. Ro +12:5. +15:7.

the Lord hearkened. 2 S 7:1-4. 2 Ch 6:7, 8. Ps 139:4. Mt 18:19, 20. Ac 4:31-33.

a book. Est 2:23. 6:1. Jb 19:23-25. Is 65:6. Da 7:10. Mt 12:35-37. Re +3:5.

of remembrance. Ex 28:29. Nu 10:10.

feared the Lord. Ps 145:19.

that thought. Ps 5:1. 10:4. 19:14. 20:7. 37:4. 94:19. 104:33, 34. 139:17, 18. Is 26:3mg, 8. He 4:12, 13.

his name. Ps +9:10.

17 **they shall.** SS 2:16. Je 31:33. 32:38, 39. Ezk 16:8. 36:27, 28. Zc +13:9. Jn 10:27-30. 17:6, 9, 10, 24. Ro +11:1. 1 C 3:22, 23. 6:20. 15:23. Ga 5:24. 2 Th 1:7-10. Re 20:12-15.

in that day. Is +2:11. Ezk +38:14. Mt 7:22. 2 Th +1:10.

jewels. *or,* special treasures. Ex +19:5. 1 Ch 29:3. Pr 31:10. Is 62:3, 4.

and I. Ne 13:22. Ps 103:8-13. Is 26:20, 21. Je 31:20. Zp 2:2. Mt 25:34. Ro 8:32. 2 C 6:18. 1 J 3:1-3.

son. Ml 1:6. 1 P 1:13-16.

18 **shall.** ver. 14, 15. Ml 1:4. Jb 6:29. 17:10. Je 12:15. Jl 2:14. Zc 1:6.

discern. Ge +18:25. Jb +2:3. Ps 58:10, 11. 94:13. +149:7, 9. Is 3:10, 11. Je 15:19, 20. Ezk 44:23, 24. Da +12:1-3. Mt +10:15. 13:43, 48-50. +25:46. +28:19. Ro 2:5, 6. 2 Th 1:5-10. Re 20:12.

righteous. Ps 37:16, 17.

between him. Jsh 24:15. Da 3:17-26. Jn 12:26. Ac 16:17. 27:23. Ro 1:9. 6:16-22. 1 Th 1:9.

MALACHI 4

1 **the day.** ver. 5. Ml 3:2. Ezk 7:10. Jl +2:1, 31. Zp 1:14-16. Zc 14:1, 2. Lk 19:43, 44. 21:20-24. 2 P +3:7-12.

shall burn. Is +24:6. 26:11. 29:6. 31:9. Ezk 22:21, 31. Ob 18. Mt +3:12. 2 Th 1:8.

and all the proud. Ml 3:15, 18. Ex 15:7. Ps 1:4-6. +119:21, 119. Is 2:12-17. 5:24. 24:4. 40:24. 41:2. Na 1:10. Lk 1:51, 53. Re 1:7.

stubble. 1 C +3:12.

burn them up. Ps 21:9, 10. Is 24:6. +30:30-33. 47:14. Mt 13:30, 40, 42, 49, 50. Jn 15:6. 2 P +3:7.

that it. Jb 18:16. Am 2:9.

neither root nor. Hab 3:13.

2 **that fear.** Ml +3:16. Pr +3:7. Is 66:1, 2. Re 11:18.

the Sun. Ge 1:16. Jg 5:31. Ps 84:11. +112:4. Is +9:2. 30:26. 49:6, 9. Mt +4:16. Jn 1:4, 8, 14. 9:4, 5. Ac 13:47. Re +2:28.

healing. Ps 103:3. 147:3. Is 53:5. 57:18, 19. Je 17:14. 33:6. Ezk 47:12. Ho 6:1. 14:4. Mt 11:5. Re 22:2.

wings. Ru 2:12. Mt 23:37.

ye shall. Ps 92:12-14. Is 49:9, 10. 55:12, 13. 66:14. Je 31:9-14. Ho 14:5-7. Jn 15:2-5. 2 Th 1:3. 2 P +3:18.

3 **tread down.** Ge +3:15. Jsh 10:24, 25. 2 S 22:43. Jb 40:12. Ps 18:40-42. +58:10. 91:13. 101:8. +149:7, 9. Pr 2:21. 11:31. Is 17:14. 25:10. 26:6. 41:11, 12, 15. 63:3-6. Ezk 38:17-22. 39:6-16. Da 7:18, 27. Mi 4:13. 5:8. 7:10, 15, 16. Zc 9:13-16. 10:5. Jn +18:36. Ro 16:20. Re 11:15. 14:20. 19:19, 20.

ashes. Ezk 28:18.

in the day. Ml 3:17. Ezk +30:3.

4 **the law.** Ex +20:3-17, etc. Is +8:20. 42:21. Mt 5:17-20. 19:16-22. 22:36-40. Mk 12:28-34. Lk 10:25-28. 16:29-31. Jn +5:39-47. Ro 3:31. 13:1-10. Ga 5:13, 14, 24, 25. Ja 2:9-13.

Moses my servant. Nu 12:7.

in Horeb. Dt 4:10.

with the statutes. Ex ch. 21-23. Le ch. 1. Dt +4:1.

5 **I will send.** Ml 3:1. Is +40:3. Mt 11:13, 14. 17:9-13. 27:47-49. Mk 9:11-13. Lk 1:17. 7:26-28. 9:30. Jn 1:21, 25.

Elijah the prophet. 2 Ch 21:12. Mt 17:3. Re 11:3-12.

before the coming. Is 66:7. Jl 2:31. Hab +3:16. Zp 2:2. 3:8. Mt 24:29. Ac 2:20.

great and dreadful. ver. 1. Je +30:7. Ezk +30:3. Da 12:1. Ac 2:19, 20.

day of the Lord. Jl 2:1, 2. 1 C +3:13. 2 Th +1:10. Re 1:10.

6 **turn.** Lk 1:16, *17,* 76.

fathers to the children. Ml 2:13. Ge +18:19. Ex +13:8. 32:29mg. Dt +6:20. 2 S +6:20. 1 Ch +28:9. Jb +1:5. Ps 78:3, 5-8. +101:2. Pr +19:18. +22:6. Is 28:9. 38:19. 2 C 12:14. Ep 6:4. Col 3:21. 1 T 3:4. +5:8. 2 T +3:14-17.

children to their fathers. Ex +20:12. Ps 34:11. Pr 7:1. 17:6. Ec 12:1. Is 45:10. Ezk 20:18. Mi 7:6. Ph +2:12.

lest. Is 61:2. Da +9:26, 27. Zc 11:6. 13:8. 14:2. Mt 22:7. 23:35-38. 24:27-30. Mk 13:14-26. Lk 19:41-44. 21:22-27.

and smite. Is +24:6. Je +26:6. Da +9:11. Zc +5:3. 14:12. Mk 11:21. Ga 3:10. He 6:8. 10:26-31. Re 22:3, 20, 21.

THE NEW TESTAMENT

MATTHEW

MATTHEW 1

1 A.M. 4000. B.C. 5.
generation. Ge 2:4. 5:1. 37:2. Is 53:8. Lk 3:23-38. Ro 9:5.
Christ. Mt 27:17. Col 4:11.
of David. Mt 9:27. 12:23. 15:22. 20:30, 31. 21:9, 15. 22:42-45. 2 S 7:12, 13, 16. Ps 89:36. 132:11. Is 7:13, 14. +9:6, 7. 11:1. Je +23:5. 33:15-17, 26. Ezk 34:23, 24. 37:24, 25. Am 9:11. Zc 12:8. Mk 10:47, 48. 12:35. Lk 1:31, 32, 69, 70. 18:38, 39. Jn 7:42. Ac 2:30. +13:22, 23. Ro 1:3, 4. 2 T 2:8. Re 22:16.
of Abraham. Ge +12:3. +22:18. Lk +3:34. He 2:16.

2 **Abraham**. Ge 21:2-5. Jsh 24:2, 3. 1 Ch 1:28. Is 51:2. Lk +3:34. Ac 7:8. Ro 9:7-9. He 11:11, 17, 18.
begat Isaac. Ge +17:19. 21:12.
Isaac begat. Ge 25:26. Jsh 24:4. 1 Ch 1:34. Is 41:8. Ml 1:2, 3. Ro 9:10-13.
Jacob. i.e. *supplanter*, S#2384g. ver. 2, 15, 16. Mt 8:11. 22:32. Mk 12:26. Lk 1:33. 3:34. 13:28. 20:37. Jn 4:5, 6, 12. Ac 3:13. 7:8, 12, 14, 15, 32, 46. Ro 9:13. 11:26. For S#3290h, see Ge +25:26.
Jacob begat. Ge 29:32-35. 30:5-20. 35:16-19. 46:8, etc. 49:8-12. Ex 1:2-5. Nu +24:17. 1 Ch 2:1, etc. 5:1, 2. Lk 1:33. 3:23, 33, 34. Ac 7:8. He 7:14. Re 7:5, Juda.
Judas. Ge +49:10. 1 Ch +5:2. Ps +60:7. He 7:14.

3 **Judas**. Ge +35:23.
Phares. i.e. *divisions*, S#5329g. Mt 1:3. Lk 3:33. For S#6557h, see Ge +46:12, Pharez.
Zara. i.e. *a rising; clearness*, S#2196g. For S#2226h, see Ge +38:30, Zarah.
Thamar. i.e. *a palm tree*, S#2283g. For S#8559h, see Ge +38:6, Tamar. Ge 38:6, 11, 24-26, Tamar. 1 Ch 2:4.
and Phares. Ge 46:12. Nu 26:21. Ru 4:12, 18. 1 Ch 2:5. 4:1, Hezron. Lk +3:33.
Aram. i.e. *exalted*, S#689g. Lk 3:33. For S#7410h, see Jb +32:2, Ram. Ru 4:19. 1 Ch 2:9, Ram.

4 **Aminadab**. 1 Ch +15:11.
Naasson. i.e. *serpent, enchanter*, S#3476g. Lk 3:32. For S#5177h, see 1 Ch +2:10, Nahshon.

5 **Salmon**. Ru 4:21. 1 Ch 2:11, 12, Salma, Boaz.
Booz. S#1003g. ver. 5. Lk 3:32. For S#1162h, see Ru +2:1, Boaz.
Rachab. i.e. *breadth*, S#4477g. See also S#4460h: He +11:31, Rahab. Ja 2:25. For S#7343h, see Jsh +2:1, Rahab. Jsh 2:1, etc. 6:22-25. He 11:31. Ja 2:25, Rahab.
Booz. Ru 1:4, 16, 17, 22. ch. 2-4.
Ruth. i.e. *satisfied*, S#4503g. For S#7327h, see Ru +1:4, Ruth.
Obed. Ru 4:13, 21, 22.
Obed begat. Lk 3:32.
Jesse. i.e. *substance*, S#2421g. ver. 5, 6. Lk 3:32. Ac 13:22. Ro 15:12. For S#3448h, see 1 Ch +2:12, Jesse.

6 **Jesse**. 1 Ch +2:12. Is *11:1, 10*.
David. i.e. *beloved*, S#1138g. ver. 1, 6, 17, 20. Mt 9:27. 12:3, 23. 15:22. 20:30, 31. 21:9, 15. 22:42, 43, 45. Mk 2:25. 10:47, 48. 11:10. 12:35-37. Lk 1:27, 32, 69. 2:4, 11. 3:31. 6:3. 18:38, 39. 20:41, 42, 44. Jn 7:42. Ac 1:16. 2:25, 29, 34. 4:25. 7:45. 13:22, 34, 36. 15:16. Ro 1:3. 4:6. 11:9. 2 T 2:8. He 4:7. 11:32. Re 3:7. 5:5. 22:16. For S#1732h, see 1 S +16:19, David.
Solomon. i.e. *peaceableness*, S#4672g. ver. 6, 7. Mt 6:29. 12:42. Lk 11:31. 12:27. Jn 10:23. Ac 3:11. 5:12. 7:47. For S#8010h, see 2 S +5:14, Solomon. 2 S 12:24, 25. 1 Ch 3:5. 14:4. 28:5.
her. 2 S 11:3, 26, 27. 1 K 1:11-17, 28-31. 15:5. Ro 8:3.
Urias. i.e. *flame of Jehovah*, S#3774g. For S#223h, see 2 S +11:3, Uriah. 2 S 23:39. 1 Ch 11:41, Uriah.

7 **Roboam**. i.e. *enlargement of the people*, S#4497g. For S#7346h, see 1 K +14:21, Rehoboam.
Abia. i.e. *worshipper of Jehovah*, S#7g. ver. 7. Lk 1:5. For S#29h, see 1 S +8:2, Abiah. 1 Ch +3:10, Abia. 1 K 14:31, Abijam. 2 Ch 12:1, Abijah.
Asa. i.e. *curing*, S#760g. ver. 7, 8. For S#609h, see 1 Ch +9:16, Asa.

8 **Josaphat**. i.e. *Jehovah is judge*, S#2498g. For S#3092h, see 2 S +8:16, Jehoshaphat.
Joram. i.e. *height; Jehovah has exalted*, S#2496g. For S#3141h, see 1 Ch +26:25, Joram.

begat. A comparison with Old Testament history shows Matthew compressed his genealogy at this point, omitting Ahaziah (2 K 8:25), Joash (2 K 11:2), Amaziah (2 K 14:1), who belong between Joram (2 K 8:24) and Uzziah (2 Ch 26:1). 1 K +15:10.

Ozias. i.e. *strength of God,* S#3604g. ver. 8, 9. For S#5818h, see 2 Ch +26:1, Uzziah.

9　**Joatham**. i.e. *Jehovah is perfect; God showed himself wholly,* S#2488g. For S#3147h, see Jg +9:5, Jotham.

Achaz. i.e. *possessor,* S#881g. For S#271h, see 1 Ch +8:35, Ahaz.

Ezekias. i.e. *strength of God,* S#1478g. ver. 9, 10. For S#2396h, see 2 K +16:20, Hezekiah. ch. 18-20. 2 Ch 28:27. ch. 29-32. Is ch. 36-39, Hezekiah.

10　**Manasses**. i.e. *forgetfulness,* S#3128g. Re 7:6. For S#4519h, see Ge +41:51, Manasseh.

Amon. i.e. *son* or *foster-child,* S#300g. For S#526h, see Ne +7:59, Amon.

Josias. i.e. *sustained of Jehovah,* S#2502g. ver. 11. For S#2977h, see 1 K +13:2, Josiah.

11　**Josias**. "Some read, Josias begat Jakim, and Jakim begat Jechonias."

Jechonias. i.e. *whom God establishes,* S#2423g. ver. 11, 12. For S#3204h, see Je +24:1, Jeconiah. Je 22:30.

about. 2 K 24:14-16. 25:11. 2 Ch 36:10, 20. Je 27:20. 39:9. 52:11-15, 28-30. Da 1:2.

12　**Jechonias**. 2 K +24:8, Jehoiachin. Je +22:24, Coniah. Je +24:1, Jeconiah.

Salathiel. i.e. *the loan of God,* S#4528g. ver. 12. Lk 3:27. For S#7597h, see Hg +1:1, Shealtiel.

and. Ezr 3:2. 5:2. Ne 12:1. Hg 1:1, 12, 14. 2:2, 23, Shealtiel, Zerubbabel. Lk 3:27.

Zorobabel. i.e. *born at Babylon; dispelling of human illusions,* S#2216g. ver. 12, 13. Lk 3:27. For S#2216h, see Hg +1:1, Zerubbabel.

13　**Abiud**. i.e. *the honor of a father,* S#10g. For S#31h, see 1 Ch +8:3, Abihud.

Azor. i.e. *helpful,* S#107g. ver. 13, 14. Compare S#5809h, Je +28:1, Azur.

14　**Sadoc**. i.e. *righteous,* S#4524g. For S#6659h, see 2 S +8:17, Zadok.

Achim. i.e. *judicious,* S#885g. Compare S#3137h, 1 Ch +4:22, Jokim.

Eliud. i.e. *God of majesty,* S#1664g. ver. 14, 15.

15　**Eleazar**. i.e. *God has helped,* S#1648g. For S#499h, see Ex +6:23, Eleazar.

Matthan. i.e. *a gift,* S#3157g. For S#4977h, see 2 K +11:18, Mattan.

16　**Joseph**. i.e. *to progress; he shall add,* S#2501g. ver. 16, 18, 19, 20, 24. Mt 2:13, 19. Lk 1:27. 2:4, 16, 33, 43. 3:23. 4:22. Jn 1:45. 6:42. For S#3130h, see Ge +30:24, Joseph.

Mary. i.e. *myrrh of the sea,* S#3137g. For S#4813h, see Ex +15:20, Miriam.

of whom. The Greek reference is to Mary, not Joseph (compare verse +11, especially Je

22:30). Mk +6:3. Lk 1:31-35. 2:7, 10, 11.

Jesus. i.e. *Savior,* S#2424g. For S#3091h, see Ex +17:9, Joshua.

who. Mt 27:17, 22. Jn 4:25.

17　**Christ**. ver. 18. Mt +16:16.

18　**the birth**. Lk 1:27, etc.

espoused. Ge 24:53. Jg 14:8. Lk 1:26, 27. Jn 3:29.

before. Mt 26:34, 75. Ge 29:26-28. Ex 1:19. Jg 14:8. Is +7:*14*, 16. Lk 3:23. Mk 14:30, 72. Lk 2:26. 22:34, 61. Jn 4:49. 8:41, 58. 14:9. Ac 2:20. 7:2. 25:16. Ga 4:4.

came together. Ge 6:4. 38:18. Dt 20:7. Ru +4:13. 1 C 7:5.

of the Holy Ghost. Ge 1:2. +3:15. Jb 14:4. 15:14. Ps 104:30. Lk 1:25, +35. Ga 4:4, 5. He 7:26. 10:5.

19　**Joseph**. ver. 20.

her husband. Le 19:20. Dt 22:23, 24.

a just. Ge 6:9. Ps 112:4, 5. Mk 6:20. Lk 2:25. Ac 10:22.

a public. Ge 38:24. Le 20:10. Dt 22:21-24. Jn 8:4, 5.

was minded. Dt 24:1-4. Mk 10:4.

20　**while**. Ps 25:8, 9. 94:19. 119:125. 143:8. Pr 3:5, 6. 12:5. Is 26:3mg. 30:21.

the angel. Jg 13:3, 8, 9. Lk 1:10-13, 19, 26, etc. 2:8-14.

in a dream. Mt 2:13, 19, 22. Ge +31:24. Jl 2:28.

Joseph. Is 7:2, 13. Je 33:26. Lk 2:4.

fear not. Mt 28:5. Ge 46:3. Dt 22:21. 1 K 17:13. Is 51:7. Je 40:9. Lk 1:30.

for that. ver. 18. Je 31:22.

conceived. Gr. begotten. S#1080g. ver. 2 (begat). Mt 2:1 (born). 19:12. 26:24. Mk 14:21. Lk 1:13 (bear). Jn 1:13 (born). 3:3-8. 8:41. Ac 13:33. 1 C 4:15. Phm 10. He 1:5. 5:5. 11:12 (sprang), 23. 1 J 2:29. 3:9. 4:7. 5:1, 4, 18.

21　**she**. Ge 17:19, 21. 18:10. Jg 13:3. 2 K 4:16, 17. Lk 1:13, 35, 36. Ga 4:4, 5.

thou. Lk 1:31. 2:21.

JESUS. *that is,* Savior, Heb. Nu 13:16. 14:6. Ne 8:17. Hg 1:1. Zc 3:1. Lk 1:31.

for he shall save. Ps 130:7, +8. Is 12:1, 2. 45:21, 22. Je 23:6. 33:16. Ezk 36:25-29. Zc +9:9. Lk +19:10. Jn +1:29. Ac 4:12. 13:23, 38, 39. 2 C 5:19. Ep 5:25-27. Col 1:20-23. 1 T +1:15. 4:10. 1 J 1:7. 2:1, 2. Re +1:5, 6. 7:14.

from their. Mt 20:28. Ac 3:26. +10:43. Ro 8:32. 2 C 5:21. Ga 1:3, 4. Ep 5:2. Col 1:14. 1 T +2:6. T 2:14. 1 P 3:18.

sins. Le +5:6.

22　**that**. Mt 2:15, 23. 5:17. 8:17. 12:17. 13:35. 21:4. 1 K 8:15, 24. Ezr 1:1. Lk 21:22. 24:44. Jn +10:35. 12:38-40. 15:25. 17:12. 18:9. 19:24, 28, 36, 37. Ac 3:18. 13:27-29. Re 17:17.

23　**a virgin**. Is +7:*14*. +9:6. 11:1. S#3933g. ver. 23. Mt 25:1, 7, 11. Lk 1:27, 27. Ac 21:9. 1 C 7:25, 28, 34, 36, 37. 2 C 11:2. Re 14:4.

they shall call his name. *or,* his name shall be called.

Emmanuel. Is +7:14. 8:8, Immanuel.

God with us. Mt +28:20. Is 7:14. +9:6, 7. +12:2. 43:10, 11. 44:6. Mi +5:2. Lk 1:32, 33. Jn 1:1, 14. Ac +20:28. Ro 1:3, 4. 9:5. 2 C 5:19. Ph 2:5, 6. Col +1:15, 16. 2:9. 1 T 3:16. He 1:3, +8. 2 P 1:1. 1 J 3:16.

24 did as. Ge 6:22. 7:5. 22:2, 3. Ex 40:16, 19, 25, 27, 32. 2 K 5:11-14. Jn 2:5-8. +15:14. He 11:7, 8, 24-31. Ja 2:21-26.

25 knew. Ge +4:1.

till. ver. +18. Mk +6:3. Lk 2:7.

she had. Ex 13:2. 22:29. Lk 2:7. Ro 8:29.

and he. Lk 2:21.

firstborn. Ex 13:2. Lk 2:7, 21.

MATTHEW 2

1 A.M. 4001. B.C. 4. "Fourth year before the account called *Anno Domini.*"

Jesus. Mt 1:25. Lk 2:4-7.

Bethlehem. i.e. *house of bread,* **S#965g**. ver. 5, 6, 8, 16. 1 S 16:1. Mi +5:2. Lk 2:4, 11, 15. Jn 7:42. For **S#1035h**, see Jsh +19:15.

of Judaea. Jsh 19:15. He 7:14.

the days. Ps +102:11.

Herod. i.e. *mount of pride,* **S#2264g**. ver. 1, 3, 7, 12, 13, 15, 16, 19, 22. Mt 14:1, 3, 6. Mk 6:14, 16-18, 20-22. 8:15. Lk 1:5. 3:1, 19, 19. 8:3. 9:7, 9. 13:31. 23:7, 8, 11, 12, 15. Ac 4:27. 12:1, 6, 11, 19, 20, 21. 13:1. 23:35.

the king ver. 3, 19. Ge +49:10. Da +9:24, 25. Hg 2:6-9.

there came. Ps **72:10**.

wise men. Mt 12:42. Ezr 7:9. Est 1:13. Je 39:3, 13. Da 2:12, 48. 4:6.

from the east. Ge +29:1. Ps 72:9-12. Is 60:1-7, 11.

to. Lk 2:22.

Jerusalem. i.e. *foundation of peace,* **S#2414g**. ver. 1, 3. 3:5. Mt 4:25. 5:35. 15:1. 16:21. 20:17, 18. 21:1, 10. Mk 3:8, 22. 7:1. 10:32, 33. 11:11, 15, 27. 15:41. Lk 2:22, 42. 18:31. 19:28. 23:7. Jn 1:19. 2:13, 23. 4:20, 21, 45. 5:1, 2. 10:22. 11:18, 55. 12:12. Ac 1:4. 8:1, 14. 11:2, 22, 27. 13:13. 18:21. 20:16. 21:17. 25:1, 7, 9, 15, 24. 26:4, 10, 20. 28:17. Ga 1:17, 18. 2:1. See also **S#2419g**, Mk +11:1. For **S#3389h**, see Jsh +10:1.

2 born. Is +9:6, 7. 32:1, 2. Je 30:9. Lk 1:32, 33. 2:11. 23:3, 38.

King. Jn +1:49.

his star. Nu +24:17. Is 60:3. Lk 1:78, 79. 2 P 1:19. Re 2:28. 22:16.

are come. Ge +49:10.

worship. ver. 10, 11. Ps 45:11. Jn 5:23. 9:38. +20:28. He 1:6.

3 he. Mt 8:29. 23:37. 1 K 18:17, 18. Lk 2:25, 38. Jn 11:47, 48. Ac 4:2, 24-27. 5:24-28. 16:20, 21. 17:6, 7.

4 the chief. Mt 21:15, 23. 26:3, 47. 27:1. 1 Ch 24:4, etc. 2 Ch 36:14. Ezr 10:5. Ne 12:7. Ps 2:2. Lk 1:5. Jn 7:32. 18:3.

scribes. Mt 7:29. 13:52. 2 Ch 23:8. 34:13, 15. Ezr 7:6, 11, 12. Je 8:8. Mk 8:31. Lk 20:19. 23:10. Jn 8:3. Ac 4:5. 6:12. 23:9.

he demanded. Ml +2:7. Jn 3:10.

should be. The present tense is used for the future, to show that something will certainly come to pass, and is spoken of as though it were already present. For other examples of this usage see Mt 3:10. 5:46. 11:3. 17:11. 26:2, 29. Mk 9:31. Lk 13:32. 17:21. Jn 12:26, 31, 34. Ro 8:30. 1 C 15:2, 12, 42-44. 2 C 5:1. Ep 1:3. Col 1:13. He 12:28. 2 P 3:11, 12.

5 they said. Jn +6:14.

In Bethlehem. Ge 35:19. Jsh 19:15. Ru 1:1, 19. 2:4. 4:11. 1 S 16:1. Mi +5:2. Jn 7:42.

6 Bethlehem. ver. 1. Mi +5:2. Jn 7:42.

of Judah. Ge 35:16, 19. 48:7. 1 Ch +5:2. Mi +5:2. He 7:14. Re 5:5.

princes. "Princes" are put for the thousands whom they led. Jg 6:15mg. 1 S 10:19. Mi +5:2.

a Governor. Mt 28:18. Ge +17:6. +49:10. Nu +24:19. 1 Ch +5:2. Ps 2:1-6. Is +9:6, 7. Ep 1:22. Col 1:18. He 7:5. Re 2:27. 11:15.

rule. *or,* feed. Is +40:11. Ezk 37:24-26. Re +2:27.

Israel. i.e. *prince with God,* **S#2474g**. ver. 6, 20, 21. Mt 8:10. 9:33. 10:6, 23. 15:24, 31. 19:28. 27:9, 42. Mk 12:29. 15:32. Lk 1:16, 54, 68, 80. 2:25, 32, 34. 4:25, 27. 7:9. 22:30. 24:21. Jn 1:31, 49. 3:10. 12:13. Ac 1:6. 2:36. 4:8, 10, 27. 5:21, 31. 7:23, 37, 42. 9:15. 10:36. 13:17, 23, 24. 28:20. Ro 9:6, 27, 31. 10:1, 19, 21. 11:2, 7, 25, 26. 1 C 10:18. 2 C 3:7, 13. Ga 6:16. Ep 2:12. Ph 3:5. He 8:8, 10. 11:22. Re 2:14. 7:4. 21:12. For **S#3478h**, see Ge +32:28.

7 when he. Mt 26:3-5. Ex 1:10. 1 S 18:21. Ps 10:9, 10. 55:21. 64:4-6. 83:3, 4. Is 7:5-7. Ezk 38:10, 11. Re 12:1-5, 15.

8 Go. 1 S 23:22, 23. 2 S 17:14. 1 K 19:2. Jb 5:12, 13. Ps 33:10, 11. Pr +21:30. La 3:37. 1 C 3:19, 20.

that. Mt 26:48, 49. 2 S 15:7-12. 2 K 10:18, 19. Ezr 4:1, 2. Ps 12:2, 3. 55:11-15. Pr 26:24, 25. Je 41:5-7. Lk 20:20, 21.

9 the star. ver. 2. Ps 25:12. Pr 2:1-6. 8:17. 2 P 1:19.

10 they rejoiced. Dt 32:43. Ps 67:4. 105:3. Lk 2:10, 11, 20. Ac 13:46-48. Ro 15:9-13.

11 they saw. Lk 2:16, 26-32, 38.

fell. Ge +17:3.

worshipped. ver. 2. Mt +4:9, 10. +8:2. +14:33. Ps 2:12. 95:6. Is *49:7*. Jn 5:22, 23. Ac 10:25, 26. He 1:6. Re +19:10. +22:8-10.

presented. *or,* offered. Jg +3:15. Ps **72:10, 15**. Is **60:6**.

gold. Ps 72:15. Is 60:6.

frankincense. Ex 30:34. Le 2:1, 2, 15. 5:11.
6:15. 24:7. Nu 7:14, 86. 1 Ch 9:29. Ne 13:5. SS
3:6. 4:6, 14. Is 60:6. Ml 1:11. Re 5:8mg. 18:13.
myrrh. Ge 37:25. 43:11. Ex 30:23. Est 2:12.
Ps 45:8. Pr 7:17. SS 1:13. 3:6. 4:6, 14. 5:1, 5,
13. Mk 15:23. Jn 19:39.

12 **warned**. ver. 22. Lk 2:26.
in a dream. ver. 13, 19, 22. Mt 1:20. 27:19.
Ge +31:24.
they departed. Ex 1:17. Ac 4:19. +5:29. 1 C
3:19.

13 **the angel**. ver. 19. Mt 1:20. Ac 5:19. 10:7,
22. 12:11. He 1:13, 14.
Arise. Mt 10:23. Pr +22:3. Re 12:6, 14.
Egypt. i.e. *tribulation*, **S#125g**. ver. 14, 15, 19.
Ac 2:10. 7:9, 10-12, 15, 17, 34, 36, 39, 40.
13:17. He 3:16. 8:9. 11:26, 27. Ju 5. Re 11:8.
be thou there. Ex 1:17, 19-21. Da 6:10. Ac
5:29.
until. ver. 19, 20. Jsh 3:13, 17. 4:10, 18. Da
3:25, 26. Ac 16:36.
for. ver. 16. Ex 1:22. 2:2, 3. Jb 33:15, 17. Ac
7:19. Re 12:4.
destroy. Ex 1:22. Gr. *apollumi*, **S#622g**.
Rendered (1) *destroy*: ver. 13. Mt +10:28.
12:14. 21:41. 22:7. 27:20. Mk 1:24. 3:6. 9:22.
11:18. 12:9. Lk 4:34. 6:9. 9:56. 17:27, 29.
19:47. 20:16. Jn 10:10. Ro 14:15. 1 C 1:19.
10:9, 10. 2 C 4:9. Ja 4:12. Ju 5. (2) *lose*: Mt
10:39, 42. 16:25. Mk 8:35, 35. 9:41. Lk 9:24,
25. 15:4, 8, 9. 17:33, 33. Jn 6:39. 12:25.
17:12. 18:9. 2 J 8. (3) *be lost*: Mt 18:11. Lk
15:4b, 6. 19:10. 2 C 4:3. (4) *lost*: Mt 10:6.
15:24. Lk 15:24, 32. Jn 6:12. (5) *perish*: Mt
5:29, 30. 8:25. 9:17. 18:14. 26:52. Mk 4:38.
Lk 5:37. 8:24. 11:51. 13:3, 5, 33. 15:17. 21:18.
Jn 3:15, 16. 6:27. 10:28. 11:50. Ac 5:37. Ro
2:12. 1 C 1:18. 8:11. 15:18. 2 C 2:15. 2 Th
2:10. He 1:11. Ja 1:11. 1 P 1:7. 2 P 3:6, 9. Ju
11. (6) *be marred*: Mk 2:22. (7) *die*: Jn 18:14.

14 **he took**. ver. 20, 21. Mt 1:24. Ac 26:19.
into Egypt. Ge 37:28.

15 **until**. ver. 19. Ac 12:1-4, 23, 24.
that. ver. 17, 23. Mt 1:22. 4:14, 15. 8:17.
12:16-18. 21:4. 26:54, 56. 27:35. Lk 24:44. Jn
19:28, 36. Ac 1:16.
Out. Ge 37:36. Ex 4:22, 23. Nu 24:8. Ho *11:1*.
He 11:27.

16 **when**. Ge 39:14, 17. Nu 22:29. 24:10. Jg
16:10. Jb 12:4.
was exceeding. Pr 27:3, 4. Da 3:13, 19, 20.
and slew. Ge 49:7. 2 K 8:12. Pr 28:15, 17. Is
+26:20, 21. 59:7. Ho 10:14. Re 17:6.
according. ver. 7.

17 **fulfilled**. ver. 15. Je *31:15*.
Jeremy. i.e. *exalted of the Lord*, **S#2408g**. Mt
2:17. 16:14. 27:9. For **S#3414h**, see Je +1:1.

18 **Rama**. i.e. *height*, **S#4471g**. For **S#7414h**, see Je
+31:15, Ramah.
a voice. Je *31:15*.

lamentation. Je 4:31. 9:17-21. Ezk 2:10. Re
8:13.
Rachel. i.e. *a ewe*, **S#4478g**. For **S#7354g**, see Ge
+29:28. Ge 35:16-20. 48:7. 1 S 10:2. Je *31:15*.
would. Ge 37:30, 33-35. 42:36. Jb 14:10.
are not. Ge 37:30. 42:13, 36. Je 10:20. La
5:7.

19 **Herod**. Ps 76:10. Is 51:12. Da 8:25. 11:45.
an angel. ver. 13. Mt 1:20. Ps 139:7. Je
30:10. Ezk 11:16.

20 **Arise**. ver. 13. Pr +3:5, 6.
for. Ex 4:19. 1 K 11:21, 40. 12:1-3.
child's. Mt +10:28. 26:38. Ge +12:13. Mk 3:4.
14:34. Lk 6:9. 17:33. Jn 12:25. Ac 3:23. Ro
11:3. He 10:39. Ja 5:20. Re 6:9. 8:9. 12:11.
16:3.
life. Gr. *psuche* or *psyche*, **S#5590g**. The uses of
psyche may be classified as follows: (1) The
natural life of the body, ver. 20. Mt 6:25, 25.
10:39, 39. 16:25, 25. 20:28. Mk 3:4. 8:35, 35.
10:45. Lk 6:9. 9:56. 12:22, 23. 14:26. 17:33a.
Jn 10:11, 15, 17. 12:25a, 25b. 13:37, 38.
15:13. Ac 15:26. 20:10, 24. 27:10, 22. Ro
11:3. 16:4. Ph 2:30. 1 J 3:16, 16. Re 8:9.
12:11. Rendered "soul," Mt 16:26, 26. Mk
8:36, 37. Lk 12:20. 1 Th 2:8. (2) The immaterial, invisible part of man: Mt 10:28. Ac 2:27,
31. 1 Th 5:23. He 4:12. (3) The disembodied
man (2 C 5:3, 4. 12:2): Re 6:9. 20:4. (4) The
seat of personality: Lk 9:24, 24. He 6:19.
10:39. (5) The seat of perception, feeling,
desire: Mt 11:29. Lk 1:46. 2:35. Ac 14:2
(mind), 22. 15:24. (6) The seat of will and
purpose: Mt 22:37. Mk 12:30, 33. Lk 10:27.
Ac 4:32. Ep 6:6. Ph 1:27. Col 3:23. He 12:3.
(7) The seat of appetite: Re 18:14. (8) Soul
put for person: an integral part of man (individually) is put for the whole person. Used of
persons or individuals: Ac 2:41, 43. 3:23.
7:14. 27:37. Ro 2:9. 13:1. Ja 5:20. 1 P 3:20. 2
P 2:14. Re 18:13. (9) The expression "my
soul," "his soul," etc., is an idiom for *me*,
myself, himself, etc. Used to emphasize the personal pronoun (a) in the first person: Mt
12:18. 26:38. Mk 14:34. Lk 12:19, 19. Jn
10:24 (us). 12:27. 2 C 1:23. He 10:38 (soul);
(b) in the second person: 2 C 12:15mg. He
13:17. Ja 1:21. 1 P 1:9, 22. 2:25; (c) in the
third person: 1 P 4:19. 2 P 2:8. (10) "Soul"
(Gr. *psyche*) is also used of animals. An ani-
mate creature, human or other: 1 C 15:45. Re
16:3. (11) The "inward man," seat of the new
life: Lk 21:19. 1 P 2:11. 3 J 2. Compare the
classification of the corresponding Old
Testament term *nephesh* at Ge +2:7.

21 **he arose**. Ge 6:22. He 11:8.

22 **Archelaus**. i.e. *ruling the people*, **S#745g**.
he was. Ge 19:17-21. 1 S 16:2. Ac 9:13, 14.
being. ver. 12. Mt 1:20. Ps 48:14. 73:24.
107:6, 7. 121:8. Is 30:21. 48:17, 18.

into. Mt 3:13. Lk 2:39. Jn 7:41, 42, 52.

Galilee. i.e. *circuit*, **S#1056g**. Mt 3:13. 4:12, 15, 18, 23, 25. 15:29. 17:22. 19:1. 21:11. 26:32. 27:55. 28:7, 10, 16. Mk 1:9, 14, 16, 28, 39. 3:7. 6:21. 7:31. 9:30. 14:28. 15:41. 16:7. Lk 1:26. 2:4, 39. 3:1. 4:14, 31, 44. 5:17. 8:26. 17:11. 23:5, 6, 49, 55. 24:6. Jn 1:43. 2:1, 11. 4:3, 43, 46, 47, 54. 6:1. 7:1, 9, 41, 52. 12:21. 21:2. Ac 9:31. 10:37. 13:31. For **S#1551h**, see Jsh +20:7.

23 Nazareth. i.e. *guarded*, **S#3478g**. Mt 4:13. 21:11. Mk 1:9, +24. Lk 1:26. 2:4, 39, 51. 4:16, 34. 18:37. Jn 1:46.

He shall. Mt 26:71. Nu 6:13. Jg 13:5. 1 S 1:11. Ps 69:9, 10. Is 11:1. 53:1, 2. Am 2:10-12. Jn 1:45, 46. Ac 24:5.

Nazarene. i.e. *kept, guarded, preserved; a flower*, **S#3480g**. ver. 23. Mt 26:71. Mk 10:47. Lk 18:37. 24:19. Jn 18:5, 7. 19:19. Ac 2:22. 3:6. 4:10. 6:14. 22:8. 24:5. 26:9.

MATTHEW 3

1 those. Lk 3:1, 2.

John. Mt 11:11. 14:2, etc. 16:14. 17:12, 13. 21:25-27, 32. Mk 1:4, 15. 6:16-29. Lk 1:13-17, 76. 3:2-20. Jn 1:6-8, 15-36. 3:27-36. Ac 1:22. 13:24, 25. 19:3, 4.

John. Lk 1:13. Jn 1:6, 7.

Baptist. Gr. *baptistees*, **S#910g**. ver. 1. Mt 11:11, 12. 14:2, 8. 16:14. 17:13. Mk 6:24, 25. 8:28. Lk 7:20, 28, 33. 9:19.

preaching. Is 40:3-6. Mk 1:7. Lk 1:17.

the wilderness. Mt 4:1. 11:7. Jsh 14:10. 15:61, 62. Jg 1:16. Lk 7:24.

2 Repent. Mt 12:41. 21:29-32. 1 K 8:47. Jb 42:6. Ml 4:5, 6. Lk 1:16, 17. 3:3. +13:3. 16:30. 2 C 7:10. 2 T 2:25. He 6:1. 2 P 3:9.

kingdom of. Mt +4:17. 6:10, 33. Mk +1:15.

heaven. Ps +73:9.

at hand. Mt 4:17. 10:7. +21:43.

3 by. Is *40:3*. Mk 1:3. Lk 3:3-6. Jn 1:23.

Esaias. i.e. *salvation of Jehovah*, **S#2268g**. ver. 3. Mt 4:14. 8:17. 12:17. 13:14. 15:7. Mk 7:6. Lk 3:4. 4:17. Jn 1:23. 12:38, 39, 41. Ac 8:28, 30. 28:25. Ro 9:27, 29. 10:16, 20. 15:12. For **S#3470h**, see Is +1:1, Isaiah.

The voice. Jn 1:23.

Prepare. Ps 68:4. Is *40:3*. 57:14, 15. Ml 3:1. Lk 1:17, 76. 3:4.

the Lord. Ne +9:6. Is *40:3*, Jehovah. Jn 8:24. 1 C 12:3.

4 John had. Is 63:1-6. Ezk 16:4-26.

his raiment. Mt 11:8. 2 K 1:8. Is 20:2. Zc 13:4. Ml 4:5. Mk 1:6. Lk 1:17, 76. 7:25. He 11:37. Re 11:3.

and his. Mt 11:18. Le 11:22. Lk 7:33.

wild. Dt 32:13. 1 S 14:25-27. Ps 81:16.

5 went out. Mt 4:25. 11:7-12. Mk 1:5. Lk 3:7. 16:16. Jn 3:23. 5:35.

Jerusalem. Ge +47:15.

and all. Ex +9:6. 2 Ch 29:36.

Judea. Ge +47:15.

region. Ge 13:10, 11. 1 K 7:46. 2 Ch 4:17.

round about. Mt 19:1.

Jordan. i.e. *the descender*, **S#2446g**. ver. 5, 6, 13. Mt 4:15, 25. 19:1. Mk 1:5, 9. 3:8. 10:1. Lk 3:3. 4:1. Jn 1:28. 3:26. 10:40.

6 were. ver. 11, 13-16. Ezk 36:25. Mk 1:8, 9. Lk 3:16. Jn 1:25-28, 31-33. 3:5, 23-25. 4:2. Ac +1:5. +2:38-41. 8:13, 23. 9:17, 18. 10:36-38. 11:16. 19:4, 5, 18. +22:16. Ro 6:3, 4, 11. 1 C 1:14-17. 6:11. 7:19. 10:2. Ga 3:26, 27. Ep 4:5. 5:25, 26. Col 2:12. T 3:5, 6. He 6:2. 9:10. 1 P 3:21.

baptized. Gr. *baptizo*, **S#907g**. ver. 6, 11, 13, 14, 16. Mt 20:22, 23. 28:19. Mk 1:4, 5, 8, 9. 6:14 (Baptist). +7:4. 10:38, 39. 16:16. Lk 3:7, 12, 16, 21. 7:29, 30. 11:38. 12:50. Jn 1:25, 26, 28, 31, 33. 3:22, 23, 26. 4:1, 2. 10:40. Ac 1:5. +2:38, 41. 8:12, 13, 16, 36, 38. 9:18. 10:47, 48. 11:16. 16:15, 33. 18:8. 19:3-5. +22:16. Ro 6:3, 3. 1 C 1:13-17. 10:2. 12:13. +15:29. Ga 3:27.

in Jordan. 2 K 5:14. Mk +1:9.

confessing. Le 16:21. 26:40. Nu 5:7. Jsh 7:19. Jb 33:27, 28. Ps 32:5. Pr 28:13. Da 9:4. Mk +1:5. Lk 15:18-21. Ac +19:18. Ja 5:16. 1 J 1:9.

7 the Pharisees. i.e. *separatist, expounders; self-righteousness*, **S#5330g**. Mt 5:20. 9:11, 14, 34. 12:2, 14, 24, 38. 15:1, 12. 16:1, 6, 11, 12. 19:3. 21:45. 22:15, 34, 41. 23:2, 13-15, 23, 25-27, 29. 27:62. Mk 2:16, 18, 24. 3:6. 7:1, 3, 5. 8:11, 15. 10:2. 12:13. Lk 5:17, 21, 30, 33. 6:2, 7. 7:30, 36, 37, 39. 11:37-39, 42-44, 53. 12:1. 13:31. 14:1, 3. 15:2. 16:14. 17:20. 18:10, 11. 19:39. Jn 1:24. 3:1. 4:1. 7:32, 45, 47, 48. 8:3, 13. 9:13, 15, 16, 40. 11:46, 47, 57. 12:19, 42. 18:3. Ac 5:34. 15:5. 23:6-9. 26:5. Ph 3:5.

Sadducees. i.e. *just, justified; the righteous*, **S#4523g**. Mt 16:1, 6, 11, 12. 22:23, 34. Mk 12:18. Lk 20:27. Ac 4:1. 5:17. 23:6-8.

baptism. Gr. *baptisma*, **S#908g**. ver. 7. Mt 20:22, 23. 21:25. Mk 1:4. 10:38, 39. 11:30. Lk 3:3. 7:29. 12:50. 20:4. Ac 1:22. 10:37. 13:24. 18:25. 19:3, 4. Ro 6:4. Ep 4:5. Col 2:12. 1 P 3:21.

O generation. Mt 12:34. 23:33. Ge +3:15. Ps 58:3-6. Is 57:3, 4. 59:5. Lk 3:7-9. Jn 8:44. 1 J 3:10. Re 12:9, 10.

of vipers. Ps 58:4. 140:3.

who. Je 6:10. 51:6. Ezk 3:18-21. 33:3-7. Ac 20:31. Ro 1:18. He 11:7.

flee. Ro 5:9. Ep 5:6. Col 3:6. 1 Th +1:10. 2 Th 1:9, 10. He 6:18. Re 6:16, 17.

wrath to come. Jn 3:36. 1 Th +1:10.

8 forth. Mt 21:28-30, 32. Is 1:16, 17. 55:7. Lk 3:8, 10-14. Ac 26:20. Ro 2:4-7. 2 C 7:10, 11. 2 P 1:4-8.

fruits. Mt 21:25. Lk 7:30. Ga 5:22, 23. Ep 5:9. Ph 1:11.

meet. etc. *or*, answerable to amendment of life. Je +35:15. Jon 3:10.

9 think. Gr. *dokeo*, **S#1380g.** To form an estimate or opinion, which may be right, (Jn 5:39; Ac 15:28; 1 C 4:9; 7:40) but which may be wrong, (Mt 6:7; Mk 6:49; Jn 16:2. Ac 27:13). Rendered (1) *think*: Mt 3:9. 6:7. 17:25. 18:12. 21:28. 22:17, 42. 24:44. 26:53, 66. Lk 10:36. 12:40. 13:4. 19:11. Jn 5:39, 45. 11:13, 56. 13:29. 16:2. Ac 12:9. 26:9. 1 C 4:9. +7:40. 8:2. 10:12. 12:23. 14:37. 2 C 11:16. 12:19. Ga 6:3. Ph 3:4. Ja 4:5. (2) *seem*: Lk 8:18. Ac 17:18. 25:27. 1 C 3:18. 11:16. 12:22. 2 C 10:9. Ga 2:6, 6, 9. He 4:1. 12:11. Ja 1:26. (3) *suppose*: Mk 6:49. Lk 12:51. 13:2. 24:37. Jn 20:15. Ac 27:13. He 10:29. (4) *seem good*: Lk 1:3. Ac 15:25, 28. (5) *please*: Ac 15:22, 34. (6) *be accounted*: Mk 10:42. Lk 22:24. (7) *trow*: Lk 17:9. (8) *be of reputation*: Ga 2:2. (9) *own pleasure*: He 12:10.

say within. Mk 7:21. Lk 3:8. 5:22. 7:39. 12:17.

We. Ezk 33:24. Lk 16:24. Jn 8:33, 39, 40, 53. Ac 13:26. Ro 2:28, 29. 4:1, 11-16. 9:6-8. Ga 4:22-31.

God. Mt +8:11, 12. Lk 19:40. Ac 15:14. Ro 4:17. 1 C 1:27, 28. Ga 3:27-29. Ep 2:12, 13.

these stones. Mt 4:3. 7:9. Lk 19:40.

10 now. Is 5:7. Ml 3:1-3. 4:1. Ac 17:30, 31. He 3:1-3. 10:28-31. 12:25.

the axe. Dt 20:20. Lk 3:9. 23:31.

therefore. Ps 1:3. 92:13, 14. Is 61:3. Je 17:8. Jn 15:2. 1 P 4:17.

good fruit. Mt 7:16-20.

is hewn. Mt 7:19. 21:19. Ps 80:15, 16. Is 5:2-7. 27:11. Ezk 15:2-7. Lk 13:6-9. Jn 15:6. He 6:8. 1 P 4:17, 18.

and cast. Je 11:16. Jn +15:6.

11 baptize. ver. 6. Mk 1:4, 8. Lk 3:3, 16. Jn 1:26, 33. Ac +1:5. 11:16. 13:24. 19:4.

with. Mt 7:2, 6. Mk 3:22. Lk 11:20. 22:49. Re 1:5. 5:9.

water. Mk 1:8. Lk 3:16. Jn 1:33. Ac +1:5. 2:33. 11:16.

unto. Gr. *eis*. Mt 28:19. 1 C 1:13. 10:2.

repentance. ver. 2, 8. Ac 13:24. 19:4.

but. Lk 1:17. Jn 1:15, 26, 27, 30, 34. 3:23-36. Ac 13:25.

whose. Mk 1:7. Lk 7:6, 7. Ac 13:25. Ep 3:8. 1 P 5:5.

he shall. Is 4:4. 44:3. 59:20, 21. Zc +13:9. Ml 3:2-4. Mk 1:8. Lk 3:16. Jn 1:33. Ac +1:5. 2:2-4. 11:15, 16. 1 C 12:13. Ga 3:27, 28.

with. Jn 3:5. Ac 2:4. 1 C 12:13.

Ghost. Gr. *pneuma*, Mt +1:18. Jn 7:39. Ac 1:5. 11:15, 16. 1 C 12:13.

fire. Dt 4:24. Ps 21:9. 50:3. +97:3. +149:9. Is 1:27. 4:4. 5:24. 9:5. 10:16, 17. 30:27, 33. 62:1.

66:15, 16. Am 1:4. 5:6. Zc 12:6. Ml 3:2, 3. 4:1. Lk 12:49. Ac 2:3. 1 C 3:13-15. +6:2. He 10:27. 12:29. 2 P +3:7. Re 2:26, 27. 14:18.

12 fan. Is 30:24. 41:16. Je 4:11. 15:7. 51:2. Lk 3:17. 22:31.

he will throughly. Mt 13:41, 49, 50. Ml 3:2, 3. 4:1. Jn 15:2.

floor. Ge +50:10.

and gather. Mt +13:30, 40, 43. Am 9:9. 2 Th 2:1.

but. Is +24:6. Ml 3:18. 4:1. Lk +3:17. 2 P 3:7.

with unquenchable. 2 K 22:17. Is 1:31. 34:10. +66:24. Je 4:4. 7:20. 17:27. 21:12. Ezk 20:47, 48. Am 5:6. Mk 9:43-48. Lk 3:17.

fire. ver. 10, +11. Mt +25:41, 46. Jb 15:30.

13 from Galilee. Mt +2:22. Lk 3:21.

to Jordan. lit. upon (Gr. *epi*) Jordan. i.e. upon the bank of the Jordan. Mk 1:4, 5, 9.

baptized. He 7:11-14.

14 John. Lk 1:43. Jn 13:6-8.

I have. Jn 1:16. 3:3-7. Ac 1:5-8. Ro 3:23, 25. Ga 3:22, 27-29. 4:6. Ep 2:3-5. Re 7:9-17.

15 Suffer. Jn 13:7-9.

for thus. Ps 40:7, 8. Is 42:21. Lk 1:6. Jn 4:34. 8:29. 9:4. 13:15. 15:10. Ph 2:7, 8. He 7:26. 1 P 2:21-24. 1 J 2:6.

to fulfill. Mt 5:17. 8:4. 17:24-27. Lk 2:39, 41, 42. 17:14. Nu 8:5-7 with He 7:13, 14.

16 Jesus. Mk 1:10.

when. Lk 3:23.

up. Mk 1:10.

out of. Gr. *apo*, lit. from. ver. 7. Ge 17:22, LXX. SS 3:6, LXX. 6:5, 6 (4, 5, LXX). Lk 2:4. Re 7:2.

lo. Ezk 1:1. Lk 3:21. Jn 1:51. Ac 7:56.

and he saw. Mt 12:18. Ps *45:7*. Is *11:2*. 42:1. 59:21. *61:1*. Lk 3:22. 4:18, 21. Jn 1:31-34. 3:34. Ac 10:38. Col 1:18, 19. I J 5:6, 8.

the Spirit. Gr. *pneuma*. The Holy Spirit himself (commonly called the Third Person of the Trinity), symbolized by the bodily form of a dove. Mt 1:20. 4:1. 10:20. 12:28, 31, 32. 22:43. 28:19. Mk 1:10, 12. 3:29. 12:36. 13:11. Lk 2:26, 27. 3:22. 4:1b, 14. 10:21. 12:10. Jn 1:32, 33a. 3:6a, 8, 34. 6:63a. 14:17, 26. 15:26. 16:13. Ac 1:16. 2:4b, 33, 38. 5:3, 9. 7:51. 9:31. 10:45. 11:28. 13:2, 4. 15:28. 16:6, 7. 20:23, 28. 21:4. 28:25. Ro 8:16a, 26, 27. 15:16, 19, 30. 1 C 2:10, 11b, 14. 3:16. 6:11. 12:3a, 4, 7-9, 11, 13a. 2 C 13:14. Ga 3:14. 5:22. 6:8b. Ep 2:18. 3:5, 16. 4:3, 4, 30. 5:9, 18. 6:17, 18. 2 Th 2:13. 1 T 4:1a. He 3:7. 9:8, 14. 10:15, 29. 1 P 1:2, 11, 22. 3:18. 4:14. 1 J 4:2a. 5:6-8. Re 1:10. 2:7, 11, 17, 29. 3:6, 13, 22. 4:2. 14:13. 17:3. 21:10. 22:17. For the other uses of *pneuma*, see Mt +8:16.

17 lo. Jn 5:37. 12:28-30. Re 14:2.

a voice. Mk 1:11.

This. Mt 12:18. 17:5. Ps 2:7. Is 42:1, 21. Mk 1:11. 9:7. Lk 3:22. 9:35. Ga 4:4, 5. Ep 1:6. Col 1:13. 2 P 1:17. 1 J 5:9.

my beloved. Ge 37:3.

Son. Mt +14:33. Jn 3:16. 17:24. Ep 1:4. Note all three persons of the Trinity. Mt +28:19. Ge +1:26. Is 6:8. +42:1. 48:12, 16. Ro 15:30. 1 C 12:4-6. 2 C 13:14. Ep 2:18. 4:4-6. 5:18-20. He 9:14. 1 P 1:2. Ju 20, 21.

well pleased. Ps 40:7, 8. Jn 4:34. 5:30. 6:38. 8:29, 49. 17:4.

MATTHEW 4

1 **was**. Mk 1:12, 13, etc. Lk 4:1, etc. Ro 8:14.

led. Ezk +8:3.

of the spirit. Gr. *pneuma*, Mt +3:16.

into. Mk 1:12. Lk 4:1.

the wilderness. Mt 3:1.

to. Ge +3:15. Jn +14:30. He 2:18. 4:15, 16.

tempted. He 2:18. +4:15. Ja 1:13.

devil. i.e. *accuser, adversary*, **S#1228g**. Gr. *diabolos*. ver. 1, 5, 8, 11. Mt 13:39. 25:41. Lk 4:2, 3, 5, 6, 13. 8:12. Jn 6:70. 8:44. 13:2. Ac 10:38. 13:10. Ep 4:27. 6:11. 1 T 3:6, 7, 11 (slanderers). 2 T 2:26. 3:3 (false accusers). T 2:3 (false accusers). He 2:14. Ja 4:7. 1 P 5:8. 1 J 3:8, 10. Ju 9. Re 2:10. 12:9, 12. 20:2, 10.

2 **fasted**. Ex 24:18. 34:28. Dt 9:9, 18, 25. 18:18. 1 K 19:8. Ezr 8:21-23. Da +9:3. Jon 3:5-10. Lk 2:36, 37. 4:2. Ac 10:30. 13:2, 3. 14:23. 2 C 6:5. 11:27, 28.

forty. Ex 34:28. Jon +3:4. Mk 1:13. Lk 4:2.

he was. Mt 21:18. Mk 11:12. Jn 4:6, 7. 19:28. He 2:14-17.

3 **the tempter**. Mt 10:1. +13:38, 39. Ge 3:1-7. 1 Ch 21:1. Jb 1:9-12. 2:4-7. Is 27:1. Mk 5:9. Lk 11:15. 22:31, 32. Jn 8:44. +14:30. 2 C 4:4. Ep 2:2. 6:12. 1 Th 3:5. 1 P 5:8. Re 2:10. 9:10, 11. 12:9-11.

If. 1 C +15:2. This kind of "if" assumes the condition to be true. By the use of "if," Satan was not calling into question whether in fact Jesus is the Son of God; rather, he assumes this to be true. Mt 3:17. 27:40. Lk 4:3, 9.

Son of God. ver. 6. Mt +14:33.

command. Ge 3:1-5. 25:29-34. Ex 16:3. Nu 11:4-6. Ps 78:17-20. He 12:16, 17.

bread. Mt 7:9. Lk 11:11.

4 **It is written**. ver. 6, 7, 10. Mk 12:10. Lk 4:4, 8, 12. Jn 7:42. Ro +15:4. Ep 6:17.

Man. Dt *8:3*. Lk 4:4. Jn 4:34. 6:49-51.

bread. Mt 6:11. +24:45. Ge +3:19.

but. Mt 14:16-21. Ex 16:8, 15, 35. 23:15. 1 K 17:12-16. 2 K 4:42-44. 7:1, 2. Hg 2:16-19. Ml 3:9-11. Mk 6:38-44. 8:4-9. Jn 6:5, etc., 31, etc., 63.

by. Dt 8:3.

every word. Dt 32:47. Jsh +1:8. 1 S 21:9. Jb +23:12. Ps 17:4. 119:11. Je +15:16. Jn +5:39.

6:63. 1 C 3:15. Ep 6:17. He 4:12. 1 P 4:18. Re 19:15.

5 **taketh**. Lk 4:9. Jn 19:11.

the holy. Mt 5:35. 27:53. Ne 11:1, 18. Ps 46:4. 48:1. Is 48:2. 52:1. Da 9:16, 24. Re 11:2. 21:2. 22:19.

on. 2 Ch 3:4.

6 **saith**. Ge 3:4, 5. Jb 1:9-11. Ga +1:8. 2 Th +2:13. 1 T 4:1-3.

If thou. 1 C +15:2.

Son of God. ver. +3.

for. ver. 4. 2 C 11:14. 2 P +3:16.

He shall. Ps *91:11, 12*. Lk 4:9-12. He 1:14.

lest. Jb 1:10. 5:23. Ps 34:7, 20. 37:24. Pr 3:23.

7 **It**. ver. 4, 10. Mt 21:16, 42. 22:31, 32. Pr +22:3. Is +8:20.

Thou shalt not. Ex +17:2. Dt *6:16*.

tempt. Mt +16:1.

8 **the devil**. ver. 5. Lk 4:5-7.

mountain. Mt +5:1.

and showeth. Mt 16:26. Est 1:4. 5:11. Ps 49:16, 17. Da 4:30. Lk 4:5. 2 C 4:18. Ep 2:2. He 11:24-26. 1 P 1:24. 1 J 2:15, 16. Re 11:15.

all the kingdoms. Ps 2:8.

world. Gr. *kosmos*, **S#2889g**. Rendered (1) *world*: ver. 4:8. Mt 5:14. 13:35, 38. 16:26. 18:7. 24:21. 25:34. 26:13. Mk 8:36. 14:9. 16:15. Lk 9:25. 11:50. 12:30. Jn 1:9, 10, 29. 3:16, 17, 19. 4:42. 6:14, 33, 51. 7:4, 7. 8:12, 23, 26. 9:5, 39. 10:36. 11:9, 27. 12:19, 25, 31, 46, 47. 13:1. 14:17, 19, 22, 27, 30, 31. 15:18, 19. 16:8, 11, 20, 21, 28, 33. 17:5, 6, 9, 11-16, 18, 21, 23, 24, 25. 18:20, 36, 37. 21:25. Ac 17:24. Ro 1:8, 20. 3:6, 19. 4:13. 5:12, 13. 11:12, 15. 1 C 1:20, 21, 27, 28. 2:12. 3:19, 22. 4:9, 13. 5:10. 6:2. 7:31, 33, 34. 8:4. 11:32. 14:10. 2 C 1:12. 5:19. 7:10. Ga 4:3. 6:14. Ep 1:4. 2:2, 12. Ph 2:15. Col 1:6. 2:8, 20. 1 T 1:15. 3:16. 6:7. He 4:3. 9:26. 10:5. 11:7, 38. Ja 1:27. 2:5. 3:6. 4:4. 1 P 1:20. 5:9. 2 P 1:4. 2:5, 20. 3:6. 1 J 2:2, 15-17. 3:1, 13, 17. 4:1, 3-5, 9, 14, 17. 5:4, 5, 19. 2 J 7. Re 11:15. 13:8. 17:8. (2) *adorning*: 1 P 3:3.

9 **All**. Mt 26:15. Ps 2:8. Jn 13:3.

I give. 1 S 2:7, 8. Ps 72:11. 113:7, 8. Pr 8:15. Je 27:5, 6. Da 2:37, 38. 4:32. 5:18, 19, 26-28. Lk 22:53. Jn +12:31. Re 13:2. 19:16.

if. This kind of "if" indicates that if the contingency or circumstance is met, certain results will follow. Compared to verse 3 and 6 where "if" may almost be taken to mean "since," because no doubt is expressed, this "if" indicates Satan is not sure the condition he suggests will be fulfilled. For other examples of this *Third Class* (or *Condition*) of conditional sentence see Mt 5:13, 19, 20, 23, 32, 46, 47. 6:14, 15, 22, 23. 7:9, 12. 8:2, 31. 9:21. 10:13. 12:11, 28, 29. 15:14. 16:19, 25, 26. 17:20. 18:3, 12, 13, 15, 16, 17, 19, 35. 21:3, 21, 22, 24, 25, 26. 22:24. 24:26, 28, 48. 26:35.

28:14. Mk 1:40. 3:24, 25. 4:26. 5:28. 7:11.
8:3, 36. 9:43, 45, 47, 50. 10:12. 11:3, 31, 32.
12:19. 14:21, 31. 16:18. Lk 4:7. 5:12. 6:33.
9:13. 10:6. 11:12. 12:45. 13:3, 5, 9. 14:34.
15:8. 17:3, 4. 19:31. 20:5, 6, 28. 22:68. Jn 3:2,
3, 5, 12, 27. 5:31, 43. 6:44, 51, 62, 65. 7:17,
37, 51. 8:16, 24, 31, 36, 51, 52, 54, 55. 9:22,
31. 10:9. 11:9, 10, 40, 48, 57. 12:24, 26, 32,
47. 13:8, 17, 35. 14:3, 14, 15, 23. 15:4, 6, 7,
10, 14. 16:7. 19:12. 20:23. 21:22, 23, 25. Ac
5:38. 9:2. 13:41. 26:5. Ro 2:25, 26. 7:2, 3, 20.
9:27. 10:9. 11:22, 23, 24. 12:20. 13:4. 14:8,
23. 15:24. 1 C 4:15, 19. 5:11. 6:4. 7:11, 28,
36, 39, 40. 8:8, 10. 9:16. 10:28. 11:14, 15.
12:15, 16. 13:1, 2. 14:5, 6, 7, 9, 11, 14, 23, 24,
28, 30. 16:4, 7, 10. 2 C 5:1. 9:4. Ga 1:8. 5:2.
6:1. Ph 3:11, 12. Col 3:13. 4:10. 1 Th 5:10. 1 T
1:8. 2:15. 3:15. 2 T 2:5, 21. He 3:6, 7, 14, 15.
4:7. 6:3. 10:38. 12:20. 13:23. Ja 2:2, 14, 15,
16, 17. 4:15. 1 P 3:13. 1 J 1:6, 7, 8, 9, 10. 2:1,
3, 15, 24, 29. 3:20, 21. 4:12, 20. 5:14, 16. 3 J
10. Re 3:3, 20, 21. 11:5. 22:18, 19. For the
other kinds or classes of the conditional "if"
sentence, see for the *First Condition* (no doubt
expressed), 1 C +15:2; for the *Second Condition*
(assumption contrary to fact in present time),
Lk +7:39; (contrary to fact or impossible in
past time), Mt +11:21; (contrary to fact or
impossible, unclassified time), Mt +23:30; for
the *Fourth Condition* (highly unlikely, remote
possibility of realization, involving the "if" or
conditional clause), Lk +22:67; (highly
unlikely, remote possibility of realization,
involving the "then" clause or conclusion), Lk
+1:62.
fall down. Da 3:5. Lk 4:7mg.
and worship. 1 C 10:20, 21. 2 C 4:4. 1 T 3:6.
1 P 5:8, 9. Re +19:10. +22:8, 9.

10 **Then saith**. He 11:24, 25.
Get. Mt 16:23. Ja 4:7. 1 P 5:9.
Satan. 1 Ch 21:1. Jb 1:6, 12. 2:1. Ps 109:6. Zc
3:1, 2. Gr. *Satanas*, i.e. *an adversary*, **S#4567g**.
Mt 4:10. 12:26. 16:23. Mk 1:13. 3:23, 26.
4:15. 8:33. Lk 4:8. 10:18. 11:18. 13:16. 22:3,
31. Jn 13:27. Ac 5:3. 26:18. Ro 16:20. 1 C 5:5.
7:5. 2 C 2:11. 11:14. 1 Th 2:18. 2 Th 2:9. 1 T
1:20. 5:15. Re 2:9, 13, 13, 24. 3:9. 12:9. 20:2,
7. See **S#4566g**, 2 C 12:7. For **S#7854h**, see Jb
1:6, Satan.
Thou shalt. Dt 6:13, 14. 10:20. Jsh 24:14. 1 S
7:3. Lk 4:8.
worship. Mt +14:33. Ex +20:2, 3, 5. 34:14.
Dt 11:16. Ps +22:28. 96:4, 5, 8, 9. Ec +12:13.
Lk 4:8. Ac 14:15. Col +2:18. Re +19:10.
+22:8, 9.
shalt thou. Dt 10:20. 13:4. Jsh +22:5. 1 S
7:3. 1 Ch 29:11. Ps +22:28.

11 **the devil**. Lk 4:13. 22:53. Jn 14:30. 2 C 4:4.
Ep 6:12.
behold. ver. 6. Mt 26:53. 28:2-5. 1 K 19:5.

Mk 1:13. Lk 22:43. Jn 12:29. 1 T 3:16. He 1:6,
14. Re 5:11, 12.

12 **when**. Mt 11:2. 14:3. Mk 1:14. 6:17. Lk 3:19,
20. Jn 3:24. 4:43, 54. Ac 10:37.
cast. *or*, delivered up. Mt 10:17, 19.
into Galilee. Is 9:1, 2. Lk 4:14, 31.

13 **leaving**. Mt 16:4. Lk 4:30, 31.
Nazareth. Mt +2:23.
came and dwelt. Mt 9:1. Mk 1:21. Lk 4:31.
Jn 2:12.
Capernaum. i.e. *village of comfort*, **S#2584g**. Mt
8:5. 11:23. 17:24. Mk 1:21. 2:1. 9:33. Lk 4:23,
31. 7:1. 10:15. Jn 2:12. 4:46. 6:17, 24, 59.
upon the sea coast. ver. 18. Mt 8:24. Jn 6:1.
Zabulon. i.e. *abiding*, **S#2194g**. ver. 15. Ge
+30:20, Zebulun. Re 7:8.
Nephthalim. i.e. *my wrestlings*. Ge +30:8,
Naphtali. **S#3508g**. ver. 15. Re 7:6.

14 **it**. Mt 1:22. 2:15, 23. 8:17. 12:17-21. 26:54,
56. Lk 22:37. 24:44. Jn 15:25. 19:28, 36,
37.
Esaias. Mk 1:2.
saying. Is 9:1, 2.

15 **The land**. ver. +10. Is 9:1, 2.
Galilee. Mt +2:22. Is 9:1, 2.

16 **which sat**. Is +42:7.
in darkness. Mt 6:23. Ps 107:10-14. Is +9:2.
42:6, 7. 60:1-3. Mi 7:8. Lk 1:78, 79. 2:32. Jn
3:19. 8:12. Ep 5:8, 14. 1 P 2:9.
region and. Ge +1:26. Is 9:1, 2.
shadow. Ps +23:4.

17 **that**. Mk 1:14.
began. Ac 1:22. 10:37.
Repent. Mt 10:7. Lk 9:2. 10:11-14. +13:3. 2
T 2:25, 26. He 6:1.
kingdom of heaven. Mt 3:2. 5:3, 10, 19, 20.
7:21. 8:11. 10:7. 11:11, 12. 13:11, 19, 24, 31,
33, 44, 45, 47, 52. 16:19. 18:1, 3, 4, 23. 19:12,
14, 23. 20:1. 22:2. 23:13. 25:1. Mk +1:15.
at hand. Mt 10:7. +21:43. Is 56:1.

18 **walking**. Mk 1:16-18. Lk 5:2.
sea. Mt 15:29. Nu 34:11. Dt 3:17,
Chinnereth. Lk 5:1, lake of Gennesaret. Mk
7:31. Jn 6:1. 21:1, sea of Tiberias.
two. Mt 10:2. Lk 6:14. Jn 1:40-42. 6:8.
Simon. i.e. *a hearing; obeying*, **S#4613g**. ver. 18.
Mt 10:2, 4. 13:55. 16:16, 17. 17:25. 26:6.
27:32. Mk 1:16, 29, 30, 36. 3:16, 18. 6:3.
14:3, 37. 15:21. Lk 4:38. 5:3, 4, 5, 8, 10. 6:14,
15. 7:40, 43, 44. 22:31. 23:26. 24:34. Jn 1:40-
42. 6:8, 68, 71. 12:4. 13:2, 6, 9, 24, 26, 36.
18:10, 15, 25. 20:2, 6. 21:2, 3, 7, 11, 15-17.
Ac 1:13. 8:9, 13, 18, 24. 9:43. 10:5, 6, 17, 18,
32. 11:13.
called Peter. Mt 10:2. Jn 1:42.
Andrew. i.e. *manly*, **S#406g**. ver. 18. Mt 10:2.
Mk 1:16, 29. 3:18. 13:3. Lk 6:14. Jn 1:40, 44.
6:8. 12:22. Ac 1:13.
casting. Mt 13:47. Ge +24:27. Ezk 47:10. Am
7:15.

for. Ex 3:1, 10. Jg 6:11, 12. 1 K 19:19-21. Ps 78:70-72. Am 7:14, 15. 1 C 1:27-29.

19 Follow. Mt 8:22. 9:9. 16:24. 19:21. Mk 2:14. Lk 5:27. 9:59. Jn 1:43. 12:26. 21:22.
I will. Ezk 47:9, 10. Mk 1:17, 18. Lk 5:10, 11. 1 C 9:20-22. 2 C 12:16.
fishers. Mt 13:47. Je 16:16.

20 they. ver. 22. Mt 10:37, 38. 19:27. 1 K 19:21. Ps 110:3. 119:60. Mk 10:28-31. Lk 18:28-30. Ga 1:16. Ph 3:7, 8.
their nets. Jn 21:6.
and followed. Mk 10:37, 38.

21 other. Mt 10:2. 17:1. 20:20, 21. 26:37. Mk 1:19, 20, 29. 3:17. 5:37. 10:35. Lk 5:10, 11. 9:54. Jn 21:2. Ac 12:2.
mending. Lk 5:2.

22 immediately left. ver. 20. Mt 10:37. 19:27. Dt 33:9, 10. Mk 1:20. 10:28. Lk 5:11. 9:59, 60. 14:26, 33. 18:28. 2 C 5:16.

23 Jesus. Mt 9:35. Mk 6:6. Jn 7:1. Ac 10:38.
all Galilee. Is *9:1, 2*.
teaching. Mt 12:9. 13:54. Ps 74:8. Mk 1:21, 39. 3:1. 6:2. Lk +4:15, 16, 31, 33, 44. 6:6. 13:10. Jn 6:59. 18:20. Ac +14:1.
preaching. Mt 7:28, 29. 9:35. 13:54. Mk 1:14, 15. Lk 4:43. Jn 7:14, 15, 46.
the gospel. Mt 13:19. 24:14. Mk 1:14. Lk 4:17, 18. 8:1. 20:1. Ro 10:15.
the kingdom. Da 2:44. Mt 24:14.
healing. Mt 8:14-17. 9:35. 10:1, 7, 8. 11:5. 12:15. 14:14. 15:30, 31. Ps +103:3. Mk 1:32-34. 3:10. 6:13, 56. Lk 4:40, 41. 5:15, 17. 6:17. 7:22. 9:2, 11. 10:9. Ac 5:15, 16. 10:38. 28:8.
and all. Ac 10:12.
among the people. Ac 5:12. 6:8.

24 his fame. lit. hearing. Mt 9:26, 31. 14:1. Jsh 6:27. 1 K 4:31. 10:1. 1 Ch 14:17. Mk 1:28. Lk 4:14, 37. 5:15.
Syria. Ac +15:23.
all sick. ver. +23. Mt 14:35. Ex +15:26.
taken. Lk 4:38.
torments. Mt 8:6.
possessed. Mt 8:16, 28, 33. 9:32. 12:22. 15:22. 17:18. Mk 1:32. 5:2-18. Lk 4:33-35. 8:27-37. Jn 10:21. Ac 10:38.
lunatic. Mt 17:15.
those that. Mt 8:6, 13. 9:2-8. Mk 2:3-5, 9, 10. Lk 5:18, 24. Ac 8:7. 9:33. He 12:12.

25 followed. Lk +5:15.
from Galilee. ver. +15.
Decapolis. i.e. *ten cities*, **S#1179g**. Mk 5:20. 7:31.

MATTHEW 5

1 seeing. Lk +5:15.
into a mountain. Mt 4:8. +14:23. 15:29. 17:1. +21:1. 28:16. Mk 3:13, 20. 6:46. 9:2. Lk 6:12, 17. 9:28. Jn 6:3, 15.

was set. Lk 4:20.
his. Mt 4:18-22. 10:2-4. Lk 6:13-16.

2 he opened. Jg +11:35. Lk 6:20, etc. Ep 6:19.

3 Blessed. ver. 4-11. Mt 11:6. 13:16. 24:46. Ps +1:1. 2:12. 32:1, 2. 41:1. 84:12. 112:1. 119:1, 2. 128:1. 146:5. Pr 8:32. Is +30:18. Lk 6:20, 21, etc. 11:28. Jn 20:29. Ro 4:6-9. Ja 1:12. Re 1:3. 19:9. 20:6. 22:14.
the poor. Mt 11:25. 18:1-3. Le 26:4, 41, 42. Dt 8:2. 2 Ch +7:14. 33:12, 19, 23. 34:27. Jb 42:6. Ps +51:17. Pr 16:19. 29:23. Ec 7:3, 8. Je 31:18-20. Da 5:21, 22. Mi +6:8. Lk 4:18. 6:20. 18:14. 1 C 1:28, 29. 2 C 6:10. Ja 1:10. 2:5. 4:9, 10. Re 3:17.
in spirit. Gr. *pneuma*, Mt +8:16; Ps +51:10. "Spirit" put for character as being in itself invisible, and manifested only in one's actions. Lk 9:55. Ro 8:15, 15. 11:8. 1 C 4:21. Ga 6:1. 1 T 4:12. 2 T 1:7. 1 P 3:4. Re 19:10.
for theirs. Mk 10:14. Lk 12:32. Ja 2:5.
kingdom of heaven. Mt +4:17.

4 that mourn. Jb 30:28. Ps 6:1-9. 13:1-5. 30:7-11. 32:3-7. 35:14. 38:6. 40:1-3. 42:9. 43:2. 55:2. 69:29, 30. 88:9. 116:3-8. 126:5, 6. Ec 7:3, 4. Is 30:19. 38:14-19. 57:17, 18. 59:11. 61:2, 3. +65:19. 66:10. Je 31:9-12, 15-17. Ezk 7:16. 9:4. Jl 2:12. Zc 12:10-14. 13:1. Lk +6:21, 25. 7:38, 50. Jn 16:20-22. 2 C 1:3-7. 6:10. 7:9, 10. Ja 1:12. 4:9.
comforted. Is 12:1. Lk 16:25. Re 7:14-17. 21:4.

5 the meek. Mt +11:29. Nu 12:3. Ps 22:26. 25:9. 37:11. 69:32mg. 76:8, 9. 147:6. 149:4. Pr 14:29. 15:1, 18. 16:32. 19:11. 20:3. Ec 7:8. Is 11:4. 29:19. 61:1. Am 2:7. Zp +2:3. Lk 18:9-14. Ga 5:23. Ep 4:2. Col 3:12. 1 T 6:11. 2 T 2:25. T 3:2. Ja 1:21. 3:13. 1 P 3:3, 4, 15.
inherit the earth. Ge +22:17. Ps 25:13. 27:13. 37:9, 11, 22, 29, 34. +106:4, 5. 115:16-18. Pr 2:21, 22. 10:30. 11:31. 12:7. Is 11:9. 26:6. 45:18. 54:17. +55:3. 57:13. +60:21. 66:22. Da +7:14, 18. Ac +7:5. +20:32. Ro 4:13. He 11:16. Re 5:10.

6 are. Ps 42:1, 2. 63:1, 2. 84:2. 107:9. Is 26:9. Am 8:11-13. Lk 1:53. 6:21, 25. Jn 6:27.
hunger. Jb 23:12. Ps 81:10. 119:103. Is 49:10. 55:1, 2. 65:13. Je 15:16. Am +8:11. Lk 1:53. 6:21. Jn 6:35. Re 21:6. 22:17.
thirst. Ps 42:2. 63:1. Is 26:9. 44:3. Jn 7:37, 38. Re 22:17.
for they. Ps 4:6, 7. 16:11. 17:14, 15. 36:8. 63:5. 65:4. 81:10, 16. 90:14. 103:5. 107:9. 132:15. 145:19. SS 5:1. Is 25:6. 41:17, 18. 44:3. 49:9, 10. +55:1-3. 65:13. 66:11, 12. Je 31:14, 25. Lk 1:53. 6:21. Jn 4:10, 14. 6:35, 48-58. 7:37, 38. Ep 3:19. Re 7:16, 17.

7 merciful. Mt 6:14, 15. 18:33-35. 25:34-36. Dt 24:12, 13, +14. 2 S 22:26. Jb 31:16-22. Ps +12:5. 18:25. 37:26. 41:1-4. +58:11. 112:4, 5, 9. Pr 3:3, 4. 11:17. 14:21. 19:17. 22:9. Is 57:1,

2. 58:6-12. Ezk +16:49. Da 4:27. Mi +6:8. Mk 11:25, 26. Lk 6:35, 36, +38. Ga 6:9, 10. Ep 4:32. 5:1, 2. Col 3:12. T +1:8. He +13:3. Ja 2:13. 3:17.

for they. Mt 7:2. 25:35. Pr 11:24-26. Ho 1:6. 2:1mg, 23. Ro 11:30, 31. 1 C 7:25. 2 C 4:1. 1 T 1:13, 16. 2 T 1:16-18. He 4:16. 6:10. Ja 2:13. 1 P 2:10.

8 pure. Mt 23:25-28. 1 Ch 29:17-19. Ps 15:2. 18:26. 24:3, 4. +51:6, 10. 73:1. Pr 22:11. Ezk 18:5, 6, 9. 36:25-27. Ac 15:9. 24:16. 2 C 7:1. 1 T 1:5. 3:9. +4:12. 2 T 2:21, 22. T 1:15. He 9:14. 10:22. Ja 1:8. 3:17. 4:8. 1 P 1:22.

in heart. 1 K +8:18. Pr +4:23. 22:11.

for they. Ge 32:30. Jb 19:26, 27. Ps 11:7. 15:1. +17:15. 42:2. 140:13. 1 C 13:12. He 12:14. 1 J 3:2, 3. Re 22:4.

9 peacemakers. Ge 13:8. 1 Ch 12:17, 18. Ps +34:14. +122:6-8. Pr 12:20. Ac 7:26. 1 C 6:6-8. 2 C 5:20. Ep 4:1-3. Ph 2:1-3, 14. 4:2. Col 3:13-15. 1 Th 5:23. He 12:14. Ja 1:19, 20.

for. ver. 45, 48. 1 P 1:14-16. 1 J +3:1.

10 persecuted. Mt 10:23, 39. 19:29. Ps 37:12, 13. 69:7, 9. Is 51:7, 8. Mk 10:30. Lk 6:22, 23. 21:12, 13. Jn 15:20, 21. Ac 5:40, 41. 8:1. 9:4. Ro 8:17, 35-39. 1 C 4:9-13. 2 C 4:8-12, 17. Ph 1:28, 29. 2 T 2:12. 3:11, 12. He 10:34, 35. Ja 1:2-5. 5:11. 1 P 3:13, 14, 17. 4:12-16. 1 J 3:12. Re 2:10.

for. ver. 3. Mt +4:17. 2 Th 1:4-7. Ja 1:12.

11 when. Mt 10:25. 27:39. Ps +9:10. 35:11. 37:40. 55:22. 69:7, 9. 118:6. Pr 29:25. Is 51:7, 8. 63:9. 66:5. Je 1:19. Zc 2:8. Lk 6:22, 26. 7:33, 34. 21:18, 19. Jn 9:28. Ro 8:35. 2 C 12:10. Ga 4:29. Ph 1:28, 29. He 11:26. 12:3. +13:5, 6. 1 P 2:23.

falsely. Gr. lying. Lk 3:14. 2 T 3:3. 1 P 3:16. 4:14.

for my sake. Mt 10:18, 22, 39. 19:29. 24:9. Ps 44:22. Mk 4:17. 8:35. 13:9, 13. Lk 6:22. 9:24. 21:12, 17. Jn 15:21. Ac 9:16. Ro 8:36. 1 C 4:10. 2 C 4:11. Re 2:3.

12 Rejoice. Lk 6:23. Ac 5:41. 13:52. 16:25. Ro 5:3. 2 C 4:17. 6:10. 7:4. 12:10. Ph 1:29. 2:17, 18. Col 1:11, 24. 1 Th 1:6. He 10:34. Ja 1:2. 1 P 1:6. 4:13.

for great. Mt 6:1, 2, 4, 5, 6, 16. 10:41, 42. 16:27. 25:21, 23, 40. Ge 15:1. Ru 2:12. Ps 19:11. 58:11. Pr 11:18. Is 3:10. Da +12:3. Mk +10:30. Lk 6:23, 35. +12:47, 48. +14:14. 18:30. 1 C 3:8, 12-15. 9:17, 18. 2 C 4:17. 9:6. Ph 3:14. Col 3:24. 1 T +4:8. He 6:10. 11:6, 26. Ja +1:12. 2 P +1:11. 2 J 8. Re 11:18. 22:12.

in heaven. Mk +10:21. He 10:34-37. 1 P +1:4.

for so persecuted. Mt 21:34-38. 23:31-37. 1 K 18:4, 13. 19:2, 10, 14. 21:20. 22:8, 26, 27. 2 K 1:9. 2 Ch 16:10. 24:20-22. 36:16. Ne 9:26. Je 2:30. 26:8, 9, 21-23. 43:2, 3. Lk 6:23. 11:47-51. 13:34. Ac 7:51, 52. 1 Th 2:15. Ja 5:10.

13 the salt. Le +2:13. Ep 4:29.

but if. Mt +4:9. Lk 14:34, 35. He 6:4-6. 2 P 2:20, 21.

14 the light. Ps 119:105. Pr +4:18. Je 5:1. Ezk 22:29, 30. Da +10:12. Lk 2:32. Jn 1:4, 9. 5:35. 8:12, 29. 9:5. 12:35, 36. Ro 2:19, 20. 15:21. 2 C 6:14. Ep 5:8-14. Ph 2:15. 1 Th 5:5. 1 J 1:5. Re 1:20. 2:1.

world. Gr. *kosmos*, Mt +4:8.

A city. Ge 11:4-8. Ps 48:2. Re 21:14, etc.

set on a hill. Jsh 20:7.

15 Neither do. Mk 4:21, 22. Lk 8:16, 17. 11:33.

candle. Pr 31:18.

put it under. Mt +6:2. +25:27, 29. Lk 19:23.

a bushel. "A measure containing about a pint less than a peck."

but on. He 9:2. Re 1:12.

it giveth. Ex 25:37. Nu 8:2. 1 C 12:7.

16 your light. Pr +4:18. 31:18. Is 58:8. 60:1-3. Ro 13:11-14. Ep 5:8. Ph 2:15, 16. 1 Th 2:12. 5:6-8. 1 P 2:9. 1 J 1:5-7.

that they. Mt 6:1-5, 16. 23:5. Ac 9:36. Ep 2:10. 1 T 2:10. 5:10, 25. 6:18. T 2:7, 14. 3:1, 7, 8, 14. Phm 6. He 10:24. 1 P 2:12. 3:1, 16.

see. Ge +30:27. 39:3. Ps 34:2. Ja +1:22. 2:18, 20.

and glorify. Mt +9:8. 1 C 14:25.

your Father. ver. 45, 48. Mt 6:9. 23:9. Lk 11:2.

17 Think not. Mt 10:34. 22:29.

to destroy. S#2647g. Mt 24:2 (thrown down). 26:61. 27:40.

the law. Mt 7:12. Lk 16:16, 17. Jn 8:5. Ac 6:13. 18:13. 21:28. Ro 3:21, 31. 10:4. Ga 3:17-24.

but to fulfill. Mt +3:15. 8:4. 17:24-27. Ps 40:6-8. Is 42:21. Lk 2:39, 41, 42. 17:14. Jn 1:17. Ro 8:4. 10:4. Ga 4:4, 5. Ph 3:3. Col 2:16, 17. He 10:3-12.

18 verily. ver. 26. Mt 6:2, 5, 16. 8:10. 10:15, 23, 42. 11:11. 13:17. 16:28. 17:20. 18:3, 13, 18. 19:23, 28. 21:21, 31. 23:36. 24:2, 34, 47. 25:12, 40, 45. 26:13, 14. Mk 3:28. 6:11. 8:12. 9:1, 41. 10:15, 29. 11:23. 12:43. 13:30. 14:9, 18, 25, 30. Lk 4:24. 11:51. 12:37. 13:35. 18:17, 29. 21:32. 23:43. Jn +1:51.

heaven. Mt 24:35. Ps 102:26. Is 51:6. Lk 16:17. 21:33. He 1:11, 12. 2 P 3:10-13. Re 20:11.

one jot. Jn +10:35.

no wise. Repeated Negation or emphatic negative. For other examples of this usage see ver. 20, 26. Mt 13:14. 16:22, 28. 18:3, 39. 22:29. 24:34, 35. 26:29, 35. Mk 14:25. Lk 1:15. 6:37. 10:19. 18:7, 30. 21:18. 22:18, 34, 67, 68. Jn 3:18. 4:14, 48. 6:35, 37. 8:12, 51. 10:5, 28. 11:26. 13:8, 38. 20:25. Ac 28:26. Ro 4:8. 1 Th 4:15. 5:3. He 8:12. 10:17. 13:5. 1 P 2:6. 2 P 1:10. Re 3:12.

pass. Ps 119:89, 90, 152. Is 40:8. 1 P 1:25.
fulfilled. Mt 24:35. Is +42:21. Lk 16:17. 24:44. Jn 10:35. Ac 1:16. 3:18.

19 **Whosoever**. Mt +4:9.
shall break. Dt 27:26. Ps 119:6, 128. Mk 7:11. Lk 11:42. 1 C 3:12-15. Ga 3:10-13. Ja 2:10, 11.
these. Mt 23:23. Dt 12:32. Lk 11:42.
shall teach. Mt 15:3-6. 23:16-22. Ml 2:8, 9. Ro 3:8. 6:1, 15. 1 T 6:3, 4. Re 2:14, 15, 20.
be called. Mt +16:27.
the least. Mt 11:11. 18:1-4. 1 S 2:30.
shall do. Mt 7:24-27. 28:20. Dt +26:16, 18. Lk 8:21. 10:25, 26. Jn +13:17. Ac 1:1. Ro 13:8-10. Ga 5:14-24. Ph 3:17, 18. 4:8, 9. 1 Th 2:10-12. 4:1-7. 1 T 4:11, 12. 6:11. T 2:8-10. 3:8. Ja 1:22. Re 22:14.
and teach. Pr 27:9. Da +11:33. Ro 12:7. 1 Th +5:11. 1 T +4:16. 2 T +2:2.
great. Mt 19:28. 20:26. Da +12:3. Lk 1:15. 9:48. 22:24-26. 1 P 5:4.
kingdom of heaven. Mt +4:17.

20 **except**. Mt +4:9.
your righteousness. Jb 27:6. Ph 3:9.
exceed. ver. +48. Mt 23:2-5, 23-28. Lk 11:39, 40, 42, 44. 12:1. 16:14, 15. 18:10-14. 20:46, 47. Ro 6:15. 9:30-32. 10:2, 3. 2 C 5:17. +7:1. Ph 3:9.
scribes and Pharisees. Mt 16:12.
ye shall. Mt 3:10. +7:21. He 12:14.
in no case. ver. +18.
enter. Mt +7:21-23. 10:33. +12:31, 32. +13:30, 49. 25:10-12, 31, +32, 33. Ps 95:11. Pr +16:4. Lk +9:24. +12:10. +16:26. 1 C 6:9, 10. Ga 5:19-21. Ep 5:5, 6. He 12:14. Ja +1:15.

21 **it**. ver. 27, 31, 33, 38, 43. 2 S 20:18. Jb 8:8-10. Jn 12:34. Ac 15:21. Ga 4:21.
by them. *or*, to them.
Thou. Mt 19:18. Ge 9:5, 6. Ex +20:13. Le 24:21. Dt 5:17. Mk 10:19. Lk 18:20. Ro 13:9. Ja 2:11.
and. Ex 21:12-14. Nu 35:12, 16-21, 30-34. Dt 21:7-9. 1 K 2:5, 6, 31, 32.
the judgment. Dt 16:18. 17:9. 2 Ch 19:5, 6.

22 **I say**. ver. 28, 34, 44. Mt 3:17. 17:5. Dt 18:18, 19. Ac 3:20-23. 7:37. He 5:9. 12:25.
That. Ge 4:5, 6. 37:4, 8. 1 S 17:27, 28. 18:8, 9. 20:30-33. 22:12, etc. 1 K 21:4. 2 Ch 16:10. Est 3:5, 6. Ps 37:8. Da 2:12, 13. 3:13, 19. Ep 4:26, 27, 31. Col 3:8. Ja 1:19.
his brother. ver. 23, 24, 47. Mt 18:21, 35. Dt 15:11. Ne 5:8. Ob 10, 12. Ro 12:10. 1 C 6:6. 1 Th 4:6. 1 J 2:9. 3:10, 14, 15. 4:20, 21. 5:16.
without a cause. Ps 7:4. 25:3. 35:19. 69:4. 109:3. La 3:52. Jn 15:25. Ro 12:18. 13:4. Ep 4:26.
be. ver. 21.
the judgment. ver. 29. Mt 10:28. 18:9. 23:15, 33.
whosoever. Mt 11:18, 19. 12:24, 37. 1 S

20:30. 2 S 16:7. Jn 7:20. 8:48. Ac 17:18. 1 C 6:10. Ep 4:31, 32. T 3:2. 1 P 2:23. 3:9. Ju 9.
Raca. *that is*, vain fellow. 2 S 6:20. Ne +5:13. Ja 2:20.
in danger. Gr. *enokos*, liable or obnoxious to, from *enekomai*, to bind, oblige. Pr 13:3. Ja 3:2-12.
the council. Mt 10:17. 26:59. Mk 14:55. 15:1. Jn 11:47. Ac 4:15. 5:27.
fool. Ps 14:1. 49:10. 53:1. 92:6. Pr 14:16. 18:6. Je 17:11. or, *Moreh*, a Hebrew expression of condemnation. Nu 20:10.
in danger. Lk +9:24.
hell. Gr. *gehenna*, **S#1067g**. Mt 5:22, 29, 30. Mt 10:28. 18:9. 23:15, 33. Mk 9:43, 45, 47. Lk 12:5. Ja 3:6. See Jsh +15:8. For **S#86g**, *hades*, see Mt +11:23. 2 P 2:4.
fire. Mt 18:8. +25:41. Dt +32:22. Ps 88:11. Is +66:24. Lk +16:23, 24. Re 20:14. Re +21:8.

23 **if**. Mt +4:9. Mt 6:15. Mk 11:25.
thou. Mt 8:4. 23:18, 19. Dt 16:16, 17. 1 S 15:22. Is 1:10-17. Ho 6:6. Am 5:21-24.
to the altar. The brazen altar, before the porch of the Temple (Wordsworth, *Greek Testament*), the altar of burnt offering. Mt 23:18, 35. Ex 27:1, 2. 2 Ch +4:1. Am +9:1. Lk 11:51. 1 C 9:13. 10:18. He 7:13. 13:10.
rememberest. Ge 41:9. 42:21, 22. 50:15-17. Le 6:2-6. 1 K 2:44. La 3:20. Ezk 16:63. Lk 19:8. 1 C 11:28.
ought against. Mk 11:25. Re 2:4, 14, 20.

24 **there**. Mt 18:15-17. Jb +42:8. Pr 25:9. Mk 9:50. Ro 12:17, 18. 1 C 6:7, 8. 1 T +2:8. Ja 3:13-18. 5:16. 1 P 3:7, 8.
be reconciled. 1 S 29:4. 1 C 7:11.
and then. Mt 23:23. 1 C 11:28.

25 **agree with**. Ge 32:3-8, 13-22. 33:3-11. 1 S 25:17-35. Pr 6:1-5. 25:8. Lk 12:58, 59. 14:31, 32.
thine adversary. Lk 12:58. 18:3.
whiles. Jb 22:21. Ps 32:6. Is 55:6, 7. Lk 13:24, 25. 2 C 6:2. He 3:7, 13. 12:17.
and the judge. 1 K 22:26, 27.
officer. Mt 26:58.

26 **Thou**. Mt 18:34. 25:41, 46. Lk 12:59. 16:26. 2 Th 1:9. Ja 2:13.
by no means. ver. +18.
uttermost farthing. Mk 12:42.

27 **Thou**. Mt 19:18. Ex +20:14. Le 18:20. 20:10. Dt 5:18. 22:22-24. Pr 6:32. Mk 10:19. Lk 18:20. Ro 13:9. 1 C +6:9. He +13:4.

28 **I say**. ver. 22, 39. Mt 7:28, 29.
That. Ge 34:2. 39:7, etc. Ex 20:17. 2 S 11:2. Jb 24:15. 31:1, 9. Ps +101:3. 119:37. Pr 6:25. Is 33:15. Ja 1:14, 15. 2 P 2:14. 1 J 2:16.
looketh. Ezk +23:16.
to lust. Gr. *epithumeo*, **S#1937g**. ver. 28. Mt 13:17 (desired). Lk 15:16 (would fain). 16:21 (desiring). 17:22. 22:15. Ac 20:33 (coveted).

Ro 7:7. 13:9. 1 C 10:6 (lusted). Ga 5:17. 1 T 3:1 (desireth). He 6:11. Ja 4:2 (lust). 1 P 1:12 (desire). Re 9:6. Compare related noun, *epithumia*, **S#1939g**, 1 Th +4:5.

hath. Ps 119:96. Ro 7:7, 8, 14.

heart. Mt 12:35. Pr +4:23. Je +6:19. Mk +7:21.

29 if. 1 C 15:2. Mt 18:8, 9. Mk 9:43-48.

right eye. Ex 29:20. 1 S 11:2. Zc 11:17.

offend thee. *or*, do cause thee to offend. Mt +17:27.

pluck. Mt 19:12. Ezk 23:34. Ro 6:6. 8:13. 1 C 9:27. Ga 5:24. Col 3:5. 1 P 4:1-3.

for. Mt 16:26. Pr 5:8-14. Mk 8:36. Lk 9:24, 25.

hell. Gr. *gehenna*, ver. +22.

30 if. 1 C +15:2.

right hand offend. Mt +11:6.

cut it off. Ezk 23:34. Mk 9:43, 44.

cast. Mt 22:13. +25:30. Lk +12:5.

31 Whosoever. Mt 19:3, 7, 9. Dt *24:1-4*. Is 50:1. Je 3:1, 8. Mk 10:2-9.

32 I say. ver. 28. Lk 9:30, 35.

whosoever. Mt 19:8, 9. Ml 2:14-16. Mk 10:5-12. Lk 16:18. Ro 7:3. 1 C 7:4, 10, 11.

fornication. Gr. *porneia*, **S#4202g**. Mt 15:19. 19:9. Mk 7:21. Jn 8:41. Ac +15:20, 29. 21:25. Ro 1:29. 1 C 5:1. 6:13, 18. 7:2. 2 C 12:21. Ga 5:19. Ep 5:3. Col 3:5. 1 Th 4:3. Re 2:21. 9:21. 14:8. 17:2, 4. 18:3. 19:2.

and whosoever. Mt +4:9.

33 it hath. Mt 23:16.

Thou. Ex 20:7. Le 19:12. Dt 5:11. Jg +11:35. 1 T 1:10.

shalt perform. Nu +30:2. Dt *23:21*. Jb 22:27. Na 1:15.

34 Swear. Dt 10:20. 23:21-23. Ec 9:2. Ja 5:12.

not at all. Ex +20:10.

heaven. Mt 23:16-22. Is +57:15. *66:1*.

throne. Ps +11:4.

35 footstool. Is +*66:1*.

the city. Mt 4:5. 2 Ch 6:6. Ps *48:2*. 87:2. Re 21:2, 10.

great King. Ps +47:2.

36 shalt. Mt 23:16-21.

because. Mt 6:27. 10:30. Lk 12:25.

37 let. 2 C 1:17-20. Col 4:6. Ja 5:12.

whatsoever. Mt 12:36, 37. Pr 10:19.

cometh. Mt 13:19. 15:19. Jn 8:44. Ep 4:25. Col 3:9. Ja 5:12.

evil. ver. 39. Mt 6:13. 12:35. Lk 6:45.

38 An eye. Ex *21:22-27*. Le *24:19, 20*. Dt 19:19, 21.

39 That. Le 19:18. 1 S 24:4-6, 10-15. 25:31-34. *26:8-10*. Jb 31:29-31. Pr 20:22. 24:29. Lk 6:29. Ro 12:17-19. 1 C 6:7. 1 Th 5:15. He 12:4. Ja 5:6. 1 P 3:9.

resist not. Mt 26:52. Ge 26:22. Pr +19:25. Lk +22:36. Jn 18:11, 36. Ro +12:19.

evil. Dt 19:19. 1 C 5:13.

whosoever. Mt +27:30. Lk +22:36. Ac 16:37. Ro 12:17. 1 P 2:20-23.

40 will sue. Pr 19:11. Lk 6:29. 1 C 6:1, 6, 7.

thy cloak. Mt 24:18. Mk 13:16.

41 compel. Mt 27:32. Mk 15:21. Lk 23:26.

42 Give to him. Mt 10:8. 25:8, 9, 35-40. 26:11. Dt 15:7-14. Jb 31:16-20. Ps 37:21, 25, 26. 112:5-9. Pr 3:27, 28. 11:24, 25. 19:17. 21:26. Ec 11:1, 2, 6. Is 58:6-12. Da 4:27. Lk 3:11. 6:30-36, +38. 11:41. 12:33. 14:12-14. Ac 18:20. 20:35. Ro 12:20. 2 C 9:6-15. Ga +6:10. 1 T 6:17-19. He +6:10. +13:16. Ja 1:27. 2:15, 16. 1 J 3:16-18.

from him. Dt +15:8.

turn not. Le 25:35. Dt 15:8, 10.

43 Thou. Le +*19:18*.

and hate. Ex 17:14-16. Dt 23:6. 25:17, 19. 1 S 24:19. Ezr 9:12. Ps 41:10. 139:21, 22.

44 Love your enemies. Ex 23:4, 5. Le 19:18. 2 K 6:22. 2 Ch 28:9-15. Ps 7:4. 35:13, 14. Pr 25:21, 22. Lk 6:27, 28, 34, 35. 23:34. Ac 7:60. Ro 12:14, 20, 21. 1 C 4:12, 13. 13:4-8. 1 Th 5:15. 1 P 2:23. 3:9.

do good. 1 S 24:17, 18. Ga 6:10.

pray for. Ps 35:13, 14. Je 29:7. Lk 6:27, 28. 23:33, 34. Ac 7:59, 60. 2 T +4:14, 16. 1 P 3:9.

persecute. Je 29:7. 1 C 4:12.

45 ye. ver. 9. Lk +6:35. Jn 13:35. Ep 5:1. Ph 2:15. 1 J 3:9, 10.

your Father. ver. 16, 48. Mt 6:9. 23:9.

for he maketh. Mt 6:26, 28-30. Dt 10:18. Jb 2:10. 25:3. Ps 104:14, 21, 27, 28. 145:9. Lk +6:35. Ac 14:17. 17:26.

the evil and. Jb +9:22. Ec +9:2. Am +3:6.

and sendeth. Le 26:4. Jb 2:10. Is 55:9-11. La 3:38. Ac 14:17.

46 if. Mt +4:9. Mt 6:1. Lk 6:32-35. 1 P 2:19-23.

publicans. Mt 9:10, 11. 11:19. 18:17. 21:31, 32. Mk 2:15, 16. Lk 3:12. 5:29, 30. 7:29, 34. 15:1. 18:10, 11, 13. 19:2, 7.

47 if. Mt +4:9.

salute. Mt 10:12. Lk 6:32. 10:4, 5.

your brethren. ver. 22.

what. ver. 20. 1 P 2:20.

do not even. Mt 6:7, 32. Je +10:2. 3 J 7.

48 perfect. Mt 19:21. 22:37-39. Ge 6:9. +17:1. Le +19:2. Dt *18:13*. 1 K 8:61. 2 K +20:3. Jb 1:1, 8. 2:3. 9:20, 21. Ps +37:18, 37. 119:1mg. Pr +21:3. 23:17. Ec 7:16. Zp 3:13. Lk 6:36, 40. Jn 17:23. 1 C 2:6. 10:31. 2 C +7:1. 13:9, 11. Ph 3:12-15. Col 1:28. 4:12. He 13:21. Ja 1:4. 3:2. 1 P 5:10. 2 P 3:11, 12. 1 J 3:2. Ju 21.

even. ver. 16, 45. Ep 3:1. 4:32. 5:1, 2. 1 J 3:3.

MATTHEW 6

1 heed. Mt 16:6. Mk 8:15. Lk 11:35. 12:1, 15. He 2:1.

ye do. 1 J 2:29.

alms. *or,* righteousness. Dt 24:13. Ps 112:9. Da 4:27. 2 C 9:9, 10.

to be seen. ver. 5, 16. Mt 5:16. 23:5, 15, 28-30. 2 K 10:16, 31. Ezk +33:31. Zc 7:5, 6. 13:4. Lk +16:15. Jn 5:44. 12:43. Ga 6:12, 13.

otherwise. ver. 4, 6. Mt +5:12, 46.

of your. *or,* with your. ver. 9, 26, 32. Mt 5:16, 48. 23:9.

2 when. Ge 47:29. Jb 31:16-20. Ps 37:21. 112:9. Pr 19:17. Ec 11:2. Is 58:7, 10-12. Lk 11:41. 12:33. Jn 13:29. Ac 9:36. 10:2, 4, 31. 11:29. 24:17. Ro 12:8. 1 C 13:3. 2 C 9:6-15. Ga 2:10. Ep 4:28. 1 T 6:18. Phm 7. He 13:16. Ja 2:15, 16. 1 P 4:11. 1 J 3:17-19.

do not sound a trumpet. *or,* cause not a trumpet to be sounded. Pr 20:6. Ho 8:1.

as the hypocrites. ver. 5, 16. Mt 7:5. 15:7. 16:3. 22:18. 23:13-29. 24:51. Jb +8:13. Mk 7:6. Lk 6:42. +12:1, 56. 13:15.

in the synagogues. ver. 5. Mt 23:6. Mk 12:39. Lk 11:43. 20:46.

glory. 1 S 15:30. Lk 16:15. Jn 5:41, 44. 7:18. 1 Th 2:6.

Verily. ver. 5, 16. Mt +5:18.

I say. Note Christ's effective use of incongruity and contrast to evoke humor. Pr 17:22. For other instances of humor see Mt 6:5, 16, 26, 34. 7:1-4, 6, 16. 8:22. 11:16-19. 12:27.

They have. ver. +5, 16. Ps 17:14. Lk 6:24. Ph 4:18. Phm 15.

3 But when. Mt 10:42. 19:21. 25:35, 37-40. Lk 6:38. 14:12-14. Ro 12:8.

doest alms. ver. 2. Ps 112:9.

let not. ver. 2. Mt 8:4. 9:30. 12:19. +23:23. Mk 1:44. Jn 7:4.

right hand. Ge +48:13. Dt 15:7. Ps 104:28. 145:16. Pr 3:27. 31:20. Ezk 21:21. Ac 3:7.

4 alms. ver. 1. Ac 10:2, 4, 31.

seeth. ver. 6, 18. 2 K 17:9. 1 Ch +28:9. Ps 17:3. 44:21. 139:1-3, 12. Je +17:10. 23:24. He 4:13. Re 2:23.

reward. Mt +5:12. 1 S 2:30. Lk 8:17. +14:14. 1 C 4:5. Ju 24.

5 when. Mt 7:7, 8. 9:38. 21:22. Ps 5:2. +55:17. Pr 15:8. Is 55:6, 7. Je 29:12. Da +6:10. 9:4, etc. Lk 18:1. Jn 16:24. Ep 6:18. Col 4:2, 3. 1 Th 5:17. Ja 5:15, 16.

prayest. Dt +19:5.

not be as. ver. 2. Mt 23:14. Jb 27:8-10. Is 1:15. Mk 12:40. Lk 18:10, 11. 20:47.

for. Mt 23:6. Mk 12:38. Lk 11:43.

love. Ps +11:5.

seen of men. ver. 1, 16. Mt 23:5.

Verily. ver. 2. Pr 16:5. Lk 14:12-14. Ja 4:6.

They have. ver. +2. Jb 12:6. 21:7-15. Ps 17:14. +42:10. 73:3-7, 12. 92:7. +103:10. Je 12:1, 2. Ezk 18:4. Lk 6:24-26. 16:25. 2 Th 1:4-8.

6 enter. Mt +14:23. 26:36-39. Ge 32:24-29. 2 K 4:33. Is *26:20.* Jn 1:48. Ac 9:40. 10:9, 30.

closet. or, inner chamber. Mt 24:26. Ge 43:30. 1 K 20:30mg. 2 K 4:10. Lk 12:3.

shut thy door. ver. 1, 18. 2 K 4:33. Is +26:20.

pray. Ps 34:15. Is +65:24. Jn 20:17. Ro 8:5. Ep 3:14.

which is in secret. Mt 14:23. 26:36-39. Ge 32:24-26. 2 K 4:32, 33. Is 26:20. Jn 1:48. Ac 9:40. 10:9, 10.

shall reward. ver. 4, 18. Mt +5:12.

7 use not. 1 K 18:26-29. Ec 5:2, 3, 7. Ac 19:34.

vain repetitions. Mt 26:39, 42, 44. 1 K 8:26-54. Da 9:18, 19.

the heathen. ver. 32. Mt 5:47. 18:17. Je +10:2. 3 J 7.

they think. 1 K 18:26, 29.

much speaking. Pr 10:19. Ec 5:2. Is 1:15mg.

8 Be not. Mt 23:3. 2 K 17:15. Je +10:2.

your Father. ver. 9, 32. Ps 38:9. 69:17-19. Is 63:15, 16. 64:7, 8. Lk 12:30. Jn 16:23-27. Ph 4:6.

before. Is +65:24. Da 2:21-23. Mk 11:24.

9 this manner. Lk 11:1, 2.

Our. ver. 1, 6, 14. Mt 5:16, 45, 48. 7:11. 10:29. 26:29, 42. Dt 32:6. 1 Ch ?29:10. Ps 68:5. Is 63:16. 64:8. Lk 15:18, 19, 21. Jn 14:6, 13. 16:23. 20:17. Ro 1:7. 8:15, 16. Ga 1:1. 4:6. 1 T 2:5. 1 P 1:17.

Father. Jn 4:23. 16:23. Ep 4:6. 1 J 3:1.

which art. Mt 7:21. 23:9. 2 Ch +20:6. Jb 22:12. Ps 2:4. 11:4. 102:19. 103:19. 115:3. 123:1. Is 40:22. +57:15. 66:1. Ac 7:49, 55, 56. 1 T +6:16.

Hallowed. 2 S 7:26. 1 K 8:43. 1 Ch 17:24. Ne 9:5. Ps 72:18, 19. 111:9. 103:20-22. 113:2, 3. Is 6:3. +8:13. 37:20. Hab 2:14. Zc 14:9. Ml 1:11, 14. Lk 1:49. 2:14. 11:2. 1 T 6:16. 1 P +3:15. Re 4:11. +5:12.

thy name. Ex +6:3. Le 18:21. 20:3. 21:6. +22:32. Ps 5:11. +9:10. Ml 1:11, 12. Jn 17:6.

10 Thy kingdom. ver. 13, 33. Mt +4:17. 13:43. 16:28. 20:21. 25:31, 34. +26:29. Ps 2:6-12. 22:28. 103:19. 145:11, 13. Is 2:2-4. 9:7. Je +23:5, 6. Da 2:44. +7:13, 14, 27. Ob 21. Zc +9:9. 14:9. Mk 11:10. Lk 12:29-32. 19:11, 38. 22:29, 30. 23:42. Ac 1:3, 6. Col 1:13. 2 T 4:1, 18. He 12:28. Ja 2:5. 2 P 1:11. Re 11:15. 12:10. 19:6. 20:4, 6.

come. Mt 7:22. 19:28. 25:34. 26:29. Ps +82:8. Mk 14:25. 15:43. Lk 12:32. +17:20, 21. 19:11. 22:18, 29, 30. 23:42. Ac +1:6. 1 Th 2:12. 2 Th 3:5. 2 T +4:1.

Thy will. Mt 26:39, 42, 44. Jg +10:15. Jb 1:20, 21. Ps 31:14, 15. +40:8. 143:10. Je 42:5, 6. Mk 14:36. Lk 22:42. Jn 6:40. 7:17. Ac 13:22. 21:14. 22:14. 1 Th +4:3. 1 J +5:14.

in earth. Mt +5:5. Dt +11:21.

as it is. Mt 28:18. Ne 9:6. Ps 103:19-21. Da 4:35. Lk 2:14. He 1:14.

11 Give us. ver. 26. Mt 4:4. 7:7. Ex 16:16-35. Jb

23:12. Ps 33:18, 19. 34:10. Pr 30:8, 9. Is 33:16. Lk 11:3. Jn 6:31, etc. 2 Th 3:12. 1 T 6:8.

daily. Mt 4:4. 24:45. 2 K 25:30. Is +58:11. Je 37:21.

bread. Mt 7:9-11. Ge +3:19. 28:20, 21. Nu 11:18, 19. Jb 38:41. Ps 78:27-29. +145:15, 16. Pr 30:8, 9. Is 33:16. La 1:11. 2:11, 12. 5:6-9. Jn 4:34.

12 forgive us. Ge 50:17. Ex 34:6-9. 2 S 24:10. 1 K 8:30, 34, 39, 50. Ps 32:1, 2. 51:1-9, 14. +103:3, 8-12. 130:1-7. Is 1:18. 30:18-20. 43:25, 26. 55:6, 7. Da 9:17-19. Ho 14:1, 2. Mi +7:18, 19. Lk 11:4. 18:13. Ac 8:22-24. 13:38. Ep 1:7. Col 2:13. Ja 5:14, 15. 1 J 1:7-9. 2:1, 2. 5:16.

debts. Mt 18:21-27, 34. Lk 7:40-48. 11:4.

as we. ver. 14, 15. Mt 18:21, 22, 28-35. Dt 15:7-11. Ne 5:12, 13. Mk 11:25, 26. Lk 6:37. 17:3-5. Ep 4:32. Col 3:13.

forgive our. Mk 11:25, 26. Lk 23:34. Ep +4:32.

debtors. Mt 18:24. Lk 11:4. 13:4mg.

13 lead. Mt 26:41. Ge 22:1. +31:7. Dt 8:2, 16. 1 Ch +4:10. Ps 141:4. Pr 30:8, 9. Mk 14:38. Lk 11:4. 22:31-46. 1 C 10:13. 2 C 12:7-9. He 11:36, 37. Ja 1:2. 1 P 5:8. 2 P 2:9. Re 2:10. +3:10.

temptation. Mt 26:41. Ps 28:3. 40:1, 2. Jn 17:15.

deliver us. 1 Ch +4:10. Ps +39:8. 40:11-13. 121:7, 8. Je 15:21. Lk +21:36. Jn 17:15. Ro 15:31. 2 C 12:7-9. Ga 1:4. 1 Th +1:10. 2 Th 3:1-3. 2 T 4:17, 18. He 2:14, 15. 1 J 3:8. 5:18, 19. Re 7:14-17. 21:4.

from evil. Ro 12:9. 1 Th 5:22. or, the evil one. Mt 13:19.

For thine. ver. 10. 1 Ch +29:11, 12. Da 4:25, 34, 35. 1 T 1:17. 6:15-17. Re 5:13. 19:1.

is the kingdom. Hendiatris; or, Three for One: three words used, but one thing meant, Je +4:2; i.e. powerful, glorious kingdom. Ps +22:28. 145:11, 13. Re +11:15.

the power. 2 Ch 14:11. 20:6, 7. Je 32:16, 17.

the glory. 1 Ch 16:35. Ps +79:9. 145:11. Zc 2:8. +6:13. Jn +14:13. 1 P +1:11.

for ever. lit. unto the ages, as in Lk 1:33. Ro 1:25. 9:5. 11:36. 16:27. 2 C 11:31. He 13:8. Greek *aion*, **S#165g**, rendered (1) *ever*: ver. 13. Mt 21:19. Mk 11:14. Lk 1:33, 55. Jn 6:51, 58. 8:35, 35. 12:34. 14:16. Ro 1:25. 9:5. 11:36. 16:27. 2 C 9:9. Ga 1:5, 5. Ph 4:20, 20. 1 T 1:17b, 17c. 2 T 4:18, 18. He 1:8, 8. 5:6. 6:20. 7:17, 21, 24. 13:8, 21, 21. 1 P 1:23, 25. 4:11, 11. 5:11, 11. 2 P 2:17. 3:18. 1 J 2:17. 2 J 2. Ju 13. Re 1:6, 6. 4:9, 9, 10, 10. 5:13, 13, 14, 14. 7:12, 12. 10:6, 6. 11:15, 15. 14:11, 11. 15:7, 7. 19:3, 3. 20:10, 10. 22:5, 5. For the various usages, see Ga 1:5 (unto the ages of the ages); Mt 21:19 (unto the age); Mt +12:32 (this

age); Mt 6:13 (unto the ages); Mt 13:39 (end of the age); Lk 1:70 (from the age).

Amen. Mt 28:20. Je +11:5mg. 1 C 14:16. 2 C 1:20. Ju 25. Re 1:18. 3:14. 5:14. 7:12. 19:4. 22:20.

14 if. Mt +4:9. Mt 16:24, 26. Ge +4:7. Je +7:5. Lk 14:26, 33, 34. Jn 8:31, 36, 39, 42, 46, 51. 7:17. 14:15, 23. 15:6, 10. 2 P +1:10.

ye forgive. ver. 12. Mt 7:2. 18:21-35. Pr 21:13. Mk 11:25, 26. Ep 4:32. Col 3:12, 13. Ja 2:13. 1 J 3:10.

15 But if. Mt +4:9. Mt 5:23. 18:35. Ja 2:13.

16 when ye fast. ver. 17, 18. Mt +4:2. 9:14, 15. Jg 20:26. 1 S 7:6. 2 S 12:16, 21. 2 Ch 7:14. 20:3. Ezr 8:21, 23. 10:6. Ne 1:4. 9:1. Est 4:1-3, 16. Ps +35:13. 69:10. 109:24. Is 58:3, 5-9. Je 36:9. Da +9:3. Jl 1:14. 2:12. Jon 3:5-9. Zc 7:5. +8:19. Lk 2:37. Ac 10:30. 13:2, 3. 14:23. 1 C 7:5. 2 C 6:5. 11:27.

be not. ver. 2, 5. 1 K 21:27. Is 58:3-5. Zc 7:3-5. Ml 3:14. Mk 2:18. Lk 18:12.

sad countenance. Lk 24:17.

disfigure. 2 S 15:30. Est 6:12.

appear unto men. ver. 1, 5. Mt 23:5.

They have. ver. 2, 5. Lk 6:24. Ph 4:18. Phm 15.

17 anoint. Ex +28:41. 2 S 12:20. Is 1:6. Zc 7:5. Mk 6:13. Lk +7:46. 10:34. Ja 5:14.

wash. Gr. *nipto*, **S#3538g**. Mt 15:2. Mk 7:3. Jn 9:7, 11, 15. 13:5, 6, 8, 10, 12, 14. 1 T 5:10.

18 appear not. ver. 2. 2 C 5:9. 10:18. Col 3:22-24. 1 P 2:13.

in secret. 2 K 17:9.

shall reward. ver. 4, 6. Ro +2:6, 7. 1 P 1:7.

19 Lay not. Mt 19:21. Ge 45:20. Jb 31:24, 25. Ps 39:6. 62:10. Pr 11:4. 16:16. 23:4, 5. Ec 2:26. 5:10-14. Je +45:5. Zp 1:18. Lk 12:15, 21, 33, 34. 18:22, 24, 25. Jn 6:27. Ph 4:5. Col 3:1-3. 1 T 6:8-10, 17-19. He 10:34. +13:5. Ja +5:1-3. 1 J 2:15, 16.

treasures. ver. 20.

moth and rust. Ja 5:2, 3.

thieves break through. Mt 24:43. Ex 22:2. Jb 24:16. Je 2:34. Ezk 12:5. Lk 12:39.

20 lay up. Mt 19:21. Pr 19:17. 30:25. Is 33:6. Lk 12:33. +16:9. 18:22. Ph 3:20. +4:17. 1 T 6:17, 19. He 10:34. 11:26. Ja +2:5. 1 P 1:4. 5:4. Re 2:9.

treasures. Mt 10:40-42. Dt +28:12. Mk 10:21. Lk 14:14. 16:9. 1 C 13:13. Ph 4:8, +17. Col 3:23, 24. 1 T +4:8. Re +11:18.

in heaven. 2 T +4:1, 18. He +11:16. 1 P +1:4.

where neither. Mt 22:30. 25:46. Is 60:20. 1 C +15:50. 1 P +1:4, 5.

21 where. Is 33:6. Lk 12:34. 1 C 7:32-34. 2 C 4:17, 18. Col 3:2.

there. Mt 12:34, 35. Pr +4:23. Je 4:14. 22:17. +45:5. Ac 8:21. Ro 7:5-7. Ph 3:19, 20. Col 1:5. 3:1-3. He +3:12. 1 J 2:15-17.

22 light of. Lk 11:34-36.

if therefore. Mt +4:9.
single. Ac 2:46. 2 C 11:3. Ep 6:5. Col 3:22.
23　**But if**. 1 C +15:2.
thine eye. Mt 20:15. Dt 15:9. 28:54, 56. Pr 23:6. 28:22. Is 44:18-20. Mk 7:22. Ep 4:18. 5:8. 1 J 2:11.
If. Mt +4:9. Mt 23:16, etc. Jb 38:15. Pr 26:12. Is 5:20, 21. +8:20. Je 4:22. 8:8, 9. Lk 8:10. Jn 9:39-41. Ro 1:22. 2:17-23. 1 C 1:18-20. 2:14. 3:18, 19. Ga 3:1. Re 3:17, 18.
the light. Mt +15:14. 23:15. 24:24. Jb 10:22. Pr +16:25. Is 5:20. Ezk 14:10. Jn +9:41. 1 C +3:18. Ga 6:3. Ep +4:14. 2 T 3:6, 7, 13. 2 P 2:18. 2 J 9, 10.
be darkness. Jb +22:6. Pr +4:19. Is +9:2.
how great. Pr 20:20. Is +8:20. 17:14.
24　**can serve**. Mt +4:10. 1 K 18:21. 2 K 17:33, 34, 41. Ezk 20:39. Zp 1:5. Lk 16:13. Ro 6:16-22. Ga 1:10. 2 T 4:10. Ja 4:4. 1 J 2:15, 16.
two masters. Mt 12:30.
hate the one. Ge 29:30, 31. Pr 13:24. Ml 1:2. Lk 14:26. 16:13. Ro +9:13.
hold to. T 1:9.
the other. Mt +11:3.
Ye cannot. Ga 1:10. Ja 4:4. 1 J 2:15.
mammon. Lk 16:9, 11, 13. 1 T 6:9, 10, 17.
25　**I say**. Mt 5:22, 28. Lk 12:4, 5, 8, 9, 22.
Take no thought. Mt +13:22. 1 S 9:5. 10:2. Ps 55:22. Mk 4:19. 13:11. Lk 8:14. 10:40-42. 12:11, 22, 25, 26, 29, 30. 1 C 7:32-34. +12:25. Ph 2:20. 4:6. 1 T 6:8. 2 T +1:7. 2:4. He +13:5, 6. 1 P 5:7.
Is not. Lk 12:23. Ro +8:32.
life. Gr. *psyche*, Mt +2:20; Ge +9:5. Mt +10:28. Ge +2:7. Ec 12:7 w 1 C 5:3, 5.
than raiment. ver. 30-32.
26　**the fowls**. Mt 10:29-31. Ge 1:29-31. Jb 12:7-9. 35:11. 38:41. Ps 104:11, 12, 27, 28. 145:15, 16. 147:8, 9. Lk 12:6, 7, 24, etc. Ac 10:12.
barns. Lk 12:18.
your heavenly. ver. 32. Mt 7:9-11. Lk 12:32.
Are ye not. Mt 10:31. 12:12.
27　**by taking thought**. ver. 25. Mt 5:36. Ps 39:5, 6. Ec 3:14. Lk 12:25, 26. 1 C 12:18.
stature. or, age. Ps 139:5. Lk 2:52. Jn 9:21.
28　**why**. ver. 25, 31. Mt 10:10. Lk 3:11. 22:35, 36.
the lilies. Ho 14:5. Lk 12:27.
29　**even Solomon**. 1 K 10:5-7. 2 Ch 9:4-6, 20-22. 1 T 2:9, 10. 1 P 3:2-5.
one of these. Mt 18:10. 25:40, 45. Lk 15:7, 10.
30　**if God**. 1 C +15:2.
clothe. 1 P +1:24.
O ye. Mt 8:26. 14:31. 16:8. 17:17, 20. Mk 4:40. 9:19. 16:14. Lk 8:25. 9:41. 12:28. 17:6. 24:25. Jn 20:27. He +3:12, 13.
31　**take no thought**. ver. 25. Ph 4:6. 1 P 5:7.
What shall we eat. Mt 4:4. 15:33. Le 25:20-

22. 2 Ch 25:9. Ps +37:3. 55:22. 78:18-31. Lk 12:29.
32　**after**. Mt 5:46, 47. 20:25, 26. Ps 17:14. Lk 12:30. Ep 4:17. 1 Th 4:5.
seek. Lk 12:30.
for your. ver. 8. Ps 84:11. 103:13. Lk 11:11-13. 12:30. 1 C 3:22.
33　**seek ye**. Mt +5:6, 20. 1 K 3:11-13. 17:13. 2 Ch 1:7-12. 31:20, 21. Pr 2:1-9. 3:9, 10. Hg 1:2-11. 2:16-19. Lk 12:31. Jn 6:27.
first. Mt 7:5. 23:26.
the kingdom. ver. 10. Mt +12:28. Col 1:13, 14. 2 P 1:11.
his righteousness. Mt 5:6, 20. 22:36-39. Is 45:24. Je 23:6. Mi +6:8. Lk 1:6. Ro 1:17. 3:21, 22. 10:3. 14:17. 1 C 1:30. 2 C 5:21. Ph 3:9. 2 P 1:1.
and all. Mt 19:29. Le 25:20, 21. Dt 33:11. Ps 37:3, 4, 18, 19, 25. +84:11. Mk +10:29, 30. Lk 18:29, 30. 1 P 3:9.
shall be added. Mt 5:6. 1 S 2:30. 1 K 3:11-14. Lk 10:42.
34　**no thought**. ver. 11, 25. Ex 16:18-20. La 3:23.
for the morrow. Dt 33:25. 1 K 17:4-6, 14-16. 2 K 7:1, 2. Pr +22:3. Lk 11:3. 14:28-30. He +13:5, 6.
Sufficient. Jn 14:27. 16:33. Ac 14:22. 1 Th 3:3, 4. Ja 4:13, 14.

MATTHEW 7

1　**Judge not**. ver. 5. Is 66:5. Ezk 16:52-56. Lk 6:37. 7:43. Jn +7:24. Ro 2:1, 2. 14:3, 4, 10-13. 1 C 2:15. 4:3-5. 10:15. Ja 3:1. 4:11, 12. 5:9.
that ye. Mt 6:14. 18:23-35. 1 C 11:31. 2 C 5:10. 13:5. Ja 2:13. 3:1.
2　**For with**. Ps 18:25, 26. Je +50:15. 51:24. Ob 15. Mk 4:24. Lk +6:38. Ro 2:1, 3. 14:10. 2 C 9:6. 2 Th 1:6, 7. Ja 4:11, 12.
and with. Mt +6:2. Le 24:19. Mk 4:24. Lk 6:37.
3　**why**. Lk 6:41, 42. 18:11.
but. 2 S 12:5, 6. 2 Ch 28:9, 10. Ps 50:16-21. Jn 8:7-9. Ga 6:1.
5　**Thou hypocrite**. Mt +6:2.
first. Mt 6:33. 23:26. Ps +51:9-13. Lk 4:23. 6:42. Ac 19:15. Ro 2:21-23.
6　**Give not**. Mt +6:2. 7:9, 10. 10:5, 11. 15:26. 2 Ch 19:2. Ps 39:1. Pr 9:7, 8. 13:1. 14:7. +16:4. 23:9. Je 7:16. Lk 19:20. 1 C 14:38. 1 J 5:16.
that. Mt 10:14, 15. 15:26. Pr 9:7, 8. 23:9. 26:11. Lk +12:10. Ac 13:45-47. Ph 3:2. He 6:6. 10:29. 2 P 2:22.
dogs. Mt 15:26. Ps 22:16. 1 K 22:38. 2 K 9:10, 36. Is 56:10, 11. 66:3. Ph 3:2. 2 P 2:2. Re 22:15.
neither cast. 1 S +25:17, 25. Pr 11:22. 14:7. +16:22. +22:3. 23:9. 29:9.
pearls. Mt +13:46.

before swine. 2 P 2:22.

turn. Mt 22:5, 6. 24:10. 2 C 11:26. 2 T 4:14, 15.

and rend. Mk 9:18.

7 **Ask**. ver. 11. Mt +18:19. Ge 32:26. 1 K 3:5. Ps 86:5. Is 55:6, 7. Je 33:3. Mk 11:24. Lk 11:9, 10, 13. 18:1. Jn 4:10. Ro 8:26, 27. He +4:16. Ja +1:5, 6, 17. 4:2. 1 J +5:14, 15. Re 3:17, 18.

seek. Ps 10:4. 27:8. 32:6. 70:4. 105:3, 4. 119:2. SS 3:2. Je +29:13. Ro 2:7. 3:11.

knock. Lk 12:36. 13:25. Re 3:20.

8 **For every one**. Mt 15:22-28. 2 Ch 33:1, 2, 19. Ps 81:10, 16. Jon 2:2. 3:8-10. Lk 23:42, 43. Ac 9:11. Ja 4:3.

9 **what man**. Lk 11:11-13.

if. Mt +4:9.

a stone. Mt 4:3. Lk 4:3.

10 **a serpent**. Je 29:11. Lk 6:35. Ja 1:17.

11 **If**. 1 C +15:2.

being evil. Mt 12:34. Ge 6:5. 8:21. Jb 15:14, 16. Je 17:9. Ro 3:9-19, 23. Ga 3:22. Ep 2:1-3. T 3:3.

know. Is +53:11.

how much. Ex 34:6, 7. 2 S 7:19. Ps 86:5, 15. 103:11-13. Is 49:15. 55:8, 9. Ho 11:8, 9. Mi 7:18. Ml 1:6. Lk 3:21. 11:11, etc. Jn 3:16. Ro 5:8-10. 8:32. Ep 2:4, 5. 1 J 3:1. 4:10.

your Father. Mt 23:9.

good things. Ps 34:10. 84:11, 12. 85:12. Je +29:11. 33:14. Ho 14:2mg. Lk 2:10, 11. 11:13. 2 C 9:8-15. T 3:4-7.

12 **all**. Pr 18:24. 24:29. Lk 6:31.

whatsoever. Mt +4:9.

do ye. T 3:2.

for this. Mt 5:17. 11:13. 22:39, 40. Le 19:18. Is 1:17, 18. Je 7:5, 6. Ezk 18:7, 8, 21. Am 5:14, 15. Mi +6:8. Zc 7:7-10. 8:16, 17. Ml +3:5. Mk 12:29-34. Lk 16:16. Ro 13:8-10. Ga 5:13, 14. 1 T 1:5. Ja 2:10-13.

13 **Enter**. 1 Ch +28:9.

at the strait. Mt 3:2, 8. 18:2, 3. 23:13. Pr 9:6. Is 55:7. Ezk 18:27-32. Mk 10:24. Lk 9:23. 13:24, 25. 14:33. Jn 10:7, 9. 14:6. Ac 2:38-40. +3:19. 14:22. 2 C 6:17. Ga 5:24.

for wide. Ge 6:5, 12. Ps 14:2, 3. Is 1:9. Ro 3:9-19. 2 C 4:4. Ep 2:2, 3. 1 J 5:19. Re 12:9. 13:8. 20:3.

gate. Ge +14:7.

that leadeth. Mt 25:41, 46. Pr 7:27. 14:12. 16:25. Ro 9:22. Ph 3:19. 2 Th 1:8, 9. 1 P 4:17, 18. Re 20:15.

destruction. Gr. *apoleia*, **S#684g**. lit. the destruction. Mt 26:28 (waste). Mk 14:4. Jn 17:12 (lit. the perdition). Ac 8:20 (perish. lit. be to destruction). 25:16 (die. lit. to destruction). Ro 9:22. Ph 1:28 (perdition). 3:19. 2 Th 2:3 (lit. the perdition). 1 T 6:9. He 10:39. 2 P 2:1 (damnable. lit. heresies of *perdition*), 1 (destruction), 2 (pernicious), 3 (damnation). 3:7, 16. Re 17:8, 11. W. J. Eerdman estab-

lishes that "destruction" is equivalent to "abaddon," the lowest pit of Sheol, the "deep" or the "abyss" (*The Unseen World: A Concordance with Notes*, p. 22). Jb 26:6 (**S#11h**). Re 9:11mg.

14 **Because**. *or*, How.

gate. Ge +14:7.

narrow. Mt 16:24, 25. Pr 4:26, 27. 8:20. Is 30:21. 35:8. 57:14. Je 6:16. Mk 8:34. Jn 15:18-20. 16:2, 33. Ac 14:22. 1 Th 3:2-5.

the way. Mt 18:8. Ps 16:11. Jn 14:6.

which leadeth. Ro 8:13.

life. Gr. *dzoe*, **S#2222g**. Rendered (1) *life*: Mt 18:8, 9. 19:16, 17, 29. 25:46. Mk 9:43, 45. Lk 12:15. Jn 3:15, 16, 36. 4:14, 36. 5:24, 26, 29, 39, 40. 10:10, 28. 14:6. 17:2, 3. 20:31. Ac 13:46, 48. Ro 6:23. Ga 6:8. 1 T 4:8. T 1:2. 2 P 1:3. 1 J 5:11, 12, 13, 16, 20. Re 3:5. 13:8. 20:12, 15. 21:6, 27. (2) *lifetime*: Lk 16:25.

and few. Mt 18:19, 20. 20:16. 22:14. 25:1-12. Ge 6:11, 12. 7:1. 18:32. Nu 14:23, 24. Is 1:5-9. +24:16. Je 5:1. Ezk 22:17, 18, 30. +33:31. Ml +3:16. Mk 10:24, 25. Lk 9:26. 12:32. 13:23-30. 18:8. Jn 1:11. 3:18, 36. 5:40. 10:1, 7, 9. 14:6. Ac 4:12. 14:22. 28:22. Ro 9:27-29, 32. 11:4-6, 14. 12:2. 1 C 1:26. +6:9, 10. Ga 5:21. Ep 2:2, 3. 2 T 1:15. 3:5. T 1:16. He 6:11, 12. 10:39. Ja 2:13. 4:17. 1 P 3:20, 21. 4:18. 2 P +1:10. 1 J 2:3, 4. Re 3:4. 7:9. +20:4.

15 **Beware**. Mt 10:17. 16:6, 11. Pr +14:15. Mk 12:38. Lk 12:1, 15. Ac 13:40. Ro 14:12. Ph 3:2. Col 2:8. 2 P 3:17.

false prophets. Mt 24:4, 5, 11, 24, 25. Dt 13:1-3. Jb +1:7. 1 K 13:18. Ps +5:9. Is 9:15, 16. Je 6:14. 14:14-16. 23:13-16. 28:15-17. 29:21, 32. Ezk 13:10, 16, 18, 22. 14:10. Mi 3:5-7, 11. Mk 13:22, 23. Lk 6:26. Ac 13:6. 20:29, 30. 1 T 4:1. T 1:10, 11. 2 P 2:1-3. 1 J 4:1. Re 2:2. 16:13. 19:20. 20:10.

which. Zc 13:4. Mk 12:38-40. Ro +16:17, 18. 2 C 11:13-15. Ga 2:4. Ep 4:14. 5:6. Col 2:8. 1 T 4:1-3. 2 T 3:5-9, 13. 4:3. 2 P 2:1-3, 18, 19. Ju 4. Re 13:11-17.

are ravening. Is 56:10, 11. Ezk +22:25, 27. Mi 3:5. Zp 3:3, 4. Jn 10:12. Ac 20:29-31. Re 17:6.

16 **Ye shall**. ver. 20. Mt +6:2. 12:33. Lk 6:37, 44. Ga 5:19-22. Ja 2:18. 2 P 2:10-18. Ju 10-19.

know. Gr. *epiginosko*, Mt +11:27.

Do. Lk 6:43-45. Ac 10:47. Ja 3:12.

thorns. He 6:8.

17 **every**. Ps 1:3. 92:13, 14. Is 5:3-5. 61:3. Je 11:19. 17:8. Lk 6:45. 13:6-9. Ro 6:22. Ga 5:22-24. Ep 5:9. Ph 1:11. Col +1:10. Ja 3:17, 18.

but. Mt 12:33-35. Ga 5:19-21. Ju 12.

18 **cannot**. Lk 6:43. Ro 8:7, 8. Ga 5:17. 1 J 3:9, 10.

neither can. Jb 14:4. Je 13:23. Mt 12:33.

19 **bringeth**. Mt 3:10. 21:19, 20. Is 5:5-7. 27:11.

Ezk 15:2-7. Lk 3:9. 13:6-9. Jn 15:2-6. He 6:8. Ju 12.

cast into. Jn 15:6.

20 **by their fruits**. ver. 16. Ac 5:38.
know. Gr. *epiginosko*, Mt +11:27.

21 **saith**. Mt 25:11, 12. Ho +8:2, 3. Lk 6:46. 13:25. Ac 19:13, etc. Ro 2:13. 1 C +12:3. T 1:16. Ja 1:22. 2:20-26.
Lord, Lord. Mt 25:11. Is 48:1, 2. Lk +6:46.
shall enter. Mt 5:20. 18:3. 19:23, 24. 21:31. 25:11, 12, 21. Mk 9:47. 10:15, 23-25. Lk 13:24. 18:17, 25. Jn 3:5. Ac 14:22. He 4:6. 2 P 1:11. Re 21:27.
kingdom of heaven. Mt +4:17.
that doeth. ver. 24-27. Mt 5:19. +6:10. 21:29-31. 26:42. Lk +11:28. 22:42. Jn 4:23. 6:38, 40. 9:31. +13:17. Ro 2:13. 12:2. Ep 2:10. T 3:8. He 10:7, 9. 13:21. Ja +1:22. 1 J 3:21-24. Re 22:14.
the will. 1 S +16:7. Ps 75:6, 7. Jn 6:38. 7:17. 1 Th +4:3.
my Father. Mt 10:32, 33. 12:50. 15:13. 16:17. 18:10, 14, 19, 35. 26:39, 42. Jn 5:17, 18. 10:29, 30. 14:7. 15:23. Re 2:27. 3:5.
in heaven. Mt +6:9.

22 **Many**. ver. 13. Mt 25:11, 12. Lk 10:20. 13:25-27.
to me. ver. +21. Mt 24:36. Ml 3:17, 18. Lk 10:12. Jn 5:22. 1 Th 5:4. 2 T 1:12, 18. 4:8. 1 P 4:18.
in that day. Is +2:11. Ml 3:17. Ac +17:31. 2 Th +1:10.
Lord. ver. 21. Mt 25:11. Ac 19:13. 1 C 12:3.
have we. Mt 10:5-8. Nu 24:4. 31:8. 1 K 22:11, etc. Je 23:13, etc. Lk 13:26. Jn 11:51. Ac 19:13-15. 1 C 13:1, 2. He 6:4-6.
prophesied. Je *14:14*. 27:15.
thy name. Le 19:12. Mk 9:38. Lk 9:49. Ac 4:18. 19:13-15. Ja 5:10.
cast out. Mt 12:27. Mk 9:38.

23 **I never knew**. Mt 10:33. 15:13. 25:12. 1 S +16:7. Ps 1:6. 31:7. 37:18. 101:4. 144:3. Ho 8:4. 13:5. Am 3:2. Mk 4:16, 17. Jn 6:70. 10:14, 27, +28, 29, 30. 17:12. Ro +8:34. 2 C +1:22. 13:5. 2 T 2:19. 2 P +2:20. 1 J 2:19.
depart. Mt +13:41. Ps 5:5. +6:8. +50:16. 75:6, 7. Hab 1:13. Re 22:15.
work iniquity. Ps 5:5. 92:7, 9. 94:4. 101:8. 125:5.

24 **whosoever heareth**. ver. 7, 8, 13, 14. Mt 5:3, etc., 28-32. 6:14, 15, 19, etc. 12:50. Lk 6:47-49. +11:28. Jn +13:17. 14:15, 22-24. 15:10, 14. Ro 2:6-9. Ga 5:6, 7. 6:7, 8. Ja 1:21-27. 2:17-26. 1 J 2:3. 3:22-24. 5:3-5. Re 22:14, 15.
and doeth. ver. 21. Lk +11:28. Ja +1:22.
liken. Ps +1:3.
a wise. Mt 25:2. Jb 28:28. Ps 111:10. 119:99, 130. Pr 10:8. 14:8. Ja 3:13-18.
which. 1 C 3:10, 11.

25 **And**. Ge +8:22.
the rain. Ezk 13:11, etc. Ml 3:3. Ac 14:22. 1 C 3:13-15. Ja 1:12. 1 P 1:7.
for it. Mt 16:18. Ps 92:13-15. 125:1, 2. Ep 3:17. Col 2:7. 1 P 1:5. 1 J 2:19.

26 **doeth them not**. 1 S 2:30. Pr 14:1. Je 8:9. Lk 6:49. Ja 2:20.
foolish. Ezk 13:10-14.

27 **the rain**. Mt 12:43-45. +13:19-22. Ezk 13:10-16. 1 C 3:13. He 10:26-31. 2 P 2:20-22.
and great. Am 6:11.

28 **came to pass**. Mt 11:1. 13:53. 19:1. 26:1. Lk 7:1.
people were astonished. Mt 13:54. 22:33. Ps 45:2. Mk 1:22, 27. 6:2. 11:18. Lk 2:47. 4:22, 32, 36. 19:48. Jn 7:15, 46. Ac 13:12.
doctrine. Mk +4:2.

29 **having**. Mt 5:20, 28, 32, 44. 21:23-27. 28:18. Dt 18:18, 19. Ec 8:4. Is 50:4. Je 23:28, 29. Mi 3:8. Mk 1:22. Lk 21:15. Jn 7:46. Ac 3:22, 23. 6:10. He 4:12, 13.
and not. Mt 15:1-9. 23:2-6, 15-24. Mk 7:5-13. Lk 20:8, 46, 47.

MATTHEW 8

1 **come**. Mt 5:1.
great. ver. 18. Lk +5:15.

2 **behold**. Mk 1:40, etc. Lk 5:12.
a leper. Mt 26:6. 2 K +5:1. Lk +7:22.
worshipped. Mt 2:2, 8, 11. 4:9. 9:18. +14:33. 15:25. 18:26. 20:20. 28:9, 17. Jsh +5:14. Mk 1:40. 5:6, 7. 15:19. Lk 5:12. 24:52. Jn 9:38. Ac 10:25. 1 C 14:25. He 1:6. Re +5:12. 19:10. 22:8, 9.
if. Mt +4:9. Mt 9:18, 28, 29. 13:58. 15:25. 18:26. 28:9. Mk 9:22-24.

3 **And Jesus**. ver. 28-34. 9:1-8, 18-26, 20-22, 27-31, 32-35. 12:9-13, 22. 15:21-28. 17:14-18. 20:29-34. 26:51. Mk 1:40-45. 6:53-56. Lk 5:12-14. 13:10-17. 14:2-6. Jn 4:46-54. 5:1-15. 9:1-39. 11:17-46.
put. Mk +5:23.
I will. Ge 1:3. Ps 33:9. Mk 1:41. 4:39. 5:41. 7:34. 9:25. Lk 5:13. 7:14. Jn 5:21. 11:43. 15:24.
immediately. Mt 11:4, 5. 2 K 5:11, 14. Lk 17:14, 15.
leprosy. Le 13:44.

4 **See**. Mt 6:1. Lk 5:14. Jn 5:41. 7:8, 18.
show. Mt 3:15. +5:17. Is 42:21. Mk +1:44.
Moses. i.e. *drawn out of the water*, **S#3475g**. Mt 17:3, 4. 19:7, 8. 22:24. Mk 1:44. 7:10. 10:3, 4. 12:19. Lk 5:14. 9:30. 20:28, 37. Jn 1:45. 3:14. 5:45, 46. 6:32. 7:19, 22. 8:5. 9:29. Ac 3:22. 6:11. 7:20, 22, 29, 31, 32, 40, 44. 15:21. 26:22. Ro 9:15. 10:5, 19. 1 C 10:2. 2 C 3:13, 15. He 3:2, 3, 5. 7:14. 8:5. 11:23, 24. 12:21.
Also **S#3475g**. Mt 23:2. Mk 9:4, 5. 12:26. Lk 2:22. 9:33. 16:29, 31. 24:27, 44. Jn 1:17. 7:22,

23. 9:28. Ac 13:39. 21:21. 28:23. Ro 5:14. 1 C
9:9. 2 C 3:7. He 3:16. 10:28. Ju 9. Re 15:3.
Also **S#3475g**. Ac 6:14. 7:35, 37. 15:1, 5. 2 T
3:8. He 9:19. For **S#4872h**, see Ex +2:10.
for. Mt 10:18. 24:14. 2 K 5:7, 8. Is 42:21. Mk
1:44. 6:11. 13:9. Lk 5:14. 9:5. 21:13. Jn 10:37,
38. 1 C +1:6. Ja 5:3.

5　entered. Mt 4:13. 9:1. 11:23. Mk 2:1. Lk 7:1.
a centurion. Mt 27:54. Mk 15:39. Lk 7:2,
etc. Ac 10:1, etc. 22:25. 23:17, 23. 27:13, 31,
43.

6　my. Jb 31:13, 14. Ac 10:7. Col 3:11. 4:1. 1 T
6:2. Phm 16.
palsy. Mt +4:24.

7　I will. Mt 9:18, 19. Mk 5:23, 24. Lk 7:6.

8　not worthy. Mt 3:11, 14. 15:26, 27. 25:37-
39. Ge 32:10. Ps 10:17. 51:3. 139:23, 24. Lk
5:8. 7:6, 7. 15:19, 21. +18:14. Jn 1:27. 13:6-8.
1 J +1:8.
but speak. ver. 3. Nu 20:8. Ps 33:9. 107:20.
Mk 1:25-27. Lk 7:7.

9　Go. Jb 38:34, 35. Ps 107:25-29. 119:91.
148:8. Je 47:6, 7. Ezk 14:17-21. Mk 4:39-41.
Lk 4:35, 36, 39. 7:8.
Do. Ep 6:5, 6. Col 3:22. T 2:9.

10　he marvelled. Mk 6:6. Lk 7:9.
I have. Mt +9:2.

11　That many. Mt +19:30. 21:41. 24:31. Ge
+12:3. 22:18. 28:14. Ps 98:3. Is +11:10. 52:10.
Je 16:19. Da 2:44. Lk 13:28-30. 14:23, 24. Ac
11:18. 14:27. 15:9. Ro 10:12. 11:30-36. Ga
3:28, 29. Ep 2:11-14. 3:6. Col 3:11. Re 7:9.
east and west. Is 11:14. 45:6. 59:19.
shall sit. Mt 19:28. Lk 12:37. 13:29. 14:15.
16:22. 22:30. Re 3:20, 21. 19:9.
with Abraham. Mt 22:32. Mi +7:20. Mk
12:26. 13:28. 20:37. Ac 3:13. 7:32. Ro 15:8.
and Jacob. Is +29:23.
in. Mt 3:2. Je 3:18, 19. Lk 13:28. Ac 14:22. 1
C +6:9. 15:50. 2 Th 1:5.
the kingdom. Mt +4:17. Ps 2:8.
of heaven. Mt 5:11, 12. 2 T +4:18. He 11:13,
+16. 1 P 1:4.

12　the children. Mt 3:9, 10. 7:22, 23. 21:43. Je
+28:5. Ac 3:25. Ro 9:4, 5.
be cast. Mt 3:10. +13:30, 41, 42, 50. 21:43.
22:12, 13. 24:51. 25:30. Lk 13:28. 17:30-37. 2
P 2:4, 17. Ju 13.
outer darkness. Mt 22:13. 25:30. Je 13:16.
Zp 1:15. 2 Th 1:9. 2 P 2:4, 17. Ju 6, 13.
weeping and. Mt +25:30. Re 21:4.

13　centurion. Lk 7:1-10.
Go. ver. 4. Ec 9:7. Mk 7:29. Jn 4:50.
and as. Mt 9:29, 30. 15:28. 17:20. Mk 9:23.
And his. Jn 4:52, 53.
selfsame hour. Mt 9:22. Ps 107:20. Jn 4:53.

14　into. ver. 20. Mt 17:25. Mk 1:29-31. Lk 4:38,
39.
wife's. Mk 1:30. 1 C 9:5. 1 T 3:2. 4:3. He
13:4.

15　touched. ver. 3. Mt 9:20, 29. 14:36. 20:34. 2
K 13:21. Is 6:7. Mk 1:41. Lk 8:54. Ac 19:11-
13.
and ministered. Lk 4:38, 39. Jn 12:1-3.

16　the even. Mk 1:32-34. Lk 4:40, 41.
they brought. Ac +5:16.
possessed. Mt +4:24.
and he. Mt 12:22. Mk 1:25-27, 34. 5:8. 9:25.
Ac 19:13-16.
spirits. 1 S 18:10. Gr. *pneuma*, **S#4151g**. Here
used of demons or evil spirits, as at Mt 10:1.
12:43, 45. Mk 1:23, 26, 27. 3:11, 30. 5:2, 8,
13. 6:7. 7:25. 9:17, 20, 25, 25. Lk 4:33, 36.
6:18. 7:21. 8:2, 29. 9:39, 42. 10:20. 11:24, 26.
13:11. Ac 5:16. 8:7. 16:16, 18. 19:12, 13, 15,
16. 2 C 11:4. Ep 2:2. 6:12mg. 2 Th 2:2. 1 T
4:1b. 1 J 4:1, 1, 3, 6b. Re 16:13, 14. 18:2. The
word *pneuma*, spirit, is used of (1) God, Jn
4:24a. (2) Christ, 1 C 6:17. (3) The Holy
Spirit, Mt +3:16. (4) The operations of the
Holy Spirit, Lk +1:17. (5) The New Nature, Ro
+8:1. (6) Psychological uses: 1) the principle
of life, of which death is described as giving
up or commending to God the spirit, Mt
+27:50. 2) the distinctive, self-conscious,
inner life of man: 1 C +2:11. 3) "life" in the
physiological sense, but drawing rather to the
meaning of "soul," Lk +8:55. (7) Spirit is put
for character, as being in itself invisible and
manifested in one's actions, Mt +5:3. (8)
Spirit is put for what is invisible, etc. Mt
+26:41. (9) Spirit, an integral part of man
individually, is put for the whole man, Mk
+2:8. (10) Adverbial use, whereby spirit
implies essence, or whatever is spoken of as
possessed or done, as being so in the highest
degree, Ac +18:25. (11) Spirit is used of
angels or spirit-beings, Lk +24:37. (12) Spirit
is used of demons or evil spirits, Mt +8:16.
(13) Spirit is used of neutral beings, 1 J +4:2b.
(14) Spirit is used of the resurrection body, Ro
+1:4. (15) Spirit in the phrase *pneuma hagion*,
Holy Spirit, without the Greek articles, is put
for the various gifts of the Spirit, "power from
on high," Mt +1:18. Compare the classification of the corresponding Old Testament
Hebrew word, *ruach*, Ge +6:3.
and healed. Mt +4:23.

17　it might. Mt 1:22. 2:15, 23.
Himself. Is 53:4. 63:9. He 4:15. 1 P 2:24.
sicknesses. Ex +23:25. Ac 10:38.

18　saw. ver. 1. Mk 1:35-38. Lk 4:42, 43. Jn 6:15.
great multitudes. Ps 2:8.
unto. Mt 14:22. Mk 4:35. 5:21. 6:45. 8:13. Lk
8:22.

19　a certain. Mt 9:18. 16:14. 18:24, 28.
21:19mg. 26:69. Mk 10:17. 12:42. Lk 5:12,
17. Jn 6:9. 7:21. 20:7. Re 8:13.
scribe. Ezr 7:6. Mk 12:32-34. Lk 9:57, 58. 1 C
1:20.

I will. Jsh 1:16. 2 S 15:15. Ps 2:8. Lk 14:25-27, 33. 22:33, 34. Jn 13:36-38. Re 14:4.

20 **have nests**. Ps 84:3. 104:17. Mt 6:26. 10:29, 31.

the Son of man. Mt 9:6. 10:23. 11:19. 12:8, 32, 40. 13:37, 41. 16:13, +27, 28. 17:9, 12, 22. 18:11. 19:28. 20:18, 28. 24:27, 30, 37, 39, 44. 25:31. 26:2, 24, 45, 64. Ps 80:17. Mk +2:10. Lk +5:24. Jn +1:51.

hath not. Mt 16:24. Ps +40:17. Is 53:2, 3. Lk 2:7, 12, 16. 8:3. Ro 15:2, 3. 1 C 4:11. 2 C 8:9. Ph 2:7, 8. He 12:2.

21 **another**. Mt +11:3. Lk 9:59-62.

suffer. Mt 19:29. Le 21:11, 12. Nu 6:6, 7. Dt 33:9, 10. 1 K 19:20, 21. Hg 1:2. 2 C 5:16.

22 **Follow**. Mt 4:18-22. 9:9. Jn 1:43.

and let. Mt +6:2. Je 16:5. Lk 9:60. 15:32. Ep 2:1, 5. 5:14. Col 2:13. 1 T 5:6.

23 **entered into a ship**. Mt 9:1. Mk 4:36. Lk 8:22.

24 **there**. Ps 107:23-27. Is 54:11. Jon 1:4-6, 13-16. Mk 4:37, 38. Ac 27:14, etc. 2 C 11:25, 26.

but. Lk 8:23. Jn 6:17, 18. 11:5, 6, 15.

25 **and awoke**. Ps 10:1. 44:22, 23. Is 51:9, 10. Mk 4:38, 39. Lk 8:24.

save. 2 Ch 14:11. 20:12. Jon 1:6.

perish. Gr. *apollumi*, Mt +2:13. Ps 80:14-16. Jon 1:6, 14. Mk 4:38.

26 **Why**. Mt +6:30. Is 30:7, 15. Ro 4:20.

fearful. Ge +15:1. Ps +34:4. 2 T +1:7. Re +21:8.

and rebuked. ver. 27. Mt 14:32. Jb 38:8-11. Ps 65:7. 89:8, 9. 93:3, 4. 104:6-9. 107:28-30. 114:3-7. Pr 8:28, 29. Is 63:12. Hab 3:8. Mk +4:39, 41. 6:48-51. Re 10:2.

27 **the men marvelled**. Mt 9:8, 33. 14:33. 15:31. Mk 1:27. 2:12. 4:41. 5:42. 6:51. 7:37. Jn 9:32. Ac 3:10-13.

What manner. Ex 14:21. Is 40:13, 14. Je +10:6. Mt +28:19. Lk 8:25. Ph 2:5-11. He 1:1-12.

that even. Mt 28:18, +19. Lk 5:9. Jn 5:21.

28 **when**. Mk 5:1, etc. Lk 8:26, etc. Ac 10:38.

Gergesenes. i.e. *those come from pilgrimage*, S#1086g, only here. Ge 10:16. 15:21. Dt 7:1.

there met. Mt 5:1-20. Lk 8:26-39.

two. Mk 5:2. Lk 8:27.

possessed. Mt +4:24.

coming. Mk 5:2-5. Lk 8:27, 29.

tombs. S#3419g. Mt 8:28. 23:29. 27:52, 53, 60, 60. 28:8. Mk 5:2, 3. 6:29. 15:46, 46. 16:2, 3, 5, 8. Lk 11:44, 47, 48. 23:55. 24:2, 9, 12, 22, 24. Jn 5:28. 11:17, 31, 38. 12:17. 19:41, 42. 20:1, 2, 3, 4, 6, 8, 11, 11. Ac 13:29.

so. Jg 5:6.

29 **cried out**. Mk 1:23, 24, 26, +34. Lk 4:33, 41. Ac 8:7.

What have. Jg +11:12.

thou Son of God. Mt +14:33. Ac 16:17. Ja 2:19.

torment. Mt 25:41. Jb 21:30. Mk 5:6-10. Lk +16:24. Ja 2:19. 2 P 2:4. Ju 6. Re 20:10.

before the time. Jb 21:30. Re 12:12.

30 **an herd**. Le 11:7. Dt 14:8. Is 65:3, 4. 66:3. Mk 5:11. Lk 8:32. 15:15, 16.

31 **devils besought**. Mk 5:7, 12. Lk 8:30-33. Re 12:12. 20:1, 2.

If. Mt +4:9.

suffer us. Jb 1:12. 2:6.

32 **Go**. 1 K 22:22. Jb 1:10-12. 2:3-6. Ac 2:23. 4:28. Re 20:7.

the whole. Jb 1:13-19. 2:7, 8. Mk 5:13. Lk 8:33.

33 **they that**. Mk 5:14-16. Lk 8:34-36. Ac 19:15-17.

34 **whole**. Ex +9:6.

they besought. ver. 29. Dt 5:25. 1 S 16:4. 2 S 6:9. 1 K 17:18. 18:17. Jb +21:14. 22:17. Ho 9:12. Mk 1:37. 5:17, 18. Lk 4:29, 42. 5:8. 8:28, 37-39. 9:53. Jn 4:40. Ac 16:39.

MATTHEW 9

1 **he**. Mt 7:6. 8:18, 23. Mk 5:21. Lk 8:37. Re 22:11.

his. Mt 4:13. Mk 2:1.

2 **they brought**. Mt 4:24. 8:16. Mk 1:32. 2:1-3. Lk 5:18, 19. Ac 5:15, 16. 19:12.

sick. Mt +4:24.

on a bed. Mk 2:4. 6:55. Lk 5:18.

seeing their faith. ver. 22, 29. Mt 8:10, 13. 15:28. 17:20. Mk 2:4, 5. 9:23. 10:52. Lk 5:19, 20. 7:9, 50. 17:19. 18:42. Jn +2:25. Ac 3:16. 14:9. Ja 1:6, 7. 2:18. 5:15.

Son. ver. 22. Mk 5:34. Jn 21:5. Lk +15:31.

good cheer. ver. 22. Ps 32:1, 2. Ec 9:7. Is 40:1, 2. 44:22. Je 31:33, 34. Lk 5:20. 7:47-50. Jn +16:33. Ac 13:38, 39. Ro 4:6-8. 5:11. Col 1:12-14.

thy sins. Lk +7:48. Jn 5:14. Ja 5:15.

3 **certain**. Mt 7:29. Mk 2:6, 7. 7:21. Lk 5:21. 7:39, 49.

said within. Lk +16:3.

This. Mk +14:64.

4 **knowing**. Mt +11:27. +28:19. Ps 44:21. Lk 7:40. 10:22. Jn +2:25.

Wherefore. Mt 15:19. Je +17:9, 10. Ezk 38:10. Mk 7:21. Ac 5:3, 4, 9. 8:20-22.

5 **whether**. Mk 2:9-12. Lk 5:23-25.

Arise. Is 35:5, 6. Jn 5:8-14, 17, 18. Ac 3:6-11, 16. 4:9, 10. 9:34. 14:8-11.

6 **the Son of man**. Mt +8:20.

hath power. Mt 28:18.

to forgive. Is 43:25. Mi 7:18. Mk 2:7, 10. Lk 5:21. Jn 5:21-23. 10:28. 17:2. 20:21-23. Ac 5:31. 7:59, 60. 2 C 2:10. 5:20. Ep 4:32. Col 3:13.

Arise. ver. 5. Lk 13:11-13. Jn +5:8. Ac 9:34.

8 **they marvelled**. ver. +33. Lk 2:20. 5:26. 7:16. 23:47. Ac 2:43.

glorified. Mt 5:16. 15:31. Ps 22:23. 50:15, 23. 86:9, 12. Is 61:3. Mk 2:12. Lk 2:20. 5:25, 26. 7:16. 13:13. 17:15, 18. 18:43. 23:47. Jn +13:31. 15:8. Ac 4:21. 11:18. 21:20. Ro 15:6, 9. 2 C 9:13. Ga 1:24. Ph 1:11. 2 Th 1:10, 12. 1 P 2:12. 4:11, 14. Re 15:4.
such power. Mk 2:1-12.

9 named. Mt 21:31, 32. Mk 2:14, etc. Lk 5:27, 28, Levi. 15:1, 2. 19:2-10.
Matthew. i.e. *gift of God*, **S#3156g**. ver. 9. Mt 10:3. Mk 3:18. Lk 6:15. Ac 1:13.
sitting. Ge +24:27. Am 7:15.
Follow. Mt 4:18-22. 1 K 19:19-21. Jn +1:43. Ga 1:16.

10 sat. Mk 2:15.
many. Mt +5:46. Jn +9:31. 1 T 1:13-16.

11 they said. Mk 2:16. 9:14-16.
Why. ver. 14. Mt 11:19. 15:2. 21:23. Is +65:5. Mk 2:24. Lk 5:29, 30. 6:2. 15:1, 2. 19:7. 1 C 5:9-11. Ga 2:15. He 5:2. 2 J 10.
your Master. Mt +22:24.
with. Lk 11:37. 14:1.

12 They that be whole. Ps 6:2. 41:4. 147:3. Je 17:14. 30:17. 33:6. Ho 14:4. Mk 2:17. Lk 5:31. 8:43. 9:11. 18:11-13. Ro 7:9-24. Re 3:17, 18.
are sick. Ro 3:9.

13 go. Mt 12:3, 5, 7. 19:4. 21:42. 22:31, 32. Mk 12:26. Lk 10:26. Jn 10:34.
what that meaneth. Mt 12:7. Lk +24:27.
I will. Mt +23:23. 1 S 15:22. Pr 21:3. Ec 5:1. Is 1:11. Ho 6:6. Mi +6:6-8. Mk 12:33. He 13:16.
for. Mt 12:12.
I am. Mt 10:34, 35. Mk 1:38. Lk 9:56. 12:49, 51. 13:7. +19:10. Jn 5:43. 6:38. 8:42. 9:39. 12:27, 46, 47. 18:37.
to call. Mt 18:11-13. Mk 2:17. Lk 5:32. 15:3-10. +19:10. Ro 3:10-24. 1 C +6:9-11. 1 T 1:13-16.
righteous. Je 28:5.
but sinners. Mt 21:28-32. Is 55:6, 7. Lk +13:3. Ro 2:4-6. 1 T +1:15. 2 T +2:25, 26. 2 P 3:9.

14 the disciples. Mt 11:2. 14:12. Lk 7:18. 11:1. Jn 1:35. 3:25. 4:1. Ac 18:25. 19:3.
Why. ver. +11. Mt 6:16. 11:18, 19. Pr 20:6. Mk 2:18-22. Lk 5:33-39. 18:9-12.
but thy. ver. 10. Mk 2:15. Lk 5:29, 30.

15 Can. Mt 25:1-10. Jg 14:11, etc. Ps 45:14, 15. Jn 3:29. Re 19:9. 21:2.
the children. Mt 8:12. 13:38. 1 S +20:31mg. Mk 2:19. Lk 5:34. +10:6.
mourn. Is 22:12. Jn 16:20.
days will come. Mt +26:11. Lk +17:22.
when. Lk 24:13-21. Jn 16:6, 20-22. Ac 1:9, 10.
and then. Ac 13:1-3. 14:23. 1 C 7:5. 2 C 11:27.

16 No man. Jn 1:17.
new cloth. *or*, raw, *or* unwrought cloth.

for. Ge 33:14. Ps 125:3. Is 40:11. Jn 16:12. 1 C 3:1, 2. 13:13.

17 old. Ge 21:14. Mk +2:22.
perish. Gr. *apollumi*, Mt +2:13.

18 behold. Mk 5:22, etc. Lk 8:41, etc.
a certain. Mt +8:19.
ruler. Mk 5:22, 35. Lk 8:41, 49. 13:14. 18:18. Ac 13:15. 18:8, 17.
worshipped. Mt +8:2. +14:33. 15:25. 17:14. 20:20. 28:17. Mk 5:22. Lk 17:15, 16. Ac 10:25, 26. Re +5:12.
My daughter. ver. 24. Mk 5:23. Lk 7:2. 8:42, 49. Jn 4:47-49.
but come. Mt 8:8, 9. 1 K 17:19-22. 2 K 4:27-35. 5:11. Jn 11:21, 22, 25, 32.
lay thy hand. Mk +5:23.

19 arose. Mt 8:7. Jn 4:34. Ac 10:38. Ga 6:9, 10.

20 behold. Mk 5:25-34. Lk 8:43-48.
an issue. Le 15:25, etc.
touched. Mt 14:36. Mk +3:10. 5:28. 6:56. 8:22. Ac 5:15. 19:12.
hem. Mt 14:36. 23:5. Nu 15:38, 39. Dt 22:12. Mk +5:27. 6:56. Lk 8:44.

21 If. Mt +4:9. Mk 5:26-33. Lk 8:45-47. Ac 19:12.
touch. Mk 3:10.
be whole. Ps 42:11. 67:2. Mk +10:52.

22 turned. Lk +22:61.
Daughter. ver. +2. Mk 5:34. Lk 8:48.
thy faith. ver. +2, 29. He 4:2.
from. Mt 8:13. 15:28. 17:18. Jn 4:53. Ac 16:18.

23 into. ver. 18, 19. Mk 5:35-38. Lk 8:49-51.
the minstrels. Mt 11:17. Ge 23:2. 1 S 25:1. 2 S 19:35. 2 Ch 35:25. Ezr 2:65. Ne 7:67. Jb 3:8. Ec 12:5. Je 9:17-20. 16:6. Ezk 24:17. Am 5:16. Mk 5:38-40. Lk 7:32. 8:52. 23:27. Jn 11:31, 33. Ac 9:39. Re 18:22.

24 give. 1 K 17:18-24. Ac 9:40. 20:10.
the maid. Ac 20:10.
not dead. Ho 13:14. Jn 11:4, 11-13, 25.
but sleepeth. Da 12:2. Jn 11:4, 11, 25.
And. Lk +8:53.

25 the people. 1 K 17:19, 20. 2 K 4:32-36. Ac 9:40, 41.
and took. Mt 8:15. Mk +1:31. 5:41. 8:23. 9:27. Lk 8:54.

26 the fame hereof. *or*, this fame. ver. 31. Mt +4:24. Mk 1:45. 6:14. Ac 26:26.

27 two. Mt +11:5.
of David. Mt +1:1. Ro 9:5.
have mercy. Mt 15:22. 17:15. 20:30, 31. Ps +4:1. Mk 9:22. 10:47, 48. Lk 16:24. 17:13. 18:13, 38, 39.

28 come. Mt 8:14. 13:36.
Believe. ver. 2, 22. Mt 9:28. 13:58. Mk 1:40. 9:23, 24. Jn 4:48-50. 9:35. 11:26, 40.
am able. Is 42:6, 7.

29 touched. Mt 20:34. Mk +1:41. 8:25. Jn 9:6, 7.
According. ver. +2. Mt 8:6, 7, 13. Ph 4:19.

30 **their**. Ps +119:18. Is 52:13.
straitly. Mk +1:43. Jn 11:33, 38.
no man know. Lk +5:14. Jn 7:8.
31 **spread**. ver. 26. Mt 4:24. 28:15. Mk 1:44, 45. 7:36.
32 **a dumb**. ver. +33.
possessed. Mt +4:24.
33 **the dumb**. Mt 12:22. 15:30, 31. Ex 4:11, 12. Is 35:6. Mk 7:32-37. 9:17-27. Lk 11:14.
marvelled. Mt +8:27.
It. 2 K 5:8. Ps 76:1. Je 32:20. Lk 7:9. Jn +15:24.
34 **Pharisees said**. Jn +1:24. 3:20.
he casteth. Mk +3:22.
the prince. Lk +11:15.
35 **Jesus went**. Mt +4:23, 24. 11:1, 5. Mk 1:32-39. +6:6, 56. Lk 4:43, 44. 13:22. Ac 2:22. 10:38.
the kingdom. Mt +13:19.
healing every sickness. Mt +4:23.
36 **when**. Lk +5:15.
moved with compassion. Mt 14:14. 15:32. 20:34. Is +63:15. Mk 1:41. 5:19. 6:34. 8:2. 9:22. Lk 7:13. 10:35. 15:20. He 2:17. 4:15. 5:2.
fainted, etc. or, were tired and lay down. Is 32:18. Je 50:6mg. Lk +7:6.
scattered. Mt 15:24. 1 P 2:25.
as sheep. Nu +27:17. Is 56:9-11. Zc 11:16. Jn 10:11.
37 **The harvest**. Mt 28:19. Mk 16:15. Lk 10:2. 24:47. Jn 4:35, 36. Ac 16:9, 10. 18:10.
but. Ps 68:11. 1 C 3:9. 2 C 6:1. Ph 2:19-21. Col 4:11. 1 Th 5:12, 13. 1 T 5:17.
38 **Pray**. Lk 6:12, 13. Ac 13:2. 2 Th 3:1.
the Lord. Mt 10:1-3. Jn 20:21. Ep 4:11.
that. Ps 68:11, 18. Je 3:15. Mi 5:7. Mk 1:12. Lk 10:1, 2. Jn 10:4. Ac 8:4. 1 C 12:28.

MATTHEW 10

1 **called**. Mt 19:28. 26:20, 47. Mk 3:13, 14. 6:7, etc. Lk 6:13. Jn 6:70. Re 12:1. 21:12-14.
he gave. Mt 6:13. 28:18, 19. Mk 3:15. 16:17, 18. Lk 9:1, etc. 10:19. 21:15. 24:49. Jn 3:27, 35. 17:2. 20:21-23. Ac +1:8. 3:15, 16. 19:15.
power. Mt 16:19. 18:18, 19. Jn 20:23. Ac 8:17-19. 15:28, 29. 2 C 12:12. Ja +5:15.
against. or, over. Mk 6:7. Jn 17:2. Ro 9:21.
spirits. Gr. pneuma, Mt +8:16.
to heal. Ac 9:34.
2 **apostles**. Lk 6:13. 9:10. 11:49. 22:14. Ac 1:26. Ep 4:11. He 3:1. Re 18:20.
Simon. Mt 4:18. 16:16-18. Mk 1:16, 17. 3:16. Lk 6:14. Jn 1:40-42. Ac 1:13. 1 P 1:1. 2 P 1:1.
Andrew. Mk 1:29. 3:18. 13:3. Jn 6:8, 12:22.
James. i.e. supplanter, **S#2385g**. ver. 3. Mt 4:21. 13:55. 17:1. 20:20. 26:37. 27:56. Mk 1:19, 29. 3:17, 18. 5:37. 6:3. 9:2. 10:35, 41. 13:3. 14:33. 15:40. 16:1. Lk 5:10. 6:14-16. 8:51. 9:28, 54.

24:10. Jn 21:2. Ac 1:13. 12:2, 17. 15:13. 21:18. 1 C 15:7. Ga 1:19. 2:9, 12. Ja 1:1. Ju 1.
John. Lk 22:8. Jn 13:23. 20:2. 21:20, 24. Ac 3:1. 1 J 1:3, 4. 2 J 1. 3 J 1. Re 1:1, 9. 22:8.
3 **Philip**. Mk 3:18. Lk 6:14. Jn 1:43-46. 6:5-7. 12:21, 22. 14:9.
Bartholomew. i.e. son that suspends the waters; a furrow, **S#918g**. Mk 3:18. Lk 6:14. Ac 1:13.
Thomas. Lk 6:15. Jn 11:16. 20:24-29. 21:2.
Matthew. Mt 9:9. Mk 2:14. Lk 5:27, Levi. 6:15. Ac 1:13.
publican. Mt 5:46.
James. Mt 27:56. Mk 3:18. Lk 6:15, 16. Ac 1:13. 12:17. 15:13. 21:18. Ga 1:19. 2:9. Ja 1:1.
Alphaeus. i.e. produce, gain, **S#256g**. Mk 2:14. 3:18. Lk 6:15. Ac 1:13.
Lebbeus. i.e. courageous, **S#3002g**, only here. Mk 3:18. Lk 6:16, Judas the brother of James. Jn 14:22, Judas, not Iscariot. Ac 1:13. Ju 1.
Thaddaeus. i.e. that praises or confesses, **S#2280g**. Mk 3:18.
4 **Simon**. Mk 3:18. Lk 6:15, Simon Zelotes. Ac 1:13.
Canaanite. i.e. zealous, acquired, **S#2581g**. Mk 3:18.
and Judas. Mt 26:14, 47. 27:3. Mk 3:19. 14:10, 43. Lk 6:16. 22:3, 47. Jn 6:71. 13:2, 26-30. 18:2-5. Ac 1:16-20, 25.
Iscariot. i.e. man of murder, he will be hired, **S#2469g**. Mt 26:14. Jsh +15:25. Mk 3:19. 14:10. Lk 6:16. 22:3. Jn 6:71. 12:4. 13:2, 26. 14:22.
betrayed. Mt +20:18.
5 **sent**. Mt 22:3. Lk 9:2. 10:1. Jn 20:21.
Go not. Mt 4:15. 15:24. Jn 7:35. Ac 10:45-48. 11:1-18. 22:21-23. Ro 15:8, 9. 1 C 10:32. Ga 3:28. 1 Th 2:16. 1 Th 4:2. 2 T 2:15.
the way. Ac 11:19.
of the Samaritans. i.e. guardianship, prison, **S#4541g**. 2 K 17:24, etc. Ezr 4:10. Lk 9:52-54. 10:33. 17:16. Jn 4:5, 9, 20, 22-24, 39, 40. 8:48. Ac +1:8. 8:1, 5, etc., 25.
6 **go**. Ac +3:26.
lost. Gr. apollumi, Mt +2:13. Nu +27:17. Is 53:6. Lk +19:10.
7 **As ye go**. Mt 3:1.
preach. Mt 4:17. 11:1. Is 58:1. 61:1. Jon 3:2. Mk 6:12. Lk 9:60. 16:16. Ac 4:2.
kingdom of heaven. Mt +4:17. Mk +1:15.
at hand. Mt 3:2. 4:17. +21:43. Is 56:1. Lk 21:31.
8 **Heal**. ver. 1. Mt +4:23. Mk 16:18. Ac 4:9, 10, 30.
freely ye. Mt 5:42. 2 K 5:15, 16, 20-27. Is 55:1. Lk 3:11. 6:38. 12:33. Jn 15:25. Ac 3:6. 8:18-23. 20:33-35. Ro 3:24. 2 C 8:7, 9. 9:8. 11:7. Ga 2:21. Re 21:6. 22:17.
freely give. ver. +42. Mt 5:42. 6:1-4. 25:34-36, 40-46. Le +25:35. Pr 21:13. 22:9. 28:27. Ec 11:1, 2. Lk 3:11. +11:41. 12:33, 34. 16:9,

11, 13, 14. Ac 20:35. Ro 12:8, 10, 20. 2 C 8:7. 9:6. Ga 6:9, 10. Ep 4:28. 1 Th +3:12. 1 T 6:17-19. He 13:16. 1 J 3:17.

9 **Provide**. *or*, Get.
neither. Mk 6:8. Lk 9:3. 10:4. 22:35. 1 C 9:7, etc.
gold. Ge +23:9.

10 **scrip**. 1 S 9:7. 17:40. Mk 6:8. Lk 22:35, 36.
two. Lk 3:11. 2 T 4:13.
staves. Gr. a staff. Ex +25:13.
for the. Le +19:13. Nu 18:31. Dt +24:15. Lk 10:7, etc. 1 C 9:4-14. Ga 6:6, 7. 1 T 5:17, 18. 2 T 2:6.

11 **enquire**. Ge 19:1-3. Jg 19:16-21. 1 K 17:9, etc. Jb 31:32. Lk 10:38-42. 19:7. Ac 16:15. 18:1-3. 3 J 7, 8.
worthy. Mt 8:8. 22:8. Ac 16:15.
and there. Mk 6:10. Lk 9:4. 10:7, 8. Ac 16:15. 1 T 5:13.

12 **salute it**. Jg 19:20. 1 S 25:6. 1 Ch 12:18. Lk 10:5, 6. Ac 10:36. 2 C 5:20. 3 J 14.

13 **And if**. Mt +4:9.
worthy. Is 45:23. 2 C 2:16.
let your. Je +29:7.
return. Ps 35:13. Lk 10:6.

14 **whosoever**. ver. 40, 41. Lk 10:10, 11. Ro +15:7. 1 Th 4:8.
shake. Mt +7:6. Ne 5:13. Ac 13:51. 18:6. 20:26, 27.

15 **verily**. Mt +5:18.
more tolerable. Mt 11:22, 24. 23:14, 15. Ps 86:13. La 4:6. Ezk +16:49. Mk 6:11. 12:40. Lk 10:12, 14. +12:48. 20:47. Jn 15:22-24. 19:11. Ro 2:12, 16. He 2:3. 10:28, 29. Ja 3:1.
the land. Ge 18:20. 19:28.
Sodom. i.e. *burning, fettered*, **S#4670g**. ver. 15. Mt 11:23, 24. Mk 6:11. Lk 10:12. 17:29. Ro 9:29. 2 P 2:6. Ju 7. Re 11:8.
Gomorrha. i.e. *bondage*, **S#1116g**. Ro 9:29. 2 P 2:6. Ju 7.
in the day of judgment. Mt 11:22, 24. 12:36, 41, 42. 13:40-42. Ps +7:8. Ezk +20:35. Lk 10:12, 14. 11:31, 32. Jn 12:48. Ac 10:42. 17:31. 24:25. 1 C 11:32. 2 T 4:1, 8. He 9:27. 2 P 2:4, 9. 3:7. 1 J 4:17. Ju 6. Re 14:7. 20:12-15.

16 **I send**. ver. 5. Jn 17:18.
as sheep. Lk 10:3. Jn 10:12. Ac 20:29. Ro 16:19.
wise. Mt 25:2. Ge 3:1, 13. Ne 6:3. Pr +31:4. Je +23:2. Ezk 28:3. Lk 21:15. Ac 6:4. 20:28-31. Ro 2:21. 16:19. 1 C 9:25-27. 14:20. 2 C 11:3, 14. Ep 5:15-17. Ph 2:15. Col 1:9. 4:5. 1 Th 2:10. 1 T 4:12-16. 6:20, 21. 2 T 1:13. 2:3, 4, 22, 23. 4:5, 7. T 2:7, 8.
harmless. *or*, simple. Mt +11:29. Pr +16:7. Ro 16:18, 19. 1 C 4:12. 13:4, 7. 14:20. 2 C 1:12. 8:20. 11:3. Ga 5:22, 23. +6:1. Ph 2:15. 1 Th 2:10. 5:22. He 10:34. +12:14. Ja 5:6.
doves. Le 1:14. Is 38:14. 59:11. Ho 7:11.

17 **beware**. Mi 7:5. Mk 13:9, 12. Jn 15:19.

17:14. Ac 14:5, 6. 17:14. 23:12-22. 2 C 11:24-26. Ph 3:2. 2 Th 3:2. 2 T 4:15.
deliver you. Mt 24:9, 10. Mk 13:9, 11. Lk 12:11, 12. 21:12, 13. Jn 16:2. Ac 4:6, etc. 5:26, etc. 14:5. 23:1, etc.
councils. Mt 5:22. 26:59. Jn 11:47.
scourge. Mt 23:34. Dt 25:2, 3. Mk 13:9. Lk 21:12. Jn +19:1. Ac 5:40. 16:22, 23. 22:19, 24, 25. 26:11. 2 C 6:5. 11:23-25. He 11:36.

18 **be**. Ps 2:1-6. Ac 5:25-27. 12:1-4. 16:19. 23:33, 34. ch. 24-26. 2 T 4:16, 17. Ja 2:6.
for my sake. ver. 22, 39. Ac 9:15, 16.
for a testimony. Mt +8:4. Ph 1:13. 1 C +1:6.

19 **when**. Mk 13:11-13. Lk 12:11. 21:14, 15.
take. Mt 6:25, 31, 34. Ph 4:6. Ja +1:5.
it shall. Ex 4:12, 15. Nu 23:5. Dt 18:18. 2 S 23:2. Is 50:4. Je 1:7-9. Da 3:16-18. Jn 14:26. 15:26. Ac 4:8-14. 5:29-33. 6:10. 13:9. 26:2, etc. 1 C 2:4. 15:10. 2 C 13:3. 1 Th 2:13. 2 T 4:17. He 1:1. 2 P 1:21.

20 **but**. 2 S 23:2. Mk 12:36. Lk 11:13. 21:15. Ac 2:4. 4:8. 6:10. 7:55, 56. 28:25. 1 P 1:12. 2 P 1:21.
Spirit. Gr. *pneuma*, Mt +3:16. Jn 14:16, 26.
your Father. Mt 6:32. Lk 12:30-32.
which speaketh. Je 1:2, 9. 2:1. 25:3, 4. 26:12, 15. Ezk 1:3. Da 2:19. Mi 3:8.

21 **the brother shall**. ver. 34-36. Mt 24:10. Mi 7:5, 6. Zc 13:3. Mk 13:12, 13. Lk 12:51-53. 21:16, 17.
the children. 2 S 16:11. 17:1-4. Jb 19:19.

22 **shall be hated**. Mt 24:9. Is 66:5, 6. Mk 13:13. Lk 6:22, 23. 21:17. Jn 7:7. 15:18, 19, 21. 17:14. 1 J 3:13.
of all. Ex +9:6.
for. ver. 39. Mt 5:11. Jn 15:21. Ac 9:16. 2 C 4:11. Re 2:3.
but he. Mt 24:13. Da 12:12, 13. Mk 13:13. Lk 8:15. Ro 2:7. Ga 6:9. He 3:14. 6:11. 10:36. Ja 1:12. Ju 20, 21. Re 2:7, 10, 17, 26. 3:21.
endureth. 1 C 1:8. 2 C 1:13. Ga 6:9. He 3:6, 14. Re 2:10.
the end. Gr. *telos*, **S#5056g**. Mt 17:25. 24:6, 13, 14. 26:58. Mk 3:26. 13:7, 13. Lk 1:33. 18:5 (continual coming. lit. unto the end). 21:9. 22:37. Jn 13:1. Ro 6:21, 22. 10:4. 13:7 (custom), 7. 1 C 1:8. 10:11 (ends). 15:24. 2 C 1:13. 3:13. 11:15. Ph 3:19. 1 Th 2:16 (uttermost). 1 T 1:5. He 3:6, 14. 6:8, 11. 7:3. Ja 5:11. 1 P 1:9. 3:8 (Finally). 4:7, 17. Re 1:8 (ending). 2:26. 21:6. 22:13. Contrast **S#4930g**, *sunteleia*, Mt +24:3.

23 **when**. Mt 2:13. 4:12. 12:14, 15. 23:34. Lk 4:29-31. Jn 7:1. 10:39-42. 11:53, 54. Ac 8:1. 9:24, 25. 13:50, 51. 14:6, 7, 19, 20. 17:10, 14. 20:1.
flee. Mk +3:7. Ac 8:1. 9:23-25, 30. 20:1.
another. Gr. *allos*, **S#243g**. Another quantitatively, of the same kind, in contrast to *heteros* (**S#2087g**, Mt +11:3), which means another

qualitatively, of a different kind. Vine notes that the two words are used interchangeably only in 1 C 1:16 and 6:1; 12:8-10; 14:17, 19, where the difference, though present, is not so readily discernible (*Expository Dictionary*, vol. 1, p. 60). The distinction is maintained and particularly asserted by Paul in Ga 1:6, 7. Rendered (1) *other* or *others*: Mt 4:21. 5:39. 12:13. 13:8. 20:3, 6. 21:8, 36, 41. 22:4. 25:16, 17, 20a, 22. 27:42, 61. 28:1. Mk 3:5. 4:8, 36. 6:15. 7:4, 8. 8:28b. 11:8. 12:5b, 9, 31, 32. 15:31, 41. Lk 5:29. 6:10, 29. 9:8, 19b. 20:16. 23:35. Jn 4:38. 6:22, 23. 7:12, 41a. 9:9b, 16. 10:16, 21. 12:29. 15:24. 18:16, 34. 19:18, 32. 20:2-4, 8, 25, 30. 21:2, 8, 25. Ac 4:12. 15:2. 1 C 1:16. 3:11. 9:2, 12, 27. 14:19, 29. 2 C 1:13. 8:13. 11:8. Ph 3:4. 1 Th 2:6. He 11:35. Ja 5:12. Re 2:24. 17:10. (2) *another*: Mt 2:12. 8:9. 10:23. 13:24, 31, 33. 19:9. 21:33. 26:71. Mk 10:11, 12. 12:4, 5a. 14:19, 58. Lk 7:8, 19, 20. 22:59. Jn 4:37b. 5:7, 32, 43. 14:16. 18:15. 21:18. Ac 2:12b. 19:32b. 21:34b. 1 C 3:10. 10:29. 12:8, 9, 10, 10, 10. 14:30. 15:39b, 39c, 39d, 41b, 41c. 2 C 11:4. Ga 1:7. He 4:8. Re 6:4. 7:2. 8:3. 10:1. 12:3. 13:11. 14:6, 8, 15, 17, 18. 15:1. 16:7. 18:1, 4. 20:12. (3) *some*: Mt 13:5, 7. 16:14. Mk 4:5, 7. 8:28a. Lk 9:19a. Jn 7:41b. 9:9a. Ac 19:32a. 21:34a. (4) *one*: Jn 4:37a. Ac 2:12a. 1 C 15:39a, 41a. (5) miscellaneous: *more*, Mt 25:20b. *otherwise*, Ga 5:10.

have gone over. *or*, end, *or*, finish. ver. 6, 7.

till. Mt 16:28. 17:1-13. 21:1-11. +23:39. 24:1, 2, 21, 27, 30, 34, 48. 25:13. 26:64. Is 2:1-4. +45:17. Ezk 39:25. Mk 9:1. 13:26. Lk 9:27. 18:8. 21:27. Ro +11:26.

Son of man. Mt +8:20.

24   **The disciple**. 2 S 11:11. Lk 6:40. Jn 3:30. 13:16. 15:20, 21. He 12:2-4.

master. Mt +22:24.

25   **If they**. 1 C +15:2. Mk +3:22. Ac 26:24.

Beelzebub. *or*, Beelzebul. i.e. *lord of the flies*; *dung god*, **S#954g**. Mt 12:24, 27. 2 K 1:2, 3, 6. Mk 3:22. Lk 11:15, 18, 19.

26   **Fear**. ver. +28. Pr 28:1. Is 8:12. Ac 4:13, 19. 1 P 3:14.

for. Is 45:19. 48:16. Mk 4:22. Lk 8:17. 12:2, 3. 24:47. Jn 18:20. Ac +1:8. 1 C 4:5. 1 T 5:25.

revealed. Ec 12:14.

27   **I tell**. Mt 13:1-17, 34, 35. Lk 8:10. Jn 16:1, 13, 25, 29. 2 C 3:12.

in the ear. Lk 10:23.

that preach. Pr 1:20-23. 8:1-5. Ac 5:20, 28. 17:17.

housetops. Dt +22:8.

28   **And fear not**. ver. 26. Ps +118:6. Is 8:12-14. Ezk 3:9. Ac 20:23, 24. 21:13. Ro 8:35-39. 2 T 4:6-8. He 7:25. 11:35. 1 P 3:14. Re 2:10.

body. Mt +6:25.

not able. Mt 22:31, 32. Mk 12:26, 27. Lk 12:4, 5. Ac 7:59. 2 C 4:18.

kill. Ge 37:21.

soul. Gr. *psyche*, Mt +2:20. The immaterial, invisible, eternally conscious part of man, as in Ac 2:27, 31. 1 Th 5:23. He 4:12. For the other uses of *psyche*, see Mt +2:20. Mt +6:25. Ge 25:8. 35:18. 1 K 17:21, 22. Jb +14:22. Ps +16:10. 22:26. 30:3. 49:15. Ec +12:7.

fear him. Jb 37:24. Ps 34:7. Pr 14:26, 27. 28:1. 29:25. Ec +12:13. Is 41:10. 66:2. Je +5:22. Ac 4:19. He 10:31.

able. Mt 25:46. Mk 9:43-48. Lk 16:22-26. Jn 5:29. 2 Th 1:8-10. Ja 4:12. Re 20:10-15.

destroy. Gr. *apollumi*, Mt +2:13. This Greek word never means annihilate, but rather means to render unsuitable for the use originally intended. ver. 6, 39. Mt 9:17. 18:11. Jb 19:10. Ho 13:9, 10. Lk +9:24. 1 C 15:16-18.

both. Is +10:18. Lk 12:5.

soul. Gr. *psyche*, Mt +2:20.

hell. Gr. *gehenna*, Mt +5:22. Mt +5:29. 1 S 28:19. Ps 139:8. Is +66:24.

29   **two**. Lk 12:6, 7.

farthing. "In value a halfpenny farthing, as being the tenth of the Roman penny. See Mt 18:28."

and one. Mt 6:26. Jb 38:41. Ps 50:11. +104:27-30.

without. Is 36:10.

30   **the very hairs**. Mt 5:36. 1 S 14:45. 2 S 14:11. 1 K 1:52. Da 3:27. Lk 12:7. 21:18. Ac 27:34.

numbered. Jb 14:16. 31:4. Ps +40:17.

31   **Fear ye not**. Lk 1:13.

more value. Mt 6:26. 12:11, 12. Ps +8:5. Lk 12:24. 13:15, 16. 1 C 9:9, 10.

32   **confess**. Lk 12:9. Jn 17:23. Ro 8:1. 10:9, 10. 1 J 4:15.

me before men. Ge 40:14. Ps 119:46. Lk 12:8, 9. Jn 1:49. 6:68, 69. 9:22, 25, 33. 11:27. Ac 4:7-12. 5:29-32, 42. 9:29. Ro 10:9, 10. 1 T 6:12, 13. 2 T 1:8. 4:2. He 10:35. 1 J 4:15. Re 1:9. 2:13. 20:4.

him will I. Mt 25:34. 1 S 2:30. Ml 3:17. Lk 12:8. Re 3:5.

confess. Gr. *homologeo*, **S#3670g**. Rendered (1) *confess*: ver. 32. Lk 12:8, 8. Jn 1:20, 20. 9:22. 12:42. Ac 23:8. 24:14. Ro 10:9. He 11:13. 1 J 1:9. 4:2, 3, 15. 2 J 7. (2) *profess*: Mt 7:23. 1 T 6:12. T 1:16. (3) *promise*: Mt 14:7. (4) *give thanks*: He 13:15. (5) *confession is made*: Ro 10:10. See for the related term *exomologeomai*, **S#1843g**, Mk +1:5.

before my. Mt +7:21. Mk +13:32. Jn 5:30. +14:28. Ro 8:34. 1 C 11:3. +15:28. 1 T 2:5. He 7:25. 9:24. 1 J 2:1.

33   **deny me**. Gr. *arneomai*, **S#720g**, Lk +12:9. Mt 26:70-75. Mk 8:38. Lk 9:26. 12:9. 2 T 2:12, 13. 2 P 2:1. 1 J 2:23.

deny before. Gr. *arneomai*, **S#720g**, Lk +12:9. lit. disown. To disown, reject, or repudiate one in the face of former relationship or better knowledge (See Cremer, *Lexicon*, p. 111). Mt 7:23. 25:12. Lk 12:9. 13:25.

34 Think not. Mt 5:17. Lk 12:51-53.
that I. Je 15:10. Lk 12:49-53. Jn 7:40-52. Ac 13:45-50. 14:2, 4. 28:24, 25.
but a sword. Ex +5:3. Ps 18:34. Lk +22:36. Re 6:4.

35 to set. ver. 21. Mt 24:10. Ezk 22:7. Mi 7:5, 6. Mk 13:12. Lk 21:16.

36 man's foes. ver. 21. Mt 24:10. Ge +3:15. 4:8-10. 37:17-28. 1 S 17:28. 2 S 15:12. 16:11. Jb 19:13-19. Ps 27:10. 41:9. 55:12, 13. 69:8. Je 9:4. 12:6. 20:9, 10. Mi 7:6. Mk 13:12. Lk 21:16. +24:27. Jn 13:18. 1 J 3:11, 12.

37 that loveth father. Mt 22:37. Ge 12:4. Ex 12:38. Dt 33:9. Ne 13:3. Is 51:2. Lk 14:26, 33. Jn 5:23. 21:15-17. 2 C 5:14, 15. Ph 3:7-9.
or mother. 1 K 15:13.
not worthy. ver. 38. Lk +21:36. Col +1:10.

38 taketh not. Mt 16:24, 25. 27:32. Mk 8:34. 10:21. 15:21. Lk 9:23, 24. 14:27, 33. 23:26. Jn 19:17. 2 T 3:10, 12.
followeth after. Mt 9:9. Jn 8:12. 12:26. 21:19.
not worthy. ver. +37. Lk 9:62.

39 findeth his. Mt 16:25, 26. Mk 8:35, 36. Lk 9:24. 17:33. Jn 12:25. Ac 20:24. Ro 8:17. Ph 1:20, 21. 2 T 4:6-8. Re 2:10. 12:11.
life. Gr. *psyche*, Mt +2:20; Ge +9:5.
lose. Gr. *apollumi*, Mt +2:13.
loseth. Gr. *apollumi*, Mt 2:13.
life. Gr. *psyche*, Mt +2:20; Ge +9:5.
for my sake. ver. 18, 22. Mk 13:9.

40 He that. ver. 20. Lk 10:16. Jn 20:21. Ro +15:7. 2 C 5:20. Ga 4:14. 1 Th 4:8.
and he that receiveth. Jn 5:23. 12:44-49. Ph 2:10, 11. 1 J 2:22, 23. 2 J 9.
that sent. Jn 4:34.

41 that receiveth a prophet. Ge 20:7. 1 K 17:9-15, 20-24. 18:3, 4. 2 K 4:8-10, 16, 17, 32-37. Ac 16:15. Ro +15:7. 16:1-4, 23. 2 T 1:16-18. He 6:10. 3 J 5-8.
a righteous man's. Lk 14:13, 14. 2 Th 1:6, 7.
reward. Mt +5:12.

42 shall give. ver. +8. Mt 25:34-36, 40. Dt 15:10. Ps 37:25, 26. 41:1-3. 112:5, 6, 9. Pr 11:24, 25, 27. 14:21. 19:17. 22:9. 28:8, 27. Ec 11:1, 2. Is 32:8. 58:7, 8, 10, 11. Mk 10:21. Lk 6:38. 11:41. 12:33. 14:13, 14. 16:9. 2 C 8:12. 9:6-8, 10. 1 T 6:17-19. He 13:16.
one. Mt 8:5, 6. 18:3-6, 10, 14. 25:40. Zc 13:7. Mk 9:41, 42. Lk 17:2. 1 C 8:10-13.
little ones. Mt 18:10. 1 C 3:1.
a cup. Mt 25:37, 40. Mk 9:41. 12:42, 43. 14:7, 8. 2 C 8:12.
name of a disciple. Mt 18:3, 5.
he shall. Pr 24:14. Lk 6:35. 14:14. 2 C 9:6-15. Ph 4:15-19. He 6:10. 2 J 8.

lose. Gr. *apollumi*, Mt +2:13.
his reward. Mt +5:12.

MATTHEW 11

1 came to pass. Mt 7:28. 13:53. 19:1. 26:1.
commanding. Mt 28:20. Jn 15:10, 14. Ac 1:2. 10:42. 1 Th 4:2. 2 Th 3:6, 10. 1 T 6:14.
he departed. Mt 4:23. 9:35. 12:9. Is 61:1-3. Mk 1:38, 39. Lk 4:15-21. 8:1. Ac 10:38.

2 when. Lk 7:18-23.
in the prison. Mt +4:12.
he sent. Mt 9:14. Jn 3:25-28. 4:1. Ac 19:1-3.

3 Art thou he. Mt 2:2-6. Ge +3:15. +12:3. 22:18. +49:10. Nu +24:17. Dt 18:15-18. Ps 2:6-12. 110:1-5. Is +7:14. +9:6, 7. Je +23:5, 6. Ezk 34:23, 24. Da +9:24-26. Ho 3:5. Jl +2:28-32. Am 9:11, 12. Ob +21. Mi +5:2. Zp 3:14-17. Hg 2:7. Zc +9:9. Ml 3:1. 4:2. Jn 4:21. 7:31, 41, 42.
come. Mt 3:11. 21:5, 9. 23:39. Nu 24:19. Ps 40:7. 118:26. Is +35:4. Ezk 21:27. Da 7:13. +9:26. Hg 2:7. Zc +9:9. Mk 1:7. 11:9. Lk 3:16. 18:8. 19:38. Jn 1:9. 3:31. 4:25, 26, 29. 6:14. 11:27. 12:13. Ro 5:14. He 10:37. 1 J 4:2, 3; 5:6.
look for. Lk 3:15.
another. Gr. *heteros*, S#2087g. i.e. another of a different kind. Rendered (1) *another*: Mt 8:21. 11:3. Mk 16:12. Lk 6:6. 9:56, 59, 61. 14:19, 20, 31. 16:7, 18. 19:20. 20:11. 22:58. Jn 19:37. Ac 1:20. 7:18. 12:17. 17:7. Ro 2:1, 21. 7:3, 3, 4, 23. 13:8. 1 C 3:4. 4:6. 6:1. 10:24. 12:9, 10. 15:40b. 2 C 11:4, 4. Ga 1:6. 6:4. He 7:11, 13, 15. Ja 2:25. 4:12. (2) *other*: Mt 6:24, 24. 12:45. 15:30. 16:14. Lk 4:43, 5:7. 7:41. 8:3, 8. 10:1. 11:16, 26. 16:13, 13. 17:34, 35, 36. 18:10. 23:32, 40. Ac 2:4, 13, 40. 4:12. 8:34. 15:35. 17:34. 23:6. 27:1. Ro 8:3. 13:9. 1 C 8:4. 10:29. 14:17, 21. 2 C 8:8. Ga 1:19. Ep 3:5. Ph 2:4. 2 T 2:2. He 11:36. (3) *other thing*: Lk 3:18. 22:65. 1 T 1:10. (4) *some*: Lk 8:6, 7. (5) *next day*: Ac 20:15. 27:3. (6) miscellaneous renderings: *be altered*, Lk 9:29. *another Psalm*, Ac 13:35. *else*, Ac 17:21. *another matter*, Ac 19:39. *one*, 1 C 15:40a. *another place*, He 5:6. *strange*, Ju 7. For *allos*, S#243g, see Mt +10:23.

4 Go and show. Jn 2:23. 5:36.

5 blind. Mt 9:27-30. 12:22. 15:30, 31. 20:30-34. 21:14. Jb 29:15. Ps 146:8. Is 29:18. 32:3, 4. *35:4-6*. 42:6, 7, 16, *18*. 61:1. Je 31:8. Mk 8:22-25. 10:46, 52. Lk 4:18. 7:21, 22. 18:35-43. Jn 2:23. 3:2. 5:36. 9:7, 32. 10:25, 38. 11:37. 14:11, 12. Ac 2:22. 4:9, 10. 26:18.
the lame. Mt 15:30, 31. 21:14. Is *35:6*. Lk 7:22. Ac 3:2-8. 8:7. 14:8-10.
the lepers. 2 K +5:1.
the deaf. Is *29:18, 19. 42:18*. 43:8. Mk 7:35, 37. 9:25.
the dead. Mt 9:24, 25. Is *26:19*. Mk 5:21-24, 35-43. Lk 7:14-16, 22. 8:40-42, 49-56. Jn 11:43, 44.

the poor. Mt +5:3. Ps 22:26. 72:12, 13. Is 61:1-3. 66:2. Je 52:16. Zc 11:7. Lk 4:18. 6:20. Ja 2:5.

gospel preached. Is *61:1*. 1 C 1:26.

6 **blessed**. Mt 5:3-12. Ps 1:1, 2. 32:1, 2. 119:1. Lk 11:27, 28.

whosoever. Mt 13:21, 55-57. 16:23. +17:27. 18:7. 21:44. 24:10. 26:31, 33. Is 8:14, 15. Mk 4:17. 6:3. 14:27, 29. Lk 2:34. 4:23-29. 7:23. Jn 16:1. Ro 9:32, 33. 1 C 1:22-24. 2:14. Ga 5:11. 1 P 2:7, 8.

7 **Jesus**. Lk 7:24-30.

What. Mt 3:1-3, 5. 21:25. Mk 1:3-5. Lk 1:80. 3:3-7. 8:18. Jn 1:38. 5:35.

A reed. Ge 49:4. 1 K 14:15. 2 K 18:21. Is 36:6. Ezk 29:6, 7. 2 C 1:17, 18. Ep +4:14. Ja 1:6.

8 **A man**. Mt 3:4. 2 K 1:8. Is 20:2. Zc 13:4. Mk 1:6. 1 C 4:11. 2 C 11:27. Re 11:3.

wear soft. 1 K 10:5. 2 Ch 9:4.

9 **A prophet**. ver. 13, 14. Mt 14:5. 17:12, 13. 21:24-26. Mk 6:20. 9:11-13. 11:32. Lk 1:15-17, 76. 20:6.

yea. Pr +6:16.

10 **this is he**. Ps +83:18. Lk +1:76.

of whom. Mt 3:3. Is 40:3. 57:14. Ml *3:1*. 4:5. Mk 1:2, 4. Lk 1:17, 76. 7:26, 27. +24:27. Jn 1:23.

11 **born**. Jb 14:1, 4. 15:14. 25:4. Ps 51:5. Ga 4:4. Ep 2:3.

a greater. Mt 3:11. 1 S 2:30. Lk 1:15, 7:28. Jn 5:35.

risen. Lk 7:16. Jn 7:52. Ac 13:22.

he that. Mt 5:19. Is 30:26. Zc 12:8. Lk 9:48. Jn 1:15, 27. 3:30. 1 C 6:4. 15:9. Ep 3:8.

kingdom of heaven. Mt +4:17.

greater. Mt 13:16, 17, 43. Ps 16:11. 68:13. 89:15-17. 91:11. Is 35:10. Da 12:3. Ml 3:17. Jn 7:39. 10:41. Ro +8:19. 16:25, 26. Col 1:26, 27. 2 T 1:10. He 11:40. 1 P 1:10. 4:13.

12 **from**. Mt 21:23-32. Lk 7:29, 30. 13:24. 16:16. Jn 6:27. Ep 6:11-13. Ph 2:12.

kingdom of heaven. Mt +4:17.

suffereth violence, and the violent take. *or*, is gotten by force, and they that thrust men take, etc. Je 13:22mg. Lk 16:16.

take it by force. Pr 12:24. +13:4. 14:23. Is +60:8, 11. Da 7:18. Am 5:9. Lk 5:1. 13:24. 16:16. Jn 6:15.

13 **all the prophets**. Mt +5:17, 18. Ml 4:6. Lk 24:27, 44. Jn 5:46, 47. Ac 3:22-24. 10:43. 13:27. Ro 3:21.

and the law. Lk 16:16. He 10:1.

until John. Dt 18:18. Jn 1:29, 45.

14 **if**. This "if" indicates there is very little likelihood of this happening, as also at Mk 16:18; Lk 6:32, 33, 34; Jn 8:16, 55; 1 C 4:7; 7:11; Ga 1:8; Re 11:5.

ye will. Ezk 2:5. 3:10, 11. Jn 16:12. 1 C 3:2.

receive. Pr 4:10. Zc 1:6. Lk 8:13. Ac 8:14.

11:1. 13:48. +17:11. 1 C 2:14. 2 C 8:17. 1 Th 1:6. 2:13. 2 Th 2:10. Ja 1:21.

this. Mt 17:10-13. Ml 4:5. Mk 9:11-13. Lk 1:17. Jn 1:21-23. Re 20:4.

Elias. i.e. Greek form of Elijah, **S#2243g**. ver. 14. Mt 16:14. 17:3, 4, 10-12. 27:47, 49. Mk 6:15. 8:28. 9:4, 5, 11-13. 15:35, 36. Lk 1:17. 4:25, 26. 9:8, 19, 30, 33, 54. Jn 1:21-23, 25. Ro 11:2. Ja 5:17. For **S#452h**, see 1 K +17:1. Mt 17:10-13. Ml 4:5. Mk 9:11-13. Lk 1:17. Jn 1:21.

which was. Mt 17:9-13. Ml *3:1*. *4:5*, *6*. Mk 9:13. Lk 1:15-17, 76, 77. 7:37.

15 **hath ears**. Mt +13:9. Ezk 3:27. Lk 8:8. 14:35.

16 **whereunto**. La 2:13. Mk 4:30. Lk 13:18, 20.

this. Mt +24:34.

It is. Lk 7:31-35.

markets. Je 5:1. Lk 11:43.

fellows. Mt +20:13.

17 **We**. Is 28:9-13. 1 C 9:19-23.

piped. Mt 9:15, 23. 1 K 1:40. Is 30:29. Je 9:17-20. 31:4. Lk 15:25.

ye have not. Pr 29:9.

danced. Ex +15:20.

mourned. 2 S 1:17. Lk 8:52.

lamented. Mt 24:30. Je 5:3. Na 2:7. Lk 8:52. 23:27.

18 **John**. Mt 3:4. Je 15:17. 16:8, 9. Da 10:3. Mk 1:6. 1 C 9:27.

nor drinking. Lk 1:15.

He. Mt 10:25. 2 K 9:11. Je 29:26. Ho 9:7. Jn 7:20. 8:48. 10:20. Ac 26:24.

19 **Son of man**. Mt +8:20.

came. Lk 5:29, 30. Ro 15:2.

eating and. Mt 9:10. Lk 7:36. 14:1. Jn 2:2. 12:2.

a friend. S5384g. Lk 7:6, 34. 11:5, 5, 6, 8. 12:4. 14:10, 12. 15:6, 9, 29. 16:9. 21:16. 23:12. Jn 3:29. 11:11. 15:13, 14, 15. 19:12. Ac 10:24. 19:31. 27:3. Ja 2:23. 4:4. 3 J 14.

publicans. Mt +5:46.

and sinners. Mt 9:10, 11. Mk 2:15, 16. Lk 5:30. 7:34. 15:1, 2. 19:7.

But wisdom. Ps 92:5, 6. Pr 8:1-36. 17:24. Lk 11:49. 1 C 1:24-29. Ep 3:8-10. Re 5:11-14. 7:12.

is justified. Ps +51:4. Lk 7:29, 35. Ro 3:4. 11:33. 1 C 2:14, 15.

her children. Pr 8:32. Lk 7:35. 10:6. +16:8.

20 **began**. Lk 10:13-15.

upbraid. Ps 81:11-13. Is 1:2-5. Mi 6:1-5. Mk 9:19. 16:14. Ja +1:5.

wherein. Jn 20:30.

because. Mt 12:41. 21:28-32. Je 8:6. Lk +13:3. 2 T +2:25, 26. Re 2:21. 9:20, 21. 16:9, 11.

21 **Woe**. Mt 18:7. 23:13-29. 26:24. Je 13:27. Lk 10:12-15. 11:42-52. Ju 11.

Chorazin. i.e. *woody places*, **S#5523g**. Lk 10:13.

Bethsaida. Mk 6:45. 8:22. Lk 9:10. Jn 1:44. 12:21.

for if. ver. 23. Mt 12:41, 42. Ezk 3:6, 7. Lk 11:31, 32. Ac 13:44-48. 28:25-28. This kind of "if" pertains to what is impossible or contrary to fact, often dealing with past time. Here, like saying "for if (but they were not)." Other examples of this kind of "if" are: Mt 12:7. 24:22. Mk 13:20. Lk 12:39. Jn 11:21, 32. 14:7, 28. 18:30. Ro 9:29. 1 C 2:8. 1 J 2:19.

mighty works. Is +49:26.

Tyre. i.e. *to distress*, S#5184g. ver. 22. Mt 15:21. Mk 3:8. 7:24, 31. Lk 6:17. 10:13, 14. Ac 12:20. 21:3, 7. For S#6865h, see 1 K +7:13.

and. ver. +22. Mt 15:21. Je 25:22. 47:4. Ezk 28:2-24. Am 1:9, 10. Mk 3:8. 7:24, 31. Lk 6:17. 10:13, 14. Ac 12:20.

Sidon. i.e. *hunting, fishery*, S#4605g. ver. 22. Mt 15:21. Mk 3:8. 7:24, 31. Lk 4:26. 6:17. 10:13, 14. Ac 27:3. For S#6721h, see Ge +10:19.

repented. Jb 42:6. Jon 3:5-10.

sackcloth. Jb +16:15.

ashes. Est +4:1.

22 **more tolerable**. ver. +24. He 6:4-8.

Tyre. Is ch. 23. Je 25:22. 27:3. Ezk ch. 26-28. 29:18. Am 1:9, 10. Zc 9:2, 3.

the day. Mt +10:15. 23:33. Jn 3:17-19. 5:29. 12:31. 16:8. 1 C 3:13. 1 T 5:24.

23 **Capernaum**. Mt 4:13. 8:5. 17:24. Lk 4:23. Jn 4:46, etc.

which art. Ge 11:4. Dt 1:28. Ezk 28:12-19. Ob 4. Lk 14:11. 2 P 2:4-9.

brought down. Is 14:13-15. La 2:1. Ezk 26:20. 31:14, 16, 17. 32:18, 24.

hell. Gr. *hades*, S#86g. ver. 23. Mt 16:18. Lk 10:15. +16:23. Ac 2:27, 31. 1 C 15:55mg. Re 1:18. 6:8. 20:13, 14.

for if. ver. +21. ver. 14 with Ml 4:5. Mt 23:39. Dt +32:22. 1 S 13:13, 14. 2 K 13:19. Ps 81:13, 14. Is +30:15. +48:18. Je 23:22. 51:9. Ezk 3:6. Da 3:18. Jl 2:28. Lk 4:23. 13:34. 19:42.

in Sodom. Mt 10:15. Ge +18:20. 19:24, 25. Lk 10:12. 17:29. Ro 9:29. 2 P 2:6. Ju 7.

done in thee. Lk 4:23.

24 **more tolerable**. ver. 22. Mt +10:15. He 2:3. +10:26-29. Ju 7.

land of Sodom. ver. 23. Ge +18:20. 19:28.

day of judgment. ver. +22. Mt +10:15. Ps 50:3-6. Ro 14:10, 11. 2 C 5:10. 2 T 4:1.

25 **Jesus**. Lk 10:21, etc.

answered and. Mt 17:4. 22:1. 24:2. 28:5. Mk 11:14. 12:35. Ac 3:12.

said. Mk 1:35.

I thank. 1 Ch 29:13. Da 2:23. Lk 10:21. Jn 11:41. Ro 6:17. 14:11. 15:9. 2 Th 2:13, 14.

Lord. Ge 14:19, 22. Dt 10:14, 15. 2 K 19:15. Is 66:1. Da 4:35. Ac 17:24.

because. Mt 13:11-16. Is 5:21. 29:10-14, 18, 19. Mk 4:10-12. Jn 7:48, 49. 9:39-41. 12:38-40. Ro 11:8-10. 1 C 1:18-29. 2:6-8. 3:18-20. 2 C 3:14. 4:3-6.

hast hid. Ge +31:7. 2 C 3:14. 4:3, 4.

the wise. Jb 37:24. Is 5:21. 29:14. Ro 1:22. 1 C 1:18-27. 3:18.

and hast revealed. Mt 13:11. 16:17. +18:3, 4. 21:16. 1 S 2:18. 3:4-21. Ps 8:2. 19:7. 25:9, 12. Pr +8:9. Is +8:20. 61:1. Je 1:5-8. Mk 10:14-16. Lk 8:10. 1 C 1:26, 27.

unto babes. Lk 9:47. 1 C 14:20. 1 P 2:2.

26 **for so**. Jb 33:13. Ps +115:3. Is 46:10. Ro +9:18. 11:33-36. 1 C 1:21. Ep 1:9, +11. 3:11. 2 T 1:9.

seemed good. Mt 18:14. Lk 12:32. Ga 1:15. He 13:21.

27 **are**. Mt 28:18. Jn 3:35. 5:21-29. 13:3. 17:2. 1 C 15:25-27. Ep 1:20-23. Ph 2:10, 11. He 1:2. 2:8-10. 1 P 3:22. Re 2:27.

no man. 1 S 6:19. Lk 10:22. Jn 1:18. 2:25. 6:46. 10:15. Col 2:18.

knoweth. Gr. *epiginosko*, S#1921g. Rendered (1) *know*: Mt 7:16, 20. 11:27, 27. 17:12. Mk 5:30. 6:33, 54. Lk 1:4. 7:37. 23:7. 24:16, 31. Ac 3:10. 9:30. 12:14. 19:34. 22:24, 29. 25:10. 27:39. 28:1. Ro 1:32. 1 C 13:12, 12. 2 C 13:5. Col 1:6. 1 T 4:3. 2 P 2:21, 21. (2) *acknowledge*: 1 C 14:37. 16:18. 2 C 1:13, 13, 14. (3) *perceive*: Mk 2:8. Lk 1:22. 5:22. (4) *take knowledge of*: Ac 4:13. 24:8. (5) *have knowledge of*: Mt 14:35. (6) *know well*: 2 C 6:9. The word *epiginosko*, a strengthened form of *ginosko*, means to know well, accurately, or thoroughly, not merely be acquainted with. Compare *oida*, Jn 8:55.

but the Father. Mt 24:36.

neither. Jn 1:18. 7:29. 8:19. 10:15. 14:6-9. 17:2, 3, 6, 25, 26. 1 J 2:23. 5:19, 20. 2 J 9.

whomsoever. Dt +10:15. Mk 4:11. Jn 17:9, 26. 2 T +2:25.

28 **Come**. Mt 12:20. Ge 45:18, 19. Ex 3:10. 2 Ch 10:4. Is 45:22-25. 53:2, 3. +55:1-3. Jn 5:40. 6:37. 7:37. 10:27, 28. Re 22:17.

all. Mt 23:4. Ge 3:17-19. Ex 2:11. 5:5. Jb 5:7. 14:1. Ps 32:4. 38:4. 90:7-10. Ec 1:8, 14. 2:22, 23. 4:8. Is 1:4. 61:3. 66:2. Mi +6:6-8. Lk 11:46. Ac 13:39. 15:10. Ro 7:22-25. Ga 5:1.

and I. ver. 29. Ru 2:12. Ps 94:13. 116:7. Is 11:10. 14:3. 28:12. 48:17, 18. Je 6:16. 31:25. Lk 10:42. 2 Th 1:7. He 4:1.

29 **my yoke**. Mt 7:24. 17:5. Nu 7:9. Je 9:5. 31:18. La 3:27. Ho 11:4. Jn 13:17. 14:21-24. 15:10-14. Ac 15:10. 1 C 9:21. 2 C 10:5. Ga 5:1. 1 Th 4:2. 2 Th 1:8. He 5:9.

and learn. ver. 27. Mt 23:8. 28:20. Lk 6:46-48. 8:35. 10:39-42. Jn 13:15. Ac 3:22, 23. 7:37. Ep 4:20, 21. Ph 2:5. 1 J 2:6.

meek. Mt +5:5. +10:16. 12:19, 20. 21:5. Nu 12:3. Ps 45:4. 131:1. Is 42:1-4. 50:6. 53:7. Zc +9:9. Mk 15:4, 5. Lk 9:51-56. 23:34. 2 C 10:1. Ph +2:3, 7, 8. Ja +1:4. 1 P 2:20-23.

and ye. ver. 28. Ps 116:7. Is 28:12. Je 6:16. Lk +24:27. He 4:3-11.

find rest. Ps 119:165. Is 48:22. Ro 7:23. Ph 4:7. 2 T 1:7.

souls. Gr. *psyche*. Lk 1:46. 2:35. Ac 14:2, 22. 15:24. Here the *psyche* may be regarded as the seat of perception, feeling, desire. Ps 84:2. 139:14. Is 26:9. For the other uses of *psyche*, see Mt +2:20. Other examples of this use are given at Ge +23:8.

30 my yoke. Pr 3:13, 17. Mi +6:8. Ac 15:10, 28. Ga 5:1, 13, 18. 1 P 2:24. 1 J 5:3.

burden. Mt 23:4. Ps 38:4. Lk 11:46. Jn 16:33. Ac 27:10. Ro 7:23-25. 10:3, 4. 2 C 1:4, 5. 4:17. 12:9, 10. Ga 6:5. Ph 4:13.

MATTHEW 12

1 At that time. Mt 11:25.

went. Mk 2:23-28. Lk 6:1-5.

to pluck. Dt 23:25.

2 Behold. ver. 10. Ex 20:9-11. 23:12. 31:15-17. 35:2. Nu 15:32-36. Is +58:13, 14. Mk 3:2-5. Lk 6:6-11. 13:10-13, +14, 15-17. 14:3. 23:56. Jn 5:9-11, 16, 17. 7:21-24. 9:14-16. Col 2:16.

3 Have ye not read. ver. 5. Mt 19:4. 21:16. 22:31. Mk 12:10, 26. Lk 6:3. 10:26.

what David. 1 S 21:3-6. Mk 2:25, 26.

4 the showbread. Ex +25:30. 40:23. 2 Ch 4:19.

but only. Ex 29:32, 33. Le 8:31. 24:9.

5 on the sabbath. Nu 28:9, 10. 1 Ch 9:32. Lk 10:26. Jn 7:22, 23.

profane. Ne 13:17. Ezk 24:21.

6 in this place. ver. 8, 41, 42. Mt 23:17-21. 2 Ch 6:18. Hg 2:7-9. Ml 3:1. Jn 2:19-21. Ep 2:20-22. Col 2:9. 1 P 2:4, 5.

7 if. Mt +11:21. Mt 9:13. 22:29. Ac 13:27.

what this. Lk +24:27.

I will. Mt 23:23. 1 S 15:22. Pr 21:3. Ec 5:1. Is 1:11-17. Ho 6:6. Mi +6:6-8. Mk 12:33. He 13:16.

condemned. Jb 32:3. Ps 94:21. 109:31. Pr 17:15. Ja 5:6.

8 the Son of man. Mt +8:20.

is Lord. Mt 9:6. Mk 2:10, 28. 9:4-7. Lk 5:24. 6:5. Jn 5:17-23. 1 C 9:21. 16:2. Re 1:10.

the sabbath day. Mt +5:17, 18. Ge 2:3. Ex 16:22, 23, 29, 30. +20:8-11. 23:12. 31:13-17. 34:21. 35:1-3. Le 19:3, 30. 23:3. 24:7, 8. Nu 15:32, 36. 28:9, 10. Dt +5:12-15. Ne 9:14. 10:31. 13:15-22. Is 56:2, 6, 7. Is +58:13, 14. Je 17:21, 22, 24, 25, 27. Ezk 12:12, 20. 22:8, 26. 46:1, 3. Mk 1:21. 2:27, 28. Lk +4:16. 6:1-9. 13:10-13, +14, 15-17. 14:1-6. 23:56. Jn +5:17, 18. 7:21-23. 9:14-16. 20:19, 26. Ac 13:14, 15, 44. 16:13. +17:2. 18:4. 20:7. 1 C 16:2. He 4:4, 9. Re 1:10.

9 he went. Mk 3:1-5. Lk 6:6-11.

10 which. 1 K 13:4-6. Zc 11:17. Jn 5:3.

Is it lawful. Mt 19:3. 22:17, 18. Lk 13:10-14. 14:3-6. 20:22. Jn 5:10. 9:16.

that. Ex 23:4, 5. Dt 22:4. Is 32:6. 59:4, 13. Lk 6:6, 7. 11:54. 20:20. 23:2, 14. Jn 8:6.

11 What man. Lk 13:15-17. 14:5.

and if. Mt +4:9. Ex 23:4, 5. Dt 22:4.

12 is a man better. Mt 6:26. 10:31. Lk 12:24.

it is lawful. Mk 3:4. Lk 6:9. 14:3. Jn 5:16, 17.

13 Stretch forth. 1 K 13:4.

and it. Lk 13:13. Ac 3:7, 8.

14 the Pharisees. Mt 21:46. Mk 3:6. Lk 6:11. Jn 5:18. 7:1, 19. 10:39. 11:53, 57.

went out. ver. 9. Mt 27:1.

held a council. *or*, took counsel. Mt 22:15. 26:4. 27:1, 7. 28:12. Mk 15:1. Jn 11:53. 12:10.

destroy. Gr. *apollumi*, Mt +2:13.

15 he withdrew. Mk +3:7. Jn 7:1, 6, 8, 30. 8:20.

great multitudes followed. Lk +5:15. Jn 9:4. Ga 6:9. 1 P 2:21.

healed them all. Mt +4:23.

16 charged them. Mk +1:43. Lk +5:14.

17 it might. Mt 8:17. 13:35. 21:4. Is 41:22, 23. 42:9. 44:26. Lk 21:22. 24:44. Jn 10:35. 12:38. 19:28. Ac 13:27.

saying. Is 42:1-4.

18 Behold. Is *42:1-3*. Lk +24:27.

my servant. Ps 105:26. Is 41:8. 43:10. 49:5, 6. 52:13. 53:11. Ezk 34:24. Zc 3:8. Ac 3:26. 4:27, 30. Ph 2:6, 7. He 5:5.

whom I have chosen. Ps 89:19. Is 49:1-3. Lk 9:35. 23:35. 1 P 2:4.

my beloved. Mt 3:17. 17:5. Mk 1:11. 9:7. Lk 9:35. Ep 1:6. Col 1:1, 13mg. 2 P 1:17.

my soul. Gr. *psyche*. The expression "my soul," "his soul," etc. is the idiom for *me, myself, himself*, etc. *Psyche* is used to emphasize the personal pronoun in the first person, as at Mt 26:38. Mk 14:34. Lk 12:19, 19. Jn 10:24 (us). 12:27. 2 C 1:23. He 10:38 (soul). For the other uses of *psyche* see Mt +2:20. For other instances of this idiom, see Nu +23:10. Le +26:11.

well pleased. Is 53:11.

I will put. Mt 3:16. Is 11:2. 59:20, 21. 61:1-3. Lk 3:22. 4:18. Jn 1:32-34. 3:34. Ac 10:38. Col 2:9.

spirit. Gr. *pneuma*, Lk +1:17.

shew judgment. Is +2:4. 32:15, 16.

to the Gentiles. ver. 21. Is 11:10. 42:1, 6. 49:6, 12, 23. 60:2, 3, 5. 62:2. 66:12, 19. Je 16:19. Ml 1:11. Lk 2:31, 32. Ac +9:15. 11:18. +13:46-48. 14:27. 15:7, 17. 26:17, 18, 23. 28:28. Ro 3:29. 11:11-15. 15:8-16. Ep 2:11-13. 3:1, 5-8. 1 T 2:7. 2 T 4:17.

19 not strive. Mt +11:29. Is *42:2*. Lk 17:20. Jn 18:36-38. 2 T 2:24, 25.

20 bruised. Mt +11:28. 2 K 18:21. Ps 51:17. 147:3. Is 36:6. 40:11. *42:3*. +57:15. 58:5. +61:1-3. La 3:31-34. Ezk 34:16. Lk 4:18. 2 C 2:7. 2 T 2:24. He 12:12, 13.

not quench. Is 43:17.

till he. Ps 98:1-3. Is 42:3, 4. Ro 15:17-19. 2 C 2:14. 10:3-5. Re 6:2. 19:11-21.

judgment. Zc 9:9.

unto victory. Jn 18:36. 1 C 15:54.

21 **in his name**. Ps 98:1-3. Is 11:10. 42:4. Lk +24:27. Ro 15:12, 13. Ep 1:12, 13. Col 1:27.

22 **Then was**. Mt 9:32. Mk 3:11. Lk 9:1. 11:14.

possessed. Mt +4:24.

he healed. Mk 7:35-37. 9:17-26.

blind. Ps 51:15. Mt +11:5.

and saw. Lk 7:21.

23 **the people**. Mt 9:33. 15:30, 31.

were amazed. Lk 2:47.

Is not. Mt +1:1. Jn 4:29.

24 **when**. Mk +3:22.

Pharisees heard. Jn +1:24.

Beelzebub. Gr. *Beelzebul*, and so ver. 27. Mt +10:25.

the prince. Lk +11:15.

25 **Jesus knew their thoughts**. Mk 3:24. Jn +2:25. 1 C +2:11.

Every kingdom. Is 9:21. 19:2, 3. Mk 3:23-26. Lk 11:17, 18. Ga 5:15. Re 16:19. 17:16, 17.

divided. Ac +4:32. Ro +16:17, 18. 1 C 12:24-27. Ga 5:15. 1 J 3:14, 15. 4:20.

26 **And if**. 1 C +15:2. Mk 3:23, 25, 26. Lk 11:18.

Satan. 1 C 5:5.

his. Jn 12:31. 14:30. 16:11. 2 C 4:4. Col 1:13. 1 J 5:19. Re 9:11. 12:9. 16:10. 20:2, 3.

27 **if I**. 1 C +15:2.

by. Mt +6:2. 10:25. 15:5, 14, 26. 16:18, 23. 18:28. 19:24. 23:3, 5, 13, 24, 25, 27. 24:28. 24:43. Mk 4:21. Lk 5:39. 11:8. 16:1-9. 18:5. 22:25. Ga 5:17. 1 J 4:4.

Beelzebub. ver. +24.

by whom. Mt 7:22. 1 S 16:23. Mk 9:38, 39. Lk 9:49, 50. 11:19. Ac 19:13-16.

your children. 1 K 20:35. 2 K 2:3. 4:1, 38. 5:22. 6:1. 9:1.

they. ver. 41, 42. Lk 19:22. Ro 3:19.

28 **if**. Mt +4:9.

I cast. ver. 18. Mt 10:7, 8. Mk 16:17. Lk 11:20. Ac +10:38. 1 J 3:8.

Spirit. Gr. *pneuma*, Mt +3:16.

kingdom of God. Mt +4:17. 6:33. 19:24. 21:31, 43. Is +9:6, 7. Mk 11:10. Lk +1:32, 33. +4:43. Col +1:13. He +12:28.

is come. Ge 6:13. Is 60:1. He 12:22.

unto you. Jn 5:36.

29 **how can**. Is 53:12. Lk 11:21, 22. Jn +12:31.

except. Mt +4:9.

bind the strong man. He 2:14, 15. Re 20:2.

and then. Jn 16:11.

30 *not with me*. Mt 6:24. Ex 32:26. Jsh 5:13. 24:15. 1 Ch 12:17, 18. Mk 9:40. Lk 9:50. 11:23. Jn 8:34, 44. 15:23. Ro 6:16. 1 C 10:17. 2 C 6:15, 16. 2 P 2:19. 1 J 2:19. 3:8. Re 3:15, 16.

is against. 1 K 18:21. Mk 9:40. Jn 3:17. Ga 1:9. Re 3:15.

gathereth. Ge +49:10. Ho 1:11. Jn 11:52.

31 **All manner of sin**. Is 1:18. 55:7. Ezk 33:11. Mk 3:28-30. Jn 6:37. Ac 13:38, 39. 1 T 1:13-15. He 6:4-6. +10:26, 29. 1 J 1:9. 2:1, 2.

and blasphemy. Jn 10:32, 33, 36.

but the blasphemy. Le +24:11. Ac 5:3. 7:51. 1 J +5:16.

Ghost. Gr. *pneuma*, Mt +3:16.

shall not be forgiven. Ro 11:20. He 2:3. 3:12. 10:26-29. 1 J 3:24.

32 **whosoever**. Mt 11:19. 13:55. Lk 7:34. 12:10. 23:34. Jn 7:12, 52. 9:24. Ac 3:14, 15, 19. 26:9-11. 1 T 1:13, 15.

the Son of man. Mt +8:20.

it shall be forgiven. Lk 23:34. Ac 8:18, 19, 22. 1 T 1:12, 13.

but whosoever. Jn 7:39. He 6:4-6. 10:26-29.

speaketh against. Ge +1:2. Lk +3:22. Jn 14:26. 16:13, 14. Ac 8:29, 39. 13:2. 15:28. 16:7. 20:28. 28:25. Ro 8:27. 1 C 2:10, 11. 12:8, 11. Ep 4:30.

Holy Ghost. Mt +3:16. Jn 7:39.

it shall not. God the Holy Spirit is immutable (Mt +28:19). Jb 36:13. Mk 3:29. Lk +12:10. 16:23-26.

in this world. Gr. *aion*, Mt +6:13. lit. "this age," as in Mt 13:22. Mk 4:19. 10:30. Lk 1:70. 16:8. 20:34. Jn 9:39. Ro 12:2. 1 C 1:20. 2:6, 8. 3:18. 2 C 4:4. Ga 1:4. Ep 1:21. 2:2. 6:12. 1 T 6:17. 2 T 4:10. T 2:12.

the world to come. Mt 13:39, 40, 49. 24:3. 28:20. Ezk 33:16. Mk +10:30. Lk 18:30. 20:35. Ep 1:21. He 2:5. 6:5. +9:27.

33 **make the tree good**. Mt 23:26. Ezk 18:31. Am 5:15. Lk 11:39, 40. Ep 4:23, 24. Ja 4:8.

and his fruit good. Mt 3:8-10. 7:16-20. Lk 3:9. 6:43, 44. Jn 15:4-7. Ja 3:12.

34 **generation**. Mt +3:7.

of vipers. Ps 58:4. 140:3.

how. Mt 7:11. 13:14, 15. 1 S 24:13. Jb 14:4. Ps 10:6, 7. 52:2-5. 53:1. 64:3-5. 120:2-4. 140:2, 3. Is 32:6. 59:4, 14. Je 7:2-5. Ro 3:10-14. Ja 3:5-8.

for out. Mt 13:52. 15:18, 19. Mk 7:20-23. Lk 6:45. Jn 8:43. 12:39. Ro 8:7. Ep 4:29.

heart. Pr +4:23. Je +17:9.

mouth speaketh. Ps 37:30, 31. Pr 10:20, 21. 15:4, 23, 28. 16:23, 24. Col 4:6.

35 **good man**. Mt 5:37. 13:52. Ps 37:30, 31. Pr 10:20, 21. 12:6, 17-19. 15:4, 23, 28. 16:21-23. 25:11, 12. Ep 4:29. Col 3:16. 4:6.

and an. ver. 34.

36 **every**. Ec 12:14. Ro 2:16. Ep 5:4-6, 11. Ju 14, 15. Re 20:12.

idle word. **S#692g**: ver. 36; Mt 20:3, 6, 6; 1 T 5:13, 13; T 1:12 (slow); 2 P 1:8 (barren). Ezk +33:31. Ep 4:29, 31. Col 4:5, 6.

give account. Mt 16:27. Ec 12:14. Ro 14:12. 1 P 4:5.

day of judgment. Mt +10:15.

37 For by. Mt 5:22. Pr 13:3. Ja 3:2-12.

justified. Lk 19:22. Ro 10:10. Ja 2:21-25.

and by. 1 T 5:13.

38 Master. Mt +22:24.

see a sign. Mt 16:1-4. Mk 8:11, 12. Lk 11:16, 29. 23:8. Jn 2:18. 4:48. 6:30. 1 C 1:22.

39 wicked. ver. 45. Mt 16:4. Mk 8:38. Lk 11:29.

adulterous. Mt 17:17. Nu 15:39. Ps 73:27. 106:39. Is 57:3. Ezk 16:26. 23:27. Ho 1:2. Mk 8:38. Ja 4:4. Re 2:20-22.

generation. Mt +24:34.

no sign. Mt 16:4. Lk 11:29, 30.

Jonas. i.e. *dove*, S#2495g. ver. 40, 41. Mt 16:4. Lk 11:29, 30, 32, 32. For S#3124h, see Jon +1:1, Jonah.

40 Jonas. Jon *1:17*. 2:1. Lk 11:30. +24:27.

three days. 1 S +30:12.

so shall. Mt 16:21. 17:23. 27:40, 63, 64. Mk 8:31. Jn 2:19.

Son of man. Mt +8:20.

three days and three nights. Jsh 5:11. 1 S 30:12. 1 K 16:8. Est 4:16 with 5:1. Mt 27:63, 64. Lk 24:7, 21, 46. Jn 2:19. 1 C 15:4.

in the heart. Dt 4:11mg. Ps +16:10. 63:9. Is 14:9. Jon 2:1-6. Lk 16:23. 23:43. Jn 2:19-23. Ep 4:9. Re 6:9, 10.

41 men. Mt 11:20-24. Jon 1:2. Lk 10:12-15. 11:32.

of Nineveh. Ge +10:11. Jon 1:2. 3:2-7. 4:11.

rise. ver. 42. Is 54:17. Je 3:11. Ezk 16:51, 52. Ro 2:27. He 11:7.

in judgment. ver. 32. Mt +10:15. Ob +21.

this generation. ver. +39, 45.

condemn it. Je 3:11. Ro 2:27.

because. Jon 3:5-10.

at. Gr. *eis*. Used here in the sense of "because of," Ac +2:38, or "on the basis of." Mt +26:28. Mk +1:4.

behold. ver. 6, 42. Jn 3:31. 4:12. 8:53-58. He 1:2, 3. 3:5, 6.

42 queen. 1 K 10:1, etc. 2 Ch 9:1, etc. Lk 11:31, etc. Ac 8:27, 28.

the judgment. ver. 41. Mt +10:15.

shall condemn it. ver. 41. Jn 3:19.

she came from. Ps 2:8. 72:8. Zc 9:10.

to hear the wisdom. 1 K 3:9, 12, 28. 4:29, 34. 5:12. 10:4, 7, 24. 2 Ch 1:7-12. 9:22. 1 C 1:22.

behold. ver. 6, 41. Mt 3:17. 17:5. Is +7:14. +9:6, 7. 11:1-3. Jn 1:14, 18. 1 C 1:24. Ph 2:6, 7. Col 2:3, 9. 1 T 3:16. He 1:2-4.

43 When. ver. 45.

the unclean. Mk +3:30. Ac 8:13.

spirit. Gr. *pneuma*, Mt +8:16.

gone out. Ro 8:11. 1 C 6:19, 20.

he walketh. Jb 1:7. 2:2. 1 P 5:8.

dry places. Ps 63:1. Is 13:21. 35:6, 7. 41:18. Je 2:6. Ezk 47:8-12. Am +8:11-13. Re 18:2.

seeking rest. Mt 8:29. Mk 5:7-13. Lk 8:28-32.

44 my house. ver. 29. Lk 11:21, 22. Jn 13:27. Ep 2:2. 1 J 4:4.

he findeth. Mt 13:20-22. Ps 81:11, 12. Ho 7:6. Jn 12:6. 13:2. Ac 5:1-3. 8:18-23. 1 C 11:19. 2 Th 2:9-12. 1 T 6:4, 5, 9, 10. 1 J 2:19. Ju 4, 5. Re 13:3, 4, 8, 9.

45 seven. ver. 24. Mk 5:9. 16:9. Ep 6:12.

spirits. Gr. *pneuma*, Mt +8:16.

more wicked. ver. 39. Mt 23:15. Lk 7:21.

they enter. Jn 13:27.

dwell there. Lk 22:3. Ac 5:3. Ro 8:11. 1 C 6:19, 20.

and the last. Mt 27:64. Lk 11:26. Jn 5:14. He 6:4-8. +10:26-31, 39. 2 P 2:14-22. 1 J +5:16, 17. Ju 10-13.

Even so. Mt 21:38-44. 23:32-39. +24:34. Lk 11:49-51. 19:41-44. Jn 15:22-24. Ro 11:8-10. 1 Th 2:15, 16.

46 yet talked. Mk 3:21, 31-35. Lk 8:10, 19-21.

his mother. Mt +1:16.

his brethren. Mt +13:55. Mk +6:3. Jn 2:12. 7:3, 5, 10. Ac 1:14. 1 C 9:5. Ga 1:19.

48 Who is. Mt 10:37. Dt 33:9. Mk 3:32, 33. Lk 2:49, 52. Jn 2:3, 4. 2 C 5:16.

49 his disciples. Mt 28:7. Mk 3:34. Jn 17:8, 9, 20. 20:17-20.

50 shall do. Mt 7:20, 21. 17:5. Mk 3:35. Lk +8:21. 11:27, 28. Jn 6:29, 40. +13:17. +15:14. Ac 3:22, 23. 16:30, 31. 17:30. 26:20. Ga 5:6. 6:15. Col 3:11. He +5:9. Ja +1:21, 22. 1 P 4:2. 1 J 2:17. 3:23, 24. Re 22:14.

the will. Mt +6:10. Ro 12:2. 1 Th +4:3.

the same. Mt 25:40, 45. 28:10. Ps 22:22. Jn 20:17. Ro 8:29. He 2:11-17.

and sister. SS 4:9, 10, 12. 5:1, 2. 1 C 9:5. 2 C 11:2. Ep 5:25-27.

and mother. Jn 19:26, 27. 1 T 5:2.

MATTHEW 13

1 house. Mt 23:38.

sat. Mk 2:13. 4:1.

sea. Da 7:1, 2. Mk 4:1. Re 13:1. 17:15.

2 great. Ge +49:10. Lk +5:15. 8:4-8.

so. Mk 4:1. Lk 5:3.

and sat. Lk 4:20.

3 in. ver. 10-13, 34, 35, 53. Mt 22:1. 24:32. Jg 9:8-20. 2 S 12:1-7. Ps 49:4. 78:2. Is 5:1-7. Ezk 17:2. 20:49. 24:3, etc. Mi 2:4. Hab 2:6. Mk 3:23. 4:2, 13, 33. 12:1, 12. Lk 8:10. 12:41. 15:3, etc. Jn 16:25mg.

a sower. Is 55:10. Am 9:13. Mk 4:2-9. Lk 8:5-8.

4 the way. ver. 18, 19.

5 stony places. ver. 20. Ezk 11:19. 36:26. Am 6:12. Zc 7:12.

of earth. i.e. "no deep earth."

6 when. ver. 21. Is 49:10. Ja 1:11, 12. Re 7:16.
because. Mt 7:26, 27. Lk 8:13. Ep 3:17. Col
1:23. 2:7.
they withered. Jn 15:6.

7 among thorns. ver. 22. Ge 3:18. Je 4:3, 4.
Mk 4:18, 19.

8 good. ver. 23. Lk 8:15. Ro 7:18.
some an hundredfold. ver. 23. Mk +10:30.
Jn 15:8. Ga 5:22, 23. Ph 1:11.

9 hath ears. ver. 16, 43. Mt 11:15. Dt 29:4. Jb
37:2. Ps 40:6. Je +7:2. Mk 4:9, 23. 7:14-16. Re
2:7, 11, 17, 29. 3:6, 13, 22. 13:8, 9.

10 Why. Mk 4:10, 33, 34.

11 Because. Mt 11:25, 26. 16:17. 19:11. Ps 25:8,
9, 14. Is 29:10. 35:8. Mk 4:11. Lk 8:10. 10:39-
42. Jn 7:17. Ac 16:14. 17:11, 12. 1 C 2:9, 10,
14. 4:7. Col 1:27. Ja 1:5, 16-18. 1 J 2:20, 27.
given. 2 T +2:25.
mysteries. Ro +16:25. 1 C 4:1. 13:2.
kingdom of heaven. Mt +4:17.
not given. Mt 11:27. Mk 4:11, 12. Lk 8:10.
10:22. Jn 6:44, 45, 65.

12 For whosoever hath. Mt 19:29. 25:29. Mk
+4:24, 25. 10:29, 30. Lk +8:18. 9:26. +12:48.
16:10-12. 18:29, 30. 19:24-26. Jn 15:2-5. Ja
4:6.
from him shall be taken. Mt 21:43. Is 5:4-
7. Mk 12:9. Lk 10:42. 12:20, 21. 16:2, 25.
20:16. 2 J 8. Re 2:5. 3:15, 16.

13 because. ver. 16. Dt 29:3, 4. Ps +119:18. Is
44:18. Je 5:21. Ezk 12:2. Mk 8:17, 18. Jn
3:19, 20. Ro 11:8.
see not. Ac 28:26, 27.
neither do. ver. 19. Jn 6:36. 7:16, 17. 8:43. 2
C 10:12mg.

14 fulfilled. Mt 1:22. Mk 1:2.
the prophecy. Is 6:9, 10. Lk +8:10. +24:27. 2
C 3:14, 15.
not. Mt +5:18.

15 heart. He +3:13.
is waxed. Dt +31:20.
ears. Zc 7:11. Jn 8:43, 44. Ac 7:57. 2 T 4:4.
He 5:11.
their eyes. Is 29:10-12. 44:20. Jn 5:40. 9:39,
41. 2 Th 2:10, 11.
should understand. Je 5:21. Ac 7:51, 52. Ro
10:10.
and should be. Ac +3:19. 2 T 2:25, 26. He
6:4-6.
and I. Is 57:18. Je 3:22. 17:14. 33:6. Ho 14:4.
Ml 4:2. Mk 4:12. Re 22:2.

16 blessed are your. Mt +5:3-11. 16:17. Lk
2:29, 30. 10:23, 24. Jn 8:56. 20:29. Ac 26:18.
1 C 6:11. 2 C 4:6. Ep 1:17, 18. He 6:9. 10:39.
eyes. Lk 10:23. 1 C 2:9.

17 That many. Lk 10:24. Jn 8:56. Ep 3:5, 6. He
11:13, 39, 40. 1 P 1:10-12.

18 Hear ye. ver. 11, 12. Mk 4:14, etc. Lk 8:11-
15.

19 heareth. ver. 13, 14.

the word. Mt 4:23. 24:14. Lk 8:11, etc. 9:2.
10:9. Ac 1:3. 28:31. Ep 3:8.
the kingdom. ver. 38. Mt 4:23. 8:12. 9:35.
24:14. Lk 12:32. Ac 20:25. 28:23. Ro 14:17.
and understandeth it not. Jb 34:32. Ps
25:9. Pr 1:7, 20-22. 2:1-6. 17:16. 18:1, 2. Mk
9:32. Jn 3:19, 20. 8:43. 18:38. Ac 17:32.
18:15. 24:25, 26. 25:19, 20. 26:31, 32. Ro
1:28. 2:8. 1 C 2:14. 8:2. 2 C 4:2-4. 2 Th 2:12.
He 2:1. 5:11, 12. 2 P 3:16. 1 J 5:20.
the wicked one. ver. 38. Mt 5:37. 6:13. Mk
4:15. Lk 8:12. Jn 17:15. Ep 6:16. 2 Th 3:3. 1 J
2:13, 14. 3:12. 5:18, 19.
This. ver. 4.

20 received. ver. 5, 6.
anon. 1 S 11:13-15. 2 Ch 24:2, 6, 14. Ps
78:34-37. 106:12, 13. Is 58:2. Ezk +33:31, 32.
Mk 4:16, 17. 6:20. Jn 5:35. Ac 8:13. 26:28. Ga
3:1. 4:14, 15. 5:7.

21 root in himself. ver. 6. Mt 7:22, 23, 26, 27.
Jb 19:28. Pr 12:3, 12. Lk +8:13. Jn 6:26, 61-
65, 70, 71. 15:5-7. Ac 8:21-23. Ga 5:6. 6:15.
Ep 3:17. Col +1:23. +2:7. He 4:2. 2 P 1:8, 9. 1
J 2:19, 20.
dureth for a while. Mt 10:22. 24:13. Jb
27:8-10. Ps 36:3. Ho 6:4. Lk +8:13. Ro 2:7. 1
C +15:2. Ga 5:7. Ph 1:6. 2 T 1:15. He +3:12-
14. 1 P 1:5.
for when tribulation. Mt 5:10-12. 10:37-
39. 16:24-26. Mk 4:17. 8:34-36. 13:12, 13. Lk
9:23-25. 14:26-33. 21:12-18. Jn 12:25, 26. Ac
14:22. 2 C 4:18. Ga 1:6. 6:12. 2 T 4:10. He
10:34-39. Ja 1:2. Re 2:13.
is offended. ver. 57. Mt +11:6. 2 T 1:15.

22 seed. ver. 7. Mk 4:18. Lk 8:14. 18:24. 2 T 4:10.
among the thorns. Je 4:3.
the care. Mt 6:24, 25. 19:16-24. Ge 13:10-
13. Jsh 7:20, 21. 2 K 5:20-27. Ps +26:4. Je
4:3. Mk +4:19. 10:23-25. Lk 12:15, 21, 29, 30.
14:16-24. 21:34. Ac 5:1-11. 8:18. 2 C 11:28.
Ga 1:4. Ph 3:18, 19. 1 T 6:9, 10. 2 T 4:10. 2 P
2:14, 15. 1 J 2:15, 16. Ju 11.
world. Gr. *aion*, Mt +6:13. ver. 38, 39, 40. Lk
16:8. Ro 12:2. 2 C 4:4. Ep 2:2. 6:12. 2 T 4:10.
He 1:2. 11:3.
the deceitfulness. Mt 19:23. Ps 52:7. 62:10.
Pr 11:28. 23:5. Ec 4:8. 5:10, 11, 13, 14. Zc
11:5. Mk 4:19. 10:21-23. Lk 18:24, 25. 2 Th
2:10. 1 T 6:9, 17. He +3:13. Re 3:17.
choke the word. Lk 8:14. 2 T 4:10. Ju 12.
becometh unfruitful. Lk 13:6-9. Jn 15:2-6.
2 P 1:8.

23 that received. ver. 8. Mk 4:20. Lk +8:15.
good. Pr 1:5, 6. 2:2-6. Ezk 18:31. 36:26. Mk
10:15. Jn 1:11-13. 8:47. 10:26, 27. 17:7, 8. Ac
16:14. 17:11. 2 Th 2:10, 13, 14. He 4:2. 8:10.
Ja +1:21, 22. 1 P 2:1, 2. 1 J 5:20.
heareth the word. Jb +37:2. Pr 2:10, 11.
4:7. Mk +4:24. Lk +8:18. +11:28. Jn 5:24. Ac
+17:11. Ro 10:17. Ga 3:2. 1 Th 2:13.

and understandeth. ver. 19. Lk 24:45. Jn 8:43. Ac 8:30, 31. 1 C 2:14. Ja 1:21, 22, 25. 2 P 3:16. 1 J 5:20.

beareth fruit. Mt 3:8, 10. 12:33. Ps 1:1-3. 92:13-15. Ho 14:8. Lk 6:43, 44. 13:9. Jn 15:1-8, 16. Ga 5:22, 23. Ph 1:11. 4:8, 17. Col 1:6, +10. He 6:7. 13:15, 16. 2 P +1:5-8.

some an hundredfold. ver. +8. Mt 25:14-29. 1 C 15:41. 2 C 8:1, 2. 1 Th 4:1. 2 P 1:5-8. 3:18.

24 put. Mt 21:33. Jg 14:12, 13. Is 28:10, 13. Ezk 17:2.

The kingdom. ver. 33, 44, 45, 47. Mt +4:17.

good seed. ver. 19, 37. Mt 4:23. Col 1:5. 1 P 1:23. 1 J 3:9.

25 men slept. Mt 25:5. Is 56:9, 10. Mk 13:37. Ac 20:29-31. Ro 13:11, 12. Ga 2:4. Ep 5:13-16. 1 Th 5:5-7. 2 Th 2:7. 2 T 4:3-5. He 12:15. 2 P 2:1. 1 J 2:18. 2 J +9-11. Ju 4. Re 2:14, 15, 20.

his enemy. ver. 39. Ge +3:15. 2 C 2:11. 11:13-15. 1 P 5:8. Re 12:9. 13:14.

sowed. Dt 22:9.

tares. ver. 38. Ac 20:29, 30. 2 C 11:13-15. Ga 1:7-9.

26 But when. Mk 4:26-29.

27 the servants. 1 C 3:5-9. 12:28, 29. 16:10. 2 C 5:18-20. 6:1, 4. Ep 4:11, 12.

whence. Ro +16:17. 1 C 1:11-13. 15:12, etc. Ga 3:1-3. Ja 3:15, 16. 4:4.

tares. ver. 25.

28 Wilt. Mt +15:14. Lk 9:49-54. 1 C 5:3-7. 2 C 2:6-11. 1 Th 5:14. Ju 22, 23.

29 Nay. 1 C 4:5.

30 Let both. ver. 39. Mt 3:12. 22:10-14. 25:6-13, 32. Ml 3:18. 1 C 4:5. 5:5-13. Ph 3:18, 19. 2 Th 3:6.

grow together. 1 S 25:29.

the harvest. ver. +39. Is 17:5-8. Ho 6:11. Jl 3:13. 1 C 15:20, 23. Re 14:14-20.

to the reapers. ver. 39-43. 1 T 5:4.

Gather ye. ver. 41. Mt 8:12. Mi +4:11-13. Lk 17:30-37.

first the tares. Mt 15:13. 24:40, 41. Is 8:12. Re 3:17. 18:7.

and bind. 1 S 25:29.

to burn. ver. 40. Mt +25:41. Is +24:6. 27:10, 11. Ezk 15:4-7. Ml +4:1. Jn +15:6. 2 P +3:7.

but gather. Mt 3:12. Is 27:12. +43:6. Je 31:8. Ezk 34:12. 37:12. +38:8. 39:28. Am 9:9. Lk 3:17. 1 Th 4:16, 17.

wheat. Mt 3:12. Lk 3:17. Jn 12:24.

31 put. ver. 24. Lk 19:11. 20:9.

The kingdom. Mt +4:17. Mk 4:30-32. Lk 13:18, 19.

a grain. Ac 1:15.

of mustard seed. Mt 17:20. Mk 4:31. Lk 13:19. 17:6.

32 the least. Ps 72:16-19. Is +2:2-4. Ezk 47:1-5.

Da +2:34, 35, 44, 45. Mi 4:1-3. Zc 4:10. +8:20-23. 14:7-10. Ac 1:15. 21:20. Ro 15:18, 19. Re 11:15.

becometh a tree. Jg 9:14, 15. Ezk 17:22, 23. 31:3-6. Da 4:10-12, 20-22.

the birds of the air. ver. 4, 19. Mt 8:20. Ge 15:11. +40:19. Dt 28:26. Ps 104:12. Ezk 17:23, 24. 31:6. Da 4:12, 21. Re 2:20. 18:12.

33 Another. Lk 13:20, 21.

like unto leaven. Mt 16:11, 12. Ex 12:15. 34:25. Le 2:4, 11. 7:13. +23:17. Ezk 46:11. Am +4:5. Mk 8:15. Lk 12:1. 13:21. 21:1. 1 C 5:6-8. 2 C 7:1. Ga 5:7-9. 2 Th 2:4.

a woman. 2 C 11:2. Ep 5:24. 1 T 2:11, 12. Ep 5:24. Re 2:20. 17:1-6.

and hid. ver. 25. Mt 11:27. 2 C 4:2. Ep 4:14. 5:11.

three. Ge 18:6. Jg 6:19. 1 S 1:24.

measures. Gr. "A measure containing about a peck and a half, wanting a little more than a pint."

meal. 1 K 17:14-16. Jn 6:32-35. 2 J 9.

till. Jb 17:9. Pr +4:18. Ho 6:3. Jn 15:2. 16:12, 13. Ph 1:6, 9. 2:13-15. 1 Th 5:23, 24. 2 P 3:18.

the whole. Ml 1:7. Ro 11:16. 1 C 5:6. 10:17. 15:33. 1 Th 5:23.

was leavened. 1 C 5:6. Ga 5:9.

34 these things. ver. 13. Mk 4:33, 34. Jn 16:25mg, 29mg.

35 it might be. ver. 14. Mt 21:4, 5.

open. Jg +11:35. Ps 78:2.

in parables. Nu 21:27.

I will utter. Is 42:9. Am 3:7. Lk 10:24. Ro 16:25, 26. 1 C 2:7. Ep 3:5, 9. Col 1:25, 26. 2 T 1:9, 10. T 1:2, 3. He 1:1. 1 P 1:11, 12.

from. Mt 25:34. Lk 11:50. Jn 17:24. Ac 15:18. Ep 1:4. 3:9. 2 T 1:9. He 4:3. 9:26. 1 P 1:20, 21. Re 13:8. 17:8.

world. Gr. *kosmos*, Mt +4:8.

36 Jesus sent. Mt 14:22. 15:39. Mk 6:45. 8:9.

multitudes. ver. 2. Lk 10:23, 24.

went into the house. ver. 1. Mt 9:28. Ps 73:16, 17. Mk 4:34.

Declare. ver. 11. Mt 15:15, 16. Mk 4:13, 33, 34. 7:17. Jn 16:17-20.

37 He. ver. 24, 27. Mk 4:14. Jn 4:36, 37.

that soweth. Ac 8:1.

good seed. Ps 22:30. Is 53:10. Ho 2:23. Mk 16:15, 20. Lk 24:47. Ro 10:18. Col 1:6. Ja 1:18.

is the Son of man. ver. +41. Mt 10:40. Lk 10:16. Jn 13:20. 20:21. Ac +1:8. Ro 15:18. 1 C 3:5-7. He 1:1. 2:3.

38 field. Mt 24:14. 28:18-20. Ge 37:15. Le 27:16. Mk 16:15-20. Lk 24:47. Ro 10:18. 16:26. Col 1:6. Re 14:6.

world. Gr. *kosmos*, Mt +4:8.

the good seed. Ps 22:30. Is 53:10. Ho 2:23. Zc 10:8, 9. Jn 1:12, 13. 12:24. Ro 8:17. Ja 1:18. 2:5. 1 P +1:23. 1 J 3:2, 9.

children of the kingdom. ver. 43. Mt +8:12. Mk 2:19. 1 J 3:10.

tares are. Mt 23:33. Ps +5:9. 36:1. 53:1-3. 73:6-12. Pr +5:22. Is +24:5. Ho 4:2. Jn 7:7. 8:44. 15:24, 25. +17:14. Ac 7:51. 13:10. Ro 1:30. 3:13-18. 8:7.

the children of the wicked one. ver. 19. Mt 23:15, 33. Ge +3:15. Jg +19:22. Jn 6:12. 8:44. Ac 13:10. Ph 3:18, 19. 1 J 3:8, 10, 12.

39 **enemy**. ver. 25, 28. 2 C 2:17. 11:3, 13-15. Ep 2:2. 6:11, 12. 2 Th 2:8-11. 1 P 5:8. Re 12:9. 13:14. 19:20. 20:2, 3, 7-10.

the harvest. ver. +30, 49. Is 17:5-8. 18:5-7. Ho 6:11. Jl 3:13. Re 14:15-19.

end of the. ver. 40, 49. Mt +24:3. 28:20. Da 12:13. He 9:26.

world. Gr. *aion*, Mt +6:13. lit. "end of the age," ver. 40, 49. Mt 24:3. 28:20. He 9:26.

reapers. Mt 25:31. Da 7:10. 2 Th 1:7-10. Ju 14. Re 14:15.

40 **the tares**. ver. 30.

are gathered. Mt 24:39. Is 24:22. Mi 4:11-13.

and burned. ver. 30, 42, 49, 50. Mt 3:12. +25:46. Is +24:6. Ml 3:18. +4:1. Jn 15:6. 2 P +3:7.

fire. 1 C 3:13, 15.

end of this. ver. 39.

world. Gr. *aion*, Mt +6:13.

41 **Son of man**. Mt +8:20.

send forth his angels. Mt +24:31. Ps +68:17. 103:20, 21. Is 13:3. Da 7:10. Jl 3:11. Mk 13:27. He 1:6, 7, 14. Re 5:11, 12.

and they. ver. 49. Mt 18:7. Ps 35:5, 6. Ro 16:17, 18. 2 P 2:1, 2.

gather out. ver. +30. Mt 8:12. +25:31. Ps 58:9. Lk 17:26-37.

things that offend. *or*, scandals. Mt +17:27. Zp 1:3.

and them. Mt +7:22, 23. +25:41. Lk 13:26, 27. Ac 17:31. Ro 2:8, 9, 16. 2 Th 1:7, 8. 2 P 2:1, 2. Re 21:27.

do iniquity. 1 J 3:4.

42 **shall cast**. ver. 50. Mt +25:41. Je 29:22. Ezk 23:25. Da 3:6, 15-17, 21, 22. Re 9:2.

wailing. ver. 50. Mt +25:30.

43 **Then shall**. Mt 25:34, 46. Jg +5:31. Ml 3:18. 1 C 15:24, 41-54, 58. Col 3:4. 1 J 3:2. Re 21:3-5, 22, 23.

the righteous. Ml 4:2. 2 Th 1:10.

shine forth. Is 24:23. Da +12:3.

in the kingdom. ver. 38. Mt +6:10.

Who hath ears. ver. +9.

44 **kingdom of heaven**. Ps +73:9. 2 T +4:18.

like. Mt 6:21. 25:18. Jb 3:21. Ps 19:10. Pr 2:2-5. 16:16. 17:16. 18:1. Jn 6:35. Ro +15:4. 1 C 2:9, 10. Col 2:3. 3:3, 4, 16.

treasure. Ex 19:5. Dt 4:20. 32:8. Ps 135:4. Ro 1:16.

hid. Dt 26:1-5. 32:10. Is 51:1, 2.

in a field. ver. 38. Dt 32:8-10. Jn 15:19. 17:6, 9, 11-13, 14, 15, 16.

hath found. Mt 15:24. Jn 1:11.

he hideth. Dt 32:28, 29.

for joy. Mt 19:21, 27, 29. Lk 14:33. 18:23, 24. 19:6-8. Ac 2:44-47. 4:32-35. Ph 3:7-9. He 10:34. 11:24-26. 12:2.

selleth all. ver. 46. Mt 25:9. Ps 22:1. Is 53:4-10. Lk 14:33. Jn 11:51, 52. Ro 8:32. 2 C 8:9. Ep 5:25. Ph 2:7. 3:7, 8.

buyeth. Pr 23:23. Is 55:1. 2 P 2:1. Re 3:18.

45 **like**. Mt 16:26. 22:5. Pr 3:13-18. 8:10, 11, 18-20. Re 3:18.

seeking. Jb 28:18. Ps 4:6, 7. 39:6, 7. Ec 2:2-12. 12:8, 13. Lk +19:10. Jn 15:16. Ac 15:14. Ep 2:17.

46 **one pearl**. Mt +7:6. Jb 28:18. Pr 2:4. 3:13-15. 4:7. 8:11. 20:15. 31:10. Is 33:6. La 4:7. Ml 3:17mg. Lk +10:42. 1 C 3:21-23. Ga 3:28. Ep 3:8. 5:27. Col 2:3. 2 Th 1:10. 1 T 2:9. 1 J 5:11, 12. Re 17:4. 21:21.

went. ver. 44. Mk 10:28-31. Lk 18:28-30. Ac 20:24. Ga 6:14.

sold all. Mt 19:21, 29. Lk 14:33. Ro 8:32. 2 C 8:9.

bought it. Is 55:1. 1 C 6:20. 1 P 1:18, 19.

47 **a net**. Mt 4:19. Jb 19:6. Ezk 12:13. 32:3. Ho 7:12. Hab 1:15. Mk 1:16, 17. Lk 5:10. Jn 21:6.

the sea. Ge 1:20-23. Re 17:15.

and gathered. ver. 26-30, 38. Mt 22:9, 10. 25:1-4. Lk 14:21-23. Jn 15:2-6. Ac 5:1-10. 8:18-22. 20:30. 1 C 5:1-6. 10:1-12. 11:19. 2 C 11:13-15, 26. 12:20, 21. Ga 2:4. 2 T 3:2-5. 4:3, 4. T 1:9-11. 2 P 2:1-3, 13-22. 1 J 2:18, 19. 4:1-6. Ju 4, 5. Re 3:1, 15-17.

every kind. Mt 22:10. 25:1, 2. Jn 6:70. 1 C 3:10. 2 C 12:20, 21.

48 **was full**. Jn 21:6, 11.

drew to shore. Jn 21:11.

gathered the good. ver. 30, 40-43. Mt 3:12. 25:31-46. Is 27:12, 13. Je 16:16. Ezk 34:12. Am 9:9. Jn 17:12. 21:11.

cast the bad. Mt 15:13, 14. 22:12, 13. Le 11:9. Ezk 20:38. Ro 16:17. 1 C 10:4, 5.

49 **world**. Gr. *aion*, Mt +6:13.

the angels. ver. 39. Mt +24:31.

and sever. ver. 41. 25:5-12, 19-33. 2 Th 1:7-10. Re 20:12-15.

from among. Is 52:11. 57:1. Ac 17:33. 23:10. 1 C 5:2. 2 C 6:17. Col 2:14. 2 Th 2:7.

50 **cast**. ver. 42.

furnace of fire. ver. 42. Mt +25:41.

wailing. ver. +42.

51 **Have ye understood**. ver. 11, 19. Mt 15:17. 16:11. 24:15. Mk 4:34. 7:14, 18. 8:17, 18. Lk 9:44, 45. Jn 10:6. 13:12. 16:29. Ac 8:30, 31. 1 J 5:20.

52 **every scribe**. Mt 23:34. Ezr 7:6, 10, 21. Da +11:33. Lk 11:49. 1 C 12:7. 2 C 3:4-6. Col 1:7.

1 T 3:6, 15, 16. +4:13-16. 2 T 3:16, 17. T 1:9. 2:6, 7.

instructed unto the kingdom. Mt 11:11. 28:19. Da +11:33. +12:3. Ac 14:21.

householder. Ro 12:7. 1 T 3:2. 4:11, 13, 16. 2 T 2:24. He 5:12. 13:17. Ja 3:1.

which bringeth. Mt 12:35. +24:45. Pr 10:20, 21. 11:30. 15:7. 16:20-24. 18:4. 22:17, 18. Ec 12:9-11. Je 15:16. Da +11:33. Jn +5:39. Ac 17:11. 2 C 4:5-7. 6:10. Ep 3:4, 8. Col 3:16.

treasure. 1 Ch 9:26.

things new. SS 7:13. Jn 13:34. Ep 3:3-5. He 5:12-14. 1 J 2:7, 8.

53 **came to pass**. Mt 7:28. 11:1. 19:1. 26:1.

he departed. Mk 4:33-35.

54 **when**. Mt 2:23. Mk 6:1, 2. Lk 4:16-30. Jn 1:11.

his own country. Mt 2:23. Lk 4:23.

he taught. Mt 4:23. 26:55. Ps 22:22. 40:9, 10. Ac 13:46. 28:17-29.

they were astonished. Mt +7:28.

Whence hath. Mt 21:23. Mk 11:28. Jn 7:15, 16. Ac 4:13.

wisdom. Ac 7:22.

mighty works. Mt 7:22. 11:20, 21, 23. 14:2. Mk 6:14.

55 **the carpenter's**. Ps 22:6. Is 49:7. 53:2, 3. Mk +6:3. Lk 3:23. 4:22. Jn 1:45, 46. 6:42. 7:41, 42, 48, 52. 9:29.

is not his. Mt +1:18-20. Lk 1:27. 2:5-7.

and his brethren. Mt 12:46, 48. 27:56. Ps 69:8. Mk +6:3. 15:40, 47. 16:1. Lk 24:10. Jn 19:25.

James. Ga 1:19.

Joses. i.e. *increaser, whom Jehovah helps*, **S#2500g**. Mt 27:56. Mk 6:3. 15:40, 47. Lk 3:29. Ac 4:36.

56 **Whence then hath**. Jn 7:15, 52.

57 **they were offended**. ver. 21. Mt +11:6. Is 49:7. 53:3.

A prophet. 2 K 5:8. Is 53:3. Je 11:21. 12:6. Mk 6:14. Lk 4:24. Jn 4:44. 7:5. Ac 3:22, 23. 7:37-39, 51, 52.

own country. Jn 7:41, 42.

own house. Mk 3:19, 21. Jn 7:3, 5.

58 **he did not many**. Mk 6:5, 6. Lk 4:25-29. Ro 11:20. He 3:12-19. 4:6-11.

because. Mt 17:20. Mk 9:23.

MATTHEW 14

1 **Herod**. Mk 6:14-16. 8:15. Lk 9:7-9. 13:31, 32. 23:8-12, 15. Ac 4:27.

Tetrarch. Lk 3:1.

the fame. Mt 4:24. Jn 12:38.

2 **servants**. Mt 8:6.

This. Mt 11:11. 16:14. Mk 6:15, 16. 8:28. Jn 10:41.

mighty works. Mt 13:54.

do show forth themselves in him. *or*, are

wrought by him. 1 C 12:6, 11. Ga 2:8. 3:5. Ep +1:11, 20. 2:2. Ph 2:13.

3 **Herod**. Mt +4:12.

bound. Jn 18:24.

in prison. Mt 11:2. Jn 3:24.

Herodias'. i.e. *heroic; the glory of the skin*, **S#2266g**. ver. 6. Mk 6:17, 19, 22. Lk 3:19.

his. Lk 3:1.

4 **not lawful**. Mt 22:24. Ge 38:8. Dt 25:5, 6. 1 K 21:19. 2 Ch 26:18, 19. Pr 28:1. Is +8:20. Mk 6:18. 12:19. Lk 20:28. Ac 24:24, 25.

to have her. Le 18:6, 16. 20:21. 2 S 12:7.

5 **when**. Mk 6:19, 20. 14:1, 2. Ac 4:21. 5:26.

he feared. Mt 21:26, 46.

because. Mt 11:9. 21:26, 32. Mk 11:30-32. Lk 20:6.

6 **birthday**. Ge 40:20. Est 1:2-9. 2:18. Da 5:1-4. Ho 7:5, 6. Mk 6:21-23.

the daughter. Mt 22:24.

danced. Est 1:10-12.

before them. Gr. in the midst. Jn 8:3. Ac 4:7.

7 **he promised**. Est 5:3, 6. 7:2.

with an oath. ver. +9. Nu +30:2. Jg +11:30, 31. Ezk 17:18. Ac +23:12.

8 **being**. 2 Ch 22:2, 3. Mk 6:24.

Give. 1 K 18:4, 13. 19:2. 2 K 11:1. Pr 1:16. 29:10.

head. Jg +7:25.

a charger. Nu 7:13, 19, 84, 85. Ezr 1:9.

9 **the king**. ver. 1. Mk 6:14.

sorry. ver. 5. Mt 27:17-26. 2 S 22:8. Je 28:5. Da 6:14-16. Mk 6:20, 26, 48. Lk 13:32. Jn 19:8, 12-16. Ac 24:23-27. 25:3-9.

the oath's. ver. +7. Nu +30:2, 5-8. Jg 21:1, 7-23. 1 S 25:22, 32-34. 28:10. 2 K 6:31-33. Ezk 17:18.

10 **and beheaded**. Mt 17:12. 21:35, 36. 22:3-6. 23:34-36. 2 Ch 36:16. Je 2:30. Mk 6:27-29. 9:13. Lk 9:9. Re 11:7.

11 **head**. Jg +7:25.

and given. Ge 49:7. Pr 27:4. 29:10. Je 22:17. Ezk 16:3, 4. 19:2, 3. 35:6. Re 16:6. 17:6.

12 **his disciples**. Mt 9:14.

took. Mt 27:58-61. Ac 8:2.

told Jesus. Jn 12:22.

13 **Jesus heard**. ver. 1, 2. Mk 6:30-33. Lk 9:10-17. Jn 6:1-13.

he departed. Mt 15:21. Mk +3:7.

14 **saw**. Lk +5:15.

moved. Is +63:15.

compassion. Mt +9:36. 23:37. Jb +36:7. Ps +119:68. +145:9. Lk 19:41, +42. Jn +1:12. 11:33-35. 13:34. 15:9. Ac 10:38. +20:24. Ro 5:6-8. 8:37. Ep 5:2. He 2:17. Ja +5:11. 1 J +2:12. Re +22:17.

he healed. Mt +4:23.

15 **his**. Mk 6:35, 36. Lk 9:12.

send. ver. 22. Mt 15:23. Mk 8:3.

16 **they**. 2 K 4:42-44. Jb 31:16, 17. Pr 11:24. Ec

11:2. Lk 3:11. Jn 6:5-7. 13:29. 2 C 8:2, 3. 9:7, 8.

17 **We have**. Mt 15:33, 34. Nu 11:21-23. 2 K 4:42-44. 7:2. Ps 78:19, 20. Mk 6:37, 38. 8:4, 5. Lk 9:13. Jn 6:5-9.
five. Mt 16:9. Mk 8:19.
loaves. Jn 6:9.

18 **Bring them**. Mt 17:17. 21:2. Nu 11:23. 1 K 17:10-16. 2 K 4:1-7, 42-44. Mk 6:37, 38. Jn 6:8, 9.

19 **he commanded**. Mt 15:35. Mk 6:39, 40. 8:6. Lk 9:14, 15. Jn 6:10.
looking. 2 Ch 6:13. Ps 121:1. 123:1, 2. Mk 6:41. 7:34. Lk 9:16. Jn 11:41. 17:1. Ac 7:55.
he blessed. Lk +24:30.
and brake. Is +58:7.

20 **were filled**. Mt 5:6. 15:33, 37. Ex 16:8, 12. Le 26:26. Dt 8:3, 10. 1 K 17:12-16. 2 K 4:43, 44. Ps 107:9. Pr 13:25. Ezk 4:14-16. Hg 1:6. Mk 6:42. 8:8. Lk 1:53. 9:17. Jn 6:7, 11, 12. Re 7:16, 17.
and they took. Mt 15:37, 38. 16:8-10. 2 K 4:1-7. Mk 6:42-44. 8:8, 9, 16-21. Lk 9:17. Jn 6:12-14.
that remained. 2 Ch 31:9, 10. Lk 15:17. Ph 4:18.

21 **about**. Jn 6:10. Ac 4:4, 34. 2 C 9:8-11. Ph 4:19.
women. Ne +12:43.
and children. Mt 15:38. Dt +29:11. Is 54:13. Lk +18:15.

22 **And straightway**. Mk 6:45-51. Jn 6:15-21.
Jesus. Mk 6:45.
constrained. Lk 14:23.
a ship. Mt 15:39.
other side. Mt 8:18.
while. Mt 13:36. 15:39.
sent. ver. 15.

23 **into a mountain**. Mt +5:1. Ex 3:12. 19:17. 32:1, 11. 2 S 15:30, 31. 1 K 18:42-44. 19:11-13. 2 K 1:9-15.
apart. Mt 6:6. Ps +1:2. Mk +1:35. Lk 5:16. 9:18.
to pray. Mt 26:36, 39, 42, 44. Ps 21:2. Mk 1:35. 6:46. Lk 5:16. 6:12. 9:18, 28, 29. 11:1. Jn 11:41, 42. 14:15, 16. 17:1. Ac 6:4. Ro +8:34. He 5:7-9.
the evening. Ge 24:11, 12. 1 K 18:36. 1 Ch 23:30. Ezr 9:5. Ps 55:17. Da 9:21. Mk 13:35.
he was. Jn 6:15-17.
alone. Ge 32:24. Mk +1:35. Lk 5:16. 6:12. 9:18.

24 **tossed**. Mt 8:24. Is 54:11. Mk 6:48. Jn 6:18.

25 **the fourth watch**. Mt 24:43. Mk 13:35. Lk 12:38. Jn +11:9.
walking on the sea. Jb 9:8. Ps 93:3, 4. 104:3. Mk 6:48. Jn 6:19. Re 10:2, 5, 8.

26 **they were**. 1 S 28:12-14. Jb 4:14-16. Da 10:6-12. Mk 6:49, 50. Lk 1:11, 12. 24:5, 37, 45. Ac 12:15. Re 1:17.

It is. Lk +4:30. 24:16, 39. Jn +20:14.
a spirit. or, apparition. lit. a phantom. **S#5326g**. Mk 6:49. Lk 24:37.

27 **Be of good cheer**. Mt 9:2. Jn 16:33. Ac 23:11.
it is I. Is 41:4, 10, 14. 51:12. Lk 24:38, 39. Jn 6:20. 14:1-3. Re 1:17, 18.
be not afraid. Mt 17:7. Dt 31:6. Jsh 10:25. 1 Ch 22:13. 28:20. Ps +34:4. 46:1, 2. Is 41:13. 43:1, 2. Jn 14:1. 16:33. Ph 4:13. 2 T +1:7.

28 **if**. 1 C +15:2.
bid. Mt 19:27. 26:33-35. Mk 14:31. Lk 22:31-34, 49, 50. Jn 6:68. 13:36-38. Ro 12:3.

29 **he walked**. Mt 17:20. 21:21. Mk 9:23. 11:22, 23. Lk 17:6. Jn 21:7. Ac 3:16. Ro 4:19. Ph 4:13.

30 **when he saw**. Mt 26:69-75. 2 K 6:15. Ps 93:3, 4. Is 43:2. Mk 14:38, 66-72. Lk 22:54-61. Jn 18:25-27. 2 T 4:16, 17.
boisterous. or, strong.
afraid. Ge +19:30.
sink. **S#2670g**. Mt 18:6 (drowned).
Lord. Mt 8:24-26. Ps 3:7. 69:1, 2. 107:27-30. 116:3, 4. La 3:54-57. Jon 2:2-7. Lk 8:24. 2 C 12:7-10.

31 **stretched**. Ps 138:7. Is 63:12. La 3:57. Mk 1:31, 41. 5:41. Ac 4:30.
and caught. Ge 22:14. Dt 32:36. Mk 16:7. Lk 22:31, 32. 24:34. 1 P 1:5. Ju 24.
O thou. Mt +6:30.
wherefore. Ge +19:30.
doubt. Mt 21:21. 28:17. Mk 11:23. Ro 4:18-20. 1 T 2:8. Ja 1:6-8.

32 **come**. Ps 107:29, 30. Mk 4:41. 6:51. Jn 6:21.

33 **they that**. ver. 22, 29. Mk 6:51, 52.
worshipped. Mt 2:11. 8:2. 9:18. 15:25. 20:20. 28:9, 17. Lk 14:10. 24:52. Jn 5:23. 9:38. +20:28. Ph 2:10, 11. He +1:6. Re +5:11-13.
Of a truth. Jn 6:14.
the Son of God. Mt 3:17. 4:3, 6. 8:29. 16:16. 17:5. 26:63. 27:40, 43, 54. Ps 2:7. Da 3:25. Mk 1:1. 3:11. 14:61. 15:39. Lk 1:35. 4:41. 8:28. 22:70. Jn 1:34, 49, +51. 3:18. 5:25. 6:68, 69. 9:35-38. 10:36. 11:4, 27. 17:1. 19:7. 20:31. Ac 8:37. 9:20. Ro 1:4. 2 C 1:19. Ga 2:20. Ep 4:13. He 1:2. 4:14. 6:6. 7:3. 10:20. 1 J 3:8. 4:15. 5:5, 10, 12, 13, 20. Re 2:18.

34 **when**. Mk 6:53-56. Jn 6:24, 25.
the land of Gennesaret. i.e. *garden of the prince*, **S#1082g**. Mk 6:53. Lk 5:1.

35 **had knowledge**. Mk 6:54-56.
they sent. Mt 4:24, 25. Mk 1:28-34. 2:1, etc. 3:8-10. 6:55.
all that were diseased. Mt 4:24. 8:16.

36 **besought him**. Ps +103:3. Je 17:14. 33:6.
only. Mt 9:20, 21. Mk 3:10. 6:56. Lk 6:19. 8:47. Ac 5:15. 19:11, 12.

hem. Mt 23:5. Ex 28:33, etc. Nu 15:38, 39.
perfectly. Mk 10:52. Jn 6:37. 7:23. Ac 3:16.
4:9, 10, 14-16.

MATTHEW 15

1 **came**. Mk 7:1-23.
  scribes. Mt 5:20. 23:2, 15, etc. Lk 5:30. Ac
  23:9.
  which. Mk 3:22. Lk 5:17, 21.
2 **Why**. Mt 9:11.
  transgress. Mk 7:2, 5. Ga 1:14. Col 2:8, 20-
  23. 1 P 1:18.
  tradition. ver. 3, 6. Dt 4:2. +12:32. Pr +30:6.
  Ga 1:14. Col 2:8. Re +22:18, 19.
  the elders. He 11:2.
  for they. Lk 11:38.
  bread. Ge +3:19.
3 **Why**. Mt 7:3-5. Mk 7:6-8, 13. Col 2:8, 23. T
  1:14.
  tradition. ver. +2. Mk 7:9.
4 **God**. Mt 4:10. 5:17-19. Is +8:20. Ro 3:31.
  Honor. Ge 22:6-10. 31:35. 45:9-11. 47:12. Ex
  +*20:12*. Dt *5:16*. Jg 11:36. 1 S 2:12. 3:9. 8:3. 2
  S 15:10. 1 K 1:5, 6. Est 2:20. Pr 3:1, 2. 10:1.
  13:1. 17:25. Mi 7:6. Ml 1:6. Mk 7:10.
  He that. Dt 21:18-21. Pr 20:20.
5 **ye say**. Mt 23:16-18. Am 7:15-17. Mk 7:10-
  13. Ac 4:19. 5:29.
  Whosoever. Mt +23:30.
  It is. Ge 28:22. Le 27:9, etc. Pr 20:25. Mk
  7:11, 12.
  a gift. Mt 23:18.
  thou mightest. Is +58:7. Mk 7:12.
6 **honor**. 1 C 12:26. 1 T 5:3, 4, 8, 16, 17. 1 P
  3:7.
  Thus. Ps 119:126, 127, 139. Je 8:8, 9. Ho 4:6.
  Ml 2:7-9. Mk 7:13. Ro 3:31.
  commandment of God. Lk 5:1. Jn +10:35.
  Ro 9:6. Re 1:2.
  none effect. Ro 2:23. Ga 3:17.
  tradition. ver. 2.
7 **hypocrites**. Mt 6:2.
  well. Is *29:13*. Mk 7:6. Ac 28:25-27.
8 **this people**. Lk +24:27.
  draweth. Is *29:13*. Ezk +33:31. Jn 1:47. 1 P
  3:10.
  lips. Ps +50:16, 17. Is 29:13. 58:1-3. Je 12:2.
  Ezk +33:31. Mk 7:5-7. Ro 8:26. 2 T 3:5. T
  1:16. Re 3:1.
  but. Pr 23:26. Je 12:2. Ac 8:21. He +3:12.
9 **in vain**. Ex 20:7. Le 26:16, 20. 1 S 12:21.
  25:21. Ps 39:6. 73:13. Ec 5:2-7. Is 1:13-15.
  58:1-3. Ml 3:14. Mk 7:7. 1 C 15:2. Ja 1:26.
  2:20.
  worship. Jn 4:24.
  teaching. Dt +4:2. Is 29:13. Col 2:18-22. 1 T
  1:4. 4:1-3, 6, 7. T 1:14. He 13:9. Re 22:18.
10 **he called**. 1 K 22:28. Mk 7:14, 16. Lk 20:45-
  47.

understand. Mt +13:19. 24:15. Is 6:9. +55:3.
Lk 24:45. Ep 1:17, 18. Col 1:9. Ja +1:5.
11 **that which goeth**. Mk 7:15. Lk 11:38-41. Ac
  10:14, 15. 11:8, 9. 21:28. Ro 14:14, 17, 20. 1
  T 4:4, 5. T 1:15. He 9:13. 13:9. Re 21:27.
  but. ver. 18-20. Mt 12:34-37. Ps 10:7. 12:2.
  52:2-4. 58:3, 4. Is 37:23. 59:3-5, 13-15. Je
  9:3-6. Ro 3:13, 14. Ja 3:5-8. 2 P 2:18.
12 **Knowest**. Mt +17:27. 1 K 22:13, 14. Ga 2:5.
  Ja 3:17.
  offended. Mt +11:6.
13 **Every plant**. Mt 13:40, 41. Ps 92:13. Is
  +60:21. 61:3. Jn 15:2, 6. 1 C 3:9, 12-15.
  which my. Mt 7:21.
  hath not. Mt +13:38-41.
  planted. Ps 1:3.
  rooted up. Ju 12.
14 **Let them alone**. Mt 7:15. 24:4. 2 Ch +19:2.
  Pr 19:27. Is 65:5. Ho 4:17. Mk 4:24. Lk 21:8.
  Ro +16:17, 18. 1 C +11:19. Ga 1:7-9. Ep
  +4:27. +5:11. Ph 3:2, 3. 2 T 2:19. Ja +5:20. Ju
  +3.
  they. Mt 23:16-24. Is 3:12. 9:16. 42:19.
  56:10. Je 5:31. 50:6. Ezk 3:18. Ml +2:7, 8. Lk
  6:39.
  And if. Mt +4:9. Je 5:31. 6:15. 8:12. Ezk
  14:9, 10. Mi 3:5-7. Ro 2:19. 2 P 2:1, 9, 17. Re
  19:20. 22:15.
  both. Mt 23:13, 15. Is 9:16. Ezk 14:10.
  fall into. Mt +6:2.
15 **Declare**. Mt 13:36. Mk 4:34. 7:17. Jn 16:29.
16 **Are ye also**. ver. 10. Mt 13:51. 16:9, 11. Is
  28:9, 10. Mk 6:52. 7:18. 8:17, 18. 9:32. Lk
  9:45. 18:34. 24:45. He 5:12.
  without understanding. Ro 1:21, 31. 10:19.
17 **that**. Mk 7:19, 20. Lk 6:45. 1 C 6:13. Col
  2:21, 22. Ja 3:6.
  and is. 2 K 10:27.
18 **those things**. ver. 11. Mt 12:34, 35. 1 S
  24:13. Ps 36:3. Pr 6:12. 10:32. 15:2, 28. Lk
  19:22. Ep +4:29. Ja 3:6-10. Re 13:5, 6.
  heart. 1 K +8:18.
  defile. ver. 11. Pr 10:19. 15:28. 1 C 3:17. Ja
  3:6.
19 **out**. Mt 12:34. Ge 6:5. 8:21. Ps 58:3. Pr +4:23.
  6:14. 22:15. 24:9. Ec 9:3. Je +17:9, 10. Mk
  7:21-23. Ro 1:21. 3:10-19. 7:18. 8:7, 8. Ga
  5:19-21. Ep 2:1-3. T 3:2-6.
  evil thoughts. Mt 9:4. Ps 56:5. 119:113. Is
  55:7. 59:7. Je 4:14. Ac 8:22. Ja 1:13-15. 2:4.
  murders. 1 J 3:15.
  adulteries. Ex 20:15, 16. Mt 5:28. 1 C +6:9,
  18.
  fornications. Mt +5:32.
  false witness. Pr +6:19.
  blasphemies. Ep +4:31.
20 **which**. 1 C 3:16, 17. 6:9-11, 18-20. Ep 5:3-6.
  Re +21:8, 27.
  but. ver. 2. Mt 23:25, 26. Mk 7:2-5. Lk 11:38-
  40.

21 **and departed**. Mt 12:15. 14:13. Mk 7:24-30.
Tyre. Mt 10:5, 6. +11:21-23.
Sidon. Mt +11:21.
22 **a woman**. Mt 3:8, 9. Ps 45:12. Ezk 3:6. Mk 7:26.
Canaan. i.e. *humiliation, to be low*, S#5478g, only here. Mk 7:26. Ge 10:15, 19. Jg 1:30-33. Ac 7:11. 13:19.
Have. Mt +9:27.
Son. Mt +1:1.
my. Mk 7:25. 9:17-22.
vexed. Mt +4:24. Ac +5:16.
23 **he answered**. Ge 42:7. Dt 8:2. Ps 28:1. La 3:8.
her not. ver. 26. Mt 21:29.
Send. Mt 14:15. Mk 10:47, 48.
24 **I am not**. Is 53:6. Lk 15:4-6. Ac +3:26.
lost. Gr. *apollumi*, Mt +2:13.
sheep of. Nu +27:17. Ps 79:13. 95:7. Ac 3:25, 26. Ro 9:4.
25 **came**. Mt 20:31. Ge 32:26. Ho 12:4. Lk 11:8-10. 18:1, etc. Ja 1:3.
worshipped. Mt +8:2. +14:33. Re +5:12.
Lord. Mk 9:22, 24.
help me. Ps 22:19. 30:10. 35:1, 2. 40:13. 70:1. 79:9.
26 **is not**. ver. 23. Mt +6:2. +7:6. Ex 4:22. Mk 7:27, 28. Lk 16:1-9. Ac 22:21, 22. Ro 9:4. Ga 2:15. Ep 2:12. Ph 3:2. Re 22:15.
bread. Ge +3:19.
dogs. Mt +7:6. 2 S 3:8. Ps 22:16. Pr 26:11. Re 22:15.
27 **Truth**. Mt 8:8. Ge 32:10. Jb 40:4, 5. 42:2-6. Ps 51:4, 5. Ezk 16:63. Da 9:18. Lk 7:6, 7. 15:18, 19. 18:13. 23:40-42. Ro 3:4, 19. 1 C 15:8, 9. 1 T 1:13-15.
yet. Mt 5:45. Lk 16:21. Ro 3:29. 10:12. 2 C 11:22. Ep 3:8, 19.
28 **Jesus**. Jb 13:15. 23:10. La 3:32.
O woman. Mk 14:8.
great. Mt +9:2. 14:31. 1 S 2:30. Lk 17:5. Ro 4:19, 20. 2 Th 1:3.
be it. Mt 9:29, 30. Jb 13:15. Ps 145:19. Mk 5:34. 7:29, 30. Lk 18:42, 43. Jn 4:50-53. Ro 10:12.
very hour. Mt 9:22. 17:18. Jn 4:52, 53.
29 **and came**. Mk 7:31.
unto. Mt 4:18. Jsh 12:3, Chinneroth. Is 9:1. Mk 1:16. Lk 5:1, lake of Gennesaret. Jn 6:1, 23. 21:1, Tiberias.
went. Mt +5:1. 13:2.
30 **great**. Lk +5:15.
lame. Mt +11:5. 14:35, 36. Ps +103:3. Mk 1:32-34. 6:54-56. Lk 6:17-19. Ac 2:22. 5:15, 16. 19:11, 12.
maimed. ver. 31. Mt 18:8. Mk 9:43.
31 **the dumb**. Mt +9:33.
the maimed. ver. +30. Lk 14:13, 21.
the lame. ver. +30.

the blind. Mt +11:5.
they glorified. Mt +9:8. Jn 9:24.
God. Ge 32:28. Is +29:23. Lk 1:68. Ac 13:17.
32 **Jesus**. Mt +9:36.
compassion. Is +63:15.
three. Mt 12:40. 27:63. Ac 27:33.
and have. Mt 6:32, 33. Lk 12:29, 30.
lest. 1 S 14:28-31. 30:11, 12. Mk 8:3.
33 **Whence**. Mt +14:17.
to fill. Mt 14:15. Lk 9:13. Jn 6:8, 9.
34 **How**. Mt 16:9, 10.
few. Lk 24:41, 42. Jn 21:9, 10.
35 **to sit**. Mt +14:19, etc.
36 **and gave thanks**. Mt 26:27. Mk 8:6. 14:23. Lk +24:30.
and brake. Is +58:7.
gave to. Mt 14:19.
37 **all**. ver. 33. Mt +14:20.
took up. Mt +14:20.
seven. Mt 16:9, 10. Mk 8:8, 9, 19-21.
38 **four thousand men**. Mt 14:21. 16:9, 10.
women. Ne +12:43.
children. Dt +29:11.
39 **he sent**. Mt 14:22. Mk 8:10.
Magdala. i.e. *magnificent*, S#3093g, only here. Jsh 19:38. Mk 8:10. 15:40.

MATTHEW 16

1 **Pharisees**. Mt 5:20. 9:11. 12:14. 15:1. 22:15, 34. 23:2. 27:62.
Sadducees. ver. 6, 11, 12. Mt +3:7, 8.
tempting. Mt 19:3. 22:18, 35. Ex +17:2. Mk 8:11. 10:2. 12:15. Lk 10:25. 11:16, 53, 54. 20:23. Jn 6:6. 8:6.
a sign. Mt 11:3-5. 12:38, 39. Mk 8:11-13. Lk 11:16, 29, 30. 12:54-56. +21:11. Jn 6:30, 31. 12:37. Ac 2:22. 1 C 1:22.
2 **When**. Lk 12:54-56.
weather. Ge +9:14.
3 **lowring**. S#4768g. Mk 10:22 (was sad).
O ye. Mt +6:2.
the signs. Mt 3:1-3. 4:23. 11:5. 12:28. Ge +49:10. 1 Ch +12:32. Is 35:4-6. Da +9:24. Lk 19:44.
4 **wicked**. Mt +24:34.
but. Jon 1:17. Lk 11:29, 30.
And he. Mt 4:13. +15:14. 21:17. Ge 6:3. Ho 4:17. 9:12. Mk 5:17, 18. Ac 18:6.
5 **were come**. Mt 15:39. Mk 8:13, 14.
6 **Take heed**. Lk 12:15.
beware. ver. 11. Lk 12:1. Ac 5:35. 1 Th 5:21. 1 J 4:1.
the leaven. ver. 12. Mt 13:33. Ex 12:15-19. Le 2:11. Mk 8:15. Lk 12:1. 13:20, 21. 1 C 5:6-8. Ga 5:9. 2 T 2:16, 17.
the Pharisees. ver. 1.
7 **they reasoned**. ver. 8. Mk 8:16-18. 9:10. 21:25. Lk 3:15. 9:46.
because. Mt 15:16-18. Ac 10:14.

8 when. Mt 26:10. Jn +2:25.
O ye. Mt +6:30. Mk 6:52. 8:17.
9 ye not. Mt 15:16, 17. Mk 7:18. Lk 24:25-27.
Re 3:19.
the five loaves. Mt 14:17-21. Mk 6:38-44.
Lk 9:13-17. Jn 6:9-13.
baskets. Mt +14:20. Mk +6:43.
10 Neither the seven. Mt 15:34-38. Mk 8:5-9,
17-21.
baskets. ver. +9.
11 How is it. Mk 4:40. 8:21. Lk 12:56. Jn 8:43.
beware. ver. 6.
leaven. ver. 6. Mt +13:33.
Sadducees. ver. 1.
12 Then understood. Mt 17:13.
beware. ver. 6. Lk 12:1.
of bread. Jn 6:27.
but. Mt 15:4-9. 23:13, etc. Ac 23:8.
the doctrine. Mt 5:20. 23:3. 1 C 5:6, 7. Ga
5:9.
13 When. Mk 8:27-29. Lk 9:18-20.
came. Mt 15:21. Ac 10:38.
Caesarea Philippi. S#2542g and S#5375g. Mt
16:13. Mk 8:27.
Whom. Mk 8:27. Lk 9:18-22. Jn 6:68, 69.
I the. Mt +8:20. He 2:14-18.
Son. ver. +27.
14 Some. Mt +8:19.
John. Mt 14:2. Mk 6:14. 8:28. Lk 9:7.
Elias. Mt 17:10. Ml 4:5. Mk 6:15. 9:11. Lk
9:8, 18, 19. Jn 1:21. 7:12, 40, 41. 9:17.
Jeremias. S#2408g. Mt 2:17. 27:9. For S#3414h,
see Je +1:1.
one of the prophets. Mt 21:11. Jn 6:14.
15 But. Mt 13:11. Mk 8:29. Lk 9:20.
16 Simon Peter. Jn 1:40, 42. 6:68, 69.
Thou. ver. 20. Mt 1:1. 11:2. +14:33. Ps 2:7.
Lk 2:26. 9:20. 22:67. 23:2. Jn 4:25, 26. 10:24,
25. Ac 4:27. 18:5.
Christ. i.e. *anointed, consecrated*, S#5547g. ver.
20. Mt 1:1, 17, 18. 2:4. 11:2. 22:42. 23:8, 10.
24:5, 23. 26:63, 68. Mk 8:29. 9:41. 12:35.
13:21. 14:61. 15:32. Lk 2:11, 26. 3:15. 4:41.
9:20. 20:41. 22:67. 23:2, 35, 39. 24:26, 46. Jn
1:20, 25, 41. 3:28. 4:25, 29, 42. 6:69. 7:26, 27,
31, 41, 42. 9:22. 10:24. 11:27. 12:34. 20:31.
Ac 2:30, +31. 1 J 5:1.
the son. Mt +14:33.
the living God. Jsh 3:10. 2 K 19:4, 16. Je
+10:10. Ho 1:10. Jn 6:57, 69. Ro 9:26. 14:11.
2 C 3:3. 6:16. 1 T 3:15. 4:10. He +3:12. 9:14.
12:22. 1 P 1:23. Re 4:9, 10. 7:2. 10:6. 15:7.
17 Blessed. Mt 5:3-11. 13:16, 17. Lk 10:23, 24.
22:32. Jn 20:29. Ro 10:9, 10. 1 P 1:3-5. 5:1.
Simon. Jn 1:42. 21:15-17.
Bar-jona. i.e. *son of Jonas or Jonah*, S#920g,
only here. Mt 10:3. Mk 10:46. Ac 13:6.
for. Ga 1:11, 12, 16.
flesh and blood. Lk +24:39. Jn 1:13. 1 C
15:50. Ga 1:16. Ep 6:12. He 2:14.

but. Mt 11:25-27. Is 54:13. Lk 10:21, 22. Jn
6:44, 45. 17:6-8. 1 C 1:28, 29. 2:9-12. Ga
1:15, 16. Ep 1:17, 18. 2:8-10. 3:5, 18, 19. Col
1:26, 27. 1 J 4:15. 5:20.
my Father. Jn 6:45. 1 C +12:3. 1 J 5:1, 5.
in heaven. Mt 7:11, 21.
18 thou. Mt 10:2. Jn 1:42. Ga 2:9.
Peter. Gr. *Petros*. i.e. *a stone, a piece of rock*,
S#4074g. Mt 4:18. 8:14. 10:2. 14:28, 29. 15:15.
16:16, 18, 22, 23. 17:1, 4, 24, 26. 18:21.
19:27. 26:33, 35, 37, 40, 58, 69, 73, 75. Mk
3:16. 5:37. 8:29, 32, 33. 9:2, 5. 10:28. 11:21.
13:3. 14:29, 33, 37, 54, 66, 67, 70, 72. 16:7.
Lk 5:8. 6:14. 8:45, 51. 9:20, 28, 32, 33. 12:41.
18:28. 22:8, 34, 54, 55, 58, 60-62. 24:12. Jn
1:40, 44. 6:8, 68. 13:6, 8, 9, 24, 36, 37. 18:10,
11, 15-18, 25-27. 20:2-4, 6. 21:2, 3, 7, 11, 15,
17, 20, 21. Ac 1:13, 15. 2:14, 37, 38. 3:1, 3, 4,
6, 11, 12. 4:8, 13, 19. 5:3, 8, 9, 15, 29. 8:14,
20. 9:32, 34, 38, 39, 40. 10:5, 9, 13, 14, 17-
19, 21, 23, 25, 26, 32, 34, 44-46. 11:2, 4, 7,
13. 12:3, 5, 6, 7, 11, 13, 14, 16, 18. 15:7. Ga
1:18. 2:7, 8, 11, 14. 1 P 1:1. 2 P 1:1.
upon. Is 28:16. 1 C 3:10, 11. Ep 2:19-22. Re
21:14.
rock. Gr. *Petra*. Mt 7:24-27. Dt +32:31. Is
28:16. 1 C 3:9-11. 10:4. Ep 2:20-22. Col 1:18.
1 P 2:4-6. Re 21:14.
I will build. Zc +6:12, 13. 1 C 3:9. Ga 2:9. He
3:3, 4. 1 P 2:4, 5.
my. Mt 18:17. Ac 2:47. 8:1. Ep 3:10. 5:25-27,
32. Col 1:18. 1 T 3:5, 15.
church. Ac 7:38. Ro 11:17-21. 1 C 3:16,
17. 2 C 6:16. Ep 2:11-16, 21. Ga 4:26. He
12:22.
and the gates. Ge +14:7. 22:17. 2 S 18:4. Jb
+38:17. Ps 69:12. 127:5. Pr 24:7. SS 8:6. Is
28:6. 1 C +15:55mg.
hell. Gr. *hades*, Mt +11:23.
shall not. Ps 125:1, 2. Is 28:16. 54:17. Jn
5:24. 10:27-30. 11:25, 26. Ac 5:39. Ro 8:33-
39. 1 C +15:55. He 12:28. Re 1:18. 11:15.
20:6. 21:1-4.
19 give. Ac 2:14, etc. 10:34, etc. 15:7.
the keys. Is 22:22. Lk +11:52. Ac 2:14, 41.
10:5, 6, 44, 45. 15:7, 28. 1 C 5:3-5. 2 C 5:18,
20. 2 P 1:20. Re 1:18. 3:7. 9:1. 20:1-3.
kingdom of heaven. Mt +4:17.
and whatsoever. Mt +4:9. Mt 18:18. Ml
3:18. Jn 20:23. 1 C 5:4, 5. 2 C 2:10. 1 Th 4:8.
Re 11:6.
thou. Mt 18:1. 20:21, 24. Ac 12:17. 15:13.
21:17, 18. 1 C 1:12. 2 C 1:24. 5:18. Ga 1:19.
2:9, 11, 12. Ja 1:1. 1 P 5:1-3.
shalt bind. Ac 5:3-10. 8:20-23.
shall be bound. Mt +18:18.
whatsoever. Mt +4:9.
thou shalt loose. Ac +3:19. 10:43. Ga 5:1. 1
J 1:9.
shall be loosed. lit. shall have been already

loosed in heaven. Jn 5:19, 30. 6:38. 8:26, 42. 12:49. 14:10. 17:8, 14. Ac 2:38-42. 10:45. Ro 11:22. 2 C 5:11, 19.

20 **charged**. Is 52:13. Lk +5:14. Jn 2:4. Ac 15:24. He 12:20.

Jesus. ver. 16. Jn 1:41, 45. 20:31. Ac 2:36. 1 J 2:22. 5:1.

21 **From that time**. Mt 4:17.

began. Mt 17:12, 22, 23. 20:17-19, 28. 26:2. Mk 8:31. 9:12, 30-32. 10:32-34. Lk 9:22, 31, 44, 45. 13:33. 18:31-34. 24:6-8, 26, 27, 46. 1 C +15:3, 4.

chief priests. Mt 26:47. 27:12. 1 Ch 24:1-19. Ne 12:7.

and be. Mt 27:63. Jn 2:19-21. Ac 2:23-32.

the third day. 1 C +15:4.

22 **began**. ver. 16, 17. 26:51-53. Mk 8:32. Jn 13:6-8.

Be it far from thee. Gr. Pity thyself. 2 S 20:20. 23:17. 1 K 22:13. 1 Ch 11:19. Ac 21:11-13.

23 **he turned**. Lk +22:61.

and said. An example of "double reference." Ge 3:15. Is 7:14, 15. 14:12-14. +25:8. Je 29:10-14. Ezk 28:11-17. Ho +11:1. Mk 5:7-16. Lk 4:33-35.

Get thee. Mt 4:10. Ge 3:1-6, 17. Mk 8:33. Lk 4:8. 2 C 11:14, 15.

Satan. 2 S 19:22. 1 Ch 21:1. Zc 3:1, 2. Jn 6:70. Ac 5:3. 1 C 5:5. Re 2:9.

thou art. Mt +11:6.

thou savorist. Mk 8:33. Ro 8:5-8. 1 C 2:14, 15. Ph 2:5. 3:19. Col 3:2.

24 **If**. 1 C +15:2. Mt 10:38. Mk 8:34. 10:21. Lk 9:23-27. 14:25-27. Ac 14:22. Col 1:24. 1 Th 3:3. 2 T 3:12. He 11:24-26.

come after. Mt 10:24, 25. 1 C +11:1. He 13:12, 13.

deny himself. 2 T 2:12, 13.

and take. Mt 10:38, 39. 27:32. Mk 15:21. Lk 23:26. Jn 19:17. 1 P 4:1, 2.

follow me. Jn 8:12.

25 **whosoever**. Mt +4:9. Jb +22:6.

will save. Mt 10:39. Est 4:14, 16. Mk 8:35. Lk 14:33. 17:33. Jn 12:25. Ac 20:23, 24. Re 12:11.

life. Gr. psyche, Mt +2:20; Ge +9:5.

will lose. Gr. apolumi, Mt +2:13. Ro 12:1, 2. Ga 2:20.

life. Gr. psyche, Mt +2:20; Ge +9:5.

for my sake. Mk 13:9.

shall find it. Re 2:10.

26 **for what**. Mt 5:29. Jb 2:4. Zp 1:18. Mk 8:36. Lk 9:25.

if he. Mt +4:9.

gain. Mt 4:8, 9. 18:1-5. 23:12. Jb 27:8. Mk 10:35-45. Lk 12:20. 16:25. 22:24-30. Jn 13:3-17. 1 J 2:16.

world. Gr. kosmos, Mt 4:8.

and lose. Gr. dzemoo, **S#2210g**. Rendered (1)

lose: ver. 26. Mk 8:36. (2) suffer loss: 1 C 3:15. Ph 3:8. (3) be cast away: Lk 9:25. (4) receive damage: 2 C 7:9.

soul. Gr. psyche, Mt +2:20. Ge 19:17. 35:18. Jg 9:17. Lk 9:24.

or what shall. Ps 49:7, 8. Mk 8:37.

soul. Gr. psyche, Mt +2:20.

27 **the Son of man**. ver. 13. Mt +8:20. Da +7:13. Mk 1:2. Ac +1:11. 7:56. 8:37. 1 Th 1:10. 2 Th 1:10. 1 J 4:2. 2 J 7. Re +1:7.

shall come. Mt 24:44. 26:64. Lk 12:40. 17:30. Jn 1:51. Ac +1:11.

the glory. Mt 24:30. 25:31. Ps +102:16. Is 2:19, 21. 35:2. 40:5. 60:1, 2, 19. 62:2. Zc 6:13. Mk 8:38. Lk 9:26. Jn +17:5. Col 3:4.

with his angels. Mt 13:41, 49. 25:31. Dt 33:2. Da 7:10. Zc 14:5. 1 Th 4:16. 2 Th 1:7-10. Ju 14.

and then. +Mt 10:15, 41, 42. +12:36. Ec 12:14. Mt 10:26. Lk 8:17. 12:2, 3. 14:14. Jn 5:29. Ro 2:16. 2 T 4:8. He +9:27, 28. Re 11:18. 22:12.

shall reward. Mt +5:12. Ec 9:5. 11:9. 12:14. Is 40:10. Ezk 7:27. Lk 14:14. Jn 5:29. Ac 10:42. Ep 6:8. He +9:27. Re 2:10, 23. 3:21. 11:18.

every man. Jn 5:28. 1 C 3:8.

according to. Mt 5:19. Jb 34:11. Ps +33:5. 62:12. Pr 24:12. Is 3:10, 11. Je 17:10. 32:19. Lk 14:14. 19:16-19. Ro 2:6, +11. 14:12. 2 C 5:10. 1 P 1:17. Re 2:23. 20:12. 22:12.

28 **There**. Mk 9:1. Lk 9:27.

not. Mt +5:18.

taste. Lk 2:26. Jn 8:51, 52. He 2:9.

till. Mt +23:39.

see. Mt 10:23. 17:1-13. 23:36. 24:3, 27-31, 34, 42, 44. 25:31. 26:64. Ps +102:16. Mi 3:12. ch 4. Zc ch. 14. Am 9:11-15. Mk 1:15. 13:26, 30. Lk 18:8. 21:27, 28, 31, 32.

Son of man. ver. +27.

coming. Mt +24:30. 26:64. Da 7:13, 14. Lk 23:42. 2 P 1:16-18. Re 1:7.

in his kingdom. Mt +6:10. Mk 9:1. Lk 9:27. 2 P 3:4, 13.

MATTHEW 17

1 **after**. Mk 9:2-8. Lk 9:28-36.

six days. Lk 9:28.

Peter. Mt 4:21. 26:37. Mk 5:37, 38. 9:2. 13:3. Lk 8:51. 9:28. 2 C 13:1.

an high. Dt 3:25. 2 P 1:18.

2 **transfigured**. Lk 9:29. Ro 12:2. 2 C 3:18. Ph 2:6, 7.

his face. Mt 28:3. Ex 34:29-35. Jn 1:14. 17:24. Ac 26:13-15. 2 C 3:7. Re 1:13-17. 10:1. 19:12, 13. 20:11.

raiment. Mt 28:3. Ps 104:2. Da 7:9. Mk 9:3. Re 1:14.

3 behold. Mk 9:4. Lk 9:30, 31.
appeared. Ge 37:35. 1 S 28:12. 2 S 12:23. Lk +16:23. 1 C 2:9. +13:12.
Moses. Mt 11:13, 14. Dt 18:18. 34:5, 6, 10. Lk 24:27, 44. Jn 1:17. 5:45-47. 2 C 3:7-11. Ph 1:23. He 3:1-6.
Elias. ver. 10-13. 1 K 17:1. 18:36-40. 2 K 2:11-14. Ml 4:5, Elijah. Lk 1:17. 9:33. 16:16.

4 answered. Mk 9:5, 6. Lk 9:33.
it is. Ex 33:18, 19. Ps 4:6. 16:11. 63:1-5. Is 33:17. Zc 9:17. Jn 14:8, 9. 17:24. Ph 1:23. 1 J 3:2. Re 21:23. 22:3-5.
if thou wilt. 1 C +15:2. Ac 18:14. 2 C 11:1.
tabernacles. Le +23:34, 42. Ne 8:15.

5 bright cloud. Mt +24:30. Ex +13:21. Ac 1:9. 2 P 1:17. Re 1:7.
a voice. Ex 19:19. Dt 4:11, 12. 5:22. Jb 38:1. Ps 81:7. Jn 5:37. 12:28-30. Ac 9:3-6.
out of. Ex +13:21.
This. Mt 3:17. Mk 1:11. 9:7. Lk 3:22. 9:35. Jn 3:16, 35. 5:20-23. Ep 1:6. Col 1:13mg. He 1:1, 2. 2:1-3. 2 P 1:16, 17.
in whom. Mt 12:18. Ex 33:17. Is 42:1, 21. Jn 15:9, 10.
well pleased. Is 41:8.
hear. Dt 18:15, 18, 19. Jn 1:18. Ac 3:22, 23. 7:37. He 1:1, 2. 2:1-3. 5:9. 12:25, 26.

6 heard. 2 P 1:18.
they fell. Ge +17:3.
afraid. Mt 14:27. Ge +19:30. Mk 6:50. Lk 24:37. Re 1:17.

7 touched. Da 8:18. 9:21. 10:10, 18. Re 1:17.
Arise. Lk 24:5. Ac 9:6.
afraid. Ge +19:30.

8 lifted. Ge +22:13.
they saw. Ge 45:1. Mk 9:8. Lk 9:36. Ac 12:10, 11.

9 Tell. Lk +5:14.
the vision. Lk 24:23. Ac 7:31.
until. ver. 23. Mt 16:21. Lk 18:33, 34. 24:46, 47.
Son of man. Mt +8:20.

10 Why. ver. 3, 4. Mt 11:14. 27:47-49. Ml 4:5, 6. Mk 9:11. Jn 1:21, 25.
Elias. Ml 4:5. Mt 11:14. 16:14.

11 and restore. Is +11:11. Ml 4:6. Mk 9:12. Lk 1:16, 17. 3:3-14. Ac +1:6. +3:21.

12 and they. Mt 11:9-15. 21:23-25, 32. Mk 9:12, 13. 11:30-32. Lk 7:33. Jn 1:11. 5:32-36. Ac 13:24-28.
knew. Gr. epiginosko, Mt +11:27.
but. Mt 11:2. 14:3-10. Mk 6:14-28. Lk 3:19, 20. Ac 7:52.
Likewise. ver. 22, 23. Mt 16:21. Is 53:3, etc. Lk 9:21-25. 17:25. Ac 2:23. 3:14, 15. 4:10.

13 understood. Mt 16:12.
he spake. Mt 11:14.

14 when. Mk 9:14-28. Lk 9:37-42.
kneeling. Mk 1:40. 10:17. Ac 10:25, 26.

15 have. Mt +9:27. Mk 5:22, +23.

for. Mt 4:24. Mk 9:17, 18, 20-22.
lunatic. Mt 4:24.
for oftimes. Mt 8:31, 32. Jb 1:10-19. 2:7. Mk 5:4, 5.

16 and they. ver. 19, 20. Mt 10:1. 2 K 4:29-31. Mk 6:7. Lk 9:1, 40. 10:17. Ac 3:16. 19:15, 16.

17 O faithless. Mt +6:30. 13:58. Dt 32:20. Ps 78:8. Lk 24:25. He 3:16-19.
and perverse. Dt 32:5, 20. Ac 2:40. 20:30. Ph 2:15.
generation. Mt +24:34. Ps 95:10.
how long. Ex 10:3, 7. 16:28. Nu 14:11, 22, 27. 2 S 2:26. 1 K 18:21. Jb 8:2. 18:2. Ps 4:2. 62:3. 82:2. Pr 1:22. 6:9. Je 4:14, 21. 47:6. Ho 8:5. Mk 9:19. Lk 9:41.
shall I be. Jn 8:25. 14:9. Ac 13:18.
suffer you. Mk +9:19.

18 rebuked. Mt 12:22. Mk +4:39. 5:8. Ac 16:18. 19:13-15.
from. Mt 8:13. 9:22. 15:28. Jn 4:52, 53.

19 Then came. Mk 4:10. 9:28.
Why could. Mt 10:1.

20 Because. ver. 17. Mt +9:2. 13:58. 14:30, 31. Jn 11:40. He 3:19.
unbelief. Mt 6:30.
If. Mt +4:9.
faith. Mt 21:21, 22. Mk 11:23. Lk 17:6. 1 C 12:9. 13:2.
a grain. Mt 13:31. Mk 4:31. Lk 13:19.
this mountain. ver. 1, 9. Mk 11:22-24. 1 C 13:2.
nothing. Jb 42:2. Mk 9:23. Lk 1:37. 18:27.

21 this. Mt 12:45.
but. Mk 9:29. Lk 2:37. Ac 13:2, 3. 14:23. 1 C 7:5.
by prayer. Gr. proseukee, S#4335g: Rendered (1) prayer: ver. 21. Mt 21:13, 22. Mk 9:29. 11:17. Lk 6:12. 19:46. 22:45. Ac 1:14. 2:42. 3:1. 6:4. 10:4, 31. 12:5. 16:13, 16. Ro 1:9. 12:12. 15:30. 1 C 7:5. Ep 1:16. 6:18. Ph 4:6. Col 4:2, 12. 1 Th 1:2. 1 T 2:1. 5:5. Phm 1:4, 22. 1 P 3:7. 4:7. Re 5:8. 8:3, 4; (2) pray earnestly: Ja 5:17. 1 K 17:20, 21. 2 Ch +7:14. Ezk 36:37. Da 9:3. Ep 6:18.
and fasting. Dt 9:18. Jg 20:26. 1 S 7:5, 6. 2 S 12:15-23. 1 K 21:27. 2 Ch 20:3, 4. Ezr 8:21-23. Ne 9:1-3. Ps 35:13. 69:10. 109:24-26. Is 58:3-11. Je 14:12. Da 9:3. 10:2, 3. Jl 1:14. 2:12. Jon 3:5-9. Mk 9:28, 29. Lk 2:37. 5:33, 34. Ac 10:30, 31. 13:2, 3. 14:23. 1 C 7:5. 2 C 11:27.

22 The Son. Mt +8:20.
betrayed. Mt +20:18. 24:10. Mk 9:30-32. 10:33, 34. Lk 18:31-34. 24:6, 7, 26, 46.

23 they shall. Ps 22:15, 22, etc. Is 53:7, 10-12. Da 9:26. Zc 13:7.
the third. Ps +16:10. Ac 2:23-31. 1 C +15:4.
And they were. Jn 16:6, 20-22.

24 when. Mk 9:33.
Capernaum. Mt 4:13.

tribute. "Gr. didrachma, in value fifteen pence." Ge 24:22. Ex 30:13. 38:26. 2 K 12:4. 2 Ch 24:6. Ne 10:32, 33.

Doth not. Mt +5:17.

master. Mt +22:24.

pay. Jn +4:8.

25 Yes. Mt 3:15. 22:21. Ro 13:6, 7.

prevented. Jn +2:25.

What thinkest. Mt 18:12. 21:28.

custom. Ro 13:7.

tribute. Mt 22:17, 19. Mk 12:14.

of their. 1 S 17:25.

26 strangers. Is 49:23. 60:10, 16, 17.

the children. Mt 21:43. Is 60:5. 61:6. Ezk 30:3. Mi 4:13. Zc 14:14. Jn 2:16. 14:2. Ro 11:25.

27 lest. Mt 15:12-14. Mk +12:12. Ro 14:21. 15:1-3. 1 C 8:9, 13. 9:19-22. 10:32, 33. 11:1. 2 C 6:3, 4. 1 Th 5:22. 2 T 2:24. T 2:7, 8. 1 P +3:8.

offend. Mt 5:29, 30. +11:6. 13:41. 15:12. 18:6, 8, 9. Mk 9:42, 43, 45, 47. Lk 17:1, 2. Jn 6:60, 61, 66. Ac 24:16. Ro 14:21. 16:17. 1 C 8:13. 10:32. 2 C 6:3. 11:29. Ph +1:10.

and take. Ge 1:28. 1 K 17:4. Ps 8:8. Jon 1:17. 2:10. He 2:7, 8.

a piece of money. "or, a stater, half an ounce of silver, value 2s. 6d., after 5s. the ounce."

that take. 2 C 8:9. Ja 2:5.

MATTHEW 18

1 the same. Mt 17:24. Mk 9:33-37.

Who. Mt 20:20-28. 23:11. Mk 9:34. 10:35-45. Lk 9:46-48. 22:24-27. Ro 12:10. Ph 2:3.

in. Mt 3:2. 5:19, 20. 7:21. Mk 10:14, 15.

kingdom of heaven. Mt +4:17. Ac 1:6.

2 a little child. Mt 11:25. 19:13, 14. 1 K 3:7. Je 1:7. Mk 9:36, 37, 42. 10:13-16. Lk 9:47, 48. 10:21. 17:2. +18:15, 16.

3 Verily. Mt +5:18.

Except. Mt +4:9. Ps +19:7. 119:59. 131:2. Is 6:10. Ezk 18:27. +33:11. Da +12:3. Mk 4:12. Jn 6:44. Ac +3:19, 26. +9:35. 28:27.

and become. Mt 11:25. 19:14. Ps 131:2. Mk 10:14, 15. Lk 18:16, 17. 1 C 14:20. 1 Th 2:7. 1 P 2:2.

shall not. Ps 7:11, 12. Jn 3:36.

enter. Mt +7:21. Ga 6:15.

4 humble. Mt +5:3. 11:29. 20:27. 23:11, 12. Ps 9:12. 131:1, 2. 138:6. Pr 3:34. 16:19. 18:12. 22:4. 29:23. Is +57:15. Mi +6:8. Lk 14:11. 18:14. Jn 13:14, 15. Ep 4:1, 2. Ph 2:3-9. Col 3:12. Ja 4:10. 1 P 5:5.

greatest. ver. 1. Mt 20:26, 27. Mk 10:43. Lk 4:48.

5 receive. Ro +15:7.

in my name. ver. 20. Mk +9:37.

receiveth. Mk 9:37. Jn 13:20. Ga 4:14.

6 offend. ver. 8. Mt +17:27. Jsh 22:25. Ps 105:15. Ezk 14:10. Zc 2:8. Ac 9:5. Ro 15:1-3. 2 Th 1:6-9.

little. ver. 2, 10, 14. Zc 13:7. Lk 17:2.

better for. Mk 14:21.

drowned. S#2670g, *katapontizomai*. Mt +14:30 (sink).

7 unto. Ge 13:7. 1 S 2:17, 22-25. 2 S 12:14. Lk 17:1. Ro 2:23, 24. 1 T 5:14, 15. 6:1. T 2:5, 8. 2 P 2:2.

world. Gr. *kosmos*, Mt +4:8.

offences. Mt +11:6.

for. Am +3:6. Mk 13:7. Ac 1:16. 1 C 2:8. 11:19. 2 Th 2:3-12. 1 T 1:13, 16. 4:1-3. 5:14. 6:1. 2 T 3:1-5. 4:3, 4. Ju 4.

that offences come. Ac 20:30. Ro 14:13.

but woe. Mt 13:41, 42. 23:13, etc. 26:24. Jn 17:12. Ac 1:18-20. 2 P 2:3, 15-17. Ju 11-13. Re 2:14, 15, 20-23. 19:20, 21.

8 if. 1 C +15:2. Mt 14:3, 4. +17:27. Dt 13:6-8. Lk 14:26, 27, 33. 18:22, 23. Ro 8:13. 1 C 9:27. Col 3:5.

and cast. Is 2:20, 21. 30:22. Ezk 18:31. Ro 13:12. Ph 3:8, 9.

enter into life. Mt +7:13. 19:16, 17. Mk 9:43, 45. Jn 5:24.

maimed. Mt 15:30, 31. 19:12.

everlasting. Gr. *aionios*, S#166g. Rendered (1) *eternal*: Mt 19:16. 25:46b. Mk 3:29. 10:17, 30. Lk 10:25. 18:18. Jn 3:15. 4:36. 5:39. 6:54, 68. 10:28. 12:25. 17:2, 3. Ac 13:48. Ro 2:7. 5:21. 6:23. 2 C 4:17, 18. 5:1. 1 T 6:12, 19. 2 T 2:10. T 1:2a. 3:7. He 5:9. 6:2. 9:12, 14, 15. 1 P 5:10. 1 J 1:2. 2:25. 3:15. 5:11, 13, 20. Ju 7, 21. (2) *everlasting*: Mt 18:8. 19:29. 25:41, 46a. Lk 16:9. 18:30. Jn 3:16, 36. 4:14. 5:24. 6:27, 40, 47. 12:50. Ac 13:46. Ro 6:22. 16:26. Ga 6:8. 2 Th 1:9. 2:16. 1 T 1:16. 6:16. He 13:20. 2 P 1:11. Re 14:6. (3) with S#5450g, *the world began*: 2 T 1:9. T 1:2b. (4) with S#5450g, *since the world began*: Ro 16:25. (5) *for ever*: Phm 15.

fire. Mt +25:41, 46.

9 if. 1 C +15:2.

thine eye. Mt 5:29. Jb 31:1.

to enter. Mt 19:17, 23, 24. Ac 14:22. He 4:11. Re 21:27.

rather. Mt 16:26. Lk 9:24, 25.

hell. Gr. *gehenna*, Mt +5:22. Mt 23:13-15. Is 66:22-24. Mk 9:43-47. Lk +12:5.

10 heed. ver. 6, 14. Mt 12:20. Ps 15:4. Zc 4:10. Lk 10:16. Ac 9:5. Ro 14:1-3, 10, 13-15, 21. 15:1. 1 C 8:8-13. 9:22. 11:22. 16:11. 2 C 10:1, 10. Ga 4:13, 14. 6:1. 1 Th 4:8. 1 T 4:12.

despise not. Pr 3:34. 9:12. 12:5. 14:21. 15:20. 19:29. 22:10. 29:8.

one. Mt 6:29. 25:40, 45. Lk 15:7, 10.

little ones. ver. 2, 6, 14. Mt 10:42. Zc 13:7.

in heaven. Lk 1:19.

their angels. Mt 1:20. 2:13, 19. 24:31. Ge 32:1, 2. 2 K 6:16, 17. Ps 34:7. 91:11. Da

10:13, 20. 12:1. Zc +3:7. Lk 16:22. Ac 5:19.
10:3. 12:7-11, 23. 27:23. Col 2:18. 1 T 5:21.
He 1:14. Re 1:20.

behold. 2 S 14:28. 1 K 22:19. 2 K 25:19mg.
Est 1:14. Ps 17:15. Zc 2:8. +3:7. Lk 1:19. Ac
2:28. Re 22:4.

my Father. ver. 14, 19, 35. Mt +7:21.

11 is come to. Mt 9:12, +13. 10:6. 15:24. Lk
9:56. 15:24, 32. +19:10. Jn 3:17. 10:10. 12:47.
Ga 3:13. Ep 2:1, 4, 5. 1 T 1:15.

lost. Gr. *apollumi*, Mt +2:13.

12 How. Mt 17:25. 21:28. 22:42. 1 C 10:15.

if. Mt +4:9. Mt 12:11. Nu +27:17. Is 53:6.

goeth into. 1 K 22:17. Ezk 34:6, 12.

and seeketh. ver. 11. Ps 119:176. Ezk 34:4,
11, 12, 16. Lk +19:10.

gone astray. Is 53:6.

13 if. Mt +4:9.

he rejoiceth. Ps 147:11. Is 53:11. 62:5. Je
32:37-41. Mi 7:18. Zp 3:17. Lk 15:5-10, 23,
24. Jn 4:34-36. Ja 2:13.

14 not the will. Mt 11:26. Ezk 18:32. Lk 12:32.
Jn 6:39, 40. 10:27-30. 17:12. Ro 8:28-39. Ep
1:5-7. 1 T +2:4. 1 P 1:3-5. 2 P +3:9.

your. Mt 5:16. 6:9, 32. 23:9.

one. Ge +18:27. Is 40:11. Zc 13:7. Jn 21:15. 1
C 8:11-13. 2 T 2:10. He 12:13. 2 P 3:9.

perish. Gr. *apollumi*, Mt +2:13.

15 if thy brother. Mt +4:9. ver. 35. Mt 5:23, 24.
Le 6:2-7. Lk 17:3, 4. 1 C 6:6-8. 8:12. 2 C 7:12.
Col 3:13. 1 Th 4:6.

go and tell. Le +19:17. Jsh 22:13. Ps 141:5.
Pr 15:23. 25:9, 10. 27:5, 6. Ep +5:11. 2 Th
3:15. T 3:10.

thou hast gained. Pr 11:30. Ro 12:21. 1 C
9:19-22. Ga 6:1. Col 3:13. Ja 5:16, 19, 20. 1 P
3:1.

16 But if. Mt +4:9.

take with. Nu 16:25. Jsh 22:13.

that in. Mt 26:60. Nu 35:30. Dt 17:6. *19:15*. 1
K 21:13. Jn 8:17. 2 C 13:1. 1 T 5:19. He
10:28. 1 J 5:7, 8. Re 11:3.

mouth. Dt +17:6.

17 And if. Mt +4:9.

tell it unto the church. Jsh 22:16. Ac 6:1-3.
15:6, 7. 1 C 5:4, 5. 6:1-4, 6, 7. 2 C 2:6, 7. 3 J
9, 10.

neglect to hear. 1 S +25:17.

let him be. Ro +16:17, 18.

an heathen. Mt 6:7. Ezr 6:21. Ezk 11:12. Lk
7:6. Jn 7:49. 2 C 6:14-17. Ep 4:17-19. 5:11, 12.

a publican. Mt +5:46.

18 Whatsoever. Mt 16:19. Je 18:23. Jn 20:23.
Ac 15:23-31. 1 C 5:4, 5. 2 C 2:10. Re 3:7, 8.

bound. Mt 16:19. Lk 12:52. He 2:13.

19 Again. Mt 19:24. Ga 5:3.

That if. Mt +4:9. Mt 5:24. 21:22. Mk 11:24.
Jn 15:7, 16. Ac 1:14. 2:1, 2. 4:24-31. 6:4.
12:5, 12, 16, 17. Ep 6:18-20. Ph 1:19. Phm
22. Ja 5:14-16. 1 J 3:22. 5:14-16. Re 11:4-6.

two. Dt 17:6.

agree. Ac 8:15, 17. 1 C 7:5. He 13:18. 1 P 3:7,
8. **S#4856g**: ver. 19. Mt 20:2, 13. Lk 5:36. Ac
5:9. 15:15.

any thing. Mt 21:22. Jn 14:14. Ro +8:32. Ep
+3:20. Ph +4:19. 1 J 5:14, 15.

shall ask. Lk +11:9. +18:1. Ja +1:5, 6. 4:2.

it shall. Mt +7:7. Jn 14:13, 14. 16:23, 24. 1 J
3:22. 5:14.

my Father. ver. 10, 35. Mt 7:21.

20 where two. ver. 19. 1 S 9:27. Da 3:25.
+11:33. Ml +3:16. 1 C 5:4. Phm +2.

or three. Ec 4:12. 1 Th 1:1.

gathered. Ge +49:10. Dt +12:5. Jn 20:19. Ac
4:30, 31. 11:26. 18:26. 20:7, 8. 1 C 1:10-13.
5:4. 11:20. +16:19. He +10:25. Ja 5:16.

in my name. ver. +5.

there. Mt +28:20. Ex 20:24. Zc 2:5. Jn +8:58.
20:19, 20, 26. Ro 8:9, 10. 1 C 5:3. 2 C 13:5. Ga
2:20. Ep 3:16-19. Col 2:5. Re 1:11-13. 2:1. 21:3.

in the midst. God the Son is omnipresent.
Mt +28:19, 20. Nu 1:50. 1 K +8:27. 1 Ch 9:27.
Ps 145:18. Pr +15:3. Jn 3:13. Jn 20:19, 26. Ep
1:23. Col 1:27.

21 brother sin against. ver. 15.

till. ver. 15. Lk 17:3, 4. Ep 4:32. Col 3:13.

seven times. Ps +119:164. Pr 24:16. Lk 17:4.

22 I say not. Jn 16:26.

but. Mt 6:11, 12, 14, 15. Ge 4:24. Is 55:7mg.
Mi 7:19. Mk 11:25, 26. Ro 12:21. Ep 4:26, 31,
32. 5:1. Col 3:8, 13. 1 T 2:8.

23 is the kingdom. Mt 3:2. 13:24, 31, 33, 44,
45, 47, 52. 25:1, 14.

which. Mt 25:19-30. Lk 16:1, 2. 19:12-27. Ro
14:12. 1 C 4:5. 2 C 5:10, 11.

24 owed. Lk 7:41, 42. 13:4mg. 16:5, 7.

ten thousand. 1 Ch 29:7. Ezr 9:6. Est 3:9. Ps
38:4. 40:12. 130:3, 4.

talents. "A talent is 750 ounces of silver,
which after five shillings the ounce is 187l.
10s." Mt 25:15.

25 had not. Lk 7:42.

commanded. Le +25:39.

and children. 2 K 4:1. Ne 5:5, 8.

26 worshipped him. *or*, besought him. Mt
+8:2. Ac 10:25. Re 3:9.

have. ver. 29. Lk 7:43. Ro 10:3.

27 moved. Jg 10:16. Ne 9:17. Ps 78:38. 86:5, 15.
145:8. Ho 11:8.

forgave. Lk 7:42.

28 the same. Mt +6:2.

pence. Mt 20:2, 9, 10, 13. 22:19. Mk 6:37.
12:15. 14:5. Lk 7:41. 10:35. 20:24. Jn 6:7.
12:5. Re 6:6.

and took. Dt 15:2. Ne 5:7, 10, 11. 10:31. Is
58:3. Ezk 45:9.

29 Have. ver. 26. Mt 6:12. Phm 18, 19.

30 but. 1 K 21:27-29. 22:27.

31 they. Ps 119:136, 158. Je 9:1. Mk 3:5. Lk
19:41. Ro 9:1-3. 12:15. 2 C 11:21. He 13:3.

and came. Ge 37:2. 2 K +5:13. Lk 14:21. Ep +5:11. He 13:17.

32 O thou. Mt 25:26. Lk 19:22. Ro 3:19.

33 even as I. Mt 5:44, 45. +6:12. Lk +6:35, 36. Ep 4:32. 5:1, 2. Col 3:13. 1 J 4:11.

34 was wroth. Jb 22:4-11. Ps 18:25, 26. Pr 21:13. Ezk 25:12-14. Lk 6:38. Ja 2:13.
and delivered. ver. 30. Mt 5:25, 26. Lk 12:58, 59. 2 Th 1:8, 9. Re 14:10, 11.

35 my. ver. 10, 19. Mt 7:21.
do. Mt 6:12, 14, 15. 7:1, 2. Pr 21:13. Mk 11:26. Lk +6:37, 38. Ja 2:13.
if. Mt +4:9.
from. Le +19:18. Pr 21:2. Je 3:10. Zc 7:12. Lk 16:15. Ro 6:17. Ep 4:32. Ja 3:14. 4:8. 1 P 1:22. Re 2:23.

MATTHEW 19

1 came to pass. Mt 7:28. 11:1. 13:53. 26:1.
that when. Mk 10:1. Jn 10:40.
he departed. Mt 17:24.
into the coasts. Mt 4:25. Lk 9:51. 17:11. Jn 10:40. 11:7.
Judaea. i.e. land of Juda, S#2449g. Rendered (1) Judaea: Mt 2:1, 5, 22. 3:1, 5. 4:25. 24:16. Mk 1:5. 3:7. 10:1. 13:14. Lk 1:5, 65. 2:4. 3:1. 5:17. 6:17. 7:17. 21:21. Jn 3:22. 4:3, 47, 54. 7:3. 11:7. Ac 1:8. 2:9. 8:1. 9:31. 10:37. 11:1, 29. 12:19. 15:1. 21:10. 26:20. 28:21. Ro 15:31. 2 C 1:16. Ga 1:22. 1 Th 2:14. (2) Jewry: Lk 23:5. Jn 7:1. For S#3063h, "Judah," see Ge +35:23.
beyond Jordan. Mt 3:5, +6, 13. 4:25. Mk 3:8. 10:1. Lk 3:2, 3. Jn 1:28. 3:26. 10:40.

2 great multitudes. Mt 14:35, 36. Mk 6:55, 56. Lk +5:15.

3 The Pharisees. Lk 17:20. Jn 8:3.
tempting. Mt +16:1.
Is it. Mt 5:31, 32. Ml 2:14-16.
put away. Mt 1:19. 5:31, 32. Mk 10:2, 4, 11, 12. Lk 16:18.
for every cause. ver. 9. Mt 5:28-30. Dt 22:21. 24:1-4. Ro 7:2. 1 C 7:15, 28. 1 T 3:2.

4 Have. Mt 12:3. 21:16, 42. 22:31. Mk 2:25. 12:10, 26. Lk 6:3. 10:26.
that. Ge 1:27. 2:18, 21-23. 5:2. Ml 2:15.

5 said. Ge 2:21-24. Ps 45:10. Mk 10:5-9. Ep 5:31.
shall a man. Ge 2:18. Pr 18:22. 1 C 7:2. He +13:4.
leave. Ge +2:24.
cleave. Ge 34:3. Dt 4:4. 10:20. 11:22. 1 S 18:1. 2 S 1:26. 1 K 11:2. Ps 63:8. Ro 12:9. Ep 5:33. 1 P 3:7.
wife. Ge +2:18. +4:19.
and they twain. Ge 2:24. 1 C 6:16. 7:2, 4.
one. Dt +6:4. Ml 2:15.
flesh. Ge +6:12.

6 God. Pr 2:17. Ml 2:14. Mk 10:9. Ro 7:2. 1 C 7:10-14. Ep 5:28. He 13:4.
hath joined. Mk 10:9.

7 Why. Mt 5:31. Dt 24:1-4. Je 3:1. Mk 10:4.
writing of divorcement. Is 50:1. Je 3:8.
and to. Mt 1:19. Ml 2:16.

8 Moses. Ex +24:4.
because. Ps 95:8. Zc 7:12. Ml 2:13, 14. Mk 10:5.
hardness. Dt 10:16. Mk 3:5. 6:52. 16:14. He 3:8.
suffered. Mt 3:15. 8:31. 1 C 7:6.
but. Ge 2:24. 7:7. Je 6:16.

9 Whosoever. Mt 5:32. Mk 10:11, 12. Lk 16:18. 1 C 7:10-13, 39.
put away. Mt 5:32. Mk 10:12.
except. Mt +4:9.
fornication. Mt +5:32. 2 Ch 21:11. Je 3:8. Ezk 16:8, 15, 29.
doth. Ge 12:18, 19. 20:3. Je 3:1. Ro 7:2, 3. 1 C 7:4, 11, 39.

10 If the case. 1 C +15:2. Ge 2:18. Pr 5:15-19. 18:22. 19:13, 14. 21:9, 19. 1 C 7:1, 2, 8, 26-28, 32-35, 39, 40. 1 T 4:3. 5:11-15.

11 All men cannot. 1 C 7:2, 7, 9, 17, 35.
save they. Mt 20:23.
given. Mt 13:11.

12 which were made. Le 21:20. Dt 23:1. 2 K 20:18. Is 39:7. 56:3-5.
which have. 1 C 7:1, 32-38. 9:5, 15. He +13:4.

13 little children. ver. +14. Mt 18:2-5. Ge 48:1, 9-20. 1 S 1:24. Ps 115:14, 15. Mk 10:13. Lk 9:47. +18:15. Ac +2:39. 1 C +7:14.
hands on them. Ac +8:17.
and the. Mt 16:22. 20:31. Mk 10:48. Lk 9:49, 50, 54, 55. 18:39.

14 Suffer. Ge +17:7, 8, 24-26. 21:4. Jg 13:7. 1 S 1:11, 22, 24. 2:18. Mk 10:14, 15. Lk 18:16, etc.
little children. ver. +13. Mt 11:25. 18:3-5. 21:16. Jl +2:16. 1 P 2:1, 2.
forbid them not. Mk 9:39. Lk 9:50.
for. Mt 11:25. +18:3. 1 C 14:20. 1 P 2:1, 2.

15 he laid. Is 40:11. Mk 10:16. 1 C +7:14. 2 T +3:15.

16 one came. Mk 10:17. Lk 18:18.
Good Master. Jn +3:2. 7:12.
what. Lk 10:25. Jn 6:27-29. Ac 16:30.
shall I do. Hab 2:4. Ro 3:28. 9:30, 31. 10:5. Ga 3:11, 12.
have. ver. 29. 1 J 5:13.
eternal. Gr. aionios, ver. 29. Mt +18:8. +25:46. Da +12:2. Lk 10:25. Jn 3:15, 36. 4:14. +5:39. 6:40, 47, 54, 68. 10:28. 12:25. 17:2, 3. 20:31. Ac 13:46, 48. Ro 2:7. 5:21. 6:22, 23. 1 T 1:16. 6:12, 19. T 1:2. 3:5-7. He 9:12, 15. 1 J 1:2. 2:25. 5:11-13, 20. Ju 21.

17 there. 1 S 2:2. Ps 52:1. +136:1. Ja 1:17. 1 J 4:8-10, 16.

but one. Mk 12:29. Ro 16:27.
but if. 1 C +15:2. Le +18:5. Ro 2:13.

18 **Which**. Mk 10:19. Ga 3:10. Ja 2:10, 11.
Thou shalt do. Mt 5:21-28. Ge +9:5, 6. Ex
+*20:13*. Dt +*5:17*. Mk 10:19. Lk 18:20. Ro
13:9. 1 J 3:15.
not commit adultery. Mt 5:27. Ex *20:14*. Le
18:20. Dt *5:18*. 22:22. Pr 6:32. Ro 13:9. 1 C
+6:9. He +13:4.
not steal. Ex *20:15*. Le 19:11. Dt *5:19*. Ro
13:9. Ep 4:28.
not bear false witness. Ex *20:16*. 23:1. Dt
5:20. 19:16-20. Pr 19:5, 9. 21:28. 24:28.
25:18.

19 **Honor**. Mt 15:4-6. Ex +*20:12*. Dt +*5:16*. Mk
7:10. Ep 6:1, 2.
love thy neighbor. Le +*19:18*.
as thyself. Le +19:18. Lk 6:31. Ep 5:29.

20 **All**. Mk 10:20. Lk 15:7, 29. 18:11, 12, 21. Jn
8:7. Ro 3:19-23. 7:9. Ga 3:24. Ph 3:6.
from. Ezk 4:14.
what. Mk 10:21. Lk 18:22.

21 **If**. 1 C +15:2.
perfect. Mt 5:19, 20, +48. 6:24. 16:26.
go. Mt 6:19, 20. Mk 10:21. Lk 12:33. 14:33.
16:9. 18:22. 19:8. Ac 2:44, 45. 4:32-35. 1 T
6:17-19. He 10:34.
give to the poor. Mt 5:42. Le 25:35. Dt 15:7.
Ps 41:1. Pr 3:27, 28. 22:9. 25:21. 31:20. Ezk
+16:49. 18:5-9. Mk 9:41. Lk 3:11. 1 C 13:3. 2
C 8:9. 9:6. 1 T 5:8, 16. 1 T 6:17, 18. He 6:10.
Ja 2:15, 16. 1 J 3:17, 18.
treasure in heaven. Mt 6:19, 20. Dt +28:12.
Mk +10:21. Lk 12:33, 34. He 10:34.
come. ver. 28. Mt 4:19. 8:22. 9:9. 16:24. Mk
2:14. 8:31. 10:21. Lk 5:27. 9:23. 18:22. Jn
1:43. 10:27. 12:26.

22 **But when**. Ps 62:10. Ezk +33:31.
he went. Mt 13:22. 14:9. Jg 18:23, 24. Da
6:14-17. Mk 6:26. 10:22. Lk 18:23. Jn 19:12-
16.
for. Mt 6:24. 16:26. Ex 20:17. Ps 17:14. Ezk
+33:31. Ep 5:5. Col 3:5.

23 **That**. Mt +13:22. Dt 6:10-12. 8:10-18. Jb
31:24, 25. Ps 49:6, 7, 16-19. Pr 11:28. 30:8, 9.
Mk 10:23, 25. Lk 12:15-21. 16:13, 14, 19-28.
18:24. 1 C 1:26. 1 T 6:9, 10. Ja 1:9-11. 2:6.
+5:1-4.
rich. Mk +4:19.
enter. Mt +7:21. 1 C +6:9, 10.

24 **It is easier**. ver. 26. Mt 23:24. Je 13:23. Mk
10:24, 25. Lk 18:25. Jn 5:44.
camel. Mt 23:24.
rich man. ver. 22, 23. 1 T +6:5, 9, 17-19.
kingdom of God. Mt +12:28.

25 **Who**. Mt 24:22. Mk 13:20. Lk 13:23, 24. Ro
10:13. 11:5-7.

26 **beheld them**. Mk 3:5, 34. 10:21, 23, 27. Lk
6:10. 20:17. 22:61. Jn 1:42.
with men. 2 K 7:2. Lk 18:27.

but. Jb +42:2. Ps 3:8. 62:11. Zc 8:6. Mk
11:23. 14:36. He 6:6.

27 **we have forsaken**. Mt 4:20-22. 9:9. Dt 33:9.
Mk 1:17-20. 2:14. 10:28. Lk 5:11, 27, 28.
14:33. 18:28. Ph 3:8.
what. Mt 20:10-12. Lk 15:29. 1 C 1:29. 4:7.

28 **in the regeneration**. Ps +71:20. Is +26:19.
54:1. 65:17. +66:7-9, 22. Ho +2:18. Jl 2:25.
Mi +5:3, 4. Zc 10:6. Lk 13:28. Jn 3:7. Ac
+3:19, 21. +13:33. Ro 8:19-23. 1 Th +4:16. T
3:5. 2 P 3:13. Re 21:5.
when. Mt 16:27. 25:31. Lk 9:26. 2 Th 1:7-10.
Re 20:11-15.
Son of man. Mt +8:20.
shall sit. Mt +25:31. He 8:1. 12:2.
the throne. Ps +45:6. 132:11, 12. Ezk 37:24.
Ac 2:30. Re 3:21.
ye also. Mt 20:21. Re +5:10.
judging. Mt +10:15. 1 C +6:2, 3. Re 20:11,
12.
the twelve. Ex 15:27. 24:4. 28:21. Le 24:5.
Jsh 3:12. 1 K 18:31. Ezr 6:17. Ac +26:6, 7. Ja
1:1. Re 7:4-8. 12:1. 21:12-14. 22:2.
Israel. Ge 13:15. Ro 4:13. Ga 3:16.

29 **every**. Mt 16:25. Mk 10:29, 30. Lk 18:29, 30.
1 C 2:9.
forsaken. Dt 33:9.
or brethren. Mt 8:21, 22. 10:37, 38. Lk
14:26, 33. 2 C 5:16. Ph 3:8, 9.
for my. Mt 5:11. 10:22. Mk 10:29. 13:9. Lk
6:22. 18:29. 21:12. Jn 15:19. Ac 9:16. 1 P
4:14. 3 J 7.
shall receive. Mt 13:12. Ro 8:18. 2 C 4:17. 2
T 2:12. 1 P 4:13.
an hundredfold. Mk +10:30.
inherit. ver. 16. Mt 25:34, 46. Mk 10:17. Lk
10:25. 18:18. T 3:7.
everlasting. Gr. *aionios*, Mt +18:8.
life. ver. 16.

30 **first shall be last**. Mt +8:11, 12. 20:16.
21:31, 32, 43. Mk 10:31. Lk 7:29, 30, 40-47.
13:30. 18:9, 13, 14. Ro 5:20, 21. 9:30-33. Ga
5:7. He 4:1.

MATTHEW 20

1 **the kingdom**. Mt +4:17.
a man. Mt 9:37, 38. 21:33-43. SS 8:11, 12. Is
5:1, 2. Jn 15:1.
early. If the work day was twelve hours long,
and ended at 6 P.M., the householder must
have sought his workers some time before 6
A.M. Mt 23:37. Ec 9:10. SS 8:11, 12. Je 25:3,
4.
laborers. Mk 13:34. 1 C 15:58. He 13:21. 2 P
1:5-10.
vineyard. Mt 21:28, 33.

2 **he had**. ver. 13. Ex 19:5, 6. Dt 5:27-30.
a penny. ver. 9, 10, 13. Mt +18:28.
he sent. 1 S 2:18, 26. 3:1, 21. 16:11, 12. 1 K

3:6-11. 18:12. 2 Ch 34:3. Ec 12:1. Lk 1:15. 2 T +3:15.

3 the third hour. Our 9 A.M. Mk 15:25. Jn 11:9. Ac 2:15. 23:23.
standing. ver. 6, 7. Mt 11:16, 17. Pr 19:15. Ezk +16:49. Ac 17:17-21. 1 T 5:13. He 6:12.
idle. Mt +12:36. Je +48:10.
marketplace. Mt 11:16, 17. Ge +14:7. 2 K 7:1. Je 5:1. Am +5:16. Lk 11:43.

4 Go. Mt 9:9. 21:23-31. Lk 19:7-10. Ro 6:16-22. 1 C 6:11. 1 T 1:12, 13. T 3:8. 1 P 1:13. 4:2, 3.
and whatsoever. Col 4:1.

5 sixth hour. Our 12 noon. Mt 27:45. Mt 15:33, 34. Lk 23:44-46. Jn 1:39. 4:6. +11:9. 19:14. Ac 3:1. 10:3, 9.
and ninth hour. Our 3 P.M. Mt 27:45, 46. Mk 15:33, 34. Lk 23:44. Jn +11:9. Ac 3:1. 10:3, 30.
and did. Ge 12:1-4. Jsh 24:2, 3. 2 Ch 33:12-19. He 11:24-26.

6 the eleventh hour. Our 5 P.M. ver. 9. Ec 9:10. Lk 23:40-43. Jn 9:4. +11:9. 1 C 15:8.
Why. Pr 19:15. Ezk +16:49. Ac 17:21. He 6:12.

7 Because. Ac 14:16. 17:30, 31. Ro 10:14-17. 16:25. Ep 2:11, 12. 3:5, 6. Col 1:26.
Go. Mt 22:9, 10. Ec 9:10. Lk 14:21-23. Jn 9:4.
and. Ep 6:8. He 6:10.

8 when. Mt 13:39, 40. 25:19, 31. Ro 2:6-10. 2 C 5:10. He 9:28. Re 20:11, 12.
even. Our 6 P.M., the start of the first watch (Mt 14:25. Mk 13:35). Jn 9:4.
unto. Ge 15:2. 39:4-6. 43:19. Lk 10:7. 12:42. 16:1, 2. 1 C 4:1, 2. T 1:7. 1 P 4:10.
steward. Lk 8:3. Ga 4:2.
their hire. Le +19:13. Dt +24:15. Ml +3:5. Ja +5:4.

9 were hired. or, were called. Only the first group (ver. 2) were hired by agreement for a particular wage. Those called to the vineyard agreed to be paid at the pleasure of the master of the vineyard.
eleventh hour. Our 5 P.M. ver. 6. Jn +11:9.
they received. ver. 2, 6, 7. Lk 23:40-43. Ro 4:3-6. 5:20, 21. Ep 1:6-8. 2:8-10. 1 T 1:14-16.

10 they supposed. Ezk 18:2-4.
likewise received. ver. 2, 13. Ge +18:25. Lk +6:35.

11 they murmured. Is 29:24. Ac 11:2, 3. 13:45. 22:21, 22. 1 Th 2:16. Ju +16.
against. Mk 14:14. Lk 12:39.

12 wrought but one hour. or, continued one hour only. They had worked from 5 to 6 P.M.
equal. Lk 14:10, 11. Ro 3:22-24, 30. Ep 3:6.
borne. Is 58:2, 3. Zc 7:3-5. Ml 1:13. 3:14. Lk 15:29, 30. 18:11, 12. Ro 3:27. 9:30-32. 10:1-3. 11:5, 6. 1 C 4:11. 2 C 11:23-28.
heat. or, hot wind. Ge 31:40. +41:6. Is 49:10. Ezk 17:10. Jon 4:8. Lk 12:55. Ja 1:11.

13 Friend. Gr. *hetairos*, **s#2083g**. A term of kindly address, to be distinguished from *philos* (**s#5384g**, Mt +11:19), a term of endearment (Vine, *Expository Dictionary*, vol. 2, p. 132). Mt 11:16. 22:12. 26:50.
I do. ver. +10. Ge +18:25. Dt +32:4. Jb 34:8-12, 17, 18. 35:2. 40:8. Ps 92:15. Ro 9:14, 15, 20.
no wrong. 1 C 15:58. Ga +6:9. He 6:10.

14 thine. Mt 6:2, 6, 16. 2 K 10:16, 30, 31. Ezk 29:18-20. Lk 15:31. 16:25. Ro 3:4, 19.
I will. Jn 17:2.

15 Is it not. Mt 11:25. Ex 33:19. Dt 7:6-8. 1 Ch 28:4, 5. Je 27:5-7. Jn 17:2. Ro 9:15-24. 11:5, 6. 1 C 4:7. Ep 1:5. 2:1, 5. Ja 1:18.
to do. Ps +115:3. Is +46:10. Ro +9:18. Ep +1:11.
Is thine. Mt +6:23. Dt 15:9. 28:54. Pr 23:6. 28:22. Mk 7:22. Ga 3:1. Ja 5:9.
because. Jon 4:1-4. Ac 13:45.

16 the last. Mt +19:30. Lk 7:47. 15:7. 17:17, 18. Jn 12:19-22.
for. Mt +7:13. 11:28. Mk 16:15. Lk 14:24. Jn 5:40. 6:37. 7:37. Ro +8:28, 30. 1 Th 2:13. Ja 1:23-25. 2 P +1:10. Re 22:17.
but few. Mt +7:14.
chosen. Ep 1:4.

17 Jesus. ver. +18. Jn 12:12.
took. Mt 13:11. 16:13. Ge 18:17. Jn 15:15. Ac 10:41.

18 go up. Lk +2:4.
Son of man. Mt +8:20.
betrayed. Mt 10:4. 16:21. 17:22, 23. 26:2, 16, 21-25, 46. 27:3, 4. Ps 2:1-3. 22:1. 69:1. Is ch. 53. Da 9:24-27. Mk 14:10, 18, 21, 44. Lk 22:4, 6, 21, 22, 48. Jn 6:64, 70, 71. 12:4. 13:2, 11, 18, 19, 21, 26. 18:2, 30, 31. Ac 1:16. 2:23. 3:13. 4:27, 28. 7:52. 21:11. 1 C 11:23.
they. Mt 26:66. 27:1. Mk 14:64, 65. Lk 22:71. Jn 19:7.

19 shall deliver. Mk +10:33. 1 C +15:3-7.
to mock. Mt 26:67, 68. Mk 14:65. Lk +22:63. Jn 19:1-4.
to crucify. Mt 26:2. 27:26. Lk 24:7. Jn 12:32, 33. 18:32.
the third. Is +26:19. Ho 6:2. 1 C +15:4.

20 came. Mk 10:35-45.
the mother. Mt 4:21. 27:56. Mk 15:40, Salome. Jn 19:25.
Zebedee's. Mk 10:35.
worshipping. Mt 2:11. 8:2. +14:33. 15:25. 28:17.

21 What. ver. 32. 1 K 3:5. Est 5:3, Mk 6:22. 10:36, 51. Lk 18:41. Jn 15:7.
Grant. Mt 18:1. 19:28. Je 45:5. Mk 10:37. Lk 22:24. Ro 12:10. Ph +2:3. Re 3:21.
the one. Mt 27:38. 1 K 2:19. Ps 45:9. +110:1.
in thy kingdom. Mt +6:10. Lk 24:21. Jn 18:36. Ac +1:6.

22 Ye know not. Mk 10:38. Lk 9:33. 23:34. Ro 8:26. Ja 4:3.

the cup. Mt 26:39, 42. Ps 11:6. 75:3. Is 51:17, 22. Je 25:15, etc. 49:12. Mk 14:36. Lk 22:42. Jn 18:11.
baptized with. Mk 10:39. Lk 12:50.
We are able. Mt 26:35, 56. Pr 16:18.

23 **Ye**. Mt 16:24. Zc 4:12. Jn 17:14. Ac 12:2. Ro 8:17. 2 C 1:7. Ph 3:10. Col 1:24. 2 T 2:11, 12. 3:12. Re 1:9. 11:14.
but to sit. Mt 25:31-40. Lk 19:11-27. Jn 5:22, 27. Ph 3:14. 2 P +1:11.
not mine. Lk +22:29. 1 C +11:3. +15:28.
for whom. Mt 19:11. 25:34. Mk 10:40. Jn 14:2. 17:24. 1 C 2:9. He +11:16.

24 **they**. Mt 21:15. 26:8. Pr 13:10. Mk 10:41. Lk 13:14. 22:23-25. 1 C 13:4. Ph 2:3. Ja 3:14-18. 4:1, 5, 6. 1 P 5:5.

25 **called**. Mt +11:29. 18:3, 4. Jn 13:12-17.
the princes. Mk 10:42. Lk 22:25-27.
exercise dominion. Da 2:12, 13, 37-45. 3:2-7, 15, 19-22. 5:19. 1 P 5:3.
great. Mk 6:21.

26 **it**. Mt 23:8-12. Mk 9:35. 10:43-45. Lk 9:48. 14:7-11. 18:14. 22:25, 26. Jn 18:36. 2 C +1:24. 10:4-10. Ph +2:3. 1 P 5:3. 3 J 9, 10. Re 13:11-17. 17:6.
minister. Mt 22:13. 25:44. 27:55. Ex 24:13. Ac 13:5. 1 C 3:5. 2 T 1:18. Phm 13. He 1:14. 1 P 4:11.

27 **whosoever will be**. Mt 18:4. 22:3. Mk 9:33-35. 10:44. Lk 22:26. Ac 20:34, 35. Ro 1:14. 1 C 9:19-23. 2 C 4:5. 11:5, 23-27. 12:15.
let him. Ro 12:10. Ph +2:3. He +13:17. 1 P +5:5.

28 **Son of man**. Mt +8:20.
came. Mt +9:13. Mk 10:45. Lk +19:10. 22:27. Jn 13:4-17. 2 C 8:9. Ph 2:4-8. He 5:8.
and to give. Jb 33:24. Ps 49:7. Is 44:22. 53:5, 8, 10, 11. Ezk 37:23. Jn 10:15. 11:50-52. Ga 1:4. 2:20. +3:13. 1 T 2:6. He 2:9. 9:28.
life. Gr. *psyche*, Mt +2:20; Ge +9:5.
a ransom. Ex +12:13. Mk 10:45.
for many. Mt +26:28. Is 53:4-6, 11, +12. Mk 14:24. Jn +1:9. 11:51, 52. Ro 5:15-19. 2 C 5:15. He 2:10. 9:28. 2 P +3:9. 1 J 2:2. Re 5:9. 7:9.

29 **as they departed**. Mt 9:27-31. Mk 10:46-52. Lk 18:35-43. 19:1.
Jericho. i.e. *constant fragrance*, **S#2410g**. Nu +22:1 (**S#3405h**). Mk 10:46. Lk 10:30. 18:35. 19:1. He 11:30.

30 **two**. Mt +11:5. *Is 59:10*.
way side. Mk 10:46-52.
Have mercy. Mt +9:27.
Son of David. Mt +1:1.

31 **rebuked**. Mt 15:23. 19:13. Lk 18:15.
but they cried. Mt +7:7, 8. Ge 32:25-29. Lk 11:8-10. 18:1, etc., 39. Col 4:2. 1 Th +5:17.

32 **What**. ver. 21. Ezk 36:37. Mk 10:36. Ac 10:29. Ph 4:6.

33 **Lord**. Ps +119:18. Ep 1:17-19.

34 **Jesus**. Mt +9:36. Ps 145:8. Jn 11:33-35. He 2:17. 1 P 3:8.
touched their eyes. Mt 9:29. Mk 7:33. Lk 22:51. Jn 9:6, 7.
received sight. Lk 7:21.
and they. Mt 8:15. Ps 119:67, 71. Lk 18:43. Ac 26:18.

MATTHEW 21

1 **when**. Mk 11:1. Lk 18:31. 19:28, 29. Jn 12:12-15.
Bethphage. i.e. *green fig house*, **S#967g**. ver. 1. Mk 11:1. Lk 19:29.
the mount. Mt 24:3. 26:30. 2 S 15:30. Ne +8:15. Ezk 11:23. Zc +14:4. Mk 11:1. 13:3. 14:26. Lk 19:29, 37. 21:37. 22:39. Jn 8:1. Ac 1:12.
two disciples. Mk 14:13.

2 **Go into**. Mt 26:18. Mk 11:2, 3. 14:13-16. Lk 19:30-32. Jn 2:5-8.
loose them. 1 S 8:16.

3 **if**. Mt +4:9.
The Lord. 1 Ch 29:14-16. Ps 24:1. 50:10, 11. Hg 2:8, 9. Lk 7:13. Jn 3:35. 17:2. Ac 17:25. 2 C 8:9.
straightway. 1 S 10:26. 1 K 17:9. Ezk 1:1, 5. 7:27. 2 C 8:1, 2, 16. Ja 1:17.

4 **this**. Mt 1:22. 26:56. Jn 19:36, 37.
saying. Zc 9:9. Jn 12:15.

5 **Tell ye**. Zc *9:9*. Note Zc 9:9 is quoted, but not Zc 9:10. Compare the similar break in quotation of prophecy made by Jesus at Lk 4:19, 20.
Behold. Lk +24:27.
the daughter. Nu +21:25. Ps 9:14. SS 3:11. Is 1:8. 4:4. 10:32. 12:6. 37:22. 40:9. *62:11*. Mi 4:8, 13. Zp 3:14, 15. Zc 2:10. 9:9. Jn 12:15.
thy King. Ge +49:10. Nu +24:19. Ps 45:1, etc. 72:1, etc. Is 32:1. Ezk 34:24. Da 2:44, 45. +7:13, 14. Zc *9:9*. Lk 1:32. Jn +1:49.
meek. Mt +11:29.
sitting. Dt 17:16. Jg +5:10. 12:14. 2 S 16:2. 1 K 1:33. 10:26. Ho 1:7. Mi 5:10, 11. Zc 9:10.

6 **and did**. Ge 6:22. 12:4. Ex 39:43. 40:16. 1 S 15:11. Mk 11:4. Lk 19:32-34. Jn +15:14.

7 **brought**. Mk 11:4-8. Lk 19:32-35.
put. 2 K 9:13.

8 **spread**. 2 K 9:13.
others. Le 23:40. Jn 12:13.

9 **Hosanna**. ver. 15. 2 S 14:4. Ps 118:24-26. Je 31:7. Mk 11:9, 10.
son of David. ver. 15. Mt +1:1.
Blessed. Ps +*118:26*.
in the highest. Ps 148:1. Lk 2:14.

10 **And when**. Mk 11:11.
all. Mt 2:3. Ru 1:19. 1 S 16:4. Jn 12:16-19. Ac 21:30.
Who. SS 3:6. Is 63:1. Lk 5:21. 7:49. 9:9. 20:2. Jn 2:18. Ac 9:5.

11 **This**. Mt 16:13, 14. Dt 18:15-19.
the prophet. ver. 46. Mk 6:15. Lk 7:16, 39.
9:8, 19. 13:33. 24:19. Jn 1:21, 25. 4:19. +6:14.
7:40-42, 52. 9:17. Ac 3:22, 23. 7:37.
of Nazareth. Mk +1:24.

12 **went**. Ml 3:1, 2. Mk 11:11.
and cast. Mk 11:15. Lk 19:45, 46. Jn 2:14-
17.
the temple. Hg *2:7, 9*. Ml *3:1*. Lk 2:27, 32.
moneychangers. Ex 30:13. Dt 14:24-26.
doves. Le 1:14. 5:7, 11. 12:6, 8. 14:22, 30.
15:14, 29. Lk 2:24.

13 **It is**. Mt 2:5. Lk +24:27. Jn 15:25.
My. Ps 93:5. Is *56:7*.
house of prayer. 1 K 8:29, 30, 41-43. 2 Ch
6:40.
den of thieves. Je *7:11*. Ezk 7:22. Mk 11:17.
Lk 19:46.

14 **the blind**. Mt +11:5.
lame. Mt +11:5.
healed. Mt 9:35. Ac 10:38.

15 **when**. ver. 23. Mt 26:3, 59. 27:1, 20. Is
26:11. Mk 11:18. Lk 19:39, 40. 20:1. 22:2, 66.
Jn 11:47-49, 57. 12:19.
wonderful. Is 9:6. 28:29. Ac 2:22.
Hosanna. ver. 9. Mt 22:42. Jn 7:42.
the son of David. ver. +9.
they were. Mt 20:24. 26:8. Jon 4:1. Lk
13:14.

16 **Hearest**. Lk 19:39, 40. Jn 11:47, 48. Ac 4:16-
18.
have. ver. 42. Mt 12:3, 5. 19:4. 22:31. Mk
2:25. 12:10.
Out. Mt 11:25. Ps *8:2*.
babes. Mt +11:25. Lk 9:47. 1 C 1:27.
and sucklings. 2 T 3:15.

17 **he left**. Mt 16:4. Je 6:8. Ho 9:12. Mk 3:7. Lk
8:37, 38.
went out. Mk 11:19. Lk 21:37.
Bethany. Jn +11:18.
lodged there. Lk 21:37.

18 **in**. Mk 11:12, 13.
he hungered. Mt 4:2. 12:1. Lk 4:2. Jn 4:6, 7.
19:28. He +4:15.

19 **a fig tree**. Gr. one fig tree. Mt 8:19. 26:69. Je
8:13.
and found. Is 5:4, 5. Mi 7:1. Mk 11:13. Lk
3:9. 13:6-9. 19:41-44. Jn 15:2, 6. 2 T 3:5. T
1:16.
Let. Mk 11:14. Lk 19:42-44. He 6:7, 8. 2 P
2:20-22. Re 22:11.
for ever. Gr. *aion*, Mt +6:13. lit. "unto the
age," as in Mk 3:29. 11:14. Lk 1:55. Jn 4:14.
6:51, 58. 8:35, 51, 52. 10:28. 11:26. 12:34.
13:8. 14:16. 1 C 8:13. 2 C 9:9. He 5:6. 6:20.
7:17, 21, 28. 1 P 1:23, 25. 1 J 2:17. 2 J 2. Ju
13.
the fig tree. Ju 12.

20 **How**. Is 40:6-8. Mk 11:20, 21. Ja 1:10, 11.

21 **If ye have**. Mt +23:30. Mt 17:20. Mk 11:22,
23. 16:17. Lk 17:6, 7. Jn 15:7, 16. 16:24. Ro
4:19, 20. 1 C 13:2. Ja 1:6.
and doubt not. Mk 11:23. Ac 10:20. Ro
4:20. 14:23. Ja 1:6. 2:4. 3:17. Ju 9, 22.
also if. Mt +4:9.
this mountain. ver. 1.
Be thou removed. Mt 8:12.

22 **all things**. Mt +18:19. Ps 57:2, 3. Je +33:3.
Mk 11:24. Lk 11:8-10. Ro +8:32. Ep 3:20. 1 J
+5:14, 15.
whatsoever. Mt +4:9.
receive. Ja 5:14, 15; 1 J 5:14, 15.

23 **when**. Mk 11:27, 28. Lk 19:47, 48. 20:1, 2.
the chief priests. 1 Ch 24:1, etc. Mk 11:18.
Lk 20:1-8.
as he was teaching. Mt 26:55. Ac 5:42.
15:35.
By what. Mt 9:11. 22:42-46. Ex 2:14. Jn
1:25. Ac 4:7. 7:27.

24 **I also**. Mt 10:16. Pr 26:4, 5. Lk 6:9. 1 C 3:19.
Col 4:6.
one thing. lit. word. Grk. *logos*.
if ye. Mt +4:9.

25 **baptism of John**. Mt 3:1, etc. 11:7-15.
17:12, 13. Mk 1:1-11. 11:27-33. Lk 1:11-17,
67-80. 3:2-20. 7:28-35. Jn 1:6, 15, 25-34.
3:26-36.
Whence. Mt 13:54.
from heaven. Ps +73:9. Da 4:26. Lk 15:18,
21. Jn 3:27.
from men. Ac 5:38, 39.
reasoned. Mt 16:7. Mk 8:16. Lk 3:15mg.
20:14.
If. Mt +4:9.
Why. ver. 32. Mt 3:7, 8. Lk 7:30. 20:5. Jn
3:18. 5:33-36, 44-47. 10:25, 26. 12:37-43. 1 J
3:20.

26 **But if**. Mt +4:9.
we fear. ver. 46. Mt 14:5. Is 57:11. Mk 11:32.
12:12. Lk 20:6, 19. 22:2. Jn 9:22. Ac 5:26.
for all. Mt 11:9. Ex +9:6. Mk 6:20. Lk 7:29.
Jn 5:35. 10:41, 42.

27 **We cannot tell**. Mt +15:14. 16:3. 23:16, etc.
Is 6:10. 28:9. 29:10-12. 42:19, 20. 56:10, 11.
Je 8:7-9. Ml 2:6-9. Lk 20:7, 8. Jn 9:30, 40, 41.
Ro 1:18-22, 28. 2 C 4:3, 4. 2 Th 2:9, 10.

28 **what**. Mt 17:25. 18:12. 22:17. Lk 13:4. 1 C
10:15.
A certain. Lk 15:11-32.
Son. Lk 15:31.
go work. Mt 20:5-7. Ps 40:1. Mk 13:34. Lk
12:37. 19:13. Jn 9:4. 1 C 15:58.
in my vineyard. ver. 33. Mt 20:1.

29 **I will not**. ver. 31. 1 S +15:23. Je 44:16. Ep
4:17-19.
he repented. ver. 32. Mt 3:2-8. 27:3. 2 Ch
33:10-19. Is 1:16-19. 55:6, 7. Ezk 18:28-32.
Da 4:34-37. Jon 3:2, 8-10. Lk 15:17, 18. Ac
26:20. 1 C 6:11. 2 C 7:8, 10. Ep 2:1-13. He
7:21.

30 **I go**. Mt 23:3. Ezk +33:31. Ro 2:17-25. T 1:16.
went not. 1 S +15:22, 23.

31 **did**. Mt +7:21. 12:50. Ezk 33:11. Lk 15:10. Ac 17:30. 2 P 3:9.
The first. 2 S 12:5-7. Jb 15:6. Lk 7:40-42. 19:22. Ro 3:19.
Verily. Mt +5:18.
the publicans. Mt +5:46. 9:9. 20:16. Lk 7:37-50. 19:9, 10. Ro 5:20. 9:30-33. 1 T 1:13-16.
go into. Mt +7:21.
the kingdom of God. ver. 43. Mt +12:28.
before you. ver. 32. Mt 19:30.

32 **came**. Mt 3:1-8. Is 35:8. Je 6:16. Lk 3:8-13. 2 P 2:21.
way of righteousness. Mt 3:8-12, 15. Pr 8:20. 12:28. 17:23. 2 P 2:21.
believed him not. ver. 25. Mt 11:18. Lk 7:29, 30. Jn 5:33-36. Ac 13:25-29.
the publicans. ver. +31.
repented not. Ps 81:11, 12. Je 5:1. 17:23-27. Zc 7:11, 12. Jn 5:37-40. 2 T 2:25. He +3:12. 6:6-8. Re 2:21.

33 **Hear**. Mt +13:18. 1 K 22:19. Is 1:10. Je 19:3. Ho 4:1.
There. ver. 28. Dt 32:32, 33. Ps 80:8-16. SS 8:11, 12. Is 5:1-4. 27:2-6. Je 2:21. Ezk 15:1-6. 19:10-14. Ho 10:1. Jl 1:7. Mk 12:1. Lk 20:9-19. Jn 15:1.
hedged it. Is 5:2.
let it out. SS 8:11, 12.
husbandmen. Mt 23:2. Dt 1:15-17. 16:18. 17:9-12. 33:8-10. Ml 2:4-9.
went. Mt 25:14, 15. Mk 13:34. 19:12.
far country. Mt +25:19. Lk 15:13.

34 **he sent**. 2 Ch +24:19. Zc 1:3-6.
that. SS 8:11, 12. Is 5:4.

35 **took his servants**. Mt 5:12. 22:6. 23:31-37. 1 K 18:4, 13. 19:2, 10. 22:24-27. 2 K 6:31. 21:16. 2 Ch 16:10. 24:19, 21, 22. 36:15, 16. Ne 9:26. Je 2:30. 25:3-7. 26:21-24. 37:15. 38:6. 44:4. Lk 13:33, 34. Ac 7:52. 2 C 11:24-26. 1 Th 2:15, 16. He 11:36, 37. Re 6:9.
beat one. 2 Ch 36:16. Je 20:2. Ac 5:40. 2 C 11:24, 25. He 11:36, 37.
killed another. Mt 22:6. 1 Th 2:15. He 11:37.
stoned another. Le +24:14.

36 **other servants**. Mt 22:4. Mk 12:5.

37 **last**. Mt 3:17. Mk 12:6. Lk 20:13. Jn 1:18, 34. 3:16, 35, 36. He 1:1, 2.
They. Is 5:4. Je 36:3. Zp 3:7. Lk 18:2.

38 **This**. Mt 2:13-16. 26:3, 4. 27:1, 2. Ge 37:18-20. Ps 2:2-8. Mk 12:7, 8. Lk 20:14. Jn 1:11. 11:47-53. Ac 4:27, 28. 5:24-28. Ro 8:17. He 1:2.
let us kill. Ge 37:20. 1 K 21:19.

39 **caught**. Mt 26:50, 57. Mk 14:46-53. Lk 22:52-54. Jn 18:12, 24. Ac 2:23. 4:25-27.
cast. Mk 12:8. He 13:11-13.

slew. Ac 2:23. 3:14, 15. 4:10. 5:30. 7:52. Ja 5:6.

40 **cometh**. Mt 24:50. 25:19. 2 S 12:5, 6.
what. Je 17:27. Mk 12:9. Lk 20:15, 16. He 10:29.

41 **He will**. Mt 3:12. 22:6, 7. 23:35-38. 24:21, 22. Le 26:14, etc. Dt 28:59-68. Ps 2:4, 5, 9. Is 5:5-7. Da 9:26. Zc 11:8-10. 12:12. 13:8. 14:2, 3. Ml 4:1-6. Lk 17:32-37. 19:41-44. 21:22-24. 1 Th 2:16. He 2:3. 12:25.
miserably. Mt 22:7. Lk 19:27. Ro 2:8, 9. 2 C +5:11. 2 Th 1:8, 9.
destroy. Gr. *apollumi*, Mt +2:13.
and will let out. ver. +43. Mt +8:11, 12. Is 49:5-7. +65:15. +66:19-21. Mk 12:9. Lk 13:28, 29. 14:23, 24. 20:16. 21:24. Ac 13:46-48. 15:7. 18:6. 28:28. Ro ch. 9-11. 15:9-18.
fruits. ver. 34, 43.
in their seasons. Mt +24:45.

42 **Did**. ver. +16.
in the scriptures. Mt +22:29. 26:54, 56. Mk +12:24. Lk 4:21. 24:27, 32, 45. Jn 2:22. +5:39. Ac +17:2, 11. 18:24, 28. Ro 1:2. 15:4. 16:26. 1 C +15:3, 4. 2 T +3:15. 2 P 3:16.
The stone. Ge 49:24. Ps 118:22, 23. Is +28:16. Zc 3:8, 9. Mk 12:10, 11. Lk 20:17, 18. Ac 4:11. Ep 2:20. 1 P 2:4-8.
builders rejected. Mk 8:31. Lk 22:2. Jn 7:48, 49.
head of the corner. Jb 38:6. Je 51:26. Zc 4:7. Col 1:18.
the Lord's doing. Ne 6:16. Ep 1:22, 23. 2:20. He 5:4, 5.
and it is. Hab 1:5. Ac 13:40, 41. Ep 3:3-9.

43 **The kingdom of God**. ver. +31. Mt +12:28. Is 28:2. Jl 2:28. Col +1:13.
shall be taken. ver. 41. Mt 22:8. 1 K 11:39. Je 22:5. Ho 3:4. Mi +5:3. Lk 14:24. Jn 11:48. Ac +13:46.
from you. Mt 8:11, 12. 22:1-14. Lk 13:28. 14:15-24. 17:22. 19:11-27, 41-44. +21:31.
and given. Is +65:13. Da 7:27. Lk +12:32.
a nation. Ex +19:5, 6. Dt 32:21. Is 26:2. +54:1. Jn +10:16. 2 Th 2:1. 1 P 2:9. Re 1:5, 6. 5:9, 10. 20:6.
bringing forth. ver. 41. Mt 3:10. +24:45. Le +26:40-42. Is 5:4, 7. Ho +3:5. 5:15. Ac +3:19-21. Ro 14:17. 1 C 13:2. Ep 5:9. Col +1:10.

44 **whosoever**. Ps 2:12. Is 8:14, 15. Lk 2:34. Ro 9:32, 33. 1 C 1:23. 2 C 4:3, 4. 1 P 2:8.
but. Mt 26:24. 27:25. Ps 110:5, 6. Da +2:44. Jn 19:11. 1 Th 2:16. He 2:2, 3.
it will grind. Is 17:13. Je +31:10. Am +9:9.

45 **they**. Mt +13:12-14. Mk 12:12. Lk 11:45. 20:19.

46 **But when**. Mt 26:4. Mk 11:18. 14:1. Lk 19:47, 48. 22:2. Jn 7:25, 30, 44.
they sought. Mt 12:14. 2 S 12:7-13. Pr 9:7-9. 15:12. Is 29:1. Jn 7:1, 7. 11:50.

they feared. ver. 11, 26. Mt 14:5. Mk 11:32. Ac 5:26.

because. ver. +11, 26. Mk 12:37.

MATTHEW 22

1 **answered**. Mt 11:25.
   and spake. Mt 9:15-17. 12:43-45. 13:3-11. 20:1-16. 21:28-46. Mk 4:33, 34. Lk 8:10. 14:16.

2 **kingdom**. Mt +4:17.
   which. Mt 25:1-13. Ps 45:10-16. Lk 14:16-24. Jn 3:29, etc. 2 C 11:2. Ep 5:24-32. Re 19:7-9.

3 **sent**. Mt 3:2. 10:6, 7. Est 6:14. Ps 68:11. Pr 9:1-3, 5. Is 55:1, 2. Je 25:4. 35:15. Mk 6:7-12. Lk 3:3. 9:1-6. 14:15-17. Re 22:17.
   to call. Lk 14:17.
   that were bidden. 1 S 9:13. Zp 1:7.
   and they would not. Mt 23:37. Ps 81:10-12. Pr 1:24-32. Is 30:15. Je 6:16, 17. Ho 11:2, 7. Lk 13:34. 15:28. 19:27. Jn 5:40. Ac 13:45. Ro 10:21. He 12:25.

4 **other**. Mt 21:36. Lk 10:1-16. 24:46, 47. Ac +1:8. 11:19, 20. 13:46. 28:17, etc.
   Behold. Ps +22:26. SS 5:1. Ro 8:32. 1 C 5:7, 8.
   my dinner. Jn 21:12.
   my oxen. Pr 9:2.
   and all. ver. 8. Ge 43:16. Ne 9:17. Ps 86:5. Lk 14:17.
   come. ver. 3.

5 **they**. Ge 19:14. 25:34. Ps 106:24, 25. Pr 1:7, 24, 25. Ac 2:13. 24:25. Ro 2:4. He 2:3.
   one. Mt 13:22. 24:38, 39. Lk 14:18-20. 17:26-32. Ro 8:6. 1 T 6:9, 10. 2 T 3:4. 1 J 2:15, 16.

6 **the remnant**. Mt 5:10-12. 10:12-18, 22-25. 21:35-39. 23:34-37. Jn 15:19, 20. 16:2, 3. Ac 4:1-3. 5:40, 41. 7:51-57. 8:1. 1 Th 2:14, 15.
   entreated them spitefully. Lk 11:45. 18:32. Ac 14:5. 1 C 11:24. 1 Th 2:2.
   and slew. Mt 21:35. Ac 7:58. 12:2. He 11:37, 38.

7 **he was wroth**. Mt 21:40, 41. Da +9:26. Zc 14:1, 2. Lk 19:27, 42-44. +21:21-24. 1 Th 2:16. He 2:3. 1 P 4:17, 18.
   his armies. Dt 28:49, etc. Is 10:5-7. 13:2-5. Je 51:20-23. Jl 2:11, 25. 3:2. Lk 19:27.
   destroyed. Gr. *apollumi*, Mt +2:13.

8 **The wedding**. ver. 4.
   but they. Jn 1:11.
   not worthy. Mt 10:11-13, 37, 38. +21:43. Mi 5:3. Lk +21:36. Ac 13:46. Col +1:10. Re 22:14.

9 *Go ye*. Pr 1:20-23. 8:1-5. 9:4-6. Is 55:1-3, 6, 7. Mk 16:15, 16. Lk 14:21-24. 24:47. Ac 13:47. Ep 3:8. Re 22:17.
   into the highways. Ezk 21:21. Ob 14.
   as many. Lk 14:21.
   bid. Mt 11:28. Ro 10:21.

10 **and gathered**. Mt +13:47.
   both bad and good. ver. 11, 12. Mt +13:30, 38, 47, 48. 25:1, 2. Lk +6:35. 1 C +6:9-11. 2 C 12:21. 2 P +3:9. 1 J 2:19. Re 2:14, 15, 20-23.
   and the. Mt 25:10. Re 5:9. 7:9. 19:6-9.

11 **when**. Mt 3:12. 13:30. 25:31, 32. Zp 1:12. 1 C 4:5. He +4:12, 13. Re 2:23.
   which had not. 2 K 10:22. Ps 45:13, 14. Is 52:1. 61:3, 10. 64:6. Je 11:15. Zp 1:8. Zc 3:3, 4. Lk 15:22. Ro 3:22. 13:14. 2 C 5:3. Ga 3:27. Ep 4:24. Col 3:10-12. He +12:14. Re 3:4, 5, 18. 16:15. 19:8. 22:14.

12 **Friend**. Mt 20:13. 26:50. Jn +15:14.
   how. Mt 5:20. 7:22, 23. Ac 5:2-11. 8:20-23. 1 C 4:5.
   And he was. Ps +107:42. Je 2:23, 26. Lk 4:35. T 3:11.

13 **servants**. Mt 20:26. 1 C 3:5.
   Bind. Mt 12:29. 13:30. Is 52:1. Da 3:20. Jn 21:18. Ac 21:11. Re 21:27.
   outer darkness. Mt +8:12.
   there. Mt +25:30. Ps +37:12. Ac 7:54.

14 **many are called**. Mt +7:13, 14. Lk 13:23, 24. Ro +8:28.
   few are chosen. Mt +7:14. 11:27. 24:22, 24, 31.

15 **went**. Ps 2:2. Mk 12:13-17. Lk 20:20-26.
   took counsel. Mt 12:14.
   how. Ps 41:6. 56:5-7. 57:6. 59:3. Is 29:21. Je 18:18. 20:10. Lk 11:53, 54. He 12:3.

16 **they sent**. Lk 20:20.
   their disciples. Mk 2:18.
   the Herodians. i.e. *partisans of Herod*, **S#2265g**. Mt 16:11, 12. Mk 3:6. 8:15. 12:13. Lk 23:7.
   Master. ver. 24, 26. Mt 26:18, 49. Mk 10:17. Lk 7:40.
   we know. Ps 5:9. 12:2. 55:21. Pr 29:5. Is 59:13-15. Je 9:3-5. Ezk +33:30, 31. Jn 3:2.
   true. Ml 2:6. Jn 7:18. 14:6. 18:37. 2 C 2:17. 4:2. 1 J 5:20.
   the way. 1 K 22:14. Mk 1:3. 12:14. Lk 1:76. 3:4. 20:21. Jn 1:23. Ac 9:2. 13:10. 18:25, 26. Ro 11:33. He 3:10. Re 15:3.
   in truth. Jn 17:19.
   neither. Le +19:15. Dt 33:9. Jb 32:21, 22. Mi 3:9-12. Ml 2:9. Ro +2:11. 2 C 5:16. Ga 1:10. 2:6. 1 Th 2:4. Ja 2:1, 9. 3:17.

17 **What**. Je 42:2, 3, 20. Ac 28:22.
   Is. Dt 17:14, 15. Ezr 4:13. 7:24. Ne 5:4. 9:37. Ac 5:37. Ro 13:6, 7.
   tribute. Mt 17:25. Lk 23:2. Ro 13:6, 7.
   Caesar. Jn +19:12-15.

18 **perceived**. Jn +2:25.
   Why. ver. 35. Mt +16:1-4. Ac 5:9.
   hypocrites. Mt +6:2.

19 **a penny**. Mt +18:28mg.

20 **Whose**. Ge +3:9.
   superscription. *or*, inscription. Lk 20:24.

21 **Render**. Mt 17:25-27. Pr 24:21. Lk 23:2. Ro 13:7. 1 P 2:17.

are Caesar's. Pr +22:3. Is 52:13.
and unto God. ver. 37. Mt 4:10. Da +3:16-18. +6:10, 11, 20-23. Ml 1:6-8. 3:8-10. Ac +4:19. +5:29. 1 T 2:2. 1 P 2:13-17.

22 **they marvelled**. ver. 33, 46. Mt 10:16. Pr +21:30. 26:4, 5. Mk 5:20. Lk 20:25, 26. 21:15. Jn 7:15. Ac 6:10. Col 4:6.
and left. Mk 12:12.

23 **same**. Mk 12:18, etc. Lk 20:27, etc.
the Sadducees. ver. 34. Mt +3:7.
which say. Ac 4:2. 23:8. 26:8. 1 C 15:12-14. 2 T 2:18.

24 **Master**. ver. 16, 36. Mt 7:21. 8:19. 9:11. 10:24, 25. 12:38. 17:24. 19:16. 23:8, 10. 26:18, 25, 49. Mk +4:38. Lk 6:46. +7:40. Jn +1:38.
Moses said. Ex +24:4. Mk 12:26. Lk 16:29. 20:37. Jn 1:45. 5:45, 46. 7:23. Ac 3:22. 15:21. Ro 9:15. 10:5, 19. 2 C 3:15.
If a man. Mt +4:9. Ge +38:8, 9, 11. Dt 25:5-10. Ru 1:11-13. 3:9. Mk 12:19. Lk 20:28.

25 **there were**. Mk 12:19-23. Lk 20:29-33. He +9:27.

26 **seventh**. *or*, seven.

29 **do err**. Mk 12:24, 27.
not knowing. Mt 5:18. Jb 19:25-27. Ps +16:9-11. 17:15. 49:14, 15. 73:25, 26. Is 25:8. +26:19. 57:1, 2. Da +12:2, 3. Ho 13:14. Lk 16:29-31. +24:44-47. Jn +5:39. +6:14. 7:49. 20:9. Ac 13:27. Ro +15:4. 1 C 15:34.
the scriptures. Mt 21:42.
nor the power. Ge 18:14. Je 32:17. Lk 1:37. Ac 26:8. 1 C 6:14. Ep 1:19. Ph 3:21.

30 **in the resurrection**. Mt 24:38. Is +54:1. Mk 12:24, 25. Lk 20:34-36. Jn 5:28, 29. 1 C 7:29-31. 1 J 3:1, 2.
as the angels. Mt 13:43. 18:10. Ps +8:5. 103:20. Zc 3:7. Lk +20:36. He 2:7, 9. 1 J 3:2. Re 5:9-11. 19:10.

31 **the resurrection**. Ps +49:15. Is 25:8. +26:19. Da +12:2. Ho +13:14. Lk 14:14. Jn 5:28, 29. 6:39. 11:23-26. Jn 12:24. 14:19. Ac 17:18. 24:14, 15. Ro 8:11, 23. 1 C 6:14. 15:23-56. 2 C 4:14. Col 3:4. 1 Th 4:14, 16. 2 T +1:10. 1 P 1:3.
have ye not read. Mt 9:13. 12:3, 5. 19:4. 21:16, 42.

32 **I am**. Ex 3:6, 15, 16. Ac 7:32. He 11:16.
God of Abraham. Mt +8:11. Lk 16:22. Ac 3:13.
God is. Mk 12:26, 27. Lk 20:37, 38.
the dead. Mt +10:28. Mk 12:27. Lk 9:30. 20:37. Ac 2:36. Ro 14:9. 1 C 15:18, 29. Ph 3:20, 21. He +11:16. 20:13.
the living. He 12:9, 23. Re 6:9, 10.

33 **they were astonished**. ver. 22. Mt +7:28, 29. Mk 12:17. Lk 20:39, 40.

34 **when**. Mk 12:28-33. Lk 10:25-28.
Sadducees. ver. 23.

they. Mt 12:14. 25:3-5. Is 41:5-7. Jn 11:47-50. Ac 5:24-28. 19:23-28. 21:28-30.

35 **a lawyer**. Lk 5:17. 7:30. 10:25-28. 11:45, 46, 52. 14:3. Ac 5:34. 1 T 1:7. T 3:13.
tempting. ver. +18.

36 **Master**. ver. +24.
which is. Mt 5:19, 20. 15:6. 23:23, 24. Ho 8:12. Mk 12:28-33. Lk 11:42.
in the law. Mt 12:5. Lk 10:25, 26. Jn 1:45. 8:5, 17. 10:34. 15:25.

37 **thou shalt love**. Dt +6:5. Ps +145:9. Ro 8:7. He 10:16, 17.
with all. Dt 4:29. 10:12. 11:1, 13. 13:3. 26:16. 30:2, 6, 10, 16, 20. Jsh 22:5. 1 K 2:4. 8:48. 2 K 23:3, 25. 2 Ch 6:38. 15:12, 15. 31:21. 34:31. Je +29:13. 32:41. Mk 12:30. Lk 10:27.
thy heart. 2 K +20:3. 1 Ch 12:38.
soul. Gr. *psyche*. Here *psyche* is used for the seat of will and purpose, as at Mk 12:30, 33. Lk 10:27. Ac 4:32. Ep 6:6. Ph 1:27. Col 3:23. He 12:3. For the other uses of *psyche*, see Mt +2:20. Nu 21:4. Dt 11:13.

39 **the second**. 1 J 4:21.
Thou shalt love. Le +19:18. Jn 13:34, 35. 15:12, 13, 17. Ro 12:9, 10. 1 C ch. 13. 14:1. Ep 1:15. 5:2. Ph 1:9. Col 1:3, 4. 1 Th 3:12, 13. 2 Th 1:3. 1 T 1:5. 6:11. 2 T 2:22. He 13:1. 1 P 2:17. 4:8. 1 J 4:7, 8, 11, 20, 21.
neighbor. Lk 10:29-37. Ro 15:2. Ga 6:10.
as thyself. 2 C 10:12. Ga 5:22. Ep 5:29. Ph 2:4.

40 **On these two**. Mt 7:12. Mk 12:31. Jn 1:17. Ro 3:19-21. 13:9. 1 T 1:5. Ja 2:8. 1 J 4:7-11, 19-21.
all. Mt 7:12. Ga 5:14.
law and. Lk 16:16.

41 **the Pharisees**. ver. 15, 34. Mk 13:35-37. Lk 20:41-44.
were gathered. ver. 34.

42 **What**. Mt 2:4-6. 14:33. 16:13-17. Jn 1:49. 6:68, 69. +20:28. Ph 2:9-11. 3:7-10. Col 3:11. 1 P 2:4-7. Re 5:12-14.
Christ. Mt +16:16.
The Son. Mt +1:1.

43 **David**. Ac 4:25.
in spirit. Gr. *pneuma*, Mt +3:16. 2 S 23:2. Mk 12:36. Lk 2:26, 27. Ac 1:16. 2:30, 31. He 3:7. 2 P +1:21. Re 1:10. 4:2.

44 **The Lord**. Ps 110:1. Ac 2:30, 34, 35.
my Lord. Jn +20:28. 1 C 1:2. Ph 3:8.
Sit. He +1:3.
right hand. 1 K 2:19. Ps 45:9. +110:1.
till. Ge +3:15. Ps 2:8, 9. 21:9. Is 63:1-6. Lk 19:27. 1 C +15:25, 28. Re 19:19-21. 20:1-3, 11-15.
thy footstool. Jsh 10:24. 1 K 5:3.

45 **If**. 1 C +15:2.

how. Jn +8:58. Ro 1:3, 4. 9:5. Ph 2:6-8. 1 T 3:16. He 2:14. Re 22:16.

46 **no**. Mt 21:27. Jb 32:15, 16. Is 50:2-9. Lk 13:17. 14:6. Jn 8:7-9. Ac 4:14.
neither. Mk 12:34. Lk 20:40.

MATTHEW 23

1 **to the multitude**. Mt 15:10, etc. Mk 7:14. Lk 11:43. 12:1, 57. 20:45, 46.

2 **The scribes**. 2 Ch +15:3. Ezr 7:6, 10, 11, 25. Ne 8:4-8. Ml +2:7. Mk 12:38. Lk 20:45, 46.
sit. Mt 26:55. 27:19. Ex 18:13. Dt 17:10, 11. 19:17. 33:3. Jg 5:10. Ps 29:10. 110:1. Lk 4:20. 10:39, 42. Jn 8:2. 9:28, 29. Ac 22:3.
Moses'. 1 C 10:2.
seat. ver. 8-10. Ge +49:10. 2 C +1:24.

3 **whatsoever**. Mt 15:2-9. Ex 18:19, 20, 23. Dt 4:5. 5:27. 17:9-12. 2 Ch 30:12. Is +8:20. Mk +1:44. Ac 5:29. Ro 2:21, 23. 13:1. 1 C 14:34.
but do not. Mt 5:20. Is 9:16. Je +10:2. Ml 2:7, 8.
for. Mt 21:30. Ps 50:16-20. Ro 2:19-24. 1 C 9:27. 2 T 3:5. T 1:16.

4 **they bind**. ver. 23. Mt +11:28-30. Lk 11:46. Ac 15:5, 10, 28. Ga 6:13. Re 2:24, 25.

5 **all**. Mt 6:1-16. 2 K 10:16. Lk 16:15. 20:47. 21:1. Jn 5:44. 7:18. 12:43. Ph 1:15. 2:3. 2 Th 2:4.
they make. Ex 13:9. Dt 6:8. 11:18. Pr 3:3. 6:21-23.
the borders. Mt 9:20. Nu 15:38, 39. Dt 22:12.

6 **love the uppermost**. Mt 20:21. Pr 25:6, 7. Mk 12:38, 39. Lk 11:43, etc. 14:7-11. 20:46, 47. Ro 12:10. Ja 2:1-4. 3 J 9.

7 **markets**. Mt 11:16. 20:3. 6:56. 7:4. Lk 7:32. Ac 16:19. 17:17.
Rabbi. i.e. *my master*, **S#4461g**. Rendered (1) Master: Mt 26:25, 49. Mk 9:5. 11:21. 14:45, 45. Jn 4:31. 9:2. 11:8. (2) Rabbi: Jn 1:38, 49. 3:2, 26. 6:25. (3) rabbi: Mt 23:7, 7, 8. Compare **S#4462g**: Mk 10:51. Jn 20:16.
Rabbi. Mt 7:21. Mk 14:45.

8 **be**. ver. 10. 2 C 1:24. 4:5. Ja 3:1. 1 P 5:3.
one. Mt 11:29. 17:5. +22:24. Ro 14:9, 10. 1 C 1:12, 13. 3:3-5.
all. Lk 22:32. Jn 21:23. Ep 3:14, 15. Col 1:1, 2. Phm 16. Re 1:9. 19:10. 22:9.

9 **call**. 2 K 2:12. 6:21. 13:14. Jb 32:21, 22. Ac 22:1. 1 C 1:12, 13. 3:4. 4:15. 1 T 5:1, 2. He 12:9.
for one. Mk 12:29.
your father. Mt 5:16, 45, 48. 6:1, 8, 14, 26, 32. 7:11. 18:14. Ml 1:6. Mk 11:25. Lk 11:13. Ro 8:14-17. 2 C 6:18. 1 J 3:1.
in heaven. Mt +6:9.

10 **neither be**. Mi +6:8. Lk 14:10. 22:26. Ro 12:3. Ph 2:3. Ja 4:10. 1 P 5:5.
masters. ver. 8.
for one is. Lk 5:5. 8:24, 45. 9:33, 49. 17:13.

11 **he that is greatest**. Mt 20:26, 27. Mk 10:43, 44. Lk 22:26, 27. Jn 13:1-9, 14, 15. Ro +12:3. 1 C 9:19. 2 C 4:5. 11:23. Ga 5:13. Ph +2:3, 5-8.

12 **shall exalt**. Pr 17:19. 25:6, 7, 27. Is 14:13, 14. Mk 10:37.
shall be abased. Pr 15:25. +16:5. Je 50:32. Ezk 21:26. 31:14. Lk 10:15.
shall humble. Mt +5:3. 18:4. Jb 22:29. Ps 138:6. Pr 15:33. 16:19. 18:12. Is +57:15. Ro +12:3. 2 C +1:24. Ph +2:3. 1 P 5:3.
shall be exalted. Mt +19:28. Jb 5:11. Ps +91:14. Is 33:16. 58:14. Da +12:3. Hab 3:19. Mk +10:30. Lk +14:14. 19:17. 1 C 6:2. 1 T +4:8. 2 T +4:8. Ja +2:5. 4:10. 1 P 5:6. Re +3:21. +5:10. 11:12, 18.

13 **woe**. ver. 14, 15, 27, 29. Mt +6:2. Is 5:8-22. 9:14, 15. 10:1. 33:14. Hab 2:6-17. Zc 11:17. Lk 11:43, 44, +52.
hypocrites. ver. 23, 25, 27, 29. Mt +6:2.
for ye shut. Mt 16:19. 21:31, 32. Lk +11:52. Jn 7:46-52. 9:22, 24, 34. Ac 4:5, 17, 18. 5:28, 40. 8:1. 13:8. 1 Th 2:15, 16. 2 T 3:8. 4:15. Re 3:7.
kingdom of heaven. Mt +4:17.
neither go in. Mt 5:20. 21:31. Lk 7:30.
neither suffer. Mi +3:5.

14 **for ye devour**. Ex +22:22-24. Is +1:17. Mk 12:40. Lk 11:39. 16:14. 20:47. 2 T 3:6. T 1:10, 11. 2 P 2:14, 15.
for a pretence. Mt 6:5. Ezk 33:30-33.
long prayer. Mt 6:7. Ec +5:2. Mk 12:40.
therefore. ver. 33. Mt +10:15. 2 P 2:3.

15 **for**. Ga 4:17. 6:12.
to make. Mt 6:23. Lk 11:52.
proselyte. Est 8:17. Ac 2:10. 6:5. 13:43.
ye make. Mt 6:23. Ezk 13:19, 22. Mi 3:5. Jn 8:44. Ac 13:10. 14:2, 19. 17:5, 6, 13. Ep 2:3.
more. Mt +10:15.
the child. Mt 13:38. Dt +15:9. Jg +19:22. Lk 10:6. Jn 17:12. 2 Th 2:3.
hell. Gr. *gehenna*, Mt +5:22.

16 **ye blind**. ver. 17, 19, 24, 26. Mt +15:14. Lk 4:18. Jn 9:39-41. Re 3:17.
Whosoever shall swear. Mt 5:33, 34. Ja 5:12.
by the temple. ver. 21, 35. Mt 26:61. 27:5, 40, 51. Mk 14:58. 15:29, 38. Lk 1:9, 21, 22. 23:45. Jn 2:19-21. 2 Th 2:4. Re 3:12.
it is. Mt 15:5, 6. Mk 7:10-13.
he is. Ga 5:3.

17 **Ye fools**. Mt 5:22. 25:2. Ps 94:8.
and blind. ver. 16.
or. ver. 19. Ex 30:26-29. Nu 16:38, 39.

18 **swear by**. Mt 5:34, 35.
the altar. Mt +5:23. Ex 29:37.
guilty. *or*, debtor. ver. 15.
the gift. Mt 5:23, 24. 8:4. 15:5. Lk 21:1, 4. He 5:1. 8:4.

19 **or**. Ex 29:37. 30:29.

21 **the temple**. ver. 16.
and by him. Ex 15:17. 1 K 8:13, 27. 2 Ch
6:2. 7:2. Ps 26:8. 132:13, 14. Ep 2:22. Col 2:9.
22 **by heaven**. Mt 21:25.
by the throne. Ps +11:4.
by him. Re 4:2, 3.
23 **hypocrites**. ver. 13.
for. Lk 11:42.
pay tithe. Ge +14:20. 1 C +9:13, 14. +16:2.
Gr. *apodekatoo*, **S#586g**: Mt 23:23. Lk 11:42.
18:12. He 7:5.
anise. Gr. *anathon*, dill. Is 28:25, 27.
the weightier. Mt 9:13. 12:7. 22:37-40. 1 S
15:22. Pr 21:3. Je 22:15, 16. Ho +6:6. Mi
+6:8. Mk 12:31. Ga 5:22, 23.
judgment. Ps 33:5. Is 5:7. Je 5:1. Mi +6:8.
Hab +1:4. Zc 7:9.
mercy. Mt 9:13. 12:7. 25:43. Ps 109:16. Pr
21:13. Ezk 34:4. Ho +6:6. Zc 7:9. 11:16. Lk
16:20, 21. Ja +4:17. 1 J 3:17.
and faith. or, stedfastness. 1 Ch +28:9. 2 Ch
+20:20. Lk +8:13. 18:8. Ac 3:16. 15:9. Ro
3:25. 4:9, 14, 19, 20. 5:2. 10:8, 17. 11:20.
12:6. 1 C +15:2, 58. Ga 6:9. Ep 2:8. Col +1:23.
+2:7. 1 T 1:19. He +3:12-14. 6:10, 11. 11:6,
39. 12:15. 2 P 1:5-10. 3:17.
these ought. Mt 5:19, 20. Le 27:30. Nu
18:21. Dt 14:22-29. Lk 11:41, 42. Jn 1:17. Ro
6:14. 10:4. Ep 2:15. Col 2:14.
24 **blind guides**. ver. 16. Mt +15:14.
Which strain. Mt +6:2. 7:4. 15:2-6. 19:24.
27:6-8. Lk 6:7-10. Jn 18:28, 40.
camel. Mt 19:24. Le 11:4. Mk 10:25. Lk
18:25.
25 **for**. Mt 15:19, 20. Mk 7:4, etc. Lk 11:39, 40. T
1:15.
the cup. Mk 7:4.
full. Is 28:7, 8.
extortion. Lk 16:14. 20:47.
and excess. 1 C 7:5.
26 **cleanse**. Mt 12:33. Is 55:7. Je 4:14. 13:27.
Ezk 18:31. Lk 6:45. 2 C 7:1. He 10:22. Ja 4:8.
first. Mt 6:33. 7:5.
27 **like**. Is 58:1, 2. Lk 11:44. Ac 23:3.
sepulchres. Nu 19:16.
are within. Ps 45:13. 51:10.
bones. 2 K +23:14.
all uncleanness. 2 K 23:16. Ezk 39:14, 15.
Ep 5:3.
28 **ye also**. ver. 5. 1 S +16:7. Ps 51:6. Je +17:9,
10. Lk 16:15. He +4:12, 13.
outwardly appear. Ps 45:13.
but. Mt 12:34, 35. 15:19, 20. Mk 7:21-23.
29 **ye build**. Lk 11:47, 48. Ac 2:29.
garnish. Mt 12:44. 1 P 3:5.
30 **If we had**. This kind of "if" speaks of what is
contrary to fact or impossible. Here, "If we
were, which is not the case." For other examples of this Second Class Condition (unclassified as to time) of "if" see Mt 5:13. 6:1. 15:5.

21:21. 24:24, 43. 25:27. 26:24. Mk 9:42.
12:49. 13:22. 14:21. Lk 17:6. 19:23, 42. Jn
4:10. 8:19, 39. 14:2. 15:24. 18:36. 19:11. Ac
18:14. 24:19. 26:32. Ro 7:7. 1 C 12:19. Ga
2:17. 4:15. He 4:8. 7:11. 8:4, 7. 9:26. 10:2.
Compare Lk +7:39; Mt +11:21.
the blood. ver. 34, 35. Mt 21:35, 36. 2 Ch
36:15, 16. Je 2:30.
31 **witnesses**. Jsh 24:22. Jb 15:5, 6. Ps 64:8. Lk
19:22.
children. Pr 27:19. Ec 1:15. +7:20. Da
+12:10. Re +22:11.
which killed. Lk 11:48. Ac 7:51, 52. 1 Th
2:15, 16.
32 **the measure**. Ge 15:16. Nu 32:14. Da 8:23.
Zc 5:6-11. 1 Th 2:15, 16.
your fathers. Jg 2:19. Je 16:12. 2 T 3:13.
33 **serpents**. Mt +3:7. 21:34, 35. Jn 10:14. Ac
20:29. 2 C 11:3.
vipers. Ps 58:4. 140:3.
how. ver. 14. He 2:3. 10:29. 12:25.
the damnation. Mt +10:15. Lk 10:14.
hell. Gr. *gehenna*, Mt +5:22.
34 **I send**. Mt 10:16. 28:19, 20. Lk 11:49. 24:47.
Jn 20:21. Ac +1:8. 1 C 12:3-11. Ep 4:8-12.
prophets. Ac 11:27. 13:1. 15:32. 1 C 12:28.
Re 11:10.
and wise. Pr 11:30. 1 C 2:6. 3:10. Col 1:28.
scribes. Mt +13:52.
ye shall kill. Mt 10:16, 17. 21:35. 24:9. Mk
13:12. Lk 21:16. Jn 16:2. Ac 7:51, 52, 58, 59.
9:1, 2. 12:2. 14:19. 22:19, 20. 1 Th 2:16. He
11:37.
scourge. Mt +10:17. Lk 12:11.
persecute. Mt 10:23. Ac 8:1. 14:5, 6. 17:13,
14.
35 **upon**. Mt 27:25. Ge +9:5, 6. Nu 35:33. Dt
21:7, 8. 2 K 21:16. 24:4. Is 26:21. Je 2:30, 34.
26:15, 23. La 4:13, 14. Re 18:24.
righteous blood. Mt 27:4. Ps 94:21. Jl 3:19.
Jon 1:14.
the blood. Lk 11:51. He 12:24. 1 J 3:12. Ju
11.
righteous Abel. **S#6g**: ver. 35. Lk 11:51. He
11:4. 12:24. For **S#1893h**, see Ge +4:2. Ge 4:8.
1 J 3:11, 12.
unto. 2 Ch 24:20-22. Zc 1:1. Lk 11:51.
Barachias. i.e. *blessing of the Lord*, **S#914g**, only
here. For **S#1296h**, see Zc +1:7.
the temple. ver. 16. 1 K 6:2.
the altar. Mt +5:23.
36 **All these**. Mt +24:34. Ezk 12:21-28.
this generation. Mt +24:34. Je +7:29.
37 **O Jerusalem**. 1 S +22:19. Je 4:14. 6:8. Lk
13:34. 19:41-44. Re 11:8.
Jerusalem. Ge +22:11.
thou. ver. 30. Mt 5:12. 21:35, 36. 22:6. 2 Ch
24:21, 22. Ne +9:26. Je 2:30. 26:23. Mk 12:3-
6. Lk 13:33. 20:11-14. Ac 7:51, 52. 1 Th 2:15.
Re 11:7. 17:6.

stonest. Le +24:14.

how often. Mt 26:55. 2 Ch 36:15, 16. Ps 81:8-14. Je 6:16, 17. 11:7, 8. 25:3-7. 35:15. 42:9-13. 44:4. Zc 1:4. Lk 4:44.

gathered. Mt 24:31. Ps 106:47. 107:3. 147:2. Pr 1:24. Mk 13:27.

thy children. Lk 23:28.

wings. Ps +91:4. Is 31:5. Ml 4:2.

and ye. Mt 22:3. Pr 1:24-31. Is 30:15. 50:2. Je 6:17. Ho 11:2, 7. Lk 14:17-20. 15:28. 19:14-44. Jn 1:5, 10, 11. 5:40.

38 **your house**. Mt 24:2. 1 K 9:7, 8. 2 Ch 7:20, 21. Ps 69:24, 25. Pr +17:13. Is 64:10-12. Je 7:9-15. 12:7. 22:5. Ezk 10:18, 19. 11:23. Da +9:26. Zc 11:1, 2, 6. 14:1, 2. Mk 13:14. Lk 13:35. 19:43, 44. 21:6, 20, 24. Ac 6:13, 14.

desolate. Le 26:31. Ps 69:25. Mi 3:12. 4:1.

39 **Ye shall not**. Ho 3:4. Lk 2:26-30. 10:22, 23. 13:35. 17:22. Jn 8:21, 24, 56. 14:9, 19.

till. Mt 10:23. +16:28. 24:34. 1 S +12:22. Is +52:8. +60:10. 62:4. +65:24. Je +4:27. Ho 3:4, 5. +5:15. 6:1. Mi +2:13. Zc 9:14. 10:6. Ml +3:6. Jn +21:22, 23. Ac +3:19-21. Ro +11:25, 26. 2 C 3:15, 16.

ye shall say. Ps 118:26. Is 30:19. Ho 8:2. 14:2. Jl 2:17. Zc 13:9.

Blessed. Ps +118:26. Is 40:9-11. Zc 12:10. Ro +11:25, 26. 2 C 3:14-18.

MATTHEW 24

1 **went out**. Mt 21:17. Lk 21:1, 27, 28, 37.

departed. Mt 21:23. 23:39. Je 6:8. Ezk 8:6. 10:17-19. 11:22, 23. Ho 9:12. Ac 13:46. He 10:26, 27.

show. Mk 13:1, 2. Lk 21:5, 6. Jn 2:20.

2 **said**. Mt 11:25.

There. 2 S 17:13. 1 K 9:7, 8. Ps 79:1. Is 64:11. Je 7:4. 26:18. Ezk 7:20-22. Da +9:26, 27. Mi 1:6. 3:12. Lk 19:44. 2 P 3:11.

3 **he sat**. Mt +21:1.

the disciples. Mt 13:10, 11, 36. 15:12. 17:19.

privately. Mk 4:34.

Tell. Da +12:6-8. Lk 21:7. Jn 21:21, 22. Ac +1:6, 7. 1 Th 5:1, etc.

when shall. Lk 17:20-27. 21:12-24.

and what shall. ver. 4-26, 37-39.

the sign. ver. 30, 32, 33, 43.

coming. Gr. *parousia*, S#3952g. Rendered (1) *coming*: ver. 3, 27, 37, 39; 1 C 15:23; 16:17; 2 C 7:6, 7; Ph 1:26; 1 Th 2:19; 3:13; 4:15; 5:23; 2 Th 2:1, 8, 9; Ja 5:7, 8; 2 P 1:16; 3:4, 12; 1 J 2:28; (2) *presence*: 2 C 10:10; Ph 2:12. ver. 30. Mt +16:27, 28. Da +7:13. Zc 9:14. +12:10. Mk 1:2. Jn +1:51. Ac 1:11. 2 T +4:1. T 2:13. Re 1:7.

and of. ver. 27-31, 40-51. Mt 25:1-46.

the end. Gr. *sunteleia*, S#4930g. The joining of

two ages (Mt 12:32). Mt +13:39, 40, 49. 28:20. He 9:26.

world. Gr. *aion*, Mt +6:13.

4 **Take heed**. Je +29:8. Col 2:8, 18. 2 P 2:1-3. 1 J 3:7. 4:1.

5 **many shall come**. ver. 11, 24. Je 14:14. 23:21, 25. 27:15. Jn 5:43. Ac 5:36, 37. 8:9, 10. 1 J 2:18. Re 13:8.

in my name. Mk +9:37.

Christ. ver. 23. Mt +16:16.

deceive many. ver. 11, 24.

6 **ye shall hear**. Je 4:19-22. 6:22-24. 8:15, 16. 47:6, 7. Ezk 14:17-21. 21:9-15, 28. Da ch. 11. Lk 21:9. Re 6:2-4.

rumors. lit. hearing. Le +13:55. Is 52:7. Je +49:14. Mk 4:24.

see. Ps 27:1-3. 46:1-3. 112:7. Is 8:12-14. 12:2. 26:3, 4, 20, 21. Hab +3:16-18. Lk 21:19. Jn 14:1, 27. 2 Th 2:2. 1 P 3:14, 15.

must. Lk +13:33.

but. ver. 14. Da +9:24-27. 1 P 4:7.

7 **nation shall**. 2 Ch 15:6. Is 5:25. 9:19-21. 19:2. Ezk 21:27. Hg 2:21, 22. Zc 14:2, 3, 13. He 12:27. Re 6:4.

kingdom against. Jg +7:22.

famines. 1 K +8:37.

pestilences. Ezk +38:22.

earthquakes. Is 13:13. 24:19-23. Zc +14:4. Lk 21:11, 25, 26. Ac 2:19, 20. Ro 8:20-23. He +12:26. Re +6:12.

8 **beginning**. Le 26:18-29. Dt +28:59. Is 9:12, 17, 21. 10:4. 1 Th 5:3. 1 P 4:17, 18.

sorrows. lit. birth pangs. ver. 15-21. Is 66:7, 8. Je +4:31. 30:4-7. Da 7:21. 8:9-14, 23-26. 9:27. 11:40-45. 12:1, 7. Mi 4:9, 10. 5:3. Zc 12:10-14:21. Mk 13:8. Jn 16:21. Ac 2:24. Ro 8:22. 11:25-27. Ga 4:19, 27. 1 Th 5:3. Re 12:2.

9 **shall they**. Mt 5:11. 10:17, 21, 22. 22:6. 23:34. Mk 13:9-13. Lk 11:49. 21:12, 16, 17. Jn 15:19, 20. 16:2. Ac 4:2, 3. 5:40, 41. 7:59. 12:1, 2, etc. 21:31, 32. 22:19-22. 28:22. 1 Th 2:14-16. 1 P 4:16. Re 2:10, 13. +6:9-11. 7:14.

to be afflicted. ver. 21, 29. Re 2:10.

shall kill. Mt +23:34. Jn 16:2.

be hated. Mt 10:22. Ps 44:22. Lk 6:22. Jn 15:18-21. 17:14. Re 11:9, 10.

all. Ex +9:6.

for my. Jn 15:21.

10 **And then**. 2 T 3:1.

shall many. Mt +11:6. 2 T 1:15. 4:10, 16.

betray. Mt +10:21, 35, 36. 26:21-24. Mi 7:5, 6. Mk 13:12. Lk 12:53. 21:16.

11 **false prophets**. ver. 5, 24. Mt 7:15. Je 14:14. Mk 13:22. Ac 20:29, 30. 1 T 4:1, 2. 2 P 2:1. 1 J 2:18, 26. 4:1. 2 J 7. Ju 4. Re 13:11. 19:20.

deceive many. ver. 5, 24. Ezk 14:10. 2 Th 2:10, 11.

12 **because**. Lk 18:7. Ja 4:1-4. 5:1-6.

iniquity. 2 Th 2:6-8.

the love. 2 Th 2:10. 2 T 3:1-5. Re 2:4, 5, 10. 3:15, 16.

shall wax cold. 2 Th 2:3, 4.

13 **shall endure**. ver. 6. Mt 10:22. Pr 16:17. Da 12:12, 13. Mk 4:16, 17. 13:13. Lk +8:13, 15. Jn +8:31. +15:6. Ro 2:7. 11:22. 1 C 1:8. 9:27. 10:12. 15:58. Ga 6:9. Ep 4:30. He 3:6, 14. 6:4-6. 10:36, 39. Ja 1:12. 1 P 1:23. 1 J 2:27. Ju 24. Re 2:10, 26. 3:5.

unto the. Ro 5:10. 6:14. 8:30. 1 C 1:8. 2 C 1:13. Ga +6:9. Col +1:21-23. 1 Th 5:23, 24. 2 Th 3:3. 2 T 4:6, 8. He 3:6, 14. 6:11. 1 P 1:5. 1 J 2:19. Ju 1. Re 2:26.

end. Gr. *telos*, **S#5056g**, Mt +10:22. The actual end of anything. Here, of life or the age. Compare "end" (Gr. *sunteleia*, ver. +3).

shall be saved. Jb 17:9. Ps 37:24, 28. 138:8. Pr +4:18. Je 32:40. Zc 13:8, 9. Lk 12:32. 22:32. Jn 5:24. 6:39, 51. 11:26. 14:19. 17:12, 24. Ro 8:38, 39. 11:26. Ph 1:6. 2 T 1:12. 4:18. He 7:25. 9:28. 10:14. 1 J 2:17.

14 **this gospel**. Mt 4:23. 9:35. 10:7. Ac 20:25. 1 C +1:17.

the kingdom. Mt 13:19. +21:43. +25:34. Ps 102:22. Zc 14:9. Ac +1:6. 28:31. 1 C +15:50. Ep +1:11. Col +1:13. 2 T +4:1, 18. 1 P 1:4. Re +5:10. 11:15.

shall be. Mt 28:19. Ps +68:11. Is +27:6. +66:19. Mk 14:9. 16:15, 16. Lk +24:47. Ac +1:8. Ro 10:18. 15:18-21. 16:25, 26. Col 1:6, 23. 1 T +2:6. Re 11:3. 14:6, 7.

in all. Mk 16:15. Lk 2:1. 4:5. Ac 11:28. Ro 1:8. 10:18. 1 P 1:1, 2. Re 3:10. 12:9. 16:14.

the world. Gr. *oikoumene*, **S#3625g**. Lk 2:1. 4:5. 21:26 (earth). Ac 11:28. 17:6, 31. 19:27. 24:5. Ro 10:18. He 1:6. 2:5. Re 3:10. 12:9. 16:14. Not the same as ver. 3 (world, lit. age, Mt +13:39, *aion*) or ver. 21 (world, *kosmos*, Mt +4:8).

for a witness. Mt +8:4. Ac +1:8.

unto all nations. Mt 25:32.

and then. ver. 3, 6. Mt 10:23. Ezk 7:5-7, 10.

15 **When ye**. Da +9:27. 11:40-45. 12:1, 7. Mk 13:14. Lk 19:43. 21:20. 2 Th 2:4. Re 11:1, 2.

abomination of desolation. Da 8:13. +9:25-27. 11:45. *12:11*. Re 13:14-17.

by Daniel. Da +9:27. 11:31. 12:11. Lk +24:27. 2 Th 2:3, 4.

the holy place. Da +9:27. Mk 13:14. Jn 11:48. Ac 6:13, 14. 21:28. 2 Th 2:4.

whoso. Ezk 40:4. Da +9:22, 23, 25. 10:12-14. Je 23:20. He 2:1. Re 1:3. 3:22.

16 **Then**. Da 9:27. 11:41.

let them. Ge 19:15-17. Ex 9:20, 21. Pr +22:3. Je 6:1. 37:11, 12. Lk 21:21, 22. He 11:7.

in Judea. ver. 13 with Da 12:12, 13; Jl 2:31, 32; Zc 13:9; Ro 11:26. ver. 14 with Is 27:6. ver. 15 with Da 9:27. ver. 20 with Je 17:27. ver. 21 with Je 30:7; Da 12:1. ver. 28 with

Ezk 39:4. ver. 31 with Is 27:12; 43:6; Je 31:8; Ezk 34:12; 38:8; Am 9:9.

flee. Pr +22:3. Is +16:3, 4. Re 12:6, 14.

mountains. Ps 60:8-12. Is 16:1-5. +26:20, 21. 63:1-6. Ezk 20:35-38. Ho 2:14, 20-23. Zc 14:5.

17 **which**. Mt 6:25. Jb 2:4. Pr 6:4, 5. Mk 13:15, 16. Lk 17:31-33.

the housetop. Dt +22:8.

not come. Lk 9:59-62.

18 **let him**. Lk 17:23.

his clothes. Mt 5:40.

19 **woe unto them**. Le +26:29. 2 S 4:4. 2 K +8:12. Mk 13:17. Lk 21:23. 23:28-30. 1 C 7:26.

20 **But pray**. Lk 18:1. 21:36.

winter. Jn 10:22. Ac 27:12. 2 T 4:21.

neither. Ex 16:23-30. +20:8-12. 23:12. 31:13-17. 34:21. 35:3. Le 23:3. 26:2. Dt 5:12-15. Is +58:13, 14. Je 17:21, 22, 27. Lk 23:56. Ac 1:12. Col 2:16.

21 **great tribulation**. Dt +4:30. Ps 69:22-28. Is 65:12-16. 66:15, 16. Je +30:7. Da +9:26. *+12:1*. Jl 1:2. 2:2. Zc 11:8, 9. 14:2, 3. Ml 4:1. Mk 13:19. Lk 19:43, 44. +21:23, 24. 1 Th 2:16. 2 Th 1:4-7. He 10:26-29. Re +3:10. +6:17. +7:14.

was not. Ex 10:14. Jl 2:2. Re 16:18.

world. Gr. *kosmos*, Mt +4:8.

22 **except**. Mt +11:21. Mk 13:20.

those days. Lk 21:22.

shortened. 1 C 7:29.

no flesh. Lk +3:6.

but for. Is 6:13. 44:1. Zc 13:8, 9. 14:2, 3. Lk 18:7. Ac +13:48. Ro 9:11. 11:25-31. 2 T 2:10.

elect's sake. ver. 24, 31. Dt +10:15. Is 45:4. 65:8, 9, +22. Mk 13:22, 27.

be shortened. Je +4:27. 30:11. 46:28. Am 9:8, 9. Zc 10:6. Re 12:12.

23 **Then if**. Mt +4:9. ver. 5, 22. Dt 13:1-3. Mk 13:21. Lk 17:23, 24. 21:8. Jn 5:43.

Christ. ver. +5. 2 C 11:13-15.

24 **there**. ver. 5, 11. 2 P 2:1-3. 3:17.

false Christs. 1 J 2:18.

false prophets. ver. 11. Ho 2:17. Zc 13:2. 2 Th 2:9-11.

and shall. Dt 13:1-3. Ac 8:9. 2 Th 2:9-11. Re 13:13, 14. 16:14. 19:20.

great. Da 8:24. 2 Th 2:9, 10.

signs and wonders. Dt 13:1-3. Jn 4:48. 2 Th 2:9-12.

insomuch. Jn 6:37, 39. 10:28-30. Ro 8:28-39. 2 T 2:19. 1 P 1:5. 1 J 5:18. Re 12:9-11. 13:7, 8, 14.

if. i.e. contrary to fact or impossible, Mt +23:30. Mk 13:22. Ac 20:16. Ro 12:18. Ga 4:15.

were possible. Mt 18:14. Jn 10:28, 29. Ro 8:28-30. 2 T 2:19.

deceive. ver. 5, 11. 1 C 6:9. Ep 5:6. 2 Th 2:3. 2 T 3:13. 2 P 3:17. 1 J 4:1.

the very elect. ver. 22.

25 **I have told you before**. Is 44:7, 8. 46:10, 11. 48:5, 6. Lk 21:13. Jn 13:19. 14:29. 16:1, 4. 2 P 3:17.

26 **Wherefore**. Ac 21:38.

if. Mt +4:9.

they shall say. ver. 5, 23. Lk 12:20.

he is in the desert. Mt 3:1. Dt +33:2. Is 40:3. Lk 3:2, 3. Ac 21:38. Re +12:6, 14.

go not. Mt 11:7-9.

secret chambers. ver. 3. Is +26:20. Mt 6:6. Lk 12:3, 24.

believe it not. ver. 23. Ep +4:14. 1 J 4:1. 1 P 3:15. 2 P 1:16.

27 **as the lightning**. Jb 37:3. 38:35. Is 30:30. Ezk 1:14. Zc 9:14. Lk 17:24, etc. 1 Th 5:1-3.

the coming. Gr. *parousia*, ver. +3. 37, 39. Mt +16:27, 28. Ml 3:2. 4:5. 1 Th 4:14-18. 2 Th 2:8. Ja 5:8. 2 P 3:4.

Son of man. Mt +8:20.

28 **wheresoever**. Mt +4:9. Dt +28:49. Jb 39:27-30. Je 16:16. Am 9:1-4.

the carcass. 1 S 17:46. Is +66:24. Ezk 39:4, 11-16. Mk 6:29. Lk +17:37.

the eagles. Dt +28:49. 1 S 17:44, 46. Hab 1:8. Lk +17:37. Jn 11:48.

be gathered. Pr 30:17. Ezk 39:17. Re 19:17, 18.

29 **Immediately after**. ver. 8. Da 7:11, 12. Mk 13:24, 25.

the tribulation. ver. +21.

shall the sun. Is 13:9, 10, 15. +24:21, 23. 34:4, 5. Je 4:23-28. Ezk 32:7, 8. Jl 2:2, 10, 30, 31. 3:15. Zc 14:6. Lk 21:11, 25, 26. Ac 2:19, 20. Re 6:12-17. 8:12. 16:8.

darkened. Ex +10:22.

and. Ge +8:22.

the stars. Is 14:12. 34:4. Re 6:13.

shall fall. Is 2:12.

the powers. Mt 8:6. Here, *dunameis, powers,* means really *armies*, from the Hebrew *chayeel* which has both meanings.

shaken. Jb 26:11. He +12:26. 2 P 3:10.

30 **And**. Ge +8:22.

shall appear. Da +7:13. Lk 21:28.

the sign. ver. 3. Da 7:13. Mk 13:4. Re 1:7.

the Son of man. Mt +8:20. +16:27. Da *7:13*.

and then shall all. Ge +12:3. 28:14.

mourn. Mt +11:17. Zc 12:10, 12. Re 1:7. 6:15-17.

shall see. ver. 3. Mt 16:27, 28. +23:39. 26:64. Mk 13:26. 14:62-64. Lk 21:27. 22:69. Ac 1:11. 2 Th 1:7, *8. Re 1:7.*

coming. ver. 3. Mt +16:28. Ps 98:9. Da 7:13. Zc +14:4, 5. Lk 18:8. Jn 14:3. 16:22. Ac +3:19-21. 1 C 1:7. 4:5. 11:26. 15:23. Ph 3:20, 21. Col 3:4. 1 Th 1:10. 2:19. 3:13. 4:14-17. 5:2-4, 23. 2 Th 1:7. 3:5. 4:5. 1 T 6:14. 2 T 4:1,

8. T 2:13. He 9:28. 10:37. Ja 5:8, 9. 1 P 1:7, 13. 5:4. 2 P 3:3, 4, 9-12. 1 J 2:28. 3:2. Ju 14, 15. Re 2:25. 16:15. 22:12, 20.

the clouds. Mt +17:5. 26:64. Ge +9:13. Ex +13:21. 2 K 2:11. 2 Ch +5:13. Ps +68:17. Da 7:13. Mk 13:26. 14:62. Ac 1:9. 1 Th 4:17.

with power. Is 24:21-23. Da 7:21, 22. Mk 9:1. 14:62. Lk 21:27. Ro +11:26. 2 Th 1:9. 2 P 1:16.

and. Ge +1:26. By Hendiadys, great and glorious power.

great glory. Mt 16:27. +25:31. Ex 24:16. Ps +102:16. Zc +2:5. 6:13. Mk 8:38. Jn +1:14. 2 Th 1:9. 2:8. 2 P 1:17, 18.

31 **And**. Ge +8:22.

he. Mt 28:18. Mk 16:15, 16. Lk 24:47. Ac 26:19, 20.

shall send. Ps 50:4, 5. Mk 13:27. 1 Th 4:16-18.

his angels. Mt +13:41, 49. 25:31. Dt 30:4. Mk 8:38. 2 Th 1:7. Re 1:20. 2:1. 14:6-9.

with. Nu 10:1-10. Ps 81:3. Is 27:13. 1 C 15:52. 1 Th 4:16.

a great sound of a trumpet. *or*, a trumpet and a great voice. Ge +1:26.

sound. Le 23:23-25. 1 Th 4:16.

trumpet. Le +23:24. 25:9. 1 S 13:3. 2 S 2:28. Is 18:3. 27:13. Zc +9:14. 1 C 15:51, 52. 1 Th 4:16. Re 11:15.

gather. Mt +23:37. 25:32. Ps +147:2. Is 11:12. +27:12. 43:6. 49:18. 60:4, 9. Je 29:14. Ezk +34:12. 37:12. +39:28. Am 9:9. Zc 14:5. Mk 13:27. Jn 11:52. Ep 1:10. 2 Th 2:1.

his elect. ver. 22. Ne +1:9. Ezk 39:28.

from. Ps 22:27. 67:7. Is 13:5. 42:10. +43:6. 45:22. Je +31:8. Ezk +38:8. 39:28. Zc 9:10. Ro 10:18.

the four winds. Je 49:36. Ezk 37:9. Da 7:2. 8:8. 11:4. Zc 2:6. Re 7:1.

end of heaven. Dt 4:32. 30:4. 2 S +22:8. Ps 19:6.

32 **a parable**. Mk 13:28, 29. Lk 21:29, 30.

When. Mk 11:13.

33 **when**. ver. 3, 15.

know. Ezk 7:2, etc. Lk 21:31. Ep 5:16. 1 Th 5:1-5. He 10:37. Ja 5:8, 9. 1 P 4:7. Re 1:3.

it. *or,* he.

at the doors. Ja 5:9. Re 3:20.

34 **This generation**. Mt +3:7. 11:16. +12:39, 41, 42, 45. 16:4, +28. 17:17. 23:36. Nu 32:13. Dt 32:5, 20. Ps 22:30. 24:6. 78:8. Mk 8:12, 38. 9:19. 13:30, 31. Lk 7:31. 9:41. 11:29-32, 50, 51. 17:25. 21:32, 33. Ac 2:40. 1 P 2:9.

not pass. Mt +5:18. Ps +102:28. Am 9:8, 9.

till. Mt +16:28. +23:39. Lk 9:27.

35 **Heaven**. Mt 5:18. Ps +89:37. 102:26. Is 34:4. *51:6.* 54:10. Je 31:35, 36. +33:25. Lk 16:17. He 1:11, 12. 12:27. 2 P 3:7-13. Re 6:14. 20:11. 21:1.

my words. Nu +23:19. Ps 19:7. 89:34. 119:89, 152. Pr +30:5. Is 40:8. 55:11. T 1:2. 1 P 1:23, 25. Re 3:14.

not. Mt +5:18.

36　**of that day**. 2 Th +1:10.
knoweth no. ver. +42, 44. Mt 25:13. Zc 14:7. Mk +13:32. Ac 1:7. 1 Th 5:1, 2. 2 P 3:10. Re 3:3. 16:15.
my Father. Mt +10:32. Jn +14:28.

37　**days of Noe**. Ge 6:5, 11-13. 7:7. Jb 22:15-17. Am 6:3-6. Lk 17:26, 27. 1 Th 5:3. He 11:7. 1 P 3:20, 21. 2 P 2:5. 3:5, 6.
so shall. ver. 27.
the coming. Gr. parousia, ver. +3.

38　**they were eating**. Ge 6:2. 1 S 25:36-38. 30:16, 17. Is 22:12-14. Ezk +16:49, 50. Am 6:3-6. Lk 12:19, 45. 14:18-20. 17:26-28. +21:34, 35. Ro 13:13, 14. 1 C 7:29-31.
marrying. Mt 22:30.
Noe entered. Ge 7:13-24.

39　**knew not**. Mt 13:13-15. Jg 20:34. Pr 23:35. 24:12. 29:7. Is 1:3. 42:25. 44:18, 19. Lk 19:44. Jn 3:20. Ac 13:41. Ro 1:28. 1 Th 5:3. 2 P 3:5.
the coming. Gr. parousia, ver. +3. 2 Th 2:8.

40　**the one**. Mt +13:30, 40. 2 Ch 33:12-24. Lk 17:34-37. 23:39-43. 1 C 4:7. 2 P 2:5, 7-9.
taken. Mt 24:31. Pr 14:32. Is 57:1. Je 11:11. Mi +4:12. Re 14:14-16.
left. Ps 37:9-11. 101:5, 6. Lk 18:8. 1 Th 4:17. 2 Th 2:1.

41　**Two**. Ex 11:5.
grinding. Jg 16:21. Jb 31:10. Ec 12:3.
at the mill. Ex 11:5. Is 47:2.
taken. ver. 39. Mt +13:30, 40. Je 11:11. Mi 4:12. Lk 17:34, 37.
and the other. Mt 21:44. Ex 14:20. 1 S 5:11. Ho 14:9. 1 P 2:6-8.
left. Is 24:6. Lk 18:8. 1 Th 4:15, 17.

42　**Watch**. ver. 44. Mt 25:13. 26:38-41. Ps 127:1. Pr 8:34. Mk 13:33-37. 14:34-38. Lk 12:35-40. 18:1. +21:36. Ac 20:31. Ro 13:11. 1 C 16:13. Ep +6:18. Col 4:2. 1 Th 5:6. 2 T 4:5. He 13:17. 1 P 4:7. 5:8. Re 3:2, 3. 16:15.
for. ver. 36, 44. Mk 13:33-35.
ye know not. ver. 36, 44. Mt 25:13. Da +9:27. 12:7. Mk 13:33. Ac 1:6, 7. 1 Th 5:1, 2. Re 12:6, 14. 13:5.
your Lord. Jn 13:13.

43　**But know**. Lk 12:39-46.
if. Mt +23:30.
goodman. Mt 20:11. Pr 7:19.
had. Lk 12:39. 1 Th 5:2-6. 2 P 3:10, 11.
in what watch. Mk 13:35.
the thief. Jl 2:9. 1 Th 5:2, 4. 2 P 3:10. Re 3:3. 16:15.
have watched. ver. 42.
would not. Ex 22:2, 3.
broken. Mt 6:19.

44　**be ye also ready**. ver. +42. Mt 25:10, 13. Ph

4:5. 1 Th 5:6. T 3:1. Ja 5:9. 2 P 3:12. Re 19:7. 22:14.
think not. Je 17:15. Lk 12:40. 2 P 3:4.
Son of man. Mt +8:20.
cometh. ver. +3. Mt 16:27. Lk 17:30. 18:8.

45　**Who then is**. Lk 12:41-43. 16:10-12. 19:17. Ac +20:28. 1 C 4:1, 2. 1 T 1:12. 2 T 2:2. He 3:5. 1 P 4:10, 11. Re 2:13.
faithful. Mt +13:52. +25:21. Ge +18:19. 2 K 12:15. Ps 101:2, 6. Je +23:28. Ezk 13:7. 1 C +4:2. Col +1:7. 2 T +2:2. He 3:5. 1 P 4:10.
wise. Mt 25:2. Da +11:33. 12:3. Col 1:28.
servant. Mt +10:24, 25. +20:27. +23:11. Mk 13:34. Ro 12:3. Ph 2:3.
ruler. Mt 25:21. Ps +149:9. 2 C 1:24. 1 T 3:5. 5:17. 2 T 2:12. He 13:7, 17, 24. 1 P 5:1-3. Re 2:27.
household. Ro +16:5. Ga 6:10. Ep 2:19. He 3:5, 6.
to give. Mt +13:52. 25:35-40. Pr 31:15. Ezk 34:2. Jn 21:15-17. Ac +20:28. 1 C 3:1, 2. Ep +4:11-13. 1 P 5:1-3.
meat. Mt 4:4. 6:11. 2 K 25:29. Jb 36:31. Ps +104:27. 145:15. Pr +27:27. 31:15. Je 3:15. Da +11:33. 1 C 3:2.
due season. Mt +21:41, 43. Ge 17:21. Le 23:2. Nu 28:2. 2 K 25:30. 1 Ch +12:32. Ps 104:27. Ec 10:17. Je 8:7. Da 12:4, 7, 9, 10. Lk +12:42. 2 T 4:2. He +3:13. +4:16.

46　**Blessed**. Mt 25:34. Lk 12:37, 43. Ph 1:21-23. 2 T 4:6-8. 1 P 5:4. 2 P 1:13-15. 1 J 3:17. Re 2:19. 16:15.
find so doing. 2 Ch 35:15.

47　**ruler over**. Ps +149:5-9. Da +12:3. Lk 12:37, 44. Jn 12:26. Re +5:10. 21:7.

48　**if**. Mt +4:9. Mt 18:32. 25:26. Lk 19:22.
say. Dt 9:4. 15:9. 2 K 5:26. Is 32:6. Mk 7:21. Lk +12:45. Jn 13:2. Ac 5:3. 8:22.
delayeth. Mt 25:5. Ex 9:4. 15:9. 32:1. 2 K 5:26. Ec +8:11. Is 32:6. Ezk 12:22, 27. Hab 2:3. Mk 7:21. Lk +12:45. Jn 13:2. Ac 5:3. 8:22. He 10:36, 37. 2 P 3:3-5. Re 22:7, 12, 20.

49　**to smite**. Is 66:5. 2 C +1:24. 11:20. 1 P +5:3. 3 J 9, 10. Re 13:7. 16:6. 17:6. 19:2.
and to. Mt 7:15. 1 S 2:13-16, 29. Is 56:12. Ezk 34:3. Mi 3:5. Ro 16:18. Ph 3:19. T 1:11, 12. 2 P 2:13, 14. Ju 12.
drink. Jn 2:10. 1 Th 5:7.

50　**come**. ver. 42-44. Mt 25:19. Pr 29:1. Lk 20:16. 1 Th 5:2, 3. Re 3:3.
in a day. Mt 25:13. 2 P 3:12.

51　**cut him asunder**. or, cut him off. 2 S 12:31. 1 Ch 20:3. Am 1:3. He 11:37.
and appoint. Jb 20:29. Ps 11:6. Is 33:14. Lk 12:46.
portion. 1 C 9:23.
hypocrites. Mt +6:2. 7:21-27. 25:3, 11, 12. Lk 12:46. Jn 10:28, 29. 2 P 2:20-22.
there shall. Mt +25:30. Re 14:3.

MATTHEW 25

1 Then. Mt 24:42-51. Lk +21:34-36.
the kingdom. Mt +4:17.
ten. Ps 45:14. SS 1:3. 5:8, 16. 6:1, 8, 9. Lk 19:13. 1 C 11:2. Re 14:4.
which. Mt 5:16. Lk 12:35, 36. Ph 2:15, 16.
lamps. Jn 18:3. Ac 20:8. Re 4:5. 8:10.
went. 2 T 4:8. T 2:13. 2 P 1:13-15. 3:12, 13.
the bridegroom. Mt 9:15. 22:2. Ps 45:9-11. Is 54:5. 62:4, 5. Ho 2:19. Mk 2:19, 20. Lk 5:34, 35. Jn 3:29. 2 C 11:2. Ep 5:25-33. Ja 4:4. Re 19:7. 21:2, 9.

2 And five. Mt 7:24-27. 13:19-23, 38-43, 47, 48. 22:10, 11. Je 24:2. 1 C 10:1-5. 1 J 2:19. Ju 5.
foolish. Mt 7:26. 23:17. 1 C 1:18.
wise. Mt 7:24. +10:16. +24:45. Ge 41:39. Lk +16:8. 1 C 4:10.

3 foolish. Mt 23:25, 26. Is 48:1, 2. 58:2. Ezk +33:31. Ro 8:9. 2 T 3:5. He +12:15. Re 3:1, 15, 16.

4 oil. Ps +45:7. Zc 4:2, 3. Jn 1:15, 16. 3:34. Ro 8:9. 2 C 1:22. Ga 5:22, 23. 1 J 2:20, 27. Ju 19.

5 tarried. ver. +19. +24:48. Hab 2:3. Lk 12:45. 20:9. He 10:36, 37. 2 P 3:4-9. Re 2:25.
they. Mt 26:40, 43. SS 3:1. 5:2. Is 5:27. Jon 1:5, 6. Mk 13:35, 37. 14:37, 38. Lk 18:8. Ro 13:11, 12. Ep 5:14. 1 Th 5:6-8. 1 P 5:8.

6 at midnight. Mt 24:44. Ex 11:4, 6. Mk 13:33-37. Lk 12:20, 38-40, 46. 1 Th 5:1-3. Re 16:15.
a cry. Mt 24:31. Jn 5:28, 29. 1 C 15:52. 1 Th +4:16. 2 P 3:10.
Behold. ver. 31. Ps 50:3-6. 96:13. 98:9. 2 Th 1:7-10. Ju 14, 15.
go. ver. 1. Is 25:9. Am 4:12. Ml 3:1, 2. Re 19:7-9.

7 Then all. Lk 12:35. Ro 13:12. 2 P 3:14. Re 2:4, 5. 3:2, 19, 20.

8 Give us. Mt 3:9. 5:42. Lk 16:24. Ac 8:24. Re 3:9.
for. Mt +13:20, 21. +24:13. Jb 8:13, 14. 18:5. 21:17. Pr +4:18, 19. +13:9. 20:20. Lk +8:18. 12:35. Col 1:23. He +3:14. Re 2:10.
gone out. *or*, going out. He 4:1.

9 Not so. Mt 5:42.
lest. Ps 49:7-9. Je 15:1. Ezk 14:14-16, 20. 18:20.
but. Is 55:1-3, 6, 7. Ac 8:22. Re 3:17, 18.
buy for yourselves. Mt 13:44.

10 the bridegroom. ver. 6. Re 1:7. 22:12, 20.
ready. ver. 20-23. Mt 24:44. Am 8:12, 13. Lk 12:36, 37. 13:24, 25. Col 1:12. 2 T 4:8. 1 P 1:13.
with him. Is 40:10.
to the marriage. Mt 22:2. Re 19:7, 9.
door was shut. Ge 7:16. Nu 14:28-34. Ps 95:11. Lk 13:25. He 3:18, 19. Re 22:11.

11 saying. Mt +7:21-23. He 12:16, 17.

12 I know you not. Mt 7:23. 10:33. Ps 1:6. 5:5.

6:8. +50:16. Hab 1:13. Lk 13:25-30. Jn 9:31. 10:14, 27. 1 C 8:3. Ga 4:9. 2 T 2:19.

13 Watch. Mt +24:42. Lk +21:34-36.
know neither. Mt 24:37-39, 50. Ec +9:12. Mk 13:32-36. Lk 17:24, 28-30. +21:35, 36. Ac +1:7.

14 as. Mt 21:33. Mk 13:34. Lk 17:22. 19:12, 13. 20:9.
far country. ver. +19. Mt 21:33. 26:11. Lk 15:13.
and delivered. Lk 16:1-12. Ro 12:6-8. 1 C 3:5. 4:1, 2. 12:4, 7-29. Ep 4:11, 12. 1 P 4:9-11.

15 talents. Mt 18:24. Lk +12:48. 19:13, 14.
to every. Ro 12:6. 1 C 4:2. 12:7, 11, 29. 2 C 6:1. Ep 4:7. 2 T 1:6. 1 P 4:10. 2 P 1:8.

16 went. 2 S 7:1-3. 1 Ch 13:1-3. ch. 22-26. 28:2, etc. 29:1-17. 2 Ch 1:9, 10. 15:8-15. 17:3-9. 19:4-10. 31:20, 21. 33:15, 16. ch. 34, 35. Ne 5:14-19. Is 23:18. 49:23. 60:5-16. Ac 13:36. Ro 15:18, 19. 1 C 9:16-23. 15:10. 1 T 6:17, 18. 2 T 2:6. 4:5-8. Phm 6, 7. 3 J 5-8.

17 he also. Ge +18:19. 2 S 19:32. 1 K 18:3, 4. 2 K 4:8-10. Jb 29:11-17. 31:16-22. Pr 3:9, 10. Ec 11:1-6. Mk 14:3-8. Ac 9:36-39. 10:2. 11:29, 30. 2 C 8:12. 9:11-14. Ga 6:9, 10. Ep 5:16. Col 4:17. 1 T 5:10. 2 T 1:16-18. He 6:10, 11. 1 P 4:10.

18 and hid. Pr 18:9. 26:13-16. Hg 1:2-4. Ml 1:10. Lk 19:20. He 6:12. 2 P 1:8.

19 a long. ver. 5, 14. Mt 9:15. 21:33. 24:48. Dt 28:59. Ps 102:13, 16. Is 32:10. La 5:20, 21. Ezk +38:8. Mk 13:31-37. Lk 5:35. 13:35. 17:22. 19:12. 20:9. Jn 7:33-36. 8:21-24. 12:35. 13:33. 16:5-7, 16-22. 17:11-13.
cometh. Mt 24:50. Lk 20:16.
reckoneth. Mt +10:15. 18:23, 24. Lk 16:1, 2, 19, etc. Ro 14:7-12. 1 C 3:12-15. 2 C 5:10. Ja 3:1.

20 behold. Lk 19:16, 17. Ac 20:24. 1 C 15:10. Col 1:29. 2 T 4:1-3. Ja 2:18.

21 Well done. 2 Ch 31:20, 21. Lk 16:10. Ro 2:29. 1 C 4:5. 2 C 5:9. 10:18. 1 P 1:7.
faithful servant. ver. 23. Mt +24:45. 2 K 12:15.
a few things. Lk 16:10. 1 C +4:2. 1 T 3:13.
I will. ver. 34-40, 46. Mt +5:12. +24:47. Pr 12:24. Lk 12:44. 22:28-30. Re 2:10, +26-28. 3:21. 21:7.
enter. ver. 23. Ne 8:10. Ps 16:10, 11. Jn 12:26. 14:3. 15:11. 17:24. Ro 8:17. Ph 1:23. 2 T 2:12. He 12:2. 1 P 1:8. 2 P 1:11. Re 7:17.

22 I have. Lk 19:18, 19. Ro 12:6-8. 2 C 8:1-3, 7, 8, 12.

23 Well. ver. 21. Mk 12:41-44. 14:8, 9.
been faithful. ver. 29. Mt +13:12.

24 and said. Ezk +33:20.
Lord. Mt 7:21. Lk 6:46.
I knew. Mt 20:12. 1 S 25:3. Jb +1:22. +2:10. 21:14, 15. Ps +9:10. Pr +19:3. Is +29:24. 58:3. Je 2:31. 44:16-18. Ezk +18:25-29. Ml 1:12,

.13. 3:14, 15. Lk 15:29. 19:20-22. Ro 8:7.
+9:14, 20.

reaping where. 2 C 8:12.

gathering. Is 18:5.

25 **I was afraid**. Ge +19:30. 2 S 6:9, 10. Ps
+9:10. Pr 26:13. Is 57:11. Ro 8:15. 2 T 1:6, 7.
Re +21:8.

and went. ver. 18.

thou hast. Mt 20:14.

26 **Thou wicked**. Mt 18:32. Jb 15:5, 6.

and slothful. Pr 19:15. 20:4. Ec +10:18. Je
+48:10. Ro +12:11. He 6:12.

27 **oughtest**. Is +24:2. Ro 3:19. Ju 15.

should. Mt +23:30.

with usury. Dt 23:19, 20. Is +24:2.

28 **Take therefore**. Lk 10:42. 19:24.

29 **unto**. Mt +13:12. Lk 16:9-12. Jn 1:16.

shall be taken. Mt 21:41. La 2:6. Ho 2:9. Lk
10:42. 12:19-21. 16:1-3, 20-25. Jn 11:48. Re
2:5.

30 **cast**. Mt 3:10. 5:13. Je 15:1, 2. Ezk 15:2-5. Lk
14:34, 35. Jn 15:6. T 3:14. He 6:7, 8. Re 3:15,
16.

unprofitable servant. Lk 17:10.

outer darkness. Mt +8:12. Re +21:8.

gnashing. Mt 8:12. 13:42, 49, 50. 22:13.
24:51. Ps 112:10. Is 65:14. 66:24. Lk 13:28.
Re 16:10, 11.

31 **Son of man**. ver. 6. Mt +8:20. 16:27. 19:28.
26:64. Da 7:13, 14. Zc 14:5. Mk 8:38. 14:62.
Lk 9:26. 22:69. Jn 1:51. 5:27-29. Ac +1:11. 1
Th 4:16. 2 Th 1:7, 8. He +1:8. Ju 14. Re +1:7.

shall come. Mt +24:30. Re +1:7.

in his glory. Mt 16:27. +24:30. Lk 9:26. Jn
+1:14. Col +3:4.

angels with him. Zc +14:5. Lk 12:8. Ju 14.

then. Mt 19:28. Ps 9:7. Re 3:21. 20:11.

sit upon. Jl 3:12.

the throne. 2 S 12:30. Zc 6:13. Lk +1:32. Ac
+2:30. Re +3:21.

of his glory. Ps 102:15, 16. Zc 6:13. Col +3:4.
1 Th 2:12.

32 **before**. Ps +7:8.

gathered. Mt +24:31. 2 S 12:31. Is 34:8-12.
Jl 3:2, 11, 12. Zp +3:8.

all nations. Mt 24:14. 28:19, 20. Jl +3:12. Ro
14:10. 16:26.

he shall separate. Mt 3:12. +5:20. +13:30,
42, 43, 49. 22:11-13. Ge 30:33. 2 S 12:31. Ps
1:5. 50:3-5. Je +43:11. Ezk 20:38. 34:17-22.
Ml 3:18. Lk 16:26. 1 C 4:5.

as. Ps 78:52. Jn 10:14, 27.

33 **the sheep**. Ps 79:13. 95:7. 100:3. Jn 10:26-
28. 21:15-17.

his right. Ge +48:13, 14, 17-19. Ps 45:9.
110:1. Ec 10:2. Mk 16:19. Ac 2:34, 35. Ep
1:20. He 1:3.

34 **the King**. ver. 40. Mt 22:11-13. 27:37. 1 S
12:12. Ps 24:7-10. Is 6:5. 32:1, 2. 33:17, 22. Je
+10:10. Lk 1:31-33. Jn +1:49.

right hand. 1 K 2:19. Ps 45:9. 110:1.

Come. ver. 21, 23, 41. Mt 5:3-12. Ge +12:2,
3. Dt 11:23-28. Ps 37:22. 115:13-15. Is 65:23.
Lk 11:28. Ac 3:26. Ga 3:13, 14. Ep 1:3. 1 Th
2:12. 1 P 1:3.

inherit. Mt 19:29. Zc 2:12. Ac +20:32. Ro
4:13. 1 C +6:9. Ga 5:21. 2 T 2:12. 4:1, 8. T 3:7.
He 1:14. 6:12, 17. 12:28. Ja 2:5. 1 P 3:9. Re
+5:10. 21:7.

the kingdom. Mt +6:10. +24:14.

prepared. Mt 20:23. Mk 10:40. Jn 14:2, 3. 1
C 2:9. He 11:16.

from. Mt +13:35.

world. Gr. *kosmos*, Mt +4:8.

35 **I was an hungered**. ver. 40. Mt 10:40-42.
26:11. Dt 15:7-11. Jb 29:13-16. 31:16-21. Ps
112:5-10. Pr 3:9, 10. 11:24, 25. 14:21, 31.
19:17. 22:9. Ec 11:1, 2. Is 58:7-11. Ezk 18:7,
16. Da 4:27. Mi +6:8. Mk 14:7. Lk 11:41.
14:12-14. Jn 13:29. Ac 4:32. 9:36-39. 10:31.
11:29. 2 C 8:1-4, 7-9. 9:7-14. Ga 6:10. Ep
4:28. 1 T 6:17-19. Phm 7. He 6:10. 13:16. Ja
1:27. 2:15, 16. 1 P 4:9, 10. 1 J 3:16-19.

thirsty. ver. 42. Pr 25:21. Ro 12:20.

gave me drink. Mt +10:42.

I was a stranger. ver. 43. Ge 18:2-8. 19:1-3.
22:21. 23:9. Dt 1:16. +26:11. Jg 19:20, 21. Ml
+3:5. Ac 16:15. Ro 12:13. +15:7. 16:23. 1 T
3:2. T 1:8. 1 P 4:9.

36 **Naked**. Jb 31:19, 20. Lk 3:11. Jn 21:7. Ja
2:14-16.

clothed. 2 Ch 28:15. Pr 31:20.

was sick. ver. 43. Ps 41:6-8. Ezk 34:4. Lk
10:33, 34. Ac 20:35. 28:8, 9. Ja 1:27. 5:14, 15.

I was in prison. Ph 4:10-14. 2 T 1:16-18. He
10:34. 13:3.

37 **when**. Mt 6:3. 1 Ch 29:14. Pr 15:33. Is 64:6.
1 C 15:10. 1 P 5:5, 6.

40 **the King**. ver. 34. Pr 25:6, 7.

Inasmuch. Mt +10:42. 2 S 9:1, 7. Pr 14:31.
19:17. Mk 9:41. Jn 19:26, 27. 21:15-17. 1 C
16:21, 22. 2 C 4:5. 5:14, 15. 8:7-9. Ga 5:6, 13,
22. 1 Th 4:9, 10. 1 P 1:22. 1 J 3:14-19. 4:7-12,
20, 21. 5:1, 2.

unto one. Mt 6:29. 18:10. Lk 15:7, 10.

the least. Mt +10:42. 12:49, 50. 18:5, 6, 10.
28:10. Mk 3:34, 35. Jn 20:17. Ro 8:29. 1 C
12:26, 27. He 2:11-15. 6:10.

ye have done it unto me. Mt 27:55. Ge
40:14. Nu 3:6. Ac 9:4, 5. 1 C 12:26, 27. Ep
5:30. He 6:10.

41 **them**. ver. 33.

Depart. Mt +7:23. Ps +6:8. +9:17.

ye cursed. Ge +12:3. Dt 27:15-26. 28:15, 20.
Ps 37:22. 119:21. Pr +3:33. Is 24:6. 65:15, 20.
Je 17:5. +26:6. La +3:65. Zc +5:3. 1 C 16:22.
Ga 3:10, 13. He 6:8.

everlasting. Gr. *aionios*, Mt +18:8. ver. +46.
Mt +3:12. 13:30, 40, 42, 50. 18:8. Ps 21:9. Is
30:33. 33:14. +66:24. Mk 9:43-48. Lk +16:23,

24. 2 Th 1:8, 9. Ju 7. Re 14:10, 11. 20:10-15.
21:8.

fire. Re 19:20.

prepared for. Mt 8:29. Ja 2:19. Re 14:11.
20:10.

the devil. Jn 8:44. Ro 9:22, 23. 2 P 2:4. 1 J
3:10. Ju 6. Re 12:7-9.

his angels. 2 C 12:7. 2 P 2:4. Ju 6.

42 I was an hungered. ver. 35. Mt 10:37, 38.
12:30. Jb 22:7. Am 6:6. Jn 5:23. 8:42-44.
14:21. 1 C 16:22. 2 Th 1:8. Ja 2:15-24. 1 J
3:14-17. 4:20.

43 stranger. Dt 27:19. Je 7:6. He 13:2.

took me not in. Dt 23:4. Jg 19:15. 1 S 25:10.
Lk 2:7. 9:53. Ro +15:7. 3 J 9, 10.

naked. ver. 36.

clothed me not. Ps +12:5. Ezk +16:49. Ja
2:15, 16. 1 J 3:17.

visited me not. Mt 8:15. 27:55. Ps 109:16.
Pr 21:13. Ezk 34:4. Zc 11:16. Lk 8:3. 16:20,
21. Ja 4:17.

44 when. ver. 24-27. Mt +7:22. 1 S 15:13-15,
20, 21. Je 2:23, 35. Ml 1:6. 2:17. 3:13. Lk
10:29.

45 Inasmuch. ver. 40. Ge +12:3. Ps 105:15. Pr
14:31. 17:5. 21:13. Zc +2:8. Jn 15:18, 19. 1 J
3:12-20. 5:1-3.

did it not. Lk 10:16. Ac 9:5. 1 C 8:12. Ja
+4:17.

46 everlasting. Gr. *aionios*, Mt +18:8.

punishment. ver. 41. Mt +13:30, 38, 40, 42.
26:24. 1 Ch +28:9. Jb +8:13. +27:8. Da +12:2.
Mk 3:29. 9:43, 44, 46, 48, 49. 14:21. Lk 3:17.
+9:24. +16:26. Jn 3:36. 5:29. Ac 24:15. Ro
2:5-9. 11:22. 2 C 5:11. +6:2. Ph 3:18, 19. 2 Th
1:7-9. He 10:31. Ja +1:15. Ju 6, 7, 13. Re
14:9-11. 20:10, 15. +21:8.

the righteous. Mt +13:43. 19:16. Ps +16:10,
11. Ro 5:19, 21.

into life. Lk 20:36. Jn 3:15, 16, 36. 4:14.
6:47, 51, 54. 10:27, 28. 11:25, 26. Ro 2:7.
6:23. Ga 6:8. T 1:2. 1 J 2:25. 5:11-13. Ju 21.

eternal. Gr. *aionios*, Mt +18:8.

MATTHEW 26

1 came to pass. Ge +38:1.

when. Mt 7:28. 11:1. 13:53. 19:1.

2 know. Mk 14:1, 2. Lk 22:1, 2, 15. Jn 13:1.

the feast. Ex 12:11-14. 34:25. Jn 2:13. 6:4.
11:55. 12:1.

passover. Le +23:5.

Son of man. Mt +8:20.

betrayed. ver. 24, 25. Mt +20:18.

crucified. Lk 24:6, 7.

3 assembled. Mt 21:45, 46. Ps 2:1, 2. 56:6.
64:4-6. 94:20, 21. Je 11:19. 18:18-20. Jn
11:47-53, 57. Ac 4:25-28.

the palace. ver. 58, 69. Je 17:27. Mk 14:54,
66. 15:16. Lk 11:21. 22:55. Jn 18:15. Re 11:2.

Caiaphas. i.e. *searcher, depression*, **S#2533g**. ver.
3, 57. Lk 3:2. Jn 11:49. 18:13, 14, 24, 28. Ac
4:6.

4 consulted. Mt 21:46. Ps 2:2. Jn 11:53.

by. Mt 23:33. Ge 3:1. Ac 7:19. 13:10. 2 C
11:3.

5 Not. Ps 76:10. Pr 19:21. +21:30. Is 46:10. La
3:37. Mk 14:2, 12, 27. Lk 22:7. Jn 18:28. Ac
4:28.

lest. Mt 14:5. 21:26, 46. 27:24. Lk 20:6. 22:6.

6 in Bethany. Jn +11:18.

Simon. Mk 14:3.

leper. 2 K +5:1.

7 came. Jn 12:2, 3.

very. Ex 30:23-33. Ps 133:2. Ec 9:8. 10:1. SS
1:3. Is 57:9. Lk 7:37, 38, 46.

ointment. Ex +30:1. 1 Ch +9:30. SS +1:12.
Jn 12:3.

poured. Gr. *katacheo*, **S#2708g**. Mk 14:3.

8 they. Mt 20:24. 21:15. 1 S 17:28, 29. Ec 4:4.
Mk 14:4. Lk 13:14. Jn 12:4-6.

To. Ex 5:17. Am 8:5. Hg 1:2-4. Ml 1:7-10, 13.

9 this ointment. Jsh 7:20, 21. 1 S 15:9, 21. 2
K 5:20. Mk 14:5. Jn 12:5, 6. 13:29. 2 P 2:15.

sold. Dt +28:33.

10 understood. Mt 16:8.

Why. Jb 13:7. Mk 14:6. Lk 7:44-50. 11:7. Ga
1:7. 5:12. 6:17.

a good. Ne 2:18. 2 C 9:8. Ep 2:10. Col +1:10.
2 Th 2:17. 1 T 3:1. 5:10. 2 T 2:21. T 1:16.
2:14. 3:1, 8, 14. He 13:21. 1 P 2:12.

11 ye have. Mt 25:34-40, 42-45. Dt 15:11. Mk
14:7. Jn 12:8. Ga 2:10. 1 J 3:17.

the poor. Ex +23:3.

but. Mt 18:20. 25:14. 28:20. Jn 13:33. 14:19.
16:5, 28. 17:11. Ac +3:21.

ye have not. Mt 9:15. Mk 2:20. Lk 5:35.
Jn 7:33. 12:35. 13:33. 14:19. 16:5, 16-19,
28.

always. Gr. *pantote*, **S#3842g**. Rendered (1)
always: ver. 11. Mk 14:7, 7. Lk 18:1. Jn 8:29.
11:42. 12:8, 8. 18:20b. Ro 1:9. 1 C 1:4. 15:58.
2 C 2:14. 4:10. 5:6. 9:8. Ga 4:18. Ep 5:20. Ph
1:4, 20. 2:12. Col 1:3. 4:12. 1 Th 1:2. 3:6. 2 Th
1:3, 11. Phm 4. (2) *ever*: Lk 15:31. Jn 18:20a.
1 Th 4:17. 5:15. 2 T 3:7. He 7:25. (3) *alway*: Jn
7:6. Ph 4:4. Col 4:6. 1 Th 2:16. 2 Th 2:13. (4)
evermore: Jn 6:34. 1 Th 5:16.

12 For in that. 2 Ch 16:14. Mk 14:8. 16:1. Lk
23:56. 24:1. Jn 12:7. 19:39, 40.

13 Wheresoever. Mt 24:14. 28:19. Ps 98:2, 3. Is
52:10. Mk 13:10. 16:15. Lk 24:47. Ro 10:18.
15:19. Col 1:6, 23. 1 T 2:6. Re 14:6.

this gospel. Ac 20:24. Ep 1:13. 6:15.

world. Gr. *kosmos*, Mt +4:8.

there. 1 S 2:30. Ps 112:6. Pr 10:7. Mk 14:9. 2
C 10:18. He 6:10.

memorial. Ex +12:14. Ac 10:4.

14 one. Mk 14:10. Lk 22:3-6. Jn 13:2, 27, 30.

Judas. ver. 25, 47. Mt 10:4. 27:3. Mk 3:19.

Lk 6:16. Jn 6:70, 71. 12:4. 18:2. Ac 1:16, 17, 25.

Iscariot. Jsh 15:25. Je 48:24, 41.

15 **What**. Ge 38:16. Jg 16:5. 17:10. 18:19, 20. Is 56:11. Lk 22:5, 6. Jn 11:57. 1 T 3:3. 6:9, 10. 2 P 2:3, 14, 15.

covenanted with. or, weighed unto him. Ge 23:16. Je 32:9.

thirty. Mt 27:3-5, 9. Ge 37:26-28. Ex 21:32. Zc *11:12, 13*. Ac 1:18.

16 **he**. Mk 14:11. Lk 22:6.

to betray. Mt +20:18.

17 **the first**. Ex 12:6, 18-20. 13:6-8. Le 23:5, 6. Nu 28:16, 17. Dt 16:1-4. Mk 14:12. Lk 22:7.

unleavened. Le +23:6.

Where. Mt 3:15. 17:24, 25. Lk 22:8, 9.

the passover. Ex +12:21. Ac 12:3, 4.

18 **Go**. Mk 14:13-16. Lk 22:10-13.

The Master. ver. 49. Mt 21:3. +22:24. Mk 5:35. Jn 11:28. 20:16.

My time. ver. 2, 45. Jn +2:4.

keep the passover. Mt 3:15. He 11:28.

19 **the disciples**. Mt 21:6. Jn 2:5. 15:14.

and they. Ex 12:4-8. 2 Ch 35:10, 11.

passover. Le +23:5. Dt 16:6.

20 **when**. Mk 14:17-21. Lk 22:14-16. Jn 13:21.

he. Ex 12:11. SS 1:12.

21 **Verily**. ver. +2, 14-16. Ps 55:12-14. He 4:13. Re 2:23.

22 **exceeding sorrowful**. ver. 38. Mk 14:19, 20. Lk 22:23. Jn 13:22-25. 21:17.

23 **He that**. Ru 2:14. Ps 41:9. Mk 14:20. Lk 22:21. Jn 13:18, 26-28.

dippeth. Gr. *embapto*, **S#1686g**. Mk 14:20. Jn 13:26.

24 **Son of man goeth**. The present tense used for something which will soon be past. Mt 26:28, 45. Mk 14:24, 41. Lk 22:19, 22. 24:49. Jn 20:17. 1 C 11:24. 2 T 4:6.

written. ver. 54, 56. Ge +3:15. Ps ch. 22. 69:1-21. Is 50:5, 6. ch. 53. Da +9:26. Zc 12:10. 13:7. Mk 9:12. Lk 18:31. 22:22. 24:25-27, 44, 46. Jn 7:33. 8:21, 22. 14:12. 16:28. 19:24, 28, 36, 37. Ac 2:23. 4:28. 13:27-29. 17:2, 3. 26:22, 23. 28:23. 1 C +15:3. 1 P 1:10, 11.

but. Mt 18:7. 27:3-5. Ps 55:15, 23. 109:6-19. Ob 7. Mi 7:6. Mk 14:21. Lk 17:1. 22:22. Jn 17:12. Ac 1:16-20.

good for. Mt 18:6. Jb 3:1-19. Je 20:14-18. Jn 17:12.

if he. Mt +23:30.

25 **Judas**. ver. 14. 2 K 5:25. Pr 30:20.

Master. ver. 49. Jn 1:38.

Thou hast said. "Thou sayest" is not an idiom which conveys a simple affirmation or consent, but means "thou (and not I) hast said it," denoting "those are your words, not mine." ver. 64. Mt +27:11. Lk 22:70. Jn 18:37.

26 **as**. Mk 14:22-25. Lk 22:18-20. 2 C 11:23-25.

Jesus. Lk 24:30. 1 C 11:23-25.

blessed it. "Many Greek copies have *gave thanks*." Lk +24:30.

and brake. Is +58:7. Ac 2:46. 20:7. 1 C 10:16, 17.

Take. Mk 14:22. Jn 6:33-35, 47-58. 1 C 11:26-29.

this. Ezk 5:4, 5. Lk 22:20. Jn 6:53. 1 C 10:4, 16. Ga 4:24, 25.

is. Ge +49:9.

my body. Jn 6:51.

27 **he took**. Mk 14:23, 24. Lk 22:20.

gave thanks. Mt 15:36.

Drink. Ps 116:13. SS 5:1. 7:9. Is 25:6. 55:1. Mk 14:23. 1 C 10:16. 11:28.

ye all. Ex 12:47. Lk 22:17.

28 **For this**. Mk 14:24.

my. Ex 24:7, 8. Le +17:11. Je 31:31. Zc 9:11. Mk 14:24. Lk 22:19. 1 C 11:25. He 9:14-22. 10:4-14, 29. 13:20.

blood. Ex 12:13. +24:8. Ac 20:28. Ep 1:7. Col 1:14. Re +1:5. 5:9.

the new. Ex 19:5. Je 31:31. Mk 14:24. Lk 22:20. 1 C 11:25. 2 C 3:6. He 8:8, 13. 9:14-18. 12:24.

testament. He 9:15.

shed for. Mt 1:21. Mk 10:45. Jn 10:11. 11:50-53. Ro 8:32-34. Ep 5:25-27. He 2:17. 3:1. 9:28.

many. Notice that when "many" is used in a contrast (as with *one*, or one person, Christ), it clearly means *all* (Ro 5:12, 15, 19). Mt +20:28. Is +53:12. Jn +1:9. Ro 5:12, 15, +18, 19. Ep 1:7. Col 1:14, 20. He 9:22, 28. 1 J 2:2. Re 7:9, 14.

for. Mk 1:4mg. Lk 1:77mg.

remission. Ro 3:25. He 9:22.

sins. Le +5:6.

29 **I will**. Ps 4:7. 104:15. Is 24:9-11. Mk 14:25. Lk 22:15-18.

not. Mt +5:18.

until. Mt 6:10. 7:21, 22. 18:20. 19:28. 28:20. Ps 40:3. SS 5:1. Is 53:11. Zp 3:17. Zc 9:17. Mk 14:25. Lk 14:15. 15:5, 6, 23-25, 32. 22:18, 29, 30. Jn 15:11. 16:22. 17:13. Ac +1:6. 10:41. He 12:2. Re 5:8-10. 14:3. 19:9.

drink it. Is 25:6. Zc 10:7.

with you. Mt +19:28. Is 25:6, 34. Jn +14:3. Re 3:20. 7:17.

Father's kingdom. Mt +6:10. Jn +14:2.

30 **when**. Ps 81:1-4. Mk 14:26. Ep 5:19, 20. Col 3:16, 17.

hymn. *or*, psalm.

they went. Ex 12:22. Jn 14:31. 18:1-4.

mount of Olives. Mt +21:1.

31 **All**. ver. 56. Mt +11:6. Lk 22:31, 32. Jn 16:32.

I will. Is 53:10. Zc *13:7*.

and the. Jb 6:15-22. 19:13-16. Ps 38:11. 69:20. 88:18. La 1:19. Ezk 34:5, 6.

32 I am. Mt 16:21. 20:19. 27:63, 64. Mk 9:9, 10. Lk 18:33, 34.
I will. Mk +16:7.

33 Though. 1 C +15:2; Lk +11:8. Mt 23:12. Mk 14:29. Lk 22:31, 33. Jn 13:36-38. 21:15.
yet. Ps 17:5. 119:116, 117. Pr 16:18, 19. 20:6. 28:25, 26. Je +17:9. Ro 12:10. Ph +2:3. 1 P 5:5, 6.

34 Jesus said. Lk 22:31-34. Jn 13:38.
That. ver. 75. Mk 14:30, 31. Lk 22:34. Jn 13:38.

35 Peter said. Lk 22:33. Jn 13:36, 37.
Though. Mt +4:9. Mt 20:22, 23. Pr 28:14, 26. 29:23. Je +17:9. Mk 14:31. Jn 11:16. Ro 11:20. 1 C 10:12. Ph 2:12. 1 P 1:17.
not. Mt +5:18.
Likewise. Mt 20:24. Ex 19:8.

36 a place. Mk 14:32-35. Lk 22:39-46. Jn 18:1, etc.
Gethsemane. i.e. *press for olives, oil press,* **S#1068g**. Mt 26:36. Mk 14:32. Compare **S#1660h**, *gath*, Jg +6:11 and **S#8081h**, *shemen*, Ge +20:18. Ex +29:40.
while. ver. 39, 42. Ps 22:1, 2. 69:1-3, 13-15. He 5:7.

37 Peter. Mt 4:18, 21. 17:1. 20:20. Mk 5:37.
sorrowful. Ps 42:5, 6. 43:5. Mk 14:33, 34. Lk 22:44. Jn 12:27. Ph 2:26.

38 My soul. Gr. *psyche*, Mt +12:18.
sorrowful. Jb 6:2-4. Ps 69:20. 88:1-7, 14-16. 116:3. Is 53:3, 10. Lk 18:23. Ro 8:32. 2 C 5:21. Ga +3:13. 1 P 2:24. 3:18.
unto death. 2 K 20:1. 2 Ch 32:24. Is 38:1. Jon 4:9.
tarry. ver. 40. Mt 25:13. 1 P 4:7.
and watch. ver. 41. Mt 24:42.

39 he went. Lk 22:41, 42, 44.
and fell. Ge +17:3.
and prayed. Mk 1:35. 14:35, 36. Lk 22:41, 42. He 5:7.
O my Father. ver. 42. Lk +22:42.
if. 1 C +15:2. Mt 24:24. Mk 13:22.
let this. Mt 20:22. Lk 22:41, 42. Jn 18:11.
cup. Mt 20:22. Lk 12:50. He 2:10.
pass from. Ex 12:23, LXX.
not as I will. ver. 42. Mt 6:10. 2 S 15:26. Jn 5:30. 6:38. 12:28. 14:31. Ro 15:1-3. Ph 2:8.

40 and findeth. ver. 43. Mt 25:5. SS 5:2. Mk 13:36. 14:37. Lk 9:32. 22:45.
What. ver. 35. Jg 9:38. 1 S 26:15, 16. 1 K 20:11.
watch. Mt 24:42.

41 Watch. Mt 6:13. +24:42. Pr 1:10. Lk +21:36. 22:40, 46. Ep +4:27.
enter. Mt 6:13. Pr 4:14, 15. Lk 8:13. 11:4. 1 C 10:13. 2 P 2:9. Re +3:10.
temptation. Ge 32:24-26. Ex 17:3, 4. Jb 1:20-22. 23:8-10. 34:31, 32. Ps 57:1-3. La 3:53-57. Da 6:10. Zc 13:9. Lk 22:31, 32. 2 C 12:7, 8. Ep 6:16-18. He 4:15, 16. 1 P 5:8-10.

the spirit. Gr. *pneuma*. "Spirit" put for that which is invisible as opposed to the flesh, whether in reference to the will, mind, what is spiritual in contrast with what is out-ward and corporate, or in reference to supernatural judgment. Mk 14:38. Ac 17:16. 18:5. 1 C 5:4. 2 C +12:18. Ph 1:27. 2:1. 2 Th 2:8. "Spirit" is also put for living or life-giving food, Jn 6:63b; for the gospel, 2 C 3:6; for the reason, 1 C 2:12a. For the other uses of *pneuma* see Mt +8:16.
is willing. Ps 119:4, 5, 24, 25, 32, 35-37, 115, 117, 173, 174. Is +26:8, 9. Ro 7:18-25. 8:3. 1 C 9:27. Ga 5:16, 17, 24. Ph 3:12-14.
but the flesh. Ps 103:14. Ph 4:10.

42 the second. ver. 39. Ge +22:15. Ps 22:1, 2. 69:1-3, 17, 18. 88:1, 2. Mk 14:39, 40. He +4:15. 5:7, 8.
O my Father. ver. 39. Mt 6:10. Ro 5:19.
if. 1 C +15:2.

43 for. Pr 23:34. Jon 1:6. Lk 9:32. Ac 20:9. Ro 13:1. 1 Th 5:6-8.

44 prayed. Mt +6:7. Da 9:17-19. Lk 18:1. 2 C 12:8.
third time. 1 S +23:4.
saying the same. ver. 39, 42.

45 Sleep on. 1 K 18:27. Ec 11:9.
the hour. ver. 2, 14, 15, 18. Jn +2:4.
Son of man. Mt +8:20.
is betrayed. ver. +24. Mt 17:22. 20:18. Mk 9:31. 10:33. Lk 9:44. 18:32.

46 let us be going. 1 S 17:48. Lk 9:51. 12:50. 22:15. Jn 14:31. Ac 21:13.

47 lo. ver. 14, 55. Mk 14:43. Lk 22:47, 48. Jn 18:1-8. Ac 1:16.

48 Whomsoever. 2 S 3:27. 20:9, 10. Ps 28:3. 55:20, 21.
hold. Mk 14:44.

49 Hail. Mt 27:29, 30. Mk 15:18. Jn 19:3.
master. ver. 25.
kissed him. Ge +27:27.

50 Friend. Mt +20:13. 22:12. 2 S 16:17. Ps 41:9. 55:12-14. Lk 22:48. Jn 7:4. 13:27.

51 one of them. ver. 35. Mk 14:47. Lk 9:55. 22:36-38, 49-51. Jn 18:10, 11, 36. 2 C 10:4.
his sword. Lk +22:36, 38.
his ear. Lk 22:50.

52 Put up. Mt 5:39. Ge 49:5-7. Ex 20:13. Le 19:18. Nu +32:23. Jb +27:13. Ps 5:6. +58:11. Pr 17:14. 18:6. 20:22. +21:7. 24:29. 26:17. 30:33. Ezk +22:29. 25:12-14. 35:5, 6. Ho 4:2, 3. Am 1:11. Hab 2:12. Lk 3:14. 18:20. +22:36. Jn +18:11. Ro 12:17, 19. 1 C 4:11, 12. 2 C 10:4. 1 Th 5:14, 15. Ja 2:11. 3:16. 4:1, 12. 1 P 2:21-23. 3:9. Re 13:10.
they. Mt 23:34-36. Ge 9:6. 1 S 15:33. Ps 55:23. Ezk 35:5, 6. Re 11:18. 13:10. 16:6.
perish. Gr. *apollumi*, Mt +2:13.

53 Thinkest thou. Jn 10:18.
I cannot. Mt +11:23.

my Father. Jn 5:17.
and he. Mt 4:11. 25:31. 2 K 6:17. Ps +68:17.
Da 7:10. Jl 2:11. Lk 22:43. Jn 18:36. 2 Th 1:7.
Ju 14.
twelve. Mt 10:1, 2.
legions. Mk 5:9, 15. Lk 8:30.

54 **But how then**. ver. 24. Mt 1:22. Ps ch. 22,
69. Is ch. 53. Da +9:24-26. Zc 13:7. Lk 24:25,
26, 44-46. Jn +10:35. Ac 1:16.
the scriptures. ver. 56. Mt 21:42.
that thus. ver. 31, 56. Ps 88:8, 18. Is 53:7-10.
Jn 18:11.
must. Lk +13:33.

55 **Are ye come**. Mk 14:48-50. Lk 22:52, 53.
a thief. Mt 21:13. Mk 11:17. Lk 10:30. 19:46.
Jn 18:40.
I sat. Mk 12:35. Lk 2:46. 4:20. 21:37, 38. Jn
8:2. 18:20, 21.
with you. Ac 26:26. 2 P 1:16.
teaching. Mt 4:23. 9:35. 13:54. 21:23. Mk
1:21. 11:17. 12:35. Lk 19:47. 20:1. 21:37. Jn
7:14, 28. 8:20. 10:23. 18:20.

56 **that**. ver. 54. Mt 1:22. Ge +3:15. Is 44:26. La
4:20. Da +9:24, 26. Zc 13:7. Jn 6:45. Ac 1:16.
2:23.
Then. ver. 31. Ps 88:8, 18. Is 63:3. Mk 14:50-
52. Jn 16:32. 18:8, 9, 15, 16. 2 T 4:16.

57 **they that**. Ps 56:5, 6. Mk 14:53, 54. Lk
22:54, 55. Jn 11:49. 18:12-14, 24.
away to. Ac 16:40.
Caiaphas. ver. +3.

58 **afar off**. Pr 29:25.
palace. ver. 3, 57.
and went. Jn 18:15, 16, 25.
and sat. Ps +1:1.
the servants. Mt 5:25. Mk 14:54, 65. Jn
7:32, 45, 46. 18:3, 12, 22. 19:6. Ac 5:22, 26.

59 **all**. Mk 1:33. 14:55. Ac 2:47. 7:10. 15:22. Ph
1:13.
council. Mt 5:22.
sought. Ps 94:20, 21. Pr +6:19. Mk 14:55, 56.
Ac 24:1-13.

60 **found none**. Da 6:4, 5. T 2:8. 1 P 3:16.
At. Dt 19:15. Mk 14:57-59.
though many. Ps 27:12. 35:11.
found they none. He 7:26. 1 P 2:22.
came two. Mt 18:16. Dt 17:6. 19:15.

61 **This**. ver. 71. Mt 12:24. Ge 19:9. 1 K 22:27. 2
K 9:11. Ps 22:6, 7. Is 49:7. 53:3. Lk 23:2. Jn
9:29. Ac 6:14. 17:18. 18:13. 22:22.
I am. Mt 27:40. Je 26:8-11, 16-19. Mk 15:29.
Jn +2:19-21. Ac 6:13.
destroy. Mt 27:40.
the temple. Mt 23:16, 35. 27:5.
three days. Mt 16:21. 27:63. Mk 14:58, 59.
Jn +2:19.

62 **Answerest**. Mt 27:12-14. Mk 14:60. Lk 23:9.
Jn 18:19-24. 19:9-11.

63 **Jesus**. Ps +38:13. Da 3:16. Mk 14:61. 15:3-5.
Lk 23:9. Jn 19:9. 1 P 2:23.

I adjure. Le 5:1. 19:12. Nu 5:19-21. 1 S 3:17,
18. 14:24, 26, 28. 1 K 22:16. 2 Ch 18:15. Pr
29:24. Mk 5:7.
living God. Mt 16:16.
that. Mk 14:61. Lk 22:66-71. Jn 8:25. 10:24.
18:37.
the Christ. Mt +16:16. Is +9:6, 7.
the Son of God. Mt +14:33.

64 **Thou**. ver. 25. Mt 27:11. Mk 14:62. Lk 22:70.
Jn 18:37.
Hereafter. Mt +16:27. +24:30. +25:31. Da
+7:13. Lk 21:27. 25:31. Jn 1:50, 51. Ac +1:11.
Ro 14:10. 1 Th 4:16. Re +1:7. 20:11.
see. Mt +16:27. +24:3, 30. Ac +1:11. Re +1:7.
Son of man. Mt +8:20. Da 7:13, 14.
sitting. He +1:3.
the right hand. Ps +110:1.
coming. Mt +24:30. Jn 14:3. 1 Th 4:16. Re 1:7.
clouds. Ge +9:13. 2 Ch +5:13.

65 **the high priest**. Le 21:10. 2 K 18:37. 19:1-3.
Je 36:24. Mk 14:63, 64.
rent his clothes. Le 10:6. 21:10. 2 K +18:37.
blasphemy. Mk +14:64.

66 **He**. Le 24:11-16. 1 K 21:10, 13. Jn 10:33.
19:7. Ac 7:52. 13:27, 28. Ja 5:6.
guilty. or, worthy, or liable to. Mk 3:29.

67 **spit**. Mt 27:30. Nu 12:14. Dt 25:9. Jb 30:9-11.
Is 50:6. 52:14. 53:3. Mk 10:34. 14:65. 15:19.
Lk 18:32. 1 C 4:13. He 12:2.
smote him. Mt +27:30. Ps 69:20. He 5:7, 8.
the palms of their hands. or, rods. Mi 5:1.

68 **Prophesy**. Mt 27:39-44. Ge 37:19, 20. Jg
16:25. Mk 14:65. Lk 7:39. 22:63-65.
thou. Mt 27:28, 29. Mk 15:18, 19. Jn 19:2, 3,
14, 15. 1 P 2:4-8.
Christ. ver. +63.
Who is. Lk 7:39.

69 **Peter**. ver. 58. 1 K 19:9, 13. Ps +1:1. Mk
14:66-68. Lk 22:55-57. Jn 18:16, 17, 25. 2 P
2:7-9.
and a. Mt +8:19.
Jesus. ver. 71. Mt 2:22, 23. 21:11. Jn 1:46.
7:41, 52. Ac 5:37.

70 **he denied**. ver. 34, 35, 40-43, 51, 56, 58. Ps
119:115-117. Pr 28:26. 29:23, 25. Is 57:11. Je
+17:9. Ro 11:20. 1 C 10:12. Re +21:8.

71 **when**. Mk 14:68, 69. Lk 22:58. Jn 18:25-27.
the porch. Lk 16:20. Ac 10:17. 12:13, 14.
14:13. Re 21:12, 13, 15, 21, 25. 22:14.
This. ver. 61.
with Jesus. Ac 4:13.
of Nazareth. Mk +1:24.

72 **with**. Mt 5:34-36. Ex 20:7. Is 48:1. Zc +5:3, 4.
8:17. Ml +3:5. Ac +5:3, 4.
I do not. ver. 74. Lk 22:34.

73 **they that stood by**. Lk 22:59. Jn 18:26.
Surely. Lk 22:59, 60. Jn 18:26, 27.
for. Jg 12:6. 2 K 8:21. Ne 13:24. Mk 14:70.
Ac 2:6, 7.
speech. Jn 4:42. 8:43.

74 **began**. Mt 27:25. Jg 17:2. 21:18. 1 S 14:24-28. Mk 14:71. Ac 23:12-14. Ro 9:3. 1 C 16:22.
saying. Mt +10:28, 32, 33. Jn 21:15-17. Re 3:19.
And. Mk 14:30, 68, 72. Lk 22:60. Jn 18:27.

75 **remembered**. ver. 34. Lk 22:61, 62. Jn 13:38.
deny. Mt 10:28. Pr 29:25. Ac 3:13, 14.
And he. Mt 27:3-5. Lk 22:31-34. Ro 7:18-20. 1 C 4:7. Ga 6:1. 1 P 1:5.
wept bitterly. Ps 51:17. Is 22:4. Je 9:1. Mi 1:8. Jn 21:17. 2 C 7:9, 10.

MATTHEW 27

1 **the morning**. Jg 16:2. 1 S 19:11. Pr +4:16-18. Mi 2:1. Lk 22:66. Ac 5:21.
all. Mt 23:13. 26:3, 4. Ps 2:2. Mk 15:1. Lk 23:1, 2. Jn 18:28. Ac 4:24-28.
took counsel. Mt 12:14. 22:15. 28:12. Ge 37:18. Jn 11:53.

2 **bound**. Ge 22:9. 39:20. Jn 18:12, 24. Ac 9:2. 12:6. 21:33. 22:25, 29. 24:27. 28:20. 2 T 2:9. He 13:3.
they led. Lk 23:1. Jn 18:28.
delivered. Mk +10:33.
Pontius Pilate. Pilate. i.e. *close pressed*, **S#4091g**. ver. 2, 13, 17, 22, 24, 58, 58, 62, 65. Mk 15:1, 2, 4, 5, 9, 12, 14, 15, 43, 44. Lk 3:1. 13:1. 23:1, 3, 4, 6, 11-13, 20, 24, 52. Jn 18:29, 31, 33, 35, 37, 38. 19:1, 4, 6, 8, 10, 12, 13, 15, 19, 21, 22, 31, 38. Ac 3:13. 4:27. 13:28. 1 T 6:13.
the governor. ver. 11, 14, 15, 21, 27. Ac 23:24.

3 **Judas**. Mt +20:18.
repented. Mt 21:29. Jb 20:5, 15-29. 2 C 7:10.
thirty pieces. Mt 26:15.

4 **I have sinned**. Ge 42:21, 22. Ex 9:27. 10:16, 17. 12:31. Nu +22:34. 1 S 15:24, 30. 1 K 21:27. Jb 20:5. Ro 3:19.
the innocent. ver. 19, 23, 24, 54. Dt +19:10. Je 26:15. Lk 23:22, 41, 47. Jn 19:7. Ac 13:28. He 7:26. 1 P 1:19.
blood. Ps +94:21.
What. ver. 25. Ac 18:15-17. 1 T 4:2. T 1:16. 1 J 3:12. Re 11:10.
see. ver. 24. 1 S 28:16-20. Jb 13:4. 16:2. Lk 16:25, 26. Ac 18:15.

5 **cast down**. Pr +12:25.
the temple. ver. 40, 51. Lk 1:9.
and departed. Jg 9:54. 1 S 31:4, 5. 2 S +17:23. 1 K 16:18. Jb 2:9. 7:15. Ps 55:23. Ac *1:18, 19*.

6 **It is not**. Mt 23:24. Lk 6:7-9. Jn 18:28.
to put. Dt 23:18. Is 61:8.
the treasury. Mk 7:11. 12:41, 43. Lk 21:1. Jn 8:20.

7 **potter's**. Zc *11:13*.

8 **that**. Ac 1:19.
unto. Mt 28:15. Ge +19:38.

9 **fulfilled**. Mt 1:22. Lk +24:27.
by. Mt 24:15. Lk +4:18.
Jeremy. Je *18:18. 32:6*. Zc 11:13.
And they. Je *32:6-9*. Zc *11:12, 13*.
thirty. Mt 26:15. Ex 21:32. Le 27:2-7.
pieces of silver. Ge 37:28. Zc *11:13*.
of the children of Israel did value. or, bought of the children of Israel.

10 **the potter's field**. Je 18:2.

11 **Jesus stood**. Mt 10:18, 25. Mk 15:2. Lk 23:3. Jn 18:33-36.
governor. ver. 2.
King of the Jews. ver. 29, 37, 42. Mt 2:2. Mk 15:2, 9, 12, 18, 26, 32. Lk 23:3, 37, 38. Jn 18:33, 39. 19:3, 14, 15, 19, 21.
Thou sayest. Mt 26:25, 64. 27:11. Mk 14:62. 15:2. Lk 22:70. 23:3. Jn 18:37. 1 T 6:13.

12 **answered nothing**. ver. 14. Ps +38:13. Is *53:7*. Mk 15:3-5. Jn 19:9-11. 1 P 2:23.

13 **Hearest**. Mt 26:62. Jn 18:35. 19:10. Ac 22:24.

14 **never a word**. Is *53:7*.
marvelled. Ps 71:7. Is 8:18. Zc 3:8. 1 C 4:9.

15 **feast**. Mt 26:5. Mk 15:6, 8. Lk 23:16, 17. Jn 18:38, 39. Ac 24:27. 25:9.

16 **a notable**. Mk 15:7. Lk 23:18, 19, 25. Jn 18:40. Ac 3:14. Ro 1:32. 16:7.
Barabbas. i.e. *son of his father*, **S#912g**. ver. 16, 17, 20, 21, 26. Mk 15:7, 11, 15. Lk 23:18. Jn 18:40.

17 **Whom**. ver. 21. Jsh 24:15. 1 K 18:21.
or Jesus. ver. 22. Mt 1:1. Mk 15:9-12. Jn 19:15.

18 **he**. 1 S 18:7-11. Is 26:11.
envy. Ps +37:1. Jn 11:47, 48. 12:19. 1 J 3:12.

19 **judgment seat**. Jn 19:13. Ac 12:21. 18:12, 16, 17. 25:6, 10, 17.
his wife. Ge 20:3-6. 31:24, 29. Jb 33:14-17. Pr 29:1.
nothing to do. Jg +11:12. 2 Ch 35:21. Jn +2:4.
that just. ver. 4, 24. Is 53:11. Zc +9:9. Lk 23:41, 47. 1 P 2:22. 1 J 2:1.
in a dream. Mt 2:12. Jb 33:14-16.

20 **persuaded**. Mk 15:11. Ac 14:18, 19. 19:23-29.
should. Lk 23:18-20. Jn 18:40. 19:15, 16. Ac 3:14, 15.
destroy. Gr. *apollumi*, Mt 2:13.

21 **release unto**. Lk 23:18. Jn 18:40. Ac 3:14.

22 **What**. ver. 17. Jb 31:31. Ps 22:8, 9. Is 49:7. 53:2, 3. Zc 11:8. Mk 14:55. 15:12-14. Lk 23:20-24. Jn 19:14, 15. Ac 13:28.

23 **Why**. Ge 37:18, 19. 1 S 19:3-15. 20:31-33. 22:14-19.
what evil. Lk 23:41. Jn 8:46.
But. Mt 21:38, 39. Ac 7:57. 17:5-7. 21:28-31. 22:22, 23. 23:10, 12-15.

24 **a tumult**. Mt 26:5.
  and washed. Gr. *aponipto*, **S#633g**, only here.
  Ex 30:19-21. Dt 21:6, 7. Jb 9:30, 31. Ps 26:6.
  73:13. Je 2:27, 35.
  innocent of. Ge 37:22. Ac 20:26.
  just. ver. 4, 9, 19, 54. Lk 23:4. Jn 19:4. Ac
  3:14. 2 C 5:21. 1 P 2:22. 3:18. 1 J 2:1.
  see ye. ver. 4.

25 **His blood**. Mt 21:44. 23:30-37. 24:21. Ge
  4:10. 42:22. Nu 35:33. Dt +19:10. Jsh 2:19. Ps
  109:12-19. Is 59:3, 4. Je 2:34. Ezk 22:2-4.
  24:7-9. Mi 3:12. Lk 11:50. Ac 5:28. 7:52.
  +18:6. 1 Th 2:15, 16. He 10:28-30.
  on us. Ge 27:13.
  on our children. Ex +20:5. Dt 5:9. La 5:7.
  Ezk 18:4, 14, etc., 20. Ac +2:39.

26 **released**. Mk 15:15. Lk 23:25.
  scourged. Is *50:6*. Jn +19:1.

27 **common hall**. *or*, governor's house. Mk
  15:16. Jn 18:28, 33. 19:8, 9. Ac 23:35. Ph
  1:13.
  band. Jn 18:3. Ac 10:1. 21:31. 27:1.

28 **stripped**. Ge 37:23. Mk 15:17. Lk 23:11. Jn
  19:2-5.
  a scarlet robe. Lk 23:11. Re 17:4. 18:12,
  16.

29 **platted**. Mt 20:19. Ps 35:15, 16. 69:7, 19, 20.
  Is 49:7. 53:3. Je 20:7. He 12:2, 3.
  bowed the knee. Mk 1:40.
  mocked him. ver. 31, 41. Lk +22:63.
  Hail. ver. 37. Mt 26:49. Mk 15:18. Lk 23:36,
  37. Jn 19:3.
  King. ver. 11.

30 **they spit**. Mt +26:67. Is 49:7. *50:6*.
  smote. Mt 5:39. 26:31, 67. 1 K 22:24. 2 Ch
  18:23. Jb 16:10. Is 50:6. Je 20:2. 37:15. La
  3:30. Mi *5:1*. Zc 13:7. Mk 14:27, 65. 15:19. Lk
  6:29. 22:63, 64. Jn 18:22. 19:3. Ac 23:2, 3. 2
  C 11:20.

31 **had mocked**. ver. 29.
  and led. Mt 20:19. 21:39. Nu 15:35. 1 K
  21:10, 13. Is 53:7. Jn 19:16, 27. Ac 7:58. He
  13:11, 12.

32 **as**. Mt 21:39. Le 4:3, 12, 21. Nu 15:35, 36. 1
  K 21:10, 13. Ac 7:58. He 13:11, 12.
  they found. Mt 16:24. Mk 15:21. Lk 23:26.
  Cyrene. Ac +2:10.
  compelled. Mt 5:41.

33 **Golgotha**. i.e. *place of a skull*, **S#1115g**. Mk
  15:22. Lk 23:27-33. Jn 19:17.

34 **vinegar**. ver. 48. Ps +*69:21*.
  with gall. Dt +29:18. Ps *69:21*.

35 **they crucified**. Ps 22:16. Jn 20:20, 25, 27.
  Ac 4:10. Ga 3:13. Ph 2:8. Col 1:20. 1 P 2:24.
  parted. Ps *22:18*. Mk 15:24, etc. Lk 23:34. Jn
  19:23, 24.
  that it. Ps 22:18.

36 **sitting down**. ver. 54. Ge 37:25. Mk 15:39,
  44.
  they watched. ver. 54. Ps 22:17.

37 **his accusation**. Mk 15:26. Lk 23:38. Jn
  19:19-22. Ac 25:18, 27.
  KING. ver. +42. Is 32:1.

38 **two thieves**. ver. 44. Is 53:12. Mk 15:27, 28.
  Lk 22:37. 23:32, 33, 39-43. Jn 18:40. 19:18,
  31-35.
  one on. Mt 20:21. Mk 10:37.

39 **reviled**. Ps 22:6, 7, 17. +31:11. 35:15-21. La
  1:12. 2:15-17. Mk 15:29, 30. Lk 22:65. 23:35-
  39. Ja 2:7. 1 P 2:22-24.
  wagging. Je +18:16.

40 **saying**. Ge 37:19, 20. Re 11:10.
  that destroyest. Mt 26:61. Lk 14:29, 30. Jn
  +2:19-22.
  temple. ver. 5, 51. Lk 1:9.
  If. 1 C +15:2. Ge +37:19.
  the Son of God. ver. 43, 54. Mt +14:33.
  come. Mt 16:4. Lk 16:31.

41 **mocking**. ver. +29. Jb 13:9. Ps *22:7, 8, 12,
  13*. Is 28:22. Zc 11:8. Lk 4:23. 22:52. 23:35,
  39.

42 **saved others**. Mk 5:41. Lk 7:14. Jn 9:24.
  11:43, 47. Ac 4:14.
  himself he cannot. Mt 26:53, 54. Jn 10:18.
  If. 1 C +15:2.
  the King. ver. 37. Lk 23:35, 37. Jn +1:49.
  let him. Mt 12:38. Lk 11:16.
  we will believe. Jn 4:48.

43 **trusted**. Ps 3:2. 14:6. *22:8*. 37:5. 42:10. 71:11.
  Pr 16:3. Is 36:15, 18. 37:10.
  deliver him. Ps 91:14.
  if he will have him. Or, "if he delight in
  him." 1 C +15:2. Ps *18:19*. 41:11.
  I am. ver. 40. Jn 3:16, 17. 5:17-25. +10:30,
  36. 19:7.
  Son of God. Ex 4:22. Ps 89:26, 27. 2 S 7:14.
  1 Ch 22:10. Lk 3:38. Jn 1:12, 13. Ro 8:14, 17.
  Ph 2:14, 15.

44 **thieves**. ver. 38. Jb 30:7-9. Ps 35:15. Mk
  15:32. Lk 23:39-43.

45 **from**. Mk 15:25, 33, 34. Lk 23:44, 45. Jn
  19:14.
  sixth hour. Our 12 noon. Mt +20:5. Jn +11:9.
  darkness. Ex +10:22. Is 50:3. Re 8:12. 9:2.
  ninth hour. Our 3 p.m. Mt +20:5. 1 K 18:29.
  Jn +11:9. Ac 3:1.

46 **ninth hour**. Our 3 p.m. ver. +45.
  Jesus. Mk 15:34. Lk 23:46. Jn 19:28-30. He
  5:7.
  cried. Lk 23:33, 34, 42, 46.
  Eli. i.e. *my God*, **S#2241g**, only here. Ps *22:1*.
  71:11. Is 53:10. La 1:12.
  sabachthani. i.e. *hast thou forsaken me?*
  S#4518g. Mt 27:46. Mk 15:34.
  why hast. 2 C 13:4.
  forsaken. Ps *22:1*. Hab 1:13. 2 C 5:21.

47 **This**. Mt 11:14. Ml 4:5. Mk 15:35, 36.

48 **and filled**. ver. 34. Ps 69:21. Lk 23:36. Jn
  19:29, 30.
  vinegar. Ru 2:14.

49 **let us**. ver. 43.

50 **when**. Mk 15:37. Lk 23:46. Jn 19:30.
yielded. Mt +20:28. Ge +25:8, 17. 35:29. 49:33. Jb 3:11. 10:18. 11:20. 13:19. 14:10. Ps 22:14, 15. 31:5. Is 53:9-12. Je 15:9. La 1:19. Da 9:26. Lk 8:55. Jn 10:11, 15, 18. Ac 5:5, 10. 7:59. 12:23. Ro 6:8-11. He 2:14. 9:14.
ghost. or, spirit. Gr. *pneuma*. The "spirit" put for: (1) "spirit" as the principle of life, of which death is described as (a) giving or commending to God of the "spirit": Mt 27:50. Mk 15:39. Lk 23:46. Jn 19:30. Ac 7:59. (b) of departed persons as Ac 23:8. He 12:9, 23. (2) the distinctive, self-conscious inner life of man, as in 1 C 2:11. Lk 1:80. 2:40. 1 C 2:11. 5:3, 5. 6:20. 7:34. 1 Th 5:23. He 4:12. Ja 4:5. (3) "life" in the physiological sense, but drawing rather to the meaning of "soul" (John Laidlaw, *The Biblical Doctrine of Man*, p. 132) as in Lk 8:55. Ja 2:26. Re 11:11. 13:15. For the other uses of *pneuma*, see Mt +8:16.

51 **the veil**. Ex 26:31-37. 40:21. Le 16:2, 12-15. 21:23. 2 Ch 3:14. Is 25:7. Mk 15:38. Lk 23:45. Ep 2:13-18. He 6:19, 20. 9:7, 8. 10:19-22.
temple. ver. 5, 40. Lk 1:9.
the earth did quake. ver. 54. Mt 28:2. Ps +97:4.

52 **graves**. Mt +8:28 (S#3419g).
many. Is 25:8. +26:19. Ho +13:14. Jn 5:25-29. 1 C 15:20.
bodies. Mt 28:6. Da +12:2. Jn +2:19, 21, 22.
the saints. Da 7:18, 22. Ac 9:32.
which slept. Da +12:2. Jn 11:11-13. Ac 7:60. 13:36. 1 C 7:39. 11:30. 15:6, 18, 20, 51. 1 Th 4:13-15. 5:10. 2 P 3:4.
arose. Mt 28:6.

53 **graves**. Mt +8:28 (S#3419g).
after his. Ac 26:23. 1 C 15:20.
holy. Mt 4:5. Ne 11:1. Is 48:2. Da +9:24. Re 11:2. 21:2. 22:19.

54 **the centurion**. ver. 36. Mt 8:5. Ac 10:1. 21:32. 23:17, 23. 27:1, 43.
watching. ver. 36.
saw. ver. 51. Mk 15:39. Lk 23:47, etc.
feared. 2 K 1:13, 14. Ac 2:37. 16:29, 30. Re 11:13.
Truly. ver. 40, 43. Mt +14:33. Lk 23:47.
the Son of God. ver. 40. Lk 4:3, 9.

55 **many**. Lk 23:27, 28, 48, 49. Jn 19:25-27.
women. Pr 31:20, 26-28. Mk 12:43, 44. Lk 24:1, 10.
afar off. Ps 38:11. Lk 23:49.
ministering. Mt 25:40, 44. Nu 3:6. Lk 8:2, 3. He +6:10.

56 *Mary Magdalene*. ver. 61. Mt 15:39. 28:1. Mk 15:40, 41, 47. 16:1, 9. Lk 8:2. 24:10. Jn 20:1, 18.
Mary the. Mk 15:47. 16:1. Jn 19:25.
James. Mt 13:55. Mk 15:40. 16:1. Lk 6:15.
the mother. Mt 20:20, 21.

57 **there**. Mk 15:42, 43. Lk 23:50, 51. Jn 19:38-42.
rich man. Is 53:9.
Arimathea. i.e. *a high place*, S#707g. Je +31:15. Mk 15:43. Lk 23:51. Jn 19:38.

58 **and begged**. Mk 15:44-46. Lk 23:52, 53. Jn 19:38.

59 **wrapped**. Mk 15:46. Jn 19:39, 40. 20:5.

60 **in his**. Is 53:9.
new tomb. Jn 19:41, 42.
hewn. 2 Ch 16:14. Is 22:16.
rolled. Ge 29:3, 8, 10.
a great. ver. 66. Mt 28:2. Mk 16:3, 4. Lk 24:2. Jn 11:38. 20:1.

61 **Mary Magdalene**. ver. 56.
the other. Mt 10:23.
Mary. ver. 56. Mt 28:1.
sitting over against. Mk 15:47.

62 **the day**. Mt 26:17. Mk 15:42. Lk 23:54-56. Jn 19:14, 31, 42.
the chief priests. ver. 1, 2. Ps 2:1-6. Ac 4:27, 28.

63 **that deceiver**. Lk 23:2. Jn 7:12, 47. 2 C 6:8.
After three days. ver. 64. Mt 28:6. 1 C +15:4.

64 **until the third day**. ver. 63.
and steal. Mt 28:13.
so the last. Mt 12:45. 2 S 13:16. Lk 11:26.

65 **have a watch**. ver. 66. Mt 28:11.
make. Mt 28:11-15. Ps 76:10. Pr +21:30. Ju 9.

66 **sealing**. Da 6:17. 2 T 2:19. Re 20:3.
the stone. ver. 60. Mt 28:2.
setting a watch. ver. 65.

MATTHEW 28

1 **end of the sabbath**. Mk 16:1, 2. Lk 18:12. 23:56. 24:1, 22. Jn 20:1, etc. Ac 13:42mg. 1 C 16:1.
began to dawn. Lk 23:54.
first. Gr. *mia*, "one," is the Greek cardinal numeral, but it is used here for the ordinal, *first*, like the Hebrew *echad*, which has both meanings (See Ge 1:5, etc. Mk 16:9. Dt +6:4).
Mary Magdalene. Mt 27:56, 61.
the other Mary. Mt 27:56, 61.

2 **was**. *or*, had been.
earthquake. Mt 27:51-53. Re +6:12.
angel of. Mk 16:3-5. Lk 2:9. 24:2-5. Jn 20:1, 12, 13. 1 T 3:16. He 1:14. 1 P 1:12.
rolled. Mt 27:60, 66. Ge 29:10. Mk 16:4, 5.

3 **countenance**. Mt 17:2. Ps 104:4. Ezk 1:4-14. Da 1:15. 10:5, 6. Re 1:14-16. 10:1. 18:1.
his raiment. Mt 17:2. Da 7:9. Mk 9:3. 16:5. Lk 9:29. Ac 1:10. Re 3:4, 5.

4 **the**. ver. 11. Mt 27:65, 66.
shake. Jb 4:14. Ps 48:6. Da 10:7. Ac 9:3-7. 16:29. Re 1:17.

5 **answered**. Mt 11:25.

Fear. Ge +15:1. He 1:14.
ye seek. Ps 105:3, 4. Lk 24:5. Jn 20:13-15. He 1:14.
which was. Mt 27:35.

6　**risen**. Mt +27:52. Jn +2:21, 22.
as he said. Mt +12:40. 16:21. 17:9, 23. 20:19. 26:31, 32. 27:63. Mk 8:31. Lk 24:6-8, 23, 44. Jn +2:19. 10:17.
Come. Mk 16:6. Lk 24:12. Jn 20:4-9.
the Lord. Lk 7:13. Jn 4:1.

7　**go**. ver. 10. Mk 16:7, 8, 10, 13. Lk 24:9, 10, 22-24, 34. Jn 20:17, 18.
he goeth. ver. 16, 17. Mk +16:7. Lk 24:6.

8　**with**. Ezr 3:12, 13. Ps 2:11. Mk 16:8. Lk 24:36-41. Jn 16:20, 22. 20:20, 21.
to. Mt 24:25. Is 44:8. 45:21. Jn 14:29. 16:4.

9　**as**. Is 64:5. Mk 16:9, 10. Jn 20:14-16.
All hail. Lk 1:28. Jn 20:19. 2 C 13:11.
and held. 2 K 4:27. SS 3:3, 4. Lk 7:38. 10:39. Jn 12:3. 20:17. Re 3:9.
worshipped. ver. 17. Mt +8:2. +14:33. Lk 24:52. Jn +20:28. Re +5:11-14.

10　**Be not afraid**. ver. 5. Mt 14:27. Ge 45:4. 50:19. Lk 24:36-38. Jn 6:20.
go tell. ver. 7. Jg 10:16. Ps 103:8-13. Mk 16:7. Jn 20:18.
my brethren. Mt 12:48-50. 25:40, 45. Ps 22:22. Mk 3:33-35. Jn 20:17. 21:23. Ro 8:29. He 2:11-18.
go into. ver. +7.

11　**some**. ver. 4. Mt 27:65, 66.

12　**assembled with**. Mt 26:3, 4. 27:1, 2, 62-64. Ps 2:1-7. Jn 11:47, 48. 12:10, 11. Ac 4:5-22. 5:33, 34, 40.
taken counsel. Mt 12:14.

13　**and stole**. Mt 27:64.

14　**And if**. Mt +4:9.
governor's. Mt 27:2.
we. Ac 12:19, 20.

15　**they took**. Mt 26:15. 1 T 6:10.
reported. Mt 9:31. Mk 1:45.
until. Mt +27:8.

16　**the eleven**. Mk 16:14. Jn 6:70. Ac 1:13-26. 1 C 15:15.
went. ver. 7, 10. Mt 26:32.
into a mountain. Mt +5:1.

17　**when**. Mt 16:28.
worshipped. ver. 9. Mt 8:2. +14:33. Ps 2:12. 45:11. Jn 5:23. Re +5:12.
but some. 1 C 15:6.
doubted. Mt 14:31. Mk 16:11. Lk 24:11, 37, 41. Jn 20:25.

18　**All power**. Mt 9:6. 11:27. 16:28. Jb 23:6. 25:2. 2 Ch 20:6. Ps 2:6-9. 62:11. 78:38. 89:19, 27. 110:1-3. Is +9:6, 7. Da +7:13, 14. Lk 1:32, 33. 4:6. 10:22. 22:29. Jn 3:35. 5:22-27. 13:3. 17:2, 5. Ac 2:36. 10:36. Ro 14:9. 1 C 15:27. Ep 1:10, 20-22. Ph 2:9-11. Col 1:16-19. 2:9, 10. He 1:2. 2:8. 1 P 3:22. Re 11:15, 17. 17:14. 19:13, 15, 16.

is given. Gr. was given. Mt 17:5.
in heaven and. Mt 6:10. Lk 2:14. 11:2.

19　**Go ye therefore**. Ps 22:27, 28. 98:2, 3. Is 42:1-4. 49:6. 52:10. 66:18, 19. Mk +16:15, 16. Lk 24:47, 48. Ac +1:8. 13:46, 47. 28:28. Ro 10:18. Col +1:23.
and teach. Mt +4:23. Jsh +1:8. Ne 8:8. Je 1:17. 23:28. 26:2. Ezk 2:7. 3:10, 11. Ac 5:42. 20:18, 20, 26-28. 1 C +1:17. 4:1, 2. 9:16. 2 C +1:24. 2:17. 4:1, 2. 1 Th 2:3-5. 2 T 2:15. 4:1-5. T 2:1. 1 P 4:11. Ju +3. *or*, make disciples, *or* Christians, of all nations. Mt +13:52. Ac 14:21mg.
all nations. Mt 24:14. Mk 11:17. 16:15. Lk +24:47. Ro 1:5.
baptizing them. Jn 3:22. Ac +2:38, 39, 41. 8:12-16, 36-38. 9:18. 10:47, 48. 16:14, 15, 33. 19:3-5. +22:16. 1 C 1:13-16. 15:29. 1 P 3:21.
in. Ac 2:38 ("in the name of Jesus Christ"); 8:16 ("in the name of the Lord Jesus"); 10:48 ("in the name of the Lord"); 19:5 ("in the name of the Lord Jesus"). Ga 3:27.
the name. Mt +3:16, 17. Ge +1:26. Nu 6:24-27. Is +42:1. 48:16. Zc +14:9. Jn +1:2. 15:26. 16:15. Ro 8:9. 15:30. 1 C 12:4-6. 2 C 13:14. Ga 4:6. Ep 2:18. 4:4-6. 2 Th 3:5. 1 P 1:2. 1 J 5:7. Ju 20, 21. Re 1:4-6. 4:8.
the Father. Mt 24:36.
Holy Ghost. Mt +3:16. Careful study of Scripture demonstrates that all three (and only these three, and no others)—Father, Son, and Holy Spirit—are the persons of the Godhead, who are associated on an equality of being, and possess the attributes and prerogatives of Deity: The Father, Son, and Holy Ghost are each (1) called God: Ex 20:1, 2 (Father); Jn +20:28 (Son); Ac 5:3, +4 (Holy Spirit). (2) called Lord: Ro 10:12. Lk +2:11. 2 C 3:17. (3) everlasting: Ro +16:26. Re +22:13. He 9:14. (4) called holy: Re 4:8 with 15:4. Ac +3:14 with 1 J 2:20. Mt 12:32. (5) called true: Jn +7:28. Re +3:7. 1 J +5:6. Each is (6) omniscient: He +4:13. Jn +21:17. 1 C 2:10, 11. (7) omnipresent: Je 23:24. Ep 1:23. Ps 139:7. (8) omnipotent: Jb +42:2. 1 C +1:24. Ac 10:38. (9) almighty: Ge 17:1. Re +1:8. Ro 15:19. (10) powerful: 1 Ch +29:12. He 1:3. Lk +1:35. They each (11) give strength: Is 40:28, +29. Ph 4:13. Ep 3:16. (12) create: Ge 1:1. Jn 1:2, +3. Jb 33:4. (13) sanctify: Ju 1. He 2:11. 1 P +1:2. (14) give eternal life: Ro 6:23. Jn 10:28. Ga 6:8. (15) are life: Dt +30:20. Col +3:4. Ro 8:10. (16) teach: Is +48:17. Lk 21:15. Jn +14:26. (17) impart knowledge: Is 54:13. Ga 1:12. 1 J 2:20. (18) raise the dead: Jn 5:21a. Jn 5:21b. 1 P 3:18. (19) raised Christ bodily from the dead: 1 C 6:14. Jn 2:19. 1 P 3:18. (20) comfort: 2 C 1:3. Ph 2:1, 2. Jn 15:26. (21) distribute spiritual gifts: Ja 1:17. Ep 4:8. 1 C 12:11. (22) divinely inspire God's

prophets and spokesmen: He 1:1. 2 C 13:3. Mk 13:11. (23) send pastors: Je 3:15. Mt 10:5. Ac 13:2. (24) send gifted servants: Je 26:5. Ep 4:11. Ac 20:28. (25) may be tempted: Dt 6:16. 1 C 10:9. Ac 5:9. (26) indwell believers: 2 C 6:16. Ep 3:17. 1 C 3:16. (27) indwell individual believers: Ep 2:22. Col 1:27. 1 C 6:19. (28) fellowship with believers: 1 J 1:3a. 1 J 1:3b. Ph 2:1. (29) work in us: He 13:20, 21. Col 1:28, 29. 1 C 12:11. They each are (30) sovereign: Ep +1:11. Mt 8:27. 1 C 12:11. (31) immutable: Ml +3:6. He 13:8. Mt 12:32. Possess the attribute of (32) immensity: Je 23:24. Jn 3:13. Ps 139:7. They each share the attributes of (33) truth: Ex 34:6. Jn 14:6. 1 J 5:6. (34) benevolence: Ro 2:4. Ep 5:25. Ne 9:20. (35) wisdom: Jb +12:13. Col 2:3. Is +11:2. (36) invisibility: 1 T +6:16. Col 1:27. Lk 24:39. (37) incomprehensibility: Ro +11:33. Ep +3:8, 19. 1 C 2:10, 11, 14. (38) being unequaled: Je +10:6. Mt 8:27. Is 40:13, 14. (39) justice: Ge 18:25. Ac 3:14. Jn 16:8. (40) goodness: Mk 10:18. Jn 10:11. Ps 143:10. (41) love: 1 J 4:16. Ep 5:2. Ro 5:5. (42) mercy: Ep 2:4. Ju 21. Ga 5:22, 23. (43) grace: Ps +84:11. 2 C +8:9. He 10:29. (44) faithfulness: Ps +36:5. He +2:17. Ep 4:30. Several divine attributes are incommunicable: they belong to God exclusively, and cannot be communicated, delegated, or given to a cre-

ated being. These include eternity (3), omniscience (6), omnipresence (7), sovereignty (30), immutability (31), and immensity (32). Since only God can possess the incommunicable attributes, yet Scripture ascribes them to Jesus and to the Holy Spirit, all three persons must be God. There is no other explanation which properly agrees with all the statements of Scripture.

20 Teaching them. Mt 7:24-27. Dt 5:32. 12:32. Je 26:2. Ac 2:42. 14:3. 20:20, 21, 27. 1 C 11:2, 23. 14:37. Ep 4:11-17, 20, etc. Col 1:28. 1 Th 4:1, 2. 2 Th 3:6-12. 1 T 6:1-4. T 2:1-10. 1 P 2:10-19. 2 P 1:5-11. 3:2. 1 J 2:3, 4. 3:19-24. Re 22:14.

to observe. Dt 33:9. Jn +14:15. Ro 15:18, 19.

all things. Je 26:2.

commanded. Ac 1:2. 1 C 11:2. 14:37. 2 Th 3:6. 1 J +2:3.

with you. Mt 18:20. Ge 39:2, 3, 21. Ex 3:12. Ru 2:4. 1 Ch 28:21. Is +43:2. Mk 16:20. Jn 12:26. 14:3, 18-23. 17:24. 2 C 13:14. Ph 4:13. He +13:5, 6. Re 22:21.

alway. lit. all the days. Lk 1:75.

unto. Mt 13:39, 40, 49. +24:3. Dt 1:31. Ps 77:20.

end. Gr. *suntelia*, **S#4930g**, Mt 24:3.

world. Gr. *aion*, Mt +6:13. lit. "end of the age," as in Mt +13:39. Mt +12:32.

Amen. Mt +6:13.

MARK

MARK 1

1 beginning. Lk 1:2, 3. 2:10, 11. Ac 1:1, 2.
gospel. Mk 16:15, 16. Is 52:7. Mt 4:23. 24:14.
Lk 2:10, 11. 24:47. Jn 3:16. Ac 20:24. Ro
1:16, 17. 2:16. 10:8. 16:25. 1 C 1:18. +15:1-4.
2 C 3:8, 9. 4:3, 4, 6. 5:18, 19. Ga 1:8. Ep 1:13.
3:4. 6:15, 19. 1 Th 2:9. 2 T 1:10. 1 P :1:25. Re
14:6.
Christ. Jn 20:31. Ro 1:1-4. 1 J 1:1-3. 5:11,
12.
son. Mt +14:33. Jn 3:16. Ro 8:3, 32.

2 written. Ps 40:7. Mt 2:5. 26:24, 31. Lk 1:70.
18:31.
in. Mt 27:9.
prophets. Ge +46:7.
Behold. Ml *3:1*. Ne +9:6. Ps 110:1. Is 40:3. Mt
11:10. Lk 1:15-17, 76. Lk +4:18. 7:27, 28. Ac
2:34-36.
before thy face. Ezk 20:35. Mt 11:10.
+16:27. 18:10. +24:3, 30. Lk 1:76. 2:31. 7:27.
Jn +1:51. Ac +1:11. 1 C 13:12. 1 J 3:2. Re
+1:7.

3 voice. Is *40:3-5*. Mt 3:3. Lk 3:4-6. Jn 1:15, 19-
34. 3:28-36.
Prepare. Lk 1:76.

4 did baptize. Mt 3:1, 2, 6, 11. Lk 3:2, 3. Jn
3:23. Ac 10:37. 13:24, 25. 19:3, 4.
in the wilderness. ver. 9. Jn 3:23.
repentance. Lk 13:3. Ac +3:19.
for. *or*, unto. Gr. *eis*. Mt 10:41. 12:41. 26:28.
Ac +2:38.
remission. Mt 26:28. Lk 1:77. Ac 10:43.
13:38, 39. +22:16. Ro 3:25. Ep 1:7. He 9:22.

5 there. Mt 3:5, 6. 4:25.
Judea. 1 S +22:19.
baptized. Jn 1:28. 3:23.
in the river. ver. 9. Jsh 3:15.
confessing. Gr. *exomologeomai*, **S#1843g**.
Rendered (1) *confess*: ver. 5. Mt 3:6. Ac 19:18.
Ro 14:11. 15:9. Ph 2:11. Ja 5:16. Re 3:5. (2)
thank: Mt 11:25. Lk 10:21. (3) *promise*: Lk
22:6. See for *homologeo*, **S#3670g**, Mt +10:32. Le
26:40-42. Jsh 7:19. Ps 32:5. Pr 28:13. Ac 2:38.
+19:18. 1 J 1:8-10.

6 clothed. 2 K 1:8. Zc 13:4. Mt 3:4.
eat. Le 11:22.

7 There cometh. Mt 3:11, 14. Lk 3:16. 7:6, 7.
Jn 1:27. 3:28-31. Ac 13:25.
latchet. Ge 14:23. Is 5:27. Lk 3:16. Jn 1:27.

8 have. Mt 3:11.
with water. Mt 3:11. Ac +1:5.
he shall. ver. 10. Pr 1:23. Is 32:15. 44:3. Ezk
36:25-27. 39:29. Jl 2:28, 29. Jn 1:33. Ac +1:5.
2:4, 16, 17, 33. 10:45. 11:15, 16. 19:4-6. 1 C
12:13. T 3:5, 6.
Holy Ghost. Gr. *pneumati hagio*, Mt +1:18.

9 came to pass. Ge +38:1.
that. Mt 3:13-15. Is 42:21. Lk 3:21.
in Jordan. ver. 4. Jn 1:28. 3:23. 10:40.

10 coming. Mt 3:16. Jn 1:31-34.
out. Mt +3:16.
opened. *or*, cloven, *or* rent. Is 64:1.
the Spirit. Gr. *pneuma*, Mt +3:16. Is 11:2, 3.
42:1.
like a dove. Lk 3:22. Jn 1:32.

11 there. Mt 3:17. Is 64:1. Jn 5:37. 12:28-30. 2 P
1:17, 18.
Thou. Mk 9:7. Ps 2:7. Is 42:1. Mt 17:5. Lk
9:35. Jn 1:34. 3:16, 35, 36. 5:20-23. 6:69. Ro
1:4. Col 1:13.

12 the spirit. Gr. *pneuma*, Mt +3:16. 4:1.
Lk 4:1.
driveth. Mt 9:38. Jn 10:4.

13 forty. Ex 24:18. 34:28. Dt 9:11, 18, 25. 1 K
19:8.
tempted. He 2:17, 18. +4:15.
and the. 1 K 19:5-7. Mt 4:11. 26:53. 1 T
3:16.
ministered. Mt 4:11. He 1:14.

14 A.M. 4031. A.D. 27.
after. Mt +4:12.
preaching. Is 61:1-3. Mt 4:23. 9:35. 24:14.
Lk 4:17-19, 43, 44. 8:1. Ac 20:25. 28:23. Ep
2:17.

15 The time. Da 2:44. *9:22-27*. Lk 3:15. 21:8. Jn
7:8. Ro +5:6. Ga 4:4. Ep 1:10.
kingdom of God. Mk 4:11, 26, 30. 9:1, 47.
10:14, 15, 23-25. 12:34. 14:25. 15:43. Mt +4:17.
+12:28. 16:28. Lk +4:43. Jn +3:3. Ac +1:3.
at hand. Mt 4:17. 10:7. +21:43.
repent. Mt 21:31, 32. Lk +13:3, 5. 2 T +2:25,
26.

believe. Mk 16:16. Ge 15:6. 2 Ch +20:20. Ac 16:30, 31. 19:4. 20:21. Ro 4:24. 16:26. Ga 3:6. He 6:1.

the gospel. Ro 1:9. 1 C 15:1-4. 2 C 8:18. 10:14. Ga 3:8. 1 Th 3:2.

16 **as he**. Mt 4:18, etc. Lk 5:1, 4, etc.
Simon. Mk 3:16, 18. Mt 10:2. Lk 6:14. Jn 1:40-42. 6:8. 12:22. Ac 1:13.

17 **Come**. 1 C 1:26-29.
fishers. Ezk 47:10. Mt 4:19, 20. Lk 5:10. Ac 2:38-41.

18 **forsook**. Mk 10:28-31. Mt 19:27-30. Lk 5:11. 14:33. 18:28-30. Ph 3:8.

19 **James**. Mk 3:17. 5:37. 9:2. 10:35. 14:33. Mt 4:21. Ac 1:13. 12:2.

20 **they left**. Mk 10:29. Dt 33:9. 1 K 19:20. Mt 4:21, 22. 8:21, 22. 10:37. Lk 14:26. 2 C 5:16.

21 **they went**. Mk 2:1. Mt 4:13. Lk 4:31. 10:15.
Capernaum. Mk 6:53. Mt 4:13. Lk 4:31-37. Jn 6:59.
he entered. ver. 39. Mt +4:23.

22 **they were**. Je 23:29. Mt +7:28, 29. Lk 21:15. Ac 6:10. 9:21, 22. 2 C 4:2. He 4:12, 13.
as the. Mk 7:3-13. Mt 23:16-24.

23 **a man**. ver. 34. Mk +3:30.
spirit. Gr. *pneuma*, Mt +8:16.

24 **Saying**. Mk 3:11, 22. 5:7. Ps +50:16. Mt 8:29. Lk 4:41. 8:28. Ac 16:17. 19:15.
Let. Mk 5:7. Ex 14:12. Mt 8:29. Lk 8:28, 37. Ja 2:19.
what. Jg +11:12.
Jesus of Nazareth. Mk 10:47. 14:67. 16:6. Mt +2:23. 21:11. 26:71. Lk 4:34. 18:37. 24:19. Jn 1:45. 18:5, 7. 19:19. Ac 2:22. 3:6. 4:10. 6:14. 10:38. 22:8. 26:9.
destroy. Gr. *apollumi*, Mt +2:13. Da +9:24. Mt +8:29. 1 J 3:8.
the Holy One. Ps +16:10. Jn 6:69.

25 **rebuked**. Mk +4:39. 2 Ch +19:2. Ps +50:16. Ac 16:17, 18.
Hold. ver. +34.

26 **spirit**. Gr. *pneuma*, Mt +8:16.
torn. Mk 9:20, 26. Lk 9:39, 42. 11:22.
came out. Ex 2:12.

27 **all amazed**. ver. 22. Mt 8:27.
new doctrine. Gr. *kainos*, Mk 2:22. Ac 17:19. He 13:9.
for. Lk 4:36. 9:1. 10:17-20.
spirits. Gr. *pneuma*, Mt +8:16.

28 **his fame**. ver. 45. Mi 5:4. Mt +4:24.

29 **entered**. Mt 8:14, 15. Lk 4:38, 39. 9:58.

30 **wife's**. 1 C 9:5.
lay sick. Mt 8:14. Lk 4:38.
they tell. Mk 5:23. Jn 11:3. Ja 5:14, 15.

31 **by the hand**. ver. +41. Mk 5:41. Ac 9:41.
ministered. Mk 15:41. Ps 103:1-3. 116:12. Mt +27:55. Lk 8:2, 3.

32 **at even**. ver. 21. Mk 3:2. Mt 8:16, 17. Lk 4:40.
possessed. Mt +4:24.

33 **all**. ver. 5. Ex +9:6. Mt +26:59.

the city. ver. 21. Ge +19:4. 1 S +22:19. Ac 13:44.

34 **healed**. Mt +4:23.
suffered not. ver. 25. Mk 3:12. Ps +50:16. Lk 4:41. Ac 16:16-18.
speak, because they. *or*, say that they.

35 **morning**. Mk +13:35. 16:2. Ge +19:27. Ps +119:147. Lk 24:1. Jn 20:1.
rising up. Mk 6:46-48. Ps 5:3. 109:4. Lk 4:42. 6:12. 22:39-46. Jn 4:34. 6:15. Ep 6:18. Ph 2:5. He 5:7.
before day. 1 S 1:19. Ps 63:1. 78:34. Is 26:9.
went out. Lk 6:12.
solitary place. Ps 107:4-7. Mt 14:23. Lk 5:16. 9:18.
there prayed. Mk 6:46. Ps 109:4. Mt 11:25. 26:39. Lk 3:21. 10:21. 11:1. 22:32. 23:34, 46. Jn 11:41. 17:9. He 5:7.

37 **All**. ver. 5. Zc 11:11. Jn 3:26. 11:48. 12:19.

38 **Let**. Lk 4:43.
for. Is 61:1-3. Lk 2:49. 4:18-21. Jn 9:4, 5. 16:28. 17:4, 6, 8.

39 **preached**. ver. 21. Mt 4:23. Lk 4:43, 44.
Galilee. Mt +2:22.
and cast. Mk 7:30. Ge +3:15. Lk 4:41.

40 **there**. Mt 8:2-4. Lk 5:12-14.
a leper. Le ch. 13, 14. 2 K +5:1.
beseeching. Nu 12:10-13. Mt 8:2, 3. Lk 5:12. 17:12, 13.
kneeling. Mk 10:17. 2 Ch 6:13. Mt 17:14. Lk 22:41. Ac +7:60. Ep 3:14.
if thou. Mt +4:9. Mk 9:22, 23. Ge 18:14. 2 K 5:7.

41 **moved**. Mt +9:36. He 2:17.
and touched. ver. 31. Mk 3:10. 5:23, 27, 41. 6:5. 7:33. 8:22, 23, 25. 9:27. 10:13, 16.
I will. Mk 4:39. 5:41, 42. Ge 1:3. Ps 33:9. He 1:3.

42 **immediately**. ver. 31. Mk 5:29. Ps 33:9. Mt 15:28. Jn 4:50-53. 15:3.

43 **straitly charged**. Mk 3:12. 5:43. 7:36. Mt 9:30. 12:16. Lk 5:14. 8:56.

44 **say nothing**. Lk +5:14.
show. Le 4:2-32. 13:2, *49.* 14:2-4, 10, 11. Dt 24:8. Mt +8:4. 23:2, 3. Lk 5:14. 17:14.
for a testimony. Mt +8:4. Ro 15:4. 1 C 10:11.

45 **and began**. Mk 7:36. Ps 77:11. T 1:10.
blaze abroad. Mt +4:24. 28:15.
could. Mk 2:1, 2, 13.
the city. 2 C 11:26.
they came. Mk 2:2, 13. 3:7. Lk 5:17. Jn 6:2.

MARK 2

1 **again**. Mk 1:45. Mt 9:1. Lk 5:18.
and it. Mk 7:24. Lk 18:35-38. Jn 4:47. Ac 2:6.

2 **straightway**. ver. 13. Mk 1:33, 37, 45. 4:1, 2. Lk 5:17. 12:1.
and he. Mk 1:14. 6:34. Ps 40:9. Mt 5:2. Lk

8:1, 11. Ac 8:25. 11:19. 14:25. 16:6. Ro 10:8. He 2:3. 2 T 4:2.

3 **bringing**. Mt 9:1, 2, etc. Lk 5:18, etc.

4 **they uncovered**. Dt +22:8. Ga 4:15.

5 **saw**. Ge 22:12. Jn +2:25. Ac 11:23. 14:9. Ep 2:8. 1 Th 1:3, 4. Ja 1:6, 7. 2:18-22.
he said. ver. 9, 10. Is 53:11. Mt +9:2. Lk 5:20. 7:47-50. Ac 5:31. 2 C 2:10. Col 3:13.
Son. Mk 5:34. Mt 9:22. Lk 8:48.
sins. Jb 14:4. 33:17-26. Ps 32:1-5. 90:7-9. +103:3. Is 38:17. 43:25. Da 9:9. Mi +7:18. Jn 5:14. 1 C +11:30. Ja 5:15.

6 **and reasoning**. Mk 8:17. Mt 16:7, 8. Lk 5:21, 22. 2 C 10:5mg.

7 **speak**. Mk +14:64.
who can. Jb 14:4. Ps 130:4. Is 43:25. Da 9:9. Mi +7:18. Lk 5:21. 7:49. Jn 20:20-23.
but God. Lk 18:19. Jn 20:21.

8 **when**. Lk 7:39, 40. Jn +2:25.
perceived. Gr. *epiginosko*, Mt +11:27.
in his. In the following texts, "spirit" refers to the sentient element in man, that by which he perceives, reflects, feels, and desires (Vine, *Dictionary*, vol. 4, p. 62): Mk 8:12. Ge 26:35. +41:8. Da 7:15. Jn 13:21. Ac 17:16. 20:22. 1 C +2:11. 2 C 7:1. 1 P 3:4.
spirit. Gr. *pneuma*. An integral part of man (individually) is put for the whole man, *pneuma* is put for one's self. Mk 8:12. Lk 1:47. Jn 11:33. 13:21. 1 C 14:14. 16:18. 2 C 2:13. 7:1, 13. Ga 6:18. Ph 4:23. 2 T 4:22. Phm 25. For the other uses of *pneuma* see Mt +8:16.
Why. Mk 7:21. Ps 139:2. Pr 15:26. 24:9. Is 55:7. Ezk 38:10. Lk 24:38. Ac 5:3. 8:22.
your hearts. 1 S 16:7.

9 **is it**. Mt 9:5. Lk 5:22-25.
Thy sins. ver. 5.

10 **Son of man**. ver. 28. Mk 8:31, 38. 9:9, 12, 31. 10:33, 45. 13:26. 14:21, 41, 62. Da +7:13, 14. Mt +8:20. Lk +5:24. Jn +1:51.
hath power. ver. 28. Mt 12:8. 28:18. Lk 6:5. Jn 5:20-27.
to forgive. Mt 9:6-8. Ac 5:31. 1 T 1:13-16.

11 **Arise**. Mk 1:41. Jn 5:8-10. 6:63.

12 **insomuch**. Mk +1:27.
glorified. Mt +9:8.
We never. Mt 9:8, 33. Jn 7:31. 9:32.

13 **by**. Mt 9:9. 13:1.
and all. ver. 2. Mk 3:7, 8, 20, 21. 4:1. Pr 1:20-22. Lk 19:48. 21:38.

14 **he saw**. Mt 9:9. Lk 5:27.
Alpheus. Mk 3:18. Lk 6:15. Ac 1:13.
receipt of custom. *or*, place where the custom was received.
Follow me. Mk 1:17-20. Mt 4:19-22.

15 **as Jesus sat**. Mt 9:10, 11. 21:31, 32. Lk 5:29, 30. 6:17. 15:1.

16 **How**. ver. 7. Is +65:5. Lk 15:2, etc. 1 C 2:15. He 12:3.
publicans. Mt 18:17.

17 **They that are whole**. Mk 7:20-23. Mt 9:12, 13. Lk 5:31, 32. 15:7, 29. 16:15. Jn 9:34, 40, 41.
I came. Is +1:18. +55:7. Lk +19:10. Ac 20:21. 1 T +1:15. T 3:3-7.

18 **disciples of John**. Mt 9:14-17. 11:2. 14:12. Lk 5:33-39. 7:18. 11:1. Jn 1:35. 3:25. 4:1. Ac 18:25. 19:3.
Why. Mk 7:5. Mt 6:16, 18. 23:5. Lk 18:12. Ro 10:3.
fast. Lk 18:12.
fast not. ver. 15. Mt 9:10. Lk 5:30.

19 **Can**. Ge 29:22. Jg 14:10, 11. Ps 45:14. SS 6:8. Mt 25:1-10.

20 **the bridegroom**. Ps 45:11. SS 1:4. 3:11. Is 54:5. 62:5. Jn 3:29. 2 C 11:2. Re 19:7. 21:9.
be taken. Zc 13:7. Mt 26:31. Jn 7:33, 34. 12:8. 13:33. 16:7, 28. 17:11, 13. Ac 1:9. +3:21.
and. Ac 13:2, 3. 14:23. 1 C 7:5. 2 C 6:5. 11:27.

21 **seweth**. Ps 103:13-15. Is 57:16. Jn 16:12. 1 C 10:13.
new. *or*, raw, *or*, unwrought. Mt 9:16.

22 **bottles**. Jsh 9:4, 13. Jb 32:19. Ps 119:80, 83. Mt 9:17. Lk 5:37, 38.
marred. Gr. *apollumi*, Mt +2:13.
new. "New" wine is *neos*; "new" skins is *kainos*. The two Greek words for "new," while generally synonymous, may be distinguished here: *neos* is new in the sense of brand new, new as opposed to old, referring to age; *kainos* is new in quality or condition, the sense of fresh, not yet used, but with no reference to age—the new wineskins conceivably could have remained unused for a long time. Perhaps this distinction holds at 2 P 3:13, where "new" heavens and a "new" earth may be understood as new in quality, not in time, for Scripture elsewhere states that the "earth abideth forever" (Ec +1:4). For *neos*, **S#3501g**: rendered (1) *new*: ver. 22. Mt 9:17, 17. Lk 5:37, 37, 38, 39. 1 C 5:7. He 12:24. (2) *new man*: Col 3:10. (3) *young woman*: T 2:4. For *kainos*, **S#2537g**: Mt 9:17. 13:52. 26:28, 29. 27:60. Mk 1:27. 2:21, 22. 14:24, 25. 16:17. Lk 5:36, 36, 38. 22:20. Jn 13:34. 19:41. Ac 17:19, 21. 1 C 11:25. 2 C 3:6. 5:17, 17. Ga 6:15. Ep 2:15. 4:24. He 8:8, 13. 9:15. 2 P 3:13, 13. 1 J 2:7, 8. 2 J 5. Re 2:17. 3:12, 12. 5:9. 14:3. 21:1, 1, 2, 5.

23 **that**. Mt 12:1-8. Lk 6:1-5.
to pluck. Dt 23:24, 25.

24 **why**. ver. 7, 16. Mt 7:3-5. 15:2, 3. 23:23, 24. He 12:3.
that. Ex 20:10. 31:15. 35:2, 3. Nu 15:32-36. Ne 13:15-22. Is 56:2, 4, 6. +58:13. Je 17:20-27.

25 **Have**. Mk 12:10, 26. Mt 19:4. 21:16, 42. 22:31. Lk 10:26.
what. 1 S 21:3-6.

26 **Abiathar.** 1 S 14:3, Ahiah. 1 S 21:1. +22:20.
did eat. 1 S *21:6*.
which is not lawful. Ex 25:30. 29:32, 33. Le 24:5-9. Mt 12:2-7.

27 **The sabbath.** Ex +20:8. 23:12. Lk 6:9. Jn 7:23. 1 C 3:21, 22. 2 C 4:15. Col 2:16.

28 **Son.** Mt 16:27.
is Lord also of. Mk 3:4. Mt 12:8. Lk 6:5. 13:15, 16. 14:5, 6. Jn 5:9-11, 16, 17. 9:5-11, 13, 14, 16. 20:19, 26. Ep 1:22. Re 1:10.

MARK 3

1 **he entered.** Mk 1:21, 23, 29. Mt 12:9-14. Lk 6:6-11.
withered. 1 K 13:4, 6. Zc 11:17. Jn 5:3.

2 **they watched.** Ps 37:32. Is 29:20, 21. Je 20:10. Da 6:4. Lk 6:7. 11:53, 54. 14:1. 20:20. Jn 9:16. Ac 9:24. Ga 4:10.
that. Lk 11:54. 20:20. Jn 8:6.

3 **he saith.** Is 42:4. Da +6:10. Lk 6:8. Jn 9:4. 1 C 15:58. Ga 6:9. Ph 1:14, 28-30. 1 P 4:1.
Stand forth. *or*, Arise, *stand forth* in the midst. Lk 6:8.

4 **Is it lawful.** Mk 2:27, 28. Ho +6:6. Mt 12:10-12. Lk 6:9. 13:13-17. 14:1-5. Jn 5:16, 17.
sabbath. Mk 2:23-28. +6:2. Mt 12:1-5, 11-13. 24:20. Lk 6:1-10. 13:11-17. Jn 5:8-10, 16, 17.
life. Gr. *psyche*, Mt +2:20; Ge +9:5.
But. Mk 9:34. Lk 14:6.

5 **looked.** ver. 34. Mk 5:32. 10:21, 23. 11:11.
with anger. Ex 11:8. Mt 5:22. Lk 6:10. 13:15. Ep 4:26. Re 6:16, 17.
grieved. Ge 6:6. Jg 10:16. Ne 13:8. Ps 95:10. Is 63:9, +10. Lk 19:40-44. Ac 7:51. Ep +4:30. 1 Th 5:19. He 3:10, 17.
hardness. *or*, blindness. Mk +6:52. 16:14. Is 6:9, 10. 42:18-20. 44:18-20. Mt 13:14, 15. Ro 11:7-10, 25. 2 C 3:14. Ep 4:18.
Stretch. 1 K 13:4, 6. Mt 12:13. Lk 6:10. 17:14. Jn 5:8, 9. 9:7. He 5:9.

6 **Pharisees.** Ps 109:3, 4. Mt 12:14. +21:46. Lk 6:11. 20:19, 20. 22:2. Jn 5:18. 7:1, 19. 11:53.
went forth. ver. 1.
took counsel. Mk 15:1. Mt 22:15. 27:1. 28:12.
Herodians. Mk 8:15. 12:13. Mt 22:16. Lk 23:7.
how. Jn 7:30.
destroy. Gr. *apollumi*, Mt +2:13.

7 **Jesus withdrew.** Pr +22:3. Is *42:2*. Mt 10:23. 12:15. 14:13. Lk 6:12. Jn 10:39-41. 11:53, 54. Ac 14:5, 6. 17:10, 14.
and a. Mk 1:45. Lk +5:15.
Galilee. Mk 10:1. Mt +2:22.

8 **from Jerusalem.** Lk 6:17.
Idumea. i.e. *earthy*, **S#2401g**, only here. For **S#123h**, see Is +34:5. Ezk 35:15. 36:5. Ml 1:2-4, Edom.

beyond Jordan. Mk +10:1. Nu 32:33-38. Jsh 13:8, etc. Mt 4:25.
Tyre. 1 K +7:13. Ezk ch. 26-28. Mt +11:21.

9 **small ship.** Mk 4:1. 6:32, 45. 8:10. Lk 5:3.
because. Mk 5:30, 31. Jn 6:15.
throng him. Mk 5:24, 31.

10 **healed many.** Mt +4:23.
pressed. *or*, rushed.
touch. Mk 5:27, 28. 6:56. Mt 9:20, 21. 14:36. Lk 6:19. Ac 5:15. 19:11, 12.
as many. Mk 5:29, 34. Ge 12:17. Nu 11:33. Lk 7:2, 21. Ac 22:24. He 11:36. 12:6.

11 **unclean.** ver. +30. Mk 1:23, 24, 26, 34. 5:5, 6. Mt 8:31. Lk 4:41. Ac 16:17. 19:13-17. Ja 2:19.
fell down. Ge +17:3.
and cried. Mk +1:24. 5:7.
the Son. Mt +14:33.

12 **straitly charged.** Mk +1:43.
should not. Mk +1:34. Ps 50:16. Lk +5:14.

13 **he goeth.** Mt 10:1, etc. Lk 6:12-16.
whom he would. Dt 18:5. 21:5. 1 Ch 15:2. 16:41. 2 Ch 29:11. Jn 13:18. 15:16, 19. Ac 9:15. Ep 1:4. 1 P 2:9.

14 **he ordained.** Jn 15:16. Ac 1:24, 25. 13:2, 3. 14:23. Ga 1:1, 15-20. 1 T +5:22. 2 T 2:2. T 1:15.
twelve. Dt 1:23.
be with. 1 Ch 4:23.
and. Lk 9:1-6. 10:1-11. 24:47. Ac +1:8.

15 **have power.** Mt 10:1. Lk 9:1. 10:19. 12:12. Ac 4:33. 6:10.
to heal. Mk 16:18. Mt 10:1. Lk 9:6. Ac 3:7. 5:16. 9:34. 14:10. 16:18. 19:12. 28:8. 1 C 12:9.
cast out devils. Mk 6:7. 9:38. 16:17. Mt 12:43-45. Lk 10:17. Ac 5:16. 8:7. 19:13-16.

16 **Simon.** Mk 1:16. Mt +16:16-18. Jn 1:42. 1 C 1:12. 3:22. 9:5. Ga 2:7-9, Cephas. 2 P 1:1.

17 **James.** Mk 1:19, 20. 5:37. 9:2. 10:35. 14:33. Jn 21:2, 20-25. Ac 12:1.
he surnamed. Is 58:1. Je 23:29. He 4:12. Re 10:11.
Boanerges. i.e. *commotion; sons of thunder*, **S#993g**, only here.
which is. Mt +6:2. Lk 9:54.
sons of thunder. Lk 10:6. Ac 4:36.

18 **Andrew.** Jn 1:40. 6:8. 12:21, 22. Ac 1:13.
Philip. Jn 1:43-45. 6:5-7. 14:8, 9.
Bartholomew. Mt 10:3. Lk 6:14. Ac 1:13.
Matthew. Mk 2:14. Mt 9:9. Lk 5:27-29, Levi. 6:15.
Thomas. Jn 11:16. 20:24-29. 21:2. Ac 1:13.
James. Mk +6:3. Mt 10:3. +13:55. Lk 6:15. Ac 15:13. 21:18. 1 C 9:5. 15:7. Ga 1:19. 2:9. Ja 1:1.
Alpheus. Mk 2:14.
Thaddeus. Mt 10:3. Lk 6:16. Jn 14:22. Ac 1:13, Judas the brother of James. Ju 1.
Simon. Mt 10:4. Lk 6:15. Ac 1:13, Simon Zelotes.

19 **Judas.** Mt 26:14-16, 47. 27:3-5. Jn 6:64, 71,

72. 12:4-6. 13:2, 26-30. Ac 1:16-25.
Iscariot. Jsh 15:25. Je 48:24, 41.
into an house. *or*, home. Mk 2:1. 7:17. 9:28.

20 **so that**. ver. 9. Mk 6:31. Lk 6:17. Jn 4:31-34.

21 **And**. ver. 21-35. Ge +8:22.
friends. *or*, kinsmen. ver. 31. Jn 7:3-10.
He is beside. 2 K 9:11. Je 29:26. Ho 9:7. Jn
10:20. Ac 26:24. 2 C 5:13. 2 T +1:7.

22 **which**. Mk 7:1. Mt 15:1. Lk 5:17.
said. Mk +1:24.
He hath. Ps 22:6. Mt 9:34. 10:25. 12:24. Lk
11:15. Jn 7:20. 8:48, 52. 10:20.

23 **in parables**. Ps 49:4. Mt 13:34, 35.
How. Mt 12:25-30. Lk 11:17-23.

24 **And**. Ge +8:22.
if. Mt +4:9.
divided against. Jg 9:23, etc. 12:1-6. 2 S
20:1, 6. 1 K 12:16, etc. Is 9:20, 21. 19:2, 3.
Ezk 37:22. Zc 11:14. Jn 17:21. 1 C 1:10-13.
Ep 4:3-6.

25 **if**. Mt +4:9.
a house. Ge 13:7, 8. 37:4. Ps 133:1. Ga 5:15.
Ja 3:16.

26 **if**. 1 C +15:2.
be divided. Lk 4:6. 2 C 11:13, 14. Ep 6:12.
hath an end. Lk 22:37.

27 **can enter**. Is 27:1. 53:12. 61:1. Jn +12:31. Ro
16:20.

28 **Verily**. Mt +5:18.
All sins. Is +1:18. Mt +12:31, 32. Lk 12:10.
Ac 8:18, 19, 22. 13:38, 39. He 6:4-8. 10:26-
31. 1 J 1:9. +5:16.
sons. Ep 3:5.
and blasphemies. Le +24:11.

29 **blaspheme against**. Ac 7:51. He 10:29.
Ghost. Gr. *pneuma*, Mt +3:16.
hath never. Gr. *aion*, Mt +6:13. Lk +12:10.
but is. Mk 12:40. Mt +25:46. 2 Th 1:9. Ju 7,
13.
in danger. Mk 14:64. Mt 5:21, 22. 26:66. 1 C
11:27. He 2:15. Ja 2:10.
eternal. Gr. *aionios*, Mt 18:8.

30 **they said**. ver. 22. Jn 10:20.
unclean. ver. 11. Mk 1:23, 26, 27. 5:2, 8, 13.
6:7. 7:25. 9:25. Mt 10:1. 12:43. Lk 4:33, 36.
6:18. 8:29. 9:42. 11:24. Ac 5:16. 8:7. Re
16:13. 18:2.
spirit. Gr. *pneuma*, Mt +8:16.

31 **There came**. Mt 12:46-48. Lk 8:19-21.
his brethren. Mk +6:3. Ps 69:8, 9. Mt
+13:55. Jn 2:12. 7:3, 5, 10. Ac 1:14. 1 C 9:5.
Ga 1:19.
his mother. Mt +1:16.

32 **thy mother**. Mt 1:16.
thy brethren. ver. +31. Mk +6:3. Jn 7:3.
seek for thee. ver. 21. Lk 4:42. 8:19. 19:3. Jn
6:24. 12:21.

33 **Who is**. Dt 33:9. Mt 12:48. Lk 2:49. Jn 2:4. 2
C 5:16.
or my brethren. ver. 21. Mk +6:3. Jn 7:3-5.

34 **looked**. ver. +5.
Behold. Ps 22:22. SS 4:9, 10. 5:1, 2. Mt
12:49, 50. 25:40-45. 28:10. Lk 11:27, 28. Jn
20:17. Ro 8:29. He 2:11, 12.

35 **whosoever**. Mt 12:50. Jn +15:14.
shall do. Mt +7:21. Lk +11:28. Ja +1:25. 1 J
3:22, 23.
the will of God. Lk 8:21. 1 Th +4:3.
the same is my. Ro 8:29. He 2:11.

MARK 4

1 **he began**. Mk 2:13. Mt +13:1, 2, etc. Lk 8:4,
etc.
so that. Lk 5:1-3.

2 **by parables**. ver. 11, 34. Mk 3:23. Ps 49:4.
78:2. Mt +13:3, 10, 34, 35.
in his doctrine. Mk 11:18. 12:38. Mt +7:28.
Jn 7:16, 17. 18:19. 2 T +3:10, 16.

3 **Hearken**. ver. 9, 23. Mk 7:14, 16. Dt 4:1. Ps
34:11. 45:10. Pr 7:24. 8:32. Is 46:3, 12. 55:1,
2. Ac 2:14. He 2:1-3. Ja 2:5. Re 2:7, 11, 29.
there. ver. 14, 26-29. Ec 11:6. Is 28:23-26.
Mt +13:3, 24-26. Lk 8:5-8. Jn 4:35-38. 1 C
3:6-9.

4 **the fowls**. ver. 15. Ge 15:11. Mt +13:4, 19.
Lk 8:5, 12.

5 **stony ground**. ver. 16, 17. Ezk 11:19. 36:26.
Ho 10:12. Am 6:12. Mt +13:5, 6, 20, 21. Lk
8:6, +13.

6 **the sun**. SS 1:6. Is 25:4. Jon 4:8. Ja 1:11. Re
7:16.
no root. Ps +1:3, 4. 92:13-15. Je +17:5-8. Ep
3:17. Col +2:7. 2 Th 2:10. Ju 12.

7 **fell among thorns**. ver. 18, 19. Ge 3:17, 18.
Je 4:3. Mt 13:7, 22. Lk 8:7, 14. 12:15. 21:34. 1
T 6:9, 10. 1 J 2:15, 16.

8 **fell on good**. ver. 20. Is 58:1. Je 23:29. Mt
+13:8, 23. Lk 8:8, 15. Jn 1:12, 13. 3:19-21.
7:17. 15:5. Ac 17:11. Col 1:6. He 4:1, 2. Ja
1:19-22. 1 P 2:1-3.
an hundred. Mk +10:30. Ge +26:12. Jn 15:5.
Ph 1:11.

9 **hath ears**. ver. 3, 23, +24. Ezk 3:27. 12:2. Mt
+13:9. 15:10. Lk +8:18.

10 **when he was alone**. ver. 34. Mk 7:17. Pr
+13:20. Mt +13:10, etc., 36. Lk 8:9, etc.
asked of him. Pr 4:7.

11 **Unto you**. Mt 11:25. +13:11, 12, 16. 16:17.
Lk 8:10. 10:21-24. 1 C 2:10. 4:7. 2 C 4:6. Ep
1:9. 2:4-10. T 3:3-7. Ja 1:16-18. 1 J 5:20.
them. 1 C 1:18. 5:12, 13. Col 4:5. 1 Th 4:12.
1 T 3:7.
all these. Mt 13:13.

12 **That seeing**. Is *6:9, 10*. Lk +8:10.
lest. Jn 5:40. 6:36, 37. 2 C 3:15.
be converted. Ac +3:19. 2 T 2:25. He 6:6.

13 **Know**. Mk 7:17, 18. Mt +13:51, 52. 15:15-
17. 16:8, 9. Lk 8:11. 24:25. 1 C 3:1, 2. He
5:11-14. Re 3:19.

14 **sower**. ver. 3. Ps +19:7. Pr 6:23. Ec 11:6. Is 32:20. Mt +13:19, 37. 20:1. Lk 8:11. 10:2. Jn 4:35, 36. 1 C 3:8, 9.
 the word. Mk 2:2. Col 1:5, 6. 1 P +1:23-25.

15 **these**. ver. 4. Ge 19:14. Is 53:1. Mt 22:25. Lk 8:12. 14:18, 19. Ac 17:18-20, 32. 18:14-17. 25:19, 20. 26:31, 32. He 2:1. 12:16.
 Satan. Jb 1:6-12. Zc 3:1. Mt +13:19. Ac +5:3. 2 C 2:11. 4:3, 4. 2 Th 2:9. 1 P 5:8. Re 12:9. 20:2, 3, 7, 10.

16 **stony ground**. Mk 6:20. 10:17-22. Ezk +33:31, 32. Mt 8:19, 20. +13:20, 21. Lk +8:13. Jn 5:35. Ac 8:13, 18-21. 24:25, 26. 26:28.

17 **have no root**. ver. 5, 6. Jb 19:28. 27:8-10. Ezk +33:31, 32. Mt 12:31. Lk 6:49. 12:10. Jn 6:66. +8:31. 15:2-7. Ep +4:14. 2 T +1:15. +2:17, 18. 4:10. 1 J 2:19.
 endure. Mt 10:22. 24:13. Lk +8:13.
 but for a time. Ho 6:4. Lk +8:13. Jn 5:35. Ac 26:28. 1 C +15:2. 2 C 4:18. Ga 1:6. 5:7. Col +1:23. 2 P +1:10.
 when affliction. 1 C 10:12, 13. Ga 6:12. 1 Th 3:3-5. 2 T 4:16. He 10:29. Ja 1:2. Re 2:10, 13.
 are offended. Mt +11:6.

18 **sown among thorns**. ver. 7. Je 4:3. Mt +13:22. Lk 8:14.

19 **the cares**. Mk 10:21-23. Ps 39:6. 127:2. Ec 1:13. 2:26. 8:16. Mt 6:25, 31. +13:22. Lk 8:14. 10:40, 41. 12:17-21, 29, 30. 14:18-20. 21:34. 2 C 11:28. Ph 4:6. 2 T +4:10. 1 P 5:7.
 of this. Mt +12:32.
 world. Gr. *aion*, Mt +6:13. lit. "age," Mt +13:22. 2 T 4:10.
 the deceitfulness of riches. Mk 10:23. Pr +23:4, +5. 28:20. 30:8, 9. Ec 4:8. 5:10-16. Je 22:21. Ezk +16:49, 50. Mt +13:22. 19:23, 24. Ac 5:1-11. 1 T 6:9, 10, 17, +18. He +3:13.
 the lusts. 1 Th +4:5. 1 P 4:2, 3. 1 J 2:15-17.
 unfruitful. Is 5:2, 4. Mt 3:10. +13:22. +25:24. Lk 13:6. 19:20. Jn 15:2. He 6:7, 8. 2 P 1:8. Ju 12.

20 **which**. ver. 8. Mt +13:23. Lk 8:15. Jn 15:4, 5. Ro 7:4. Ga 5:22, 23. Ph 1:11. Col +1:10. 1 Th 4:1. Ja +1:21, 22. 2 P 1:8.
 an hundred. ver. 8. Mk +10:30. Ge +26:12.

21 **Is a candle**. Is 60:1-3. Mt 5:15, 16. +6:2. Lk 8:16. 11:33. Ac 10:47. 1 C 12:7. Ep 5:3-15. Ph 2:15, 16.
 bushel. Mt 5:15mg.

22 **nothing hid**. Ps 40:9, 10. 78:2-4. Ec 12:14. Mt 10:26, 27. Lk 8:17. 12:2, 3. Ac 4:20. 20:27. Ro 2:16. 1 C 4:5. 1 T 5:25. 1 J 1:1-3.

23 **have ears**. ver. +9, +24.

24 **Take heed**. Pr +19:27. Je 17:21. Ezk 14:10. *Mt +15:14*. Lk +8:18. Ac 17:11. He 2:1. 1 J 4:1. 1 P 2:2. 2 P 2:1-3.
 what ye hear. Mk 8:15. Ps +119:63. Pr +19:27. 20:12. Is +8:20. 65:5. Ezk +14:10. Mt 16:12. Lk +8:18. 1 T 1:4. +4:16. 2 T 4:3. 1 J 4:1. 2 J 9-11. Ju +3.

with what measure. Le 24:19. Jg +1:7. 1 S 15:33. Mt 7:2. Lk +6:37, 38. 2 C 9:6.
that hear. Mk 9:7. Is +55:3. Jn 5:25. 10:16, 27.

25 **he that hath**. Mt +13:12. Lk 16:9-12.
 from him. Mk 6:11. Je 5:25.

26 **So is**. Mk +1:15.
 as if. ver. 3, 4, 14, etc. Pr 11:18. Ec 11:4, 6. Is 28:24-26. 32:20. Mt +13:3, 24. Lk 8:5, 11. Jn 4:36-38. 12:24. 1 C +3:6-9. Ja 3:18. 1 P 1:23-25.

27 **night and day**. Mk 5:5. La 2:18. Lk 2:37. 18:7. Ac 9:24. 20:31. 26:7. 1 Th 2:9. 3:10. 2 Th 3:8. 1 T 5:5. 2 T 1:3.
 should spring. Is 61:11.
 and grow. Ec 8:17. 11:5. Jn 3:7, 8. 1 C 15:37, 38. 2 Th 1:3. 2 P 3:18.

28 **the earth**. Ge 1:11, 12. 2:4, 5, 9. 4:11, 12. Is 61:11. 1 C 3:7, 9.
 fruit. Ge 1:12. Jn +15:16.
 first. ver. 31, 32. Ps +1:3. 92:13, 14. Pr +4:18. Ec 3:1, 11. Ho +6:3. Ph 1:6, 9-11. Col +1:10. 1 Th 3:12, 13.
 blade. Mt 13:26.

29 **brought forth**. *or*, ripe. Jb 5:26. 2 T 4:7, 8.
 he putteth. Is 57:1, 2. Jl *3:13*. Mt +13:30, 39-43. Re 14:13-17.

30 **Whereunto**. Is 40:18. La 2:13. Mt 11:16. Lk 13:18, 20, 21. 1 C 3:1, 2.

31 **like**. Mt +13:31-33. Lk 13:18, 19.
 is less than. Ge 22:17, 18. Ps 72:16-19. Is 2:2, 3. +9:7. 49:6, 7. 53:2, 12. 54:1-3. 60:22. Ezk 17:22-24. Da 2:34, 35, 44, 45. Am +9:11-15. Mi 4:1, 2. Zc 2:11. 8:20-23. 12:8. 14:6-9. Ml 1:11. Mt 13:32. Ac 2:41. 4:4. 5:14. 19:20. 21:20. Re 11:15. 20:1-6.

32 **it groweth**. Da *4:9*.
 and becometh. Pr +4:18. Is 11:9. Ac 2:41. 4:4. 5:14. 19:20. 21:20.
 shooteth. Ps 80:9-11. Ezk 31:3-10. Da 4:10-14, 20-22.
 fowls. Ezk *17:23*. 31:6. Da *4:12*.
 lodge. Ps 91:1. SS 2:3. Is 32:2. La 4:20. Mi 4:1.

33 **with many**. Mt +13:34, 35.
 as they. Jn 16:12. 1 C 3:1, 2. He 5:11-14.

34 **when**. ver. 10, 11. Mk 7:17-23. Mt +13:36, etc. 15:15. Lk 8:9, etc. 24:27, 44-46.

35 **the same**. Mt 8:23. Lk 8:22.
 Let. Mk 5:21. 6:45. 8:13. Mt 8:18. 14:22. Jn 6:1, 17, 25.

36 **even**. ver. 1. Mk 3:9.

37 **there arose**. Mt 8:23, 24. Lk 8:22, 23.
 great storm. Jb 1:12, 19. Ps 107:23-31. Jon 1:4. Ac 27:14-20, 41. 2 C 11:25.

38 **in the**. Ps 4:8. Jn 4:6. He 2:17. +4:15.
 and they. 1 K 18:27-29. Ps +3:7. Mt 8:25. Lk 8:24.
 Master. Mk 5:35. 9:17, 38. 10:17, 20, 35. 12:14, 19, 32. 13:1. 14:14, 45. Mt +22:24. Lk +7:40. Jn +1:38.

carest. Ge +19:30. Ps 10:1, 2. 22:1, 2. 77:1-10. Is 40:27, 28. 49:14-16. 54:6-8. 63:15. 64:12. La 3:8. Jon 1:6. 1 P 5:7.
perish. Gr. *apollumi*, Mt +2:13.

39 he arose. Ex 14:16, 22, 28, 29. Jb 38:11. Ps 29:10. 93:3, 4. 104:7-9. 107:29. 148:8. Pr 8:29. Je 5:22.
rebuked. Mk 1:25. 5:7, 8. 9:25. Ps 106:9. Ec 8:4. Is 50:2. Na 1:4. Zc 3:2. Mt 8:26. 17:18. Lk 4:35, 39, 41. 8:24. 9:42. Ac 10:38. Ju 9.
be still. Mk 1:25.
the wind. Ps 89:9. La 3:31.
great calm. Mk 6:51. Jb 38:11. Ps 65:7. 89:9. 93:4. Mt 14:32.

40 Why. Ps 46:1-3. Is 42:3. 43:2. Mt 8:26. 14:31. Lk 8:25. Jn 6:19, 20.
fearful. Ps +118:6. 2 T +1:7. Re 21:8.
no faith. Mt +6:30.

41 feared. 1 S 12:18-20, 24. Ps 33:8. 89:7. Jon 1:9, 10, 14-16. Ml 2:5. Lk +1:65. He 12:28. Re 15:4.
What manner. Mk +16:20. Jb 38:11. Mt +8:27. Lk 4:35, 36. Jn 2:23. 5:36. 7:31. 10:37, 38. 11:42-45, 47, 48. 20:30, 31.
that even. Lk 5:9.

MARK 5

1 came over. Mk 4:35. Mt 8:28-34. Lk 8:26, etc.
Gadarenes. i.e. *fortified*, **S#1046g**. Lk 8:26, 37.

2 out. Is 65:4. Lk 8:27.
with. ver. 8. Mk +3:30.
spirit. Gr. *pneuma*, Mt +8:16.

3 dwelling. Mk 9:18-22. Is 65:4. Da 4:32, 33. Lk 8:29.

4 tame. Ja 3:7, 8.

5 tombs. Gr. *mnema*, **S#3418g**. Lk 8:27. 23:53 (sepulchre). 24:1. Ac 2:29. Re 11:9 (graves).
crying. 1 K 18:26. Jb 2:7, 8. Jn 8:44.
cutting. Le +19:28.

6 he ran. Ps 66:3mg. 72:9. Lk 4:41. Ac 16:17. Ja 2:19.
worshipped. Mt +8:2.

7 What. Jg +11:12.
Jesus. Ph 2:10.
Son. Mk 3:11. 14:61. Mt 16:16. Jn 20:31. Ac 8:37. 16:17.
most high God. Mk 11:10. Nu 24:16. Ps +7:17. Is 14:14. 57:15. Mi 6:6. Lk 1:32. 6:35. Ro 9:5. 1 C 10:9. 1 Th 3:13.
I adjure. 1 K 22:16. Mt 26:63. Ac 19:13. 1 Th 5:27mg.
that. Ge +3:15. Mt 8:29. Lk 8:28. Ro 16:20. He 2:14. Ja 2:19. 2 P 2:4. 1 J 3:8. Ju 6. Re 12:12. 20:1-3.

8 Come out. Mk 1:25. 9:25, 26. Ac 16:18.
spirit. Gr. *pneuma*, Mt +8:16.

9 What is. Lk 8:30. 11:21-26.
Legion. i.e. a division of the Roman army,

S#3003g. ver. 9, 15. Lk 8:30. Mt 26:53.
we are many. Mt 12:45.

10 he besought. ver. 13. Mk 3:22. Lk 8:31.

11 herd. Le 11:7, 8. Dt 14:8. Is 65:4. 66:3. Mt 8:30. Lk 8:32.

12 all the devils. Jb 1:10-12. 2:5. Lk 4:41. 22:31, 32. 2 C 2:11. 1 P 5:8.
besought. Ro +1:4.
Send us. Ac +5:32. Ro +1:4.

13 gave them leave. 1 K 22:22. Jb 1:12. 2:6. Am +3:6. Mt 8:32. Col 2:9. 1 P 3:22. Re 13:5-7. 20:7.
spirits. Gr. *pneuma*, Mt +8:16.
the herd. Jn 8:44. Re 9:11.

14 they that fed. Mt 8:33. Lk 8:34.

15 him that. ver. 4. Is 49:24, 25. Mt 9:33. 12:29. Lk 8:35, 36. 10:39. Col 1:13.
right mind. 1 C 6:11. 2 T +1:7.
and they. 1 S 6:20, 21. 16:4. 1 Ch 13:12. 15:13. Jb 13:11. Ps 14:5. 2 T +1:7.

16 possessed. ver. 18. Mt 4:24.
swine. Lk 8:32.

17 pray him to depart. ver. 7. Mk 1:24. Ge 26:16. Dt 5:25. 1 K 17:18. Jb +21:14, 15. Mt 8:34. Lk 5:8, 9. 8:37. Ac 16:39. 2 C 2:14.

18 prayed. ver. 7, 17. Ps 116:12. Lk 8:38, 39. 17:15-17. 23:42, 43. Ph 1:23, 24.
be with. Lk 9:61, 62. Ph 1:23.

19 Go home. Ge +16:9. Ps 66:16. Is 38:9-20. Da 4:1-3, 37. 6:25-27. Jon 2:1, etc. Jn 4:29. Ac 22:1-21. 26:4-29.
tell them. Ps 107:2. Lk 12:8, 9. Jn 1:41. Ac 4:19, 20. 2 T 1:8. 1 P 3:15.

20 began to publish. Ps 51:12, 13. 66:16. Is 38:9, 19. Jn 1:40-42.
Decapolis. Mt +4:25.

21 passed over. Mt 9:1. Lk 8:40.
people gathered. Lk 8:40.

22 rulers. Mt +9:18.
Jairus. i.e. *running water*, **S#2383g**. Lk 8:41. See **S#2971h**, Nu +32:41, Jair.
he fell. Ge +17:3.

23 besought. Mk 7:25-27. 9:17-24. 2 S 12:15-23. Ps +50:15. Mt 8:5. 15:22-28. 17:14-18. Lk 4:38. 7:2, 3, 4, 12. 8:41. 9:38. Jn 4:46-50. 11:3, 21.
of death. Ge 32:9-11. 2 S 12:15, 16. 1 Ch 21:16, 17. Ps 39:11-13. 107:17-19. Lk 7:2, 3. 8:41, 42.
lay thy hands. Mk 6:5, 6, 13. 7:32. 8:25. 16:18. 2 K 5:11. Jb 5:18. Mt 8:3. 9:18. Lk 4:40. 13:13. Ac +8:17. 9:12, 17. 28:8. Ja 5:14, 15.

24 went. Lk 7:6. Ac 10:38.
and thronged. ver. 31. Mk 3:9, 10, 20. Lk 8:42, 45. 12:1. 19:3.

25 a certain. Mt 9:20-22. Lk 8:43, 44.
an issue. Le 15:19, 20, 25-27.
twelve. Lk 13:11. Jn 5:5, 6. Ac 4:22. 9:33, 34.

26 **had suffered**. Jb +13:4. Je 51:8.
spent all. Ge 47:18. Lk 15:14. 21:4.
nothing. Ps 108:12.

27 **touched**. Mk 6:56. 2 K 13:21. Mt 14:36. Ac
5:15. 19:12.

28 **be whole**. or, saved. ver. 23, 34. Mk 10:52.

29 **straightway**. Ex +15:26. Jb 33:24, 25. Ps
30:2. +103:3. 107:20. 147:3.
fountain. Le 20:18.
felt. lit. knew. Is +53:11.
plague. ver. 34. Mk 3:10. 1 K 8:37. Lk 7:21.

30 **knowing**. Gr. *epiginosko*, Mt +11:27.
virtue. Lk 6:19. 8:46. 1 P 2:9mg.

31 **Thou seest**. Lk 8:45. 9:12.

32 **he looked**. Mk 3:5.

33 **the woman**. Mk 4:41. Lk 1:12, 29. 8:47.
fearing. Ge +19:30.
and told. Ps 30:2. 66:16. 103:2-5. 116:12-14.

34 **Daughter**. Mt 9:2, 22. Lk 8:48.
thy faith. Mk 9:23, 24. Mt 9:2, 28, 29. 13:58.
15:28. 21:22. Lk 17:19. Jn 4:50, 51. Ac 14:8-
10.
go. Lk +7:50.

35 **there came**. Lk 8:49.
house certain. ver. 38. Ro 16:10, 11. 1 C 1:11.
Thy daughter. Jn 5:25. 11:25.
why. Lk 7:6, 7. Jn 11:21, 32, 39.
the Master. Mk +4:38.

36 **heard**. Ge +18:10.
only believe. ver. 34. Mk 9:23. 2 Ch +20:20.
Mt 9:28, 29. +17:20. Lk 8:50. Jn 4:48-50.
11:40. Ro 4:18-24.

37 **he suffered no**. Lk 8:51. Ac 9:40.
save. Mk 9:2. 14:33. 2 C 13:1.

38 **and seeth**. Mt +9:23, 24.

39 **not dead**. Da +12:2. Jn 11:11-13. Ac 20:10. 1
C +11:30. 1 Th 4:13, 14. 5:10.

40 **they laughed**. Ps 123:3, 4. Lk +8:53.
when. Mk 7:33. 8:23. 1 K 17:19. 2 K 4:33.
Mt +7:6. 9:24, 25. Lk 8:53, 54. Ac 9:40.
he taketh. Ac 26:26. 2 P 1:16.

41 **took**. Mk 1:31. Ac 9:40, 41.
Talitha cumi. S#5008g, only here. This is pure
Syriac, the same as in the Syriac version, the
proper translation of which is given by the
evangelist. Compare S#2924h, *taleh*, 1 S 7:9
(lamb). Is 65:25 (lamb).
interpreted. Ps +7:13. S#3177g, *mether-
meeneuomai*. Mk 15:22, 34. Mt 1:23. Jn 1:41.
Ac 4:36. 13:8. Compare the related words
S#1329g, *diermeeneuo*, Lk +24:27; S#2058g, *her-
meenia*, 1 C +12:10; S#2059g, *hermeenuo*, Jn
+1:38.
Damsel. Mk 1:41. Ge 1:3. Ps 33:9. Lk 7:14,
15. 8:54, 55. Jn 5:28, 29. 11:43, 44. Ro 4:17.
Ph 3:21.

42 **damsel**. ver. 41.
astonished. Mt +8:27. Ac 3:10-13.

43 **he charged**. Mk +1:43. Is 52:13. Lk +5:14. Jn
5:41. 7:8.

and commanded. Mt 14:16.
given. Lk 24:30, 42, 43. Ac 10:41.

MARK 6

1 **and come**. Mt 13:54-58. Lk 4:16-30.
own country. Mt 2:23. Lk 4:23.

2 **sabbath**. Mk +3:4. Le 19:30. Ps 84:1-10.
132:7. Is +58:13. 66:23. Ezk 46:3. Lk 4:16, 31.
13:10, +14. Ac 13:14-16, 42, 44. 15:21. 17:2.
18:4. 1 C 16:2. He 10:25.
he began. Mt +4:23.
astonished. Mt +7:28.
From. Mk 11:28. Mt 21:23. Jn 6:42. 7:15, 52.
Ac 4:13, 14.
wisdom. Ac 7:22.

3 **this**. Mt +13:55, 56. Lk 4:22. Jn 6:42.
carpenter. Is 49:7. *53:2, 3*. 1 P 2:4.
Mary. Mt 1:16. Jn 6:42.
the brother of. Mk +3:31. Ps +69:8. Mt 1:18,
25. +13:55. Lk 2:7. Ac 1:14.
James. Mk 15:40. Mt 12:46. 1 C 9:4. Ga 1:19.
Juda. Jn 14:22. Ju 1.
Simon. Mk 3:18. Ac 1:13.
offended. Is 53:3. Mt +11:6.

4 **A prophet**. Je 11:21. 12:6. Mt 13:57. Lk
4:24. Jn 4:44. 7:5.
own country. Jn 7:41, 42.
own house. Mk 3:19, 20. Jn 7:3.

5 **he could**. Mk 9:23. Ge 19:22. 32:25. Is 59:1,
2. Mt 13:58. He 4:2.
laid his hands. Mk +5:23.

6 **marvelled**. Mk 5:20. Is 59:16. Je 2:11. Mt
8:10. Lk 7:9. Jn 9:30.
their unbelief. Mt 17:20.
And he went. Mt 4:23. 9:35. 11:1. Lk 4:31,
44. 8:1. 13:22. Ac 10:38.

7 **the twelve**. Mk 3:13, 14. 9:35. Mt 10:1, etc.
Lk 6:13-16. 9:1-6. 10:3, etc. 22:35.
to send. Jn 17:18.
by two. Mk 11:1. 14:13. Ex 4:14, 15. Ec 4:9,
10. Re 11:3.
and two. ver. 39, 40. Lk 9:14. 10:1. 2 C
4:16.
power. Mk 16:17. Mt 10:9. Lk 10:17-20.
unclean. Mk +3:30.
spirits. Gr. *pneuma*, Mt +8:16.

8 **take**. Mt 10:9, 10. Lk 10:4. 22:35.
staff. Ex +25:13.
scrip. 1 S 17:40. Mt 10:10. Lk 22:35, 36.
money. Mk 12:41. Mt 10:9, 10. Lk 9:3.

9 **be shod**. Mt 10:10. Ac 12:8. Ep 6:15.
sandals. Ac 12:8.
not put on. Lk 5:14. Jn 5:44. Ac 1:4. 17:3.
two coats. Mk 14:63. Lk 3:11.

10 **there abide**. Mt 10:11-13. Lk 9:4. 10:7; 8. Ac
16:15. 17:5-7. 1 T 5:13.

11 **shall not**. Ne 5:13. Ro +15:7.
shake. Ac 13:50, 51. 18:6.
for a testimony. Mt +8:4. 2 Th 1:10.

more tolerable. Mt +10:15. He 6:4-8. 10:26-31. 2 P 2:6. Ju 7.
and. Gr. or.
in the day. Mt 12:36. Ro 2:5, 16. 2 P 2:9. 3:7. 1 J 4:17.

12 went out. Lk 9:6.
preached. Mk 1:3, 15. Lk 11:32. +13:3, 5. 2 C 7:9, 10. 2 T +2:25, 26.

13 cast. ver. 7. Mt 10:7, 8. Lk 10:17.
anointed. Jn 9:6, 7. 1 C 12:9. Ja 5:14, 15. 1 J 2:20.

14 king Herod. ver. 22, 26, 27. Mt 14:1, 2. Lk 3:1. 9:7-9. 13:31. 23:7-12.
of him. or, of these mighty works.
his name. Mk 1:28, 45. 2 Ch 26:8, 15. Mt 9:31. 1 Th 1:8.
John the Baptist. Mk 8:28. Mt 16:14.
risen from the dead. Mt +11:14. +27:52.
mighty works. Mt +13:54.
show forth. 1 C 12:6, 11. Ga 2:8. 3:5. Ep 1:11, 20. 2:2. Ph 2:13.

15 it is Elias. Mk 8:28. 9:12, 13. 15:35, 36. Ml 4:5, Elijah. Mt 16:14. 17:10, 11. Lk 1:17. 9:8, 19. Jn 1:21, 25.
a prophet. Mt +21:11.

16 It is. Ge 4:10, 11. Ps 53:5. Mt 14:2. 27:4. Lk 9:9. Re 11:10-13.

17 A.M. 4032. A.D. 28.
Herod. Mt +4:12.
Philip's. Lk 3:1.

18 It is. Le 18:16. 20:21. 1 K 22:14. Ezk 3:18, 19. Mt +14:3, 4. Ac 20:26, 27. 24:24-26.

19 Herodias. Ge 39:17-20. 1 K 21:20.
a quarrel. or, an inward grudge. Ge 49:23. Ec 7:9. Lk 11:53. Ep 4:26, 27.

20 feared. Mk 11:18. Ex 11:3. 1 S 18:14. 1 K 21:20. 2 K 3:12, 13. 6:21. 13:14. 2 Ch 24:2, 15-22. 26:5. Ezk 2:5-7. Da 4:18, 27. 5:17. Mt 14:5. 21:26. Lk 8:37. Ac 24:25.
observed him. or, kept him, or saved him. 1 S 19:11. Ps 37:32. Zc 3:9. Lk 9:7. 20:20.
and heard. Mk 4:16. Ps 106:12, 13. Ezk +33:31, 32. Jn 5:35.
gladly. Mk 4:16. 12:37. Mt +13:20.

21 when. Ge 27:41. 2 S 13:23-29. Est 3:7. Ps 37:12, 13. Ac 12:2-4.
his birthday. Ge 40:20. Est 1:3-7. 2:18. Pr 31:4, 5. Da 5:1-4. Ho 7:5. 1 P 4:3. Re 11:10.
made a supper. 1 K 3:15. Est 1:3. 2:18.
to his lords. Re 6:15.
high captains. Mk 10:42. Ac 21:31. Re 18:23.
chief. Lk 19:47. Ac 13:50. 17:4. 25:2. 28:7, 17.
Galilee. Lk 3:1.

22 the daughter. Est 1:10-12. Is 3:16, etc. Da 5:2. Mt 14:6.

23 he. 1 S 28:10. 2 K 6:31. Mt 5:34-37. 14:7.
Whatsoever. Est 5:3, 6. 7:2. Pr 6:2. Mt 4:9.

24 said. Ge 27:8-11. 2 Ch 22:3, 4. Ezk 19:2, 3. Mt 14:8.

The head. Jb 31:31. Ps 27:2. 37:12, 14. Pr 27:3, 4. Ac 23:12, 13.

25 with haste. Pr 1:16. Ro 3:15.
a charger. Nu 7:13, 19, etc.

26 was exceeding. Mt 14:9. 27:3-5, 24, 25. Lk 18:23.
his oath's. ver. 23. Jg +11:30, 31, 35.
their sakes. Is 8:13.

27 the king. Mt 14:10, 11.
an executioner. or, one of his guard.

29 his disciples. Mt 9:14.
they came. 1 K 13:29, 30. 2 Ch 24:16. Mt 14:12. 27:57-60. Ac 8:2.

30 the apostles. Mt 10:2. Lk 6:13. 9:10. 17:5. 22:14. 24:10. Jn 13:16. Ac 1:2.
gathered. ver. 7, etc. Lk 9:10. 10:17.
and told. Lk 14:21. Jn 15:15. Ac 14:27.
both. Ac 1:1. 20:18-21. 1 T 4:12-16. T 2:6, 7. 1 P 5:2, 3.

31 Come. Mk 1:45. 3:7, 20. Mt 14:13. Jn 6:1, 2.
apart. Ex +3:1. Pr +18:1. Mt 14:23. 15:29. 17:1. 20:17. Lk 9:10. 22:41. Ga 1:17, 18. Re 1:9.
and rest. Ge 18:4. Ex 16:23. 23:12. Dt 33:12. Jb 11:19. Ps +127:2. Ec +2:23. Mt 8:18, 24. 11:29.

32 they departed. Mt 14:13.
privately. Ge 32:24. Ex +3:1. Ps 55:7. Je 9:2. Mt 28:16. Lk 5:16. Ga 1:17, 18.

33 knew. Gr. *epiginosko*, Mt +11:27. ver. 54, 55. Mt 15:29-31. Jn 6:2. Ja 1:19.

34 saw. Mt +9:36. Lk 9:11. Ro 15:2, 3.
moved. Is +63:15.
because. Nu +27:17. Ezk 34:5.
and he. Is 61:1-3.

35 when the day. Mt 14:15, etc. Lk 9:12, etc. Jn 6:5, etc.
far spent. Jg 19:8mg, 9mg, 11. Je 6:4. Lk 24:29.

36 Send them away. ver. 45. Mk 3:21. 5:31. Mt 15:23. 16:22.

37 Give. Mk 8:2, 3. Mt 14:16. 15:32.
Shall. Mt +14:17.
pennyworth. Mt +18:28.

38 Five. Mk 8:5, 19. Mt 14:17, 18. 15:34. 16:9. Lk 9:13. Jn 6:9.

39 all sit down. 1 K 10:5. Est 1:5, 6. Mt +14:19. 1 C 14:33, 40.

40 by hundreds. Lk 9:14, 15.

41 looked up. Mt +14:19.
blessed. Lk +24:30. 1 C 10:31.

42 all did eat. Ps 145:15, 16. Mt +14:20, 21.

43 twelve baskets. Mk 8:8, 19, 20. Mt 14:20. 15:37. 16:9. Lk 9:17. Jn 6:13. Ac 9:25.

45 straightway. Mt 14:22-32. Jn 6:15-17, etc.
constrained. Mt 8:18. Lk 14:23.
the ship. ver. 32, 51. Mk 3:9.
unto Bethsaida. i.e. *house of provision, house of hunting*, **S#966g**. ver. 45. Mk 8:22. Mt 11:21. Lk 9:10. 10:13. Jn 1:44. 12:21. See **S#6719h**,

tsayad, Je 16:16, hunters. *or*, over against Bethsaida. Mk 8:22. Mt 11:21, 23. Lk 9:10. 10:13. Jn 6:17. 12:21.

he sent. ver. 36.

46 **had sent.** Lk 9:61. 14:33. Ac 18:18, 21. 2 C 2:13.

he departed. Mk +1:35. Mt 6:6. 14:23. Lk 5:16. 6:12. 1 P 2:21.

mountain. Mt +5:1.

47 **when even.** Mk +13:35. Mt 14:23. Jn 6:16, 17.

48 **he saw.** Is 54:11. Jon 1:13. Mt 14:24.

the fourth watch. Our 3 a.m. to 6 a.m. Mk 13:35, morning. Ex 14:24. 1 S 11:11. Mt +14:25. Lk 12:38.

he cometh. Jb 9:8. Ps 93:4. 104:3.

would have. Ge 19:2. 32:26. Lk 24:28.

49 **they saw.** Ge +21:19. Jb 9:8. Lk +24:16.

supposed. Jb 4:14-16. Mt 14:25, 26. Lk 24:37.

50 **were troubled.** Lk 24:37.

good cheer. Dt 31:6. Jsh 10:25. 1 Ch 22:13. 28:20. Jn 16:33.

it is I. Is 43:2. Mt 14:27. Lk 24:38-41. Jn 6:19, 20. 20:19, 20.

be not afraid. Is 41:13. 43:1. Mt 17:7.

51 **the ship.** ver. 32, 45. Mk 3:9.

wind ceased. Mk 4:39. Ps 93:3, 4. 107:28-30. Mt 8:26, 27. 14:28-32. Lk 8:24, 25. Jn 6:21.

and they. Mt +8:27.

52 **they.** Mk 7:18. 8:17, 18, 21. 9:32. Mt 16:9-11. Lk 24:25.

their. Mk 3:5. 16:14. Is 63:17.

hardened. Mk 8:17. Jn 12:40. Ro 11:7. 2 C 3:14.

53 **the land.** Mt 14:34-36. Lk 5:1. Jn 6:24.

54 **knew.** Gr. *epiginosko*, Mt +11:27. ver. 33. Ps +9:10. Ph 3:10.

55 **ran through.** Mk 2:1-3. 3:7-11. Mt 4:24.

in beds. Mk 2:4. Mt 9:2. Lk 5:18.

sick. Mt 4:24. 8:16.

56 **they laid.** Ac 5:15.

in the streets. Mk 7:4. SS 3:2. Am +5:16. Mt 6:5. Lk 11:43.

touch. Mk 3:10. 5:27, 28. 2 K 13:21. Mt 14:36. Lk 6:19. 8:47. 22:51. Ac 5:15. 19:12.

the border. Nu 15:38, 39. Dt 22:12. Mt 9:20. 14:34-36. Lk 8:44.

him. *or*, it.

made whole. Mk 10:52.

MARK 7

1 **the Pharisees.** Mk 3:22. Mt 15:1. Lk 5:17. 11:53, 54. Ph 3:5, 7.

2 **defiled.** *or*, common. ver. 5. Ac 10:14, 15, 28. 11:8. Ro 14:14mg. He 10:29. Re 21:27.

they found. Da 6:4, 5. Mt 7:3-5. 23:23-25.

3 **wash.** Gr. *nipto*, **S#3538g.** Mt 6:17. 15:2. Jn 9:7,

11, 15. 13:5, 6, 8, 10, 12, 14. 1 T 5:10. For **S#3068g,** *louo,* see Jn +13:10. For **S#3067g,** *loutron,* see Ep +5:26. For **S#4150g,** *pluno,* see Re +7:14. For **S#628g,** *apolouo,* see Ac +22:16. For **S#633g,** *aponipto,* see Mt 27:24. For **S#637g,** *apopluno,* see Lk 5:2. For **S#1026g,** *breko,* see Lk +7:38.

oft. *or,* diligently. Gr. *pugma,* **S#4435g,** only here. i.e. with the fist; up to the elbow.

the tradition. ver. 7-10, 13. Dt +4:2. Ga 1:14. Col 2:8, 21-23. 1 P 1:18.

the elders. He 11:2.

4 **the market.** Mk 6:56. Lk 11:43.

except. Jb 9:30, 31. Ps 26:6. Is 1:16. Je 4:14. Mt 27:24. Lk 11:38, 39. Jn 2:6. 3:25. He 9:10. Ja 4:8. 1 J 1:7.

wash. lit. baptize. Gr. *baptizo,* **S#907g,** Mt +3:6. Lk 11:38. Ex 29:4. Le 8:5, 6. Nu 8:5-7. Dt +23:11. Lk 11:38. Ac 1:5. He 6:2. 9:10.

washing. Gr. *baptismos,* lit. baptizing. **S#909g.** ver. 4, 8. He 6:2. 9:10.

cups. Mt 23:25. Lk 11:39.

pots. "Gr. *Sextarious;* about a pint and a half."

tables. *or,* beds. Gr. *klinee,* **S#2825g.** ver. 4, 30. Mk 4:21. Mt 9:2, 6. Lk 5:18. 8:16. 17:34. Ac 5:15. Re 2:22.

5 **the Pharisees and.** Mk 2:16-18. Mt 15:2. Ac 21:21, 24. Ro 4:12. 2 Th 3:6, 11.

tradition. ver. 3. Col 2:8.

but eat. Lk 11:38.

unwashen. ver. 2.

6 **Well.** Is *29:13.* Mt 15:7-9. Lk +24:27. Jn 28:25.

Esaias. Mk 1:2.

hypocrites. Mt +6:2.

honoreth. Is *29:13.* Ezk +33:31. Ho 8:2, 3. Jn 5:42. 8:41, 42, 54, 55. 15:24. 2 T 3:5. T 1:16. Ja 2:14-17.

their heart. 1 S +16:7. Pr 23:26.

7 **in vain.** 1 S 12:21. Ml 3:14. Mt 6:7. 15:9. 1 C 15:14, 58. T 3:9. Ja 1:26. 2:20.

worship. Dt 4:24. Na 1:2. Lk +14:10. Jn 4:24. Ac 16:14. 18:7, 13. 19:27. Ro 1:25. Ph 3:3.

teaching. Is +8:20. Je 23:21, 22, 29. 1 P 1:18.

doctrines. Col 2:22. T 1:14.

the commandments. Dt 12:32. Je 23:21, 22, 29. Col 2:22. 1 T 4:1-3. Re 14:11, 12. 22:18.

8 **laying.** Is 1:12.

commandment. 1 C 7:19. Re 12:17. 14:12.

the traditions. ver. 3, 4.

9 **Full.** 2 K 16:10-16. Is 24:5. 29:13. Je 44:16, 17. Da 7:25. 11:36. Mt 15:3-6. 2 Th 2:4.

reject. *or,* frustrate. ver. 13. Ps 119:126. Je +8:9. Lk 7:30. Ro 3:31. Ga 2:21. 3:15. He 10:28.

10 **Honor.** Ge 45:9-11. Ex +*20:12.* Dt *5:16.* Mi 7:6.

Whoso. Pr +20:20.

11 **But.** Mt 5:19.

If. Mt +4:9.

It is Corban. i.e. *offering*, **S#2878g**. ver. 11. Mt 27:6. Hebrew **S#7133h**, *corban, offering*, as at Le 1:2. Nu 5:15. Ezk 20:28. 40:43. Le 1:2. 2:1. 7:13. 19:5. Mt 15:5. 23:18. 27:6. 1 T 5:4-8.

whatsoever. Mt +4:9.

12 **no more**. Is +58:7.

to do ought. 1 T 5:4.

13 **the word**. ver. 9. Is +8:20. Je 8:8, 9. Ho 8:12. Mt 5:17-20. 15:6. T 1:14.

of God. Lk 5:1. Jn 10:35. Ro 9:6. Re 1:2.

none effect. Ro 2:23. Ga 3:17.

tradition. Lk 12:1.

such. Ezk 18:14. Ga 5:21.

14 **when**. 1 K 18:21. 22:28. Ps 49:1, 2. 94:8. Mt 15:10. Lk 12:1, 54-57. 20:45-47.

and understand. ver. 18. Pr 8:5. Is 6:9. Mt 13:51. 15:16. Ac 8:30.

15 **nothing**. ver. 18-20. Le 11:42-47. Ac 10:14-16, 28. 11:8-10. 15:20, 21. 21:28. Ro 14:17. 1 C 10:25. 1 T 4:3-5. T 1:15. He 9:10, 13. 13:9. Re 21:27.

but. ver. 20-23. Pr 4:23. Mt 12:34, 35. 15:16-20.

16 **If**. 1 C +15:2.

have ears. Mt +13:9. Lk 8:8. 14:35.

17 **when he was entered**. Mk 3:19. 4:10, 34. 9:28.

disciples asked. Mt 13:10, 36. 15:15.

18 **without understanding**. ver. 14. Mk 4:13. 8:17, 18. Is 28:9, 10. Je 5:4, 5. Mt 15:16, 17. 16:11. Lk 24:25. Jn 3:10. Ro 1:21, 31. 10:19. 1 C 3:2. He 5:11, 12.

defile. ver. 15.

19 **entereth not**. Mt 15:17. 1 C 6:13. Col 2:21, 22.

purging all meats. Lk 11:41. Ac 10:14, 15. 11:9. Ro 14:17. Ga 2:12. Col 2:16-23. 1 T 4:3. T 1:15. He 9:10. 13:9.

20 **That which**. ver. 15. Ps 41:6. Ho 7:6. Mi 2:1. Mt 12:34-37. 15:11. Ep 4:29. Ja 1:14, 15. 3:6. 4:1.

21 **From within**. Mt 12:34. 15:19.

out of the heart. Ge 6:5. 8:21. Jb 14:4. 15:14-16. 25:4. Ps 14:1, 3. 53:1, 3. 58:2, 3. Pr +4:23. Ec 9:3. Je 4:14. +17:9. Mt 15:19. 23:25-28. Lk 16:15. Jn 3:19. Ac 5:4. 8:22. Ro 1:21. 7:5, 8. 8:7, 8. 1 C 2:14. Ga 5:19-21. Ep 4:17-19. 5:8. T 1:15. 3:3. Ja 1:14, 15. 4:1-3. 1 P 4:2, 3.

evil thoughts. Dt 15:9. Ps 56:5. Pr 15:26. 23:7. 24:9. Is 59:7. Je 4:14. +6:19. Ezk 38:10. Mt 9:4. Ja 2:4.

adulteries. Ex +20:14.

fornications. Mt +5:32. 1 C +6:9, 18.

murders. Ex +20:13.

22 **thefts**. Ex +20:15. Ep 4:28.

covetousness. Gr. covetousnesses. Ps +10:3. **S#4124g**; Lk 12:15. Ro 1:29. 2 C 9:5. Ep 4:19 (greediness). 5:3. Col 3:5. 1 Th 2:5. 2 P 2:3,

14. Compare **S#4123g**: 1 C 5:10, 11. 6:10. Ep 5:5.

wickedness. Gr. wickednesses. **S#4189g**. Mt 22:18. Lk 11:39. Ac 3:26. Ro 1:29. 1 C 5:8. Ep 6:12.

deceit. Pr 11:18. 12:17. 24:28. 26:24-28. Mt 19:18. 2 C 4:1, 2. Ep 5:6. Col 2:8. 1 P 2:1, 2. 3:10. **S#1388g**: Mk 14:1 (craft). Mt 26:4 (subtilty). Jn 1:47 (guile). Ac 13:10. Ro 1:29. 2 C 12:16 (guile). 1 Th 2:3. 1 P 2:1, 22. 3:10. Re 14:5. Compare **S#1389g**, 2 C 4:2 (handling deceitfully).

lasciviousness. **S#766g**. Ro 13:13 (wantonness). 2 C 12:21. Ga 5:19. Ep 4:19. 1 P 4:3. 2 P 2:7 (filthy), 18. Ju 4.

an evil eye. Dt 15:9. +28:54, 56. 1 S 18:8, 9. Ps +37:1. Pr 23:6. 28:22. Mt 6:23. 20:15. 2 P 2:14.

blasphemy. **S#988g**. Mk 2:7. 3:28. 7:22. 14:64. Mt 12:31, 31. 15:19. 26:65. Lk 5:21. Jn 10:33. Ep +4:31 (evil speaking). Col 3:8. 1 T 6:4 (railings). Ju 9 (railing). Re 2:9. 13:1, 5, 6. 17:3.

pride. 2 Ch 32:25, 26, 31. Pr +16:5. 2 C 10:5.

foolishness. Pr 12:23. 22:15. 24:9. 27:22. Ec 7:25. 2 C 11:1, 17, 21. Ep 5:17. 1 P 2:15.

23 **All these**. 1 C +6:9, 10.

evil things. Lk 1:79. Ga 5:19.

defile. ver. 15, 18, 23. 1 C 3:17. T 1:15. Ju 8.

24 **from**. Mt 15:21, etc.

Tyre. Mt +11:21.

Sidon. Ge +49:13.

and would. Mk 2:1. 3:7. +6:31, 32. Is 42:2. Mt 9:28. 1 T 5:25.

could not. SS 1:3, 12. Jn 12:3.

25 **a certain woman**. Mt 15:22.

whose. Mk 9:17-23.

unclean. Mk +3:30.

spirit. Gr. *pneuma*, Mt +8:16.

at. Mk 1:40. Ge +17:3.

26 **Greek**. *or*, Gentile. i.e. *non-Jewish*, **S#1674g**. Used here and at Ac 17:12. Is 49:12. Ro 1:16. 1 C 12:13. Ga 3:28. Col 3:11.

a Syrophenician. i.e. *exalted palm, purple*, **S#4949g**, only here. Mt 4:24. 15:22. Ac 21:2, 3.

27 **Let**. Mt +7:6. Ac 22:21, 22. Ep 2:12.

first be filled. Ac +3:26. Ro 3:29.

not meet. Mt 10:6.

cast it. Mt +7:6.

28 **yet**. Ps 145:16. Is 45:22. 49:6. Mt +5:45. Lk 7:6-8. 15:30-32. Ac 11:17, 18. Ro 3:29. 10:12. 15:8, 9. Ep 2:12-14. 3:8.

crumbs. Lk 16:21.

29 **For this**. Is +57:15, 16. 66:2. Mt +5:3. 8:9-13. 1 J 3:8.

go thy way. Mt 8:13. Jn 4:50.

30 **she was**. Jn 4:50-52.

she found. 1 J 3:8.

31 **from**. ver. 24. Mt 15:29, etc.

Decapolis. Mt 4:25.

32   **bring**. Mt +9:33.
    deaf. Is 35:5, 6.
    put his hand. Mk +5:23.
33   **took him aside**. Mk +5:40. 8:23. 1 K 17:19-
    22. 2 K 4:4-6, 33, 34. Jn 9:6, 7.
    and put. 2 K 13:17.
    he spit. Jn 9:6.
    touched. Mk 1:41.
34   **looking**. Mt +14:19.
    he sighed. Mk 8:12. Ps +12:5. Is 53:3. Ezk
    21:6, 7. Lk 19:41. Jn 11:33, 35, 38. He +4:15.
    Ephphatha. i.e. *opened*, **S#2188g**, only here.
    Mk 5:41. 15:34.
    Be opened. Mk 1:41. Lk 7:14. 18:42. Jn
    11:43. Ac 9:34, 40.
35   **straightway**. Mk 2:12. Ps 33:9. Is 32:3, 4.
    35:5, 6. Mt 11:5.
36   **he charged**. Mk +1:43. Is 42:2. Lk +5:14.
37   **were**. Ps 139:14. Mt +8:27. Ac 2:7-12. 14:11.
    He hath done. Ge 1:31. 2 S 3:36. Ps 39:9.
    98:1. Is 12:5. 38:15. Ezk 14:23. Lk 13:17.
    23:41. Jn 13:7.
    he maketh. Ex 4:10, 11.

MARK 8

1   **the multitude**. Mt 15:32, etc.
2   **compassion**. Mk 5:19. Ps 103:13. 145:8, 15.
    Mi 7:19. Mt +9:36.
    and have. Mt 4:2-4. 6:32, 33. Jn 4:6-8, 30-
    34.
3   **if**. Mt +4:9.
    they will faint. Jg 8:4-6. 1 S 14:28-31.
    30:10-12. Ps 103:14. Is 40:31.
4   **From**. Mt +14:17.
5   **asked**. Mk 11:13. Jn +2:25. 11:34.
    How. Mt +14:17.
6   **to sit**. Mt +14:19. Lk 12:37. Jn 2:5.
    gave thanks. Lk +24:30.
    brake. Is +58:7.
    before the people. 2 K 4:43.
7   **fishes**. Lk 24:41, 42. Jn 21:5, 8, 9.
    he blessed. Mk 6:41. Mt 14:19.
8   **and were**. ver. 19, 20. Ps 132:15. 145:16. Mt
    +14:20. 15:28. 16:10. Jn 6:11-13, 27, 32-35,
    47-58.
    they took. 1 K 17:14-16. 2 K 4:2-7, 42-44.
    Mt +14:20.
10   **straightway**. Mt 15:39.
    Dalmanutha. i.e. *leanness*, **S#1148g**, only here.
11   **Pharisees**. Mk 2:16. 7:1, 2. Mt 12:38. 16:1-4.
    19:3. 21:23. 22:15, 18, 23, 34, 35. Lk 11:53,
    54. Jn 7:48.
    seeking. Lk 11:16. 12:54-57. Jn 4:48. 6:30. 1
    C 1:22, 23.
    a sign. Dt 13:1. 18:18.
    tempting. Mt +16:1.
12   **he sighed**. Mk 3:5. 7:34. 9:19. Is 53:3. Lk
    19:41. Jn 11:33-38.
    spirit. Gr. *pneuma*, Mk +2:8.

    Why. Mk 6:6. Lk 16:29-31. 22:67-70. Jn
    12:37-43.
    There. Mt 12:39, 40. 16:4. Lk 11:29, 30.
13   **he left**. Ps 81:12. Je 23:33. Ho 4:17. 9:12. Zc
    11:8, 9. Mt +7:6. +15:14. Lk 8:37. Jn 8:21.
    12:36. Ac 13:45, 46. 18:6.
14   **had forgotten**. Mt 16:5.
15   **he charged**. Nu 27:19-23. 1 Ch +28:9, 10,
    20. 1 T 5:21. 6:13. 2 T 2:14.
    Take. Pr +19:27. Mt 16:6, 11, 12. Lk 12:1, 2,
    15.
    the leaven of the. Ex 12:18-20. Le 2:11. Mt
    16:6. 1 C 5:6-8.
    Pharisees. Jn +1:24.
    of Herod. Mk 12:13. Mt 22:15-18.
16   **reasoned**. Mt 16:7, 8. Lk 9:46. 20:5.
17   **knew**. Jn +2:25.
    perceive. Mk 3:5. 6:52. 16:14. Is *6:9, 10*. 63:17.
    Mt 15:17. 16:8, 9. Lk 24:45. He 5:11, 12.
18   **see**. Mk 4:12. Dt 29:4. Ps 69:23. 115:5-8. Is
    6:9, 10. 42:18-20. 44:18. Je *5:21*. Ezk *12:2*. Mt
    13:14, 15. Jn 12:40. Ac 28:26, 27. Ro 11:8.
    do. 2 P 1:12.
19   **brake**. Is +58:7.
    the five. Mk 6:38-44. Mt 14:17-21. Lk 9:12-
    17. Jn 6:5-13.
20   **the seven**. ver. 1-9. Mt 15:34-38.
21   **How**. ver. 12, 17. Mk 6:52. 9:19. Ps 94:8. Mt
    16:11, 12. Jn 14:9. 1 C 6:5. 15:34.
22   **Bethsaida**. Mk 6:45. Mt 11:21. Lk 9:10.
    10:13. Jn 1:44. 12:21.
    they bring. Mk 2:3. 6:55, 56.
    to touch. Mk 1:41. 5:27-29. Mt 8:3, 15. 9:29.
23   **he took**. Mk 7:33.
    by the. Is 51:18. Je 31:32. Ac 9:8. He 8:9.
    out. Mk 7:33. Is 42:2.
    spit. Jn 9:6, 7. Re 3:18.
    put his hands. Mk 5:23.
24   **I see**. Jg 9:36. Is 29:18. 32:3. 1 C 13:9-12.
25   **hands**. Mk +5:23.
    and saw. Pr 4:18. Mt 13:12. Lk 7:21. Ph 1:6.
    1 P 2:9. 2 P 3:18.
26   **Neither**. ver. 23. Lk +5:14.
27   **the towns**. Mt 16:13, etc.
    and by. Lk 9:18, 19, etc.
    Whom. Mt 16:13. Lk 9:18-21. Jn 6:68, 69.
28   **John**. Mk 6:14-16. Mt 14:2. 16:14. Lk 9:7-9.
    Elias. Mk 9:11-13. Ml 4:5, Elijah. Jn 1:21.
29   **But**. Mk 4:11. Mt 16:15. Lk 9:20. 1 P 2:7.
    Thou. Mt +16:16. Jn 1:41, 49. 1 J 4:15.
30   **he charged**. ver. +26.
31   **he began**. Mk 9:31, 32. 10:33, 34. Mt 16:21.
    17:22, 23. 20:17-19. Lk 9:22. 18:31-34. 24:6,
    7, 26, 44.
    rejected. Ps 118:22. Jn +12:48. Ac 3:13-15.
    7:35, 51, 52.
    and after. Ho 6:2. Jon 1:17. 1 C +15:4.
32   **openly**. Jn 16:25, 29.
    Peter. Mk 4:38. Mt 16:22. Lk 9:21. 10:40. Jn
    13:6-8.

33 turned. Mk 3:5, 34. Lk +22:61.
and looked. Ac 6:15. 7:55, 56.
he rebuked. Le +19:17. 2 S 19:22. Ps 141:5.
Pr 9:8, 9. Mt 16:23. Lk 9:55. 1 T 5:20. T 1:13.
Re 3:19.
Get. Ge 3:4-6. Jb 2:10. Mt 4:10. Lk 4:8. 1 C
5:5.
savorest. Mt 6:31, 32. Ro 8:5-8. 1 C 2:14. Ph
3:19. Ja 3:15-18. 1 P 4:1, 2. 1 J 2:15, 16.
34 called. Mk 7:14. Lk 9:23. 20:45.
Whosoever. Mk 9:43-48. Mt 5:29, 30. 7:13,
14. 16:24. Lk 13:24. 14:27, 33. Ro 15:1-3. 1 C
8:13. 9:19. Ph 3:7, 8. T 2:12.
take. Mk 10:21. Mt 10:38. 27:32. Jn 19:17.
Ac 14:22. Ro 6:6. 8:17, 18. 1 C 4:9-13. 15:31.
2 C 4:17. Ga 2:20. 5:24. 6:14. Ph 3:10. Col
1:24. 3:5. 2 T 3:11. 1 P 4:1, 13. Re 2:10.
follow. Nu 14:24. 1 K 14:8. Lk 14:26. 18:22.
Jn 10:27. 13:36, 37. 21:19, 20. He 13:13. 2 P
1:14. 1 J 3:16.
35 will save. Est 4:11-16. Je 26:20-24. Mt
10:39. 16:25. Lk 9:24. 17:33. Jn 12:25, 26. Ac
20:24. 21:13. 2 T 2:11-13. 4:6-8. He 11:35. Re
2:10, 11. 7:14-17. 12:11.
life. Gr. *psyche*, Mt +2:20; Ge +9:5.
lose. Gr. *apollumi*, Mt +2:13.
lose. Gr. *apollumi*, Mt +2:13.
life. Gr. *psyche*, Mt +2:20; Ge +9:5.
for. Mt 5:10-12. 10:22. 19:29. Lk 6:22, 23. Jn
15:20, 21. Ac 9:16. 1 C 9:23. 2 C 12:10. 2 T
1:8. 1 P 4:12-16.
36 what. Jb 2:4. Ps 49:17-19. 73:18-20. Mt 4:8-
10. 16:26. Lk 9:25. 12:19, 20. 16:19-23. Ph
3:7-9. Re 18:7, 8.
profit. Jb 22:2. Ml 3:14. Ro 6:21. He 11:24-
26. Ja 1:9-11.
if he. Mt +4:9.
world. Gr. *kosmos*, Mt +4:8.
lose. Mt +16:26 (**S#2210g**).
soul. Gr. *psyche*, Mt +2:20.
37 Or what. Ps 49:7, 8. 1 P 1:18, 19.
soul. Gr. *psyche*, Mt +2:20.
38 ashamed. Mt 10:32, 33. Ps 119:46. Lk 9:26.
12:8, 9. Ac 5:41. Ro +1:16. Ga 6:14. 2 T 1:8,
12, 16. 2:12, 13. He 11:26. 12:2, 3. 13:13. 1 J
2:23.
adulterous. Mt +12:39. 16:4. Ja 4:4.
the Son. Mk +2:10. Mt +25:31. Jn 1:14.
when. Dt +33:2. Ps 102:16. Da 7:10. Zc
+14:5. Mt +13:41. Jn 1:51. 2 Th 1:7, 8. Ju 14,
15.

MARK 9

1 That. Mt +16:28.
taste. Lk 2:26. Jn 8:51, 52. He 2:9.
the kingdom. ver. 47. Mk +1:15. Mt +24:30.
25:31. Lk 22:18, 30. Jn 21:23. Ac 1:6, 7.
2 after. Mt 17:1, etc. Lk 9:28, etc.
Peter. Mk 5:37. 14:33. 2 C 13:1.

an high. Ex 24:13. 1 K 18:42, 43. Mt 14:13.
Lk 6:12.
apart. Mk 5:37. Mt 26:37.
transfigured. Mk 16:12. Ex 34:29-35. Is
33:17. 53:2. Mt 17:2. Lk 9:29. Jn 1:14. Ro
12:2. 2 C 3:7-10. Ph 2:6-8. 3:21. 2 P 1:16-18.
Re 1:13-17. 20:11.
3 his raiment. Ps 104:1, 2. Da 7:9. Mt 28:3. Ac
10:30. Re 1:14.
exceeding. Ps 51:7. 68:14. Is 1:18. Re 7:9,
14. 19:8.
no. Ml 3:2, 3.
4 appeared. Mt 11:13. 17:3, 4. Lk 9:19, 30, 31.
24:27, 44. Jn +5:39, 45-47. Ac 3:21-24. 1 P
1:10-12. Re 19:10.
Elias. 2 K 2:11, 12, Elijah.
Moses. Dt 34:5, 6.
5 it is. Ex 33:17-23. Ps 63:2, 3. 84:10. Jn 14:8,
9, 21-23. Ph +1:23. 1 J 3:2. Re 22:3, 4.
tabernacles. Le +23:42.
6 wist not. Mk 16:5-8. Da 10:15-19. Re 1:17.
afraid. Mt 17:6, 7.
7 a cloud. Ex +13:21. Da +7:13. Mt 26:64. Ac
1:9. Re +1:7.
This is. Mk 1:11. Ps 2:7. Mt 3:17. 26:63.
27:43, 54. Lk 3:22. Jn 1:34, 49. 3:16-18. 5:18,
22-25, 37. 6:69. 9:35. 15:26. 19:7. 20:31. Ac
8:37. Ro 1:4. 2 P 1:17. 1 J 4:9, 10. 5:11, 12,
20.
hear. Ex 23:21, 22. Dt 18:15-19. Ac 3:22, 23.
7:37. He 2:1. 12:25, 26.
8 suddenly. Lk 9:36. 24:31. Ac 8:39, 40. 10:16.
9 he charged. Lk +5:14.
till. ver. 30, 31. Mk 8:31. 10:32-34. Mt
+12:40. 16:21. 27:63. Lk 24:46.
10 they. Ge 37:11. Lk 2:50, 51. 24:7, 8. Jn
16:17-19.
what. ver. 32. Mt 16:22. Lk 18:33, 34. 24:25-
27. Jn +2:19-22. 12:16, 33, 34. 16:17, 29, 30.
Ac 17:18.
11 Why say. ver. 4. Ml 3:1. 4:5. Mt 11:14. 17:10,
11.
12 Elias. Ml *4:5*.
restoreth. Mk 1:2-8. Is 40:3-5. Ml 4:6. Mt
3:1, etc. 11:2-18. Lk 1:16, 17, 76. 3:2-9. Jn
1:6-36. 3:27, etc. Ac +1:6. +3:21.
he must. Ps ch. 22. 69:1, etc. Is ch. 53. Da
+9:24-26. Zc +13:7.
set. Ps 22:6, 7. 69:12. 74:22. Is 49:7. 50:6.
52:14. 53:1-3. Da +9:26. Zc 11:13. +13:7. Lk
23:11, 39. Ac 4:11. Ph 2:7, 8.
13 Elias. Mt +11:14. 17:12, 13. Lk 1:17.
and they. Mk 6:14-28. Mt 14:3-11. Lk 3:19,
20. Ac 7:52.
14 when. Mt 17:14, etc. Lk 9:37.
the scribes. Mk 2:6. 11:28. 12:14. Lk 11:53,
54. He 12:3.
15 were. ver. 2, 3. Ex 34:30.
greatly amazed. Mk 10:32. 14:33. 16:5, 6.
running to. Ex 34:3.

16 **What**. Mk 8:11. Lk 5:30-32.
with them. *or*, among yourselves.
17 **Master**. ver. 38. Mk +4:38.
I have brought. Mk +5:23. 10:13.
a dumb. ver. +25.
spirit. Gr. *pneuma*, Mt +8:16.
18 **teareth him**. *or*, dasheth him. ver. 26. Mt 7:6. 15:22. Lk 9:39.
he foameth. ver. 20. Ju 13.
gnasheth. Jb 16:9. Ps 112:10. Mt 8:12. Ac 7:54.
and they. ver. 28, 29. Mk 6:7. 11:23. 2 K 4:29-31. Mt 10:1. 17:16, 19-21. Lk 9:1, 40. 10:17.
19 **O faithless**. Ps 106:21-25. Mt +6:30.
generation. Mt +24:34.
how long. Mt +17:17.
suffer you. Mt 17:17. Lk 9:41. Ac 13:18. 18:14. Ro 2:4. 2 C 11:1, 4, 19, 20. Ep 4:2. Col 3:13. 2 T 4:3.
20 **the spirit**. Gr. *pneuma*, Mt +8:16. ver. 18, 26. Mk 1:26. 5:3-5. Jb 1:10, etc. 2:6-8. Lk 4:35. 8:29. 9:42. Jn 8:44. 1 P 5:8.
21 **How**. Mk 5:25. Jb 5:7. 14:1. Ps 51:5. Lk 8:43. 13:16. Jn 5:5, 6. 9:1, 20, 21. Ac 3:2. 4:22. 9:33. 14:8.
22 **destroy**. Gr. *apollumi*, Mt +2:13.
if. 1 C +15:2. Mk 1:40-42. Mt 8:2, 8, 9. 9:28. 14:31.
have. Mk 7:26. Mt +9:36. 15:22-28.
23 **If**. 1 C +15:2. Mk 11:23. 2 Ch +20:20. Mt 17:20. 21:21, 22. Lk 17:6. Jn 4:48-50. 11:40. Ac 14:9. 2 Th 1:11. He 11:6.
all things. Mk 10:27. Ex +9:6.
24 **with**. 2 S 16:12mg. 2 K 20:5. Ps 39:12. 126:5. Je 14:17. Lk 7:38, 44. Ac 20:19, 31. 2 C 2:4. 2 T 1:4. He 5:7. 12:17.
help. Lk 17:5. Jn 12:27. Ro +10:17. 14:4. Ga 3:2, 5. Ep 2:8. Ph 1:29. 2 Th 1:3, 11. He 11:6. 12:2.
25 **he rebuked**. Mk +4:39. 1 J 3:8.
foul. *or*, unclean. Mk +3:30.
spirit. Gr. *pneuma*, Mt +8:16.
Thou. Mt +9:33.
spirit. Gr. *pneuma*, Mt +8:16.
I charge. Lk 8:29. Ac 16:18.
26 **cried**. ver. 18, 20. Mk 1:26. Ex 5:23. Re 12:12.
27 **took him**. Mk 1:31, 41. 5:41. 8:23. Is 41:13. Ac 3:7. 9:41.
28 **asked**. Mk 4:10, 34. Mt 13:10, 36. 15:15.
Why. Mt 17:19, 20.
29 **This**. Mt 12:45. Lk 11:26.
by prayer. Mk 5:2-8. 1 K 17:20-22. 2 K 4:33, 34. Mt 15:21-28. 17:21. Ac 9:40, 41. 2 C 12:8. Ep 6:18. Ja 5:15.
fasting. Jg 20:26. 2 Ch +7:14. Da +9:3. Lk 2:37. Ac 14:23. 1 C 9:27. 2 C 6:5. 11:27.
30 **through**. Mt 27:22, 23. Jn 7:1-9.
he. ver. 9. Mk +6:31, 32.

31 **The Son**. ver. 12. Mk +2:10. Mt 16:21. 21:38, 39. Lk 19:44. 24:26, 44-46. Jn +2:19. 3:14. 10:18. Ac 2:23, 24. 4:27, 28. 2 T 2:12.
delivered. Mt +2:4.
the third day. Mk 8:31. Ho 6:2. Mt +12:40.
32 **they**. ver. 10. Mk 6:52. Mt 13:19. 17:13. Lk 2:50. 9:45. 18:34. 24:25, 26, 45. Jn 8:27, 28. 10:6. 12:16. 14:5-9. 16:17-19.
were. Mk 7:18. 8:17, 18, 33. 16:14. Jn 4:27. 16:19.
33 **he came**. Mt 17:24.
What. Mk 2:8. Ps 139:1-4. Jn +2:25. 21:17. He 4:13. Re 2:23.
34 **they had**. Mt 18:1, etc. 20:21-24. Lk 9:46-48. 22:24, etc. Ro 12:10. Ph 2:3-7. 1 P 5:3. 3 J 9.
35 **the twelve**. Mk 4:10. 6:7. 10:32. 11:11. 14:10, 17, 20, 43. Lk 8:1. 9:1, 12. 18:31. 22:3, 47. Jn 6:67, 70, 71. 20:24. Ac 6:2. 1 C 15:5.
If. 1 C +15:2. Mk 10:42-45. Pr 13:10. Je 45:5. Mt 20:25-28. 23:11, 12. Lk 14:10, 11. 18:14. 22:26. Ja 4:6.
and servant. Gr. *diakonos*, **S#1249g**. Mk 10:43. Mt 20:26. 22:13. 23:11. Jn 2:5, 9. 12:26. Ro 13:4, 4. 15:8. 16:1. 1 C 3:5. 2 C 3:6. 6:4. 11:15, 23. Ga 2:17. Ep 3:7. 6:21. Ph 1:1 (deacons). Col 1:7, 23, 25. 4:7. 1 Th 3:2. 1 T 3:8, 12. 4:6.
of all. Mk 10:43-45. Jn 13:12-15. Ro 15:1-3. 1 C 9:19-22. 10:24, 32, 33. 2 C 8:9. Ga 6:9, 10. Ep 6:5-8. Ph 2:3, 4.
36 **took a child**. ver. 42. Mk 10:16. Mt 18:2, 6. 19:14, 15. 21:16. Lk 9:48. 10:21. 17:2. 18:16.
taken him. Mk 10:16. Mt 18:2. Lk 9:48.
37 **receive one**. Ro +15:7.
in my name. ver. 39. Mk 13:6. Mt 18:5. 24:5. Lk 1:59. 9:48, 49. 21:8. 24:47. Ac 4:17, 18. 5:28, 40. +15:26.
receive me. Lk 10:16. Jn 5:23. 10:30. 12:44, 45. 14:21-23. 1 Th 4:8.
38 **Master**. Nu 11:26-29. Lk 9:49, 50. 11:19.
casting out. Mk 16:17. Mt 7:22. 12:27. Lk 10:17. Ac 3:6. 16:18. 19:13.
we forbad. Mk 10:14. Mt 19:14. Lk 9:50. 18:15.
39 **Forbid**. Mk 10:13, 14. Mt +13:28, 29. Ph 1:18.
there. Mt 7:22, 23. Ac 19:13-16. 1 C 9:27. 13:1, 2.
lightly. 1 C 12:3.
40 **he that**. Mt 6:24. 12:30. Lk 9:50. 11:23. 2 C 6:15, 16.
41 **whosoever**. Mt +10:42. 25:35, 40. 1 C 13:3. He 6:10.
because. Jn 19:25-27. Ro 8:9. 14:15. 1 C 3:23. 15:23. 2 C 10:7. Ga 3:29. 5:24. 1 P 4:14.
lose. Gr. *apollumi*, Mt +2:13.
42 **offend**. Is 9:16. Mt +17:27. 1 T 5:14, 15. 2 P 2:2.
little ones. ver. 36. Zc +13:7.

it is better. Mk 14:21. Mt 25:45, 46. Ac 9:4. 26:11-14. 2 Th 1:6-9. Re 6:9, 10. 16:6, 7.
that a. Mt +23:30.

43 **if**. Mt +4:9. Dt 13:6-8. Mt +17:27. Ro 8:13. 1 C 9:27. Ga 5:24. Col 3:5. T 2:12. He 12:1. 1 P 2:1.
offend thee. or, cause thee to offend: and so ver. 45, 47.
enter into. ver. 45. Mt +7:14. 18:8, 9. 19:17. Jn 5:24.
maimed. Mt 15:30, 31. Lk 14:13, 21.
hell. Gr. gehenna, Mt +5:22.
quenched. ver. 48. Mt +3:12. +25:41.

44 **their**. ver. 46, 48. Is +66:24. Lk +24:27.
the fire. Mt +25:41, 46.

45 **And if**. Mt +4:9.
thy foot. ver. 43, 44. Mt 18:8.
hell. Gr. gehenna, Mt +5:22.

46 **their worm**. Lk 16:24-26.

47 **And if**. Mt +4:9.
thine. Ge 3:6. Jb 31:1. Ps 119:37. Mt 5:28, 29. 10:37-39. Lk 14:26. Ro 8:13. Ga 4:15. Ph 3:7, 8.
offend thee. or, cause thee to offend. ver. 43mg.
enter. Mt +7:21.
kingdom of God. ver. +1.
hell. Gr. gehenna, Mt +5:22.

48 **their worm**. ver. 44, 46. Jb +14:22. Is +66:24.
the fire. ver. 43. Lk 16:24.

49 **every one**. 2 C 2:16.
salted. Dt +29:23. 2 C 2:16. He 12:29.
with fire. 1 C 3:13. 1 P 4:12.
and every sacrifice. Le +2:13. 1 C 3:15.

50 **Salt is good**. Jb 6:6. Mt 5:13. Lk 14:34, 35.
but if. Mt +4:9.
Have salt. Le 2:13. Ezk +24:10. 43:24. Da +11:33. Ep 4:29. Col 4:6. He +3:12, 13.
have peace. Jn 13:34, 35. 15:17, 18. 2 C 13:11. Ga 5:14, 15, 22. Ph 1:27. 2:1-3. 2 T 2:22. He +12:14. Ja 1:20. 3:14-18. 1 P 3:8, 9.
another. Ro +12:5.

MARK 10

1 A.M. 4033. A.D. 29.
he arose. Mt 19:1, etc.
by. Mk +3:8. Mt 3:5. 4:25. 19:1. Lk 3:3. Jn 1:28. 3:26. 10:40. 11:7.
resort. Ps 71:3. Jn 10:41.
as he was wont. Lk +4:16. 22:39.
he taught. Ec 12:9. Je 32:33. Jn 18:20.

2 **the Pharisees**. Jn +1:24.
Is it. Mt +19:3. 1 C 7:10, 11.
tempting. Mt +16:1.

3 **What**. Is +8:20. Lk 10:25, 26. Jn +5:39. Ga 4:21.
Moses. Ex +24:4.

4 **Moses suffer**. Dt 24:1-4. Is 50:1. Je 3:1. Mt 1:19. 5:31, 32. 19:7.

5 **For**. Dt 9:6. 31:27. Ne 9:16, 17, 26. Mt 19:8. Ac 7:51. He 3:7-10.

6 **the beginning**. Ge 1:1. 2 P 3:4.
God. Ge 1:27. 2:20-23. 5:2. Ml 2:14-16. Mt 19:4.

7 **this cause**. Ge 2:24. Ps 45:10. Mt 19:5, 6. Ep 5:31.

8 **one flesh**. 1 C 6:16. Ep 5:28.

9 **hath joined**. Ro 7:1-3. 1 C 7:10-13.

10 **in the house**. Mk +4:10. 9:28, 33.

11 **Whosoever**. Mt 5:31, 32. +19:9. Lk 16:18. Ro 7:3. 1 C 7:4, 10, 11. He 13:4.

12 **And if**. Mt +4:9.
a woman. Mk 6:17. 1 C 7:11, 13.
she committeth. Ge 2:24. Ps 45:10. Mt 19:5, 6. 1 C 6:16. Ep 5:31.

13 **they**. Mt 19:13-15. Lk 18:15, 16.
disciples. ver. 48. Mk 9:38. Ex 10:9-11. Dt 31:12, 13. Jl 2:16.

14 **he was**. Mk 3:5. 8:33. Lk 9:54-56. Ep 4:26.
Suffer. Dt 4:37. +29:11, 12. 1 S 1:11, 22, 27, 28. Ps 78:4. 115:14, 15. Ac 3:25. Ro 11:16, 28. 1 C +7:14. 2 T 1:5. 3:15.
for. Ps 131:1, 2. Mt 18:4, 10. 19:14. 1 C 14:20. 1 P 2:2. Re 14:5.

15 **Whosoever**. Mt 18:3-5. Lk 18:17. Jn 3:3-6.
enter. Mt +7:21.

16 **he took**. Ge 48:14-16. Dt 28:3. Is 40:11. Lk 2:28-34. 24:50, 51. Jn 21:15-17.

17 **when**. Mt 19:16, etc. Lk 18:18, etc.
running. Mk 9:25. Mt 28:8. Jn 20:2-4.
kneeled. Mk 1:40. Da 6:10. Mt 17:14.
Good. Mk 12:14. Jn 3:2. 7:12.
what shall. Jn 6:28. Ac 2:37. 9:6. 16:30, 31. Ro 10:2-4, 9, 10. T 3:5-7.
inherit. Mt 19:16, 29. 25:34. Lk 10:25. 18:18. T 3:7.
eternal. Gr. aionios, Mt +18:8. 25:46. Lk 10:25. Jn 4:14. +5:39. 6:27, 40. Ac 13:46, 48. Ro 2:7. 6:23. 1 J 2:25. 5:11-13.

18 **Why**. Mt 19:17. Lk 18:19. Jn 5:41-44. Ro 3:12.
none good but one. Ex +34:6. Ps 33:5. 143:10. Mt +28:19. Jn 10:11. Ro 2:4. +11:22. 16:27. Ep 2:7. 2 Th 1:11. 1 T 6:16. T 3:4. Re 15:4.
that is. 1 S 2:2. Ps 36:7, 8. 86:5. 119:68. Ja 1:17. 1 J 4:8, 16.

19 **knowest**. Mk 12:28-34. Is +8:20. Mt 5:17-20. 19:17-19. Lk 10:26-28. 18:20. Ro 3:20. Ga 4:21.
commit. Ex 20:12-17. Dt 5:16-24. Ro 13:9. Ga 5:14. Ja 2:11.
adultery. Ex 20:14.
kill. Ex 20:13.
false. Ex 20:16. Ep 4:25.
Defraud. Le +19:13. Mi 2:2. Ml +3:5. 1 C 6:7-9. 1 Th +4:6.
honor. Ex +20:12. Mt 19:19. Ep 6:2.

20 **all these**. Is 58:2. Ezk 5:14. +33:31, 32. Ml
3:8. Mt 19:20. Lk 10:29. 18:11, 12. Ro 3:20,
23. 7:9. Ph 3:6. 2 T 3:5.
from my youth. Ezk 4:14.

21 **loved**. Ge 34:19. Is 63:8-10. Lk 19:41. 2 C
12:15.
One thing. Ps 27:4. Ec 3:19. Lk +10:42.
18:22. Jn 9:25. Ph 3:13. Ja 2:10. 2 P 3:8. Re
2:4, 14, 20.
sell. Pr 23:23. Mt 13:44-46. 19:21. Lk 12:33.
Ac 2:44, 45. 4:34-37.
give. Is 58:7. Mt +19:21. Lk 14:13, 14.
treasure. Dt +28:12. Mt +5:12. 6:19-21.
16:26. Lk +14:14. +16:9. Ph 3:20. Col 1:5. 1 T
6:17-19. 2 T 4:8. He 10:34-37. 11:16. 1 P
+1:4, 5. Re 11:18.
take. Mk 8:34. Mt 16:24. Lk 9:23. Jn 12:26.
16:33. Ro 8:17, 18. 2 T 3:12.

22 **sad**. Mk 6:20, 26. Ezk +33:31. Mt 19:22. 27:3,
24-26. Lk 18:23. 2 C 7:10. 2 T 4:10.
for. Ge 13:5-11. Dt 6:10-12. 8:11-14. Jb 21:7-
15. Ps 62:10. Ezk +33:31. Mt 13:22. Lk 12:15.
Ep 5:5. 1 T 6:9, 10. 1 J 2:15, 16.

23 **looked**. Mk 3:5. 5:32.
How hardly. Mt 19:23-26. Lk 18:24. 1 C
1:26. Ja 2:5. 4:4.
have riches. Mt +13:22. 1 T +6:9.
enter. ver. +15.

24 **astonished**. Mt 19:25. Lk 18:26, 27. Jn 6:60.
Children. Jn 13:33. 21:5. Ga 4:19. 1 J 2:1.
4:4. 5:21.
how hard. Mt +7:14.
trust. Jb 31:24, 25. Ps 17:14. 49:6, 7. 52:7.
62:10. Pr 11:28. 18:11. 23:5. Je 9:23. Ezk
28:4, 5. Hab 2:9. Zp 1:18. Lk 12:16-21. 16:14.
1 T 6:17. Ja +5:1-3. Re 3:17.

25 **easier**. Je 13:23. Mt 7:3-5. 19:24, 25. 23:24.
Lk 18:25.

26 **out**. Mk 6:51. 7:37. 2 C 11:23.
Who. Lk +13:23. 18:26. Ac 16:31. Ro 10:9-
13.

27 **With men**. Ge +18:14. 2 K 7:2. Zc 8:6.
for. Jb +42:2. Ph 3:21. He 7:25. 11:19.
all things. Mk 9:23. 14:36. Ge 18:14.

28 **Lo**. Mk 1:16-20. Mt 19:27-30. Lk 14:33.
18:28-30. Ac 14:22. Ph 3:7-9.
followed. Mt 19:28.

29 **There**. Ge +12:1-3. 45:20. Dt 33:9-11. Lk
22:28-30. He 11:24-26.
for. Mk 8:35. Mt 5:10, 11. 10:18. 1 C 9:23. Re
2:3.

30 **shall receive**. Mt +5:7. 19:29. Ps +58:11. Lk
+6:38.
an hundredfold. Ge +26:12. 2 Ch 25:9. Jb
42:10. Ps 84:11. Pr 3:9, 10. 16:16. Is 40:2.
61:7. Ml 3:10. Mt +13:8, 23, 44-46. 19:29. Lk
18:30. 2 C 6:10. 9:8-11. Ph 3:8. 2 Th 2:16. 1 T
6:6. 1 J 3:1. Re 2:9. 3:18.
now in this time. Mt 6:33. Lk 18:30. Ro
3:26. 8:18. 1 T +4:8. He 9:9. 1 J 5:13.

house. Mt 19:29. Lk 18:29.
brethren. Mk 3:35.
with persecutions. Mt 5:11, 12. Jn 15:20.
16:22, 23. Ac 5:41. +14:22. 16:25. Ro 5:3.
8:35. 2 C 12:10. Ph 1:29. 2 Th 1:4. 2 T 3:11,
12. He 12:6. Ja 1:2-4, 12. 5:11. 1 P 1:6. 4:12-
16. 5:10.
world. Gr. *aion*, Mt +6:13.
to come. Mt +12:32. Lk 18:30. 20:35. Ep
1:21. 2:7. He 6:5.
eternal. Gr. *aionios*, Mt +18:8. ver. 17. Jn
10:23. Ro 6:23. 1 J 2:25. 5:11-13.

31 **But many**. Mt +19:30. Ac 13:46-48.

32 **they were in**. Mt 20:17, etc. Lk 18:31, etc.
they were amazed. Zc 3:8. Lk 9:51. Jn 11:8,
16.
And he. Mk 4:34. Mt 11:25. 13:11. Lk 10:23,
24.

33 **we go**. Lk +2:4. Ac 20:22.
and the Son. Mk +2:10. Mt 16:21.
condemn. Mk 14:64. Mt 26:66. Ac 13:27. Ja
5:6.
deliver. Mk 15:1. Mt 20:19. 27:2. Lk 18:32.
20:20. 23:1, 2, 21. 24:20. Jn 18:28, 35. 19:11.
Ac 2:23. 3:13, 14. 21:11.

34 **mock**. Lk +22:63. Jn 19:2, 3.
scourge. Jn +19:1.
spit. Mt +26:67.
third day. Ps 16:10. Ho 6:2. Jon 1:17. 2:10. 1
C +15:4.

35 **James**. Mk 1:19, 20. 5:37. 9:2. 14:33.
come. Mt 20:20-28.
Master. Mk +4:38.
we would. lit. we desire. 2 S 14:4-11. 1 K
2:16, 20. 1 T +6:9.

36 **What**. ver. 51. 1 K 3:5, etc. Jn 15:7.

37 **may sit**. 1 K 22:19. Ps 45:9. +110:1. Mt
+19:28.
in. Mk 8:38. Mt 25:31. Lk 24:26. 1 P 1:11.

38 **Ye know not**. 1 K 2:22. Je 45:5. Mt 20:21,
22. Ro 8:26. Ja 4:3.
drink of the. Mk 14:36. Ps 75:8. Is 51:22. Je
25:15. Mt 26:39. Lk 22:42. Jn 18:11.
baptized with the. Lk 12:50.

39 **We can**. Mk 14:31. Pr 16:18. Mt 26:35, 56. Jn
13:37.
Ye shall. Mk 14:36. Mt 10:25. 16:24. Jn
15:20. 17:14. Ac 12:2. Col 1:24. Re 1:9.

40 **to sit**. ver. +37. Mt 25:34. Jn 17:2, 24. He
+11:16.
not mine. Mt 20:23. 1 C +15:28.
for whom. Mt 19:11. Ro 8:17. Col 1:5.
prepared. Mt 25:34. Jn +14:2. 17:24. 1 C
2:9. 2 C 5:2. Ph 3:20. 2 T 4:8. T 2:13. He
10:34-37. +11:16. 1 J 3:2, 3. Re 21:2.

41 **they**. Mk 9:33-36. Pr 13:10. Mt 20:24. Lk
22:24. Ro 12:10. Ph +2:3. Ja 4:5, 6.

42 **Ye know**. Mt 20:25. Lk 22:25. 1 P 5:3.
are accounted. *or*, think good.

43 **But**. Mt 20:26.

so. Jn 18:36. Ro 12:2.
whosoever. Mk 9:35. Mt 20:26, 27. 23:8-12. Lk 9:48. 14:11. 18:14. Jn 13:13-18. 1 C 9:19-23. Ga 5:13. 1 P 5:5, 6.

44 And whosoever. Mt 20:27.

45 came. Mt 11:29. 20:28. Lk +19:10. 22:26, 27. Jn 13:14. Ph 2:5-8. He 5:8.
and to give. Mk 14:22. Jn 10:18. 11:51, 52. Ga +3:13. 1 T 2:4-6.
life. Gr. *psyche*, Mt +2:20; Ge +9:5.
ransom. Mt 20:28. 1 T 2:6.
for many. Mt +26:28. He 9:28.

46 they came. Mt 20:29, etc. Lk 18:35, etc.
blind Bartimeus. i.e. *son of one esteemed; son of one unclean*, **S#924g**.
Timeus. i.e. *highly prized; polluted*, **S#5090g**.
begging. Lk 16:20, 22. Jn 9:8. Ac 3:2, 3.

47 Jesus. Mk +1:24.
thou. Mt +1:1.
have. Mt +9:27.

48 many. Mk 5:35. Mt 19:13. 20:31. Lk 18:39.
but. Mk 7:26-29. Ge 32:24-28. Je +29:13. Mt 15:23-28. Lk 11:5-10. 18:1, etc. Ep 6:18. He 5:7.
have. Ps 62:12.

49 stood. Ps 86:15. 145:8. Mt 20:32-34. Lk 18:40. He 2:17. +4:15.
Be. Jn 11:28.
rise. Pr 6:9. SS 2:10. Is 60:1. Lk 22:46. Jn 5:8. Ep 5:14.

50 casting away. Ph 3:7-9. He 12:1.

51 What. ver. 36. 2 Ch 1:7. Mt 6:8. 7:7, 8. Lk 18:41-43. Ph 4:6.
Lord. Dt 4:7. Ph 4:5.

52 thy faith. Mk 5:34. Mt 9:22, 28-30. 15:28. Lk 7:50. 8:48.
made thee whole. *or,* saved thee.
he received. Mk 8:25. Ps 33:9. Mt +11:5. Jn 9:5-7, 32, 39.
followed. Mk 1:31. Lk 8:2, 3.
in the way. Ge +24:27. Ac 26:13.

MARK 11

1 when. Mt 21:1, etc. Lk 19:29, etc. Jn 12:14, etc.
Jerusalem. **S#2419g**. Mt 23:37. Lk 2:25, 38, 41, 43, 45. 4:9. 5:17. 6:17. 9:31, 51, 53. 10:30. 13:4, 22, 33, 34. 17:11. 19:11. 21:20, 24. 23:28. 24:13, 18, 33, 47, 49, 52. Ac 1:8, 12, 19. 2:5, 14. 4:6, 16. 5:16, 28. 6:7. 8:25-27. 9:2, 13, 21, 26, 28. 10:39. 12:25. 13:27, 31. 15:2, 4. 16:4. 19:21. 20:22. 21:4, 11-13, 15, 31. 22:5, 17, 18. 23:11. 24:11. 25:3, 20. Ro 15:19, 25, 26, 31. 1 C 16:3. Ga 4:25, 26. He 12:22. Re 3:12. 21:2, 10. See also **S#2414g**, Mt +2:1.
Bethphage. Mt +21:1.
Bethany. Jn +11:18.
mount of Olives. Mt +21:1.
he. Mk +6:7. 14:13.

2 Go your way. Mt 21:2, 3. Lk 19:30, 31.
whereon never. Nu 19:2. Dt 21:3. Jg 15:13. 16:11. 1 S 6:7. Ps 8:6. +104:30. Lk 19:30. 23:53. Jn 19:41.
loose him. 1 S 8:16.

3 if. Mt +4:9.
the Lord. Mk 12:35-37. Ps 24:1. Mt 7:21. Lk 7:13. Ac +10:36. 17:25. 1 C 8:5, 6. +12:3. 16:22. 2 C 8:9. Ga 1:19. He 2:7-9.
and straightway. Mk 14:15. 1 Ch 29:12-18. Ps 110:3. Ac 1:24.

4 and found. Mt 21:6, 7. 26:19. Lk 19:32-34. Jn 2:5. He 11:8.
without. Je 17:27. 49:27.

5 What do ye. Ep +5:11.

6 had commanded. Mt 4:20. 7:24. 9:9. 21:6. 26:19. Lk 5:5. 6:47. Jn 2:7. 11:29. 14:21. 21:6.

7 the colt. Zc +9:9. Mt 21:4, 5. Lk 19:35.
and cast. 2 K 9:13. Mt 21:7, 8. Lk 19:36. Jn 12:12-16.

8 spread. 2 K 9:13.
cut. Le 23:40.

9 Hosanna. 2 S 14:4. Je 31:7. Jn 19:15.
Blessed. Ps +118:26.
that cometh. Is 62:11.

10 the kingdom. Is +9:6, 7. Je 33:15-17, 26. Ezk 34:23, 24. 37:24, 25. Ho 3:5. Am 9:11, 12. Lk +1:31-33.
our father David. Ac 2:29.
in the highest. Ps 148:1. Lk 2:14. 19:38-40. Jn 12:12-15.

11 Jesus. Ml 3:1. Mt 21:10-16. Lk 19:41-45.
when. Ezk 8:9. Zp 1:12.
he went. Mt 21:17. Lk 21:37, 38. Jn 8:1, 2.

12 on. Mt 21:18, etc.
he was. Mt 4:2. Lk 4:2. Jn 4:6, 7, 31-33. 19:28. He 2:17. +4:15.

13 seeing. Mt 21:19. Lk 13:6-9.
if. 1 C +15:2. Mk 8:5. Jn 11:34.
haply. Ru 2:3. 1 S 6:9. Lk 10:31. 12:6, 7.
might find. Jn 15:8.
he found. Is 5:7.
yet. Mk 5:13. Le 19:9, 10. 23:22. Dt 23:24. 24:19-21. Mt 21:19.

14 answered and said. Mk 9:5. 10:24. 12:35. 14:48. 1 S 14:28. Mt 11:25. Lk 13:14. 14:3. 22:51. Jn 2:18. 5:17. 10:32. Ac 3:12.
No. ver. 20, 21. Is 5:5, 6. Mt 3:10. 7:19. 12:33-35. 21:19, 20, 33, 44. Jn 15:6. He 6:4-8. 10:26-31. 2 P 2:20-22. Re 22:11.
ever. Gr. *aion*, Mt +6:13.

15 and Jesus. Mt 21:12-16. Lk 19:45, 46. Jn 2:13-17.
the tables. Dt 14:25, 26.
moneychangers. Ex 30:13.
doves. Le 1:14. 5:7. 12:8. 14:22. Lk 2:24.

16 would not suffer. Mk 7:29. Jn 5:27.
vessel through. Ex 3:5. 1 T 3:15.
the temple. Hab +2:20.

17 Is it. 1 K 8:41-48. Is 56:7. 60:7. Zc 8:22. Lk

19:46. +24:27.

of all nations the house of prayer. *or*, an house of prayer for all nations.
a den. Je 7:11. Ho 12:7. Mt 21:13. Lk 19:46. Jn 2:16.

18 **and sought**. Mk 3:6. 12:12. 14:1, 2. Is 49:7. Mt 21:15, 38, 39, 45, 46. 26:3, 4. Lk 19:47. Jn 11:53-57.
destroy. Gr. *apollumi*, Mt +2:13.
feared. ver. 32. Mk 6:20. 1 K 18:17, 18. 21:20. 22:8, 18. Mt 21:46. Ac 24:25. Re 11:5-10.
astonished. Mt +7:28.
doctrine. Mk +4:2.

19 **when even**. ver. 11. Lk 21:37. Jn 12:36.

20 **they saw**. ver. +14. Jb 18:16, 17. 20:5-7. Is 5:4. 40:24. Mt 13:6. 15:13. 21:19, 20. Jn 15:6. He 6:8. Ju 12.

21 **cursedst**. Pr +3:33. Zc +5:3, 4. Mt +25:41. 1 C 16:22.

22 **Have**. ver. 24. Mk 9:23, 24. 10:46-52. 2 Ch +20:20. Ps 6:8, 9. 17:6. 18:3. 20:6. 22:9, 10. 37:4-7. 55:16. 56:9-11. 60:12. 62:8. 71:1-5. 73:28. 86:6, 7. 121:1, 2. Is 7:9. Mi 7:7-9. Hab 3:17, 18. Mt 8:10, 13. 9:28-30. 15:21-28. 17:19-21. 21:21, 22. Jn 14:1. 15:7. T 1:1. He 4:16. 10:21, 22. 11:6. Ja 1:5-7. 5:14, 15. 1 J 5:14, 15.
faith in God. *or*, the faith of God. Ac 3:16. Ro 3:22. Ga 2:20. 3:22. Ep 3:12. Ph 3:9. Col 2:12.

23 **whosoever**. Mt 17:20. 21:21, 22. Lk 17:6. 1 C 13:2.
this mountain. Dt +19:5. Zc 4:7.
Be thou removed. Ps 46:2. 1 C 13:2. Re 8:8.
and shall. Mt 14:31. Ro 4:18-25. He 11:17-19. Ja +1:5, 6.
not doubt. 2 K 7:2. Mt 21:21. Ac 10:20. Ro 4:20, 21. 14:23. Ja 1:6. 2:4. Ju 9, 22.
but shall believe. Mk 9:23. 16:17. Jn 14:12.
shall have. Mt 19:26.
whatsoever. Ps 37:4. Jn 14:13. 15:7.

24 **What things**. Mt 18:19. Lk 11:9-13. 18:1-8. Ja 1:5, 6. 1 J +5:14, 15.
ye desire. Col 1:9.
believe. Mk 5:36. 9:23. Ex 4:30, 31. Ps 116:10. 119:66. Jon 3:5. Mt 8:13. 9:28, 29. 21:21, 22. Jn 4:49, 50. 6:68, 69. 11:22. Ro 10:14. He 11:6. 1 J 5:14, 15.
receive. *or*, have received. Is +65:24. Mt 6:8.

25 **stand**. Ex 9:29. 1 K 8:22. 1 Ch +17:16. 2 Ch 6:13. Zc 3:1. Mt 26:39. Lk 18:11, +13. 22:41, 42. Ac 20:36. Re 11:4.
forgive. Pr 20:22. 25:21, 22. Mt 5:44, 45. 6:12, 14, 15. 18:23-35. *Lk 6:35*, 37. 11:4. Ro 12:20. Ep 4:32. Col 3:13. Ja 2:13. 1 P 3:9.
if. 1 C +15:2.
have ought against. Mt 5:23. 6:15. Col 3:13. Re 2:4, 14, 20.
your Father. Mt 23:9.

26 **But if**. 1 C +15:2. Mt 6:15. 18:28, 34, 35. Ro 1:31. Ja 2:13.

27 **as he**. Ml 3:1. Mt 21:23-27. Lk 20:1-8. Jn 10:23. 18:20.
the chief. Mk 14:1. Ps 2:1-5. Ac 4:5-8, 27, 28.

28 **By what**. Mk 6:2. Ex 2:14. Nu 16:3, 13. Mt 9:11. 21:23. Jn 1:25. 7:52. Ac 4:7. 7:27, 28, 38, 39, 51.

29 **I will**. Is 52:13. Mt 21:24. Lk 20:3-8.
question. *or*, thing.

30 **baptism of John**. Mk 1:1-11. 9:13. Mt ch. 3. Lk 3:1-20. Jn 1:6-8, 15-36. 3:25-36.
from heaven. Da 4:26. Lk 15:18, 21. Jn 3:27.
from men. Ac 5:38, 39. Ga 1:10-12.

31 **they reasoned**. Mk 8:16. Mt 16:7. Lk 20:14.
If. Mt +4:9.
Why. Mt 11:7-14. 21:25-27, 31, 32. Lk 7:30. Jn 1:15, 29, 34, 36. 3:29-36.

32 **But if**. Mt +4:9.
they. Mk 6:20. 12:12. Mt 14:5. 21:46. Lk 20:19. 22:2. Ac 5:26.
for. Mt 3:5, 6. 11:9. 21:31, 32. Lk 7:26-29. 20:6-8. Jn 5:35. 10:41.

33 **We**. Is 1:3. 6:9, 10. 29:9-14. 42:19, 20. 56:10. Je 8:7-9. Ho 4:6. Ml 2:7, 8. Mt +15:14. 23:16-26. Jn 3:10. Ro 1:18-22, 28. 2 C 3:15. 4:3, 4. 2 Th 2:10-12.
Neither. Jb 5:13. Pr 26:4, 5. Mt +7:6. 16:4. 21:27. Lk 10:21, 22. 20:7, 8. 22:66-69. Jn 9:27.

MARK 12

1 **he began**. Mk 4:2, 11-13, 33, 34. Ezk 20:49. Mt 13:10-15, 34, 35. 21:28-33. 22:1-14. Lk 8:10. 22:9.
A certain. Mt 21:33-40. Lk 20:9-15.
planted. Dt 32:32, 33. Ps 80:8-16. Is 5:1-4. 27:2-6. Je 2:21. Ezk 15:1-6. 19:10-14. Ho 10:1. Jl 1:7. Mt 21:28. Lk 13:6-9. Jn 15:1-8. Ro 11:17-24.
and set. Ne 9:13, 14. Ps 78:68, 69. 147:19, 20. Ezk 20:11, 12, 18-20. Ac 7:38, 46, 47. Ro 3:1, 2. 9:4, 5.
and digged. Jl 3:13.
and let. SS 8:11, 12. Is 7:23.
and went. Mk 13:34. Mt 25:14. Lk 15:13. 19:12.

2 **at**. Ps +1:3.
he sent. 2 Ch +24:19.
a servant. Jg 6:8-10. Ezr 9:11. Mi 7:1. Zc 1:3-6. 7:7. Lk +12:48. Jn 15:1-8. He 1:1.

3 **they**. 1 K 18:4, 13. 19:10, 14. 22:27. 2 K 6:31. 21:16. 2 Ch 16:10. 24:19-21. 36:16. Ne 9:26. Je 2:30. 20:2. 26:20-24. 29:26. 37:15, 16. 38:4-6. 44:4. Mt 5:12. 22:6. 23:34-37. Lk 11:47-51. 13:33, 34. Ac 7:52, 59. 2 C 11:24-26. 1 Th 2:15. He 11:36, 37.
and sent. 2 Ch +24:19. Da 9:10, 11.

5 **and him**. Mk 9:13. Ne 9:30. Je 7:25, etc. Mt 5:12. 21:35, 36. 22:6. 23:37. Lk 6:22, 23, 26.

6 **one**. Ps 2:7, 8. Mt +1:23. 11:27. 26:63. Jn 1:14, 18, 34, 49. 3:16-18. Ro 8:3. 1 J 4:9. 5:11, 12.
his. Mk 1:11. 9:7. Ge 22:2, 12. 37:3, 11-13. 44:20. Is 42:1. Mt 3:17. 17:5. Lk 3:22. 9:35. Jn 3:35. He 1:1, 2.
They. Ps 2:12. Jn 5:23. He 1:6. Re 5:9-13.

7 **This**. ver. 12. Ge +3:15. 37:20. 1 K 21:19. Ps 2:2, 3. 22:12-15. Is 49:7. 53:7, 8. Mt 2:3-13, 16. Jn 1:11. 11:47-50. Ac 2:23. 5:28. 7:52. 13:27, 28. Ro 8:17. He 1:2.

8 **killed**. Mt 21:35. Ac 2:23. 7:52. 1 Th 2:15.
cast. Mt 21:33, 39. Lk 20:15. He 13:11-13.

9 **shall**. Mt 21:40, 41. Lk 19:27.
he will. Le 26:15-18, 23, 24, 27, 28. Dt 4:26, 27. +28:15, etc., 61. Jsh 23:15. 2 S 12:5, 6. Pr 1:24-31. Is 5:5-7. Da +9:26, 27. Zc 13:7-9. Mt 3:9-12. 12:45. 22:7. 23:34-38. 24:50. 25:19. Lk 19:27, 41-44. 20:15, 16.
destroy. Gr. *apollumi*, Mt +2:13.
and will. Is 29:17. 32:15, 16. 65:15. Je 17:3. Ml 1:11. Mt +8:11-13. 21:43. Lk 20:16. Ac 13:46-48. 18:6. 28:23-28. Ro 9:30-33. 10:20, 21. 11:1, etc.

10 **have**. ver. 26. Mk 2:25. 13:14. Mt 12:3. 19:4. 21:16. 22:31. Lk 6:3.
The stone. Ps *118:22, 23*. Mt +21:42. Col 1:18.

11 **This was**. Nu 23:23. Hab 1:5. Ac 2:12, 32-36. 3:12-16. 13:40, 41. Ep 3:8-11. Col 1:27. 1 T 3:16.

12 **feared**. Mk 11:18, 32. Mt 21:26, 45, 46. Lk 20:6, 19. Jn 7:19, 25, 30, 44.
people. Mt 21:8, 9. Mk 11:8-10. Lk 4:14, 15. 5:15. Jn 6:15. 11:47, 48. 12:19.
knew. 2 S 12:7, etc. 1 K 20:38-41. 21:17-27.

13 **they send**. Ps 38:12. 56:5, 6. 140:5. Is 29:21. Je 18:18. Mt 22:15, 16. Lk 11:54. 20:20, etc.
Herodians. Mk 3:6. 8:15. Mt 16:6.

14 **Master**. Mk 14:45. Ps 12:2-4. 55:21. 120:2. Pr 26:23-26. Je 42:2, 3, 20.
we know. Jn 7:18. 2 C 2:2, 17. 4:2. 5:11. 1 Th 2:4.
carest. Dt 33:9, 10. 2 Ch 18:13. Is 50:7-9. Je 15:19-21. Ezk 2:6, 7. Mi 3:8. 2 C 5:16. Ga 1:10. 2:6, 11-14.
for thou. Ex 23:2-6. Ro +2:11.
Is it. Ezr 4:12, 13. Ne 9:37. Mt 17:25-27. 22:17. Lk 20:22. 23:2. Ro 13:6, 7.

15 **knowing**. Jn +2:25.
Why tempt. Mt +16:1. Lk +1:35, 22:28.
a penny. Mt +18:28.

16 **image**. Mt 22:19-22. Lk 20:24-26. 2 T 2:19. Re 3:12.

17 **Render**. Pr 24:21. Mt 17:25-27. Ro 13:7. 1 P 2:13, 17.
and to. ver. 30. Pr 23:26. Ec 5:4, 5. Da 3:16. +6:10. Ml 1:6. Ac +4:19, 20. +5:29. Ro 6:13. 12:1. 1 C 6:19, 20. 2 C 5:14, 15.

And they. Jb 5:12, 13. Mt 22:22, 33, 46. 1 C 14:24, 25.

18 **come**. Mt 22:23, etc. Lk 20:27, etc.
say. Ac 4:1, 2. 23:6-9. 1 C 15:13-18. 2 T 2:18.

19 **If**. Mt +4:9. Ge 38:8. Dt 25:5-10. Ru 4:5.
that. Ru 1:11, 13.
his brother. Dt *25:5*.

20 **were seven**. Mt 22:25-28. Lk 20:29-33.

24 **Do ye**. Is +8:20. Je 8:7-9. Ho 6:6. 8:12. Mt 22:29. Jn +5:39. 20:9. Ac +17:11. Ro 15:4. 2 T 3:15-17.
not err. ver. 27. Jb 6:24. Pr +19:27. Is 9:16.
because. Jb 19:25-27. Ps +9:10. Is 25:8. +26:19. Ezk 37:1-14. Da +12:2. Ho 6:2. 13:14.
know not. 1 Ch 28:19. Jb 24:16. Is +8:20. Ho 4:1, 6. Mt 22:29. Jn +5:39, 46. 20:9. 1 C 15:34.
the scriptures. Mt +21:42. 1 Th 2:13. 2 T +3:15-17.
neither. Mk 10:27. Ge 18:14. Je +32:17. Lk 1:37. 1 C 6:14. Ep 1:19, 20. Ph 3:21.

25 **shall rise**. Da +12:2. 1 C 15:42, 49, 52.
neither marry. Mt 22:30. 24:38. Lk 17:27. 20:34-36. 1 C 15:42-54. He 12:22, 23. 1 J 3:2.
as the angels. Ps +8:5. Lk 20:36. He 2:7, 9.

26 **have**. ver. 10. Mt 21:16. 22:31, 32.
in the book. ver. 19. Ex 3:2-6, 16. Lk 20:37. Ac 1:20. 7:30-32. Ro 11:2mg.
of Moses. Ex +24:4.
I am. Ge +17:7, 8. 33:20mg. Ex *3:6*.
of Abraham. Is 41:8. 63:16. Mt 8:11. Lk 16:22-31. Ac 3:13.

27 **is not**. Ro 4:17. 14:9. He 11:13-16.
ye. ver. 24. Pr +19:27. He 3:10.

28 **one**. Mt 22:34-40.
Which. Mt 5:19. 19:18. +23:23. Lk 11:42.

29 **hear**. ver. 32, 33. Dt +6:4. 10:12. 30:6. Pr 23:26. Mt 10:37. Lk 10:27. 1 T 1:5.
is one. Mt 19:17. 23:9. Jn 5:44. 17:3, Ro 3:30. 1 C 8:4, 6. Ga 3:20. Ep 4:6. 1 T 1:17. +2:5. Ja 2:19. 4:12. Ju 25.

30 **shalt love**. Dt +6:5.
with all. Je +29:13.
soul. Gr. *psyche*, Mt +22:37.

31 **Thou**. Le +*19:18*. Mt 7:12. 1 C 13:4-8. 1 J 4:7, 8, 11, 21.
greater. Mt +23:23.

32 **Master**. ver. 14, 19. Mk +4:38.
one God. ver. 29. Dt 4:35, 39. 5:7. +6:4. Is 44:8. 45:5, 6, 14, 18, 21, 22. 46:9. Je 10:10-12.
none other. Dt *4:35, 39*. 1 S 2:2. 2 S 22:32. Ps 18:31. Is 43:3, 10, 11. 44:6, 8. 45:5, 18, 22. 46:9. Zc 14:9. Ml 2:10. Jn 17:3. Ro 16:27. 1 C +8:4, 6. Ep 4:5, 6. 1 T +2:5.

33 **the understanding**. Dt 4:6. Lk 2:47. Ro 1:21, 31. 1 C 1:19. Col 1:9. 2:2. 2 T 2:7.
soul. Gr. *psyche*, Mt +22:37.
to love. Dt +*6:5*.

neighbor as. Le *19:18*.

is more. 1 S +*15:22*. Ps 50:8-15, 23. +51:16, 17. Pr 15:8. 21:3. Is 1:11-17. 58:5-7. Je 7:21-23. Ho 6:6. Am 5:21-24. Mi +6:6-8. Mt 9:13. 12:7. 1 C 13:1-3.

whole burnt. Ps 40:6. He 10:6, 8.

34 Thou. Mt 12:20. Ro 3:20. 7:9. Ga 2:19, 20.

the kingdom. Mk +1:15.

And no. Jb 32:15, 16. Mt 22:46. Lk 14:6. 20:40. Ro 3:19. Col 4:6. T 1:9-11.

35 answered and said. Mk 11:14.

while. Mk 11:27. Lk 19:47. 20:1. 21:37. Jn 18:20.

in the temple. Mt 26:55.

How. Mt 22:41, 42. Lk 20:41-44. Jn 7:42.

36 David. Ac 2:34, 35. 4:25.

by. 2 S 23:2. Ne 9:30. Mt 22:43-45. Lk 10:21. Ac 1:16. 28:25. 1 C 12:3. 2 T 3:16. He 3:7, 8. 4:7. 1 P 1:11. 2 P 1:21.

Ghost. Gr. *pneuma*, Mt +3:16.

The Lord. Ps +*110:1*. 1 C 15:25.

Sit. 1 K 2:19. Ps 45:9.

till. 1 C +15:28.

thy footstool. Jsh 10:24. 1 K 5:3. Is 66:1. Ac 7:49.

37 David. ver. 36.

and whence. Mt 1:23. Ro 1:3, 4. 9:5. 1 T 3:16. Re 22:16.

And the. Mt 11:5, 25. 21:46. Lk 19:48. 21:38. Jn 7:46-49. 12:9, 12. Ja 2:5.

heard. Mk 6:20. Lk 5:1. 15:1. 1 C 1:26.

38 said. Mk +4:2.

Beware. Ezk 22:25. Mt 10:17. 23:1-7, 14. Lk 20:45-47.

which. Mt 6:5. Lk 11:43. 14:7-11. 3 J 9.

marketplaces. Mk 6:56. 7:4. Mt 11:16. 20:3. Lk 7:32. Ac 16:19. 17:17.

39 chief seats. Lk 11:43. Ja 2:2, 3.

uppermost rooms. Lk 14:7, 8.

40 devour. Ezk 22:25. Mi 2:2. 3:1-4, 11. Zp 3:4. Ml +3:5. Mt +23:14.

widows'. Ja 1:27.

long. Mt 6:5, 7. +23:14.

greater. Dt +32:22. Mt +10:15. 23:33.

41 sat. Mt 27:6. Lk 21:1-4, etc.

against the treasury. ver. 43. Mt 27:6. Jn 8:20.

cast. 2 K 12:9. 2 Ch 24:8, 10.

money. "A piece of brass money, see Mt 10:9." Mk 6:8.

the treasury. 2 K 12:9.

42 a certain. Mt 8:19.

two mites. "It is the seventh part of one piece of that brass money." *Lk 12:59*.

farthing. Mt 5:26.

43 Verily. Mt +5:18.

That. Ex 35:21-29. Jg 19:20. Ps 34:9. Mt 10:42. Ac 11:29. 2 C 8:2, 12. 9:6-8.

44 cast in of. Mk 14:8. 1 Ch 29:2-17. 2 Ch

24:10-14. 31:5-10. 35:7, 8. Ezr 2:68, 69. Ne 7:70-72. 2 C 8:2, 3. Ph 4:10-17.

but she. 1 K 17:12. Lk 4:26. 6:38. 19:8, 9.

all her. Dt 24:6. Lk 8:43. 15:12, 30. 21:2-4. 1 J 3:17.

MARK 13

1 as he. Mt +24:1, etc. Lk 21:5, etc.

out. Ezk 7:20-22. 8:6. 10:4, 19. 11:22, 23. Ml 3:1, 2.

2 there. 2 S 17:13. 1 K 9:7, 8. 2 Ch 7:20, 21. Je 26:18. Mi 1:6. 3:12. Mt +24:2. Lk 19:41-44. 21:6. Ac 6:14. Re 11:2.

3 as. Mt +24:3.

Peter. Mk 1:16-19. 5:37. 9:2. 10:35. 14:33. Mt 10:2. 17:1. Jn 1:40, 41.

privately. Mk 4:34. Mt 13:10, 36.

4 when shall. Da 12:6, 8. Mt +24:3. Lk 21:7. Jn 21:21, 22. Ac +1:6, 7. 1 Th 5:1, 2, 4.

5 Take. ver. 9, 23, 33. Je +29:8. 1 C 15:33. Col 2:8. 1 Th 2:3. 1 J 3:7. 4:1. Re 20:7, 8.

6 many. ver. 21, 22. Je 14:14. 23:21-25. 27:15. Mt +24:23, 24. Jn 5:43. 1 J 2:18. 4:1.

in my name. Mk +9:37.

I am. Jn +8:24.

and shall. ver. 22. Mt +24:5, 11, 23, 24. Ac 5:36-39.

7 when. Ps 27:3. 46:1-3. 112:7. Pr 3:25. Is 8:12. Je 4:19-21. +49:14. Mt +24:6, 7. Lk 21:9-11. Jn 14:1, 27.

rumors. lit. hearing. Le +13:55.

not troubled. 2 Th 2:2.

must. 2 S 14:14. Da *2:28*. Mt 18:7. Lk +13:33. Ac 17:3.

come to pass. Re 1:1.

the end. Mt +24:14. 1 P 4:7.

not yet. Mt +24:6, 14. 2 Th 2:2, 3, 7, 8.

8 nation shall. 2 Ch 15:6. Is *19:2*. Je 25:32. Hg 2:22. Zc 14:13. Re 6:4.

kingdom against. Is 19:2.

earthquakes. Re +6:12.

famines. 1 K +8:37.

these. Mt +24:8.

sorrows. Is 37:3. Mt +24:8.

9 take. ver. 5. Mt 10:17, 18. 23:34-37. +24:9, 10. Lk 21:16-18. Jn 15:20. 16:2. Ac 4:1-21. 5:17-40. 6:11-15. +7:54-60. 8:3. 9:1, 2, 13, 14, 16. 12:1-3. 16:20-24. 21:11, 31-40. 22:19, 20. 23:1, 2. 24:1, etc. ch. 25, 26. 1 C 4:9-13. 2 C 11:23-27. Ga 6:1. Ph 1:29. 2 Th 1:5. 2 J 8. Re 1:9. 2:10, 13. 6:9-11.

councils. Mt 5:22. Ac 4:15.

synagogues. Mt 23:34.

before rulers. Ac 17:6. 18:12. 24:1. 25:6.

and kings. Ac 25:23. 27:24. 2 T 4:16, 17.

for my sake. Mk 8:35. 10:29. Mt 5:11. 10:18, 29, 39. 16:25. +24:9. Lk 6:22. 9:24. 18:29. 21:12.

for a testimony. Mt +8:4.

10 **the gospel**. Mk 14:9. 16:15. Mt +24:14. 28:18, 19. Ro 1:8. 10:18. 15:19. 16:25, 26. Col 1:6, 23. Re 14:6.

11 **and deliver**. ver. 9. Mt 10:17, 21. Ac 3:13.
take no thought. Ex 4:10-12. Je 1:6-9. Da 3:16-18. Mt 6:25. 10:19, 20. Lk 12:11, 12. 21:14, 15. Ac 2:4. 4:8, etc., 31. 6:10, 15. 7:55.
shall be given. Nu 23:5. Dt 18:18. Is 50:4. Jn 3:27. Ep 6:19, 20. Ja +1:5.
for it. Lk 21:15. Ac 4:8. 6:10. 13:9. 1 C 15:10. 2 C 13:3. 1 Th 2:13. He 1:1.
but. 2 S 23:2. 1 C 2:13. Ep 3:5. 1 P 1:12.
Ghost. Gr. *pneuma*, Mt +3:16.

12 **shall betray**. Ezk 38:21. Mi 7:4-6. Mt 10:21, 35, 36. +24:10, 12. Lk 12:52, 53. 21:16.
children. Mi 7:6.
put to death. Mt 23:34. Lk 11:49. Jn 16:2.

13 **ye**. Mt +5:11, 12. +24:9. Dt 11:12. 2 Ch 16:9. Lk 6:22, 23. 21:17-19. Jn 15:18, 19. 17:14. 1 J 3:13.
for my. ver. 9. Jn 15:21.
but. Da +12:12, 13. Mt 10:22. +24:13. Ro +2:7. Ga 6:9. He 3:14. 10:36, 39. Ja 1:12. Re 2:10. +3:10.
unto the end. 1 C 1:8. 2 C 1:13. Ga 6:9. He 3:6, 14. 6:11. Re 2:26.

14 **the abomination**. Da +8:13. +9:27. 11:31. +*12:11*. Mt +24:15, etc. Lk 21:20-22.
spoken. Lk +24:27.
where. La 1:10. Ezk 44:9.
let him. Da +9:22, 23, 25-27. Mt +13:51. Ac 8:30, 31. 1 C 14:7, 8, 20. Re 1:3. 13:18.
then. Lk 21:20-24.
flee. Ge 17:17, 19.

15 **let him**. Ge 19:15-17, 22, 26. Jb 2:4. Pr 6:4, 5. +22:3. Mt +24:16-18. Lk 17:31-33. Ac 27:18, 19, 38. Ph 3:7, 8. He 11:7.
housetop. Dt +22:8.

16 **his garment**. Mk 10:50. Mt 5:40.

17 **woe to them**. Le +26:29. Ho 9:14. 13:16. Mt +24:19-21. Lk 21:23. 1 C 7:26.

19 **in those**. ver. 24. Dt 28:59. 29:22-28. Is 65:12-15. La 1:12. 2:13. 4:6. Da 9:12, +26. +*12:1*. Jl 2:2. Mt +24:21. Lk 21:22-24.
such as. Jl +2:2. Re 16:18.
from the beginning. Mk 10:6. Dt 4:32.
God created. Ge 1:1.

20 **except**. Mt +11:21.
no flesh. Lk +3:6.
for the elect's. ver. 22, 27. Is 1:9. 6:13. 65:8, 9. Zc 13:8, 9. Mt 22:14. +24:22. Lk 18:7. Ro 11:5-7, 23, 24, 28-32. Re 7:14.
hath chosen. Dt +10:15. Jn 13:18. 15:16, 19. Ep 1:4. 2 Th 2:13. 2 T 1:9. Ja 2:5. Re 13:8. 17:8.

21 **if any**. Mt +4:9. ver. 6. Dt 13:1-3. Mt +24:5, 23-25. Lk 17:23, 24. 21:8. Jn 5:43.
here is. Mt 24:26-28.
Christ. Mt +16:16.

22 **false Christs**. 1 J 2:18.

false prophets. Dt *13:1-5*. Mt 7:15. 1 T 4:1, 2. 2 P 2:1.
shall show. Dt 13:1-3. Ac 8:9. 2 Th 2:9-11. Re 13:13, 14. 16:14. 19:20.
signs. Jn 4:48.
to seduce. ver. 6.
if it were possible. Mt +23:30. ver. 6. Mt +24:24. Jn 10:27-29. 2 Th 2:8-14. 2 T 2:19. 1 J 2:19, 26, 27. Re 13:8, 13, 14. 17:8.
the elect. ver. 20. Mt 24:22.

23 **take**. ver. 5, 9, 33. Mt 7:15. Lk 21:8, 34. 2 P 3:17.
behold. Is 44:7, 8. Mt +24:25. Jn +13:19. 14:29. 16:1-4. 2 P 3:17.

24 **in those days**. Is *13:10*. 24:20-23. Je 4:23-25, 28. Da 7:10. 12:1. Ac 2:19, 20. 2 P 3:10, 12. Re 6:12-14. 20:11.
after. Mt +24:29.
that tribulation. ver. 19. Je +30:7.
the sun shall. Is 24:23. Je 4:23, 24. Jl 3:15. Zc 14:6. Ac 2:20. Re 6:12. 8:12.
darkened. Ex +10:22.

25 **the stars**. Is 14:12. 34:4. 2 P 3:10. Re 6:13.
the powers. Ep 6:12.
shaken. Jb 26:11. Is *34:4*. He +12:26.

26 **they**. The shift from the grammatical "second person" of the preceding context (ver. 14 "ye," 21 "you," 23 "ye") to the "third person" *they* of this verse marks a corresponding shift in time from what could have applied to the disciples and Christians of the first century fulfilled in part at the fall of Jerusalem to events which are to occur long after at the end of the age.
shall see. Mt +16:27, 28. Re +1:7.
Son of man. Mk +2:10. Da *7:13*.
coming. Mk 8:38. 14:62. Da 7:9-14. Mt 16:17, +27. 24:30. +25:31. 26:64. Ac +1:11. 1 Th 4:16. 2 Th 1:7-10. Re +1:7.
clouds. Ge +9:13. 2 Ch +5:13.
great. Mk 5:40, 42. Lk 1:64.
power. Mk 9:1. Mt +25:31. 26:64.
and glory. Ps 68:17. Ac 7:55.

27 **shall he send**. Mt +13:41, 49. +24:31. Lk 16:22. Re 7:1-3. 15:6, 7.
shall gather. Ge +49:10. Dt *30:4*. Zc 2:6. Mt 23:37. +24:31. 25:31, 32. Jn +10:16. 11:52. 1 Th 4:14-17. 2 Th 2:1. Re 7:5-9.
his elect. ver. 20, 22. Is 65:9. Mt +24:22, 24, 31. Lk 18:7. Ro 8:33. Ep 1:4. Col 3:12. 2 T 2:10. 1 P 1:2.
four winds. Je 49:36. Ezk 37:9. Da 7:2. 8:8. 11:4. Zc 2:6. Mt 12:42. Re 7:1.
from the uttermost. Dt 30:4. Ac 1:8.
to the uttermost. Dt 4:32. 30:4. Ps 19:6.

28 **learn a parable**. Mt +24:32, 33. Lk 21:29-31.
When her branch. Mk 11:13.

29 **know**. Ezk 7:10-12. 12:25-28. He 10:25-37. Ja 5:9. 1 P 4:17, 18.
at the doors. Ja 5:9. Re 3:20.

30 **Verily**. Mt +5:18.
this generation. Mt +24:34.

31 **Heaven**. Ps +89:37. 102:25-27. Is 34:4. 51:6. Je +33:25. Mt +5:18. +24:35. Lk 16:17. He 1:10-12. 12:27. 2 P 3:10-12. Re 20:11. 21:1.
my words. Nu 23:19. Jsh 23:14, 15. Ps 19:7. 119:89, 152. Is 40:8. Zc 1:6. Lk 21:33. 2 T 2:13. T 1:2. 1 P 1:23, 25.

32 **of that day**. ver. 26, 27. Mt +24:36-42. 25:6, 13, 19. Jn 14:11. Ac 1:7. 1 Th 5:2. 2 P 3:10. Re 3:3.
knoweth. Dt +29:29. Mt 25:13. Jn 13:7. 16:12. Ro 13:11. 1 C 13:12. Ep 3:5. 1 Th 5:1, 2, 4.
neither the Son. Is 42:6. Mt 11:27. +14:23, 33. 24:36. +28:19. Lk 10:22. Jn 3:35. 5:19-23, 25, 26, 30. +6:38, 57. 8:28, 29. +10:30. 14:10. 20:17. Ac 1:4. 1 C +15:28. 2 C 13:4. Ph 2:6, 7. Re 1:1. 19:12.
but the Father. Ho +8:4. Zc 14:7. Mt +10:32. Jn 5:20. +14:28. Ac 1:7.

33 **Take ye heed**. ver. 5, 23, 35-37. Mt +24:42. Lk 21:34-36. He 12:15.
watch and pray. Ne 4:9. Mt +24:42. Lk +21:36.
ye know not. ver. 32. Ro 13:11.

34 **as a**. Mt +24:45. +25:14-30. Lk 12:36-38. 19:12-17.
far journey. Mk 12:1. Mt 21:33. +25:19.
left his house. He 3:6.
gave authority. Mt +16:19. +18:18. Ac +20:28. He 13:17. 1 P 5:3, 5.
his servants. Mk +9:35. Da +11:33. 1 C 4:1, 2.
and to every man. Nu 4:19. Mt +24:45. Ro 12:4-8. 13:6. 1 C 3:5-10. 12:4-31. 15:58. Col 3:24. 4:1.
his work. Ps 62:12. Lk 19:13.
and commanded. Ezk 3:17-21. 33:2-9. Mt +24:45-47. Lk 12:36-40. Ac 20:29-31.
the porter. 1 Ch 9:22, 19. Ps 84:10. Ezk 44:11. Mt 16:19. Lk 12:36. Jn 10:3. Re 3:7.
to watch. ver. 33, 37.

35 **Watch**. ver. 33. Mt +24:42, 44. Lk +21:36.
when. Mt 24:43.
at even. The first watch, our 6 p.m. to 9 p.m. Mk 1:32. 11:11, 19. Mt 20:8.
midnight. The second watch, our 9 p.m. to 12 midnight. Jg 7:19. 16:3. Ps 119:62. Is 59:10. Mt 25:6. Lk 11:5. +12:38. Ac 16:25. 20:7.
cockcrowing. The third watch, our 12 midnight to 3 a.m. Mk 14:30, 68, 72. Jg 7:19. Lk 12:38.
morning. The fourth watch, our 3 a.m. to 6 a.m. Mk 1:35. 6:48. Ex 14:24. Ps 130:6. Mt 14:25.

36 **coming suddenly**. Mt 24:44. 1 Th 5:1-6.
he find. Mk 14:37, 40. Pr 6:9-11. 24:33, 34.

SS 3:1. 5:2. Is 56:10. Mt +24:48-51. 25:5. 26:40. Lk 21:34. 22:45. Ro 13:11-14. Ep 5:14. 1 Th 5:6, 7.

37 **I say**. ver. 33, 35. Lk 12:41-46.

MARK 14

1 **two**. Mt 26:2. Lk 22:1, 2. Jn 11:53-57. 13:1.
the passover. Ex 12:6-20. Le +23:5. Nu 28:16-25. Dt 16:1-8. Jn 6:4.
unleavened bread. Ex 23:15. 34:18. Le +23:6. Dt 16:16. 2 Ch 8:13. 30:13, 21. 35:17. Ezr 6:22.
chief. Ps 2:1-5. Jn 11:47. Ac 4:25-28.
sought. Mk 12:12. Jn 11:53.
by craft. Ps 52:3. 62:4, 9. 64:2-6. Mt 26:4.

2 **Not**. Pr 19:21. +21:30. La 3:37. Mt 26:5.
lest. Mk 11:18, 32. Mt 27:24. Lk 20:6. 22:6mg. Jn 7:40. 12:19.

3 **being**. Mt 26:6, 7. Jn 11:2. 12:1-3.
of ointment. SS 4:13, 14. 5:5. Lk 7:37, 38.
spikenard. *or*, pure nard, *or* liquid nard.

4 **there**. Ec 4:4. Mt 26:8, 9. Jn 12:4, 5.
Why. Ex 5:4-8. Ml 1:12, 13.

5 **pence**. Mt +18:28mg.
given to. Jn 12:5, 6. 13:29. Ep 4:28.
And they. Ju 16.

6 **Let**. Jb 42:7, 8. Is 54:17. 2 C 10:18.
a good. Mt 26:10. Jn 10:32, 33. Ac 9:36. 2 C 9:8. Ep 2:10. Col +1:10. 2 Th 2:17. 1 T 5:10. 6:18. 2 T 2:21. 3:17. T 2:7, 14. 3:8, 14. He 10:24. 13:21. 1 P 2:12.

7 **ye have**. Dt *15:11*. Mt 25:35-45. 26:11. Jn 12:7, 8. 2 C 9:13, 14. Phm 7. Ja 2:14-16. 1 J 3:16-19.
the poor. Ex +23:3.
ye may do. 2 C 9:7. Ga 6:10.
but. Mk 2:20. Mt 9:15. Jn 7:33. 12:35. 13:33. 14:19. 16:5, 16-19, 28. 17:11. Ac +3:21.

8 **hath done**. 1 Ch 28:2, 3. 29:1-17. 2 Ch 31:20, 21. 34:19-33. Ps 110:3. Lk 7:45. 2 C 8:1-3, 12.
what she could. Mk 12:43. Mt 15:28. Lk 21:3.
she is. Mk 15:42-47. 16:1. Lk 23:53-56. 24:1-3. Jn 12:7. 19:32-42.
to the burying. Mt 26:12. Re 12:11.

9 **Wheresoever**. Mk 16:15. Mt 26:12, 13.
this gospel. Mk 13:10. Mt 24:14. Ac 20:24. Ep 1:13. 6:15.
world. Gr. *kosmos*, Mt +4:8.
a memorial. Ex +12:14. Ps 112:6-9.

10 **Judas**. Mt 26:14-16. Lk 22:3-6. Jn 13:2, 30.
Iscariot. Jsh 15:25. Je 48:24, 41.
one. Ps 41:9. 55:12-14.
the twelve. Mk 9:35.
to betray. Mt +20:18.

11 **they heard**. Jn 11:57.
they were. Ho 7:3. Lk 22:5.
and promised. 1 K 21:20. 2 K 5:26. Pr 1:10-

16. 28:21, 22. Mt 26:15. 1 T 6:10. 2 P 2:14, 15. Ju 11.

he sought. Lk 22:5, 6.

conveniently. 2 T 4:2.

12 **the first**. Ex 12:6, 8, 18. 13:3. Le 23:5, 6. Nu 28:16-18. Dt 16:1-4. Mt 26:17. Lk 22:7.

killed. *or*, sacrificed. Dt 16:6, 7. Ac 14:13, 18. 1 C 5:7, 8. 10:20.

the passover. Ex +12:21. Le +23:5. Ac 12:3, 4.

Where. Mt 3:15. Lk 22:8, 9. Ga 4:4.

13 **two**. Mk 11:2. Mt 21:2. Lk 19:29. 22:8.

Go. Mk 11:2, 3. Mt 8:9. 26:18, 19. Lk 19:30-33. 22:10-13. Jn 2:5. +15:14. He 4:13. 5:9.

14 **The Master**. Mk +4:38.

guestchamber. Lk 2:7. 22:11.

where I. Re 3:20.

passover. ver. +12.

15 **he will**. 2 Ch 6:30. Ps 110:3. Pr 16:1. 21:1, 2. Jn +2:24, 25. 21:17. 2 T 2:19. He 4:13.

upper. Lk 22:12. Ac 1:13. 20:8.

16 **and found**. Lk 19:32. 22:13, 35. Jn 16:4.

17 **in the evening**. Mt 26:20. Lk 22:14.

18 **as they sat**. Ex 12:11. Mt 26:21.

Verily. ver. 9, 25. Mt +5:18.

One. ver. +10. Ps *41:9*. 55:13, 14.

eateth with me. Ru 2:14. Jn 13:18, 26.

19 **and to**. Mt 26:22. Lk 22:21-23. Jn 13:22.

one by one. Jn 8:9.

and another said. Mt 26:25.

20 **It is**. ver. 43. Mt 26:47. Lk 22:47. Jn 6:71.

the twelve. ver. 10.

dippeth. ver. 18. Ru 2:14. Ps 41:9. Mt 26:23. Jn 13:26.

21 **Son of man**. Mk +2:10.

goeth. ver. 49. Ge +3:15. Ps 22:1, etc. 69:1, etc. Is 52:14. ch. 53. Da 9:24, 26. Zc 13:7. Mt 26:24, 54, 56. Lk 22:22. 24:26, 27, 44. Jn 7:33. 8:21, 22. 14:12. 16:28. 19:28, 36, 37. Ac 2:23. 4:27, 28. 13:27-29.

as it is written. ver. 49. Mk 9:12. Lk 18:31. 24:25-27, 46. Ac +17:2, 3. 26:22, 23. 1 C +15:3. 1 P 1:10, 11.

but. Ps 55:15. 109:6-20. Mt 18:7. 27:3-5. Lk 17:1. 22:22. Ac 1:16-20, 25.

by whom. Ob 7. Mi 7:6.

good were. Mt 18:6, 7. 26:24, 25. Mk 9:42. Jn 17:12.

if. Mt +23:30.

never been born. Jb 3:1-19. Je 20:14-18.

22 **as**. Mt 26:26-29. Lk 22:19, 20. 1 C 10:16, 17. 11:23-29.

took bread. Jn 6:35.

and blessed. Lk 24:30.

brake. Is +58:7.

Take. Jn 6:48-58.

this is. ver. +24. Ge 41:26, 27. +49:9. Ex 12:11. Da 7:24. Zc 5:7, 8. Mt 13:38, 39. Lk 8:9. 15:26. 18:36. 22:20. Jn 7:36. 10:6. Ac

10:17. Ga 4:25. Re 1:20. 5:6, 8. 11:4. 17:12, 18. 19:8.

my body. Jn 6:51, 53.

23 **when**. ver. 22. Mt 15:36. Lk 22:17. Ro 14:6. 1 C 10:16.

and they all. Mt 26:27.

24 **This is**. ver. +22. Ex *24:8*. Zc *9:11*. Jn 6:53. 1 C 10:4, 16. He 10:29. 13:20, 21.

new. Mt +26:28.

which. Mk 10:45. Re 5:8-10. 7:9-17.

is shed. Mt +26:24.

for many. Mt 20:28. 26:28.

25 **I will**. Ps 104:15. Mt 26:29. Lk 22:16-18, 29, 30.

no more. Mt +5:18.

until. Mt +26:29. Lk 22:18. Ac 10:41.

new. Jl 3:18. Am +9:13, 14. Zc 9:17.

in the kingdom. Mk +1:15. Is 25:6. Mt +8:11. Lk 14:15. 22:18, 30. Jn 16:22. Re 7:17. 19:9.

26 **sung**. Ps 47:6, 7. Ac 16:25. 1 C 14:15. Ep 5:18-20. Col 3:16. Ja 5:13. Re 5:9.

hymn. *or*, psalm. Ps ch. 113-118.

they went. Mt 26:30. Lk 22:39. Jn 18:1-4.

27 **All**. Lk 22:31, 32. 2 T 4:16.

offended. Mt +11:6.

for it is written. Lk +24:27.

I will smite. Zc *13:7*.

28 **after**. Mk +16:7. Mt 16:21. 1 C +15:4-6.

29 **Although**. Lk +11:8. Pr 28:14, 26. Je +17:9. Mt 26:33-35. Lk 22:33, 34. Jn 13:36-38. 21:15. 1 C 10:12.

30 **That**. Lk 4:21; 19:9.

this day. Ge 1:5, 8, 13, 19, 23. Mt 21:28. Lk 22:34. +23:43.

before. ver. 66-72. Mt 26:69-75. Lk 22:54-62. Jn 18:17, 25-27. 1 C 10:12.

crow twice. ver. 68, 72. Mt 26:34, 75. Lk 22:34, 60. Jn 13:38. 18:27.

31 **he spake**. 2 K 8:13. Jb 40:4, 5. Ps 30:6. Pr 16:18. 28:26. 29:23. Je 10:23. +17:9. Jn 13:36-38.

If. Mt +4:9.

Likewise. Ex 19:8. Dt 5:27-29.

32 **they came**. Mt 26:36, etc. Lk 22:39. Jn 18:1, etc.

while. ver. 36, 39. Ps 18:5, 6. 22:1, 2. 88:1-3. 109:4.

33 **Peter**. Mk 1:16-19. 5:37, 38. 9:2. Mt 17:1.

and began. Ps 38:11. 69:1-3. 88:14-16. Is 53:10. Mt 26:37, 38. Lk 22:44. He 5:7.

34 **My soul**. Gr. *psyche*, Mt +12:18. Ps *42:5, 6*. 43:5. Is 53:3, 4, 12. La 1:12. Jn 12:27.

exceeding sorrowful. Mk 6:26. Mt 26:38. Lk 18:23.

unto death. 2 K 20:1. 2 Ch 32:24. Is 38:1. Jon 4:9.

and watch. ver. 37, 38. Mt +24:42.

35 **went forward**. Lk 22:41, 42.

and fell. Ge +17:3. He 5:7.

the hour. Jn 12:27.
if. 1 C +15:2.
might pass. ver. 41. Lk 22:53. Jn 2:4. 12:23, 27. 13:1. 16:4. 17:1.

36 **Abba**. i.e. *father*, **s#5g**. Mt +6:9. Ro 8:15, 16. Ga 4:6.
Father. Lk +22:42.
all. Mk 10:27. Ge +18:14. Jb +42:2. Je +32:27. Mt 19:26. 2 T 2:13. T 1:2. He 5:7. 6:18.
take. Lk 22:41, 42.
this cup. Mk 10:38. Mt 20:22.
nevertheless. Mt +6:10. Jn 5:30. 6:38, 39. 12:27. 18:11. Ph 2:8. He 5:7, 8.

37 **and findeth**. ver. 40, 41. Mk 13:36. Lk 9:31, 32. 22:45, 46.
Simon. ver. 29-31. 2 S 16:17. Jon 1:6. Mt 25:5. 26:40. 1 Th 5:6-8.
couldest. Je 12:5. He 12:3.
watch. Mt +24:42.

38 **Watch**. ver. 34. Ne 4:9. Ps 102:7. 119:147. 130:6. 141:2, 3. Mt +24:42. Lk +21:36. 22:40, 46.
enter into. Mt +6:13.
The spirit. Gr. *pneuma*, Mt +26:41. Ro 7:18-25. Ga 5:17. Ph 2:12.
the flesh. He 5:2.

39 **he went**. Mt 6:7. 26:42-44. Lk 18:1. 22:43, 44. 2 C 12:8.
the same. ver. 36.

40 **eyes were heavy**. Lk 9:32.
neither. Mk 9:6, 33, 34. Ge 44:16. Lk 9:33. Ro 3:19.

41 **third time**. 2 C 12:8.
Sleep. Mk 7:9. Jg 10:14. 1 K 18:27. 22:15. 2 K 3:13. Ec 11:9. Ezk 20:39. Mt 26:45, 46.
it is enough. Lk +22:38.
the hour. ver. 35. Jn +2:4.
Son of man. Mk +2:10.
is betrayed. ver. 10, 18. Mk 9:31. 10:33, 34. Mt 17:22. 20:18. 26:2. Lk 9:44. 18:32. Jn 13:2. Ac 7:52.

42 **Rise up**. Mt 26:46. Jn 13:1. 14:31. 18:1, 2.

43 **while**. Mt 26:47. Lk 22:47, 48. Jn 18:3-9. Ac 1:16.
and with. Ps 2:1, 2. 3:1, 2. 22:11-13.

44 **a token**. Ex 12:13. Jsh 2:12. Ph 1:28. 2 Th 3:17.
Whomsoever. 2 S 20:9, 10. Ps 55:20, 21. Pr 27:6. Mt 26:48-50.
and lead. 1 S 23:22, 23. Ac 16:23.

45 **Master**. Mk +4:38. Is 1:3. Ml 1:6.
and kissed him. Ge +27:27. Mt 26:49, 50.

46 **they laid**. Jg 16:21. La 4:20. Mt 26:50. Jn 18:12. Ac 2:23.

47 **one of them**. Mt 26:51-54. Lk 22:49-51. Jn 18:10, 11.
sword. Lk +22:38.

48 **answered and said**. Mk 11:14.

Are ye. 1 S 24:14, 15. 26:18. Mt 26:55. Lk 22:52, 53.
a thief. Mk 11:17. Mt 21:13. Lk 10:30. 19:46. Jn 18:40.

49 **was daily**. Mk 11:15-18, 27. 12:35. Mt 21:23, etc. Lk 19:47, 48. 20:1, 2. 21:37, 38. Jn 7:28-30, 37. 8:2, 12. 10:23. 18:20.
in the temple. Lk 2:46. Jn 18:20.
teaching. Mk 1:21. 11:17. 12:35. Mt 4:23. 9:35. 13:54. 21:23. Lk 19:47. 20:1. 21:37. Jn 7:14, 28. 8:20. 10:23. 18:20.
the scriptures. Ps ch. 22, 69. Is ch. 53. Da 9:24-26. Zc 13:7. Mt 26:54, 56. Lk 22:37. 24:25-27, 44, 45.
must be. Mt 26:54. Lk 22:37. 24:44. Ac 1:16.
fulfilled. Mt 1:22.

50 **they all forsook**. ver. 27. Jb 19:13, 14. Ps 38:11. 88:7, 8, 18. Is 63:3. Jn 16:32. 18:8, 9. 2 T 4:16.

51 **linen cloth**. Mk 15:46. Jg 14:12. Pr 31:24.

52 **he left**. Mk 13:14-16. Ge 39:12. Jb 2:4.
fled. Am 2:16.
naked. Is +20:2.

53 **they led**. Is 53:7. Mt 26:57, etc. Lk 22:54, etc. Jn 18:13, 14, 24.
and with. Mk 15:1. Mt 26:3. Ac 4:5, 6.

54 **Peter**. ver. 29-31, 38. 1 S 13:7. Mt 26:58.
even. ver. 68. Jn 18:15, 16.
the palace. ver. 66. Mt 26:3.
and he. 1 K 19:9, 13. Pr 28:14. Mt 6:13. Lk 22:55, 56. Jn 18:18, 25. 1 C 10:12.
the servants. ver. 65. Mt 5:25. Jn 7:32, 45, 46. 18:3, 12, 22. 19:6. Ac 5:22, 26.
and warmed. ver. 67. Is 44:16. Je 36:22. Lk 22:44. Jn 18:18.

55 **all**. Mt +26:59.
the council. Mt 5:22.
sought. 1 K 21:10, 13. Ps 27:12. 35:11. Mt 26:59, 60. Ac 6:11-13. 24:1-13.
and found. Da 6:4. 1 P 3:16-18.

56 **false witness**. Ps 27:12. 35:11.
agreed not. ver. 59. Dt 17:6. 19:15.

57 **and bare**. Mk 15:29. Je 26:8, 9, 18. Mt 26:60, 61. 27:40. Jn +2:18-21. Ac 6:13, 14.

58 **heard him say**. Ac 6:14.
I will. Mk 15:29. Mt 27:40. Jn +2:19.
this temple. Mk 15:29, 38. Mt 23:16.
with hands. Ac 7:48. 17:24. Ep 2:11. He 9:11, 24.
three days. Mt 16:21. Jn 2:19.
made without hands. Da 2:34, 45. Ac 7:48. 17:24. 2 C 5:1. Col 2:11. He 9:11, 24.

59 **neither**. ver. 56.

60 **Answerest thou nothing**. Mk 15:3-5. Mt 26:62, 63. Jn 19:9, 10.

61 **he held his peace**. Mk 15:4, 5. Ps 39:1, 2, 9. Is 53:7. Mt +26:63. 27:12-14. Jn 19:9. Ac 8:32, 33. 1 P 2:23.
Art thou. Mk 15:2. Mt 11:3-5. Jn 18:37.
the Christ. Mt +16:16.

the Son. Ps 119:12. Is +9:6, 7. Mt +14:33.
the Blessed. Lk 1:68. Ro 1:25. 9:5. 2 C 1:3.
11:31. Ep 1:3. 1 T 1:11. 6:15. 1 P 1:3.

62 I am. Mk 15:2. Mt 26:64. +27:11. Lk 22:70.
23:3. Jn +8:24.
ye shall see. Mt +16:27. +24:30. Lk 21:27.
the Son of man. Mk +2:10. Ac 1:9-11. 2 Th
1:7-10. Re +1:7. 20:11.
sitting. He +1:3.
right hand. Ps +110:1, 2.
coming. Da 7:13. Re +1:7.
the clouds. Ge +9:13. 2 Ch +5:13. Mt
+25:30. Re +1:7.

63 rent his clothes. Le 10:6. 21:10. 2 K
+18:37.

64 heard the blasphemy. Mk 2:7. Le +24:11,
16. 1 K 21:9-13. Mt 9:3. 26:65, 66. Lk 5:21.
22:71. Jn 5:18. 8:58, 59. 10:31-33, 36. 19:7.
Ac 6:11, 13.
all condemned. Lk 23:50, 51.
guilty. Mk 3:29.
of death. Le 24:16.

65 began to spit. Is *50:6*. Mt +26:67.
cover his face. Est 7:8. Jb 9:24. Is 53:3.
the servants. ver. 54.
strike him. Is 52:14. 53:3. Mt +27:30.

66 as Peter. ver. 54. Mt 26:58, 69, 70. Lk 22:55-
57.
the palace. ver. 54. Mt 26:3.
one of the maids. Jn 18:15-18.

67 Jesus of Nazareth. Mk +1:24.

68 he denied. ver. 29-31. Jn 13:36-38. 2 T 2:12,
13.
know not. Ju 10.
neither. Pr 29:25. Mt +10:28, 33.
he went. Mt 26:71, 72.
and the. ver. 30, 72.

69 a maid. Mt 26:71. Jn 18:17.
and began. ver. 38. Lk 22:58. Jn 18:25. Ga
6:1.

70 a little after. Mt 26:73, 74. Lk 22:58-60. Jn
18:26, 27.
for thou art. Jg 12:6. Ac 2:7.
and thy speech. Jg 12:6. 2 K 8:21. 1 Ch
6:36. Ne 13:24. Mt 26:73. Ac 2:6, 7.

71 he began. 2 K 8:12-15. 10:32. Je +17:9. 1 C
10:12.

72 the second. ver. 30, 68. Mt 26:34, 74.
Peter. 2 S 24:10. Ps 119:59, 60. Je 31:18-20.
Ezk 16:63. 36:31. Lk 15:17-19. 22:60, 61.
deny me. Ac 3:13, 14.
when he thought thereon, he wept. *or*, he
wept abundantly, *or* he began to weep. Ezk
7:16. Mt 26:75. Lk 22:62. 2 C 7:10.

MARK 15

1 straightway. Ps 2:2. Mt 27:1, 2. Lk 22:66. Ac
4:5, 6, 25-28.
a consultation. Mk 3:6. Ps 71:10.

and delivered. Mk +10:33.
Pilate. Lk 3:1. 13:1. Ac 3:13. 4:27. 1 T 6:13.

2 Art thou. Mt 2:2. 27:11. Lk 23:3. Jn 18:33-
37. 19:19-22. 1 T 6:13.
King of the Jews. ver. 9, 12, 18, 26, +32. Mt
2:2. 27:29, 37. Lk 23:37, 38. Jn 18:33, 39.
19:3, 19, 21.
Thou sayest. Mt +27:11. Lk 22:70.

3 the chief. Mt 27:12. Lk 23:2-5. Jn 18:29-31.
19:6, 7, 12.
but. ver. 5. Mk 14:60, 61. Is 53:7.
answered nothing. Mt +26:63.

4 Answerest. Mt 26:62. 27:13. Jn 19:10.

5 Jesus. Is 53:7. Jn 19:9, 10.
answered nothing. Mt +26:63.
Pilate. Ps 71:7. Is 8:18. Zc 3:8. Mt 27:14. 1 C
4:9.

6 at the feast. Mt 26:2, 5. 27:15. Lk 23:16, 17.
Jn 18:39, 40. Ac 24:27. 25:9.

7 Barabbas. Mt 27:16. Lk 23:18, 19, 25. Jn
18:40.
made insurrection. Ac 5:36, 37.
committed murder. Ac 3:14.

8 ever. S#104g. Gr. *aei*, rendered (1) *alway*: 2 C
4:11. 6:10. T 1:12. He 3:10. (2) *always*: Ac
7:51. 1 P 3:15. 2 P 1:12. (3) *ever*: ver. 8.

9 Will. Mt 27:17-21. Jn 18:39. 19:4, 5, 14-16.
Ac 3:13-15.
King of the Jews. ver. +2.

10 for envy. Ge 4:4-6. 1 S 18:8, 9. Ps +37:1. Jn
11:47, 48. 12:19. 1 J 3:12.

11 chief priests. Ho 5:1. Mt 27:20. Jn 18:40. Ac
3:14.

12 What. Mt 27:22, 23. Lk 23:20-24. Jn 19:14-16.
whom. ver. 1, 2. Mk 11:9-11. Ps 2:6, 7. Is
+9:6, 7. Je +23:5, 6. Zc 9:9. Mt 2:2-4. 21:5. Lk
23:2. Jn 19:15. Ac 5:31.

13 And they. Re 16:15.
Crucify him. Ac 13:28.

14 Why. Is 53:9. Mt 27:4, 19, 24, 54. Lk 23:4,
14, 15, 21, 22, 41, 47. Jn 18:38. 19:6. He
7:26. 1 P 1:19.
And they. Ps 69:4. Is 53:3. Mt 27:23-25. Lk
23:23, 24. Jn 19:12-15. Ac 7:54-57. 19:34.
22:22, 23.
what evil. Lk 23:41. Jn +8:46.
Crucify. Ge 37:20.

15 willing. Pr 29:25. Is 57:11. Mt 27:26. Lk
23:24, 25. Jn 19:1, 16. Ac 24:27. 25:9. Ga
1:10.
when. Jn +19:1.

16 the soldiers. Mt 27:27.
Pretorium. Mt 27:27. Jn 18:28, 33. 19:9. Ac
23:35. Ph 1:13.
band. Jn 18:3, 12. Ac 10:1. 21:31. 27:1.

17 clothed. Mt 27:28-30. Lk 23:11. Jn 19:2-5.
purple. Re 17:4. 18:12, 16.

18 Hail. ver. 29-32. Ge 37:10, 20. Mt 27:42, 43.
Lk 23:36, 37. Jn 19:14, 15.
King of the Jews. ver. +2.

19 **they smote**. Mk 9:12. Mt +27:30.
spit upon. Mt +26:67.
and bowing. Ge 41:43. 43:28. 1 K 19:18. Est 3:2-5. Is 45:23. Ro 11:4. 14:10, 11. Ph 2:10.
worshipped. Mt +8:2.

20 **mocked him**. Lk +22:63.
and led. Is 53:7. Mt 27:31. Jn 19:16.

21 **they compel**. Mt 5:41. 27:32. Lk 23:26. Jn 19:17.
a Cyrenian. i.e. *belonging to Cyrene* (i.e. *wall; coldness; hitting*), **S#2956g**. Ac +2:10.
Alexander. i.e. *man defender; helper of men*, **S#223g**. Ac 4:6. 19:33, 33. 1 T 1:20. 2 T 4:14.
and Rufus. i.e. *red*, **S#4504g**. Ro 16:13.
to bear. Lk 14:27. Jn 19:17-20.

22 **Golgotha**. Mt 27:33, etc. Lk 23:27-33, Calvary. Jn 19:17, etc.
interpreted. Mk +5:41. Ps +7:13.

23 **they**. Ps +69:21.
myrrh. Mt +2:11.
but. Mk 14:25. Mt +26:29. Lk 22:18.

24 **crucified**. Dt 21:23. Ps 22:16, 17. Is 53:4-8. Ac 5:30. 2 C 5:21. Ga 3:13. 1 P 2:24.
they parted. Ps *22:18*. Mt 27:35, 36. Lk 23:34. Jn 19:23, 24.
casting lots. Jsh +14:2.

25 **third hour**. Our 9 a.m. Mt 20:3. Jn +11:9. Ac 2:15.
and they. ver. 33. Mt 27:45. Lk 23:44. Jn 19:14. Ac 2:15.

26 **the superscription**. Dt 23:5. Ps 76:10. Pr 21:1. Is 10:7. 46:10.
his accusation. Lk 23:2. Jn 19:12. Ac 25:18, 27.
was written. Ac 17:23.
THE KING OF THE JEWS. ver. +2. Ps 2:6. Zc 9:9. Mt 2:2. 27:37. Lk 23:37, 38. Jn 19:18-22.

27 **with him**. Mt 27:38. Lk 23:32, 33. Jn 19:18.
two thieves. Is 53:12. Jn 18:40.
one on. Mk 10:37. Mt 20:21.

28 **fulfilled**. Is *53:12*. Lk 22:37. 2 C 5:21. He 12:2.

29 **passed by**. La 1:12.
railed. Ps *22:7, 8, 12-14*. +31:11. 35:15-21. La 1:12. 2:15. Lk 22:65. 23:39. Ja 2:7.
wagging. Ps *109:25*. Je +18:16.
Ah. Ps 35:21, 25. 40:15.
destroyest. Mk 14:58. Ge 37:19, 20. Mt 26:61. Jn +2:18-22.
the temple. ver. 38. Lk 1:9.

31 **also**. Ps 2:1-4. 22:16, 17. Mt 27:41-43. Lk 23:35-37.
He. Lk 4:23. 7:14, 15. 23:39. Jn 11:43, 44, 47-52. 12:23, 24. 1 P 3:17, *18*.
himself. Mt 26:53, 54. Jn 10:18.

32 **Christ**. Mt +16:16. Jn 20:25-29.
King of Israel. ver. +2. Jn +1:49.
that. Ge 37:20. Ro 3:3. 2 T 2:18.
see and believe. Lk 16:31. Jn 4:48. 6:30.

20:8, 29. 2 C 5:7.
And. Mt 27:44. Lk 23:39-43.

33 **when**. ver. 25. Mt 27:45. Lk 23:44, 45.
sixth hour. Our 12 noon. Mt +20:5. Jn +11:9.
darkness. Ex +10:22. Is 50:3, 4.
ninth hour. 1 K 18:29. Ac 3:1.

34 **at**. Da 9:21. Lk 23:46. Ac 10:3.
Eloi. i.e. *my God*, **S#1682g**, only here. Ps *22:1*. Mt 27:46. He 5:7.
interpreted. Mk +5:41. Ps +7:13.
why. Ps 27:9. 42:9. 71:11. Is 41:17. La 1:12. 5:20. 2 C 13:4.

35 **he**. ver. 23. Mk 9:11-13. Ps 69:21. Mt 17:11-13. 27:47-49. Lk 23:36. Jn 19:28-30.

36 **and filled**. ver. 23. Ru 2:14. Ps *69:21*. Lk 23:36. Jn 19:28-30.

37 **Jesus cried**. Ps 31:5. Mt 27:50. Lk 23:46. Jn 19:30.
gave up. ver. 39. Ge +25:8, 17. 35:29. 49:33. Jb 3:11. 10:18. 11:20. 13:19. 14:10. Je 15:9. La 1:19. Lk 23:46. Jn 10:18. Ac 5:5, 10. 7:59. 12:23.

38 **the veil**. Ex 26:31-34. 40:20, 21. Le 16:2, etc. 2 Ch 3:8-14. Mt 27:51-53. Lk 23:45. Ep 2:13-16. He 4:14-16. 6:19. 9:3-12. 10:19-23.
temple. ver. 29. Lk 1:9.

39 **the centurion**. ver. 44. Mt 8:5-10. Ac 10:1, 2. 27:1-3, 43.
ghost. Gr. *pneuma*, Mt +27:50.
he said. Mt 27:43, 54. Lk 23:47, 48.
the Son of God. Da 3:25. Mt +14:33.

40 **women**. Ps 38:11. Mt 27:55, 56. Lk 23:49. Jn 19:25-27.
Mary Magdalene. ver. 47. Mk 16:1, 9. Mt 27:56, 61. 28:1. Lk 8:2, 3. 24:10. Jn 19:25. 20:1, 11-18.
Mary the. ver. 47. Mk 16:1. Mt +13:55. 27:55, 61. Jn 19:25. 1 C 9:5. Ga 1:19. Ja 1:1.
James. Lk 6:15.
the less. Lk 19:3.
Salome. i.e. *peaceable*, **S#4539g**. Mk 16:1. Mt 27:56.

41 **ministered**. Mt 25:44. 27:56. Lk 8:2, 3.
came up. Lk +2:4.

42 **now when**. Mt 27:57, 62. Lk 23:50-54. Jn 19:38.
the preparation. Mt 27:62.

43 **an honorable**. Mk 10:23-27. Lk 23:50. Ac 13:50. 17:12.
waited for. Mk 14:25. Mt 6:10. 7:21, 22. 19:28. 26:29. Lk 2:25, 38. 11:2. 22:18, 29, 30. 23:51. +24:21. Ac +1:6.
kingdom of God. Mk +1:15.
and went. Mk 14:54, 66, etc. Mt 19:30. 20:16. Ac 4:8-13. Ph 1:14.

44 **marvelled**. Jn 19:31-37.
if. 1 C +15:2.
centurion. ver. 39.

45 **he gave**. Mt 27:58. Jn 19:38.

46 fine linen. Mk 14:51.
and took. Mt 27:59, 60. Lk 23:53. Jn 19:38-42.
and laid. Is 53:9.
hewn. 2 Ch 16:14. Is 22:16.
and rolled. Mk 16:3, 4. Ge 29:3, 8, 10. Mt 27:60. 28:2. Jn 11:38.
47 Mary Magdalene. ver. 40. Mk 16:1. Mt 27:61. 28:1. Lk 23:55, 56. 24:1, 2.

MARK 16

1 when. Mk 15:42. Mt 28:1, etc. Lk 23:54, 56. 24:1, etc. Jn 19:31. 20:1, etc.
sabbath was past. Mk 1:32.
Mary Magdalene. Mk 15:40, 47. Lk 24:10. Jn 19:25.
sweet. Mk 14:3, 8. 2 Ch 16:14. Lk 23:56. Jn 19:40.
anoint. Mk 14:8. Jn 11:2. 12:3.
2 very early. Mt 28:1. Lk 24:1, 10. Jn 20:1.
the first day. ver. 9.
3 Who. Mk 15:46, 47. Mt 27:60-66.
4 they saw. Mt 28:2-4. Lk 24:2. Jn 20:1.
rolled. Ge 29:10. Mt 28:2.
very great. Mt 27:60.
5 entering. Lk 24:3. Jn 20:8.
a young. Da 10:5, 6. Mt 28:1, 3. Lk 24:4, 5. Jn 20:11, 12.
clothed. Mk 9:3. Da 7:9. Jn 20:12. Ac 1:10.
white garment. Mt 28:3. Re 6:11. 7:9.
and they. Mk 6:49, 50. Ge +19:30. Da 8:17. 10:7-9, 12. Lk 1:12, 29, 30.
6 Be not. Ge +15:1. Mt 14:26, 27.
Ye seek. Ps 105:3, 4. Pr 8:17.
Jesus. Mk +1:24.
was crucified. Mk 15:24.
he is risen. Mk 9:9, 10. 10:34. Ps 71:20. Mt +12:40. 28:6, 7. Lk 24:4-8, 20-27, 46. Jn +2:19-22. 1 C +15:3-7.
they laid. Mk 15:46.
7 tell. Mk 14:50, 66-72. Mt 28:7. 2 C 2:7.
into Galilee. Mk 14:28. Mt 26:32. 28:7, 10, 16.
there. Mt 28:17. Jn 21:1. Ac 13:31.
1 C 15:5.
8 they went. Mt 28:8. Lk 24:9-11, 22-24.
for they trembled. ver. 5, 6. Lk 24:37.
neither. 2 K 4:29. Lk 10:4.
were afraid. Mk 9:6.
9 the first day. Ps 118:24. Mt 28:1, 8, 9. Jn 20:19. Ac 20:7. 1 C 16:2. Re +1:10.
he appeared. Mk 15:40, 47. Mt 28:9. Lk 24:10. Jn 20:14-18.
Magdalene. i.e. *of Magdala; magnificent,*
S#3094g. ver. 1, 9. Mk 15:40, 47. Mt 27:56, 61. 28:1. Lk 8:2. 24:10. Jn 19:25. 20:1, 18. Compare S#3093, Mt 15:39.
out. Lk 8:2.
10 she went. Mt 28:10. Lk 24:10. Jn 20:18.

as. Mk 14:72. Mt 9:15. 25:75. Lk 24:17. Jn 16:6, 20-22.
mourned. Lk 6:25. Ja 4:9. Re 18:11, 15, 19.
11 believed not. ver. 13, 14, 16. Mk 9:19. Ex 6:9. Jb 9:16. Lk 24:11, 23-35.
12 he appeared. ver. 14. Lk 24:13-32. Jn 21:1, 14.
another form. Ge 27:16. Lk 9:29. +24:13, 16.
unto two. Lk 24:13-31.
13 they went. Lk 24:33-35.
neither. Lk 16:31. Jn 20:8, 25.
14 he appeared. ver. 12.
unto the eleven. Lk 24:36-43. Jn 20:19, 20, 36. 1 C 15:5-8.
at meat. *or,* together.
and upbraided. Mk 7:18. 8:17, 18. Mt +6:30. 11:20. 15:16, 17. Lk 22:32. 24:25, 38, 39. Re 3:19.
unbelief. Nu 14:11. Ps 95:8-11. Lk 24:41. He 3:7, 8, 15-19.
hardness. Mk 3:5. 10:5. Mt 19:8. He 3:8.
believed not. ver. 11, 13.
15 Go. 2 K +16:3. Ps 9:17. 74:20. Mt 10:5, 6. +28:19, 20. Lk +10:1. 14:21-23. 24:47, 48. Jn 15:16. 20:21. Ro 2:12. 10:14, 15. 1 J 4:14.
into all. Mk 13:10. Ps 22:27. 67:1, 2. 96:3. Is 42:10-12. 45:22. 60:1-3. Lk +3:6. Ac +1:8. Ro 10:18. 16:26. Ep 2:17. Col 1:6, 23. Re 14:6.
world. Gr. *kosmos,* Mt +4:8.
to every. Ro 8:22. Col 1:23.
16 that believeth and. Mk 1:15. Lk 7:50. 8:12. Jn 1:12, 13. 3:15, 16, 18, 36. 5:24. 6:29, 35, 40. 7:37, 38. 11:25, 26. 12:46. 20:31. Ac 10:43. 13:38, 39. 16:30-32. Ro 3:6. 4:5, 24. 10:9. He 10:38, 39. 1 P 1:21. 3:21. 1 J 5:10-13.
is baptized. Mt +28:19. Jn 3:3, 5. Ac +2:38, 41. 8:36-39. 10:48. 13:24. +22:16. Ro 6:3, 4. 10:9-14. 1 C 12:13. Ga 3:27. Col 2:12. 1 P 3:20, 21.
shall be saved. Ac 16:31. Ro 10:9. Ep 2:8. T 3:5. 1 P 3:21.
but he. Jn 3:18, 19, 36. +8:24. 12:47, 48. Ac 13:46. 2 C 4:3, 4. 2 Th 1:8. 2:8, 12. Re 20:15. +21:8.
believeth not. ver. 11. Lk 24:11, 41. Ac 28:24. Ro 3:3. 2 Th 2:12. 2 T 2:13. 1 P 2:7.
17 these signs. Mk 11:23. Jn 14:12.
shall follow. Lk 1:3.
In my name. Mk 6:13. 9:38. Lk 10:17. Ac 5:16. 8:7. 16:18. 19:12-16.
shall speak. Ac 2:4-11, 33. 10:46. 19:6. 1 C 12:10, 28, 30. 13:1, 8. 14:2, 5-27, 39.
tongues. Ac 2:4. 1 C 14:18.
18 shall take. Ge +3:15. Ps 91:13. Lk 10:19. Ac 28:3-6. Ro 16:20.
if. Mt +4:9. 2 K 4:39-41.
they shall lay hands. Mk +5:23. Ac 3:6-8, 12, 16. 4:10, 22, 30. 5:15, 16. 8:17-19. 19:12. 1 C 12:9.

19 **after**. Mt 28:18-20. Lk 24:44-50. Jn 21:15, 22. Ac 1:2, 3.

he was received. 2 K 2:1-3, 11. Lk 9:51. 24:50, 51. Jn 6:62. 13:1. 16:5, 28. 17:4, 5, 11, 13. 20:17. Ac 1:2, 3, 9-11. 2:33. +3:21. Ep 1:20-22. 4:8-11. 1 T 3:16. He 4:14. 6:20. 7:26. 9:24. 10:12, 13, 19-22. 1 P 3:22.

and sat. He +1:3.

right hand. Ps +110:1.

20 **they went**. Ac ch. 2-28.

every where. Ge +7:19. 1 K 18:10. Lk 18:1. 24:53. Ac 28:22. 1 C 4:17.

the Lord. Ac 4:30. 5:12. 8:4-6. 14:3, 8-10. Ro 15:19. 1 C 2:4, 5. 3:6-9. 2 C 6:1. He 2:3, 4.

working with. 1 Ch 28:21. Mt 18:20.

confirming. Mk +4:41. Ex 4:4, 5. 14:31. 19:9. 1 K 18:38, 39. Jn 3:1, 2. Ac 8:6. 14:3. He 2:4.

the word. Mk 2:2. 4:14, 20, 33. Mt 13:19-23. Lk 1:2. 8:11-15. Ac 8:4. Ja 1:21-23. 1 J 2:7.

with signs. Ac 2:43. 4:29, 30. 5:12. 6:8. 8:6. 14:3. 15:12. 19:11. Ro 15:19. 1 C 2:4, 5. 2 C 12:12. He 2:3, 4.

following. 1 T 5:10, 24. 1 P 2:21.

LUKE

LUKE 1

1 A.M. 3998. B.C. 6.

those. Jn 20:31. Ac 1:1-3. 1 T 3:16. 2 P 1:16-19.

most surely. Ac 3:18. Ro 4:21. 14:5. Col 2:2. 4:12. 1 Th 1:5. 2 T 4:5, 17. He 6:11. 10:22.

2 **delivered**. 1 C 11:2, 23. 15:3.

which. Lk 24:48. Mk 1:1. Jn 15:27. 16:4. Ac 1:3, 8, 21, 22. 4:20. 10:39-41. 11:15. He 2:3. 1 P 5:1. 1 J 1:1-3.

eyewitnesses. Ac 4:20. 1 P 5:1. 2 P 1:16. 1 J 1:1, 3.

and ministers. Ac 26:16. Ro 15:16. 1 C 4:1. Ep 3:7, 8. 4:11, 12. Col 1:23-25.

the word. Mt 21:24. Mk 4:14. Ac 6:2. 10:29, 44. 19:38. 1 C 15:2.

3 **seemed**. Ac 15:19, 25, 28. 1 C 7:40. 16:12.

having. Mk 16:17. Ac 1:1-3. 1 T 4:6. 2 T 3:10.

from the very first. Ac 26:5.

in order. ver. 1. Ps 40:5. 50:21. Ec 12:9. Ac 11:4. 18:23.

most. Ac 1:1. 23:26. 24:3. 26:25.

Theophilus. i.e. *God-given*, **S#2321g**. Ac 1:1.

4 **mightest know**. Gr. *epiginosko*, Mt +11:27. Jn 20:31.

the certainty. 1 P +3:15. 2 P 1:15, 16.

instructed. Ac 18:25. 21:21, 24. Ro 2:18. 1 C 14:19. Ga 6:6.

5 **Herod**. Mt 2:1.

Judea. Lk 4:44.

Zacharias. i.e. *remembered of Jah*, **S#2197g**. ver. 5, 12, 13, 18, 21, 40, 59, 67. Lk 3:2. 11:51. Mt 23:35. For **S#2148h**, see Zc +1:1.

of the course. ver. 8. 1 Ch 24:10, 19. 2 Ch 8:14. Ne 12:4, 17, Abijah.

Elizabeth. i.e. *oath of God*, **S#1665g**. ver. 5, 7, 13, 24, 36, 40, 41, 41, 57. For **S#472h**, see Ex +6:23.

6 **righteous**. Lk 2:25. 16:15. 23:50. Ge 6:9. 7:1. 17:1. Jb 1:1, 8. 9:2. Mt 23:35. Mk 6:20. Ac 4:19. 8:21. 10:22. Ro 3:9-25. 8:4. Ph 3:6-9. T 3:3-7.

walking. Ge +17:1. Dt 28:9. 1 K 9:4. Ps 119:1, 6. Ac 23:1. 24:16. 1 C 11:2. 2 C 1:12. Ph 3:6. Col +1:10. T 2:11-14. 1 J 2:3, 29. 3:7.

blameless. Jn +17:6. Ph 2:15. 3:6. Col 1:22. 1 Th 2:10. 3:13. 5:23. 2 P 3:14.

7 **they had**. Ge 15:2, 3. 16:1, 2. 25:21. 30:1, 2. Jg 13:2, 3. 1 S 1:2, 5-8.

no child. Ge +11:30.

barren. ver. 36. Ge +11:30.

well stricken. ver. 18. Lk 2:36. Ge 17:17. 18:11. 1 K 1:1. 2 K 4:14-16. Ro 4:19, 20. He 11:11, 12.

8 **he executed**. Ex 28:1, 41. 29:1, 9, 44. 30:30. Nu 18:7. 1 Ch 24:2, 19. 2 Ch 11:14.

in. ver. 5. 1 Ch 24:19. 2 Ch 8:14. 31:2, 19. Ezr 6:18.

9 **his lot**. Ex 30:7, 8. 37:25-29. Nu 16:40. 1 S 2:28. 1 Ch 6:49. 23:13. 2 Ch 26:16-18. 29:11. He 9:6, 7.

burn incense. Ex 30:1-6.

the temple. ver. 21, 22. Lk 11:51. Mt 23:16, 35. 27:5, 40, 51. He 9:2, 3. Re 11:2, 19.

10 **praying without**. Le 16:17. He 4:14-16. 9:24.

incense. Ps +141:2.

11 **appeared**. ver. 19, 28. Lk 2:9, 10. Jg 13:3, 9. Ac 5:19. 10:3, 4. He 1:14.

right side. Ac 7:55, 56.

altar of incense. Ex 30:1-6, 10. 37:25-29. 39:38. 40:5, 26, 27. Le 4:3, 7, 13, 18. 16:13, 18. Nu 4:11. 1 S 2:28. 1 K 6:20, 22. 1 Ch 28:18. 2 Ch 4:19. +13:11. 26:16. Ps 141:2. Ezk 41:22. Ml 1:11. Re 5:8. 6:9. 8:3, 4. 9:13. 11:1. 14:18. 16:7.

12 **he was troubled**. ver. 29. Lk 2:9, 10. 9:34. Jg 6:22. +13:22. Jb 4:14, 15. Da 10:7, 8, 17. Mk 16:5. Ac 10:4. 19:17. Re 1:17.

fear. Ge +19:30.

13 **the angel**. ver. 11.

Fear not. ver. 30. Lk 5:10. 8:50. 24:36-40. Ge +15:1. Jg 6:23.

thy prayer. Ge 15:2-5. 25:20, 21. 30:22, 23. 1 S 1:9-11, 20-23. Ps 118:21. Ac +10:4, 31.

and thy. Ge 17:10. 18:14. Jg 13:3-5. 1 S 2:21. 2 K 4:16, 17. Ps +113:9. +127:3-5.

thou. ver. 60-63. Lk 2:21. Ge 17:19. Is 8:3. Ho 1:4, 6, 9, 10. Mt 1:21.

name. Ge +4:26.

John. i.e. *grace; dove*, **S#2491g**. ver. 13, 60, 63. 3:2, 15, 16, 20. Lk 5:33. 7:18-20, 22, 24, 28, 29, 33. 9:7, 9, 19. 11:1. 16:16. 20:4, 6. Mt 3:1, 4, 13, 14. 4:12. 9:14. 11:2, 4, 7, 11-13, 18.

14:2-4, 8, 10. 16:14. 17:13. 21:25, 26, 32. Mk 1:4, 6, 9, 14. 2:18. 6:14, 16-18, 20, 24, 25. 8:28. 11:30, 32. Jn 1:6, 15, 19, 26, 28, 29, 32, 35, 40. 3:23, 24, 25, 27. 4:1. 5:33, 36. 10:40, 41, 41. Ac 1:5, 22. 10:37. 11:16. 13:24, 25. 18:25. 19:3, 4.

14 **have joy**. ver. 58. Ge +21:6, 7. Pr 15:20. 23:15, 16, 24, 25.

15 **he shall**. ver. 32. Je 1:5. Ga 1:15.
great. Lk 7:28. Ge 12:2. 48:19. Jsh 3:7. 4:14. 1 Ch 17:8. 29:12. Mt 11:9-19. Jn 5:35.
shall drink neither. Mt +5:18. Lk 7:33. Nu 6:2-4. Jg 13:4-7, 14. Mt 11:18. Ep +5:18.
filled. ver. 41, 67. Zc 9:15. Ac 2:4, 14-18. 11:24. Ep 5:18.
Ghost. Gr. *pneuma*, Mt +1:18.
even. Ps 22:9. Is 49:1, 5. Je 1:5. Ga 1:15.

16 **many**. Lk +4:18. ver. 76. Is 40:3-5. 49:6. Da +12:3. Ml 3:1. Mt 3:1-6. 21:32.
children of Israel. Ac 5:21.

17 **go before**. ver. 16, 76. Is *40:3-5*. Ml *3:1*. Jn 1:13, 23-30, 34. 3:28.
in the. Ml 4:5, 6. Mt 11:14. 17:11, 12. Mk 9:11-13. Jn 1:21-24. Re 20:4.
spirit. Gr. *pneuma*, Nu +11:17. Spirit put for gifts and operations of the Spirit: Lk 4:18. Mt 12:18. Jn 3:5, 6b. 4:23, 24b. 7:39. Ac 2:17, 18. 5:32. 6:10. 10:44, 47. 11:15. 15:8. 1 C 2:4. 7:40. 12:13b. 14:2, 12, 32. 2 C 1:22. 3:3. 4:13. 5:5. Ga 5:5. Ep 1:13, 17. Ph 1:19. 1 Th 4:8. 5:19. 1 J 4:13. Re 22:6. For the other uses of *pneuma* see Mt +8:16.
power. 1 K 17:1. 18:18, 21. 21:20. 2 K 1:4-6, 16, Elijah. Mt 3:4, 7-12. 11:14. 14:4. 17:11.
turn. Lk 3:7-14. Is 63:16. Ml 4:6.
disobedient. Is 29:24. Mt 21:29-32. Ro 10:21. 1 C +6:9-11.
to. *or*, by.
the wisdom. Pr 4:7. Da +11:33. +12:3. Ho +14:9. Ep 1:8. 2 T 3:15. Ja 3:17.
of the just. Ge 6:9. Ps 111:10. Jn 1:29. Ac 3:14. Col 2:3.
to make. Ge +10:1. Lk 7:27. 1 S 7:5. 1 Ch 29:18. 2 Ch 29:36. Ps 10:17. 78:8. 111:10. Am 4:12. Ml 3:1. Mt 11:10. Mk 1:2. Jn 1:29. Ac 10:33. Ro 9:23. Col 1:12. 2 T 2:21. 1 P 2:9. 2 P 3:11-14. 1 J 2:28.
prepared. Lk 2:31. 2 Ch 29:36.

18 **the angel**. ver. 11.
Whereby. ver. 34. Ge 15:8. 17:17. 18:12. Jg 6:17, 36-40. 2 K 20:8. Is 38:22.
for. ver. 7. Nu 11:21-23. 2 K 7:2. Ro 4:17, 19-21. T 2:2.

19 **I am**. ver. 26. Da 8:16. 9:21-23. Mt 18:10. He 1:14.
Gabriel. *i.e. strength of God*, **S#1043g**. ver. 19, 26. For **S#1403h**, see Da +8:16.
that stand. Dt +10:8. 1 K 17:1. 18:15. 2 K 3:14. 5:16. Est 1:14. Jb 1:6. Is 63:9. Mt 18:10.
and to. Lk 2:10.

20 **thou shalt**. ver. 22, 62, 63. Ex 4:11. Ezk 3:26. 24:27.
because. ver. 45. Ge 18:10-15. Nu 20:12. 2 K 7:2, 19, 20. Is 7:9. Mk 9:19. 16:14. Re 3:19.
which. Ro 3:3. 2 T 2:13. T 1:2. He 6:18.

21 **waited**. ver. 10. Nu 6:23-27.
the temple. ver. 9.

22 **perceived**. Gr. *epiginosko*, Mt +11:27.
he beckoned. ver. 62. Jn 13:24. Ac 12:17. 19:33. 21:40.

23 **the days**. ver. 8. 2 K 11:5-7. 1 Ch 9:25. 2 Ch 23:8.
ministration. Ac 13:2. Ph 2:17. He 1:7. 8:6. 9:21. 10:11.

25 **hath**. ver. 13. Ge 21:1, 2. 25:21. 30:22. 1 S 1:19, 20. 2:21, 22. He 11:11.
to take. Ge 30:23. 1 S 1:6. Ps +113:9. +127:3. Is 4:1. 54:1-4.

26 **the sixth**. ver. 24.
the angel. ver. 19.
a city. Mt +2:23. Jn 7:41, 42.

27 **a virgin**. Lk 2:4, 5. Ge +3:15. Is +7:14. Je 31:22. Mt 1:16, 18, 21, 23.
Joseph. Lk 2:4, 16. 3:23. 4:22. Mt ch. 1, 2. 13:55. Jn 1:45. 6:42.
house of David. Lk 2:4. Mt 1:16, 20.
Mary. Mt +1:16.

28 **Hail**. Da 9:21-23. 10:19.
highly favored. *or*, graciously accepted, *or* much graced. ver. 30. Ps 45:2. Da 9:23. Ho 14:2. Ep 1:6.
the Lord. Is +43:2. Je 1:8, 19.
blessed. ver. 42. Lk 11:27, 28. Jg 5:24. Pr 31:29-31. Mt 12:48-50.

29 **she was**. ver. 12. Mk 6:49, 50. 16:5, 6. Ac 10:4.
and cast. ver. 66. Lk 2:19, 51.
what. Jg 6:13-15. 1 S 9:20, 21. Ac 10:4, 17.

30 **Fear not**. ver. +13. Ro +8:31, 32.
found favor. Ge 6:8. Ac 7:46. He 4:16.

31 **And**. Ge +8:22.
thou. ver. 27. Is +7:14. Mt +1:23. Ga 4:4.
and shalt. ver. 13. Lk 2:21. Mt 1:21, 25. 1 T 3:16.

32 **shall be great**. ver. 15. Lk 3:16. Mi 5:4. Mt 3:11. 12:42. Ph 2:9-11.
and. Ge +8:22.
shall be called. Mt 16:16. 27:54. Jn 1:34.
the Son. ver. 35. Mt +14:33. Mk 5:7. 14:16. Ac 16:17.
the Highest. ver. 35, 76. Lk 6:35. Mk 5:7. Ac 7:48.
shall give. ver. 69. Lk 19:12, 15. 2 S 7:11-13, 16. Ps 89:4. +132:11. Is +9:6, 7. 11:1, 10. 16:5. Je +23:5, 6. +30:9. 33:15-17. Ezk 17:22-24. 34:23, 24. +37:24, 25. Da 7:14. Ho +3:5. Am +9:11-15. Mt 28:18. Jn 3:35, 36. 5:21-29. 12:34. Ac 2:30, 36. 15:16. Ep 1:20-23. He 1:1-8. Re 3:7.

the throne. Ac +2:30. He 10:12, 13. Re +3:21.

David. Is +55:3. Mt 1:1. Ac +13:23. Re 22:16.

33 **he shall reign**. Ps 89:35-37. Is +24:23. Ob +21. 1 C 15:24, 25. Re +11:15.

the house. Ps 118:26. Mt 23:37, 38. Lk 13:35. Jn 1:11, 12. Ro 9:6. Ga 3:29. 6:16. Ph 3:3.

of Jacob. Lk 3:23, 34. Le 26:42, 44. Nu +24:17. Dt 32:9. Ps 59:13. 135:4, 12, 21. Is 49:5, 6. 62:1, 2. Ezk 34:11-13. Ob +17. Zc 2:12. Mt 1:2. Ac 2:36.

for ever. Gr. *aion*, Mt +6:13. Ge +9:12. 2 S 7:16. Ps +72:5. Ep 2:7. 3:21. Re +11:15.

of his kingdom. Jn 12:34. 1 C 15:24-28. 2 T +4:1. Re +11:15.

no end. Ps +45:6, 7. 145:13. Da 7:14. Mi 4:7. 1 C 15:25. 1 T 1:17. 2 T +4:18. He 12:28. 1 P 4:11. 2 P 1:11. Re 1:6. 11:15. 22:3, 5.

34 **How shall**. Jg 13:8-12. Ac 9:6.

know not. Ge 19:8. Nu 31:17. Jg 11:39.

35 **The Holy**. ver. 27, 31. Mt 1:20.

Ghost. Gr. *pneuma*, Mt +1:18.

the power. Lk 5:17. +24:49. Ac +1:8. Ro 8:11.

the Highest. ver. 32.

overshadow. Ps +121:5. 1 K 8:12.

holy thing. Jb 14:4. 15:16. 25:4. Ps 51:5. 58:3. Mk 1:12, 13, 24. +12:15. 15:23. Jn 8:46. 14:30. Ac 3:14. Ro 1:3, 4. 5:12. 10:5. 2 C 5:21. Ep 2:3. He 2:17, 18. +4:15. 7:26-28. Ja 1:17. 1 P 2:22. 1 J 1:5. 2:16. 3:5.

the Son of God. ver. 32. Lk 4:34. Mt +14:33. Jn 1:14, 18, 34, 49. 20:31. Ga 2:20. He 1:5, 6.

36 **thy cousin**. ver. 24-26.

conceived. Ge +29:31.

barren. ver. 7. Ge +11:30.

37 **with**. Jb +42:2. Zc 8:6. Ro 4:20, 21. Ph 3:21.

38 **Behold**. 2 S 7:25-29. Ps 116:16. Ro 4:20, 21.

be. 1 S 3:18. Ps 119:38.

angel departed. Jg 6:21. Ac 12:10.

39 **into**. ver. 65. Jsh 10:40. 15:48-59. 20:7. 21:9-11.

city. Jsh 11:21. 21:11, 13.

41 **the babe**. ver. 15, 44. Lk +18:15. Ge 25:22. Ps 22:10.

filled. ver. 15, 67. Lk 4:1. Ac 2:4. 4:8. 6:3. 7:55. Ep 5:18. Re 1:10.

Ghost. Gr. *pneuma*, Mt +1:18.

42 **Blessed art**. ver. 28, 48. Lk +11:28. Jg 5:24.

blessed is. Lk 19:38. Ge 22:18. Dt 28:4. Ps 21:6. 45:2. 72:17-19. Ac 2:26-28. Ro 9:5. He 12:2.

the fruit. Ge 30:2. Ps +127:3. La 2:20.

43 **whence**. Lk 7:7. Ru 2:10. 1 S 25:41. Mt 3:14. Jn 13:5-8. Ph +2:3.

my Lord. Lk 2:11. 20:42-44. Ps 110:1. Jn 13:13. +20:28. Ph 3:8.

44 **the babe**. ver. 41.

leaped. ver. 41. Lk 6:23.

45 **blessed**. ver. 20, 48. Lk 11:27, 28. 1 Ch +20:20. Jn 11:40. 20:29.

that believed: for there. *or*, which believed that there, etc. Ac 27:25.

46 **My soul**. Gr. *psyche*, Mt +11:29; Ge +4:23; Ps +16:10. Ge +41:8. Ps 34:2, 3. 35:9. 103:1, 2. Is 24:15, 16. 45:25. Hab 3:17, +18. Mk 12:30. 1 C 1:31. 2 C 2:14. He 6:19. Ja 1:21. 1 P 1:8.

magnify. Ps 34:3. 69:30. Ac 10:46.

47 **spirit**. Gr. *pneuma*, Mk +2:8.

rejoiced. Ps 35:9. Hab +3:18.

God. Lk 2:11. Ps 14:7. +88:1. 106:21. Is +12:2, 3. 25:9. 43:11. 45:21, 22. Zp 3:14-17. Zc 9:9. 1 T 1:1. 2:3. 4:10. 2 T +1:9. T 1:3. 2:10, 13. 3:4-6. Ju 25.

48 **regarded**. Lk 9:38. 1 S 1:11. 2:8. 2 S 7:8, 18, 19. 16:12. Ps 25:18. 102:17. 113:7, 8. 136:23. 138:6. Is 66:2. 1 C 1:26-28. Ja 2:5, 6.

all generations. ver. 28, 42, 45. Lk 11:27. Ge 30:13. Ps 72:17. Ml 3:12.

49 **he**. Ge 17:1. Ps 24:8. 89:8, 19. Is 1:24. 63:1. Je 10:6. 20:11. Zp 3:17.

hath. Ps 71:19-21. 126:2, 3. Mk 5:19. Ep 3:20.

and holy. Dt 28:58. Ps +99:3. Mt +6:9.

50 **his mercy**. Ge +17:7. Ex +20:6. +34:6, 7. Dt 7:9. Ps 33:18. 145:19. Ml +3:16-18. Re 19:5.

that fear him. Pr +3:7. Ro 11:22. 1 P 1:17.

51 **showed**. Ex 15:6, 7, 12, 13. Dt 4:34. Ps 63:5. 118:15, 16. Is 63:12. Re 18:8.

arm. Ex +15:16.

he hath scattered. Ge +10:32. 11:8. Ex 15:9-11. 18:11. 1 S 2:3, 4, 9, 10. Jb 40:9-12. Ps 2:1-6. 33:10. 89:10. Is 8:10. 10:12-19. Je 48:29, 30.

the proud. Pr +16:5. Mk 7:22. Ro +1:30.

the imagination. Ge 6:5. 8:21. Dt 29:19, 20. Jb 5:12. Ro 1:21. 2 C 10:5.

52 **put down**. Lk 14:11. 18:14. 1 S 2:4, 6-8. Jb 5:11-13. 12:19. 34:24-28. Ps 75:7. 107:40, 41. 113:6-8. 147:6. Ec 4:14. Ezk 17:14, 24. 21:26. Da 4:30. Am 9:11. Mk +6:3. Ja 1:9, 10. 4:10.

the mighty. Ac 8:27.

and exalted. Lk 6:25. 16:25. Ge 45:26. Ps 78:70, 71. Am 5:9. Mk 10:31.

low degree. Mt +5:3-5. 1 C 1:26-29. Ph +2:3. Ja +2:5. 1 P 5:6.

53 **filled**. 1 S 2:5. Ps +37:3. Ezk 34:29. Mt +5:6. +14:20. Ja 2:5.

the rich. Lk 6:24. 12:16-21. 16:19-25. 18:11-14, 24, 25. 1 C 1:26. 4:8. Ja 2:6. 5:1-6. Re 3:17, 18.

sent empty. Lk 6:24. 18:10-14. 20:11. Jb 22:9. Mt +6:5.

54 **He hath**. ver. 70-75. Ps 98:3. Is +41:8, 9. 44:21. 46:3, 4. 49:14-16. +54:6-10. 63:7-16. Je 31:3, 20. +33:24-26. Mi +7:20. Zp 3:14-20. Zc 9:9-11. Ro 11:26-29. He 2:16.

servant Israel. Is 41:8, 9. 42:1. 44:1, 2, 21. 45:4. 49:3.

remembrance. ver. 72, 73. Ps 98:3.
Mi 7:20.
his mercy. Zc 10:6.

55 he spake. Ge +12:3. 17:19. Ps 132:11-17. Mi
+7:20.
his seed. Ge 17:7.
for ever. Gr. *aion*, Mt +6:13. Ge 9:12.

57 full time. ver. 13. Lk 2:6, 7. Ge 21:2, 3. Nu
23:19.

58 her neighbors. ver. 25. Ru 4:14-17. Ps
+113:9.
showed great mercy. Ge 19:19.
they rejoiced. ver. 14. Ge 21:6. Is 66:9, 10.
Ro 12:15. 1 C 12:26.

59 eighth day. Lk 2:21. Ge 17:12. 21:3, 4. Le
12:3. Ac 7:8. Ph 3:5.

60 Not. ver. 13, 63. 2 S 12:25. Is 8:3. Mt 1:25.

62 made signs. ver. 22.
how he. That is, what he might wish his son
to be called. This conditional sentence is like
having an if/then statement, here, assuming
the remote possibility he just might have a
concern for naming his son. Other examples
of this "if" construction are: Lk 6:11. 9:46.
18:36. Ac 5:24. 8:31. 10:17. 17:18. 26:29.

63 writing table. Pr 3:3. Is 8:1. 30:8. Je 17:1.
Hab 2:2.
His name. ver. 13, 60.

64 his mouth. ver. 20. Ex 4:15, 16. Je 1:9. Ezk
+24:27. Mt 9:33. Mk 7:32-37.
opened. Jg +11:35.
and he. Ps 30:7-12. 118:18, 19. Is 12:1. Da
4:34-37.
and praised. Lk 2:28. 24:53.

65 fear. Lk 5:26. 7:16. 8:37. Est 8:17. Ps 40:3. Je
+5:22. Mt 28:8. Mk 4:41. 5:15, 33. Ac 2:43.
5:5, 11. 19:17. Re 11:11.
sayings. *or*, things.
hill country. ver. 39. Jsh 10:6, 40.

66 laid. Lk 2:19, 51. 9:44. Ge 37:11.
Ps 119:11.
And the. ver. 80. Lk 2:40. Ge 39:2. Jg 13:24,
25. 1 S 2:18. 16:18. 1 K +18:46. Ps 80:17.
89:21. Ac 4:28, 30. 11:21. 13:11.

67 filled. ver. 15, 41. Nu 11:25. 2 S 23:2. Jl 2:28.
2 P 1:21.
Ghost. Gr. *pneuma*, Mt +1:18.

68 Blessed. Ge 9:26. 14:20. 1 K 1:48. 8:15. 1 Ch
29:10, 20. Ezr 7:27. Ps 41:13. 72:17-19. 89:52.
106:48. 150:6. Ep 1:3. 1 P 1:3.
God of Israel. Mt 15:31.
he. Lk 7:16. 19:44. Ex 3:16, 17. 4:31. Ps
111:9. Ep 1:7.
visited. Lk 7:16. 19:44. Ex 4:31. Ps 8:4. Ac
15:14. He 2:6.
and redeemed. ver. 71. Lk 2:38. 21:28.
24:21. Ps 19:14. 111:9. 130:7, 8. Is 43:1.
59:20. Ac 7:35. Ro 3:24. He 9:12.

69 raised up. Jg 3:9, 15.
an horn. Ps +92:10.

in the house. 2 S 7:26. 1 K 11:13. Ps 89:3,
20, etc. Mt +1:1. Mk 11:10.
David. ver. 32. Ac +13:23.

70 spake. 2 S 23:2. Je +23:5, 6. 30:10. Mk
12:36. Ac 28:25. Ro 1:2. He 1:1. 3:7. 2 P 1:21.
Re 19:10.
which. Lk 24:26, 27, 44. Ge +3:15. +12:3.
+49:10. Da +9:24-27. Ac 3:21-24. 1 P 1:12. 2
P 3:2.
world. Gr. *aion*, Mt +6:13. lit. "from the age,"
as in Jn 9:32. Ac 3:21. 15:18. Col 1:26.

71 we. ver. 74. Ex 18:10. Dt 33:29. Ps 18:17.
106:10, 47. Is 14:1-3. 44:24-26. 51:22, 23.
54:7-17. +59:19, 20. Je 23:6. 30:9-11. 32:37.
Ezk 28:26. 34:25, 28. +38:8. Jl 2:20. Zp 3:15-
20. Zc 9:9, 10, 14. +12:8. Ac +3:19-21. Ro
+11:26. 1 J 3:8.

72 perform. ver. 54, 55. Ps 98:3. Mi +7:20.
the mercy. Dt +32:43. Is 49:10. +55:3. Mi
7:20.
and. ver. 54, 55. Ge 17:4-9. Le +26:42. Ga
3:15-17.
covenant. Ro 9:4. 15:8.

73 The oath. Ge +12:3. 17:4. 24:7. Ex 2:24. Dt
7:8, 12. Ps 105:9. Je 11:5.

74 that we. ver. 71. Is 35:9, 10. 45:17. 54:13,
14. 65:21-25. Ezk 34:25-28. +39:28, 29. Jl
+3:17. Zp 3:15-17. Zc 9:8-10. Ml 4:1-3. Ro
5:1. 6:18, 22. 8:15. 2 T +1:7. He 2:15. 9:14. Re
2:10.
might serve. Dt 28:47. Ne 8:10. Ps 100:2.
without fear. Jb 9:34, 35. Ps +34:4. 64:1. Zp
3:15.

75 In holiness. Dt 6:2. Ps 105:44, 45. Je 31:33,
34. +32:39, 40. Ezk 36:24-27. Mt 1:21. Ro
12:1, 2. 2 C 7:1. Ep 1:4. 2:10. 4:24. Ph 1:10,
11, 27. 4:8. Col +1:10. 1 Th 2:10. 4:1-3, 7. 2
Th 2:13. 2 T +1:9. T 1:8. 2:11-14. 3:8. He
12:14. 1 P 1:14-16. 2:24. 2 P 1:4-8. 1 J 2:6,
15-17. 3:3, 6, 7.
before him. Nu 8:22. Ac 24:16.
all the days. Je 32:39. Mt 28:20.

76 shalt be. Lk 7:26, 28. 20:6. Mt 11:9. 14:5.
21:26. Mk 11:32.
Highest. ver. 32, 35. Lk 6:35. Ps +7:17. Ro
9:5. 1 C 10:5. 1 Th 3:13.
thou shalt. ver. 16, 17. Lk 3:4-6. 7:27. Dt
31:3. Is 40:3-5. Ml 3:1. 4:5. Mt 3:3, 11. 11:10.
Mk 1:2, 3. Jn 1:23, 27. 3:28. Ac 13:24, 25.
the Lord. Jn 10:30. 1 C 2:8. +12:3. Ph 2:11.
his ways. Lk 20:21.

77 give. Lk 3:3, 6. Je 31:34. Mk 1:3, 4. Jn 1:7-9,
15-17, 29, 34. 3:27-36. Ac 19:4.
knowledge. Is +53:11.
by. *or*, for.
the remission. Lk 7:47-50. Mk 1:4. Ac
+2:38. +3:19. 5:31. 10:43. 13:38, 39. Ro 3:25.
4:6-8. Ep 1:7.

78 tender. *or*, bowels of the. Is +63:15. Jn 3:16.
Ep 2:4, 5. 1 J 4:9, 10.

dayspring. *or,* sunrising, *or* branch. Is +11:1. Re +2:28.

from on high. Lk 24:49. Is 32:15.

hath visited. ver. 68.

79 **give light**. Is +9:2. Ml +4:2. Mt +4:16.

darkness. Lk 5:31, 32. Is +9:2. Col 1:13.

shadow of death. Ps +23:4.

to guide. Ps +32:8. 85:10-13. Pr 3:17. Is 48:17, 18, 22. 57:19-21. 59:8. Mt 11:28, 29. Ro 3:17.

peace. Lk 2:14. Is 59:8. Ro +5:1.

80 **the child**. ver. 15. Lk 2:40, 52. Jg 13:24, 25. 1 S 3:19, 20.

waxed strong. Ep 3:16.

spirit. Gr. *pneuma,* Mt +27:50; Nu +11:17.

and was. Mt 3:1. 11:7. Mk 1:3, 4.

the deserts. Lk 3:2. 5:16.

his showing. Lk 10:1. Jn 1:31.

LUKE 2

1 **came to pass**. Ge +38:1.

in those days. ver. 2, 7. Ge *49:10*. Ml *3:1*.

decree. Ac 17:7.

Caesar. Jn +19:12.

Augustus. i.e. *majestic,* **S#828g**, only here.

all. Ex +9:6. Mt 24:14. Mk 14:9. 16:15. Ac 11:28. 19:27. Ro 1:8.

world. lit. "habitable world." Gr. *oikoumene,* Mt +24:14.

taxed. *or,* enrolled. Ac 5:37.

2 **taxing**. Ac 5:37.

Cyrenius. i.e. *spearman, warrior,* **S#2958g**, only here.

governor. Lk 3:1. Ac 13:7. 18:12. 23:26. 26:30.

Syria. Ac +15:23.

3 **all went**. Ro 13:7.

every one. ver. 4.

4 **Joseph**. Lk 1:26, 27. 3:23.

went up. ver. 42. Lk 18:31. 19:28. Mt 20:17, 18. Mk 10:32, 33. 15:41. Jn +2:13. Ac +18:22.

from Galilee. Lk 1:26.

city of Nazareth. ver. 39, 51. Mt +2:23.

into Judea. Lk 23:5.

unto. ver. 11. Ge 35:19. 48:7. Ru 1:19. 2:4. 4:11, 17, 21, 22. 1 S 16:1, 4. 17:12, 58. 20:6. 2 S 5:7, 9. 1 Ch 11:5, 7. Mi +5:2. Mt 2:1-6. Jn 7:42.

Bethlehem. ver. 15. Mt 2:1.

he was. Lk 1:27. 3:23-31. Mt 1:1-17, 20.

lineage. Ac 3:25. Ep 3:15.

of David. Ac +13:23.

5 **Mary**. Dt 22:22-27. Mt 1:18, 19.

6 **A.M. 4000. B.C. 4.**

so. Ps 33:11. Pr 19:21. Mi +5:2.

while. Mt 2:1.

the days. Lk 1:57. Re 12:1-5.

7 **she**. Is +7:14. Mt 1:25. Ga 4:4.

firstborn. Mk +3:31. +6:3. Col +1:15. He 1:6.

and wrapped. ver. 11, 12. Jb 38:9. Ps 22:6. Is 53:2, 3. Mt 8:20. +13:55. Jn 1:14. 2 C 8:9.

manger. ver. 16.

no room. Jn 14:3.

the inn. Lk 10:34. 22:11. Ge 42:27. 43:21. Ex 4:24. Mk 14:14.

8 **there were**. Ge 35:21. Mi 4:8.

abiding. Ge 31:39, 40. Ex 3:1, 2. 1 S 17:34, 35. Ps 78:70, 71. Ezk 34:8. Jn 10:8-12.

watch over their flock by night. *or,* the night watches.

9 **lo**. Lk 1:11, 28. Jg 6:11, 12. Mt 1:20. Ac 27:23. 1 T 3:16.

the angel. Lk 1:11. Mt 28:2. Ac 5:19.

came upon. or, stood by. ver. 38. Lk 20:1. 24:4. Ac 12:7. 23:11.

and the glory. Lk 9:31, 32. Ex 16:7, 10. 24:16, 17. 40:34, 35. Le 9:6, 23. Nu 14:10. 16:19, 42. 20:6. 1 K 8:11. Is 6:3. 35:2. 40:5. 60:1. Ezk 3:23. Jn 12:41. Ac 7:55. 2 C 3:18. 4:6. Re 18:1.

and they. Lk 1:12. Is 6:4, 5. Ac 22:6-9. 26:13, 14. He 12:21. Re 20:11.

10 **the angel**. Lk 24:4-7.

Fear not. Ge +15:1.

I bring. Lk 1:19. 8:1. Is 40:9. 41:27. 52:7. 61:1. Ac 13:32. Ro 10:15.

good tidings. Ac 10:43. Ro 1:4.

great joy. Lk 15:7. Ac 8:8. Ro 5:11. 1 P 1:8.

to all. ver. 31, 32. Lk +3:6. Ge +12:3. Ps 67:1, 2. Da +9:26. Zc 9:9. Mt 28:18, 19. Mk 1:15. Jn 11:50. Ro 15:9-12. Ep 3:8. Col 1:23.

11 **unto**. Lk 1:69. Is +9:6. Mt 1:21. Ga 4:4, 5. 2 T 1:9, 10. T 2:10-14. 3:4-7. 1 J 4:14.

is born. Mt 2:2.

in the city. ver. 4. Mt 1:21.

a Savior. Mt 1:21. Jn 4:42. Ac 5:31. 13:23. Ph 3:20. 2 T 1:10.

which is. ver. 26. Lk 1:43. Ge +3:15. +49:10. Ps 2:2. Da +9:24-26. Ac 2:36. 17:3.

Christ. La 4:20. Mt +16:16.

the Lord. Lk 1:43. 19:31. 20:42-44. Ac 2:36. 10:36. Ro 14:9. 1 C +2:8. 8:6. 12:3. 15:47. 2 C 4:5. Ph 2:11. 3:8. Col 2:6. Re 19:16.

12 **a sign**. Ex 3:12. 1 S 2:34. 10:2-7. 2 K 19:29. 20:8, 9. Ps 22:6. Is +7:11, 14. 53:1, 2.

wrapped. ver. 7.

13 **a multitude**. Ge 28:12. Jb 38:7. Ps 68:17. +103:21. Is 6:2, 3. Ezk 3:12. Da 7:10. Lk 15:10. Ep 3:10. He 1:14. 1 P 1:12. Re 5:11, 12.

heavenly host. Ac 7:42.

14 **Glory**. Lk 19:38. Ps 69:34, 35. 85:9-12. 96:11-13. Is 44:23. 49:13. Jn +13:31.

in the highest. Lk 10:21. Ps 148:1. Mt 6:10. 21:9. 28:18. Ac 7:49. Ep 3:15. Ph 2:10. Col 1:16, 20. Re 5:13.

on earth. Is 26:9. Mt 6:10. Jn 17:4.

peace. Lk 1:79. Ps 29:11. 119:165. Is +9:6, 7. Je 14:13. +23:5, 6. Mi 5:5. Hg 2:9. Ro +5:1.

good will. Gr. *eudokia.* Lk 3:22. Ps 106:4. Mt

3:17 (*eudokessa*, well pleased). 12:18. 17:5. Mk
1:11. Jn 3:16. Ep 2:4, 7. 2 Th 2:12, 16. T 3:4-
7. He 10:6, 8, 38. 2 P 1:17. 1 J 4:9, 10.
toward. Lk 3:22. 12:32. Ep 1:5, 9. Ph 2:13.

15 **into**. Lk 24:51. 2 K 2:1, 11. 1 P 3:22.
shepherds. Gr. men the shepherds. Is
+40:13mg.
Let. ver. 4. Ex 3:3. Ps 111:2. Mt 2:1, 2, 9-11.
12:42. Jn 20:1-10.

16 **with**. Lk 1:39. Ec 9:10.
found. ver. 7, 12. Lk 19:32. 22:13.

17 **made known**. ver. 38. Lk 8:39. Ps 40:9, 10.
66:16. 71:17, 18. Ml 3:16. Jn 1:41-46. 4:28,
29. Ac 4:20. 1 J 1:3.
the saying. ver. 10-12.

18 **wondered**. ver. 33, 47. Lk 1:65, 66. 4:36.
5:9, 10. Is 8:18.

19 **Mary kept**. ver. 51. Lk 1:66. 9:43, 44. Ge
37:11. 1 S 21:12. Ps 119:11. Pr 4:4. Ho +14:9.

20 **glorifying**. Lk 19:37, 38. 1 Ch 29:10-12. Ps
72:17-19. 106:48. 107:8, 15, 21. Is 29:19. Mt
+9:8. Ac 2:46, 47.

21 **eight**. Lk 1:59. Ge 17:12. Le 12:3. Mt 3:15.
Ro 15:8. Ga 4:4, 5. Ph 2:8.
his name was. Lk 1:31. Mt 1:21, 25. Ac 4:12.
before. Mt 1:21, 25.

22 **her purification**. Le 12:2-6.
according. ver. 21, 27. Ga 4:4.
law of Moses. Jn 7:23.
present. 1 S 1:22, 24.

23 **law of the Lord**. ver. 24, 39. Ex 13:9. 2 Ch
31:3. Ro 7:22.
Every. Ex 13:2, 12-15. 22:29. 34:19. Nu 3:13.
8:16, 17. 18:15.
holy. Lk +1:35.

24 **law of**. ver. 23.
A pair. Le 1:14. 5:7. *12:2, 6-8*. 23:12, 19. 2 C
8:9.

25 **just**. Lk 1:6. Ge +6:9. Jb 1:1, 8. Da 6:22, 23.
Mi +6:8. Ac 10:2, 22. 24:16. T 2:11-14.
devout. Ac 2:5. 8:2. 22:12. He 5:7. 12:28.
waiting for. ver. 38. Lk 23:51. Ps +25:3. Is
40:1. 49:23. Mk 15:43. 1 Th 1:10.
consolation. Lk 6:24. Is 40:1. 49:13. 51:3,
11, 12. 52:9, 10. 57:18. Ho 6:2, 3. Jn 11:24,
25. 1 C +14:3. 2 Th 2:16.
of Israel. Ac 26:6, 7. 28:20.
Holy. Lk 1:41, 67. Nu 11:25, 29. 2 P 1:21.
Ghost. Gr. *pneuma*, Mt +1:18.

26 **revealed**. Ps 25:14. Am +3:7. Mt 2:12, 22. Ac
10:22. 11:26. Ro 7:3. He 8:5. 11:7. 12:25.
Ghost. Gr. *pneuma*, Mt +3:16.
see death. Lk 9:27. Ps 89:48. Jn 8:51. Ac
2:27. He 11:5.
the Lord's. Lk 9:20. 23:35. 1 S 24:6. Ps 2:2,
6. Is 61:1. Da +9:24-26. Jn 1:41. 4:29. 20:31.
Ac 2:36. 9:20. 10:38. 17:3. He +1:8, 9.
Christ. ver. +11.

27 **by**. Lk 4:1. Mt 4:1. Ac 8:29. 10:19. 11:12.
16:7. Re 1:10. 17:3.

Spirit. Gr. *pneuma*, Mt +3:16.
the parents. ver. 33, 41, 43, 48, 51. Lk 3:23.
to. ver. 22.

28 **took**. Mk 9:36. 10:16.
and. ver. 13, 14, 20. Lk 1:46, 64, 68. 24:53.
Ps 32:11. 33:1. 105:1-3. 135:19, 20.

29 **Lord**. Ac 4:24. 2 P 2:1. Ju 4. Re 6:10.
servant. Ja 1:1.
depart. Ge +15:15. 46:30. Ph +1:23.
in peace. Ps 37:37. Is +57:1, 2. Re +14:13.
according. ver. 26.

30 **mine eyes have**. ver. 10, 11. Lk 3:6. Ge
49:18. 2 S 23:1-5. Is 40:5. 49:6. 52:10. Ac
4:10-12.
thy salvation. Gr. *to soterion*, not the usual
soteria. Used of Jehovah Himself (not merely
of salvation as such). Lk +3:6. Ps 14:7. 27:1.
85:7. +88:1. 132:16. Is 62:11.

31 **prepared**. Lk 1:17. 24:47. Ps 96:1-3, 10-13.
97:6-8. 98:2, 3. Is 42:1-4, 10-12. 45:21-25.
62:1, 2.

32 **light**. Is 52:10. 61:1-3. Ml +4:2. Mt +4:16. Ac
26:23. 28:28. Ro 15:8, 9.
to lighten. Is 25:7. 60:2.
the Gentiles. Ps 98:2.
and the glory. Ps 85:9. Is 4:2. +40:5. 45:25.
46:13. Hg *2:7, 9*. Zc 2:5. 1 C 1:31.
thy people. ver. 10. Dt +32:43.

33 **Joseph and**. ver. 27, 48. Lk 1:65, 66.
Is 8:18.

34 **blessed**. Ge 14:19. 47:7. Ex 39:43. Le 9:22,
23. He 7:1, 7.
is set. Is 8:14, 15. Ho +14:9. Mt 21:44. Jn
3:20. 9:29. Ro 9:32, 33. 1 C 1:23. 2 C 2:15,
16. Ph 1:16. 1 Th 3:3. 1 P 2:7.
the fall. Is 8:14. Mt 21:44. Jn 9:39. 1 C 1:23,
24. 2 C 2:16. 1 P 2:7-9.
and rising. Da +12:2. Ac 2:36-41. 3:15-19.
6:7. 9:1-20.
of many. Da *+12:2*. 1 Th +4:16.
for a sign. Ps 22:6-8. 69:9-12. Is 8:18. Mt
11:19. 26:65-67. 27:40-45, 63. Jn 5:18. 8:48-
52. 9:24-28. Ac 4:26, 27. 13:45. 17:6, 7. 24:5.
28:22. 1 C 1:23. He 12:1-3. 1 P 4:14.

35 **a sword**. Ps 42:10. Jn 19:25.
soul. Gr. *psyche*, Mt +11:29.
that the thoughts. Lk 5:22. 6:8. 9:46, 47.
16:14, 15. 24:38. Dt 8:2. Jg 5:15, 16. Mt
12:24-35. Jn 8:42-47. 9:16. 15:22-24. Ac
8:21-23. 1 C 11:19. 1 J 2:19.

36 **Anna**. i.e. *gracious*, **S#451g**, only here. For
S#2584h, see 1 S +1:2, Hannah.
a prophetess. Ex +15:20. Ac 2:17, 18. 1 C
12:1.
Phanuel. i.e. *face of God*, **S#5323g**, only here.
For **S#6439h**, see 1 Ch +4:4, Penuel.
Aser. i.e. *happy*, **S#768g**. Lk 2:36. Re 7:6. For
S#836h, see Ge +30:13, Asher. Jsh 19:24.
she. Lk 1:7, 18. Jb 5:26. Ps 92:14.

37 **widow**. 1 T 5:3, 5.

which. Ex 38:8. 1 S 2:22. Ps 23:6. 27:4. 84:4, 10. 92:13. 135:1, 2. Re 3:12.

departed not. Lk 24:53. Ex 33:11. Pr 8:34. Am +3:7. Re 7:15.

but served. Ps 22:2. Ac 26:7. Ph 3:3. 1 T 5:5. He 9:9. 10:2. 12:28. Re 7:15.

fastings. Lk 5:33. Mt +6:16-18.

prayers. 1 Th +5:17.

night and day. Mk 4:27.

38 **coming**. ver. 9, 27. Lk 20:1.

gave thanks. ver. 28-32. Lk 1:46, etc., 64, etc. Is 52:9. 2 C 9:15. Ep 1:3.

looked. ver. 25. Lk 23:51. 24:21. Is 40:1. Mk 15:43. 1 C 1:7. T 2:13. He 9:28.

redemption. Lk 1:68. Is 52:9.

Jerusalem. *or*, Israel.

39 **performed**. ver. 21-24. Lk 1:6. Dt 12:32. Mt 3:15. Ga 4:4, 5.

they returned. ver. 4. Mt +2:22.

Nazareth. ver. 4, 51. Mt +2:23.

40 **the child**. ver. 52. Jg 13:24. 1 S 2:18, 26. 3:19. Ps 22:9, 10. Is 53:1, 2.

grew. Lk 1:80. Ex 2:1, 2. Ac 7:20. He 11:23.

strong. Lk 1:80. Ep 6:10. 2 T 2:1.

spirit. Gr. *pneuma*, Mt +27:50.

filled. ver. 47, 52. Is 11:1-5. Col 2:2, 3.

wisdom. ver. 52. Lk 3:2.

the grace. Ps 45:2. Jn 1:14. Ac 4:33.

upon him. Is 40:5.

41 A.M. 4012. A.D. 8.

his parents. ver. 27.

went. Ex 23:14-17. 34:23. Dt 12:5-7, 11, 18. 16:1-8, 16. 1 S 1:3, 21.

the feast. Ex 12:14. 23:15. Le +23:5. Nu 28:16. Dt 16:1, 16. Jn 2:13. 6:4. 11:55. 13:1.

42 **went up**. ver. +4. Jn 11:55.

43 **fulfilled**. 2 Ch 30:21-23. 35:17.

the days. Lk 2:15, 16. Le 23:6-8. Dt 16:3.

44 **in**. Ps 42:4. 122:1-4. Is 2:3.

acquaintance. Lk 23:49.

46 **after three**. ver. 44, 45. 1 K 12:5, 12. Mt +12:40. 16:21. 27:63, 64.

temple. Jn 18:20.

sitting. Mt 26:55.

the doctors. Lk 5:17. Jn 3:10. Ac 5:34.

both. Is 49:1, 2. 50:4.

47 **were astonished**. Ps 119:99. Mt +7:28. Jn 7:14, 15, 46. Ac 2:7.

his understanding. Ge 41:39. Is 50:4. Mk 12:33.

48 **Son**. Lk 15:31.

thy father. ver. 27, 49.

sorrowing. Lk 16:24, 25. Ac 20:38. Ro 9:2. 1 T 6:10.

49 **I must**. Lk +13:33.

my. ver. 48. Ps 40:8. Ml 3:1, 2. Mt 10:37. 21:12. Jn 2:16, 17. 4:34. 5:17. 6:38. 8:29. 9:4. 14:2.

business. 1 S 21:8. Jn 9:4. 17:4. 19:30. 1 C 3:12.

50 **understood not**. Lk 9:45. 18:34. 24:25. Mk 9:32. Jn 10:6.

51 **came**. ver. 39.

Nazareth. ver. +4.

and was subject. Ge +16:9. Mt 3:15. 15:4. Mk +6:3. Ep 5:21. +6:1, 2. Ph 2:5, 7, 8. 1 T +3:4. 1 P 2:21.

kept. ver. 19. Lk 1:66. Ge 37:11. Da 7:28.

52 **Jesus**. ver. 40. Lk 1:80. 1 S 2:26.

increased. Ex 2:1, 2. 2 S 5:10. Ac 7:20. He 11:23.

stature. or, age. Lk 12:25. 19:3. Ps 39:5. Mt 6:27. Jn 9:21, 23. Ep 4:13. He 11:11.

and in favor. ver. 40. Ge 39:4, 6. 1 S 2:26. Pr 3:3, 4. Ac 7:9, 10. 24:16. Ro 14:17, 18.

LUKE 3

1 A.M. 4030. A.D. 26.

Tiberius. i.e. *watching, from the Tiber*, S#5086g.

Caesar. Jn +19:12.

Pontius. i.e. *bridged; of the sea*, S#4194g. Mt 27:2. Ac 4:27. 1 T 6:13.

Pilate. Lk 23:1-4, 24, 25. Ge +49:10. Mt 27:2. Ac 4:27. 23:26. 24:27. 26:30.

governor. Lk 2:2.

Herod. ver. 19. Lk 8:3. 9:7, 9. 13:31. 23:6-11. Mk 6:14. 8:15. Ac 4:27.

tetrarch. i.e. *ruler of the fourth part of a realm*, S#5075g. Also S#5076g: ver. 19. Mt 14:1. Lk 9:7. Ac 13:1.

his. Mt 14:3. Mk 6:17.

Iturea. i.e. *encircled*, S#2484g.

Trachonitis. i.e. *rocky region; cruel*, S#5139g.

Lysanias. i.e. *grief dispelling*, S#3078g.

Abilene. i.e. *the father of mourning*, S#9g.

2 **Annas**. i.e. *one who answers*, S#452g. Jn 11:49-51. 18:13, 14, 24. Ac 4:6.

and Caiaphas. Mt 26:3. Jn 18:13, 24. Ac 4:6.

high priests. Je 52:24.

the word. Lk 1:59-63. Ge 15:1. 1 S 15:10. 2 S 7:4. 24:11. 1 K 12:22. Je 1:2. 2:1. Ezk 1:3. Ho 1:1, 2. Jon 1:1. Mi 1:1. Zp 1:1.

came. Lk 1:80. 2:40.

unto John. Lk 1:13. Jn 1:6, 7.

in. Lk 1:80. 7:24. Jsh 15:61. Jg 1:16. 1 S 23:19. Is 40:3. Mt 3:1. 11:7. Mk 1:3. Jn 1:23.

3 **the country**. Mt 3:5, 6. Mk 1:4, 5. Jn 1:28. 3:26.

preaching. Mt 3:6, 11. Mk 1:4. Jn 1:31-33. Ac 13:24. 19:4. +22:16.

baptism. Gr. *baptisma*, Mt +3:7.

of repentance. Ac +3:19. 5:31.

for the remission. Lk 1:77. 24:47. Mt 3:11. Ac +2:38. +22:16.

4 **The voice**. Is *40:3-5*. Mt 3:3. Mk 1:3. Jn 1:23.

Prepare. Lk 1:16, 17, 76-79. Is *40:3*. 57:14. 62:10. Ml *3:1*. 4:6. Jn 1:7, 26-36. 3:28-36.

5 **valley**. Lk 1:51-53. Is 2:11-17. 35:6-8. *40:4*. 49:11. 61:1-3. Ezk 17:24. Ja 1:9-11.

and the crooked. Is 42:16. 45:2. He 12:12, 13.

6 all flesh. Lk +24:47. Ge +6:12. Ps 136:25. Is *40:5*. 66:16, 23. Je 32:27. 45:5. Jl 2:28. Zc 2:13. Mt 24:22. Mk 13:20. Jn 17:2. Ac 2:17. Ro 3:20. 10:12, 18. 1 C 1:29. Ga 2:16. 1 P 1:24.

the salvation. Lk 1:69, 71, 77. 2:10, 11, 30-32. Ps 98:2, 3. Is 49:6. 52:10. Mk 16:15, 16. Ac 28:28. T 2:11.

7 O generation. Mt +3:7-10. Ac 13:10.

to flee. Ro 1:18. 2:8, 9. 1 Th +1:10. He 6:18. Re 6:16.

8 fruits. Is 1:16-18. Ezk 18:27-31. Ac 26:20. 2 C 7:10, 11. Ga 5:22-24. Ph 1:11. He 6:7, 8.

worthy of. *or*, meet for.

We have Abraham. Lk 13:28, 29. 16:23-31. Is 48:1, 2. Je 7:4-10. Mt 3:9. Jn 8:33, 39. Ro 4:16. 9:6, 7.

of these. Lk 19:40. Jsh 4:3-8. Mt +8:11, 12. 21:43. Ga 3:28, 29. 6:15.

9 the axe. Lk 13:7, 9. 23:29-31. Is 10:33, 34. Ezk 15:2-4. 31:18. Da 4:14, 23. Mt 3:10. 7:19. Jn +15:2, 6. He 10:28, 29. 12:29. Re +21:8.

10 What shall. ver. 8, 11-14. Lk 18:18-23. Ac 2:37. 9:6. 16:28-31. 22:10.

11 He that hath. 2 C 8:13-15.

two coats. Lk 9:3. 11:41. 18:22. 19:8. Ex +23:4. Is 58:7-11. Ezk 18:7. Da 4:27. Mt 10:10. 25:40. Mk 6:9. 14:5-8, 63. Jn 13:29. Ac 10:2, 4, 31. 2 C 8:3-14. Ep 4:28. 1 T 6:18. He 6:10. Ja 1:27. 2:15-26. 1 J 3:17. 4:20.

impart. Lk 18:22. Mt 5:42. 10:8. Lk +6:38. 12:33. Ac 20:35. 1 Th 2:8.

12 publicans. Mt +5:46.

what shall. ver. 10.

13 Exact. Lk 19:8. Ps 18:23. Pr 28:13. Is 1:16, 17. 55:6, 7. Ezk 18:21, 22, 27, 28. Mi +6:8. Mt 7:12. 1 C 6:10. Ep 4:28. T 2:11, 12. He 12:1.

14 the soldiers. Mt 8:5, 6, 10. Mk 6:27. Ac 10:1, 2, 7. 1 C 7:20. 2 T 2:4.

And what shall we do. Lk +22:36. 1 Ch +12:32. Pr 30:6. Is 8:20. Mk 7:9. 1 C 7:20. Ac 10:7.

Do violence to no man. *or*, Put no man in fear. Le 19:11. Jb 24:9. Je 22:3. Ro 13:9, 10. Ph 2:15.

accuse. Lk 19:8. Ex +20:16. 23:1. Le 19:11. T 2:3. Re 12:10.

and be content. Mt 20:10-15. Ph 4:11. 1 T 6:8-10. He 13:5, 6.

wages. *or*, allowance. Je +22:13. Ml +3:5. 1 C 9:7. 2 C 11:8.

15 expectation. *or*, suspense. Mk +1:15. Jn +6:14. 10:24.

mused. *or*, reasoned, *or* debated. Jn 1:19, etc. 3:28, 29.

whether. Jn 1:19, 20.

the Christ. Mt +16:16. Ac +2:31.

16 I indeed. Mt 3:11. Mk 1:7, 8. Jn 1:26, 33. Ac +1:5. 11:16. 13:24, 25. 19:4, 5.

with water. Is 44:3, 4. Jl 2:28, 29. Ac +1:5. 10:47.

mightier. Mk 1:7, 8.

cometh. Jn 1:15, 27. 3:30, 31. Ac 7:33. 13:25.

latchet. Is 5:27. Jn 1:27.

he shall. Pr 1:23. Is 32:15. 44:3, 4. Ezk 36:25. Jl 2:28, 29. Jn 7:38. Ac 2:33. 10:44. 11:15. 1 C 12:13.

with. Jn 1:33. Ac +1:5. 11:15, 16. 1 C 6:11.

Ghost. Gr. *pneuma*, Mt +1:18.

and with fire. Lk 12:49. Is 4:4. Zc 13:9. Ml 3:2, 3. Ac 2:3, 4, 17, 18.

17 fan. Mt +3:12.

gather the wheat. Lk 22:31. Am 9:9. Mi 4:12. Mt +13:30. 2 Th 2:1.

but the chaff. Jb 21:18. Ps +1:4. 35:5. Is 5:24. 17:13. 29:5. 41:15, 16. Je 23:28. Da 2:35. Ho 13:3. Zp 2:2. Mt 3:12. 1 J 2:19.

he will burn. Is +24:6. Mt +13:30. 2 P +3:7.

unquenchable. Mt +3:12. +25:46.

18 many other things. Jn 1:15, 29, 34. 3:29-36. 20:30. 21:25. Ac 2:40.

19 But Herod. Pr 9:7, 8. 15:12. Mt +4:12.

20 Added yet this. Lk 13:31-34. 2 K 21:16. 24:4. 2 Ch 24:17-22. 36:16. Ne +9:26. Je 2:30. Mt 21:35-41. 22:6, 7. 23:31-33. 1 Th 2:15, 16. Re 16:6.

prison. Ge +1:28.

21 that. Mt 3:13-15. Mk 1:9. Jn 1:32, etc.

baptized, and praying. Lk 9:28, 29. Mk 1:35. Jn 12:27, 28. Ac +22:16.

the heaven. Mt 3:16, 17. Mk 1:10, 11. Jn 1:32-34.

22 Ghost. Gr. *pneuma*, Mt +3:16. Mt 12:32. +28:19. Jn 14:16. 2 C 13:14. Ep 2:18. Ep +4:30. 1 P 1:2. 1 J 5:7.

descended. Jn 1:32.

bodily. S#**4984**g. ver. 22. 1 T 4:8.

shape. S#**1491**g. ver. 22. 9:29 (fashion). Jn 5:37. 2 C 5:7 (sight). 1 Th 5:22 (appearance).

a voice. Ex 19:17-19. 1 K 19:13. Mt 3:17. Mk 1:11.

from heaven. Lk 11:13. Mt 7:11. Jn 12:27, 28.

Thou art. Lk 9:34, 35. Ps 2:7. Is 42:1. Mt 12:18. 17:5. 27:43. Col 1:13. 1 P 2:4. 2 P 1:17, 18. 1 J 5:9.

beloved Son. Mk 9:7. Jn 15:26. 17:24. Ro 1:4. Ep 1:6.

23 began to be. Mt 3:16. 4:17. Ac 1:1, 2.

thirty. Ge 41:46. Nu 4:3, 35, 39, 43, 47.

being. Lk 2:27. 4:22. Mt +13:55. Mk +6:3. Jn 1:45. 6:42.

Heli. i.e. *ascending*, S#**2242**g. Compare S#**5941**h, 1 S +1:3, Eli.

24 Matthat. i.e. *gift*, S#**3158**g. ver. 24, 29.

Levi. i.e. *to adhere*, S#**3017**g. ver. 24, 29.

Melchi. i.e. *the Lord is king*, S#**3197**g. ver. 24, 28.

Janna. i.e. *answering*, S#**2388**g.

25 Amos. i.e. *a burden*, **S#301g**.
Naum. i.e. *ease*, **S#3486g**. For **S#5151h**, see Na +1:1.
Esli. i.e. *reserved*, **S#2069g**.
Nagge. i.e. *clearness*, **S#3477g**.

26 Maath. i.e. *fearing*, **S#3092g**.
Mattathias. i.e. *gift of Jehovah*, **S#3161g**. ver. 25, 26. For **S#4993h**, see Ezr 10:43, Mattithiah.
Semei. i.e. *obeys*, **S#4584g**. For **S#8096h**, see 2 S +16:5, Shimei.

27 Joanna. i.e. *Jehovah is gracious giver*, **S#2490g**.
Rhesa. i.e. *will; course*, **S#4488g**.
son of Zorobabel. Mt 1:12.
Salathiel. 1 Ch 3:17. Ezr 3:2.
Neri. i.e. *light of God*, **S#3518g**.

28 Addi. i.e. *my witness*, **S#78g**.
Cosam. i.e. *diviner*, **S#2973g**.
Elmodam. i.e. *God of measure*, **S#1678g**.
Er. i.e. *watch*, **S#2262g**.

29 Jose. i.e. *a savior*, **S#2499g**.
Eliezer. i.e. *God of help*, **S#1663g**.
Jorim. i.e. *the height*, **S#2497g**.

30 Simeon. i.e. *hearkening*, **S#4826g**. ver. 30. Lk 2:25, 34. 3:30. Ac 13:1. 15:14. 2 P 1:1. Re 7:7.
Juda. i.e. *praise; confession*, **S#2455g**.
Jonan. i.e. *pigeon*, **S#2494g**.
Eliakim. i.e. *my God arises*, **S#1662g**. Mt 1:13.

31 Melea. i.e. *filling*, **S#3190g**.
Menan. i.e. *enchanted; soothsayer*, **S#3104g**.
Mattatha. i.e. *gift of the Lord*, **S#3160g**.
of Nathan. i.e. *a giver*, **S#3481g**. For **S#5416h**, see 2 Ch +9:29.

32 was the son of Jesse. 1 Ch +2:12. Is +*11:1, 2*.
which was the son of Obed. i.e. *serving*, **S#5601g**. Mt 1:5. For **S#5744h**, see Ru +4:17.
Salmon. i.e. *he that rewards; clothing*, **S#4533g**. Mt 1:4, 5. For **S#8012h**, see Ru 4:21. 1 Ch 2:51, 54.
Naasson. 1 Ch +2:10. Mt 1:4.

33 Aminadab. i.e. *noble nation*, **S#284g**. Mt 1:4. For **S#5992h**, see 1 Ch +15:11.
Esrom. i.e. *dart of joy*, **S#2074g**. Mt 1:3. For **S#2696h**, see Ge +46:9. Ge 46:12. Nu 26:20, 21, Hezron.
Phares. Ge +48:12.
of Juda. Ge 29:35. 49:8, Judah. Mt 1:2, Judas.

34 of Jacob. Lk 1:33. Ge 29:35. Nu +*24:17*. Mt 1:2.
which was the son of Isaac. Ge +*17:19*. 21:3, *12*. 25:26. *26:2-5*. 1 Ch 1:34. Mt 1:2. Ac 7:8. Ro 9:6-8. He 11:17-19.
Abraham. i.e. *faithfulness; father of a great multitude*, **S#11g**. ver. 8. Lk 1:55, 73. 13:16, 28. 16:22-25, 29, 30. 19:9. 20:37. Mt 1:1, 2, 17. 3:9. 8:11. 22:32. Mk 12:26. Jn 8:33, 37, 39, 40, 52, 53, 56-58. Ac 3:13, 25. 7:2, 16, 17, 32. 13:26. Ro 4:1-3, 9, 12, 13, 16. 9:7. 11:1. 2 C 11:22. Ga 3:6-9, 14, 16, 18, 29. 4:22. He 2:16.

6:13. 7:1, 2, 4-6, 9. 11:8, 17. Ja 2:21, 23. 1 P 3:6. For **S#85h**, see Ge +17:5. Ge +12:3. 21:3. +*22:18*. 26:4. 28:14. Mt 1:1. Lk 1:54, 55. Jn 11:51, 52. Ac 3:25. Ro 4:13. Ga 3:8, 16.
Thara. i.e. *late*, **S#2291g**. For **S#8646h**, see Ge +11:26, Terah.
Nachor. i.e. *snoring*, **S#3493g**. For **S#5152h**, see Ge +11:22, Nahor.

35 Saruch. i.e. *a branch; intertwined*, **S#4562g**. For **S#8286h**, see Ge +11:20, Serug. Ge 11:18-21, Serug, Reu.
Ragau. i.e. *fellowship*, **S#4466g**. For **S#7466h**, see Ge +11:18, Reu.
Phalec. i.e. *to cut*, **S#5317g**. For **S#6389h**, see Ge +10:25, Peleg.
Heber. i.e. *companion*, **S#1443g**. For **S#5677h**, Ge +10:24, Eber.
Sala. i.e. *branch*, **S#4527g**. For **S#7974h**, see Ge +10:24, Salah.

36 Cainan. i.e. *fixed*, **S#2536g**. ver. 37. Ge 11:12.
Arphaxad. i.e. *one that heals*, **S#742g**. For **S#775h**, see Ge +10:22.
Sem. i.e. *fame*, **S#4590g**. For **S#8035h**, see Ge +5:32, Shem.
Noe. i.e. *consolation*, **S#3575g**. Lk 17:26, 27. Mt 24:37, 38. He 11:7. 1 P 3:20. 2 P 2:5. For **S#5146h**, see Ge +5:29, Noah.
Lamech. i.e. *wild man*, **S#2984g**. For **S#3929h**, see Ge +4:18.

37 Mathusala. i.e. *man of a dart*, **S#3103g**. For **S#4968h**, see Ge +5:21. Ge 5:6-28. 1 Ch 1:1-3, Methusaleh, Mahalaleel.
Enoch. i.e. *dedicated*, **S#1802g**. Lk 3:37. He 11:5. Ju 14. For **S#2585h**, see Ge +5:21.
Jared. i.e. *descended*, **S#2391g**. For **S#3382h**, see Ge +5:15.
Maleleel. i.e. *praise of God*, **S#3121g**. For **S#4111h**, see Ge +5:12, Mahalaleel.
Cainan. i.e. *fixed*, **S#2536g**. ver. 36. For **S#7018h**, see Ge +5:9.

38 Enos. i.e. *a mortal*, **S#1800g**. For **S#583h**, see Ge +4:26.
Seth. i.e. *appointed*, **S#4589g**. For **S#8352h**, see Ge +4:25.
which was the son of Adam. i.e. *red earth, earthy*, **S#76g**. Ro 5:14, 14. 1 C 15:22, 45, 45. 1 T 2:13, 14. Ju 14. For **S#120h**, see Ge +2:19. Ge 4:25, 26. 5:3.
of God. Ge 1:26, 27. 2:7. 5:1, 2. Is 64:8. Ac 17:26-29. 1 C 15:45, 47. He 12:9.

LUKE 4

1 A.M. 4031. A.D. 27.
Jesus. Mt 4:1, etc.
full. ver. 14, 18. Lk 3:22. Is 11:2-4. 61:1. Mt 3:16. Jn 1:32. 3:34. Ac 1:2. 10:38.
Ghost. Gr. *pneuma*, Mt +1:18.
and was led. Lk 2:27. Ezk +8:3. Mt 4:1. Mk 1:12, etc. Ac 8:39. Ro 8:14.

Spirit. Gr. *pneuma*, Mt +3:16.
the wilderness. 1 K 19:4. Mk 1:13.
2 **forty**. Ex 24:18. 34:28. Dt 9:9, 18, 25. 1 K
19:8. Mt 4:2. Mk 1:13.
tempted. Ge +3:15. 1 S 17:16. He 2:18.
he did. Est 4:16. Jon 3:7.
he afterward. Mt 4:2. 21:18. Jn 4:6. He
+4:15.
3 **If thou be**. 1 C +15:2. Lk 3:22. Mt 4:3.
4 **It**. ver. 8, 10. Is +8:20. Jn 10:34, 35. Ep 6:17.
That. Lk 22:35. Ex 23:25. Dt *8:3*. Jb +23:12.
Je +15:16. 49:11. Mt +4:4. 6:25, 26, 31.
word of God. Ep 6:17.
5 **taking**. Mt 4:8, 9. 1 C 7:31. Ep 2:2. 6:12. 1 J
2:15, 16.
world. Gr. *oikoumene*, Mt +24:14.
in a moment. Jb 20:5. Ps 73:19. 1 C 15:52. 2
C 4:17.
6 **All**. Jn 8:44. 2 C 11:14.
and the. Est 5:11. Is 5:14. 23:9. 1 P 1:24.
and to. Jn +12:31. Re 13:2, 7.
7 **If thou**. Mt +4:9.
worship me. *or*, fall down before me. Lk
8:28. 17:16. Ex +34:14. Ps 72:11. Is 45:14.
46:6. Mt 2:11. Re 4:10. 5:8. 22:8.
8 **Get**. Mt 4:10. 16:23. Ja 4:7. 1 P 5:9.
for. ver. 4. Ex 34:14. Dt 6:13. 10:20. Mt 4:10.
Ep 6:17. Re 19:10. 22:9.
only. 1 S 7:3. 2 K 19:15. Ps 83:18. Is 2:11.
9 **brought**. Jb 2:6. Mt 4:5.
on. 2 Ch 3:4.
If. 1 C +15:2. ver. 3. Mt 4:6. 8:29. Ro 1:4.
10 **It is written**. ver. 3, 8. 2 C 11:14. Ep 6:17.
He. Ps *91:11, 12*. He 1:14.
11 **And in**. Ps *91:12*.
12 **Thou**. Ex +17:2. Dt 6:16.
13 **devil had ended**. Mt 4:11. Jn +14:30. He
2:17, 18. +4:15. Ja 4:7.
for a season. Lk 22:53. Ac 13:11.
14 **returned**. Mt 4:12. Mk 1:14. Jn 4:43. Ac
10:36, 37.
in. ver. 1. Ac 1:8.
Spirit. Gr. *pneuma*, Mt +3:16.
and there. ver. 37. Mt +4:24.
15 **he**. ver. 16, 31, 33, 44. Lk 13:10. Mt +4:23.
9:35. 13:54. Ac 13:5, 14. +14:1.
being. Is 55:5. Mt 9:8. Mk 1:27, 45. Jn 4:45.
16 **to**. Mt +2:23. 13:54. Mk 6:1.
as his custom was. ver. 15. Lk 2:42. 22:39.
Mk 10:1. Jn 18:20. Ac +17:1, 2.
went into. Ps 22:22. 40:9, 10.
and stood. Ac 13:14-16. 17:2.
to read. Ac 13:15, 27. 15:21. 2 C 3:15. Col
4:16. 1 Th 5:27.
17 **the book**. Lk 3:4. 20:42. Ac 7:42. 13:15,
27.
the place. Is *61:1, 2*. Lk +24:27.
18 **Spirit**. Gr. *pneuma*, Lk +1:17. Ps 45:7. Is 11:2-
5. 42:1-4. 48:16. 50:4. 59:21. Mt 12:18. Mk
1:10. Ac 1:2. 10:38.

anointed. Jn +1:41mg.
to preach. Lk 6:20. 7:22. Is 29:19. 66:2. Zp
3:12. Zc 11:11. Mt +5:3. 11:5. Ja 2:5.
hath sent. Is *61:2*. Lk 1:78. Jn 3:34. Col 2:9.
to heal. 2 Ch 34:27. Ps +51:17.
to preach deliverance. Ps +146:7. Is 45:13.
52:2, 3. Mt 4:16. +11:28. Jn 8:36. Col 1:13. 2
T 2:26.
and recovering. Is 60:1, 2. Ml 4:2. Mt 4:16.
+11:5. Jn 9:39-41. 12:46. Ep 5:8-14. 1 Th 5:5,
6. 1 P 2:9. 1 J 2:8-10.
sight. Ge +3:7.
to set. Our Lord cites Is *58:6* with his reading
from Is 61:1, 2, thus forming a composite
quotation. Our Lord compared Scripture with
Scripture in expounding its meaning (Lk
+24:27, 44, 45. Jn +5:39. Ac +17:11), as did
Paul (Ac 17:3). For other examples of composite quotations see Mt 21:5, 13. 27:9. Mk
1:2, 3. Lk 1:16, 17. 3:4, 5. Ac 1:20. Ro 3:10-
12, 13-18. 9:33. 11:8, 26, 27. 1 C 15:54, 55. 2
C 6:16. Ga 3:8. He 9:19, 20. 1 P 2:7, 8.
at liberty. Ro 6:13, 14, 18.
bruised. Ge +3:15. Is 42:3. Mt 12:20.
19 **To preach**. Lk 19:42. +24:27. Le 25:8-13, 50-
54. Nu 36:4. Is 49:8. 61:2. 63:4. 2 C 6:1, 2.
acceptable. Ps 69:13.
20 **and he**. ver. 17. Mt 20:26-28.
closed the book. Our Lord ended his reading
at Is 61:2, in the middle of the sentence. His
stopping point is most instructive, for the rest
of the prophecy pertains to what will transpire
at the Second Advent. Thus, between clauses
of the same sentence is an unannounced time
interval. For other unannounced prophetic
time intervals, see Is +61:2. Compare Mt 21:4,
5, with Zc 9:9 but not Zc 9:10.
and sat. Lk 5:3. Mt 5:1, 2. 13:1, 2. 26:55. Mk
4:1. Jn 8:2. Ac 13:14-16. 16:13.
And the. Lk 19:48. Ac 3:4, 12.
21 **This day**. Lk 10:23, 24. Mt 13:14. Jn 4:25,
26. +5:39. Ac 2:16-18, 29-33. 3:18.
this scripture. Mt 21:42. Mk 12:10. Jn 2:22.
Ac 1:16. 8:32, 35. Ro 4:3. 9:17. 10:11. 11:2.
Ga 3:8, 22. 4:30. 1 T 5:18. 2 T 3:16. Ja 2:8, 23.
4:5. 1 P 2:6. 2 P 1:20.
fulfilled. Mt 1:22.
22 **wondered**. Mt 13:54, 55. Mk 6:2, 3.
Jn 6:42.
the gracious. Lk 2:47. 21:15. Ps 45:2, 4. Pr
10:32. 16:21. 25:11. Ec 12:10, 11. SS 5:16. Is
50:4. Mt 13:54. Mk 6:2. Jn 1:14. 7:46. Ac
6:10. T 2:8.
proceeded. Re 19:21.
Is not. Mt 13:55, 56. Mk +6:3. Jn 6:42.
Joseph's son. Lk 2:27. 3:23.
23 **Physician**. Lk 6:42. 23:39. Mt 27:42. Mk
15:31. Ro 2:21, 22.
whatsoever. Mt 4:13, 23. +11:23, etc. Mk
2:1-12. Jn 2:12. 4:48.

do. Jn 2:3, 4. 4:28. 7:3, 4. Ro 11:34, 35. 2 C 5:16.
thy country. ver. 16. Mt 13:54. Mk 6:1.
24 **Verily**. Mt +5:18.
No prophet. Mt 10:36. 13:57. Mk 6:4, 5. Jn 4:41, 44. Ac 22:3, 18-22.
is accepted. Dt 33:24. Ac 10:35.
25 **many**. Lk 10:21. Is 55:8. Mt 20:15. Mk 7:26-29. Ro 9:15, 20. Ep 1:9, 11.
when the. 1 K 17:1. 18:1, 2, Elijah. Ja 5:17. Re 11:6.
26 **save**. 1 K 17:9, etc., Zarephath. Ob 20.
Sarepta. i.e. *she hath refined*, **S#4558g**. For **S#6886h**, see 1 K +17:9.
Sidon. Ac 12:20.
unto. 1 K 17:12.
widow. Mk 12:42.
27 **many lepers**. 2 K 7:3.
Eliseus. i.e. *God of my salvation*, **S#1666g**. For **S#477h**, see 1 K +19:16, Elisha. 1 K 19:19-21.
saving. Mt 12:4. Jn 17:12. Ro +9:15.
Naaman. i.e. *pleasantness*, **S#3497g**. For **S#5283h**, see Ge +46:21. 2 K ch. 5. Jb 21:22. 33:13. 36:23. Da 4:35.
28 **were**. Lk 6:11. 11:53, 54. 2 Ch 16:10. 24:20, 21. Je 37:15, 16. 38:6. Ac 5:33. 7:54. 13:46, 50. 22:21-23. 1 Th 2:15, 16.
29 **and thrust out**. Le +4:12. Mt 8:34. Jn 8:37, 40, 59. 15:24, 25. Ac 7:57, 58. 16:23, 24. 21:28-32.
brow. *or*, edge.
that. 2 Ch 25:12. Ps 37:14, 32, 33.
30 **passing through**. Lk +24:16. Jg 18:20. Pr +22:3. Is +53:2. Je 37:12. Mt 26:48. Mk 14:44. Jn 8:59. 10:39. 18:6, 7. Ac 12:18.
the midst. Ge +27:16.
went his way. Ps 18:29. 37:32, 33. Jn 7:30.
31 **came**. Mt 4:13. Mk 1:21.
taught. ver. 15, 16. Mt 4:23. 10:23. Ac 13:50-52. 14:1, 2, 6, 7, 19-21. 17:1-3, 10, 11, 16, 17. 18:4. 20:1, 2, 23, 24.
on the sabbath. Mk 6:2.
32 **astonished**. ver. 36. Je 23:28, 29. Mt +7:28, 29. Jn 6:63. 1 C 2:4, 5. 14:24, 25. 2 C 4:2. 10:4, 5. 1 Th 1:5. T 2:15. He 4:12, 13.
33 **in the synagogue**. Mk 1:23.
unclean. Mk +3:30.
spirit. Gr. *pneuma*, Mt +8:16.
cried out. Mt 8:29.
34 **Let us alone**. *or*, Away. Lk 8:37. Ac 16:39.
what have. ver. 41. Jg +11:12. Ja 2:19.
of Nazareth. Mk +1:24.
art thou come. Ge +3:15. Mt +8:29. He 2:14. 1 J 3:8. Re 20:2.
destroy. Gr. *apollumi*, Mt +2:13.
I know thee. Mk 1:34. Ac 19:15. Ja 2:19.
the Holy One. Ps +16:10. Jn 6:69.
35 **Jesus**. ver. 39, 41. Ps +50:16. 17:18. Mk 3:11, 12. +4:39. Ac 16:17, 18.
Hold thy peace. Mt 22:12. Mk 1:25.

thrown. Lk 9:39, 42. 11:22. Mk 1:26. 9:26. Re 12:12.
36 **they were**. ver. 32. Lk 8:25. Mt 8:27. 9:33. 12:22, 23. Mk 1:27. 4:41. 7:37.
What. ver. 32. Lk 10:17-20. Mk 16:17-20. Ac 19:12-16.
and power. Lk 5:17.
unclean. ver. 33. Mk +3:30.
spirits. Gr. *pneuma*, Mt +8:16.
they come. 1 P 3:22.
37 **the fame**. ver. +14. Is 52:13. Mk 6:14.
38 **he arose**. Mt 8:14, 15. Mk 1:29-31. 1 C 9:5.
taken with. Mt 4:25.
they besought. Mk +5:23. Ja 5:14, 15.
39 **stood over**. Lk 20:1.
and rebuked. ver. 35.
and ministered. Lk 8:2, 3. 10:40. Ps 116:12. Jn 12:2. 2 C 5:14, 15.
40 **when**. Mt 8:16, 17. Mk 1:32-34.
laid his hands. Mt +4:23. Mk +5:23. Ac 19:12.
41 **crying out**. ver. 33-35. Mk 1:25, 26, 34. 3:11. 5:12.
Thou art. Mt 8:29. 26:63. Mk 1:24. Jn +5:39. 20:31. Ac +10:43. 16:17, 18. Ja 2:19.
Son of God. Mt +14:33.
rebuking. ver. 35. Mt 12:16.
suffered them not. Mk +1:34.
speak, etc. *or*, say that they knew him to be Christ. Mt +16:16.
42 **when**. Lk 6:12. Mt 12:15-21. Mk +1:35. Jn 4:34.
into a desert place. Lk 5:16.
and the. Mt 14:13, 14. Mk 1:37, 45. 6:33, 34. Jn 6:24.
and stayed. Lk 8:37, 38. 24:29. Jn 4:40. Ro 1:18. 2 Th 2:6mg.
43 **I must**. Lk +13:33. Mk 1:14, 15, 38, 39. 2 T 4:2.
kingdom of God. Lk 6:20. 7:28. 8:1, 10. 9:2, 11, 27, 60, 62. 10:9, 11. 11:20. 12:31, +32. 13:18, 20, 28, 29. 14:15. 16:16. 17:20, 21. 18:16, 17, 24, 25, 29. 19:11. 21:31. 22:16, 18. 23:51. Da 2:44. 7:14, 27. Mt +12:28. Mk +1:15. Jn +3:3. Ac +1:3. Ro +14:17.
therefore am I sent. ver. 18. Lk 9:48. 10:16. Is 42:1-4. 48:16. 61:1-3. Jn 4:34. 6:38-40. 20:21.
44 **he**. ver. 15. Mt 4:23. Mk 1:39.
Galilee. Lk 23:5. Is 2:19. 9:1, 2. Jn 3:22. 5:1.

LUKE 5

1 **it**. Lk 8:45. 12:1. Mt 4:18, etc. 11:12. Mk 1:16, etc. 3:9. 5:24.
to hear. Lk +8:18, 21. Mk 2:13. 4:1. Jn 5:24. 12:48. 14:23. Ac 8:25. 13:26. 14:3, 15:7. 1 C 1:18. Ep 1:13. Ph 2:16. Col 1:25. 3:16. 2 T 2:15. Ja 1:19, 21-25.
the word of God. Lk 8:11, 21. 11:28. Mt

15:6. Mk 4:14-20. 7:13. Jn +10:35. Ac 4:31.
6:2, 7. 8:14. 11:1. 12:24. 13:5, 7, 46, 48.
16:32. 17:13. 18:11. Ro +9:6. 10:17. 1 Th
2:13. Re 1:2.

the lake. Lk 8:22, 23, 33. Jsh +11:2. Mt
+4:18. 14:34. Mk 6:53.

2 **washing**. Gr. *apopluno*, **S#637g**, only here. Mt
4:21. Mk 1:19.

3 **which**. Mt 4:18. Jn 1:41, 42.
he sat. Lk +4:20. Mt 5:1. 13:1, 2. Mk 4:1, 2.
Jn 8:2.

4 **Launch**. Mt 17:27. Jn 21:6.

5 **Master**. Lk 8:24, 45. 9:33, 49. 17:13.
we. Ps 127:1, 2. Ezk 37:11, 12. Jn 21:3.
nevertheless. Lk 6:46-48. 2 K 5:10-14. Ezk
37:4-7. Jn 2:5. 15:14.

6 **they inclosed**. 2 K 4:3-7. Ec 11:6. Jn 21:6-
11. Ac 2:41. 4:4. 1 C 15:58. Ga 6:9.

7 **partners**. Jb 41:6. 2 C 6:1.
that they should. Ex 23:5. Pr 18:24. Ac
11:25, 26. Ro 16:2-4. Ga 6:2. Ph 4:3.
sink. Gr. *bathizo*. **S#1036g**. 1 T 6:9 (drown).

8 **he fell down**. ver. 12. Ge +17:3.
Depart. Ex 20:19. Jg 13:22. 1 S 6:20. 2 S 6:9.
1 K 17:18. 1 Ch 13:12. Da 10:16, 17. Mt
+8:34. 17:6.
I am. Jb 40:4. 42:5, 6. Is 6:5. Da 10:16. Mt 8:8.

9 **he**. Lk 4:32, 36. +8:25. Ps 8:6, 8. Mk 9:6.
draught of the fishes. Mt +13:47.

10 **James**. Lk 6:14. Mt 4:21. 20:20.
partners. ver. 7. 2 C 3:5, 6. 8:23.
Fear not. ver. 26. Lk +1:13.
from. Ezk 47:9, 10. Mt 4:19. 13:47. Mk 1:17.
Ac 2:4.
catch. 2 T 2:26mg.

11 **they forsook all**. Lk 18:28-30. Mt 4:20.
10:37. 19:27. Mk 1:18-25. 10:21, 28-30. Ph
3:7, 8.
and followed. Nu +32:11, 12. Dt 13:4. 1 K
14:8. +18:21. Ps 68:3. Jn 8:12. 10:27. 12:26.
Ep 5:1. Re 14:4.

12 **a man**. Mt 8:2-4. Mk 1:40-45.
full. Ex 4:6. Le ch. 13, 14. 2 K +5:1.
fell. ver. +8.
besought. Lk 17:13. Ps +50:15. 91:15. Mk
5:23.
if. Mt +4:9. Ge +18:14. Mt 8:8, 9. 9:28. Mk
9:22-24. He 7:25.

13 **touched**. Lk 22:51. Mt 8:3, 15. +9:29. Mk
1:31. +5:23. 7:33. 8:22.
I will. Ge 1:3, 9. Ps 33:9. 2 K 5:10, 14. Ezk
36:25-27, 29. Ho 14:4. Mt 9:29, 30.
immediately. Lk 4:39. 8:54, 55. Jn 4:50-53.

14 **he charged**. Mk +1:43.
tell no. Lk 8:56. 9:21, 36. Mt 8:4. 9:30.
12:16-19. 16:20. 17:9. Mk +1:34, 44. 5:43.
7:36. 8:26, 30. 9:9. Jn 8:50.
and show. Mk +1:44.
and offer. Le 14:4, 10, 21, 22.
for. Mt +8:4.

15 **so**. Pr 15:33. Mk 1:45. 1 T 5:25.
went. Mt +4:24.
great multitudes. Lk 6:17. 12:1. 14:25. Mt
4:25. 5:1. 8:1. 12:15. 13:2. 14:14. 15:30, 31.
19:2. 20:29. Mk 1:34. 2:1, 2. 3:7. 4:1. Jn 6:2.

16 **withdrew**. Mk +3:7. Jn 6:15.
wilderness. Lk 1:80. 8:29. Ge 21:14-16. Ex
14:10, 11. Nu 21:5-7. 1 K 19:4. Ps 107:4-6.
Mk 1:45.
prayed. Lk 6:12. 9:28. Mt 14:23. Mk 1:35,
36. 6:46.

17 **it came**. Lk 8:22. 20:1.
teaching. Lk +9:11.
that there. ver. 21, 30. Lk 7:30. 11:52-54.
15:2. Jn 3:21.
doctors of. Lk 2:46. Mt 22:35. Ac 5:34. 1 T
1:7.
Jerusalem. Mt 15:1. Mk 3:22. 7:1.
power. Lk 1:35. 4:36. 6:19. 8:46. 24:49. Mt
11:5. Mk 16:18. Ac 4:30. 6:8. 10:38. 19:11, 12.

18 **men brought**. Mt 9:2-8. Mk 2:3-12. Jn 5:5,
6. Ac 9:33.
in a bed. Mk 6:55.

19 **not find**. Lk 8:20.
they went. Mk 2:4.
housetop. Dt +22:8.
through. Mk 2:4.

20 **he saw**. Ge 22:12. Mt +9:2, 22, 29. Jn +2:25.
Ac 11:23. Ep 2:8.
Man. Lk +12:14.
thy sins. Lk +7:48. Ps 90:7, 8. 107:17, 18. Is
38:17. Mt 9:2. Mk 2:5. Jn 5:14. 2 C 2:10. Col
3:13. Ja 5:14, 15.

21 **scribes**. ver. 17. Lk 7:49. Mk 2:6, 7.
began to reason. Lk 3:8. 13:25, 26. 14:9.
Who. Lk 7:49. Jn 5:12.
blasphemies. Mk +14:64.
Who can. Ex 34:6, 7. Jb 14:4. Ps 32:5. 35:5.
51:4. 86:5. +103:3. 130:4. Is 1:18. 43:25.
44:22. Da 9:9, 19. Mi 7:19. Mk 2:7. Ro 8:33.
but God. Lk 18:19. Jn +20:28.

22 **perceived**. Gr. *epiginosko*, Mt +11:27. Pr
15:26. Is 66:18. Ezk 38:10. Jn +2:25.
their thoughts. Lk +2:35.
What. Lk 24:38. Mk 8:17. Ac 5:3.

23 **is easier**. Mt 9:5. Mk 2:9.
and walk. Is 35:6. Jn 5:8.

24 **Son of man**. Lk 6:5, 22. 7:34. 9:22, 26, 44,
56, 58. 11:30. 12:8, 10, 40. 17:22, 24, 26, 30.
18:8, 31. 19:10. 21:27, 36. 22:22, 48, 69. 24:7.
Da 7:13. Mt +8:20. Mk +2:10. Jn +1:51. Re
1:13.
power. Is 53:11. Mt 9:6. 28:18. Jn 5:8, 12,
22, 23. 17:2. 20:22, 23. Ac 5:31.
I say. ver. 13. Lk 7:14. 8:54. Jn 11:43. Ac 3:6-
8. 9:34, 40. 14:10.
Arise. Jn +5:8.
and take. Jn 5:8-12.

25 **immediately**. ver. 13. Lk 8:44, 55. 18:43. Ge
1:3. Ps 33:9.

glorifying. Ps 103:1-3. 107:20-22. Mt +9:8. Jn 9:24.

26 and they. Lk 1:65. 9:43. 13:17. Mt 12:23.
glorified. Mt +9:8.
and were. ver. 8. Lk +1:65.

27 saw a publican. Lk +3:12.
named Levi. Mt 9:9, etc. 10:3, Matthew. Mk 2:13, 14. 3:18. 6:15. Ac 1:13.
Follow me. Lk 18:22. Mt 4:19-21. 8:22. Jn 1:43. 12:26. 21:19-22.

28 left all. ver. 11. Lk 9:59-62. 14:33. 1 K 19:19-21. Ps 110:3. Mt 19:22-27.
and followed. Lk 9:23. Mt 4:19.

29 made. Lk 7:34. 14:1, 13. Mt 10:32, 33. 11:19. Jn 1:41. 4:28, 29. 12:2.
and there. Mt +5:46. 1 C 5:9-11. 10:27.

30 their scribes and. ver. 17, 21. Lk 7:29, 30, 34, 39. 18:11. Is +65:5. Mt 21:28-32. 23:13. Mk 2:16. 7:3. Ac +23:9.
murmured. Ju +16.
publicans. Mt +5:46.

31 They that. Je 8:22. Mt 9:12, 13. Mk 2:17. Re 3:17, 18.
but they. Jn 1:12. Ro 3:10, 23. 6:23. 1 T 1:15. Re 3:20.

32 came not. Lk 4:18, 19. 9:56. 18:10-14. +19:10. Is 55:6, 7. +57:15. Jn 9:39. 1 C +6:9-11. 1 T 1:15, 16.
but sinners. Jsh 6:25.
to repentance. Lk +13:3. Pr 28:13.

33 Why. Mt 18:12. Is 58:3-6. Zc 7:6. Mt 6:16. 9:14-17. Mk 2:18-22.
disciples of John. Mt 11:2. 14:12. Jn 1:35. 3:25. 4:1. Ac 18:25. 19:3.
fast often. Lk 2:37. 18:1, 12.
and make. Lk 11:1. 20:47. Pr 28:9. Is 1:15. Mt 6:5, 6. 23:14. Mk 12:40. Ac 9:11. Ro 10:2, 3. 1 T 2:1.
but. ver. 30. Lk 7:34, 35.

34 the children. Lk +10:6. Jg 14:10, 11. Ps 45:14. SS 2:6, 7. 3:10, 11. 5:8. 6:1. Mt 25:1-10. Re 19:7-9.
bridegroom. Ps 45:10-16. Is 54:5. 62:5. Zp 3:17. Mt 22:2. +25:1. Jn 3:29. 2 C 11:2. Ep 5:25-27.
is with them. Jn 16:16.

35 the days. Lk +17:22.
when. Lk 24:17-21. Da +9:26. Zc 13:7. Mt +26:11. Jn 12:8. 13:33. 14:3, 4. 16:4-7, 16-22, 28. 17:11-13. Ac 1:9. 3:21.
then shall they fast. Is 22:12. Mt 6:17, 18. Jn 16:20. Ac 13:2, 3. 14:23. 1 C 7:5. 2 C 11:27.

36 a parable. Mk 4:33. Jn 16:12.
No man. Mt 9:16, 17. Mk 2:21, 22. Jn 1:17.
if. 1 C +15:2.
agreeth. Le 19:19. Dt 22:11. 2 C 6:16.

37 old bottles. Mt +9:17.
perish. Gr. *apollumi*, Mt +2:13.

38 new wine. Ezk 36:26. 2 C 5:17. Ga 2:4, 12-

14. 4:9-11. 5:1-6. 6:13, 14. Ph 3:5-7. Col 2:19-23. 1 T 4:8. He 8:8-13. 13:9, 10. Re 21:5.

39 desireth. Mt +6:2.
The old is. Je 6:16. Mk 7:7-13. Ro 4:11, 12. 7:6. 2 C 3:6. He 11:1, 2, 39.

LUKE 6

1 the second. Ex 12:15, 16. Le 23:7, 10, 11, 15. Dt 16:9.
that. Mt 12:1, etc. Mk 2:23, etc.
and his. Dt 23:25.

2 Why. ver. 7-9. Lk 5:33. Mt 12:2. 15:2. +23:23, 24. Mk 2:24. Jn 5:9-11, 16. 9:14-16.
not. Ex 20:10. 31:15. 35:2. Nu 15:32-35. Is +58:13.

3 Have. Mt 12:3, 5. 19:4. 21:16, 42. 22:31. Mk 2:25. 12:10, 26.
what. 1 S 21:3-6. Mt 12:3, 4. Mk 2:25, 26.

4 which. Le 24:5-9.

5 Son. Mt +8:20.
Lord also of. Mt 12:5-8. Mk 2:27, 28. 9:7. Re 1:10.
sabbath. Lk 13:14.

6 it came. Mt 12:9-14. Mk 3:1-6.
he entered. Mt +4:23. Jn 9:16.
there. 1 K 13:4. Zc 11:17. Jn 5:3.

7 watched. Lk 13:14. 14:1-6. Ps 37:32, 33. 38:12. Is 29:21. Je 20:10. Mk 3:2. Jn 5:10-16. 9:16, 26-29.
on the sabbath. Lk 13:14.
that. Lk 11:53, 54. 20:20. Mt 26:59, 60.

8 But. Lk 7:40. Ps 44:21. Jn +2:25.
Rise. Is 42:4. Jn 9:4. Ac 20:24. 26:26. Ph 1:28. 1 P 4:1.
stand forth. Mk 3:3.

9 Is it lawful. Lk 14:3. Mt 12:11-13. Mk 3:4. Jn 7:19-24.
to save. Lk 9:56.
life. Gr. *psyche*, Mt +2:20; Ge +12:5; Ge +9:5.
destroy. Gr. *apollumi*, Mt +2:13.

10 looking. Mk 3:5.
Stretch. Ex 4:6, 7. 1 K 13:6. Ps 107:20. Jn 5:8.

11 they. Lk 4:28. Ps 2:1, 2. Ec 9:3. Ac 5:33. 7:54. 26:11.
communed. Mt 12:14, 15. 21:45, 46. Mk 3:6. Jn 7:1. 11:47, 48. Ac 4:15, 16. 5:33, 34.
what. Lk +1:62.

12 that. Lk 5:16. Ps 55:15-17. 109:3, 4. Da +6:10. Mt 6:6. Mk +1:35. 14:34-36. He 5:7.
into a mountain. Lk 22:39.
continued all night. Ge 32:24-26. 1 S 15:10, 11. 2 S 12:16. Ps 22:2. Jl 1:13. Mt 14:23-25. Mk 6:46. Col 4:2.
in prayer. Ps 5:3. 109:4. Mk +1:35. He 5:7.

13 when. Lk 9:1, 2. Mt 9:36-38. 10:1-4. Mk 3:13-19. 6:7.
twelve. Lk 22:30. Mt 19:28. Re 12:1. 21:14.
apostles. Lk 11:49. 2 C 5:20. Ep 2:20. 4:11. He 3:1. 2 P 3:2. Re 18:20.

14 **Simon.** Lk 5:8. Jn 1:40-42. 21:15-20. Ac
1:13. 2 P 1:1.

Andrew. Mt 4:18. Jn 6:8.

James. Lk 5:10. Mt 4:21. Mk 1:19, 29. 5:37.
9:2. 14:33. Jn 21:20-24. Ac 12:2.

Philip. Mt 10:3. Jn 1:45, 46. 6:5. 14:8, 9. Ac
1:13.

15 **Matthew**. Lk 5:27, Levi. Mt 9:9.

Thomas. Jn 11:16. 20:24-29.

James. Ac 15:13. Ga 1:19. 2:9. Ja 1:1.

Alpheus. Mt 10:3. Mk 2:14. 3:18. Ac 1:13.

Simon. Mt 10:4. Mk 3:18, Simon the
Canaanite. Ac 1:13.

Zelotes. i.e. *zealous, jealous*, **S#2208g**. Ac 1:13.

16 **Judas**. i.e. *praised, confession*, **S#2455g**.

the brother. Mt 10:3, Lebbeus, Thaddeus.
Mk 3:18, Thaddeus. Jn 14:22. Ju 1.

Judas Iscariot. "Iscariot" probably means *Ish
Kerioth*, "the man from Kerioth," a town of
Judah, Jsh 15:25. Mt 10:4. 26:14-16, 25, 47.
27:3-10. Mk 3:19. 14:10, 43. Lk 6:16. 22:3,
47, 48. Jn 6:70, 71. 12:4. 13:2, 26, 29. 18:2, 3,
5. Ac 1:16-20, 25.

the traitor. Ps 41:9. 1 J 2:19.

17 **and a**. Lk +5:15.

the sea. Mt +11:21.

to be. Mt +4:23.

18 **vexed**. Ac +5:16.

unclean. Mk +3:30.

spirits. Gr. *pneuma*, Mt +8:16.

19 **sought**. Nu 21:8, 9. 2 K 13:21. Mt 9:20, 21.
14:36. Mk 3:10. 6:56. 8:22. Jn 3:14, 15. Ac
5:15, 16. 19:12.

for. Lk 8:45, 46. Mk 5:30. 1 P 2:9.

20 **he lifted**. Lk 16:23. 18:13. Ge +22:13. Mt
5:2, etc. 12:49, 50. 17:8. Mk 3:34, 35. Jn 4:35.
6:5. 11:41. 17:1.

Blessed. ver. 24. Lk 4:18. 16:25. 1 S 2:8. Ps
37:16. 113:7, 8. Pr 16:19. 19:1. Is 29:19.
+57:15, 16. 61:1. 66:2. Zp 3:12. Zc 11:11. Mt
11:5. Jn 7:48, 49. 1 C 1:26-29. 2 C 6:10. 8:2,
9. 1 Th 1:6. Ja 1:9, 10. +2:5, 6. Re 2:9.

poor. Ps 9:12, 18. 10:2, 9, 12. +12:5. 40:17.
69:29. 72:2, 4, 12, 13. 82:3, 4. 86:1. 109:22.
113:7.

for. Lk +4:43. Mt +5:3, 10. 1 C 3:21-23. 2 Th
1:5. Ja 1:12.

21 **ye that hunger**. ver. 25. Ps 42:1, 2. 132:15.
143:6. Mt +5:6. 1 C 4:11. 2 C 11:27. 12:10.

for ye shall be filled. Mt +5:6. Jn 6:35.

ye that weep. ver. 25. Lk 23:28. Ge +29:11.
1 S 20:41. 2 S 15:30. 16:12mg. 2 K 20:3, 5.
Ezr 10:1. Jb 2:12. Ps 42:3. +56:8. 80:5. 102:9.
+119:136. Is 38:3, 5. Je 31:9, 13, 18-20. Mt
+5:4. *Jn 11:35*. Ac 20:37. 1 P 1:6-8. Re 21:3,
4.

ye shall laugh. Ge 17:17. +21:6. Ps 28:7.
30:11, 12. Is +12:1, 2. 65:14.

22 **when men**. Mt 5:10-12. 10:22. Mk 10:29,
30. 13:9-13. Jn 7:7. 15:18-20. 17:14. 2 C

11:23-26. Ph 1:28-30. 1 Th 2:2, 14, 15. 2 T
3:11, 12. 1 P 2:19, 20. 3:14. 4:12-16.

separate. Lk 20:15. 2 Ch 13:9. Is +65:5. 66:5.
Jn 9:22-28, 34. 12:42. 16:2. Ac 22:22. 24:5.

reproach. Ps +31:11. Is 66:5.

cast out. Dt 22:19. Jn 9:34.

for. Lk 21:17. Mt 10:18, 22, 39. Jn 15:21. Ac
9:16. 1 C 4:10, 11.

23 **Rejoice**. Mt +5:12. Ac 5:41. 13:52. Ro 5:3. 2
C 6:10. 7:4. 12:10. Ph 1:29. 2:17. Col 1:11, 24.
1 Th 1:6. He 10:34. 13:13. Ja 1:2, 3. 1 P 1:6.
4:13.

leap. Lk 1:41, 44. 2 S 6:16. Is 35:6. Ac 3:8.
14:10.

your reward. ver. 35. Mt +5:12. Ro 8:18. 2
Th 1:5-7. 2 T 2:12. 4:7, 8. 1 P 4:13. Re 2:7, 10,
11, 17, 26. 3:5, 12. 21:7.

for in. 1 K 18:4. 19:2, 10, 14. 21:20. 22:8, 27.
2 K 6:31. 2 Ch 16:10. 24:20, 21. 36:16. Ne
+9:26. Je 2:30. 26:8, 20, 23. Mt 21:35, 36.
23:31-37. Ac 7:51, 52. 1 Th 2:14, 15. He
11:32-39.

24 **woe**. Lk 12:15-21. 18:23-25. Jb 21:7-15. Ps
49:6, 7, 16-19. 73:3-12. Pr 1:32. Je 5:4-6.
22:21. Am 4:1-3. 6:1-6. Hg 2:9. 1 T 6:17. Ja
2:6. 5:1-6. Re 18:6-8.

have received. Lk 16:19-25. Mt 6:2, +5, 16.

25 **full**. Dt 6:11, 12. 1 S 2:5. Pr 30:9. Is 28:7.
65:13. Ezk +16:49. Ph 4:12, 13. Re 3:17.

shall hunger. Is 8:21. 9:20. 65:13.

laugh. Lk 8:53. 16:14, 15. Ge +21:6. Jb 20:5.
Ps 22:6, 7. Pr 14:13. Ec 2:2. 7:3, 6. Ep 5:4. Ja
4:9.

mourn. Lk 12:20. 13:28. Jb 20:5-7. 21:11-13.
Ps 49:19. Is 21:3, 4. 24:7-12. Da 5:4-6. Am
8:10. Na 1:10. Mt 22:11-13. 1 Th 5:3. Re
18:7-11.

26 **when**. Je 45:5. Mi 2:11. Jn 7:7. 15:19. Ro
16:18. 2 Th 2:8-12. Ja 4:4. 2 P 2:18, 19. 1 J
4:5, 6. Re 13:3, 4.

so. 1 K 22:6-8, 13, 14, 24-28. Is 30:10. Je
5:31. 2 P 2:1-3.

27 **unto**. Lk 8:8, 15, 18. Mk 4:24.

Love. ver. 35. Lk 23:34. Jb 31:29-31. Pr
24:17. Mt +5:44. Ac 7:60. Ro 12:17-21.

do. ver. 22. Ac 10:38. Ga 6:10. 3 J 11.

28 **Bless**. Lk 23:34. Mt 5:44. Ac 7:60. Ro 12:14.
1 C 4:12. Ja 3:10. 1 P 3:9.

pray for. Lk 23:34. Ac 7:60. 1 C 4:12. 2 T
4:16. 1 P 3:9.

despitefully. Ezk 25:15. 36:5. Ac 14:5. 1 P
3:16.

29 **unto him**. Pr +19:25. Ro 12:17. 1 P 2:19-23.

smiteth. Lk +22:36. 1 Ch +12:32. Pr +22:3.
Mt +27:30. 1 C 4:11.

and him. 2 S 19:30. Mt 5:40, 41. 1 C 6:7. He
10:34.

cloak. Mt 24:18. Mk 13:16.

30 **Give**. ver. 38. Lk 11:41. 12:33. 18:22. Dt
15:7-10. Ps 37:21, 26. 41:1. 112:5, 9. Pr 3:27,

28. 11:24, 25. 19:17. 21:26. 22:9. Ezk 11:1, 2. Is 58:7-10. Ec 18:16. Mt 5:42, etc. 25:8, 9. Ac 20:35. 2 C 8:9. 9:6-14. Ep 4:28. 1 J 3:17.
and him. Ex 22:26, 27. Ne 5:1-19. Mt 6:12. 18:27-30, 35.

31 as ye would. Pr 18:24. 24:29. Mt 7:12. 22:39. Ga 5:14. Ja 2:8-16.

32 if. 1 C +15:2. Mt 5:46, 47.
what. ver. 33, 34. 1 P 2:19, 20.

33 And if. Mt +4:9. Mt 5:47.
what thank. ver. 32. Lk 17:9, 10.

34 if ye lend. Mt +4:9. ver. 35. Lk 14:12-14. Dt 15:8-11. Ps 37:26. Pr 19:17. Mt 5:42.

35 love. ver. 27-31. Le 25:35-37. Ps 37:26. 112:5. Pr 19:17. 22:9. Ro 5:8-10. 2 C 8:9.
do good. Mi +6:8. Ro 12:20, 21. Ga +6:10. T 3:8. He 6:9, 10. Ja 1:27. 2:15, 16. 1 J 3:17.
and lend. ver. +30. Dt 15:7-11. Ps 37:26. 112:5. Pr 19:17.
hoping for nothing. ver. 33. Pr 1:19. 15:27. 22:16. 28:22. Is +24:2. 1 T 3:3, 8. +6:5.
your reward. 1 T +4:8. Re 11:18.
great. Lk +12:48.
and ye. Mt +5:44, 45. Jn 13:35. 15:8. 1 J 3:10-14. 4:7-11.
the Highest. Lk 1:32, 35, 76. Mk 5:7. Ac 7:48.
for he is kind. Ge 18:25. Dt 20:20. 2 Ch 15:7. Ps 34:8. 68:18. 112:4. +145:9. Is +27:4. Mt +5:45. 10:42. Ac 14:17. 17:25, +30. 1 T 6:17.

36 merciful. ver. +35. Ex +34:6. Is +27:4. Mt +5:7, 48. Ep 4:31, 32. 5:1, 2. Ja 3:17. 1 P 1:15, 16.
is merciful. Ps 112:4. 2 C 1:3. Col 3:12. Ja 5:11.

37 Judge not. ver. 41, 44. Is +65:5. Mt +6:2. +7:1. Jn +7:24. Ro 2:1, 2. 14:3, 4, 10-16. 1 C 4:3-5. 5:3. Ja 4:11, 12. 5:9.
shall not. Mt +5:18.
condemn not. Jb 15:6. Pr 17:15. 30:10. Mk 3:2. Ro 2:1. +14:4, 22.
not be condemned. Is 50:9. Jn 3:18. 5:24. Ro 8:1, 34. 14:22. 1 J 3:21.
forgive. Lk 17:3, 4. Mt +5:7. 6:14, 15. 18:35. Mk 11:25, 26. 1 C 13:4-7. Ep 4:32. Col 3:13.

38 Give. Lk 3:11. 12:33. Mt 5:42. 6:1-4, 23. 10:8. 25:8, 9.
and it. ver. 30. Lk +18:28. Dt 15:10. 2 Ch 31:10. Ezr 7:27, 28. Jb 31:16-20. 42:11, 12. Ps 37:3, 25, 26. +58:11. 112:5, 6. Pr 3:9, 10. 10:22. 11:24-26. 13:7. 19:17. 22:9. Ec 11:1, 2. Is 32:8. Ml 3:9-12. Mt +5:7. 10:42. Mk +10:30. Ac 20:35. 2 C 8:14, 15. 9:6-8. Ph 4:17-19.
bosom. Ps 79:12. Pr 6:27. Is 65:6, 7. Je 32:18.
with. Le 24:19. Dt 19:16-21. Jg 1:7. 1 S 15:33. Est 7:10. 9:25. Ps 18:25, 26. 41:1, 2. Mt 7:2. Mk 4:24. Ja 2:13. Re 16:5, 6.

39 Can. Pr +19:27. Mt +15:14. Mk +4:24. 1 T 6:3-5. 2 T 3:13.
shall. Je 14:15, 16. Zc 11:15-17. Mt 23:33.

40 The disciple. Lk 22:27. Mt 10:24, 25. Jn 13:16. 15:20. He 12:3.
master. Mt 22:24.
that is perfect shall be as his master. or, shall be perfected as his master. Mt +5:48. 23:15. 1 C 1:10. 2 C 3:18. 2 T 3:17.

41 why. Mt 7:3-5. Ro 2:1, 21-24.
but. 2 S 12:5-7. 20:9, 10, 20, 21. 1 K 2:32. 1 Ch 21:6. Ps 36:2. Je +17:9. Ezk 18:28. Jn 8:7, 40-44. Ja 1:24.

42 hypocrite. Mt +6:2. Ac 8:21. 13:10.
cast. Lk 22:32. Ps 50:16-21. 51:9-13. Pr 18:17. Mt 26:75. Ac +2:38. 9:9-20. Ro 2:1, 21, etc. 2 C 5:18. 1 Th 2:10-12. Phm 10, 11.
first. Mt 6:33. 23:26.
see. Mt 6:22, 23. 2 T 2:21. 2 P 1:9. Re 3:17, 18.

43 good tree. Ps 92:12-14. Is 5:4. 61:3. Je 2:21. Mt 3:10. 7:16-20. 12:33.

44 For of. Ga 5:19-23. T 2:11-13. Ja 3:12. Ju 12.
grapes. Gr. a grape.

45 good man. Ps 37:30, 31. 40:8-10. 71:15-18. Pr 10:20, 21. 12:18. 15:23. 22:17, 18. Mt +12:35. Jn 7:38. 15:1, 5. Ep 4:29. 5:3, 4, 19. Col 4:6.
treasure. Mt +13:52. 2 C 4:6, 7. Ep 3:8. Col 3:16. He 8:10.
and an evil. Ps 12:2-4. 41:6, 7. 52:2-4. 59:7, 12. 64:3-8. 140:5. Is 32:6. Je 9:2-5. Mt 15:18, 19. Mk 7:20-23. Jn 8:43. 12:39. Ac +5:3. 8:19-23. Ro 3:13, 14. 8:7. Ja 3:5-8. Ju 15.
for. Mt +12:34-37.

46 why call. Lk 13:25-27. Ml 1:6. Mt 7:21-23. 25:11, 12, 24, 44. Jn 13:13-17. Ga 6:7. 1 P 3:6.
Lord, Lord. Mt 7:21.
and do not. Ezr +7:10. Ezk +33:31, 32. Jn +13:17. Ja +1:22.

47 cometh. Lk 14:26. Is +55:3. Mt 11:28. Jn 5:40. 6:35, 37, 44, 45. 1 P 2:4.
heareth. Mt 7:24, 25. 17:5. Jn 8:52. 9:27, 28. +10:27.
doeth them. Lk +8:8, 13. +11:28. Mt 11:29, 30. 12:50. Jn +13:17. 14:15, 21-24. 15:9-14. Ro 2:7-10. He 5:9. Ja 1:22-25. 4:17. 2 P +1:10. 1 J 2:29. 3:7. Re 22:14.

48 and laid. Pr 10:25. Is 28:16. Mt 7:25, 26. 1 C 3:10-12. Ep 2:20. 2 T 2:19.
digged deep. lit. dug and deepened.
rock. Dt 32:15, 18, 31. 1 S 2:2. 2 S 22:2, 32, 47. 23:3. Ps 95:1. Is 26:4. 1 P 2:4-6.
the flood. 2 S 22:5. Ps 32:6. 93:3, 4. 125:1, 2. Is 59:19. Na 1:8. Jn 16:33. Ac +14:22. Ro 8:35-38. 1 C 3:13-15. 15:55-58. 2 P 3:10-14. 1 J 2:28. Re 6:14-17. 20:11-15.

could not. 2 P +1:10. Ju +24.
for. Ps 46:1-3. 62:2.
49 **that heareth**. ver. 46. Lk 8:5-7. 19:14, 27. Je
44:16, 17. Ezk +33:31. Mt 21:29, 30. 23:3. Jn
15:2. Ja 1:22-26. 2:17-26. 2 P 1:5-9. 1 J +2:3,
4.
built. Ezk 13:10-14.
against. Mt +13:20-22. +24:10. Ac 20:29.
26:11. 1 Th 3:5.
immediately. Pr 28:18. Ho 4:14. Mt 12:43-
45. Mk 4:17. 1 J 2:19.
the ruin. Lk 10:12-16. 11:24-26. +12:47. Am
6:11. He +10:26-29. 2 P +2:20-22.

LUKE 7

1 **when**. Mt 7:28, 29.
he entered. Mt 8:5-13.
2 **centurion's**. Lk 23:47. Mt +27:54. Ac +10:1,
2. 22:26. 23:17. 27:1, 3, 43.
who. Ge 24:2-14, 27, 35-49. 35:8. 39:4-6. 2
K 5:2, 3. Jb 31:15. Pr 29:21. Ac 10:7. Col
3:22-25. 4:1.
was sick. Lk 8:42. Mt 8:6. Jn 4:46, 47. 11:2, 3.
3 **beseeching**. Mk +5:23. Phm 10.
4 **worthy**. ver. 6, 7. Lk 20:35. Mt 10:11, 13, 37,
38. Ga 5:6. Re 3:4.
5 **he loveth**. 1 K 5:1. 2 Ch 2:11, 12. Ga 5:6. 1 J
3:14. 5:1-3.
and. 1 Ch 29:3, etc. Ezr 7:27, 28. 1 J 3:18, 19.
6 **Jesus**. Mt 20:28. Mk 5:24. Ac 10:38.
trouble. Lk 8:49.
for. ver. 4. Lk 5:8. 15:19-21. Ge 32:10. Pr
29:23. Mt 3:11. 15:26, 27. Ja 4:6, 10.
not worthy. Jn 7:49. 1 C 13:4. Ro 12:3. Ph
2:3, 4.
enter. Lk 14:1. Mt 18:17. Ac 10:28.
7 **worthy**. ver. 6. 1 C 13:4.
but. Lk 4:36. 5:13. Ex 15:26. Dt 32:39. 1 S
2:6. Ps 33:9. 107:20. Mt 8:16. Mk 1:27.
8 **under**. Ac 22:25, 26. 23:17, 23, 26. 24:23.
25:26.
one. Gr. this man.
and he goeth. Ac 10:7, 8. Col 3:22. 1 T 6:1,
2.
9 **he marvelled**. Mt 8:10. 15:28.
not in. Ps 147:19, 20. Mt 9:33. Ro 3:1-3. 9:4,
5.
10 **found**. Mt 8:13. 15:28. Mk 9:23. Jn 4:50-53.
11 **And**. Ge +8:22.
he went. Ac 10:38.
Nain. i.e. *beautiful*, **S#3484g**, only here.
Compare Heb. *naah*, **S#4999h**, Ps +23:2 (pastures).
12 **the only**. Gr. *monogenes*, **S#3439g**. Lk 8:42.
9:38. Ge 22:2, +12. Jg 11:34. 2 S 14:7. 1 K
17:9, 12, 18, 23. 2 K 4:16, 20. Ps 25:16, LXX.
Je 6:26. Am 8:10. Zc 12:10. Jn 1:14, 18. 3:16,
18. He 11:17. 1 J 4:9.
and. Ge +8:22.

a widow. Jb 29:13. Ac 9:39, 41. 1 T 5:4, 5. Ja
1:27.
and much. Lk 8:52. Jn 11:19. Ac 11:24, 26.
19:26.
13 **And**. Ge +8:22.
the Lord. ver. 19. Lk 10:1, 39. 11:39. 12:42.
13:15. 17:5, 6. 18:6. 19:8, 31, 34. 22:61. 24:3,
34. Mk 16:19. Jn 4:1.
had compassion. Jg 10:16. Ps 86:5, 15.
103:13. Is 63:9. Je 31:20. La 3:32, 33. Mt
+9:36. Jn 11:33-35.
Weep not. Lk 8:52. Je 31:15, 16. Jn 20:13,
15. 1 C 7:30. 1 Th 4:13.
14 **And**. Ge +8:22.
bier. *or*, coffin. 2 S 3:31.
Young. 1 K 17:21. Jb 14:12, 14. Ps 33:9. Is
+26:19. Ezk 37:3-10. Jn 5:21, 25, 28, 29.
11:25, 43, 44. Ro 4:17. Ep 5:14.
Arise. ver. 22. Lk 8:54, 55. Mt 10:8. 11:5.
27:42. Mk 5:41. Jn 11:43. Ac 9:40, 41.
15 **And**. Ge +8:22.
sat up. Ac 9:40.
he delivered. Lk 9:42. 1 K 17:23, 24. 2 K
4:32-37. 13:21. Jn 19:27. Ac 9:41. Col 4:1. He
11:35.
16 **And**. Ge +8:22.
a fear. Lk +1:65.
they glorified God. Mt +9:8.
a great prophet. ver. 39. Dt 18:15. Mt
+21:11.
is risen. Mt 11:11. Jn 7:52. Ac 13:22.
God hath visited. Lk 1:68. 19:44. Ge
+49:10. Ex 4:31. Ps 65:9. 106:4, 5. Zc 9:9. Jn
3:2.
17 **And**. Ge +8:22.
this rumor. Lk 4:14. Mt 4:24. 9:31. Mk 1:28.
6:14.
18 **And**. Ge +8:22.
disciples of John. Mt 11:2-6. Jn 3:26.
19 **two**. Lk 10:1. Jsh 2:1. Mk 6:7. Ac 10:7, 8. Re
11:3.
Art thou. Lk 18:8.
that cometh. Lk 3:16. Ge +3:15. 22:18.
+49:10. Dt 18:15-18. Ps 40:7. 110:1-4.
118:26. Is +7:14. +9:6, 7. 11:1. 40:10, 11.
59:20, 21. Je +23:5, 6. Da 7:13. +9:24-26. Mi
+5:2. Hg 2:7. Zc 9:9. Ml 3:1-3. 4:2. Mt 3:11.
Mk 1:7. Jn 4:25. +6:14. 11:27. Ro 5:14. He
10:37.
or look we. Lk 3:15.
20 **Art thou he**. ver. +19.
21 **he cured**. Mk 1:34.
plagues. 1 K 8:37. Ps 90:7-9. Mk 3:10. 5:29,
34. Ac 22:24. 1 C 11:30-32. He 11:36. 12:6. Ja
5:14, 15.
evil spirits. *Pneumata ponara*, are here clearly
distinguished from bodily disorders. Gr.
pneuma, Mt +8:16. Lk 8:2. 11:26. Mt 12:45.
Ac 19:12-16.
gave sight. Mt +11:5.

22 **Go**. Jn 1:46. 2:23. 5:36.
  how that. ver. +21. Jn 3:2.
  the lame. Mt +11:5.
  the lepers. 2 K +5:1.
  the deaf. Is +29:18.
  the dead are. ver. 14, 15. Lk 8:53-55. Is
  26:19.
  to the poor. Lk +4:18. 6:20. Is 60:1-3. 61:1.
  Zp 3:12. Mt +5:3. Ja 2:5.
23 **blessed**. Ps 118:22. Mt +11:6. Ac 4:11. Ro
  9:32, 33.
24 **What**. Mt 11:7, 8.
  wilderness. Lk 1:80. 3:2. Mt 3:1-5. Mk 1:4,
  5. Jn 1:23.
  A reed. Ge 49:4. 1 K 14:15. 2 K 18:21. Is
  36:6. Ezk 29:6, 7. 2 C 1:17-20. Ep 4:14. Ja
  1:6-8. 2 P 2:17. 3:17.
25 **A man**. 2 K 1:8. Is 59:17. Mt 3:4. Mk 1:6. 1 P
  3:3, 4.
  are in. 2 S 19:35. 1 K 10:5. 2 Ch 9:4. Est 1:3,
  11. 4:2. 5:1. 8:15. Mt 6:29.
26 **A prophet**. Lk 1:76. 20:6. Mt 14:5. 21:26.
  Mk 6:20. 11:32.
  and. Lk 16:16. Mt 11:9-14. Jn 3:26, etc. 5:35.
27 **This is he**. Mk 1:2, 4.
  written. Lk +24:27.
  Behold. Lk 1:15-17, 76. Ne +9:6. Is 40:3.
  57:14. Ml *3:1*. 4:5, 6. Jn 1:23. Col 1:16.
28 **Among**. Lk 1:14, 15. 3:16.
  born of women. Jb 14:1. 15:14. 25:4. Ga
  4:4.
  not a greater. Lk 1:15. Mt +11:11, 14. Jn
  5:35.
  but. Lk 9:48. 10:23, 24. Mt 11:11. 13:16, 17.
  Jn 7:39. 10:41. Ep 3:8, 9. Col 1:25-27. He
  11:39, 40. 1 P 1:10-12.
  kingdom of God. Lk +4:43.
29 **all the people**. Lk 20:6.
  the publicans. Mt +5:46.
  justified God. ver. 35. Jg 1:7. Ps +51:4, 5. Ro
  3:4-6. 10:3. Re 15:3. 16:5.
  being baptized. Lk 3:12. Mt 3:5, 6. 21:31, 32.
  baptism of John. Ac 18:25. 19:3.
30 **Pharisees and**. ver. 16, 33. Mt 21:25, 32.
  23:13. Mk 11:31.
  lawyers. Mt 22:35.
  rejected. *or*, frustrated. Lk 13:34. 20:6. Dt
  18:15, 19. Je 8:8. Mt 21:32. Mk 7:9. Ro 10:21.
  2 C 6:1. Ga 2:21. 3:15. He 10:28.
  the counsel. Ps 33:11. 107:11. Pr 1:25.
  19:21. Ac 2:23. 13:36. 20:27. Ep +1:11. 1 T
  +2:4. He 6:17.
  against. *or*, within.
  being not baptized. Lk 20:5. Mt 3:5-12.
  21:25. Mk 11:30, 31.
31 **Whereunto**. Lk 13:18, 20. La 2:13. Mt 11:16,
  etc. Mk 4:30.
  liken. ver. 25. Mt 11:16-19.
32 **are like**. Pr 17:16. Is 28:9-13. 29:11, 12. Je
  5:3-5. Mt 11:16-19.

children. Zc 8:5.
  the marketplace. Lk 11:43. Mt +11:16.
  have piped. Pr 29:9.
  have mourned. Mt +9:23.
33 **came neither**. Lk 1:15. Je 16:8-10. Da 10:3.
  Mt 3:4. 11:18. Mk 1:6.
  eating. Pr +31:4.
  nor drinking wine. Lk 1:15.
  He. Mt 10:25. Jn 7:20. 8:48, 52. 10:20. Ac
  2:13.
34 **Son of man**. Lk +5:24.
  eating. ver. 36. Lk 5:29. 11:37. 14:1. Mt 9:10.
  Jn 2:2. 12:2.
  a friend. Lk 15:2. 19:7. Mt 9:11.
  publicans and. Mt +5:46.
35 **wisdom**. Lk 11:49. Ro 11:33.
  is justified. ver. 29. Ps 92:5, 6. 107:43. Pr
  8:32-36. 17:16. Ho +14:9. Mt 11:19. Ro 3:4. 1
  C 2:14, 15.
  her children. Lk 10:6. 16:8. Pr 8:32. Jn 3:33.
  Ro 1:16. 1 C 1:21.
36 **one**. Mt 26:6, etc. Mk 14:3, etc. Jn 11:2, etc.
  And he. ver. 34. Lk 11:37. 14:1.
  sat down. ver. 34. Jn 4:6.
37 **which**. ver. 34, 39. Lk 5:30, 32. 18:13. 19:7.
  Mt 21:31. Jn 9:24, 31. Ro 5:8. 1 T 1:9, 15. 1 P
  4:18.
  a sinner. Lk 15:7. Mt 21:32.
  knew. Gr. *epiginosko*, Mt +11:27.
  an alabaster. Mt 26:7. Mk 14:3. Jn 11:2.
  12:2, 3.
38 **And**. Ge +8:22.
  stood at his feet. ver. 37. Ac 22:3.
  weeping. Lk +6:21. 22:62. Mt +5:4.
  wash. Gr. *brecho*, **S#1026g**. ver. 44. Ge 18:4. Jn
  13:4, 5.
  did wipe. ver. 44. Jn 11:2. 12:3.
  and kissed. ver. +45.
  and anointed. ver. 45, 46. Ec 9:8. SS 1:3. Is
  57:9.
39 **spake within**. Lk 3:8. 12:17. 16:3. 18:4. 2 K
  5:20. Pr 23:7. Mk 2:6, 7. 7:21.
  This man. ver. 16. Lk 15:2. Jn 7:12, 40, 41,
  47-52. 9:24.
  if he were. This kind of "if" assumes the prem-
  ise is contrary to fact, impossible, or unreal,
  although in actual fact it may be true, in present time. For other examples of this kind of "if"
  see Jn 5:46. 8:42. 9:33, 41. 15:19, 22. 18:36. 1
  C 11:31. Ga 1:10. 3:21. He 4:8. 11:15.
  a prophet. ver. +16.
  would. ver. 37. Lk 15:2, 28-30. 18:9-11.
  22:64. Is +65:5. Mt 9:12, 13. 20:16. 21:28-31.
40 **answering**. Lk 5:22, 31. 6:8. Mt 17:25. Jn
  +2:24, 25. 16:19, 30.
  Master. Lk 8:49. 9:38. 10:25. 11:45. 12:13.
  18:18. 19:39. 20:21, 28, 39. 21:7. 22:11. Mt
  +22:24. Mk +4:38. Jn +1:38.
  say on. Lk 18:18. 20:20, 21. Ezk +33:31. Ml
  1:6. Mt 7:22. 26:49. Jn 3:2. 13:13.

41 **a certain**. Lk 11:4. 13:4mg. Is 50:1. Mt 6:12. 18:23-25.
debtors. Lk 16:5.
the one. ver. 47. Ro 5:20. 1 T 1:15, 16.
pence. Mt +18:28mg.
the other. Lk +12:48. Nu 27:3. Je 3:11. Jn 15:22-24. Ro 3:23. 1 J 1:8-10.

42 **when**. Ps 49:7, 8. Mt 18:25, 26, 34. Ro 5:6. Ga 3:10.
nothing to pay. Ge 47:18. Ep 2:8, 9. 2 T 1:9.
he frankly forgave. Ps 32:1-5. +51:1-3. +103:3. Is 43:25. 44:22. Je 31:33, 34. Da 9:18, 19. Ho 14:4. Mi 7:18-20. Mt 6:12. Ac 13:38, 39. Ro 3:24. 4:5-8. 8:32. 11:6. 2 C 2:7, 10. 12:13. Ep 1:7. 4:32. Col 2:13. 3:13.
love. ver. 41.

43 **I**. ver. 47. 1 C 15:9, 10. 2 C 5:14, 15. 1 T 1:13-16.
Thou. Lk 10:28. Ps 116:16-18. Mk 12:34.
rightly judged. Mt 7:1. Jn 7:24. 1 C 2:15. 10:15.

44 **he turned**. ver. 9, 38. Lk +22:61.
Seest. ver. 37-39.
thou gavest me no water. Ge +18:4. Ja 2:6.
for my feet. lit. "Water upon my feet thou didst not give." Ex 30:19, 21. 2 K 3:11. SS +5:3. Is 44:3.
but she. 1 S +17:7.
and wiped. ver. 38.

45 **gavest me no kiss**. Ge +27:27. Mt 26:48, 49. Ro 16:16. 1 C 16:20. 2 C 13:12. 1 Th 5:26. 1 P 5:14.
this woman. Mk 14:8.
to kiss. ver. 38.

46 **with oil**. Ru 3:3. 2 S 14:2. Ps 23:5. 92:10. 104:15. 141:5. Ec 9:8. Da 10:3. Am 6:6. Mi 6:15. Mt 6:17.

47 **Her sins**. ver. 42. Lk 5:20, 21. Ex 34:6, 7.
which are many. ver. 37, 39. Is 1:18. 55:7. Ezk 16:63. 36:29-32. Mi 7:19. Ac 5:31. Ro 5:20. 1 C +6:9-11. 1 T 1:14, 15. 1 J 1:7.
are forgiven. Mk 2:7-10.
she loved much. ver. 43. Mt 10:37. Jn 21:15-17. 2 C 5:14. Ga 5:6. Ep 6:24. Ph 1:9. 1 J 3:18. 4:10, 19. 5:3.
little is forgiven. Ps 5:4. Is +57:15. 64:6. Hab 1:13. Lk 12:48. Ro 3:10, 19, 23. Ga 3:22. Ja 2:10.
loveth little. Ps +9:10. Mt 25:26. Jn 3:30. Jn +14:15. Ro 5:8. 7:13, 18. 10:3. 2 C 5:13-15. Ep 3:8. 2 J +2:3-5. 4:19.

48 **Thy sins**. Lk 5:20. Mt 9:2. Mk 2:5. Jn 20:23. Ac 2:38. Ja 5:15. 1 J 2:12.

49 *Who is this*. Lk 5:20, 21. Mt 9:3. Mk 2:7.

50 **Thy faith**. ver. 9, 47. Lk 8:12, +18, 42, 48. Hab +2:4. Mt +9:2, 22. Mk 5:34. Ro 10:17. Ep 2:8-10. 1 T 1:14. Ja 2:14-26.
go in peace. Lk 8:48. Ex 4:18. Jg 18:6. 1 S

1:17. 20:13, 42. 25:35. 29:7. 2 S 15:9. 2 K 5:19. Ec 9:7. Mk 5:34. Ac 15:33. 16:36. Ro 5:1, 2. Ja 2:16.

LUKE 8

1 **that**. Lk 4:43, 44. Mt 4:23. 9:35. 11:1. Mk 1:39. Ac 10:38.
the glad. Lk 2:10, 11. +4:18. Is +61:1-3. Mt +13:19. Ac 13:32. Ro 10:15.
the kingdom. Lk +4:43. Ro 14:17. Col 1:13.
and the. Lk 6:14-16. Mt 10:2-4. Mk 3:16-19.

2 **certain women**. Lk 23:27, 49, 55. Mt 27:55, 56. Mk 15:40, 41. 16:1. Jn 19:25. Ac 1:14.
spirits. Gr. *pneuma*, Mt +8:16. Lk 7:21.
Mary. Lk 24:10. Mt 27:56, 61. 28:1. Mk 15:40, 47. 16:1, 9. Jn 19:25. 20:1, 18.
Magdalene. Lk 7:45. Mt 15:39.
out. ver. 30. Mk 16:9.

3 **Joanna**. i.e. *whom Jehovah has graciously given*, **S#2489g**. Lk 24:10.
Chuza. i.e. *prophet*, **S#5529g**.
Herod's. Lk 9:7-9. Jn 4:46-53. Ac 13:1. Ph 4:22.
Susanna. i.e. *lily*, **S#4677g**.
which ministered. Lk 7:37, 38. 2 K 4:10. Pr 31:20. Mt 27:55, 56. Mk 14:3. Ac 21:9. Ro 16:1-3, 6, 12. 1 T 5:10.
of their substance. Lk 21:2-4. Ex 35:25. 1 Ch 29:14. Pr 31:20. Is 23:18. Mt 2:11. 25:40. 26:11. Jn 12:3. Ac 9:36-39. 2 C 8:9. Ph +4:17. 1 T 5:10.

4 **when much**. Mt 13:2-13, 18-23. Mk 4:1-20.

5 **sower**. ver. 11. Mt +13:3, 4, 18, 19, 24-26, 37. Mk 4:2-4, 15, 26-29.
fell. ver. 12. He 2:1. Ja 1:23, 24.
it. Ps 119:118. Mt 5:13.
and the. Ge 15:11.

6 **a rock**. ver. 13. Je 5:3. Ezk 11:19. 36:26. Am 6:12. Mt +13:5, 6, 20, 21. Mk 4:5, 6, 16, 17. Ro 2:4, 5. He 3:7, 8, 15.

7 **thorns**. ver. 14. Lk 21:34. Ge 3:18. Je 4:3. Mt +13:7, 22. Mk 4:7, 18, 19. He 6:7, 8.

8 **other**. ver. 15. Mt +13:8, 23. Mk 4:8, 20. Jn 1:12, 13. 3:3-5. Ep 2:10. Col +1:10.
an hundredfold. Ge +26:12. Mt +13:8, 23. 19:29. Mk +10:30.
He that. Pr 1:20-23. 8:1. 20:12. Je 13:15. 25:4. Mt +13:9.

9 **What**. Ho +6:3. Mt +13:10, 18, 36. 15:15. Mk 4:10, 34. 7:17, 18. Jn 15:15.

10 **Unto**. Lk 10:21-24. Ps 25:14. Pr 20:12. Am +3:7. Mt 11:25. +13:11, 12. 16:17. Mk 4:11, 12. Ro 16:25, 26. 1 C 2:7-11. 12:11. Ep 3:3-9. Col 1:26-28. 2:2. 1 T 3:16. 1 P 1:10-12.
kingdom. Lk +4:43.
that seeing. Dt 29:4. Is *6:9, 10*. 29:14. 43:8. 44:18. Je 5:21. Ezk 12:2. Mt +13:14-17. Mk 4:12. Jn 12:40. Ac 28:26, 27. Ro 11:7-10. 1 C 2:14. Ep 4:18.

11 **The seed**. Is +8:20. Mt +13:19. Mk 4:14, etc. 1 C 3:6, 7, 9-12. Col 1:5, 6. Ja 1:21. 1 P +1:23-25.

12 **by the wayside**. ver. 5. Pr 1:24-26, 29. Mt +13:19. Mk 4:15. Ja 1:23, 24.
then cometh. Pr 4:5. Is 65:11. Mt +13:19. Mk 4:15. 2 Th 2:9-14. He 2:1. Re 12:9.
believe. Mk 16:16. Ac 14:9. 15:11. 16:31. Ro 10:9. Ep 2:8.

13 **receive**. Ps 106:12-14. Is 58:2. Ezk +33:22. Mt +13:20, 21. Mk 4:16, 17. 6:20. 10:15. Jn 5:35. Ga 3:1, 4. 4:15-20. Ja 1:21.
with joy. Ps 106:12, 13. Is 58:2. Ezk +33:31, 32. Mk 6:20. Jn 5:35.
and these. Jb 19:28. Pr 12:3, 12. Ep 3:17. Col 2:7. Ju 12.
for a while believe. Lk 22:31, 32. Dt +29:18. Ps 106:12. Ho +4:10. 6:4. Jn +2:23-25. 6:66. 8:30-32. 12:42, 43. 15:2, 6. Ac 8:13-23. 1 C 13:2. +15:2. Ga 1:6. +4:11. 5:7. Col +1:23. 1 Th +3:5. 1 T +1:19. 2 T 2:18, 19. He 10:39. Ja 2:26. 2 P 2:20, 22. 1 J 2:19.
in time. Pr 24:10. Je +12:5. Da 11:33, 35. Ja 1:2.
fall away. Je +1:16. Ezk +33:18. 1 T +4:1.

14 **and are choked**. ver. 7. Lk 16:13. Mt 6:24, 25. +13:22. Mk +4:19. 1 T 6:9, 10, 17. 2 T +4:10, 16. 1 J 2:15-17.
cares. Lk 17:26-30. 21:34.
riches. Lk 18:24, 25.
pleasures. Gr. *heedonee*, **S#2237g**. T 3:3. Ja 4:1, 3. 2 P 2:13.
this life. Mk +4:19.
and bring. Lk 13:6-9. Jn 15:6.
no fruit. 2 P +1:8. Ju 12.
to perfection. Pr 11:30. He 6:1, 9.

15 **in an honest and**. Lk 6:45. Dt 30:6. 2 K +20:3. 1 Ch 12:38. Ps +51:10. Je 31:33. 32:39. Ezk 36:26, 27. Ro 7:18. Ep 2:8. He 4:2. Ja 1:16-19. 1 P 2:1, 2.
heard. Jn 8:47.
the word. Mt +13:23. Jn +8:31. Ac +17:11.
keep. Lk +11:28. Jb +23:11, 12. Ps +1:1-3. 119:11, 127-129. Pr 3:1. Je +15:16. Jn 14:15, 21-24. 15:10. Ro 1:18. 2:7. 1 C 7:19. He 2:1. +3:14. Ja +1:22-25. 1 J 2:3.
bring forth fruit. Ho 14:8. Jn 15:5, 16. Ro 6:22. 7:4. Ga 5:22-26. Ph 1:11. Col +1:6, 10.
with patience. Lk 21:19. Mt +24:13. Ro 2:7. Ph 3:13-15. He +6:11, 12. 10:36. 12:1. Ja 1:4. 5:7, 8, 11.

16 **when**. Lk 11:33. Mt 5:14-16. Mk 4:21, 22. Ac 26:18. Ph 2:15, 16. Re 1:20. 2:1. 11:4.

17 **nothing is secret**. Lk 12:2, 3. Ec 12:14. Mt 10:26, 27. 1 C 4:5. 1 T 5:25.

18 **Take heed**. Lk 9:44. Dt 32:46, 47. Pr 2:2-5. Je 17:21. Mk +4:23, 24. 13:14. Ac 10:33. 17:11. He 2:1. Ja 1:19-25. 1 P 2:1, 2.
how ye hear. Lk 11:28. Dt 28:1, 2, +15. Jb

+37:2. Pr 4:20-22. 23:19. Je +29:19. Mk +4:24. Ja +1:25.
for whosoever hath. Mt +13:12.
from him. Lk 19:24, 26. Mt 7:22, 23. 1 C 13:1-3.
seemeth to have. *or*, thinketh that he hath. Pr +14:12. Ro +12:3. 1 C 3:18. 8:2. 14:37. Ph 3:4. Ja 1:26.

19 **Then came**. Mt 12:46-50. Mk +3:21, 31-35.

20 **thy brethren**. Mt +13:55, 56. Mk +6:3. Jn 7:3-6. Ac 1:14. 1 C 9:5. Ga 1:19.

21 **My mother**. Lk 11:27, 28. Mt 12:49, 50. 25:40, 45. 28:10. Jn +15:14, 15. 20:17. 2 C 5:16. 6:18. He 2:11-13.
which hear. ver. 15. Mt 7:21-26. 17:5. Jn 6:28, 29. 13:17. Ja 1:22. 1 J 2:29. 3:22, 23. 3 J 11.
and do it. Lk +11:28. Ps 119:67. Mt +5:19. +7:21. Jn 14:21. +15:14. 17:6. Ga 5:6. Ja +1:22, 25.

22 **that**. Mk 8:18, 23-27. Mk 4:35-41. Jn 6:1.
Let. Mt 14:22. Mk 5:21. 6:45. 8:13.

23 **he fell**. Ps 44:23. Is 51:9, 10. He +4:15.
came. Ps 93:3, 4. 107:23-30. 124:2-4. 148:8. Is 54:11. Ac 27:14-20.

24 **Master**. Ps 69:1, 2. 116:3, 4. 142:4, 5. La 3:54-56. Jon 2:2-6. Mt 14:30. 2 C 1:9, 10.
perish. Gr. *apollumi*, Mt +2:13.
he arose. Ps 65:7. 104:6-9. 107:25-29. Je 5:22.
and rebuked. Mk +4:39.

25 **Where**. Mt +6:30. Is 43:2. Jn 11:40.
being afraid. Ge 1:9, 10. Jsh 10:12-14. Jb 38:8-10. Pr 8:29. 30:4.

26 **Gadarenes**. Mt 8:28, etc., Gergesenes. Mk 5:1, etc.

27 **met**. Mk 5:2-5.
and ware. 1 S 19:24.
but. Nu 19:16. Is 65:4.

28 **he cried**. Lk 4:33-36. Mt 8:29. Mk 1:24-27. 5:6-8. Ac 16:16-18.
fell. Ge +17:3.
What have. ver. 37, 38. Jg +11:12. Ac 19:15. Ja 2:19.
Son. Mt +14:33.
most high. Ps +7:17. Mt 11:10. Ro 9:5. 1 C 10:9. 1 Th 3:13.
I beseech. Is 27:1. Ja 2:19. 2 P 2:4. 1 J 3:8. Ju 6. Re 20:1-3, 10.
torment. Mt +8:29.

29 **commanded**. Mk 5:8. Ac 19:12-16.
unclean. Mk +3:30.
spirit. Gr. *pneuma*, Mt +8:16.
caught. Lk 9:39, 42. Mk 5:3-5. 9:20-26. 2 T 2:25, 26.

30 **Legion**. Mt 26:53. Mk 5:9.
many. ver. 2. Mt 8:29. Mk 16:9.

31 **they besought**. ver. 28. Jb 1:11. 2:5. Mk 5:10. Ph 2:10, 11.
not command. Mk 5:10.

the deep. S#12g. Mt +25:41. Ro 10:7. Re 9:1, 2, 11. 11:7. 17:8. 19:20. 20:1-3, 14, 15.

32 there an. Le 11:7. Is 65:4. 66:3. Mt 8:30-33. Mk 5:11-13.

besought. Jb 1:10. Ps 62:11. Jn 19:11. 1 J 4:4.

he suffered. 1 K 22:22. Jb 1:12. 2:6. Re 20:7.

33 the herd. Jn 8:44. 1 P 5:8. Re 9:11.

34 they fled. Mt 8:33. 28:11. Mk 5:14. Ac 19:16, 17.

35 and found. Is 49:24, 25. 53:12. He 2:14, 15. 1 J 3:8.

sitting. Lk 2:46. 10:39. Mk 5:15. Ac 22:3.

clothed. ver. 27. Lk 15:17.

in his. Ps +51:10.

right mind. Lk 15:17. Col 1:13. 2 T +1:7.

37 besought. ver. 28. Lk 5:8. Dt 5:25. 1 S 6:20. 2 S 6:8, 9. 1 K 17:18. Jb 21:14, 15. Mt 8:34. Mk 5:17. Ac 16:39.

fear. Lk +1:65.

and he went. Lk 9:5, 56. 10:10, 11, 16. 1 S 18:14. Mk 6:20. Ac 24:25.

38 besought. ver. 28, 37. Dt 10:20, 21. Ps 27:4. 32:7. 116:12, 16. Mk 5:18. Ph 1:23.

saying. Ex 12:25-27. 13:8, 9, 14-16. Ps 71:17, 18. 78:3-6. 107:21, 22, 31, 32. 111:2-4. 145:3-12. Is 63:7-13. Mk 5:19, 20. Ac 9:13-16. Ga 1:23, 24. 1 T 1:13-16.

39 Return. 1 T 5:8.

and published. Lk 17:15-18. Dt 10:21. Ps 66:16. 126:2, 3. Da 4:1-3, 34-37. Mk 1:45. Jn 4:29.

40 that. Mt 9:1. Mk 5:21.

the people. Lk 5:1. 19:6, 37, 38, 48. Mk 6:20. 12:37. Jn 5:35.

received. Ac 2:41. 15:4. 18:27. 24:3. 28:30. Ro +15:7.

waiting. Pr 8:34. Ac 10:33.

41 a ruler. Mt +9:18.

and he fell. ver. +8.

and besought. Mk +5:23. Ac 9:38.

42 one. Lk 7:12. Ge 44:20-22. Jb 1:18, 19. Zc +12:10.

and she. Jb 4:20. Ps 90:5-8. 103:15, 16. Ec 6:12. Ezk 24:16, 25. Ro 5:12.

But. ver. 45. Mk 5:24.

43 having. Le 15:25, etc. Mt 9:20-22. Mk 5:25.

twelve. ver. 27. Lk 13:11, 16. Mk 9:21. Jn 5:5, 6. 9:1, 21. Ac 3:2. 4:22. 14:8-10.

had spent all. Lk 15:14. Ps 108:12. Is 2:22. +55:1-3. Mk 9:18, 22.

neither. Jb +13:4.

44 behind. Lk 7:38.

touched. Dt 22:12. Mt 9:21. Mk 5:27, 28. 6:56. Ac 5:15. 19:12.

immediately. Lk 13:13. Ex +15:26. Ml 4:2. Mt 8:3. 20:34. Lk 13:13.

45 the multitude. Lk 6:19. 9:13. Mk 5:30-32.

46 for. Lk 6:19. 1 P 2:9mg.

47 when. Ps 38:9. Ho 5:3.

she came. 1 S 16:4. Ps 2:11. Is 66:2. Ho 13:1. Hab 3:16. Mt 28:8. Mk 5:33. Ac 16:29. 1 C 2:3. 2 C 7:15. Ph 2:12. He 12:28.

she declared. Lk 17:15, 16. Ps 66:16.

touched him. Mt 14:36. Mk 6:56.

48 Daughter. Mt 9:2, 22. 12:20. 2 C 6:18.

thy faith. Lk 17:19. Mt 8:13. Ac 14:9. He 4:2.

go. Lk +7:50.

49 he. ver. 41-43. Mt 9:23-26. Mk 5:35.

Master. Lk +7:40.

50 believe. ver. 48. Is 50:10. Mk 5:36. 9:23. 11:22-24. Jn 11:25, 40. Ro 4:17, 20.

51 he suffered. 1 K 17:19-23. 2 K 4:4-6, 34-36. Is 42:2. Mt 6:5, 6. Mk +5:40. Ac 9:40.

save. Lk 6:14. 9:28. Mk 5:37-40. 9:2. 14:33.

52 all. Ge 23:2. 37:34, 35. 2 S 18:33. Zc +12:10. Mt +9:23.

she. Mk 5:38, 39. Jn 11:4, 11-13.

53 laughed. Lk +16:14. 2 Ch 30:10. Ne 2:19. Jb 12:4. 17:2. Ps 22:7. 80:6. Is +53:3. Mt 9:24. Mk 5:40. He +11:36.

knowing. Mk 15:44, 45. Jn 11:39. 19:33-35.

54 he put. ver. 51. Mk 5:40.

took. Je 31:32. Mt 9:25. Mk 1:31. 5:41. 8:23. 9:27.

Maid. Lk 7:14, 15. Jn 5:21, 28, 29. 11:43. Ac 9:40. Ro 4:17.

55 her spirit. Gr. *pneuma*, Mt +27:50. 1 K 17:21-23. Ec +12:7. Jn 11:44. Ac 7:59. 1 C 5:5. Ja 2:26.

came again. Ge 45:27. Jg 15:19. 1 S 30:12.

and he. Lk 24:41-43. Mk 5:43. Jn 11:44.

56 were astonished. Lk 2:47. Ac 2:7, 12.

he charged. Mk +1:43.

tell no. Lk +5:14.

LUKE 9

1 he. Lk 6:13-16. Mt 10:2-5. Mk 3:13-19. 6:17-13.

gave. Lk 10:19. Mt 10:1. 16:19. Mk 6:7. 16:17, 18. Jn 14:12. Ac +1:8. 3:16. 4:30. 9:34.

2 to preach. Mk 6:12. 16:15.

the kingdom. Lk +4:43. Mt 3:2. 10:7, 8. 13:19. 24:14. Mk 1:14, 15. He 2:3, 4.

3 Take. Lk 10:4, etc. 12:22. 22:35. Ps 37:3. Mt 10:9, 10. Mk 6:8, 9. 2 T 2:4.

two. Lk 3:11. 5:29. 12:28. Mk 14:63.

4 whatsoever house. Lk 10:5-8. Mt 10:11. Mk 6:10. Ac 16:15.

there abide. 1 T 5:13.

5 whosoever. ver. 48. Ro +15:7.

shake. ver. 53-56. Ne 5:13. Ac 13:50, 51. 18:6.

a testimony. Mt +8:4.

against. 2 Th 1:10. Ja 5:3.

6 preaching the gospel. ver. 1, 2. Mk 6:12, 13. 16:20. Ac 4:30. 5:15.

7 A.M. 4036. A.D. 32.

Herod. Jb 18:11, 12. Ps 73:19. Mt 14:1-12. Mk 6:14-28.

he was perplexed. Lk 21:25. Is 22:5. Mi 7:4. Ac 2:12. 5:24. 10:17.

8 of some. ver. 19. Mt 17:10. Mk 6:15. 8:28. Jn 1:21.

Elias had appeared. Ml 4:5.

prophets. Mt 4:3. 14:2. +21:11. Jn 1:45. 3:2.

9 John. ver. 7.

And he. Lk 13:31, 32. 23:8.

10 the apostles. Lk 10:17. Zc 1:10, 11. Mk 6:30. He 13:17.

he took. Mt 14:13. Mk 2:7. +6:31, 32.

Bethsaida. Mt 11:21. Mk 6:45. Jn 1:44.

11 And. Jn 6:5-14.

when. Mt 14:14. Mk 6:33, 34. Ro 10:14, 17.

and he. Is 61:1. Jn 4:34. 6:37. Ro +15:7. 2 T 4:2.

the kingdom. Lk 8:1, 10. Mt 21:31, 43. Ac 28:31.

healed. Lk 1:53. 5:31. He 4:16.

12 when. Mt 14:15, etc. Mk 6:35, 36, etc. Jn 6:1, 5, etc.

wear away. Lk 24:29. Jg 19:8, 9, 11. Je 6:4.

Send. Mt 15:23, 32.

and lodge. Lk 19:7.

for. Ps 78:19, 20. Ezk 34:25. Ho 13:5.

get victuals. Ps 34:10. 1 T 4:8.

13 Give. Mt +14:17.

have. Pr 11:24, 25.

except. Mt +4:9.

14 Make. Mt +14:19. 1 C 14:40.

16 and looking. Mt +14:19.

he blessed. Lk +24:30.

17 eat. Ps 37:16. Mt +14:20, 21.

were. Ps 107:9.

and there. Mt +14:20. Ph 4:18, 19.

18 as. Lk 11:1. 22:39-41. Mt 26:36.

Whom. Mt 16:13, 14. Mk 8:27-30. Jn 6:68, 69.

19 John. ver. 7, 8. Ml 4:5. Mt 14:2. Mk 6:14. Jn 1:21, 25.

Elias. ver. 8. Mt 17:10. Mk 6:15. 9:11. Jn 1:21.

old. Mt +21:11.

20 whom. Mt 5:47. 16:15. 22:42.

The Christ of God. Mt +16:16.

21 straitly charged. Lk +5:14.

22 Son of man. ver. 26, 44, 56, 58. Lk +5:24.

must suffer. ver. 44. Lk 18:31-34. 24:7, +26. Ge +3:15. Ps ch. 22, 69. Is ch. 53. Da 9:26. Zc 13:7. Mt 16:21. 17:12, 22, 23. Mk 8:31. 9:30, 31. 10:33, 34. Ac 4:25-28. 13:27-29. 1 C 15:4. 1 P 1:11.

be rejected. Jn +12:48.

the third day. 1 C +15:4.

23 If. 1 C +15:2. Lk 14:26, 27. Mt 10:38, 39. 16:22-25. Mk 8:34-38. Jn 8:31. 12:25, 26. Ro 8:13. Col 3:5. 2 T 3:12.

deny. 2 T 2:12, 13. T 2:12.

take up. Ac 14:22. Col 1:24. 1 P 4:13.

daily. Ro 8:36. 1 C 15:30, 31.

follow me. Jn 8:12.

24 will save. Lk 17:33. Jn 12:25. Ac 20:23, 24. He 11:35. Re 2:10. 12:11.

life. Ge +9:5. Gr. *psyche*, here used for the seat of personality, as in He 6:19. 10:39. For the other uses of *psyche*, see Mt +2:20. Is 53:10 with 1 T 2:6.

lose. Gr. *apollumi*, Mt +2:13. Lk 12:4, 5. 13:23, 24. Mt 5:22. +10:28. 16:25, 26. 18:8. Mk 9:43-48. 2 T 2:11, 12. He 4:1. 1 P 4:17, 18. Re +2:11.

his life. Ge +9:5.

25 what. Lk 4:5-7. 12:19-21. 16:24, 25. Ps 49:6-8. Mt 16:26. Mk 8:36. 9:43-48. Ac 1:18, 25. 2 P 2:15-17. Re 18:7, 8.

if he. Mt +5:29.

world. Gr. *kosmos*, Mt +4:8.

lose. Gr. *apollumi*, Mt +2:13.

be cast away. Mt 13:48, 50. +16:26 **(S#2210g)**. Mk 8:36. 1 C 3:15. 9:27. 2 C 7:9. Ph 3:8.

26 whosoever. Lk 12:8, 9. Ps 22:6-8. Is 53:3. Mt 10:32, 33. Mk 8:38. Jn 5:44. 12:43. Ro 1:16. 2 C 12:10. Ga 6:14. 2 T 1:8, 12, 16. 2:12. He 11:16, 26. 13:13. 1 P 4:14-16. Re 3:5.

of him. Lk 13:25-27. Mt 7:22, 23. 1 C 3:15. 2 P 1:11. 1 J 2:28. Re +21:8.

when he cometh. Dt 33:2. Da 7:10, 13. Zc 14:5. Mt 16:27. +24:30, 31. +25:31. 26:64. Jn 1:51. Ac +1:11. 2 Th 1:8-10. 4:16. Ju 14. Re +1:7. 20:11.

his own glory. Lk 24:26. Mt 19:28. 25:31. Mk 10:37. Jn 17:24.

his Father's. Ac 1:4.

holy angels. Zc +14:5. Mt 13:41. 16:27. Mk 8:38. Ac 10:22. Re 14:10.

27 I tell. Mt +16:28. Jn 14:2. 16:7.

some. Jn 21:22, 23.

taste. Lk 2:26. Jn 8:51, 52, 59. He 2:9.

till. ver. 28-35. Lk 21:31, 32. Mt 10:23. 16:28—17:8. 23:36. 24:34. Mk 1:15. 9:1-8. 13:30. 2 P 1:16-18.

see. Lk 22:18. Mt 24:14, 15, 30. Mk 14:25.

the kingdom. Lk +4:43. Ho 12:9.

28 about. Mt 17:1, etc. Mk 9:2, etc.

eight. Le 23:39. Mt 17:1.

sayings. *or*, things.

he took. Lk 8:51. Mt 26:37-39. Mk 14:33-36. 2 C 13:1.

into. ver. 18. Lk 6:12. Ps 109:4. Mk +1:35. 6:46. He 5:7.

29 the fashion. Ex 34:29-35. Ps 104:2. Is 33:17. 53:2. Da 7:9. Mt 17:2. 28:3. Mk 9:2, 3. Jn 1:14. Ac 6:15. Ph 3:7, 8. 2 P 1:16-18. Re 1:13-16. 20:11.

altered. Mk 16:12.

30 two men. Mt 22:32.

with him. Ph 1:23.

which. Lk 24:27, 44. Mt 17:3, 4. Mk 9:4-6. Jn 1:17. Ro 3:21-23. 2 C 3:7-11. He 3:3-6.

Elias. ver. 19. Lk 1:17. Ja 5:17, 18.

31 appeared. 2 C 3:18. Ph 3:21. Col 3:4. 1 P 5:10.

spake. ver. 22. Lk 13:32-34. Jn 1:29. 1 C 1:23, 24. 1 P 1:11, 12. Re 5:6-12. 7:14.
decease. lit. exodus. Dt 3:25-27. 2 P 1:15.

32 **were heavy**. Lk 22:45, 46. Da 8:18. 10:9. Mt 26:40-43. Mk 14:40.
saw his glory. Ex 33:18-23. Is 60:1-3, 19. +66:18. Jn 1:14. 17:24. 2 P 1:16. 1 J 3:2. Re 22:4, 5.

33 **it is**. Ps 4:6, 7. 27:4. 63:2-5. 73:28. Jn 14:8, 9. 2 C 4:6.
and let. Mt 17:4. Mk 9:5, 6.
tabernacles. Le +23:34, 42. Ne 8:15.
not knowing. Mt 20:22. Mk 9:6. 10:38. 14:40.

34 **a cloud**. Ex +13:21. 2 P 1:17.
and they. Jg 6:22. 13:22. Da 10:8. Re 1:17.

35 **a voice**. Lk 3:22. Jn 12:28. 2 P 1:17, 18.
out of the cloud. ver. +34.
This. Lk 3:22. Mt 3:17. Jn 3:16, 35, 36. 2 P 1:17, 18.
hear. Dt 18:15, 18, 19. Is +55:3, 4. Jn 5:22-24. Ac 3:22, 23. He 2:3. 3:7, 8, 15. +5:9. 12:25, 26.

36 **found**. 1 S +13:15.
And they. Lk +5:14. Ec 3:7.

37 **on the next day**. Mt 17:14-21. Mk 9:14-29.

38 **beseech**. Ne +1:5.
look. Mk +5:23.
for. Ge 44:20. Zc +12:10.

39 **lo**. Lk 4:35. 8:29. Mt 17:15. Mk 5:4, 5. 9:20, 26. Jn 8:44. 1 P 5:8. Re 9:11.
spirit. Gr. *pneuma*, Mt +8:16.

40 **and they**. ver. 1. Lk 10:17-19. 2 K 4:31. Mt 17:20, 21. Ac 19:13-16.

41 **O faithless**. Mt +6:30. He 3:19. 4:2, 11.
perverse. Ac 20:30. Ph 2:15.
generation. Mt +24:34.
how long. Mt +17:17.
and suffer. Mk +9:19. He 3:9-11.
Bring. 2 K 5:8. Mt 11:28. Mk 10:14, 49. He 7:25.

42 **the devil**. ver. 39. Mk 1:26, 27. 9:20, 26, 27. Re 12:12.
rebuked. Mk +4:39.
spirit. Gr. *pneuma*, Mt +8:16.
and delivered. Lk 7:15. 1 K 17:23. 2 K 4:36, 37. Ac 9:41.

43 **amazed**. Lk 4:36. 5:9, 26. 8:25. Ps 139:14. Zc 8:6. Mk 6:51. Ac 3:10-13.
mighty. Is +49:26.

44 **these**. Lk 1:66. 2:19, 51. Is 32:9, 10. Jn 16:4. 1 Th 3:3, 4. He 2:1. 12:2-5.
for. ver. 22. Lk 18:31. 24:6, 7, 44. Mt 16:21. 17:22, 23. 20:18, 19. 21:38, 39. 26:2. Mk 8:31. 9:31. Jn +2:19-22. 19:11. Ac 2:23. 3:13-15. 4:27, 28.
into. 2 S 24:14.

45 **understood not**. ver. 46. Lk 2:50. 18:34. 24:25, 26. Mt 13:19. 16:22. 17:13. Mk 6:52. 8:16-18, 32, 33. 9:10, 32. Jn 8:27, 28. 10:6.

12:16, 34. 14:5. 16:17, 18. 2 C 3:14-16.
was hid. Lk 18:34. 24:16.

46 **arose a reasoning**. Lk 14:7-11. 22:24-27. Mt 18:1, etc. 20:20-22. 23:6, 7. Mk 9:33-37. Ro +12:3, 10. Ga 5:20, 21, 25, 26. Ph +2:3, 14. 3 J 9.
should. Lk +1:62.

47 **perceiving**. Lk 7:39, 40. Jn +2:25.
took. Mt +18:2-4. 19:13-15. Mk 10:14, 15. 1 C 14:20. 1 P 2:1, 2.
a child. Lk 10:21. 17:2. 18:16. Mt 11:25. 18:6. 19:13-15. 21:16. Mk 9:42. 10:13-16. 1 C +7:14.

48 **Whosoever shall receive this**. Lk 10:16. Mt 18:5, 6, 10, 14. Jn 12:44, 45. 14:21. Ro +15:7. 1 Th 4:8.
in my name. ver. 49. Mk +9:37.
he that is least. Lk 7:28. 14:11. 22:30. Pr 18:12. Mt +19:28. 23:11, 12. Ph +2:3. 1 P 5:3, 4, 6. Re 3:21. 21:14.

49 **we saw**. Nu 11:27-29. Mk 9:38-40. 10:13, 14. Ac 4:18, 19. 5:28. 1 Th 2:16. 3 J 9, 10.
casting out. Lk 10:17. Mt 7:22. 12:27. Mk 16:17. Ac 3:6. 16:18. 19:13.
we forbad. Nu 11:28. Mt 19:14.

50 **Forbid him not**. Jsh 9:14. Pr 3:5, 6. Mt 13:28-30. 17:24-26. Lk 15:28. Ac 11:2. 2 C 2:7, 10. Ph 1:15-18.
for. Lk 11:23. 16:13. Mt 6:24. 12:30. Mk 9:40, 41. 1 C +12:3. 2 C 6:15, 16.

51 **received up**. Mk +16:19. Jn 17:11. He 12:2.
he stedfastly. Lk 12:50. Is 50:5-9. Ac 20:22-24. 21:11-14. Ph 3:14. 1 P 4:1.
set his face. Ge 31:21. 2 K 8:11. 12:17. Is 50:7. Je 21:10. 42:15. 44:12. Ezk 6:2. 13:17. 20:46. 21:2. 25:2. 28:21. 29:2. 35:2. 38:2. Da 11:17.
to go. Lk 13:22. 17:11. 18:31. 19:11, 28. Mk 10:32.

52 **sent**. Lk 7:27. 10:1. Ml 3:1.
and they. Mt 10:5.
the Samaritans. Lk 10:33. 17:16. 2 K 17:24-33. Ezr 4:1-5. Jn 8:48.
make ready. i.e. to prepare a reception for him.

53 **did not receive him**. ver. 48. Jn 4:9, 40-42.

54 **wilt thou**. 2 S 21:2. 2 K 10:16, 31. Ja 1:19, 20. 3:14-18.
fire. 2 K 1:10-14. Ps +104:4. Mk 3:17. Ac 4:29, 30. Re 13:13.

55 **and rebuked**. Lk 24:25. 1 S 24:4-7. 26:8-11. 2 S 19:22. Jb 31:29-31. Pr 9:8. Mt 16:23. Ro 9:20. Re 3:19.
Ye know. Nu 20:10-12. Jb 2:10. 26:4. 34:4-9. 35:2-4. 42:6. Je +17:9. Mt 26:33, 41, 51. 16:9. Ac 23:3-5. 26:9-11. Ro 12:14, 19. Ja 1:19, 20. 3:10, 16, 17. 1 P 3:9.
spirit. Gr. *pneuma*, Mt +5:3. Nu 14:24.

56 **the Son**. Lk +19:10. Mt 18:11. 20:28. Jn 3:17. 10:10. 12:47. 1 T 1:15.

destroy. Gr. *apollumi*, Mt +2:13.
lives. Gr. *psyche*, Mt +2:20; Ge +9:5.
but to save. Jn 12:47.
And. Lk 6:27-31. 22:51. 23:34. Mt 5:39. Ro 12:21. 1 P 2:21-23.

57 a certain. Ex 19:8. Mt 8:19, 20. Jn 13:37.

58 Jesus. Lk 14:26-33. 18:22, 23. Jsh 24:19-22. Jn 6:60-66.
Foxes. Ps 84:3. 2 C 8:9. Ja 2:5.
hath not. Ge 37:15. 1 C 4:11.

59 Follow me. Mt 4:19-22. 9:9. 16:24.
suffer. 1 K 19:20. Hg 1:2. Mt 6:33. 8:21, 22.

60 Jesus said. Mt +6:2.
Let. Lk 15:32. Je 16:5. Mt 8:22. Ep 2:1, 5. 1 T 5:6. Re 3:1.
the dead. Jn 5:25. Ro 6:18.
but. Jn 21:15-17. 1 C 9:16. 2 C 5:16-18. 2 T 2:3, 4. 4:2, 5.

61 but. Lk 14:18-20, 26. Dt 33:9. 1 K 19:20. Ec 9:10. Mt 10:37, 38. Mk 5:18, 19.
bid them. Is +38:1. Mk 6:46.

62 No. Ge +22:14. Lk 17:31, 32. Ps 45:10. 78:8, 9. Mt +13:20, 21. Jn 6:66. Ac 15:37, 38. Ph 3:13. 2 T 4:10. He 6:1. 10:38. Ja 1:6-8. 2 P 2:20-22.
having put. Lk 10:2.
looking back. Lk +8:13. Ge 19:17. Ex 2:12. Pr 4:25. Ezk 18:24. He 10:38, 39.
is fit. Lk 14:35. He 6:7.
for. Gr. *eis*. Ac +2:38. Col 1:13.
the kingdom. Lk +17:20, 21. Mt 8:11, 12. Jn 18:36. Re 11:15.

LUKE 10

1 these. Mt 10:1, etc. Mk 6:7, etc.
appointed. Is 62:6. Ml 2:7. Ac 20:24, 28. 26:16-18. Ro 12:6-8. 1 C 1:1. 12:7-11. 2 C 5:18. Col 4:17. 1 T 1:12. T 1:3.
other seventy. Ge +46:27.
two and. Ec 4:9-12. Ac 13:2-4. Re 11:3-10.
whither. Lk 1:17, 76. 3:4-6. 9:52. Ml 3:1.

2 The harvest. Mt 9:37, 38. Jn 4:35-38. 1 C 3:6-9.
the laborers. Mt 20:1. Mk 13:34. 1 C 15:10. 2 C 6:1. Ph 2:25, 30. Col 1:29. 4:12. 1 Th 2:9. 5:12. 1 T 4:10, 15, 16. 5:17, 18. 2 T 2:3-6. 4:5. Phm 1.
are few. 1 K 18:22. 22:6-8. Is 56:9-12. Ezk 34:2-6. Zc 11:5, 17. Mt 9:36. Ac 16:9, 10. Ph 2:21. Re 11:2, 3.
pray. 2 Th 3:1.
the Lord. Lk 9:1. Nu 11:17, 29. Ps 68:11. Je 3:15. Mk 16:15, 20. Ac 8:4. 11:19. 13:2, 4. +20:28. 22:21. 26:15-18. 1 C 12:28. Ep 4:7-12. 1 T 1:12-14. He 3:6. Re 2:1.
send forth. Mk 1:12. Jn 10:4.

3 Go. Jn 15:16.
I send. Ps 22:12-16, 21. Ezk 2:3-6. Mt 10:16, 22. Jn 15:20. 16:2. 17:18. Ac 9:2, 16.
wolves. Zp 3:3. Mt 7:15. Jn 10:12. Ac 20:29.

4 neither. Lk 9:3, etc. 22:35. Mt 10:9, 10. Mk 6:8, 9.
and salute. Lk 9:59, 60. Ge 24:33, 56. 1 S 21:8. 2 K 4:24, 29. Pr 4:25.

5 into whatsoever. Lk 19:9.
Peace be. Je +29:7.

6 And if. Mt +4:9.
the Son. Lk 5:34. 7:35. 16:8. 20:34, 36. 1 S 20:31. +25:17. 2 S 7:10. 12:5. Ps 89:22. Is +9:6. Mt 23:15. Mk 2:19. 3:17. Jn 12:36. 17:12. Ac 3:25. 4:36. Ep 2:2, 3. 5:6, 8. Col 3:6. 1 Th 5:5. 2 Th 2:3. 3:16. Ja 3:18. 1 P 1:14. 2 P 2:14.
if. 1 C +15:2.
it shall. Ps 35:13. Is 45:23. 2 C 2:15, 16.
turn. Ps 35:13.

7 in. Lk 9:4. Mt 10:11. Mk 6:10. Ac 16:15, 34, 40.
for the laborer. Ge +29:15. Le +7:7. Dt 12:12, 18, 19. Ps 90:17. 128:2. Pr 14:23. 22:29. Ec 2:24. Mt 10:10. 1 C 9:4-15. Ga 6:6. Ph 4:17, 18. 1 T *5:17, 18*. 2 T 2:6. 3 J 5-8.
his hire. Le +19:13. Nu 18:31. Dt +24:15. Je +22:13. 1 C 9:4, 7-14.
Go not. Mt 10:11. 1 T 5:13.

8 receive you. ver. 10. Ro +15:7.
eat. Ge 43:31, 32. 1 S 28:22-25. 2 S 12:20, 21. 2 K 6:22, 23. 1 C 10:27.

9 heal. Lk 9:2. Mt 10:8. Mk 6:13. Ac 28:7-10.
The kingdom. ver. 11. Lk +4:43.

10 go. Lk 9:5. Mt 10:14. Ac 13:51. 18:6.

11 the very dust. Ne 5:13. Ac 13:51. 18:6.
notwithstanding. ver. 9. Dt 30:11-14. Ac 13:26, 40, 46. Ro 10:8, 21. He 1:3.

12 more tolerable. Mt +10:15.
in that day. Lk 21:34. Is +2:11. Mt 7:22.
for Sodom. Lk 17:29. Mt 10:15. 11:23, 24. Ro 9:29. 2 P 2:6. Ju 7. Re 11:8.

13 unto. Mt 11:20-22.
Bethsaida. Lk 9:10. Mt 11:21. Mk 6:45. 8:22. Jn 1:44. 5:2. 12:21.
for if. 1 C +15:2. Lk 11:31, 32. Ezk 3:6, 7. Mt +11:23. 12:41, 42. Jn 9:41. Ac 28:25-28. Ro 9:29-33. 11:8-11. 1 T 4:2. Ja 4:17.
Tyre. Ezk ch. 26-28. Am 1:9, 10. Mt +11:21.
which. Lk 9:10-17. Mk 8:22-26.
repented. Est +4:1. Jb +16:15.

14 more tolerable. ver. +12. Am 3:2. Jn 3:19. Ro 2:1, 27.
at the judgment. Mt +10:15. 23:33. Jn 5:29. 12:31. 16:8. 1 T 5:24.

15 Capernaum. Lk 4:23, 31. 7:1, 2. Mt 4:13.
which. Ge 11:4. Dt 1:28. Is *14:13-15*. Je 51:53. Ezk 28:12-14. Am 9:2, 3. Ob 4. Mt 11:23.
thrust. Lk 13:28. Is 5:14. 14:15. La 2:1. Ezk 26:20. 31:14, 16-18. 32:18, 20, 24, 27. Mt +10:28. 2 P 2:4.
hell. Gr. *hades*, Mt +11:23.

16 heareth you. Lk 9:48. Mt 10:40. 18:5. Mk

9:37. Jn 12:44, 48. 13:20. 1 Th 4:8.
despiseth you. Ex 16:7, 8. Nu 14:2, 11.
16:11. 1 S 8:7. Mt 25:45. Jn 12:48. Ac 5:4. 1
Th 4:8.
despiseth him. Ml 1:6. Jn 5:22, 23. 1 Th 4:8.
17 **returned**. ver. 1-9. Lk 9:1. Ro 16:20.
even. Mk 16:17.
through thy name. Jn 14:13.
18 **I beheld Satan**. Jn +12:31. Re 9:1.
fall from. Is 14:12. Re 12:9, 12. 20:3, 10.
19 **I give**. Ge +3:15. Ps 91:13. Is 11:8. Ezk 2:6.
Mk 16:18. Ac 28:5. Ro 16:20.
serpents and. Lk 11:12. Dt 8:15. Re 9:3.
the enemy. Mt 13:25, 28, 39. 1 P 5:8.
and nothing. Mt +5:18. Lk 21:17, 18. Is
11:8, 9. Jn 10:28, 29. Ro 8:28, 31-39. He
+13:5, 6. Re 11:5.
hurt. Ro 8:31.
20 **in this**. Mt 7:22, 23. 10:1. 26:24. 27:5. 1 C
13:2, 3.
spirits. Gr. *pneuma*, Mt +8:16.
your names. Ps 87:6. Is 56:5. Je 17:13. Ph
+4:3. Re +3:5.
written. Ex +32:32. Ezr 2:62, 63.
in heaven. Je 17:13. Ph 3:20.
21 **Jesus rejoiced**. Lk 15:5, 9. Is 53:11. 62:5. Zp
3:17.
spirit. Gr. *pneuma*, Mt +3:16. "Spirit" (Gr.
pneuma) denotes that whatever is spoken of
as possessed or done, as being so in the highest degree. Here, "rejoiced in spirit" means
rejoiced exceedingly. For other examples of
this usage see Ac +18:25. 19:21. 20:22. Ro
1:9.
I thank. Mt 11:25, 26. Jn 11:41, 42. 17:24-
26. Ro 14:11. 15:9. Re 7:12.
Father. Lk +22:42.
Lord. Ps 24:1. Is 66:1. Ac 17:24.
thou hast hid. Lk 8:10. Jb 5:12-14. 37:24. Is
29:14. Mt 13:11. 18:3. Mk 4:11. Jn 9:39. Ro
1:22. 1 C 1:19-26. 2:6-8. 3:18-20. 2 C 3:14.
4:3, 4. Col 2:2, 3.
revealed. Lk 8:10. Ps 8:2. 19:7. 25:14. Pr
+8:9. Is 29:18, 19. 35:8. Mt 11:25. 13:11-16.
16:17. 21:16. Mk 10:15. 1 C 1:27-29. 2:6, 7.
Ja 1:5. 1 P 2:1, 2.
unto babes. Lk 9:47. Mt 18:3, 4. 1 C 14:20.
even so. Je 11:5. Ep 1:5, +11.
seemed good. Lk 12:32. Mt 18:14. Ga 1:15.
He 13:21.
22 **All things**. "Many ancient copies add, And
turning to his disciples he said." Mt 11:27.
28:18. Jn 3:35. 5:22-27. 13:3. 17:2, 10. 1 C
15:24. Ep 1:21, 22. Ph 2:9-11. He 2:8.
and no. Jn 1:18. 6:44-46. 7:29. 8:19. 10:15.
14:6-9. 17:5, 25, 26. 2 C 4:6. 1 J 5:20. 2 J 9.
to whom. Jn 17:6, 9, 26.
23 **he turned**. Lk +22:61.
Blessed. Mt 13:16, 17. 16:17.
eyes. Mt +13:16.

24 **many**. Jn 8:56. Ep 3:5, 6. He 2:1. 11:13, 39. 1
P 1:10, 11.
25 **a certain**. Lk 7:30. 11:45, 46. Mt 22:35.
tempted him. Mt +16:1.
Master. Lk +7:40.
what shall. Lk 18:18. Mt 19:16. Mk 10:17-
19. 12:28-32. Jn 6:28. Ac 16:30, 31.
to inherit. Mt 19:16, +29. Ga 3:18.
eternal. Gr. *aionios*, Mt +18:8.
life. Gr. *zoe*, Mt +7:14. Mt +10:28.
26 **What is written**. Is +8:20. Mt 5:19. Ro 3:19.
4:14-16. 10:5. Ga 3:12, 13, 21, 22.
in the law. Mt 12:5. 22:36. Jn 1:45. 8:5, 17.
10:34. 15:25.
27 **Thou**. Dt +6:5. He 8:10.
with all. Mt +22:37.
heart. 2 K +20:3. 1 Ch 12:38.
and. Ge +8:22.
soul. Gr. *psyche*, Mt +22:37.
and thy. Le +19:18.
28 **Thou hast**. Lk 7:43. Mk 12:34.
this do. Le +18:5. Ps +19:11. Mt 19:17. Ro
2:13. 3:19-22. 7:10, 18. Ga 3:12, 13, 21, 22.
Ja 3:2.
29 **willing**. Lk 16:15. 18:9-11. Le 19:34. Jb 32:2.
Ro 4:2. 10:3. Ga 3:11. Ja 2:24.
justify. Lk 16:15.
And. ver. 36. Mt 5:43, 44.
neighbor. Mt 22:39. Jn 1:27. Ro 13:10.
30 **went down**. Jon 1:3. Lk 18:31. 19:28.
Jericho. Lk 18:35. 19:1. Mt 20:29. Mk 10:46.
He 11:30.
fell among. Je 3:2.
stripped him. Mi 3:8.
wounded. Ps 88:4, 5. Je 51:52. La 2:12. Ezk
30:24.
31 **by chance**. Ge +24:44. Ru 2:3mg. 2 S 1:6. Ec
9:11. Mt 10:29, 30.
priest. Nu 8:19. Je 5:31. Ho 5:1. 6:9. Ml 1:10.
Jn 1:19.
he passed. Jb 6:14-21. Ps 38:10, 11. 69:20.
142:4. Pr 21:13. 24:11, 12. Ml 2:7-9. Ja 2:13-
16. 1 J 3:16-18.
32 **Levite**. i.e. *joined, cleaving to*, **S#3019g**. Jn 1:19.
Ac 4:36.
and looked. Ps 109:25. Pr 27:10. Ac 18:17. 2
T 3:2.
33 **Samaritan**. Lk 9:52, 53. 17:16-18. Pr 27:10.
Je 38:7-13. 39:16-18. Mt 10:5. Jn 4:9. 8:48.
came. Le 14:3. He 13:13.
had compassion. Ex 2:6. 32:31-33. 1 S 24:16-
18. 1 K 8:50. Jb 1:9, 21. 13:15. 29:12, 13. Da
3:16-18. 6:10. Mt +9:36. 18:33. Ac 2:44, 45.
4:32-35. Ro 9:1-3. 2 C 8:9. 12:14. He 11:24-26.
34 **went**. ver. 34. Ex 23:4, 5. Pr 24:17, 18. 25:21,
22. Mt 5:43-45. Ro 12:20, 21. 1 Th 5:15.
bound. Ps 147:3. Is 1:5, 6. Mk 14:8.
pouring. Gr. *epicheo*, **S#2022g**, only here.
oil. Dt 28:40. Ps 23:5. Is 1:6. Mk 6:13. Ja
5:14. Re 3:18.

and wine. Jg 19:19. Pr 17:22. 1 T 5:23.
his own. 1 K 1:33.
an inn. Lk 2:7. Ge 42:27. Ex 4:24.
took care. Ac 18:26.

35 **two pence**. Mt +18:28mg.
the host. Ro 16:23.
Take care. Le 19:18. Mt 19:19. Mk 12:31.
Phm 18. Ja 2:8.
whatsoever. Lk 14:13, 14. Pr 19:17.
come again. Lk 19:15.

36 **thinkest**. Lk 7:42. Mt 17:25. 21:28-31. 22:42.
was. ver. 29.

37 **He that**. Pr 14:21. Ho 6:6. Mi +6:8. Mt 20:28.
+23:23. 2 C 8:9. Ep 3:18, 19. 5:2. He 2:9-15.
Re +1:5.
Go. Lk +6:32-36. Mt 5:44. Jn 13:15-17. 1 P
2:21. 1 J 3:16-18, 23, 24. 4:10, 11.

38 **a certain**. Jn 11:1-5, 19, 20. 12:1-3.
Martha. i.e. *who becomes bitter; she was rebellious; lady*, **S#3136g**. ver. 38, 40, 41. Jn 11:1, 5,
19-21, 24, 30, 39. 12:2.
received. Lk 8:2, 3. 19:6. Jn 1:38, 39. Ac
16:15. 17:7. Ro +15:7. Ja 2:25. 2 J 10.

39 **sat at**. Lk 2:46. 8:35. Dt 33:3. Pr 8:34. SS 2:3.
Jn 11:20, 29, 32. 12:3. Ac 22:3. 1 C 7:32, etc.
the Lord's. Lk 7:13.
feet. Lk 7:37, 38. 8:35. Mt 15:30. Mk 5:22,
23. 7:25. Jn 11:32. Re 1:17.
and heard his word. Ho 14:8. Mt +13:23.

40 **cumbered**. Lk 12:29. Jn 6:27. 1 C 7:35.
much serving. Jn 12:2.
came to. Lk 20:1.
dost. Mt 14:15. 16:22. Mk 3:21. 4:38.
Ju +16.
my sister. Lk 9:55. Jon 4:1-4.
serve alone. Mt 8:15. Jn 12:2.
bid her. Lk 12:13. Ro 16:2. Ph 2:14. 4:2.

41 **thou art**. Lk 8:14. 21:34. Mk 4:19. 1 C 7:32-
35. Ph 4:6.
careful. Lk 12:11. Mt 6:25.
many. Ec 6:11. Mt 6:25-34.

42 **one thing**. Lk 18:22. Ps 27:4. 73:25, 28. Ec
3:19. Mk 10:21. Jn 9:25. Ph 3:13. 2 P 3:8.
needful. Ec 12:13. Mt 6:33. 16:26. Mk 8:36.
Jn 6:27. 17:3. 1 C 13:3. Ga 5:6. Col 2:10, etc.
1 J 5:11, 12.
chosen. Dt 30:19. Jsh 24:15, 22. Ru 2:12. Ps
17:15. 119:30, 111, 173. Mt 11:28.
good. Ps 16:5, 6. 73:26. 119:57, 72, 162.
142:5. La 3:24.
which. Lk +8:18. 12:20, 33. 16:2, 25. Mt
+5:6. Mk 14:9. Jn 4:14. 5:24. 10:27, 28. Ro
8:35-39. Ph 1:6. Col 3:3, 4. 1 P 1:4, 5.

LUKE 11

1 **that**. Lk 6:12. 9:18, 28. 22:39-45. Mt 14:23.
Mk +1:35. He 5:7.
teach. Jb 37:19. Ps 10:17. 19:14. Zc 12:10. Ro
8:26, 27. Ep 2:18. 6:18. Ja 4:2, 3. Ju 20.

as John. Lk 5:33.
his disciples. Mt 9:14.

2 **When**. Ec 5:2. Ho 14:2. Mt 6:6-8.
Our. Is 63:16. Mt 6:9, etc. Ro 1:7. 8:15. 1 C
1:3. 2 C 1:2. Ga 1:4. Ep 1:2. Ph 1:2. 4:20. Col
1:2. 1 Th 1:1, 3. 3:11-13. 2 Th 1:1, 2. 2:16.
which. 2 Ch 20:6. Ps 11:4. Ec 5:2. Da 2:28.
Mt 5:16. 10:32.
Hallowed. Lk 1:49. Le 10:3. 22:32. Nu 20:12.
1 K 8:43. 2 K 19:19. Ps 57:11. 72:18, 19.
108:5. Is 8:13. 29:23. Ezk 20:41. 28:22. 36:23.
38:16, 23. Hab 2:14. 1 P 3:15. Re 15:4.
thy name. Le 18:21. 20:3. 21:6. +22:32. Ps
5:11. +9:10. Ml 1:11, 12. Jn 17:6.
Thy kingdom. Lk 10:9-11. Is +2:2-5. Da
2:44. 7:18, 27. Mt 3:2. +4:17. 6:33. +26:29.
Mk +1:15. Ro 14:17. Re 11:15. 19:6. 20:4.
Thy will. Lk 22:41, 42. Jg 10:15. 2 S 15:25,
26. Ps 103:20. Is 6:2, 3. Mt +6:10. 26:39, 42.
Mk 14:35, 36, 39. Ac 21:14.

3 **Give**. Ex 16:15-22. Jb +23:12. Pr 30:8. Is
33:16. Mt 6:11, 34. Jn 6:27-33.
day by day. *or*, for the day. Ne 11:23. Ac
17:11. 2 C 4:16.

4 **forgive us**. Lk 7:48. Ge 50:17. Ex 32:32. Nu
14:19. 1 K 8:34, 36. Ps 25:11, 18. 32:1-5.
+51:1-3. 130:3, 4. Is 43:25, 26. Da 9:19. Ho
14:2. Mt +6:12. 1 J 1:8-10.
our sins. Mt 6:12.
for we. Mt +6:14, 15. 18:35. Mk 11:25, 26.
Ep 4:31, 32. Col 3:13. Ja 2:13.
lead. Lk 8:13. 22:40, 46. Ps 5:4. Je +29:11.
Mt 6:13. 26:41. Mk 14:38. 1 C 10:13. 2 C
12:7, 8. Ja 1:2, 13-17. Re 2:10. +3:10.
but deliver. Ge 48:16. Ps 121:7. Jn 17:15. 2
Th 3:3. 2 T 4:18.

5 **Which of you**. Lk 18:1-8.
at midnight. Mk 13:35.

6 **in his journey**. *or*, out of his way.
have nothing. Ex 4:2. Ps 62:5. Jn 6:9. 2 C 12:9.

7 **Trouble**. Lk 7:6. Mt 26:10. Mk 14:6. Ga 6:17.
the door. Lk 13:25. Mt 25:10.
I cannot. SS +5:3.

8 **Though**. The logical concession signaled here
by "though" is assumed to be a fact. For other
examples of this see Lk 18:4. Mt 26:33. Mk
14:29. 2 C 4:16. 7:8, 12. 11:6. 12:11. Ph 2:17.
Col 2:5. He 6:9.
because of his importunity. Lk 18:1-8.
22:44. Ge 18:32. 32:26. Ex 17:11. Dt 9:18. Is
62:6, 7. Mt 15:22-28. Jn 4:49. Ac 12:5. Ro
15:30. 2 C 12:8. Col 2:1. 4:12. Ja 5:16, 17.
give him. Ps 37:3, 4. Ro 8:32. 2 C 8:9. 9:8. Ph
4:19. Ja 4:2, 3. 2 P 1:3.

9 **I say**. Lk 13:24. Mt 6:29. 21:31. Mk 13:37. Re
2:24.
Ask. 1 K 3:5. Ps 118:5. Je 33:3. Zc 10:1. Mt
18:19. Mk +11:24. Jn 4:10. Ro 12:12. 2 C
12:8, 9. Ep 6:18. Col 4:2. He 4:16. Ja +1:5, 6.
+4:2, 3. 1 J +5:14, 15.

it shall be given you. Ps 84:11. Pr 10:24. Jn 15:7. Ac 10:4. 2 C 1:20. 1 P 3:12. 1 J 3:22.

seek. Lk 13:24. Ps +9:10. 27:4, 8, 9. 32:6. +34:4, 10. 105:3, 4. Pr 2:4. SS 3:1-4. 5:6. Je +29:13. Da 9:3. Jn 1:45-49. Ac 10:4-6. Ro 2:7.

ye shall find. 2 Ch +7:14. Jb 22:27. 33:26. Pr 2:5. Je 33:3.

knock. ver. +8. Lk 12:36. 13:25. 1 S +23:4. 2 K 13:18, 19. Ps +40:17. Is 45:11. 62:6, 7. Ac 12:5-17. Re 3:20.

be opened. Ps +34:15. 143:8. Pr 3:5, 6. 15:8. Jn 1:38, 39. Ac 5:19. 12:10. 2 C 6:2. Col 4:3.

10   **every one**. Lk 18:1. Ps 31:22. La 3:8, 18, 54-58. Jon 2:2-8. Ja 4:3. 5:11.

seeketh. Je 29:13.

knocketh. ver. +8. Lk 12:36. 13:25.

11   **a son**. Is 49:15. Mt 7:9, 10.

ask bread. Lk 4:3. Mt 4:3.

father. Ps 103:13.

or if. 1 C +15:2.

12   **if**. Mt +4:9.

offer. Gr. give.

a scorpion. Lk 10:19. Ezk 2:6. Re 9:3, 10.

13   **If ye**. 1 C +15:2. Lk 18:6, 7.

being evil. Ge 6:5, 6. 8:21. Jb 15:14-16. Ps 51:5. Je +17:9. Mt 7:11. 12:34. Jn 3:5, 6. Ro 3:23. 7:18. T 3:3.

know. Is 49:15. Mt 7:11. He 12:9, 10.

how. Mt 6:30. Ro 5:9, 10, 17. 8:32. 2 C 3:9-11.

your. Mt +23:9.

heavenly. ver. 2. Lk 15:30-32. Mt 5:16, 45. 6:14, 32.

give the. Lk 3:21. Pr +1:23. Is 44:3, 4. Ezk 36:26, 27, 37. Jl +2:28. Mt 7:11. Jn 4:10. 7:37-39. 14:16, 17. Ac 1:4, 5, 14. 2:38. 4:31. 8:15. 2 C 1:21, 22. Ga 4:6. Ep 3:14-19. He 12:9, 10. Ja 1:13, 17.

Spirit. Gr. *pneuma*, Mt +1:18; Jn +3:34.

14   **dumb**. Mt +9:33.

people wondered. Mk +5:20.

15   **He**. Mk +3:22.

Beelzebub. Gr. Beelzebul, and so ver. 18, 19. Mt +10:25.

the chief. Mt 9:34. 12:24. Jn 12:31. +14:30. 16:11. Ep 2:2.

16   **tempting him**. Mt 12:38, 39. +16:1-4. Jn 6:30. 1 C 1:22.

a sign. Lk 21:11.

17   **knowing**. Jn +2:25.

Every. 2 Ch 10:16-19. 13:16, 17. Mt +12:25.

18   **If**. 1 C +15:2.

Satan. Mt 12:26. 1 C 5:5.

ye say. ver. 15. Mt 12:31-34. Ja 3:5-8.

19   **if**. 1 C +15:2.

by whom. Lk 9:49. 1 S 16:23. Mt +6:2. 7:22. 12:27, 28. Mk 9:38. Ac 19:13.

your sons. 1 K 20:35. 2 K 2:3. 4:1, 38. 5:22. 6:1. 9:1.

shall. ver. 31, 32. Lk 19:22. Jb 15:6. Mt 12:41, 42. Ro 3:19.

20   **if I**. 1 C +15:2. Ac 10:38. 1 J 3:8.

the finger. Ex +31:18.

no doubt. Lk 17:21. Mt 19:24. 21:31, 43.

the kingdom. Lk +4:43.

is come. Lk 16:16. +17:20, 21. Mt 4:17. 11:12. 12:28. 21:43. Mk 1:14, 15.

21   **a strong man**. Pr 11:16. Mt +12:29. Mk 3:27.

his palace. Mt 26:3.

22   **when a stronger**. Is 27:1. 53:12. 63:1-4. Jn +12:31.

overcome. Mt 12:29. Jn 16:33. Col 2:15.

his armor. Ep 6:11, 13.

divideth. Is 53:12.

23   **not with me**. Lk 9:50. 18:17. Ex 32:26. Mt 12:30. Mk 9:40. Jn 11:52. He 13:13. Re 3:15, 16.

24   **the unclean**. Mt 12:43-45. Mk +3:30.

spirit. Gr. *pneuma*, Mt +8:16.

he walketh. Jb 1:7. 2:2. 1 P 5:8.

dry places. Lk 8:29. Jg 6:37-40. Ps 63:1. Is 13:21. 35:1, 2, 7. 41:17-19. 44:3. Je 2:6. Ezk 47:8-11. Ep 2:2. Re 18:2.

seeking rest. Pr 4:16. Is 48:22. 57:20, 21.

I will. Mk 5:10. 9:25.

25   **he findeth**. 2 Ch 24:17-22. Ps 36:3. 81:11, 12. 125:5. Mt 12:44, 45. 2 Th 2:9-12. 2 P 2:10-19. Ju 8-13.

26   **spirits**. Gr. *pneuma*, Mt +8:16. Lk 7:21.

more wicked. Mt 23:15.

last state. Zp 1:6. Mt 12:45. 27:64. Jn 5:14. He 6:4-8. 10:26-31. 2 P 2:20-22. 1 J 5:16. Ju 12, 13.

27   **certain woman**. Lk 12:13.

lifted. Lk +6:20. 17:13. Ge +22:13. Jg 21:2. 1 S 11:4. Ac 2:14. 4:24. 14:11. 22:22.

Blessed. Lk 1:28, 42, 48. 1 K 10:8. 2 Ch 9:7.

28   **Yea rather**. Lk 6:47, 48. +8:21. Ps +1:1-3. 119:1-6. Is 48:17, 18. Mt 7:21-25. 12:48-50. Jn +13:17. Ja +1:21-25. 1 J 3:21-24. Re 1:3. 22:7, 14.

blessed. Ja 1:25.

that hear. Lk +8:18. Jb +37:2. Mk +4:24.

the word of God. Lk +5:1. Ac +17:11. 1 Th 2:13.

and keep. Lk 6:46. Le 19:37. 22:31. Nu 15:40. Dt 4:40. +26:16. Ps 119:105. Mt 7:21. Jn +13:17. Ro 2:13. 2 T +3:15-17. Ja 1:22.

29   **when**. Lk 12:1. 14:25, 26.

This is. ver. 50. Is 57:3, 4. Ac 7:51, 52.

generation. Mt +24:34.

they seek. Mt 12:38, 39. 16:1-4. Mk 8:11, 12. Jn 2:18. 6:30. 1 C 1:22.

30   **as Jonas**. Lk 24:46, 47. Jon 1:17. 2:10. 3:2, etc. Mt +12:40.

Ninevites. i.e. inhabitants of Nineveh. **S#3536g**. ver. 30. Mt 12:41.

Son of man. Lk +5:24.

31   **queen**. 1 K 10:1, 2, etc. 2 Ch 9:1. Mt 12:42.

rise. Lk 10:13-15. Is 54:17. Je 3:11. Mt 11:20-24. Ro 2:27. He 11:7.

the judgment. Lk 10:14.
and condemn. Je 3:11. Ezk 16:51, 52. Ro 2:27. He 11:7.
uttermost parts. Ps 2:8. 72:8. Zc 9:10.
to hear. 1 C 1:22.
the wisdom. 1 K 4:29-34. 5:12. 10:23, 24. 2 Ch 1:7-12. 9:22.
a greater. ver. 32. Lk 3:22. 9:35. Is +9:6, 7. Mt 12:6. Col 1:15-19.

32 **men**. Jon 3:5-10.
of Nineve. i.e. *agreeable*, **S#3535g**. only here. For **S#5210h**, Ge +10:11.
in the judgment. Ob +21. Mt +10:15.
they repented. Jon 3:5.
a greater. ver. 31. Jon 1:2, 3. 4:1-4, 9. Mt 12:6. He 7:26.

33 **when**. Lk 8:16, 17. Mt 5:14, 15. Mk 4:21, 22.
a candle. Pr 20:27.
a bushel. Mt 5:15mg.
may see. Mt 5:16. 10:27. Jn 11:9. 12:46. Ph 2:15, 16.

34 **light of**. Ps 119:18. Mt +6:22, 23. Mk 8:18. Ac 26:18. Ep 1:17, 18.
single. Ac 2:46. 2 C 1:12. 11:3. Ep 6:5. Col 3:22.
but. Ge 19:11. Dt 15:9. 28:54, 56. 2 K 6:15-20. Ps 81:12. Pr 23:6. 28:22. Is 6:10. 29:10. 42:19, 20. 44:18. Je 5:21. Mt 20:15. Mk 4:12. 7:22. Ac 13:11. Ro 11:8-10. 1 C 2:14. 2 C 4:4. Ga 3:1. 2 Th 2:9-12.

35 **Take heed**. Pr 16:25. 20:27. 26:12. Is 5:20, 21. Je 8:8, 9. Mt +6:23. Jn 7:48, 49. 9:39-41. Ro 1:22. 2:19-23. 1 C 1:19-21. 3:18-20. Ja 3:13-17. 2 P 1:9. 2:18, 19. Re 3:17.

36 **If**. 1 C +15:2.
no part dark. Jb 11:15. SS 4:7. Je +10:2. Mt +6:23. Ac 20:26. 24:16. 1 C 5:6. 2 C +6:17. 7:1. Ep +5:8, 11, 27. 1 Th 4:4. +5:22, 23. 2 T 2:21. 1 P 3:16. 2 P 3:14.
the whole. Ps 119:97-105. Pr 1:5. 2:1-11. 4:18, 19. 6:23. 20:27. Is +8:20. 42:16. Ho +6:3. Mt 13:11, 12, 52. Mk 4:24, 25. 2 C 4:6. Ep +4:14. Col 3:16. 2 T 3:15-17. He 5:14. Ja 1:25. 2 P 3:18.
the bright shining of a candle. Gr. a candle by its bright shining. Mt 5:16.

37 **a certain Pharisee**. Lk 7:36. 14:1. 1 C 9:19-23.
to dine. Gr. "to breakfast." Lk 14:1. Jn 21:12, 15.

38 **he marvelled**. Mt 15:2, 3. Mk 7:2-5. Jn 3:25.
washed. Gr. *baptizo*, Mk +7:4.

39 **the Lord**. Lk 7:13.
Now. Lk 20:47. Mt 23:25, 26. Ga 1:14. 2 T 3:5. T 1:15, 16.
the cup. Mk 7:4.
but. Lk 16:15. Ge 6:5. 2 Ch 25:2. 31:20, 21. Pr 26:25. 30:12. Je 4:14. Mt 12:33-35. 15:19, 20. Jn 12:6. 13:2. Ac 5:3. 8:21-23. Ja 4:8.
ravening. Lk 16:14. Ps 22:13. Ezk 22:25, 27. Zp 3:3. Mt 7:15.

40 **fools**. Lk 12:20. 24:25. Ps 14:1. 75:4, 5. 94:8, 9. Pr 1:22. 8:5. Je 5:21. Mt 23:17, 26. 1 C 15:36. Ep 5:17.
did. Ge +1:26. +2:7. Nu 16:22. Ps 33:15. 94:9, 10. Zc 12:1. He 12:9.

41 **rather**. Lk 12:33. 14:12-14. 16:9. 18:22. 19:8. Dt 15:8-10. Jb 31:16-20. Ps 41:1. 112:9. Pr 14:31. 19:17. Ec 11:1, 2. Is 58:6-11. Da 4:27. Mt 5:42. 6:1-4. 25:34-40. 26:11. Ac 9:36-39. 10:31, 32. 11:29. 24:17. 2 C 8:7-9, 12. 9:6-15. Ep 4:28. He +6:10. 13:16. Ja 1:27. 2:14-16. 1 J 3:16, 17.
give alms. Mt 6:1.
of such things as ye have. *or*, as you are able. ver. 42. Le 5:7. 14:30. 27:8. Dt 16:17. Ezr 2:69. Ne 5:8. Mt 23:23. Ac 9:36. 11:29. Ro 12:8. 13:8. 1 C 16:2. 2 C 8:12, 14. 9:7. Ga 6:6, 10. 1 T +5:8, 17. He 13:16.
all things. Mt 15:10-20. Mk 7:14, 15, 18-23. Ac 10:15. Ro 14:14-18. 2 C 7:1. 1 T 4:4, 5. T 1:15. Ja 4:8.

42 **woe**. Mt 23:13, +23, 27.
for ye tithe. Lk 18:12. Dt 14:22. Mt 6:19-21. +23:23. Ph +4:17. Col 2:16-23.
and all. i.e. herb of every (tithable) kind.
and pass over. Dt 10:12, 13. 1 S 15:22. Pr 21:3. Is 1:10-17. 58:2-6. Je 7:2-10, 21, 22. Mi +6:8. Ml 1:6. 2:17. Jn 5:42. T 2:11, 12. 1 J 4:20, 21.
judgment. Ps 33:5. Je 5:1. Mi +6:8. Zc +7:9.
the love of God. 1 J 3:17.
these ought. 1 S +15:22. Mt 5:19.
and not. Le 27:30-33. 2 Ch 31:5-10. Ne 10:37, 38. Ec 7:18. Ml 3:8-10.

43 **for**. Lk 14:7-11. 20:46. Pr 16:18. Mt 23:6, 7. Mk 12:38, 39. Ro 12:10. Ph +2:3. Ja 2:2-4. 3 J 9.
love. Ps +11:5.
markets. Lk 7:32. Mt 11:16. 20:3. Mk 6:56. 7:4. Ac 16:19. 17:17.

44 **for**. Nu 19:16. Ps 5:9. Ho 9:8. Mt 23:27, 28. Ac 23:3.
graves. Mt +8:28 (**S#3419g**).
not aware. Nu 19:16. Ep 5:3.

45 **lawyers**. ver. 46, 52. Mt +22:35.
thou reproachest. Lk 18:32. 1 K 22:8. Ps +31:11. Am 7:10-13. Jn 7:7, 48, 49. 9:40, 41. Ac 14:5.

46 **Woe**. Is 10:1. Mt 23:2-4. Mk 7:7, 8. Ga 6:13.
lawyers. ver. 45, 52. Mt 22:35.
lade. Mt 11:28-30. Ac 15:10.
with burdens. Mt 11:30.
grievous. Pr 27:3.
ye yourselves. Is 58:6.

47 **for**. Mt 23:29-33. Ac 7:51, 52. 1 Th 2:15, 16.

48 **Truly**. Mt 23:31.
ye bear. Jsh 24:22. Jb 15:6. Ps 64:8. Ezk 18:19.
allow. Ro 1:32.
your fathers. Ac 7:51, 52.

for. 2 Ch 36:16. Mt 21:35-38. He 11:35-38. Ja 5:10.

49 the wisdom. Lk 7:35. Pr 1:2, etc., 20. 8:1-12, 22, 23, 30. 9:1-3. Mt 11:19. 1 C 1:24, 30. Col 2:3.

I will send. Lk 24:47. 2 Ch +24:19. Ac +1:8. Ep 4:11. Re 16:6.

prophets. 1 C 12:28. Re 18:20.

and some. Lk 21:16, 17. Mt 21:35. 22:6. Jn 16:2. Ac 7:57-60. 8:1, 3. 9:1, 2. 12:1, 2. 22:1, 2, 4, 5, 20. 26:10, 11. 2 C 11:24, 25.

slay and. Mt 5:12. 1 Th 2:15.

50 the blood. Ge 9:5, 6. Nu 35:33. 2 K 24:4. Ps 9:12. Is 26:21. Re 18:20-24.

all the prophets. Ac 10:43.

the foundation. Mt +13:35.

world. Gr. *kosmos*, Mt +4:8.

may. Ex 20:5. Je 7:29. 51:56.

required of. Ge 9:5. 42:22. Dt 18:19. Jsh 22:23. 2 S 4:11. 1 K 2:32. 2 Ch 24:22. Ps 9:12. 10:13. Ezk 3:18. 33:6, 8.

this generation. Lk 21:22. Mt +24:34.

51 the blood of Abel. Ge 4:8-11. He 11:4. 12:24. 1 J 3:12. Ju 11.

Zacharias. 2 Ch 24:20-22. Zc 1:1. Mt 23:35.

perished. Gr. *apollumi*, Mt +2:13.

the altar. Ex +40:6.

the temple. lit. house. Ac 7:47. 2 Ch 35:5. Ezk 40:47.

It shall. Ex +20:5. Je 7:28. 51:56.

52 for. Lk 19:39, 40. Ml 2:7. Mt 23:13. Mk 7:13. Jn 7:42-52. 9:24-34. Ac 4:17, 18. 5:40.

taken away. Je 18:15. Ezk 22:26. Ml 2:7, 8. Mt 23:15.

key. Ps 119:97-105. 1 Ch 9:27. Is +8:20. Je 23:28-30. Ml 2:7, 8. Mt 16:19.

of knowledge. 1 Ch +12:32. Jb +21:14. Ps +49:20. Pr 4:13. +8:10. 23:23. Je +8:7. Da 12:4, 9, 10. Ro 2:20.

ye enter not. Lk 7:30. Mt 5:20. 21:31.

were entering. Lk 14:23.

hindered. *or*, forbad. Ne 4:8. 1 Th 2:18.

53 to urge. Ge 49:23. Ps 22:12, 13. Is 9:12. Mk 6:19.

to speak. Lk 20:20, 27. Je 18:18. 20:10. 1 C 13:5.

54 Laying wait. Lk 20:20. Dt 19:11. Is 29:21. La 4:19. Mt 12:10. Mk 3:2. Jn 8:6. Ac 23:21.

seeking. Ps 37:32, 33. 56:5, 6. Mt 22:15, 18, 35. Mk 12:13.

LUKE 12

1 mean time. Ac 26:12.

when. *Lk 11:29*.

an innumerable. Lk +5:15. Ps 3:6. Ac 21:20. 1 C 4:15.

trode. 2 K 7:17.

first. 1 C 15:3. Ja 3:17.

Beware. Mt 16:6-12. Mk 8:15, etc. Ac 5:35.

the leaven. Lk 13:20, 21. Mt +13:33. 1 C 5:6-8. Ga 5:9.

which. ver. 56. Lk 11:44. Jb +8:13. Mt +6:2. 23:28. Mk 12:15. Ga 2:13. 1 T 4:2. Ja 3:17. 1 P 2:1.

2 nothing covered. Lk 8:17. Ec 12:14. Is 45:19. 48:16. Mt 10:26. Mk 4:22. Jn 15:15. 18:20. Ro 2:16. 1 C 4:5. 2 C 5:10. 1 T 5:25. Re 20:11, 12.

3 whatsoever. Jb 24:14, 15. Ec 10:12, 13, +20. Ezk 33:30. Mt 12:36. Ju 14, 15.

in closets. Ge 43:30. Jg 16:9. 1 K 20:30. 22:25. 2 K 9:2. 2 Ch 18:24. Mt +6:6. 24:26.

housetops. Dt +22:8.

4 my friends. SS 5:1, 16. Is 41:8. Jn 15:14, 15. Ja 2:23.

Be not afraid. Ps +34:4. Pr 29:25. Is 8:12, 13. 51:7-13. Je 1:8, 17. 26:14, 15. Ezk 2:6. 3:9. Da 3:16, 17. Mt +10:28. Ac 4:13. 20:24. Ph 1:28. 2 T +1:7. He +13:6. 1 P 3:14. Re 2:10.

5 forewarn. Mk 13:23. 1 Th 4:6.

Fear him. Dt +6:2.

after he hath killed. Mt 10:28. Ja 4:12.

power. Ps 9:17. Mt +10:28. 25:41, 46. 2 P 2:4. Re 20:14.

hell. Gr. *gehenna*, Mt +5:22. Re +20:15.

6 five. Mt 10:29mg.

and not one. ver. 24, 27. Jb 38:41. Ps 50:10, 11. 113:5, 6. 145:15, 16. 147:9.

forgotten. Ps +13:1.

7 the very hairs. Lk 21:18. 1 S 14:45. 2 S 14:11. 1 K 1:52. Da 3:27. Mt 10:30. Ac 27:34.

Fear not. ver. +32. Ps +34:4. 2 T +1:7.

ye are. ver. 24. Jb 35:11. Ps 8:6. Is 43:3, 4. Mt 6:26. 10:31. 12:12. 1 C 9:9, 10.

8 Whosoever. 1 S 2:30. Ps 119:46. Mt +10:32, 33. Ro 10:9, 10. 2 T 2:12. He 10:35. 1 J 2:23. Re 2:10, 13. 3:4, 5.

him shall. Ml 3:17.

Son of man. Lk +5:24.

confess before. Lk 15:10. Mt 10:32, 33. 25:31-34. 1 T 5:21. Ju 24, 25. Re 3:5.

angels. Lk 16:22.

9 he. Lk 9:26. Mt 10:33. Mk 8:38. Ac 3:13, 14. 2 T 2:12. 2 P 2:1. 1 J 2:23. Re 3:8, 10, 12.

that denieth. Gr. *arneomai*, **S#720g**. Rendered (1) *deny*: Mt 10:33. 26:70, 72. Mk 14:68, 70. Lk 8:45. 12:9. 22:57. Jn 1:20. 18:25, 27. Ac 3:13, 14. 4:16. 1 T 5:8. 2 T 2:12, 13. 3:5. T 1:16. 2:12. 2 P 2:1. 1 J 2:22, 23. Ju 4. Re 2:13. 3:8. (2) *refuse*: Ac 7:35. He 11:24.

shall. Lk 13:25-27. Mt 7:23. 25:12, 31, 41. 1 J 2:23, 28.

be denied. Gr. *aparneomai*, **S#533g**. lit. utterly denied. Mt 16:24. 26:34, 35, 75. Mk 8:34. 14:30, 31, 72. Lk 9:23. 12:9. 22:34, 61.

before the angels. ver. 8.

10 whosoever shall. Lk 23:34. Mt +12:31, 32. He 6:4-8. +10:26-31. 1 J 5:16.

against. Lk 7:34. Mt 11:19. Jn 7:12. 9:24.

Son of man. Lk +5:24.
shall be forgiven. 1 T 1:12, 13.
blasphemeth. Le +24:11.
Ghost. Gr. *pneuma*, Mt +3:16. Is +63:10.
shall not. Mt +12:31, 32. Mk 3:28, 29. He 3:7-11. +10:26-29. 1 J +5:16.

11 **when they**. Lk 21:12-14. Mt 10:17-20. 23:34. Mk 13:9-11. Ac 4:5-7. 5:27-32. 6:9-15.
magistrates. Lk 20:20. T 3:1.
and powers. Ro 13:1.
no thought. ver. 22. Lk 21:14. Mt 6:25.
shall answer. Ac 19:33.

12 **shall teach**. Lk 21:15. Ex 4:11, 12. Mt 10:19, 20. Mk 13:11. Jn 14:26. 15:26. Ac 4:8. 6:8, 10. 7:2, etc., 55. ch. 26. 2 T 4:17.

13 **And one**. Lk 11:27.
Master. Lk 6:45. Ps 17:14. Ezk 33:31. Ac 8:18, 19. 1 T 6:5.

14 **Man**. Lk 5:20. 22:58, 60. Mi +6:8. Ro 2:1, 3. 9:20.
who made. Ex 2:14. Jn 5:27. 6:15. 8:11. 18:35, 36. Ac 7:27.

15 **Take heed**. Lk 8:14. 16:14. 21:34. Jsh 7:21. Jb 31:24, 25. Ps +10:3. 62:10. 119:36, 37. Pr 23:4, 5. 28:16. Je 6:13. 22:17, 18. Mi 2:2. Hab 2:9. Mt +13:22. Mk 7:22. 1 C 5:10, 11. 6:10. Ep 5:3-5. Col 3:5. 1 T 6:6-11. 2 T 3:2. He +13:5. 2 P 2:3, 14.
for. ver. 22. Jb 2:4. Ps 37:16. Pr 15:16. 16:16. Ec 4:6-8. 5:10-16. Mt 6:25, 26. 1 T 6:6-8.
abundance. Pr 23:4.

16 **The ground**. Ge +26:12-14. 41:47-49. Jb 12:6. Ps 49:16-20. 73:3, 12. Ho 2:8. Mt +5:45. Ac 14:17. Ja +5:1-3.

17 **What**. ver. 22, 29. Lk 10:25. 16:3. Ac 2:37. 16:30.
shall. ver. 33. Lk 3:11. 11:41. 14:13, 14. 16:9. 18:22. 19:17. Ec 5:10. 11:2. Is 58:7. Mt 5:42. Ro 12:13. 2 C 9:6-15. 1 T +6:17, 18. 1 J 3:16, 17.

18 **This will**. ver. 21. Lk 16:4, 6. Ps 17:14. Ja 3:15. 4:15.
barns. ver. 24. Mt 6:26.

19 **soul**. Gr. *psyche*, Mt +12:18; Nu +23:10. Ps +103:1, 2. 104:1. 146:1. Is 42:1.
Soul. Gr. *psyche*, Mt +12:18. The absurdity of the assertion of some, that "soul" invariably means "breath," or "life," can be seen by the use of "soul" here. Dt 6:11, 12. 8:12-14. Jb 31:24, 25. Ps 49:5-13, 18. 52:5-7. 62:10. Pr 18:11. 23:5. Is 5:8. Ho 12:8. Hab 1:16. Mt 6:19-21. 1 T 6:17. Ja +5:1-3.
much goods. Dt 8:17.
for many. Jb 14:1. Pr 27:1. Ja 4:13-15.
take. Lk 16:19. 21:34. Jb 21:11-13. Ec 2:24. 11:9. Is 5:11, 12. 22:13, 14. Am 6:3-6. 1 C 15:32. Ph 3:19. 1 T 5:6. 2 T 3:4. Ja 5:5. 1 P 4:3. Re 18:7.
be merry. Lk 15:23.

20 **God**. Lk 16:22, 23. Ex 16:9, 10. 1 S 25:36-38. 2 S 13:28, 29. 1 K 16:9, 10. Jb 20:20-23. 27:8.

Ps 73:19, 20. 78:30, 31. Da 5:1-6, 25-30. Na 1:10. Mt 24:48-51. 1 Th 5:3.
Thou fool. Lk 11:40. Je +17:11. Mt 16:26. Ja 4:14.
this night. Ps +102:24. 1 C 11:30.
thy soul shall be required of thee. *or*, do they require thy soul. Jb 27:8. Ps 49:19.
soul. Gr. *psyche*, Mt +2:20.
then. Est 5:11. 8:1, 2. Jb 27:16, 17. Ps 39:6. 49:6-10, 16-19. 52:5-7. Pr 11:4. 28:8. Ec 2:18-22. 4:8. 5:14-16. Je 17:11. Da 5:28. 1 T 6:7.

21 **he**. ver. 33. Lk 6:24. Ps 52:7. Ho 10:1. Hab 2:9. Mt 6:19-21. Ro 2:5. 1 T 6:19. Ja +5:1-3.
rich. Lk 16:11. 2 C 6:10. 1 T 6:17-19. Ja +2:5. Re 2:9.

22 **Take**. ver. 11, 25, 26, 29. Lk 10:41. 1 S 9:5. 10:2. Ps 55:22. Mt 6:25, 27, 28, 31, 34. 10:19. 13:22. Mk 13:11. 1 C 7:32-34. 12:25. Ph 2:20. 4:6. 1 T +5:8. He +13:5. 1 P 5:7.
life. Gr. *psyche*, Mt +2:20; Ge +9:5. Lk 9:24. 14:26. Le 17:11. 2 S 14:7. Est 8:11.

23 **life**. Gr. *psyche*, Mt +2:20; Ge +9:5.
is more. Ge 19:17. Jb 1:12. 2:4, 6. Pr 13:8. Ac 27:18, 19, 38.

24 **the ravens**. 1 K 17:1-6. Jb 12:7-9. 38:41. Ps 145:15, 16. 147:9. Mt 6:26.
God feedeth. Ro 8:32. 1 T 5:8.
how. ver. 7, 30-32. Jb 35:11. Mt 10:31.

25 **taking thought**. ver. +22. Mt 5:36. 6:27.
stature. Lk 2:52. 19:3. Ps 39:5.

26 **If**. 1 C +15:2.
not able. Je +12:5.
why. ver. 29. Ps 39:6. Ec 7:13. 1 P 5:7.

27 **the lilies**. ver. 24. Ho 14:5. Mt 6:28-30. Ja 1:10, 11.
that. 1 K 10:1-13. 2 Ch 9:1-12.
not arrayed. Jn 13:4.
like one. Lk 15:7, 10. Mt 18:10. 25:40, 45.

28 **If**. 1 C +15:2.
which. 1 P +1:24.
how much more. Ps 23:1. +37:3. 84:11. Ro 8:32. Ph 4:19. He +13:5.
O ye. Mt +6:30.

29 **seek**. ver. 22. Lk 10:7, 8. 22:35. Mt 6:31.
neither, etc. *or*, live not in careful suspense. Ja 1:6.

30 **all**. Mt 5:47. 6:32. Ep 4:17. 1 Th 4:5. 1 P 4:2-4.
the nations. Mt 6:7, 8.
world. Gr. *kosmos*, Mt +4:8.
seek. Mt +6:22.
your. ver. 32. Mt 6:1, 8, 32. 10:20. 18:14. Jn 20:17.

31 **rather seek**. Lk 10:42. 1 K 3:11-13. Ps 34:9, 10. 37:3, 19, 25. 84:11. Is 33:15, 16. Mt 5:6, 20. 6:33. Jn 6:27. Ro 8:31, 32. 14:17. 1 C 12:31. 1 T 4:8. He +13:5.
the kingdom. Lk +4:43. 11:2. Mt 6:10.
be added. 1 K 3:11-14. Ps 37:4, 25. Mk +10:29, 30. 1 T 4:8. 1 P 3:9.

32 Fear not. ver. 7. Ge +15:1.
  little flock. Ps 23:1. Is 41:14mg. 53:6. Ezk +34:31. Zc +13:7. Mt +7:14, 15. 18:12-14. 20:16. 26:31. Jn 10:16, 26-30. Ac 20:28, 29. 1 P 5:2, 3.
  it is. Lk 2:14. 10:21. Mt 11:25-27. Ep 1:5-9. Ph 2:13. 2 Th 1:11.
  good pleasure. Mt 18:14.
  to give. Lk 3:11. +6:38. Mt 5:42. 10:8. 21:43. Mk 10:40. Ac 20:35. 2 C 5:2. Ph 3:20. Col 1:5. 2 T 4:8. T 2:13. He 10:34-37. 1 P 1:4, 5, 7. 1 J 3:2, 3. Re 21:2.
  the kingdom. Lk 6:20. 13:29. 22:28-30. Je 3:19. Mt +5:5. +8:11. +13:19, 43. 25:34. Jn +14:2. 18:36. Ro 5:17. 6:23. 8:28-32. 1 C 6:2. Ep +1:11, 18. 1 Th 2:12. 2 Th 1:5. 2 T 4:1. He 12:28. Ja +2:5. 1 P 1:3-5. 2 P 1:10, 11. Re 1:6. 2:26-28. 3:21. 20:4. 22:5.

33 Sell. Lk 18:22. Mt 19:21. Ac 2:45. 4:34, 35. 1 C 7:30. 2 C 8:2.
  give alms. Lk 11:41.
  provide. Lk 16:9. Hg 1:6. Mt 6:19-21. Jn 12:6. 1 T 6:17-19. Ja +5:1-3.
  a treasure. Dt +28:12. ver. 21. Mt 6:20. 1 P 1:4.
  faileth not. Lk 16:9.
  neither moth. Ja 5:2, 3.

34 where. Mt 6:21. 1 C 7:32-34. 2 C 4:17, 18. Ph 3:20. Col 1:5. 3:1-3. 1 J 2:15-17.

35 your loins. 1 K 18:46. 2 K 4:29. 9:1. Jb 12:21mg. 38:3. 40:7. Pr 31:17. Is 5:27. 11:5. Jn 13:4. 21:7, 18. Ac 12:8. Ep 6:14.
  be girded. Lk 17:8. Ex 12:11. Ps +18:32. Je 1:17. Ph 3:20. 2 T 2:4. 1 P 1:13.
  your lights. Mt 5:16. 25:1, 4-10. Ph 2:15.

36 men. Lk 2:25-30. Ge 49:18. Is 64:4. La 3:25, 26. Mt 24:42-44. Mk 13:34-37. Ja 5:7, 8. 2 P 1:13-15. Ju 20, 21.
  that wait. Lk 23:51. Ps 40:1. Ph 3:20. 1 Th 1:10. 2 P 3:12.
  return. Mt 22:1, etc. 25:1, etc. Ph 1:23. 2 T 4:6.
  when. SS 5:5, 6.
  and knocketh. Lk 11:10. 13:25. Re 3:20.
  open. 1 Ch 9:19, 22. Mk 13:34.

37 Blessed. ver. 43. Lk +21:36. Mt +24:45-47. 25:20-23. Ph 1:21, 23. 2 T 4:7, 8. 1 P 5:1-4. 2 P 1:11. 3:14. Re +14:13.
  watching. Lk +21:36. Mt +15:14. 1 C 10:12. Ep +4:27. 5:15, 16. 6:10. 1 T 6:12. 2 T 2:3.
  verily. Mt +5:18.
  that. Is 62:5. Je 32:41. Zp 3:17. Jn 12:26. 13:4, 5. 1 C 2:9. Re 3:21. 7:17. 14:3, 4. 19:9.
  gird himself. ver. +35. Lk 17:8.
  sit down. Lk 22:27.
  and serve. Mt 21:28.

38 And if. Mt +4:9.
  shall come. Mt 25:6. 1 Th 5:4, 5.
  second watch. Our nine o'clock till midnight. Ex 14:24. Jg 7:19. Mt +14:25. Mk 13:35.

third watch. Our midnight to 3 a.m. Mk 13:35, cockcrowing.

39 this know. Mt +6:2. +24:43, 44.
  if. Mt +11:21.
  the thief. 1 Th 5:2-4. 2 P 3:8-10. Re 3:3. 16:15.
  broken through. Ex 22:2. Jb 24:16. Je 2:34. Ezk 12:5. Mt 6:19, 20. 24:43.

40 ready. ver. 47. Lk +21:34-36. Mt 24:42, 44. 25:10, 13. Mk 13:33-36. Ro 13:11, 14. 1 Th 5:6. 2 P 3:12-14. Re 19:7.
  Son of man. Lk +5:24.
  cometh. Lk 21:27. Mt +16:27.
  when ye think not. Lk +21:34, 36. Mk +13:32, 33.

41 Lord. Mk 13:37. 14:37, 38. 1 P 4:7. 5:8.
  unto all. ver. 47, 48. Mk 13:37.

42 the Lord. Lk 7:13.
  Who then is. Lk 19:15-19. Mt +24:45, 46. 25:20-23. 1 C 4:1, 2. T 1:7.
  faithful. Ge +18:19. Ps 101:2, 6. Is +32:20. Je +23:28. Mt +24:45. +25:21.
  wise. Gr. *phronimos*, **S#5429g**. ver. 42. Lk 16:8. Da +11:33. 12:3. Mt 7:24. 10:16. 24:45. +25:2, 4, 8, 9. Ro 11:25. 12:16. 1 C 4:10. 10:15. 2 C 11:19.
  steward. Lk 16:1-12. Mt 20:8. 1 C 4:1, 2. 1 P 4:10.
  ruler. 1 T 3:15. 5:17. He 3:5. 13:7, 17.
  to give. Je 23:4. Ezk 34:3. Mt +13:52. Jn 21:15-17. Ac +20:28. 1 P 5:1-4.
  portion. 2 Ch 31:14-16. Ne 13:13. Pr 31:15.
  in due season. Ge +17:21 (**S#4150h**). Le 23:2. Nu 28:2. Pr 15:23. Ec 10:17. Is 50:4. Mt +24:45. 2 T 4:2.

43 Blessed. Jn 13:17. Re 16:15.
  whom. ver. 37.
  so doing. Mt 5:16. Jn 15:8. Ac 10:38. T 3:8.

44 that he will. Lk 19:17-19. 22:29, 30. Ps +149:6-9. Da +12:2, 3. Mt +24:47. 25:21, 23. Re 3:21.

45 and if. Mt +4:9. Ezk 12:22, 27, 28. Mt 24:48-50. 2 P 2:3, 4.
  his heart. Mt +5:8.
  delayeth. Ec 8:11. Hab 2:3. Mt 25:5. He 10:37. 2 P 3:4, 9.
  and shall. Ge +8:22. He 12:14. 2 P 3:14.
  to beat. Is 65:5. Je 20:2. Ezk 34:3, 4. Mt 22:6. 2 C 11:20. 3 J 9, 10. Re 13:7-10, 15-17. 16:6. 17:5, 6. 18:24.
  to eat. Is 56:10-12. Ezk 34:8. Jn 2:10. Ro 16:18. Ph 3:18, 19. 2 P 2:13, 19. Ju 12, 13. Re 18:7, 8.
  be drunken. Ec 10:17. 1 Th 5:7.

46 lord. ver. 19, 20, 40. 2 P 3:12, 14. Re 16:15.
  and. Ge +8:22.
  cut him in sunder. *or*, cut him off. 2 S 12:31. 1 Ch 20:3. Ps 37:9. 94:14. Is +33:14. Am 1:3. Mt +24:51. 2 Th 2:8, 12. He 6:8. 11:37. 2 P 2:1-3. Ju 4, 13. Re 6:16.

and will appoint. Jb 20:29. Ps 11:5. Mt 7:22, 23. +13:41, 42, 49, 50.

portion with. Ro +2:12. Re 21:8.

the unbelievers. Mt 24:51.

47 knew. Lk 10:12-15. Nu 15:30, 31. 2 Ch 33:9. Mt 11:22-24. Jn 9:41. 12:48. 15:22-24. 19:11. Ac 17:30. 22:14. 2 C 2:15, 16. Ja 4:17. 2 P 2:21.

prepared not. ver. 40. Ge 18:25. Ezk 18:4, 20. Am +4:12. Ro 2:12. He +9:27.

shall. Dt 25:2, 3.

with many. Mk 12:40. Re 18:6, 7.

48 knew not. Le 5:17. Nu 15:29, 30. Dt 11:2. Ac 17:30. Ro 1:19, 20. 2:12-16. 1 T 1:13.

few stripes. Jon 4:11. Mt +10:15. Ac 17:30. 1 T 1:13.

For. Ge 39:8, etc. Mt +13:12. Jn 15:22. 1 C 9:17, 18. 1 T 1:11, 13. 6:20. T 1:3. Ja 3:1.

49 am come. ver. 51-53. Lk +19:10.

send fire. Lk +3:16. Is 11:4. Jl +2:30, 31. Mt +3:11. 10:34-36. 2 P 3:7, 10-12.

and what. Lk 11:53, 54. 13:31-33. 19:39, 40. Jn 9:4. 11:8-10. 12:17-19.

if it. Mt +23:30.

kindled. Ps 78:21. Ml 3:2.

50 I have. Mt 20:17-22. Mk 10:32-38.

and how. Ps 40:8. Jn 4:34. 7:6-8, 10. 10:39-41. 12:27, 28. 18:11. 19:30. Ac 20:22.

straitened. *or*, pained. Ac 18:5. 2 C 5:14. Ph 1:23.

till. Jn 12:27. 19:28, 30.

51 give peace. ver. 49. Zc 11:7, 8, 10, 11, 14. Mt 10:34-36. 24:7-10.

Nay. Re 6:4.

division. Lk 11:17. Jn 7:12, 43. 9:16, 10:19. 17:23. 1 C 1:10.

52 there shall be. Ps 41:9. Mi 7:5, 6. Jn 7:41-43. 9:16. 10:19-21. 15:18-21. 16:2. Ac 13:43-46. 14:1-4. 28:24.

house divided. Jsh 23:12. 2 P 2:21.

53 son against the father. Lk +24:27. Ezk 22:7. Mi 7:6. Zc 13:2-6. Mt 10:21, 22. 24:10.

54 When. Ge +9:14. 1 K 18:44, 45. Mt 16:2, etc.

cloud. Ge +9:13. 1 K 18:43, 44.

55 when ye see. Ge +9:14. Jb 37:17.

will be heat. Ge 31:40. Is 49:10. Ezk 17:10. Jon 4:8. Mt 20:12. Ja 1:11.

56 hypocrites. Mt +6:2.

ye can discern. Ge +9:14. 1 Ch +12:32. Mt 11:25. 16:3. 24:32, 33.

face. Ge +1:2.

not discern this time. Lk 19:42-44. Ge +49:10. 1 Ch +12:32. Ps 32:6. +74:9. Da +9:24-26. Is 35:4-6. 55:6. Hg 2:7. Ml 3:1. 4:2. Mt 3:1-3. Ac 3:24-26. Ga 4:4.

57 why even. Dt 32:29. Mt 15:10-14. 21:31, 32. Ac 2:40. 13:26-38. 1 C 11:14.

of yourselves. Lk 21:30. Jb 32:8. Ps +102:18. Pr 18:1. Is +8:20. Je 23:28. Da +11:33. Jn +6:14. 7:49. Ro +1:19. 1 P 1:20. 1 J 2:27.

judge ye. Jn +5:39. +7:24. Ac 4:19. +17:11 1 C 10:29. 11:13. 14:29. 1 Th 5:21. 1 J 4:1.

58 thou goest. ver. 13, 14. Pr 25:8, 9. Mt 5:23-26.

thine adversary. Lk 18:3. Mt 5:25. 1 P 5:8.

give diligence. Lk 14:31, 32. Ge 32:3-28. 1 S 25:18-35. Jb 22:21. 23:7. Ps 32:6. Pr 6:1-5. Is 55:6. 2 C 6:2. He 3:7-13.

the judge. Lk 13:24-28. Jb 36:17, 18. Ps 50:22.

into. Mt 18:30. 1 P 3:19. Re 20:7.

59 thou shalt. Lk 16:26. Mt 18:34, 35. 25:41, 46. 2 Th 1:3.

mite. Lk 21:2. Mk 12:42mg.

LUKE 13

1 the Galileans. i.e. *a circuit, rolling, revolution*, S#1057g. ver. 2. Lk 22:59. 23:6. Mt 26:69. Mk 14:70. Jn 4:45. Ac 1:11. 2:7. 5:37.

Pilate. Lk 23:1.

mingled. La 2:20. Ezk 9:5-7. 1 P 4:17, 18.

2 Suppose. ver. 4. Jb 4:7. 8:20. 22:5-16. Jn 9:2. Ac 28:4.

3 Nay. Nu +32:23. Jb +9:22. Jn 9:3. He 12:5.

except. Mt +4:9.

ye repent. ver. 5. Lk 5:32. 15:7, 10. 24:47. 2 Ch +7:14. Je +35:15. Ezk 14:6. 18:30. Mt 3:1, 2, 10-12. 4:17. 9:13. 11:20. Mk +1:15. 6:12. Ac 2:38-40. +3:19. 5:31. 8:22. 11:18. 17:30. 20:21. 26:20. 2 T 2:25, 26. Ja +4:10. 2 P +3:9. Re 2:5, 21, 22.

ye shall. Lk 19:42-44. 21:22-24. 23:28-30. Mt 12:45. 22:7. 23:35-38. 24:21-29.

perish. Gr. *apollumi*, Mt +2:13.

4 in Siloam. Ne 3:15. Is 8:6. Jn 9:7, 11.

fell. 1 K 20:30. Jb 1:19.

sinners. *or*, debtors. Lk 7:41, 42. 11:4. Mt 6:12. 18:24.

5 except. Mt +4:9.

ye repent. ver. +3. Is 28:10-13.

perish. Gr. *apollumi*, Mt +2:13.

6 fig tree. Ps 80:8-13. Is 5:1-4. Je 2:21. Ho 9:10. Jl 1:7. Mt 21:19, 20. Mk 11:12-14.

and he came. Lk 20:10-14. Mt 21:34-40. Jn +15:16. Ga 5:22. Ph 4:17.

7 three years. Le 19:23. 25:21. Ro 2:4, 5.

cut it down. Lk 3:9. +12:46. Ex 32:10. Da 4:14. Mt 3:10. 7:19. Jn +15:2, 6. Ro 11:20-23. 2 P 2:9, 17. 3:7, 9.

why. Ex 32:10. Mt 3:9.

8 Lord, let. Ex 32:11-13, 30-32. 34:6, 9. Nu 14:11-20. Jsh 7:7-9. Ps 106:23. Je 14:7-9, 13, etc. 15:1. 18:20. Jl 2:17. Ro 2:4. 10:1. 11:14. 2 P 3:9, 15.

9 And if. Mt +4:9. Lk 19:42. Ex 32:32. Ezr 9:13-15. Is 5:5-7. Da 3:15.

if not. Mt +4:9. Ezr 9:14, 15. Ps 69:22-28. Da 9:5-8. Jn 15:2. 1 Th 2:15. He 6:8. Re 15:3, 4. 16:5-7.

10 **was teaching**. Lk +4:15, 16, 44.
11 **a spirit**. Gr. *pneuma*, Mt +8:16. ver. 16. Lk 8:2. Jb 2:7. Ps 6:2. Mt 9:32, 33. Ac 16:16. 1 J 4:6.
eighteen. Lk 8:27, 43. Mk 9:21. Jn 5:5, 6. 9:19-21. Ac 3:2. 4:22. 14:8-10.
bowed. Ps 38:6. 42:5mg. 145:14. 146:8.
in no wise. He 7:25.
12 **Woman**. Lk 6:8-10. Ps 107:20. Is 65:1. Mt 8:16.
loosed. ver. 16. Jl 3:10.
13 **he laid**. Mk +5:23.
and immediately. Lk 17:14-17. 18:43. Ps 103:1-5. 107:20-22. 116:16, 17.
made straight. Le 26:13.
glorified. Mt +9:8.
14 **the ruler**. Mt +9:18.
answered. Mk 11:14.
with indignation. Lk 6:11. Mt 20:24. 21:15. 26:8. Mk 10:14, 41. 14:4. Jn 5:15, 16. Ro 10:2. 2 C 7:11.
because. Jn 5:15, 16. Ro 10:2.
healed on the sabbath. Lk 4:16-22, 31-37, 38-41. 6:1-5. 14:3. Ps 119:128. Is +58:13. Mt 12:2, 9-21. 24:20. Mk 6:1-6. Jn 5:5, etc. 7:21, etc. 9:16. Ac 15:10. Ro 7:22. 14:1, 5. 1 C 9:20. 2 C 3:3. Ga 4:7-11. 5:1. Col 2:14-17. He 8:10. 1 J 5:3.
There are six. Ex +20:9. 23:12. 34:12. 35:2. Le 23:3. Dt 5:13. Ezk 20:12. 46:1.
and not. Lk 6:7. 14:3-6. Mt 12:10-12. Mk 3:2-6. Jn 5:16. 9:14-16.
15 **The Lord**. Lk 7:13.
Thou hypocrite. Jb +8:13. Mt +6:2. Ac 8:20-23. 13:9, 10.
doth not. Lk 14:5. Mt 12:11. Jn 7:21-24.
16 **being**. Lk 3:8. 16:24. 19:9. Mt 15:24. Ac 13:26. Ro 4:12-16.
whom. ver. 11. Jb 2:6, 7. Jn 8:44. 2 T 2:26.
Satan hath bound. ver. 11. Mt 4:10. Ac 10:38. 1 C 5:5. 2 C 12:7.
be loosed. ver. 12. Mk 2:27. 7:35.
17 **all his**. Lk 14:6. 20:40. Ps 40:14. 109:29. 132:18. Is 45:24. 2 T 3:9. 1 P 3:16.
and all. Lk 19:37-40, 48. Ex 15:11. Ps 111:3. Is 4:2. Mk 12:37. Jn 12:17, 18. Ac 3:9-11. 4:21.
rejoiced. Lk 5:26. 18:43. Ps 98:1. Is 12:5. Mk 7:37.
glorious things. Ex 34:10. Dt 10:21. Jb 5:9. 9:10.
18 **Then said**. Mt 13:31, 32. Mk 4:30-32.
Unto. ver. 20. Lk 7:31. La 2:13. Mt 11:16. +13:31. Mk 4:30.
the kingdom. Lk +4:43.
19 *like*. Lk 17:6. *Mt* +13:31, 32. 17:20. Mk 4:31, 32.
cast. SS 4:12, 16. 5:1. 6:2. 8:13. Is 58:11. 61:11. Je 31:12.
and it. Ps 72:16, 17. Is +2:2, 3. +9:7. 49:20-25. 51:2, 3. 53:1, 10-12. 54:1-3. 60:15-22. Ezk

17:22-24. 47:1-12. Da 2:34, 35, 44, 45. Mi 4:1, 2. Zc 2:11. 8:20-23. 14:7-9. Ac 2:41. 4:4. 15:14-18. 21:20. Ro 15:19. Re 11:15.
and the fowls. Ps 104:12. Ezk 17:23. 31:6. Da *4:12, 21*. Mt 8:20. +13:32.
20 **And again**. Mt 13:33.
Whereunto. ver. 18. Mt 11:16.
the kingdom. ver. 18.
21 **like leaven**. Lk 12:1. Mt +13:33mg.
three measures. Ge 18:6. Jg 6:19. 1 S 1:24.
till. Jb 17:9. Ps 92:13, 14. Pr +4:18. Ho +6:3. Jn 4:14. 15:2. 1 C 5:6. 10:5. Ga 5:9. Ph 1:6, 9-11. 1 Th 5:23, 24. Ja 1:21.
22 **through**. Lk 4:43, 44. 8:1. Mt 9:35. 11:1. Mk 6:6. Ac 10:38.
journeying. ver. 33. Lk +9:51. SS 7:1. Is +2:2. 60:5. Ep 6:15.
23 **are there few**. Mt +7:14. 19:25. 20:16. 22:14. Re 7:9.
that be saved. Ac 2:47. 1 C 1:18. 2 C 2:15.
And. Lk 12:13-15. 21:7, 8. Mt +24:3-5. Mk 13:4, 5. Jn 21:21, 22. Ac +1:7, 8.
24 **Strive**. Lk 9:23. 14:33. +21:36. Ge 32:25, 26. Mt 11:12. Mk 10:24. Jn 6:15, 27. Ac 14:22. 1 C 9:24-27. Ep 6:12-18. Ph 2:12, 13. Col 1:29. 4:12. 1 T 4:10. 6:12. 2 T 4:7. He 4:11. 12:4. 1 P 4:7. 2 P 1:10. Ju +3.
the strait. Mt +7:13, 14.
for many. Pr 1:24-28. 14:6. 21:25. Ec 10:15. Is 1:15. 58:2-4. Ezk +33:31. Mk 6:18-20. Jn 7:34. 8:21. 13:33. Ro 9:31-33. 10:3.
shall not. Lk +9:24. Pr 1:27. 2 C +6:1, 2. He 12:17. Re 6:16.
25 **once**. Ps 32:6. Is 55:6. 2 C 6:1, 2. He 3:7, 8, 15. 12:17.
risen up. He 10:12.
hath shut. Lk 19:42. Ge 7:16. Mt 25:10. Re +22:11.
begin. ver. 25. Lk 3:8. 5:21. 14:9.
to knock. Lk 11:10. 12:36.
Lord. Lk 6:46. Mt 7:21, 22. 25:11, 12.
I know. ver. 27. Lk 12:9. Mt 7:23. 10:33. +25:41.
26 **begin**. ver. +25.
We. Ge 31:54. Ex 18:12. 24:11. Is 58:2. 2 T 3:5. T 1:16.
taught in. Is 42:2. Mt 12:19.
27 **I tell**. ver. 25. Ps +1:6. Mt 7:22, 23. 25:12, 41. 1 C 8:3. Ga 4:9. 2 T +2:19.
know. ver. 25.
depart. Ps 5:4-6. +6:8. 28:3. 101:8. 125:5. Ho 9:12. Mt 7:23. +25:41.
workers of. Ps 92:7, 9. 94:4. 101:8. 125:5. Mt +13:41.
28 **weeping**. Mt +25:30.
when. Mt +8:11.
shall see. Lk 16:23. Is +66:24. Da +12:2. Mt +25:32. Jn 7:34. Re 14:10.
Abraham. Lk 20:37. Mt +8:11. +19:28. 22:32. Mk 12:23. Ac 3:13. 7:32.

all the prophets. Ac +10:43. Re +11:18.
in the kingdom. Lk +4:43. 23:42, 43. 2 P 1:11.
you. Lk 10:15. Re +21:8. 22:15.

29 **they shall come**. Ge 28:14. Ps 107:3. Is 43:5, 6. 45:6. 49:6, 12. 54:2, 3. *59:19*. 66:18-20. Je 3:18. Ml *1:11*. Mt 19:30. Mk 10:31. 13:27. Ac 28:28. Ep 3:6-8. Col 1:6, 23. Re 7:9, 10.
from the east. 1 Ch 9:24. Ps 107:3.
sit down. Lk 14:15. 22:30. Re 19:9.
the kingdom. Lk +4:43.

30 **there are last**. Mt 3:9, 10. +19:30. Ep 3:6.

31 **Get**. Ne 6:9-14. Ps 11:1, 2. Pr +22:3. Je +36:19. Am 7:12, 13.
depart hence. Mt 19:1. Mk 10:1.
for Herod. Lk 3:1.

32 **Go ye**. Jn 8:44. 1 J 3:10.
that fox. Lk 3:19, 20. 9:7-9. 23:8-11. Ezk 13:4. Mi 3:1-3. Zp 3:3. Mk 6:26-28.
I cast. Lk 7:22. 9:7. Mk 6:14. Jn 10:32. 11:8-10.
the third day. 1 C +15:4.
I shall be. Jn 17:4, 5. 19:28, 30. He +2:10. 5:9. 7:28.

33 **I must**. Lk 2:49. 4:43. 9:22. 17:25. 19:5. 21:9. 22:37. 24:7, 26, 44. Mt 24:6. 26:54. Mk 13:7. Jn 3:14. 4:4. 9:4. 10:16. 12:34. 20:9. Ac 1:16, 22. 3:21. 9:6. 10:38. 17:3. 27:24-26. 1 C 15:25. Re 1:1.
following. Ac 20:15. 21:26.
for. Lk 9:53. Mt 20:18. Ac 13:27.
a prophet. Mt +21:11.
perish. Gr. *apollumi*, Mt +2:13.
out of Jerusalem. ver. 22.

34 **Jerusalem**. Lk 19:41, 42. Mt 23:37-39.
killest. ver. 33. 2 Ch 24:21, 22, 36:15, 16. Ne +9:26. Je 2:30. 26:23. La 4:13. Mt 5:12. 21:35, 36. 22:6. Ac 7:52, 59. 8:1. 1 Th 2:15. Re 11:8.
and stonest. Le +24:14.
how often. Dt 5:29. 32:29. Ps 81:10, 13. Is 48:17-19. 50:2. Mt 26:55.
would I have. Je 51:9.
gathered. Ps 106:47. 107:3. 147:2. Pr 1:24. Mt 24:31. Mk 13:27.
thy. Lk 19:44. 23:28. Ps 149:2. La 1:16. Jl 2:23. Ga 4:25, 26.
as. Ps +91:4.
and ye. Lk 15:28. Ne 9:30. Ps 81:11. Pr 1:24-30. Is 30:15. Je 6:16. 7:23, 24. 35:14. 44:4-6. Ho 11:2, 7. Zc 1:4. Mt 22:3. Jn 1:5, 10, 11. 5:40. Ac 3:14, 15.

35 **your house**. Lk 11:51. 21:5, 6, 24. Le 26:31, 32. 1 K 9:7, 8. Ps 69:25, 26. Is 1:7, 8. 5:5, 6. 64:10, 11. Je *12:7*. *22:5*. Ezk 10:18, 19. 11:23. Da +9:26, 27. Mi 3:12. Zc 11:1, 2. 14:2. Mt +23:38. Jn +14:2. Ac 6:13, 14.
Ye shall not. Ho +3:4, 5. Mt +23:39. Jn 7:34-36. 8:22-24. 12:35, 36. 14:19-23.
until. Mt +23:39.

Blessed. Ps +*118:26*. Is 40:9-11. 52:7. Zc +12:10. Ro 10:9-15. 2 C 3:15-18.

LUKE 14

1 **went into**. Lk 7:34-36. 11:37. 13:31. 1 C 9:19-22.
chief. Jn 3:1. 7:50. 19:39. Ac 5:34.
to eat. Lk 7:34. Mt 11:19. Jn 2:2. 12:2.
they watched. Lk 6:7. 11:53, 54. 17:20. 20:20. Ps 37:32. 41:6. 62:4. 64:5, 6. Pr 23:7. Is 29:20, 21. Je 20:10, 11. Mk 3:2.

3 **answering**. Mk 11:14.
the lawyers. Lk 11:44, 45. Mt 22:35.
Is it lawful. Lk 6:9. 13:14-16. Mt 12:10, 12. Mk 3:4. Jn 5:16, 17. 7:23.

4 **they held their peace**. Mt 21:25-27. 22:46. Ac 11:18.

5 **Which of**. Lk 13:15. Ex 23:4, 5. Dt 22:4. Mt 12:11, 12.
a pit. Gr. *phrear*, S#5421g. ver. 5; Jn 4:11 (well), 12; Re 9:1 (pit), 2. Ge +16:14.

6 **could not answer**. Lk 13:17. 20:26, 40. 21:15. Mt 22:46. Mk 3:4. 12:34. Ac 6:10.

7 **put**. Jg 14:12. Pr 8:1. Ezk 17:2. Mt 13:34.
they. Lk 11:43. 20:46. Mt 23:6. Mk 12:38, 39. Ac 8:18, 19. Ro +12:3. Ph +2:3. 3 J 9.

8 **When**. Pr 25:6, 7. Ph +2:3.

9 **and thou**. Est 6:6-12. Pr 3:35. 11:2. 16:18. 25:6, 7. Ezk 28:2-10. Da 4:30-34.
begin. Lk 3:8. 5:21. 13:25, 26.

10 **go**. 1 S 15:17. Pr 15:33. 25:6, 7.
room. 1 S 9:22.
Friend. Pr 25:7.
then. Is 60:14. Re 3:9.
have worship. Ge 37:7, 9. 42:6. Ex 18:7. 1 K 1:23. 18:7. 1 Ch 29:20. Ps 45:11. Is 49:23. Da 2:46. Mt +8:2. +14:33. 18:26. Mk 7:7. Jn 4:23, 24. Ac 10:25.

11 **whosoever**. Lk 10:15. 1 S 15:17. Jb 5:11. Pr 15:33. +16:5. 18:12. 29:23. Is +57:15. Ezk 21:26. Mt 18:4. Ju 10.

12 **to him**. ver. 1.
When. Lk 1:53. Pr 14:20. 22:16. Ja 2:1-6.
a dinner. Jn 21:12.
and a recompense. Lk 6:32-36. Zc 7:5-7. Mt 5:46. 6:1-4, 16-18.

13 **a feast**. Lk 5:29.
call. ver. 21. Lk 11:41. Dt 14:29. 16:11, 14. 26:12, 13. 2 S 6:19. 2 Ch 30:24. Ne 8:10, 12. Est 9:22. Jb 29:13, 15, 16. 31:16-20. Pr 3:9, 10. 14:31. 31:6, 7. Is 58:7, 10. Mt 14:14-21. 15:32-39. 22:10. 25:35. Ac 2:44, 45. 4:34, 35. 9:39. Ro 12:13-16. 1 T 3:2. 5:10. T 1:8. Phm 7. He 13:2. 1 J 3:17.
the poor. ver. 21. Ps 41:1. Pr 14:21. 19:17. 28:27. Mt 19:21. Ga 2:10.
the maimed. ver. 21. Ge +10:1.

14 **be blessed**. Jb 42:10. Pr 11:25. 2 C 5:10. Re 20:6.

they cannot. Lk 6:35. Mt 5:46.
be recompensed. Pr 19:17. Mt +5:12. Mk
10:21. Ro 2:6, 16. 14:10. 1 C 3:11-15. 4:5. Ga
6:9, 10. Ep 6:8. Ph +4:17-19. 1 T 6:17-19. He
9:15. 10:35. Re 11:18.
at. Is 3:10, 11. 40:10. 62:11. Mt 16:27. Ro
2:16. 14:10. 1 C 3:8, 13. 15:23, 2 C 5:10. Col
3:24. 1 Th 4:16, 17. 2 Th +1:10. 2 T +4:1. Re
22:12.
the resurrection. Lk 20:35, 36. Da +12:2, 3.
Mt +10:15. Jn 5:29. Ac 24:15. Ro 8:11, 23. 1
C 3:8, 13. He 11:35. Re +11:18. 22:12.
of the just. Lk 20:35, 36. Jn 6:39, 40, 44, 54.
11:24. Ac 24:15. 1 C 6:14. 15:22-24, 52. Ph
+3:11. 1 Th +4:16. Re 20:4, 5.

15 **Blessed**. Lk 12:37. 13:29. 22:16, 30. Ps
+22:26. Mt +8:11. 25:10. Jn 6:27, etc. Re
19:9.
eat bread. Ex +18:12.
the kingdom. Lk +4:43.

16 **Then said**. Mt ch. 13. 25:1-12. Lk ch. 15, 16.
A certain. Pr 9:1, 2. Is 25:6, 7. Je 31:12-14.
Zc 10:7. Mt 22:2-14.
bade. SS 5:1. Is 55:1-7. Mk 16:15, 16. Re
3:20. 22:17.

17 **his**. Lk 3:4-6. 9:1-5. 10:1, etc. Est 6:14. Pr
9:1-5. Mt 3:1, etc. 10:1, etc. Ac 2:38, 39. 3:24-
26. 13:26, 38, 39.
bidden. Zp 1:7.
Come. SS 2:4. Is 55:1, 2. Mt 11:27-29. 22:3,
4. Jn 7:37. 2 C 5:18-21. 6:1. He 3:15. Re 19:9.
22:17.

18 **all**. Lk 20:4, 5. Is 28:12, 13. 29:11, 12. Je 5:4,
5. 6:10, 16, 17. Mt 22:5, 6. 23:37. Jn 1:11.
5:40. Ac 13:45, 46. 18:5, 6. 28:25-27.
make excuse. Ex 3:11, 13. 4:1, 10, 13. SS
+5:3.
I have. Lk 8:14. 17:26-31. 18:24. Dt 20:5, 6.
Mt 24:38, 39. 1 T 6:9, 10. 2 T 4:4, 10. He
12:16. 1 J 2:15, 16.

20 **have married**. ver. 26-28. Lk 18:29, 30. Dt
20:7. 24:5. 1 C 7:29-31, 33.

21 **and showed**. Lk 9:10. 1 S 25:12. Mt 15:12.
18:31. Mk 6:30. He 13:17.
being. ver. 24. Ps 2:12. Mt 22:7, 8. He 2:3.
12:25, 26. Re 15:1, etc. 19:15.
Go. Lk 24:47. Pr 1:20-25. 8:2-4. 9:3, 4. Je 5:1.
Zc 11:7, 11. Mt 21:28-31. Jn 4:39-42. 7:47-
49. 9:39. Ac 8:4-7. Ja 2:5. Re 22:17.
the poor. ver. 13. Lk 7:22, 23. 1 S 2:8. Ps
113:7, 8. Mt 11:5, 28. 22:9, 10. Mk 12:37.
and the maimed. ver. 13. Ge +8:22.
and the halt. ver. 13 (lame). ver. 19. Ps 38:7.
Is 33:23. 35:6.
and the blind. ver. 18.

22 **it is**. Ac ch. 1-9.
and yet. Ge 24:23. Ps 103:6. 130:7. Jn +14:2.
Ep 3:8. Col 2:9. 1 T 2:5, 6. 1 J 2:2. Re 7:4-9.

23 **Go**. Ps 98:3. Pr 1:21. Is 11:10. 19:24, 25.
27:13. 49:5, 6. 66:19, 20. Zc 14:8, 9. Ml 1:11.

Mt 21:43. 22:9, 10. +28:19, 20. Mk 16:15. Ac
9:15. 10:44-48. 11:18-21. 13:47, 48. 18:6.
22:21, 22. 26:18-20. 28:28. Ro 1:16. 10:18.
15:9-12. Ep 2:11-22. Col 1:23.
compel. Ge 43:16. Ps 110:3. Mt 14:22. Mk
6:45. Ac +16:15. Ro 11:13, 14. 1 C 9:19-23. 2
C 5:11, 20. 6:1. Col 1:28. 2 T 4:2.
to come in. Lk 11:52.

24 **That none**. Pr 1:24-32. Mt 21:43. 22:8.
23:38, 39. Jn 3:19, 36. 8:21, 24. Ac 3:46.
13:46. Ro +11:1. He 12:25, 26.

25 **there went**. Lk +5:15. Jn 6:24-27.
he turned. Lk +22:61.

26 **If any**. 1 C +15:2. ver. 33. Dt 13:6-8. 33:8, 9.
Ps 73:25, 26. Mt 10:37. 19:29. Ph 3:8.
hate. Lk 5:28. 16:13. 21:16. Ge 29:30, 31. Dt
21:15. 33:9. Jb 7:15, 16. Ec 2:17-19. Ml 1:2,
3. Mt 6:24. 10:37. Jn 12:25. Ro +9:13.
yea. Lk 9:23. Ac 20:24. Re 12:11.
life. Gr. *psyche*, Mt +2:20; Ge +9:5. Lk 9:24.
12:23.

27 **doth**. Lk 9:23-25. Mt 10:38. 16:24-26. Mk
8:34-37. 10:21. 15:21. Jn 19:17. 2 T 3:12.
cannot. Mt 13:21. Ac 14:22. 2 T 1:12.

28 **intending**. Ge 11:4-9. Pr 24:27.
sitteth. Ps +112:5. Pr +22:3.
first. ver. 31. Lk 12:33. 16:8-10. Pr 6:8. 13:16.
+22:3. 24:27. Mt 16:25, 26. 2 C 6:2. He 2:3.
counteth. ver. 33. Jsh 24:19-24. Mt 8:20.
10:22. 20:22, 23. Ac 21:13. 1 Th +3:4, 5. 2 P
1:13, 14.
to finish. Mt +13:20, 21.

30 **began to build**. Mt 7:27. 27:3-8. Ac 1:18, 19.
1 C 3:11-14. He 6:4-8, 11. 10:38. 2 P 2:19-22.
2 J 8.

31 **make war**. 2 S +11:1. 1 K 20:11. 2 K 18:20-
22. Pr 20:18. 25:8. Ac 17:18.
first. ver. 28. Pr 13:16.
consulteth. 2 K 14:10.

32 **great way**. Dt 20:11-15.
ambassage. Jsh 9:4.
and desireth. Lk 12:58. Jsh 9:6. 1 K 20:31-
34. 2 K 10:4, 5. Jb 40:9. Mt 5:25. Ac 12:20. Ja
4:6-10.

33 **whosoever**. ver. 26. Lk 5:11, 28. 18:22, 23,
28-30. Ac 5:1-5. 8:19-22. Ph 3:7, 8. 2 T 4:10.
He 11:26. 1 J 2:15, 16.
forsaketh. Lk 9:61. Mt 10:37. Mk 6:46. 8:35.
Ac 18:18, 21. 2 C 2:13. Ph 3:6-8.

34 **Salt**. Le +2:13. Dt +29:23.
but if. Mt +4:9. He 2:4-8.

35 **but**. Jn 15:6.
He. Lk 8:8. 9:44. Mt +13:9.

LUKE 15

1 **drew near**. Lk 5:29-32. 7:29. 13:30. Ex
33:21. Dt 5:31. Ezk 18:27, 28. Mt 9:10-13.
21:28-31. Ro 5:20. 1 T 1:15.
all. Ex +9:6.

publicans. Mt +5:46.
to hear. Mk 12:37.

2 **Pharisees and scribes murmured**. ver. 29, 30. Lk 7:34, 39. Jsh 9:18. 1 C 5:9-11. Ju +16.
This man. Lk 7:39.
receiveth sinners. Ro +15:7. 16:2. Ph 2:29.
eateth with. Lk 5:30. Mt 9:11. Mk 2:16. Ac 11:3. 1 C 5:9-11. Ga 2:12.

4 **man**. Lk 13:15. Mt 12:11. 18:12. Ro 2:1.
having. Nu +27:17. Is 53:6. Ezk 34:8, 11, 12, 16, 31. Jn 10:11, 15, 16, 26-28.
lose. Gr. *apollumi*, Mt +2:13.
wilderness. Ex 3:1. 1 S 17:28.
lost. Gr. *apollumi*, Mt +2:13.
go after. Lk +19:10. Ge 37:17. Ezk 34:4, 11, 12, 16.
until. Ga 6:1. 1 T 4:13-16. 2 T +2:12. He +3:13, 14. Ja +5:19. 1 J 5:16. Ju 23.

5 **when**. Lk 19:9. 23:43. Is 62:12. Jn 4:34, 35. Ac 9:1-16. Ro 10:20, 21. Ep 2:3-6. T 3:3-7.
he layeth. Is 40:10, 11. 46:3, 4. 49:22. 60:4. 63:9. 66:12. Mi 5:4. Ep 1:19, 20. 2:10. 3:7. 1 Th 1:5. 2 T 2:26. 1 P 1:5.
rejoicing. ver. 23, 24, 32. Dt +30:9. Is 53:10, 11. Ezk 18:23. 33:11. Mi +7:18. He 12:2.

6 **his friends**. ver. 7, 10, 24. Lk 2:13, 14. Is 66:10, 11. Jn 3:29. +15:14. Ac +11:23. 15:3. Ph 1:4. 2:17. 4:1. 1 Th 2:19. 3:7-9.
Rejoice. Ps 22:22. Mt 18:13. Ju 24.
for. Ps 119:176. 1 P 2:10, 25.
lost. Gr. *apollumi*, Mt +2:13. ver. 4.

7 **joy**. ver. 10, 32. Lk 2:10. 5:32. Mt 18:13, 14.
one sinner. ver. 10. Lk 7:37. Ezk 33:11. Mt 6:29. 18:10. 25:40, 45.
that repenteth. ver. 10. Lk +13:3, 5.
just. Lk 5:32. 16:15. 18:11, 12. Pr 30:12. Mt 9:13.
which. ver. 29. Lk 16:15. 18:9-11. Pr 30:12. Ro 7:9. Ph 3:6, 7, 9.

8 **pieces**. "'Drachma,' here translated a piece of silver, is the eighth of an ounce, which cometh to 7 1/2 d., and is equal to the Roman penny. Mt 18:28." Dt 22:15.
if. Mt +4:9.
lose. Gr. *apollumi*, Mt +2:13.
and seek. Lk +19:10. Ezk 34:12. Jn 10:16. 11:52. Ep 2:17.
till. ver. 4.

9 **Rejoice**. ver. 6, 7.
neighbors. Ru 4:17.
lost. Gr. *apollumi*, Mt +2:13.

10 **there**. Lk 2:10-14. Ezk 18:23, 32. 33:11. Mt 18:10, 11. 28:5-7. Ac 5:19, 20. 10:3-5. He 1:14. Re 5:11-14.
the angels. Lk 12:8.
one. Lk 7:47. 13:5. 2 Ch 33:13-19. Mt 18:14. Ac 11:18. 2 C 7:10. Phm 15.
repenteth. Lk +13:3.

11 **A certain man**. Mt 21:23-31.

12 **give**. Dt 21:16, 17. Ps 16:5, 6. 17:14.
And he. Mk 12:44.

13 **and took**. 2 Ch 33:1-10. Jb 21:13-15. 22:17, 18. Ps 10:4-6. 73:27. Pr 27:8. Is 1:4. 30:11. Je 2:5, 13, 17-19, 31. Mi 6:3. Mt 21:33. Ep 2:11-13, 17.
wasted. ver. 30. Lk 16:1, 19. Jb 20:14, 15. Pr 5:8-14. 6:26. 18:9. 21:17, 20. 23:19-22. 28:7. 29:3. Ec 11:9, 10. Is 22:13. 56:12. Am 6:3-7. Ro 13:13, 14. 1 P 4:3, 4. 2 P 2:13.
riotous living. Ep 5:18. T 1:6. 1 P 4:4.

14 **spent all**. Lk 8:43. Ge 47:18. Pr 21:20.
arose. 2 Ch 33:11. Pr 21:20. Ezk 16:27. Ho 2:9-14. Am 8:9-12.
famine. Ge +12:10. 41:56, 57. Is 55:2. Am +8:11, 12.
be in want. 2 C 11:9. Ph 4:12.

15 **he went**. ver. 13. Ex 10:3. 2 Ch 28:22. Is 1:5. 9:10-13. 57:17. Je 5:3. 8:4-6. 31:18, 19. 2 T 2:25, 26. Re 2:21, 22.
joined himself. 2 Ch 20:36.
to feed. Lk 8:32-34. Ezk 16:52, 63. Na 3:6. Ml 2:9. Ro 1:24-26. 6:22. 1 C 6:9-11. Ep 2:2, 3. 4:17-19. 5:11, 12. Col 3:5-7. T 3:3.

16 **he would**. Lk 16:21. Pr 23:21. Is 44:20. 55:2. La 4:5. Ho 12:1. Ro 6:19-21.
husks. Ex 16:31. Pr 27:7.
that. Ps 73:22.
no. Ps 142:4. Is 57:3. Jon 2:2-8.

17 **when**. Lk 8:35. 16:23. 1 K 8:47. 2 Ch 6:37. Ps 73:20. Ec 9:3. Je 31:19. Ezk 18:28. Ac 2:37. 16:29, 30. 26:11-19. Ep 2:4, 5. 5:14. T 3:4-6. Ja 1:16-18.
came to himself. Lk 8:35. Ac 12:11. 2 T +1:7.
How. ver. 18, 19. La 1:7.
hired servants. Le 25:50. Jb 7:1.
and to spare. 2 Ch 31:9, 10. Mt 14:20. Ph 4:18.
perish. Gr. *apollumi*, Mt +2:13.
with hunger. Le 22:4, 6, 7. 1 J 1:6, 7.

18 **will arise**. 1 K 20:30, 31. 2 K 7:3, 4. 2 Ch 33:12, 13, 19. Ps 32:5. 116:3-7. Je 31:6-9. 50:4, 5. La 3:18-22, 29, 40. Ho 2:6, 7. 14:1-3. Jon 2:4. 3:9.
will say. Ho +14:2.
Father. Lk 11:2. Is 63:16. Je 3:19. 31:20. Mt +6:9, 14, 15. 7:11.
I have. Lk 18:13. Ex 10:16. Le 26:40, 41. 1 K 8:47, 48. Ne 1:6. Jb 33:27, 28. 36:8-10. Ps 25:11. 32:3-5. 51:3-5. Pr +28:13. Is 55:7. Je 3:12, 13. Mt 3:6. 1 J 1:8-10.
against. ver. 21. Da 4:26. Mt 21:25. Jn 3:27.
heaven. Ex 9:22. Ps +73:9. Mt 14:19.

19 **no**. Lk 5:8. 7:6, 7. Ge 32:10. Jb 42:6. 1 C 15:9. 1 T 1:13-16.
make. Ge 48:20. Jsh 9:24, 25. Ps 84:10. Is 41:15. Mt 15:26, 27. Ja 4:8-10. 1 P 5:6.
hired servants. Le 22:10. Jn 15:15.

20 **And**. Ge +8:22.

he arose. Is 55:7.
But. Dt 30:2-4. Jb 33:27, 28. Ps +32:5. 103:8-13. Is 49:15. 55:6-9. 57:18. Ezk 16:6-8. Ho 11:8. Mi +7:18, 19. Ac 2:39. Ep 2:13, 17.
had compassion. Ho +11:8. Mk 8:2.
and fell. Ge 33:4. 45:14, 15. 46:29. Ac 20:37.
and kissed. Ge +27:27.

21 Father. ver. 18, 19. Le 26:40. Ps 32:5. 51:4. 130:3, 4. Je 3:13. Ezk 16:63. Ro 2:4.
against. Ps 51:4. 143:2. 1 C 8:12.

22 the best. Ex +28:2. Ps 45:13. Ezk 16:9-13. Mt 22:11, 12. Ep 4:22-24. Re 3:4, 5, 18. 6:11. 7:9, 13, 14.
and. Ge +8:22.
a ring. Ge 38:18, 25. 41:42. Est 3:10. 8:2. Ro 8:15. Ga 4:5, 6. Ep 1:13, 14. Ja 2:2. Re 2:17.
and shoes. Ps 18:33. Ezk 16:10. Ep +6:15.

23 And. Ge +8:22.
the fatted. Ge 18:7. 1 S 28:24. Ps 63:5.
eat. Ru 1:22. 2 Ch 30:21. Ps +22:26.
be merry. ver. 24, 29, 30. Lk 12:19. 16:19. Re 11:10.

24 this. ver. 32. Mk 8:22. Jn 5:21, 24, 25. 11:25. Ro 6:11, 13, 21. 8:2. 11:15. 2 C 5:14, 15. Ep 2:1, 5. 5:14. Col 2:13. 1 T 5:6. Ju 12. Re 3:1.
he. ver. 4, 8. Lk +19:10. Ge 45:28. Je 31:15-17. Ezk 34:4, 16. Mt 18:11-13.
lost. Gr. apollumi, Mt +2:13.
they. ver. 7, 9, 10, 23. Ge 43:34. Ec 9:7. 10:19. Is 35:10. 66:11. Je 31:12-14. Ro 12:15. 1 C 12:26.

25 his elder son. ver. 11, 12.
heard music. Lk 7:32.
dancing. Ex +15:20. Ps 126:1.

27 Thy brother. ver. 30. Ac 9:17. 22:13. Phm 16.
and thy. ver. 23.
he hath received. Ro 11:28, 31.

28 he was angry. ver. 2. Lk 5:30. 7:39. 1 S 17:28. 18:8. Is 65:5. 66:5. Jon 4:1-3. Mt 20:11. Ac 13:45, 50. 14:2, 19. 22:21, 22. Ro 10:19. 1 Th 2:16.
would not. Lk 9:50. Ac 11:3. 2 C 2:7, 10.
therefore. Lk 13:34. 24:47. Ge 4:5-7. Jon 4:4, 9. 2 C 5:20.

29 Lo. Lk 17:10. 18:9, 11, 12, 20, 21. 1 S 15:13, 14. Is 58:2, 3. 65:5. Zc 7:3. Mt 20:12. Ro 3:20, 27. 7:9. 10:3. Ph 3:4-6. 1 J 1:8-10. Re 3:17.
yet. ver. 7. Lk 19:21. Ml 1:12, 13. 3:14. Re 2:17.
make merry. ver. 23.

30 this. ver. 32. Lk 18:11. Ex 32:7, 11.
devoured. ver. 13, 22, 23. Pr 29:3.
thy living. ver. 12. Mk 12:44.

31 Son. Lk 2:48. 16:25. 19:22, 23. Mt 9:2. 11:19. 20:13-16. 21:28. Mk 2:5. 7:27, 28. 10:24. Ro 9:4, 5. 11:1, 35. Ep 6:1. Col 3:20. 1 T 1:18. 2 T 2:1.
thou art. Jn 8:35.
and all. ver. 12.

32 was meet. Lk 7:34. Ps 51:8. Is 35:10. Ho 14:9. Jon 4:10, 11. Ac 11:18. Ro 3:4, 19. 15:9-13.
make merry. ver. 23.
for this. ver. 24. Ep 2:1-10.
was dead. ver. 24. Ep 5:14. 1 T 5:6. Re 3:1, 2.
lost. Gr. apollumi, Mt +2:13.

LUKE 16

1 a certain. Mt 18:23, 24. 25:14, etc.
a steward. Lk 8:3. 12:42. Ge 15:2. 43:19. 1 Ch 28:1. 1 C 4:1, 2. T 1:7. 1 P 4:10.
rich man. Ja 2:6-9. +5:1-6.
accused. Gr. diaballo, S#1225g, only here. lit. maliciously charged. Le +19:15. Pr 17:4, 15. +18:13. Jn +7:24, 51. Ep 6:9. Ja 2:6-9.
wasted. ver. 19. Pr +18:9. Ho 2:8. Ja 4:3.

2 How. Ge 3:9-11. 4:9, 10. 18:20, 21. 1 S 2:23, 24. 1 C 1:11. 1 T 5:24.
give. Lk 12:42. Ec 11:9, 10. 12:14. Mt 12:36. 25:19. Ro 14:12. 1 C 4:2, 5. 2 C 5:10. 1 P 3:15. 4:5, 10. 1 T 4:14. Re 20:12.
stewardship. ver. 3, 4. 1 C 9:17. 1 T 1:4.
for. Lk 12:20. 19:21-26.

3 said. Lk 7:39. 18:4. Est 6:6. Mt 9:3.
What shall. Lk 12:17. Is 10:3. Je 5:31. Ho 9:5. Ac 9:6.
I cannot. Pr 13:4. 15:19. 18:9. 19:15. 21:25, 26. 24:30-34. 26:13-16. 27:23-27. 29:21. 2 Th 3:11.
to beg. Lk 16:20, 22. Jb 15:23. Ps 109:10. Pr 20:4. Mk 10:46. Jn 9:8. Ac 3:2.

4 resolved. Pr 30:9. Je 4:22. Ja 3:15.
put out. Ac 13:22.

5 his. Lk 7:41, 42. Mt 18:24.

6 measures. "The word Batos in the original containeth nine gallons three quarts. See Ezk 45:10-14."
Take. ver. 9, 12. T 2:10.

7 An hundred. Lk 20:9, 10, 12. SS 8:11, 12.
measures. "The word here interpreted a measure, in the original containeth about fourteen bushels and a pottle. Gr." 1 K 4:22mg. Ezr 7:22mg. Ezk 45:14.

8 unjust steward. i.e. accountant. ver. 9, 10. Lk 18:6. Mt 6:24. Ac 1:18. 1 T 6:10. Ja 1:25.
done. ver. 4. Ge 3:1. Ex 1:10. 2 S 13:3. 2 K 10:19. Pr 6:6-8.
wisely. Pr +22:3. Mt 25:2.
children of this. Lk 10:6. 20:34. Ps 17:14. Mt 13:38. Jn 8:23. 1 C 3:18, 19. Ga 1:4. Ph 3:19.
world. Gr. aion, Mt +6:13. lit. "this age," Mt +12:32. +13:22.
in their generation. Ps 49:10-19. Mt 17:26.
wiser. Mt +11:19.
children of light. Is 42:18. Jn 12:35, 36. Ep 5:8. 1 Th 5:5-8. 2 Th 2:3. 1 P 2:9. 1 J 3:10.

9 I say. Mt +6:2. 15:26. Mk 7:27.

Make. Lk 11:41. 12:33. 14:14. Pr 10:2. 11:4. 19:17. Ec 11:1. Is 58:7, 8. Ezk 7:19. Da 4:27. Mt 6:19, 20. 19:21. 25:35-40. Ac 10:4, 31. 2 C 9:12-15. 1 T 6:17-19. 2 T 1:16-18.
of the. ver. 11, 13. Mt 6:24.
mammon. *or*, riches. ver. 11, 13. Pr 23:5. Mt 6:24. 1 T 6:9, 10, 17.
of unrighteousness. ver. 8. Pr 22:16. Je 17:11. Mk 10:24.
when. Ps 73:26. Ec 12:3-7. Is 57:16.
receive you. Lk 6:38. 15:20-24. Ps +126:6. Ec 11:1. Da +12:3. 1 Th +2:19, 20. He 10:34. 2 P +1:10.
into. 2 C 4:17, 18. 5:1. 1 T 6:18, 19. Ju 21.
everlasting. Gr. *aionios*, Mt +18:8. Da +12:3. He +10:34.
habitations. Lk 12:33. Mt 19:21. Jn +14:2. 2 C 5:1.

10 **faithful in**. ver. 11, 12. Lk 19:17. 1 K +12:7. 2 K 12:15. 2 Ch 31:12. Je +12:5. +48:10. Mt 25:21, 23. 1 C 4:2. 11:31. Ep +1:1. Ph +2:12. He 3:2. 3 J 5.
he that is unjust. 1 K +12:10. Ps +12:5. Pr 29:12. Ec +5:8. Ezk +16:49. Mi +6:8. Ml +3:5. Mt +23:23. Jn +7:24, 51. 12:6. 13:2, 27.

11 **If**. 1 C +15:2.
in. ver. 9.
mammon. *or*, riches. ver. 9mg. Mt 6:24.
commit. Jn 2:24.
true. Lk 12:33. 18:22. Pr 8:18, 19. Ep 3:8. Ja 2:5. Re 3:18.

12 **if**. 1 C +15:2.
been faithful. Da 6:4.
in that. Lk 19:13-26. 1 Ch 29:14-16. Jb 1:21. Ezk 16:16-21. Ho 2:8, 9. Mt 25:14-29.
that which is your. Lk 10:42. Col 3:3, 4. 1 P 1:4, 5.

13 **servant**. Ac 10:7. Ro 14:4. 1 P 2:18.
can serve. ver. 9, 11. Lk 9:50. 11:23. Jsh 24:15. Mt 4:10. 6:24. Ro 6:16-22. 8:5-8. Ga 1:10. 2 T +4:10. Ja 4:4. 1 J 2:15, 16.
hate. Lk +14:26. Ro +9:13.
Ye cannot. Ps +7:13.
serve God. ver. 9. Ja 1:1.
and mammon. ver. 9, 11. Mt 6:24.

14 **who**. Lk 11:39. 12:15. 20:47. Is 56:11. Je 6:13. 8:10. Ezk 22:25-29. +33:31. Mt 23:14.
covetous. Ps +10:3. Mt 23:25. 1 T 6:10. 2 T 3:2. He 13:5.
derided. Lk +8:53. 23:35. Jb 30:1. Ps 22:7. 35:15, 16. 44:13. 79:4. 119:51. Is 53:3. Je 20:7, 8. 48:27. La 3:14. Ezk +33:31. 36:4. Ga 6:7. He +11:36. 12:2, 3.

15 **Ye are**. Lk 18:9-12. 2 K 10:16. Ps +10:2. 39:6. Pr 3:35. +16:5. 20:6. Hab 2:16. Mt 6:5, 16. 23:5-7. 2 C 10:12. Ph +2:3. 3:19.
justify yourselves. Lk 10:29. 11:39. 18:11, 14, 21. 20:20, 47. Pr 20:6. Mt 6:2, 5, 16. 23:5, 25-27. Ro 3:20. Ja 2:21-25.
before men. Mt 6:2, 5, 16. 23:5, 7.

God knoweth. 1 S +16:7. Jb 10:4. Ps 138:6. Pr 21:2. Mt 23:25. Jn +2:25. Ro 8:27. 1 C 4:5.
for that. 1 S 2:30. Ps 10:3. 49:13, 18. Pr 16:5. Is 1:10-14. Am 5:21, 22. Ml 3:15. 1 P 3:4. 5:5.
is abomination. Pr 6:16, 17. 8:13.

16 **Law**. ver. 29, 31. Lk +24:27, 44. Mt 5:17. 7:12. 11:9-14. 22:40. Jn 1:45. 6:45. 7:23. Ac 3:18, 24, 25. Ac 10:43. 13:15. 24:14. 26:22. 28:23. Ro 3:21.
were until. Mt 11:13. Col 2:17.
the kingdom of God. Lk +4:43.
and every. Lk 7:26-29. 15:1. Mt 21:32. Mk 1:45. Jn 11:48. 12:19.
presseth into it. i.e. pressed against, or resisted. Lk 7:30. Mt 11:11, 12. 23:13. Jn 1:11. 12:37. Ro 11:8, 11, 12.

17 **it**. Lk 21:33. Ps 102:25-27. Is 51:6. Mt +5:18. 2 P 3:10. Re 20:11. 21:1, 4.
than. Is 40:8. Ro 3:31. 1 P 1:25.
to fail. Jsh 23:14. 1 S 3:19. Est 6:10. Ro 9:6. 1 C 13:8.

18 **putteth away**. Ge 2:23, 24. Ml 2:15, 16. Mt 5:32. +19:3-9. Mk 10:2-12. Ro 7:2, 3. 1 C 7:4, 10-12.

19 **There was**. ver. 1.
rich. Lk 12:16-21. 18:24, 25. 1 T 6:17-19. Ja +5:1-5.
clothed. ver. 1. Lk 15:13. Jb 21:11-15. Ps 73:3-7. Ezk +16:49. Am 6:4-6. Re 17:4. 18:7, 16.
purple. Jg 8:26. Est 8:15. Pr 31:22. Ezk 16:13. 27:7. Mk 15:17, 20. Re 18:12, 16.
fine linen. Ex +26:1.
fared sumptuously. Lk 15:23. Ja 5:5.

20 **a certain**. Lk 18:35-43. 1 S 2:8. Ja 1:9. 2:5.
Lazarus. Jn 11:1, 2, 14, 43. 12:1, 2, 9, 10, 17.
was laid. Ac 3:2.
his gate. Mt 26:71.
full. ver. 21. Dt +28:35. Jb 2:7, 8. Ps 34:19. 38:7, 8. 73:14. Is 1:6. Je 8:22.

21 **desiring**. Lk 15:16. 1 C 4:11. 2 C 11:27.
crumbs. Mt 15:27. Mk 7:28. Jn 6:12.
moreover. Ro 7:7. 8:37.

22 **that**. Jb 3:13-19. Is 57:1, 2. Re 14:13.
was carried. Ps 91:11, 12. Mt +13:38-43. 24:31. Ep 4:8. He 2:14.
the angels. Lk 12:8. 15:10. 2 K 6:17. Ps 34:7. Mt 18:10. Ac 12:15. He 1:13, 14.
Abraham's. Mt +8:11. Jn 13:23. 21:20.
the rich. Lk 12:20. Jb 21:13, 30-32. Ps 49:6-12, 16-19. 73:18-20. Pr 14:32. Mk 8:36, 37. Ja 1:11. 1 P 2:24.
died. Jb 4:21. 27:19. Ps +146:4.
and was buried. 2 K 9:34, 35. Jb 4:21. 21:13. 27:19. Ec 8:10. Is 14:18. 22:16.

23 **in hell**. Gr. *hades*, Mt +11:23. Ps +9:17. +16:10. 49:15. +55:15. 86:13. Pr 5:5. 7:27. 9:18. 15:24. Is +14:9, 15. 50:11. +66:24. Da 12:2. Mt 5:22, 29. 11:23. +12:40. 18:9. 23:33. +25:41, 46. Ac 2:27. 1 C 15:55mg. 2 P 2:4. Re 20:13, 14.

in torments. ver. 28. Lk 8:28. Mt 8:29. Ja 2:19. Re 14:10, 11. 20:10.

seeth. Lk 13:28, 29. Is +63:16. +66:24. Mt +17:3. Re 14:10.

Abraham. Lk 13:28. Mt +8:11, 12. Mk 12:26, 27.

in his. Lk 23:43. Jn 13:23. 2 C 5:6-8. Ph +1:23.

24 **Father Abraham**. ver. 30. Lk 3:8. 19:9. Mt 3:9. Jn 8:33-39, 53-56. Ro 4:12. 9:7, 8.

have mercy. Lk 17:13. 1 S 28:16. Is 27:11. Ja 2:13.

send Lazarus. ver. 27.

dip. Gr. *bapto*, **s#911g**. ver. 24. Jn 13:26. Re 19:13. For related words see Mk +7:4.

in water. Is 41:17, 18. 65:13, 14. Jn 4:10, 14. 7:37. Re 7:16, 17. 22:1.

and cool. Zc 14:12. Ja 3:6.

for. Mt +25:41.

tormented. Lk 2:48. Is +33:14. Mt +8:29.

flame. Ps +9:17. 21:9. Is +30:33. +33:14. +66:24. 2 Th 1:8. Re 9:2. 20:10. +21:8.

25 **Son**. ver. 24. Lk 15:31.

remember. ver. 23. Pr 5:11-14. Je 8:20. La 1:7. Da 5:22, 23, 30. Mk 9:46. Ro +3:19. 2 C +1:12.

receivedst. Lk 6:24. Jb 21:13. 36:11, 12.

thy good. Lk 6:24. Jb 21:13, 14. 22:18. Ps 17:14. 37:35, 36. 49:11, 17. 73:7, 12-20. Ro 8:7. Ph 3:19. 1 J 2:15, 16.

likewise. ver. 20. Jn 16:33. Ac 14:22. 1 Th 3:3, 4. He 11:25, 26. Re 7:14-17.

but now. 1 S 2:8. Pr +16:5. Je +20:11.

is comforted. Re +14:13.

and thou. Mt 19:23.

26 **between**. 1 S 25:36. Ps 49:14. Ezk 28:24. Ml 3:18. 2 Th 1:4-10. Ja 1:11, 12. 5:1-7.

cannot. Lk 13:26, 27. Jb +27:8. Is 38:18. Mt +25:46. 2 C +6:2. He +9:27. Re +22:11, 12.

they pass. Lk 12:59. Ps 50:22. Mt 25:46. Jn 3:36. 2 Th 1:9. Re 20:10. 22:11.

28 **testify**. Ac 2:40. 8:25. 10:42. 18:5. 20:21, 23, 24, 26. 23:11. 26:22. 28:23. 1 C +1:6. Ep +4:17. 1 Th +4:6.

lest. Ge 4:13, 14. Ex 10:16, 17. 32:10-12. Jg 10:9, 10. 1 S 12:19. 2 K 1:13, 14. Ps 49:12, 13. Jon 1:14. 3:6-9. Ac 8:22-24.

29 **They have**. ver. 16. Is +8:20. 34:16. Ml 4:2-4. Jn +5:39-45. Ac 15:21. 17:11, 12. 2 T 3:15-17. 2 P 1:19-21.

Moses. ver. 31. Lk +24:27. Ex +24:4. Jn 5:46. Ac 15:21. 21:21. 26:22. 28:23. 2 C 3:15.

the prophets. Ac 10:43.

let them hear. Jn 5:45-47. Ga 4:21.

30 **father**. ver. 24.

but if. 1 C +15:2.

repent. Lk +13:3, 5. Re 16:9-11.

31 **If they**. 1 C +15:2. Ps +19:7. Je +23:28, 29. 2 C 10:4, 5. He 4:12.

hear not Moses. ver. 29. Jn 5:46. Ro 15:4, 8. 2 T 3:15-17.

and the prophets. Ac 13:40, 41.

neither. Ex +9:30. Jn 5:47. 11:43-53. 12:10, 11. 2 C 4:3.

be persuaded. Ge 9:27mg. Ac 19:8. 26:28. 28:23. 2 C 5:11.

rose from. Mt 28:11-15. Jn 12:10, 11. Ac 4:10, 17.

LUKE 17

1 **It is**. Ac 20:30. 1 C 11:19. 2 Th 2:10-12. 1 T 4:1, 2. Re 2:14, 20. 13:14, etc.

offenses. Mt +17:27.

but woe. Lk 22:22. Mt 26:24. Mk 14:21.

2 **better**. Mt 18:6. 26:24. Mk 9:42. 1 C 9:15. 2 P 2:1-3.

that a. lit. if a. 1 C +15:2.

one. Is 40:11. Zc 13:7. Mt 18:3-5, 10, 14. Jn 21:15. 1 C 8:11, 12. 9:22.

little ones. Lk +9:47. +18:15. 1 J 2:12, 13.

3 **heed**. Lk 21:34. Ex 34:12. Dt 4:9, 15, 23. 2 Ch 19:6, 7. Ac 5:35. Ep 5:15. He 12:15. 2 J 8.

If. Mt +4:9. Mt 18:15-17, 21, 22.

rebuke. Le +19:17. Ps 141:5. Pr 9:8, 9. +17:10. 27:5, 6. Ga 2:11-14. 2 Th 3:15. 1 T +5:19, 20. 2 T 4:2. T 3:10. Ja 5:19, 20.

4 **if**. Mt +4:9. Mt 18:21, 22, 35. 1 C 13:4-7. Ep 4:31, 32. Col 3:12, 13.

seven times. Ps +119:164. Pr 24:16. Mt 18:21.

turn again. Lk +22:32.

I repent. Mt 5:44. 6:12, 14, 15. 18:16, 17. Ro +12:20, 21. 2 Th 3:13, 14.

5 **the apostles**. Lk 9:10. Mk 6:30.

the Lord. Lk 7:13.

Increase. Ps +138:3. Mk 9:24. 2 C 12:8-10. Ph 4:13. 2 Th 1:3. He 12:2. 1 P 1:22, 23. 2 P 3:18.

faith. Lk 22:31, 32. Mt 17:20. Mk 9:23, 24. 11:23. Ac 6:8. 11:24. Ro 4:20, 21. 10:17. Ep 2:8. 6:23. 1 Th 3:10.

6 **If**. 1 C +15:2. Mt 17:20, 21. 21:21. Mk 9:23. 11:22, 23. 1 C 13:2.

as a grain. Lk 13:19. Mt 13:31, 32.

ye might. Mt +23:30.

sycamine tree. Lk 19:4. 2 S 5:23. 1 Ch 14:15. 27:28. 2 Ch 1:15. 9:27. Ps 78:47. Am 7:14.

it should. This is an example of the use of more than one kind of "if," called a mixed condition. The "if" clause is the First Class Condition (1 C 15:2); the "then" clause, expressing result, is Second Class (Mt 23:30). Other examples of such mixed conditions are Jn 8:39. 13:17. Ac 5:38, 39. 8:31. 24:19. 1 C 7:28. 9:11.

7 **which of you**. Lk 13:15. 14:5. Mt 12:11.

8 **Make**. Ge 43:16. 2 S 12:20.

and gird. Lk +12:35, 37. Ex 28:39. Is 22:21.

9 **the things**. Lk 3:13. Ac 23:31.

10 **when ye shall.** 1 Ch 29:14-16. Jb 10:15. 22:2, 3. 35:6, 7. 41:11. Ps 16:2, 3. 35:6, 7. Pr 9:12. Is 6:5. 64:6. Je +48:10. Ezk +16:49. Mt +25:26, 30, 37-40. Ro 3:12. 11:35. 1 C 9:16, 17. 15:9, 10. Ph 3:8, 9. Phm 11. 1 P 5:5, 6.
We are. Jb 10:15. Ro +12:3. Ph +2:3.
unprofitable. Ps 143:2. Is 64:6. Ro 3:27. 1 C 4:7.
have done. 1 C 10:12. 1 P 4:18.
our duty. 1 C 15:58.
11 **as he went.** Lk +9:51, 52.
passed through. 1 K 16:24. Mt 19:1. Jn 4:4.
12 **lepers.** Lk 7:22.
which stood. Lk 5:12. 18:13. 2 K +5:1. La 4:15.
13 **lifted.** Lk 11:27. Ge +22:13. Jg 21:2. 1 S 11:4. Ac 2:14. 4:24. 14:11. 22:22.
Master. Lk 5:5.
have. Mt +9:27.
14 **Go show.** Mk +1:44.
as. 2 K 5:14. Is 65:24. Mt 8:3. Jn 2:5. 4:50-53. 9:7. 11:40.
15 **one of them.** ver. 17, 18. 2 Ch 32:24-26. Ps 30:1, 2, 11, 12. 103:1-4. 107:20-22. 116:12-15. 118:18, 19. Is 38:19-22. Jn 5:14. 9:38.
glorified God. Mt +9:8.
16 **fell.** Ge +17:3. Jn 5:23.
and he. Lk 9:52-56. 10:32-35. Mt 10:5. Jn 4:9, 21, 22, 39-42. 8:48. Ac +1:8. 8:5, etc.
17 **ten.** ver. 12.
but. Ge 3:9. Ps 106:13. Jn 8:7-10. Ro 1:21.
18 **not found.** 2 Ch 32:25.
to give. Ps 29:1, 2. 50:23. Re +11:13.
save. 2 K 17:24. Is 61:5. Mt +8:10, 11. 15:24-28. 19:30. 20:16. 1 J 5:20.
19 **thy faith.** Lk 7:50. 8:48. 18:42. Mt 9:22. Mk 5:34. 10:52.
20 **when the.** Lk +19:11, 12. +21:31. Mt +23:39. Mk +13:32. Ac +1:6, 7.
kingdom of God. Lk +4:43. +22:29, 30. Mt +21:43. Jn +18:36. Re 11:15.
cometh not. Lk 12:39. 14:1. +21:31. Mt 25:13. Jn 18:36. 1 Th 5:2, 3. 2 T +4:1.
observation. *or,* outward show. ver. 23, 24. Lk 12:31, 32. 16:16. Da 2:44. Zc 4:6. Mk +13:32. Jn 18:36. Ac +1:6, 7. Ro 14:17. 1 C 4:20. Col 1:13. He 12:22, 23. Re 1:9.
21 **Lo here.** ver. 23. Lk 21:8. Mt 24:23-28. Mk 13:21-23.
the kingdom. ver. +20. Col 1:27.
is. Mt +2:4. 26:2. 1 C 15:42-44.
within you. *or,* among you. Lk 10:9-11. 11:20. Mt 12:28. 23:26. Mk +1:15. Jn 1:26. 12:35.
22 **days.** Dt +4:32.
will come. Lk 19:43. 21:6. 23:29. Mk 2:20. Jn 4:21.
when. Lk 5:35. 13:35. Mt 9:15. 25:19, 24. Jn 7:33-36. 8:21-24. 12:35. 13:33. 16:5-7, 16-22. 17:11-13.

to see. Am 5:18. Jn 8:56.
days of. ver. +24. 1 C 1:8. 2 C 1:14. Ph 1:6. 1 Th 5:2.
shall not. Mt 25:14, +19.
23 **See here.** ver. 21. Lk 21:8. Mt +24:23-26. Mk 13:21-23.
24 **as the lightning.** Jb 37:3, 4. Ezk 1:14. Zc 9:14. Mt 24:27.
in his day. Ml 3:1, 2. 4:1, 2. Mt +24:30. +25:31. 26:64. 1 C 1:8. 1 Th 5:2. 2 Th 2:2, 8. Ja 5:8. 2 P 3:10.
25 **must he suffer.** Lk +13:33. 18:31, 33. 24:25, 26, 46. Mt 16:21. 17:22, 23. 20:18, 19. Mk 8:31. 9:31. 10:33.
be rejected. Jn 1:11. +12:48. 1 P 2:4.
26 **as it was.** Mt +24:37-39.
the days of the Son. ver. 22, 24. Lk 18:8. 1 C 1:8.
27 **did eat.** Lk 12:19, 20. 16:19-23. Dt 6:10-12. 8:12-14. 1 S 25:36-38. Jb 21:9-13. Is 21:4. 22:12-14. Mt 24:38, 39. 1 Th 5:1-3.
they drank. Ge +10:1.
in marriage. Lk 20:35. Mt 22:30. Mk 12:25.
until the day. Ge 7:7.
the flood came. Ge 7:17-24.
destroyed. Gr. *apollumi,* Mt +2:13.
28 **days of Lot.** i.e. *protection,* S#3091g. ver. 29, 32. 2 P 2:7. For S#3876h, see Ge +11:27. Ge 13:13. 18:20, 21. 19:4-15. Ezk +16:49, 50. Ja +5:1-5.
they drank. Ge +10:1.
29 **same day.** Ge +19:24. Re 11:8.
rained fire. 2 Th 1:8. 2 P 3:7.
Sodom. Lk +10:12.
destroyed. Gr. *apollumi,* Mt +2:13.
30 **in the day.** ver. 24. Lk 21:22, 27, 34-36. Mt 16:27. +24:3, 27-31, 44. 26:64. Mk 13:26. 1 C 1:7. 2 Th 1:7. 1 P 1:7, 13. 4:13. Re 1:7.
is revealed. 2 Th +1:7.
31 **he which.** Lk 21:21. Mt 24:17, 18. Mk 13:15, 16.
the housetop. Dt +22:8. Jb 2:4. Je 45:5. Mt 6:25. 16:26. Ph 3:7, 8.
not return. Ge 19:26.
32 **Remember.** Ge 19:17, 26. 1 C 10:6-12. He +10:38, 39. 2 P 2:18-22.
33 **shall seek.** Lk 9:24, 25. Mt 10:39. 16:25. Mk 8:35-37. Jn 12:25. Re 2:10.
to save. Ac 20:28. Ep 1:14. 1 Th 5:9. 2 Th 2:14. 1 T 3:13. He 10:39. 1 P 2:9.
life. Gr. *psyche,* Mt +2:20; Ge +9:5.
lose. Gr. *apollumi,* Mt +2:13.
life. Gr. *psyche,* Mt +2:20; Ge +9:5.
preserve it. Ac 7:19. 1 T 6:13. 2 T 4:6-8.
34 **I tell you.** Lk 13:3, 5, 24. Is 42:9. Mt 24:25. Mk 13:23. Jn 14:29.
in that night. Mt 24:40, 41.
two. Ps 26:9. 28:3. Je 45:5. Ezk 9:4-6. Ml 3:16-18. Ro 11:4-7. 1 Th 4:16, 17. 2 P 2:9.

one shall be taken. ver. 37. Je 11:11. Mi +4:12. Mt 8:12. +13:30, 41. +24:41.

35 Two women. Mt 24:41.
grinding. Ex 11:5. Jg 16:21. Jb 31:10. Ec 12:3. Is 47:2.
taken. ver. +34. Je 11:11. Mt 8:12. +13:30, 41.

36 Two men. "This verse is wanting in most of the Greek copies." Mt 24:40.
taken. ver. +34. Mt 8:12. +13:30, 41.

37 Wheresoever. Jb 39:29, 30. Is +66:24. Ezk 39:4, 5, 11, 12-18. Da +9:26, 27. Jl 3:2, 9-16. Am 9:1-4. Zp +3:8. Zc 13:8, 9. 14:2. Mt 24:28. Jn 11:48. Ro 2:8, 9, 16. 1 Th 2:16. Re 16:14-16. 19:17-21.
the body. Ezk 39:11-15. Da 7:11. Mt +24:28. Re 19:18.
the eagles. Dt 28:49. Jb 39:27-30. Pr 30:17. Is 18:6. +40:31. Je 16:4. Ezk 39:17-21. Ho 8:1. Hab 1:8. Mt +24:28. Re 4:7. 19:17-21.
be gathered together. 1 S 17:44, 46. Ezk 39:4, 17.

LUKE 18

1 ought always. Lk 11:5-8. +21:36. Ge 32:9-12, 24-26. 1 S +7:8. Jb 27:8-10. Ps 55:16, 17. 65:2. 86:3mg. +102:17. 142:5-7. Is 62:6, 7. Je +10:25. 29:12, 13. Ac 10:2. Ro 12:12. Ep 6:18. Ph 4:6. Col 4:2, 12. 1 Th 5:17.
to pray. Jb 42:8. Pr 4:6. Is 55:6. Ezk 36:37. Mt 5:44. 6:9-13. +14:23. 26:41. 1 Th 3:10. 1 T 2:1-3, 8. He 4:15, 16. Ja 5:13, 16. 1 P 4:7.
and not to faint. Ps 27:13. Jon 2:7. 2 C 4:1, 16. Ga 6:9. Ep 3:13. 2 Th 3:13. He 12:3-5.

2 city. Gr. certain city. Is 1:10. Ezk 16:26, 46. 20:7. Re 11:8.
which. ver. 4. Ex 18:21, 22. 2 Ch 19:3-9. Jb 29:7-17. Ps 82:1-4. Is 10:1, 2. Je 22:16, 17. Ezk 22:6-8. Mi 3:1-3. Ro 3:14-18. 2 C 8:21.
regarded. ver. 4. Lk 20:13. Pr 29:7. Is 33:8. Mt 21:37. Mk 12:6. He 12:9.

3 a widow. 2 S 14:5, etc. Is +1:17. 54:4, 5.
Avenge. ver. 7, 8. Ps 79:1-3, 5. 54:5. 55:9. 143:12. Is 63:15. Ro +6:10. 13:3, 4.
adversary. Lk 12:58.

4 he said. Lk 12:17. 16:3. He 4:12, 13.
Though. Lk +11:8.
fear not. Ex +9:30.
nor regard. Lk 11:8.

5 because. Lk 11:8. Jg 16:16. 2 S 13:24-27.
continual coming. Is 62:7.
weary. ver. 39. Mt 15:23. Mk 10:47, 48. 1 C 9:27.

6 the Lord. Lk 7:13.
unjust judge. lit. judge of unrighteousness. Lk 16:8, 9. Ja 2:4.

7 shall not. Mt +5:18. Lk 11:13. Mt 7:11. 15:22-28. Mk 7:24-30. 2 P 3:9.
avenge. Jg 16:27-30. 1 S 24:11-15. 26:10, 11.

Dt +32:35. Ps 9:8, 18. 10:15-18. 54:1-7. +58:10. Je +10:25. 20:11-13. 2 Th 1:6.
elect. Dt +10:15. Mk 13:20. Ro +8:28-30, 33. 2 T +2:10. 1 P 1:1, 2. 2 P +1:10.
which cry. Lk 2:37. Ex +22:23. Ps 9:12. 22:2. 88:1. 1 Th 3:10. 1 T 5:5. 2 T 1:3. Re 7:15.
day and night. Ps 32:4. 42:3. La 2:18. Mk 4:27. 5:5. Ac 9:24. Re 4:8. 7:15. 12:10. 14:11. 20:10.
though. Ps 13:1, 2. Hab 2:3. He 10:35-37. Ja 5:7. 2 P 3:9.

8 he will avenge. Dt +32:35. Ps 46:5. 143:7-9. Ro +12:19. 2 P 2:3. +3:7-9. Re 6:10. 19:2.
speedily. Hab 2:3. He 10:37. Re 1:1.
when. Lk 7:19. Mt 11:3. 24:9-13, 24, 44. 25:5. 1 Th 5:1-3. He 10:23-26. Ja 5:1-8.
Son of man. Lk +5:24.
cometh. Mt +16:28. +24:3, 30.
find. Lk 17:26-30. Dt 32:20. Je 5:1. Ezk 22:30. +33:31. Mt +7:14. 24:12, 22, 38, 39. 1 Th 4:15, 17.
faith. or, the faith. Lk 17:5. Ac +6:7. 1 T +1:19. Re 2:19. 13:10.
on the earth. Re +5:10. +6:10.

9 which trusted. ver. 14. Lk 10:29. 15:29. 16:15. Pr 30:12. Is +65:5. 66:5. Mt 5:20. Jn 9:28, 34. Ro 7:9. 9:31, 32. 10:3. Ph 3:4-6.
in themselves. Lk 11:22. 2 C 1:9. He 2:13.
that they were righteous. or, as being righteous. Pr 30:12. Is +65:5. Jn 7:48, 49.
and despised. ver. 11. Lk 7:39. 15:2, 30. 19:7. 23:11. Is +65:5. Jn 7:47-49. 8:48. Ac 4:11. 22:21, 22. Ro 14:3, 10. 3 J 9.

10 Two men. Lk 1:53.
into. ver. 14. Lk 1:9, 10. 19:46. 1 K 8:30. 10:5. 2 K 20:5, 8. 2 Ch 9:4. Jn 7:14. Ac 3:1. 10:9.
a Pharisee. Lk +7:29, 30. Mt 21:31, 32. Ac 23:6-8. 26:5. Ph 3:5.
a publican. Mt +5:46.

11 stood and. ver. 13. 1 S 1:26. 1 K 8:14, 22. 2 Ch 6:12. Ps 134:1. 135:2. Mt 6:5. Mk 11:25. Ac 27:21.
God. Is 1:15. 58:2, 3. Je 2:23, 35. Ezk +33:31. Mi 3:11. 1 C 4:7, 8. 15:9, 10. 1 T 1:12-16. Re 3:17, 18.
as. Lk 20:47. Is +65:5. Mt 3:7-10. 19:18-20. Ga 3:10. Ph 3:6. Ja 2:9-12.
extortioners. Lk 11:39. Mt 23:25. 1 C 5:10, 11. 6:10.

12 fast. Lk 5:33. +17:10. Nu 23:4. 1 S 15:13. 2 K 10:16. Jb +21:15. Ps +106:13. Is 1:15. 58:2-5. Zc 7:5, 6. Mt 6:1, 5, 16. 9:14. 15:7-9. Mk 2:18. Ro 3:27. 10:1-3. 1 C 1:29. 2 C +7:10. Ga 1:14. +4:17. Ep 2:9. 1 T 4:8. 2 T +3:5.
week. lit. sabbath. Mt +28:1.
I give. Lk 11:42. Le 27:30-33. Nu 18:24. Ml 3:8. Mt +23:23, 24.
tithes of all. Lk +11:41, 42. Ge 28:22. Dt 14:22, 23. 2 Ch 31:5. Ml 3:10. Mt 23:2, 3, +23. Mk 12:42.

13 standing. ver. 11. Ge 24:12-14. Ex 33:10. 1 K 8:14, 22, 55. 2 K 23:3. 1 Ch +17:16. 2 Ch 20:9, 13, 19. Ne 9:4, 5. Mk 11:25.
afar off. Lk 5:8. 7:6, 7. 17:12. 23:49. Ezr 9:6. Jb 42:6. Ps 40:12. Is 6:5. Ezk 16:63. Da 9:7-9. Ac 2:37.
not lift. Jb 22:29mg.
his eyes. Lk 6:20. Ps 40:12. Jn 6:5. 17:1.
but smote. Lk 23:48. Je 31:18, 19. Mt 11:17. 2 C 7:11.
God. Ps 25:7, 11. 41:4. +51:1-3. 86:15, 16. 119:41. 130:3, 4, 7. Da 9:5, 9-11, 18, 19. He 4:16. 8:12.
merciful. Ezr 9:6, 7. Ps +4:1. 25:11. 40:12. 41:4. 51:1-17. 79:9. Ezk 16:63. Da 9:8, 19. He 2:17. 1 J 2:2. 4:10.
a sinner. Lk 15:18-21. 23:40-43. Ex 10:16, 17. 34:8, 9. Jg 10:10. 2 Ch 33:12, 13, 19, 23. Ps 51:1-9. 106:6. Is 1:18. 55:6, 7. 64:5, 6. Jon 3:4, 5. Mt 9:13. Mk +11:25. Ac 8:22. Ro 5:8, 20, 21. 1 T 1:15. 1 J 1:8-10.

14 went. Lk 5:24, 25. 7:47-50. 1 S 1:18. Ec 9:7.
justified. Lk 7:35. 10:29. 16:15. Jb 9:20. 25:4. 33:32. Ps 143:2. Is 45:25. 50:8. 53:11. Hab 2:4. Ro 3:20. 4:5. 5:1, 9. 8:33. Ga 2:16. Ja 2:21-25.
for every. Lk 1:52. 14:11. Ex 18:11. Jb 22:29. 40:9-13. Ps 138:6. Pr 3:34. 15:33. 16:18, 19. 18:12. 29:23. Is 2:11-17. +57:15. Da 4:37. Hab 2:4. Mt +5:3. 18:4. 23:12. Ja 4:6, 10. 1 P 5:5, 6.
he that humbleth. Lk 14:11. Jg +10:15. 2 Ch +7:14. 33:12, 13. Ps 9:12. Pr +28:13. 29:23. Mt +8:8. Ph 2:5-11. Ja 4:6, +10. 1 P 5:5, 6.

15 they brought. 1 S 1:24. Mt 19:13-15. Mk 10:13-16.
infants. Dt +29:11. 1 C +7:14. **S#1025g**: Lk 1:41, 44 (babe). 2:12, 16. Ac 7:19 (children). 2 T +3:15 (child). 1 P 2:2 (babes).
they rebuked. ver. 39. Lk 9:49, 50, 54. Mt 20:31. Mk 10:48.

16 Suffer. Ge 17:10-14. 21:4. Dt 29:11. 31:12. 2 Ch 20:13. Je 32:39. Mt 18:3, 4. Ac +2:39. 1 C +7:14.
little children. Lk 9:47. 1 C +7:14.
forbid them not. Lk 9:50. Mk 9:39.
for. Mt 18:3, 4. 1 C 14:20. 1 P 2:2.
the kingdom. Lk +4:43.

17 Verily. ver. 29. Mt +5:18.
Whosoever. Ps 131:1, 2. Mk 10:15, 16. Jn 3:3, 5. 1 P 1:14.
receive. Lk +8:13. Jn 1:12. Ja 1:21.
as. Mt 18:3.

18 a certain. Mt +9:18. 19:16, etc. Mk 10:17, etc. Jn 3:1.
Good Master. Lk 6:46. +7:40. Ezk +33:31. Ml 1:6. Jn 7:12. 13:13-15.
what. Lk 10:25. Jn 6:28. Ac 2:37. 16:30.
inherit. ver. 30. Mt 19:16, 29.

eternal. Gr. *aionios*, Mt +18:8. Ro 6:22, 23. 1 J 5:11-13.

19 Why callest. Lk +1:35. 11:13. Jb 14:4. 15:14-16. 25:4. 1 T 3:16. He 7:26. Ja 1:17. 1 J 3:5.
good. Hab 1:12. Mk 2:7. Jn 10:14. Ac 2:27. 3:14.
none is. Ge +6:5. Ro 3:23.
save one. 1 S 2:2. Ps 89:6. 119:68. Ro 16:27. Re 15:4.

20 knowest. Lk 10:26-28. Is +8:20. Mt 19:17-19. Mk 10:18, 19. Ro 3:20. 7:7-11.
Do not commit. Ex 20:12-17. Dt 5:16-21. Ro 13:9. Ga 3:10-13. Ep +6:2. Col 3:20. Ja 2:8-11.
adultery. Ex +20:14. Le 18:20. Dt 5:18. 22:22. Pr 6:32. Mt 5:27. Ro 13:9. 1 C +6:9. He +13:4.
kill. Ge +9:5, 6. Ex +20:13. Dt 5:17. Mt 5:21. Ro 13:9. 1 J 3:15.
steal. Ex +20:15. Le 19:11. Dt 5:19. Ro 13:9. Ep 4:28.
bear false witness. Ex +20:16. 23:1. Dt 5:20. 19:16-20. Pr 19:5, 9. 21:28. 24:28. 25:18.
Honor thy. Ex +20:12.

21 All these. ver. 11, 12. Lk 15:7, 29. 17:10. Mt 5:20. 19:20, 21. Mk 10:20, 21. Ro 10:2, 3. Ph 3:6.
from. Ezk 4:14.

22 Yet lackest. T 1:5. 3:13.
one thing. Lk +10:42. Ps 27:4. Ph 3:13. Ja 2:10. 2 P 3:8.
sell. Lk 12:33. 16:9. Mt 6:19, 20. Ac 2:44, 45. 4:34-37. 1 T 6:17-19.
treasure. Dt +28:12.
in heaven. Mt 6:19, 20.
and come. Lk 9:23, 57-62. Mt 19:21, 27, 28.
follow me. Jn 1:43. Ph 3:6-9.

23 when he heard. Ezk +33:31.
he was very sorrowful. Jg 18:23, 24. Mt 19:22. 26:38. Mk 6:26. 10:22. 14:34.
very rich. Lk +8:14. 12:15. 19:8. 21:34. Jb 31:24, 25. Ps 62:10. Mt 6:24. Mt +13:22. 16:26. Ep 5:5. Ph 3:8. Col 3:5. 1 J 2:15, 16.

24 he was. Mk 6:26. 2 C 7:9, 10.
How hardly. Dt 6:10-12. 8:11-17. Ps 10:3, 4. 73:5-12. Pr 11:28. 18:11. 30:9. Je 2:31. 5:5. Mt +13:22. 19:23-25. Mk 10:23-27. 1 C 1:26, 27. 1 T 6:9, 10. Ja 2:5-7. +5:1-6.
the kingdom. Lk +4:43.

25 easier. Mk 10:25.
a camel. Mt 23:24.
enter. Mt +7:21.

26 Who. Lk 13:23.

27 The things. Jb +42:2. Da 4:35. Zc 8:6. Mk 14:36. Ep 1:19, 20. 2:4-10. He 6:6.

28 Lo. Lk 5:11. Mt 4:19-22. 9:9. 19:27. Mk 10:28. Ph 3:7-9.
left all. Lk 5:11, 28. 14:33. Ge 22:10, 12. Jg +10:15. Mt 4:20, 22. 10:37-39. 16:24-26. 19:29. Mk 1:18, 20. 8:34-37. +10:28-30. Lk 14:26, 27, 33.

29 Verily. ver. +17.
There. Lk 14:26-28, 33. Dt 33:8, 9, 11. Mt
10:37-39. 19:28-30. Mk +10:29-31.
for the kingdom. Mt 19:29. Mk 10:29.

30 not. Mt +5:18.
manifold more. Lk 12:31, 32. Ps 37:16.
63:4, 5. 119:72, 103, 111, 127, 162. Ro 6:21-
23. Ph 4:7. 6:6. He +13:5, 6. Re 2:10, 17. 3:21.
present time. Ge +6:13. Mt +12:32. Mk
+10:30.
world. Gr. *aion*, Mt +6:13; +12:32. Lk 20:35.
Ep 1:21. 2:7. 2 T 4:8. He 6:5.
everlasting. Gr. *aionios*, Mt +18:8. ver. 18. Mt
19:16.

31 the twelve. Mk 9:35.
Behold. Lk 9:22. 24:6, 7. Mt 16:21. 17:22,
23. 20:17-19. Mk 8:31. 9:30, 31. 10:32-34.
we go. Lk +9:51.
up to. Lk +2:4.
and. Lk 21:22. 24:44-46. Ps ch. 22, 69. Is ch.
53. Da +9:26. Zc 13:7. Mt 1:22. 26:24. Jn
6:45.
Son of man. Lk +5:24.

32 delivered. Mk +10:33.
unto the Gentiles. Lk 23:11, 12. Ac 4:27.
21:11.
mocked. Lk +22:63. Jn 18:22. 19:1-5.
spitefully. Ac 14:5.
and spitted on. Mt +26:67.

33 scourge. Jn +19:1.
and put. Mk 8:31.
third day. Ac 2:29-32. 1 C +15:4.

34 understood none. Lk 2:50. 9:45. 24:25, 45.
Ps 139:6. Mk 9:32. Jn 10:6. 12:16. 16:1-19. 1
C 2:10, 11.
was hid. Lk 2:50. 9:45. 24:16.

35 as. Mt 20:29, 30. Mk 10:46, 47.
Jericho. Lk 10:30.
begging. Lk 16:20, 21. 1 S 2:8. Jn 9:8. Ac 3:2.

36 he. Lk 15:26. Mt 21:10, 11.
what it. Lk +1:62.

37 they. Mk 2:1-3. Jn 12:35, 36. 2 C 6:2.
Jesus. Mt +2:23.
of Nazareth. Mk +1:24.

38 Jesus. Mt +1:1.
have mercy. Ps 62:12. Mt +9:27.

39 rebuked. ver. 15. Lk 8:49. 11:52. 19:39. Mt
19:13.
but. Lk 11:8-10. 18:1. Ge 32:26-28. Ps 141:1.
Je 29:12, 13. Mt 7:7. 26:40-44. 2 C 12:8.

40 stood. Mt 20:31-34. Mk 10:48-52.

41 What. 1 K 3:5, etc. Mt 7:7. 20:21, 22. Mk
10:36. Ro 8:25. Ph 4:6.

42 Receive. Lk 7:21. Ps 33:9. 107:20. Mt 8:3.
15:28.
thy faith. Lk 7:50. 8:48. 17:19. Mt 9:22. Mk
5:34.
hath saved. Lk 7:3. 8:36, 48, 50. Mk 10:52.
Jn 11:12. Ac 4:9. Ja 5:15.

43 immediately. Lk 5:25. 8:44, 55.

he. Ps 30:2. Mt +11:5. Jn 9:5-7, 39, 40.
followed. Lk 4:39. Ps 103:1-3. 107:8, 15, 21,
22, 31, 32. Is 43:7, 8, 21. 1 P 2:9.
glorifying. Mt +9:8.
all the people. Lk 5:26. 19:37.
gave praise. Lk 13:17. 17:18. Ro 4:20. Re 4:9.

LUKE 19

1 entered. Lk 18:35. Mt 20:29. Mk 10:46.
Jericho. Lk 10:30. Jsh 2:1. 6:1, etc., 26. 1 K
16:34. 2 K 2:18-22.

2 Zacchaeus. i.e. *just, pure*, **S#2195g**. ver. 5, 8.
the chief. *Arkitelonees*, rather, "a chief publican," or tax gatherer. Mt +5:46.
and he. Lk 18:24-27. 2 Ch 17:5, 6.
was rich. 1 T 6:17.

3 he sought. Lk 9:7-9. 23:8. Jn 1:38. 12:21.
because. Lk 12:25.
stature. Lk 2:52.

4 climbed. Lk 5:19.
a sycamore. Lk +17:6. 1 K 10:27. 1 Ch
27:28. 2 Ch 1:15. 9:27. Is 9:10. Am 7:14.

5 he looked. Ps 139:1-3. Ezk 16:6. Jn 1:48.
4:7-10.
Zaccheus. Ec 9:10. 2 C +6:1, 2.
for. ver. 10. Ge 18:3-5. 19:1-3. Ps 101:2, 3. Jn
10:3. 14:23. Ep 3:17. He 13:2. Re 3:20.
I must. Lk +13:33.
abide. Jn 1:38, 40. Ac 16:15.

6 he. Lk 2:16. Ge 18:6, 7. Ps 119:59, 60. Ga
1:15, 16.
received. Lk 10:38.
joyfully. Lk 5:29. Is 64:5. Ac 2:41. 16:15, 34.

7 they all murmured. Lk 7:34, 39. 18:9-14.
Mt 9:4, 11-13. 21:28-31. Ju +16.
guest. Lk 9:12.

8 the Lord. Lk 7:13.
Behold. Lk 3:8-13. 11:41. 12:33. 16:9. 18:22,
23. Ps 41:1. Mt 3:8. Ac 2:44-46. 4:34, 35. 2 C
8:7, 8. 1 T 6:17, 18. Ja 1:10, 11.
the half. Mk 12:44.
I give. Lk 18:22.
and if. 1 C +15:2.
by false. Lk 3:14. Ex 20:16.
accusation. Ge +43:18mg.
I restore. Ex 22:1-4, 7. Le 5:16. 6:1-6. Nu
5:7. 1 S 12:3, 2 S 12:6. 1 K 20:34. 2 K 8:6. Ne
5:6-13. Pr 6:31. Ezk +33:15. Mt 5:23, 24, +26.
Ep +4:28.

9 unto him. or, concerning him.
This day. Lk 2:30. 13:30. Jn 4:38-42. Ac
16:30-32. 1 C +6:9-11. 2 C +6:2. 1 P 2:10.
salvation come. Jn 4:26. 9:37. Ac 16:31. 1 T
6:19.
house. Ge +7:1.
forsomuch. Lk 3:8. 13:16. 16:24, 25, 27, 30.
Jn 8:33. Ac 3:25. Ro 4:11, 12, 16. Ga 3:7, 14,
29.
son. Mt 3:9. Ga 3:7.

10 **Son of man**. Lk +5:24.
come to. Lk 5:31, 32. 15:4-7, 9, 10, 32. Ge
37:16. Je 31:20. Ezk 34:11, 16. Mi 7:19. Mt
1:21. 5:17. +9:12, 13. 10:6. 15:24. +18:11.
20:28. Mk 2:17. 10:45. Jn 5:14. 10:10. Ro 5:6.
1 T +1:15. He 7:25. 1 J 3:8. 4:9-14.
to save. Is 53:11. Mt 1:21.
lost. Gr. *apollumi*, Mt +2:13. Ps 119:176. Mt
+10:28.

11 **was nigh**. ver. 28. Lk +9:51.
to Jerusalem. Is +24:23.
they thought. Lk +17:20. +24:21. Mk 1:15.
Ac +1:6, 7. 2 Th 2:1-3.
kingdom of God. Lk +4:43. +22:29, 30. Mt
+21:43. Jn +18:36.
immediately appear. Lk +21:31.

12 **A certain**. Mt 25:14-30. Mk 13:34-37.
a far country. Lk 20:9. 24:51. Mt 21:38.
+25:19. Mk 12:1. 16:19. Ac 1:9, 10.
to receive. ver. 15. Mt 28:18. Da +7:13, 14.
Lk +1:32. Jn 18:37. 1 C 15:25. Ep 1:11, 20-23.
Ph 2:9-11. 2 T 4:18. He 12:28. 1 P 3:22. Re
11:15, 18.
a kingdom. Da 2:44. Mt 25:34. Lk 22:29, 30.
2 T +4:1.
and to return. Mt 16:27. 19:28. 24:30.
25:31. Ac +1:11. 17:31. He 9:28. Re +1:7.

13 **his ten**. Mt 25:2, 14. Jn 12:26. Ga 1:10. Ja
1:1. 2 P 1:1.
delivered. Mt 25:15. Ro 12:6-8. 1 C 12:7-11,
28, 29. 1 P 4:9-11.
pounds. "Mina, here translated a pound, is
12 1/2 oz. which, according to 5s the ounce,
is 3l. 2s. 6d."
Occupy. Ezk 27:15, 21mg, 27. Da 8:27. Mt
25:16.
till I come. Jn 21:22, 23. 1 C 11:26.

14 **his citizens**. ver. 27. 1 S 8:7. Ps 2:1-3. 35:19.
69:4. Is 49:7. Zc 11:8. Jn 1:11. 15:18, 23-25.
19:14, 15. Ac 3:14, 15. 4:27, 28. 7:51, 52.
We will not. ver. 27. Ge 37:8. Nu 16:12. 1 K
+11:4. Jb 21:14. 27:22. Ps 12:4. +14:1. Is
30:11. Je +6:16. Ezk +33:20. Mt +23:37. Jn
+5:40. Ro 1:28. 2 P +3:5.

15 **was returned**. Lk 10:35.
having received. ver. 12. Ps 2:4-6. Da 7:14.
Lk +1:32. 1 C 15:24.
money. Gr. silver, and so ver. 23.
that he. Lk +12:48. 16:2, etc. Mt 18:23, etc.
25:19. Ro 14:10-12. 1 C 4:1-5.

16 **Lord**. 1 Ch 29:14-16. 1 C 4:7. 15:10. Col
1:28, 29. 2 T 4:7, 8. Ja 2:18-26.

17 **Well**. Ge 39:4. 1 S 2:30. Mt 25:21. Ro 2:29. 1
C 4:5. 2 T 2:10. 1 P 1:7. 5:4. Re 20:12.
been faithful. Lk 16:10. 22:30. Da +12:3. Mt
25:21. 1 C 4:2. 15:41. 1 T 3:13. Re 2:26-29.
authority. ver. 19. Lk 12:44. Ps +49:14. Mt
20:25. 24:47. Ep 6:9. Ja 5:6. Re +5:10.

18 **thy pound**. Mt +13:23. Mk 4:20. 2 C 8:12.
hath gained. ver. 16. 1 C 4:7. 15:10.

19 **Be**. ver. 17. Lk 12:44. Is 3:10. Mt 24:47. 1 C
3:8. 15:41, 42, 58. 2 C 9:6. 2 J 8.

20 **Lord**. ver. 13. Lk 3:9. 6:46. Pr 26:13-16. Mt
25:24. Ja 4:17.
napkin. lit. sweat-rag for wiping perspiration
from face. Mt +6:2. 7:15. Lk 10:21. 13:32.
14:8-11, 16-24. 18:11, 12. 22:25. Jn 11:44.
20:7. Ac 19:12.

21 **I feared**. Ex 20:19, 20. 1 S 12:20. Ps +9:10.
18:23, 26. Mt +25:24, 25. Ro 8:15. 2 T +1:7.
Ja 2:19. 1 J 4:18. Re +21:8.
because. 1 S 6:19-21. 2 S 6:9-11. Jb 21:14,
15. Ezk 18:25-29. Ml 3:14, 15. Ro 8:7.
Ju 15.
austere. 1 S 25:3.
thou takest. Lk 21:3. Mk 12:43, 44. 2 C
8:12. 9:7.

22 **Out**. 2 S 1:16. Jb 9:20. 15:5, 6. Mt 12:37.
22:12. Ro 3:19.
wicked servant. Mt 18:32.
Thou knewest. Mt +25:24, 26, 27.

23 **Wherefore**. Ro 2:4, 5.
bank. Mt 21:12.
might. Mt +23:30.
required. Lk 3:13.
mine own. Mt 25:27.
usury. Is +24:2.

24 **that stood by**. 1 K 10:8. 2 Ch 9:7. Est 4:5.
Take. Lk 12:20. 16:2. Mt 21:43.
and give. ver. 16. Lk 8:18. Ac 13:46.

25 **Lord**. Lk 16:2. 2 S 7:19. Is 55:8, 9.

26 **That unto**. Mt +13:12.
and from. That is, the *poor man*, who possesses but *little*. Lk 16:3. 1 S 2:30. 15:28. 2 S
7:15. Ps 109:8. Ezk 44:12-16. Mt 21:43. Ac
1:20. 2 J 8. Re 2:3. 3:11.

27 **mine enemies**. ver. 14, 42-44. Lk 21:22, 24.
Nu 14:36, 37. 16:30-35. Ps 2:3-5, 9. 21:8, 9.
69:22-28. Is 66:6, 14. Na 1:2, 8. Mt 21:37-41.
22:7. 23:34-36. 1 C 15:25. 1 Th 2:15, 16. He
10:13. Re 19:11-21.
would not. ver. +14. Nu 16:12. Jb 21:14. Ro
+9:20.
and slay. Lk 20:16. 1 S 15:33. Mt 21:41.
22:7. Mk 12:9.

28 **he went**. Lk +9:51. 12:50. Jsh 3:11. Ps 40:6-
8. Jn +10:4. 18:11. He 12:2. 1 P 4:1.
ascending. ver. 11. Lk +2:4. 10:30.

29 **when**. Zc 9:9. Mt 21:1, etc. Mk 11:1, etc. Jn
12:12-16.
Bethany. Jn +11:18.
mount of Olives. ver. 37. Mt +21:1.
sent two. Lk 22:8. Mk 14:13.

30 **Go ye**. ver. 32. Lk 22:8-13. 1 S 10:2-9. Jn
14:29.
whereon yet. Lk 23:53. Nu 19:2. Dt 21:3. Jg
15:13. 16:11. 1 S 6:7. Ps 8:6. +104:30. Mk
11:2. Jn 19:41.
loose him. 1 S 8:16.

31 **And if**. Mt +4:9.

the Lord. Lk +7:13. Ps 24:1. 50:10-12. Mt 21:2, 3. Mk 11:3-6. Ac 10:36.
hath need. ver. 34. Ps 50:10.

32 went. Lk 5:5. 6:47. Jn 2:5, 7.
as he had said. Lk 21:33. 22:13. 1 K 8:56. Ps 93:5. 111:7. Ezk 12:25. Da 9:12. Mt 5:18. 17:27. Ro 4:16.

33 the owners. Mk 11:5.

34 The Lord hath need. Zc 9:9. Mk 11:6. Jn 10:35. 12:16. 2 C 8:9.

35 they cast. 2 K 9:13. Mt 21:7, 8. Mk 11:7, 8. Jn 12:14, 15. Ga 4:15, 16.
they set. Zc 9:9.

36 as he went. Mt 21:8.
they spread. 2 K 9:13.

37 at the descent. ver. 29. Mk 13:3. 14:26.
the mount. ver. +29.
the whole. Lk 7:16. 18:43. Ex 15:1, etc. Jg 5:1, etc. 2 S 6:2-6. 1 K 8:55, 56. 1 Ch 15:28. 16:4, etc. 2 Ch 29:28-30, 36. Ezr 3:10-13. Ps 106:12, 13. Jn 12:12, 13.
for all. Jn 12:17, 18.

38 Blessed. Ps 72:17-19. +118:26.
the King. Jn +1:49.
peace. Ps 148:1. Ro +5:1.
glory. Ep 1:6, 12. 3:10, 21. 1 T +1:17. 1 P 1:12. He 5:9-14. 19:1-6.

39 And some. Mt 21:15, 16.
Master. Lk +7:40.
rebuke. Is 26:11. Mt +23:13. Jn 11:47, 48. 12:10, 19. Ac 4:1, 2, 16-18. Ja 4:5.

40 if these. 1 C +15:2.
the stones. Ps 96:11. 98:7-9. 114:1-8. Is 55:12. Hab 2:11. Mt 3:9. 21:15, 16. 27:45, 51-54. 2 P 2:6.

41 beheld the city. Lk 13:34, 35. 23:28-31. Mt 23:37-39. Ac 17:16.
and wept. Ge +42:24. 2 K 8:11. Ps 119:53, +136, 158. 126:6. Is +22:4. Je 17:16. Ho 11:8. Mk 3:4.

42 If. Mt +23:30. Lk 13:9. Dt 5:29. 32:29. Ps 47:7. 81:13-15. 107:43. +119:68. +145:9. Is 48:18. Je 5:3. Ezk 18:31, 32. 33:11. Jon +4:2.
in this. ver. 44. Ps 32:6. 95:7, 8. Is 55:6. Jn 12:35, 36. 2 C 6:1, 2.
thy day. Dt +4:32.
the things. Lk 1:77-79. 2:10-14. 10:5, 6. Ac 10:36. 13:46. He 3:7, 13, 15. +10:26-29. 12:24-26.
peace. Ge +25:22.
but now. Is 6:9, 10. 29:10-14. 44:18. Mt 13:14, 15. Jn 12:38-41. Ac 28:25-27. Ro 11:7-10. 2 C 3:14-16. 4:3, 4. 2 Th 2:9-12.

43 the days. Lk 17:22. +21:20-24. 23:29. Dt 28:49-58. Ps 37:12, 13. Da +9:26, 27. Mt 22:7. 23:37-39. Mk 13:14-20. 1 Th 2:15, 16.
cast. 2 K 19:32. Ec 9:14. Is 29:1-4. 37:33. Je 6:3-6. Ezk 4:2. 21:22. 26:8. Hab 1:10.
and compass. Lk 21:20. Je 4:17. 6:3.

44 lay. Lk 21:6. 1 K 9:7, 8. 2 K 8:12. Ps 137:9. Is

13:16, 18. Ho 10:14. 13:16. Mi 3:12. Na 3:10.
thy children. Lk 13:34, 35. Mt 23:37, 38.
leave. Lk 21:6. 2 S 17:13. Mi 1:6. Mt 24:2. Mk 13:2.
because. ver. 42. Lk 1:68, 78. La 1:8. Da 9:24. Jn 3:18-21. 1 P 2:12.
time of. Lk 12:56. Je +8:12. Mt 16:3.
visitation. Lk 1:68, 69, 77-79. Ge 50:24. Jb 29:2. Je 6:6. 1 P 2:12.

45 went. Mt 21:12, 13. Mk 11:15-17. Jn 2:13-17.
sold. Dt 14:25, 26.

46 It is written. Ps 93:5. Is 56:7. Je 7:11. Ezk 43:12. Ho 12:7. Mt 23:14. Lk +24:27.
house of prayer. 1 K 8:29, 30, 41-43. 2 Ch 6:40.
den of thieves. Je 7:11. Ezk 7:22. Mt 21:13. Mk 11:17.

47 taught. Lk 20:1. 21:37, 38. Mt 21:23. 26:55. Mk 11:27, etc. Jn 18:20.
the chief priests. Mt 21:15. 26:3, 4. Mk 11:18. 12:12. 14:1. Jn 7:19, 44. 8:37-40. 10:39. 11:53-57.
the chief. Mk 6:21.
sought. Lk 20:19. Mt 21:46.
destroy. Gr. apollumi, Mt +2:13.

48 could. Lk 20:19, 20. 22:2-4. Mt 22:15, 16.
the people. Mt 7:28, 29.
were very attentive to hear him. or, hanged on him. lit. "they hung upon him hearing." Ne 8:3. Mk 12:37. Jn 7:46-49. Ac 16:14.

LUKE 20

1 that. Lk 19:47, 48. Mk 11:27. Jn 18:20.
taught. Ac 5:42. 15:35.
the chief. 1 Ch ch. 24.
came upon. Lk 2:9, 48. 4:39. 10:40. 21:34. 24:4. Ac 4:1. 6:12. 10:17. 11:11. 12:7. 17:5. 22:13, 20. 23:11, 27. 28:2.

2 Tell. Lk 19:35-40, 45, 46. Mt 21:23-27. Mk 11:28-33. Jn 7:15.
who. Ex 2:14. Jn 2:18. 5:22-27. Ac 4:7-10. 7:27, 35-39, 51.

3 I will. Lk 22:68. Mt 15:2, 3. Col 4:6.

4 baptism. Lk 7:28-35. Mt 11:7-19. 17:11, 12. 21:25-32. Jn 1:6, 19-28.
from. Lk 15:18. Da 4:25, 26.

5 If. Mt +4:9.
Why. Lk 7:30. Jn 1:15-18, 30, 34. 3:26, 36. 5:33-35. Ac 13:25.

6 if. Mt +4:9.
all. Mt 21:26, 46. 26:5. Mk 12:12. Ac 5:26.
for. Lk 1:76. 7:26-29. Mt 14:5. 21:26. Jn 10:41.

7 that. Is 6:9, 10. 26:11. 29:9-12, 14. 41:28. 42:19, 20. 44:18. Je 8:7-9. Zc 11:15, 17. Ml 2:7-9. Jn 3:19, 20. 9:39. 2 Th 2:10-12. 2 T 3:8, 9. 2 P 3:3.

8 Neither tell. Lk 22:68. Jb 5:12, 13. Pr 26:4,
5. Mt +15:14. 16:4. 21:27. Mk 11:33.

9 this. Mt 21:33, etc. Mk 12:1, etc.
planted. Dt 32:32, 33. Ps 80:8-14. Is 5:1-7.
27:2-6. Je 2:21. Ezk 15:1-6. 19:10-14. Ho
10:1. Jl 1:7. Mt 21:28. Jn 15:1-8. 1 C 3:6-9.
and let. SS 8:11, 12.
husbandmen. Dt 1:15-18. 16:18. 17:8-15.
went. Lk 15:13. 19:12. Mt 25:14, 15. Mk 13:34.
long time. Dt 28:59. Ho 3:4, 5. Mt +25:19.

10 the season. Ps +1:3. Je 5:24. Mt 21:34-36.
Mk 12:2-5.
sent. Jg 6:8-10. 2 Ch +24:19. Ho 6:4-6. Zc
1:3-6. Jn 15:16. Ro 7:4.
beat. Lk 11:47-50. 13:34. 1 K 18:13. 22:24-
27. 2 K 6:31. 21:16. 2 Ch 16:10. 24:19-21.
26:15, 16. Ne 9:26. Je 2:30. 20:2. 26:20-24.
29:26, 27. 37:15, 16. 38:4-6. 44:4. Mt 5:12.
22:6. 23:34, 37. Ac 7:52. 2 C 11:24-26. 1 Th
2:15. He 11:36, 37.

11 sent another. Mt 22:4.
entreated. Mt 23:30-37. Ac 5:41. 7:52. 1 Th
2:2. He 11:36, 37.
and sent. Lk 1:53. Ge 31:42. Dt 15:13. 1 S
6:3. Jb 22:9. Ho 10:1.

12 wounded. Lk 10:34. Ac 19:16.
cast. Lk 13:33, 34. 1 K 22:24-27. 2 Ch 24:19-
22. Ne 9:26. Ac 7:52. 1 Th 2:15. He 11:36, 37.

13 What. Is 5:4. Ho 6:4. 11:8.
I will send. Lk 9:35. Ge 37:13. Mt 3:17. 17:5.
Jn 1:34. 3:16, 17, 35, 36. Ro 8:3. Ga 4:4. 1 J
4:9-15.
my beloved son. Mt 3:17. Mk 12:6.
it may. Je 36:3, 7.
reverence. Lk 18:2.

14 reasoned. ver. 5. Mt 16:7. 21:25.
the heir. Ps 2:1-6, 8. 89:27. Mt 2:2-16. Jn
1:11. Ro 8:17. He 1:2.
let. ver. 19. Lk 19:47. 22:2. Ge 37:18-20. 1 K
21:19. Mt 27:21-25. Jn 11:47-50. Ac 2:23.
3:15.

15 they. He 13:12.
cast him out. 2 Ch 13:9.
What. Mt 21:37-40. Mk 12:6-9.

16 come. 2 S 12:5, 6. Mt 24:50. 25:19.
destroy. Gr. *apollumi*, Mt +2:13. Lk 19:27. Ps
2:8, 9. 21:8-10. Mt 21:41. 22:7. Ac 13:46.
shall give. Ne 9:36, 37. Mt 8:11, 12. 21:43.
Mk 12:9. Ac 13:46. 18:6. 28:28.
to others. Jn 10:16.
God forbid. Ge 44:7, 17. Jsh 22:29. 24:16. 1
S 12:23. 14:45. 20:2. 24:6. 26:11. 1 K 21:3. 1
Ch 11:19. Jb 27:5. Ro 3:4, 6, 31. 6:2, 15. 7:7,
13. 9:14. 11:1, 11. 1 C 6:15. Ga 2:17. 3:21.
6:14.

17 beheld. Lk 19:41. 22:61. 2 K 8:11. Mt 19:26.
Mk 3:5. 10:23.
What. Lk 22:37. 24:44. Jn 15:25.
The stone. Ps *118:22.* Mt +21:42.
the head. Jb 38:6. Je 51:26. Zc 4:7.

18 shall fall. Lk 2:34. Da +2:44. Ro 9:32, 33. 1 C
1:23, 24. 1 Th 2:16. 1 P 2:8.
grind. Is 17:13. Je 31:10. Am 9:9.

19 the same. ver. 14. Lk 19:47, 48. Mt 21:45,
46. 26:3, 4. Mk 12:12.
they feared. Lk 22:2. Mt 14:5. 21:11, 26. Mk
11:32. Ac 5:26.

20 they watched. 1 S 19:11. Ps 37:32, 33.
38:12. Is 29:20, 21. Je 11:19. 18:18. 20:10. Zc
3:9. Mt 22:15, 18. Mk 6:20. 12:13, 15.
feign. 2 S 14:2. 1 K 14:2-6. Ps 66:3. 81:15mg.
2 P 2:3.
take hold. ver. 26. Lk 11:54. Ps 56:5. Mk 3:2.
they might deliver. Mk +10:33.
power and. Lk 12:11. 1 C 15:24.
the governor. Mt 27:2, 11. 28:14. Ac 23:24.

21 Master. Ps 12:2. 55:21. Je 42:2, 3. Mt 22:16.
26:49, 50. Mk 12:14. Jn 3:2.
sayest. 2 C 2:17. Ga 1:10. 1 Th 2:4, 5.
acceptest. Ro +2:11.
the way. Lk 1:76. 3:4. Ps 27:11. Mt 3:3.
22:16. Mk 1:3. 12:14. Jn 1:23. Ac 9:2. 13:10.
18:25, 26. Ro 11:33. He 3:10. Re 15:3.
truly. *or,* of a truth.

22 lawful. Dt 17:15. Ezr 4:13, 19-22. 9:7. Ne
5:4. 9:37. Mt 22:17-21. Mk 12:14-17. Ac 5:37.
give tribute. Lk 23:2. Mt 17:25. Ro +13:6.
unto Caesar. Jn +19:12, 15.

23 he perceived. Jn +2:25.
craftiness. 1 C 3:19. 2 C 4:2. 11:3. 12:16. Ep
4:14.
Why. ver. 20. Mt +16:1.

24 a penny. Mt +18:28mg.
Caesar's. ver. +22.

25 Render. Pr 24:21. Mt 17:27. 22:21. Mk
12:17. Ro 13:6, 7. 1 P 2:13-17.
unto God. Pr 23:26. Ac +4:19, 20. +5:29. 1 C
6:20. 10:31. 1 T 2:2. 1 P 4:11.

26 they could. ver. 20, 39, 40. Jb 5:12, 13. Pr
+21:30. 26:4, 5. 2 T 3:8, 9.
and they marvelled. Lk 13:17. Mt 22:12,
22, 34. Mk 5:20. Jn 7:15. Ro 3:19. T 1:11.

27 the Sadducees. Mt +3:7.
which deny. Ac 4:1, 2. 23:8. 1 C 15:12. 2 T
2:17, 18.

28 Master. ver. 21, 39. Lk +7:40.
Moses wrote. ver. 37. Lk 16:29. Ge 38:8, 11,
26. Dt 25:5-10. Ru 1:11, 12. 3:9. Jn 1:45. 5:45,
46. 7:23. Ac 3:22. 15:21. Ro 9:15. 10:5, 19. 2
C 3:15.
If. Mt +4:9.

29 and died. Le 20:20. Je 22:30.

32 died. Jg 2:10. Ec 1:4. 9:5. He +9:27.

33 in the resurrection. Mt 22:24-28. Mk
12:19-23.

34 The children. Lk 10:6. 16:8.
world. Gr. *aion*, Mt +6:13.
marry. Lk 17:27. 1 C 7:2, etc. Ep 5:31. He
+13:4.

35 accounted worthy. Lk +21:36.

to obtain. Da +12:2, 3. Jn 5:29. Ac 24:15. He 11:35.
that. Mt +12:32.
world. Gr. *aion*, Mt +6:13. Lk 18:30. Is 64:5. Mk +10:30.
the resurrection. Lk +14:14.
from. Ac 4:2. Ph +3:11. 1 P 1:3.
neither. Lk 17:27. Is +54:1. Mt +22:29. 24:38. Mk +12:24.

36 **Neither can**. Is 25:8. Ho 13:14. Jn 11:25. Ro 6:9. 1 C 15:26, 42, 53-55. Ph 3:21. 1 Th 4:13-17. Re 20:6. 21:4. 22:2-5.
they are. Ge 1:26. Zc 3:7. Mt 22:30. Mk 12:25. 1 C 15:49, 52. Re 5:6-14. 7:9-12. 22:9.
equal unto. Ps +8:5. 1 C +6:3.
the children of God. 1 J +3:1.
being the children. Lk +10:6.
of the resurrection. Lk +14:14. Is +26:19. 54:1. Ro 8:23. 1 C 15:52.

37 **even Moses**. ver. 28. Ex 3:2-6. Dt 33:16. Ac 7:30-32.
when. Ge +17:7. Ro 11:2.
he calleth. Ex 3:15. Ac 7:32.
the God. Lk 16:22. Mt +8:11. Ac 3:13.

38 **For he**. Mt +22:32.
a God. Ps 16:5-11. 22:23-26. 23:4. 145:1, 2. He 11:16.
for all. Jn 6:57. 11:25, 26. 14:19. Ro 6:10, 11, 22, 23. 14:7-9. 2 C 5:15. 6:16. 13:4. Ga 2:19. Col 3:3, 4. 1 Th 5:10. He 9:14. 1 P 4:2. Re 7:15-17. 22:1.

39 **thou**. Mt 22:34-40. Mk 12:28-34. Ac 23:9.

40 **durst not ask**. Lk 14:6. Pr 26:5. Mt 22:46. Mk 12:34.

41 **How**. Mt 22:41, 42. Mk 12:35, etc.
Christ. Is +9:6, 7. 11:1, 2. Je +23:5, 6. 33:15, 16, 21. Mi +16:16.
David's son. Lk 18:38, 39. Mt 1:1. Re 22:16.

42 **himself**. Lk 24:44. 2 S 23:1, 2. Mt 22:43. Mk 12:36, 37. Ac 1:20. 13:33-35. He 3:7.
The Lord. Ps +110:1.
Sit. He +1:3.
right hand. 1 K 2:19. Ps 45:9. +110:1.

43 **thine enemies**. Lk 19:27. Ps 2:1-9. 21:8-12. 72:9. 109:4-20. 110:5, 6. Ac 4:25. 1 C 15:25. Re 19:14-21.
thy footstool. Jsh 10:24. 1 K 5:3. Is 66:1. Ac 7:49.

44 **how**. Lk 1:31-35. 2:11. Is +7:14. Mt +1:23. Ro 1:3, 4. 9:5. Ga 4:4. 1 T 3:16. Re 22:16.

45 **in the audience**. Ezk 22:25. Mt 15:10. 23:1. Mk 8:34. 12:38. 1 T 5:20.

46 **Beware**. Lk 12:1. Mt 16:6. Mk 8:15. 2 T 4:15.
which desire. Lk 11:43. 14:7. Pr 29:23. Mt 23:5-7. Mk 12:38, 39. *Ro 12:10.* Ph +2:3-5. 3 J 9.
love greetings. Lk 11:43.
the markets. Lk 7:32. Mt 11:16. 20:3. Mk 6:56. 7:4. Ac 16:19. 17:17.
chief rooms. Lk 14:7, 8.

47 **devour**. Is +1:17. Am +2:7. 8:4-6. Mi 2:2, 8, 9. 3:2, 3. Mt +23:14. 2 C 11:20.
for a show. Lk 12:1. Ezk +33:31. Mt 6:5, 7. 23:26-28. 1 Th 2:5. 2 T 3:2-5. T 1:16.
the same. Mt +10:15.

LUKE 21

1 **and saw**. Mk 7:11-13. 12:41-44.
casting. 2 K 12:9. 2 Ch 24:10.
the treasury. Jsh 6:19, 24. 1 K 14:26. 2 K 24:13. 2 Ch 36:18. Ne 13:13. Mt 27:6. Jn 8:20.

2 **widow**. Is +1:17.
mites. Lk 12:59. Mk +12:42mg.

3 **Of**. Lk 4:25. 9:27. 12:44. Ac 4:27. 10:34.
more than. Lk 11:41mg. Ex 35:21-29. Jg 19:20. Ps 34:9. Mk 12:43, 44. 14:8, 9. 2 C 8:2, 3, 12. 9:6, 7.

4 **of**. Ep 2:8.
of her penury. Ph 4:11.
all the living. Lk 8:43. 15:12, 30. 1 Ch +21:24. Ac 2:44, 45. 4:34. 1 J 3:17.

5 **as some spake**. Mt 24:1, etc. Mk 13:1, etc. Jn 2:20.

6 **days will come**. Lk 17:22.
there shall not. Lk 19:44, etc. 1 K 9:7-9. 2 Ch 7:20-22. Is 64:10, 11. Je 7:11-14. 26:6, 9, 18. La 2:6-8. 4:1. 5:18. Ezk 7:20-22. Da +9:26, 27. Mi 3:12. Zc 11:1. 14:2. Mt 24:2. Mk 13:2. Ac 6:13, 14.

7 **Master**. Lk +7:40.
when. ver. 32. Da 12:6, 8. Mt +24:3. Mk 13:3, 4. Jn 21:21, 22. Ac +1:6, 7.
what. ver. 20, 21, 27, 28. Mt 24:15, 16. Mk 13:14.

8 **Take heed**. Je +29:8. Col 2:8. 1 J 3:7. 4:1. Re 12:9.
for many. Je +14:14. Mt 24:23, 24. Mk 13:21, 22. Jn 5:43. Ac 5:36, 37. 8:9, 10. 1 J 2:18.
in my name. Mk +9:37.
I am. Jn +8:24.
and the time. *or*, and, The time. Mt 3:2. 4:17. Mk 1:15. Re 1:3.

9 **when**. ver. 18, 19. Ps 27:1-3. 46:1, 2. 112:7. Pr 3:25, 26. Is 8:12. 51:12, 13. Je 4:19, 20. Mt +24:6-8. Mk 13:7, 8.
commotions. 1 C 14:33. 2 C 6:5. 12:20. Ja 3:16.
terrified. Lk 24:37.
must. Lk +13:33.
come to pass. Da 2:28. Re 1:1.
but. ver. 8, 28.
the end. Je 4:27. Mt 24:14. 1 P 4:7.

10 **Nation shall**. 2 Ch 15:5, 6. Is 19:2. Hg 2:21, 22. Zc 14:2, 3, 13. Mk 13:8. Ac 2:19, 20. 11:28. He 12:27. Re 6:2-12.

11 **earthquakes**. Re +6:12.
famines. 1 K +8:37.

pestilences. Je 27:13. Ezk +38:22.
fearful sights. Is 19:17.
and great signs. ver. 25-27. Lk 11:16. Mt
16:1. 24:29, 30. Mk 8:11. Re 12:1, 3. 13:13.
15:1.

12 **before**. Lk 11:49-51. Mt 10:16-25. 22:6.
23:34-36. +24:9, 10. Mk 13:9-13. Jn 15:20.
16:2, 3. Ac 4:3-7. 5:17-19, 40. 6:12-15. 7:57-
60. 8:3. 9:4. 12:1-4. 16:22-26. 21:30, 31.
22:30. 24:1, etc. 25:1, 2, 11, 12, 22-25. 26:2,
etc. 1 Th 2:15, 16. 1 P 4:12-14. Re 2:10.
they shall. Lk 12:11, 12. Mt 10:17-22.
persecute. Jn 15:20. 16:2, 3. Re 2:10.
synagogues. Ac 22:19. 26:11.
prisons. Ac 4:3. 5:18. 8:3. 12:4-7. 16:24.
24:27. 2 C 11:23. He +11:36.
being brought. Ac 16:19.
before kings. Ac 25:23. 27:24. 2 T 4:16, 17.
rulers. Ac 17:6. 18:12. 24:1. 25:6.
for my. 1 P 2:13.

13 **shall turn**. Ph 1:13, 14, 19, 28. 1 Th 3:3, 4. 2
Th 1:5.
testimony. Mt +8:4.

14 **Settle**. Lk 9:44. 12:11, 12. Mt 10:19, 20.
meditate. Mk 13:11.

15 **I will**. Lk 12:12. 24:45. Pr 2:6. Je 1:9. Ezk
+24:27. Mt 10:19. Mk 13:11. Ac 2:4. 4:8-13,
31-33. Ja +1:5.
wisdom. 1 S 18:30. Da 1:20. Ja 1:5.
which. Ac 6:10. 24:25. 26:28. 2 T 4:16, 17.
to gainsay. Lk 14:6. 20:40. Mt 22:46. Mk
12:34. Ac 4:14.

16 **ye shall**. Je 9:4. 12:6. Mi 7:5, 6. Mt 10:21.
Mk 13:12.
parents. Lk 12:53. 14:26, 33. Mt 10:35.
and some. Lk 11:49. Mt 23:34. Jn 16:2. Ac
7:59. 12:2. 26:10, 11. Re 2:13. +6:9. 12:11.

17 **be hated**. Lk 6:22. Mt 10:22. 24:9. Mk 13:13.
Jn 7:7. 15:19. 17:14. 1 J 3:12.
for. Lk 6:22. Mt +5:11. Jn 15:20, 21. Ac 9:16.
2 C 4:5, 11. 12:10. Ph 1:29. 1 P 4:14. Re 2:3.

18 **not**. Mt +5:18.
an hair. Lk 10:19. 12:7. 1 S 14:45. 25:29. 2 S
14:11. Da 3:27. Mt 10:30. Jn 10:28. Ac 27:34.
perish. Gr. apollumi, Mt +2:13.

19 **patience**. Lk 8:15. Ps 27:13, 14. 37:7. 40:1.
Mt 10:22. 24:13. Ro 2:7. 5:3. 8:25. +15:4, 5. 1
C 10:13. 1 Th 1:3. 2 Th 3:5. He 6:11, 12, 15.
10:36. Ja 1:3, 4. 5:7-11. Re 1:9. 2:2, 3. +3:10.
13:10. 14:12.
possess. Lk 9:24. He 10:34.
souls. Gr. psyche, used here of the "inward
man," seat of the new life, as in 1 P 2:11. 3 J
2. For the other uses of psyche, see Mt +2:20;
Ge +23:8; Mt +11:29. Mt +10:28.

20 **when ye shall see**. ver. 7. Lk 19:43. Da
+9:27. Mt +24:15. Mk 13:14.

21 **flee**. Lk 17:31-33. Ge 19:17, 19, 26. Ex 9:20,
21. Pr +22:3. Mt +24:16-18. Mk 13:15, 16.
and let them. Nu 16:26. Je 6:1. 35:11.

37:12, 13. Re 18:4.
depart out. Je 37:12.
the countries. Lk 17:31. Mt 24:18. Mk
13:16. Jn 4:33. Ja 5:4.

22 **days of vengeance**. Lk 18:7, 8. Ps +58:10. Je
5:29. +50:15. Ho 9:7. Ro 2:5. 2 P 2:9. +3:7.
all. Lk 4:21. 18:31. 22:37. +24:44. Le 26:14-
33. Dt 28:15-68. 29:19-28. 32:34, 43. Ps
69:22-28. +149:7-9. Is 65:12-16. Da +9:26,
27. Zc 11:1, etc. 14:1, 2. Ml 4:1. Mt +1:22. Mk
13:19, 20. Jn 13:18. Ac 1:16. 3:18. 13:27. Re
17:17.

23 **woe**. Le +26:29. Ho 9:12-17. Mt +24:19.
great distress. Lk 19:27, 43, 44. Mt 21:41,
44. 1 Th 2:16. He +10:26-31. Ja 5:1. 1 P 4:17,
18.
the land. ver. 25, 35.
and wrath. 1 Th 2:16.

24 **shall fall**. Je 29:18.
edge. lit. mouth. Ge 34:26. Jsh 6:21. 8:24.
10:28. He 11:34.
led. Le 26:33. Dt 4:27. 28:64-68. Ne 1:8. Ps
44:11. Je 9:16. Ezk 12:15. 20:23. 22:15. Zc
7:14.
Jerusalem. Ps 79:1. Is 5:5. 63:3, 18. La 1:15.
Da 8:10, 13. Re 11:2.
trodden down. Ps 79:1. Is 63:18. Da 8:10. Zc
12:3.
until. Is 66:12, 19. Ezk +34:13. Da +9:27.
12:7. Ml 1:11. Ro +11:25.
times of. Ezk +30:3.

25 **signs**. ver. 11. Ex +10:22. Mt +24:29. 2 P
3:10-12. Re 20:11.
stars. Is 14:12. 34:4. Re 6:13.
upon the earth. ver. 23, 35. Da +12:1.
distress. Lk 12:50. 19:43. Zp +1:15. 2 C 2:4.
with perplexity. Lk 8:45. Is 22:4, 5. Mi 7:4.
the sea. Ps 46:3. 65:7. 88:7. Is +5:30. 28:2, 15,
18. 29:6. 30:30. 51:15. Ezk 38:22. Hab 3:8-10.

26 **hearts failing**. Ge 42:28. Le 26:36. Dt 28:32-
34, 65-67. Ps 112:7. Pr 1:33. He 10:26, 27.
for looking. Ac 12:11.
earth. Gr. oikoumene, Mt +24:14.
for the powers. 2 P 3:10-12.
of heaven. Ps 33:6. Is 34:4. 40:26.
shaken. He +12:26.

27 **see**. Da 7:10, 13. Mt +24:30. 26:64. Mk
13:26. Ac 1:9-11. Re +1:7. 14:14.
coming. Lk 12:40. Da 7:13. Mk 14:62. 1 Th
4:16. 2 Th 2:8.
with power. Mt 16:27, 28. 25:31. Mk 9:1.
Re 19:11-16.
great glory. Ps +102:16.

28 **And when**. 2 Th +1:7.
look up. Lk 13:11. Ps 98:5-9. Is +12:1-3.
25:8, 9. 30:19. 60:1, 2. Zc 9:14. 12:8. Jn 8:7,
10. Ac 7:55. He +9:28.
lift up. Jg +8:28. Lk 13:11. Jb 10:15. Ps 3:3.
34:5. 121:1. 123:1. Is 40:26. Da 4:34. Jn 8:7,
10. 11:41. 17:1. Ac 1:10. 7:55. 1 C 1:7.

for your. Lk +18:7. Pr 23:18. Is +59:19, 20. Jn 16:16, 19, 20, 22. Ac 3:20. Ro +11:26. 1 Th 1:10.

redemption. Lk 1:68. Ro 3:24. 8:19, 23. Ep 1:14. +4:30. Col 1:14.

draweth nigh. Ps 25:14. Da +11:33. Am +3:7. Ml 4:5, 6. Mt 25:6. Ro 13:11. 1 Th 5:4. Re 16:15.

29 **Behold**. Mt 24:32-35. Mk 13:28-30.

30 **of your own selves**. Lk +12:57. Mt 16:3.

31 **when**. Lk 12:51-57. 17:22. Mt 16:1-4. 23:39. Ezk 32:7. 34:27. +39:28.

these things. ver. 7, 17, 20, 22, 24, 25-27. Mt 24:33.

the kingdom of God. Lk +4:43. 2 T +4:1.

nigh at hand. ver. +28. Mt +10:7. +21:43. 24:33. He 10:37. Ja 5:9. 1 P 4:7.

32 **Verily**. Mt +5:18.

This generation. Mt +24:34.

33 **Heaven**. Lk 16:17. Ps 89:37. 102:25, 26. Ec +1:4. Is 34:4. 51:6. Je +33:25. Mt +5:18. +24:35. Mk 13:31. He 1:11, 12. 12:27. 1 P 1:25. 2 P 3:7-14. Re 20:11. 21:1.

my words. Nu 23:19. Ps 119:89, 152. Is 40:8. 1 P 1:23, 25.

34 **take**. ver. 8. Lk 17:3. Mk 13:9. Ac 5:35. He 12:15. 2 P 3:14.

lest. Ro 13:13. 1 Th 5:6-8. 1 P 4:7.

your hearts. Lk 12:45. Ge +31:20. Le 10:9, 10. Pr 21:4, 5. Is 28:7, 8. 56:10-12. Ho 4:11, 12. Ac 14:17. Ro 13:11-13. 1 Th 5:6-8. Ja 5:5. 1 P 4:3-7.

surfeiting. Dt 29:19, 20. 1 S 25:36. Is 28:1-3. 1 C 5:11. 6:10. Ga 5:20, 21.

drunkenness. Ro 13:13. 1 C +6:10. Ga +5:21. 1 Th 5:7.

cares. Lk 8:14. 10:41. Mt +13:22. Mk 4:19. 1 C 6:3, 4. Ph 4:6.

that day. Lk 10:12. 12:40, 46. Ps 35:8. Mt 24:39-50. Mk 13:35-37. 1 Th 5:2-4. 2 P 3:10, 14. Re 3:3.

come upon. Lk 20:1g. 1 Th 5:3.

35 **as a snare**. Ps 11:6. 69:22. 73:19, 20. Ec 9:12. Is *24:17, 18*. Je 48:43, 44. La 3:47. Ro 11:9. 1 Th 5:2, 3. 1 T 6:9. Re 3:3. 16:15.

all them. 1 Th 5:3.

dwell. Lk 17:37. Ge 7:4. Je 25:29. Ac 17:26.

the face. Ge +1:2.

of the whole earth. Ge 41:57. Is 13:5. Ho 1:2.

36 **Watch**. Mt +24:42.

pray always. Lk +18:1. Ps 40:1.

accounted worthy. Lk 20:35. Zp +2:3. Mt 10:37. 22:8. Ac 5:41. Col +1:10. 2 Th 1:5, 11. 2 T 4:8. T 2:13. *He 9:28*. Re 3:4. or, prevail. Lk 23:23. Ho 12:4. Ja 5:16.

to escape. Ge 19:29. Ps 32:6, 7. 37:38-40. 71:2. 83:3. +94:13. Pr 3:25, 26. +11:8. 14:26. Is 4:2. 16:1-5. +26:20. +57:1. Je 11:11. 15:21. 44:14, 28. Jl +2:32. Ob +17mg. Hab +3:16. Zp

+2:3. Ml 3:17. Mt +6:13. Ro 2:3. 1 Th +1:10. 5:3. He 2:3. Re +3:10.

stand. Dt +10:8. Ezr 9:15. Ps +1:5. 76:7. Pr +22:29. Je 15:19. 35:19. 40:10mg. Da +1:5. 7:10. +12:13. Ml 3:2. Ep 6:13, 14. 1 Th 2:19. 1 J 2:28. Ju 24. Re 6:17.

before. Is 24:23. Ho 6:2.

Son of man. Lk +5:24.

37 **the day time**. Lk 22:39. Mt 21:17. 26:55. Mk 11:12. Jn 12:1.

teaching in. Jn 8:2.

at night. Mt 21:17. Mk 11:19.

abode. Mt 21:17.

mount. Mt +21:1.

38 **all the people**. Jn 8:1, 2.

to hear. Lk 19:48.

LUKE 22

1 **the feast**. Ex 12:6-23. Le 23:5, 6. Mt 26:2. Mk 14:1, 2, 12. Jn 11:55-57. 1 C 5:7, 8.

unleavened. Lk 2:41. Ex 23:15. 34:18. Le +23:6. Dt 16:16. 2 Ch 8:13. 30:13, 21. 35:17. Ezr 6:22.

Passover. Le +23:5. Jn 6:4.

2 **the chief priests**. Lk 19:47, 48. 20:19. Ps 2:1-5. Mt 21:38, 45, 46. 26:3-5. Jn 11:47-53, 57. Ac 4:27.

they feared. Lk 19:48. 20:19. 21:38. Ac 5:26.

3 **entered**. Mt 26:14. Mk 14:10, etc. Jn 6:70, 71. 12:6. 13:2, 27, 30. Ac 5:3. 1 C 5:5.

Judas. Lk 6:16. Mt 27:3. Jn 6:71. 12:4. Ac 1:16.

Iscariot. Jsh +15:25. Je 48:24, 41.

being. ver. 21. Lk 6:16. Ps 41:9. 55:12-14. Mt 26:23. Mk +9:35. 14:18-20. Jn 13:18, 26.

4 **went**. Mt 26:14. Mk 14:10, 11.

captains. ver. 52. 1 Ch 9:11, etc. Ne 11:11. Ac 4:1. 5:24, 26.

5 **were glad**. Jn 20:29.

and covenanted. Zc 11:12, 13. Mt 26:15, 16. 27:3-5. Ac 1:18. 8:20. 1 T 6:9, 10. 2 P 2:3, 15. Ju 11.

6 **betray**. Mt +20:18.

in the absence of the multitude. *or*, without tumult. Mt 26:5. Mk 14:2. Ac 24:18.

7 **the day of**. ver. 1. Ex 12:6, 18. Mt 26:17. Mk 14:12.

unleavened bread. Ex 12:18. Le +23:5. Nu 28:16. 1 C 5:7.

8 **he sent**. Mk 14:13-16.

Go. Lk 1:6. Mt 3:15. Ga 4:4, 5.

prepare. Jn 14:3.

passover. Ex +12:21. Le +23:5. Ac 12:3, 4.

10 **Behold**. Lk 19:29, etc. 1 S 10:2-7. Mt 26:18, 19. Jn 16:4. Ac 8:26-29.

11 **The Master**. Lk +7:40. 19:31, 34. Mt 21:3.

Where is. Lk 2:7. 19:5. Re 3:20.

passover. Ex +12:21.

12 **he**. Jn +2:25. 21:17. Ac 16:14, 15.

a large. Mk 14:15. Ac 1:13. 20:8.

13 they went. Lk 21:33. Jn 2:5. 11:40. He 11:8.
as he had said. Lk 19:32.

14 when. Dt 16:6, 7. Mt 26:20. Mk 14:17.
the hour. Jn +2:4.
sat down. ver. 69. Ex 12:6, 11.
apostles. Mk 6:30.

15 With desire I have desired. *or*, I have
heartily desired. Lk 12:50. SS 7:10. Jn 4:34.
13:1. 17:1.
passover. Ex +12:21. He 11:28.

16 I will not. ver. 18-20.
until. ver. 30. Lk 12:37. 14:15. Jn 6:27, 50-
58. Ac 10:40, 41. 1 C 5:7, 8. He 10:1-10. Re
19:9.
the kingdom. Lk +4:43.

17 took. Ps 23:5. 116:13. Je 16:7. Mt 26:27. Mk
14:23.
cup. Je +49:12.
gave thanks. ver. 19. Lk +24:30.

18 I will not. ver. 16. Mt +5:18. 26:29. Mk
14:25. 15:23.
the fruit. Jg 9:13. Ps 104:15. Pr 31:6, 7. SS
5:1. Is 24:9-11. 25:6. 55:1. Zc 9:15, 17. Ep
+5:18, 19.
until. Lk 9:27. 21:31. Da 2:44. Mt 16:18.
+26:29. Mk 9:1. Ac +1:6. 2:30-36. Col 1:13.
kingdom of God. Mk 15:43.

19 he took. Mt 26:26-28. Mk 14:22-24. 1 C
10:16. 11:23-29.
gave thanks. ver. +17. 1 Th 5:18.
brake. Is +58:7.
is my. ver. 20. Ge 41:26, 27. Ezk 37:11. Da
2:38. 4:22-24. Zc 5:7, 8. 1 C 10:4. Ga 4:25.
body. 1 C 10:16.
given. Jn 6:51. 1 C 11:24, 25. Ga 1:4. Ep 5:2.
T 2:14. 1 P 2:24.
this do. Ps 78:4-6. 111:4. SS 1:4.
remembrance. Ex +12:14. 1 C 11:24, 25. 1 C
4:17. 2 T 1:6. He 10:3.

20 the cup. ver. 17. Je +49:12.
This. Ex 24:8. Zc 9:11. 1 C 10:16-21.
the new. Mt +26:28.
testament. He 10:29. 13:20.
for you. Mt 26:28. Mk 14:24.

21 the hand. Jb 19:19. Ps 41:9. Mi 7:5, 6. Mt
+20:18.

22 truly. Lk 24:25-27, 46. Ge +3:15. Ps ch. 22,
69. Is ch. 53. Da +9:24-26. Zc 13:7. Mt 26:24,
53, 54. Mk 14:21. Ac 2:23. 4:25-28. 13:27, 28.
26:22, 23. 1 C +15:3, 4. 1 P 1:11.
Son of man. Lk +5:24.
goeth. Mt +26:24. Jn 7:33. 8:21, 22. 14:12.
16:28.
determined. Ac 2:23. 4:28. 10:42. 17:26, 31.
Ro 1:4. Re 13:8.
but. Ps 55:12-15. 69:22-28. 109:6-15. Ob 7.
Mi 7:6. Mt 27:5. Jn 17:12. Ac 1:16-25. 2 P 2:3.
woe unto. Lk 17:1. Mt 18:7.

23 inquire. Mt 26:22. Mk 14:19. Jn 13:22-25.
should do. 2 S 15:15. Jn 2:5.

24 a strife. Lk 9:46-48. Mt 20:20-24. Mk 9:34,
50. 10:37-41. Ro 12:10. 1 C 3:3. 13:4. Ph
+2:3-5. Ja 4:5, 6. 1 P 5:5, 6.

25 The kings. Mt 20:25-28. Mk 10:41-45.
lordship. Ro 14:9. 2 C 1:24. 1 T 6:15.
1 P 5:3.
benefactors. Mt +6:2.

26 ye shall not. Lk 9:48. Mt 18:3-5. 23:8-12. Ro
12:2. 1 P 5:3. 3 J 9, 10.
is greatest. Ro +12:3. 1 P 5:3.
the younger. 1 P 5:5.
is chief. Mt 2:6. Ac 7:10. 14:12. 15:22. He
13:7, 17, 24.
doth serve. Mt 20:26, 27. Mk 10:43, 44. Jn
13:14. Ga 5:13. 6:2, 10. He 13:17, 24.

27 is greater. Lk 12:37. 17:7-9. Mt 20:28. Jn
13:5-16. 2 C 8:9. Ph 2:7, 8.
but I am. Ge 40:4. Ps +145:9. Mt 9:11, 12.
19:14, 15. 20:27, 28. Mk 10:45. Jn 13:5, 13,
14. 2 C 8:9. Ph 2:5-8. He 2:11, 12, 16.

28 continued. Ru 1:16. 2 K 2:2. Mt 19:28, 29.
24:13. Jn 6:67, 68. 8:31. 13:1. Ac 1:25. Ro
16:4. 2 T 1:16.
my temptations. Lk 4:2. Mt 4:1. He 2:18.
+4:15. Ja 1:2.

29 I appoint. Lk +12:32. 19:17. Mt +24:47.
25:34. 28:18. Jn 17:18. Ac 14:22. 1 C 9:25. 2
C 1:7. 1 Th +2:12. 2 T 2:12. Ja 2:5. 1 P 5:4. Re
1:6. 21:14.
a kingdom. Lk +12:32. +13:28, 29. Ezk
37:21, 22. Da 7:18, 27. Mi 4:6-8. 7:20. Mt
+5:5. +8:11. 16:27. 25:34. Mk 11:10. Ro 5:17.
2 Th 1:5.
as my Father hath appointed unto me. Lk
1:32. 19:15. Ps 2:8. Is 49:5-12. Da +7:13, 14.
Ph 2:9-11.

30 eat. ver. 16-18. Lk 12:37. 13:29. 14:15. 2 S
9:9, 10. 19:28. Mt +8:11. Re 19:9.
my table. Ps 23:5. Is 25:6. Ezk 39:17-22. Re
19:17, 18.
my kingdom. Mt 13:41. 1 C +15:24. 2 T 4:1.
2 P 1:11.
and sit. Ps 49:14. Mt +19:28. Ro 5:17. 1 C
6:2, 3. Re 1:6. 2:26, 27. 3:21. 4:4. 20:4.
judging. 1 C 6:2.
twelve tribes. Ac 26:7. Ja 1:1. Re 21:12.

31 Simon. Lk 10:41. Ac 9:4.
Satan. Jb 1:8-11. 2:3-6. Zc 3:1. 1 C 5:5. 2 C
2:11. 1 P 5:8, 9. Re 12:10.
hath desired. Jb 1:8mg.
to have you. Mt 26:31, 56. Mk 14:27, 50.
sift. Am 9:9.
as wheat. Mt +3:12. Jn 16:32.

32 I have prayed for. Is 53:12. Zc 3:2-4. Mk
+1:35. Jn 14:19. 17:9-11, 15-21. Ro 5:9, 10.
8:32-34. He 7:25. 9:24. 1 P 1:5. 1 J 2:1, 2.
thy faith. Lk +8:13. +17:5. 2 T 2:18. T 1:1.
He 12:15. 2 P 1:1. 1 J 2:19.
and when. ver. 61, 62. Mt 18:3. 26:75. Mk
14:72. 16:7. Ac +3:19.

converted. Lk 17:4. Ps 19:7. 23:3. Jn 14:19. 21:17. Ac +3:19. 1 P 5:8, 10.
strengthen. Ps 32:3-6. 51:12, 13. Jn 21:15-17. 2 C 1:4-6. Ga 6:2. 1 Th 3:2. 1 T 1:13-16. He 10:25. 12:12, 13. 1 P 1:13. 5:8-10. 2 P 1:10-12. 3:14, 17, 18.

33 I am. 2 K 8:12, 13. Pr 28:26. Je 10:23. +17:9. Mt 20:22. 26:33-35, 40, 41. Mk 14:29, 31, 37, 38. Jn 13:36, 37. Ac 20:23, 24. 21:13. 1 C 10:12.
prison. Ac 12:4.
death. Jn 21:19.

34 the cock. Mt 26:34, 74. Mk 14:30, 71, 72. Jn 13:38. 18:27.
shall not. Mt +5:18.

35 When. Lk 9:3. 10:4. Mt 10:9, 10. Mk 6:8, 9.
scrip. 1 S 17:40. Mt 10:10. Mk 6:8.
lacked. Lk 12:29-31. Ge 48:15. Dt 8:2, 3, 16. 1 K 4:27. Ne 9:21. Ps 23:1. +37:3.

36 But now. Lk 9:3. 10:3. Pr 17:3. Is 48:10. Mt 10:22-25. Jn 15:20. 16:33. 17:15. 1 Th 2:14, 15. 3:4. 1 P 4:1.
scrip. ver. +35.
no sword. ver. 38. Nu 31:3. Jg 3:2. 1 Ch +5:22. Ne 4:13. Ps 18:34. Pr +20:18. Mt +5:39. 10:34. Jn 18:11, 36. Ac 22:25-29. 23:23.

37 this. ver. 22. Lk 18:31. 21:22. 24:25, 26, 44-46. Mt 1:22. 26:54-56. Jn 10:35. 19:28-30. Ac 1:16. 13:27-29.
must. Lk +13:33.
And he. Lk 23:32. Is 53:12. Mk 15:27, 28. 2 C 5:21. Ga 3:13.
for the things. Jn 17:4. 19:30.
an end. Mk 3:26.

38 two swords. ver. +36, 49. Mt 26:51. Mk 14:47.
It. Dt 3:26. Mt 26:52-54. Mk 14:41. Jn 18:36. 2 C 10:3, 4. Ep 6:10-18. 1 Th 5:8. 1 P 5:9.

39 he came. Mt 26:30, 36-38. Mk 14:26, 32-34. Jn 18:1, 2.
as he was wont. Lk 1:9. 2:42. 4:16. Mk 10:1. 11:11, 19. Jn 18:2. He 5:7.
mount of Olives. Mt +21:1.

40 the place. Jn 18:2.
Pray. ver. 46. Lk 11:4. 1 Ch 4:10. Ps 17:5. 19:13. 119:116, 117, 133. Pr 30:8, 9. Mt 6:13. 26:41. Mk 14:38. 2 C 12:7-10. Ep 6:18, 19. 1 P 4:7. 5:8, 9. Re +3:10.
enter not. Lk 11:4. Mt 6:13.

41 withdrawn. Ac 21:1.
stone's cast. Ge +21:16.
and kneeled. Mt 26:39. Mk 14:35. Ac 7:60.

42 Father. Lk 10:21. 23:34, 46. Mt 11:25. 26:39, 42, 44. Mk 14:36. Jn 11:41. 12:27, 28. 17:1, 5, 11, 21, 24, 25. He 5:7.
if thou. 1 C +15:2.
willing, remove. Gr. willing to remove.
cup. ver. 17-20. Is 51:17, 22. Je 25:15. Mt 20:22. Jn 18:11.
not. Mt +6:10. Jn 5:30. 6:38.

43 an angel. Lk 1:11-13. 4:10, 11. Ge 21:17. Nu 20:16. Jg 6:11. 13:9. 1 K 19:5-8. 2 Ch 32:20, 21. Ps 91:11, 12. Da 9:20-23. 10:2-6, 12. Zc 1:9. Mt 4:6, 11. 26:53. Jn 12:29. Ac 10:1-4, 30, 31. 12:5-9. 1 T 3:16. He 1:6, 14.
strengthening. ver. 32. Dt 3:28. Jb 4:3, 4. Is 35:3, 4. Da 10:16-19. 11:1. Ac 18:23. He 2:17.

44 being. Ge 32:24-28. Ps 22:1, 2, 12-21. 40:1-3. 69:14-18. 88:1-18. 130:1, 2. 143:6, 7. La 1:12. 3:53-56. Jon 2:2, 3. Jn 12:27. 2 C 5:21. He 5:7, 8.
agony. Ps *22:14, 15*.
prayed more earnestly. Ac 12:5mg.
his. Is 53:10. La 1:12. Ro 8:32.

45 sleeping. Mt 26:40, 43. Mk 13:36. 14:37, 40, 41.
for sorrow. Mt 17:23. Mk 14:19.

46 Why sleep ye. ver. 40. Lk +21:34-36. Pr 6:4-11. Jon 1:6.
rise. Pr 6:9. SS 2:10. Is 60:1. Mt 26:41. Mk 10:49. Jn 5:8. Ep 5:14.

47 while. Mt 26:45-47. Mk 14:41-43. Jn 18:2-9.
Judas. ver. 3-6. Mt 26:14-16, 47. Mk 14:10, 43. Ac 1:16-18.

48 betrayest. Ps 41:9. 55:21. Pr +26:23.
Son of man. Lk +5:24.
kiss. Ge +27:27.

49 shall. lit. If we shall.
with the sword. ver. 38.

50 smote a servant. Mt 26:51-54. Mk 14:47. Jn 18:10, 11. Ro 12:19. 2 C 10:4.

51 answered and. Mk 11:14.
Suffer. Jn 17:12. 18:8, 9.
And he. Mk 1:41. Ro 12:21. 2 C 10:1. 1 P 2:21-23.

52 Jesus. Mt 26:55. Mk 14:48, 49.
captains. ver. 4. 2 K 11:15. Jn 18:12. Ac 5:26.
a thief. Lk 10:30. 19:46. Mt 21:13. Mk 11:17. Jn 18:40.

53 I was. Lk 21:37, 38. Mt 21:12-15, 23, 45, 46. Jn 7:25, 26, 30, 45.
in the temple. Lk 2:46. Jn 8:2. 18:20.
but. Jg 16:21-30. Jb 20:5. Jn 12:27. 16:20-22.
your hour. Jb 20:5. Mk 14:35, 41. Jn 8:44. 12:27. 16:4.
the power. Lk 4:6, 13. Jn 13:30. +14:30. Ac 26:18. 2 C 4:3-6. Ep 6:12. Col 1:13. Re 12:9-12. 20:10.
darkness. Ge +1:2. Mi 7:8. Ac 26:18. Ep 6:12. Col 1:13. 1 Th 5:5.

54 took. Mt 26:57, 58. Mk 14:53, 54. Jn 18:12-17, 24.
And Peter. ver. 33, 34. 2 Ch 32:31.

55 had. ver. 44. Mt 26:69. Mk 14:66. Jn 18:17, 18.
the hall. Mt 26:3.
Peter sat. Ps +26:4. 28:3.

56 a certain maid. Mt 26:69. Mk 14:6, 17, 66-68. Jn 18:17.
earnestly looked. Lk 4:20. Ac 3:4.

57 **he denied**. ver. 33, 34. Lk 12:9. Mt 10:33. 26:70. Jn 18:25, 27. Ac 3:13, 14, 19. 1 C 10:12. 2 T 2:10-12. 1 J 1:9.

58 **another**. Mt 26:71, 72. Mk 14:69, 70. Jn 18:25.
　　Man. ver. 60. Lk 12:14.

59 **confidently**. Mt 26:73, 74. Mk 14:69, 70. Jn 18:26, 27. Ac 12:15.

60 **Man**. ver. 58. Lk 12:14.
　　the cock. ver. 34. Mt 26:74, 75. Mk 14:71, 72. Jn 18:27.

61 **turned**. Lk 7:9, 13, 44. 9:55. 10:23, 41. 14:25. 23:28. Mt 9:22. 16:23. Mk 5:30. 8:33. Jn 1:38.
　　looked. Lk 20:17. Jb 33:27. Is 57:15-18. Je 31:18-20. Ho 11:8. Zc +12:4. Mk 10:21. Ac 5:31.
　　And Peter. Ezk 16:63. 36:31, 32. Ac 11:16. 20:35. Ep 2:11. Re 2:5.
　　the word. Jn 15:3.
　　Before. ver. 34. Mt 26:34, 75. Jn 13:38.
　　deny. Ac 3:13, 14.

62 **and wept**. Ps 38:18. 126:5, 6. 130:1-4. 143:1-4. Is 22:4. Je 9:1. 31:18. Ezk 7:16. Mi 1:8. Zc 12:10. Mt +5:4. 26:75. Mk 14:72. 1 C 10:12. 2 C 7:9-11.

63 **the men**. Mt 26:59-68. Mk 14:55-65. Jn 18:22.
　　mocked. Lk 18:32. 23:11, 36. Jb 11:3. 12:4. 13:9. 16:9, 10. 17:2. 21:3. 30:9-14. Ps 22:6, 7, 13. 35:15, 16, 25. 69:7-12, 19, 20. Is 49:7. 50:6, 7. 52:14. 53:3. Je 20:7. Mi 5:1. Mt 20:19. 27:28-31, 39-44. Mk 10:34. 15:16-20, 27-32. He +11:36. 12:2, 3. 1 P 2:23.

64 **blindfolded**. Jg 16:21, 25.
　　struck him. Mt +27:30.
　　Prophesy. Lk 7:39.

65 **blasphemously**. Le +24:11. Mt 27:39.

66 **as soon**. Mt 27:1. Mk 15:1. Jn 18:24, 28.
　　elders. Ps 2:1-3. Ac 4:25-28. 22:5.
　　council. Ac 4:15. 5:21, 27, 34, 41. 6:12, 15. 22:5, 30. 23:1, 6, 15, 20, 28. 24:20.

67 **Art thou**. lit. If thou art. 1 C +15:2. Mt 11:3-5. 26:63, etc. Mk 14:61, etc. Jn 10:24.
　　the Christ. Mt +16:16.
　　If I tell. This kind of "if" expresses a considerable degree of uncertainty: an unlikely assumption or a possibility not very likely to happen. It is known as a Hypothetical Proposition in the form of a Conditional ("if") Sentence called the Fourth Condition; or, Mere Assumption with Remote Idea of Realization, involving the Protasis ("if," or conditional clause). For other instances of this construction see Ac 17:11, 27. 20:16. 24:19. 25:20. 27:12, 39. 1 C 14:10. 15:37. 1 P 3:14, 17.
　　ye will not. Mt +5:18. Lk 16:31. Jn +5:39-47. 8:43-45. 9:27, 28. 10:25, 26. 12:37-43.

68 **if I also**. Mt +4:9. Lk 20:3-7, 41-44. Je 38:15.
　　will not. Mt +5:18.

69 **shall**. Mt 26:64. Mk 14:62.
　　Son of man. Lk +5:24. Da +7:13, 14.
　　sit on. Ps 110:1. Ep 4:8-10. He +1:3.
　　right hand. Ps +110:1.
　　the power. Ac 8:10. Re 22:1.

70 **the Son of God**. Mt +14:33.
　　Ye say. Lk 23:3. Mt 26:25, 64. +27:11. Mk 14:62. 15:2. Jn 18:37.

71 **What need**. Mt 26:65, 66. Mk 14:63, 64.

LUKE 23

1 **whole multitude**. Lk 22:66. Mt 27:1, 2, 11, etc. Mk 15:1, etc. Jn 18:28, etc.
　　Pilate. Lk 3:1. 13:1. Ac 3:13. 4:27. 1 T 6:13.

2 **they**. Zc 11:8. Mk 15:3-5. Jn 18:30.
　　perverting. ver. 5, 14. 1 K 18:17. Je 38:4. Am 7:10. Ac 16:20, 21. 17:6, 7. 24:5.
　　forbidding. Lk 20:20-25. 1 K 21:10-13. Ps 35:11. 62:4. 64:3-6. Je 20:10. 37:13-15. Mt 17:27. 22:15, 17, 21. 26:59, 60. Mk 12:13, 14, 17. 14:55, 56. Ac 24:13. 1 P 3:16-18.
　　Caesar. Jn +19:12.
　　that. Lk 22:69, 70. Jn +18:36.
　　is Christ. Mt +16:16.
　　a king. Ps 2:2, 6mg. Mk 15:32. Jn +1:49. 6:15. 19:12. Ac 17:7.

3 **Pilate**. Mt 27:11. Mk 15:2. Jn 18:33-37. 1 T 6:13.
　　the King. ver. 38. Lk 1:32, 33. 19:38-40. Mk 15:18, 32. Jn 1:49. 18:36, 37. 19:3, 19-21.
　　he answered. 1 T 6:13.
　　Thou sayest it. Mt +27:11. Lk 22:70.

4 **I find**. ver. 14, 15, 22. Mt 27:19, 24. Mk 15:14. Jn +8:46. 18:38. 19:4-6. He 7:26. 1 P 1:19. 2:22. 3:18.

5 **they**. ver. 23. Lk 11:53. Ps 22:12, 13, 16. 57:4. 69:4. Mt 27:24. Jn 19:15. Ac 5:33. 7:54, 57. 23:10.
　　all Jewry. Lk 1:5. 2:4. 4:44. 7:17. Ac 1:8. 2:9. 8:1. 10:37. 11:1, 29.
　　beginning. Lk 4:14, 15. Mt 4:12-16, 23. Mk 1:14. Jn 1:43. 2:11. 7:41, 52. Ac 10:37.

6 **a Galilean**. Lk 13:1. Ac 5:37.

7 **knew**. Gr. *epiginosko*, Mt +11:27.
　　Herod's. Lk 3:1. 13:31.

8 **for**. Lk 9:7-9. 19:3. Mt 14:1. Mk 6:14. Jn 12:21.
　　and he. Lk 4:23. 2 K 5:3-6, 11. Mt 12:38. Ac 8:19.

9 **but**. Lk 13:32. Ps 38:13, 14. 39:1, 2, 9. Is 53:7. Mt +7:6. 27:14. Ac 8:32. 1 P 2:23.
　　answered him. Mt +26:63.

10 **and vehemently**. ver. 2, 5, 14, 15. Lk 11:53. Ac 18:28. 24:5.

11 **Herod**. Ac 4:27, 28.
　　set. Lk 18:9. 22:64, 65. Ps 22:6. 69:19, 20. Is 49:7. 53:3. Mt 27:27-30. Mk 9:12. 15:16-20. Ga 4:14.
　　mocked. Lk +22:63.

arrayed. Mt 27:28. Mk 15:17. Jn 19:5.
gorgeous. Ja 2:2.

12 **Pilate and**. Ps 2:2. 83:4-6. Mt 16:1. Ac 4:27.
Re 17:13, 14.

13 **And Pilate**. Mt 27:21-23. Mk 15:14. Jn
18:38. 19:4.
the rulers. Lk +24:20.

14 **as one**. ver. 1, 2, 5.
having examined. Ac 3:13. 12:19.
have found. ver. 4. Da 6:4. Mt 27:4, 19, 24,
54. Ac 13:28. He 7:26.

15 **nothing worthy**. Lk 12:48. Dt 19:6. 21:22. 1
S 26:16. 1 K 2:26. Je 26:11, 16. Ac 23:29.
25:11, 25. 26:31. Ro 1:32.

16 **chastise**. ver. 22. Is 53:5. Jn +19:1-4. Ac
5:40, 41.

17 **of necessity**. Mt 27:15. Mk 15:6. Jn 18:39.

18 **they**. Mt 27:16-23. Mk 15:7-14. Jn 18:40. Ac
3:14.
Away. Dt 17:7. 19:19. Jn 19:15. Ac 21:36.
22:22.

19 **sedition**. ver. 2-5.
for murder. Ac 3:14.

20 **willing**. Mt 14:8, 9. 27:19. Mk 15:15. Jn 19:12.

21 **But**. Ac 3:13.
they cried. Ac 12:22. 21:34. 22:24.
Crucify. ver. 23. Mt 27:22-25. Mk 15:13, 14.
Jn 19:15.

22 **Why**. ver. 14, 20. 1 P 1:19. 3:18.
what evil. ver. 41. Jn 8:46.
found no. ver. 14, 15.
I will. ver. 16.

23 **instant**. ver. 5. Ps 22:12, 13. 57:4. Zc 11:8.
prevailed. Lk 21:36. Mt 27:24, 25.

24 **Pilate**. Mt 27:26. Mk 15:15. Jn 19:1, 16, 17.
gave sentence. *or*, assented. Ex +23:2. Pr
17:15.
it should be. Ex +23:2.

25 **for sedition and**. ver. 2, 5, 19. Mk 15:7. Jn
18:40.
whom. ver. 18. 1 S 12:13. Mk 15:6. Ac 3:14.
but. Mt 27:26. Mk 15:15. Jn 19:16.

26 **they laid**. Mt 27:32, etc. Mk 15:21, etc. Jn
19:16, 17.
a Cyrenian. Ac +2:10.
that. Lk 9:23. 14:27.

27 **and of**. ver. 55. Lk 8:2. Mt 27:55, 56. Mk
15:40.
bewailed. Mt +9:23.

28 **turning**. Lk +22:61.
daughters. SS +1:5.
weep. Lk +6:21.
children. Mt 23:37.

29 **the days**. Lk 17:22. 19:43. 21:23, 24. Mt
24:19. Mk 13:17-19.
Blessed. Lk 1:24, 25. Le +26:29. *Ho 9:12-16.*
13:16.

30 *begin to say*. Pr 1:24-33. Is 2:19. Ho *10:8.* Re
6:16. 9:6.

31 **if**. 1 C +15:2.

in a green tree. Ps 1:3. Pr 11:31. Is +4:2. Je
25:29. Ezk 15:2-7. 20:47, 48. 21:3, 4. Da
+9:26. Mt 3:12. Jn 15:6. He 6:8. 1 P 4:17, 18.
Ju 12.
what shall. Je +12:5. Ml 4:1. Mt 3:10.

32 **two other**. Lk 22:37. Ge 40:2, 3. Is 53:9, 12.
Mt 20:21. 27:38. Mk 10:37. 15:27, 28. Jn
19:18. He 12:2.

33 **when**. Mt 27:33, 34. Mk 15:22, 23. Jn 19:17,
18. He 13:12, 13.
Calvary. *or*, the place of a skull. **S#2898g**. Mt
27:33 (skull). Mk 15:22. Jn 19:17.
they crucified. Lk 24:7. Dt 21:23. Ps 22:16.
Zc 12:10. Mt 20:19. 26:2. Mk 10:33, 34. Jn
3:14. 12:33, 34. 18:32. Ac 2:23. 5:30. 13:29.
Ga 3:13. 1 P 2:24.

34 **Then said**. 2 Ch 24:22. Ac 3:17. 7:60. 2 T
4:16.
Father. ver. 46, 47, 48. Lk +22:42. Ge 50:17.
Ps 106:16-23. Mt +5:44. Mk 1:35. Ac 7:60. Ro
12:14.
forgive. Is *53:12*. Mt 5:44. Ac 7:59, 60.
they know not. Lk +12:47, 48. Mk 10:38. Jn
15:22-24. 19:11. Ac 3:17. 13:27. 1 C 2:8. 1 T
1:13.
And they. Ps *22:18, 19*. Mt 27:35, 36. Mk
15:24. Jn 19:23, 24.
lots. Jsh +14:2.

35 **the people**. Ps 22:12, 13, 17. Zc 12:10. Mt
27:38-43. Mk 15:29-32.
the rulers. Lk +24:20.
derided. Lk +16:14. Ge 37:19, 20. Ps 4:2.
22:7. 71:11. Ga 6:7.
He saved. Lk 4:23. 7:14, 15. Jn 3:16. 11:43.
let him. Mt 26:53, 54. Jn 10:18.
if he be. 1 C +15:2. Lk 4:3, 9.
Christ. Ps 22:6-8. Is 42:1. Mt +16:16.
the chosen. Lk 9:35. 1 K 8:16. Ps 89:3, 19. Is
42:1. 49:7. Mt 3:17. 12:18. 1 P 2:4.

36 **mocked him**. ver. 11. Lk +22:63.
vinegar. Ps +69:21.

37 **If thou be**. 1 C +15:2. ver. 35.
king of the Jews. ver. 3. Mt 27:11.

38 **a superscription**. ver. 3. Mt 27:11, 37. Mk
15:18, 26, 32. Jn 19:3, 19-22.
Latin. i.e. *of Rome's strength*, **S#4513g**, only
here.
THIS IS. Jn 14:1.
THE KING. ver. 3. Mt 27:11.

39 **one of the malefactors**. Lk 17:34-36. Mt
27:44. Mk 15:32.
railed on him. Mt 27:39.
if. 1 C +15:2.
save thyself and. ver. 35, 37.

40 **rebuked**. Le +19:17. Ep +5:11.
Dost. Lk +12:5. Ps 36:1. Re 15:4.
fear God. Pr 1:7. Ro 3:18.
seeing. 2 Ch 28:22. Je 5:3. Re 16:11.

41 **we indeed**. Lk 15:18, 19. Le 26:40, 41. Jsh
7:19, 20. 2 Ch 33:12. Ezr 9:13. Ne 9:3. Da

9:14. Ja 4:7. 1 J 1:8, 9.

due reward. Ge 41:9, 12. Ex 15:1, 6, 7. Dt +32:43. Ps 28:4, 5. 94:1, 2. Zp +3:14. Re 6:9, 10. 15:3, 4. 18:20. 19:1-7.

but. ver. 47. Lk 22:69, 70. Mt 27:4, 19, 24, 54. 1 P 1:19.

done nothing. ver. 22. Jn +8:46.

amiss. Ac 25:5. 28:6.

42 **Lord**. Lk 18:13. Ps 106:4, 5. Jn +20:28. Ac 16:31. 20:21. Ro 10:9-14. 1 C 6:10, 11. 1 P 2:6, 7. 1 J 5:1, 11-13.

remember. Lk 12:8. Ge 40:14. Jg 16:28. Ne 5:19. 13:14, 22, 29-31. Jb 7:7, 8. 10:9, 12. Ps 13:1, 2. 42:9. 74:2. 106:4, 5. 132:1. Je 15:15. La 5:1, 2. Mt 10:32. Ro 10:9, 10. He 6:10.

when. Lk 14:14. +21:31. 22:18. Ps 49:14. 90:14. +102:16. 143:8. Mt +23:39. +26:29. Ac +1:3, 6. +3:19-21. 1 P +1:11.

comest into. Lk 19:12. Mt +16:27, 28.

thy kingdom. Lk +17:20, 21. +21:31. +22:29, 30. 24:26. Ps 2:6. Is +9:6, 7. 53:10-12. Da +7:13, 14. Mt +21:43. Jn +1:49. +18:36. 2 T +4:1, 18. 1 P 1:11. 2 P +1:11.

43 **Verily**. Mt +5:18.

To day. Dt +4:26. Je 42:21. Mk +14:30.

shalt thou. Lk 15:4, 5, 20-24. +19:10. Ge 40:13. Jb 33:27-30. Ps 32:5. +50:15. Is 1:18, 19. 53:11. 55:6-9. +65:24. Mi 7:18. Mt 20:15, 16. Ro 5:20, 21. 1 T 1:15, 16. He 7:25.

with me. Zc 3:2. Jn +14:3. 17:24. 2 C +5:8. Ph +1:23.

in paradise. Lk 16:22. Ge 2:8. Ne 2:8. Ec 2:5. SS 4:12, 13. Is 51:3. Ac 2:31. 2 C 12:2, 4. Ep 4:9. Re 2:7. +14:13.

44 **sixth hour**. Our 12 noon. Mt +20:5. 27:45. Mk 15:33. Jn +11:9. 19:14.

there. Ex +10:22. Hab 3:8-11. Ac 2:20.

earth. *or*, land.

ninth hour. Our 3 p.m. Le 23:11. 1 K 18:29. Ps +141:2. Da 9:25, 26. Mt +20:5. 27:45, 46. Jn +11:9. Ac 3:1. 10:3, 30. 1 C 15:4.

45 **and the veil**. Ex 26:31. Le 16:12-16. 2 Ch 3:14. Mt 27:51-53. Mk 15:38. Ep 2:14-18. He 6:19. 9:3-8. 10:19-22.

temple. Lk 1:9.

46 **cried**. Mt 27:46-49. Mk 15:34-36. Jn 19:30.

Father. ver. 34. Lk +22:42. Ps 31:5. Jn 10:18. Ac 7:59. 1 P 2:23.

commend. 2 T 1:12. 1 P 4:19.

spirit. Gr. *pneuma*, Mt +27:50. Ec +3:21. +9:5. +12:7. Ac 7:59. +23:8, 9. He 12:23. 1 P 3:19.

having. Mt 27:50, etc. Mk 15:37, etc. Jn 19:30.

gave up. Jn 10:18.

Ghost. S#1606g: ver. 46; Mk 15:37, 39. Ge +25:8, 17. 35:29. 49:33. 2 K +24:6. Jb 3:11. 10:18. 11:20. 13:19. 14:10. Je 15:9. La 1:19. Mt 27:50. Jn 19:30. Ac 5:5, 10. 12:23.

47 **centurion**. Lk 7:2, 6. Mt +8:5.

he glorified God. Mt +9:8. Mt 27:54. Mk

15:39. Jn 19:7.

righteous man. ver. 41. Mt 27:19, 24.

48 **smote**. Lk 18:13. Je 31:19. Mt 11:17. Ac 2:37.

49 **acquaintance**. Lk 2:44. Jb 19:13. Ps 38:11. 88:8, 18. 142:4.

the women. ver. 27, 55. Lk 8:2. Mt 27:55, 56, 61. Mk 15:40, 41, 47. Jn 19:21-27. Ac 1:14.

afar off. Lk 18:13. Ps 38:11. 88:8.

50 **there**. Mt 27:57, 58. Mk 15:42-45. Jn 19:38.

a counsellor. Mk 15:43.

a good. Lk 2:25. Ac 10:2, 22. 11:24.

51 **had not**. Ge 37:21, 22. 42:21, 22. Ex +23:2. Pr 1:10. Is 8:12. Mk 14:64.

Arimathea. 1 S 1:1.

waited for. ver. 42. Lk 2:25, 38. Ge 49:18. Mk 15:43.

the kingdom of God. Lk +4:43.

52 **went unto Pilate**. Jn 19:38-42.

53 **and wrapped**. Is 53:9. Mt 27:59, 60. Mk 15:46.

hewn in stone. 2 Ch 16:14. Is 22:16.

wherein. Lk 19:30. Mk 11:2. Jn 19:41.

54 **the preparation**. Mt 27:62. Jn 19:14, 31, 42.

drew on. lit. began to dawn. Mt 28:1.

55 **the women**. ver. 49. Lk 8:2. Mt 27:61. Mk 15:47.

beheld the sepulchre. Mk 15:47.

56 **prepared**. Lk 24:1. 2 Ch 16:14. Mk 16:1. Jn 19:39.

rested. Ex 12:16. +20:8-10. 35:2, 3.

LUKE 24

1 **upon**. Mt 28:1-8. Mk 16:1, 2. Jn 20:1, 2.

first day. Ac 20:7. 1 C 16:2. Re 1:10.

they came. ver. 10. Lk 8:2, 3. 23:55, 56. Mt 27:55, 56. Mk 15:40.

bringing. Lk 23:56.

spices. Mk 16:1.

2 **they found**. Mt 27:60-66. 28:2. Mk 15:46, 47. 16:3, 4. Jn 20:1, 2.

the stone. Mt 27:60. Mk 15:46. Jn 11:38. 20:1.

rolled away. Ge 29:3, 8, 10.

3 **they entered in**. ver. 23. Mk 16:5. Jn 20:6, 7.

the Lord Jesus. Lk 7:13. Mk 16:19.

4 **much perplexed**. Ga 4:20.

two. Mt 28:2. Mk 16:5, 6. Jn 20:12.

men. Lk 2:9. Ac 1:10. 10:30.

stood by. Ge 18:2. Mt 28:2-6. Mk 16:5. Jn 20:11, 12. Ac 1:10.

5 **they**. ver. 37. Lk 1:12, 13, 29. Da 8:17, 18. 10:7-12, 16-19. Mt 28:3-5. Mk 16:5, 6. Ac 10:3, 4. 24:25. Re 11:13.

the living. *or*, him that liveth. Is 8:19. Jn 6:57. He 7:8. Re 1:17, 18. 2:8.

6 **is risen**. Ps 16:10.

remember. ver. 44-46. Lk 9:22, 44. 18:31-33. Mt +12:40. 16:21. 17:22, 23. 20:18, 19. 27:63. 28:6. Mk 8:31. 9:9, 10, 31, 32. 10:33, 34.

7 **Saying**. ver. 6. Lk 9:22, 44.
Son of man. Lk +5:24.
must be delivered. ver. 26, 44. Lk +13:33.
be crucified. Mt 20:19.
third day. ver. +46.

8 **they remembered**. Jn 2:19-22. 12:16. 14:26. 16:4.

9 **returned from**. ver. 22-24. Mt 28:7, 8. Mk 16:7, 8, 10.
and told. Jn 20:18.

10 **Mary Magdalene**. Lk 8:2, 3. Mk 15:40, 41. 16:9-11. Jn 20:11-18.
Joanna. Lk 8:2, 3.
Mary. Mt 27:56. Mk 15:40, 41.

11 **idle tales**. ver. 25. Ge 19:14. 2 K 7:2. Jb 9:16. Ps 126:1. Ac 12:9, 15.
believed them not. Ge 45:26. Mk 16:11, 16.

12 **arose Peter**. Jn 20:3-10.
stooping down. Jn 20:5, 6.
linen clothes. Jn 19:40. 20:5-7.
departed. Jn 20:10.

13 **two**. ver. 18. Mk 16:12, 13.
Emmaus. i.e. *in earnest longing, warm springs, obscure*, **S#1695g**. Compare Jsh 19:35, Hammath.

14 **they talked together**. Lk 6:45. Dt 6:7. Ml +3:16. Ac 20:11. 24:26.

15 **Jesus**. ver. 36. Ge 45:15. Mt 18:20. Jn 14:18, 19.

16 **eyes were holden**. ver. +31. Lk 9:45. 18:34. Ge +19:11. 21:19. 1 Ch 21:16. Ps +119:18. Mk 16:12. Jn 20:14. 21:4.
that. Ge +27:16.
should not. Lk +4:30. Is +53:2. Mt 26:48. Mk 14:44. 16:12.
know. Gr. *epiginosko*, Mt +11:27.

17 **and are sad**. Ge 40:7. Ezk 9:4-6. Mt 6:16. Jn 16:6, 20-22.

18 **Cleopas**. i.e. *the whole glory; famed of all*, **S#2810g**, only here. Jn 19:25.

19 **Concerning**. Jn 3:2. +6:14.
of Nazareth. Mk +1:24.
a prophet. Mt +21:11.
mighty. Ac 7:22. 18:24.
in deed. Ac 2:22.

20 **chief priests**. Lk 22:66-71. 23:1-5. Mt 27:1, 2, 20. Mk 15:1. Ac 2:23. 3:13-15. 4:8-10, 27, 28. 5:30, 31. 13:27-29. 1 Th 2:15.
our rulers. Lk 18:18. 23:13, 35. Mt +9:18. Jn 3:1. 7:26, 48. 12:42. Ac 3:17. 4:5, 8. 13:27. 1 C 2:8.
delivered. Mk +10:33.

21 **we trusted**. Lk 2:38. Mt 20:21. Mk +15:43. Ac 1:6.
redeemed Israel. Lk 1:68. Ps +130:8. Is +59:20. Ac +1:6. Ro +11:26. 1 P 1:18, 19. Re

5:9.
the third day. 1 C +15:4.

22 **and certain women**. ver. 9-11. Mt 28:7, 8. Mk 16:9, 10. Jn 20:1, 2, 18.
early at. ver. 1.

23 **found not his body**. ver. 3.
vision of angels. ver. 4, 5, 9.

24 **went**. ver. 12. Jn 20:1-10.

25 **O fools**. Mt +6:30. Mk 7:18. 8:17, 18. Ga 3:1, 3. He 5:11, 12.
slow of heart. Lk 9:45.

26 **suffered**. ver. 7, 44, 46. Lk 18:31-33. Ps ch. 22, 69. Is ch. 53. Zc 13:7. Mt 26:54. Jn 11:49-52. 12:24, 32. Ac 3:18. +17:3. 1 C +15:3, 4. He 2:8-10. 9:22, 23. 12:2. 1 P 1:3, +11.
his glory. Zc +6:13. Lk 9:26. 1 C 15:17. 1 P +1:11.

27 **beginning**. ver. 44. Ge +3:15. 12:3. 18:18. 22:18. 26:4. 28:14. +49:10. Ex 12:3-28, 43-51. Le ch. 16. Nu 20:11. 21:6-9. 24:17. Dt 18:15. Jn +5:39, 45-47. Ac 3:22. 7:37. 8:35. 28:23.
at Moses. Lk 16:16, +29. Jn 1:45. 3:14. +5:39, 45-47. Ac 3:22. 7:2-53. 8:35. 13:27. 28:23.
and all. ver. 25. 2 S 7:12-16. Ps 16:9, 10. 132:11. Is +7:14. +9:6, 7. 40:10, 11. 50:6. 52:13, 14. ch. 53. 61:1. Je +23:5, 6. 33:14, 15. Ezk 34:23. 37:25. Da 7:13, 14. +9:24-26. Jon 1:17. 3:5. Mi +5:2-4. 7:20. Zc 6:12. 9:9. 12:10. 13:7. Ml 3:1-3. 4:2. Jn 1:45. Ac 3:24. 10:43. 13:27-30. 28:23. Re 19:10.
the prophets. Christ's actual citations from the prophets given in the gospels are: (1) Mt 9:13 with Ho 6:6. (2) Mt 10:35, 36 w Mi 7:6. (3) Mt 11:10 w Ml 3:1. (4) Mt 11:28-30 w Je 6:16. (5) Mt 12:7 w Ho 6:6. (6) Mt 12:18 w Is 42:1-3. (7) Mt 12:21 w Is 42:4. (8) Mt 12:39-42 w Jon 1:17. (9) Mt 13:14 w Is 6:9, 10. (10) Mt 15:8 w Is 29:13. (11) Mt 21:5 w Zc 9:9. (12) Mt 21:13 w Je 7:11. (13) Mt 24:15 w Da 9:27. (14) Mt 27:9 w Zc 11:13. (15) Mk 7:6 w Is 29:13. (16) Mk 9:44 w Is 66:24. (17) Mk 11:17 w Is 56:7. (18) Mk 13:14 w Da 9:27. (19) Mk 14:27 w Zc 13:7. (20) Lk 4:18 w Is 61:1, 2 and 58:6. (21) Lk 7:27 w Ml 3:1. (22) Lk 12:53 w Mi 7:6. (23) Lk 19:46 w Is 56:7 and Je 7:11. (24) Jn 6:45 w Is 54:13.
expounded. Ac 17:2, 3. **S#1329g**, *diermeeneuo*. Ac 9:36 (by interpretation). 1 C 12:30 (interpret). 14:5, 13, 27. See **S#1328g**, 1 C 14:28 (interpreter). For related words, see Mk +5:41.
all the scriptures. ver. 32, 45. Mt 21:42.
concerning himself. Jn +5:39.

28 **whither they went**. ver. 13.
he made. Ge 19:2. 32:26. 42:7. 1 S 16:2. Mk 6:48.

29 **constrained**. Ge 32:26. Ac +16:15.
Abide. Jn 4:40, 41. He 13:2.

far spent. Lk 9:12. Jg 19:9, 11. Je 6:4.

30   **he took**. ver. 35. Mt 15:36. Mk 8:6.
and blessed. Lk 9:16. 22:17, 19. Dt +8:10.
Jsh 9:14. 1 S 9:13. Mt +14:19. +15:36. 26:26.
Mk 6:41. 8:6, 7. 14:22. Jn 6:11, 23. Ac 27:35.
Ro 14:6. 1 C 10:16, 30, 31. 11:24. 14:16. Col
3:17. 1 Th 5:18. 1 T 4:3-5.
and brake. Is +58:7.

31   **their eyes**. ver. 16. Jn 20:13-16.
opened. ver. +16, 45. Lk +4:18. Ge +21:19. 1
Ch 21:16. Ps +119:18. Jn 20:16. 21:7. Ac
9:17, 18.
knew. Gr. *epiginosko*, Mt +11:27. i.e. fully rec-
ognized him. Ge 45:1.
vanished out of their sight. *or*, ceased to be
seen of them. Lk 4:30. Jn 8:59. 10:39.

32   **Did**. Jb 32:18, 19. Ps 39:3. 104:34. Pr 27:9,
17. Is 50:4. Je +15:16. 20:9. 23:29. Jn 6:63.
He 4:12.
while he talked. Ge 3:10. Ps 45:2. Jn 7:46.
opened. ver. 45. Ge 41:56. Ac +17:2, 3.
28:23.
the scriptures. ver. 27, 45. Mt 21:42.

33   **and found**. Mk 16:13. Jn 20:19-26.
and them. Ac 1:14.

34   **Saying**. Mk 16:13.
the Lord. Lk 7:13.
hath appeared. Lk 22:54-62. Mk 16:7. 1 C
15:5.

35   **they told**. Mk 16:12, 13.
was known. Ge 45:1.
breaking of bread. Is +58:7. Ac 2:42.

36   **Jesus himself**. Mk 16:14. Jn 20:19-23. 1 C
15:5.
Peace. Ge +43:23. Ro +5:1.

37   **terrified**. Lk 16:30. 21:9. 1 S 28:13. Jb 4:14-
16. Mt 14:26, 27. Mk 6:49, 50. Ac 12:15.
affrighted. ver. 5. Mt 17:7.
supposed. Mt 14:26. Mk 6:49.
spirit. Gr. *pneuma*, put for a spirit being or an
angel, as in ver. 39. A "spirit" is distinguished
from an angel in Ac 23:8; this context shows
the apostles thought what they saw was a disembodied spirit, not the actual person of
Christ himself, a misconception Christ immediately and emphatically corrects. ver. 39. Ac
8:29, 39. 10:19. 11:12. He 1:7, 14. 1 P 3:19. 1
J 4:6a. Re 1:4. 3:1. 4:5. 5:6. For the other uses
of *pneuma*, see Mt +8:16.

38   **and why**. Je 4:14. Da 4:5, 19. Mt 16:8. 17:7.
He 4:13.
thoughts. Lk 2:35. Ro 14:1.
arise. Ac 7:23. 1 C 2:9.

39   **Behold**. Mt +27:52. 28:6. Jn +2:19, 21, 22.
20:27.
my hands. Jn 20:20, 25, 27. Ac 1:3. 1 J 1:1.
it is I myself. Ge 45:12. Ac +1:11. 2:32, 36. 1
Th 4:16.
handle me. Jn 20:27. 1 J 1:1.
for. Lk +23:46. Nu 16:22. Ec +12:7. Ac 23:8.

1 Th 5:23. He 12:9.
spirit. ver. +37.
hath not. A spirit is therefore an intelligent
entity, and like God the Father and God the
Holy Spirit, must be invisible. Mt +28:19. Jn
4:24. 14:17. 1 C 3:16. 6:19.
flesh and bones. Mt +16:17. 1 C 15:50. Ep
5:30. 6:12.

40   **And when**. Jn 20:20.
he showed. Ac 1:3.
hands and. Ps 22:16.

41   **believed not**. Ge 45:26-28. Jb 9:16. Ps 126:1,
2. Mk 16:16. Jn 16:22.
for joy. Ac 12:14.
Have. Jn 21:5, 10-13.

43   **and did eat**. Jn 21:12, 13. Ac 1:4. 10:40, 41.

44   **These are the words**. ver. 6, 7. Lk 9:22.
18:31-33. Mt 16:21. 17:22, 23. 20:18, 19. Mk
8:31, 32. 9:31. 10:33, 34. Jn +2:18-22.
while I. Jn 16:4, 5, 16, 17. 17:11-13. Ac 9:39.
that all. ver. 26, 27, 46. Lk 21:22. Mt 26:54,
56. Jn 19:24-37. Ac 3:18. 13:29-31, 33. 1 C
+15:3, 4.
must. Lk +13:33.
in the law. Ge +3:15. 14:18. +22:18. +49:10.
Le 16:2, etc. Nu 21:8, 9. 35:25. Dt 18:15-19.
Jn 3:14, 15. 5:46, 47. 7:23. Ac 3:22-24. 7:37.
He 3:5. 7:1-3. 9:8-12. 10:1.
in the prophets. ver. +27. Is +7:14. +9:6, 7.
11:1-10. 28:16. 40:1-11. 42:1-4. 49:1-8. 50:2-
6. 52:13-15. ch. +53. 61:1-3. Je +23:5, 6.
33:14, 15. Ezk 17:22-24. 34:23, 24. Da 2:44.
7:13, 14. +9:24-27. Ho 1:7-11. 3:5. Jl +2:28-
32. Am 9:11, 12. Mi +5:1-4. Hg 2:7-9. Zc
6:12, 13. 9:9. 11:8-13. 12:10. 13:7. 14:4. Ml
3:1-3. 4:2-6. Ac 28:23.
in the psalms. Ps ch. 2. +16:9-11. ch. 22.
34:20. 40:6-8. 68:18. ch. 69. 72:1-19. ch. 88.
109:4-20. ch. 110. 118:22-26. 132:11. Jn
+5:39. Ac +17:2, 3. 1 P 1:11. Re 19:10.

45   **opened**. Ex 4:11. Jb 33:16. 36:10. Ps
+119:18. Jn 2:22. Ac 16:14. 1 C 2:11. Ep 5:14.
1 J 5:20. Re 3:7.
the scriptures. ver. 27, 32. Mt 21:42.

46   **Thus it is written**. ver. 7, 26, 27, 44. Ps ch.
22. Is 50:6. 53:2, etc. Mt +26:24. Ac 4:12.
17:3. 1 P 1:3.
behoved. Is 53:5.
to rise. Jn 20:9. Ac 5:31.
third day. 1 C +15:4.

47   **that repentance**. Lk +13:3. Da +9:24. Mt
3:2. 9:13. Ac 13:38, 39, 46. 1 J 2:12.
in his name. Lk +9:48. Ac 4:12.
among. Lk +3:6. Ge +12:3. Ps 22:27. 67:2-4,
7. 86:9. ch. 117. Is 2:1-3. 11:10. 19:24, 25.
42:6. 60:1-3. 66:18-21. Je 31:34. Ho 2:23. Mi
4:2. Ml 1:11. Mt 8:10, +11. +28:19. Ac 13:46-
48. 18:5, 6. Ro 10:12-18. 15:8-16. *Ga* 3:8. Ep
3:8. Col 1:27.
beginning. ver. 49. Lk 13:34. Is 5:4. Ho 11:8.

Ac 1:4. 2:14-47. +3:26. 10:37. Ro 5:20. 11:26, 27. Ep 1:6.

48 **ye are witnesses**. Jn 15:27. Ac +1:8, 22. +2:32. 3:15. 4:33. 5:32. 10:39, 41. 13:31. 22:15. 1 C 15:15. He 2:3, 4. 1 P 5:1. 2 P 1:16. 1 J 1:2, 3.

49 **I send**. Is 44:3, 4. 59:20, 21. Ezk 36:27. Jl +2:28, etc. Zc 12:10. Jn 14:16, 17, 26. 15:26. 16:7-16. Ac 2:16, 17, 33. Ep 1:13.
promise. Ge 1:2. Ac 1:4, 5.
my Father. Lk 10:22. 22:29. Mt 7:21. Jn 5:17.
but tarry. Is 32:15. Ac 1:4, 8. 2:1-21.
in the city. ver. 47.
endued. Jb 8:22. 29:14. 39:19. Ps 35:26. 93:1. 132:9. Is 52:1. 61:10. Ro 13:12, 14. 1 C 15:53, 54. 2 C 5:2, 4. Col 3:12. 1 P 5:5.
power from. Lk 5:17. Ge 1:2. Mi 3:8. Mt

+1:18. Ac 1:5, 8.
on high. Lk 1:78. Is 32:15.

50 **as far**. Mk 11:1. Ac 1:12.
to Bethany. Jn +11:18.
he lifted. Ge 14:18-20. 27:4. 48:9. 49:28. Nu 6:23-27. Mk 10:16. He 7:5-7.

51 **blessed them**. Dt 33:1. Ac 3:26.
he was parted. Mk +16:19. He 1:3.
carried up. Ps *68:18*. Jn 3:13.

52 **they worshipped him**. Mt +8:2. +14:33. 28:9, 17. Jn +20:28. He +1:6.
returned. ver. 49.
with great joy. Ps 30:11. Jn 14:28. 16:7, 22. 1 P 1:8.

53 **in the temple**. Ac 2:46, 47. 3:1. 5:21, 41, 42.
blessing God. Lk 1:64. 2:28. 13:13.
Amen. Mt 28:20. Mk 16:20. Re 22:21.

JOHN

JOHN 1

1 **the beginning.** Jn 8:58. 17:5. Ge 1:1. Pr 8:22-31. Is 9:6. Mi +5:2. Ep 3:9. Col 1:17. He 1:10. 7:3. 13:8. 1 J 1:1. Re 1:2, 4, 8, 11, 17. 3:14. 21:6. 22:13.

the Word. ver. 14. He 4:12. 1 J 1:1, 2. 5:7. Re 19:13.

with. ver. 18. Jn 16:28. 17:5. Pr 8:22-30. 1 J 1:2.

and the Word. Jn 10:30-33. +20:28. Ps +45:6. Is +7:14. +9:6. 40:9-11. Mt 1:23. Ro 9:5. Ph 2:6. 1 T 3:16. T 2:13. He 1:8-13. 2 P 1:1. 1 J 5:7, 20.

was God. Jn 5:18. +8:35, 58, 59. +10:30, 33, +34. 14:7. +20:28. Dt +32:39. Jb +19:26. Is 43:10. 44:6. Je 23:5, 6. Mi +5:2. Mt 27:54. Ac 12:22. 20:28. Ro 9:5. 2 C 4:4. Ep 5:5. Ph 2:6. 2 Th 1:12. T 2:13. He +1:8. 2 P 1:1. Re 21:7.

2 **in the beginning.** Ge 1:1. He 1:10.

with God. Jn 8:56. Ge 17:1. Ex +6:3. Dt 32:39. Is 44:6. Da +7:13. Lk 3:22. Ac 7:38. Re +1:8. 15:3.

3 A.M. 1. B.C. 4004.

All things. ver. 10. Jn 5:17-19. Ge 1:1, 26. Jb +26:13. Ps 33:6, 9. 102:25. 146:6. Is 37:16. 40:26, 28. 44:24. 45:12, 18. 66:2. Je 10:10-12. 32:17. 1 C 8:6. Ep 3:9. Col 1:16, 17. He 1:2, 3, 10-12. 2:10. 3:3, 4. Re 1:5. 3:14. 4:11. 10:6.

4 **life.** Jn 3:16. 4:14. 5:21, 26. 6:57. 10:10, 28. 11:25. 14:6. 17:2. Ge 2:9. Ac 3:15. Ro 6:23. 1 C 15:45. Col 3:4. 2 T 1:10. 1 J 1:2. 5:1, 11, 12. Re 1:18. 4:9, 10. 22:1.

the life. ver. 5, 8, 9. Jn 8:12. 9:5. 12:35, 46. Ps 84:11. Is 35:4, 5. 42:6, 7, 16. 49:6. 60:1-3. Ml 4:2. Mt 4:16. Lk 1:78, 79. 2:32. Ac 26:23. Ep 5:14. 1 J 1:5-7. Re 21:23. 22:16.

5 **the light.** ver. 10. Jn 3:19, 20. 12:36-40. Jb 24:13-17. Pr 1:22, 29, 30. Ro 1:28. 8:7. 1 C 2:14.

darkness. Jn 8:12. Is 9:2.

comprehended. Ep 3:18.

6 A.M. 3999. B.C. 5.

a man. ver. 33. Jn 3:28. 17:18. Is 40:3-5. Ml 3:1. 4:5, 6. Mt 3:1, etc. 11:10. 21:25. Mk 1:1-8. Lk 1:15-17, 76. 3:2, etc. Ac 13:24, 25.

John. Mt 3:1. Mk 1:4. Lk 1:13, 61-63. 3:2.

7 **a witness.** ver. 15, 19, 26, 27, 29, 32-34, 36. 3:26-36. 5:33-35. 10:41. 15:27. Ac 19:4.

bear witness. ver. 32. Jn 6:69. Mk +1:24. Ac +5:32. +10:43. Ro +1:4.

that. ver. 9, 12. Jn 3:26. Ac 19:4. Ep 3:9. 1 T 2:4. T 2:11. 2 P 3:9.

believe. Jn 5:44.

8 **that light.** ver. 20. Jn 3:28. Ac 19:4.

9 **That was the.** ver. 4. Jn 6:32. 14:6. 15:1. Is 49:6. Mt 6:23. 1 J 1:8. 2:8. 5:20.

true. Jn 4:23. 6:32. 15:1. 17:3. 19:35.

light. Jn 12:46. 1 J 1:5.

which lighteth. Jn 3:19. Ps 119:105. Mt 5:14.

every. ver. 7. Jn 8:12. 12:46. Is +8:20. 1 Th 5:4-7. T 2:11.

that cometh. Jn 3:19. 11:27. 12:46.

world. Gr. *kosmos*, Mt +4:8. ver. +29.

10 **was in.** ver. 18. Jn 5:17. Ge 11:6-9. 16:13. 17:1. 18:33. Ex 3:4-6. Ac 14:17. 17:24-27. He 1:3.

world. Gr. *kosmos*, Mt +4:8.

and the world. Gr. *kosmos*, Mt +4:8.

made. Gr. *ginomai*, **S#1096g.** ver. 10, 14. Jn 2:9. 5:4, 6, 9, 14a. 8:33. 9:39. Ga 3:13. 4:4, 4. Ph 2:7b. T 3:7. Ja 3:9. 1 P 2:7.

by him. ver. +3. Je 10:11, 12. Col 1:16. He 1:2, 3, 10-12. Re 3:14.

world. Gr. *kosmos*, Mt +4:8. Jn 3:17. 6:33, 51. 7:7. 14:17, 31. 15:19. 16:20, 33. 17:9, 14, 21. Ac 17:6. 19:27. 1 C 11:32. 1 J 3:1. 4:5. 5:4, 5.

knew him not. ver. 5. Jn 16:3. 17:25. Ge 42:8. Mt 11:27. 1 C 1:21. 2:8. 1 J 3:1.

11 **came.** Mt 15:24. Ac 3:25, 26. 13:26, 46. Ro 9:4, 5. 15:8. Ga 4:4.

his own. Mt 21:38.

and. Jn 3:32. 13:1. Is 53:2, 3. Lk 19:14. 20:13-15. Ac 7:51, 52.

his own. 1 C 2:13. 2 C 9:8.

not. Jn 3:11, 32. 5:40, 43. 12:37. Ge 37:18. Ps *69:8.* Is *63:3.* Je +25:4. Lk 19:14. Ac 7:25. 13:46.

12 **as many.** T 1:4. Ju 3.

received. Dt 30:19. Mt 10:40. 18:5. Lk 18:17 with Mt 18:3. Col 2:6, 7. Re 3:20.

to them. Is 56:5. Je 3:19. Ho 1:10. Ro 8:14, 15. 2 C 6:17, 18. Ga 3:26. 4:6. 2 P 1:4. 1 J 3:1. 5:1.

gave he. Mt +27:43. Ph 2:13.
power. *or*, the right, *or*, privilege.
to become. Mt 5:45. T 1:4. 1 J 3:1.
the sons. Jn 11:52. 1 J +3:1, 2.
even. Jn 2:23. 3:18. 20:31. Mt 12:21. Ac
3:16. 1 J 3:23. 5:12, 13.
believe. Jn 3:16, 18, 36. 6:28, 29, 40, 53, 54.
8:24, 47. 11:25, 26. Ac +3:19. 10:43. 16:31.
Ro 10:4. Ga 2:16. 2 Th 2:10-12. He 11:6. Ja
+5:20. 1 J 2:23. 5:10-13. 2 J 9-11. 3 J 4.
his name. Jn 2:23. 3:18. 14:13, 14, 26. 15:16.
16:23, 24, 26. 20:31. Dt +28:58. 1 J 2:12.
3:23. 5:13. 3 J 7. Re 2:3, 13. 3:12. 14:1.

13 **were born**. Jn 3:3, 5, 7. Ja 1:18. 1 P 1:3, 23.
2:2. 1 J 2:29. 3:9. 4:7. 5:1, 4, 18.
not. Jn 8:33-41. Mt 3:9. Ro 9:7-9. 1 P 1:23.
of the will of the. Jn 3:6. Ge 25:22, 28.
27:4, 33. Ps 51:5. Ro 7:18. 9:10-16.
Ga 5:17.
nor of the will of man. Ps 110:3. Ro 9:1-5.
10:1-3. 1 C 3:6. Ph 2:13. Ja 1:18.
of God. Jn 3:6-8. 1 C 3:7. T 3:5. 1 J 2:28, 29.

14 **the Word**. ver. 1. Is +7:14. Mt 1:16, 20-23.
Lk 1:31-35. 2:7, 11. Ro 1:3, 4. 9:5. 1 C 15:47.
Ga 4:4. Ph 2:6-8. 1 T 3:16. He 2:11, 14-17.
10:5. 1 J 4:2, 3. 2 J 7.
was made. Jn 6:51. Is +7:14. +9:6. Mt +1:23.
Ro 1:3. 8:3. Ga 4:4. Ph 2:7, 8. Col 1:22. He
2:14. 1 J 4:2. 2 J 7.
flesh. Jn 6:53. 1 T 3:16. He 10:20. 1 P 3:18. 1
J 4:2.
and dwelt. Jn 2:21. Zc 2:10, 11. Re 7:15.
among us. Ps +68:17.
we beheld. Jn 2:11. 11:40. 12:40, 41. 14:9. Is
40:5. 53:2. 60:1, 2. Mt 17:1-5. Lk 9:32. 2 C
4:4-6. 1 T 3:16. He 1:3. 1 P 2:4-7. 2 P 1:16,
17. 1 J 1:1, 2. 4:12, 14.
his glory. Jn +7:39. Mt 17:2. +25:31. 2 P
1:16-18.
the glory. Ex 16:10. Is 4:2mg. +40:5. Ezk
1:28. Lk 2:32. He 1:3.
as. Ps 122:3. Ho 4:4. Mt 14:5. Ro 1:21. 3:7.
9:32. 1 C 3:1. 4:1. 7:25. 8:7. 2 C 3:18. Phm 9.
He 3:5, 6. 1 P 1:19. 2 P 1:3.
the only. ver. 18. Jn 3:16, 18. Ps 2:7. Ac
13:33. He 1:5. 5:5. 11:17. 1 J 4:9.
of the Father. Jn 6:46. 7:29. 16:27.
full. ver. 16, 17. Ps 45:2. 2 C 12:9. Ep 3:8, 18,
19. Col 1:19. 2:3, 9. 1 T 1:14-16.
grace. ver. 16, 17. Ro 5:21. 6:14.
truth. ver. 17. Jn 3:21. 5:33. 8:32, 40. 14:6.
16:13. 17:17. 18:37. Ep 4:21. 2 J 1.

15 A.M. 4030. A.D. 26.
bare witness. ver. 7, 8, 29-34. Jn 3:26-36.
5:33-36. Mt 3:11, 13, etc. Mk 1:7. Lk 3:16.
and cried. Jn 7:28, 37. 12:44.
he was before. *ver. 1, 2*, 27, +30. Jn 8:58.
17:5. Pr 8:22. Is +9:6. Mi +5:2. Ph 2:6, 7. Col
1:17. He 13:8. Re 1:11, 17, 18. 2:8.
16 **of his**. Jn 3:34. 10:10. 15:1-5. Mt 3:11, 14. Lk

21:15. Ac 3:12-16. Ro 8:9. 1 C 1:4, 5. Ep 3:19.
4:7-12. Col 1:19. 2:3, 9, 10. 1 P 1:11.
fulness. ver. 14. Ge 42:25. Is 45:24. Ac 5:31.
1 C 1:30. Ep 1:23. 3:19. 4:13. Col 1:19. 2:9.
all we. Le 7:10.
and grace. Is 57:19. Zc 4:7. Mt 13:12. 25:29.
Ro 5:2, 17, 20. Ep 1:6-8. 2:5-10. 4:7. 1 P 1:2.
17 **the law**. Jn 5:45. 7:19, 23. 9:29. Ex 20:1, etc.
Dt 4:44. 5:1. 33:4. Ac 7:38. 28:23. Ro 3:19,
20. 5:20, 21. 2 C 3:7-10. Ga 3:10-13, 17. He
3:5, 6. 8:8-12.
grace. ver. 14. Jn 8:32. 14:6. Ge +3:15. 22:18.
Ps 85:10. 89:1, 2. 98:3. Mi 7:20. Lk 1:54, 55,
68-79. Ac 13:34-39. Ro 3:21-26. 5:21. 6:14.
15:8-12. 2 C 1:20. He 9:22. 10:4-10. 11:39,
40. Re 5:8-10. 7:9-17.
Jesus Christ. Jn 17:3. Mt 1:1.
18 **seen God**. Jn 5:37. 6:46. 12:45. Ge +32:30.
Ex 33:20. Dt 4:12. 1 K +22:19. Ec 3:11. Mt
11:27. Lk 10:22. Col 1:15. 1 T 1:17. +6:16. 1 J
4:12, 20. 3 J 11.
the only. 1 T 1:17. 6:16. 1 J 4:9.
begotten. ver. 14. Jn 3:16, 18. Is +9:6. 1 J
4:9.
Son. Ps 2:7. Pr 30:4. Is 9:6. 1 J 4:14.
in the bosom. Jn 13:23. 14:6, 9. Dt 13:6. Ps
+74:11. Pr 8:30. Is 40:11. La 2:12. Mt 11:27.
Lk 16:22, 23.
he hath. Jn 3:11, 32. 12:41. 14:9. 17:6, 26.
Ge 16:13. 18:33. 32:28-30. 48:15, 16. Ex 3:4-
6. 23:21. 33:18-23. 34:5-7. Nu 12:8. Jsh 5:13-
15. 6:1, 2. Jg 6:12-26. 13:20-23. Is 6:1-3. Ezk
1:26-28. Ho 12:3-5. Mt 11:27. Lk 10:22. 1 J
5:20.
19 **when**. Jn 5:33-36. Dt 17:9-11. 24:8. Mt
21:23-32. Lk 3:15, etc.
Levites. Lk 10:32. Ac 4:36.
from Jerusalem. Mt 15:1.
Who. Jn 8:25. 10:24. Ac 13:25. 19:4.
20 **confessed**. ver. 8. Jn 3:28. Lk 3:15. Ac 13:25.
am not. Jn 3:28-36. Mt 3:11, 12. Mk 1:7, 8.
Lk 3:15-17.
the Christ. ver. 25, +41. Mt +16:16.
21 **Art thou Elias**. Ml 4:5. Mt +11:14. 16:14.
17:10-12. Lk 1:17.
Art thou that. *or*, Art thou a. ver. 25. Jn
+6:14. Mt 11:9-11. 16:14. +21:11.
22 **that we may**. 2 S 24:13.
23 **I am**. Jn 3:28. Mt 3:3. Mk 1:3. Lk 1:16, 17,
76-79. 3:4-6.
Make straight. Lk 1:76.
as said. *Is 40:3-5*. Mk 1:2.
24 **were of**. Jn 3:1, 2. 4:1. 7:32, 45, 47-49. 8:3,
13. 9:13. 11:46-48, 57. 12:19, 42. Mt 9:34.
12:23, 24. 15:12. 23:13-15, 26. Mk 8:15. 10:2.
Lk 5:30. 6:7. 7:30. 11:39-44, 53. 16:14. Ac
23:8. 26:5. Ph 3:5, 6.
25 **Why**. Mt 3:6. 21:23. Mk 1:4. Lk 3:3, 7. Ac
4:5-7. 5:28.
if. 1 C +15:2.

but. Ps 104:15. Pr 9:1-6, 16-78. Lk 16:25. Re 7:16, 17.

thou hast. Jn 14:27.

11 **beginning**. Jn 1:17. Ex 4:9. 7:19-21. Ec 9:7. Ml 2:2. 2 C 4:17. Ga 3:10-13.

miracles. ver. 18, 23. Jn 3:2. 4:48, 54. 6:2, 14, 26, 30. 7:31. 9:16. 10:41. 11:47. 12:18, 37. 20:30. Mt 12:38. Lk 21:11.

did. Jn 1:50, 51. 3:2. 4:46.

Cana. ver. 1.

Galilee. Jn 1:43.

manifested. Jn 1:14. 5:23. 7:4. 12:41. 14:9-11, 13. Dt 5:24. Ps 96:3. Is +40:5.

his glory. Jn 1:14.

and his. ver. 2.

believed. Jn 4:39. 11:15. 20:30, 31. 1 J 5:13.

12 **went down**. Jn 4:47, 49, 51.

Capernaum. Jn 4:46. 6:17, 24, 59. Mt 4:13. 11:23.

his mother. ver. 1.

and his brethren. Jn 7:3-5. Mt 12:46. +13:55, 56. Mk +6:3. Ac 1:13, 14. 1 C 9:5. Ga 1:19.

his disciples. ver. 2.

13 **passover**. ver. 23. Jn 5:1. 6:4. 7:2. 11:55. Ex 12:6-14. Le +23:2. Nu 28:16-25. Dt 16:1-8, 16. 1 S 15:22. Is 1:14. Lk 2:41.

went up. Jn 5:1. 7:8, 10. 11:55. 12:20. Lk +2:4.

14 **And found**. Dt 14:23-26. Zc 14:20, 21. Ml 3:1-3. Mt 21:12. Mk 11:15. Lk 19:45, 46. Re 11:2.

oxen. Le 22:19.

doves. Le 1:14. 5:7. 12:8. Lk 2:24.

15 **cords**. Ac 27:32.

he drove. Jn 18:6. Zc 4:6. Mk 11:15. 2 C 10:4.

poured. Gr. *ekcheo*, **S#1632g**. Rendered (1) *pour out*: Ac 2:17, 18. Re 16:1, 2, 3, 4, 8, 10, 12, 17. (2) *shed*: Ac 22:20. Ro 3:15. T 3:6. Re 16:6. (3) *shed forth*: Ac 2:33. (4) *spill*: Mk 2:22. (5) *run out*: Mt 9:17.

16 **make**. Is 56:5-11. Je 7:11. Ho 12:7, 8. Mt 21:13. Mk 11:16, 17. Ac 19:24-27. 1 T 6:5. 2 P 2:3, 14, 15.

my. Jn 5:17, 18. 8:49. 10:29, 30. 20:17. Lk 2:49.

Father's house. Jn 14:2. Lk 2:49.

house of merchandise. Mt 21:13. Mk 11:17. Lk 19:46.

17 **The zeal**. Ps 69:9. 119:139.

18 **the Jews**. Jn +5:10.

What. ver. 11. Jn 4:48. 6:30. Ex 4:1, 8. 7:9. Mt 12:38, etc. 16:1-4. Mk 8:11. Lk 11:29.

seeing. Jn 1:25. Mt 21:23. Mk 11:27, 28. Lk 20:1, 2. Ac 4:7. 5:28.

19 **Destroy**. Mt 26:60, 61. 27:40. Mk 8:31. 14:58. 15:29. Lk 9:22. Ac 6:14.

temple. Mt 23:16.

and in. Mt +12:40. 27:63.

three days. 1 S +30:12. Mt 26:61.

I will raise it. Jn 5:19. 10:17, 18. 11:25. Jb +19:25, 26. Is +26:19. Mk 8:31. Ac +2:24. 1 C 15:3, 4, 12. 1 P 3:18.

20 **Forty and**. Ezr 5:16.

temple. Mt 12:6. 26:61.

three days. Ho 6:2.

21 **he spake**. Jn 1:14. Col 1:19. 2:9. He 8:2.

temple. Mt +23:16. 1 C 3:16. 6:19. 2 C 6:16. Ep 2:20-22. Col 2:9. 1 P 2:4, 5.

his body. Jn 20:25, 27. Ps +16:10. 49:15. Is 43:10. Da +12:2. Mt +27:52. *28:6*. Lk 24:39. Ro 8:11. Ph 3:21. 1 T 2:5. 1 J 3:2.

22 **risen from**. Jn 20:27. Mt +27:52, 53. 28:6. Lk 24:39. Ac 13:29, 30, 34. Ro 8:11. 10:9, 10. Ph 3:21.

his. ver. 2, 17. Jn 12:16. 14:26. 16:4. Lk 24:7, 8, 44. Ac 11:16.

had said. Ge 41:54.

and they believed. ver. 11. Jn +5:47. 20:8, 9.

the scripture. Jn +5:39, 46, 47. 7:38, 42. 10:35. 13:18. 17:12. 19:24, 28, 36, 37. 20:9. Ps 16:10. Mt 21:42. Lk 4:21. +24:27, 44, 45. Ac +17:11. Ro 9:17.

23 **at the passover**. ver. 13.

many. Jn 3:2. 6:14. 7:31. 8:30, 31. 12:42, 43. Mt 13:20, 21. Mk 4:16, 17. Lk +8:13. Ga 5:6. Ep 3:16, 17. Ja 2:19, 20. 1 J 5:13.

name. Ge +4:26.

when they saw. ver. 11. Jn 3:2. 4:45, 48. 7:31. 11:45, 47, 48. 12:37. 20:30. Mt 11:4-6. Ac 8:6.

the miracles. Jn 6:2. 20:30. Mk 1:34.

24 **did**. Jn 6:15. Mt 10:16, 17.

not commit. 1 K 13:7-24. Ps 89:34. Lk 16:11. He 6:18.

because he knew. ver. +25. 1 C 1:24, 30. Col 2:3.

25 **needed not**. ver. 4. Jn 4:32. 6:15. Mt 17:4. Mk 6:48. Lk 20:8. 22:49.

knew. Jn 1:42, 47, 48. 4:16-19, 29. 5:42. 6:61, 64, 71. 8:14. 10:14, 27. 13:1, 11, 27, 28. 16:19, +30. 18:4. 19:28. 21:17. Ge 42:7, 8. 1 K 8:39. 1 Ch 28:9. 29:17. 2 Ch 6:30. Jb 42:2. Ps 1:6. 7:8, 9. +40:17. 44:21. 139:2-4. Is 66:18. Ezk 11:5. Am 4:13. Na 1:7. Mt 9:4. 12:25. 16:8. 17:25-27. 22:18. Mk 2:8. 8:17. 12:15. Lk 5:22. 6:8. 9:47. 11:17. 16:15. 20:23. Ac 1:24. 15:8. 2 T 2:19. He 4:13. 1 J 3:20. Re 2:23.

what was in. Je +17:10. 20:12. Mk 7:21. Ac 1:24.

JOHN 3

1 **of the Pharisees**. ver. 10. Jn +1:24.

Nicodemus. i.e. *innocent blood; conqueror of the populace; victorious among his people*, **S#3530g**, (ver. 4, 9. Jn 7:50. 19:39). Jn 7:47-49. 19:39.

ruler. Lk +24:20.

the Jews. Jn +5:10.

2 came. Jn 7:50, 51. 12:42, 43. 19:38, 39. Jg 6:27. Is 51:7. Ph 1:14.
Rabbi. ver. 26. Jn 1:38. 20:16.
we know. Mt 19:16. Ac 17:22. 22:3-6. 26:2, 3.
thou art. Jn 4:19. 9:24, 29. Mt 22:16. Mk 12:14. Lk 20:21.
come from God. Jn 16:27.
for. Jn 5:36. 7:31. 9:16, 30-33. 11:47, 48. 12:37. 15:24. Ac 2:22. 4:16, 17. 10:38.
miracles. Jn 2:11.
except. Mt +4:9. Jn 5:36. 9:33. 10:38. 14:10, 11. 1 S 18:14. Ac 2:22. 10:38.

3 Verily. Jn +1:51. 2 C 1:19, 20. Re 3:14.
Except. Mt +4:9. ver. 5, 6. Jn 1:13. Mt 18:3. 1 C 2:14. Ga 6:15. Ep 2:1, 4, 5. T 3:5. Ja +1:18. 1 P +1:3, 23. 1 J 2:29. 3:9. 5:1, 18.
again. *or*, from above. ver. 7, 31. Jn +1:13. 19:11. 2 C 5:17. Ga 4:9. 6:15. Ja 1:17. 3:15, 17. 1 P 1:23.
he cannot see. ver. 5, 36. Jn 1:5. 12:40. Dt 29:4. Je 5:21. Mt 13:11-16. 16:17. Mk +16:16. 1 C +6:9, 10. +15:50. 2 C 4:4. He +12:14.
the kingdom of God. Jn +18:36, 37. 1 Ch 28:4, 5. Mt +12:28. 25:34. Mk +1:15. Lk +4:43. +22:29, 30. Ac +1:3, 6. Ro 9:8. +14:17. Ja +2:5. 2 P 1:11. Re +5:10.

4 How. ver. 3. Jn 4:11, 12. 6:53, 60. 1 C 1:18. 2:14.

5 Verily. Jn +1:51.
Except. Mt +4:9.
born. ver. 3. Is 44:3, 4. Ezk 36:25-27. Mt 3:11. Mk 16:16. Ac +2:38. Ep 5:26. T 3:4-7. 1 P 1:2. 3:21. 1 J 5:6-8.
of water. Jn 1:33. 7:38. 13:10. Ps 119:9, 11. Ezk 36:25. Mk 16:16. Ac +1:5. +2:38. 8:36. 10:47. 11:16. +22:16. Ep 5:26. T 3:5. He +10:22. 1 P 1:23. 3:20. 2 P 3:5, 6. 1 J 5:6, 8. Re 22:1, 17.
and. or, even. Two words used (water, Spirit), one thing meant (Spirit), Ge +1:26. ver. 6, 8. Jn 7:38, 39. Ro 8::9. 1 C 12:13.
of the. Jn 1:13. 6:63. Mt 3:11. Mk 16:16. Ro 8:2. 1 C 2:12. 6:11. 1 J 2:29. 5:1, 6-8.
Spirit. Gr. *pneuma*, Lk +1:17. Jn 6:63. Ezk 36:26, 27. Mt 3:16. 1 C 15:45.
cannot enter. Mt +7:21. 28:19. Ac 2:38. +3:19. Ro 14:17. 1 C +6:9, 10. 2 C 5:17, 18. Ga 6:15. Ep 2:4-10. 2 Th 2:13, 14.
the kingdom. ver. +3. Mt +8:11, 12. 21:43.

6 born of the flesh. Jn 1:13. Ge 5:3. 6:5, 12. Pr +20:9. Ro 8:1, 4, 5-9, 13. 1 C 15:47-49, +50. 2 C 5:17. Ga 5:16-21, 24. Col 2:11.
is flesh. Jn 6:63. 1 P 3:18. 4:6.
that. Ezk 11:19, 20. 36:26, 27. Ro 8:5, 9. 1 C 6:17. Ga 5:17. 1 J 3:9.
born. Jn +1:13.
the Spirit. Gr. *pneuma*, Mt +3:16. Jn 7:39.
is spirit. Gr. *pneuma*, Lk +1:17; Ps +51:10. Jn 4:24. Ps +119:59. Ga 5:22. 6:8. Ep 4:22, 23. 1 J 4:7.

7 Marvel. ver. 12. Jn 5:28. 6:61-63. 1 J 3:13.
Ye must. ver. 3. Jn 4:24. Jb 14:4. 15:14. Mt 13:33-35. Ac 4:12. Ro 3:9-19. 8:5, 7. 9:22-25. 12:1, 2. 1 C 2:14. Ep 4:22-24. Col 1:12. He 12:14. 1 P 1:14-16, 22. Re 21:27.
be born. Ac +13:33. Ga 6:15. 1 P 2:2.
again. *or*, from above. ver. 3mg. Jn 1:12, 13. Ezk 36:27. 37:14. Mt +19:28. 2 C 5:17. 1 P +1:3, 23.

8 wind. or, spirit. Gr. *pneuma*, Mt +3:16. Jb 37:10-13, 17, 21-23. Ps 107:25, 29. 135:7. Ec 11:4, 5. Ezk 37:9. Ac 2:2. 4:31. 1 C 2:11. 12:11.
the sound. Ac 2:6.
so. Jn 1:13. Is 55:9-13. Mk 4:26-29. Lk 6:43, 44. Ro 9:15, 16. 1 C 2:11. 1 J 2:29. 3:8, 9.
Spirit. Gr. *pneuma*, Mt +3:16.

9 How. ver. 4. Jn 6:52, 60. Pr +4:18. Is 42:16. Mk 8:24, 25. Lk 1:34.

10 Art. Is 9:16. 29:10-12. 56:10. Je +8:8, 9. Mt 11:25. +15:14. 22:29.
master. Lk 2:46. 5:17. Ac 5:34. Ro 2:20.
Israel. Jn 1:31.
and knowest not. Jn 9:30. Ex 33:19. Dt 10:16. 30:6. 1 Ch 29:19. Ps 51:6, 10. 73:1. Is 11:6-9. 66:7-9. Je 31:33. 32:39, 40. Ezk 11:19. 18:31, 32. 36:25-28. 37:23, 24. Mt 22:29. Ro 2:28, 29. Ph 3:3. Col 2:11.

11 verily. ver. 3, 5. Jn +1:51.
We speak. ver. 13, 32-34. Jn 1:18. 7:16. 8:14, 28, 29, 38. 12:49. 14:24. Is 55:4. Mt 11:27. Lk 10:22. 1 J 1:1-3. 5:6-12. Re +1:5. 3:14.
ye. ver. 32. Jn 1:11. 5:31-40, 43. 12:37, 38. Is 49:4, 5. 50:2. 53:1. 65:2. Mt 23:37. Ac 22:18. 28:23-27. 2 C 4:4.

12 If. 1 C +15:2.
earthly. ver. 3, 5, 8. Ezk 36:25-27. 1 C 3:1, 2. 15:40. 2 C 5:1. Ph 2:10. 3:19. Col 3:2. He 5:11, 12. Ja 3:15. 1 P 2:1-3.
if I tell. Mt +4:9.
heavenly. ver. 13-17, 31-36. Jn 1:1-14. 6:51-53. +8:58. +10:30. 1 C 2:7-9. Ep 1:3, 20. 2:6. 3:10. 6:12. Ph 2:10. 1 T 3:16. 1 J 4:10, 14.

13 no man. Jn 1:18. 6:46. Dt 30:11, 12, 14. Pr 30:4. Ac 2:34. Ro 10:6-8. 1 C 15:50. Ep 4:9, 10.
hath ascended. Jn 6:62. Ge 5:24 w He 11:5. 2 K 2:11. Mt 22:32. Lk 23:43. 24:51. 2 C 5:8. 12:1-4. 1 T 2:5. Re 4:1.
but he. ver. 31. Jn 6:33, 38, 42, 51, 62. 8:42. 13:3. 16:28-30. +17:5. Ge +11:5. 1 C 15:47.
even. Jn 1:18. Mt 28:20. Mk 16:19, 20. Ac 20:28. Ep 1:23. 4:10.
Son of man. Jn +1:51. Ps 80:17. Is +55:3. Ezk +37:24. Da +7:13.
which is in heaven. Jn 1:18. 7:34. Ps 139:7. Je 23:24. Mt +28:19. Ro 8:34. He 7:25. 9:24. 1 J 2:1.

14 And as. Nu 21:7-9. 2 K 18:4.

even. Jn 8:28. 12:32-34. Ps 22:16. Mt 26:54. Lk 18:31-33. 24:20, 26, 27, 44-46. Ac 2:23. 4:27, 28.

must. ver. 30. Lk +13:33.

lifted up. Jn 8:28. 12:32, 34. Ac 2:33. 5:31. Ph 2:9.

15 **whosoever**. ver. 16, 36. Jn 1:12. 6:40, 47. 11:25, 26. 12:44-46. 20:31. Is 45:22. Mk 16:16. Ac 8:37. 10:34, 35. 16:30, 31. Ro 4:23-25. 5:1, 2. 10:9-14. Ga 2:16, 20. 3:11. He 7:25. 10:39. 1 J 5:1, 11-13.

believeth. Jn +5:44.

in him. Jn 15:4. 16:33. 1 J 5:12, 20.

not. Jn 5:24. 10:28-30. Mt +18:11. Lk +19:10. Ac 13:41. 1 C 1:18. 2 C 4:3.

perish. Gr. *apollumi*, Mt +2:13.

but have. Jn 5:24. 1 J 5:13.

eternal. Gr. *aionios*, Mt +18:8. Jn 17:2, 3. Ro 5:21. 6:22, 23. 1 J 2:25. 5:13, 20.

16 **God**. Je 31:3. Lk 2:14. Ro 5:8. 2 C 5:19-21. Ep 2:4-7. 2 Th 2:16. T 3:4-7. 1 J 3:1. 4:9, 10, 14, 19. Re 1:5.

loved. 1 J 4:9.

world. Gr. *kosmos*, Mt +4:8. Jn +1:29. 7:4. Ac 17:31. 1 J 2:2.

gave. Jn 1:14, 18. Ge 22:12. Is +9:6. Mk 12:6. Ro 5:10. 8:32.

only. ver. 18. Jn 1:14. Ge 22:2, +12. Lk +7:12.

begotten. Gr. *monogenes*, **S#3439g**, Lk +7:12. lit. the only one of a family, unique of its kind. Jn 1:14, 18. 3:18. 20:21. Ge 16:15. 21:12. 22:2, 12, 16. 25:1-4. 1 Ch 1:32, 33. Ps 2:7. Is 9:6. Mt 17:5. 21:37. Ga 4:23. Col 1:15. He 1:8. 11:17. 1 J 4:9. 5:18.

Son. ver. 35. Jn +5:25. Is +9:6.

that whosoever. ver. 15. Mt 9:13. 1 T 1:15, 16. Re 22:17.

believeth. In the NT, belief that leads to eternal life is always expressed (in the present tense, as here) as continuous or continuing belief, never a single or one time action. ver. 18, 36. Jn 1:12. +4:39. +5:24, 44. 6:35, 47. 12:46. 20:29. Is 28:16. 45:22. Mt 11:28. Mk 9:23. Lk 7:50. Ac 10:43. 16:31. Ro 1:16. 4:5. 9:33. 10:4. Ga 3:7, 9, 22. Ep 2:8-10. 1 T 4:10. He 6:12. 10:38, 39. 1 P 2:4-6.

in him. Jn 15:4. 16:33. 1 J 5:12, 20.

perish. Gr. *apollumi*, Mt +2:13. Jn +10:28. Lk +19:10. 23:35. 2 P 3:9.

everlasting. Gr. *aionios*, Mt +18:8.

17 **God**. Jn 5:45. 8:15, 16. 12:47, 48. Lk 9:56.

sent. ver. 34. Jn 4:34. 5:36, 38. 6:29, 38, 57. 7:29. 8:42. 10:36. 11:27, 42. 17:3, 8, 18, 21, 23, 25. 20:21. Ro 8:3. 1 J 4:9, 10, 14.

his Son. ver. 35.

to condemn. Jn 4:42. 5:22, 45. 8:11, 15. 12:47. Lk 9:55.

world. Gr. *kosmos*, Mt +4:8.

but. Jn 1:29. 6:40. Is 45:21-23. 49:6, 7.

53:10-12. Zc 9:9. Mt 1:23. +18:11. Lk 2:10, 11. +19:10. 1 T +2:5, 6. 1 J 2:2. 4:14.

world. 1 J +2:2.

18 **He that**. Lk 2:34, 35.

believeth. Jn 5:24. 1 J 5:13.

is not condemned. ver. 36. Jn 5:24. 6:40, 47. 20:31. Ro 5:1. 8:1, 34. 1 J 5:12.

he that believeth not. Pr +1:29. Is +66:4. Mk 16:16. He 2:3. 12:25. 1 J 5:10.

is condemned. Ge 2:17. Ga 3:10. 2 Th 2:12.

hath not. Mt +5:18.

the name. Jn +1:12.

only begotten. ver. 16.

Son of God. Mt +14:33.

19 **this is the condemnation**. Jn 9:39-41. 15:22-25. Ex +6:6. Mt 11:20-24. Lk 10:11-16. +12:47. Ro 1:32. 2 C 2:15, 16. 2 Th 2:12. He +3:12, 13. Ex +6:6.

light. Jn 1:4, 9-11. 8:12.

world. Gr. *kosmos*, Mt +4:8. Jn +1:9. 12:46.

men loved. 2 S 13:9. Ps +11:5. Is 30:10. Je 5:31. Ep 5:12.

darkness. Jn 1:5, 6. 8:12. 12:35, 46. 1 J 1:5. 2:8, 9, 11.

rather than. Jn 12:43, 48. Mt 7:26, 27. 11:20-24. 12:41. Lk 11:31, 32. 12:47, 48. Ro +5:13. Ep +4:30. He 10:26-29.

because. Jn 5:44. 7:7. 8:44, 45. 10:26, 27. 12:43. Ge +6:5. 37:2. Is 30:9-12. Je +17:9. Mk 7:21-23. Lk 16:14, 15. Ac 24:21-26. Ro 2:8. 1 P 2:8. 2 P 3:3.

20 **every**. Jn 7:7. 1 K 22:8. Jb 24:13-17. Ps 50:17. 64:4. Pr 1:29. +4:18. 5:12. 15:12. 22:8. Am 5:10, 11. Lk 11:45. Ro 13:12. Ja 1:23-25.

that doeth. or, practiseth. Jn 5:29. 1 J 3:9.

reproved. *or*, discovered. Jn 16:8. Ep +5:11-13mg. Re 3:19.

21 **he that**. Jn 1:47. +5:39. Ne 9:33. Jb 13:6. Ps 1:1-3. 119:80, 105. 139:23, 24. Is +8:20. Ac 17:11, 12. 1 J 1:6.

cometh. Ps 139:23, 24.

that his. Jn 9:3. 15:4, 5. Is 26:12. Ho 14:8. 1 C 15:10. 2 C 1:12. Ga 5:22, 23. 6:8. Ep 5:9, 13. Ph 1:11. 2:13. Col 1:29. He 13:21. 1 P 1:22. 2 P 1:5-10. 1 J 2:27-29. 4:12, 13, 15, 16. Re 3:1, 2, 15.

they are. 3 J 11.

in God. Ro 16:12. Ph 2:13. 1 J 3:24.

22 **these**. Jn 2:13. 4:3. 7:3.

disciples. Jn 2:2.

and baptized. ver. 26. Jn 4:1, 2.

23 **was baptizing**. Mt 3:5, 6. Mk 1:4, 5.

Aenon. i.e. *fountains, springs; to praise; cloud, darkness*, **S#137g**, only here. Ezk 47:17. 48:1, Hazar Aenon, *the Village of Fountains*. "Aenon" is the plural form of the singular *En* or *Ain*, "fountain" or "eye" (**S#5869h**, Ge +24:13).

near to Salim. i.e. *a fox; tossing; completed*, **S#4530g**, only here. For **S#8004h**, see Ge +14:18.

Ge 33:18, Shalem. 1 S 9:4, Shalim.
much water. lit. "many springs." Ex 15:27.
Nu 24:7. 2 S 22:17, 18. 2 Ch 32:3, 4. Ps 18:16.
77:19. 93:4. 107:23. Is 17:13. Je +9:1. 51:13,
36. La 2:11, 18, 19. 3:48, 49. Ezk 1:24. 19:10.
43:2. Re 1:15. 14:2. 17:1. 19:6.
and they. Mt 3:5, 6. Mk 1:4, 5. Lk 3:7.

24 **John**. Jn 5:35. Mt 4:12. Lk 9:7-9.

25 **disciples**. Jn 1:35.
about purifying. Jn 2:6. Nu 19:7. Mt 3:11.
Mk 7:2-5, 8. Lk +11:38. He 6:2. 9:8-10, 13,
14, 23. 1 P 3:21.

26 **Rabbi**. ver. 2. Jn 1:38.
he that. Nu 11:26-29. Ec 4:4. 1 C 3:3-5. Ga
5:20, 21. 6:12, 13. Ja 3:14-18. 4:5, 6.
beyond Jordan. Jn 1:28. 10:40. Mt 19:1.
to whom. Jn 1:7, 15, 26-36.
the same. ver. 22.
and all. Jn 1:7, 9. 11:48. 12:19. Ps 65:2. Is
45:23. Ac 19:26, 27.

27 **A man**. Nu 16:9-11. 17:5. 1 Ch 28:4, 5. Je
1:5. 17:16. Am 7:15. Mt 25:15. Mk 13:34. Ro
1:5. 12:6. 1 C 1:1. 2:12-14. 3:5. 4:7. 12:11.
15:10. Ga 1:1. Ep 1:1. 3:7, 8. 1 T 2:7. Ja 1:17.
1 P 4:10, 11.
receive. *or*, take unto himself. He 5:4, 5.
except. Mt +4:9.
be given. Jn 4:10. 6:65. 17:2. 1 Ch 29:14. Is
55:11. Ro 9:16. 1 C 3:7. 4:7. Ph 2:12, 13. Ja
1:17, 18. 1 P 4:10. 1 J 5:20.
from heaven. Jn 19:11. Ps +73:9. Mt 21:25.
Mk 11:30, 31.

28 **I said**. Jn 1:20, 25, 27.
but. Jn 1:6, 15, 23. Ml 3:1. 4:4, 5. Mt 3:3, 11,
12. Mk 1:2, 3. Lk 1:16, 17, 76. 3:4-6. Ac 19:4.

29 **hath**. Ps 45:9-17. SS 3:11. 4:8-12. Is 54:5.
62:4, 5. Je 2:2. Ezk 16:8. Ho 2:19, 20. Mt
22:2. 25:1. 2 C 11:2. Ep 5:25-27. Re 19:7-9.
21:9.
the friend. Jg 14:10, 11, 20. Ps 45:14. SS 5:1.
Mt 9:15.
this. Jn 15:11. Is 66:11. Lk 2:10-14. 15:6. 1 P
1:8.

30 **must increase**. Ps 72:17-19. Is +9:7. 53:2, 3,
12. Da 2:34, 35, 44, 45. Mt 3:11. +13:31-33.
Lk 7:47. Re 11:15.
but. Ac 13:36, 37. 1 C 3:5. 2 C 3:7-11. Col
1:18. He 3:2-6.
decrease. Ro 12:3. Ph +2:3.

31 **that cometh**. ver. 13. Jn 6:33. +8:23, 24. 1 C
2:8. 15:47. Ep 1:20, 21. 4:8-10. Ph 2:6. Ja 2:1.
is above all. ver. 35. Jn 1:15, 27, 30. 5:21-25.
Ne +9:6. Ps 97:9. Mt 28:18. Ac 10:36. Ro 9:5.
1 C 1:30. +12:3. Ep 1:21. Ph 2:9-11. 1 P 3:22.
Re 19:16.
he that is. ver. 12. Mt 16:23. 1 C +15:47, 48.
He 9:1, 9, 10.
and speaketh. 1 J 4:5.
he that cometh. ver. 13. Jn 6:33, 51. 16:27,
28.

above all. Jn 1:15. Ps 89:27. Ac +10:36. 1 C
+2:8. +15:47. Col 1:15, 18. He 1:4-6. Re 1:5.
3:14.

32 **what**. ver. 11. Jn 1:18. 5:20. 7:16. 8:26, 28,
38, 40. 12:49. 14:24. 15:15. 18:37. Re 1:5.
and no man. ver. 11, 19, 26, 33. Jn 1:11.
5:43. 12:37. Is 50:2. 53:1. Ro 10:16-21. 11:2-
6.

33 **hath set**. Ro 3:3, 4. 4:11, 18-21. 2 C 1:18. T
1:1, 2. He 6:17, 18. 1 J 5:9, 10.
seal. Ne 9:38. Ro 15:28. 1 C 9:2. Ep +4:30.
God is true. Jn 8:26. Ro 3:4. 1 J 5:10.

34 **he**. ver. 32. Jn 7:16. 8:26-28, 40, 47.
hath sent. ver. 17. Jn 20:21. 1 J 4:14.
speaketh. Ezk 3:4.
the words. Jn 8:47.
for God. ver. 17. Jn 1:16. 5:26. 7:37-39.
15:26. 16:7. Nu 11:25. 2 K 2:9. Ps +45:7. Is
11:2-5. 59:21. 62:1-3. Ro 8:2. Ep 3:8. 4:7-13.
Col 1:19. 2:9, 10. Re 21:6. 22:1, 16, 17.
Spirit. Gr. *pneuma*, Mt +3:16. Jn 6:63. Ge
+1:2. Ps *45:7*. Is *11:2*. *61:1*, Lk 11:13. Ac 19:2.
1 C 14:12mg, 32. Ga 3:2. Ep 5:18. 1 Th 5:19.
by measure. Ezr 7:22. Ezk 4:11, 16. 12:19. 2
C 1:22. 5:5. Ep 1:13, 14. 4:7. 5:18. 1 J 2:20,
27.

35 **Father**. Jn 5:20-23. 15:9. 17:23, 24, 26. Pr
8:30. Is 42:1. Mt 3:17. 17:5.
the Son. ver. 17, 36. Jn 5:19-26. 6:40. 8:36.
14:13. 17:1. Mt 24:36. 1 J 2:22. 4:14. 2 J 3, 9.
and. Jn 13:3. 17:2. Ge 41:44, 55. Ps 2:8.
110:1, 2. Is +9:6, 7. Mt 11:27. 28:18. Lk
10:22. 11:22. 1 C 15:27. Ep 1:22. Ph 2:9-11.
He 1:2. 2:8, 9. 1 P 3:22.
all things. Jn 5:20. Ge 39:4, 8.

36 **he that believeth on**. ver. 15, 16. Jn 1:12.
5:24. 6:40, 47-54. 10:28. 11:25, 26. 20:31.
Hab +2:4. Mt 19:16. Ro 1:17. 6:22. 8:1. 1 J
3:14, 15. 5:10-13.
everlasting. Gr. *aionios*, Mt +18:8.
believeth. or, obeyeth. He +5:9.
not the Son. Jn +8:24. Ac 4:12. Ro 5:1.
not see. ver. 3. Jn 8:51. Nu 32:11. Jb 33:28.
Ps 36:9. 49:19. 106:4, 5. Lk 2:30. 3:6. Ro 8:24,
25. Re +21:8.
but the wrath. Jn 9:39. 12:40. 2 K 22:13. Ps
2:12. Na 1:2. Mt 3:7. 22:7, 12. 24:28, 30.
25:12. Lk 19:27. Ro 1:18. 2:4-9, 17. 4:15. 5:9.
+11:22. 2 C +5:11. Ga 3:10. Ep 5:6. Col 3:6. 1
Th 1:10. 2:16. 5:9. He 2:3. 10:29. Ju 15. Re
6:16, 17. 11:18.
abideth. Is 55:7. Jon 4:2. Mt 12:31, 32.
+25:46. He +9:27. Re +22:11.

JOHN 4

1 **the Lord**. Jn 6:23. 11:2. 13:13, 14. 20:2, 18,
20, 25. 21:7, 12. Lk 1:76. 2:11. 7:19. 19:31,
34. Ac +10:36. 1 C 2:8. 15:47. 2 C 4:5. Ja 2:1.
Re 19:16.

40 **they**. Ge 32:26. Pr 4:13. SS 3:4. Je 14:8. Lk 8:38. 10:39. 24:29. Ac 16:15.
he abode. Lk 19:5-10. 2 C 6:1, 2. Re 3:20.

41 **many**. Ge +49:10. Ac +1:8. 8:12, 25. 15:3.
believed. ver. 39, 42, 48, 53. Jn 5:44.
because. Jn 6:63. 7:46. 8:30. Mt 7:28, 29. Lk 4:32. 1 C 2:4, 5. He 4:13.

42 **we believe**. ver. +41.
thy saying. Jn 8:43. Mt 26:73.
for. Jn 1:45-49. 17:8. Ac 17:11, 12.
and know. ver. 29. Jn 1:29. 3:14-18. 6:68, 69. 11:27. Is 45:22. 52:10. Lk 2:10, 11, 32. Ac 4:12. Ro 10:11-13. 2 C 5:19. 2 T 1:12. 1 J 4:14. 5:20.
the Savior. Jn 3:17. 5:34. 12:47. Lk 2:11. 1 T 1:15. 2:4. 4:10.
world. Gr. *kosmos*, Mt +4:8. Jn +1:29. Mt 20:28.

43 **two**. ver. 40. Mt 15:21-24. Mk 7:27, 28. Ro 15:8.
and. ver. 46. Jn 1:43. Mt 4:13.

44 **testified**. Jn 18:37.
that. Mt 13:57. Mk 6:4. Lk 4:24.
own country. Jn 7:41, 42.

45 **the Galileans**. Mt 4:23, 24. Lk 8:40.
having. Jn 2:13-16, 23. 3:2.
for. ver. 20. Dt 16:16. Lk 2:42-44. 9:53.

46 **Cana**. Jn 2:1-11. 21:2. Jsh 19:28.
nobleman. *or*, courtier, *or*, ruler.
whose. Ps +50:15. 78:34. Ho +5:15. Mt 9:18. 15:22. 17:14, 15. Lk 7:2. 8:42.
Capernaum. ver. 49, 51. Jn 2:12.

47 **he heard**. Mk 2:1-3. 6:55, 56. 10:47.
was come. ver. 3, 54.
besought him. Ge 21:14-16. La 2:19. Mk 5:22, +23.
that he. Lk 11:21, 32. Ps 46:1. Lk 7:6-8. 8:41. Ac 9:38.

48 **Except**. ver. 41, 42. Jn 2:18. 6:30. 12:37. 15:24. 20:29. Nu 14:11. Mt 16:1. 27:42. Lk 10:18. 16:31. Ac 2:22. 1 C 1:22.
signs and. Jn 2:11. Ex 7:3. Da 4:2, 3. 6:27. Mt 24:24. Mk 13:22. Ac 2:19, 22, 43. 4:30. 5:12. 6:8. 7:36. 8:13. 14:3. 15:12. Ro 15:19. 1 C 1:22. 2 C 12:12. 2 Th 2:9. He 2:4.
will not. Mt +5:18.
believe. ver. +41.

49 **The nobleman**. Mk 9:24.
come. ver. 47, 51. Ps 40:17. 88:10-12. Mk 5:23, 35, 36.
ere my child die. Jn 11:21, 32. Mk 5:35. Lk 8:49.

50 **Go**. Jn 11:40. 1 K 17:13-15. Mt 8:13. Mk 7:29, 30. 9:23, 24. Lk 17:14. Ac 14:9, 10. Ro 4:20, 21. He 11:19.
believed the word. Jn 5:47. 2 Ch 32:8.

51 **Thy**. ver. 50, 53. 1 K 17:23.

52 **seventh hour**. Our 1 p.m. Jn +11:9.

53 **at the**. ver. 50. Ps 33:9. 107:20. Mt 8:8, 9, 13.

and himself believed. ver. 41. Lk 19:9. Ac +2:39. 16:15, 34. 18:8.
whole house. Ac 11:14. 16:34. 18:8.

54 **This is**. Jn 2:11 with ver. 45-47.
the second. Jn 2:1-11.
miracle. Jn 2:11.
come out. ver. 45, 46.

JOHN 5

1 **a feast**. Jn 2:13. 6:4. Ex 23:14-17. 34:23. Le 23:2, etc. Dt 16:16. Mt 3:15. Ga 4:4.

2 **market**. *or, gate*. Ne 3:1, 32. 12:39.
pool. Is 22:9, 11.
Hebrew. Jn 19:13, 17, 20. Ac 21:40. Re 9:11. 16:16.
Bethesda. i.e. *house of mercy*, **S#964g**.

3 **of blind**. Mt 15:30, 31. Lk 7:22.
withered. 1 K 13:4. Zc 11:17. Mt 12:10. Mk 3:1-4. Lk 6:6, 8.
waiting. Pr 8:34. La 3:26. Ro 8:25. Ja 5:7.

4 **an angel**. Re 16:5.
first. Ps 119:60. Pr 6:4, 5. 8:17. Ec 9:10. Ho 13:13. Mt 6:33. 11:12. Lk 13:24-28. 16:16.
was made. 2 K 5:10-14. Ezk 47:8, 9. Zc 13:1. 14:8. 1 C 6:11. 1 J 1:7.

5 **thirty**. ver. 14. Jn 9:1, 21. Mk 9:21. Lk 8:43. 13:16. Ac 3:2. 4:22. 9:33. 14:8.

6 **and knew**. Jn +2:24, 25. 21:17. Ps 142:3. He 4:13, 15.
Wilt. Is 65:1. Je 13:27. Lk 18:41.

7 **I have**. Dt 32:36. Ps 72:12. 142:4. Ro 5:6. 2 C 1:8-10.
when. ver. 4.
is troubled. Ezk 32:2.
before. ver. 4. 1 C 9:24.

8 **Rise**. Pr 6:9. SS 2:10. Is 60:1. Mt 9:6, 7. Mk 2:9, 11, 12. 10:49. Lk 5:24, 25. 22:46. Ac 9:34. Ep 5:14.
bed. Mk 2:4, 9, 11, 12. 6:55. Ac 5:15. 9:33.

9 **immediately**. ver. 14. Mk 1:31, 42. 5:29, 41, 42. 10:52. Ac 3:7, 8.
and on. ver. 10-12. Jn 7:23. 9:14. Mt 12:10-13. Mk 3:2-4. Lk +13:10-16.

10 **The Jews**. ver. 15, 16, 18. Jn 1:19. 2:6, 18, 20. 3:1, 25. 4:22. 6:4, 41, 52. 7:1, etc. 8:22, etc. 9:18, 22. 10:19, 24, 31, 33. 11:8, etc. 12:9, 11. 13:33. 18:12, etc., 20, 33, 36. 19:7, 21, 42. 20:19.
it is not lawful. Jn 7:23. 9:16. Ex +20:8-11. 31:12-17. Ne 13:15-21. Is +58:13. Je 17:21, 22, 27. Mt 12:2, etc. Mk 2:24. 3:4. Lk 6:2. +13:14. 23:56.

11 **He that**. Jn 9:16, 17. Mk 2:9-11.

12 **What**. Jg 6:29, 30. 1 S 14:38, 39. Mt 21:23. Ro 10:2.

13 **he that**. Jn 14:9.
for Jesus. Jn 6:15.
conveyed himself away. Jn 8:59. Lk +4:30. +24:31.

a multitude being. *or*, from the multitude that was.

14 Jesus. Jn 1:43. 9:35.
in the temple. Le 7:12. Ps 9:13, 14. 27:6. 66:13-15. 107:20-22. 116:12-19. 118:18, 19. Is 38:20, 22.
sin. Jn 8:11. Ezr 9:13, 14. Ne 9:28. Mt 9:2, 5. Mk 2:5. 1 P 4:3.
lest. ver. 5. Le 26:23, 24, 27, 28. 2 Ch 28:22. Ezr 9:14. La 3:22. Mt 12:45. 1 C +11:30. Re 2:21-23.

15 and told. Jn 4:29. 7:21. 9:11, 12. Mk 1:45.
which. ver. 12. Jn 9:15, 25, 30, 34.

16 persecute. Jn 15:20. Ac 9:4, 5.
and sought. ver. 13. Jn 7:19, 20, 25. 10:39. Mt 12:13, 14. Mk 3:6. Lk 6:11.
because. Jn 7:23. 9:16. Lk +13:14.

17 answered. ver. 19. Mt 12:2-8. Mk 2:24-28. +11:14. Lk 13:14-17.
My Father. ver. 43. Jn 2:16. 6:32, 40. 8:19, 49, 54. 10:18, 25, 29, 37. 14:2, etc. 15:1, etc. 17:1. 20:17. Mt +7:21.
worketh. Jn 9:4. 14:10. Ge 2:1, 2. Ps 65:6. Is 40:26. Mt 10:29. Ac 14:17. 17:28. 1 C 12:6, 7. Col 1:16, 17. He 1:3.
I work. Jn 9:4. Lk 2:49.

18 the Jews. ver. 10. Jn 7:19.
sought. Jn 7:1.
broken the sabbath. ver. 16. Jn 7:22, 23. 10:35. Mt 12:5. Lk +13:14.
God was. ver. 23. Jn 8:54, 58. 10:30, 33. 14:9, 23. Zc 13:7. Ph 2:6. Re 21:22, 23. 22:1, 3.
his Father. Ro 8:32.
making himself. Jn 10:33. 19:7.
equal. ver. 17. Jn +10:30, 33. 14:9, +28. 17:5, 10. Mt +10:32. +27:43. Mk +13:32. 1 C 11:3. +15:28, 45, 47. Ph 2:5, 6.

19 answered. ver. 17.
Verily. ver. 24, 25. Jn +1:51.
The Son. ver. 30. Jn 3:35. 8:28. 9:4. 12:49. 14:10, 20.
do nothing. Jn 16:13. Ge 41:16.
of himself. (1) Jn 1:1, 3. Ge 1:1. (2) Ne 9:6. Col 1:17. (3) Ac 2:24. Jn 2:19. (4) Jn 6:44. 12:32. (5) Jn 5:22, 23. Ps 50:6. (6) Ro 8:11. Ph 3:20, 21. (7) Ps 27:14. 2 C 12:9. (8) Pr 2:6, 7. Lk 21:15. (9) Je 23:24. Ep 1:23. (10) Jn 6:45. Ga 1:12. (11) Ju 1. He 2:11. (12) Je 17:10. Re 2:23. (13) Is 43:11. Jn 4:42. (14) T 1:3. 1:4. Mt +28:19.
but what. Ge 41:25.
for. (1) Jn 14:16-23. Ge 1:1, 26. Is 44:24. Col 1:16. (2) ver. 22 with Ps 50:6. 2 C 5:10. (3) Jn 2:19. 10:18, with Ac 2:24. Ro 6:4. 1 C 15:12. 1 P 3:18. (4) and ver. 21, 25, 26, with Ep 1:18, 19. 2:5. (5) and ver. 28, 29. Jn 11:25, 26, with Ro 8:11. 2 C 4:14. Ph 3:21. 1 Th 4:14. (6) Ps 27:14. 138:3. Is 45:24, with 2 C 12:9, 10. Ep 3:16. Ph 4:13. Col 1:11. (7) Ex

4:11. Pr 2:6, with Lk 21:15. (8) Je 17:10, with Re 2:23.

20 the Father. Jn 3:35. 10:17. 15:9, 10. 17:23, 24, 26. Mt 3:17. 17:5. Mk 1:11. 9:7. Lk 3:22. 9:35. Ep 1:6. Col 1:13. 2 P 1:17.
and showeth. Jn 1:18. 10:32. 15:15. Ge 41:39. Ps 103:7. Pr 8:22-31. Mt 11:27. Lk 10:22.
all things. Jn 3:35. +14:28. Mt +10:32. Mk +13:32. Lk 2:52.
greater. ver. 21, 25, 29. Jn 12:45-47. 14:12.
works. ver. 17, 36. Jn 4:34. 9:3, 4. 10:32, 37. 14:10. 17:4. Mt 11:2.

21 as. Dt +32:39. 1 S 2:6. 1 K 17:21, 22. 2 K 4:32-35. 5:7. Ac 26:8. Ro 4:17-19.
even. Jn 11:25, 43, 44. 17:2. Lk 7:14, 15. 8:54, 55.
the Son. Jn 6:33. 11:25. 1 C 15:45.
quickeneth. Ps +71:20. 80:17, 18. Ro 4:17. 8:11, 23. Ep 2:5. Col 2:13. 1 T 6:13.
whom. Ro 9:18.
he will. Jn 17:24. 21:22.

22 the Father. ver. 27. Jn 3:35. 17:2. Mt 11:27. +16:27. 28:18. Ac 10:42. 2 Th 1:7-10. 2 T 4:1. 1 P 4:5.
hath committed. ver. 27. Jn 3:17. 9:39. 17:2. Ac 10:42.
all judgment. ver. 27. Ps +7:8. 2 T 4:1.

23 That all. Da 7:13, 14. 1 C 8:6. Ph 2:10.
men should. (1) Jn 14:1. Ps 146:3-5. Je 17:5-7. Mt 12:21. Ro 15:12. 2 C 1:9. Ep 1:12, 13. 2 T 1:12mg. (2) Ps 2:12. Is 42:8. 43:10. 44:6. Mt +28:19. Ro 1:7. 1 C 1:3. 2 C 13:14. 1 Th 3:11-13. 2 Th 2:16, 17. He 1:6. 2 P 3:18. Re 5:8-14. (3) Mt 10:37. 22:37, 38. 1 C 16:22. Ep 6:24. (4) Lk 12:8, 9. Ro 6:22. 14:7-9. 1 C 6:19. 10:31. 2 C 5:14, 15. T 2:14. (5) Is 43:11. 45:15, 21. Zc 9:9. T 2:13. 3:4-6. 2 P 1:1.
honor the Son. Mt +14:33. Nu 12:8. Re +5:12.
even as. Jn 14:1. 16:15. Is 42:8. Mt 4:10. +14:33. 1 J 2:23.
honor the Father. Jn 8:49. Is 48:11. +58:13. 1 T +1:17.
He that. Jn 15:23, 24. 16:14, 15. 17:10. Mt 11:27. Lk 10:16. Ro 8:9. 1 J 2:23. 2 J 9.
hath sent. ver. 30, 37. Jn 4:34.

24 Verily. Jn +1:51.
He that. Jn 3:16, 18, 36. 6:40, 47. 8:51. 11:26. 12:44. 20:31. Mk 16:16. Ro 10:11-13. 14:12. 1 P 1:21. 1 J 5:1, 11-13.
heareth. Jn 8:43. Lk +8:18.
believeth. Jn 20:31. Ac 16:34. 1 J 5:9-13.
hath. Eternal life is a present possession. 1 J 5:13.
everlasting. Gr. *aionios*, Mt +18:8.
and shall not. Jn 10:27-30. +17:6. Ro 8:1, 16, 17, 28-30, 33, 34. Ep 4:30. 1 Th 5:9. 2 Th 2:13, 14. 1 P 1:5. Ju 24.
but. Mt 18:8. 1 J 3:14.

25 **The hour**. Jn 4:23. 13:1. 17:1.
when. ver. 21, 28. Lk 9:60. 15:24, 32. Ro 6:4.
Ep 2:1, 5. 5:14. Col 2:13. 3:4. Re 3:1.
shall hear. Jn 10:16. 11:43.
Son of God. Mt +14:33.

26 **hath life**. Jn 6:57. Ex 3:14. Dt 32:40. Ps 36:9.
90:2. Je 10:10. Ac 17:24, 25. 1 T 1:17. 6:15,
16. Re 1:17, 18.
so hath. Jn 1:4. 4:10. 7:37, 38. 8:51. 11:26.
14:6, 19. 17:2, 3. 1 C 15:45. Col 3:3, 4. 1 J
1:1-3. Re 7:17. 21:6. 22:1, 17.
have life. Mt +28:19.

27 **hath**. ver. +22. Jn 17:2. Ps 2:6-9. Mt +28:18.
Ac 10:42. 1 C 15:25. Ep 1:20-23. 1 P 3:22.
judgment. ver. 22. Ex 18:13. Mt 5:21, 22.
12:41, 42. Lk 12:14.
because. Da +7:13, 14. Ph 2:7-11. He 2:7-9.
the Son of man. Jn +1:51. Da 7:13. Mk
15:39. Re 1:13. 14:14.

28 **Marvel**. ver. 20. Jn 3:7. Ac 3:12. 1 J 3:13.
for the hour. ver. 25. Jn 4:23. 6:39, 40.
11:24, 25. Jb +19:25, 26. Is +26:19. Ezk 37:1-
10. Ho 13:14. Mt 9:22. Mk 13:11. Lk 10:21. 1
C 15:22, 42-54. Ph 3:21. 1 Th 4:14-17. 1 J
2:18. Re 20:12.
in which all. ver. 29. Is 24:21-23. Da 12:2. 1
C 15:23.
graves. Mt +8:28 (**S#3419g**).
shall hear. Jn 11:43-45.

29 **come forth**. Jn 6:39, 40, 54. 11:25. Jb 19:25-
27. Ps 16:9, 10. 71:20. Is +26:19. Da +12:2, 3.
Mt 25:31-46. Lk 20:35, 36. Ac 24:15. Ro 8:11.
1 C 6:2, 3. 15:21, 42-44, 49-54. 2 C 4:14. 5:1-
4, 10. Ph 3:21. 1 Th 4:14-17. 2 T 1:10.
done good. Gr. *agatha poieesantes*, do good. Lk
14:14. Ac 16:30, 31. Ro 2:6-10. Ga 6:8-10. Ep
2:8, 9. 1 T 6:18, 19. T 3:4-8. He 13:16. Ja
2:17. 1 P 3:11. 1 J 3:9.
resurrection of life. Jn 6:39, 40, 44, 54. Lk
+14:14. 1 C 15:23. Ph +3:11. 1 Th +4:16. He
11:35. Re +20:5.
done evil. Gr. *phaula praxantes*, practice evil.
The distinction between 'have done' (*poieo*)
and 'have practiced' (*prasso*) lies in this, that
poieo denotes an act complete in itself, while
prasso denotes a habit. Compare Jn 3:20, 21,
where the same distinction is made (Vine,
Commentary on John, p. 44). The words are
associated in Jn 3:20, 21. 5:29. Ac 26:9, 10.
Ro 1:32. 2:3. 7:15, 19, etc. 13:4, etc.
resurrection of damnation. ver. 24. Is
+24:22. Da 12:2. Ac +24:15. Re 20:5, 11-15.

30 **can**. ver. 19. Jn 7:17, 18. 8:28, 42. 10:18.
14:10.
I judge. Jn 8:15, 16. Ge +18:25. Ps 96:13. Is
11:3, 4. Ro 2:2, 5.
because. Jn 4:34. 6:38. 7:18. 8:50. 17:4.
18:11. Ps 40:7, 8. Mt 26:39. Ro 15:3. He 10:7-
10.
which hath. ver. 23, 37. Jn 4:34. Mt +10:32.

31 **If**. Mt +4:9.
bear witness. Jn 8:13, 14, 18, 54. Jn 18:37.
Pr 27:2. Re 3:14.

32 **is another**. ver. 36, 37. Jn 1:33. 8:17, 18.
12:28-30. Mt 3:17. 17:5. Mk 1:11. Lk 3:22. 1 J
5:6-9.
and I. Jn 7:28, 29. 12:50.

33 **sent**. Jn 1:7, 19-27.
he. Jn 1:6-8, 15-18, 29-34. 3:26-36. 18:37.

34 **I receive**. ver. 32, 37, 41. Jn 8:54. 1 C 4:3. 1
Th 2:6. 1 J 5:9.
that. Jn 3:17. 4:22, 42. 10:9. 20:31. Mt 1:21.
3:7. Lk 13:34. 19:10, 41, 42. 24:47. Ro 3:3.
10:1, 21. 12:21. 1 C 9:22. 1 T 2:3, 4. +4:16.

35 **was**. Jn 1:7, 8. Nu 25:13. 2 S 21:17. Ps
132:17. Mt 11:11. Lk 1:15-17, 76, 77. 7:28. 2
P 1:19.
light. Mt 5:16. Ph 2:15, 16.
and ye. Jn 6:66. Ezk +33:31. Mt 3:5-7. 11:7-
9. 13:20, 21. 21:26. Mk 1:6. 6:20. Ga 4:15, 16.

36 **I have**. ver. 32. 1 J 5:9, 11, 12.
witness. ver. +39. Jn 10:25. Ac +10:43. Ro
+1:4.
the works. ver. 20. Jn 2:23. 3:2. 9:30-33.
10:25, 37, 38. 11:37, 38. 14:10, 11. 15:24.
17:4. Mt 11:4, 5. Lk 7:22. Ac 2:22.
to finish. Jn 4:34.
bear witness. Jn 3:2.
sent. Jn 3:17.

37 **borne**. ver. 32. Jn 6:27. 8:18. 12:28. Mt 3:17.
17:5. Mk 1:11. 9:7. Lk 3:22. 9:35. 24:27.
his voice. Dt 4:12. Ac 7:31. 9:4. 10:13. 2 P
1:17.
nor seen. Jn +1:18. 14:9. 15:24. Ex 20:19. 1 J
1:1, 2.

38 **ye have**. ver. 42, 46, 47. Jn 8:37, 46, 47.
15:7. Dt 6:6-9. Jsh +1:8. Ps 119:11. Pr 2:1, 2.
7:1, 2. Col 3:16. Ja 1:21, 22. 1 J 1:10. 2:14.
5:10.
his word. Jn 8:31.
for. ver. 43, 46, 47. Jn 1:11. 3:18-21. 12:44-
48. Is 49:7. 53:1-3.

39 **Search**. **S#2045g**: ver. 39; Jn 7:52; Ro 8:27; 1 C
2:10; 1 P 1:11; Re 2:23. ver. 46. Jn 7:52. Dt
11:18-20. 17:18, 19. 32:46, 47. Jsh +1:8. Ps
1:2. 119:11, 97-99. Pr 6:23. 8:33, 34. Is +8:20.
29:18. 34:16. Je 8:9. Mt 22:29. Mk 12:10. Lk
16:29, 31. Ac 8:32-35. +17:11. Ro 2:17, 18.
3:2. Col 3:16. 2 T 3:14-17. 1 P 1:11. 2 P 1:19-
21.
the scriptures. Mt +21:42.
in them. 1 C 15:2. 1 Th 2:13. 2 T 3:15. Ja
1:18. 1 P 1:23.
ye think. Gr. *dokeo*, **S#1380g**, Mt +3:9. ver. 46.
Dt 32:47. Ps 16:11. 21:4. 36:9. 133:3. Da
+12:2. Mt 19:16-20. Mk 7:7-9. 12:24. Lk
10:25-29. 16:31. Ac 15:28. 1 C 4:9. +7:40. 2 T
3:15, 16. He 11:16, 35. Ja 1:18. 1 P 1:23.
ye have. ver. 24. Jn 3:36. 4:14. 1 J 5:13.
eternal. Gr. *aionios*, Mt +18:8.

which testify. ver. 32, 36. Jn 1:45. Dt 18:15, 18. Lk +24:27, 44. Ac 10:43. 18:28. 26:22, 23, 27. Ro 1:2. 1 C 15:3. 1 P 1:10, 11. Re 19:10.

40 **will not**. ver. 43, 44. Jn 1:11. 3:19. 8:45, 46. 12:37-41. Ps 81:11. Is 49:7. 50:2. 53:1-3. Je 27:13. Ezk 33:11, 31, 32. Mt 22:3. 23:37. Lk 13:34. 14:18. +19:14. Re 22:17.
come. Jn 6:35. Is 45:22-24. 55:3. Je 3:22. Mt 11:28. Re 22:16, 17.
that. ver. 26, 39. Jn 6:27, 37, 40, 68, 69. 7:37, 38. 11:25, 26. 20:31. Ro 6:23. He 7:25. 1 J 5:11-13.

41 **receive not honor**. ver. 34, 44. Jn 6:15. 7:18. 8:50, 54. 12:43. 16:33. 18:36. Mt 6:1, 2. 1 Th 2:6. 1 P 2:21. 2 P 1:17.

42 **I know**. Jn +2:25.
that. ver. 44. Jn 8:42, 47, 55. 15:23, 24. Ro 8:7. 1 J 2:15. 3:17. 4:20.
the love. Dt +6:5.
in you. Jn 6:53. 1 J 2:15. 5:10.

43 **come**. Jn 3:16. 6:38. 8:28, 29. 10:25. 12:28. 17:4-6. Ex 23:21. Dt 18:18. He 5:4, 5.
Father's name. Jn 5:43. 10:25. 12:13, 28. 14:13. 17:6, 11, 12, 26.
receive me not. Jn 1:11. 3:11, 32. 12:37.
if. Mt +4:9. Mt +24:5, 24. Mk 13:5, 6, 22. Lk 21:8. Ac 5:36, 37. 21:38. 2 Th 2:2, 3, 8-12.
another. Gr. *allos*, Mt +10:23. Da 7:24. 8:9, 23, 24. 9:27. 11:35-45. Mt 24:15. 2 Th 2:2, 3, 8-12. 1 J 2:18. Re 13:8, 14, 18.
him. Da 8:25. 9:27.
ye will receive. Is 2:6, 8. Je 5:30, 31. Ezk +14:10. Da 8:25. 9:27. Ho +14:8. Ac 20:29, 30. 2 T 4:2-4. 1 J 5:21. Re 13:8, 14, 18.

44 **How can ye**. Jn 3:20. 8:43. 12:43. Je 13:23. Ro 8:7, 8. He +3:12.
believe. Jn 1:7, 50. 3:15. 4:39, 41, 42, 48, 53. 6:36, 47, 64. 11:15, 40. 12:39. 14:29. 19:35. 20:8, 25, 29, 31. Ac 13:12. Ro 4:11.
which receive. lit. receiving. Note the cause/effect relationships implied in this verse (Ps +9:10). Mt 23:5. Ga 5:19-21. Ph +2:3.
honor. ver. 41.
seek not. Jn 7:13. 12:43. 1 S 2:30. 2 Ch 6:8. Mt 25:21-23. Lk 19:17. Ro 2:7, 10, 29. 1 C 4:5. 2 C 10:18. He 11:6. Ja 2:1. 1 P 1:7.
only. Jn 17:3. Ro 16:27. 1 T 6:15, 16. Ju 25.

45 **Do not think**. Jn 3:17. 12:47, 48.
there. Jn 7:19. 8:5, 9. Ro 2:12, 17, etc. 3:19, 20. 7:9-14. 2 C 3:7-11. Ga 3:10.
Moses. Mk +12:19.
in whom. Jn 8:5, 6. 9:28, 29. Mt 19:7, 8. Ro 2:17. 10:5-10.
ye trust. 2 C 1:10. 1 T 4:10. 5:5. 1 J 3:3.

46 **For had ye believed**. Lk +7:39. ver. 38. Lk 16:29-31. Ga 2:19. 3:10, 13, 24. 4:21-31.
for. Jn 1:45. Ge +3:15. +12:3. 18:18. 22:18. 28:14. +49:10. Nu 21:8, 9. 24:17, 18. Dt 18:15, 18, 19. Ac 26:22. Ro 10:4. He ch. 7-10.
he wrote. Ex +24:4.

47 **But if**. 1 C +15:2.
ye believe not. Lk 16:29, 31.
writings. Jn 7:15.
believe my words. ver. 24, 38, 46. Jn 2:22. 4:50. 6:30. 8:31, 45, 46. 10:37, 38. 14:11. Ac 18:8. 1 J 3:23.

JOHN 6

1 A.M. 4036. A.D. 32.
these. Mt 14:13, 15, etc. 15:32-38. Mk 6:31, 32, 34, 35, etc. 8:1-10. Lk 9:10-12, etc.
the sea. Jsh +11:2. Mt +4:18. 15:29.
Tiberias. i.e. *good vision*, S#5085g. ver. 23. Jn 21:1.

2 **a great multitude**. Mk 6:33. Lk +5:15.
miracles. ver. 14, 26, 30. Jn 2:11, 23.

3 **Jesus went**. ver. 15. Mt +5:1.

4 **the passover**. Jn 2:13. 5:1. 11:55. 12:1. 13:1. Ex 12:6, etc. Le 23:5, 7. Dt 16:1. 1 C 5:7, 8.
feast. Jn 2:23. 12:1. 13:1. 18:28, 39. 19:14. Ex ch. 12. 23:15. Dt 16:1-6. Mt 26:2, etc. Mk 14:1, etc. Lk 2:41. 22:1, etc. Ac 12:4. He 11:28.
the Jews. Jn +5:10.

5 **lifted**. Ge +22:13. Lk 6:20.
saw. Jn 4:35. Mt 14:14, 15. Mk 6:34, 35. Lk 9:12.
Philip. Jn +1:43.
Whence. Mt +14:17.

6 **prove**. Ge 22:1. Dt 8:2, 16. 13:3. 33:8. 2 Ch 32:31. 2 C +13:5.

7 **Two**. Nu 11:21, 22. 2 K 4:43.
pennyworth. Mt +18:28mg.

8 **disciples**. Jn +2:2.
Andrew. Jn 1:40-44. Mt 4:18. Mk +13:3.

9 **which**. Mt 14:17. 16:9. Mk 6:38. 8:19. Lk 9:13.
barley. Dt 8:8. 32:14. Jg 7:13. 1 K 4:28. 2 K 4:42, 43. 7:1. Ps 81:16. 147:14. Ezk 13:19. 27:17. 2 C 8:9. Re 6:6.
fishes. ver. 11. Jn 21:9, 10, 13.
but. ver. 7. Jn 11:21, 32. 2 K 4:42-44. Ps 78:19, 20, 41.

10 **Make**. Mt +14:19.
Now. ver. 4. Mk 6:39.

11 **given thanks**. ver. 23. Jn 11:41. Pr 10:21. Lk +24:30.
as much. Ge 44:1.

12 **they**. Ne 9:25. Mt +14:20.
Gather. Le 23:22.
remain. Is 1:9.
that nothing. Ge 41:35, 36. Ne 8:10. Pr 18:9. 21:20. Lk 15:13. 16:1.
lost. Gr. *apollumi*, Mt +2:13.

13 **and filled**. 1 K 17:15, 16. 2 K 4:2-7. 2 Ch 25:9. Pr 11:24, 25. 2 C 9:8, 9. Ph 4:19.
baskets. Mk +6:43.

14 **miracle**. ver. 2.
This is. Jn 1:21, 41, 45, 49. 7:31, 40-42, 52.